EUROPE
1450 TO 1789
ENCYCLOPEDIA OF THE EARLY MODERN WORLD

EDITORIAL BOARD

Europe, 1450
40°E
FINLAND
(Sweden)
Abo
Stockholm
Tornea/lven
Umea/lven
Lake Onega
Lake Ladoga
Volkhov
Saaremaa
Gotland
Baltic Sea
TEUTONIC KNIGHTS
Neman
Dvina
Danzig
Minsk
POLAND-LITHUANIA
Vistula
Warsaw
Bug
Silesia
Oder
Kiev
Dnieper
Southern Bug
Dniester
Prut
Moscow
Volga
RUSSIAN STATES
URAL MTS.
Don
Donets
Kuban&
Caspian Sea
CAUCASUS MTS.
Carpathian Mts.
Buda
Pest
Tisza
HUNGARY
MOLDAVIA
Siret
Maros (Mures*)
Drava
Belgrade
BOSNIA
WALLACHIA
Bucharest
Danube
Black Sea
Morava
SERBIA
Bulgaria
Balkan Mts.
Alps
Venice
Maritsa
Vardar
Constantinople
Sea of Marmara
OTTOMAN EMPIRE
Aegean Sea
Ionian Sea
Athens
Crete (Venice)
Cyprus
ASIA
N
0 200 400 mi.
0 200 400 km
For Reference
Not to be taken from this room

EUROPE
1450 TO 1789
ENCYCLOPEDIA OF THE EARLY MODERN WORLD

Volume 3
Gabrieli to Lyon

Jonathan Dewald, Editor in Chief

CHARLES SCRIBNER'S SONS®

THOMSON
GALE™

New York • Detroit • San Diego • San Francisco • Cleveland • New Haven, Conn. • Waterville, Maine • London • Munich

THOMSON
GALE

Europe 1450 to 1789:
Encyclopedia of the Early Modern World

Jonathan Dewald, Editor in Chief

For more information, contact
Charles Scribner's Sons
An imprint of The Gale Group
300 Park Avenue South
New York, NY 10010

LIBRARY OF CONGRESS CATALOGING-IN-PUBLICATION DATA

Europe 1450 to 1789 : encyclopedia of the early modern world / Jonathan Dewald, editor in chief.
p. cm.
Includes bibliographical references and index.
ISBN 0-684-31200-X (set : hardcover) — ISBN 0-684-31201-8 (v. 1) — ISBN 0-684-31202-6 (v. 2) — ISBN 0-684-31203-4 (v. 3) — ISBN 0-684-31204-2 (v. 4) — ISBN 0-684-31205-0 (v. 5) — ISBN 0-684-31206-9 (v. 6)
1. Europe—History—15th century—Encyclopedias. 2. Europe—History—1492–1648—Encyclopedias. 3. Europe—History—1648–1789—Encyclopedias. 4. Europe—Intellectual life—Encyclopedias. 5. Europe—Civilization—Encyclopedias. I. Title: Encyclopedia of the early modern world. II. Dewald, Jonathan.
D209.E97 2004
940.2—dc22

2003015680

This title is also available as an e-book.
ISBN 0-684-31423-1 (set)
Contact your Gale sales representative for ordering information.
Printed in United States of America
10 9 8 7 6 5 4 3 2 1

CONTENTS OF THIS VOLUME

VOLUME 3

I

J

CONTENTS OF OTHER VOLUMES

VOLUME 1

B

C

VOLUME 2

N

VOLUME 5

VOLUME 6

T

U

V

USING THE ENCYCLOPEDIA

Tables of contents. Each volume contains a table of contents for the entire *Encyclopedia*. Volume 1 has a single listing of all volumes' contents. Volumes 2 through 6 contain "Contents of This Volume" followed by "Contents of Other Volumes."

Maps of Europe. The front of each volume contains a set of maps showing Europe's political divisions at six important stages from 1453 to 1795.

Alphabetical arrangement. Entries are arranged in alphabetical order. Biographical articles are generally listed by the subject's last name (with some exceptions, e.g., Leonardo da Vinci).

Royalty and foreign names. In most cases, the names of rulers of French, German, and Spanish rulers have been anglicized. Thus, Francis, not François; Charles, not Carlos. Monarchs of the same name are listed first by their country, and then numerically. Thus, Henry VII and Henry VIII of England precede Henry II of France.

Measurements appear in the English system according to United States usage, though they are often followed by metric equivalents in parentheses. Following are approximate metric equivalents for the most common units:

1 foot = 30 centimeters
1 mile = 1.6 kilometers
1 acre = 0.4 hectares
1 square mile = 2.6 square kilometers
1 pound = 0.45 kilograms
1 gallon = 3.8 liters

Cross-references. At the end of each article is a list of related articles for further study. Readers may also consult the table of contents and the index for titles and keywords of interest.

Bibliography. Each article contains a list of sources for further reading, usually divided into Primary Sources and Secondary Sources.

Systematic outline of contents. After the last article in volume 6 is an outline that provides a general overview of the conceptual scheme of the *Encyclopedia,* listing the title of each entry.

Directory of contributors. Following the systematic outline of contents is a listing, in alphabetical order, of all contributors to the *Encyclopedia,* with affiliation and the titles of his or her article(s).

Index. Volume 6 concludes with a comprehensive, alphabetically arranged index covering all articles, as well as prominent figures, geographical names, events, institutions, publications, works of art, and all major concepts that are discussed in volumes 1 through 6.

MAPS OF EUROPE, 1453 TO 1795

The maps on the pages that follow show political boundaries within Europe at six important stages in the roughly three hundred and fifty years covered by this *Encyclopedia:* 1453, 1520, 1648, 1715, 1763, and 1795.

1453. In the years around 1450, Europe settled into relative political stability, following the crises of the late Middle Ages. France and England concluded the Hundred Years' War in 1453; the Ottoman Turks conquered Constantinople in the same year and established it as the capital of their empire; and in 1454 the Treaty of Lodi normalized relations among the principal Italian states, establishing a peaceful balance of power among Venice, Florence, the duchy of Milan, the Papal States, and the Kingdom of Naples.

1520. In 1520, the Habsburg prince Charles V was elected Holy Roman emperor, uniting in his person lordship over central Europe, Spain, the Low Countries, parts of Italy, and the newly conquered Spanish territories in the Americas. For the next century, this overwhelming accumulation of territories in the hands of a single dynasty would remain the most important fact in European international politics. But in 1520 Habsburg power already faced one of its most troublesome challenges: Martin Luther's Reformation, first attracting widespread notice in 1517, would repeatedly disrupt Habsburg efforts to unify their territories.

1648. The 1648 Peace of Westphalia ended the Thirty Years' War, one of the most destructive wars in European history. The peace treaty formally acknowledged the independence of the Dutch Republic and the Swiss Confederation, and it established the practical autonomy of the German principalities—including the right to establish their own religious policies. Conversely, the Holy Roman Empire lost much of its direct power; although its institutions continued to play some role in German affairs through the eighteenth century, the emperors' power now rested overwhelmingly on the Habsburg domain lands in Austria, Bohemia, and eastern Europe.

1715. The Peace of Utrecht (1713) ended the War of the Spanish Succession, the last and most destructive of the wars of the French king Louis XIV. The treaty ended Spain's control over present-day Belgium and over parts of Italy, and it marked the end of French hegemony within Europe. In the eighteenth century, France would be only one of five leading powers.

1763. The 1763 Treaty of Paris ended the Seven Years' War, a war that involved all the major European powers and included significant campaigns in North America and southern Asia, as well as in Europe. The war made clear the arrival of Prussia as a great power, at least the equal of Austria in central and eastern Europe.

1795. By 1795, French armies had repelled an attempted invasion by Prussia, Austria, and England, and France had begun annexing territories in Belgium and western Germany. These military successes ensured the continuation of the French Revolution, but they also meant that European warfare would continue until 1815, when the modern borders of France were largely established. Warfare with France did not prevent the other European powers from conducting business as usual elsewhere: with agreements in 1793 and 1795, Prussia, Austria, and Russia completed their absorption of Poland.

COMMON ABBREVIATIONS USED IN THIS WORK

A.D.	*Anno Domini*, in the year of the Lord
A.H.	*Anno Hegirae*, in the year of the Hegira
b.	born
B.C.	before Christ
B.C.E.	before the common era (= B.C.)
c.	*circa*, about, approximately
C.E.	common era (= A.D.)
ch.	chapter
d.	died
ed.	editor (pl., eds.), edition
e.g.	*exempli gratia*, for example
et al.	*et alii*, and others
etc.	*et cetera*, and so forth
exh. cat.	exhibition catalogue
fl.	*floruit*, flourished
i.e.	*id est*, that is
MS.	manuscript (pl. MSS.)
n.d.	no date
no.	number (pl., nos.)
n.s.	new series
N.S.	new style, according to the Gregorian calendar
O.S.	old style, according to the Julian calendar
p.	page (pl., pp.)
rev.	revised
S.	*san, sanctus, santo,* male saint
SS.	saints
Sta.	*sancta, santa,* female saint
supp.	supplement
vol.	volume
?	uncertain, possibly, perhaps

EUROPE
1450 TO 1789
ENCYCLOPEDIA OF THE EARLY MODERN WORLD

G

GABRIELI, ANDREA AND GIOVANNI (Andrea Gabrieli, c. 1532/33–1585; Giovanni Gabrieli, c. 1554/57–1612), Italian composers and organists noted for the grandeur of their sacred and ceremonial music. Andrea Gabrieli and his nephew Giovanni Gabrieli were leading figures in Venetian music and influenced the development of seventeenth-century German music as well. Most likely a native of Venice, Andrea may have been in Verona during the 1550s (as indicated by the publication there of his earliest known madrigal and his probable association with the Accademia Filharmonica of Verona), and in Munich in 1562 at the court of Albert V, duke of Bavaria, where he met Orlando di Lasso (c. 1532–1594), the most famous composer of the era. By 1566, Andrea was appointed as one of the two permanent organists at the Basilica of St. Mark's in Venice, a position he held until his death, and was followed in this position by his nephew Giovanni. Andrea established a line of native Venetian musicians working at St. Mark's after a period of dominance by northern masters.

As a composer, Andrea Gabrieli wrote in most of the musical genres of his day, including masses, psalms, motets, madrigals, and many instrumental works, most for solo keyboard. He composed both small- and large-scale works, including polychoral music employing the technique of *cori spezzati* (split choirs) that exploited the spatial separation of two or more choirs through chordal textures, syllabic text setting, and short imitative dialogues between performing groups.

Many of his compositions were published posthumously in the *Concerti* (1587), a collection of large-scale vocal works (sacred and secular) and instrumental works, edited by his nephew Giovanni Gabrieli. The collection includes madrigals as well as settings of liturgical texts for major feast days in Venice (Christmas, Easter, St. Mark's, Corpus Christi, Marian feasts). It also contains ceremonial music for events of church and state in Venice, including occasional works to Italian texts in commemoration of state visits by Archduke Charles of Austria in 1565 or 1569 and by the French king Henry III in 1574, a motet for the new Franciscan Church of the Redentore (built 1577–1592) designed by architect Andrea Palladio (1508–1580) erected to celebrate the end of a plague epidemic in 1577, and a series of mass movements perhaps written to honor the state visit of five Japanese princes in 1585.

The compositions that Andrea Gabrieli wrote for instrumental ensemble and solo keyboard are important to the development of independent instrumental genres. His *intonazioni* (preludes) and many of his toccatas are free, improvisatory pieces, while his ricercars and canzonas feature fugal writing (that is, with musical phrases imitated in two or more voices). Andrea's music remained in print until the mid-seventeenth century, published in Germany and the Low Countries as well as in Italy. He was a renowned teacher whose students included German composers Hans Leo Hassler (1564–

1612) and Gregor Aichinger (1564/65–1628), music theorist Lodovico Zacconi (1555–1627), and his own nephew Giovanni.

Giovanni Gabrieli was once thought to be of patrician origins; however, the recent discovery of the identity of his father as Piero di Fais, called Gabrieli, confirms that the family was not of Venetian nobility. Giovanni followed in the footsteps of his uncle Andrea, working first at the Munich court of Albert V under Orlando di Lasso, then returning to Venice to become organist at St. Mark's beginning in 1584 (a position made permanent in 1585) until his death in 1612. In the year 1585, the two Gabrielis served together for several months as organists at the basilica. Giovanni described himself as "little less than a son" of Andrea, whose music he edited for publication in 1587, along with some of his own compositions. Giovanni's duties included composing ceremonial music for St. Mark's, much of which was published in two monumental collections: *Sacrae Symphoniae* (1597) and *Symphoniae Sacrae* (1615). Giovanni also held the post of organist for the Scuola Grande di San Rocco from 1585 on, and some of this music served the confraternity on high feast days. Like Andrea, Giovanni was a preeminent teacher whose reputation reached far beyond the Veneto; the most famous of his northern students was German composer Heinrich Schütz (1585–1672).

The close connection between church and state in Venice, emphasized by the proximity of the ducal palace to St. Mark's, led to sumptuous religious and civic celebrations accompanied by vocal and instrumental music and splendid pageantry. Gabrieli wrote several grand motets for the feast of St. Mark, the city's patron, and for Ascension Day festivities, on which occasion the famous ceremony of the Wedding of Venice to the Sea took place, when the doge cast a ring into the lagoon to be retrieved by a young fisherman, symbolizing the domination of the Venetian Republic over the Adriatic after conquering Dalmatia in the year 1000. Francesco Sansovino, in volume 12 of his 1581 guidebook to Venice, *Venetia città nobilissima,* described one such commemoration performed with the "two famous organs of the church, and the other instruments [which] made the most excellent music, in which the best singers and players that can be found in this region took part." The description refers to performances with some musicians positioned in choir lofts on either side of the nave, each with a pipe organ, in addition to the musicians on the floor. Gabrieli's polychoral motet *O quam suavis* (1615), for two choirs and instruments, sets a text for vespers on the Feast of Corpus Christi, an occasion that called for a grandiose procession *(andata)* in St. Mark's Square in which all the clergy, confraternities, and civic dignitaries took part. The participation of singers and instrumentalists on the Feast of St. Mark's (April 25) was captured by Gentile Bellini (c. 1429–1507) in his well-known painting *Procession of the True Cross in the Piazza San Marco* (1496), commemorating this event and the miraculous healing powers of the True Cross of the Scuola di San Giovanni Evangelista.

Giovanni Gabrieli's output of instrumental music was remarkable. His ensemble canzonas and sonatas exploited the rich musical resources of St. Mark's and were meant for ceremonial performance on high feast days. Giovanni was among the first composers to specify instrumentation in his works: his *Sonate pian e forte* (1597) calls for two instrumental choirs (violin with three trombones, and cornetto with three trombones) and is one of the earliest compositions to include dynamic markings.

Although Giovanni shunned the lighter secular forms of villanella and canzonetta, his madrigals were included in a number of anthologies. Several of these works celebrate eminent acquaintances, including the powerful Augsburg banker Jacob Fugger (1542–1598), who was the dedicatee of the *Concerti* (1587).

Giovanni's later works show early baroque characteristics of florid solo writing set against larger forces, and the use of organ basso continuo. After Claudio Monteverdi (1567–1643) was appointed choirmaster at St. Mark's in 1613, the influence of Andrea and Giovanni Gabrieli began to wane in Italy, and the more dramatic, mannerist style of Monteverdi began to transform Italian music; however, their impact remained significant on musical styles in the north.

See also **Baroque; Monteverdi, Claudio; Music; Schütz, Heinrich; Venice.**

BIBLIOGRAPHY

Arnold, Denis. *Giovanni Gabrieli and the Music of the Venetian High Renaissance.* London, 1979.

Bryant, David. "The *cori spezzati* of S. Marco: Myth and Reality." *Early Music History* 1 (1981): 165–186.

———. "Gabrieli, Andrea" and "Gabrieli, Giovanni," in *The New Grove Dictionary of Music and Musicians.* 2nd ed. Edited by Stanley Sadie. Vol. 9, pp. 384–396. London, 2001.

Charteris, Richard. "Newly Discovered Works by Giovanni Gabrieli." *Music and Letters* 68 (1987): 343–363.

Morell, Martin. "New Evidence for the Biographies of Andrea and Giovanni Gabrieli." *Early Music History* 3 (1983): 101–122.

Selfridge-Field, Eleanor. *Venetian Instrumental Music from Gabrieli to Vivaldi.* 3rd ed. New York, 1994.

KRISTINE K. FORNEY

GAINSBOROUGH, THOMAS (1727–1788), English painter. Rivaling Sir Joshua Reynolds in the field of portraiture, Thomas Gainsborough's career highlights the opportunities available to a painter in eighteenth-century England. After establishing his practice in provincial cities, Gainsborough maintained close connections to the London scene through personal contacts and by regularly displaying his work at exhibition venues. His continued allegiance to the unprofitable genre of landscape painting served as a model for future generations of landscapists, such as John Constable and Joseph Mallord William Turner.

Born in Sudbury, Suffolk, Gainsborough received his early training from Francis Wynantz, probably a Dutch artist. East Anglia traditionally had close ties to the Low Countries, and Gainsborough's early landscape style reflects this influence.

Gainsborough's father was a failed clothier, who after declaring bankruptcy in 1733 became the local postmaster. Gainsborough, however, was an artistic prodigy, and around 1740 he went to London, where he studied with the French artist Hubert François Gravelot and then with Francis Hayman. Absorbing the French rococo style of Gravelot, Gainsborough also adopted his master's practice of drawing from small-scale dolls. Gravelot returned to Paris in 1745, and it is this year to which Gainsborough's independent practice is usually dated. His independence was further bolstered by his marriage in 1746 to Margaret Burr, who had an annual income of £200, which she received from the duke of Beaufort, assumed to be her natural father.

At the death of his father in 1748 and in pursuit of patronage, Gainsborough established a practice in his native Sudbury. Before leaving London, he completed the roundel *The Charterhouse* (1748; Thomas Coram Foundation for Children, London) for the Foundling Hospital. In addition, he began his early landscape masterpiece *Cornard Wood* or *Gainsborough's Forest* (c. 1746–1747; National Gallery, London). When Alderman Boydell purchased this work in 1788 for 75 guineas, Gainsborough wrote with satisfaction that "it is in some respects a little in the schoolboy stile—but I do not reflect on this without a secret gratification; for as an early instance how strong my inclination stood for Landskip."

Of necessity, however, Gainsborough had to concentrate his practice on portraiture, and in 1752 he moved to Ipswich in order to find a wider clientele. By 1759 he was increasingly traveling farther afield in search of new commissions, and by the end of that year had moved to the spa city of Bath, where he remained until 1773.

Soon after his arrival in Bath, Gainsborough raised his prices to 20 guineas for a head portrait, 40 guineas for a half-length portrait, and 80 guineas for a full-length portrait, suggesting that there was sufficient patronage in the fashionable city for the newcomer as well as the already established William Hoare. The first large work Gainsborough painted in Bath was the full-length portrait of Ann Ford (1760; Cincinnati Art Museum), the future wife of his friend Philip Thicknesse.

Gainsborough's move to Bath coincided with the establishment of annual exhibitions at the Society of Artists in London, and from 1761 onward he sent examples of his full-length portraits, such as *Robert Craggs, Earl Nugent* (1760; private collection), as well as some of his landscapes, such as *The Harvest Wagon* (1767; Barber Institute of Fine Arts, University of Birmingham). The strength of his reputation in the London art world was confirmed by his invitation in December 1768 to become a founder-member of the Royal Academy.

Gainsborough articulated his dual love of music and landscape in a letter dated 1769 to his friend

Thomas Gainsborough. *Mr. and Mrs. Andrews,* painted c. 1750. ©NATIONAL GALLERY COLLECTION; BY KIND PERMISSION OF THE TRUSTEES OF THE NATIONAL GALLERY, LONDON/CORBIS

William Jackson, the composer and organist of Exeter Cathedral, "I'm sick of Portraits and wish very much to take my Viol da Gamba and walk off to some sweet Village where I can paint Landskips and enjoy the fag End of Life in quietness and ease." Nevertheless, he continued to paint portraits, and after his 1774 move to London, Gainsborough gained important commissions from the royal family, whose patronage Reynolds was never to attain. Even so, on the death of Allan Ramsay in 1784, Reynolds was named principal painter on the basis of his presidency of the Royal Academy.

Although Gainsborough was appointed to its council the year of his move to London, his relationship with the Royal Academy was uneasy. In 1773 he had objected to the way his paintings were hung at the academy's annual exhibition, and he did not again contribute to the exhibition until 1777. In 1784 he once more complained about the hanging of his portraits; they were returned to him, and he never exhibited at the Royal Academy again. Gainsborough also advised his patrons on the best placement of his portraits, showing his attention to the effect of light on his work. Gainsborough's concern with light and its effects can be seen in his painting technique: Often he would paint by candlelight, as well as with long brushes to achieve distance from the canvas.

On Gainsborough's death in 1788, Reynolds devoted his annual lecture to the students and members of the Royal Academy to his rival, acknowledging that "all those odd scratches and marks . . . by a kind of magick, at a certain distance assumes form, and all the parts seem to drop into their proper places."

See also **Academies of Art; Britain; Art in; Reynolds, Joshua; Rococo.**

BIBLIOGRAPHY

Primary Sources

Reynolds, Sir Joshua. *Discourses on Art.* Edited by Robert R. Wark. New Haven and London, 1975.

Woodall, Mary, ed. *The Letters of Thomas Gainsborough.* London and Greenwich, Conn., 1963.

Secondary Sources

Hayes, John T. *The Landscape Paintings of Thomas Gainsborough: A Critical Text and Catalogue Raisonné.* London and Ithaca, N.Y., 1982.

Lindsay, Jack. *Thomas Gainsborough: His Life and Art.* London, 1981.

Rosenthal, Michael. *The Art of Thomas Gainsborough: "A Little Business for the Eye."* New Haven and London, 1999.

ELIZABETH A. PERGAM

GALILEO GALILEI (1564–1642), Italian scientist. Born in Pisa, Galileo was the eldest of the six or seven children of Vincenzio Galilei, a merchant and music theorist, and Giulia Ammannati. He spent his childhood in Pisa and Florence; in the fall of 1581, upon his father's advice, he enrolled at the University of Pisa as a student of medicine. Not enthusiastic about this discipline, within two years he had begun to study Euclidean and Archimedean works privately and left the university in 1585 without a degree. He offered both public and private lessons in mathematics for the next three years and sought, unsuccessfully, to obtain a professorial chair at Bologna in 1588. His various meditations on and experiments with mechanics, metrology, and musical consonance, and his participation in a Florentine academy in this period, helped him secure the chair in mathematics at the University of Pisa in the fall of 1589.

By late 1592 Galileo had won a more prestigious post in mathematics at the University of Padua, and it was here that he undertook significant work in optics and catoptrics, magnetism, tidal theory, mechanics, and instrumentation. This last area was crucial to his financial well-being: in order to meet the demands incumbent upon him as the eldest son, and to supplement his professorial salary, Galileo offered private lessons to students in Padua, many of whom were eager to learn the various uses of a calculating instrument of his design. Galileo's extant writings in mechanics in these same years likewise reflect a strong interest in combining classical problems with actual devices for lifting, lowering, and guiding solid bodies and fluids.

Galileo may have become an adherent of the heliocentric world system posited by Nicolaus

Galileo Galilei. Portrait by Justus Sustermans (1597–1681). THE ART ARCHIVE/GALLERIA DEGLI UFFIZI FLORENCE/DAGLI ORTI (A)

Copernicus (1473–1543) in the mid-1590s: so he asserted in 1597 in a letter to the German astronomer Johannes Kepler (1571–1630), discoverer of the laws of planetary motion. Certain conjectures regarding tidal theory reflect a cautious interest in the hypothesis of a mobile Earth, for tides were explained as a product of the globe's annual and diurnal motions, with variations in periodicity deriving from the particular shape of any large body of water. One might also infer Galileo's discreet support of the Copernican system through the attention he devoted in this period to speculative arguments derived from mechanics. The arena in which cosmogony and mechanics intersected was in a quantified approach to a myth mentioned in Plato's *Timaeus* involving the "creation point," or the place or places from which the Divine Architect originally dropped the various planets. These bodies, after falling toward the sun, would each reach and remain in the orbits to which they had been assigned. Scholars have suggested that around 1602–1604 Galileo did attempt to combine his still evolving understanding of the law of falling bodies and of the way such bodies behave when diverted into uniform orbital motion, with Kepler's estimated periods of revolution for Saturn, Mars, and Jupiter.

By the fall of November 1604 Galileo's attention was on the heavens, for the appearance of a new star seemed to offer strong evidence against Aristotelian conventions regarding an immutable world beyond the Moon. But his most explicitly Copernican conjectures concern the Moon; between 1605 and 1607 he and several of his closest associates had observed the ashen light reflected onto that body by Earth at the beginning and end of each lunar cycle. The rough and opaque body of Earth was, in other words, like other planets, tolerably bright; the corollary was, for some, that Earth likewise participated in "the dance of the stars." In this period Galileo was also engaged in more studies of motion and hydrostatics, and involved with additional work in magnetism.

By spring or summer 1609, Galileo was making celestial observations with the aid of a telescope at least three times more powerful than a prototype from The Hague. By November of that year, he had developed a telescope that magnified twenty times, and it was with this instrument that he undertook his observations of the lunar body. His *Starry Messenger* of 1610 shows that the telescope confirmed his earlier naked-eye impressions of both a rough lunar surface and of the ashen light, and that it allowed him to present certain of the Moon's features, most notably its peaks, valleys, and craters, in terms of their terrestrial counterparts. He used the shadows cast by a particular mountain on the Moon to calculate the average height of such formations. On the basis of these observations of the Moon's similarity to Earth, Galileo proposed a thoroughgoing revision of the Ptolemaic conception of the cosmos, and he promised to deliver such arguments in his *System of the World*, the forerunner to the eventual *Dialogue concerning the Two Chief World Systems* of 1632.

The greatest discoveries in the *Starry Messenger* lay in its final section, a description of the positions of the satellites of Jupiter from 7 January until 2 March 1610, when the treatise went to press. In these brief observations and in the spare diagrams that accompanied them, Galileo presented the orbital movements of four satellites, or Medici stars, whose very existence was new to virtually all of his audience. The fact that Jupiter had moons strongly suggested to him that Earth was neither unique nor central nor motionless: satellites revolving about a celestial body clearly did not prevent its movement.

By the end of 1610, Galileo, newly appointed as mathematician and philosopher at the court of the grand duke of Tuscany, had interpreted the phases of Venus as a confirmation of Copernican claims, and perhaps more importantly, evidence against the models of both Ptolemy and and the Danish astronomer Tycho Brahe (1546–1601), who posited that the five planets revolved around the Sun, which in turn revolved around Earth; Kepler obligingly published his letters on the matter in his *Dioptrice* of 1611. Galileo had some notion of sunspots by spring 1611, but his systematic study of the phenomena appears to date only to early 1612, when he had learned of the observations of several friends, and of the treatise of an eventual enemy, the Swabian Jesuit Christoph Scheiner (1573–1650). Galileo took immediate issue with Scheiner's initial conjecture that the spots were actually small stars orbiting and partially eclipsing the solar body, and he did not hesitate to expose both the Jesuit astronomer's ignorance of Galileo's recent findings concerning Venus, and the weakness of Scheiner's geometrical proofs. Because he saw no reason to subscribe to the Aristotelian fiction of the changeless heavens, Galileo's three letters on the subject offered the more consistent (though inaccurate) explanation of the sunspots as enormous masses of dark clouds constantly produced on the solar surface and moving uniformly over it before vanishing forever.

Galileo's next writing, the *Letter to the Grand Duchess Christina*, was of little scientific importance, for it neither offered new observations nor announced novel astronomical hypotheses, and was published only in 1636 in a Latin translation. In terms of the sort of interpretation it offered—a brilliant analysis of the Old Testament verse Joshua 10:12 as compatible with a heliocentric universe and incompatible with a geocentric one—the *Letter* was among the boldest and most ill-advised moves of Galileo's career. His confidence in his reading, for all of its economy, appears to have been misplaced, and by early 1615 a complaint had been lodged with the Inquisition. In a meeting whose general tenor and purpose are still the subject of debate, Galileo met with Robert Cardinal Bellarmine in February 1616, but was not asked to abjure his Copernican beliefs. The Edict of 1616 formally prohibited books attempting to reconcile Scripture and the hypothesis of a mobile Earth, and stipulated that Copernicus's *On the Revolutions of the Heavenly Spheres* was suspended until such passages could be struck through. While Galileo appears not to have seen the edict as of particular concern to him, rivals immediately recognized its impact on the astronomer's career.

The controversy between Galileo and the Jesuit astronomer Orazio Grassi ranged from the fall of 1618, when three comets emerged, to 1626, when Grassi published his third and final work on the phenomena. Galileo's principal discussion of the comets, the *Assayer,* appeared in 1623. Although Galileo could no longer openly defend Copernicanism, and did not have an accurate explanation of the comets, he recognized flaws in many of Grassi's arguments, particularly in the implicit support that Grassi gave to the Tychonic world system. The *Assayer* contains important discussions of the usefulness of parallax and of the causes of telescopic magnification of distant bodies, several of Galileo's clearest formulations of his own methodology, and some of the most caustic and amusing moments of any scientific controversy.

The synthesis of Galileo's decades of astronomical observations, speculation, and revision, the *Dialogue concerning the Two Chief World Systems, Ptolemaic and Copernican,* was published in Florence in 1632. Divided into four days of exchanges between the learned Salviati, the cultured Sagredo, and the tireless Aristotelian Simplicio, the *Dialogue* examines and discards traditional arguments distinguishing the motions, substance, and final purpose of celestial and terrestrial bodies, discusses the experimental and logical evidence for Earth's diurnal and annual movements, presents the particulars of the orbits and telescopic appearance of the other planets, draws on the emergent science of magnetism as well as upon observations of the new stars of 1572 and 1604, the fixed stars, Moon spots, and sunspots, and concludes with an ample discussion of Galileo's theory of tides. The tempo and variety of the *Dialogue* are surely part of its enormous appeal: the speakers move easily from minute calculations to the most abstruse philosophical speculations without losing sight of their goal of assessing the two chief world systems. But to suggest, as Galileo did, that the work involves equally qualified opponents, or recognizes the merits of aspects of both views, or presents Copernicanism as merely hypothetical, is to err: Simplicio is overmatched from the outset, a rather inept spokesman for the Ptolemaic position throughout, and effectively silenced by his companions in the last pages of the *Dialogue.*

Summoned to Rome to account for his publication, Galileo recanted on 22 June 1633. Although depressed and humiliated by this turn of events, he soon focused on the *Two New Sciences Pertaining to Mechanics and Local Motions.* Published in Leiden in 1638, his last great work is in dialogue form, and again involves Salviati, Sagredo, and Simplicio. The product of a warring age, it is set in Venice's arsenal, the site of the republic's shipbuilding and munitions production. It has as one focus the "supernatural violence" with which projectiles are fired, presents the legendary burning mirrors of antiquity as plausible weapons, discusses at length notions of impact and resistance, is dedicated to a member of the *noblesse d'épée,* and refers to the battlefield death of one of Galileo's former students and fellow experimenters. That said, the *Two New Sciences* also attend to nonmilitary matters such as the void, the speed of light, the principle of the balance, musical intervals, the role of scale in very large structures or animals, uniformly accelerated or natural motion, and the Platonic "creation point." The true fight, as Galileo's dedication and several asides suggest, is for the reestablishment of his scientific and ethical reputation, and despite the burden of illness and old age, the stricture of house arrest, and his renunciation of cosmological issues, the victory was his.

See also **Astronomy; Brahe, Tycho; Copernicus, Nicolaus; Kepler, Johannes; Optics; Scientific Instruments.**

BIBLIOGRAPHY

Primary Sources

Galilei, Galileo. *Dialogue concerning the Two Chief World Systems.* Translated by Stillman Drake. 2nd rev. ed. Berkeley, 1967.

———. *Discourse on the Comets.* In *The Controversy on the Comets of 1618.* Translated by Stillman Drake and C. D. O'Malley. Philadelphia, 1960.

———. *Sidereus Nuncius or the Sidereal Messenger*. Translated and with an introduction, commentary, and notes by Albert Van Helden. Chicago, 1989.

———. *Two New Sciences*. Translated with an introduction and notes by Stillman Drake. Madison, Wis., 1974.

Secondary Sources

Biagioli, Mario. *Galileo, Courtier: The Practice of Science in the Culture of Absolutism*. Chicago, 1993.

Drake, Stillman. *Essays on Galileo and the History and Philosophy of Science*. Selected and introduced by N. M. Swerdlow and T. H. Levere. 3 vols. Toronto, 1999.

———. *Galileo at Work: His Intellectual Biography*. Chicago, 1978.

Redondi, Pietro. *Galileo: Heretic*. Translated by Raymond Rosenthal. Princeton, 1987.

EILEEN A. REEVES

GALLEYS. Galleys, oared seagoing vessels, had been warships since ancient times but became important in Mediterranean warfare between the fifteenth and eighteenth centuries. Around 1500 galleys were fitted with centerline hull-smashing cannons firing balls of thirty to fifty pounds, giving them firepower viable against contemporary sailing vessels like carracks. Although the last large-scale military use of galleys was at the 1571 Battle of Lepanto, they continued to be important in eastern Mediterranean littoral warfare through the eighteenth century. They were eventually outmoded by ships of the line with large artillery.

STRUCTURE, CAPABILITIES, AND MANPOWER

By the fifteenth century galleys were typically at least 120 to 150 feet in length with around 25 banks of oars and crews of 200 to 300 men. Galleys had cannon that could fire at close range. Boarding parties attacked enemy ships from bow spurs that had grappling hooks and boarding bridges. Although galleys grew in size during the seventeenth century, their numbers declined.

IMPORTANT MILITARY ENGAGEMENTS

The galley was ideal for coastal waters with variable winds and few great harbors capable of receiving large ships. It gave rise to a style of Mediterranean warfare characterized by the close integration of naval operations, amphibious warfare, and siege with few full-scale battles. The sixteenth century witnessed only a few major galley battles, notably at Prevesa in 1538, at Jerba (Djerba) in 1560, and at Lepanto in 1571. Although those were massive confrontations (Lepanto included at least 150,000 people on ships), their decisiveness has been a matter of controversy. Galley fleets could be rebuilt in a few months, but the logistical limitations of galleys prevented successful exploitation of the victories they achieved. After Piyale Pasha won at Jerba, for instance, he was not able to press his attack against the Venetian fleet. Two years after the cream of Ottoman galley forces were destroyed or captured at Lepanto, the reconstituted Ottoman fleet led by Uluç Ali conducted serious fleet operations along the Apulian coast. Control of the sea with galley fleets was always temporary and localized, making them tactical, more than strategic, assets.

THE END OF THE GALLEY ERA

Some of the last consequential galley confrontations took place between Venice and the Ottoman Empire in the War of 1714–1718, in which, after naval defeats by Ottoman galley forces at Corfu, Lemnos, and Cape Matapan, Venice had to leave the Morea (in modern Greece) according to the 1718 Treaty of Passarowitz. From a technical point of view, the galley was gradually supplanted by the ship of the line with its massive artillery and high freeboard. One French ship of the line, *Le Bon*, fought off thirty Spanish galleys. Advances in naval tactics and strategy that made ships of the line their centerpieces started to develop in the North Sea and the Atlantic during the early seventeenth century as a result of technological advances during the Anglo-Dutch wars that soon spread to the Mediterranean. Even the Ottoman navy, a traditional bastion of galleys, began acquiring ships of the line to replace galleys as their main warships by the mid-eighteenth century.

See also **Armada, Spanish; Lepanto, Battle of; Navy; Passarowitz, Peace of (1718); Shipbuilding and Navigation.**

BIBLIOGRAPHY

Guilmartin, John F., Jr. *Galleons and Galleys*. London, 2002.

———. *Gunpowder and Galleys*. London and New York, 1974.

ERNEST TUCKER

GALLICANISM. The term "Gallicanism," coined in the early nineteenth century, defines a conception of church-state relations that developed in early modern France and subsequently influenced other European countries. This conception, medieval in origin, was based on two principles: separation of powers, which protected the state from any intervention from the papacy, and constitutionalism, which submitted the pope to the authority of church canons. The word also applies to an interpretation of Catholicism that places the pope under the authority of the church represented by the general council and rejects his personal infallibility.

THE CONCORDAT OF BOLOGNA AND POLITICAL GALLICANISM

Negotiated in 1516, the Concordat of Bologna between Francis I and Pope Leo X formed the legal base of church-state relations in early modern France: the papacy gave the monarchy control of most benefices, bishoprics, and abbeys, whose titulars were appointed by the king and approved by Rome. The Parlement of Paris resisted the agreement on the ground of fidelity to ancient laws, or "Gallican liberties." After its forced registration (1518), legists defended these liberties in their writings, constituting a body of references that established political Gallicanism.

Reviving a medieval tradition of resistance to the papacy and state control of the church, these authors collected traditions and precedents that asserted the independence of the French church and of the kings. *Les libertés de l'église Gallicane* (1594; The liberties of the Gallican church), by Pierre Pithou, a lawyer in the Paris Parlement, was reprinted and commented on by Pierre and Jacques Dupuy in *Traité des droits et libertés de l'Église gallicane* (Treatise on the rights and liberties of the Gallican church) and *Preuves des droits et libertés de l'église Gallicane* (Proofs of the rights and liberties of the Gallican church), published in 1639; its arguments were extended by Pierre Toussaint Durand de Maillane in 1771. Though an attempt to impose as a fundamental article (law of the kingdom) the absolute independence of the king in secular matters was defeated by the clergy at a meeting of the Estates-General in 1615, this principle was accepted by all French canonists and theologians, though with a lesser extension than applied by legists and civil servants.

ECCLESIASTICAL GALLICANISM

Most French clerics shared the legists' respect for the ancient church, and they also sought state backing for the religious unification of the kingdom. However, they resented any form of lay control and needed papal authority to support the Catholic renewal that followed the Council of Trent. To counter this perceived shift from Gallican principles, Edmond Richer, the *syndic* (moderator) of the Sorbonne, the theological faculty of Paris, reissued works written during the conciliarist period by Pierre d'Ailly (1350–c. 1420), Jean Charlier (Jean de Gerson, 1363–1429), and Jacques Almain (c. 1480–1515). Richer's extreme views, as expressed in the 1612 pamphlet *Libellus de ecclesiastica et politica potestate* (Booklet on ecclesiastical and political power), were rejected at that time, but theological Gallicanism subsisted in the faculty, expressed in a succession of pronouncements, the most important of which are the six Articles of 1663, an exposition of official doctrine on papal authority, and the censure of the book of Jacques Vernant, also known as the Carmelite Bonavendute d'Hérédie (1612–1667), that defended papal infallibility.

By that time, another form of Gallicanism had developed, which was also the revival of an ancient model: episcopal Gallicanism. This concept derived from the question of Jansenism. The French bishops who had asked Rome to arbitrate on the issue of the Dutch theologian Cornelus Otto Jansen (Cornelius Jansenius, 1585–1638) and the "Five Propositions" attempted to balance their recourse to papal authority by the assertion of their own. Following the precedent of the early African church, they claimed to "receive," that is, to approve, the papal condemnation. As papal infallibility was also claimed to support these pronouncements, more Gallican resistance followed, rejecting this personal privilege.

These separate developments converged in the *Déclaration du Clergé de France sur la puissance ecclésiastique* (Declaration of the French clergy on ecclesiastical power; March 1682), formulated at Louis XIV's request, by a special assembly of the French clergy. The intention was to pressure Pope

Innocent XI on the dispute concerning the king's right *(regalia)* to administer a diocese during the vacancy of the see. Despite Louis's later recantation, the four articles of this declaration were to represent the official doctrine of the French church during the Old Regime.

The first article of the declaration concerned the separation of spiritual and secular powers, as noted above. The second admitted papal spiritual power but subjected it to the authority of general councils. The third article insisted that the exercise of papal power was regulated by the ancient canons and Gallican customs. The fourth acknowledged papal authority in matters of faith but rejected infallibility and demanded that in order to be irreformable his pronouncements receive the consent of the universal church.

LATER DEVELOPMENTS

In order to eradicate Jansenism, which had been revived by the works of Pasquier Quesnel (1634–1719), Louis XIV allied himself with pope Clement XI and secured the acceptation of the bull *Unigenitus* (1713). As some of the condemned propositions excerpted from the book dealt with Gallican principles, the issue of *Unigenitus* divided the Gallicans. On one side were the supporters of a condemnation requested by the king and accepted by the majority of bishops, on the other, those who rejected the censures and appealed to a future general council. From this perspective, a mutation happened that was to have serious consequence: Gallicanism divided into two branches. One, authoritarian Gallicanism, followed the hierarchical model and only transferred to the king or bishops the authority over the church claimed by the pope, being therefore a form of regalism or episcopalism. The other, participatory Gallicanism, reinterpreted the medieval concept, itself founded on Aristotle's *Politics*, which developed a democratic model structured on the notions of representation and reception. Representation is a process of formulation of truth that, starting from the community, moves through hierarchical authority in order to be expressed at the highest level; reception is the process of confirming and authenticating the decision. This reconstruction of classical university and parlement Gallicanism, applied first to the ecclesiastical structure, was soon transposed to the political level.

Though both reflected the 1682 articles, the two perspectives conflicted during the eighteenth century, ostensibly on the issue of Jansenism but in fact on that of absolutism, preparing the way for the French Revolution. The Civil Constitution of the Clergy, passed by the National Assembly in 1790, was an application of participatory Gallicanism developed by Bishop Henri Grégoire and other "constitutional" bishops. The concordat negotiated by Napoléon Bonaparte and the Holy See in 1801 marked a return to political Gallicanism, without the balancing weight of episcopal Gallicanism.

See also **Church and State Relations; Jansenism.**

BIBLIOGRAPHY

Blet, Pierre. *Le clergé du grand siècle en ses assemblées, 1615–1715.* Paris, 1995.

Bouwsma, William. "Gallicanism and the Nature of Christendom." In his *A Usable Past: Essays in European Cultural History.* Berkeley, 1990. pp. 308–324.

Gres-Gayer, Jacques M. *Le Gallicanisme de Sorbonne.* Paris, 2002.

Hayden, J. Michael. *France and the Estates General of 1614.* Cambridge, U.K., 1974.

Knecht, R. J. "The Concordat of 1516: A Reassessment." In *Government in Reformation Europe, 1520–1560.* Edited by Henry J. Cohn. London, 1971. Pp. 91–112.

Lecler, J. "Qu'est-ce que les libertés de l'église Gallicane?" *Revue des sciences religieuses* 22 (1932): 385–410, 542–568; 24 (1934): 47–87.

Martimort, Aimé Georges. *Le Gallicanisme,* Paris, 1973.

———. *Le Gallicanisme de Bossuet.* Paris, 1953.

Martin, Victor. *Le Gallicanisme et la réforme catholique.* Paris, 1919.

———. *Le Gallicanisme politique et le clergé de France.* Paris, 1929.

———. *Les origines du Gallicanisme.* Paris, 1939.

Nelson, Eric W. "Defining the Fundamental Laws of France: The Proposed First Article of the Third Estate at the French Estates General of 1614." *English Historical Review* 115 (2000): 1216–1230.

Powis, Jonathan. "Gallican Liberties and the Politics of Later Sixteenth-Century France." *Historical Journal* 26 (1983): 515–530.

Préclin, Emile. "Edmond Richer (1539–1631), sa vie, son oeuvre, le richérisme." *Revue d'histoire moderne* 55 (1930): 241–269, 321–336.

Puyol, Edmond. *Edmond Richer: Étude historique et critique sur la rénovation du Gallicanisme au commencement du XVIIe siècle.* 2 vols. Paris, 1876.

Van Kley, Dale K. *The Religious Origins of the French Revolution: From Calvin to the Civil Constitution, 1560–1791.* New Haven and London, 1996.

JACQUES M. GRES-GAYER

GAMA, VASCO DA (c. 1469–1524), Portuguese explorer, first count of Vidigueira, and "discoverer" of the sea route to India. Vasco da Gama was born in the Alentejo coastal town of Sines about 1469. His family had longstanding service ties to the crown in its struggles against Castile and Islam, and Vasco's father, Estevão, had won grants, including the post of *alcaide-mor* (governor-major) of Sines, for these services. He also became a commandery holder, or possessor of a revenue-generating land grant, in the powerful Order of Santiago, thus elevating the family's social and economic status, a process that would culminate with the career of his son. King João II (ruled 1481–1495) may have asked Estevão to undertake the search for an all-water trade route between Europe and India, but he died before he could make the voyage.

Not much is known about the early years of Vasco da Gama's life. He received a solid education in nautical matters and had also demonstrated martial skills in campaigns against Castile. In 1492, King João II had selected da Gama to confiscate French shipping in the ports of the Algarve, in retaliation for the French seizure of a Portuguese ship returning from Africa loaded with gold, and he accomplished this task with "great brevity."

In 1497, King Manuel (ruled 1495–1521) selected da Gama to command the epic expedition to India that successfully ended the search for a sea route to Asian spices begun during the days of the Portuguese Prince Henry the Navigator (1394–1460). Some say that Vasco's brother, Paulo, was first offered the opportunity but turned it down. The four-ship fleet (*São Gabriel, São Rafael, Berrio,* and a stores ship) departed Lisbon on 8 July 1497 with 170 men aboard. After stopping at São Tiago (27 July–3 August) in the Cape Verde Islands, da Gama and his fleet headed out into the Atlantic to exploit the prevailing winds. On 8 November, the fleet reached Santa Helena Bay, and on the 22 November rounded the Cape of Good Hope. In the Indian Ocean, da Gama confronted the entrenched economic power of the Arabs. This religious and economic hostility complicated his task along the East African coast during a stay at Mozambique island (March 1498), and especially at Mombasa (April 1498), where the local sultan sought to storm the fleet in a midnight raid. Da Gama received a more favorable reception at Malindi, obtaining a skilled pilot who guided the Portuguese fleet across the Arabian Sea to the pepper-rich Malabar coast of India by May 1498. His mission of arranging both a treaty and the purchase of pepper in the key port city of Calicut was complicated by the intrigues of Arab merchants with the local Hindu ruler, the Zamorin (Samudri), and da Gama's rather paltry gifts. Nevertheless, his resolve overcame these problems, and he departed in August with a respectable cargo of spices. Although the return trip to Portugal was complicated by fickle winds, the *Berrio* and *São Gabriel* reached Lisbon in July and August 1499, respectively. Da Gama, after burying his brother Paulo on Terceira in the Azores, reached home in September. He received the right to use the prestigious title "Dom," a hefty annual pension, and

Vasco da Gama. NEW YORK PUBLIC LIBRARY PICTURE COLLECTION

other rewards, including the title admiral of the Indian Seas.

To avenge the massacre of Portuguese factors left at Calicut by the fleet of Pedro Álvares Cabral (1500–1501), in 1502 King Manuel dispatched twenty well-armed ships under da Gama. He used this formidable force to intimidate the sultan of Kilwa on the east African coast into fealty (July 1502), to intercept Muslim shipping arriving on the Indian coast, and to inflict a decisive defeat on an Arab fleet in the service of the Zamorin (February 1503). His ruthless nature was revealed on this voyage when he burned several hundred Muslim pilgrims alive aboard a captured ship in September 1502. He returned to Lisbon in October 1503 and received additional rewards. During the following two decades, da Gama labored in Portugal to consolidate his social and economic position. His marriage to Dona Catarina de Ataíde produced seven children, and, despite problems with the mercurial King Manuel, da Gama at last entered the ranks of the senhorial elite in 1519 when he was created the first count of Vidigueira.

By 1524, although the Portuguese empire in Asia stretched from Mozambique to Indonesia, corruption had begun to infiltrate this impressive imperial edifice. The young king, John III, appointed Vasco viceroy in that year to address these problems. Sailing with fourteen ships in April 1524, da Gama reached India in September and undertook an impressive reform campaign that was tragically cut short by his death at Calicut on Christmas Eve 1524.

Da Gama's life and career mirrored the rise of Portugal: nautical expertise, military prowess, ruthlessness, and religious conviction entrenched his personal and familial fortune while Portugal, at the same time, achieved its Golden Age.

See also **Camões, Luís Vaz de; Exploration; Portugal; Portuguese Colonies: The Indian Ocean and Asia.**

BIBLIOGRAPHY

Ames, Glenn J. *Portuguese Pilgrim: The Life and Career of Vasco da Gama.* New York, 2003.

Subrahmanyam, Sanjay. *The Career and Legend of Vasco da Gama.* Cambridge, U.K., 1997.

Teixeira de Aragão, A. C. *Vasco da Gama e a Vidigueira.* Lisbon, 1871.

Velho, Alvaro. *A Journal of the First Voyage of Vasco da Gama, 1497–1499.* Translated and edited by E. G. Ravenstein. London, 1898.

GLENN J. AMES

GAMBLING. From the early medieval period, various forms of gambling were popular at every level of society, although the types of games played, as well as the freedom to indulge in them, was dependent on an individual's position in the social hierarchy, and subject to sustained criticism from both church and state. Blood sports such as bearbaiting and cockfighting were popular among the peasantry, and regular contests, accompanied by heavy betting, drinking, and general revelry, were a traditional part of community life.

At the other end of the social spectrum, horse racing was a pastime confined to the upper classes. The ownership and racing of horses operated within a system of royal patronage, with successive monarchs—most notably, Charles II of England (ruled 1660–1685), "the father of the British turf"—organizing races and entering horses to compete in their name. Betting was a strictly private affair conducted among the aristocracy, who regarded participation in the sport as their exclusive right.

Lotteries began during the fifteenth century, and, although popular, were governed by politically expedient legislation that made participation irregular and often arbitrarily illegal. The most widespread form of gambling, however, was dice playing, which endured as the standard game of the entire medieval period. The most ancient and simple form of gambling, it was pursued assiduously by all sections of society—including the clergy—despite being subject to innumerable bans and prohibitions. The Saxons, Danes, and Romans all introduced their own varieties of games and their own styles of playing, although most games tended to fall into one of two types: either based on moving counters around boards (such as the Spanish *alquerque,* a game similar to checkers), or guessing games based on dice throws (such as hazard). Playing cards were introduced into Europe from the East toward the end of the thirteenth century, where they grew, over the next three hundred years, from an elite pastime into a leisure activity popular with every social class.

Gambling. *The Card Players,* seventeenth-century engraving by David Teniers II. ©CORBIS

Their route of entry is uncertain: some have suggested that Marco Polo brought them back from his travels in Cathay, while others believe they were introduced by Gypsies or returning Crusaders. Whatever the case, the first mentions of cards in Europe come from Italy in 1299, from Spain in 1371, from the Low Countries (modern Belgium, Luxembourg, and Netherlands) in 1379, and from Germany in 1380. By 1465, they were sufficiently well established in Britain to be subject to an import ban.

These early cards were crafted by hand on copper and ivory as well as card and wood, usually by professional painters who found patronage in aristocratic households. The first woodcuts on paper were, in fact, playing cards. (The term *Kartenmahler* or *Kartenmacher,* 'painter' or 'maker of cards', appears in German in 1402.) At first, their expense put cards out of reach of all but the wealthiest in society, with the result that widespread playing was initially restricted to the upper classes. Gambling was fashionable among this group, with high-stakes "betting orgies" frequently lasting for days and serving as a marker of status and prestige as much as a straightforward leisure pursuit. Cards and games were symbolic systems that represented the cultural climate and social order that surrounded them. Medieval card games such as *brelan, pair, gleek,* and *primero* were based on the principals of "melds" and "murnivals"—pairing and joining cards in ranks—reflecting the hierarchical social organization, represented as the "great chain of being" in the Middle Ages.

The development of the printing press in the fifteenth century was crucial to the history of cards, transforming them from the playthings of the aristocracy into mass-produced commodities enjoyed by all ranks of society. The presses also gave cards the name they still have today. The medieval Latin *charta,* 'sheet of paper', was taken as shorthand for the playing cards, which were, for a time, the presses' main industry. The word survives as the standard term for cards throughout Europe, variously as *cart, carte, Karte, karta,* and *kartya.*

Despite its widespread popularity, attempts were continually made by both church and state to limit or outlaw gambling. Although ostensibly designed to curb the excesses of the general population, most legislation targeted the poor and was uneven in its application. Initially, prohibitions imposed by the Catholic Church were pragmatic and aimed at steering the population away from sedentary activities that were seen to encourage idleness and toward more organized exertions, such as sports. Ultimately, the aim was to create a fit workforce that could be easily rallied into an indigenous army, a definite advantage in the violent climate of the Middle Ages. As such, various edicts attempted to regulate gambling according to social position. From the time of the Crusades, dicing by any soldier below the rank of knight was forbidden.

Cardplaying on workdays had been banned since 1397, and was further outlawed when a statute of Henry VIII (ruled 1509–1547) confined all gambling among the working population to Christmas, the assumption being that, as they would be celebrating anyway, its disruptive effects would be minimal. After the Reformation, attempts to outlaw gambling were dramatically increased by the Protestant bourgeoisie, who objected to it on the ideological grounds that it undermined the work ethic and squandered time and money.

Criticism continued throughout the Enlightenment, when the emphasis shifted to the disorderly effects of gambling within rational society—again, aimed primarily at the poor. Across the continent, legislation during the seventeenth and eighteenth centuries attempted to remove gambling from the mass of the population, primarily by fiscal means: imposing taxes on cards and dice, charging hefty entrance fees for horse races, and increasing the price of lottery tickets.

At the same time, many European countries introduced laws limiting public gambling to licensed premises, while restricting the granting of licenses to members of the nobility and upper classes. The result of such legislation was the stratification of public betting and the effective outlawing of gambling for the majority of the population, with the poor restricted to playing in illegal, unlicensed taverns, and the upper classes free to indulge in a wide variety of games with impunity.

See also **Class, Status, and Order; Games and Play; Lottery; Printing and Publishing; Roma (Gypsies); Sports.**

BIBLIOGRAPHY

Ashton, John. *The History of Gambling in England.* Montclair, N.J., 1969. Originally published in 1898.

Cotton, Charles. *The Compleat Gamester.* London, 1674.

Kavanagh, Thomas. *Enlightenment and the Shadows of Chance: The Novel and the Culture of Gambling in Eighteenth-Century France.* Baltimore and London, 1993.

Reith, Gerda. *The Age of Chance: Gambling in Western Culture.* London and New York, 1999.

GERDA REITH

GAMES AND PLAY. The types of games and amusements played in early modern times ran the gamut from physical games of an athletic nature to sedentary games, like cards, which were enormously popular. Some amusements were pursued outdoors, in parks and gardens, while others were more properly confined to interior spaces. The standard edition of François Rabelais's *Gargantua* (1542) lists some 217 sports and parlor and table games, many of which were played at times of celebration and feasting. This popular aspect of play continued throughout the period, although the rise of domesticity and new concepts of the family constrained the universalizing tendencies of communal amusement, bringing games principally into the private sphere. While members of every social class played at times, play was of central importance to the noble lifestyle.

PLAY AND THE NOBILITY

The noble class of early modern Europe defined itself through warfare and leisure. Since the Middle Ages, male members of the nobility had used physical games to train for battle in times of peace. Cards and chess, often played between the sexes, additionally taught skills of strategy thought to be useful both on the battlefield and in affairs of the heart. Games and behavior at play reinforced the principles of courtly love.

From the sixteenth century onward, as the nobleman's role on the battlefield began to wane and more time was spent distinguishing oneself through codes of behavior, play became of central importance in the daily life of the elite. It was how members of the nobility spent a large portion of their day. Indeed, some scholars consider the persona of the courtier to have been invented within a framework of play.

Early modern games served an important pedagogical function, at least in terms of sociability. Conversational games—often called games of society—were a staple of noble culture, teaching many of the verbal and behavioral skills needed to survive at court. Baldassare Castiglione's *Book of the Courtier* (written between 1513 and 1524)—a book that was regarded as a handbook of behavior and a model for all future treatises on the topic throughout Europe—uses this type of game to structure a definition of the ideal attributes of a courtier. It is not only the qualities described that teach the reader, but also the example of the players who demonstrate how the games of court are played.

GAMBLING AND CARD GAMES

Dating back to medieval times, cards had long been a favorite evening occupation in court circles. This proclivity grew into a mania during the late seventeenth and eighteenth centuries, particularly in France, but also in other parts of Europe. English gentlemen on the grand tour were warned not to play in Paris, because so many young men had been fleeced by both upper-class and lower-class players. Moreover, the social problem of the gaming house expanded dramatically at this time in spite of numerous regulations and penalties designed to eliminate its existence.

The vice of gambling increasingly became a point of concern, and was believed by many to be the chief cause of moral and physical degeneration among the nobility. Much was made of the damaging effects of the dark, cavernous spaces that gamblers occupied while playing, and the sedentary requirements of play were blamed for all sorts of ailments. As an alternative to this vice, philosophers, moralists, and physicians encouraged people to play outdoors at amusements designed to exercise the body and liberate the soul. Moderately active forms of play, like swinging, were recommended as appropriate for the delicate, noble disposition.

In their card games, the nobility greatly preferred games of chance to those involving skill. Many scholars attribute this preference to the courtly idea of disinterest—to practice and employ strategies at cards would suggest that the player was overly concerned with the consequences of play, which often involved the loss of considerable sums. During the eighteenth century, as more members of the bourgeoisie began to play alongside the nobility, the aim of being an expert player became more pronounced. Treatises on play became a virtual cottage industry throughout Europe. Games of luck increasingly gave way to games of skill, as books written by the Englishman Edmund Hoyle (1672–1769) taught players strategies by which the whims of chance could be overcome.

PLAY AND CHILDHOOD

There were few distinctions between the games of childhood and adulthood. Noble children were taught games of chance at an early age, particularly as they would be expected to take a seat at gaming tables later in life. Amusements that are now considered childish—swinging, for instance—were enjoyed by people of all ages. The game of blindman's buff, which had been played by the kings of Europe in the sixteenth and seventeenth centuries, was made popular once again by Marie-Antoinette, queen of France in the final years of the Old Regime.

During the seventeenth and eighteenth centuries, however, new concepts of childhood caused moralists and philosophers to turn their attention to the safeguarding of children. Treatises on the subject of children's upbringing discussed the need to prohibit "evil" games (namely those related to gaming) and to encourage "good" games (often referring to simple, outdoor amusements or games that could be modified to teach useful lessons). Enlightenment notions of the child and work, in particular, changed the way that play was understood at the end of the period.

Children's play began to be conceptualized as something distinct and separate from that of adults. It also became an important part of the child's edu-

Games and Play. *Children's Games,* by Pieter Bruegel the Elder, 1560 (detail). ©FRANCIS G. MAYER/CORBIS

cation, different from the behavioral pedagogy that play had traditionally taught. The English philosopher John Locke theorized in *Some Thoughts concerning Education* (1693) that children would be more inclined to learn their lessons when play was built into the curriculum. If the child preferred to play with tops, he proposed, then properties of physics could be taught through that amusement.

Such ideas revolutionized pedagogical thought across Europe. Games that had once been designed to convey the principles of courtly love, such as the French board game known as the *jeu de l'oie* (game of the goose), were transformed to teach lessons in history. Similarly, cards that had been used in games of chance, played as a social obligation and expectation of class, became tools for teaching mathematics and improving memory.

At the same time, the notion of free play—that is, play that stimulated the body without specific pedagogical purpose—developed in tandem with the "new" child created by the Enlightenment. The French philosopher Jean-Jacques Rousseau's educational tract *Émile* (1762) discusses numerous games and amusements appropriate for the child at different ages, and it also puts its emphasis on the physical benefits of play. Émile (the child created by Rousseau in his book) whips a top, but he learns nothing from the process. Instead Rousseau focuses on the exercise—the strengthened arm and eye—that results.

PLAY AND ART

Leisure pursuits are a recurring subject in the visual arts, yet the specific theme of play reached a height of popularity during the early modern era. Some scholars have explained this rise in terms of audience. As a middle class came into existence, a new interest in familiar subject matter—scenes of daily life, as opposed to grand and often obscure mythological or historical stories—developed. Other scholars situate this change of preference firmly within the outlook of the aristocracy. A new emphasis on sociability in court culture altered the taste of noble viewers, who desired images reflecting their class-defining behavior.

Favorite play subjects of the Renaissance and baroque were scenes of bawdy behavior caused by gaming disputes, like the tavern brawls of the Flemish painter David Teniers the younger (1610–1690), or card sharps, such as the gypsy cheats depicted by Caravaggio (1573–1610) and Georges de La Tour (1593–1652). In general, the characters in these scenes were members of the lower classes, rather than the middle-class or noble beholders who bought these works of art. Art historians attribute this difference to a focus on ignoble behavior, which served to distance the intended viewers from their base counterparts.

Rococo images of play, in contrast, tend to picture images of polite play by noble participants. Few images depict the real-life mania of gaming. Instead, images of swinging, blindman's buff, seesaws, and other outdoor amusements were preferred—Jean-Honoré Fragonard's *Happy Hazards of the Swing* (1767; Wallace Collection, London) is the paradigmatic example. The emblematics of these scenes are largely related to the pleasures and hazards of love, and art history has tended to judge such images as a reflection of aristocratic frivolity. Recent research, however, finds the style of the rococo to be inherently playful—employing serpentine forms and harmonies of color that keep the eye in continual motion. This emphasis on visual play coincides with the discernment of a "play impulse" in aesthetic philosophy, whereby writers such as Immanuel Kant (1724–1804) and Friedrich Schiller (1759–1805) conceptualized the ideal aesthetic experience as a free play of the mind, without motive or purpose.

See also **Aristocracy and Gentry; Childhood and Childrearing; Court and Courtiers; Festivals; Gambling; Locke, John; Rousseau, Jean-Jacques.**

BIBLIOGRAPHY

Ariès, Philippe. *Centuries of Childhood: A Social History of Family Life.* Translated by Robert Baldick. New York, 1962.

Bakhtin, Mikhail. *Rabelais and His World.* Translated by Hélène Iswolsky. Bloomington, Ind., 1984.

Barolsky, Paul. *Infinite Jest: Wit and Humor in Italian Renaissance Art.* Columbia, Mo., 1978.

Black, Jeremy. *The British Abroad: The Grand Tour in the Eighteenth Century.* New York, 1992.

Isherwood, Robert M. *Farce and Fantas: Popular Entertainment in Eighteenth-Century Paris.* New York and Oxford, 1986.

Lanham, Richard A. "The Self as Middle Style: Cortegiano." In *The Motives of Eloquence: Literary Rhetoric in the Renaissance.* New Haven and London, 1976.

Motley, Mark. *Becoming a French Aristocrat: The Education of the Court Nobility, 1580–1715.* Princeton, 1990.

Schalk, Ellery. *From Valor to Pedigree: Ideas of Nobility in France in the Sixteenth and Seventeenth Centuries.* Princeton, 1986.

Stafford, Barbara Maria. *Artful Science: Enlightenment Entertainment and the Eclipse of Visual Education.* London and Cambridge, Mass., 1994.

JENNIFER D. MILAM

GARDENS AND PARKS. Long appreciated for their formal and botanical contents, the gardens and parks of early modern Europe were also products of complex historical forces and conditions. Between the mid-fifteenth and late eighteenth centuries, major trends included increasing integration of architecture and garden design; an increasing dominance of axial composition and bilateral symmetry; new emphasis on visual integration between gardens and the surrounding landscape; and, in the eighteenth century, the emergence and development of irregular design.

In Renaissance Italy, developments in garden design were greatly influenced by the rise of humanist culture and the emergence of urban-based elites. Literary works such as the *Ten Books on Architecture* (1452; published 1485), by Leon-Battista Alberti (1404–1472), and the *Hypnerotomachia Poliphili* (1499), attributed to the monk Francesco Colonna (1433–1527), promoted rural life and antiquarianism while describing alternatives to the medieval *hortus conclusus,* 'enclosed garden'. In garden design, humanist interests were discernible in new emphases on geometry, harmony, and spatial integration, in keeping with the principles of Vitruvius Pollio's *Ten Books on Architecture* (first century B.C.E., the sole treatise on architecture to survive from Roman antiquity); in forms drawn from literary descriptions of ancient gardens, such as those found in the letters of Pliny the Younger (first century C.E.), and from archaeological sites, such as the Temple of Fortuna Primigenia (80 B.C.E.) at

Gardens and Parks. La Salle des Festins in the gardens of the Château de Versailles c. 1688; painting by Etienne Allegrain. THE ART ARCHIVE/MUSÉE DU CHÂTEAU DE VERSAILLES/DAGLI ORTI

Gardens and Parks. South parterre at the Palace of Versailles, with gardens designed by André Le Notre. ©ADAM WOOLFITT/ CORBIS

Praeneste (modern Palestrina), east of Rome; and in arrangements that reflected scientific interests in the collection, classification, and management of natural specimens. *Villeggiatura,* 'retreat to country life', practiced by urban elites such as the Medici of Florence and the papal court in Rome, led to the development of important villa complexes in the vicinities of Italy's major urban centers. Notable examples include the Medici villas at Fiesole (c. 1455), Pratolino (1560), and other settings near Florence, many of which were depicted in lunette panels by the Flemish painter Giusto Utens (d. 1609); the Villa d'Este, Tivoli (begun in 1550), by the architect and antiquarian Pirro Ligorio (c. 1500–1583); the Villa Lante, Bagnaia (begun in 1564), attributed to the architect Giacomo da Vignola (born Giacomo Barozzi, 1507–1573); the mannerist Villa Orsini, Bomarzo, Lazio (1552–1580); and the Villa Aldobrandini, Frascati (1598–1603).

The ideas and practices cultivated in Italy spread north to France beginning in the late fifteenth century, in part through the diffusion of texts and images and in part through the migration of patrons, artists, and technicians. During the reign of Francis I (ruled 1494–1547), the royal château at Fontainebleau became a major center of artistic innovation, dominated first by Italian artists and later by native Frenchmen. Typical features of Renaissance garden design in France included large compartmentalized planting beds arranged in geometric patterns; elaborate arbors and trelliswork galleries; and prominent, classically themed fountains and sculptures. The integration of architecture and garden design pursued in Italy was initially resisted in France. For example, at Blois (begun c. 1500) and Gaillon (begun in 1506)—among many important sites represented in Jacques Androuet du Cerceau's *Les plus excellents bastiments de France* (1576–1579)—the main gardens were surrounded by walls and completely detached from the residential buildings. Greater integration and openness were found at Saint-Germain-en-Laye (new château and terrace

Gardens and Parks. A pavilion designed by Jules Hardouin-Mansart in 1673 is a feature of the gardens of the Château de Dampierre in western France. THE ART ARCHIVE/DAGLI ORTI

gardens begun c. 1550) and the Tuileries (1564–1572), the latter having been created at the edge of Paris for Henry II's wife, Catherine de Médicis (1519–1589). Important examples of Renaissance design elsewhere in the north included the gardens created for Henry VIII at Hampton Court Palace (1531–1534), west of London; designs published by the Netherlands painter and engineer Hans Vredeman de Vries (1527–c. 1606) in his *Hortorum viridariorumque* (1587); and the Hortus Palatinus, Heidelberg (c. 1615), by the architect and engineer Salomon de Caus (1576–1626).

Beginning around the turn of the seventeenth century, the scale and visual organization of elite gardens and parks began to increase throughout Europe, reflecting the growing power of centralized forms of governments and the rising importance of scientific culture with its emphasis on visual perception. In and around Rome, those developments were reflected in the formation of substantial estate properties by papal families, most notably the Villa Borghese (1606–1633) and the Villa Pamphili (1630–1670). In France, the scale and visual power of axial design were expanded to unforeseen extremes in the work of André Lenôtre (1613–1700), first for Louis XIV's minister of finance Nicolas Fouquet (1615–1680) at Vaux-le-Vicomte (1656–1661) and subsequently for the king himself at Versailles (begun in 1663). The construction of such gardens required vast natural, technical, and human labor resources. Their realization drew upon expertise developed in military and civil engineering, and their forms referred implicitly to the power of their patrons to manipulate resources on regional and territorial scales. Versailles became a model for princely gardens throughout Europe, impossible to duplicate but nevertheless often emulated, with guidance from Dézallier d'Argenville's *La théorie et la pratique du jardinage* (first published in 1709). Noteworthy examples included the renovations at Hampton Court (begun in 1689) and Chatsworth (1690–1703) in England; Het Loo (begun in 1686; enlarged 1692) in the Netherlands; Drottningholm (begun during the 1680s), near Stockholm; the Peterhof (1713–1725), St. Petersburg; La Granja (1719–1740), San Ildefonso, Spain; and Caserta (1752–1754), near Naples.

The dominance of regular design was first challenged in England through influential writings about nature and irregular form by Anthony Ashley Cooper, 3rd earl of Shaftesbury (1671–1713), the essayist and statesman Joseph Addison (1672–1719), the theorist and designer Stephen Switzer (1682–1745), and the poet Alexander Pope (1688–1744). During the first half of the eighteenth century, a new approach emerged in which axial composition was replaced by forms that were ostensibly more natural although, in truth, equally artificial. The English version of irregular design—demonstrated at properties such as Castle Howard (begun in 1701), Stourhead (1735–1783), and Painshill (1738–1771)—privileged broad views and drew inspiration, in part, from landscape paintings by Claude Lorrain (born Claude Gellée, 1600–1682), Gaspard Poussin (born Gaspard Dughet, 1615–1675), and Salvator Rosa (1615–1673). Designers such as Charles Bridgeman (d. 1738), William Kent (c. 1686–1748), and Lancelot "Capability" Brown (1715–1783) made frequent use of the ha-ha, a sunken fence that facilitated visual integration between the estate garden and the larger landscape. Important examples include Stowe (c. 1715–c. 1776), Kent's designs for Chiswick (c. 1730) and Rousham (1738), and the renovated grounds of Blenheim Palace (begun in 1764). Investigations of irregular design began to take place on the Continent during the last third of the eighteenth century, most notably in and around Paris, where the approach flourished in gardens such as Ermenonville (begun in 1766), the Jardin de Monceau (c. 1771–1789), the Désert de Retz (1774–1794), and the Petit Trianon at Versailles (1774). Most French examples bore little resemblance to English precedents, being of smaller scale and considerably more eclectic. They nevertheless proved equally influential in the diffusion of irregular design throughout the Continent. Eventually, many of the gardens around Paris also contributed to the rise of public parks through their confiscation and use as festival spaces during the French Revolution.

See also **Architecture; Britain, Architecture in; City Planning; Estates and Country Houses; France, Architecture in; Rome, Architecture in.**

BIBLIOGRAPHY

Benes, Miroslava, and Dianne Harris, ed. *Villas and Gardens in Early Modern Italy and France.* New York, 2001.

Hunt, John Dixon, and Peter Willis, ed. *The Genius of the Place: The English Landscape Garden, 1620–1820.* London, 1975.

Laird, Mark. *The Formal Garden: Traditions of Art and Nature.* New York, 1992.

Mosser, Monique, and Georges Teyssot, eds. *The Architecture of Western Gardens: A Design History from the Renaissance to the Present Day.* Cambridge, Mass., 1991.

Thacker, Christopher. *The History of Gardens.* Berkeley, 1979.

David L. Hays

GASSENDI, PIERRE (1592–1655), French Catholic priest and philosopher. Born in Provence on 22 January 1592, Gassendi was admitted to the clerical state in 1604 and received his doctor of theology degree at the University of Avignon in 1614. He studied philosophy and theology at the college of Aix-en-Provence, where he later taught from 1616 to 1622. He published his first book, *Exercitationes Paradoxicae adversus Aristoteleos,* in 1624, a work in which he criticized Aristotelianism by using the skeptical arguments of the ancient philosopher Sextus Empiricus (fl. c. 200 C.E.). Having rejected Aristotelianism, Gassendi undertook the task of creating a new, complete philosophy, one that included the three traditional areas: logic, physics, and ethics. Writing in the style of the Renaissance humanists, Gassendi chose the ancient atomist and hedonist Epicurus (341–271 B.C.E.) as his model. Before European intellectuals could accept the philosophy of Epicurus, it had to be purged of various heterodox notions, such as materialism and the denial of creation and providence.

Gassendi worked on his Epicurean project from the 1620s until his death. The massive, posthumous *Syntagma Philosophicum* (1658) is the culmination of this project. It consists of three parts: "The Logic," "The Physics," and "The Ethics." In "The Logic," Gassendi presented his theory of knowledge, which he had first articulated in the *Exercitationes.* His empiricist theory of knowledge was an outgrowth of his response to skepticism. Accepting the skeptical critique of sensory knowledge, he denied that we can have certain knowledge of the real essences of things. Rather than falling into skeptical despair, however, he argued that we can acquire knowledge of the way things appear to us. This "science of appearances" is based on sensory experience and can only attain probability. It can, nonetheless, provide knowledge useful for living in the world. Gassendi denied the existence of essences in either the Platonic or Aristotelian sense and identified himself as a nominalist.

In "The Physics," Gassendi presented a Christianized version of Epicurean atomism. Like Epicurus, he claimed that the physical world consists of indivisible atoms moving in void space. Unlike the ancient atomist, Gassendi argued that there exists only a finite, though very large, number of atoms, that God created these atoms, and that the resulting world is ruled by divine providence rather than blind chance. Deeply involved in the natural philosophy of his time, Gassendi tried to provide atomistic explanations of all the phenomena in the world, including the qualities of things, inanimate bodies, plants, and animals. In contrast to Epicurus's materialism, Gassendi enriched his atomism by arguing for the existence of an immaterial, immortal soul. He also believed in the existence of angels and demons. His theology was voluntarist, emphasizing God's freedom to impose his will on the creation.

Adopting the hedonistic ethics of Epicurus, which sought to maximize pleasure and minimize pain, Gassendi reinterpreted the concept of pleasure in a distinctly Christian way. He believed that God endowed humans with free will and an innate desire for pleasure. Thus, by utilizing the calculus of pleasure and pain and by exercising their ability to make free choices, they participate in God's providential plans for the creation. The greatest pleasure humans can attain is the beatific vision of God after death. Based on his hedonistic ethics, Gassendi's political philosophy was a theory of the social contract, a view that influenced the writings of Hobbes and Locke. His emphasis on free will—both human and divine—led him to reject astrology, which he considered absurd, and other forms of divination that entailed any kind of hard determinism in the world.

Gassendi was an active participant in the philosophical and natural philosophical communities of his day. He corresponded with Galileo during his troubles with the church, and interacted with both Hobbes and Descartes. He conducted experiments on various topics in natural philosophy, wrote extensively about astronomy, corresponded with important natural philosophers, and wrote a treatise defending Galileo's new science of motion. Gassendi's version of the mechanical philosophy rivaled that of Descartes, with whom he engaged in an extensive controversy following the publication of the latter's *Meditations* in 1641.

Gassendi's philosophy was promulgated in England in several books published in the 1650s by Walter Charleton (1620–1707) and in France by François Bernier's *Abrégé de la philosophie de Gassendi* (1674). A younger generation of natural philosophers, including Robert Boyle (1627–1690) and Isaac Newton (1642–1727), who accepted the mechanical philosophy, faced a choice between Gassendi's atomism and Descartes's plenism. John Locke (1632–1704) absorbed many of Gassendi's ideas about epistemology and ethics, which thus had considerable influence on the subsequent development of empiricist epistemology and liberal political philosophy.

See also **Aristotelianism; Astronomy; Boyle, Robert; Cartesianism; Charleton, Walter; Descartes, René; Determinism; Empiricism; Epistemology; Free Will; Galileo Galilei; Hobbes, Thomas; Humanists and Humanism; Locke, John; Logic; Mechanism; Natural Philosophy; Neoplatonism; Newton, Isaac; Philosophy; Physics; Political Philosophy; Reason; Scientific Method; Scientific Revolution; Skepticism: Academic and Pyrrhonian.**

BIBLIOGRAPHY

Primary Sources

Gassendi, Pierre. *Opera Omnia.* Lyon, 1658; reprinted Stuttgart-Bad Canstatt, 1964.

———. *The Selected Works of Pierre Gassendi.* Translated by Craig Brush. New York, 1972.

Secondary Sources

Osler, Margaret J. *Divine Will and the Mechanical Philosophy: Gassendi and Descartes on Contingency and Necessity in the Created World.* Cambridge, U.K., and New York, 1994.

Sarasohn, Lisa T. *Gassendi's Ethics: Freedom in a Mechanistic Universe.* Ithaca, N.Y., 1996.

MARGARET J. OSLER

GATTINARA, MERCURINO (1465–1530), grand chancellor of the Holy Roman Empire. Mercurino Arborio de Gattinara was born to a noble family in the town of Vercelli, in the territory of Savoy (northern Italy). He received an excellent humanist education, followed by rigorous training in Roman law; the works of Justinian I (ruled 527–565) and Dante (1265–1321) had a particular impact on him. In 1502 he entered the service of Margaret of Austria (1480–1530), archduchess of Savoy and daughter of Holy Roman Emperor Maximilian I (ruled 1493–1519). From this point on Gattinara tied his fortunes to those of the house of Habsburg. In 1507 he accompanied Margaret to the Netherlands, where she ruled as regent. From 1508 to 1518 Gattinara acted as Margaret's chief legal adviser and president of Burgundy, an important administrative position. During this period Gattinara was exposed to Burgundian courtly and chivalric traditions, which would be an important influence on his intellectual development. In the Netherlands he also met Margaret's nephew Charles (1500–1558)—the future Spanish king (as Charles I, ruled 1516–1556) and Holy Roman emperor (as Charles V, ruled 1519–1556)—to whom Gattinara devoted the rest of his life.

In 1518 Charles appointed Gattinara his grand chancellor, a position of great responsibility in both foreign and domestic affairs. For the next twelve years Gattinara was one of Charles's closest advisers. He often traveled with Charles's itinerant court, following his master as he visited the various lands of his multinational empire. In Spain, Gattinara reformed the government's administrative structure and helped create the conciliar system that served the Spanish monarchy for the next several centuries. But Gattinara's greatest legacy was his contribution to the development of a Habsburg ideology of empire.

Gattinara was greatly responsible for the theory and practice of Charles V's empire. He wove together Roman imperial concepts, Burgundian chivalric traditions, and Christian ideology borrowed from his Dutch contemporary Desiderius Erasmus (1466?–1536) to create a new understanding of empire, focused on the unique character of Charles V's reign. Through dynastic inheritance, Charles acquired an unprecedented empire that stretched from the Low Countries to Vienna, and thanks to Christopher Columbus and the conquistadores, he also ruled an entire "New World." Many of Charles's subjects, particularly Gattinara, perceived divine intervention in these circumstances. Gattinara saw Charles as a man destined to unite Christendom, defeat the Muslim infidels, and create the earthly paradise. Gattinara wrote a number of propagandistic tracts that cited Scripture as well as classical and legal texts, claiming that Charlemagne (Charles the Great) was about to be outdone by his namesake Charles the Greater and that God was on his side.

It is not clear to what extent Charles himself subscribed to these notions. But it is evident that the emperor heeded Gattinara's advice about the importance of Italy as the strategic and symbolic foundation of his empire. Gattinara revived Ghibellinism, the medieval Italian belief that the Holy Roman emperor represented the highest authority in Europe, particularly in Italy, even including the papacy. He emphasized to Charles that control of Italy was vital to the security and the legitimacy of his empire and that anyone who challenged that hegemony must be crushed. Charles's foreign policies clearly reflected this conviction; in his famous "Political Instructions" to his son Philip II (ruled 1556–1598), he too stressed the importance of Italy for the Spanish Empire.

Gattinara and Charles did not always agree on everything. In the period 1522–1525 Gattinara attempted to broaden the executive powers of his office and exert greater influence over the young emperor, causing a strain in the relationship. In 1526 Gattinara became so angry about a proposed peace treaty with King Francis I of France (ruled 1515–

1547), arguing that Charles should put his trust in Italian princes rather than the slippery Francis, that he refused to affix the chancellery seals to the document. The following year he left the court altogether. Nevertheless Gattinara continued to have an impact on Charles's policies. He had encouraged Charles to think of Pope Clement VII (reigned 1523–1534) as a political antagonist rather than a spiritual leader, an attitude that became useful after imperial troops sacked Rome (1527). Gattinara was responsible for much of the imperial propaganda that followed this event, which argued that the papacy deserved what it got by opposing Charles. Gattinara, however, was also instrumental in arranging the Treaty of Barcelona (1529), which healed the rift between Charles and Clement. The pope was so pleased with Gattinara's assistance that he made him a cardinal.

The peace between Charles and Clement paved the way for Charles's imperial coronation by Clement VII at Bologna (1530). This symbolic triumph marked the culmination of Gattinara's dreams for his master, but sadly he died that same year. Charles did not replace him; he was the last imperial grand chancellor.

See also **Charles V (Holy Roman Empire); Habsburg Dynasty; Holy Roman Empire; Spain.**

BIBLIOGRAPHY

Brandi, Karl. *The Emperor Charles V.* Translated by C. V. Wedgwood. London, 1939.

Brunelli, G. "Gattinara, Mercurino Arborio marchese di." In *Dizionario biografico degli Italiani,* edited by Alberto M. Ghisalberti, vol. 52, pp. 633–643. Rome, 1960–.

Headley, John M. *The Emperor and His Chancellor: A Study of the Imperial Chancellery under Gattinara.* Cambridge, U.K., 1983.

——. "The Habsburg World Empire and the Revival of Ghibellinism." In *Theories of Empire, 1450–1800,* edited by David Armitage, pp. 45–79. Aldershot, U.K., 1998.

——. "Rhetoric and Reality: Messianic, Humanist, and Civilian Themes in the Imperial Ethos of Gattinara." In *Prophetic Rome in the High Renaissance Period,* edited by Marjorie Reeves, pp. 241–269. Oxford, 1992.

MICHAEL J. LEVIN

GDAŃSK (German, Danzig). A Slavic village founded in the second half of the tenth century at the mouth of the Vistula on the Baltic, Gdańsk became a largely German-speaking Hansa city, serving as the major port for trade between the Commonwealth of Poland-Lithuania and western Europe, especially Holland. The Teutonic Knights, welcomed in 1226 by the rulers of the Polish principality of Mazovia, occupied Gdańsk in 1308. German immigrants began to reside in the suburbs by the second half of the thirteenth century. After the defeat of the Teutonic Knights by Polish-Lithuanian forces at the Battle of Grunwald (Tannenberg, 1410), Gdańsk swore allegiance to the Polish crown. In response to the Knights' continued threats, gentry, clergy, and nineteen towns formed the Prussian Union in 1440. The order's rule ended definitively in Gdańsk in 1454, and the Prussian estates again swore allegiance to the Polish crown.

The *privilegia casimiriana* (for King Kazimierz IV Jagiellończyk, ruled 1444–1492) laid the foundation for the city's rights and freedoms until 1793. Gdańsk was now linked via the Vistula with the Polish-Lithuanian hinterland, where it had the right of free trade; the king promised to respect the city's autonomies. Gdańsk flourished, together with the commonwealth, until the wars of the mid-seventeenth century. Population rose from about 20,000 in 1450 to a peak of c. 70,000 in 1650, making it the leading city of Poland-Lithuania. The port became the link between two major trading partners, Poland and Holland, with Gdańsk merchants reaping profits from the grain trade. Imports included salt, salt herrings, spices, and wine.

The Reformation came to Gdańsk against the background of challenges to the patriciate's monopoly of power in the years 1522–1526. King Zygmunt I restored order in 1526, again banning Lutheran teachings. Residents may have remained crypto-Lutherans, and the ideas soon resurfaced. Sigismund II Augustus in 1557 allowed Communion in both kinds, and in 1577 Stephen Báthory granted a privilege for the practice of Lutheranism. By the seventeenth century the city was divided into a Calvinist patriciate and a Lutheran commonality. Some Catholics, some of them Slavs, lived in the city and suburbs. Jews, Mennonites, and Quakers competed with the city's artisans and merchants, al-

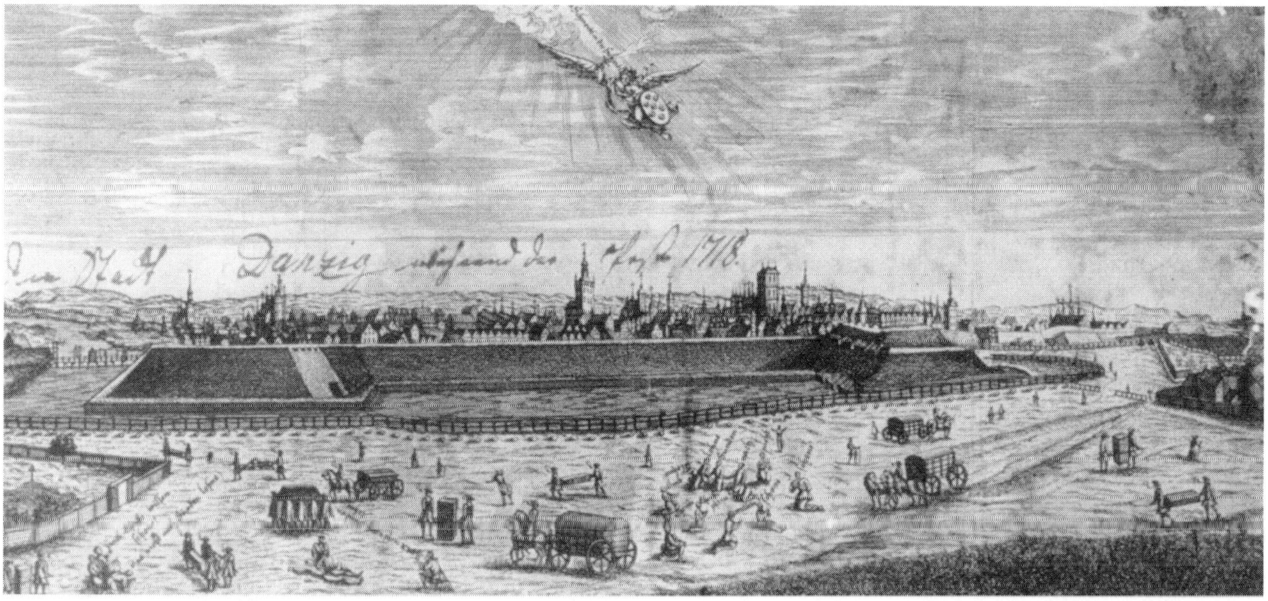

Gdańsk. A view of the Danzig riverfront, 1718. In the foreground are workers transporting the bodies of victims of a plague epidemic which struck the city that year. NATIONAL LIBRARY OF MEDICINE, BETHESDA, MD.

though they were restricted to residence in the suburbs, where other sorts of non-guild commercial activities throve.

Printing began in Gdańsk in 1499, and by the seventeenth century local houses were producing books in German, Dutch, Polish, French, Latin, Greek, and Hebrew. An Academic Grammar School stood at the peak of the city's education system and drew students from abroad (including Poles, Lithuanians, and Hungarians); it offered a course in Polish from 1589. Members of the merchant patriciate emulated the lives of Polish nobles, and residents sent their children to the hinterland to acquire the language. The Collegium Medicum founded in 1614 was the first such institution in the commonwealth.

The city defended its independence from foreign powers (Prussia, Sweden, Russia) just as tenaciously as it guarded its ties with, and privileges and rights vis-à-vis, the Polish crown. It shared in the upheavals and decline that met the commonwealth and the grain trade from the middle of the seventeenth century (including the Swedish "Deluge" of 1655–1660; the Northern War of 1700–1721; and the 1734 Saxon and Russian siege of the city). The population had declined to 36,000 by 1793. Although spared occupation in the first partition of Poland (1772), Gdańsk was subjected to a Prussian economic embargo for the next twenty years. Prussian troops entered the city on 4 April 1793, and the second partition of Poland put an end to Gdańsk's status as port to a now moribund Polish-Lithuanian Commonwealth.

See also **Hansa; Northern Wars; Poland to 1569; Poland-Lithuania, Commonwealth of, 1569–1765; Prussia.**

BIBLIOGRAPHY

Bogucka, Maria. *Das alte Danzig: Alltagsleben vom 15. bis 17. Jahrhundert.* Munich, 1987.

Cieślak, Edmund, ed. *Historia Gdańska.* Vol. 2, *1454–1655.* Vol. 3, pt. 1, *1655–1793.* Gdańsk, 1982, 1993.

Cieślak, Edmund, and Czesław Biernat. *History of Gdańsk.* Gdańsk, 1995.

Simson, Paul. *Geschichte der Stadt Danzig bis 1626.* 3 vols. Gdańsk, 1913–1924. (Reprint: Aalen, 1967.)

DAVID FRICK

GELLÉE, CLAUDE. *See* **Claude Lorrain (Gellée).**

GENDER. Until the 1980s, "gender" was a word used primarily in the realm of linguistics. The women's movement changed that, as it changed so much else. Advocates of women's rights in the present looked at what they had been taught about the past and realized that it described only the male experience, though often portraying this as universal. This realization, combined with increasing numbers of women going into the field of history, led to investigation of the lives of women in the past. Women were first fitted into existing conceptual categories—nations, historical periods, social classes, religious allegiances—but focusing on women often disrupted these classifications, forcing a rethinking of the way history was organized and structured.

This disruption of well-known categories and paradigms ultimately included the topic that had long been considered the proper focus of all history—man. Viewing the male experience as universal had not only hidden women's history, it had also prevented the analysis of men's experiences as those of men. Historians familiar with studying women increasingly began to discuss the ways in which systems of sexual differentiation affected both women and men, and by the early 1980s they began to use the word "gender" to describe these systems. They differentiated primarily between "sex," by which they meant physical, morphological, and anatomical differences (what are often called "biological differences") and "gender," by which they meant a culturally constructed, historically changing, and often unstable system of differences. Historians interested in this new perspective asserted that gender was an appropriate category of analysis when looking at all historical developments, not simply those involving women or the family. Every political, intellectual, religious, economic, social, and even military change had an impact on the actions and roles of men and women, and, conversely, a culture's gender structures influenced every other structure or development.

Historians of the early modern period figured prominently in the development of both women's and gender history and continue to be important voices in their subsequent growth and that of related areas of study such as the history of sexuality. Though summarizing their conclusions in a brief article goes against the central premise of the field—that gender issues should be a part of every historical analysis—three main areas can serve as examples of the way in which thinking about gender challenges understandings of the early modern era: gender and periodization, gender and political power, gender and the social order.

GENDER AND PERIODIZATION

One of the most important insights in women's and then gender history began with a simple question—Did women have a Renaissance?—first posed by the historian Joan Kelly in 1977. Her answer, "No, at least not during the Renaissance," led to intensive historical and literary research as people attempted to confirm, refute, modify, or nuance her answer. This question also contributed to the broader questioning of the whole notion of historical periodization. If a particular development had little, or indeed a negative, effect on women, could it still be called a "golden age," a "Renaissance," or an "Enlightenment"? Can the seventeenth century, during which hundreds or perhaps thousands of women were burned as witches on the European continent, still be described as a period of "the spread of rational thought"?

Kelly's questioning of the term "Renaissance" has been joined more recently by a questioning of the term "early modern." Both historians and literary scholars note that there are problems with this term, as it assumes that there is something that can unambiguously be called "modernity," which is usually set against "traditional" and linked with contemporary Western society. The break between "medieval" and "early modern" is generally set at 1500, roughly the time of the voyages of Columbus and of the Protestant Reformation, but recently many historians argue that there are more continuities across this line than changes. Some have moved the decisive break earlier—to the Black Death in 1347 or even to the twelfth century—or have rejected the notion of periodization altogether. Gender historians, most prominently Judith Bennett, have been among those questioning the validity of the medieval/modern divide, challenging, in Bennett's words, "the assumption of a dramatic change in women's lives between 1300 and 1700" and asserting that historians must pay more attention to continuities along with changes.

GENDER AND POLITICAL POWER

During the fifteenth through the seventeenth centuries male and female writers in many countries of Europe wrote both learned and popular works debating the nature of women. Beginning in the sixteenth century, this debate also became one about female rulers, sparked primarily by dynastic accidents in many countries that led to women serving as advisers to child kings or ruling in their own right. The questions vigorously and at times viciously disputed directly concerned the social construction of gender: could a woman's being born into a royal family and educated to rule allow her to overcome the limitations of her sex? Should it? Or stated another way: which was (or should be) the stronger determinant of character and social role, gender or rank?

The most extreme opponents of female rule were Protestants who went into exile on the Continent during the reign of Mary Tudor (ruled 1553–1558), most prominently John Knox, who argued that female rule was unnatural, unlawful, and contrary to Scripture. Being female was a condition that could never be overcome, and subjects of female rulers needed no other justification for rebelling than their monarch's sex. Their writings were answered by defenses of female rule which argued that a woman's sex did not automatically exclude her from rule, just as a boy king's age or a handicapped king's infirmity did not exclude him. Some theorists asserted that even a married queen could rule legitimately, for she could be subject to her husband in her private life, yet monarch to him and all other men in her public life. As Constance Jordan has pointed out, defenders of female rule were thus clearly separating sex from gender and even approaching an idea of androgyny as a desirable state for the public persona of female monarchs.

Jean Bodin (1530–1596), the French jurist and political theorist, stressed what would become in the seventeenth century the most frequently cited reason to oppose female rule: that the state was like a household, and just as in a household the husband/father has authority and power over all others, so in the state a male monarch should always rule. Male monarchs used husbandly and paternal imagery to justify their assertion of power over their subjects, though criticism of monarchs was also couched in paternal language; pamphlets directed against the crown during the revolt known as the Fronde in seventeenth-century France, for example, justified their opposition by asserting that the king was not properly fulfilling his fatherly duties.

This link between royal and paternal authority could also work in the opposite direction to enhance the power of male heads of household. Just as subjects were deemed to have no or only a very limited right of rebellion against their ruler, so women and children were not to dispute the authority of the husband/father, because both kings and fathers were held to have received their authority from God; the household was not viewed as private, but as the smallest political unit and so part of the public realm.

Many analysts see the Protestant Reformation and, in England, Puritanism as further strengthening this paternal authority by granting male heads of household a much larger religious and supervisory role than they had under Catholicism. The fact that Protestant clergy were themselves generally married heads of household also meant that ideas about clerical authority reinforced notions of paternal and husbandly authority; priests were now husbands, and husbands priests. After the Reformation, the male citizens of many cities and villages increasingly added an oath to uphold the city's religion to the oaths they took to defend it and support it economically. For men, faith became a ritualized civic matter, while for women it was not. Thus both the public political community and the public religious community—which were often regarded as the same in early modern Europe—were for men only, a situation reinforced in the highly gendered language of the reformers, who extolled "brotherly love" and the religious virtues of the "common man."

Religious divisions were not the only development that enhanced the authority of many men. Rulers intent on increasing and centralizing their own authority supported legal and institutional changes that enhanced the power of men over the women and children in their own families. In France, for example, a series of laws were enacted between 1556 and 1789 that increased both paternal and state control of marriage. Young people who defied their parents were sometimes imprisoned by what were termed *lettres de cachet,* documents that families obtained from royal officials authorizing the imprisonment without trial of a family member who was seen as a source of dishonor. Men occasionally used *lettres de cachet* as a means of solving marital disputes, convincing authorities that family honor demanded the imprisonment of their wives, while in Italy and Spain a "disobedient" wife could be sent to a convent or house of refuge for repentant prostitutes. Courts generally held that a husband had the right to beat his wife in order to correct her behavior as long as this was not extreme, with a common standard being that he not draw blood, or that the diameter of the stick he used not exceed that of his thumb.

Access to political power for men as well as women was shaped by ideas about gender in early modern Europe. The dominant notion of the "true" man was that of the married head of household, so that men whose class and age would have normally conferred political power but who remained unmarried did not participate to the same level as their married brothers; in Protestant areas, this link between marriage and authority even included the clergy.

Notions of masculinity were important symbols in early modern political discussions. Both male and female rulers emphasized qualities regarded as masculine—physical bravery, stamina, wisdom, duty—whenever they chose to appear or speak in public. A concern with masculinity pervades the political writings of Machiavelli, who used "effeminate" to describe the worst kind of ruler. (Effeminate in the early modern period carried slightly different connotations than it does today, however, for strong heterosexual passion was not a sign of manliness, but could make one "effeminate," that is, dominated by as well as similar to a woman.) The English Civil War (1642–1649) presented two conflicting notions of masculinity: Royalist cavaliers in their long hair and fancy silk knee-breeches, and Puritan parliamentarians with their short hair and somber clothing. Parliamentary criticism of the court was often expressed in gendered and sexualized terminology, with frequent veiled or open references to aristocratic weakness and inability to control the passions.

GENDER AND THE SOCIAL ORDER

The maintenance of proper power relationships between men and women served as a basis for and a symbol of the functioning of society as a whole. Women or men who stepped outside their prescribed roles in other than extraordinary circumstances, and particularly those who made a point of emphasizing that they were doing this, were seen as threatening not only relations between the sexes, but the operation of the entire social order. They were "disorderly," a word that had much stronger negative connotations in the early modern period than it does today, as well as two somewhat distinct meanings—outside of the social structure and unruly or unreasonable.

Women were outside the social order because they were not as clearly demarcated into social groups as men. Unless they were members of a religious order or guild, women had no corporate identity at a time when society was conceived of as a hierarchy of groups rather than a collection of individuals. One can see women's separation from such groups in the way that parades and processions were arranged in early modern Europe; if women were included, they came at the end as an undifferentiated group, following men who marched together on the basis of political position or occupation. Women were also more "disorderly" than men because they were unreasonable, ruled by their physical bodies rather than their rational capacities, their lower parts rather than their upper parts. This was one of the reasons they were more often suspected of witchcraft; it was also why they were thought to have nondiabolical magical powers in the realms of love and sexual attraction.

Disorder in the proper gender hierarchy was linked with other types of social upheaval and viewed as the most threatening way in which the world could be turned upside down. Carnival plays, woodcuts, and stories frequently portrayed domineering wives in pants and henpecked husbands washing diapers alongside professors in dunce caps and peasants riding princes. Men and women involved in relationships in which the women were thought to have power—an older woman who married a younger man, or a woman who scolded her husband—were often subjected to public ridicule, with bands of neighbors shouting insults and banging sticks and pans in their disapproval. Adult male journeymen refused to work for widows although this decreased their opportunities for employment. Fathers disinherited disobedient daughters more often than sons. The derivative nature of an adult woman's authority—the fact that it came from her status as wife or widow of the male household head—was emphasized by referring to her as "wife" rather than "mother" even in legal documents describing her relations with her children. Of all the ways in which society was hierarchically arranged—class, age, rank, race, occupation—gender was regarded as the most "natural" and therefore the most important to defend.

See also **Family; Marriage; Patriarchy and Patriarchalism; Sexual Difference, Theories of; Sexuality and Sexual Behavior; Women.**

BIBLIOGRAPHY

Amussen, Susan Dwyer. *An Ordered Society: Gender and Class in Early Modern England.* London, 1988.

Bennett, Judith. "Medieval Women, Modern Women: Across the Great Divide." In *Culture and History 1350–1600: Essays on English Communities, Identities and Writing,* edited by David Aers, pp. 147–175. London, 1992.

Breitenberg, Mark. *Anxious Masculinity in Early Modern England.* Cambridge, U.K., 1996.

Hanley, Sarah. "The Monarchic State in Early Modern France: Marital Regime, Government and Male Right." In *Politics, Ideology, and the Law in Early Modern Europe. Essays in Honor of J. H. M. Salmon,* edited by Adrianna Bakos, pp. 27–52. Rochester, 1994.

Hardwick, Julie. *The Practice of Patriarchy: Gender and the Politics of Household Authority in Early Modern France.* University Park, Pa., 1998.

Jordan, Constance. *Renaissance Feminism: Literary Texts and Political Models.* Ithaca, N.Y., 1990.

Kelly, Joan. "Did Women Have a Renaissance?" In *Becoming Visible: Women in European History,* edited by Renate Bridenthal and Claudia Koonz, pp. 138–164. Boston, 1977.

Pateman, Carole. *The Sexual Contract.* Stanford, 1988.

Perry, Mary Elizabeth. *Gender and Disorder in Early Modern Seville.* Princeton, 1990.

Pitkin, Hannah Fenichel. *Fortune is a Woman: Gender and Politics in the Thought of Niccolò Machiavelli.* Berkeley, 1984.

Wiesner-Hanks, Merry E. *Gender in History.* London, 2001.

MERRY WIESNER-HANKS

GENERATION. *See* **Sexual Difference, Theories of.**

GENEVA. The only European city to become an independent republic in the sixteenth century and remain so for over 250 years (1536–1798), Geneva became best known as the seat of John Calvin's (1509–1564) Reformation. These two distinctions are closely connected. Calvinist austerity gave a durable imprint to Geneva's character, and many of the republic's leading families descended from French religious refugees who were drawn by Calvin's fame. Thanks partly to its university, founded in 1559 to train pastors for the Reformed Church in France, Geneva maintained a disproportionate intellectual role in early modern Europe from the Reformation through the Enlightenment. However, the city that attracted Voltaire (1694–1778) and repelled its illustrious native son Jean-Jacques Rousseau (1712–1778) seems significantly different from the place where Calvin settled two centuries earlier. Worldly prosperity had undermined the relatively impoverished austerity of its heroic Reformation period. After the fall of Napoléon I, Geneva became a Swiss canton in 1814 and continued its international vocation in the nineteenth century through the Red Cross (founded by a Genevan) and in the twentieth century as host to the League of Nations.

Geneva's political history as a successful independent urban republic was unique in early modern Europe. Its independence, exemplified by its proud new motto *Post Tenebras Lux* (After Darkness, Light) and a coat of arms displaying half of the imperial eagle and half of the papal keys (the modern flag of the Swiss canton of Geneva), survived many serious threats. After 1559 two great Catholic neighbors, the duchy of Savoy and the kingdom of France, surrounded its minuscule territories on land. Geneva sustained its independence only through permanent political alliances with two Swiss cantons, Bern and Zurich; the city remained physically connected to its Bernese political allies only via Lake Geneva. The most serious threat came from an attempted escalade by the Savoyards on the longest night of the year in 1602, whose successful repulse is still celebrated annually in Geneva on 12

December, the pre-Gregorian and thus "Protestant" date of the winter equinox in 1602. Geneva narrowly avoided annexation by Louis XIV (ruled 1643–1715) after the revocation of the Edict of Nantes in 1685, but the republic survived for over another century until it was annexed by revolutionary France. As Peter Gay pointed out in 1959, one of the last champions of Genevan civic republicanism was none other than Voltaire, who was often assumed to prefer enlightened absolutism but who on this point largely agreed with his philosophical rival Rousseau.

Of course Calvin dominates Geneva's religious history, just as his statue dominates the Wall of the Reformation near the University of Geneva. In early modern Europe, Geneva quickly developed a reputation for austere righteousness that was unparalleled in a place of this size. Rival myths about Geneva's peculiarities developed by the mid-sixteenth century. Enthusiastic Protestants described it as a kind of earthly Jerusalem, while Catholics saw it as a sink of iniquity where renegade priests engaged in orgies. As John Knox (1513–1572), himself a byword for austerity and once the minister of an English refugee church in Geneva, put it, "manners and religion so sincerely reformed I have not yet seen in any other place." A related tribute came from a different source a generation after Calvin's death, when a visiting Jesuit

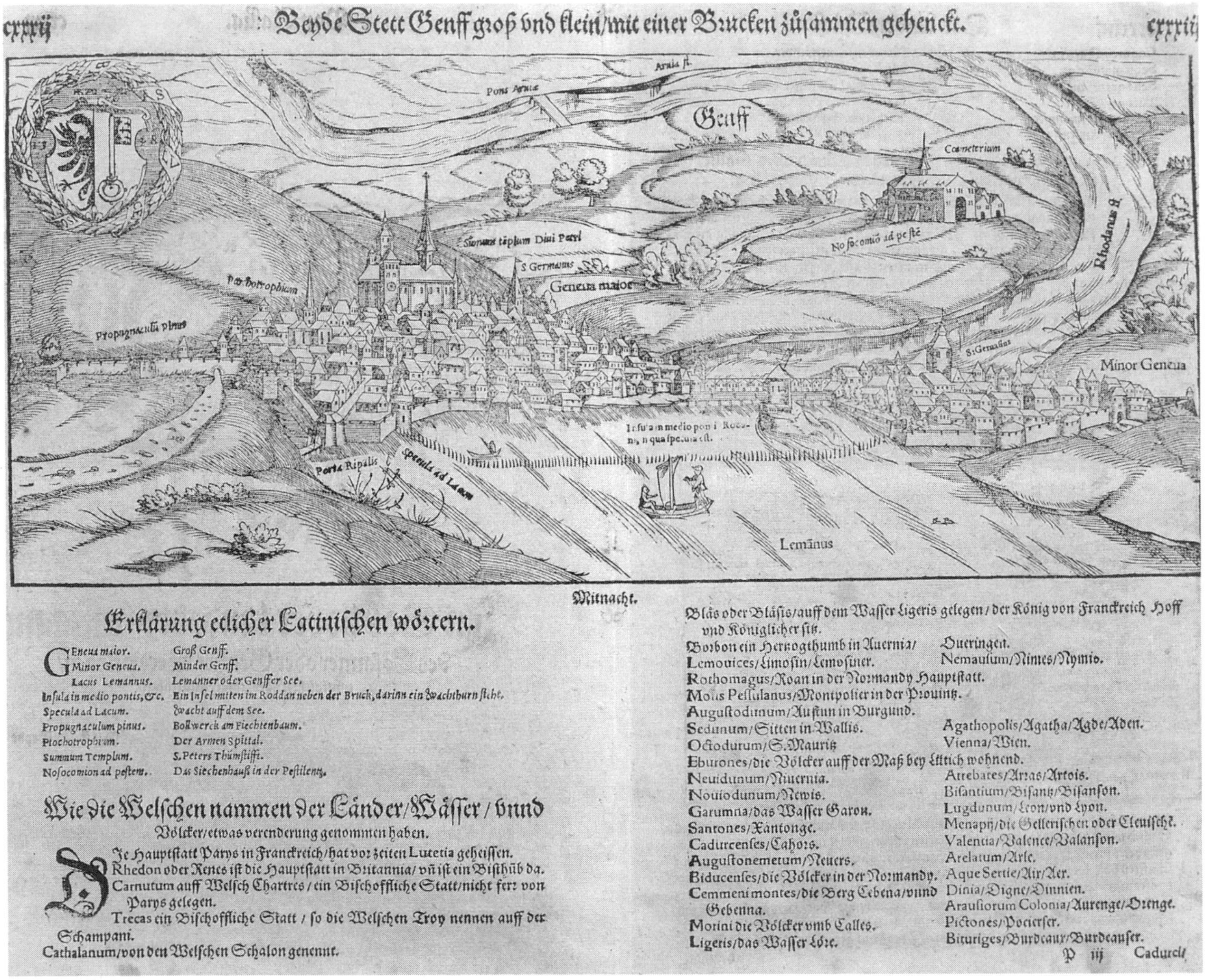

Geneva. City view, with Latin place names and German equivalents, sixteenth century, from *Cosmographia* by Sebastian Münster. THE ART ARCHIVE/UNIVERSITY LIBRARY, GENEVA/DAGLI ORTI

remarked enviously that no one dared to blaspheme anyplace in Geneva.

The most important religious institution affecting the daily lives of Genevans after the Reformation was the Consistory, which Calvin introduced in 1541 to enforce ecclesiastical discipline. Within a year it systematically required troublemakers to "give an account of their faith," that is, it tested them for what came to be called confessional orthodoxy. Traces of Catholic practices disappeared within a generation. The Consistory's moral severity remained largely unchallenged until Voltaire's day.

Geneva has never been a major European city. At the peak of the Calvinist refuge around 1560, the city-republic held about twenty-five thousand people. By the 1580s the population had fallen by nearly half, and it remained below fifteen thousand until the early eighteenth century, gradually regaining its earlier peak by the time the city finally lost its independence. Geneva's economic history is almost as distinctive as its religious or political history. A highly successful printing industry, developed by French religious refugees like Jean Crespin and Laurent de Normandie, made religious propaganda the city's leading export in Calvin's time. Conventional wisdom correctly links vernacular printing to the spread of the French Reformation in the mid-sixteenth century. Although Geneva—Europe's only Protestant Francophone publishing center—remained intellectually significant far into the following century, most Genevan books were printed in Latin after 1585.

However, by 1590 Geneva entered a prolonged depression. The city emerged gradually in the late seventeenth century thanks to the growth of two new leading export-oriented trades, watchmaking and banking, both of which long outlived the republic (Rousseau was the son of a Geneva watchmaker). One invention of Geneva's eighteenth-century financiers involved investment in one-life annuities issued by the French crown. Using local genealogical data, they made actuarial tables that showed that girls past the age of five from wealthy families had the longest life expectancies. These bankers then created collective shares based on the lives of thirty selected Genevan girls—a scheme that worked well until the French Revolution destroyed the state that paid these annuities.

See also **Bèze, Théodore de; Calvin, John; Calvinism; Knox, John; Reformation, Protestant; Switzerland; Zurich.**

BIBLIOGRAPHY

Among the recent achievements of Genevan scholarship, one must mention three ongoing critical editions, all published locally by Librairie Droz: the European-wide correspondence of Calvin's successor, Théodore de Bèze (22 volumes to date, through 1582); the minutes of Geneva's Company of Pastors (thirteen volumes so far, covering 1546–1618), and the early records of Geneva's Consistory (two volumes to date).

Gay, Peter. *Voltaire's Politics.* Princeton, 1959.

Guichonnet, Paul, ed. *Histoire de Genève.* 3rd ed. Toulouse and Lausanne, 1986.

Monter, E. William. *Calvin's Geneva.* New York, 1967.

Naphy, William G. *Calvin and the Consolidation of the Genevan Reformation.* Manchester, U.K., 1994.

WILLIAM MONTER

GENOA. Genoa, the major port city of northwestern Italy, is situated at the center of the Ligurian coast and protected by a rugged mountain range and an easily defensible harbor. In the early modern period, Genoa's territory stretched from La Spezia in the east to Ventimiglia in the west, and included portions of the Lombard plain north of the coastal range. The Genoese also controlled the island of Corsica, which they administered as a colony.

The early modern Genoese state emerged in 1528, following an aristocratic revolt that put an end to the medieval regime that had endured since the early tenth century. The revolt, backed by the Spanish and led by the Genoese admiral Andrea Doria (1466–1560), established a republican constitution in which eligibility for political office was predicated on membership in one of twenty-eight *alberghi*—extended aristocratic kinship networks based on clientage rather than strict consanguinity. The 1528 constitution expanded the opportunity to hold office to newer aristocratic families whose wealth was based on commerce instead of banking. Strife between the new families and the older established aristocrats became one of the defining features of the Genoese republic, and led to a pair of constitutional reforms. The first, in 1547, was de-

Genoa. Woodcut of Genoa from *Liber Chronicarum,* 1493. RARE BOOK DIVISION, LIBRARY OF CONGRESS

signed to ensure that the older families maintained control of the higher councils of government by filling key positions through appointment rather than election. The second, occasioned by the threat of civil war in 1576, resulted in the abolition of the *alberghi* as formally recognized groups, and the declaration that all aristocrats were equal in status and privilege before the law.

Despite the waning of the republic's naval power in the sixteenth century, the city remained an important economic center. To maintain their hold on goods carried by northern European ships, the Genoese declared themselves a free port in 1669. No longer actively involved in maritime trade, the city's oligarchs turned their attention to other commercial opportunities. The Genoese were among the European leaders in banking, at one point in the late sixteenth century holding most of the Spanish crown's public debt. The sparse population and difficult terrain of the Ligurian coast did not permit the agricultural speculation that other Italian cities engaged in, but the rural population was put to work as wage laborers for traditionally urban industries, especially textile manufacturing. Moving urban industries to the countryside created a large class of indigent poor in the city. In 1656, to combat what was increasingly seen as a threat to public order, the city created the Albergo dei Poveri, a combination prison and workhouse. The Albergo was the first of its kind in Europe, and the institution was widely imitated in the coming centuries.

Despite the fact that the Genoese oligarchs found new avenues for investment, the republic's military and political power steadily declined. Both the Spanish and French crowns had designs on Genoa's port, forcing the Genoese to play the two rivals against each other in an effort to retain their own liberty. In the end, however, the lack of a standing army or large fleet meant that the Genoese were unable to resist a gradual loss of their territory. In 1746 the city was briefly occupied by an Austrian army, but a popular revolt reestablished the republic. In 1768 financial problems forced the Genoese to sell Corsica to the French. It was a sign of things to come, as in 1797 the French army under the command of a Corsican general, Napoléon Bonaparte, put an end to Genoa's tenuous independence.

See also **Italy.**

BIBLIOGRAPHY

Costantini, Claudio. *La repubblica di Genova nell'età moderna.* Vol. 9 of *Storia D'Italia,* edited by Giuseppe Galasso. Turin, 1978.

Epstein, Steven A. *Genoa and the Genoese, 958–1528.* Chapel Hill, N.C., 1996.

Grendi, Edoardo. *La repubblica arsitocratica dei genovesi: Politica, carità e commèrcio fra Cinque e Seicento.* Bologna, 1987.

KARL APPUHN

GENTILESCHI, ARTEMISIA (1593–c. 1654), Italian painter. Artemisia Gentileschi is known for her early dramatic biblical narratives presenting forceful female protagonists. Her less-known later paintings feature pensive heroines and classically composed groupings.

She was the daughter of Orazio Gentileschi, a Tuscan painter who trained her to paint in his style combining the artificial contrivance of mannerism with a naturalism inspired by the revolutionary vision of Caravaggio (born Michelangelo Merisi, 1573–1610). Although some scholars have dated her earliest work to 1609, based on Orazio's 1612 boast that she had achieved remarkable successes in only three years, she probably began painting in 1605, apprenticing at age twelve as did many male painters. In 1611 she was raped by Orazio's colleague Agostino Tassi. Testimony from the ensuing trial provides valuable information on Artemisia's early life, including her own account of the assault. She worked in Rome until late 1612 or early 1613, when she married a Florentine and moved to Florence. On returning to Rome in 1620, she entered one of her most successful periods. In 1627 she visited Venice, although the duration of her stay is unknown. She settled in Naples by August 1630, her home for the rest of her life except for a sojourn in London around 1639. Her patrons included major contemporary collectors such as Michelangelo Buonarroti, nephew to the great Renaissance artist; the grand duke of Tuscany; the kings of England and Spain; the Roman scholar Cassiano dal Pozzo; and Don Antonio Ruffo of Sicily.

Famous in her own day, she was generally ignored until the twentieth century when the reevaluation of Caravaggio and seventeenth-century naturalism extended to his followers, including Artemisia, his sole female disciple. Roberto Longhi, the great Caravaggio scholar, wrote the first serious account of both Gentileschis in 1916. Focus on Artemisia as caravaggista was later supplanted by attention to her role as feminist heroine, beginning with Anna Banti's 1946 novel *Artemisia,* a personal homage to Artemisia's life and art that highlighted the rape and subsequent trial. Later twentieth century studies have championed Artemisia as a strong female artist who, having overcome violence, created paintings that asserted women's power over their own lives and expressed revenge against male domination.

Her first signed and dated painting, the 1610 *Susanna and the Elders,* has been interpreted as a statement of women's strength and courage in the face of male oppression. Among the most compelling images of the story ever painted, it reveals Artemisia as one of the most gifted practitioners of baroque exuberance and an astute interpreter of dramatic narrative. Although it has been disputed whether Artemisia painted the entire canvas or whether her father helped (some claim Orazio alone created it), most scholars accept it as primarily Artemisia's work. Several other early paintings from her

Artemisia Gentileschi. *Judith Beheading Holofernes.* ©ALINARI/ART RESOURCE, N.Y.

Roman period have been attributed to Orazio. There is at present no clear scholarly consensus.

Evaluating Artemisia among Caravaggio's followers has highlighted pictures that emphasize bold lighting, surface texture, and aggressive naturalism (*Judith Beheading Holofernes* [Uffizi]; *Lucretia* [Milan]; *Judith and Her Maidservant* [Detroit]) and led to her being credited with bringing Caravaggio's style to Naples. However, this Caravaggio-dominated paradigm no longer holds. From the trial records, we understand her early life to have been severely restricted, with little opportunity to explore Rome's treasures, resulting in limited knowledge of Caravaggio other than through his influence on her father. It is also now clear that Caravaggio's realist style had reached Naples earlier than Artemisia's arrival. In fact, recent discoveries have revealed Artemisia's work as far more varied and less stylistically coherent than the caravaggesque model implies. Although her earliest pictures (1609–1613) demonstrate a debt to Caravaggio, her Florentine paintings move beyond this influence in their freer use of paint and color. Furthermore, her later works, often subdued and poetic, exhibit widely disparate expressive forms. In spite of recent suggestions that Artemisia adopted the style in vogue in the city in which she worked, her surviving paintings reveal a broader and more varied visual response. Having been trained to paint in the style of her father, she continued to demonstrate a remarkable ability to draw from others as she fashioned pictures that ranged from the rich color and compositional power of early Guercino (born Giovanni Francesco Barbieri, 1591–1666) to the restrained idealism of Guido Reni (1575–1642). Her assimilation of disparate styles may have been related to gender. Surviving letters, some thirty in number, reveal her awareness of her difficult position in a male-dominated profession. She may also have understood the impact of her gender on patrons who commissioned female nudes, her presumed specialty.

See also **Caravaggio and Caravaggism; Naples, Art in; Women and Art.**

BIBLIOGRAPHY

Primary Sources

Baldinucci, Filippo. *Notizie de' professori del disegno da Cimabue in qua.* 6 vols. Florence, 1681–1728. 5 vols., edited by F. Ranalli, Florence, 1845–1847. Edition by P. Barocchi, with annotations and 2 vols. of appendices, Florence, 1974–1975.

Bellori, Giovan Pietro. *Le vite de' pittori, scultori e architetti moderni.* Rome, 1672. Artemisia is discussed in the life of Orazio.

Menzio, Eva, ed. *Artemisia Gentileschi/Agostino Tassi: Atti di un processo per stupro.* Milan, 1981. Partial transcription of testimonies in Tassi's 1612 rape trial.

Secondary Sources

Bissell, R. Ward. *Artemisia Gentileschi and the Authority of Art: Critical Reading and catalogue raisonné.* University Park, Pa., 1999.

Christiansen, Keith, and Judith W. Mann. *Orazio and Artemisia Gentileschi.* New York, 2001.

Florence, Casa Buonarroti. *Artemisia.* Exh. cat., edited by Roberto Contini and Gianni Papi. Rome, 1991.

Garrard, Mary D. *Artemisia Gentileschi: The Image of the Female Hero in Italian Baroque Art.* Princeton, 1988. Includes most of Gentileschi's letters and an English translation of some of the trial testimony.

Lapierre, Alexandra. *Artemisia: Un duel pour l'immortalité.* Paris, 1998. Although a novel, the footnotes contain the results of important archival research.

Longhi, Roberto. "Gentileschi padre e figlia." *L'arte* XIX (1916): 245–314.

Spear, Richard E. "Artemisia Gentileschi: Ten Years of Fact and Fiction." *Art Bulletin* 82 (2000): 568–579.

JUDITH W. MANN

GENTLEMAN. The word "gentle" is derived from the Latin word *gentilis,* an adjective meaning 'of or belonging to the same clan, stock, or race'. Throughout the early modern era noble birth would largely define the gentleman, but the ideal of gentlemanly behavior changed dramatically from the sixteenth through the eighteenth centuries.

From the Middle Ages to the sixteenth century, a gentleman was expected to be a warrior. Military service was the main source of ennoblement. The gentleman was to receive training in arms, and to engage in activities reflecting a martial quality. In the absence of combat, the gentleman engaged in hunting or tournaments. Private violence was acceptable within the community of nobles, who used it often to defend their honor. Recognition by peers was in many ways the foundation of noble identity.

Gentleman. *Portrait of a Young Man* by Agnolo Bronzino. This is one of Bronzino's best-known portraits, typical in its dispassionate depiction of a clearly self-assured aristocrat. ©FRANCIS G. MAYER/CORBIS

The king was also a gentleman who adhered to the code of gentlemanly conduct. As a member of the society of nobles, he was considered the first among equals, or simply the most powerful of lords. Throughout the sixteenth century, kings were expected to lead troops into battle and engage in other pursuits related to combat such as hunting and tournaments.

By the seventeenth century, the martial aspect of gentlemanly behavior began to decline. The ideal gentleman was no longer a warrior but a courtier, although these roles often overlapped. The two ideals are represented in Baldassare Castiglione's *Il Cortegiano* (The courtier; 1528). Written in 1518, but enjoying enormous popularity throughout the sixteenth and seventeenth centuries, Castiglione's book outlines the qualities of an ideal courtier: trained in arms and loyal to his prince, but also exhibiting noble birth, grace, and talent. Good manners, wit, and education became important attributes for a gentleman who increasingly resided at court rather than in his own domains.

A major factor in the transformation of the ideal of the gentleman was the rise of the state. This in turn was precipitated by changes in the technology of warfare. The "gunpowder revolution" ensured the obsolescence of the knight on horseback and the increased importance of the mass infantry. Whereas in the Middle Ages nobles could often afford to field armies against the king, by the sixteenth century, no noble could compete with the king's army, which was equipped and trained by means of taxation. In the newly created state, the king did not need as many nobles to fight for him; rather he needed bureaucrats and administrators to ensure the efficient mobilization of resources. That, more than noble valor, increasingly determined the outcome of war. Nobles filled lucrative offices in the state administration, spending less time in their feudal domains and more time at court. Here they retained their social prominence, but they declined in their political power in relation to the king. The king increasingly distanced himself from his fellow nobles through propaganda aimed at his glorification. By the late seventeenth century, most kings no longer led their troops into battle. The king hired non-nobles to government offices, sometimes rewarding them with titles of nobility. In order to distance themselves from these newly ennobled officials, the old nobility focused on their genealogies. Pedigree became more important than valor in the definition of a gentleman. However, the conflict between the new nobility and the old, as well as the conflict between the nobility and the king, has been downplayed by recent historians who stress that nobles had much to gain from the state. Life at court offered intellectual stimulation, the society of women, and a certain kind of political power that operated through networks of patronage.

Attendance at court required "civility," and the code of gentlemanly conduct placed a new emphasis on self-discipline. A proliferation of etiquette manuals occurred in the sixteenth and seventeenth centuries, regulating behavior in a courtly environment. Claiming a monopoly on violence, the state no longer tolerated private violence between nobles. The gentleman distinguished himself through culture and refinement rather than through military prowess or political domination.

The nature of the gentleman changed again in the eighteenth century in response to a new economic reality: the capitalist economy. Whereas in the past the gentleman derived his income from land or government offices, by the eighteenth century the gentleman was permitted to engage in certain forms of trade. Thus nobles adapted to the new capitalist economy, while simultaneously maintaining their position at the top of the social and economic hierarchy.

In terms of culture, the seventeenth-century concern with "civility" gave way to the eighteenth-century emphasis on "sociability." Whereas civility dictated relations among people of unequal status in the hierarchical world of the court, sociability was a bond of friendship between equals. Sociability governed relationships outside the court, especially in the setting of the salon, a social environment often dominated by women. Increasingly, the ideal gentleman inhabited private spaces untouched by the state. There was a new emphasis on intimacy that appeared in the architecture of country houses. These reflected the individuality of their owners. Private rooms testified to an increased desire for private space. The courtier's proper appearance and conduct, so important in the seventeenth century, became less important than introspection and consciousness of self. This interiority is reflected in the rise of the novel, a genre made possible by the new emphasis on individuality.

A debate going back to the Italian Renaissance posed the question whether birth or virtue defined the true gentleman. The debate continued throughout the early modern era, despite major changes in the meaning of the word "virtue." Whether he exhibited superior valor, refinement, or sensitivity, the gentleman retained his position at the top of the cultural hierarchy throughout the early modern era.

See also **Aristocracy and Gentry; Class, Status, and Order; Court and Courtiers; Duel; Estates and Country Houses; Hunting.**

BIBLIOGRAPHY

Ariès, Philippe, and Georges Duby, eds. *A History of Private Life.* Vol. 3, *Passions of the Renaissance.* Edited by Roger Chartier. Translated by Arthur Goldhammer. Cambridge, Mass., 1989.

Clark, Samuel. *State and Status: The Rise of the State and Aristocratic Power in Western Europe.* Montreal, 1995.

Dewald, Jonathan. *The European Nobility 1400–1800.* Cambridge, U.K., 1996.

Duindam, Jeroen. *Myths of Power: Norbert Elias and the Early Modern European Court.* Translated by Lorri Granger and Gerard T. Moran. Amsterdam, 1994.

Elias, Norbert. *The Court Society.* Translated by Edmund Jephcott. New York, 1983.

Schalk, Ellery. *From Valor to Pedigree: Ideas of Nobility in France in the Sixteenth and Seventeenth Centuries.* Princeton, 1986.

REBECCA BOONE

GENTRY. *See* **Aristocracy and Gentry.**

GEOFFRIN, MARIE-THÉRÈSE

(Marie-Thérèse Rodet Geoffrin; 1699–1777), French Enlightenment *salonnière* ('host of literary salons'). Mme Geoffrin hosted intellectual conversations for important philosophes (writers and thinkers of the French Enlightenment), artists, musicians, and writers on Mondays and Wednesdays at her home on the fashionable rue Saint-Honoré in Paris. Born in Paris, the daughter of a valet to the dauphine and orphaned in her youth, Marie-Thérèse was raised by her grandmother, Mme Chemineau, who valued self-education. She prepared Marie-Thérèse religiously, morally, and socially for society. Although pedagogy did not concern Chemineau, she cultivated independent thought and reason in her granddaughter, characteristics later integral to the foundation of her renowned salon.

On 19 July 1713, the aging, and thus concerned, Chemineau, married fourteen-year-old Marie-Thérèse to the fifty-year-old Peter Francis Geoffrin, a wealthy manufacturer, and the prestigious director and a shareholder in the royal glassworks, Compagnie de Saint-Gobain. Geoffrin gave birth to two children, her namesake and a son who died at the age of ten. Her daughter, Mme de la Ferté-Imbault, wrote later of her parents' marital strife, her filial competition with Geoffrin, and the ultimate blessing of growing up among "great minds."

Marie Thérèse Geoffrin. *An Evening at the Home of Mme Geoffrin in 1755,* by Anicet Charles Gabriel Lemonnier. THE ART ARCHIVE/MALMAISON MUSÉE DU CHATEAU/DAGLI ORTI (A)

Geoffrin attended the salons of her neighbor, Mme Tencin, a celebrated *salonnière* who attracted many of the leading intellectuals of the day, including Helvétius and Montesquieu. Tencin was an undisputed mentor to Geoffrin, yet Geoffrin's letters emphasize her gratitude to Chemineau for encouraging her erudition. Geoffrin's instincts, her grandmother's guidance, and her exposure to the intellectual discourse at Mme Tencin's salons combined to fashion her probing mind. Geoffrin's husband did not share Geoffrin's intellectual drive, yet his financial support contributed to her initial success in 1748. Following the deaths of Tencin and her husband in 1749 and 1750, respectively, Geoffrin joined the board and management of the Saint-Gobain glassworks and welcomed the habitués of her mentor to her own salons. Geoffrin distinguished herself from her colleagues by the unparalleled and elevated exchange in her salons.

The diversity of intellects drawn to Mme Geoffrin's salons and her correspondence testify to the esteem in which prominent artistic, literary, and political circles held her. She established a serious purpose for the gatherings over which she presided, and her guests noted her skill in drawing worldly and erudite minds to her salons, a challenge to her brilliant rival, Mme du Deffand. Her contemporaries describe her integrity, distaste for conflict, and incomparable brilliance in navigating thorny subjects. On Mondays one found artists and sculptors including Carle Van Loo, François Boucher, and Étienne Maurice Falconet. On Wednesdays men of letters, including Denis Diderot, the art critic and editor of the *Encyclopédie,* and the editor Friedrich Melchior von Grimm were frequently in attendance.

Though Geoffrin shunned discord, she respected the process of civilized conversation and she harnessed runaway egos, maintaining a strict focus. Her motto, *donner et pardonner,* "to give and to pardon," describes the role she seemed born to play within the Republic of Letters (the intellectual and rational discourse of the Enlightenment facilitated by the polite conversation and letter-writing of salon culture). Geoffrin counted Catherine the Great, tsarina of Russia (ruled 1762–1796), and Stanisław Poniatowski, the last king of Poland (ruled 1764–1795), among her friends, and her letters to both rulers demonstrate the personal and political rapport they shared. In 1766 Geoffrin visited Poniatowski in Poland, a rare trip outside her beloved Paris.

Recent scholarship has reassessed Geoffrin's role, eschewing eighteenth-century views of women seeking recognition in the shadows of famous men. Geoffrin may have demonstrated what her friend André Morellet called "a little vainglory," yet she did not desire the celebrity she achieved through her salons. Her passion was education, and her goal was to propagate Enlightenment thought, evidenced particularly by assisting in the *Encyclopédie*'s rescue from its censors in 1759, paying 200,000 livres to facilitate production. Artistic images of her gatherings, for example, A. C. G. Lemonnier's *An Evening at the Home of Mme Geoffrin in 1755*, reveal a sophisticated Parisian woman who inspired intellectual risks and helped to govern the civilizing discourse of the French Enlightenment.

By 1777, her daughter, Mme Ferté-Imbault, had zealously insulated Geoffrin, who was suffering from erysipelas, a skin disorder, from her indebted following. Ferté-Imbault viewed this intellectual coterie as nothing more than a group of depraved infidels. Patronage of the Enlightenment did not mitigate Geoffrin's unyielding devotion as a Christian. She was humored by her daughter's fierce protection and determination to giver her a proper Christian burial. Shortly before her death, Geoffrin and Ferté-Imbault repaired the ancient enmity that had divided them. Saint-Beuve recalled Geoffrin's peerless influence, and the artist Mme Vigée-Lebrun described her unique legacy as remarkable for a woman of the eighteenth century. Geoffrin died in Paris on 6 October 1777.

See also **Catherine II (Russia); Diderot, Denis; *Encyclopédie;* Enlightenment; Helvétius, Claude-Adrien; Montesquieu, Charles-Louis de Secondat de; Philosophes; Poniatowski, Stanisław II Augustus; Republic of Letters; Salons.**

BIBLIOGRAPHY

Primary Source

[Poniatowski, Stanisław, king of Poland, and Marie-Thérèse Geoffrin]. *Correspondance inédite du roi Stanislas-Auguste Poniatowski et de Madame Geoffrin (1764–1777).* Paris, 1875.

Secondary Sources

Goodman, Dena. *The Republic of Letters: A Cultural History of the French Enlightenment.* Ithaca, N.Y., 1994.

Gutwirth, Madelyn. *The Twilight of the Goddesses: Women and Representation in the French Revolutionary Era.* New Brunswick, N.J., 1992.

ROSAMOND HOOPER-HAMERSLEY

GEOGRAPHY. *See* **Cartography and Geography.**

GEOLOGY. Geology was only in the process of becoming a recognized science near the close of the eighteenth century. Tracing geology's root sources, during the several centuries prior to its emergence as a distinct science, requires attention to varied forms of activity and knowledge, including (1) practical activities such as quarrying, mining, surveying, and the metallurgical arts; (2) descriptive and classificatory inquiries in fields of natural history such as mineralogy and physical geography; (3) philosophical explorations of the causes of the formation of minerals, stones, and crystals; (4) history proper, which is to say chronological and antiquarian research; and (5) efforts to construct a theory of the earth, a genre that began to flourish especially after the middle of the seventeenth century.

VARIED MODES OF PURSUIT OF EARTH SCIENCE

Growing confidence in the practical value of systematic knowledge lay behind efforts to survey mineral resources and promote their exploitation. The writings of the German mining physician Georgius Agricola (1494–1555) are representative of increasingly acute descriptions and rationalizations of technical procedures for extracting and treating those resources. By the seventeenth century, under state ownership or patronage of mining authorities in several Continental countries, formalized institutes were being founded as centers for instruction and analysis in the extraction industries. The leading eighteenth-century example was the Saxon *Bergakademie* (Mining Academy) at Freiberg, where Abraham Gottlob Werner (1749–1817) achieved fame as both teacher and theoretician. Similar practical and economic motives lay behind royal support for a French mineralogical survey launched in the 1760s.

Until well into the eighteenth century, the term *fossil* referred comprehensively to things found in or dug out of the ground. Renaissance naturalists such as the Swiss physician Conrad Gessner (1516–1565) undertook to codify knowledge of fossils, through both observation of specimens and study of texts from Greco-Roman antiquity. Such efforts at literary compilation were echoed by the enthusiasm of collectors (such as the Dane Ole Worm [1588–1654] and the Jesuit polymath Athanasius Kircher [1601?–1680]) for assembling displays of stones, gems, and other "natural antiquities." How stones form, and the possible causative roles played by water or generative seeds in that process, was a central question of early modern natural philosophy. It was perhaps most prominently posed in chemical cosmogonies from Jean Baptiste van Helmont (1579–1644) to Georg Ernst Stahl (1660–1734), and physicians regularly addressed it when explaining the formation of bladder stones. Of obvious relevance was assaying of mineral waters, one of the most frequently treated topics of geological investigation during the sixteenth and seventeenth centuries.

Related to these problems was the prolonged debate concerning the origins of "figured stones," or fossil bodies of regular form. One group of theories attributed these bodies to generative powers or seeds indigenous to the earth—the mineral domain being considered capable of engendering "intrinsic fossils" through its own specific powers, analogous to those of plants or animals. Such theories were effectively modified toward the end of the seventeenth century, particularly by the Danish anatomist Niels Stensen (Nicolaus Steno, 1638–1686) and some contemporaries. While employed at the Tuscan court, Steno recognized that the fossils known as *glossopetrae* resembled sharks' teeth. In his examination of "solid bodies contained naturally within solids," Steno developed a lucid analysis of the processes of sedimentation and petrifaction whereby an actual tooth or other durable organic part might become preserved within solid rock, thus making it an "extrinsic" fossil object. Extrinsic fossils were treated by many naturalists as relics of the biblical Flood, but such "diluvial" interpretations came under broad attack during the eighteenth century as difficulties multiplied for those viewing fossils as remnants of a single event within the time constraints of orthodox biblical chronology.

Advances in antiquarian scholarship during the seventeenth century, meanwhile, provided new standards for authenticating, dating, and interpreting historical relics and records, whether sacred, civil, or natural (terms such as *monument* or *inscription* were commonly applied to both human and natural productions). Thus, increasingly rigorous and critical analytical procedures used to study the human past—often with the aim of confirming historical knowledge found in the Bible—were applied simultaneously to comprehension of the earth's history, extending backward in time from the reconstructed physical geography of the classical era. Finally, as European scholars took Chinese historical records and New World inhabitants into consideration, comparisons of biblical chronology with archaeological and historical discoveries about non-Western peoples yielded doubts about the sufficiency of classical texts, including the Bible, as sources of historical information applicable to all of humanity. Such developments promoted lines of investigation that eventually led to a separation of natural history from civil history, and conviction grew that nature has had a long prehuman history.

Notwithstanding various challenges posed by geological activities and thinking to traditional religious doctrines, pursuit of geological questions up through 1800 proceeded with wide acceptance—often with hearty endorsement—of the presumed consistency of natural knowledge with revealed knowledge. It remained unusual for geological writers to dispute the compatibility of their scientific endeavor with religiously sanctioned belief in the divine superintendence of nature; few geological authors distanced themselves very far from a vision of nature laden with moral meaning.

EIGHTEENTH-CENTURY DEVELOPMENTS

While much early modern study of minerals and fossils consisted of examining specimens in the cabinet or museum, an ethos grew emphasizing travel and field observation, especially during the eighteenth century. Notable among the results were sustained efforts to discern the configurations of mountains and the patterns of distribution in their constituent rock masses. Around 1750 a consensus began to develop, distinguishing relatively unstructured and nonfossiliferous "primary" rocks, often found in the core districts of mountain ranges, from the stratified and frequently fossiliferous "secondary" rocks. Whether systematic distinctions between these types of rocks might promise access to a satisfactorily inclusive account of the earth's history since its inception was contested; some thought the evidence indicated a series of changes ("revolutions") of perhaps indeterminate number and scope. In general, a broadly shared sense of satisfaction with real progress in precise description of geological phenomena was not matched with agreement about which phenomena mattered most, or about their proper causal explanation. A strong preference existed for explaining the origins and transformations of most geological features through the agency of water ("Neptunism"), although field investigations were gradually yielding information warranting expanded roles for "fire" or heat. Aqueous agency tended to be seen as ordered and constructive (the organized strata of the earth's crust were, after all, mainly sedimentary), whereas fire was commonly viewed as a cause of disorder and disfigurement. The eighteenth century also witnessed a widening adoption of interpretive attitudes that have in retrospect been called "actualistic": this entailed the presumption that causal explanations should rely only on natural agents of types empirically known to operate. ("Actualism" thus differed from nineteenth-century uniformitarianism, which in addition to presuming continuity of kinds or types of cause also assumed continuity in the rate or intensity of their operation.)

Notwithstanding nineteenth-century attacks on the intellectual consequences of theories of the earth—Charles Lyell argued in *Principles of Geology* (vol. 1, 1830) that they promoted intellectual indolence—in their post-Cartesian heyday such syntheses or systems tended to serve geological investigation as both motivators for and receptacles of new information and drew attention to geological problems. Whether comprehensive theories constituted good science became increasingly controversial in the second half of the eighteenth century, especially in debates over the merits of theories published by Georges Louis Leclerc Buffon (1707–1788). Late Enlightenment skepticism about geological "systems" helps explain the generally inhospitable reception given the *Theory of the Earth* (1788, 1795) offered by the deistic Scottish philosopher James Hutton (1726–1797). His was a synthetic perspective on the maintenance of geological conditions propitious for support of life on the earth's surface, through a dynamic equilibrium between internal processes of heat-driven rock consolidation and elevation on one hand and external processes of erosion and deposition on the other (the original expression of what has since come to be known as the geostrophic cycle).

In the last quarter of the eighteenth century the science of geognosy (German *Geognosie*) made a bid for recognition as the leading means of analyzing mineral phenomena on a local and by extension even a global scale. Geognosy was a method or doctrine taught by Werner, at Freiberg, to an international cadre of students, most of whom were preparing for careers in their respective mining establishments. It elaborated on the litho-stratigraphic insights traceable back to Steno (since adapted and extended by other naturalists), and on skills in mineral identification, to develop recognition of how distinct rock masses relate to one another in subterranean space. Wernerian geognosy produced a key new geological concept, the "formation," defined essentially as a rock mass distinguishable in its lithological character and evident mode of origin, and thus as presumably formed at a given point in time. The formation, as a time-specific rock entity, became the focus of research on the relative positions of differentiated geological elements in the earth's crust (stratigraphy), and thus on their relative ages.

Geology's emergence as a distinct science around 1800 marked a momentous transformation in the history of Western science: an unprecedentedly definitive investment in nature with a sense of historical development. The classic aim of natural philosophy, prior to this shift of conception, had been confined mainly to the delineation of a presumably fixed order of nature, acting through processes usually believed not to have generated substantially altered configurations in the natural framework or in the objects furnishing it. With the advent of historical geology, the sciences added to their agenda the objective of tracing nature's successive changes. A portentous outcome of this new kind of research was the dawning cognizance, at the end of the eighteenth century, of the reality of biological extinction.

HISTORIOGRAPHY

The complications of disciplinary history apply with special force to geology in the early modern period; during most of this time no geological discipline existed. At least until recently, histories of geology have most often been written as retrospective accounts of the science's ancestry. Leading historical interpretations, founded by nineteenth- and twentieth-century geologists wishing to understand how their science came to take its modern form (or to use history as a tool to advance their particular conception of the science), tended to yield Whiggish historical accounts assigning credit or blame in accord with the degree to which various figures or scientific approaches contributed to, or obstructed, geology's progress. This kind of history thus tended also to obscure the motivations and intentions of many of the relevant actors, since few of them (at least until the late eighteenth century) conceived of the establishment of geology as their purpose. Genuinely historical recovery of geology's antecedents requires consultation of research literatures addressing the diverse fields in which, looking back, geological topics are seen to have been treated. Some of the better modern historical research—carried out largely within the "retrospective" tradition, but in calculated avoidance of Whig history—has called into question a long-standing Anglophone tendency to honor British over Continental strands in early geology's development, and to redress heavy emphasis on the physical and historical features of certain theories of the earth as preludes to geology, in favor of greater roles for descriptive and chemical-mineralogical enterprises (cf. Laudan). Modern scholarship has also tended to draw back from an earlier inclination to identify a single founder or "father" of geology—Hutton was long a British favorite, Werner a Continental one—and to see in geology, instead, a creature of multiple parentage.

See also **Buffon, Georges Louis Leclerc; Earth, Theories of the; Gessner, Conrad; Scientific Method; Steno, Nicolaus.**

BIBLIOGRAPHY

Ellenberger, François. *Histoire de la géologie.* 2 vols. Paris, 1988–1994.

Gohau, Gabriel. *Les sciences de la terre aux XVIIe et XVIIIe siècles: Naissance de la géologie.* Paris, 1990.

Jardine, N., J. A. Secord, and E. C. Spary, eds. *Cultures of Natural History.* Cambridge, U.K., and New York, 1996.

Laudan, Rachel. *From Mineralogy to Geology: The Foundations of a Science, 1650–1830.* Chicago, 1987.

Oldroyd, David R. *Thinking about the Earth: A History of Ideas in Geology.* Cambridge, Mass., 1996.

Porter, Roy. *The Making of Geology: Earth Science in Britain, 1660–1815.* Cambridge, U.K., and New York, 1977.

Rappaport, Rhoda. "The Earth Sciences." In *The Cambridge History of Science.* Vol. 4: *Eighteenth-Century Science,* edited by Roy Porter, pp. 417–435. Cambridge, U.K., and New York, 2003.

———. *When Geologists Were Historians, 1665–1750.* Ithaca, N.Y., 1997.

Rossi, Paolo. *The Dark Abyss of Time: The History of the Earth and the History of Nations from Hooke to Vico.* Chicago, 1984. Translation of *I segni del tempo* (1979) by Lydia G. Cochrane.

Rudwick, Martin J. S. *The Meaning of Fossils: Episodes in the History of Palaeontology.* 2nd ed. Chicago, 1985.

Schneer, Cecil J., ed. *Toward a History of Geology.* Cambridge, Mass., 1969.

KENNETH L. TAYLOR, KERRY V. MAGRUDER

GEORGE I (GREAT BRITAIN) (1660–1727; ruled 1714–1727), king of Great Britain and Ireland. George I, who was also elector of Hanover (1698–1727), was the first of the Hanoverian dynasty to rule in Britain. Unlike William III (ruled 1689–1702), who seized power in 1688–1689 and who was familiar with English politics and politicians from earlier visits, marriage into the English royal family, and extensive intervention in English domestic politics, George knew relatively little of England. His failure to learn English and his obvious preference for Hanover further contributed to this sense of alien rule. It was exacerbated by a sense that the preference for Hanover entailed an abandonment of British national interests, as resources

George I. Equestrian portrait by Godfrey Kneller. ©ARCHIVO ICONOGRAFICO, S.A./CORBIS

were expended for the aggrandizement of Hanover and as the entire direction of British foreign policy was set accordingly. Within five years of his accession, George was at war with Spain, was close to war with Russia, and, having divided the Whigs and proscribed the Tories, was seeking to implement a controversial legislative program. Allied with France from 1716, George pursued a foreign policy that struck little resonance with the political experiences and xenophobic traditions of his British subjects.

On the other hand, George's reign was not so much the wholesale Hanoverian takeover that some feared. Despite periodic rows about Hanoverian interests, George did not swamp Britain with German ministers or systems. Instead, he adapted to British institutions, conforming to the Church of England despite his strong Lutheranism. Even his dispute with his son, later George II (ruled 1727–1760), in 1717–1720 fitted into a parliamentary framework with court and Leicester house parties at Westminster. And the failure of the Jacobite rising of the Old Pretender, James Edward Stuart (1688–1766), in 1715 indicated early in his reign that the establishment on which George depended was determined in turn to maintain his rule.

George's place in politics was not of his choosing but was instead a consequence of the limitations in royal authority and power that stemmed from the Glorious Revolution of 1688–1689 and subsequent changes. George was sensible enough to adapt and survive. Unlike James II (ruled 1685–1688), he was a pragmatist who did not have an agenda for Britain other than helping Hanover. In part this was a sensible response to circumstances and in part a complacency that arose from diffidence, honesty, and dullness. George lacked the decisiveness, charisma, and wiliness of Louis XIV (ruled 1643–1715) of France and Peter the Great (ruled 1682–1725) of Russia.

As an individual George was a figure of suspicion because of the incarceration of his adulterous wife, Sophia Dorothea, and the disappearance in 1694 of her lover, Philipp Christoph von Königsmarch, and because of rumors about his own personal life. His choleric quarrel with the future George II also attracted attention. George I enjoyed drilling his troops and hunting. When he could, he had fought, including in 1675–1678 in the Dutch war against Louis XIV and in 1683–1685 against the Turks in Hungary. He had led forces into Holstein in 1700, led an invasion of Wolfenbüttel in 1702, and commanded on the Rhine against Louis XIV's forces in the War of the Spanish Succession (1701–1714).

George's reliance on the Whigs and antipathy toward the Tories was more important, as it limited his room for political maneuver. In 1720 George had to accommodate himself to Robert Walpole (1676–1745), the leading opposition Whig, but it is also clear that Walpole had to adapt to George. In 1720 George was also reconciled with his son, but only to the extent of a mutual coldness. George refused to have his son as regent in England during his trips to Hanover in 1723, 1725, and 1727, on the last of which he died en route. He also turned down his son's request for a military post in any European conflict that might involve Britain.

George showed both political skills and a sense of responsibility during his reign. An incompetent and unyielding monarch might well have led to the end of Hanoverian rule in Britain, but at George's death in 1727 there was no question that the succession would pass anywhere other than to his son.

See also **George II (Great Britain); Hanoverian Dynasty (Great Britain); Jacobitism.**

BIBLIOGRAPHY

Beattie, John M. *The English Court in the Reign of George I.* London, 1967.

Hatton, Ragnhild. *George I: Elector and King.* Cambridge, Mass., 1978.

Marlow, Joyce. *George I: His Life and Times.* London, 1973.

Plumb, J. H. *The First Four Georges.* Rev. ed. London, 1974.

JEREMY BLACK

GEORGE II (GREAT BRITAIN)

GEORGE II (GREAT BRITAIN) (1683–1760; ruled 1727–1760), king of Great Britain and Ireland. George II, who was also elector of Hanover (1727–1760), was the second of the Hanoverian dynasty to rule Britain. He was the son of George I (ruled 1714–1727). It is not easy to evaluate George II, as he left relatively little correspondence. In his youth he took an active role in the War of the Spanish Succession (1701–1714) with France, and he never lost his love of military matters. In 1705 he married the vivacious Princess Caroline of Ansbach (1683–1737), who exercised considerable influence on him until her death in 1737. The contrast between the queen's bright, sparkling, witty nature and George's more dour, boorish demeanor led contemporaries to underrate the influence of the latter. George accompanied his father to London in 1714 and became Prince of Wales. Relations between the two were difficult, and in 1717 this led to a rift that was closely linked to a serious division within the Whig Party. Relations were mended in 1720, although they remained difficult.

Succeeding to the throne in 1727, George II kept his father's leading minister, Sir Robert Walpole (1676–1745), in office and supported him until his fall in 1742. George's attitudes were important in politics, but he was not always able to prevail. Thus in 1744 and 1746 George failed to sustain John, Lord Carteret (1690–1763) in office, while in 1746 and 1755–1757 George could not prevent the entry into office of William Pitt the Elder (1708–1778), later first earl of Chatham. Pitt had angered George by his criticism of the degree to which British policies favored George's native electorate of Hanover, and that indeed was central to George's concerns. He spent as much time as possible in the electorate and actively pressed its territorial expansion. This was not to be, however. Instead, George's hated nephew, Frederick II (Frederick the Great, ruled 1740–1786) of Prussia, became the leading ruler in North Germany, and George had to face the humiliation of a French conquest of the electorate in 1757.

George's reign also saw the defeat in 1746 of a Jacobite attempt, under Charles Edward Stuart (1720–1788), "Bonnie Prince Charlie," to overthrow Hanoverian rule. George did not panic in December 1745 when the Jacobites advanced as far as Derby. After George's second son, William Augustus (1721–1765), duke of Cumberland, was victorious over the Jacobites at Culloden, not only was the Protestant establishment affirmed, but the Hanoverian dynasty was also finally and explicitly accepted as representing the aspirations and security of the realm.

George II was not noted as a patron of the arts, although he was interested in music. He was despised as a boor by his wife's influential favorite, John Lord Hervey (1696–1743). In fact George, as king, was happiest in 1743, when at Dettingen he became the last British monarch to lead his troops into battle. George displayed great courage under fire, and the battle was a victory. It was celebrated by George Frideric Handel (1685–1759) in *Dettingen Te Deum*. As a young man George had also participated in 1708 in the battle of Oudenaarde, where he had charged the French at the head of the Hanoverian dragoons and had his horse shot from under him. He was keen on the army, enjoyed the company of military men, and was determined to control military patronage. George had the guards' regimental reports and returns sent to him personally every week, and when he reviewed his troops, he did so with great attention to detail. George's personal interest in the army (but not the navy) could be a major nuisance for his British ministers, since as a result they had less room for concession and parliamentary maneuvering over such issues as the size of the armed forces and the policy of subsidies paid to secure the use of Hessian forces.

George II. Portrait by Thomas Hudson. ©BETTMANN/CORBIS

The impact of George's martial temperament upon his conduct of foreign policy also concerned the government. In Britain, however, George had no particular political agenda, and this was important to the development of political stability. His pragmatism was both a sensible response to circumstances and the consequence of a complacency that arose from diffidence, honesty, and dullness, albeit also a certain amount of choleric anger.

With Caroline, George had eight children, three boys and five girls. His relations with his eldest son, Frederick Louis (1707–1751), Prince of Wales, were particularly difficult, mirroring those of George II with his father. The prince's opposition was crucial to the fall of Walpole. After Caroline died, George settled into a domestic relationship with his already established mistress, Amalia Sophie Marianne von Walmoden. George made her countess of Yarmouth, and she became an influential political force because of her access to him.

By the close of George's reign, Britain had smashed the French navy and taken much of the French Empire to become the dominant European power in South Asia and North America. The direct contribution of the by then elderly king to this process was limited, but the ability of William Pitt the Elder to direct resources to transoceanic goals was a consequence of the way he, his ministerial colleague the duke of Newcastle, and George II operated parliamentary monarchy in the late 1750s.

See also **Hanoverian Dynasty (Great Britain); Jacobitism; Pitt, William the Elder and William the Younger.**

BIBLIOGRAPHY

De-la-Noy, Michael. *The King Who Never Was: The Story of Frederick, Prince of Wales.* London and Chester Springs, Pa., 1996.

van der Kiste, John. *King George II and Queen Caroline.* New York, 1997.

Whitworth, Rex. *William Augustus Duke of Cumberland: A Life.* London, 1992.

JEREMY BLACK

GEORGE III (GREAT BRITAIN)

(1738–1820; ruled 1760–1820), king of Great Britain and Ireland. George III was also elector of Hanover (1760–1815), king of Hanover (1814–1820), and the last monarch to rule the thirteen colonies that became the United States of America. George III's father, Frederick Louis (1707–1751), the son of George II (ruled 1727–1760), died in 1751, leaving his eldest son to succeed him first as Prince of Wales and then as king. As prince George III developed a sense of antagonism toward the prevailing political system, which he thought oligarchical and factional. The young prince and his confidant, John Stuart (1713–1792), third earl of Bute, favored the idea of politics without party and a king above faction.

Succeeding his grandfather, George II, in 1760, George III was a figure of controversy from the outset because of his determination to reign without party. Unlike George I (ruled 1714–1727) and George II, George III was not a pragmatist, and he

George III. Portrait by Thomas Gainsborough. ©ARCHIVO ICONOGRAFICO, S.A./CORBIS

did have an agenda for Britain. He thought that much about the political system was corrupt and ascribed this in part to the size of the national debt. As a consequence George's moral reformism, which drew on his piety, was specifically aimed against faction and luxury. Like other rulers, George found it difficult to create acceptable relationships with senior politicians at his accession, and this contributed powerfully to the ministerial and political instability of the 1760s. Nevertheless, there was no fundamental political crisis, and after George found an effective political manager in Frederick North (1732–1792) in 1770, the political situation within Britain became far more quiescent. However, George's determination to maintain royal authority played a major role in the crisis of relations with the American colonies that led to revolution there in 1775. In turn failure there brought down the North ministry in 1782, beginning a period of instability that lasted until 1784.

George matured in office, becoming a practiced politician and a man more capable of defining deliverable goals. His conscientious nature shines through his copious correspondence. George felt the monarch could reach out, beyond antipathy and factional self-interest on the part of politicians, to a wider, responsible, and responsive public opinion.

George remained politically influential during the long ministry of William Pitt the Younger (1759–1806), but his ill health in 1788 led to a serious political crisis. George's attack of porphyria, which led to symptoms of insanity, caused the regency crisis. George's recovery in 1789 ended the crisis, and he again became a factor to reckon with. His obduracy created problems for his ministers when in the 1790s he opposed the extension of rights to Catholics in Ireland or Britain. Arguing that such moves would breach his coronation oath, George stated that he would not give royal assent to such legislation. This helped precipitate Pitt's resignation in 1801 and the fall of the ministry of William Wyndham Grenville (1759–1834) in 1807.

George's attitude also made religious issues even more central in the politics of the early nineteenth century than they might otherwise have been. His firmness, not to say rigidity, contrasted with the more flexible attitude of his non-Anglican predecessors, George II, George I, William III (ruled 1689–1702), and arguably Charles II (ruled 1660–1685). It also helped focus the defense of order, hierarchy, and continuity much more on religion than would otherwise have been the case in a period of revolutionary threats. George was motivated not only by his religious convictions but also by the argument that the position of the Church of England rested on fundamental parliamentary legislation. Any repeal would also thus challenge the constitutional safeguards that were similarly founded and secured. It is not surprising therefore that Edmund Burke's emphasis, in his *Reflections on the Revolution in France* (1790), on continuity and the value of the Glorious Revolution found favor with George III.

The monarchy became a more potent symbol of national identity and continuity in response to the French Revolution. In 1809, when George celebrated his jubilee, the public event not only symbolized the stability he had provided in an age of volatile politics but also expressed the genuine affection and admiration his subjects now had for the monarch. The social elite and the bulk of public opinion had rallied around the themes of country, crown, and church.

George's health broke down permanently in 1811. The following year his eldest son, George, Prince of Wales, became regent; in 1820 he succeeded his father as George IV (ruled 1820–1830).

George III was a keen family man. His wife, Charlotte of Mecklenburg-Strelitz, whom he married in 1761, struck up a genuinely close relationship with him, but as their numerous children grew to adulthood (Charlotte bore a total of nine sons and six daughters), there arose a conflict between George's own sense of propriety and the dissolute lifestyle adopted by most of his boys. The members of the younger generation were especially loath to accept the king and queen's choices of marriage partners and entered into liaisons that, while often stable and personally fulfilling, hardly redounded to the increasingly prudish image George wished to promote. The alienation between the generations was represented most strikingly in the endless disputes between the king and the Prince of Wales.

George was a major art collector and a supporter of the astronomer Sir William Herschel (1738–1822). His cultural preferences, particularly his interest in the work of George Frideric Handel (1685–1759), were related to his moral concerns. George was interested in farming and was known as "Farmer George." Although this led to satire at his expense, his domestication of the monarchy and his lack of ostentatious grandeur was important to a revival in popularity for the monarchy that served it well in the political crisis of the 1790s caused by the French Revolution. He was the originator of the emphasis on domesticity in the British royal family. The contrast between the fates of the British and French monarchies was due to many factors, but the differences between the personalities and attitudes of George III and Louis XVI (ruled 1774–1792) were important. Similarly George was subsequently favorably contrasted by British commentators with the apparently tyrannical and bellicose Napoléon I.

See also **American Independence, War of (1775–1783); George II (Great Britain); Handel, George Frideric; Hanoverian Dynasty (Great Britain); Pitt, William the Elder and William the Younger; Revolutions, Age of.**

BIBLIOGRAPHY

Black, Jeremy. *Eighteenth-Century Britain, 1688–1783.* Basingstoke, U.K., 2001.

Ditchfield, G. M. *George III: An Essay on Monarchy.* Basingstoke, U.K., 2002.

Newman, Gerald. *Britain in the Hanoverian Age, 1714–1837: An Encyclopedia.* New York and London, 1997.

Pares, Richard. *George III and the Politicians.* Oxford, 1953.

Thomas, P. D. G. *George III: King and Politicians, 1760–1770.* Manchester, U.K., 2002.

JEREMY BLACK

GERMAN LITERATURE AND LANGUAGE.

GERMAN LITERATURE AND LANGUAGE. German literature of the early modern period is as heterogeneous as the patchwork of principalities constituting the Holy Roman Empire at this time. The variety of literary forms, particularly during the Renaissance, reflects a panoply of political, social, and confessional interests among contemporary patrons and audiences.

LITERATURE FROM 1450 TO 1700

When compared with German literature around 1200 or 1800, few works of this "middle" period have entered the canon of world literature. To explain this deficit, many scholars point to the Protestant Reformation and its seventeenth-century progeny, the Thirty Years' War (1618–1648), both of which diverted substantial creative energy toward theological debate, political diatribe, and at times sheer survival. However, the lack of a cohesive polity played an equal role, depriving authors of a central focal point for literary activities, such as a royal court or an emerging capital as found in England or France. Nonetheless, German literary works of the Late Middle Ages, Renaissance, and Baroque reward their readers with intimate views of a society shaped by the opposing forces of city and court, Protestantism and Catholicism, and high and low culture.

The late medieval inheritance. Medieval literature proved especially long-lived in Germany. Some traditions or genres lasted well into the sixteenth century, although they frequently underwent substantial transformations as they adapted to changing tastes and audiences. For example, the meistersingers of Nuremberg and other cities considered the minnesinger Wolfram von Eschenbach one of their forebears and adhered strictly to the tripartite barform stanzas practiced around 1200, even if Wolfram sang of secular love for the nobility, as opposed to the primarily religious songs composed by the meistersingers for their bourgeois audience. The prestige of aristocratic models remained strong, prompting urban authors to adapt them to their own uses.

This is most evident in the continuing popularity of knightly tales of combat, romance, and exotic encounters. Medieval verse epics, such as Gottfried von Straßburg's *Tristan und Isolt,* Wirnt von Grafenberg's *Wigalois,* or the anonymous *Nibelungenlied,* retained broad appeal and appeared as some of the earliest chapbooks, both in prose (*Tristrant und Isalde,* 1484; *Wigoleis,* 1472, by Ulrich Füetrer) and in newly versified forms (*Das Lied vom Hürnen Seyfrid,* or The Song of Horned Siegfried; c. 1530). Other chapbooks presented stories adapted from French sources, such as *Melusine* (1456) by Thüring von Ringoltingen (1410/1415–1483) or *Huge Scheppel* (c. 1437) by Elisabeth von Nassau-Saarbrücken (c. 1393–1456). Later works introduced bourgeois heroes such as *Fortunatus* (1509), who succeeds with the aid of a magic purse. Meanwhile, clever peasant protagonists got the better of other social classes in works like *Salomon und Markolf* (c. 1482) and *Till Eulenspiegel* (c. 1510). Nonetheless, chivalry remained strong, as evidenced by Emperor Maximilian I (ruled 1493–1519), often known as "the last knight." With the aid of court ghostwriters, Maximilian produced *Theuerdank* (1517; Lofty thinker), a rhymed allegory of his courtship of Mary of Burgundy. He is also responsible for the *Ambraser Heldenbuch* (1504–1516; Ambras book of heroes), a compilation of twenty-five medieval courtly epics.

Perhaps the most lingering literary legacy of the Middle Ages was that of medieval theater, which encompassed both religious drama, such as Passion, Easter, and Last Judgment plays, as well as the secular tradition of *Fastnachtspiele,* or Carnival plays. Easter plays focused on Christ's Crucifixion and Resurrection, while Passion plays treated the totality of salvation history from the Creation to the martyrdom of saints. These texts are generally grouped according to "families" such as the Rhine-Hesse group, whose related scenes suggest some form of theatrical exchange among the communities involved. Carnival plays traditionally transgressed social mores and are similarly grouped into regional traditions. In Nuremberg, performances took place in inns, while in Lübeck, Sterzing (Tyrol), southwest Germany, and Switzerland, these were open-air events. The tradition grew less ribald following the Reformation. The Nuremberg plays of Hans Sachs (1494–1576) are perhaps the best-known *Fastnachtspiele* from the sixteenth century, but Lucerne produced important late Catholic examples of the genre alongside the *Lucerne Passion Play,* performed until 1616 and the best-documented play of its type.

Renaissance humanism. Following the development of movable type in the 1440s and 1450s, books became more affordable, leading to widespread changes in reading habits and the dissemination of knowledge. Illiteracy and the high cost of manuscripts had meant that literary works were most frequently read aloud in a group, but now an increasingly educated bourgeoisie began to read in private. Education itself, once the domain of the church, expanded to secular institutions with the proliferation of municipal schools and the continued expansion of universities. As a result, an educated, nonclerical class developed, nourished by towns' and territorial rulers' growing need for administrators. This group proved especially receptive to the rediscovery of classical learning and arts at the heart of the Italian Renaissance.

The resulting humanist movement had a far-reaching impact on learning and literature. Although Latin was the humanists' primary language, their adaptation of classical models established the course of "high" German literature for much of the early modern period. Early humanists, such as the Swabian scholars Niklaus von Wyle (c. 1415–1479), Albrecht von Eyb (1420–1475), and Heinrich Steinhöwel (1411/12–1479), focused on translations in an effort to cultivate their "barbaric" native tongue. Members of the next generation engaged predominantly in imitation, producing Neo-Latin works intended to rival those of antiquity.

Conrad Celtis or Celtes (1459–1508), Germany's "arch-humanist" and first poet laureate (1487), followed Horatian models for his *Quatuor Libri Amorum* (1502; Four books of *Amores*), while Johannes Reuchlin (1455–1522) wrote *Scaenica Progymnasmata* or *Henno* (1497), the first successful Terentian comedy north of the Alps. By the early 1500s, northern humanists were producing original works of lasting influence, such as the sublimely humorous *Moriae Encomium* (1509; Praise of folly) by Desiderius Erasmus of Rotterdam (1466?–1536) or the poetically supple *Basia* (published 1539; Kisses) by another Dutchman, Janus Secundus (1511–1536).

A humanist also produced the single most successful German literary work prior to the Enlightenment: *Das Narrenschiff* (1494; Ship of fools) by Sebastian Brant (c. 1457–1521). In the 112 chapters of the original edition, each accompanied by an illustrative woodcut with a three- to four-line motto, the author moralizes against all manner of "follies" ranging from gluttony and greed to excessive ecclesiastical benefices. Four unauthorized editions of the work appeared within its first year of publication, but it was not until its Latin adaptation by Brant's protégé Jacob Locher (*Stultifera Navis*, 1497) that it became a true pan-European sensation. In its wake, a tradition of *Narrenliteratur* (Fools' literature) emerged, with authors such as Thomas Murner (1475–1537), Jörg Wickram (c. 1505–c. 1562), and Hans Sachs among Brant's direct or indirect heirs. The *Narrenschiff*'s "Sankt Grobian" (Saint Uncouth) was to provide a model for sixteenth-century conduct books, and the work's melding of text and image anticipates later emblem books.

Reformation. While some early humanists seemed to prize poetry over piety, later proponents of the *studia humanitatis* eagerly applied the motto *ad fontes* ('to the sources') to religious texts. Johannes Reuchlin was the first to promote Greek and Hebrew studies, considering the latter so important that he cautioned the emperor against an effort to destroy Jewish writings. Scholastic opponents charged Reuchlin with heresy, and the resulting dispute became a humanist cause célèbre, producing the *Epistolae Obscurorum Virorum* (1515–1517; Letters of obscure men), a satire of Reuchlin's ineloquent adversaries written by Crotus Rubeanus (c. 1480–c. 1545), Ulrich von Hutten (1488–1523), and others. Erasmus became the leading Christian humanist, editing the writings of St. Jerome, along with other church fathers, and following in his footsteps as biblical translator by producing the *Novum Instrumentum* (1516), a Greek edition of the New Testament with an accompanying Latin translation distinct from the Vulgate.

In 1522, another translator of the Bible, Martin Luther (1483–1546), based his German translation of the New Testament on the second edition of Erasmus's work. Beyond its religious significance, the Lutheran Reformation had a profound impact on vernacular literature. For the first time, the power of printing became manifest, with Protestant authors churning out broadsides, dialogues, plays, and songs to promote the new faith. Catholic authors responded in kind, but not in quantity, since many considered the common vernacular inappropriate for theological debate. Luther's hymns and above all his Bible stand as lasting artistic achievements. His success as a translator lay in his ability to render biblical Hebrew and Greek in the idiomatic German spoken by "the mother at home, the children in the street, and the common man at market," as described in his *Sendbrief vom Dolmetschen* (1530; Letter on translation), which defends Luther's rendition of contested passages against Catholic detractors.

Despite an initial alliance, humanist support for Luther was mixed at best. By the mid-1520s, the debate between Luther and Erasmus over free will signaled a break between the two movements. Still, Protestants embraced humanist educational ideals, and Luther's colleague Philipp Melanchthon (1497–1560) is known to posterity as the "Teacher of Germany" for his widely influential reforms.

Mid- to late sixteenth century. In adapting countless classical, medieval, and Renaissance works for a bourgeois audience, Hans Sachs embodied the humanists' belief in the edifying power of literature. Although his meistersongs far outweigh his other production, Sachs remains best known for Carnival plays such as *Der fahrende Schüler im Paradies* (1550; The traveling scholar in paradise) or *Das Narrenschneiden* (1536; The Foolectomy), later produced by Goethe in Weimar. He was also a leading author of confessional literature, producing

Reformation dialogues, numerous broadsheets, and "Die Wittenbergische Nachtigall" (1523), which compared Luther's preaching of the Gospel to the song of a nightingale.

Other important authors from the latter half of the century include Jörg Wickram, like Sachs a meistersinger and playwright, but best known for his prose works. His *Rollwagenbüchlein* (1555; Stagecoach stories) became a model of short, entertaining fabliaux, while *Der Goldfaden* (1557; The golden thread) is considered the first German novel based on a plot of the author's own creation. Johann Fischart (c. 1547–1590) produced the exuberant *Geschichtklitterung* (1575; revised second edition 1582), a playfully punning translation of François Rabelais's *Gargantua et Pantagruel.* Leading playwrights are Nicodemus Frischlin (1547–1590), known for his Neo-Latin biblical plays, and Duke Heinrich Julius von Braunschweig (1564–1613), whose vernacular works show the mark of itinerant English troupes active on the Continent.

In terms of lasting influence, however, no late-sixteenth-century work can compare with the *Historia von D. Johann Fausten* (1587; History of Dr. Johann Faust), a purported biography of this part-historical, part-legendary necromancer. In typical humanist fashion, Faust desires to recreate antiquity, but the pursuit of knowledge for knowledge's sake is now demonized. Soon after its publication, the chapbook found it way to England, where playwright Christopher Marlowe created *The Tragicall History of Dr. Faustus* (1588; published 1604). Goethe began to occupy himself with this material around 1775, with *Faust I* published in 1808 and *Faust II,* posthumously, in 1832.

The baroque period. Seventeenth-century Germany saw a resurgence of courtly patronage and Catholicism. The Jesuit order worked actively to restore the old faith, adapting popular genres as Protestants had done before them. Jesuit drama proved especially effective: the eternal damnation portrayed in *Cenodoxus* (1602) by Jakob Bidermann (c. 1577–1639) drove fourteen spectators into spiritual retreat in 1609 to take up the *Exercises of St. Ignatius.* The leading author of Catholic hymns was Friedrich Spee von Langenfeld (1591–1635), also a member of the Society of Jesus. Protestants pursued an inner spirituality as well, apparent in the poetry of Catharina Regina von Greiffenberg (1633–1694) and Johannes Scheffler, who became Angelus Silesius (1624–1677) upon his conversion to Catholicism in 1653. Nonetheless, Protestant literary traditions remained strong, as demonstrated by the hymns of Paul Gerhardt (1607–1676).

The publication of *Das Buch von der deutschen Poeterey* (1624; The book of German poetics) by Martin Opitz (1597–1639) marked the true beginning of baroque literature in Germany. The work is a concise handbook with practical recommendations for versification, rhetorical devices, and genre distinctions. The significance of Opitz's metrical reform cannot be overstated. Long schooled on Latin and French verse, which were based either on vowel length or syllable counting, German authors ignored the natural alternation of accented and unaccented syllables. Opitz restored this rhythm with the result that the Alexandriner—iambic hexameter with a central caesura—became the standard verse form for the German baroque. The four-beat doggerel *Knittelvers* of Hans Sachs and others became a thing of ridicule, as illustrated by Andreas Gryphius's *Absurda Comica oder Herr Peter Squentz* (1658; Comic absurdities or Mr. Peter Squentz).

Lyric poets also embraced Opitz's recommendations. In addition to those mentioned above, among the most talented poets were Paul Fleming (1609–1640), Simon Dach (1605–1659), Georg Philipp Harsdörffer (1607–1658), Christian Hofmann von Hofmannswaldau (1617–1679), and Caspar Stieler (1632–1707). Together they introduced a highly ornamented language replete with tropes and figures. Faced with the horrors of the Thirty Years' War, such authors frequently treated the themes of *vanitas* (the vanity of worldly pursuits) and *carpe diem* (seize the day). Amatory poetry was equally in vogue, as found in the Petrarchism of Fleming or the gallant poetry of Hofmannswaldau. Popular forms were the sonnet, the epigram, and figural or concrete poetry, in which the printed text evoked the item described.

Opitz did not include the novel in his handbook, but by 1700 it had become an acknowledged genre. Baroque authors produced three basic novel types. *Arminius* (1689–1690) by Daniel Casper von Lohenstein (1635–1683) and *Aramena* (1669–1673) by Duke Anton Ulrich von Braunschweig (1633–1714) are prime examples of the heroic-gallant novel, which treated seventeenth-century dynastic politics in Roman guise. *Die adriatische Rosemund* (1645) by Philipp von Zesen (1619–1689) is considered Germany's prime pastoral novel, although Rosemund's idyllic existence as a shepherdess is a mere interlude in an otherwise tragic story set in a bourgeois milieu. Representing the *Schelmenroman* (picaresque novel) is the most famous German baroque novel of all, *Der abenteuerliche Simplicissimus* (1668; The adventurous Simplicissimus; *Continuatio,* 1669; Continuation) by Hans Jakob Christoffel von Grimmelshausen (1622?–1676). Like Grimmelshausen himself, the novel's protagonist leads a peripatetic life marked by the vicissitudes of war. Forced from home by marauding soldiers, Simplicissimus begins as a simpleton and moves through several stages of life and experience before finally withdrawing from the world.

Baroque vernacular theater is inextricably linked to the contemporary culture of court pageantry. Elaborate stage machinery allowed for striking visual effects, and baroque playwrights employed these to delight or disarm their audiences, particularly in the popular tragedies (*Trauerspiele,* literally 'sad plays') of Andreas Gryphius (1616–1664) and Daniel Casper von Lohenstein. Gryphius is known for martyr dramas such as *Catharina von Georgien* (c. 1647), but also for *Cardenio und Celinde* (c. 1648), in which the lovers, unlike Romeo and Juliet, renounce their love before it leads to a tragic end. Gryphius, along with Harsdörffer and others, also composed opera libretti, such as *Majuma,* performed for the coronation of Ferdinand IV of Habsburg in 1653. None other than Opitz founded German opera with *Daphne* (1627), adapted from an Italian libretto by Ottavio Rinuccini, although the corresponding score by Heinrich Schütz (1585–1672) is unfortunately lost. In its combination of word, image, and music, opera became the most celebrated performance genre of the century.

Toward a standard language. Linguistically, early modern Germany was as disparate as its political landscape. As today, the Low German dialects of the north differed substantially from southern German variants, but in 1450 no well-established standard existed to allow easy communication between them. The emergence of New High German by the late seventeenth century was a slow and complicated process, and the transitional period between roughly 1350 and 1650 is known as *Frühneuhochdeutsch,* or Early New High German.

Unlike the Middle High German of medieval authors, which was rooted in the language of the Hohenstaufen court in southwest Germany, *Frühneuhochdeutsch* was not based on any one regional dialect. However, some areas exerted more linguistic influence than others, in particular through the chancelleries of cities and leading courts, which gradually abandoned Latin in favor of a "common" German stripped of specific regionalisms. The Prague chancellery of Emperor Charles IV, the Habsburg chancellery in Vienna, and the Saxon chancellery in Meißen are all important in this regard. Indeed, Luther himself followed the model of the Saxon chancellery, and the ubiquity of Luther's Bible did much to hasten the development of a standard language. However, Luther did not singlehandedly create the basis for New High German, as Jakob Grimm and others once claimed. Rather, recent research has demonstrated that Luther, the chancelleries, and early printers all adopted linguistic trends in process around them.

As the need for a unified language became increasingly apparent, humanists and their successors strove to normalize orthography, lexicon, and grammar. Sixteenth century efforts, such as the dictionaries of Petrus Dasypodius (*Dictionarium Latino-Germanicum,* 1525) and Josua Maaler (*Die Teütsch Spraach,* 1561), or Johannes Clajus's *Grammatica Germanicae Linguae* (1578; Grammar of the German language), were produced primarily for foreigners familiar with Latin. Later, baroque *Sprachgesellschaften* (literary societies) worked to cultivate the language by freeing it from foreign influence. Philipp von Zesen (1619–1689) and others created German neologisms to replace borrowed terms, while Justus Schottel (1612–1676) produced his *Ausführliche Arbeit von der Teutschen Haubt Sprache* (1663), considered by many the first systematic grammar of the German language.

Recent research. Early modern German literature is the most under-researched period of German literary history. However, its transitional position between Middle Ages and modernity, once considered a disadvantage, has now become its asset, attracting fresh research on shifts in political, social, and intellectual paradigms. As in other fields, recent work has turned from an emphasis on canonical works to an exploration of the margins that bounded and defined "high" literature. Representations of gender and minorities have generated substantial interest, with women authors gaining a new appreciation. Popular literature, such as Carnival plays, has also enjoyed a positive reassessment. Much work is interdisciplinary in nature, due in no small part to authors' polymathic interests, which included medicine and alchemy.

LITERATURE FROM 1700 TO 1780

German literature of the eighteenth century is usually thought of as being a break with the traditions of the period from 1450 to 1700. At last, such thinking goes, German emerged as a literary language easily read by modern readers. In addition, many of the earlier writers were considered to be nothing more than precursors of Schiller and Goethe. By 1780, literary culture in Germany was on the threshold of its golden age, the *Klassik* (1785–1830), and all that preceded it was but a prelude to greatness. Such views of German literature and language of the period are not entirely invalid, yet the creative achievement of eighteenth-century writers may be measured as much by its continuity with the past as by its own accomplishments. In each genre—lyric poetry, drama, epic verse, and prose—German literary culture in the years 1700–1780 stood on its own, even as it pointed in the direction of modernity.

Intellectual foundations. The foundation of the intellectual ferment that became the German Enlightenment, the *Aufklärung,* was constructed by Gottfried Wilhelm von Leibniz (1646–1716). A truly cosmopolitan intellect in the mold of early modern scholars, he laid the philosophical groundwork for eighteenth-century rationalism. His disciple, Christian Wolff (1679–1754), popularized his master's thinking even as he freed philosophical discourse from the strictures of theology. His watchword, *Vernunft,* meaning systematic reasoning, became a significant component of the century's mindset. In the writings of Johann Christoph Gottsched (1700–1766) such rationalist thinking was applied to literature, specifically in his *Versuch einer Critischen Dichtkunst vor die Deutschen* (1730; Attempt at a critical poetics for the Germans). There, Gottsched replaced early modern descriptions of literary forms by Martin Opitz (1597–1639) and others with logical discourse, which rationally defined literature's didactic and social functions. Comic drama, for example, was to instruct bourgeois viewers about human foibles by means of *Verlachen,* satiric laughter about a comic figure's lack of *Vernunft.* Literature and theater served to perfect human behavior, a view reflected in Gottsched's espousal of the exemplary quality of French classicist drama.

Pietism was an equally important component of the eighteenth-century mindset in Germany. Believing participants in this early modern movement within Lutheranism sought a one-to-one, often emotionally charged relationship to their God. The heart rather than the mind governed this mode of perception. The individual mattered. Even though Johann Jakob Breitinger (1701–1776) and Johann Jakob Bodmer (1698–1783) were not Pietists, their focus on imagination and illusion, on literary description, which inspires and affects the heart of the reader, was analogous to this strain of religious experience. Friedrich Gottlieb Klopstock's (1724–1803) daring epic poem *Der Messias* (1748/1773; The Messiah) was the culmination of such spirituality. For Klopstock, writing poetry was the celebration of the sacred. The writer undertook a transcendent, even prophetic, act. To the extent that the text ecstatically inspired the reader, literature achieved its desired result.

Literary developments. German culture of the early modern period saw the proliferation of literary forms, a wide array of stylistic experimentation, the struggle for the creation of language fit for differentiated expression. Additionally, German literature was highly derivative: dramas derived from Greek and Roman models; lyric poetry looked to classical Rome and contemporary France, Italy, and the Netherlands; novels were modeled on Spanish and French forebears. During the eighteenth century, German writers looked to external models (specifically to England), but also found their own voice. An examination of historical developments within each genre from 1700 to 1780 bears this out.

Poetry. Barthold Hinrich Brockes (1680–1747) focused in his collection, *Irdisches Vergnügen in Gott* (in nine volumes 1721–1748; Worldly joy of God), on God's rational order even in the smallest of plants. Albrecht von Haller's (1708–1777) *Die Alpen* (1732; The Alps) described Switzerland's landscape set among the towering mountains as the locus of virtuous life and human fulfillment. Countless Pietist hymn writers, notably Gerhard Tersteegen (1697–1769), extolled their religious vision, while Christian Friedrich Henrici (1700–1764) wrote cantata texts and the libretti of the *St. Matthew* and *St. Mark Passions* for Johann Sebastian Bach (1685–1750). All of these, along with Klopstock's uplifting odes and the magisterial verse epic *Messias,* itself inspired by the grandeur of John Milton's *Paradise Lost,* spoke to the function of poetry as a purveyor of religious values and a full range of human experiences.

Other lyric poets turned their attention to worldly matters. With stylistic grace, Friedrich von Hagedorn (1708–1754) wrote of youthful love and friendship and the virtues of the rural life, adapting Horace to the times. Christian Fürchtegott Gellert's (1715–1769) immensely popular fables and tales in verse (from 1741 on) appeared in the periodical press and reinforced bourgeois values. Anna Luisa Karsch (1722–1791) astounded her readers with lyric virtuosity. Johann Wilhelm Ludwig Gleim (1719–1803) recognized Karsch as being a natural, even as he himself adroitly refined the ancient conventions of lilting verses on wine, women, and song (*Versuch in scherzhaften Liedern;* 1744, Attempt at witty songs). Every young poet of the age tried his hand at such verse in imitation of the ancient Greek poet Anacreon. Poets of the *Göttinger Hain* (Göttingen Circle), an assembly of kindred young spirits, picked up on Anacreon as well as experimenting with ballads. Gleim had introduced the ballad (1756) to the German-language repertoire, and Johann Gottfried von Herder (1744–1803) collected and translated ballads from the English in his *Volkslieder* (1777/78: Folk songs). Herder's work inspired Johann Wolfgang von Goethe (1749–1832) and the writers of German Romanticism.

Drama. Dramatists in 1700 wrote for three venues, each a holdover from traditions that originated in the sixteenth century—princely courts, schools, and open-air stages. This was slow to change, but by 1780 permanent theaters with scheduled public performances and professional actors in cities like Hamburg, Mannheim, and Vienna had been established, often only temporarily. Gotthold Ephraim Lessing's (1729–1781) *Hamburgische Dramaturgie* (1767–1769; The Hamburg dramaturgy), a collection of reviews of performances and interpretations of Aristotle's theory of tragedy, documented the state of the theatrical arts in Germany, as tenuous as it was.

An examination of the career of Lessing as a dramatist may serve as a touchstone for the development of drama during the period. He had participated in schoolboy drama, *Schuldrama,* in his provincial hometown Kamenz near Dresden in Saxony. His studies took him to Leipzig, where he fell in with players in the troupe of Friederike Caroline Neuber (1679–1760), a woman whose productions had for a while featured those French dramatists most favored by Gottsched, namely Corneille, Racine, Voltaire, and Molière. She had fallen out with the professor of poetics, all the more reason for the young Lessing to have her produce his comedy about a preposterously erudite fool, *Der junge Gelehrte* (1747; The young scholar). He perfected the conventions of the so-called *sächsische Komödie* (Saxon comedy) to expose the irrational. Later, Lessing excoriated Gottsched for his predilection for formulaic French drama. He himself championed Shakespeare's authentic language and true-to-life dramatic plots and inaugurated Germany's admiration of Shakespeare.

In Berlin, Lessing's journalistic critiques of the literary scene and his interest in the theory of drama resulted in a tragedy situated in the bourgeois milieu, *Miß Sara Sampson* (1755; Miss Sara Sampson), arguably the first *bürgerliches Trauerspiel* (bourgeois tragedy) in Germany. The heroine was not of high social station, not a princess, and her tragic fate moved audiences to tears. Performed to this day, *Minna von Barnhelm* (1767), a comedy, bordering on tragedy, extended the limits of the dramatic form. As earnest as it was, it was the first modern German comedy. *Emilia Galotti* (1772), a tragedy born of the conflict between virtuous bourgeois Emilia and a lecherous prince, criticized the reality of absolutist society. Its first performance was in a court theater, where the message was sure to prick the conscience of the listeners.

In *Nathan der Weise* (1779; Nathan the wise), his last play, Lessing continued to break new ground. He introduced blank verse to German literature; the unrhymed iambic pentameter flowed as naturally as the prose speech of his other plays. The protagonist was a Jewish merchant, another first. Nathan was as rich in humane wisdom as he was in economic terms, a break with stereotypical characterization. The action was set in medieval Jerusalem at the time of the Crusades and it was the wise Jew, rather than his Christian and Moslem counterparts, who forwarded a vision of *Toleranz,* the mutual acceptance of religious beliefs. The play delivered the central message of the *Aufklärung* as the emancipation of the German Jews commenced and just prior to Immanuel Kant's philosophical definition of the process of human enlightenment.

By 1780, then, German drama had emerged as a truly progressive cultural force. The works of women playwrights such as Luise Gottsched (1713–1762) (and also those who wrote under male names) appeared. That they were writing and publishing exemplified the emancipatory aspirations of the Enlightenment. The hotheaded playwrights of the Sturm und Drang (Storm and stress), a cultural phase (1765–1785) often seen as the radicalization of the Enlightenment's idealistic pursuit of life, liberty, and happiness, was a further case in point. The plays of Jakob Michael Reinhold Lenz (1752–1792) and Friedrich Maximilian Klinger (1752–1831), but especially Friedrich Schiller's *Die Räuber* (1781; The robbers), were revolutionary in both form and content. Dynamic and larger-than-life types called loudly for the immediate reform of a corrupt society largely made up of emasculated weaklings. The language was as brashly explicit as the message. The works of these women and men signaled that German drama had arrived.

Epic prose. Early modern epic prose from the satiric chapbooks and didactic novels of the sixteenth century to the satiric picaresque, the cloying pastoral, and the complex allegorical political novels of the seventeenth century gradually lost relevance for eighteenth-century readers. Early prose was eventually supplanted by novels modeled on English sentimental forms that tell of bourgeois family life of the landed gentry. A growing interest in the depiction of human psychology, rather than the grand sweep of adventure, reflected both the effects of Pietism and the didactic intentions of Enlightenment authors.

Johann Gottfried Schnabel's (1692–c. 1750) four-volume *Insel Felsenburg* (1731–1743; The island Felsenburg), a transitional work, combined elements of Robinson Crusoe adventures and utopian thinking. It depicted an ideal bourgeois spiritual community situated far from European realities, one founded on the principles of Pietist virtue and God-given *Vernunft.* Gellert's *Das Leben der Schwedischen Gräfin von G**** (1746; The life of the Swedish countess G***), a biographical treatment of horrific personal trauma, depicted the personal depravities of an imperfect world. The moralizing impulse implicit in both novels became the era's stock in trade. For example, Sophie von La Roche's (1730–1807) *Geschichte des Fräuleins von Sternheim* (1771/72; The story of Miss von Sternheim) told of the uplifting triumph of personal virtue, while Johann Heinrich Jung-Stilling's (1740–1817) *Heinrich Stillings Jugend* (1777 and sequels 1778–1804; Heinrich Stilling's youth) engagingly traced the life of a Pietist soul. The ups and downs chronicled in Ulrich Bräker's (1735–1798) true-to-life *Lebensgeschichte und natürliche Ebentheur des Armen Mannes im Tockenburg* (1789; The biography and real adventures of the unfortunate man in Toggenburg) implied that the day-to-day struggle of the provincial commoner was noteworthy, even noble.

What Lessing was to drama, Christoph Martin Wieland (1733–1813) was to the novel. He early turned his attention to the philosophy of the Enlightenment, and his later interaction with Bodmer attuned him to the strains of literary *Empfindsamkeit* (sentimentality) and ecstatic religiosity. His first novel, *Der Sieg der Natur über die Schwärmerei, oder Don Sylvio von Rosalva* (1774; The triumph of nature over enthusiasm or Don Sylvio von Rosalva), a fantastic story modeled on the Spanish novelist Cervantes, dealt with the central categories of the century, true-to-life reality versus inspirational illusion. Don Sylvio was an updated Don Quixote, a German dreamer. An embedded fairy-tale narrative led to the novel's appeal. Wieland's *Geschichte des Agathon* (1766–1767, with revisions 1773 and

1798; The story of Agathon) investigated the same issues as they played themselves out in an imagined ancient Greece. The whole vocabulary of sentimentalism appeared in the novel; sentimental souls were those who feel most accurately, feeling was their test of truth. Love was not desire, but a condition based on *Empfindung* (sentiment).

Lessing considered *Agathon* to be the century's best novel, even as he rejected Goethe's European bestseller *Die Leiden des jungen Werthers* (1774; The sorrows of young Werther), because of Werther's excessive, ultimately suicidal desire. The threshold crossed between Wieland and Goethe marked the German novel's true coming of age.

The achievement of the era 1700–1780. German-language literary culture of the eighteenth century was unlike that of the years preceding 1700 on several counts. While the canon of texts enumerated above is generally well-known internationally, the dramas of Lessing are routinely staged in Germany and elsewhere. The phrase "Lessing, Schiller, Goethe" resonates with any German. Each author has at least one museum (such as the Lessing Museum in Kamenz), a named journal (*The Lessing Yearbook* in Cincinnati), and a named institution of scholarship (Lessing Akademie in Wolfenbüttel) devoted to the author's achievement. The triumvirate is as much a component of German cultural memory as the familiar "Three B's"—Bach, Beethoven, Brahms. Not coincidentally, it was the eighteenth century that saw the emergence of such notable figures who pointed the way into the long nineteenth century. Along with literature and music, modern western philosophy originated in the mind of the stylistically effective writer Immanuel Kant (1724–1804).

Any answer as to why this period of cultural achievement came about is speculative. Some would pin it on the transition from the priority of theology to the priority of science and philosophy, on curious questioning rather than on believing acceptance. This explanation emphasizes, correctly, the remarkable extent to which German thinkers were sensitive to religion, in contrast to those in many other countries. Others would look to the gradual shift to a bourgeois ethics in line with the emancipatory values of life, liberty, and the pursuit of happiness. While the controlling administrative institutions of the Holy Roman Empire might still have been in place, a self-confident citizenry in cities like Berlin, Leipzig, and Hamburg was a match for the long-entrenched aristocratic social order. Lessing, for example, sought to earn his keep in the marketplace of publishing. Even though he was ultimately unsuccessful in freeing himself from courtly patronage, the attempt to earn a living by writing was part of the cultural process that eventually led to modernity.

See also **Brant, Sebastian; Drama: German; Dutch Literature and Language; Enlightenment; Erasmus, Desiderius; Goethe, Johann Wolfgang von; Grimmelshausen, H. J. C. von; Herder, Johann Gottfried von; Humanism; Kant, Immanuel; Klopstock, Friedrich Gottlieb; Lessing, Gotthold Ephraim; Luther, Martin; Melanchthon, Philipp; Nuremberg; Pietism; Reformation, Protestant; Schiller, Johann Christoph Friedrich von; Wieland, Christoph Martin.**

BIBLIOGRAPHY

Primary Sources

Bidermann, Jakob. *Cenodoxus.* Edited and translated by D. G. Dyer. Austin, Tex., 1974. Translation of *Cenodoxus* (1602).

Blackwell, Jeannine, and Susanne Zantop. *Bitter Healing: German Women Writers from 1700 to 1830: An Anthology.* Lincoln, Neb., 1990.

Brant, Sebastian. *The Ship of Fools.* Translated by Edwin H. Zeydel. New York, 1944. Translation of *Das Narrenschiff* (1494).

Browning, Robert M., ed. *German Poetry from 1750 to 1900.* German Library, vol. 39. New York, 1984. Translations of German poetry into English; the companion volume to Walsoe-Engel (below).

Celtis, Konrad. *Selections.* Edited and translated by Leonard Forster. Cambridge, U.K., 1948.

Erasmus, Desiderius. *Praise of Folly and Letter to Martin Dorp.* Translated by Betty Radice. Introduction by A. H. T. Levi. Harmondsworth, U.K., 1971. Translation of *Moriae Encomium* (1509).

The German Lyric of the Baroque in English Translation. Translated by George C. Schoolfield. Chapel Hill, N.C., 1961.

Goethe, Johann Wolfgang von. *The Sufferings of Young Werther and Elective Affinities.* Edited by Victor Lange. German Library, vol. 19. New York, 1990. Translations of the epoch-making novels.

Grimmelshausen, Hans Jakob von. *The Adventures of Simplicius Simplicissimus.* Translated by George Schulz-Behrend. 2nd ed. Columbia, S.C., 1993. Translation of *Der abenteuerliche Simplicissimus* (1668).

Kant, Immanuel. *Philosophical Writings.* Edited by Ernst Behler. German Library, vol. 13. New York, 1986. A translation of various writings including "An Answer to the Question: What Is Enlightenment?"

Leidner, Alan C., ed. *Sturm und Drang.* German Library, vol. 14. New York, 1992. Translations of various dramas of the period to include Klinger's play *Sturm und Drang.*

Lessing, Gotthold Ephraim von. *Nathan the Wise, Minna von Barnhelm, and other Plays and Writings.* Edited by Peter Demetz. German Library, vol. 12. New York, 1991.

Oakes, Edward T., ed. *German Essays on Religion.* German Library, vol. 54. New York, 1994. Selections from essays by Kant and Lessing are translated.

Schiller, Friedrich. *Plays.* Edited by Walter Hinderer. German Library, vol. 15. New York, 1983. A translation of *Kabale und Liebe* and *Don Carlos.*

Shookman, Ellis, ed. *Eighteenth-Century German Prose.* German Library, vol. 10. New York, 1992. Translations of selected passages from Sophie von La Roche, Christoph Martin Wieland, Ulrich Bräker, among others.

Till Eulenspiegel: His Adventures. Translated by Paul Oppenheimer. New York, 1991. Translation of *Till Eulenspiegel* (c. 1510).

Ulrich von Hutten, et al. *On the Eve of the Reformation: Letters of Obscure Men.* Translated by Francis Griffin Stokes. New York, 1964. Translation of *Epistolae Obscurorum Virorum* (1515–1517).

Walsoe-Engel, Ingrid, ed. *German Poetry from the Beginnings to 1750.* German Library, vol. 9. New York, 1992. Translations of German poetry into English; the companion volume to Browning's (above).

Wickram, Jörg. *The Golden Thread.* Translated by Pierre Kaufke. Pensacola, Fla., 1991. Translation of *Der Goldfaden* (1557).

Secondary Sources

Baldwin, Claire. *The Emergence of the Modern German Novel: Christoph Martin Wieland, Sophie von La Roche, and Maria Anna Sagar.* Rochester, N.Y., 2002.

Baron, Frank. *Doctor Faustus: From History to Legend.* Munich, 1978. Best study of the Faust legend in English.

Bernstein, Eckhard. *German Humanism.* Boston, 1983. A survey of leading humanist authors and their activities.

Brown, F. Andrew. *Gotthold Ephraim Lessing.* Twayne World Authors Series 113. New York, 1971. A good introduction to Lessing's life and works.

Browning, Robert M. *German Poetry in the Age of the Enlightenment: From Brockes to Klopstock.* University Park, Pa., 1978. A useful overview of the genre.

Correll, Barbara. *The End of Conduct: Grobianus and the Renaissance Text of the Subject.* Ithaca, N.Y., 1996. An analysis of Renaissance conduct literature and its role in reshaping normative identity after the Middle Ages.

Daphnis. The leading journal of early modern German literature.

Dawson, Ruth. *The Contested Quill: Literature by Women in Germany, 1770–1800.* Newark, Del., 2002. Useful scholarship on Friderika Baldinger (1739–1786), Sophie von La Roche, and Philippine Engelhard (1756–1831), Marianne Ehrmann (1755–1840), and Sophie Albrecht (1757–1840).

Dünnhaupt, Gerhard. *Personalbibliographien zu den Drucken des Barocks.* 2nd ed. Stuttgart, 1990–. Definitive reference work in German on the authors of the baroque.

Fick, Monika. *Lessing-Handbuch: Leben—Werk—Wirkung.* Stuttgart, 2000. An excellent introduction to Lessing's life and works.

Hardin, James, ed. *German Baroque Writers, 1580–1660.* Vol. 164, *Dictionary of Literary Biography.* Detroit, 1996. Recent biographies of the leading German authors of the early baroque; includes select bibliographies.

———. *German Baroque Writers, 1661–1730.* Vol. 168, *Dictionary of Literary Biography.* Detroit, 1996. Recent biographies of the leading German authors of the late baroque; includes select bibliographies.

Hardin, James, and Max Reinhart, eds. *German Writers of the Renaissance and Reformation, 1280–1580.* Vol. 179, Dictionary of Literary Biography. Detroit, 1997. Recent biographies of leading German authors from the Late Middle Ages through the Reformation; includes select bibliographies.

Hardin, James, and Christoph E. Schweitzer, eds. *German Writers from the Enlightenment to Sturm und Drang, 1720–1764.* Detroit, 1990. Up-to-date scholarship and bibliographies on all the major authors of the period.

Jørgensen, Sven-Aage. *Christoph Martin Wieland: Epoche—Werk—Wirkung.* Munich, 1994. An excellent introduction to Wieland's life and works.

Kleinschmidt, Erich. *Stadt und Literatur in der frühen Neuzeit: Voraussetzungen und Entfaltung im südwestdeutschen, elsässischen und schweizerischen Städteraum.* Cologne, 1982. Important study on the interactions between urban culture and literature in early modern Germany.

Kord, Susanne. *Little Detours: The Letters and Plays by Luise Gottsched (1713–1762).* Rochester, N.Y., 2000. An excellent introduction to Luise Gottsched's life and works.

McCarthy, John A. *Christoph Martin Wieland.* Twayne's World Authors Series 528. Boston, 1979. A good introduction to Wieland's life and works.

Parente, James A., Richard E. Schade, and George C. Schoolfield, eds. *Literary Culture in the Holy Roman Empire, 1555–1720.* Chapel Hill, N.C., 1991.

Pascal, Roy. *German Literature in the Sixteenth and Seventeenth Centuries: Renaissance, Reformation, Baroque.* New York, 1968. Dated but useful survey in English of early modern German literature.

Pelikan, Jaroslav, with Valerie R. Hotchkiss and David Price. *The Reformation of the Bible—The Bible of the Reformation.* New Haven, London, and Dallas, 1996. Exhibition catalogue cum monograph on humanist sacred philology and the resulting Renaissance of Bible translations and editions during the Reformation.

Ruh, Kurt, et al., eds. *Die deutsche Literatur des Mittelalters: Verfasserlexikon.* 2nd ed. 11 vols. to date. Berlin and New York, 1977–. Definitive reference work on medieval German literature; includes authors and anonymous works through the early sixteenth century.

Schade, Richard E., managing ed. *The Lessing Yearbook/Jahrbuch.* Vol. 1 (1969)–34 (2002) ongoing. Scholarship in English and German on Lessing and his era. Complete listing of articles available at http://asweb.artsci.uc.edu/german/lessing.

Scholz Williams, Gerhild, and Stephan K. Schindler. *Knowledge, Science, and Literature in Early Modern Germany.* University of North Carolina Studies in the Germanic Languages and Literatures, vol. 116. Chapel Hill, N.C., 1996. Recent conference proceedings in English on the period, including the emergence of natural science and medicine.

Scribner, R. W. *For the Sake of Simple Folk: Popular Propaganda for the German Reformation.* 2nd ed. Oxford and New York, 1994. Definitive study of Protestants' exploitation of popular media.

Wilson, W. Daniel, and Robert C. Holub, ed. *Impure Reason: Dialectic of Enlightenment in Germany.* Detroit, 1993. Important essays in English on the German Enlightenment.

Glenn Ehrstine, Richard E. Schade

GERMANY, IDEA OF. The idea of Germany as a single ethnic and linguistic entity was created by German humanists around 1500. The form "German" *(deutsch)* was in common medieval use, usually as an adjective, rarely as a noun. The term "German lands" designated the post-Carolingian duchies of Bavaria, Swabia, Franconia, Saxony, and soon other lands as well. As a plural its medieval meaning was the community of German-speaking peoples as distinct from Romance-speakers (especially the French). As a singular term was needed, "Alemannia," "Germania," and "Theutonia," for which no vernacular equivalent existed, were used interchangeably. During the fifteenth century a new collective term appeared, "the German nation," which was borrowed from academic and ecclesiastical usage to designate the community of the German lands that bore the Roman imperium. The two terms merged in a title, "the Holy Roman Empire of the German Nation" *(das Heilige Römische Reich deutscher Nation),* first recorded in 1492. Their duality expressed the collaborative regime captured in the common sixteenth-century formula, *Kaiser und Reich,* 'emperor and empire', which distinguished between the monarch and the imperial Estates. In popular usage the terms could be interchangeable, as when Saxons heading westward said that they were going "into the empire." The terms "nation" and "fatherland" in both German and Latin could be used for a native city, district, or region, so that one could speak of the city of Basel as a "fatherland" and of a Swabian or Westphalian "nation."

"Germany" as an idea was created by the humanists around 1500. The key event in its genesis was Gian Francesco Poggio Bracciolini's (1380–1459) discovery at Hersfeld Abbey of a unique manuscript of Tacitus' *Germania.* It was brought to Rome by 1455 and printed in Latin at Venice in 1470 and Nuremberg in 1473. Its publication sparked the interest around 1500 in the deeper German past among an entire generation of German writers. Those figures who shared and nourished this interest included such leading humanists as Conrad Celtis (1459–1508) and Jakob Wimpheling (1450–1528), each of whom wrote a work entitled *Germania* (published in 1500 and 1501 respectively), and the Alsatian Beatus Rhenanus (1485–1547).

A single "Germany" *(Germania)* is therefore a humanist creation, and its vernacular equivalent *(Deutschland)* was fixed by the polemical writings of the noble humanist Ulrich von Hutten (1488–1523), who gave a new, political edge to the term that played an important role in the Reformation movement. From this time onward, "Germany" became a term current in both Latin and German. What and where this Germany was remained a topic for debate, however, and the geographer and cartographer Matthias Quad (1557–1613) concluded that "there is no country in all of Christendom which embraces so many lands under one name" (Sheehan, p. 40).

Between 1600 and 1800, the idea of the Holy Roman Empire began to be filled with the meaning of "Germany." The process advanced in two stages. In the first, seventeenth-century, stage the Protestant jurist Hermann Conring (1606–1681) stripped away the empire's claim to be a continuation of the ancient Roman Empire, contending that the Roman and Holy Roman empires had no common history. Meanwhile, he and other Protestant jurists denied the sacrality, the holiness, of the empire and searched for secular, utilitarian sources of its legitimacy that did not depend on the Catholicity of the monarch. Cartographers accepted and spread the new usage, which was supported by secular and utilitarian tendencies in philosophy, political thought, and jurisprudence. Once the confessional schism had been formally regulated by the Peace of Westphalia in 1648, the Protestants in particular were free to examine the legal strengths and weaknesses of the polity, the Catholic loyalty of its monarch notwithstanding. The imperial chancellery at Vienna continued, for good reasons, to use the old formulae, less because of the monarch's piety than because the unity of the emperor's hereditary lands—Austria, Bohemia, and Hungary—consisted

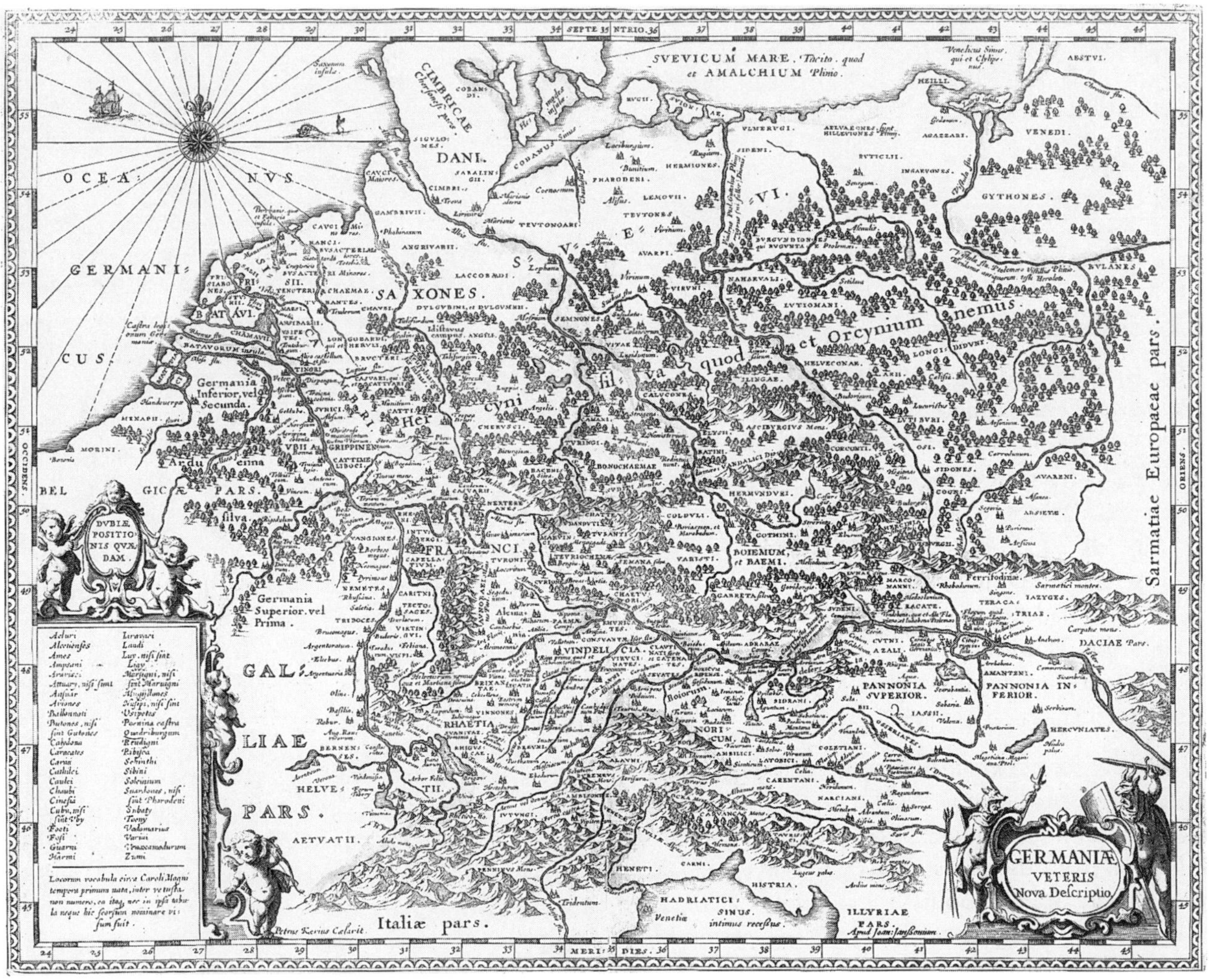

Germany. A map of ancient Germania in Roman times, from a Dutch atlas first issued by Jan Jansson in Amsterdam, circa 1645. Historical maps were often added to general atlases published at this time, and Jansson included this one in a separate atlas of historical maps issued in 1652. Filled with the names of ancient Germanic tribes, the map covers the area from Gaul in the west to part of Sarmatia in the east. MAP COLLECTION, STERLING MEMORIAL LIBRARY, YALE UNIVERSITY

solely in their common ruler and his official Roman Catholic religion.

In the second, eighteenth-century, stage, cartographers and others accepted a new usage: "German Empire" in the place of "Holy Roman Empire." This shift expressed acknowledgment of a historical fact, the empire's loss since the fifteenth century of most of its non-German subjects—French, Italian, Dutch, and Slavic. While the empire as a whole had become an overwhelming German polity, the Habsburg Monarchy's lands retained their ethnic and linguistic diversity under a weakly articulated state.

Astute foreigners noted that the Germans were becoming more like one another. Baron de Montesquieu's comment about the German love of liberty inherited from the forests of ancient Teutonia and Madame de Stäel's about "the energy of their personal beliefs" attest to the growth of an estimate of the Germans far different from the old Italian and French prejudices concerning Germans' drunkenness, crudity, and belligerence. Still, the bewildering variety of the German lands and their pasts tempted both foreigners and Germans themselves to greatly exaggerate the unity of German "national" culture. Most of the important misuses of German histories in modern times have arisen from a desire to intensify or to frustrate a greater sense of German unity and nationhood.

Looking back on the empire of his youth, Goethe put this verse into the mouth of a student named Frosch, a carouser in Auerbach's Cellar at Leipzig (*Faust,* Part I): "The dear old Holy Roman Empire, lads, / What keeps its carcass going?" (*"Das liebe heil'ge Röm'sche Reich, / Wie hält's nur noch zusammen?")* A German historian recently provided this pithy answer: "In the beginning was Napoleon."

See also **Holy Roman Empire.**

BIBLIOGRAPHY

Alter, Peter. *The German Question and Europe: A History.* London and New York, 2000.

Gagliardo, John G. *Reich and Nation. The Holy Roman Empire as Idea and Reality, 1763–1806.* Bloomington, Ind., 1980.

Sheehan, James J. "What Is German History? Reflections on the Role of the Nation in German History and Historiography." *Journal of Modern History* 53 (1981): 1–23.

Strauss, Gerald. *Sixteenth-Century Germany: Its Topography and Topographers.* Madison, Wis., 1959.

THOMAS A. BRADY, JR.

GESSNER, CONRAD (also Konrad Gesner, 1516–1565), polymath, philologist, theologian, naturalist, and town physician of Zurich from 1554. Gessner was born in 1516 into a family originally from Nuremberg. His father, Urs, was a furrier from Solothurn, Switzerland, who moved to Zurich, becoming a citizen there in 1511. Conrad's mother was Agathe Fritz (or Frick). He received a humanistic education at the Fraumünster School, and attended the Carolinum for theology. He was then tutored by Johann Jacob Ammann (1500–1573), a friend of Desiderius Erasmus (1466?–1536), and became a protégé of Huldrych Zwingli (1484–1531) shortly before the reformer's death in the Battle of Kappel (1531).

Patronage allowed him to study Hebrew and give Greek lessons in Strasbourg in 1532. Thanks to Zwingli's successor, Heinrich Bullinger (1504–1575), and later to Johannes Steiger (1518–1581) of Berne, Gessner was able to travel to Basel and Paris, where he read Latin and Greek literature, rhetoric, and natural and moral philosophy. In 1534, because of persecution of Protestants, he left Paris for Strasbourg and Zurich, where he made an unhappy marriage to Barbara Singerin in 1536, and was obliged to teach elementary school. Further patronage enabled him to study medicine in Basel.

On the basis of his *Lexicon Graecolatinum* (1539; Greek-Latin dictionary), he was appointed professor of Greek at the Academy of Lausanne, where he also continued his studies. In 1540 he moved to Montpellier to study at the medical school and met the naturalists Guillaume Rondelet (1507–1566) and Pierre Belon (1517–1564). He received his medical degree at Basel in February 1541 and returned to Zurich to lecture on mathematics, physics, astronomy, philosophy, and ethics at the Carolinum, to practice medicine, and to write and publish prolifically in many areas. He made one trip to Spain and Italy in 1543, studying manuscripts and meeting naturalists, and another to Augsburg in 1545, where he read the Greek naturalist Aelian (fl. c. 175–c. 235 C.E.) in manuscript; he was later to edit the text (1556). Gessner's *Bibliotheca Universalis* (1545; Universal Bibliography) and *Pandectarum libri* (1548; Universal Bibliography, Vol. 2) brought him fame, which increased with his later works. He became a European clearinghouse, gathering and juxtaposing with his own natural historical information from such people as William Turner (c. 1508–1568) and John Caius (1510–1573) of England, Ippolito Salviani (1514–1572) and Pierandrea Mattioli (1501–1578) of Italy, Leonhard Fuchs (1501–1566) and Valerius Cordus (1515–1544) of Germany, and Belon and Rondelet in his five-volume *Historiae Animalium* (1551–1587; Histories of animals) and its three-volume picture book version, *Icones* (1553–1560; Images). He also published a *Historia Plantarum* (History of plants, 1541), and prepared botanical manuscripts, published partially by Casimir Christoph Schmiedel (1718–1792), Gessner's biographer in the eighteenth-century, and wholly in a recent edition (*Conradi Gesneri Historia Plantarum Faksimileausgabe* [Conrad Gessner's history of plants, facsimile edition], 1972–1980, 1987–1991). He died ministering to victims of the plague in Zurich on 13 December 1565.

Gessner epitomizes the scientific and philological spirit of fifteenth- and early-sixteenth-century humanism, in which the search for historical truth meets the search for truth about the world around us. In his case, these interests focused on natural history. He has been called the father of modern bibliography, and of modern zoology as well.

See also **Biology; Botany; Bullinger, Heinrich; Erasmus, Desiderius; Humanists and Humanism; Natural History; Natural Philosophy; Nature; Rhetoric; Zoology; Zwingli, Huldrych.**

BIBLIOGRAPHY

Fischer, Hans, Georges Petit, Joachim Staedtke, Rudolf Steiger, and Heinrich Zoller. *Conrad Gessner, 1516–1565: Universalgelehrter, Naturforscher, Arzt.* Zürich, 1967.

Leu, Urs B. *Conrad Gesner als Theologe: ein Beitrag zur Zürcher Geistesgeschichte des 16. Jahrhunderts.* Bern and New York, 1990.

Pyle, C. M. "Conrad Gessner on the Spelling of his Name." *Archives of Natural History,* 27 (2000): 175–186.

Wellisch, Hans. *Conrad Gessner: A Bio-bibliography.* Zug, Switzerland, 1984.

CYNTHIA M. PYLE

GHENT, PACIFICATION OF (1576).

See Dutch Revolt (1568–1648).

GHETTO.

From their earliest days in the Diaspora, Jews chose voluntarily to live close together, reflecting a practice commonly adopted by groups dwelling in foreign lands. Their quarters, often referred to as the Jewish quarter or street, initially were almost never compulsory, and they continued to have contacts on all levels with their Christian neighbors. However, the Catholic church looked askance at such relationships, and in 1179 the Third Lateran Council stipulated that Christians should not dwell together with Jews. This vague policy statement had to be translated into legislation by the secular authorities, and only infrequently in the Middle Ages were laws enacted confining Jews to compulsory, segregated, and enclosed quarters. The few such Jewish quarters then established, such as that of Frankfurt, were never called ghettos, since that term originated in Venice and became associated with the Jews only in the sixteenth century.

THE GHETTO OF VENICE

In 1516, as a compromise between allowing Jews to live anywhere they wished in Venice and expelling them, the Venetian government required them to dwell on the island known as the Ghetto Nuovo (the New Ghetto), which was walled up with only two gates that were locked from sunset to sunrise. Then, when in 1541 visiting Ottoman Jewish merchants complained that they did not have enough room in the ghetto, the government ordered twenty dwellings located across a small canal walled up, joined by a footbridge to the Ghetto Nuovo, and assigned to them. This area was already known as the Ghetto Vecchio (the Old Ghetto), thereby strengthening the association between Jews and the word "ghetto."

Clearly, the word "ghetto" is of Venetian rather than of Jewish origin, as sometimes conjectured. The Ghetto Vecchio had been the original site of the municipal copper foundry, called "ghetto" from the Italian verb *gettare,* 'to pour or to cast', while the island across from it, on which waste products had been dumped, became known as *il terreno del ghetto,* 'the terrain of the ghetto', and eventually the Ghetto Nuovo.

Although compulsory, segregated, and enclosed Jewish quarters had existed in a few places prior to 1516, since the term "ghetto" had never been applied to them before 1516, the oft-encountered statement that the first ghetto was established in Venice in 1516 is correct in a technical linguistic sense but very misleading in a wider context, while to apply the term "ghetto" to an area prior to 1516 would be anachronistic. The most precise formulation is that the compulsory segregated and enclosed Jewish quarter received the designation "ghetto" as a result of developments in Venice in 1516.

THE SPREAD OF THE GHETTO

The word "ghetto" did not long remain confined to the city of Venice. In 1555, Pope Paul IV issued his restrictive bull, *Cum Nimis Absurdum.* Its first paragraph provided that the Jews of the Papal States were to live together on a single street, or should it not suffice, then on as many adjacent ones as necessary, with only one entrance and exit. Accordingly, the Jews of Rome were moved into a new compulsory, segregated, enclosed quarter, which apparently was first called a ghetto seven years later. Influenced by the papal example, local Italian authorities established special compulsory quarters for the Jews in most places in which they were allowed to reside. Following the Venetian nomenclature, these new residential areas were called "ghetto" in the legislation that established them.

In later years, the Venetian origin of the word "ghetto" in connection with the foundry came to be forgotten, as it was used exclusively in its secondary meaning as referring to compulsory, segregated, and enclosed Jewish quarters and then in a looser sense to refer to any area densely populated by Jews, even if they had freedom of residence and lived in the same districts as Christians.

Although the segregated, compulsory, and enclosed ghettos were abolished under the influence of the ideals of the French Revolution and European liberalism (as in Venice, 1797; Frankfurt, 1811; and Rome, where the gates and walls were removed in 1848 although the Jews were basically confined to that area until the city became a part of the Kingdom of Italy in 1870), the word "ghetto" lived on as the general designation for areas densely

Ghetto. A modern aerial view of the Jewish ghetto area of Venice. ©Fulvio Roiter/Corbis

inhabited by members of minority groups, almost always for socioeconomic reasons rather than for legal ones, as had been the case with the initial Jewish ghetto.

AMBIGUOUS USAGE OF THE WORD "GHETTO"

It must be noted that the varied uses of the word "ghetto" have created a blurring of the Jewish historical experience, especially when employed loosely in phrases such as "the age of the ghetto," "out of the ghetto," and "ghetto mentality." Actually, the word can be used in its original sense of a compulsory, segregated, and enclosed Jewish quarter only in connection with the Jewish experience in Italy and a few places in the Germanic lands, and not at all with that in Poland-Russia. If it is to be used in its original sense in connection with Eastern Europe, then it must be asserted that the age of the ghetto arrived there only after the Nazi invasions of World War II. However, there was a basic difference: unlike ghettos of earlier days, which were designed to provide Jews with clearly defined permanent space in Christian society, twentieth-century ghettos constituted merely temporary stages on the planned road to total liquidation.

Finally, to a great extent because of the negative connotations of the word "ghetto," the nature of Jewish life in the ghetto is often misunderstood. The establishment of ghettos did not lead to the breaking off of Jewish contacts with the outside world on any level. Additionally, from the internal Jewish perspective many evaluations of the ghetto's alleged impact upon the life of the Jews and their mentality require substantial revision. In general, the decisive element determining the nature of Jewish life was not so much whether or not Jews were required to live in a ghetto, but rather the nature of the surrounding environment and whether it constituted an attractive stimulus to Jewish thought and offered a desirable supplement to traditional Jewish genres of intellectual activity. In all places, Jewish life must be examined in the context of the external environment, and developments, especially those subjectively evaluated as undesirable, should not be attributed solely to the alleged impact of the ghetto.

See also **Jews and Judaism; Jews, Attitudes toward; Jews, Expulsion of (Spain; Portugal); Venice.**

BIBLIOGRAPHY

Bonfil, Robert. *Jewish Life in Renaissance Italy.* Translated by Anthony Oldcorn. Berkeley, 1994.

Calabi, Donatella. "Les quartiers Juifs en Italie entre 15e et 17e siècle. Quelques hypotheses de travail." *Annales* 52 (1997) 4: 777–797.

Ravid, Benjamin. "From Geographic Realia to Historiographical Symbol: The Odyssey of the Word *Ghetto.*" In *Essential Papers on Jewish Culture in Renaissance and Baroque Italy,* edited by David Ruderman, pp. 373–385. New York, 1992.

Benjamin C. I. Ravid

GIAMBOLOGNA (Giovanni da Bologna; 1529–1608), Flemish sculptor and architect, active in Italy. Born in Douai, Giambologna received his early training in the shop of Jacques Du Broeucq, a Flemish sculptor, engineer, and minor architect who had spent time in Italy. Probably with his master's encouragement, the young artist traveled around 1551 to Rome, where he made wax and clay sketches after the city's best artworks. Around 1553, while passing through Florence on his way back to Flanders, he met the banker Bernardo Vecchietti, who brought the young sculptor into his household. Through Vecchietti's connections, Giambologna began around 1558 to receive Medici commissions; by 1561, he was a salaried court artist, and soon thereafter he became the dukes' preeminent sculptor. Though he traveled to Bologna in 1562 (to work on his Neptune Fountain), to Rome in 1572 (to study and acquire antiquities), and to Genoa in 1579 (to accept the commission for the Grimaldi family chapel in the subsequently destroyed church of S. Francesco di Castelletto), Giambologna spent most of the remainder of his life in the Tuscan capital.

Giambologna's enormous success and productivity depended in part on his flexibility as an artist—his ability to fulfill commissions ranging from buildings to sugar sculptures—and in part on the talents of the other major sculptors who worked in his shop. Much in demand as a Counter-Reformation artist, Giambologna designed a number of innovative altarpieces, the most important of which was the Altar of Liberty, made for the church of S. Martino in Lucca. Here the sculptor responded to new christocentric devotional currents with a central freestanding marble image of the Risen Savior. Giambologna also designed unified, multimedia decorative programs for several chapels. The best surviving example of these is the Capella Salviati in the church of San Marco in Florence, which the sculptor reoutfitted to promote the relics of S. Antonino, one of that church's most important historical figures.

Better known today than these works are the independent sculptures on secular themes that Giambologna made for the Medici and other clients. These included figures of Venus, of various scales and in various materials, and of Hercules—including the impressive, monolithic *Hercules and the Centaur,* formerly at the Canto dei Carnesechi and now in the Loggia de' Lanzi. His most famous statue in this category was and is the *Rape of the Sabine Women,* commissioned to serve as a pendant to Benvenuto Cellini's *Perseus and Medusa* in the same loggia. The *Sabine* cleverly adapted the triumphal themes of the statues that already occupied the piazza to a subject of love and possession. It allowed the duke to identify himself with the statue's hero, even as it, like many of Giambologna's other Florentine public works, avoided direct glorification of the current ruler. Also typical of many of Giambologna's works was the ambiguity of the *Sabine*'s subject matter; in this case, at least, that ambiguity was deliberate, as it provoked writers to unpack the statue's numerous possible meanings in encomiastic poems.

In addition to these works, Giambologna also designed a number of witty fountains, including a *Bacchus,* at the end of Florence's Borgo San Jacopo, which poured water from its lifted cup; a *Mercury* for the Villa Medici in Rome, which represented the flying god as the terminus of a windy exhalation; and the *Appenine* for the Villa Medici (now Demidoff) at Pratolino, which fused a prisoner type and a grotto format. Much desired, in Giambologna's time, were also the sculptor's smaller statuettes, many of which were produced as multiples, so that

Giambologna. *Rape of the Sabine Women,* 1583, marble sculpture in the Loggia dei Lanzi, Florence. ©ALINARI/ART RESOURCE, N.Y.

they could be acquired by private collectors or sent as diplomatic gifts to foreign courts. Giambologna was also a skilled architect, as is witnessed in his elegant Palazzo Vecchietti and in his design for the facade of Florence's cathedral.

On Giambologna's death, in 1608, he was buried in the extraordinary chapel he had decorated for himself in the Church of the SS. Annunziata, largely using new casts of bronzes he had previously exported to Genoa and Munich. Though this death came just one year before Annibale Carracci's and just two before Caravaggio's, Giambologna, unlike these founders of the "baroque," is usually considered a late sculptural representative of the "mannerist" period. The designation reflects the awkwardness of transferring period styles in painting to sculpture, and of considering the Roman sculpture of Bernini as normative: with figures like Pietro Tacca (1577–1640) in Tuscany, Francavilla (1548–1615) in France, and Adriaan de Vries (c. 1546–1626) in Germany all emulating his inventions, Giambologna's manner, no less than Annibale's or Caravaggio's, remained dominant in Europe well into the seventeenth century.

See also **Caravaggio and Caravaggism; Florence; Florence, Art in; Mannerism; Medici Family.**

BIBLIOGRAPHY

Avery, Charles. *Giambologna: The Complete Sculpture.* Mt. Kisco, N.Y., 1987.

Giambologna, 1529–1608: Sculptor to the Medici. Exh. cat. London, 1978.

Gibbons, Mary Weitzel. *Giambologna: Narrator of the Catholic Reformation.* Berkeley, 1995.

MICHAEL COLE

GIANNONE, PIETRO (1676–1748), Italian reformer, historian, and jurist. Born in Ischitella, Italy, and educated at the University of Naples, Giannone cultivated early ties with the Accademia Medina Celi, the famous academy sponsored by the duke of Medina Celi, of which Giambattista Vico was a member. He began a career in law, but his associations with the Neapolitan reforming jurists soon involved him in the antifeudal battle against the local nobility and the jurisdictional battle with Rome. Even his work as a historian took on a powerful polemical tone.

His ideas for the *Istoria civile del Regno di Napoli* (1723; *Civil history of the kingdom of Naples*) developed from his work as a jurist, which he evaluated in the light of the English civil lawyer Arthur Duck's 1653 history of Roman law in Europe. The resulting masterwork was an innovative fusion of legal history, cultural history, and social history. Conceived over a period of some twenty years, it aimed to combine erudition (often borrowed from sixteenth- and seventeenth-century authors possessing firsthand experience with the documents) and a philosophical outlook in harmony with the virulent anti-ecclesiastical program characteristic of the Enlightenment. A major purpose was to provide the new Austrian rulers of Naples with a basis for correcting the social and political problems caused by what he viewed as the excessive influence of Rome and the Catholic Church in Neapolitan civic affairs. Translated into French in 1742, the work eventually earned the praise of Montesquieu, Voltaire, and Edward Gibbon.

At the time, however, it launched its author into a sea of troubles. Giannone was excommunicated by the local archbishop and forced to leave Naples, while the work was placed on the Index of Forbidden Books. In the Vienna of Emperor Charles VI, Giannone found a secure asylum in which to undertake and publish detailed responses (later issued together in 1755 as *Apologia del'istoria civile* [Apology of the civil history]) to the many polemics provoked by his writings. Meanwhile, he worked on an unfinished history of the origins of civilization (the *Triregno,* complete edition of the manuscript published only in 1895), developing many of the themes in the *Istoria civile* and adding others, in part inspired by Baruch Spinoza, Pierre Bayle, and John Toland, concerning the abolition of ecclesiastical hierarchy and the institution of a natural religion.

The promise of a new regime in Naples under the Spanish Bourbons attracted Giannone back to Italy in 1734. In Venice he found a congenial environment for study and discussion, but he soon became a victim of Italian religious politics. Betrayed by his Venetian associates, chased out of Modena, tricked into leaving relatively safe Geneva and delivering himself into the hands of the Savoy police, he ended up in jail in Piedmont, where he remained from 1736 until the end of his life in 1748, in spite of having submitted to a forced abjuration of his beliefs. In this last period, among other works exploring the themes of politics, philosophy, and religion that had long interested him, he wrote a vivid account describing his intellectual development amid personal tragedy, entitled *Vita di Pietro Giannone* (The life of Pietro Giannone; complete edition first published in 1904).

See also **Bayle, Pierre; Charles VI (Holy Roman Empire); Enlightenment; Gibbon, Edward; Montesquieu, Charles-Louis de Secondat de; Naples, Kingdom of; Vico, Giovanni Battista; Voltaire.**

BIBLIOGRAPHY

Primary Source

Opere di Pietro Giannone. Edited by Sergio Bertelli and Giuseppe Ricuperati. Milan, 1971.

Secondary Source

Ricuperati, Giuseppe. *L'esperienza civile e religiosa di Pietro Giannone.* Milan-Naples, 1970.

BRENDAN DOOLEY

GIBBON, EDWARD (1737–1794), the leading English historian of the eighteenth century, famous for his *History of the Decline and Fall of the Roman Empire.* The affluent only son of Edward Gibbon, a member of Parliament and country gentleman, Gibbon was briefly at Magdalen College, Oxford. The formative experience was his years in Lausanne (1753–1758). There he received an important introduction to Enlightenment thought and also defined his political judgments with reference to the various government structures and practices of the Swiss cantons, leading to his unpublished *Letter on the Government of Berne.* In 1758, Gibbon began the *Essai sur l'étude de la littérature* (Essay on the study of literature), a work that focused on the controversy of the ancients and moderns, providing a clear defense of the former.

After he had spent some time in England, Gibbon's next formative experience was a visit to Italy in 1764–1765. At Rome in 1764, he "trod, with a lofty step, the ruins of the Forum; each memorable spot where Romulus stood, or Tully spoke, or Caesar fell . . . it was at Rome . . . as I sat musing amidst the ruins of the Capitol, while the barefooted friars were singing Vespers in the Temple of Jupiter, that the idea of writing the decline and fall of the city first started to my mind."

As a member of Parliament in 1774–1784, Gibbon was a supporter of the government of Lord North against the American Revolution and was a member of the Board of Trade in 1779–1782. Not a natural speaker, Gibbon did not enjoy being in Parliament, and preferred retirement to Lausanne.

Gibbon's *History* (6 vols., 1776–1788) was a masterpiece of scholarship and skepticism and led to his being regarded in England as the leading historian of his generation. Based on formidable reading across a range of languages, and supported by over 8,300 references and a sound knowledge of the geography of the Classical world, the work contrasted with the less profound and philosophical character of most contemporary historical work.

Gibbon attributed the fall of Rome in part to the rise of Christianity, although he was cautious about providing a general model of change and preferred to focus on a detailed narrative of developments. He contrasted the degenerate Roman Empire with the vigor of the barbarian invaders. Rather than focusing only on Rome and its successor states, Gibbon extended his scope to a history of Eurasia. He was particularly interested in the displacement of the Greek and Syrian world by the Arabs and Islam. While Gibbon was writing, the banners of the Ottoman Empire still waved above the walls of Belgrade. He sought to understand the past that foreshadowed the modern world and to explain the world of post-Roman power, ecclesiastical authority, and Scholastic philosophy against which eighteenth-century civil society had been constructed.

Gibbon was convinced of the general benefit of history and of modern European civilization:

> Since the first discovery of the arts, war, commerce, and religious zeal have diffused among the savages of the Old and New World these inestimable gifts . . . every age of the world has increased and still increases the real wealth, the happiness, the knowledge, and perhaps the virtue of the human race. The merit of discovery has too often been stained with avarice, cruelty, and fanaticism; and the intercourse of nations has produced the communication of disease and prejudice.

The *History* was critically and commercially successful, although his critical account of Christianity was attacked by many. Nevertheless, Gibbon's remained the best history of the rise of Christianity in English into the following century.

Gibbon's apparent ambivalence toward Christianity was such that he can scarcely be cited as typifying the values of his age. This was also true of his cosmopolitanism, opposition to war and martial glory, and disapproval of imperial expansion. In his *History,* Gibbon made his cosmopolitanism clear:

> It is the duty of a patriot to prefer and promote the exclusive interest and glory of his native country; but a philosopher may be permitted to enlarge his views, and to consider Europe as one great republic, whose various inhabitants have attained almost the same level of politeness and cultivation.

In later years, Gibbon condemned the French Revolution, which threatened his concept of enlightened Europe and forced him to return home from Lausanne. He never married. The irony of Gibbon's authorial voice was linked to moral and moralistic concerns: rulership, governance, and political life were seen as moral activities. Gibbon's *History* reflects the scholarship of his age in being essentially a political account, but it is also a great work of literature.

See also **Ancient World; English Literature and Language; Enlightenment; Historiography.**

BIBLIOGRAPHY

Primary Source

Gibbon, Edward. *The History of the Decline and Fall of the Roman Empire.* Edited by J. B. Bury. 7 vols. 2nd ed. London, 1909–1914.

Secondary Sources

Pocock, J. G. A., *Barbarism and Religion.* Vol. I, *The Enlightenments of Edward Gibbon.* Cambridge, U.K., 1999.

Porter, Roy. *Edward Gibbon: Making History.* London, 1988.

JEREMY BLACK

GILBERT, WILLIAM (1544–1603), English scientist and physician. Gilbert is best known for his revolutionary theories on magnetism, published in his book *De Magnete* (or *De Magnete, Magneticisque Corporibus, et de Magno Magnete Tellure*; On the loadstone and magnetic bodies, and on the great magnet the Earth) in 1600. Remarkably little is known of Gilbert's life. Born in Colchester to a prosperous magistrate, he received a B.A. from Cambridge University in 1561, an M.A. in 1564, and an M.D. in 1569. By the mid-1570s, he was practicing medicine in London, where he became a member of the Royal College of Physicians (and was elected president of the group in 1600). There, he also came into contact with navigators, compass makers, and practical mathematicians, and pursued his research on magnetism. In his successful medical practice, he was consulted by members of the aristocracy, was appointed as one of Elizabeth I's personal physicians (1600–1603), and, after her death in 1603, served as James I's physician until a plague epidemic that November took his own life.

Navigational accuracy assumed greater importance with the overseas explorations by the Spanish and Portuguese in the fifteenth century, and during the sixteenth century Dutch and English navigators compiled observations that were of significant use to Gilbert. It was not lost on Gilbert or his contemporaries that discoveries about magnetism would be politically and commercially useful. Despite the widespread use of nautical compasses on Spanish, English, Dutch, and French ships, none of his contemporaries understood why compass needles behaved as they did: attraction, repulsion, variation, dip, bipolarity, and the discovery of latitude were recognized empirically, but poorly understood. Through his experiments on magnets and magnetic bodies (especially the lodestone, that is, naturally magnetized iron ore), Gilbert methodically investigated a wide range of magnetic behaviors.

In fact, Gilbert's book went far beyond being a useful navigational treatise, and represented the first comprehensive analysis of magnetism, featuring a revolutionary new theory about the Earth's magnetic force. In formulating his views, Gilbert insisted on using his own empirical data rather than relying on past scientific authorities. His book is full of carefully contrived laboratory experiments that he urged his readers to replicate. He assailed credulous acceptance of myths (such as the power of a magnet to detect adultery), rejected Aristotelian explanations, and invented his own language to describe magnetic phenomena, including the terms *electricity, electric force, electric attraction,* and *magnetic pole.* To explain the phenomena he investigated, he concluded that the Earth was alive with magnetic potency or force, and he likened this to sexual attraction. Hence, for him, magnetism was an immaterial, innate force operating in the universe, with occult and vital properties.

The stunning claim of Gilbert's book was that the Earth behaves in the heavens as a spherical magnet does on earth. He based this assertion on his experiments with spherical magnets and on his deduction that the Earth itself was a giant spherical magnet. Reasoning by analogy, he stated boldly that the Earth rotated daily on its own axis by its magnetic power, just as a perfectly spherical lodestone aligned with the Earth's poles would spin on its axis. Declaring himself an adherent of astronomer Nicolaus Copernicus (1473–1543), whose theory about the Earth's rotation around the heavens had been published in 1543, Gilbert added new magnetic arguments to the arsenal of the Copernican polemic.

INFLUENCE ON LATER SCIENCE

Subsequent natural philosophers including Francis Bacon (1561–1626) and Galileo Galilei (1564–1642) hailed Gilbert's handling of empirical and experimental evidence, and others applauded his rejection of Aristotle's erroneous ideas about physics and astronomy. Johannes Kepler (1571–1630) and Sir Isaac Newton (1642–1727) pondered Gilbert's magnetic forces before devising their own physical explanations of astronomical motions. And, although many parts of Gilbert's new magnetic theories were soon rejected, including his analogy of the Earth and the spherical lodestone, he is still acknowledged for some of his discoveries about electricity and magnetism (such as the distinction between magnetic and static electricity), and for correctly recognizing that the fixed stars are not all the same distance from the earth.

See also **Astronomy; Bacon, Francis; Copernicus, Nicolaus; Exploration; Galileo Galilei; Kepler, Johannes; Newton, Isaac; Shipbuilding and Navigation.**

BIBLIOGRAPHY

Gilbert, William. *On the Loadstone and Magnetic Bodies, and on the Great Magnet the Earth.* Translated by P. Fleury Mottelay. New York, 1958.

Pumfrey, Stephen. *Latitude and the Magnetic Earth.* Cambridge, U.K., 2002.

Roller, Duane H. D. *The De Magnete of William Gilbert.* Amsterdam, 1959.

MARTHA BALDWIN

GIORGIONE (Giorgo da Castelfranco; 1477–1510), Italian painter, master of the Venetian school. Although little is known about Giorgione, it is clear that in the course of a brief career curtailed by the plague in the autumn of 1510 he transformed the field of painting in Renaissance Venice. In a number of small-scale devotional works (e.g., the *Allendale Nativity,* c. 1500, National Gallery of Art, Washington, D.C.), the young artist responded in brilliant fashion to the pictorial innovations of his master, Giovanni Bellini (c. 1438–1516). In these paintings, Giorgione demonstrated his understand-

Giorgione. *Sleeping Venus* (c. 1510). ©Erich Lessing/Art Resource, N.Y.

ing of Bellini's tonal and atmospheric approach to pictorial composition in which individual forms are loosely bound together through the unifying play of warm golden light. Also derived from Bellini is the placement of human and sacred protagonists within a broadly articulated natural landscape.

Giorgione broadly relied on the established painting types and iconographies of late-fifteenth-century Venice in his earlier work. But his uniquely expressive artistic personality is already very evident in the dreamlike atmosphere that pervades each painting. This air of moody introspection is most noticeable in the Castelfranco altarpiece (c. 1500–1502, Castelfranco, Duomo), Giorgione's first and only monumental religious commission. Here, the rigorously defined rational space of the early Renaissance altarpiece is undermined by a perspective scheme that makes little logical sense. Works such as two well-known male portraits (both c. 1500–1502, one at the Staatliche Museum, Berlin, the other at the San Diego Museum of Art) are undoubtedly commissioned portraits, but their lack of reference to the trappings of social rank makes them very unlike the average fifteenth-century painting of this type. *Col Tempo* (c. 1505, Accademia, Venice), *Laura* (1506, Kunsthistorisches Museum, Vienna), and the *Boy with an Arrow* (c. 1505–1507, Kunsthistorisches Museum, Vienna) cannot really be understood as "portraits" at all, although the artist very deliberately drew on the conventions of the genre. In each painting, Giorgione presents a strongly lit form emerging out of dark shadow, indicating his awareness of the art of Leonardo da Vinci, who had briefly visited Venice in 1500. But Giorgione's fluid and varied application of paint goes beyond Leonardo's smooth blending, pushing the limits of the malleable oil medium. In *Col Tempo,* it is the realization of the woman's weathered skin through the use of broadly applied impasto touches that breathes life into the *vanitas* theme. Both *Laura* and the *Boy* are more conceptually ambiguous. Despite the portraitlike arrangement, we are shown a real individual in neither case. These works are characterized by a simmering (yet understated) eroticism wholly unprecedented in Italian Renaissance art. Texture and touch are the means by which Giorgione creates the sensual mood: in *Laura* by the juxtaposition of fingers, fur, and secret flesh; in the *Boy* by the softly melting treatment of one physical substance into another.

Paintings such as these set the tone for much of Giorgione's later work, which is typically intimate and secular in tone, as well as boldly original in style, technique, and exposition of subject. Little is known of the circumstances in which these paintings were commissioned. But in the 1520s and 1530s *The Three Philosophers* (c. 1508–1510, Kunsthistorisches Museum, Vienna) was owned by Taddeo Contarini, *The Tempest* (c. 1509–1510, Accademia, Venice) by Gabriele Vendramin, and the *Sleeping Venus* (c. 1510, Gemäldegalerie, Dresden) by Girolamo Marcello. These men are likely to have been the original patrons, and recent studies have revealed that they formed an intimate and sophisticated private circle of Venetian patricians. Giorgione's artistic response to the primarily poetic and esoteric interests of this circle may help to explain both the formal originality and the iconographic ambiguity characteristic of his work for them.

The subject matter of both *The Three Philosophers* and *The Tempest* has been hotly disputed by scholars, but such arguments may have been anticipated by the painter who, conceiving his paintings as complex visual and iconographic "puzzles," intended to stimulate interpretation. X-rays of *The Three Philosophers,* for example, indicate that details revealing the subject as that of the three Magi were concealed in the final version. Technical examination of *The Tempest* suggests a less deliberate procedure altogether: rather than veiling a preconceived subject, Giorgione seems to have invented the picture as he went along, his final composition being radically different from that revealed by the x-ray. The many modern attempts to read the painting in terms of a specific mythological, biblical, or allegorical subject seem to sell the painting short. It might be better to think of *The Tempest* as a pictorial attempt to rival the open-ended associative power of the pastoral poetry then so in vogue with Gabriele Vendramin and his select circle.

The vastly influential *Sleeping Venus,* completed by Titian following Giorgione's death, brings together many of the themes and qualities of his art. The subject matter, so typical in its combination of classical and erotic elements, is not on this occasion in doubt. But the Venus once again suggests Giorgione's fundamental conception of painting as a kind of "poetry," which works its magic less through the "logical" or scientific description of the object observed than through its ability to encourage the free association of ideas. It is perhaps for this reason that the anatomical impossibility of Giorgione's goddess has failed to disturb the many who have found in her fluid form the perfect realization of an aesthetic ideal.

See also **Venice, Art in.**

BIBLIOGRAPHY

Anderson, Jaynie. *Giorgione: The Painter of "Poetic Brevity."* Paris and New York, 1997.

Lucco, Mauro. *Giorgione.* Milan, 1995.

Pignatti, Terisio. *Giorgione.* Venice, 1969.

Settis, Salvatore. *Giorgione's Tempest: Interpreting the Hidden Subject.* Cambridge, U.K., 1990.

TOM NICHOLS

GLISSON, FRANCIS (1598 or 1599–1677), English physician and natural philosopher. Glisson enrolled at Caius College, Cambridge, at the age of eighteen. Finally turning to medical studies in his late twenties, he went on to a distinguished career in medicine and natural philosophy. He became a fellow of the Royal College of Physicians in 1635 and held numerous offices there, including that of reader in anatomy in 1639, and of president from 1667 to 1669. His success as a physician was also reflected in the fact that he was appointed Regius Professor of Physic ("Medicine") at Cambridge in 1636, a post he held until his death. He was a member of the group of experimental natural philosophers who met in London in the period after the execution of Charles I in 1649, and which has been identified as a precursor of the Royal Society. Although he subsequently became one of the earliest fellows of the society, his own research led him to develop a natural philosophy that was at odds with the prevailing views in the society, so he was never prominent.

After an initial publication, *De Rachitide* (On rickets, 1650), which was then believed to be a new disease, all Glisson's works were devoted to understanding human physiology in the light of William

Harvey's (1578–1657) discovery of the circulation of the blood (1628). Before Harvey, the liver was seen as the source of the venous system, and of venous blood, so when the discovery of circulation showed that the veins were continuous with the arterial system and converged on the heart, it became obvious that the role of the liver was completely misunderstood. Glisson's *Anatomia Hepatis* (Anatomy of the liver, 1654) sought to put this right. An important outcome of this research was the concept of irritability, an idea he pursued by turning his attention to the stomach and intestines. Glisson began by establishing that sensitivity, which he saw as an ability to perceive, was inherent in living tissue even where no nerves were present, but he went on to believe that all matter, animate and inanimate, was perceptive and endowed with appetite and motility. He deferred publishing on the stomach in favor of a major account of these ideas in his *Tractatus de Natura Substantiae Energetica* (Treatise on the energetic nature of substance, 1672). The subsequent *Tractatus de Ventriculo et Intestinis* (Treatise on the stomach and intestines, 1677) appeared in the year of his death.

The medical importance of Glisson's discovery of irritability remained unnoticed until the theory was established by Albrecht von Haller (1708–1777) in 1753, but it raised immediate controversy in natural philosophy. The prevailing mechanical philosophy promoted a view of matter as completely passive and inert, and Glisson's research ran counter to this. Because the passivity of matter was frequently used to ensure a role for God's providence, Glisson's active matter was seen as a support for atheism. Consequently, his works were explicitly attacked by the Cambridge Platonists Henry More (1586–1661) and Ralph Cudworth (1617–1688).

See also **Anatomy and Physiology; Haller, Albrecht von; Harvey, William; Mechanism; Medicine; More, Henry; Natural Philosophy; Neoplatonism.**

BIBLIOGRAPHY

Giglioni, Guido. "Anatomist Atheist? The 'Hylozoistic' Foundations of Francis Glisson's Anatomical Research." In *Religio Medici: Medicine and Religion in Seventeenth-Century England,* edited by O. P. Grell and A. Cunningham, pp. 115–135. Aldershot, U.K., 1996.

Henry, John. "Medicine and Pneumatology: Henry More, Richard Baxter, and Francis Glisson's Treatise on the Energetic Nature of Substance." *Medical History 31* (1987): 15–40.

Pagel, Walter. "Harvey and Glisson on Irritability, with a Note on Van Helmont." *Bulletin of the History of Medicine 41* (1967): 497–514.

JOHN HENRY

GLORIOUS REVOLUTION (BRITAIN).

The Glorious Revolution was the term contemporaries coined to refer to the events of 1688–1689 that led to the overthrow of the Catholic James II (ruled 1685–1688) in England (and thereby also in Ireland and Scotland) and his replacement by the Protestant William III and Mary II (ruled 1689–1702). Some historians see the Glorious Revolution as a Whig victory that established limited monarchy in England; others have emphasized the important role of the Tories in bringing down James II and stressed the compromise nature of the revolution settlement; still others have seen it as little more than a foreign invasion, a dynastic coup brought about from outside and from above (within the royal family), not from below. One thing is certain: the Glorious Revolution was not "bloodless," as it was once styled. Not only was there some blood shed in England, but the overthrow of James II provoked bloody wars in both Scotland and Ireland, which left a bitter and long-lasting legacy.

THE OVERTHROW OF JAMES II

James II inherited a strong position when he came to the throne in 1685. The Tory reaction of Charles II's (ruled 1660–1685) last years had not only seen a ruthless campaign against all forms of political and religious dissent (with Whigs being purged from local office and Nonconformist conventiclers harried in the law courts) and an effective bolstering of the powers of the crown, but also witnessed a marked swing in public opinion. People rallied behind the crown and the legitimate heir against what they saw as a threat to the existing establishment in church and state posed by the Whigs and their Nonconformist allies. James's accession in February 1685 was broadly popular, as evidenced by numerous loyalist demonstrations and addresses, and when he met his first Parliament in May, a mere 57 members of Parliament (out of a total of 513) were known Whigs, thanks in part to Charles II's interference in borough franchises during his final years, but also due to a shift in opinion in favor of the Tories. Although James Scott, the duke of Monmouth, and a few radical Whigs did launch a rebellion that summer to try to overthrow James, it met with very little support.

Nevertheless, despite promises at the beginning of his reign that he would respect his subjects' rights and liberties and protect the existing Protestant establishment in the church, James immediately set about advancing the interests of his fellow Catholics through the royal prerogative. Thus he issued dispensations to Catholics from the provisions of the Test Act of 1673, which restricted political office to communicating members of the Church of England, winning a decisive test case in favor of the dispensing power—*Godden v. Hales*—in June 1686 (though only after a purge of the judicial bench). He also promoted the public celebration of the Mass; sought to undermine the Anglican monopoly of education by forcing the universities to admit Catholics; issued a Declaration of Indulgence (April 1687), which in one fell swoop suspended all penal laws against Protestant and Catholic nonconformists; and engaged in a campaign to pack Parliament so that he could establish Catholic toleration by law.

His initiatives, however, met with considerable obstruction from the Tory–Anglican interest. His loyalist Parliament of 1685 called for a strict enforcement of the laws against Catholics and condemned the dispensations given to Catholic officers in the army and had to be prorogued before the end of the year; the Anglican clergy began delivering fiery sermons against popery, which led the king to set up an Ecclesiastical Commission to keep them in line; and the Tory–Anglican squierarchy, in response to a poll conducted by the crown, overwhelmingly refused to commit themselves to support a repeal of the penal laws in a forthcoming Parliament. When in April 1688 James tried to make the clergy read a reissue of his Declaration of Indulgence from the pulpit, most refused, and seven bishops petitioned the crown against the Indulgence on the grounds that it was against the law. The crown brought a prosecution against the seven bishops for seditious libel, but in June 1688 they were found not guilty by a King's Bench jury. In that same month, when James's second wife, Mary of Modena (1658–1718) gave birth to a son, who would take precedence in the succession over James's Protestant daughters by his first marriage, the prospect of a never-ending succession of Catholic kings led a group of seven politicians to invite the Dutch stadtholder William of Orange, husband of James's eldest daughter and fourth in line to the throne in his own right, to come and rescue English political and religious liberties. In the face of William's invasion, James began to backtrack and, following the advice of his bishops, agreed to abandon the dispensing and suspending power and his Ecclesiastical Commission and to restore things to the way they had been at the time of his accession. In short, it was the Tory–Anglican interest who defeated the drift toward popery and arbitrary government under James.

Following William's landing at Torbay on 5 November 1688, members of the ruling elite and even sections of the army began to desert James, while anti-Catholic rioting broke out in many parts of the country. Although William invaded with a sizeable and well-trained professional army (estimates vary from between 14,000 and 21,000 men), James was able to send nearly 30,000 men to meet him at Salisbury Plain and had another 8,000–10,000 men ready to bring into action. However, James was not defeated by an invading army; he panicked in the face of desertions by his subjects and opted to flee the country. Although his first attempt, in the early hours of 11 December, was unsuccessful, he did leave on 23 December, after William had already occupied the capital.

THE REVOLUTION SETTLEMENT

In January 1689, a Convention Parliament, which was evenly balanced between Whigs and Tories, met to settle the state of the nation. Most Tories hoped to preserve the hereditary principle either by keeping James as king with a regent ruling in his name or by settling the throne on his eldest daughter, Mary (taking comfort in the myth that the Prince of Wales had not really been delivered by the queen but had been smuggled into the bedchamber in a warming-pan). The Convention determined, however, that James, by breaking his contract with the people (a Whig doctrine) and withdrawing himself from the kingdom, had abdicated the government, and proceeded in early February to fill the vacancy by declaring William and Mary king and queen jointly (though with full regal power vested in William alone). The Convention then determined what powers they should give the new monarchs. Twenty-eight Heads of Grievances were drawn up, some of which were articulations of existing rights, others demands for constitutional reform. In the end, the Convention decided to leave out those grievances that would have required fresh legislation, and instead agreed to a Declaration of Rights (12 February) that purported to do no more than vindicate and assert ancient rights and liberties. There has been considerable controversy over whether or not the Declaration of Rights in fact made new law under the guise of proclaiming the old, especially with regard to its declarations that the suspending power, the dispensing power (as exercised under James), the Ecclesiastical Commission, and a standing army in time of peace without parliamentary consent were illegal. What can be said with confidence is that the framers of the Declaration of Rights genuinely believed that the powers they condemned were illegal, and that the Declaration reflected the concerns of both the Whigs and Tories.

William and Mary were proclaimed king and queen in London and Westminster on 13 February and shortly thereafter in the rest of the country; they were crowned on 11 April 1689. The Declaration of Rights was not the totality of the revolution settlement, however. Several of the reforms in the original Heads of Grievances that did not make it into the Declaration were enacted during William's reign: in April 1689, a Toleration Act secured limited toleration for Protestant nonconformists; in December, the Declaration of Rights was passed into law with the Bill of Rights, which also barred Catholics from the succession and prevented any future king or queen from marrying a Catholic; a Triennial Act of 1694 secured frequent Parliaments (the act stipulated that Parliaments must meet at least once every three years and that no Parliament was to last for more than three years without a dissolution), while the Act of Settlement of 1701, in addition to determining that the succession should pass to the Hanoverians once the Protestant Stuart line became extinct, also ensured the independence of the judiciary. Yet more than anything else, it was the revolution in foreign policy that accompanied the dynastic shift in 1688–1689 that changed the nature of the monarchy in England. The nation became involved in an expensive war against France, which resulted in the setting up of the Bank of England (1694) and the establishment of a national debt that had to be serviced by regular grants of taxation. This increased the monarchy's dependence on Parliament, while William's repeated absences from England in the 1690s, as he led the war effort on the Continent, led to the emergence of the cabinet system of government.

Whereas the revolution in England was a bipartisan affair, the same was not true for the other two kingdoms under Stuart rule. In Scotland, the Whigs and Presbyterians were able to forge a more radical settlement in church and state, overturning episcopacy and stripping the crown of many of the powers it possessed under Charles II and James II. The government did not succeed in putting down Jacobite resistance until May 1690, though Jacobite sentiment in the Highlands and among the Episcopalians of the northeast remained strong, helping to fuel further Jacobite rebellions in 1715 and 1745. In Ireland, the Catholic majority declared for James II, who went there in March 1689 with the intention of trying to use the kingdom as base from which to reconquer Scotland and England. An overwhelmingly Catholic Parliament that met in Dublin in the spring of 1689 passed a legislative package restoring political and economic power to the Catholics; but this was undone by Williamite victory in the ensuing war—the turning point coming with William's victory at the Boyne on 1 July 1690 (after which James fled), although Jacobite resistance continued until the final surrender at Limerick on 3 October 1691. Following the peace, successive Protestant Parliaments passed a series of repressive penal laws designed to guarantee the Protestant ascendancy and make it extremely difficult for Catholics to exercise their religion, inherit property, engage in trade or practice a profession.

See also **Church of England; England; Jacobitism; James II (England); Stuart Dynasty (England and Scotland); William and Mary.**

BIBLIOGRAPHY

Beddard, Robert, ed. *A Kingdom without a King: The Journal of the Provisional Government in the Revolution of 1688.* Oxford, 1988.

———. *The Revolutions of 1688: The Andrew Browning Lectures 1988.* Oxford, 1988.

Cruickshanks, Eveline. *The Glorious Revolution.* London, 2000.

Harris, Tim. "The People, the Law and the Constitution in Scotland and England: A Comparative Approach to the Glorious Revolution." *Journal of British Studies* 38 (1999): 28–58.

———. *Politics under the Later Stuarts: Party Conflict in a Divided Society 1660–1715.* London and New York, 1993.

Holmes, Geoffrey, ed. *Britain after the Glorious Revolution, 1689–1714.* London, 1969.

Israel, Jonathan I., ed. *The Anglo-Dutch Moment: Essays on the Glorious Revolution and its World Impact.* Cambridge, U.K., 1991.

Pincus, Steven, "'To Protect English Liberties': The English Nationalist Revolution of 1688–1689." In *Protestantism and National Identity: Britain and Ireland, c. 1650–c. 1850.* Edited by Tony Claydon and Ian McBride. Cambridge, U.K., 1998, pp. 75–104.

Schwoerer, Lois G. *The Declaration of Rights, 1689.* Baltimore, 1981.

Simms, J. G. *Jacobite Ireland, 1685–91.* London and Toronto, 1969.

Speck, W. A. *Reluctant Revolutionaries: Englishmen and the Revolution of 1688.* Oxford, 1988.

TIM HARRIS

GLUCK, CHRISTOPH WILLIBALD VON (1714–1787), Austrian composer of Bohemian birth. Gluck is important for his "reform" of the Metastasian opera seria in works written for Vienna and Paris. The son and grandson of gamekeepers, Gluck studied music (singing and violin), and at the age of thirteen or fourteen, faced with his father's determination that he follow the paternal vocation, fled to Prague, where he supported himself by various musical activities (notably as organist at the Týn Church). In Prague he had the opportunity to hear contemporary Italian opera by Vivaldi, Albinoni, and others. After briefly serving Prince Lobkowitz in Vienna, in 1737 he accepted employment as a violinist in Prince Melzi's service in Milan. Four years later his first Italian opera, *Artaserse,* to a libretto by Pietro Metastasio (1698–1782), had its premiere. For the next dozen years he followed a career path typical of moderately successful composers of Italian opera. He traveled extensively, for a while as music director of the Mingotti company and later for Locatelli's company, and wrote operas on commission for cities in Italy, as well as Dresden, Copenhagen, Vienna, and London. In these he gained a mastery of current conventions in opera structure, forms, expression of emotions, florid melodic writing, text setting, and orchestral scoring (although sometimes with brusque and unexpected results). In 1745 he became resident composer at the King's Theatre in London. The first of his two works written for production there, *La caduta de' giganti,* contains clear allusions to the current political situation in forecasting allegorically the suppression of the Jacobite rebellion. Both London operas include much music revised from earlier works, as would remain Gluck's custom throughout his career (and, indeed, it was standard practice for Italian opera composers to borrow from works of their own heard only elsewhere and, often at the behest of singers, to include music of others in their scores). While in England the composer became acquainted with George Frideric Handel's music and David Garrick's "realistic" style of dramatic acting, whose aesthetics were to mark his subsequent approach.

By 1748 Gluck was back in Vienna, where the court commissioned him to compose the music for Metastasio's *La semiramide riconnosciuta* to celebrate the birthday of Empress Maria Theresa. Two years later he married Maria Anna Bergin, whose dowry and personal wealth gave him financial stability. The couple remained based in her native Vienna, although in the early years of their marriage Gluck continued to accept foreign commissions that required travel. He also became Konzertmeister and later Kapellmeister to Prince Joseph Friedrich von Sachsen-Hildburghausen. For the imperial couple's visit to his estate outside Vienna, the composer wrote *Le cinesi,* a clever parody of contrasting dramatic genres as well as an address to tastes for the "exotic." These operas and other musical activities doubtless brought the composer to the attention of Count Durazzo, who in 1756 hired him to supervise concerts and French opéras comiques at the court-controlled Burgtheater (four years later the production of ballet music was added to his duties). Several commissions of Italian operas, French opéras comiques and ballet scores for the theater and for the court soon followed. Of these the most

Christoph von Gluck. Portrait by Carl Jaeger, 1881.

significant musically is the *ballet d'action, Don Juan* (1761, choreography by Gasparo Angiolini). Because he was busy with Viennese projects and because travel was hindered by the War of the Austrian Succession (1740–1748) and its aftermath, Gluck seldom ventured elsewhere during this period. One important exception was the opera for Rome, *Antigono* (1756); during his visit there the pope named him *cavaliere dello sperone d'oro* (knight of the golden spur), a title that the composer took pride in using.

By 1760 Gluck was well established as the leading opera composer in Vienna. While during the decade he continued to compose opéras comiques, serenatas, and other works for the court (often to texts by the venerable Metastasio) and was awarded a court pension in 1763, he is remembered today for his "reform" of opera seria in his *Orfeo ed Euridice* (1762) and *Alceste* (1767). Significantly, the librettist for both was Raniero Calzabigi, an Italian familiar with French theatrical and operatic dramaturgy and probably the anonymous critic of the Metastasian model (*Lettre sur le méchanisme de l'opéra italien,* 1756). Operatic change was in the air: Gluck and other Italian opera composers and librettists had already anticipated some of the directions that the "reform" would take. Still, *Orfeo* and *Alceste* mark the most thoroughgoing development of a new aesthetic, a "noble simplicity" according to contemporaries: the drama comes first and unfolds in a logical, straightforward way; aria structures are more varied and flexible and avoid lengthy orchestral introductions *(ritornelli);* florid vocal display is avoided in favor of a more direct expression in often syllabic settings; the chorus has a heightened role; integration of chorus, soloists, aria, accompanied recitative, and dance in impressive tableaux match requirements of the plot and give the work greater musical continuity (though the divisions remain clear). In performance, acting by the soloists, including their gestures, became more "natural"; the first Orfeo, the castrato Gaetano Guadagni, had studied with Garrick, and the music historian Charles Burney later recounted that Gluck himself told him that he had insisted on numerous repetitions during rehearsals until all aspects of the performance met his standards. *Alceste,* in addition, broke with tradition in omitting castrati from the soloists' ranks (original version).

As several of the innovations were inspired by the model of the French *tragédie* and the *tragédie lyrique,* Gluck decided to try to conquer Paris, then the cultural capital of Europe. Preceded by a clever publicity campaign mounted by C. L. G. L. du Roullet, the librettist for several of his French operas, Gluck arrived there in late 1773. With the support of his former student, Marie Antoinette (dauphine, shortly to become queen), he soon gained a contract with the Académie Royale de Musique. After six months of intensive rehearsal his first opera for the Académie, *Iphigénie en Aulide,* was a success, followed shortly by *Orphée et Euridice,* a revision of *Orfeo,* performed to even greater acclaim. *Alceste* (1776) differs substantially from its Italian predecessor. In choosing to reset Jean-Baptiste Quinault's libretto written for Jean-Baptiste Lully, Gluck sought in *Armide* (1777) to align himself explicitly with the French tradition. His *Iphigénie en Tauride* (1779) is his masterpiece.

These five operas show the composer's growing mastery of French declamation and his substantial advance in the "reform" agenda. In *Alceste,* for example, the two principal characters and the chorus are portrayed more convincingly as a loving couple and grieving people, compared to the Italian version. In *Armide* Gluck not only exploited spectacular stage effects, but also achieved a more fluid musical construction. *Iphigénie en Tauride* builds on this in an unusually high number of ensembles matching the drama.

After having divided his time between Paris and Vienna for six years, Gluck returned to the Austrian capital for good in 1779. His final major operatic effort was to revise a translation into German of *Iphigénie en Tauride* (1781). *Orfeo/Orphée* (often in various hybrid versions) and his French *tragédies lyriques* were an important legacy. Not only were these operas part of the repertory throughout the nineteenth century, although they were sometimes revised to meet current casts and audience tastes by musicians such as Berlioz (*Orphée,* 1859; *Alceste,* 1861, both Paris), Wagner (*Iphigénie en Aulide,* 1847, Dresden) and Richard Strauss (*Iphigénie en Tauride,* 1889, Weimar), they have continued to be revived in the twentieth and twenty-first centuries.

See also **Lully, Jean-Baptiste; Music; Opera; Vienna.**

BIBLIOGRAPHY

Brown, Bruce A. *Gluck and the French Theatre in Vienna.* Oxford, 1991.

Brown, Bruce Alan, and Julian Rushton. "Gluck, Christoph Willibald Ritter von." In *The New Grove Dictionary of Music and Musicians.* 2nd ed. London, 2001.

Gluck, Christoph Willibald. *Sämtliche Werke.* Edited by Rudolf Gerber, et al. Kassel and Basel, 1951–.

Howard, Patricia. *Christoph Willibald Gluck: A Guide to Research.* 2nd ed. New York, 2003.

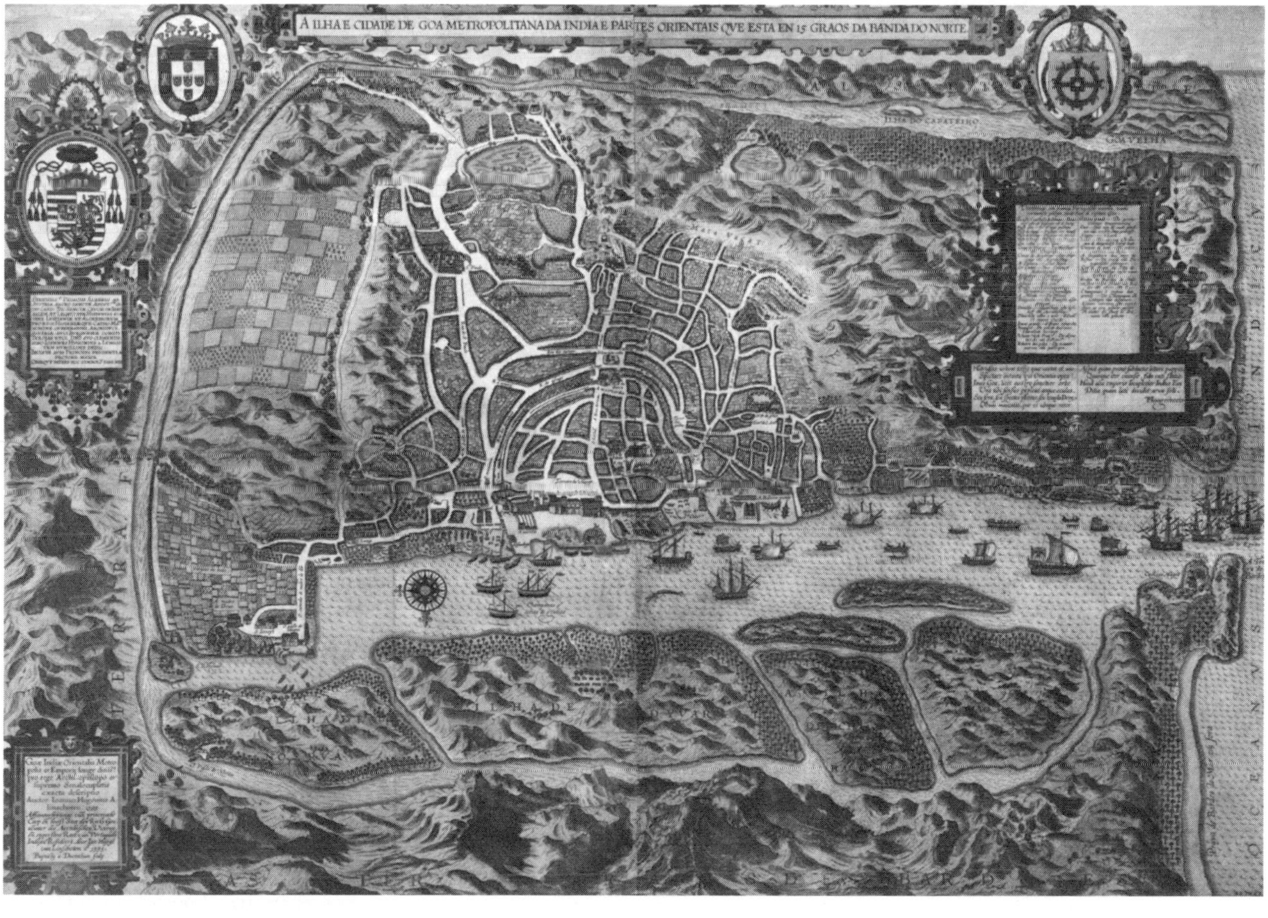

Goa. Map of Goa, engraved by Johannes Baptista van Doetechum the Younger, 1595. PRIVATE COLLECTION/THE STAPLETON COLLECTION/BRIDGEMAN ART LIBRARY

———. *Gluck: An Eighteenth-Century Portrait in Letters and Documents.* Oxford, 1995.

Lesure, François, ed. *Querelle des Gluckistes et des Piccinnistes.* Geneva, 1984. Facsimiles of eighteenth-century pamphlets and other materials.

Rice, John A. *Antonio Salieri and Viennese Opera.* Chicago, 1998.

M. ELIZABETH C. BARTLET

GOA. Goa was the administrative and religious capital of the Portuguese Asian empire. Located on the west coast of India, Goa had been an important center of Indian Ocean trade under the sultan of Bijapur well before the arrival of the Portuguese. After 1510 it became the center of Portuguese activities in Asia and by 1600 its population grew to seventy-five thousand. As in Macau and other cities in Portuguese Asia, the Portuguese always formed a small percentage of the total population. Goa is the name of both the city and the area surrounding it. By the 1630s the region had a population of 250,000. During the sixteenth century and part of the seventeenth century Goa reached its zenith, becoming one of the jewels in the Portuguese crown. Long-distance trade with Lisbon brought New World gold and silver to trade for Asian spices (such as pepper, cloves, and cinnamon) as well as tea and Chinese silks. Trade within the Indian Ocean region was based on exchanging prized Arabian horses in South Asia for Indian cotton and rice.

In Goa's heyday travelers remarked on the many large buildings and the highly evolved urban nature of the city, in which the Portuguese had built a number of large churches and an important convent (Santa Mónica). A slow decline began by 1650, and the city was eventually abandoned because of reoccurring health concerns (malaria and cholera). The urban population moved several miles west to Panaji, the modern capital of the Indian state of Goa.

See also **Macau; Portuguese Colonies: The Indian Ocean and Asia.**

BIBLIOGRAPHY

Pearson, M. N. *The Portuguese in India.* Cambridge, U.K., 1987. A succinct summary of Portuguese interactions in India, especially Goa.

Souza, Teotonio R de. *Medieval Goa.* New Delhi, 1979. Pathbreaking study that discusses Goa in the Indian context, focusing on the local Goan population under Portuguese rule.

Souza, Teotonio R. de, ed. *Indo-Portuguese History: Old Issues, New Questions.* New Delhi, 1985. A collection of essays outlining the newer issues raised in the field.

TIMOTHY J. COATES

GOETHE, JOHANN WOLFGANG VON (1749–1832; elevated to the nobility as von Goethe in 1782), German writer, scientist, and statesman. The dominant figure of the German Classicist-Romantic period, and for many still the most influential of all German writers, Goethe was often referred to as the last Renaissance man. He successfully cultivated a multitude of extraordinary talents, while his works, especially *Faust* and his novels, expressed and helped shape modern individualism. He brought radical subjectivity to German poetry and expressed a modern view of history: history revealed in the exceptional individual. The cult of Goethe as the eminent icon of German culture (in the much-lamented absence of a nation-state) and his canonization began during his lifetime, which also saw the beginnings of German philology and literary historiography. Recent scholarship has examined and reevaluated the diverse cultural production in Goethe's "shadow," especially the writing of Charlotte von Stein (1742–1827) and Marianne von Willemer (1784–1860), who had previously been of interest in numerous biographies of Goethe merely as his beloved and as the inspiration and models for his fictional characters.

Goethe was the first child of a patrician couple in Frankfurt am Main, the coronation city of the Holy Roman Empire. Retired imperial councillor Johann Caspar Goethe (1710–1782) and Katharina Elisabeth, née Textor (1731–1808), a major's daughter, led a cultured life and valued artistic endeavors. The only surviving son, Goethe enjoyed a privileged humanistic education at home together with his sister Cornelia (1750–1777). In 1765 Goethe was sent to study law at Leipzig University, where he also cultivated his interests in art and literature. He was exposed to Enlightenment thinkers and the new English literature of sensibility, and he wrote elegant erotic poetry and a pastoral play. After a severe case of tuberculosis in 1768 and a subsequent return to Frankfurt, he continued his studies in Strasbourg in 1770. There he met the young East Prussian writer Johann Gottfried Herder (1744–1803), later a theologian in Weimar. They shared criticism of rationalism and the prevailing French taste and enthusiasm for Jean-Jacques Rousseau, German folk song, and medieval architecture, and each found in Shakespeare and Homer models for original creativity. Goethe graduated in 1771 with a *Lizentiat* (doctoral degree) and became an attorney for the Frankfurt juridical court; increasingly, though, he devoted his efforts to writing and drawing. He initiated a radically subjective style, commonly referred to as "Sturm und Drang" (storm and stress), that marked the beginning of German Romanticism. He soon became famous across Europe through his love poems, his Shakespearean chronicle play *Götz von Berlichingen* (published 1773) based on the controversial knight of that name (c. 1480–1562) during the Peasants' War, and his scandalous epistolary novel *Die Leiden des jungen Werthers* (1774; The sufferings of young Werther). In the fall of 1775 young Carl August of Saxe-Weimar (1757–1828) invited Goethe to Weimar. Although his Thuringian duchy was small, it was nonetheless an important cultural center thanks to the endeavors of Carl August's mother, Anna Amalia (1739–1807; regent 1756–1775). In June 1776 Goethe became a member of the duke's cabinet and his privy councillor. Except for Goethe's "flight" to Italy from his many bureaucratic obligations (1786–1788), a journey to Venice (1790), the German campaign against revolutionary France, and shorter travels, he remained in the small province for the rest of his long life. In 1806 he married the lowborn Christiane Vulpius (1765–1816) with whom he had lived since 1788, much to the outrage of Weimar society.

Goethe, best known for his wide range of poetry, plays, and novels, was also a respected administrator, knowledgeable art collector, and successful director of the Weimar Hoftheater (court theater, including opera) from 1791 to 1813. He admired Napoleon and recognized the genius of Beethoven. His interest in the sciences ranged from osteology and botany to optics and mineralogy; he believed strongly in his theory of colors (*Zur Farbenlehre;* 1810), which contradicted Newton's.

Johann Wolfgang von Goethe. ©Bettmann/Corbis

Goethe's extensive correspondence is an endless resource for insights into his intense relationships with contemporaries. Most important was the friendship and collaboration with Friedrich Schiller (1759–1805) from 1794 to 1805, when both wrote in a Classicist style and theorized on the central function of art in human life and in society. Their rigorously pedagogical aesthetics met with resistance, and Goethe's own earlier works remained much more popular. Literary history, however, established Goethe's and Schiller's works from those years as Weimar Classicism.

Only very few works from Goethe's rich œuvre can be mentioned here. His poetry was so innovative and is so rich and multifaceted that any mention of single titles does not do justice to it. It ranges from stormy nature and love poems, hymns, classical elegies and satirical epigrams, and ballads, to the idyllic epic poem *Hermann und Dorothea* (1797) and his adaptation of Oriental traditions in *West-Östlicher Divan* (1819). Numerous poems have been set to music by composers from Mozart and Schubert to contemporary ones. Dramas such as *Egmont* (1788), *Iphigenia auf Tauris* (1787; Iphigenia on Tauris), and *Torquato Tasso* (1790) draw on (literary) history and mythology for models and reinterpretations of harmonious and autonomous individuals; yet the emotional struggle is merely contained, not overcome, in an equilibrium. Thus the dichotomy between Classicist (recent research prefers this term over "classical" and its hierarchical implications) and Romantic writers is not as sharp as previously believed. The novel *Wilhelm Meisters Lehrjahre* (1795–1796; Wilhelm Meister's apprenticeship years), long regarded as the exemplary German "Bildungsroman" (novel of individual organic development or self formation), was most influential for the Romantics and the nineteenth and twentieth centuries in general. Whether the protagonist achieves the alleged goal of character formation and a well-rounded education or whether the novel criticizes and undermines such a goal remains controversial.

Interpretation of Goethe's universal life work situates him within various tendencies of his time, a critical period in the development of the modern world, but also stresses that he anticipated modernist (and even postmodern) fractured structures, especially in his last novel *Wilhelm Meisters Wanderjahre, oder Die Entsagenden* (1829; Wilhelm Meister's travel years, or the renunciants) where he wrote critically on developments such as industrialization and specialization. Goethe pursued a lifelong interest in the subject of Faust, the sixteenth-century alchemist, scholar, and magician, and rendered the pact-with-the-devil legend into an original tragedy of human striving and complex symbolism of human life, society, and politics. Goethe's *Faust* (fragment published 1790; *Faust,* Part I of the tragedy, 1808; *Faust,* Part II, posthumously 1832) is a masterpiece of world literature; Part II is a plethora of mythology and heterogeneity. Interpretations of it and its influence on literature and music are innumerable. In his autobiographical writings (*Dichtung und Wahrheit* [Poetry and truth], 1811–1814; *Italienische Reise* [Italian journey], 1816–1817, 1829, etc.), which were very influential for the genre of autobiography, he styled himself as a German classical writer and Olympian.

See also **Drama: German; Frankfurt am Main; German Literature and Language; Herder, Johann Gottfried von; Schiller, Johann Christoph Friedrich von.**

BIBLIOGRAPHY

Primary Sources

Goethe, Johann Wolfgang von. *Collected Works.* Edited by Cyrus Hamlin. Translated by Cyrus Hamlin, Walter Arndt, Michael Hamburger, Frank Ryder, et al. 12 vols. New York, 1983–1988 and 1994–.

———. *Faust.* Edited by C. Hamlin. Translated by Walter Arndt. New York, 2000. Excellent German/English edition in the Norton Critical Editions Series with extensive notes and introductory and supporting material.

———. *Sämtliche Werke, Briefe, Tagebücher und Gespräche.* 39 vols. Frankfurt, 1985–. The most inclusive edition in German available, edited by a wide range of scholars.

Secondary Sources

Boyle, Nicholas. *Goethe: The Poet and the Age.* 2 vols. Oxford and New York, 1991 and 1999. Interpretative biography.

Boyle, Nicholas, and John Guthrie, eds. *Goethe and the English-Speaking World: Essays from the Cambridge Symposium for His 150th Anniversary.* Rochester, N.Y., 2002.

Sharpe, Lesley, ed. *The Cambridge Companion to Goethe.* Cambridge, U.K., and New York, 2002. Scholarly yet accessible chapters on his works by genre and on relations to the contemporary world as well as reception.

Wagner, Irmgard. *Goethe.* New York, 1999. Concise introduction to major literary works.

WALTRAUD MAIERHOFER

GOLDONI, CARLO (1707–1793), Italian dramatist. Carlo Goldoni was born in Venice to a family that had immigrated from Modena and that had members in both the professional class and the nobility. Fascinated by the theater from an early age, Goldoni wrote his first play before he was ten. While attending school in Rimini, he became friendly with a comedy troupe that included women, banned from the stage in much of Italy, and departed with them for Chioggia. In 1723 he undertook the study of law at the University of Pavia, but he was expelled in 1725 for a satire of the city's women. After his father died in 1731, Goldoni completed his degree at the University of Padua, but he departed for Milan in 1732 to avoid financial and sentimental obligations.

Carlo Goldoni. Undated portrait engraving.

In 1734 he began his association with the Imer troupe of actors. By the late 1730s he was working regularly in theaters in Venice and other cities and had begun his reform of the improvised commedia dell'arte tradition. He wrote out individual parts and then entire plays, blending Tuscan-speaking aristocratic characters of the erudite tradition with dialect-speaking nonaristocratic characters. While retaining some elements of commedia dell'arte masks and writing a masterpiece in *Il servitore di due padroni* (1747; Servant of two masters) Goldoni endowed his characters with new psychological depth and realism. *La vedova scaltra* (The artful widow) of 1748, the first comedy fully implementing these reforms, was favorably received by many. It was also criticized by others, especially Goldoni's rival and imitator Pietro Chiari, the polemic resulting in the censure of theaters by the Venetian government.

Goldoni responded with plays in a wide range of styles, including the famous sixteen comedies of the 1751 Carnival season and his memorable dialect comedies. *Mirandolina* (The mistress of the inn), staged in 1753, tells of a young proprietress of an inn who exercises great freedom in her dealings with aristocratic suitors. The *Villeggiatura* (The country vacation) trilogy (1761) pokes fun at city aristocrats who take their artifice-filled habits with them on country vacations. In *Le baruffe chiozzotte* (Chioggian quarrels) (1762) a girl whose needlework earns her good money attracts rival suitors. Opposition to Goldoni's work intensified, with accusations by the satirist and author of theatrical fables Carlo Gozzi (1720–1806) that Goldoni was inverting the social order by associating aristocratic characters with vice and the popular classes with virtue. Gozzi mounted a successful theatrical alternative, a series of exotic tales set in a world of aristocratic privilege.

In 1762, worn down by polemics, Goldoni moved to Paris to work with the Comédie italienne. The French public's expectation that Italian comedy conform to the traditional commedia dell'arte style left him few professional satisfactions. He nevertheless remained in Paris, writing a number of well-received plays and his memoirs.

The strength of Goldoni's theater lies in its inclusion of divergent and even conflicting elements that occur in daily life and that are part of theatrical tradition. The complicated relations of men and women, the generations, and social classes fascinated him. His most consistent focus is on forces that strengthen those bonds or that, on the contrary, break them by setting individuals on destructive paths. While Goldoni appreciated the vitality of the lower social orders, he feared their violence, and while he appreciated aristocrats' elegance, he feared their arrogant vanity. What remained was the sober and directed energy of the middle social orders.

As the plots of his plays show, Goldoni understood that bad choices often result either from indulgence in pleasure or from despair. He also knew that human beings favor those who attract them, and that this causes them to neglect those to whom they are obligated. Thus his plays include husbands who abandon their wives for their drinking companions, wives who prefer their husbands to the children who depend upon them, and servants more interested in gossip than work.

Goldoni experimented with a variety of measures designed to maintain prudent behavior, both internalized social rules, such as an acceptance of authority figures, and severe consequences for irregular behavior, such as the poverty that results from gambling and the damage and death that result from violence. He also showed how authority figures, including fathers and members of the aristocratic class, bring their subordinates into line through both kind and harsh measures, as he kept his characters in line by writing out the parts rather than continuing the improvisation of the commedia dell'arte.

At the same time Goldoni understood that subordination to men creates difficulties and even dangers for women. While most of his numerous and prominent female characters accept and even embrace submissiveness to men, a few of them enjoy a combination of financial security and a lack of male relatives that permits an unprecedented emotional independence. Mirandolina the innkeeper's marriage to her servant rather than to a misogynistic nobleman shows that she intends to remain mistress of her life.

See also **Commedia dell'Arte; Drama: Italian.**

BIBLIOGRAPHY

Primary Sources

Goldoni, Carlo. *Four Comedies.* Translated by Frederick Davies. Harmondsworth, U.K., 1968. Translations of *I due gemelli Veneziani* (1750), *La vedova scaltra* (1748), *La locandiera* (1753), and *La casa nova* (1761).

———. *Memoirs of Carlo Goldoni.* Translated by John Black, edited by William A. Drake. New York and London, 1926. Translation of *Mémoires* (1787).

———. *The Servant of Two Masters.* Translated and adapted by Frederick H. Davies. London, 1961. Translation of *Il servitore di due padroni* (1747).

———. *Tutte le opere.* Edited by Giuseppe Ortolani. Milan, 1935–1956.

———. *Carlo Goldoni's Villeggiatura Trilogy.* Translated by Robert Cornthwaite. Lyme, N.H., 1994. Translation of *Le smanie della villeggiatura, Le avventure della villeggiatura,* and *Il ritorno dalla villeggiatura.*

Secondary Sources

Angelini, Franca. *Vita di Goldoni.* Rome, 1993.

Baratto, Mario. *La letteratura teatrale del Settecento in Italia: studi e letture su Carlo Goldoni.* Vicenza, 1985.

Branca, Vittore, and Nicola Mangini, eds. *Studi goldoniani.* Venice, 1960. The acts of an important conference with papers by respected scholars.

Ferroni, Giulio. *Storia della letteratura italiana dal Cinquecento al Settecento.* Milan, 1991.

Fido, Franco. *Guida a Goldoni: Teatro e società nel Settecento* Turin, 1977.

———. *Nuova guida a Goldoni: Teatro e società nel Settecento.* Turin, 2000.

Günsberg, Maggie. *Playing with Gender: The Comedies of Goldoni.* Leeds, U.K., 2001.

Siciliano, Enzo. *La letteratura italiana.* 3 vols. Milan, 1986–1988.

Spezzani, Pietro. *Dalla commedia dell'arte a Goldoni: studi linguistici.* Padua, 1997.

Linda L. Carroll

GÓNGORA Y ARGOTE, LUIS DE

(1561–1627), Spanish poet of the late sixteenth and early seventeenth centuries. Luis de Góngora y Argote was born into a privileged family in Córdoba on 11 July 1561. Góngora was destined for a career in the church from childhood. He took minor orders in 1575, studied canon law at the University of Salamanca 1576–1581, and became a deacon of the Cathedral of Córdoba in 1585. As a representative of the cathedral, Góngora traveled widely in Spain, and made frequent trips to the court of Philip III. He finally moved to the court at Madrid in 1617, was ordained in 1618, and subsequently became chaplain to the king. During his years at the court of Philip III and Philip IV, Góngora enjoyed powerful patrons, became a member of the cultural elite, gained access to the innermost circles of the crown, and acquired the reputation of a gifted poet and esteemed man of letters. Ill health and financial exigency forced him to leave the capital in 1626 to return to Córdoba, where he died on 23 May 1627.

Góngora was a lifelong experimenter with poetry who composed in a variety of poetic forms—ballads, songs, rondelets, and sonnets, among others. He also was the author of the play *Las firmezas de Isabela* (1610) as well as the unfinished drama *El doctor Carlino* (1613). Góngora is primarily known, and remembered, however, as the creator of *gongorismo,* a style of discourse identified with his poetic masterpieces the *Fábula de Polifemo y Galatea* (1612) and the *Soledades* (1612–1614). Both are hybrid works, difficult to classify by type. The *Polifemo* is based on the story in Book Thirteen of Ovid's *Metamorphoses* that tells of the ill-fated love of the cyclops Polyphemus for the nymph Galatea, enamored of the handsome Acis. The *Soledades* mix epic and pastoral motifs in two poems totaling about two thousand lines in length that detail the wanderings of a mysterious, shipwrecked pilgrim through the dreamlike countryside of an unknown land. Góngora authorized the publication of only a few of his poems during his lifetime, although collections of his works started to appear shortly after his death.

When the *Polifemo* and *Soledades* first circulated at court, they unleashed a firestorm of controversy over the innovative poetic language employed by Góngora. *Gongorismo,* also called *cultismo* or *culteranismo,* that is, the cultured or cultivated style, refers to elegant discourse replete with rhetorical ornamentation: hyperbata (inversions of natural word order), neologisms, latinate words and syntax, elaborate conceits, mythological allusions, and so forth. Gongorism is a self-consciously challenging and at times enigmatic style directed at an erudite, aristocratic audience, able and willing to decipher the linguistic puzzles posed in verse. Góngora's vociferous detractors, who included such important writers as Lope de Vega and Francisco Quevedo, objected to what they saw as the affectation and deliberate obscurantism of Gongorine style. The great Góngora debate, which played out in well-known exchanges in caustic letters, satirical verse, and at the literary academies, was essentially a battle over which kind of poetic style would become the predominant one—a simpler, clearer type of discourse, more accessible to a wide range of readers, or the more ornate language of Gongorism, which appealed to a smaller, more intellectually engaged audience. *Cultismo,* often associated with mannerism and the baroque, and frequently compared to marinism in Italy and euphuism, the elegant and artful style identified with the Elizabethan English writer John Lyly, ultimately won the day and many disciples. The powerful influence of Gongorism was eclipsed in the eighteenth century, only to be resurrected by Spain's Generation of 1927 poets, a group so-named in honor of the tricentennial anniversary of the death of Góngora, whose complex metaphors they particularly admired.

Over the years, Góngora has been called both the "Prince of Darkness" and the "Angel of Light."

Luis de Góngora y Argote. LIBRARY OF CONGRESS

Not surprisingly, to this day, the poet's works and Gongorism remain a subject of considerable debate. While some critics see in Gongorism the construction of an independent world of words that has nothing to do with the realm of everyday experience, and in some ways anticipates postmodern literature, others envision in the poet's *cultismo* a cryptic language employed to create allegories critical of imperial Spain. Still another group of scholars views Gongorism as an attempt to restore to poetic language the visionary power of the *vates,* the poet-prophet of classical antiquity, and to make poetry a vehicle for exploring the mysteries of the universe. Although these critical viewpoints differ greatly, they all show a heightened interest in Góngora and Gongorism as a poet and poetic style closely tied to the court culture of Habsburg Spain and of Europe in general at the time.

See also **Philip III (Spain); Philip IV (Spain); Spanish Literature and Language; Vega, Lope de.**

BIBLIOGRAPHY

Primary Sources

Góngora, Luis de. *Polyphemus and Galatea.* Introduction by Alexander A. Parker. Translated by Gilbert F. Cunningham. Austin, 1977. Translation of *Fábula de Polifemo y Galatea* (1612).

———. *The Solitudes.* Translated by Gilbert F. Cunningham. Baltimore, 1968. Translation of *Soledades* (1612–1614).

Rivers, Elias L., intro. and ed. "Luis de Góngora." In *Renaissance and Baroque Poetry of Spain,* pp. 157–198. New York, 1966. Prospect Heights, Ill., 1988. Selection of poems with prose translations.

Secondary Sources

Beverley, John. *Aspects of Góngora's "Soledades."* Amsterdam, 1980.

Collins, Marsha S. *The "Soledades," Góngora's Masque of the Imagination.* Columbia, Mo., 2002.

Gaylord [Randel], Mary. "Metaphor and Fable in Góngora's *Soledad primera.*" *Revista Hispánica Moderna* 40 (1978–1979): 97–112.

McCaw, R. John. *The Transforming Text: A Study of Luis de Góngora's "Soledades."* Potomac, Md. 2000.

Smith, Paul Julian. "Barthes, Góngora, and Non-Sense." *PMLA* 101 (1986): 82–94.

Terry, Arthur. "Luis de Góngora: The Poetry of Transformation." In *Seventeenth-Century Spanish Poetry: The Power of Artifice,* pp. 65–93. Cambridge, U.K., and New York, 1993.

MARSHA S. COLLINS

GOYA Y LUCIENTES, FRANCISCO DE (1746–1828), Spanish painter and printmaker. Born on 30 March 1746 in the village of Fuendetodos, Francisco Goya received his earliest artistic training in the provincial capital of Saragossa, under the Neapolitan-trained painter José Luzán y Martínez. In 1766 Goya competed unsuccessfully in a drawing competition at the Royal Academy of San Fernando. Documents reveal his entry into another academic competition in Parma, Italy, in 1771, where he received an honorable mention for the painting *Hannibal Crossing the Alps* (Fundación Selgas-Fagalda, Cudillero, Spain).

On his returning to Saragossa in 1772, Goya undertook religious commissions for private patrons and religious organizations. In 1773 he married the sister of the court painter, Francisco Bayeu y Subías (1734–1795), and it was probably through Bayeu's influence that the artist was invited to the court of Madrid in 1774 to paint designs (also known as cartoons) for the royal tapestry factory. Goya's ability was soon recognized, and he was given permission to paint tapestry cartoons "of his own invention"—that is, he was allowed to develop original subjects for these images. He painted three series of tapestry cartoons for rooms in the royal residences before the tapestry factory cut back production in 1780 because of a financial crisis engendered by Spain's war with England. The decade of the 1780s was nevertheless one of great advancement for the artist, beginning with his election to the Royal Academy of Fine Arts of San Fernando in 1780 and continuing as he won patronage for religious paintings and portraits from the grandest families in Spain, including the duke and duchess of Osuna and the count and countess of Altamira. His appointment as court painter in April 1789, four months after Charles IV had acceded to the throne, cemented his fortunes.

Documents and paintings of the early 1790s suggest the artist's growing unease with the limitations imposed on painters by traditions and patronage. Images in his final series of cartoons, such as *The Straw Mannikin* (1792; Museo del Prado, Madrid), betray an increasingly cynical view. As one of several academicians asked in 1792 to report on the institutional curriculum, he responded that "there are no rules in painting." Thus, although the turn in Goya's art to a more liberated exploration of unprecedented subject matter is often credited to a serious illness suffered in 1792–1793, such a change might have occurred in any case. From 1793 onward, in addition to his work as a painter of commissioned portraits and religious paintings, Goya explored experimental subjects—ranging from shipwrecks to scenes of everyday life in Madrid—in uncommissioned paintings, prints, and drawings. This experimentation led to the publication in 1799 of a series of eighty aquatint etchings known as *Los Caprichos,* whose subjects encompass witchcraft, prostitution, fantasy, and social satire. It is wrongly thought that these etchings jeopardized Goya's relationship with his patrons; that this is not the case is proven by Goya's promotion to first court painter eight months after their publication. The artist would continue to paint portraits including *The Family of Charles IV* (1800–1801, Prado), as

Francisco de Goya y Lucientes. *The Second of May 1808.* THE ART ARCHIVE/MUSEO DEL PRADO MADRID/THE ART ARCHIVE

well as works for the king and queen's close confidant, Manuel Godoy, that include portraits, allegories, and probably the *Naked Maja* and the *Clothed Maja* (c. 1797–1805; Prado).

In 1808 Napoleonic forces invaded Spain, the royal family abdicated, and Napoleon's brother, Joseph Bonaparte, assumed the Spanish throne. In 1810 Goya undertook etchings documenting the atrocities of war, today known as the *Disasters of War*. Goya probably continued work on these etchings even after the Spanish government of Ferdinand VII was restored in 1814, although the series of eighty plates was published only in 1863, thirty-five years after Goya's death. On the restoration of the Spanish monarchy, Goya depicted *The Second of May* and *The Third of May* (1813–1814; Prado) to commemorate the Spanish uprising against French troops; although these are among Goya's most famous works, little is known of their original function or placement, or of their early reception.

Goya continued in his position as first court painter under the restored monarch, who nevertheless preferred the neoclassical style of the younger Vicente López. In 1819 Goya purchased a villa on the outskirts of Madrid and painted on the walls of its two main rooms images of witchcraft, religious ceremonies, and mythical subjects today known as the *Black Paintings* (1819–1823; Prado). In 1824 the artist left Spain and after a brief trip to Paris settled in Bordeaux among a colony of Spanish exiles. Here he continued to paint and draw, and also to experiment with the technique of lithography—leading to the publication of *The Bulls of Bordeaux*, a masterpiece in that medium. He died in Bordeaux on 26 April 1828.

See also **Spain, Art in.**

BIBLIOGRAPHY

Gassier, Pierre, and Juliet Wilson. *The Life and Complete Works of Francisco Goya*. New York, 1971.

Tomlinson, Janis. *Francisco Goya y Lucientes, 1746–1828*. 2nd ed. London, 1999.

———. *Goya in the Twilight of Enlightenment*. New Haven and London, 1992.

JANIS TOMLINSON

GRANADA. Located in the southeastern sector of the Iberian Peninsula, the city of Granada lies in the northern foothills of the Sierra Nevada, some sixty kilometers from the Mediterranean. It rose to prominence in the mid-thirteenth century as capital of the Muslim kingdom of Granada, the last surviving state of medieval Al-Andalus or Islamic Iberia. During the latter half of the fifteenth century, Granada faced growing internal instability and the increasing militancy of its northern neighbor, the Christian kingdom of Castile.

Granada's capitulation in 1492 to the forces of Ferdinand V and Isabella I (ruled 1474–1504), king and queen of Aragón and Castile, signaled the end of independent Muslim power on the Iberian Peninsula. Though the treaty of surrender guaranteed Granadans their traditional religion, forced conversions in 1499 drove the Muslim community to insurrection. The crown responded by rescinding the treaty and demanding mass baptisms. By 1501 the city's Muslim population—estimated at fifty thousand souls in 1492—either emigrated to North Africa or became Moriscos (Muslim converts to Christianity). Thousands of "Old Christian" newcomers from southern and central Castile soon replaced the émigrés. By 1561, immigrants to the city numbered around thirty thousand, perhaps twice the dwindling Morisco population. Both Moriscos and immigrants found employment in Granada's lucrative silk industry. Granadan Moriscos dyed the raw silk produced by rural Morisco peasants; immigrants, however, dominated the weaving process.

Granada. A seventeenth-century view of the city from *Civitates Orbis Terrarum*, by Braun and Hogenberg. THE ART ARCHIVE/ BIBLIOTECA NAZIONALE MARCIANA VENICE/DAGLI ORTI (A)

Merchants—often Genoese—exported raw silk to textile centers in the Castilian interior and finished cloth to Italy, North Africa, Flanders, and the Americas.

New local and national institutions marked Granada's incorporation into the crown of Castile and signaled the city's rising national stature. Internal security and coastal defenses were the province of the captain general, headquartered in the Alhambra, Granada's famed medieval Muslim fortress. The 1505 transfer to Granada of the *Chancillería,* one of two permanent high courts of appeal, established the city as one of Castile's principal bureaucratic centers. A new municipal council, chaired by a royal representative, the *corregidor,* governed civic affairs. Two council members represented Granada at the Castilian *Cortes,* a parliamentary body representing a select group of prominent cities. Granadans' spiritual welfare was the province of the Roman Catholic Church, led by the archbishop and the cathedral chapter. The crown exercised unusual control over church appointments in Granada through its *Real Patronato,* a papal concession of 1486 later extended to all of Spanish America.

These new institutions joined in converting and acculturating the subject Morisco population. In 1567, however, the Catholic authorities' growing intolerance of Morisco rejections of Castilian culture and religion resulted in stringent laws against Morisco cultural practices. The desperate Morisco revolt of 1568 was quelled with equal violence and forced resettlements to the Castilian interior. The expulsions reduced Granada's population by a third, devastated the silk industry, and exacerbated Granada's share of the general economic troubles of late sixteenth-century and seventeenth-century Europe. Seville, gateway to the Americas, soon surpassed Granada in population, prosperity, and prominence, and Granada was relegated to only regional importance for the remainder of the early modern period.

See also **Ferdinand of Aragón; Isabella of Castile; Islam in the Ottoman Empire; Moriscos; Moriscos, Expulsion of (Spain); Spain.**

BIBLIOGRAPHY

Barrios Aguilera, Manuel. *Granada morisca, la convivencia negada.* Granada, Spain, 2002. Analytic essays and primary texts on ethnic relations during the sixteenth century.

Cortés Peña, Antonio Luis, and Bernard Vincent. *Historia de Granada.* Vol. 3: *La época moderna, siglos XVI, XVII y XVIII.* Granada, Spain, 1986.

Peinado Santaella, Rafael G., ed. *Historia del Reino de Granada.* 3 vols. Granada, Spain, 2000. Excellent collection of essays on all aspects of Granada's past from prehistory to 1833.

A. Katie Harris

GRAND TOUR. Protracted travel for pleasure was scarcely unknown in classical and medieval times, but it developed greatly in the sixteenth, seventeenth, and eighteenth centuries, becoming part of the ideal education and image of the social elite as well as an important source of descriptive and imaginative literature and art. As tourism developed, its patterns became more regular, and the assumptions about where a tourist should go became more predictable. Literary conventions were also established. The term the "grand tour" reflects a subsequent sense that this was an ideal period of the fusion of tourism and social status as well as a contemporary desire to distinguish protracted and wide-ranging tourism from shorter trips.

The grand tour is commonly associated with aristocratic British travelers, more particularly with the eighteenth century. But travel for pleasure did not begin then, and it was not restricted to the British. There was a more general fascination with southern Europe among northern Europeans. The vast majority of those who had traveled to Italy over previous centuries had done so for reasons related to their work or their salvation. Soldiers and those seeking employment had shared the road with clerics discharging the tasks of the international church and pilgrims. Such travel was not incompatible with pleasure, and in some cases it fulfilled important cultural functions as travelers bought works of art or helped spread new tastes and cultural interests. This was not the same, however, as travel specifically and explicitly for personal fulfillment, both in terms of education and of pleasure, the two being seen as ideally linked in the exemplary literature of the period.

Such travel became more common in the seventeenth century, although it was affected by the religious (and political) tensions that followed the Protestant Reformation of the previous century. The war with Spain that had begun in 1585 ended in 1604, and England had only brief wars with France, Spain, and the Dutch over the following seventy years. It was no accident that the earl and countess of Arundel went to Italy in 1613–1614 or that a series of works on Italy, including Fynes Moryson's *Itinerary* (1617), appeared in the years after the Treaty of London of 1604.

However, divisions culminating in civil wars (1642–1646, 1648, 1688–1691) in the British Isles forced people to focus their time and funds on commitments at home and also made travel suspect as in some fashion indicating supposed political and religious sympathies. Concern about Stuart intentions in large part focused on the real and alleged crypto-Catholicism of the court, and this made visits to Italy particularly sensitive. The situation for tourists eased with the Stuart Restoration of 1660, and Richard Lassels, a Catholic priest who acted as a "bearleader" (traveling tutor), published in 1670 his important *Voyage of Italy; or, A Compleat Journey through Italy.*

The expansion of British tourism from 1660 was part of a wider pattern of elite cosmopolitan activity. Throughout Europe members of the elite traveled for pleasure in the late seventeenth century and the eighteenth century. The most popular destinations were France, which meant Paris, and Italy. Italy held several important advantages over Paris. The growing cult of the antique, which played a major role in the determination to see and immerse oneself in the experience and repute of the classical world, could not be furthered in Paris, although Paris was seen as the center of contemporary culture. There was little tourism to eastern Europe, Iberia, and Scandinavia let alone beyond Europe.

There was no cult of the countryside. Tourists traveled as rapidly as possible between major cities and regarded mountains with horror, not joy. The contrast with nineteenth-century tourism and its cult of the "sublime" dated from Romanticism toward the close of the eighteenth century, not earlier. The Italian cities offered a rich range of benefits, including pleasure (Venice), classical antiquity (Rome and its environs, the environs of Naples), Renaissance architecture and art (Florence), the splendors of baroque culture (Rome and Venice), opera (Milan and Naples), and warm weather (Naples). Once tourism had become appropriate and fashionable, increasing numbers traveled, a growth interrupted only by periods of war, when journeys, although not prohibited, were made more dangerous or inconvenient by increased disruption and lawlessness. The outbreak of the French Revolutionary War in 1792, however, led to a major break in tourism that was exacerbated when French armies overran Italy in 1796–1798. Thereafter tourism did not resume on any scale until after the final defeat of Napoleon in 1815.

See also **Art: The Art Market and Collecting; Italy; Paris; Travel and Travel Literature.**

BIBLIOGRAPHY

Black, Jeremy. *The British Abroad: The Grand Tour in the Eighteenth Century.* New York, 1992.

JEREMY BLACK

GRAUNT, JOHN (1620–1674), English statistician and demographer. Born in London, John Graunt was the son of a draper. He was apprenticed to a haberdasher and became a successful merchant, serving as warden of the Drapers' Company in 1671–1672. He also served the city government in various capacities, reaching the level of a common councilman. Late in life, Graunt converted to Roman Catholicism; he died in 1674 at the age of 54.

Graunt's fame rest on his short book *Natural and Political Observations Made upon the Bills of Mortality* (1662). The book was immediately popular and went through five editions (two in the first year alone). Translations and reprints appeared throughout the eighteenth century. Because of this book, Graunt was elected fellow of the Royal Society upon direct recommendation of Charles II, an unusual honor for a London merchant. Graunt's friend Sir William Petty (1623–1687) labeled his work political arithmetic—a term that stuck throughout the eighteenth century.

Graunt was the first to analyze society numerically. Troubled by exaggerated claims about the size of London, he created methods to calculate the population from the annual numbers of christenings and burials listed in the London bills of mortality. (He reckoned London's population at 384,000, far smaller than contemporary estimates of two million.) To bring clarity to his calculations, Graunt created a series of tables. In one, he summarized the causes of death for a twenty-year period and found the mortality rates of acute and chronic diseases, especially of the plague. In another table, Graunt showed how many individuals out of a population of one hundred would be alive at specific ages. This was the first life table (or mortality table) ever constructed and was an entirely new way to conceptualize life expectancy. Mathematicians such as Edmund Halley (1656–1742) and Antoine de Parcieux refined Graunt's life table over the course of the late seventeenth and eighteenth centuries. They remain essential tools of modern demography and actuarial science.

In his analysis of the bills of mortality, Graunt identified several numerical regularities. For every fourteen males christened, for example, there were thirteen females christened; thus, there was a constant ratio between male and female births. (Graunt used this ratio to argue against polygamy.) He defined chronic diseases as those that maintained a fixed portion of the total number of burials and included in this category jaundice, gout, rickets, and, somewhat surprising, suicides. For Graunt, the prevalence of chronic diseases was a measure of the salubrity of a community. Graunt also identified a high infant mortality rate, a significant characteristic of early modern societies (one-third of all infants born died before age six).

Graunt's book laid the foundations for modern statistics and demography. His life table stimulated the application of probability mathematics to life expectancy. His use of mortality figures to evaluate the incidence and constancy of different diseases encouraged eighteenth-century physicians to apply statistics to medicine, most notably in the debates surrounding the introduction of smallpox inoculation. His efforts to provide accurate population figures spawned a tradition of political arithmetic that was only eclipsed when regular national censuses were instituted around 1800.

See also **Census; Petty, William; Statistics.**

BIBLIOGRAPHY

Glass, David V. "John Graunt and His Natural and Political Observations." *Proceedings of the Royal Society,* Series B, 159 (1963): 2–37.

Kreager, Philip. "Histories of Demography." *Population Studies* 47 (1993): 519–539.

———. "New Light on Graunt." *Population Studies* 42 (1988): 129–140.

Pearson, Karl. *The History of Statistics in the 17th and 18th Centuries against the Changing Background of Intellectual, Scientific and Religious Thought.* Edited by E. S. Pearson. London, 1978.

Rusnock, Andrea. *Vital Accounts: Quantifying Health and Population in Eighteenth-Century England and France.* Cambridge, U.K., 2002.

Sutherland, Ian. "John Graunt: A Tercentenary Tribute." *Journal of the Royal Statistical Society,* Series A, 126 (1963): 537–556.

ANDREA RUSNOCK

GREECE. Greece is a country in the south of the Balkan Peninsula, bordering on the east with Turkey, on the north with Bulgaria and the Republic of Macedonia, and on the northwest with Albania. Greece is a mountainous country with ragged littoral and few plains. A large part of its territory consists of islands. The bulk of Greek lands entered early modern times as part of two states, the Ottoman Empire and the Venetian Republic.

TERRITORIES UNDER OTTOMAN RULE

Under Ottoman rule, cities were modest and of only regional importance except for a few provincial capitals and ports (Patra, Livadia, Ioannina, Larissa, Serres). The biggest city was Salonica; in the sixteenth century, it evolved into a large manufacturing center, and in the eighteenth became a major commercial port. Most of the population in the territories, especially in the country, was Orthodox Christian. Cities usually had large Christian and Muslim communities and small Jewish ones (except for Salonica, a Jewish metropolis). Some Muslims were originally settlers from Anatolia, but most were descendants of local converts. Muslims were predominantly Turkish-speaking except in Crete and Epirus, where large-scale conversions had taken place. Christian townspeople were mostly Greek-speaking; in the country, alongside ethnic Greeks (the majority in central and southern Greece, Crete, and the Islands), there also existed large Slavic, Aromunian, and Albanian populations. Jewish communities were predominantly Sephardic, but there also existed several Romaniot ones.

The Ottoman conquest of mainland Greece was essentially completed by 1460, that of the Aegean Islands by 1570. Crete was conquered in 1669. In general, the conquest of the mainland was rapid and did not cause major disruption in local life. The sixteenth century witnessed considerable demographic and economic growth. Large-scale construction projects, usually financed by imperial funds, together with religious, commercial, and learning establishments, supported by endowments, provided urban infrastructure; churches and monasteries were rebuilt and renovated. By the end of the century, a demographic decline was seen, accompanied by small-scale migratory movements. The mid-seventeenth century brought a severe economic crisis. This was followed by a large-scale demographic crisis that continued well into the eighteenth century and affected the settlement pattern. The eighteenth century witnessed major socioeconomic changes: consolidation of large estates in private—mainly Muslim—hands in the fertile parts of the country; growth of cattle breeding, manufacture, and commerce; intensification of trade with western Europe; establishment of commercial networks in central and eastern Europe; an explosion of banditry. Economic growth, together with changes in patterns of consumption, increasing mobility, and contact with Europe, led to cultural flourishing in many towns and cities.

The Greek lands were integrated in the Ottoman prebendal system and divided in provinces with a dual judicial/civil and executive/military administration. Towns were the seats of *kadis,* who combined judicial and administrative authority; provincial capitals were also the seats of military governors. Beneficence and welfare were provided by pious foundations, some of which were major owners of urban and rural property, while others were involved in moneylending. Craftsmen and traders were organized in guilds. The suppression of banditry was entrusted to—usually Christian—paramilitary troops *(martolos/armatoloi).*

Alongside the *kadi,* the governor and various officials, a body of "notables" (Muslim *ayan;* Christian *prokritoi* or *kocabaşi*) was involved in local administration. The *prokritoi* were usually elected every year by the heads of households and ran the affairs of the community. During the eighteenth century wealthy landowners and guildsmen became dominant in the election process, and oligarchic community leaderships emerged in many towns. At the same time, the *ayan,* consisting mainly of wealthy landowners and tax farmers, brought local administration under their control and acquired an institutional role in provincial decision making.

A fundamental misconception of the role of the church together with the presence of elaborate communal institutions led to the thesis of the "autonomy" or "self-government" of the Greek Orthodox under Ottoman rule. Actually, Christians were an integral part of the Ottoman society and made full use of Ottoman institutions, including that of the *kadi* court, to which they did not even hesitate to take members of the clergy. Communities, irrespective of their supposed origins, were in their structure and functions a product of Ottoman institutions and socioeconomic realities and emerged mainly as a means to cope with the administration of collectively assessed taxes. Admittedly, in some places the Ottoman authority was either weak or nonexistent. These included communities that were granted "privileges" at the time of the conquest, districts without resident Ottoman authorities, and regions that the state could not effectively control. But these self-governing communities were the exception, not the rule.

The consolidation of the Ottoman Empire led to the emergence of interregional networks that enabled the movement of people, goods, and ideas and reestablished a connection between Greece and southeastern Europe and the Near East. Greeks were also actively involved in the growing export-oriented commerce with the West, either acting as local agents for European merchants or trading in European cities. During the eighteenth century, a wave of emigration began from Greek regions to western Anatolia. The same century witnessed the growth of old diaspora communities and the creation of new ones, especially in central Europe. Relations with Russia also intensified, especially after the Ottoman-Russian treaty of Kuchuk Kainarji (1774), among the ramifications of which was the emergence of a Greek commercial marine under the

Russian flag transporting goods in the Mediterranean and the Black Sea.

Commercial activity also led to cultural interaction. Constantinople (Istanbul) seat of the Ottoman sultan and the Orthodox Christian patriarch, soon after its conquest became a center of Greek culture with empirewide influence. Greek reinforced its position as the language of religion, education, and commerce, which led to its spreading among the middle and upper classes of Orthodox Christians. In the eighteenth century, Smyrna (Izmir), Bucharest, and Jassy (Iaşi) emerged as major cultural centers outside Greece, while Greek books were printed in Venice and Vienna. By the end of the century, an Enlightenment movement had evolved in the diaspora communities and filtered into the commercial towns of Greece, often confronting the reaction of "traditionalists" and the church.

In the seventeenth and especially the eighteenth century, Greece captured European imagination both because of its ancient past and as part of the Ottoman Orient. Some Western travelers were disappointed by what they perceived as the uncivilized descendants of glorious ancestors; but, in the main, Philhellenism prevailed and helped create a romanticized view of noble Greece and Greeks suffering under the barbarous Turkish yoke. European perceptions led Greeks, especially in the diaspora, to a new awareness concerning their identity and place within European nations.

Notwithstanding nationalistic interpretations, prior to the Greek revolution (1821–1830) the Ottoman rule had not been challenged in most of the mainland. The only major Christian rebellion was the involvement of several regions and bands of *martolos* (paramilitary troops, usually Christian) from the Morea and Central Greece in the abortive enterprise of the Russian fleet under the Orloff brothers (1770). The eighteenth century, however, had witnessed the deterioration of relations between Christians and Muslims, generated by major socioeconomic changes. Intercommunal tensions heightened after the military defeats of the empire and the emergence of Russians as protectors of Orthodox Christians. By the early nineteenth century, several vague revolutionary plans circulated in the hope of exploiting the Russo-Ottoman confrontation, and a secret society after the model of the Carbonari based in Odessa, the *Philike Hetaireia* (Friendly Society), established a widespread network of prospective revolutionaries. In February 1821, the fear of imminent betrayal of the society's plans to the Ottomans led to a dual insurrection in the Danubian Principalities and the Morea, which soon spread in most Greek regions. Though the rebellion was soon suppressed in the north, it gained momentum in the south, and in January 1822 the Greek Republic was proclaimed.

TERRITORIES UNDER VENETIAN RULE

In the fifteenth century, Venice held several ports and coastal areas in central Greece the Morea, and some Aegean islands, as well as Corfu, Euboea, and Crete. At the turn of the century, it annexed most of the Ionian Islands, but by 1550 it had lost most of its other possessions to the Ottomans. In 1669 Crete also passed into Ottoman hands. The Morea came briefly under Venetian occupation (1685–1715), but the only Greek territories to remain under its rule until 1797 were the Ionian Islands. The bulk of the population consisted of Greek-speaking Orthodox Christians, but among the gentry, many were of Venetian or Italian origin, professing the Catholic faith. In the towns there also existed Jewish communities.

Venetian possessions were administered by governors appointed by the metropolis under the supervision of a high official called the general *provveditor* for the east. Local administrative institutions were not uniform, mainly because the various territories were annexed at different times. The Venetian-held territories, however, underwent similar socioeconomic developments, which differed substantially from those in the regions under Ottoman rule. The most prominent differences include the preservation of serfdom and other feudal institutions, especially in Crete and Corfu, the inferior position of the Orthodox Church, and the division of urban population in estates: burghers *(cittadini)* and common people *(popolani)*, in Crete also noblemen *(nobili)*.

Differences between Venetian and Ottoman territories are especially obvious in the cultural domain. Venice, the metropolis, seat of a thriving Greek community, and a cultural center of the Greek-speaking world, was a mediator of Western culture to Greeks. The University of Padua became a major learning center for Greeks. Direct contact with developments in Italy led to a boost in literary, theatrical, and artistic production in Crete that bears the stamp of Renaissance and baroque, while in the eighteenth century, poetry and drama flourished in the Ionian Islands.

See also **Orthodoxy, Greek; Ottoman Dynasty; Ottoman Empire; Venice.**

BIBLIOGRAPHY

Clogg, Richard. "Elite and Popular Culture in Greece under Turkish Rule." In *Hellenic Perspectives,* edited by John T. A. Koumoulides, pp. 107–144. Lanham, Md., 1980.

———. "The Greek Millet in the Ottoman Empire." In *Christians and Jews in the Ottoman Empire,* edited by Benjamin Braude and Bernard Lewis, vol. 1, pp. 185–208. New York, 1982.

Gara, Eleni. "In Search of Communities in Seventeenth-Century Ottoman Sources: The Case of the Kara Ferye District." *Turcica* 30 (1998): 135–162.

Greene, Molly. *A Shared World: Christians and Muslims in the Early Modern Mediterranean.* Princeton, 2000.

Holton, David, ed. *Literature and Society in Renaissance Crete.* Cambridge, U.K., 1991.

Kitromilides, Paschalis M. *The Enlightenment as Social Criticism: Iosipos Moisiodax and Greek Culture in the Eighteenth Century.* Princeton, 1992.

Roudometof, Victor. "From Rum Millet to Greek Nation: Enlightenment, Secularization, and National Identity in Ottoman Balkan Society, 1453–1821." *Journal of Modern Greek Studies* 16, no. 1 (1998): 11–48.

Tsigakou, Fani-Maria. *The Rediscovery of Greece: Travelers and Painters of the Romantic Era.* New Rochelle, N.Y., 1981.

Eleni Gara

GREEK ORTHODOXY. *See* **Orthodoxy, Greek.**

GREUZE, JEAN-BAPTISTE (1725–1805), French painter. Born in Tournus (Burgundy) to a prosperous middle-class family, Greuze studied art in Lyon in the late 1740s with the portrait painter Charles Grandon. In about 1750, he sat in on drawing classes at the Académie Royal in Paris, and in 1755 became an associate member of the academy as a genre painter after presenting *A Father Reading the Bible to His Family, The Blindman Deceived,* and *The Sleeping Schoolboy.* These moralizing narratives that deal with social and familial issues of contemporary life among the lower and middle classes (reminiscent in certain ways of William Hogarth) announced principal themes the artist would become most celebrated for throughout his career.

Aristocratic patrons in *ancien régime* France took great interest in genre subjects and encouraged French painters to revive this tradition. Thus, Greuze found ready patronage for his paintings. Like many fellow genre painters, Greuze was influenced by seventeenth-century Dutch predecessors whose genre images were accessible through prints as well as original works in private collections. He also studied Rubens and Rembrandt, both of whom had an indelible impact on his style. In addition, Greuze was influenced by the style of the esteemed rococo court painter François Boucher (1703–1770) and the celebrated genre painter Jean-Baptiste-Siméon Chardin (1699–1779), who was a peer as well as a rival.

Greuze traveled in Italy in 1755–1757 as a guest of Louis Gougenot, Abbé de Chezal-Benoît. He stayed at the French Academy in Rome in 1756–1757 thanks to the intercession of the Marquis de Marigny, superintendent of buildings for Louis XV. While in Rome Greuze seemed impervious to an emerging neoclassicism and continued to work on moralizing subjects in a style he had developed in France. Upon returning to France in 1757 he exhibited at the salon "Four Pictures in Italian Costume": *Indolence, Broken Eggs, The Neapolitan Gesture,* and *The Fowler.* All present moralizing narratives and commentary on contemporary mores with didactic implications. *Indolence,* for example, is an emblem or allegory of sloth; it inaugurated a series of admonitory works in which Greuze represented sensual young women as single figures with emblematic objects or surroundings such as in *The Broken Mirror* (1763), somewhat unusual in its depiction of a wealthier interior. Often the compositions communicate the erotic accessibility of servants, as in *The Laundress* (1761), or the loss of virginity in young adolescent girls, as in the variations on the theme of a young girl mourning her

Jean-Baptiste Greuze. *The Marriage Contract.* THE ART ARCHIVE/MUSÉE DU LOUVRE PARIS/DAGLI ORTI

dead bird (1759, 1765) or *The Broken Pitcher* (1773). These paintings, often moralizing in theme, nonetheless emphasize an eroticism and sensuality that belong to the French rococo tradition. Greuze also specialized in depicting the beauty of children, as in *Girl Playing with a Dog* (1767), *Young Shepherd Boy with a Basket of Flowers* and its pendant, *Simplicity* (1761), *Boy with Lessonbook* (1757), and commissioned children's portraits such as the *Comtesse Mollien with Puppies at Age Six* (1791).

Broken Eggs, another in the 1757 series of "Italian Costume" paintings, signaled an important direction in Greuze's art, that of the moralizing narrative in which a larger social group of the rustic lower classes is involved. Greuze also depicted more complex narratives involving familial and social situations. One of his best-known works, *The Marriage Contract* (1761), depicts a bride reluctant to leave her family as her father hands over her dowry to her betrothed and a notary records the transaction. This painting was hailed by the great Enlightenment philosophe and art critic Denis Diderot (1713–1784), who often praised the artist. He saw this and similar paintings by Greuze as visual correspondents to his psychological family dramas known as the *drame bourgeois.*

Although Greuze sometimes represented familial devotion, as in *The Paralytic Father* (1763) and *The Well-Loved Mother* (1765), his most dramatic compositions depict unhappy families, as in his well-known pendants, *The Father's Curse* and *The Punished Son* (1778). In these works, gesture and body language communicate the tragic familial narrative. In the first painting, the aging father of a large family curses his son, who abandons the family to join the army in spite of the pleas of his mother and siblings. In the pendant, the wounded son returns to his father's deathbed. He is a broken man, his father has just died, and his grief-stricken family is impoverished.

Greuze was also well known for intimate scenes of young mothers of the lower class with their children, as in *Silence!* (1759), in which a beautiful young mother with bared breast (she is ostensibly breastfeeding her infant), admonishes her son to stop blowing his horn, which will awaken the sleeping siblings. Here, simplicity, poverty, and familial intimacy are combined with erotic elements that emphasize sensuality and fertility.

Although Greuze enjoyed great success as a genre painter, he aspired to history painting, the top of the hierarchy of genres in French academic art. In 1769 he submitted a historical subject as his reception piece for full admittance to the academy, *Septimius Severus Reproaching His Son Caracalla for Having Wanted to Assassinate Him,* a composition influenced by Poussin and painted in the neoclassical style. The academy ridiculed the painting and rejected Greuze as a history painter, admitting him instead only in the category of genre painting. Greuze was so embittered by this decision that he did not exhibit at the salon again until 1800. Late in his career he returned to history painting with such works as *Psyche Crowning Cupid* (1792) and his last major painting, the strange and enigmatic religious composition, *St. Mary of Egpyt* (1801).

Greuze also established a solid reputation as a portrait painter. One of his most insightful studies of character is the subtle portrait of the academy model Joseph (1755). Other expressive and lively portraits include those of his patron, *Ange-Laurent La Live de Jully* (1759), *The Marquise de Bezons Tuning Her Guitar* (1759), and *Benjamin Franklin* (c. 1777).

Greuze's impact on the development of French painting in the late eighteenth and early nineteenth centuries helped ensure the continued popularity and importance of genre painting as a means of conveying moral, psychological, and social narratives of everyday life, influencing such painters as Louis-Léopold Boilly (1761–1845). His immediate students and followers, Wille the Younger and Nicolas-Bernard Lépicié (1735–1784), enjoyed success, and Greuze also encouraged his female students, who included Constance Mayer and his daughter Anna Greuze.

See also **Art: Artistic Patronage; Diderot, Denis; France, Art in.**

BIBLIOGRAPHY

Bailey, Colin. *Jean-Baptiste Greuze: The Laundress.* Los Angeles, 2000.

Brookner, Anita. *Greuze: The Rise and Fall of an Eighteenth-Century Phenomenon.* Greenwich, Conn., 1972.

Ledbury, Mark. *Sedaine, Greuze and the Boundaries of Genre.* Oxford, 2000.

Munhall, Edgar. *Jean-Baptiste Greuze, 1725–1805.* Hartford, Conn., 1976.

Sahut, Marie Catherine, and Nathalie Volle, eds. *Diderot et l'art de Boucher à David.* Paris, 1984.

DOROTHY JOHNSON

GRIMM, FRIEDRICH MELCHIOR VON (1723–1807), German-born critic of French culture. Friedrich (later Frédéric) Melchior Grimm was born in Regensburg into a family of modest circumstances. While studying law, philosophy and literature in Leipzig, he wrote a tragedy, *Banise.* In Paris from 1748 on, he served as tutor or secretary to a succession of German aristocrats, allowing him entry into Parisian society as well as relations with dignitaries from many European courts. He quickly gained a solid reputation for his quick wit and fine taste (*bon goût*). His friendship with Jean-Jacques Rousseau (1712–1778), albeit brief (the two became bitter enemies beginning in 1757), led to more long-lasting alliances with other French philosophers, such as Denis Diderot (1713–1784) and Voltaire (1694–1778). In 1753 the abbot Guillaume Raynal (1713–1796) charged Grimm with composing the *Correspondance littéraire, philosophique et critique,* a handwritten newsletter about French literature and culture. It was copied by hirelings and sent to a limited, select body that included King Stanislaw II of Poland (1732–1798), Queen Louise Ulrica of Sweden (1720–1782), and Empress Catherine II of Russia (1729–1796). In this effort he was helped by Diderot, Mme Louise-Florence d'Epinay (1726–1783), and later the Swiss Jacques-Henri Meister (1744–

1826), as they kept the European courts informed of artistic and social events in Paris. In the 1770s Grimm was named a baron of the Holy Roman Empire. He continued writing the unpublished, and therefore uncensored, missives twice monthly until 1793. The turbulent course of the French Revolution finally forced him to flee Paris and end his *Correspondance,* and he spent his final years as a Russian minister to Lower Saxony and finally a courtier at Gotha.

The *Correspondance,* which was first made public in 1812–1813 and published in reliable texts from 1877 to 1882, provides a uniquely privileged insight into aesthetic and historical events in late-eighteenth-century France. Grimm incarnated the elegant, witty, cosmopolitan ideals of thought and expression of the time; he was an elitist writing to an elite audience. His *Correspondance* had a varied content, consisting of several pages of criticism of current works, polemical defenses of the philosophers, and short, original works. A few of these had been previously published, although most had not, and while most authors submitted their work for inclusion in the *Correspondance,* not all authors were aware that Grimm used their material. Unlike his contemporaries, he did not include long extracts to fill his pages. By its tone and liberty of expression the *Correspondance* was distinguished from, and often opposed to, the print media (the *journaux,* such as the *Mercure de France, L'année littéraire,* and the *Journal encyclopédique*). He was quite hostile to the eminent French critic Élie Fréron (1718–1776) and fanatics in general, but quick to praise Voltaire, whose words and deeds he often reported to his interested subscribers. Grimm championed the cause of classical theater but recognized the value of Diderot's more modern conception of drama. Rousseau's novel, *La nouvelle Héloïse,* occasioned a lively attack in 1761, as Grimm found it to be implausible and poorly structured, indicating an author "deprived of genius, imagination, judgment and taste." Able to offer a firsthand perspective on major cultural events, his originality lay perhaps even more in his personal taste, which he was able to freely and elegantly express to an eager and appreciative audience.

See also **Diderot, Denis; Philosophes; Rousseau, Jean-Jacques; Voltaire.**

BIBLIOGRAPHY

Monty, Jeanne R. *La critique littéraire de Melchior Grimm.* Geneva and Paris, 1961.

Pizer, John. "Friedrich-Melchior Grimm's Views on French Seventeenth Century Literature." *Papers on French Seventeenth Century Literature* 11, no. 20 (1984): 167–181.

Schwartz, Leon. "F. M. Grimm and the Eighteenth-Century Debate on Women." *The French Review* 58, no. 2 (1984): 236–243.

Waldinger, Renée. "The *Correspondance littéraire*: A Document on French Cosmopolitanism in the Eighteenth Century." *Studies on Voltaire and the Eighteenth Century* 304 (1992): 910–913.

Allen G. Wood

GRIMMELSHAUSEN, H. J. C. VON

(Johann [Hans] Jakob Christoffel von Grimmelshausen; 1622?–1676), German writer. Grimmelshausen was born in Gelnhausen in Hesse to a family that descended from the lower nobility but had long practiced bourgeois trades. This sometime soldier, secretary, steward, innkeeper, and village mayor belongs to the handful of seventeenth-century German writers of enduring fame whose work continues to influence German cultural production. His masterpiece, *Der abenteuerliche Simplicissimus* (1669; The adventurous Simplicissimus), has been translated into many languages, and it, along with his lesser-known works, has influenced such German writers as the Grimm Brothers, Bertolt Brecht, and Günter Grass. As Grimmelshausen typically published under pseudonymous anagrams of his name, his identity as author of a vast prose corpus remained hidden until German philologists uncovered it in 1837/1838.

Scholars generally divide Grimmelshausen's works into four groups. Three satirical novels set in the Thirty Years' War, and the two parts of *Der wunderbarliche Vogel-Nest* (1672, 1675; The marvelous bird's nest) comprise the "Simplician works," a label Grimmelshausen himself provided. These satirical narrative works, loosely connected by the recurrence of characters and such motifs as a bird's nest that renders its bearer invisible, castigate the folly of the world. Two love stories, *Dietwalts und Amelinden anmuthige Lieb- und Leids-Beschreibung* (1670; Pleasant description of the love and sorrow of Dietwalt and Amelinde) and *Des Durchleuchtigen Printzen Proximi, und seiner ohnvergleichlichen Lympidae Liebs-Geschicht-Erzählung* (1672; The love story of the illustrious Prince Proximus and his incomparable Lympida), based on Christian legends, along with a rendering of the biblical Joseph story and a sequel, *Musai* (1666/1667, 1670), constitute a second group consisting of edifying works that present ideal types. *Des Abenteuerlichen Simplicissimi Ewig-währender Calender* (1670/71; The adventurous Simplicissimus' perpetual calendar) in the genre of the almanac and a symposium on husbanding wealth, *Rathsstübel Plutonis* (1672; Plutus' council chamber), number among the ten lesser works that form the third group. The fourth group consists of four tractates, including the anti-Machiavellian *Simplicianischer Zweyköpffiger Ratio Status* (1670; Simplician two-headed reason of state) and *Deß Weltberuffenen Simplicissimi Pralerey und Gepräng mit seinem Teutschen Michel* (1673; The boasting and showing off of the world-famous Simplicissimus with his German Michael), a polemic on language that, while itself displaying nationalistic tendencies, mocks overzealous purists who would purge German of foreign words.

Grimmelshausen's graphic detailing of violence and the vicissitudes of war in *Simplicissimus, Trutz Simplex: Oder ausführliche und wunderseltzame Lebensbeschreibung der Ertzbetrügerin und Landstörtzerin Courasche* (1670; translated as The runagate courage), and *Der seltzame Springinsfeld* (1670; The strange Hop-in-the-Field) offers a compelling look at a period when the economic and social fabric of the German territories was rent by armed conflict in the name of religion. The Peace of Westphalia that ended the Thirty Years' War in 1648, leaving the German empire divided into sixty-one imperial cities and around three hundred sovereign states, offered an autocratic solution to religious strife by ordaining that the religion of the ruler dictate the religion of the territory. Grimmelshausen, who had converted to Catholicism sometime before 1649, would devote his voluminous oeuvre to railing against the venality and horrors of this world, asserting ideals of good rulers and proper husbandry of personal and public wealth, and writing both exemplary and cautionary tales of redemptive import, and to literary experimentation with mending the broken world by incorporating and piecing together its diverse texts in his writing.

Grimmelshausen's linguistic virtuosity and searing critique of contemporary mores made him a popular author in his own time, as evidenced by the proliferation of imitations, most notably by Johann Beer (1655–1700), and by accounts of reading his books by members of both the nobility and the urban middle classes. Although the scant biographical information about Grimmelshausen provides no indication of extended education, his work evidences broad reading of (pseudo)scientific, philosophical, religious, and literary texts and displays encyclopedic knowledge. His oeuvre indicates, furthermore, engagement with the literary and cultural production and debates of his day as they had been recorded and transmitted across Europe.

As is typical of seventeenth-century prose, hybridity characterizes Grimmelshausen's writings. Indeed, he dabbled in and mixed genres. The three aforementioned wartime novels reveal in their pseudoautobiographical stance affinities to the Spanish picaresque novel; the rapscallion protagonists struggle to survive in a harsh world while sharing in its corruption. These same novels, however, draw on a variety of traditions, both fiction and nonfiction.

Grimmelshausen's oeuvre shares in the nascent cultural nationalism of the period when, for example, it ridicules those who ape French manners or facetiously notes that the entry of a foreign word into the German language always means trouble, as, for example, the militant word *marschieren,* 'to march'. Grimmelshausen thus remarks on the linguistic dominance of the French in the art of war, and war, he will remind his readers repeatedly, gives humankind license to do its worst.

Grimmelshausen's Nuremberg publisher, Wolf Eberhard Felsecker, advertised these works as delightful and entertaining but also affirmed their didacticism. In fact, the energy, unruliness, and transgressiveness of Grimmelshausen's narratives, derived from the literary arsenal of the Renaissance at its bawdiest—bodily excess, cross-dressing, pranks, and farce—exert a fascination over readers that can obscure the yearning in these texts for stable social arrangements, divine justice, and Christian redemption.

See also **German Literature and Language; Thirty Years' War (1618–1648).**

BIBLIOGRAPHY

Primary Sources

Grimmelshausen, Hans Jakob Christoph von. *Gesammelte Werke in Einzelausgaben.* Edited by Rolf Tarot. 13 vols. Tübingen, 1967–1976.

———. *The Life of Courage, the Notorious Thief, Whore, and Vagabond.* Translated by Michael Mitchell. Sawtry, U.K., 2001. Translation of *Trutz Simplex; Oder ausführliche Beschreibung der Ertzbetrügerin und Landstörtzerin Courasche* (1670).

———. *Simplicissimus.* Translated by Michael Mitchell. Sawtry, U.K., 1999. Translation of *Der abenteuerliche Simplicissimus* (1669).

———. *Tearaway.* Translated by Michael Mitchell. Sawtry, U.K., 2003. Translation of *Der seltsame Springinsfeld* (1670).

———. *Werke.* Edited by Dieter Breuer. 3 vols. Frankfurt am Main, 1989–1997.

Secondary Sources

Breuer, Dieter. *Grimmelshausen Handbuch.* Munich, 1999.

Menhennet, Alan. *Grimmelshausen the Storyteller: A Study of the "Simplician" Novels.* Columbia, S.C., 1997.

Negus, Kenneth. *Grimmelshausen.* Twayne World Author Series, no. 291. New York, 1974

Otto, Karl F., Jr., ed. *A Companion to the Works of Grimmelshausen.* Rochester, N.Y., 2003.

Tatlock, Lynne, ed. *Seventeenth Century German Prose.* The German Library, no. 7. New York, 1993.

Wagener, Hans. "Johann Jacob Christoffel von Grimmelshausen." In *German Baroque Writers, 1661–1730,* edited by James Hardin. *Dictionary of Literary Biography,* vol. 168. Detroit, 1996.

Lynne Tatlock

GROTIUS, HUGO (Huigh de Groot; 1583–1645), Dutch jurist, classical scholar, theologian, and ambassador for Sweden, traditionally known as the father of modern international law. Born in Delft on 10 April 1583, Grotius was the son of Jan de Groot, a burgomaster of Delft, who had studied under Justus Lipsius and was curator of the University of Leiden. After early schooling in Delft, he was taught by Johannes Uyttenbogaert, a preacher and theologian in The Hague. At the age of eleven he entered the University of Leiden, where he studied under the famous classical scholar Joseph Scaliger. At fifteen he accompanied Johan van Oldenbarneveldt, grand pensionary of Holland, on a mission to the court of Henry IV of France, remaining in the country to earn the degree of doctor of laws from the University of Orléans in 1598. In 1599 he returned to Holland and was admitted to the bar in The Hague. In 1601 the Estates of Holland appointed him official historiographer with the request that he write about the Dutch struggle with Spain. This historical work, begun that year and titled the *Annales et Historiae de Rebus Belgicis* (Annals and histories of Belgian affairs), was not published until after 1657, thirteen years after Grotius's death. On the model of Tacitus's major works, it was organized in two sections, the "Annals," treating 1559–1588, and the "Histories," which covered the period from 1588 to the Twelve Years' Truce of 1609–1621. Grotius's work as a classical scholar included editions of Martianus Capella, Lucan, the *Phaenomena* of Aratus of Soli, Tacitus, a *History of the Goths, Vandals and Lombards,* a New Testament commentary, and Latin translations of Theocritus (with Daniel Heinsius) and Euripides' *Phoenician Women.* His writings of a literary nature included a great deal of Latin verse and a number of well-received plays *(Adam in Exile, The Suffering Christ, Joseph at the Court).*

In 1604–1605, at the request of the Dutch East India Company, he wrote a treatise *On the Law of Prize and Booty,* a work he himself knew as *On the Indies (De Indis).* The treatise defended access to the ocean by all nations against the claims of particular powers to control the seas. One chapter of this work, published anonymously in 1609 under the title *Mare Liberum* (The Freedom of the seas), was widely influential and frequently reprinted. In 1607 Grotius was appointed advocate general of the fisc of the provinces of Holland, Zeeland, and Friesland. In 1613 he was named pensionary of Rotterdam. Politically he was closely tied to Oldenbarneveldt, the leader of resistance by the province of Holland against the absolutist ambitions of Prince Maurice of Nassau (1567–1625). Grotius's support for the Estates of Holland against Prince Maurice in the Arminian controversy (involving aspects of the Calvinist doctrine of predestination) resulted in 1618 in a trial in which he was condemned to life imprisonment and sent to the castle of Loevestein. (His patron, Johan van Oldenbarneveldt, was put to death.) In prison he wrote *Bewijs van den waren Godsdienst* (On the truth of the Christian religion) and began the composition of a work on the law of Holland that was published in 1631. Hiding in a chest of books, Grotius escaped from the castle in 1621 and fled to France, where he was received by Louis XIII (ruled 1610–1643), who gave him a pension that was paid in fits and starts.

In Parisian exile Grotius published his greatest work, *De Jure Belli ac Pacis* (1625; On the law of war and peace). The work was dedicated to the French king in the hope of receiving steady employment; Cardinal Richelieu, however, successfully opposed this. In his book Grotius argued that all laws can be distinguished between primary laws of nature, which express the divine will, and secondary laws, which lie within the realm of human reason. International society, Grotius argued, belongs to this second sphere. Its laws may be scientifically deduced from the rational and social nature of man, without reference to religious beliefs. Grotius was famously criticized by Rousseau in *Du contrat social* (1762; The social contract) for being a defender of slavery and a flatterer of tyrants. Although there are indeed defenses in particular instances of slavery and absolute rule, Grotius believed that slavery and absolute rule were exceptions and somehow against nature, although under certain circumstances they may be legitimate. As one of the great theorists of religious toleration, Grotius saw in the common principles of the various confessions (belief in the existence and unity of God and God's creation of the world) the basis of natural religion, from which Christianity differentiates itself by other elements that find their justification not in natural reason but only in faith. This is conferred by the mysterious help of God. Hence it is contrary to reason to impose Christianity by arms on those to whom God has not given that help. Grotius is also believed to have established a new basis for ethics, since he affirmed it to be a tenet of natural law that all men are permitted to attempt to preserve themselves against death and harm.

Grotius devoted himself to his writing in Paris until 1631, when, six years after the death of Prince Maurice in 1625, he went home to Holland. Threatened again with imprisonment, he left for Hamburg, where acquaintance with the chancellor of Sweden, Axel Oxenstierna, resulted in his appointment in 1634 by Queen Christina as Swedish ambassador to France. Returning to Paris, Grotius proved personally incompatible both with his old foe, Richelieu, and then with Richelieu's successor, Cardinal Jules Mazarin; all the same, it was on the negotiations of these men that Swedish-French relations depended for ten crucial years of the Thirty Years' War (1618–1648). Only in 1644 did Queen Christina recall Grotius to Sweden, relieving him of his ambassadorship. Grotius was offered a position in Sweden, but he declined it and decided to return to Paris. On his way back, however, a ship that was carrying him to Lübeck was wrecked on the Pomeranian coast, sixty miles from Rostock. After a journey of two days he arrived in Rostock with a fever and died there on 26 August 1645.

See also **Diplomacy; Dutch Republic; Dutch Revolt (1568–1648); Law: International; Natural Law; Oldenbarneveldt, Johan van.**

BIBLIOGRAPHY

Primary Sources

Grotius, Hugo. *The Annals and History of the Low-Countrey Warrs.* London, 1665. English translation.

———. *Briefwisseling.* Edited by P. C. Molhuysen. The Hague, 1928–2001. Rich correspondence in several languages.

———. *De Dichtwerken.* Edited by B. L. Meulenbroek. Assen, 1970–. Latin verse with Dutch translation and commentary.

———. *De Iure Belli ac Pacis Libri Tres.* 2 vols. Translated by Francis W. Kelsey. Oxford, 1925. Latin text and English translation.

———. *De Iure Praedae Commentarius: Commentary on the Law of Prize and Booty.* 2 vols. Trans. Gwladys L. Williams and Walter H. Zeydel. Oxford, 1950. Latin text and English translation of the work Grotius knew as *De Indis.*

Secondary Sources

Haakonssen, Knud. "Hugo Grotius and the History of Political Thought." *Political Theory* 13 (1985): 239–265.

———. *Natural Law and Moral Philosophy: From Grotius to the Scottish Enlightenment.* Cambridge, U.K., and New York, 1996.

Knight, W. S. M. *Life and Works of Hugo Grotius.* London, 1925. Reprinted New York and London, 1962.

Ter Meulen, Jacob, and P. J. J. Diermanse. *Bibliographie des écrits imprimés de Hugo Grotius.* The Hague, 1950.

Tuck, Richard. *The Rights of War and Peace: Political Thought and the International Order from Grotius to Kant.* Oxford and New York, 1999.

WILLIAM J. CONNELL

GUICCIARDINI, FRANCESCO

(1483–1540) Florentine historian and political thinker. Francesco Guicciardini was the greatest historian of the Renaissance. His family rose to prominence under the Medici regime (a nascent *principate* operating behind a republican facade). During his lifetime the Medici were expelled from Florence and a republican regime restored (1494–1512), two members of the Medici family were elected to the papacy (Leo X and Clement VII), the Medici regained control of Florence (1512–1527) but lost it again briefly (1527–1530), and finally established themselves as hereditary princes. In external affairs, a French army invaded Italy in 1494, and the Valois monarchy subsequently attempted to establish hegemony there, but was challenged and ultimately defeated by the supranational Habsburg empire of Charles V, which from c. 1530 exercised hegemony in the peninsula. Guicciardini, who was trained as a lawyer, served the Medici papacy as a senior administrator, and was a participant in the vicissitudes of the Habsburg-Valois wars in Italy, which he narrated in his last and greatest work, the *Storia d'Italia* (History of Italy), composed in the late 1530s. Within Florence, the pressure of events and the conflict of interests created a political debate of such intensity that a cohort of Florentines led by Niccolò Machiavelli (1469–1527), and including Guicciardini, virtually founded the modern tradition of political thought. During the early modern period, Guicciardini was known throughout Europe for his *History of Italy,* and for his *Ricordi* (Maxims and reflections). In the nineteenth and twentieth centuries all of his writings were published, providing a much more complex picture of the man, and at the beginning of the twenty-first century new editions, translations, and studies continue to appear.

Guicciardini's early *Storie fiorentine* (Florentine histories) deals mainly with the Florentine experiment in broadly based republican government that began in 1494 and, despite many difficulties, was still in existence at the time of writing (1508–1509). Over three thousand Florentine males were permanent members of the voting assembly on which the political system was based—an extraordinarily high number in comparison to most other European states at that time, though a small fraction of the population. But political participation and influence were strongly correlated to social position, so most of the leading individual actors were members of prominent families, had aristocratic views, and favored a stronger role for the executive and the creation of a permanent senate to represent their interests, while a few supported the Savonarolan movement and others collaborated secretly with the Medici.

In 1512 Guicciardini drafted his first political treatise, the *Discorso di Logrogno* (Discourse composed in Logrogno), a set of proposals for refining the republican government. Guicciardini's outlook was broadly that of his fellow aristocrats, but his real concern was to ensure that perceptive and experienced men would prevail over the foolish and the inexperienced in the business of government. Like Machiavelli, Guicciardini tried throughout his life to gain an intellectual grasp of how political and military events are determined. They did not have modern social science to aid them, or any experience of parliamentary government by organized political parties, but they were imbued with ancient Greek and Roman literature on war, politics, and conquest, and their own experience of war and politics was much closer to that of the ancient world than it was to that of people living in the nineteenth, twentieth, or twenty-first centuries. Hence they placed great emphasis on the character of individual leaders and their advisors, and the process of deliberation. Guicciardini did exercise power directly, but not in the context of Florentine politics. He was a senior administrator in the northern part of the Papal States (somewhat like a Roman proconsul, or a colonial governor), and his *Ricordi* are largely based on that experience. Each of them is a gem of insight into character and conduct, prudent choice of course of action, and the mutability of fortune.

Yet the problem of Florence never left Guicciardini's mind, and in the 1520s he returned to it yet again in his *Dialogo del reggimento di Firenze* (Dialogue on the government of Florence), which is set in late 1494. Four Florentine leaders debate the good and bad aspects of Medici rule and the prospects for the current broadly based republican regime, and the one with the most foresight (i.e., the one whom Guicciardini endows with his own hindsight) is also the most pessimistic. Machiavelli in the *Discourses on the First Ten Books of Livy* (written c. 1514–1520) used the ancient Roman republic, the most successful conquest state in European history, as a standard against which to assess the situation of the states of modern Italy; Guicciardini responded with a short set of *Considerations on Machiavelli's Discourses* (written c. 1530), in which he emphasized the uniqueness of every historical situation and the consequent illegitimacy of analysis and prescription based on a paradigm case.

The theme of the *History of Italy* is not politics as such but European interstate conflict during the epochal period from 1494 to about 1530. The modern state was coalescing throughout western Europe, and the European state system was assuming the dynamic form it was to retain throughout the early modern period. Italy became the theater and victim of Habsburg-Valois conflict because its own sophisticated state system was too small in scale to withstand the impact of the large armies led there, or sent there, by the monarchs of France and Spain. One reason for the work's classic status is Guicciardini's ability to marshal the tumult of events into a vast narrative. Another is his profound insight into the complex, systemic way overall outcomes are determined, as numerous individual decision makers and their advisors throughout Italy and Europe, with all their personal idiosyncrasies, continually assess the intentions, capacities, words, and deeds of all the others, and choose their own courses of action.

See also **Florence; Habsburg-Valois Wars; Historiography; Machiavelli, Niccolò; Political Philosophy; Republicanism.**

BIBLIOGRAPHY

Primary Sources

Guicciardini, Francesco. *Dialogue on the Government of Florence.* Translated with introduction and notes by Alison Brown. Cambridge, U.K., and New York, 1994. In the same year a new, thoroughly annotated edition of the original text was published: *Dialogo del reggimento di Firenze.* Edited by Gian Maria Anselmi and Carlo Varotti. Turin, 1994.

———. *The History of Florence.* Translated by Mario Domandi. New York, 1970. Translation of the *Storie fiorentine dal 1378 al 1509.* The most recent edition of the original text is *Storie fiorentine dal 1378 al 1509.* Edited by Alessandro Montevecchi. Milan, 1998.

———. *The History of Italy.* Translated and abridged by Sidney Alexander. New York, 1969; Repr., Princeton, 1984. A number of good, annotated editions of the original, *Storia d'Italia,* are available from Italian publishers.

———. *Maxims and Reflections of a Renaissance Statesman.* Translated by Mario Domandi. Introduction by Nicolai Rubenstein. New York, 1965; Philadelphia, 1972. Translation of *Ricordi politici e civili.*

Machiavelli, Niccolò, and Francesco Guicciardini. *The Sweetness of Power: Machiavelli's Discourses and Guicciardini's Considerations.* Translated with introduction by James V. Atkinson and David Sices. Dekalb, Ill., 2002.

Secondary Sources

Gilbert, Felix. *Machiavelli and Guicciardini: Politics and History in Sixteenth-Century Florence.* Princeton, 1965.

Moulakis, Athanasios. *Republican Realism in Renaissance Florence. Francesco Guicciardini's* Discorso di Logrogno. Lanham, Md., 1998. A wide-ranging assessment of Guicciardini from the perspective of the history of political thought, with an English translation of the *Discorso.*

WILLIAM MCCUAIG

GUILDS. The guild, a formal organization of craftspeople, held an important place in a theoretical system of order called corporatism that emerged in the late Middle Ages in Europe and survived until the late eighteenth and early nineteenth centuries. Medieval guilds began as devotional and mutual aid societies, but by the early modern period they had become identified with governance as well as with the regulation of economic activities. Guild masters responded to indiscipline in the workplace by drafting statutes or guild bylaws. Municipalities, and eventually monarchs, sanctioned these statutes for a fee, oversaw their enforcement by imposing fines for transgressions, and increasingly conferred legal status upon the guilds.

Corporatism laid out organizing principles that shaped social, political, and economic organization, embracing the concept of paternalism and restricting competition to preserve the livelihood of artisans and channel quality goods, fairly priced, to the consuming public. In keeping with these principles, monopoly over the manufacture and sale of particular items was a privilege widely protected by guild statutes. Statutes also frequently regulated the labor supply to reduce competition among masters, restricting the allowable number of journeymen a master might employ.

Guilds also had a social function. Membership placed an artisan—master, journeyman, apprentice, or widow—in the finely graded hierarchy that structured Old Regime society. Such a system was equally a power structure, and distinction and difference issued from a concern among male masters for subordination of inferiors, be they journeymen, apprentices, wageworkers, or women. Numerous provisions in guild statutes throughout Europe focused on status, above all by strictly regulating the access of workers to the corporation and to mastership within it. They also increasingly excluded women. Escalating fees, extended periods of apprenticeship, and the continuing refinement of masterpieces all pointed to a mounting preoccupation with discipline and a growing hierarchization in the world of work; the barriers between male and female, master and journeyman (that is, a worker with some institutional claim to guild membership), and journeyman and nonguild worker (those with no guild membership whatsoever) were being raised higher than ever before. Master guildsmen and the political authorities shared these values of institutionalization, and their common interests came together in the formulation of the corporate regime, enshrined in part in guild statutes.

EXPANSION OF THE GUILD REGIME

Guilds proliferated throughout Europe from the fifteenth to the seventeenth centuries; in some places such as Sweden and Austria the high point was reached in the eighteenth century. The fifteenth century was a time of corporate expansion in most French towns, and the sixteenth century witnessed a similar development in the towns of the southern Netherlands and England, where expansion continued into the seventeenth century. The towns of the new United Provinces in the northern Netherlands, for example, had few guilds before the seventeenth century, but by 1700 there were about two thousand. The German "home towns" of the seventeenth and early eighteenth centuries—polities that were relatively independent of external political authority and held between one thousand and five thousand inhabitants—epitomize the early modern European guild system. The guilds in these locations were political, economic, and social entities. All possessed statutes that stipulated, as elsewhere, the nature and duration of apprentice training, regulations for recruitment of workers and their distribution among the shops of the town, and monopolies. Guild masters enforced these rules with the sanctioning of the municipality. Regulating economic competition had the higher goal, however, of securing community peace and maintaining the social order. This order was rooted in social position defined by *Ehrbarkeit* or 'honorable status'. Guild masters everywhere, not just in the home towns, possessed this quality, characterized by "the respect of the respected," and jealously guarded it, for it defined one's exclusive position at the upper levels of society.

GUILDS AND ECONOMIC REGULATION

Determining the role that regulation played in economic practice has formed the research agenda of many historians of the early modern period, and the function of guilds is a central concern in this inquiry. Guilds were empowered and enjoined by municipal, ducal, ecclesiastical, or royal governments to regulate the economy—workshop inspections and access to courts are evidence of this. Many instances of artisans' workshops being searched for illegal materials or unacceptable workmanship can be cited, as can examples of litigation between guilds over encroachment of monopolies. The high-water mark of regulation came in the late seventeenth century and is best illustrated by the policies of the French finance minister Jean-Baptiste Colbert (1619–1683) and his immediate successors. Between 1673 and 1714 in France, the crown enacted 450 *règlements,* or rulings, on manufacture, and another 500 on the policing of the guilds and on jurisdictions between them. Similar regulatory policies were imitated by nearly every state in eighteenth-century Europe.

Historians have long been aware of this regulatory system but only recently have they probed its actual impact on economic activity. Indeed, historians now point to overwhelming evidence that reveals that in many places, normal economic practice was largely beyond regulation, as it comprised a flexible and spontaneous mixture of licit and illicit

Guilds. The sign of the Venetian Weavers' Guild, painted in the eighteenth century. Museo Correr, Venice, Italy/Bridgeman Art Library

activity in production, distribution, and consumption. The early modern craft economy was too dynamic to be contained by regulation, since illegal activities such as operating multiple shops, smuggling, unlicensed peddling, and clandestine workers working outside of guilds proliferated. In 1748 in Amsterdam, for instance, nonguild workers—both male and female—were making more clothes than master tailors.

So what can we conclude about guild regulation and the craft economy? Certainly guilds did not suffocate the free-market economy. The regulatory regime, however, was not totally ineffective or irrelevant. Rather, it was extremely flexible, responding to the various needs of artisans and governments. There were different kinds of markets in the early modern economy, and regulation fit differently in them. There was the sprawling, heterogeneous, and unregulated clandestine and illegal craft economy. Alongside this economy there was the licensed one, but even here within the official organization of the guild we find ample room for flexibility and economic growth. Indeed, within this official, "regulated" structure, masters of the same guild competed with one another, even inviting regulation of their products as a form of advertising their quality precisely so that they could have an advantage over fellow guildsmen.

FROM CORPORATISM TO LIBERALISM: THE END OF GUILDS

Corporatism and guilds were embodied in most polities of early modern Europe. Guilds were simultaneously empowered by political authorities and rendered vulnerable to them, and so if these political authorities abandoned corporatism, guilds would disappear. In the eighteenth century, corporatism was increasingly challenged by a rival system, liberalism, and as governments came to embrace the principles of free trade and unregulated markets, corporatism was eventually displaced. Such a displacement, however, was hardly rapid or unconflicted. There was considerable ambivalence within the ranks of political authority about just what liberalism was and how it might be implemented. An episode involving the French controller general of finance, Anne-Robert-Jacques Turgot (1727–1781), illustrates this confusion. Turgot attempted to abolish the guilds in February 1776 and was abruptly dismissed in May. An advocate of free trade and therefore an opponent of the regulatory corporate regime, he saw guilds as impediments to growth in the French economy and asserted that abolishing them would liberate commercial and industrial activity. Turgot, however, was not thinking in simply narrow economic terms; nor were his opponents, the staunch defenders of corporatism. Both parties were fundamentally concerned with preserving social order, but equally fundamentally disagreed on how best to secure such order. Turgot sought to replace what he thought was the unnatural and stultifying hierarchy of corporatism with a natural and free one, and so he had no sympathy for his opponents, who clamored that his edict would dissolve the bonds of subordination and invite anarchy. Turgot assumed that masters and workers would form natural hierarchical relationships in the marketplace, that the natural law of the market would maintain order. Corporatists countered that Turgot's natural hierarchy was a dangerous illusion, and because the principle of incorporation linked all of France in a chain that led directly to the throne, to sever one link (as with the abolition of the guilds) would cut the chain and ultimately destroy the entire system and even the monarchy itself.

Turgot lost the battle, but liberalism eventually won the war. Over the long run liberalism did prove corrosive to corporatism in general and to guilds in particular, as attested by the liberal-inspired legislation in the late eighteenth and nineteenth centuries abolishing guilds all across Europe. The assault on corporations may have been largely inspired by demands for free trade and unregulated markets, but guilds were more than simply economic entities; rather, they were a fundamental unit of the entire early modern system of social representation and social control. Their dissolution, therefore, had widely felt cultural ramifications. As guilds disappeared, the very nature of the artisanry, and the identity of the artisan, was redefined.

See also **Artisans; Liberalism, Economic; Proto-Industry.**

BIBLIOGRAPHY

Black, Antony. *Guilds and Civil Society in European Political Thought from the Twelfth Century to the Present.* Ithaca, N.Y., 1984.

Chevalier, Bernard. "Corporations, conflits politiques et paix sociale en France aux XIVe et XVe siècles." *Revue historique* 268 (1982):17–44.

Crossick, Geoffrey, ed. *The Artisan and the European Town, 1500–1900.* Aldershot, U.K., 1997.

Farr, James R. *Artisans in Europe, 1300–1914.* Cambridge, U.K., and New York, 2000.

Kaplan, Steven L. *The Bakers of Paris and the Bread Question, 1700–1775.* Durham, N.C., 1996.

Mackenney, Richard. *Tradesmen and Traders: The World of the Guilds in Venice and Europe, c. 1250–c. 1650.* Totowa, N.J., 1987.

Prothero, I. J. *Artisans and Politics in Early Nineteenth-Century London: John Gast and His Times.* Baton Rouge, La., 1979.

Sewell, William H., Jr. *Work and Revolution in France: The Language of Labor from the Old Regime to 1848.* Cambridge, U.K., and New York, 1980.

JAMES R. FARR

GUISE FAMILY. The Guise lineage was the product of the dynastic convolutions of the Houses of Lorraine and Anjou in the fifteenth century. René II, duke of Lorraine (1451–1508), passed his lands in the kingdom of France to his second son, Claude I, count of Guise (1496–1550), who was naturalized French in 1506, but the Guise never forgot their dynastic claims to Scotland, Provence, and Naples. Claude made a good marriage in 1513 to Antoinette de Bourbon, eldest daughter of François de Bourbon-Vendôme. Although he was not an intimate of King Francis I (1494–1547), he was rewarded with the elevation of the county of Guise to a duchy in 1526; his credit peaked around 1538

Guise Family. *Three Men of the de Guise Family,* sixteenth-century painting. THE ART ARCHIVE/CHÂTEAU DE BLOIS/DAGLI ORTI

when he married his eldest daughter, Marie (1515–1560), to James V, king of Scotland (1512–1542). Control of ecclesiastical patronage was at the heart of Guise power throughout the sixteenth and seventeenth centuries. It was under René's third son, Jean (1498–1550), that the foundations of a formidable ecclesiastical empire were laid. Jean possessed six abbeys and six dioceses, including the archbishopric of Reims, the most prestigious in France, which was held by various members of the family from 1533 until 1641.

On his death, Claude I de Guise left ten children to be provided for, and the favored position enjoyed by his brother in the French church was exploited to the full in order to prevent the fragmentation of the patrimony. The eldest son, François (1519–1563), became duke of Guise and shared the temporal inheritance with his younger brothers, Claude II, duke of Aumale (1526–1573), and René, marquis of Elbeuf (1536–1566), each of whom founded important lineages. The remaining sons and daughters were designated for the church at an early age; Charles (1525–1574), the second son, inherited the benefices of his uncle Jean, and the fourth son, Louis (1527–1578), became bishop of Troyes in 1545 and later cardinal of Guise.

François de Guise and his brother Charles, cardinal of Lorraine, were well provided for in the palace revolution that marked the accession of Henry II. Although both were admitted to the privy council, they did not achieve the intimacy that marked the relationship between Henry and Constable Anne de Montmorency. The king's mistress, Diane de Poitiers, sought to counterbalance her lover's dependency on Montmorency by patronizing the Guise. Rivalry between the factions was at its most bitter over control of foreign policy. François's military reputation, first signaled at the siege of Metz (1552) and crowned by his capture of Calais (1558), was complemented by Charles's skills as a financier—he was reputed to be the richest man in France—and diplomat. Guise influence reached its height with the marriage of their niece Mary Stuart to the dauphin in 1558. When he ascended to the throne as Francis II a year later, the Guise dominated power. However, their authority was challenged by the opposition of the Bourbon princes of the blood, the spread of heresy, and the collapse of royal finances. When Francis II died in

December 1560, the Guise were disgraced. Their reaction to heresy was mixed: the cardinal of Lorraine was a Catholic moderate interested in concord, but his brother, François, was more hard-line, and his retinue's massacre of Protestants at Wassy in March 1562 signaled the start of the Wars of Religion. François's own assassination by a Huguenot in 1563 hardened the family's attitude to the Protestants and began a vendetta with the Montmorency clan that dominated the politics of the 1560s, ending with the murder of Admiral Coligny by François's son, Henri (1550–1588), an act that sparked the Massacre of St. Bartholomew.

Financial difficulties and growing estrangement from Henry III led the Guise into alliance with Spain in the 1570s. When the heir to the throne died in 1584, Henri de Guise resurrected the Catholic League with Spanish money to combat the claim of Henry of Navarre to the throne. Henri de Guise mobilized a popular urban power base and took control of large parts of France, but he and his brother Louis II, cardinal of Guise (1555–1588), were murdered by the king at the height of their power. The Catholic League, now headed by the surviving Guise brother, Charles, duke of Mayenne (1554–1611), was weakened after initial success by war weariness and polarization between radical and moderate factions. Mayenne, unable to find a suitable Catholic candidate to replace Henry III, who had been murdered in 1589, compromised with Navarre in 1595, signaling the end of the league. The dynasty continued to be important in the seventeenth century but suffered through its conspiracies against Cardinal Richelieu, resulting in the exile of Charles, duke of Guise (1572–1640), in the 1630s and of his son Henri, the archbishop of Reims (1614–1664), in the 1640s.

See also **Catholic League (France); Coligny Family; France; Lorraine, Duchy of; Richelieu, Armand-Jean Du Plessis, cardinal; St. Bartholomew's Day Massacre; Wars of Religion, French.**

Guise Family. Portrait of Claude of Lorraine, duke of Guise, by Jean Clouet. ©ARTE & IMMAGINI SRL/CORBIS

BIBLIOGRAPHY

Bergin, Joseph. "The Decline and Fall of the House of Guise as an Ecclesiastical Dynasty." *Historical Journal* 25 (1982): 781–803.

———. "The Guises and their Benefices, 1588–1641." *English Historical Review* 99 (1984): 34–58.

Carroll, Stuart. "The Revolt of Paris, 1588: Aristocratic Insurgency and the Mobilization of Popular Support." *French Historical Studies* 23 (2000): 301–337.

———. *Noble Power during the Wars of Religion: The Guise Affinity and the Catholic Cause in Normandy.* Cambridge, U.K., and New York, 1998.

———. "The Guise Affinity and Popular Protest during the Wars of Religion." *French History* 9 (1995): 125–152.

Evennett, Henry Outram. *The Cardinal of Lorraine and the Council of Trent: A Study in the Counter-Reformation.* Cambridge, U.K., 1930.

Nugent, Donald. *Ecumenism in the Age of Reformation: the Colloquy of Poissy.* Cambridge, Mass., 1974.

Sutherland, N. M. "The Cardinal de Lorraine and the Colloque of Poissy: A Reassessment." In *Princes, Politics and Religion: 1547–1589.* London, 1984.

STUART CARROLL

GUNPOWDER PLOT. *See* **James I and VI (England and Scotland).**

GUSTAVUS II ADOLPHUS (SWEDEN) (1594–1632; ruled 1611–1632), king of Sweden. Gustavus was the son of Sweden's Charles IX and Christina of Holstein-Gottorp. He grew up in a particularly troubled time in Sweden's history, during which his father led a successful rebellion to depose his nephew, Sigismund I Vasa, (1599) and then ruthlessly established his place as king. Gustavus was raised as his heir. He received a humanistic education, primarily from his tutor, Johan Skytte, and was schooled in the emerging Dutch ideas in warfare. Charles IX introduced him to political affairs early, and Gustavus represented the ailing king at the 1609 meeting of the parliament.

Only seventeen when his father died in October 1611, Gustavus's succession was not entirely secure. Sigismund, who was king of Poland as Sigismund III Vasa, still hoped to regain the throne, and his half-brother, John, also had a claim. Gustavus's younger brother, Charles Philip, was also a factor. More important, the high nobles were eager to recover the influence Charles IX had denied them. An ongoing war with Denmark made a decision vital. Gustavus paid for his recognition by agreeing to an accession charter that assured an elite in the nobility a share in governing through the Council of State *(riksråd)* and guaranteed the historic privileges of the noble estate, including tax exemption and a monopoly on offices. This deal embodied the ideas of aristocratic constitutionalism and was written by Axel Oxenstierna, the chancellor and a member of the council.

Two themes dominated Gustavus's reign: war abroad and developments at home to support war. Peace was concluded with Denmark at Knäred in 1613, but on unfavorable terms that included a huge ransom for the return of Älvsborg, Sweden's window on the west. War with Russia ended in 1617 with the Treaty of Stolbova, which assured Sweden's control of the Gulf of Finland. The sporadic conflict with Poland in the 1620s was suspended by a truce, negotiated in 1629, which recognized Sweden's gains on the south Baltic coast.

It was during this period that Gustavus introduced changes in recruitment, training, equipment, and battle tactics that earned him a place in the so-called military revolution of the seventeenth century. Realizing the problems inherent in mercenary armies, he created a force based heavily on Swedish provincial regiments, which were well trained and regularly paid. He adopted line formations in place of the traditional squares and drilled his troops for greater mobility. Firepower was crucial, he believed, and he increased the number of guns over pikes in the infantry and added numbers and mobility to his artillery. He preferred the defensive in battle, and his forces gained repeated victories by standing their ground and cutting attacking opponents to bits.

Gustavus II Adolphus. Contemporary portrait, Dutch School. THE ART ARCHIVE/GRIPSHOLM CASTLE SWEDEN/DAGLI ORTI (A)

Alarmed by the Holy Roman Empire's gains in Germany, Gustavus entered the Thirty Years' War (1618–1648) in June 1630. At first his presence was unwelcome to the Protestants. Following the Battle of Breitenfeld (September 1631), however, he garnered more support and became increasingly central to the struggle. What he hoped to accomplish is unclear. Overthrow of the Habsburgs, the imperial crown, a Brandenburg-Vasa dynasty, security for Swedish interests in the Baltic, continued German disunity, territory, security for Germany's Lutherans, and the legitimacy of his own claim to the throne in Sweden are all on the list. Whatever the case, the issue became moot when Gustavus was killed in the Battle of Lützen in November 1632. He was succeeded by his only surviving heir, his six-year-old daughter Christina. Thereafter, direction of Sweden's policy in Germany fell to Axel Oxenstierna.

During Gustavus's reign, reforms that were designed to strengthen Sweden and provide the political and economic base for empire were instituted at home. A new royal court (*Svea hovrätt,* 1614) was introduced and similar courts created in Åbo and Dorpat. At the central level, government was organized around five "colleges" (chancery, treasury, justice, war, and navy). Regional government was based on districts *(län)* headed by governors to whom local officials were responsible. The organization and procedures of the parliament *(riksdag),* which increasingly became the point of contact between the king and the estates *(ständer)* (clergy, nobles, burghers, and farmers), were more carefully defined. New secondary schools *(gymnasier)* were established, and the country's one university at Uppsala given better support. Economic development, especially trade, mining, and manufacturing, was encouraged, as was immigration, particularly by experts in government, business, and technology.

Long a subject of debate is the extent of Gustavus's role in all of these developments. Excepting the army reforms, Axel Oxenstierna was probably the author of most of them, but they had Gustavus's support. The chancellor, who believed in a powerful aristocracy, and Gustavus, who believed in a strong monarchy, worked together in harmony, each contributing to Sweden's emergence as the major power in northern Europe.

See also **Charles X Gustav (Sweden); Christina (Sweden); Military; Oxenstierna, Axel; Sweden; Thirty Years' War (1618–1648); Vasa Dynasty (Sweden).**

BIBLIOGRAPHY

Ahnlund, Nils. *Gustav Adolf the Great.* Translated by Michael Roberts. Princeton, 1940. Originally published in Sweden in 1932.

Oredsson, Sverker. *Gustav Adolf Sverige och Trettioåriga kriget.* Lund, 1992.

Ringmar, Erik. *Identity, Interest and Action. A Cultural Explanation of Sweden's Intervention in the Thirty Years' War.* Cambridge, U.K., 1996.

Roberts, Michael. *Gustavus Adolphus.* London and New York, 1992.

———. *Gustavus Adolphus and the Rise of Sweden.* London, 1973.

BYRON J. NORDSTROM

GUTENBERG, JOHANNES (Johannes Gensfleisch zur Laden; c. 1400–1468), the first European printer, inventor of movable type. Throughout the Middle Ages texts continued to be created and transmitted the way they had been in ancient Greece and Rome: by handwriting. Each manuscript (literally, 'written by hand') was a unique and individually made object. If one copy of a text existed, and a second was needed, it required a fresh round of handwork, taking about as much time to complete as the first copy had. Then about 1450, an entirely new technique of text-creation, typographic printing, was developed in Mainz by Johannes Gutenberg. Through his invention, multiple copies of the same text, whether of a single-page document such as a church indulgence, or of a massive book such as the Bible, could be produced in a workshop as part of a single, mechanized process of production. Within the next quarter century Gutenberg's invention took firm root in Europe, and printed books became familiar objects for educated readers. Printing radically changed the tempo and scale of bookmaking: contemporaries remarked in amazement that as much could be printed in a day as a scribe could write in a year. This in turn affected the systems of book sales and distribution, book prices, readers' expectations for the appearance of their books, and eventually all aspects of book culture.

In their layouts and letterforms the earliest printed books closely resemble, as they were meant to do, professionally written manuscripts of their time. Yet the way in which they were made is so different from handwriting that, although we know almost nothing about Gutenberg's personality, we must believe that he had a rarely creative mind. The underlying idea of typography is the creation, in cast metal alloy, of multiple copies of every letter form in reverse, each standing on a rectangular shaft of about one-inch height so that they could be easily picked up and placed side by side to form lines of words, which then were arranged and blocked together to form entire type-pages of words. These type-pages were dabbed with a sticky black oil-based ink; a sheet of paper (or vellum, as the case may be) was laid over the page; and the paper and types were put under the plate of a screw-action press. The plate pressed the inked, reverse-image types strongly into the paper, leaving a sharp, forward-reading image of a full page of text in the paper. By successive inkings, as many copies as desired of that same type-page could be printed off, and gradually, multiple copies of a complete book were created, page by page.

The critical feature of Gutenberg's invention was that after all the needed copies of a given page had been printed off, the types were cleaned of ink, loosened, and returned, one by one, into the type cases, each character going into its appropriate box, ready for setting more text. By means of this constant recycling, a relatively small amount of type, and thus a relatively small investment in time, labor, and metal, was sufficient to print hundreds of copies of a book of any length. For instance, a single type-page of the Gutenberg Bible would have amounted to about twenty pounds of metal, and a typical full case of type in one of the early printing shops may have weighed about sixty-five pounds. However, if the entire text of the Gutenberg Bible had been set in standing pages, the total weight of the types needed would have been more than twelve tons.

Fragments survive of several crudely produced editions of a Latin grammar, *Donatus,* and of a German prophetic poem, the *Sibyllenbuch,* which are probably the results of Gutenberg's earliest typographic experiments. The massive Latin Bible commonly called the Gutenberg Bible, completed in 1455, was a much more expensive and ambitious project: a two-volume work, beautifully printed, of more than 1,200 large pages (approximately 16 by 11 inches). The Italian humanist Aeneas Sylvius Piccolomini, the future Pope Pius II (reigned 1458–1464), saw sample sheets of the Bible in Frankfurt am Main in the fall of 1454 and wrote enthusiastically to a friend in Rome about the high quality of the workmanship. He was told that some 180 copies were being made.

The chief investor in the Bible project was a wealthy Mainz citizen, Johann Fust (d. 1466). After the Bible was completed, Fust brought a successful lawsuit against Gutenberg, claiming that his investment had been partly diverted to other projects of Gutenberg's. Fust and his son-in-law Peter Schoeffer went on to form their own successful printing shop in Mainz.

After the breakup with Fust, Gutenberg was able, with the aid of another Mainz investor, to continue his experiments in typography into the late 1450s. A potential drawback of his first invention was that, because the pages of type were only temporary, if a new edition of a text was called for, it had to be reset from the beginning, with time and costs equal to that of the first edition. In response to this, Gutenberg developed a second system of printing, whereby the composed pages of type were not printed from directly. Instead, the set types were used to make moulds, into which were cast thin metal strips, each bearing on its surface the raised impression of two lines of text. These strips were blocked together to make up type-pages, which went under the printing press. When the printing was done, the strips could be stored, page-by-page, so that if a new edition was called for, they could be quickly reassembled, without the time and cost of new composition.

Using this system, Gutenberg and his workers produced in 1460 two brief religious tracts and a massive Latin dictionary, the *Catholicon.* After Gutenberg's death, the strips of the tracts were printed from once again (1469), and of the *Catholicon* twice again (1469 and 1473). Unlike the first invention of recycling types, this second invention of "frozen" types did not spread to other printing shops. Its near equivalent, stereotyping, was not developed until some 250 years later.

THE SPREAD OF PRINTING

In Gutenberg's lifetime the technology of printing spread slowly, to Strasbourg, Bamberg, Cologne, and into Italy, reaching Rome in 1467. In the year he died, 1468, it may not have been clear to contemporary eyes that printing would soon become a substantial replacement for, rather than just a parallel alternative to, the traditional system of handwritten books. A much broader and more rapid spread began in 1469 and after, when printing was first introduced to the great trading city of Venice. By 1500, printing shops had been introduced to more than 250 European cities and towns, although many of these were the sites for only brief experiments. Concurrently, a strong consolidation of shops began to form in a dozen or so cities—Venice, Paris, Milan, Strasbourg, Nuremberg, and others—which among them produced nearly two thirds of the approximately 28,000 surviving printed editions of the fifteenth century. By contrast, from about 1475 onward, there was a rapid fall-off in the production of manuscript books.

In essence, the fifteenth-century printers and publishers produced, in the totality of their output, a kind of résumé of all the written culture of the western world that still had a wide currency in their own age: ancient authors and the Bible; the major writings and commentaries on theology, law, and medicine; sermon collections; liturgical and devotional books; confessionals and other manuals for priests. Many of the "best-selling" authors of the period, such as Cicero, St. Augustine, and St. Thomas Aquinas, had been dead for centuries. At the same time, the printers were capable of giving quick and wide currency to the events and concerns of the day. When Columbus returned from his first voyage to the New World in 1493, his report to King Ferdinand and Queen Isabella was rapidly translated into Latin and published in three Rome editions as a kind of brief newsletter.

The role of printing, from the earliest years, in creating a mass circulation of almanacs, prognostications, indulgences, and small vernacular writings of many kinds has often been underestimated because of the very low survival rate of these genres. For example, we know from a document that in 1500 a printer in Messina had produced more than 130,000 copies of indulgences for the bishop of Cefalù, yet not a single copy is known to survive.

See also **Bible: Translations and Editions; Caxton, William; Printing and Publishing.**

BIBLIOGRAPHY

Davies, Martin. *The Gutenberg Bible.* London and San Francisco, 1996.

Ing, Janet. *Johann Gutenberg and His Bible: A Historical Study.* New York and London, 1988.

PAUL NEEDHAM

GUYON, JEANNE-MARIE DE LA MOTTE. *See* **Quietism.**

GYPSIES. *See* **Roma (Gypsies).**

H

HABSBURG DYNASTY

This entry includes two subentries:
AUSTRIA
SPAIN

AUSTRIA

The Habsburgs were the princely family that provided the dukes and archdukes of Austria starting in 1282, the kings of Hungary and Bohemia from 1526 onward, and the emperors of Austria from 1804 to 1918. From 1438 to 1806 (with one interruption, 1742–1745) the Habsburgs were emperors of the Holy Roman Empire and from 1516 to 1700 kings of Spain. All dynastic politics hinge on fertile marriages. Without legitimate heirs, dynasties regularly fall into civil war or foreign conquest. While this was true for all the early modern monarchies, the House of Habsburg seemed for a time to have perfected dynastic practice. Emperor Maximilian I (ruled 1493–1519) cultivated the motto, *"Bella gerant alii, tu felix Austria nube"* (What others achieve by war, let you, happy Austria, achieve by marriage). This policy was most evident in the arrangements made by Emperor Frederick III (ruled 1440–1493) for his son Maximilian I, who first married Mary of Burgundy (1457–1482) in 1477 and produced a son, Philip I (called "The Handsome," ruled Castile 1504–1506). Maximilian's marriage to Mary created claims to the Burgundian inheritance in the Low Countries as well as the duchy of Burgundy itself. After Mary's death in 1482, Maximilian married Anne of Brittany (1477–1514) by proxy in 1490, but this marriage was never consummated because in 1491 King Charles VIII of France (ruled 1483–1498) took Anne for himself. So in 1493 Maximilian married Bianca Maria Sforza, niece of Lodovico Sforza of Milan (1452–1508).

In all of these efforts one sees evidence of careful dynastic planning, which is even more obvious in the advantageous marriage Maximilian I arranged in 1496 for his son Philip I to Joanna (Juana) of Castile (ruled Castile 1504–1555; Aragón 1516–1555), the daughter of Ferdinand II of Aragón (ruled Sicily 1468–1516; Castile 1474–1504; Aragón 1479–1516; Naples 1504–1516) and Isabella of Castile (ruled 1474–1504). Although the unfortunate Joanna became mentally disordered in the early sixteenth century and was queen in name only, she bore six children, including the future Emperor Charles V (ruled 1519–1556; Charles I of Spain 1516–1556), who continued his family's dynastic planning by marrying Isabel of Portugal (1503–1539) in 1526. Thus it was that, without major military conquests, Charles V came to inherit the Austrian and southwest German homelands of the Habsburgs, the Low Countries, Burgundy, Spain, and all the Spanish possessions (including Spain's New World colonies and the Kingdom of Naples and Sicily). In 1519, after intense lobbying, he was also elected Holy Roman emperor, bringing sovereignty over most of the German lands. Such a family empire was obviously too large to control, and Charles spent much of his life fighting the kingdom of France and the Turks in the Mediterranean. He turned his Austrian homelands over to his brother

Ferdinand I (ruled 1558–1564), who pursued his own dynastic politics by marrying Anne, the daughter of Wladislav II, king of Hungary and Bohemia. Meanwhile his sister Mary married the son of Wladislav, King Louis II (ruled 1516–1526), who died childless at the battle of Mohács in 1526. This left Ferdinand I with a legitimate claim to both kingdoms, and from then until 1918 the Habsburgs were rulers of Austria, Bohemia, and those parts of Hungary not controlled by the Ottoman Turks.

What marriage could assemble, however, its failures could also destroy. This first became clear with Emperor Rudolf II (ruled 1576–1612), who failed to marry and was succeeded by his brother Matthias (ruled 1612–1619). Matthias married late in life but did not have children. When Matthias died, the stage was set for a bitter controversy over succession, especially in the Bohemian lands, where the crisis marked the beginning of the Thirty Years' War (1618–1648). Habsburg dynastic policy ran into another snag when Emperor Charles VI (ruled 1711–1740) died with no surviving male heirs in 1740. Using a "Pragmatic Sanction," he had arranged that his hereditary lands should go to his daughter, Maria Theresa (1717–1780), but this international agreement did not restrain King Frederick II of Prussia (ruled 1740–1786) from seizing Silesia and exciting the War of the Austrian Succession (1740–1748). Although Silesia was lost for good, Maria Theresa and her husband, Francis Stephen of Lorraine (Emperor Francis I, ruled 1745–1765), reestablished Habsburg rule over the Holy Roman Empire as well as in the Austrian, Bohemian, and Hungarian hereditary lands. Thus despite dynastic crises, strategic marriages decisively shaped the history of central Europe and nowhere more than among the Habsburgs.

See also **Charles V (Holy Roman Empire); Charles VI (Holy Roman Empire); Ferdinand I (Holy Roman Empire); Ferdinand II (Holy Roman Empire); Ferdinand III (Holy Roman Empire); Francis II (Holy Roman Empire); Frederick III (Holy Roman Empire); Habsburg Territories; Holy Roman Empire; Joseph I (Holy Roman Empire); Joseph II (Holy Roman Empire); Leopold I (Holy Roman Empire); Maria Theresa (Holy Roman Empire); Matthias (Holy Roman Empire); Maximilian I (Holy Roman Empire); Maximilian II (Holy Roman Empire); Rudolf II (Holy Roman Empire).**

BIBLIOGRAPHY

Hamann, Brigitte, ed. *Die Habsburger: Ein biographisches Lexikon.* 2nd ed. Vienna, 1988. Reprint, Munich, 2001.

Ingrao, Charles W. *The Habsburg Monarchy, 1618–1815.* 2nd ed. New York, 2000.

Mamatey, Victor S. *The Rise of the Habsburg Empire, 1526–1815.* New York, 1971.

Tanner, Marie. *The Last Descendant of Aeneas: The Hapsburgs and the Mythic Image of the Emperor.* New Haven, 1993.

H. C. ERIK MIDELFORT

SPAIN

Known to contemporaries as the House of Austria, the Habsburg dynasty succeeded the Trastámara dynasty (1369–1516) and ruled Spain from 1516 to 1700. Its earliest title, count of Habsburg, provides the name now used for it. Spanish kings placed "count of Habsburg" after their royal and ducal titles, which included king of Castile and León, Aragón, Valencia, Navarre, Sicily, Sardinia, Naples, and Jerusalem; archduke of Austria; duke of Burgundy, Brabant, Luxembourg, Milan, and more. Other titles with the status of count included Barcelona, Flanders, Holland, Tyrol, and Franche Comté, all preceding such lordships as the Basque Country and Indies East and West.

Their titles gave the Habsburgs a conviction of divine favor, with its concomitant obligations. The first Habsburg in Spain, Philip I (1504–1506), duke of Burgundy, was king-consort of Castile as husband of Queen Joanna I ("Joanna the Mad," 1479–1555), third child of Ferdinand of Aragón (ruled 1479–1516) and Isabella of Castile (ruled 1474–1504). In 1496, Ferdinand, for diplomatic purposes, married Joanna to Philip, son of Holy Roman Emperor Maximilian I (ruled 1493–1519), and his own son, Prince John (1478–1497), to Maximilian's daughter Margaret. He hardly expected that Joanna would inherit Spain, and that her son Charles I (Carlos I, ruled 1516–1556) would succeed to the Spanish thrones. Charles was born in 1500 in Ghent, where Maximilian influenced his upbringing. Maximilian and his father, Emperor Frederick III (ruled Holy Roman Empire 1452–1493; ruled Germany 1440–1493), developed a mystique about their dynasty, which included fictive genealogies tracing descent from Roman caesars and kings of Israel. Maximilian promoted the ideals of chivalry and crusade, also dear to Ferdinand. To Spain's court Charles bequeathed the elaborate etiquette of Burgundy.

On Maximilian's death, Charles became Holy Roman Emperor Charles V (ruled 1519–1558). He vowed to uphold the Roman Catholic Church when he confronted Martin Luther at Worms. Differences with France involved him in dynastic wars; only in 1530–1541 did he find opportunity to crusade. He continued the marriage strategies of his grandfathers. His sisters married into Portugal, Hungary-Bohemia, France, and Denmark; his brother Ferdinand (1503–1564), to whom Charles ceded his Austrian holdings in 1522, also married into Hungary-Bohemia and founded the Austrian Habsburg line. The Spanish line remained senior. Charles's sister Mary of Hungary acted as arbiter between Charles and Ferdinand, and succeeded their aunt Margaret as Charles's regent of the Low Countries. Serving the absent ruler as viceroy or regent in his chief holdings became a family obligation.

Charles married Isabel of Portugal. Their eldest daughter, Maria, married her Austrian cousin, future emperor Maximilian II (ruled 1564–1576). Their youngest, Joanna, married the prince of Portugal. Maria, Maximilian, and Joanna served as regents in Spain. Charles acknowledged two bastards. The first, Margaret (1522–1586), eventually married the duke of Parma, grandson of Pope Paul III (1534–1549). Both she and her son Alexander Farnese served as regents in the Low Countries, as did Charles's natural son, John of Austria (1547–1578), who also commanded Spain's Mediterranean fleet. Male bastards, potential threats to the legitimate line, did not marry.

Charles's heir, Philip II of Spain (ruled 1556–1598), married successively Maria Manuela of Portugal, mother of the unfortunate Don Carlos (1545–1568); childless Mary Tudor of England; Elisabeth de Valois of France; and his niece Ana of Austria, who mothered Philip III (1598–1621). Philip's eldest daughter by Elisabeth, named Isabel, married her cousin Archduke Albert. Philip endowed them with the Low Countries, but when Albert died childless, title reverted to Spain, while Isabel continued as regent. Her sister Catalina (1567–1597) married Charles Emmanuel I of Savoy (1580–1630).

Philip brought four of Maximilian II's sons to Spain for their education. Private instructions penned by him and Charles V became part of the family heritage. His monastery-palace, El Escorial, remains Spain's enduring monument to the Habsburg dynasty.

Europe's division between Catholic and Protestant limited Spain's Habsburgs to marriages with consanguineous Catholic dynasties, primarily Austria and France. (Portugal ceased being an option while annexed to Spain [1580–1640].) Philip II considered marriage to Elizabeth I of England (ruled 1558–1603) for himself or an Austrian archduke if she became Catholic. In the early 1620s, Spanish diplomats dangled the prospect of marriage to an infanta, or princess, before Protestant Charles Stuart (ruled 1625–1649), who, as prince of Wales, traveled to Madrid only to be rejected.

Philip III married his second cousin Margaret of Austria. His heir, Philip IV (ruled 1621–1665), married French princess Elisabeth de Bourbon, but only a daughter, Maria Teresa (1638–1683), survived to marry Louis XIV of France (ruled 1643–1715), son of Louis XIII (ruled 1610–1643) and Philip IV's sister Anne of Austria (1601–1666). Another sister married Emperor Ferdinand III (1637–1657), whose daughter Mariana married Philip after Elisabeth's death. Mariana bore Charles II (ruled 1665–1700), and Margarita, who married her uncle Emperor Leopold I (ruled 1658–1705).

Philip IV embellished his court with the art of the Spanish painter Velázquez (1599–1660). He also sired bastards. One, Juan José de Austria (1629–1679; also known as John Joseph of Austria) served in military and viceregal offices for his father, and as minister to Charles II. Because Charles was sickly from birth, Juan José hinted that he should marry Margarita and reign if Charles died, outraging Philip. Charles first married Marie Louise d'Orléans, niece of Louis XIV, then Mariana of Neuburg, daughter of the elector palatine and sister of Leopold's second wife, Eleanor.

Philip IV and Charles continued to employ brothers and Austrian relations as viceroys and regents, particularly in the Spanish Netherlands. Charles's last representative there, Elector Max Emmanuel of Bavaria, married Maria Antonia, daughter of Margarita and Leopold.

Habsburg Dynasty: Spain. Standing: Maximilian I with his first wife, Mary of Burgundy,and at center their son Philip I of Spain and King of Castile (the Fair). Seated, from left: Charles V, Ferdinand I, and Ludwig II of Hungary, Maximillian's grandson-in-law. KUNSTHISTORISCHES MUSEUM, VIENNA, AUSTRIA/BRIDGEMAN ART LIBRARY

Charles did not conceive an heir. Some thought him bewitched and tried exorcisms as a cure. Questions remain about his genes; his parents were uncle and niece, his grandparents cousins, his great-grandparents, all but one, Habsburgs. Austrian Leopold took charge of Habsburg fortunes, irritating Madrid, anxious about Spain's future. Leopold considered the Spanish monarchy Habsburg patrimony, and promoted his second son by Eleanor, Archduke Charles, to succeed Charles. Louis XIV promoted his and Maria Teresa's grandson Philip, duke of Anjou. Outside Spain and Austria, most favored a partitioned inheritance, with the son of Max Emanuel and Maria Antonia, Joseph Ferdinand, receiving Spain and the Indies, while Philip and Charles divided the rest. Charles accepted Joseph Ferdinand but not partition.

In 1699 Joseph Ferdinand died. Pressured by his council of state, Charles willed his inheritance to the Bourbon Philip of Anjou. When Charles died on 1 November 1700, the Spanish Habsburg dynasty became extinct. Spain's fundamental law of female succession validated Philip V's (ruled 1700–1724, 1724–1746) descent from Philip IV through Maria Teresa, regardless of her renunciation, toppling Leopold's claim that Habsburg possessions passed only through the male line.

See also **Anne of Austria; Charles I (England); Charles II (Spain); Charles V (Holy Roman Empire); Holy Roman Empire; Isabel Clara Eugenia and Albert of Habsburg; Joanna I, "the Mad" (Spain); Juan de Austria, Don; Leopold I (Holy Roman Empire); Louis XIV (France); Maximilian I (Holy Roman Empire); Maximilian II (Holy Roman Empire); Netherlands, Southern; Parma, Alexander Farnese, duke of; Philip II (Spain); Philip III (Spain); Philip IV (Spain); Spain; Spanish Succession, War of the (1701–1714).**

BIBLIOGRAPHY

Brown, Jonathan, and John H. Elliott. *A Palace for a King: The Buen Retiro and the Court of Philip IV.* New Haven, 1980.

Elliott, John H. "The Court of the Spanish Habsburgs: A Peculiar Institution?" In *Spain and Its World, 1500–1700: Selected Essays,* pp. 142–161. New Haven, 1989.

Koenigsberger, Helmut G. *The Habsburgs and Europe, 1516–1660.* Ithaca, 1971.

Martínez Millán, José, ed. *La corte de Felipe II.* Madrid, 1994.

Redworth, Glyn, and Fernando Checa. "The Courts of the Spanish Habsburgs." In *The Princely Courts of Europe,* edited by John Adamson, pp. 43–65. London, 1999.

Tanner, Marie. *Last Descendant of Aeneas: The Habsburgs and the Mythic Image of the Emperor.* New Haven, 1993.

Wheatcroft, Andrew. *The Habsburgs: Embodying Empire.* London, and New York, 1995.

PETER PIERSON

HABSBURG TERRITORIES.

HABSBURG TERRITORIES. The Habsburg territories of central Europe were a diverse and far-flung assortment of lands ruled by the Austrian line of the House of Habsburg. Sometimes dubbed the Habsburg Monarchy by historians, this collection comprised an informal dynastic union of the Austrian Habsburg hereditary lands, or *Erblande* (acquired by the house in 1278), and the independent crownlands of both the Bohemian and the Hungarian Monarchies (added to its holdings in 1526). Less a state than a political agglutination occasioned by marriage alliances and international pressures, the Habsburg Monarchy was unlike any other.

LANDS AND PEOPLES

The medieval core of the Habsburg Monarchy, the Austrian hereditary lands, consisted of several large principalities and related smaller territories. Situated along the Danube River, "Austria" proper included the duchies of Upper and Lower Austria. To the south, "Inner Austria" included the nearby duchies of Styria, Carinthia, and Carniola, while the smaller principalities of Gorizia, Istria, and Trieste extended the realm to the Adriatic. Located far to the west were the county of Tyrol and "Further Austria," or the *Vorlande,* consisting of the county of Vorarlberg (in the east), the Sundgau, the Breisgau, and Freiburg (in the west), and approximately one hundred scattered enclaves ruled by the Habsburgs in Swabia (in between), which included the oldest ancestral lands. Though largely German, the hereditary lands were by no means linguistically or ethnically homogeneous. To the west and south, segments of the population spoke various Romance languages: Ladin in Vorarlberg, Romansch in western Tyrol, and Italian in Trieste and southern Tyrol. Some areas to the south contained significant Slavic populations: Slovene was spoken in Carniola, as well as parts of Styria, Carinthia, and Gorizia, while Croatian was spoken in Istria. More significant, the Habsburgs ruled each of these territories individually, rather than collectively, and despite some grander pretensions, at times showed little interest in doing otherwise in the face of resistance—a pattern they would repeat elsewhere.

The five Bohemian crownlands had existed independent of Habsburg rule for close to five hundred years. They, like the Austrian lands, were politically diverse. Located to the north of the Austrian lands, they consisted of the largely Slavic kingdom of Bohemia and margravate of Moravia, in the south, and the largely German duchy of Silesia and margravates of Upper and Lower Lusatia, in the north. Nonetheless, each territory was linguistically and ethnically mixed. Bohemia and Moravia were predominantly Czech-speaking, with German-speaking minorities in some urban areas and along the western and northern periphery. Nearly all of the nobles and much of the populace in Lusatia and Silesia spoke German, although the Lusatian margravates contained significant numbers of Sorbs, Europe's smallest Slavic ethnic group, and Silesia was home to a large Polish minority, as well as a smaller Czech one.

Like the Bohemian lands, Hungary had a long history as a medieval kingdom before Habsburg rule. The crownlands consisted of the central kingdom on the Danubian plain, mountainous Upper Hungary (Slovakia) to the north along the Carpathians, and Transylvania to the east. Closely associated with Hungary through a centuries-long personal union were the southwestern kingdoms of Croatia and Slavonia. Each territory was quite distinct from the others, with its own estates, laws, and linguistic or ethnic groups. Magyars (Hungarians) predominated in the Danubian plain, while Slavs did elsewhere. Regardless of their ethnic identity or location, political elites usually adopted Magyar speech and customs (less so in Croatia than elsewhere). In contrast, outside of the central kingdom, the peasantry spoke Slovak and Ruthene in the Carpathians; Croatian in to the southwest; and Romanian in Transylvania, where Magyars, Magyar-speaking Szekels, and "Saxon" Germans were also found. In addition, German-speakers could predominate in more urban areas throughout Hungary, and Serbs entered Croatian territory in increasing numbers as the Ottoman Turkish threat increased in 1529.

POLITICS AND GOVERNMENT

The Habsburg Monarchy of the early modern period had humble roots in the reign of Rudolf I (ruled 1273–1291), whose election as emperor of Germany signaled the slow rise of a minor noble house, and whose acquisition of Austria provided the core of his successors' hereditary dominions. Although subsequent Habsburgs obtained the imperial title, few dramatic changes in the dynasty's fortunes occurred until political marriages arranged by Emperor Maximilian I (ruled 1493–1519) began to bear fruit. In 1482 his son Philip I (ruled 1482–1506) inherited the Burgundian territories in the Low Countries from his mother. In 1516 Maximilian's grandson Charles V (ruled 1519–1556)—who would inherit the Austrian territories and become emperor in 1519—added his mother's Spanish kingdoms (along with their Italian and overseas possessions) to his father's Burgundian holdings. In 1526 another grandson of Maximilian, Ferdinand I (ruled 1558–1564), to whom Charles had ceded the Austrian territories in 1521, secured his own elections to the Bohemian and Hungarian crowns when his brother-in-law King Louis II of Bohemia (ruled 1516–1526) died without an heir in battle with the Turks. Ferdinand would later become German emperor upon his brother's abdication in 1556. It thus came to pass that the House of Habsburg had become divided into two lines, the Spanish and the Austrian, ruling lands far in excess of Maximilian's late-fifteenth-century dreams.

Yet, the central feature of Habsburg rule over these territories was that it proceeded from a different constitutional basis in each one. For this reason, it is important to distinguish the central European Habsburg territories from the Spanish and Burgundian territories and from the German Holy Roman Empire. The successors of Charles V in Spain never ruled the central European lands, despite continuing family alliances, and the empire was a separate political entity that never became a Habsburg possession, even though the Austrian line provided it with a string of elected emperors. They played an important role in German affairs, and since portions of the central European lands belonged to the empire, they were simultaneously territorial princes within it, but the Habsburg Monarchy was not the same as the Holy Roman Empire of the German Nation. Instead, it was a wildly heterogeneous group of politically independent territories owing allegiance to the Habsburg dynasty.

Remarkably, the house managed to rule each land through traditional rather than centralized institutions, bringing each into a dynastic union with the others only by virtue of providing them with monarchs. Although this union created a limited

sense of shared purpose, the individual lands preserved their own identities, political forms, and administrative practices. Thus, in most cases, each land had a system of estates and a territorial diet, along with its own laws, privileges, and customs, all confirmed by succeeding Habsburg rulers.

In the Austrian hereditary lands, governors nominated by the estates and appointed by the prince served as the heads of territorial governments. Yet, greater power lay with the executive councils *(die Verordneten)* appointed by the estates of each land to oversee affairs whenever the diets were not in session. Ultimately, even more important to the functioning of government were local nobles, who were charged with implementing governmental decrees within their jurisdiction *(Herrschaft),* and who protected this responsibility as a right.

Rule in the Bohemian and Hungarian crownlands followed a similar pattern, with the diets enjoying even greater control over taxation, the appointment of officials, and the implementation of policy. The Bohemian Court Chancery, an estates' institution staffed by Czech nobles, remained the chief governmental organ of the kingdom. In Hungary, where significant noble privileges limited the scope of Habsburg initiatives, the diet retained control over the implementation of policy. Of course, in both kingdoms, the diets had the right to elect the monarch, although the so-called Renewed Constitution of 1627 abrogated this right in Bohemia, and the Hungarian Diet suspended it for as long as the House of Habsburg could produce a male heir. As was the case in the Austrian lands, the Habsburgs seldom challenged noble power in the estates (excepting Bohemia during the Thirty Years' War), let alone at the local level, until well into the eighteenth century.

Other than the Habsburg court itself, the monarchy simply lacked transterritorial institutions, let alone a general assembly for all its lands. In the sixteenth century, Ferdinand I made a limited attempt to establish a more centralized government in Vienna when he created a Privy Council for policy, a Court Chamber for finance, and Court War Council for defense. In practice, however, only the Privy Council was truly transterritorial, but it was a consultative organ, lacking the power to enforce its decrees. Finance and defense were issues too entangled with territorial privileges for the Court Chamber and Court War Council to have any real effect; their authority in these areas could only be shared with their territorial counterparts. Complicating matters further, of course, were similar institutions in the German empire. In attempting to centralize, Habsburg rulers really had no choice but to create an additional level of administration—the household—to complement the imperial and territorial institutions already in place. Ferdinand's successors did so, but structural realities always constrained their effectiveness. In any case, Ferdinand himself undermined hopes for lasting change when he divided his territories among his three sons in 1564, passing Bohemia and Hungary (along with the imperial title) to Maximilian II (ruled 1564–1576), Tyrol and Further Austria to Ferdinand, and the Inner Austrian territories to Charles. Only in 1619 would the territories again be united in personal union under Charles's son Ferdinand II (ruled 1619–1637).

Nevertheless, despite the centrifugal forces at work, several centripetal forces contributed to the monarchy's perseverance, not the least of which were the needs of international politics and the dynasty's own attempts to foster a shared political culture around its own court. The Habsburg territories provided a bulwark against growing French power in the west and against a persistent threat from the Ottoman Turks in the southeast. The fact that the monarchy was decentralized only increased its appeal to its external allies and its internal nobility, since this status ensured that it would not become a greater threat to the status quo or territorial prerogatives. In fact, early attempts to centralize and consolidate Further Austria into a Swabian duchy by Maximilian I were thwarted, as were later attempts by Charles V and Ferdinand II to increase Habsburg authority in the German empire. Given this state of affairs, Habsburg rulers eventually forged an imperial ideology within their own territories by allying themselves with the Catholic Church and their landed nobility, fostering the interests of a universal church and the territorial estates (following the suppression of Protestantism) in order to secure the dynasty's own interests. The result was a gradual increase in central authority, achieved through existing political institutions and increased reliance upon the court's prestige. As R. J. W. Evans has argued in *The Making of the Habsburg Monarchy,* this alliance of crown, church, and estates facilitated the processes of Habsburg state building, even if the resulting polity little resembled the more homogeneous nation-states to the west.

AUSTRIAN PIETY AND ENLIGHTENED ABSOLUTISM

Habsburg attempts to consolidate authority proceeded in fits and starts, always limited by difficult political realities. In the sixteenth and early seventeenth centuries, Charles V, Ferdinand I, Maximilian II, Rudolf II (ruled 1576–1612), and Matthias (ruled 1612–1619) were all constrained by the Reformation in Germany. Nominally Catholic, each sought to support the Catholic Church against Protestantism, but each did so in ways that took into account not only genuine desires for compromise, but also their own reliance upon Protestant nobility in the empire and in the monarchy to turn back the Turkish threat.

Only Matthias's successor, his cousin Ferdinand II, threw his unrestrained support behind the Catholic cause when religious affairs in the empire had reached a point of crisis at the outbreak of the Thirty Years' War (1618–1648), and Habsburg rule in Bohemia was threatened by a rival claimant to the throne. Pursuing harsh measures against the Bohemian rebels, Ferdinand also sought to secure Habsburg authority within the German empire. Although his attempts in the empire eventually fell short, measures against Protestant nobility in the Austrian hereditary lands and Bohemia proved lasting—a feat that makes him one of the most influential rulers in Austrian history. By the mid-seventeenth century, his son Ferdinand III (ruled 1637–1657) had effectively eliminated the Protestant threat in the Habsburg domains. Although noble privileges remained secure throughout the territories, they were enjoyed by nobles markedly different from the recalcitrant Protestants of the late sixteenth century.

From the crucible of religious antagonisms emerged a Catholic baroque culture that was integral to Habsburg absolutism. Still a bulwark against both France and the Ottoman Empire, the Habsburg Monarchy experienced both successes and failures, but the threat of internal dissent decreased with the consolidation of an invigorated imperial ideology. For during the reigns of Ferdinand II, Ferdinand III, Leopold I (ruled 1658–1705), Joseph I (ruled 1705–1711), and Charles VI (ruled 1711–1740), the Catholic piety of the Habsburg Monarch was turned into a public cult. Catholicism thus provided the language and form of state ritual and served to legitimate Habsburg rule within existing political structures. By creating a governmental ethos, "Austrian Piety" provided a model of religious and political practice to be emulated at court, bound the populace to the cause of Catholic baroque imperialism, and secured the foundations of the Habsburg state.

Ironically, from this context of Catholic ideology and traditional hierarchies emerged the top-down reforms of enlightened absolutism during the second half of the eighteenth century. During the reigns of Maria Theresa (ruled 1740–1780) and her son Joseph II (ruled 1780–1790), the ideas and institutions of baroque absolutism proved old and weak in comparison to new programs and structures in place elsewhere in Europe. Yet, neither Maria Theresa nor the bolder Joseph eliminated the traditional forms of Habsburg rule. Instead, they adapted them to increase their rationality, efficiency, and effectiveness. In maintaining the dynasty's alliance with the Catholic Church and the estates, they preserved territorial autonomy and relied upon the prestige of the imperial court. With greater or lesser success, they transformed absolutism from a conservative force to a progressive one. Viewed from the nineteenth century, their actions were clearly not enough, but it is easy to underestimate their contemporary successes. Their reforms went both too far and not far enough. It should surprise no one that they were undermined not only by a resurgent traditionalism but also by an advancing modernism.

THE MYTH OF CRISIS AND DECAY

Confronted with the extreme diversity of the Habsburg Monarchy and its failure to embody western European political paradigms, some historians choose to depict it as doomed to unceasing crisis and decay. Yet, the monarchy not only withstood the difficulties confronting it during the sixteenth, seventeenth, and eighteenth centuries, weathering

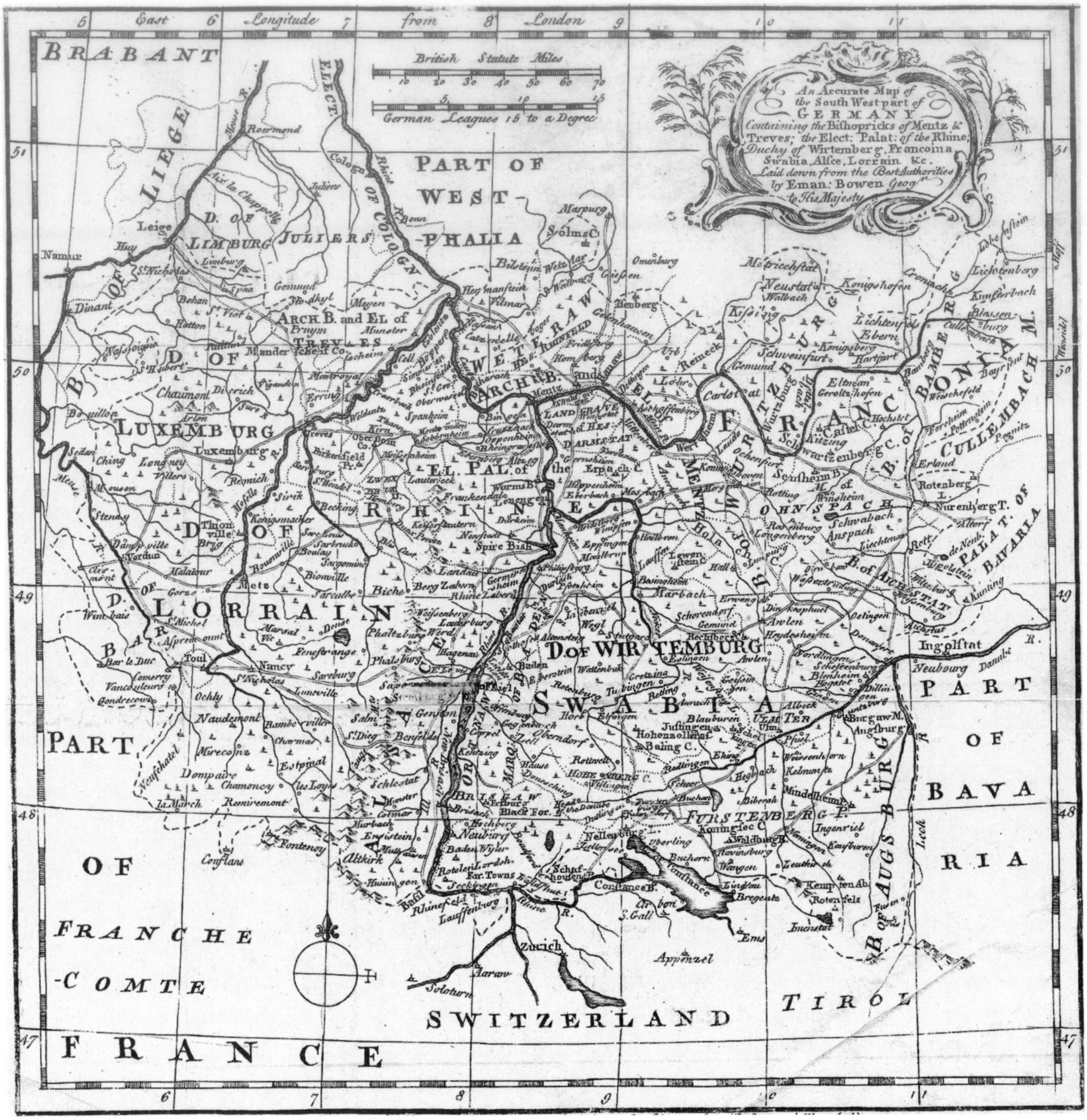

Habsburg Territories. This map, from the British periodical *General Magazine of Arts and Sciences* of November 1756 (although the map is dated 1757), gives testimony to the plethora of German states that made up the Habsburg territories. The subtitle of the map reads "Containing the Bishopricks of Mentz & Treves; the Elect[orate of the] Palat[inate] of the Rhine, Duchy of Wirtemberg, Franconia, Swabia, Alsce, Lorrain &c." MAP COLLECTION, STERLING MEMORIAL LIBRARY, YALE UNIVERSITY

the storms of Turkish invasions, religious discord, internal dissent, and continental wars, but also thrived, introducing political, social, and economic reforms and leaving a lasting cultural legacy. The monarchy's problems were real enough, but it offered practical solutions in a part of the world unaccustomed to uniformity and largely unwilling to pursue it.

Despite enjoying less wealth and facing greater problems than other states, by the second half of the eighteenth century, the monarchy was still expanding its reach, fielded Europe's largest army, possessed a stable yet innovative government, led the way in public education, and was without peer in the world of music. By the beginning of the next century, it was poised to play a central role in reversing the military conquests of Napoleon following the French Revolution. Through a transterritorial alliance with the Catholic Church and the estates of its diverse lands, the Habsburg dynasty fostered a political and cultural allegiance during the early modern period that allowed it to outlast all other monarchies in terms of longevity and continuity. Only the nationalism of the nineteenth century would erode that allegiance, and only a world war in the twentieth would eliminate it entirely in 1918.

See also **Austria; Bohemia; Charles V (Holy Roman Empire); Charles VI (Holy Roman Empire); Dutch Republic; Ferdinand I (Holy Roman Empire); Ferdinand II (Holy Roman Empire); Ferdinand III (Holy Roman Empire); Habsburg Dynasty; Holy Roman Empire; Holy Roman Empire Institutions; Hungary; Joseph I (Holy Roman Empire); Joseph II (Holy Roman Empire); Maria Theresa (Holy Roman Empire); Maximilian I (Holy Roman Empire); Maximilian II (Holy Roman Empire); Netherlands, Southern; Rudolf II (Holy Roman Empire); Spain.**

BIBLIOGRAPHY

Brunner, Otto. *Land and Lordship: Structures of Governance in Medieval Austria.* Translated from the 4th rev. ed. by Howard Kaminsky and James Van Horn Melton. Philadelphia, 1992.

Evans, R. J. W. *The Making of the Habsburg Monarchy, 1550–1700: An Interpretation.* Oxford, 1979.

Evans, R. J. W., and T. V. Thomas, eds. *Crown, Church and Estates: Central European Politics in the Sixteenth and Seventeenth Centuries.* New York, 1991.

Ingrao, Charles W. *The Habsburg Monarchy, 1618–1815.* Cambridge, U.K., 1994.

Ingrao, Charles W., ed. *State and Society in Early Modern Austria.* West Lafayette, Ind., 1994.

Johnson, Lonnie R. *Central Europe: Enemies, Neighbors, Friends.* New York, 1996.

Kann, Robert A., and Zdenek V. David. *The Peoples of the Eastern Habsburg Lands, 1526–1918.* Seattle, 1984.

Louthan, Howard. *The Quest for Compromise: Peacemakers in Counter-Reformation Vienna.* Cambridge, U.K., 1997.

Melton, James Van Horn. *Absolutism and the Eighteenth-Century Origins of Compulsory Schooling in Prussia and Austria.* Cambridge, U.K., and New York, 1988.

Okey, Robin. *The Habsburg Monarchy: From Enlightenment to Eclipse.* New York, 2001.

Szabo, Franz A. J. *Kaunitz and Enlightened Absolutism, 1753–1780.* Cambridge, U.K., and New York, 1994.

Edmund M. Kern

HABSBURG-VALOIS WARS. The Habsburg-Valois Wars of 1494–1559 were for a long time crucially intertwined with the Italian Wars. The latter arose from the instability of the Italian peninsula, which was divided among a number of vulnerable powers, but also from a new willingness of outside rulers to intervene. Initially, the most important was Charles VIII of France (ruled 1483–1498), who invaded Italy in 1494, capturing Naples the following March. Charles's artillery particularly impressed contemporaries. Mounted on wheeled carriages, his cannon used iron shot, allowing smaller projectiles to achieve the same destructive impact as larger stone shot. This permitted smaller, lighter, and thus more maneuverable cannon.

Charles's initial success aroused opposition both in Italy and from two powerful rulers who had their own ambitions to pursue: Maximilian I (ruled 1493–1519), the Holy Roman emperor, who ruled Austria and the other Habsburg territories, and Ferdinand of Aragón (ruled Sicily 1468–1516; Aragon 1479–1516; Naples as Ferdinand III 1504–1516; Castile, with Isabella, 1474–1504). Ultimately, Maximilian's grandson, Emperor Charles V (ruled 1519–1558; ruled Spain 1516–1556 as Charles II), was to succeed to the Habsburg, Burgundian, Aragonese, and Castilian inheritances, creating a formidable rival to the Valois dynasty of France and ensuring that the wars are known as the Habsburg-Valois wars.

Ferdinand's forces intervened in southern Italy in 1495, while Charles VIII was forced by Italian opposition to retreat, although an attempt to cut off his retreat failed at Fornovo (6 July 1495); the Italian forces of the League of St. Mark had numerical superiority but were poorly coordinated. Charles VIII's successor, Louis XII (ruled 1498–1515), in turn invaded the Duchy of Milan in northern Italy in 1499, claiming it on the grounds that his grandmother had been a Visconti. Disaffection with French rule led to a rallying of support to Ludovico Sforza (1451–1508), but Louis was able to reimpose his power in Milan and to partition the kingdom of Naples with Ferdinand in 1500. They fell out in 1502, and the French tried to take the entire kingdom, only to be defeated by the Spaniards at Cerignola (28 April 1503). The French-held positions were then captured, and Louis XII renounced his claims to Naples by the Treaty of Blois of 12 October 1505.

Cerignola was the first in a series of battles in which a variety of weapons, weapon systems, and tactics were tested in the search for a clear margin of military superiority. The state of flux in weaponry entailed a process of improvisation in the adoption and adaptation of weapons and tactics. In addition, perceived "national" differences were linked to fighting methods. The Swiss and Germans were noted as pikemen, equally formidable in offense and defense, but vulnerable to firearms. The French put their emphasis on heavy cavalry and preferred to hire foreign pikemen.

Italy was increasingly dominated by France and/or Spain, the only powers with the resources to support a major military effort. In contrast, other powers, especially Venice, defeated by Louis XII, Milan, the Swiss, and the papacy, took less important and independent roles. Pope Julius II (ruled 1503–1513) had formed the League of Cambrai in 1508 to attack Venice, but it was France's role that was decisive in that war. The French defeated the Venetians at Agnadello (14 May 1509) and then overran much of the Venetian mainland. Italian rulers lacked the resources to match French or Spanish armies readily in battle. Instead, they adapted to the foreign invaders and sought to employ them to serve their own ends. Thus, there was no inherent conflict between these local rulers and foreign powers. Instead, the latter were able to find local allies.

At the same time, weaker powers could help affect the relationship between France and Spain. In 1511, Pope Julius II's role in the formation of the Holy League with Spain, Venice, and England to drive the French from Italy led to a resumption of Franco-Spanish hostilities. The French beat the Spaniards at Ravenna on 11 April 1512, but opposition to the French in Genoa and Milan helped the Spaniards to regain the initiative, as did Swiss intervention against France. The French retreated across the Alps, while Ferdinand of Aragón conquered the kingdom of Navarre, which was to be a permanent gain.

In 1513, the French invaded again, only to be defeated by the Swiss at Novara on 6 June; the advancing Swiss pikemen took heavy casualties from the French artillery before overrunning the poorly entrenched French position. Left without protection, the French harquebusiers were routed.

Soon after coming to the French throne, the vigorous Francis I (ruled 1515–1547) invaded anew. He was victorious at Marignano (13–14 September 1515), the French cannon, crossbows, harquebusiers, cavalry, and pikemen between them defeating the Swiss pikemen, and occupied Milan until 1521, reaching a settlement with the future Emperor Charles V at Noyon in 1516.

However, the election of Charles as Holy Roman emperor in 1519 seemed to confirm the worst French fears of Habsburg hegemony, and in 1521 Francis declared war. The main theater of conflict was again northern Italy, although there was also fighting in the Low Countries and the Pyrenees. After their defeat at Bicocca (27 April 1522), the French position in northern Italy collapsed. In 1523 Venice felt that it had to ally with Charles. That year, however, invasion attempts on France from Spain, Germany, and England all failed to make an impact. In turn, Francis sent an army into northern Italy, which unsuccessfully besieged Milan before being driven out in early 1524 by the Habsburg forces.

In 1524 Charles again attempted to mount a concerted invasion of France with Henry VIII (ruled 1509–1547) of England and Charles, duke of Bourbon (1490–1527), a rebel against France. Such concerted invasions reflected the ambitious scope of strategic planning in the period although their lack of adequate coordination and failure testified to the limitations of operational execution.

In response, Francis invaded Italy again in October 1524, captured Milan, and besieged Pavia. The arrival of a Spanish relief army, however, led to the battle of Pavia (24 February 1525), in which the French were defeated and Francis captured. This was a battle decided by the combination of pikemen and harquebusiers, although it is not easy to use Pavia to make definitive statements about the effectiveness of particular arms. Even more than most battles, it was confused, thanks to the effects of heavy early morning fog; in addition, many of the advances were both small-unit and uncoordinated, and the surviving sources contain discrepancies. As in most battles of the period, it would be misleading to emphasize the possibilities for, and extent of, central direction. Nevertheless, Spanish success in defeating repeated attacks by the French cavalry was crucial. Francis had attacked in a way that enabled the Spaniards to use their army to maximum advantage.

The captured Francis signed the Treaty of Madrid (14 January 1526) on Charles's terms, enabling Charles to invest his ally Francesco Sforza (1495–1535) with the Duchy of Milan. Nevertheless, once released, Francis claimed that his agreement had been extorted, repudiated the terms, agreed with Pope Clement VII (ruled 1523–1534), Sforza, Venice, and Florence to establish the league of Cognac (22 May 1526), and resumed the war. This led to the sack of Rome by Charles's unpaid troops in 1527, but repeated French defeats, especially at Landriano (20 June 1529), led Francis to accept the Treaty of Cambrai (3 August 1529), abandoning his Italian pretensions. Francesco Sforza was restored to Milan, but with the right to garrison the citadel reserved to Charles. The high rate of battles in this period in part reflected the effectiveness of siege artillery.

War that resumed after the death of Sforza in November 1535 led to a disputed succession in Milan. Francis invaded Italy in 1536, conquering Savoy and Piedmont in order to clear the route into northern Italy. However, the inability of either side to secure particular advantage led to an armistice in 1537, which became a ten-year truce in 1538. As this was on the basis of *uti possidetis* ('retaining what was held'), Francis was left in control of Savoy, while in 1540 Charles invested his son (later Philip II of Spain) with the Duchy of Milan.

The rivalry between Francis and Charles continued and was stirred by Charles's suspicion of links between Francis and the Ottomans. Francis, in turn, was encouraged by the failure of Charles's expedition against Algiers in late 1541. Francis attacked northern Italy the following year, beginning a new bout of campaigning. The French defeated the Spaniards at Ceresole in Piedmont (11 April 1544). As at Pavia, any summary of the battle underplays its confused variety. As a result of both the hilly topography and the distinct formations, the battle involved a number of struggles. Each side revealed innovation in deployment in the form of interspersed harquebusiers and pikemen, the resulting square formations designed to be both self-sustaining and mutually supporting, although it is probable that, as yet, this system had not attained the checkerboard regularity seen later in the century. Bringing harquebusiers into the pike formations drove up the casualties when they clashed. The French cavalry played a key role in Francis's victory.

Combined arms tactics are far easier to outline in theory than to execute under the strain of battle. The contrasting fighting characteristics of the individual arms operated very differently in particular circumstances, and this posed added problems for coordination. So also did the limited extent to which many generals and officers understood these characteristics and problems. The warfare of the period was characterized by military adaptation rather than the revolution that is sometimes discerned.

However, after Ceresole, a lack of pay made Francis's Swiss mercenaries unwilling to fight for Milan. Indeed, the Spaniards retained their fortified positions in Lombardy. Instead, the decisive campaigning, although without a battle, took place north of the Alps. An invasion of eastern France by Charles V led Francis to accept the Peace of Crépy in September 1544. This success, and a truce with the Ottomans in October 1545, enabled Charles to turn on and defeat the German Protestants in 1546–1547. In this he was helped by French neutrality, a consequence of the secret terms of the Peace of Crépy.

However, Charles was unable to produce a lasting religious settlement and this led to a French-supported rising in Germany in 1552. Francis I's successor, Henry II (ruled 1547–1559), exploited the situation to overrun Lorraine, while campaigning began in Italy. A truce negotiated in 1556 was short-lived, and conflict resumed in both Italy and the Low Countries in 1557. Spanish victories in the latter part of 1557 and 1558 at St. Quentin (10 August 1557) and Gravelines (13 July 1558) led Henry to accept the Treaty of Cateau-Cambrésis in

1559, which left Spain and her allies dominant in Italy. The Habsburgs had won the Italian Wars.

As in earlier periods, the wars of the 1550s in Italy saw not only a clash between major powers, but also related struggles involving others. Thus, Spain fought Pope Paul IV (ruled 1555–1559), and also supported Florence in attacking the republic of Siena in 1554; after a ten-month siege, Siena surrendered, to be annexed by Florence. This was an example of the extent to which divisions within Italy had interacted with those between the major powers; in 1552, Siena had rebelled against Spanish control and, in cooperation with France, seized the citadel from the Spaniards. Florence under the Medicis was, from the late 1520s, an ally of the Habsburgs.

The significance of the wars cannot be captured by a brief rendition of the fighting. The wars were more important for their political and cultural significance. They underlined the centrality of conflict in European culture and society and also helped ensure that Europe would have a "multipolar" character, with no one power dominant. The Habsburgs won, but France was not crushed. Thus Europe was not to be like China under the Ming and, later, the Manchu, or India under the Moguls.

See also **Charles V (Holy Roman Empire); Charles VIII (France); Francis I (France); Habsburg Dynasty; Habsburg Territories; Italian Wars (1494–1559); Louis XII (France); Naples, Kingdom of; Valois Dynasty (France).**

BIBLIOGRAPHY

Abulafia, David, ed. *The French Descent into Renaissance Italy, 1494–95: Antecedents and Effects.* Aldershot, U.K., and Brookfield, Vt., 1995.

Black, Jeremy. *European Warfare, 1494–1660.* New York, 2002.

JEREMY BLACK

HAGIOGRAPHY. In the wake of the Protestant and Catholic Reformations, when attitudes to the cult of saints provided one of the clearest boundaries marking the confessional divide for the people of early modern Europe, hagiographers were forced to refurbish and discipline their skills. However, the external spur of Protestant polemic (expressed most brilliantly and influentially perhaps in John Calvin's *Traicté des reliques* [Treatise on relics] of 1543) was not alone responsible for this development. Far more significant than even the humanist critique by Juan Luis Vives (1492–1540) and other medieval collections of saints' lives such as the *Golden Legend* (1265) was Roman Catholic liturgical reform. This principally took the form of an extensive pruning of the calendar of saints and lay at the center of the revision of service books such as the Roman Breviary (1568), the missal (1570), and the Roman Martyrology (1584). This was accompanied by extensive rewriting, in the spirit of concision and greater chronological precision, of the short Latin accounts of saints' deeds read out at matins and by the more centralized control of the cult of saints.

Supervised jointly by the two papal standing committees of cardinals, the Congregation of the Holy Office (founded 1542) and the Congregation of Rites and Ceremonies, the reform of sanctity centered on the tightening up of canonization procedure and the closely related imposition of a clear hierarchy of devotion between "saints," who could be universally venerated, and the "blessed," who were only permitted local or regional public veneration. Whereas central regulation had previously been focused primarily on universal cults, particular devotions were now also subject to careful control. This compelled local churches (and religious orders) throughout the Roman Catholic world to account for their cults and devotions.

They did so for the most part by adopting a polemical weapon that had initially been unsheathed by the Protestants—history. The years 1552–1559 saw the publication of four major Protestant martyrologies by Ludwig Rabus, Jean Crespin, Adriaen van Haemstede, and John Foxe. All of them attempted to make sense of the persecution of their fellow coreligionists by inserting their experience in a firmly historical interpretative template. In the case of Foxe (1516–1587), his first English edition of the *Actes and Monuments* (1563) traced the contemporary Roman Catholic persecution of true believers back from the reign of "Bloody Mary"—Queen Mary Tudor (ruled 1553–1558)—to 1000 C.E.

Similarly, to evoke and justify the antiquity of their devotions, regional and local Catholic counterparts to Foxe and his colleagues deployed not just straightforward saints' lives but also the full range of historico-literary conventions, which contemporaries grouped together under the umbrella term *historia sacra* (sacred history). Written in both Latin and the vernacular, these included civic chronicle, episcopal calendar, collective biography, sacred drama (both spoken and sung), and topographical description as well as individual saints' lives (which not uncommonly appeared together with hagiographical readings from the relevant office—the religious service chanted or read by monks, nuns, and priests—by way of an appendix).

This renaissance in local or regional hagiography had its universal counterpart in the massive Jesuit initiative that is the ongoing *Acta sanctorum* (1643ff.; Deeds of the saints). The origins of this work lie with Héribert Rosweyde (1569–1629), in whose regional survey of holy men and women of his native Belgium (at that time ruled as the Southern Netherlands by the Spanish Habsburgs), the *Fasti sanctorum quorum vitae in belgicis bibliotecis manuscriptae* (1607; Deeds of saints whose manuscript lives are in Belgian libraries), he outlined his idea for what became the *Acta sanctorum.*

Proceeding according to the calendar year beginning on 1 January, the *Acta sanctorum,* under the direction of Jean de Bolland (1596–1665), sought to provide its users with the most authentic, philologically accurate (multiple) accounts of the lives of the saints treated (1,170 for January alone). Each account was prefaced by a historical commentary and followed by exhaustive explanatory notes. However, the very scale and learning of this project (fifty-three volumes from 1643 to 1794, providing coverage down to 14 October) should not detract from its utilitarian, down-to-earth purpose. Rosweyde sought to reassert the Roman Catholic identity of the southern provinces, which were then a "frontier" zone bordering the Calvinist northern provinces controlled by Holland, through the celebration of their saintly heritage. What he sought to achieve for Belgium in the *Fasti,* he hoped to achieve for the entire Christian world (including, by implication, those areas that had recently been lost to the Protestant heretics) in the *Acta.*

Robert Bellarmine (1542–1621), the leading Catholic controversialist of his age, criticized Rosweyde's plan on the grounds that the *Acta,* through their very comprehensiveness, would provide too many hostages to fortune for the benefit of Protestant polemicists. Bellarmine held up as models the more selective, if still substantial, saints' life collections by Luigi Lippomano (1500–1559) and Laurentius Surius (1522–1578). The former's eight-volume *Sanctorum priscorum patrum vitae* (1551–1560; Lives of ancient and holy fathers) provided the basis for the latter's even larger *De probatis sanctorum historiis* (1570–1573; Proven histories of the saints). Significantly, both authors had been intimately involved with combating Protestantism; Lippomano as papal nuncio to Germany (1548–1550) and Surius as a convert from Lutheranism. Each volume of Lippomano's work contained an index relating particular passages to Roman Catholic dogma, while Surius sought to reclaim for Roman Catholicism its monopoly on the miraculous. Accordingly, the 699 lives he collected included accounts of no fewer than 6,538 miracles.

The latest scholarship has clearly demonstrated the protean role played by hagiography in early modern Europe as a focus of local, regional, or national pride as well as of confessional distinctiveness and spiritual food. To do justice to the very variety of the cultural work it carried out, it is more helpful to consider hagiography as a cluster of related literary genres than as a single one. Similarly, during this (or any earlier or later) period, the writing of saints' lives is more easily defined by its content than its forms, which were as various as its uses. Rather than ask what it was, it is more helpful to ask what hagiography did in early modern Europe (and beyond).

See also **Bellarmine, Robert; Biography and Autobiography; Martyrs and Martyrology; Reformation, Catholic.**

BIBLIOGRAPHY

Cochrane, Eric W. *Historians and Historiography in the Italian Renaissance.* Chicago, 1981. See especially Chapter 16, "Sacred History."

Ditchfield, Simon. *Liturgy, Sanctity and History in Tridentine Italy.* Cambridge, U.K., 1995.

Gregory, Brad S. *Salvation at Stake: Christian Martyrdom in Early Modern Europe.* Cambridge, Mass., 1999.

Soergel, Philip M. *Wondrous in His Saints: Counter-Reformation Propaganda in Bavaria*. Berkeley, 1993.

SIMON DITCHFIELD

HALLER, ALBRECHT VON (1708–1777), Swiss physician, anatomist, and poet. Haller was born in Bern, Switzerland, the youngest son of a lawyer. He began his medical studies in Tübingen in 1724, then moved to Leiden to continue his training under the famed Herman Boerhaave (1668–1738). After receiving his degree in 1727, Haller traveled in England, where he was enormously impressed with English science and literature; Paris, which he left in haste when pursued by authorities for dissecting cadavers in his rooms; and Basel, where he sojourned for two years, studying mathematics with the renowned Johann Bernoulli I (1667–1748) and teaching anatomy. Haller returned to Bern to practice medicine, but he was unsuccessful in obtaining an academic position and served as a librarian in the state library. During these early years Haller journeyed frequently through the Alps, collecting botanical specimens that led later to several publications on Swiss botany. Another result was Haller's most well-known poem, "Die Alpen" (1728), which was published in 1732 in *Versuch Schweizerischer Gedichte,* a collection of his poems that went through several editions.

When the University of Göttingen opened its doors in 1736, Haller was selected as professor of anatomy, surgery, and medicine. He remained at Göttingen for seventeen years, during which he published his most significant work in physiology, proposing the concept of muscular "irritability," in 1753. He developed one of the leading medical centers of Europe in Göttingen, was first president of its scientific society, and served as editor of an academic journal, in which he published some nine thousand book reviews.

One of Haller's greatest ambitions was to be elected to the ruling governing council (the "small council") in Bern, which would have catapulted him into the aristocracy. In 1753 he abruptly resigned his post in Göttingen to accept a minor administrative position in Bern. Named director of the saltworks in Roche five years later, Haller busied himself with public service but never advanced any further up the political scale.

Haller's scientific work continued to advance, however, particularly through his observations on chick development. These led in 1758 to his conversion to the theory of preexistence of germs (the idea that God had created all future organisms at once). Haller had previously supported the opposing theory of epigenesis (the theory of gradual development at each instance of reproduction). Over the next few years Haller published his masterful eight-volume *Elementa physiologiae corporis humani* (1757–1766; Elements of the physiology of the human body), which furthered his program of uniting anatomy and physiology under *anatomia animata* (living anatomy).

Haller has been characterized as "the last universal scholar" of the Enlightenment. As a scientist he contributed to medicine, physiology, anatomy, embryology, and botany. He wrote articles for over thirty academic journals and published poetry, three political novels, and works on political theory and religious apologetics. Never one to shy away from controversy, he was involved in numerous disputes in science and philosophy. Throughout his life Haller held fast to a Newtonian vision of nature deeply rooted in morality and religion and rejected the more radical facets of Enlightenment thought.

See also **Anatomy and Physiology; Boerhaave, Herman; Enlightenment; Scientific Revolution.**

BIBLIOGRAPHY

Primary Source

Haller, Albrecht von. *The Natural Philosophy of Albrecht von Haller*. Edited by Shirley A. Roe. New York, 1981. Collection of primary and secondary sources.

Secondary Sources

Toellner, Richard. *Albrecht von Haller: Über die Einheit im Denken des letzten Universalgelehrten*. Sudhoffs Archive Beihefte, no. 10. Wiesbaden, 1971.

Wiswall, Dorothy Roller. *A Comparison of Selected Poetic and Scientific Works of Albrecht von Haller*. Bern, 1981.

SHIRLEY A. ROE

HALS, FRANS (c. 1581/85–1666), Dutch painter. Born in Antwerp, Hals emigrated to Haarlem with his family before 1591. There, he learned his trade from the painter, theorist, and historian Karel van Mander (1548–1606) prior to van Mander's death in 1606. As Hals did not enter the painters' guild in Haarlem until 1610, it is possible that he trained with, or worked as a journeyman for, an additional master in the interim. Shortly before joining the guild, Hals married Anneke Harmensdochter, but was widowed in 1615. Two years later, Hals wedded Lysbeth Reyniers, with whom he raised fourteen children from both marriages. Perhaps in part to ease the strain of supporting his large family, Hals taught an unusually large number of pupils, many of whom went on to enjoy accomplished careers. Yet despite painting actively until the end of his life, Hals required subsistence from the Old Men's Almshouse in Haarlem, whose regents he painted in 1664, before dying destitute in 1666.

During his long career Hals painted individual portraits, primarily of the Haarlem elite; group portraits of the local militia officers and regents of charitable institutions; and single figure genre paintings. In the 1610s and 1620s, Hals produced genre imagery and portraits concurrently. His portraits from this period were highly finished and crafted in fine detail, while his genre images were much more roughly executed. Hals's pendants of Jacob Pietersz Olijcan and Aletta Hanemans from 1625 show precisely rendered embroidered damask patterning and elegantly transcribed lace borders at both the cuff and the collar. In contrast, the allegorical representation of hearing, *Boy Holding a Flute (Hearing)*, (1626–1628; Staatliches Museum, Schwerin) displays a summary description of the youth's garments. Here, Hals employed broad sweeps rather than delicate lines to mark the white cuff, and the left shoulder between collar and jerkin is so roughly painted that the anatomical structure blurs into a series of juxtaposed swatches of color. When he devoted himself entirely to portraiture (from the late 1630s onward), Hals increasingly favored constructing his paintings from assemblages of unblended brushstrokes. In *Claes Duyst van Voorhout* (c. 1638; Metropolitan Museum, New York) Hals captured the play of light on the sitter's gray jacket by layering short horizontal jabs of white and light yellow pigments rather than blending his brushwork to craft supple color gradations, as he had in his earlier portraits. By the 1660s, Hals's

Frans Hals. *The Merry Drinker,* c. 1628–1630. ©Francis G. Mayer/Corbis

Portrait of a Man (Museum of Fine Arts, Boston) presents the sitter's red kimono as a nearly flat surface of frenetic brushwork that shows little concern for the delineation of the body beneath it. Though not as rough as the sleeve, Hals composed the man's face as a patchwork of largely unmodulated color on which shadow and highlight are set side by side but not blended together, leaving each individual touch exposed. Unlike the works of his contemporaries that exhibited meticulous surfaces of seamlessly woven brushwork, Hals's late portraits recall the sketchy appearance of his earlier genre paintings.

Hals offered his viewers a naturalistic yet artful manner. As the historian Theodorus Schrevelius wrote in 1648, "His paintings are imbued with such force and vitality that he seems to surpass nature herself with his brush. This is seen in all his portraits . . . which are colored in such a way that they seem to live and breathe" (Schrevelius, p. 383). Hals's distinct manner, seen, for example, in his sketchy contours, heightened the sense of the sitters' activity, capturing not only his subjects' appearance but also their vivacity. In his group portraits, such as *The*

Officers of the St. Hadrian Civic Guard from 1627 (Frans Halsmuseum, Haarlem), Hals further activated these pieces by dispersing the bustle across the canvas through a series of uniquely posed and engaged sitters. In both his group and individual portraits Hals's unblended, broad strokes also exhibited the artist's masterful facility in handling paint. It is highly likely that seventeenth-century audiences perceived Hals's flourishes as marks of his virtuosity. In this way, Hals's paintings could have been appreciated both as representations of individuals and as objects of art.

Regard for Hals's paintings plummeted throughout the eighteenth century as his rough manner clashed with the period's more refined aesthetic. It was not until the late nineteenth century that appreciation for Hals's work was resurrected. At that time, painters like Manet and Van Gogh perceived Hals's style to be highly individualized and thus modeled their own approaches upon his direct relationship to his sitters and admired his visible, bravura brushwork. This emulation of Hals by pioneering artists demonstrates the important role that Hals played in the construction of modern conceptions of art and artistry.

See also **Netherlands, Art in the.**

BIBLIOGRAPHY

Grimm, Claus. *Frans Hals: The Complete Work*. Translated by Jürgen Riehle. New York, 1990.

Schrevelius, Theodorus. *Harlemias ofte, om beter te seggen, de eerste stichtinghe der stadt Haerlem*. Haarlem, 1648.

Slive, Seymour. *Frans Hals*. 3 vols. Washington, D.C., 1970–1974.

Slive, Seymour, ed. *Frans Hals*. Exh. cat. Munich and New York, 1989.

CHRISTOPHER D. M. ATKINS

HAMBURG. Located along the Elbe River in northern Germany, Hamburg developed into one of the largest cities of the Holy Roman Empire. Between the latter half of the fifteenth century and the era of the Thirty Years' War (1618–1648), it grew from about 10,000 to 50,000 inhabitants. In the early eighteenth century that number had risen to 75,000. By 1787 it reached 100,000, and in the era of French expansion, 130,000. The growth was not steady; for example, the plague years 1712 and 1713 cost many thousands of lives.

The city was a largely independent republic governed by a council of citizens, predominantly merchants and lawyers by profession. Since 1483 the right of political participation had been granted to eligible property-owning male inhabitants who swore an oath of citizenship. The year 1528 marked the successful and peaceful establishment of Lutheranism as the city's official religion, after which only Lutherans enjoyed full political privileges. The reformer Johann Bugenhagen (1485–1558) composed a church ordinance for Hamburg, which was adopted in 1529. That year the city also underwent a major constitutional reform. Thereafter, the government was composed of a council *(Rat* or *Senat)* of twenty-four members and a college *(Kollegium)* of 144 citizens' representatives, who came in equal numbers from the four parish districts of St. Jacobi, St. Nikolai, St. Petri, and St. Katarinen. With the addition in 1685 of a fifth district, St. Michaelis, the citizens' college grew to 180 members.

Constitutional tensions grew throughout the seventeenth century because some factions of the citizenry felt the council wielded power autocratically. A major crisis came in 1699 when the traditional constitutional order was suspended under pressure from the guilds. The period of political experimentation ended in 1708 when imperial troops arrived to reestablish the old order. The result was the constitutional recess of 1712, in which council and citizens' college were declared equal partners in Hamburg's governance. This arrangement lasted until 1806.

Since the late fifteenth century the Danish monarchy had had hopes of forcing Hamburg to submit to its authority, and Danish forces even laid siege to the city unsuccessfully in 1686. The 1626 completion of the city's modern fortress walls proved an advantage against Danish challenges, as well as against the conflicts of the Thirty Years' War, during which Hamburg remained neutral and unscathed. Although Hamburg was ostensibly in the imperial orbit for most of the early modern era, it was not until 1768, when Denmark recognized the city's independence, that it officially joined the ranks of the imperial free cities. Throughout its history Hamburg has been a major commercial port. Until

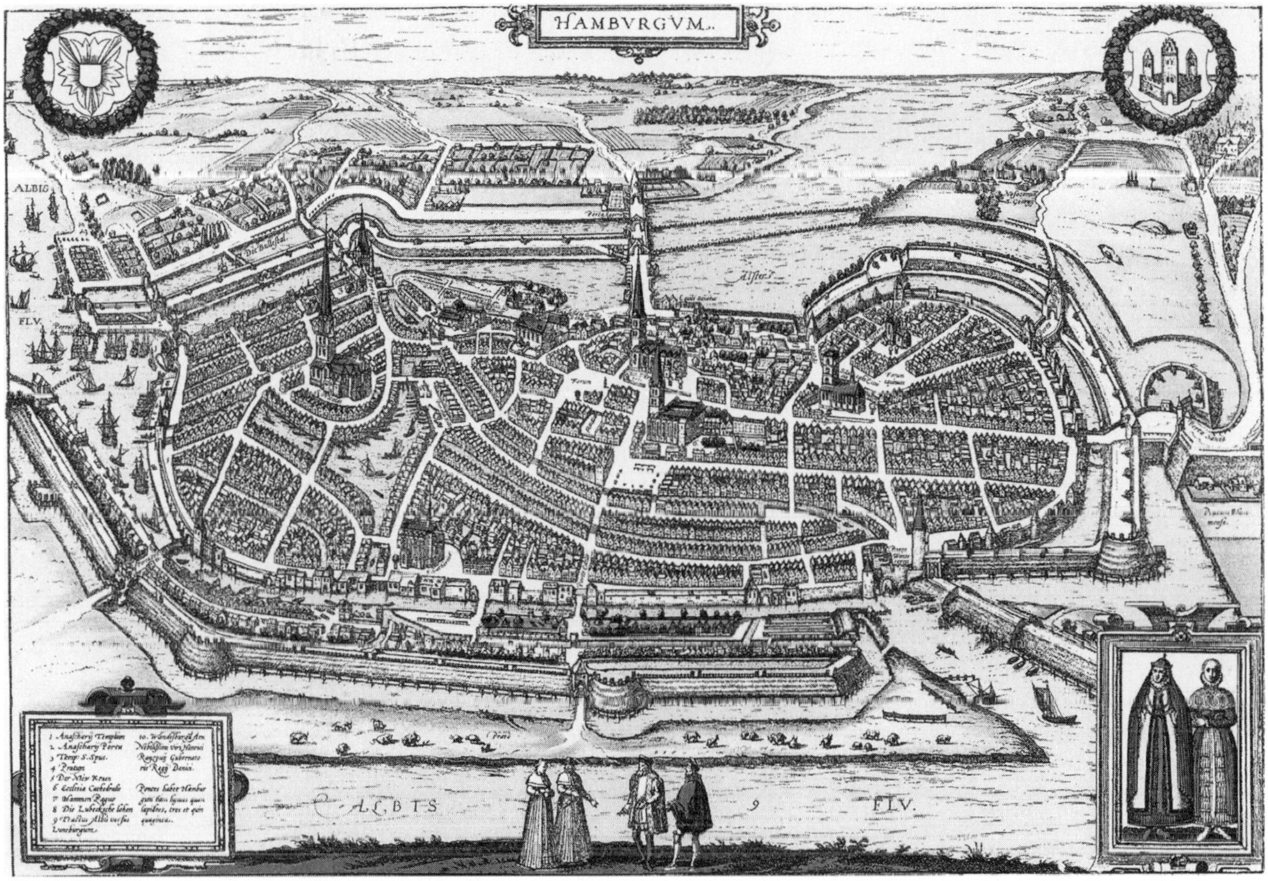

Hamburg. A reproduction of a map of Hamburg from Georg Braun and Franz Hogenberg's *Civitates Orbis Terrarum,* the first collection of printed town plans, originally published in 1573. MAP COLLECTION, STERLING MEMORIAL LIBRARY, YALE UNIVERSITY

the Hansa dissolved in the seventeenth century, Hamburg was one of the long-standing members of the loose economic and political alliance. In 1558 it opened its stock exchange, the first in a German territory, and in 1619 its first merchant bank was founded. The city's merchants shipped goods all across Europe, and by the end of the eighteenth century destinations included ports worldwide. Other major economic activities included whaling, insurance, sugar refining, textile production, and tobacco preparation.

By the seventeenth century confessional outsiders made up a significant minority of the city's population, and non-Lutherans contributed in important ways to the city's economy. For political and economic reasons the council allowed members of the best established of non-Lutheran communities (Calvinists, Catholics, Jews, and Mennonites) to settle in Hamburg. Nonetheless, because of pressure from Lutheran clergymen, religious minority communities were denied the privilege of practicing religious rites publicly in the city; non-Lutheran religious services were usually held in nearby Altona. This restriction on public worship was removed in 1785 for Calvinists and Catholics only. Non-Lutheran Christians could become citizens, albeit with limited rights of political participation. Probably the city's best-known non-Lutheran resident was the Jewish diarist Glueckel von Hameln (1646–1724).

Among the city's cultural leaders were Gerhard Schott (1641–1702), founder of the first public opera in the German territories; the organ builder Arp Schnitger (1648–1719); and the composers Georg Philipp Telemann (1681–1767) and Carl Philipp Emanuel Bach (1714–1788). Founded in 1765, the Hamburger Gesellschaft zur Beförderung der Künste und nützlichen Gewerbe (Hamburg society for the encouragement of the arts and useful crafts; also known as the Patriotische Gesellschaft or Patriotic Society) stands out among many institutions of

Enlightenment-era public life. Its founding members included the mathematics professor Johann Georg Büsch (1728–1800), the philosopher Hermann Samuel Reimarus (1694–1768), and the architect Ernst Georg Sonnin (1713–1794). The literary masters Gotthold Ephraim Lessing (1729–1781) and Friedrich Gottlieb Klopstock (1724–1803) both spent time in Hamburg. Philipp Otto Runge (1777–1810) is one of Hamburg's best-known painters.

See also **Free and Imperial Cities; Hansa; Holy Roman Empire; Lutheranism.**

BIBLIOGRAPHY

Jochmann, Werner, and Hans-Dieter Loose, eds. *Hamburg: Geschichte der Stadt und ihrer Bewohner.* 2 vols. Hamburg, 1982.

Kopitzsch, Franklin. *Grundzüge einer Sozialgeschichte der Aufklärung in Hamburg und Altona.* Hamburg, 1982. Reprint, 1990.

Kopitzsch, Franklin, and Daniel Tilgner, eds. *Hamburg-Lexikon.* Hamburg, 1998. Reprint, 2000.

Lindemann, Mary. *Patriots and Paupers: Hamburg, 1712–1830.* New York, 1990.

Whaley, Joachim. *Religious Toleration and Social Change in Hamburg, 1529–1819.* Cambridge, U.K., 1985. Reprint, 2002.

Zeitschrift des Vereins für Hamburgische Geschichte. 1841–.

MICHAEL D. DRIEDGER

HANDEL, GEORGE FRIDERIC

HANDEL, GEORGE FRIDERIC (1685–1759), German-born musician eventually hailed as "England's national composer." He was the first great composer who broke free of church and court patronage and earned a living directly from the public; England was perhaps the only country that could provide such support in his time.

Born Georg Friedrich Händel at Halle, Lower Saxony, on 23 February 1685, he was the son of a sixty-three-year-old barber-surgeon. His early talents persuaded his father to let him study music as well as law, and he took lessons from the local organist, Friedrich Wilhelm Zachau (1663–1712). After a year as organist of the Calvinist Domkirche (cathedral), he traveled to Hamburg, where he gained his first experience of opera, playing violin and harpsichord under the distinguished composer Reinhardt Keiser (1673–1739) and later composing operas and concertos. He then traveled to the fountainhead of music, Italy, where he stayed for nearly four years (1706–1710), dividing his time between Florence, Rome, Venice, and Naples. There he composed and performed music in many forms, developing the extroverted, cosmopolitan manner that so clearly distinguishes him from his contemporary Johann Sebastian Bach (1685–1750).

In January 1710 he took up an appointment as *Kapellmeister* (director of music) at the court of George, elector of Hanover (soon to become George I of England). In that year he paid his first visit to London, where he was commissioned to write an opera, *Rinaldo,* for the Queen's Theatre in the Haymarket.

In the spring of 1712 Handel left Hanover for England, which was to be his home for the rest of his life, despite frequent visits to the Continent. He rapidly became the most sought-after composer in London. *Rinaldo* had been an astonishing success, and was decisive in the establishment of Italian opera as the chief entertainment of the British aristocracy. His *Te Deum,* performed on 7 July 1713, to celebrate the Peace of Utrecht, at once displaced Henry Purcell's as the standard piece for royal and national celebrations. After a period as private musician to the earl of Carnarvon, later duke of Chandos (1717–1718), at Cannons, his recently built mansion at Edgware, Handel was engaged as the chief composer in a series of London opera schemes. The most brilliant was the Royal Academy of Music (1719–1727), which sponsored several of his greatest operas, including *Giulio Cesare* (1724) and *Rodelinda* (1725). He enjoyed the strong support of King George II and Queen Caroline, but became a political pawn in the running feud between the king's Whig administration and the rival faction surrounding Frederick, Prince of Wales. He continued to produce operas until 1741, composing forty-two in all, but with fitful success.

Looking for a more stable source of support, Handel chanced on the oratorio. A pirated version of his *Esther,* written for Cannons in 1718, was mounted at a London tavern in 1733. Always a keen businessman, Handel competed, putting on a rival performance at the opera house with additional mu-

George Frideric Handel. Contemporary drawing by an unknown artist. ©BETTMANN/CORBIS

sic. The bishop of London would not allow acting or costumes to represent a sacred subject, but *Esther* was still conceived as a drama, and was sung on stage against a scenic backdrop. It allowed plenty of scope for Handel's dramatic genius, as expressed in the operatic forms of recitative and aria. The public liked the use of the English language, the biblical stories familiar to all, and the choruses in the English ceremonial style they knew and loved.

Handel developed this formula in such masterpieces as *Saul* (1739), *Samson* (1744), *Solomon* (1748), and *Jephtha* (1751). He varied it by choosing mythological subjects in *Semele* (1744) and *Hercules* (1745), and, on the other hand, by using librettos compiled directly from the Bible in *Israel in Egypt* (1738) and *Messiah* (1742). In his later performances of *Messiah* at the Foundling Hospital chapel he took the first step that moved his oratorios away from the theater toward the church. The gigantic Handel Commemorations at Westminster Abbey (1784–1791) presented his works as monuments of the religious sublime, playing down the subtle interplay of human character that had always been an important inspiration of his greatest dramatic music.

Handel's ceremonial music epitomizes the grandeur and brilliance of the baroque. The *Royal Fireworks Music* and *Water Music* have proved to be the most durable occasional music ever written. He also contributed fine orchestral concertos, chamber works, keyboard music, and organ voluntaries, and was responsible for a new form, the organ concerto, originally played between the acts of his oratorios.

See also **Music; Opera.**

BIBLIOGRAPHY

Dean, Winton. *Handel's Dramatic Masques and Oratorios.* London, 1959.

Lang, Paul Henry. *George Frideric Handel.* New York, 1966.

Smith, Ruth. *Handel's Oratorios and Eighteenth-Century Thought.* Cambridge, U.K., 1995.

NICHOLAS TEMPERLEY

HANOVER. Hanover was one of the most important territories in the Holy Roman Empire, situated in the Lower Saxon region *(Kreis)* of northern Germany. It was ruled from the twelfth century by the Guelphs (Welfen), a once-powerful family that declined through frequent dynastic partitions. There were generally two major lines, designated by their principal duchies in Lüneburg and Wolfenbüttel. The latter was initially more important and became more generally known as Brunswick (Braunschweig) by the eighteenth century. Both lines frequently subdivided, with the Lüneburg branch splitting into the duchies of Celle and Calenberg in 1641. Hanover developed from the latter, taking its name from its principal town where the ruling branch set up residence in 1636. The entire area was flat and primarily agrarian, particularly with the decline of the Lüneburg salt springs and the mining region bordering the Harz Mountains after the sixteenth century.

The introduction of the Reformation was violently opposed by Duke Henry of Brunswick-Wolfenbüttel (ruled 1514–1568) until he was defeated by the Protestant Schmalkaldic League between 1542 and 1547. Thereafter, the Guelphs were solidly Lutheran and hoped to extend their regional influence by secularizing the neighboring prince bishoprics of Hildesheim, Osnabrück, and Paderborn. These ambitions drove them to ally first with Denmark, 1625–1629, and then with Sweden after 1631 during the Thirty Years' War, but they lacked the strength for a truly independent policy and shared the local defeats of their allies. Forced to make peace with the emperor in 1641, the Hanoverians had to be satisfied with partial control of Osnabrück, where their rule alternated with that of a local Catholic bishop.

The groundwork for Hanover's subsequent rise was laid by Duke John Frederick (1625–1679), who seized control of the duchy from his relations in 1665 and initiated a ruthless policy of military expansion, hiring troops to Venice, France, Spain, England, the Dutch Republic, and the emperor. His brother, Ernst August (1629–1698), continued this strategy after 1679, culminating in an alliance with Holy Roman emperor Leopold I. In return for substantial financial and military support against the Ottomans, Leopold made Ernst August an elector *(Kurfürst),* greatly increasing his prestige and influence within the empire. The ensuing controversy dominated imperial politics into the 1720s when an agreement was reached with the Wolfenbüttel line allowing them to inherit the new title if the Hanoverians died out. The other princes formally recognized it in 1708. Leopold also confirmed Ernst August's introduction of primogeniture, paving the way for his successor, George Louis (1660–1727), to inherit Celle when that line died out in 1705, doubling his territory. Within ten years, the new elector, whose mother was the granddaughter of James I of England, was catapulted into the front rank of European royalty when he inherited the British crown as George I with the backing of the English Parliament in 1714. He continued to pursue a primarily Hanoverian policy, joining the war against Sweden to capture its German possessions of Bremen and Verden in 1715. With the acquisition of the tiny county of Bentheim in 1752, Hanover reached its maximum extent of 10,214 square miles (26,455 square kilometers), and its population climbed slowly to 800,000 by 1803.

While the king-electors still visited Hanover, they became progressively more British than German, leaving government to the local nobles, who had a strong sense of responsibility, self-esteem, and corporate identity. Their rule was slow, orderly and mild. Although the new university at Göttingen, founded in 1734 and opened in 1737, rapidly became a model of enlightened learning, government remained conservative. Hanover remained a strategic liability for Britain until it was seized by France in 1803. The connection to Britain was severed in 1837 when Hanover became an independent kingdom until its annexation by Prussia in 1866.

See also **George I (England); Hanoverian Dynasty (England); Saxony.**

BIBLIOGRAPHY

Birke, Adolf M., and Kurt Kluxen, eds. *England und Hannover= England and Hanover.* Munich, 1986.

Chance, John Frederick. *George I and the Northern War. A Study of British-Hanoverian Policy in the North of Europe in the Years 1709 to 1720.* London, 1909.

Dann, Uriel. *Hanover and Britain 1740–1760: Diplomacy and Survival.* Leicester, U.K., and Irvington, N.Y., 1991.

Hatton, Ragnhild. *George I: Elector and King.* Cambridge, Mass., 1978.

Hodgskin, Thomas. *Travels in the North of Germany: Describing the Present State of the Social and Political Institutions* . . . 2 vols. Reprint. New York, 1969. Originally published Edinburgh, 1820.

Schnath, Georg. *Geschichte Hannovers im Zeitalter der neunten Kur und der englischen Sukzession 1674–1714.* 5 vols. Hildesheim, 1938–1982.

PETER H. WILSON

HANOVERIAN DYNASTY (GREAT BRITAIN). Under the terms of the 1701 Act of Settlement, on the death of Queen Anne on 1 August 1714 the joint crowns of England and Scotland fell to George Ludwig, elector of Hanover, a north German territory of medium size and power. He was the son of Sophie, the granddaughter of James I of England. George I, as he was styled in Britain, spoke no English and throughout his reign remained more attached to his native land (to which he frequently returned) than to his adopted kingdom, which he ruled until his death in 1727. He was succeeded by his son George II (ruled 1727–1760), now chiefly remembered for his military valor. He became the last British monarch to lead his troops into battle in person, but at home he also had to fend off a serious challenge to his rule in the uprising led by Charles Edward Stuart ("Bonnie Prince Charlie") in 1745. George II's eldest son, Frederick, Prince of Wales, predeceased him, leaving the king's 22-year-old grandson to succeed him as George III. George was the first of the Hanoverians to be born in England, and he was to enjoy an exceptionally long reign of sixty years, which was, however, punctuated by crises overseas such as the loss of the American colonies in 1783 and the outbreak of the French Revolution in 1789. George III was followed on the throne by two of his sons (George IV [ruled 1820–1830] and William IV [1830–1837]) and his granddaughter (Victoria [1837–1901]), making the Hanoverian dynasty one of the most enduring in British history. Despite uprisings seeking the restoration of the male line of the house of Stuart in 1715 and 1745, the Hanoverian age marked a long period of relative domestic stability, which allowed Britain to become a major imperial power.

See also **Anne (England); George I (Great Britain); George II (Great Britain); George III (Great Britain); Jacobitism.**

BIBLIOGRAPHY

Ayling, Stanley. *George the Third.* London, 1972.

Brooke, John. *King George III.* London, 1972.

Hatton, Ragnhild. *George I: Elector and King.* London, 1978.

Newman, Gerald, ed. *Britain in the Hanoverian Age, 1714–1837.* New York, 1997.

Owen, John B. "George II Reconsidered." In *Statesmen, Scholars and Merchants,* edited by Anne Whiteman, John S. Bromley, and Peter G. M. Dickson, pp. 113–134. Oxford, 1973.

Trench, Charles Pocklington Chenevix. *George II.* London, 1973.

HANNES KLEINEKE

HANSA. The Hansa was a league of northern European cities that emerged in the fourteenth century. Along with other town leagues that predate the Hansa, such urban leagues became a common means for townsmen to extend their influence and establish favorable trading conditions at a time when broader state authority was generally too weak to provide needed assistance. The extremely loose Hanseatic confederation was made up largely of towns in the Holy Roman Empire, which enjoyed a great deal of political autonomy. The Hansa acted in concert to protect and promote the commercial position of the members. Lübeck was the leader and often the site of meetings of the assembly of town representatives, the *Hansetag.* It began to take joint action certainly by the late thirteenth century, gaining concessions in Flanders and Norway. The league developed its enduring organization during the 1367–1370 war against Denmark. After that it was a major political force in the Baltic and North Seas. A tax voted by the towns on their trade paid for a fleet, which brought naval victory and, with the subsequent Peace of Stralsund, special trading rights in Danish markets. The Hansa had "factories" (trading centers) in Bruges, London, Bergen, and Novgorod. Merchants from member towns could trade and live there, enjoying immunity from local taxes and laws, important concessions won by the Hansa. In the fifteenth century internal divisions became clear as the towns of the Rhine Valley led by Cologne and the Prussian towns led by Gdańsk (Danzig) did not always find their commercial and political interests coinciding with those of the Wendish towns in northeastern Germany and especially with the most powerful one, Lübeck. Wars against the dukes of Burgundy, ending in peace in 1441, and against England, ending in peace in 1474, illustrated these divisions as many towns refused to follow the lead of Lübeck. Conscious of the disadvantages to domestic merchants and to their own incomes from concessions forced on them by the Hansa, sixteenth-century centralizing monarchs from England to Russia and everywhere in between worked to undermine the power of the confederation. The factories were closed, tariff advantages were rescinded, and then the naval power of the Hansa—which meant that of Lübeck and a few nearby towns—was broken as the navies of Denmark and Sweden became much more powerful. The Hansa shrank in numbers, and its political influence declined. Though most Hanseatic towns were Lutheran, the league played little role in the religious wars and could not form a consistent policy. The prosperity of the Hansa was based on the export of a limited range of primary goods, grain but also forest products and salted herring from the

Baltic to western Europe in exchange for manufactures and for silver. Already by 1400 western Europeans were gradually supplanting production of beer, a major export of Bremen and Hamburg, and production of salted herring, a major export from Scania in southern Sweden. As western Europeans found themselves able to meet their own needs for food grains in the second half of the seventeenth century, the economic advantages of the Hanseatic towns were further eroded. After a hiatus of thirty-nine years, the last meeting of the Hansetag was held in 1668. It ended indecisively and after that the Hansa in effect no longer existed. Despite the end of its political influence, the towns that belonged or had belonged to the Hansa still enjoyed in the eighteenth century a level of prosperity as great as or greater than in the past.

See also **Commerce and Markets; Hamburg; Lübeck; Shipping.**

BIBLIOGRAPHY

Dollinger, Philippe. *The German Hansa.* Translated and edited by D. S. Ault and S. H. Steinberg. Stanford, 1970.

Glete, Jan. *Warfare at Sea 1500–1650: Maritime Conflicts and the Transformation of Europe.* London, 2000.

Hammel-Kiesow, Rolf. *Die Hanse.* Munich, 2000.

Unger, Richard W. *Ships and Shipping in the North Sea and Atlantic, 1400–1800.* Aldershot, U.K., 1997.

RICHARD W. UNGER

HANSEATIC LEAGUE. *See* Hansa.

See **Hansa.**

HAREM. The Arabic term *harem* means a forbidden and sacred space that describes inviolable sanctuaries like the holy cities of Mecca and Medina *(haremeyn-i sharifeyn)* and the Muslim household, which were off limits to outsiders who were non-Muslims in the former case and unrelated men in the latter. In the ordinary meaning of the word *harem* usually refers to the extended household and may or may not refer to a polygamous household. Ruling-class harems, however, were usually polygamous and contained several servants and slaves in addition to close relatives.

The institution of the imperial harem can be traced back to the ancient Near East. It became firmly established under the Abbasid caliphs of Baghdad (750–1258) and became associated in the West with the Ottoman (1300–1923), Mamluk (1250–1517), Safavid (1501–1732), and Mughal (1526–1739) imperial and ruling-class households during the early modern period.

The notions of Muslim sexuality and harem life were exaggerated if not completely inaccurate in western artistic and literary representations. European artists like Jean-Auguste-Dominique Ingres *(La grande odalisque* and *The Turkish Bath),* John Fredrick Lewis *(Life in the Harem),* Jean-Leon Gérôme *(The Bath),* and Anton Ignaz Melling *(Interior of the Palace of Hatice Sultana* and *The Royal Harem)* depicted the harem life in numerous paintings in the eighteenth and nineteenth centuries. Ottoman images of harem life by indigenous artists like Levnî, Buharî, and Enderunî Fazil Bey, on the other hand, were more realistic and less obsessed with nudity and overt sexuality than the European artists. Sexuality and reproduction were only one aspect of harem life in the Muslim East. Some Ottoman sultans displayed an insatiable appetite for women, but even they had to follow the rigid rules of conduct associated with the imperial harem. The *valide-sultan* ('queen mother') set these rules and wielded great power as the head of the harem hierarchy. She chose the sexual partners for her sons and was in charge of training all the women. The chief black eunuch *(kizlar ağasi)* guarded the harem and worked closely with the *valide-sultan.* He was also in charge of all imperial religious and charitable foundations and became an important personality in harem politics. He represented the link between the imperial harem and the outside world. However, not all palace women remained completely confined to the harem. Some women graduated from their palace training and were manumitted and married to high dignitaries in the empire. They maintained their ties with the palace and played an important role in Ottoman politics. In the eighteenth century Ottoman princesses were able to move out of the Topkapi Palace harem and set up private mansions along the Bosphorus. Although not really independent of the sultan, they had large retinues and held enormous wealth as tax farmers and landowners.

Harem. The throne room in the Topkapi Palace harem. Built by Mehmed II in 1453, Topkapi served as the home of the Ottoman sultans. ©WOLFGANG KAEHLER/CORBIS

Slavery and polygamy were the backbone of this institution, which received sanction in Islamic practice. The Koran allowed Muslim men to marry four legal wives and have an unlimited number of concubines. The prophet Mohammed himself had eleven legal wives and several concubines. Despite this Koranic injunction, only 2 to 3 percent of Muslim men practiced polygamy in the Ottoman Empire. However, concubinage was probably more widespread, at least in the cities, due to the ready availability of female slaves. Many households in Istanbul contained at least one female slave who performed household duties. Slaves had limited legal rights but could move to better positions once they converted to Islam and bore children. The Koran encouraged Muslim men to marry their slaves (Sura 24:30). Muslim men were permitted to marry non-Muslim women, including their concubines, while Muslim women could not marry anyone but free Muslim men. Moreover, Muslim women were forbidden from having more than one husband at the same time. The Koran considered the children of concubines legitimate and equal in rights to children born to free women. It also banned the prostitution of female slaves by their master and promoted their fair treatment and manumission. However, these proscriptions could not always be enforced.

The institution of the imperial harem as it developed in the Ottoman Empire was an abrogation of Islamic principles although it received religious sanction from the Hanafi *ʿulema* ('scholars'). The Koran encouraged the manumission of slaves and discouraged concubinage. The Ottoman sultans fully adopted this institution when the empire became centralized in the fifteenth century. The flow

Harem. *Turkish Women in the Harem,* a print from the *Encyclopedia of Voyages* by Jacques Grasset de St. Saveur, 1796. Grasset's somewhat fanciful depictions of characters from around the world focus particularly on the subjects' mode of dress. ©GIANNI GAGLI ORTI/CORBIS

of male and female slaves increased with military victories in the Balkans. The sultan claimed one-fifth of the war booty, which included male and female slaves. The palace also purchased slaves from the slave market. A good proportion of the population of Istanbul was of servile background during the early modern period. The Ottomans incorporated many male slaves into the military system, while female slaves ended up in domestic households, with the youngest and most beautiful entering the royal household. These women received training in various skills and a salary depending on their rank within the harem.

Some of the women attracted the attention of the sultan and became his *haseki,* or favorite concubine (see Peirce). If a haseki bore the sultan a son, she moved up in the hierarchy and ultimately could become the *valide-sultan* if her son inherited the Ottoman throne. The Ottoman sultans adopted a "one concubine, one son" policy to avoid the concentration of power in the hands of one concubine and to prevent succession crises, which had become endemic to the empire. Supposedly the sultan stopped sleeping with a concubine once she bore him a son.

The *haseki* played an important role in ensuring succession for her son. Some favorites like Hürrem, Nurbanu, and Kösem, who became valide-sultans, wielded enormous power and prestige in the harem and even shaped the direction of Ottoman politics. They formed networks of power with their sons, daughters, and sons-in-law within and outside the palace. Sometimes, this led to intense rivalry and political tensions that could end up in the murder of the *valide-sultan* if her faction lost out. The *valide-sultans* received the highest salary in the harem and amassed great fortunes. They set up numerous charitable foundations all over the empire that carried their name and imperial legacy. Because of the *valide-sultans*' influence over the sultans and their active role in politics, they received bad reputations in Ottoman chronicles.

The Ottoman princesses, blood relatives of the dynasts, fared better and became repositories of Ottoman legitimacy and prestige. Many married grand viziers and high officials and set up their own households outside the Topkapi palace. Their husbands were required to give up their polygamous households before the marriage to an Ottoman princess could take place. They also had to provide a rich bride price and support the opulent lifestyle of their princess-wives. The Ottoman princesses lived in elaborate mansions and had their own female retinue made up of slaves. Lady Mary Montagu, the wife of the English ambassador to the Ottoman Empire, visited the young Fatma Sultan, the daughter of Ahmed III (1703–1730) in Edirne and was impressed by her charming hostess in 1717. She became a regular visitor to the harem of great ladies and tried to correct the distorted view of her compatriots in her letters to her friends and relatives in London. She commented about the status of Muslim women and the great prestige and freedom enjoyed by upper class Ottoman women. The western image of oppressed and confined Muslim women, however, gained more currency in the writings of Enlightenment philosophers and European travelers.

See also **Ottoman Dynasty; Ottoman Empire; Sultan; Topkapi Palace.**

BIBLIOGRAPHY

Alderson, A. D. *The Structure of the Ottoman Dynasty.* Oxford, 1956.

Arberry, A. J. *The Koran Interpreted.* New York, 1973.

Montagu, Lady Mary. *Letters from the Levant during the Embassy to Constantinople, 1716–18.* New York, 1971.

Peirce, Leslie P. *The Imperial Harem: Women and Sovereignty in the Ottoman Empire.* Oxford and New York, 1993.

Penzer, N. M. *The Harem.* London. 1936.

Stevens, Mary Anne, ed. *The Orientalists: Delacroix to Matisse.* New York, 1984.

Uluçay, Çağatay. *Harem II.* Ankara, 1992.

Zarinebaf-Shahr, Fariba. "The Wealth of Ottoman Princesses during the Tulip Period." In *The Great Ottoman-Turkish Civilization.* Vol 2, edited by Kemal Çiçek. Ankara, 2000.

FARIBA ZARINEBAF

HARLEY, ROBERT (1661–1724), British politician. Robert Harley headed the Tory ministry from 1710 to 1714. Although by background a Whig and dissenter, he eventually changed his political affiliation, becoming leader of the Tory and Anglican governing regime.

Born in London on 5 December 1661, the eldest son of Sir Edward Harley and Abigail Harley, daughter of Nathaniel Stephens, Robert Harley received a private education and was admitted to the Inner Temple on 18 March 1682, though never called to the bar. During the Glorious Revolution of 1688 he assisted his father in raising a regiment of cavalry and took part in capturing the city of Worcester on behalf of William III (ruled 1689–1702). In March 1689 Harley was appointed high sheriff of Herefordshire and was elected to Parliament for the borough of Tregoney until 1690, when he became member of Parliament for New Radnor, a seat he retained until his elevation to a peerage. In this position he advanced numerous legislative measures, including the Triennial Bill, which provided that elections be held at intervals no longer than three years, the National Land Bank, and the reduction in army strength following the Treaty of Ryswick (1697). Harley was speaker of the commons between 1701 and 1705 and served as secretary of state from 1704 to 1708, when, due to political intrigues, he was forced to resign.

With the collapse of the Marlborough Godolphin coalition in 1710, Harley returned to office as chancellor of the exchequer. After the Tory election landslide of 1710, he became head of a reconstructed administration and in 1711 was elevated to an earldom (Oxford). He launched the South Sea Company in 1711 and initiated the complex deliberation with France that resulted in the Treaties (or Peace) of Utrecht of 1713, which laid the foundation of Britain's imperial hegemony. Harley played a key role not only in the initial negotiations of the Treaty of Utrecht but also in the concluding stages until October 1712. These initiatives brought him into conflict with his colleague Henry St. John, first viscount Bolingbroke (1678–1751), whose ambition for supreme office was fanned by Harley's growing alienation from Queen Anne (ruled 1702–1714) and declining support within Tory ranks. Harley's tenuous political position was further eroded by increasing apathy, excessive drinking, and his questionable (if not treasonous) correspondence with the Jacobite Old Pretender James Edward (1688–1766). Dismissed on 27 July 1714 and excluded from power, Harley's influence ended with the Hanoverian succession (August 1714). He was impeached for corruption, sedition, and other misdemeanors and languished for two years in the Tower of London pending trial. For lack of evidence he was eventually acquitted. Harley spent his last years banished from court but attending the House of Lords, speaking in opposition to the Mutiny Bill in 1718 and protesting the Peerage Bill the following year.

Harley died at his home on Albermarle Street in London on 21 May 1724. He was buried at Brampton Bryan, Herefordshire, where a memorial was erected to his memory.

Excelling at political intrigue and manipulation, Harley was an intelligent, moderate, and pragmatic minister with the ability to attract and conciliate followers from both the Whig and the Tory ranks. His positive achievement lay in promoting measures of the highest national importance while providing the resourceful leadership required to steer them through Parliament during a time of chronic partisan divisions. Committed to political independence, Harley invariably strove to maintain an administration that functioned autonomously, free from dictation by parties and party leaders. So secretive was his nature and political strategy that they ultimately became a liability, confirming a reputation for deviousness and bad faith that cost him the support of vital Whig political groupings that distrusted his intentions.

Appreciating the influence of the press in contemporary politics, Harley recruited many notable pamphleteers, including Daniel Defoe (1660–1731), Jonathan Swift (1667–1745), and Charles Davenant (1656–1714) to manipulate national opinion on his ministry's behalf. He also had broad literary and cultural interests. Over the years he assembled a sizable collection of books and manuscripts that form the nucleus of the Harleian Collection in the British Library.

See also **Anne (England); Churchill, John, duke of Marlborough; Defoe, Daniel; Glorious Revolution (Britain); Parliament; Swift, Jonathan; Utrecht, Peace of (1713); William and Mary.**

BIBLIOGRAPHY

Biddle, Sheila. *Bolingbroke and Harley.* New York, 1974.

Dickinson, William Calvin. *Sidney Godolphin, Lord Treasurer, 1702–1710.* Lewiston, N.Y., 1990.

Gregg, Edward. *Queen Anne.* London, 1980.

Hill, Brian. "Oxford, Bolingbroke, and the Peace of Utrecht." *Historical Journal* 16 (1973): 241–263.

——. *Robert Harley: Speaker, Secretary of State, and Premier Minister.* New Haven, 1988.

KARL W. SCHWEIZER

HARRINGTON, JAMES (1611–1677), English political theorist. James Harrington was born at Upton, Northamptonshire, the eldest son of Sir Sapcote Harrington and his first wife Jane (née Samuel). Most of our knowledge about Harrington's life comes from three seventeenth-century sources: John Aubrey's *Brief Lives,* Anthony Wood's *Athenae Oxonienses,* and John Toland's "Life of James Harrington," which served as an introduction to his edition of Harrington's works. Since Wood drew on Aubrey, and Toland drew on Wood, there is some overlap between these three sources.

Harrington entered Trinity College, Oxford, as a gentleman commoner in 1629 but did not take his degree. Instead he traveled extensively on the Continent. There is little evidence about Harrington's involvement during the first Civil War (1642–1646), though Wood claims that he sided with the Presbyterians and tried, unsuccessfully, to win a seat in Parliament. In May 1647, however, he was appointed Gentleman of the Bedchamber to Charles I, who was being held at Holdenby House. The ambiguity of Harrington's position—employed by Parliament to serve the king—perhaps explains the ambiguity of his political views, particularly his attitude toward the king. Despite the republican tone of Harrington's works, it was said that he got on well with Charles and that the latter's execution, on 30 January 1649, affected him profoundly.

Harrington's major work, *The Commonwealth of Oceana* (1656), was written and published under the Protectorship of Oliver Cromwell. The work was dedicated to Cromwell, but the sincerity of that dedication is questionable. The work can be divided into two main parts: "The Preliminaries," in which Harrington set out his political theory, and "The Model of the Commonwealth," in which that theory was applied in the context of Oceana (England). The first part of the preliminaries deals with what Harrington called "Ancient Prudence"—the politics of the ancient world or "the [government] of laws, and not of men." The second part concerns "Modern Prudence"—the politics of the period since the fall of the Roman Empire, or "the [government] of men, and not of laws." The aim of the work as a whole was to show how to bring about a return to "Ancient Prudence" in the modern world. On the basis of his theory of the economic underpinnings of political power, Harrington argued that the time was ripe for such a revival in England.

"The Model of the Commonwealth" consists of a series of "orders" by which the new regime was to be established. At the national level Harrington advocated a variation on the conventional mixed system of government, with the magistrate (the one) executing the laws, the senate (the few) debating the laws, and the popular assembly (the many) voting on the laws. The system also involved rotation of office, a complex balloting process based on the Venetian model, and a network of assemblies running from the parish to the national level to ensure that the whole country would be governed effectively.

Harrington's subsequent works are less well-known than *Oceana*. They were aimed either at responding to critics of that work or at restating the theory presented there. But Harrington's ideas were of practical as well as theoretical interest. In July 1659 a petition was submitted to Parliament which proposed that certain of Harrington's ideas be adopted there. And in the autumn and winter of 1659–1660 Harrington and his friends formed the Rota Club, which met at Miles's Coffee House in New Palace Yard, Westminster. There Harrington's ideas were discussed and his system of balloting practiced. At the Restoration, the ambiguity of Harrington's position again brought him under scrutiny. He was arrested, interrogated, and finally sent to the Tower, later being transferred elsewhere. Though eventually released, his mind had been affected by his imprisonment, and he did not fully recover before his death in 1677.

Harrington's ideas continued to be influential after his death. During the eighteenth century they had an impact on such diverse figures as Thomas Gordon, David Hume, and Thomas Spence. Moreover, through the influence of men like Thomas Hollis, Harrington's works also found their way to America, where they influenced the revolutionary generation, and to France, where a model constitution based on *Oceana* appeared in 1792 and translations of Harrington's works in 1795. Harrington seems to have faded from view during the nineteenth century, but he became popular again in the twentieth century through the uses made of his works by R. H. Tawney in the debate over the rise of the gentry and by Caroline Robbins and J. G. A. Pocock in their accounts of eighteenth-century Commonwealthmen and neo-Harringtonians.

See also **Constitutionalism; English Civil War and Interregnum; Political Philosophy.**

BIBLIOGRAPHY

Primary Sources

Aubrey, John. *Brief Lives: A Modern English Version*. Edited by Richard Barber. Woodbridge, U.K., 1982.

Harrington, James. *The Political Works of James Harrington*. Edited by J. G. A. Pocock. Cambridge, U.K., and New York, 1977. Pocock's introduction provides further details concerning the sources on Harrington's life and works, as well as providing the most detailed recent account.

Toland, John. "The Life of James Harrington." In *The Oceana of James Harrington and His Other Works*. Edited by John Toland. London, 1700. Reprinted in *James Harrington and the Notion of a Commonwealth*. Edited by Luc Borot. Collection "Astraea," 6. Montpellier, France, 1998.

Wood, Anthony. *Athenae Oxonienses: An Exact History of All the Writers and Bishops Who Have Had Their Education in the University of Oxford*. Edited by P. Bliss. 4 vols. London, 1967.

Secondary Sources

Pocock, J. G. A. *The Machiavellian Moment: Florentine Political Thought and the Atlantic Republican Tradition*. Princeton, 1975.

Robbins, Caroline. *The Eighteenth-Century Commonwealthman: Studies in the Transmission, Development, and Circumstance of English Liberal Thought from the Restoration of Charles II until the War with the Thirteen Colonies*. Cambridge, Mass., 1959.

Russell Smith, H. F. *Harrington and His Oceana: A Study of a Seventeenth-Century Utopia and Its Influence on America*. Cambridge, U.K., 1914. Good on Harrington's posthumous influence in America and France.

Worden, Blair. "James Harrington and 'The Commonwealth of Oceana,' 1650" and "Harrington's 'Oceana': Origins and Aftermath, 1651–1660." In *Republicanism, Liberty, and Commercial Society, 1649–1776*. Edited by David Wootton. Stanford, 1994.

Rachel Hammersley

HARTLIB, SAMUEL (Samuel Hartlieb; c. 1600–1662), English reformer. Samuel Hartlib was a scientific "intelligencer" who helped to place England on the map of the emerging Republic of Letters. He was born at Elbing (Elblag) in Poland around 1600 into a distinguished mercantile family, and received an extensive education in Germany and at Cambridge (1625–1626) under John Preston (1587–1628), master of Emmanuel College. He retreated to London in 1628 as the Habsburg armies advanced toward the Baltic coast and, after 1630, spent the rest of his life there.

Hartlib began to cultivate his international network of correspondents, assisted by his friend John

Dury (1596–1672), a Calvinist minister whom he had met at Elbing. Together they shared the vision of reconciling Protestant divisions and consorting with a fraternity whose goal was to establish a model Protestant religious community. Hartlib's manuscript diary delineates his obsession for the processes of learning that had already led him to admire and reflect on the works of Francis Bacon. His correspondence with the Czech educational philosopher Jan Amos Comenius (1592–1670) had begun in 1632, and one of Hartlib's earliest publications was a sketch of *pansophy* (or encyclopedic learning) that Comenius had sent him. His second, expanded edition of this work (*Pansophia Prodromus,* 1639), became a prospectus for Comenius in England.

This involvement with Comenius established Hartlib's reputation as an agent of learning. Hartlib believed that Christian solidarity arose out of relations of exchange. God had given all humans a "talent" that should not be "hidden under a bushel" but distributed for the common good. These talents would best be released by a reformation of learning (or *Reformation of Schooles* as Hartlib entitled his translation of Comenius's *Prodromus* in 1642). In October 1641, Hartlib published a small utopian treatise entitled *Macaria* (after an offshore island in Thomas More's *Utopia,* 1515). Its authorship used to be ascribed to him, but it was evidently written by Gabriel Plattes (1600–1655). It described a commonwealth in which government and people collaborated in prosperity generated by the practical application of diffused knowledge. Pansophy's ultimate goal was a millennial recovery of the knowledge that humanity had lost after Eden. In a pact signed by Comenius, Hartlib, and Dury on 13 March 1642, they committed themselves to a secret fraternity for the advancement of religious pacification, education, and the reformation of learning. This delineated Hartlib's goals for the rest of his life.

During the English Civil War (1642–1649), Hartlib stayed in London, acting as an agent for the parliamentary cause. His proposed reformation of learning induced John Milton (1608–1674) to write his treatise *On Education* (1644), which he dedicated to Hartlib. Following the parliamentary victory in 1646, Hartlib devoted himself to establishing an "Office of Address" with elements borrowed from a similar agency established in Paris. It was designed as a labor exchange and a means of spreading knowledge on "matters of religion, of learning, and ingenuities." Although never officially instituted, Hartlib was voted an annual pension by the Commonwealth and became "a conduit pipe towards the Publick. . . ." He employed scriveners and translators to copy letters and treatises to others. What is sometimes now called the "Hartlib Circle" was a diverse group of enthusiasts who shared interests in the possibilities of technical change. His surviving papers, rediscovered in London in 1933, testify to the extent of Hartlib's network, although his influence remained mostly behind the scenes. His most visible impact lay in the numerous pamphlets that he published. Their greatest effect was in agriculture, where the advantages of planting new leguminous crops, experimenting with fertilizers and manures, using seed drills and new plows, and advocating the possibilities of apiculture (raising bees) and silk cultivation (in Virginia) were advocated. It is difficult to determine Hartlib's overall impact, because he readily adopted the dominant ideas and language of others and his agenda evolved over time, but his adoption of other people's ideas also involved the perception that, by spreading knowledge, the public good would be served and the coming of the millennium achieved. His commitment to that goal was distinctive, even though it would eventually be carried forward in very different ways after his death by the Royal Society of London.

See also **Agriculture; Bacon, Francis; Comenius, Jan Amos; Education; English Civil War and Interregnum; English Civil War Radicalism; Milton, John; More, Thomas; Republic of Letters; Utopia.**

BIBLIOGRAPHY

Greengrass, M. "Samuel Hartlib and the Commonwealth of Learning." In *The Cambridge History of the Book in Britain,* edited by John Barnard and D. F. McKenzie. Vol. 4, pp. 304–322. Cambridge, U.K., 2002.

Greengrass, M., and M. P. Leslie, eds. *The Hartlib Papers on CD-ROM.* 2nd ed. Sheffield, U.K., 2002.

Leslie, Michael, and Timothy Raylor. *Culture and Cultivation in Early Modern England: Writing and the Land.* Leicester, U.K., 1992.

Turnbull, G. H. *Hartlib, Dury, and Comenius: Gleanings from Hartlib's Papers.* Liverpool, U.K., 1947.

Webster, Charles. *The Great Instauration: Science, Medicine, and Reform, 1626–1660.* London, 1975.

———. *Samuel Hartlib and the Advancement of Learning.* Cambridge, U.K., 1970.

MARK GREENGRASS

HARVEY, WILLIAM (1578–1657), English physician and anatomist. William Harvey was born at Folkestone, on the south coast of England. He matriculated at Gonville and Caius College, Cambridge, in 1593 and studied anatomy in Padua under Girolamo Fabrizi d'Aquapendente. Harvey received his degree as doctor of medicine in 1602. Returning to England, he settled in London, where he started a medical practice. In 1607 he became a fellow of the College of Physicians and was formally appointed physician to St. Bartholomew's Hospital in 1609. In 1613 he was elected censor in the College and in 1615 Lumleian Lecturer of Surgery with the principal duties of giving a series of lectures on set texts and performing an annual public anatomy in the hall of the College. Some of the anatomical lecture notes survive and have been edited by the College of Physicians (1886); by C. D. O'Malley, F. N. L. Poynter, and K. F. Russell (1961); and by G. Whitteridge (1964).

In 1618 Harvey was appointed court physician to James I and later to Charles I (1625), and as a member of the royal entourage, he was involved in a number of political and diplomatic activities. In 1629 he attended the duke of Lennox in his travels abroad on the orders of Charles I. On several occasions (in 1633, 1639, 1640, and 1641) he was asked to accompany the king to Scotland. In 1635 he traveled with the earl of Arundel on a diplomatic mission to the Emperor Ferdinand II's court at Regensburg. After the Battle of Edgehill (1642), Harvey followed Charles I to Oxford. He remained there for three years and was made warden of Merton College in 1643. During the Civil War, his lodgings at Whitehall were plundered by Parliamentary troops, and he lost all his notes on the generation of insects and natural history. In 1646, when the city surrendered to Parliament, Harvey returned to London, where he lived in learned retirement. He died in 1657, at the age of seventy-nine.

THEORIES OF CIRCULATION

In the *Exercitatio Anatomica de Motu Cordis et Sanguinis in Animalibus* (Anatomical study on the motion of the heart and blood in animals), published in Frankfurt in 1628, Harvey announced his epoch-making discovery of the circulation of the blood. According to the old view, as it had been systematized by Galen in the second century C.E., blood originated in the liver from the assimilation and transformation of food and then ebbed and flowed through the veins in order to nourish the various parts of the body. A part of the venous blood was thought to seep through the interventricular septum of the heart (considered to be porous) and, upon arrival in the left ventricle, was supposed to undergo further elaboration as a result of being mixed with air coming from the lungs. Galen believed that the veins and the arteries were separate systems that carried fluids of different natures: thick, nutritive blood in the former, and spirituous, energizing blood in the latter. By means of a series of close arguments and experimental proofs, Harvey demonstrated that the blood was continuously and rapidly transmitted from the veins to the arteries, was driven into every part of the body in a far greater quantity than was needed for nourishment, and was finally drawn from the periphery to the heart to start the same cycle again.

A long and complex genealogy of anatomical findings and physiological speculations underlies Harvey's discovery. Realdo Colombo (1516?–1559?) discovered pulmonary circulation, but failed to put it in the wider context of systemic circulation; Andrea Cesalpino (1519–1603) caught a glimpse of the capillaries, but by circulation he meant a series of distillations occurring in the blood; Girolamo Fabrizi (1537–1619) detected the venous valves but did not understand their role in the centripetal venous flow. Unlike his predecessors, who reached only partial conclusions and remained entangled in the theoretical constraints of older accounts, Harvey managed to find an elegant and consistent solution for a whole series of interrelated problems: the correct interpretation of the systole and diastole of the heart (the former viewed as an active contraction, the latter as a passive distension), the clear demonstration of the pulmonary transit of the blood (from the right to the left ventricle by way of the pulmonary artery, the lungs, and the pulmonary vein), the understanding of the actual role of the venous valves (which serve to prevent the blood driven into the veins from being regurgitated back into the arteries). The experimental demonstration of circulation rested on the correct understanding of two key insights: the uses of ligatures of varying tightness and the calculation of the rate of blood passing through the heart at each beat.

THEORETICAL ELABORATIONS, ANATOMY, AND SPIRIT

In *Exercitationes Anatomicae Duae de Circulatione Sanguinis* (1649; Two anatomical exercitations on the circulation of the blood), written in response to some objections put forward by Jean Riolan, he distanced himself from René Descartes's explanation of the heartbeat. In addition, Harvey took the opportunity to define his idea of spirit as an inherent and material component of blood. In so doing, he rejected Jean Fernel's belief in the existence of transcendent and immaterial spirits governing the vital functions of the body.

The theory presented in *De Motu Cordis* and *De Circulatione* offered an alternative and revolutionary account of the anatomy and physiology of the human body. By disentangling the function of respiration from the motion of the heart and arteries and by separating the purpose of the circulation from the processes of concoction and nutrition, Harvey initiated a process of conceptual and factual reorganization in which the respiratory, digestive, and nervous apparatuses began to assume the characteristic features that they still have today. Inevitably, though, Harvey's model was also confronted with a crucial objection: why had the blood to circulate rapidly and incessantly throughout the body if nourishment of the parts was not one of the functions of that circulation and if no exchange of vital properties contained in the inhaled air took place in the lungs? The ultimate purpose of circulation and the difference between arterial and venous blood remained two unsolved points in Harvey's system.

In *Exercitationes de Generatione Animalium* (1651; Anatomical exercitations concerning the generation of living creatures), Harvey addressed the question of the generation of oviparous and viviparous animals. In embryology he advanced the theory that the parts of higher animals were successively formed out of the undifferentiated matter of the egg (a process he called "epigenesis"). Harvey's main concern in the treatise was the explanation of the origin and mechanism of conception. Unable to observe the initial stages of pregnancy in dissected hinds and does, he failed to understand the part played by the male's semen in fecundating the female. He argued that the process of fertilization could be compared to a transmission of vital energy at a distance.

In *De Generatione* Harvey also argued in favor of the preeminence of the blood, as an inherently animate matter, over the other parts of the body. His theory of epigenesis demonstrated the original nature of the blood. Its intrinsically spirituous substance confirmed the existence of a vital matter endowed with the ability to move, perceive, and respond to external stimuli. Harvey went so far as to identify the soul with the blood. His interest in the responsive nature of living matter dated back to the beginnings of his natural investigations. An unfinished treatise entitled "De Motu Locali Animalium" (On the local motion of the animals) testifies to his interest in studying the difference between voluntary and involuntary motions and the interplay of muscles, nerves, and the organs involved in locomotion and sensation.

The first to accept the circulatory model was Harvey's friend and colleague at the College of Physicians, Robert Fludd (1574–1637), who looked at the discovery of circulation as a confirmation of his speculations on the correspondence of microcosm and macrocosm. René Descartes (1596–1650) accepted Harvey's discovery of the circulation of the blood but disagreed with his explanation of the movement of the heart. Whereas Harvey maintained that the movement was the result of a vital contraction, Descartes explained it as a mechanical impulse determined by the ebullition and consequent rarefaction of the blood. Thomas Willis (1621–1675) and Richard Lower (1631–1691) refined and supplemented Harvey's circulatory model. Both mechanical anatomists like Marcello Malpighi (1628–1694) and chemical physiologists like Franciscus de la Boë (called Sylvius; 1614–1672) made Harvey's discovery an integral part of their physiological schemes. Francis Glisson (1597–1677) took the Harveian thesis of the inherently active and sentient nature of the blood as the starting point for a comprehensive theory of irritability.

See also **Anatomy and Physiology; Biology; Descartes, René; Matter, Theories of; Medicine; Scientific Method.**

BIBLIOGRAPHY

Primary Sources

Harvey, William. *The Circulation of the Blood and Other Writings.* Translated by K. J. Franklin. London, 1990.

———. *The Works of William Harvey.* Translated by R. Willis. London, 1847.

Secondary Sources

Bono, James. "Reform and the Languages of Renaissance Theoretical Medicine: Harvey versus Fernel." *Journal of the History of Biology* 23 (1990): 341–387.

Frank, Robert G. *Harvey and the Oxford Physiologists: A Study of Scientific Ideas.* Berkeley, 1980.

French, Roger. *William Harvey's Natural Philosophy.* Cambridge, U.K., 1994.

Keynes, Geoffrey. *The Life of William Harvey.* Oxford, 1966.

Lawrence, T. *Gulielmi Harveii Opera Omnia: A Collegio Medicorum Londinensi Edita.* London, 1766.

Pagel, Walter. *New Light on William Harvey.* Basel, 1976.

———. *William Harvey's Biological Ideas.* Basel, 1967.

GUIDO GIGLIONI

HASIDISM. *See* **Messianism, Jewish.**

HASKALAH (JEWISH ENLIGHTENMENT).

"Haskalah" is the Hebrew term for the Enlightenment movement and ideology that began in European Jewish society in the 1770s and continued until the 1880s. A proponent of the Haskalah was known as a *maskil* ('an enlightened Jew'; pl. *maskilim*). The Haskalah shared many aspects of the European Enlightenments, but as a national variant of the general movement it also addressed specific Jewish concerns of the period. The Haskalah was a feature of Ashkenazic Jewish society, the branch of world Jewry with origins in medieval French and German lands whose descendents inhabited German lands, the Polish-Lithuanian Commonwealth, and the partitioned lands of Poland. Beginning in Prussia, and spreading eastward to Austrian Galicia and tsarist Russia, the Haskalah, like the European Enlightenment, was an optimistic, self-conscious intellectual movement that urged European Jews to dare to liberate themselves from their past and fashion their own lives, in the spirit of Immanuel Kant's well-known answer to the question, "*Was ist Aufklärung?*"; in the Jewish case, *maskilim* exhorted their brethren to unfetter themselves from and transform the culture of early modern Ashkenazic Judaism. *Maskilim,* like other European enlighteners, turned back to a classical era in search of an unbenighted rational past free of superstition and religious intolerance. But, in contrast to philosophes and *Aufklärer,* who, in Peter Gay's interpretation, found their model in the ancient Greco-Roman world, Jewish enlighteners favored the "golden age" of medieval Iberian-Jewish culture, seeking to remake early modern Ashkenazic Jewish culture in its image.

THE CRITIQUE OF EARLY MODERN ASHKENAZIC JEWISH SOCIETY AND CULTURE

Contemporary European Jewish society, in the minds of the *maskilim,* had become insular, valorizing the study of Talmud and its commentaries to the exclusion of the Hebrew Bible, biblical grammar, Hebrew poetry, and humanistic subjects, such as mathematics, geography, natural science, and history, that were indispensable to modern European life. According to the *maskilim's* critique, the ideal of the Torah Sage *(talmid hakham),* together with the exclusionary legislation of the non-Jewish political authorities, had resulted in a distorted Jewish economic profile concentrated solely in trade and other "unproductive" professions. Moreover, early modern Ashkenazic Jewry's attachment to *minhag* (religious custom), in addition to its observance of traditional Jewish law, had deepened its parochialism, leading to an explosion of new Jewish rituals that hindered participation in broader European society. *Maskilim* resoundingly judged Yiddish, Ashkenazic Jewry's capacious vernacular composed of German, Hebrew, Slavic, and Romance-language components, as incapable of elevating Jewish culture and unsuitable for expressing the values of modern Jewish life. Perforce, the Haskalah was decidedly male, for early modern Jewish life was gendered, and only Jewish men received the requisite education in traditional Jewish languages and texts for a full-scale enlightened critique of their culture.

Marked by a didactic commitment to regenerate and revitalize Ashkenazic Jewish culture as a means of preserving Jewish life in the modern world, the Haskalah gave voice to a new kind of

European Jew, a secular *intelligent.* The worldview of the *maskilim,* individuals in the process of "enlightening" themselves, was shaped by an ideology of creative tension between the worlds of traditional Jewish culture and European society and values, what the Prussian *maskil* Naphtali Herz Wessely (1725–1805) called *Torat ha-Adam* (secular knowledge) and *Torat ha-Elohim* (sacred knowledge) in his programmatic educational pamphlet, *Divrei Shalom ve-Eme* (Words of peace and truth, 1782). In contrast to activists in the European Enlightenment who were already Europeans, the *maskilim* not only waged a self-conscious battle to regenerate Ashkenazic Jewish culture, but also struggled to justify Jewish participation in European society as men, like all other men, endowed with the universal faculty of reason. The Haskalah, in its defense of Jewish particularism, qualified the universalism of the Enlightenment.

The figure of Moses Mendelssohn (1729–1786), son of a poor Jewish scribe from Dessau who settled in Berlin, the center of the Prussian Enlightenment, epitomized the new type of European Jew. Mendelssohn remained devout throughout his life, yet acquired a vast reservoir of secular and non-Jewish knowledge that he applied to philosophical, political, and exegetical writings, penned in both flawless German and impeccable Hebrew. His *Jerusalem, or on Religious Power and Judaism* (1783), a philosophic defense of the compatibility of the observance of Jewish law with the ideals of Enlightenment natural religion, expressed the Haskalah's conservative attitude toward revelation and inherited traditions, a posture characteristic of the moderate German *Aufklärung*'s debt to the philosophy of Christian Wolff. Shaped in the Prussian context, the Haskalah lacked the anticlericalism and critique of the religious establishment that motivated the French philosophe's conception of Enlightenment.

The generation of Prussian *maskilim* after Mendelssohn institutionalized the movement by establishing periodicals *(Ha-Me'assef*/the Gatherer), publishing houses (Hevrat Hinukh Ne'arim/Society for the Education of the Youth), reading circles (Hevrat Dorshei Leshon Ever/The Society for the Promotion of the Hebrew Language, 1782, Königsberg), and schools (Jüdische Freischule/Jewish Elementary School, 1778), with new textbooks (*Lesebuch für jüdische Kinder*/Reader for Jewish children, 1779), activities supported by the *maskilim* and a small group of economically elite Jews with privileges to live in Prussia's cities. By the 1790s, the Haskalah in Prussia encountered the political demands of the centralizing absolutist state, which sought to dissolve all premodern corporations, including the Jewish communal authority *(kahal),* and the acculturating aspirations of the rising Jewish bourgeoisie, resulting in its radicalization. Prussian Jewish intellectuals soon focused their efforts on political emancipation and cultural acceptance, rather than on inner reform, embodied by the *maskil* David Friedländer's 1799 letter to Pastor Teller asserting his willingness to convert to Christianity with the provision that he not accept the divinity of Christ. The shift in emphasis was tellingly marked by the failure of Hebrew periodical literature to sustain itself in Prussian lands, giving way to new German periodicals *(Sulamith)* focused on the struggle for political rights.

THE EASTWARD TURN OF THE HASKALAH

The social and political environment of central and eastern Europe, with their demographically rich Ashkenazic Jewish populations and laggard state-building multiethnic empires, became fertile ground for the dissemination of the Jewish Enlightenment. Although subject to the centralizing political demands of absolutist Austria and Russia to integrate the Jewish community into the life of the state, the quest for political emancipation and religious reform was largely absent among *maskilim* in the East. Rather, the Haskalah in Austrian Galicia and Russia focused on communal regeneration, particularly as it faced the entrenchment of traditional Jewish culture by Hasidism, the extraordinarily successful Jewish spiritual movement that, born in the mid-eighteenth century, had transformed eastern European Jewry. Using the didactic tools of the general Enlightenment (periodical literature, satire, ethical anthologies, curriculum reform), the battle of east European *maskilim,* such as Mendel Lefin (1749–1826), Joseph Perl (1773–1839), Nachman Krochmal (1785–1840), and Isaac Baer Levinsohn (1788–1860), against Hasidism gave birth to modern secular Hebrew and Yiddish prose literature, new forms of Bible commentary, and historical writing.

Although always a self-selected intellectual minority within Ashkenazic Jewry, the *maskilim* represented a radical break with traditional patterns of Jewish life and engendered sharp opposition from traditional rabbinic authorities in central and eastern Europe. Nonetheless, recent scholarly interpretations of the Jewish Enlightenment emphasize its conservatism in comparison with the other responses of European Jewry to modernity (that is, Jewish nationalism, socialism, revolution, migration, political emancipation, and communal self-liquidation/assimilation). Flowering almost a full century after the European Enlightenments, the Haskalah's Hebraism and religious moderation laid the foundation for contemporary constructions of liberal Jewish identity.

See also **Enlightenment; Jews and Judaism; Mendelssohn, Moses; Philosophes; Prussia.**

BIBLIOGRAPHY

Breuer, Edward. *The Limits of Enlightenment: Jews, Germans and the Study of Scripture in the Eighteenth Century.* Cambridge, Mass., and London, 1996.

Feiner, Shmuel. *Haskalah and History: The Emergence of a Modern Jewish Historical Consciousness.* Translated by Chaya Naor and Sondra Silverston. Oxford and Portland, Ore., 2002.

Feiner, Shmuel, and David Sorkin, eds. *New Perspectives on the Haskalah.* Oxford, 2001.

Katz, Jacob, ed. *Toward Modernity: The European Jewish Model.* New York and Oxford, 1987.

Mahler, Raphael. *Hasidism and the Jewish Enlightenment: Their Confrontation in Galicia and Poland in the First Half of the Nineteenth Century.* Philadelphia and New York, 1985.

Sorkin, David. *Moses Mendelssohn and the Religious Enlightenment.* Berkeley, 1996.

Stanislawski, Michael F. *For Whom Do I Toil?: Judah Leib Gordon and the Crisis of Russian Jewry.* New York, 1988.

Nancy Sinkoff

HASTINGS, WARREN (1732–1818), first governor-general of India. Warren Hastings was a competent, honorable, and farsighted administrator whose policies, some controversial, decisively shaped and stabilized future Anglo-Indian relations. The controversy surrounding his administration made him the subject of impeachment and trial in Great Britain.

Warren Hastings was born at Daylesford, Worcestershire, on 6 December 1732, the son of a country solicitor whose family had fallen into poverty. When his mother, Hester Warren, died soon after his birth, his father departed for the West Indies. Warren was raised by an uncle who sent him to school, first at Newington and then to Westminster, where he became the first king's scholar of his year in 1747.

In October 1750, Hastings entered service as a clerk in the East India Company. Able and ambitious, he advanced rapidly, becoming the company's resident (1757). From 1761 to 1764, he served on the Calcutta Council, the chief governing body in Bengal. During this period he attempted to reform abuses in the transit system, specifically the practice whereby British officials passed private consignments free of duty, resulting in disproportionate fiscal burdens on the Mughul nabob Mir Kasim and his subjects. Hastings's compromise proposal proved ineffectual and a brief war erupted, ending in the defeat of Mir Kasim and restoration of the former nabob, Mir Jaffier.

In 1764 Hastings returned to England, but financial need forced him to seek reemployment with the Company, which, in 1769, appointed him to the Council of Madras. Two years later he was promoted to the governorship of Bengal.

From 1772 to 1774, Hastings consolidated British control over native authorities, restored order to the province's judicial system, abolished the pension that Lord Clive had paid to the Mughul, and created a new, more efficient procedure for collecting the land revenues, a major source of the company's financial solvency. The English collectors, being inexperienced and extortionate, were removed and replaced with native officers of proven knowledge and ability. Six divisions were created by grouping the districts and subordinating them to provincial councils under the control of non-Indian administrators. This arrangement, like so many of Hastings's ideas, was to become an enduring part of the British ruling tradition in India.

Lord North's Regulating Act of 1773 placed India under three presidencies, with one governor-general, a position held by Hastings from 1774 to

1784, assisted by a newly created council of five, three of whom—strangers to India—were hostile to his policies. Given only a single vote, Hastings frequently found himself overruled in his efforts to curb further corruption and introduce reforms. Eventually his fellow councillors, led by Sir Phillip Francis, conspired against him, fabricating charges of corruption and cruelty that were to culminate in his impeachment. Despite such obstructionism, Hastings launched military expeditions to defeat the Mahrattas conspiracy that threatened Britain's imperial governance, quelled provincial revolts, continued his financial reforms, and founded the Asiatic Society of Bengal and the Calcutta Madrisa, a vital center of Muslim culture. He also had to confront the danger posed by the sultanate of Haidar Ali, who (with the connivance of the French and Dutch) plotted insurrection against British rule. On his own authority, Hastings removed the incompetent governor of Madras and replaced him with the veteran militarist Sir Eyre Coote, who defeated Ali's forces at Porto Novo. Parallel naval action drove the rebels out of the Carnatic (a region in southeastern India). On the death of Haidar Ali in 1782, Hastings negotiated the treaty of Salbai, which acknowledged British supremacy throughout India and calmed the situation in Madras.

Hastings resigned his office in December 1784 and returned to England on 13 June the following year. In 1787 he faced impeachment charges initiated by Edmund Burke (working with Hastings's enemies), whose outrageous conduct evoked numerous rebukes from the House of Lords. The lengthy trial, beginning in 1788 and lasting until 1795, ended in Hastings's acquittal, but severely compromised his reputation, ruined his health, and cost him £50,000.

In his later years, Hastings campaigned for a peerage and a parliamentary reversal of the impeachment, neither of which ever materialized. He received a doctorate of civil law from Oxford in 1813, was sworn privy councillor in May 1814, and died, a rural recluse, on 22 August 1818.

Although Hastings's conduct of affairs tended at times to be high-handed, if not unscrupulous, his motives were invariably patriotic, not self-interested. He expanded the territorial scope of British dominion in India, honored and preserved indigenous cultures, and introduced many needed and lasting reforms. The prince regent (the future George IV) put it best when, in 1814, he called Hastings "the most deserving yet also one of the worst used men in the empire."

See also **British Colonies: India; Burke, Edmund; Colonialism; George II (Great Britain); George III (Great Britain); Mercantilism; Trading Companies.**

BIBLIOGRAPHY

Bowen, H. V. *Revenue and Reform: The Indian Problem in British Politics, 1757–1773.* Cambridge, U.K., and New York, 1991.

Feiling, K. *Warren Hastings.* London and New York, 1954.

Forrest, G. W. *India under Hastings.* New Delhi, 1984.

Marshall, P. J. *The Impeachment of Warren Hastings.* London, 1965.

Turnbull, P. *Warren Hastings.* London, 1975.

KARL W. SCHWEIZER

HAYDN, FRANZ JOSEPH (1732–1809),

Austrian composer considered the founder of Vienna classicism. Born in modest circumstances as the son of a wheelwright in the Lower Austrian town of Rohrau, Haydn was by 1800 the most celebrated composer in Europe. He is sometimes called the father of both the symphony and the string quartet.

Haydn was raised in a devoutly Catholic household and his parents had hopes of his entering the clergy. He showed an early aptitude for music, which was noticed by a visiting schoolmaster who convinced his parents to send the six-year-old Joseph to a parish school in the neighboring town of Hainburg. Catholic parish schools had traditionally emphasized music (the schoolmaster usually doubled as the church organist) since pupils were needed to sing or perform in the parish's annual cycle of regular masses, baptisms, funerals, and processions. Haydn acquired his first formal training in music at the Hainburg school, and at the age of eight left to continue his musical education as a pupil at the choir school of St. Stephen's Cathedral in Vienna. He remained a pupil at St. Stephen's for almost ten years until he was forced to leave around 1749—not, as legend has it, to escape castration but because his voice broke.

Haydn's early years as a composer and musician illustrate the crucial importance of aristocratic musical patronage in eighteenth-century Europe. After struggling for several years as a teacher, freelance musician, and occasional composer for the popular Viennese stage, Haydn finally obtained a measure of financial security when Count Karl Joseph Franz Morzin took him into his household as music director around 1757. Haydn's first symphonies as well as his earliest string quartets date from this period. Decisive for his career was his entry a few years later (1761) into the service of Prince Paul Anton Esterházy, scion of the wealthiest magnate family in Hungary. Haydn, in his capacity as Vice-Kapellmeister (1761–1765) and later Kapellmeister (1761–1790), was in charge of supervising, if not composing, the music performed at the prince's palace at Esterháza. There Haydn was responsible for providing both vocal and instrumental music, including operas performed in the prince's lavish theater. Although Haydn's operas are today the least regarded part of his musical oeuvre—perhaps because they would soon be so overshadowed by Mozart's—Haydn devoted much of his musical energy in the years between 1766 and 1783 to operatic compositions. Best known today are his comic (or *buffa*) operas, such as those based on librettos by the eighteenth-century Italian playwright Carlo Goldoni (*Lo speziale* [1768)], *Le pescatrici* [1769–1770], and *Il mondo della luna* [1777]). But they also included dramatic pieces like *Armida* (1783), adapted from the late-humanist poet Torquato Tasso, which was the last opera Haydn produced. In the meantime Haydn continued to experiment with the symphonic form, moving from the syncopated eccentricities of his Sturm und Drang ('storm and stress') phase (1768–1772) to the exquisite sublimity of his later symphonies. During Haydn's years at Esterháza his string quartets also acquired the quintessentially conversational style that would be their hallmark, evoking the atmosphere of the Enlightenment salons he frequented during visits to Vienna in the 1770s and 1780s.

Franz Joseph Haydn. LIBRARY OF CONGRESS

By the 1780s Haydn had begun to free himself financially from dependence on his Esterházy patrons. He did this partly by successfully marketing his compositions to publishing houses in Vienna, London, and Paris, and partly through commissions like *Die sieben letzten Worte unseres Erlösers am Kreuze* (1785–1786; Seven last words of our Redeemer on the cross), an oratorio composed for the cathedral of Cádiz in southern Spain for performance during Holy Week. But it was above all the financial success of Haydn's triumphal London tours (1791–1792, 1794–1795) that sealed his economic independence. Haydn skillfully exploited the opportunities for performance and composition offered by the city's commercialized musical culture with its theaters, subscription concerts, and public pleasure gardens. All in all, Haydn's London visits earned him some 24,000 gulden, the equivalent of twenty years' salary at Esterháza. His "London symphonies" (nos. 93–104) achieved particular success in the British capital. His succeeding years in Vienna, where he spent the remainder of his life, won him popular acclaim as well. *Die Schöpfung* (1797; The creation) and *Die Jahreszeiten* (1801; The seasons), oratorios that remain two of his most beloved compositions today, served especially to crown his broad popularity in the Austrian capital.

In this respect Haydn's career epitomized the transition from aristocratic patronage to public performance that had begun to characterize the social history of music during his day. The legend of "Papa Haydn," the good-natured and self-effacing figure known for his generous encouragement of Mozart and Beethoven, can obscure the attention Haydn devoted to promoting the public reception of his own music. Commercially savvy, Haydn was keenly attuned to the tastes of his public. He often incorporated folk themes into his music, and the playful and mischievous qualities that came to be a hallmark of many of Haydn's compositions doubtless contributed to his broad appeal. As his "Surprise" Symphony (no. 94) or "Joke" Quartet (op. 33, no. 2) illustrate, Haydn loved musical gags, sudden reversals of tempo, the injection of a humorous moment into an ostensibly serious one. Critics of his day sometimes attacked this aspect of Haydn's music, noting his penchant for shifting unexpectedly between refinement and coarseness, the elevated and the vulgar. Yet Haydn's success in blurring the boundaries between high and low was a key element of his popularity, attesting to his ability to appeal to a wide audience.

See also **Goldoni, Carlo; Mozart, Wolfgang Amadeus; Music; Vienna.**

BIBLIOGRAPHY

Gotwals, Vernon. *Haydn: Two Contemporary Portraits.* Madison, Wis., 1963.

Landon, H. C. Robbins. *Haydn: Chronicle and Works.* 5 vols. London, 1976–1980.

Landon, H. C. Robbins, and David Wyn Jones. *Haydn: His Life and Music.* London and Bloomington, Ind., 1988.

Webster, James. "Haydn, (Franz) Joseph." In *The New Grove Dictionary of Music and Musicians,* edited by Stanley Sadie, vol. 11, pp. 171–271. London and New York, 2001.

JAMES VAN HORN MELTON

HELMONT, JEAN BAPTISTE VAN

(1579–1644; also known as Johannes von Helmont), Flemish chemist. Born at Brussels, Helmont studied at the University of Louvain, where dissatisfaction with the curriculum in philosophy led him to pursue medicine. He obtained a medical degree in 1599 but soon grew critical as well of ancient medical authorities. After seven years of travel and independent study he emerged as an iatrochemist, mixing chemistry with natural philosophy and medicine. In this regard Helmont followed in the tradition of Paracelsus, although with notable differences. He rejected symbolic analogies linking the macrocosm with the microcosm and considered that the Paracelsian first principles (sulfur, salt, and mercury) were created through chemical processes rather than being preexistent in material substances. While accepting the existence of sympathies in nature, he believed these to occur naturally and not as a result of supernatural forces. This last view brought him into an already raging controversy concerning the so-called weapon salve (an ointment that supposedly cured wounds after being applied not to the wound itself but to the weapon that had caused it). Although disparaging magical or diabolic explanations, Helmont thought that a certain magnetic sympathy nevertheless existed not between the weapon and the wound, but between the wound and the blood left on the weapon that had caused it. The same type of magnetic sympathy, he believed, also accounted for the effects of sacred relics. "Propositions" such as this led to his condemnation by the Spanish Inquisition and, thereafter, to his imprisonment. His collected works came to light after his death, edited and published (1648) by his son, Franciscus Mercurius (1614?–1699; also known as Francisco Mercurio van Helmont).

Much of Helmont's medical philosophy was concerned with the activity of a vital spirit in nature. All things in nature, he believed, arose from spiritual seeds planted into the medium of elementary water. By means of a ferment, which determined the form, function, and direction of all animals, vegetables, and minerals, the seed mingled with water to become an individual entity. To find the invisible seeds of bodies he studied the chemical nature of smoke arising from combusted solids and fluids. It was this "specific smoke" that he termed *gas,* a name that for Helmont carried spiritual and religious connotations within a vitalist cosmology. Another term, *blas,* represented a universal motive power, present in nature and in every human being.

Like Paracelsus, Helmont believed that the key to understanding nature was to be found in chemistry, and a good deal of his attention was given to techniques of quantification and to determining the weights of substances in chemical reactions. In his famous tree experiment he compared the weight of water given to a growing tree with respect to the weight of the tree itself. Against Aristotle, and on the basis of observations of a burning candle surrounded by a glass container resting in water, he argued that air could be diminished or contracted, thus making possible the existence of a vacuum in nature. He also advanced techniques for various chemical preparations, especially chemical medicines involving mercury, and advocated a corpuscularian, or particulate, view of matter. Following upon earlier suggestions, Helmont determined that acid was the digestive agent of the stomach and defended the Paracelsian idea of a medicinal liquor alkahest, which, it was claimed, could reduce every body into its first matter.

See also **Alchemy; Chemistry; Medicine; Paracelsus.**

BIBLIOGRAPHY

Primary Source

Helmont, Johannes von. *Ortus Medicinae*. Edited by Francisco Mercurio van Helmont. Amsterdam, 1648. Reprint. Brussels, 1966.

Secondary Sources

Clericuzio, Antonio. "From van Helmont to Boyle . . . ," *British Journal for the History of Science* 26 (1993): 303–343.

Debus, Allen. *The Chemical Philosophy*. New York, 1977. Reprint. Mineola, N.Y., 2002, pp. 295–343.

Pagel, Walter. *Joan Baptista van Helmont: Reformer of Science and Medicine*. Cambridge, U.K., and New York, 1982.

BRUCE T. MORAN

HELVÉTIUS, CLAUDE-ADRIEN

(1715–1771), French philosopher. Claude-Adrien Helvétius was one of the most audacious writers of the French Enlightenment. The uproar surrounding the publication of his first book, *De l'esprit* (1758), was so sensational that he was forced to recant three times. Only the conflict between the parlements and the court over control of censorship, along with his ties at court to Madame de Pompadour and the duc de Choiseul, saved him, and he decided that his second book, *De l'homme* (1773), would not be released until after his death.

Helvétius had an uncanny knack for taking thoughts common to all the philosophes and presenting them in a scandalous form that provoked all-out counterattacks from the Catholic Church. Philosophical empiricism and hedonism, denials of original sin, repudiations of the repressive ethics of Christianity—these were doctrines not of Helvétius alone but of almost all members of "the party of humanity." But whereas other philosophes asserted the aforesaid views without calling down upon their movement the full-blown wrath of the church, Helvétius sparked a controversy that almost led to the suppression of the *Encyclopédie*—the great collective enterprise in research and propaganda undertaken by Denis Diderot (1713–1784), Jean Le Rond d'Alembert (1717–1783), and the "society of men of letters."

Both in his empiricism and in his hedonism, Helvétius vigorously argued for a position that the exasperated philosophes regarded as impolitic, needlessly inflammatory, and a reductio ad absurdum of their own philosophy. Virtually all the philosophes agreed with Helvétius that, under cover of the Cartesian notion of innate ideas, the church had conspired to place its dogmatic assertions above criticism. The philosophes in general borrowed John Locke's notion that our ideas are acquired rather than given, that they are the result of the interaction of the human senses with the external world, and that a supposedly innate idea is simply one whose origins in early childhood have been lost to human memory.

Helvétius went further than his comrades, however, in his dogmatic assertions that the human mind is completely passive and absolutely determined by the environment. He maintained that we are what our surroundings have made us, nothing more. The upshot of his thought was that the only difference between a genius and a fool was one of environment, which led Diderot to remark that Helvétius apparently believed his kennelman could have written *De l'esprit.* Equally disturbing, the doctrine of natural rights, so central to the Enlightenment, obviously could not survive Helvétius's claim that there is no such thing as human nature. The final embarrassment was that Helvétius seemed to have vindicated the church's claim that the philosophes were the champions of an uncompromising philosophical materialism.

Another charge that the church regularly lodged against the philosophes was that they were proponents of free love and enemies of the family; and here again Helvétius—to the consternation of his comrades—seemed to prove the clergy correct. It was one thing for the philosophes to contend that the search for pleasure is an inevitable and legitimate human quest; it was quite another for Helvétius to suggest that all pleasures are bodily joys, sexual in nature. An admirer of ancient Sparta, Helvétius held that Lycurgus had utilized the sexual favors of women to transform ordinary men into heroic beings. Young Spartan females danced naked in front of the soldiers, praising the brave men, and shaming the cowards. If Helvétius had not existed, the church would have had to invent him.

Diderot, too, had dreamed of a sexual paradise, but he placed it in Tahiti rather than Europe, and refrained from publishing his tantalizing thoughts. The official Diderot was the author of *Le fils naturel* (1757; The natural son) and *Le père de famille* (1758; The father of the family), two plays that praised conventional familial ideals in exclamatory language. Helvétius, by contrast, failed to understand that discretion is sometimes the better part of enlightened valor.

Although the philosophes distanced themselves from Helvétius, some among their numbers learned to take seriously his thoughts on the arts. What Helvétius added to their discussions was the recognition that the study of culture must be linked to the study of politics. Under monarchies comedy is the most flourishing genre because the public, excluded from public affairs, is frivolous and desperate for laughter. Under republics there is a genuine public, attentive to public affairs and hungry for the ennobling passions of tragedy. England, despite its monarch, is a modern republic, the one country where an author can write for an enlightened audience.

Diderot and Paul Thiry, baron d'Holbach (1723–1789) were two of the most prominent of the philosophes who learned from Helvétius that "the dignity of the republic of letters" would remain an empty expression unless France, like England, evolved in a more republican direction. Helvétius played a crucial role in politicizing the Enlightenment.

See also **Atheisim; Holbach, Paul Thiry, baron d'; Diderot, Denis; Locke, John; Mechanism; Philosophes.**

BIBLIOGRAPHY

Primary Sources

Helvétius, Claude-Adrien. *De l'esprit.* Paris, 1988.

———. *De l'Homme.* 2 vols. Paris, 1989. The English translations dating from the eighteenth century are unreliable.

Secondary Sources

Andlau, Beatrix. *Helvétius, Seigneur de Voré.* Paris, 1939. For information about his life and family.

Smith, D. W. *Bibliography of the Writings of Helvétius.* Ferney, 2001.

———. *Helvétius, a Study in Persecution.* Oxford, 1965. For the politics of censorship.

MARK HULLIUNG

HENRY VII (ENGLAND) (1457–1509; ruled 1485–1509), king of England. Henry Tudor, later earl of Richmond, was born in Pembroke Castle, Wales, on 28 January 1457, the son of Edmund Tudor and Margaret Beaufort. He was directly related to the Lancastrian royal family through both his mother and his father and, as such, became a key figure in the dynastic struggles of the Wars of the Roses. In 1471, with his uncle Jasper, he was forced to flee to the Continent when the Yorkist Edward IV (ruled 1461–1470; 1471–1483) recaptured the throne from Henry VI (ruled 1422–1461; 1470–1471). The next fourteen years of his life were spent in exile, first in Brittany, then in France, before he set sail at the head of a small band of English exiles and French mercenaries in August 1485 to capture the English throne. On 22 August he defeated Richard III at the Battle of Bosworth Field and was crowned king of England.

On 18 January 1486 Henry married Elizabeth of York, daughter of Edward IV, to fulfill a promise made in exile to unite the warring houses of York and Lancaster. Despite this, Henry still faced challenges to his rule from disaffected Yorkists. The first serious rebellion came in 1487 when Lambert Simnel, claiming to be the Yorkist earl of Warwick, was crowned king of England in Dublin. Henry defeated Simnel and his followers at the Battle of Stoke in June. A more serious challenge came in the person of Perkin Warbeck, who claimed to be Edward IV's youngest son, Richard. Aided by Margaret, dowager duchess of Burgundy, and the Scottish king, James IV (ruled 1488–1513), Warbeck attempted invasions of England in 1495 and 1497 but was eventually captured and imprisoned in the Tower. The Tudor succession was, however, further threatened in April 1502 by the death of Henry's eldest son, Arthur (born 19 September 1486), and by a continuation of Yorkist claims in the person of Edmund de la Pole, earl of Suffolk. Most of the diplomatic efforts of the latter part of Henry's reign were designed to secure the succession: first, by ensuring that foreign princes did not support his dynastic opponents, and second, by arranging a marriage between his second son, Henry, and Arthur's widow, Catherine of Aragon.

Traditionally, the reign of Henry VII has been seen as the end of the Middle Ages in England and the beginning of the "New Monarchy" of the Tudors. In three ways the monarchy of Henry VII was seen to be significantly new. First, Henry was alleged to have broken the power of the "overmighty" nobility, largely responsible for the Wars of the Roses. Second, he introduced "modern" bureaucratic methods of government, rescuing the crown from the financial crisis of the mid-fifteenth century and putting the monarchy on a secure fiscal base. Finally, Henry rejected the traditional bellicosity of English kings and sought to strengthen England's position in Europe through diplomatic and trading alliances. More recent accounts, however, have stressed the continuity of Henry's reign, especially with his Yorkist predecessor, Edward IV. His continued reliance on his nobility as the essential link between the crown and the localities has been stressed, while the novelty of his financial policies has been downplayed. Moreover, by invading France in 1492 and waging war with Scotland in 1496, Henry could be seen to be continuing the traditional policies of English medieval kings.

Nevertheless, Henry's policies represented, in some respects, a significant break from the past. He used the crown's landed patrimony, augmented through forfeitures and dynastic accident in the fifteenth century, to build up the crown's military and political strength in the localities, at times riding roughshod over local sensibilities. Henry's willingness to tax his subjects led to rebellion in 1489 and 1497, and his use of suspended financial penalties ensured that most of the nobility and much of the wider political nation were bound to the king by the early 1500s. At his death Henry had amassed a fortune, probably in excess of one million pounds. While these policies may have caused resentment and unrest in certain parts of the realm, there were no significant plots or rebellions within England after 1499.

Henry died on 22 April 1509, although his death was kept secret while his unpopular ministers, Empson and Dudley, were deposed in a palace coup. A measure of his success in establishing a new dynasty on the English throne must be that he was the first English king since Henry V (ruled 1413–1422) to pass the throne undisputed to his son and heir, who was to reign as Henry VIII (ruled 1509–1547).

See also **Henry VIII (England); Tudor Dynasty (England).**

BIBLIOGRAPHY

Carpenter, Christine. "Henry VII and the End of the Wars." In *The Wars of the Roses: Politics and the Constitution c. 1437–1509,* edited by Christine Carpenter. Cambridge, U.K., and New York, 1997. Hostile analysis of Henry's reign.

Chrimes, S. B. *Henry VII.* New Haven and London, 1999. Standard biography of Henry, strong on administration but lacking in analysis of politics.

Condon, Margaret. "Ruling Elites in the Reign of Henry VII." In *The Tudor Monarchy,* edited by John Guy. London, 1997.

Cunningham, S. "Henry VII and Rebellion in North-Eastern England, 1485–1492: Bonds of Allegiance and the Establishment of Tudor Authority." *Northern History* 32 (1996): 42–74.

Grummitt, David. "'For the Surety of the Towne and Marches': Early Tudor Policy towards Calais 1485–1509." *Nottingham Medieval Studies* 44 (2000): 184–203.

———. "Henry VII, 'Chamber Finance and the New Monarchy': Some New Evidence." *Historical Research* 72 (1999): 229–243.

Gunn, S. J. "The Accession of Henry VIII." *Bulletin of the Institute of Historical Research* 64 (1991): 278–288.

———. "The Courtiers of Henry VII." *English Historical Review* 108 (1993): 23–49; reprinted in *The Tudor Monarchy,* edited by John Guy (1997).

———. "Sir Thomas Lovell (c. 1449–1524): A New Man in a New Monarchy?" In *The End of the Middle Ages,* edited by John L. Watts, pp. 117–153. Stroud, U.K., 1998.

Jones, M. K., and M. G. Underwood. *The King's Mother: Lady Margaret Beaufort, Countess of Richmond and Derby.* Cambridge, U.K., and New York, 1992. Biography of Henry's mother and analysis of her important role in the formation of the Tudor regime.

Luckett, D. A. "Crown Office and Licensed Retinues in the Reign of Henry VII." In *Rulers and Ruled in Late Medieval England,* edited by Rowena Archer and Simon Walker, pp. 223–238. London, 1995.

———. "Crown Patronage and Political Morality in Early Tudor England: The Case of Giles, Lord Daubeney." *English Historical Review* 110 (1995): 578–595.

Pugh, T. B. "Henry VII and the English Nobility." In *The Tudor Nobility,* edited by G. W. Bernard, pp. 49–101. Manchester, 1992.

Thompson, B., ed. *The Reign of Henry VII.* Stamford, 1995. Especially the introduction and the contributions of Christine Carpenter, Dominic Luckett, and John Watts.

DAVID GRUMMITT

HENRY VIII (ENGLAND) (1491–1547; ruled 1509–1547), king of England. Henry VIII has a good claim to be regarded as England's most important monarch. It was he who initiated and pushed through the seminal event in the nation's history, the break with the church of Rome. Though historians have long debated the king's motivations and the depth of his control over the policy-making process, few would question his fundamental importance to the English Reformation; nor indeed that of the English Reformation to the subsequent historical development of England, Britain, and the British Empire.

Born at Greenwich Palace on 28 June 1491, the child of Henry VII (Henry Tudor; ruled 1485–1509) and Elizabeth of York, Henry was second in line to the throne. He became heir apparent after his elder brother, Arthur, died of consumption in 1502. On 22 April 1509 Henry's respected but unloved father died; the young prince ascended the throne amid popular rejoicing, the first uncontested succession in over half a century.

The new king quickly disposed of his father's chief ministers, Richard Empson and Edmund Dudley (both executed for constructive treason in 1510). Their place was taken by the brilliant and ostentatious commoner Thomas Wolsey (c. 1475–1530). Henry ruled through Wolsey, who became his lord chancellor, from 1514 to 1529, making him the principal influence on the formulation of royal policy and giving him authority over the day-to-day affairs of government. The main focus of policy during the first half of the reign was foreign affairs. The early years were taken up by war with France and Scotland (1511–1514). In France, Henry achieved his first success on the field of battle (the Battle of the Spurs, 1513); in the same year King James IV of Scotland (ruled 1488–1513) was defeated and killed at the head of an invading army at Flodden. Glorious though it might be, war was a drain on the nation's finances. Wolsey had a more realistic appreciation than his master of England's limited resources and inferior status to the Continent's leading powers; instead of war he pursued diplomacy as a cost-effective means of retaining the place of the king at the forefront of European relations, largely through acting as a peace broker in the conflicts between France, Spain, and the Holy Roman Empire. Henry tired of the passive role in the early 1520s, invading France once again in 1523. This invasion was an ignominious failure, ending in retreat and a severe depletion of the crown treasury; it would be the last such enterprise for almost two decades.

THE DIVORCE

On 11 June 1509, Henry married Arthur's widow, Catherine of Aragón (1485–1536). The marriage failed to provide Henry with a male heir; only a girl born in 1516, the future Queen Mary, survived beyond infancy. For a long time a sequence of renewed pregnancies and the distractions of Wolsey's diplomatic schemes concealed the problem, but the unhappy cycle of miscarriages and stillborn infants would not cease, aging Catherine prematurely and turning Henry increasingly suspicious of the marriage. Henry's concerns were not idle: as a child of the Wars of the Roses he was acutely aware of the danger to the stability of the nation that a contested succession could bring; and as the child of the founder of the Tudor dynasty he knew that posterity would compare him with his father principally by his success in perpetuating the line. A male heir would certainly have saved the marriage, but by the early 1520s it was clear that Catherine could become pregnant no more.

Around mid-decade the substantial concerns over the succession combined with two related developments: the king's infatuation with a clever and desirable lady of the court named Anne Boleyn (1507?–1536) and his discovery of two texts in the Book of Leviticus that cast doubt on the theological probity of a marriage to a dead brother's wife. Henry soon decided that his marriage to Catherine was cursed by God and must be annulled forthwith; he would then marry Anne Boleyn, who would provide him with a son. Had Catherine been English, the papal dissolution of the marriage would have been granted immediately. But Catherine was the aunt of the Holy Roman Emperor Charles V (ruled 1519–1556), whose army had recently sacked and occupied Rome (1527); under the circumstances the pope could not help the king.

Henry VIII. Painting by Hans Holbein.

THE BREAK WITH ROME

Yet the king would not be deflected. Wolsey, unable to advance the matter sufficiently and detested by Anne, was discarded and died on his way to a final reckoning with his master in 1529. The cardinal's place was taken by new men sympathetic to Anne's cause and, like the woman who would be queen herself, attracted to the incipient Protestant ideas that had emanated from Germany over the previous decade. Chief among them were Wolsey's erstwhile assistant Thomas Cromwell (1485?–1540), soon to replace his lord as the king's minister, and Thomas Cranmer (1489–1556), appointed archbishop of Canterbury in 1533. These two worked with the king and his mistress on a radical solution to the great matter: if the pope would not dissolve the marriage and allow Henry to marry Anne, then the king would follow his chosen course independently of Rome. The king was determined that the process should have the appearance of legitimacy; thus it was that Parliament was called into service to provide the legal apparatus that permitted Henry to have his way.

The Parliament that sat from 1529 to 1536 is rightly known to history as the Reformation Parliament. Though it had no program at the outset for making the break with Rome and establishing an independent Church of England, that is what it did. A succession of legislative instruments deprived Rome of its authority over the English spiritual estate, redirected its finances and property to the crown, and established the king as the supreme head of the English Church. At the same time, Henry was provided with his divorce and married to Anne in 1533; a child followed the same year, though to Henry's chagrin it was a daughter (the future Queen Elizabeth) rather than the expected son. By the middle of the decade Henry might have wondered if it had all been necessary: early in 1536 Catherine died of natural causes, and later the same year Anne, transformed from the enchanting mistress of the early days to a shrew of a wife, was executed on trumped-up charges of adultery and witchcraft, almost certainly the result of a contest between court factions seeking to make the best out of the king's growing dislike for his second marriage.

But by now the soap opera–like succession of events had been overtaken by a much greater story. Though the king was and remained for the rest of his life conservative in his theological beliefs (with some idiosyncratic exceptions), the repudiation of the authority of Rome provided the opportunity for those of more reformist belief to make the newly established church one whose theology owed more to the emerging Protestant faith than to that of the Roman Church. During the 1530s Cromwell and Cranmer urged the king not to stop at assuming the supreme headship of the church and subsuming the institution into the state, but to appoint Protestants to key clerical positions, to issue the first officially sanctioned English Bible (published in 1539), and even to adopt a Protestant theological code for the church.

CONSERVATISM

Yet the advances came at a price. Henry's innate conservatism asserted itself more strongly in the wake of Anne's execution, as he married the religiously conventional Jane Seymour (1509?–1537) and soon after faced a huge popular rebellion, known as the Pilgrimage of Grace, against the religious changes in the north of England. Though the rebellion was extinguished in 1537, Henry's concern at the pace of religious change became plain thereafter, and the momentum of reform slowed. Jane provided Henry with the much-desired son, the future Edward VI, in 1537, but she died days after giving birth.

As reform stagnated, Cromwell saw an opportunity to restore the initiative by pursuing the marriage of Henry to a German duchess with Protestant connections, Anne of Cleves (1515–1557). However, the plan backfired when the king set eyes on Anne for the first time just before the wedding in early 1540 and found her repulsive. Though the diplomatic situation was such that Henry had to go ahead with the marriage, Cromwell's position was fatally compromised: his enemies persuaded the king that he was disloyal, and he was executed in the summer of 1540.

The remainder of the reign saw few developments to match those of the 1530s, as the king put a stop to further doctrinal innovation and refocused his kingship on the pastime of his younger days, foreign policy. Henry ruled in the closing years without a minister, executing policy instead through a small body of elite advisors, the Privy Council. Foreign affairs were dominated by wars with Scotland and France. Scotland was invaded in 1542 and France in 1544; though both conflicts were concluded honorably (the Treaty of Greenwich with Scotland in 1543 and the Treaty of Ardres with France in 1546), there was little in the way of diplomatic compensation for the ruinous expenses incurred. All the while the king's marital adventures continued. In July 1540 Henry divorced Anne; less than three weeks later (on the same day as Cromwell's execution) he married Catherine Howard (1520?–1542). Accused of adultery, she was beheaded in 1542. Henry married Catherine Parr (1512–1548), his sixth and last wife, in 1543. The oldest of Henry's brides and previously married herself, she proved adept at managing the failing and increasingly irascible king in his dotage, not only to her own profit, but also to that of the Protestant cause, restraining the persecution of reformers and ensuring that the young prince Edward was educated by men of reformed views. King Henry VIII died on 28 January 1547, leaving behind him an independent English church, a son and regency council who would over the next five-and-a-half years put England on a course of radical religious reform, and a daughter in Elizabeth who would consolidate and defend the national church and associated national identity that her father had done so much to establish.

See also **Church of England; Cromwell, Thomas; Divorce; Edward VI (England); Elizabeth I (England); Julius II (pope); Mary I (England); More, Thomas; Reformation, Protestant; Tudor Dynasty (England).**

BIBLIOGRAPHY

Primary Source

Letters and Papers, Foreign and Domestic, of the Reign of Henry VIII, 1509–1547. Edited by J. S. Brewer, J. Gairdner, and R. H. Brodie. London, 1862–1910.

Secondary Sources

Elton, Geoffrey R. *Reform and Reformation: England, 1509–1558.* London, 1977.

Guy, John. *Tudor England.* Oxford, 1988.

MacCulloch, Diarmaid. *Thomas Cranmer: A Life.* New Haven, 1996.

McEntegart, Rory. *Henry VIII, the League of Schmalkalden, and the English Reformation.* Woodbridge, U.K., and Rochester, N.Y., 2002.

Scarisbrick, J. J. *Henry VIII.* London, 1968.

Starkey, David. *The Reign of Henry VIII: Personalities and Politics.* London, 1985.

———. *Six Wives: The Queens of Henry VIII.* London, 2003.

Weir, Alison. *Henry VIII: The King and His Court.* New York, 2001.

RORY MCENTEGART

HENRY II (FRANCE)

HENRY II (FRANCE) (1519–1559; ruled 1547–1559), king of France. The second son of Francis I (ruled 1515–1547) and Claude of France, Henry was born on 31 March 1519. He was seven years old when he and his older brother Francis were sent to Spain as hostages for their father, who had been captured at Pavia in February 1525. Henry felt that the Spanish mistreated him during the four years he was a prisoner and bore a lifelong grudge against both his father and Emperor Charles V (ruled 1519–1556). In October 1533 he wedded Catherine de Médicis (1519–1589) as part of an alliance with the Medici pope, Clement VII (reigned 1523–1534). The pope soon died, ending the political value of the marriage, which also came under strain because of the lack of children for the first ten years. Henry and Catherine eventually had seven children who survived childhood. Henry's love for Diane de Poitiers further strained the marriage. Henry first met Diane when he returned from Spain in 1530, and he loved her until his death, although she was twenty years his senior.

When his older brother died in 1536, Henry became dauphin, and he ascended the throne on 31 March 1547 at the death of his father. He already had a cadre of close advisers—the constable Anne, duke of Montmorency (1493–1567); François de Lorraine, duke of Guise (1519–1563), and his brother, Charles de Lorraine, cardinal of Lorraine (1524–1574); and Marshal Jacques D'Albion de Saint-André—who now dominated the royal council. Diane also wielded broad influence over her royal lover. In government Henry largely carried on trends begun under his father; his major innovation was creating the offices of the four secretaries of state, each having responsibility for a different area of administration. The selling of royal offices was

Henry II. Portrait by François Clouet, c. 1555. ©ARTE & IMMAGINI SRL/CORBIS

already an important source of royal revenue, but Henry greatly increased the number of venal offices.

The war against the Habsburgs continued during Henry's reign, and he allied with the German Lutherans and the Ottoman Turks against them. With the approval of the Lutheran princes, he occupied the three bishoprics of Lorraine, and in cooperation with the Ottoman fleet, he seized Corsica from Charles V's ally Genoa in 1553. Henry's alliance with the Lutherans prevented him from being as severe on the French Protestants as he wished, but he took seriously his oath to protect the Catholic Church. Shortly after becoming king, he created a new chamber in the Parlement of Paris to deal with heresy. Called the *chambre ardente* ("zealous chamber") for its zealous pursuit of Protestants, it condemned thirty-seven persons to death in three years. The Catholic hierarchy's objections to its loss of jurisdiction over heresy persuaded him to close it down in 1550. The rivalry between the parlement and the episcopate over heresy prosecution rendered ineffective such harsh edicts against heresy as the Edict of Châteaubriand in 1551. This problem and Henry's perception that heresy was lower-class sedition led him to overlook Protestantism in the French elite, and it flourished despite his resolve to rid his realm of religious dissent.

Like his father, Henry was a patron of Renaissance culture, although he preferred to patronize French talent. He completed several projects begun by Francis, including the château of Fontainebleau and the reconstruction of the Louvre, while putting his own stamp on them. The major building project under Henry was the château of Anet, done for Diane de Poitiers by Philibert Delorme (de L'Orme; 1515?–1570). In literature, Henry's reign saw a reaction against the emphasis on using Latin and a greater effort to use French, as Joachim Du Bellay (c. 1522–1560) argued in his *Defense and Illustration of the French Language* (1549). Du Bellay was a member of the Pléiade, a group of poets who wrote in French. The most famous among them was Pierre de Ronsard (1524–1585).

The end of Henry's reign was shadowed by economic problems, a huge royal debt amounting to 2.5 times the annual royal revenues, an upsurge in religious dissent, and continued war with the Habsburgs. When he sent an army under the duke of Guise to Italy to reclaim Naples and Milan at the urging of Pope Paul IV, Philip II (ruled 1556–1598) invaded northern France and defeated Montmorency at Saint-Quentin in August 1557. When Philip failed to push his forces on to attack Paris, Henry sent the army assembled for defending the city to take Calais in January 1558. With the fortunes of war balanced, both rulers agreed to the Peace of Cateau-Cambrésis in 1559. Henry, jousting in a tournament celebrating the peace and the marriage by proxy of his daughter Elisabeth to Philip, was fatally wounded when his opponent's shattered lance struck him in the face. He died on 10 July 1559, leaving his fifteen-year-old son Francis II (ruled 1559–1560) a realm beset with problems, the most serious of which was the religious division.

See also **Cateau-Cambrésis (1559); Renaissance.**

BIBLIOGRAPHY

Primary Source

Baudouin-Matusek, M. N., and Anne Merlin-Chazelas, eds. *Catalogue des actes de Henri II.* 6 vols. Paris, 1979–2002.

Secondary Sources

Baumgartner, Frederic J. *Henry II, King of France, 1547–1559.* Durham, N.C., 1988. Scholarly biography, only recent one in English.

Cloulas, Ivan. *Henri II.* Paris, 1985. Especially strong on Henry's patronage of art and culture.

FREDERIC J. BAUMGARTNER

HENRY III (FRANCE) (1551–1589), king of France. Henry III was the last of the Valois dynasty and has claim to be the only intellectual to have ruled France. Unfortunately he had the double misfortune of ruling at time of prolonged civil war and of failing to produce an heir, ensuring that during his reign monarchical authority plumbed new depths of impotence. He was the sixth child and the third surviving son of Henry II (ruled 1547–1559) and Catherine de Médicis (1519–1589). His political role began early with the death of his eldest brother Francis II (1544–1560) in 1560 and the accession of Charles IX (ruled 1560–1574), making him next in line to the throne. In 1566 he became duke of Anjou and entered the royal council, where he soon made his mark as a champion of the Ultra-Catholic faction and an enemy of the prince of Condé (1530–1569), leader of the Protestant party.

Henry was a more talented and cultured man than King Charles and was less interested than his brother in traditional aristocratic pursuits such as hunting. He was the favorite son of Catherine de Médicis, and when the Wars of Religion broke out once more in 1567, she secured his appointment as commander in chief of the royal armies. Aided by a council of experienced captains, his tenure was initially successful, defeating the Protestants at Jarnac (March 1569) and Moncontour (October 1569). These victories sealed his reputation as the youthful hero of renascent Catholicism. But otherwise outright victory remained elusive, and the war ended in a compromise peace. Henry's Ultra-Catholic sensibilities in this period gave him a vengeful streak. He transgressed chivalric convention in 1569 by ordering the murder of Condé, who had been captured at Jarnac. His role in the Massacre of Saint Bartholomew (24 August 1572) is obscure, but he was deeply implicated in the conspiracy to eliminate the Protestant leadership.

Henry's sojourn as king of Poland in the winter of 1573–1574 and his extensive travels on his return to France to claim the throne on the death of his brother (May 1574) were a turning point. Henry now believed that Protestantism would never be defeated militarily and that civil war merely served to weaken royal authority. The fortunes of the monarchy had reached their lowest ebb, and only thoroughgoing reforms of church and state could rebuild its power. Crucial to this project were the favorites, or *mignons,* who had shared his exile and who were rewarded with royal patronage; they were a valuable core of support at a time of political instability. Henry embarked on a series of reforms of the court, of royal administration, and of finances, and by the early 1580s he had succeeded in reestablishing royal authority and balancing the books. His devout Catholicism was now redirected to combating the threat posed by the Catholic League by promoting Counter-Reformation piety within his administration and to combating schism by winning lost souls back to the faith. A supporter of the new religious orders, he encouraged his subjects to greater piety through extravagant displays of public devotion and encouraged his nobles through the foundation of the Order of the Holy Spirit.

Henry III (France). Equestrian portrait c.1580, French school. THE ART ARCHIVE/MUSÉE CONDÉ CHANTILLY/DAGLI ORTI (A)

Henry was a controversial figure in his own lifetime. He improved royal finances through the unpopular practices of selling offices and by interfering in provincial administration. Henry's baroque piety was seen as undignified for a king, and many aristocrats were alienated by the favoritism shown to his *mignons.* Opposition would have remained marginal and Henry's private life the subject of harmless gossip had he not been childless. In 1584 his younger brother and heir died, leaving the Protestant Henry of Navarre (1553–1610) as his successor. Henry III believed he could outmaneuver the revived Catholic League as he had before, but support for the movement led by Henry, duke of Guise, and his brother Cardinal Louis II melded intense popular religiosity with the defense of the traditional rights under attack from the rejuvenated monarchy. Particular vituperation was reserved for Henry's beloved *mignons* the duke of Epernon and Joyeuse. Henry's lukewarm support for war against the Protestants led to an uprising in Paris (May 1588), which left the king at the mercy of the Guise brothers and their supporters in the Catholic League. In December 1588 Henry had the Guise brothers murdered and joined forces with Navarre, ensuring that most of northern France rebelled against him. Henry was assassinated by a Catholic fanatic while besieging Paris in August 1589.

Henry III was largely dismissed in the centuries after his death as too pious, too ineffectual, and responsible for the collapse of royal authority. However, his reputation has been revived by historians who see his reforming zeal as a precursor to the religious and political changes of the seventeenth century, and as a complex and intelligent man struggling against forces beyond his control.

See also **Condé Family; Guise Family; Valois Dynasty (France); Wars of Religion, French.**

BIBLIOGRAPHY

Cameron, Keith. *Henri III: A Maligned or Malignant King?* Exeter, U.K., 1978.

Holt, Mack P. *The French Wars of Religion, 1562–1629.* Cambridge, U.K., 1995.

Martin, A. Lynn. *Henri III and the Jesuit Politicians.* Geneva, Switzerland, 1973.

Potter, David. "Kingship in the Wars of Religion: The Reputation of Henri III." *European History Quarterly* 25 (1995): 485–528.

Salmon, J. H. M. *Society in Crisis: France in the Sixteenth Century.* London, 1975.

Yates, Frances A. *Astraea: The Imperial Theme in the Sixteenth Century.* London, 1993.

———. *The French Academies of the Sixteenth Century.* London, 1988.

STUART CARROLL

HENRY IV (FRANCE) (1553–1610; ruled 1589–1610), king of France and Navarre. Henry IV helped to end the Wars of Religion and established the foundation for France's emergence as a major power in early modern Europe. He was the first of the Bourbon kings, and his family ruled until the French Revolution of 1789 and again during the Restoration (1815–1830). Much admired by contemporaries for his bravery and his gallantry, Henry IV was known as the Gallic Hercules and endures to this day as one of France's most popular rulers.

FAMILY AND EARLY LIFE (1553–1572)

Henry was born 14 December 1553 at the château of Pau in Béarn. His father, Antoine de Bourbon, the duke of Vendôme (1518–1562), was a prince of the blood and headed the powerful Bourbon-Vendôme household, whose vast domains stretched from central to southwestern France. The Bourbons' lineage went back to Robert, count of Clermont (1256–1318), the sixth son of Louis IX (ruled 1226–1270). This remote royal ancestry assumed huge significance as Henry II's (ruled 1547–1559) sons each failed to sire an heir to continue the Valois dynasty. Henry IV's mother, Jeanne d'Albret, queen of Navarre (ruled 1555–1572), ruled a tiny kingdom straddling the Pyrenees. Her public embrace of Calvinism in 1555 soon introduced her young son and her daughter, Catherine, to the faith. Members of the Condé branch of the Bourbon-Vendôme family also converted, most notably Louis, Prince of Condé, who led the Huguenot movement until his violent death in 1569. Henry received his formal education from Pierre Victor Palma-Cayet and François de La Gaucherie, who reinforced his Calvinist upbringing in what was otherwise a typical Renaissance curriculum that combined book learning with training in horsemanship and the handling of arms. He also frequented the royal court, which schooled him in the ways of intrigue and gallantry. Although not intellectually inclined, Henry matured to become a keen judge of character and prone to decisive, frequently impulsive acts of will to overcome the many obstacles that he faced during his eventful life. These qualities served him well as the country slipped into the chaos of the Wars of Religion (1562–1598).

HUGUENOT LEADER AND HEIR TO THE THRONE (1572–1589)

In a bid to end factional strife, the queen mother, Catherine de Médicis (1510–1589), arranged a marriage between her daughter, Marguerite of Valois (1553–1615), and Henry on 17 August 1572. The wedding, which was held in Paris, instead led to the St. Bartholomew's Day Massacre, during which thousands of Huguenots died, including the movement's leader, Gaspard de Coligny (1519–1572), admiral of France. Henry escaped death by renouncing his Calvinist faith and becoming a prisoner at the Valois court until his escape in February 1576. After recanting his forced conversion, Henry consolidated his leadership of the Huguenots during the course of the three wars that broke out over the next eight years. Henry's status dramatically changed when, according to the Salic law of succession, he became heir presumptive to the French throne as a result of the death on 10 June 1584 of Francis, Duke of Alençon (1555–1584). The specter of a Huguenot succession caused a clash between the rules governing a hereditary succession and the monarchy's long and close affiliation with Catholicism. As a result, the question of Henry of Navarre's confessional allegiances became the central issue of the day. Militant Catholics rallied to the Holy League revived in 1584 by Henry of Lorraine, duke of Guise (1550–1589), especially after Pope Sixtus V (ruled 1585–1590) excommunicated Navarre the next year. The inability of Henry III (ruled 1574–1589) to maintain order following his humiliating expulsion from Paris on the Day of the Barricades (12 May 1588)

Henry IV (France). Henry IV grants regency to Marie de Médicis as he leaves for war in Germany, 1610. Painting by Peter Paul Rubens. THE ART ARCHIVE/MUSÉE DU LOUVRE PARIS/DAGLI ORTI (A)

culminated in his calamitous decision on 24 December 1588 to order the murders of Henry, duke of Guise, and his brother, Louis, the cardinal of Guise. Rather than restore royal authority, the move sparked a general insurrection across the kingdom that eventually resulted in the king's own assassination at the hands of a fanatical monk on 1 August 1589. The regicide brought Henry of Navarre to the throne as Henry IV, though it was five years before he was able to command the obedience of his rebellious Catholic subjects.

WINNING THE KINGDOM (1589–1598)

Henry IV's promise in the Declaration of St. Cloud (4 August 1589) to consider in the near future a possible Catholic conversion, coupled with decisive military victories at Arques (21 September 1589) and Ivry (14 March 1590), shored up public support for him. The grueling siege of Paris (summer 1590) demonstrated that Catholic League resistance could not be overcome by sheer force, however. Three years later, while an Estates-General met in Leaguer Paris to contemplate the election of a new French ruler, Henry IV finally decided to convert to Catholicism amidst much fanfare on 25 July 1593 at St. Denis. The advice of Maximilien de Béthune, baron of Rosny and duke of Sully (1559–1641), himself a Protestant, and of Henry IV's Catholic mistress, Gabrielle d'Estrées (1573?–1599), are thought to have heavily influenced the king's decision to make this "perilous leap." The famous phrase "Paris is worth a Mass" actually came from Catholics who wanted to impugn the sincerity of Henry IV's conversion. Crowned in accordance with Catholic ceremony on 27 February 1594 at Chartres, Henry IV triumphantly entered Paris on 24 March 1594. In 1595, Pope Clement VIII affirmed the converted king's standing as a Catholic by bestowing a papal absolution upon him. Assassination attempts came close to ending Henry IV's life on several occasions and eventually resulted in the expulsion of the Jesuits from the kingdom in 1595. Over the next three years, Henry IV gradually pacified the kingdom more by kindness than by force, winning the allegiance of former Catholic Leaguers through generous peace accords and allaying Huguenot fears in 1598 with the royal guarantees enshrined in the celebrated Edict of Nantes. The year 1598 also saw the signing of the Treaty of Vervins, which brought to a favorable conclusion France's long war with Spain.

RECOVERY AND RENEWAL (1598–1610)

With peace finally at hand, Henry IV initiated a program to restore the kingdom's well-being and the monarchy's authority. First he had to secure his dynasty's future. Against the better judgment of his advisors, Henry IV actively pursued the possibility of making Gabrielle his queen after the pope annulled his marriage to Marguerite of Valois in February 1599. Gabrielle had borne the king three children, all of whom he had legitimized by acts of the parlement. They were César, duke of Vendôme (1594–1665), Catherine-Henriette (1596–1663), and Alexandre, later grand prior of France (1598–1629). Gabrielle's death in childbirth on 10 April 1599, however, dashed Henry's hopes of marrying the woman he most adored and had come to rely upon during the early years of his reign. The king instead married Marie de Médicis (1573–1642), daughter of the Duke of Tuscany, in October 1600. On 27 September 1601, she bore him the future Louis XIII (d. 1643), who continued the Bourbon line.

Henry IV's military successes and dashing manner won him strong admiration from the nobility, whose support was crucial in pacifying the country. With the aid of Sully, who served as *surintendant* of finances, the king put the crown's fiscal house back in order through prudent expenditures, an overhaul of municipal finance, and the consolidation of the state's debt. By 1608, Sully estimated that the royal treasury had accumulated reserves totaling 32.5 million livres. Henry IV also introduced a ministerial style of government that restricted the judicial prerogatives claimed by the parlements and provincial privileges claimed by local representative assemblies. In 1604, Henry IV regularized the heritable nature of venal offices by the payment of a special fee known as the Paulette. He also cultivated close relations with the old nobility by showering them with pensions and titles; those aristocrats who conspired against him felt his full wrath, however, as demonstrated by the execution of Charles, duke of Biron (1562–1602). Henry IV also encouraged the beginnings of Catholic reform among both churchmen and the lay public, working hard at the same time to uphold the protections recently granted to the Huguenots. On the economic front, the king entrusted to Barthélemy de Laffemas (c. 1545–1611) the execution of innovative measures to restore commerce and living standards—a campaign reflected in the contemporary slogan of a "chicken in every pot" *(la poule au pot)*.

Henry also initiated a major urban renewal project in Paris with the building of the Pont-Neuf, the Place Royale (now Place des Vosges), the Place Dauphine, a new Hôtel de Ville, the great gallery of the Louvre, and the completion of the Tuileries garden. During his reign, the eclecticism of the late French Renaissance gradually gave way to the more grandiose, royally inspired movement known as Classicism. Militarily, the king secured territorial gains for France in the southeast at the expense of the Duchy of Savoy; with Sully's help, he also substantially upgraded the country's armaments industry and invested heavily in fortification construction along the frontiers in the north and east.

As France became more unified and strengthened under his leadership, Henry thought it increasingly necessary to challenge Habsburg hegemony in Europe. An occasion to do so arose in 1609 in the lower Rhineland over the disputed succession to Jülich-Clèves. On the eve of his planned invasion, 14 May 1610, however, the king was struck down in the streets of Paris by the blade of a fanatical Roman Catholic assassin. He died a martyr in the eyes of his subjects and of later writers, such as Voltaire and Jules Michelet, who came to identify Henry IV as the very embodiment of what was best about the French. The style of rule and policy directions introduced by Henry IV led to France's rise under his successors as Europe's preeminent power during the next century.

See also **Absolutism; Bourbon Dynasty (France); Catherine de Médicis; France; Huguenots; Marie de Médicis; Nantes, Edict of; St. Bartholomew's Day Massacre; Wars of Religion (France).**

BIBLIOGRAPHY

Buisseret, David. *Henry IV.* London and Boston, 1984. An excellent biography that traces the course of Henry IV's life and contributions.

Finley-Croswhite, S. Annette. *Henry IV and the Towns: The Pursuit of Legitimacy in French Urban Society, 1589–1610.* Cambridge, U.K., and New York, 1999. Studies the problems and eventual solutions shaping Henry IV's relations with urban elites during times of war and peace.

Greengrass, Mark. *France in the Age of Henri IV: The Struggle for Stability.* 2nd ed. London and New York, 1995. A brilliant analysis of France's evolution under the first Bourbon king.

Love, Ronald. *Blood and Religion: The Conscience of Henry IV, 1553–1593.* Montreal and Ithaca, N.Y., 2001. A sensitive study that argues Henry IV remained a lifelong Calvinist even after 1593.

Wolfe, Michael. *The Conversion of Henri IV: Politics, Power, and Religious Belief in Early Modern France.* Cambridge, Mass., 1993. Examines the struggles sparked by the issue of Henry IV's religion during the 1580s and 1590s.

Michael Wolfe

HERALDRY. "Heraldry" is a term that was coined in the late sixteenth century to designate the profession of the heralds of arms, a profession that originated in the twelfth century, reached the height of its prestige and influence in the fifteenth and sixteenth, declined slowly in the seventeenth, and reached its historical nadir in the eighteenth century. The heralds have been aptly described as the priesthood of the secular religion of chivalry. Their duties included a knowledge of the emblems, identity, ancestry, dignities, precedence, and deeds of all of the members of the nobility of their district or "march of arms" (usually corresponding to a large province or a small kingdom), and of the rituals to be observed not only in knightly sports, but in the investiture of new knights, barons, princes, and kings, and in all other forms of secular ritual involving members of the noble order, especially funerals. By the early fourteenth century, the heralds had come to be permanently attached to the households of kings and princes, and divided into the ascending grades of pursuivant, herald, and king of arms. Those of the last grade—the senior heralds of kings and sovereign princes—had also been given jurisdiction over particular marches. Between 1415 and about 1520, these marches were increasingly grouped into regnal or comparable jurisdictions under a "principal king of arms," usually attached to the corresponding order of knighthood (the Garter in England, St. Michael in France, the Golden Fleece in the Burgundian lands), and the heralds placed under the authority of a principal king might also be incorporated in a college under his presidency.

Of course, the field with which the heralds were most closely identified throughout their history was that concerned with the family of iconic emblems (two-dimensional identity signs) employed exclusively (in countries including those of Britain and Iberia) or primarily (in all other countries) by nobles and noble corporations. This field came to be known in English by 1489 as "armory," since the original and always essential species of emblem used in this way—a formal design of fixed elements in fixed numbers, colors, attitudes, and arrangements most commonly displayed covering the surface of a shield (though also displayed on flags and surcoats)—had been given the name "arms," and the other species that came gradually to be formally associated with it came to be referred to by 1567 as "armorial bearings." Persons and corporations endowed with arms were now called "armigers" and described as "armigerous."

Down to about 1350 the science of armory seems to have been passed on orally, but from about that date forward, armory came to be the subject of brief treatises, composed both by heralds and by "heraldists" learned in the lore of heraldry. Such works were very rare before 1390, but from about that date they were produced in growing numbers in a growing number of countries, and they increased significantly in length and sophistication after 1520. These treatises were at first aimed primarily at heralds, but from about 1450 they were aimed at an audience that also included noblemen of all ranks, lawyers, court officials, and artisans who might need to paint arms on shields and flags. From about 1410 the treatises on armory were joined in many manuscripts by similar treatises on other aspects of heraldry, which soon included the imagined historical origins of the heralds and their profession (placed on the field before Troy), the qualities and knowledge ideally required of the three ranks of herald, the rights and duties of the heralds in particular ceremonies, the ranks of the nobility and how they could be acquired, the current holders of each of the higher ranks of lordly status and their arms, and the like. The heralds who composed these works were at pains to promote the dignity of their office and mystery, and in order to assimilate the latter to the growing Renaissance interest in esoteric symbolism and allegory, either borrowed or invented a vast array of symbolic implications and associations for the figures and colors of existing arms, which previously had borne little or no symbolic meaning. These fantastic ideas were only finally put to rest in the later seventeenth century, when learned antiquarians demonstrated their falsity.

Although the arms remained central to the mystery of armory, from the later fifteenth century the heralds took a steadily growing interest in the other types of armorial bearing—which included both secondary emblems and insignia (signs of nature, status, and rank)—that had come to be formally associated with the arms in the compound emblem known in English by 1548 as the "armorial achievement." Distinct emblematic and insignial forms of achievement evolved in a largely separate fashion in the fourteenth and fifteenth centuries. The former gradually attracted to it the more important emblems of the paraheraldic system that had emerged in the 1360s (livery colors, livery badges of several types, ciphers, mottoes, and combinations of the motto and badge now called "devices"), while the insignial form incorporated the more distinctive forms of headgear, staves, and collars introduced to indicate status and rank in both the ecclesiastical and nobiliary hierarchies. The period from 1500 to 1700 saw the full fusion of the insignial and emblematic types of achievement, the completion and generalization of national systems of coronets and a universal system of clerical hats, and the assignment of insignial significance to the form, metal, and orientation of the helmet. After about 1520, achievements increasingly displaced arms from their traditional places of display, including flags and the surcoats (or "tabards") of heralds.

Not surprisingly, both the conceptual design of armorial bearings and the artistic styles in which they were represented underwent considerable change during the course of the three centuries after 1480. The simple, generally dichromatic designs of classic armory gradually gave way to more complex, polychromatic designs involving numerous different forms of charge often set on partitions and geometrical subfields, the number of which multiplied steadily. The new forms of charge included many new monsters and figures drawn from both Christian and classical mythology. In keeping with the artistic trend of the period, all such figures were increasingly represented in natural forms and natural colors, and this contributed to the sharp decline in the standards of both design and representation characteristic of the period after 1660.

The armorial functions of the heralds in a number of countries (including those of the British Isles) were both increased and institutionalized in the fif-

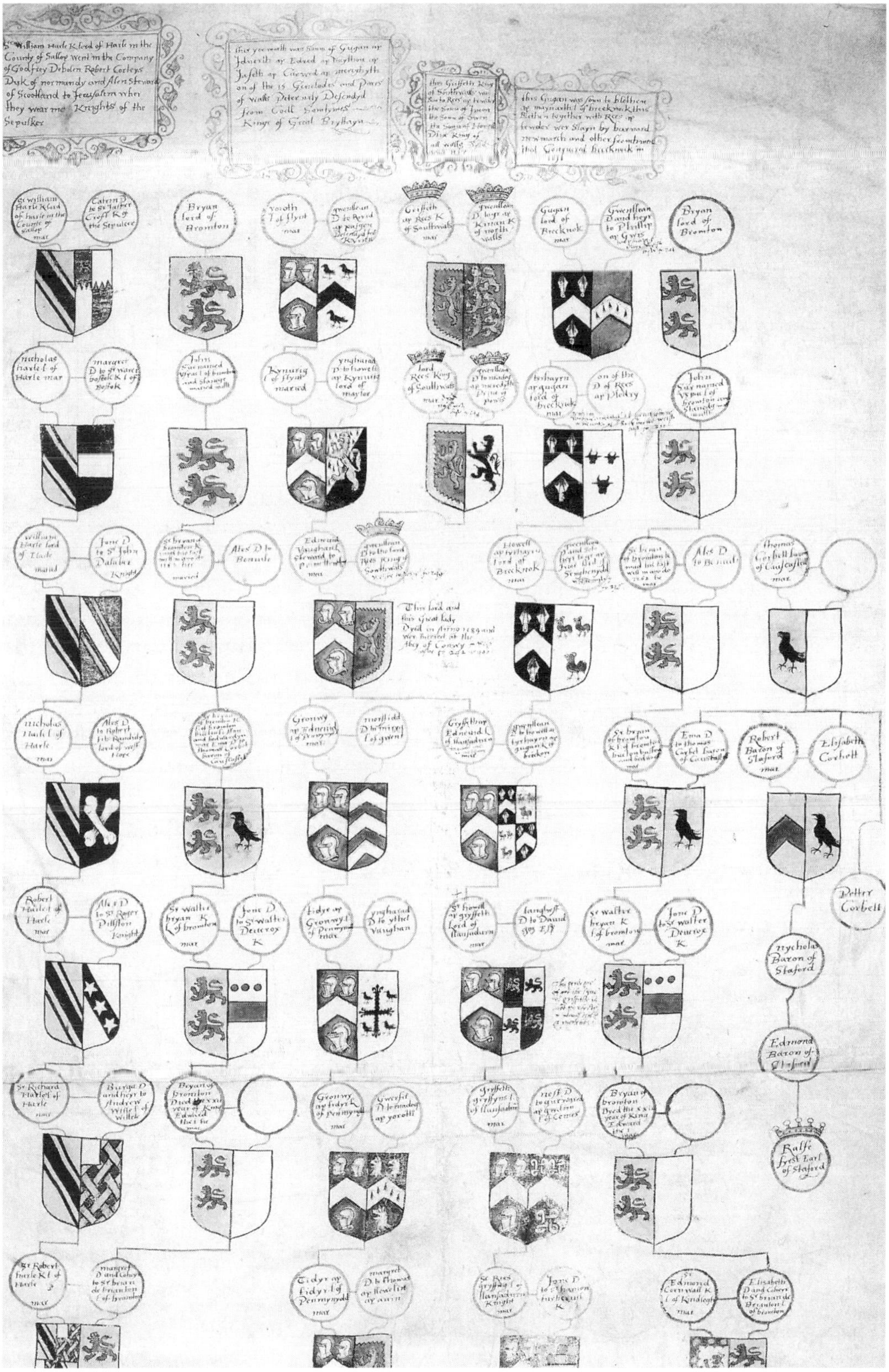

Heraldry. Pedigree roll of Anne Harle of Brompton by Thomas Jones, 1593, showing her lineage and the coats of arms of her ancestors. THE ART ARCHIVE/NATIONAL LIBRARY OF WALES/THE ART ARCHIVE

teenth and sixteenth centuries in order to maintain some royal control over admission to the nobility. Royal or princely edicts forbidding non-armigers to assume new arms (the principal mark of nobiliary status in many countries) were followed by letters conferring on the kings of arms the right to register existing arms and to confer new arms and other bearings on those they deemed worthy, making them the gatekeepers of the noble order. The earliest letters patent making grants of this sort date from the middle years of the fifteenth century, and they become steadily more numerous over the next century or so, marking very clearly the upward social mobility characteristic of that period. At some point, the heralds of some of these countries were also ordered to make visitations of the houses of all those living nobly, and of all armigerous corporations, to determine their right to arms; in England the recorded visitations began in 1530 and continued to 1687. Both heraldry and armory followed very different paths in other countries, however. In France, for example, the heralds were never given the right to grant or record arms or establish rules for usage, and no comparable authority was established until 1615, when the office of Juge d'armes (Judge of Arms) was created outside the College of Heralds—which as a result lost all connection to armory.

The value of armorial bearings in the eyes of all ranks of society throughout the Renaissance period is clear from the extent to which those who lacked them sought them and those who had them flaunted them. The period between about 1400 and 1650 was the heyday of heraldic display throughout Latin Europe, and both armorial and paraheraldic emblems were displayed by those who had them in every possible environment. Thereafter, the display of such emblems tended to become more restrained, but it remained important throughout the eighteenth century.

See also **Aristocracy and Gentry.**

BIBLIOGRAPHY

Dennis, Rodney. *The Heraldic Imagination.* London, 1975. An excellent introduction to the cultural world of the heralds.

Neubecker, Ottfried. *Heraldry: Sources, Symbols, and Meaning.* New York, 1976. The best general work on heraldry available in English.

Pastoureau, Michel. *Traité d'heraldique.* 3rd ed. Paris, 1997. The best scholarly introduction to heraldry from a Continental perspective.

Wagner, Sir Anthony. *Heralds of England: A History of the Office and College of Arms.* London, 1967. The only detailed history of the Office of Arms in England.

Woodcock, Thomas, and John Martin Robinson. *The Oxford Guide to Heraldry.* Oxford and New York, 2001. The best survey of English heraldic practice available.

D'A. J. D. BOULTON

HERDER, JOHANN GOTTFRIED VON (1744–1803), German philosopher and theologian. Born in Mohrungen, East Prussia (now Morag, Poland), the son of a schoolteacher, Herder studied at the university of Königsberg for two years, where he began a lifelong friendship and correspondence with Johann Georg Hamann (1730–1787) and heard lectures by Immanuel Kant (1724–1804), then a private lecturer, not yet famous or even a professor. In 1764 Herder began a career as a Lutheran pastor, first at Riga (1764–1769), then at the court of Schaumberg-Lippe in Bückeburg (1771–1776), and finally at the court of Sachsen-Weimar in Weimar (1776–1803). Twice he nearly joined the theological faculty at the University of Göttingen, but in 1776 when the Hanoverian court in London required that he submit to a test of religious orthodoxy, he opted to follow Johann Wolfgang von Goethe (1749–1832), whom he had met in Strasbourg in 1770, to Weimar. In 1789 the Weimar court promoted him as an inducement to decline Göttingen's offer.

During his travels in France and western Germany between his positions at Riga and Bückeburg, Herder learned of the annual essay competition sponsored by the Royal Prussian Academy of Sciences in Berlin on the topic of the origin of language. The Academy had been debating the question for nearly twenty-five years, and in December of 1770 as he convalesced from unsuccessful eye surgery in Strasbourg, Herder dashed off an entry in advance of a 1 January 1771 deadline. He won the competition, and the academy published the essay, which inaugurated a prolific literary career.

Herder's thesis, that the difference between humans and animals was language and that language was the vehicle of cognition, was not distinctly original. Others had pointed out that, since the orangutan possessed speech organs similar to those of humans but could not freely manipulate abstract concepts in the mind apart from what they represented in space and time, the seat of language had to be not in the mouth, but in the soul. The difference, argued Herder in *Abhandlung über den Ursprung der Sprache* (Essay on the origin of language), was in the purposes of man. "The bee was a bee as soon as it built its first cell," he wrote, "but a person was not human until he had achieved completeness. People continued to grow as long as they lived. . . . We are always in process, unsettled, unsatiated. The essence of our life is never satisfaction, rather always progression, and we have never been human until we have lived to the end."

Unlike animals, children were uniquely vulnerable, but that weakness was by design. Children must learn to speak, and the family was the social unit charged with educating children in that most basic and essential of all human capacities—language. More than teaching a child language, the family also imparted the individual's sense of identity and made him or her part of a group. Herder took it as a natural law that "man is by destiny a creature of the herd, of society." Where Jean-Jacques Rousseau had said in *Émile* that the child had more to say to the mother than the mother to the child, Herder countered that by teaching children language, the family's manner of thinking and set of values were developed and preserved. The education of the human race occurred in the bosom of the family. "Why does the mute child so weakly and unwittingly depend on his mother's breasts and his father's knee? So that he might be hungry for learning and learn language. He is weak so that his race may be strong." The treasury of the family heritage was preserved through the family language. As the clan expanded into a tribe, it celebrated the deeds of its forefathers. All heroic poetry—Germanic, Ossianic, Homeric—was tribal, that is, familial, in origin.

Through the 1770s and 1780s Herder explored the formation of national character in the primitive state. *Die ältesten Urkunden des Menschengeschlechts* (1774; The oldest documents of the human race) and *Auch eine Philosophie der Geschichte zur Bildung der Menschheit* (1774; Yet another philosophy of history for the education of humanity) were comparative studies of the primitive mind in society, while *Von deutscher Art und Kunst* (1773; On the German type and art) and *Vom Geist der hebräischen Poesie* (1782–1783; The spirit of Hebrew poetry) celebrated the unique spirit of primitive Germanic and Hebrew literature. Although his prose essays drew together much of the leading scholarship of the day, Herder reflected the innovations of other scholars more than he advanced his own. His real genius was as a translator of poetry, and here he influenced Goethe and secured his reputation as an author of national import in the Romantic period. He collected two volumes of *Volkslieder* (Folksongs; 1778–1779, reissued posthumously with a third volume as *Stimmen der Völker in Liedern* [Voices of the peoples in song]), and his version of the Spanish heroic epic *El Cid* went through literally dozens of editions and reprintings in the nineteenth century. In what is now his most famous work, *Ideen zur Philosophie der Geschichte der Menschheit* (1784–1791; Ideas for the philosophy of the history of humanity, 4 vols.), he insisted that the education of the human race was tantamount to the education of individuals. The goal of the individual was to develop his or her personhood or humanity, and as individuals developed their faculties, so did the family, the community, the nation, and humanity as a whole. There was such a thing as what Gotthold Ephraim Lessing called "the education of the human race" but not in the Neoplatonic sense of individuals participating in some unified World Soul. Instead each individual, community, and nation developed according to its own internal logic, which was unique and valuable in its own right. Herder hated all forms of centralization and imperialism, whether ancient Roman or modern European, as these suppressed the unique genius of both the conquerors and the vanquished.

His notion of the uniqueness of cultural groups and the particular manifestations of mind in human history brought him into conflict with Kant's critical philosophy. Toward the end of his life Herder offered a *Metacritique* (1799) of Kant's *Critique of Pure Reason* (1781) arguing that there was no such thing as pure reason, only human reason. If language was the vehicle of reason, and if languages differed between nations, then so must reason also differ. Reason existed only in particular historical circumstances as it was exercised by particular peoples, nations, and communities. Just as he wrote in

Ideen zur Philosophie der Geschichte der Menschheit that each society must find its own unique form of happiness, and within a society each generation must do the same, so in the *Metacritique* he said that each nation defines reason and rationality in its own terms, terms that do not necessarily correspond to those of eighteenth-century Europe.

See also **German Literature and Language; Germany, Idea of; Goethe, Johann Wolfgang von; Kant, Immanuel; Lessing, Gotthold Ephraim; Neoplatonism; Romanticism.**

BIBLIOGRAPHY

Primary Sources

Herder, Johann Gottfried. *Essay on the Origin of Language.* Translated by John H. Moran and Alexander Gode. New York, 1967. Together with Jean-Jacques Rousseau's *Essay on the Origin of Languages.*

———. *J. G. Herder on Social and Political Culture.* Edited and translated by F. M. Barnard. Cambridge, U.K., 1969. This most widely available English edition of Herder contains loose and misleading translations and should be carefully verified with the German.

———. *Outlines of a Philosophy of the History of Man.* Translated by T. O. Churchill. London, 1800. Abridged as *Reflections on the Philosophy of the History of Mankind.* Edited by Frank E. Manuel. Chicago, 1968.

———. *Philosophical Writings.* Translated and edited by Michael N. Forster. Cambridge, U.K., and New York, 2002.

———. *Sämtliche Werke.* Edited by Bernhard Suphan et al. 33 vols. Tübingen, 1877–1913.

———. *The Spirit of Hebrew Poetry.* Translated by James Marsh. Burlington, Vt., 1833.

———. *Werke in zehn Bänden.* Edited by Martin Bollacher et al. 10 vols. Frankfurt am Main, 1985–2000.

Secondary Sources

Beiser, Frederick C. *The Fate of Reason: German Philosophy from Kant to Fichte.* Cambridge, Mass., 1989.

Berlin, Isaiah. *Vico and Herder: Two Studies in the History of Ideas.* London, 1976.

Clark, Robert T. *Herder: His Life and Thoughts.* Berkeley, 1955.

Ergang, Robert Reinhold. *Herder and the Foundations of German Nationalism.* New York, 1931.

Koepke, Wulf. *Johann Gottfried Herder.* Boston, 1987.

Zammito, John. *Kant, Herder, and the Birth of Anthropology* Chicago, 2001.

MICHAEL CARHART

HERMETICISM. Hermeticism was a philosophical movement that arose in Alexandria around the first century C.E. Influenced by Platonism, Gnosticism, Egyptian thought, and probably both Jewish and early Christian thought, Hermeticism represented a syncretistic response to foreign domination, appropriating and transforming philosophical ideas in a manner congenial to native Egyptians. The most influential texts for the Renaissance, the Hermetic Corpus, purported to be conversations between Hermes Trismegistus (Thrice-Great Hermes), an ancient Egyptian priest, and various interlocutors, particularly Pimander (the demiurge), Hermes' son Tat (a Romanized form of the Greek Thoth and the Egyptian Theuth), and Asclepius (to the Romans, Aesculapius). These texts proposed a theurgical (god-influencing), mystical, and magical philosophy similar to Neoplatonism. Many early thinkers believed Hermes to be approximately contemporary with Moses; most importantly, Lactantius (c. 240–320), Clement of Alexandria (c. 150–211 or 215), and Augustine (354–430) granted his antiquity, though the latter considered him "amicably disposed towards [the] mockeries of the demons" (*City of God* VIII, 23). The Greek texts, long lost, were rediscovered in 1460 in Macedonia, whence they were transported to Cosimo de' Medici in Florence, who in 1463 commissioned Marsilio Ficino (1433–1499) to translate them, interrupting the latter's work on Plato. Ficino too accepted Hermes' claims, and later thinkers generally followed his opinion; many considered Hermes the fountainhead of pagan learning, even claiming that all learning derived ultimately either from the tradition of Moses or from that of Hermes.

Renaissance Hermeticism had its heyday in the sixteenth century, when references to "the divine Hermes" became commonplace, often marking anti-Aristotelian and otherwise counter-mainstream philosophies. One early exemplar was Giovanni Pico della Mirandola (1463–1494), who drew on both Hermeticism and Cabala and argued that the two might bring about a renovation of learning.

An essential doctrine for Renaissance Hermeticism was the idea of the microcosm, which suggested that between universe and man existed a powerful analogy, such that each could be interpreted in light of the other. This bore fruit in alchemy, in which transmutation of base metals into gold within a universelike crucible effected a parallel transmutation of the alchemist's soul. Thus the name of Hermes became a banner for occult and mystical philosophies.

Hermeticism clearly encouraged the Renaissance interest in Egypt, which influenced speculations on language and linguistic philosophy, particularly in the seventeenth century, when the Jesuit Athanasius Kircher (1601–1680) published voluminous works on hieroglyphs. More generally, Hermes served as an inspiration and justification for radical explorations of nature and divinity, notably by Paracelsus (1493–1541), Giordano Bruno (1548–1600), and John Dee (1527–1608).

The English scholar Dame Frances Yates famously proposed that the Hermetic revival also encouraged the success of the scientific revolution, arguing that Egyptian sun worship promoted Copernican heliocentrism, and that theurgy encouraged emphasis on "man as operator" upon nature. While scholars now agree that Yates overstated somewhat, the "Yates Thesis" has merit; a notable example is the immediate acceptance of William Harvey's 1628 presentation of the circulation of the blood by the English physician and mystic Robert Fludd (1574–1637), who believed that this demonstrated the microcosm because the heart was like the sun, with blood circulating like the planets.

Despite the 1614 proof of the late origin of the Hermetic texts by the French scholar Isaac Casaubon (1559–1614), Hermeticism continued to influence thinkers as late as the Enlightenment, although this effect shifted largely (as seen in the cases of Rosicrucianism and Freemasonry) into the political sphere.

See also **Alchemy; Cabala; Freemasonry; Magic; Occult Philosophy; Paracelsus; Rosicrucianism.**

BIBLIOGRAPHY

Primary Source

Hermetica: The Greek Corpus Hermeticum and the Latin Asclepius in a New English Translation with Notes and Introduction. Translated by Brian P. Copenhaver. Cambridge, U.K., 1992. The most useful of many translations.

Secondary Sources

Faivre, Antoine. *The Eternal Hermes: From Greek God to Alchemical Magus.* Translated by Joscelyn Godwin. Grand Rapids, Mich., 1995. Translation of six separate articles in French, covering a wide range of historical, philosophical, and bibliographical material.

Fowden, Garth. *The Egyptian Hermes: A Historical Approach to the Late Pagan Mind.* Rev. ed. Princeton, 1993. Brilliant study of the Hermetic texts in their original context.

Yates, Frances A. *Giordano Bruno and the Hermetic Tradition.* London, 1964. The most important and influential of Yates's many works.

CHRISTOPHER I. LEHRICH

HESSE, LANDGRAVIATE OF. The Hessian landgraviate, a precarious political amalgam in the west central part of the Holy Roman Empire, exemplified the changing fortunes of German territorial organization over the early modern period. General notice of the territory's history is usually focused at the apex of its development as a strong, unified principality under Landgrave Philip the Magnanimous (ruled 1509–1567), who played a major role in the Protestant Reformation. Philip's medieval predecessors had ruled various regional configurations shaped and reshaped more by historical contingencies than by any consistent program, and four such units constituted the major divisions of the landgraviate: the two traditional regions of Lower Hesse focused on Kassel, and Upper Hesse consisted of Marburg (contiguous only after inheritance of the county of Ziegenhain in 1437) and the county of Katzenelnbogen, itself divided into two noncontiguous regions around Rheinfels and Darmstadt.

By 1500 these (and other) parts of the landgraviate already formed a unified territorial base for the dynamic politics Philip undertook after 1518 that would leave a singular imprint on European history. After he helped to defeat Franz von Sickingen's "knights' revolt" in 1523, internal noble opposition to strong landgravial rule dissolved, and Philip went on to crush several peasant uprisings in 1525. His introduction of Protestantism in 1526 was notable for charitable and educational achievements (hospitals, preparatory schools, Marburg University) and a moderate stance between

Lutheranism and Zwinglianism, but Philip failed in his effort to foster doctrinal accord among Protestants at his Marburg Colloquy of 1529. To resist Charles V's reimposition of Catholicism, Philip helped forge the Schmalkaldic League in 1531 and led its victorious restoration of the deposed Duke Ulrich of Württemberg in 1534. His notorious bigamy of 1540 weakened his leadership in the Protestant camp, however, and exposed him to the imperial ban. After his five-year imprisonment following Protestant defeat in 1547, Philip emerged ill and politically cautious, even as he continued to promote doctrinal compromise among Protestants.

The scandal caused by Philip's bigamy carried fateful consequences for his landgraviate. To appease sons from both of his marriages, he abandoned his original intention of primogeniture, made lesser provisions for the seven illegitimate heirs, and divided his unified territory among the four sons from his first marriage: half went to the oldest, William IV (ruled 1567–1592) in Kassel, a quarter went to Ludwig IV in Marburg, while sons Philip and George I each got an eighth in Rheinfels and Darmstadt, respectively. Although they maintained many common institutions and managed to cooperate, gradually the heirs moved apart, especially on religious issues. Ludwig espoused an orthodox Lutheranism, also embraced by his brother George and nephew Ludwig V in Darmstadt, while his nephew Moritz the Learned (landgrave 1592–1627) moved Hesse-Kassel toward Calvinism. The childless deaths of all but two of Philip's sons brought territorial adjustments and eventual survival of two Hessian landgraviates centered in Kassel and Darmstadt, which engaged in bitter disputes over their joint inheritance of Hesse-Marburg in 1604. Their decades-long conflict merged with the disastrous Thirty Years' War (1618–1648), with its confusing reversals of military and political fortunes, economic devastation, and an estimated 40 to 50 percent population loss for Hesse. As Lutheran Darmstadt tied itself firmly to the emperor's cause and the Calvinist line barely survived political elimination through resolute leadership and alliances with foreign powers, they set patterns for their two distinct histories thereafter.

While they faced similar challenges after 1648—demographic and economic recovery, extreme indebtedness, limited resources—Hesse-Darmstadt and Hesse-Kassel developed rather different profiles as middle-sized German states. The Lutheran landgraviate maintained limited foreign policy objectives within the Habsburg orbit, suffered heavily from Louis XIV's aggression, and never managed debt relief. Nor could the administratively weak territory (organized as ten noncontiguous holdings) assert sovereignty over its collateral line in Hesse-Homburg. While it fostered education and attempted cameralist policies, Hesse-Darmstadt's endemic poverty coexisted with a sometimes flourishing high culture, as at Countess Caroline's court (1765–1774), admired throughout the German states for its musical and literary patronage.

Distinguished for its line of vigorous, highly competent Calvinist rulers, Hesse-Kassel reestablished its sixteenth-century reputation as a well-administered state. Its wartime experience led the seventeenth-century landgraves to enlarge their armies and to supplement their limited resources by leasing troops to other rulers, a common practice that they exploited consistently and successfully. From the 1680s onward this military trade enabled the dynasty to assume a subsidiary but noticeable role in European power politics, particularly within Protestant alliances among Britain, the Netherlands, Sweden, and north German states like Brandenburg-Prussia (Hesse-Kassel's closest ally and model). Military and cameralist policies combined to increase resources, provide a modicum of public welfare and tax relief for an overburdened populace, and support the artistic and intellectual patronage that made eighteenth-century Kassel a striking home for Enlightenment institutions.

See also **Calvinism; Germany, Idea of; Holy Roman Empire; Lutheranism; Schmalkaldic War (1546–1547); Thirty Years' War (1618–1648).**

BIBLIOGRAPHY

Demandt, Karl E. *Geschichte des Landes Hessen*. Rev. reprint of 2nd ed. Kassel, 1980.

Fox, George Thomas. "Studies in the Rural History of Upper Hesse, 1650–1830." Ph.D. diss., Vanderbilt University, 1976.

Heinemeyer, Walter, ed. *Das Werden Hessens*. Marburg, 1986.

Hillerbrand, Hans J. *Landgrave Philipp of Hesse, 1504–1567: Religion and Politics in the Reformation*. St. Louis, Mo., 1967.

Ingrao, Charles W. *The Hessian Mercenary State: Ideas, Institutions, and Reform under Frederick II, 1760–1785.* Cambridge, U.K., 1987.

Schwind, Fred, ed. *Geschichtlicher Atlas von Hessen.* Marburg, 1984.

Taylor, Peter. *Indentured to Liberty: Peasant Life and the Hessian Military State, 1688–1815.* Ithaca, N.Y., 1994.

Theibault, John. *German Villages in Crisis: Rural Life in Hesse-Kassel and the Thirty Years' War, 1580–1720.* Atlantic Highlands, N.J., 1995.

Wright, William John. *Capitalism, the State, and the Lutheran Reformation: Sixteenth-Century Hesse.* Athens, Ohio, 1988.

GERALD L. SOLIDAY

HETMANATE (UKRAINE). A Ukrainian Cossack polity (1648–1781) ruled by a hetman, the Hetmanate is also referred to as "Little Russia." The Hetmanate emerged as a result of the Khmelnytsky Uprising (1648), which swept Polish authority from central Ukraine. In order to consolidate his position, Hetman Bohdan Khmelnytsky was forced to seek the protection of the Muscovite tsar (by the Pereiaslav Agreement of 1654). Khmelnytsky's successor, Hetman Ivan Vyhovskyi, repudiated the Muscovite arrangement and negotiated the Hetmanate's adherence, as the Rus' princedom, to a triune Polish-Lithuanian-Rus' Commonwealth (Treaty of Hadiach, 1658). Such an arrangement was not acceptable to Muscovy, parts of Ukrainian society, or the Polish elite, and it was only partially implemented. As a result, the Hetmanate split into pro-Polish and pro-Muscovite factions, each with its own hetman, army, and administration. Attempts by competing hetmans and their foreign allies to take control of Ukraine resulted in a period of continuous warfare and anarchy known as the "Ruin" (1659–1679). With the final sanctioning of the Hetmanate's partition (the "Eternal Peace" between Poland and Muscovy in 1686) and the elimination of the pro-Polish hetmans on the Right Bank (the western bank of the Dnieper), the Hetmanate stabilized on the Left Bank of the Dnieper.

This truncated Left-Bank Hetmanate remained under tsarist authority on the basis of the Pereiaslav Agreement. It maintained its own military, administrative, fiscal, and judicial system. Under the rule of the hetmans Ivan Samoilovych (1672–1687) and Ivan Mazepa (1687–1709), Cossack officers established themselves as a landed gentry, creating a more dynamic administration and an invigorated cultural life, including a distinctive political thought and historical literature. However, the Petrine reforms increasingly clashed with Ukrainian autonomy and drove Hetman Mazepa to break with Russia and side with Sweden, resulting in defeat at Poltava (1709).

In the eighteenth century, the Ukrainian elite developed a political outlook that combined a strong commitment to "Little Russian rights and liberties" with loyalty to the "all-Russian" tsar. Such a loyalist stand did little, however, to mitigate the leveling of Ukrainian autonomy. The first attempt to rule the Hetmanate directly, initiated by Tsar Peter I the Great (1722), was a failure, and the Hetmanate's autonomy, including the election of a hetman, was restored in 1727. Between 1727 and the 1760s the local administration and judicial system of the Hetmanate functioned without interference, but the imperial authorities vacillated in their dealings with the Hetmanate's central administration, at times merely supervising it and at other times assuming some of its functions.

Between 1750 and 1764, the Hetmanate experienced another respite. Because of his good connections with the imperial court (his brother was closely linked with Empress Elizabeth), Hetman Kyrylo Rozumovsky was able to restore Ukrainian autonomy virtually to the level exercised by Mazepa. But Catherine II the Great, the new empress (ruled 1762–1796), envisioned the empire as a well-ordered police state, an ambition entirely at odds with the concept of regional autonomy. Thus, the office of hetman was abolished in 1764, and with the creation of the Kiev, Chernihiv, and Novhorod-Siver'skyi vicegerencies (1781), the Hetmanate ceased to exist as a political entity.

See also **Cossacks; Khmelnytsky, Bohdan; Khmelnytsky Uprising; Mazepa, Ivan; Ukraine; Ukrainian Literature and Language.**

BIBLIOGRAPHY

Gajecky, George. *The Cossack Administration of the Hetmanate.* 2 vols. Cambridge, Mass., 1978.

Kohut, Zenon E. *Russian Centralism and Ukrainian Autonomy: Imperial Absorption of the Hetmanate, 1760s–1830s.* Cambridge, Mass., 1988.

Okinshevich, Leo. *Ukrainian Society and Government, 1648–1781.* Munich, 1978.

Plokhy, Serhii. *The Cossacks and Religion in Early Modern Ukraine.* Oxford, 2001.

Ševčenko, Ihor. *Ukraine between East and West: Essays on Cultural History to the Early Eighteenth Century.* Edmonton and Toronto, 1996.

Subtelny, Orest. *The Mazepists: Ukrainian Separatism in the Early Eighteenth Century.* Boulder, Colo., 1981.

ZENON KOHUT

HISTORIOGRAPHY. The early modern era witnessed enormous changes in historiography, both in the quantity and variety of works written about the past and in the status of history within intellectual and social life. At the dawn of the Reformation, history was still a minor genre, read principally in manuscript or in small printed editions. The Renaissance had enriched the medieval chronicle tradition, especially in Italy, by revisioning selected periods and subjects (the history of particular city-states first and foremost) according to humanist principles and in Latin that aspired to Ciceronian purity, while also focusing on the political lessons to be gleaned from the past, as done most famously by Niccolò Machiavelli (1469–1527). The changes of the next two centuries would be considerably more profound and would be driven by two engines: ideology (both religious and political), which sought to make command over the interpretation of the past a weapon in present struggles, and print, which enabled the replication and dissemination of historical works in ever-increasing numbers and, especially in the seventeenth and early eighteenth centuries, in forms accessible to an expanding readership below the level of the most affluent classes.

REFORMATION, CATHOLIC, AND NATIONAL TRADITIONS

In the German Reformation, Martin Luther's vision of a medieval past that was not simply that of a dark time of poor learning and bad Latin (the humanist position) but of a church corrupted and led astray by unwritten traditions and papal monarchy, set the polemical tone of much sixteenth-century historical writing. Among the most noteworthy books to be produced by German Reformation scholars was *Commentaries on the State of Religion and the Empire under Charles V* by Johannes Sleidanus (1506–1556), which made use of documentary sources and information from reformers. Sleidanus's later *Chronicle of World Empires* popularized the idea, derived from the Book of Daniel, that history had unfolded in an apocalyptic series of four major "empires," of which the Roman would be the last. Johann Carion (1499–1537 or 1538) also produced a chronicle that would be completed by Luther's adherent Philipp Melanchthon (1497–1560). Most significant and influential, though riddled with error, was the vast *Magdeburg Centuries,* a multivolume effort initiated by the Croatian Matthias Flacius Illyricus (1520–1575), one of Luther's more radical disciples.

With some variation according to doctrine, this reinterpretation of the past was taken up by Protestant (Calvinist, Anglican, and Reformed) churches elsewhere in Europe. In England, where Sleidanus's works were issued in translation, the divorce of King Henry VIII (ruled 1509–1547) from Catherine of Aragon and his break with Rome were both defended through historical research, while a series of Protestant chroniclers from Edward Hall (d. 1547) through Richard Grafton (d. 1572) and Raphael Holinshed (d. 1580?) rewrote England's past to establish its adherence to "primitive" or pure Christianity prior to the corruption of the medieval church. The fires of persecution in several parts of Europe also ignited a new genre, the Protestant martyrology: John Foxe in England (1516–1587), Heinrich Pantaleon (1522–1595) in Basel, Adriaan Cornelis van Haemstede (1526–1562) in the Netherlands, and Jean Crespin (d. 1572) in France were among its major practitioners, their accounts of the deaths of Protestant martyrs at the hands of popish persecutors creating a strongly anti-Catholic version of history for subsequent generations.

Protestants held no monopoly on historical writing. Catholic Europe responded to the challenge of the Reformation in different ways. The Italian tradition of urban and official historiography continued through the sixteenth century, surviving the collapse of the medieval and early Renaissance city-state regime in the era of grand duchies and Spanish rule over much of the peninsula. Spain itself produced a series of able historians such as the Jesuit Juan de Mariana (1536–1624). Though many of these reflected a Castilian perspective, other parts of the monarchy also developed historiographically, in particular Aragon, represented by the *Annals* of Jerónimo de Zurita y Castro (1512–1580), and Catalonia, by Francisco de Moncada (1586–1635). The mid-seventeenth-century Spanish crisis served as a further stimulus to the development of rival traditions there and in the Basque region. Perhaps most significant in the longer run were the works of Spanish missionaries abroad, since they introduced to European readers lands and pasts previously unknown. Following earlier works by Portuguese visitors to South and Southeast Asia such as João de Barros (c. 1496–1570) and Fernão Lopes de Castenheda (c. 1500–1559), Spaniards now wrote accounts of the Americas, in particular the Dominican Bartolomé de las Casas (1474–1566) and the Jesuit José de Acosta (1540–1600). One of the first indigenous writers, Garcilaso de la Vega, El Inca (1539–1616), son of an Inca princess and a Spanish soldier, contributed *Royal Commentaries of the Incas,* which provided a valuable corrective to earlier Spanish representations of the Inca Empire.

In Italy, Counter-Reformation scholars such as Cardinal Cesare Baronio (1538–1607) sought to repudiate Protestant historical writing through scholarship as well as rhetoric. Baronio's *Ecclesiastical Annals,* which reverted to the year-by-year format favored by medieval chroniclers, repudiated the *Magdeburg Centuries* only to be attacked in turn by a Huguenot scholar, Isaac Casaubon (1559–1614), who had significantly greater philological skills than Baronio. In Venice, which was one of the few cities to retain its independence and was itself under a papal interdict in the early seventeenth century, a moderate priest named Paolo Sarpi (1552–1623) captured, in his *History of the Council of Trent,* the lost moment in the mid-sixteenth century when Christendom might have been put back together. Himself nearly the victim of assassination, Sarpi's critical stance toward Rome and his shrewd, Tacitean appreciation of the motives of political behavior led to his book having to be published pseudonymously in London, where it was well received by Protestant readers.

In Bohemia, early Czech nationalism was integrated with a Catholic perspective in the Czech *Chronicle* by the priest Vaclav Hajek (d. 1553); a century later he was followed by Bohuslav Balbín (1621–1688), another Catholic but one who regretted the decline in Czech culture since the Battle of White Mountain in 1620. Elsewhere, Latin historiography was initiated in the Hungarian Renaissance by the Italian Antonio Bonfini (1427–1502) and followed in the sixteenth century by István Szamosközy (c. 1565–1612), a contemporary historian of his own semi-independent Transylvania, and by Miklós Istvánffy (1538–1615), who covered events from the late fifteenth to the early sixteenth century in the Habsburg-controlled parts of Hungary.

There were significant contributions to historical writing in parts of Europe relatively unaffected by the main conflicts of the Reformation and Counter-Reformation. In Poland, for instance, the heirs of the late medieval chronicler Jan Długosz (1415–1480), who had written in Latin, eventually included some vernacular authors, for instance Maciej Stryjkowski (1547–c. 1582) and Reinhold Heidenstein (1556–1620); a full synthesis of Polish history would first be produced by Marcin Kromer (1512–1589) in the late sixteenth century. Romanian and Moldavian historiography emerged slightly later in the work of Romanian-language aristocratic exponents such as the executed boyar conspirator Miron Costin (1633–1691). Further east, Russian historiography began to mature in Andrei Mikhailovich Kniaz Kurbskii's (1528–1583) *History of the Muscovite Grand Prince,* written in the 1560s and largely an account of the reign of Ivan IV the Terrible (1530–1584). Seventeenth-century Russian historians were faced with a new challenge, that of integrating their own history with that of the newly absorbed Ukraine, a task accomplished by Innokentii Gizel (d. 1683) in his *Synopsis* (1674). Finally, altogether outside Christian Europe, Ottoman historiography also developed during this period in the hands of Ibrahim Peçevi (1574–1649 or 1650), a historian of the era since Suleiman the Magnificent (d. 1566), and Mustafa Naima (1655–1716), whose *Annals of the Turkish Empire from 1591 to 1659 of the Christian Era* is the outstanding record of the Ottomans during that period.

THE DEBATE OVER NATIONAL MYTHS

The establishment of national churches and of state-supported confessional regimes stimulated a tendency to promote national and ethnic myths (many of which had medieval or classical origins) and then to produce debate over their veracity. In Germany, humanists such as Beatus Rhenanus (1485–1547) seized on the ancient historian Tacitus's *Germania,* a text that had praised primitive German virtue while criticizing imperial corruption. In Scotland Presbyterian scholars such as George Buchanan (1506–1582) wrote accounts of their national past fiercely defending that realm's independence from its wealthier southern neighbor, England; the myth of an ancient line of Scottish kings going back to pre-Christian times would prove durable until undermined by the relentless scholarship of a much later Scot, the emigré Catholic priest Thomas Innes (1662–1744). In Sweden, the Vasa regime produced Olof Petersson's (Olaus Petri, 1493–1552) *Swedish Chronicle* in the 1530s (though King Gustav Vasa disliked this and prevented its publication), while Catholic Swedish exiles such as Archbishop Johannes Magnus (1488–1544) wrote the anti-Vasa *History of the Gothic Kingdom of Sweden.* The particular role of the Goths as European and especially Swedish ancestors was foregrounded by Magnus's brother Olaus or Olof (1490–1557) in his *History of the Nordic People;* it was given new life in the late seventeenth century in *Atlantica,* a peculiar work by Olof Rudbeck (1630–1702) that identified Sweden with the lost kingdom of Atlantis. The old medieval myth of the founding of Rome and other states by Trojan refugees was reenergized in western Europe during the sixteenth century, as Gallican French writers argued for a foundation of their country by Francus or Francio, and English writers theirs by Brutus or Brute (a Trojan foundation being preferable to a medieval one since it would precede the establishment of the city and empire of Rome).

Most of these accounts did not stand up to scrutiny. In England, an émigré Italian named Polydore Vergil (c. 1470–1555) wrote the first full-length history of England in humanist Latin, evincing skepticism both about Brutus and about the historicity of a late-Romano-British hero, King Arthur; he was widely criticized by Welsh and English writers, including able scholars such as John Leland (c. 1506–1552) and John Bale (1495–1563). The French attack on myth was much more formidable and, for a time, decisive. The end of the sixteenth century witnessed a flourishing of scholarly activity on the past, much of it affiliated with study of the law, and Estienne Pasquier (1529–1615), among others, expressed considerable doubt about the Trojan descent and many other venerable myths in his series of *Researches on France.* Pasquier's own teacher, the Huguenot lawyer François Hotman (1524–1590), argued for the national affiliation of the Franks and the Germans (an unpopular position in the absolutist France of the next century), his position reached by a combination of comparative legal scholarship and hatred of the royalist regime that had committed the atrocity of St. Bartholomew's Day in 1572. It is significant that Hotman's and Pasquier's findings were endorsed by the Catholic antiquaries Jean du Tillet (d. 1570) and Nicolas Vignier (1530–1596): by 1600 the Trojan myth seemed all but demolished in France, and even English scholars were now handling it with cautious skepticism.

ANTIQUARIANISM, SKEPTICISM, AND THE THEORY OF HISTORY

As the work of these French *érudits* suggests, one of the most significant developments in historical writing at this time was the advent of antiquarianism. This had several origins, and its practitioners often had little to do with the writing of history as a formal genre; they were thus not bound by the prescribed rules for the writing of history laid down in classical and Renaissance *artes historicae* (see below). Many antiquaries approached the past through study of the law: in France, a long tradition of legal scholars from Guillaume Budé (1468–1540) and François Baudouin (1520–1573) to Hotman and Jean Bodin (1530–1596) applied the humanist concern for accurate editing of texts to the study of the law (the so-called *mos gallicus* or French method). Bodin in particular was able to rise above his sources to achieve a philosophical perspective on history, most clearly articulated in his *Method for the Easy Comprehension of History* (1566). A work that was widely read elsewhere in Europe, the *Method* attacked well-worn schemes for interpreting the past such as the "four empires" propagated by earlier historians like Sleidanus.

Other antiquaries focused on the study of words, of objects, and of places: a prominent genre from the late sixteenth century was chorography, which studied the history of particular regions or towns but used place rather than time as the organizing principle. Continental chorographers included the Brescian Ottavio Rossi (1570–1630), Guillaume Catel of Toulouse (1560–1626), and the Provençal Cesar de Nostredame (1553–1629). Their contemporary William Camden (1551–1623), the greatest English practitioner of this genre, followed the lead of his predecessor John Leland, who had journeyed about England in the 1530s and 1540s and recorded his observations in a series of unpublished *Itineraries.* Camden's own *Britannia* (1586) was a much-reprinted work in Latin and English editions. The group of scholars of whom he was a leading member, including a short-lived Society of Antiquaries, had close ties with Continental scholars, both Protestant and Catholic, such as the numismatist and librarian Janus Gruter (1560–1627), the chronologer and philologist Joseph Justus Scaliger (1540–1609), the Dutch writer Gerhard Vossius (1577–1649), and the French contemporary historian Jacques-Auguste de Thou (1553–1617). The wealth of Latin and vernacular correspondence, a good deal of which was published at the time, and which is now held by European and English libraries, testifies to the existence of a western European "republic of letters" that could transcend confessional divisions in the pursuit of an accurate understanding of the past.

The multiplication of forms of historical writing and the tension between a belief in the unity of truth and the inescapable fact of disagreement about the past produced in the late sixteenth century a series of attempts to make some sense of historical genres and to prescribe principles for the writing, or at least the reading, of history. A variety of works of uneven sophistication, collectively known as *artes historicae* ('arts of history') were produced all across Europe by authors such as the Spaniard Melchor Cano (1509–1560) and the German Bartholomew Keckerman (c. 1571–c. 1608). Many, following the ancient writer Dionysius of Halicarnassus, were little more than summaries of what had been written from antiquity to the current era, with critical comments. A number of such works were published together by the Swiss printer Johann Wolf in 1579. A few, such as Bodin's *Method,* Francesco Patrizi's (1529–1597) *Ten Dialogues on History,* and Francis Bacon's (1561–1626) somewhat later *Advancement of Learning* (which dealt with many other subjects than history), aspired to a more systematic view and borrowed from educational theorists such as the Frenchman Petrus Ramus (1515–1572). Among the most interesting products of this time was the *History of Histories, with the Idea of Perfect History and the Design for a New History of France* (1599) by the Frenchman Henri Lancelot Voisin de la Popelinière (1541–1608). La Popelinière espoused the goal of an accurate history that would be "perfect" or complete in the sense of resting on firm scholarly foundations and would not be subject to constant revision. This notion seems foreign today, but in La Popelinière's time it amounted to a bulwark against confessional polemic and unjustified nationalist myth. It was also an answer to credulity's opposite extreme, a rising "pyrrhonist" doubt (associated with the followers of the ancient skeptic Pyrrho) that the past could ever actually be known with any accuracy.

THE SEVENTEENTH CENTURY: ERUDITION AND IDEOLOGY

Ideology continued to influence the writing of history in the seventeenth and early eighteenth centuries, for instance in Scotland, where rival Presbyterian and Episcopalian interpretations of the ecclesiastical past were represented respectively by David Calderwood (1575–1650) and Archbishop John Spottiswoode (1565–1637). But though religion remained the preeminent point of difference, ideological disagreements were not always exclusively religious, especially as the century wore on and the era of confessional warfare was displaced by one of contending commercial empires. In England, a period of bloody civil strife and regicide in the middle of the century led to a virtual explosion of historical writing from various points of view ranging from the absolutist position of Thomas Hobbes (1588–1679) to the republicanism of the Machiavellian-influenced James Harrington (1611–1677) to the radicalism of the Leveller and Digger movements, with their view that England had been enslaved not by a Roman but by a Norman yoke at the Conquest of 1066. On the Continent, the solidification of absolutist regimes, especially in France, led to a retreat from the kind of open-ended inquiry practiced in Bodin's and Pasquier's day, as a series of crown-sponsored historiographers royal became instead "artisans of glory." The Trojan myth, once thoroughly discredited, returned in full force, and the scholar Nicolas Fréret (1688–1749) went to the Bastille in 1714 for the crime of maintaining the ancient connection between the Franks and the Germans. Despite such instances of persecution, however, the "erudite" tradition remained strong in Europe, assisted by the establishment of national academies of learning and by early examples of scholarly journals. Cultural exchange between scholars of different religions and countries continued after the end of the religious wars by about the middle of the seventeenth century and into the early eighteenth. This scholarly community was not always as civilized and friendly as it has often been portrayed; the language of scholarly dispute was often heated and rhetorical to a degree that would embarrass even a scathing modern book reviewer. In this the later seventeenth-century *érudits* were simply following the lead of some of their illustrious predecessors, in particular the polymath Scaliger, possibly the most learned scholar of his own day, and John Selden (1584–1654), his younger English admirer, both of whom were also vituperative critics of those they perceived as guilty of willful error.

A century of publication and a much more widespread interest in the past meant that by the late seventeenth century, history had established itself as a printed genre much in demand: publishers in the next decades would use devices such as serial publication and advance subscription to extend history's readership far beyond its previous social bounds. At the same time, the youth of Europe acquired both an understanding of the past (thought to be useful both in civilized discourse and in future political or legal careers, or even in the mundane matter of running estates), and a sensitivity to its difference from the present. Many students followed the grand tour that took in famous historic sites and monuments across Europe. Along the way, they collected coins and artifacts, for which a vigorous market had developed, a virtual "archaeological economy" that saw the trade and export of ancient and medieval curiosities. By the end of the century this interest had extended to natural remains such as fossils, and many scholars were shifting their attention from the explanation of physical objects according to ancient texts toward their systematic observation, collection, and comparison. Although still constrained by a scriptural chronological framework that ran no further back than six thousand years, the study of fossils and the conclusion to which it led, that there might once have lived species no longer extant, when put together with a century of awareness of New World and East Asian societies, produced a renewed wave of skepticism. Among the products of this "crisis" in belief was some searching criticism of the literal truth of the Old Testament account of the Creation, Patriarchal descent, and the Flood, especially by the Frenchman Richard Simon (1638–1712) and the Englishman Thomas Burnet (1635–1715). The skepticism and anticlericalism of Enlightenment figures such as Voltaire would be built on such foundations as these.

As the eighteenth century dawned, historiography flourished in a number of different traditions. The erudite tradition, associated with the republic of letters, continued to mix philological scholarship (the continuous improvement of editions of earlier writers) with antiquarian observation, the latter now blending with natural philosophy or science, as it did notably in the work of the Welshman Edward Lhuyd (1660–1709) and the Scot Sir Robert Sibbald (1641–1722). The polymathic ideal of seamless learning was represented perhaps most strikingly by the mathematician, philosopher, and scholar Gottfried Wilhelm Leibniz (1646–1716). Within this broad erudite tradition, the activity of producing precise, learned texts ruled by rigorous scholarship remained prominent, and in several different spheres. These included sacred history, best represented in the activities of the seventeenth-century Bollandists (whose *Acta Sanctorum* continues to this day) and Maurists, especially the founder of systematic paleography and diplomatics, Jean Mabillon (1632–1707). Late antique history was set on a new critical footing by the likes of Louis-Sebastien Le Nain de Tillemont (1637–1698). Further strides were made in administrative and legal history—the Polish *Volumina Legum* of the first half of the eighteenth century, for instance, or the studies and texts of two English antiquaries, Thomas Rymer (1641–1713) and Thomas Madox (1666–1727). National collections of historical documents were printed and annotated by a number of scholars, for instance the medieval sources of Italian history published by Ludovico Antonio Muratori (1672–1750) and the Hungarian records produced by his slightly younger contemporary, Matthias or Matyas Bél (1684–1749).

The second grand tradition, mainstream political history writing, continued to produce accounts of the national past in each land, with a few outstanding examples setting the pace, for instance Edward Hyde, earl of Clarendon's (1609–1674) *History of the Rebellion and Civil Wars*, modeled on an earlier account of the French religious wars by the Italian Arrigo Caterino Davila (1576–1631) and François Eudes de Mézeray's (1610–1683) *History of France*. The first Russian history to be based on detailed analysis and critical annotation of medieval sources was Vasilii Nikitich Tatishchev's (1686–1750) *Russian History from Antiquity*, though it remained in manuscript until the late eighteenth century. Full-length national histories such as this were much in vogue, perhaps the most durable being the Scottish historian and philosopher David Hume's (1711–1776) mid-eighteenth-century *History of England*.

Finally, the third tradition, a more philosophical one (though often based on learning as sophisticated as that of the *érudits*) stretches back to Bodin and forward to Voltaire and Herder in the Enlightenment proper. The Moldavian prince Dmitrie Cantemir (1673–1723), whose *History of the Growth and Decay of the Ottoman Empire* combines deep knowledge of Ottoman society with a cyclical view of history, belongs to this tradition, as does the Croatian proto-nationalist Pavao Vitezovic (1652–1713). Perhaps the greatest practitioners of erudite philosophical history were two Italians, the jurist Pietro Giannone (1676–1748), who wrote a *Civil History of the Kingdom of Naples* combining profound learning with an understanding of the development of culture and society, and Giambattista Vico (1668–1744), author of *New Science*. Vico conceived of three major ages of history, each with a distinctive mode of knowledge and communication, and of a series of recurring cycles in civilization. The originality and innovative perspective of his book would largely be ignored until its rediscovery in the nineteenth century, but the *New Science* now stands as the climactic achievement of early modern historical thought on the eve of the Enlightenment.

See also **Archaeology; Bossuet, Jacques-Bénigne; Budé, Guillaume; Condorcet, Marie-Jean Caritat, marquis de; Gibbon, Edward; Grand Tour; Guicciardini, Francesco; Hagiography; Herder, Johann Gottfried von; Machiavelli, Niccolò; Martyrs and Martyrology; Muratori, Ludovico Antonio; Robertson, William; Sarpi, Paolo; Sleidanus, Johannes; Vasari, Giorgio; Vico, Giovanni Battista.**

BIBLIOGRAPHY

Allan, David. *Virtue, Learning, and the Scottish Enlightenment: Ideas of Scholarship in Early Modern History*. Edinburgh, 1993.

Cochrane, Eric W. *Historians and Historiography in the Italian Renaissance*. Chicago, 1981. Mainly on the Renaissance, but extends into the seventeenth century.

Franklin, Julian H. *Jean Bodin and the Sixteenth-Century Revolution in the Methodology of Law and History*. New York, 1963.

Goldgar, Anne. *Impolite Learning: Conduct and Community in the Republic of Letters, 1680–1750*. New Haven, 1995.

Gregory, Brad S. *Salvation at Stake: Christian Martyrdom in Early Modern Europe*. Cambridge, Mass., 1999. Useful material on the martyrologies.

Huppert, George. *The Idea of Perfect History: Historical Erudition and Historical Philosophy in Renaissance France*. Urbana, Ill., 1970.

Johannesson, Kurt. *The Renaissance of the Goths in Sixteenth-Century Sweden: Johannes and Olaus Magnus as Politicians and Historians*. Translated and edited by James Larson. Berkeley, 1991.

Kelley, Donald R. *Faces of History: Historical Inquiry from Herodotus to Herder*. New Haven, 1998.

———. *Foundations of Modern Historical Scholarship: Language, Law and History in the French Renaissance*. New York, 1970.

Knowles, David. *Great Historical Enterprises. Problems in Monastic History*. London and New York, 1963. Essential account of Bollandists and Maurists.

McCuaig, William. *Carlo Sigonio: The Changing World of the Late Renaissance*. Princeton, 1989.

Momigliano, Arnaldo. "Ancient History and the Antiquarian." In his *Studies in Historiography*. New York, 1966. Seminal article on the division between erudition and narrative history writing.

Pocock, J. G. A. *The Ancient Constitution and the Feudal Law: A Study of English Historical Thought in the Seventeenth Century*. Cambridge, U.K., 1987. Revised edition of classic 1957 study of English legal historical thought.

Pompa, Leon. *Vico: A Study of the "New Science."* 2nd ed. Cambridge, U.K., and New York, 1990.

Ranum, Orest A. *Artisans of Glory: Writers and Historical Thought in Seventeenth-Century France*. Chapel Hill, N.C., 1980.

Schiffman, Zachary. *On the Threshold of Modernity: Relativism in the French Renaissance*. Baltimore, 1991.

Woolf, D. R. *The Idea of History in Early Stuart England: Erudition, Ideology, and "The Light of the Truth" from the Accession of James I to the Civil War.* Toronto, 1990.

Woolf, D. R., ed. *A Global Encyclopedia of Historical Writing.* 2 vols. New York, 1998. Includes survey articles by various authors on a variety of national historical traditions and biographical entries on representative historians.

D. R. Woolf

HOBBES, THOMAS (1588–1679), English philosopher. Thomas Hobbes, perhaps the greatest of the English philosophers, was born in Malmesbury, Wiltshire, in 1588. The son of the disreputable vicar of Westport, he was raised by a wealthy uncle who saw to his education and his admission to Magdalen Hall, Oxford (B.A., 1608). After Oxford, Hobbes became tutor to the son of William Cavendish, the earl of Derbyshire, and remained attached to the Cavendish family throughout his life.

Hobbes's early association with Francis Bacon (1561–1626) strengthened what would become a lifelong dislike of Aristotelian philosophy that he had acquired at Oxford in opposition to his tutors. But he retained an interest in classical literature and published a translation of Thucydides' *History of the Peloponnesian War* in 1629 and a translation of Homer in quatrains in 1674–1675. Hobbes's discovery of geometry, his association with Marin Mersenne (1588–1648), and the friendship of Pierre Gassendi (1592–1655) and Galileo Galilei (1564–1642) provided him with the analytic scheme and scientific method for which he had been searching to undergird a complete philosophy of nature and society. An association with the Great Tew circle (a group of men of letters who met at Great Tew, Lord Falkland's house north of Oxford) seems to have helped to move him from a humanistic and classical view of the world to one that was—in contrast to the appeals to the Bible that charged the outlooks of so many of his contemporaries—decidedly juridical and modern and drawn from the political crises that led to the English Civil War. His *Elements of the Law,* circulated in manuscript in 1640 and published in two parts in 1650, was the first statement of the darkly pessimistic view of human nature and call for undivided, absolute sovereignty for which he is known.

In late 1640—fearing for his life, he claimed, when the Long Parliament began its work—Hobbes fled to France, where he was welcomed by Mersenne's circle and where he served briefly as tutor to the Prince of Wales (the exiled and future King Charles II). In France, he enjoyed his most productive philosophic period, culminating in the publication of his masterpiece, *Leviathan; or the Matter, Form, and Power of a Commonwealth, Ecclesiastical and Civil,* in 1651 shortly before he returned to England.

The aim of *Leviathan,* as announced in the Preface and in the Review and Conclusion, was to demonstrate, in the context of the recently concluded Civil War, the necessity of strong, overarching, unchallengeable government. The work was a distillation and an extension of Hobbes's quest for a comprehensive philosophy that moved from accounts of ultimate reality and human nature, through logic and reason, to a radically new understanding of politics that was also an attack on virtually all religious beliefs and practices. The political genius of *Leviathan* was its use of the emerging natural law, natural rights, and social contract theories and a radically individualistic conception of human nature in conjunction with the new science rather than the more conventional divine right doctrines to defend political absolutism. In one of the most memorable phrases in the history of political thought, Hobbes described life in the pre-political state of nature as "solitary, poore, nasty, brutish, and short" (*Leviathan,* ch. 13), the only remedy for which was the agreement to form a civil society with an absolute ruler at its head. For his efforts Hobbes was rewarded with the scorn of his contemporaries, especially for his apparent atheism, although the earliest critic of political theory, the divine right patriarchal royalist Sir Robert Filmer praised his conclusions while objecting to their foundations.

After the publication of *Leviathan,* Hobbes continued to work on his systematic philosophy and to attract critics. He enjoyed the patronage and probably the protection of the restored King Charles II, but he was attacked by Parliament after the Great Fire of 1666 and ultimately forbidden the right to publish. Nonetheless, he wrote *Behemoth, or the Long Parliament,* an account of English history during the period of the Civil War and Interregnum viewed from the perspective of his conceptions of human nature and politics, and an uncompleted *Dialogue between a Philosopher and a Student of the Common Law,* which offered a conception of law and sovereignty that is suggestive of the theories of J. L. Austin (1911–1960). Both works were published posthumously, in 1681 and 1682 respectively.

Hobbes's philosophic system, pointedly anti-Scholastic and anti-Aristotelian, was naturalistic and mechanistic; knowledge and understanding were rooted in experience. His metaphysics is often summarized as "matter in motion," and he was untroubled by some of the pressing problems of his day—and of subsequent philosophy—including accounting for the non-perceptual existence of phenomena and causation. Human beings, while capable of reason, are driven by their passions and motivated by fear, especially of one another. They are irreducibly self-interested and will cooperate only when they believe that it is to their advantage. All this was demonstrated by Hobbes's theory of the state of nature as altogether without institutions and relationships and as a condition in which everyone enjoyed an equal, natural freedom and had the natural right to all things and no corresponding obligations or duties, leading to the famous "war of every man against every man" (*Leviathan,* ch. 13)—hence, the description of life in that situation that was quoted above.

Although he believed that there was a law of nature, Hobbes's conception was altogether unlike the traditional view. His law of nature did not bind human actions in the absence of sufficient security, did not contain a body of moral and ethical principles, and was not truly the product of divine will. It was, however, discernable through reason, and its first principle was self-preservation. According to Hobbes, natural law commanded that people seek peace but only when others were willing to do so as well. It dictated that they agree to a social compact instituting an absolute sovereign who would maintain this conventionally established peace and to whom everyone was politically obligated because they had agreed to his rule because he "personated" them and their institutes, and because he had the legitimate power to punish their disobedience with death, which was their greatest fear. Although Hobbes believed that the establishment of a strong ruler would eventually lead to a less brutal and anxious life for the members of civil society, the psychology of the state of nature remained just beneath the surface of all human endeavors, kept in check by habits of forbearance maintained by fear of the sovereign.

Thomas Hobbes. Portrait by William Dobson. GETTY IMAGES

Hobbes died in 1679 in the Cavendish home, Hardwick Hall in Derbyshire, and was buried nearby. Witty to the end, he composed epitaphs for himself, his favorite of which was, "This is the true Philosopher's Stone." It was not used.

See also **Aristotelianism; Atheism; Bacon, Francis; Divine Right Kingship; English Civil War and Interregnum; Galileo Galilei; Gassendi, Pierre; Mathematics; Mersenne, Marin; Natural Law; Philosophy; Political Philosophy; Scientific Method.**

BIBLIOGRAPHY

Johnston, David. *The Rhetoric of Leviathan: Thomas Hobbes and the Politics of Cultural Transformation.* Princeton, 1986.

Malcolm, Noel. *Aspects of Hobbes.* Oxford and New York, 2002.

Martinich, A. P. *Hobbes: A Biography.* Cambridge, U.K., and New York, 1999.

Rogers, G. A. J., and Alan Ryan, eds. *Perspectives on Thomas Hobbes.* Oxford and New York, 1988.

Skinner, Quentin. *Reason and Rhetoric in the Philosophy of Hobbes.* Cambridge, U.K., and New York, 1996.

GORDON SCHOCHET

HOGARTH, WILLIAM (1697–1764), English painter and engraver. Famous for his biting and satirical visual commentaries on urban life, William Hogarth had a particularly profound impact on the development of print culture, especially political cartoons and the modern comic strip.

Born in London to the schoolmaster Richard Hogarth and Anne Gibbons, Hogarth served an apprenticeship in 1713 to a silver-plate engraver before becoming an independent engraver in 1720. By this time he had also taken up painting, attending the academy in St. Martin's Lane. During the 1720s and 1730s, Hogarth emerged as an important portraitist, producing several impressive "conversation pieces"—small-scale informal group portraits of members of a family or friends in social gatherings—and a number of sensitive portraits of individual sitters. Hogarth, however, pursued his goal of history painting, achieving his first major success in 1729 with *The Beggar's Opera,* the repre-

William Hogarth. *A Harlot's Progress,* plate 2: *Quarrels with Her Jew Protector,* 1732. ©BURSTEIN COLLECTION/CORBIS

sentation of a scene from John Gay's popular satirical ballad opera. In his *Biographical Anecdotes,* Hogarth later explained that he conceived of his pictures as stages, and men and women his players, "who by means of certain actions and gestures, are to exhibit a dumb shew" (Hogarth, 1955, p. 209). It was, above all, with his so-called modern moral subjects that Hogarth developed his ideals of pictorial drama. In this innovative genre, Hogarth related moralizing tales drawn from contemporary life in a sequence of narrative paintings, which were subsequently engraved and circulated widely. Satirical in tone, these modern moral subjects offered tart critiques of virtually all social groups.

The first of these sequential narratives, *A Harlot's Progress* (1732), comprised six scenes that followed the misfortunes of a country girl in London. Scene two shows her dominating a Jewish lover, having adopted the flamboyant lifestyle of an aristocratic lady, complete with gossiping servants and a tea-bearing black servant. In subsequent scenes, the woman declines into prostitution and finally dies of syphilis. A similar trajectory can be witnessed in Hogarth's *A Rake's Progress* (1735), which tracks the fate of its spendthrift protagonist from inheritance to the madhouse. Hogarth's most lavish modern moral subject was, however, *Marriage à la Mode* (1745). This set of images—Hogarth's only series to take place completely indoors—comments directly on the evils that stem from greed and a continual quest for status. Scene four shows the consequences of a doomed arranged marriage. At a morning reception, the newly wed countess presides over a colorful group of hangers-on, including a French hairdresser, who fusses with her hair, and an Italian castrato. *Marriage à la Mode* also addresses artistic taste by lampooning contemporary fashion for Continental finery, including baroque painting and Palladian architecture.

Hogarth set forth his thoughts on aesthetics systematically in his 1753 treatise *The Analysis of Beauty.* In this illustrated text, Hogarth drew on everyday life and often comic examples to argue that the judgment of beauty was not the prerogative of the connoisseur, whose pretensions he despised, but rather a set of qualities available to a wider public.

Hogarth's serious works offered fresh perspectives on the persistent social ills—substance abuse, poverty, and moral decay—that plagued life in eighteenth-century London. Operating within the lively paper culture that was transforming the early modern public sphere, Hogarth's successful pictorial dramas both reflected these ills and developed visual critiques of their causes. In so doing, Hogarth produced a socially, morally, and politically engaging art that addressed issues of class, gender, and race in an age of colonial expansion. The artist's skepticism left few unscathed; he ruthlessly poked fun at politicians (as in *The Times, The Lottery,* and *The Election* series), industrialists (*The South Sea Scheme),* clerics, the lower, middle, and upper classes. However, Hogarth also offered strikingly sympathetic representations of, for example, professional women: seamstresses, milkmaids, ballad-sellers, fish-girls, and actresses. His engaging *Strolling Actresses Dressing in a Barn* (1738), issued with the *Four Times of Day* print series, can be regarded as an icon of working-class women. His lucidly executed painting *The Shrimp Girl* (c. 1745; National Gallery, London) expresses the natural virtue of "common people" and, possibly, the nation. Hogarth's social didacticism emerged most strongly in his graphic series *Industry and Idleness* (1747) and the diptych *Beer Street and Gin Lane* (1751), which offer the viewer a rhetorical choice between good and evil.

Although one may recognize the moral thrust of Hogarth's works, it is difficult to align them with a single authorial voice. His work established a mode of British urban narrative marked by multiplicity, ambiguity, and trenchant humor.

See also **Britain, Art in; Caricature and Cartoon; Prints and Popular Imagery.**

BIBLIOGRAPHY

Primary Sources

Hogarth, William. *Autobiographical Notes* (c. 1764). In *The Analysis of Beauty.* Edited by John Burke, pp. 201–236. Oxford, 1955.

Nichols, John. *Biographical Anecdotes of William Hogarth and Catalogue of His Works Chronologically Arranged.* London, 1781.

Secondary Sources

Bindman, David. *Hogarth.* London, 1981.

Dabydeen, David. *Hogarth's Blacks: Images of Blacks in Eighteenth Century English Art.* Kingston-upon-Thames, U.K., 1985.

Fort, Bernadette, and Angela Rosenthal, eds. *The Other Hogarth: Aesthetics of Difference.* Princeton, 2001.

Hallett, Mark. *Hogarth.* London, 2000.

Paulson, Ronald. *Hogarth.* 3 vols. New Brunswick, N.J., 1991–1993.

———. *Hogarth's Graphic Works.* 2 vols. 3rd ed. New Haven and London, 1989.

ANGELA H. ROSENTHAL

HOHENZOLLERN DYNASTY. The ruling house of Brandenburg-Prussia, the House of Hohenzollern is most famous for providing rulers of the kingdom of Prussia and later of the German empire. The ancestral home of the House of Hohenzollern is in Swabia near the sources of the Danube and Neckar Rivers, about eighty miles south of today's Stuttgart. The Hohenzollerns began their climb to dynastic fame in 1417 when Holy Roman emperor Sigismund of Luxembourg awarded the Mark of Brandenburg in what was then the far northeast to Frederick of Hohenzollern as a reward for loyal service. Although Frederick found his new land to be poor, unproductive, and exposed to danger, he decided to stay. This land, in which Berlin later rose, was the foundation of the Hohenzollern dynasty.

The second major property to come into Hohenzollern possession was the province of East Prussia. In the early thirteenth century a Polish prince invited the Teutonic Knights, an order that emerged during the Third Crusade (1189–1192), to subdue and convert the pagan Balts in the area that would become East Prussia. The Teutonic Knights did so and settled there. In 1511 the Knights chose as their grand master a Hohenzollern, and, when the Protestant Reformation swept through northern Germany, this Hohenzollern prince dissolved the order and became simply duke of Prussia, a vassal of the king of Poland.

The third major property that enhanced the family's power and made it a force in western Germany was the acquisition of Cleves and Mark on the Rhine, which the Hohenzollerns gained on a dynastic claim in 1609. In 1618 all three of these areas—Brandenburg, Prussia, and Cleves and Mark—came under the rule of a single Hohenzollern, John Sigismund (ruled 1608–1619), the grandfather of Frederick William, the Great Elector (ruled 1640–1688), who is credited with laying the foundations of the modern Prussian state.

See also **Brandenburg; Frederick I (Prussia); Frederick II (Prussia); Frederick William (Brandenburg); Frederick William I (Prussia); Frederick William II (Prussia); Prussia; Teutonic Knights; Utrecht, Peace of (1713).**

BIBLIOGRAPHY

Carsten, F. L. *The Origins of Prussia.* Oxford, 1954.

KARL A. ROIDER

HOLBACH, PAUL THIRY, BARON D' (1723–1789), French philosopher, scientist, man of letters, founder of a salon, and critic of the *ancien régime.* Holbach's life and literary career are somewhat shadowy because he published his books clandestinely to avoid persecution and did not write a memoir, diary, or a great number of letters.

Holbach was born in the village of Edesheim in the Palatinate, a German-speaking area close to France and its culture. His parents, non-noble landowners, raised him as a Catholic. In childhood, he was influenced greatly by his uncle François-Adam d'Holbach, a rich financier ennobled in Vienna in 1720 and made a baron in 1728. His uncle arranged for the young boy to leave his parents' home and live with him in Paris. Little is known about Holbach's education except that in 1744 he began his legal studies at the eminent University of Leiden in the Dutch Republic and spent several years there and at his uncle's estate in that country.

Holbach settled in Paris and became a French citizen in 1749 and a barrister before the Parlement of Paris, one of the highest courts of France. But his legal career proved short-lived, for he took much more interest in his social and intellectual life. He organized a salon, holding regular Thursday and Sunday dinners at which he provided excellent food and wine and encouraged the frankest exchange of ideas. Such freethinkers as Denis Diderot, Jean Le Rond d'Alembert, Jacques-André Naigeon, and Marie-Jean Caritat, marquis de Condorcet, became members of his social circle, as did many others of varied beliefs. The salon lasted in Paris and at Holbach's country estate nearby into the 1780s.

Holbach could afford such entertaining. His uncle had given him valuable property in 1750 and, at his death in 1753, left his nephew a large legacy in addition to the title of baron of the Holy Roman Empire. Moreover, in 1750 he married his cousin, Basile-Geneviève-Suzanne d'Aine, a daughter of the wealthy Nicolas and Suzanne d'Aine. Two years after his wife's death in 1754, he married one of her sisters, Charlotte-Suzanne d'Aine. Holbach's fortune was enlarged by these marriages; and in 1756 he purchased the office of secretary to the king, an expensive sinecure conferring automatic French nobility.

Holbach also aspired to be a man of letters. In the early 1750s he wrote a pamphlet favoring Italian over French music and started his collaboration on the *Encyclopédie* edited by Diderot and d'Alembert, to which he contributed hundreds of signed and anonymous articles on science, technology, religion, politics, geography, and other topics. In addition, from 1752 to 1771, he translated anonymously into French more than ten important German and Scandinavian books on chemistry, mineralogy, and metallurgy. In these books and in his articles for the *Encyclopédie,* he helped prepare the way for advances in the emerging science of geology and the revolution in chemical theory initiated by Antoine-Laurent Lavoisier and his colleagues.

Holbach's passion for chemistry and mineralogy, his esteem for Epicurus, Lucretius, Cicero, Seneca, and other classical writers, and his admiration for the thought of French and English deists and atheists led him to forsake Catholicism and champion a deterministic, materialistic, and atheistic view of the universe. He thought matter in motion to be the sole reality and believed that men and women were purely physical beings moved by self-interest, yet capable of a humane secular morality. From 1759 to 1770, he secretly translated, edited, and authored many books that denounced all religions and their clergy for fostering illusory supernatural beliefs in God, the soul, miracles, and immortality, all of which Holbach thought increased human suffering. Several of these works sold well, especially *Le système de la nature* (1769, with a 1770 imprint; The system of nature). Naigeon and a few other members of his circle assisted him in his literary enterprise. In 1770 the Parlement of Paris and

Paul Thiry, baron d'Holbach. ©BETTMANN/CORBIS

the royal administration condemned some of these works, but Holbach escaped prosecution. He concealed his authorship of these writings from all but a few trusted friends, and the government did not zealously seek to discover the identity of the author. He seems to have had protectors in high office.

In the early and mid-1770s, Holbach elaborated on his politics. In several books he asserted that rulers should maximize happiness for the greatest number of their subjects rather than allowing them to suffer from poverty and humiliation. To accomplish this, he rejected divine right absolute monarchy, enlightened despotism, rule by an aristocracy, and democracy. Instead, in the anonymous *La politique naturelle* (1773; Natural politics), he supported a monarchy that encouraged a wide distribution of land ownership and that was checked by representative bodies of landowners. How much power would be given to these bodies is unclear, but he believed France should not replicate the British House of Commons, which he visited in 1765 and considered corrupt. He also lacked confidence in change by revolution, and in 1776 dedicated his anonymous *Éthocratie* (Government based on morality) to the recently crowned Louis XVI.

After 1776 Holbach largely stopped writing for publication and did not reveal his opinions of the American Revolution and the calling of the Estates-General in France. He died in January 1789, six months before the fall of the Bastille. During the French Revolution, he became publicly known as the author of controversial works, for Naigeon and Condorcet either republished or wrote commentaries about several of them and identified them as having been written by Holbach. Since then his works have often been reprinted. He deserves to be remembered as the host of a brilliant salon, the writer and translator of important scientific works, and a fervent polemicist for materialistic atheism and political reform. His life exemplifies the French philosophes—their sociability, passion for natural science, and criticism of existing religious and political institutions.

See also **Alembert, Jean Le Rond d'; Atheism; Diderot, Denis; *Encyclopédie;* Enlightenment; Philosophes; Salons.**

BIBLIOGRAPHY

Primary Source

Holbach, Paul Thiry d'. *Oeuvres philosophiques.* Edited by Jean-Pierre Jackson. Paris, 1998–. A modern French edition of many of Holbach's important books. There is no equivalent edition in English, but there are translations of some of his books.

Secondary Sources

Kors, Alan Charles. "The Atheism of d'Holbach and Naigeon." In *Atheism from the Reformation to the Enlightenment,* edited by Michael Hunter and David Wooton, pp. 273–300. Oxford and New York, 1992. On Holbach's irreligious beliefs.

——. *D'Holbach's Coterie: An Enlightenment in Paris.* Princeton, 1976. A valuable study of the salon and its members.

Ladd, Everett C. "Helvétius and D'Holbach . . ." *Journal of the History of Ideas* 23 (1962): 221–236. On Holbach's politics.

Naville, Paul. *D'Holbach et la philosophie scientifique au XVIIIe siècle.* Rev. ed. Paris, 1967. The standard study of his life and works.

Rappaport, Rhoda. "Baron d'Holbach's Campaign for German (and Swedish) Science." *Studies on Voltaire and the Eighteenth Century* 323 (1994): 225–246. On Holbach's science.

Wickwar, W. H. *Baron D'Holbach: A Prelude to the French Revolution.* London, 1935. Informative on Holbach's life and thought.

FRANK A. KAFKER

HOLBEIN, HANS, THE YOUNGER

(1497/98–1543), German portrait painter. Hans Holbein the Younger, a painter and designer of stained glass, woodcuts, and jewelry, was born in Augsburg to a family of artists. His father Hans the Elder (active c. 1490–1523) was probably his first teacher, and his uncles Sigmund Holbein and Hans Burgkmair the Elder (1473–c. 1531) were important early influences. He left Augsburg at eighteen to join his elder brother Ambrosius (1493/94–1519?) in Basel as journeymen in the workshop of the leading painter there, Hans Herbst, or Herbster (1470–1552), and collaborated on the marginal drawings in Oswald Myconius's famous copy of Erasmus's *Praise of Folly.* Commissions from Basel humanists and city officials soon ensued: portraits of Erasmus's publisher, Johannes Froben; Erasmus's attorney and heir, Bonifacius Amerbach (1519; Basel); three portraits of Erasmus himself (1523; Longford Castle, Ireland; Louvre, Paris; and Basel); a diptych portrait of the mayor Jakob Meyer and his wife Dorothea Kannegiesser (1516), who also commissioned *The Meyer Madonna* (1526–1530; Darmstadt); a madonna with standing saints for the then city clerk Johannes Gerster (1522, *The Solothurn Madonna*); and an altarpiece for a Basel city council member, Hans Oberried.

During 1517–1519 Holbein assisted his father with illusionistic decorations for the facade of the Jakob Hertenstein house (Lucerne) and the Haus zum Tanz in Basel. Admitted to the Basel painters' guild Zum Himmel on 25 September 1519, that same year he married Elsbeth Binzenstock, a tanner's widow. On 20 July 1520 he secured Basel citizenship, and a year later he received a commission to decorate the new council chamber. Further religious works included a Passion altarpiece, a Last Supper scene, and *The Body of the Dead Christ in the Tomb* (1521; all in Basel). This last work, a panel for use from Good Friday until Easter morning, is so radical a representation of death that the nineteenth-century Russian author Dostoevsky would later declare, "This picture could rob many a man of

Hans Holbein the Younger. *Jean de Dinteville and Georges de Selve* ("The Ambassadors"), by Hans Holbein the Younger, 1533. ©NATIONAL GALLERY COLLECTION; BY KIND PERMISSION OF THE TRUSTEES OF THE NATIONAL GALLERY, LONDON/CORBIS

his faith," creating its effect with an imaginary painting in his novel *The Idiot.* Designs for the woodcut *Dance of Death* series were also made during these years (1522–1525).

Holbein traveled to France (1524), perhaps hoping to find employment with Francis I, and may have seen works by Leonardo da Vinci and Andrea del Sarto at Amboise, as well as three-color chalk drawings by Jean Clouet, a technique that he adapted for his own use in portrait work. His paintings of Venus and Cupid and of *Lais of Corinth* (1526; Basel) show the strong influence of the Franco-Italian Renaissance.

Erasmus, concerned for the welfare of his favorite painter, recommended Holbein by letter to his friend Sir Thomas More in London, and the artist departed from Basel for England, by way of Antwerp, on 29 August 1526. While there, he painted a group portrait of the More family, for which only the individual chalk studies (Windsor Castle) and the preliminary sketch (Basel) with the artist's notes have survived—the latter was presented to Erasmus. He also finished portraits of Sir Thomas More (1527; Frick Collection, New York); the Archbishop of Canterbury William Warham (1527; Louvre, Paris); the comptroller of Henry VIII's household, *Sir Henry Guildford,* and his wife, *Lady Guildford* (both 1527; Windsor and St. Louis); Henry's privy councillor Sir Henry Wyatt (1527/28; Louvre, Paris); and a drawing of his son, the poet Sir Thomas Wyatt (undated). Before leaving England, Holbein also painted a portrait of the king's German astronomer Nicolas Kratzer (1528; Louvre, Paris). Unlike his Basel paintings, which are a mixture of tempera and oil on pine or lindenwood, the British portraits were completed on oak panels.

Returning to Basel, Holbein bought two houses, painted on paper a group portrait of his wife and children, *The Artist's Wife and Her Two Children, Philip and Catherine* (1528, Basel; silhouetted and mounted on panel), and made adjustments to the *Meyer Madonna,* which by then was to become an epitaph. In 1528 and 1529, during the wave of iconoclasm that accompanied the Reformation in Basel under the influence of Ulrich Zwingli, religious works of art were removed from the churches and many were destroyed. Consequently, Holbein left for England once again. Thomas More now being out of favor at court, Holbein found clients among the young German merchants of the Steelyard, including Georg Gisze of Danzig (1532; Berlin), Hermann Wedigh of Cologne (1533; New York) and Dierick Born (1533; Vienna). His double portrait of the French ambassador Jean de Dinteville and his houseguest Georges de Selve, bishop of Lavour, entitled *The Ambassadors* (1533; London) also dates from this period. Soon afterward he was made part of Henry VIII's court, portraying Henry himself, Queen Jane Seymour (1536; Vienna), Christina of Denmark (1538; London), Anne of Cleves, and the future King Edward VI, the two-year-old Prince of Wales (1539; Washington). The King's physician Sir John Chambers was Holbein's last client. The artist died, probably of the plague, in 1543, leaving behind a mistress and two young children in England.

See also **Britain, Art in; Erasmus, Desiderius; Henry VIII (England); More, Thomas.**

BIBLIOGRAPHY

Bätschmann, Oskar, and Griener, Pascal. *Hans Holbein.* Princeton, 1997.

Ganz, Paul. *Dessins de Hans Holbein le jeune.* Geneva, 1939.

Hervey, Mary F. S. *Holbein's 'Ambassadors', the Picture and the Men. An Historical Study.* London, 1900.

Michael, Erika. *Hans Holbein the Younger: A Guide to Research.* New York and London, 1997.

Roberts, Jane. *Holbein. Zeichnungen vom Hofe Heinrichs VIII.* Exh. cat. Hamburg and Basel, 1988.

Rowlands, John. *Holbein: The Paintings of Hans Holbein the Younger.* Oxford, 1985.

Strong, Roy. *Holbein and Henry VIII.* London, 1967.

JANE CAMPBELL HUTCHISON

HOLY LEAGUES. Several military alliances that arose between 1495 to 1699 in the turbulent conditions of Europe were given the name "Holy League." Three of the most significant were the Holy Leagues formed to fight the Ottoman Empire by the Habsburgs, the papacy, and other states such as Venice, Genoa, and Poland. This article will discuss these anti-Ottoman alliances that were formed in 1538–1540, 1571–1573, and 1679–1699 because they were all similarly characterized as "crusades." They were mainly financed by the increased wealth of the Habsburg empire in order to check Ottoman expansion in Europe. The increasing success of each alliance was partly the result of rising prosperity in Europe, owing to the influx of precious metals from the New World into the European economy, simultaneous with Ottoman economic decline.

THE HOLY LEAGUE OF 1538–1540

Venice, the Habsburg emperor Charles V, and the papacy formed the first of this type of Holy League in early 1538 to counter a wave of Ottoman expansion in Europe that had begun with the accession of Sultan Suleiman I to the throne in 1520. However, this coalition was marred from the outset by rivalry between the Venetians and Charles, who had different goals in fighting the Ottomans. As a result of this disunity, the Ottoman fleet was able to overcome the Holy League fleet at the battle of Prevesa in 1538. The Venetians left this league in 1540. Although Charles sent his own fleet in 1541 to attack the Ottomans at Algiers, weather destroyed it before it arrived, curtailing Christian plans to reassert dominance at that time over the Mediterranean.

THE HOLY LEAGUE OF 1571–1573

The next such Holy League was formed in 1571 by Pope Pius V between Spain, Venice, Genoa, and the papacy to respond to Ottoman attacks against Tunis and Cyprus. It achieved a significant victory at Lepanto, at the mouth of the Gulf of Patras (in modern Greece), in October 1571, but came to an end with the death of Pius in 1572 and Venice's financial troubles, which drove the league to make peace with the Ottomans in 1573. This Holy League was also hampered by the disparate goals of its major participants.

THE HOLY LEAGUE IN THE LONG WAR (1679–1699)

After a few other attempts to form coalitions against the Turks, the Holy League of 1679–1699 was the most successful and secured the first enduring Ottoman withdrawal from European territory for several centuries. It was formed to counter the threat of Kara Mustafa Pasha against Vienna in 1683. The Polish king John III Sobieski was an important commander in this force. Although this last alliance had a naval component, its most important dimension was the advance of Habsburg forces into the Balkans for the first time, resulting in the Peace of Carlowitz in 1699, signed by the Ottoman sultan Mustafa II and the Habsburg emperor Leopold I and viewed by later historians as an important sign of the actual decline of the Ottoman Empire.

See also **Charles V (Holy Roman Empire); Lepanto, Battle of; Ottoman Empire; Suleiman I; Vienna, Sieges of.**

BIBLIOGRAPHY

Ingrao, Charles W. *The Habsburg Monarchy, 1618–1815.* Cambridge, U.K., 2000.

Lane, Frederic C. *Venice: A Maritime Republic.* Baltimore: 1973.

ERNEST TUCKER

HOLY ROMAN EMPIRE. The Holy Roman Empire was a feudal monarchy that encompassed present-day Germany, the Netherlands, Belgium, Luxembourg, Switzerland, Austria, the Czech and Slovak Republics, as well as parts of eastern France, northern Italy, Slovenia, and western Poland at the start of the early modern centuries. It was created by the coronation of the Frankish king Charlemagne as Roman emperor by Pope Leo III on Christmas Day in the year 800, thus restoring in their eyes the western Roman Empire that had been leaderless since 476. Charlemagne's Frankish successor emperors faltered under political and military challenges, and his inheritance was permanently divided in 887. After 924 the western empire was again without an emperor until the coronation of Otto I, duke of Saxony, on 2 February 962. This coronation was seen to transfer the Roman imperial office to the heirs of the East Franks, the Germans. The position of emperor remained among the Germans until the Holy Roman Empire was abolished in the aftermath of the Napoleonic Wars in 1806.

In 1512 the name "Holy Roman Empire of the German Nation" *(Heiliges römisches Reich deutscher Nation)* became the official title of the empire, which spanned central Europe between the kingdom of France to the west and the kingdoms of Hungary and Poland to the east. In the north it was bounded by the Baltic and North Seas and by the Danish kingdom; in the south, it reached to the Alps. At no time in its long history did the empire possess clearly defined boundaries; its people, perhaps fifteen million in 1500, spoke a variety of languages and dialects. German predominated, but the advice of the Golden Bull of 1356 that future princes of the empire should learn the "German, Italian, and Slavic tongues" remained apposite. The multilingual empire stood at the crossroads of Europe and its emerging national cultures; it also included significant Jewish communities in the south and west. European trade and communication moved along the mighty rivers within the empire—the Rhine, the Main, the Danube, and the Elbe. On these rivers stood some of its most important cities: Cologne, the largest in the empire with about thirty thousand inhabitants, as well as Frankfurt, Vienna, and Hamburg. By 1500 there were about a dozen big cities with over ten thousand inhabitants each, and about twenty with between two and ten thousand people. Visitors to the empire from Italy, such as Niccolò Machiavelli, noted the size and wealth of these great German cities.

The history of the term "Holy Roman Empire of the German Nation" illustrates several key developments on the path to the early modern empire. The medieval "Roman Empire," ambiguously created through the imperial coronation of Charlemagne, was first given the adjective "holy" *(sacrum imperium Romanum)* by the Imperial Chancellery of Frederick I Barbarossa (ruled 1152–1190) in 1157. The term "Holy Roman Empire," used regularly from 1184, challenged the monopoly on the sacred presented by the papacy of the "Holy Roman Church" *(sancta Romana Ecclesia)* and presented the empire as an equal heir to the legacy of Rome. The first official use of the full term "Holy Roman Empire of the German Nation" in 1474 acknowledged that the empire had been for some time a German political unit in all practical terms. At the

same time, the term also underscored a sense that it was the unique destiny of the Germans to rule the universal sacred empire of Christendom. In this way the term limited claims to the empire from ambitious French rulers such as Francis I (ruled 1515–1547), who campaigned for election to the imperial throne in 1519, only to be defeated by the Habsburg Charles of Ghent, Emperor Charles V (ruled 1519–1556).

The Holy Roman Empire developed a complex legal and political structure. Its central figure was the emperor, whose position combined ancient Roman pretensions of universal, divinely sanctioned rule with the Germanic tradition of elected kingship, overlaid with efforts to define the emperor as a feudal overlord and his leading princes as his vassals. The position of emperor was elected, a characteristic the empire shared with other European monarchies such as the papacy. Just as the cardinals, princes of the church, chose each new pope, so the leading princes of the empire, called electors, chose their emperor. Technically, each emperor was first chosen "king of the Romans," signifying his popular claim to the Roman Empire, by the leading nobles of the empire. The right of these princes to choose their king was precisely codified in 1356 by a proclamation of Emperor Charles IV (ruled 1346–1378) called the "Golden Bull." This bull, the fundamental law of the empire, limited the right to elect the king of the Romans to seven leading princes: three ecclesiastical electors, the archbishops of Mainz, Trier, and Cologne; and four lay electors, the king of Bohemia, the duke of Saxony, the margrave of Brandenburg, and the count Palatinate of the Rhine. Originally, the king of the Romans received the title of emperor only through coronation by the pope. This tradition was set aside by Maximilian I (ruled 1493–1519), who assumed the title "Elected Roman Emperor." His successor Charles V was the last emperor to be crowned in Italy; subsequent emperors were still elected and crowned king of the Romans by the electors and simply assumed the title of emperor without a separate coronation. Only males were allowed to hold the imperial office.

In 1438 Albert II of Habsburg was elected to the imperial throne; he was succeeded by his cousin Frederick III (ruled 1440–1493). From their base of power in Austria, the House of Habsburg outmaneuvered other leading families of the empire to secure their election to the imperial throne again and again; from the reign of Albert in 1438 forward, a Habsburg was always elected (except for a brief interlude from 1742 to 1745 when the Wittelsbach Prince Charles Albert of Bavaria was elected as Emperor Charles VII), and the office of the emperor became quasi hereditary. This is less surprising when one realizes that by the mid-fifteenth century only a leading prince of the empire could benefit from the imperial title, as the prestige of the emperor's position far surpassed its actual power. In legal terms the emperor was "administrator of the empire" rather than "lord of the empire." The empire was divided into a patchwork of principalities, some large and powerful like Wittelsbach Bavaria, others small but independent, like the imperial abbeys in the southwest. In each of these principalities rulers exercised many of the functions associated by early modern and modern political theorists with sovereignty. In the first instance the princes of the empire—rather than the emperor—collected taxes, administered justice, minted coins, and claimed responsibility for the material and spiritual salvation of their subjects. Many of the principalities of the empire had their own parliamentary bodies representing the estates of the territory.

The territorial ambitions of the princes, alongside their predilection for partible inheritance, created a patchwork of German principalities that grew bewilderingly complex. By 1450 the empire contained the seven electoral principalities; twenty-five major secular principalities, such as the duchies of Austria, Bavaria, and Brunswick; about ninety archbishoprics, bishoprics, and imperial abbeys; over one hundred independent counties of very unequal importance; and seventy free imperial cities such as Cologne, Bremen, Lübeck, and Hamburg in the north; Strasbourg, Nuremberg, Ulm, and Augsburg in the south; and Frankfurt and Mühlhausen in central Germany. These cities were subject to no one but the emperor, which made them effectively independent. In his pathbreaking analysis of the empire's constitution in 1667, Samuel Pufendorf explained the fragmentation of political authority in the empire: "in the course of time, through the negligent complaisance of the emperors, the ambition of the princes, and the scheming of the clergy" the empire had developed from "an ordered monarchy" to "a kind of state so disharmonious" that it stood somewhere between a limited monarchy and a federation of sovereign principalities. Scholars today would explain the development in different terms but agree that the imperial monarchy had traded away considerable power and authority to the princes and the church during the medieval period.

Few European political units seem as remote and confusing as the Holy Roman Empire. At the start of the early modern period, the supranational, multiethnic structure of this feudal state made perfect sense, of course, to the people who lived in it and shaped its development. Indeed, in the period from 1450 to 1555 the Holy Roman Empire was a dynamic political unit of crucial importance to the growth of the Habsburg empire and the Protestant Reformation. It survived the chaos of the Thirty Years' War (1618–1648) to emerge as a guarantor of peace, if not progress, in central Europe. By the mid-eighteenth century, however, Europeans saw the Holy Roman Empire in a very different light. In a Europe of centralized, hereditary monarchies consolidating their nation-states, its polycentric, supranational structure, elected emperor, and ponderous parliament had become ever more difficult to understand and explain. When it ceased to exist in 1806, few understood its significance.

IMPERIAL INSTITUTIONS IN THE RENAISSANCE

At the end of the fifteenth century the empire entered a period of institutional growth and increased political importance. The focus of the empire had shifted to its German-speaking lands, especially the wealthy southern area known as Upper Germany, which saw the birth and growth of effective imperial institutions. Foremost was its parliament, the Imperial Diet *(Reichstag)*. The diet emerged from medieval political struggles that obligated the emperor to consult with his leading princes (in feudal terms, the holders of imperial fiefs) on decisions affecting the empire. These leading princes, including the seven electors, dukes and counts, bishops and abbots, and autonomous cities became known collectively as the "imperial estates" *(Reichsstände)* and their assembly as the Imperial Diet. The diet became the most important site of communication, conflict, and negotiation between the emperor and the estates.

The emperor did not rule as an autocrat but was bound by the resolutions of the Imperial Diet. As was typical of early modern statecraft, the diets often passed resolutions that could not be enforced (the Edict of Worms of 1521 is the most famous example), but its organization helped define the empire through its estates. From 1489 on, the diet met in three colleges, similar to the houses of the English Parliament: the college of the imperial electors, in which the three ecclesiastical and four lay electors each had a vote; the college of the imperial princes; and the college of the imperial free cities. The diet was summoned by the emperor only when needed; sessions were held in the leading imperial cities of the south, usually Augsburg, Nuremberg, Regensburg, or Speyer. When the diet met, the emperor presided, flanked by six of the electors, with the archbishop of Trier seated directly in front of the imperial throne. Along the sides of the hall sat the representatives of the college of imperial princes, and facing the emperor at the back of the hall were the representatives of the imperial free cities. Each college deliberated separately, voted within the college, and then cast one vote in the assembled diet. After 1663 the diet transformed itself into a body of representatives sitting permanently in Regensburg.

Frustration during the long reign of the neglectful Emperor Frederick III led to calls for imperial reform, and Emperor Maximilian I was willing to work with the estates to modernize the empire's institutions. The Imperial Diet in Worms in 1495 marked a turning point. Led by the archbishop-elector of Mainz, Berthold von Henneberg (1484–1504), the diet outlawed all private wars and noble feuding and established the Imperial Cameral Court *(Reichskammergericht)* to replace violence with arbitration. The imperial estates gathered in Worms in 1495 also voted to establish a new form of direct imperial taxation, the "Common Penny" *(gemeiner Pfennig)*, to fund the Imperial Cameral Court. The tax was collected from all male inhabitants, regardless of status, for a period of four years and was renewed in 1512 and in 1542 to pay for the defense of the empire. The division of the empire into administrative districts called Imperial Circles *(Kreise)* was another innovation of the reign of Maximilian. Initially these districts served to enforce the imperial peace, but later their competence was extended to include imperial taxation and defense. From 1512, the empire was divided into ten Imperial Circles: the Austrian and Burgundian regions; the circle of the Rhenish electors; the Upper Saxon, Franconian, Bavarian, and Swabian circles; and the Upper Rhenish, Lower Rhenish-Westphalian, and Lower Saxon circles. The territories of the Bohemian crown, the Swiss Confederation, and the Italian imperial fiefs were not included in this plan.

These Circles and the Imperial Diet came to define the empire by the early sixteenth century and can help us distinguish between two conceptions of the empire. The greater empire was based on theoretical claims of universal dominion and historical claims of rule over Italy, Burgundy, and Germany. This greater empire encompassed all of Italy north of the Papal States (except Venice) as fiefs of the empire and included the kingdom of Bohemia, the Swiss Confederation, and the Habsburg Netherlands. Within these broad claims based on medieval precedent, feudal law, and dynastic connections, a second, more concentrated empire ("Reichstags-Deutschland") actually participated in the growth of imperial institutions in the fifteenth and sixteenth centuries. This empire, culturally German, found its political and institutional base in the southwest of the empire and in the electoral principalities. The diet was largely ignored by the Swiss Confederation, the Netherlands, and the kingdom of Bohemia (despite its king's position as an elector). The treaties of the Peace of Westphalia of 1648 confirmed the independence of the Netherlands and Switzerland from the empire; Bohemia, on the other hand, where the Thirty Years' War had begun, was firmly integrated into the dominion of its Austrian Habsburg rulers.

The threat to the empire posed by the dynamic Ottoman Empire stood on the agenda of almost every Imperial Diet during the reigns of Maximilian I and Charles V. Habsburg Austria was constantly threatened by Turkish invasion, and the Habsburg emperors called the estates together to request aid. The threat was especially clear when the Ottoman Turks conquered most of Hungary in 1526: Austria would be next. Vienna was besieged by an army led by Suleiman the Magnificent (ruled 1520–1566) in 1529. The dependence of the Habsburg emperors on the support of the imperial estates in their struggle against Turkish expansion deeply affected their response to the next great challenge of imperial politics, the Reformation.

EMPIRE AND REFORMATION

The Protestant Reformation did not cause the division of Germany into dozens of independent territories; in fact, the reverse is true. The extraordinarily diverse and divided political landscape of the empire in the early sixteenth century was the single most important factor in the spread of evangelical ideas and the adoption of church reforms. As it became clear to Martin Luther that the Church of Rome would not accept his theological and pastoral reforms (referred to as "evangelical"), he turned "to the Christian Nobility of the German Nation" (the title of his important treatise of 1520, *An den christlichen Adel deutscher Nation*) and exhorted them to take up their responsibility to reform the church. Their response was varied. Luther's own territorial ruler, Elector Frederick III the Wise of Saxony (ruled 1486–1525), was willing to allow the ideas of his unruly theologian to circulate in Saxony and in the empire; other princes and free imperial cities eagerly read, creatively interpreted, and put into practice the ideas coming out of Wittenberg. Emperor Charles V, like most of the German princes, appreciated Luther's criticism of the papacy and the Roman curia but wanted no part of Luther's fundamental theological challenge to the authority of the Church of Rome. Charles stated clearly that he would not "deny the religion of all his ancestors for the false teachings of a solitary monk."

The young emperor and the rebellious theologian met at the Diet of Worms in 1521. Luther's refusal to recant his teachings prompted the Edict of Worms, which threatened his supporters with the imperial ban and outlawry and prohibited his writings. Protected from arrest and trial for heresy by his prince, Frederick the Wise, and frightened by the disorder unleashed by the spread of evangelical ideas, Luther looked to the leading secular authorities of the empire to implement his ideas. This they did, taking advantage of the fragmentation of imperial and territorial authority across the empire. Individual principalities and city-states became "laboratories" for church reform and religious innovation. Because the builders of the first Protestant institutions were leaders among the estates of the empire, the conflict over reform and Reformation was played out in the institutions of the empire, above all in the Imperial Diets. It was at the Diet of Speyer in 1529 that the a group of princes including the elector of Saxony and the landgrave of Hesse and fourteen imperial free cities submitted an official protest against the suppression of the evangelical movement. The name "Protestant" arose from their action. The next Imperial Diet at Augsburg in 1530 produced a definitive Protestant statement of faith, the Augsburg Confession of Philipp Melanchthon, and a reinforcement of the Edict of Worms. Tensions rose and in 1531 the empire's leading Protestant princes and free cities formed a defensive alliance, the Schmalkaldic League. This alliance was not formally directed against the empire or its Catholic ruling house of Habsburg, but its confessional politics held an immense potential to disrupt the institutions of the empire.

WAR AND PEACE IN THE CONFESSIONAL ERA

The Protestant princes and free cities of the empire created their own territorial churches by seizing the lands of monasteries and churches, severing all links with Rome, and overseeing the doctrine and morals of their subjects. Scholars have labeled this process "confessionalization," and it is the defining characteristic of the empire in the period from the 1530s through the end of the seventeenth century. Confessionalization meant the doctrinal and organizational consolidation of the diverging Christian Reformations into established churches with mutually exclusive creeds, constitutions, and forms of piety. The power and authority of the princes was naturally reinforced by this new level of spiritual administration.

In the confessional era the line between insider and outsider became much sharper. Subjects and rulers together deployed the new scope of territorial authority to accuse, try, and burn witches; expel Jews and Christians of other confessions; and police the poor and the criminal. The cruel work of the great European witch persecutions reached its peak in the years between 1580 and 1660, and about half of the forty to fifty thousand executions took place in the empire. The promulgation of countless church and police ordinances allowed territorial rulers to envision (though not create) a land of godly, orderly, and obedient subjects. Geographically and politically, these territories resembled modern sovereign states, and this gain in power and authority by the individual estates of the empire proved irreversible.

The first evidence that power had shifted came in the aftermath of the Schmalkaldic War (1546–1547). Despite the military victory of Charles V over the Protestant princes, he was unable to roll back the progress of the Reformation before shifting alliances forced him to flee Germany in 1552. Exhausted by the struggle to return the German princes to the Catholic faith, Charles handed all responsibility for German affairs over to his brother, Archduke Ferdinand of Austria (ruled as emperor 1558–1564), who negotiated the Religious Peace of Augsburg in 1555. This agreement established the legal equality of the Evangelical and Catholic churches and the right of princes of the empire to choose either of these confessions for their territories. With the Religious Peace of Augsburg, the empire was divided among two mutually hostile Christian confessions: Roman Catholic and Evangelical (Lutheran). After 1563, Reformed (Calvinist) churches were also established. These divisions strained the imperial institutions described above, but they continued to function. The right of reform granted by the Peace of Augsburg strengthened the estates but also secured peace in the empire just as the Netherlands and France were engulfed in wars of religion.

The Peace of Augsburg lasted for sixty-three years, and the devastating Thirty Years' War (1618–1648) that followed was not an inevitable result of the political and confessional division of the empire. The weakness of the Habsburg emperors Rudolf II (ruled 1576–1612) and Matthias (ruled 1612–1619) paralyzed the very imperial institutions that had served to prevent war within the empire since 1555. The initial goals of Emperor Ferdinand II (ruled 1619–1637) were territorial rather than imperial; following the disorganization of his two predecessors, he sought to reimpose Habsburg authority in their hereditary lands, especially Bohemia, touching off the Bohemian revolt of 1618. This regional conflict rapidly spread as both Ferdinand and his opponents sought support (based on religion or reason of state) from within the empire and abroad. This raised a set of constitutional questions about the emperor's power to invite external (in this case, Spanish) forces into the empire, and the rights of the estates to resist the emperor. Some scholars have argued that these fundamental constitutional questions, as much as confessional hatred and international intervention, made the war so protracted and difficult to conclude.

Despite their successes in the Thirty Years' War, the Habsburgs did not shift the distribution of power in the empire from the princes to the emperor. Like Charles V before them, Ferdinand II and Ferdinand III (ruled 1637–1657) could not develop an imperial monarchy. The Westphalian treaties of 1648 that ended the war left the empire in the form established in 1555, "a monarchy caged by constituted aristocratic liberties," in the words of Thomas A. Brady, Jr. The Peace of Westphalia legitimized the Reformed confession in the empire and restored the territorial and confessional status of the empire to the year 1624, the "normal year" of the treaties.

The Westphalian settlement tied the longstanding balance between emperor and estates to an international agreement designed to bring lasting peace to Europe. France and Sweden stood as guarantors of the treaty's terms, and their purpose was to hold the empire as a whole passive in European affairs. The peace confirmed the broader European trend toward a system of fully sovereign, independent states but left the empire, with its fragmented sovereignty, and the imperial estates, with their lesser, territorial sovereignty within the empire, as exceptions that proved the rule.

Given the consolidation of the power and authority of the individual estates by the Peace of Westphalia, was the Holy Roman Empire a state after 1648? Historians of the nineteenth and most of the twentieth centuries, focused on the modern nation-state, answered in the negative, and critically. The origins of the modern state in Germany were seen in the larger territories of the empire, especially Brandenburg-Prussia. The apotheosis of the nation-state meant the condemnation of the Old Empire, which was denied any significant contribution to the modern state. Early modern political theorists offer a different perspective. Samuel Pufendorf described the empire as "resembling a monster" in his 1667 treatise on the empire's constitution, but Pufendorf, like most of his contemporaries, did not deny that the empire was a state—albeit a state with a complex and irregular constitution that did not fit with any classical model or modern system.

ART AND CULTURE IN THE POLYCENTRIC EMPIRE

In the century after the Peace of Westphalia, the fundamental acceptance of the existence of the empire by the other European powers led to a period of relative peace and prosperity. During this period German art, music, and learned culture once again flourished. Eighteenth-century observers lamented the empire's lack of a capital city that could serve as a cultural center, but the polycentric structure of the empire had its benefits for the cross-pollination of ideas and cultures. As noted above, the spread of Reformation ideas and their implementation benefited from the variety of religious orders, universities, independent city-states, and centers of printing in the empire. From the mid-seventeenth century, the polycentric empire offered an array of careers, patrons, and stimuli for the arts, especially architecture and music. The flowering of German baroque architecture after 1700 can be seen in the works of Johann Bernhard Fischer von Erlach and Johann Lucas von Hildebrandt in the Habsburg lands, Balthasar Neumann in Würzburg, Matthäus Daniel Pöppelmann in Saxony, and Andreas Schlüter in Berlin. These baroque palaces and churches, each testifying to the glory of a prince of the empire, rang with the music of the age, composed by Johann Sebastian Bach in Saxony, George Frideric Handel in Hanover and London, and Franz Joseph Haydn and Wolfgang Amadeus Mozart in Vienna. The careers of these men were shaped by the variety of courts and confessions unique to the empire.

AUSTRO-PRUSSIAN DUALISM AND THE END OF THE EMPIRE

The revival of the Habsburgs' military power and imperial authority began during the reign of Emperor Leopold I (ruled 1658–1705), as the empire was threatened by French and Turkish aggression. These threats resulted in the loss of imperial cities like Strasbourg to France (1681) and the Ottoman siege of Vienna (1683), but without imperial leadership the damage could have been much worse. This demonstrated to even the most powerful princes of the empire that its central institutions, including the emperor, were indispensable to the defense and organization of the empire and its constituent territories. By 1700 the estates focused on strengthening the Imperial Circles and the Imperial Army and supported legislation such as the Imperial Trades Edict of 1731, which regulated the craft guilds of the empire. The two highest courts of the empire, the Imperial Cameral Court and the Imperial Aulic Court *(Reichshofrat)* also grew more effective. These courts settled several major interterritorial disputes through peaceful arbitration in the late seventeenth and eighteenth centuries. They also resolved disputes within territories between princes and their estates. In a case cited by Peter H. Wilson, Duke William Hyacinth, ruler of Nassau-Siegen, was exiled from his tiny principality in 1707 by soldiers from Cologne acting on the instructions of the Imperial Aulic Court, which had ruled that he had forfeited his throne through his autocratic and irrational policies. In the free imperial city of Hamburg, a century-long dispute between the city council and the citizenry was settled in 1712 through an imperial commission. In 1719 the estates of Mecklenburg obtained a verdict and military intervention to prevent their prince's use of his standing army against his own subjects, and in 1764 the Württemberg estates secured an injunction against their duke's attempt to collect new taxes by force. At least a quarter of all cases heard by the Imperial Aulic Court in the period 1648–1806 were brought by subjects against their rulers, a clear sign of the relevance of imperial institutions to subjects and princes in the last 150 years of the empire.

By the mid-eighteenth century the creation of standing armies divided the empire into "armed" and "unarmed" territories. Brandenburg-Prussia led the way with a standing army established by Frederick William I, the Great Elector (ruled 1640–1688). The Hohenzollern electors of Brandenburg, who were also the dukes of Prussia (which lay outside the empire), acquired the title of "king in Prussia" in 1701—an elevation sanctioned by Emperor Leopold I in return for military support from Brandenburg-Prussia. By the reign of Frederick II the Great (ruled 1740–1786), Brandenburg-Prussia had joined the great powers of Europe and pursued its own foreign policy. For Brandenburg-Prussia, as for Austria, the empire was now only one political factor among many.

Historians speak of the "centrifugal forces" that pulled the empire apart in the late eighteenth century. Its two largest principalities, Habsburg Austria and Hohenzollern Brandenburg-Prussia, expanded eastward in the seventeenth and eighteenth centuries, each tapping sources of authority and power outside the empire; the rulers of Saxony and Hanover did the same by accepting crowns in Poland and Great Britain. The lesser territories of the empire, the so-called "Third Germany," focused more attention on the empire, but competition between Austria and Brandenburg-Prussia, the rigidity of the treaties of Westphalia, and the ponderous pace of imperial institutions combined to leave the empire politically impotent. A series of reforms in 1803 came too late to restore political relevance to the empire and could not prevent its elimination, through the abdication of Emperor Francis II (ruled 1792–1806), at the instigation of Napoleon. The tradition of the empire died, and its revival was not seriously discussed at the Congress of Vienna in 1815.

See also **Augsburg, Religious Peace of (1555); Austro-Ottoman Wars; Charles V (Holy Roman Empire); Charles VI (Holy Roman Empire); Ferdinand I (Holy Roman Empire); Ferdinand II (Holy Roman Empire); Ferdinand III (Holy Roman Empire); Francis II (Holy Roman Empire); Frederick III (Holy Roman Empire); Free and Imperial Cities; Habsburg Dynasty: Austria; Habsburg Territories; Joseph I (Holy Roman Empire); Joseph II (Holy Roman Empire); Matthias (Holy Roman Empire); Maximilian I (Holy Roman Empire); Maximilian II (Holy Roman Empire); Peasants' War, German; Reformation, Protestant; Representative Institutions; Schmalkaldic War (1546–1547); Thirty Years' War (1618–1648); Westphalia, Peace of (1648).**

BIBLIOGRAPHY

Primary Sources

Lindberg, Carter, ed. *The European Reformations Sourcebook.* Oxford and Malden, Mass., 2000. Good documentation of the Protestant Reformation in the empire.

Macartney, C. A., ed. *The Habsburg and Hohenzollern Dynasties in the Seventeenth and Eighteenth Centuries.* New York, 1970.

Pufendorf, Samuel. *Die Verfassung des deutschen Reiches.* Translated and edited by Horst Denzer. Frankfurt am Main, 1994. Translation of *De statu imperii Germanici* (1667).

Scott, Tom, and Robert W. Scribner, eds. and trans. *The German Peasants' War: A History in Documents.* Atlantic Highlands, N.J., 1991. Hundreds of documents never before translated into English on the largest rebellion in the history of the empire.

Secondary Sources

Aretin, Karl Otmar, Freiherr von. *Das alte Reich, 1648–1806.* 4 vols. Stuttgart, 1993–2000. Fundamental to any discussion of the empire after the Peace of Westphalia.

Asch, Ronald G. *The Thirty Years War: The Holy Roman Empire and Europe, 1618–1648.* Basingstoke, U.K., 1997.

Blickle, Peter. *Obedient Germans? A Rebuttal: A New View of German History.* Translated by Thomas A. Brady, Jr. Charlottesville, Va., 1997.

Brady, Thomas A., Jr. "Settlements: The Holy Roman Empire." In *Handbook of European History, 1400–1600: Late Middle Ages, Renaissance, and Reformation.* 2 vols. Edited by Thomas A. Brady, Jr., Heiko A. Oberman, and James D. Tracy. Leiden and New York, 1994–1995.

———. *Turning Swiss: Cities and Empire, 1450–1550.* Cambridge, U.K., and New York, 1985.

Carsten, F. L. *Princes and Parliaments in Germany, from the Fifteenth to the Eighteenth Century.* Oxford, 1959. Still valuable for its detail and comparative breadth.

Evans, R. J. W. *Rudolf II and His World: A Study in Intellectual History, 1576–1612.* Oxford, 1973. Reprint, Oxford, 1994.

Fichtner, Paula S. *The Habsburg Monarchy, 1490–1848: Attributes of Empire.* New York, 2003.

Gagliardo, John G. *Germany under the Old Regime, 1600–1790.* London and New York, 1991.

Heer, Friedrich. *The Holy Roman Empire.* Translated by Janet Sondheimer. New York, 1968. Reprint, New York, 2002. Well-illustrated.

Hsia, R. Po-chia. *Social Discipline in the Reformation: Central Europe, 1550–1750.* London and New York, 1989.

Hughes, Michael. *Early Modern Germany, 1477–1806.* Basingstoke, U.K., 1992.

Mann, Golo. *Wallenstein: His Life Narrated.* Translated by Charles Kessler. New York, 1976. Classic biography of one of the central figures of the Thirty Years' War.

Moeller, Bernd. *Imperial Cities and the Reformation: Three Essays.* Edited and translated by H. C. Erik Midelfort and Mark U. Edwards, Jr. Durham, N.C., 1982.

Press, Volker. "The Habsburg Lands: The Holy Roman Empire, 1400–1555." In *Handbook of European History, 1400–1600: Late Middle Ages, Renaissance, and Reformation.* Edited by Thomas A. Brady, Jr., Heiko A. Oberman, and James D. Tracy. 2 vols. Leiden and New York, 1994–1995.

Schindling, Anton, and Walter Ziegler, eds. *Die Territorien des Reichs im Zeitalter der Reformation und Konfessionalisierung: Land und Konfession, 1500–1650.* Katholisches Leben und Kirchenreform im Zeitalter der Glaubensspaltung, 49. 7 vols. Münster, 1989–1997. An invaluable reference work, especially for the smaller territories of the empire.

Scribner, Robert W., and Sheilagh C. Ogilvie, eds. *Germany: A New Social and Economic History.* 2 vols. London and New York, 1996. Vol. 1, *1450–1630,* is edited by Robert W. Scribner; vol. 2, *1630–1800,* by Sheilagh Ogilvie.

Vierhaus, Rudolf. *Germany in the Age of Absolutism.* Translated by Jonathan B. Knudsen. Cambridge, U.K., and New York, 1988.

Walker, Mack. *German Home Towns: Community, State, and General Estate, 1648–1871.* Ithaca, N.Y., 1971.

Wilson, Peter H. *The Holy Roman Empire, 1495–1806.* New York, 1999. A concise and effective summary of the history and institutions of the early modern empire in light of current revisionist scholarship.

Zophy, Jonathan W., ed. *The Holy Roman Empire: A Dictionary Handbook.* Westport, Conn., 1980.

CRAIG KOSLOFSKY

HOLY ROMAN EMPIRE INSTITUTIONS.

HOLY ROMAN EMPIRE INSTITUTIONS. Though the German monarchy existed from late Carolingian times, the Holy Roman Empire as an institutionalized structure of governance was created between 1495 and 1555, and, with modifications following the Peace of Westphalia (1648), it endured until abolished by Napoleonic decree in 1803.

The imperial reform encompasses the institutions created through negotiations at the imperial diets. Its main phase began at Worms in 1495 and culminated there in 1521; following an interruption by the Reformation, a final phase of reform occurred at Augsburg in 1555. The reform provided for new organs of justice (the Imperial Chamber Court) and peacekeeping (Perpetual Peace) and a regionally based police and military structure (the Circles) and system of taxation (the Common Penny), none of which functioned more than desultorily before the 1550s. An executive commission (the Imperial Governance Council), which functioned briefly and poorly, was also created. The most important of the later additions were the Religious Peace of Augsburg of 1555, which enabled imperial governance to function despite the religious schism, the emergence of the Imperial Aulic Council as an imperial court of justice, and the creation of the Imperial Treasurer's office (1570s–1590s), followed in the seventeenth century by a permanent parliamentary body (the Perpetual Diet) with a fixed seat at Regensburg and formal confessional caucuses in religious matters *(itio in partes).*

The early modern empire was characterized by the absence of a comprehensive royal administration. The central administrative functions were divided among the imperial chancellery of the emperor, which was not entirely distinct from the Austrian chancellery; the imperial chancellery at Mainz, under the elector of Mainz, who served as arch-chancellor of the empire; and the imperial diet. From the mid-sixteenth century most administrative, fiscal, police, and military matters were handled either through the Circles or by delegated princes.

In addition to the monarchy, the principal imperial governing institution was the parliament (diet), which took institutionalized form during the last third of the fifteenth century. Until the Thirty Years' War, the monarch called the parliament to meet in one of several (mainly southern) free cities to deliberate, advise, and decide on measures described in his agenda (referred to as the Proposition). After 1663 the diet met in continuous session at Regensburg (hence the label "Perpetual Diet"), with the Estates represented by envoys. From beginning to end, the diet deliberated in three councils: the first of the several imperial electors, the second of around fifty spiritual and thirty temporal

princes (plus one representative each for the imperial abbots and imperial counts), and the third representing the fifty-five or so free cities. Territorial (i.e., nonimperial) nobles, prelates, and towns or districts did not participate in the imperial diet, but rather in their respective territorial parliaments, if such existed.

The empire's fiscal system remained, by European standards, primitive. Twice, in 1495 and again in the early 1540s, futile attempts were made to introduce a general property tax (the Common Penny), which, in the absence of any local imperial officials, parish priests were delegated to collect. Otherwise, taxes were levied according to registers, based on the lists of 1521, which apportioned the levies to the individual estates, based on occasionally revised estimates of their relative wealth.

The imperial church possessed no superior jurisdiction or organs. Around 1500 it consisted of around fifty prince-bishops and eight archbishops, who held lands as temporal lords, bore the title of imperial prince, and held seats in the imperial diets (although one archbishop and sixteen bishops had no such privileges). Twelve bishoprics, nine of them prince-bishoprics, were lost to the Protestants between the 1540s and 1648.

The imperial electors were fixed at seven by the Golden Bull in 1356; these were the archbishops of Mainz, Cologne, and Trier; the electors of the Palatinate, Saxony, and Brandenburg; and the king of

Bohemia. The empire's political aristocracy consisted of the princes (dukes, margraves, landgraves, and princes, plus a few counts), who dominated the diet, while the imperial counts, barons, and knights were represented barely or not at all, though in the sixteenth century they formed important corporate organizations on a regional basis. The nobility, great and small, dominated the bishoprics (and great abbeys), thanks to their predominance in the electing bodies, the cathedral chapters. This power, with which both Vienna and Rome had to come to terms, was not broken until the end of the empire.

The strengths of imperial governance lay in its stability and flexibility. Its stability rested on a fundamental understanding that neither the monarchy nor the Estates could rule alone, an arrangement that encouraged negotiation and compromise. This rule, fixed between 1495 and 1521, was threatened only twice—first between 1546 and 1552 and then during the Thirty Years' War—by insurrection and civil war. Once the political consequences of the religious schism were contained, the system remained remarkably stable during its last 150 years. The flexibility of imperial governance arose from its dependence for the enforcement of law not on a central, royal apparatus of officials but on the Estates in their regions, organized into the Circles.

The greatest weakness of imperial governance lay in the area of defense. For defense against the Ottomans in Hungary until 1681 and for offensive action thereafter, the empire depended on the Habsburg Monarchy and the defensive system of the Austrian lands. It was powerless to prevent Spanish, Danish, Swedish, and French incursions during the Thirty Years' War and equally helpless to act in concert during the wars of Louis XIV and those of the eighteenth century. A second weakness consisted in the inability of the empire's weakly articulated central government to promote economic growth.

Recent literature on imperial governance has contradicted the earlier, highly unfavorable estimates of the empire's functioning as a state. It emphasizes the imperial policy of protecting small Estates from the expansionist aims of the great princes and affording access to courts of law on several levels. Currently, there is a tendency to idealize the empire as a precursor of modern Germany, governed by the rule of law. This said, perhaps no premodern European political system has benefited more from the decline in the reputation of the modern nation-state.

See also **Augsburg, Religious Peace of (1555); Habsburg Territories; Taxation; Thirty Years' War (1618–1648); Westphalia, Peace of (1648).**

BIBLIOGRAPHY

Angermeier, Heinz. *Die Reichsreform 1410–1555: Die Staatsproblematik in Deutschland zwischen Mittelalter und Gegenwart.* Munich, 1984.

Gagliardo, John G. *Reich and Nation: The Holy Roman Empire as Idea and Reality, 1763–1806.* Bloomington, Ind., 1980.

Hartung, Fritz. "Imperial Reform, 1485–1495: Its Course and Character." In *Pre-Reformation Germany.* Edited by Gerald Strauss. New York, 1972.

Press, Volker. "The Holy Roman Empire in Germany History." In *Politics and Society in Reformation Europe: Essays for Sir Geoffrey Elton on His Sixty-Fifth Birthday.* Edited by E. I. Kouri and Tom Scott. Basingstoke, U.K., 1987.

Strauss, Gerald. "The Holy Roman Empire Revisited." *Central European History* 11 (1978): 290–301.

Vann, James A., and Steven W. Rowan, eds. *The Old Reich. Essays on German Political Institutions, 1495–1806.* International Commission for the History of Representative and Parliamentary Institutions. Studies, 48. Brussels, 1974.

THOMAS A. BRADY, JR.

HOMOSEXUALITY. Like modern homosexuality, early modern homosexuality is better understood in the plural than in the singular. Homosexualities in different parts of early modern Europe were profoundly divergent, with equally profound differences existing between rural and urban settings and between diverse social groups in the same geographic areas. Class and other hierarchical differences added further dimensions to this divergence. Just as modern male and female homosexualities may be seen as the outcome of historical processes, their histories, despite their occasional intersections, are quite different. Until the eighteenth century, there were no societal, psychological, or self-identifying concepts of "gay" and "lesbian" as we know them today. But the eighteenth century was an era of transition that gave rise to modern homosexualities, in particular in northern France, England, and the Dutch Republic.

TERMINOLOGY AND SOURCES

The words "homosexuality" and "lesbianism" were first coined in the second half of the nineteenth century. Previously, aside from words in the vernacular, the common European term for homosexuality was "sodomy," which had profound theological and legal connotations. The term derived from the biblical story of the destruction of Sodom and Gomorrah, and of God's wrath for presumably widespread homosexual practices in those cities. Religious connotations affected words in the vernacular as well. "Buggery" and "bugger" (which had derivations in different languages, like the French *bougre* or Dutch *bogger*) came from Latin *bulgarus* and connected sodomy with heresy; this is because Bulgaria supposedly had been a center of Manichaeism, which espoused an indulgence in heterosexual and homosexual sodomy. Sodomy was also referred to as *crimen nefandum,* the 'umentionable vice', the crime not to be known or mentioned among Christians.

From a strictly legal or penal perspective, sodomy did not refer exclusively to a same-sex configuration. The term could refer to anal intercourse, sets of prohibited sexual acts between men or between men and women, bestiality, and in some instances or places, sodomy referred to sexual contacts between Christians and Jews or Christians and Muslims. Although the word sodomy, at least in legal practice, was sometimes applied to sex between women, usually the terms "tribady" or "sapphism," as well as the more obscure Latin terms *fricatrices, subigatrices,* and *clitorifantes,* were used in vernaculars and in legal discourse. These words lacked the negative social and moral connotations of the term sodomy and instead referred specifically to sexual acts. By the end of the early modern period, the term sodomy referred to homosexual intercourse and bestiality in the general parlance. Throughout the era, a "sodomite" was a man who engaged in same-sex behavior. By the end of that period, words like "sapphist" and "sapphism," referring to same-sex female relations, had gained such currency in popular parlance in England. Early modern documents, such as love letters, that provide unmitigated personal accounts of men or women with same-sex orientations are extremely rare. However, some of these have survived, mainly as components of court records from the seventeenth and eighteenth centuries. The latter provide the most substantial (if somewhat problematic, having been filtered by judicial systems) documentation on same-sex behavior and desires in early modern Europe. Although there certainly was no impunity for women who engaged in lesbian acts, the numbers of women prosecuted for same-sex behavior are small in comparison to men, and consequently documents on lesbian behavior are rare indeed.

LEGISLATION

Presumably, the East Roman emperor Justinian, in his sixth century writings against sodomy, had been the first to justify legislation against homosexuality. He claimed that natural disasters, like floods and earthquakes, diseases, and the negative outcome of wars, were collective penalties for homosexual behavior. Those ideas would affect legislation and legal practices in many parts of Europe for centuries to come. In 1120, the Council of Nablus turned sodomy in canonical law into a capital offense. Those convicted of the crime were punished by burning at the stake. The council also designated sodomy a crime that could be prosecuted by ecclesiastical and civil authorities. Local and regional laws in the next centuries provided a variety of penalties for sodomy, ranging from fines and mutilations for repeat offenders to death.

At the beginning of the early modern period, more penal unity was achieved in continental Europe with the enforcement of the *Constitutio Criminalis Carolina* of Holy Roman Emperor Charles V (ruled 1519–1558) in 1532, followed a year later in England by Henry VIII's (ruled 1509–1547) "buggery" act. In many places prosecutors or judges deciding in sodomy cases could still call upon custom, local or regional laws, mosaic law, or rather arbitrary interpretations of Roman laws such as the *Lex Scantinia* from the third century B.C.E. and the *Lex Julia de Adulteriis Coercendis* from the first century B.C.E.

The *Carolina* and the English act both placed the death penalty on sodomy offenders: the first stipulated burning at the stake, the latter called for hanging or decapitation. Joost de Damhouder

(1507–1581), an advisor to Charles V, in his *Praxis Rerum Criminalium* (1554), a commentary on the *Carolina* that was authoritative in many parts of Europe into the first half of the eighteenth century, once again invoked the Sodom story and claimed that natural disasters and pestilence would be God's wrath for the existence of sodomy. Although the main focus was on male homosexual and heterosexual sodomy, commentators on legal issues at the time often did include female same-sex relations as well.

Enlightenment writers like Beccaria in Italy, Montesquieu in France, and Bentham in England rejected (in their works on penal reform) the penalties for same-sex behavior. With the exception of Bentham (who never published his most radical writings on this issue), they had nothing positive to say about same-sex love, yet they rejected the idea that the inherent harm in homosexual behavior was so great that it warranted interference of the state through punitive action. Pursuing a separation of church and state, radical penal reformers also rejected antisodomy laws because those were believed to originate in theology. Reformers emphasized the political abuse of antisodomy laws and maintained that confessions of defendants were all too often obtained through torture. While rejecting the death penalty for sodomy, not all Enlightenment legal reformers rejected penalization, and in many places some form of punishment remained in place. At the end of the early modern period, those countries that adopted the French Napoleonic penal code (or had that code forced upon them) decriminalized same-sex behaviors.

PROSECUTIONS

The late Middle Ages also saw prosecutions and executions of individuals in Europe who were charged with same-sex intimate behavior. Sometimes legal actions were politically inspired, like the accusations in England against Edward II in 1372, or those against the Knights Templar. Prior to the early modern period, accusations of homosexual or heterosexual sodomy were also leveled against groups of heretics who at times faced extreme persecution.

In the late Middle Ages and at the beginning of the early modern period, religious and civil authorities in cities in Tuscany tried to stamp out widespread practices of so-called age-based homosexuality. Venice, Lucca, and Florence created special courts to deal with the offenders. In its seventy years of existence, the court in Florence dealt with over 10,000 cases. Although death penalties and incarcerations were sometimes applied in Venice, in Florence most cases offenders were merely fined, creating the belief (especially later in Protestant countries) that Italians considered sodomy to be a *peccadillo,* a minor sin. A century later, cities like Geneva and Ghent saw serious persecutions, yet in both places mostly foreigners, and especially Italians, faced trial. In Ghent, as in some other places in Flanders at the beginning of the Reformation, a number of monks were burned at the stake after having been found guilty of sodomy. Autos da fé (the public burning of offenders) occurred on the Iberian Peninsula especially during the sixteenth and seventeenth centuries.

Sodomy trials in rural parts of Europe like Prussia and Sweden usually involved charges of bestiality. This was the most common sexual offense in Sweden well into the twentieth century. No serious persecutions have been reported in eastern European countries. In Denmark sodomy seems to have been a crime without offenders: there have been no sodomy trials in that country.

France had witnessed limited numbers of sodomy trials in the sixteenth and seventeenth centuries. In the eighteenth century the Parisian police documented and policed sodomites' lives in a way unheard of before, but this hardly ever resulted in trials. However, such observations did provide ample documentation on sodomite subcultures in Paris. England and the Dutch Republic also had few sodomy trials up to the late seventeenth century. From that time on and well into the next century, there is ample documentation on raids on "molly houses" (from Latin *mollis,* referring to softness and effeminacy) in London. Offenders often were seriously injured by being put on the pillory for their crimes.

After the 1670s in the Dutch Republic, the number of sodomy trials gradually increased until a major wave of arrests erupted in 1730, which was to be repeated several times during the eighteenth century. Persecutions here turned into the most severe in early modern Europe. Between 1730 and 1811, when the French penal code was enforced in the Netherlands, some 800–1,000 sodomy trials were held there, resulting in about 200 death penalties and as many (often de facto lifelong) solitary confinements when mutual masturbation was the only proven offense. Most of the rest of the men prosecuted were forever expelled from their countries, often after they had already taken refuge abroad.

Trials against women for same-sex activities were rare. Occasionally, cross-dressing women who had sex with other women were brought to trial. Only in a three-year period in late-eighteenth-century Amsterdam were lower-class women prosecuted regularly for having sex with one another. They faced up to several years of incarceration.

EARLY MODERN HOMOSEXUALITIES

Divergent patterns of male same-sex behavior dominated different parts of Europe and the rest of the world at different times; upon closer examination, several patterns of behavior—cross-gender, class-based, intergenerational (age-based), and equal-status—could be distinguished. These patterns could also be mixed. The first three patterns, generally speaking, were related to assigned passive and active roles. Only in the equal-status pattern could adult men interchange active and passive roles with one another. Patterns of same-sex behavior could be permanent or temporary. Unlike in the modern West, these patterns did not necessarily represent an alternative sexuality, but were part of male social bonding and also of the socialization process from boyhood into adult masculinity.

In the cross-gender pattern, men dressed as women and took on a female role. Although crossing class barriers (which is what the second pattern is about) is a persistent and apparently enticing feature of same-sex behavior, traditionally the class-based homosexuality is mostly relevant to societies in which free-born men engaged in sexual activities with male slaves. European colonizers met the first among indigenous populations of the Americas, and may have engaged themselves in the second form.

The two most dominant patterns of male homosexual behavior in early modern Europe are the age-based and equal-status homosexualities, although the latter only began to emerge in the later part of the seventeenth century in northwestern Europe—England, northern France, and the Dutch Republic—and may have been present in urbanized western parts of Germany. Age-based homosexuality was the most dominant pattern in southern Europe throughout the early modern period, in particular in Italy; adult men strictly upholding active and passive roles sought sex with pubescent and sometimes prepubescent boys. Those boys, on reaching adulthood, switched from passive to active roles, started to have sex with women (mostly prostitutes), and ideally left all of that behind them when they were married in their late twenties or early thirties. Florence had gained such a reputation in Europe that "to Florence" had become a verb in German and Dutch, referring to same-sex activities. By the late Middle Ages, Italy had already earned a reputation for its apparent widespread homosexual activities: during most of the early modern period in western Europe, the word "Italian" was synonymous with "sodomite." Although documentation on homosexuality in eastern European countries is still scant, reports suggest that in a city like Moscow in the seventeenth century, patterns of behavior existed that were not unlike those in Tuscan cities. Once St. Petersburg started its ascendancy as capital and as window to the West, more "modern" patterns of homosexual behavior may have emerged here.

Prior to the emergence of equal-status homosexuality in northwestern Europe, far more hierarchical forms were dominant there, usually taking the forms of class- and age-based same-sex behavior, or some combination thereof. Homosexual behavior could manifest itself between masters and apprentices, or officers and privates. Such hierarchical and age-based forms involving young cabin boys show up persistently in documents of ship councils far into the eighteenth century.

The rise of the equal-status homosexuality in the late seventeenth century marked the beginning of a period of transition into modernity, which would eventually result in modern homosexualities and identity formations. This rise went hand in hand with the emergence of same-sex subcultures. Meeting sites for sodomites have been reported since the late Middle Ages in cities like Cologne, but they meant little compared to the numerous places—pubs, brothels, parks, gardens, and urban sites like city halls, commodity exchanges, and theaters—that show up in court documents from the late seventeenth and eighteenth centuries in cities like Paris, London, and Amsterdam, and some smaller cities.

In Amsterdam, sodomites who had met someone could go to any number of public toilets underneath bridges. Some of those toilets had a reputation as places where sodomites could pick up partners, too. European societies with a dominant age-based homosexuality have also documented some sites at which men used to meet, yet those were typical places where men used to socialize and bond. The meeting sites frequented by sodomites in Holland and elsewhere from the late seventeenth century onwards were often the places where female prostitutes picked up their customers.

The rise of the sodomitical subcultures was accompanied by the development of a distinct homosexual role. Sodomites developed an often effete body language and deportment, and used gestures and an argot that sometimes resembled that of prostitutes. At one of the most notorious meeting sites for sodomites in Amsterdam, men used to walk to and fro with their arms akimbo and hit another man with their elbow if they were interested in him. Prostitutes of the time may have used similar tactics. In London's so-called molly houses sodomites staged plays and rituals in which they mocked marriage ceremonies and childbirth. While in the age-based same-sex pattern men could be infatuated with particular boys, in this equal-status homosexuality some men engaged in jealously guarded love affairs. By the end of the early modern period, to have a lover had become a definite goal for many members of these subcultures.

While in previously dominant patterns male desires were generally not directed exclusively towards other males, but were epitomized by the literary and also printed image of a man holding a boy on one arm and a woman on the other, in the eighteenth century the "new" effete sodomitical role became more solely geared toward males. Upon being arrested, some of these men in northwestern Europe would acknowledge that they never had had any desire for women. For some that would also mean acknowledging a preference for a passive role in sex.

Patterns of female same-sex behavior are far more difficult to discern. As with some male homosexualities, some forms of lesbian behavior must be looked at from a wider perspective. One of these is the tradition of amply documented female transvestism. Throughout the early modern period, women cross-dressed to masquerade as soldiers, sailors, pirates, or sometimes just to travel safely. Whether some of these women originally dressed up for sexual reasons is unknown, yet there is also documentation of women who in their male attire courted and even married other women. Some had sex while using artificial penises they had made. Women who cross-dressed had to adopt a male role in such a way that even people in close quarters like ship bunks did not become suspicious.

Women did not have subcultures like those men had in northwestern Europe, that is, clandestine spots and physical cues that exclusively served male-to-male desires. There is some evidence, especially from the Netherlands, that lower-class women did have subcultures, in which (although not exclusively) female-to-female desires could be fulfilled. These women, often widowed, abandoned, or left behind by sailor husbands, formed mutual support networks in which (sometimes through prostitution) they could pursue sex with men but also with one another. These women may have lived together in inconspicuous manners. Upper-class women and, for instance, actresses, although not cross-dressing, sometimes dressed in sufficiently ambiguous ways, mixing male and female attire, to raise suspicions if not of same-sex behavior, at least of having loose ways.

PERCEPTIONS

Separating theological from penal views is difficult, since the latter were mostly based upon theological perspectives on sexuality. Thomas Aquinas's thirteenth-century distinction between natural and unnatural sexual offenses (even though Thomism temporarily lost its influence) bore upon the early modern consciousness. In his morphology of sex crimes, rape and adultery were at least natural because they did not stand in the way of procreation and therefore were not as heinous as sodomy. While later Protestant writers would not refer to Aquinas, they by and large adhered to the same morphology. For Aquinas as much as for these writers, the only thing worse than sex between men or between women was sex with an animal.

The acknowledgment by Protestants and Catholics after the Counter-Reformation that sexual pleasure was a means for strong bonding between spouses, and was therefore primarily an environment to create offspring, probably engendered even more virulent rejections of same-sex behavior. After all, by bringing pleasure into the equation, a dangerous border was crossed that required constant vigilance. Since the Middle Ages and perhaps before, same-sex behavior had already been seen as the ultimate form of hedonism.

Such hedonism began with indulgence in other, corporeal pleasures, the *luxuria*. Indulgence in fine or copious food and drink, in dancing and smoking, in fine clothes, and also abuse of leisure through card playing or gambling was thought to provoke desires and lust for more pleasure and worse acts, such as womanizing, adultery, whoring, and, ultimately, homosexual acts. Unnatural behavior could thus originate in natural needs for food, drink, dress, and rest, and then only deteriorate from there. This was supposedly what had happened in Sodom and Gomorrah, which had been located on a fertile plain. The riches of these cities led to indulgence in all kinds of debauchery and, eventually, to God's wrath.

Women were considered to have less perfect bodies than men and were supposed to be, by nature, insatiable; thus submitting to the hierarchy of the sexes was seen as the only way for women to control their cravings. However, men could also lose control and become as insatiable as women were supposed to be, resulting in effeminate behavior and indulgence in all kinds of sexual vices. Hence, effeminacy in the eighteenth century was still seen as the hallmark of a womanizer. Womanizing was, after all, seen as only one step away from sodomy with men. This potential for sodomy was seen as destructive not just on the individual level, but on a national level as well. People feared eventual destruction by fire and sulfur, just as God had once destroyed Sodom and Gomorrah. Hedonism, abuse, and loss of control represented chaos, and chaos could eventually become the undoing of society and creation, as the very purpose of creation had been to bring order into chaos.

To the extent that this way of thinking was a psychological theory about the causes of same-sex behavior, it attributed little if any agency to the mind, and it was profoundly distrustful of the temptations the body put in the way of even the righteous. In its prediction of individual and collective behaviors, of the rise and fall of nations, this theory was also social and political. It explained the demise of southern European countries as well as the ascendancy of the Dutch Republic in the seventeenth century. Sodomy supposedly did not exist there until the sobriety that had characterized its inhabitants gave way to indulgence in the wealth that God had once bestowed upon them as a reward for their sober ways.

In the course of the eighteenth century, although remaining largely implicit, more individualized theories took hold; some commentators began to speak of inner proclivities rather than of bodies that had run amok. In a sense, the historical paths of male and female homosexualities also met around the 1750s. Lesbian activities at the time were attributed to "whores," that is, women who were not necessarily prostitutes but who had loose morals. Whereas previously effeteness among males had been the characteristic of womanizers, after the mid-eighteenth century it became more and more the hallmark of sodomites. The effete sodomite was like a he-whore, an English author wrote at the time, and that was also the way sodomites were perceived in the Dutch Republic. Consequently, fears of the spread of same-sex practices diminished somewhat in the course of the eighteenth century, although among some groups they persist to this very day. Nevertheless, authorities—and as indicated before, penal reformers—in many parts of Europe felt the need to "contain" the vice, no longer because they feared God's immediate wrath, but because they feared that the male sex was undermined, and with it nations' capacity to pursue political, economic, and military power.

SELF-PERCEPTIONS

By the late eighteenth century, sodomites in northwestern Europe had not only developed a distinctive societal role, but also perceived themselves as a separate category from men and women. They also talked about these issues among one another. Early in the eighteenth century they would refer to other sodomites as men who liked to do this kind of thing as well. Some seventy years later sodomites talked about "being a member of the family," "people like us," and "you and me and thousands like us." It especially allowed devout men to look upon themselves as morally responsible human beings. From the 1750s onward sodomites arrested in the Dutch Republic would refer to the biblical story of David and Jonathan, and increasingly they would claim to have been born with their inclinations intact. More than half a century before Karl Heinrich Ulrichs in Germany in the 1860s formulated the theory of the existence of a third sex—men born with a female soul—sodomites in the Netherlands spoke among one another of their "condition" or "way of being" as an inborn weakness. There is no documentation about women who clearly spoke in such a way of themselves. For men, one might say this newfound homosexual identity culminated in the contents of a love letter from one Dutch male servant to his male lover early in the nineteenth century. He used still-current terms for boyfriend, talked about "being of the family," and he called upon innate weaknesses to explain their desires, while also legitimizing those desires by telling his lover that God had not created any human being for its own damnation.

See also **Crime and Punishment; Gender; Sexual Difference, Theories of; Sexuality and Sexual Behavior.**

BIBLIOGRAPHY

Bray, Alan. *Homosexuality in Renaissance England.* London, 1982.

Everard, Myriam. *Ziel en zinnen. Over liefde en lust tussen vrouwen in de tweede helft van de achttiende eeuw.* Groningen, 1994.

Faderman, Lilian. *Surpassing the Love of Men: Romantic Friendship and Love Between Women from the Renaissance to the Present.* New York, 1983.

Greenberg, David. *The Construction of Homosexuality.* Chicago and London, 1988.

Halperin, David. *How to Do the History of Homosexuality.* Chicago and London, 2002.

Healey, Dan. *Homosexual Desire in Revolutionary Russia: The Regulation of Sexual and Gender Dissent.* Chicago and London, 2001.

Liliequist, Jonas. "Peasants against Nature: Crossing the Boundaries between Man and Animal in Seventeenth- and Eighteenth-Century Sweden." In *Forbidden History: The State, Society and the Regulation of Sexuality in Modern Europe,* edited by John Fout, pp. 57–87. Chicago and London, 1992.

Merrick, Jeffrey W., and Michael Sibalis, eds. *Homosexuality in French History and Culture.* New York and London, 2001.

Monter, William. "Sodomy and Heresy in Early Modern Switzerland." In *Historical Perspectives on Homosexuality,* edited by Salvatore J. Licata and Robert P. Petersen, pp. 41–55. New York, 1981.

Mott, Luiz. "Loves Labors Lost: Five Letters from a Seventeenth-Century Portuguese Sodomite." In *The Pursuit of Sodomy: Male Homosexuality in Renaissance and Enlightenment Europe,* edited by Kent Gerard and Gert Hekma, pp. 91–101. New York and London, 1989.

Rey, Michel. "Parisian Homosexuals Create a Lifestyle, 1700–1750: The Police Archives," *Eighteenth Century Life* 9, no. 3. *Unauthorized Sexual Behavior During the Enlightenment.* Edited by Robert P. Maccubbin. (1985): 179–191.

Rocke, Michael. *Forbidden Friendships: Homosexuality and Male Culture in Renaissance Florence.* New York and Oxford, 1996.

Trumbach, Randolph. *Sex and the Gender Revolution.* Vol. 1, *Heterosexuality and the Third Gender in Enlightenment London.* Chicago and London, 1998.

Van der Meer, Theo. "Sodomy and the Pursuit of a Third Sex in the Early Modern Period." In *Third Sex/Third Gender: Beyond Sexual Dimorphism in Culture and History,* edited by Gilbert Herdt, pp. 137–212. New York, 1994.

Von Rosen, Wilhelm. "Sodomy in early modern Denmark: a crime without victims." In *The Pursuit of Sodomy: Male Homosexuality in Renaissance and Enlightenment Europe,* edited by Kent Gerard and Gert Hekma, pp. 177–204. New York and London, 1989.

THEO VAN DER MEER

HONOR. Honor was an ethical system whose prescriptions varied according to one's place in the social hierarchy. Rank, gender, age, and a host of other personal qualities determined what types of behavior were honorable, and what degree of respect and deference one could expect from others. Tension existed, however, between how honor was defined in the abstract and how people used honor. Jurists and moralists in early modern Europe conceived of honor as part of a rigid structure of values and conduct, an almost tangible possession that one could gain or lose. In practice honor was more fluid and served as a rhetoric flexible enough for individuals to adapt to their own purposes. For example, the laws of the state and the morals of the church labeled prostitutes in sixteenth-century Rome as dishonorable, but court records show that prostitutes used the language of honor to make claims for respect from their clients, patrons, and neighbors.

THE ROLES OF HONOR

Despite its equivocal meanings, honor was a crucial aspect of culture and conduct at every level of society. Notions of honor varied by region, gender, status, and time, but these differences were all variations on a theme that maintained remarkable similarity as it stretched across Europe, reached back into the Middle Ages, and persisted in some form into the nineteenth century. Everywhere honor depended on one's reputation for proper behavior, as judged by one's peers and neighbors, so personal honor was always vulnerable to gossip and slander that could redefine one's estimation in the eyes of others. While honor was meant to be a moral code, in reality its concerns had as much to do with preventing, masking, or redressing humiliation than with encouraging virtue.

Individual communities used honor to define membership and to enforce the responsibilities of members. For example, if a young woman defied custom and married an old man, disappointed young men might defend the honor of their village by staging raucous and even violent protests, called *charivaris* in France and "rough music" in England. Artisan guilds acted against guild members who threatened their corporate honor through dishonest business practices. In Venice, groups of young men engaged in bouts of ritual combat over the city's bridges to assert the honor of one neighborhood against another. Honor also demarcated castes in society, as in Germany where executioners were considered dishonorable and were not allowed to intermarry with other, honorable groups.

One aspect of honor that remained constant throughout early modern Europe was its strong connection to patriarchy, sex, and gender. Honor codes universally prescribed appropriate sexual behavior for both women and men. Women needed to be chaste in order to be honorable, and "whore" was usually the most damning affront one could level against a woman. Men were held responsible for the sexual conduct of women under their protection, including their wives, daughters, and sisters. This left male honor dangerously vulnerable to the actions of women. If a man failed to control "his" women, he invited neighbors to brand him a cuckold. Because male honor and female chastity were so thoroughly intertwined, men might take violent revenge against anyone who threatened, in word or deed, the sexual honor of "their" women—if they did not direct their violence against the women themselves. While honor's sexual component is associated most closely with the underdeveloped Mediterranean basin, historians have found similar patterns in vanguards of modernity like Holland and in regions as far removed from the Mediterranean as Muscovy. Even for women, however, sexuality was never the sole determinant of personal honor. In England, for example, a woman's honor rested partly on her skills as a housewife and mother.

Honor also embraced social hierarchy. Nobles enjoyed a more honorable standing than commoners, and they reinforced their claims to honor through the ceremony of the duel. Dueling arose first in Italy as part of the Renaissance's developments in courtesy and manners, and then spread throughout Europe. Dueling became the accepted means of redressing an affront, thereby distancing noblemen from brawling commoners. Dueling manuals did not recognize the right of plebeian men to duel, but nevertheless popular duels did exist. Sailors in Amsterdam and peasants in Castile invested their knife fights with rituals similar to elite dueling practices, and their contests even arose from similar causes, such as precedence, lying, and women, even if non-nobles sometimes preferred terms like "honesty" and "reputation" instead of "honor" when describing their claims to respect and good treatment. Throughout the early modern period, as elite customs and manners continued to draw away from the behavior of the nonelite, the honor of the nobility became increasingly distant from that of their inferiors. Vendettas, brawls, and *charivaris* gave way to politeness and civility as components of honor for gentlemen, especially in the eighteenth century. Even aristocratic duels became less violent. As the elite became less tolerant of violence, the duelist's aim became the demonstration of his courage rather than the destruction of his opponent.

Throughout the early modern period, honor had its critics. No matter how courteous the etiquette of dueling became, in the eyes of the civil and religious authorities assault and murder remained crimes and sins. Moralists declared that true honor resided in Christian virtue and in the conscience, not in the estimation of one's peers. Just as often, however, honor fit hand in glove with other values and historical trends. By attacking debauched clerics who preyed on good Christian women, and by expelling prostitutes from Christian communities, Protestant reformers appealed to honor to win popularity in sixteenth-century German cities. Honor helped foster the scientific revolution by allowing gentlemen to trust the word of peers who conducted experiments hundreds of miles away. Honor helped shape diplomacy and warfare, for example preventing seventeenth-century Spanish statesmen from reining in Madrid's imperial overreach because they could not bear to abandon obligations they had made to defend Catholicism and preserve the Habsburg inheritance. Honor even played a role in the revolution that brought the early modern period to a close, as illicit pornographic writings circulated in Old Regime France that undermined respect for Louis XVI, depicting him as an impotent cuckold. Honor did not pass away during the French Revolution, however. Well into the nineteenth century statesmen, capitalists, and journalists adapted honor to suit their new social circumstances.

See also **Class, Status, and Order; Duel; Gentleman; Sexuality and Sexual Behavior.**

BIBLIOGRAPHY

Cohen, Elizabeth S. "Honor and Gender in the Streets of Early Modern Rome." *Journal of Interdisciplinary History* 22 (1992): 597–625.

Farr, James R. *Hands of Honor: Artisans and Their World in Dijon, 1550–1650.* Ithaca, N.Y., and London, 1988.

Kollmann, Nancy Shields. *By Honor Bound: State and Society in Early Modern Russia.* Ithaca, N.Y., and London, 1999.

Muir, Edward. *Mad Blood Stirring: Vendetta & Factions in Friuli during the Renaissance.* Baltimore and London, 1993.

Shoemaker, Robert B. "The Taming of the Duel: Masculinity, Honour and Ritual Violence in London, 1660–1800." *The Historical Journal* 45, no. 3 (2002): 525–545.

SCOTT TAYLOR

HOOKE, ROBERT (1635–1703), English natural philosopher, microscopist, experimenter, surveyor and architect, and pioneer palaeontologist. A sickly child who grew into a crookbacked, pale, lean, and anxious hypochondriac, Hooke was a gifted mechanic who became, arguably, the leading natural philosopher in England before Isaac Newton, perhaps rivaled only by his patron, Robert Boyle. Hooke attended Westminster School before entering Christ Church, Oxford, as a chorister in 1653. He soon became part of the circle of experimental natural philosophers brought together by John Wilkins, warden of Wadham College. Here he met, and in 1658 became assistant to, Robert Boyle, and embarked upon his career as an experimental philosopher. The work they did together, using an air pump designed and built by Hooke, proved important and highly influential. In 1662 Boyle allowed Hooke to take up the post of curator of experiments for the newly founded Royal Society of London. Hooke's brief was not only to try experiments suggested by the fellows, but also to bring three or four "considerable Experiments" to each meeting. Few could have managed this at all, but Hooke made an astonishing success of it, and was quite literally the mainstay of the society for well over a decade. In 1666 Hooke was appointed by the city as one of the surveyors on the rebuilding committee established after the Great Fire of London. His friend Sir Christopher Wren was appointed by the king. Like Wren, Hooke did not confine his activities to surveying but also proved to be a highly gifted architect, although never achieving the recognition accorded to Wren. In the early 1670s Hooke became embroiled first with Newton and then with the leading Dutch mathematician, Christiaan Huygens, and the secretary of the Royal Society, Henry Oldenburg, in bitter priority disputes. Even though the fellows tended to support Oldenburg, after his death in 1677 they appointed Hooke to succeed him. However, this seems to have marked the point of Hooke's intellectual decline. He was ejected from the post after five years and received scant consideration in 1686 when he tried (with some justification) to claim priority for the planetary dynamics expounded in Newton's soon-to-be-published *Principia Mathematica* (1687). In 1687 his niece and mistress, Grace, died and left Hooke emotionally devastated and reclusive. He produced no more significant work and died embittered and alone even though he left over £9,000 in cash (money that he must have accrued as surveyor for the City of London).

Hooke's scientific achievements were considerable. He developed, but never fully expounded, a unique system of mechanical philosophy that depended upon supposed incessant vibrations of matter. Ingeniously explaining solidity, for example, in terms of particles vibrating so rapidly that they could beat off any intruding body; and chemical reactions in terms of vibrations of two substances in harmony (in cases of combination) or in discord (in cases of disaggregation), Hooke's main problem was to explain such putative vibrations. Although he never succeeded in this, he was led to many suggestive experiments on the nature of vibrations and what he called "simple harmonic motions." His theory and practice was closely linked not only to the first statement of what is now known as Hooke's Law (stress is proportional to strain), and his awareness of the dynamic equivalence of vibrating springs and pendulums, but also to his insight in 1658 that a clock might be driven by a spring instead of a pendulum—an idea that was first made to work in practice by Huygens in 1674 but that Hooke believed should have been acknowledged as his invention. The influence of his vibratory physics can even be seen in Hooke's recognition that light was a periodic phenomenon, as demonstrated in his analysis of colors produced in soap bubbles and other thin films. Hooke was inspired by his optical theories to develop the idea that planetary motions could be explained in terms of a single attractive force from the sun bending the straight-line motion of a planet into an elliptical orbit. Furthermore, he guessed that this force would vary in inverse proportion to the square of the distance between the sun and the planet. He published this speculation in 1666 and drew it to Newton's attention in correspondence in 1679. Hooke couldn't prove it mathematically, but when Newton subsequently proved it, at the request of Edmund Halley in 1684, he did not correct Halley's assumption that Newton had hit on the idea himself. This proof, of course, was to be the centerpiece of Newton's *Principia Mathematica,* which Halley now persuaded him to write. Small wonder that Hooke was outraged when he heard that his original idea was not acknowledged in the *Principia.*

Hooke was undoubtedly an insightful and ingenious theorist of great influence even though he never quite succeeded in establishing the truth of any of his theoretical ideas. His industry and ingenuity has, nevertheless, ensured his position in the history of science. He invented the universal joint, the iris diaphragm, a calibrated screw adjustment for telescopes, and the wheel barometer. He was also one of the first to take seriously the idea that fossils represented the genuine remains of ancient creatures (previously it was assumed they were simply features in the rocks which accidentally mimicked living forms), and was led by his knowledge of them to conclude that the surfaces of the earth could change, land giving way to sea and vice versa, and that the number and kinds of species of plants and animals were not fixed. Perhaps his most lasting monument, however, is his one major book, *Micrographia* (1665), the first major work of microscopy. Although justly famous for its meticulous and genuinely surprising descriptions of microscopic phenomena, and for its superb illustrations, *Micrographia* also includes some of Hooke's most fruitful theoretical speculations and his most profound comments upon good practice in natural philosophy.

See also **Academies, Learned; Boyle, Robert; Chemistry; Huygens Family; Newton, Isaac; Physics; Scientific Illustration; Scientific Instruments; Scientific Method; Wren, Christopher.**

BIBLIOGRAPHY

Bennett, Jim, M. Cooper, M. Hunter, and L. Jardine. *London's Leonardo: The Life and Work of Robert Hooke.* Oxford, 2003.

'Espinasse, Margaret. *Robert Hooke.* Berkeley, 1956.

Gal, Ofer. *Meanest Foundations and Nobler Superstructures: Hooke, Newton and the "Compounding of the Celestial Motions of the Planetts."* Dordrecht, 2002.

Hunter, Michael, and Simon Schaffer, eds. *Robert Hooke: New Studies.* Wolfeboro, N.H., 1989.

John Henry

HOOKER, RICHARD (1553 or 1554–1600), English theologian and legal scholar. Richard Hooker's major work, *Of the Laws of Ecclesiasti-*

cal Polity (1593–1662), quickly became the authoritative text legitimating the Elizabethan Settlement and defending it from Catholic and Puritan attacks. Hooker, born about 1554 near Exeter, entered Corpus Christi College, Oxford, in 1569 (B.A. 1574; M.A. 1577) under the sponsorship of Bishop John Jewel (1522–1571). Hooker remained at Oxford until 1584, becoming a fellow, teaching logic and Hebrew, and becoming an Anglican priest. With the help of his patron, Archbishop Edwin Sandys (1516?–1588), Hooker in 1585 was appointed master of the Temple in London, a position akin to dean and chief pastor. The Temple was one of the premier English centers of legal study and training. As master Hooker began his public defense of Anglicanism against Puritanism, delivering his sermons to the Temple congregation in the morning only to be rebutted by the afternoon lectures of his colleague Walter Travers (c. 1548–1635), a prominent Puritan scholar.

In London, Hooker lived with his good friend John Churchman. In 1588 Hooker married Joan Churchman, John's daughter. They had six children. Hooker resigned as master in 1591, perhaps at the instigation of Archbishop John Whitgift (c. 1530–1604), to devote himself to the composition of his *Laws.* He delegated his new clerical duties as subdean of Salisbury and rector of Boscombe and remained in London at Churchman's home. In 1595 the crown rewarded Hooker's 1593 publication of Books 1–4 of the *Laws* with residency in Bishopsbourne, Kent. There he continued to work on the *Laws* until his death in 1600. He published Book 5 of the *Laws* in 1597, but Books 6–8 were still in draft form when he died. Portions of these drafts circulated in manuscript before they were eventually published in 1648 (Books 6 and 8) and 1662 (Book 7).

The English Puritanism opposed by Hooker in the *Laws* asserted that there is only one true law, God's law; that Scripture clearly and adequately states this law; and that this law has exclusive authority in all things. Hooker, drawing upon Thomas Aquinas (1225–1274) and Aristotle (384–322 B.C.E.), responded that Scripture clearly is neither intended nor sufficient to address matters of ecclesiastical or civil government; where Scripture was found wanting, recourse must be made to tradition and human reason. And in England, Scripture, tradition, and human reason supported the 1559 Elizabethan Settlement, which established Anglicanism as the state religion and adopted for it the Book of Common Prayer.

The general, Books 1–4 of the *Laws* lay the groundwork for the more specific Books 5–8. Book 1, the most widely read, deals with the fundamental characters of and the relations among divine, natural, and human laws. Book 2 contains proofs that Scripture does not contain laws governing all things. Along these same lines, Book 3 denies that Scripture designates an absolute form of polity. Book 4 defends the overlaps between Anglican and Catholic practice and ceremony attacked by the Puritans.

Book 5, the central and largest, seeks to conserve the Christian Commonwealth established by the settlement by defending the Book of Common Prayer—especially its role in shaping the moral character of the people. Book 6 rejects the Puritan claim that lay elders must govern the church, while Book 7 defends the continued church governance by bishops (episcopacy). Book 8, which has attracted the most critical scholarly attention, deals with the royal supremacy in religious matters and the impossibility of rigidly separating church and state.

Hooker's continued fame derives largely from Izaak Walton's biography and the anthologization of portions of Book 1 as the premier example of Elizabethan prose style. However, beginning in the early twentieth century critics assailed Hooker's three-hundred-year reputation as "judicious" and unbiased. While these attacks were justified to the extent that Hooker, with immense success, created the impression that his positions were uncontroversial, they failed to credit him for raising the standards for Renaissance controversialist tracts with his restrained style, reasoned argument, and consistent resort to first principles. Subsequent critical attention has focused on the three long-neglected yet profound limitations Hooker attached to the royal supremacy in religious matters: God's power is superior to the monarch's; the monarch's power is subject to human law, if derived from it; and the monarch is inferior to his or her realm united in opposition. Contemporary debate also surrounds whether or not the appeal by John Locke

(1632–1704) to Hooker as the inspiration for his doctrine of the state of nature was disingenuous. Opinions are mixed as to whether to characterize Hooker's thought as essentially medieval and conservative or as more modern—as containing innovative and radical elements.

See also **Church of England; Elizabeth I (England).**

BIBLIOGRAPHY

Primary Sources

Hooker, Richard. *The Folger Library Edition of the Works of Richard Hooker.* Edited by W. Speed Hill. Cambridge, Mass., 1977–1990. The definitive edition of Hooker's words; includes a volume containing his early sermons.

———. *Of the Laws of Ecclesiastical Polity: Preface, Book I, Book VIII.* Edited by Arthur Stephen McGrade. Cambridge Texts of Political Thought. Cambridge, U.K., 1989. One of a widely available, popular series. This volume contains the most commonly read passages from the *Laws* and has an excellent introduction.

Secondary Sources

Archer, Stanley. *Richard Hooker.* Twayne's English Authors series. Boston, 1983.

Faulkner, Robert K. *Richard Hooker and the Politics of a Christian England.* Berkeley, 1981.

Hill, W. Speed, ed. *Studies in Richard Hooker: Essays Preliminary to an Edition of His Works.* Cleveland, Ohio, and London, 1972.

Kirby, W. J. Torrance. *Richard Hooker's Doctrine of Royal Supremacy.* Leiden and New York, 1990.

McGrade, Arthur Stephen, ed. *Richard Hooker and the Construction of Christian Community.* Medieval and Renaissance Texts and Studies, vol. 165. Tempe, Ariz., 1997.

ANDREW MAJESKE

HOSPITALS. From their inception in Byzantium, hospitals evolved within a Christian religious framework of hospitality and charity, providing primarily shelter, food, and a good death with spiritual salvation. Often, medical services were marginal, contracted to deal with associated physical disabilities and pain. With poverty endemic by the late fifteenth century in many areas of Europe, the emphasis shifted away from broadly dispensed hospitality to the "poor of Jesus Christ." Charity was no longer conceived as either private or religious. With almsgiving dwindling because of wars and economic crises, social welfare needed to be reformed and rationed, a function increasingly delegated by the church to the contemporary secular powers. Thus, after 1500, new welfare policies cut across religious boundaries and followed patterns closely tailored to local urban conditions. Charitable assistance was channeled through existing social structures such as parishes, confraternities, and municipalities to benefit schools and several types of hospitals.

Institutions such as almshouses and retirement homes retained their traditional custodial functions while leper and pesthouses functioned primarily as segregation tools for persons suffering from particular diseases considered contagious. At the same time, the hospital's role was recast on the basis of ideas derived from Renaissance humanism as one aiding physical recovery and restoration. This change affected certain urban hospitals of northern Italy, reflecting a more positive vision of health and its importance in Europe's new economy. Acutely ill patients were admitted and subjected to medical treatments for the purpose of rehabilitation and possible complete cures in larger establishments such as the 250-bed Santa Maria Nuova Hospital in Florence. Patient populations were composed of young, unattached laborers whose economic well-being was closely linked to physical health. The regular presence of practitioners in the wards signaled a decisive shift toward a greater institutional role for medicine and surgery. Physicians visited regularly, experimented on patients with traditional and new remedies, and preserved their newly gained clinical experience in casebooks. They also created disease classifications, occasionally instructed medical students, and subjected deceased and unclaimed inmates to anatomical dissections. In 1539, for example, Giovanni B. da Monte (1498–1561), professor of medicine at the University of Padua, began taking his apprentices to the local Ospedale di San Francesco for the purpose of seeing patients afflicted with diseases he was lecturing on.

By the late 1400s, several cities in southwest Germany established special hospitals—the so-called "pox houses"—for the care of men and women afflicted by a seemingly new disease variously referred to by Germans and Italians as "morbus gallicus" or French disease. Fear of an impending epidemic, together with the dramatic symptoms and lethal outcome of what was presumably an acute and highly lethal form of venereal syphilis, mobilized municipal authorities, private philanthropists, and specialized physicians. They opened a number of facilities exclusively devoted to a series of medical treatments, including the 122-bed "pox house" in Augsburg founded in 1495. Like their Italian counterparts, these institutions were located within urban walls and featured permanent medical staffs represented by physicians, barber-surgeons, and apothecaries.

The Protestant Reformation created a new relationship to both God and the community. Individuals were given the right to charitable assistance together with obligations to contribute and assist others through local and national systems of relief financed by subscriptions or taxes. Divine Providence, not the quest for indulgences, was to be the path toward salvation, leading to the collapse of hospital patronage as an instrument of salvation. In Protestant countries, institutionalized health care became restricted to smaller infirmaries and dispensaries supported by local governments or community organizations. In Catholic Europe, the Council of Trent (1545–1563) made specific efforts to eliminate widespread administrative fraud perpetrated by religious personnel, including hospital administrators. Thus the church reorganized religious hospitals and closed small, poorly endowed institutions, accelerating an ongoing, two-century-old consolidation process. In their place rose privately endowed, large general hospitals or shelters, often run by local confraternities. These establishments were designed to house together diverse groups of needy people, including orphans, chronic sufferers, mentally ill individuals, and the elderly. The sick poor found medical care in "God's hostels" (*Hôtels Dieu*) and other institutions.

Placed under civic authority, most European hospitals became involved in novel schemes of social control and medical assistance. A work ethic adopted by both Protestants and the Catholic Counter-Reformation viewed daily labor as a spiritually fulfilling communal obligation. In selecting its welfare recipients, modern European society thus sought to identify those it considered deserving of assistance—including medical care—through a series of means tests. Most of the deserving poor were modest and law-abiding working people, stable residents seemingly content with their status in society as bestowed by Divine Providence. By contrast, homeless paupers and strangers, as well as drifters, vagrants, and beggars were characterized as undeserving of social welfare, identified with social unrest and crime. In the eyes of the Catholic Church, however, the distinction between worthy and unworthy poor remained blurred. All were considered sinners who needed to be saved. Indeed, spiritual salvation remained the ultimate objective of Catholic hospitalization, and religious ceremonies continued to be central to hospital life, leading to tensions with medical caregivers.

To fulfill their social contract and be productive, early modern European workers needed to remain physically healthy, or, if sick, be assisted in their recovery. Living in crowded and unhygienic conditions, urban populations increasingly fell prey to an expanding panorama of diseases affecting especially the young and the aged. Although Protestant values conferred an active role on individuals pursuing their own healing, help and assistance was to be always available. Outpatient relief in the form of home care and provision of medicines by visiting nurses were furnished to support the "deserving" poor's legitimate status in society. Local efforts designed to stem such assaults on health were encouraged and greatly valued. Belief in Divine Providence encouraged medical activities considered divinely approved instruments to assist in recovery. In turn, hospitals were now considered places of early rather than last resort.

During the seventeenth century, the medicalization of hospitals accelerated, as Europe witnessed the emergence of modern national states. Within the new mercantilist context a growing and physically able population was believed to be essential for achieving political, military, and economic goals. With labor viewed as the key source of power and wealth, efforts to enhance the productivity of a country's citizenry inevitably included the workers' health. Prevention and rehabilitation became national goals. The result was an impressive network of general, military and naval hospitals as well as institutions for housing individuals classified as invalids. Reformers such as William Petty (1623–1687) stressed the importance of medicine and the participation of physicians and surgeons in such care.

Writing in the eighteenth century, Enlightenment thinkers crafted an optimistic view concerning the preservation and rehabilitation of human health. Despite popular perceptions about the fateful inevitability of sickness and disability, French philosophes and others insisted that disease could be controlled, removed, and even prevented by the prompt and deliberate application of traditional dietary, medicinal, and behavioral means. In Protestant countries, belief in Divine Providence supported medical assistance, while Catholic Europe continued to stress spiritual salvation over bodily rehabilitation. Merging traditional religious and secular philanthropic motives, however, state and municipal governments, voluntary associations, and corporate bodies all joined forces to implement a program of public assistance designed to mend bodies while still saving souls. In Britain, local "alliances against misery" comprising private individuals, including businessmen, bankers, lawyers, physicians, and surgeons, came together to establish new voluntary hospitals. Governmental and private organizations aimed at better infant and maternal health, creating lying-in and children's institutions.

By the 1770s, the British voluntary hospital movement was already in full swing, while Continental establishments expanded their services. Hospitals became ideal settings for a greater medical presence, providing physicians with access to vast sectors of the population hitherto left outside the scope of mainstream medicine. Early leaders of this hospital development were John Aikin (1747–1822) who considered the hospitalized sick poor as ideally suited for "experimental practice," John Howard (1726–1790), a widely traveled prison and hospital reformer, and Jacques Tenon (1724–1816), who viewed hospitals as symbols of Enlightenment civilization. Others provided the necessary impetus for bedside medical research and improved clinical skills. Indeed, hospitals were now seen as "nurseries" capable of "breeding" better medical professionals. Informal methods of clinical teaching, brought from Italy to Holland a century earlier, became part of academic instruction pioneered by the University of Leiden. There, at the St. Caecilia Gasthuis, Herman Boerhaave (1668–1738) held "practical exercises," making rounds, questioning, examining, and prescribing remedies for the carefully selected patients. The routine also included the questioning of students, performance of autopsies on those who had died, and efforts to correlate specific postmortem findings with previously detected symptoms. Later, other academic institutions in London, Edinburgh, and Pavia followed this model, although the potential inherent in hospitals to furnish new clinical and pathological knowledge capable of revolutionizing medicine was only fully realized after 1800 in Parisian institutions. In sum, the early modern period witnessed the decisive transformation of the hospital from a religious shelter to a space exclusively devoted to medical interventions.

See also **Apothecaries; Boerhaave, Herman; Catholic Spirituality and Mysticism; Catholicism; Charity and Poor Relief; Medicine; Poverty; Public Health; Reformation, Protestant.**

BIBLIOGRAPHY

Primary Sources

Aikin, John. *Thoughts on Hospitals.* London, 1771.

Blizard, William. *Suggestions for the Improvement of Hospitals and Other Charitable Institutions.* London, 1796.

Tenon, Jacques. *Memoirs on Paris Hospitals.* Translated and edited by D. Weiner. Canton, Mass., 1996. Originally published 1788.

Vives, Juan L. *Concerning the Relief of the Poor.* Translated by M. M. Sherwood. New York, 1917. Originally published 1526.

Secondary Sources

Brockliss, Lawrence, and Colin Jones. *The Medical World of Early Modern France.* Oxford, 1997.

Finzsch, Norbert, and Robert Jütte, eds. *Institutions of Confinement: Hospitals, Asylums, and Prisons in Western Europe and North America, 1500–1950.* Cambridge, U.K., and New York, 1996.

Foucault, Michel. *The Birth of the Clinic.* Translated by A. M. Sheridan Smith. London, 1973.

Granshaw, Lindsay, and Roy Porter, eds. *The Hospital in History.* London, 1989.

Grell, O. P., and Andrew Cunningham, eds. *Health Care and Poor Relief in Protestant Europe, 1500–1700.* London, 1997.

Risse, Guenter B. *Hospital Life in Enlightenment Scotland: Care and Teaching at the Royal Infirmary of Edinburgh.* New York, 1986.

———. *Mending Bodies—Saving Souls: A History of Hospitals.* New York, 1999.

GUENTER B. RISSE

HOUSEHOLD. *See* **Family.**

HOUSING. The ancient Greek word for household, *oikos,* is the root of the modern word "economy." In early modern Europe, housing was associated both with living and working, consuming and producing. This combined function shaped the outward form and internal organization of houses during the era. It also introduces complications to explicating the theme of housing, because the focus could be equally on the domicile itself or on the groups of people who inhabited it. Contemporary officials often used the term *hearth* to refer to households, though the term refers to the structure used to heat a room as well. A lack of sources makes it difficult to determine who actually lived together in the early modern era: in some cases, several households lived together under one roof, perhaps in separate rooms or all together. It is also difficult to determine how people used space inside the house: there are very few descriptions of house interiors and little way of knowing how representative those descriptions are.

There was no single "typical" house of the early modern era. For one thing, there was a strong tendency toward regional cultural patterns, both among and within linguistic and political units, which were expressed in housing styles. Few things more readily distinguish different regions than the prevailing style of houses, especially in the countryside. Regional differences resulted in part from local variations in building materials, but they clearly had deeper cultural roots as well. Housing types were also shaped by the fundamental difference between urban and rural living conditions. Though the overwhelming majority of Europeans lived in the countryside, the urban world was often more dynamic and exhibited a greater variety of living conditions. Town size magnified those differences. A few great cities, such as Paris or London, had a completely different housing mixture from the typical "large" city of about 20,000 inhabitants, not to mention the numerous small towns of the era. Variation in status and the work people performed also affected how and where they lived. The houses of nobles and patricians were quite different from those of peasants and artisans. Higher status homes certainly displayed a greater variety of styles than did lower status homes. Even more importantly, however, higher status homes comprise the greater body of evidence about what was in early modern homes and how they were used. Thus, while one may talk about some general trends in all housing during the era, the key features of housing must be viewed in wider social and geographical contexts.

BUILDING HOUSES

There were no significant technological changes affecting living conditions in early modern Europe. Building materials and practices did not change much. As a rule, the types of houses that people lived in at the end of the eighteenth century would have been familiar to those of the early sixteenth century, aside from external ornamentation. Indeed, many houses remained standing for the entire period, though wood-frame houses typically needed replacing every century or so. This continuity of building styles was particularly pronounced in the housing of peasants and artisans. However, elite housing did change in function and style over the period, so that a noble palace at the end of the early modern era would have appeared quite different from one at the beginning of the era.

There were three main building materials for houses: wood, stone, and brick. One may divide European housing into three zones according to which of those materials was predominant in buildings because of local availability of that material. There was, however, a status hierarchy of building materials, so that some towns would include a few stone or brick buildings in among a majority of wood-frame houses. In the great cities, homes of the elite were constructed of stone or brick, while homes in poorer districts were built of wood. Stone and brick also became more prevalent building materials over time. By the seventeenth century, Paris had (poorly enforced) regulations prohibiting wood construction. London also built more extensively in stone and brick after the devastating fire of 1666. The progress of stone building in large cities was varied. The French city of Cambrai had numerous stone houses by the middle of the seventeenth century. Nearby Rouen did not begin to build in stone until the end of the eighteenth century. The German city of Nuremberg built houses with stone first floors and half-timbered upper stories.

Wood was the favored building material in both the towns and countryside of the heavily forested parts of northern and central Europe. It was unusual for houses to be built entirely from logs. Instead, most structures were half-timbered: large hewn logs formed the frame for the house, while the spaces within the frame were filled with wattle and daub (a mixture of sticks with mud or plaster), with bricks, or stucco. Timber for housing construction was not, in fact, a highly developed industry in the era. Timber exports were more likely to be sent for shipbuilding than housing, so half-timbering eased demand for large logs. Indeed, in some port towns, the primary source of timber for house construction was old ships. Half-timbering created a distinctive colorful urban landscape, remnants of which exist today in some German, French, and English towns. By the late eighteenth century, however, half-timbered town houses were often considered excessively rustic. The facades of such houses were plastered over to create a more classical effect.

A major danger of the widespread use of wood in construction was fire. Fires leveled many towns, such as Stockholm, Sweden, in 1625. Fear of arsonists was a common concern of householders and town officials alike.

In most of southern Europe, and some parts of northern Europe, timber was much scarcer than stone, so stone and mortar were the preferred building materials for both towns and the countryside. The quality of stone used in construction could vary widely. Almost all structures were constructed from stone quarried locally. Small towns and villages took on a unified landscape from the color and texture of the locally quarried stone. For example, the all-red sandstone of the village of Collonges-la-Rouge in France distinguished it from the mostly golden or gray stone of neighboring towns. More elegant housing might rely on stone imported from a greater distance, but most quarries were small operations that depended on major public projects such as churches to drive most of their activity.

In the coastal regions of northern Europe and in the larger cities of southern Europe, brick was the preferred building material. Brick making was a significant industrial operation, the center of which was usually located in the countryside near a town. Unlike stone and wood, brick was used almost exclusively for urban housing. Farmhouses in regions where urban brick houses predominated were usually half-timbered or wattle and daub. Bricks were well designed for constructing geometrically proportioned, stable houses, which produced regimented streetscapes. In northern European cities in the Netherlands and coastal Holy Roman Empire, exposed brickwork helped define the city landscape in the same way that colored stone defined some southern European towns. In the southern European cities that used bricks instead of stones, the bricks were usually covered with stucco, so that it was not immediately apparent that brick rather than stone was the primary building material.

Roofing material was equally subject to the interplay of local availability and a slight status hierarchy of materials. In the countryside, both stone and half-timbered houses were usually roofed with thatch. More substantial houses in the countryside and most urban houses were covered with shingles, which might be made of wood, locally quarried slate, or kiln-dried tiles. Only the houses of the wealthiest people would be sheathed in lead or copper.

The building trades themselves also underwent little change during this era. Most rural houses and houses of artisans were built by guild craftsmen, masons, and carpenters, without the assistance of architects. Some towns enforced building regulations to ensure effective design. In sixteenth-century Nuremberg, for example, the town building department acquired many drawings of new structures and additions that were to be built, few of which were created by architects. By the end of the early modern era, architects began to play a more prominent role in constructing housing for urban professionals as well as noblemen.

PEASANT HOUSES

The majority of the European population lived in villages. Most villages exhibited a uniform housing type, because there were only small disparities of wealth and work among most peasants. Nevertheless, one can find some differentiation between the houses of the rural poor and those of the more substantial farmers. The most common dwelling for the rural poor was a one-room house, sometimes called a "long house," where the residents slept, ate, and worked in the same space. In its most basic form, it had an open hearth in the middle of the room and a hole in the ceiling to let the smoke out. The house was built on the ground, which served as the floor. Straw or grass was strewn on the floor to reduce dampness. Light could enter the house through windows, which lacked glass but could be closed by wooden shutters. More advanced houses had a brick or stone hearth with a chimney located on one side of the house instead of a centrally located firepot. Such houses had glass windows to let in light and keep out the cold. It also became increasingly common for even simple farmhouses to be built on excavated foundations and wood plank floors rather than simply resting on the ground.

For modern observers, and even for some contemporaries, one of the most striking features of the single-room house was that animals would be housed under the same roof as people. Writers who stayed at such rural farmsteads commented on being kept awake by the noises of the cows. However, animals did not have free rein of the house: there was usually a barrier between the human inhabited space and the stalls for the animals.

Sometimes, more than one family shared the one-room house. In any case, privacy was very rare. The poorest households possessed a very small repertoire of furniture. The most important item in a peasant household after the hearth was the bed. It consisted of a frame, a mattress, and usually a canopy whose curtains could be closed to attain some privacy. There was usually a long table for eating, with benches rather than chairs for seating. Many benches served double service as chests. Extra clothing, linens, and personal effects were kept in chests or armoires, which were rudimentary in the poorest households and more elaborate in wealthier ones. Though almost all parts of Europe had colorful folk-art traditions in furniture or pottery, the overall appearance of the interior of most peasant houses would have been dark and unadorned.

Many peasants lived in a slightly more elaborate version of the long house. Instead of consisting of a single room, the house was divided into two spaces: a foyer and rooms. Cooking, eating, and work all took place in the foyer. The rooms were separated from the foyer by walls, with doors that could be closed and locked for at least some privacy from the work environment. Such houses might also have a separate cellar and storeroom for grain and an upstairs room, which could be used as a bedroom. This room was usually accessible by a trapdoor and ladder rather than a stairwell. It was less common for animals to be housed under the same roof as humans in these larger houses; instead they had stalls in a barn.

The main work of rural households was, of course, agriculture. So the main house was usually built as part of a larger courtyard in which the everyday tools of farming were kept: wagons, plows, harnesses, a dung heap. More prosperous peasants might have several buildings built around the courtyard, such as grain storerooms, separate stalls for animals, sheds, possibly even a baking oven, though that was usually a communal building rather than part of an individual's property. The courtyard itself might be separated from the street by a large gate or doorway that could be closed. Some of these gateways provided an opportunity for self-expression. In Germany, it was fairly common for a married couple to inscribe their names, the date of construction, and a pious statement over the entryway of a new house.

There were also some specialized forms of housing in the rural world. There were three structures which, while not present in every village, were central to peasant life: the parsonage, the tavern, and the mill. The parsonage, or priest's house, was usually just a large version of the typical peasant house of the region. Throughout the early modern era, the pastor or priest participated in the broader agricultural economy as well as attending to his spiritual duties, so his house had to be arranged to perform both kinds of tasks. Rural inns, like their urban counterparts, had to provide lodging and meals to travelers, but relied primarily on a local customer base for support. Mills were fundamentally important for rural society because they converted grain to flour; their living space was subordinated to their economic function. The sites of both windmills and water mills depended on geography. Building a mill was a greater capital investment than building a house, so most mills were built with higher quality materials with the intention that they would last for several generations. Millers, innkeepers, and pastors were usually the wealthiest members of the community, so their housing was the most elaborate in the village.

In most parts of Europe, peasants lived in nucleated villages. It was possible to survive in a village with only a one-room house and no elaborate courtyard because much work was done communally, so one's house did not have to have all the required work materials. But large isolated farmhouses were characteristic of Alpine lands, in which raising animals was more important than tending cereal crops. Isolated farmsteads had to be self-sufficient because there were no neighbors to rely on. As a result, the houses of isolated farmsteads were significantly bigger than those in villages, even if the farmstead occupants were sometimes poorer than some of the more successful inhabitants of villages. The farmstead houses almost invariably consisted of two or even three stories, with stalls for animals in the lower story. Since these houses were often built in hilly country, they were arranged with ground access to the upper story, which was a large open space for storing grain and supplies.

URBAN ARTISAN HOUSING

Perhaps the most important distinction within the towns of early modern Europe was between citizens and noncitizens. In almost all towns, ownership of a house in town was a prerequisite for citizenship. The single-family–owned house, therefore, was the norm for merchants, professionals, and most independent craftsmen, the bulk of the citizens in urban Europe during this era. Not everyone aspired to or acquired citizenship, however. Many of the working poor lived crowded together with other families in single houses. For example, in seventeenth-century Augsburg, 70 percent of the households lived in houses containing an average of four families. Though there was some tendency for the houses of the wealthiest citizens to concentrate in the center of town near the public buildings, different trades were usually mixed together throughout town. This mixing of wealth and occupation was one of the most striking characteristics of the small- and medium-sized towns of the era.

Space was at a premium in urban areas. House facades directly abutted the street and were built one on top of the other. The characteristic urban street was a narrow alley with houses built close enough to block out the sun on the street. In some towns, the upper stories of houses overhung their entrances, almost touching the houses across the street. Houses generally showed a narrow front to the street and extended deeply to the rear. In the far rear, there was usually a garden or courtyard. In smaller towns (and earlier in the sixteenth century) ordinary houses tended to be only two stories tall. The first story was taller than the second. In those cities that experienced strong population growth, houses tended to be built upward, though it was very rare for them to reach more than five stories.

The interior of an artisan's house was organized for craft production, not as a haven from work. It often made sense to have one fairly undifferentiated room on the main floor of the house. That room would serve as kitchen, eating area, and workspace. Sometimes journeymen and apprentices would also sleep in the work area, rolling up their bedding at the start of the workday. There was usually at least some sense of separation between work areas and living areas, even in the large rooms, but that separation sometimes blurred. As late as the eighteenth century, one could still find blacksmiths' houses where the kitchen hearth also served as the foundry for the iron. The specific craft of the homeowner influenced home design and location. Tanners, for example, had to be located near a watercourse (and tended to produce unpleasant odors), so they were concentrated in the same neighborhood. Their houses' interiors included built-in vats for soaking and treating of hides, which had to be separate from living spaces. Such occupational needs placed constraints on housing design.

Most artisan houses had two or three rooms on each floor. There was often a parlor on the first floor, in addition to the main work area or shop. This room was also a public space of the household. The upstairs rooms were usually for sleeping. It is possible that one could find greater privacy in a typical urban home than in its rural equivalent, but it was still mostly a shared rather than isolated living situation.

Though it is unlikely that conditions were quite as squalid as they would become in the first decades of the industrial revolution, it is clear that many urban workers throughout the early modern era lived in dingy, crowded conditions, with little that could be considered luxuries or even comforts. Furnishings in artisan households were mostly comparable to those of the peasantry: sturdy furniture and supplies with perhaps a smattering of folk-art coloring. Studies of inventories at death show that the most important piece of personal property of the poor was the bed and accompanying linens. Urban houses differed from rural ones in some other respects. Most rooms in the urban house had fireplaces to keep them warm in the winter. Latrines inside the house became commonplace in the sixteenth century; in some cities, such as in Rouen in 1519, interior latrines were mandated by law. These comforts suggest that urban housing was more advanced than rural housing, even for the poor.

URBAN ELITE HOUSING

Dutch genre paintings by Vermeer, Steen, and de Hooch, among others, show sumptuous interiors that are not at all like the rather drab artisan households. The Dutch Republic was in the forefront of a broader based development of a self-confident "bourgeois" culture. Indeed, the explosion of genre painting in the Netherlands was partly a symptom of the new culture that it portrayed. Urban elites, and even those who possessed above-average wealth, no matter what their status, began to decorate their homes in a more elaborate style, akin to that of the nobility. Inventories show that paintings and prints were some of the decorations that became commonplace in bourgeois homes.

The interiors of urban elite homes reflected two important cultural trends. The first was a sharper separation of public and private lives. Unlike in the houses of urban artisans, the kitchen, storerooms, and servants' quarters were in the basement of the houses of merchants and members of the professions, separate from the general living and working space. A modern eighteenth-century town house consisted of ten to fifteen rooms spread over three or four stories. The first floor was mostly for interaction with the public. The key room was the parlor, where guests were greeted. Merchant houses also included a counting room or study that could be a place of repose but also a place to meet clients. The second floor contained the main dining room for entertaining guests, but also semi-private rooms such as the drawing or dressing room. Architects recognized that homeowners might conduct some business in the drawing room and thus advocated separating the drawing room from the bedrooms, which were often placed on the third floor.

The second cultural trend reflected in urban elite homes was the emergence of a consumer culture. Simple comforts that characterized most artisan homes by the eighteenth century, such as hearths in every room, internal latrines, and glass windows, were widespread in elite homes at the beginning of the early modern era. In addition, the rooms of bourgeois town houses were decorated profusely with moldings, wainscoting, marble mantlepieces, carpets, drapery, and mirrors. The increasing importance of new decorative objects such as mirrors, clocks, and sofas can be traced through inventories. Again, these trends were most conspicuous in large cities such as London and Paris, but they also extended to medium-sized towns. The Dutch were particularly noted for their comfortable and clean houses. In Germany, clocks were becoming an accessory in professional homes by the 1720s. A building boom in the late eighteenth century, exemplified in towns like Bath, created town houses appropriate for such conspicuous consumption.

NOBLE HOUSING

Housing in towns and villages in the early modern era consisted primarily of elaborations on medieval forms. But noble housing underwent a conspicuous change between the medieval and early modern eras, caused mostly by changes in the quintessential noble activity: warfare. Gunpowder weapons and artillery rendered the fortified castle useless as a safe haven for nobles. Some saw their castles destroyed during royal pacification campaigns; others decided that castles were uncomfortable and incompatible with the kind of splendor that went with living nobly. So noble housing became oriented toward display rather than defense.

Already in the Renaissance, urban nobles in Italy had revived the country villa as a retreat from urban life. The villa was modeled on the ancient Roman estate, but without the slaves. Architecturally, it incorporated classical notions of proportion and harmony that typified the Renaissance. In northern Europe, some royal palaces were built as a retreat from the hectic pace of urban life. Many were used primarily as hunting lodges. But many northern nobles were already primarily based in the rural world. The palace replaced the castle as the house from which nobles exerted their control over the countryside. The pace of the conversion of castles or construction of noble palaces in the countryside varied from region to region in Europe. Poorer noblemen had to be content with modest additions or remodeling of already existing castles. The largest concentration of new construction was in France and England. In England, the secularization of the monasteries opened large properties to development by regional elites. A wave of "great houses" went up beginning in the early sixteenth century. In eastern Europe, by contrast, rural palaces continued to exhibit clearly their function as agricultural centers as well as centers of noble power.

Part of the function of noble housing was the extravagant display of wealth and authority. A rural palace was symbolic as well as domestic architecture. It achieved its impact by its setting as well as by its facade and furnishings. Noble landowners might divert a river or extend a moat to make the approach to the main buildings more dramatic. Extensive formal gardens were an important accompaniment to the main structure.

The impact created by the approach to the building was then reinforced by its interior layout and decoration. In the country houses of England, the centerpiece of display was the hall, which one entered from the front door of the house. This was the most public space in the house and was decorated to focus attention on the head of the house, even when he was not present. Placing a great stairway in the hall became increasingly common, turning what had been a necessary but decidedly secondary architectural feature into another element of prominent display. Great houses had innumerable other rooms branching off from the hall, with increasing degrees of privacy associated with them.

The most prominent room in the house after the hall was the great chamber. Originally, it had been a general-purpose sleeping, eating, and meeting room of the head of the house. Increasingly, the sleeping area of the householder developed into a suite of rooms, including an antechamber and dressing room. An important part of the work of a nobleman was entertaining other noblemen. Great houses and palaces contained apartments in the family's own wing of the house and also in other wings to accommodate visitors. The status of visitors could be seen by where they were lodged in the house. An apartment consisted of four rooms: a sleeping chamber, a dressing room, an antechamber, and a room for personal servants.

As in bourgeois houses, the service rooms of the house were generally kept separate from both the public and private spaces. Some servants, of course, lived in rooms adjacent to their masters' or mistresses' chambers, but others slept in a separate section of the house, often dormitory style, when they were not on duty. Undoubtedly the central service room of the house was the kitchen. Along with the pantry, buttery, bakehouse, larder, and brewery, kitchens were kept out of the way of regular traffic. There was almost no space devoted exclusively to children, though most great houses had a separate nursery for the very young.

Noble houses experienced the same expansion of domestic comforts as bourgeois homes did. By the eighteenth century, it was commonplace for palaces to have running water, interior latrines, and fixed lighting. Instead of a single public room, such as the parlor, noble houses had a library or study, galleries, and a chapel. Formal gardens and outbuildings such as an orangerie (akin to a greenhouse) or folly (akin to a gazebo) provided another setting for nobles to meet or enjoy privacy. Indeed, gardens, in addition to their function as display, played an important role in noble intimacy and escape from the very public activity of much of the house.

The growth of the state drew more and more nobles to capital cities. The same issues of display and representation affected the housing nobles chose to live in or build in cities such as Paris and London. City layouts made it difficult to recreate the dramatic effect of the approach to a rural palace. Instead, the interiors and courtyards became the primary areas for dramatic display. Italy, which already had an established urban nobility in the Middle Ages, set the initial standards for the urban palazzo. In most respects, they followed the same internal organization as their rural counterparts. The architectural principles of "classicism" established in Paris became the norm for urban noble housing throughout Europe. In the eighteenth century, court cities such as Berlin, Vienna, and Munich experienced a building boom of noble houses based on variants of the classical and baroque styles.

HOUSING AS PROPERTY

The populated areas of Europe had already developed clear property lines at the beginning of the early modern era. New buildings were visibly constrained by these legal boundaries. This situation was particularly acute in urban areas, where the existing structures meant that the only way to increase the area of one's house was to build it upward, with additional stories, or to purchase a new plot of land with greater space. But even in villages, property lines defined housing spaces in the core of the village that were clearly differentiated from the croplands and pasture. Houses were restricted to that core. Once built, a house was expected to survive for a long time before being replaced. Increasing population in the countryside spurred the construction of new housing in the eighteenth century, often on subdivided plots. But, except in cases of a major catastrophe, such as fire, building a house was an infrequent phenomenon in most villages. Many structures built in the early modern era survived into the industrial era. The most extensive building projects for new housing were in the expanding suburbs of major cities or in newly founded court cities such as Versailles, Karlsruhe, or Turin, built explicitly on a grid pattern on property made available by the prince for the purpose of dynastic display.

Relatively clear property boundaries fostered a real estate market. One can, of course, find many instances of a single family residing on a piece of property for several generations. But some property became available because a lineage died out, and still more became available because of a change in the economic fortunes of a lineage. So purchasing a house was not at all a rare occurrence. Prices, of course, varied greatly. Even within the peasantry and artisan class, there were clear gradations in the quality of housing. Fancier peasant houses were worth about five times as much as cheaper ones in the housing market. Joint ownership of houses was also possible.

In the great cities, urban expansion was fostered by speculation in real estate. Urban elites invested in numerous building projects in suburbs and occasional renovation projects in the center of town. Some of these projects, the most famous of which is probably the Place Royale in Paris, completed in 1612, attracted elite buyers. Many others appealed primarily to people of middling means. Still others were rented out, either short term for noncitizens or long term for the working poor. The Fuggerei in Augsburg is perhaps the best-known example of housing for the working poor built by elite investors, but it was exceptional in being built primarily as a charitable institution rather than as an investment. In some cities, rental housing was a significant part of the housing stock. Fifteen percent of the population of Lübeck lived in rented cellars or rented row houses in alleys. The owners of such rental properties were often the urban elites of the towns.

By the end of the eighteenth century, urban housing was beginning to take on characteristics that would become widespread in the nineteenth century. Increasing population in towns such as Manchester put pressure on the housing stock for the working poor. At the same time, town house developments targeted at the upper middle classes, such as New Town, Edinburgh, became an important economic factor reshaping cities. They fostered speculation in both land and houses, which in turn fed urbanization on an unprecedented scale.

See also **Architecture; Aristocracy and Gentry; Artisans; Cities and Urban Life; City Planning; Daily Life; Engineering: Civil; Estates and Country Houses; Peasantry; Technology; Villages.**

BIBLIOGRAPHY

Baumgarten, Karl. *Das Deutsche Bauernhaus.* East Berlin, 1980.

Collomp, Allain. "Families: Habitations and Cohabitations." In *A History of Private Life.* Vol. 3, *Passions of the Renaissance,* edited by Roger Chartier, pp. 493–530. Translated by Arthur Goldhammer. Cambridge, Mass., and London, 1989.

Cooper, Nicholas. *Houses of the Gentry, 1480–1680.* New Haven and London, 1999.

Cruikshank, Dan, and Neil Burton. *Life in the Georgian City.* New York and London, 1990.

Dirlmeier, Ulf, ed. *Geschichte des Wohnens.* Vol. 2, *Hausen, Wohnen, Residieren.* Stuttgart, 1998.

Girouard, Mark. *Life in the English Country House.* New Haven and London, 1978.

Goldthwaite, Richard. *The Building of Renaissance Florence: An Economic and Social History.* Baltimore, Md., 1980.

Mohrmann, Ruth-Ellen. *Alltagswelt im Land Braunschweig.* 2 vols. Münster, 1990.

JOHN THEIBAULT

HUGUENOTS. "Huguenot" was the pejorative name given to Calvinist French Protestants by their Catholic opponents in the sixteenth century. The etymology of the word is obscure and contested. Henri Estienne (Latin Stephanus) was among several contemporaries to attribute it to the name given around 1560 to Protestants in Tours, after the neighborhood and city gate in which they held their religious services. Estienne may well have been correct, but an alternative derivation from *Eidgenossen* ('Confederates') that had become *Eigenotz,* or the supporters of the Swiss Protestant canton of Bern against the supporters of Catholic Savoy in the factional politics of Geneva in the 1530s, is still widely accepted. French Protestants preferred to call themselves *l'église réformée,* 'the Reformed church', and the French crown normally referred to them officially as "those of the so-called Reformed religion" after 1560.

French Protestantism emerged from the deeper wells of biblical humanism, reforming Gallicanism, inflected Lutheranism, and religious heterodoxy. But, under the influence of persecution, many Protestants were exiled to Strasbourg, Basel, and Geneva, which is where John Calvin established himself permanently from 1541. Increasingly in the 1550s, the influence of Calvin's writings and the model of the Genevan church came to exercise a dominant impact upon French-speaking Protestants, first among the communities of exiles in the Rhineland and elsewhere and then, from 1555 onward, in France itself. The Genevan Company of Pastors (Compagnie des Pasteurs) began to train and dispatch a limited number of ministers back to France in response to a deluge of requests from particular communities. In this period, French Protestantism became, in its theology and organization, irreducibly Calvinist. Although there had been at least one earlier gathering of French churches in 1557, the first generally recognized synod of the French Protestant church took place secretly in Paris in 1559. The delegates endorsed the "Confession of Faith" and "Discipline" which, taken together, provided a constitution and a creed for the Reformed communities. In church organization, this meant that the powers, selection, and responsibility of church officers (the familiar elders, pastors, deacons, and doctors of the Genevan new order) were vested in individual churches in the form of a consistory, composed of these officials and often made up of its notability. A contrary view, that power be vested in the congregation at large, still found its echoes in the documents of 1559, but they were gradually eliminated from Huguenot thought and practice in the course of the 1560s, culminating in the modifications at the synod of La Rochelle in 1571. Thereafter, the Confession and Discipline proved enduring statements of what the Huguenots stood for over the next two centuries. For their opponents, however, the movement was defined by the Huguenot Psalter, the Genevan metrical translation begun by Clément Marot and completed by Théodore de Bèze, Calvin's successor in Geneva, and by the French vernacular Bible, most notably the Neuchâtel Bible, originally translated by Pierre Robert Olivétan (French Olivier, Latin Olivetanus) and the basis for all subsequent French Protestant Bibles (including the Geneva Bible) in the sixteenth century.

French Protestantism found itself at what would be the height of its influence in the early 1560s. The political circumstances of a royal minority and regency, and the emergence of powerful protectors at court, especially Gaspard III de Coligny (1519–1572) and his cousin, a younger prince of the blood, Louis I de Bourbon, prince of Condé (1530–1569), assisted the chaotic and dramatic growth in Protestant numbers in these years. In March 1562, Coligny is supposed to have presented a list of the 2,150 churches then extant in France to the regent Catherine de Médicis. His figure may, however, have been exaggerated, and later historians can only document the existence of around 1,200–1,250 churches in this decade, or less than 4 percent of the Catholic parishes of the kingdom. If we allow for 1,500 communicating members of each church, we arrive at an adult Protestant population of under two million, perhaps not far from 10 percent of the total population of the French kingdom. These churches were, however, unevenly distributed, reflecting on the one hand its literate, urban constituency and, on the other, its seigneurial

Huguenots. An engraving by Hogenberg depicts the execution of members of the Amboise conspiracy, who planned in 1560 to abduct Francis II to separate him from the anti-Protestant Guise family. The plot failed and the conspirators were executed. THE ART ARCHIVE/UNIVERSITY LIBRARY GENEVA/DAGLI ORTI

heartland. Although there were many Reformed churches in Normandy, they remained quite widely scattered through the rest of northern France. Only south of the Loire, and especially in the crescent of communities stretching from La Rochelle through the southern provinces of Guyenne, Languedoc, and Dauphiné to Geneva, would there be a critical mass sufficient to provide an enduring basis for the forthcoming military struggle against the French crown.

That struggle was sustained and grueling. The Huguenots mobilized the resources of the churches in the early civil wars and seized royal revenues and ecclesiastical wealth in order to fund their campaigns. The civil wars lasted off and on from 1562 to 1598, and then again from 1622 to 1629. Without their naval strength off the Atlantic coast, mercenary German reinforcements, and the leadership of their most skilful "protector," Henry of Navarre, later Henry IV, king of France (ruled 1589–1610), they would probably not have succeeded in winning the limited degrees of toleration that the French crown reluctantly conceded them in edicts of pacification that culminated in the pacification of Nantes (April 1598), modified by the peace of Alais (1629). From the early civil wars, however, the antipathy of the Catholic majority in France toward the Huguenots was manifested by aristocratic feud and sectarian hatred. Both culminated in the famous St. Bartholomew's Day Massacre (August 1572) in Paris, an event that was mirrored in a score of provincial cities in the following weeks. The experience permanently

Huguenots. A seventeeth-century engraving shows Huguenot families fleeing the French city of La Rochelle in 1661. La Rochelle had been a Protestant stronghold, but a seige in 1627–1628 by the forces of Louis XIV had reestablished Catholic control. THE ART ARCHIVE/MUSÉE DES BEAUX ARTS LA ROCHELLE/DAGLI ORTI

eroded Protestant support, especially in northern France. It also cemented the emerging defensive and stoic mentality of French Protestantism, in which earlier persecution (recalled in successive and enlarged editions of Jean Crespin's famous French martyrology, the *Histoire des martyrs* [1554]) became the pattern of the way in which God repeatedly tested his faithful French elect.

The sixteenth-century Catholic perception of Huguenot political engagement has created an enduring view that they were republicans, determined to resist monarchical authority, who sought to establish a federal state in France after the model of the Swiss cantons or the emerging Dutch Republic. In reality, the basis for Huguenot "resistance theory" was laid among Protestant refugee reformers from a variety of backgrounds and found its echoes later in the sixteenth century among Catholics who were themselves similarly at odds with French monarchical authority. And, although French Protestants had a political assembly that met on an irregular basis to provide credibility to its military and financial organization, it was never the basis for a republican movement. In reality French Huguenots continued to adhere to the principles of monarchy, even though they preferred (like many of their Catholic counterparts) to see it in less than absolutist terms. Their great spokesman and one-time advisor to Henry IV, Philippe Duplessis Mornay, repeatedly defended his coreligionists against those who accused them of wanting to set up a "state within a state," to "diminish royal authority," or "establish a democracy." A comparable distillation, that the Huguenots stood for the principle of religious toleration, has also to be seen as something of a retrospective myth, born of the inevitable apologetic of a minority religious movement and incarnated by the Enlightenment and liberal nineteenth-century historiography.

The Edict of Nantes granted French Protestants limited rights of worship, access to royal offices, legal redress before special royal courts (known as *chambres de l'édit* or 'Chambers of the Edict'), and rights to establish their own academies. Royal letters *(brevets)* accompanying the edict granted subsidies for their troops, pastors, and schools and allowed them to garrison certain towns. The *brevets* were not maintained beyond 1629, and the terms of the edict were interpreted by royal officials in an increasingly restrictive way, especially after 1661, until the edict was revoked by Louis XIV in the Edict of Fontainebleau (October 1685). Of the 873 pastors remaining in France at that time, about 140 abjured; but the remainder chose to defy the edict and take up exile in the Dutch Republic (43 percent), Switzerland (27 percent), England (23 percent) and Germany (7 percent). More surprising to the authorities was the degree of illegal emigration of lay Huguenots—latest estimates suggest a figure of around 200,000. The Huguenot diaspora made the revocation a European phenomenon and cemented the French Protestant sense of a separate identity. The cultural and economic influence of the exiled Huguenots was far from negligible, spreading beyond Europe to colonial North America and the Dutch colonies, even if it has sometimes been exaggerated. Protestantism survived underground in eighteenth-century France and was once more officially tolerated on the eve of the Revolution.

See also **Bèze, Théodore de; Bible; Calvin, John; Calvinism; Coligny Family; Condé Family; Gallicanism; La Rochelle; Lutheranism; Martyrs and Martyrology; Nantes, Edict of; Reformation, Protestant; Resistance, Theory of; St. Bartholomew's Day Massacre; Wars of Religion, French.**

BIBLIOGRAPHY

The *Bulletin de la Société de l'Histoire du Protestantisme Français,* and the equivalent *British Proceedings of the Huguenot Society of Great Britain and Ireland* are an indispensable starting point for all those wishing to trace their Huguenot ancestry.

Benedict, Philip. *The Faith and Fortunes of France's Huguenots, 1600–1685.* St. Andrews Studies in Reformation History. Aldershot, U.K., and Burlington, Vt., 2001.

Butler, Jon. *The Huguenots in America: A Refugee People in New World Society.* Cambridge, Mass., and London, 1983.

Garrisson, Janine. *Les Protestants au XVIe siècle.* Paris, 1988.

Gray, Janet. "The Origin of the Word Huguenot." *Sixteenth Century Journal* 14, no. 3 (1983): 349–359.

Greengrass, M. *The French Reformation.* Oxford, 1987.

Gwynn, Robin D. *Huguenot Heritage: The History and Contribution of the Huguenots in Britain.* London, 1985.

Kingdon, Robert McCune. *Geneva and the Coming of the Wars of Religion in France, 1555–1563.* Travaux d'humanisme et renaissance, vol. 22. Geneva, 1956.

———. *Geneva and the Consolidation of the French Protestant Movement, 1564–1572.* Travaux d'humanisme et renaissance, vol. 92. Geneva, 1967.

Léonard, Émile G. *A History of Protestantism.* Edited by H. H. Rowley. 2 vols. London, 1965–1967.

Magdelaine, Marie, and R. von Thadden, eds. *Le refuge huguenot (1685–1985).* Paris, 1985.

Prestwich, Menna, ed. *International Calvinism, 1541–1715.* Oxford, 1985.

Wolff, Philippe, ed. *Histoire des protestants en France, de la réforme à la révolution.* Toulouse, 1977.

MARK GREENGRASS

HUMAN RIGHTS. *See* Rights, Natural.

HUMANISTS AND HUMANISM.

Humanism was the dominant intellectual movement among the educated classes of Europe from the Renaissance to the seventeenth century. The term reflects the belief that certain academic subjects known since ancient times as the *studia humanitatis* (humanistic studies) must shape the education and culture of those who rule society. Humanism was closely linked to the Renaissance desire to broaden knowledge about antiquity as a means of recovering not only more information but also the inner spirit that had made Greece and Rome flourish. The "humanistic" subjects were five in number: grammar (chiefly Ciceronian Latin), rhetoric (the art of persuasive speaking and writing), moral philosophy (the guide to making responsible choices in personal and political life), history, and poetry. The first three of these were taught in medieval universities, though humanists charged that they had been eclipsed by the inordinate attention given to dialectic. Those who promoted humanism contended that the mastery of the "humanities" was essential for the intellectual and moral development of an educated man.

This definition of humanism is based on the work of Paul Oskar Kristeller (1905–1999), who believed that the nineteenth-century historian Jacob Burckhardt (1818–1897) introduced confusion into Renaissance studies when he defined humanism as a new philosophy of life even though he never succeeded in defining a coherent set of philosophical ideas held by all humanists. Kristeller defined humanists as essentially grammarians and rhetoricians who regarded the languages and literatures of ancient Greece and Rome as a precious heritage that they must recover. Some scholars still follow Burckhardt and define humanism as a secular philosophy of life that foreshadows the modern world, but Kristeller's approach predominates.

ORIGINS OF ITALIAN HUMANISM

The roots of humanism lie in the unique social and political conditions of Italy about 1300. Northern Italy had become a commercial society dominated by independent city-republics. Chivalric literature and scholastic learning were remote from the primary concerns of urban laymen. But lawyers and notaries developed a professional subculture that led some individuals to become interested in ancient literature, and about 1300 a Paduan judge, Lovato dei Lovati (c. 1240–1309) and his friend Albertino Mussato (1261–1329), a notary, produced Latin works that imitated ancient Roman models.

Although these Paduan classicists may be the first humanists, the true founding figure was the poet Petrarch (1304–1374), the first humanist to gain international fame and to lead a group of disciples. The son of a Florentine notary attached to the papal curia at Avignon, Petrarch was attracted to poetry and classical literature. His father sent him to study law, but he devoted his life to poetry and Latin literature. His vernacular poems established his literary fame. He also wrote Latin poetry and produced a collective biography of famous Romans and an epic poem inspired by Virgil's *Aeneid.* Petrarch's dismay at the physical and moral decay of contemporary Rome led him to a new conception of ancient history. Unlike medieval thinkers, who never fully realized that they lived in post-Roman times, he saw that the Rome he loved had died a thousand years ago. In his opinion, the intervening millennium was a Dark Age. Good learning had perished. His goal was to restore knowledge of ancient Rome through study of its literature and thus to recapture the inner secret of Rome's greatness. So Petrarchan humanism was associated with a desire to bring about a "renaissance" of civilization. Petrarch was far more troubled by religious concerns than were most of his Italian contemporaries. His *Secretum* (Secret book) displays his awareness of discord between his desire for eternal salvation and his desire for worldly fame. He favored the contemplative over the active life and disdained the worldly concerns (politics, family, wealth) that captivated his Italian contemporaries. Hence his early following was limited to admirers of his poetry and of ancient literature.

The association of humanist learning with contemporary life was the work of Coluccio Salutati (1331–1406), chancellor of the Florentine republic. Salutati gained fame as an advocate for the republic at a time of political crisis. As the person who conducted the city's diplomatic correspondence, he created a network of humanist friends scattered throughout Italy. His activity made Florence the center of Italian humanism. In 1397 he persuaded the city to hire the Byzantine scholar Manuel Chrysoloras (1350–1415) to teach Greek, thus creating Italy's first generation of Hellenists and initiating the recovery of Greek literature. Salutati contributed to the triumph of humanism as the common culture of the ruling classes, first at Florence but eventually throughout Italy. A growing number of Florentine fathers chose humanistic education for their sons because they believed that the skills it taught and its Roman ethos of citizenship would prepare their heirs to assume their rightful place in society.

THE QUATTROCENTO

By the early Quattrocento (fifteenth century), humanism had become the dominant culture of educated Italians. Salutati's disciples at Florence made secular interests—especially politics—the focus of humanism. Leonardo Bruni (c. 1370–1444) associated Florentine republicanism with the cause of liberty for all Italians. His *History of the Florentine People* (1415–1444) explicitly proclaimed the superiority of a republican constitution to a monarchy. He attributed the greatness of Rome to its republican constitution and its later decline to the tyranny of the emperors. His republican ideology and his ideal of political involvement became the hallmark of Florentine humanism. Yet humanistic skills could also be useful in the service of a monarch, and humanism thus became the prevailing culture in Italy's princely courts as well as in its republics.

The fashion for humanism is reflected in a series of educational revolutions in fifteenth-century Italy and sixteenth-century France, Spain, Portugal, Germany, and England. Many of the town schools of Italy, which had taught traditional subjects, were transformed during the fifteenth century because ambitious city councillors wanted humanistic education for their sons. They hired humanists as headmasters and specified that instruction should be based on classical authors. In the sixteenth century, the municipal colleges of France and Spain experienced a similar transformation. Humanistic reform of northern universities proved far more difficult than reform of grammar schools and produced bitter conflicts in the early sixteenth century, but eventually humanists succeeded in winning an important place in most universities.

Since humanists admired classical literature, they were eager to discover lost works of ancient authors. Petrarch hunted for manuscripts and made important finds, including many of Cicero's letters; but the early fifteenth century was the golden age for rediscovery of Latin authors. The recovery of Greek literature was even more striking. Italian humanists brought back from Constantinople hundreds of previously unknown Greek books. Since relatively few Western students learned to read Greek well, the crucial moment in the availability of a Greek book was its translation into Latin. During the fifteenth century, the work of translation advanced rapidly. The most influential addition to the body of translations was the previously little-known works of Plato, translated by the Florentine philosopher Marsilio Ficino (1433–1499). By 1600, most of the Greek literature now known was available in printed Latin translations.

Fifteenth-century humanists also defined new standards for editing texts. Early humanist textual scholarship was driven more by enthusiasm than by rational criticism. Lorenzo Valla (1407–1457) was a pioneer in the development of a critical spirit. His greatest achievement was his realization that language itself is a product of history and changes with the passage of time. This idea is the foundation of modern philological scholarship. It was the basis of Valla's influential guide to good Latin style, *Elegances of the Latin Language* (1471). He demonstrated its power to evaluate texts in his treatise on the "Donation of Constantine" (c. 750–800), which he proved to be a forgery, and in his annotations on the New Testament, which showed how the ability to read Greek could aid the study of Scripture.

HUMANISM CROSSES THE ALPS

Since northern culture remained far more traditional than Italian, at first only scattered individuals in the north displayed interest in humanism. Many northerners who spent time in Italy, especially students of law or medicine, became interested in humanism and continued to pursue this interest after returning home. Not until about 1450 did their interests begin to spread. Several Germans who studied in Italy became itinerant lecturers, moving from university to university to lecture on humanistic subjects. The most influential was Peter Luder (1415–1472). After returning from Italy in 1456, he lectured at several universities. His announced goal was to restore the purity of the Latin language, which had declined into "barbarism." Early German humanists presented humanism in the secularized form that they had found in Italy. They were classicists, educational reformers, even German patriots, but they did not associate humanism with religious revival. Yet a longing for spiritual renewal had become a powerful force in northern Europe.

The movement called "Christian humanism" explicitly applied humanist studies as a means to regenerate Christian faith. In Germany, an early example was Johann Reuchlin (1455–1519), who became expert in the biblical languages, Greek and Hebrew, and sought to apply Neoplatonism and Jewish mysticism (Cabala) to deepen his understanding of Scripture. In France the chief figure was Jacques Lefèvre d'Étaples (1455–1536). His initial goal was to improve the teaching of Aristotelian philosophy at the University of Paris. But in 1508 he retired from teaching and devoted himself to study of the Bible. His biblical publications included his *Fivefold Psalter* (1509) and his commentary on the Epistles of St. Paul (1512).

By far the greatest Christian humanist was Desiderius Erasmus of Rotterdam (1466?–1536). As a young man he won attention for his elegant Latin style, and as a student of theology at Paris, he became close to Parisian humanists. Erasmus became known as a Latin poet, an editor of classical authors, and the author of a collection of classical proverbs. From about 1500 he also published on religion. His book of spiritual counsel to laymen, *Enchiridion Militis Christiani* (1503; Handbook of the Christian warrior), became a religious best-seller. Erasmus concluded that mastery of Greek was essential for study of the New Testament and of the church fathers. Reexamination of the scriptural and patristic sources of Christian faith could liberate both theology and spiritual life from the spiritual morbidity of the unreformed church. He called his ideal "the Philosophy of Christ." Although this ideal of a religion expressed in righteous living rather than in dogma and ritual might seem to have little connection with scholarship, Erasmus found the connection in the need of the Christian community to recapture the inspiration that had made the early church spiritually powerful. His goal was a renaissance of genuine Christianity to match the other humanist goal of a renaissance of classical learning. His scholarship culminated in his edition of the Greek New Testament (1516). Between about 1516 and 1521, he became the leader of a humanist campaign to effect gradual and peaceable religious reform through scholarship and the education of a new generation of leaders.

THE REFORMATION DIVIDES HUMANISM

The outbreak of the Protestant Reformation in 1517 thwarted these hopes. Although Martin Luther also favored humanistic studies as a preparation for the reform of the church, and at Wittenberg led a university reform that made humanistic subjects the center of the curriculum, humanism split apart over the Reformation. Erasmus and the older generation of humanists were appalled at the prospect of a divided church, and ultimately nearly all of them remained Catholic. Many of the young humanists, however, had come to admire Luther even more than Erasmus; they became leading Protestant clergymen. Although they accused Erasmus of lacking the courage to follow his own best principles, Protestant humanists still admired him. The humanists who remained in the old church, including Erasmus himself, came under attack by conservative Catholics who accused them (Erasmus in particular) of being the source of Luther's heresies. The religious upheaval that followed did not destroy humanism but did narrow its scope. As denominational barriers hardened, humanists of the later sixteenth century tended to avoid trouble by putting aside aspirations for sweeping spiritual renewal and institutional reform. They narrowed the scope of their studies to classical scholarship and the perfection of the philological tools of textual criticism; religion they left to the theologians.

POST-REFORMATION HUMANISM

On the purely technical side, post-Reformation humanism remained productive. The scholar-printer Robert Estienne (1503–1559) produced an authoritative Latin dictionary (1531) that was used for centuries. His son Henri (1528–1598) published an edition of Plato that still governs scholarly citation practices. He also compiled a dictionary of Greek (1572) to match his father's Latin one. Comparable in importance was Josephus Justus Scaliger (1540–1609), whose work on ancient chronology, *Opus Novum de Emendatione Temporum* (1583), was a pioneering effort to integrate the dating systems of various ancient cultures. As a Protestant, Scaliger felt free to apply his critical skills to demolish the traditional authority of the patristic author known as Dionysius the Areopagite (first century C.E.), proving that Dionysius was not converted by St. Paul but lived centuries later. Isaac Casaubon (1559–1614) performed a similarly destructive criticism of the tracts attributed to Hermes Trismegistus, supposedly a divinely inspired treasury of Egyptian religion but actually a jumble of unrelated and unimportant texts.

Late Renaissance humanism also produced a challenge to the jurisprudence of the medieval universities, attacking the commentaries of medieval professors as a distortion of Roman law and calling for a fresh look at the original text of the laws. This "legal humanism" was foreshadowed by the critical scholarship of Valla, the Florentine humanist Angelo Poliziano (1454–1494), and the French humanist Guillaume Budé (1468–1540); it reached maturity in the teaching of Andrea Alciati (1492–1550) at Avignon and Bourges. But as French legal humanists probed the legal foundations of their own society, they discovered that French institutions and much of French law did not come from Rome at all. François Hotman (1524–1590) concluded that French laws originated not with Rome but with the customs of the early Franks and the legislation of the medieval kings. Humanism provided the linguistic method used by Hotman, but French patriotism was what drove him to discover the medieval origins of his nation. In a sense, he and other legal humanists invented medieval history by discovering the documentary sources of medieval French law. Another special direction of later humanism was patristic scholarship. In Catholic Europe this became a specialty of the monastic orders. The Benedictine Congregation of St. Maur in France became famous for editions of the church fathers and for development of important tools of scholarship, such as Jean Mabillon's (1632–1707) *De Re Diplomatica* (1681) and the *Paleographia Graeca* (1708) by Bernard de Montfaucon (1655–1741).

By the seventeenth century, humanism in the sense understood by its Renaissance creators was gone. The Renaissance dream of applying classical learning in order to revitalize civilization and the church perished in the conflicts of the Reformation. Humanism survived in three forms: the specialized field of classical scholarship, especially classical philology; the recovery of nearly the whole body of Latin and Greek literature; and the educational changes that transformed schools and universities from centers for the study of scholastic logic and metaphysics into centers for teaching the classical languages and the literary curriculum that dominated Western schools from the fifteenth to the twentieth century.

See also **Education; Erasmus, Desiderius; Luther, Martin; Reformation, Protestant; Universities.**

BIBLIOGRAPHY

Baron, Hans. *The Crisis of the Early Italian Renaissance: Civic Humanism and Republican Liberty in an Age of Classicism and Tyranny.* Rev. ed. Princeton, 1966.

Burckhardt, Jacob. *The Civilization of the Renaissance in Italy: An Essay.* Translated by S. G. C. Middlemore. 3rd ed. London, 1950. The best of many editions. Translation of *Die Cultur der Renaissance in Italien: Ein Versuch* (1860). The classic study of the Renaissance and humanism. Though often criticized, it still dominates all discussion of the period.

Garin, Eugenio. *Italian Humanism: Philosophy and Civic Life in the Renaissance.* Translated by Peter Munz. New York, 1965. Translation of *L'umanesimo italiano* (1958).

Grafton, Anthony. *Defenders of the Text: The Traditions of Scholarship in an Age of Science, 1450–1800.* Cambridge, Mass., 1991. Traces the emergence and development of classical philology.

Grafton, Anthony, and Lisa Jardine. *From Humanism to the Humanities: Education and the Liberal Arts in Fifteenth- and Sixteenth-Century Europe.* Cambridge, Mass., 1986. Challenges the humanists' own claims for the cultural significance of their program of education.

Grendler, Paul F. *Schooling in Renaissance Italy: Literacy and Learning, 1300–1600.* Baltimore, 1989. A study of the "educational revolution" caused by Italian humanism.

King, Margaret L. *Women of the Renaissance.* Chicago, 1991. Studies the relatively few Renaissance women who attempted (with limited success) to participate in humanistic culture.

Kristeller, Paul Oskar. *Renaissance Thought: The Classic, Scholastic, and Humanist Strains.* New York, 1961. One of several collections of essays by Kristeller. This volume contains the most influential of the essays in which he develops his definition of humanism and its relationship to ancient and medieval culture.

Nauert, Charles G. *Humanism and the Culture of Renaissance Europe.* Cambridge, U.K., 1995. A synthesis of recent scholarship on humanism, both Italian and non-Italian.

Rabil, Albert, Jr., ed. *Renaissance Humanism: Foundations, Forms, and Legacy.* 3 vols. Philadelphia, 1988. Massive collection of essays by specialists on many aspects of humanism.

Rummel, Erika. *The Confessionalization of Humanism in Reformation Germany.* Oxford, 2000. Discusses the mutual interaction of the Reformation and German humanism.

Trinkaus, Charles. *"In Our Image and Likeness": Humanity and Divinity in Italian Humanist Thought.* 2 vols. London and Chicago, 1970. Study of Italian humanists' views on human nature.

Witt, Ronald. *"In the Footsteps of the Ancients": The Origins of Humanism from Lovato to Bruni.* Leiden, 2001. Reexamination of the origins and nature of early Italian humanism.

CHARLES G. NAUERT

HUME, DAVID (1711–1776), Scottish philosopher and historian. Hume was born in the Scottish border country near Edinburgh into an old family of prosperous provincial lawyers. His father died when he was an infant. His mother never remarried and devoted herself to raising Hume and his brother and sister. Throughout his life Hume was deeply attached to his family and proud of its traditions. He studied at the University of Edinburgh until the age of fourteen or fifteen. For the next ten years he pursued a rigorous plan of independent study that surveyed the whole of humanistic learning and cost him a temporary nervous breakdown. From this period, Hume conceived two projects, the later fulfillment of which would complete his career as a writer—a philosophical science of human nature (comprehending all the sciences) and the writing of history. Hume is unique in being both a great philosopher and a great historian. He is commonly ranked, along with William Robertson, Edward Gibbon, and Voltaire as one of the four most important eighteenth-century historians.

By the age of twenty-six Hume had composed his philosophical masterpiece, *A Treatise of Human Nature* (1739–1740). The work was not well received, and Hume quickly began recasting its ideas into the more readable form of essays. Most of these were published from 1741 to 1752 and were warmly received in Britain and America and translated into French, German, and Italian. The most important works from this period are *Essays: Moral, Political, and Literary* (1752), *An Enquiry Concerning Human Understanding* (1748), and *An Enquiry Concerning the Principles of Morals* (1751). These essays contain important contributions to epistemology, aesthetics, economics, and moral and political philosophy. *The Natural History of Religion* (1757) and *Dialogues Concerning Natural Religion* (published posthumously in 1779), arguably establish Hume as the founder of the philosophy of religion.

Around 1752 he turned to the second project set for himself in his youth, namely the writing of history. *The History of England* appeared in six volumes over the years 1754–1762. It achieved the status of a classic in Hume's lifetime, was viewed as the standard work on the subject for nearly a century, and was in print down to the end of the nineteenth century, passing through at least 160 posthumous editions. Hume had now achieved a European reputation as one of the great writers of his age, and he enjoyed friendships with such illustrious figures as Adam Smith, Jean-Jacques Rousseau, Anne Robert Jacques Turgot, Denis Diderot, Jean d'Alembert, and Benjamin Franklin.

In 1983 *The History of England* was republished after having been out of print for nearly a century. During that period Hume had been narrowly thought of as a technical philosopher. The early skeptical and negative interpretation of *The Treatise of Human Nature* put forth by James Beattie, Thomas Reid, Immanuel Kant, and John Stuart Mill persisted far into the twentieth century. Hume's historical work was considered irrelevant to his philosophy and almost entirely forgotten. Hume, however, thought of the *History* as an integral part of his philosophical work. This can best be appreciated by considering his skepticism. The ancient Pyrrhonians taught that the main source of misery for highly cultivated people is the attempt to guide life by philosophical speculation. Hume denied that the disposition to philosophize could or should be purged, but he agreed with the Pyrrhonians that philosophical speculation can be a source of disorder in the soul. The first problem for Hume's science of human nature, then, was to distinguish what he called "true philosophy" from its corrupt and corrupting forms. Hume used skeptical tropes to make this distinction. His intention was neither to subvert (Beattie, Reid, Mill) nor to raise skeptical challenges for others to solve (Kant). His goal was to purge the philosophical intellect of its corrupt forms.

False philosophy seeks radical autonomy and imagines itself emancipated from the pre-reflective customs and prejudices of common life. True philosophy knows this to be a psychological and conceptual impossibility. True philosophy may still speculate about reality but only by critically passing through, and rendering more coherent, the inheri-

David Hume. Portrait by David Martin. ©CHRISTIE'S IMAGES/CORBIS

ted prejudices of common life. Hume went beyond the Pyrrhonians in teaching that false philosophy has a corrupting effect not only on the soul but on social and political order as well—and especially so under modern conditions where, for the first time in history, the disposition to philosophize was becoming a mass phenomenon. He narrated the tragedy of the English Civil War in the *History* as just such a corruption. His critique of philosophical rationalism in all its forms (in science, morals, politics, religion, and philosophy itself) is the one theme that unites his philosophical and historical work. And it establishes Hume as the first to work out a systematic critique of modern ideologies.

See also **Alembert, Jean Le Rond d'; Diderot, Denis; Historiography; Kant, Immanuel; Philosophy; Rousseau, Jean-Jacques; Skepticism, Academic and Pyrrhonian; Smith, Adam.**

BIBLIOGRAPHY

Primary Sources

Hume, David. *David Hume's Enquiries Concerning Human Understanding and Concerning the Principles of Morals.* Edited by L. A. Selby-Bigge. 3rd ed. revised, edited by P. H. Nidditch. Oxford, 1975.

——. *Essays, Moral, Political, and Literary.* Edited by Eugene F. Miller. Indianapolis, 1985.

——. *Principal Writings on Religion, Including Dialogues Concerning Natural Religion and The Natural History of Religion.* Edited by J. C. A. Gaskin. Oxford and New York, 1993.

——. *A Treatise of Human Nature.* Edited. by L. A. Selby-Bigge. 2nd ed. with text revised and variant readings by P. H. Nidditch. Oxford and New York, 1978.

Secondary Sources

Bongie, Laurence L. *David Hume, Prophet of the Counter-Revolution.* Indianapolis, 2000. Shows how important Hume's *History* was in shaping the ideological conflict in France shortly before, during, and after the French Revolution.

Forbes, Duncan. *Hume's Philosophical Politics.* Cambridge, U.K., and New York, 1975. Views Hume's *History* as an integral part of his political philosophy.

Livingston, Donald W. *Hume's Philosophy of Common Life.* Chicago, 1984. Argues against the reading of Hume as a radical empiricist; shows how his philosophical and historical writings are internally connected.

——. *Philosophical Melancholy and Delirium: Hume's Pathology of Philosophy.* Chicago, 1998. Fully explores Hume's distinction between true and false philosophy.

Norton, David Fate. *David Hume: Common-Sense Moralist, Sceptical Metaphysician.* Princeton, 1982.

Penelhum, Terence. *Themes in Hume: The Self, the Will, and Religion.* Oxford and New York, 2000.

Stewart, John B. *Opinion and Reform in Hume's Political Philosophy.* Princeton, 1992.

DONALD W. LIVINGSTON

HUMOR. Aristotle, in *De partibus animalium,* defined man as a being capable of laughter, but laughter is not, as some optimists have claimed, a universal language. Its function and importance differed so widely, even during our historical period, depending on national, social, and other variables, that it is far easier to ask questions than to answer them. Why did (and do) some Christians, like Jacques-Bénigne Bossuet (1627–1704), strongly disapprove of laughter? Is there any common element uniting the hearty, even crude, laughter provoked by carnival merrymaking and slapstick comedy (French farces and *sotties,* Spanish *pasos,* the Italian commedia dell'arte) and the urbane wit called *festivitas* by Desiderius Erasmus (1466?–1536) and Thomas More (1478–1535) and exemplified by the noble speakers in Baldassare Castiglione's *Book of the Courtier* (1528)? Can we clearly separate "popular" from "refined" or "learned" humor? And why is the terminology of humor not easily translated from one language to another?

Laughter was often considered more important in the Renaissance than it has been since. Several Renaissance princes, including Lorenzo de' Medici (1449–1492) and Louis XII of France (ruled 1498–1515), were reputed to enjoy jokes, even those directed against themselves, whereas France's Louis XIV (ruled 1643–1715) is said to have made only one joke in his life. Unfortunately, even today no explanation of why we laugh is universally endorsed. Sixteenth-century theorists about humor were mainly medical authorities (Laurent Joubert [1529–1582], Ambroise Paré [1510–1590]) interested in physiology; in the seventeenth century Thomas Hobbes (1588–1679), following Aristotle, articulated the first of the three commonest modern explanations of laughter: superiority, incongruity, and release from restraint. If we can usually see why satire provokes laughter, we are at a loss when we try to compare the humor of Molière (1622–1673) and Shakespeare (1564–1616), or of Miguel de Cervantes (1547–1616) and Laurence Sterne (1713–1768).

THE SIXTEENTH CENTURY

The Renaissance and the Reformation inspired a remarkable variety of verbal and visual humor. The great humanist Erasmus, in his *Colloquies* (1518), produced both biting anti-church satire ("The Funeral"), and sly and charming wit ("The Abbot and the Learned Lady"). Reformation and anti-Reformation satirists created an explosion of comic caricature in broadsheets attacking either Luther and his cohorts or the venal priests and hypocritical monks of the Roman Catholic Church. Humanist polemic did not shrink from scatological invective that would horrify most readers today (the *Eccius Dedolatus*), and French farce characters could urinate on stage. Much humanist wit, like the *Epistles of Obscure Men*, is incomprehensible to readers with no knowledge of Latin.

The century apparently reveled in jokes (*facetiae* in Latin) and in comic short stories, as numerous anthologies in England, France, Italy, and Germany attest. The most influential were those of Poggio Bracciolini in Italy (1438–1452) and Heinrich Bebel in Germany (1508–1512), both written in Latin. Later collections became larger and more inclusive; there are 981 *facezie* in the 1574 edition of Ludovico Domenichi, written in Italian. An Erasmian love of humor inspired both François Rabelais (*Gargantua and Pantagruel*, 1532–1564), who used wit and hyperbole to convey his humanist message, and Shakespeare, whose comedies radiate a smiling acceptance of human frailty. Comic theater came to life again in most European countries in the sixteenth century, stimulated by the rediscovery of Aristotle's dramatic principles and of Plautus and Terence. National differences in comic outlook are strikingly illustrated by the German adaptation of Rabelais (1575–1590) by Johann Fischart, which is much cruder than its model and much less humanistically inclined. Comic visual art includes not only a wealth of satirical engravings, but the compelling visual grotesques of Pieter Bruegel (1525?–1569) and Hieronymus Bosch (1450?–1516) and the whimsical portraits of Giuseppe Arcimboldo (c. 1530–1593), which are created exclusively of fruit, flowers, or fish.

THE SEVENTEENTH CENTURY

Whereas much literature of the previous century was still written in Latin, this one saw the flowering of vernacular literatures; it is Spain's Golden Age, and France's Age of Classicism. Cervantes's *Don Quixote* (1615), generally recognized as the first novel, has comic moments, but its prevailing tone is ironic rather than frankly humorous. Comic theater flourished, with some common elements; for instance, the classical clownish slave lived on as the Spanish *gracioso,* as Molière's *soubrette,* as the *zanni* (crafty servant) of the commedia dell'arte, and as numerous characters in the plays of Shakespeare and Ben Jonson (1573–1637).

The century's great comic dramatists were not primarily satirists. Shakespeare's dramatic worlds are more imaginary than real. Molière's minor comedies owe more to literary sources than to real life (*Les Fourberies de Scapin,* 1671), and his best plays only occasionally reveal his scorn for stupid minor nobles, or for dangerous religious hypocrites (*Le Tartuffe,* 1667). Their genius, like Shakespeare's, lies in revealing character through comedy, though Shakespeare was freer to include farce in his plays.

England's Restoration drama (after 1660) was much more satirical; William Wycherley (1640–1716), John Vanbrugh (1664–1726), John Farquhar (1678–1707), and William Congreve (1670–1729) delighted in skewering stupidity and pretentiousness, as Jonson had before them. Critics continued to discuss the form and function of stage comedy, and comic opera became a popular genre.

THE EIGHTEENTH CENTURY

The Age of Enlightenment specialized in satire, though less in the theater than in other genres. Carlo Goldoni's (1707–1793) comedies continue the tradition of comedy of intrigue, while those of Pierre de Marivaux (1688–1763) are more interested in human emotions than in social mores. In Russia, Denis Fonvizin (1745–1792) showed members of the nobility in a comic light (*The Brigadier,* 1769).

England produced some satirical giants: Henry Fielding (1707–1754), whose sprawling novel *Tom Jones* (1749) has comic moments; Richard Sheridan (1751–1816), whose Mrs. Malaprop in *The School for Scandal* (1777) is a comic type to rival Shakespeare's Falstaff; William Hogarth, whose moralizing series (*Marriage à la mode,* 1745) prefigured the modern cartoon; the verse satires of John Dryden (1631–1700) and Alexander Pope (1688–1744), and above all, Jonathan Swift (1667–1745). Compared to his mentors, Erasmus and Rabelais, Swift is sometimes too ferocious to be comic, as when he recommends relieving the famine in Ireland by eating babies (*A Modest Proposal,* 1729), but *Gulliver's Travels* (1726) remains a humorous and readable indictment of the society of his time.

France's Voltaire (1694–1778) is often both subtler and funnier than Swift, especially in his masterpiece, *Candide* (1759), a comprehensive attack on the aristocracy, religion, and general prejudices of his time (a battle is a "heroic butchery"; a Spanish grandee demonstrates "pride suitable in a man with so many names"). A new element in this century is the connection between laughter and eroticism, in works by Charles-Louis de Secondat de Montesquieu (1689–1755), Denis Diderot (1713–1784), and Pierre Choderlos de Laclos (1741–1803) (*Les liaisons dangereuses,* 1782).

See also **Caricature and Cartoon; Castiglione, Baldassare; Cervantes, Miguel de; Commedia dell'Arte; Dryden, John; Erasmus, Desiderius; Jonson, Ben; Molière; Pope, Alexander; Rabelais, François; Shakespeare, William; Sheridan, Richard Brinsley; Swift, Jonathan; Voltaire.**

BIBLIOGRAPHY

Primary Source

Bowen, Barbara C. ed. *One Hundred Renaissance Jokes: An Anthology.* Birmingham, Ala., 1988. Latin jokes with English translations.

Secondary Sources

Bremmer, Jan, and Herman Roodenburg, eds. *A Cultural History of Humor: From Antiquity to the Present Day.* Malden, Mass., 1997.

Ménager, Daniel. *La Renaissance et le rire.* Paris, 1995.

BARBARA C. BOWEN

HUNGARIAN LITERATURE AND LANGUAGE.

HUNGARIAN LITERATURE AND LANGUAGE. Hungarian, or Magyar, spoken by some 14 to 15 million Hungarians in Hungary and elsewhere by the beginning of the twenty-first century, is a Finno-Ugric language. Together with the Vogul-Ostiak, Finnish, and other Finno-Ugric tongues, Hungarian belongs to the Uralic linguistic family, which, according to certain scholars, had close contacts with the Altaic languages (Turkic, Mongolian, and Manchu-Tungus). It is an agglutinative tongue, and its richness in vowel sounds renders it especially suitable for poetry. Apart from major early modern European political and cultural trends, the evolution of Hungarian and its literature was significantly influenced by the division of the country and its relationship to the Austrian empire. Between 1541 and 1699 Hungary was divided into three parts, ruled by the Austrian Habsburgs, the Ottomans, and the Ottomans' vassal Hungarian princes in Transylvania; from 1684 to 1699 the Habsburgs "reconquered" Hungary, and throughout the eighteenth century they attempted to subjugate Hungary and integrate it into the Habsburg Monarchy.

ADMINISTRATIVE AND SCHOLARLY LANGUAGE

Although Latin was the official language of legislation in Hungary until 1844, from the 1540s onward Hungarian spread rapidly in all three parts of the country as a language of both administration and literature. By 1565 it had become the language of legislation and administration in the Principality of Transylvania. Around the same time, with the help of their Hungarian notaries, Ottoman governors residing in Buda started to use Hungarian in their dealings with the Viennese authorities, the princes of Transylvania, and local Hungarian officials. Latin served as the language of education until 1792, when Hungarian became an obligatory subject in secondary schools. Despite the influence of Latin, Turkish, German, and various Slavic languages, this period witnessed the homogenization of the vernacular and the appearance of two main regional dialects. It also marked the beginning of the formation of a Hungarian literary language that stood above regional dialects.

Apart from translations of the Bible (the New Testament in 1541; the first complete Protestant and Catholic translations in 1589 and 1626), the sixteenth and seventeenth centuries saw the publication of the first Hungarian-language studies of Magyar orthography (1535 and 1655) and grammar (1610 and 1682) and the first Hungarian dictionary (1604). There was also an attempt to create a new vocabulary that would render Hungarian suitable for scientific literature. To that end, books were published in the vernacular on logic, medicine, arithmetic, physics, geography, and mineralogy. The first general encyclopedia in Hungarian was published in 1653 by János Apáczai Csere (1625–1659), the principal representative of Hungarian Puritanism, while the first lexicon of Hungarian writers, Péter Bod's *Magyar Athénas* (Hungarian Athenaeum), appeared in 1766. Yet some of the most important works were still published in Latin. Of these, the most notable were Mátyás Bél's (1684–1749) multivolume historical-geographical description of Hungary and the monumental histories of the Magyars by two Jesuit professors at the University of Pest, György Pray (1723–1801) and István Katona (1732–1811), the latter's in forty-two volumes.

HUNGARIAN AS A LITERARY LANGUAGE

The first continuous Hungarian text is the *Halotti beszéd* (Funeral oration) from around 1200, while the oldest known Hungarian poem, the *Ómagyar Mária-siralom* (Old hymn to the Virgin Mary), is known from a Latin codex dated about 1300. Until the early sixteenth century Hungarian literature, mainly religious, was cherished in the monasteries and recorded in codices. The representatives of Renaissance literature—Archbishop János Vitéz (de Zredna), Bishop Janus Pannonius, and others—worked in the court of King Matthias I Corvinus (ruled 1458–1490). His court also housed the famous Bibliotheca Corviniana, one of the richest manuscript libraries of fifteenth-century Europe.

Along with the typical genres of Protestant literature, the first exemplars of popular and court poetry also appeared in the sixteenth century. Sebestyén Tinódi Lantos (1510?–1556) recorded the struggle of the Hungarians against the Ottoman conquerors in a series of rhymed chronicles. The greatest lyric poet of the century was Bálint Balassi (1554–1594). By combining the motifs of Hungarian and east-central European love songs with the European tradition of Petrarchan love poetry, Balassi elevated Hungarian love poetry to a much higher standard than it had previously reached. He also penned the first Hungarian play about love, and he wrote heroic and religious poetry as well.

The two towering figures of baroque literature in seventeenth-century Hungary were Archbishop Péter Pázmány (1570–1637), the leader of the Hungarian Catholic renewal, and Count Miklós Zrínyi (1620–664), a military commander, statesman, and writer. Pázmány's theological synthesis *Isteni igazságra vezérlo kalauz* (1613; Guide to divine truth) represents Hungarian baroque prose at its best. Zrínyi's *Szigeti veszedelem* (1651; Siege of Sziget), which chronicles the heroic and ultimately unsuccessful defense of Szigetvár by Zrínyi's great-grandfather and namesake against Sultan Suleiman's army in 1566, is the most polished epic in Old Hungarian. Memoirs (by Miklós Bethlen, János Kemény, Péter Apor, and Mihály Cserei) are perhaps the strongest genre of Transylvanian literature of the period. Dramas, in both Hungarian and Latin, were performed mainly in the schools of the religious orders.

In the late baroque period (1690–1772), literature was often used by members of the Magyar nobility to express their criticism of Vienna's absolutist policies. While these works were usually of modest literary value, the *Törökországi levelek* (Letters from Turkey) by Kelemen Mikes (1690–1761) represents the finest example of this genre. Mikes, Ferenc Rákóczi II's faithful companion during his exile in Turkey, addressed his letters to a fictitious female relative who symbolizes his longing for the motherland as well as unfulfilled love.

The first notable representative of the Hungarian Enlightenment was Gyorgy Bessenyei (1747–1811). As a member of Maria Theresa's (ruled 1740–1780) Hungarian Guard in Vienna, Bessenyei mastered French and German and introduced new ideas into Hungarian literature, using familiar literary genres (poetry, drama) along with new ones (the travel novel, the enlightened epos, etc.). Another "bodyguard writer," János Batsányi (1763–1845), promptly greeted the French Revolution, realizing its significance. Aside from these two writers, the Jesuits Dávid Baróti Szabó (1739–1819) and József Rájnis (1741–1812) and the Piarist friar Miklós Révai (1750–1807) played major roles in polishing the Hungarian literary language through their classical metric poems, translations (from Virgil), and passionate literary debates. Their efforts were facilitated by the newly established literary journals of the late eighteenth century as well as by the expanding book industry. Between 1712 and 1790 some fifteen thousand works appeared in the country. Under Austrian Emperor Joseph II (ruled 1780–1790) the percentage of books printed in Hungarian and German had risen from 27 to 34 percent and from 17 to 23 percent, respectively, whereas the percentage of books in Latin decreased from 50 to 36 percent. This was the beginning of a new era. The works of a younger generation of poets and writers of the Hungarian Enlightenment, including Mihály Csokonai-Vitéz (1773–1805) and Ferenc Kazinczy (1759–1831), among others, ushered in a revival of Hungarian language and literature.

See also **Budapest; Habsburg Territories; Hungary; Ottoman Empire.**

BIBLIOGRAPHY

Czigány, Lóránt. *The Oxford History of Hungarian Literature from the Earliest Times to the Present.* Oxford and New York, 1984.

Kósa, László, ed. *A Companion to Hungarian Studies.* Budapest, 1999.

———. *A Cultural History of Hungary: From the Beginnings to the Eighteenth Century.* Budapest, 1999.

Kosáry, Domokos. *Culture and Society in Eighteenth-Century Hungary.* Budapest, 1987

Szentpéteri, József. *Magyar kódex.* Vol. 3, *Magyarország muvelodéstörténete, 1526–1790.* Budapest, 2000.

Gábor Ágoston

HUNGARY. Hungary's history from 1450 through 1790 can be divided into three periods. The century from 1450 was the last phase of the independent Hungarian Kingdom, whose major political concern was the Ottoman advance. Hungary lost her long struggle at the battle of Mohács in 1526 and was divided into three parts by the mid-sixteenth century. The second period (1541–1699) is often labeled as the era of the tripartite division of the country. Royal Hungary in the west was under Habsburg rule and Ottoman Hungary in the middle was ruled, at least partly, from Constantinople (Istanbul), whereas the Principality of Transylvania in the east, although an Ottoman satellite state, had considerable autonomy, especially in its domestic affairs. While hostilities and rivalries often divided the Hungarian political elite, with regard to socioeconomic, religious, cultural, and even political developments, the three parts were connected on many levels. The next era can be described as the integration of Hungary into the Habsburg Monarchy that reconquered the country from the Ottomans by the end of the 17th century. This period witnessed a new political compromise between Vienna and the Hungarian estates, as well as visible economic and demographic growth and cultural flourishing.

In the mid-fifteenth century, the Kingdom of Hungary was a regional power in Central Europe. It had an estimated territory of 300,000 square kilometers, a population of 3.1–3.5 million, and annual revenues of 500,000 gold florins under King Matthias (Mátyás) Corvinus of the Hunyadi family (1458–1490). Protected by the natural boundaries of the Carpathian Mountains in the north and in the east, Hungary was bordered by Poland in the north, Bohemia in the northwest, and Habsburg Austria in the west. In the south, the Danube and Sava Rivers—and the southern border defense system built along those rivers—separated the country from the Ottoman Empire.

The Ottoman threat fostered military reforms and centralization in Hungary. Relying on the

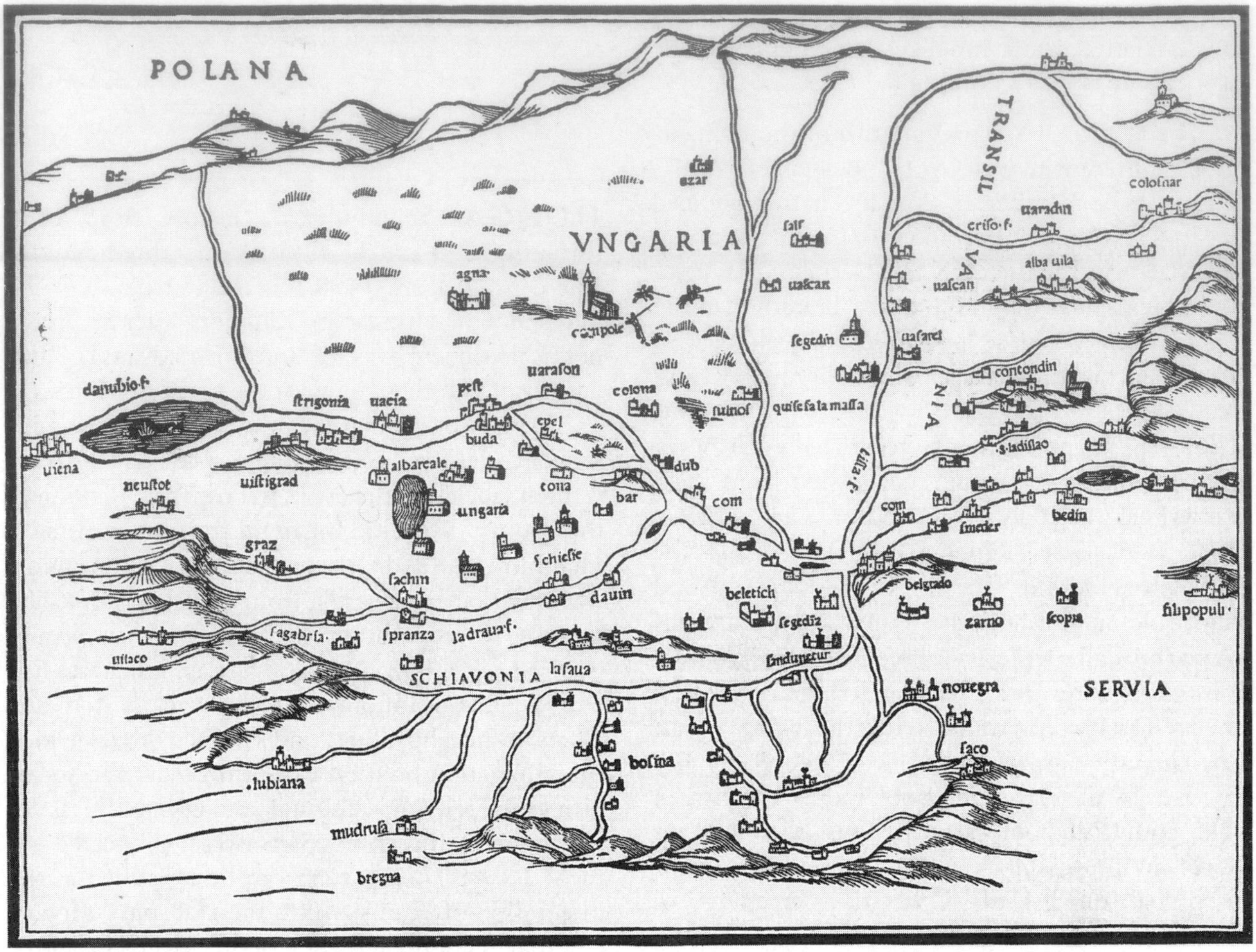

Hungary. A small reproduction of one of the earliest printed maps of Hungary by the Venetian Giovanni Vavassore. It was originally published in 1526, the year that the Hungarians were defeated by the Turks at Mohács, beginning 150 years of Ottoman domination. On the Danube River, which flows through the center of the map, are shown the cities of Buda and Pest. Schiavonia, in the bottom center between the Drava and Sara rivers, is Slovonia. MAP COLLECTION, STERLING MEMORIAL LIBRARY, YALE UNIVERSITY

towns and the lesser nobility, a reformed tax system, a secular bureaucracy, and a mercenary army of thirty thousand strong, King Matthias curtailed the influence of the aristocracy. Although the king strengthened and reorganized the country's southern defenses, vast resources were spent on his wars against Austria and Bohemia in pursuit of a Danubian monarchy, as well as on the king's lavish court and patronage of the arts and sciences.

During the rules of King Matthias's Jagiello successors (1490–1526), the power-hungry nobility strengthened its position vis-à-vis both the crown and the rest of the society. An influential compilation of Hungarian customary law, called the Tripartitum (1514), codified the rights and privileges of the nobility, including the right to resist the king. The book perceived the nobility, whose members supposedly enjoyed equal rights *(una et aedem nobilitas),* as "the mystical body" of the "holy crown" that is, the sole representatives of the "political nation." Following the rebellion of 1514, the nobility subjected the peasants to "eternal servitude." Although the Tripartitum was never promulgated and the decrees of the Diet of 1514 were often suspended, they provided the nobility with a legal framework until 1848 and were largely responsible for Hungary's unhealthy social structure.

The annihilation of the Hungarian army at the battle of Mohács (1526) not only meant the end of the medieval Kingdom of Hungary but also marked the beginning of Habsburg-Ottoman military confrontation in Central Europe. Following the Ottomans' withdrawal from Hungary in 1526, competing factions of the nobility elected two kings, János Szapolyai (John Zapolya, 1526–1540), the royal Hungarian governor (or *vajda*) of Transylvania, and Ferdinand of Habsburg (1526–1564). With Ottoman military assistance, Szapolyai controlled the eastern parts of the country, while Ferdinand ruled the northern and western parts of Hungary. When the death of Szapolyai (1540) upset the military equilibrium between the Habsburgs and Ottomans, Sultan Suleiman I annexed central Hungary to his empire (1541). Hungary's strategically less significant eastern territories were left in the hands of Szapolyai's widow and were soon to become the Principality of Transylvania, an Ottoman vassal state. Throughout the sixteenth and seventeenth centuries, the Habsburgs, who remained on the Hungarian throne until 1918, had to content themselves with northern and western Hungary, known as Royal Hungary.

Although the Ottomans launched multiple campaigns against Hungary and the Habsburgs (1529, 1532, 1541, 1543, 1551–1552, 1566, 1663–1564) and the two empires waged two exhausting wars in Hungary (1593–1606 and 1683–1699), the buffer-zone-turned-country saved Habsburg central Europe from Ottoman conquest. Successive peace treaties (1547, 1568, 1606, and 1664) maintained the tripartite division of the country, which ended only in 1699, when, in the treaty of Karlowitz, the Ottomans ceded most of Hungary and Transylvania to the Habsburgs. The country's unity was only partially restored, however, for Vienna administered Transylvania as a separate imperial territory until 1848.

The price of being the "bastion of Christendom" was the dismemberment of the country and constant warfare along the Muslim-Christian divide with severe economic and social consequences. However, the endurance of Hungarian society and its economy proved to be much stronger than expected. Despite continuous skirmishes and protracted wars, famine, and epidemics, Hungary's population had increased from 3.1 million in the 1490s to 4 million by the early 1680s. In spite of double taxation (Hungarian and Ottoman), many towns in the Great Plain (Alföld) under Ottoman rule profited from the Hungaro-Ottoman condominium and succeeded in strengthening their privileges and self-government. The sixteenth century was the golden age of manorial agriculture and cattle trade. From the 1570s, Hungary exported some eighty thousand to one hundred thousand head of cattle annually to Vienna and to the German and Italian cities through an elaborate chain of cattle keepers and merchants. While defending the border was a major burden on the society, many profited from feeding and supplying imperial armies and Ottoman and Hungarian garrisons.

The tripartite division of the country and the limits of Habsburg authority also fostered the spread of Protestant Reformation. In Transylvania, Catholicism, Lutheranism, Calvinism, and Unitarianism were declared accepted denominations *(recepta religio)* in 1568. In the 1580s, half of Hungary's population was Calvinist, another quarter followed the Augsburg Confession, and the remaining 25 percent belonged to the Unitarian, Catholic, and Orthodox churches.

Angered by Vienna's lukewarm Turkish policy and aggressive Counter-Reformation, Protestant Magyar nobles rebelled repeatedly against the Catholic Habsburgs in the seventeenth century. They were aided by the princes of Transylvania, which, under the able rule of Gábor Bethlen (1613–1629) and György Rákóczi I (1630–1648) flourished economically and culturally. Allied with the Protestant states in the Thirty Years' War (1618–1648), the princes launched several campaigns against the Habsburgs and extended the principality's territories at the expense of Royal Hungary. When the Habsburgs conceded further Hungarian territories to the Ottomans in the treaty of Vasvár in 1664 in spite of the former's victory at St. Gotthard, even the loyal Catholic magnates of Royal Hungary were outraged and many joined the anti-Austrian "magnate conspiracy" of 1670–1671. The severe punishment of the members of the plot and Emperor Leopold's "confessional absolutism" triggered new waves of anti-Habsburg rebellions, of which the most serious was the revolt of Imre Thököly's *kurucs* (a group of Hungarian "national crusaders" or insurgents) in 1681–1683. Thököly's war led to the creation of yet another pro-Ottoman vassal state in Upper Hungary at a critical moment when the Ottomans' failed siege of Vienna (1683)

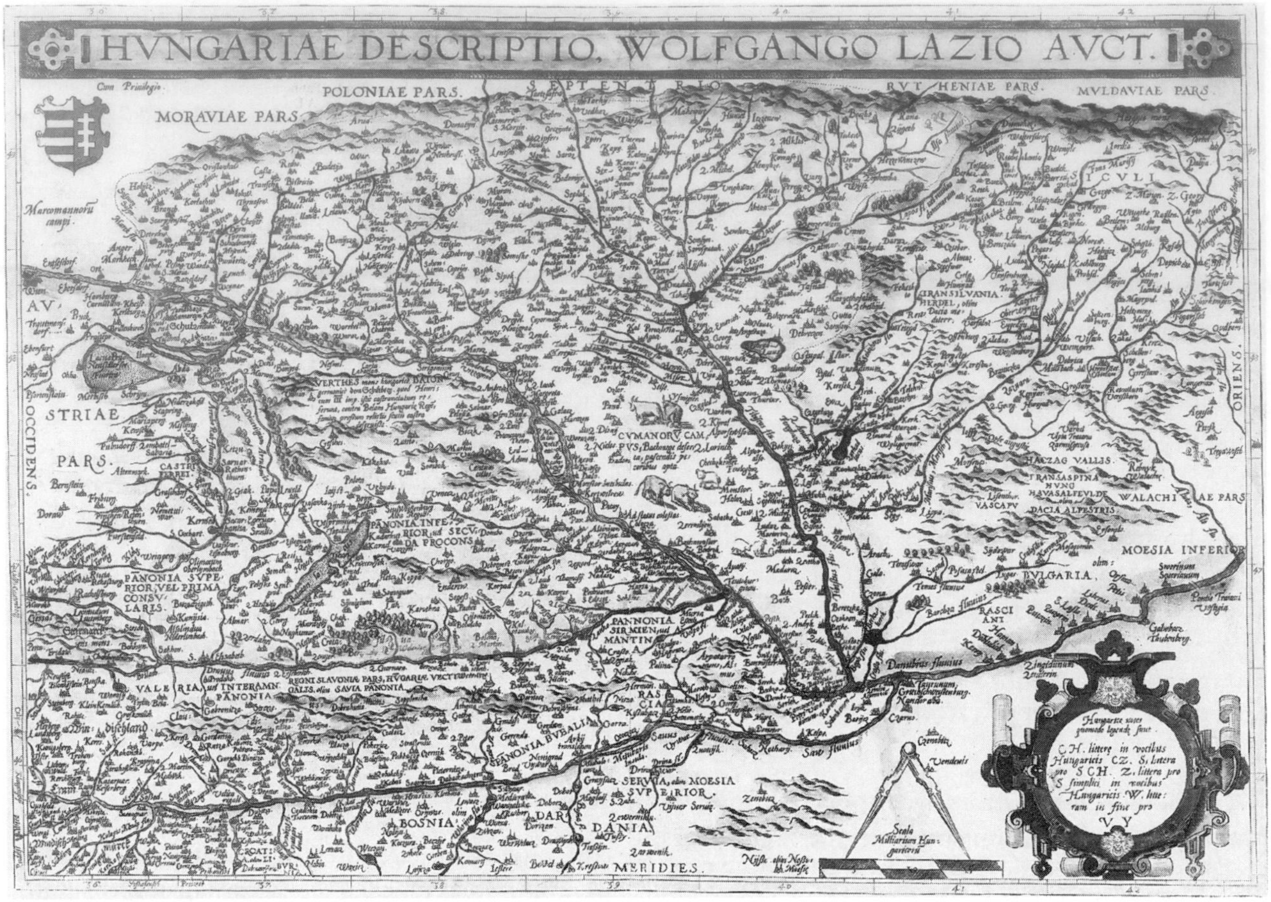

Hungary. Abraham Ortelius's map of Hungary, first issued in his *Theatrum Orbis Terrarum* of 1570, was based on an earlier wall map by Wolfgang Lazius published in Vienna in 1556. MAP COLLECTION, STERLING MEMORIAL LIBRARY, YALE UNIVERSITY

set off an international counteroffensive, which, by the end of the century, had reconquered most of Hungary from the Ottomans.

After 1699, the Habsburgs treated Hungary as a conquered and subjugated province, thus provoking another revolt of the Magyars. The peace treaty of Szatmár (1711), which ended Ferenc Rákóczi's defeated War of Independence (1703–1711), was a wise compromise for both parties. It altered initial Habsburg designs regarding Hungary's incorporation into the monarchy, leaving the county-level administration and jurisdiction in the hands of the Hungarian nobility, which also retained many of its former privileges including tax exemption. On the other hand, Charles VI (Charles III as king of Hungary, 1711–1740) restored Habsburg rule over Hungary, whose Estates recognized his daughter's succession (the Pragmatic Sanction) in the Diet of 1722/23, making Hungary a hereditary Habsburg kingdom.

Within two generations, the population of the country (including Croatia and Transylvania) had doubled, reaching nine million by the late 1780s. This was partly due to voluntary immigration and state-organized settlement policy through which hundreds of thousands of Romanians, Croatians, Slovaks, and Germans arrived in Hungary. This significantly changed the ethnic composition of the country, where the Hungarians lost their absolute majority and comprised less than 40 percent of the inhabitants in the end of the century.

Led by ideas reflecting the Enlightenment and by absolutistic and physiocratic principles, Maria Theresa (ruled 1740–1780) and Joseph II (ruled 1780–1790) initiated important administrative, economic, legal, and cultural reforms, issued as royal patents and carried out by royal commissioners to avoid their blocking by the Estates in the Diet. Many of these reforms were beneficial for Hungary. The Urbarial Patent of 1767 regulated the size of peasant holdings and obligations in order to eliminate inequalities and overtaxation, whereas the *Ratio educationis* of 1777 reformed the educational system. Joseph II's Edict of Tolerance (1781) permitted the "free practice" of religion for all denominations, enabling their members to become guild masters, earn university diplomas in Hungary, and serve in state offices. However, Maria Theresa's discriminatory tariff regulations (1754), which separated Hungary from the rest of the monarchy and its traditional German and Italian markets, negatively affected Hungary, reinforcing the country's agrarian supplier status and hindering the development of domestic industries. Joseph II's decision to replace Latin with German as the official language of administration was perceived as "Germanization" and, along with his patents that abolished Hungary's old administrative structure, infuriated the Estates. By the end of Joseph II's rule, the country, which was feeling overwhelmed by the severe burden of a new Turkish war (1787–1790), was again on the brink of an insurrection. Facing possible armed rebellion in Hungary, growing Prussian pressure, a changing international order because of the French Revolution, and military defeat in his Turkish war, Joseph II decided to appease his Magyar nobility. In January 1790, the emperor revoked all his reforms, except for his Edict of Toleration and his decrees that benefited the peasantry and parishes.

After the compromise in 1711, loyal Hungarian magnates and the Catholic hierarchy were among the richest people in the monarchy. They were also instrumental in the cultural life of the country. The palaces built by the Esterházy, Károlyi, Pálffy, and Festetics families at Fertõd, Erdõd, Királyfalva, and Keszthely respectively are, along with magnificent churches, the best examples of Hungarian baroque. Many of the magnates were not only patrons of the arts and of literature, but were themselves active writers spreading the ideas of Enlightenment, the most radical of which were discussed in the twenty-some lodges of the Freemasons. While the eighteenth century saw spectacular population growth, solid, though uneven, economic development, and cultural revival, it also witnessed the preservation of the country's medieval and anachronistic "constitution" and social structure. All this, along with the radically changed ethnic composition of Hungary, would considerably complicate the country's history in the nineteenth century.

See also **Habsburg Dynasty: Austria; Hungarian Literature and Language; Joseph II (Holy Roman Empire); Maria Theresa (Holy Roman Empire); Ottoman Empire; Rákóczi Revolt; Suleiman I.**

BIBLIOGRAPHY

Balázs, Éva H. *Hungary and the Habsburgs, 1765–1800.* Budapest, 1997.

Ingrao, Charles. *The Habsburg Monarchy, 1618–1815.* Cambridge, 1994.

Köpeczi, Béla, ed. *History of Transylvania.* Budapest, 1994.

Lendvai, Paul. *The Hungarians.* Princeton, 2003.

Sugar, Peter F., et al., eds. *A History of Hungary.* Bloomington, Ind., 1994.

GÁBOR ÁGOSTON

HUNTING. Early modern Europe was a settled agricultural and commercial society. As such, hunting played a secondary or negligible role in supplying the nutritional needs of all but a handful of Europeans. Yet hunting had a symbolic importance in European society out of proportion to its economic importance because it was closely linked to the culture of monarchy. In most of Europe, hunting was a privilege restricted to the nobility. In general, the noble monopoly of hunting derived from seignorial control over the forests in which hunting took place. In some lands, such as England, the king exercised exclusive seignorial jurisdiction over all forests; in other lands, such as France, seignorial jurisdiction over forests came with jurisdiction over the neighboring villages and so could be "owned" by anyone. Such control enabled kings and aristocrats to restrict hunting to a very narrow social stratum. Even some nobles were prevented from participating in the hunt.

Most of the social history of hunting revolves around the justifications for and enforcement of noble monopoly. Non-nobles sometimes chafed at being prevented from hunting for sport, but they were more frequently troubled by the fact that the noble monopoly on hunting for sport prohibited

Hunting. *Hunt in Aranjuez,* seventeenth-century painting by Juan Bautista Mazo. In this formalized Spanish version of the hunt, game is driven into a narrow enclosure to be pursued by members of the royal court. ©ERICH LESSING/ART RESOURCE, N.Y.

commoners from hunting for food or stopping wild animals from damaging their crops. Conflicts over hunting were, therefore, part of a larger negotiation over relations of power between nobles and peasants. The three main types of hunting—hunting vermin, hunting for food, and hunting for sport—touched on different aspects of those relations.

ERADICATING VERMIN

Hunting vermin, animals that posed a threat to crops or livestock, was the least contested area of hunting in the early modern era. Common people were allowed, even encouraged, to destroy vermin and they were eager to do so. The main kinds of vermin hunted in early modern Europe were stoats, otters, foxes, and wolves.

The treatment of wolves is most emblematic of early modern European attitudes toward vermin. Throughout Europe, rulers or their officials offered bounties for wolf hides or other evidence of the destruction of wolves. Criminals were sometimes permitted to pay off fines or debts by supplying wolf pelts. Wolves were to be killed whenever and by whatever means. They were feared not just for the threat they posed to livestock, but also (though with how much justification remains an open question) as a threat to humans. The policy of wolf eradication was very successful in some parts of Europe. Already by 1560, wolves were extinct in England. The last confirmed killing of a wolf in Scotland took place in 1691. Wolves were extinct in Ireland by 1770. On the other hand, wolves continued to survive on the Continent throughout the early modern era.

Initially, foxes were treated in the same manner as wolves. But in the eighteenth century, hunting foxes began to take on the character of sport hunting rather than vermin hunting. Until that time, the prime small game animal for "coursing" had been the hare. Aristocrats discovered that foxes made a very good target for coursing hounds. So, they began to foster the stability of fox populations by building fox shelters and even importing foxes from other regions; thus there was a continuing source of sporting pleasure. It was not until the nineteenth century that foxhunting lost its significance as a means of controlling vermin and became the main sporting pastime of the English aristocracy.

HUNTING FOR FOOD

Game animals played a larger and more diverse role in the diet in the early modern era than they would in later centuries. Wild boar and venison, sometimes killed by the king himself, were a regular feature of royal feasts. Since the royal table could be amply supplied with meats by domesticated animals, these dishes were more important symbolically than nutritionally. For example, Francis I (ruled 1515–1547) of France sent venison pasties (a type of meat pie) from a deer he had personally hunted as a gesture of good will to Henry VIII (ruled 1509–1547) of England. For commoners, there were few restrictions on catching marginally edible fare such as badgers or starlings, but they were usually barred from hunting prime edible game animals such as wild boar and deer. Some resorted to poaching to provide meat for their diet or to sell at market.

Poaching was illegal in early modern Europe, but it was not uncommon. Forest account books show numerous fines for illegal capture or killing of game. In rare cases, poaching was a capital offense, but in most of Europe, the most widespread punishment was a stiff fine. Some cases of poaching were clearly as much symbolic protest acts as efforts to get something to eat. In seventeenth-century England, it was not at all rare for gentry to poach on the lands of their neighbors. Most historians assume that forest officials were often bribed to look the other way. Perhaps the best-known effort to suppress poaching was the Black Act in England in 1724, which, among other things, made deer-stalking in royal forests a capital crime. The numbers of animals taken in the areas affected by the Black Act were small. It is impossible to say how frequently poachers were caught in early modern Europe and, by extension, how important game was for the livelihoods of villagers in the vicinity of forests.

HUNTING FOR SPORT

Hunting explicitly for sport had been a noble, and especially a royal, prerogative since ancient times. It was considered an important test of bravery and skill with arms that would carry over into battle. The early modern era continued practices that had been prevalent in the Middle Ages. Hunting adapted readily to gunpowder weapons, though crossbows and longbows, and even swords or knives, remained common weapons even into the seventeenth century. Though early modern royalty continued to keep falcons as they had in the Middle Ages, the most prominent form of sport hunting in the early modern era was coursing with hounds. The dog became the prized adjunct to the hunt. Hunting literature, such as George Gascoigne's *The Noble Art of Venery and Hunting* (1575), proliferated in the early modern era. Much of it was written for or dedicated to notable royal hunters. Tales of kings or noblemen finishing off an enraged animal that charged the hunters, endangering their lives, became a trope of royal propaganda.

The early modern era was suffused with a casual cruelty toward animals. Hunting for sport partook of some of that same casual cruelty. It was common to round up wild animals, sometimes in large numbers, and herd them to a place where the hunters could easily slaughter them. Contemporary depictions of the hunt often show the hunters standing behind a blind or shooting stand while drivers chased dozens of animals in front of their waiting guns.

Certain creatures were especially prized for their ability to create an exciting chase. The three animals most frequently prized for their coursing were red deer, fallow deer, and hares. For the latter, the sport was primarily to watch the chasing hounds in action. Hares were fast and nimble and so made for an exciting spectacle. The hunter did not shoot the animal, but instead allowed the dogs to tear the animal to pieces once it had been caught. Deer, on the other hand, could be flushed out using hounds, but the object was for the hunter to shoot them. Red deer stags were the most prized target because they combined a noble bearing with an exciting chase. Wild boar were less prized for the chase, but

Hunting. *Hunting Coots and Waterfowl,* painting of the Flemish school, c. 1600–1620. THE ART ARCHIVE/ROSENBORG CASTLE COPENHAGEN/DAGLI ORTI (A)

remained a fit target because they were dangerous when cornered.

The royal or noble hunt was, in part, a performance—a demonstration of mastery over nature as a justification for monarchical authority. Sometimes, the hunt would be a small affair, with the king or nobleman and a few intimates; other times it would be a large public occasion with hundreds of participants and spectators. The hunt encouraged ritual gestures that reinforced the sense that it was an expression of royal majesty. For example, when James I of England (ruled 1603–1625) successfully shot a red deer in an aristocratic hunting party, he would personally slit the throat of the dying animal to begin dressing it; he then would insist that all of the members of the shooting party smear the blood of the animal on their faces. Since the king shed the animal's blood, this gesture brought royal favor to the participants. Though hunting was primarily a masculine activity, women also participated as spectators and hunters. Elizabeth I of England (ruled 1558–1603), for example, hunted avidly. On one occasion her hunt consisted of repeatedly firing a crossbow into a paddock filled with deer, killing three or four of them. The slaughter was accompanied by tunes played by the queen's musicians and a singing nymph who placed the crossbow into her hands.

A literature of forest management arose alongside the literature on the aristocratic virtues of hunting. Royal gamekeepers made sure that royal forests were continuously stocked, just as demesne officials made sure that royal demesnes were planted and harvested. Indeed, sometimes deer had to be imported to maintain population levels. One hundred head were sent from Haughton Forest to Windsor Forest in 1711, for example. In densely populated parts of Europe, game reserves were walled or fenced off to keep game in and poachers out. Palaces served as hunting lodges for the king.

The burdens that fell on peasants who lived in or near forests were connected to forest management. Peasants were usually prohibited from owning hunting dogs of their own. Instead, some were required to board the king's or a nobleman's dogs and make them available whenever the owner wanted to hunt, with only part of the costs defrayed by the owner. Peasants might also be called on to perform *corvée* ('unpaid labor') during the hunt as beaters or carters of slaughtered animals. It was often galling for peasants forced to perform such services to watch as the hunters ran their horses through the fields, destroying the peasants' own crops. There are innumerable supplications seeking to modify the obligations to perform such duties and protect the crops during the hunt. The frequency of such supplications underscores how little they changed hunters' behavior.

In the seventeenth and eighteenth century, there was a small groundswell of antihunting sentiment, primarily amongst religious thinkers. Hunting for sport was considered wasteful, an indulgence in luxury. These criticisms did not merge with the criticisms by peasants of the damage caused to their own crops by the hunt, so there was never any sustained effort to change hunting practice during the era, just a small decline in the numbers of aristocrats who enjoyed the sport. Nevertheless, hunting retained its aristocratic character at the end of the eighteenth century and would only be opened to commoners with the French Revolution.

See also **Aristocracy and Gentry; Class, Status, and Order; Enclosure; Food and Drink; Forests and Woodlands; Games and Play; Sports.**

BIBLIOGRAPHY

Berry, Edward. *Shakespeare and the Hunt: A Cultural and Social Study.* Cambridge, U.K., 2001.

Eckardt, Hans Wilhelm. *Herrschaftliche Jagd, bäuerliche Not und bürgerliche Kritik.* Göttingen, 1976.

Manning, Roger B. *Hunters and Poachers: A Social and Cultural History of Unlawful Hunting in England, 1485–1640.* Oxford and New York, 1993.

Salvadori, Philippe. *La chasse sous l'ancien régime.* Paris, 1996.

Schindler, Norbert. *Wilderer im Zeitalter der französischen Revolution: Ein Kapitel alpiner Sozialgeschichte.* Munich, 2001.

Thompson, E. P. *Whigs and Hunters: The Origin of the Black Act.* New York, 1975.

JOHN THEIBAULT

HUSSITES. The Hussite revolution was a protest movement for sociopolitical freedom and religious reform in fifteenth-century Bohemia. Visible in several manifestations prior to the Thirty Years' War, the term identifies followers of the martyred priest Jan Hus (c. 1372/73–1415), whose distinguishing and unconventional practices involved celebrating the Eucharist in species of both bread and wine.

The instability of the House of Luxembourg in Prague and repeated interference by Sigismund, aspiring Holy Roman emperor, created political uncertainty. Ecclesiastical affairs were no better; the papal schism directly affected Prague, and Czech resentment toward foreign religious domination escalated. Ecclesiastical property included up to fifty percent of Bohemia. Heavy taxation, a declining silver industry, static wages, rising prices, peasant devastation, and an impoverished gentry comprised a host of social and economic grievances. Conflicts between church and state, monarch and barons, and Czechs and Germans exacerbated the climate of discontent. Heretical movements like that of the Waldensians and the teachings of John Wycliffe (c. 1330–1384), combined with native reform movements, heightened the potential for protest and dissent.

HUSSITE BEGINNINGS, VICTORIES, AND DEFEATS

The leading personality was university professor and preacher Jan Hus, who facilitated reform aimed at correcting abuses. Hus exerted unusual influence from his pulpit and wrote prolifically, but ran afoul of the Prague episcopal see, lost favor with the king, and was excommunicated and later accused of heresy. He attended the Council of Constance (1414–1415) hoping for a fair hearing, but was seized and executed. After his death, and the inability of King Wenceslas (Václav) IV (ruled 1378–1419) to govern effectively, university masters and Czech barons assumed political power. A league formed in 1415 to protect Hussite interests. Hussite ideologues led by Jakoubek of Stříbro (d. 1429) and Nicholas of Dresden (d. 1417) inaugurated Utraquism, the practice of Communion using both bread and wine. As Utraquism constituted a rejection of Roman ecclesiastical authority, it was condemned by the Council of Constance. Later, Utraquism included all the baptized, including infants. The chalice became the Hussite symbol. Crisis loomed when radical preachers and their followers engaged in thoroughgoing protests against religious and political establishments.

By 1417 Bohemia faced economic blockade. Prague's archbishop commenced active repression, refusing to ordain Hussite priests while evicting incumbents, but the Hussites struck back. The university ratified Utraquism while dissenters forced a suffragan bishop to perform ordinations. Catholic clerics were ejected and replaced with Hussites. The king undertook a largely ineffectual royal repression. By 1419 a crusade aimed at crushing resistance received papal approbation. The Hussites refused to submit and Reformation became revolution. Radical priest Jan Želivský (d. 1422) incited public demonstrations. Resistance rallies formed on hilltops in rural Bohemia throughout 1419, attended by thousands. In July a mob, led by Želivský, overthrew the Prague civil authorities. The king was forced to accept the Hussite coup, but died within a month.

In 1420 the radical community at Tábor began to contravene religious and social mores: vernacular replaced Latin, liturgical vestments and accessories were abandoned, and preaching and simple eucharistic piety predominated. Simultaneous communal experiments developed: private property was forbidden, taxes abolished, equality proclaimed, and community chests established. Radicals elected their own bishop. Originally pacifists, the Táborites became "warriors of God."

Greatly alarmed, Sigismund marched on Prague, suffering ignominious defeat at the hands of Jan Žižka's (c. 1360–1424) peasant forces. Four subsequent crusades were scattered. Throughout the 1420s the Hussites attempted social and religious reform. Refusing to accept Sigismund as king, they sought a ruler from the Polish-Lithuanian dynasty. The Hussite wars continued, spreading to neighboring regions after Žižka's death. The Four Articles of Prague functioned as a charter, calling for free preaching, Utraquism, divestment of church wealth, and punishment of serious sins. A massive propaganda campaign followed. Radicals advocated seizing property from the wealthy, correcting religious abuses wherever encountered, and promoting "saint" Jan Hus, the chalice, and the law of God. This latter component possessed both theological and social implications.

Forced to negotiate, the Council of Basel (1433) implemented strategic divide-and-conquer policies. When initial talks disintegrated and crisis gripped the Hussite leadership, conservative Utraquist barons colluded with Catholic forces, captured Prague, and forced a confrontation with the radicals in 1434. The Táborites were crushed. Bohemian had outwitted Bohemian in the interests of Rome. Jan Roháč of Dubá (d. 1437) and confederates resisted Sigismund until 1437.

AFTERMATH AND INFLUENCE OF HUSSITISM

Petr Chelčický (c. 1390–c. 1460) a Táborite separatist, summarized Hussitism as a rejection of medieval society with its tripartite divisions. He exerted formative influence on the Unity of Brethren, a group that survived into the seventeenth century. Jan Rokycana (d. 1471) dominated the Utraquist party. The Hussite movement, together with the nobles organized in the Estates, remained the chief force in Bohemia until their disastrous defeat by the Habsburgs at the Battle of White Mountain (1620). Before White Mountain, Bohemian society and politics took the Hussites seriously. The political reality of the fifteenth-century revolution was a strengthened nobility. During the militant period, army captains Žižka and Prokop Holý (c. 1375–1434) exerted enormous political influence, while Tábor's bishop Mikuláš of Pelhimov (d. 1460) provided leadership for three decades. After 1440 two main Hussite groups continued: the Utraquists, who inclined toward Lutheranism after 1520, and the Calvinist Unity of Brethren.

Hussite strength and achievement are measured by the standardization of the Czech language (undertaken by Hus), restoration of lay Communion using both bread and wine, and survival through five imperial crusades. In the process, the Hussites achieved formal recognition by the official church (1433), a triumph of toleration exemplified in the "Peace of Kutná Hora" (1485), a common religious confession (1575), and maintained their uniqueness despite Lutheran and Calvinist Reformations. In 1609 the "Letter of Majesty" was published, recognizing the right of Hussite traditions to exist, and in 1596 the vernacular Bible of Kralice was produced. The Hussites thus reformed their religion before the age of the European Reformations. Their greatest weakness was twofold: a tendency toward internal dissension contributing to a major defeat in 1434, and their proclivity for negotiating with the official church, a stance that prevented full implementation of Hussite doctrine. Their defeat at White Mountain was total. During the Thirty Years' War Bohemia was forcibly re-Catholicized. Hussites were exiled or driven underground. A century later, however, the spiritual descendants of Hussites emerged: the Moravian Brethren, who persist to the present day. It cannot be maintained that Hussite ideals survived, except in very limited ways in small communities in eastern Moravia.

The Hussite ethos lasted two hundred years, shaping the Bohemian nation. Its influence on movements within the Protestant Reformation was considerable. Hussites were the first to produce a full-fledged reformation from a movement of heresy and protest, and in this way altered European civilization.

See also **Bohemia; Prague; Reformation, Protestant; Schmalkaldic War (1546–1547); Thirty Years' War (1618–1648).**

BIBLIOGRAPHY

Primary Source

Fudge, Thomas A. *The Crusade against Heretics in Bohemia, 1418–1437: Sources and Documents for the Hussite Crusades.* Aldershot, U.K., 2002. Over 200 documents illustrating the radical period.

Secondary Sources

Bartoš, František Michálek. *The Hussite Revolution, 1424–1437.* Edited by John Klassen, translated by J. Weir. New York, 1986. Translation of *Husitská revoluce.* Study by a leading Czech scholar.

David, Zdeněk V. *Finding the Middle Way: The Utraquists' Liberal Challenge to Rome and Luther.* Baltimore, 2003. Definitive study of the Hussite tradition during the Reformation.

Fudge, Thomas A. *The Magnificent Ride: The First Reformation in Hussite Bohemia.* Aldershot, U.K., 1998. Emphasis on heresy, propaganda, and theological motifs up to 1437.

Heymann, Frederick G. *George of Bohemia: King of Heretics.* Princeton, 1965. Political history of the movement up to the 1470s.

———. *John Žižka and the Hussite Revolution.* New York, 1969. Fully documented with 11 sources appended.

Holeton, David R., and Zdeněk V. David, eds. *The Bohemian Reformation and Religious Practice.* 5 vols. Prague, 1996–2004. Wide-ranging collection of essays by international scholars of Hussitism.

Kaminsky, Howard. *A History of the Hussite Revolution.* Berkeley, 1967. The definitive study; history-of-ideas approach that stops at 1424.

Klassen, John M. *The Nobility and the Making of the Hussite Revolution.* New York, 1978. Insightful perspective with emphasis on the barons and political aspects of the movement.

Odložilík, Otakar. *The Hussite King: Bohemia in European Affairs 1440–1471.* New Brunswick, N.J., 1965. Contextual study of Hussite Bohemia with emphasis on politics.

Říčan, Rudolf. *The History of the Unity of Brethren.* Translated by C. Daniel Crews. Bethlehem, Pa., 1992. Translation of a Czech work and essential for understanding the larger dimensions of the Hussites up to the 1620s.

Šmahel, František. "The Idea of the 'Nation' in Hussite Bohemia." Translated by R. F. Samsour. *Historica* 16 (1969): 143–247 and 17 (1970): 93–197. Vigorous assessment of ideological and political aspects of national identity.

Wagner, Murray L. *Petr Chelčický: A Radical Separatist in Hussite Bohemia.* Scottdale, Pa., 1983. Excellent monograph emphasizing radical theology and political thought.

THOMAS A. FUDGE

HUYGENS FAMILY. Influential in Dutch politics and culture, the Huygens family served the House of Orange, and thus, its political fortunes rose and fell with those of its patrons. Christiaan the Elder (1551–1624) served William of Orange (William the Silent; 1533–1584) until the latter's assassination, at which point he became secretary to the Council of State that oversaw the newly formed United Provinces of the Netherlands. His firstborn, Maurits (1595–1642), was secretary to William's successor, Maurits (1567–1625), and then the council; his second son, Constantijn (1596–1687), was secretary to Maurits's younger brother Frederik Hendrik (1584–1647), then the latter's son William II (1626–1650), and finally to the council. During the 1640s, as the princes of Orange consolidated power in the United Provinces, Constantijn enjoyed immense authority and accumulated the lands and monies that go with such a relationship. Conversely, during the minority of William III (1650–1702), with the government controlled by the Republicans and the Orangists in disarray, Constantijn concentrated on the young prince's education and made sure that his eldest son, Constantijn, Jr. (1627–1697), eventually became William's secretary. When a grown William regained power during war with France (1672) and moved to England to share the throne (1689), Constantijn, Jr., followed. Because William III had no brothers, Constantijn's younger sons had no parallel patrons to serve, even though their father had trained them for civil service. Indeed, the youngest, Philips (1633–1657), died while on a diplomatic mission. The third son, Lodewijk (1631–1699), did remain in politics, serving in minor positions and embarrassing the family in a bribery scandal. Constantijn's second son, Christiaan (1629–1695), made early contact with the scientific communities on both sides of the English Channel while traveling as a diplomatic clerk, even being elected the first foreign member of the Royal Society of London during one such trip in 1663. In 1666 Christiaan abandoned the family profession to follow his natural talent as a scientist, going to Paris to lead the newly formed Académie Royale des Sciences of Louis XIV (ruled 1643–1715).

Constantijn Huygens, poet, musician, and patron, lived a full life outside of politics. Tutored at home in languages, music, mathematics, and logic, he spent 1616–1617 studying law at Leiden before setting off as clerk in the diplomatic missions that would foster his career. Repeated visits to England (in 1622 he was even knighted) broadened his early training by exposing him to the experimental science of Francis Bacon (1561–1626) and Cornelius Drebbel (1572–1633). Enamored of John Donne's (1572–1631) poetry, he translated nineteen poems into Dutch even before they had been published in English. Today Constantijn is primarily remembered as one of the leading poets of the Dutch Golden Age, who contributed to the growth of the Dutch language through his verses, such as those included in the collection he called his "cornflowers" (*Korenbloemen,* 1658). His works range from birthday poems to a comic play (*Trijntje Cornelis,* 1653) to epic autobiographies (*Daghwerck* [1638; A day's work], and *De Vita Propria Sermonum inter Liberos Libri Duo* [1678]). He was a member of the Muiden Circle that gathered around the great Dutch poet and historian Pieter Corneliszoon Hooft (1581–1647), discussing literature and setting style. A noted composer (only his *Pathodia Sacra et Profana* survive) and musician, Constantijn argued for the reintroduction of the organ into the Reformed Church. He befriended René Descartes (1596–1650) when the philosopher settled in Holland during the 1640s, and the two seem to have formed a mutual admiration society. As the arbiter of court patronage, he encouraged the artistic careers of Rembrandt van Rijn (1606–1669) and Jan Lievens (1607–1674). Throughout his life he maintained a dilettante's interest in science, particularly the work of his son.

Christiaan Huygens, mathematician, physicist, astronomer, and inventor, was one of the leading scientists of the seventeenth century, most particularly as a founder of the field of applied mathematics. Educated at home, he demonstrated his analytical prowess early on by extending results in classical mathematics, particularly the work of Archimedes, including developing an improved method for determining pi. At the University of Leiden, he studied with Frans van Schooten (c. 1615–1660) and contributed to the latter's *Geometria,* a codification of Descartes's mathematics. He accepted the basic principles of Cartesian physics throughout his life but was frequently at odds with the particulars. Thus, he always believed that mechanical theory must be rooted in explanations involving matter in relative motion, but his first major study on moving bodies disproved Descartes's fundamental rules for collisions. Likewise, he opposed the Cartesian explanation of refraction and of the speed of light. On the other hand, he continued to seek a vortex explanation of gravity, even after Isaac Newton (1642–1727) had undermined Descartes's theory in the *Principia*. He never achieved his own unified mathematical system of the world, even though he had written many treatises that mathematically analyzed physical problems. Thus, when he invented the first accurate pendulum clock and developed an improved version that made the bob follow a cycloidal path, his description of the successor is wrapped in an elegant theory of curves called evolutes that proved why it was theoretically precise (*Horologium Oscillatorium,* 1673). Likewise, when he developed his wave theory of light, its justification was a mathematical extension of evolutes to the phenomenon of double refraction, including his assertion, now called the Huygens Principle, that a wave front is the curve (envelope) that is tangent to all the secondary waves emanating pointwise from along the previous front (*Traité de la lumière* [1690; Treatise on light]). But, although he discovered Saturn's largest moon, Titan (1658), and explained that Saturn's odd appearance could be accounted for by a ring (*Systema Saturnium* [1659; The system of Saturn]), he never mathematically extended this early work to an analysis of planetary systems, even though he worked extensively on the problem of circular motion. He wrote a treatise on expectations in probability, contributed to the discussions that led to the calculus, designed telescopes and ground their lenses with his older brother, and participated in the development of the air pump, spiral spring watch, and microscope. Unfortunately, many important works only appeared posthumously, including a massive treatise on the refraction of light through lenses (*Dioptrica,* 1703), and a popularization of cosmology written for his older brother in which he speculated on the possibility of extraterrestrial life. Without publications to assert his priority, his influence depended on his correspondence network, and much of what he accomplished was unwittingly redone by others. Nevertheless, both Newton and Gottfried Wilhelm Leibniz (1646–1716) considered him the most important precursor of their own work in physics and mathematics.

See also **Academies, Learned; Astronomy; Bacon, Francis; Clocks and Watches; Cosmology; Descartes, René; Donne, John; Dutch Literature and Language; Dutch Republic; Leibniz, Gottfried Wilhelm; Mathematics; Newton, Isaac; Optics; Physics; Rembrandt van Rijn; Scientific Instruments; Scientific Method; Scientific Revolution; Technology.**

BIBLIOGRAPHY

Primary Sources

Huygens, Christiaan. *The Celestial Worlds Discover'd.* Translated by Timothy Childe, 1698. Reprint, London, 1968. Translation of *Cosmotheōros* (1698).

———. *Oeuvres complètes de Christiaan Huygens.* 22 vols. Edited by a committee of Dutch scholars. The Hague, 1888–1950.

———. *The Pendulum Clock or Geometrical Demonstrations Concerning the Motion of Pendula as Applied to Clocks.* Translated by Richard J. Blackwell. Ames, Ia., 1986. Translation of *Horologium Oscillatorium* (1673).

Huygens, Constantijn. *De gedichten van Constantijn Huygens.* 9 vols. Edited by J. A. Worp. Groningen, Netherlands, 1892–1899.

———. *A Selection of the Poems of Sir Constantijn Huygens (1596–1687).* Translated by Peter Davidson and Adriaan van der Weel. Amsterdam, 1996.

Secondary Sources

Bos, H. J. M., et al. *Studies on Christiaan Huygens: Invited Papers from the Symposium on the Life and Work of Christiaan Huygens.* Amsterdam, 22–25 August 1979. Lisse, Netherlands, 1980.

Colie, Rosalie L. *"Some Thankfulnesse to Constantine": A Study of English Influence upon the Early Works of Constantijn Huygens.* The Hague, 1956.

Daley, Koos. *The Triple Fool: A Critical Evaluation of Constantijn Huygens' Translations of John Donne.* Nieuwkoop, Netherlands, 1990.

Yoder, Joella G. *Unrolling Time: Christiaan Huygens and the Mathematization of Nature.* Cambridge, U.K., and New York, 1988.

JOELLA G. YODER

HYMNS. Hymns, original religious poems intended for singing in public or private, were very widely known and used in early modern Europe. As well as embodying communal religious feeling across class barriers, they were the sole form of musical expression in many a devout family and institution.

THE LATIN HYMN

The familiar metrical form in several stanzas is credited to St. Ambrose (c. 340–397). Medieval hymns were sung by priest and choir at mass or office. Their plainsong tunes, repeated with each stanza, later became the basis of polyphonic compositions in several vocal parts. In the sixteenth century and after, many composers published hymn settings. Instruments were generally added after 1600: an outstanding example is "Ave maris stella" (Hail, star of the sea) from Claudio Monteverdi's *Vespers* (1610).

THE LUTHERAN HYMN

A key aspect of Martin Luther's theology was the praise of God with understanding, and (following Jan Hus) he promoted a kind of singing in worship that could be understood, and if possible, joined by the congregation. The texts must be in the vernacular and in simple diction; the tunes were often adapted folk songs, or were composed in a popular style by Luther himself or by one of the skilled musicians among his followers. In hymns like "Ein' feste Burg ist unser Gott" (A mighty fortress is our God) Luther literally planted the Christian message, as he saw it, in the people's mouths and hearts. Many of his hymns ("chorales"), and those of a distinguished line of successors including Philipp Nicolai (1556–1608) and Paul Gerhardt (1607–1676), have been in continuous use, firmly wedded to their early tunes. Like their medieval precursors, they were used as a basis for more elaborate compositions by such men as Michael Praetorius (1571–1621) and Samuel Scheidt (1587–1654). Above all, Johann Sebastian Bach (1685–1750) displayed a seemingly inexhaustible creativity in the treatment of hymn melodies in his organ chorales (often misnamed "chorale preludes"), fantasias, cantatas, and passions.

THE ENGLISH HYMN

Because of the predominantly Calvinist theology of the early Church of England, hymns of "human composure" had to give way to metrical paraphrases of the psalms in Anglican worship. Thomas Sternhold and John Hopkins's *The Whole Booke of Psalmes* (London, 1562) did, however, include a few anonymous hymns in an appendix, nominally for domestic use, and there is evidence that the pre-Reformation custom of the communion hymn survived in Anglican worship. The now widely sung hymns of George Herbert (1593–1633) and Thomas Ken (1637–1711) were intended for private use only, or even for silent reading. Hymns in worship were championed by the Independent Isaac Watts (1674–1748), and by the founder of Methodism, John Wesley, whose brother Charles (1707–1788) has a claim to be the greatest hymn writer in the English language. These leaders championed a vigorous, heartfelt singing by women as well as men, which was in striking contrast to the then-current Anglican mode of singing. The Wesleys adapted tunes from any available source, including theater pieces, concert music, and folk song.

See also **Church of England; Luther, Martin; Lutheranism; Methodism; Wesley Family.**

BIBLIOGRAPHY

Anderson, Warren, et al. "Hymn." In *The New Grove Dictionary of Music and Musicians,* edited by Stanley Sadie, 29 vols. 2nd ed. London, 2001, vol. 12, pp. 17–35.

Benson, Louis F. *The English Hymn: Its Development and Use in Worship.* Richmond, Va., and London, 1915.

NICHOLAS TEMPERLEY

I

IDEALISM. As a philosophical concept, idealism can be employed both in a broad sense and in a much narrower, more specific form. Broadly speaking, idealism encompasses any philosophy that treats ideas—rather than, for example, matter—as primary. Plato's theory of forms is perhaps the first example of this approach. When applied more specifically, idealism is the notion that the only things that exist are minds and their contents (ideas). This theory was first fully developed by Bishop George Berkeley (1685–1753).

Plato drew a clear distinction between the sensory world and the intelligible world, which we can only apprehend through reason. He argued that the objects of the sensory world are mere copies of universal, ideal "forms," that make up the realm of what is intelligible. Plato's theory was subsequently taken up and developed by the Neoplatonists, especially Plotinus and St. Augustine. To some extent, Berkeley's idealism built on these earlier theories, but it also drew on and challenged scientific understandings of the world that had been developed during the sixteenth and seventeenth centuries. Berkeley set out his philosophy in his *Treatise concerning the Principles of Human Knowledge* (1710). Three years later he published his *Three Dialogues between Hylas and Philonous,* a more accessible version of the theory, in which Philonous ('lover of mind') convinces and converts Hylas ('matter') to his point of view. Both works were, in part, a response to John Locke's (1632–1704) *Essay concerning Human Understanding* (1689). Locke's explanation of the world relied on four key elements, God, matter, ideas, and minds. While Berkeley expressed great respect for Locke, he rejected the doctrine of matter that Locke, along with many others, accepted. According to Berkeley matter in itself is unintelligible; it is impossible for us to either observe or imagine matter alone, devoid of all other qualities or characteristics. Moreover, Berkeley argued that an adequate explanation of the world could be given on the basis of the other three elements alone, in Berkeley's terminology God, finite spirits, and their ideas. Berkeley defined "ideas" as the objects of perception and "spirits" as the entities that exercise perception. Within this system the existence of an infinite spirit, God, which is both omniscient and omnipresent, is crucial.

Berkeley's theory had a mixed reception. The story is that Samuel Johnson (1709–1784) claimed to be able to refute it simply by kicking a stone, but others took it more seriously. There has been much discussion as to whether (and to what extent) Berkeley influenced Immanuel Kant (1724–1804). In his *Kritik der reinen Vernunft* (1781; Critique of pure reason) Kant attacked Berkeley's traditional version of idealism and advocated a combination of "empirical realism" and "transcendental idealism." Both philosophers saw all experience as mind-dependent. However, for Berkeley there was nothing beyond or outside of mind, whereas Kant retained the regulative idea of "things-in-themselves" lying behind experience.

Idealism continued to be important beyond the early modern period. During the nineteenth century the ideas of Berkeley and especially of Kant provided a basis for the absolute idealism of Johann Gottlieb Fichte (1764–1814) and Georg Wilhelm Friedrich Hegel (1770–1831). Despite a subsequent collapse in the influence of this position, idealism continues to be advocated into the twenty-first century, though usually in forms that are closer to Kant than to Berkeley.

See also **Berkeley, George; Kant, Immanuel; Philosophy.**

BIBLIOGRAPHY

Primary Sources

Berkeley, George. *Principles of Human Knowledge and Three Dialogues.* Edited by Howard Robinson. Oxford and New York, 1996.

Kant, Immanuel. *Critique of Pure Reason.* Translated and edited by Paul Guyer and Allen W. Wood. Cambridge, U.K., and New York, 1998. Translation of *Kritik der reinen Vernunft* (1781).

Secondary Sources

Urmson, J. O. *Berkeley.* Oxford and New York, 1982.

Vesey, Godfrey, ed. *Idealism Past and Present.* Cambridge, U.K., and New York, 1982. See especially the foreword and the first three chapters.

RACHEL HAMMERSLEY

IGNATIUS OF LOYOLA (1491–1556), Spanish religious leader. Founder of the Society of Jesus, known as the Jesuits, Ignatius of Loyola was born Iñigo de Oñaz y Loyola in 1491 in Azpeitia in the Basque province of Guipúzcoa in northeastern Spain. He was the youngest of thirteen children in a family of lesser nobility but not lacking in social contacts or high prestige. Ignatius's father, just before his death, situated his youngest son in the household of Juan Velázquez de Cuéllar, the chief treasurer of King Ferdinand (1452–1516) and Queen Isabella (1451–1504). There young Ignatius learned courtly manners and sophistication, skills that served him well throughout his life. King Ferdinand's death brought about the downfall of Ignatius's patron, and through friends and family Ignatius received a position with the duke of Nájera, don Antonio Manrique de Lara.

Ignatius's life at either of these courts could not be held up as an example of Christian virtue. In May 1521 the simmering conflict between King Francis I (1491–1547) of France and King Charles I (1500–1558) of Spain erupted when the French forces attacked Pamplona. While Ignatius was defending the city against the French siege, a cannonball struck him in the leg. The French victors assured transport of the wounded man back to his family's castle. During his convalescence, Ignatius requested books on chivalry, particularly those with the character of Amadis of Gaul. Instead his sister-in-law gave him two works, *Life of Christ,* authored by Ludolph of Saxony and translated by Ambrosio Montesino, and a Spanish version of *Lives of the Saints* by Jacobus de Voragine (Jacopo de Varazze) translated by Gauberto María Vagad. Contemplating these books, Ignatius underwent a conversion, rejected his past, and chose to live as a hermit in Jerusalem.

On his way to Jerusalem, Ignatius visited Montserrat, a Marian shrine near Barcelona managed by the Benedictines; he then spent just over a year in the nearby village of Manresa (April 1522 to February 1523). There he created the framework of the *Spiritual Exercises.* In the *Exercises,* Ignatius presented various methods by which a person could move systematically through the three traditional steps of spiritual growth: purgation, illumination, and union with God. Although completed in substance in Manresa, the work took on additional features until its final form received papal approval in 1548. Leaving Manresa, Ignatius arrived in Jerusalem in September 1523, but his plans to stay were thwarted by the Franciscan custodians, who wisely perceived such a strong-willed pilgrim as a liability.

Returning to Barcelona in 1524, Ignatius set his course on a new project. Changing his desire to live as a spiritual recluse, he discerned his vocation as "helping souls." This conversion grew from religious fervor and not from a specific desire to defeat Protestantism, and therefore he stands with other Catholic reformers of the early sixteenth century. To help souls he realized he needed a formal education, and for the first time he took up a serious study of Latin, the necessary tool for academic progress. After two years of study in Barcelona, his teachers recommended he continue at the new university at Alcalá, near Madrid. Arriving at the university in March 1526, he took courses in an indiscriminate fashion. He experienced discouraging attempts to study at Alcalá and later in Salamanca, but at both locations he was imprisoned in 1527 under the suspicion of the Inquisition. Ignatius continued his education in a more methodological way at the University of Paris, where he earned both his licentiate and a master's in philosophy between 1528 and 1535. The name "Ignatius" is inscribed in the school's role for 1534, and from this time forward, with few exceptions, he referred to himself as Ignatius, giving up the "Iñigo" of his early years.

In Paris, Ignatius gathered six men who together decided upon lives of poverty and chastity. They also desired to make a pilgrimage to the Holy Land and there decide their futures. If such a trip were impossible, they would make themselves available to the Roman pontiff. The trip proved impossible, and the group, wishing to remain together, formed a religious order that received the oral approval of Pope Paul III (1468–1549) in 1539 and written approval in 1540. Elected as the order's first superior general in 1541, Ignatius witnessed its growth from a few men to one thousand members at his death on 31 July 1556. He supervised the creation of thirty-three schools, wrote the order's constitutions, and governed the ever-expanding Society of Jesus in South America, Africa, Europe, and Asia. Successfully grafting humanism, Catholic reform, and the missionary opportunities created by the New World economies onto medieval Europe's religious and philosophical heritage, Ignatius was one of the principal forces behind the transition from the medieval church to early modern Catholicism.

See also **Ferdinand of Aragón; Isabella of Castile; Jesuits; Missions and Missionaries; Religious Orders.**

Ignatius of Loyola. Portrait by Peter Paul Rubens.
©BETTMANN/CORBIS

BIBLIOGRAPHY

Primary Sources

Saint Ignatius of Loyola. *Constitutions of the Society of Jesus.* Edited and translated by George E. Ganss. St. Louis, 1970.

———. *Ignatius of Loyola: The Spiritual Exercises and Selected Works.* Edited by George E. Ganss. New York, 1991. This edition includes the full text of the *Spiritual Exercises,* the *Autobiography of Ignatius,* selected letters, and parts of the constitutions.

———. *Letters of Saint Ignatius of Loyola.* Selected and translated by William Young. Chicago, 1959.

———. *Letters to Women.* Collected by Hugo Rahner. New York, 1960.

Monumenta Ignatiana. Exercitia spiritualia Sancti Ignatii de Loyola et eorum directoria. 2nd ed. rev., 2 vols. Monumenta Historica Societatis Iesu (MHSI). Madrid, 1919; Rome, 1969. The Institutum Historicum Societatis Iesu, formerly in Madrid and now in Rome, has edited the early documents of the Society of Jesus. These scholarly editions appear as a series with various contents or themes in the Monumenta Historica Societatis Iesu (MHSI).

Monumenta Ignatiana. Fontes documentales de Sancti Ignatio de Loyola. Monumenta Historica Societatis Iesu (MHSI). Rome, 1977.

Monumenta Ignatiana. Sancti Ignatii de Loyola Constitutiones Societatis Jesu. 3 vols. Monumenta Historica Societatis Iesu (MHSI). Rome, 1934–1938.

Monumenta Ignatiana. Sancti Ignatii de Loyola Societatis Jesu fundatoris epistolae et instructiones. Monumenta Historica Societatis Iesu (MHSI). Madrid, 1903–1911.

Monumenta Ignatiana. Scripta de Sancto Ignatio de Loyola, Societas Jesu fundatore. 2 vols. Monumenta Historica Societatis Iesu (MHSI). Madrid, 1904–1918.

Polgár, László. *Bibliographie sur l'histoire de la Compagnie de Jésus, 1901–1980.* 3 vols. Rome, 1981–1990. The most extensive bibliography dealing with Ignatius.

Secondary Sources

De Dalmases, Cándido. *Ignatius of Loyola: Founder of the Jesuits.* Translated by Jerome Aixalá. St. Louis, 1985.

Ganss, George E. *Saint Ignatius' Idea of a Jesuit University.* Milwaukee, 1954.

O'Malley, John W. *The First Jesuits.* Cambridge, Mass., 1993.

Ravier, André. *Ignatius of Loyola and the Founding of the Society of Jesus.* Translated by Maura Daly, Joan Daly, and Carson Daly. San Francisco, 1987.

Tellechea Idígoras, José Ignacio. *Ignatius of Loyola: The Pilgrim Saint.* Edited and translated by Cornelius Michael Buckley. Chicago, 1994.

MICHAEL W. MAHER

IMPERIAL CITIES. *See* **Free and Imperial Cities.**

IMPERIAL EXPANSION, RUSSIA. The transformation of the tiny principality of Moscow into a Eurasian empire took place over several centuries, but by the end of the seventeenth century Russia had become the largest country in the world. No single motivation ("urge to the sea," fear of foreign invasion or domination, control of trade routes, unbridled expansionism) explains all Russian territorial acquisitions in the early modern period, and the process is best viewed as a series of ad hoc decisions, opportunities, and actions. Recent commentators have concluded that no messianic ("theory of the Third Rome") or programmatic (the spurious "testament of Peter I") texts guided Russian expansion.

Between the thirteenth and fifteenth centuries, the Grand Principality of Moscow (called Muscovy by European observers) expanded primarily at the expense of other Rus' principalities by conquering, inheriting, purchasing, and annexing the lands of other Rurikid princes. The rise of Moscow was marked by cooperation with Tatars rather than struggle against them. Monasteries (which doubled as forts and centers of economic activity) played a considerable role in advancing Russian settlement into areas originally inhabited by Finno-Ugric peoples.

The conquests of Novgorod (1478) and Kazan' (1552) were central to the course of Russian expansion. While the former signified Moscow's triumph over the other Rus' principalities, the latter solidified its position vis-à-vis the Chingissid successor states and the steppe. In both cases Russian diplomats advanced historic claims to neighboring territories, but strong economic interests and rivalries over trade routes played key roles. Conquest was preceded by decades of diplomatic maneuvering, Muscovite intervention, and struggles between factions within those political structures. Novgorod gave Muscovy a trading emporium in proximity to the Baltic basin and control over vast northern hinterlands. The conquest of Kazan' facilitated an advance into the middle and lower Volga regions, the North Caucasus, and Siberia. In both cases lands were confiscated and redistributed to Muscovite military men, but this was a policy of selective, rather than wholesale, displacement of traditional elites.

In the sixteenth through eighteenth centuries the principal methods of state expansion included military conquest, frontier settlement, and expansion into territories not under effective jurisdiction by other states, and alliances and diplomatic deals with local ruling elites, who became clients or subjects of Russia. Throughout the early modern period, decisions about western strategy had to be carefully correlated with developments in the south to avoid coordinated actions by Russia's rivals. Along its open southern and eastern frontiers the Russian state pursued a strategy of annexing lands, building settlements, constructing fortified lines to impede nomadic attacks, and concluding flexible alliances with groups in the outer zones of the frontier (Cossacks and/or pastoralist groups such as the Nogays, Kalmyks, etc.) to further interests in the steppe. Fortified lines expanded steadily into the steppe, Siberia, and the Northern Caucasus from the second half of the sixteenth century to the mid-eighteenth. They incorporated forts, wooden and earthen ramparts, ditches, watchtowers, and steppe patrols.

The conquest of Siberia (1581–1649) was clearly one of the largest, swiftest, and most durable imperial conquests in global history. After establish-

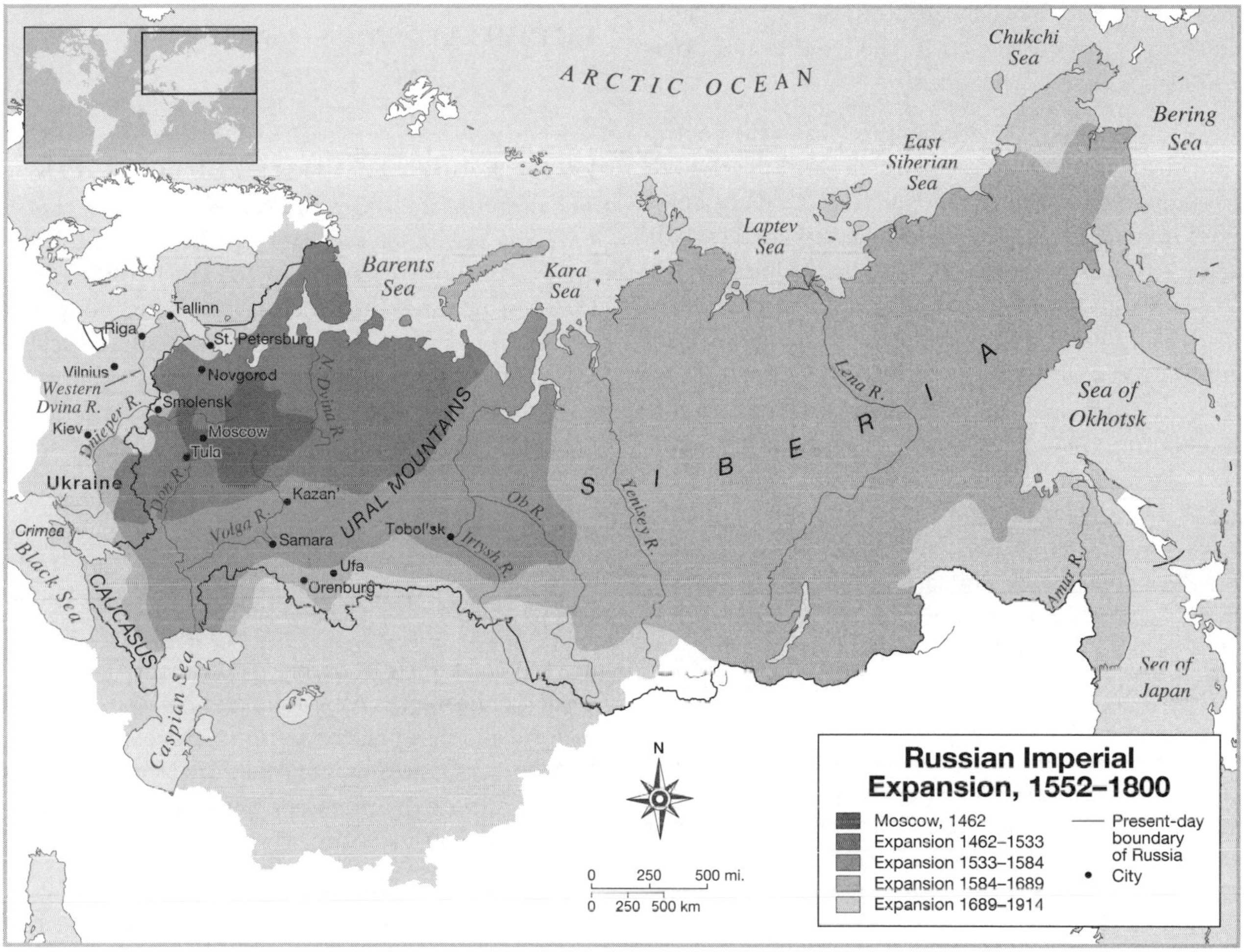

ing themselves in Western Siberia, Cossacks and government forces advanced along the course of major river systems (Ob-Irtysh by 1605, Yenisey by 1628, Lena by 1640, and Amur in the 1640s) until all of Siberia was under Russian control. By 1689, in spite of the fact that Russia maintained only a few thousand armed men in eastern Siberia, the Chinese state recognized the bulk of Russia's eastern conquests in the Treaty of Nerchinsk.

In the west, protracted wars and treaty negotiations defined the process of Russian expansion. In contrast to other expansion into other regions, western expansion primarily involved the introduction of Russian garrisons, administrators, and merchants to towns in the Baltic region and Dnieper basin, but it did not result in the migration of Russian agriculturalists. Struggles over adjacent lands served as a constant source of cross-border conflict between Moscow and its western neighbors. Traditional rivalries with Sweden and the Polish-Lithuanian Commonwealth escalated into a major international conflict when Russia attempted to contest control of the Baltic coast during the Livonian Wars (1558–1583). The conflict failed to give Russia a foothold on the Baltic, and during the Time of Troubles (1603–1613) Polish and Swedish borders expanded at the expense of Russia. The alliance between Tsar Alexis Mikhailovich and Bohdan Khmelnytsky in 1654 initiated a long struggle for domination of Ukraine that raged intermittently until the partitions of Poland in the late eighteenth century. As a result of its deepening military commitments in Ukraine, Russia abandoned its longstanding policy of friendship toward the Ottoman Empire and concluded its first anti-Ottoman alliance (1667). During the Great Northern War (1700–1721) Tsar Peter I established a permanent Russian presence on the Baltic coast and succeeded in annexing much of modern-day Latvia and Estonia. In a series of agreements negotiated between local elites and Russian administrators, the Baltic Germans were confirmed in their rights and privileges over local populations.

Outside the predominantly Russian central provinces of the empire (in which serfdom, the old Muscovite service class, and the Law Code of 1649 predominated) a mosaic of local arrangements characterized Russian rule. While the peoples of the Volga region were incorporated into the Russian landholding and legal systems, several regions were administered under separate deals with the tsar and retained their own legal traditions and considerable local autonomy: the Hetmanate (Ukraine), the Baltic Provinces, and the Cossack Hosts. Siberian peoples came under differing levels of government control: groups such as the Yakuts came under intense pressure to convert and acculturate while groups living in the far north continued their traditional ways and sporadically provided tribute. Russian rulers claimed sovereignty over certain peoples of the North Caucasus, but the state had little effective authority over the region in the early modern period. Nomadic groups in the steppe often received subsidies and provided occasional services to the tsar but were not under direct control. Although conversion to Orthodoxy was encouraged, few resources were actively committed to the goal of Christianization. Orthodox Christians were prohibited from converting to other religions. Although the term *Rus'* continued to be employed to refer to the Orthodox heartland of the empire, in the seventeenth century the term *Rossiia* (Russia) was increasingly employed to designate the diverse territories under Romanov jurisdiction.

See also **Andrusovo, Truce of (1667); Black Sea Steppe; Cossacks; Fur Trade: Russia; Khmelnytsky, Bohdan; Livonian War (1558–1583); Northern Wars; Russia; Time of Troubles (Russia); Ukraine.**

BIBLIOGRAPHY

Kappeler, Andreas. *The Russian Empire: A Multiethnic History.* Translated by Alfred Layton. Harlow, U.K., 2001.

Liubavskii, Matvei Kuz'mich. *Obzor istorii russkoi kolonizatsii s drevneishikh vremen i do XX veka.* Moscow, 1996.

Rieber, Alfred J. "Persistent Factors in Russian Foreign Policy: An Interpretive Essay." In *Imperial Russian Foreign Policy.* Edited by Hugh Ragsdale. Cambridge, U.K., and New York, 1993.

BRIAN BOECK

IMPERIALISM. *See* **Colonialism.**

INDEX OF PROHIBITED BOOKS.

The origin of the Index of Prohibited Books *(Index librorum prohibitorum)* dates to the 1520s, following Martin Luther's revolt in 1517, when the printing press became the principal means for the spread of the Protestant Reformation. Universities, ecclesiastical and civil authorities, and local inquisitors published many lists of condemned books and authors that paved the way for the Index.

The first printed Index of Prohibited Books was published in 1544 by the Faculty of Theology of the University of Paris, followed by editions appearing in 1545, 1547, 1549, 1551, and 1556. The Faculty of Theology of the University of Louvain published its own catalogues in 1546, 1551, and 1558. These academic initiatives were followed by lists compiled by local and national inquisitions, especially in Italy, with Indices issued at Venice in 1549 and 1554, in Portugal, with editions appearing in 1547, 1551 and 1561, and in Spain, with Indices published in 1551 and 1559.

The Inquisition in Rome prepared the first Roman Index, issued by Paul IV in 1559. It contained more than a thousand interdictions divided into three classes: authors, all of whose works were to be prohibited; individual books that bore the names of their authors; and anonymous writings. The Index compiled by a commission established by the Council of Trent, published by Pius IV in 1564, was distinguished principally by the ten general rules it promulgated, which became the basis of Catholic censorship policy for the entire modern period. In 1571 Pius V created the Congregation of the Index as a permanent organ of government in the Church. The Index published in 1596 by Clement VIII added more than eleven hundred condemnations to those contained in the Tridentine Index.

From the early seventeenth century, the Congregation of the Index conducted the prohibition of books through the promulgation of particular decrees that combined the congregation's own condemnations with those pronounced by the Holy Office of the Inquisition and the pope. Editions of the Index appeared at intervals incorporating the new titles prohibited in these decrees. Two catalogues published in the seventeenth and eighteenth centuries are of special significance.

For the entire modern era, the Spanish and Portuguese Inquisitions also issued their own catalogues, which had authority in the Iberian Peninsula as well as in their American, African, and Asian colonies. The Spanish and Portuguese Indices were at the same time prohibitory and expurgatory, while the Roman Indices, with rare exceptions, were exclusively the former.

Prefacing the different editions of the Roman Index are the papal documents and general rules proscribing in an absolute manner various categories of works and determining the modalities according to which control over the printed book must be exercised. The general rules contained in the Tridentine Index prohibit in their entirety all books by heretical authors treating religious subjects, lascivious and obscene writings, and works of astrology, divination, and the occult arts. The reading of the Bible in the vernacular was permitted only to persons holding a written license issued by an inquisitor or bishop. Other rules added to the Index in the course of the centuries prohibited other categories of books as well. The Index of Benedict XIV, published in 1758, by its constitution "Sollicita ac Provida" reorganized the condemned materials and considerably liberalized the procedures for the inclusion of new works.

The number of writers and works placed on the Roman Index from the mid-sixteenth century to the end of the eighteenth amounted to about four thousand.

Brought into being to prevent the circulation of Protestant writings, the Index evolved over time, always maintaining a twofold objective: to defend the Catholic Church against external attacks and to protect the homogeneity of the faith and of morality against dangers occurring from within. The defense against Protestantism always remained a major preoccupation of Roman censors. Protection of the political and juridical rights and privileges of the church, the pope, and the hierarchy also find a notable echo in the Index. Thus, writings favoring Gallicanism and those advocating the right of civil authorities to intervene in ecclesiastical affairs appear prominently, alongside polemical works dealing with the political intervention of the Holy See, such as during its conflict with the Republic of Venice in 1606–1607, or the oath of loyalty in England during the pontificate of Paul V (1605–1621).

Writings favorable to Jansenism represent an important part of the seventeenth and eighteenth century condemnations, just as one finds a considerable number of works concerning the debates over casuistry and probabilism. Mystical literature is represented by numerous titles, such as those supporting the Quietism of Miguel de Molinos (1628–1696) and the pure love of Madame de Guyon (1648–1717) and of Archbishop Fénelon (1652–1715). The struggle against popular superstitions explains the prohibition of countless prayers, false indulgences, novenas, apocryphal histories, and legends of the saints.

The presence in the Index of works by the great philosophers is quite remarkable, such names as Blaise Pascal, René Descartes, Nicolas de Malebranche, Baruch Spinoza, Immanuel Kant, Francis Bacon, Thomas Hobbes, John Locke, David Hume, George Berkeley, and of the greatest French writers of the Enlightenment, Pierre Bayle, Denis Diderot, Jean d'Alembert, Voltaire, and Jean-Jacques Rousseau. The interdiction of the writings of Nicolaus Copernicus in 1616 and of Galileo Galilei in 1634, not removed from the Index until 1822, is the most glaring example of the chasm separating the church and science.

The moral obligation to submit to the Index has unfailingly been opposed by heterodox and progressive groups, and especially by intellectuals. But if one examines the attitudes of Catholics as a whole, it would appear that the constraints imposed on the written word gradually came to be considered acceptable practices in the pastoral mission of the church.

Censorship and the Index have undoubtedly hindered literary productivity and the expression of original ideas. Many Catholic authors, Pascal among them, practiced self-censorship and renounced embarking on some projected works. It can also be maintained that the close surveillance imposed by the Index over printing and the book placed a brake on the growth of publishing in the Catholic world, and we can query the effect that censorship and the Index exerted on the religious, cultural, and social development of the modern world. But it is also possible to ask whether the Church of Rome could have succeeded in neutralizing the many centrifugal forces pulling against it, maintained religious unity within Catholicism, and reaffirmed its authority without the weapons of censorship and the Index.

See also **Censorship; Copernicus, Nicolaus; Enlightenment; Galileo Galilei; Gallicanism; Inquisition, Roman; Inquisition, Spanish; Jansenism; Papacy and Papal States; Printing and Publishing; Quietism.**

BIBLIOGRAPHY

Primary Sources

Bujanda, Jésus Martinez de. *Index des livres interdits.* 10 vols. Sherbrooke, Canada, and Geneva, 1984–1996. Vol. 1, *Index de l'Université de Paris,* 1544, 1545, 1547, 1549, 1551, 1556. Vol. 2, *Index de l'Université de Louvain,* 1546, 1550, 1558. Vol. 3, *Index de Venise, 1549, et de Venise et Milan, 1554.* Vol. 4, *Index de l'Inquisition portugaise, 1547, 1551, 1561, 1564, 1581.* Vol. 5, *Index de l'Inquisition espagnole, 1551, 1554, 1559.* Vol. 6, *Index de l'Inquisition espagnole, 1583, 1584.* Vol. 7, *Index d'Anvers, 1569, 1570, 1571.* Vol. 8, *Index de Rome, 1557, 1559, 1564.* Vol. 9, *Index de Rome, 1590, 1593, 1596.* Vol. 10, *Thesaurus de la littérature interdite au seizième siècle.* Historical surveys, analyses of the expurgations, and critical editions of all sixteenth-century Indexes of Prohibited Books.

———. *Index librorum prohibitorum* (1600–1966). Montreal and Geneva, 2002. This volume offers succinct biographical information on approximately 3,000 authors as well as a brief description and the location of the editio princeps for more than 5,000 forbidden books.

Secondary Sources

Fragnito, Gigliola. *La Bibbia al rogo: La censura ecclesiastica e i volgarizzamenti della Scrittura (1471–1605).* Bologna, 1997. Based on assiduous research in civil and ecclesiastical repositories, especially the Archive of the Holy Office in Rome, presents a detailed history of the prohibition and control of vernacular biblical translations and commentaries.

Fragnito, Gigliola, ed. *Church, Censorship and Culture in Early Modern Italy.* Cambridge, U.K., 2001. Collaborative volume containing nine studies devoted to ecclesiastical censorship activity in Italy.

Grendler, Paul F. *The Roman Inquisition and the Venetian Press, 1540–1605.* Princeton, 1977. Influential study based on the large collection of Venetian Holy Office trials and other primary documents. Examines the impact of Inquisition and Index on the book trade and the reactions on all fronts to the invasive controls and prohibitions.

Rozzo, Ugo, ed. *La censura libraria nell'Europa del secolo XVI.* Udine, Italy, 1997. Conference volume containing thirteen studies devoted to the Indexes, the activities of the congregations of the Inquisition and Index, and ecclesiastical censorship activity in various European countries.

J. M. De Bujanda

INDUSTRIAL REVOLUTION. To the end of the early modern period, Europe remained a preindustrial society. Its manufactured goods came from small workshops, and most of its machinery was powered by animals, wind, falling water, or human labor. These two facts reinforced each other, and together they constricted Europe's economic development. Water-powered manufacturing, for instance, could develop only in favored regions and remained constantly subject to weather-related interruptions; with limited supplies of power, there was little reason to concentrate manufacturing processes in large workshops. By 1850, however, these descriptions no longer applied to large areas of western Europe, and by 1914 the European economy as a whole was dominated by large factories, many of them employing thousands of workers. Both manufacturing and transportation now relied on steam power, and gasoline and electric motors were becoming common. The quantity and variety of goods manufactured rose accordingly, a transformation suggested by the development of the British iron industry: Britain produced about 30,000 tons of pig iron in 1760, about one million tons in 1810. Contemporary awareness of change advanced even more quickly than the reality. In his 1848 *Manifesto of the Communist Party,* written at a time when most Europeans still worked in agriculture and when even British manufacturing was still evenly divided between factories and small workshops, Karl Marx (1818–1883) presented industrialization as the obvious destiny of all European society. The rapidity of these changes and their far-reaching effects amply justify historians' designation of the period as the "industrial revolution." In the century after 1780, European life was transformed.

Industrialization thus numbers among the most important processes that brought the early modern period to a close, and as such it raises important questions about the period itself. Signs of dramatic economic and technological change were already apparent in later eighteenth-century Britain, prompting historians to ask how this phase of rapid change could have emerged from the relatively stable early modern economy and why it emerged first in Britain. More broadly, historians have asked why Europe industrialized ahead of other regions of the globe, and what contributions Europe's empires in the Americas and elsewhere made to its industrialization. Answers to these questions have been varied and surprising. Though the concept of industrialization itself remains unchallenged, recent historical research has overturned much conventional wisdom about how the process took place.

MANUFACTURING BEFORE INDUSTRIALIZATION

Though it lacked factories and steam engines, preindustrial Europe did not have a static economy, and manufacturing counted for a significant share of its total economic activity—about one-fourth of France's gross national product and almost 40 percent of Britain's in the early eighteenth century, one historian has estimated. In some regions, such as the Netherlands and northern Italy, the percentages might have been even higher, but the difficulties of early modern transportation meant that manufacturing was widely dispersed; with transportation costs high, producers had a strong incentive to establish their workshops near the sources of their raw materials and to focus on meeting the needs of regional markets. Despite this fragmentation, early modern producers regularly introduced new products and adopted new techniques. In the thirteenth century, for instance, Italian craftsmen learned how to make silk cloth, and their techniques spread north of the Alps in the fifteenth and sixteenth centuries, so that by the eighteenth century the French city of Lyon numbered several thousand silk weavers. The technology of silk weaving changed as well, most dramatically with the invention of the Jacquard loom in the 1720s. The new loom had mechanical codes that governed the weaving process, allowing a relatively unskilled weaver to produce a complex product. In an early version of a process that would be frequently repeated during the industrial revolution, the balance between machine and worker had shifted; knowledge could be embedded in the machine, rendering differences among workers less important. Likewise, calico cloths from India created a sensation when first introduced in later seventeenth-century England. They were quickly imitated by British manufacturers, who effectively established an altogether new industry.

A stream of inventions thus changed manufacturing over the early modern period, but the most important changes that the period witnessed had to do with the organization of work rather than its technology. Most European cities restricted manufacturing work, limiting access to some trades so that those already established in them could continue to enjoy respectable incomes and controlling the amounts that workshops might produce to prevent any one manufacturer from acquiring too dominant a position. Impatient with such restrictions, from the seventeenth century on, merchants in many regions organized new forms of production in the countryside. Labor there was cheap and abundant since contemporary agriculture left many peasants underemployed, and economic restrictions were weak. Cloth merchants were especially well placed to take advantage of this opportunity. They supplied villagers with raw materials, transported goods from one stage of production to the next, and finally marketed the finished product, taking as well the largest share of the profits. Other goods too could be manufactured in this way: in eastern France and Switzerland, merchants organized clock making on these lines. By the mid-eighteenth century, the balance between agriculture and manufacturing had shifted in many regions; for most villagers, farm work had become a supplemental source of income, and they relied mainly on spinning, weaving, and other artisanal activities for their livelihoods.

Historians have applied several names to this process. The term *cottage industry* accurately captures the fact that this system of manufacturing left unchanged the basic conditions of its workers' lives. Spinners, weavers, and others continued to live in small villages and continued to work according to their own preferences, as independent contractors who owned their equipment. But historians have also spoken of this process as *proto-industrialization,* a term that emphasizes the new economic relationships and expectations, as well as the demographic consequences, created by this system. Though they set their own pace of work, those involved in cottage industry nonetheless depended on far-flung economic networks; their goods were produced for national and international markets, and the workers were subject to the economic power of the merchants who sold what they produced. The proto-industrial workforce was in some sense a proletariat, whose economic fate rested with others; some historians have suggested that these workers were in effect learning the habits that they would eventually need to work in the factories of the nineteenth century.

But as important as its implications for work discipline were, the rise of cottage industry also changed European buying. As the historian Jan de Vries has argued, seventeenth- and eighteenth-century families were working harder than they had in the past in exchange for the ability to buy more goods: cottage industry allowed women and children to earn cash incomes, and it converted what had been the family's leisure time—especially the slow phases of the agricultural cycle—into cash as well. Well before the onset of industrialization, European manufacturers thus had available to them a large consumer market, one eager for small luxury goods. Historians have turned to probate inventories to demonstrate the breadth of the consumer revolution that these centuries brought to England, the Netherlands, France, and Germany. Even backward areas showed the effects of these changes, with families buying mirrors, clocks, brightly printed clothing, prints, and a variety of other manufactured goods. But the effects were most visible in the developing cities of the age. The largest city of early modern Europe, London, by itself concentrated about 16 percent of England's population—an enormous, conveniently centralized and accessible market for manufactured goods. Paris was smaller in absolute numbers and much smaller relative to total French population, but it too offered manufacturers an enormous, fashion-conscious market for new goods.

TOWARD THE NEW ECONOMY

A critical aspect of the industrial revolution was the effort of manufacturers to take advantage of these markets, most visibly in the clothing industry. By the early eighteenth century, a fundamental step had already been taken: clothing manufacturers increasingly devoted their attention to lightweight, cheap, easily-colored fabrics, rather than the high-quality woolens that had dominated the medieval textile industry. In the early seventeenth century, they shifted to producing the lightweight woolen fabrics known in Britain as "new draperies"; later in the century, the arrival of cotton calicoes and muslins from India produced enormous enthusiasm among consumers and led to efforts both to exclude such imports and to replace them with British-made cotton goods. Over the eighteenth century, manufacturers produced a variety of fabrics that mixed cotton with other fibers, because British thread was usually too weak for producing all-cotton cloths. Throughout, popular demand played a crucial role, and in mid-eighteenth-century Britain cotton producers could not keep up with the demand for their products. In response they introduced a series of technological innovations designed to speed up the manufacturing process and to create other attractive new cotton products. Improvements in weaving starting in the 1730s created pressure on the spinning process, which produced cotton thread; at this point it took eight spinners to produce enough thread to supply one weaver, and several inventors sought to produce machines that could do the job more quickly. Solutions came in the 1760s and 1770s, with the spinning jenny, the water frame, and the spinning mule, all devices that allowed a single operator to manage multiple spindles—and that produced a higher-quality, more even thread than hand spinning. Contemporaries immediately recognized the value of these machines, and they spread rapidly, transforming the relationship between spinning and weaving. With spinning increasingly mechanized, there was now pressure to mechanize weaving—a more difficult task, with a first power loom invented in 1787 but not widely used until the early nineteenth century. But though handloom weaving remained dominant, a revolution in the cotton industry had already occurred by the end of the eighteenth century: between 1770 and 1800 imports of raw cotton to Britain increased twelvefold.

New machinery encouraged new ways of organizing work. The spinning jenny was designed as a hand-operated device, and could be adapted to the needs of cottage industry. But the water frame was larger and from the beginning required an external power source to drive it. Richard Arkwright (1732–

1792), who held the patent on it, immediately established a set of water-driven mills to exploit the new invention, and the economies of scale that these factories enjoyed meant that by 1800 cottage spinning had largely disappeared. The larger machinery also required a new approach to managing labor. Necessarily centralized around a single source of power, the new machines required close management in order to repay their heavy costs. The factory thus encouraged a new degree of labor discipline, with workers required to report to work at exact hours and labor at a pace set by the factory's managers. The Arkwright mills and their competitors made an immediate impression on contemporaries; the artist Joseph Wright of Derby (1734–1797) painted them, and the poet William Blake (1757–1827) in about 1805 already spoke of "dark Satanic Mills" transforming the British landscape.

Blake found the mills "Satanic" partly because by his time a growing number of them relied on steam power. The development of steam technology represented a second critical strand in the industrial revolution, and, as with the development of cotton manufacturing, its origins lay in the seventeenth century, in a combination of scientific, technological, and ecological developments. As late as the mid-seventeenth century, scientists such as René Descartes (1596–1650) doubted that a vacuum was even possible, but his contemporary, the Italian physicist Evangelista Torricelli (1608–1647), and others demonstrated both the possibility and its practical implications. Inventors developed a series of pumps based on this idea, and in 1698 the Englishman Thomas Savery (c. 1650–1715) developed the first working steam engine, essentially a machine for creating a vacuum and using its suction to lift water. A much-improved version was developed by the Englishman Thomas Newcomen (1663–1729), and in 1712 a Newcomen engine was set to work pumping out coal mines in northern England; by the 1730s such engines were in operation in several European countries. As the economic historian Joel Mokyr has observed, this was the world's first economically viable mechanism for transforming heat into regular motion, the artificial power that would be at the center of industrialization. The Newcomen engine performed its task very inefficiently, though, and in 1776 the first of James Watt's (1736–1819) engines was put into commercial operation, allowing a fourfold improvement in efficiency. By 1800, about 2,500 steam engines had been built in Britain, most of them used in mines, but many powering iron foundries, cotton-spinning machines, and other industrial processes. Contemporaries understood that a technological revolution was underway, and despite the inefficiency of the early engines, inventors immediately began exploring new ways to use them. Steam hammers, rolling mills, and bellows revolutionized the British iron industry from the 1760s on; in 1783 a first steamboat was constructed (in France), and in 1803 a first steam locomotive. By the 1820s, railway construction had begun, and a steam-powered ship had crossed the Atlantic.

This sequence of inventions and applications was closely bound up with the availability of cheap fuel, yet another element of the early modern economy that came to full development during the industrial revolution. Coal had long been known as a fuel, but contemporaries disliked its smoke and smell. By the mid-seventeenth century, however, Britons had little choice but to make use of it, for the country was running short of wood and it was becoming too expensive to use as fuel for even the basic needs of heating, let alone for novel industrial uses. The enormous size of seventeenth-century London, over half a million people within easy reach of cheap water transport, and its insatiable demand for fuel ensured that coal mining could be profitable even in the face of technological obstacles. As mines became deeper, for instance, there was the problem of removing the water that seeped into them—the problem that steam-driven pumps eventually answered. Steam-driven vehicles and carts that moved along rails (radically reducing friction) were first employed in the British coal fields as well. The economics of coal-mining made even the inefficiencies of early steam power acceptable; operating in the coal fields themselves, the first steam engines had a readily available supply of cheap fuel and could even use some of the waste from the mining process. With a fully developed coal-mining industry, and increasingly sophisticated means of using the energy that coal contained, Britain suddenly increased its supply of power many times over. The historian Kenneth Pomeranz has argued that only with this step did Europe move clearly ahead of Asian technology, setting the stage for Europe's domination of the world economy during the nineteenth and twentieth centuries. This interpretation probably understates the significance of other differences, but it accurately captures an important aspect of the industrial revolution: during the eighteenth century, Britain acquired a seemingly limitless supply of power.

Coal played an especially important role in the iron industry, which constituted the fourth strand of industrialization. Iron and steel had been important to European technology since the Middle Ages, but expensive production processes limited their uses. Like other early modern manufacturing, ironmaking relied on the experience and skill of a mass of individual artisans, whose small foundries permitted close inspection of each piece that they produced. Steel was even more clearly a specialized product, requiring superior iron ore found mainly in Sweden; forged by hand, it was reserved for such uses as weaponry, and was much too expensive for more mundane products. But starting in the early eighteenth century, the availability of coal and steam engines to power blowers (to create very high temperatures) and hammers (to remove impurities) stimulated a sequence of new iron-making processes, and these dramatically changed the industry's economics. Because expensive machinery was essential to these techniques, iron production was increasingly concentrated in huge enterprises, most dramatically that of the ironmaster John Wilkinson (1728–1808); but once the machinery was in place, it allowed the use of lower-grade, cheaper ores. Costs fell accordingly, and by the late eighteenth century, the availability of cheap iron made it possible to envision an entirely new range of uses for it.

This enthusiasm for spreading innovations to new economic domains was a further characteristic of the later eighteenth century, and it meant that the industrial revolution transformed numerous areas of the British economy, not just cotton, ironmaking, and steam power. Cheap iron, for instance, allowed for the creation of new machine tools, and when combined with steam power, these made possible mechanized production of numerous products that once had been made by hand. Steam power and coal fuel allowed the potter Josiah Wedgwood (1730–1795) to establish mass production processes in making porcelain, until then a luxury good. Inventors began to think about the possibilities of using iron in buildings and ships. Economic transformations of these kinds did not mean the end of small workshops or skilled artisans. On the contrary, the development of machine making required more workshops and highly skilled laborers, and many consumer products lent themselves to small-scale production. Even after the advent of power looms, handloom weavers remained numerous and prosperous well into the nineteenth century. But by 1800 it was clear to all that dramatic change was likely to affect all domains of the economy; technological advances had become normal, and contemporaries expected that it would transform new areas of economic activity.

GEOGRAPHIES

Overwhelmingly, the technological innovations that marked eighteenth-century industrialization took place in Britain. Understanding this British dynamism has been an enduring historical problem, producing both classic answers and intense debate among historians. Geographical accidents offer one explanation for British success. Britain had abundant supplies of coal of a quality especially well suited to iron production, and its lack of wood forced it to exploit this resource from the seventeenth century on; in contrast, France had plenty of wood and relatively little coal, and Holland had only peat, which could not produce the high temperatures needed for large-scale iron production. As a relatively small island with numerous navigable rivers, Britain also enjoyed the advantages of cheap water transportation, which allowed the development of an unusually well-integrated national market. The remarkable development of seventeenth-century London offered further economic advantages; as the British historian Anthony Wrigley pointed out a generation ago, London offered a large, concentrated market for industrial products, far more important as a share of the nation's population than contemporary Paris, and it provided a laboratory for new social practices, encouraging both producers and consumers to try out new products. Historians have also noted the chronological accidents that aided British industrial development. During most of the eighteenth century, French economic growth roughly equaled British, but the generation of political chaos that followed the French Revolution of 1789 gave British manufacturers a chance to establish themselves in new markets, with little competition from continental industry. By the end of the Revolutionary Wars, in 1815, Britain had fully established its economic supremacy in Europe.

Efforts to explain British economic successes in terms of culture, politics, and social organization have stimulated more debate among historians. In its social structure, Britain was as aristocratic as other European countries, and its merchants were as eager as merchants elsewhere to achieve acceptance among the landed gentry. But the British aristocracy was probably unusual in the respect that it accorded commerce and manufacturing, and the gentry-dominated British Parliament energetically defended commercial and manufacturing interests against foreign competition. British law was certainly unusual in the protections it gave inventors and property holders. Between 1624 and 1791, Britain was the only European nation with a system of patent laws, designed to give inventors the profits of their achievements. The system both encouraged innovation and expressed British society's admiration for it. In other respects, however, differences between Britain and other countries were less significant. Acquisitive, profit-oriented economic attitudes characterized most of eighteenth-century Europe; and Britain was like other Protestant countries of the early modern period in having a relatively well-educated working class. As for advanced education in the sciences and engineering, eighteenth-century Britain lagged well behind France.

By the late eighteenth century, Britain was also Europe's leading imperial power, holding territories in North America, the Caribbean, and India, and benefiting from the trade in African slaves. Many historians have seen in this global power a further important explanation for British industrialization. Colonies, they have argued, offered raw materials at a discount and ready markets for industrial goods, and the high profits generated by colonial trade permitted British merchants to make expensive investments in machines and factories. But recent scholarship has tended to present colonial markets and materials as only a secondary cause of British economic successes. Few historians would deny the rapacity of eighteenth-century imperialism or the determination of British governments to use any means that might advance the country's economic interests; to protect domestic cotton manufacturers, for instance, importation of Indian cloth was rigorously prohibited. As the Spanish empire of the sixteenth century had demonstrated, however, colonial possessions were no guarantee of industrial development; and the profits of colonial trade were not especially high in the seventeenth and eighteenth centuries. The critical fact in Britain's economic development seems to have been the demand for goods within the country itself and the readiness of manufacturers to use novel means to meet that demand. Colonialism perhaps mattered less as a source of capital than as a source of economic novelties, encouraging Europe as a whole and Britain in particular to undertake business innovations. Such colonial products as tea, coffee, tobacco, and sugar were among the early mass-market luxuries that became the model for later industrial production. More substantial goods like Chinese ceramics and Indian cotton fabrics stimulated determined, and eventually successful, efforts at imitation. The eighteenth-century global economy thus helps to explain Britain's industrialization; indeed, based on a product that did not grow in Europe, the cotton industry itself was only conceivable in the setting of a global economy. But the critical fact was manufacturers' readiness to respond to opportunities that the global economy presented.

THE EXPERIENCE OF WORK AND THE ORGANIZATION OF SOCIETY

"Everything that is solid melts into air," wrote Karl Marx to describe the changes that he saw accompanying the industrialization of Europe. Until well after World War II, most historians of the industrial revolution shared Marx's sense of the period as one of overwhelming social change, both positive and negative. Like contemporaries, historians have been dazzled by the wave of new products and processes that the period brought forth during what Mokyr has called "the age of miracles." Historians have also been struck by the new kinds of work organization that machines required. Preindustrial work tended to be individualistic, with workers setting their own pace; in cottage industry, moments of intense activity alternated with moments of relaxation, and as independent contractors, workers could take on as much work as they chose. Factory work allowed for no such freedoms. Work had to be continuous and coordinated if investments in steam engines, machinery, and buildings were to pay off. Labor discipline thus represented an important aspect of the transition to the factory system; for many ordinary people, this was the point at which clock time became an essential component of daily life and the pocket watch the sign of one's responsibility. The role of skill also diminished in the factory setting. What was needed was someone to tend machines, and this could just as easily be children as adults. Deskilling of this kind represented a loss of both status and income to workers who had been used to the freedom of working on their own. Having reduced the role of skill, factory owners could effectively control the wages they paid; an unskilled worker dissatisfied with his income could easily be replaced by another.

On the other hand, much recent scholarship has drawn attention to continuities between the preindustrial world and what followed, and to the complexities of industrial development itself. As a result, this line of scholarship has offered more nuanced views of the society that early industrialization produced than were previously available. One reason for this caution has been historians' growing knowledge of preindustrial economies, both in Europe and in the world at large. These economies were capable of considerable growth, and they offered their inhabitants considerable material abundance. Rather than a complete break with the past, therefore, the industrial revolution in significant ways represented a culmination of earlier developments. Historians have also given more attention to the survival of small workshops and skilled work during the industrial revolution. Because the factory system relied so heavily on complex machinery, it created whole new forms of skilled labor in the trades that built and maintained machinery. Small workshops thrived in many other developing trades as well, notably those that produced small metal goods like buttons, buckles, cheap jewelry, guns, and so on, trades that employed about half the workforce of Birmingham, one of Britain's most important industrial cities. The historian Maxine Berg has shown that even the introduction of steam power did not bring the factory system to these trades; instead, several small workshops could share the power of a single steam engine, for instance by renting space in a large building. Even the early textile factories retained some aspects of preindustrial work organization. Family relations continued to count in the factory, and for many manufacturing processes small groups needed to work closely together.

In one respect, however, traditional depictions of industrialization retain their full force: already in late eighteenth-century Britain, early industrialization had created zones of intensive industrial activity that grouped together mining, metallurgy, and a variety of related trades, creating a new kind of physical environment and new social relations. Coal was expensive to transport, and breakage during shipment made it useless in the blast furnaces that produced wrought iron. It thus proved economical to concentrate iron making near the coal fields, and other industrial processes tended to follow. Cotton textiles tended to concentrate also, around the fast-growing city of Manchester, while metal working developed in the city of Birmingham. With the expansion of these highly developed industrial centers, the more evenly dispersed industrial activity of the early eighteenth century tended to disappear. A number of regions that had been important manufacturing centers in the early modern period returned to purely agricultural pursuits, while the new industrial zones became crowded with manufacturing activities, reducing any mixture with agriculture to mere vestiges. Contemporaries found these new industrial regions appalling. As rapidly growing new towns, they lacked basic services and traditional forms of social organization. The combination of haphazard development, inadequate water supplies, coal smoke, and industrial wastes made them unhealthy, and contemporaries believed that the social conditions of industrial life added to the problem. Young people, for instance, earned wages that freed them from the controls that parents earlier exercised over them, and allowed them to indulge in a variety of unwholesome pastimes; they had little or no time for school. Industrial zones like these were genuine challenges to the established order of European society. They offered the spectacle of new disorder among laborers—and of new wealth among factory owners. From a modest background, Richard Arkwright became extremely wealthy from his cotton-spinning mills, and made a point of displaying his wealth in conspicuous ways. He was only one of many industrialists to do so.

But historians have become cautious in interpreting descriptions of this sort, and more alert to the ideological commentaries they contained. If observers were impressed at the forms of misbehavior that characterized the new industrial towns, this to some extent reflected their fears of social change and their inability to see the social relationships that in fact characterized them. It also reflected their limited attention to the evils of preindustrial work, which was altogether ready to employ women and children. Despite their unhealthy conditions, the new industrial centers paid high wages and attracted workers. In the same way, the dramatic rise of new fortunes from industry to some extent obscured from contemporary observers the ability of old elites to profit from economic innovation. Britain's great aristocrats were especially well placed to benefit from the development of mining and metallurgy, controlling as they did many of the country's coal deposits; during the eighteenth and early nineteenth centuries, they showed themselves alert and inventive in profiting from these opportunities, so that their wealth rose in tandem with that of the new industrialists—allowing them to continue dominating Britain's politics down to the eve of World War I. Historians have demonstrated similar adaptations in continental Europe, with old ruling groups effectively profiting from industrialization. If the industrial revolution helped bring the early modern period to a close, it thus also preserved some of that period's characteristic forms of social organization.

See also **Clocks and Watches; Industry; Laborers; Mining and Metallurgy; Proto-Industry; Textile Industry.**

BIBLIOGRAPHY

Adas, Michael. *Machines as the Measure of Men: Science, Technology, and Ideologies of Western Dominance.* Ithaca and London, 1989.

Berg, Maxine. *The Age of Manufactures, 1700–1820.* New York and Oxford, 1986; 2nd edition, 1994.

de Vries, Jan. *The Economy of Europe in an Age of Crisis, 1600–1750.* Cambridge, U.K., 1976.

———. "The Industrial Revolution and the Industrious Revolution." *Journal of Economic History* 54, no. 2 (June 1994): 249–270.

Deane, Phyllis. *The First Industrial Revolution.* Cambridge, U.K., 1965; 2nd edition, 1979.

Gutmann, Myron. *Toward the Modern Economy: Early Industry in Europe, 1500–1800.* Philadelphia, 1988.

Landes, David. *The Unbound Prometheus: Technological Change and Industrial Development in Western Europe from 1750 to the Present.* Cambridge, U.K., 1969.

Mokyr, Joel. *The Lever of Riches: Technological Creativity and Economic Progress.* New York and Oxford, 1990.

Pomeranz, Kenneth. *The Great Divergence: China, Europe, and the Making of the Modern World Economy.* Princeton, 2000.

Reddy, William. *The Rise of Market Culture: The Textile Trade and French Society, 1750–1900.* Cambridge, U.K., and New York, 1984.

Thompson, E. P. *The Making of the English Working Class.* London, 1963; 2nd edition, 1972.

JONATHAN DEWALD

INDUSTRY. The subject of industry is part of the general pattern of economic development in the early modern period. This development had three basic phases: the first, a period of expansion running from the middle of the fifteenth century through to the very end of the sixteenth; the second, a long stagnation during the seventeenth century that lingered well into the eighteenth; the third, an upswing beginning no earlier than 1730 and perhaps as late as 1750.

The first period began with signs of recovery from the long recession associated with the Black Death (1348–1350) and its recurrent visitations. Among the most significant of those signs were population growth and overseas expansion, particularly the influx of precious metals from the New World. The stagnation of the seventeenth century was marked by the disruption of markets in central Europe by the Thirty Years' War (1618–1648), and by the continued decline of the Mediterranean region. Nevertheless, England and Holland enjoyed continuing economic growth during this period, especially in manufactures, which held significant implications for the future. The upturn of the eighteenth century was sustained by the breaking of the vicious circle of uncertainty created by war, famine, and plague in the preindustrial era. The eighteenth century is the only one to which the term *industrialization* may reasonably be applied, and then perhaps only to the machine tool inventions and eventually the steam power that were beginning to change the processes of production in Britain.

It is also vital to take careful account of fundamental continuities throughout the period in order to keep the scale of industrial activity in proper proportion. An industrial sector did not exist in its own right but was part of a complex network linking the needs of people in different regions. Villagers needed their cobbler, smith, miller, and butcher. The workshops of the towns were much smaller in scale than the industries of the mountains—mining, smelting, and quarrying. Some urban merchants employed and thus controlled large numbers of workers in rural areas. Throughout the following discussion, it is essential to remember that industry cannot be viewed in isolation from the gradual unfolding of commercial and agricultural circumstance or from social and political evolutions, both planned and unplanned, for industry was in part shaped by these and in turn helped to shape them.

RURAL ECONOMY

In seeking to locate industry in the early modern economy, therefore, several observations must be made. First, whatever the signs of industrial growth, it was the condition of the rural economy that most affected everyday life. Moreover, concentrations of labor on a truly "industrial" scale were to be found not in the cities but in the serf-based manorial estates of the landlords of eastern Europe. Harvest failure was the trigger of social unrest—as was to be proved in 1789 and 1848. Even in the nineteenth century, something like 70 percent of the urban wage was spent for bread. Second, industrial activity must be seen in relation to the predominance of commerce at the international level and to artisan manufacture in urban workshops. Put another way, the possibilities of "mass production" were very limited. The only goods produced mechanically in identical form were coins and printed books. Third, evidence of "industrialization" was patchy and confined to specific regions and cannot be seen as a truly European phenomenon until well into the nineteenth century.

In turn, this means that the idea of "the rise of the bourgeoisie" as a social phenomenon in the early modern period must be used with great caution—if at all. The social structure fundamentally lacked the plasticity that began to manifest itself only in eighteenth-century Britain. Put more directly, society was still essentially composed of estates, and the old feudal vision of the three orders—clergy, nobility, and those who lived by their labor—still prevailed. Those who prayed *(oratores)* sanctioned the social predominance of those who fought *(bellatores)*, while those who worked *(laboratores)* owed their masters labor in return for protection and prayer. The overthrow of this model was the aim—very imperfectly achieved—of the revolutionaries of 1789. Even at that late date, there seemed to be little room in the recognizable social hierarchy for the towns, the state, or the women. Status was a question of function or of birth rather than of money. The church was suspicious of profit, and nobles disdained commerce and handicrafts as unworthy. It is essential to be aware of the social matrix as resistant and often overtly hostile to capital and manufacture. This overrides—and in many ways overwhelms—any scattered examples of the confrontation of capital and labor. By this reasoning, any connection between the "Protestant ethic" and the "spirit of capitalism" must be set in the context of a world in which something approaching 90 percent of the population were peasants.

THE ROLE OF THE STATE

There is also a fundamental paradox in the subject. While industrial activity is usually linked to capitalist free enterprise, the concentration of human and material resources on an unprecedented scale in the early modern period was usually the work of the state. The growth of European armies in the period was staggering, and the state's monopoly on the means of destruction is far more noticeable than the ownership of the means of production by a capitalist entrepreneur. In their scale and power, the new militarized states of the early modern era dwarf any industrializing tendencies in manufacture at that time. Louis XIV of France (ruled 1643–1715) had something like 400,000 men under arms in 1700. The unit of manufacturing production, the urban workshop, rarely exceeded a dozen members. When Louis's minister Jean Baptiste Colbert sought in 1673 to reform manufactures with an edict and with policies often described as "mercantilist," armaments and gun foundries began to employ hundreds of workers. Even so, they did not form anything approaching an industrial proletariat. Instead, they were a privileged category of labor subsidized by the state.

The theme of paradox may be extended and strengthened. Too often, and for too long, historians have sought the seeds of the industrial world in the early modern era, and terms such as *preindustrial* and *proto-industrialization* imply some sort of primitive rehearsal for the real thing, which is unhelpful. When considering industrial activity before the industrial revolution, it is essential to be aware of two abiding problems: teleology and anachronism. The teleology insists upon the gradual but inevitable development of a capitalist "world system" and a capitalist civilization, ideas that identify the early modern period as marking a "transition from feudalism to capitalism" in the European economy. Instead, industry in the early modern era should be understood in relation to precedents, precocities, false dreams, and blind alleys. The Middle Ages had experienced its own "industrial revolutions": in the smelting of base metals in the later twelfth century, for instance, and in the introduction of the fulling mill in textile manufacture at about the same time. Moreover, the great cloth towns of Flanders and Italy had witnessed, in the later fourteenth century, startlingly "modern" confrontations of the labor force and the bosses as wage laborers and owners of the means of production clashed in conflicts that bore the features of "class war." Anachronism—the application of terminology and concepts inappropriate to the early modern period—is a common fallacy in our own "post-industrial" era. The modern tendency to describe virtually any economic activity as an industry—for example "farming industry," "food industry," "tourism industry," "music industry," or "film industry"—has no relevance to the early modern era and can prove very misleading. In the early modern world, "industry" was a quality, not a sector of the economy. In the Renaissance, an *ingegnere* was not so much an "engineer" in the modern sense as someone marked out by their *ingegno,* which meant "talent" or "genius."

LARGE-SCALE INDUSTRY

With those qualifications in mind, "industry"—meaning a large-scale enterprise concentrating a numerous work force that is dependent on the owner of the means of production—is applicable in the early modern era to three major economic activities: mining, building (including shipbuilding), and textiles. These were not exclusively urban activities: mining and some processes of textile production were carried out in rural areas, and the workforce often consisted of peasants. Indeed, concentrations of peasant labor—as in the case of the millions of serfs in the great manorial estates of central and eastern Europe—often seem to provide the prototype for the exploitation of labor on a truly "industrial" scale. More starkly still, the mines in the New World, where millions of people from the indigenous population were literally worked into the ground at the will of their Spanish lords, set a pattern for factory production that was perhaps re-exported to Europe via the plantation.

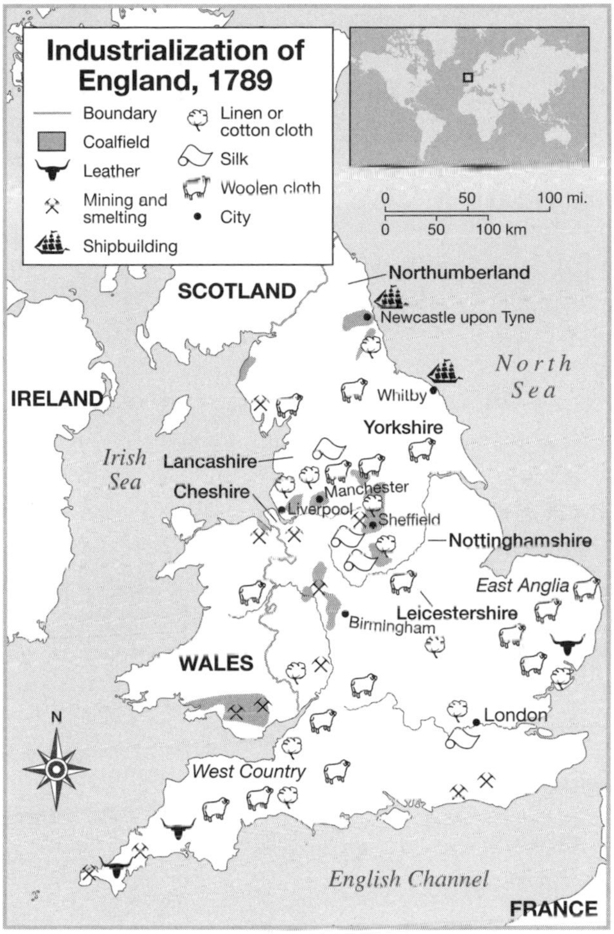

Both in eastern Europe and in the New World, therefore, large-scale enterprises were run by essentially "feudal" lords. Somewhat surprisingly, in western Europe at the same time, industrial activity involved the state in a central coordinating role. The most precocious example of this pattern is to be found in the Arsenal of Venice, which concentrated resources on a scale impossible for private enterprise. The Arsenal was the largest industrial complex in the preindustrial era. It employed some five thousand workers (some estimates are three times that figure) as carpenters, caulkers, and makers of sails (many of whom were women), rope (in a factory of some one hundred workers), and oars. Rather than being a repressed proletariat, the workers known as the *Arsenalotti* were highly skilled and were something approaching an "aristocracy of labor." They formed the personal bodyguard of the doge on ceremonial occasions. The shipyards produced more than half the Christian fleet of more than two hundred galleys that defeated the Turks at Lepanto in 1571. Three years later, the workforce demonstrated that they could fit out a galley in the time it took for the Republic's honored guest—on his way to being crowned Henry III of France in 1574—to dine.

Venetian warships protected and advanced the material interests of the republic in a precocious colonial empire run along mercantilist lines in the Middle Ages. However, the first phase of economic expansion in the early modern period, sometimes referred to as the "long" sixteenth century, witnessed significant developments in patterns of demand that had new implications for manufacture. The increase in population was especially marked in towns, and city-dwellers were, in some important ways, the material beneficiaries of the Renaissance and the Reformation.

LUXURY GOODS

The mercantile wealth of cities and the new educational opportunities for the laity brought about a considerable increase in demand for inessentials—goods that went beyond the fundamentals of food, clothing, and shelter. There were new delights in household furnishings and the embellishments of the interior: compare the cool and simple lines of an interior in fresco by Giotto from the fourteenth century with the swaggering opulence of a Holbein from the sixteenth. From the fifteenth century onward, tapestries, furniture, tableware, paintings, porcelain, and metal goods were symptoms of changes in material culture, which scholars now see as significant generalized manifestations of the cultural achievements of the Renaissance. In Florence, a wedding chest for the bride or a birth tray for the newborn child might be decorated by Ghirlandaio or Botticelli, and the fireplace or the dining room might be graced with majolica inspired by the designs of Andrea and Luca della Robbia. Candelabra, lanterns, locks, scales, and weights, along with warming pans and scissors, were the specialist wares of Nuremberg. Moreover, as the period unfolded, such developments were not confined to towns. As the power of the state advanced, the country house came to replace the fortress in the lifestyle of the nobility. In terms of demand and manufacture, we might ponder the significance of replacing defensive walls with glass windows.

GUILDS

Whatever the changes in taste and demand, it is essential to bear in mind that the processes of production remained in traditional patterns associated with medieval guilds and the workshops that they regulated. The complexity and rigor of a workshop training ensured passage from apprenticeship to mastery through the submission of a "masterpiece" for examination, using materials inspected by the officers of the guild. This was an assurance of the quality of workmanship. Thus, in Nuremberg, clockmakers had to produce a standing timepiece that struck the quarters and the hours with different rings, with mobile representations of the Sun and Moon along with the date and the positions of the heavenly bodies, as well as a watch that was worn round the neck and operated as an alarm clock. Each master had to be able to practice a trade with his own hands. Handicraft training thereby acted as protection against overconcentration of labor in dependence on a single capitalist. Day laborers worked as "journeymen" within the workshop. Their position was more vulnerable than that of the apprentice, and they could easily join the ranks of the poor in the event of a sudden downturn in demand. In Lyon and in Venice, however, there is plenty of evidence to suggest that journeymen had their own robust organizations and social networks.

The traditional structures of guilds and workshops were not as hostile to technical innovation as once supposed. Nuremberg provides a fascinating case history of technological changes in the production of metal goods and the development of new possibilities in the making of scientific instruments and weaponry, still very much within the traditions of the corporate structures of guilds. However, the printing of books marked the beginning of a revolution in communications that has persisted through the industrial and postindustrial eras. In the workshop of Aldus Manutius (c. 1450–1515) in Venice in the early sixteenth century, artisans rubbed shoulders with great writers such as Erasmus in an extraordinary combination of the refinedly learned and the strictly practical. Manutius's invention of the elegant italic script made possible the pocket edition with important implications for price and accessibility. The revolutionary quality of book production demanded a new organization of labor. Market forces began to intrude on the workshop. In Lyon in the 1560s fierce competition between groups of journeymen drove wages down as each group sought to outdo the other. Their conflicts were exacerbated by religious differences, a feature that sets them firmly in their time, but there was a clear pointer to the future in the recasting of relations between workers and bosses.

While the printed word is rightly seen as crucial to the spread of the Reformation, one should also bear in mind the significance of the press in spreading new techniques and ideas. Among the most notable works in this category were the *De Re Metallica* (Concerning metals) of Georgius Agricola (1494–1555), and Vannoccio Biringuccio's (1480–1539) studies of industrial chemistry in *Pirotechnia* (1540; The art of fireworks). This influential work included studies of gunpowder technology and typecasting, which can still be regarded as the symbols of a new age. Other works spread knowledge of precision instruments: one thinks here of Galileo's writings on telescopes.

PATTERNS OF PRODUCTION

However, most such treatises were not strictly instructional manuals but aimed to flatter their princely dedicatees. There is no simple causal connection to be made between the new ideas of the seventeenth century and changing patterns of production. Indeed, it should be emphasized that the scientific revolution of the seventeenth century occurred in a period of economic stagnation and had little immediate impact on production processes. Moreover, in some places, traditional structures took on a new social and political significance. Guilds were organizations that could offer young, unattached males (a group vulnerable to natural decrease) shelter, training, and work. That work might be shared, a further safeguard against abject poverty. In Nuremberg in 1556, eleven workshops of cloth shearers deposited their profits with the Sworn Master who divided up the total "in such a way that the highest producer and the lowest producer get each an appropriate share." In seventeenth-century Leiden, guild structures remained buoyant and vital during the city's growth from twelve thousand people in 1582 to seventy thousand by 1660. By that time, its workshops were producing 130,000 pieces of cloth per year. The provision of work and forms of social insurance took considerable pressure off the limited welfare available from the city authorities. Within the age of economic stagnation, demand for luxuries continued to expand. A vast concentration of labor and materials produced Versailles for Louis XIV, and Christopher Wren (1632–1723) was to remark that scarcely a surface could be found in the palace that did not support some decorative object. The extraordinary project, far from looking forward to a new age, looks back to the two thousand or so workers on site for the building of the new St. Peter's in Rome in the mid-sixteenth century. Versailles itself was to become a symbol of the *ancien régime*.

At a much more humdrum level, many of the most important changes in patterns of production in the seventeenth century are summarized by the term *proto-industrialization*. This is a term to be used with caution, since its explicit sense of being a rehearsal for industrialization "proper" is strongly tinged with the teleology mentioned above. However, it is a concept that takes careful account of new forms of the organization of production associated especially with "putting out" or the "domestic system" in the manufacture of cloth. This is helpful to an understanding of early modern industrial activity because it seeks to trace economic change over the broad long term rather than in relation to technological invention. The new organization of production took shape roughly in the following manner. As economic conditions tightened, merchants sought ways to avoid the overheads—particularly high wages—that guilds jealously protected in towns. Instead merchants offered work—especially spinning and weaving—to people who worked at home in rural areas, where such work was a welcome source of supplementary income. The decline of certain urban centers was sometimes startling. In 1612

Augsburg had more than three thousand master weavers, but barely four hundred by 1720. However, there were clear logistical limitations to putting out work in this way. Quality was difficult to control (a serious disadvantage when compared with urban workshops and guild regulation), pilfering was widespread, and the coordination of the delivery of raw materials and the collection of finished products over relatively long distances was slow and difficult.

Nevertheless, "putting out" was an important underpinning of the production of the so-called "new draperies" in England and the United Provinces. These cloths were light kerseys and worsteds that proved much cheaper than the heavier traditional broadcloths and enabled northern merchants to penetrate the markets of the Levant, to the detriment of centers such as Venice. In fact, Venetian broadcloths remained competitively priced throughout the seventeenth century—but for the tax that the government imposed upon them. That said, during the early modern period, the Venetian economy experienced a huge shift (which its guild system seems to have fostered) from manufacture to retail and services. In terms of production, the balance of economic predominance moved to the north.

The emergent capitalism of seventeenth-century Amsterdam was tied to the extension of the vast serf estates in all the lands that might send grain to Gdańsk (Danzig) in the willing barges of the Dutch. Having thrown off the yoke of the Spanish monarchy in 1648, the Dutch developed the most enterprising, tolerant, "bourgeois" society of the early modern era. And—within the context of their times—they were great industrialists. Peter I the Great of Russia (ruled 1682–1725) visited Amsterdam to find out how to build his ships. Leiden was one of Europe's leading centers of textile production. Dutch entrepreneurs organized the exploitation of the copper mines and iron foundries of Sweden. Dutch printing presses produced some of the seminal works of the scientific revolution and the Enlightenment, and Dutch telescopes and maps furthered overseas commercial interests.

However, the interiors painted by the great Dutch artists show a cultivated taste for comfort—clothing, drapes, tiles, wall hangings, musical instruments, furniture and glass—that only the highest standards of manufacture could sustain. Workshops continued to depend on the appropriate guild's stipulations for training, and the units of production remained small: a workforce as large as fifty people in a glassworks was quite exceptional. In some ways, then, the expansion of the Dutch economy in the seventeenth century may be seen as the culmination of the "material Renaissance" rather than a foreshadowing of the industrial world. The United Provinces played no significant role in the launching of the industrial revolution. The chief reason for this appears to be environmental accident. The Dutch had plenty of peat, but no coal, and peat cannot generate sufficient heat to smelt iron. In England, by contrast, albeit from a very small initial base, domestic coal output rose by 1,400 percent between 1560 and 1690. This was the basis of what is sometimes known as "carboniferous capitalism."

THE EIGHTEENTH CENTURY

Many more statistics and data are available from the eighteenth century than from the preceding period. It is important, therefore, not to exaggerate the nature and scale of change in the era because in reviewing the evidence we may not always be comparing like with like. Yet some cautious generalizations are possible. First, wars became more disciplined, and a clearer distinction developed between military and civilian spheres. Climatic conditions marked a distinct improvement over the "Little Ice Age" of the seventeenth century, making for fewer disastrous harvests. Plague made its last visitation (though no one could have known that it would not return). The chances of survival were greater, and the resultant population expansion known as the "vital revolution" has continued into modern times. There were new concentrations of demand for products, and again the political dimension is essential here since urban growth was particularly marked in the case of capital cities. Following its foundation in 1703, St. Petersburg grew to 220,000 people by 1789, Berlin grew from 8,000 people to 180,000, Paris had more than 500,000 inhabitants by the late eighteenth century, and by then perhaps 900,000 people lived in London. Such expansion dramatically increased the available labor force, and challenged guild monopolies (which were often limited in jurisdiction to the area within the old city walls). Considerable improvements were made in communication and distribution between such centers, too, brought about in Britain in particular by vast programs of canal building and road construction. The broader potential of expansion was boosted by the underpinning of state banks—in England in 1694, Scotland 1695, Prussia 1765, and France 1776.

However, the new concentrations of labor in the same workplace provide the most potent signs of industrialization. Whether we cite the two thousand people who worked for the Wilkinson foundry at Bersham, or the 300,000 workers in the mines and forges of the Urals, such numbers are considerably higher than what was usual in the earlier part of our period. However, it is in textile production that the reorganization through concentration was most marked. Nowhere was it especially sudden, and it is important to acknowledge its beginnings in the seventeenth century in regions such as northeastern France, Westphalia, Silesia, Saxony, Flanders, and the West Riding of Yorkshire in England. The rural dimension of production remained highly significant. Even in the 1780s, 73 percent of all the looms in Picardy in France were located in rural areas. In 1748 in Silesia, 81 percent of all the linen produced was made in the countryside. By mid-century in Sedan, twenty-five merchants were employing around 15,000 people. In 1765, one Prussian *Manufaktur* employed more than 750 workers in the same place. In Abbeville, after Anne Robert Jacques Turgot's abolition of France's old corporations in 1776, the Van Robais Company had ten thousand employees in domestic industry, but also eighteen hundred working under one roof.

Striking evidence can be found of dramatic increases in textile production. French cloth production rose 126 percent between 1700 and 1785, and Scottish linen production increased sevenfold between 1730 and the end of the century. While the production of English woolen cloth doubled, it soon became clear that cotton would be king. Britain imported a million pounds of it in 1700, and 15 million in 1780, a figure that had doubled to 30 million by 1789. Cotton cloth was to be the first sizeable industry of the industrial revolution, depending as it did on mechanical inventions, notably James Hargreaves's spinning jenny (c. 1764; patented 1770), Richard Arkwright's waterframe (patented 1769), and Samuel Crompton's mule-jenny (1779). However, the china factories of Dresden prove that new patterns of production were not entirely confined to textiles in Britain, and signs of the development of industrial regions can be found not just in the north of England, but also in Biscay and in Catalonia.

Soaring production was accompanied by falling prices. It is appropriate to quote Adam Smith, who remarked in *Inquiry into the Nature and Causes of the Wealth of Nations* (1776) on the price of a watch, for it seems to symbolize a reshaping of the relationship between time and money. At the beginning of the early modern period, merchants were still hemmed in by church teaching—and laws—on usury. Traditionally, time belonged to God, and to make money over time was to appropriate what belonged to God. Such action was an expression of pride, the capital sin of Lucifer. By the last quarter of the eighteenth century, trade and manufacture, with the profit and prosperity they generated, were celebrated as an expression of humanity's control over the world and its resources. This in turn was the result of the scientific revolution of the seventeenth century with its new emphasis on direct observation and material demonstration. In the Enlightenment of the eighteenth century, these ideas began to find more extensive application. Smith wrote, "the diminution of price has, in the course of the present century, been most remarkable in those manufactures of which the materials are the coarser metals. A better movement of a watch, that about the middle of the last century would have been bought for 20 pounds, may now perhaps be had for 20 shillings."

This confidence in the direction of things seemed to be reflected in the physical environment. Apothecaries' shops and candlemakers continued in their traditional ways in Shropshire, but they now stood in the shadow of a coal mine and close to Europe's first iron bridge—which gave its name to the town (Ironbridge). However, as the new era of mechanical progress opened, abrupt changes in the workplace and in the natural landscape made the new mills—at least to Luddites and saboteurs—look dark and satanic.

See also **Agriculture; Capitalism; Commerce and Markets; Feudalism; Guilds; Industrial Revolution; Laborers;**

Mercantilism; Peasantry; Proto-Industry; Scientific Revolution.

BIBLIOGRAPHY

Braudel, Fernand. *Civilization and Capitalism, 15th–18th Century.* Translated from the French by Siân Reynolds. 3 vols. New York, 1981–1984.

Cipolla, Carlo M. *Before the Industrial Revolution: European Society and Economy, 1000–1700.* New York, 1976.

Continuity and Change, vol. 8, no. 2 (1993) is devoted to proto-industrialization.

De Vries, Jan. *The Economy of Europe in an Age of Crisis, 1600–1750.* Cambridge, U.K., 1976.

DuPlessis, Robert S. *Transitions to Capitalism in Early Modern Europe.* Cambridge, U.K., 1997.

Farr, James R. *Artisans in Europe, 1300–1914.* Cambridge, U.K., 2000.

Goldthwaite, Richard A. *Wealth and the Demand for Art in Italy, 1300–1600.* Baltimore, 1993.

Kriedte, Peter. *Peasants, Landlords and Merchant Capitalists: Europe and the World Economy, 1500–1800.* Translated from the German by Volker Berghahn. Leamington Spa, U.K., 1981.

Léon, Pierre. *Économies et sociétés préiundustrielle.* Tome 2, *1650–1780: Les origines d'une acceleration de l'histoire.* Paris, 1970.

Mackenney, Richard. *Tradesmen and Traders: The World of the Guilds in Venice and Europe, c. 1250–c. 1650.* London, 1987.

Miskimin, Harry A. *The Economy of Later Renaissance Europe, 1460–1600.* Cambridge, U.K., 1977.

Nef, John U. *Industry and Government in France and England, 1550–1640.* Ithaca, N.Y., 1957.

Parker, William N. "Industry." In *New Cambridge Modern History,* vol. 13, edited by Peter Burke, pp. 43–79. Cambridge, U.K., 1979.

Rapp, Richard T. *Industry and Economic Decline in Seventeenth-Century Venice.* Cambridge, Mass., 1976.

Safley, Thomas Max, and Leonard N. Rosenband, eds. *The Workplace before the Factory: Artisans and Proletarians, 1500–1800.* Ithaca, N.Y., 1993.

Schama, Simon. *The Embarrassment of Riches: An Interpretation of Dutch Culture in the Golden Age.* New York, 1987.

Wilson, Charles, and Geoffrey Parker. *An Introduction to the Sources of European Economic History, 1500–1800.* Ithaca, N.Y., 1977.

RICHARD MACKENNEY

INFANTRY. *See* **Military: Battle Tactics and Campaign Strategy.**

INFLATION. Inflation is a long-term, sustained rise in the general level of prices, as measured by a consumer price index. For early modern European history, the best known of these are the "basket of consumables" indexes devised by Earl Hamilton for Spain (for the period 1501–1650), by Henry Phelps Brown and Sheila Hopkins for southern England (1264–1954), and by Herman van der Wee for the Antwerp-Lier-Brussels region of Brabant (1401–1700). In European economic history, undoubtedly one of the longest and certainly the best-known era of inflation was the so-called price revolution of circa 1515–1650 (See Table 1). If we take the decade 1501–1510 as the base, for which the average price index in all three regions equals 100, and then calculate five-year means of these price indexes, we would find, by the final quinquennium 1646–1650, that the Spanish index had risen to 457.09; the English index to 697.54; and the Brabantine index to 845.07 (i.e., an 8.45-fold increase). Thus, one may observe that, during this 135-year period, inflation was a Europewide phenomenon, but that its intensity and impact varied by region, according to local circumstances. Thereafter, prices fell in most of western Europe, as, by 1656–1660, to an index of 614.45 in Brabant and to 569.56 in England.

REAL (DEMOGRAPHIC) AND MONETARY FACTORS IN INFLATION: THE EQUATION OF EXCHANGE

In the literature of early modern economic history, the predominant though quite misleading explanation for this inflation has been population growth. To be sure, population growth, acting upon relatively fixed (inelastic) land and other natural resources, resulting in diminishing returns and rising marginal costs, may well explain the rise in the relative prices of some specific commodities, such as grain and timber (whose English prices did rise the most over this 130-year period). But demographic factors alone cannot explain a rise in the price level; for inflation is fundamentally though not uniquely monetary in origin and character. Indeed, since England's population in the early 1520s was only

TABLE 1.

Composite Price Indexes for Brabant, Southern England, and Spain (Castile)

IN QUINQUENNIAL MEANS: 1501–05 TO 1646–50
INDEX: MEAN OF 1501–10 = 100

Years	Brabant 1501–10=100	England 1501–10=100	Spain 1501–10=100 Silver-Based	Spain 1501–10=100 Vellon from 1597*
1501–05	104.43	101.43	92.43	92.43
1506–10	95.57	98.57	107.57	107.57
1511–15	114.80	103.08	98.98	98.98
1516–20	125.09	114.40	104.28	104.28
1521–25	149.79	138.72	122.14	122.14
1526–30	148.61	149.45	131.57	131.57
1531–35	144.85	147.83	132.44	132.44
1536–40	154.54	144.69	138.73	138.73
1541–45	173.44	167.69	147.90	147.90
1546–50	166.01	218.12	165.89	165.89
1551–55	216.87	261.63	176.02	176.02
1556–60	250.34	300.00	194.01	194.01
1561–65	261.34	274.80	223.43	223.43
1566–70	264.97	277.63	227.73	227.73
1571–75	352.49	281.24	246.77	246.77
1576–80	400.18	319.61	247.82	247.82
1581–85	513.98	320.58	269.07	269.07
1586–90	665.77	367.74	274.97	274.97
1591–95	573.01	395.14	284.42	284.42
1596–00	626.80	513.42	320.97	320.98
1601–05	509.74	438.12	349.92	352.43
1606–10	512.71	472.06	330.11	335.31
1611–15	529.56	506.11	316.81	322.68
1616–20	521.93	494.28	328.56	335.64
1621–25	679.09	503.14	317.85	344.72
1626–30	765.57	498.72	328.04	410.81
1631–35	756.32	577.86	329.91	395.13
1636–40	805.55	584.26	323.47	409.67
1641–45	821.78	532.37	313.50	432.48
1646–50	845.07	697.54	343.36	457.09

* Vellon was a largely copper-based coinage, with little but diminishing amounts of silver. The high-denomination and basically pure silver and gold coins were not debased. From 1597 this index is based on actual Spanish prices, while the silver-based index is based on Hamilton's estimates of prices based on the silver contents of the entire coinage (i.e., as if the vellon coinage had been excluded).

about 2.25 million, evidently less than half the late-medieval peak of about 5.0 million in 1300, it is inconceivable that any renewed population growth in the following three decades could have produced the ensuing inflation, by which the mean price index more than doubled, to a mean of 218.12, in the quinquennium 1546–1550.

The relationship between monetary and so-called "real factors" (population, investment, technology, trade) can be best expressed by the Equation of Exchange, M.V = P.y, which is a modified version of the famous Fisher Identity. On the right-hand side, P stands for the price level, as measured by one of the aforementioned "basket of consumables" indexes; and y represents the real (deflated) value of net national income (NNI) = net national product (NNP = Gross National Product minus depreciation), replacing the unmeasurable T (total transactions) in the original Fisher Identity. On the left-hand side, M is the total stock of available money, which, in this era meant gold and silver coins, supplemented by some credit instruments; and V represents the income velocity of money: the rate at which a unit of money (e.g., the silver penny) circulates in producing aggregate national income y.

A much earlier generation of economists had quite fallaciously believed that both V and T (or y) were fixed, at least in the short run, so that changes in the quantity of money M necessarily produced a proportional change in the price level P. But since all four of these variables are in fact always variable, an increase in M need not produce any inflation, because it could be offset by a fall in V and a corresponding rise in y, that is, by stimulating real economic growth. Indeed, Keynesian economists believe that, since a high level of V reflects society's efforts to economize on scarce stocks of money, an increase in M should be offset by some fall in V, a theorem that can be historically demonstrated for much of western Europe from the thirteenth to nineteenth centuries, with one significant exception: the price revolution era, when V may have doubled.

For this era, we may conclude that the product of M.V ultimately expanded to a greater extent than did the real growth of national income y (or NNP), so that inflation (rising P) ensued. Population growth (more than doubling, in England, to 5.60 million by 1651) may have played a dual role in this inflation: by inducing diminishing returns and rising marginal costs in the agricultural and extractive industries, thus restricting the rate of economic growth; and by inducing a rise in V (income velocity), through changes in demographic structures (higher dependency ratios) and market structures, with increased urbanization and commercialization.

THE CAUSES OF THE EUROPEAN PRICE REVOLUTION, 1515–1650

But if the crude quantity theory of money is historically fallacious, nevertheless changes in money stocks and money instruments do remain paramount in explaining the price revolution. Monetary expansion in fact had begun far earlier, with Portuguese imports of West African gold from the 1460s, but most especially with the central European silver-copper mining boom, also from the 1460s. It may have increased European silver stocks fivefold by the 1540s (to possibly 90,000 kg per year); and a considerable stock of underutilized resources may explain why inflation did not ensue until after 1510. Only from the 1540s did an influx of Spanish American silver become truly important, with imports rising from an annual mean of 16,816 kg in 1541–1545 to a peak of 273,705 kg in 1591–1595 (223,027 kg in 1621–1625). But of equal monetary importance was a veritable financial revolution in negotiable credit, established in the Habsburg Netherlands and England from the 1520s: with effective institutions for legally enforceable transactions in negotiable bills of exchange, bills obligatory (promissory notes), and government annuities *(rentes)*. Indeed in Habsburg Spain the issue of negotiable annuities *(juros)* (many of which were traded on the Antwerp Bourse) rose from 3.6 million ducats in 1516 to 80.4 million ducats in 1598 (death of Philip II). The impact of such changes in both private and public credit increased both the effective money supply and certainly its velocity of circulation.

One may therefore wonder why the degree of inflation was so much less in Spain than in the Netherlands (Brabant) and England. The principal reason lies in another monetary factor. For coinage debasements were absent in Spain before 1597 but had become quite drastic in sixteenth-century England ("Great Debasement" of 1542–1552) and in the southern Netherlands (less drastic, though more prolonged). Furthermore, credit undoubtedly played a smaller role in the relatively undeveloped Spanish economy.

THE CONSEQUENCES OF THE EUROPEAN PRICE REVOLUTION

Only a summary of the consequences of inflation may be suggested here. In general, inflation redistributes income from wage earners and those living on fixed incomes, especially landowners with many hereditary tenures, or leaseholds on long-term contracts, to merchants and industrialists, in particular. Many in the latter group certainly benefited from a general lag of wages behind prices, even if industrial prices rose much less than did grain prices; and, given the vital importance of capital in the economy, most merchants and industrialists benefited from a fall in real interest costs, all the more so since nominal as well as real interest rates fell over this entire period throughout western Europe. Many peasants or small landholders also gained, insofar as their rents remained fixed, while the prices of the products that they sold in the market continued to rise. On the other hand, some undoubtedly did suffer the consequences of population growth, at least in areas of partible inheritance, which thus meant a significant subdivision of holdings. A balance sheet of winners and losers from inflation would be most difficult to construct for the price revolution era.

See also **Capitalism; Economic Crises; Landholding; Money and Coinage; Peasantry.**

BIBLIOGRAPHY

Fisher, Douglas. "The Price Revolution: A Monetary Interpretation." *Journal of Economic History* 49 (December 1989): 883–902.

Goldstone, Jack A. "Urbanization and Inflation: Lessons from the English Price Revolution of the Sixteenth and Seventeenth Centuries." *American Journal of Sociology* 89 (1984): 1122–1160.

Lindert, Peter. "English Population, Wages, and Prices: 1541–1913." *Journal of Interdisciplinary History* 15, no. 4 (spring 1985): 609–634.

Mayhew, Nicholas. "Population, Money Supply, and the Velocity of Circulation in England, 1300–1700." *Economic History Review*, 2nd ser., 482 (May 1995): 238–257.

Munro, John. "The Monetary Origins of the 'Price Revolution': South German Silver Mining, Merchant-Banking, and Venetian Commerce, 1470–1540." In *Global Connections and Monetary History, 1470–1800.* Edited by Dennis O. Flynn, Arturo Giráldez, and Richard von Glahn. Aldershot, U.K., 2002.

Outhwaite, R. B. *Inflation in Tudor and Early Stuart England.* Studies in Economic and Social History series, 2nd ed. London, 1982.

Ramsey, Peter H., ed. *The Price Revolution in Sixteenth Century England.* London, 1971.

JOHN H. MUNRO

INHERITANCE AND WILLS. For the overwhelming mass of the population, both rural and urban, early modern material life was anchored in the ownership of fixed capital assets, above all land and buildings. The perpetuation of society depended upon the transmission of these assets from one generation to another, making inheritance (together with marriage, for which inheritance was usually an implicit, and in some cases an explicit, requirement) one of the essential social processes in early modern Europe. Inheritance also had significant, though equivocal, implications for patterns of demographic growth and long-term economic change. Relative to its importance, early modern inheritance remains a subject about which we know embarrassingly little. The prescriptive rules of postmortem succession, codified with increasing frequency from the sixteenth century across the entirety of Europe, have been well studied. At the same time, it has become obvious not only that formal norms were heavily modified by actual practice, but also that postmortem succession was normally only the final stage of a more drawn-out process of generational replacement.

PARTIBILITY

The classic point of reference for the analysis of European inheritance customs is the issue of partibility. Nineteenth-century investigations of peasant inheritance customs in western and central Europe divided the continent into regions of partible inheritance (East Anglia and Kent, Aragon-Castile, Italy, the French Riviera, northern France, the Low Countries, and much of Rhineland Germany) and impartible inheritance (most of the British Isles, Catalonia, southern France, northeastern and southeastern Germany, Austria, and Scandinavia), although there was considerable small-scale regional variation. The historicity of this division is uncertain. It can certainly be dated back to c. 1550–1600, but in some impartible zones like Upper Swabia there is clear evidence of partibility during the later Middle Ages. At least among the European aristocracy (whose inheritance practices are admittedly only an uncertain guide to the customs of commoners), there was a definite drift toward impartibility during the sixteenth century, a trend underscored by a burgeoning legal literature on the practice and ethics of unigeniture (inheritance by a single heir). The reasons for the partibility/impartibility division are less clear. There is considerable truth to the suggestion that impartibility was usually a product of strong feudal overlordship (and the attendant pressure to preserve the integrity of rent-paying units) in regions of arable agriculture, but this is hardly a universal association.

For all the attractive simplicity of the partibility/impartibility division, the reality on the ground was much more complex, and the seemingly stark opposition of the two regimes was in practice mitigated by a host of qualifications. Systems of partible inheritance often explicitly advantaged one heir over the others, a custom known as *préciput* in northeastern France. Even in Normandy, the "egalitarian" obligation to return any premortem endowment to ensure the absolutely even division of family property at the parent's death was modified by the exclusion of daughters from inheriting land. Conversely, impartible arrangements in both England and Germany typically required the heir to buy out or otherwise compensate the other siblings ("yielding heirs," as they were often called in Bavaria) for their exclusion from the family farm. Most inheritance systems, in other words, attempted to strike a balance (often at the expense of the weaker members of the kindred, especially women) between security and equity, between preserving an ancestral property and providing the foundation for the next generation of kin.

Partibility and impartibility are thus best understood as the poles of a continuum of strategies for the regulation of household formation in conformity with the socioeconomic context. Impartibility, however modified, tended to limit the creation of new households by restricting access to property, which helps to explain the spread of such inheritance practices during the demographic surge of the sixteenth century. Partibility imposed fewer restrictions on household formation, and in the case of the German territory of Lower Saxony, it has been demonstrated that regions of partible inheritance experienced significantly higher rates of population growth than regions of impartibility. Variations in inheritance customs had similarly divergent implications for household structure. Despite the overall dominance of nuclear households in early modern Europe, impartible inheritance often led to an extended phase of the household's life cycle, with either a retired parent living with the principal heir (as in central Europe), or with a number of brothers co-owning an undivided ancestral property (as in Italy or southern France). Regions of partible inheritance were less likely to evince this pattern, as the facility with which children could establish independent households militated against coresidence.

SPOUSAL RIGHTS

The recognition that postmortem transfers from parent to child were only one facet of the dynamics of inheritance has in recent years redirected scholarly attention to other aspects of the nexus between kinship and property, in particular to the property rights of widowed spouses. In many regions, especially in urban areas, the property brought by each spouse to a marriage was merged indivisibly, so that in the event of one partner's death, an irreducible fraction, and sometimes the entirety, of the property devolved upon the survivor (in some regions this merger only took place if there had been issue from the marriage). In some areas (for example, England) the widow's estate was an interest for her lifetime only, but in many places on the continent (for example, Wallonia) a widow could remarry in situ and effectively disinherit the children from the first marriage. Allowing as it did for the inheritance (albeit temporary, in some cases) of property by women, this widespread custom of "conjugal community" was a characteristic feature of European inheritance practices, marking them off sharply from customs in sub-Saharan Africa and many parts of Asia.

WILLS

Given the complex and drawn-out nature of generational replacement in early modern Europe, the will turns out (ironically) to be a much less important instrument of inheritance than might be expected, especially outside of cities. In continental Europe the peasant will was more important for the registration of pious legacies than for the disposition of land. In much of Germany, this latter allocation was normally accomplished by premortem conveyance, while in northern France, a householder was explicitly forbidden to dispose of more than a fraction (one-third in Picardy, Artois, Touraine, Anjou, Maine, and Brittany; one-fifth in the Paris Basin, the Beauvaisis, the Nivernais, and the Orléanais) of his property by will, with the kindred retaining an inextinguishable claim to the remaining "reserve." Even in southern France, where a Roman Law regime contributed to a more absolute conception of private property, the customs of Gascony and Aquitaine prohibited the alienation of more than a fraction of the testator's property (in Languedoc, however, a testator was free to convey his property to whomsoever he wished). The most important exception to these restrictions on testator freedom was England, where a long tradition of individualistic property rights was enshrined in the 1540 Statute of Wills, which for the first time legalized the conveyance of land by will. Nevertheless, the theoretical power of an English father to disinherit his children was only rarely resorted to in practice.

See also **Family; Gender; Law; Property.**

BIBLIOGRAPHY

Actes à cause de mort=Acts of Last Will. Receuils de la société Jean Bodin pour l'histoire comparative des institutions LX–LXII. 3 vols. Brussels, 1992.

Goody, Jack, Joan Thirsk, and E. P. Thompson, eds. *Family and Inheritance: Rural Society in Western Europe, 1200–1800.* Cambridge, U.K., and New York, 1976.

Howell, Martha C. *The Marriage Exchange: Property, Social Place, and Gender in Cities of the Low Countries, 1300–1550.* Chicago, 1998.

Sabean, David. *Kinship in Neckarhausen, 1700–1870.* Cambridge, U.K., and New York, 1998.

Seccombe, Wally. *A Millennium of Family Change: Feudalism to Capitalism in Northwestern Europe.* London and New York, 1992.

GOVIND P. SREENIVASAN

INQUISITION. Scholars distinguish between the medieval, or papal, Inquisition, which evolved in the thirteenth century to combat the Cathar heresy in southern France, and the modern Inquisition, reestablished in parts of Europe during the fifteenth and sixteenth centuries.

FOUNDATIONS

The first two modern Inquisitions were established in Spain (1478) and Portugal (1536) to deal with a heresy peculiar to the Iberian Peninsula, Cryptojudaism, or a reversion to Judaism among converts to Christianity *(conversos).* To punish this form of apostasy, the Catholic monarchs Ferdinand and Isabella obtained authorization in 1478 from Pope Sixtus IV to establish a new Inquisition in Castile, and later, in 1483, to revive Aragón's medieval tribunals. Nonetheless, cases of Judaizing continued to occur, so the Catholic monarchs took the extreme decision in 1492 of ordering all Jews to either convert to Christianity or leave Castile. Many Jews crossed the border to Portugal to join the large numbers of *conversos* who had already fled there from Spain. In 1496, the king of Portugal, John II, ordered the expulsion of Jews from his territory, and in 1497, the conversion of any who remained, who joined ranks with the Spanish refugees. The presence of this group of New Christians eventually forced John III to bring the Inquisition to Portugal in 1536.

Pope Paul III, who had authorized the foundation of the Portuguese Inquisition, six years later (1542) revived the Holy Office of the Inquisition in the Italian Papal States. Here, however, the Roman Inquisition's concern was not Judaizing, but the threat to Italy from Protestantism. Soon, other states in the Italian peninsula reinstated local tribunals of the Inquisition: Naples and Venice in 1547, and Milan in 1562.

INSTITUTIONAL STRUCTURE AND PROCEDURE

The modern Inquisitions generally followed the body of jurisprudence developed by the medieval Inquisition, compiled in 1376 by Nicolau Eimeric into the *Directorium inquisitorum,* revised in the late sixteenth century by Francisco Peña. Unlike their medieval predecessor, however, the Spanish and Portuguese Inquisitions were controlled by the crown, and in Italy, there was considerable secular oversight as well, except in the Papal States. In Spain, Ferdinand created a government board, the Council of the Supreme and General Inquisition, which established policies and procedures, oversaw the appointment of officials and functioning of tribunals throughout the Spanish realms, and served as the court of appeals. Until 1560, the number and territories of the Spanish districts fluctuated considerably; thereafter they remained stable at fourteen peninsular tribunals and four island tribunals (Mallorca, Sardinia, Sicily, and the Canaries). Additional tribunals were added as the empire expanded: Mexico, Lima, Cartagena de Indias, Manila, and finally, the royal court at Madrid.

Portugal's Inquisition was also placed under the direction of a royal board, known as the General Council. Ultimately, there were tribunals in Lisbon, Coimbra, and Evora, plus another in Goa, the Portuguese colony in India.

In Italy, the papacy attempted to exert some control over the Inquisitions outside the Papal States; this process culminated in the establishment of the Congregazione del Sant' Ufficio in 1588. As was the case in Portugal and Spain, the Congregation functioned as the supreme appellate court for the tribunals in Italy. In each of the states with Inquisitions, the network of local tribunals followed the preexisting structure of bishoprics. For example, in the Republic of Venice, aside from the head tribunal in Venice itself, there were tribunals at Brescia, Padua, Udine, Treviso, Cyprus, Rovigo, Picenza, Bergamo, Vicenza, Verona, and Capo d'Istria.

Thanks to a shared legal tradition, the operation of the Inquisition in each area was similar. In Spain each tribunal consisted of one or two inquisitors, a fiscal prosecutor, defense attorney, various employees who were charged with record keeping and care of the prisoners, unpaid theological and legal consultants, and a network of local legal representatives *(comisarios)* and messengers/jailors *(familiars),* also unpaid, who created an inquisitorial presence in the hinterland. Strict guidelines established the qualifications for various members of the tribunal. Inquisitors had to be at least forty years old, licentiates or doctors in theology or canon law. After the fifteenth century, few Spanish inquisitors were drawn from the religious orders such as the Dominicans, who had once dominated the medieval institution. *Comisarios* were drawn from the local secular clergy, and familiars were laymen of uncontested Christian ancestry. Portugal's tribunals were structured along the same lines, while in Italy, often only one inquisitor led the court (in Iberia there were two), while the local legal representatives, known as *vicarii,* held more power than their Iberian counterparts. Unlike their Iberian counterparts, both the inquisitors and the vicars came from the ranks of the regular religious orders, primarily the Dominicans and Franciscans.

A tribunal generated its cases in a variety of ways. The standard method was for the inquisitor to go on a visitation of his district. First, the inquisitor would issue the Edict of Grace, a sermon that defined the heresies sought after and promised leniency for those who confessed within thirty days. The follow-up sermon, the Edict of Faith, offered no leniency but continued the exhortations to confess. Voting members of the tribunal would examine the resulting confessions and issue a warrant for arrest. Once detained, the prisoner disappeared to the outside world: in order to inspire fear and prevent reprisals, the courts attempted to conduct their business in the strictest secrecy. Similar secrecy within the proceedings kept the prisoner at a disadvantage. Not until well into the trial did the prisoner learn the charges against him, and never was the accused allowed to know who had given evidence against him—or, once freed, to speak about his experiences. With the inquisitor acting as both judge and investigator, the prosecution presented its case first, and the defendant, with the aid of a court-appointed lawyer, could respond. At this point, if the defendant's confession was not seen as sufficient, the tribunal would vote on the question of torture: what kind and how much. In reality, torture was employed rarely (in less than 3 percent of cases) and frequently was overcome. The large majority of cases ended in guilty verdicts. In Spain and Portugal, the final act in the trial was the public auto-da-fé, where prisoners were sentenced amid great ceremony; actual punishments were carried out separately. An important tool of the Iberian Inquisition was public humiliation: those convicted of serious offenses were required to wear the *sanbenito,* a distinctive outer tunic that was also displayed in the convict's parish church.

Abolition came slowly, with the advance of the Enlightenment and then French troops to southern Europe. Generally, the Italian tribunals were disbanded between 1774 and 1800, and the Iberian ones disappeared between 1812 and 1834, although the Spanish and American tribunals effectively ended operation in 1820. The fate of each tribunal's archives is capricious: some survive virtually intact, while others disappeared during the Napoleonic Wars. Major repositories exist in the Archivo General de la Nación (Mexico), Arquivo Nacional da Torre do Tombo (Lisbon), Archivo Histórico Nacional (Madrid), and in the Archivi dell'Inquisizione Romana (The Vatican, opened in 1998), but substantial numbers of trials and other papers remain outside these repositories.

Considerable controversy exists over how many individuals were tried and executed by the courts, but the loss of so many records makes precise accounting impossible. A survey of nineteen Spanish tribunals from 1540 to 1700 yielded 49,092 cases. The Portuguese Inquisition tried 44,817 cases between 1536 and 1767, the most active court being Goa. Naples between 1564 and 1740 tried 3,038 cases, and Venice between 1547 and 1794 tried 3,592 cases. The death sentence was invoked in less than 5 percent of all trials. In Spain and Portugal the first victims were *conversos,* many of whom were sentenced to death (often in absentia), while the Italian courts pursued Protestants. With time, the tribunals changed their focus and moderated their severity: in Spain, converted Muslims *(Moriscos)*, homosexuals, Protestants, witches, and ordinary Spaniards guilty of making crude theological statements all at some point became the focus of the tribunals' attention. Indeed, relatively minor crimes such as blasphemy accounted for much of the Spanish Inquisition's caseload. In addition to punishing religious crimes, all of the Inquisitions were responsible for enforcing censorship of printed materials and searching for contraband.

IMPACT AND LASTING SIGNIFICANCE

Because of the Inquisition's role in censorship, many have accused the institution of curbing scientific inquiry, dampening literary creativity, and even hindering economic growth. Historians now reject these charges. A few cases achieved notoriety in their day and continue to define the image of the Inquisition in the public's mind. Most infamous is the case of Galileo Galilei (1564–1642), who was summoned before the Roman Inquisition in 1632 to account for his public defense of the Copernican system, earlier deemed heretical by the church. He was condemned to perpetual house arrest and silence on the issue. For many, this trial epitomizes the conflict between scientific reason and free speech on the one hand, and religious fanaticism on the other. The philosopher Giordano Bruno (1548–1600) was not so lucky as Galileo; he was burned at the stake for his radical ideas about revealed religion and the possibility of an infinite universe with multiple worlds. In Spain, fear of religious experimentation led the inquisitors to target some of the leading mystics of the sixteenth century—St. Theresa of Jesus, St. John of the Cross, and Luis de León—although none was executed. Such cases, added to the Inquisition's role in censorship, the stream of Protestant propaganda directed against the papacy, and the Enlightenment's championship of basic freedoms, combined to create a lasting image of an arbitrarily cruel and inhumane institution. In the last twenty-five years, however, new scholarship has done much to mitigate the fearsome image of the Inquisition and to place the institution in its proper historical context.

See also **Censorship; *Conversos;* Ferdinand of Aragón; Galileo Galilei; Index of Prohibited Books; Isabella of Castile; Moriscos; Papacy and Papal States; Persecution.**

BIBLIOGRAPHY

Primary Sources

Del Col, Andrea, ed. *Domenico Scandella Known as Menocchio: His Trials before the Inquisition (1583–1599).* Translated by John Tedeschi and Anne C. Tedeschi. Binghamton, N.Y., 1996.

Eimeric, Nicolau, and Francisco Peña. *Le manuel des inquisiteurs.* Translated and with introduction by Louis Sala-Molins. Paris, 1973.

Firpo, Massimo, and Dario Marcatto, eds. *Il processo inquisitoriale del Cardinal Giovanni Morone: Edizione critica.* 6 vols. Rome, 1981–1995.

Simancas, Diego de. *Institutiones catholicae quibus ordine ac brevitate discritur quicquid ad praecavendas et extirpandas haereses necessariium est.* Valladolid, 1552.

Secondary Sources

Bethencourt, Francisco. *La Inquisición en la época moderna: España, Portugal, e Italia, siglos XV–XIX.* Madrid, 1997.

Grendler, Paul F. *The Roman Inquisition and the Venetian Press, 1540–1605.* Princeton, 1977.

Henningsen, Gustav, and John Tedeschi in association with Charles Amiel, eds. *The Inquisition in Early Modern Europe: Studies on Sources and Methods.* De Kalb, Ill., 1986.

Kamen, Henry. *The Spanish Inquisition: An Historical Revision.* London, 1997.

Lea, Henry Charles. *A History of the Inquisition of Spain.* 4 vols. New York, 1906–1908.

———. *The Inquisition in the Spanish Dependencies.* New York, 1908.

Netanyahu, Benzion. *The Origins of the Inquisition in Fifteenth-Century Spain.* New York, 1995.

Perry, Mary Elizabeth, and Anne J. Cruz, eds. *Cultural Encounters: The Impact of the Inquisition in Spain and the New World.* Berkeley, 1991.

Peters, Edward. *Inquisition.* New York and London, 1988.

Vekene, Emil van der. *Bibliotheca bibliographica historiae sanctae Inquisitionis. Bibliographisches Verzeichnis des gedruckten Schrifftums zur Geschichte und Literatur der Inquisition.* 3 vols. Vaduz, Liechtenstein, 1982–1992.

Sara Tilghman Nalle

INQUISITION, ROMAN. The Roman Inquisition was a penal and judicial institution brought into being by the Catholic Church in midsixteenth century Italy as a response to the Protestant challenge in that country. Prior to this time, a loosely knit, decentralized network of individual clerics drawn from the early-thirteenth-century mendicant orders investigated specific instances of heresy. Neither the Roman Inquisition nor its medieval predecessor should be confused with the more famous Spanish Inquisition, which started in 1478, was controlled by the crown, had a separate history, and operated in virtual independence of the papacy.

ORIGIN AND STRUCTURE

The chief features the reorganization set in motion in Rome by Paul III (1534–1549) with his bull *Licet ab Initio* of July 1542 were as follows: a centralized authority for the pursuit of heresy in the form of a commission of cardinals, which appointed and closely supervised the work of the local inquisitors; the expansion of local tribunals throughout the peninsula, the seats of which were usually Dominican and Franciscan convents; and the repeal of privileges that exempted from prosecution regular clergy who previously had to answer only to their superiors in the religious orders, a measure that preceded the major reorganization by a few months.

The addition of new tribunals took place gradually over the course of the century, with new seats erected at intervals or elevated to full status only after existing for many years. Concurrently, the definition of what was heretical and proper for the Inquisition to prosecute was also expanded to include such offenses as apostasy from the religious orders, blasphemy, and bigamy, among others; this resulted in squabbles between the Inquisition and competing authorities, episcopal courts, and secular magistracies.

The customary provincial tribunal consisted of an inquisitor, his vicar, a notary, and such "familiars" as prison guards and messengers. A network of lesser officials called *vicari foranei*, 'external vicars', selected from the ranks of the regular clergy and parish priests, represented the parent tribunal in the small towns under its jurisdiction. The judicial role of the *vicari foranei* was generally limited to conducting preliminary inquiries and receiving depositions. The presence of a bishop or, usually, an episcopal vicar was required when the court wanted to proceed to such grave stages as judicial torture or final sentencing.

Every court was assisted in its deliberations by a body of "consultors" drawn from the ranks of prominent lawyers and theologians. Except in the most ordinary of cases, a local tribunal would not reach the point of final sentencing until the Supreme Congregation in Rome, which received and closely scrutinized copies or summaries of trials in progress, had expressed its binding opinion.

JURISDICTION

The jurisdiction of the reconstituted tribunal was limited to the Italian peninsula, excluding Sicily and Sardinia, where the Spanish Inquisition prevailed. It was also barred from working openly in Naples, part of the Spanish empire, where Rome had to act under the cover of the episcopal courts. The island of Malta and the city of Avignon in France fell under Roman purview. As for the rest of Italy, although inquisitors were able to proceed in their duties freely in the states of the church, their activities were curtailed to varying degrees in independent principalities and republics where arrests, incarceration, confiscations, and extraditions to Rome were dependent on the approval of the local ruler. Although they had no official roles, lay functionaries appointed by the secular government sat on the tribunals to guarantee the correctness of the proceedings. Venice, perhaps more than any other state, limited the Inquisition by a series of special dispositions.

PROCEDURES

Recent research has overturned many long-standing assumptions connected with the Roman Inquisition, framing its juridical theory and procedures in a new, more favorable light. For example, it has been determined that in trials conducted under the Inquisition's jurisdiction, accusers had to make their depositions under oath. Other findings include the following: the arraigned had the benefit of a defense attorney; transcripts of the proceedings were provided to prisoners in writing; and an appropriate interval allowed for the preparation of counterarguments and the summoning of friendly witnesses. Judicial torture (universally practiced by all courts in Europe) could be applied only after the defense had made its case and where the indicia (the evidence of heresy) were compelling. Appeals were also permitted and were made regularly to a higher court, namely the Supreme Congregation in Rome. First offenders were dealt with much more leniently than recidivists. A sentence to *carcere perpetuo*, 'life imprisonment', by the Holy Office meant parole after a few years (generally three) subject to good behavior; house arrest, which often included permission to work outside one's home, was frequently imposed, especially given the lack of secure prisons outside Rome. Sentences pronounced by provincial tribunals were scrutinized by the Supreme Congregation of the Inquisition in Rome, and implausible confessions that contradicted the defendant's testimony during the trial were unacceptable. There were many additional safeguards in witchcraft proceedings, not the least of which was the Supreme Congregation's 1588 decision that alleged participants at Sabbaths were not allowed to implicate supposed accomplices, a measure that spared Italy (and Spain) the panics that swept through northern Europe until well into the seventeenth century.

PUNISHMENT

The stake, incarceration, and galley sentences are dramatic forms of penal procedure that are associated with inquisitorial practice. But a survey of the thousands of surviving sentences shows that milder forms of punishment actually prevailed, the most common being the wearing of the penitential garment (the *sanbenito*), abjurations read on the cathedral steps on feast days, and such salutary penances as fines, communal service, and the recital of prayers and devotions.

Death by burning at the stake was reserved for three categories of offenders: the obstinate and unrepentant who refused to be reconciled to the church; the relapsed, namely those who had suffered a previous sentence for formal heresy; and, following bulls promulgated by Paul IV (1555–1559) in July 1556 and February 1558, persons convicted of an attempt to overturn such central doctrines as the virgin birth and the full divinity of Christ.

Although there are serious lacunae in the documentation, the available numbers of those executed by the Roman Inquisition suggest that there were fewer than has generally been believed. For example, only four of the first thousand defendants who appeared before the Friulan tribunal of Aquileia-Concordia (1551–1647) were put to death, and only one, in 1567, for religious heresy in Modena, out of the hundreds of trials conducted in that city. And of the more than 200 sentences contained in the Trinity College manuscripts for parts of 1580–1582, only three called for condemnations to the stake.

SOURCES

Existing knowledge of the Roman Inquisition is based on a broad array of surviving sources. Even before the 1998 opening of the central archives of the old Roman Holy Office (now the Congregation for the Doctrine of the Faith) to the scholarly public, there was no shortage of original inquisitorial documents. Numerous printed legal manuals written between the early fourteenth and mid-seventeenth centuries are still in existence.

Large quantities of dispersed manuscript records are also available. The suppression of the Inquisition throughout the Italian peninsula in the eighteenth century, in addition to the closing of many of the religious establishments that had housed the local tribunals, brought about the transfer of long runs of inquisitorial records to public repositories and to episcopal archives. Thousands of trials have survived intact in Udine, Venice, Modena, Rovigo, Naples, and elsewhere; extensive series of correspondence between the Supreme Congregation of the Inquisition in Rome and its outlying outposts in Bologna, Modena, Naples, and Udine still exist; and a large body of sentences spanning a century and a half (c. 1556–c. 1700) found their way in the nineteenth century to Trinity College, Dublin, as part of the considerable archival material that changed hands during the time of Napoleon.

An important new infusion of pertinent documents became available with the opening of the previously inaccessible Roman Archive of the Holy Office. Scholars now could consult the archive of the Congregation of the Index, which was transferred intact to the Holy Office in 1917; the complete, original, sixteenth-century trials of a few highly placed ecclesiastics, such as Cardinal Giovanni Morone, Bishop Vittore Soranzo, and the prothonotary Pietro Carnesecchi (thousands of "lesser" trials were consciously destroyed in Paris after the fall of Napoleon); the long runs of the *Acta Sancti Officii,* namely the decrees coming out of the weekly meetings of the Roman Congregation, at which the pope generally presided, ranging in date from 1548 to the twenty-first century (with lacunae); the correspondence from provincial inquisitors to Rome, numbering some 225 volumes (previously only the letters from Rome were available in local repositories); and the records of the Sienese Inquisition, which were transferred to the Supreme Congregation in 1911 from the episcopal archive in Siena.

See also **Index of Prohibited Books; Inquisition; Papacy and Papal States; Paul III (pope); Persecution.**

BIBLIOGRAPHY

Primary Source

Del Col, Andrea. *Domenico Scandella Known as Menocchio: His Trials before the Inquisition (1583–1599).* Translated by John and Anne C. Tedeschi. Binghamton, N.Y., 1996. The original Italian edition of the proceedings against the celebrated Friulan miller was published in 1991.

Secondary Sources

Borromeo, Agostino. "The Inquisition and Inquisitorial Censorship." In *Catholicism in Early Modern History: A Guide to Research,* edited by John W. O'Malley, pp. 253–272. St. Louis, 1988. Historiographical survey.

Henningsen, Gustav, and John Tedeschi, eds., in association with Charles Amiel. *Inquisition in Early Modern Europe: Studies on Sources and Methods.* De Kalb, Ill., 1986. Volume based on several papers presented at a Danish symposium, September 1978.

Romeo, Giovanni. *L'Inquisizione nell'Italia moderna.* Bari, 2002. The best comprehensive treatment in brief compass.

Tedeschi, John. *The Italian Reformation of the Sixteenth Century and the Diffusion of Renaissance Culture: A Bibliography of the Secondary Literature.* Modena, 2000. Devotes ample attention to the role of the Inquisition in the suppression of the Reformation in Italy.

———. *The Prosecution of Heresy: Collected Studies on the Inquisition in Early Modern Italy.* Binghamton, N.Y., 1991. *Il giudice e l'eretico: Studi su l'Inquisizione romana.* Revised and updated Italian translation. Milan, 1997. Pioneered the new perspective on the Roman Inquisition.

Vekene, Emil van der. *Bibliotheca Bibliographica Historiae Sanctae Inquisitionis. Bibliographisches Verzeichnis des gedruckten Schrifttums zur Geschichte und Literatur der Inquisition.* 3 vols. Vaduz, Liechtenstein, 1982–1992. The standard bibliography on the Inquisition in general, listing both the primary and secondary literature.

JOHN TEDESCHI

INQUISITION, SPANISH. Since its inception the Spanish Inquisition has been controversial. In 1478 Ferdinand of Aragón (ruled 1471–1504) and Isabella of Castile (ruled 1474–1504) requested papal permission to establish the religious tribunals in Castile. Unlike the medieval papal Inquisition, the Spanish Inquisition was a hybrid religious-secular institution under the authority of the crown, which appointed its officials and supervised its operation. The tribunals employed judicial procedures that were both contrary and offensive to existing Castilian legal practice. The establishment of the Spanish Inquisition in the kingdom of Aragón, which already had its own (albeit moribund) papal Inquisition, was seen as an affront to the kingdom's privileges, and one inquisitor was assassinated in the cathedral of Zaragoza in 1485. During the sixteenth century northern Protestants used the Inquisition as a cornerstone of the anti-Spanish propaganda campaign later dubbed the Black Legend. Even in its abolition the Inquisition was controversial, as it took three attempts to suppress the court, which lingered until 1834.

Since the fifteenth century the Inquisition has inspired a lively and sometimes lurid debate over the nature of its policies and practices.

EARLY YEARS OF THE INQUISITION

The first inquisitors arrived in Seville in November 1480. Their mission was to extirpate heresy and punish the guilty. Court procedures drew on medieval inquisitorial practice, distilled into the *Directorium Inquisitorum* by Nicolau Eimeric in 1376. The medieval Inquisition had been founded to combat Catharism, but the Spanish Inquisition's special target was the new heresy of "Judaizing." During the fifteenth century, either by force or choice, many Spanish Jews had converted to Christianity. Some of these New Christians *(conversos)* continued to practice Judaism secretly while advancing rapidly in Christian society. Seville, the first city targeted by the Spanish Inquisition, was home to a large and wealthy *converso* community. Several hundreds of people were tried and punished in a short period of time, and similar scenes were repeated in Córdoba, Ciudad Real, Toledo, and Valencia.

The Inquisition used several degrees of sentencing. For those found guilty of heresy, there was relaxation to the secular arm of justice (for death by burning), relaxation in effigy for those heretics who had fled or previously had died, and reconciliation for those who abjured and promised to return to the Christian fold. In all cases, the property of those found guilty of heresy was confiscated. Both during and after public humiliation and sentencing at the ceremony known as the *auto da fe*, the condemned were obligated to wear a distinctive penitential tunic (the *sanbenito*) over their clothes, and they and their male descendants were banned from holding public office for several generations. Undoubtedly, for those Old Christians who were determined to eliminate unwanted competition from the *converso* class, the Inquisition was an efficient weapon.

The Inquisition's formative phase lasted until 1517. A well defined institutional structure took shape. At the top were the inquisitor general (also called the grand inquisitor; the first was Friar Tomás de Torquemada [1420–1498]) and the royal council, known as La Suprema. Several permanent tribunals emerged at this time, while others functioned briefly and then disappeared. During the formative years the tribunals focused almost exclusively on Judaizers. The limited evidence that survives from this period suggests that perhaps as many as 15,000 to 20,000 people were tried during this time, nowhere near the 340,592 suggested in 1808 by the Inquisition's critic and former secretary Juan Antonio Llorente (1756–1823). One must remember furthermore that a great many of the sentences were handed out in absentia or posthumously, so even during this period of fierce persecution about 30 to 40 percent of those arrested ultimately faced the death penalty.

PERIOD OF GREATEST INFLUENCE

The Inquisition's period of greatest influence occurred in 1569–1621, during the reigns of Philip II (ruled 1556–1598) and Philip III (ruled 1598–1621). Before then, under Charles V (ruled 1517–1556), the Inquisition had suffered from a lack of direction. Prosecution of Judaizers had run its course, and aside from prosecuting the heretics known as *alumbrados* and the followers of Desiderius Erasmus (1466?–1536) in the 1520s and 1530s, the tribunals were left without a well-defined mission. The decade of the 1550s changed all that, however, when Protestants were found in Seville and at the royal court at Valladolid. Under inquisitor general Fernando de Valdés (1483–1568), the tribunals were reformed and redirected toward combating Protestantism.

Eventually numbering a total of sixteen tribunals in Spain, two in Italy, and three in the New World, the Inquisition took over responsibility for censorship and contraband and greatly expanded its prosecution of various religious crimes. In addition to Protestants, *conversos,* Moriscos (converted Muslims), and foreigners, ordinary Spaniards were drawn into the tribunals, as even the most casual religious oaths and statements became worthy of scrutiny and correction. Detailed questioning of prisoners, once limited to those accused of the most heinous heresies, now was applied to the most unlikely suspects, who were usually fined a ducat or two (a heavy fine for most) and sent on their way without further ado. The large majority of all cases undertaken by the Inquisition took place during this period.

During this period each tribunal functioned at a high level of efficiency thanks to the efforts of two groups of officials, one consisting of professional, salaried career men and the other made up of unpaid volunteers. The professional core of each tribunal included two inquisitors, lawyers for the prosecution, secretaries, a jailor, a bailiff, and a doorman. Periodically one inquisitor was required to go on a circuit (the *visita*) of his district, while the other inquisitor remained at home to handle business there. The tribunals relied heavily on various types of unpaid officials. First, there were the two networks of familiars and *comisarios.* The familiars were laymen charged with carrying messages and arresting suspects and delivering them to the Inquisition, but they were not spies and informers. The *comisarios* were priests who assisted in the gathering of evidence at the local level. To assess the heretical content of the accusations, the inquisitors were advised by theologians known as *calificadores.* At key stages in a trial inquisitors were required to consult with voting members of the tribunal, who voted on whether or not to indict, torture, and convict. Cases involving the death penalty were sent to the Suprema for review and approval, and each tribunal

TABLE 1

Cases in the Spanish Inquisition, 1540–1700

(Excludes the tribunals of Cuenca, Cerdaña, and Palermo)

Judaizers	Moriscos	Protestants	All Others	Total	Total Relaxed
4,397	10,817	3,646	25,814	44,674	1,604
9.8%	23.2%	8.1%	57.8%	100.0%	3.5%

Adapted from Jaime Contreras and Gustav Henningsen, "Forty-four Thousand Cases of the Spanish Inquisition (1540–1700): Analysis of a Historical Data Bank," in Henningsen and Tedeschi, 116. Included in the category "All Others" are propositions and blasphemy (27.1%), bigamy and solicitation (8.4%), acts against the Inquisition (7.5%), superstition (7.9%), and various (6.8%). The "Total Relaxed" involves only those sentenced to death in person.

was required to maintain detailed correspondence with the Suprema about all of its affairs.

The period 1569–1621 also witnessed a series of controversial trials. First, the archbishop of Toledo and primate of Spain, Bartolomé de Carranza (1503–1576), was sucked into the vortex of court intrigue that consumed the early years of Philip II's reign. Carranza's trial, which lasted from 1559 to 1576, started in Spain and ended in Rome. He was all but exonerated of the charges of heresy in 1576 but died shortly thereafter. A second politically motivated trial was the case of Philip II's secretary Antonio Pérez (1539–1611), who was implicated in the murder of another secretary. After Pérez escaped to Aragón in 1590, Philip tried to recapture him using the Inquisition of Zaragoza. The use of the Inquisition in this manner provoked such widespread discontent in Aragón that Philip was forced to order in the army. Despite these two famous cases, such overt political abuse of the Holy Office's power was rare. However, the Inquisition believed it was entirely justified in closely monitoring Spain's spiritual writers and preachers, who were suspected of having Protestant tendencies. Nowadays the list of those tried or called in for questioning reads like a who's who of Spain's most famous religious men and women, including, among others, Saint Ignatius of Loyola, Saint John of Ávila, Friar Luis de Granada, Saint Francisco de Borja, Friar Francisco de Osuna, Saint Teresa of Ávila, and Friar Luis de León.

DECLINE OF THE INQUISITION

The Inquisition declined with the Spanish empire in the seventeenth century. As the tribunals pulled back from their ambitious program of vigilance, caseloads and revenue fell. The tribunals focused on cases of Portuguese *conversos* living in Spain, witchcraft and superstition, and censorship. In the eighteenth century the Inquisition could not stop the slow spread of Enlightenment ideas to Spain, and the country's intellectuals increasingly began to see the tribunals as out of step with the times. With the Napoleonic invasion of 1808, the courts were suppressed for the first time, at the hands of French officials and Spanish liberals. Conservative nationalists, however, fighting for independence and the return of Ferdinand VII (ruled 1808, 1814–1833), claimed that the court was the guardian of Spanish identity and morals. The Inquisition was restored without powers in 1814, only to undergo a lingering death between 1820 and 1834.

The Holy Office was suppressed for the final time by official decree in 1834, but historians have argued about its significance ever since. In the nineteenth century Protestant historians and Spanish liberals blamed Spain's backwardness on the Inquisition and the Catholic Church, which were seen as having terrorized the country, suppressed the basic rights of freedom of speech and religion, and retarded economic growth and scientific thought. In the twentieth century, with the advent of murderous anti-Semitic and totalitarian regimes, the focus shifted to understanding the Inquisition's role in the long history of the persecution of Jews and repression of entire populations. Under the pro-Catholic dictatorship of Francisco Franco (1892–1975; ruled 1939–1975), censorship prevented Spaniards from freely evaluating the Inquisition's legacy, and in the 1970s the most objective work was carried out by foreign historians interested in the new social history and history of *mentalités.* After the collapse of the regime in 1975, Spaniards in the 1980s and 1990s joined in a renaissance of Inquisition studies to understand their country's complex history. The large body of scholarship produced since 1975 has considerably modified and fleshed out understandings of the Holy Office, which has come to be seen as considerably less monolithic and ruthless than was previously thought.

See also **Catholicism; *Conversos;* Ferdinand of Aragón; Isabella of Castile; Persecution; Philip II (Spain); Spain.**

BIBLIOGRAPHY

Primary Sources

Beinart, Haim, ed. *Records of the Trials of the Spanish Inquisition in Ciudad Real.* 3 vols. Jerusalem, 1974.

Eimeric, Nicolau, and Francisco Peña. *Le manuel des inquisiteurs.* Translated and introduced by Louis Sala-Molins. Paris, 1973.

Jiménez Monteserín, Miguel, ed. *Introducción a la Inquisición española: Documentos básicos para el estudio del Santo Oficio.* Madrid, 1980.

Secondary Sources

Alcalá, Ángel, ed. *The Spanish Inquisition and the Inquisitorial Mind.* Boulder, Colo., 1987.

Bennassar, Bartolomé. *L'Inquisition espagnole: XVe–XIXe siècle.* Paris, 1979.

Contreras, Jaime. *El Santo Oficio de la Inquisición en Galicia, 1560–1700.* Madrid, 1982.

Dedieu, Jean-Pierre. *L'administration de la foi: L'Inquisition de Tolède, XVIe–XVIIIe siècles.* Madrid, 1989.

García Cárcel, Ricardo. *Orígenes de la Inquisición española: El tribunal de Valencia, 1478–1530.* Barcelona, 1976.

Haliczer, Stephen. *Inquisition and Society in the Kingdom of Valencia, 1478–1834.* Berkeley, 1990.

Henningsen, Gustav, and John Tedeschi, eds. *The Inquisition in Early Modern Europe: Studies on Sources and Methods.* DeKalb, Ill., 1986.

Kamen, Henry. *The Spanish Inquisition: A Historical Revision.* London, 1997.

Lea, Henry Charles. *A History of the Inquisition of Spain.* 4 vols. New York, 1906–1907.

Monter, William. *Frontiers of Heresy: The Spanish Inquisition from the Basque Lands to Sicily.* Cambridge, U.K., 1990.

Nalle, Sara Tilghman. *Mad for God: Bartolomé Sánchez, the Secret Messiah of Cardenete.* Charlottesville, Va., 2001.

Starr-LeBeau, Gretchen D. *In the Shadow of the Virgin: Inquisitors, Friars, and Conversos in Guadalupe, Spain.* Princeton, 2003.

SARA TILGHMAN NALLE

INSURANCE. Insurance is a contract of indemnification in which an underwriter agrees to compensate a policyholder for specified losses during a certain length of time, or term, in return for a payment, or premium. Insurers hedge their financial exposure by adjusting premiums to the perceived likelihood that a policy will result in a claim and by underwriting a number of policies, thereby dispersing individual risks among many. During the early modern period insurance evolved from a specialized device utilized mainly by merchants and financiers to a firmly established industry offering marine, life, and fire insurance to a rapidly growing market.

ORIGINS

While insurance-like mechanisms for distributing risk have been identified in the ancient world, the first recognizable policies of insurance originated in Florence and other northern Italian towns in the early fourteenth century. These early policies, the first surviving example of which was issued at Genoa in 1347, covered losses at sea. In the following decades Italian merchants transmitted the practice of marine insurance across the Mediterranean basin and into northern Europe. By the early sixteenth century the marine insurance business, still largely under Italian control, had spread to Flanders and the Netherlands, and thence by mid-century to England and the Baltic countries. Marine insurance was by far the largest and most widely practiced branch of underwriting in early modern Europe.

Life insurance appeared, around the year 1400, as an incidental circumstance when marine insurance policies covered embarked travelers or slaves. It was quickly adapted to the money-lending business to collateralize loans by insuring the debtor's life, as was done on the life of Pope Nicholas V in 1454. The growth of life insurance was hindered, however, by its increasing use as a device for wagering on human longevity and by the concomitant suspicion that it incited fraud and murder. The alleged immorality of life insurance led to its prohibition, from the fifteenth through the seventeenth centuries, everywhere in Europe except Florence, Naples, and the British Isles. Its use as a long-term device guaranteeing family welfare had to await the formation, at the end of the seventeenth century, of the first life insurance societies in England, the most enduring of which was the Amicable Society (1706–1866).

A system of fire insurance that went beyond the traditional mutual aid arrangements of guildsmen was first established on a municipal basis in Hamburg's General Feuerkasse as early as 1591. Similar town-sponsored offices were founded in London (1682), Altona (1713), Berlin (1718), and in French cities in the same period. These public initiatives proved less successful than the private provision of fire insurance, which began in London in the years following the Great Fire of 1666. The earliest of these companies were transient, but Nicholas Barbon's pioneering Fire Office (1680) demonstrated the long-term viability of the fire insurance business. Other notable ventures included the Hand-in-Hand (1696), the Sun Fire Office (1710), and the Royal Exchange Assurance and London Assurance Corporations (both 1720). In France, the use of fire insurance was slower to develop. The first large company insuring against fire losses was the Compagnie d'assurances générales (1753), later joined by the Compagnie royale d'assurance (1786).

ORGANIZATION

Unlike marine insurers, whose risks were short-term and dispersed on various sea routes, fire and life insurers faced the daunting challenge of providing long-term coverage against contingencies that sometimes occurred catastrophically, such as urban conflagrations or outbreaks of epidemic disease. As a consequence, marine insurance remained overwhelmingly the preserve of underwriters working individually or in partnerships, even if they also entered into larger associations like Lloyd's (originally Lloyd's Coffee House, established in 1688), whereas fire and whole life underwriting required a corporate or mutual structure in order to ensure the payment of claims. Many of the early fire and life companies were mutual associations in which members contributed as need arose, with the result that either the cost of membership or the amount of compensation for loss was variable. This arrangement was necessitated by a lack of reliable statistical data from which the liabilities attached to life or fire risks might be calculated. Although Edmond Halley in 1693 published a mortality table (giving the average expectation of life at different ages), life insurers were very slow to place much trust in mortality statistics. Instead, they excluded the very young, the very old, and the obviously infirm or drunken. Similarly, fire insurers discriminated among "common," "hazardous," and "doubly hazardous" risks based more on intuition than hard data, and until the foundation of the Phoenix Assurance Company in 1782 simply refused to insure fire-prone sugar bakers. By the second half of the eighteenth century insurance was acquiring a more secure statistical basis. The Equitable Life Assurance Society (1762) was the first insurer to graduate policy premiums according to age at purchase, although it continued, conservatively, to price its policies above their actuarial value.

SOCIAL AND ECONOMIC IMPACT

Insurance played a major role in European economic expansion and in the social management of risk. Marine underwriting reduced the risks of maritime commerce, especially during wartime. Fire insurers during the eighteenth century provided increasing coverage for commercial stocks and industrial plants, thereby fostering the expansion of industrial capitalism. The provision of life insurance protected the fortunes of middle-class families against the premature death of a breadwinner. Insurers also lowered economic losses more subtly by disciplining risk-taking, since ship captains who failed to sail in convoys during wartime or manufacturers who practiced hazardous trades in timber-framed buildings were subject to higher premiums or the withdrawal of coverage altogether. Fire insurance companies contributed to a generally safer urban environment by organizing fire brigades to protect the properties that they insured. With time, these brigades were amalgamated into municipal squads. Insurance furthermore had an important mental influence on early modern society by serving as a major conduit (along with gambling) for the transmission of probabilistic and statistical thinking to the eighteenth-century public. Despite its power, this new statistical worldview supplemented rather than supplanted older magical or religious beliefs, even among practitioners of insurance. Seventeenth-century English merchants queried the famous astrologer, William Lilly, whether ships overdue in port could be insured for profit, while a century later underwriters in Barcelona still had masses sung for the deliverance of ships they insured.

See also **Commerce and Markets; Shipping.**

BIBLIOGRAPHY

Primary Sources

Magens, Nicolas. *An Essay on Insurances.* 2 vols. London, 1755. A valuable summary of European insurance practices and laws, with incisive commentary.

Park, James Allan. *A System of the Law of Marine Insurances, with Three Chapters on Bottomry, on Insurances on Lives, and on Insurances against Fire.* London, 1789. A classic legal compendium of British insurance law with occasional reference to Continental codes.

Secondary Sources

Clark, Geoffrey. *Betting on Lives: The Culture of Life Insurance in England, 1695–1775.* Manchester, U.K., and New York, 1999. A study of the birth and early growth of the first substantial life insurance market, with European background.

Halpérin, Jean. *Les assurances en Suisse et dans le monde, leur rôle dans l'evolution économique et sociale.* Neuchâtel, 1946. A thought-provoking examination of the role of insurance in the development of financial and commercial capitalism.

Raynes, Harold E. *A History of British Insurance.* London, 1964. Originally published, 1950. A comprehensive account of insurance in the country where it flourished most.

Stefani, Giuseppe. *Insurance in Venice from the Origins to the End of the Serenissima.* 2 vols. Trieste, 1958. Collection of archival documents.

Geoffrey Clark

INTENDANTS. The term *intendant* usually refers to provincial administrators in seventeenth- and eighteenth-century France. The term also had other meanings: there were between one and ten *intendants des finances*—financial administrators who worked at the highest level with the controller-general, or superintendent of finances; There were also administrators often qualified as "intendants" in the French naval, military and colonial administrations, but the latter were not normally concerned with the fiscal matters that so preoccupied the provincial intendants.

ORIGINS

In the sixteenth and the early seventeenth centuries, junior members of the king's royal council, known as masters of requests *(maîtres des requêtes),* were commonly sent to deal with specific problems of justice or administration in the provinces. However, with the fiscal crisis caused by France's warlike foreign policy in the 1630s and the consequent increases in direct taxes (the *taille* and associated levies), these officials became resident commissioners in most provinces, usually under the name of "intendants of justice, police, and finances." Traditionally, in each province, local venal officeholders *(élus* and *trésoriers)* had been responsible for dividing the total amount of direct tax to be assessed among subregions and parishes, and for hearing complaints about assessments. They often used their powers to favor their clients and tenants; this impeded the war effort. Intendants now worked side-by-side with the local financial officials, and their royal commissions gave them power to impose their will. Unlike the officeholders, they were the king's creatures; they held a revocable royal commission; their careers depended on success and loyalty to the ruler and his ministers. Suits against them were directed to the king's council, thereby bypassing local courts and the parlements, where local influence might have blunted their effectiveness. Although their concerns were principally fiscal, intendants had extensive police and extraordinary judicial powers.

The civil war known as the Fronde (1648–1652) was fueled in part by officeholder resentment against the intendants and the higher taxes; the grievances drawn up by the Paris "sovereign courts" in the spring of 1648 forcefully echoed these complaints. Cardinal Jules Mazarin (1602–1661) and the regent, Anne of Austria (1601–1666), gave way and abolished the intendants, but subsequently brought them back, at first surreptitiously, then openly when the Fronde was over.

REFORM

The end of the long conflict with Spain in 1659, the death of Mazarin, and Louis XIV's (ruled 1643–1715) assumption of personal power in 1661 did not bring the use of intendants to an end. Jean-Baptiste Colbert (1619–1683), who became Louis's chief financial adviser, had made up his mind that the intendants would be essential to carrying out any program of reform. Before 1661, the chancellor, the chief law officer of the crown, gave most orders to the intendants; after that date, Colbert and his successors in the post of controller general became their effective superior, and although the intendants continued to have some judicial functions, they became primarily fiscal and administrative agents. They were used, particularly in the eighteenth century, to implement schemes for economic development and social reform and control: welfare, hospitals, road building, industrial development, poor relief, managing the food supply, and mobilizing the peasantry through the royal *corvée* to build a national road network.

One of Louis XIV's main declared aims was to reform justice. This meant drawing up new law codes and streamlining the courts, but it also implied a quantum leap in the statistical information and intelligence of all kinds to be supplied to government at the local and national levels. Among other projects, Colbert wanted to improve the tax yield by imposing lower but fairer levies, reducing the number of privileged persons exempt from tax, and rooting out corrupt officials. In the 1660s and 1670s, the intendants usually played the major role in the numerous purges of recent or fake nobles, putting them back on the assessment rolls, thereby gaining a powerful hold over local notables in the process. When large-scale war became quasi-permanent after 1672, their original function as fiscal supervisors made them even more necessary, particularly when the direct tax base was widened by wartime emergency taxes (*capitation,* 1695; *dixième,* 1710) to take in nobles and privileged people of all kinds.

Colbert's measures to control spending by town and parish governments culminated in the edict of April 1683, which made all changes in town and village government spending subordinate to the intendant's approval. A regular police presence was also needed to keep down resistance to wartime taxation and to the policy of religious uniformity that culminated with Louis's revocation of the Edict of Nantes (1685). All this required the continued presence of the intendants and longer stays in their provinces. Under Cardinal Richelieu (Armand-Jean du Plessis; 1585–1642) and Mazarin they had only remained three years on the average; between 1666 and 1716 the average stay was five years; in the eighteenth century it was seven.

With the increased activity (under Louis XIV and later) came the strengthening of the intendants' local control and accountability to their superiors. The practice grew up whereby intendants informally co-opted local officials, called "subdelegates" *(subdélégués),* usually from among the lesser local officeholders. Colbert did not like this, but the logic of the system he was building required it. The numbers of permanent subdelegates increased impressively: by 1700 there were probably between four and five hundred subdelegates; by the 1780s, there were about seven hundred. In larger intendancies, the intendants often appointed *subdélégués généraux* as executive assistants who could replace them during absences and built up a little staff of secretaries and domestics. The growth and development of the intendancy as a regular institution, and the intendant as a bureaucratic functionary, is evident when we compare the sporadic, often frantic or desperate correspondence of the intendants of Richelieu and those of Louis XIV. The latter reveal a central administration with an agenda, enforcing frequent correspondence with the offices of the controller general, demanding replies to uniform and regularly recurring questionnaires, and a yearly work cycle built around annual reports on the economic state of the intendancy and the routine administration of direct tax collection. The degree of control was always weaker in the *pays d'États* like Brittany, Languedoc, and so forth, where local institutions still assumed some of these tasks and the intendant's role was often more political than administrative.

SELECTION

Intendants were usually chosen among the seventy or eighty-odd masters of requests in the royal council. In the eighteenth century, these recruits were supposed to be thirty years of age, to have a law degree or equivalent legal experience, and to serve six years as a junior member *(conseiller)* of a parlement or other high court; the length of this study and service was often reduced by dispensation. Throughout the period, 40 to 50 percent of masters of requests had sat previously as junior members in the Parlement of Paris, around a third (until 1774) came from the Grand Conseil, a specialized high court. At the time, critics of the intendants, such as financier and statesman Jacques Necker (1732–1804), said that they were too young to bear such responsibilities. But the average age of a beginning master of requests under Louis XV (ruled 1715–1774) was twenty-nine, not inordinately young (though it appeared to be falling somewhat toward the end of the Old Regime). In any event, throughout the entire period from Richelieu onward, the overwhelming majority did not get their first posting as intendants until their mid-thirties or later. Intendancies were often a springboard to higher functions as royal councillors *(conseillers d'état)*, or even as secretaries of state and ministers. The Royal Council was a good training ground. It had a certain collective mentality: councillors worked harder than the members of the parlement; they were self-effacing, career-oriented, consensus-minded. Working there gave future intendants wide experience in preparing and judging disputed issues in taxation, administrative law, jurisdictional disputes, and the like—the sort of administrative and political problems that they would later face in the provinces.

The nineteenth-century historian and writer Alexis de Tocqueville (1805–1859), misled perhaps by the diatribes of Claude-Henri de Rouvroy, comte de Saint-Simon (1760–1825), said that Louis XIV's intendants were bourgeois, whereas those of Louis XVI (ruled 1774–1792) were nobles. This was wrong. Even in the days of Richelieu and Mazarin, all the intendants claimed noble status. At that time, the families of about a third of them had acquired transmissible nobility by the purchase of the offices of *secrétaire du roi,* one-third by hereditary office, and the rest by letters of nobility, and so forth, and all of them held personal nobility by virtue of their offices of masters of requests. This pattern continued. The true quality of nobility, however, was measured by the number of generations it had been in a family. Paradoxically, at the end of the eighteenth century more intendants were sons and grandsons of "new nobles" than at the end of the seventeenth, so in a sense the institution had become more open. But the truly significant social ties of the intendants and masters of requests were to the Parisian and financier milieu. Fully two-thirds of the councillors of state and masters of requests under Louis XIV were born in Paris, and this trend continued; they generally came from wealthy families and tended either to intermarry or to find wives in the milieu of royal financiers. They were thus true representatives of the Old Regime state elite; the families that waxed wealthy and powerful and gained prestige from the king's service, and their loyalty to the Colbertian model and service ethic was never in question.

At the end of Louis XIV's reign, criticism of the intendants' powers resumed. Their jurisdiction was the target of increasingly bold attacks from provincial parlements and estates from the 1750s onward. From the days of François de Salignac de La Mothe-Fénelon (1651–1715) and his coterie at the end of Louis XIV's reign through Victor Riqueti, marquis de Mirabeau (1715–1789) and René Louis de Voyer de Paulmy, marquis d'Argenson (1694–1757) at mid-century to Anne-Robert-Jacques Turgot (1727–1781) and Jacques Necker in the 1770s, there were projects to create or restore provincial estates or assemblies, which would have reduced or eliminated the role of intendants. A couple of provincial assemblies were created by Necker as pilot projects in the 1780s. Étienne-Charles de Loménie de Brienne (1727–1794), in the monarchy's last desperate reforms of 1787, actually set up advisory boards filled by prominent landowners in each intendancy to work with the intendant. When the Constituent Assembly reorganized France in 1789, it assumed from the outset that the intendants had to go. The division of France into eighty-three self-administering departments on 15 February 1790 left no place for them; but Napoleon's prefects, created by the law of 28 Pluviôse Year VIII (17 February 1800) regained most of the intendants' powers within the framework of an authoritarian regime sanctioned by popular sovereignty, and many of them still survive today.

See also **Absolutism; Colbert, Jean-Baptiste; France; Fronde; Louis XIV (France); Louis XV (France); Louis XVI (France); Mazarin, Jules; Parlements; Provincial Government; Richelieu, Armand-Jean Du Plessis, cardinal; State and Bureaucracy; Taxation.**

BIBLIOGRAPHY

Antoine, Michel. *Le cœur de l'État: Surintendance, contrôle général, et intendances des finances, 1552–1791.* Paris, 2003.

——. *Le dur métier de roi.* Paris, 1986.

——. *Le gouvernement et l'administration sous Louis XV: Dictionnaire biographique.* Paris, 1978.

Bonney, Richard. *Political Change in France under Richelieu and Mazarin, 1624–1661.* Oxford, 1978.

Bordes, Maurice. *L'administration provinciale et municipale en France au XVIIIe siècle.* Paris, 1972.

Esmonin, Edmond. "Les origines et les débuts des subdélégués des intendants." In *Etudes sur la France des XVIIe et XVIIIe siècles,* pp. 131–166. Paris, 1964.

Goubert, J.-P., G. Arbellot, and A. Laclau. "Les subdélégations à la veille de la Révolution de 1789." In *Atlas de la Révolution française,* edited by Serge Bonin and Claude Langlois, vol. 5, pp. 47–52, 81, and Map 4. Paris, 1989.

Gruder, Vivian R. *The Royal Provincial Intendants: A Governing Elite in Eighteenth-Century France.* Ithaca, N.Y., 1968.

Mousnier, Roland. "État et commissaire: Recherches sur la création des intendants des provinces (1634–1648)." In *La plume, la faucille et le marteau: Institutions et société en France du moyen âge à la Révolution,* pp. 170–199. Paris, 1970.

Smedley-Weill, Anette. *Les intendants de Louis XIV.* Paris, 1995.

T. J. A. Le Goff

INTEREST. Usury laws, inspired both by Scripture and by a misunderstanding of monetary economics, have probably never prevented lenders from charging interest. Throughout early modern Europe, not only states, businesses, and private individuals, but even religious institutions from mosques to monasteries commonly lent and borrowed with interest. Nonetheless, usury laws have shaped the history of credit by forcing contracting parties to disguise interest payments as something else. No one, of course, is fooled by the subterfuge, but it has often determined the nature of monetary institutions and severely limited the survival of documentation through which historians might study the movement of the interest rate. By the eighteenth century, as religious objections weakened, the debate over usury laws became utilitarian rather than doctrinal. At the same time, a new debate over the determination of the interest rate became central to the economic theory of the Enlightenment, and to the rejection of earlier mercantilist policies.

USURY LEGISLATION

"Lend without expecting any return," counsels Jesus in the Sermon on the Mount (Luke 6:34–35), and though the context would suggest that one should not even expect repayment of the principal, the medieval church read his statement as a prohibition on interest. The lesson was reinforced by certain passages of the Old Testament that denounce "usury" without clearly defining the word (Exodus 22:25; Deuteronomy 23:19–20; Psalms 15:5), as well as Aristotle's doctrine that money is sterile (*Politics* 1:10; *Ethics* 5:5). Jews were often permitted to lend to Christians at interest since they fell outside the spiritual authority of the church, thus demonstrating that the original purpose of usury legislation was to protect the lender from sin, not to protect the borrower from exploitation. The reputation of Jews as moneylenders was greatly exaggerated, however, and they never played more than a minor role in credit markets before the rise of the Rothschild Bank in the nineteenth century.

A papal bull of 1425 permitted Catholics to buy and sell perpetual annuities, at least when mortgaged against real property (a distinction that was eventually ignored). The Orthodox Church also relaxed usury laws by the sixteenth century. Though the Koran also denounces usury (2:275, 3:130, 4:161, 30:39), in the early fifteenth century the Ottomans came to allow a form of perpetual annuity known as the *cash waqf.* Originally created to fund charitable institutions such as schools and mosques, it became a common form of private investment by the sixteenth century.

In western Europe in the sixteenth century, Protestant reformers began to chip away at the remaining religious prohibitions on interest, which they associated with Scholasticism. Luther, Calvin, and Zwingli variously argued that interest is not usurious so long as the rate charged is moderate and the contract is in accordance with the Golden Rule ("Do unto others as you would have them do unto you"). Luther, moreover, insisted that one should submit to the laws of the state and not invoke biblical usury prohibitions as an excuse for default. In Catholic Europe, the Jesuits played a similar role in promoting the toleration of interest. The effect of such teachings was not so much to extinguish as to secularize discussions of usury law, so that by the eighteenth century the debate had become almost entirely utilitarian rather than exegetical.

Some Enlightenment writers, including John Locke and Jeremy Bentham, insisted on the complete deregulation of interest. Adam Smith believed that a legal ceiling on interest rates was justified to prevent consumption loans to spendthrifts, since lenders would consider them a bad risk at the legal rate. He agreed, however, that if the ceiling were set below the market rate for commercial loans, it would be counterproductive since merchants would be forced to borrow outside the law. Without the security provided by the law courts, lenders would charge a risk premium, thus actually raising, not lowering, interest rates. Anne-Robert-Jacques

Turgot made much the same point when he described an incident in Angoulême in 1769, in which a group of insolvent debtors brought financial panic, and thus extraordinarily high interest rates, on the entire city by attempting to prosecute their creditors for usury.

LONG-TERM INTEREST

Long-term bonds in early modern Europe usually took the form of perpetual annuities. The purchaser of the annuity (that is, the lender) paid a lump sum, in return for which the seller (or borrower) promised to pay a fixed coupon once a year forever. On the Continent the contract of sale had to pass before a notary (thus incurring notarial fees), as did any resale to a third party. The lender could not require the borrower to repay the principal, though the borrower could do so voluntarily at any time, and thus extinguish the loan. Throughout Europe, permissible coupon rates tended to fall from 10 percent or more in the sixteenth century to 5 percent or less in the eighteenth century. In any given period, coupon rates recorded in notarized contracts were usually simply the maximum allowed by law, and thus seemed to represent a legal fiction. That is, contracting parties presumably varied the yield rate of the bond simply by agreeing to a sales price somewhat higher or lower than that stated in the contract. For historians, the fluctuation of long term interest rates on private bonds is thus largely unrecoverable.

European states also borrowed primarily through perpetual annuities, the most famous being the Consols with which Britain consolidated its national debt after the Glorious Revolution (1688–1689). By the eighteenth century state bonds were actively traded on national stock exchanges, and yield rates can often be inferred from the quotations printed in commercial newspapers. In Britain and the Netherlands, where representative assemblies managed the national debt to the advantage of their wealthy constituents, the risk on state bonds was essentially zero, and yield rates fell as low as 3 percent. In France, on the contrary, the monarchy issued partial defaults on its debt every few decades and could only continue to borrow by offering exceptionally high interest rates (which, of course, rendered future defaults more likely). The need for cheap credit to finance increasingly costly wars thus seems to have worked to the advantage of representative regimes, a fact that goes a long way toward explaining the widespread movement for constitutional reform in the second half of the century.

SHORT-TERM INTEREST

Starting in northern Italy at the end of the thirteenth century, merchants developed a variety of new forms of short-term credit that bore hidden interest. By far the most important were the promissory note and the bill of exchange. A promissory note is little more than an IOU by which the debtor (who in most cases is purchasing merchandise on credit rather than actually borrowing cash) promises to pay to the creditor, "or his order," a given sum on a given date. Typically written at term of two to six months, rarely more than a year, such notes make no mention of interest, but the interest is in fact included in the face value. At any given moment the market value of a promissory note is thus its face value minus the "discount," or interest over the remaining term. If, for instance, the discount rate is currently 8 percent per year (0.08), then a promissory note with a face value of 100 ducats payable in six months (0.50 year) is worth:

$$100 \text{ ducats} - [(0.50)(0.08)(100 \text{ ducats})] = 96 \text{ ducats}$$

The discount rate thus expresses interest not as a percentage of the principal borrowed, but as a percentage of the final payment (interest plus principal). If r is the interest rate as conventionally calculated, d is the discount rate and t is the term, then:

$$r = d/(1 - dt)$$

At short term, however, the difference between r and d is negligible.

Through the bill of exchange, a merchant sells the right to collect a sum of money from his correspondent in a different city. Rather than an IOU, it is thus a sort of "he-owes-you" used to transfer funds between two geographically distant locations, either within the same country (inland bills) or in different countries (foreign bills). The value of the bill of exchange depends on the going exchange rate, expressed as a percentage premium or loss for inland bills, and as a rate of exchange between two national currencies in the case of foreign bills. As with the promissory note, the bill of exchange nowhere mentions interest, but merchants openly charged less for bills written at longer term. Even sight bills (technically payable one day after acceptance by the party on whom they were drawn) included a small amount of hidden interest, since it would take them several weeks to reach their destination through the mail. Bills payable one, two, or more months after acceptance sold at correspondingly more advantageous exchange rates. One of the curious results is that the going rate of exchange at any city A on another city B was consistently different from the rate of exchange at B on A. If a merchant purchased a bill of exchange at A on B, sent it to B, instructed his correspondent to use the funds to purchase another bill at B on A, and finally cashed the latter in A, he would end up with more than he started with, the difference corresponding to the interest on his initial outlay.

Bills of exchange and promissory notes did not require notarization. By the seventeenth century (and probably earlier) they were negotiable throughout Europe by simple endorsement. Issued by businesses large and small, they circulated widely. Unlike cash, commercial paper, with its hidden interest, constantly gained value until it came due. The portfolio of credits outstanding thus came to replace cash as the largest reserve of liquid wealth, not only for wholesale merchants but even for humble artisans and shopkeepers. The movement of the interest rate therefore directly concerned all business people.

THE MOVEMENT OF INTEREST RATES

The economic history of Europe has been written largely on the basis of grain prices. The movement of interest rates, though equally important, is less well known, largely because the habit of disguising interest makes the rates so difficult to recover. Eighteenth-century economists asserted that interest rates had fallen steadily from about 10 percent in the sixteenth century, to 6 to 8 percent in the seventeenth century, and to 5 percent or less in the eighteenth century. This long-run movement has been substantiated by the research of Sidney Homer and Richard Sylla.

The short-run movement of the discount rate at Paris and Amsterdam came to light suddenly in the eighteenth century, thanks to exchange rate quotations in *The Course of the Exchange*. Beginning in 1723, this British commercial newspaper printed two exchange rates at London on Amsterdam, one for sight bills and one for two-month bills. The percentage difference between the rates corresponds to the discount rate in Amsterdam, at least as it was known to London exchange agents. The newspaper similarly printed twin rates on Paris from 1740. For the period through 1789, discount rates in Paris averaged 5 percent and tended to peak in the autumn months as grain merchants borrowed heavily to finance the purchase of the harvest. Discount rates at Amsterdam averaged 4.5 percent and were not clearly tied to the agricultural cycle. Discount rates at Paris correlated poorly with those at Amsterdam, demonstrating that the two markets were not highly integrated. The most pronounced feature of each series was the sharp rise of interest rates during financial panics that tended to occur two or three times a decade.

Several studies have demonstrated that the London and Amsterdam capital markets were highly integrated with each other in the eighteenth century, and that one of the principal mechanisms of integration was interest rate arbitrage. That is, speculators frequently used the exchange market to move funds between these two cities in order to take advantage of the higher rate of return. London and Amsterdam were probably the exception, however. Interest rate arbitrage appears to have been far less significant at Paris, and the same was probably true in other financial centers.

THE EIGHTEENTH-CENTURY DEBATE

The economists of the Enlightenment shared with their mercantilist predecessors the conviction that high interest rates are a disincentive to invest, since any investment earning less than the interest rate will be unprofitable. Early modern economic policy was thus largely a set of strategies for reducing the interest rate. Enlightenment writers came to differ sharply from the mercantilists, however, in their theory of the determination of the interest rate, and thus in the specific strategies that they considered advisable.

Mercantilist writings of the seventeenth and early eighteenth centuries, including those of John Locke, are marked by a belief that the rate of interest is an inverse function of the money supply. Though often poorly articulated, this quantity theory of interest, suggestive of John Maynard Keynes's "liquidity curve," was clearly central to monetary thought and went largely unchallenged until the mid-eighteenth century. Like many late mercantilists, Montesquieu, in his *Spirit of the Laws* (1748), saw proof of the quantity theory of interest in the decline of interest rates from roughly 10 percent to 5 percent since the discovery of the Americas, which he thought was due to the resulting influx of silver. Thus, to encourage investment, mercantilists sought to draw bullion into the country by means of a favorable balance of trade. At times they also proposed more creative devices for increasing the money supply, such as John Law's 1705 scheme to issue a paper currency based on the value of land.

Inspired in part by the early eighteenth-century writings of Richard Cantillon and Pierre de Boisguilbert, the Enlightenment subjected the quantity theory of interest to systematic critique. Boisguilbert had pointed out that most of the money supply was quasi-money in the form of commercial paper, and that its quantity was not dependent on stocks of coin. Cantillon argued effectively that an increase in the money supply would raise prices and thus leave the real money supply unaltered, with no long-run effect on interest rates. Adam Smith, David Hume, and the French Physiocrats repeated and developed these arguments. As Hume pithily remarked in 1752, "Silver is more common than gold; and therefore you receive a greater quantity of it for the same commodities. But do you pay less interest for it?"

Enlightenment writers came thus to argue that the rate of interest is an inverse function not of the supply of money, but of the supply of productive capital. The new theory, like the old one, offered a plausible explanation of the gradual decline of interest rates since the sixteenth century. Since the supply of capital was thought also to determine the rate of profit, the hope was now that at equilibrium the interest rate would fall below the profit rate, rendering all regulation of the interest rate unnecessary. Smith asserted that in England the profit rate was currently about 10 percent, and the interest rate about 5 percent. Though he acknowledged that the relationship was not strictly linear, he believed that the interest rate would rise or fall with the profit rate in such a way as to leave investors with a reasonable net profit. Still, the Physiocrats feared that excessive government borrowing might crowd out private investment by artificially bidding up the interest rate, and consequently sought to persuade the French monarchy to reduce budget deficits.

See also **Banking and Credit; Capitalism; Hume, David; Law's System; Locke, John; Mercantilism; Physiocrats and Physiocracy; Smith, Adam.**

BIBLIOGRAPHY

Primary Sources

Hume, David. "Of Interest." In *Essays Moral, Political and Literary*. Revised ed. Edited by Eugene F. Miller. Indianapolis, 1987.

Smith, Adam. *An Inquiry into the Nature and Causes of the Wealth of Nations.* Edited by Edwin Cannan. New York, 1937.

Turgot, Anne-Robert-Jacques. *Ecrits économiques.* Edited by Bernard Cazes. Paris, 1970.

Secondary Sources

De Roover, Raymond. "What Is Dry Exchange? A Contribution to the Study of English Mercantilism." *Journal of Political Economy* 52 (1944): 250–266.

Eagly, Robert V., and V. Kerry Smith. "Domestic and International Integration of the London Money Market, 1731–1789." *Journal of Economic History* 36 (1976): 198–212.

Ferguson, Niall. *The Cash Nexus: Money and Power in the Modern World, 1700–2000.* New York, 2001.

Heckscher, Eli F. *Mercantilism.* 2nd ed. 2 vols. Translated by Mendel Shapiro. New York, 1955.

Hoffman, Philip T., Gilles Postel-Vinay, and Jean-Laurent Rosenthal. *Priceless Markets: The Political Economy of Credit in Paris, 1660–1870.* Chicago, 2000.

Homer, Sidney, and Richard Sylla. *A History of Interest Rates.* 3rd ed. New Brunswick, N.J., 1991.

Mandaville, Jon E. "Usurious Piety: The Cash Waqf Controversy in the Ottoman Empire." *International Journal of Middle Eastern Studies* 10 (1979): 289–308.

Neal, Larry. *The Rise of Financial Capitalism: International Capital Markets in the Age of Reason.* Cambridge, U.K., 1990.

Rist, Charles. *History of Monetary and Credit Theory from John Law to the Present Day.* Translated by Jane Degras. New York, 1940.

Taeusch, Carl F. "The Concept of 'Usury': The History of an Idea." *Journal of the History of Ideas* 3 (1942): 291–318.

THOMAS M. LUCKETT

INTERNATIONAL LAW. *See* **Law: International Law.**

IRELAND. Ireland's history has been shaped by the inescapable facts of geography. A small island at the western edge of Europe, barely within the mainstream of Continental experience, it lay beyond the reach of the Roman Empire (with all that that entailed for the development of law and modes of administration) yet would later become one of the great depositories of Christian art, spirituality, and learning. The European context is crucial to an understanding of Ireland's past, but the critical geographical fact is the island's proximity to Britain. On a clear day, the Mull of Kintyre in southwest Scotland is visible from the Antrim coast in northeast Ireland. Gaelic civilization, moreover, extended like an arc along the western and northern coasts of Ireland into the Scottish Highlands. Scottish Lowlanders and the English referred to Scots Gaelic as the "Irish language." From the importation by Gaelic lords of Highland mercenary soldiers—the gallowglass and the redshanks—to the role of Scots settlers in the Ulster plantation and the Scots army in the North in the 1640s, a strong Scottish dimension runs through early modern Irish history, though ultimately Ireland's troubled relationship with its larger neighbor, England, would have the greater impact.

THE FALL OF THE HOUSE OF KILDARE

In 1450 Ireland was a lordship, and the king of England its lord. The English crown's claim to sovereignty over the whole island had never been vindicated in practice, however, and during the later Middle Ages English power and jurisdiction were in retreat. Effectively, the king's writ and the common law were confined to the Pale, the area of English settlement around Dublin, capital city and seat of royal authority. Beyond the Pale and the towns, the great Anglo-Norman magnates negotiated the shifting frontiers of Gaeldom through "march law," a bastardized amalgam of common and Irish *brehon* (native) laws and customs. Even the levers of royal authority began to slip from the king's grasp. The crown in Ireland was represented either by a lord lieutenant, a lord deputy, or, in the absence of one or the other, by lords justices. Between 1447 and 1460, Richard of York's (1411–1460) political standing conferred stature upon the lord lieutenancy and, equally important, kept it within the orbit of the court. Then, between the 1470s and 1520, successive earls of Kildare virtually monopolized the office, using it as a source of patronage to extend their local power base and network of alliances.

The local autonomy enjoyed by the "Kildare ascendancy" has struck some historians of the old nationalist school as part of a wider pattern of incipient Anglo-Irish separatism. But it is surely anachronistic to attribute proto-nationalist ambitions to a political community, the descendants of the original Anglo-Norman settlers, that had no concept of an Irish "nation" in the modern sense. It did, however, have a strong sense of English identity, albeit "English by blood" rather than by birth. Nevertheless, from Parliament's declaration that Ireland was "corporate of itself" (1460) to its declaration of legislative independence in 1782, Anglo-Irish constitutional relations provides a major framework for Irish political history. Subordination of Ireland to England (and, after 1707, Great Britain) and Irish resistance to subordination, though rarely rising to outright separatist aspirations, runs like a leitmotiv through these centuries.

The ascendancy of the earls of Kildare entailed a sometimes spectacular loss of royal control over Irish affairs, most vividly in 1487 when the Yorkist eighth earl, Garrett Mor, crowned the pretender, Lambert Simnel (c. 1475–1535), king of England in Christ Church Cathedral, Dublin. Kildare's survival in office, despite his treason, underlines the weakness of the English crown in the fifteenth century. From a position of greater strength and internal stability, however, Henry VIII would not countenance such overmighty subjects anywhere within his realm. Thus, when the ninth earl was summoned to London under the shadow of the executioner in 1534, his son, Lord Offaly, "Silken Thomas," led his followers in the Geraldine League into rebellion. The Geraldine revolt, which lasted until 1540, opened a new, blood-drenched chapter in Irish history. The advent of a new era was signaled by the first ever use of artillery—against the Kildare stronghold of Maynooth—by the ruthless suppression of the rebellion, and by the first stirrings of anti-Reformation Catholicism among the rebels.

The fall of the house of Kildare also inaugurated a prolonged phase of direct rule from London. That practice became the sine qua non of England's Irish policy, and several illustrious names among En-

Ireland A modern reproduction of a map of Ireland that appeared in editions of Abraham Ortelius's *Theatrum Orbis Terrarum* from 1573 to about 1606. The map, oriented with north to the right, identifies many of the leading families and their holdings. As the heading indicates, this was a time of bitter conflict as Elizabeth I, who reigned from 1558 to 1603, faced several rebellions in her attempt to impose Protestantism and British rule on Ireland. MAP COLLECTION, STERLING MEMORIAL LIBRARY, YALE UNIVERSITY

gland's governing elite occupied Dublin Castle, namely the earls of Essex (1599), Strafford (1633–1640), and Chesterfield (1745–1747). There were notable exceptions to the rule: the Irish-born Protestant first duke of Ormond served as lord lieutenant under both Charles I and Charles II, while the Irish-born old English Catholic, the earl of Tyrconnell, held the office under James II in the 1680s. But after the first decade of the eighteenth century (when the second duke, Ormond's grandson, served) occupation of Dublin Castle was reserved for Englishmen. Until the very end of that century, and the appointments of John Fitzgibbon as lord chancellor and Viscount Castlereagh as chief secretary, Englishmen monopolized all senior executive posts, including the lord lieutenancy, chief secretaryship, lord chancellery, and the archbishopric of Armagh. On one level, official Ireland, especially its established church, functioned merely as a patronage outpost for a British political system oiled by the disbursement of places, preferments, pensions, promotions, titles, and favors. On another level, control of the executive rested on British security considerations.

ENGLAND'S DIFFICULTY, IRELAND'S OPPORTUNITY

Security underpinned England's Irish policy. In essence, the concern was strategic. As Thomas Waring put it in the wake of the Cromwellian reconquest of 1649–1650, "humane reason and policie dictate's that the hous cannot bee safe so long as the back door is open." Ireland served as England's "back door" as early as 1497, when another Yorkist pretender, Perkin Warbeck, landed at Cornwall with a retinue of Irish supporters. Then, as Reformation and Counter-Reformation Europe split into warring camps, the vulnerability of Protestant England's western seaboard (and the dangers of Spain's sponsorship of Irish Catholic rebels) concentrated the Tudor mind. Spain (and the papacy) twice intervened in Ireland, landing troops at Smerwick, County Kerry (1580), and, in greater force, at Kinsale, County Cork (1601). Strategic necessity lent urgency to the Tudor reconquest of the sixteenth century and galvanized English determination to hold onto Ireland thereafter. Enemies changed, geography did not: French soldiers fought in Ireland in 1690 and 1798.

England's dominance depended, at bottom, on coercive force. Beyond that, Whitehall and Westminster exercised an array of political, legislative, and administrative controls. These included the retention in English hands of key public offices and the imposition of restrictive laws limiting the autonomy of the Irish Parliament and regulating Irish trade. A few legislative landmarks plot the troubled course of Anglo-Irish relations. First, "Poynings's Law" (1494), aimed originally at too-powerful lord deputies of the Kildare type, evolved into a procedure whereby all Irish parliamentary bills were subject to amendment—amounting to a veto—by the English Privy Council. The repeal of Poynings's Law constitutes the so-called revolution of 1782. Second, the Irish Parliament's subordinate status, institutionalized under Poynings, received confirmation in the Declaratory Act of 1720, a forthright assertion of Westminster's supremacy in the Kingdom of Ireland. Finally, Westminster used its claim of jurisdiction to impose laws prohibiting the import of Irish cattle to England (1667) and the export of Irish wool (1699). Both laws long caused bitter resentment in Ireland, the preliminary controversy surrounding the latter provoking the classic defense of Ireland's historic right to legislative independence, William Molyneux's *The Case of Ireland Being Bound by Acts of Parliament in England, Stated* (London, 1698).

The roots of England's perennial "Irish problem" lay in the failures of England's Irish policies. By 1450, although the territory of the Pale had contracted, it still boasted the most densely populated, intensively cultivated, and economically diverse region of the country. Yet Gaeldom had also demonstrated its military and cultural vitality. And, as Sir John Davies recognized in his *Discovery of the True Causes Why Ireland Was Never Entirely Subdued* (1612), the Irish problem would remain intractable for so long as the Gael remained outside—and indeed resistant to—the boon of common law, civility, and, by Davies's time, Protestantism or "true religion." "All the world knows their barbarism," Cromwell remarked of his Irish enemies. Only the adoption of English customs, Reformed religion, language, and law—in a word, anglicization—could save them from their wretched condition.

GAELIC IRELAND

The Gaelic Irish saw matters differently, and while the story of English-Irish conflict supplies the historian with a ready, dramatic, and compelling narrative structure, it is vital that historians not view the past solely in terms of that conflict. Early modern Ireland, viewed from the Atlantic shores of Donegal, looks rather different from the anglophone Ireland mapped and preserved in the Public Record Office. For the historian, the question of perspective is precisely about rescuing the Gaelic-speaking O'Donnell retainer and MacSweeny swordsman from the enormous condescension of the state papers. Gaelic politics, economy, and society are more difficult to reconstruct than Anglo-Ireland because they never generated the sorts of records—tax rolls, bureaucratic memoranda, even paintings—upon which historians usually rely. The Gaelic world has thus either remained hidden, or, as recently as 1988, been caricatured on the basis of the naive or hostile reportage of outsiders. Fortunately, the dearth of conventional sources has been circumvented somewhat by the mining of a rich, if tricky, lode of nontraditional evidence: Irish-language poetry. Excavations (and cataloguing) are still in the heroic phase, but already the findings of scholars working with these hitherto underused sources have altered and enhanced our understanding of, for example, the depth and range of Irish Jacobite sentiment in the eighteenth century.

English late medieval society, including the Irish Pale, was organized around legally binding principles of mutual obligation and services based on land tenures. In contrast, in Gaelic society land ownership and inheritance, obligation, and political

Thomas Gainsborough. *Cornard Wood,* c. 1746–1747. Although he made his living as a portrait painter, Gainsborough was devoted to the landscape genre. Of this early masterpiece, he wrote: "It is in some respects a little in the schoolboy stile — but I do not reflect on this without a secret gratification; for as an early instance how strong my inclination stood for Landskip."

RIGHT: Artemisia Gentileschi. *Saint Catherine.* Taught by her father, Orazio, Gentileschi absorbed the naturalistic tenets of Caravaggism and became renowned for her large-scale paintings on biblical themes. She is widely praised for her sensitive presentation of female protagonists, both in the dramatic biblical paintings and in later, more personal scenes.

BELOW: Gambling. *The Cheat with the Ace of Clubs* by Georges de la Tour, late 1620s. This painting presents a moral lesson on the perils of gambling: the well-dressed young man on the right is being cheated by a trio of cardsharps.

LEFT: Francisco de Goya y Lucientes. *The Straw Mannikin,* tapestry cartoon, 1792. In this cartoon, one of a series Goya created for the Spanish royal tapestry factory, the artist presents a comment on the power of women in his society. THE ART ARCHIVE/MUSEO DEL PRADO MADRID

BELOW: Giorgione. *Portrait of a Young Woman (Laura),* 1506. The subtle eroticism of this work was unprecedented in Renaissance art and is just one of the many innovations that distinguished the career of the renowned Giorgone. ©ERICH LESSING/ART RESOURCE, N.Y.

OPPOSITE PAGE: Frans Hals. *Portrait of a Woman,* c. 1640. Of Hals, the historian Theodorus Schrevelius wrote in 1648, "His paintings are imbued with such force and vitality that he seems to surpass nature herself with his brush. This is seen in all his portraits...which are colored in such a way that they seem to live and breathe." ©NATIONAL GALLERY COLLECTION; BY KIND PERMISSION OF THE TRUSTEES OF THE NATIONAL GALLERY, LONDON /CORBIS

TOP: Jean-Baptiste Greuze. *Broken Eggs,* 1757. In his many skillful genre paintings, Greuze helped popularize the use of that medium as a source of moral instruction. Here, the broken eggs clearly symbolize the loss of purity of the young woman. ©FRANCIS G. MAYER/CORBIS

CENTER: Harem. The harem sitting room in Topkapi Palace. ©CRAIG LOVELL/CORBIS

BOTTOM: William Hogarth. *The Countess's Morning Levee,* scene 4 from *Marriage à la mode,* 1745. Hogarth's satirical commentaries on urban life exerted great influence in the development of print culture in the eighteenth century. Here, the newlywed countess entertains a group of fawning hangers-on. ©NATIONAL GALLERY COLLECTION; BY KIND PERMISSION OF THE TRUSTEES OF THE NATIONAL GALLERY, LONDON/CORBIS

TOP: Inigo Jones. A 1760 view of Covent Garden Market painted by an unknown artist shows Jones's St. Paul's Church, center, before the 1795 fire and restoration. THE ART ARCHIVE/LONDON MUSEUM/SALLY CHAPPEL

CENTER: Angelica Kauffmann. *The Sellers of Love (Cupids).* Kauffmann was one of the first artists to paint in a neoclassical style and one of few women to gain fame from historical paintings. ©GIRAUDON/ART RESOURCE, N.Y.

BOTTOM: Charles Le Brun. *Louis XIV, 1638–1715, King of France, Armed on Land and Sea,* 1671, sketch for the ceiling of the Hall of Mirrors at the Château of Versailles. THE ART ARCHIVE/MUSÉE D'ART ET D'HISTOIRE AUXERRE/DAGLI ORTI

OPPOSITE PAGE: Leonardo da Vinci. *Ginevra de Benci,* c. 1474. In this relatively early portrait, the artist's skill is most evident in the detail of the curls that surround the subject's face. THE ART ARCHIVE/NATIONAL GALLERY OF ART WASHINGTON/ALBUM/JOSEPH MARTIN

Louis XIV. *Louis XIV, King of France, with His Family in Olympia,* by Jean Nocret. Louis's reign represented the zenith of French monarchical power; in this painting by one of his official court painters, he and his extended family are depicted as classical deities. THE ART ARCHIVE/MUSÉE DU CHÂTEAU DE VERSAILLES/DAGLI ORTI

succession were determined by kinship. A chief's power rested on his ability to enforce it, and under the system of "tanistry" his designated heir was as likely a brother or cousin as an eldest son. Kinship, alliances through marriage and fosterage and the receipt of tribute from lesser clans defined a great chief's status more than territory or even cattle—the staple of the Gaelic pastoral economy. Certain families, notably the O'Neills and O'Donnells in Ulster, the O'Connors in Connacht, and the MacCarthys and O'Briens in Munster, predominated. They inhabited a world of insistent, low-intensity warfare and comparative political instability. Exactions of tribute—in kind, or in military or labor services—lacked regulation, and by the early modern period were epitomized by the abuses of "coign and livery"—the billeting at free quarters by a chief of his dependants on his tenants.

The crown and the Dublin administration were not prepared to leave the natives to their own ways for three reasons. First, the inevitable processes of intermarriage, cultural interaction, and linguistic borrowings (in both directions) of the Gaedhil (or Irish) and the Gaill (or foreigners)—which historians call gaelicization but which the English called degeneracy—could not be permitted to continue. Second, the English "common law mind" embraced legal uniformity and abhorred local particularism. Ireland, reported an early-sixteenth-century English observer, comprised a patchwork of over sixty "countries" ruled by captains, each of whom "maketh war and peace for himself, and holdeth by the sword, and hath imperial jurisdiction within his room, and obeyeth to no other person." Worse still, degenerate "captains of English noble family . . . followeth the same Irish order." The gaelicized Anglo-Norman House of Desmond cast its shadow across the common law mind. Finally, particularistic march law and Gaelic custom rooted in local power bases challenged royal sovereignty as well as legal uniformity.

CONQUEST AND "REFORM"

Whereas conventional nationalist histories of sixteenth-century Ireland focused on reconquest, revisionist historians have recovered the Tudor commitment to reform, although conquest and, in Brendan Bradshaw's terminology, "the catastrophic dimension of Irish history" are now being reintroduced to a more complicated picture. The set pieces of reform are the Act of Kingly Title (1541), which upgraded Ireland from a lordship to a kingdom, and "surrender and regrant," under which Gaelic chieftains surrendered their titles to the crown and were regranted them in English law. Several leading figures were ennobled, for example "the O'Neill" now became Earl of Tyrone, and succession and inheritance were at least theoretically stabilized by the extension of primogeniture. In the longer run, however, the prospects for reform were dashed by the rise of confessional conflict.

In Ireland, the Protestant Reformation assumed the character of an alien imposition. Decisively, the old English, as well as the native Irish, remained Catholic. Protestants were—and remained—a minority. When the Tudors completed the reconquest by the subjugation of Hugh O'Neill (1603), Gaelic Ireland had suffered military defeat but retained its cultural identity. Ethnic origin divided the Gael from his fellow Catholic old English almost as much as from the Protestant new English, yet shared adversity during the first decades of the seventeenth century conspired to forge a common Catholic identity. The defeat of O'Neill was followed by "the flight of the Earls" (1607) when O'Neill and others fled to Catholic Europe. Interpreted as an act of rebellion, the fugitives' lands escheated to the crown and were redistributed to English and Scottish settlers in the plantation of Ulster. The last bastion of Gaelic civilization thereby became the beachhead of British Protestantism in Ireland. The Scottish communities, moreover, laid the seedbed for Presbyterianism.

Stuart Ireland thus hosted four major ethnoreligious groups: native Irish Catholics, old English Catholics, new English Protestants of the established church, and (before 1642, informally) Scots Presbyterians. Intra-denominational relations, already tense, strained to breaking point with the crisis of the Stuart monarchies in the late 1630s. Ireland, in fact, helped detonate the wars of the three kingdoms with the Ulster rebellion of 1641. Many Protestant planters were killed by insurgents, and lurid tales of massacre swept England, deepening the rage against popery and suspicion of the king, in whose defense the rebels claimed to act. Ireland, like England and Scotland, experienced the trauma of civil war in the 1640s. Alliances and allegiances shifted bewilderingly but, crucially, the old English were forced into military coalition with their Gaelic coreligionists. When Cromwell arrived in 1649 once more to subjugate the Irish and to revenge 1641, he made no ethnic distinctions among his papist enemies.

The land confiscations begun in the Tudor era and continued by the Ulster plantation reached unprecedented levels with the Cromwellian settlement. In 1603 Catholics owned more than 60 percent of the land; by 1659 that figure had been reduced to about 9 percent. During the reign of Charles II, Catholic ownership climbed back to around 25 percent, thanks to successful pleas in the court of claims, but fell again to 14 percent by the end of the century as a result of the forfeitures that followed the second defeat of Catholic Ireland in 1691. This time there would be no court of claims, but rather a relentless chipping away, by the implementation of penal laws, at the remaining Catholic-owned land. By 1775 it stood at 5 percent. The political nation, like the landowning elite, of eighteenth-century Ireland was Protestant. But the Protestants were a minority, and if anything is inevitable in history, the Catholics could not be excluded from public life and political power forever. A rising Catholic mercantile class had already begun to articulate its grievances by the 1780s, but once more it was events outside the island that catalyzed Irish politics, including the "Catholic question." With the storming of the Bastille on 14 July 1789, a new epoch opened in European—and Irish—history.

See also **Cromwell, Oliver; Dublin; England; Landholding; Law; Nationalism; Provincial Government; Revolutions, Age of.**

BIBLIOGRAPHY

Brady, Ciaran, and Raymond Gillespie, eds. *Natives and Newcomers: Essays on the Making of Irish Colonial Society, 1534–1641.* Dublin, 1986.

Connolly, Sean J. *Law, Religion and Power: The Making of Protestant Ireland, 1660–1760.* Oxford, 1992.

Ellis, Steven G. *Ireland in the Age of the Tudors, 1447–1603: English Expansion and the End of Gaelic Rule.* London and New York, 1998.

Moody, T. W., F. X. Martin, and F. J. Byrne, eds. *A New History of Ireland III: Early Modern Ireland, 1534–1691.* Oxford, 1976.

JIM SMYTH

ISABEL CLARA EUGENIA AND ALBERT OF HABSBURG

ISABEL CLARA EUGENIA AND ALBERT OF HABSBURG (Isabel Clara Eugenia, 1566–1633; Albert of Habsburg, 1559–1621), archdukes of Austria, governors and sovereigns of the Spanish Netherlands. Isabel Clara Eugenia, eldest daughter of Philip II of Spain and Elisabeth de Valois, learned statecraft at her father's side. While her sister Catalina Micaëla (1567–1597) married the duke of Savoy in 1585, Philip found no suitable husband for Infanta Isabel. Sebastian of Portugal perished in battle, and Emperor Rudolf II proved too eccentric. In 1590–1593, when Philip vainly pressed Isabel's claim to the French throne, he considered Charles, duke of Guise (1571–1640) for her hand before settling on Archduke Ernst of Habsburg (1553–1595), who was appointed governor-general of the revolt-torn Netherlands in 1593. Ernst died in 1595, and in 1597, Philip decided that Isabel would marry Ernst's brother, Cardinal-Archduke Albert, who had succeeded Ernst in the Netherlands, and arranged the necessary dispensations with Rome.

Isabel Clara Eugenia. Portrait by Atelier of Pourbus. THE ART ARCHIVE/MUSÉE DU CHÂTEAU DE VERSAILLES/DAGLI ORTI

Albert, sixth son of Emperor Maximilian II and Philip II's sister Maria, had gone from Austria to Spain in 1570 with his sister Ana when she married Philip II. Groomed for the church, Albert was nominated cardinal in 1577 and was soon designated archbishop of Toledo to follow the aged Gaspar de Quiroga, who did not die until 1594. Cardinal-Archduke Albert meantime filled political offices. Appointed viceroy of Portugal in 1583, he learned about military matters during preparations for the Spanish Armada and the defense of Portugal in 1589 against the English counterattack led by Sir Francis Drake. In 1593 Philip brought Albert to Madrid to assist him and guide Prince Philip, who later became Philip III. Appointed governor of the Netherlands in 1595, Albert had mixed success in his battles with the Dutch stadtholder Maurice of Nassau, the son of William of Orange, and with Henry IV of France. In May 1598 Albert achieved the treaty of Vervins with France. The same month, Philip II bestowed sovereignty of the Netherlands on him and Isabel, with the proviso that if either died childless, the Netherlands would return to the Spanish crown.

Albert of Habsburg. Portrait by Atelier of Pourbus. THE ART ARCHIVE/MUSÉE DU CHÂTEAU DE VERSAILLES/DAGLI ORTI

Philip II died that September, and his son Philip III (1598–1621) had come to the throne when Albert, never priest and no longer cardinal, married Isabel at Valencia in May 1599. Together the "archdukes" returned to Brussels. Maurice invaded Flanders briefly in 1600 and defeated Albert in battle. Albert's army became mutinous without pay, yet with Isabel's encouragement in 1601 he laid siege to Ostend, the remaining rebel stronghold in Flanders. He also achieved peace with England. Ambrogio Spinola (1569–1630), Genoese banker turned soldier, repaired the army's finances and took over the siege. Pressured by Madrid, Albert gave him command of the army. In 1604, Ostend surrendered.

In the same years Albert, in collaboration with Isabel, sought through diplomacy to end the Dutch revolt and reunite the provinces of the Dutch Republic with the "obedient" provinces known as the Spanish Netherlands. Isabel and Albert were often at odds with Madrid. In religion they favored persuasion and Catholic revival rather than fire and the stake. But religious differences remained profound and talk of toleration too vague for either Catholic or Calvinist. The archdukes' centralization of government, however efficient, and their ignoring of the southern States General after 1600, ran contrary to Dutch republican ideals. Amsterdam did not want Antwerp as a rival. Trade concessions in Spain's empire seemed too conditional, its plunder more appealing. Refugees who moved their businesses to the Dutch Republic did not relish a revived Flanders. And all knew that the archdukes remained dependent on funds from Spain and a consideration in Spanish strategy.

The fortunes of war seesawed, and both sides became exhausted, while France and England tired of the cost of backing the Dutch. In 1609 a compromise Twelve Years' Truce was achieved. The years of peace proved unsettled. Industry languished though urban oligarchs prospered, and the nobility tightened its hold on the countryside. Culture flourished. Louvain and Douai became centers of Catholic learning while the baroque style inspired the arts. The archdukes became patrons of Peter Paul Rubens.

International crises, such as the Jülich-Cleves dispute of 1609–1610, proved frequent. In 1618, the Thirty Years' War commenced, and Albert sent Spinola to devastate the Rhine (or Lower) Palatinate. In 1621, Albert died as the Twelve Years' Truce with the Dutch, which he had tried to extend, expired. The Spanish Netherlands reverted to Spain. Infanta Isabel became governor for her nephew Philip IV while Spinola remained in command of the army.

In the field Spinola capped his successes in 1625 when Breda surrendered, but in 1628 he was called to Italy. The war turned against Isabel, and sedition spread although she was personally beloved for her works of charity. In vain she sought peace for the Spanish Netherlands. She summoned the States General in 1632 and employed subtle diplomacy using Rubens. Disheartened, she died in Brussels after a brief illness on 1 December 1633.

See also **Dutch Republic; Henry IV (France); Marie de Médicis; Netherlands, Southern; Philip II (Spain); Philip III (Spain); Philip IV (Spain); Rubens, Peter Paul; Thirty Years' War (1618–1648).**

BIBLIOGRAPHY

Allen, Paul C. *Philip III and the Pax Hispanica 1598–1621: The Failure of a Grand Strategy.* New Haven, 2000.

Caiero, Francisco. *O Arquiduque Alberto de Austria Vice-Rei e Inquisidor-mor de Portugal.* Lisbon, 1961.

Terlinden, Charles. *L'Archiduchesse Isabelle.* Brussels, 1943.

Thomas, Werner, and Luc Duerloo, eds. *Albert and Isabella 1598–1621; Essays.* Turnhout, Belgium, 1998.

PETER PIERSON

ISABELLA OF CASTILE (1451–1504), queen of Castile and joint ruler of Aragón. Isabel I was born in medieval Castile; she died in early modern Spain, having had much to do with the transition from medieval to modern. She was three years old in 1454 when her father, King John II (ruled 1406–1454) of Castile, died and her older half-brother, Henry IV (ruled 1454–1474), succeeded him. That year too another event paved her way to the crown and did much to determine the course of her reign: Constantinople, the eastern capital of Christendom, fell to Muslim Turks, causing widespread fear of Turkish advance into the West and a papal call for crusade. Henry IV responded to it by renewing war against Granada, the last Muslim kingdom in Iberia. Some powerful nobles, already perceiving themselves shunted aside by the king, adjudged his pursuit of that war halfhearted. Civil war erupted in the 1460s, ending only when Henry named Isabel, whom the dissidents favored, his heir.

Against Henry's wishes, Isabel in 1469 contacted, met, and married Ferdinand, prince of Aragón, in what proved a love match and lifelong partnership, and put Spain on the road to national unity. The couple were cousins, their goals similar and their personalities complementary. On Henry's death in 1474 civil war again broke out. Two years later, it was clear the couple had won. Isabel emerged as reigning queen in Castile with Ferdinand as her consort. Yet from the outset, the reign was publicized as joint at Isabel's insistence, attesting to her sensitivity to the popular temper and mind cast and her recognition of a queen's limitations even while she overcame them. A medieval ruler was expected to do justice, lead in war, and lead subjects to God, guiding them to salvation. Having triumphed in war, Isabel immediately and effectively presided over a court of law in Seville, Castile's largest city. She chose her closest advisers from the two most educated groups, clergy and lawyers (most lawyers were also clergy). In medieval Europe, and especially in Spain, the monarch traditionally headed the church, while the clergy represented rulers as divinely sanctioned and were looked to as intermediaries linking the crowned heads and the people.

Isabel herself exhibited piety, but less the lady-praying-on-her-knees variety often ascribed to her than the militant Christianity of Spain's greatest kings, those who showed themselves as finding their highest purpose in the crusading endeavor to reconquer Spanish territory held by Muslims since 711. In announcing that such was her intent and thereby also reinforcing her own initially shaky right to rule, Isabel put traditional imagery to work. During her coronation she had a double-edged sword, perceived as the sword of justice, of God's warriors, and of divine wrath and vengeance, carried before her. As one of her first acts as queen, she commissioned tombs for her parents at Miraflores outside Burgos, their prominent display of the well-understood symbols of star and sun announcing her dynastic commitment to achieving Spain's cosmic destiny. She sponsored the Toledo church dedicated to her patron saint, San Juan—St. John the Evangelist, whose Book of Revelation promised salvation to the godly and a messianic end to history, promises often interpreted among the Spanish as made to themselves, the new Israel. When she gave birth in 1478 to a son, Juan, the prince was greeted in messianic terms in attendant ceremonies and by chroniclers and clergy. Moreover, it was expected that Juan, as heir to the crowns of both Castile and Aragón, would one day in his person unite Spain.

Isabel grew up in wartime, and war remained central to her evolving reign; no war was more popularly unifying, or of more transcendental purpose, or more capable of centralizing royal power than the by then traditional religious and national mission of reconquest. Resumption of war against Granada was announced in 1480, along with such other centralizing measures as codifying laws and reclaiming crown lands from nobles. Concurrently, Isabel also asserted royal religious authority in instituting the Spanish Inquisition (1478), designed to find and punish religious heretics and apostates. Its focus was those converted Jews, *conversos,* who still held to Jewish beliefs. Thereafter, Isabel's Spain waged religious warfare on two fronts, both internally and against the Muslim kingdom of Granada.

For nearly a decade, year after year, she relentlessly directed campaigns against the sprawling and mountainous kingdom of Granada. She oversaw recruitment, finances, and supplies, conferred on strategy, and on occasion cajoled Fernando into keeping to the field as military commander, or herself joined Spanish armies at the front during long sieges. On 1 January 1492, she and Ferdinand rode ceremoniously into the city of Granada. It was not simply happenstance that Isabel sent out Christopher Columbus that same year with instructions to find a sea route to the rich East and through it to the goal of all crusaders, Jerusalem, then under Muslim control; nor that in 1492 she and Fernando expelled Spain's Jews and, in 1502, Castile's Muslims. Rather, each of those measures was spoken of as advancing Christian conquest in accord with Spain's mandate.

Veterans of the Granada wars fought on, in Navarre, and in Italy against France and for the

Isabella of Castile. Portrait by the Circle of Juan de Flandres, c. 1496–1519. ©CHRISTIE'S IMAGES/CORBIS

papacy, which in appreciation designated Spain's rulers "Los Reyes Católicos," The Catholic Kings. Many helped establish Spanish rule in the Caribbean islands and explored mainland coasts. Isabel looked on the peoples encountered as her subjects; she directed that they be instructed in the Spanish language and ways and in the Christian faith and that, if peaceful, they be well treated, but that those who warred on the Spanish be enslaved. A codicil to her will instructed her heirs that "if [the Indians] were receiving any harm, to remedy it, so that it did not exceed the apostolic order of concession." Arguably, nothing more succinctly expresses a piety that linked the royal role, morality, law, and national interest, and viewed all of them in an international context regulated and guaranteed through a religion and its titular head on earth.

In what was Isabel's last decade, Spain experienced aspects of the Renaissance. Isabel acquired paintings and tapestries by Flemish masters and pietistic devotional books from the new printing presses. Increasingly ill, she appears to have become more introspective, more concerned with her immortal soul and those of her subjects, and more averse to men dying in wars with no religious aim. And she repeatedly suffered personal loss. She had made grand dynastic marriages for her five children—encircling France and creating an alliance with the powerful Habsburgs who ruled the Lowlands and much of Germany and Austria through the double marriage of her son Juan to the Princess Margaret and her daughter Joanna to the Habsburg heir, Philip. She married her daughter Isabel to the Portuguese King Manuel, and, when young Isabel died in childbirth, had another daughter, María, wed Manuel. And she sent her youngest child, Catherine, to England to wed Prince Arthur. She did not live to see Arthur die and his brother, becoming King Henry VIII, marry the widowed Catherine of Aragón. Probably of greatest impact on Isabel was the death of her son Juan, leaving as heir to Castile her oldest surviving child, the unstable Joanna, known to history as "La Loca" ('The Mad'). Nor did she live to see Joanna's son Charles I (Holy Roman emperor Charles V) unite Castile and Aragón as well as inherit Habsburg lands and new dependencies in America to make real what she fully expected to be Spain's future, a globe-encircling empire.

Spain came into modernity as one of Europe's most powerful and esteemed monarchies, but selectively, as a society closed to all aspects of modernity at odds with its dominant, nation-building religious beliefs.

See also **Charles V (Holy Roman Empire); Ferdinand of Aragón; Inquisition, Spanish; Spain.**

BIBLIOGRAPHY

Boruchoff, David A., ed. *Isabel la Católica, Queen of Castile: Critical Essays.* New York, 2003.

Ladero Quesada, Miguel Ángel. *La España de los Reyes Católicos.* Madrid, 1999.

Liss, Peggy K. "Isabel of Castile: Her Self-Representation and Its Context," In *Queenship in Early Modern Spain,* edited by Theresa Earenfight. New York, 2003.

———. *Isabel the Queen: Life and Times.* New York, 1992. Spanish language edition *Isabel la Católica.* Madrid, 1999.

———. "Isabel I of Castilla, reina de España." In *Isabel la Católica,* edited by Pedro Navascués. Madrid, 2002.

PEGGY K. LISS

ISLAM IN THE OTTOMAN EMPIRE. The Ottoman Empire was an Islamic polity that originated in early-fourteenth-century Anatolia. Islam had been established in Anatolia before the emergence of the empire, but between the fourteenth and sixteenth centuries the religion spread with Ottoman conquest to the Balkan Peninsula and central Hungary. This does not mean that the population was uniformly Muslim. In many parts of the Ottoman Empire, most notably in the Balkan Peninsula, Christians formed a majority of the population, and even in areas where Muslims formed a majority there was usually also a minority of non-Muslim inhabitants. Unlike some of the rulers of western Europe, the Ottoman sultans never attempted to impose religious uniformity. Islam was, however, the dominant religion, and the political structure of the empire reflected this fact. The dynasty itself was Muslim and, before the reforms of the nineteenth century, with rare exceptions, non-Muslims could not hold regular political office or military command. Christians and Jews were able to participate in the maintenance of the empire by serving as tax farmers or contractors supplying, for example, cloth for Janissary uniforms or materials to the naval arsenals, but they could not serve as viziers, provincial governors, or army commanders. In the fourteenth and fifteenth centuries a few Christian fief holders in the Balkans retained their positions in the years immediately after the Ottoman conquest but, as their descendants converted to Islam, this phenomenon disappeared within a generation. In the Balkans, too, some Christian groups served as military auxiliaries into the sixteenth century. More important in the day-to-day lives of the sultan's subjects, the system of law courts also reflected the dominant position of Islam. The Christian and Jewish communities maintained their own courts for regulating intracommunal affairs, but only the network of Muslim courts covered the entire empire, and only Muslim courts were open to all the sultan's subjects, irrespective of religion. Any cases involving Muslims or a Muslim and a non-Muslim had to be heard in the Muslim court and, in principle, a non-Muslim could not testify against a Muslim. The exclusion, therefore, of non-Muslims from political office and the supremacy of Islamic law guaranteed the hegemonic position of Islam within the Ottoman Empire. At the same time, the imposition of *jizya,* a poll tax on adult non-Muslim males, and the occasional short-lived imposition of dress restrictions on non-Muslims, symbolized the inferior position of Christians and Jews.

FORMS OF ISLAM

By the time of the emergence of the Ottoman Empire in the fourteenth century, Islam was fully formed as a system of belief with its associated intellectual, legal, and cultural attributes. The central concept of the religion was "knowledge," or *ʿilm,* meaning specifically the knowledge of God through revelation. God had revealed himself to mankind through the missions of the prophets, among whom Abraham (Ibrahim), the monotheistic founder of the Kaʿba at Mecca, Moses (Musa), and Jesus (ʿIsa) held especially revered positions. The recognition of Abraham, Moses, and Jesus as prophets before the final revelation of Islam justified the tolerated but subordinate positions of Jews and Christians within the Ottoman Empire and other Islamic polities. God's final and most perfect revelation was through the prophet Muhammad, "the Seal of the Prophets." The primary text of revelation is the Koran. This is regarded by Muslims as the literal word of God transmitted to mankind through the medium of the Prophet. The record of the sayings and actions—the hadith—of the Prophet, as an exemplar to mankind, form the second text of the revelation. It is through the Koran and hadith, therefore, that man can know God and, in principle, these form the foundation of knowledge, or *ʿilm.*

A seeker after knowledge had first to study Arabic, the language of revelation and the language of science, which acquired a role in the Ottoman Empire and in the Islamic world as the universal language of religion, somewhat similar to the role of Latin in western Christendom. The study of the sacred texts and the sciences in general also required a grounding in logic and rhetoric. With these tools at his disposal, a scholar could embark on any of the specialized branches of *ʿilm,* which developed as discrete, though interrelated genres: the interpretation of the Koran *(tafsir),* the study of hadith, theology *(kalam),* dogma *(ʿaqaʾid)* or law *(fiqh).* These were the sciences through which one acquired a knowledge of God, and which therefore formed the central curriculum of Ottoman and other Islamic colleges. Subsidiary sciences—for example, the life of the Prophet *(sira),* history *(taʾrikh),* the vitae of saints or scholars by generation *(tabaqat)*—served to strengthen sectarian or dynastic identity, and all came to form genres of Ottoman literature. Of the sciences, it was the study of law *(fiqh)* that enjoyed the greatest prestige and made the greatest impact on communal and individual lives. It represented not exactly God's commands to mankind, as these are ultimately unknowable, but the best that humankind can achieve in its efforts to discover God's law. It regulated not only secular affairs, notably in the sphere of family law, but also rituals such as ablution, prayer, fasting, and forbidden foods. The basics of the law, popularized as the "five pillars of Islam"—the profession of faith, prayer five times daily, charity, fasting during Ramadan, and the pilgrimage to Mecca—are something that every Muslim must know. In many respects, therefore, it was the adoption of Islamic law—the *sharʿ* or *shariʿa*—that gave Ottoman, and other Islamic societies, their distinctive form.

A person who had studied *ʿilm* was an *ʿalim* ('one who knows [God]') and enjoyed great prestige. The plural of *ʿalim* is *ʿulama,* and the ulema came to form a respected class within all Muslim societies, often, as in the Ottoman Empire, wielding political as well as legal and spiritual power.

ʿIlm was not, however, the only route to knowing God. Already in the early centuries of Islam some claimed to know God through direct revelation, a condition exemplified by the saying of al-Sarraj (d. 988): "There is no *ʿilm* that is known and nothing that is understood except what exists in the Book of God, or is transmitted from the Messenger of God, or in what is revealed in the hearts of saints." In order to distinguish the knowledge of God acquired by direct revelation "in the hearts of saints," its adepts, the Sufis, referred to it not as *ʿilm,* but as *ʿurf or maʾrifa,* both words having the sense of "knowledge." This doctrine had revolutionary potential, since a person claiming knowledge via direct divine inspiration could claim to be above the divine law as professed by the ulema. Indeed some Sufis, notably al-Hallaj (d. 909), who reputedly suffered death for declaring "I am God," did emerge, in the Ottoman Empire and elsewhere, as opponents of the religious and political order.

What is more remarkable, however, is how *tasawwuf*, the faith of the Sufis—radically different from the religion of the ulema—came to form a branch of orthodox Islam.

In principle, *ʿilm* and *ʿurf* are antagonistic in their fundamental beliefs. In orthodox belief, God created the world ex nihilo; he revealed himself through his prophets; the world will end with the Resurrection and the Judgment, where individuals will be judged and assigned in eternity to Heaven or Hell. In Sufi belief, all creation was originally one with God. God created mankind and the universe because "He was a hidden treasure and wished that He should be known." Since this separation from the Creator, all Creation has yearned to return to its Maker. The Sufi therefore yearns to be reunited with God, as the lover yearns for union with the beloved. In orthodox Islam, knowledge of God comes through written revelation whose interpretation is the preserve of the ulema. In Sufi belief, knowledge of God is acquired through direct experience, or "taste" of God.

There has at all times been antagonism between some of the orthodox ulema and the Sufis. For example, in the Ottoman Empire of the mid-sixteenth century, the jurist Ibrahim of Aleppo (d. 1549) and the Ottoman chief mufti, Çivizade Mehmed (d. 1542), adopted anti-Sufi positions, while the Sufis for their part conducted a literary polemic against these orthodox opponents. The poet Khayali (d. 1556/57) compared the orthodox ulema who could not recognize that God was in the world around them to "fish who are in the sea, but do not know what the sea is." Nonetheless, opponents of the Sufis remained a minority and *tasawwuf* in practice became an important strand of mainstream Islam in the Ottoman Empire.

Tasawwuf grew in importance through doctrinal development. In the developed Sufi theory of knowledge, the first rule that a Sufi must follow is obedience to the *shariʿa*. This precept brought *tasawwuf* within the bounds of orthodoxy. Second, the spiritual goal of most Sufis was not to declare "I am God," but to seek "annihilation of the self in God": the Sufi's soul became like "a drop of wine in the ocean of God's love." In other words, *tasawwuf* became quietist rather than activist. At the same time, *tasawwuf* became institutionalized. Different orders of Sufis formed around the memories of Sufi saints, and these organizations acquired properties and endowments, to preserve which they had to remain acceptable to orthodox Islamic regimes. Finally, the favorable opinions of al-Ghazali (d. 1111), perhaps the most influential Islamic thinker, made *tasawwuf* acceptable to most orthodox opinion. Some orders, it is true, remained unacceptable. In the Ottoman Empire, an offshoot of the Bayrami order of Sufis, which formed after 1450, adopted the activist belief that God is manifest in the human form, thus putting men—or at least their members—above the dictates of the *shariʿa*. These Sufis constituted an underground and ineffective, though persecuted, opposition to orthodox Islam and the Ottoman sultanate.

THE POLITICAL STRUCTURE OF OTTOMAN ISLAM

Although *tasawwuf* may have been the strongest influence on the beliefs of many, if not most, Ottoman Muslims and permeated Ottoman literature, music, and visual art, it was the Islam of the ulema that was significant in determining the structures of the empire. A few surviving literary fragments suggest that in the fourteenth century, the level of Islamic learning in the Ottoman Empire was very low. Persons wishing for an advanced Islamic education at this period traveled to the old Islamic world, especially to Damascus or Cairo, and it was largely these returning scholars who transferred Islamic doctrine and law to the Ottoman realms and trained the early generations of Ottoman ulema. By the mid-fifteenth century, with the establishment of a system of colleges within the empire and the formation of a learned class, there was no further need for such learning journeys.

The religious colleges (madrasas) attached to mosques throughout the empire, established on the model of the madrasas in the old Islamic world, were the institutions that trained the ulema. The most prestigious colleges were royal foundations, with the Eight Colleges of Mehmed II (1451–1481) and the colleges attached to the mosque of Suleiman I (1520–1566), completed in 1557, enjoying the highest rank, and the foundations of senior statesmen occupying the second tier. Each college was an independent institution with a separate endowment. In the sixteenth century, however, Suleiman I and later Mehmed III (1595–1603) made efforts to formalize the hierarchy of colleges and, to a degree, to control the curriculum, which remained firmly based on the medieval Islamic classics. By the seventeenth century there seems to have been a well-recognized hierarchy, based on the wealth of the endowment and the level of the curriculum. From the late seventeenth century, when the empire began to lose territories, some colleges suffered as the lands that provided their endowments passed into foreign hands.

It was the colleges that maintained the level of Islamic learning in the empire. A graduate might find a position as imam in an important mosque; he might stay in the system as a teacher *(mudarris);* or he might choose a career as a judge *(qadi)*. However, if he opted for a legal career immediately on graduating, he would, at least between the sixteenth and eighteenth centuries, find his career confined to the judgeships of small towns. Judgeships of the great cities, especially of Istanbul, Edirne, and Bursa, were reserved for *mudarris*es from the Eight Colleges or other high-ranking madrasas. Furthermore, between the sixteenth and the eighteenth centuries, a few ulema families monopolized these prestigious teaching positions and judgeships. It was also from the judges of the great cities that the sultan chose the two military judges *(kadiaskers),* the senior judges of the empire, who sat on the Imperial Council. Below the level of the great cities, however, most of the judges and religious officials tended to be local men, who from the sixteenth century would normally have received part of their education in Istanbul.

The judges, at all levels, administered Islamic law, and in continuing to exercise this function at all times, including times of crisis, they played the major role in ensuring the stability and continuity of Ottoman government. Of the four schools of law within Sunni Islam—the Shafiʿi, Maliki, Hanbali, and Hanafi—the Ottomans adopted the Hanafi school, presumably because this is the school that was already established in pre-Ottoman Anatolia. As the Hanafi jurists typically offer more than one acceptable solution to each legal problem, the Hanafi was perhaps the most flexible of the schools and, for this reason, the most suitable to form the basis of a working legal system. After their formative period in the early Islamic centuries, the four schools remained mutually exclusive. According to Hanafi theorists, for example, a person could have recourse to a Shafiʿi judge only in the two cases for which the Hanafi school offered no solution: the dissolution of an oath or when a deserted wife seeks a dissolution of marriage. The Ottomans endorsed this exclusivity, although among the general population in the Arab lands there was some movement between schools.

Judges in the Ottoman Empire as elsewhere put the law into effect by virtue of the delegation to them of sultanic power. Above the judges stood the muftis. A mufti is a religious authority with the competence to issue *fatwa*s, authoritative opinions on any religious-legal problems that questioners may ask. A *fatwa* is not an executive command: it requires a judge's or sovereign's decree to put it into effect. It also differs from a judge's decree, in that the judge's decree is valid only for the case in hand, while the *fatwa* has a universal validity. Ottoman *fatwa*s reflect this understanding by reformulating each question so as to conceal the identity of the questioner, even if the questioner was the sultan himself, to remove specific details of the case such as time, locality, or personal identities, and to eliminate details not relevant to the case in question. Between the sixteenth and eighteenth centuries, Ottoman *fatwa*s in their content, format, and anonymity came increasingly to resemble the classical juristic texts which were the source of their authority.

The mufti in theory remained above and apart from the secular power, a concept embodied from the sixteenth century in Ottoman ceremonial, where the sultan stands in the presence of the chief mufti. His authority derived from his role as interpreter of the Holy Law in its application to mundane realities, including the realities of political power. In much of the Islamic world, muftis acquired their role through public recognition rather than official appointment, and really did stand apart from the secular power. In the Ottoman Empire, however, the muftis were effectively part of the government. The chief mufti, or *sheikh al-islam* as he came to be known by the seventeenth century, was the senior figure in the religious-legal establishment, and usually achieved the position by serving first as a senior judge and then as a military judge; like these offices, the chief muftiship after the mid-sixteenth century came to be the preserve of a very few ulema families. The chief mufti owed his exalted position partly to the Islamic view that accorded greater dignity to muftis than to judges, but also to the prestige of two sixteenth-century holders of the office, Kemal Pashazade (1525–1534) and Ebu's-su'ud Mehmed (1545–1574). Ebu's-su'ud in particular systematized the chief mufti's major function of issuing *fatwas*, ensuring that his office was able to undertake a great volume of work to a high standard. The system that he established remained in its essentials intact until the end of the empire.The chief mufti came to have an important, if informal, role in the Ottoman government. Outside the capital, muftis were sometimes official appointees, but did not enjoy high status of the chief mufti, and their function could often be fulfilled by the *mudarris* of a local college.

TASAWWUF IN THE OTTOMAN EMPIRE

By the time of the establishment of the Ottoman Empire, *tasawwuf* was well established in the Islamic world and accepted, within limits, as a form of orthodox Islam. Groups of Sufis had established and continued to establish their own orders *(tariqas)* throughout the Islamic world, each with its own saints and distinctive beliefs and rituals. Many of the orders that originated outside the empire found disciples in Ottoman territories. For example, the Khalveti order, named after the eponymous saint 'Umar al-Khalwati, originated in late-fourteenth-century Azerbaijan. During the fifteenth century the disciples of the Khalveti sheikh Yahya al-Shirvani (d. c. 1463) brought the order to Anatolia. When he was governor of Amasya, the future sultan Bayezid II (1480–1512) was initiated as a Khalveti and established the order in Istanbul after he became sultan. Later, Murad III (1574–1595) was also initiated. Other orders originated within the Ottoman Empire itself. For example, the Bayrami order was the creation of Hajji Bayram (d. 1429/30), who established the fraternity originally among the craftsmen of Ankara. His successor Ak Shemseddin (d. 1459) became a spiritual mentor to Mehmed II.

Once established, Sufi orders sometimes split into smaller groups, the Khalvetis, for example, giving birth to ten or more subgroups during the sixteenth and seventeenth centuries. The Bayramis, too, split into two groups after 1450, the orthodox group following Ak Shemseddin, the "heretical" group, the Melamis, coming under the leadership of 'Ömer the Cutler (d. 1475/6). This group became particularly active in Bosnia. By the late seventeenth century, however, the Melamis had reemerged as an orthodox order, although distinct from the original Bayramis. Conversely, different groups could merge. The Bektashi order, which took its name from a fourteenth century saint, Hajji Bektash, formed as a coherent order under the leadership of Balim Sultan about 1500, and absorbed and syncretized a wide range of Sufi and other popular beliefs. The Bektashis became particularly well established in Albania.

Many Muslims in the Ottoman Empire belonged to a Sufi order, giving these an essential role not only in disseminating popular faith but also in establishing networks and social solidarity among members. In some orders membership included women, giving them a role not available in orthodox Islam. The orders could also acquire charitable functions, the rural lodges of the Bektashis, for example, providing accommodation for travelers. Above all, they influenced the cultural life of the empire. Each order had its own liturgy and ceremonies, usually involving music, recitation, singing, and sometimes dancing, and to preserve their traditions the orders had to train adepts in these arts, many of whom acquired fame beyond the confines of the organization. The Mevlevi order—the so-called whirling dervishes—had a particular educational role. The sacred text of the order, the lengthy mystical poem known as the Mesnevi, by its eponymous saint, Mevlana Celaleddin Rumi (d. 1273), is written in Persian, a language that Mevlevis therefore had to learn. Since Persian was not taught in Ottoman madrasas, it was above all the Mevlevi lodges that provided instruction and were instrumental in maintaining the enormous prestige of Persian culture in the Ottoman Empire. They also acted as musical and literary academies. The most celebrated Ottoman composers and many Ottoman poets from the seventeenth to the nineteenth century were Mevlevis. While the Mevlevi order was a repository of Ottoman high culture, the Bektashis played a similar role in transmitting popular culture, for example in preserving and adding to the corpus of Turkish religious poetry attributed to the semi-mythical Sufi of the thirteenth or fourteenth century, Yunus Emre.

ORTHODOXY AND HETERODOXY

Although *tasawwuf* had an intellectual tradition and a structure of "knowledge" that imitated *ʿilm,* its primary appeal was aesthetic rather than intellectual. The liturgies of the orders, which aimed to produce a state of ecstasy in participants as they "became drunk with the wine of God's love," offered a religious and theatrical experience that was not available in the impressive but austere ceremonies in the mosques. What was equally important is that the orders, and particularly those with a popular following, institutionalized popular piety, with its appetite for saints and miracles. The hagiographies of Sufi saints, such as Enisi's early sixteenth-century vita of the Bayrami Ak Shemseddin, formed a branch of popular literature that provided entertainment, edification, and a focal point for people's loyalties as adherents to a particular Sufi order. At the same time the shrines of saints, whether or not they had an association with a particular order, became sites of pilgrimage, offering cures for diseases or other of life's problems. It was at this level that beliefs of Ottoman Muslims and Christians often became indistinguishable, with formerly Christian shrines, such as the Sufi lodge at Seyyid Gazi in Anatolia, becoming sites of Muslim veneration. Other sites attracted both Muslim and Christian pilgrims. An example of this was the shrine of St. George on the island of Levitha near Patmos, which became a site of Greek Orthodox, Catholic, and Muslim pilgrimages, St. George also acquiring the Turkish name Koç Baba.

Popular practices, notably visiting saints' tombs and the liturgical use of music and dancing, always aroused the opposition of a section of the ulema. Hostility to these practices became particularly intense in mid-seventeenth-century Istanbul, when Mehmed Kadizade (d. 1635) and his followers, disciples of the fundamentalist scholar Mehmed of Birgi (d. 1575), preached against them in public, attacking in particular the rituals of the Khalvetis. Such attacks, however, never had a lasting effect, and most of the many *fatwa*s issued on the subject of the Sufi orders are in fact tolerant of their practices, the higher ulema on the whole espousing a latitudinarian understanding of Islam. The affiliation of several sultans and many members of the political elite with the orders ensured that, in general, they enjoyed political protection. Furthermore, popular belief was ineradicable, and permeated even the sultan's palace. As examples of this, the sultans provided employment for makers of talismans, and in 1640, the advice writer Kochi Bey urged the new sultan Ibrahim I (1640–1648) to carefully preserve a loaf of bread whose grain revealed the name Allah.

Nonetheless, despite the latitude of tolerated belief and practice, an official definition of heresy did emerge and became a matter of concern especially during the sixteenth century. This development was closely linked to the claims of the Ottoman dynasty, which drew on Islamic themes to legitimize its rule. Until about 1500, these legitimizing elements came primarily from folk religion. Through dreams, God had promised sovereignty to the first sultan Osman and his father; the dynasty had gained a spiritual descent from Osman's marriage to the daughter of a saint; saints led the sultan's warriors in battle. In the sixteenth century, however, the dynasty came to derive its legitimacy from orthodox Islamic tradition. This was partly a consequence of the increasing influence of classically trained ulema in the empire, but partly also a consequence of external events. In 1516/17, the conquest of the Mamluk empire made Selim I (1512–1520) and his successors lords of Mecca and Medina, the holy cities of Islam. This gave the Ottoman sultan the prestigious title of "Servitor of the Two Holy Places," and also the responsibility for the safety of the pilgrimage routes to Mecca. He could now, as the upholder of the religion, claim primacy among Islamic sovereigns. At the same time, the rise to power in Iran of the Safavid dynasty, which claimed spiritual power as leaders of the Safavid Sufi order, and whose Shiʿism contrasted with the Sunnism of the Ottomans, presented a religious and political threat to the Ottoman Empire, especially since the Safavids found many adherents to their order among the sultan's subjects in Anatolia. The Ottomans countered Safavid propaganda by declaring the Safavids and their followers to be worse than infidels, and by presenting the Ottoman dynasty as the only defenders of Sunni Islam against this mortal danger. By the mid-century, Suleiman I was declaring himself to be "the one who makes smooth the path for the precepts of the *shariʿa*" and the one "who makes manifest the Exalted Word of God" and who "expounds the signs of the luminous *shariʿa*." He was also the first Ottoman sultan to assume the title of caliph, implying the leadership of the entire Islamic world. With these developments the dynasty identified itself so closely with orthodox Sunni Islam that disloyalty to one implied disloyalty to the other.

It was particularly during Suleiman's reign, and partly as a result of his claim to be the defender of the faith, that heresy acquired a clear definition. In identifying heresy, the ulema were not concerned with a person's inner belief or private actions. These are matters between the individual and God. Their concern was with stated belief, certain tenets of the Holy Law or Sunni dogma providing the test. If, for example, a Sufi declared that the ceremonies of his order constituted an act of worship *(ʿibada),* a term which in the *shariʿa* refers only to the obligatory purification, prayer, fasting, and alms-giving, then he was a heretic, because in claiming the ceremonies to be "obligatory" he was claiming an authority in prescribing ritual that only the *shariʿa* possessed. It was this test that the sultan used to execute the Melami Oğlan Şeyh and his followers in 1528. Provided, however, the Sufi did not declare his practices to be an act of worship, he remained within the bounds of orthodoxy. Since the *shariʿa* forbids Muslims to drink wine, if a Muslim declares wine to be licit, he has abjured the *shariʿa,* and become liable to death. If, however, he drinks wine without believing it to be licit he is not a heretic. In Ottoman religious "trials" the key to identifying heresy was the accused's statements on what is canonically forbidden, permitted, and obligatory. A heretic was someone whose stated beliefs did not conform with the *shariʿa*. However, in the more merciless pursuit of Safavid sympathizers within the Ottoman realms a key indicator was whether or not the accused cursed the Orthodox caliphs, the denunciation of the first three successors to the prophet Muhammad being a tenet in Shiʿite belief. Public behavior could also indicate heresy. It was for this reason that Suleiman I decreed in 1537 that the authorities should build mosques in all villages that lacked one and note who failed to attend the obligatory congregational prayers. In this way the sultan not only enforced Sunni ritual, in his capacity as protector of the faith, but could also, by their refusal to perform obligatory prayers, identify heretics. Since by this time the sultan identified his own legitimacy with Sunni orthodoxy, disavowal of the commands of the *shariʿa* was also identified as an act of rebellion against the dynasty.

In practice, therefore, the definition of heresy served to identify political opponents of the dynasty, and with changing political circumstances certain heretical beliefs became more acceptable. The persecution of Ottoman Shiʿites, for example, seems to have stopped when, from the mid-seventeenth century, the Safavids of Iran no longer presented a political and ideological danger. Furthermore, since the Ottoman government demanded of Muslims no more than verbal adherence to certain tenets of the *shariʿa* and the outward performance of its obligatory rituals, and did not examine inward faith, a huge variety of beliefs and practices were able to flourish unmolested within Ottoman Islam.

See also **Mehmed II (Ottoman Empire); Ottoman Dynasty; Ottoman Empire; Suleiman I.**

BIBLIOGRAPHY

Birge, John Kingsley. *The Bektashi Order of Dervishes.* London, 1937.

Clayer, Nathalie. *Mystique, État et société: Les Halvetis dans l'aire balkanique de la fin du XVe siècle à nos jours.* Leiden and New York, 1994.

Faroqhi, Suraiya. *Der Bektaschi-Orden in Anatolien: Vom späten fünfzehnten Jahrhundert bis 1826.* Vienna, 1981.

Gerber, Haim. *Islamic Law and Culture, 1600–1840.* Leiden, 1999.

———. *State, Society and Law in Islam: Islamic Law in Comparative Perspective.* Albany, N.Y., 1994.

Heyd, Uriel. "Some Aspects of the Ottoman Fetva." *Bulletin of the School of Oriental and African Studies* 32 (1968): 35–56.

———. *Studies in Old Ottoman Criminal Law.* Edited by V. L. Ménage. Oxford, 1973.

Imber, Colin. *Ebu's-suʿud: The Islamic Legal Tradition.* Edinburgh, 1997.

Johansen, Baber. *The Islamic Law on Tax and Rent.* London, 1988.

Lifchez, Raymond, ed. *The Dervish Lodge: Architecture, Art and Sufism in Ottoman Turkey.* Berkeley, 1990.

Mandaville, Jon E. "Usurious Piety: The Cash *Waqf* Controversy in the Ottoman Empire." *International Journal of Middle Eastern Studies* 10 (1979): 289–308.

Popovic, A., and G. Veinstein. *Les Voies d'Allah: Les ordres mystiques dans le monde mussulman des origines à aujourd'hui.* Paris, 1996.

Repp, R. C. *The Müfti of Istanbul: A Study in the Development of the Ottoman Learned Hierarchy.* Oxford, 1986.

Tucker, Judith E. *In the House of the Law: Gender and Islamic Law in Ottoman Syria and Palestine.* Berkeley, 1998.

Uğur, Ahmed. *The Ottoman ʿUlemâ in the Mid-17th Century.* Berlin, 1986.

Zarinebaf-Shahr, Fariba. "Qizilbash 'Heresy' and Rebellion in Ottoman Anatolia during the Sixteenth Century." *Anatolia Moderna* 7 (1997): 1–15.

Zilfi, Madeline C. *The Politics of Piety: the Ottoman Ulema in the Postclassical Age (1600–1800).* Minneapolis, 1988.

COLIN IMBER

ISLANDS. Islands played a larger role in European history during the early modern period than at any other time before or since. They were crucial to economic and political development, and were no less significant culturally. One must consider not only the physical islands that Europe explored, claimed, and colonized, but also those it imagined and fictionalized.

Until the fifteenth century, Europe had been a sea-fearing, inward-looking civilization, which envisioned itself as but one part of an earth island girdled by a terrifying, impassable river, known to southern Europeans as Oceanus and to the Norse as Uthaf. Whatever the Vikings had learned during their expeditions to the west around the year 1000 had been lost. Knowledge of the oceanic isles was secondhand and largely the product of ancient and medieval legends. But the accumulating tales of rich and paradisiacal isles had become so compelling by the fifteenth century that mariners were venturing into the near Atlantic; and it was but one short step for Christopher Columbus to attempt to reach the fabulous archipelagos of the Indies by extending his voyage west of the Azores. Using maps and texts that assured him that the sea was filled with a vast archipelago, he believed he could island-hop all the way to the Indies. Islands also figured prominently in his apocalyptic visions of bringing nearer the Second Coming of Christ. As far as Columbus was concerned, the isles he reached were the far side of his own earth island. He had no idea he had discovered a new world, and it would be a very long time before geographers decided that the Americas were continents rather islands.

Islands were vital to the age of discovery, not just as provisioning and watering stops, but as cognitive and psychological bridges across a vast, empty oceans. It was imagined as much as real islands that account for Europe's unprecedented seaborne expansion. Exploration expanded the horizons of the known world, but it also produced vast new terrains of terra incognita, filled with unknown isles that excited further speculation. For most of the early modern period Europe's attention was focused on islands rather than continents.

Europe's early modern political ambitions were also insular. Instead of concentrating on the creation of territorial nation-states, rulers extended their sovereignty archipelagically, incorporating many noncontiguous lands and peoples. The period produced a series of island empires, beginning in the Mediterranean and then reaching out into the near Atlantic before incorporating the islands and littorals of the New World. After the initial period of continental conquest led by the Spanish, islands and coasts became the greater political and economic prize. The initial goal had been trade and control of trade routes to the Old World in any case. In the sixteenth and seventeenth centuries islands proved vital not only to the fur trade and to fishing in the North Atlantic, but also to the slave trade on the African coast and the plantation economies in both the Caribbean and the Pacific.

The growth of commercial capitalism was inextricably bound up with islands. Its most profitable enterprise of the early modern period, sugar production, had originated on Mediterranean islands in the Middle Ages. Transferred to the islands of the eastern Atlantic, it was then perfected in the Caribbean. The slave trade on which it depended for labor was organized from islands on Africa's western coast. Islands were natural prisons, and slave populations became involuntary consumers for European manufactures. If Europe accumulated enormous riches during this period, it owed a good deal of its accumulated capital to islands.

Islands were no less important to early modern culture. They provided a space onto which a Europe that was fragmenting politically and religiously could project a multitude of powerful desires and deep fears. Dreams of paradise, previously focused on golden ages of the past, took on new life on islands located in the distant present. The vast new terra incognita became the location for numerous island edens, first in the Atlantic and later in the Pacific. An unknown island provided Sir Thomas More with the opportunity to outline the first modern utopia in 1516. In the next two centuries, dozens of island utopias and dystopias were written. The remote and bounded nature of islands made them ideal for imagining alternative worlds, and it was no accident that the first modern novel, Daniel Defoe's *Robinson Crusoe* (1719), used an island setting to construct the foundation myth of modern masculine individualism. What Europe could not yet conceive of on its own territories, it invented in insular settings. In a certain sense, Europe constructed its modernity archipelagically, using island microcosms to try out new ideas it found more difficult to contemplate on its own shores.

By the eighteenth century European science had become heavily reliant on islands for its understanding of nature. The scientific expeditions of Captain James Cook and Louis Antoine de Bougainville to the isles of the south Pacific paved the way for Charles Darwin's later voyage to the Galápagos Islands (1835). Islands were already being used as laboratories for testing new crops and extending Europe's control over natural resources. They were also the places where Europeans first became aware of the environmental damage caused by ruthless capitalist exploitation of soils and forests. Islands provided a glimpse of the negative as well as the positive sides of economic development long before these were visible in the context of larger landmasses. In the course of the early modern period there came into being an Atlantic world in which islands played a central role. Once remote and isolated from the continent, islands were anything but insular by the eighteenth century. Populated by peoples drawn from the Atlantic littorals, they were perhaps the most cosmopolitan places on earth. Africans, Europeans, and Native Americans commingled, producing new creolized island cultures and societies that had a dynamic all their own. The world of islands was better known and more highly prized than the interiors of mainlands, and for a time it seemed that the future belonged to islands rather than continents. But the political and industrial revolutions of the late eighteenth century changed all that. Capitalism concentrated its productive capacity on the European and North American continents, while states concentrated their power within continental territorial boundaries. Islands became politically peripheral and isolated from modern economic industrial development. They continued to serve as laboratories for science and field stations for anthropology, but they ceased to be places where Europe imagined its future. On the contrary, islands came to be associated with backwardness and primitivism, imagined as fossilized remnants of lost worlds.

See also **Atlantic Ocean; British Colonies; Capitalism; Cartography and Geography; Colonialism; Columbus, Christopher; Commerce; Defoe, Daniel; Dutch Colonies; Environment; Exploration; French Colonies; Fur Trade: North America; More, Thomas; Pacific Ocean; Portuguese Colonies; Slavery and the Slave Trade; Spanish Colonies; Sugar; Triangular Trade Pattern; Utopia.**

BIBLIOGRAPHY

Duncan, T. Bentley. *Atlantic Islands: Madeira, the Azores, and the Cape Verdes in Seventeenth-Century Commerce and Navigation*. Chicago, 1972.

Flint, Valerie I. J. *The Imaginative Landscape of Christopher Columbus*. Princeton, 1992.

Grove, Richard H. *Green Imperialism: Colonial Expansion, Tropical Island Edens, and the Origins of Environmentalism, 1600–1800*. Cambridge, U.K., 1991.

Lestringant, Frank. *Mapping the Renaissance World: The Geographical Imagination in the Age of Discovery*. Translated by David Fawcett. Cambridge, U.K., 1994.

JOHN R. GILLIS

ITALIAN LITERATURE AND LANGUAGE. Italian literature entered an active and important phase in the late fifteenth century that was stimulated by the revival of classical literature, a flourishing popular culture, and the growth of courts. Among the genres developed were the comic epic, lyric poetry, the pastoral, and comic theater. Intruding onto the cultural scene were worries about trade competition, Turkish aggression, and domination by outside powers. Although France initially seemed likely to succeed in such conquests, by 1530 Holy Roman emperor Charles V (ruled

1519–1556) had gained control of most states, except Venice, through a series of wars fought on Italian soil.

POETRY: THE COMIC EPIC AND THE COURTLY LYRIC

Three important comic epics were written during the late fifteenth and early sixteenth centuries: *Morgante* (1478, 1482 or 1483) by Luigi Pulci, a member of the Medici circle; *Orlando innamorato* (1483, 1495) by Matteo Maria Boiardo; and *Orlando furioso* (1516, 1521, 1532) by Ludovico Ariosto, the latter two at the Este court in Ferrara. The works continued the Italian tradition of adding local color to the medieval epic that narrated the defense of France by Charlemagne and his nephew Roland against Saracen attack. An infusion of comedy and fantasy qualified these works as mock or comic epics.

Morgante recounts the adventures of Charlemagne's knights and a giant, for whom it is named, and the betrayal of Roland and the aged Charlemagne's inability to discern the betrayal. *Orlando innamorato* creates a French origin for the Este dynasty, which in the work is said to be the progeny of Ruggiero, a Saracen convert to Christianity, and his French bride Bradamante. Ruggiero, like Virgil's Aeneas, is descended from a Trojan soldier, further strengthening Este claims to legitimacy. Boiardo's poem also introduced Roland's love for the Chinese princess Angelica, an enemy of France. In Ariosto's *Orlando furioso,* Roland's passion costs him his sanity. Discovering that Angelica has married a lowly Saracen foot soldier, he hurls to the heavens the trees on which the history of their love is carved.

A renewed interest in lyric poetry was sparked in Italian courts by Spanish performers who followed the Aragonese and the Borgia to Italy. Pietro Bembo, who frequented several of those courts, spearheaded the revival of Petrarchan poetry dedicated to Platonic love, the most influential movement in lyric poetry. A fondness for pageantry is evident in Angelo Poliziano's *Stanzas for the Joust of the Magnificent Giuliano* (1475–1478), which glorified a Medici family member's winning of a tournament. The pastoral, prominent in Roman and medieval literature, inspired the *Arcadia* (1504) of Jacopo Sannazaro, which was set in an idealized countryside of shepherds tending their flocks and was marked by the practical subtext of court patronage.

COMEDY: CONTINUATION OF TRADITIONS, REVIVAL OF THE ANCIENTS, AND CREATION OF NEW GENRES

Theater developed along several lines during the late fifteenth and early sixteenth centuries. Continuing from the Middle Ages was the religious play or *sacra rappresentazione,* which was particularly popular in Tuscany. Folk plays celebrating marriages and seasonal festivities such as Carnival were staged in rural and urban Italy. States, especially Venice, utilized folk genres to influence the popular classes' opinions on political questions. Urban life among the popular classes of Naples was the subject of several comic compositions by Sannazaro. The pastoral tradition inspired the first known vernacular nonreligious drama, Poliziano's *Orpheus* (1480).

Toward the end of the fifteenth century, theatrical developments gained momentum. The Este rulers of Ferrara staged the comedies of Plautus and Terence in Latin and in Italian translation. Playwrights in Venice composed their own comedies in Latin about contemporary subjects. In the early sixteenth century, a new genre began to form: the learned comedy. Taking its general framework from ancient comedy, learned comedy was also influenced by Giovanni Boccaccio's (1313–1375) *Decameron* (1348–1353), which was written in the vernacular and emphasized characters' ingenious and fair solutions to the contemporary social conflicts in which they were caught up. Comedies were performed at Carnival and wedding festivities; they explored the conflicts between parents arranging financially advantageous marriages for their children and the young people's dedication to the contemporary vogue for love. Typical of the genre are Ariosto's *The Coffer, The Pretenders,* and *The Necromancer* or *The Magician* (all written in 1508–1520), *The Mandrake Root* (1504–1518) by Niccolò Machiavelli, and *The Follies of Calandro* (1513) by Bernardo Dovizi (Il Bibbiena).

The lower classes and undignified behavior subsequently assumed greater importance in comedy. The works of several Sienese playwrights and those of Angelo Beolco (Il Ruzante), who wrote between about 1516 and 1536, mixed Arcadian shepherds with real peasants, exploiting their mutual misunderstandings to comic effect. Beolco's plays of the late 1520s concentrated on peasant life and the terrible sufferings inflicted by a wave of war, famine, and disease. Ariosto's final play, *Lena* (1528–1529), presents a bleak picture of the moral compromises called for by impoverished urban life that was probably influenced by Beolco, with whom he was working. Aretino's comedies *The Courtesan* (1525) and *The Stablemaster* (1526–1527) satirized urban and courtly life. The anonymous work *The Venetian Woman* (1510–1517 or 1536) depicted the clandestine and forbidden erotic rivalry of two Venetian patrician women.

THE NOVELLA

The most popular genre of nondramatic prose was the novella, which favored plot variety and armchair travel. Inspired by Boccaccio's *Decameron* and a strong indigenous tradition, Florentine writers of the late fifteenth century created popular and aristocratic variants of the novella. Tommaso Guardati (Masuccio Salernitano) ushered in a new phase marked by pessimism and moralizing. His 1476 collection, whose title *Il Novellino* is a pun on 'little novel' and 'novice', introduced the convention of dedicatory letters to aristocrats. The mid-sixteenth century saw the publication of numerous novella collections. Matteo Bandello's *Novelle* and Giovanni Battista Giraldi Cinzio's *Hecatommiti,* the latter including a philosophical dialogue on civil life, share a somber tone and assign tragic outcomes to transgressive actions. Shakespeare employed a number of the novellas as the bases of his plays. *The Pleasurable Nights* of Giovan Francesco Straparola, tales supposedly told during Carnival on the Venetian island of Murano, return to the bawdy tone of the earlier tradition and the magic realism of the comic epics. The Renaissance novella, like its medieval counterpart, emphasized restraint, analysis, and intelligent deployment of resources. Added to those features were the new conventions of strengthened support for social hierarchy and the inclusion of a chorus that commented on the actions of the protagonists. The latter convention was perhaps derived from theater, for which many authors of novellas also wrote.

NEW PROSE GENRES

Expository prose developed several new vernacular genres. Leonardo da Vinci (1452–1519) provided an illustrious beginning for scientific writing. The behavioral manual, indispensable in a period of changing social relations, was embodied by *The Courtier* (1528) by Baldassare Castiglione. A somewhat subversive variant was Aretino's *Dialogues* (1534), some of which teach the arts of eroticism. Normativity returned with Giovanni Della Casa's *Galateo* (1558), whose title became synonymous with good deportment.

LITERARY THEORY AND ARISTOTELIANISM

One of the most important results of the humanistic search for lost classical texts was the rediscovery of Aristotle's *Poetics.* The translation of the *Poetics* into Latin in 1498 and into Italian in 1549 initiated a theoretical debate about the classifications and definitions of various literary genres. Of special interest was poetry's relationship to history, ethics, and moral philosophy. The two parts of Gian Giorgio Trissino's *Poetics* opened the topic with the first part (1529) and closed it with the second (1562); other participants included Giovanni Pontano, Francesco Robortello, Benedetto Varchi, Alessandro Piccolomini, and Lodovico Castelvetro. Over the decades of debate, Aristotle's concern with civic order caused a shift in emphasis from poetry as a solitary and pleasurable activity to poetry as bearer of civic responsibilities.

Among the genres most affected by this rediscovery were comedy and tragedy. Renaissance theorists formulated a set of norms for each on the basis of Aristotle's observations on art as imitation, on the nature of genres, and on appropriate and effective forms of representation. These were combined with Roman drama criticism to produce a value-based literary hierarchy; a series of rules governing plot, character, sentiment, and diction; a progressive five-act structure; and the renowned unities of time, place, and action (plot), which require that a play be based on one action occurring in one place on one day. Important contributions to this movement included Trissino's *Poetics,* Francesco Robortello's *On Comedy* (1548), Madius's *On the Ridiculous* (1550), and Giraldi Cinzio's *On Composing Comedies and Tragedies* (1543).

At the same time, theatrical presentations acquired established sites, with a permanent theater becoming a requirement of a ruler's palazzo.

TRAGEDY

The first tragedies were written during the War of the League of Cambrai (1509–1517): Gian Giorgio Trissino's *Sophonisba* (1515), in which a queen defeated by the Romans commits suicide, and Giovanni Rucellai's *Rosmunda*. Aristotle believed that tragedy's concentration on rulers and on the emotions of horror and compassion made it superior to comedy. The rediscovery of his theories promoted respect for tragedy, which was staged exclusively for aristocratic audiences. Although Renaissance authors adhered to the strict rules that classical theoreticians developed for tragedy, they also included contemporary issues in their works. The Este court in Ferrara undertook the first staging of a vernacular tragedy, Giraldi Cinzio's *Orbecche,* in 1541. The Paduan Academy of the Enflamed's performance of Sperone Speroni's *Canace,* planned for 1542, was postponed by Beolco's death and never rescheduled. The first generation of tragic performances shocked aristocratic audiences with depictions of ruling families as bloodthirsty, ruthless, and incestuous.

THE *QUESTIONE DELLA LINGUA*

Related to literary theory was the *questione della lingua,* the question of which form of the vernacular to employ in various writings. The Italian peninsula's political and vernacular fragmentation and the extensive use of Latin made this a complicated and thorny issue. Early in the sixteenth century a group of literary courtiers, including Baldassare Castiglione, proposed a contemporary language that would both transcend and respect regional differences by allowing local variation and foreign terms. Pietro Bembo opposed their suggestion in his *Prose della volgar lingua* (Vernacular writings), advancing instead fourteenth-century literary Tuscan, for which he provided a detailed grammar. Florentine writers including Machiavelli, resisting such archaic usage, favored contemporary Florentine. Northern Italian writers Trissino and Speroni unsuccessfully attempted to revive the proposal of an eclectic language that would draw upon the vernaculars of all regions.

Bembo's proposal prevailed, an early sign of which was Ariosto's Tuscanization of *Orlando furioso.* Bembo's success was due to his own printed grammar and the many printed copies of the texts of Petrarch and Boccaccio, his models for poetry and prose, respectively. Also influential were the power of the Florentine popes Leo X (1513–1521) and Clement VII (1523–1534) and the pressures on the publishing industry to increase the market with a standard language. Although some viewed Bembo's solution as aristocratic, it encouraged the spread of reading, as the popularity of printed chapbooks and grammars attests.

THE LATE SIXTEENTH CENTURY: VARIATIONS ON ESTABLISHED THEMES

Literary developments during the second half of the sixteenth century largely consisted of variations on the themes established in the preceding years. Lyric poetry in the Petrarchan tradition enjoyed renewed vitality in the middle decades of the century: the appeal of its interiority and allusive language increased in a time of uncertainty in the civic and religious spheres. Women began to write in this style, their numbers including courtesans such as Gaspara Stampa and Veronica Franco, women of the popular class such as Modesta Pozzo, and upper-class women such as Vittoria Colonna and Chiara Matraini. Themes of the love of woman for man and the love of God were added to the traditional theme of the Platonic love of man for woman. Some genuine, rather than comic, epics appeared as a result of the high value accorded to the epic by Aristotle. These included Trissino's *Italia liberata dai Goti* (1547–1548) and Torquato Tasso's great *Jerusalem Delivered* (1581), which celebrated the recapture of Jerusalem by Christian knights during the Crusades.

Comedy, which Aristotle confined to the lowest sphere of society and values, became associated largely with the nascent commedia dell'arte. Performances were conducted not by courtiers but by the first professional troupes, who abandoned scripts for type characters and conventional plot devices. Only Venice and Florence, with their republican governments, maintained a robust scripted tradition with the comedies of playwrights such as Andrea Calmo and Anton Francesco Grazzini. The pastoral, which reached its zenith with Tasso's *Aminta* (1573), provided courtly entertainment.

In the final decades of the century, doubts about the validity and sustainability of strict Aristotelian categories crept in. New mixed genres appeared, along with interest in nonaristocratic and female characters, and subversive and distorted language. The comedies of Giovan Battista Della Porta and Giordano Bruno's *The Candlebearer* (1582) embody these developments. Both playwrights' restless questioning of religious orthodoxy led to investigations by the Inquisition; Bruno was burned at the stake. Tragedy, after a brief absence from the stage, developed along more moderate lines. The tensions generated by the absolute power of God and inescapable human guilt were softened in the new genre of the tragedy with a happy ending. Kings, while still all-powerful, owed their ill deeds to advisers rather than their own defects, and horror-inducing actions no longer occurred onstage. The pastoral continued in Ferrara as a mixed genre with Giovanni Battista Guarini's *Faithful Shepherd,* written in a tragicomic style. Other popular blended forms included the melodrama and the serious or dark comedy. The Aristotelian debate underwent a final shift toward a view of poetry as art. In the linguistic sphere, archaic Tuscan, that is, the fourteenth-century Tuscan of Dante, Petrarch, and Boccaccio, suffered a setback when Tasso eschewed it for his epic.

THE SEVENTEENTH CENTURY

Seventeenth-century Italian literature continued a number of important late-sixteenth-century trends. Many of the most significant developments occurred in academies, which were selective private groups of learned men. Scientific rationalism produced great though isolated monuments in the writings of Galileo Galilei (1564–1642), a member of the Accademia dei Lincei (Academy of the Lynx-like). Scientific rationalism was applied by Paolo Sarpi to human affairs in his works on church–state relations and by the Accademia Della Crusca (Academy of the Bran) to language in a Florentine dictionary that they compiled under Medici patronage. The dictionary was a milestone in the *questione della lingua,* its affirmation of archaic Tuscan stimulating much debate and instigating a countertrend in the use of local dialects in literary compositions. Theatrical productions abounded, led by the commedia dell'arte, a variety of mixed genres, and melodrama. The construction of theaters to which the public was admitted for a fee opened a profitable enterprise, while the leading family acting troupes such as the Andreini attracted a large public following. The novella, with its variety of characters, locations, and outcomes, experienced continued popularity. Poetry comprised both the floridity of the baroque, with its love of the bizarre and the marvelous, and the severity of classicism. The leading figure in the former style was Giovan Battista Marino, whose *Adone* (Adonis), the longest poem in Italian literature, recounted the loves of Venus and Adonis. His followers, the Marinisti, wrote numerous love poems.

THE EIGHTEENTH CENTURY

The eighteenth century, known as the Age of Enlightenment for its emphasis on secular rationalism, saw the growth of scientific research. Learned men wrote the first histories of literature and the theater and compiled collections of historical documents. In his *New Science* (1725, 1730, 1744), Giambattista Vico studied human society in a systematic manner for the first time. Newspapers brought discussions and debates on many topics to a wider audience. The backdrop of many of these developments was a reform of the aristocratic regime, most of whose proponents aimed to eliminate excesses and restore the aristocracy to a role of leadership, but whose egalitarianism and respect for work and the law contained the seeds of a new order.

Aristocratic life received comic treatment in Giuseppe Parini's *The Day* (1763 and 1765). The last of the mock epics, it recounts a day in the life of a young Milanese nobleman, a day dedicated entirely to his pleasure. Implicitly in *The Day* and explicitly elsewhere, Parini expressed his admiration for the sobriety, practicality, and work ethic of the lower classes who produced the items consumed by the young nobleman. Yet Parini was not a revolutionary, preferring that the aristocracy reform itself and earn its privileges, not vanish entirely.

The stage attracted the interest of many talented writers. Most renowned among them was one of the world's great playwrights, the Venetian Carlo Goldoni (1707–1793). While his early plays conformed to the typed characters and plot devices of the commedia dell'arte, Goldoni soon spearheaded a move toward realism that appealed to many theatergoers. The plays of his reform period recognize the worth of middle- and lower-class characters, depicting the impoverished aristocracy as arrogant and frivolous. Opposition came from many, including Carlo Gozzi, whose exotic tales filled with aristocratic wealth and privilege also attracted a large following. Venetian authorities censured the theater and required Goldoni to rewrite some of his plays. In 1762, Goldoni left for Paris, where he worked with the Comédie Italienne and wrote his memoirs.

A desire to liberate the states of the Italian peninsula from the tyranny of foreign rule inspired the tragedies of Vittorio Alfieri (1749–1803). After extensive travels outside the peninsula, Alfieri took up residence in Florence, where he wrote plays and the treatise *Of Tyranny* (1777) to expose the defects of tyrannical rule. Yet Alfieri's works showed that he was unable to completely renounce the old order. He chose tragedy, the most conservative, aristocratic genre, and he deposes no ruler in his plays. The innermost sentiments of the characters are conveyed in lyrical language. His masterpiece *Saul* depicts King Saul's struggles with the knowledge that David will soon replace him as ruler, yet the old king maintains his dignity throughout the work.

Autobiography, which began with the poets Dante and Petrarch in the fourteenth century and reemerged in the sixteenth century with Benvenuto Cellini's *Life,* reached its culmination in the eighteenth century. With the old social order weakened and under scrutiny, personal reinvention through prose was more possible than at any time since the fourteenth century, and more useful. The unusually large number of authors seeking public affirmation by creating a written persona included Goldoni, Gozzi, Casanova, Alfieri, and Vico.

The gathering momentum for the liberation of Italy from foreign rule breathed life into the *questione della lingua.* Alfieri preferred contemporary Tuscan, while the Verri brothers, associated with the newspaper *The Caffé,* opposed it. Goldoni typified the open approach, writing plays both in Tuscan and in the dialects of Venice and the neighboring fishing town of Chioggia. In his influential *Essay on the Philosophy of Language* (1785), Melchiorre Cesarotti advanced the view that all Italians possessed their language, and that control of it should pass from a closed local academy to a committee of learned men from all regions.

See also **Castiglione, Baldassare; Cellini, Benvenuto; Drama: Italian; Galileo Galilei; Goldoni, Carlo; Leonardo da Vinci; Machiavelli, Niccolò; Tasso, Torquato.**

BIBLIOGRAPHY

Primary Sources

Alfieri, Vittorio. *Of Tyranny.* Translated by Julius A. Molinaro and Beatrice Corrigan. Toronto, 1961. Translation of *Della tirannide* (1777).

Aretino, Pietro. *Aretino's Dialogues.* Translated by Raymond Rosenthal. New York, 1971. Translation of *Ragionamenti* (1534).

———. *The Marescalco.* Translated by Leonard G. Sbrocchi and J. Douglas Campbell. Ottawa, 1986. Translation of *Il Marescalco* (1533).

Ariosto, Lodovico. *The Comedies of Ariosto.* Translated and edited by Edmond M. Beame and Leonard G. Sbrocchi. Chicago, 1975. Translations of *The Coffer* [in prose], *The Pretenders, The Necromancer, Lena, The Coffer* [in verse], *The Students, The Scholastics* (1508–1533).

———. *Orlando furioso.* Translated by Guido Waldman. Oxford and New York, 1998. Translation of *Orlando furioso* (1532).

Beolco, Angelo (Il Ruzante). *L'Anconitana. The Woman from Ancona.* Translated by Nancy Dersofi. Berkeley, 1994. Translation of *L'Anconitana* (1536).

———. *La Moschetta.* Translated by Antonio Franceschetti and Kenneth R. Bartlett. Ottawa, 1993. Translation of *La Moscheta* (1528–1530).

———. *Ruzzante Returns from the Wars.* In *The* Servant of Two Masters *and Other Italian Classics.* Edited by Eric Bentley. New York, 1958. Translation of *Il Parlamento (Il Reduce)* (1529).

Boiardo, Matteo Maria. *Orlando innamorato.* Translated by Charles Stanley Ross. English verse edited by Anne Finnigan. Berkeley, 1989. Translation of *Orlando innamorato* (1482 or 1483, 1495).

Bruno, Giordano. *Candlebearer.* Translated by Gino Moliterno. Ottawa, 1999. Translation of *Il candelaio* (1582).

Casanova, Giacomo. *History of My Life.* Translated by Willard R. Trask. Baltimore, 1997. Translation of *Mémoires* (1797).

Castiglione, Baldassare. *The Book of the Courtier.* Translated by Charles Singleton. Edited by Daniel Javitch. New York, 2002. Translation of *Il libro del cortegiano* (1528).

Cellini, Benvenuto. *My Life.* Translated by Julia Conaway Bondanella and Peter Bondanella. New York, 2002. Translation of *La vita* (1562).

Della Casa, Giovanni. *Galateo: A Renaissance Treatise on Manners.* Translated by Konrad Eisenbichler and Kenneth R. Bartlett. Toronto, 1994. Translation of *Galateo* (1558).

Della Porta, Giambattista. *Gli duoi fratelli rivali.* Edited and translated by Louise George Clubb. Berkeley, 1980. Translation of *Gli duoi fratelli rivali* (1601).

Dovizi, Bernardo (Il Bibbiena). *The Follies of Calandro.* Translated by Oliver Evans. In *The Genius of the Italian Theater.* Eric Bentley, ed. New York, 1964. Translation of *La Calandria* (1513).

Galilei, Galileo. *Dialogue Concerning the Two Chief World Systems, Ptolemaic and Copernican.* Translated by Stillman Drake. New York, 2001. Translation of *Dialogo dei massimi sistemi* (1632).

———. *Discoveries and Opinions of Galileo: Including* The Starry Messenger *(1610),* Letter to the Grand Duchess Christina *(1615), and Excerpts from* Letters on Sunspots *(1613),* The Assayer *(1623).* Translated by Stillman Drake. New York, 1990. Translation of *Siderius nuncius, Lettera alla Gran Duchessa Cristina, Lettere, Il saggiatore.*

———. *Galileo against the Philosophers in His* Dialogue of Cecco di Ronchitti *(1605) and* Considerations of Alimberto Mauri *(1606).* Translated by Stillman Drake. Los Angeles, 1976. Translation of *Dialogo de Cecco di Ronchitti da Bruzene in perpuosito de la stella nuova, Considerazioni di Alimberto Mauri.*

Goldoni, Carlo. *Four comedies [by] Goldoni.* Translated by Frederick Davies. Harmondsworth, U.K., 1968. Translation of *I due gemelli Veneziani* (1750), *La vedova scaltra* (1748), *La locandiera* (1753), and *La casa nova* (1761).

———. *Memoirs of Carlo Goldoni.* Translated by John Black. Edited by William A. Drake. Westport, Conn., 1926. Translation of *Mémoires* (1787).

———. *The Servant of Two Masters.* Translated and adapted by Frederick H. Davies. London, 1961. Translation of *Servitore di due padroni* (1747).

———. *Villeggiatura Trilogy.* Translated by Robert Cornthwaite. Lyme, N.H., 1994. Translation of *Le smanie della villeggiatura, Le avventure della villeggiatura, Il ritorno dalla villeggiatura* (1761).

Guarini, Battista. *The Faithful Shepherd.* Translated by Thomas Sheridan. Edited and completed by Robert Hogan and Edward A. Nickerson. Newark, Del., and Cranbury, N.J., 1989. Translation of *Il pastor fido* (1589).

Machiavelli, Niccolò. *The Comedies of Machiavelli.* Edited and translated by David Sices and James B. Atkinson. Hanover, N.H., 1985. Translations of *Mandragola* (1504–1518), *Andria* (1517/1518), *Clizia* (1524/1525).

Poliziano, Angelo. *A Translation of the* Orpheus *of Angelo Politian and the* Aminta *of Torquato Tasso.* Translated by Louis E. Lord. Reprint. Westport, Conn., 1986. Translation of *Orfeo* (1480).

———. *The Stanze of Angelo Poliziano.* Translated by David Quint. Amherst, Mass., 1979. Translation of *Stanze cominciate per la giostra del Magnifico Giuliano de' Medici* (1475–1478).

Pulci, Luigi. *Morgante: the Epic Adventures of Orlando and His Giant Friend Morgante.* Translated by Joseph Tusiani. Introduction and notes by Edoardo A. Lèbano. Bloomington, Ind., 1998. Translation of *Morgante* (1478, 1482 or 1483).

Sannazaro, Jacopo. *Arcadia, & Piscatorial Eclogues.* Translated by Ralph Nash. Detroit, 1966. Translation of *Arcadia* (1504).

Sermini, Gentile, et al. *Renaissance Comic Tales of Love, Treachery, and Revenge.* Edited and translated by Valerie Martone and Robert L. Martone. New York, 1994. Translation of tales by Gentile Sermini, Giovanni Gherardo da Prato, Lorenzo de' Medici, Matteo Bandello, Masuccio Salernitano, and Anton Francesco Grazzini.

Tasso, Torquato. *A Translation of the* Orpheus *of Angelo Politian and the* Aminta *of Torquato Tasso.* Translation by Louis E. Lord. Reprint. Westport, Conn., 1986. Translation of *Aminta* (1573).

———. *Jerusalem Delivered.* Edited and translated by Anthony M. Esolen. Baltimore, 2000. Translation of *Gerusalemme liberata* (1581).

Vico, Giovan Battista. *New Science: Principles of the New Science Concerning the Common Nature of Nations.* London and New York, 1999. Translation of *Scienza nuova* (1744).

Secondary Sources

Andrews, Richard. *Scripts and Scenarios: The Performance of Comedy in Renaissance Italy.* Cambridge, U.K., 1993.

Angelini, Franca. *Vita di Goldoni.* Rome, 1993.

Ascoli, Albert Russell. *Ariosto's Bitter Harmony: Crisis and Evasion in the Italian Renaissance.* Princeton, 1987.

Asor Rosa, Alberto. *Storia della letteratura italiana.* Florence, 1985.

Attolini, Giovanni. *Teatro e spettacolo nel Rinascimento.* Rome 1988.

Baratto, Mario. *La letteratura teatrale del Settecento in Italia: studi e letture su Carlo Goldoni.* Vicenza, 1985.

———. *Tre studi sul teatro: Ruzante, Aretino, Goldoni.* Venice, 1964.

Carroll, Linda L. *Angelo Beolco (Il Ruzante).* Boston, 1990.

Clubb, Louise George. *Giambattista della Porta, Dramatist.* Princeton, 1965.

———. *Italian Drama in Shakespeare's Time.* New Haven, 1989.

Croce, Benedetto. *La Spagna nella vita italiana durante la Rinascenza.* Bari, 1949.

Di Maria, Salvatore. *The Italian Tragedy in the Renaissance: Cultural Realities and Theatrical Innovations.* Lewisburg, Pa., 2002.

Ferroni, Giulio. *Storia della letteratura italiana dal Cinquecento al Settecento.* Milan, 1991. Vol. 4 of *Storia della letteratura italiana.*

Fido, Franco. *Guida a Goldoni. Teatro e società nel Settecento.* Turin, 1977.

———. *Nuova guida a Goldoni. Teatro e società nel Settecento.* Turin, 2000.

Hall, Robert Anderson. *The Italian questione della lingua, an Interpretative Essay.* Chapel Hill, N.C., 1942.

Herrick, Marvin Theodore. *Comic Theory in the Sixteenth Century.* Urbana, Ill., 1950.

———. *Italian Comedy in the Renaissance.* Urbana, Ill., 1960.

———. *Italian Tragedy in the Renaissance.* Urbana, Ill., 1965.

Marinelli, Peter V. *Ariosto and Boiardo: the Origins of* Orlando furioso. Columbia, Mo., 1987.

Oreglia, Giacomo. *The Commedia dell'Arte.* Translated by Lovett F. Edwards. London, 1968.

Panizza, Letizia, and Sharon Wood, eds. *A History of Women's Writing in Italy.* Cambridge, U.K., and New York, 2000.

Radcliff-Umstead, Douglas. *The Birth of Modern Comedy in Renaissance Italy.* Chicago, 1969.

Sabbatino, Pasquale. *La "Scienza" della scrittura: Dal progetto del Bembo al manuale.* Florence, 1988.

Siciliano, Enzo. *La letteratura italiana.* 3 vols. Milan, 1986–1988.

Weinberg, Bernard. *A History of Literary Criticism in the Italian Renaissance.* 2 vols. Chicago, 1961.

LINDA L. CARROLL

ITALIAN WARS (1494–1559).

Renaissance Italy lacked a strong institutional framework that enjoyed a broad consensus. The medieval wars pitting proponents of imperial supremacy (the Ghibellines) against those who advocated papal supremacy (the Guelfs) were fought to a stalemate. Neither the emperor nor the pope enjoyed much real power over the mosaic of city-republics, territorial principalities, or fiefs in central and northern Italy. In the kingdom of Naples, which was theoretically a fief of the church, control passed from a French (Angevin) dynasty to one linked to Aragón without much interference from the rest of Italy. Much internecine warfare wracked the peninsula, as aristocrats fought each other for primacy in their respective cities, as larger towns conquered their rural hinterlands, and as the larger territorial states attempted to absorb the smaller ones around them. The Peace of Lodi in 1454 inaugurated an era of relative peace for forty years, but it did not extinguish the various pretexts of territorial ambition, dynastic ambition, or autonomist sentiment that could engulf Italy in new large-scale hostilities.

FRENCH ADVENTURES

The entry into Italy of the French king's army in his quest to make good his claims to the throne of Naples in 1494 ignited many simultaneous conflicts. The French king Charles VIII (ruled 1483–1498) was assisted by the "tyrant" of Milan, Ludovico Sforza (ruled 1494–1499), who was losing his grip on power in Lombardy. Florence swept the Medici out of power and restored a real republic, but it needed French support to survive, and subject cities rebelled against it. The Aragonese Pope Alexander VI Borgia (reigned 1492–1503) had no army able to oppose the French, so the great force of Charles VIII advanced to Naples virtually unopposed and chased away the local branch of the Aragonese dynasty. But within a year the pope, the Republic of Venice, the duke of Mantua, King Ferdinand of Aragón (monarch in Sicily; ruled 1468–1516), and the Emperor Maximilian I (ruled 1493–1519) drew together and threatened to bottle up the French king's army in southern Italy. Only a fighting retreat in 1495 allowed Charles VIII to regain France, and his Neapolitan regime collapsed behind him.

His successor Louis XII (ruled 1498–1515) launched a new army into Italy in 1500, this time laying claim to Milan as well as Naples. With Genoese and Venetian help, the French army quickly seized most of northwest Italy, but the king would not rest on this success. By secret treaty with Ferdinand of Aragón, he agreed to split the kingdom of Naples between the two of them. Fighting soon broke out between Spaniards and French over their respective shares, and the latter were driven out. The new spoiler was now Venice, exploiting tensions everywhere in order to extend its hold in the Adriatic basin. A new alliance of Aragón, France, the Holy Roman Empire, and the pope crushed Venetian ambitions in 1509. But Venice allied with the pope, with Ferdinand, with the Swiss cantons,

Italian Wars. *The Battle of Pavia, Feb. 24 1525,* painting by Joachim Patnir. ©Erich Lessing/Art Resource, N.Y.

and with the emperor to expel the French from Milan soon after. By the end of 1512, the French were ejected from Italy a second time.

Francis I (ruled 1515–1547), successor to Louis XII, sent a fresh army in 1515 to occupy Milan and its territory. This time the pope, and even the new king of Aragón, Charles I, recognized the French king's conquest, but the French position deteriorated rapidly as Charles became king of Spain in 1516 and then Holy Roman emperor in Germany in 1519. As Emperor Charles V, the young Habsburg monarch and his allies expelled the French from Milan in 1521 and defeated renewed attempts to recapture it. In 1525 Francis I was captured at the battle of Pavia. The wars were far from over, but this turn in the fighting marked the onset of a new and durable phase of Habsburg ascendancy in Europe.

HABSBURG CONSOLIDATION

The union of large territories under the sway of a single monarch was a dynastic accident, but Charles was able to harness the wealth of Spain, the Low Countries, the German principalities, and almost half of Italy to keep the French at bay. Soon he would be king in Mexico and Hungary as well. In each of these realms he inherited monumental problems, but after each crisis he appeared more powerful than ever. In 1527 a new French league against him came apart after an imperial army besieged and sacked Rome itself, an event whose impact on the people of Rome and on European public opinion was catastrophic. Genoa, with its fleet and its commerce, swung over to Charles in 1528. The emperor then supported the restoration of the Medici as absolute princes in Florence. After a brief truce, French armies occupied Savoy and most of Piedmont in an attempt to reconquer Milan. Intermittent campaigning in Italy and over half of Europe could not break the stalemate, however. The new French king Henry II (ruled 1547–1559) would not let Italy out of his sights. France intervened in Parma in 1551 to expel papal forces there and in 1552 backed a Sienese uprising against its imperial garrison; in 1555 France supported the extremist Pope Paul IV (1555–1559), who called for Spain's removal from Naples, and yet again a French army descended on the peninsula to occupy the territory. But Habsburg armies won victories everywhere in those years, until France consented to the Peace of Cateau-Cambrésis in 1559.

The Italian Wars were but one theater in a continental struggle involving most of western Europe, with France and the Habsburg territories constituting the eternal adversaries. The 1559 treaty might only have been a truce had not religious divisions led to a French civil war that lasted intermittently for three generations. Habsburg territorial ascendancy in Italy was complete, with the conquest of Milan, Naples, Sicily, and Sardinia. The duke of Piedmont-Savoy, the princes of Mantua, Parma, Ferrara, and Florence, and the rich republic of Genoa were reduced to satellite status. Moreover, Charles (who retired in 1555) followed a policy of encouraging stability in the peninsula, allowing the minor princes to impose greater control over their subjects, and stifling any Protestant sentiment. The enduring legacy of these wars was a long Pax Hispanica that underlay the renewed prosperity and heightened influence of Italy in the world until the next great disruption after 1620.

See also **Cateau-Cambrésis (1559); Charles V (Holy Roman Empire); Italy; Naples, Kingdom of; Rome, Sack of.**

BIBLIOGRAPHY

Hale J. R., and M. E. Mallett. *The Military Organization of a Renaissance State: Venice c. 1400 to 1617.* Cambridge, U.K., and New York, 1984.

Hall, Bert S. *Weapons and Warfare in Renaissance Europe: Gunpowder, Technology and Tactics.* Baltimore, 1998.

Pepper, Simon, and Nicholas Adams. *Firearms and Fortifications: Military Architecture and Siege Warfare in Sixteenth-Century Siena.* Chicago, 1986.

Taylor, Frederick Lewis. *The Art of War in Italy, 1494–1529.* Westport, Conn., 1973.

GREGORY HANLON

ITALY. The early modern period following the Renaissance is only now emerging from long neglect by historians, who once considered the period one of unbroken decline. This neglect is paradoxical considering that it was in the period of the late Renaissance and the Counter-Reformation that Italy attained its greatest influence in the Western world and a degree of wealth and sophistication that gave it the pilot role in European civilization. The two-and-a-half centuries following the end of the Italian wars in 1559 do not constitute a single period, however.

ITALIAN STATES

Unlike France, England, and Castile, which were relatively centralized monarchies with deep roots in the Middle Ages, and unlike Germany, which was a loose-knit confederation of a myriad of relatively stable states under the benign leadership of the Holy Roman emperor, Italy lacked a simple overarching political framework that enjoyed a wide consensus. Medieval wars between Guelphs and Ghibellines, partisans of papal and imperial authority, respectively, were fought to a stalemate where the reality of power lay with each major city and each great lord in central and northern Italy. Then a gradual and fairly rapid process of elimination of the small states by the larger ones resulted in a political map articulated around less than a dozen territorial states by the time of the Peace of Lodi in 1451. The large-scale Italian wars beginning in 1494 simplified this situation even more after a half-century of intermittent fighting. When the wars were over, the king of Spain, Philip II (ruled 1555–1598), was duke of Milan and king of Naples, Sicily, and Sardinia. A handful of Italian princes seated in Turin, Mantua, Ferrara, Parma, Florence, and Urbino were reduced to satellite status. The pope had now become effective ruler over all the Papal States in central Italy by eliminating the virtual independence of city-states like Perugia or Bologna. Three medieval city-republics still survived: the powerful Venetian state jealous of its independence, the rich but subservient Genoese republic, and the almost insignificant Luccan state. Once the French threat was definitively removed by a long succession of religious conflicts (1561–1629), Italy enjoyed the fruits of a Pax Hispanica that underpinned its economic growth and its new institutional stability.

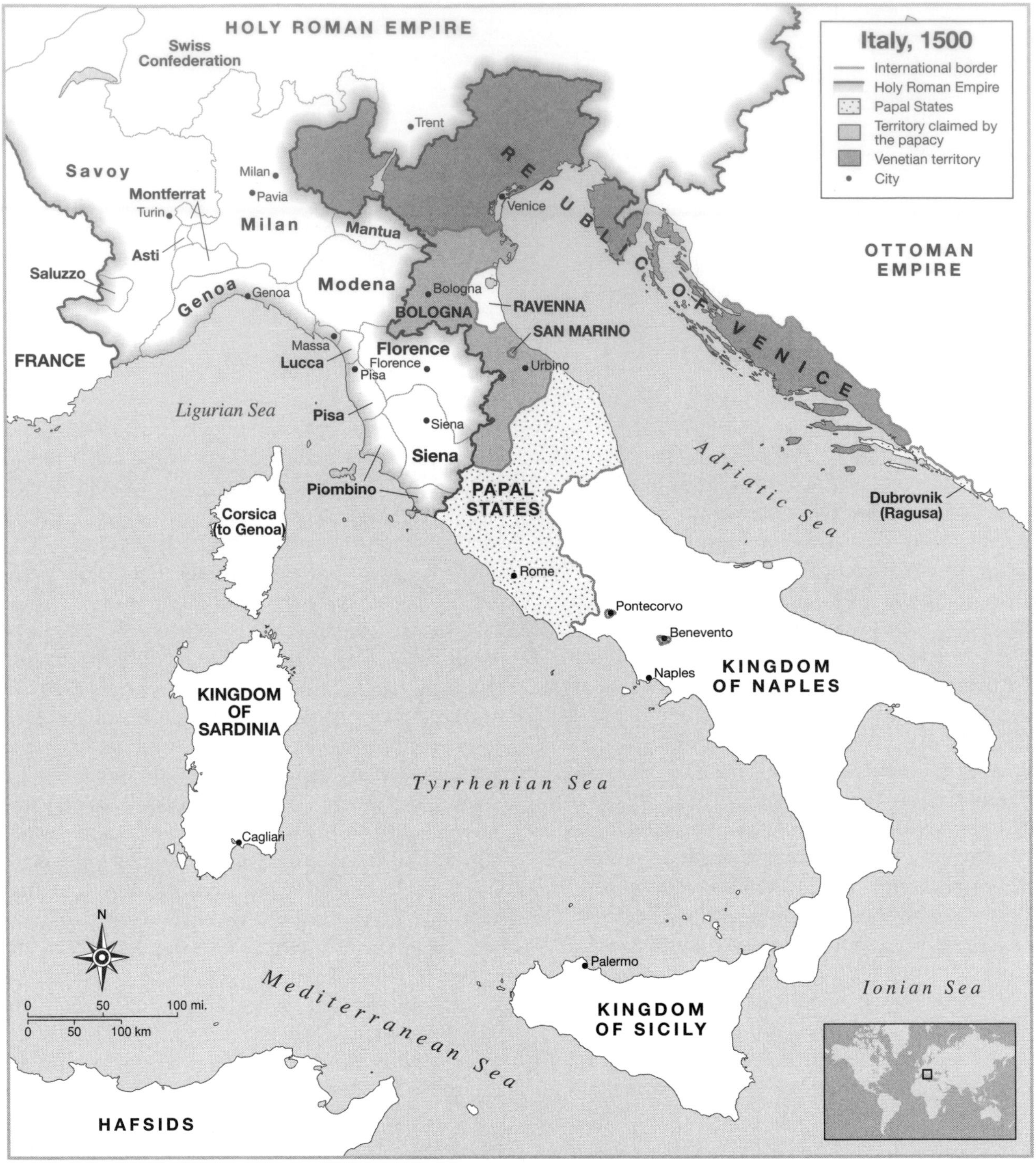

The new principalities themselves were significant improvements over the unstable coalitions of interests in small city-states. Dynasties like the Medici in Florence, the Farnese in Parma, and the Savoy in Turin gradually reined in the privileges and the autonomy of feudal lords and ensured greater stability by offering more impartial justice. Italian urban governments were as efficient as those anywhere, and the political prerogatives enjoyed by established families in the towns and cities of central and northern Italy enabled them to govern conjointly with their princes. These princes also took the first steps to empower the elites of subject towns in their bureaucracies and employed them at their courts. While most princes built citadels to guarantee the docility of local nobles, they also entrusted the peasantry with arms and training as territorial militia. With time, even the new, upstart dynasties planted roots in the territories they ruled, cajoled the aristocracy to cooperate with them, wove alliances, and multiplied marriages with other dynasties in Europe. In short, they acquired legitimacy in the eyes of their subjects.

Similarly, the king of Spain held Neapolitan and Sicilian barons on a tighter leash and kept them from each others' throats. These aristocrats readily admitted the usefulness of a strong foreign monarch who served as a safety valve against overbearing and ambitious members of their own group. Spain held out many rewards for their compliant obedience and granted noble families ample autonomy in their fiefs. Spanish imperial ventures in the New World, in the Mediterranean, and in Flanders gave Italian elites almost everywhere a worthy theater in which to display their bravura and achieve their most lofty ambitions. Spanish power also kept the peace in Italy by barring the way to invaders and mediating the tensions arising between Italian states. Most of Italy lived contentedly in the Spanish shadow, and its elites joined the great Catholic crusades against heresy in Flanders, in France, and against the Turks in Hungary and the Mediterranean. More pacific Italians enriched themselves by helping finance the great Spanish military machine.

THE SIXTEENTH CENTURY

This long sixteenth century, lasting until 1620, marked the creation of the first truly global economy with ramifications in Asia and the Americas. Much of the great flow of silver from the Spanish New World was diverted to the coffers of Italian businessmen who then reinvested it in large-scale trade. Italy enjoyed a number of cultural advantages it had accumulated since the Middle Ages. With Arabic numerals, with widespread numeracy, and commonplace recourse to paper transactions, Italians developed the most sophisticated financial and credit mechanisms anywhere. Italy's high-quality urban manufactures dominated the lucrative luxury sectors of international commerce, the skills to produce them protected and enhanced continually in each city. Venice was probably the most important industrial city in Europe, if not the world. Milan was a vast workshop fed from the great Po valley and provisioned, like the manufacturing cities around it in Lombardy, from much of Europe. Cities like Florence, Bologna, and Naples were also notable centers of manufacturing in a broad range of activities. This economy was directed, at the top, by large-scale bankers, dominated by the Genoese, meeting annually in Piacenza to sort out the exchange and credit needs of all of Europe. The man-

TABLE 1.

Italian Ruling Dynasties

Duchy of Mantua

Francesco II Gonzaga (1484–1519)
Federico II (1519–1540)
Francesco III (1540–1550)
Guglielmo (1550–1587)
Vincenzo I (1587–1612)
Francesco IV (1612)
Ferdinando (1612–1626)
Vincenzo II (1626–1627)
Carlo I (1627–1637)
Carlo II (1637–1665)
Carlo Ferdinando (1665–1708)

Duchy of Ferrara, Modena & Reggio

Alfonso I d'Este (1476–1534)
Ercole II (1534–1559)
Alfonso II (1559–1597)
Cesare (1597–1628): bastard branch, minus Ferrara
Alfonso III (1628–1644)
Francesco I (1644–1658)
Alfonso IV (1658–1662)
Francesco II (1662–1694)
Rinaldo (1694–1737)
Francesco III (1737–1780)
Ercole III (1780–1803)

Duchy of Urbino

Guidobaldo I Montefeltro, (1503–1508)
Francesco Maria I Della Rovere (1508–1516 & 1521–1538)
Guidobaldo II (1538–1574)
Francesco Maria II (1574–1631)

Duchy of Parma and Piacenza

Pier Luigi Farnese (1545–1547)
Ottavio (1547–1586)
Alessandro (1586–1592)
Ranuccio (1592–1622)
Odoardo (1622–1646)
Ranuccio II (1646–1694)
Francesco (1694–1727)
Antonio (1727–1731)
Philippe de Bourbon (1748–1765)
Ferdinando (1765–1802

ufacturing economy was complemented by one of the most efficient agricultural economies in the Western world, giving Italy the highest population density in Europe. The successful integration of livestock-raising, tree and vine crops, and cereals in central and northern Italy permitted landlords to utilize scant resources more rationally. If the country was not quite self-sufficient in food supplies, ruling elites adopted complex administrative measures to avert urban famine.

Italy was not least the seat of the Catholic Church. Despite the challenge to its hold over western Europe with Protestant reformations in Germany, France, and England, the great and complex institution survived and gradually recovered. The long and intermittent Council of Trent (1545–1563) enhanced the unity of the institution, while new religious orders like the Jesuits bolstered the power of the pontiff. The new Roman Inquisition (founded in 1542) quickly crushed any hint of nonconformity in Italy, while an array of committees rejuvenated the basic texts and doctrines of the faith. The Roman Curia grew to become one of the great courts of Europe, and the city of Rome grew with it, largely rebuilt and deploying modern concepts and tools of urbanism that made the Eternal City the most modern metropolis on the continent and a great repository of both sacred and secular architecture. The Council of Trent had far-reaching consequences for the practice of Catholicism throughout the world, but Italy was its motor, the area of recruitment of its most active proponents. It took decades for the central organs of the church to apply the council's decisions to the urban and rural hinterland, and much longer for these changes to bear fruit. Nevertheless by 1600 the reforms were everywhere in full swing, with the aim of Christianizing Italians in depth. One effect was to make the church an ever more powerful political entity that expanded its jurisdiction and its taxing power with respect to the state. Members of the social elite flocked to enter both old and new religious orders, or saw the church as a coveted career choice. Clerical discipline and doctrine were then relayed to men and women in both city and country via ever more numerous confraternities.

CULTURAL LEADER OF EUROPE

Italy's cultural inventions provided the standards to which Europeans complied in literature, architecture, art, and music until the end of the nineteenth century, although the country lost some of its pilot role by 1650. The era is synonymous with the baroque aesthetic, fashioned in Rome in the late 1500s, and often closely associated with the Catholic Church. Italian spectacles and festive activities were something of a magnet for Europeans, who imitated its styles. In music, both the small-scale madrigal and the large-scale opera were inventions of the period with a long future. Italian cities invented the modern conservatory to train professional musicians, as they invented the art academy as a place to master the techniques and the theory of painting, sculpture, and architecture. Rome and Venice witnessed the emergence of the first art "market" where buyers and sellers exchanged artworks as commodities. Over time, the baroque aesthetic gradually simplified to announce the basic principles of what would become neoclassicism in the eighteenth century. Italy remained the favorite destination of painters and architects seeking models elaborated in both modern and ancient times.

The proponents of all these reforms and inventions were very largely aristocrats. Urban living had given them a patina of urbanity that combined gentle birth, good breeding, a high level of education, and the ability to choose among a wide array of professional and amateur activities without equal in Europe. The humanist models of *virtù* exercised in this world were taught formally to nobles in Jesuit-run colleges created first in Italy and then exported throughout the Catholic world and beyond. At first, little prevented the active involvement of noblemen in commerce and manufacture, but as aristocratic mores formed a proper doctrine by the late sixteenth century, they began to withdraw from the active role to celebrate a more genteel *otium* ('leisure'). Yet it was precisely this detachment from mundane affairs that other Europeans found compelling. The pomp and formality of aristocracy defined the early modern elite, and even the age.

THE SEVENTEENTH CENTURY

The Italian pilot role was snatched away suddenly around 1620. The country was never fully protected from foreign threats. During all of the early modern

age, Barbary pirates infested the Mediterranean and the Adriatic seas, seizing ships laden with merchandise belonging to Italians. Worse, flotillas of Muslim pirates raided coastal villages and carried off the population into slavery in North Africa or the Middle East. At times, even substantial cities like Reggio Calabria could be sacked by the largest of such flotillas. Italians and Spaniards responded by building a vast network of coastal fortresses and towers, manned with troops and backed with militia to rally threatened districts. The great Ottoman fleets were smashed at Lepanto in 1571, but insecurity reigned thereafter, checked only by the expansion or creation of Catholic crusading flotillas of the knights of

Saint John of Jerusalem and of Santo Stefano, operating out of Malta or Livorno, or the small papal and Savoyard squadrons combined with Spanish vessels based in Genoa, Naples, or Sicily.

WARS AND POLITICS

The corsair raids were mere pinpricks next to the eruption of large-scale warfare in Italy and Europe after about 1613, which engulfed first the northern states and then gradually all the others. The Thirty Years' War, which began in 1618, widened to include France intermittently after 1625 and permanently after 1635. Northern Italy became a frequent battleground for contending armies, while other territories contributed troops and money, mostly in support of Habsburg Austria and Spain. The consequences of large-scale, long-term warfare threw the Italian economies into upheaval, destroying networks of credit and exchange, closing off markets, closing workshops, weakening survivors to the point of making them more vulnerable to contagious diseases. By the 1640s, mounting taxes and a dizzying public debt triggered a massive uprising in the kingdom of Naples that imperiled the Spanish regime. If the region saw the rapid recovery by Spain, the kingdom of Naples was too exhausted to remain a pillar of Spanish strength. During the seventeenth century, King Philip IV (ruled 1621–1665) privatized most of his assets in southern Italy in a desperate attempt to find cash to fight the war, reducing royal power in that region to a shadow. It would be decades before Spanish viceroys could muster enough strength in the form of tax revenue to impose their control over the mountainous hinterland and impose obedience on the most turbulent feudal lords. In Sicily, too, the number of troops in the coastal fortresses contracted to the edge of insignificance. Even Venice was drawn into a long and costly defense of its overseas empire against the Ottoman Turks in three very costly wars (1645–1670, 1684–1699, 1714–1718) that reduced its presence in the Middle East to a mere shadow. Hundreds of Venetian patricians died on the ramparts of Candia (present-day Hania), the capital of Crete, or in desperate sea battles with the Turks in the Aegean or the Dardanelles, or of typhus and plague contracted during military operations.

With the eclipse of Spanish power everywhere in Europe, Italian states became pawns in the new European state system articulated around a handful of emergent great powers. Challenged repeatedly by France, Spain was hard pressed to defend its overseas colonies and its European possessions. It almost lost Sicily in the 1670s in the aftermath of an urban revolt at Messina (1674–1678), and Naples and Sardinia escaped conquest only due to French lack of initiative. French pressure on Italian states convinced those princes and republics to let lapse their ties and alliances with Madrid. Only in 1690 did a challenge to French ambitions emerge with the Habsburg emperor Leopold I's (ruled 1657–1705) dispatch of an army to northern Italy, intent on filling the Spanish vacuum with an Austrian one. Leopold I intended to impose his jurisdiction (and his claims to Italian taxes) on the whole of northern and central Italy, as Charles V (ruled 1519–1556) had been briefly able to do in the sixteenth century. The demilitarization of most of the Italian states after the end of the Thirty Years' War in 1648 forced the smaller states without large standing armies, like Genoa, Mantua, Florence, and Modena, to comply reluctantly with imperial ultimatums. This crisis came to a head during the War of the Spanish Succession (1701–1714) when the extinction of the Spanish Habsburg line opened a succession contested between France and the rest of Europe. Most of Spain acclaimed Louis XIV's grandson Philip as king and heir of all the Spanish dominions in 1700. However, the prospect of combining the weak global empire of Spain with the powerful and populous kingdom of France was too horrible to contemplate for the Austrian Habsburgs and their allies in England, Germany, and the Netherlands. Spanish territories in Italy meekly accepted the Bourbon candidate, Philippe d'Orléans, and most accepted the presence of French armies in Italy to defend the inheritance. The Gonzaga rulers of Mantua openly sided with the "Gallispans," as they were called. Piedmont was dragged into the French alliance at the outset of the war but changed sides in 1704. Campaigning on a scale never before seen, between the Gallispan forces and the imperial and Piedmontese in northern Italy, culminated in the perilous siege of Turin by the French in 1706. A victory there would probably have entrenched the Bourbon dynasty in Italy. At the last minute, an imperial army under Prince Eugene of Savoy

(1663–1736) maneuvered its way to Piedmont and routed the Gallispan army and chased it out of Italy. In the subsequent campaigns, Austrian armies occupied all of Lombardy and the kingdom of Naples and imposed imperial tutelage on all the smaller states. Over the subsequent decades, Vienna would patiently extend its authority over them all, with the exception of Piedmont and Venice, which had substantial armies of their own.

ECONOMY AND SOCIAL CONDITIONS

The legacy of war in the seventeenth century included both disease and ruin. Hard times magnified the impact of diseases like the plague that swept away a quarter of the population of northern Italy in 1630 and then a quarter of southern Italy in 1656. The decline of food prices in the aftermath of the plagues also served to depress the entire economy, with the result that most peasants lost the land they owned due to insufficient revenues in hard times. Widespread misery took a lethal toll in frequent outbreaks of typhus, which killed hundreds of thousands of people each time there was a general harvest failure. Widespread poverty drove prices downward for at least a century, between 1620 and 1730, forcing all to curtail spending and investment. The urban manufactures lost their markets abroad and then increasingly their markets at home, too. Instead of importing food and raw materials and exporting high-quality manufactured goods, as in the past, Italians imported ever more manufactured goods from France, the Netherlands, and England, and sold agricultural commodities and semifinished products in exchange. From what we can measure, standards of living in Italian cities and villages declined along with the population. This was not an economic crisis, per se, preparing a rapid recovery. Rather, Italy fell quickly and enduringly behind its northern European neighbors and became the very example of stagnation and decline.

Italy lost its cultural ascendancy in the same period. After spearheading the mathematization of the universe, Italian philosophers formulated the first serious challenge to the Aristotelian worldview that the church supported. However, the church grew in strength throughout this crisis period, and with the active support of Italian princes, it mobilized against new currents in philosophy and science in an enduring manner. If Italy retained a larger number of universities and academies compared to other countries, these were gradually coopted by religious authorities vigilant against dangerous novelties. Italian elites ceased their campaign to spread literacy in cities and villages. Europe's cultural center of gravity shifted away from northern Italy to settle on the triangle of Paris-London-Amsterdam, which became the fulcrum of the Enlightenment.

THE EIGHTEENTH CENTURY

The eighteenth century nevertheless witnessed a partial recovery of Italy, though it did not begin to close the gap with northwest Europe. The long depression of the European economy ended around 1730 as the newly rising population began to raise prices and intensify commercial exchanges. Italy's once-prized urban manufactures continued to lose ground, and the country ruralized further, while in northern Europe the cities gained ground absolutely and relatively. Nevertheless, famines became less frequent as large-scale maize and rice cultivation introduced these high-yield crops into the staple diet. A new interest in agricultural questions among the elite sparked an era of innovation and experiment, and investments aimed to reclaim farmland from marshes and hillsides. The Italian population increased from thirteen million to eighteen million at the end of the century, but European population increase was stronger outside Italy. Fortunes were made supplying grain and other foodstuffs to the cities, and the country exported food and other agricultural products like raw silk. Economic thinkers began to suggest lifting the number of restrictions hedging agricultural production and distribution, in the expectation that landlords would produce more food as prices rose. The widespread famines of the mid-1760s constitute a watershed in that governments everywhere began to liberalize the economy, and the grain trade in particular. Production did indeed rise, but prices rose relentlessly, too, and with them, misery proved irrepressible.

The same liberalizing trends were introduced into manufacturing, with the same mixed results. State monopolies and privileges protecting specific industries did not prove very successful. After mid-century, governments began to turn a blind eye to breaches in the regulations. Governments contributed to the expansion by investing effort in roads, canals, and monetary stability. More typically, new initiatives scattered to the countryside and used peasant labor that was abundant and cheap in the off-season. By the late eighteenth century, the future geography of Italian industry was already perceptible in Piedmont, northern Lombardy and the Veneto, Liguria, and northern Tuscany, producing cheap goods for popular markets in Italy and beyond. As the price of manufactured goods declined, something of a consumer revolution began to reach a large portion of the population, in central and northern Italy particularly.

RELIGION

The same secularizing trends at work north of the Alps began to weaken the monolithic nature of Tridentine Catholicism in the peninsula. In order to contest the challenges to their jurisdiction coming from France, Spain, and Austria, the popes gave new impetus to the study of church history, armed with the new tools of chronology and diplomatics. The unintended result was to have church scholars lead an assault on over a thousand years of church legends. A more critical form of erudition, a study of history, law, and institutions, made intellectual elites in Italy more suspicious of receiving tradition uncritically. After more than a century of active Counter-Reformation, the Italian clergy had never been so well educated or disciplined, but this meant that they were open to fresh intellectual currents, too. The church sometimes excoriated secular tendencies and arrested some of the early Freemasons (members of a philanthropical secret society who tolerated unorthodox religious views), but it could not reverse the trend. In the 1720s and 1730s Piedmont began to limit the church's jurisdiction, and took a more active role in education and charity, areas in which church institutions had been more active than the state. States began to invoke the need to appoint their own censors. Inquisition activities began to be curtailed, since they had always operated with the state's cooperation, and this was no longer automatically forthcoming. Italian states began to impose new taxes on church incomes, to reduce the tax immunities of clergymen, to reduce the number of priests and monks in their territories, and to abolish mortmain, which had prevented church land from being sold to secular landowners. Between 1750 and 1770 a spate of laws limiting the church's jurisdiction was issued all across Italy, sometimes accompanied by new concordats. Nevertheless, this did not entail the more profound dechristianization that was beginning in France. Popular attendance at church services was still very high everywhere. Over most of Italy, the late seventeenth and the entire eighteenth century witnessed missionary activity on an unprecedented scale over the entire countryside, instilling a more modern individual piety despite the theatrical flourishes typical of Mediterranean religiosity. If anything, the eighteenth century witnessed an unprecedented cultural gulf between urban cultural elites and the illiterate majority of Italians.

INTELLECTUAL CURRENTS

The intellectual dynamism in eighteenth-century Italy was considerable, across the gamut of genres. Increasing numbers of books were published in Italy, and ever more were imported, legally or as contraband. While censorship was still the norm, censors often intervened with a light hand. The church's index of prohibited books of 1758 was less severe than those preceding it, and was perhaps less severe than that of some Italian states. A great many forbidden works lined the bookshelves of Italian homes or libraries, often published in French. The publication of books was complemented by the multiplication of periodicals. While they rarely reached more than a couple of thousand subscribers each in northern and central Italy, they usually passed through more hands. These made known books published throughout Italy and the rest of Europe with very little time lag. Italian elites became conversant with French Enlightenment principles and with English ideas, too, spread by young aristocrats on the grand tour. By the 1760s and 1770s, the Italian authors who were members of academies and contributors to philosophical and literary journals began to disseminate their ideas close to the realm of power in Milan and Turin, Parma and Modena, Florence and Naples.

PIEDMONT

More often than not, Italian governments were friendly to such developments, which never encompassed much more than an urban elite. Many of the academies functioned with the blessing of princely governments. These governments evolved gradually in the direction of more discretionary power in the hands of the prince and his court, and a dwindling role for the noble heirs of the urban governments whose institutions reached back into the Middle Ages. The model was largely French, fashioned over several centuries by kings who gradually subjected great lords and autonomous regions to their authority. Piedmont applied these lessons most effectively with perfect continuity through the dukes of Savoy from Emanuel Philibert (ruled 1559–1580) onward. The house of Savoy domesticated its nobility by making service a condition of fiefholding. Nobles served in the army and at court, in both cases enhancing the power of the prince. Noblemen strove to be admitted to bureaucratic institutions in Turin. The dukes also adopted the French employment of

powerful commissioners, called *intendants,* entrusted with the strict application of the duke's decisions in every district capital. With a more efficient government hierarchy, the dukes could afford to raise taxes and establish a standing army, which could be used to enforce its will on recalcitrant subjects. During the long reign of Victor Amadeus II (1683–1730), the duke single-mindedly pushed back provincial, aristocratic, and ecclesiastical privilege with the aim of increasing his revenues. These he spent principally on warfare. Aided by British and Dutch subsidies, Victor Amadeus fashioned a large and effective military force that helped tilt the balance against Louis XIV and resulted in the expansion of the state in Lombardy and the acquisition of Sardinia (1720) with its royal title. Along with Venice, but with more ambitious expansion aims, Piedmont possessed the only serious Italian army on the peninsula. By committing its army to one side or the other in the rivalry between the Bourbons and the Habsburgs, the Savoy dynasty was able to increase the size and power of the state.

NAPLES

Piedmont was eventually isolated after 1756 once Habsburgs and Bourbons decided to make peace to confront other threats. Both dynasties applied absolutist principles in the Italian areas they governed, although these were not completely novel in the eighteenth century. The French Bourbon kings considered Italy to be a sideshow and did not seek major gains there during the eighteenth century. Their sole durable initiative was to purchase the rebellious island of Corsica from Genoa in 1767 and to crush the rebels there. Ejected from the peninsula after 1707, the Spanish Bourbons returned in 1734 when a seaborne army enabled the adolescent Charles III (ruled in Naples 1734–1759) to take Naples and Sicily from Austria. Charles was long dependent upon instructions from his parents, who gave him an army composed chiefly of Spanish and other foreign troops. True to Bourbon principles, Charles sought to domesticate the Neapolitan aristocracy and rule through civil servants steeped in royalist tradition. Charles was forced by family allegiance to commit the kingdom to war against the Habsburgs after 1740. With luck, his army defeated an Austrian attempt at reconquest in 1744, and Neapolitan notables resigned themselves to the Bourbon regime. The chief minister in Naples, Bernardo Tanucci (ascendant 1740–1776), adopted principles long followed in France, then Spain, to curtail baronial and ecclesiastical jurisdictions and liberties to the benefit of royal government, and to recover the direction of tax offices alienated to private investors during the preceding century. The place of the church was drastically curtailed during the latter half of the eighteenth century, in part due to a new concordat. Feudal power receded more gradually, though baronial excesses and violence were largely things of the past after 1750. There was even some progress in enhancing royal control over the tax machinery and in streamlining government procedures. After Tanucci retired, and the crown settled on Charles's son Ferdinand I (ruled 1767–1825) and his Habsburg queen Maria Carolina, absolutist policies designed by aristocratic Freemasons hemmed in baronial power in Sicily, too. The Bourbons tried to maintain a credible army and rally the aristocracy around it, and in the 1780s they created a navy, too, with which to combat Barbary corsairs. In Naples the regime established a panoply of royal institutions, including a palace at Caserta modeled on Versailles. The regime was fairly deeply rooted in the kingdom when French revolutionaries overthrew it in 1799, and it was restored largely through popular rebellion.

NORTHERN ITALY AND THE HABSBURGS

Austrian Habsburgs applied the same general principles in the areas they governed after winning the War of the Spanish Succession in 1714. Initially they scooped up most of the Spanish territories in Italy: Milan, Naples, and Sardinia (exchanged with Piedmont for Sicily in 1720). Habsburg ambitions did not end there. Mantua was confiscated from the Gonzaga dukes for backing the Bourbons. The emperor Charles VI (ruled 1711–1740) also intended to incorporate into the empire the other Italian principalities: Parma on the extinction of the Farnese in 1731; Tuscany on the extinction of the Medici in 1737. Italians constituted about one-third of the emperor's direct subjects in those years.

But the incipient "Austrian" empire was a ramshackle conglomeration of territories articulated around the Austrian and Bohemian heartland, with its peripheries responding poorly to directives from the center. Its vulnerability in Italy was demonstrated during the War of the Polish Succession in 1733–1735 as Gallispan armies supported by Piedmont ejected imperial troops from both Lombardy and Naples, losing the latter definitively. When in 1740 a Prussian attack gave birth to a new coalition aimed at breaking up the Austrian Habsburg empire, triggering the War of the Austrian Succession, the new Habsburg regime headed by Maria Theresa had never looked weaker. The Danubian territories rallied around the dynasty, however, permitting the levy of new Habsburg armies for fighting in Italy, Germany, and the Low Countries. A new Spanish army operating in Emilia with Neapolitan support was beaten back. When Piedmont and Britain joined Austria soon after, the

Habsburg Monarchy was able to mount better odds. Maria Theresa briefly lost Milan and Parma in 1745 to Gallispan troops but soon after recovered sufficiently to put the Bourbons on the defensive. French successes elsewhere finally allowed a Spanish Bourbon to become duke of Parma in 1748, but it was a limited success. Maria Theresa spent the rest of her reign reinforcing imperial institutions in Milan. As in Piedmont, the crucial initiative was to undertake a meticulous cadastre of landed property that allowed it to assess taxes more equitably and efficiently. Gradually, the monarchy took over the business of raising taxes, which was novel for the *ancien régime*. After 1765, Maria Theresa was aided by her eldest son, Joseph, who reigned as emperor between 1780 and 1790. As a result of their initiatives to stimulate the economy and streamline the administration, Milanese patricians gradually lost their hold over the region, to the benefit of Italians nominated from Vienna.

The Habsburg influence spread throughout Italy in the eighteenth century, prefiguring the predominance of Metternich's age in the early nineteenth century before Italian unification. Genoa relied on imperial troops to retain its shaky hold on Corsica. Maria Theresa's husband, emperor Francis I (ruled 1737–1765), succeeded the Medici to the grand-ducal throne of Florence, and ruled it from Vienna through the intermediary of Lorrainer officials, until his son Leopold (ruled 1765–1790) went to rule there directly after 1765. The Este line in Modena eventually merged with a Habsburg prince, extending Vienna's influence into Emilia. Once Habsburgs and Bourbons formed an alliance in 1756, it was cemented in place through a series of marriages, and queen Maria Carolina effectively brought Naples into the Austrian sphere of influence at the end of the century, displacing the Spanish connection of her Bourbon husband.

Habsburg reforms tended to be most drastic with respect to the Catholic Church. Maria Theresa was content to impose Vienna's jurisdiction in her territories, at the expense of the pope. It can be argued that she was following the Bourbon lead in this area, imposing ultimate state control over papal functionaries. Reforms to church structures under her sons Joseph II (in Lombardy and the Trentino) and Leopold (in Tuscany) were intentionally more fundamental, as both princes sponsored the spread of Jansenist principles at the expense of traditional Catholicism. Bishops nominated from Vienna were henceforth all selected with a view to uprooting "superstition" and "fanaticism." Priests were trained at great seminaries under state control, using a Jansenist catechism. The great majority of religious houses were closed by government order and their property confiscated. Most of these measures irritated most Italians, and the Tuscan reformers were challenged by traditional bishops and popular riots in 1787. Leopold decreed a pause in these and other reforms, but they marked the real end of the Counter-Reformation era in Italy, just before the arrival of French revolutionary troops in 1796.

See also **Florence; Habsburg Dynasty: Austria; Habsburg Dynasty: Spain; Maria Theresa (Holy Roman Empire); Papacy and Papal States; Savoy, duchy of; Venice.**

BIBLIOGRAPHY

Berce, Yves-Marie, Gerard Delille, Jean-Michel Sallmann, and Jean-Claude Waquet. *L'Italie au XVIIe siècle.* Paris, 1989.

Bianconi, Lorenzo. *Music in the Seventeenth Century.* Cambridge, U.K., and New York, 1987.

Black, Christopher. *Early Modern Italy: A Social History.* London and New York, 2001.

Braudel, Fernand. *The Mediterranean and the Mediterranean World in the Age of Philip II.* Translated by Sian Reynolds. New York and London, 1976.

Cochrane, Eric. *Florence in the Forgotten Centuries, 1527–1800: A History of Florence and the Florentines in the Age of the Grand Dukes.* Chicago and London, 1973.

———. *Italy, 1530–1630.* Edited by J. Kirshner. New York and London, 1988.

Cohen, Elizabeth S., and Thomas V. Cohen. *Daily Life in Renaissance Italy.* Westport, Conn., and London, 2001.

Delumeau, Jean. *L'Italie de Botticelli à Bonaparte.* Paris, 1974.

Gross, Hans. *Rome in the Age of Enlightenment.* Cambridge, U.K., and New York, 1990.

Hanlon, Gregory. *Early Modern Italy: Three Seasons in European History.* London and New York, 2000.

———. *The Twilight of a Military Tradition: Italian Aristocrats and European Conflicts, 1560–1800.* New York, 1998.

Mackenney, Richard. *Tradesmen and Traders: The World of the Guilds in Venice and Europe, c. 1250–c. 1650.* London, 1987.

Malanima, Paolo. *La fine del primato: Crisi e riconversione nell'Italia del Seicento.* Milan, 1998.

Marino, John, ed. *Early Modern Italy, 1550–1796.* Oxford and New York, 2002.

Marino, John, and Antonio Calabria, eds. and transl. *Good Government in Spanish Naples.* New York, 1990.

Pastor, Ludwig von. *The History of the Popes, from the Close of the Middle Ages.* 40 vols. London, 1936–1967.

Ricuperati, Giuseppe, and Dino Carpanetto. *Italy in the Age of Reason, 1685–1789.* New York and London, 1987.

Sella, Domenico. *Crisis and Continuity: The Economy of Spanish Lombardy in the 17th Century.* Cambridge, Mass., 1979.

———. *Italy in the Seventeenth Century.* New York and London, 1997.

Smith, Denis Mack. *A History of Sicily.* 2 vols. New York, 1969.

Symcox, Geoffrey. *Victor Amadeus II: Absolutism in the Savoyard State, 1675–1730.* Berkeley, 1983.

Venturi, Franco. *Italy and the Enlightenment: Studies in a Cosmopolitan Century* Translated by Susan Corsi. New York, 1972.

Woolf, Stuart J. *A History of Italy, 1700–1860: The Social Constraints of Political Change.* London and New York, 1986.

GREGORY HANLON

IVAN III (MUSCOVY) (1440–1505; ruled 1462–1505), grand prince of Muscovy. Ivan III Vasil'evich grew up during the dynastic civil war of his father's reign and went on to lay the foundations of Russian statehood and ethnographic territory.

After ascending the throne in 1462, Ivan expanded the territory of the Grand Principality of Moscow by annexing the small but crucial principalities of Yaroslavl' (1463), Rostov (1474), Tver' (1485), Vyatka (1489), and most importantly, the Novgorod republic (1478). Exploiting internal rivalries among the ruling elite of Novgorod, Ivan was able to annex it without serious fighting. He thus acquired the main Russian emporium for the Hanseatic League and the vast Russian north, rich in furs, salt, and forest products. Defections to Moscow of Russian princes on the Lithuanian border led to two wars (1487–1494 and 1501–1503) and the addition of Chernigov (Chernihiv), Novgorod-Seversk, and Byansk to Moscow. In 1480 Ivan's army confronted the Great Horde, a successor state to the Golden Horde, but the Horde retreated without a battle. The event provided a symbolic end to the supremacy of the heirs of the Mongols, by now weakened by internal feuds. After the death of his first wife, Maria of Tver', Ivan married Sofiia Paleologue, a Byzantine princess living in Rome. The 1472 marriage, encouraged by the Venetian Pope Paul II, brought new prestige to Moscow and, in Sofiia, a powerful figure to its court, where she remained until her death in 1503.

Ivan's policy rested on new state institutions that evolved from the princely household. Foremost in importance was the duma, the council of some ten or twelve men of the great aristocratic clans who ruled with the prince. The center of administration was the treasury, headed by a boyar from the Greek Khovrin family of the Crimea and comprising half a dozen secretaries and lesser staff. It not only kept and recorded revenues but acted as an archive of treaties, charters, and foreign policy, whose administration it handled. The court was headed by the majordomo, who managed Ivan's household as well as taking on larger judicial functions. These aristocrats worked well with Ivan until the 1490s, when the death of his eldest son occasioned a succession crisis. At first Ivan favored his grandson Dmitrii, who was even crowned in 1498. Almost immediately, however, Dmitrii fell from favor, and Ivan chose in his place Vasilii, his second son by Sofiia. As a result the greatest of the boyars, the princes Patrikeev, went into exile.

Under Ivan the army came to rest less on the retinues of the great aristocrats than on the new gentry cavalry, each given a *pomest'e,* a land grant conditional on military service. Lands confiscated in the 1490s from the old Novgorod nobility formed a large part of these grants. The law code of 1497 began the process of writing down Muscovite law, although it was still more of a procedural handbook for judges than a code.

Ivan's reign coincided with a period of ferment in the church. Autocephalous since 1448, the Russian Orthodox Church maintained correct, if strained, relations with the Greeks. The first challenge to its authority came from a small group of Novgorod clergy and Moscow lay officials called "Judaizers" by their opponents. They seem to have questioned monastic institutions, the devotion to icons, and some aspects of trinitarian doctrine. After some hesitation from Ivan, they were condemned and executed in 1504–1505. Their principal opponent, the abbot Joseph of Volokolamsk, was a staunch proponent of traditional monasticism and, after Ivan rejected the heretics, of princely power as well. At the same time the hermit Nil Sorskii advocated a more individual monastic piety and rejected the punishment of the heretics.

Ivan was the motivating force behind the construction of one of Russia's greatest architectural achievements, the Moscow Kremlin as we see it today. Almost entirely the work of Italian architects, the new building began with Aristotele Fioravanti's Dormition Cathedral (1475–1479), followed by the work of the Milanese Marco Ruffo and Pietro Antonio Solari, who built the Kremlin walls (1485–1495) in imitation of the Sforza castle in Milan. At the same time they constructed the princely palace, of which the Faceted Palace (1487–1491) still remains. Russian architects from Pskov built the Annunciation Cathedral as the palace church (1484–1489).

The new palace, churches, and fortifications reflected the Moscow principality's new position in the world. During these years the usage *Rossiia* ('Russia'), reflecting Greek antecedents, began to replace the older "Rus'" and to refer to the lands under Ivan's rule. Informal usage of the term "tsar" appears in some documents. Ivan III, more than any other ruler, laid the foundations for the later Russian state.

See also **Duma; Ivan IV, "the Terrible" (Russia); Russia; Russia, Architecture in; Russia, Art in; Vasilii III (Muscovy).**

BIBLIOGRAPHY

Alef, Gustave. *The Origins of Muscovite Autocracy: The Age of Ivan III.* Forschungen zur osteuropäischen Geschichte 39. Berlin, 1986.

Fennell, J. L. I. *Ivan the Great of Moscow.* London, 1963.

Soloviev, Sergei M. *History of Russia.* Vol. 7, *The Reign of Ivan III the Great.* Translated by John D. Windhausen. Gulf Breeze, Fla., 1978. Vol. 8, *Russian Society in the Age of Ivan III.* Translated by John D. Windhausen. Gulf Breeze, Fla., 1979.

PAUL BUSHKOVITCH

IVAN IV, "THE TERRIBLE" (RUSSIA) (1530–1584; ruled 1533–1584), grand prince of Muscovy and, from 1547, first tsar of Russia. The early achievements of Ivan IV Vasil'evich, known as "the Terrible," were clouded by failure in war and repression at home in his later years. The son of Grand Prince Vasilii III and Princess Elena Glinskaia, Ivan was only three when his father died. His mother led a regency with Prince Ivan Telepnev-Obolenskii, but on her death in 1538, a boyar regency took over and proved to be dominated by vicious factional struggles. At first the princes Shuiskii ousted Obolenskii and Metropolitan Daniil (1539), then the princes Bel'skii rose to power, only to be replaced by the Vorontsovs and then once again by the Glinskiis, the relatives of Ivan's mother. In 1547 Metropolitan Makarii crowned the young Ivan tsar. The new official title signified a claim to equality in rank with the Holy Roman emperor, the Ottoman sultans, and the Chingisid Tatar khans, as well as the Byzantine emperors of the past. Shortly afterwards, Ivan married Anastasiia Romanova, a woman of one of the major boyar clans. After a major riot in Moscow against the Glinskii clan led to their fall from favor, the Romanovs became the closest boyar clan to the throne.

The next decade was one of major accomplishments on all fronts. Historians dispute how much influence Ivan's inner circle of informal advisers wielded. It is certain that, along with the boyars, Aleksei Adashev, the tsar's chamberlain and head of the Petitions Office, and Ivan's chaplain Sil'vestr advised Ivan about policy. After several expeditions down the Volga, Ivan conquered the Tatar khanate of Kazan' in 1552 and the Astrakhan' khanate in 1556, giving Russia control of the whole length of the river and the steppe around it. In a few years the Russians had built a fort on the Terek River near present-day Grozny. These spectacular successes changed the balance of power in western Eurasia, as Russia was the first sedentary power to break into the steppe, cutting off its western extension from Central Asia. These conquests laid the foundation for Russian settlement of the Urals and, at the very end of Ivan's reign, the expedition of the Cossack Yermak Timofeyevich into Siberia (1581–1584), which began the Russian conquest and settlement of northern Asia.

Ivan IV. Portrait engraving c. 1680s. THE ART ARCHIVE/RUSSIAN HISTORICAL MUSEUM MOSCOW/DAGLI ORTI (A)

Ivan's internal measures, often anachronistically called reforms, built up the Russian state apparatus on new foundations. In these years new state offices *(prikazy)*—no longer household offices—came into being, with an army office *(razriad)*, one for landed estates, and others for bandits, petitions, and other functions. The Ambassadorial Office split off from the treasury in 1549. At the same time, the government continued the policy of ordering local gentry to elect elders to deal with crime and public order, and it replaced the older system of direct collection of taxes by local governors to support their work (*kormlenie,* or 'feeding') with the requirement for the village community to collect taxes. The older type of provincial government gave way to a more centralized state. In 1550 the government issued a new law code *(Sudebnik),* really a procedural manual for trials and investigation. In 1551 Ivan called a council of the church that resulted in a series of enactments called the Hundred Chapters, which tried to correct administrative, liturgical, and moral abuses by strengthening episcopal administration as well as the tsar's control.

In 1553 Ivan fell ill and seemed on the point of death, and he tried to guarantee the succession for his infant son. Some boyars supported him, but others feared a regency that would only empower the Romanovs. A third group favored Ivan's cousin, Vladimir of Staritsa, an incapable but certainly legitimate possibility. Fortunately Ivan recovered, but the episode poisoned relations between the tsar and his cousin, as well as with many of the boyars. The poison began to work a decade later.

In 1558 Ivan, confident in his power after the victories over the Tatars, decided to invade and attempt to conquer Livonia, founded in the thirteenth century by a German crusading order on the territory of present-day Estonia and Latvia. The Reformation had destroyed the rationale and unity of the order, and Poland and Russia both craved its lands and trading cities. For Russia, they were the main artery of commerce with Europe. Ivan's army was quickly successful, but the entrance of Poland into the war provided a new enemy. At first victorious over the Poles, Ivan's army bogged down in a long stalemate that lasted until the 1570s, when Poland and Sweden expelled the Russians and divided Livonia between themselves. The failed war was a major burden on the Russian treasury and ruinous for the peasantry, who paid the taxes to support it.

The war also caused discontent among the elite, and in 1564 Prince Andrei Mikhailovich Kurbskii defected to Poland-Lithuania, inaugurating a famous exchange of polemics with Ivan and also contributing to the establishment of the *oprichnina.* The executions and exactions of the following years struck the boyar elite as well as the gentry and townspeople in Novgorod. In 1575 Ivan suddenly placed a converted Tatar prince, Semen Bekbulatovich, on the throne for a few months, but the strange episode had no consequences. A return to near normalcy failed to improve Russia's position in the war, and a truce with Poland in 1582 brought Ivan no gains for his enormous effort. The one accomplishment was the beginning of the conquest of Siberia under Yermak, but this was sponsored by the Stroganov merchants rather than the government. At the end of Ivan's reign the clans began to return to court and to power, a process completed after Ivan's death.

Ivan's reign was a vivid time, full of light and dark, a reign that saw massive and permanent expansion alongside defeat in war, the foundations of the Russian state apparatus, and enormous political and organizational chaos. The agrarian crisis caused by the Livonian War contributed to the beginnings of serfdom, while trade with England and Holland began and thousands of peasants moved to new and better lands in the south and east. The problems at the core of Ivan IV's reign and his legacy are highly complex, and many aspects remain highly controversial.

See also **Baltic Nations; Boris Godunov (Russia); Imperial Expansion, Russia; Law: Russian; Livonian War (1558–1583); Oprichnina; Russia; Russo-Polish Wars; Serfdom in Russia; Vasilii III (Muscovy).**

BIBLIOGRAPHY

Camphausen, Hans-Walter. *Die Bojarenduma unter Ivan IV: Studien zur altmoskauer Herrschaftsordnung.* Frankfurt am Main, 1985.

Platonov, S. F. *Ivan the Terrible.* Translated by Joseph L. Wieczynski. Gulf Breeze, Fla., 1974.

Skrynnikov, R. G. *Ivan the Terrible.* Translated by Hugh F. Graham. Gulf Breeze, Fla. 1982.

Soloviev, Sergei M. *History of Russia.* Vol. 10, *The Reign of Ivan the Terrible: Kazan, Astrakhan, Livonia, the Oprichnina and the Polotsk Campaign.* Translated by Anthony L. H. Rhinelander. Gulf Breeze, Fla., 1995.

Zimin, A. A. *Oprichnina.* 2nd ed. Moscow, 2001.

PAUL BUSHKOVITCH

J

JACOBITISM. Jacobitism was the underground cultural and dynastic movement that supported the restoration of the main line of the Stuart dynasty to the thrones of England, Scotland, and Ireland.

DEVELOPMENT

Jacobitism took its name from Jacobus, the Latin form of James, and stemmed directly from the Revolution of 1688 (also known as the Glorious Revolution, the English Revolution, or the Bloodless Revolution), in which the Catholic James II (ruled 1685–1688) was overthrown by a Dutch invasion (led by his Protestant nephew and son-in-law William of Orange, subsequently William III [ruled 1689–1702]) and widespread rebellion in England. James II, who became convinced he was liable to be murdered by the supporters of the Revolution, known as Revolutioners, fled to France in December 1688. There he found a refuge at the royal palace of St. Germain en Laye and (at least intermittent) support from Louis XIV (ruled 1643–1715), who saw in James's cause an opportunity to display his credentials as an upholder of both monarchical government and the Counter-Reformation. When support for James and the Jacobite cause did not conflict with his other objectives, Louis provided substantial military resources to back attempts to restore James II and subsequently his only surviving son, "James III" (the Old Pretender, a sobriquet fixed on him by Whig propagandists). These attempts began in March 1689 when James II and a small French force landed at Kinsale in Ireland. The Catholicizing regime brought in while James was king was at that point still in control of most of the island, but serious rebellions had broken out against his authority in Ulster, where Irish Protestant rebels had seized the towns of Londonderry and Enniskillen and were holding out for the newly proclaimed King William III. Despite the goodwill of the great majority of his Catholic Irish subjects, James proved unable to construct the administrative and military infrastructure necessary to maintain the large army of volunteers he found waiting for him in Ireland. This was in part the result of Ireland's relative poverty and in part that of a rift between James's objectives and those of the leaders of the Irish Catholic community. Whereas James simply sought to turn Ireland into a steppingstone for his reconquest of England, the Irish Catholic political nation wanted the overturning of the post-1660 land settlement, which had left nearly 80 percent of Ireland in the hands of the descendants of earlier Protestant colonists, and the sharp attenuation of the constitutional power of the English Parliament to dictate policy and law to Ireland's Parliament. The upshot was that Londonderry and Enniskillen were never retaken, and the Irish Jacobite army was in a poor state to face William III when he landed in Ireland with a large veteran army in the summer of 1690. At the battle of the Boyne on 1 July, William defeated James and routed his army. James fled the country on 3 July, ungratefully (and unfairly) blaming the Irish for the disaster. With the help of French reinforcements, resistance continued in the west of Ireland until 12 July 1691, when the Jacobite army was again defeated at the battle of Aughrim and forced to fall back on its last stronghold at Limerick. After a brief siege, the defenders of Limerick surrendered on 3 October 1691 on generous terms that allowed the evacuation of 12,000 of them to France, where they subsequently became the basis of the elite Irish brigade that served the Bourbons until 1789. With the collapse of Irish Jacobite resistance, the Highland rebellion it had inspired in Scotland also came to an end. There, after an unexpectedly good start when James Graham, Viscount Dundee, defeated a Williamite army at Killiecrankie on 17 July 1689 (despite the fact that he himself was killed in the closing moments of the battle), the war in Scotland had settled into a bitter pattern of raid and counterraid that bankrupted the Scottish state and ravaged the Highlands without reaching any conclusion. Hearing of the surrender of Limerick and with it the end of any hope of reinforcement from Ireland, the Scottish Jacobites negotiated a cessation in the autumn of 1691. Brinksmanship over the taking of oaths of loyalty to the Williamite regime by several clan chieftains, and bad faith combined with malice on the part of key government officials, then led to a punitive expedition against the technically holdout Macdonalds of Glencoe. The troops entrusted with the operation duplicitously quartered themselves on the Macdonalds and then on the night of 13 February 1692 perpetrated an infamous massacre on their hosts that shocked the Scottish political nation.

From 1691 until the death of Louis XIV in 1715 Jacobitism in the British Isles revolved around plotting for risings against the new order. Louis several times (1692, 1696, and 1708) provided troops and ships to support and/or precipitate a Jacobite rising, but on each occasion matters went awry. The major obstacles to a French invasion were the Royal Navy, the unpredictability of the weather, and the difficulty of coordinating a rising in England or Scotland with a French invasion. Basically, the Jacobites wanted a French landing first, after which they would rise, while the French wanted a Jacobite rising first, after which they would land. In addition, the French navy, facing mounting odds in its struggle with the Royal Navy and its Dutch allies in both the War of the League of Augsburg (1688–1697) and the War of the Spanish Succession (1702–1714), was increasingly reluctant to undertake an operation that would be tantamount to a death ride for the ships and crews involved. In between plotting for invasions, the Jacobites sought with equal energy to subvert and undermine the post-Revolution political order through propaganda and conventional politics, both at Westminster and on the streets. Throughout the reign of Queen Anne (1702–1714), the Jacobites were somewhat more restrained in their plotting than under William III, partly out of liking for the pious Tory queen, and partly out of the mistaken belief that she favored the restoration on her death of the main line of the Stuarts, in the shape of her half-brother, the Old Pretender.

As she lay dying in August 1714, however, Anne ensured that the Act of Succession of 1702 would be enforced, and rather than the Old Pretender succeeding, her Parliament-approved successor, George, elector of Hanover (a distant, but reliably Protestant, relative) peacefully inherited the throne. For Continental political reasons George I (ruled 1714–1727) had aligned himself with the Whigs in the bitter parliamentary struggles of Queen Anne's last years, and when it subsequently became clear that he would continue to favor the Whigs, the Tories rapidly became alienated. The process began when the Whigs took the first opportunity to be revenged on their old enemies in a series of parliamentary impeachments of members of Queen Anne's last, Tory, ministry. This drove a significant minority of the Tories into the arms of the Jacobites. Meanwhile, in Scotland support for the Jacobite cause had been boosted by the constitutional union of Scotland and England (which was primarily driven by English determination to ensure that Scotland adhered to the Hanoverian succession), forced through the Scots Parliament in 1706–1707, which had outraged a great many Scots. Thus when England erupted in Tory/Jacobite rioting in the summer of 1715, the Scots Jacobites, led by John Erskine, the earl of Mar, felt emboldened to rebel in September. The rebels rapidly won control of most of northern Scotland, more by dint of the fact that the Whig ministry was determined to secure southern England and so kept the bulk of the army there, than by their own abilities. Though Mar was able to build up a formidable force at Perth that far outnumbered the government army at Stirling, he was paralyzed by indecision. It appears that he expected to be quickly reinforced and replaced as commander by Jacobite professional officers in French pay, most notably James Fitzjames, duke of Berwick and marshal of France, and had no idea what to do in the interim. When forced by a conclave of Jacobite leaders to march south, he was met by the government army under John Campbell, duke of Argyll, at Sherrifmuir on 13 November. A battle ensued which Argyll may be said to have won insofar as the core of his army survived despite being outnumbered in the region of three to one. Mar retreated north, back to Perth. He was joined there at the end of December by the Old Pretender, who had finally managed to slip through a dragnet of British agents and Royal Navy warships to get to Scotland. The Old Pretender's arrival, however, closely coincided with the commencement of a winter campaign by Argyll, which took Perth in three days and chased the dwindling Jacobite army north. On 4 February 1716 at Montrose, Mar and the Old Pretender took ship for the Continent. What was left of the Jacobite army retreated north into the Highlands, and within a month the government was back in control of the whole of Scotland. A small Jacobite rising in northern England in October–November 1715 was trapped and forced to surrender at Preston on 14 November.

The collapse of the 1715 rebellion initiated a long period of fruitless plotting and dashed hopes. For thirty years plots were hatched in the British Isles while Jacobite diplomats from the shadow court sought the military backing of a European great power. At various times Sweden, Spain, the Habsburgs, Russia, and France negotiated with them, either to put diplomatic pressure on Britain or out of genuine sympathy. Only Spain, in a moment of desperate crisis during the War of the Quadruple Alliance (1718–1720), actually attempted an invasion of Britain, but it was forced back by storms on 18 March 1719. A separate, diversionary Spanish force led by the Earl Marischal managed to reach Lewis on 9 April, and subsequently raised a small rebellion in the Highlands, but the Jacobite army was defeated at Glenshiel on 5 June, which put an end to the affair. Only in the 1740s, as virtually all of the great powers became involved in the War of the Austrian Succession, did real openings for Jacobite diplomacy reemerge. Negotiations inaugurated by the leaders of a faction among the Tories led in due course to French preparations for an invasion, to be backed up by a Tory/Jacobite rising, in February 1744. Once again a storm and the Royal Navy prevented French and Jacobite plans from coming to fruition.

The Old Pretender's oldest son, though, had been secretly invited to France from Rome, where his father was by this time in exile, to head the invasion force. Charles Edward Stuart (the Young Pretender or Bonnie Prince Charlie) was a young man in a hurry, and when the French abandoned their invasion plans in favor of renewed campaigning in Flanders he opted to try and go it alone. With the help of Irish merchants, well established in the ports of western France, he surreptitiously gathered a force of volunteers from the Irish brigades and arms for many more and invaded Scotland in the summer of 1745. By various mishaps he arrived on Eriskay in the Hebrides on 23 July with only one ship, few arms, and little money, and was promptly advised to go home by local Jacobite leaders. Using his considerable charm Charles Edward broke down their resistance, and within a month was on the march with a small, but growing, force composed primarily of Highland clansmen. In a whirlwind campaign commanded mainly by Lord George Murray, the Jacobites were able to capture Edinburgh, apart from the castle, and rout a government army at Prestonpans on 21 September. After gathering further recruits, Charles Edward cajoled the Scots Jacobite leaders into undertaking an invasion of England that swept as far south as Derby by 5 December, causing panic in London and a crisis of confidence in the Whig ministry. The premise of the campaign was, however, that if they were shown what the Scots could achieve, the French would invade and the English Jacobites would rise. Neither transpired. The French government was desperately throwing together another invasion force, but it was not ready to depart until the very end of December, and the English Jacobites dithered until the opportunity had passed. So at a council of war in Derby on 5 December 1745 Charles Edward was forced to turn back by his commanders. Despite the Jacobite prince's sour obstructionism, the Jacobite army reached Scotland safely on 20 December, and there regrouped in time to defeat another government army at Falkirk on 17 January 1746. The victory could not, though, hold back the numbers of government troops converging on southern Scotland,

and the Jacobites were forced to retreat into northern Scotland. At the insistence of Charles Edward, the Jacobite army ill-advisedly tried to make a stand at Culloden on 16 April 1746 and was badly defeated there by a government force commanded by William Augustus, duke of Cumberland, second son of George II. Even so, the Jacobite army rallied at Ruthven and offered to fight on, but was abandoned by Charles Edward, who chose to try to escape to France. The Jacobite army dispersed and when several Highland chieftains refused to comply with Cumberland's demand that they surrender unconditionally, Cumberland launched a savage campaign of repression that ravaged the Highlands and is still bitterly remembered throughout Scotland and the Scottish diaspora. Charles Edward was meanwhile sheltered by sympathizers in the Highlands and eventually escaped to France, arriving there on 30 September 1746.

The failure of the '45 is usually taken as the death knell of the Jacobite movement, but in fact Jacobite plotting and negotiations with great powers such as France, Prussia, and Spain continued into the late 1750s. The defeat of the rebellion sapped the Jacobites' strength and credibility in Scotland, yet there was still a strong Jacobite diaspora loyal to the Stuart cause in France and Spain. The last Jacobite invasion attempt, which was largely the brainchild of Arthur Tollendal, comte de Lally, commander of the Irish brigade, was only defeated by the victory of the Royal Navy at the battle of Quiberon Bay on 20 November 1759. Charles Edward eventually succeeded his father as the Jacobite "Charles III" in January 1766, by which time he was a paranoid, bitter alcoholic. Though he lingered until 30 January 1788, the Jacobite cause may fairly be said to have been dead by that time.

THE JACOBITE THREAT

The threat to the post-Revolutionary order posed by the Jacobites is the subject of much debate among historians. The debate ultimately revolves around the level of support they enjoyed in the three kingdoms. Since those who expressed Jacobite sympathies in any form were liable to severe punishment, we can never know exactly how many English, Welsh, Scots, and Irish truly favored the restoration of the Stuarts. Our only tangible measures are the numbers who turned out to fight in rebellions, and records of crown prosecutions of suspected Jacobites. Moreover, the numbers yielded by even these sources are obviously flawed. How many Jacobite soldiers were obliged to fight against their own inclinations, by their clan chieftains or landlords, or, conversely, would have joined a Jacobite army if one had passed nearby? How many Jacobite ballad singers, roisterers, or rioters escaped prosecution by the crown? We have, therefore, to assume that both the numbers of Jacobites in arms and the numbers caught committing Jacobite crimes are merely the tip of an iceberg. That said, it seems likely that the strongest support for Jacobitism lay in Scotland and Ireland. In England and Wales there was a small Nonjuror church that split with the Church of England over its acceptance of William III as monarch in 1689. This church remained loyal to the Stuarts to the very end, and its adherents shaded over into the more extreme, High Church wing of the Church of England, but the best guess would put their numbers combined at less than 5 percent of the English and Welsh population. To this we must add the small Catholic minority, which comprised around 2.5 percent of the population by the eighteenth century. There may well have been further sympathizers, but it is impossible to even guess at their numbers, which makes an estimate of 5–10 percent of the English population inclined to Jacobitism as good as we can get.

In Scotland the situation was quite different. The Episcopal clergy forced out of the Presbyterian Kirk in the 1690s soon established their own independent church that from the start adhered to the Stuarts. In large parts of the Highlands and in Lowland Scotland north of the Tay, this church probably included a majority of the population, and may have amounted to 30–40 percent of the population of Scotland as a whole in the early eighteenth century. In addition, the tiny Catholic minority (1–2 percent of the population), which tended to be concentrated in particular clans, were steadfast Jacobites. To this number we should add a small minority of Presbyterians who were so incensed by the Union of England and Scotland bulldozed through the Scottish Parliament in 1706–1707 that they tended to be inclined to Jacobitism thereafter. Deducting neutralist/loyalist Episcopalians, maybe as many as 30 percent of Scots were inclined to support the Jacobites.

Ireland, by contrast, was a Jacobite hotbed. Because there were no further Jacobite rebellions there after 1691, many historians have been skeptical about the depth of Irish Jacobitism, mainly because they based their analyses on partial, and misleading, English-language sources. In fact, Irish (Gaelic) sources reveal a general enthusiasm for the Jacobite cause among the majority, Catholic, population despite the shabby treatment of the Catholic Irish by James II and the Stuart dynasty as a whole. Since it is generally accepted that about 75 percent of the Irish population was Catholic in the period 1692–1800, this would make Ireland the key bastion of Jacobitism in the British Isles. This assessment is underscored by the flow of recruits out of Ireland to join the Irish brigades in French and Spanish service. Though some of them were seeking only adventure or an escape from poverty and discrimination, many more were recruited with the promise that they would soon return to the British Isles as part of a victorious army led by their rightful (Stuart) king. The Irish brigades were, in spirit, the Stuarts' army in exile, and certainly tens of thousands of young Irishmen slipped overseas to join them between 1692 and 1760.

THE IMPACT OF JACOBITISM

Jacobitism was the bane of the post-Revolutionary political order for the first seventy years of its existence. The new order was no more certain of the number of secret Jacobites than we are and oscillated between a general concern and outright panic with respect to how to deal with the threat they posed. Jacobite plotting and invasion attempts in concert with one or another European great power punctuated political life. On average there was a Jacobite-related political "event" every one or two years between 1689 and 1730 and one every three or four years between 1730 and 1760. Always lurking on the fringes of possibility was the chance that the Jacobites would get a European great power's backing, successfully land in Britain, and coordinate a general uprising in support of the Stuart cause. Rather than run the risk of this nightmare scenario ever happening, the ministers of successive post-Revolution regimes worked to forestall Jacobite diplomacy in Europe by alliances and treaties, built up their military forces, and ferreted out conspiracy in the British Isles. In terms, then, of both the dynamics of politics and the development of the British fiscal-military state Jacobitism had a profound influence. Though it started as an expression of dynastic loyalty, Jacobitism came to act as a vehicle for nationalistic aspirations. In Scotland and Ireland a Stuart restoration was linked to the restoration of lost sovereignty and the reattainment of a golden age. If for no other reason, Jacobitism's acting as a conduit for such sentiments among the subsumed polities of the British Isles justifies its inclusion among the most important phenomena of the eighteenth century.

See also **Anne (England); George I (Great Britain); George II (Great Britain); Glorious Revolution (Britain); Hanoverian Dynasty (Great Britain); Scotland.**

BIBLIOGRAPHY

Baynes, John. *The Jacobite Rising of 1715.* London, 1970.

Bennett, Gareth V. *The Tory Crisis in Church and State: The Career of Francis Atterbury, Bishop of Rochester 1688–1730.* Oxford, 1975.

Black, Jeremy. *Culloden and the '45.* New York, 1990.

Clark, Jonathan C. D. "On Moving the Middle Ground: The Significance of Jacobitism in Historical Studies." In *The Jacobite Challenge,* edited by Eveline Cruickshanks and Jeremy Black, pp. 177–188. Edinburgh, 1988.

Cruickshanks, Eveline. *Political Untouchables: The Tories and the '45.* London, 1979.

Fritz, Paul S. *The English Ministers and Jacobitism between the Rebellions of 1715 and 1745.* Toronto, 1975.

Gregg, Edward. "The Jacobite Career of John, Earl of Mar." In *Ideology and Conspiracy: Aspects of Jacobitism, 1689–1759,* edited by Eveline Cruickshanks, pp. 179–200. Edinburgh, 1982.

Hopkins, Paul. *Glencoe and the End of the Highland War.* Edinburgh, 1986.

Jarvis, Rupert. *Collected Papers on the Jacobite Risings.* 2 vols. Manchester, U.K., and New York, 1972.

Lenman, Bruce. *The Jacobite Risings in Britain 1689–1746.* London, 1980.

Macinnes, Allan I. *Clanship, Commerce and the House of Stuart, 1603–1788.* East Linton, Scotland, 1996.

McLynn, Frank J. *Charles Edward Stuart: A Tragedy in Many Acts.* London and New York, 1988.

———. *France and the Jacobite Rising of 1745.* Edinburgh, 1981.

Monod, Paul K. *Jacobitism and the English People 1688–1788.* Cambridge, U.K., and New York, 1989.

ó Ciardha, Éamonn. *Ireland and the Jacobite Cause, 1685–1766: A Fatal Attachment.* Dublin, 2002.

Pittock, Murray G. *The Myth of the Jacobite Clans.* Edinburgh, 1995.

———. *Poetry and Jacobite Politics in Eighteenth-Century Britain and Ireland.* Cambridge, U.K., 1994.

Szechi, Daniel. *George Lockhart of Carnwath, 1689–1727: A Study in Jacobitism.* East Linton, Scotland, 2002.

———. *The Jacobites. Britain and Europe, 1688–1788.* Manchester, U.K., 1994.

———. *Jacobitism and Tory Politics, 1710–14.* Edinburgh, 1984.

DANIEL SZECHI

JADWIGA (POLAND) (Hungarian: Hedvig; German: Hedwig; c. 1374–1399; ruled 1384–1399), queen of Poland, wife of Władysław II Jagiełło. The youngest daughter of Louis of Anjou, king of Hungary and Poland, and Elizabeth of Bosnia, Jadwiga was betrothed as early as 1378 to William of Habsburg. When the Polish lords rejected the candidacy of Jadwiga's elder sister, Maria, for the Polish crown (because she had ascended the Hungarian throne in 1382), Elizabeth decided that Jadwiga would be queen of Poland. Jadwiga arrived in Poland in 1384 and was crowned on 16 October of that same year. Her engagement to William, disliked by the Poles, was annulled (1385) and on 15 February 1386, on the initiative of the lords of Little Poland, she was married to the Lithuanian grand duke Jogaila, known after his baptism as Władysław Jagiełło. Their marriage fulfilled a condition of Poland's union with the Grand Duchy of Lithuania, concluded at Krewo in 1385.

The position of Jadwiga, heiress to the Polish throne (as great-granddaughter of Władysław I the Short) was equal to that of Jagiełło (who was elected king), but because of her young age she did not play an independent political role for a long time and was mainly a symbol for the supporters of the Polish-Lithuanian union. In 1387 Jadwiga accompanied the troops that took over Red Ruthenia from Hungary. Probably influenced by the lords who surrounded her, she was an advocate of a peaceful solution to the conflict with the Order of Teutonic Knights, and in 1397–1398 she conducted unsuccessful negotiations with the grand master of the Order, Konrad von Jungingen, in an attempt to recover the duchy of Dobrzyñ. She also mediated in Jagiełło's diplomatic talks with the Lithuanian princes.

A well-educated woman, Jadwiga was surrounded by scholars. It was also said that she had an aura of saintliness. In her last will (1399) she bequeathed some of her jewels to Cracow Academy (later the Jagiellonian University), which made possible its renovation in 1400. She died giving birth to a daughter, who also died. Her death weakened Jagiełło's position as king of Poland and left the question of succession open. Jadwiga was buried in the cathedral on Wawel Hill in Cracow. Her cult began to grow soon after her death, and she was canonized by Pope John Paul II on 8 June 1997.

See also **Poland to 1569; Władysław II Jagiełło.**

BIBLIOGRAPHY

Halecki, Oskar. *Jadwiga of Anjou and the rise of East Central Europe.* Edited by Thaddeus V. Gromada. Boulder, Colo., and Highland Lakes, N.J., 1991.

Wyrozumski, Jerzy. *Królowa Jadwiga: Między epoką piastowską i jagiellońską.* Cracow, 1997.

MARCIN KAMLER

JAGIELLO (POLAND). *See* **Władysław II Jagiełło (Poland).**

JAGIELLON DYNASTY (POLAND-LITHUANIA), the dynasty that ruled the Grand Duchy of Lithuania, Poland, and at times Hungary and Bohemia, from the fourteenth to the sixteenth century. Its progenitor was Gediminas, grand duke of Lithuania (ruled 1316–1341), the founder of the Lithuanian-Ruthenian state and father of Grand Duke Algirdas (ruled 1345–1377). The founder of the dynasty in Poland was Algirdas's son and successor Jogaila. As a result of a Polish-Lithuanian agreement signed at Krewo on 14 August 1385, which envisaged the Christianization of Lithuania and its union with Poland, Jogaila married the Polish queen Jadwiga of Anjou and was baptized and crowned king of Poland, becoming Władysław II Jagiełło (1386–1434).

The Jagiellon dynasty ruled in the Grand Duchy of Lithuania from 1377 to 1401 and from 1440 to 1572, in Poland from 1386 to 1572, in Hungary from 1440 to 1444 and from 1490 to 1526, and in Bohemia from 1471 to 1526. Władysław II had two sons by his fourth marriage with Sophia, a Lithuanian princess: Władysław III Warneńczyk, king of Poland (1434–1444) and Hungary (as Ulászló I; 1440–1444), who was killed in battle against the Turks at Varna; and Casimir IV (called Jagiellończyk), grand duke of Lithuania (1440–1492) and king of Poland (1447–1492).

By his marriage to Elizabeth of Austria, daughter of Albrecht II of Habsburg, king of Germany, Bohemia, and Hungary, Casimir IV had six sons: Vladislav II, king of Bohemia (1471–1516) and Hungary (as Ulászló II; 1490–1516); Casimir, canonized in 1602; John I Albert, king of Poland (1492–1501); Alexander I, king of Poland (1501–1506); Sigismund I, later called the Old, king of Poland (1506–1548); and Frederick, archbishop of Cracow (1488) and cardinal (1493). Casimir IV also had daughters: Jadwiga was married to the Bavarian duke; Georg (1475), Sophia to the Brandenburg margrave, Frederick (1479); Anna to the Pomeranian duke Boguslaus X (1491); Barbara to the duke of Saxony, Georg (1496); and Elizabeth to the duke of Liegnitz, Frederick II (1515).

At the zenith of their power under Casimir IV in the 1490s, the Jagiellons ruled Poland, Lithuania, Bohemia, and Hungary. But at the Treaty of Vienna in 1515 an agreement was concluded with the Habsburgs regarding the marriage of King Vladislav II's children with Holy Roman emperor Maximilian I's grandchildren. Louis II, king of Hungary and Bohemia from 1516, married Maria, daughter of the king of Castile, Philip I the Handsome (1522). Anna married Ferdinand, who later became emperor as Ferdinand I, in 1521. When Louis fell in the battle against the Turks at Mohács (1526), Bohemia and Hungary came under the rule of Habsburgs.

The Kings John Olbracht and Alexander died without issue. By his marriage with Barbara, daughter of the Transylvanian *Voivode* Stephen Zápolya, Sigismund I the Old had a daughter, Jadwiga, who married the Brandenburg elector, Joachim II (1535). By his second marriage to Bona Sforza, an Italian, Sigismund had six children: his son Sigismund II Augustus became king of Poland and the Grand Duchy of Lithuania in 1548; Isabella was married to the king of Hungary, János Szapolyai, in 1539 and after his death (1540) ruled Transylvania for eleven years on behalf of her underage son, John Sigismund; Sophia became the wife of Henry, duke of Brunswick (1556); Anna became queen of Poland (1575) and wife of Stephen Báthory (1576); and Catherine married John, who later became king of Sweden as John III Vasa (1562).

The death without issue of Sigismund II Augustus in 1572 and of his sister Anna in 1596 meant the end of the dynasty. Its descendants by distaff survived much longer. The mother of Sigismund III Vasa, king of Poland (1587–1632) and Sweden (1592–1599), was a Jagiellon. Thanks to the marriages of Casimir IV's daughters all European monarchs at the beginning of the twenty-first century—the queen of Great Britain and Northern Ireland, Elizabeth II; the king of Belgium, Baudouin I; the queen of Denmark, Margarethe II; the queen of Holland, Beatrix; the king of Norway, Harald V; the king of Sweden, Carl XVI Gustaf; the prince of Lichtenstein, Hans Adam II; the grand duke of Luxembourg, Jean; and the prince of Monaco, Rainier III—could claim Casimir IV as their ancestor.

The Jagiellon dynasty ruled Poland and the Grand Duchy of Lithuania for nearly two hundred years. The Jagiellons concluded a union between Poland and Lithuania, which was endorsed by the Polish Diet (Sejm) at Lublin in 1569, that changed the political structure of east central Europe. They sought to unite all old Polish territories and incorporated Gdańsk Pomerania (known as Royal Prussia, 1466) and Mazovia (gradually from 1462 and fully in 1526–1529) into Poland. At the summit of the Jagiellons' power at the end of the fifteenth century and the first quarter of the sixteenth, the dynastic policy pursued by Casimir IV—whose ambition was that his sons should ascend the thrones of Bohemia and Hungary—resulted in the Jagiellons ruling over nearly the whole of east central Europe, from the Dvina and the Baltic in the north to the upper Elbe, the Adriatic, and the Black Sea in the south. Their successes laid the foundations for the "Jagiellonian idea," developed by Polish historiography in the nineteenth and twentieth centuries—a concept of a multiethnic state and a federal union of states and nations in east central Europe.

Under the Jagiellons, Poland's political system was transformed from an estate-based monarchy to a democracy of the nobility, unique in Europe. The principles of religious toleration were confirmed by the Compact of Warsaw (1573), which proclaimed freedom of religion, guaranteed peace between followers of different religions and equality of rights to dissidents, and forbade religious persecution by secular authorities. Official toleration also included the Jews, who in the sixteenth century flowed into Poland in great numbers (mainly from Germany) and set up large communities in many towns. The principles of civil rights, parliamentary government, and religious toleration were observed by the Jagiellons in all countries under their rule. But the Jagiellons did not succeed in strengthening royal power in Poland or carrying out the fiscal, military, and political reforms that in western Europe laid the foundations for modern state structures and opened the way to absolutism.

See also **Jadwiga (Poland); Lithuania, Grand Duchy of, to 1569; Poland to 1569; Sigismund II Augustus (Poland, Lithuania); Władysław II Jagiełło.**

BIBLIOGRAPHY

Duczmal, Małgorzata. *Jagiellonowie: Leksykon biograficzny.* Cracow, 1996.

Kolankowski, Ludwik. *Polska Jagiellonów: Dzieje polityczne.* 3rd ed. Olsztyn, 1991.

Łowmianski, Henryk. *Polityka Jagiellonów.* Poznań, 1999.

Mączak, Antoni, ed. *Dynastie Europy.* Wrocław, 1997.

Wdowiszewski, Zygmunt. *Genealogia Jagiellonów.* Warsaw, 1968.

MARCIN KAMLER

JAMES I AND VI (ENGLAND AND SCOTLAND)

JAMES I AND VI (ENGLAND AND SCOTLAND) (1566–1625), king of England (as James I, 1603–1625) and Scotland (as James VI, 1567–1625). Born in June 1566, James was the son of Mary, Queen of Scots, and Henry Stewart, Lord Darnley. Rumors abounded from his birth that he was in fact the son of Mary's lover, her Italian secretary David Riccio. Although these were probably unfounded, Mary's marriage to Darnley was certainly an unhappy one: in February 1567 she was involved in the assassination of the feckless Darnley by Scottish lords, led by James Hepburn, earl of Bothwell, at Kirk O'Fields near Edinburgh. Bothwell then divorced his own wife and married Mary. The Protestant Scottish lords were outraged by their behavior, and Mary was deposed. On 19 July 1567 her thirteen-month-old son was crowned James VI of Scotland.

James's minority was dominated by his various noble regents, two of whom were killed in the political violence that characterized Scottish politics during this period, and by his tutors, the strict Calvinist George Buchanan and the more sympathetic Peter Young. In August 1582 James was lured into Ruthven castle and held captive for more than a year by the Protestant earls of Gowrie and Angus. This led to the downfall of James's friend and regent, the pro-French Esmé Stewart, duke of Lennox, and made an indelible mark on the young king. In June 1583 James escaped from his captors and began to assert his authority as king. Chief among his targets was the Scottish Kirk, or assembly of the Presbyterian Church, which the king never forgave for rejoicing in the fall of his friend Lennox. The struggle for control of the Scottish church was a defining feature of James's rule in Scotland, and he continually strove to enforce the so-called Black Acts of 1584, which asserted royal authority over the church. James was only moderately successful; he did not succeed, for example, in appointing any new bishops (the counterweight to the authority of the Kirk) in Scotland between 1585 and 1600. In 1592 the Golden Acts recognized the Kirk's authority in religious matters but retained the king's right to summon it when and where he wished. James also struggled to overcome a factious nobility, notably Francis Stewart, earl of Bothwell (nephew of the third husband of Mary, Queen of Scots) and George Gordon, earl of Huntly. Nevertheless, by 1600 James had established royal control over the Scottish nobility, and his relations with the Scottish Parliament were generally good.

James's international and dynastic standing was increased in October 1589 by his marriage to Anne of Denmark (1574–1619). James traveled to Denmark to collect his bride and only returned to Scotland the following April. Anne bore him three sons and four daughters: Henry, Elizabeth, Margaret, Charles, Robert, Mary, and Sophia. James had made

James I. Portrait by Paul van Somer, c. 1577–1622. ©Archivo Iconografico, S.A./Corbis

only token gestures against the execution of his mother by Elizabeth I of England in 1587, and was careful to maintain his position as the obvious successor to the English throne. When Elizabeth died in March 1603, James was named as her successor and arrived in London the following month.

Almost immediately, however, James came into conflict with his new subjects. Two issues in particular stood out: first, the English disliked the Scottish courtiers who accompanied their new king, and second, James's wish for political union between England and Scotland was opposed by the English Parliament. On 20 October 1604 he assumed the "name and style of King of Great Britain" but by November had confided to his ministers that full union of the kingdom should be left to "the maturity of time." James's major achievement of the first year of his reign was the ending of the long and costly war with Spain in August 1603.

As king of England James enjoyed both successes and failures. Perhaps his most successful area of policy was toward the church. James ensured that the English episcopacy and clergy were well-educated and administered a broad, national church, although tensions with the persecuted Catholic minority surfaced in the Gunpowder Plot of 1605. This conciliatory tone was also apparent in his relations with the Scottish church after 1603. Less successful was his management of English political society, particularly Parliament. When he acceded to the English throne James considered himself an experienced ruler who knew how to manage his subjects' concerns, but he failed to appreciate the differences between his realms. He was unable to tackle the principal problem facing his English realm, that of the inadequacy of the fiscal system and the spiraling costs of England's involvement in European affairs. James thus clashed with his Parliaments: the so-called Great Contract of 1610 (an attempt to replace the crown's ancient fiscal rights with an annual income tax) failed, and the king closed Parliament in anger in 1610, 1614, and 1621. James also clashed with the Parliament over the management of his household, his extravagant spending, and the influence of his favorites, most notably George Villiers, duke of Buckingham.

James died of a stroke on 27 March 1625. He left a considerable literary legacy including political works and poetry. His first book of poetry was published in 1584; in 1599 he set out his theory of kingship in *Basilikon Doron;* in 1611 he oversaw the translation of the King James Version of the Bible. His historical legacy is mixed. For centuries the hostile contemporary portrait by Sir Anthony Weldon (in *The Court and Character of King James,* 1650) of a lazy, unhygienic, and homosexual king devoted to his favorites to the detriment of his kingdoms held sway. More recent historians have stressed that James must be judged first as a largely successful king of Scotland who rescued that realm from political and religious turmoil and, second, as a king of three kingdoms (England, Scotland, and Ireland) who struggled manfully with the unique problems of multiple monarchy. They argue that James strove to avoid entanglement in the developing Thirty Years' War (1618–1648) in Europe and thus saved the lives and purses of his subjects. Although in some areas, such as the settling of Protestants in Ulster and his failure to reach accord with the English Parliament, James contributed to the problems that would beset his son, Charles I, there was nothing in James's reign that made the English Civil War (1642–1649) inevitable.

See also **Bible: Translations and Editions; Charles I (England); English Civil War and Interregnum; Scotland; Stuart Dynasty (England and Scotland).**

BIBLIOGRAPHY

Barroll, Leeds. *Anne of Denmark, Queen of England: A Cultural Biography.* Philadelphia, 2001.

Cogswell, Thomas. *The Blessed Revolution: English Politics and the Coming of War, 1621–1624.* Cambridge, U.K., 1989.

Croft, Pauline. *King James.* Basingstoke, U.K., 2003. Most accessible recent account of James's reign, stressing his role as monarch of three kingdoms.

Fincham, Kenneth. *Prelate as Pastor: The Episcopate of James I.* Oxford, 1990.

Fischlin, Daniel, Mark Fortier, and Kevin Sharpe. *Essays on Royal Subjects: The Writings of James VI and I.* Detroit, 2002.

Galloway, Bruce R. *The Union of Scotland and England, 1603–1608.* Edinburgh, 1986.

Goodare, Julian, and Michael Lynch, eds. *The Reign of James VI.* East Linton, U.K., 2000.

Lee, Maurice Jr. *Great Britain's Solomon: James VI and I in His Three Kingdoms.* Urbana, Ill., and Chicago, 1990.

Lockyer, Roger. *Buckingham: The Life and Political Career of George Villiers, First Duke of Buckingham, 1592–1628.* London, 1981.

Peck, Linda Levy, ed. *The Mental World of the Jacobean Court.* Cambridge, U.K., 1991.

Sommerville, Johann P., ed. *King James VI and I: Political Writings.* Cambridge, U.K., 1994.

Wormald, Jenny. "Gunpowder, Treason and Scots." *Journal of British Studies* 24 (1985): 141–168.

———. "James VI and I: Two Kings or One?" *History* 68 (1983): 187–209. Seminal article, the first to tackle the problem of James ruling simultaneously over more than one kingdom and the beginning of the reinterpretation of James's reign.

DAVID GRUMMITT

JAMES II (ENGLAND) (1733–1701; ruled 1685–1688), king of England, Scotland, and Ireland. James II was born on 14 October 1633, the second son of Charles I (ruled 1625–1649), and was created duke of York and Albany in January 1634. Following his father's defeat in the civil war, James spent 1648–1660 in exile on the Continent, where he fought in the service of the French and Spanish crowns, earning a reputation for bravery. Returning to England in 1660 with the Restoration of the monarchy under his brother, Charles II (ruled 1660–1685), he became lord high admiral and oversaw a period of expansion for the navy. He converted to Catholicism sometime in the late 1660s and was forced to resign all of his offices in 1673 following his noncompliance with the Test Act of that year. In 1679–1681 the parliamentary Whigs launched an attempt to exclude him from the succession on the grounds of his religion (he was next in line to the throne due to his brother's failure to father any legitimate children). Exiled to Scotland by his brother while the exclusion crisis unfolded, James had two successful stints as head of the government there, where he showed himself a firm friend of the Episcopalian interest against the Presbyterian menace.

Recalled to England in 1682, James enjoyed a surge of popularity during the Tory reaction that followed the defeat of the exclusion movement. His accession in February 1685 was greeted with numerous loyal addresses and widespread rejoicing across England, Scotland, and Ireland. A few diehard radicals rose with Archibald Campbell (1629–1685), earl of Argyll (in Scotland), and James Scott (1649–1685), duke of Monmouth, Charles II's eldest illegitimate son (in England), that summer, but both rebellions failed miserably for lack of support.

James made a public commitment at the beginning of his reign to rule by law and protect the Protestant establishment, but he soon proved that his word could not be relied upon. He began issuing Catholics dispensations from the Test Act so they could hold commissions in the army, prompting the ire of his newly elected Parliament (an overwhelmingly Tory-Anglican body), which he dismissed in November 1685. He achieved a judicial ruling in favor of the dispensing power in the feigned action of *Godden v. Hales* in June 1686 (though only after removing six of the twelve judges), which allowed him to bring Catholics into his privy council. He encouraged Catholics to celebrate Mass openly, promoted Catholic schools, and used the press to try to convince people of the merits of converting, though his missionary efforts met with limited success. When the Anglican clergy refused to heed his demand that they refrain from anti-Catholic sermonizing, James set up an Ecclesiastical Commission to discipline recalcitrant clergymen. Realizing that the Tory-Anglican interest would not assist him in his efforts to help his coreligionists, he tried to forge an alliance with the Protestant Nonconformists, hiring former Whig publicists, such as Henry Care and the Quaker William Penn, to promote the cause of religious toleration in the press. In April 1687 he issued his first Declaration of Indulgence, suspending all the penal laws against Nonconformists by dint of his royal prerogative, and embarked upon a campaign to secure the return of a packed Parliament so he could turn this toleration into law.

James also built up a sizable standing army, increasing the less than nine thousand troops he inherited from his brother to twenty thousand by the end of 1685 and adding a further fourteen to fifteen thousand over the course of 1688. On the foreign policy front, he tried to adopt a middle position between the French and Dutch interests, though his failure to take a stance against the aggressions of Louis XIV (ruled 1643–1715) toward the Protestant interest on the Continent led to widespread suspicions that he was in cahoots with the French king.

James made a serious miscalculation in trying to force the clergy to read his second Declaration of Indulgence of April 1688. Seven bishops petitioned against the royal suspending power, and though charged with sedition by the crown, were found not guilty by a King's Bench jury. When James's second wife, Mary of Modena (1658–1718), gave birth to the Prince of Wales on 10 June 1688, raising the prospect of a never-ending succession of Catholic kings, a group of seven Whig and Tory politicians invited William of Orange (William III, ruled 1689–1702) to come from Holland to rescue English liberties and the Protestant religion. William landed at Torbay on 5 November, meeting little resistance. James fled the country for France in December 1688, after first throwing the great seal into the River Thames, thereby effectively abdicating the government (although his first attempt at leaving the country was foiled by fishermen in Kent, and it took a second attempt later that month before he made it to the Continent).

James II. Portrait by Sir Godfrey Kneller, 1665. ©BETTMANN/CORBIS

James's pursuit of similar pro-Catholic policies in Scotland and Ireland alienated Protestant opinion in his other two kingdoms, though Jacobite sentiment remained strong in Ireland, where 80 percent of the population was Catholic. Hence James went to Ireland in March 1689 to launch a bid to reclaim his British thrones, but he was defeated by William at the battle of the Boyne (1 July 1690) and withdrew again to France. He died at Saint-Germain-en-Laye, outside Paris, on 6 September 1701.

See also **Charles II (England); Glorious Revolution (Britain); Jacobitism; William and Mary.**

BIBLIOGRAPHY

Primary Source

Beddard, Robert, ed. *A Kingdom without a King: The Journal of the Provisional Government in the Revolution of 1688.* Oxford, 1988.

Secondary Sources

Childs, John. *The Army, James II, and the Glorious Revolution.* Manchester, U.K., 1980.

Miller, John. *James II: A Study in Kingship.* London and New Haven, 2000.

Pincus, Steven. "'To Protect English Liberties': The English Nationalist Revolution of 1688–1689." *In Protestantism and National Identity: Britain and Ireland, c. 1650–c. 1850,* edited by Tony Claydon and Ian McBride, pp. 75–104. Cambridge, U.K., 1998.

Speck, W. A. *James II.* Harlow, U.K., 2002.

———. *Reluctant Revolutionaries: Englishmen and the Revolution of 1688.* Oxford, 1988.

Turner, Francis Charles. *James II.* London, 1948.

Western, J. R. *Monarchy and Revolution: The English State in the 1680s.* Basingstoke, U.K., 1985.

TIM HARRIS

JANISSARY. The Janissaries (from *yeniçeri,* meaning 'new soldier' in Turkish) were an elite standing force of infantrymen, first formed by the Ottoman Sultan Murad I around 1380. Legally slaves *(kul)* of the sultan, they served over the centuries as bowmen, crossbowmen, and musketeers. The Janissaries were distinguished from the main body of the army, which was made up of cavalrymen *(sipahis)* drawn from the freeborn retinues of provincial officials and notables. Janissary recruits were chosen from groups of boys who were taken into Ottoman service in periodic levies on Christian peasant families, predominantly those in the Balkans. The boys were brought to Istanbul, converted to Islam, despite Islamic prohibitions against the forcible conversion of Christians, and then trained for military service.

ORGANIZATION AND TACTICS

The Janissary corps was originally organized in the late fourteenth century when a group of prisoners of war were converted to Islam and personally attached to the sultan. It grew from approximately 20,000 men in the late sixteenth century to well over 100,000 by the early nineteenth century, even though it came to include many non-combatants in later years.

The organization became an important Ottoman military force soon after it was established because the Janissaries were perceived to be the sultan's most trustworthy soldiers as well as disciplined troops with particular small arms skill. They received special privileges and benefits to secure their sole allegiance to the ruler, with their group solidarity reinforced by the way they were organized into small companies of celibate warriors living in barracks and receiving constant military training.

The colonel of each company was called the *çorbaci* ('soup cook') and wore a soup ladle as his rank insignia to symbolize humility before the sultan although he never actually served food himself. The head of the whole Janissary force was the *agha,* one of the most important officials in the realm. He served on the Imperial Divan, ranking just below the main Ottoman viziers (ministers) but above other military commanders. The Janissaries lived together in large barracks within the cities in which they were stationed. They were forbidden to marry until they retired from active duty. Several Ottoman grand viziers and admirals had served as members of the Janissary corps during their careers.

The Janissaries' military technique was to rush very quickly into battle after a breach had been made in fortress walls or to outflank an enemy cavalry force that had already charged first. They would then attack with handguns or rifles as appropriate. In peacetime, Janissaries served as guards in fortresses and towns and as firefighters in major Ottoman cities. Although Janissaries were principally a land force, there were naval Janissaries who helped man Ottoman ships.

The Janissaries were famous for their distinctive marching style and headgear. Their special military bands are believed to have inspired military bands all over Europe. The Janissary corps was closely connected with Bektashi dervishes, a popular mystical order regarded by many Muslims as heterodox. To commemorate the Islamic millennium in 1591–1592, the sultan allowed the master of the Bektashi order and eight dervishes to become part of the Janissaries.

JANISSARIES IN WAR

The Janissaries made significant contributions to many important Ottoman victories, among them the conquest of Constantinople in the spring of 1453, the battle against the Iranian Safavids at Chaldiran in 1514, and the defeat of the Mamluk armies at Marj Dabik in 1516. In all these confrontations, the Janissaries administered the final decisive blow after a series of preliminary assaults, usually in swift gunfire attacks. Each of these encounters fueled European perceptions of the Janissary corps as a kind of Ottoman "secret weapon" able to use firearms more effectively than any adversary. Perhaps the greatest moment of Janissary victory was at the battle of Mohacs in 1526, when Janissaries were able to mow down scores of Hungarian cavalry with precise rifle volleys. Many contemporary observers believed that the quality of the Janissary corps diminished in the late sixteenth century when the sons of Janissaries, and freeborn Muslims generally, were permitted to join, and the corps' slave discipline was compromised. This assessment, however, is belied by subsequent Janissary victories in the seventeenth century. Many strains weighed on this group, including inflation and the continual devaluation of Ottoman money, which substantially lowered salary values.

JANISSARIES IN THE SEVENTEENTH AND EIGHTEENTH CENTURIES

In the early seventeenth century, when economic and social unrest threatened the stability in the empire, the Janissaries became more deeply involved in royal politics. The young sultan in 1621, Osman II, blamed the Janissaries for the Polish defeat of the Ottomans at Khotin. Osman did not trust their loyalty since he associated them with his uncle and rival, the previous sultan Mustafa I, who had just been deposed. Within a year, Mustafa became Sultan again (with his mother behind the throne), and the Janissaries killed Osman II. Many of the regicides were hunted down and executed in retribution for Osman's death, but the Janissaries' kingmaker role was in no way diminished.

Throughout the seventeenth century, the Janissaries had a fearsome reputation for fomenting unrest instead of fighting in combat. The distinction between the urban craft guilds and the Janissaries had already started to blur, a development that reduced unit cohesion and undermined the Janissaries' fighting capacity. The Janissaries came to be blamed for a series of military defeats, beginning with unsuccessful Ottoman campaigns against the Habsburgs in the 1690s that led to the Treaty of Carlowitz, the first permanent Ottoman surrender of territory to European powers.

The "Tulip Era" of the 1720s was a time when European ideas and fashions became extremely popular in the Ottoman Empire, challenging the traditional system in the wake of a string of Ottoman military failures. This era of social change, combined with the financial weakness and inept administration of the government at that time, produced tensions that culminated in a popular revolt to overthrow Sultan Ahmed III (1703–1730). Patrona Halil, a noncombatant, illiterate Janissary, led this uprising.

JANISSARIES IN THE ERA OF OTTOMAN MILITARY REFORM

Count Alexandre de Bonneval was assigned in the 1730s to modernize the Janissaries. Despite slight improvements in their military capabilities, the Janissaries still had great difficulties adapting to modern warfare and did not receive adequate funding. Further disasters were in store, such as Janissary mismanagement of naval forces that led to a terrible defeat at Chesme in 1770 during the Russo-Ottoman War.

The Ottomans then turned to another European adviser, Baron de Tott, to begin modernizing the military by establishing a naval engineering school in the 1790s. This began an educational transformation in the Ottoman military that totally left out the Janissaries. New army units with no connection to them were organized under Sultan Selim III (ruled 1789–1807) in a military and financial program called the *Nizam-i Cedid* ('New Order').

By the late eighteenth century, though, the Janissaries would prove difficult to dislodge. As their importance as soldiers waned, they had developed considerable economic and coercive power in major Ottoman cities and were able to thwart reformers' direct assaults on their status for several decades. When they were ordered in 1807, for example, to wear European-style uniforms, the Janissaries staged a revolt and put a new sultan, Mustafa IV, on the throne.

However, general reform trends worked against them. Another sultan, Mahmud II, took power in 1808, and gradually developed strong alliances with advocates of change that resulted in drastic action against the Janissaries eighteen years later. During the so-called "Auspicious Event" in 1826, Mahmud carried out a secret plan to surround the Janissary barracks with artillery and kill everyone inside. The Bektashi order, so closely associated with the Janissaries, was outlawed in the Ottoman Empire in December 1826. This incident, which occurred as enemies with more modern armies were trouncing the Ottomans, ushered in the era of profound military and social reform that extended over the next few decades.

See also **Islam in the Ottoman Empire; Ottoman Dynasty; Ottoman Empire; Sultan; Tulip Era (Ottoman Empire); Vizier.**

BIBLIOGRAPHY

Goodwin, Godfrey. *The Janissaries.* London, 1997.

Inalcik, Halil. *The Ottoman Empire: The Classical Age, 1300–1600.* Translated by Norman Itzkowitz and Colin Imber. New York, 1973.

Itzkowitz, Norman. *Ottoman Empire and Islamic Tradition.* Chicago, 1972.

ERNEST TUCKER

JANSENISM. Jansenism was a religious movement in the Catholic Church, named after Cornelis Jansen (Latin, Cornelius Jansenius, 1585–1638), bishop of Ypres, which originated in Spanish Flanders and in France, and spread to other European countries. In their struggle to assert and defend their positions, its members exerted a deep influence over church, society, and politics until the end of the eighteenth century.

HISTORY

Jansen's *Augustinus* presented the teaching of Saint Augustine on salvation and grace, though disputes between theologians on these matters had been forbidden by the Holy See (1611, 1625). Posthumously published in Louvain (1640), the book was immediately attacked by the Jesuits, who denounced it as heretical. In France, where it was reprinted (1641, 1643), the work was well received, especially by the group under the influence of Jansen's friend, Jean Duvergier de Hauranne (1581–1643), abbot of Saint-Cyran. Their center was the convent of Port-Royal in Paris, reformed by the abbess Angélique Arnauld, which attracted influential members of the nobility and the bourgeoisie; later, a group of laymen, the *solitaires,* lived next to the nuns. Under the pen name of Petrus Aurelius, Saint-Cyran asserted the authority of local bishops over members of religious orders; his attacks on moral permissiveness (laxism) irked Cardinal Richelieu, who was also weary of his criticism of French alliance with Protestant states in the Thirty Years' War. In 1638, he was imprisoned for alleged heresy in Vincennes and his writings examined for errors.

Following a general papal condemnation of the book (*In Eminenti,* dated 1642, published 1643), for breach of the directive of silence on these matters, Richelieu initiated a campaign against *Augustinus* that focused on the accusation of Calvinism. Saint-Cyran's disciple, Antoine Arnauld (1612–1694), brother of Angélique Arnauld, responded in 1644 with a defense of Jansenius. He had already expanded the controversy by attacking the Jesuits on their laxity concerning reception of the Eucharist (*De la fréquente communion,* 1643) and morality (*Théologie morale des Jésuites,* 1643). During the rebellion that followed Richelieu's death, members of the Port-Royal circle were perceived as supporters of the Fronde (the revolt of the nobles and the parlement against the monarchy); to weaken them, his successor, Cardinal Mazarin, supported by the queen regent, Ann of Austria, sought a new and stronger condemnation. For that purpose, theological assertions disputed in Paris were sent to Rome, after attempts to have them censured by the Faculty of Theology (1649) or the assembly of the French Clergy (1650) did not succeed. Alexander VII's bull *Cum Occasione* (31 May 1653) condemned as heretical five of these propositions, but despite an introductory reference to the book, did not explicitly indicate their origin.

Against Jesuit claims that in this document the pope had condemned *Augustinus* as heretical and even disapproved Augustinian theology, Antoine Arnauld disputed the presence of the propositions in the book. Following a classical theological dis-

Jansenism. Portrait engraving of Cornelis Otto Jansen. GETTY IMAGES

tinction, he asserted his compliance to the *droit* (right or principle): condemnation of possible Calvinist doctrine in the propositions, and his rejection of the *fait* (fact): that they were extracted from Jansenius's book. In reaction, French bishops, influenced by Mazarin, added to the papal condemnation an oath or formulary (1655) that asserted explicitly that the five condemned propositions were to be found in *Augustinus.* Arnauld's renewed objections caused the Sorbonne to censure and expel him with more than one hundred of his confreres (1656), after a long debate, heavily influenced by political pressure. He was defended by a member of the Port-Royal circle, Blaise Pascal (1623–1662), who, in his *Provincial Letters* (1656–1657), mocked the expulsion procedure and wittily attacked Jesuit moral laxism.

Two Roman pronouncements confirmed the bishops' ruling: *Ad Sanctam* (October 1656), which specified the presence of the propositions in the book; and *Regiminis Apostolici* (February 1665), which prescribed the pope's own formulary. The weight claimed for these decisions introduced into the debate the issue of papal authority, and more precisely the existence of infallible judgments, dealing not only with doctrine but with mere facts. As this prerogative was not yet defined (it would be, in a very limited way, at Vatican I, 1871), many French theologians rejected it in accordance with their Gallican principles, which reserved infallibility for the Ecumenical Council. Four bishops declared that they could not endorse the formulary in their dioceses; when Rome started to proceed against them, nineteen of their colleagues offered their support. In order to prevent division, even schism, Louis XIV allowed the negotiation of a secret clause of conscience allowing "obsequious silence," that is, private dissent, on the "fact." This "Peace of the Church," authorized by Clement IX (14 January 1669), allowed the Port-Royal circle to extend its influence in biblical (Bible of Sacy, 1672), patristic, liturgical, and historical studies; it also took an important part in religious controversy with Protestants (*Perpétuité de la foi,* 1669–1672). By that time, the Jansenist movement had acquired its distinctive features, above all its strong individualism, that could be perceived as a sectarian menace to the church and the state. In their obstinacy to defend their right of conscience, the Jansenists dissociated themselves from the moderate participants in the Catholic Renewal; at the same time, they provoked Roman misgivings for their defiance and government resentment for their political tactics, especially their appeal to public opinion. Under suspicion in Paris and in Rome, the leaders, Antoine Arnauld and Pasquier Quesnel (1634–1719), took refuge in the Spanish Netherlands (1685). The publication in 1702 of a *Case of Conscience* submitted to the Sorbonne was perceived as a breach of the 1669 agreement since, approved by forty theologians, it brought back the issue of the "fact" of the five propositions. The evidence produced a few months later by Quesnel's arrest (May 1703) of an extensive Jansenist network, active even in Rome, incited Louis XIV to seek a renewal of the condemnations. Clement XI obliged with the bull *Vineam Domini* (1705), which condemned the *Case* and reiterated the earlier pronouncements. As it proved ineffective, the king requested another document considering Jansenism as a whole; for that purpose were denounced excerpts from Quesnel's spiritual book, *Réflexions morales sur le Nouveau Testament* (Moral reflections on the New Testament), a verse-by-verse presentation of the biblical text, followed by adapted meditations. The Apostolic Constitution *Unigenitus Dei Filius* (1713) censured 101 passages from Quesnel's work, presented in a thematic order that explicitly established Jansenism as opposed to orthodox Catholicism, not only on the matter of salvation and grace, but on many aspects of religious life. As the specific degree of error of each passage was not indicated (the censure was *in globo,* "as a whole"), different interpretations were possible. This imprecision stirred opposition to the papal document by a minority of bishops, clergy, and laity, headed by the archbishop of Paris, cardinal Louis Antoine de Noailles (1651–1729), who demanded a clarification. Louis XIV moved to crush the protest but he died (1715) before the national council he had summoned over papal reluctance could meet.

THE CRISIS OF *UNIGENITUS*

Despite the limited areas of resistance and the low numbers of opponents, *Unigenitus* generated a crisis that was to have ripple effects. The papal constitution became exemplary of a type of Catholicism that was rejected both for its doctrinal deficiencies and its authoritarianism. This rejection also took on political tones, because of the involvement of the secular power in the conflict. After Louis XIV's death, extremist bishops, clergy, and laity, emboldened by the support offered by the regent, Philip of Orléans, in 1717 appealed against *Unigenitus* to a future General Council. Soon, however, the state turned against them, under the ministry of Cardinal Fleury, who exiled or jailed them. In 1730, *Unigenitus* was registered as law of the land, which meant that opposition to it became a civil crime. In 1749, the archbishop of Paris, Christophe de Beaumont (1703–1781), decided to deny the sacraments (and therefore Catholic burial) to those who did not assent to the bull and did not produce a certificate of confession. These measures contributed to a weakening and dispersion of the Jansenists. Many continued in their opposition, appealing to public opinion and seeking support from the parlements. Some became more extreme, as manifested in the "miracles" of Saint-Médard cemetery and the *Convulsionaries,* who associated pain with spiritual experience (1730–1760). In these instances, the spiritual confusion of the believers was expressed through miraculous cures and self-imposed suffering; at the theological level, "figuratism" or a reinterpretation of history through biblical images (J. J. Duguet and J. B. d'Etemare) was another way to voice disillusion or even despair. The expulsion of the Jesuits from France (1761–1764), and the suppression of the Society of Jesus in 1773, were perceived as a victory of the Jansenists. The events certainly demonstrated the influence of the movement, diffused through numerous pamphlets, books, and the clandestine newsletter, *Nouvelles ecclésiastiques* (1728–1803), an influence that spread through most European Catholic countries.

EUROPEAN JANSENISM

Jansenism was already present in the United Provinces, where many Appellants had settled; in 1723, the consecration of a bishop elected by the clergy without Rome's approval established a schismatic church that still survives (Old Catholic Church). In Mediterranean and Middle European countries, many of the Jansenist themes surfaced in various expressions of the "Catholic Enlightenment," which developed under the protection of the state. Though opposed to the philosophes, they favored a critical renewal of Christianity, modeled on the early church and based on the writers of the Port-Royal circle. The decrees of the Synod of Pistoia (1786), condemned by Pius VI in *Auctorem Fidei* (1794), represent this perspective. This last document, carefully prepared, avoided the imprecisions of the former ones, and condemned with precise qualifications every aspect of Jansenism.

JANSENISM AND REVOLUTION

In their resistance to the state in the name of their religious convictions, members of the Jansenist movement influenced the opposition to absolutism that prepared the way for the French Revolution, both in actions and in words. Some were directly involved in the first stages of the Revolution, but they soon disagreed on the issue of the *Civil Constitution of the Clergy* (1790). Very few actually adhered to the Constitutional church, but as its leaders, especially Bishop Henri Grégoire (1750–1831), came to see themselves as the heirs of Port-Royal, they manifested in the early nineteenth century what can be seen as the last coherent form of Jansenism.

WHAT IS JANSENISM?

During the past fifty years the issue of Jansenism has been the object of extensive research, the results of which modify considerably the classic historical perspective. Contrary to the traditional acceptation of the word, the association with Calvinism has been disproved as well as the puritanical connotation of rigorism. With their common Augustinian background, the five condemned propositions could represent a certain proximity with Protestantism, but this proximity was explicitly rejected by those concerned. As to the opposition to laxism, it was an early feature of the Catholic Renewal adopted by many, especially in the French church, against the practice of religious orders. The Jansenist movement, on the other hand, had important repercussions on early modern European history at the religious and political levels.

Religious Jansenism. Jansenism is to be understood within the larger context of the Catholic renewal that followed the Council of Trent (1545). It represents a traditional and rather conservative element that wanted to reform the church in order to recompose Christian unity. It was also a reaction against the progressive version of Catholicism offered by the Jesuits and their disciples. Jansenius's *Augustinus* was an attempt to counter Molinism (an optimistic interpretation of the salvation process) by the assertion of strict Augustinianism. His reconstruction, in contravention of the Roman ban, was presented as a defiance of the authority of the church. When the Port-Royal circle defended the book against early papal condemnations, they provided a confirmation of this perception. Later bickering on the five propositions and resistance to episcopal and pontifical judgments reflected their sectarian position. Inevitably, these difficulties with the magisterium of the church accentuated a form of individualism inherent to any reform movement. Taking as their reference an idealized early church, the Jansenists could not embrace the centralized post-Tridentine structure; instead, they favored a hierarchical system where the rule of the pope would be balanced by that of bishops, and the rule of bishops by that of their clergy. Hence there was a notable drift toward Gallican Episcopalism, and later Richerist Presbyterianism.

This divergence on ecclesiastical structures was not the only one. The other deviations condemned by the bulls *Unigenitus* and *Auctorem Fidei* suggest that, in an abstract way, Jansenism came to represent an alternative to Tridentine Catholicism, distinct by its doctrine of salvation, its conception of the church, as well as its exigence on sacramental reception, moderate devotions, access to the Bible, and liturgical participation. This ideal attracted clergy and laity, who regrouped in parishes and religious communities, eventually forming a network of faithful who shared the same goals of purification and reform, and undertook to impose it on others. This perception explains why, as they insisted on their Catholic orthodoxy, the hierarchy strove to identify their errors and to eradicate them.

Political Jansenism. The political ideal of Jansenius and of his French supporters was that of a Catholic monarch promoting the interests of the church. Their objections to the modern state account for their early difficulties and the mistreatment they had to endure. These difficulties excited a spirit of resistance, combining a "mentality of opposition" with an energetic defense of their ideas. They looked for support in the higher circles of church and state, constituted systems of influence, attacked their adversaries, and appealed to public opinion. This activism in turn developed and nuanced their "political theology." Augustinian in principle, it grew stronger in its opposition to absolutism; by the middle of the eighteenth century, some started to envision in the state the participatory polity they advocated in the church.

As a social group, the Jansenists appear more diverse than was long thought. Though significant, the participation of the nobility was limited, mostly to those who had an allegiance to the Port-Royal community, through family connections, education, and religious objectives. Especially in times of crisis, the Jansenist cause received the support of an "old style middle class," the *bourgeoisie de robe.* This social group had the education and time to be engaged in spiritual life and theological reflection. They also were concerned with the religious reform of society, primarily through education, social action, and political involvement. It is not surprising, therefore, that many of the active members of the movement, male and female, belonged to that group. But this does not support a once favored political interpretation of the Jansenist phenomenon. If undeniably Jansenist exaltation of the right of conscience represented values attractive to bourgeois ideals, Jansenist morality with its rejection of temporal achievement and its dramatic appeal to perfection could not appeal to the same bourgeoisie. Recent historiography has evidenced Jansenist influence in the lower classes, especially in towns, mostly the result of education and pastoral care. The presence and influence of women in these different groups—often decried by the adversaries—has also been documented, confirming a new perception of the movement, less elitist, both traditional and modern in its perspectives.

See also **Absolutism; Arnauld Family; Calvinism; Clergy: Roman Catholic Clergy; Gallicanism; Jesuits; Louis XIV (France); Reformation, Catholic; Reformation, Protestant; Trent, Council of.**

BIBLIOGRAPHY

Bolton, Charles A. *Church Reform in 18th Century Italy (The Synod of Pistoia, 1786).* The Hague, 1969.

Ceyssens, Lucien. "Les cinq propositions de Jansenius à Rome." *Revue d'histoire ecclésiastique* 66 (1971): 449–501, 821–886.

Ceyssens, Lucien, and Joseph A. G. Tans. *Autour de l'Unigenitus.* Louvain, 1987.

Golden, Richard M., ed. *Church and Society under the Bourbon Kings.* Lawrence, Kans., 1982.

Gres-Gayer, Jacques M. *Le Jansénisme en Sorbonne, 1643–1656.* Paris, 1996.

———. "The *Unigenitus* of Clement XI: A Fresh Look at the Issues." *Theological Studies* 49 (1988): 259–282.

Hamscher, Albert N. "The Parlement of Paris and the Social Interpretation of Early French Jansenism." *Catholic Historical Review* 63 (1977): 392–410.

Kolakowski, Leszek. *God Owes Us Nothing: A Brief Remark on Pascal's Religion and on the Spirit of Jansenism.* Chicago, 1995.

Kreiser, B. Robert. *Miracles, Convulsions and Ecclesiastical Politics in Early Eighteenth Century Paris.* Princeton, 1978.

Maire, Catherine L. "Port-Royal: The Jansenist Schism." In *Realms of Memory. Rethinking the French Past.* Vol. 1. Edited by P. Nora, pp. 301–351. New York, 1996.

Plongeron, Bernard. "Recherches sur l'Aufklärung catholique en Europe occidentale (1770–1830)." *Revue d'histoire moderne et contemporaine* 16 (1969): 555–605.

Sedgwick, Alexander. *Jansenism in Seventeenth Century France: Voice from the Wilderness.* Charlottesville, Va., 1977.

Van Kley, Dale. *The Jansenists and the Expulsion of the Jesuits from France, 1757–1765.* New Haven, 1975.

———. *The Religious Origins of the French Revolution: From Calvin to the Civil Constitution (1560–1791).* New Haven and London, 1996.

Weaver, F. Ellen. "Erudition, Spirituality and Women: The Jansenist Contribution." In *Women in Reformation and Counter-Reformation Europe: Public and Private Worlds.* Edited by Sherrin Marshall, pp. 189–206. Bloomington, Ind., 1989.

JACQUES M. GRES-GAYER

JENKINS' EAR, WAR OF (1739–1742). The War of Jenkins' Ear, an armed conflict between Britain and Spain, arose from longstanding Anglo-Spanish antagonism fostered by illicit British trading activities in the Spanish Caribbean and the determined, often brutal, attempts by Spain's colonial *guarda costa* ('coast guard') vessels to suppress such ventures. Popular feeling, incited by opponents of the Walpole ministry in London and a vigorous merchant lobby opposed to diplomatic efforts, further intensified pressures conducive to war.

The immediate events that precipitated open hostilities were the alleged sinking of several British merchant ships by Spanish privateers, the suspension of the *asiento* or slave supply contract, and the intensification of Spain's search and seizure claims against British smuggling vessels, and, marginally, the ill usage suffered by one Capt. Robert Jenkins, Master of the brig *Rebecca.* Legitimately bound for London from Jamaica with a cargo of sugar, Jenkins's ship was plundered and his ear severed by the commander of a Spanish coast guard vessel near Havana on 9 April 1731.

The case received brief publicity, subsided, but then was revived (together with other, similar incidents) during a stormy Commons debate in March 1738. Although modern research has established that, contrary to historical tradition, Jenkins never appeared personally to present the missing ear, his plight was highly dramatized and contributed to the momentum of the political opposition campaign urging an immediate offensive against Spain. This appealed to national sentiment and commercial interests alike. Temporizing, Walpole arranged the Convention of Pardo with Spain, which provided compensation for vessels lost but avoided the crucial issue: Spain's continued determination to suppress all smuggling attempts. Confronted with growing public and parliamentary indignation, Walpole finally had to yield and war was declared on 19 October 1739.

In the lackluster naval operations that followed, Admiral Vernon (1684–1757) sacked Porto Bello (in modern Panama) in November 1739, but the attack on Cartagena (Colombia) in early March 1741 failed due to spirited Spanish resistance, tropical disease, and dissension between British army and navy commanders. Commodore George Anson, operating with a small squadron off Chile, marauded coastal areas, then circumnavigated the globe in the HMS *Centurion* (1740–1744), capturing Spanish treasure along the way. Attempts to seize Cuba in December 1741 and raids along the Florida coast were largely fruitless, resulting in heavy British casualties. Gradually the war overseas petered out into desultory forays against Spanish shipping and ineffectual attempts to isolate Spain from her colonies before becoming enveloped and overshadowed by hostilities in Europe (War of the Austrian Succession, 1740–1748) in which Britain, by means of mercenary forces, supported Austria against France (who had joined Spain) and her German allies.

While in its altered, Continental dimension the war enabled Britain to contain threatening Bourbon expansionism in key strategic areas abroad during the period 1742–1748, overseas it failed to achieve the initially anticipated sweeping victory over Spain. Small-scale Anglo-Spanish clashes in Caribbean and Mediterranean waters produced little monetary or strategic gain, clearly indicating that naval action was not the solution to Britain's commercial grievances at this time, nor the key to much-needed political stability.

See also **Austrian Succession, War of the (1740–1748); Spanish Colonies: The Caribbean; Spanish Colonies: Other American Colonies; Walpole, Horace.**

BIBLIOGRAPHY

Black, Jeremy. *British Foreign Policy in the Age of Walpole.* Edinburgh and Atlantic Highlands, N.J., 1985.

Harding, Richard. *Amphibious Warfare in the 18th Century: The British Expedition to the West Indies, 1740–1742.* London and Rochester, N.Y., 1991.

McLachlan, Jean. *Trade and Peace with Old Spain, 1667–1750: A Study of the Influence of Commerce on Anglo-Spanish Diplomacy in the First Half of the Eighteenth Century.* Cambridge, U.K., 1940.

Nelson, George. "Contraband Trade under the *Asiento,* 1730–1739." *American Historical Review* 51 (1945–1946): 55–67.

Temperley, Harold. "The Causes of the War of Jenkins' Ear." *Transactions of the Royal Historical Society,* 3rd ser. III (1909): 197–236.

Woodfine, Philip. *Britannia's Glories: The Walpole Ministry and the 1739 War with Spain.* Woodbridge, U.K., and Rochester, N.Y., 1998.

KARL W. SCHWEIZER

JESUITS. The Society of Jesus (the Jesuits) is a religious order of men within the Roman Catholic Church formed under the inspiration of Ignatius of Loyola (1491–1556) and his companions and given approval by Pope Paul III (1468–1549) on 27 September 1540. A dramatic conversion from a less than pious life encouraged Ignatius's desire to further his education to "help souls," a desire that brought him to the University of Paris in 1528. In Paris, Ignatius gathered like-minded men who followed his Spiritual Exercises to attain interior peace and a clearer idea of their vocation. Together they decided on lives of poverty and chastity. On 15 August 1534 they promised to go to the Holy Land and there decide their futures with the stipulation that, if the Jerusalem trip proved impossible, they would make themselves available to the Roman pontiff. The war between Venice and its allies against the Turks prohibited the Jerusalem trip, and while waiting for any possible entry to the Holy Land, Ignatius and some from the group were ordained priests in Venice on 24 June 1537.

In January 1538 the companions—as they called themselves—gathered in Rome, where they were suspected of harboring Lutheran tendencies. Ignatius protected his orthodox reputation by seeking legal justice against his detractors. Declared innocent of all charges on 18 November 1538, the companions offered themselves to Pope Paul III for service in the church. They then faced another question. Should they remain as a group, that is, form a religious order, or should they be missioned for service as individuals? They conferred from March to June 1539, and from these deliberations the companions elected to form a religious order. Ignatius composed a "way of life," to which the pontiff gave oral approval on 3 September 1539, reputedly saying, "The finger of God is here." This rule was unique in the history of religious life in making no mention of lifelong residence in one community, the singing of the divine office in common, and the choosing of a superior by election of the local community. Ignatius incorporated these radical changes believing that this "company of Jesus" should be free to spend "a great part of the day and even of the night in comforting the sick both in body and spirit." Ignatius also composed rules that favored a more absolutist form of government with structures for its implementation. Although Cardinal Gasparo Contarini (1483–1542), Ignatius's personal friend, advocated the rule's quick approbation, the cardinal designated to formulate these rules into a papal bull, Giralomo Ghinucci (d. 1541), saw in these novelties the very criticisms Martin Luther (1483–1546) had lodged against the Roman church. Another cardinal, Bartolomeo Guidiccioni (1469–1549), also raised issue with the plan since previous church legislation outlawed new orders.

Ignatius surmounted these objections, and on 27 September 1541 Pope Paul III signed the new order into existence with the bull *Regimini militantis ecclesiae.* Pope Julius III (1487–1555) reconfirmed this "way of life" in *Exposcit debitum,* promulgated on 21 July 1550, and this is the version the Society of Jesus considers its founding document. This "way of life" or *Formula of the Institute* defined the company of men as those who desire to be designated by the name of Jesus, to serve the Lord alone and his church under the Roman pontiff, and to strive especially for the defense and propagation of the faith and for the progress of souls in Christian life and doctrine. The *Formula* specified how these goals were to be carried out: preaching, administration of the sacraments, reconciling the estranged, and providing for the poor in hospitals and prisons, works to be performed throughout the world, "even in the region called the Indies." From its inception the order's vision extended beyond the European peninsula.

GOVERNANCE

Soon after the pope approved the *Formula,* Ignatius composed a more detailed constitution that included rules concerning the order's governance and the training of its men. Jesuit formation was rigorous for its time. Legislation required those preparing for priesthood to study courses in humanities, philosophy, and theology according to the "method of Paris," a system characterized by a well-ordered approach to education that held Thomistic philosophy as the best system in which reason could defend the truths of the faith. The *Constitutions* established a governing system that placed the superior general as the head, area provincials directly under the general, and local superiors under the provincials. To promote unity within its membership, which by 1773 numbered 22,589 members working from Tibetan mountains to South American jungles, Jesuits were to write frequently to report their successes and failures and to seek advice from their superiors and provincials. Provincials in turn were to write annual reports to their headquarters in Rome. Jesuits rewrote and published these letters to promote vocations and inspire financial donations for their overseas efforts. These annual reports provide a wealth of information for historians, natural scientists, and ethnographers. The annual letters from New France, compiled by Reuben Gold Thwaites as *Jesuit Relations and Allied Documents* (1896–1901), provide one important example.

SCHOOLS

Although the Jesuits embraced a singular goal, the members employed means as varied as the countries and cities in which they labored. Though schools were not mentioned specifically in the *Formula,* Ignatius soon realized that they would be one of the best means "to aid our fellowmen to the knowledge and love of God and to the salvation of their souls." (*Constitutions,* part 4, chapter 12, paragraph 446) Since his own education benefited from the organized "method of Paris," he legislated these organizational principles in part 5 of the *Constitutions.* Although a few schools predated it, the Roman College, founded in 1551, received a great part of Ignatius's attention. This school and its method of studies, or *ratio studiorum,* served as a template for Jesuit schools throughout the world. Constantly modified, the initial ratio embedded in part 5 of the

Constitutions received a definitive articulation in the *Ratio Studiorum,* published under superior general Claudio Aquaviva (1543–1615) in 1599. Under the inspiration of this *Ratio,* by 1773 the Jesuits ran 669 colleges, 179 seminaries, and 61 houses of study for their members in formation in addition to partial or full governance of 24 universities.

Within these academic walls the order's greatest minds taught and did their research. A few names speak for many. Christoph Clavius's (1537–1612) astronomical observations provided the basis for the Gregorian calendar. Athanasius Kircher (1601–1680), one of the seventeenth century's more eclectic minds, did pioneering work in linguistic theory, archaeology, and pharmacology. Pietro Pallavicino (1607–1667), in his *History of the Council of Trent* (1656–1657), set a higher standard for historical writing, as did Heribert Rosweyde (1569–1629) and Jean van Bolland (1596–1665), historians who developed hagiography into a modern discipline. Jesuit philosophers and theologians dominated the field in the late sixteenth century and the seventeenth century. Catholic apologists, such as Cardinal Robert Bellarmine (1542–1621) and Peter Canisius (1521–1597), wrote catechisms used throughout the Catholic world, old and new. Francisco Suárez (1548–1617) wrote leading works on international law and statecraft. Luis de Molina (1535–1600) attempted a Catholic response to the complex relationship between God's power and foreknowledge and human free will.

Jesuit artists frequently traveled to create works for Jesuit colleges and their chapels. Andrea Pozzo (1642–1709) excelled as the master of perspective, particularly in his portrayal of a light-filled dome painted on a flat canvas for the ceiling of Saint Ignatius Church in Rome. In China, Giuseppe Castiglione (1688–1766) combined Western techniques with Chinese brushwork for the pleasure of the Ch'ing court. Baroque spectacle filled the Jesuit school stages, where rhetoric, drama, choreography, set design, and lighting combined to produce a moral message that moved souls toward love of the good and fear of hellfire—which the Jesuits frequently portrayed in great detail. Just as some Jesuits excelled in directing the drama on stage, others directed the drama within the individual soul. To this end they preached from the pulpit, persuaded others with books and pamphlets, and served as confessors and spiritual directors, all activities undertaken to help move souls toward their supernatural end. Louis Bourdaloue (1632–1704), Paolo Segnari (1624–1694), John Regis (1597–1640), and Edmund Campion (1540–1581) were a few of the order's great preachers.

Just as the *Ratio* provided a template for promoting education, the Marian Congregations, established in 1563 by Jean Leunis at the Roman College, served as a model for implementing spiritual reform among the laity throughout the world. Under Jesuit direction, these congregations provided spiritual counsel and structured guidance for frequent reception of the sacraments and participation in good works. Limited first to students, the groups quickly comprised all aspects of male society and became a successful means for Jesuits to implement Tridentine Catholicism's ideals and their own spirituality. Jesuits also promoted specific devotions, rituals, and practices intended to bring souls to a greater love of Christ. The Jesuits established the devotion to the merciful heart of Jesus in France during the late seventeenth century specifically to counter the rigors of Jansenism. Increased mortality in Europe during the mid-seventeenth century encouraged the Jesuits to develop the *bona mors* devotion: Friday lectures and prayers that focused on preparation for a "good death." During the late seventeenth century the Jesuits promoted devotion to the Holy Family and to Saint Joseph in an attempt to emphasize the family's dignity, especially the responsibilities of husbands and fathers. The Jesuits advanced these congregations and devotions because they best implemented the advice given by Ignatius in the *Constitutions:* the most practical and best use of personnel occurs when one Jesuit influences or has a great effect on many. Keeping this advice in mind, the Jesuits seized the opportunity to act as confessors to Europe's Catholic ruling houses.

MISSIONS

Since the Jesuits identified saving souls as their purpose, they quickly responded to the challenge of converting "undiscovered" populations of the New World and the non-Christian populations of the Indies. Francis Xavier (1506–1552), one of Ignatius's first companions, inaugurated the order's missionary endeavors by accompanying Portuguese merchants into India, the Moluccas, and Japan. Alesandro Valignano (1539–1606) inaugurated tremendous success in the Asian missionary field with his *Mission Principles* (1574–1606), a set of recommendations that encouraged the adaptation of Christian thought to Indian, Japanese, and Chinese cultures. His former student and missionary companion Matteo Ricci (1552–1610) institutionalized these adaptations by formulating Christianity within a vocabulary understood by Chinese intellectuals. His *T'ien-chu Shih-i* [1603; The true meaning of the lord of heaven] explained basic metaphysical foundations of Christian truths using a Confucian vocabulary. The mission to Japan began with Xavier's arrival in 1549 and proceeded with some success. Because the Jesuits were not able to discern the shifts in political power while confronting fierce persecutions fueled by suspicion of Western traders, Christianity was all but eradicated in Japan by 1614.

Although Christianity existed in India prior to European expansion, Xavier initiated Jesuit contact in 1542. Again where Xavier left off others followed, in part because Akbar (1542–1605), ruler of the Mogul court, in 1579 requested Jesuits to explain the Christian faith. Like Ricci in China, Roberto de Nobili (1577–1656) in India studied the documents that shaped local culture. Nobili's understanding of Sanskrit and the Hindu Vedas provided an opportunity for a deeper insight into indigenous culture and means by which Catholicism could be expressed in a non-European vocabulary. The Jesuits arrived in the New World first in Brazil in 1549 and operated extensive missions in that Portuguese colony. In South America the most spectacular Jesuit missionary success was the transfer of thousands of Guaraní Indians away from the reach of costal slave traders and into small inland cities of approximately thirty-five hundred persons known as "reductions." Dominico Zipoli (1688–1726) composed music for voices, lutes, and viols for the reductions. Sung and played by natives, the music echoed from magnificent baroque structures and amazed European visitors, who had been told on some occasions that these natives had no souls. In North America the Jesuits labored for the most part in New France but also in what became the United States, particularly in the upper Midwest, on the East Coast, and in the Southwest.

CONTROVERSIES AND SUPPRESSION

Controversies followed the Jesuits along with success. From the foundation of the order, the Jesuits had always emphasized that human nature, despite its fallen state, still had as its deepest orientation the desire to be with God, an outlook grounded in Ignatius's *Spiritual Exercises*. This emphasis on the goodness of the will situated most Jesuits in opposition to some other Catholics, who accentuated the effects of original sin and disparaged a person's ability to choose to do good outside of God's direct action. This issue touched upon a difficult theological point that attempted to distinguish the extent of a person's free will in light of God's providence and power. Known as the controversies concerning nature and grace, these controversies raged into the early years of the seventeenth century. The Jesuits' frequent acceptance of non-European rituals as a means of expressing Catholic truths further emphasized their implicit belief in the goodness of human nature. Holding that nature, human and otherwise, was not intrinsically evil, the Jesuits granted greater latitude in the performance of certain indigenous practices by converts. Nobili in India and Ricci in China allowed those indigenous rituals not perceived as injurious to the faith. Reports of native Christians wearing Brahmin designations or Chinese converts bowing before ancestor tablets left some missionaries (including some Jesuits) and theologians disturbed. They feared such practices jeopardize the efficacious action of the sacraments or could lead to synchronistic and superstitious practices.

These debates were commonly referred to as the rites controversies since they involved the propriety of indigenous ritual among new converts. The Jesuit emphasis on the probity of the will also set the order against the Jansenists, a group of Catholics who embraced the more pessimistic writings of Augustine (354–430) concerning the human condition. The Jansenists saw in the Jesuits' theology a laxity that would lead the faithful away from truly coming to grips with their sinful condition. The Jansenist Blaise Pascal (1623–1662), in his *Provincial Letters* (1656), ridiculed Jesuit theologians for what he believed was their attempt to soften moral rigor and their efforts to find causes for laxity. By the eighteenth century the Jesuits, with their strong propapal stance and resolute defense of the Catholic faith, came head to head with the Enlightenment's intellectual powers that saw organized religion as the true enemy of the rights of people.

Accusations of financial mismanagement and rumored hoarding of vast treasures fueled distrust among European leaders. Sebastião José de Carvalho e Mello, the marquês de Pombal (1699–1782), orchestrated the Jesuits' eviction from Portugal and its colonies in 1759. Other Catholic countries followed: France in 1764, Spain in 1767. The universal suppression of the Society of Jesus occurred on 21 July 1773 with the papal bull *Dominus ac Redemptor,* signed by Clement XIV (1705–1774). Because of Poland's partition in 1772, 201 Jesuits formally working there became subjects of Catherine the Great (1729–1796) of Russia, who never allowed the papal bull of suppression to be promulgated. A novitiate and headquarters for the society survived in Poland, and future popes allowed Jesuits from other areas to join this group. The papacy officially restored the Society of Jesus in 1814.

See also **Ignatius of Loyola; Jansenism; Trent, Council of.**

BIBLIOGRAPHY

Primary Sources

Backer, Augustin de. *Bibliothèque de la Compagnie de Jésus.* Edited by Carlos Sommervogel. Brussels, 1890–1932. Identifies books written by Jesuits from the order's beginning into the nineteenth century.

Burrus, Ernest J., ed. and trans. *Jesuit Relations, Baja California, 1716–1762.* Los Angeles, 1984.

Correis-Alfonso, John, ed. *Letters from the Mughal Court: The First Jesuit Mission to Akbar (1580–1583).* St. Louis, Mo., 1981.

Ignatius of Loyola. *The Constitutions of the Society of Jesus.* Translated with an introduction and a commentary by George E. Ganss. St. Louis, Mo., 1970.

Nobili, Roberto de. *Preaching Wisdom to the Wise.* Translated and introduced by Anand Amaladass and Francis X. Clooney. St. Louis, Mo., 2000.

Padberg, John W., Martin D. O'Keefe, and John L. McCarthy, eds. *For Matters of Greater Moment: The First Thirty Jesuit General Congregations: A Brief History and a Translation of the Decrees.* St. Louis, Mo., 1994. General congregations provided legislative interpretations of the *Constitutions.* An important complement to the order's fundamental documents.

Polgár, László. *Bibliographie sur l'histoire de la Compagnie de Jésus: 1901–1980.* 3 vols. Rome, 1981–1990. Bibliography of Jesuit subject matter authored in the twentieth century.

Ricci, Matteo. *The True Meaning of the Lord of Heaven.* Edited by Edward J. Malatesta, translated with introduction and notes by Douglas Lancashire and Peter Hu Kuo-chen. St. Louis, Mo., 1985.

Rienstra, M. Howard, ed. and trans. *Jesuit Letters from China, 1583–84.* Minneapolis, Minn., 1986.

Ruiz de Montoya, Antonio. *The Spiritual Conquest.* Edited and translated by C. J. McNaspy. St. Louis, Mo., 1993. A contemporary description of the reductions.

Simons, Joseph. *Jesuit Theater Englished: Five Tragedies of Joseph Simons.* Edited by Louis Oldani and Philip Fischer, translated by Richard Arnold. St. Louis, Mo., 1989.

Thwaites, Reuben Gold, ed. and trans. *Jesuit Relations and Allied Documents.* 66 vols. Cleveland, Ohio, 1896–1901. The compiled annual letters from New France.

Xavier, Francis. *The Letters and Instructions of Francis Xavier.* Translated and introduced by M. Joseph Costelloe. St. Louis, Mo., 1992.

Secondary Sources

Aldama, Antonio M. de. *An Introductory Commentary on the Constitutions.* Translated by Aloysius Owen. St. Louis, 1989.

Bangert, William V. *A History of the Society of Jesus.* St. Louis, Mo., 1972.

Chatellier, Louis. *The Europe of the Devout: The Catholic Reformation and the Formation of a New Society.* Translated by Jean Birrell. New York and Cambridge, U.K., 1989.

Codina Mir, Gabriel. *Aux sources de la pédagogie des Jésuites: Le "modus parisiensis."* Rome, 1968.

Elison, George. *Deus Destroyed: The Image of Christianity in Early Modern Japan.* Cambridge, Mass., 1973.

Gernet, Jacques. *China and the Christian Impact.* Translated by Janet Lloyd. Cambridge, U.K., and New York, 1985. Provides an alternative view of Jesuit "success" in the China mission.

Guibert, Joseph de. *The Jesuits: Their Spiritual Doctrine and Practice.* Translated by William J. Young. Chicago, 1964.

Maher, Michael. *Devotion, the Society of Jesus, and the Idea of St. Joseph.* Philadelphia, 2000.

O'Malley, John W. *The First Jesuits.* Cambridge, Mass., 1993.

Schurhammer, Georg. *Francis Xavier: His Life, His Times.* 4 vols. Translated by M. Joseph Coselloe. Rome, 1973–1982.

Schütte, Josef Franz. *Valignano's Mission Principles for Japan.* Translated by John J. Coyne. St. Louis, Mo., 1980–1985.

Smith, Gerald, ed. *Jesuit Thinkers of the Renaissance.* Milwaukee, Wis., 1939.

MICHAEL W. MAHER

JEWELRY. Until about the mid-eighteenth century, both men and women wore significant quantities of jewelry. Sixteenth-century portraits, for example of Robert Dudley, show men wearing the popular hat badges *(enseignes)* and pins *(agraffes),* an occasional earring, gold chains, often adorned with pendants or lockets, and several rings. Women could wear such pieces in even greater quantity, pinning pendants to their sleeves and starched collars and into their hairdos as well as layering shorter and longer necklaces. While certain types were gender-specific—jeweled daggers and sword hilts for men, pairs of bracelets, girdles, and marten or sable pelts with jeweled heads for women—the earlier period stands out for the types and designs they had in common. The clothing of both sexes was adorned with rows of pearls, stone-set rosettes, pairs of tassel-like aglets, or larger sets of small jewels sewn onto fabric, indicating jewelry's close connection to costume and fashion.

In the course of the eighteenth century, as men's fashion grew simpler, their jewelry was reduced to buttons, buckles, rings, and, occasionally, medals, hat jewels, and ceremonial weapons. Women wore quantities of pearls dangling from their ears and in necklaces, elaborate pins or bodice jewels (stomachers), and hair jewelry, as forms of jewelry became increasingly specialized and gendered. The quantity and quality of jewelry denoted status, yet the frequency and repetitiveness of sumptuary laws mainly proves how ineffectual such regulations were. The most expensive and elaborate jewels belonged to monarchs and the high nobility, who, however, did not hesitate to pawn them for money when necessary. Displaying fabulous jewels at ceremonial or special public occasions was required to maintain rank and standing among their peers and in the eyes of the general public. The rising merchant class and bourgeoisie developed their own, only slightly less elaborate, versions; basically, everyone wore similar forms of jewelry, but in lesser materials according to what one could afford. Costume jewelry, which always existed but does not survive in quantity from earlier periods, became a more widespread alternative during the eighteenth century. As manufacturing techniques advanced, so did the use of glass paste, rhinestones, gilt silver and brass, and prefabricated, stamped, or other types of hollow jewelry worn by larger segments of the population.

Jewelry. Bodice ornament, gold openwork in scroll and leaf design, set with diamonds and decorated with enamel, with five pendants, possibly Dutch, c. 1630. ©VICTORIA & ALBERT MUSEUM, LONDON/ART RESOURCE, NY

Important jewelry-making centers existed in all the major trade and court cities of Europe. There was such a great exchange of objects, artists, and designs that attributions to individuals, and even to particular regions, are often impossible to determine. Stylistically, the early modern period saw a fundamental transition around 1600 from narrative and colorful gold and enamel jewelry to more monochromatic, abstract, and often geometric, forms. Such designs were driven by an emphasis on glittering rows of faceted stones as gem-cutting techniques advanced and greater quantities of stones, especially diamonds and pearls, became available. The pendant, perhaps the most popular Renaissance jewel, displayed a range of subjects, from religion and mythology to miniature portraits, while the characteristic motifs of later centuries focused on large glittering rosettes, sets of graduated bows, or stylized plant forms.

See also **Aristocracy and Gentry; Bourgeoisie; Class, Status, and Order; Clothing; Diamond Necklace, Affair of; Sumptuary Laws; Technology; Women.**

BIBLIOGRAPHY

Bury, Shirley. *Jewellery, 1789–1910: The International Era.* Woodbridge, U.K., 1991.

Cocks, Anna Somers, ed. *Princely Magnificence: Court Jewels of the Renaissance, 1500–1630.* Exh. cat. London, 1980.

Een eeuw van schittering: Diamantjuwelen uit de 17de eeuw = A Sparkling Age: 17th-Century Diamond Jewellery. Exh. cat. Antwerp, 1993.

STEFANIE WALKER

JEWS, ATTITUDES TOWARD. A number of the most important shifts in European Christian treatment of Jews overlap with the early modern period but transcend its chronological boundaries. For instance, the Jewish expulsions from western and southern Europe had already begun in the thirteenth century, would peak at the end of the fifteenth, and begin to peter out only toward the end of the sixteenth century. Or, to cite another case, decisive shifts in Jewish legal status, ones rooted in the processes of early modern European state building, persisted well into the nineteenth century, not just in eastern Europe but in many parts of western and central Europe too. Furthermore, some of the distinct patterns marking how intellectuals perceived Jews or Judaism cannot be fitted into a discrete "early modern" category either. For example, the Christian Hebraist movement (Christian scholarly inquiry into post-biblical Jewish texts in Hebrew or cognate languages), though it certainly climaxed during the sixteenth and seventeenth centuries, began as early as the thirteenth century. In the meantime, popular notions about and images of Jews (to the extent that they were distinct from elite ones) appear to have changed relatively little between the late Middle Ages and the modern era. Finally, since Jews lived in different regions of Europe, there was little simultaneity in terms of their status, treatment, or relationships with non-Jews. The ritual murder trials that began to die out in late-sixteenth-century Germany, for instance, reemerged with a vengeance in seventeenth-century Poland.

These caveats aside, the early modern label is an apt one in at least one major respect: the period 1450–1750 effectively traces the years during which Renaissance humanism came to exert a profound effect on Christian perceptions of Jews and Judaism and then declined in influence. Humanism became the source of a great variety of disparate approaches to Judaism—from Christian cabala to "mercantilist philo-Semitism." One might say that humanism became the single most important *new* factor influencing intellectual perceptions of Jews during this era, until it was itself eventually superceded by the equally decisive ideologies of the Enlightenment.

CHRISTIAN HEBRAISM AND CABALA

Appropriately enough, the first domain that felt the impact of humanism was the scholarly world. Christian Hebraism did not dictate a uniform attitude toward Jews or Judaism, but it often entailed a paradoxical one. Hebraists justified their interest in Judaism by asserting that only through the Christian scholar's mastery of Jewish texts could he hope to persuade Jews of the Gospels' saving truth. This was essentially the conviction underlying the medieval *Pugio Fidei* of Raymond Martini (c. 1220–after 1284), which attempted to expose the proofs of Christ's messianic identity that Martini believed were secreted in early rabbinic works, such as the Babylonian Talmud (c. 500 C.E.).

When Christian Hebraism fell under the influence of Renaissance humanism, it perpetuated this syllogistic presumption. But now the missionary aim had to compete with another element that had been absent from the polemical writings of medieval Dominican scholars. This was the belief that a true (that is, Christological) understanding of rabbinic texts would serve not only to convert Jews but also to enlighten Christians. In other words, rabbinic literature contained information about God that was not available from the New Testament itself—a remarkable humanist gloss on the patristic justification for tolerating Jews as unwitting witnesses to scriptural truth. Such a conception reflected a number of factors: the general humanist regard for antiquity and its languages (Hebrew included), the instrumentality of the *studia humanitatis* to a genuine Christian piety, and the belief in the existence of an esoteric body of divine wisdom (including the writings of Hermes Trismegistus, Pythagoras, Plato,

Dionysius the Areopagite, and Moses) that had been lost to medieval Christians but preserved by Jews. This so-called *prisca theologica* contained not only doctrinal truths regarding the inner life of the divinity and its relation to the cosmos, the soul, and the natural world, but also coded information that would enable man to access divine secrets and harness their theurgic and magical power.

All of these elements—humanist, Hebraist, and hermetic—converged in the arguments put forward to Pope Leo X (reigned 1513–1521) in 1512 by the Christian Hebraist, Johannes Reuchlin (1455–1522). By this time, the "Battle of the Books" was in full swing, with Reuchlin and his humanist allies arrayed against the convert Johann Pfefferkorn (1469–1522), who with Dominican support had sought to suppress the Talmud and other rabbinic works as a prerequisite for bringing about the mass apostasy of the Jews. Reuchlin too was interested in Jewish conversion, but it is more accurate to say that he believed in conversion as a mode of reconciliation, one in which the ancient wisdom recovered through humanist scholarship would redefine Christianity and make it faithful to its original creed. In this "truer" Christianity, the cabala would come to play a decisive role, for as Reuchlin informed the pope, cabala was the axis around which both Hebraic and Hellenistic wisdom revolved.

Yet Reuchlin, building on the earlier Christian cabala of Giovanni Pico della Mirandola (1463–1494), represented only a minority tendency within humanism generally and Hebraism in particular. Most humanists were not Hebraists and evinced only a modest enthusiasm for Hebrew studies (witness the case of Erasmus himself). And the majority of that minority known to us as Christian Hebraists eschewed the hermetic speculations of the Christian cabalists in favor of more stolid fare: biblical exegesis undertaken with the aid of medieval Jewish grammarians and commentators whose theological "blindness" was seen to be partly compensated for by their relatively greater Hebraic competence.

Christian Hebraism came to thrive during a period when the Hebrew print industry (driven more by Jewish than Christian consumption) had come into its own, with centers emerging in Venice, Salonika (Thessaloniki), Istanbul, Cracow, Prague, Alsace, and Bavaria by the 1550s. The availability of Bibles adorned with Hebrew commentaries by such medieval luminaries as Rashi (Rabbi Solomon ben Isaac), Abraham Ibn Ezra, and David Kimhi made the "Jewish" Bible accessible to an ever-widening circle of Christians.

Yet one of the contradictory effects of this expansion was the progressive (if never complete) decline of face-to-face contacts between rabbinic and Christian Hebraic scholars. Leading sixteenth-century Hebraists like Egidio da Viterbo, Guillaume Postel, Sebastian Münster, and Paul Fagius had all benefited from studies with a Jewish teacher (in fact, all of them were students of the same teacher, Rabbi Elias Levita [1468–1549]). But once Hebraic learning became institutionalized through universities, and once an array of grammars, primers, bibliographies, and translations became available, Christian Hebraists would come to feel less of a need for rabbinic tutelage. Many became convinced they had surpassed their Jewish contemporaries (if not predecessors) as Hebrew philologists and linguists and had made Scripture their own. One might say that mastery of Hebrew thus made possible a second Christian appropriation of the Old Testament. In this light, and aside from the important though ambiguous case of Jewish apostates, Christian Hebraism did not in the long run bring Jews and Christians into appreciably greater proximity. Lacking Reuchlin's ecumenical vision, the aims of rabbinic Jews and Christian Hebraists (one or two joint millenarian adventures aside) revealed themselves to be disparate and incommensurate.

EXPULSIONS

The birthplaces of humanist Hebraism and Christian cabala—late fifteenth-century Italy and Germany—were also the two locales west of the Oder that still contained pockets of Jews. Germany and Italy constituted partial exceptions to the pattern of expulsions that by 1500 had erased the licit Jewish presence from England, France, and Iberia. What differentiated these two "countries" was that neither had produced a unified state capable of carrying out comprehensive expulsion policies. Even so, from the late fourteenth through the first half of the sixteenth centuries, German Jews endured waves of local persecutions and banishments, while Italian Jews underwent similar if less bloody ordeals between the 1490s and the 1560s.

While no single cause accounted for all of these expulsions, social and religious factors were foremost. Rulers generally favored a Jewish presence for fiscal reasons, yet governmental encroachment on the prerogatives of the estates (quasi-feudal corporate groups, such as nobility or burghers) through Jewish tax farming or money lending led to popular demands for the Jews' removal. In the imperial cities of late-fifteenth-century Germany, urban commercial decline and guild domination of municipal government made the Jews direct objects of contention between city councils, which were vying to restore judicial independence, and the emperor, who was ready to pawn such rights to the local nobility or patriciate in his relentless pursuit of cash. In this setting, an imperial concession permitting the expulsion of the Jewish population would be regarded by the local burghers as a triumph for the cause of urban Christian freedom.

In Italy as in Germany, hostility to Jews was rooted in forms of social conflict that became inseparable from and aggravated by religious antagonism. Jews, many of them migrants from the south or refugees from France and Germany, had become a principal source of credit in small towns scattered throughout the papal states, Tuscany, Ferrara, Modena, and Mantua. But with the decline of local handicrafts industries, the policy of relegating banking functions to Jews came under intense fire from Franciscans, who clamored to replace the infidel usurers with interest-free or low-interest banks *(Monti di Pietà)*. As in the German case, here too the struggle against Jewish economic power made ample use of blood libel accusations, charges that Jews kidnapped and murdered Christians (usually children) for the purpose of ritually consuming their blood. Such accusations (most notably in Trent, 1475) helped to bring about local expulsions, with the result that Jews increasingly sought the protection of powerful urban oligarchs like the Este, Gonzaga, and Medici.

REFORMATION

How did the Reformation affect phenomena such as blood libel accusations and expulsions that were already manifest when it emerged? Clearly, the Jews' demographic situation in the German lands was not profoundly altered by the Reformation, which arrived after two centuries of attrition had already taken a profound toll. In Wittenberg, where no Jews could reside, Martin Luther (1483–1546) waited in vain for a mass conversion to his restored apostolic creed (as he reasoned, given the choice between popery and Judaism, he too would have remained a Jew). What did gradually change, as historian R. Po-chia Hsia has argued, was that the reformers' systematic campaign against saintly cults, relics, and salvational "works" inadvertently undercut the association between Jews and demonic practices, such as host desecration and black magic (if not in the public mind, then at least in the juridical processes responsible for translating accusations into legal actions). This factor appears to have reduced the quantity and efficacy of blood libel trials in central Europe, even as the frequency of the charge climbed in Hungary, Poland, and Lithuania.

Such a shift is clearly apparent in the debate over the blood libel between Johann Eck (1486–1543), Luther's lifelong antagonist, and the Nuremberg Evangelical Andreas Osiander (1498–1552). It is true that neither participant exactly typified the respective attitudes of the Catholic and Protestant camps. Since the thirteenth century, popes and emperors had consistently denounced the ritual murder charge, while in the sixteenth century any number of Protestant divines subscribed to it. But Osiander's systematic refutation of the blood libel, his careful demolition of accompanying biological myths regarding Jews (for example, the Jews' supposed physiological *need* for Christian blood, as attested to by Eck), and his insistence that blood libel charges often reflected an effort to cover up Christians' crimes by leveling charges against their *economic* competitors, represented a milestone in the Protestant demystification of belief.

Though Luther himself denounced Osiander's anonymously published pamphlet, his own 1543 anti-Jewish polemic *(On the Jews and Their Lies)*, while appearing to endorse each and every fantastic claim that had been leveled against Jews since the late Middle Ages, in fact shifted the locus of Jewish criminality from the supernatural to the social psychological plane. "They have been bloodthirsty bloodhounds and murderers of all Christendom for more than fourteen hundred years in their intentions and would undoubtedly prefer to be such with their deeds." Here Luther implied that the Jews' hatred was entirely mortal, if no less dangerous, inveterate, and infernal for that. Indeed, there was nothing secret or concealed about their conniving, he maintained. The proof of it could be found in the prayers they uttered daily for the arrival of an avenging messiah and in the usury they practiced, which enabled these "lazy rogues" to "idle away their time, feasting and farting, and on top of all, boasting blasphemously of their lordship over the Christians by means of our sweat."

Luther's diatribe had little immediate impact on Jewish status; Jews were already excluded from Saxony and other regions where he enjoyed influence. Nor did his tract become doctrinal for the Evangelical Church as a whole: it was denounced by Osiander, derided by Philipp Melanchthon (1497–1560), and downplayed by most of the other reformers. Still, its echoes are apparent in later guild documents, in Christian Hebraist compilations of Jewish ritual "curiosities," and even in the anti-emancipation propaganda of post-Napoleonic German nationalists. Luther's characterization of Jews as a faux nobility, reifying their status as descendents of the chosen Hebrews in order to legitimate their usurious economic exploitation of German laborers, reverberated in a society intensely riven by social and economic divisions.

COUNTER-REFORMATION

If most of the Reformation's repercussions for Jews were inadvertent and indirect, the Counter-Reformation's shift in attitudes appears as something of a delayed reaction. The relaxed spirit of Renaissance papal policy toward Jews, permissive of Hebraist-rabbinic contacts and opposed, on both doctrinal and pragmatic grounds, to inquisitorial harassment of relapsed Iberian New Christian refugees in Italy, persisted through the 1540s. But Julius III (reigned 1550–1555), though continuing to tolerate the Judaizing New Christian merchants settled in the port of Ancona, could not withstand the mounting pressure to extend church censorship to Jewish as well as heretical Christian texts. In 1553, through the impetus of Cardinal Giovanni Pietro Caraffa (1476–1559), possession of the Talmud became prohibited and its volumes were incinerated in cities under papal domination.

The Counter-Reformation managed to resolve the church's longstanding ambivalence toward the Talmud: on the one hand, as a blasphemous, anti-Christian, and anthropomorphic abomination, and on the other, as a backhanded rabbinic attestation to Christian truth (and therefore a useful missionary tool). Even Hebraists like Pico and Reuchlin approved the Talmud less in its own right than as a repository of exegetical techniques deployed in cabala. But by mid-century the church had rendered its verdict: the Talmud was an obstacle—perhaps the main one—to Jewish conversion. When Caraffa succeeded to the throne of St. Peter as Paul IV (reigned 1555–1559), he determined to either convert the Jews or take decisive measures to prevent them from corrupting Christians (both the pope and Luther lived in dread of Jewish proselytizing). In fact, both of these ends would be pursued through the same policies. Thirteenth-century mandates such as the "Jewish badge" would now be restored and the Jews' segregation from Christians fully enforced—excluding, of course, their obligatory attendance at Christian sermons. If this degree of separation proved too utopian to be realized in its entirety, it still extended well beyond the medieval precedents, many of which had been poorly enforced and none of which had entailed the creation of walled ghettos (the impossibly congested mandatory Jewish residential quarters, surrounded by a wall with gates locked at night). Despite momentary reversals by some of Paul IV's successors, this Counter-Reformation papal Jewish policy of segregation and repression persisted through the late nineteenth century. Though it qualitatively increased the number of converts, like Luther's Reformation it failed to win over the bulk of the Jewish population. Instead papal Jewish policy resolved itself into a stalemate (or war of attrition) with its erstwhile Jewish adversary, and through the perpetuation of the ghetto appeared to render Jewish-Christian relations frozen in time.

RAISON D'ÉTAT, MERCANTILISM, AND ABSOLUTISM

One might go further and assert that the institution of the ghetto facilitated the partial revival of Italian Jewry between the late sixteenth and the mid-seventeenth centuries. In a period when Sephardic Jews came to play an increasingly prominent role in Mediterranean and Atlantic trade, any device that made possible a Jewish presence in one locale had the potential to feed its expansion into another. Twenty-three ghettos were established in northern

Italy between 1555 and 1779, and with the economic shift of sixteenth-century Italian Jews from predominance in money lending to concentration in international trade, justifications could readily be found for employing new groups of Jews, even relapsed "New Christians," to fertilize local exchange. As Counter-Reformation pressures mounted, Italian rulers rationalized their invitations to settle foreign Jews by emphasizing the contribution they would make to the commonweal. In 1593 Ferdinand I de' Medici, the grand duke of Tuscany, advertised his "worthy motives" and "hope to benefit all Italy, Our subjects and especially the poor" when he accorded generous privileges to "Levantine" Jewish merchants who consented to populate his new port city of Livorno.

Economic benefit, whether rooted in trade, credit, tax farming, or estate management, had long functioned as a sine qua non for the Jews' presence within various quarters of Christendom—witness the justification offered in 1086 by Bishop Rudiger, who, by attracting Jewish merchants to Speyer, intended "that the glory of our town would be augmented a thousand fold." What proved unique to the circumstances of late sixteenth- and seventeenth-century western and central Europe, however, was that Jews had been absent from these territories for generations or sometimes centuries. This had the effect of weakening the estates' resistance to the small-scale readmission of Jews, so long as this resettlement could be justified as fulfilling only certain limited and targeted economic duties that no other group could. Although exercised by the very fact of a renewed Jewish presence, guilds won assurances that Jews would traffic solely in commodities already excluded from regulation. It was no small irony, then, that such new goods in which the Jewish merchants specialized—including tobacco, sugar, and coffee from the New World—were among the era's most profitable.

Still, this detailed specification within governmental privileges of the exact purview of Jewish settlement and the precise limits of their commerce marked the period when absolutist government came to impose itself as the ultimate arbiter of permissible Jewish activity. What could better express the seventeenth-century apotheosis (or distortion) of humanist *raison d'état* than the baroque manner in which absolutism translated limited resettlement privileges into tortuous and seemingly arbitrary "Jews' Regulations"? Frederick II's 1750 Revised General Code *(Revidiertes Generalprivilegium und Reglement),* to cite a classic example, reveals the bind in which the absolutist state found itself. It was caught between, on the one hand, its impulse to incorporate Jews into ever more homogenous categories of subject status (a process likewise driven by the state's increasing importation of Roman law), and on the other, its institutional loyalty to the functionalist and mercantilist rationales that had made a renewed Jewish presence possible in the first place. Although there were improvements in Jewish status in the second half of the eighteenth century (for example, the abolition of the onerous *Leibzoll,* 'toll'), it took the cataclysm of the French Revolution to eventually cut this Gordian knot.

PHILO-SEMITISM

In Calvinist Holland and Puritan England, economic and Hebraist rationales for Jewish toleration combined to create an atmosphere that was distinctive from the claustrophobic regulatory regimes of Lutheran and imperial Germany or the ghettos of Catholic Italy. The Jewish community of Amsterdam had been founded by the immigration of Iberian New Christians, many of whom eventually openly reverted to Judaism. It was one of these former New Christians, Rabbi Manasseh ben Israel (1604–1657), who made a famous appeal to Oliver Cromwell, shrewdly combining mercantilist and messianic arguments on behalf of a Jewish restoration to England. Proclaiming that "the opinion of many Christians and mine doe concurre herein" that Jews will be restored to their ancient homeland only after being first restored to England, Manasseh made Jewish readmission dependent upon English recognition of the spiritual and worldly benefits Albion would accrue from the presence of a skillful population of Jewish "merchandizers."

Such arguments found a receptive audience within a segment of the Puritan and remonstrant communities of mid-seventeenth-century England and Holland. Calvinism, though at its inception an unlikely impetus to Jewish-Christian rapprochement, did exhibit at least one promising trait: a rejection—as the historian Salo Baron once put it—of "Pauline antinomianism in favor of Old Testament legalism." Yet this relative fondness for biblical law was in itself no assurance of philo-Semitism. Also required was a type of millenarian conviction entirely lacking in the patristic heritage, namely, the expectation that the prophesied conversion of the Jews would occur only through their restoration to the Holy Land. This factor theoretically made feasible what had never before been even conceivable: the possibility that *two* chosen peoples could coexist—a national Protestant one and a resuscitated Jewish one. As the widow Johanna Cartwright and her nephew Ebenezer put it in their 1649 petition to the Puritan general Thomas Lord Fairfax, "this Nation of England, with the inhabitants of the Netherland, shall be the first and readiest to transport Izraells Sons and Daughters in their Ships to the Land promised to their fore-Fathers, Abraham, Isaac, and Jacob, for an everlasting Inheritance." Truly, this was as close to a revival of Reuchlin's grand vision as any latter-day and millenarian version of Hebraism was likely to come.

CONCLUSION

But philo-Semitism is a relative term; there were, in fact, few "unconditional" philo-Semites in early modern Europe. A prejudice in favor of the Jews necessarily came with certain strings attached to it, whether it was the wealth that would be generated by the Jews' commerce or the millennium that would be inaugurated by their conversion. Philo-Semitism of this variety flowered in mid-seventeenth-century Holland and England but remained dormant through much of the eighteenth century. In this period weariness with Puritanism and all forms of "enthusiasm"—including not just Quakers but Jewish followers of the apostate messiah, Shabbetai Tzevi (also Sabbatai Sevi) (1626–1676), as well—went hand in hand with the ascent of a more "polite and commercial" Britain. Similarly, Holland's loss of successive wars and overseas markets to England augured economic hard times, a fact that could not help but dull the mercantile sheen of Amsterdam Jewry. Even so, and without minimizing the widespread enmity manifested toward Catholicism or the occasional flare-ups of anti-Semitic invective, Augustan England justly earned the sort of reputation for religious toleration in the eighteenth century that the Dutch had enjoyed in the seventeenth.

This nondoctrinal adherence to toleration, hard fought for but comfortably worn, was one of the features that Voltaire, ensconced in London between 1726 and 1729, found most attractive about English life. Yet despite their embrace of toleration and condemnations of anti-Jewish violence, Voltaire and other philosophes, like most of the deists before them, evinced a deep hostility to Judaism itself, one that reflected the spirit of the criticism they leveled at, or perhaps to diverted to, the Old Testament. This had important repercussions for eighteenth-century Jews. In premodern Europe, Jews were essentially defined by their religion. Converts might be cruelly reminded of the "Jewish malice still in their hearts," but the specimen of the secular Jew was still unknown. Humanism, short of actually converting the Jew, was not interested in abstracting him from his Judaism. Enlightenment ideology changed that. The philosophes held that the Jew was redeemable only to the extent that he distanced himself from Talmudic Judaism, without at the same time necessarily succumbing to Christianity. "As you are a Jew remain so, but be a philosopher!" Voltaire counseled the Sephardic Jew, Isaac de Pinto. Christian Wilhelm von Dohm (1751–1820), in his influential *Über die bürgerliche Verbesserung der Juden* (On the civic improvement of the Jews), put it somewhat differently: the Jew is capable of enjoying civic equality, Dohm insisted, but only to the extent that he regards himself as "more man than Jew."

In eighteenth-century Enlightenment circles, the termination of religious hatred of Jews was therefore thought to require not just Christian toleration of the practice of Judaism, but paradoxically, the Jews' own partial detachment from a faith widely regarded as a primary source of religious intolerance. The Jew's vices, his materialism, chauvinism, and greed—though in themselves universally acknowledged—were seen not as biologically determined traits but rather as by-products of the narrowness of the Jewish creed. While not at all synonymous with popular anti-Semitism, this secularist antipathy to Judaism would prove readily compatible with it. For when the Jews' behavioral characteristics refused to fade with the reform or even abandonment of the ancestral faith, the mystery of how Jews could exist without Judaism seemed to demand a solution. Modern anti-

Semitism, a product of the nineteenth century, arose to fill precisely that need.

See also **Cabala; *Conversos;* Ghetto; Haskalah (Jewish Enlightenment); Jews, Expulsion of (Spain; Portugal); Jews and Judaism; Messianism, Jewish; Reformation, Protestant; Reformations in Eastern Europe: Protestant, Catholic, and Orthodox; Toleration.**

BIBLIOGRAPHY

Baron, Salo W. "John Calvin and the Jews." In *Essential Papers on Judaism and Christianity in Conflict: From Late Antiquity to the Reformation,* edited by Jeremy Cohen. New York, 1991.

Coudert, Allison P. "Seventeenth-Century Christian Hebraists: Philosemites or Antisemites?" In *Judaeo-Christian Intellectual Culture in the Seventeenth Century,* edited by Allison P. Coudert, Sarah Hutton, Richard Popkin, and George M. Weiner. Dordrecht, 2003.

Dan, Joseph, ed. *The Christian Kabbalah: Jewish Mystical Books and Their Christian Interpreters: A Symposium.* Cambridge, Mass., 1997.

Ettinger, Shmuel. "The Beginnings of the Change in the Attitude of European Society towards the Jews." In *Studies in History, Scripta Hierosolymitana,* vol. 7, edited by Alexander Fuks and Israel Halpern, pp. 193–217. Jerusalem, 1961.

———. "Jews and Judaism in the Eyes of the English Deists of the Eighteenth Century" (Hebrew). In *Zion,* xxix/3–4, pp. 182–207. Jerusalem, 1964.

Hsia, R. Po-chia. *The Myth of Ritual Murder: Jews and Magic in Reformation Germany.* New Haven, 1988.

Luther, Martin. *Works.* Vols. 45 and 47. Edited by Helmut T. Lehman. Philadelphia, 1955–1986.

Manuel, Frank E. *The Broken Staff: Judaism through Christian Eyes.* Cambridge, Mass., 1992.

Menasseh ben Israel. *Menasseh ben Israel's Mission to Oliver Cromwell.* Edited by Lucien Wolf. London, 1901.

Mendes-Flohr, Paul, and Jehuda Reinharz, eds. *The Jew in the Modern World: A Documentary History.* 2nd ed. New York, 1995.

Peuckert, Will-Erich. "Ritualmorde." In *Handwörterbuch des Deutschen Aberglaubens,* edited by Hanns Bächtold-Stäubli and E. Hoffmann-Krayer, vol. 7, pp. 727–735. Berlin and Leipzig, 1927–1942.

Stow, Kenneth. "The Burning of the Talmud in 1553, in Light of Sixteenth-Century Catholic Attitudes toward the Talmud." In *Essential Papers on Judaism and Christianity in Conflict: From Late Antiquity to the Reformation,* edited by Jeremy Cohen. New York, 1991.

JONATHAN KARP

JEWS, EXPULSION OF (SPAIN; PORTUGAL). The Iberian kingdoms were neither the first nor the last to expel their Jewish populations: England expelled its Jews in 1290, France expelled its Jews in 1306, and periodic expulsions of the Jews took place across Europe throughout the early modern period. But the expulsion of the Jews from Spain in 1492, from Portugal in 1497, and from Navarre in 1498 has long been seen as a critical turning point in the history of Iberia and in the history of Sephardic or Spanish Jewry.

CAUSES

Historians continue to debate the causes of the expulsions in Iberia. Ferdinand and Isabella's actions in Spain regarding the Jews served as the catalyst for expulsions in the rest of Iberia, and so all the Iberian expulsions must be seen in the broader context of the reforms of their reign. Isabella fought a civil war with her niece to gain the crown of Castile after her half-brother, Henry (Enrique) IV, died in 1474. Isabella's husband, Ferdinand, inherited the crown of Aragon in 1479. Through their marriage they united their two kingdoms in what became known as Spain, but civil unrest continued for years. Only in the 1480s did Isabella and Ferdinand begin to exert authority over their dominions and to institute new methods of legal, bureaucratic, and institutional control. Furthermore, by 1482, Ferdinand and Isabella had begun a fierce war against the Muslims of Granada. In Castile, Isabella also engaged in an extensive propaganda war, justifying the legitimacy of her own reign at the expense of her half-brother's

Jews and *judeoconversos* (Jews who converted to Christianity and their descendents; also known as New Christians) came to occupy an important place in Isabella and Ferdinand's program of reform. Not only were there many Jews and *conversos* in Ferdinand and Isabella's court, but anxiety about the place of Jews and *conversos* in society was growing in the second half of the fifteenth century. Isabella and Ferdinand received permission from the pope to found their own Inquisition in 1478 precisely to punish and reform those New Christians who were believed to observe Jewish rites in secret. Many so-called "Old Christians" feared—rightly or wrongly—that *conversos* were not genuine Christians and could not be trusted in religious or political terms. Some Old Christians at the time laid the blame for this at the feet of the Jews who might encourage New Christians to Judaize as well as serve as a source of information on the details of Jewish observance. At the same time, Isabella in particular was convinced that the Apocalypse was nearing, an event that would involve mass conversion of the Jews. Most scholars, therefore, have explained the motivation for the expulsion in the context of anxiety about Jews and *conversos*. Many scholars affirm that the true motive was not expulsion per se, but rather to encourage conversion of the remaining Jews in Iberia. Others hypothesize that the expulsion was a measure designed to help New Christians avoid the temptation to revert to Judaism. Once there were no Jews to encourage *conversos* to practice Judaism, New Christians might assimilate more fully to Christianity. Still other scholars have posited that *converso* officials encouraged the expulsion of Jews to protect their own position in society, but this could not be the sole explanation of the expulsion.

THE EXPULSION IN SPAIN

The decree ordering the expulsion of the Jews from Spain was issued 31 March 1492, though it was not officially announced in many cities until several weeks later. Jews were given six months to leave. The decree met with immediate protest in some quarters by those who thought that the kingdoms should not have expelled such "industrious" people. Indeed, some of Ferdinand and Isabella's most important advisers, such as Don Isaac Abravanel, emigrated. Others worried that the decree might provoke anti-Jewish violence, which was against the statutes of the church. Many Spaniards, though, applauded the decree of expulsion and leapt at the opportunity to take advantage of it. Jews were required to sell their property and could not even take jewels or coins with them; as a result, unscrupulous Old Christians bought the property of desperate Jews for a fraction of its true value. Once on the road toward the border towns and ports that would be their last stopping place in Spain, the Jews' troubles continued. One contemporary chronicler, Andrés Bernáldez, described the sad families walking in slow procession to the border, lamenting their fate.

Despite the number of Jews who fled before the edict of expulsion, it is not clear that Ferdinand and Isabella expected or wanted the Jews to leave. In fact, it appears that many, if not most, Jews converted to Christianity to stay in the country. Perhaps the most notable convert was the chief rabbi of Castile, Don Abraham Seneor, who was baptized at the shrine of the Virgin of Guadalupe in Extremadura, with Isabella and Ferdinand standing as godparents. Exact numbers of those who stayed and those who left are difficult to ascertain, but Henry Kamen estimates that there were no more than 70,000 Jews in Castile (about 1.6 percent of the population) and no more than 10,000 Jews in Aragon (about 1.2 percent of the population). Of those, the best evidence suggests that most converted rather than emigrated. Over ten thousand Jews left via the Mediterranean coast in 1492–1493 (including Aragonese and Castilian Jews), and possibly as many as forty to fifty thousand left overall, traveling west to Portugal and north to Navarre, as well as south to Africa, east to Italy and—over time—to Ottoman territory in the eastern Mediterranean. Yet even the figure of fifty thousand may well be high, since many of those who left in 1492 had returned and converted by 1499. Isabella and Ferdinand encouraged conversion and return, promising in a decree that houses, property, and goods would be returned to their former owners for the price for which they were sold. Enforcement of this decree was inconsistent, but, nonetheless, evidence from many sources suggests that many exiles returned, particularly after Portugal and Navarre expelled or converted their Jewish populations, too.

THE EXPULSIONS IN PORTUGAL AND NAVARRE

Portugal received the clear majority of Spain's exiled Jews. Its proximity, cultural similarity, and economic ties made it an ideal destination for the unwilling exiles. Yet Portugal would not prove to be a permanent haven. When King Manuel wished to marry the daughter of Ferdinand and Isabella, the Spanish monarchs demanded that Portugal expel its Jews. Manuel agreed, and five days after the marriage agreement was signed, on 5 December 1496, he issued a decree giving Portugal's Jews eleven months to leave the country. Again, the long delay between publication of the edict and the date in which it took effect suggests a lack of enthusiasm for the project, and Manuel's actions emphasize that his primary concern was conversion. Initially, he instructed the Jews to leave from one of three ports, but soon he restricted them to leaving from Lisbon only. When October 1497 arrived, the thousands of Jews assembled there were forcibly converted. Portugal's mass forced baptisms precipitated another exodus, this time of Spanish Jews returning home.

Tiny Navarre, in the north of the Iberian Peninsula, also suffered dual pressure, first from trying to assimilate Spanish Jewish exiles, and later from the Spanish government to expel or convert its Jewish population. Benjamin Gampel estimated that in the mid-1490s Navarre had approximately 3,550 Jews (about 3.5 percent of the population). That relatively high percentage, compared to the percentages in Castile and Aragon, was certainly due to the presence of Spanish exiles in Navarre. Even more so than with Portugal, Ferdinand and Isabella exerted much pressure on the small neighboring kingdom, and the threat of Spanish annexation was constant. The decree, which has not survived, was public knowledge by the beginning of 1498 and required that Navarrese Jewry convert or leave by sometime in March 1498.

CONSEQUENCES

The economic costs to Spain of the expulsion, once thought to be significant, now seem to have been relatively minor. The number of exiles was less than previously imagined, and the Jewish communities of Spain, already reduced in size by a century of conversions, did not command the wealth of previous generations. The social costs, both in terms of the loss of individual talents and in terms of the loss of a more pluralistic society, were much greater. Contemporaries may not have acknowledged the latter; but critics of the decree lamented the expulsion of so many industrious, esteemed Spaniards. But most traumatic was the terrible cost to Jewish individuals and families, who were faced with the horrific choice of giving up their faith or their home and whose families were often painfully divided in the upheaval that followed.

See also ***Conversos;*** **Jews, Attitudes toward; Jews and Judaism; Moriscos, Expulsion of (Spain); Portugal; Spain.**

BIBLIOGRAPHY

Primary Source

"Charter of the Expulsion of the Jews." In *Medieval Iberia. Readings from Christian, Muslim, and Jewish Sources,* edited by Olivia Remie Constable, pp. 352–356. Philadelphia, 1997.

Secondary Sources

Gampel, Benjamin R. *The Last Jews on Iberian Soil: Navarrese Jewry, 1479/1498.* Berkeley, 1989.

Kamen, Henry. "The Mediterranean and the Expulsion of Spanish Jews in 1492." *Past and Present* 119 (1988): 3–55.

Meyerson, Mark. "Aragonese and Catalan Jewish Converts at the Time of the Expulsion." *Jewish History* 1–2 (1992): 131–149.

Peters, Edward. "Jewish History and Gentile Memory: The Expulsion of 1492." *Jewish History* 9 (1995): 9–34.

GRETCHEN D. STARR-LEBEAU

JEWS AND JUDAISM. The term *early modern* applies differently to Jewish than to general European history. Jews experienced no Reformation or Counter-Reformation of their own, nor for that matter were all Jews geographically "European" (between the sixteenth and eighteenth centuries approximately 30 to 40 percent lived outside of Europe proper). Perhaps for these reasons, nineteenth-century Jewish historians tended to view the modern era of Jewish history as proceeding immediately from a long Middle Ages (akin to the period Marxists traditionally ascribed to European "feudalism," roughly from the Christianization of the Roman Empire until the French Revolution). Modernity thus marked a sharp and sudden break with the past, a Reformation, Renaissance, and Revolution rolled into one. Meanwhile, the period between the expulsion of Jews from Spain and the era of the Enlightenment was cast in dark hues, a nadir in both mundane and spiritual terms, marked by intensive persecution and religious stagnation.

This depiction changed in the mid-twentieth century with a growing scholarly interest in the history of Jewish mystical and messianic movements, spurred by the writings of Gershom Scholem (1897–1982). Yet while Scholem's focus on the mystical cabala (kabbalah) and the great messianic pretender Shabbetai Tzevi (also Sabbatai Sevi) (1626–1676) gave the Jewish early modern period a distinctive cast, it also reinforced the earlier emphasis on external persecution and internal crisis. Indeed, in this new rendering, the expulsion of Jews from Spain in 1492 came to be seen as the root cause of virtually all changes in Jewish life in subsequent centuries.

In the last several decades—building on the earlier research of figures like Salo W. Baron, H. H. Ben-Sasson, Cecil Roth, Jacob Katz, and Selma Stern—Jewish historians have complicated this picture considerably. Among other things, they have offered a multifarious portrait of Jewish culture in early modern Italy and a more coherent picture of the key role played by mercantilist policies in shaping Jewish demography, economic activities, and political fortunes. The spiritual plight, economic importance, and cultural contribution of Iberian *conversos* (forced converts to Christianity in the period 1391 to 1497, many of whom secretly practiced Judaism) have also received renewed scholarly attention. These advances have tended to underscore the utility of the designation "early modern," albeit only when appropriately adjusted to fit the Jews' distinctive geographic and cultural-religious experiences.

DEMOGRAPHY AND GEOGRAPHY

The Jewish early modern period is marked by dramatic demographic shifts. The Iberian expulsions of the late fifteenth century left only small pockets of Sephardic Jews within Christendom and spurred new Jewish settlement in North Africa, Greece, Turkey, and Palestine. The Ashkenazic Jews of Germany likewise declined through expulsions and migrations between the late fourteenth and mid-sixteenth centuries, a factor that contributed to the explosive expansion of Polish Jewry from the mid-sixteenth century on. Moreover, from the late sixteenth to the early eighteenth century, small numbers of Jews were readmitted to France, Holland, Germany, and England. Part of this latter process involved a segment of the Portuguese *converso*, or "New Christian," population, a number of whom had retained familial and commercial ties with the expelled Jews. Some of these—the so-called Marranos, who continued secretly to practice Judaism in Iberia—migrated to Spanish or Portuguese colonies in the New World, or fled to towns along the European Atlantic seaboard, where they were often eventually able to revert openly to Judaism. The consequence of these population movements, as historian Jonathan Israel has remarked, was to ensure the distribution of Jews and New Christians to many of the key nodes of Western trade (Iberia, Italy, the Balkans, Poland, central Europe, the Atlantic seaboard, and the New World). This, in turn, made it possible for Jews to become a leading commercial force from the middle of the sixteenth to the end of the seventeenth century.

Expulsions and migrations. Expulsions from Spain (Castile and Aragon in 1492) and neighboring regions (Navarre in 1498, Provence in 1500, Sicily in 1492, and the Kingdom of Naples in 1541), as well as the forced conversion of the entire Jewish population of Portugal (including tens of thousands of Spanish refugees) in 1497, shifted the Jewish center of gravity, demographically and culturally, into the eastern zones of both the Mediterranean (North Africa, Palestine, Turkey, Bulgaria, and Greece) and Europe (Poland). The Ottoman conquest of the Balkans, Bulgaria, and large portions of Hungary complemented this eastward (or southeasterly) movement by opening avenues of migration into the Turkish hinterlands (and, to a lesser extent, facilitating the movement of Sephardic Jews to Buda and other Ottoman-controlled Hungarian locales). At the same time, due to the lack of state centralization, Jewish expulsions in sixteenth-century Germany and Italy resulted in a significant degree of "internal migration." In the German and central European case, this meant dispersion into the countryside and villages; in the Italian, it entailed an increased concentration within the provinces of Mantua and Tuscany, in Ferrara, and in the cities of Venice and Livorno, in many cases within walled ghettos.

It is important to keep in mind that not all Jewish population movements resulted from expulsions. Voluntary migration had accounted for the Jews' original presence in many parts of Europe and recurred throughout the Middle Ages. The most notable case during the sixteenth century was Poland. With the 1569 Union of Lublin formally uniting Poland and Lithuania (confirming a dynastic union of 1386), the nobility dangled extensive privileges to lure Jews to the frontier regions of the east. Large numbers of Jews shifted from more urbanized western and central Poland to the regions of Lithuania, Little Russia, and western Ukraine ("borderlands"). It is estimated that between 1568 and 1648 the Jewish population of eastern Poland increased twelvefold. Moreover, beginning in the second half of the seventeenth century, a reverse trend of sorts came into effect, with Polish Jews trickling back to the West, a phenomenon that increased with the exponential growth of the eastern European Jewish population, and that reached its climax in the late nineteenth century.

It should also be noted that an account of Jewish expulsions, migrations, and resettlements does not readily fit into a single schematic sequence. Although the most sustained wave of expulsions extended from 1470 to 1570, local ones persisted through the seventeenth and eighteenth centuries, including the notorious cases of Vienna (1670) and Prague (1745). Even the period's general eastward trend was counteracted by a tendency, already apparent by the middle of the sixteenth century, to draw so-called "Levantine" Jewish merchants back from Turkey and the Balkans into Italy and to lure Iberian "New Christians" into southwestern France (Bordeaux and Bayonne), an increasingly attractive prospect with the intensification of the Portuguese Inquisition in 1579. A year later, Portugal's union with Spain intensified the exodus of Jews from Iberia to Livorno, Venice, Brazil, and Antwerp. A community of *converso* Jews had remained in Antwerp throughout the first half of the century, growing steadily in numbers and prosperity until the mid-1580s, while after the 1595 Dutch blockade against Spanish shipping, *conversos* sought refuge elsewhere, establishing new trading centers in Amsterdam, Rouen, and (though as yet only as New Christians) in London. Even the Hanseatic port city of Hamburg, long prohibited to Jews, permitted a *converso* settlement at this time. The Hamburg city council insisted upon the *conversos'* commercial value despite a public clamor to expel them for crypto-Judaizing activities. At the same time, the new Sephardic presence encouraged Ashkenazic Jews to trickle into the Netherlands, as well as Altona and eventually Hamburg itself.

International trade. As a consequence of these population shifts, Jews became positioned as key players in the burgeoning international trade of the late sixteenth and early seventeenth centuries. Commerce linked the far-flung Jewish diaspora from the Jewish communities in the Ottoman lands and Poland in the East to the New Christian merchants in Iberia and South America and their Jewish Marrano cousins in southwest France, Amsterdam, and Hamburg. (Sincere "New Christians" often continued to do business with crypto-Judaizers or returned Jews, even when bitterly at odds religiously.) Between 1550 and 1630 Jews dominated the important overland commerce through the Balkans and played an important role in the Vistula lumber, grain, and fur trade. They likewise had a hand in overseas commodity trades, including tobacco, sugar, Brazil wood, alcohol, and slaves, as well as brokerage and the refinement of imported raw materials, such as diamond cutting and tobacco processing in Amsterdam and coral polishing in Livorno. By the seventeenth century the mere appearance of Jewish commercial prominence in so wide a range of locales often functioned to persuade rulers to open their territories to Jews, who operated not just as merchants but also increasingly as lenders and financial agents to crowns.

Court Jews. These developments helped make possible the rise of the court Jews *(Hofjuden)* in western and central Europe, a phenomenon that reached its acme in the period 1650–1750. The political aftermath of the Peace of Westphalia (1648), with its fractured sovereignties and attendant proliferation of state bureaucracies and armies, created a crushing need for cash on the part of states both large and small. Jewish financiers not only paid troops but also mastered the art of supplying armies in the field. The Hanover court factor, Leffmann Behrens, for instance, started as a financial intermediary between Louis XIV (ruled 1643–1715) and his ally Duke John Frederick (1625–1679), then served as a military supplier and financier to John's brother Ernest Augustus (1629–1698) (along the way helping him raise the colossal funding needed to purchase a position as the ninth elector of the imperial college), and then, in a final incarnation, became an unofficial finance minister for George Louis (1660–1727), later George I of Great Britain (ruled 1714–1727).

Jews like Behrens formed the top echelon of an elaborate network of money, credit, and supplies, linked by religion, skills, and marriage. Yet the court Jews' demise was often as remarkable as their rise. Samuel Oppenheimer (1630–1703) brilliantly served Emperor Leopold I (ruled 1658–1705) as banker and military supplier through the War of the League of Augsburg (1688–1697) before his master (never an admirer of the Jews) abandoned him to the angry Viennese mobs. A similar fate befell the still more flamboyant and reviled Joseph Süss ("Jew Süss") Oppenheimer (1698–1738) who, much to the chagrin of his Protestant subjects, became the virtual viceroy to the Catholic Duke Karl Alexander of Württemberg. With the duke's death, Jew Süss was summarily tried and executed, his remains left on public display in an iron cage. In earning extensive privileges for themselves by strengthening royal centralization against the jealous local estates (quasi-feudal corporate groups), the court Jews rendered their own circumstances intensely vulnerable. Still, no matter how precarious their individual fortunes, the entitlement to settle their Jewish entourages usually endured, such settlements becoming beachheads for many a fledgling Jewish community in the seventeenth century, scattered through Germany, Austria, Holland, Denmark, and Hungary.

Eastern Europe. In Poland, where by the 1600s a majority of European Jews lived, the court Jew phenomenon found its counterpart in the institution of the *arendator,* a lessee of economic privileges on noble estates in Poland, Lithuania, and Ukraine. The opening up of latifundia during the fifteenth and sixteenth centuries—making possible a Baltic grain trade whose vast expansion facilitated the enserfment of the Ukrainian peasantry—drew Jews into the towns and villages of Lithuania and western Ukraine to assist the nobility's economic exploitation of the eastern territories. In return for their services to the magnates, Jews won increasing religious, residential, and occupational freedoms, including protections against collective punishments and ritual murder accusations, limited rights to own real estate, and freedom to engage in a widening array of professions. With an expanding population, the Jewish economy became increasingly complex, diversifying well beyond the Jews' traditional banking and tax farming activities into crafts, transport, and estate administration. The price for all this, however (in addition to mounting taxes), was the Jews' insinuation into the dangerous and oppressive *arenda* regime.

The 1648 peasant backlash against the exploitative system, aggravated by religious tensions among Greek Orthodox, Catholics, and Jews, and inflamed by Ukrainian Cossacks' resentment against their misuse by the Polish crown, led to a ferocious rebellion under the generalship of Ukrainian hetman Bohdan Khmelnytsky (1595–1657). The Cossack phase of the conflict lasted until 1655 and exacted a devastating toll on Jewish population centers throughout Podolia, Volhynia, southwestern Lithuania, and even part of Galicia and central Poland. While contemporary chronicles exaggerated the extent of the loss, as many as 40,000 people—a quarter of Polish Jewry—may have perished. The Khmelnytsky uprising became the largest Jewish massacre before the twentieth century. But while the devastation created a drastic refugee crisis (the Cossack rebellion was followed by invasions from Sweden and Muscovy lasting through 1667) and accelerated Jewish migration to the West, it did not stem the tide of overall Jewish economic and demographic expansion in eastern Europe. On the contrary, within a century of the uprising the Jewish population reached one half million, with Jews becoming a key commercial force in an eighteenth-century Poland beset by economic woes.

Economic decline. In contrast to the early sixteenth century, Jews in the eighteenth century found themselves residing throughout the Continent, though in small numbers in western Europe. Yet now the mechanisms that had allowed for their restoration and distribution—the overland Balkan trade; Dutch overseas commerce with the New World, North Africa, and India; war and state building in the petty sovereignties of central Europe—had diminished in importance or were no longer operative. Jews were ill placed to take advantage of the new commercial centers and dynamic forces fueling a changing European economy, such as British colonial trade, early industrialization, and regional, intrastate as opposed to trans-European or intercontinental trade. Even the growing importance of Jews in Poland seemed to go hand in hand with that land's political and economic decline, or so many anti-Semites believed. Polish Jewry's demographic growth fed emigration and itinerancy, thus aggravating the existing poverty of sister communities in central and western Europe. By the end of the early modern period a widespread perception emerged in the European press of an internal Jewish social crisis, leading to demands for Jewish political and occupational reform at the dawn of the modern age.

JEWISH SELF-GOVERNMENT

The autonomous community. In the wake of the Khmelnytsky massacres, Rabbi Nathan Hanover (d. 1693), himself a Polish refugee living in Livorno, concluded his chronicle of the devastation with an extensive elegy for the golden era of Polish Jewry, which he believed had now come to an end. In this idealized portrait, Hanover praised the features of Polish Jewry that made it so exemplary: its devotion to religious learning and scholarship, its highly developed and meritocratic system of religious education, its generous charitable institutions, and, finally, its extensive network of religious and civil courts and local, regional, and national administration. According to Hanover's depiction, Jews lived in a self-enclosed world, sealed off from all corrupting non-Jewish influences. "Never was a dispute among Jews brought before a Gentile judge or before a nobleman, or before the King . . . and if a Jew took his case before a Gentile court he was punished and chastised severely."

Despite Hanover's exaggerated claims (in seventeenth-century Poland, powerful Jewish interests—merchants, tax farmers, *arendators*—rarely hesitated to enlist non-Jewish authorities on their own behalf), Polish Jewry did enjoy a degree of autonomy almost unprecedented in the history of the diaspora, with self-governing institutions that extended from the municipal to the federal level. In earlier centuries the Polish crown had appointed chief rabbis for the entire Jewish community; such efforts died out by the middle of the sixteenth century when Jews won the right to administrative autonomy, even at the "national" level. Indeed, the crown benefited fiscally and the Jews administratively from the establishment of the Council of the Four Lands (first documented in 1581) and the Council of the Land of Lithuania (1623). Both were annual or biannual synods composed of delegates from regional Jewish councils who were entrusted with formulating general policies and recommendations for the Jewish population as a whole. Indeed, these councils exerted an influence well beyond their own lands, intervening on occasion in the internal disputes of other Ashkenazic communities (for example, Frankfurt, 1615–1628, and Amsterdam, 1660–1673), a development that underscored Polish Jewry's newfound preeminence in the early modern period numerically, institutionally, and intellectually.

The autonomous Jewish community had derived its historic legitimacy from two sources: the consensus of its constituent members, made sacred through oaths and rights of excommunication *(herem)* and the independent, quasi-corporate standing conferred upon it in governmental charters, such as that granted by Casimir the Great in 1364 and renewed periodically by his successors. Membership rights in the community *(kehillah)* were the prerogative of the Jewish municipal government *(kahal),* rooted in local custom and conditioned by changing economic circumstances. Such membership, though normally heritable, did not automatically transfer to a new spouse; on the contrary, despite the premium placed on marriage in Judaism, communities exercised strict control over marriage and settlement. The medieval formula, according to which one acquired town citizenship by residence for "a year and a day," did not apply to the Jewish community of this period, which imposed waiting periods of between six and twenty-five years on prospective members, again depending on economic circumstances. On the other hand, visitors remaining for longer than several weeks were subject to special taxes—the city of Kassel, for example, required outsiders lingering more than a month to pay all of the taxes normally imposed on residents, in addition to the tolls to which travelers and merchants were otherwise subject. Itinerants might receive initial assistance with food and shelter, but they would be sent packing after a few days. Especially in northern and eastern Europe, by the second half of the seventeenth century, when population growth, war, and increased regional economic integration vastly multiplied the number of Jewish beggars, communities felt forced to impose strict rules against sheltering wanderers. In 1623 the Council of the Land of Lithuania insisted that "no beggar whatsoever shall be given anything except transportation to send him away; neither shall he be kept in one's house for more than twenty-four hours." The Jewish community was responsible for its own poor (if no kin were able) and could not support outsiders too, a factor that further aggravated the problems of homelessness and mendicancy.

Oligarchy. As social divisions widened, particularly in the larger communities, a trend toward oligarchic rule emerged. In theory, ultimate authority resided in the consensus or majority rule of the entire community, meaning, essentially, all married male taxpayers. Yet by the sixteenth century, Jewish communities throughout Europe entrusted the election of municipal officers to "the majority of wealth." Indirect election became the rule, with taxpayers of sufficient property choosing an initial assembly that in turn elected—depending on the community's size—two or three tiers of officers (in Poland: *tovim,* 'good men'; *zekenim,* 'elders'; and *parnasim,* 'pillars') for an annual term. The position of community executive was usually rotated on a monthly basis. Stiff regulations against reappointment and nepotism were enacted, though increasingly observed in the breach. Indeed, private money was an essential ingredient of community government. At times offices might be directly purchased—though this abuse was vigorously condemned in community record books *(pinkasim)* and rabbinic preachments. But even short of such extreme cases, serving as an officer was a privilege of wealth, indeed, one that might carry numerous costs. The privilege of self-government came at a price, since every appointment of new officers had to be ratified by the ruler or his agent, entailing the payment of a sizable fee on each occasion. Rulers generally made officers personally responsible for unpaid community debts and taxes, imprisoning them to extort the fine if necessary. For this reason, communities felt justified in imposing penalties on wealthy individuals who declined to serve.

Institutions. The religious prerequisites for the existence of a Jewish community were a prayer quorum *(minyan)* of ten adult males, a cemetery, a kosher slaughterer *(shochet),* and a ritual bath *(mikvah).* If a community's small size made any of these prohibitive, it would seek to affiliate with its nearest neighbor. A rabbi was not strictly necessary so long as a lay member possessed a respectable mastery of Jewish law. If no man was able, knowledgeable women would also sometimes serve as unofficial guides to the law and (in early modern Italy, at least) ritual slaughterers. The rabbinate became professionalized throughout Europe in the late Middle Ages, but financial arrangements for hiring rabbis differed according to region; in Poland, for instance, the rabbi received a salary as well as specified tax exemptions and monopoly rights; in Italy, on the other hand, he earned merely a nominal fee, which he had to supplement through teaching, preaching, writing, or business. Still, any community that could afford to have a rabbi did so, for he epitomized its highest values and embodied its authority. He was both teacher and judge—even if in reality his personal power was often subordinate to that of the lay communal leadership.

Once the framework of local government was in place, its chief functions were to collect taxes (for its own administration and on behalf of the government); to maintain good relations with the authorities (often entailing a special functionary, the *shtadlan,* as "lobbyist," and always requiring the allocation in the budget of special funds for "gifts"); to ensure internal order and observance of the law (civil and religious); to appoint clerical officials (a rabbi and religious teachers) and lay judges to oversee local courts; to provide essential services, such as health facilities and teachers for the children of the poor; to appoint and supervise special officers, such as those responsible for tax assessment or truancy enforcement; and to oversee committees *(hevrahs)* engaged in specific activities (both ritual and civic), such as the burial society *(hevrah kadisha)* or artisan fraternities, as well as those engaged in poor relief and other charitable pursuits (for example, providing dowries to enable poor girls to marry). With the expansion of the size and complexity of Jewish communities and the intrusion of class polarities, such *hevrahs* proliferated. They allowed for participation by the middling ranks in community bodies otherwise inaccessible to them. In fact, though most *hevrahs* were restricted to males, a minority also offered a rare channel for women to participate in self-governing organizations. *Hevrahs* were mutual aid societies in life and death, providing charitable funds to help the family of a deceased member, as well as intercessory prayers on behalf of their souls. They were vehicles for the expression of new forms of spiritual creativity, even quasi-autonomous loci for an emergent Jewish civic society. But whatever their specific functions, it is important to keep in mind that such *hevrahs* were viewed as religious institutions and not political ones.

Education. Public education at the elementary level, to the extent that it existed, was for the children of the poor alone. Poor but promising scholars were objects of private charity; it was considered a great religious virtue *(mitzvah)* to feed and house a penurious Talmudist. While valued as an end in its own right, scholarship also provided an avenue of social mobility and could secure a marriage into a wealthy family. Such meritocratic virtues served to elevate scholars and denigrate the illiterate. Promising children were urged to advance through the curriculum as rapidly as possible. Pedagogical theory held that the earlier something was learned, the longer it would be retained, and for this reason, ambitious parents sought to teach their sons to read Hebrew from as early as the age of two. As a proud father recorded in sixteenth-century Italy, at three his son began his religious studies, at four he chanted from Scripture, at five he learned to write, at eight he studied the legal codes, and at twelve he learned ritual slaughtering and led the morning service in synagogue. A childhood so attenuated—the process completed, as the historian Roberto Bonfil notes, even prior to any bar mitzvah rite of passage—expressed the premium placed by Jewish society on boys' achieving early intellectual maturity. Maturity for girls, on the other hand, meant early marriage (from twelve or thirteen up). The community placed no value on a girl's religious education (and only a wealthy family might train a girl in some secular arts), except that pertaining to the dietary rules and laws of ritual purity. Schools for girls, such as the one established in Rome in 1475, were rare. Nevertheless, learned women, self-taught or instructed by a parent, appear repeatedly in the early modern sources. Women's spirituality—exclusive of their domestic roles—found expression in special Yiddish prayers *(tekhines)* and moralistic stories, and through the communal experience of the *hevrahs* and their charitable and devotional activities.

Finances and taxes. The Jewish community was as much an economic institution as a social and religious one. What this meant in practice was that the *kahal,* in its corporate status, frequently engaged in business transactions, loans (as both lender and borrower), and the leasing of franchises. (A Jewish community in early modern Poland-Lithuania might be a general *arendator,* subletting specific functions to individual community members.) In late medieval Germany, entire communities, ostensibly the "property" of the crown, were pawned to princes, nobles, or municipalities to generate cash. Jewish communities frequently found themselves deeply in debt—to individual members of their own communities or to Christians (in Poland-Lithuania, monasteries in particular thrived on loans to Jewish communities for periods often lasting generations). The trend toward oligarchic rule tended to dampen the fortunes of the *kahal,* since corruption, tax exemptions for the wealthy, the growing burden of poor relief, and mounting interest on community debts placed communal financial burdens increasingly on the backs of the middle stratum of "householders" *(ba'ale batim).*

Paying for communal services and privileges entailed a wide array of taxes. The Jewish community received assessments from state and local governments based on its ascribed population size and then apportioned the fiscal responsibility of its individual members. This created considerable overlap between "external" and "internal" taxation, with the former generally taking the form of capitation and property taxes and the latter sales taxes on commodities and fees on services. The *kahal*'s ingenuity was continuously tested by increased demands from above. Taxes on kosher meat and candles for the Sabbath and holidays proved particularly onerous, since these items were religiously obligatory. These taxes began as community imposts but were eventually seized upon by governments as their own. Ritual items like citrons (for the autumnal "Festival of Booths" [Sukkoth]) as well as "luxury" items like tobacco were likewise taxed. The community imposed sales taxes not just on types of commodities but on the types of professions that produced them. For instance, eighteenth-century Cracow taxed all transactions by peddlers, jewelers, bakers, and tailors, among others, at fixed rates, regardless of their character or size. Indeed, marriage, death, and taxes went hand in hand since dowries and burials were often taxed as well.

Eighteenth-century developments. The imposition of tax upon tax mandated by indebtedness and state demands, interference in the *kehillah's* internal affairs by overweening magnates, increased oligarchic manipulation of the instruments of Jewish self-government, growing economic and social differentiation within the Jewish community, jurisdictional disputes between large Jewish communities and their numerous suburban satellites, and the eventual emergence of a strong Jewish artisan class jealous of its fraternal ties all conspired to transform if not destroy the traditional autonomous Jewish community in eastern Europe by the eighteenth century. In 1764, in an effort to extract more funds from the Jewish population, the Polish *sejmiki* dissolved the Council of Four Lands, thus ending one of the more remarkable experiments in the history of Jewish diaspora autonomy. With the Polish partitions of 1772, 1793, and 1795, the bulk of Polish Jewry fell under the administration of Prussia, Austria, and Russia, each with different policies affecting the future of the self-governing Jewish community.

Central, southern, and western Europe. Since medieval times the Jews of Germany and central Europe had made periodic use of rabbinic synods to deal with pressing political, economic, or religious problems. As absolutism became the order of the day, these interregional synods waned and were eventually replaced by regional councils or *Landjudenschaften,* backed, or sometimes even created, by the princes. Indeed, court Jews—acting as both agents of the crown and community lobbyists—would frequently play decisive roles in these bodies, at times even occupying the position of "state rabbi" *(Landesrabbiner).* Crown interference in the internal mechanism of the *Landjudenschaften,* a phenomenon that intensified in the eighteenth century, was not the only curb on their power and prestige, however. Perhaps more significant was the fact that a number of the major Jewish communities of central Europe—Vienna, Berlin, Prague—lay outside their jurisdiction. The increased independence of large urban communities in central Europe offered greater opportunities toward the end of the eighteenth century for institutional experimentation and religious reform.

A similar situation presented itself in Italy, where regional and peninsula-wide synods were held in the fifteenth century (Bologna, 1415; Florence, 1428; Ravenna, 1442–1443), but where localization was becoming the norm in the seventeenth. In Italian cities, as in Amsterdam, Hamburg, and Paris (not to mention throughout the Balkans and the Ottoman lands), Jewish community life was also fragmented by other centrifugal forces, such as linguistic and cultural divisions between Castilian, Aragonese, Portuguese, German *(tedesco),* Romaniot (Greek-speaking Jews), and other ethnic enclaves. In these settings communal solidarity transcending country of origin would have been unlikely, to say the least. Different rites and customs and endogamous marriages usually went together with different synagogues, cemeteries, and communal administrations. While each communal leadership demanded absolute obedience from its constituency, such institutional multiplicity and functional overlap tended in the long term to undermine the authority and prestige of autonomous Jewish institutions.

If these factors—state interference in the functioning of the super-communities, major urban communities that increasingly went their own way, and internal ethnic divisions—weakened Jewish self-government throughout Europe, they did not in themselves destroy it. On the contrary, in the "backward" societies of eastern Europe, unaffected by the French Revolution or liberal capitalism, the Jewish community persisted well into the nineteenth century, despite social divisions and frequent attacks on its legal basis and moral character.

RELIGIOUS AND INTELLECTUAL DEVELOPMENTS

Jewish law **(halakhah).** In the early modern as in the medieval period, Jews assumed that the proper and necessary expression of Jewish life was through the observance of Jewish law *(halakhah).* This was true even of the Marranos or crypto-Jews: their "Jewishness" expressed itself, inter alia, as the unfulfilled aspiration to observe the commandments of the Torah. For this reason, meaningful discussion of the inner life of the Jews of the early modern period must begin with the *halakhah.*

The *halakhah* was a highly elaborated system of study and praxis, based on the Mosaic law, alongside the "oral law" that, according to ancient custom, had been passed down from generation to generation as part of the original revelation at Mount Sinai. Scriptural and oral law were reintegrated, so to speak, both as a literary corpus and as a practical system of observance by scholars (rabbis) active between the second and sixth centuries in Palestine and Babylonia. The laconic Mishnah (c. 200 C.E.) and the vast "sea" of the Babylonian Talmud (c. 500 C.E.)—the latter a compendium of scriptural and Mishnaic commentary, lore, and rabbinic hagiography—defined much of rabbinic Judaism and constituted the broad ideological and practical foundation for Jewish existence. Mastery of the Talmud—meaning not just its numerous tractates but also the successive layers of commentary and analysis that had evolved over generations—was also the prerequisite for entrance into the rabbinic class. Talmudic principles had to be applied and adapted to the specific circumstances of daily life as they emerged in different historical settings. Thus, a great deal of rabbinic literature is a literature of legal analysis, including commentaries on one or another aspect of the Talmudic corpus, codes of Jewish law, *hiddushim* (collections of legal *novellae* inferred from Talmudic literature and precedent), and *responsa* (answers by leading scholars to queries sent by letter from local rabbis regarding specific practical *halakhic* problems).

Responsa *literature and legal codes.* Because of the upheavals caused by wars, expulsions, migrations, and resettlements, the sixteenth and seventeenth centuries abounded in *responsa* literature. Much of it concerned banal or not particularly topical issues, for instance, the use of embroidered images on a synagogue curtain, the legality of employing non-Jewish musicians at weddings or of divorcing a wife for her refusal to relocate to the land of Israel. But a considerable number of *responsa* from this period reflect larger historical changes: disputes over jurisdiction and custom that arose when new settlements of exiles developed side by side with older established communities, for example, or uncertainty over the status of marriages, divorces, and inheritances when one or several members of a family had converted to Christianity—as was not infrequently the case with Jews leaving Iberia. In Poland, topical problems such as population growth, the rise of the *arenda,* the subsequent spread of novel economic relationships, and, later, as a consequence of the Khmelnytsky massacres, the proliferation of widows ineligible for remarriage (because Jewish witnesses could not attest to the deaths of their husbands, as required by *halakhah)* prompted penetrating investigation into the legal sources.

Despite the urgency surrounding the content of much of this literature, the stylistic convention of rabbinic *responsa* became increasingly intricate and scholastic (one is tempted to say, baroque) in character by the sixteenth century. Far more *responsa* have endured from this period than from the preceding era. Yet despite their great quantity and weighty contents, they abound in deferential pieties that insist upon the superior understanding of the juristic giants who came before. Indeed, it is from the sixteenth century that *halakhic* scholars begin referring to themselves as *aharonim* ('later authorities') and their predecessors as *rishonim* ('primary authorities').

Such terminology attests to an emergent consciousness among Jewish legal scholars in the sixteenth century of a temporal divide between their own and the preceding era. This was not conceived of in terms of "ancients and moderns." Rather, a wide array of sources attests to a growing sense within Jewish life that the providential plan had taken a decisive turn. In *halakhah* its clearest evidence emerges from the compulsion felt simultaneously by scholars in widely different places to devise a new and definitive code of Jewish law that would offer practical guidance to a people afflicted by seemingly continuous upheaval. The *Shulhan Arukh* (1564–1565; The prepared table) authored by Joseph Karo (1488–1575), a Spanish exile who lived first in Turkey and then in northern Palestine (Safed), appeared to answer that need. Its success derived from its pithy and accessible quality, no doubt. But backing this up was the unimpeachable authority of Karo's lengthier and far more academic legal code, the Bet Yosef. Still more decisive was the fact that the *Shulhan Arukh* was soon supplemented by the *Mapah* (Tablecloth) of the Polish rabbi Moses ben Israel Isserles (1525 or 1530–1572), who glossed the Sephardic Karo in the light of Ashkenazic jurisprudence and custom.

Initially, Karo's compendium had provoked strong opposition in eastern Europe, on the grounds that a legal code so devoid of argumentation would attenuate direct study of the Talmudic sources, diminishing the stature of the rabbis and undermining local and regional usage *(minhag).*

Why then did Polish rabbis eventually reconcile themselves to Karo's enterprise? The answer lies in the character of the problems generated by the mode of Ashkenazic legal studies in the early modern period. Polish Jewry had become perhaps the outstanding locus of *halakhic* scholarship by the sixteenth century. Its chief innovation was *hiluk* (both a form of pedagogy and a method of textual analysis), characterized by the continuous comparison of disparate Talmudic texts to uncover their underlying conceptual principles. While often denigrated as "casuistic," this dialectical approach made possible increased legal flexibility, a great virtue in the face of the many conundrums confronting early modern Jewish communities. At any rate, though the method of *hiluk* was antithetical to the spirit of codification, many Polish scholars came to realize that the vast amount of legal commentary and custom that had accumulated in recent generations necessitated a new and systematic organization of the law. (Note that similar controversies surrounding codification efforts were taking place among non-Jews in sixteenth-century Europe.) Broadly speaking, then, and despite the original controversy that surrounded it, the *Shulhan Arukh* triumphed because it addressed a range of pressing needs through its unique combination of practicality, scholarship, and universality.

Cabala (Kabbalah). Karo was no pedantic legalist, but a mystic and a visionary, the recipient, in fact, of nightly visitations from a heavenly messenger *(maggid)* who revealed divine secrets to him through the mechanism of automatic speech. His *maggid* aside, as a devotee of the cabala or kabbalah (a body of Jewish mystical thought and practice dating from twelfth-century Provence and Spain), Karo was hardly unusual—even among *halakhic* scholars. By the sixteenth century, cabala had become widely disseminated in almost every diaspora locale, due in part to the dispersion of Judeo-Spanish refugees throughout the Mediterranean and beyond. With roots in gnostic and Neoplatonic thought, and a core conception of divine ontology as corresponding to and interacting with human activity, cabala helped to invest Jewish ritual with fresh meaning and magical potency. Although cabalistic theosophy achieved its classical expression in the thirteenth-century *Zohar* (a pseudepigraphic work traditionally attributed to the second-century sage Rabbi Simeon bar Yochai), the sixteenth-century Safed cabalists Moses Cordovero (1522–1570) and Isaac Luria (1534–1572) lent it greater systematization and a new set of topical emphases. Cordovero's mystical fraternity produced instructional guides to moral behavior *(hanhagah)* that reified mystical abstractions into concrete practices and lifestyles accessible to such fraternities *(hevrahs)* throughout the diaspora. Luria, according to the formulation of the historian Gershom Scholem, took over the gnostic myth of an originary crisis existing within the godhead and highlighted its correspondence to the specific condition of Jewish exile, thereby focusing attention on the cosmic process of messianic redemption within Jewish collective consciousness.

Abetted by the new print revolution, the cabalistic currents emanating from Safed and elsewhere fused with the existing pietistic temperament of sixteenth-century Poland, the latter a legacy of that community's origins in medieval Ashkenaz and of its own syncretistic folk culture. Asceticism, strict penances, self-flagellation, and elaborate demonologies, though hardly alien to diaspora Jewish life elsewhere at this time, became especially pronounced in early modern Poland. Both pietistic and eschatological interests found expression in cabalistically inspired Bible commentaries that reveled in numerological interpretations of scriptural terms and calculations of the anticipated date of messianic redemption. In addition, *musar* literature, a genre dating to the early Middle Ages that aimed at guiding the reader to a life of mental and spiritual perfection through the adoption of an ascetic behavioral regimen, now came to function as an apt vehicle for transmitting cabala to a wider readership. *Musar* works took on a strongly cabalistic flavor, infusing prayer, Sabbath observance, study, and sexuality (or the strict avoidance of sexual sin, particularly masturbation)—indeed, nearly all areas of life—with a core of mystical symbolism. But cabala could also be disseminated orally through preaching, sermons, and homilies; through group study and recitation, as conducted by *hevrahs*; or simply through the complex if unconscious processes by which new customs, such as midnight vigils, alterations in the order of prayer recitation, prohibitions on sons attending their father's funerals, and countless other *tikkunim* ('corrections' of the cosmos), become sanctioned and sanctified. There can be little doubt that the explosion of such practices signaled a heightened sensitivity to the new spiritual possibilities engendered by the contemporary moment.

Renaissance trends. In early modern Italy, however, cabala seemed to take an altogether different turn. There it became linked to Renaissance trends, of both a Neoplatonic and a hermetic variety. In contrast to Isaac Luria's mythical and intensely anti-Gentile formulations, the Florentine Johanan ben Isaac Allemanno (c. 1435–c. 1504) constructed an enduring synthesis of cabala and Neoplatonism, reflective of and conducive to a Jewish-Christian dialogue. Allemanno exerted an important influence on Giovanni Pico della Mirandola (1463–1494) and on the development of Christian cabala more generally. Indeed, in Italy—despite the proselytizing aims of its Christian practitioners—Christian and Jewish cabala shared many features, reflecting a common philosophical vocabulary and devotion to the ancient wisdom lying beneath the surface meaning of the scriptural text.

Italian cabala functioned as one component of a Jewish Renaissance humanism that embraced the aesthetic values of the general environment. Italian Jews were active in every sphere of Renaissance literary production—biographical, linguistic, poetic, and philosophic. Strikingly, the Aristotelianism that since the time of Maimonides (1135–1204) had created deep fissures in the Jewish world was now deployed in a failed rearguard action against the rising forces of cabala and Neoplatonism. The latter—with Jewish roots in eleventh- and twelfth-century Spain—achieved its highest Italian-Jewish expression in the *Dialoghi di Amore* of León Hebreo (also Judah León Abrabanel, c. 1460–after 1523).

Sixteenth-century Italy (though the phenomenon extended beyond the peninsula) also experienced a brief efflorescence of Jewish historical writing, a genre that possessed rather shallow roots in post-biblical Jewish culture. Some of these works exhibited a decidedly apocalyptic character—again, suggesting a widespread sense of approaching cosmic crisis—but others, like the *Me'or 'Enayim* (The light of the eyes) of Azariah ben Moses dei Rossi (c. 1511–c. 1578), were produced with an unmistakably humanist orientation. Indeed, Jewish humanists viewed the pagan arts then being revived in Italy as derivative of their own ancient creed. As the geographer Abraham Farissol (1451–c. 1525) explained, "at the foot of Mt. Sinai God crowned us with the Torah in its entirety: it contained all the sciences, natural sciences, logic, theology, law, politics, and it was here that the whole World slaked its thirst." Such one-upmanship served Jews well. In a milieu where acculturation offered opportunities and enticements, the claim of Judaic priority in the humanistic curriculum enabled Jews to act as their own cultural gatekeepers.

"CRISIS" OR "INCIPIENT MODERNITY"?

Italian ghettos. Though the broad humanist curriculum was the province of a relative handful of Jews, the adoption of Italian names, folkways, melodies, delicacies, and pastimes permeated the Italian Jewish community as a whole, even when secluded behind ghetto walls. Indeed, the impact of Italian ghettoization—few Jewish communities outside of Italy lived in ghettos proper—did not necessarily mandate inwardness or insularity. The famous Venetian rabbi Leone Modena (1571–1648), although admittedly an exceptional case, records that during the December festival of Hanukkah, the friar whom he called "Satan," "duped me into playing games of chance . . . by the following [May holiday of] *Shavuot,* I lost more than three hundred ducats." At the same time, while ghettos did not seal Jews hermetically from the outside world, they did offer protection from physical attack (though not plague and wrenching poverty), and a defined if circumscribed and degraded place within Christian society. That for many historians "the ghetto" became a catchall for the premodern Jewish experience in Europe as a whole is unfortunate, since it violates the actual ghetto's historical specificity as well as misconstrues its paradoxical value to those Jews who experienced it.

This paradoxical nature of ghetto life manifested itself in a psychological need to define the moral and conceptual boundaries of Judaism within a Christian society. Indeed, ghetto existence appears to have given rise to a number of apologetic works that defended Judaism and advertised the purported benefits of maintaining a Jewish presence to Christian state and society. In a work by the aforementioned Leone Modena, written in Hebrew but readily accessible to a host of contemporary Christian Hebraist scholars, the author brought forth a penetrating analysis of the New Testament, depicting Jesus as a Pharisee whose later epigones had distorted his original Jewish message. In 1638 Modena's younger Venetian colleague, Simone Luzzatto (d. 1663), offered Christians a quite different message, unabashedly insisting that Jews act to enrich the gentile polity with their unmatched commercial skills. Luzzatto's argument on behalf of "mercantilist philosemitism" influenced debates on Jewish readmission to England in 1654–1655 and continued to have an impact well into the eighteenth century.

Marranism and messianism. The ghetto was not the only stimulus to such literature, however. The return of many Iberian New Christians to Judaism prompted a number of them to produce treatises, addressed not just to Christians but to wavering fellow Marranos as well, that attested to what the former New Christian Isaac Cardoso (1603 or 1604–1683) called "the excellences of the Hebrews." Such former New Christians constituted a volatile addition to the Jewish communities of Italy, Amsterdam, Hamburg, and London during the seventeenth century. Unlike their sixteenth-century predecessors, a number of whom retained a living memory of open Jewish practice in Iberia, many of these Marranos possessed only the most rudimentary knowledge of rabbinic Judaism, its observances, doctrines, and mentalities. Their subjection to the discipline of the Sephardic *kahal* government (the *Mahamad*), its alien customs, and *halakhic* regimen sometimes evoked in the minds of these "returnees" comparisons with the very tyranny they had fled. Even an insincerely felt Christianity might leave an enduring impression on the soul. When combined with a sense of disappointment with their recovered faith, this could lead in the most varied directions. The roughly contemporaneous Uriel Acosta (1585–1640) and Abraham Miguel Cardoso (c. 1630–1706)—brother of the above-mentioned Isaac—demonstrate the polar range of alternatives. Acosta fled the Portuguese Inquisition in 1615, but was later excommunicated by the Amsterdam Jewish community for his increasingly radical criticisms of the oral law. His case dramatically illustrates how the abandonment of Christianity could feed a religious skepticism irreconcilable with an equally powerful need for membership within a Jewish community. Abraham Cardoso, however, seemingly presented the opposite phenomenon. His intense hostility to his former Christian faith manifested itself in a dogged adherence to the cause of the messianic pretender Shabbetai Tzevi, even justifying on cabalistic grounds the latter's conversion to Islam. The fact that these cases are extreme ones should not obscure the intimate and complex connections between Marranism and messianism in the Jewish history of the seventeenth century. Messianic pretenders had not been lacking during the previous century. But figures like Asher Lemlein and Solomon Molcho (c. 1500–1532), however great the fascination they engendered, secured relatively few actual followers, whereas the messianic fervor surrounding Shabbetai Tzevi appears at its height to have seized the hearts of close to a majority of Jews worldwide. The messiah's appeal cannot be attributed to any single historical cause; neither the expulsion of 1492, nor the dissemination of Lurianic cabala, nor the rough phenomenological equivalents that appeared simultaneously within Christendom are sufficient to account for a movement that swept from Adrianople to Amsterdam—sweeping up all types and classes of Jews along its path.

Less speculative are the reasons why the modest achievements and erratic and sometimes psychotic behavior of the pretender himself did not induce a greater skepticism. The momentous announcement in the summer of 1665 of the messiah's advent, emanating from the holy land and in the guise of a solemn appeal from his "prophet," Nathan of Gaza (1643/1644–1680), for mass repentance, appears to have successfully undercut competing reports of Shabbetai Tzevi's bizarre sexual behavior and evidence of the physical thuggery that his followers unleashed upon "infidel" dissenters. Concerns raised by reports of his February 1666 arrest at the hands of the sultan were likewise dampened by word that the messiah's prison was actually a palace where the "king" hosted emissaries from throughout the exile. Only the profound shock of Shabbetai's apostasy on 15 September 1666, once absorbed, transformed joy into disappointment, and elation into rage or despair. Cooler heads among the community leaders now emerged to supervise a systematic effort to cover up the extent of official collusion with the movement and to root out lingering pockets of belief.

If in most cases the status quo ante was restored relatively quickly, two minority tendencies also made themselves felt: conversion from Judaism, on the one hand, and participation in the heretical Shabbetean movement, on the other. In the first instance, Christian missionaries proved adept at capitalizing on the disillusionment Shabbetai had inspired in many Jews. As for the case of Jewish heresy, Shabbetai's propagandists (including Abraham Cardoso and Nathan of Gaza) succeeded in formulating doctrines to demonstrate that the apostasy actually "proved" Shabbetai's messianic or (in extreme versions) divine nature. It seems that such claims may have found a particular resonance among former Marranos. For them, after all, the outward conversion and crypto-Judaizing that Shabbetai and some of his followers now engaged in constituted the very crux of their own past religious experience.

Shabbeteanism would cast a shadow over the next century of Jewish intellectual and religious life in Europe. This did not occur because the heresy was itself so widespread. Admittedly, respected community leaders such as the Sephardic chief rabbi of Amsterdam, Solomon ben Jacob Ayllon (1655–1728), and even a revered Talmudist, Jonathan Eybeschuetz (1690–1754), were secret though moderate Shabbeteans, while at the other end of the spectrum, the shocking heretical messianism of Jacob Frank (1726–1791) seems to have taken the form of a perverse experiment to see if the original shabbatean debacle could be outdone. Yet while these instances should not be overlooked, more significant still was the degree to which self-appointed heresy hunters in the decades following Shabbetai Tzevi's demise claimed to see incarnations of Shabbeteanism extremism almost everywhere they looked—in the pietistic conventicle of the brilliant Italian mystic Moses Hayyim Luzzatto (1707–1747), in the acrobatic "enthusiasm" of the fledgling Hasidic movement, and even in some of the mild pedagogic reforms advocated by the early Jewish Enlightenment. The Shabbetean scare, in short, seems to have produced a form of reductionism within some orthodox circles, which in itself helped to determine the dynamic interplay of "tradition and crisis" in the Judaism of the eighteenth century.

Conclusion. If heresy calls forth inquisition, skepticism dogma and laxity enforcement, then it is plain why some historians have depicted early modern era Judaism as engendering a crisis. The crisis they describe pits the irresistible force of acculturation, antinomianism, and apostasy against the immovable object of cultures and communal institutions turned inward and rigid. According to this view, by the middle of the eighteenth century, such tensions proved too powerful to contain, leaving the fabric of traditional Judaism exposed and vulnerable to the simultaneous eruption of Enlightenment in the West and Hasidism in the East. However, more recently, an alternative narrative has vied for dominance, one that emphasizes a comparatively seamless transition to modernity. According to this view, an "incipient modernity" was engineered, more or less unconsciously, by representatives of a moderate tradition within Judaism—philosophical in medieval Spain, humanistic in the Renaissance, and scientific in the Enlightenment—who were at home in both the world of Jewish observance and that of commerce and culture. However, if both scenarios possess merit, they likewise equally exaggerate, particularly with regard to the degree of autonomy they accord to European Jewish history. Modernity did not "arrive" at all Jewish communities simultaneously. Rather, as was the case with most minorities within Europe—as well as most populations outside of it—modernity imposed itself as an alien but ineluctable force that left no choice but to react, resist, or adapt.

See also **Cabala; *Conversos;* Ghetto; Inquisition, Spanish; Jews, Attitudes toward; Jews, Expulsion of (Spain; Portugal); Khmelnytsky Uprising; Messianism, Jewish; Shabbetai Tzevi.**

BIBLIOGRAPHY

Baron, Salo Wittmayer. *The Jewish Community: Its History and Structure to the American Revolution.* 3 vols. Philadelphia, 1942.

Bonfil, Roberto. *Jewish Life in Renaissance Italy.* Translated by Anthony Oldcorn. Berkeley, 1994.

Halpern, Israel. *The Jews of Poland* (Hebrew). 2 vols. Jerusalem, 1948–1953.

Hannover, Nathan Nata. *The Abyss of Despair: The Famous Seventeenth Century Chronicle Depicting Jewish Life in Russia and Poland during the Chmielnicki Massacres of*

1648–1649. Translated by Abraham J. Mesch. New Brunswick, N.J., 1983.

Idel, Moshe. *Kabbalah: New Perspectives.* New Haven, 1988.

Israel, Jonathan I. *European Jewry in the Age of Mercantilism, 1550–1750.* London and Portland, Ore., 1998.

Kaplan, Yosef. "The Portuguese Community in Seventeen-Century Amsterdam and the Ashkenazi World." In *Dutch Jewish History II,* edited by Jozeph Michman, pp. 23–45. Jerusalem, 1989.

Katz, Jacob. *Tradition and Crisis: Jewish Society at the End of the Middle Ages.* Translated by Bernard Dov Cooperman. New York, 1993.

Modena, Leone. *The Autobiography of a Seventeenth-Century Venetian Rabbi: Leon Modena's Life of Judah.* Translated and edited by Mark R. Cohen. Princeton, 1988.

Ruderman, David B., ed. *Essential Papers on Jewish Culture in Renaissance and Baroque Italy.* New York, 1992.

Scholem, Gershom Gerhard. *Sabbatai Sevi: The Mystical Messiah, 1626–1676.* Translated by R. J. Zwi Werblowsky. Princeton, 1973.

Shochat, Azriel. *Changing Times: The Beginning of the Haskalah among German Jews* (Hebrew). Jerusalem, 1960.

Stern, Selma. *The Court Jew; A Contribution to the History of the Period of Absolutism in Central Europe.* Translated by Ralph Weiman. Philadelphia, 1950.

JONATHAN KARP

JOANNA I, "THE MAD" (SPAIN)

(1479–1555), third child and second daughter of Isabella of Castile and Ferdinand of Aragón, and mother of the Emperor Charles V. The marriage agreement of Isabella and Ferdinand had stipulated that Ferdinand could not inherit the crown of Castile if Isabella died before him. It would pass instead to their legitimate heirs, who could include their daughters since in Castile women were allowed to exercise sovereign power. Intelligent and well educated, Joanna also showed signs of rebelliousness and mental instability that troubled her parents. Nonetheless, in 1502 Isabella and Ferdinand secured the cooperation of the Castilian Cortes in recognizing Joanna as proprietary heiress of Castile (her older siblings Isabel and Juan had both already died) and her husband, the Habsburg Philip the Handsome, as her legitimate consort.

When Isabella died in 1504, Joanna and Philip were not in Castile. This allowed Ferdinand to engage in political machinations that portrayed Joanna as mentally unsound and convinced the Cortes to appoint him in her place. A power struggle emerged between Ferdinand and Philip. Philip died in 1496, plunging Joanna into a period of profound mourning (which only exacerbated her tendency toward mental instability). By 1509 Ferdinand had "exiled" his daughter to Tordesillas, where she lived until her death in 1555.

Some recent scholarship has attempted to separate Joanna's image from the unfortunate appellation of "the Mad," seeking to demonstrate that she was the victim of the political ambitions of both her father and husband. Despite her exclusion from power, Joanna remained the queen of Castile, reigning jointly after 1516 with her son Charles I (Charles V of the Holy Roman Empire).

Joanna I. Portrait by Juan de Flandes, 1500. KUNSTHISTORISCHES MUSEUM, VIENNA, AUSTRIA/BRIDGEMAN ART LIBRARY

See also **Charles V (Holy Roman Empire); Ferdinand of Aragón; Isabella of Castile.**

BIBLIOGRAPHY

Altayó, Isabel. *Juana I: La reina cautiva.* Madrid, 1985.

Aram, Bethany. "Joanna 'the Mad's' Signature: The Problem of Invoking Royal Authority, 1505–1507." *Sixteenth Century Journal* 29: 2 (1998), 331–358. The revisionist view.

Fernández Alvarez, Manuel. *Juana la Loca: La cautiva de Tordesillas.* Madrid, 2000.

ELIZABETH A. LEHFELDT

JOHNSON, SAMUEL (1709–1784), English writer, lexicographer, and critic. Known as "Dr. Johnson," Samuel Johnson was one of the most complex and important figures of eighteenth-century culture. Renowned particularly for his personality, his contribution to eighteenth-century writing is important both for his scholarly knowledge and for his insight into humanity in its moral and social complexity.

Samuel Johnson. Portrait by Sir Joshua Reynolds. THE ART ARCHIVE/COURAGE BREWERIES/EILEEN TWEEDY

EARLY LIFE AND EDUCATION

The son of Michael Johnson, a bookseller with intellectual ambitions in Lichfield, Staffordshire, Samuel Johnson was born in 1709. When he was three, he was taken to London to be touched by Queen Anne to cure his scrofula, which, along with smallpox, caused lasting disfiguration. Johnson was educated at Lichworth Grammar School and read prodigiously, enjoying Latin authors and Renaissance literature. While at school, he wrote several English and Latin poems and essays, and a distant cousin, the Reverend Cornelius Ford, whom he visited in Worcestershire, encouraged his interests in poetry and classical culture. As a student at Pembroke College, Oxford, Johnson translated Alexander Pope's "Messiah" into Latin verse, and the poem was published in 1731.

Due to the family's increasing poverty, Johnson completed only one year toward his degree at Oxford, a prevailing source of unhappiness throughout his life. Faced with unemployment, Johnson grudgingly helped in his father's bookshop for two years. The drudgery was compensated for by his friendship with the Reverend Gilbert Walmesley of Lichfield, who encouraged Johnson's literary ambitions. Johnson taught briefly at Market Bosworth Grammar School in Leicestershire but quarreled with his employer and moved to Birmingham in 1733. He lived with a former school friend, Edmund Hector, and earned money writing for the *Birmingham Journal.* He translated the Portuguese Jesuit Jeronymo Lobo's *Voyage to Abyssinia* in 1735. In the same year he married Elizabeth Porter, a widow twenty-five years his senior, and opened a boarding school in Edial, near Lichfield; the school failed, perhaps as a result of the combination of Johnson's indifference to teaching and his physical deformity.

LONDON, JOURNALISM, AND BIOGRAPHY

In 1737 Johnson traveled with David Garrick (a former pupil who was to become the most famous actor of his time) to London, where Johnson was to spend the rest of his life. He found employment as a journalist with the printer Edward Cave, the founder of *The Gentleman's Magazine,* and later commented, "No one but a blockhead wrote except for money." Johnson almost certainly influenced the journal's development as an authoritative source of information. He contributed book reviews on several subjects and wrote reports of parliamentary debates (a forbidden practice) under the title of *Debates of the Senate of Magna Lilliputia,* which was a blend of both fact and Johnson's own views presented in his own words. After writing satirical pamphlets that were critical of Prime Minister Robert Walpole, Johnson went into hiding in Lambeth under a false name because his arrest had been ordered.

Johnson secured literary success with *London,* a satirically exuberant poem on the excesses and corruption of London life. Between 1738 and 1744 he also wrote short biographies of historical and naval figures. He helped to catalogue the Harleian library, a collection of books by the first earl of Oxford, writing an influential preface on cataloguing as essential in helping scholarly investigation. Johnson collated *The Harleian Miscellany,* a series of pamphlets on the political controversies in sixteenth- and seventeenth-century Britain, and wrote a preface to his collation. In 1744 he wrote an extended biography, *A Life of Richard Savage,* a passionately written defense of his friend, a struggling poet who had died in poverty in 1743.

LEXICOGRAPHER, LITERARY CRITIC, AND POET

Johnson's ambition to be an authority on language and literature is realized in his most important work. In 1747, he produced a plan for *A Dictionary of the English Language* addressed to statesman Philip Dormer Stanhope (Lord Chesterfield), who ignored Johnson and sent him £10. Johnson wished to provide a work of reference "for the use of such as aspire to exactness of criticism, or elegance of style" (Preface, 1756). His intention was to stabilize the language, for example in usage and pronunciation, but not to impose rigid rules like the dictionaries of the continental academies. Johnson's dictionary elucidates the different meanings of words through close examination of the use of quotations from celebrated and authoritative authors. The dictionary's diversity reflects Johnson's wide reading to find illustrative quotations, which were transcribed with the help of six amanuenses. In a famous letter to Lord Chesterfield, Johnson refused his offer of patronage after the dictionary was published to high critical acclaim in 1755 and an abridgment published in 1756. The abridged version became the standard dictionary until the publication of Noah Webster's in 1828.

The Vanity of Human Wishes, an imitation of the Latin poet Juvenal's tenth satire, was published in 1749; the tone and vision of the poem has been debated by critics as reflecting either pessimism at human vanity or hope for humanity's redemption. Although Johnson was disillusioned with the judgment of theater producers about its value as a tragedy, his play *Irene* was produced by David Garrick in 1749. It earned Johnson £300. Johnson also established a twice-weekly periodical, *The Rambler* (1750–1752), writing critical essays on many topics such as the English novel. Between 1758 and 1760, he produced for the *Universal Chronicle, or Weekly Gazette* a series of essays called *The Idler* that were lighter in tone. He also edited and wrote reviews for *The Literary Magazine.* Opposed to the Seven Years' War, Johnson wrote sporadic pieces attacking the war. To pay the expenses of his mother's illness, Johnson rapidly wrote *Rasselas, Prince of Abyssinia,* (1759) a philosophical "Oriental" novella. Because of his scholarly successes, Johnson was awarded an honorary M.A. by Oxford University in 1755 and an LL.D. by Dublin University in 1765. The need to support himself by writing was relieved in 1762, when he (controversially) accepted an annual pension of £300 from Lord Bute's ministry.

JAMES BOSWELL AND LATER YEARS

In 1763, Johnson became acquainted with a young Scot named James Boswell, who became his friend and his biographer. Johnson's expanding social life saved him from the bouts of melancholia and depression he suffered. Acquainted with almost all the leading political and literary figures of the time, in 1764 he formed the Literary Club, whose members included Joseph Banks, Edmund Burke, David Garrick, Edward Gibbon, Richard Brinsley Sheridan, Adam Smith, and James Boswell, who recorded their conversations. Johnson befriended Robert Chambers, a lawyer, who asked his help in composing a course of lectures on common law to deliver to Oxford undergraduates. The degree to which Johnson helped write the fifty-six lectures remains undetermined. In the same year he met the Welsh writer Hester Lynch Thrale (later Piozzi), with whom he developed a close friendship, and traveled to Wales and to France with her family. Her *Anecdotes of*

Johnson (1786) and *Letters to and from Johnson* (1788), as well as her diaries, have provided rich material for Johnson's biographers. In 1765, Johnson finally published an edition of Shakespeare's plays, which is the first variorum edition, providing the notes of previous editors to aid or sometimes correct interpretation. His preface to the edition demonstrates Johnson's excellence at close critical reading.

In 1773, Johnson traveled with Boswell to the Hebrides, recorded in his *Journey to the Western Islands of Scotland* (1775) and in Boswell's *Journal of a Tour to the Hebrides* (1785). At the urging of a number of London booksellers, Johnson agreed in 1777 to write *Prefaces, Biographical and Critical to the Works of the English Poets* (later known as *The Lives of the Poets*), which was published 1779–1781. The monumental work discussed fifty-two of the most celebrated English writers and displayed Johnson's powers of literary criticism and insight.

Johnson died in December 1784 and was buried in poets' corner in Westminster Abbey. His fame followed him with the appearance of his letters and several biographies after his death, most notably James Boswell's *The Life of Samuel Johnson* (1791).

See also **Boswell, James; Dictionaries and Encyclopedias; English Literature and Language.**

BIBLIOGRAPHY

Primary Sources

Johnson, Samuel. *A Dictionary of the English Language.* London, 1755.

———. *Early Biographical Writings of Dr. Johnson.* Edited by J. D. Fleeman. Farnborough, U.K., 1973.

———. *The History of Rasselas, Prince of Abyssina.* Edited by J. P. Hardy. Oxford, 1999.

———. *Journey to the Western Islands of Scotland.* Edited by J. D. Fleeman. Oxford, 1985.

———. *The Letters of Samuel Johnson.* Edited by Bruce Redford. 5 vols. Princeton, 1992.

———. *Samuel Johnson: Political Writings.* Edited by Donald J. Greene. New Haven, 2000.

———. *Samuel Johnson: The Major Works.* Edited by Donald J. Greene. Oxford, 2000.

———. *The Yale Edition of the Works of Samuel Johnson.* 16 vols. currently published. New Haven, 1958–.

Secondary Sources

Boswell, James. *Boswell's Life of Johnson, together with Boswell's Journey of a Tour of the Hebrides and Johnson's Diary of a Journey into North Wales.* Edited by George Birkbeck Hill and revised by L. F. Powell. Oxford, 1934–1964. Important posthumous biographies of Johnson, invaluable for its detail.

Clingham, Greg. *The Cambridge Companion to Samuel Johnson.* Cambridge, U.K., 1997. Fifteen essays discussing politics, religion, travel, women, imperialism and many other topics.

Greene, Donald. *Samuel Johnson.* Boston, 1989. Useful introductory guide to the range of Johnson's work and influence. See also Greene's critical introduction to *Samuel Johnson: A Critical Edition of the Major Works.* Oxford, 1984.

Hart, Kevin. *Samuel Johnson and the Culture of Property.* Cambridge, U.K., 1999. Explores the critical emergence of "The Age of Johnson" in relation to Johnson's literary reputation as a public commodity.

Korshin, Paul J., and Jack Lynch, eds. *The Age of Johnson: A Scholarly Annual.* New York, 1987–. Periodical published once a year focusing on Johnson and his influence.

Venturo, David F. *Johnson the Poet: The Poetic Career of Samuel Johnson.* Newark, N.J., 1999. First monograph focusing on all of Johnson's poetry.

Max Fincher

JOINT STOCK COMPANIES. *See* **Trading Companies.**

JONES, INIGO (1573–1652), English architect. Inigo Jones was important for introducing Italian design into a country that was only haphazardly acquainted with the forms of Renaissance architecture. He was also responsible, from 1605 to 1640, for staging over fifty masques and plays for the royal court, often in collaboration with Ben Jonson; many surviving drawings show how well acquainted he was with stage designs from Florence and the Medici court. Jones was born in London, the son of a Welsh clothworker. Nothing is known of his early life but he is first recorded in 1603 as a picture-maker, working for the 5th earl of Rutland, with whom he perhaps went on a diplomatic mission to Denmark. But it was also about this time that he first traveled to Italy, perhaps in the entourage of Frances Manners, the earl's brother.

Jones's first architectural designs date from about 1606 and show that by then he had already

Inigo Jones. Queen's House, Greenwich, England, designed by Inigo Jones, 1619–1635. ©GILLIAN DARLEY; EDIFICE/CORBIS

acquired a knowledge of the work of architects like Andrea Palladio and Sebastiano Serlio. In 1610 he was appointed surveyor to Henry, Prince of Wales, and it was during this period that he may have worked on some internal alterations at St. James's Palace. In 1612, after the death of the prince, Jones came into contact with the duke of Arundel, an important patron and collector of art, in 1613–1614 accompanying him to Italy, to deepen further his knowledge of architecture. It was on this trip that Jones acquired his first drawings by Palladio. When, in 1615, he was appointed surveyor of the king's works, he was now ready to design works of his own. Through the generous patronage of King James I, he was able to design a small, but important, number of buildings: the Queen's House at Greenwich (1619–1635), the Queen's Chapel at St. James's Palace (1617–1618), and the Banqueting House, Whitehall (1619–1622). Nothing like these buildings, in their strict, spare Italianate forms, had ever been seen in England, and their style was perhaps at first difficult for many to appreciate.

From about 1618 to 1640 Jones was also busy on two other major projects: the repair of St. Paul's Cathedral, London, and the square and houses that he built for the Earl of Bedford on property the earl owned at Covent Garden. The work Jones did at St. Paul's Cathedral was destroyed in the fire of 1666, but, especially in its vast Corinthian portico, it represented a new and grander Roman style of architecture, defining church architecture in ways that would be especially important for Christopher Wren when he also worked at St. Paul's and later designed other London churches. At Covent Garden, where Jones designed St. Paul's Church, the first classical church in England, his opportunities were limited. But in the plan, and in the design of the houses around the square, borrowed from what he had seen in Paris and Livorno, Jones defined a pattern of urban architecture that would be used widely in England for the next two centuries.

Jones's grandest project was for a vast palace at Whitehall, modeled on both the Escorial in Spain and the Louvre in Paris. And if nothing came of his plans because of the financial and political difficulties of King Charles I, what Jones suggested, as documented in his preparatory drawings, affected all the later designs done on this important site. Jones was also involved with several projects for country houses, the most important being Wilton House, Wiltshire, where the south front, begun by Isaac de Caux about 1636, was much influenced by his ideas. In a series of designs from this time, none of which were executed, Jones defined a restrained, undecorated style that was used in many of the buildings of this kind designed in England after the Revolution of 1688–1689.

The political misfortunes of Charles I affected Jones very directly; in 1643 he was dismissed as surveyor of the king's works. He received no further commissions after this, but when he died, he was able to leave a considerable sum of money to John Webb, his pupil and assistant, who had married one of his relatives. It was also to Webb that Jones bequeathed his drawings, which were later acquired by Lord Burlington in the 1720s and then used to define the revival of Palladio in England in the eighteenth century. Over forty volumes from Jones's library, many with his annotations, now reside at Worcester College, Oxford, and have been used extensively by scholars; many of his drawings for masques and stage designs passed through Lord Burlington to the dukes of Devonshire and are presently preserved at Chatsworth.

See also **Britain, Architecture in; London; Palladio, Andrea, and Palladianism; Wren, Christopher.**

BIBLIOGRAPHY

Primary Sources

Chaney, Edward. *Inigo Jones' Roman Sketchbook.* Facsimile of the original manuscript at Chatsworth. Forthcoming.

Harris, John, and Gordon Higgott. *Inigo Jones: The Complete Architectural Drawings.* New York, 1989.

Peacock, John. *The Stage Designs of Inigo Jones: The European Context.* Cambridge, U.K., and New York, 1995.

Secondary Sources

Summerson, John. *Inigo Jones.* London, 1966. Reprinted, New Haven and London, 2000.

———. "The Surveyorship of Inigo Jones, 1615–43." In *History of the King's Works,* edited by H. M. Colvin, vol. 3, pp. 129–160. London, 1975.

DAVID CAST

JONSON, BEN (1572–1637), English playwright and poet. A highly influential dramatist of Jacobean London and the court of his day, Jonson was a colorful character of early theater history. His plays communicate much about the vicissitudes of life for those who shared the playwright's time and place. Jonson's father was a clergyman; his death a month before Jonson's birth was to affect the playwright's early life, for Jonson's mother soon married a master bricklayer, Robert Brett. Jonson was educated at Westminster School, where the antiquary William Camden, who was the master, became his intellectual inspiration. It is not certain, however, how long Jonson remained at school. According to the Scottish poet William Drummond of Hawthornden (1585–1649), friend and recorder of his conversations, Jonson was "taken" from Westminster and began an apprenticeship in bricklaying. He left London briefly to serve as a soldier in the Low Countries, but by 1594 he had returned. He married, and in 1595 he entered the Tylers and Bricklayers Company.

Soon after this he was writing and performing as an actor with the Earl of Pembroke's Men. In 1597 the company got into trouble for presenting *The Isle of Dogs* (now lost), a seditious play that Jonson finished for Thomas Nashe, and subsequently they had to disband. Jonson was constantly at odds with the authorities. In 1598, the same year that he produced his highly successful comedy, *Every Man in His Humour,* for Shakespeare's company, the Chamberlain's Men, he killed an actor called Gabriel Spencer in a duel. When arraigned for the offense, he successfully pleaded "benefit of clergy"—that is, he escaped a hanging due to his ability to read. While in prison for this offense, he became a Catholic, though he reverted to the Protestant faith twelve years later.

Jonson was frequently punished for the subject matter of his plays, which were often interpreted as being too satirically interested in national or court politics. In response to his tragedy *Sejanus His Fall,* performed at the Globe in 1603 and published in 1605, he was suspected of portraying the political crimes of Robert Devereux, the earl of Essex. He was jailed in 1605 with George Chapman (1559–1634) and possibly John Marston (c. 1575–1634), collaborators with him on the London satire, *Eastward Ho!,* because it alluded to King James I's acceptance of payments for knighthoods. Despite these troubles, Jonson always seemed to emerge unharmed, and ultimately he excelled within the context of court entertainment. This is borne out by the success of his many masques, written for members of the court to perform. Some of these were produced in collaboration with the designer and architect Inigo Jones (1573–1652). In 1616 he was given a royal pension that was similar, in today's terms, to being granted the post of "poet laureate" in England. Thereafter he styled himself "the King's Poet."

His principal dramatic works, other than those already mentioned, include satirical pieces like *Cynthia's Revels* (1600) and *Poetaster* (1601)—both contributing to a perceived dialogue among the playwrights, or what has been called "the war of the theaters" played out between Jonson, Marston, and Thomas Dekker. Other satires include *Every Man Out of His Humour* (1599), *Epicene, or the Silent Woman* (1609), *The Devil Is an Ass* (1616), and the rumbustuously carnivalesque *Bartholomew Fair* (1614). The most famous of the playwright's works are undoubtedly *Volpone, or the Fox* (1606) and *The Alchemist* (1610), which are regularly produced on the stage to this day.

Jonson also wrote poetry including his *Epigrams* and a selection called *The Forrest.* These were published in his collected *Works* of 1616. Another selection of verse called *Underwoods* was published in a collection in 1640. This also included *Timber; or Discoveries made upon Men and Matter,* a prose work that comprised some personal musings on texts he had read. Jonson is best remembered for plays that, while showing his audience the world in which they lived, drew heavily on classical influences. These sources were often noted in the margins of Jonson's published works—nowhere more so than in the collection that he himself put together, the folio of 1616. Never before had there been such a publication, which included dramatic works written in English, and it was this endeavor that probably inspired the production of Shakespeare's First Folio of plays in 1623. Jonson demonstrated perceptiveness and foresight concerning the universal nature of Shakespeare's work when he wrote in a prefatory poem to his dead friend's collection that Shakespeare's plays were "not of an age, but for all time!" Jonson's plays belonged to early modern London and to England's court, and therefore to his age.

In 1623, Jonson suffered the catastrophe of seeing many of his papers burned in a fire. Although he continued to write into the Caroline period, he never regained the favor he had once won at court. In 1628 this extraordinary personality suffered a paralytic stroke, and he died in 1637 plagued by ill health and financial insecurity. He is buried in Westminster Abbey under a tombstone bearing the inscription, "O rare Ben Jonson."

See also **Drama: English; English Literature and Language; Shakespeare, William.**

BIBLIOGRAPHY

Primary Sources

Jonson, Ben. *The Poetaster, or, The Arraignment; Sejanus, His Fall; The Devil Is an Ass, The New Inn, or, The Light Heart.* Edited by Margaret Jane Kidnie. Oxford and New York, 2000.

———. *Three Comedies: Volpone, The Alchemist, Bartholomew Fair.* Michael Jamieson, ed. London and New York, 1966.

Jonson, Ben, George Chapman, and John Marston. *Eastward Ho!* Edited by C. G. Petter. London and New York, 1994. Originally published London, 1973.

Secondary Sources

Kay, W. David. *Ben Jonson: A Literary Life.* Basingstoke, U.K., and London, 1995.

Shakespeare, William. *The First Folio of Shakespeare.* Prepared by Charles Hinman; 2nd ed. New York and London, 1996.

EVA GRIFFITH

JOSEPH I (HOLY ROMAN EMPIRE)

(1678–1711; ruled 1705–1711), Habsburg emperor. Joseph I's reign was dominated by the War of the Spanish Succession (1701–1714), which pitted Bourbon France and Spain against the "Grand Alliance" led by Austria and the Maritime Powers. Born to Emperor Leopold I and Eleonore of the

Palatinate-Neuburg, Joseph's upbringing was notable for the absence of Jesuit influence and the resurgence of German patriotism during lengthy struggles against France and the Ottoman Empire. In 1699 he married Wilhemine Amalie of Brunswick-Lüneburg, who his parents hoped would tame his youthful excesses, which included wild parties and a string of indiscriminate sexual escapades. He was soon admitted to the privy council, where he became the center of a "young court" of reform-minded ministers eager to resolve the daunting financial and military crises that confronted the monarchy during the opening years of the war, which Leopold had entered to secure the far-flung Spanish inheritance for his second son, Archduke Charles (the future Holy Roman emperor Charles VI). Their first victory came in 1703, with the appointments of Prince Eugene of Savoy and Gundaker Starhemberg to head the war council *(Hofkriegsrat)* and treasury *(Hofkammer)*. Shortly afterward, John Churchill, the duke of Marlborough, was induced to march a British army into southern Germany, where it combined with imperial troops in destroying a Franco-Bavarian force at Blenheim (August 1704).

Joseph I. Portrait engraving, late seventeenth century. ©BETTMANN/CORBIS

Although the great victory saved the monarchy from imminent defeat, Joseph had to overcome a succession of new challenges after succeeding his father (5 May 1705), which included the need to wage war on multiple fronts in Germany, the Spanish Netherlands, Italy, the Low Countries, and Spain, while simultaneously suppressing a massive rebellion in Hungary led by Prince Ferenc II Rákóczi. Joseph's strong German identity informed vigorous initiatives within the empire, including reform of the Imperial Aulic Council *(Reichshofrat)* and the banning of several renegade German and Italian princes who had sided with the Bourbons. Yet he gave little assistance to the imperial army fighting along the Rhine frontier or to the Maritime Powers campaigning in the Low Countries. Instead, he focused his resources (together with considerable Anglo-Dutch loans) on Italy, which Prince Eugene delivered in a single stroke at the battle of Turin (1706), after which the French evacuated northern Italy, much as they had abandoned Germany after Blenheim. A small force expelled Spanish forces from Naples the following spring. Joseph's other principal concern was Hungary, where Rákóczi had aroused widespread support against Leopold's regime of heavy taxation and religious persecution. Although Joseph dissociated himself from his father's policies and promised to respect Hungary's liberties, he refused Rákóczi's demand that he cede Transylvania as a guarantee against future Habsburg tyranny. As a result, the war dragged on for eight years, as Joseph committed roughly half of all Austrian forces to the difficult process of reconquering the country. Once victory was assured, relatively generous terms were granted the rebels at the peace of Szatmár (April 1711), signed just ten days after Joseph's death.

With Italy secured and the Hungarian rebellion under control, Joseph shifted his attention to the last and least pressing of his war aims—his brother's acquisition of the rest of Spain's European and American empire. Prince Eugene and a small force were sent to join Marlborough's Anglo-Dutch army in the Spanish Netherlands, most of which fell after their victory at Oudenarde (1708). Joseph also instigated a short war with Pope Clement XI at the end of 1709, forcing him to recognize Charles as king of Spain. By 1710, the first Austrian troops were fighting alongside their British, Dutch, and Portuguese allies in Spain itself. Nonetheless, a combination of logistical difficulties, timely French reinforcements, and the Spanish people's dogged support for the Bourbon claimant, Philip V, doomed the allied effort. Unsuccessful peace negotiations at The Hague (1709) and Gertruydenberg (1710) failed to deliver what the allies could not win for themselves. Finally, a new British cabinet initiated secret peace talks with Louis XIV at the beginning of 1711, foreshadowing the Peace of Utrecht two years later.

Despite his untimely death from smallpox (17 April 1711), Joseph attained his two main objectives: securing an Italian glacis to the southwest and reconciling Hungary to Austrian domination, albeit with constitutional safeguards. Indeed, both achievements endured until 1866. Much of his success rested with a talent for choosing and managing able ministers to whom he could delegate much of the responsibility for realizing policy objectives. At the same time, Joseph jeopardized these gains through extramarital liaisons, which prevented his wife from bearing children after he gave her a venereal infection in 1704. Although he was survived by two daughters, the absence of a male heir foreshadowed the dynasty's extinction in 1740.

See also **Habsburg Dynasty; Leopold I (Holy Roman Empire); Rákóczi Revolt; Spanish Succession, War of the (1701–1714); Utrecht, Peace of (1713).**

BIBLIOGRAPHY

Hengelmüller von Hengervár, Ladislas, Freiherr. *Hungary's Fight for National Existence; Or, the History of the Great Uprising Led by Francis Rakoczi II, 1703–1711.* London, 1913.

Ingrao, Charles W. *In Quest and Crisis: Emperor Joseph I and the Habsburg Monarchy.* West Lafayette, Ind., 1979.

McKay, Derek. *Prince Eugene of Savoy.* London, 1977.

CHARLES INGRAO

JOSEPH II (HOLY ROMAN EMPIRE) (1741–1790; ruled 1765–1790), the eldest son of Empress Maria Theresa (ruled 1740–1780) and Francis of Lorraine (ruled 1745–1765), succeeded his father on the imperial throne in 1765, after which he acted as co-regent with his mother in ruling the Habsburg domains. Although the imperial dignity meant little in the non-Habsburg lands of the Holy Roman Empire, it was of real importance within the Austrian domains. These were held together constitutionally only by the person of the emperor and the Pragmatic Sanction of 1713, in which Emperor Charles VI (ruled 1711–1740) had declared the Austrian lands to be indivisible and that the various titles and thrones would descend to his daughter Maria Theresa. To this minimal constitutional framework Maria Theresa added the Council of State (Staatsrat) in 1762, part of a continuing effort to strengthen the central administration of her lands. Her constant policy, which her son would accelerate, was to increase royal power at the expense of provincial autonomy.

The domains that Maria Theresa and Joseph II ruled were the most diverse in all of Europe. Belgium belonged to the Habsburgs, as did some Italian provinces, the Duchies of Austria, Styria, Carniola, Carinthia, the kingdom of Bohemia, Croatia, the kingdom of Hungary, and other assorted lands and duchies. All spoke different languages, had different histories, laws, and customs, and were accustomed to being ruled according to their own traditions. Maria Theresa and Joseph II made it their overriding political aim to bring together administratively provinces and kingdoms that were otherwise separate, and which defended local privileges and immunities with tenacity and vigor.

Maria Theresa and Joseph II had two aims in their efforts to strengthen the central monarchy at the expense of provincial autonomy. The first, and easier to obtain, was centralization, which involved transferring political decision-making power from local notables to the royal councils. The second, much more difficult aim was uniformity, which meant treating all provinces and all social and legal classes alike in matters of law and administration. These policies constituted the core of enlightened despotism, in which reforms and modernization were imposed from above upon often hostile and unappreciative subjects. As enlightened despots, Maria Theresa and Joseph II had good intentions. For Maria Theresa, the difficulties in achieving centralization and especially uniformity had made her cautious, but Joseph was impatient, and his enlightened rationalism was as absolute as his despotism.

In 1780, the courteous, modest, diligent, and likeable Joseph II became sole ruler of Austria at the death of his mother, which enabled him to push his aims as hard and fast as he liked. He had several programs, which he instituted quickly throughout all of his diverse domains. Joseph disliked the independent power of the Roman Catholic Church. He began his reign with an edict of religious toleration (13 October 1781), fulfilling the Enlightenment ideal that religious persecution was squalid, loathsome, and beneath the moral dignity of a modern monarch. This followed the Edict on Idle Institutions (1780), which began the closure of monasteries—ultimately about seven hundred of them—with their property seized to support secular state schools and charitable institutions. Joseph believed in religious liberty for everyone. His general religious opinions may be discerned from his comment that service to God was the same as service to the state.

Joseph combined secularism with reform of the courts and law within the Austrian crownlands. Centralization and uniformity were the basic principles he used to bring order and coherence to the chaos of multiple legal inheritances. He abolished the law that made mixed marriages a crime against religion, and he closed a number of ecclesiastical courts. Beyond these particular changes, Joseph simply nationalized the judicial system. Manorial and municipal courts had their jurisdiction circumscribed, and they came under much closer governmental scrutiny. He established new appellate courts, which were uniform throughout all his lands. He engaged in a favorite project of enlightened rulers and philosophers: codification of the existing welter of medieval law into a modern and coherent code that would apply uniformly to all the realm. He continued the work begun by Maria Theresa, who in 1770 had issued a criminal code, the Nemesis Theresiana. Joseph reformed this further with the Penal Code of 1787 and the Code of Criminal Procedure in 1788. A notable feature of this code was a substantial reduction in the death penalty. He also reformed civil law, with a code of the law of persons and of property in 1786. Finally, he abolished the patrimonial courts in the kingdom of Hungary, establishing new courts of first instance and bringing Hungarian procedure in line with the rest of the Austrian crownlands. Such judicial reform is rarely easy. Joseph's reforms deeply angered

Joseph II. Portrait by Joseph Hickel. The Art Archive/Historisches Museum (Museen de Stadt Wein) Vienna/Dagli Orti

the Hungarian rural nobility, who complained about the loss of their ancestral privileges.

Joseph II departed most dramatically from his mother's pattern of cautious reform in the area of land and the abolition of serfdom. On 1 November 1781, he abolished some of the worst disabilities of serfdom in the lands of Bohemia and Austria, and he extended these reforms to Transylvania in 1783 and Hungary in 1785. In 1789 he abolished the remaining obligations of serfdom and changed the existing tax structure into a single tax on land. This was the culmination of his social reforms, which turned the serfs from patrimonial into royal subjects.

Joseph had tried to reform everything, never learning that politics is the art of the possible, not the perfect. He appears to have been convinced that imperial power was sufficient to change virtually every aspect of social and communal relationships in the crownlands. A flood of decrees would improve everything. In Joseph's world, however, inertia had greater power than command. He attempted to use central power to create the state, whereas it was the state that must come first for the central power to be effective.

See also **Austria; Bohemia; Holy Roman Empire; Hungary; Maria Theresa (Holy Roman Empire).**

BIBLIOGRAPHY

Beales, Derek Edward Dawson. *Joseph II.* Cambridge, U.K., and New York, 1987.

Bernard, Paul P. *Joseph II and Bavaria: Two Eighteenth-Century Attempts at German Unification.* The Hague, 1965.

Gagliardo, John G. *Reich and Nation: The Holy Roman Empire as Idea and Reality, 1763–1806.* Bloomington, Ind., 1980.

Krieger, Leonard. *The German Idea of Freedom: History of a Political Tradition.* Chicago, 1972.

Padover, Saul K. *The Revolutionary Emperor: Joseph the Second, 1741–1790.* New York and London, 1934.

JAMES D. HARDY, JR.

JOSEPHINISM. The meaning of the term, as well as the origins and nature of Josephinism, have been the objects of one of the most savage controversies in Central European historiography. Initially coined in the nineteenth century to describe the reform program implemented in the Habsburg Monarchy during the reign of Emperor Joseph II (co-regent 1765–1780, ruled 1780–1790), "Josephinism" came increasingly to apply specifically to the measures undertaken against the social, economic, political, and cultural position of the Catholic Church in the monarchy. Definitions have ranged across a broad spectrum, from seeing it as a general ideology of reform—a kind of Austrian variant of the Enlightenment—to interpreting it narrowly as state control over the ecclesiastical sphere. All interpretations have come to agree, however, that the roots of the reform momentum go back to the early eighteenth century, and that the reign of Empress Maria Theresa (ruled 1740–1780) was the critical era during which reform ideas crystallized.

In the seventeenth-century Counter-Reformation, Catholicism was in many ways the integrating ideology of the highly pluralistic patrimony of the Habsburgs. It involved not only a set of confessional dogmas, but broader patterns of thought and culture inextricably intertwined with a social and political infrastructure that had grown out of the economic and social upheavals of the era. When this polity proved unequal to the challenges it faced in the first half of the eighteenth century, the remedial measures undertaken identified confessional issues among the central problems to be addressed. Because of the degree of integration between political and confessional issues in the Counter-Reformation state, however, these reforms were not effected in discrete confessional spheres but had broad social, economic, and political consequences. Political economists argued that confessional policies were responsible for the relative economic underdevelopment of the Habsburg lands, while various ecclesiastical reform movements within the church became increasingly disenchanted with most ritualized form of baroque piety and advocated more internalized forms of worship. Secular, rational, and utilitarian values and a simpler, internalized religious ethos thus came to constitute the backbone of Josephinism.

By the time Joseph II became sole ruler of the Habsburg lands in 1780, all the main features of the "Josephinist" program were already in place. Both the pace and scope of reform accelerated, but even then its most prominent aspects remained those that touched on the religious sphere: the dissolution of about one-third of the monarchy's monastic institutions with its concomitant confiscation of church property, the proclamations of confessional tolerance for Protestants and Jews, the effective establishment of a civil constitution for the Austrian clergy through state control of seminaries and the wide-ranging reorganization of parishes, and the promulgation of civil marriage and austere burial ordinances. Attitudes underlying these reforms remained alive well into the next century, despite the monarchy's sharp turn to political conservatism during the Revolutionary and Napoleonic Wars and the subsequent Age of Metternich. Josephinism can thus be seen as one of the most important roots of nineteenth-century Austrian liberalism.

See also **Bohemia; Enlightenment; Habsburg Dynasty: Austria; Joseph II (Holy Roman Empire); Maria Theresa (Holy Roman Empire).**

BIBLIOGRAPHY

No study specifically devoted to Josephinism exists in the English language. The reform momentum of the eighteenth century with its central ecclesiastical dimension, which culminated in the reign of Joseph II, can best be approached through Ernst Wangermann, *The Austrian Achievement, 1700–1800* (London, 1973). More recent discussions can be followed in the relevant chapters of Derek Beales, *Joseph II, Vol. 1: In the Shadow of Maria Theresa, 1741–1780* (Cambridge, U.K., 1987) and Franz A. J. Szabo, *Kaunitz and Enlightened Absolutism, 1753–1780* (Cambridge, U.K., 1994). The major studies in German are by Fritz Valjavec, Eduard Winter, and Ferdinand Maass.

FRANZ A. J. SZABO

JOURNALISM, NEWSPAPERS, AND NEWSSHEETS. The earliest printed periodical news publications appeared shortly after 1600. By the end of the seventeenth century, newspapers were being published in every major European country. Together, they constituted a phenomenon new in European history and unique in the world: a system of communication that made the most up-to-date information available, not just to members of government bureaucracies or wealthy elites, but to a socially diverse public that included even those of modest means. Printed periodicals tied Europe's "Republic of Letters" together, promoted the diffusion of knowledge and of new cultural models, and offered a source of income to the period's increasing number of writers. As a medium for advertising, periodicals helped promote the growth in consumption that was one of the striking phenomena of the eighteenth century. By 1804, the German journalist and scholar August Ludwig von Schlözer could write that the periodical press was "one of the great instruments of culture through which we Europeans have become what we are."

Broadsheets (French *canards,* German *Flugblätter* or *Neue Zeitungen*), the earliest printed news publications, began to appear in the sixteenth century, carrying news of unusual occurrences such as battles, royal deaths, and "wonders" such as two-headed calves. Printers produced them irregularly, as the flow of events dictated, and used illustrations and headlines set in oversized type to attract readers. Around the same time, manuscript newsletters, particularly common in Italy, began to offer subscribers a regular flow of reports. Such handwritten newspapers continued to circulate in many parts of Europe until the period of the French Revolution, but soon after the beginning of the seventeenth century, the development of dependable postal systems encouraged the creation of the first printed publications issued on a regular periodical schedule. The earliest known printed newspapers were published in Germany in 1605. In the course of the seventeenth century, the press spread throughout the European continent. The first newspapers appeared in Holland in 1618, England in 1622, France in 1631, Spain in 1641, and Russia in 1702. Events such as the Thirty Years' War, the Puritan Revolution in England, and the wars of Louis XIV promoted the spread of newspaper publication, producing a flow of constantly changing reports and generating an audience with an intense interest in the latest developments.

Unlike the broadsheets, early modern news gazettes lacked pictures and headlines, and their content consisted largely of dry chronicles of events from the major courts, battlefronts, and trading cities. The earliest news publications appeared at relatively long intervals, sometimes only once a year, but it did not take long for weekly and twice-weekly gazettes to dominate the market. A daily newspaper appeared in Bremen as early as 1650, and although daily publication remained rare before the French Revolution, there was a general trend toward more frequent issues and a greater total volume of content. Publishers quickly learned to help their readers make sense of the news by numbering and dating each issue of the paper, and giving the date and place of origin of each news bulletin they printed. Readers often preserved their newspapers as a permanent chronicle of events, and publishers sometimes provided title pages and even indexes so that the annual collections could be bound as books.

Throughout the early modern period, newspapers continued to be produced on hand-operated wooden printing presses. This technology limited the number of copies that could be printed: a single press could produce at most 3,000 copies of a paper in a day, so that expanding the press run required paying compositors to set a second form of type. In contrast to the leisurely and irregular pace of work in most enterprises of the period, newspaper printers were subjected to strict time constraints and

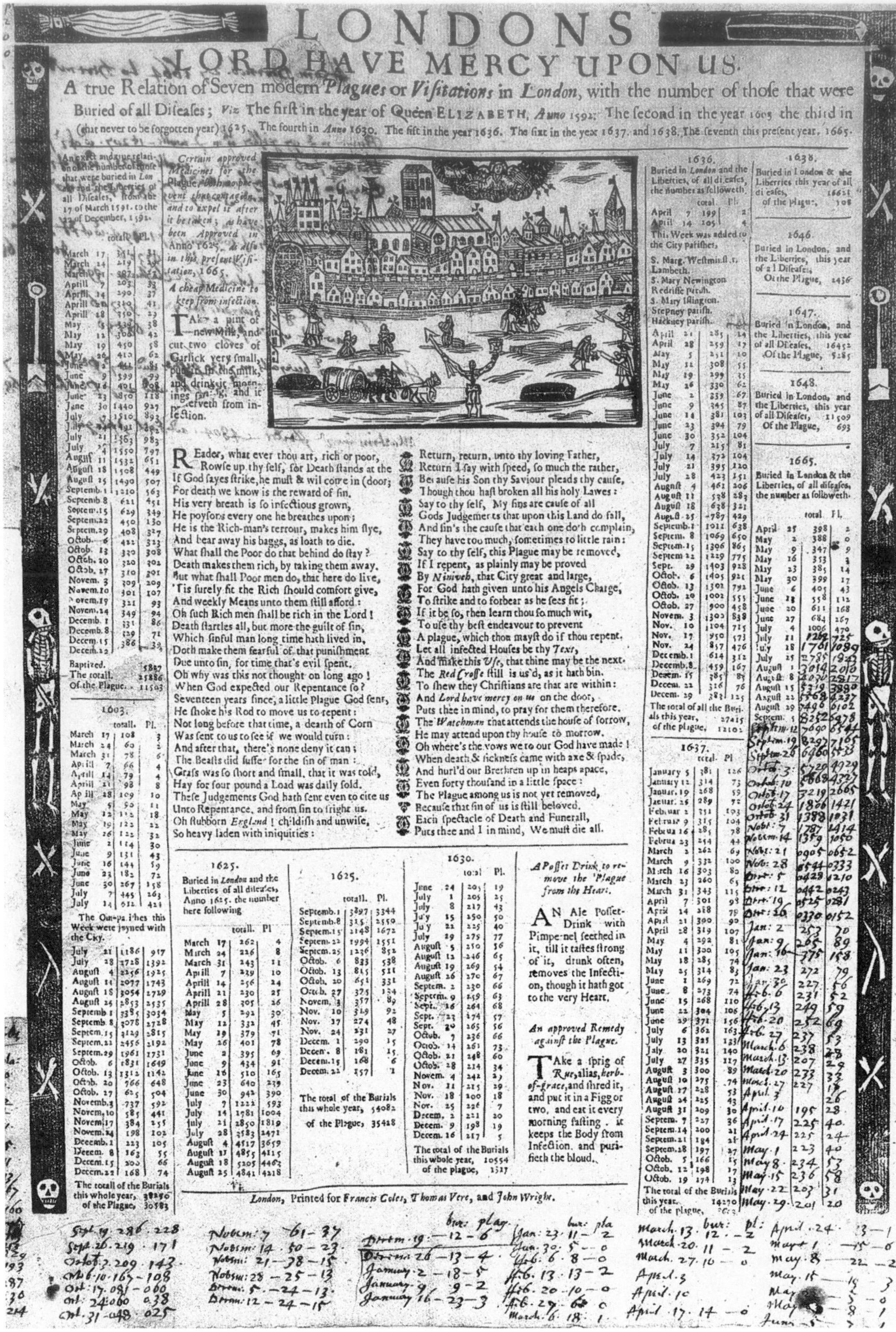

LONDONS
LORD HAVE MERCY UPON US.

A true Relation of Seven modern *Plagues* or *Visitations* in *London*, with the number of those that were Buried of all Diseases; *Viz.* The first in the year of Queen ELIZABETH, *Anno* 1592. The second in the year 1603 the third in (that never to be forgotten year) 1625. The fourth in *Anno* 1630. The fift in the year 1636. The sixt in the year 1637. and 1638. The seventh this present year, 1665.

An exact and true relation of the number of those that were buried in London and the Liberties of all Diseases, from the 17 of March 1591. to the 22 of December, 1592.

		totall.	Pl.
March	17	351	31
March	24	219	29
March	31	307	27
Aprill	7	203	33
Aprill	14	290	37
Aprill	21	310	41
Aprill	28	350	29
May	5	339	38
May	12	300	42
May	19	450	58
May	26	410	62
June	2	441	81
June	9	399	99
June	16	401	108
June	23	850	118
June	30	1440	927
July	7	1510	893
July	14	1491	892
July	21	1563	983
July	28	1550	797
August	11	1532	651
August	18	1508	449
August	25	1490	507
Septemb.	1	1210	563
Septemb.	8	621	451
Septem.	15	629	349
Septem.	22	450	130
Septem.	29	408	327
Octob.	6	422	323
Octob.	13	330	308
Octob.	20	320	302
Octob.	27	310	301
Novem.	3	309	209
Novem.	10	301	107
Novem.	17	321	93
Novem.	24	349	94
Decemb.	1	331	86
Decemb.	8	329	71
Decem.	15	386	39
Decem.	22		

Baptized. 5837
The totall. 25886
Of the Plague. 11503

1603.

		totall.	Pl.
March	17	108	3
March	24	60	2
March	31	78	6
Aprill	7	66	4
Aprill	14	79	4
Aprill	21	98	8
Aprill	28	109	10
May	5	90	11
May	12	112	18
May	19	122	22
May	26	122	32
June	2	114	30
June	9	131	43
June	16	144	59
June	23	182	72
June	30	267	158
July	7	445	263
July	14	612	421

The Out-parishes this Week were joyned with the City.

July	21	1186	917
July	28	1728	1392
August	4	2256	1925
August	11	2077	1743
August	18	3054	2729
August	25	2853	2535
Septemb.	1	3385	3034
Septemb.	8	3078	2728
Septem.	15	3129	2815
Septem.	22	2456	2192
Septem.	29	1961	1731
Octob.	6	1831	1649
Octob.	13	1312	1142
Octob.	20	766	648
Octob.	27	625	504
Novemb.	3	737	592
Novem.	10	585	441
Novem.	17	384	255
Novem.	24	198	102
Decemb.	1	223	105
Decem.	8	163	55
Decem.	15	200	66
Decem.	22	168	74

The totall of the Burials this whole year, 38250
of the Plague, 30583

Certain approved Medicines for the Plague, both to prevent that contagion, and to expel it after it be taken; as have been Approved in Anno 1625. as also in this present Visitation, 1665.

A cheap Medicine to keep from infection.

TAke a pint of new Milk, and cut two cloves of Garlick very small, put it in the milk, and drink it mornings fasting, and it preserveth from infection.

Reader, what ever thou art, rich or poor,
Rowse up thy self, for Death stands at the (door;
If God sayes strike, he must & wil come in
For death we know is the reward of sin.
His very breath is so infectious grown,
He poysons every one he breathes upon;
He is the Rich-man's terrour, makes him flye,
And bear away his baggs, as loath to die.
What shall the Poor do that behind do stay?
Death makes them rich, by taking them away.
But what shall Poor men do, that here do live,
'Tis surely fit the Rich should comfort give,
And weekly Means unto them still afford:
Oh such Rich men shall be rich in the Lord!
Death startles all, but more the guilt of sin,
Which sinful man long time hath lived in,
Doth make them fearful of that punishment
Due unto sin, for time that's evil spent.
Oh why was this not thought on long ago!
When God expected our Repentance so?
Seventeen years since, a little Plague God sent,
He shoke his Rod to move us to repent:
Not long before that time, a dearth of Corn
Was sent to us to see if we would turn:
And after that, there's none deny it can;
The Beasts did suffer for the sin of man:
Grass was so short and small, that it was told,
Hay for four pound a Load was daily sold.
These Judgements God hath sent even to cite us
Unto Repentance, and from sin to fright us.
Oh stubborn *England*! childish and unwise,
So heavy laden with iniquities:
Return, return, unto thy loving Father,
Return I say with speed, so much the rather,
Because his Son thy Saviour pleads thy cause,
Though thou hast broken all his holy Lawes:
Say to thy self, My sins are cause of all
Gods Judgements that upon this Land do fall,
And sin's the cause that each one doth complain,
They have too much, sometimes to little rain:
Say to thy self, this Plague may be removed,
If I repent, as plainly may be proved
By *Niniveh*, that City great and large,
For God hath given unto his Angels Charge,
To strike and to forbear as he sees fit;
If it be so, then learn thou so much wit,
To use thy best endeavour to prevent
A plague, which thou mayst do if thou repent.
Let all infected Houses be thy *Text*,
And make this *Use*, that thine may be the next.
The *Red Crosse* still is us'd, as it hath bin.
To shew they Christians are that are within:
And *Lord have mercy on us* on the door,
Puts thee in mind, to pray for them therefore.
The *Watchman* that attends the house of sorrow,
He may attend upon thy house to morrow.
Oh where's the vows we to our God have made!
When death & sickness came with axe & spade,
And hurl'd our Brethren up in heaps apace,
Even forty thousand in a little space:
The Plague among us is not yet removed,
Because that sin of us is still beloved.
Each spectacle of Death and Funerall,
Puts thee and I in mind, We must die all.

1625.

Buried in *London* and the Liberties of all diseases, Anno 1625. the number here following

		totall.	Pl
March	17	262	4
March	24	226	8
March	31	243	11
Aprill	7	239	10
Aprill	14	256	24
Aprill	21	230	25
Aprill	28	305	26
May	5	292	30
May	12	332	45
May	19	379	71
May	26	401	78
June	2	395	69
June	9	434	91
June	16	510	165
June	23	640	239
June	30	942	390
July	7	1222	593
July	14	1781	1004
July	21	2850	1819
July	28	3583	2471
August	4	4517	3659
August	11	4855	4115
August	18	5205	4463
August	25	4841	4218

1625.

		totall.	Pl.
Septemb.	1	3897	3344
Septemb.	8	3157	2550
Septem.	15	2148	1672
Septem.	22	1994	1551
Septem.	29	1236	852
Octob.	6	833	538
Octob.	13	815	511
Octob.	20	651	331
Octob.	27	375	134
Novem.	3	357	89
Nov.	10	319	92
Nov.	17	274	48
Nov.	24	231	27
Decem.	1	290	15
Decem.	8	181	15
Decem.	15	168	6
Decem.	22	157	1

The total of the Burials this whole year, 54082
of the Plague, 35428

1630.

		total	Pl.
June	24	205	19
July	1	205	25
July	8	217	43
July	15	250	50
July	22	225	40
July	29	275	77
August	5	250	56
August	12	246	65
August	19	269	54
August	26	270	67
Septem.	2	230	66
Septem.	9	259	63
Sept.	16	264	68
Sept.	23	174	57
Sept.	30	265	56
Octob.	7	236	66
Octob.	14	261	73
Octob.	21	248	60
Octob.	28	214	34
Novem.	4	242	27
Nov.	11	215	29
Nov.	18	200	18
Nov.	25	226	7
Decem.	2	221	20
Decem.	9	198	19
Decem.	16	217	5

The total of the Burials this whole year, 10554
of the plague, 1317

A Posset Drink to remove the Plague from the Heart.

AN Ale Posset-Drink with Pimpernel seethed in it, till it tastes strong of it, drunk often, removes the Infection, though it hath got to the very Heart.

An approved Remedy against the Plague.

TAke a sprig of *Rue*, alias, *herb-of-grace*, and shred it, and put it in a Figg or two, and eat it every morning fasting, it keeps the Body from Infection, and purifieth the bloud.

1636.

Buried in *London* and the Liberties, of all diseases, the number as followeth.

		total.	Pl.
April	7	199	2
April	14	205	4

This Week was added to the City parishes,
S. Marg. Westminster.
Lambeth.
S. Mary Newington
Redriffe parish.
S. Mary Islington.
Stepney parish.
Hackney parish.

April	21	285	24
April	28	259	17
May	5	251	10
May	12	308	55
May	19	299	35
May	26	330	62
June	2	339	67
June	9	345	87
June	16	381	103
June	23	394	79
June	30	352	104
July	7	215	81
July	14	372	104
July	21	395	120
July	28	423	151
August	4	461	206
August	11	538	283
August	18	638	321
August	25	787	429
Septemb.	1	1011	638
Septem.	8	1069	650
Septem.	15	1306	865
Septem.	22	1229	775
Sept.	29	1403	928
Octob.	6	1405	921
Octob.	13	1302	792
Octob.	20	1002	555
Octob.	27	900	458
Novem.	3	1303	838
Nov.	10	1104	715
Nov.	17	950	573
Nov.	24	857	476
Decemb.	1	614	312
Decemb.	8	459	167
Decem.	15	385	83
Decem.	22	316	76
Decem.	29	383	125

The total of all the Burials this year, 27415
of the plague, 12102

1637.

		total.	Pl
January	5	381	126
January	12	314	73
Januar.	19	268	59
Januar.	26	289	72
Februar	2	351	103
Februar	9	315	104
Februa	16	285	78
Februa	23	254	44
March	2	262	69
March	9	332	100
March	16	303	80
March	23	260	65
March	31	343	115
April	7	301	98
April	14	288	78
April	21	300	90
April	28	319	107
May	4	292	81
May	11	300	105
May	18	285	74
May	25	314	83
June	1	269	72
June	8	273	74
June	15	268	110
June	22	304	106
June	29	371	156
July	6	362	163
July	13	325	133
July	20	321	140
July	27	335	117
August	3	300	89
August	10	275	74
August	17	228	53
August	24	225	43
August	31	209	30
Septem.	7	227	36
Septem.	14	200	21
Septem.	21	184	21
Septem.	28	197	27
Octob.	5	166	15
Octob.	12	198	17
Octob.	19	174	13

The total of the Burials this year, 14270
of the plague, [illegible]

1638.

Buried in London & the Liberties this year of all diseases, 16621
of the plague, 308

1646.

Buried in London, and the Liberties, this year of all Diseases,
Of the Plague, 2436

1647.

Buried in London, and the Liberties, this year of all Diseases, 16452
Of the Plague, 5285

1648.

Buried in London, and the Liberties, this year of all Diseases, 11509
Of the Plague, 693

1665.

Buried in London & the Liberties, of all diseases, the number as followeth.

		total.	Pl.
April	25	398	2
May	2	388	0
May	9	347	9
May	16	353	3
May	23	385	14
May	30	399	17
June	6	405	43
June	13	558	112
June	20	611	168
June	27	684	267
July	4	1006	470
July	11	1269	725
July	18	1761	1089
July	25	2785	1843
August	1	3014	2010
August	8	4030	2817
August	15	5319	3880
August	22	5568	4237
August	29	7496	6102
Septem.	5	8252	6978

London, Printed for *Francis Coles*, *Thomas Vere*, and *John Wright*.

Journalism, Newspapers, and Newssheets. A 1665 English broadsheet laments an outbreak of the plague. THE ART ARCHIVE

had to "frequently work as if on a forced march," as an eighteenth-century typographer put it: the papers had to be ready to be mailed at fixed times. Although the work was demanding, skilled workers could earn more than in ordinary printing shops, and even before the end of the eighteenth century, some publishers offered enticements such as pensions to keep a loyal work force. For the owners of printing shops, newspaper publishing was a way of ensuring a regular income, particularly since most periodicals were sold by subscription, and readers therefore had to pay in advance, in contrast to the purchasers of books. In small provincial towns, a newspaper might be just one of a local printer's many ways of keeping his presses occupied. At the opposite extreme, the eighteenth century already saw the rise of the first great "press barons," entrepreneurs who brought together a group of periodicals aimed at different market niches. In the 1770s and 1780s, the French publisher Charles-Joseph Panckoucke (1736–1798) managed to gain control of most of the French national press, including the venerable *Gazette de France* and the country's leading literary journal, the *Mercure de France,* and to create a "stable" of writers dependent on his patronage.

The news carried in the gazettes attracted a large and varied audience: rulers and their courtiers, military officers, bankers and merchants, all of whom had professional reasons for wanting to know about wars, treaty negotiations, and unusual developments in foreign states, as well as general readers motivated by simple curiosity. Kaspar Stieler (1632–1707), whose *Zeitungs Lust und Nutz* (1695) was the first book about newspapers, claimed that they were read by many artisans and also discussed their influence on women. Newspapers were the most popular reading matter in the coffeehouses, cafés, and reading rooms that began to spring up in major European cities in the late seventeenth century and then spread across the continent. Numerous sources describe the animated discussions that resulted from this kind of public reading: newspapers were the essential fuel for the verbal interactions that produced the phenomenon of public opinion.

Early journalists, such as Théophraste Renaudot (1586–1653), creator of the *Gazette de France,* had recognized that the newspaper could also serve an important economic function by carrying advertising. In addition, many newspapers regularly reported the prices of commodities and other economic information. In most continental countries, advertising was printed primarily in newspapers licensed specially for that purpose (French *affiches,* German *Intelligenzblätter*), but in eighteenth-century England, a tradition developed of newspapers combining commercial advertising and political news. These mixed publications had a stronger revenue base than most of their continental rivals and pointed toward the form that the newspaper would take throughout the world in the nineteenth and twentieth centuries.

Whereas gazettes dealt largely with political news, periodical magazines, of which the first was the French *Journal des Sçavans,* founded in 1665, showed that the periodical form could also be adapted to carry many kinds of cultural information. Whereas newspapers did not change greatly in form and function before the end of the eighteenth century, magazines became increasingly varied. Less tied to the immediate flow of events than newspapers, they appeared at less frequent intervals and were often aimed at more limited audiences. Book reviews, literary journals, periodicals aimed at particular professions and at audiences such as women and peasants all appeared in the course of the eighteenth century. Joseph Addison (1672–1719) and Richard Steele's (1672–1729) *Spectator* (1711–1714), which offered witty commentary on middle-class urban life, served as a model for dozens of imitators throughout Europe.

The profession of journalist developed more slowly than the press itself. Early news gazettes were frequently compiled by entrepreneurs who also engaged in other activities, such as postmasters, who had privileged access to incoming news, or printers. By the eighteenth century, some writers were able to make a living from editorial work alone, but journalists were disparaged as mercenaries who prostituted their talents for pay, and they therefore had a strong incentive to present themselves as "men of letters" rather than identifying themselves with the periodical industry. Voltaire's article in Diderot's *Encyclopédie* urging that "a good gazetteer should be promptly informed, truthful, impartial, simple, and correct in his style" shows that the elements of what would later become journalism's professional ethic were taking shape, but Voltaire also complained that few journalists measured up to these standards. In spite of its low prestige, newspaper work provided an important source of income for many eighteenth-century writers, and positions such as the editorship of the *Gazette de France* were much-coveted patronage plums. Editing journals and magazines generally paid less well, but by the end of the seventeenth century it had become one way in which individuals could establish important positions in the "Republic of Letters." Pierre Bayle's *Nouvelles de la République des lettres,* founded in 1684, provided one of the first demonstrations of this possibility and inspired imitators throughout the eighteenth century.

Rulers took a strong interest in the press from the outset. Throughout most of Europe, publishers needed a license or privilege to create a periodical. They were usually required to submit to censorship and to pay an annual fee to publish, but in exchange they enjoyed a protected monopoly on publication in their native region. Although governments routinely censored the press to prevent the circulation of items that might cause unrest in the population or embarrassment at court, their interest in the press also had a positive side. At a time when the notion of the reporter was unknown, publishers often depended on their local government to furnish them with foreign news culled from diplomatic dispatches. Each major government sponsored its own official gazette to present the news in the fashion most favorable to its own interests. By the eighteenth century, most rulers saw that periodicals could serve useful functions by publicizing new laws and edicts and by circulating economic information; French *intendants* often played key roles in establishing provincial *affiches.* Through the fees they paid for their privileges and for postal delivery, periodicals were also a source of income for governments.

The development of the press in England differed from the pattern on the continent. In 1695, the Licensing Act that had restricted press freedom was allowed to lapse, making England the only country where publishers could establish periodicals without prior permission. As a result, England became the only country where the press took on a clear political coloration, with Whigs and Tories subsidizing editors to promote their points of view. The absence of restrictions also gave free reign to entrepreneurial initiative in England. Many of the country's provincial newspapers, for example, were established by local bookstore owners, who used them to advertise their wares. The British press was not completely unfettered: a stamp tax on printing paper kept prices high and discouraged the poor from subscribing, and frequent libel prosecutions had a deterrent effect on most journalists and publishers. Summaries of debates in Parliament were not permitted until the 1780s. Continental visitors were nevertheless struck by the outspokenness of British periodicals and their wide audience.

Although the absence of regulation made the English press unique, its influence on the Continent was limited. In international affairs, the most important newspapers of the eighteenth century were the so-called *gazettes d'Hollande,* journals published in French but produced in the Netherlands or in other parts of Europe where the censorship systems of the major powers did not reach. Although they depended on privileges granted by their city governments, publications such as the *Gazette d'Amsterdam* and the *Gazette de Leyde* were normally accorded considerable latitude in their coverage of events in other countries. Founded in many cases by members of the Huguenot diaspora during Louis XIV's reign (1643–1715), they remained a major part of public life in Europe throughout the eighteenth century. Unable to prevent their circulation, rulers sought to influence them instead by courting their editors, offering them confidential information, and negotiating favorable postal rates. Since French was an international language, these gazettes found readers throughout the European world. Under the editorship of Étienne Luzac from 1738 to 1772 and his nephew Jean Luzac from 1772 to 1798, the *Gazette de Leyde* occupied the position of Europe's "newspaper of record." "By water and land it was sent to the most distant countries; it was read with the same intense interest at the gates of the Seraglio and on the banks of the Ganges, and copied from by almost all other newspaper editors . . . ," wrote one observer.

Censorship restrictions kept newspapers published in the Holy Roman Empire from reporting as comprehensively as the international French-language press, but more newspapers were published in the German-speaking world than in any other part of Europe: at least 93 in 1750, and 151 by

1785. The most successful of these, the *Hamburgische Unparteyische Correspondent,* may have reached a press run of 20,000 by the time of the French Revolution. The large number of newspapers in Germany, and the correspondingly impressive number of journals and magazines, reflected both the area's division into many political units and the relatively high level of literacy in the population. By the 1780s, some German publishers were even putting out newspapers aimed explicitly at the peasant population.

Under normal conditions, governments throughout Europe were able to control the periodical press more easily than certain other forms of printing, such as pamphlets, which could be circulated anonymously. Anxious not to jeopardize their privileges and dependent on postal systems to deliver their products, publishers had strong incentives not to antagonize the authorities. The century saw few genuine examples of underground or subversive periodicals. The outstanding example was the French *Nouvelles ecclésiastiques,* the voice of that country's Jansenist religious minority, which successfully defied the police from 1728 down to the Revolutionary era. This feat was only possible, however, because the paper spoke for a well-organized and strongly committed group that included many influential elite members.

When public authority broke down, however, the door was opened for "media revolutions" in which periodicals became instruments for political agitation. The poet John Milton (1608–1674) served as a newspaper editor during the English Civil Wars of the 1640s, and the impact of his contemporary Marchamont Needham's (1620–1678) journalism was still remembered by the journalists of the French Revolution. Periodicals played important roles in the "democratic revolutions" of the second half of the eighteenth century, particularly the revolt in Britain's North American colonies and the Dutch Patriot movement of the 1780s. The greatest example of the press's role in a crisis was the French Revolution of 1789. At the start of that year, there had been only four newspapers published in Paris, only one of them a daily; before the end of 1789, 140 new titles had been founded, and readers had a choice of several dozen dailies representing a wide spectrum of political views and writing styles. This journalistic explosion increased readership; newspapers read aloud even reached illiterate sections of the population. Leading journalists commanded salaries that dwarfed what pre-Revolutionary writers had made from their books, and many of them, most notably Jean-Paul Marat (1743–1793), used their papers to launch political careers.

The French Revolution and the wars that resulted from it brought about fundamental changes in Europe's press. Although Napoleon restored censorship and licensing of newspapers, press freedom became a central part of liberal programs throughout the Continent. Public demand for news led publishers to experiment with new technologies that would allow larger press runs: in 1814, the London *Times* put the first steam-powered press into service. Such machines allowed periodicals to overcome the limitations on press runs that had characterized the "typographical old regime" of the early modern period and made the development of a true mass press possible. The growth of the press after 1800 was so striking that its early modern predecessors were largely forgotten. Modern scholarship has made it possible to appreciate the important roles that periodical publications played in the politics, culture, and economic life of the seventeenth and eighteenth centuries.

See also **Censorship; Literacy and Reading; Printing and Publishing; Public Opinion.**

BIBLIOGRAPHY

Barker, Hannah. *Newspapers, Politics, and Public Opinion in Late Eighteenth-Century England.* Oxford and New York, 1998. A study of the press in the country where it enjoyed the greatest political freedom in the early modern period.

Censer, Jack R. *The French Press in the Age of Enlightenment.* London and New York, 1994. A survey covering the eighteenth century.

Feyel, Gilles. *L'annonce et la nouvelle: La presse d'information en France sous l'ancien régime (1630–1788).* Oxford, 2000. This detailed study of the French regional press demonstrates its important role in the early modern economy.

Lindemann, Margot. *Geschichte der deutschen Presse.* Part 1, *Deutsche Presse bis 1815.* Berlin, 1969. A comprehensive survey of the press in the German-speaking world.

Popkin, Jeremy D. *News and Politics in the Age of Revolution: Jean Luzac's Gazette de Leyde, 1772–1798.* Ithaca, N.Y., 1989. An analysis of the international news system of the eighteenth century and of its political and cultural impact.

Solomon, Howard M. *Public Welfare, Science, and Propaganda in Seventeenth-Century France.* Princeton, 1972. The life of the creator of the first French newspaper.

Tucoo-Chala, Suzanne. *Charles-Joseph Panckoucke et la librairie française, 1736–1798.* Pau, France, 1977. Biography of the first great "press baron."

JEREMY D. POPKIN

JOURNALS, LITERARY. Literary journals appeared in the seventeenth and eighteenth centuries to provide a growing readership with news and gossip about literary matters and a sampling of contemporary writings. Like novels, coffeehouses, and salons, literary journals appealed to an emerging public keen on fashioning its own cultural tastes and literary opinions.

Though the best-known literary journals, such as *The Tatler* and *The Spectator* in England, were independent publications launched by enterprising men of letters, others, especially early periodicals, originated from official sponsorship. The *Journal des savants,* for example, was created by Jean-Baptiste Colbert in 1665 and combined scientific and technical information with the most noteworthy news from "the Republic of Letters." The *Mercure galant,* founded in 1672, was also a quasi-official publication: its editor was provided lodgings in the Louvre and received a royal pension. It furnished readers with news of the court and Parisian society, as well as commentary on literary, theatrical, and scientific events. France was not the only nation to give rise to literary journals in the seventeenth century. In Italy the *Journal des savants* served as a model for several *Giornali dei letterati,* which began appearing in 1668.

It was in the eighteenth century that this type of periodical, like newspapers in general, began to appear throughout western Europe, becoming an important feature of urban culture and sociability. Germany had its *Litteratur-Zeitung;* Spain its *Espiritu de los mejores diarios;* Italy its *Giornale dei letterati d'Italia,* published in Venice starting in 1710. Many of these newspapers, especially those in Germany and Spain, had a very limited circulation of only several hundred readers. The *Mercure galant,* however, was distributed in twenty-six provincial towns in 1748 and fifty-five by 1774.

By far the most successful and influential literary newspapers were *The Tatler* (1709–1711), edited by the playwright Richard Steele, and *The Spectator* (1711–1712), a joint venture of Steele and the poet Joseph Addison. Though in part literary in nature, they were "moral" in spirit, aimed at improving manners and fostering sociability in a society increasingly dominated by the competitive spirit of commercialism. The success of these periodicals was enormous: *The Spectator* went from a circulation of 4,000 to around 30,000 in a few months. They also inspired emulators on the Continent despite the fact that the conditions for publication, such as censorship and a limited reading public, were clearly less favorable. The French writer Pierre de Marivaux (1688–1763) took Addison's journal as his model for the *Spectateur français* (1722). The first German weekly, the *Hamburg Vernunftler* (1713–1740), was also fashioned after the English newspapers. Justus van Effen (1684–1735) began publishing the journal *Le misantrope* in Holland and also published *De Hollandsche Spectator* (1731–1735).

Literary newspapers were integral to the culture of the Enlightenment. Indeed, well-known men of letters, such as Jean-François Marmontel, who edited the *Mercure de France* in 1758–1760, helped transform these publications into organs of Enlightenment, offering fellow philosophes popular and convenient outlets for their ideas. They also served as agents of national integration, bringing the fashion, language, and news of the court and capital to the provinces. But these journals were not simply one-way instruments: they invited readers' comments and printed their letters, thus fostering discussion and debate. Many of their readers were women. Nearly half of the articles appearing in Addison and Steele's newspapers addressed female concerns. In France the *Journal des dames,* which specifically aimed at a female readership, was inaugurated in 1759.

Literary journals scrupulously avoided the contentious topics of politics and religion. It was in part because of this that they were able both to flourish and to create a public out of readers who might otherwise find themselves at odds.

See also **Addison, Joseph; Colbert, Jean-Baptiste; Journalism, Newspapers, and Newssheets; Steele, Richard.**

BIBLIOGRAPHY

Goodman, Dena. *The Republic of Letters: A Cultural History of the French Enlightenment.* Ithaca, N.Y., and London, 1994.

Melton, James van Horn. *The Rise of the Public in Enlightenment Europe.* Cambridge, U.K., and New York, 2001.

ROBERT A. SCHNEIDER

JOURNALS, SCIENTIFIC. *See* Communication, Scientific.

JUAN DE AUSTRIA, DON (1547–1578), Spanish admiral and governor, known to Elizabethans as Don John. Born in Regensburg, Germany, to commoner Barbara Blomberg, Don Juan, the natural son of Emperor Charles V, was brought to Brussels, where his mother married. In 1550 Charles had the boy, called Jeromín, taken to Spain by a servant couple, and then, in 1554, transferred to the castle of his chief of household, Don Luis de Quijada, and his wife, Doña Magdalena de Ulloa, at Villagarcía de Campos. Before his death, Charles saw Jeromín but did not openly acknowledge his parentage. In 1559 Philip II embraced Jeromín as his brother and renamed him Juan de Austria. Philip did not accord him royal status, though he was ranked before the grandees, but in 1575 he yielded to Don Juan's being addressed as "Highness." Charles hoped Don Juan might enter the clergy, but during his education in statecraft alongside Prince Don Carlos and Alexander Farnese, future duke of Parma, he revealed his martial inclinations. When he reached twenty-one in 1568, Philip appointed him Captain General of the [Mediterranean] Sea.

Don Juan returned from his summer at sea to find the court mourning the deaths of the mentally unstable Don Carlos and the queen. Differing with Philip over his place at the queen's funeral, he withdrew to a monastery. When the Morisco revolt erupted in Granada, Don Juan volunteered to serve as supreme commander over feuding local grandees in March 1569 to suppress it. Quijada, assigned to guide him, was mortally wounded in a skirmish, and a musket ball grazed his own helmet. In subduing the rebellion, he became a skilled general. Blond and handsome, he also became a womanizer. He sired two natural daughters, one in Spain, the other in Naples.

When Philip agreed to a Holy League with Venice and Pope Pius V against the Ottoman Turks in 1570, he sought supreme command for Don Juan. Philip hoped the league might recover Tunis and conquer Algiers, after saving Cyprus for Venice. Don Juan sailed from Barcelona in July 1571 and had the League armada assembled at Messina by September. Unknown to him, Cyprus had been lost. Despite arguments that the season was late, he took the league armada to sea. The 207 galleys of the distrustful allies he mixed in the center, two wings, and rearguard, so that none dared desert. On 7 October 1571 he won a heady victory over the Turks at Lepanto and became a hero to all Christendom.

He hoped to complete the destruction of Turkish sea power in 1572, but Philip II, nervous about developments in France and the Netherlands, kept him and his galleys in the western Mediterranean. Not until September did Don Juan join the Venetian and papal galleys off the Peloponnesus, where forts and cavalry prevented him from destroying the beached Turkish fleet.

Venice quit the league in March 1573, and Don Juan recovered Tunis in October. Advised to dismantle the fortress of La Goleta, which dominated Tunis's harbor, and level Tunis, Don Juan chose instead to hold La Goleta and erect a citadel in the city. (Critics claimed he hoped the pope would make him king of Tunis.) In summer 1574, while Don Juan was distracted by Genoese politics and French threats, a huge Turkish armada took Tunis and La Goleta. In 1575 Philip declared bankruptcy, limiting Don Juan to raids against Turkish Barbary.

In May 1576 he received orders to proceed directly to the rebellious Netherlands as governor-general and restore peace. In correspondence with his half-sister, Margaret of Parma, once regent there, he expressed fear of such assignment. Other than duty, the only lure, nurtured by the papacy, was the possibility of invading England to liberate Mary Stuart, queen of Scots, and join her on England's throne. Uncertain about funds and authority, he detoured to see Philip in Spain. Continuing through France in disguise, he reached Luxembourg in November to find that the sack of Antwerp

Don Juan de Austria. Anonymous portrait engraving, undated. ©Image Select/Art Resource, N.Y.

by mutineers had united the Estates-General (the Netherlands' parliament) against him. Only by dismissing Philip's army, (and, thus, the chance to free Mary Stuart), temporizing on religion, and trading on his personal charm did he win acceptance. In May 1577 he entered Brussels. As his instructions allowed no real concessions regarding religion, the Protestant provinces remained defiant. Fearing assassination, in July Don Juan seized Namur in the southern Netherlands and dispatched secretary Juan de Escobedo to Spain to beg the return of the army. Having just received fresh treasure from America, Philip reluctantly agreed.

In December 1577 the army returned with the prince of Parma. In January 1578 they routed the Estates-Generals' army at Gembloux. In Spain, the king's unscrupulous and ambitious secretary, Antonio Pérez, bred unjustified suspicions of Don Juan in Philip's mind, and in March had Escobedo murdered (probably with Philip's approval). Again, inadequately funded, Don Juan failed before Brussels in July. With success eluding him and unsure of Philip's trust, he regrouped outside Namur, where, health failing, he died on 1 October 1578. He had served Philip faithfully and, if he failed, it was due to their shared opposition to religious toleration.

See also **Charles V (Holy Roman Empire); Lepanto, Battle of; Moriscos; Moriscos, Expulsion of (Spain); Parma, Alexander Farnese, duke of; Philip II (Spain).**

BIBLIOGRAPHY

Dennis, Amarie. *Don Juan of Austria.* Madrid, 1966.

Ibañez de Ibero, Carlos, Marqués de Mulhacén. *Don Juan de Austria.* Madrid, 1944.

Stirling-Maxwell, William. *Don John of Austria, or Passages from the history of the sixteenth century.* 2 vols. London, 1883.

Peter Pierson

JUDAISM. *See* **Jews and Judaism.**

JÜLICH-CLEVES-BERG.

The duchy of Jülich-Cleves was a shifting agglomeration of principalities on the Lower Rhine, a location that, despite its lack of large cities, gave it strategic significance as the gateway from the Low Countries to central and southern Germany. During the late Middle Ages the county of Jülich was raised to the dignity of a duchy in 1356 and expanded by adding the county of Ravensberg in 1346 and the county of Berg in 1348. Meanwhile the county of Cleves was taken over by the county of Mark in 1368 and was then raised to the dignity of a duchy in 1417. In 1511 a strategic marriage joined the duchies of Jülich-Berg-Ravensberg in a personal union with Cleves Mark, creating a territory almost the size of the landgraviate of Hesse or Württemberg.

In an effort to consolidate and expand these holdings, Duke William V ("the Rich," ruled 1539–1592) took advantage of the death of Charles of Egmont (1467–1538), the last duke of Gelderland, in 1538 and took over lordship of this important province as well, a move that could have had major political and religious implications, creating as it did a direct link between Cleves (on the Netherlandish frontier) and Jülich (between Aachen and Cologne). Duke William also seemed to welcome Lutheran ideas in his lands. In preparation for a possible contest over this expansion, William had pursued a calculated dynastic policy by marrying Jeanne d'Albret of Navarre, the thirteen-year-old niece of Francis I of France (ruled 1515–1547), while giving his sister Anne of Cleves (1515–1557) to Henry VIII of England (ruled 1509–1547) in 1540. An older sister, Sybilla, had married Elector John Frederick I of Saxony in 1526. However, Emperor Charles V (ruled 1519–1556) reacted energetically to counter such an expansion by exercising a claim that Gelderland belonged to his Burgundian inheritance. Diplomatically he secured the neutrality of France and England and crushed Duke William at Düren in 1543. William the Rich had to subject himself to the emperor, give up all claims to Gelderland, and give up his wife (the marriage with Jeanne d'Albret was annulled in 1545).

In 1546 William married Mary, a daughter of King Ferdinand I of Austria (ruled 1521–1564; emperor 1558–1564), and he learned to practice a more cautious religious policy over the next thirty years. It was long thought that his moderate rule along with the influence of his skeptical physician, Johann Weyer (Wier), protected the duchies from severe witchcraft trials. But research has shown that over a span of 240 years well over two hundred persons were executed as witches, including two as late as 1737–1738.

In 1592, with the death of the duke, the succession of Jülich-Cleves-Berg went to William's only surviving son, Johann Wilhelm I (ruled 1592–1609), who was already suffering from severe madness. Despite increasingly desperate measures, Johann Wilhelm's marriage to Jacobe of Baden remained childless, as did his subsequent marriage to Antoinette of Lorraine. It seemed obvious that there would be no direct male heir, and claimants began jockeying for position already in the 1590s. When Johann Wilhelm died in 1609, the two *Possidentes* (that is, the two claimants already in place at the ducal court in Düsseldorf) were Elector Johann Sigismund of Brandenburg (1572–1619) and Pfalzgraf Wolfgang Wilhelm of Pfalz-Neuburg, both of whom were Lutherans. Emperor Rudolf II (ruled 1576–1612) reacted to prevent an important portion of the empire from going Protestant, and in 1610 the War of the Jülich Succession broke out (with reinforcements on the Protestant side from England, the Netherlands, France, and the Protestant Union). With the assassination of Henry IV of France (ruled 1589–1610), the anti-Habsburg coalition collapsed, but the two Protestant claimants prevailed. Soon enough their collaboration broke down, however, especially after Johann Sigismund converted to Calvinism (1613) and Wolfgang Wilhelm converted to Catholicism (1614).

In the Treaty of Xanten (1614, reconfirmed in 1666) it was agreed that the duchy should be divided, with Cleves, Mark, and Ravensberg going to Brandenburg and Jülich and Berg going to Pfalz-Neuburg. This division was fateful in many ways, for while it extinguished an independent power on the Lower Rhine, it also guaranteed the involvement of two major dynasties in that region: the Hohenzollern of Brandenburg Prussia and the Wittelsbach of the Palatinate and Bavaria. Their rivalry punctuated the history of this region to the end of the eighteenth century. On the death of Elector Maximilian III (Joseph of Bavaria; 1727–1777; elector 1745–1777) in 1777, the presumptive heir Charles Theodore (Karl Theodor) of Pfalz-Sulzbach (1724–1799) even made plans with Emperor Joseph II (ruled 1765–1790) in 1777–1778 to exchange Bavaria for the Austrian Netherlands, which, along with Jülich and Berg, would have once again created a major power on the Lower Rhine and a greatly expanded and consolidated Habsburg territory in the southeast. But Frederick the Great of Prussia (Frederick II, ruled 1740–1786) successfully opposed these plans in the War of the Bavarian Succession (1778–1779, also ridiculed as the "Potato War" because of its military maneuvers without battles). The Prussian-sponsored League of Princes (1785) guaranteed that the Wittelsbach dynasty would remain in possession of Bavaria and would not expand on the Lower Rhine. The Hohenzollern possessions in Cleves and Mark provided a western outpost and later an industrial powerhouse that balanced their overwhelmingly agrarian interests in the German Northeast.

See also **Bavaria; Brandenburg; Hohenzollern Dynasty; Palatinate; Prussia; Wittelsbach Dynasty (Bavaria).**

BIBLIOGRAPHY

Anderson, Alison D. *On the Verge of War: International Relations and the Jülich-Kleve Succession Crises (1609–1614).* Boston, 1999.

Midelfort, H. C. Erik. *Mad Princes of Renaissance Germany.* Charlottesville, Va., 1994.

Stadtmuseum Düsseldorf, ed. *Land im Mittelpunkt der Mächte: Die Herzogtümer Jülich, Kleve Berg*. 2nd ed. Kleve, 1984.

H. C. ERIK MIDELFORT

JULIUS II (POPE) (Giuliano della Rovere; 1443–1513; reigned 1503–1513), Italian pope. Born at Albissola near Savona in 1443, Giuliano was a vigorous man, suited to a life of action, not contemplation, and destined for an ecclesiastical career under the aegis of his uncle, Francesco della Rovere, who became a cardinal in 1467. Like him, Giuliano was a Franciscan; he studied at a Franciscan friary in Perugia.

The election of his uncle to the papal throne as Sixtus IV (reigned 1471–1484) was swiftly followed in December 1471 by his own promotion to cardinal. Important benefices were bestowed on him, including the see of Avignon, as well as the major curial office of Grand Penitentiary. He welcomed the opportunities for action, including participation in military campaigns, offered by legations to Umbria in 1474 and to France in 1480–1482. His wealth, energy, increasing experience, and taste for politics made him one of the most powerful figures in the College of Cardinals; he was an influential adviser to Pope Innocent VIII (reigned 1484–1492) and a leader of the opposition to the Borgia pope, Alexander VI (reigned 1492–1503). Justifiably fearing arrest, he went into exile in France in 1494, and, after accompanying King Charles VIII of France (ruled 1483–1498) on his campaign to conquer the kingdom of Naples in 1494 to 1495, he did not return to Rome during Alexander's lifetime. He was elected pope on 31 October 1503, taking the title Julius II.

His choice of title has been seen as a desire to identify himself and the papacy with the imperial traditions of ancient Rome, an ambition that is often associated with his artistic commissions as pope. Although there is no direct evidence for this link, Julius II was undoubtedly one of the most important cultural patrons of Renaissance Italy. Among the major artists who worked for him were Michelangelo Buonarroti (1475–1564), from whom he commissioned the Sistine Chapel ceiling and his own tomb, Raphael Sanzio (1483–1520), who decorated Julius's apartments in the Vatican and painted his portrait, and Donato Bramante (1444–1514), whose projects for the pope included the Vatican courtyard and the new St. Peter's, which replaced the crumbling old basilica.

His most consistent political aim as pope was to bring the Papal States more firmly under the control of the papacy; he took personal command of some of the military operations that these aims involved. His efforts to prevent the Venetians from extending their influence in the northern Papal States brought him to participate in the League of Cambrai of 1509, and the subsequent war against Venice in 1509–1510. Having achieved his aims, he made peace with Venice and turned his attention to reducing the power in Italy of his former ally, Louis XII of France (ruled 1498–1515); he was a member of the coalition that drove the French out of the duchy of Milan in 1512.

Julius's initiatives in Italian politics and his personal participation in military campaigns shaped his reputation, both among his contemporaries and posthumously. He has been criticized by some patriotic Italians for his part in the war against Venice and lauded by others for his reputed determination to expel the "barbarians" from Italy. In practice, he was prepared to ally himself with the "barbarians" of France, Spain, and Germany when it suited his purposes, but he did not want them to form independent links with his own subjects. His penchant for military life was seen as unfitting for a pope, although his resolution and physical courage were admired by some. The image of Julius leading an army to the gates of heaven to demand entrance and being turned away by St. Peter, in the c. 1513 satirical dialogue *Julius Exclusus* 'Julius Excluded from Heaven' attributed to Desiderius Erasmus (1466?–1536), has had an enduring influence.

Julius himself regarded the recovery of the territory of the church and the defense of the independence of the Papal States, by war if need be, as prime duties of the pope. Although his outbursts of rage and heavy drinking attracted ridicule, he was conscious of the dignity of his office and careful to fulfill his religious duties. Nevertheless, his behavior gave Louis XII and the Emperor Maximilian I (ruled 1493–1519) an opportunity to seek his deposition from the papacy. They used dissident cardinals to call a general council of the church that opened in Pisa in 1511; this attracted little support. The summons by Julius of the Fifth Lateran Council may have been a riposte to this, but once it assembled in 1512, he insisted that it should give serious consideration to the reform of the church. Julius died during the night of 20 February 1513.

See also **Cambrai, League of (1508); Charles VIII (France); Louis XII (France); Michelangelo Buonarroti; Papacy and Papal States; Raphael.**

BIBLIOGRAPHY

Primary Source

Sowards, J. Kelley, ed. *The* Julius Exclusus *of Erasmus.* Bloomington, Ind., 1968.

Secondary Sources

Partridge, Loren, and Randolph Starn. *A Renaissance Likeness: Art and Culture in Raphael's "Julius II."* Berkeley, 1980.

Shaw, Christine. *Julius II: The Warrior Pope.* Oxford, 1993.

CHRISTINE SHAW

JUSTICE. *See* **Law: Courts.**

K

KALMAR, UNION OF. The Union of Kalmar, which combined the three crowns of Denmark, Norway, and Sweden under one sovereign, was founded in 1397 in the Swedish city of Kalmar and lasted, with some exceptions, until 1520. The union established internal peace under a strong union king, supported by the nobility. It became a reality at a time when other unions in Europe were founded, such as the union in 1386 between Poland and Lithuania. Earlier unions had also existed in Scandinavia. A union between Norway and Sweden was established in 1319, and Scania and Sweden had a common king from 1332 to 1360.

Denmark and Norway united in 1380 when the young Danish King Olof, son of Haakon VI of Norway and Queen Margaret of Denmark (1353–1412), succeeded to the throne of Norway on the death of his father. Margaret had served as regent of Denmark since 1376, and she now became regent of Norway for her son. Olof died in 1387, but Margaret continued to rule Denmark and Norway. At the same time a group of Swedish nobles who opposed the Swedish king, Albert of Mecklenburg, asked for Margaret's help and made her regent of Sweden. The power struggle ended in 1389 when Margaret's forces defeated and captured Albert at Falköping.

Eric of Pomerania, Margaret's fifteen-year-old grandnephew, had been recognized as heir to the Norwegian throne in 1388 and was elected king in Denmark and in Sweden in 1396, but Margaret continued to govern. In the summer of 1397 she invited nobles from Denmark, Norway, and Sweden to Kalmar. The meeting resulted in the formation of the Kalmar Union with Eric as its king. The coronation document presented a strong royal political program *(regimen regale),* whereas the "Letter of the Union," the written record of the proceedings, expressed aristocratic constitutional interests *(regimen politicum).*

Queen Margaret and Eric of Pomerania governed the three Nordic states as a unity until her death in 1412. Denmark was the most prominent country in the union, and the Øresund (The Sound, the straits between Denmark and Scania) became an economic center. Danes and Germans were placed in several Swedish castles. Eric followed an active foreign policy toward the Teutonic Order and fought the dukes of Holstein for many years in order to secure the Duchy of Schleswig for Denmark. From 1426 the king was also at war with the Hanseatic cities. The centralized royal system created opposition in the church and among the peasants and the nobility in Sweden. Under the leadership of Engelbrekt Engelbrektsson, the Swedish peasants rioted in 1434 and were soon supported by the nobility and the church. At a meeting in Kalmar in 1436 Eric had to agree to govern with more respect for the constitution, but he soon tried to restore his old position and was removed from the throne in Denmark in 1439 and in Sweden in 1440, forcing Norway to follow in 1441. King Eric lived on the island of Gotland in the Baltic Sea until 1449.

The new elected union king was Christopher of Bavaria, son of King Eric's sister Katarina; he governed the three countries together with their Councils of State. After his death in 1448, the Swedes elected the nobleman Karl Knutsson (Bonde) as King Charles VIII, whereas the Danes elected Duke Christian I of Oldenburg as king. The two monarchs fought over Norway and Gotland, with the conflict ending in favor of Christian I, who was king of Denmark and Norway.

During the union wars beginning in 1452, portions of the Swedish nobility supported Christian I, and in 1457 the union was reinstated with Christian as king, but this lasted for only a few years. A noble faction rioted in 1464, and Karl Knutsson became the Swedish king 1464–1465 and again 1467–1470. After his death, his nephew Sten Sture the Elder took over as regent and defeated King Christian in a battle at Brunkeberg in 1471; the subsequent negotiations did not restore the union.

King Hans succeeded his father Christian I in 1481 as king of Denmark and Norway. In 1483 the Swedish Council of State supported a renewal of the union (Kalmar Recess). Sten Sture the Elder managed to stay in power, however, until King Hans allied with his opponents in 1497 and was recognized as king of Sweden. The union was restored, but in 1501 a faction of Swedish noblemen rioted, and Sten Sture took over his old position.

The following two decades were marked by negotiations and war. The confrontation sharpened when Christian II became king of Denmark and Norway in 1513. Finally, in 1520, Christian II invaded Sweden, won a decisive military victory, and became king of Sweden. In spite of having promised amnesty, in November 1520 he in the end ordered the execution of all the Swedish nobles who had opposed him, the so-called Stockholm Bloodbath. This act stiffened Swedish resistance to Christian and to the Kalmar Union, which came to a definitive end when Gustav Eriksson became king of Sweden as Gustav I Vasa in 1523.

See also **Denmark; Northern Wars; Sweden; Vasa Dynasty.**

BIBLIOGRAPHY

The Cambridge History of Scandinavia. Vol. 1, *Prehistory to 1520*. Edited by Knut Helle. Cambridge, U.K., forthcoming.

Christensen, Aksel E. *Kalmarunionen og nordisk politik 1319–1439*. Copenhagen, 1980.

Enemark, Poul. *Fra Kalmarbrev til Stockholms Blodbad: Den Nordiske Trestatsunions Epoke 1397–1521*. Copenhagen, 1979.

Larsson, Lars-Olof. *Kalmarunionens tid. Fraan Drottning Margareta til Kristian II*. Stockholm, 1997.

Margrete I. Regent of the North. The Kalmar Union 600 Years. Danish National Museum, exhibition catalogue. Copenhagen, 1997.

Jens E. Olesen

KANT, IMMANUEL (1724–1804), German philosopher.

Immanuel Kant was born 24 April 1724 in Königsberg (now Kaliningrad) in East Prussia. He attended a Pietist school and the University of Königsberg and in 1755, after six years as a private tutor, obtained a position at his university. Promoted to professor there in 1770, he taught and served in administrative posts until 1798 and died 12 February 1804.

CENTRAL IDEAS

Kant's predecessors had treated knowledge as beginning from data about the world that the mind passively receives from the senses or through immediate insight into eternal truths or ideas. Kant, by contrast, made the activity of the mind central both to the world as we live in it and to our knowledge of it.

Kant built his systematic theoretical philosophy around the idea that the world as we experience it does not exist independently of us. Our own minds, he argued, are responsible for its form and structure. This idea constituted his "Copernican revolution." Before Copernicus, astronomical data were explained by assuming that the sun revolves around the earth. Reversing this, Copernicus explained the data by taking the earth to revolve around the sun. Kant explained experience by denying that our knowledge conforms to objects, instead holding that objects in experience conform to our knowledge—to the way our mind necessarily works.

In moral philosophy Kant proposed an equally revolutionary idea. In morality, he held, we are not required to obey laws imposed by God or eternal moral principles or Platonic forms; instead we must understand morality as resting on a law that springs from our own practical rationality. We are "autonomous" because we legislate the moral law we are to obey. The form of the moral world results from the mind's activity.

These views were designed to protect scientific knowledge from skeptical attacks such as that of David Hume (1711–1776) and also to show how morality and responsibility could be preserved in a Newtonian deterministic universe. Kant's theoretical philosophy laid the foundations for the whole enterprise.

THEORETICAL PHILOSOPHY

In the *Kritik der reinen Vernunft* (1781; Critique of pure reason) Kant criticized his predecessors for not seeing that there is a deep difference between perceptual experiences and abstract concepts. The mind accepts the "percepts" that things outside it cause in it, but the mind itself imposes a framework of both time and space even on such given data. Concepts are rules by which the mind organizes percepts, and they show the mind's activity. The mind of any rational agent is equipped with several basic "categories," which are fundamental ways of organizing the data accepted through the senses. Nothing can be part of our experience, therefore, unless it is temporal and spatial and is organized by categories like those of continuing physical object and cause and effect. Percepts and concepts together yield the world as we live in it. The mind's structure explains how we can attain necessary truth in our knowledge of this world.

Kant allows that we can think of a thing as it is in itself *(Ding an sich)* outside experience—a noumenon—but insists that we can know only things as they are for us—as phenomena. Because percepts as well as concepts are necessary for knowledge, we cannot know anything at all about what goes beyond possible experience. Hence we cannot have answers, either positive or negative, to what were then the main questions of religion and metaphysics: Does God exist? Are we immortal? Are we free?

MORAL PHILOSOPHY

In the *Grundlegung zur Metaphysik der Sitten* (1785; Groundwork of the metaphysics of morals) and the *Kritik der praktischen Vernunft* (1788; Critique of practical reason) Kant claimed that, in

Immanuel Kant. Undated portrait. LIBRARY OF CONGRESS

the practical realm, our desires are the counterpart to given sensory data in theoretical knowledge. But we are not causally determined to accept desires as giving us reasons to act. We are free because our will enables us to affirm or reject the claim of any desire to be a reason. Only what the will accepts is a reason to act. And the will, which Kant defines as practical reason, imposes its own forms prior to allowing a desire to count as a reason.

The forms the will imposes on desires include the master form, which is the moral law. As it applies to us, the moral law is an imperative or directive that cannot reasonably be flouted: it is the "categorical imperative." It tells us to act only on plans we could rationally allow everyone to act on. Hence morality, under the categorical imperative, would create a harmonious moral world out of desires that would naturally all too often lead us into conflict.

RELIGION

Because he denied that we could know anything that goes beyond experience, Kant seemed to his contemporaries to have eliminated all hope for a rational religion. But he said that he had destroyed knowledge to make room for faith. He tried to justify a religion safe from scientific criticism by arguing that the categorical imperative gives us practical or moral reason to believe in the essential religious tenets: God, freedom, and immortality. If few philosophers have been convinced by his moral arguments for God and immortality, many think that his account of freedom still has great appeal.

SIGNIFICANCE

Kant aimed to limit naturalism—the view that a single system of causation explains all human activity as well as all other events. To do so, he made philosophy the master discipline that sets boundaries to the cognitive claims of all other thinking. Science is the judge of beliefs about experience, but it can say nothing about claims concerning morality or religion, or (as Kant also argued) about aesthetic taste. His remarkable theory that the mind helps construct the world in which we live opened the way for the radical idealisms of Friedrich Wilhelm Joseph von Schelling (1775–1854), Johann Gottlieb Fichte (1762–1814), and Georg Wilhelm Friedrich Hegel (1770–1831). Kant's assertion of "the primacy of practical reason"—that practical reason can answer questions that theoretical reason cannot—was suggestive for the development of pragmatism. His moral philosophy has been and still is both widely used and hotly contested. Kant's work has had an influence on Western thought unsurpassed by that of any other modern philosopher.

See also **Hume, David; Moral Philosophy and Ethics; Natural Law.**

BIBLIOGRAPHY

Primary Sources

The Cambridge Edition of the Works of Immanuel Kant, edited by Paul Guyer and Allen W. Wood, Cambridge, U.K., 1992–. Contains the best translations of Kant's works, from the early "pre-critical" writings through the *Opus Postumum,* and including extensive selections from student lecture notes.

Kant, Immanuel. *Gesammelte Schriften.* Vols. 1–27. Berlin, 1969–.

Secondary Sources

Guyer, Paul, ed. *Cambridge Companion to Kant.* Cambridge, U.K., 1992. Contains articles covering most aspects of Kant's philosophy and a good bibliography.

Kuehn, Manfred. *Kant: A Biography.* Cambridge, U.K., 2001. Excellent scholarly bibliography.

J. B. SCHNEEWIND

KAUFFMANN, ANGELICA

KAUFFMANN, ANGELICA (1741–1807), Swiss neoclassical painter. The Swiss-born painter was considered a child prodigy, achieving attention for her works as early as age eleven. She was trained by her father, Johann Josef Kauffmann, whose family accompanied him to Italy, where he executed decorative schemes for churches. The Kauffmann family lived in Como, Milan, Parma, Florence, and eventually Rome, where Angelica copied the works of famous Old Masters. These included her richly colored version of Domenichino's *Cumaean Sibyl* (1763, National Museum of Women in the Arts, Washington, D.C.) that was probably purchased by the 4th duke of Gordon, one of her many aristocratic patrons. Others included Catherine the Great of Russia, Emperor Franz Joseph of Austria, and John Parker II, Lord Boringdon.

During her first stay in Rome (1765–1766), Kauffmann became an integral part of the circle of artists that gathered around the German theorist Johann Joachim Winckelmann, who served as librarian to Cardinal Albani. This group, which included Pompeo Girolamo Batoni, Anton Raphael Mengs, Benjamin West, Sir Nathaniel Dance, and Giambattista Piranesi, was instrumental in promoting a neoclassical stylistic approach in art that remained fashionable in both Europe and America well into the nineteenth century. Kauffmann, in fact, was one of the first artists to paint in a neoclassical style and one of few women to gain fame from historical paintings. Her classically inspired historical works include *Venus Directing Aeneas and Achates to Carthage* (1768, The National Trust, England, Saltram collection); *Venus Persuading Helen to Accept the Love of Paris* (1790, Hermitage Museum, St. Petersburg, Russia); *Zeuxis Selecting Models for His Picture of Helen of Troy* (1778, Brown University, Providence, R.I.); and *Sappho* (1775, John and Mabel Ringling Museum, Sarasota, Florida).

It is believed that Kauffmann used self-portraits in her representations of Helen and Sappho, as well as many more of her historical figures, since they often resemble her. This may be judged by comparing them to her identified self-portraits, such as the one she contributed to the famous de Medici self-portrait collection at the Uffizi (1787, Uffizi Gal-

Angelica Kauffmann. *Zeuxis Selecting Models for His Picture of Helen of Troy,* 1778. BROWN UNIVERSITY LIBRARY

lery, Florence). Looking much like a classical goddess, Kauffmann wears a white muslin dress, belted just below the bodice. It is secured by a cameo that, according to Louise Rice and Ruth Eisenberg, represents the battle between Minerva and Neptune for control of Athens—a battle significantly won by the female goddess. Kauffmann's stylistic approach combines the linearity and order of neoclassicism with a pastel lushness characteristic of the English rococo. This is not surprising since Kauffmann spent from 1766 to 1782 in London, where she was named one of the founding members of the Royal Academy of Art (1768). She painted a portrait of the academy's first director, Sir Joshua Reynolds, in 1767 (The National Trust, England, Saltram collection). Reynolds praised Kauffmann's talent, but there were many who criticized her weak rendering of anatomy. It was difficult for a woman to gain skill in this area because she was generally barred from drawing nude models.

Kauffmann was skillful enough in her historical works to be invited to contribute to the decorative scheme of Somerset House, a building designed by William Chambers to house the Royal Academy. Kauffmann's contribution included four oval compositions entitled *Invention, Composition, Design,* and *Color* using iconographic references from Cesare Ripa's *Iconologia or Moral Emblems* (1611). These works are now located at Burlington House, London. She was also asked to participate in a scheme to decorate the dome of St. Paul's Cathedral, although this was never realized.

Kauffmann had many admirers in both her personal and professional life. Contemporaries praised her beauty, talent, intelligence, and wit. Not surprisingly, she attracted a number of suitors, which included Reynolds, Dance, and the early Romantic painter Henry Fuseli. She rejected the attention of these artists to marry a Swedish rogue named Brandt, who charaded as the Count de Horn. After his death (1767), she married the Italian artist Antonio Zucchi and returned with him to Rome in 1782. There she was an active member of the Academy of St. Luke and maintained a studio that was often visited by fellow artists. These included Elisabeth Vigée-Lebrun, who visited Kauffmann while in exile after the French Revolution. Kauffmann died in Rome on 5 November 1807. After a magnificent funeral, she was buried in the church of Sant'Andrea delle Fratte. Three years after her death, her good friend Giovanni Gherardo de Rossi published his *Vita di Angelica Kauffmann* (Life of Angelica Kauffmann), which serves as a major source of information with regard to her life and career.

See also **Reynolds, Joshua; Women and Art.**

BIBLIOGRAPHY

Primary Source

De Rossi, Giovanni Gherardo. *Vita di Angelica Kauffmann, pittrice 1741–1807.* Florence, 1810.

Secondary Sources

Adam, Malise Forbes, and Mauchline, Mary. "Neoclassical Furniture in the Palace of Pavlovsk with Designs after Angelica Kauffmann." *Apollo* 155, no. 479 (Jan. 2002): 42–46.

Gerard, Frances. *Angelica Kauffmann.* London, 1892.

Manners, Victoria, and G. C. Williamson. *Angelica Kauffmann, R. A.: Her Life and Her Works.* London, 1924. Reprinted New York, 1976.

Mayer, Dorothy. *Angelica Kauffmann R. A. 1741–1807.* Gerrards Cross, U.K., 1972.

Pomeroy, Jordana. "The Uncommon Genius of Angelica Kauffmann." *Women in the Arts* 15 (Winter 1997): 2–4.

Rice, Louise, and Ruth Eisenberg. "Angelica Kauffmann's Uffizi Self-Portrait." *Gazette des Beaux Arts* 117 (March 1991): 123–126.

Rosenthal, Angela. *Angelika Kauffmann: Bildnismalerei im 18. Jahrhundert.* Berlin, 1996.

Roworth, Wendy Wassyng. *Angelica Kauffmann: A Continental Artist in Georgian England.* London, 1992.

———. "Biography, Criticism, Art History: Angelica Kauffmann in Context." In *Eighteenth Century Women and the Arts,* edited by Frederick M. Keener, pp. 209–221. New York and London, 1988.

KATHLEEN RUSSO

KEPLER, JOHANNES (1571–1630), German astronomer and mathematician; discoverer of the laws of planetary motion. Born into the Protestant minority in the free city of Weil der Stadt, within the Lutheran duchy of Württemberg, Kepler's family was poised at the boundary between the aristocracy and the artisan class. His father and brother Heinrich both served as soldiers; his youngest brother worked as a tinsmith. Kepler was educated at religious schools supported by the duke of Württemberg, and at the University of Tübingen. Here he studied with theologians trained by Philipp Melanchthon (1497–1560), the great German religious and educational reformer, and began a lifelong friendship with his mathematics teacher, the Copernican astronomer Michael Mästlin (1550–1631).

Unable to follow a church career because his scruples prevented him from signing the Formula of Concord, Kepler began his professional life as a teacher in the Protestant gymnasium at Graz, in southern Austria. From here he rose to become an imperial courtier, and achieved lasting fame as an innovator in astronomy. Kepler married twice (1597 and 1613). He was a devoted father who suffered deeply at the early deaths of many of his children, and he seems to have used mathematical research as a solace. Kepler's publication of the *Mysterium Cosmographicum* (1596; The secret of the universe) began a meteoric rise. Compelled to leave Graz with other Protestants in 1598, he attached himself to the court of Emperor Rudolf II (ruled 1576–1612) in Prague, and succeeded Tycho Brahe as imperial mathematician in 1601. Thus, in only three years, Kepler ascended from the position of a provincial schoolteacher to become the astrological and astronomical adviser to the most powerful monarch in the Christian world, although the emperor proved unreliable as a source of financial support. Kepler immediately began to produce a series of major works, especially the *Optics* (*Astronomiae pars Optica,* 1604) and the *New Astronomy* (1609), which extended and refounded their subjects. Other works (1601, 1610) attempted to reform astrology. In 1612, after the forced abdication and death of Rudolf, Kepler left Prague, but retained his title of imperial mathematician under later emperors. From 1612 to 1626 he and his family made their home in Linz, in Upper Austria, although Kepler traveled widely. While in Linz he produced the *Epitome of Copernican Astronomy* (1618–1621) and the *Harmony of the World* (1619). The latter precipitated a violent exchange with the English theosophist Robert Fludd (1574–

1637), but Kepler declined an invitation to visit England despite his long-standing admiration for King James I (ruled 1603–1625). During this period his mother was accused of witchcraft. Kepler directed the defense that led to her acquittal in 1620–1621. The work that had secured the favor of the imperial house for so long, the *Rudolfine Tables,* was completed in 1627.

With the increasing violence and disorder of the Thirty Years' War, Kepler again sought the protection of a powerful patron, and he became astrological adviser to A. W. E. von Wallenstein, the leading Catholic general, in 1628. His patron's fall from power immediately preceded his own death, at Regensburg, in 1630. In the *Mysterium Cosmographicum,* Kepler presented the most important defense of Sun centered astronomy since the appearance of Nicolaus Copernicus's *De Revolutionibus Orbium Coelestium* in 1543. Uniting ideas from his education in mathematics and religion, Kepler proposed that God had employed each regular geometrical solid exactly once in the plan of the world. Nesting the solids within each other, the orbs defining the limits of the planets' motions could be inscribed between them. The five regular solids provided the spacing between six orbs, explaining both their relative distances and the number of planets (the Earth-Moon system forms one unit). On both counts Kepler's Sun-centered model could be argued to be superior to the Earth-centered Ptolemaic system. But Kepler's defense of Copernicus faced another rival: the newly proposed hybrid system of Tycho Brahe, in which Earth was central and stationary, the Moon and Sun went around the Earth, but all the other planets circled the Sun.

On arriving in Prague in 1600, Kepler was effectively subordinated to Brahe, who first set him to writing an attack on an earlier imperial mathematician *(A Defense of Tycho against Ursus).* Although not actually published during Kepler's lifetime, this work gives valuable insights into both the state of astronomy and Kepler's novel methodological ideas. Brahe had presented Kepler to Rudolf II as the man who would distill Brahe's decades of observations into new astronomical tables that would carry the emperor's name. When Brahe died unexpectedly in 1601, the importance of this project helped Kepler to succeed Brahe as imperial mathematician. Kepler used the superlatively accurate and complete observations to show that Brahe's cosmic scheme was untenable, and to replace Copernicus's circle-based models with elliptical orbits.

In 1604 Kepler published an important work on optics, which treated the nature of light and vision, the phenomena of refraction, and the applications of optics in astronomy. During the same period he established that the path of Mars was an ellipse and introduced a new way of calculating the planet's position based on the novel concept of an orbit with the Sun at one focus (a principle now called the first law of planetary motion). He showed that his new approach was superior not only to the models of Ptolemy and Brahe, but also to the original form of Copernicus's system. Also improving on Copernicus, he was able to show that the planes of the planet's orbits intersected in the Sun. He also suggested that the Sun was the origin of a quasi-magnetic force responsible for the planets' motions. Based on these physical ideas, he argued for a connection between the speed of a planet along its path and the area swept out by the line connecting it to the Sun (now called the second, or area, law). He demonstrated this result first for a circular path, then for an ellipse. Although originally presented only for the case of Mars, the elliptical orbit and the mathematical principles governing its motion were intended to extend to all planets, based on universal physical principles. Kepler advertised the new connection between physics and astronomy in his book's title, *A New Astronomy, Based on Causes, or Celestial Physics.* It appeared in 1609 after a delay caused by Brahe's heirs.

In Prague, Kepler also produced two important works attempting to reform astrology, *On More Certain Foundations for Astrology* (1601) and *Tertius Interveniens* (1610; The intermediary third position [between two extremes]). He rejected the traditional astrological machinery of houses, but retained the idea that geometrical configurations of celestial objects influenced human judgment and caused terrestrial weather. Also in 1610 he gave enthusiastic support to Galileo Galilei (in *Conversation with the Sidereal Messenger,* 1610, and preface to the *Dioptrice,* 1611), and confirmed the latter's telescopic discovery of the moons of Jupiter.

During his time in Linz, Kepler's two most important productions were the *Harmony of the*

World (1619) and the *Epitome of Copernican Astronomy* (which appeared in several volumes, 1617–1621). The former attempted a grand synthesis of geometry, harmonics, astrology, and astronomy, and presented the music of the spheres, in the form of tones generated as planets vary in speed throughout their orbits. Here also Kepler stated the third law of planetary motion, connecting the square of the planetary year with the cube of its mean distance. The *Epitome of Copernican Astronomy* was a systematic presentation of Kepler's version of the Copernican system, intended as a textbook, and as a basis for understanding Kepler's approach in the *Rudolfine Tables.* Appearing in 1627, the tables successfully predicted that Mercury would pass across the face of the sun in November 1631, showing that Kepler had improved the accuracy of positional calculations by a factor of ten.

Kepler was an innovator where Copernicus was a renovator. Copernicus had re-centered the planetary system, but his calculations of planetary positions took as their geometrical center the mean sun, a constructed point, located elsewhere than the Sun itself. The Sun played no physical role in Copernicus's system and he retained celestial spheres to move the planets. Like Ptolemy, Copernicus continued to use circles carrying circles to predict the positions of planets against the background of fixed stars, and although distances were calculable in his system, they played no role in predicting positions. Kepler introduced the modern form of Copernicanism. His planets moved freely through the heavens, propelled by a force originating in the Sun, along orbits that intersected at the Sun. They obeyed mathematical laws that united physics and astronomy in a new way. Their path through space was an ellipse, not a circle, and their distances and velocities were linked in the second law.

Kepler's insights were not immediately accepted by contemporaries, but they were vindicated by Isaac Newton (1642–1727), who replaced Kepler's solar force with universal gravitation, and demonstrated that the three laws of planetary motion followed from his own more general laws of motion in the case of a planet moving around the Sun. Although the laws of planetary motion became central results of the later mechanical philosophy, Kepler himself was not a mechanical philosopher. Kepler's sun rotates because of an animating spirit; the planet Earth has a spirit that perceives celestial alignments and creates weather; in the 1609 presentation of Kepler's theory, planets are capable of directing their own motion of approach to or recession from the Sun. In his last work, the *Somnium,* published posthumously in 1634, another kind of spirit narrates the appearance of the heavens as seen from the Moon. In Kepler's cosmos, mathematical regularities are evidence of controlling minds, and the structure of the universe, which Kepler spent his life uncovering, testifies to the architectonic mind of its Creator.

See also **Astrology; Astronomy; Brahe, Tycho; Copernicus, Nicolaus; Galileo Galilei.**

BIBLIOGRAPHY

Primary Sources

Kepler, Johannes. *Apologia Tychonis contra Nicolaum Raymarum Ursum.* Prague, 1600.

——. *De Fundamentis Astrologiae Certioribus.* Prague, 1601.

——. *Dioptrice.* Augsburg, 1611. Reprint, Cambridge, U.K., 1962.

——. *Epitome of Copernican Astronomy Books IV and V, and Harmony of the World Book V.* Translated by C. G. Wallis. New York, 1995. Translation of *Epitome Astronomiae Copernicanae* (1617–1621).

——. *Harmony of the World.* Translated by E. J. Aiton, A. M. Duncan, and J. V. Field. Philadelphia, 1993. Translation of *Harmonice Mundi* (1619).

——. *Kepler's Conversation with Galileo's Sidereal Messenger.* Translated by E. Rosen. New York, 1965. Translation of *Dissertatio cum Nuncio Siderio* (1610).

——. *Mysterium Cosmographicum: The Secret of the Universe.* Translated by A. M. Duncan. Norwalk, Conn., 1981. Translation of *Prodromus Dissertationem Cosmographicarum, continens Mysterium Cosmographicum* (1596).

——. *New Astronomy.* Translated by William H. Donahue. Cambridge, U.K., 1992. Translation of *Astronomia Nova Aitiologetos, sev Physica Coelestis* (1609).

——. *Optics: Paralipomena to Witelo and the Optical Part of Astronomy.* Translated by William H. Donahue. Santa Fe, N.M., 2000. Translation of *Ad Vitellionem Paralipomena, quibus Astronomiae pars Optica Traditur* (1604).

——. *Somnium.* Translated by E. Rosen. Madison, 1967. Translation of *Somnium, sive Astronomia Lunaris* (1634).

——. *Tabulae Rudolfinae.* Ulm, 1627.

——. *Tertius Interveniens.* Frankfurt am Main, 1610.

Secondary Sources

Barker, Peter, and Bernard R. Goldstein. "Theological Foundations of Kepler's Astronomy." *Osiris* 16 (2001): 88–113. On the religious background of Kepler's thought.

Caspar, Max. *Kepler.* Translated and edited by C. Doris Hellman. New York, 1993. The most important scholarly biography of Kepler.

Field, J. V. "A Lutheran Astrologer: Johannes Kepler." *Archive for History of Exact Sciences* 31 (1984): 189–272. Translation, with commentary, of Kepler's *On More Certain Foundations of Astrology.*

Gingerich, O., and W. Walderman. "Rudolfine Tables: Introduction." *Quarterly Journal of the Royal Astronomical Society* 13 (1972): 360–373.

Jardine, N. *The Birth of History and Philosophy of Science: Kepler's* A Defense of Tycho against Ursus *with Essays on its Provenance and Significance.* Cambridge, U.K., and New York, 1984. Latin and English versions of *Apologia Tychonis contra Nicolaum Raymarum Ursum* (1600).

Methuen, Charlotte. *Kepler's Tübingen: Stimulus to a Theological Mathematics.* Aldershot, U.K., and Brookfield, Vt., 1998. Examines the University of Tübingen at the time of Kepler's education. Valuable for translations of primary sources.

Simon, Gérard. *Kepler astronome astrologue.* Paris, 1979. A balanced presentation of Kepler's work in both astronomy and astrology. Still the best single book on Kepler.

Stephenson, Bruce. *The Composition of Kepler's Astronomia Nova.* Princeton, 2001. Details Kepler's tribulations on the way to his most important book.

———. *Kepler's Physical Astronomy.* 2nd ed. Princeton, 1994. Detailed study of the *Mysterium Cosmographicum* and *New Astronomy.*

———. *The Music of the Heavens: Kepler's Harmonic Astronomy.* Princeton, 1994.

Voelkel, James R. *Johannes Kepler and the New Astronomy.* Oxford and New York, 1999. Brief, accessible, and accurate biography.

PETER BARKER

KHMELNYTSKY, BOHDAN (c. 1595–1657), hetman of the Zaporozhian Cossack Host (1648–1657) and founder of the Hetmanate (Cossack state). Born into a family of Orthodox petty gentry, Khmelnytsky received a Jesuit education. Khmelnytsky took part in the Battle of Cecora (1620) and was taken as a prisoner to Istanbul for two years. He enlisted in the Chyhyryn Cossack regiment near his family holding of Subotiv and emerged during the Cossack revolts of 1637–1638 as military chancellor of the Zaporozhian Host, signing the capitulation of 27 December 1637. It is possible that he served among Cossack mercenary troops in France in 1644. In 1646, as captain of the Chyhyryn regiment, he accompanied a Cossack delegation to King Władysław IV Vasa (ruled 1632–1648), who sought to win the Cossacks over to his secret plans for a war against the Ottomans.

Khmelnytsky's life as an established Cossack took a radical turn in 1647 because of a personal and property dispute with a magnate's servitor. Khmelnytsky found no redress for the seizure of his estate and was arrested in November 1647. He escaped and fled to the traditional Cossack stronghold or *sich,* where he was proclaimed hetman in February 1648. He rallied the Cossacks, who smarted under the harsh Polish regime, to his cause and came to an agreement with the Crimean Khanate that ensured cavalry support for the Cossack infantry. In May, Khmelnytsky defeated the Polish armies sent after him. The death of the king in the same month threw the Polish-Lithuanian Commonwealth, an elective monarchy, into crisis.

Although some historians believe that from the first Khmelnytsky had sought to overthrow Polish rule, in the initial phase of the revolt his demands centered on Cossack rights. Throughout 1648, as social war reigned in much of Ukraine and the commonwealth's elite fell into factional struggles over the election, Khmelnytsky energetically organized a military force and an administration of the territory he controlled. Defeating what remained of the commonwealth's forces in September, Khmelnytsky forces reached the limit of Ukrainian ethnic territory and influenced the election of John II Casimir Vasa (Jan II Kazimierz; ruled 1648–1668) as a pro-peace candidate. At the end of the year Khmelnytsky marched east, entering the ancient Ukrainian capital of Kyiv to the acclamation of the clergy and the other inhabitants that he was a Moses and a liberator from the "Polish bondage." He announced his plans to liberate the Ruthenian (Ukrainian-Belarusian) nation and declared that God had raised him up to be the autocrat of Rus'. These declarations of intentions to be the ruler of a new state could only be resolved by military victory. The Battle of Zboriv (August 1649) proved inconclusive because of the desertion of the Crimean

Bohdan Khmelnytsky. A monument to Khmelnytsky stands near St. Sophia Cathedral in Kiev. ©DEAN CONGER/CORBIS

khan, who was troubled by the rising power. Khmelnytsky was recognized as hetman with sweeping privileges, above all as the leader of a Cossack Host of forty thousand. But this fell far short of his earlier aspirations and endangered his position because the masses rejected the terms and the depredations of his Tatar allies.

From mid-1649 Khmelnytsky sought to keep the unwieldy coalition supporting him in Ukraine together as he searched for foreign allies and protectors against the commonwealth in a program to entrench his rule. Initially the Ottoman Empire seemed the most likely source, and the hetman sought to create a dynasty by marrying his son Tymish to the daughter of the Moldavian hospodar, an Ottoman vassal. Defeated by the Poles at Berestechko (June 1651), Khmelnytsky in turn defeated the Poles in June 1652 on an expedition to marry off his son. His Balkan policy ultimately ended in ruin and the death of his son (September 1653). Khmelnytsky then turned more seriously to the Muscovite tsar, taking an oath of loyalty to him in January 1654 at Pereiaslav but failing to receive an oath from him. Retaining far greater power in Ukraine than the terms negotiated, Khmelnytsky came to be disillusioned with Muscovy, especially after the truce between Muscovy and the commonwealth in November 1656. He joined a coalition with Sweden and Transylvania against the commonwealth (and Muscovite desires), but news of the failure of a Transylvanian-Ukrainian invasion reached him on his deathbed.

Khmelnytsky's major problem in his final years was the question of succession because his remaining son Iurii was a weak figure. Iurii initially succeeded him, but the Host soon turned instead to his chancellor Ivan Vyhovsky.

In a ten-year period the hetman had managed to create an effective army and civil administration and to turn his capital Chyhyryn into a center of international diplomacy. Khmelnytsky had not, however, found a secure place for the Hetmanate in the East European state system or a way to prevent foreign intervention in Cossack affairs. Contemporary and subsequent evaluations of him differed, with some seeing him as a brilliant state builder and diplomat, an equal of Oliver Cromwell (1599–1658) or Armand-Jean du Plessis, Cardinal Richelieu (1585–1642), while others saw him as chimerical, rash (above all in the terms he negotiated with Muscovy), given to bouts of drunkenness, and even a destructive despot similar to Tamerlane (Timur; 1336–1405) or Batu Khan (died 1255). Eighteenth-century Ukrainian historiography created a cult of Khmelnytsky as founder of the Hetmanate. Opinions varied in the nineteenth century, with the Ukrainian national poet Taras Shevchenko (1814–1861) chiding him for his agreement with the Russians. Soviet historiography beginning in the 1950s praised him for bringing about the "reunification" of Ukraine and Russia. In the Jewish tradition he is decried as responsible for massacres of Jews during the uprising. He figures prominently in Polish historical imagination as an enemy of the Polish state.

See also **Cossacks; Khmelnytsky Uprising; Poland-Lithuania, Commonwealth of, 1569–1795; Ukraine.**

BIBLIOGRAPHY

Hrushevsky, Mykhailo. *History of Ukraine-Rus'*. Vol. 8. Translated by Marta D. Olynyk. Edmonton and Toronto, 2002.

Sysyn, Frank E. "Bohdan Chmel'nyc'kyj's Image in Ukrainian Historiography since Independence." In *Ukraine,* edited by Peter Jordan et al., pp. 179–188. Wien, 2001.

——. "The Changing Image of the Hetman: On the 350th Anniversary of the Khmel'nyts'kyi Uprising." *Jahrbücher für Geschichte Osteuropas* 46 (1995): 531–545.

——. "Grappling with the Hero: Hrushevs'kyi Confronts Khmel'nyts'kyi." *Harvard Ukrainian Studies* 22 (1998): 589–609.

——. "The Political Worlds of Bohdan Khmel'nyts'kyi." *Palaeoslavica* 10, no. 2 (2002): 197–209.

Vernadsky, George. *Bohdan, Hetman of Ukraine*. New Haven, 1941.

FRANK E. SYSYN

KHMELNYTSKY UPRISING. The uprising in the Ukrainian territories against the Polish-Lithuanian Commonwealth began in early 1648 under the leadership of Bohdan Khmelnytsky (c. 1595–1657), a Cossack officer proclaimed hetman. The secret negotiations of King Władysław IV Vasa (ruled 1632–1648) with the Cossacks to begin a war with the Ottomans against the will of the diet stirred them to action. Initiated because of injustices against Khmelnytsky and discontent among the Cossack stratum with their treatment by the Polish authorities, the revolt rapidly succeeded because it enlisted Crimean Tatar support. The rebels destroyed the Polish standing army, and the confusion and dissension following the death of the king in May 1648 gave them the advantage.

The Cossack revolt turned into a general uprising drawing upon peasant resistance to the imposition of serfdom and manorial duties, Eastern Orthodox anger at discrimination by the Catholic authorities, Ruthenian (Ukrainian-Belarusian) antagonism toward the Poles, and the Ukrainian frontier population's opposition to the magnates and their servitors and leaseholders. In the first months a bloody social war raged with attacks on landlords, Catholic clergy, and Jews. Where they had the means, the magnates took brutal reprisals. The disparate coalition assembled around the Cossack Host did not have a united social or political program, but the Cossack hetman professed to support the monarch against the willful high nobility. Yet negotiations failed with the new king, John II Casimir Vasa (Jan II Kazimierz; ruled 1648–1668), elected in November, and by early 1649 the rebels had greatly expanded their Cossack Estate demands to a broad political-national program that would have virtually overturned the old order in Ukraine. Certainly by this time the leadership envisaged a break with the commonwealth and entered into negotiations with foreign powers for support. A battle at Zboriv in August 1649 wrung major concessions from the government, but the betrayal of the Crimean khan deprived the rebels of a decisive victory.

By 1649 a new political structure, the Cossack Hetmanate, had emerged out of the Cossack Host in the central Ukrainian territories, but it could not come to an accommodation with the commonwealth's magnate elite, which would not accept sweeping changes in the economic and political order. Defeated at the Battle of Berestechko in 1651, the Cossack authorities, despite subsequent victories, could not fully triumph over the commonwealth in battle, thus leading them to redouble their search for foreign protectors.

Although surrounding states feared the radical nature of the revolt and distrusted the Cossack parvenu elite, they soon sought to take advantage of the commonwealth's distress and the opportunities offered by the revolt. The Ottoman sultan accepted the new polity under his protection in 1650–1651, but tied down by the War of Candia, he did not provide essential military support. The Porte also found Cossack intervention among its Danubian vassals troublesome, though this Ukrainian policy ended in a fiasco in 1653, offering new opportunity for Polish revanche. The need for military support led the Cossack hetman to accept the sovereignty of the Muscovite tsar, a coreligionist, in January 1654, though from the first the political cultures of the autocratic Russian state and the Cossack Hetmanate, derived from the traditions of the Cossack Host and the Polish monarchical republic, clashed. The commonwealth continued to struggle to regain its control of Ukraine, even coming to an agreement with Muscovy in 1656. The Muscovite officials attempted to assert control in Ukraine, but Hetman Khmelnytsky continued to rule over the new order he had established up until his death in 1657. He sought to change the political position of the Hetmanate and to partition the commonwealth through alliances with Sweden, which had invaded the weakened commonwealth in 1655, and Transylvania.

There is no clear ending to the Khmelnytsky Uprising because the consequences of the rebellion unfolded over decades. Although the commonwealth eventually won back the Ukrainian territories to the west of the Dnieper (1667, confirmed in 1686), the political and social order established by the revolt endured to the end of the eighteenth century. The Khmelnytsky Uprising stands out among early modern revolts for its success in overturning the social order and in setting up a new polity, thereby motivating some to call it a revolution. It also had great impact in setting off conflicts among the neighboring states and remaking the international order, above all by weakening the commonwealth, transforming Muscovy into the Russian Empire, and inciting the Ottomans' last great thrust into central Europe. It has also served as a focal point for modern Ukrainian identity and relations with Poles, Russians, and Jews.

See also **Cossacks; Khmelnytsky, Bohdan; Poland-Lithuania, Commonwealth of, 1569–1795; Ukraine.**

BIBLIOGRAPHY

Basarab, John. *Pereiaslav 1654: A Historiographical Study.* Edmonton, 1982.

"Gezeirot Ta"h: Jews, Cossacks, Poles, and Peasants in 1648 Ukraine." Special issue. *Jewish History* 17, no. 2 (2003).

Hrushevsky, Mykhailo. *History of Ukraine-Rus'.* Vol. 8. Translated by Marta D. Olynyk. Edmonton and Toronto, 2002.

Raba, Joel. *Between Remembrance and Denial: The Fate of the Jews in the Wars of the Polish Commonwealth during the Mid-Seventeenth Century as Shown in Contemporary Writings and Historical Research.* Boulder and New York, 1995.

Sysyn, Frank E. *Between Poland and the Ukraine: The Dilemma of Adam Kysil, 1600–1653.* Cambridge, Mass., 1985.

———. "The Khmelnytsky Uprising and Ukrainian Nation-Building." *Journal of Ukrainian Studies* 17, nos. 1–2 (Summer–Winter 1992): 141–170.

———. "Ukrainian-Polish Relations in the Seventeenth Century: The Role of National Consciousness and National Conflict in the Khmelnytsky Movement." In *Poland and Ukraine: Past and Present,* edited by Peter J. Potichnyj, pp. 58–82. Edmonton and Toronto, 1980.

———. "Ukrainian Social Tensions before the Khmel'nyts'kyi Uprising." In *Religion and Culture in Early Modern Russia and Ukraine,* edited by Samuel H. Baron and Nancy Shields Kollmann, pp. 52–70. DeKalb, Ill., 1997.

———. "War der Chmel'nyćkyj-Aufstand eine Revolution? Eine Charakteristik der 'großen ukrainischen Revolte' und der Bildung des kosakischen Het'manstaates." *Jahrbücher für Geschichte Osteuropas* 53, no. 1 (1995): 1–18.

FRANK E. SYSYN

KIEV (Ukrainian, Kyiv; Polish, Kijów). Capital of the Rus' principality (tenth to thirteenth centuries), Kiev arose on the Dnieper River at the intersection of the Varangian trade route connecting the north by river with Constantinople and overland routes connecting the Caucasus and the Crimea with Galicia and western Europe. This religious and trade

Kiev. The cathedral of St. Sophia in Kiev. ©Dean Conger/Corbis.

center of medieval eastern Europe was sacked in 1240 by the Mongol-Tatar army of Batu Khan. In 1362 Lithuanian Grand Duke Algirdas annexed Kiev, and in 1471 it became the capital of the Kiev palatinate of the Grand Duchy of Lithuania. A modest revival began in the early fifteenth century, culminating in the confirmation of the Magdeburg law for municipal self-government by Grand Duke Alexander in the years 1494–1497. By this time, however, the Crimean Khan Mengli Giray had again plundered Kiev (1482), and the "Upper City" lay in ruins for over a century.

With the Union of Lublin in 1569, the Kiev palatinate was transferred from the Grand Duchy of Lithuania to the direct rule of the Polish crown, opening the door more widely to Polish immigration and cultural influences. In the first half of the seventeenth century, Kiev again experienced renewal, and it eventually became the political, religious, and cultural capital of Rus'-Ukraine, overtaking existing centers of early modern Ruthenian culture that had arisen in Vilnius and Lviv. Cossack hetman Petro Sahaidachnyi resided there (c. 1610–1622) and was a member of the Kiev Orthodox Brotherhood of the Epiphany (founded 1615). A printing house was established at the Kiev Monastery of the Caves by 1615. In 1620, Patriarch of Jerusalem Theophanes III, stopping off in Kiev on his way home from Moscow, restored an Orthodox Ruthenian hierarchy to sees occupied by Uniate bishops since the Union of Brest in 1596. The Orthodox metropolitan again took up residence in Kiev. The Moldavian nobleman Peter Mohyla (archimandrite of the Caves Monastery 1627–1632, metropolitan of Kiev 1633–1647) launched a wide-ranging renovation of the city's old monuments (including the St. Sophia Cathedral) and began new construction. The school he founded at the Caves Monastery in 1631 was joined in 1632 with the older Brotherhood school (established c. 1615) to form the Kiev College (renamed the Kievan Mohyla Academy in 1701). It was the premier center of higher learning for the Orthodox of the Polish-Lithuanian Commonwealth, and it would later help propagate Western learning in the Russian empire.

The triumphant entry of Bohdan Khmelnytsky into Kiev in December 1648 confirmed the city's status as the spiritual capital of a new Cossack polity. With the 1654 Treaty of Pereiaslav, a Muscovite garrison was established in the town. The Muscovite-Polish Treaty of Andrusovo (1667) granted Kiev to Muscovy for two years only, but the city never returned to Polish rule, and the 1686 Eternal Peace acknowledged the status quo. Until the second partition of Poland in 1793, Kiev remained an autonomous border town, severed from its former hinterland in Polish right-bank Ukraine. The city experienced a brief reflourishing under the hetmancy of Ivan Mazepa (1687–1709), but the Russian tsars of the eighteenth century progressively curtailed Kiev's autonomies along with those of the Hetmanate, making Kiev more and more into a provincial Russian city. In 1797 it became the capital of the Kiev province of the Russian empire.

See also **Cossacks; Mohyla, Peter; Orthodoxy, Russian; Ukraine; Uniates.**

BIBLIOGRAPHY

Alferova, G. V., and V. A. Kharlamov. *Kiev vo vtoroi polovine XVII veka: Istoriko-arkhitekturnyi ocherk.* Kiev, 1982.

Hamm, Michael F. *Kiev: A Portrait, 1800–1917.* Princeton, 1993.

Kondufor, Iu. Iu., ed. *Istoriia Kieva.* Vol. 1, *Drevnii i srednevekovyi Kiev,* and vol. 2, *Kiev perioda pozdnego feodalizma i kapitalizma.* Kiev, 1982–1983.

David Frick

KINGSHIP, DIVINE RIGHT.

See **Divine Right Kingship.**

KIRCHER, ATHANASIUS (1602–1680),

German Jesuit polymath and collector. Considered by many to be the greatest polymath in an encyclopedia age, Athanasius Kircher was a scholar who aspired to expertise in many different domains of knowledge and sought connections among them in a quest to recover ancient *pansophia* (universal wisdom). He corresponded with scholars, princes, popes, and missionaries, and his books traveled to virtually every corner of the globe.

Born in the German town of Geisa, Kircher entered the Society of Jesus in 1616; he completed his novitiate in 1620 and was ordained in Würzburg in 1628. That same year he requested to be sent as a missionary to China (he would make the same request in 1637). The Superior General turned down his request because he felt that Kircher's unique talents would best serve the society closer to home. After teaching mathematics, philosophy, and Syrian at the Jesuit college in Würzburg for several years and developing a reputation as an inventor of sundials, Kircher found himself caught in the vicissitudes of the Thirty Years' War (1618–1648) and fled Germany. He spent almost two years in Avignon, teaching at the Jesuit college there and cultivating a relationship with the French savant and antiquarian Nicolas-Claude Fabri de Peiresc. During this period, he convinced Peiresc that he was the person most capable of deciphering Egyptian hieroglyphs through the study of Coptic. Peiresc urged his Roman acquaintances, principally the pope's nephew, Cardinal Francesco Barberini, to find a position for Kircher in the Eternal City in order to realize this project.

Kircher arrived in Rome in November 1633, only months after the condemnation of Galileo for his advocacy of heliocentrism. He succeeded Christoph Scheiner in the prestigious chair of mathematics at the Collegio Romano, the leading educational institution of the Society of Jesus. Save for a brief excursion to Malta and Sicily in 1637–1638 to accompany a recently converted German prince on his travels, Kircher remained in Rome for the rest of his life. During his long and productive career, he published over thirty encyclopedic works on virtually every imaginable subject, not including the works of disciples such as Kaspar Schott, Giuseffo Petrucci, Johann Kestler, and Francesco Lana Terzi, who published his ideas—and often his exact words—under their own names. By 1646 his intellectual work had become so valuable and his fame so great the Jesuits relieved him of his teaching duties at the Collegio Romano, allowing him to devote himself fully to his research.

Kircher began his intellectual career with two principal interests: physico-mathematics and ancient Eastern languages and cultures. His earliest publications concerned various mathematical instruments such as the sundial he created in the Jesuit college in Avignon and a multipurpose measuring, calculating, and observational device that he invented during his trip to Malta. By 1636 his first work on Egypt, the *Prodromus Coptus sive Aegyptiacus* (Coptic or Egyptian forerunner), appeared. During the next two decades, Kircher published a series of works on Egyptian language, philosophy, history, and religion, culminating in his massive *Oedipus Aegyptiacus* (Egyptian Oedipus) of 1652–1655. In such works, he demonstrated his mastery of hieroglyphs—based on his Neoplatonic understanding of Egyptian as a symbolic and divine language, which bore little resemblance to the early-nineteenth-century decipherment of the Rosetta Stone—and argued strongly that Egypt was a universal source of culture and civilization that had anticipated Christianity with its strong Trinitarian symbolism. Kircher parlayed his expertise into a series of famous interpretations of the principal obelisks of Rome, namely the obelisk erected at the center of the sculptor Gian Lorenzo Bernini's famous fountain in Piazza Navona and the one atop Bernini's elephant in front of Santa Maria sopra Minerva. Kircher assisted Bernini in devising the words beneath each obelisk and published his interpretations of them in 1650 and 1666 respectively.

In addition to his work on Egypt, Kircher was equally prolific and bold in his account of the natural world. In 1641, his popular *Magnes sive de Arte Magnetica* (The magnet or the magnetic art) appeared, one of several publications in which Kircher argued that magnetism was the principal force organizing and controlling nature. At the same time, he began to develop his ideas on optics, leading to his *Ars Magna Lucis et Umbrae* (Great art of light and shadow) of 1646—a work filled with numerous optical demonstrations such as Kircher's famous magic lantern. Kircher complemented his work on optics with similarly intensive studies of acoustics in such works as his *Musurgia Universalis* (Universal music making) of 1650. The hydraulic organ in the Quirinale in Rome still today bears traces of his skills at designing ingenious musical machines that created sound without regular human intervention. Finally, Kircher spent over twenty years developing an explanation of earthquakes, after witnessing the eruption of Mount Etna in his youth. His *Mundus Subterraneus* (Subterranean world) of 1664–1665 attempted a comprehensive portrait of all the natural forces that organized the earth, just as his controversial *Iter Ecstaticum* (Ecstatic journey) of 1656 sought to explain what the cosmos looked like in an imaginative dialogue between an angel and a philosopher who discussed its composition while traveling throughout the heavens.

Kircher's reputation as a man who knew almost everything emanated not only from his publications but from his role as custodian of one of the most famous museums in Europe. Founded in 1651, the museum of the Collegio Romano flourished under his guidance. Kircher filled it with natural objects, machines, antiquities, paintings, and curiosities brought back by missionaries from all over the world. Visitors were enthralled by dancing demons, talking automata, sunflower clocks, Japanese scrolls, Chinese stone rubbings, Greco-Roman and Egyptian fragments, and a seemingly endless series of demonstrations of the powers of the magnet. Kircher parlayed his ability to gather objects and information into expertise on subjects about which he otherwise knew very little. His popular *China Illustrata* (China illustrated) of 1667, for example, was written without once traveling to Asia or knowing much about its languages, customs, and religions.

Kircher relied upon his ability to command the resources of the entire Jesuit order in the service of a universal account of the presence of Christianity in every corner of the world. His boundless curiosity and energy, a source of wonder in his own lifetime, made him a figure of fun in a later age when scholars such as Leibniz declared that Kircher had written much but known nothing about virtually every interesting subject of his age. He was one of the last great humanistic scholars of the seventeenth century, a man of faith whose vision of the world was as global as the missionary networks of his religious order.

See also **Dictionaries and Encyclopedias; Galileo Galilei; Jesuits; Leibniz, Gottried Wilhelm; Museums; Peiresc, Nicolas-Claude Fabri de.**

BIBLIOGRAPHY

Beinlich, Horst, et al. *Spurensuche. Wege zu Athanasius Kircher*. Dettelbach, Germany, 2002.

Findlen, Paula. *Possessing Nature: Museums, Collecting, and Scientific Culture in Early Modern Italy.* Berkeley, 1994.

Findlen, Paula, ed. *Athanasius Kircher: The Last Man Who Knew Everything.* New York, 2003.

Godwin, Joscelyn. *Athanasius Kircher: A Renaissance Man and the Quest for Lost Knowledge.* London, 1979.

Leinkauf, Thomas. *Mundus Combinatus: Studien zur Struktur der barocken Universalwissenschaft am Beispeil Athanasius Kircher SJ (1602–1680).* Berlin, 1993.

Lo Sardo, Eugenio, ed. *Athanasius Kircher S. J. Il Museo del Mondo.* Rome, 2001.

Marrone, Caterina. *I geroglifici fantastici di Athanasius Kircher.* Viterbo, Italy, 2002.

Rowland, Ingrid. *The Ecstatic Journey: Athanasius Kircher in Baroque Rome.* Chicago, 2000.

Stolzenberg, Daniel, ed. *The Great Art of Knowing: The Baroque Encyclopedia of Athanasius Kircher.* Stanford, 2002.

PAULA FINDLEN

KLOPSTOCK, FRIEDRICH GOTTLIEB (1724–1803), German poet. Friedrich Gottlieb Klopstock was the oldest of seventeen children born into an impoverished Pietist family of attorneys and pastors in Quedlinburg (Saxony-Anhalt). After receiving a humanistic education at the princely college in Schulpforta, he studied theology and philosophy at the universities of Jena and Leipzig, where he began writing the first songs of his monumental religious epic *Der Messias* (The Messiah; published in 4 volumes between 1748 and 1773, final version in 1799/1800). In 1751, he accepted an invitation from the Danish king, Frederick V, who sponsored the completion of the *Messias.* Shortly after his arrival in Denmark, Klopstock married Margarethe (Meta) Moller from Hamburg, the "Cidli" of his odes, who died four years later. After living in Denmark for almost twenty years, Klopstock resided in Hamburg for the rest of his life, married his first wife's niece, the widow Johanne Elisabeth von Winthem, and published poems, plays, and theoretical writings on German literature, language, and culture.

Klopstock became one of the most celebrated poets of his time and revolutionized German poetic language and its function within the theoretical debate about the possibility of a German national culture. Inspired by Johann Jakob Bodmer's and Johann Jakob Breitinger's literary theory of the poetic use of imagination, he rejected the dominant German aesthetic theory, the rationalist poetics of Johann Christoph Gottsched with its rigid literary conventions. Klopstock aspired to create a new poetry that could live up to the stylistic qualities of masterpieces such as Homer's *Iliad* or John Milton's *Paradise Lost.* His vision of the poet as "genius" or prophetic "creator" rather than "imitator" of nature led to the invention of a new lyrical language. Written in classical hexameters instead of the traditional German alternating verse forms, the first three cantos of the *Messias* signaled a departure from grammatical and syntactical rules and introduced an innovative, complex style. The pathetic use of inversions, repetitions, neologisms, comparisons, and metaphors infused enthusiasm, passion, and sentiment into the biblical story. In this way Klopstock transformed the culture of religious dogma into an inner world of sensitive experience. Although composed and perceived as a devotional work, the *Messias* evoked readers' or listeners' emotional responses and let them experience the religious sublime through the new aesthetic form. In his following poems, odes of enthusiasm, patriotic hymns, and elegies, Klopstock continued his formal experiments and was the first to introduce free verse into German poetry. His search for an emotional and yet sacred poetic language that manifested the experiences of the inner self combined expressive subjectivity with poetic autonomy and resulted in the interdependence of the secular and the spiritual. In this way, Klopstock instilled religious pathos into the poetic representation of friendship, nature, love, leisure, and the nation.

While Klopstock wrote spiritual songs (*Geistliche Lieder* [1757, 1769]), and religious and patriotic tragedies (*Der Tod Adams* [1757; The death of Adam] and *David* [1772]), his most influential work was probably the play *Hermanns Schlacht* (1769; The battle of Arminius). However, it did not receive the same attention as his poetic work—after all, Klopstock and the *Messias* had become synonyms. His collection of theoretical and fictional texts, *Die deutsche Gelehrtenrepublik* (1774; The German Republic of Letters) added a new dimension to his publications. This utopian historiography of a German national culture in the making launched the idea that national identity could be generated through shared values and transmitted by cultural artifacts and institutions. Drawing on Greek ideals, Klopstock envisioned a German republic in which the humanist tradition would unite political and cultural and public and private spheres. While the esoteric montage of different text genres did not receive the same attention as the *Messias,* its form of dissemination was quite remarkable in the history of publishing. Being concerned to receive fair compensation as an author, Klopstock circumvented the established book trade through publishers and booksellers by advertising his work via subscription and successfully launched a new means of profitable distribution.

Klopstock's contemporaries celebrated him as Germany's national poet. His poetic focus on feeling and experience influenced the young poets of the Sturm und Drang (Storm and Stress) movement; Johann Wolfgang von Goethe, Johann Gottfried Herder, and Friedrich Hölderlin praised him as Germany's leading lyric poet, and the Romantics embraced his cultural patriotism. Klopstock's poetic legacy was soon surpassed by that of Goethe, who dominated Germany's cultural landscape throughout the nineteenth century, and it was not until the twentieth century that German poets and authors such as Rainer Maria Rilke, Arno Schmidt, and Peter Rühmkorf rediscovered the power of Klopstock's lyrical voice. Recent scholarship has established a continuing interest in Klopstock through the production of a historical-critical edition of his works.

See also **Drama: German; German Literature and Language; Germany, Idea of; Goethe, Johann Wolfgang von; Herder, Johann Gottfried; Pietism.**

BIBLIOGRAPHY

Primary Sources

Klopstock, Friedrich Gottlieb. *Werke und Briefe: Historisch-kritische Ausgabe.* Edited by Horst Gronemeyer et al. Berlin and New York, 1974–.

Swales, Martin, ed. *German Poetry: An Anthology from Klopstock to Enzensberger.* Cambridge, U.K., and New York, 1987.

Secondary Sources

Hilliard, Kevin. *Philosophy, Letters, and the Fine Arts in Klopstock's Thought.* London, 1987.

Hilliard, Kevin, and Katrin Kohl, eds. *Klopstock an der Grenze der Epochen. Mit Klopstock-Bibliographie 1972–1992.* Berlin and New York, 1995.

Kohl, Katrin M. *Friedrich Gottlieb Klopstock.* Stuttgart, 2000.

—. *Rhetoric, the Bible, and the Origins of Free Verse: The Early "Hymns" of Friedrich Gottlieb Klopstock.* Berlin and New York, 1990.

Lee, Meredith. *Displacing Authority: Goethe's Poetic Reception of Klopstock.* Heidelberg, 1999.

Stephan K. Schindler

KNOWLEDGE, DISSEMINATION OF. *See* Dissemination of Knowledge.

KNOX, JOHN

KNOX, JOHN (c. 1513–1572), Scottish church reformer. Born in Haddington (Lothian), Knox studied at Glasgow University and probably also at St. Andrews. After his ordination to the priesthood in 1536, he became a notary apostolic (a church lawyer); as tutor to Lothian gentry, the Douglases and Cockburns, he met the Scottish reformer George Wishart and was converted to evangelical views around 1545. When Wishart was burned at the stake in 1546, Knox took refuge with the Protestant garrison in St. Andrew's Castle and began his preaching career. Although he had not been involved in the garrison's murder of Cardinal David Beaton, when the French captured the castle in July 1547, he was taken to France and made a galley slave, which permanently undermined his health. After his release in 1549, he went to England, where he actively promoted official Protestant changes, first in the northeast; he inevitably came into conflict with the conservative bishop of Durham Cuthbert Tunstall, but also captivated an enthusiastic evangelical gentlewoman, Elizabeth Bowes. In autumn 1551 he was made a royal chaplain, and John Dudley, duke of Northumberland, brought him south, probably hoping to exploit his religious radicalism to strip the church of its wealth. However, their relations deteriorated, and Knox was among the leading clergy who in early 1553 denounced politicians' worldliness. He failed to persuade the Privy Council to modify the 1552 Book of Common Prayer to forbid kneeling at holy communion, although his protests prompted Archbishop of Canterbury Thomas Cranmer to insert a last-minute instruction (the "black rubric") explaining that kneeling did not signify adoration of the bread and wine.

Mary I's accession in 1553 interrupted Knox's preaching ministry in Buckinghamshire. He fled abroad, followed by Elizabeth Bowes (who abandoned her Catholic husband) and her daughter Marjorie, whom he soon married. Knox championed thoroughgoing Calvinist reform among English exiles at Frankfurt am Main, resulting in his expulsion in 1555; he returned to John Calvin's Geneva, which he called "the most perfect school of Christ on earth since the days of the Apostles." In 1555–1556 he made a clandestine preaching tour in Scotland; back in Geneva in 1556 he drew up a directory of worship for the English congregation, the basis of the Church of Scotland's *Book of Common Order.* After Scottish bishops burned him in effigy in Edinburgh, he abandoned a planned return visit to Scotland in 1557. His attack on the two Catholic rulers Mary Tudor in England and Mary of Guise in Scotland, *The First Blast of the Trumpet against the Monstrous Regiment of Women* (1558), asserted that it was unnatural ("monstrous") for women to hold political power ("regiment"). Unfortunately this soon also applied to the Protestant Elizabeth I. Furious, she ended Knox's hopes of resuming his English career, refusing even to let him pass through England on his way back to Scotland. He was appointed minister of Edinburgh in 1559. He became the most prominent clerical leader of the Protestant and anti-French revolution and successfully pressed Elizabeth's adviser, William Cecil, Lord Burghley, for English military support. In August 1560 he was one of a team of ministers ("the six Johns") who drew up a Confession of Faith for the Kirk (the new Protestant Church of Scotland); they also prepared a scheme to reorganize the Kirk on Calvinist lines, the first *Book of Discipline,* which, because of political uncertainty and lack of resources, was not fully implemented. From 1561 he bitterly opposed Mary, Queen of Scots and preached violent sermons against her; after she was deposed in 1567, he preached at her son's coronation as James VI. He also preached at the funeral of the murdered regent James Stewart, earl of Moray, in 1570, but Stewart's death and the resulting civil war lessened his influence. One of his last contributions to the Reformation cause was, in spite of having suffered a stroke, to preach one of his classic sermons on the St. Bartholomew's Day massacre of French Protestants.

Knox's *History of the Reformation of Religion within the Realm of Scotland* (published 1587, then in full in 1644) remains an essential witness to the Reformation although it carefully conceals much of his own early career. He is a potent symbol of a militant and uncompromisingly Presbyterian Scottish Reformation, yet with his English wife and live-in mother-in-law, he was more Anglophile and flexible than either his detractors or his Presbyterian near-idolators have recognized. The contemporary Roman Catholic controversialist Ninian Winzet sneered at Knox that he had forgotten "our auld plane Scottis quhilk your mother lerit you" because his language was so Anglicized: at the height of the Scottish political crisis in 1566, he spent six mysterious months in England of which we know nothing. Without the accidents of English politics, John Knox might well have become the first in a long troop of Scotsmen to end up a bishop of the Church of England.

See also **Calvinism; Church of England; Elizabeth I (England); Reformation, Protestant; Scotland.**

BIBLIOGRAPHY

Primary Source

Knox, John. *The Works of John Knox.* Edited by David Laing. 6 vols. Edinburgh, 1846–1864. Reprint, New York, 1966.

Secondary Sources

Mason, Roger A., ed. *John Knox and the British Reformation.* Aldershot, U.K., and Brookfield, Vt., 1998.

Ridley, Jasper. *John Knox.* Oxford, 1968.

Diarmaid MacCulloch

KOCHANOWSKI, JAN (1530–1584), Polish and Neo-Latin poet, humanist, royal secretary and courtier, arguably the outstanding literary figure of the Slavic world before the Romantic age. Kochanowski was born to a middling gentry family of Little Poland. He matriculated at the standard age of fourteen in the Cracow Academy in 1544, then spent 1551–1552 at the Lutheran university in

Königsberg, where he once returned (1555–1556), perhaps in search of a patron at Duke Albert Frederick's court. Over the years 1552–1559, Kochanowski spent three longer periods at the University of Padua, where he studied with one of Italy's leading humanist scholars, Francesco Robortello. He completed his study years with a tour of France (1558/1559), where he came into contact with the poet Pierre de Ronsard.

Upon his return to Poland in 1559, Kochanowski began a fifteen-year period of activities connected with politics and the royal court. We find him among the clients of Little Polish magnates, including the Calvinist palatine of Lublin, Jan Firlej, and crown vice-chancellor (later bishop of Cracow) Piotr Myszkowski, thanks to whose patronage he became one of King Sigismund II Augustus's secretaries and courtiers. Around 1571 Kochanowski's ties with court life began to loosen, and he retreated more and more to his country estate at Czarnolas in Little Poland, where he lived from 1575 until his death in 1584.

Kochanowski began as a Neo-Latin poet, but his place in literary history is secured by his pioneering work in Polish. This "father of Polish literature" attempted to establish Polish models for the entire canon of classical and humanistic genres. During his court period, Kochanowski focused on poetry in an epic tonality (*Susanna,* c. 1562; *Chess,* between 1562 and 1566) and occasional poetry, as well as political poetry (*Harmony,* 1564; *Satyr, or the Wild Man,* c. 1564). He gradually shifted toward what would be his strength, lyric poetry. A central work here was his *Songs* (published posthumously in 1585), composed over nearly twenty years and based on Horatian and Petrarchan models. Over the same years Kochanowski worked on his *Trifles,* a collection of mostly short poems, often of personal or topical content, ranging in style from epic to anacreontic. They continue to find imitators among Polish poets. Kochanowski was the author of Poland's first Renaissance tragedy, *The Dismissal of the Grecian Envoys* (written probably c. 1565 but first performed in 1578, before King Stephen Báthory, and published that year). From the last, rural period come his *Laments* (1580) on the death of his beloved daughter Urszula. Kochanowski began work on his masterpiece—a versified *Psalter,* based on the model of George Buchanan's Latin version (among others)—while still at court, but he did the lion's share of the work at Czarnolas, publishing it only in 1579.

Kochanowski received recognition as the premier Polish poet during his lifetime, and traditions of reading and imitation of his work have continued uninterrupted. His *Psalter* was issued twenty-five times by the middle of the seventeenth century, and it influenced similar projects in Russian, Romanian, Lithuanian, German, Hungarian, Czech, Slovak, and Lusatian. Polish Catholics and Protestants sang his versions of the Psalms in their churches (often without realizing whose they were), and seventeenth-century Polish Catholics sought to make him into an orthodox post-Tridentine Catholic, evidently troubled by the tonalities of Horatian epicureanism, Senecan stoicism, and Erasmian irenicism in his life and work.

See also **Polish Literature and Language.**

BIBLIOGRAPHY

Fiszman, Samuel, ed. *The Polish Renaissance in its European Context.* Bloomington, Ind., and Indianapolis, 1988.

Langlade, Jacques. *Jean Kochanowski: L'homme, le penseur, le poète lyrique.* Paris, 1932.

Pelc, Janusz. *Jan Kochanowski: Szczyt renesansu w literaturze polskiej.* Warsaw, 1980.

DAVID FRICK

KOŁŁĄTAJ, HUGO (1750–1812), Polish cleric, reformer of education, politician, promoter of Enlightenment thought, historian, and philosopher. Born in Dederkały (Volhynia), the youngest son of an impoverished gentry family, he soon chose the clerical path of material and social advancement. He began studies at the Cracow Academy in 1761 and continued in Vienna (1771–1772) and Italy, especially Rome (1772–1774); during these travels he studied French, canon law, and theology and made his first contacts with Enlightenment thought.

Upon his return to Cracow in 1775, Kołłątaj took priestly orders and soon joined in the work of the Commission of National Education. From 1775 to 1786 he directed the reform of the Cracow Academy, Poland's oldest university, serving as rector from 1783 to 1786. In the years immediately preceding the Second Partition of Poland (1786–1792), Kołłątaj resided in Warsaw, playing a leading role in attempts to reform Polish politics and society. He achieved high office (becoming Lithuanian spiritual referendary in 1787 and crown vice-chancellor in 1791) and led a movement to transform Poland's feudal, magnate-dominated society into a modern bourgeois nation led by propertied gentry and burghers, governed by a parliament in permanent session, and with a now hereditary but much weakened monarch. From "Kołłątaj's Smithy" (a term coined by his opponents) came a stream of reformist writings by various authors. Among his concerns was the status of burghers and Jews in a reformed state. Kołłątaj was a coauthor of the constitution of 3 May 1791.

In the face of the catastrophe of 1792, Kołłątaj took up a conciliatory stance, urging King Stanisław II August Poniatowski to find a modus vivendi with the Russian-sponsored Confederation of Targowica—although Kołłątaj himself was anathema to the Polish conservatives of the confederation. The Second Partition (1793) found him in Saxony, where he helped prepare the Kościuszko uprising of 1794. Contacts with revolutionary France radicalized some of his ideas. Kołłątaj returned to Warsaw in May 1794, where he became a focal point for supporters of the uprising, burghers, and Jacobins, although he was certainly not the "Polish Robespierre" that the king and others saw in him.

After the Russian conquest of Warsaw in early November 1794, Kołłątaj fled south and was arrested by the Austrians near Przemyśl. He remained incarcerated in Moravian Olomouc until November 1802. During this time he continued his scholarly work, gathering materials and sketching an outline for an ambitious historical and ethnographic project. Upon release, Kołłątaj settled in Russian Volhynia, where, under discreet police surveillance, he continued his scholarly projects and worked on the organization of a lyceum at Kremenets.

Summoned to Warsaw under Napoleon in 1806, Kołłątaj delayed. This delay, plus the emperor's distrust of former "Jacobins," increased his isolation. He was arrested by the Russians in 1807 and interned in Moscow until the next year, when he returned to Warsaw. He failed, however, in his attempts to play a role in the politics and culture of Napoleonic Poland. A late work, *Nil Desperandum* (1808), offered a vision of a modernized, liberal Poland restored to its old borders, in alliance with France, in a Europe divided into two empires, west (France) and east (Russia).

See also **Poland, Partitions of; Poland-Lithuania, Commonwealth of, 1569–1795; Poniatowski, Stanisław II Augustus; 3 May Constitution.**

BIBLIOGRAPHY

Jobert, Ambroise. *La Commission d'Education Nationale en Pologne, 1773–1794, son oeuvre d'instruction civique.* Paris, 1941.

Lech, Marian J. *Hugo Kołłątaj.* Warsaw, 1973.

Leśnodorski, Bogusław. *Les Jacobins polonais.* Paris, 1965.

DAVID FRICK

KRAKÓW. *See* **Cracow.**

L

LA BRUYÈRE, JEAN DE (1645–1696), French moralist, social commentator, and satirist. Jean de La Bruyère was baptized in Paris. His parents were bourgeois. Other than these facts, little is known about his early years before he obtained a law degree from the University of Orléans in 1665. He did not practice, however, and led a life of leisure, made possible by a modest inheritance from an uncle in 1671. In 1684 he obtained a position as one of the tutors to Louis de Bourbon, grandson of the Grand Condé, Louis II de Bourbon (1621–1686), a royal prince. When the latter died three years later, the young Louis quit his studies, but La Bruyère remained attached to the household. The role of domestic servant did not suit his temperament, although it allowed him to observe closely the court and all of its foibles.

His wounded pride and the injustices he witnessed due to the disparity of social status are often considered crucial to the creation of his only literary work, a collection of sarcastic observations and caricatures entitled *Les caractères* (1688; The characters). The work was immediately and immensely successful, going through seven editions in four years, with each edition bringing additions to previous texts as well as new passages. He was received into the Académie française (French Academy) in 1693, and can be considered one of the last "Anciens" in the quarrel between ancients and moderns. He wrote a polemical tract, *Dialogues sur le Quiétisme* (1696; Dialogues on Quietism), against the contemporary vogue for religious mysticism, assailing with vigor François Fénelon (1651–1715). He died suddenly at Versailles in May, 1696.

In *Les caractères,* ('portraits' or 'caricatures'), La Bruyère established his work within the tradition of classical Greco-Roman literature. He presented first a French translation of the Greek text by Theophrastus (d. 278 B.C.E.) with some of his own *caractères* and satiric observations drawn from his own time and society. These were divided into sixteen different chapters, covering such diverse topics as literary criticism, life in town and country, the court, women, judgment, and taste. With each successive edition came an increase of entries in all categories, until La Bruyère's text far surpassed that of Theophrastus. The opening passage to his own work, in which he switches from translator to author, begins with the often-cited phrase, "Everything has been said. . . ." a paradoxical beginning perhaps, but one that indicates the contemporary view of imitation. Novelty is to be sought less in substance than in style, in how a work is expressed.

His text is a compendium of brief forms—maxims, observations, thoughts, portraits—that often lack external connections or transitions. The coherence, or organic unity, of the whole is not apparent, although certain themes and perspectives, such as superficiality, vanity, and righteous indignation, reappear. Some critics have argued that the entire work should be read in light of the final chapter—a Christian defense—although others consider him more a pessimist or satirist than a Christian reformer. He does stress the virtues of retreat from society. Within a textual entry, elliptical, paratactical structures make for a rapid and vivid description, as nouns and verbs come shooting forth, separated by punctuation marks, a simple "and" or "but" rather than complex constructions joined by direct causal links ("because"). The age of King Louis XIV (1638–1715) prized an oral, theatrical style, and many of the *caractères* read like small scenes, presented without authorial comment. To this extent the reader plays a role in supplying the criticism or condemnation implicit within the text, such as that found in the chasm that separates Giton, who is rich, from Phédon, who is poor.

Following his literary model, La Bruyère used Greek pseudonyms for his portraits, and keys soon circulated that claimed to identify the real identities of Ménalque, the scatterbrain, Gnathon, the gourmand, Ornulphre, the religious hypocrite patterned after Molière's Tartuffe, and dozens of other individuals. He was much imitated in the eighteenth century, although without much success. Due to their short form but richly dense material, many passages were anthologized in the nineteenth and twentieth centuries, for general audiences as well as classroom exercises. Gustave Flaubert (1821–1880), Marcel Proust (1871–1922), and André Gide (1869–1951) were influenced by his style, and recent literary criticism has found an affinity for the open, "readerly" nature of the texts. As for his content, his comments on women have brought him some approbation, but his indictment is primarily against the way society treats them and how they are obliged to behave. In addition, La Bruyère was one of the few writers of the seventeenth century even to allude to the plight of the poor and the peasants.

See also **Ancients and Moderns; Condé Family; Fénelon, François; French Literature and Language; Louis XIV (France); Molière (Jean-Baptiste Poquelin); Quietism.**

BIBLIOGRAPHY

James, Edward. "La Bruyère: A traditionalist in an age of change." In *Seventeenth-Century French Studies* 14 (1992); 69–79.

Knox, Edward C. *Jean de La Bruyère.* New York, 1973.

Parkin, John. "La Bruyère: A Study in Satire." In *French Humour,* edited by John Parkin. Amsterdam, 1999.

Van Delft, Louis. *La Bruyère moraliste.* Geneva, 1971.

Allen G. Wood

LA FAYETTE, MARIE-MADELEINE DE

LA FAYETTE, MARIE-MADELEINE DE (Marie-Madeleine Pioche de la Vergne, countess of La Fayette; 1634–1693), French novelist. Born in Paris to a family of the lower nobility with close ties to the court of King Louis XIII (ruled 1610–1643), Marie-Madeleine Pioche de la Vergne became a lady-in-waiting at the age of fifteen to Anne of Austria, the French queen. She received a broad education in the classics and languages, was an enthusiastic reader of the popular new novels of her day, and, from an early age, was close to prominent figures including the moralist and philosopher François de la Rochefoucauld, the cardinal of Retz, and the writers Gilles Ménage and Madeleine de Scudéry. In 1655 she married Francis Motier, count of La Fayette, and moved with him to his property in the Auvergne. The first of her two sons was born in Poitou in 1658, but after three years in the provinces Marie-Madeleine moved back to Paris, leaving her husband behind to manage his country estates. She lived independently in Paris for the rest of her life in her home next to the Luxembourg palace, where she remained closely involved with the intellectual and political life of the court and the salons of the capital.

Literary history has traditionally designated Madame de La Fayette as the originator of the modern novel. She turned to writing fiction soon after her return to Paris, and in 1662 anonymously published a short historical fiction, *La princesse de Montpensier* (The princess of Montpensier) followed by two novels, *Zaïde* (1670) and *La princesse de Clèves* (1678; The princess of Clèves). La Fayette's great innovation was her particular way of blending history, romance, and psychological analysis. In her fiction she incorporated some of the features of pastoral and epic narrative into a framework more closely resembling memoirs and historical documents. In her most important and influential novel, *La princesse de Clèves,* she designed a plot drawn from events at the French court of the sixteenth century. Into a group of characters including Catherine de Médecis, the duc of Guise, and the young Mary Stuart, she placed a central figure of her own invention, presenting the story of the psychological development of a young woman maturing in the oppressive atmosphere of courtly intrigue. Madame de La Fayette's first readers recognized in her novel more a reflection of their own time than that of history. The book precipitated a major literary quarrel, conducted in print via a popular gazette of the day, *Le Mercure galant* (The gallant Mercury). Readers argued passionately about the novel's realism, the plausibility of the heroine's behavior, and the moral implications of her story. The controversy extended to La Fayette's readers in England, where each of her novels was published in translation within a year of its appearance in France.

Themes central to *La princesse de Clèves* are examined in all of La Fayette's fiction: the difficulty of sincere communication, the fugitive quality of love, the tensions between religious principles and worldly demands, and the constraints of marriage. Retreat from the world is the solution that holds the strongest appeal for her female characters, but the difficulty of decisions such as these, and their slow maturation in the minds of the protagonists, are what most fascinate La Fayette: exemplary behavior is achieved at a great cost. In the darkest of La Fayette's scenarios, as in the posthumously published *La comtesse de Tende* (1724; The princess of Tende), the heroine's urge for escape is suicidal. In *La princesse de Clèves,* retreat is a solution that is closer to a form of religious devotion.

Also published posthumously were historical memoirs of the court of King Louis XIV, *Mémoires de la cour de France* (1731; Memoirs of the French court). La Fayette used the memoir genre to dramatize the inevitable confrontation with death in her more personal historical memoir, *Histoire de Madame Henriette d'Angleterre* (The Story of Madame Henrietta of England) begun as a biography at the request of her friend Henrietta of England and transformed by the princess's abrupt death in 1670.

In the last decade of her life Madame de La Fayette withdrew from Parisian society but continued to engage in social life through letter correspondence. Her closest friend, after the death of her companion La Rochefoucauld, was Madame de Sévigné, whose letters are an important source for our knowledge of La Fayette's life. Their correspondence also provides documentation of Madame de La Fayette's ambivalent attitude toward her own status as an author and her strategic use of the practice of anonymous publication. Sévigné's letters record the popularity of La Fayette's writings.

Madame de La Fayette has remained a canonical figure in French literary history. The innovative aspects of her fictional plots are increasingly explored in literary criticism, with particular interest in her invention of new models for describing women's psychological and social development.

See also **French Literature and Language; La Rochefoucauld, François, duc de; Louis XIII (France); Scudéry, Madeleine de; Sévigné, Marie de.**

BIBLIOGRAPHY

Primary Sources

La Fayette, Madame de. *La princesse de Clèves; La princesse de Montpensier; La comtesse de Tende.* Translated by Terence Cave. Oxford and New York, 1999.

———. *The Secret History of Henrietta, Princess of England, First Wife of Philippe, Duc d'Orléans; Together with, Memoirs of the Court of France for the Years 1688–1689.* Translated by J. M. Shelmerdine. New York, 1993.

Secondary Sources

Green, Anne. *Privileged Anonymity: The Writings of Madame de Lafayette.* Oxford, 1996.

Henry, Patrick, ed. *An Inimitable Example: The Case for the* Princesse de Clèves. Washington, D.C., 1992.

ELIZABETH C. GOLDSMITH

LA FONTAINE, JEAN DE (1621–1695), French poet and fable writer. Jean de La Fontaine grew up in a bourgeois family in rural France, where his grandfather, father, and finally he himself held the local charge of master of waters and forests. In his youth he quit the study of theology to pursue and obtain a law degree. He married and had a son, but cared little for his family and soon lived separately, in Paris. The poems "Adonis" (1658) and "Elegie aux nymphes de Vaux" (1661; The dream of Vaux) impressed Nicolas Fouquet (1615–1680), Louis XIV's superintendent of finances and a patron of the arts, who granted the poet a pension in 1659. The disgrace and imprisonment of Fouquet (1662) disrupted La Fontaine's life and finances and caused the king to be suspicious of the poet for many years. He entered into the service of the king's widowed aunt, where he again had access, albeit limited, to the rich bourgeoisie and the aristocracy. He began to frequent literary salons and published *Contes et nouvelles en vers* (1665; Tales and stories in verse), which were shockingly indecorous to precious ladies and followers of classicism because of their bawdy

Jean de La Fontaine. Portrait by Nicolas de Largilliere. THE ART ARCHIVE/MUSÉE DU CHATEAU DE VERSAILLES/DAGLI ORTI

topics, and which were closer in subject and style to medieval fabliaux or the works of François Rabelais (c. 1483–1553).

In 1668 La Fontaine published the first of a collection of *Fables choisies mises en vers* (Selected fables set in verse; books 1–6), dedicated to the dauphin, which became extremely popular. Fables and other short poetic forms had been practiced in the literary salons for a while by a number of noted writers, but not with the style, wit, or power that La Fontaine displayed. As the guest and protégé of Mme Marguerite de la Sablière (c. 1640–1693) he enjoyed modest personal and financial comfort. He continued to write and publish new *Tales,* but with less success, and eventually incurred a police ban. He wrote the libretto for an opera *(Daphné)* by Jean-Baptiste Lully (1632–1687), but the two fought and parted. Although actively writing, he only found approbation with a second set of *Fables* (books 7–11) in 1678–1679. When he was elected to the French Academy in 1683, the king complicated matters for the former client of Fouquet and withheld royal approval until after Nicolas Boileau-Despréaux (1636–1711) had been admitted several months later. Leading a libertine life well into his sixties, La Fontaine did not change his life or renounce his more scandalous works until after he fell gravely ill in 1693. The next year saw a final book of *Fables,* a year before his death in Paris.

La Fontaine had the nickname of the "butterfly of Parnassus," as he was often considered to be flighty and disorganized. Anecdotes abound related to his naïveté, lack of seriousness, and inability to hold a decent conversation. But more recently this view has been challenged, and he has been seen as a capable courtier possessed of more skills than previously thought. Meanwhile, his superb mastery of poetic technique has never been doubted.

The two hundred and forty or so fables that he wrote can be considered as various overlapping scenes in the drama of human life. This is presented generally by a brief story of animal conflicts, making the poems allegorical. They need to be applied to human behavior (the wolf represents a certain kind of individual, or even a particular person) before instruction can be drawn. The morals, which are often (but not always) stated, can seem contradictory, or at least tied to a certain situation, when the entire body of fables are read, but the didactic purpose frequently lies in citing one fable for a unique real-life case. The fables are appealing to both children and adults and are linked to the seventeenth century by numerous specific details, but they attain universal pertinence by the general character traits and morals revealed.

The first set of *Fables* was inspired mainly by the Greek writer Aesop and the Roman Phaedrus, while later works were modeled after Bilpay and other non-Western sources. The conflicts between the grasshopper and the ant, the wolf and the lamb, and the tortoise and the hare, among many others, were part of both an oral tradition and a literary one. La Fontaine did not alter the basic stories or outcomes from these sources, but elaborated both the narrative and poetic aspects. A bit of conversation or some detail of clothing or place makes them more dramatic, picturesque, and plausible. As for poetic technique, at a time that valued the alexandrine couplet, La Fontaine displayed great irregularity, as he varied his line lengths and rhyme schemes within each fable, making them less artificial and predictable.

Both Jean-Jacques Rousseau (1712–1778) and Alphonse Marie Louis de Prat de Lamartine (1790–1869) criticized the *Fables* as being too violent for children or even for adults, who also might mistakenly follow the vices, rather than the virtues, depicted. It is true that the poems often teach by negative example, but their charm has captivated most critics, teachers, and parents for more than three hundred years.

See also **Boileau-Despréaux, Nicolas; Folk Tales and Fairy Tales; French Literature and Language; Lully, Jean-Baptiste.**

BIBLIOGRAPHY

Calder, Andrew. *The Fables of La Fontaine.* Geneva, 2001.

Danner, Richard G. *Patterns of Irony in the Fables of La Fontaine.* Athens, Ohio, 1985.

Lapp, John C. *The Esthetics of Negligence: La Fontaine's Contes.* Cambridge, U.K., 1971.

Rubin, David Lee. *A Pact with Silence: Art and Thought in the Fables of Jean de La Fontaine.* Columbus, Ohio, 1991.

Runyon, Randolph Paul. *In La Fontaine's Labyrinth: A Thread through the Fables.* Charlottesville, Va., 2000.

Slater, Maya. *The Craft of La Fontaine.* London, 2001.

Sweetser, Marie-Odile. *La Fontaine.* New York, 1987.

Vincent, Michael. *Figures of the Text.* Amsterdam and Philadelphia, 1992.

ALLEN G. WOOD

LA METTRIE, JULIEN OFFROY DE

(1709–1751), French physician and philosopher. Julien Offroy de La Mettrie is best known for his work of materialist philosophy, *L'homme-machine* (1747). His philosophical works were written early in the French Enlightenment but are among some of the most radical works of that period.

La Mettrie was born in Saint-Malo in Brittany on 19 December 1751, the son of a textile merchant wealthy enough to give him a good education. He attended several provincial colleges, where he was influenced by Jansenism. In 1725 he enrolled in the College d'Harcourt, the first academic institution to make Cartesianism central to the curriculum. La Mettrie then spent five years at the University of Paris studying medicine. To avoid graduation fees at Paris, he took his degree at the University of Reims. He found his education insufficient preparation for the actual practice of medicine and went to the University of Leiden to study with Hermann Boerhaave (1668–1738), a renowned teacher of physiology and chemistry and an innovative practitioner of clinical medicine. La Mettrie translated many of Boerhaave's most significant works, and in his commentaries on those works, he emphasized the materialistic strand he found in them that provided the foundation for his own medical philosophy. La Mettrie also wrote five medical treatises on specific diseases and public health. His medical experiences led him to lampoon the ignorance and venality of Parisian medical practitioners in thinly veiled medical satires. From these satirical counterexamples, La Mettrie developed his notion of the *médecin-philosophe* who incorporated the astute empirical observation of a surgeon, the thorough training in physiology of an idealistic physician, and the zeal of the reform-minded philosophe. The *médecin-philosophe* could be an agent for reform based on scientific knowledge.

The critical perspective of the *médecin-philosophe* was gleaned from an understanding of the human being based in medicine and physiology. La Mettrie's philosophical works all approached philosophical issues from this perspective. *L'histoire naturelle de l'âme* (1745), his first philosophical work, was a rather conventional discussion of the philosophical treatment of the vegetative and animal souls combined with a materialist view of the human, rational soul, using a materialist reading of John Locke's (1632–1704) *An Essay concerning Human Understanding* (1690) as its source. La Mettrie argued that the human soul could be completely identified with the physical functions of the body and that any claims about the existence of the soul must be substantiated by physiology. Consequently his books were banned, and he was exiled to Holland in 1745. In *L'homme-machine*, La Mettrie not only adopted the engaging style of Enlightenment philosophes, he also applied a thoroughgoing materialism to human beings. Using evidence drawn from anatomy, physiology, and psychology, he demonstrated the effects of the body on the soul and the comparability between humans and animals. His man-machine was active, organic, and self-moving; his materialism did not distinguish between conscious, voluntary movement and unconscious, instinctive movement. This work was deemed so radical that the tolerant Dutch exiled La Mettrie. He sought refuge at the court of Frederick the Great (1712–1786) of Prussia, where he remained until his early death in 1751.

Several other philosophical works, including *L'homme plante* (1747) and *Le système d'epicure* (1751), compared humans to lower creatures and placed all creatures in the context of the unfolding of matter and motion in an evolutionary process. La Mettrie insisted that the physician's approach to questions, usually treated by theologians and metaphysicians, would be more productive, even on ethical issues. In *Le discours sur le bonheur* (1748) La Mettrie examined the implications of materialism for moral values. He questioned whether moral systems corresponded to human nature as corroborated by his physiological understanding of human beings. Vice and virtue, he concluded, were arbitrarily constructed by society to serve its interests, but those interests were often at odds with the physiological constitution of the individual. He hoped that, by recognizing the arbitrary nature of its moral notions, society would reward a greater array of human behaviors and so alleviate the sufferings of those who were ill disposed to seek happiness in what society deemed virtuous. La Mettrie was particularly critical of both stoicism and Christianity as moral systems, which, he claimed, were based on a distorted understanding of human nature.

La Mettrie saw the *médecin-philosophe* as an agent of rational analysis and social progress and identified with the goals of the early Enlightenment. The philosophes, however, found his materialism, moral relativism, hedonistic ethics, and atheism much too dangerous to espouse. Even other materialists, such as the Baron d'Holbach (1723–1789) and Denis Diderot (1713–1784), did not acknowledge their debt to such a radical thinker. La Mettrie's medical materialism, grounded in the scientific issues of his day, is his most significant contribution to the French Enlightenment and the history of philosophy.

See also **Boerhaave, Herman; Medicine; Philosophes; Philosophy.**

BIBLIOGRAPHY

Thomson, Ann. *Materialism and Society in the Mid-Eighteenth Century: La Mettrie's "Discours Préliminaire."* Geneva, Switzerland, 1981.

Vartanian, Aram. *La Mettrie's "L'homme machine": A Study in the Origins of an Idea.* Princeton, 1960.

Wellman, Kathleen. *La Mettrie: Medicine, Philosophy, and Enlightenment.* Durham, N.C., 1992.

KATHLEEN WELLMAN

LA RAMÉE, PIERRE DE. *See* **Ramus, Petrus.**

LA ROCHEFOUCAULD, FRANÇOIS, DUC DE

LA ROCHEFOUCAULD, FRANÇOIS, DUC DE (1613–1680), French writer. A peer of France who later became a leading moralist in the French classical age, La Rochefoucauld, the eldest son of a provincial nobleman and courtier from the Angoumois in western France, was groomed early to inherit the family name, title, and estate. His formative reading centered more upon popular romance than the classical canon, as he acquired his nickname from a character in the serialized novel *Astrée.* Married at fifteen when he was still the prince of Marcillac, he soon embarked upon a military career. Starting in the middle 1630s, he fell in with noble opposition to the ministries first of Cardinal Richelieu (1624–1642) and then of Cardinal Mazarin (1642–1660). During the civil upheavals known as the Fronde (1648–1652), he sided with the rebels against the regency government, and was wounded in battle 9 February 1649. At the unsuccessful conclusion of the Fronde, he made a wary peace with the government, receiving a pension in exchange for renouncing further political intrigue.

From the end of the Fronde until his death, La Rochefoucauld spent his time principally in the social world of Paris, where he was a frequent guest in the salons and where he developed his very considerable talents as a writing stylist. Among his friends and collaborators were the salon hostess the Marquise de Sablé, the novelist Mme de La Fayette, and the worldly Jansenist Jacques Esprit. La Rochefoucauld is known today as the author of three significant works. The *Réflexions diverses* (Diverse reflections), which was only discovered and published posthumously and has never been translated into

English, is a series of essays on taste, sociability, and moral psychology. His *Mémoires* (1662) offer one of the most important accounts of the political factionalism in noble circles in the period up to and including the Fronde. His subtle and nuanced attacks on the motives of some of the principal players of his time, including Cardinals Richelieu and Mazarin and Louis de Bourbon, the prince of Condé, made the work a scandal when it first appeared in the 1660s.

His most important work was the *Maximes.* Growing out of a collaborative salon pastime, this work went through considerable elaboration between its first appearance in 1665 and its most polished edition of 1678. In the *Maximes,* most of the traditional resources of self-control and moral responsibility are depicted as illusory. Fortune triumphs over fortitude, the humors and temperaments win out over character, the passions interfere with reason, and self-love rules all. Even in the least likely corners of the heart and soul, the author traces the effects of self-deception and hidden self-aggrandizement. Some of the maxims seem to debunk the possibility of noble virtues such as courage and perseverance. Others unravel the more private sentiments such as love and friendship. Still others erode the social affections such as gratitude and generosity. "Self-love is the greatest flatterer of them all" (Maxim 2) is a fair sample of the genre.

The sheer scale of the unmasking enterprise, and the prominent role of self-love in it, led contemporaries to a disagreement that has not abated since. Some observers associated La Rochefoucauld with Blaise Pascal (1623–1662), Pierre Nicole (1625–1695), and other Jansenists, that austere movement of religious and moral revival that adopted St. Augustine's view that grace alone brought salvation, and that what appear to be human virtues are in reality merely variations on the hidden pride and self-interest that move fallen man. Other readers felt that La Rochefoucauld's systemic, lynx-eyed suspicion covered sacred as well as secular, religious as well as worldly ideals, and that his moral psychology therefore is best seen as a form of reductionism, perhaps even nihilism.

In the eighteenth century, there was a tendency to accept the premise of La Rochefoucauld's views on the pervasiveness of self-love while drawing more hopeful conclusions from it. Writers from Bernard Mandeville (1670–1733) to Claude-Adrien Helvétius (1715–1771) saw in the *Maximes* support for an emerging liberal view of society in which the pursuit of private self-interest is conducive to the public good, a view that perhaps culminated in Adam Smith's *An Inquiry into the Nature and Causes of the Wealth of Nations* (1776). In the nineteenth century, La Rochefoucauld's most noteworthy influence was exerted on German aphoristic philosophers such as Arthur Schopenhauer (1788–1860) and Friedrich Nietzsche (1844–1900). Nietzsche saw in La Rochefoucauld an admirable specimen of uncorrupted European aristocracy, as well as a method of psychological insight and moral honesty far preferable to the democratizing utilitarianism of his day.

See also **Fronde; Jansenism; Mazarin, Jules; Paris; Richelieu, Armand-Jean Du Plessis, cardinal; Salons.**

BIBLIOGRAPHY

Primary Sources

La Rochefoucauld. *Maxims.* Translated and introduced by Leonard Tancock. New York, 1959. Long the standard English translation of the 1678 edition of the *Maximes.*

———. *Maxims: La Rochefoucauld.* Translation, introduction, and notes by Stuart D. Warner and Stéphane Douard. South Bend, Ind. 2001. Bilingual edition of the *Maximes.*

Secondary Sources

Bénichou, Paul. "The Destruction of the Hero." In *Man and Ethics: Studies in French Classicism.* Translated by Elizabeth Hughes. Garden City, N.Y., 1979. Translation of *Morales du grand siècle* (1948). Standard account of the social implications of the *Maxims* and other contemporary works.

Bishop, Morris. *The Life and Adventures of La Rochefoucauld.* Ithaca, N.Y., 1951. The only book-length biographical account in English.

Clark, Henry C. *La Rochefoucauld and the Language of Unmasking in Seventeenth-Century France.* Geneva, 1994. Argues for a secular, nonreligious interpretation of the moralist's work.

Holman, Robyn, and Jacques Barchilon, eds. *Concordance to the "Maximes" of La Rochefoucauld.* Boulder, Colo., 1996.

Lafond, Jean. *La Rochefoucauld: Augustinisme et littérature.* Paris, 1977. Leading statement of a religious interpretation of the *Maximes.*

HENRY CLARK

LA ROCHELLE. The primary characteristic of La Rochelle was its isolation. Situated on the Bay of Biscay, the city was all but cut off from the interior by marshland. Yet this very isolation allowed La Rochelle to become one of France's most prosperous towns by the end of the Middle Ages. At the beginning of the twelfth century the port barely existed. It blossomed into prominence with the subsequent expansion of the export trade in wine and salt, a salt yielded in abundance by the encircling marshes. The city also profited from seigneurial rivalries and ambitions to secure an unusual degree of municipal autonomy. It barely paid any royal taxes, and the economic life of the commune was regulated by its one hundred–member council headed by the mayor.

The most dynamic elements of La Rochelle's population of twenty thousand consisted of merchants, shopkeepers, and artisans. Royal authority was nominally represented by the *senechal* (who had the honor of selecting the mayor from three names offered by the council) and from 1553 by a diminutive corps of legal officers. Despite the existence of a number of monastic houses, La Rochelle boasted only five parish churches, and the ecclesiastical hierarchy was weak compared with that of many other towns.

This social physiognomy helps explain the receptiveness of the Rochelais to the Reformed Church. Clerics, artisans, merchants, and municipal and royal officers all adopted the Protestant doctrines, and by 1570 the municipality was firmly attached to the Huguenot cause, providing a virtually impregnable retreat for the Huguenot grandees in times of difficulty. La Rochelle withstood a siege lasting six months in 1573 and emerged from the Wars of Religion with its privileges bolstered. The resulting sense of security almost certainly explains why, as in the southern Huguenot towns of Montauban and Nîmes, the Huguenots sustained their congregations, which embraced the overwhelmimg majority of the population.

By the 1620s, however, La Rochelle's privileges had become an intolerable barrier to the government's plans to enhance its fragile control of the Atlantic seaboard, an ambition that dovetailed with the renewal of war against the Huguenots. The two processes reached a spectacular climax with a fourteen-month blockade that culminated in the entry of Louis XIII (ruled 1601–1643) into the city at the head of his troops on All Saints' Day 1628. Reduced by death and desertion to a mere five thousand survivors, La Rochelle emerged into a different world. La Rochelle's municipal institutions and autonomy were destroyed along with most of the city walls. The wealth of its merchants was subject to the soaring fiscal exigencies of the crown, a fact most strikingly brought home by the progressive abandonment of the heavily taxed salt marshes.

It is testimony to the power of the Atlantic economy that the decline in La Rochelle's fortunes was relative rather than catastrophic. By 1675 the population had returned to its former level, and expanding colonial trade together with the growth of the brandy trade compensated for the decline in the quality of the local wines. By 1720 brandy formed 37 percent of total exports, while the West Indian slave trade gave the merchant community a new lease on life.

Yet the effects of royal taxation on a modestly sized town with an inadequate harbor and no major river ultimately could not be avoided. As the populations of Nantes and Bordeaux soared in the decades after 1720, that of La Rochelle declined once more. Although the value of its trade had risen, its share of France's colonial trade declined from 20 percent in 1730 to 7 percent in the 1770s.

See also **Huguenots; Richelieu, Armand-Jean Du Plessis, cardinal; Wars of Religion, French.**

BIBLIOGRAPHY

Clark, John G. *La Rochelle and the Atlantic Economy during the Eighteenth Century.* Baltimore and London, 1981.

Meyer, Judith Chandler Pugh. *Reformation in La Rochelle: Tradition and Change in Early Modern Europe, 1500–1568.* Geneva, 1986.

Parker, David. *La Rochelle and the French Monarchy: Conflict and Order in Seventeenth-Century France.* London, 1980.

Pérouas, Louis. *Le diocèse de La Rochelle de 1648 à 1724.* Paris, 1964.

Robbins, Kevin C. *City on the Ocean Sea, La Rochelle, 1530–1650: Urban Society, Religion, and Politics on the French Atlantic Frontier.* Leiden, 1997.

Trocmé, Étienne, and Marcel Delafosse. *Le commerce Rochelais de la fin du XV siècle au début du XVIIe.* Paris, 1952.

DAVID PARKER

LA TOUR, GEORGES DE. *See* **Caravaggio and Caravaggism.**

LABORERS. Overtime, output schedules, and standardized wares suggest both rapid and regular production. Steady, fast-paced toil also conjures up the factory and mechanized work—and workers. Craft shops and even many mills, with the languid splash of their waterwheels, evoke a more leisurely rhythm of labor, a human pace governed by the hand and readily disturbed by the seductions of the tavern or carnival. A vast divide supposedly separated these two worlds of work, one modern and the other traditional, one in which time is spent and the other in which time was passed (Thompson, p. 359). There is much to commend in this conventional depiction. But the intensification of labor did not await the machine, and in many trades and settings, time became money without Watt's engine.

WORKSHOP ORDER AND CONTROL

Fashioning a saddle, a wig, or a pewter cup in early modern Europe was often frustrating. When markets turned inviting, petty craftsmen and substantial manufacturers frequently faced idle workbenches and inadequate inventories. Locating ample raw materials, since many were perishable, could be maddening. Papermakers, for instance, engaged in an endless search for white rags, the material base of their reams, but knew that most bales of discarded linen would be streaked with dirt or human filth. At the other end of the process, successful producers of sheets of paper or panes of glass relied on cumbersome, risky portage. Teamsters turned into thieves, or simply abandoned fragile wares in the rain and dropped them on muddy roads. Above all, when demand surged, securing a group of skilled hands or a single man with indispensable know-how was an art in itself. And, once hired, said the masters, these workers rarely toiled with a proper sense of urgency.

Apprentices in the skilled crafts learned their trades slowly, with formal indentures generally lasting from three to seven years. Since employment was fleeting, they also learned quickly to labor slowly, which stretched hours and spread work and wages around. After completing their terms, these youths entered restless, spot labor markets, in which bosses discharged printers and stonecutters as soon as they completed a press run or a building. Ever boastful, Benjamin Franklin surely failed to endear himself to his brother workers in a London printing house by sometimes "carr[ying] up and down Stairs a large Form of Types in each hand, when others carried but one in both Hands." His "constant Attendance" and abstention from Saint Monday, usually observed by pressmen and compositors at an alehouse, "recommended [him] to the Master," but never to his fellows. When he violated yet another of his comrades' rules, the "Chapel Ghost," the guardian of their properties, exacted revenge by "mixing [his] Sorts, transposing [his] Pages, breaking [his] Matter" (Franklin, p. 99–101). In every mechanical art, skilled men sweated mightily to keep their ranks thin, familial, and initiated. Ensuring the appropriate duration of their toil was a crucial element of this mastery. Moreover, the men who enjoyed it did not depend on a foreman's watch. Legislation from fourteenth-century Verona reveals that the town bell sounded the time to leave for work, the start and conclusion of the noon meal break, the afternoon respite, and the close of the workday (Goldthwaite, p. 290). At the building site of Santo Spirito, a clock chimed every thirty minutes, thereby empowering the workers as much as their masters (King, p. 51).

In 1796, the English Parliament mandated that paperworkers should take thirty minutes to fashion each post of paper, the trade's production measure, and fabricate twenty posts per day. This clause was never enforced; papermaking went on as it always had, until the pulp ran dry. Meanwhile, French paperworkers traditionally commenced their day's work in the middle of the night, from midnight to three A.M., and labored into the early afternoon. To economize on candles and oil, the master papermakers of Thiers decided to shut their mills until just before daybreak. Incensed, the paperworkers stayed away from the shops, leaving their bosses surrounded by vatfuls of perishing pulp. The manufacturers turned to youngsters, women, and "workers foreign to the province," but the scabs

Laborers. A seventeenth-century drawing depicts workers in a printing shop. (See also the cover of Volume 3.) THE ART ARCHIVE/MUSÉE DES BEAUX ARTS DÔLE/DAGLI ORTI

decamped quickly, the masters dismissed the women, and the producers' pleas to innkeepers "to cut off credit to the rebels" failed to bring the strikers to their knees. Despite the state's edict that the journeymen's workdays were to be divided equally around noon, a local official, Mignot, intervened in vain, for the paperworkers bent "neither to threat nor to persuasion." After two months of trouble and idled vats, the Thiernois masters threw in the towel: the paperworkers continued to start their day at three A.M. (Gachet, p. 130). "This is probably not the right hour to pursue a rigorous policy" toward the journeymen paperworkers, Mignot concluded (ibid.). Yet skilled paperworkers toiled within a complex division of labor and had an active, stiff-necked association.

Of course, the distance between the skilled man and the unskilled, the *gagne-deniers,* 'penny earners', in France, was not always great and, especially in hard times, could close rapidly. Witness the twin definitions in eighteenth-century Paris of the term *tonnelier,* at once a cooper and a longshoreman unloading casks of wine (Haim Burstin, "Unskilled Labor in Paris at the End of the Eighteenth Century" in Safley and Rosenband, p. 68). That said, the hod carrier and street sweeper inevitably lacked many of the rights and powers of the skilled guild member, and doubtless possessed less mastery over the time and hours of their work. Still, it was widely recognized that the Auvergnat immigrant to the capital often became a water carrier, the Lyonnais served as a porter, the Savoyard shined shoes and swept out chimneys, and the Norman broke stones. Equally, in 1786, Parisian penny-earners dared to rise against a new company destined to monopolize the delivery of packages in the city and hence displace "established" porters (Burstin in Safley and Rosenband, p. 71). Such men did not expect to labor regularly and likely would have been thrilled with two hundred days (even partial days) of work in a year. Quotas were certainly distant from their orbit of toil, but they, too, evidently put a price on their labor and knew how to secure—and protect—these precious hours.

THE PACE OF LABOR

So the length of the average early modern European workday will continue to be hard to determine. Unstable employment, seasonal patterns of production, and complicated accounting of time at the bench mandate cautious, cross-trade comparisons. London tailors, after all, labeled their slow summers "cucumber time," when they could afford little else on which to subsist (Rule, p. 51). In printing, papermaking, and leather breech making, a "day" represented a closely negotiated amount of work rather than a fixed set of hours. Just to assess the earnings of the shipwrights in the royal dockyards of England, John Rule observed, involves the deciphering of the meaning of "treble days, double days, day-and-a-half, two for one, task, job, common hours, nights and 'tides.'" Worse yet, these words, and hence the toil they depict, often defied conventional definitions (Rule, p. 63). At the far edge of this terminological thicket, consider this vague, but eloquent, rendering of the hatter's day: "a man goes early and works late" (Rule, p. 55). In fact, when work was available, journeymen on both shoulders of the Channel routinely put in twelve- and fourteen-hour days, and sometimes labored even longer. Parisian blacksmiths endured workdays of fourteen hours in the eighteenth century, while bookbinders sweated for sixteen (Sonenscher, p. 95). Still, in 1776, the willful Josiah Wedgwood admitted, "Our men have been at play 4 days this week, it being Burslem Wakes. I have rough'd & smoothed them over, & promised them a long Xmass, but I know it is all in vain, for Wakes must be observed though the World was to end with them" (Pollard, p. 182). Wedgwood was both angered and puzzled by a problem, from the masters' perspective, that extended far beyond his pot-bank: why did the laboring poor, so often desperate for work and familiar with punishing hours of toil, respond so peculiarly to the carrots and sticks he proferred? The issue, known to economists as "leisure preference," can be reduced to a paradox, at least to modern readers responsive to the lure of high pay and other incentives: early modern Europeans tended to cut back on hours and effort when work was plentiful, wages high, and grain prices low. Long ago, Max Weber provided an explanation for this practice: the worker "did not ask: how much can I earn in a day if I do as much work as possible? but: how much must I work in order to earn the wage which I earned before and which takes care of my traditional needs?" (Rule, p. 52). Eighteenth-century observers were less charitable, instead condemning the dissolute ways of the working classes. Restif de la Bretonne explained that the "dearness of labor" actually threatened a populace that "if it can earn what it needs in three days, only works for three days and spends the other four in debauchery" (Michael Sonenscher, "Work and Wages in Paris in the Eighteenth Century," in Berg et al., p. 150). An English clothier put it bluntly: elevated rewards had rendered his hands "scarce, saucy and bad" (Rule, p. 54).

High wages, however, had yet to become the order of the day. Put another way, relatively few among the laboring poor enjoyed the chance to respond to the carrot while all too many still felt the compulsion of the stick. This circumstance suited those "low-wage thinkers" who celebrated long hours at flinty pay as the surest means to combat indolence and intemperance. But enlightened thinkers like Adam Smith had reached a different conclusion: "That a little more plenty than ordinary may render some workmen idle, cannot well be doubted; but that it should have this effect on the greater part . . . seems not very probable." Indeed, Smith added, "Where wages are high, accordingly, we shall always find the workmen more active, diligent, and expeditious" (Smith, pp. 81–83).

CONSUMER CULTURE AND THE "INDUSTRIOUS REVOLUTION"

For high pay to work its magic, however, the laboring poor had to sacrifice their leisure in favor of consumption. Even the butcher, baker, and candlestick maker, who lacked internal promptings to maximize and accumulate, took pleasure in finery or an extra dram. As the Old Regime progressed, the wants of the past—goods that journeymen and penny earners had once dreamed about—were becoming needs. In an era when appearance still remained the measure of a man (and a woman), bourgeois and nobleman alike grumbled about the pretensions of their inferiors. An anonymous memoir from Montpellier, penned in 1768, raged that "The most vile artisan behaves as the equal of the most eminent artiste or anyone who practices a trade superior to his. They are indistinguishable by their expenditures, their clothes, and their houses" (Darnton, p. 134). Shopgirls now wore silk stockings, and, to the horror of their betters, might be mistaken for persons of quality.

Perhaps the blurring of certain social lines during the twilight of the Old Regime accounted for an exaggerated concern over the ostentation and "luxury" of the laboring poor. If the plight of the casual laborer Louis Bequet, who crowded into one Parisian bed with his wife and five children in 1779, was unusual, cradles and children's beds remained rare among the common sorts. Nevertheless, cheap knockoffs of muffs, snuffboxes, umbrellas, and countless other items increasingly figured among the inheritances of eighteenth-century workers. As Daniel Roche commented, they were "learning to be consumers" (Roche, p. 127). Nothing symbolized this education more than the prevalence of mirrors in working-class quarters. Here was evidence of a newfound attention to appearance among the popular classes, and possibly a willingness to exchange leisure for adornments. This was fertile soil for the manufacture of time-discipline at the workbench, both inside the factory and outside its gates.

The penetration of this "consumer revolution" into the lower ranks of European society, however incomplete, poses a critical question: if real wages in the eighteenth century were stagnant at best, how shall we account for the widening array of wares present in the inventories of the laboring poor? Jan De Vries has worked out an ingenious solution to this conundrum, which he termed the "industrious revolution" (De Vries, p. 255). This approach rests on careful consideration of the early modern European household as a site of production and as a source of labor power, as well as a web of consumption and distribution. De Vries contends that laboring households in England, northwestern Europe, and colonial America made decisions that enhanced both the supply of commodities and muscle outside the home and the demand for goods purchased in the marketplace. Thus peasants intensified their production for the market, unemployed hands in agrarian regions were increasingly put to work at the loom and the spinning wheel, and women and children performed more waged labor.

BUREAUCRACY, EXPLOITATION, AND EFFICIENCY

While an internal impulse to consume blossomed, it is also likely that a measure of exploitation, especially of women and children, accompanied the secondhand tapestries hanging in ever more households. Wages, however, also may have granted some independence to these women. Perhaps this relatively free hand, plus a taste for what a few extra sous could buy, helped prepare them for their role in the mills and factories of the industrial revolution—a role that submitted them to wearying, regular workdays (when the machines did not break down) of twelve hours or more, six days a week.

To reduce theft and coordinate the sweat and skills of a large number of hands, substantial workshops had systems of labor discipline, including time management, well before the turn to mechanized production and steam power. Unlike lesser hand papermakers, the Montgolfiers, one of the largest producers in late-eighteenth-century France, installed a precisely bounded workday, with quotas for each of the sections of a proper day's work (Rosenband, p. 108). Consider, too, the Venetian state shipyards, better known as the Arsenal. By 1600, a battalion of administrators supervised this enterprise. They included at least a score of clerks and bookkeepers, as well as nearly one hundred technical and disciplinary figures who oversaw every facet of production. (Of course, all this should not be construed to mean that skilled and unskilled hands alike gave up their dodges, pranks, and capacity to steal rope and timber.) As a result of its organization of production and the Republic's resources, the Arsenal was renowned for its capacity to turn out considerable numbers of battle-ready warships in a matter of months or even weeks (Robert C. Davis, "Arsenal and Arsenalotti: Workplace and Community in Seventeenth-Century Venice" in Safley and Rosenband, p. 180). Yet much of the work in these yards revolved around traditional skills, with their conventional nomenclature and custom.

A very different project took shape in the English dockyards under Samuel Bentham. Appointed inspector-general of the naval works in 1795, he embraced the quantifying spirit of the Enlightenment, particularly as a tool for the creation of orderly shops. He approached the resources at his disposal with an accountant's eye and sense of efficiency. He also intended to overthrow the journeymen's rule of thumb and settle scores with these overmighty hands. So, his proud widow explained, "He therefore began by classing the several operations requisite in the shaping and working up of materials of whatever kind, wholly disregarding the customary artificial arrangement according to trade." From there, Bentham developed machines "independently of the need for skill or manual dexterity in the workman" (Linebaugh, p. 397). He reorganized and sped up the refitting of ships, introduced a new method for joining wood, and adopted the steam-powered sawmill for the handling of rough timber. This last innovation helped put an end to "chips," the right of journeymen to the shavings and flakes from recently worked wood, which frequently justified the disappearance of much larger pieces from the yards. And he installed the principle of "INCESSANT WORK," as he scripted it—twenty-four-hour shiftwork (Linebaugh, p. 399). Lastly, like the Montgolfiers, who had locked out their veteran hands (and, they hoped, their custom) and trained a bevy of newcomers in the art, Bentham attempted to drown the old ways of the dockyards in a deepened pool of workers. "It is well known," he claimed, "that an increase of the number of workpeople in any business is the most effectual bar to combinations [trade unions]" (Linebaugh, p. 400).

In the Netherlands, guild regulations around 1500 required the observance of forty-seven feast days. With the Protestant reform of religion, this number fell to six (Jan De Vries, "Between Purchasing Power and the World of Goods," in Brewer and Porter, p. 110). Later, the Montgolfiers secured lengthy workyears that doubtless earned the envy of their competitors. Many entrepreneurs, however, remained slow to press for greater time discipline, attributing Bentham's or the Montgolfiers' success to state support, advanced technology, and unusually stable markets (Pollard, p. 192). Still, the pace of manufacture quickened and became more regular at once, despite incomplete shifts and wholesale retreats. As E. P. Thompson acknowledged, "the division of labour; the supervision of labour; fines; bells and clocks; money incentives; preachings and schoolings; the suppression of fairs and sports," gradually accomplished their work (Thompson, p. 394). So did the new patterns of consumption and market behavior within the households of the laboring poor. After all, the heirs of those men and women saddled with twelve-hour workdays fought for half-Saturdays and the ten-hour day.

See also **Commerce and Markets; Consumption; Guilds; Industrial Revolution; Industry; Wages.**

BIBLIOGRAPHY

Primary Sources

Franklin, Benjamin. *The Autobiography of Benjamin Franklin.* Edited by Leonard Labaree et al. New Haven, 1964. Poor Richard in his own voice.

Smith, Adam. *An Inquiry into the Nature and Causes of the Wealth of Nations.* Edited by Edwin Cannan. New York, 1937. Endless insight, and several surprises, about production and its rewards.

Secondary Sources

Berg, Maxine, Pat Hudson, and Michael Sonenscher, eds. *Manufacture in Town and Country before the Factory.* Cambridge, U.K., 1983. A set of challenging essays about work and wages before the onset of large-scale mechanization.

Brewer, John, and Roy Porter, eds. *Consumption and the World of Goods.* London, 1993. A vast collection full of stunning detail about everyday material life, both high and low.

Darnton, Robert. *The Great Cat Massacre and Other Episodes in French Cultural History.* New York, 1984. A series of evocative depictions of eighteenth-century lives.

De Vries, Jan. "The Industrial Revolution and the Industrious Revolution." *The Journal of Economic History* 54, no. 2 (June, 1994): 249–270. A brilliant synthesis of the current debates about consumption and the coming of the industrial revolution.

Gachet, Henri. "Les grèves d'ouvriers papetiers en France au XVIIIème siècle jusqu'à la Révolution." *Eleventh International Congress of the International Association of Paper Historians.* Haarlem, 1972. Wonderful accounts of centuries of conflict in a venerable French trade.

Goldthwaite, Richard A. *The Building of Renaissance Florence: An Economic and Social History.* Baltimore, 1980. An elegant, comprehensive history, written with verve and masterly detail.

King, Ross. *Brunelleschi's Dome: How a Renaissance Genius Reinvented Architecture.* New York, 2000. A model popular account.

Linebaugh, Peter. *The London Hanged: Crime and Civil Society in the Eighteenth Century.* Cambridge, U.K., 1992. Controversial and rich in vivid detail.

Pollard, Sidney. *The Genesis of Modern Management: A Study of the Industrial Revolution in Great Britain.*

Cambridge, Mass., 1965. The classic depiction of the nature and methods of early industrial labor discipline.

Roche, Daniel. *The People of Paris: An Essay in Popular Culture in the 18th Century.* Translated by Marie Evans. Berkeley, 1987. Superb discussions of the material culture and reading habits of the common classes.

Rosenband, Leonard N. *Papermaking in Eighteenth-Century France: Management, Labor, and Revolution at the Montgolfier Mill, 1761–1805.* Baltimore, 2000. A careful account of the introduction and response to an innovative system of labor discipline.

Rule, John. *The Experience of Labour in Eighteenth Century English Industry.* New York, 1981. A brief but comprehensive account anchored firmly in rich detail.

Safley, Thomas, and Leonard Rosenband, eds. *The Workplace before the Factory: Artisans and Proletarians, 1500–1800.* Ithaca, N.Y., 1993. A collection that ranges widely across Europe and its crafts and industries.

Sonenscher, Michael. *Work and Wages: Natural Law, Politics, and the Eighteenth-Century French Trades.* Cambridge, U.K., 1989. A deeply researched discussion of guilds, work, and political economy, primarily during the twilight of the Old Regime.

Thompson, Edward P. *Customs in Common: Studies in Traditional Popular Culture.* New York, 1991. An extraordinarily rich exploration of the cultural world of the early modern English laboring poor.

LEONARD N. ROSENBAND

LACLOS, PIERRE AMBROISE CHODERLOS DE (1741–1803), French novelist. Little in the life of the military officer offers a clue that Choderlos de Laclos was destined to write one of the most controversial and influential French novels of the eighteenth century. Born in Amiens into the lower nobility, he chose an army career in the 1760s. France was at peace and barracks life was routinely dull. He wrote poetry, erotic tales, and a comic opera, *Ernestine,* which failed when it was produced (1777). In 1779, upon being upgraded to captain and sent to fortify the île d'Aix, he began to form the plan for his novel, *Les liaisons dangereuses,* composed while he was on leave in Paris, and published in 1782. It met with immediate success, and scandal. He quickly took a military assignment in La Rochelle to avoid the controversy, and there met Marie Soulange-Duperré, with whom he had a child before they were married in 1784.

His criticism of French fortifications (1786) made him equally controversial in the military, and he soon left for service as a secretary to Louis-Philippe, duke of Orléans (1725–1785). At this time he wrote several tracts on military and political topics. During the French Revolution he was protected by Georges-Jacques Danton (1759–1794)—a member of the Paris Commune and minister of justice in the new republic—imprisoned, nevertheless, during the Reign of Terror, liberated, and eventually made a brigadier general (1800) by Napoleon Bonaparte (1769–1821). Named to a post in Naples, he died in Italy of dysentery in 1803.

Laclos's reputation rests on his single novel, *Les liaisons dangereuses.* The plot involves interconnecting attempts at seduction and betrayal within a closed, elite segment of society. The vicomte de Valmont is encouraged by his former mistress, the marquise de Merteuil, to seduce the naive and innocent Cécile Volanges, engaged to a young man, Danceny, upon whom Mme de Merteuil seeks revenge. At first Valmont refuses, preferring, instead, to court the virtuous wife of the President de Tourvel. She appears to be slowly yielding, as the two libertines (Valmont, Merteuil) bitterly ridicule each other. Mme de Merteuil sends Valmont a lengthy lesson in seduction (letter 81) and pretends to be seduced by Prevan. Meanwhile, Valmont, learning that Cécile's mother warned the president's wife of his designs on her, decides to accept Mme de Merteuil's challenge and becomes Cécile's lover. The president's wife, still in love with Valmont, finally yields to him. Mme de Merteuil demands that Valmont sacrifice his love for the president's wife if he hopes to win her back, and the vicomte complies. Rather than finding love, however, the two libertines are at war with each other, and divulge each other's letters. A young man in love with Cécile is furious and kills Valmont in a duel, Cécile enters a convent, and Mme de Merteuil, disgraced and disfigured by smallpox, flees society, which she had called "that great theater."

The epistolary novel is structured as a series of personal letters exchanged between the main characters. The lack of a narrator, and the conflicting, competing perspectives presented by the different letter writers creates an open, ambiguous moral tone that shocked many contemporary readers. The work can be seen as promoting seduction through

Choderlos de Laclos. Pastel portrait by Louis Leopold Boilly. THE ART ARCHIVE/MUSÉE DU CHÂTEAU DE VERSAILLES/DAGLI ORTI

Valmont's and Merteuil's presentation of detailed tactics and a rhetoric of temptation, or as condemning this debauchery by the libertines' eventual failure and defeat. The amorality of the seducers, and their victims, is portrayed directly, with a neutrality that made the novel itself appear amoral, if not, indeed, immoral.

The exclusive use of the characters' letters also indicates effectively the hypocrisy of polite society, because they often reveal great differences between public and private conduct. On the one hand is illusion, on the other the reality of Valmont and Merteuil, whom Charles Baudelaire (1821–1867) labeled "a Satanic Eve." All the characters maintain a virtuous façade, although the tempters reveal their real intentions and devious machinations to each other. The more innocent women reveal by their letters their slow descent as they yield to Valmont. We learn that he seeks not only to corrupt them but to ruin their reputation, as he plans to use their love letters as proof. When Valmont and Merteuil reveal each other's letters near the novel's end, however, these missives serve as proof of their duplicity and corruption, ruining them and leading to their demise.

Laclos considered himself a follower of Jean-Jacques Rousseau (1712–1778), and we see this not only in the epistolary form of the novel, as in the philosopher's *Julie, ou la nouvelle Héloïse* (1761; Julie, or the new Eloise), but also in its content. Rousseau saw society and writing as corrupting influences, opposed to a natural state of purity and oral language. In Laclos's novel, moral degradation and letter writing are inextricably linked. Modern film versions of the novel have considerably extended the work's popularity and influence.

See also **French Literature and Language; Romanticism; Rousseau, Jean-Jacques.**

BIBLIOGRAPHY

Brooks, Peter. *The Novel of Worldliness: Crébillon, Marivaux, Laclos, Stendhal.* Princeton, 1969.

Conroy, Peter V. *Intimate, Intrusive, and Triumphant: Readers in the* Liaisons dangereuses. Amsterdam, 1987.

Diaconoff, Suellen. *Eros and Power in* Les liaisons dangereuses: *A Study in Evil.* Geneva, 1979.

Rosbottom, Ronald C. *Choderlos de Laclos.* Boston, 1978.

Roulston, Christine. *Virtue, Gender, and the Authentic Self in Eighteenth-Century Fiction: Richardson, Rousseau, and Laclos.* Gainesville, Fla., 1998.

Thelander, Dorothy. *Laclos and the Epistolary Novel.* Geneva, 1963.

Winnett, Susan. *Terrible Sociability: The Text of Manners in Laclos, Goethe, and James.* Stanford, 1993.

ALLEN G. WOOD

LAGRANGE, JOSEPH-LOUIS

LAGRANGE, JOSEPH-LOUIS (1736–1813), French mathematician. Lagrange, a leading mathematician of the Enlightenment, contributed to a wide range of fields and played a leading role in the establishment of the metric system. Born in Turin to a French family of high officials in the service of the dukes of Savoy, Lagrange was destined for a career in the law. While in his teens he was introduced to the study of advanced mathematics when he read a treatise on calculus by the English astronomer royal Edmond Halley (1656–1742). Lagrange's remarkable mathematical abilities were quickly recognized, and in 1755, at the age of nineteen, he was appointed professor of mathematics at the artillery school of Turin. He spent the next eleven years in his native city and established his reputation as one of the leading mathematicians in Europe. In 1766 Lagrange left Turin to become the director of the mathematics section at the Berlin Academy, taking over from Leonhard Euler (1707–1783), who had recently returned to St. Petersburg. In 1787, following the death of his patron Frederick II of Prussia (ruled 1740–1786), Lagrange moved to Paris as "veteran" member of the Paris Academy of Sciences. He remained there until his death, and during the tumultuous years that followed, he managed to stay apart from the political fray that absorbed many of his colleagues.

By the age of twenty Lagrange had already made one of his most important contributions to mathematics, the calculus of variations, which he developed along with Euler. Unlike the ordinary calculus, which analyzes the point characteristics of specific functions, the calculus of variations deals with the extremum characteristics of functions as a whole. The work quickly attracted the attention of Pierre-Louis Moreau de Maupertuis (1698–1759), president of the Berlin Academy, who used it to support his "principle of least action" against numerous critics.

Lagrange successfully applied his calculus of variations to many scientific fields. In 1759 he sided with Euler against Jean Le Rond d'Alembert (1717–1783) in the controversy on the proper mathematical representation of vibrating strings. In the late 1760s and the early 1770s Lagrange took part in several prize competitions sponsored by the Paris Academy on questions in celestial mechanics. He won the grand prize several times with essays on the orbit and rotation of the Moon, the trajectories of comets, the orbital perturbations of the moons of Jupiter, and the three body problem in general. After publishing on these and other topics in solid and fluid mechanics throughout his career, he summarized his work in *Mécanique analytique* in 1788. There he proposed to establish mechanics as a series of general formulas whose development would yield the necessary equations for the solution of each specific problem. Lagrange also contributed substantially to debates on the foundations of calculus, promoting a purely algebraic understanding of the subject as against the geometric views of colleagues such as d'Alembert.

In 1790 the French Constituent Assembly established the Committee on Weights and Measures and made Lagrange its chairman. In this position Lagrange was largely responsible for the adoption and diffusion of the decimal metric system. During the 1790s he taught at the newly established École Polytechnique, and in his later years he worked on revising and republishing his works. During the empire he came under the patronage of Napoléon I, who made Lagrange a count of the empire, a senator, and a grand officer of the Legion of Honor. On his death in 1813 Lagrange was entombed in the Pantheon.

See also **Alembert, Jean Le Rond d'; Astronomy; Enlightenment; Euler, Leonhard; Mathematics; Weights and Measures.**

BIBLIOGRAPHY

Primary Source

Lagrange, Joseph-Louis. *Analytical Mechanics.* Translated and edited by Auguste Boissonnade and Victor N. Vagliente. Dordrecht, Boston, and London, 1997. Translation of *Mécanique analytique,* nouvelle édition (1811).

Secondary Source

Itard, Jean. "Lagrange, Joseph-Louis." In *Dictionary of Scientific Biography,* edited by Charles Coulston Gillispie. 16 vols. New York, 1970–1980.

AMIR ALEXANDER

LANDHOLDING. Land was not only the source of most wealth in early modern Europe, but also a fount of political power, social status, and broad legal rights. The concentration of land in the hands of the aristocracy, the gentry, and the church (who constituted roughly 5 percent of the population but collectively owned between 50 and 70 percent of the land in many regions), was the dominant social feature of the age. Landownership of seigneuries or manors (privileged properties) conferred an array of financial and judicial powers over tenants at the local level and was indispensable to maintaining a gentle or noble lifestyle. The enduring symbolic and political functions of landholding were in turn rooted in the central economic role played by land. Agricultural commodities not only formed the mainstay of the European economy until the end of the eighteenth century, but also directly produced most of the raw materials used in manufactured goods. Within these broad outlines, however, there were significant changes in landholding patterns between 1450 and 1789. The decline of serfdom in western Europe by 1450, the rise of a new village elite of well-off peasant leaseholders by 1550, and new opportunities for investment outside of land during the eighteenth century gradually altered social relationships based on landholding.

PATTERNS OF LANDHOLDING

While the nobility seldom constituted more than 2 percent of the population in western Europe, it owned approximately 40 to 50 percent of the land in many regions. Most noble land was in fact concentrated in the hands of a small minority of that class. In Brittany, approximately 200 of the 2,000 noble families controlled 40 percent of the land. In England, the aristocracy was a tiny but immensely wealthy elite. By the late eighteenth century it comprised about 150 families, who owned 20 percent of the land. But the gentry were collectively the largest landowners in England. Gentry landownership expanded from 25 percent to roughly 50 percent of arable land between 1500 and 1700, at the expense of both church and crown. Landownership was essential for supporting the four main expenses of the gentry and the nobility: buying crown offices, marrying off children, prosecuting lawsuits, and enjoying (as well as displaying) a gentle lifestyle.

From the early sixteenth through the eighteenth centuries, the percentage of land in church hands declined in Europe as a whole. The Protestant Reformation led to the seizure and sale of many formerly Catholic properties in the Holy Roman Empire, Scandinavia, the Baltics, and the Low Countries. In England, the church had owned significantly more land than the crown in 1450, controlling between a fourth and a third of the arable. By the end of the English Reformation, only about 4 percent of the land was left in church hands; almost all properties had gone to private buyers in the gentry or merchant classes.

Despite the predominance of landless or leaseholding peasants in western Europe, there were important pockets of peasant freeholders. In Holland, cultivators enjoyed full ownership rights over extensive lands they had reclaimed from peat bogs, as did some peasants in the central Rhineland. In France, approximately one-third to two-fifths of rural land was in the hands of the peasantry before the French Revolution. But that figure includes land occupied by peasant houses and their garden closes; recent scholarship indicates that their ownership of the arable or open fields was often no more than 10 percent.

RIGHTS ATTACHED TO LANDOWNERSHIP

Landownership conferred a constellation of legal, political, and financial rights on landlords. Kaleidoscopic in their variety, these rights tended to fall into several broad categories. On seigneuries, or manors, they included the right to collect rents, crop shares, and reliefs, or entry fees (on a tenant inheriting or taking possession of a new piece of land); *corvées,* or labor obligations (requiring tenants to farm the lord's domain and repair bridges and roads); and *banalités,* or monopoly fees (for using the lord's grain mill, ovens, or winepress). Noble land held of the crown usually required homage, wardship, and relief to the crown. Across western Europe, however, these obligations generally became less onerous in both monetary and symbolic terms from the sixteenth through the eighteenth centuries. Ground rent, and in some regions, crop shares, became the central relationship between landlords and tenants.

The most politically symbolic group of rights were those of justice. Most seigneuries carried rights of low or middling justice, which allowed the landlord to adjudicate rent disputes and minor delicts. The most powerful seigneuries carried the right of high justice, which allowed them to hear cases meriting the death penalty. In some regions manorial or seigneurial justice faded in importance during the seventeenth and eighteenth centuries, especially in northwestern Germany and in England, where jurisdiction was absorbed by local justices of the peace or by the state. In other regions, like Normandy, landowners' high justices remained an important complement to the state's judicial system.

PROPERTY LAW AND PROPERTY RIGHTS

Landownership was almost always subject to the rights and usages of multiple parties in early modern Europe. Most villages included common lands that provided timber, reeds, or grazing grounds for the rural community and that were essential to the survival of the poorest inhabitants. Disputes over ownership of the village common lands and wastelands, as well as over usage rights like hunting, fishing, pasturing, and gleaning, were a source of endless litigation and frequent popular protest. In England, twin enclosure movements in the sixteenth and eighteenth centuries dramatically changed multiple property rights. Two-thirds of English arable land had been enclosed by the beginning of the eighteenth century, and most of the remainder was enclosed between 1750 and 1790. The loss of the common lands sent thousands of destitute rural laborers into London and other cities for work.

The transition from multiple-use rights to private property rights in land was gradual at best. The British Parliament passed hundreds of private bills granting clear-cut property rights to landholders in the eighteenth century. In France and Spain, however, the crown was powerless to alter provincial property laws or to enforce enclosures of common lands. Early modern legal codes prevented landowners from freely disposing of their properties in other ways, too. Customary, royal, and Roman laws on land inheritance were all carefully designed to prevent the fragmentation of estates (and of political authority) among the landed classes throughout Europe. The law of entail in England (fee entail), like the customs of France *(preciput)*, ensured that noble and gentry properties could not be willed away from the legal heir. Ultimately, laws guarding the integrity of land ensured the landowning classes' continuing political and social dominance through the eighteenth century.

See also **Agriculture; Aristocracy and Gentry; Class, Status, and Order; Enclosure; Feudalism; Law; Peasantry; Property; Serfdom; Villages.**

BIBLIOGRAPHY

Collins, James B. *Classes, Estates, and Order in Early Modern Brittany.* New York and Cambridge, U.K., 1994.

Price, J. L. *Dutch Society, 1588–1713.* New York, 2000.

Rosenthal, Jean-Laurent. *The Fruits of Revolution: Property Rights, Litigation, and French Agriculture, 1700–1860.* New York and Cambridge, U.K., 1992.

Sharpe, J. A. *Early Modern England: A Social History, 1550–1760.* London and New York, 1997.

Zoë A. Schneider

LAS CASAS, BARTOLOMÉ DE (1474–1566), Spanish historian and missionary. Bartolomé de Las Casas was a missionary, Dominican theologian, historian, and bishop of Chiapas. In 1493 he saw Christopher Columbus pass through Seville on his return from the first voyage across the Atlantic. That year Las Casas's father, Pedro de Las Casas, and his uncles sailed with Columbus on his second voyage. Las Casas first traveled to the Western Hemisphere in 1502 to manage the land Columbus gave his father. Like other colonists, Las Casas at first gave no thought to the *encomienda* system of royal land grants that included Indians to work the fields in exchange for educating them in Christianity.

Returning to Europe in 1507, Las Casas was ordained a priest in Rome. He returned to the West Indies and in 1513–1514 served as chaplain to the invaders during the conquest of Cuba. After that campaign he was awarded additional land. Upon listening to a sermon by a Dominican father denouncing the treatment of Indians, Las Casas relinquished his holdings to the governor.

Las Casas returned to Spain to plead the Indians' cause before King Ferdinand II (ruled 1479–1516). With the support of the archbishop of Toledo, Las Casas was named priest-procurator of the Indies in 1516. He returned to the Western Hemisphere as a member of a commission of investigation. During 1520 he developed an alternative to the *encomienda* system in Venezuela with a colony of farm communities. After the failure of this idealistic scheme to get Spanish farmers to work alongside free natives, Las Casas joined the Dominican order in Santo Domingo during 1522.

Over the following decades Las Casas ceaselessly promulgated an ideological position that Indians had the right to their land and that papal grants to Spain were for the conversion of souls, not the appropriation of resources. Developing into a politically astute lobbyist, he was often able to effect positive change, such as insuring a peaceful entry into Guatemala by Dominican friars. During 1544 he was named bishop of Chiapas in Guatemala to enforce the "New Laws" of Emperor Charles V (ruled 1519–1556), which prohibited slavery and limited ownership of Indians to a single generation. The settlers objected to any limits, and many clergy would not follow the new bishop's lead. After the king rescinded the prohibition on inheritance, Las Casas resigned his office in 1547 and returned to Spain.

This tireless "Defender of the Indians" crossed the Atlantic ten times in all. After he published his *Brief Relation of the Destruction of the Indies* in Seville during 1552, a flood of hectoring books followed. In 1550 he came into conflict with Juan Ginés de Sepúlveda (1490?–1572 or 1573), a scholar who was attempting to gain the right to publish a book approving war against the Indians. Las Casas appeared at a debate before the Council of Valladolid, where he spoke for five days straight. He influenced the committee not to approve his opponent's book for publication.

Las Casas's massive *History of the Indies*, finished in manuscript during 1562 but unpublished until 1875, incorporates an invaluable abstract of Columbus's now lost first logbook. The book demonstrates a prophetic intent to reveal to Spain that the injustices of its colonial rule would lead to a terrible punishment at God's hand. His example influenced both Simon Bolívar (1783–1830) during the nineteenth-century revolt against colonial rule and Mexicans during their struggles for independence.

Spanish patriots condemned Las Casas for helping create with his tireless propaganda a "Black Legend" that Spaniards were exceptionally cruel. The English published a translation of the *Brief Relation* when they were about to seize Jamaica. Another edition was issued by the U.S. government during the Spanish-American War to justify taking Spain's island possessions.

Las Casas has been applauded by proponents of human rights. In all his actions and writings he operated, however, from an unexamined theoretical foundation that maintains that Catholic Christianity is God's chosen creed for all people, and thus the argument with his opponents was primarily over the means to that conversion. In this sense the Indians were treated by him as wards who were allowed no doctrinal choice. Enemies in his time and some later scholars have argued that Las Casas shaped the truth as he wished it to be, exaggerating statistics about the loss of life and sometimes writing about places he had never been. Some recent estimates of the population of the mainland and islands argue that

Bartolomé de Las Casas. LIBRARY OF CONGRESS

the loss of life was originally higher than even Las Casas believed, and so the decline was much steeper than he estimated. It has also been shown that some of his remarks about areas outside the scope of his observation were drawn from official reports. He and his writings continue to be controversial, but he remains a key figure in historical scholarship about human rights.

See also **Colonialism; Rights, Natural; Sepúlveda, Juan Ginés de; Spanish Colonies: The Caribbean; Toleration.**

BIBLIOGRAPHY

Primary Sources

Las Casas, Bartolomé de. *History of the Indies.* Edited and translated by George Sanderlin. Maryknoll, N.Y., 1971.

———. *In Defense of the Indians: The Defense of the Most Reverend Lord, Don Fray Bartolomé de Las Casas, of the Order of Preachers, Late Bishop of Chiapa against the Persecutors and Slanderers of the Peoples of the New World Discovered across the Seas.* Translated and edited by Stafford Poole. Dekalb, Ill., 1992.

———. *A Short Account of the Destruction of the West Indies.* Edited by Nigel Griffin. New York and London, 1992.

Secondary Sources

Friede, Juan, and Benjamin Keen, eds. *Bartolomé de Las Casas in History: Toward an Understanding of the Man and His Work.* Dekalb, Ill., 1971.

Hanke, Lewis. *Aristotle and the American Indians.* London, 1959.

Wagner, Henry Raup. *The Life and Writings of Bartolomé de Las Casas.* Albuquerque, N.M., 1967.

MARVIN LUNENFELD

LASSO, ORLANDO DI (c. 1532–1594), Franco-Flemish composer. Born in Mons, in what is now southern Belgium, Lasso spent much of his youth in Italy. From about 1544 until 1549, he was in the service of Ferrante Gonzaga (1507–1557), generalissimo of Holy Roman Emperor Charles V in Italy, France, and Flanders, and traveled with him to Mantua, Palermo, and Milan, after which he worked in Naples and then Rome, where he was choirmaster at San Giovanni in Laterano in 1553–1554. According to his first biographer, Samuel Quickelberg, Lasso returned to the Low Countries in 1554 to see his ailing parents, but they had died before he reached Mons. He may have traveled to England and France with Giulio Cesare Brancaccio, a Neapolitan nobleman. By late 1554 he was in Antwerp, where he oversaw the publication in 1555 of his first music book, his so-called Opus 1, an anthology of madrigals, *villanescas,* chansons, and motets; and that same year, Lasso's first book of five-voice madrigals was printed in Venice. Lasso had found support in Antwerp from the wealthy Genoese merchant community for publishing his Opus 1, and from the powerful ecclesiastic Antoine Perrenot de Granvelle for his next publication, a book of his five- and six-voice motets, issued in 1556. Thus began a long series of active collaborations between the composer and his various publishers, in which Lasso exercised strong entrepreneurial control over the dissemination of his music.

In 1556, he was invited, on the recommendation of Granvelle and of Augsburg banker Johann Jakob Fugger, to serve in Munich at the court of Albert V, duke of Bavaria, first as a singer and by 1563 as choirmaster. Lasso remained at the Munich court until his death in 1594. In 1558 he married the daughter of a Bavarian court official; their offspring included two sons, Ferdinand and Rudolph, who became musicians. Lasso's duties at court included recruiting singers, training the choirboys, overseeing the duke's daily entertainment, and composing music for religious services and special occasions. Under Lasso's leadership, the chapel grew in size, the duke spending extravagantly on his musicians. The most celebrated event during Lasso's tenure was the 1568 marriage, after difficult negotiations, of Albert's son William V to Renée of Lorraine. Lasso wrote music and supervised performances for the festivities, and he himself played a role in a commedia dell'arte production, according to a description by chronicler Massimo Troiano. Correspondence between Lasso and his patron reveals the composer to be learned and witty, and on friendly terms with the duke. Lasso chose to stay on at the court after the death of Albert, despite a much reduced musical chapel; Albert had made provisions that Lasso would continue to receive his salary for the rest of his life. Two miniatures by court painter Hans Mielich (c. 1516–1573), included in a Munich Staatsbibliothek manuscript, provide valuable performance scenes of Lasso with his musicians.

Lasso was perhaps the most prolific and versatile composer of his era. His output of sacred music includes about sixty Masses—most modeled on motets, chansons, or madrigals—hymns, canticles (including more than one hundred Magnificats), Passions, Lamentations, and other polyphony for the Divine Offices, and more than five hundred motets that span religious works, humorous and ceremonial compositions, didactic pieces, and settings of classical or humanistic texts. Notable is his collection *Prophetiae Sibyllarum,* featuring highly chromatic settings of Latin humanistic texts preserved in a manuscript from about 1560 but published posthumously (1600), and *Dulces Exuviae* (1570), a setting of Dido's lament from Virgil. The large amount of polyphonic music written for the Divine Offices suggests that these were celebrated with great solemnity at the Munich court.

His secular works include approximately 175 Italian madrigals and lighter *villanescas,* some 150 French chansons, and about 90 German lieder. He set Italian texts by Petrarch (1304–1374), Ludovico Ariosto (1474–1533), and Jacopo Sannazaro (1456/58–1530), among others, and French poems by Clement Marot, Pierre de Ronsard (1524–1585), Joachim du Bellay (c. 1522–1560),

Orlando di Lasso. Nineteenth-century engraving. ©BETTMANN/CORBIS

and Jean-Antoine de Baïf (1532–1589). These pieces are highly varied in style, spanning most of his productive career.

Lasso's music was the most widely disseminated of any composer, his works having been reprinted frequently during and after his lifetime. He was honored just after his death with the monumental motet collection *Magnum Opus Musicum* (1604), assembled by his two sons. Lasso is noted for his close attention to expressing the meaning of words through chordal declamation, sometimes alternating with contrapuntal writing, clear harmonic progressions, and finely crafted thematic material. His influence was far-reaching: his works provided the basis for innumerable parodies, especially of his well-known spiritual chanson *Susanne un jour.* Lasso's rich use of text painting in sacred music served as a precedent for German Protestant composers during the early seventeenth century, and helped establish Germany as a mainstream compositional center. Venetian composers Andrea Gabrieli (c. 1532/33–1585) and Giovanni Gabrieli (c. 1554/57–1612) both studied in Munich under Lasso, where they assimilated his style of polychoral writing.

See also **Bavaria; Charles V (Holy Roman Empire); Gabrieli, Andrea and Giovanni; Music.**

BIBLIOGRAPHY

Bossuyt, Ignace, Eugeen Schreurs, and Annelies Wouters, eds. *Orlando Lassus and His Time: Colloquium Proceedings, Antwerpen, 1994.* Yearbook of the Alamire Foundation. Peer, Belgium, 1995.

Forney, Kristine. "Orlando di Lasso's 'Opus 1': The Making and Marketing of a Renaissance Music Book." *Revue belge de musicologie* 39–40 (1985–1986):33–60.

Haar, James. "Munich at the Time of Orlande di Lassus." In *The Renaissance, from the 1470s to the End of the 16th Century,* edited by Iain Fenlon, pp. 143–162. Man & Music Series. London, 1989.

——. "Orlande de Lassus." In *The New Grove Dictionary of Music and Musicians.* 2nd. ed., edited by Stanley Sadie. Vol. 14, pp. 295–322. London, 2001.

——. "Orlando di Lasso, Composer and Entrepreneur." In *Music and the Cultures of Print,* edited by Kate van Orden, pp. 125–162. Critical and Cultural Musicology Series, vol. 1. New York, 2000.

KRISTINE K. FORNEY

LATE MIDDLE AGES. The fourteenth and fifteenth centuries were difficult ones in European history. The demographic growth and prosperity that had characterized the High Middle Ages gave way to plague, famine, social upheaval, and rampant warfare. The crises altered the structure of European society.

PLAGUE AND FAMINE

The signal event of the era was the Black Death, which struck Europe in 1347/1348, and returned periodically for much of the next hundred years. The contagion is believed to have originated in central Asia. It moved westward along the silk route and was pushed to the Black Sea by Mongol horsemen. Genoese traders encountered the disease at their colony of Caffa in the Crimea and transported it to western Europe, to the city of Messina in Sicily, in November 1347. It subsequently appeared in Pisa and Genoa, and then spread throughout the peninsula and the rest of Europe, traveling as far north as Iceland and moving back east through Islamic lands. It did not subside until the end of the fifteenth century.

There are few precise figures for the number of deaths. Contemporary chroniclers gave graphic descriptions of heaps of dead bodies piled in public areas but often exaggerated the losses. The standard agreement is that from one-third to one-half of Europe died of the plague and its recurrences. But the disease did not strike all towns and regions the same way. The city of Florence may have lost as much as three-quarters of its population. Milan, by contrast, probably lost no more than 10 to 15 percent. Bohemia also likely lost only 10 percent of its population.

The plague struck Europe at a time when it was already suffering the effects of a series of bad harvests. During the last decades of the thirteenth century, agricultural production in numerous areas had declined significantly. The boundaries of productive land reached their limits, and peasants worked marginal plots with diminished returns. Records from the estates of Winchester, an important grain-producing area in southern England, show that there were declines in yields of wheat, barley, and rye after 1250. Wheat yields were also down in German lands and in northern France. Evidence exists that the European climate changed on the eve of the fourteenth century. Winters and summers became colder and wetter. A series of crop failures occurred at the beginning of the century, followed by a widespread famine from 1315 through 1317. The effects of this famine were felt particularly in urban areas, which relied on outside imports of food. The commercial town of Bruges lost 5 percent of its population in six months; the cloth-producing town of Ypres lost 17 to 20 percent of its population. The mortality elsewhere in Europe may have reached as high as 10 to 25 percent, though such figures are disputed. Some scholars, chief among them the English economic historian M. M. Postan and his French counterpart Emmanuel Le Roy Ladurie, have cited the decreased yields and famines as evidence that Europe experienced a "subsistence" or "Malthusian" crisis, which preceded the plague and indeed paved the way for it. The interpretation remains at the core of a lively debate.

The dramatic loss of population affected the European economy. In general, the price of labor rose, while land values declined. The former helped the peasant class, which could now demand salaries for its labor; the latter hurt the nobility, whose wealth was derived from the profits of its estates. Authorities moved to forestall the changes—which threatened the traditional structure of society—by instituting wage and price controls. King Edward III in England's famous Statute of Laborers of 1351 ordered prices and wages frozen at pre-plague levels, forbade the movement of peasants from farms, and, to augment the labor force, required beggars to find work. Governments in France, Aragon, Castile, and elsewhere issued similar legislation. Economic historians tell of a "scissors effect," particularly after 1375, in which the price of wheat fell with respect to manufactured goods. In addition, the overall volume of trade declined. Exports of wine from Bordeaux declined from 100,000 tons in the first decade of the fourteenth century to 13,000 to 14,000 tons at the end of the century. The port of Genoa, one of the most active throughout the Middle Ages, experienced dramatic declines across the board.

The European economy was also affected by two important, though less-studied, factors: a shortage of bullion and the disruption of trade routes to Asia resulting from the advance of the Ottoman Turks. By the last decades of the fourteenth century the rich silver mines of central Europe and Tyrol, the source of much of the coin that sustained the earlier economic expansion, had become exhausted. They revived only toward the end of the century, with the help of new technology, and soon became augmented by the flow of specie from the New World. The Ottomans supplanted the Mongols, the traditional middleman between Europe and the East. Despite a reputation for ferocity in war, the Mongols had long been friendly to Christian traders. The Ottomans were less so. The Turkish presence expanded steadily, and in 1453 they took the great port city of Constantinople.

Scholars have long debated the broader meaning of the demographic crises and shifts in trade. Did they bring economic "depression" or did they result in a "new equilibrium," in which the standard of living, particularly among the wage-earning classes, improved? The disagreement has been particularly heated for Italy, the most commercially sophisticated part of Europe. Evidence exists on both sides. The city of Florence, for example, compensated for a decline in the overall production of wool cloth, its principal manufacture, by moving more forcefully into higher-priced silks and luxury cloth. Florence's banking industry, the international leader, all but collapsed just prior to the plague, but restructured itself, and emerged more resilient. Florentine bankers introduced the idea of limited liability, thus protecting themselves from losing more than what they invested in their businesses, and sought new markets. They remained closely attached to the papacy, a continuous source of money even in the worst of times. On the other hand, the evidence for the city of Genoa suggests that the decline in the volume of goods passing through its ports exceeded the decline in population and was not compensated for by other business ventures.

WARFARE

Demographic crisis and economic change occurred against a backdrop of warfare. In Italy, where fighting among numerous autonomous states in close geographic proximity was already commonplace, the recourse to violence increased markedly. The city of Milan embarked on a series of aggressive campaigns that involved virtually all of the peninsula. This and other wars continued through the middle of the fifteenth century. In 1454, Italian states signed the Treaty of Lodi, bringing a temporary cessation of hostilities. But the truce was tenuous and at times ignored. The French under Charles VIII initiated a new round of warfare when they invaded Italy in 1494.

The most famous war of the era was the Hundred Years' War, which was fought between England and France in episodic fashion from 1337 until 1453. Much of the fighting took the form of destructive marches known as *chavauchées,* in which English armies rode through the French countryside burning houses and fields, inflicting heavy economic damage. The English scored impressive battlefield victories at Crécy (1346), Poitiers (1356), and Agincourt (1415). The victories resulted in large part from superior English tactics, which included taking the defensive posture, descending from horses to fight on foot, and use of the longbow. The longbow could be fired more quickly than the traditional crossbow, yet still had impressive striking power. English archers sent thick volleys of arrows, which blunted French cavalry charges. The French clung to old methods, which corresponded to established chivalric codes of behavior, and were thus slow to respond to the English challenge. Their fortunes turned with the advent of Joan of Arc (c. 1412–1431), a young peasant girl who rallied local armies. By 1453, the French had expelled the English from all but Calais.

The Hundred Years' War was followed in short order by the Wars of the Roses in England (1455–1485) and the Burgundian wars in France (1470–1493). Both were essentially dynastic struggles arising from disputes within the ruling elite. In the Holy Roman Empire a series of bitter wars broke out between the emperor and religious dissenters, the Hussites. In Spain, attempts to retake land from the Muslims, the Reconquista, were ongoing; the kingdom of Aragon was involved in the Italian Wars through connections in southern Italy. Popes spearheaded crusades against the Muslim Ottomans. The crusade to Nicopolis in 1396 ended in a humiliating defeat for the Christians.

Some scholars have directly linked the increase in warfare and violence to the crises of plague and famine. In a study of eastern Normandy, Guy Bois argues that declines in feudal rents led lords to search for additional sources of revenue. They hired themselves out as soldiers and exerted pressure on their overlords to wage wars. The wars themselves helped accentuate the effects of the other crises. Armies burned crops, which exacerbated famine, and they moved from region to region, thus spreading plague. The need to keep armies in the field for prolonged periods of time hastened the end of the old feudal system of mutual obligation and accelerated the recourse to wages. English scholars speak of a "bastard feudalism" arising from the Hundred Years' War.

SOCIAL AND POLITICAL UPHEAVAL

Europe experienced at this time numerous revolts by the lower classes. The uprisings were stimulated not by abject misery, but by a general improvement in the lot of the poor, which inclined them to seek still more from the upper classes. One of the earliest rebellions occurred in the commercially advanced region of Flanders. Artisans and peasants refused to pay taxes. The revolt, aimed at the gentry class, was soon joined by weavers in Bruges and in Ypres. The weavers briefly took control in Bruges, but the insurrection was ultimately put down by a French royal army in 1328.

A revolt known as the Jacquerie broke out in Paris in 1358. Peasants, known derisively as "Jacques," a generic name for commoners, rose up against their lords, who had been unable to protect them from the ravages of roaming bands of soldiers during the Hundred Years' War. The bands had burnt local villages and exacerbated the already profound fiscal burdens brought on the peasantry by the war. In 1356 King John II (d. 1364) had been captured by the English in battle and the nobility, obliged to ransom him, attempted to shift some of the responsibility onto the peasantry. The peasants went on a rampage and, as in Flanders, were joined by artisans. But as in Flanders, the nobles ultimately crushed the rebellion.

Perhaps the most spectacular revolt occurred in England in 1381. It too grew out of tensions over taxation. The English government imposed a series of unpopular flat or "poll" taxes to help pay for the war. These fell disproportionately on the lower classes, and with the enactment of the poll tax of 1381, artisans and peasants rose up, stormed London and outlying villages, killed the archbishop of Canterbury, and nearly toppled the young King Richard II (ruled 1377–1399). The rebels expressed egalitarian ideas, some of the most radical of the period. Their famous slogan ran thus: "When Adam delved and Eve span, who then was the gentleman?" They demanded the abolition of serfdom, the commutation of services for rents, and the elimination of the poll tax. Like their predecessors, however, they were eventually crushed by the nobility.

The most successful uprising of the period happened in Florence in 1378. Members of the lower rung of the wool cloth business, the so-called *ciompi,* rose up against the town government. They called on authorities to set minimum production levels in the cloth industry, thus ensuring their employment. They also sought representation in government, the right to form their own guild, and the elimination of monetary speculation by the wealthy classes. The uprising succeeded, and the *ciompi* dominated Florentine government for three years until it was swept aside by what some scholars have called a "patrician regime."

CHURCH CRISES

The church experienced some of the most profound crises of the era. The great institutional battle between kings and popes, with deep roots into the Middle Ages, took a dramatic turn at the beginning of the fourteenth century. The French King Philip IV (ruled 1285–1314) vied with Pope Boniface VIII (reigned 1294–1303) over the issue of taxation of the clergy. Philip sought money from the clergy to wage his wars; Boniface objected and issued the famous bull *Unam Sanctam,* stating in bald terms the primacy of papal authority over that of kings. Philip responded by repudiating the pope and sending men to intimidate the elderly pontiff. The exchange represented a low point in papal prestige. Boniface died shortly thereafter and Pope Clement V moved the papacy in 1309 to Avignon in France, initiating the so-called Babylonian Captivity. The papacy remained in Avignon for nearly seventy years. Pope Gregory XI returned to Rome in 1377, but died the next year. Under pressure from a Roman mob, the conclave chose an Italian, Urban VI. Alarmed French clerics, claiming they had been coerced, repudiated the choice and elected a Frenchman, who took the name Clement VII. There were now two popes. The English, at war with France, supported the Italian pope; the Scots, at odds with the English, supported the French claimant. A conciliar movement, rooted in the work of the Italian doctor and theorist Marsilius of Padua (c. 1280–c. 1343), sought to end the dispute by means of a church council. One such assembly met at Pisa in 1409. But the two popes refused to cede authority and for a brief time there were three popes. The schism was ended at the Council of Constance (1414–1418).

If the split in the papacy increased the cynicism of European Christians, so too did the plague, famines, and other disasters of the era. Some contemporary writers spoke of the coming of the four horsemen of the apocalypse. Giovanni Boccaccio (1313–1375) in the introduction to his *Decameron* described how some citizens in Florence let go all restraint, ate too much, drank too much, and lived for the day. Others responded in precisely the opposite way, seeking refuge in their faith. The great Dutch historian Johan Huizinga speaks of a "somber melancholy" that descended upon European society. Clerics were often the first line of defense against the plague, comforting those who fell sick and burying those who died. Consequently they themselves died in large numbers, leaving a crisis in leadership and a dearth of qualified men.

Popular religious movements flourished. Flagellants appeared in German and Spanish lands. Men and women formed long processionals, publicly whipping themselves in an effort to gain absolution from God. The groups often preached anti-Semitic doctrine, blaming Jews for the contagion. They acted without the consent of the established church and were ultimately condemned by the pope. In England and Bohemia respectively, John Wycliffe (c. 1320–1385) and Jan Hus (1372/1373–1415) preached clerical poverty, the subordination of church to state, and the primacy of scriptures in faith. Both were condemned; Hus was burned at the stake at the Council of Constance, despite royal assurances that he would not be harmed. But the doctrines of Wycliffe and Hus continued to attract followers after their deaths.

THE BALANCE

Amid all the crises and difficulties, there were positive developments. War necessitated taxes, and taxes brought complaints. But taxes also facilitated the emergence of more centralized nation states, enabling kings to consolidate their sources of revenue, expand royal bureaucracies, and strengthen court systems. France initiated a permanent army in 1422 and King Louis XI (ruled 1461–1483) set in place the first reliable system of royal taxation. Henry Tudor, the winner of the War of the Roses, became Henry VII and increased both his legal and fiscal authority. Meanwhile, the shortage of manpower resulting from the plague hastened technical labor-saving innovations, chief among them the invention of the printing press. The movements of the Ottomans and the difficulties trading with the East encouraged overseas explorations, which led to the discovery of the New World. The wars and dislocations in Italy coincided with an intellectual and cultural flowering, which produced writers such as Petrarch (1304–1374), Boccaccio, and Lorenzo Valla (1404–1457), and artists such as Masaccio (1401–1428), Donatello (1386?–1466), and Brunelleschi (1377–1446).

See also **Introduction; Economic Crises; Feudalism; Peasantry; Plague; Renaissance.**

BIBLIOGRAPHY

Allmand, C. T. *The Hundred Years War: England and France at War, c. 1300–c. 1450.* Cambridge, U.K., 1988.

Bois, Guy. *The Crisis of Feudalism: Economy and Society in Eastern Normandy, c. 1300–1550.* Cambridge, U.K., and New York, 1984. Translation of *Crise du féodalisme.*

Hay, Denys. *Europe in the Fourteenth and Fifteenth Centuries.* London and New York, 1989.

Herlihy, David. *The Black Death and the Transformation of the West.* Edited by Samuel K. Cohn, Jr. Cambridge, Mass., 1997.

Huizinga, Johan. *The Autumn of the Middle Ages.* Translated by Rodney J. Payton and Ulrich Mammitzsch. Chicago, 1996. Translation of *Herfsttij der Middeleeuwen.*

Le Roy Ladurie, Emmanuel. *The Peasants of Languedoc.* Translated by John Day. Urbana, Ill., 1974. Translation of *Les paysans de Languedoc.*

Lopez, Robert. "Hard Times and the Investment in Culture." In *The Renaissance: A Symposium,* pp. 50–61. New York, 1953.

Oakley, Francis. *The Western Church in the Later Middle Ages.* Ithaca, N.Y., 1979.

Postan, M. M. *The Medieval Economy and Society: An Economic History of Britain.* Berkeley, 1973.

Tierney, Brian. *The Foundations of Conciliar Theory: The Contribution of the Medieval Canonists from Gratian to the Great Schism.* Enl. new ed. Leiden and New York, 1998.

WILLIAM CAFERRO

LATIN.

LATIN. Latin continued to be taught, studied, and even spoken in the early modern period. Knowledge of Latin was a sign of social prestige. It was the international language used to conduct the day-to-day business of church and state. It was, above all, the language of the educated and governing classes. University courses were taught in Latin, scholars wrote in Latin, and most official correspondence was conducted in Latin.

Latin remained a living language throughout the Middle Ages and into the early modern period. Medieval Latin, however, differed considerably from the language spoken within the Roman Empire. New words had filtered their way into the language to meet the needs of political, ecclesiastical, and academic institutions, which were almost entirely medieval products. Words had changed meaning over the centuries, some of the grammatical rules had been altered, vernacular words had crept in, and spelling and pronunciation were inconsistent. Efforts were made by humanist scholars to stress the importance of classical Roman authors, particularly Cicero, Virgil, and Horace, as models for their own writings. Medieval Latin was considered by many humanists to be barbarous in comparison with the elegance of classical Latin. Not all scholars agreed, however. Many expressed their concern that an emphasis on the beauty of pagan classical Latin would corrupt the church and its theology.

Lorenzo Valla's (1407–1457) ambitious *Elegantiae linguae latinae libri sex* (printed 1471; Six books of the elegances of the Latin language) was a widely circulated work that proposed such reforms. Valla, like Desiderius Erasmus (1466?–1536), never advocated a slavish imitation of the classical authors. Other humanists, however, were proponents of Ciceronianism, the view that Cicero, considered by many to be the best Latin author of the classical world, should be the model for contemporary Latin usage. This meant that Ciceronians would only use words and constructions found in Cicero's writings. This movement was especially popular in Rome since Ciceronian language lent the majesty and authority of imperial Rome to the ideology and theology of the Renaissance papacy.

New Latin grammars were written with the hope of replacing the popular medieval grammars, such as the *Doctrinale* (c. 1199) of Alexander de Villa Dei, but this did not achieve wide success until the second half of the sixteenth century. Likewise, medieval spellings of certain words continued to be used into the sixteenth century despite efforts to restore the classical spelling. Latin pronunciation, too, varied significantly from region to region, as speakers tended to follow the norms of their mother tongue. Therefore, when Englishmen, Germans, and Italians were in the same room, they spoke Latin to each other, but with such different pronunciations that they sometimes could not be understood. The Italian pronunciation was most widely accepted because many people studied Latin in Italy, where they acquired this pronunciation.

By the seventeenth century, however, the attempts by humanists to restore classical Latin became overshadowed by the rise of the vernacular languages and the discoveries of the scientific revolution. Many European vernacular languages, such as French, English, and Italian, were highly developed and had become classical languages in their own right by this time. Each could boast of their own great writers, such as Dante (1265–1321) and Shakespeare (1564–1616). Furthermore, people still had to come up with new words to describe the new discoveries in science and technology that surpassed those of the Romans. Although scholars of the scientific revolution were trained in classical Latin, the number of academic works written in the vernacular began to increase rapidly. For example, Galileo Galilei (1564–1642) published some of his scientific results in Italian, Isaac Newton (1642–1727) in English, and Gottfried Wilhelm von Leibniz (1646–1716) in French. It took a long time before Latin was altogether replaced by the vernacular languages. In the early modern period, the choice of Latin still offered a writer several advantages. First, a work in Latin reached a broader audience since Latin was an international language. Second, Latin offered a more stable and standardized medium, while the vernacular languages were in a state of flux and changing rapidly. As society changed, the need for knowing Latin declined, and by the nineteenth century the vernacular languages had all but taken over.

See also **Classicism; Erasmus, Desiderius; Humanists and Humanism.**

BIBLIOGRAPHY

Benner, Margareta, and Emin Tengström. *On the Interpretation of Learned Neo-Latin.* Göteborg, 1977.

Grafton, Anthony. "The New Science and the Traditions of Humanism." In *The Cambridge Companion to Renaissance Humanism,* edited by Jill Kraye, pp. 203–223. Cambridge, U.K., and New York, 1996.

Jensen, Kristian. "The Humanist Reform of Latin Teaching." In *The Cambridge Companion to Renaissance Humanism,* edited by Jill Kraye, pp. 63–81. Cambridge, U.K., and New York, 1996.

The Right Way of Speaking Latin and Greek: A Dialogue. In *Collected Works of Erasmus,* vol. 26. Edited by Maurice Pope. Toronto, 1985.

Tunberg, Terence. "Neo-Latin Literature and Language." In *Encyclopedia of the Renaissance,* edited by Paul F. Grendler et al. Vol. 4, pp. 289–294. New York, 1999.

MILTON KOOISTRA

LAUD, WILLIAM (1573–1645), English clergyman and archbishop of Canterbury. The only son of a master tailor in Reading, Laud was educated at St. John's College, Oxford, of which he became a fellow in 1593. He was ordained an Anglican priest in 1601 and rapidly became controversial, being criticized by the vice chancellor of Oxford, Henry Airay (d. 1616), in 1606 for preaching sermons that were regarded as containing popish opinions. He was strongly opposed to the prevailing Calvinist trend in the Church of England and hoped to restore some of the pre-Reformation liturgy. Laud was closely associated with the Arminian tendency within the Church of England. Arminianism, an anti-Calvinist doctrine that attacked the rigid Calvinist views on predestination, was prevalent both in the Church of England and among its Puritan critics in the 1610s, and gained even more influence in the 1620s when Richard Neile, bishop of Durham, became principal church adviser to James I (ruled 1603–1625). A protégé of Neile, whose chaplain he became in 1608, Laud advanced rapidly. He was elected president of St. John's College, Oxford, in 1611, and became dean of Gloucester in 1616 and bishop of St. David's in 1621. His influence grew under Charles I (ruled 1625–1649), and he was promoted to the bishopric of Bath and Wells in 1626 and to that of London in 1628. He also became dean of the Chapel Royal and, in 1629, chancellor of the University of Oxford. In 1633 he became archbishop of Canterbury.

Once he became archbishop, the preaching of Calvinist doctrine in England was limited, as Laud sought to enforce uniformity on a church that had been, in many respects, diverse for decades. In 1633, at Laud's prompting, Charles I wrote to the bishops instructing them to restrict ordination to those who intended to undertake the cure of souls, an action that resulted in the suppression of Puritan lecturers. He was unwilling to offer to Puritan clerics the possibility of only occasional compliance with the regulations, and he insisted that parish churches should match the more regulated practice of cathedrals.

This authoritarianism compounded what was regarded by the Puritans as the offensive nature of Laudian ceremonial and doctrine—not least its stress on the sacraments and church services that emphasized the cleric, not the congregation, and made the altar rather than the pulpit the center of the service. As dean of Gloucester, Laud had moved the communion table to the east end of the choir, a measure seen as crypto Catholic. He also bowed whenever the name of Jesus was pronounced and bowed toward the east on entering a church. Arminianism was seen as crypto-Catholic (and thus conducive to tyranny) by its Puritan critics. Although Laud rejected claims that he was a crypto-Catholic, he was widely referred to by Puritans as the "pope of Canterbury."

Laud was an active opponent of Puritan views, opposing, for example, Puritan strictures on the staging of plays and on activities on Sundays. He responded harshly to Puritan criticisms and writings. Laud was also active in government and was added to the Commission of the Treasury and to the Committee of the Privy Council for Foreign Affairs in 1635. He supported the promotion of clerics in the government and was delighted in 1636 when his friend Bishop William Juxon of London was made Lord Treasurer. Laud's attitude toward the Scottish church played a major role in the breakdown of Charles I's position in Scotland, and thus in the eventual collapse of royal authority. Laud actively backed a new prayer book and new canons for the Scottish church, and, when opposition was voiced in 1637, he persisted in enforcing his reforms. In 1639–1640, he was also a supporter of war with Scotland, a war that was to prove disastrous.

Laud, who had introduced new canons proclaiming divine right kingship in 1640, was to be a victim of the reaction against Charles I. He was impeached by the Long Parliament in December 1640 and committed to the Tower of London the following March. His trial for treason did not begin until March 1644; members of the House of Lords were hesitant about the charge, which they felt had been forced on them by the Commons. As a result, proceedings were brought against Laud alleging that he had tried to subvert the fundamental laws, to alter religion as by law established, and to subvert the rights of Parliament. After his request that the harsh character of the execution for treason be commuted was finally accepted, Laud was beheaded on Tower Hill on 10 January 1645.

An obstinate and difficult man, Laud bore part of the responsibility for his own downfall; he failed to comprehend the growing trend toward Puritanism and the intense hostility aroused by his treatment of those who disagreed with him, both of which contributed to the crisis of trust that led to the outbreak of the Civil War. He became a martyr figure for the "high" tradition of the Church of England.

See also **Bible; Charles I (England); Church of England; English Civil War and Interregnum; Puritanism.**

BIBLIOGRAPHY

Carlton, Charles. *Archbishop William Laud.* London and New York, 1987.

Duncan-Jones, A. S. *Archbishop Laud.* London, 1927.

Trevor-Roper, Hugh. *Archbishop Laud, 1573–1645.* 3rd ed. Basingstoke, U.K., 1988.

Tyacke, Nicholas. *Aspects of English Protestantism c. 1530–1700.* Manchester, U.K., and New York, 2001.

JEREMY BLACK

LAVOISIER, ANTOINE (Antoine-Laurent Lavoisier; 1743–1794), considered the father of modern French chemistry and the discoverer of oxygen. Born to a family of notaries and lawyers, Lavoisier was raised in the comfort of bourgeois Paris and attended the Collège Mazarin, where he studied literature, rhetoric, and the natural sciences. Intended for a legal career (he received his law degree in 1763 and several prizes for rhetoric), he early on moved first into mineralogy, traveling with Jean Étienne Guettard of the Academy of Sciences, and then into chemistry, following especially the public courses of the controversial Guillaume-François Rouelle at the Jardin du Roi. He was accepted at a very early on into the Academy of Sciences, of which he would be a lifelong and tireless member.

At a young age, Lavoisier felt that chemistry was a science filled with unclear names and confused theories, and he was committed to resolving it into a science as systematic as Newton's physics. From 1763 to about 1770, he slowly elaborated his famous principle that "nothing is gained and nothing is lost" in chemical reactions, that is, that conservation of mass defines the conceptual closure of chemical experiments. He also demonstrated that water is not an element by separating it into hydrogen and oxygen and then reversing the process. During the "crucial year," 1772–1773, he identified oxygen (and hydrogen) as elements and set the stage for the chemical revolution that disproved the phlogiston, or fixed-fire, theory of chemistry. In 1787 he and his disciples sealed their success with the *Method of Chemical Nomenclature,* a controversial reform of the field of chemistry based on Condillac's definition of a science as a perfect analytic language. Lavoisier's *Elements of Chemistry* of 1789 united the reformed nomenclature with the principles of closure-determined experimental observation and his definition of the chemical element. From the early 1780s he also worked with Laplace (1749–1827), studying the chemistry of respiration and theorizing that metabolism is a form of combustion. In this way he prepared the way for much of nineteenth-century biochemistry.

Lavoisier's life was not limited to chemistry, however. Although he had inherited a fortune sufficient for financial independence, he was a shy, serious young man, not given to public displays of brilliance or adept at social climbing. His marriage to the fourteen-year-old Marie Paulze, daughter of one of the members of the infamous General Farm, a quasi-governmental organization that collected the taxes from the French subjects for the crown, provided him with the social connections and the additional financial resources needed to join the oligarchy of Enlightenment meritocrats attempting to reform the French state under Louis XV (ruled 1715–1774) and Louis XVI (ruled 1774–1792). Lavoisier's training as a lawyer served him well at the tax farm and as a collaborator with Turgot (1727–1781) on proposals to reform the French economy. Dupont de Nemours (1739–1817) introduced him to the Physiocrats, and Lavoisier applied his scientific and economic theories to real-world experiments in agriculture (using experimental farms in his tax region to test the utility of crop rotation), prison reforms, analyses of the quality of the water of Paris, proposals for lighting Paris, and comparisons of hot-air versus hydrogen balloons for military observations and scientific investigations.

During the French Revolution and until the 1793 abolition of the Academy of Sciences, Lavoisier turned the sciences to the service of the republic. He was tireless in establishing a Bureau of

Antoine Lavoisier. Lavoisier with his wife, Maria. Painting by Jacques-Louis David, 1788. ©BETTMANN/CORBIS

Weights and Measures and the adoption of the metric system. He ran the in-town saltpeter factory that provided France (but only after his chemical improvements) with sufficient gunpowder to fight the counterrevolutionaries. With Condorcet (1743–1794) he proposed a structure for a secular public education, in part based on his experience of the reform of chemistry through its nomenclature: He believed that a French language freed from the confusion, superstition, and historical connotations of *ancien régime* ideology would create a new type of republican citizen and guarantee the economic security of the modern technological state.

He was, nonetheless, sent to the guillotine with the other *fermiers généraux* on 8 May 1794. His wife and chemical disciples had circulated letters and petitions to show how much the "father of French chemistry," as he was called, had been useful to the Revolution. The answer given them is famous: "the Revolution has no need of scientists." The Reign of Terror fell only three months later, and the posthumous rehabilitation of Lavoisier as the ideal citizen-scientist went hand-in-hand with the dismantling of Robespierre's (1758–1794) terrorist state.

See also **Chemistry; Condorcet, Marie-Jean Caritat, marquis de; Revolutions, Age of.**

BIBLIOGRAPHY

Primary Sources

Lavoisier, Antoine Laurent. *Elements of Chemistry.* Translated by Robert Kerr. Introduction by Douglas McKie. New York, 1965. This is the standard English translation of the *Traité élémentaire de chimie,* 1789.

———. *Oeuvres de Lavoisier.* Paris, 1862. The editing of his correspondence is still not finished. This same edition is also available online at the Sorbonne's http://histsciences.univ-paris1.fr/i-corpus/lavoisier/index.php, and many of the manuscripts as well as a good overview of the location of unpublished manuscripts held around the world can be found at the Panopticon Lavoisier, established by Marco Beretta and Andrea Scotti at http://moro.imss.fi.it/lavoisier/.

Secondary Sources

Guerlac, Henry. *Lavoisier: The Crucial Year.* Ithaca, N.Y., 1961. The classic reading of Lavoisier's invention of modern chemistry.

Holmes, Frederic Lawrence. *Lavoisier and the Chemistry of Life.* Madison, Wisc., 1985. The best analysis of Lavoisier's work on animal respiration and metabolism.

Poirier, Pierre-Jean. *Lavoisier, Chemist, Biologist, Economist.* Translated by Rebecca Balinski. Philadelphia, 1996. Translation of *Antoine Laurent de Lavoisier, 1743–1794,* Paris, 1993. The best modern biography of Lavoisier in that it deals with the full scope of his scientific, technical, and public activities.

WILDA CHRISTINE ANDERSON

LAW

This entry contains seven subentries:

CANON LAW

The basic elements of canon law were the *Decretum* (c. 1140) and the *Decretales* (1234). The *Decretum* (The concordance of discordant canons), compiled by a monk named Gratian, brought together materials related to the law and the administration of the church from a wide variety of sources in a dialectic fashion, in order to create a uniform body of law for the universal church. The *Decretales* (The Gregorian decretals) consisted of approximately two thousand decretal letters, judicial decisions, that various popes issued between the mid-twelfth and the early thirteenth century. Eventually several smaller collections were added as well: the *Liber sextus* (The sixth book of decretals; 1298); the *Constitutiones Clementinae* (The Clementine constitutions; 1317), and the *Extravagantes a Johanne Papa XXII* (Decretal letters of Pope John XXII; 1325). The last brief collection was the *Extravagantes communes* compiled at the end of the fifteenth century.

In addition to texts in the *Corpus iuris canonici,* canon law also contained commentaries based on glossing the texts. Initially brief marginal comments explaining unusual words and phrases and referring the reader to related materials elsewhere, the glosses grew longer and more detailed. By the mid-thirteenth century there existed a standard commentary, a *Glossa ordinaria,* on the *Decretum* and one on the *Decretales.* These provided a kind of basic textbook based on the writings of a number of early canonists. Subsequently, many canonists wrote longer commentaries, not simply defining obscure terms and citing related materials but writing at length on substantive issues raised in the texts. Some of these commentaries contained in effect brief legal treatises on points of law and even political theory. The most extensive of these commentaries was that of Johannes Andreae (c. 1270–1348).

The period 1140–1378 was the golden age of canon law, the period when the law was fully formed and produced its greatest thinkers. Scholars judge the post-1378 period in the history of canon law as sterile, an era when commentators repeated thoughts of their predecessors without adding significantly to the law. Part of the reason for this division was that after 1325, papal judgment letters, decretals, were replaced as the basis of the law by decisions of the other papal courts, especially that known as the Rota. Nevertheless, canonists continued to produce extensive commentaries on the *Decretales,* often running to several volumes, that have received little scholarly attention although there is evidence that they deserve more extensive analysis. John F. McGovern has argued that many early modern economic concepts that Max Weber and others associated with the Protestant Reformation had in fact existed in the works of fifteenth-century Italian canonists.

During the sixteenth and seventeenth centuries, the Protestant Reformation and the Catholic response to it had a significant effect on the development of canon law. The major effect of the Reformation was that canon law was no longer the recognized law of Christian Europe. Now only Catholic countries recognized canon law, and even in those countries agreements between Catholic rulers and the papacy granted wide powers to the rulers in return for supporting the papacy, agreements that restricted the jurisdiction of the law. Such agreements, concordats, effectively limited the role of the papacy and therefore of the canon law within Catholic kingdoms. The agreements often required the papacy to seek royal permission before circulating statements on ecclesiastical law and doctrine. The climax of this development came with the Peace of Westphalia (1648), which ended the religious wars in Germany. The pope was not invited to send a representative to the negotiations that led to the peace, and Pope Innocent X (1644–1655) condemned the treaty but to no avail. This marked the end of the role of the pope and of canon law in the international relations of Europe.

Within the Catholic community, there were important developments regarding canon law. In response to calls for codifying the canon law to bring all of the disparate materials of the law into a coherent body of law, Pope Pius V (1566–1572), taking advantage of Renaissance humanist scholarship, created a commission composed of cardinals and scholars with a mandate to examine the various manuscript copies of the materials of canon law, to correct errors, and to excise materials that had been added to the original texts. The result was the *Corpus iuris canonici* (Body of canon law), the official law of the Roman Catholic Church until 1918.

Another source of development in canon law in the sixteenth century was the Council of Trent (1545–1563), which generated a series of canons designed to respond to issues that the Protestant reformers had raised. Overall, the canons and decrees of Trent reinforced the institutional structure of the church, the sacramental system, and the power of the papacy, seeing the reform of the existing church structure as central and rejecting the

Protestant argument that the entire ecclesiastical structure, including the canon law, had to be eliminated.

From the perspective of Christian daily life, the most important of the canons of Trent was Tametsi (1563) dealing with marriage law. This decree restated the Catholic position that marriage was a sacrament and subject to ecclesiastical regulation, in opposition to the Protestant view that marriage was fundamentally a civil matter. Tametsi required parental consent, witnesses, formal recording of the marriage, and a blessing by a priest. This ended the older practice of secret marriage entered into by two persons without witnesses, a situation that caused a great deal of confusion for the ecclesiastical courts. Finally, Tametsi forbade secular rulers from interfering in any way with the freedom of their subjects to marry as they wished, thus stressing the right of the individual to enter a marriage without compulsion, a right protected by the requirement that the marriage ceremony be celebrated publicly and in the presence of witnesses.

Martin Luther (1483–1546) famously illustrated the Protestant opinion about canon law when he publicly burned volumes of the law along with other materials that he saw as corrupting the Christian faith by stressing the letter rather than the spirit of Christianity. Protestants rejected the Catholic sacramental system and the entire clerical structure headed by the pope so that it was possible to reject canon law as well. Even those Protestant countries that did retain some elements of canon law rejected any papal role in its functioning.

It was not only the Protestant Reformation that affected the role of canon law in European society in the early modern era. As modern states began to emerge, secular governments also began to take responsibility for marriage and family law, for cases involving wills and probate, and other matters that had previously been within the jurisdiction of the church and canon law. The canon law connected with these activities became the basis of secular law in these areas even in Protestant countries. As a result, one of the most important areas of scholarly research in modern times has concerned the appropriation of canon law by secular lawyers and political theorists in the early modern world. This scholarship has focused attention on three aspects of the development of canon law in the early modern era: the conciliar movement, canon law in the expansion of Europe overseas, and marriage law. In each of these areas, the work of the canonists contributed to the shaping of modern political and legal concepts.

The conciliar movement, a fifteenth-century movement to reform the institutional structure of the Catholic Church, played an important role in subsequent discussion of representative government, because the canonists had wrestled with problems associated with the governance of large communities, the relation of the ruler, that is, the pope, to a representative institution, the council, and the nature of representation within a political community, issues that in the seventeenth century lay at the heart of political debate throughout Europe. Careful analysis of early modern political and legal texts has uncovered not only concepts developed by the canon lawyers but the language of the canonists as well.

A related concept that developed from the debates of the canon lawyers was the notion of the ruler as sovereign and then the application of that concept to the emerging nation-state, making the state answerable to no outside authority. This had emerged in the canonistic tradition as the canonists discussed the powers of the pope and the emperor. The canonists had rejected imperial claims to jurisdiction over all other Christian rulers, arguing instead that Christian kings possessed within their own kingdoms the power identified with the imperial office. Subsequent writers, such as Jean Bodin (1529–1596), whose *Six Books of the Republic* is usually identified as the initial modern work on the concept of sovereignty, drew heavily on the canonistic tradition in his work.

Finally, in spite of Luther's burning of volumes of the canon law, Protestant churches also employed at least some elements of the canon law tradition. The Church of England was perhaps the most notable example of continued use of the canon law and church courts in a variety of matters, but as recent scholarship has indicated, Lutherans also used elements of canon law. Elements of the medieval canon law can also be found in the major works of John Calvin, whose *Institutes* and *Ecclesiastical Ordinances* reflect a highly legal conception of church structure, a conception rooted in the writings of the thirteenth-century canonists.

See also **Calvin, John; Catholicism; Church of England; Luther, Martin; Papacy and Papal States; Reformation, Protestant; Trent, Council of.**

BIBLIOGRAPHY

Primary Source

Canons and Decrees of the Council of Trent. Original text with English translation by H. J. Schroeder. St. Louis and London, 1941.

Secondary Sources

Bernhard, Jean, Charles Lefebvre, and Francis Rapp. *L'époque de la réforme et du concile de Trente.* Vol. 14 of *Histoire du droit et des instituions de l'église en Occident.* Paris, 1989.

Brundage, James. *Medieval Canon Law.* London and New York, 1995.

Helmholz, R. H. *Roman Canon Law in Reformation England.* Cambridge, U.K., and New York, 1990.

McGovern, John F. "The Rise of New Economic Attitudes in Canon and Civil Law, A.D. 1200–1550." *The Jurist* 32 (1972): 39–50.

Ourliac, Paul, and Henri Gilles. *La période post-classique (1378–1500).* Vol. 13 of *Histoire du droit et des institutions de l'église en Occident.* Paris, 1971.

Pennington, Kenneth. *The Prince and the Law, 1200–1600: Sovereignty and Rights in the Western Legal Tradition.* Berkeley, 1993.

Tierney, Brian. *Religion, Law, and the Growth of Constitutional Thought, 1150–1650.* Cambridge, U.K., and New York, 1982.

Witte, John. *Law and Protestantism: The Legal Teachings of the Lutheran Reformation.* Cambridge, U.K., and New York, 2002.

JAMES MULDOON

COMMON LAW

The common law was generally defined as the unwritten law, or *lex non scripta,* of England. It derived its authority from immemorial usage and "universal reception throughout the kingdom," as phrased by Sir William Blackstone (1723–1780) in his *Commentaries on the Laws of England* (1765–1769). The common law was contrasted with written statutory laws enacted by Parliament. For some, like Sir John Davies (1569–1626), it was "nothing else but the Common Custome of the Realm" (preface to *Reports,* 1612). Indeed, the *De Laudibus Legum Angliae* (c. 1470; In Praise of the laws of England) of Sir John Fortescue (c. 1395–c. 1477) declared that "the realm has been continuously ruled by the same customs as it is now." Most, however, found it more accurate to describe the system as customary in origin. As Sir Edward Coke (1552–1634) put it in the preface to the eighth volume of his *Reports* (1600–1615), it was "the grounds of our common laws" that were "beyond the memorie or register of any beginning." By the mid-seventeenth century, Sir Matthew Hale (1609–1676) made it clear that the "immemoriality" of the common law did not imply that it was unchanging, it only indicated that the precise origin of institutions (such as Parliament and the jury) and rules (notably of landed property) predating 1189 could not be traced. Their continued existence carried the presumption of both original and continued popular consent. As Hale wrote in his *History of the Common Law* (1713), the common law was "singularly accommodated" to the "Disposition of the English Nation" and "incorporated into their very Temperament," while also reflecting their experience.

As Coke pointed out in the first volume of his *Institutes of the Laws of England* (1628–1644), there were "divers lawes within the realme of England," including the prerogative law of the crown, the canon law practiced in the ecclesiastical courts, and the maritime law administered in the Admiralty. However, as John Selden (1584–1654) put it, "There are no laws in England but are made laws either by custom or act of parliament" (*Commons Debates,* 1628). These "particular laws" were included in the definition of *lex non scripta,* because their authority in England derived, according to Hale, from "their being admitted and received by us" either through statute or "by immemorial Usage and Custom in some particular Cases and Courts." They were subject to the control of the common law, which sought to keep their jurisdiction within its accepted boundaries or even, as in the early seventeenth century, to restrict them. Besides these particular laws, the *lex non scripta* also encompassed local and particular customs. Local customs, which originated in local practice in derogation from the general rules of common law, were recognized and enforced in the common law courts, but only if they were immemorial, continuous in usage, certain, and reasonable. Particular customs such as the custom of merchants *(lex mercatoria)* were also said to be part of the common law. In court, if any doubt arose about what the custom was, the evidence of merchants was received to inform the court.

In the first half of the seventeenth century common lawyers fearful of the ambitions of the Stuart monarchy challenged the idea that law derived from the commands of a king, whose authority came either from divine right or conquest. For them, the common law was a "fundamental law" derived from an ancient constitution, limiting the power of the crown and guaranteeing the freedoms and rights of the English, most particularly to their property. In the case of *Prohibitions del Roy* (1607) Coke declared that the law as administered by the judges was "the golden met-wand and measure to try the causes of [the] subjects," while in the *Case of Proclamations* (1610) it was ruled that the king's proclamations did not have the force of law. The legal debate over the existence of an "absolute" power in the king to act according to his idea of what the public good required in emergencies continued to be debated in a legally inconclusive way in a number of causes célèbres in the early seventeenth century. But the vision of the constitution espoused by common lawyers prevailed in the later seventeenth century and was secured by the Bill of Rights in 1689.

Such was Coke's veneration of the common law that he stated in 1610 that it could even declare void a statute "against common right and reason" *(Dr. Bonham's Case)*. Before the outbreak of the English Civil War in 1642, lawyers sometimes described Parliament as a court, implying that statutes might be seen as judgments or declarations of the common law. More usually, however, lawyers from Coke to Blackstone described Parliament's power as "transcendent and absolute" (Coke, *Institutes*) and not liable to judicial review. In doing so they did not expect (and did not see) an active, interventionist legislature. Legislation that was passed amended and modified the common law, rather than displacing it. Parliament was therefore seen as part of the common law's world rather than as a threat to it. Just as the common law grew from the consent of the people as manifested in custom, so statute was seen to come from current consent. It was a fundamental rule of the constitution, constantly reiterated, that the crown could neither change the law nor impose taxation without consent. It was this that made England (in Fortescue's terms) "a government not only regal but also political." As Hale put it, all legislation was a "tripartite indenture" between king, lords, and commons, rather than the mere will of the king or the people. The notion of the mixed constitution, founded on a presumed ancient original contract reconfirmed in 1689 and conferring unlimited power on the crown-in-Parliament, was generally accepted in mid-eighteenth-century England. However, when Parliament began in the 1760s to tax colonists who were not represented at Westminster, American lawyers invoked Coke's rhetoric from Bonham's case, arguing for the existence of a higher law to control the legislature. Where parliamentary sovereignty became the cornerstone of the British constitution, the American constitution of 1787 recast the old ideas of a fundamental law.

THE COMMON LAW IN THE COURTS

In a narrower sense, the common law was the body of law administered in Westminster Hall by the twelve judges of the three superior courts of law. These were the Common Pleas, whose position as the prime court for civil suits had been secured by the Magna Carta (1215) and which continued to attract most civil litigation until the early eighteenth century; the King's Bench, which originally dealt with crown business (including criminal matters) and had jurisdiction to correct errors from other courts of record; and the Exchequer of Pleas, which originally dealt primarily with revenue matters. By the later Middle Ages, thanks to procedural changes designed to attract litigants, these courts had a largely concurrent jurisdiction, and the King's Bench gradually became the most popular court. The common law administered in these three courts contrasted with "equity" as administered primarily in the Court of Chancery. The Chancery was originally a court of conscience, concerned with securing justice in individual cases rather than following strict rules. There were some complaints in the sixteenth and seventeenth centuries about the certainty of the common law being undermined by the interference of the lord chancellor. It was argued that one chancellor's conscience might differ from his successor's, just as the length of their feet did. In 1614–1616 an unsuccessful attempt was made by Coke to assert the supremacy of the common law courts over the

Court of Chancery. However, after the Restoration, when Heneage Finch, earl of Nottingham, was lord chancellor (1675–1682), the court began to develop a more fixed set of principles and rules, which were further developed by Philip Yorke, earl of Hardwicke (lord chancellor, 1737–1756). By the eighteenth century, the old antagonism between the systems had gone. With a distinct procedure and set of remedies, the Chancery was able to develop a jurisdiction over matters to which the common law remained blind, most notably trusts. It thereby made up for the shortcomings of the common law, but its rules and doctrines presumed the existence of the common law, which it modified in particular contexts.

While common lawyers saw their law as based on immemorial custom, they also described it in terms of reason. As Coke put it in the *Institutes,* "reason is the life of the Law, nay the common law itself is nothing else but reason." By this he meant not the "natural reason" of every man but the "artificial reason" of lawyers, obtained by long study and experience. Knowledge of the law was a specialized enterprise, which had to be left to lawyers, and "if all the reason that is dispersed into so many several heads were united into one, yet he could not make such a law as the Law of England is." This law was seen to be both developing and unchanging. On the one hand, its core principles were seen as timeless. On the other, its details had been, as Coke stated elsewhere, "refined and perfected by all the wisest men in former succession of ages and proved and approved by continuall experience to be good & profitable for the common wealth."

Rather than directly reflecting the customary practices of the people, most of the law applied in the courts to the end of the eighteenth century had been created and developed in the judicial forum. The common law had originated in the reign of Henry II (ruled 1154–1189) not as a set of substantive rules, but as a set of institutions and procedures to enforce rights whose substance was defined by community custom. However, with the development both of a legal profession and of the jury in the thirteenth century, new legal norms emerged by which custom was rapidly turned into law, which then developed within the courtroom. Since the jury's function was to decide questions of fact, matters of the law had to be settled by lawyers and judges. In the later Middle Ages, when the process of pleading was flexible, judges avoided making clear determinations of substantive law, preferring to get the parties in uncertain cases to reformulate their claims to reflect the common understanding of what the law was. In this era, the law was often seen in terms of the "common erudition" of the lawyers, as debated at the Inns of Court as well as in the courtroom. By the sixteenth century, however, when pleading had become more formal, judges began to be more confident about making clear statements of law. Law was now often settled, after the determination of facts by the jury, by motions debated on the bench at Westminster Hall after a trial had taken place at the assizes.

In elaborating the law, judges assumed that the common law already contained within itself the answers to any questions they might be asked. They saw their function as being to declare what the law already was, rather than to make new law. In order to maintain certainty, they were expected as far as possible to follow the reasoning of earlier cases. Since cases were seen to be evidence of the law rather than law itself, no doctrine of binding precedent emerged in this period. Nevertheless, from the sixteenth century onward, law reports were produced that clearly set out the substantive decisions, in a way not done in the medieval Year Books, and lawyers such as Edmund Plowden (1518–1585) and Coke now published reports that sought to illustrate the principles of the law. Until the mid-eighteenth century most published law reports were the unreliable results of speculating publishers, but manuscript reports circulated widely and were often quoted in court. Principles, or maxims, could thus be obtained by a process of induction from the *ratio decidendi,* or reason for the decision, of earlier cases. Besides applying the principles and maxims thus obtained, judges were also expected to extend the reason of one case to another by a process of analogy. However, judges did not only derive their law from precedent or analogy, for in novel cases they were free to resort to arguments drawn from natural law, public policy, or convenience.

See also **Absolutism; Constitutionalism; English Civil War and Interregnum; Natural Law.**

BIBLIOGRAPHY

Primary Sources

Blackstone, William. *Commentaries on the Laws of England.* 4 vols. Chicago, 1979. Originally published 1765–1759.

Coke, Edward. *The First Part of the Institutes of the Laws of England, or, A Commentary upon Littleton.* Edited by Francis Hargrave and Charles Butler. 15th ed. London, 1794.

———. *The Fourth Part of the Institutes of the Laws of England: Concerning the Jurisdiction of the Courts.* London, 1644.

———. *La huictme part des reports de sr. Edw. Coke.* London, 1611.

———. *Le quart part des reportes del Edward Coke.* London, 1604.

Davies, John. *Les reports des cases & matters en ley, resolves & adjudges en les courts del roy en Ireland.* London, 1674.

Fortescue, John. *De Laudibus Legum Angliae.* Edited and translated by S. B. Chrimes. Holmes Beach, Fla., 1986.

Hale, Matthew. *The History of the Common Law of England.* Edited by Charles M. Gray. Chicago, 1971. First published 1713.

Johnson, Robert C., et al., eds. *Commons Debates, 1628.* 6 vols. New Haven, 1977–1983.

Secondary Sources

Baker, J. H. *An Introduction to English Legal History.* 4th ed. London, 2002.

Brooks, Christopher W. *Lawyers, Litigation, and English Society since 1450.* London and Rio Grande, Ohio, 1998.

Burgess, Glenn. *The Politics of the Ancient Constitution: An Introduction to English Political Thought, 1600–1642.* Houndmills, U.K., 1992.

Lobban, Michael. *The Common Law and English Jurisprudence, 1760–1850.* Oxford and New York, 1991.

Oldham, James. *The Mansfield Manuscripts and the Growth of English Law in the Eighteenth Century.* 2 vols. Chapel Hill, N.C., 1992.

Pocock, J. G. A. *The Ancient Constitution and the Feudal Law: A Study of English Historical Thought in the Seventeenth Century: A Reissue with a Retrospect.* Cambridge, U.K., and New York, 1987.

Sommerville, J. P. *Royalists and Patriots: Politics and Ideology in England, 1603–1640.* London and New York, 1999.

Stoner, James R., Jr. *Common Law and Liberal Theory: Coke, Hobbes, and the Origins of American Constitutionalism.* Lawrence, Kans., 1992.

Tubbs, J. W. *The Common Law Mind: Medieval and Early Modern Conceptions.* Baltimore, 2000.

MICHAEL LOBBAN

COURTS

Early modern law courts were multifunctional institutions whose reach extended far beyond the judicial branch of government. Throughout Europe, they held a wide range of administrative, governing, and policing powers, frequently making them a main channel of state administration. In eastern Europe, the courts were closely fused to the state bureaucracy and operated as the secure tools of crown authority. In western Europe, courts enjoyed varying levels of independence from the sovereign, but they nevertheless were active in maintaining daily order in both villages and state. Given the complex nature of early modern society, the judiciary was a key mechanism for conflict resolution not only among individuals, but among classes, estates, and orders. Law courts also served as a central elevator for social mobility. Buying or acquiring offices in the royal courts was an important stepping-stone into the gentry or the nobility, conferring honor, influence, and sometimes titles on the officeholder. Finally, judges served as the protectors of common law, customary laws, and privileges on behalf of society, and often actively defended those traditions against the encroachments of increasingly powerful sovereigns. Judges and lawyers in the courts were thus at the epicenter of several early modern rebellions and revolutions, including the French Fronde (1648–1653), the English Civil War (1642–1649), and the French Revolution (1789).

The law courts proved to be one of the most flexible and useful tools of governance available in western Europe, and the use of both elaborate law codes and a widespread court system to govern is one of the key factors in the development of the early modern state. Local seigneurial and royal courts helped to make village communities and towns largely self-governing, while provincial and regional courts often helped oversee the administration of large territories. At the pinnacle of the state, sovereign courts negotiated the privileges and competing claims of nobles, officials, and corporations. Despite the intense interest in recent decades in early modern crime and punishment, the vast majority of European courts' business was the regulation of civil society through contracts, laws, and customs. Courts thus provided limited opportunities for ordinary people to resolve their most pressing problems, especially those of family, property, and community, in a civil forum.

ORGANIZATION OF COURTS

The organization of the law courts in continental Europe was byzantine, full of overlapping jurisdictions that reflected both the organic growth of courts over time and the reality of competing claims to judicial sovereignty. Almost all European states had three major independent court systems: ecclesiastical courts to judge the religious crimes of clerics and parishioners, seigneurial or manorial courts that delivered justice to tenants (including the right to impose the death penalty for landlords exercising high justice), and state courts, which gradually began to encroach on the jurisdictions of the other two. Church jurisdiction eroded significantly from the sixteenth through the eighteenth centuries in many countries, but sovereigns faced a steeper challenge in dismantling the private jurisdictions of landlords, for whom courts were considered part of their property and family honor.

Outside of these three major systems, however, most corporations like towns, guilds, and officers' corps had the right to regulate their own members through internal courts and statutes. An enormous volume of early modern litigation was also resolved through formal and informal adjudication outside of the court system, though often brokered by notaries, lawyers, or even judges from the law courts.

SOVEREIGN OR SUPERIOR COURTS

Well before 1450, superior or sovereign courts had emerged out of the medieval king's household (the *curia regis*) in many states. They developed into professionalized resident law courts that enjoyed relatively high degrees of independence on a day-to-day basis. In France, the sovereign Parlement of Paris was installed on the Île-de-la-Cité by 1300 and remained there even when the royal court was itinerant. Peers of France had the right to have their cases heard there in the first instance, and the court's judgments were unappealable (save to the king himself). The parlement's real strength, however, lay in the extent of its geographic and legal jurisdiction. The court could judge any civil or criminal case in its extensive domain (the lands originally held by the Capetian kings, about one-third of France) and heard appeals from the lower courts, making it one of the most inclusive jurisdictions in Europe. The parlement also had the right to register royal edicts before enforcing them, which gave magistrates opportunities to delay legislation or to remonstrate with the king. Although the *parlementaires* could neither legislate nor veto royal laws, they did issue a wide variety of administrative *arrêts* ('decrees') that gave them broad authority over public order.

The system of parlements was gradually extended to new provinces as they were added to the realm. In many recently acquired provinces, like Burgundy (1477) and Normandy (1499), existing ducal courts were simply transformed into sovereign parlements. By the late eighteenth century, France had thirteen parlements, each sovereign within its own jurisdiction. The Parlement of Paris, however, remained the superior member of the court system, and was often looked to for legal precedents. France thus had an extraordinarily dense corps of sovereign magistrates; there were roughly 240 *parlementaires* in Paris in the eighteenth century, and another thousand in the other sovereign courts.

By 1400 the French crown had appointed five varieties of sovereign courts to deal with different types of cases. Apart from the parlements, there were three sovereign financial courts: the Court of Aids *(Cour des Aides)* for tax cases, the Chamber of Accounts *(Chambre de Comptes)* for royal accounting disputes, and the Court of Monies *(Cour de Monnaies)* for monetary cases like counterfeiting. (Provinces with parlements typically had one or more of these sovereign financial courts as well.) Finally, the Grand Council decided jurisdictional disputes among the other courts and heard special political cases. Outside of these formal courts, the king, in his role as God's judge, always retained the right to hear cases, render judgment, and grant pardons in exceptional circumstances. For the most part, however, early modern French sovereigns increasingly left judging to a trained corps of jurists and lawyers.

One of the most prominent features of the French sovereign courts was that judgeships were both venal (bought by the official, sometimes for princely sums) and hereditary. Repeated fiscal crises of the French crown had early on led kings to the expedient of selling offices in their own administration, a habit that proved impossible to break. In

Law: Courts. *A Judge and Three Advocates,* eighteenth-century painting by an artist of the Venetian School. GALLERIA DELL'ACCADEMIA, VENICE, ITALY/BRIDGEMAN ART LIBRARY

1604 Henry IV (ruled 1589–1610) allowed royal officers to pass offices on to their heirs or sell them in exchange for an annual fee (the *paulette*), equal to one-sixtieth of the office value. Because of the high status of judging, it became axiomatic that the highest judgeships should only be held by nobles. Judgeships in the sovereign courts (all *parlementaires* and Masters in the Chamber of Accounts, for example) endowed personal nobility on their holders and eventually hereditary nobility on their families. The result was the emergence of a powerful "nobility of the robe" (for the long robes they wore in office), which became an increasingly wealthy, educated, and sometimes politically fractious elite. Robe nobles from the sovereign courts played important roles in the revolt of the Fronde as well as in the French Revolution in 1789, but they were an essential part of the backbone of national and provincial order in less contentious times.

Other continental regions experimented with different forms of sovereign courts. In the Holy Roman Empire, the Diet of Worms (the imperial parliament) created an imperial supreme court in 1495, an appellate bench for both territorial and urban jurisdictions. The magistrates also claimed original jurisdiction over a variety of civil and criminal cases, including cases involving corporations, cities, estates, and crimes against the state. In practice, however, the more powerful states of the empire continued to claim sovereign jurisdiction and did not recognize the imperial court's authority. Below the supreme court were a series of weaker imperial courts that were often regional in jurisdiction, and whose cases were increasingly appealed to the supreme court. As in France, these multiple appellate layers provided litigants with numerous political and legal avenues for pursuing their cases, and with abundant opportunities to exploit rivalries between jurisdictions.

England's law courts were far more successfully centralized than most continental courts. Three types of superior courts were based in and around London, each specializing in a different type of law: common law courts, equity courts, and royal prerogative courts. The three main royal courts sitting at London's Westminster Hall, the King's Bench, the Court of Common Pleas, and the Exchequer, primarily practiced common law. By 1500, Common Pleas was the busiest jurisdiction in England, hearing nearly fifty thousand cases a year at its peak. The court possessed jurisdiction over most civil cases, including property, rents, and debts. King's Bench originally enjoyed criminal jurisdiction, but its civil jurisdiction was expanded after the 1530s, allowing it also to hear the common pleas from most of England. By 1600 the two courts' civil jurisdiction was similar, although King's Bench still heard only one-third as many cases as Common Pleas. The Exchequer had its own small court for revenue cases or debt, but few litigants had the right to plead there until the late 1600s. Despite the centrality of the Westminster courts, there was a remarkably small group of judges on the bench: there were only about fifteen sovereign judges in England. Once points of law had been settled by the courts at Westminster, most cases returned to the counties to be tried by jury in the assize courts. All three superior common-law courts were united in the nineteenth century.

Apart from the central common-law courts, and developed partly in opposition to them, were the crown's prerogative courts. The infamous Court of Star Chamber, along with the Court of High Commission, allowed crown and church to investigate and prosecute powerful nobles or ecclesiastics outside of common law. (Most sixteenth-century cases tried in the prerogative courts actually involved powerful subjects prosecuting one another, but the courts were notoriously used by Archbishop Laud to prosecute nonconformists in the early seventeenth century.) Lastly, the Court of Chancery in London administered equity law to litigants and appellants. Equity (considered a branch of reason) gradually evolved into a formal set of legal principles by 1700 and was integrated into the common law by 1800.

During the legal revolution of the seventeenth century, England's superior court structure was radically streamlined. In 1641 Parliament abolished the prerogative courts, including Star Chamber, High Commission, and Requests, along with the royal court of wards and legal enclaves that had long been under the jurisdiction of the Councils of the North and of Wales. This streamlining of the law courts reflected an increasingly unified sovereignty under the leadership of Parliament in England, and it furthered an increasingly dominant common law.

In eastern Europe, law courts were more firmly integrated into the bureaucracy and had considerably less freedom of action than in most western states, but in the eighteenth century both Frederick II of Prussia (1748; ruled 1740–1786) and the Habsburgs in their own provinces (1749) gave the judiciary a more independent identity. Frederick II no longer allowed the bureaucracy to involve itself in judicial cases, and the Habsburgs set up a new ministry and supreme court, the Oberste Justizstelle, to distinguish justice from administration more clearly. In both states, however, there was a far less developed structure of rights, privileges, and laws outside the control of the crown or bureaucracy than in most western states. In Russia, the senate had evolved into a judicial body under Peter I (ruled 1682–1725), but in practice it heard only cases of the nobility. Moreover, Russian *ukazy* ('imperial decrees') and government ministry orders were neither codified nor published, making it difficult for any organized study of the law to develop. Repeated attempts to codify Russian law by Peter I, Elizabeth (ruled 1741–1762), and Catherine II (ruled 1762–1796) between 1700 and 1767 all came to naught. Local justice was dispensed to Russian serfs on their estates through land courts, and landowners were essentially a law unto themselves. Under such conditions, a relatively independent judiciary never developed into a key institution of civil society.

LOCAL COURTS

Law courts frequently became the main channel of local administration in western Europe during the sixteenth and seventeenth centuries. As the nobility deserted the countryside for the allure of royal courts or cities, the mantle of daily authority settled naturally on the shoulders of royal judges in many regions. In France, a pyramidal structure of local courts spread out beneath the sovereign courts (the parlement, Cour des Aides, and Chambre des Comptes) within each province. The main line of the judiciary ran from the provincial parlement to the lower appellate courts (the *présidiaux,* established under Henry II [ruled 1547–1559]) and from there to the bailiwick courts (*bailliages* in the north of France, *sénéchaussées* in the south and in Brittany). Bailiwicks were medieval jurisdictions that varied greatly in size, but they averaged roughly a hundred parishes by the later seventeenth century.

In many regions there was a final layer of petty royal courts (*vicomtés,* or 'viscounts', or *prévotés,* 'provosts') under the bailiwick courts.

Each of these local royal courts heard both civil and criminal cases and could judge customary, royal, and Roman laws. (There were some jurisdictional distinctions between them; civil cases involving large sums of money were heard first in the *présidial* or in the parlement, for example.) Each royal court was required to have a judge *(lieutenant général)* and a royal attorney *(procureur du roi),* but most attracted a full complement of assistant judges, councillors *(conseilleurs),* and royal lawyers *(avocats du roi),* all venal offices. This meant that France's judiciary was perhaps the densest bureaucracy in early modern Europe, with provinces like Normandy or Brittany supporting several thousand officials and functionaries each.

Most royal judicial officials enjoyed considerable independence from the crown. While the state provided letters accepting candidates into office, in practice almost all local offices were passed between individual buyers, without the intervention of the crown. The king did set minimum educational requirements for judges and attorneys, but the corps accepting them was supposed to inquire into their qualifications, morals, and religious practices, allowing them to vet (and sometimes reject) candidates for a variety of reasons. Lower court offices tended to be significantly less expensive than judgeships in the sovereign courts, but they did not confer personal or hereditary nobility on their buyers. (Nevertheless, a significant number of bailiwick judges were already noble before buying a judgeship.) In theory, all lower court cases could be appealed up from the bailiwicks to the *présidial* or parlement, but in practice only infamous criminal cases and civil cases involving officers, nobles, or wealthy elites tended to be appealed there. The vast majority of litigation was settled within the bailiwick (jurisdiction of a lower-court judge).

The authority of local judges was considerable by the seventeenth century. In France, bailiwick judges and king's prosecutors were often the only resident royal officers in the countryside. They became administrators par excellence, supervising matters as diverse as the upkeep of bridges, roads, and chimneys, tavern hours, bread riots, and public order in general. They also policed markets, prices, and the guilds, performing essential economic regulation. In many regions they held minor military responsibilities, too, for raising the militia. Above the bailiwick judges, the magistrates in the provincial parlements (in tandem with the provincial Estates where they existed), also exercised a broad governing role in the countryside. But these magistrates only rarely intervened in local administration outside of the city where the parlement resided, and the bailiwick remained the central unit of local governance. Unlike in England, there was relatively little interaction between the sovereign courts of parlement and the lower courts that served the majority of the population. The professional and social gap between the two main levels of the judiciary widened after the middle of the seventeenth century, leaving local judges little role to play in national affairs.

Alongside the main royal courts in France, there were hundreds of specialized jurisdictions handling everything from tax cases (the *élections*), crimes on the high roads, and army deserters (the *maréchaussée,* or mounted constabulary courts) to woods and waters cases (*eaux et fôrets,* or water and forest courts). In one district that covered a third of Normandy, there were more than seventy special royal jurisdictions outside the main (parliamentary) branch of the judiciary. These were further complicated by more than 228 seigneurial high justices and dozens of ecclesiastical courts, but the confusion was more apparent than real by the middle of the seventeenth century. Although the tax courts remained vigorous, cases from many specialized jurisdictions were gradually swallowed up by the bailiwick courts over the course of the seventeenth century, making the bailiwick courts an increasingly important center of gravity for local governance.

Although French and other continental courts have often been criticized as despotic institutions, run by venal officeholders and lacking juries or criminal defense lawyers, the reality was considerably more nuanced. Local courts were thoroughly embedded in local society through their officials, attorneys, and functionaries. Even a relatively modest bailiwick court might have between twenty and fifty minor functionaries and lawyers drawn from the ranks of farmers, cottagers, and even weavers. Notaries, solicitors, sergeants, ushers, jailers, keepers of weights and measures—all anchored the courts in local society. Judges were typically drawn from owners of *sieuries* or *seigneuries,* the equivalent of the English gentry, and king's attorneys came from similar or slightly lower backgrounds. Criminal procedures and some civil procedures were deeply dependent on the willingness of witnesses in the community to come forward and give testimony. Finally, judges frequently used the flexible legal tools of equity (judicial reason, as opposed to statutory law), discretionary sentencing, and community reputation when deciding cases. French local courts rarely pronounced death sentences and even more rarely actually executed them, even for crimes in which capital punishment was allowed. In Spain, local judges who were also venal officials exercised considerable discretion in applying royal edicts (the *Recopilación de los Leyes de España,* or 'Compilation of Spanish Laws') and in executing a harsh penal code. Given that the primary function of these courts was to regulate property, family, and other civil cases according to customary laws, they often functioned reasonably well in stabilizing communities and families and in keeping public order.

In England, justices of the peace (JPs), like French bailiwick judges, had become the preeminent judicial and administrative officers in the counties by the late fourteenth century. Meeting four times a year in quarter sessions, usually in the county town, JPs initially heard felony indictments and judged misdemeanors. There were approximately five thousand of them in the counties. The English crown, seizing on the usefulness of these unpaid officials, passed over three hundred statutes by 1600 that expanded the justices' governing powers in every direction. They were responsible above all for keeping order in the countryside, including quelling riots, controlling vagabonds, punishing extortion, prosecuting poachers, and helping with the military muster when necessary. JPs regulated the local economy as well, setting wages and prices, licensing taverns, and regulating weights and measures. Social and religious regulation was an increasingly large part of their brief. Justices gradually became responsible for enforcing the poor laws, sumptuary legislation, and religious laws. Finally, they were essential to the financial machinery of the state, because tax collection in the counties was partly under their supervision.

During the sixteenth century, the growth of litigation and the increasing burden of their responsibilities led JPs to use petty sessions, often every six weeks, to transact business. The number of JPs also rose dramatically in the sixteenth century, to as many as eighty in some shires. Given their broad governing powers, JPs were almost universally drawn from the gentry and had to meet property qualifications in most cases. They were given their commissions annually by the crown (the Commission of the Peace), although they were usually chosen by the lord chancellor, and they could be dismissed for political reasons. By the seventeenth century, an important segment of the House of Commons was made up of local JPs, and those not serving in Parliament were still expected to play an important role during elections. Their ties to the national government, through the common law, the assize sessions, elections, and Parliament made them not only the backbone of local government, but the core of English national government.

Twice a year, judges and senior lawyers (sergeants-at-law) from the common-law courts in London held assize sessions in the counties, riding the six circuits of England. Spending one or two days in each county town, they heard both cases sent up by the local JPs and cases sent down by the common-law courts at Westminster for trial. By the sixteenth century they typically heard criminal felony cases (such as murder and treason) as well as civil lawsuits sent back for jury trial from the courts of Common Pleas and King's Bench. They asked grand juries to give presentments of any malefactors or suspects in the jurisdiction and sat with petty juries to pass judgment on civil and criminal cases. Trials were usually brief (sometimes lasting minutes), and criminal defendants were not allowed legal counsel. On the other hand, relatively few convicted criminals were actually hanged by the assizes for offenses that technically merited the death penalty. Executions in England declined dramatically after 1630.

One of the notable features of English justice was the use of petty and grand juries to establish the facts and decide on guilt or innocence in trials. Grand juries (or presentment juries) were called at each assize to present suspected criminals or crimes in the jurisdiction. Grand juries typically had twenty-three members, mostly drawn from the lesser gentry. If the members determined that there was a "true bill," or reasonable case to be heard, it was sent to the petty jury for judgment. Petty juries, comprised of twelve men (a number with religious overtones), were typically made up of yeoman farmers and occasionally husbandmen. They were impaneled by JPs at petty sessions and quarter sessions, as well as by circuit judges at the assizes. Common law required unanimity in verdicts by juries. Although possibly Norman in origin, juries were increasingly used after the church abolished trial by ordeal in 1215. The level of popular participation in the English law courts was further increased by the appointment of constables who were usually yeoman farmers and of lawyers who typically came from the small landowners or lesser gentry.

URBAN COURTS

Urban courts were often an offshoot of city councils. In cities as distinct as Amsterdam in the Dutch Republic, Venice in the Venetian Republic, and the free imperial city of Lübeck in the Holy Roman Empire, courts were run by the regents or town councillors. These were the same men who also made city laws and enforced them. Judicial, legislative, and executive functions were thus gathered into the hands of the same elites. In France, the main urban courts (the *bailliages* and *sénéchausées*, or bailiwick courts, in most cities) were instead integrated into the royal judicial system and filled with venal crown officers. Some French cities also had royal provosts who shared jurisdiction with the bailiwick courts. Many large commercial towns in Europe had merchants' courts as well. The Dutch East India Company's High Court of Justice, like French mercantile courts, allowed merchants to judge their peers. Urban guilds typically had their own internal courts to police their apprentices, journeymen, and even masters. Although these were informal courts, they were highly effective in policing the members of their crafts through a variety of fines and even banishment from the trade or from a region.

SEIGNEURIAL AND MANORIAL COURTS

During the chaos of the Middle Ages, tens of thousands of nobles across Europe won the hereditary privilege of holding law courts on their estates. These *seigneuries,* or 'privileged properties', typically were given rights of low, middle, or high justice. Low justice was considered to be inherent in the seigneury, and it allowed landlords to judge disputes over rents or other obligations with their tenants. Middle justice was hazily defined but typically included a broader civil and criminal jurisdiction over tenants. High justice endowed the seigneurial court with the right to judge almost all civil and criminal cases, including those warranting the penalty of death. They ranged dramatically in size as well as in power. Some courts held jurisdiction over only a part of one parish, while the jurisdiction of great nobles could extend over several hundred parishes and effectively function as lower-level state courts. In Brittany, an unusually dense region for seigneurial courts, there was roughly one seigneurial court per parish. Over France as a whole, there were somewhere between fifty and seventy thousand seigneurial courts. In England, these were known as manorial courts or courts leet, and their jurisdiction was largely eroded by state courts during the seventeenth century. In Spain, by contrast, landlords continued to exercise justice over their tenants well past the early modern period.

The crown always retained some residual powers over high justices. In France, a high justice could only be created by the king, and kings in fact continued to do so for the revenues (Louis XIV [ruled 1643–1715] created more than ninety high justices in Normandy alone). The crown also forbade seigneurs to judge in their own courts or to hold court in the manor house. Judges of French high justices were required to have a law degree and to be confirmed by the provincial parlement after 1680; in the 1770s Prussia also set minimum qualifications for seigneurial judges. Nevertheless, French seigneurial justice retained a high degree of independence in most regions. Despite a royal edict that required certain royal cases *(cas royaux)* like counterfeiting and treason to be heard in royal courts in the first instance, these were exceptionally rare crimes in rural areas and had very little effect on the seigneurial courts' real jurisdiction.

Despite the apparent conflict between royal courts and landlords' courts in early modern Europe, the theory that the state set out to deprive seigneurial courts of jurisdiction does not hold up on closer inspection. In France the crown was interested in regulating seigneurial justice and bringing it into line with professional standards used in the royal courts, precisely because it was so integral to the functioning of justice. Seigneurial courts, whatever their defects, were relatively cheap, accessible, and run at the expense of the seigneur rather than the crown. They were also increasingly run by the same personnel as royal courts. Many seigneurial court judgeships were actually held by officials and attorneys in the royal courts who were moonlighting in multiple jurisdictions. Last but not least, private seigneurial courts were increasingly owned by noble royal officials, including almost all the judges of the parlements by the middle of the seventeenth century. In Austria, Joseph II (ruled 1760–1790) felt compelled to order landowners to continue providing justice on their estates in 1786, because landlords were increasingly uninterested in the trouble and expense.

While French low justices gradually lost many of their clients during the seventeenth century, high justices tended to remain vigorous jurisdictions, and the largest of them sometimes operated as the bailiwick court for their districts. English manor courts (courts leet), by contrast, gradually lost both criminal and civil jurisdiction to the quarter sessions and assizes in the seventeenth century. Misdemeanors and capital crimes both went to the royal courts by about 1600.

CHURCH COURTS

Catholic and Protestant churches alike maintained their own internal courts and laws that governed the clergy and the faithful. The Catholic Church had developed an elaborate canon law based on Roman law procedures. Popes were also energetic lawmakers, adding to church law through papal bulls or decretals (papal decrees on points of canon law). Canon laws were enforced through a system of ecclesiastical courts that ran throughout the entire church hierarchy but whose center of gravity was usually the diocese or archdiocese. For serious infractions, the church could punish misbehavior with excommunication (for individuals) and interdicts (for regions or groups of people), which barred the accused from receiving most sacraments. Well before 1450, however, the jurisdiction of church courts over morals cases and crimes was being pushed back in centralizing monarchies like France and England. Judgments in church courts could increasingly be appealed to royal courts, under procedures like the *appel comme d'abus* ('abuse summons') in France, which further undermined their powers.

The church's concern with heresy had led to the establishment of exceptional tribunals using inquisitorial procedures in the high Middle Ages (1231). The Roman inquisition (and later the Spanish Inquisition) were central tribunals staffed by inquisitors, usually drawn from the Dominican and, later, the Franciscan orders. Inquisitorial procedure allowed judges to seek cases out rather than to wait for cases to be brought to them. The procedure also allowed suspects to be tried secretly, without known witnesses or defense attorneys. The Inquisition was particularly notorious, however, for approving the use of torture to extract confessions if other forms of proof were not sufficient. (Indeed, the accused could not have found lawyers in any case because it was a crime to aid heretics). Fewer than two or three thousand individuals were probably executed in Europe throughout the Inquisition's existence, but enormous amounts of property were seized, especially in Spain, where the Inquisition was used to root out both Moorish and Jewish communities.

Protestant churches also policed morals through internal courts. The Dutch Reformed church's consistories, for example, regularly issued summonses for adultery, drunkenness, suspicious bankruptcies, and disruptive behavior (even summoning Rembrandt's mistress for adultery). The penalties included exclusion from the sacraments and loss of public reputation. Ecclesiastical courts in England (sometimes called "bawdy courts") policed sexual and moral behaviors through a combination of canon law, Roman law, and ecclesiastical common law, but these cases were increasingly being handled by justices of the peace. By the late eighteenth century, ecclesiastical courts no longer had jurisdiction over the laity.

LAW CODES

Legal systems in Europe had grown up organically out of the mixture of Roman, tribal, and church law systems imposed on the landscape. Like court jurisdictions, law codes accurately reflected the divided sovereignty of most regions, in which landlords, the church, and the state all exercised some public powers. Four main legal systems stood out, however, in the mosaic of codes in use across Europe. These were Roman law (drawn particularly from Justinian's *Digests* and *Institutes,* c. 533 C.E.), customary law (derived from medieval tribal codes), positive law (created by sovereigns, parliaments, or cities), and canon law (ecclesiastical law). While Roman law tended to remain most vital in the regions of southern Europe occupied by the Roman Empire, especially Italy and the south of France, elements of Roman law seeped into numerous law codes across Europe. Most Habsburg hereditary territories as well as the Low Countries were under mixed Roman and Germanic customary laws. By corollary, Roman law in the south of France was recognized by many eighteenth-century jurists as having developed into the customary law of the south, because it had gradually been transformed through long usage.

These dominant varieties of law were typically combined with minor codes, creating distinctive legal patterns that sometimes varied from parish to parish. In England, the early-seventeenth-century jurist Sir Edward Coke identified fifteen distinct types of law practiced across the realm. Most prominent among these were the common law (the general customs of the realm), manorial and borough laws (local customs), parliamentary statutes, the law merchant, and canon law. Each of these types of law in fact corresponded closely to a separate set of English courts. The common law was thus the law administered by the main royal courts sitting at Westminster, as well by the county assizes and quarter sessions, making it the dominant legal code.

This relative legal uniformity in England was furthered by the centralization of legal training in London at the eight Inns of Chancery and four Inns of Court. The Inns of Court (Grey's, Lincoln's, Inner Temple, and Middle Temple) were residences for lawyers during the four annual sessions of the Westminster courts, but they also provided lectures and training for students. No lawyer could plead before the superior courts without being first called to the bar at one of the Inns of Court; and, by extension, no judges in the superior courts or assize circuits could practice without having trained there as well.

England's was a remarkably organized legal system by continental standards, however. The positive laws of the French crown numbered over 800,000 by 1715. Despite their impressive number, though, they primarily gave the crown legal control over state administration and taxes. The vast majority of cases heard in the kingdom were, in fact, regulated by more than three hundred provincial and local customary codes and by thousands of seigneurial privileges or microcustoms that varied from one seigneury to the next. Customary laws dominated provincial legal proceedings; in some local bailiwicks, no more than about 2 percent of all cases involved positive royal laws. Because they governed property, family, and inheritances in France, they were naturally the laws used by ordinary people engaged in litigation. Customary laws and usages were codified with the crown's permission in the late sixteenth century, but they were largely impervious to state intervention until the French Revolution.

One of the most innovative regions in Europe with respect to law was the Dutch Republic. After the seven provinces broke with Spain to form the Union of Utrecht in 1579, a new legal framework had to be established for the fledgling state. Universities with law faculties were founded in several provinces, beginning with Leiden in 1575. Roman law became the lodestone of Dutch legal practice, but it was pragmatically combined with Germanic customary law, natural law, and the new statutes of the state by jurists and scholars. The provinces each retained their traditional system of lower courts and High Courts, like the Hooge Raad (High Court) of Holland, and flexibly adapted the new legal system to existing provincial customs.

From 1450 to 1789 two main patterns emerged in European law. The first was the rising tide of positive laws issued by sovereigns and local governments, which attempted to more minutely control the political, economic, and even social behavior of their subjects. By the late seventeenth and eighteenth centuries, attempts to codify laws were under way in states as different as Prussia, Russia, Austria, and France. Prussia's was the most successful attempt, producing the *Preussisches Allgemeines Landrecht* (Prussian General Common Law) in 1794, but almost everywhere the attempt foundered on the strength of customary laws, the vested interests of prominent social groups, or the lack of police and judicial officers to enforce them. The codifiers and law commissions paved the way for Napoleon's Code Civil in 1804, however, and for numerous European legal codes that were forged in its wake.

The second pattern was the dramatic increase in litigation across much of Europe, particularly in the sixteenth and seventeenth centuries. Suits in the English courts of Common Pleas and King's Bench increased tenfold between 1500 and 1600. Litigation peaked in England and France from the mid- to late seventeenth century, then saw falling caseloads in the eighteenth century. The increase in litigation probably had multiple causes: increasingly complex laws, the growing pace of commercial and property transactions, rising literacy, and the growth of trained lawyers and jurists to handle cases. The decline of litigation in the eighteenth century is still a mysterious and ill-understood phenomenon, but the overall trends toward sophisticated law codes and increasingly large and wealthy legal classes reflected societies that had become increasingly driven by the rule of law during the early modern period.

See also **Absolutism; Crime and Punishment; Divorce; Inheritance and Wills; Inquisition; Marriage; Parlements; Provincial Government; Star Chamber; Sumptuary Laws; Torture.**

BIBLIOGRAPHY

Anderson, M. S. *Europe in the Eighteenth Century, 1713–1789.* Harlow, U.K., and New York, 2000.

Beik, William. *Absolutism and Society in Seventeenth-Century France: State Power and Provincial Aristocracy in Languedoc.* Cambridge, U.K., and New York, 1985.

Cockburn, J. S. *A History of English Assizes, 1558–1714.* Cambridge, U.K., 1972.

Collins, James B. *The State in Early Modern France.* Cambridge, U.K., and New York, 1995.

Crubaugh, Anthony. *Balancing the Scales of Justice: Local Courts and Rural Society in Southwest France, 1750–1800.* University Park, Pa., 2001.

Dawson, J. P. *A History of Lay Judges.* Cambridge, Mass., 1960.

Dewald, Jonathan. *The Formation of a Provincial Nobility: The Magistrates of the Parlement of Rouen, 1499–1610.* Princeton, 1980.

Doyle, William. *Venality: The Sale of Offices in Eighteenth-Century France.* Oxford and New York, 1996.

Hamscher, Albert N. *The Conseil Privé and the Parlements in the Age of Louis XIV: A Study in French Absolutism.* Philadelphia, 1987.

Hay, Douglas, et al., eds. *Albion's Fatal Tree: Crime and Society in Eighteenth-Century England.* London, 1975.

Kagan, Richard L. *Lawsuits and Litigants in Castile, 1500–1700.* Chapel Hill, N.C., 1981.

Kettering, Sharon. *Judicial Politics and Urban Revolt in Seventeenth-Century France: The Parlement of Aix, 1629–1659.* Princeton, 1978.

Landau, Norma. *The Justices of the Peace, 1679–1760.* Berkeley, 1984.

Moote, Lloyd A. *The Revolt of the Judges: The Parlement of Paris and the Fronde, 1643–1652.* Princeton, 1971.

Raeff, Marc. *The Well-Ordered Police State: Social and Institutional Change through Law in the Germanies and Russia, 1600–1800.* New Haven, 1983.

Ruff, Julius R. *Crime, Justice, and Public Order in Old Régime France: The Sénéchausées of Libourne and Bazas, 1696–1789.* London, and Dover, N.H., 1984.

Sharpe, J. A. *Crime in Early Modern England, 1550–1750.* New York, 1999.

Stein, Peter. *Roman Law in European History.* New York, 1999.

Strakosch, H. E. *State Absolutism and the Rule of Law: The Struggle for the Codification of Civil Law in Austria, 1753–1811.* Sydney, 1967.

Weisser, Michael. *Crime and Punishment in Early Modern Europe.* Hassocks, U.K., 1979.

ZOË A. SCHNEIDER

INTERNATIONAL LAW

Tradition has assigned the title "father of international law" to the Dutch scholar, lawyer, and diplomat Hugo Grotius (also known as Huig de Groot; 1583–1645), because his *De Iure Belli ac Pacis* (On the law of war and peace), which appeared in 1625, was the most extensive treatise on international law and relations yet written. Grotius himself recognized that there already existed a number of treatises dealing with aspects of international law and an extensive body of customary practices regulating relations between states, materials such as the law of the sea, treaties, rules of war, and treatises on the just war written by medieval scholars. These concerned relations among the states of Christian Europe, although there was some interest in the nature of relations between Christian and non-Christian, especially Muslim, societies.

A second source of writing on international law consisted of treatises, papal letters, and royal charters accompanying the European overseas expansion that began in the fifteenth century. Initially, these dealt with the legal basis for European possession of the Atlantic islands, Canaries, Azores, Cape Verde, and Madeira, as well as parts of the African mainland. Subsequently, Columbus's voyages generated even more literature about the legitimacy of European possession of the New World, beginning with three bulls that Pope Alexander VI (1492–1503) issued in 1493. These bulls drew a line of demarcation from pole to pole, dividing the New World between the Portuguese and the Spanish, assigning each monarch responsibility for sending missionaries to preach the Christian Gospel and awarding each ruler a monopoly of trade and contact with the region assigned to him.

The basis for Alexander VI's actions was the concept that all mankind formed a single community and that the pope was the judge of all mankind, judging Christians by canon (church) law, Jews by the Law of Moses, and all other people according to the natural law. The natural law consisted of that part of God's eternal law accessible to all mankind by the use of reason. While the specific terms of that law were rarely spelled out, one important element of it was the right to travel freely in peace. The refusal of an infidel society to allow Christian missionaries to enter and preach was therefore a violation of the natural law. The pope could authorize Christian rulers to protect missionaries where necessary, justifying the conquest of infidel societies. The papal conception of an international legal order was a hierarchical one with the pope serving as the ultimate judge in matters of international relations. The most extensive discussion of the Catholic conception of international order was that of the Spanish Dominican theologian Francisco de Vitoria (c. 1485–1546), whose *Relectio de Indiis* (published 1557; Concerning the American Indians) analyzed all of the arguments for and against the legitimacy of the conquest of the Americas. Vitoria was, however, only one of a number of Spanish authors who responded to the discovery of the New World with a treatise on the legal issues involved.

The Protestant Reformation changed the character of the discussion about international law because the Reformers rejected the papacy and canon law. Furthermore, Protestant scholars distinguished more clearly than did their Catholic counterparts between theological bases for international law and relations and legal ones based on human reason and experience alone. Early Protestant writers included Alberico Gentili (1552–1608), an Italian scholar who eventually became a professor at Oxford, whose *De Iure Belli* (Concerning the law of war) was a major influence on Grotius's work.

One fundamental difference between Catholic and Protestant writers concerned access to the sea and therefore access to trade between Europe and the New World. The Catholic position was that the pope had the right to judge all mankind, to punish violators of the natural law, to assign jurisdiction over the seas to specific Christian rulers in order to ensure peace among Christian nations, and to support the church's spiritual mission to the newly encountered peoples. Grotius's first work, the anonymously published *Mare Liberum* (1609; The freedom of the sea), denied that the pope or anyone else had the right to limit access to the sea. In his opinion the sea was open to all who would sail there in peace. Grotius defended the interests of Dutch merchants whose wealth depended upon access to the markets of Asia and America, restricted by papal decision to the Spanish and Portuguese and those whom these nations chose to license, as well as the interests of Dutch fishermen who desired access to the fishing grounds in the waters adjacent to Britain.

Grotius's views drew responses from Portuguese and English lawyers, who defended closing the sea, although they differed about who could do this. The Portuguese scholar Seraphinus de Freitas (d. 1622) wrote the *De Justo Imperio Lusitanorum Asiatico* (1625; Concerning the legitimate Portuguese Empire in Asia) defending Portugal's claim to a monopoly of trade with Asia based on papal authorization. William Welwood (1578–1622) and John Selden (1584–1654) wrote to defend the right of James I of England (ruled 1603–1625) to ban Dutch fishermen from the waters around the British Isles without royal license. They argued that any ruler could limit access to the adjacent waters but denied that the pope could do so universally. Eventually, European governments agreed that states possessed jurisdiction only over a zone extending three miles from the shore, a line that Cornelius Bynkershoek (1673–1743) defined as the distance that a cannon could fire.

Grotius's major work, *On the Law of War and Peace,* followed the medieval tradition of seeing mankind as a single community governed by natural law. Grotius did not base his discussion of natural law on theology or philosophy but on the actual practice of human societies as described in the historical record. Thus, while the overall principles of international law sprang from the *jus naturale* (natural law), there was also a body of specific practices and customs agreed upon by participating nations forming the *jus gentium*, the law of nations. These two laws formed the basis for a legal structure that would regulate relations among states.

Unlike his predecessors, who saw the papal court as the ultimate venue for settling international disputes, Grotius did not describe any institutions to enforce these laws. He saw each state as sovereign, that is, not subject to any external authority. He also argued, however, that it might be necessary for one state to punish the rulers of another sovereign state because they had violated the natural law. While this would seem to make Grotius a defender of expansion into the New World, in fact he showed little interest in that issue. His interest was in relations among European Christian states, not relations between the Christian and the non-Christian worlds.

The writers on international law who followed Grotius fall into two broad categories. The first continued to employ the term *natural law* but understood the term differently than Grotius. They argued that the natural law described the law that governed men when they lived in the state of nature, that is, before the formation of organized societies. They identified these societies with individuals living in a state of nature so that each human society was therefore a sovereign entity equal to all other societies, just as each man, regardless of age, strength, and intellect, was equal to every other man. There was then no basis for one society punishing another's violation of the law of nature. This school of thought included Samuel Pufendorf (1632–1694) and Emerich de Vattel (1714–1769).

The second school of international law thinkers was the positivists, who argued that international law was the product of custom and of treaties that states made with one another for the purpose of regulating their relations. This school of thought included Cornelius van Bynkershoek.

These discussions had a limited effect on the practice of European states. The flaw in such discussions was the lack of any external mechanism to enforce the law. What these works did was provide a conceptual framework and a language for creating a legal order among states. Unlike Grotius and his medieval predecessors, however, later proponents of international order restricted it to the European Christian states and did not include non-European states.

These early discussions of international law had one other effect on European thought. The Catholic writers were concerned about the relations between Christian and non-Christian societies. Was the conquest of the New World legitimate? Did the inhabitants of the Americas possess a right to govern themselves and to own property? If so, Europeans had no obvious right to conquer them. Although European thinkers did produce arguments that justified the conquest, arguing that the Indians violated the natural law, for example, they also produced arguments that defended the rights of the Indians to autonomy as well. According to these arguments, Christians could not assert a claim to all infidel lands simply on the grounds that infidels had no right to them. This became one of the bases for subsequent discussions of human rights, that is, the rights possessed by all people by virtue of their humanity.

In the final analysis, the discussion of international law in the early modern world consisted of attempts to create a legal order that would regulate relations among the various states and societies of the world. The goal was to limit, not to abolish, war and to create a framework for peaceful relations among peoples.

See also **Grotius, Hugo; Natural Law; Rights, Natural.**

BIBLIOGRAPHY

Primary Sources

Grotius, Hugo. *De Jure Belli ac Pacis Libri Tres.* Translated by Francis W. Kelsey. Washington, D.C., 1925. Reprint: Indianapolis, 1962.

Vitoria, Francisco de. *Political Writings.* Edited by Anthony Pagden and Jeremy Lawrance. Cambridge, U.K., 1991.

Secondary Sources

Brierly, J. L. *The Law of Nations: An Introduction to the International Law of Peace.* 6th ed. Oxford, 1963.

Bull, Headley, Benedict Kingsbury, and Adam Roberts, eds. *Hugo Grotius and International Relations.* Oxford, 1990.

Muldoon, James. "The Contribution of the Medieval Canon Lawyers to the Formation of International Law." *Traditio* 28 (1972): 483–497.

Tuck, Richard. *The Rights of War and Peace: Political Thought and the International Order from Grotius to Kant.* Oxford, 1999.

JAMES MULDOON

LAWYERS

The activities of early modern lawyers had much in common with those of their modern counterparts. They practiced courtroom defense, acted as political and legal counsels to princely houses, municipalities, and religious houses, and held positions in the courts and royal administration. The general economic expansion since the late Middle Ages and the accompanying growth of social and institutional complexity created a growing demand for services that could be performed only by those who possessed technical and specialized legal skills. Just as modern states employ teams of lawyers, a variety of governmental and judicial institutions of early modern states needed legally educated personnel. The functions and organization of lawyers varied over time and space, but the early modern period saw the ever-increasing presence and influence of lawyers throughout Europe.

RISE OF LAWYERS

The legal profession was already vigorous in the Italian towns of the twelfth and thirteenth centuries, fostered in part by the revival of jurisprudence in the study of Roman law. The Florentine guild of lawyers and notaries (Arte dei Giudici e Notai) dates from the early thirteenth century. The rise of lawyers in northern Europe coincided with the establishment of the supremacy of the royal courts over seigneurial and ecclesiastical jurisdictions. In France, lawyers for secular courts appeared in the mid-thirteenth century around the same time as the emergence of the sovereign court, the parlement. Feudal procedure, with its reliance on a judicial duel and ordeal, had been gradually transformed in the king's courts into accusatory procedure, where the parties were required to substantiate their claims by calling upon witnesses and producing written proof. The complexity of adversarial procedure required the intervention of legally educated personnel capable of representing the parties involved. The crowns of England and France allowed litigants in royal courts to appoint lawyers to represent them and oversee the convoluted process of trial. A legal world that became increasingly complicated thus gave rise to professional lawyers when a growing number of people depended on royal justice for vindication.

Unlike in Italy, where the legal profession was governed and regulated by the guild, lawyers in northern Europe were closely attached to the state. The French royal ordinance of 1345 set the conditions of admission to the legal profession and its duties. To become a lawyer, the candidate had to prove that he (women were excluded) had studied law at a university for years. After the judges examined candidates' learning and moral rectitude, successful candidates were sworn in and were inscribed on the official roll. Lawyers were expected to abide by certain principles of professional conduct. According to the 1345 French rule, lawyers were prohibited from assuming the defense of causes they knew to be unjust, obliged to expedite the causes they had undertaken as promptly as was possible, and prohibited from withholding evidence from the opposing parties. These injunctions, which have a familiar ring today, were apparently frequently breached. The seventeenth-century writer Bernard de La Roche Flavin deplored the fact that lawyers all too often used surprises and dirty tricks, holding the best evidence back so as to catch the opponents by surprise in front of the judge. Another rule, also repeated time and again, was to plead and write briefly. Irrepressible verbosity of lawyers—and the public's exasperation with it—goes back to the profession's formation.

DIVISION OF FUNCTIONS

The lawyers of early modern Europe were a diverse group, ranging from a small elite of learned jurists to obscure practitioners akin to legal artisans. From early on, notaries were considered to form a profession separate from lawyers. In the Italian guild of judge-lawyers and notaries, the two groups were clearly distinguished. Drawing up contracts, deeds, marriage agreements, and wills was for the most part the province of notaries. Within the practice of law a division of function developed, leading to different careers with varying qualifications and reputation. The most fundamental distinction involved the separation between those who handled the procedural aspects of a suit and those who dealt with substantive legal issues. A royal proclamation of 1547 in England restricted the right to plead before the royal courts to students of the Inns of Court. By 1600 a rigid divide had emerged between *advocati* and *procuratores* (barristers and attorneys in England, *avocats* and *procureurs* in France, *abogados* and *procuradors* in Spain). Although the distinctions between the two groups were not as clear as in the modern English or French legal profession (barrister/solicitor in England and *avocat/avoué* in France until 1971), each group held an exclusive right on a specific activity. Only the *advocatus* (hereafter 'barrister'), not *procurator* (hereafter 'attorney'), had the right to plead before the court. In England solicitors (*solicitadores* in Spain) appeared as an identifiable branch of the legal profession during the sixteenth century.

A barrister was a man formally trained in jurisprudence. He offered legal advice to clients and presented oral or written arguments to the court. Barristers' arguments touched only on questions of law supposedly requiring legal knowledge and reasoning while questions of fact were left to the attorneys. Few French *avocats,* in fact, spent much time pleading in open court, for the parlements judged most cases on the basis of written evidence. Also, French *avocats* handled only civil cases; criminal defendants were deprived of their right to counsel by the ordinance of Villers-Cotterets in 1539. The ordinance of Villers-Cotterets required the use of French in both pleadings and court rulings, but lengthy Latin quotations were not easily abandoned by the Renaissance lawyers who were all too proud of their knowledge of the classics. Less prestigious than a barrister was an attorney. His place in society was solid but lowlier. It was an attorney who was most often consulted by a client needing legal representation at the beginning of a suit. His function was to steer cases through the court and take care of the procedural details, filing motions, drawing up writs, assembling facts, and collecting evidence. The attorney handled the formalities of the lawsuits, gave clients advice, and represented their claims in court. Only when a lawsuit involved a question of law that required greater expertise would the services of a barrister be obtained. An attorney was denied the right of audience, which properly belonged to a barrister, a full-fledged jurist. In the sixteenth century there was as yet no sign of the later rule prescribing that clients contact barristers only through attorneys, but usually attorneys procured clients in the marketplace and then chose barristers. Attorneys did not necessarily train at a university, instead learning their law through clerkship or apprenticeship to other practitioners.

In the early modern period French kings openly sold royal offices to the highest bidder. In the sixteenth and seventeenth centuries the kings had forced venality upon nearly all legal occupations, magistracies included. French *procureurs* needed to purchase a venal office, but *avocats* did not become venal officers. The reason for this is not clear, but it is possible that the *avocats*' powerful clients, prominent nobles and prelates, opposed venality, lest it threaten their interests. At any rate, this exemption of *avocats* from venality conferred a certain degree of status on the bar, as admission to its ranks was perceived to emphasize learning, not money. The price of the *procureur*'s offices rose sharply during the sixteenth century when the volume of litigation increased rapidly. Established attorneys opposed creation of additional places, fearing that such expansion would decrease the value of their own offices.

BUSINESS OF LAW

The relative profitability of the legal profession and its respectable status attracted talented young men to legal careers. There are many examples of those who pursued legal studies, often pressured by their ambitious fathers, but eventually failed or abandoned them: Petrarch (1304–1374), Martin Luther (1483–1546), John Calvin (1509–1564), and Voltaire (1694–1778) were only a few. The best source of lucrative practices for barristers lay in becoming consultants to leading princely houses, ecclesiastical institutions, towns, and corporate bodies. Those who made fortunes depended heavily on the business of aristocrats, managing their vast real estate holdings and providing legal and political advice. Of those lawsuits handled by Florentine lawyers, disputes over dowries were among the most common, followed by cases dealing with the confiscation of private property due to some act of rebellion. Other cases involved litigations between religious houses or between individual clerics over benefices, disputes between local administrations, or litigations between government offices and individuals.

Little is known about legal fees. There were significant differences of income within and between members of the branches of the legal profession. From early on, lawyers claimed that the fees they charged were the result of free agreement with the clients and thus outside any state interference. The kings often attempted to prohibit excessive fees, without much success. The French Ordinance of Blois of 1579 (Art. 161) stipulated that *avocats* reveal the amount of their fees at the bottom of deliberations and court documents. In 1602 the Parlement of Paris, backed by Henry IV, revived this rule, which had fallen out of observance. Livid over what they regarded as a blow to their honor, the *avocats* waged a successful two-week boycott of the courts in protest. Faced with the collective resignation of the *avocats,* the parlement had no choice but to withdraw the measure. In general, lawyers' vested interests in the existing system and its traditions dictated their outlook and attitudes. Lawyers of early modern Europe were a tight-knit corporate group. On the eve of the French Revolution, the king simply could not break the fundamental solidarity of the jurists blocking legal reforms.

Like their modern counterparts, early modern lawyers were targets of sustained hostility. They were criticized for overcharging, fraudulently keeping clients' monies, illegally negotiating contingent fees, maliciously pursuing delays, or lodging endless appeals. Tales of shyster lawyers seem timeless. Luther, never kind to lawyers, observed that a successful jurist was a woeful Christian.

LAWYERS AND CULTURE

Men with legal training were one of the most prominent groups in early modern culture. Renaissance humanism in Italy was largely a creation of lawyers and notaries, such as Coluccio Salutati (1331–1406), Poggio Bracciolini (1380–1459), and Lorenzo Valla (c. 1406–1457). The French Renaissance displayed the close relations between humanism and the law, as represented by Guillaume Budé (1467–1540), Jean Bodin (1530–1596), Antoine Loisel (1536–1617), and Étienne Pasquier (1529–1615). Thomas More (1478–1535), Francesco Guicciardini (1483–1540), Michel de Montaigne (1533–1592), Francis Bacon (1561–1626), Giambattista Vico (1668–1744), and Montesquieu (1689–1755) were among the many lawyers who were the leading minds of their time. Equipped with humanistic education and style, and endowed with judicial dignity and political influence, lawyers were often at the forefront of intellectual inquiry and challenge in early modern Europe.

SOCIAL BACKGROUND AND CAREERS

There existed a vast social gulf within the legal profession. Historians have confirmed the overall social heterogeneity of early modern European lawyers. The commonplace observation that the law was a quick and assured means of achieving upward social mobility appears exaggerated. Social mobility was indeed possible in the legal profession, but it occurred only at a slow pace over several generations. The great majority of lawyers in Europe came from families that had acquired wealth a few generations before there was a lawyer in the household. One obvious reason that the notion of rags to riches was no more than a myth in a legal career was that education at one of the great law schools was a very expensive affair. Historians have shown that a university education in the fifteenth and sixteenth centuries was much costlier than in modern times. A doctorate in canon law normally required six years of university and in civil law seven or eight years. A large number of lawyers had doctorates in both civil and canon law, spending a minimum of ten years in study. In most cases an aspiring lawyer either had some direct contact with the profession or had grown up with material means sufficient to set off to a university in order to pursue a dignified legal career.

Recruitment from within the legal professions was common and often involved a step upward. A son of a court clerk or a notary, for example, would become an attorney, and occasionally a shopkeeper's child would enter the career of attorney. The attorney, having made his moderate fortune, was likely to send his own child to law school and to the bar. Many lawyers in the *Reichskammergericht* (imperial court of justice) in Speyer in the early sixteenth century had been *Prokuratoren* (attorneys). It was rare for a barrister's or a magistrate's son to become an attorney, moving downward in social hierarchy. Many barristers came from families already established in the law. The bar also attracted the sons of well-off merchants or urban *rentiers*. Sons of barristers used their law degrees to move even further up the hierarchy of law. In France, positions as magistrates in the inferior courts were readily open to them, and there was a chance, providing they had the money, to purchase an ennobling office in a sovereign court.

From the mid-sixteenth century the legal profession in most European countries tended to become more exclusive. Within the legal field each group was increasingly conscious of its status and took steps to protect it. Separation of attorneys from barristers was not merely a matter of the evolution of distinct procedural functions but of the differentiation of lawyers organized on the lines of education, prestige, self-perception, and family links. A doctorate required of *avocats* as well as of magistrates in the sovereign courts was one of the means to regulate entry into the higher ranks of the legal profession. Both magistrates and barristers had the strong desire to perpetuate their profession in their families, and there existed a high degree of continuity of career among families involved in the practice of law. The law faculties in early modern Europe increasingly became the preserve of students whose fathers were, in one capacity or another, men of law. Any French magistrate who wished to guard his investment in office and pass it on intact in inheritance saw to it that at least one of his sons attended a faculty of law.

In England, the gentry entered the world of justice in great numbers. In the years 1590–1640 more than half the barristers were gentry. France witnessed in the sixteenth century the emergence of noble judicial families, a *noblesse de robe*. The proportion of aristocrats among those attending law faculties in the Holy Roman Empire quadrupled at the beginning of the seventeenth century. Throughout Europe, access to higher-ranking legal offices and occupations was firmly in the possession of tightly interwoven families of lawyers, many of which formed great legal dynasties. It became rarer to rise from the ranks of attorney to barrister. Barristers from outside the close-knit network had difficulty procuring legal business and complained that certain families jealously maintained a virtual monopoly on legal practice.

AN INDEPENDENT PROFESSION

Before 1600 the French *avocats* did not have a formal bar association. The discipline of the practicing *avocats* and the protection of their collective interests were largely left to the magistrates of the parlements. Many magistrates, presidents of the parlements, and chancellors were selected from *avocats*. However, this relationship of the traditional cordiality and mutual respect between the *avocats* and magistrates began to deteriorate seriously because of venality of offices. By the early seventeenth century, high judicial offices had been made inheritable, practically becoming personal property. *Avocats* no longer had special access to magistracies; they had to purchase judgeships like others. As prices of offices increased, the prospect of becoming a judge became slim. In terms of training and social profile, barristers did not differ much from magistrates. However, the sale of offices now drew a clear line between the magistrates and *avocats*, between those who came from families of prominence and inherited wealth and who now enjoyed the title of nobility by virtue of their offices and those who saw themselves relegated into second-class citizens in the world of the law. Charles Dumoulin (1500–1566), the great French jurist of customary law, blamed his struggling career as an *avocat* at the Parlement of Paris on venality. He bitterly claimed that he, a brilliant scholar, was being ignored in his own country simply because he did not choose (rather, could not afford) to purchase a judicial office. The kings recruited the members of royal councils and administration in large part from the parlements, and the proportion of lawyers acceding to the highest public offices declined after the mid-sixteenth century. Furthermore, the *avocats* faced added competition from officeholders who, often in debt after acquiring their position, actively sought business from princely houses as counselors.

The social and moral crisis suffered by the *avocats* eventually brought about a significant redefinition and redirection of the profession. The emergence of the independent Order of Barristers in France in the 1660s represented a step toward professionalization of the lawyers. The order set down standards of conduct and disciplined its members. Aspiring *avocats* now needed to complete a two-year internship to obtain practical skills before gaining formal acceptance by the order. Lawyers, responding to a crisis in their profession, embraced a modern sense of professionalism, a concern for high ethical standards and occupational competence.

LITIGATION AND LAWYERS

The changing culture of litigation in early modern Europe overall contributed to the emergence of professional consciousness among lawyers. The favorable economic and demographic climate of the sixteenth century resulted in a marked increase in litigation and an almost explosive rise in the number of lawyers. England saw an enormous increase in central court litigation between 1560 and 1640. Business in King's Bench increased fourfold between 1560 and 1580, and more than doubled between 1580 and 1640. Historians have noted a sharp rise in litigation in Castile beginning in the late fifteenth century and continuing almost uninterrupted until the second quarter of the seventeenth century. In England the years between 1558 and 1640 witnessed a steady increase in the number of admissions to the four Inns of Court, from around fifty per year in the early sixteenth century to about three hundred in the later years of the reign of James I. Matriculations in the law faculties soared during the sixteenth century throughout Europe, more than doubling the number of graduates in less than fifty years. Between five thousand and six thousand students were enrolled each year in the law faculties of Salamanca and Valladolid; in 1617 there were five thousand law students in Naples. In France during the reigns of Louis XIII and Louis XIV, the influx of students into the faculties of law was so copious that many reformers, including Jean-Baptiste Colbert, were concerned that it would hamper the development of a commercial class.

This century-long expansion of lawyers began to recede from the mid-seventeenth century. Recent studies have linked loss of population, a stagnant economy, and rising court costs to contraction in litigation and a corresponding decrease in the number of lawyers in the late seventeenth century. The shrinking number of suits was reflected in the decline of the universities' once prosperous law faculties. From Spain and England to the provinces of the Netherlands and the Holy Roman Empire, the stream of students in law faculties fell steadily during the eighteenth century.

The downturn in legal business brought about a significant change in the legal profession. A negative economic climate and business retrenchment meant that lawyers, in order to carve out a living from the law, needed to reconfigure their activities and recast their relations with society as a whole. Faced with professional uncertainty, shrinking sources of income, and growing competition, lawyers developed a new professional model, one based on occupational competence, competitiveness, self-regulation, a heightened sense of identity, and claims to special knowledge and expertise. The study of law had attracted not only students interested in a professional legal career but also sons of the gentry and the nobility for whom legal training represented a broad preparation for life. In England, fewer than 10 percent of those attending the Inns of Court at the beginning of the seventeenth century truly aimed at practice as a barrister. In the seventeenth and eighteenth centuries fewer than half of the lawyers in the Netherlands were active in their profession. In France thousands of men held the title of *avocat* in the seventeenth century, but only a small percentage of them practiced law, many holding the title for purely decorative reasons. In the eighteenth century, however, legal study became a relentlessly practical training of vocational nature. Being a law graduate and becoming a lawyer now meant a profession, not a mere status or ornament.

The legal profession in early modern Europe underwent long-term evolution. By the end of the eighteenth century, lawyers possessed most of the criteria associated with a modern career. The increasing professionalization of this old occupation played an essential role in the development of the law itself and the differentiation of the legal systems of modern Europe.

See also **Crime and Punishment.**

BIBLIOGRAPHY

Primary Sources

La Roche Flavin, Bernard de. *Treize livres des parlemens de France.* Geneva, 1621.

Loisel, Antoine. *Pasquier; ou, Dialogue des advocats du Parlement de Paris.* Paris, 1602. Edited by André Dupin. Paris, 1844.

Secondary Sources

Acerra, Martine. "Les avocats du Parlement de Paris (1661–1715)." *Histoire, économie et société* 2 (1982): 213–225.

Amelang, James S. "Barristers and Judges in Early Modern Barcelona: The Rise of a Legal Elite." *The American Historical Review* 89 (1984): 1264–1284.

Bell, David A. *Lawyers and Citizens: The Making of a Political Elite in Old Regime France.* New York, 1994.

Berlanstein, Lenard R. *The Barristers of Toulouse in the Eighteenth Century (1740–1793).* Baltimore, 1975.

Bouwsma, William J. "Lawyers and Early Modern Culture." *The American Historical Review* 78 (1973): 303–327.

Brooks, Christopher W. *Lawyers, Litigation and English Society since 1450.* London, 1998.

Cipolla, Carlo. "The Professions: The Long View." *The Journal of European Economic History* 2 (1973): 37–52.

Delachenal, Roland. *Histoire des avocats au Parlement de Paris, 1300–1600.* Paris, 1885.

Dolan, Claire. "Entre les familles et l'état: Les procureurs et la procédure au XVIe siècle." *Journal of the Canadian Historical Association* 10 (1999): 19–36.

Kagan, Richard L. "Law Students and Legal Careers in Eighteenth-Century France." *Past & Present* 68 (1975): 38–72.

——. *Lawsuits and Litigants in Castile, 1500–1700.* Chapel Hill, N.C., 1981.

Karpik, Lucien. *French Lawyers: A Study in Collective Action, 1274 to 1994.* Translated by Nora Scott. Oxford, 1999.

Martines, Lauro. *Lawyers and Statecraft in Renaissance Florence.* Princeton, 1968.

Prest, Wilfrid, ed. *Lawyers in Early Modern Europe and America.* New York, 1981.

Ranieri, Filippo. "From Status to Profession: The Professionalisation of Lawyers as a Research Field in Modern European Legal History." *The Journal of Legal History* 10 (1989): 180–190. Translation of "Vom Stand zum Beruf: Die Professionalisierung des Juristenstandes als Forschungsaufgabe der europäischen Rechtsgeschichte der Neuzeit" in *Ius Commune* 13 (1985): 83–105.

MARIE SEONG-HAK KIM

ROMAN LAW

Roman law consists of the law of the Roman Republic and Empire, from the *Twelve Tables* (c. 451–450 B.C.E.) to the *Corpus Juris Civilis* (Body of the Civil Law) of the sixth century C.E. Within the context of Roman law, the term *civil law* is usually used specifically to refer to the *Corpus Juris Civilis,* the compilation that was ordered by Emperor Justinian I (ruled 527–565 C.E.) and directed by the jurist Tribonian.

SOURCES AND ORGANIZATION

Roman law grew amorphously from several sources over a thousand years. These sources were divided into unwritten law *(ius non scriptum)* and written law *(ius scriptum).* Unwritten law referred to custom in Roman times, although by the early modern period in Europe, customs were accepted as written law in many places. Written law for the Romans was divided into six categories: acts *(leges),* resolutions or plebeian statutes *(plebiscita),* senate resolutions *(senatus consulta),* imperial laws or constitutions *(constitutiones principium),* magistrates' edicts *(edicta),* and jurists' responses or interpretations *(responsa prudentium).* Contradictions in the laws occurred because these numerous sources were neither coordinated nor routinely collected.

The early attempts to organize Roman law included the *Institutes of Gaius* in the second century C.E. and the *Theodosian Code* under Emperor Theodosius II in 438 C.E., but these were incomplete. The final compilation of the *Corpus Juris Civilis* under Justinian in the sixth century was issued in four parts: the *Digest* (533), the collection of judicial interpretations of the laws; the *Code* (534), the imperial laws and rescripts Tribonian's committee chose to keep; the *Institutes* (533), a condensed version to be used by first-year law students; and the *Novels* (until 565), new imperial laws.

MEDIEVAL ROMAN LAW

Roman law continued to influence European law after the fall of the Western Roman Empire to Germanic tribal rule, but it did so not as territorial law but as merely the personal law of the section of the population claiming to be Roman rather than Germanic. Among the Germanic kingdoms of western Europe, rulers such as the Visigothic kings of Spain used vulgarized forms of Roman law for their Roman subjects. The basis for these laws was usually the *Theodosian Code* rather than Justinian's, since the former was disseminated before the collapse of the Western Roman Empire. Justinian's corpus was not compiled until after Roman power was largely lost in the West. Roman law also influenced western Europe, because it was used as the basis of canon (church) law in the *Corpus Juris Canonici* (Body of Canon Law), and Roman civil and canon law also became the basis of the *ius commune,* a set of legal principles generally accepted throughout Europe. Within each developing state of the late Middle Ages and the early modern period, Roman law had varying impact on local and royal laws, depending on the geographical proximity to the old Roman imperial areas and individual developments within the separate states.

Although it was taught continuously in the East, it was not until the late eleventh century that the West rediscovered the *Corpus Juris Civilis* of Justinian, and the text was then studied and taught at the medieval universities throughout western Europe beginning in the twelfth century. This new study of the *Corpus Juris Civilis* began in Bologna, Italy, at the university's law school, and it became popular for a number of reasons. The Roman Empire of Justinian and the medieval Holy Roman Empire were conflated in the minds of many. Justinian was seen as a Holy Roman Emperor and his laws as imperial legislation. In addition, twelfth-century jurists recognized that Roman law represented a high development of legal thought, and they saw Roman law as "written reason" and hence superior to other law.

University scholars not only studied the *Corpus Juris Civilis,* they also added their own explanations and interpretations, which often became as important as the original text. The earliest of these scholars were known as the glossators, who wrote marginal or interlinear comments called glosses on the entire text of Justinian. In this process they discovered some inconsistencies and contradictions that Tribonian's hurried committee had not managed to eliminate. Glossators tried to resolve such discrepancies by interpretation. Between 1220 and 1250 the glossator Franciscus Accursius compiled a collection of selected glosses, which became known as the *Glossa ordinaria* (or *Magna glossa*).

Following the glossators were the commentators (or postglossators). They did not merely continue the glossators' work but also contributed their own legal knowledge by writing original commentaries on the *Corpus Juris Civilis* and the *Glossa ordinaria.* They also applied the law to their own time by writing legal opinions in response to questions concerning real cases. Two of the most significant of the early commentators were Bartolus of Saxoferrato and Baldus of Ubaldis. The commentators were most active in the fourteenth and fifteenth centuries, and, like the glossators, most were Italian.

RENAISSANCE HUMANISM AND ROMAN LAW

New approaches to Roman law developed with Renaissance humanism in the fifteenth and sixteenth centuries. Humanists applied philological techniques to the study of the Roman law to determine what it had been meant to say, and they also studied the laws and their meaning in the original context of Rome. Although begun in Italy with the work of Andrea Alciato, this movement reached its height in the French historical school of law in the sixteenth century. Because of their humanist approach, these scholars were able to see the *Corpus Juris Civilis* in historical context, as a product of its own time and place. They saw it as useful but not infallible, and their work identified many problems in the law itself and in the medieval studies of it. Guillaume Budé, Jacques Cujas, Hugues Doneau, and François Hotman, among others, contributed to this movement in France, as did Ulrich Zasius in Germany. Hotman's *Anti-Tribonian* (1567) was particularly critical of Justinian's compilation and elevated French law in its place. These scholars established the historicity of Roman law and removed its claim to authority over contemporary societies, even though it could still be seen to a certain extent as "written reason."

ROMAN LAW IN FRANCE, GERMANY, AND GREAT BRITAIN

France. Italy and southern France were the areas most continuously influenced by Roman law because they had been governed by the Romans themselves and by Germanic versions of Roman law codes. These were also areas where universities developed early, as did Renaissance humanism. Southern France had adopted Roman law and was known as the land of the written law *(pays de droit écrit),* while the northern two-thirds of France was subject to diverse local customary laws *(pays de droit coutumier).* This caused some tension, and French legal humanists tried to resolve some of the problems by carefully applying Roman law. French kings continually tried to increase the uniformity of the country's laws in the sixteenth through eighteenth centuries. Roman law sometimes provided the source of these common laws, but so did the Custom of Paris, which was often seen as a more appropriate source for France. Partly under influence of the "written reason" of the *Corpus Juris Civilis,* the French tried to codify their customs, frequently using the organization of Roman law as a model for the structure, if not for the laws themselves. This is particularly notable in Antoine Loisel's *Institutes Coutumieres* (1607) and Étienne Pasquier's *L'interprétation des institutes de Justinian* (1609).

Germany. In Germany, the reception of Roman law began around 1500, when the *ius commune* was given precedence over local customs in the imperial supreme court. Use of Roman law in this form was particularly attractive in the Holy Roman Empire, because there were over three hundred independent local jurisdictions, some quite backward administratively. Roman law provided a model for them and also created some form of unity in the fragmented empire.

Great Britain. Scotland had introduced Roman law indirectly in the form of *ius commune,* because it was distinct from English common law, and the Scots wished to establish their independence from English control. English common law developed independently from Roman law, but some courts in England, the Equity and Admiralty Courts, for example, were influenced by Roman law, at least in the form of the *ius commune* or through canon law, which church courts continued to use in England even after the Reformation.

THE WIDER INFLUENCE OF ROMAN LAW

The growth of the influence of Roman law was a gradual and continuous historical process; the law was adapted to territories well beyond those its Roman originators could have imagined and to uses of which they had not conceived. The Spanish acceptance of Roman law meant that it spread beyond western Europe and came to the Spanish territories of the New World.

Roman law was used to support various, even opposing, ideas. For instance, its maxims could support both absolutism and popular government: while the maxim "What pleases the prince has the force of law" *(Quod principi placuit legis habet vigorem)* was used as an argument for royal absolutism in various countries, on the other hand, "What touches all must be decided by all" *(Quod omnes tangit, ab omnibus approbetur)* was used to justify representative government and even rebellion against oppressive regimes. Roman law's influence persisted beyond the end of the early modern period, as it served as the main model for Napoleon Bonaparte's Civil Code (1804).

See also **Budé, Guillaume; Humanists and Humanism.**

BIBLIOGRAPHY

Primary Sources

Krueger, Paul, ed. *Justinian's Institutes.* Translated by Peter Birks and Grant McLeod. Ithaca, N.Y., 1987. The *Institutes* is the Roman law work that is most accessible to the beginner in legal studies. This is one of several editions.

Mommsen, Theodor, and Paul Krueger, eds. *The Digest of Justinian.* 4 vols. Philadelphia, 1985. English translation edited by Alan Watson. The Latin and English texts are on opposing pages.

Scott, S. P., trans. and ed. *The Civil Law: Including the Twelve Tables, the Institutes of Gaius, the Rules of Ulpian, the Opinions of Paulus, the Enactments of Justinian, and the Constitutions of Leo.* 17 vols. in 7. Cincinnati, Ohio, 1932. Reprint, New York, 1973.

Watson, Alan, ed. *The Digest of Justinian.* 2 vols. Philadelphia, 1998. Revision of Watson's 1985 English translation.

Secondary Sources

Bellomo, Manlio. *The Common Legal Past of Europe, 1000–1800.* Translated by Lydia G. Cochrane. Washington, D.C., 1995.

Caenegem, R. C. van. *An Historical Introduction to Private Law.* Translated by D. E. L. Johnson. Cambridge, U.K., and New York, 1988.

Merryman, John Henry. *The Civil Law Tradition: An Introduction to the Legal Systems of Western Europe and Latin America.* 2nd ed. Stanford, 1985.

Watson, Alan. *Roman Law and Comparative Law.* Athens, Ga., 1991.

KATHLEEN A. PARROW

RUSSIAN LAW

During the early modern period, Russian law was modernized, that is, it became more predictable, rational, and ascertainable. There was considerable codification and ever increasing proliferation and sophistication of judicial officials. As of 1450 Russia had largely completed its transition from an archaic or dyadic legal system, characterized by no judicial officials, composition (blood-wite, or penalty for bloodshed), and irrational modes of proof, to a triadic legal system, characterized by judges, criminal law, and rational modes of proof. The judicial officials, however, were not specialists and there were no real standing courts. Judges for particular cases were appointed on an ad hoc basis from the ranks of the service class and probably decided civil cases based on their own sense of rough justice or fairness. Perhaps the most advanced aspect of Russian law at the time was that detailed records of trials, judgments, and land transactions were maintained. Most of the early trial records involve trials over the ownership of land. Written deeds were also used and maintained to record transfers of land.

Existing alongside the grand prince's courts were ecclesiastical courts. Each of approximately thirteen bishops had his own court. The church courts had jurisdiction over the clergy in all matters and over laymen in such matters as marriage, family, inheritance, sexual crimes, heresy, and witchcraft. Monasteries also exercised judicial power over those who resided on their vast landholdings.

In 1497 Ivan III of Moscow promulgated Russia's first national law code, consisting of sixty-eight articles. It was primarily a procedural guide, with numerous provisions regulating the fees that judicial officials could charge. It provided penalties for only a few crimes, such as murder. The code also provided for central courts with judges from the two highest ranks of the service class and with judicial records, to be maintained by clerks. Starting in the sixteenth century, certain permanent chancelleries, staffed primarily by clerks, became the standing central law courts. They also performed administrative functions. The chancelleries proliferated, so that by the end of the seventeenth century there were as many as 150. The jurisdiction of the chancellery courts was therefore highly fragmented. The clerks began to develop judicial expertise and kept detailed records. They also developed internal procedure manuals for judicial business. One of the chancelleries also became the repository for deeds to land.

A somewhat more comprehensive codification of civil law was issued in 1550, but this codification, like the 1497 code, was largely procedural. The 1550 code also contained further specifications of crimes and criminal penalties. But while civil trials were adversarial in nature (the two competing parties presented their evidence to a judge), criminal trials were inquisitorial; in other words, the same official was the judge and prosecutor. Criminal procedure would remain inquisitorial through the remainder of the early modern period. The clerical courts became more sophisticated as well, and in 1551 a vast codification of canon law was compiled, the so-called Hundred Chapters. As the tsar's power and bureaucracy increased, however, the independent power of the church courts was gradually circumscribed.

Legal modernization stagnated in the late sixteenth and early seventeenth centuries as the result of political turmoil, dynastic instability, and civil war. After the installation of the Romanov dynasty in 1613, the legal system and bureaucracy of the late sixteenth century was restored. The legal system, however, became the target of popular suspicion. It was perceived as subject to favoritism and corruption, particularly with respect to lawsuits over escaped serfs. In 1648 demands that the chancellery rulebooks be published became the focus of widespread civil disturbances, which culminated in the calling of an assembly to codify the laws. A vast codification was soon produced, based mainly on the chancellery rule books. The law code of 1649 was one of the most advanced codifications of its time. Its 967 articles fill over two hundred pages in a modern printed edition. For the first time the substantive law relating to landed property, serfs, slaves, and numerous other subjects was codified, along with lengthy codes of civil procedure and criminal procedure. Everyone, even slaves, had access to the courts, and legal rules were published to regulate most important relationships. The code proclaimed that it was to be applied in all cases, and it was indeed extensively cited in subsequent judgments and trial records. Among the most important, but dubious, achievements of the law code was the completion of the enserfment of the peasantry. The 1649 code was to remain Russia's basic law throughout the remainder of the early modern period.

It is important to note that this legal modernization was accomplished without lawyers or law schools and without any Western models or influences. The clerks in the chancelleries developed considerable practical expertise, but the Russian legal system and Russian law as a whole lacked the theoretical consistency of Western legal systems developed by professional lawyers.

Peter I the Great (ruled 1682–1725) substantially reformed the machinery of justice, replacing the chancelleries with nine colleges, which, like the chancelleries, performed both judicial and administrative functions. He also created the Senate, which among its other functions, served as a supreme court. These institutions remained in place throughout the remainder of the century. Peter also used law as an instrument of reform: his reforms of the civil service, armed forces, and central bureaucracy were accomplished by means of lengthy decrees and regulations. Under Peter the church courts largely lost their independence. Peter also unsuccessfully attempted to transform the law of inheritance by requiring primogeniture.

Under the influence of the Enlightenment, the idea of legal rights, particularly for the nobility, began to gain ground in the eighteenth century, culminating in the Charter to the Nobility in 1785. Throughout the early modern period, law played an important role in controlling crime and protecting the property and status of the service class. Although there were few legal rights, Russia became a state governed by elaborate published laws.

See also **Alexis I (Russia); Autocracy; Peter I (Russia); Russia.**

BIBLIOGRAPHY

Primary Sources

Dewey, H. W., trans. and ed. *Muscovite Judicial Texts, 1488–1556.* Michigan Slavic Materials, no. 7. Ann Arbor, Mich., 1966. Contains translations of the 1495 and 1550 codes.

Hellie, Richard. *The Muscovite Law Code* (Ulozhenie) *of 1649.* Irvine, Calif., and Pullman, Mich., 1988. A dual-language edition.

Secondary Sources

Weickhardt, George G. "Due Process and Equal Justice in the Muscovite Codes." *The Russian Review* 51, no. 4 (October 1992): 463–480.

———. "The Pre-Petrine Law of Property." *Slavic Review* 52, no. 4 (Winter 1993): 663–679.

GEORGE G. WEICKHARDT

LAW'S SYSTEM. A prophet of a modern credit-based economy, operating free of ties to metal currency, John Law (1671–1729) was born into a commercial family in Edinburgh, Scotland. After a rakish sojourn in London, where he narrowly escaped the hangman's noose, Law succeeded in Europe as a professional gambler, thanks to his grasp of probability theory. He also studied economics and argued in learned treatises that paper instruments should replace gold and silver as money. Only an economy free to expand its currency and fueled by credit could develop significantly. In Paris he befriended Philippe, duke of Orléans (1674–1723), himself a gambler as well as the nephew of King Louis XIV (ruled 1643–1715). When Philippe became regent of France, he turned to Law for help with the financial effects of twenty-six years of war, an empty treasury, and mountainous state debt.

Law perceived that these problems could be solved in association with each other. He planned to turn the debt into equity or shares of stock and to make the shares into paper currency, demonetizing gold and silver coin while simultaneously expanding credit. An economy thus oriented to growth would, in his view, lift itself free of debt.

Between 1716 and 1719, he created France's first national bank, the Royal Bank, and a powerful conglomerate, the Company of the West, or Mississippi Company, merging them in 1720. The former, based in Paris, established branches throughout the realm, taking in tax revenues as deposits and issuing negotiable banknotes. The latter sold shares of stock, also negotiable. It controlled tax revenues, the royal mint, and commerce with Africa, Asia, and the Americas. It assumed the state debt, turning creditors into shareholders and liabilities into assets. To encourage the public to buy company shares, some of which paid dividends of 12 percent, Law dropped interest rates to 2 percent, from 5.55 percent, a blow to fixed annuities. These elements, along with sharp restrictions on the monetary use of gold and silver, became his system.

After initial hesitations, the investing public reacted favorably. In January 1720, a share of company stock, having long since climbed nicely from its initial price of 550 livres, peaked at 10,100 livres, a real stock-market boom. Euphoric buyers, emboldened by easy credit, anticipated a share price of 20,500. Some of them became, if only briefly, "millionaires," a word coined at the time. The system took on the aspects of a Europe-wide miracle. But when Law, deeming shares overvalued, acted to reduce their price, investors turned against him in fury, and the shares tumbled in value, compromising the bank and the company. A rueful John Law left France in December 1720 and died in Venice in 1729.

Amid the ruins of the system, the state emerged as a net gainer, having lightened its debt load: urban workers, victimized by inflation, were the primary losers. The experience turned France against paper money for almost two centuries and gave historians a low opinion of the system, until recently. In the twentieth century, however, the global economy developed in the growth-oriented ways that Law anticipated, with regard to a credit base, the importance of the quantity of money, and its freedom at long last from specie.

See also **Banking and Credit.**

BIBLIOGRAPHY

Faure, Edgar. *La banqueroute de Law, 17 juillet 1720.* Paris, 1977.

Hamilton, Earl J. "Prices and Wages at Paris under John Law's System." *The Quarterly Journal of Economics* 51 (1937): 42–70.

Kaiser, Thomas E. "Money, Despotism, and Public Opinion in Early Eighteenth-Century France: John Law and the Debate on Royal Credit." *Journal of Modern History* 63 (March 1991): 1–28.

Murphy, Antoin E. *John Law: Economic Theorist and Policy-Maker.* Oxford and New York, 1997.

JOHN J. HURT

LE BRUN, CHARLES (1619–1690), French court painter and academician. After working briefly with François Perrier, Le Brun became a pupil of Simon Vouet (1590–1649). His earliest known works, such as the dynamic *Hercules and the Horses of Diomedes* of 1641 (Nottingham Castle, Nottinghamshire) reveal their influence and display a talent precocious enough to win the rare praise of Nicolas Poussin, whom Le Brun joined in 1642 on the elder artist's return to Rome. Le Brun's stay in Italy was supported for three years by the powerful Pierre Séguier, duke of Villemor and chancellor of France.

On his return to Paris, Le Brun became one of Louis XIV's painters and was one of the founders of the Académie royale de peinture et de sculpture in 1648. Not surprisingly, his patron, Séguier, was designated as the protector of the fledgling organization. Le Brun executed canvases and decorative commissions for large Parisian townhouses and religious organizations throughout the 1650s. The deaths of Perrier, Vouet, and Eustache Le Sueur by the middle of the decade—combined with the success of Le Brun's ceiling in the Galerie d'Hercule of the Hôtel Lambert—made him the unrivaled French painter of his day. A royal order of 1656 forbidding the reproduction of his works without permission provides a measure of his growing reputation.

In 1658, Le Brun began the decorations at the château of Vaux-le-Vicomte for Nicolas Fouquet, the minister of finance. His responsibilities grew to include the direction of the embellishment of the country palace. Three years later, when Louis XIV imprisoned Fouquet for embezzlement of state funds (soon after viewing the results of Le Brun's lavish efforts), the artist and most of his collaborators were quickly employed by the king in the royal household, especially at Versailles (beginning in 1669), where Le Brun would produce his most celebrated works in the Hall of Mirrors, the Ambassador's Staircase, and the Royal Chapel. Le Brun's part in the transformation of this former hunting lodge into the premier palace of Europe included supervising and supplying designs to an enormous team of painters, sculptors, gardeners, architects, and decorative artists, as well as executing vast stretches of painted surfaces glorifying his royal patron (*modello* for *The Second Conquest of Franche-Comté,* early 1680s, Musée National de Versailles). His commissions soon expanded to the Louvre and other royal residences.

Le Brun's brilliant success as both artist and administrator may be a reflection of his absorption of the effective studio organization he witnessed at first hand during his years as a student in Vouet's busy atelier. His perfect blend of talents led to his ennoblement in 1662, his appointment as director

Charles Le Brun. *Chancellor Séguier.* THE ART ARCHIVE/MUSÉE DU LOUVRE PARIS/DAGLI ORTI

of the Gobelins manufactory in 1663 (the division of the royal household that supplied most of the luxurious furniture and decorative arts for the royal residences), and his posts as first painter to the king, curator of the royal collections, and chancellor for life of the Académie in 1664.

Le Brun's role at the Académie was critical for the development of French painting and sculpture during the next two centuries. For him, drawing was the basis of the visual arts and therefore the most fundamental skill necessary for a young artist, especially one who aspired to be a painter of the historical, mythological, and religious works that Le Brun codified as the most noble type (or genre) of painting. His belief in the primary importance of drawing followed a long-established Italian tradition undoubtedly inherited from Vouet. It is also revealed in the many thousands of his own very accomplished extant sheets (*Triton,* c. 1680, Musée du Louvre). To ensure that the Académie's students attained the desired level of proficiency as draftsmen, Le Brun established and systematized a routine of study involving several years of well-defined, graduated stages of figure drawing—one that began with copies of prints or plaster casts and ended with drawings after the live model—that became the standard for academies across Europe. He also oversaw the founding of the French Academy in Rome in 1666 so that the best French students could travel for extended study in what was then the center of the European art world. And finally, beginning in 1667, he initiated his series of lectures, or *conférences,* at the Académie in Paris—including the pivotal lecture on expression (1668) that was illustrated with his own drawings (*Terror,* c. 1668, Musée du Louvre)—that quickly became obligatory reading for young French artists. During his tenure, the Académie also became the center of heated debates over issues such as perspective and, most importantly, the merits of color versus design, or Rubens versus Poussin. Without forgetting the merits of Rubens, Le Brun's opinion was made clear: the greatest historical example was Raphael, whose genius was taken to even greater heights by Poussin. As he certainly realized, his view proclaimed the primacy of the French school.

Le Brun ended his career with a remarkably detailed inventory of the paintings in the royal collection in 1683. He also produced a number of successful cabinet pictures. Between his numerous posts in the royal household, his multitude of prestigious commissions, and his pivotal role at the Académie, he trained an entire generation of students and collaborators that included Louis and Bon de Boullogne, Louis Chéron, Antoine Coypel, Charles de Lafosse, René Houasse, Jean Jouvenet, and both Michel II and Jean-Baptiste Corneille, influencing them with the richly colored, heavy (but energetic), declarative, and classicizing baroque blend of Poussin and Rubens that had earned him such success.

See also **Academies of Art; Art: Artistic Patronage; Louis XIV (France); Poussin, Nicolas; Versailles; Vouet, Simon.**

BIBLIOGRAPHY

Beauvais, Lydia. *Charles Le Brun, 1619–1690: Inventaire général des dessins.* 2 vols. Paris, 2000.

Gareau, Michel. *Charles Le Brun, premier peintre du roi Louis XIV.* Paris, 1992.

Jouin, Henri. *Charles Le Brun et les arts sous Louis XIV.* Paris, 1889.

Montagu, Jennifer. *The Expression of the Passions: The Origin and Influence of Charles Le Brun's Conférence sur l'expression générale et particulière.* New Haven and London, 1994.

Thuillier, Jacques. *Charles le Brun, 1619–1690: Peintre et dessinateur.* Exh. cat. Paris, 1963.

ALVIN L. CLARK, JR.

LEAGUE OF AUGSBURG, WAR OF THE (1688–1697). This war is also known as the War of the Grand Alliance, the Nine Years' War, and King William's War.

FRENCH POLICY IN THE 1680S AND THE COMING OF WAR

French success at the Peace of Nijmegen (1678), which concluded the Dutch War (1672–1678), was followed a decade later by a diplomatic fiasco in which Louis XIV (ruled 1643–1715) began a war in which he had no allies and was opposed by a coalition comprising almost all the European powers. Indisputable characteristics of the years following Nijmegen were overconfidence in France's capacity to pursue political aims through military force and a dangerous contempt for international opinion. The "Chambers of Reunion" active between 1679 and 1682 may initially have presented spurious justifications for absorbing substantial territories lying across France's eastern frontier, but by the time French troops occupied Strasbourg and most of the duchy of Luxembourg, it was evident that Louis and his ministers were indulging the opportunism of the powerful. The lack of effective resistance owed much to the preoccupation of Emperor Leopold I (ruled 1658–1705) with the Ottoman threat, which climaxed in the 1683 siege of Vienna. The spectacular collapse of Ottoman power following the breaking of the siege caused concern at Versailles, but no modification of policy: Spain responded to France's "reunions" by a declaration of war in 1683, and in retaliation Louis sanctioned the seizure of the city of Luxembourg and the naval bombardment of Spain's ally Genoa. Although the Spanish, vainly expecting imperial leadership of an anti-French coalition, were forced to accept a truce at Regensburg in 1684, hostility and fear about French intentions were now widespread.

In this fragile situation French actions grew more provocative. The revocation of the Edict of Nantes in 1685 completed the alienation of Protestant Europe: after 1685 no Protestant power would again make an alliance with Louis XIV. Intrigues over the archbishopric of Cologne and a ham-handed attempt to exploit the succession to the Palatine Electorate antagonized and frightened the German princes. Meanwhile the success of imperial forces in the Balkans, which culminated in the 1688 capture of Belgrade, freed Emperor Leopold to play an active role in an anti-French coalition in the West. In 1686 a number of German princes, Charles II (ruled 1665–1700) of Spain, and Leopold I signed the League of Augsburg (later known as the Grand Alliance) to coordinate resistance to France. Preoccupied by his attempt to bully Pope Innocent XI and the German princes into accepting a French client as archbishop-elector of Cologne, and convinced that a protracted civil war in England would be the most likely—and desirable—consequence of an armed challenge to James II (ruled 1685–1688), Louis and his ministers did nothing to block the invasion of England by William, the stadtholder of the Dutch Republic. Landing at Torbay in November 1688, William's forces rapidly undermined any resistance on behalf of James, and by December, William and his wife, Mary, the daughter of James II, were in London. Louis's most implacable enemy was now established at the head of both the great maritime powers.

A house of cards consisting of facile and inflexible assumptions about the international situation was collapsing; belatedly, Louis and his ministers sought to halt the momentum toward war, but a characteristic reliance on threats and violence simply compounded the crisis. Though demanding that the emperor and the German princes should convert the 1684 truce of Regensburg into a permanent peace, a simultaneous attack by French forces on the Rhineland fortress of Philippsburg ensured that the French ultimatum was ignored. Louis's response was the devastation of the Palatine cities and countryside, not by any means the only instance of such exemplary destructiveness in the period, but one that could hardly have been worse timed in the face of a hostile coalition of all the major western European powers.

THE COURSE OF THE WAR

There had been little attempt during the 1680s to prepare France for another long war, and even in 1689 Louis still hoped that it might be won quickly. The pattern of conflict had much in common with the preceding Dutch War. In the field the French armies proved superior to their opponents, and a group of capable and enterprising commanders were able to maintain the initiative during successive campaigns. French forces in the first few years of the war gained the military advantage in the Spanish Netherlands at Fleurus (July 1690), Steenkerque (August 1692), and Neerwinden (July 1693), while their victory at Staffarda (August 1690) in Piedmont threatened the collapse of allied power in northern Italy. But sustaining the war effort placed immense pressure upon France; the army was increased to at least 300,000 troops by the early 1690s. The allies could sustain heavy losses on campaign and still reinforce their army corps before the French could exploit a tactical advantage; French victories in the field and successful sieges did not, as Louis and his ministers hoped, bring the allies to the negotiating table. The French financial system and military administration were both under unprecedented strain. In 1693–1694 France suffered twin harvest failures accompanied by famine and disease, which killed upwards of 10 percent of the population. Tax revenues collapsed, much of the army went unpaid and unfed, and lingering hopes that Louis might be able to gain decisive victory evaporated. The French navy had acquitted itself impressively in 1690 with the victory over the combined Anglo-Dutch fleets at Bézeviers, and had continued to demonstrate tactical effectiveness in subsequent engagements. Yet in response to domestic crisis the navy was decommissioned (1695); some of the warships were contracted out to privateers, who continued a *guerre de course* (raiding campaign) against the allies, while the rest rotted in the dockyards.

By 1694–1695 the French government was desperate either to end the continental war outright or to reduce the scale of its military commitments; the allied capture of Namur (September 1695) provided alarming evidence that the military balance might be tipping against the French. Initiatives to divide the allies failed, and only in 1696 did Louis achieve a costly diplomatic breakthrough by a treaty (Turin) with Victor Amadeus II of Savoy (1666–1732), through which France gained the neutralization of the northern Italian theater at the price of abandoning the key French fortifications south of the Alps. Awareness that even with this scaling down of commitments in the south French forces on the northern and eastern frontiers would be heavily outnumbered during the 1696 campaign encouraged the first serious initiatives toward a general settlement.

Initial allied demands involved the restoration of all French acquisitions since Nijmegen, and negotiations foundered on Louis's refusal to return Strasbourg or to renounce any Bourbon claims in a future settlement of the Spanish succession. French negotiators finally settled with the Dutch and English representatives, recognizing William III as king of England, and conceding Dutch rights to garrison a fortress barrier in the Spanish Netherlands. The preliminary French settlement with the Dutch and English at Ryswick early in 1697 left the Austrians and the Spanish exposed diplomatically and militarily: the negotiations made major concessions to allied demands, returning most of France's conquests since 1678. Jeopardizing settlement over the refusal to surrender Strasbourg seemed disproportionate. Moreover, without the Maritime Powers' soldiers and warships, continuing the struggle against France looked less attractive. Indeed, deprived of the Anglo-Dutch navy, the Spanish were unable to prevent the French capture of Barcelona in August 1697. This provided a decisive inducement to accept the peace, signed at Ryswick by all the major combatants in September and October 1697. Although the emperor resented the abandonment of Strasbourg, and a party within Spain had wanted French concessions over earlier conquests in Flanders, Ryswick showed that France had been pushed to the limits of her resources by nine years of war.

See also **Dutch War (1672–1678); James II (England); Leopold I (Holy Roman Empire); Louis XIV (France); William and Mary.**

BIBLIOGRAPHY

Primary Source

Actes et Mémoires des Négociations de la Paix de Ryswick. 4 vols. Reprint. Graz, Austria, 1974. Originally published The Hague, 1725.

Secondary Sources

Barker, Thomas M. *Double Eagle and Crescent: Vienna's Second Turkish Siege in its Historical Setting.* Albany, N.Y., 1967.

Bluche, François. *Louis XIV.* Translated by Mark Greengrass. London, 1990. A work of indefatigable chauvinism, which seeks to defend Louis XIV's policies on the eve of the war.

Childs, John. *The Nine Years' War and the British Army, 1688–1697: The Operations in the Low Countries.* Manchester, U.K., 1991.

Lossky, Andrew. "The General European Crisis of the 1680's." *European Studies Review* 10 (1980): 177–197.

———. "Maxims of State in Louis XIV's Foreign Policy in the 1680's," In *William III and Louis XIV: Essays by and for Mark Thompson,* edited by Ragnhild Hatton and John S. Bromley, pp. 7–23. Liverpool and Toronto, 1968.

Lynn, John A. *The Wars of Louis XIV, 1667–1714.* London, 1999.

Place, Richard. "The Self-Deception of the Strong: France on the Eve of the War of the League of Augsburg." *French Historical Studies* 6 (1970): 459–473.

Rowen, Herbert H. *The Princes of Orange: The Stadtholders in the Dutch Republic.* Cambridge, U.K., 1988.

Rowlands, Guy R. *The Dynastic State and the Army under Louis XIV: Royal Service and Private Interest in France, 1661 to 1701.* Cambridge, U.K., 2002.

Spielmann, John P. *Leopold I of Austria.* London, 1977.

Storrs, Christopher. *War, Diplomacy and the Rise of Savoy, 1690–1720.* Cambridge, U.K., 1999.

Symcox, Geoffrey. *The Crisis of French Sea Power, 1688–1697: From* the guerre d'escadre *to the* guerre de course. The Hague, 1974.

———. "Louis XIV and the Outbreak of the Nine Years War." In *Louis XIV and Europe,* edited by Ragnhild Hatton, pp. 179–212. London, 1976.

Wolf, John B. *Louis XIV.* New York, 1968.

DAVID PARROTT

LEAGUE OF CAMBRAI. *See* **Cambrai, League of (1508).**

LEDOUX, CLAUDE-NICOLAS (1736–1806), French architect. Ledoux was among the most prominent architects of the final decades of the *ancien régime.* Although few of his buildings are extant, engravings of them and of his unrealized projects continue to draw the attention of architects and theorists interested in their inventive forms, symbolic expression, and social vision.

Ledoux's career exemplifies the increased social and professional mobility of architects in the second half of the eighteenth century. Born into a merchant family of modest means in a provincial town, Dormans (Marne), Ledoux received a classical education in Paris as a scholarship student at the

Claude-Nicolas Ledoux. Barrière (toll station) at La Villette, Paris, designed by Ledoux and built in 1784. ©GILLIAN DARLEY; EDIFICE/CORBIS

Collège de Dormans-Beauvais from 1749 to 1753. He subsequently apprenticed as an engraver and studied architecture at the private École des Arts, directed by the eminent architectural educator, Jacques-François Blondel (1705–1774). He reportedly completed his professional training in the atelier of Louis-François Trouard (1729–1794). Ledoux deftly established his career through contacts among alumni of the *collège,* the architects and amateurs affiliated with Blondel's school, and a circle of musicians and artists at Versailles that opened to him in 1764 when he married Marie Bureau, the daughter of an oboist in the court orchestra. From the 1760s, these overlapping networks led to a wide range of challenging and profitable private and public commissions as well as his appointment to the royal academy of architecture in 1773. His royalist associations, however, led to his professional ruin and imprisonment (1793–1795) during the French Revolution.

Ledoux began his practice as neoclassicism was emerging as the preferred style among trend-setting designers and clients, and he made a place for himself among them. In 1771–1773, he achieved fame with two commissions, a pavilion at Louveciennes for Madame du Barry (1743–1793), who had recently become Louis XV's mistress, and a house and private theater in Paris for Marie-Madeleine Guimard (1743–1816), a prominent dancer at the Opéra. Both women sought to use patronage of architecture and art to legitimize their place in society, and Ledoux responded to their ambition with buildings attesting to their (and his) discriminating and adventuresome taste. He shared the interest in Greco-Roman architecture that constitutes a defining attribute of neoclassicism, but his formal sources and theoretical intentions went beyond the revival of antiquity. His teacher, Blondel, instilled an enduring appreciation for the grandeur and compositional logic in the buildings of François Mansart

(1598–1666) and a conviction that architects must infuse their designs with an expressive character appropriate to their purpose. Ledoux pursued this attitude by exploring typology and the ways by which architecture can convey meaning. His investigations into the fundamental characteristics of building types paralleled the classificatory efforts of scientists, such as Georges-Louis Leclerc, comte de Buffon (1707–1788). His study of meaning engaged him with contemporary theories of perception, including Edmund Burke's (1729–1797) writings on the sublime. Ledoux's formal language was informed by a lifelong interest in three-dimensional geometry and also by the compositional vocabulary of Andrea Palladio (1508–1580), which he learned through study of Palladio's *Four Books on Architecture* (1570) and English neo-Palladian architecture.

Public commissions were an important part of Ledoux's practice from the beginning of his career. In 1764, he obtained a position in the royal department of water and forests (Département des Eaux et Forêts) for which he designed churches, fountains, and bridges. This experience sparked an interest in the economics, social organization, and architecture of rural life and brought him into contact with physiocratic reformers. In 1771, his patron, Madame du Barry, facilitated his appointment as architect-engineer for the saltworks *(salines)* in eastern France administered by the corporation of tax farmers (Fermiers Généraux). From 1775 to 1780, Ledoux realized a new saltworks, the Saline de Chaux, at Arc-et-Senans (Doubs). His master plan and architectural designs systematically addressed the technical, social, and symbolic dimensions of this important industry. Subsequently, he expanded the project into a visionary scheme for urban and rural development, which he presented in his treatise, published in 1804. Ledoux's work for the Fermiers Généraux included projects in Paris; notably, one of the first commissions for a large office building (begun 1783, never completed) and the master plan and buildings for a wall around the city (begun 1784) intended to regulate the collection of customs duties. Four of his toll stations *(barrières)* remain today. Among his commissions for public buildings outside Paris were the municipal theater in Besançon (1771–1784), an unrealized project for the city hall of Neuchâtel, Switzerland (1783), and the Palais de Justice and prisons for Aix-en-Provence (designed 1779–1786), begun in 1787 but completed to the designs of others.

See also **Architecture; Buffon, Georges Louis Leclerc; City Planning; France, Architecture in; Mansart, François; Neoclassicism; Palladio, Andrea, and Palladianism.**

BIBLIOGRAPHY

Primary Sources

Gallet, Michel, ed. *Claude-Nicolas Ledoux: Unpublished Projects.* Berlin, 1992. Translation of *Architecture de Ledoux: inédits pour un tome iii* (1991).

Ledoux, Claude-Nicolas. *L'architecture considérée sous le rapport de l'art, des moeurs, et de la législation.* Paris, 1804. Reprint edited by Daniel Ramée, Princeton, 1984.

Ramée, Daniel, ed. *Architecture de C. N. Ledoux.* Princeton, 1984.

Secondary Sources

Braham, Allan. *The Architecture of the French Enlightenment.* Berkeley, 1980.

Gallet, Michel. *Claude-Nicolas Ledoux: 1736–1806.* Paris, 1980.

Vidler, Anthony. *Claude-Nicolas Ledoux: Architecture and Social Reform at the End of the Ancien Régime.* Cambridge, Mass., 1990.

RICHARD CLEARY

LEEUWENHOEK, ANTONI VAN

(1632–1723), Dutch microscopist. Born the son of a basket maker on 24 October 1632 in Delft, Leeuwenhoek had little formal education. He moved when he was sixteen to Amsterdam, where he was trained and employed by a draper. In 1654 he returned to Delft, married his first wife, Barbara, and established his own drapery business. One child from this first marriage survived, his daughter Maria, who became her father's lifelong companion.

Leeuwenhoek entered civic life in 1660, when he became chamberlain to the sheriffs of Delft. In 1669 he passed the exam to become a city surveyor, and in 1679 he became official wine gauger to the city of Delft. His first wife died in 1666; Leeuwenhoek married his second wife, Cornelia, in 1671, and she died in 1695.

Leeuwenhoek's career as a tradesman and civic figure took a sharp turn in 1673, when he was introduced to the Royal Society of London by a letter from Reinier de Graaf (1641–1673), a prominent anatomist of Delft. De Graaf said that Leeuwenhoek had devised microscopes that were far superior to any then known, and he included a paper by Leeuwenhoek that offered observations of bits of mold, the eye and sting of a bee, and a louse. The secretary of the Society, Henry Oldenburg, was interested and encouraged further correspondence. Over the next fifty years, Leeuwenhoek wrote more than three hundred letters to the Royal Society. He read and wrote only Dutch, so these letters had to be translated into Latin for publication. The extracts printed in the Society's *Philosophical Transactions* constitute the bulk of Leeuwenhoek's published scientific work.

We do not know how Leeuwenhoek became interested in either microscopy or lens making. It has been suggested that his use of the draper's glass to examine woven cloth might have been a stimulus, but probably his acquaintance with de Graaf and Cornelius's Gravesande, another Delft anatomist, was more important. Whatever the stimulus, by 1671 Leeuwenhoek was making his own microscopes, and they had a unique design. Whereas the microscopes made by Robert Hooke (1635–1703) and other contemporaries were compound instruments, with both an objective lens and an eyepiece, Leeuwenhoek built simple microscopes, with a single beadlike lens mounted between two small thin metal sheets, usually brass. The object to be viewed was mounted on a pin on one side of the lens, and the eye was placed, almost touching the lens, on the other. The microscopes were successful because the tiny spherical lenses were exquisitely ground, or, in a few cases, blown. The measure of their success is what Leeuwenhoek was able to see through them.

In 1674 Leeuwenhoek examined cloudy water from a nearby lake and discovered it was teeming with tiny "animalcules," which we recognize as protozoa. Two years later, while continuing to study his tiny animals, he discovered in an infusion of pepper water some creatures that were much smaller, so small that, in his words, a million would not occupy the space of a grain of sand. Leeuwenhoek had discovered bacteria (although he never recognized them as a radically different form of life from protozoa). The Royal Society was quite excited by Leeuwenhoek's discovery of microscopic life, which he announced in his famous letters of 7 September 1674 and 9 October 1676, and other microscopists scurried to see for themselves. This was not easy, as no one had microscopes with the resolution of Leeuwenhoek's, but eventually his claims were confirmed.

Leeuwenhoek's other most notable achievement was the discovery of spermatozoa, which he announced in a letter of November 1677. He observed these first in humans, then in dogs, and eventually in more than thirty different species. After persistent study, he came to argue that each sperm was the seed of an individual creature and would give rise to the next generation if properly nourished in the womb. Since most contemporaries argued that the female provided the seed and the male merely some sort of fertilizing power, this was a radically new theory of generation. Leeuwenhoek believed that every element of an adult form was contained in a single sperm. However, he did not, as is sometimes stated, ever claim to see the form of a human within a human sperm.

Leeuwenhoek made other notable discoveries and observations. He was one of the pioneers of plant anatomy, taking a special interest in wood structure. He made a series of detailed studies of blood, observing the red blood cells, and was actually able to see single cells circulating through the capillaries in the tail of an eel, which he announced in a letter of 7 September 1688.

Leeuwenhoek became quite a famous figure in Delft (which, except for two early excursions, he never left). He entertained visitors willingly, although this proved quite time consuming in later life. The future James II of England (ruled 1685–1688) and Tsar Peter I of Russia (ruled 1682–1725) were among those who journeyed to Delft to see Leeuwenhoek and his wonders. When Leeuwenhoek had mastered a particular specimen, he would set up a permanent stand in his house, with a microscope devoted to that specimen, so that a visitor could go from station to station and observe swamp water, blood, insect parts, and other exotica without wasting time. This required a great number of microscopes, and it is estimated that Leeuwenhoek built over five hundred in his lifetime. Twenty-six, made of silver, were presented to the Royal Society after his death, with specimens attached; sadly, these have disappeared. But nine of his microscopes have survived and are the treasures of museums in Utrecht, Leiden, Rotterdam, Antwerp, and Munich.

One rather odd feature of Leeuwenhoek's life is that he was executor, in 1676, for the estate of the artist Jan Vermeer (1632–1675). Although other interaction between the two figures cannot be documented, it has been suggested that Vermeer learned optics from Leeuwenhoek, or perhaps vice versa, and it has been further suggested that Leeuwenhoek was the sitting subject for two of Vermeer's famous paintings, *The Astronomer* (1668) and *The Geographer* (1668–1669).

Although the *Philosophical Transactions* of the Royal Society was the primary forum for Leeuwenhoek's discoveries throughout his life, he did supervise the separate publication of several collections of those letters, in both Dutch and Latin, beginning in 1684 and continuing to 1722. However, he never wrote any kind of a synthesis of his work. Leeuwenhoek died in his home, at the age of ninety, on 26 August 1723, shortly after dictating a last letter to the Royal Society.

See also **Academies, Learned; Hooke, Robert; Optics; Scientific Instruments; Scientific Revolution; Technology.**

BIBLIOGRAPHY

Primary Source

Leeuwenhoek, Antoni van. *Alle de brieven.* 12 vols. Amsterdam, 1939–.

Secondary Sources

Dobell, Clifford. *Antony van Leeuwenhoek and His "Little Animals": Being Some Account of the Father of Protozoology and Bacteriology and His Multifarious Discoveries in These Disciplines.* New York, 1958.

Fournier, Marian. *The Fabric of Life: Microscopy in the Seventeenth Century.* Baltimore, Md., 1996.

Palm, Lodewijk C., and Harry A. M. Snelders, eds. *Antoni van Leeuwenhoek, 1632–1723: Studies on the Life and Work of the Delft Scientist Commemorating the 350th Anniversary of His Birthday.* Amsterdam, 1982.

Schierbeek, Abraham. *Measuring the Invisible World: The Life and Works of Antoni van Leeuwenhoek.* London, 1959.

WILLIAM B. ASHWORTH, JR.

LEIBNIZ, GOTTFRIED WILHELM

(1646–1716), German philosopher, mathematician, physicist, historian, and diplomat. Gottfried Wilhelm Freiherr von Leibniz was born at the end of the Thirty Years' War in Leipzig, a Protestant university town in Germany, where his father was a professor. His father died when Leibniz was only six, but he inherited his library and his respect for intellectual pursuits and from an early age read widely in the Latin classics, history, Christian theology, and logic. His precocious eclecticism foreshadowed the course of his later life. The sixty thousand handwritten pages that he left behind at his death (now mostly housed in the Leibniz Archives in Hanover, Germany) cover an awesome range of topics, his mastery of each one of which is stamped by the erudition of a scholar and the originality of genius. His legacy includes the invention of the infinitesimal calculus and its application to mechanics via the study of differential equations and transcendental curves; a metaphysics that reconciles mechanistic science with the inviolable integrity of human awareness; a theory of knowledge based on analysis as a search for conditions of intelligibility and guided by a prescient appreciation of formal languages; a moral theory born of his experience as a diplomat that underwrites religious and cultural tolerance and decries tyranny; and a history of the House of Hanover, exemplary in its scholarly procedures, that deepens our understanding of the Middle Ages.

After an early academic post at the University of Altdorf, Leibniz decided in favor of the practical life as an advisor to princes: in 1667 he was called to the Catholic court of the Bishop Elector in Mainz, which led to his four wonderful years in Paris, 1672–1676; thereafter he served the dukes (then electors) of Hanover until his death, service punctuated by frequent voyages in Europe, the longest of which was a sojourn in Italy from 1687 to 1690. The sojourn in Paris changed his life, for there he met the Dutch physicist Christiaan Huygens (1629–1695), who introduced him to Descartes's geometry and the new algebra, and also made the acquaintance of Nicolas de Malebranche (1638–1715) and Antoine Arnauld (1612–1694). It is fair to say that between 1672 and 1676, Leibniz recapitulated the history of Western mathematics, for he came to Paris knowing only Euclid and left with the

Gottfried Wilhelm Leibniz. LIBRARY OF CONGRESS

invention of the infinitesimal calculus, including the essential notational innovations of dx for the differential and ∫ for the integral, to his credit. The inaugural publication of his differential and integral calculus appeared in the journal *Acta Eruditorum*: "Nova Methodus pro Maximis et Minimis" (A new method for maxima and minima) in October 1684, and "De Geometria Recondita et Analysi Indivisibilium atque Infinitorum" (On a deeply hidden geometry and the analysis of indivisibles and infinites) in June 1686. Leibniz's discovery of the calculus in the 1670s occurred independently of Isaac Newton's (1642–1727) activity, though his later application of the theory of differential equations to planetary motion seems to have been directly inspired by Newton's *Principia* (1687). Johann (1667–1748) and Jakob (1654–1705) Bernoulli used Leibniz's ideas and notation to work out important problems in analysis and mechanics, which led in turn to the work of Leonhard Euler (1707–1783), Jean Le Rond d'Alembert (1717–1783), and Joseph-Louis Lagrange (1736–1813) in the eighteenth century.

In the same year, 1686, Leibniz composed his *Discours de métaphysique* (Discourse on metaphysics) and began his correspondence with the French Jansenist philosopher Antoine Arnauld, two works that display the metaphysical position of his middle years with special clarity. The *Discourse on Metaphysics* argues that we should make God's creation of the world our model in the employment of an *ars inveniendi,* though since we are finite, we must rest content with employing highly reductive formal languages ("characteristics") to investigate intelligible but infinite or infinitesimal things. Its scientific reflections are developed in the unpublished *Dynamica* (Dynamics) of 1689–1691, and "Specimen dynamicum" (A specimen of dynamics) published in 1695. The jurisprudential and political works written during Leibniz's maturity also urge that we take God's rational and charitable freedom as the model for our moral decisions, legal system, and the comportment of princes and parliaments. Voltaire could never have satirized Leibniz's philosophical views as naïve in his novel *Candide* (1759) if he had read and taken to heart the essay "Mars Christianissimus" (1683; Most Christian war god), where Leibniz attacks the aggression and autocracy of Louis XIV, then king of France, with the eloquent fury of a seasoned diplomat whose dearest wish was to see Europe reunited as a pacific confederacy. Leibniz was also one of a handful of seventeenth-century European intellectuals to entertain seriously the learning of China and to argue that Europe might profit from cultural exchange with the great Eastern empire. His later metaphysics, oriented more toward theology than science or politics, is summarized in short unpublished works written in 1714, "Principes de la nature et de la grâce, fondés en raison" (Principles of nature and grace, founded on reason) and "Monadologia" (Monadology), as well as the explicitly theological work of 1710, *Essais de Théodicée* (Essays on theodicy). Leibniz died quietly in Hanover in 1716, but his thought has enjoyed an animated afterlife ever since.

See also **Alembert, Jean Le Rond d'; Euler, Leonhard; Huygens Family; Lagrange, Joseph-Louis; Mathematics; Newton, Isaac.**

BIBLIOGRAPHY

Primary Sources

Leibniz, G. W. *Philosophical Essays.* Translated and edited by Roger Ariew and Daniel Garber. Indianapolis, 1989.

———. *Political Writings.* Translated and edited by Patrick Riley. Cambridge, U.K., 1988.

Secondary Sources

Sleigh, R. C., Jr. *Leibniz and Arnauld: A Commentary on Their Correspondence.* New Haven and London, 1990.

Wilson, Catherine. *Leibniz's Metaphysics: A Historical and Comparative Study.* Princeton, 1989.

EMILY R. GROSHOLZ

LEIPZIG. Leipzig was a center of trade, religious organization and innovation, music, printing, and education in the Holy Roman Empire. The population of the town grew from about 9,000 in 1500 to about 30,000 in 1800. Contemporaries often contrasted Leipzig's commercial atmosphere to the court-dominated atmosphere of Dresden, the other main Saxon urban center. From 1485, when the territory of Saxony was divided into electoral and ducal portions, until 1547, Leipzig was located in ducal Saxony. When Duke Maurice was awarded the electoral title in 1547, Leipzig became part of electoral Saxony.

Leipzig was influenced by the course of Saxon politics in many ways. The city's economic and cultural boom from the late seventeenth to the mid-eighteenth century was in part the result of Saxony's political prominence under the rule of Frederick Augustus I (ruled 1694–1733) and Frederick Augustus II (ruled 1733–1763). Similarly, the timing and degree of the city's involvement in the Schmalkaldic War (1546–1547), the Thirty Years' War (1618–1648), the Seven Years' War (1756–1763), and the Napoleonic Wars (1796–1815) were conditioned by territorial politics. The electoral court also influenced local politics, although historians have recently emphasized the power of local elites. The Leipzig city council was divided into three rotating groups, each typically made up of twelve councillors and one mayor, who served a one-year term as the governing or "sitting" council. About half of the councillors were merchants, and half were lawyers. Election was by co-optation (new members were chosen by the existing members). Eligibility to serve on the council was not formally restricted, but most councillors were members of well-established local merchant and professional families.

Artisanal production, the university, and the printing industry were all important sectors of the local economy. About seventy trades were represented in the city; the university's thousand-plus students helped support the entertainment, luxury, and printing trades. Also key were Leipzig's trade fairs, held three times a year. The fairs achieved dominance in Saxony and Thuringia by 1500, and from the 1680s onward, they were the largest in central Europe. Leipzig became one of the main German distribution centers for colonial goods.

Leipzig had become a cultural center by the fifteenth century. A university that became one of the most prominent in Germany was founded there in 1409. By the eve of the Reformation, the city housed numerous monasteries, and the two main churches, St. Nicholas and St. Thomas, were the object of endowments by the city council, guilds, and individuals. Some burghers were early adherents of the Lutheran doctrine preached in nearby electoral Saxony. However, the Reformation was officially introduced into the city only in 1539, when Duke Heinrich succeeded his brother George, who had remained Catholic. Leipzig's clerics soon became well-known and influential in the Lutheran world. The next major religious dispute erupted in 1689, when a group of reformist students and burghers known as Pietists challenged mainstream orthodox clerics. High baroque culture thrived in Leipzig from the 1680s onward, with a boom in public and private architecture, fashion, entertainment, and secular and sacred music, most notably represented by Johann Sebastian Bach, who served as town cantor from 1723 to 1750. Leipzig was also a center of Enlightenment printing and debate.

See also **Bach Family; Dresden; Pietism; Printing and Publishing; Saxony.**

BIBLIOGRAPHY

Bräuer, Helmut. *Der Leipziger Rat und die Bettler: Quellen und Analysen zu Bettlern und Bettelwesen in der Messestadt bis ins 18. Jahrhundert.* Leipzig, 1997.

Duclaud, Jutta, and Rainer Ducland. *Leipziger Zünfte.* Berlin, 1990.

Leipzig. Illustration from *Civitates Orbis Terrarum,* c. 1572–1618, by Braun and Hogenberg. ©ARCHIVO ICONOGRAFICO S.A./CORBIS

Kevorkian, Tanya. *Baroque Piety: Religious Practices and Society in Leipzig, 1650–1750.* Forthcoming.

———. "The Rise of the Poor, Weak, and Wicked: Poor Care, Punishment, Religion, and Patriarchy in Leipzig, 1700–1730." *Journal of Social History* 34 (2000): 163–181.

Martens, Wolfgang, ed. *Leipzig: Aufklärung und Burgerlichkeit.* Heidelberg, 1990.

Pevsner, Nikolaus. *Leipziger Barock: Die Baukunst der Barockzeit in Leipzig.* Dresden, 1928. Reprint: Leipzig, 1990.

Stiller, Günther. *Johann Sebastian Bach and Liturgical Life in Leipzig.* Translated by Herbert J. A. Bouman, Daniel F. Poellet, and Hilton C. Oswald. Edited by Robin A. Leaver. St. Louis, 1984.

Wittmann, Reinhard. *Geschichte des deutschen Buchhandels: Ein Überblick.* Munich, 1991.

TANYA KEVORKIAN

LEO X (POPE) (1475–1521; reigned 1513–1521). Second son of Lorenzo "the Magnificent" de' Medici and Clarice Orsini, Giovanni Romolo de' Medici was trained in the humanities and received a doctorate in canon law from the University of Pisa in 1492. He was appointed cardinal in 1489, and held various legations culminating in that to the Holy League, which reinstalled his family to power in Florence in 1512.

Elected pope by the younger cardinals in 1513, Leo X quietly continued the imperial and Spanish alliance against France pursued by his predecessor Julius II (reigned 1503–1513), but he made peace with the French king Francis I following the latter's military victory in 1515 and negotiated a concordat with him at Bologna, to replace the Pragmatic Sanction of Bourges (1438). He tried to create a French alliance by Medici marriages to relatives of Francis I: His brother Giuliano (1479–1516) was married to the royal aunt Philiberte de Savoy, and his nephew Lorenzo di Piero (1492–1519), to Madeleine de La Tour d'Auvergne (d. 1519), probably a royal cousin, whose orphaned daughter, Catherine (1519–1589), later became queen of France. With their deaths and the election of Charles V as Holy Roman emperor in 1519, which he opposed, Leo returned clearly to the Habsburg alliance and regained Parma and Piacenza for the Papal States once the French were defeated in 1521.

As head of the Roman Catholic Church, Leo took his responsibilities seriously. At religious ceremonies he presided with dignity and devotion. He brought to a successful conclusion the Fifth Lateran Council (1512–1517), which healed the Pisan schism, approved the abrogation of the Pragmatic Sanction, and confirmed the Concordat of Bologna; regulated relations between bishops and exempt clerics; condemned Averroistic views on the soul; ordered prepublication censorship of books; legislated various moral and curial reforms; and ordered a crusade that, given Christian rivalries, could never be launched. He tried to promote a reunion of the churches by sending a legate to the Hussites and establishing good relations with the Maronites and Ethiopians. To promote the evangelization of non-Christians, he approved in 1518 the training of non-European clergy and the episcopal consecration of Enrique (c. 1494–1531), son of the king of the Congo. To preserve orthodoxy he threatened Martin Luther (1483–1546) with penalties should he fail to recant forty-one propositions (*Exsurge Domine,* 1520); he then excommunicated the recalcitrant friar (*Decet Romanum Pontificem,* 1521). To Henry VIII he assigned in 1521 the title "Defender of the Faith" for writing against Luther. While he actively supported the observant movement in religious orders, he failed to effect a serious reform of the Roman Curia, because it would have reduced his revenues.

Leo was a lavish patron of arts and letters. He employed Michelangelo Buonarroti (1475–1564) to carve the Medici tombs in Florence, and in Rome he commissioned Raphael Sanzio (1483–1520) to work on the frescoes in the papal apartments and loggia, design the Sistine tapestries, paint his papal portrait, and supervise the construction of the new St. Peter's Basilica and excavations of Roman archeological sites. As domestic secretaries he hired the humanists Pietro Bembo (1470–1547) and Jacopo Sadoleto (1477–1547). He endowed professorships at the University of Rome and founded there a Greek college and press. Leo was on good terms with leading humanists such as Desiderius Erasmus (1466?–1536), who dedicated to him the *Novum Instrumentum* (New Testament) of 1516. He commissioned Marco Girolamo Vida (c. 1490–1566) to compose the epic poem *Christiad* (1535), begun in 1518, and in 1521 he urged Jacopo Sannazaro (1458–1530) to complete his *De Partu Virginis* (1526; "On the virgin birth"), begun in 1506.

Pope Leo X. Pope Leo X with cardinals Giulio de' Medici (later Pope Clement VII) and Luigi de Rosai. Portrait by Raphael, 1518, Uffizi Gallery, Florence.

Leo promoted numerous relatives and clients to church office, most notably in the 1517 mass creation of thirty-one cardinals following a plot to poison him, which had been provoked by his interference in Sienese political affairs. His first cousin Giulio de' Medici (1478–1534), whom he appointed archbishop of Florence, cardinal, and vice-chancellor of the church, was his closest adviser and would eventually succeed him as Clement VII (reigned 1523–1534). By his lavish expenditures on culture and warfare, and despite his efforts to raise new revenues by the sale of venal offices, dispensations, and indulgences, Leo X left the papacy deeply in debt at the time of his sudden death from pneumonia. He was eventually buried in the church of S. Maria sopra Minerva.

See also **Francis I (France); Medici Family; Papacy and Papal States.**

BIBLIOGRAPHY

Falcone, Carlo. *Leone X: Giovanni de' Medici.* Milan, 1987.

Gattoni, Maurizio. *Leone X e la geo-politica dello stato pontifico (1513–1521).* Vatican City, 2000.

Pastor, Ludwig von. *The History of the Popes from the Close of the Middle Ages.* Edited by Frederick Ignatius Antrobus, et al. 6th ed. 40 vols. Nendeln, Liechtenstein, 1969.

NELSON H. MINNICH

LEONARDO DA VINCI (1452–1519), Italian painter, sculptor, architect, and inventor. The illegitimate son of a young notary and a farm girl, both of whom married other people of their own social station shortly after his birth, Leonardo was adopted into his father's household when his stepmother remained childless. Unlike his father, Ser Pietro, who had learned Latin in connection with his profession, Leonardo, for all his evident intelligence, proved a poor and distracted student; he received the arithmetical training known as "abacus school" *(scuola di abbaco)* and then seems to have quit his formal schooling to be apprenticed to the famous Florentine sculptor Andrea del Verrocchio (1435–1488).

Leonardo's first biographer, Giorgio Vasari (1511–1574), tells how the young apprentice painted so ethereal an angel for Verrocchio's *Baptism of Christ* that the master threw up his hands and admitted defeat. But Verrocchio also helped to create Leonardo's famous sfumato or "smudged" shading technique, and encouraged his reliance on drawing as the chief medium for artistic composition, whether in painting, sculpture, architecture, or mechanics. Leonardo's first independent commission, an altarpiece for the Chapel of Saint Bernard in Palazzo della Signoria, contracted in 1478, was never completed, and this unfinished business set a pattern for the rest of his life. When his father procured for him the assignment of an altarpiece with the *Adoration of the Magi* for the Augustinian Canons Regular at San Donato in 1481, he put in several months of hard work on the ambitious painting, then abruptly left Florence for Milan in September, where he joined the court of Ludovico Sforza (duke of Milan 1481–1499).

This move represented more than a change of place; it also brought on a change in Leonardo's whole way of life. Florence, despite the heavy hand of the Medici clan in every government office and public commission, was nominally a republic, a large city-state with an elaborate set of public institutions. Ludovico, on the other hand, was a professional soldier who had seized Milan by force and aimed to keep control of the city by maintaining an efficient system of government and an active cultural life.

Leonardo seems to have applied to Ludovico Sforza with an offer to serve as a military architect. He spent much of his time with Donato Bramante (1444–1514) and the mathematician Luca Pacioli, providing the illustrations for Pacioli's popular book *On Divine Proportion* (1509), some of them originally pillaged from Piero della Francesca

Sometime between 1493 and 1495, Leonardo obtained the commission to decorate the refectory of the Dominican convent of Santa Maria delle Grazie with a *Last Supper.* The fresco was widely influential despite the failure of Leonardo's experimental formula for its paint, which began to deteriorate almost immediately.

In 1494, Charles VIII, the king of France, invaded Italy. By 1499, Milan had fallen to French troops, who imprisoned Ludovico. Leonardo, in the company of Luca Pacioli, returned to Florence, but not before he had seen the huge clay model for his never-completed statue of Francesco Sforza used for target practice by Gascon bowmen.

In 1502 Leonardo worked briefly as a military engineer in central Italy for Cesare Borgia. When Borgia's military campaigns began to be reined in by his father, Rodrigo (later Pope Alexander VI; reigned 1492–1503), Leonardo again returned to the Florentine republic, where an extensive remodeling of the great city hall, the Palazzo della Signoria, was under way. Here, in a monumental room designed to hold the republic's new representative council, Leonardo was asked to paint scenes from the battle of Anghiari, a skirmish in which Florence had gotten the best of her inveterate rival (and sometime port) Pisa. On the opposite wall, the city council had engaged Michelangelo Buonarroti, whose newly completed *David* still provides the most eloquent testimony to the indomitable spirit of this early-sixteenth-century Florentine republic.

Leonardo da Vinci. *The Virgin and Child with Saint Anne and Saint John the Baptist.* ©NATIONAL GALLERY COLLECTION; BY KIND PERMISSION OF THE TRUSTEES OF THE NATIONAL GALLERY, LONDON/CORBIS

Leonardo worked up at least part of his design for the *Battle of Anghiari* (begun 1503) to full size and transferred it to the wall of the council hall, but he decided to paint it in a medium that would lend the chalky plaster surface of the fresco something of the sheen of oil paint. The experiment failed miserably, and Leonardo never finished the work. It was finally covered by another fresco executed by Giorgio Vasari. Also in Florence, Leonardo became preoccupied with water and its motions. Another side of nature shows forth in Leonardo's sketches for his lost painting of *Leda and the Swan.*

From 1506 to 1513, Leonardo moved between Milan and Florence, evading the irate city councilmen who clamored for the rest of their *Battle of Anghiari* and also evading the violent skirmishes that plagued the area around Milan. He filled a series of notebooks with his writings, sketches, and anatomical studies. In 1512, the Florentine republic fell to a restored Medici dynasty; in 1513, Medici rule was reinforced by the election in Rome of a Medici pope, Leo X (reigned 1513–1521), son of Lorenzo the Magnificent. When the pope invested his brother, Giuliano de' Medici, with honorary Roman citizenship, Leonardo traveled with Giuliano's entourage and continued to study and write from his own special apartment in the Vatican Palace. In a city dominated by the imposing influence of Raphael, who had transformed himself from a painter to a designer *(disegnatore)* of international fame, Leonardo began to compile his own notes on painting, which would eventually be gathered together by his pupil Francesco Melzi and published in 1651 as *Treatise on Painting.*

In 1516, the aging artist accepted an invitation to become *peintre du roi* by Francis I of France and moved north with Melzi and his servant Salai. He died there in 1519 at the age of sixty-seven.

See also **Art: Artistic Patronage; Florence, Art in; Medici Family; Vasari, Giorgio.**

BIBLIOGRAPHY

Bambach, Carmen C., ed. *Leonardo da Vinci, Master Draftsman.* New York, 2003. Includes an extensive bibliography.

Bramly, Serge. *Leonardo: The Artist and the Man.* Translated by Sian Reynolds. New York, 1994.

Clark, Kenneth. *Leonardo da Vinci.* Revised edition with an introduction by Martin Kemp. Harmondsworth, U.K., 1988.

Pedretti, Carlo, ed. *The Literary Works of Leonardo da Vinci.* Berkeley, 1977.

Turner, A. Richard. *Inventing Leonardo.* Berkeley, 1993.

INGRID ROWLAND

LEOPOLD I (HOLY ROMAN EMPIRE) (1640–1705; king of Hungary and of Bohemia from 1655; Holy Roman emperor from 1658). The second surviving son of Emperor Ferdinand III (ruled 1637–1657), Archduke Leopold was destined by dynastic tradition to enter the church, where he could use the wealth and influence of high ecclesiastical office to further Habsburg dynastic interests in Europe. His older brother, the heir apparent, died in 1654, however, and Leopold, at age fourteen, had to take his brother's place and abandon clerical vows in order become the dynastic patriarch. The young archduke's education was overseen by tutors and aristocratic mentors who molded him for an ecclesiastical career. Leopold early adopted the intense Catholic piety expected of him and the gentle manners appropriate to a merely supporting role. He grew to manhood without the military ambition that characterized most of his fellow monarchs. From the beginning, his reign was defensive and profoundly conservative.

His first crisis concerned the Habsburg dynastic succession in the future, for in seven years death had reduced the living male Habsburgs to only two: Leopold and his sickly cousin Charles II of Spain. In 1666 Leopold married the younger daughter of Philip IV of Spain, the infanta Margareta (1651–1673); of their four children, only one, Maria Antonia (1669–1692) lived beyond the first year. A second marriage in 1673 to Claudia Felicitas of the Tyrol (1653–1676) brought two more daughters, both of whom died in their first year. In 1676 his third marriage to Eleanora Magdalena of Neuburg (1655–1720) finally produced a male heir in Joseph I (ruled 1705–1711) and then another son, Charles VI (ruled 1711–1740).

Two decades of dynastic crisis encouraged Leopold's neighbors to contemplate the Habsburg lands should Leopold fail to provide a male heir. France coveted the Spanish territories along the Rhenish frontier; in the east the Turks seized control of Transylvania in 1663 and invaded Hungary the next year. A coalition of imperial and Hungarian forces defeated the invaders at St. Gotthard in 1664. Leopold then surprised and disgusted his generals by concluding a hasty treaty at Vasvár accepting Turkish occupation of most of what they held and paying a large tribute to the Sublime Porte, the Ottoman government in Turkey. Leopold defended the treaty by pointing to French threats against the Low Countries. The immediate consequence, however, was the emergence of a conspiracy among Hungarian magnates who accused Leopold of wasting their blood. Leaders formed armed bands that moved about Hungary attacking both imperial and Turkish units, leading to renewed Turkish incursions. When the plot developed into a plan to murder Leopold, the court struck back, rounded up all the leaders, and executed them. Characteristically, Leopold himself favored clemency for the plotters, several of whom had been childhood friends, but sterner voices prevailed in his councils.

The imperial court at Vienna was a multilingual assembly of some two thousand persons, only about a hundred of whom participated in decision making through the judicial, financial, and military councils. Around them were small swarms of secretaries, copyists, investigators, bodyguards, lawyers, and others who were gradually coalescing into a primitive bureaucracy. Beyond them was a larger swarm of laborers, janitors, kitchen help, grooms, stable hands, laundresses, and court purveyors. All of these enjoyed the privilege of being subject to a special judiciary under the court marshall.

The aristocratic elite that dominated the governing councils generally split into two distinct factions: "westerners," who followed Leopold's own preference for appeasing the Turks in order to concentrate on the French threat, and on the other side the "easterners," who insisted that the Turks were the greater threat. That group included most of the military leaders, courtiers with great properties in Hungary or Croatia, and above all the church hierarchy, which followed the papacy's lead in the crusade against militant Islam.

It was clear that Leopold's territories could not provide the resources to allow major military campaigns in both Hungary and the Low Countries. Unrest in the east and French invasions into the Netherlands forced Leopold to enter into an alliance with the Calvinist Dutch Republic. This move unsettled his conscience for years, but the commercial wealth of the Protestant sea powers combined with the human and material resources of central Europe formed the basis on which subsequent Habsburgs built their Danubian empire. The war with France, which began in 1673, lasted beyond the end of his reign with only two brief periods of armed peace.

To deal with the eastern problems, Leopold was advised to resort to a policy of repression, revoking the privileges and freedoms guaranteed by Hungary's constitution and occupying the country with German troops, who would be paid by the local counties and the magnates. Spontaneous uprisings produced a general revolt. Vienna responded with a program of violent repression, setting up special courts that prosecuted Protestant preachers, an-gering popular opinion in Protestant states. The repression lasted until 1676, when Leopold had to remove the imperial garrisons from Hungary to fight against France. Hungary again fell into civil war between Catholic magnates loyal to the emperor and Protestant nobles defending their freedom of religion as guaranteed in their constitution. Restoration of traditional liberties in 1681 merely intensified the rebellion.

A deadly plague spreading up the Danube hit the Austrian provinces in 1679, forcing the court to move to Prague. Vienna lost about a fifth of its population. That disaster alongside the diversion of war with France led the Turkish vizier Kara Mustafa to undertake a massive onslaught against the west. In 1683, moving unexpectedly quickly, a Turkish army of nearly a hundred thousand surrounded Vienna on 16 July. Leopold fled with his councils to Passau, where the government began organizing the city's relief. A relieving force gathered above Vienna attacked the besieging forces on 12 September. With the help of King John Sobieski III of Poland, the long battle ended with the Turks in full retreat down the Danube.

The triumph of 1683 turned Leopold's attention to the east. The shift of power in Hungary came slowly. Remaining rebel forces gradually accepted Leopold's offered amnesty. By 1686 Buda fell, the next year imperial forces occupied Transylvania, and in 1688 the great fortress of Belgrade fell. Vienna had just begun celebrating when France invaded the Palatinate. This forced Leopold once again to choose between allowing France to ravage the empire and concentrating on the east, or taking the great risk of fighting a two-front war. Leopold agreed to a greater war, which is known as the War of the League of Augsburg. For nearly a decade neither front produced clear results. In 1691 the Turks retook Belgrade. In 1697, with Prince Eugene of Savoy in command, imperial forces defeated the main Turkish army at Zenta. Two years later the Treaty of Karlowitz fixed the eastern boundary of the Habsburg empire where it remained largely unchanged until the twentieth century.

The treaty of Ryswick temporarily interrupted hostilities with France, but upon the death of Charles II in 1700, war broke out again over the Spanish succession. Leopold sent his forces into northern Italy to occupy what they could of Spanish possessions there. The war soon became global, involving struggles in Germany, Flanders, Italy, Spain, Canada, New England, and the West and East Indies. Leopold died in 1705 at the peak of its intensity. He left a monarchy strengthened by military success, but in much need of institutional reform. Leopold was not a forceful personality. He believed sincerely that his conscientious piety would be sustained by divine providence, which would produce the necessary miracles for survival. He was a master at the art of representing his sovereignty on an elaborate baroque stage, staging complex allegorical productions, performing in them, and composing oratorios and incidental music for them. Vienna's premier role in the development of western music owes much to this modest emperor's cultivation of the one art form that could bridge the many languages spoken by his subjects.

See also **Habsburg Dynasty; Holy Roman Empire; Hungary; League of Augsburg, War of the (1688–1697); Spanish Succession, War of the (1701–1714); Vienna; Vienna, Sieges of.**

BIBLIOGRAPHY

Béranger, Jean. *A History of the Habsburg Empire 1273–1700.* Translated by C. A. Simpson. London and New York, 1994.

Evans, R. J. W. *The Making of the Habsburg Monarchy, 1550–1700: An Interpretation.* Oxford and New York, 1979.

Goloubeva, Maria. *The Glorification of Emperor Leopold I in Image, Spectacle, and Text.* Mainz, 2000.

Ingrao, Charles W. *The Habsburg Monarchy 1618–1815.* Cambridge, U.K., and New York, 1994.

———. *In Quest and Crisis: Emperor Joseph I and the Habsburg Monarchy.* West Lafayette, Ind. 1979.

McKay, Derek. *Prince Eugene of Savoy.* London, 1977.

Redlich, Oswald. *Weltmacht des Barock, Österreich in der Zeit Kaiser Leopolds I.* 4th edn. Vienna, 1961.

Spielman, John P. *Leopold I of Austria.* London and New Brunswick, N.J., 1977.

John P. Spielman

LEPANTO, BATTLE OF. The Battle of Lepanto took place on 6–7 October 1571 between

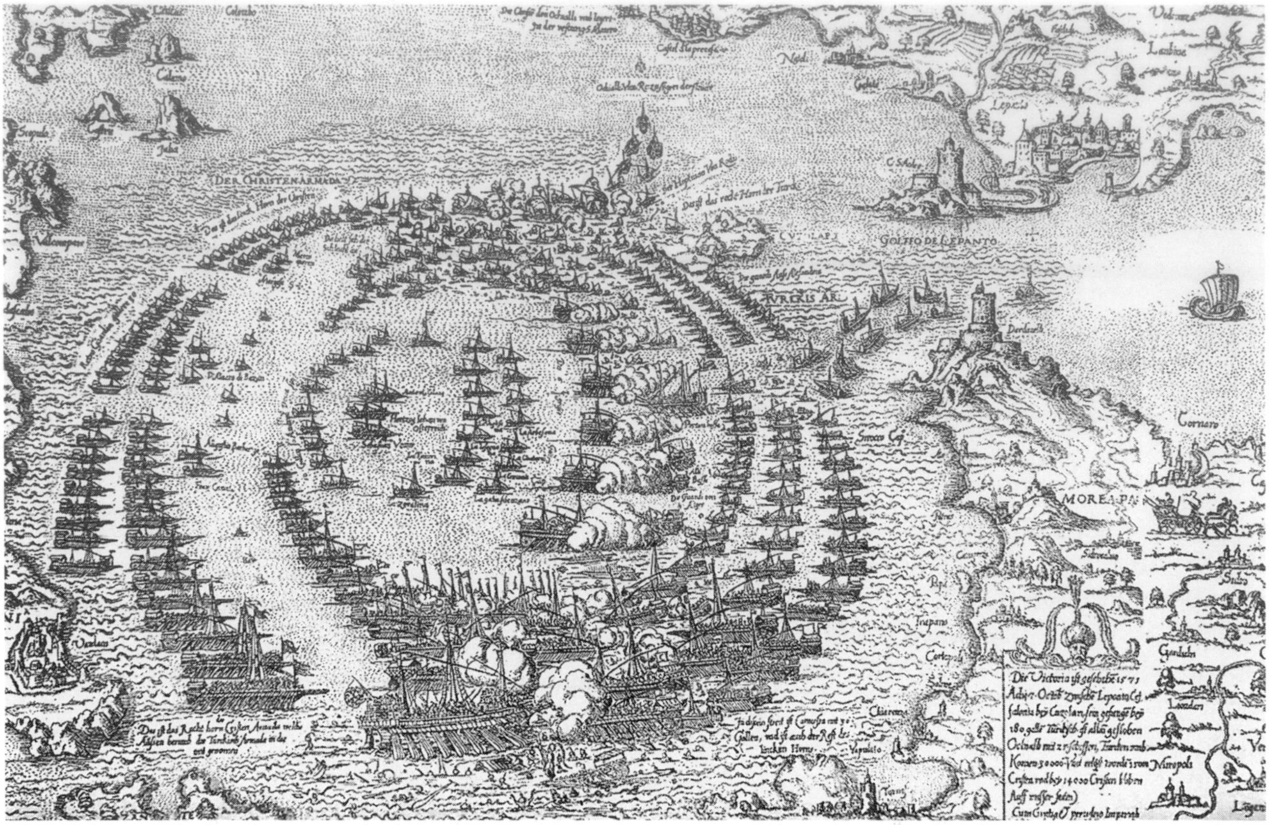

Battle of Lepanto. A sixteenth-century engraving shows the encirclement of the Turkish fleet. ©BETTMANN/CORBIS

the Catholic Holy League fleet led by Don Juan of Austria, a bastard son of Habsburg emperor Charles V, and an Ottoman fleet under Müezzinzade Ali Pasha. It occurred at the mouth of the Gulf of Patras, near where the Peloponnesian peninsula joins the mainland (now in modern Greece). An Ottoman debacle, Lepanto was the last great galley battle in the Mediterranean. The Ottomans sent about 280 ships there, and the Holy League had about the same number. The battle featured the use by the Holy League of a new naval weapon: galleasses. These were Venetian merchant ships outfitted with high cannon superstructures sent in front of the armada to pound the Ottoman fleet as it tried to sweep around them. Debate has persisted about whether it was these new ships with their improved firepower or the Ottoman failure to outflank the Christian force that caused the latter's victory. The battle resulted in about two hundred Ottoman ships being sunk or captured and thirty thousand Ottoman sailors and soldiers killed or captured with only minimal casualties on the Christian side.

A CELEBRATED BUT QUESTIONABLE MILESTONE

This defeat occurred only one month after the shattering Ottoman defeat of Venetian forces defending Cyprus, which the Ottomans then conquered and controlled for the next three centuries. Lepanto was soon celebrated in Europe as a reversal of this defeat and as the end of many years of naval defeats that the Ottomans had inflicted on the Christians. The battle came to be seen as the beginning of subsequent naval decline of the Ottoman Empire. Some modern historians have discounted this view by pointing out that the Ottoman Empire rebuilt virtually the entire fleet that it had lost at Lepanto within a year. Others have pointed out that although the Ottomans did restore their fleet, they suffered a crippling loss of manpower that was particularly harmful for galley warfare. The battle provided a psychological boost for the Catholic world then locked in numerous conflicts across Europe. It was commemorated in Europe through paintings and drawings that depicted it as evidence of a renewed crusading spirit. Miguel de Cervantes, a soldier for

Habsburg Spain, was so severely wounded in the hand at Lepanto that he became a writer. G. K. Chesterton memorialized the battle in a poem.

Lepanto proved the last great Christian-Muslim naval battle in the Mediterranean since privateers and corsairs increasingly dominated naval warfare there. Large-scale Christian-Muslim galley warfare ended in the Mediterranean, perhaps because this battle revealed to both sides the difficulties of permanently controlling this sea. The change may simply reflect, however, that the arena of naval combat had shifted to include the Atlantic and more distant oceans and seas. Ottoman, Habsburg, and Venetian acceptance of the inability of any one power to control the whole Mediterranean after Lepanto led to both a rise in piracy and more commercial activity between traditional partners like Genoa, Venice, and the Ottoman Empire, as well as newcomers like the British, the Dutch and the French.

See also **Austro-Ottoman Wars; Cervantes, Miguel de; Galleys; Holy Leagues; Juan de Austria, Don.**

BIBLIOGRAPHY

Guilmartin, John F., Jr. *Galleons and Galleys.* London, 2002.

———. *Gunpowder and Galleys: Changing Technology and Mediterranean Warfare at Sea in the Sixteenth Century.* London and New York, 1974.

———. "The Tactics of the Battle of Lepanto Clarified." In *New Aspects of Naval History,* edited by Craig L. Symonds, pp. 41–65. Annapolis, Md., 1981.

Hess, Andrew. "The Battle of Lepanto and Its Place in Mediterranean History." *Past and Present* 57 (November 1972): 53–73.

ERNEST TUCKER

LERMA, FRANCISCO GÓMEZ DE SANDOVAL Y ROJAS, 1ST DUKE OF

(1552/1553–1625), favorite of Philip III of Spain and a member of a Valencian family with a long tradition as courtiers. Lerma, about whom few historians ever have said anything kind, was the first of the seventeenth-century *validos,* or Spanish favorites, whose greatest exemplar was the Count-Duke of Olivares (1587–1645).

Philip III (ruled 1598–1621) was an unworthy successor to his grandfather, Charles V (ruled as Holy Roman emperor 1519–1556; as Charles I, king of Spain, 1516–1556), and father, Philip II (ruled 1556–1598). Lerma dominated the young monarch immediately upon his accession and for the next twenty years. Until his fall in 1618, Lerma amassed enormous wealth, elevated friends and relatives whose incompetence was matched only by their greed, oversaw economic ruin, including the sale of offices and debasement of currency, encouraged a lavish court that was a stark contrast to the austerity practiced in the sixteenth century, and engineered the costly and useless transfer of the capital to Valladolid. But he also advocated a series of peace treaties that enabled Spain (and its enemies) to spend around fifteen years in relative peace and recover from decades of warfare.

Scholars traditionally have said that Philip III, under the sway of Lerma, essentially abdicated. Lerma's contemporaries, angry that he kept the king in virtual isolation and beyond their reach, certainly thought so, but recent scholarship disagrees. Evidence is scanty, but what is clear is that Philip III's reign was the occasion for important political developments. The crisis of authority during the early seventeenth century provided theorists with ammunition for new ideas about the relationship between monarch and advisor; the economic crisis propelled the representative Cortes (parliament) and the cities into a more active political role; and even the opulent tastes of the aristocracy and the court spurred artistic production. Lerma can be blamed for these developments; he can also be credited for them. Moreover, peace allowed the government to undertake serious naval rebuilding.

Lerma owned one of the largest art collections of the period and was a patron of dramatists and architects. Peter Paul Rubens (1577–1640) painted his portrait in 1603, seating him like a king on horseback amid glorious, light-infused battle scenes. Juan Pantoja de la Cruz painted portraits of Lerma and Philip III in 1602 and 1606 that are practically identical; the implications were surely not lost on contemporaries.

By 1612, Lerma was the sole intermediary between the king and all government institutions, so much so that the king ordered the Council of State to obey the duke in all matters. His signature had the same weight as that of the king. He had skillfully

Duke of Lerma. Equestrian portrait by Peter Paul Rubens. ©DAVID LEES/CORBIS

institutionalized and legitimized this position of unprecedented power, which he capped in 1618, on the eve of his fall, by being appointed a cardinal of the Roman Catholic Church, apparently the culmination of years of indecision about joining a religious order and withdrawing from the world.

Lerma was probably the richest man in Spain, as well as the most powerful. His enemies were legion, not surprisingly, and they included most of the aristocracy and the female members of the king's family: his wife, Margaret of Austria; his grandmother, Empress Maria of Austria; and his aunt, Margaret of the Cross, a nun. Indeed, it was partly to escape their influence that Lerma moved the king to Valladolid.

Lerma's power began to wane with the Twelve Years' Truce in 1609, seen by some as capitulation to the Dutch rebels. His enemies alleged that others of his noninterventionist decisions, such as avoiding the 1612 Savoy crisis, also were defeatist. One of his closest allies, Rodrigo Calderón, was forced to leave the country in 1611, an important step along the way to dislodging Lerma. As the Twelve Years' Truce neared its end and conflict in Bohemia appeared inevitable, his chief rivals, among them Cristóbal de Sandoval y Rojas, duke of Uceda (and Lerma's own son), and Baltasar de Zúñiga, a former ambassador who was already aiming to advise the future Philip IV, rose in prominence. In September 1618, Lerma asked permission to retire, which the king granted.

As courtiers and rivals fought to divide his wealth and influence and the new regime punished his allies (Calderón was eventually executed), Lerma spent his last years in the seat of his estates, the beautiful town of Lerma, just south of Burgos. The walled town, rebuilt on the orders of the duke in 1606, is among the most outstanding examples of seventeenth-century urban design, both a ducal court and a conventional town. He died 17 May 1625 in Valladolid.

See also **Dutch Revolt (1568–1648); Olivares, Gaspar de Guzmán y Pimentel, count of; Philip III (Spain); Spain.**

BIBLIOGRAPHY

Allen, Paul. *Philip III and the Pax Hispanica, 1598–1621: The Failure of Grand Strategy.* New Haven, 2000.

Feros, Antonio. *Kingship and Favoritism in the Spain of Philip III, 1598–1621.* Cambridge, U.K., and New York, 2000.

Lynch John. *The Hispanic World in Crisis and Change, 1598–1700.* Oxford, 1992.

Phillips, Carla Rahn. *Six Galleons for the King of Spain: Imperial Defense in the Early Seventeenth Century.* Baltimore, 1986.

Sanchez, Magdalena. *The Empress, the Queen, and the Nun: Women and Power at the Court of Philip III of Spain.* Baltimore, 1998.

Tomás y Valiente, Francisco. *Los validos en la monarquía española del siglo XVII.* Madrid, 1982.

Williams, Patrick. "Lerma, 1618: Dismissal or Retirement?" *European History Quarterly* 19 (1989): 307–332.

RUTH MACKAY

LESSING, GOTTHOLD EPHRAIM (1729–1781), German dramatist, critic, theologian, and most prominent proponent of the German Enlightenment. A son of the city's chief Lutheran pastor, Lessing was born in Kamenz in the Electorate of Saxony on 22 January 1729. After attending the local Latin school and the famous ducal school of St. Afra in Meissen, Lessing entered the University of Leipzig in 1746 in order to study theology. Having discovered his love for the theater, he left the university without a degree and, to the dismay of his father, started to make a living as a freelance writer and critic, moving back and forth between the cities of Leipzig, Berlin, Wittenberg, and Breslau.

Scholars emphasize Lessing's role in the development of German theater and drama and his aesthetic theory. His earliest tragedy, *Miss Sara Sampson* (1755), which foreshadowed his rise to literary prominence, constituted a shift from the prevalent French classicist models to an advocacy of Shakespeare and the English theater. *Miss Sara Sampson* can be called an early example of bourgeois tragedy. Lessing argued that the essence of tragedy—pity—depended on the depiction of human suffering and not on the social milieu of the protagonists. It was important, however, to create situations and characters with which the audience could identify.

This new concept is best exemplified in his last tragedy, *Emilia Galotti* (1772). The play is an indictment of an immoral prince who ruthlessly pursues his love interest, the virtuous bourgeois girl Emilia. Seeing no other way of defending his daughter, her father kills her in order to preserve her morality. The play shifts the focus from the court milieu of the heroic play into the private realm of the middle-class family. Later writers such as Johann Wolfgang von Goethe (1749–1832) and Johann Gottfried Herder (1744–1803) equally acknowledged the play's success in depicting an emancipated bourgeoisie of the Enlightenment rebelling against the corruption of court society.

Lessing outlined his thoughts on theater and drama in his *Hamburgische Dramaturgie* (1767–1769; Hamburg dramaturgy), which he wrote while serving as a theater critic at the German National Theater in Hamburg from 1767 to 1769. Despite the fact that the *Hamburgische Dramaturgie* is not a systematic work, it provides many insights into Lessing's thought. Its main concern is the critique of French classical drama and the reinterpretation of Aristotle's work on tragedy.

Lessing's interest in the classics reveals itself in his work on aesthetics. In his *Laokoon: oder über die Grenzen der Malerei und Poesie* (1766; Laocoon: or the limits of painting and poetry), Lessing emphasized the differences between the visual arts and literature. According to Lessing, literature focuses on action, whereas the visual arts focus on static objects. Lessing concluded that literature is superior to painting or sculpture because it can represent the full spectrum of human emotions.

With Lessing's acceptance of the post of ducal librarian at Wolfenbüttel in 1769, theological and religious themes emerged as the overriding concerns of his writings.

During his stay in Hamburg, Lessing had become a close friend of the children of Hermann Samuel Reimarus (1694–1768), a renowned Lutheran theologian and professor of Oriental languages at the academic gymnasium in Hamburg. Influenced by English deism, Reimarus had secretly written an attack on the veracity of revealed religion. After their father's death, Reimarus's children entrusted Lessing with the manuscript, from which Lessing published several parts under the title *Fragmente eines Ungenannten* (1774–1778; Fragments from an unnamed author). Most of the fragments criticized different parts of the Old and New Testament on moral as well as historical grounds. The publication created a stir in religious circles so that Lessing's employer, the duke of Brunswick, withdrew Lessing's censorship privileges. Forced to silence, Lessing wrote his most famous play, the epic poem *Nathan der Weise* (1779; Nathan the wise). Modern scholarship views the play essentially as a call for religious tolerance. By taking characters from the three major religious denominations, Lessing stressed his conviction that religious differences obscure the fact that all belief systems share a set of moral values. Lessing's last work, his *Erziehung des Menschengeschlechts* (1780; The education of the human race) has often been viewed as his literary testament. The work addressed the theological issues raised during the *Fragmente* controversy and in *Nathan der Weise,* namely the problem of the relationship between reason and revelation. According to Lessing, religion is part of the process of the spiritual growth of mankind. Whereas ancient religions needed textual codification in order to provide human beings with guidance in their lives, eventually reason would free humankind of this necessity.

Lessing is justifiably regarded as one of the most distinguished representatives of the Enlightenment. His advocacy of basic humanitarian values such as tolerance illustrates that some proponents of the High Enlightenment not only debated their ideas and values behind the closed doors of the reading societies and salons, but also defended unpopular positions and values in public.

See also **Drama: German; Enlightenment; German Literature and Language.**

BIBLIOGRAPHY

Primary Sources

Lessing, Gotthold Ephraim. *Emilia Galotti: A Tragedy in Five Acts.* Translated by Edward Dvoretzky. New York, 1962.

——. *Gesammelte Werke.* Edited by Paul Rilla. Berlin, 1954–1958.

——. *Laocoön: An Essay on the Limits of Painting and Poetry.* Translated by Edward Allen McCormick. Indianapolis, 1962.

——. *Miss Sara Sampson: A Tragedy in Five Acts.* Translated by G. Hoern Schlage. Stuttgart, 1977.

——. *Nathan the Wise.* Translated by Walter Frank Charles Ade. Woodbury, N.Y, 1972.

———. *Sämtliche Schriften.* Edited and revised by Karl Lachmann and Franz Muncker. 3rd ed. Stuttgart, 1886–1924. Reprinted Berlin, 1968.

———. *Theological Writings: Selections in Translation with an Introduction.* Translated by Henry Chadwick. Stanford, 1956.

Secondary Sources

Albrecht, Wolfgang. *Gotthold Ephraim Lessing.* Stuttgart, 1997.

Allison, Henry E. *Lessing and the Enlightenment: His Philosophy of Religion and Its Relation to Eighteenth-Century Thought.* Ann Arbor, Mich., 1966.

Batley, Edward M. *Catalyst of Enlightenment, Gotthold Ephraim Lessing: Productive Criticism of Eighteenth-Century Germany.* Bern, 1990.

Eckhart, Jo-Jacqueline. *Lessing's* Nathan the Wise *and the Critics: 1779–1991.* Columbia, S.C., 1993.

Engel, Eva, and Claus Ritterhoff, eds. *Neues zur Lessing-Forschung. Ingrid Strohschneider-Kohrs zu Ehren am 26. August 1997.* Tübingen, 1998.

Fick, Monika. *Lessing-Handbuch: Leben-Werk-Wirkung.* Stuttgart, 2000.

Lamport, F. J. *Lessing and the Drama.* Oxford, 1981.

Ugrinsky, Alexej, ed. *Lessing and the Enlightenment.* New York, 1986.

Yasukata, Toshimasa. *Lessing's Philosophy of Religion and the German Enlightenment: Lessing on Christianity and Reason.* Oxford, 2002.

ULRICH GROETSCH

LETTRE DE CACHET. The term "lettre de cachet" refers to arrest warrants that were signed by the king and delivered at the request of royal officials or family members. These letters, whose wax seal or cachet had to be broken in order to be read, allowed individuals to be incarcerated indefinitely and without legal recourse. Although it is difficult to date their first appearance, the use of lettres de cachet accelerated in the seventeenth century with the growth of royal authority. During the mid-century rebellion known as the Fronde, the crown used lettres de cachet to arrest prominent opponents. Once the crisis had subsided, the crown extended the practice to the realm of family discipline, where it acquired its greatest influence and notoriety. The recourse to lettres de cachet, which developed in response to gaps in Old Regime justice, rested on a consensus among the king and his subjects privileging public order over personal freedom. New ideas about human nature and government that took root during the Enlightenment undermined this consensus and the institutional practices that it had sustained.

A parent or spouse submitted a request for a lettre de cachet to the king via his chief police officer, the lieutenant general. The most frequent complaints included debauchery, mental alienation, physical abuse, and financial dissipation. Individuals at all levels of French society could resort to a lettre de cachet when other options failed to resolve the problem. If the family was wealthy and willing to pay expenses, the accused was detained in a convent or a monastery. More humble subjects ended up in Old Regime prisons like the Bastille or asylums like Charenton. The procedure was extrajudicial since the accused had no access to a lawyer and never appeared before a judge. Detention time varied from several months to a lifetime, although the majority of victims were released in less than a year.

The lettre de cachet demonstrates the complicity between royal officials and subjects in the policing apparatus of the Old Regime. While police commissioners executed the arrest, they rarely initiated the request. The people turned to the police to reinforce their disciplinary capacities over an unruly individual. The monarchy complied with most requests because it viewed the family as a school of obedience and loyalty and thus as a model of political order in the kingdom. The supplicant always emphasized the socially disruptive nature of the behavior that threatened family honor while setting a bad example for others to follow. These arguments and their success in swaying the authorities reflected the value of honor in a traditional society based on hierarchy and privilege. The lettre de cachet allowed families to defend their honor without risking the damaging publicity of a trial.

During the Enlightenment intellectuals like Voltaire (1694–1778) and Simon-Nicolas-Henri Linguet (1736–1794) condemned the lettre de cachet in their campaigns for criminal law reform. The libertine writer and future revolutionary leader Mirabeau (Honoré-Gabriel Riqueti; 1749–1791) published a best-selling polemic in 1782 denouncing the lettres de cachet after his release from the Bastille. This book, along with juridical treatises, consolidated the image of the lettre de cachet as a tool of abusive authority. By 1789 popular hostility toward the practice was unanimous and targeted the Bastille as the prison most closely identified with it. The revolutionary government abolished the lettres de cachet in March 1790.

See also **Ancien Régime; Crime and Punishment; France; Fronde; Law; Police; Revolutions, Age of.**

BIBLIOGRAPHY

Primary Sources

Diderot, Denis, and Jean Le Ronde d'Alembert. *Encyclopédie, ou dictionnaire raisonné des sciences, des arts, et des métiers par une société des gens de lettres.* 36 vols. Geneva, 1778–1779. See the entries "Crime" and "Lettre de Cachet."

Linguet, Simon-Nicolas-Henri. *Mémoires sur la Bastille.* London, 1783.

Mirabeau, Honoré-Gabriel de Riquetti. *Des lettres de cachet et des prisons d'état.* Hamburg, 1782.

Secondary Sources

Andrews, Richard Mowery. *Law, Magistracy, and Crime in Old Regime Paris, 1735–1789.* Vol. 1, *The System of Criminal Justice.* Cambridge, U.K., 1994.

Donzelot, Jacques. *The Policing of Families.* Translated by Robert Hurley. New York, 1979.

Farge, Arlette. *Fragile Lives: Violence, Power, and Solidarity in Eighteenth-Century Paris.* Translated by Carol Shelton. Cambridge, Mass., 1993.

Farge, Arlette, and Michel Foucault. *Le désordre des familles: Lettres de cachet des archives de la Bastille au XVIIIe siècle.* Paris, 1982.

Lebigre, Arlette. *La justice du roi: La vie judiciare dans l'ancienne France.* Paris, 1988.

Maza, Sarah. *Private Lives and Public Affairs: The Causes Célèbres of Prerevolutionary France.* Berkeley, 1993.

Quétel, Claude. *De par le roy: Essai sur les lettres de cachet.* Toulouse, 1981.

LISA JANE GRAHAM

LEVANT. The Levant covers the eastern Mediterranean, its islands, including Crete, Cyprus, Rhodes, Chios, and Lesbos, and the lands it borders: modern-day Turkey, Syria, Lebanon, Israel, Palestine, and Egypt. Around 1300, the region was under the control of a variety of different rulers, the Turco-Circassian Mamluk dynasty in Egypt and Syria, various Turkish states in western Anatolia, and the Byzantines. The Genoese controlled Chios and Lesbos and had established themselves on the Anatolian mainland and in Constantinople, while Venice controlled Crete, Negroponte, Naxos, Andros, Mykonos, Karpathos, and Santorini. The Hospitallers ruled Rhodes and, at the beginning of the fourteenth century, built a castle on the Anatolian coast at Bodrum.

From about the mid-fifteenth century, the Ottomans became increasingly dominant. They defeated the Venetians in war from 1463 to 1479 and, in the following century, destroyed the Mamluks, capturing Syria (1516) and Egypt (1517), took Rhodes from the Hospitallers (1522), and conquered Cyprus (1571). While Ottoman control of the Levant weakened thereafter, such weakness was relative, for in 1669 the Ottomans took Crete from the Venetians. As Genoese and Venetian importance declined in the area, that of France, Britain, and Holland increased. Later, Russia also became increasingly active in the region. In 1770 the Russian navy wiped out the Ottoman fleet at Cesme.

TRADE

In the fourteenth and fifteenth centuries, Western traders, in particular those from Genoa and Venice, imported goods such as textiles, soap, cloth, wine, and war materials into the Levant and exported commodities such as slaves, grain, alum, cotton, and spices. Apart from being a producer of commodities itself, the Levant was also a central point for the transit trade in luxury items from the East.

With the Portuguese activities in the Red Sea and the opening up of the sea route to the East, the Levant suffered some decline, particularly as a region for the transit trade in luxury items such as spices, which had formed an important part of Egypt's trade. However, the area continued to be of major commercial importance into the eighteenth century and beyond.

From the late sixteenth century, the English became increasingly important in the commerce of the Levant. English trade, consisting largely of the import of woolen cloth, was to a great extent under the control of the English Levant Company in London, which was granted its first charter in 1581. Dominant through the seventeenth century, English trade went into a temporary decline in the eighteenth century, when the Marseilles merchants became the dominant European traders. The French had established close diplomatic relations with the Ottomans from the early sixteenth century. From 1661, their trade was subject to very firm royal control. The Dutch also came to play a commercial role in the Levant. The interests of these western merchants were represented by their various consuls and ambassadors, and these countries conducted much of their trade through Ottoman middlemen, who liased among the western merchants, the Ottoman authorities, and the local producers. Such middlemen tended often to be Greeks, Armenians, or Jews.

RELIGION

Throughout this period the Levant represented a world of religious plurality in which Christianity (including Greek Orthodox, Maronite, Suryani, Armenian, Catholic, and Protestant), Judaism, and Islam coexisted, and in which Muslims, Jews, and Christians very much shared a common cultural heritage. From the beginning of the seventeenth century, Catholic missionaries began to proselytize among the various eastern-rite churches. Such efforts were often successful and there were many conversions, particulary among the Suryani. The eastern churches were much concerned by the threat such missionary activity posed to their communities, and Christian authorities in Aleppo, for example, appealed to the Ottoman sultan to protect them against this religious encroachment. The Ottoman government responded, backing the local religious establishment against the interloper, less in the interests of religion than from a desire for internal stability, and they issued decrees forbidding the Christian population from changing sects.

In the eighteenth century, religion came to be used as a political lever by the great powers, each seeking to protect the interests of a particular religious community within the Ottoman Empire in an attempt to gain influence over internal Ottoman political affairs. Russia claimed to represent the interests of the Othodox community, using a clause in the Treaty of Kucuk Kaynarca, concluded between Catherine the Great (ruled 1762–1796) and the Ottoman Empire in 1774, to justify their right to intervene in favor of the Orthodox subjects of the sultan. The French claimed to represent the Catholics, and the British concerned themselves with the Protestants.

From early on, the Holy Land attracted a growing number of pilgrims, both Christian and Muslim, visiting Jerusalem, Mecca, and Medina. Protection of the pilgrimage routes and of the Holy Cities formed an important part of the Ottoman sultan's image. While the sheer number of pilgrims could create problems for the authorities, temporarily swelling the population and placing additional strain on the resources of the cities, they also brought additional revenue. For example, in Jerusalem, the Christian pilgrims paid a tax to enter the Church of the Holy Sepulchre. Relations between the Christian pilgrims were not always harmonious, reflecting the bitter hostility between the Greek and Latin churches for control of the holy places. In 1755 the Franciscans were driven out of the Holy Sepulchre by the Greek Orthodox. Despite energetic protests from France, the Ottoman authorities supported the Greek Orthodox in this dispute.

This religious plurality was also reflected in the great ethnic mix of the Levant, which was made up of a great assortment of ethnicities. While the islands had populations of Greeks and Latins, as well as Ottoman Muslims, the great trading cities such as Aleppo were populated by a variety of different ethnic groups, for example, Greeks, Armenians, Turks, Latins, Arabs, and Kurds.

The Levant was thus a mixed world, religiously, ethnically, and linguistically, which gave rise to a vibrant cosmopolitan commercial Levantine culture. Although there were trade wars and political upheavals, and divisions between different groups and religions, the overriding feature of this world was one of fluidity and accommodation, not hard-and-fast divisions and impermeable boundaries.

See also **Mediterranean Basin; Ottoman Empire.**

BIBLIOGRAPHY

Brummett, Palmira. *Ottoman Seapower and Levantine Diplomacy in the Age of Discovery.* Albany, N.Y., 1994. Interesting presentation of the Ottomans as a naval power.

Goffman, Daniel. *Izmir and the Levantine World, 1550–1650.* Seattle, 1990. Detailed study.

Greene, Molly. *A Shared World: Christians and Muslims in the Early Modern Mediterranean.* Princeton, 2000. Crete in transition from Venetian to Ottoman rule.

Hamilton, Alastair, Alexander H. de Groot, and Maurits H. van den Boogert, eds. *Friends and Rivals in the East: Studies in Anglo-Dutch Relations in the Levant from the Seventeenth to the Early Nineteenth Century.* Leiden, 2000. A collection of articles on military, diplomatic, and commercial relations.

KATE FLEET

LEVELLERS. *See* **English Civil War Radicalism.**

LEYDEN, JAN VAN (Jan Beuckelson, John of Leiden; 1509–1536), Dutch religious leader. Jan van Leyden was a prophet who became notorious as "the king of New Jerusalem" in Münster, Westphalia. Very little is known about him, except for the few years in which he rocketed to world fame. His father was a deputy sheriff; his mother hailed from the vicinity of Münster. The city of Leiden in Holland was known for its cloth. When Jan became a tailor's apprentice, his future looked bright. However, by the time he could make a start, the Netherlands was hit by an economic depression that lasted for more than a decade. Leyden fled Leiden and lived in London for a while, then wandered along the coast of Europe.

In the meantime, the Reformation had begun to spread. Yet it was neither Lutheranism nor Zwinglianism, established by Swiss religious reformer Huldrych Zwingli (1484–1531) in Zürich, that would set the Netherlands ablaze, but Anabaptism. Anabaptism originated in middle Europe and was a refuge for people who had become disenchanted with aspects of the Protestant Reformation. The Anabaptists believed that the End of Time was approaching and that they were to be admitted to God's chosen few by means of adult, not infant, baptism. It was Melchior Hofmann (c. 1495–1543/44), a German prophet, who in 1532 brought the new faith to the Dutch border. The Last Judgment, he prophesied, was to be held in Strasbourg, the city which God had chosen for his New Jerusalem (Revelations, 21:9). The Dutch responded enthusiastically and embraced Hofmann as their own prophet. The authorities, however, considered Anabaptism a dangerous heresy and sought to root it out.

Up to this time Leyden was not an Anabaptist. He had settled down after his journeys and opened a tavern in Leiden called The Three Herrings. There he performed in his own plays and satirized monks and priests. He had also been to Münster to hear a famous preacher, and even preached himself, but once back in Leiden he returned to his cheery plays. This all changed suddenly when Jan Matthijsz, the new prophet of the Dutch Anabaptists, knocked at his door. Leyden was rebaptized on 13 January 1534 and was sent by Matthijsz to baptize and organize believers in the new Israel at Münster.

The idea of going to Münster was probably Leyden's. None of the Dutch followers had ever seen Strasbourg, and after Hofman's first prediction about the date of Christ's Second Coming (end of 1533) did not materialize, they felt that since Hofman was wrong about the time, he probably was wrong about the location, too. However, there was no doubt about the reality of the approaching End of Time, so the Dutch followers began to look for cities themselves. Leyden was the first to arrive at Münster to prepare the ground for Christ's Second Coming. At this task he was very successful; in a matter of weeks he built up a huge following.

Soon it was known to Anabaptists everywhere, and especially in Holland, that "God's own people" were in Münster. On a snowy morning in February 1534 the Anabaptists, led by Matthijsz, drove out many of the Münsterites in order to make room for the thousands of newcomers. Ownership of private property and money were abolished and churches and monasteries destroyed. The Anabaptists were in a hurry to sanctify themselves because Jan Matthijsz had predicted the Apocalypse would occur at Easter. On that day he left the city unarmed, expecting the opposing forces to be crushed by the sword of the Lord. Instead, he was butchered before the eyes of his believers by the soldiers of the bishop of Münster, Franz von Waldeck. Leyden was Matthijsz's designated successor.

Leyden was now faced with a very difficult task. He had to try to restore the loss of faith among the people as well as fight Waldeck's soldiers. It was a race against the clock. The bishop grew stronger every day, but Leyden hoped his people would grow in holiness even more quickly, so that Christ would call the Last Judgment before the soldiers could conquer the city. To help achieve this, he invented all kinds of new measures, for one of which he became notorious: the "new marriage," or polygamy, for which Leyden has been derided as a disciple of lust ever since. But although he did not by any means eschew the pleasures of the flesh, his new institution of polygamy had a holy end: Of the 8,000 inhabitants of the New Jerusalem, 6,000 were female, and most people were without partners, many of them for more than six months by then. If he could not make monks out of his Israelites, he would make them polygamists, just like many of the Hebrew patriarchs of the Old Testament.

Jan had many wives. As a "second David," after becoming king, he took more. Several times a week he preached in the marketplace and administered justice. During the course of his reign, after keeping order became more difficult, death penalties became more frequent. But even under these circumstances, it was with his leadership that the city beat off two of Waldeck's attacks. When famine came, Leyden tried to mobilize support from Anabaptists in the Netherlands, but to no avail. On 12 June, 1535, the city fell by the act of a traitor. Leyden had to wait for half a year for his death, which came after prolonged torture. He and two of his companions were put in iron cages and hung high in the tower of the Lambertus Church of Münster. The cages still hang there.

See also **Anabaptism; Münster; Reformation, Protestant; Zwingli, Huldrych.**

BIBLIOGRAPHY

Cohn, Norman. *The Pursuit of the Millennium: Revolutionary Millenarians and Mystical Anarchists of the Middle Ages.* London, 1970.

Haude, Sigrun. *In the Shadow of "Savage Wolves": Anabaptist Münster and the German Reformation during the 1530s.* Boston, 2000.

Panhuysen, Luc. *De Beloofde Stad.* Amsterdam, 2000.

LUC PANHUYSEN

L'HÔPITAL, MICHEL DE (1507–1573), French lawyer and statesman. Michel de L'Hôpital, the future chancellor of France and architect of religious toleration, was the son of a physician who served the dukes of Bourbon. L'Hôpital was destined for a legal career, but in addition to studying law he had a humanist education at a number of Italian and French universities. His religious orthodoxy in his early life is attested by his marriage in 1537 to Marie Morin, daughter of Jean Morin, a Parisian royal official and fierce opponent of heresy. Councillor at the Parlement of Paris in 1544, president of the Chambre des Comptes, and councillor of the Grand Conseil, his career was greatly aided by aristocratic patronage. His father had ended his days in the service of Renée de Bourbon, wife of the duke of Lorraine, and it was through this route that Michel moved into the orbit of the Guise, the most powerful princely family in France, and became the most famous product of the irenic intellectual circle that revolved around Charles of Guise, cardinal of Lorraine. Lorraine procured for his client the office of *maître des requêtes* in 1553 and served as godparent to L'Hôpital's first grandson in 1558.

L'Hôpital's Christian humanist pacifism did not prevent him from becoming an apologist for the Guise war policy in the 1550s. When Henry II died in July 1559 he was succeeded by his sickly fifteen-year-old son, Francis II, who was dominated by his wife Mary Stuart and his Guise uncles. The new regime continued the policy of religious persecution, but the weakness of royal authority and the opposition of the princes of the blood gave encouragement to Calvinism, which was expanding rapidly. The regime was badly shaken by a bloody failed Protestant coup at Amboise in March 1560, following which the cardinal of Lorraine began to rethink the policy of repression. Catherine de Médicis, the queen mother, now began to play a greater role in the shaping of policy. When Olivier, the chancellor of France, died on 28 March 1560, the cardinal procured the appointment of his protégé L'Hôpital.

The new policy formulated by Lorraine, Catherine, and L'Hôpital aimed to promote civil peace by disentangling religious discord from sedition, making a distinction between heresy, which was to be treated more leniently, and rebellion. At the opening of the Estates-General at Orléans in December 1560 L'Hôpital spoke forcefully in favor of religious concord. Following the death of Francis II, the disgrace of the Guise, and the establishment of a regency under Catherine, L'Hôpital's intellectual authority grew, and the policy of compromise it represented was pursued more systematically. Until the end of 1561 neither L'Hôpital nor Catherine believed that toleration and the existence of two religions in a state was possible. The Colloquy of Poissy, which met in August 1561, enshrined their belief that peace could only be achieved by reaching doctrinal concord between Catholics and Protestants. L'Hôpital's move toward toleration was a realistic response to the failure of Poissy and the divisive political and religious situation facing the monarchy. The Edict of Toleration of January 1562 and the Peace of Amboise of March 1563, which followed the First War of Religion, were novel legal attempts to solve the crisis of religious schism by establishing limited rights of worship for Protestant communities.

By the end of 1563 L'Hôpital and his moderate allies had come to dominate the royal council. He combated religious conservatives in the parlements who opposed his religious policy, and he clashed openly in the council with his former patron, Lorraine, who returned from the Council of Trent opposed to his former policies. Between 1563 and 1567 L'Hôpital was concerned with the reform of the royal judiciary and administration, which had suffered from the growth of venal office-holding and the collapse of royal authority. His reforms were enacted in the Ordonnance of Moulins (1566). Catherine de Médicis had been adopting a more intransigent position toward the Protestants for a number of years, and the outbreak of the brief second civil war in 1568 and the breakdown of L'Hôpital's relations with Lorraine led to his removal from the council in June 1568. At the outbreak of the third civil war in September he was forced to give up the seals, and he retired to his residence at Vignay, dying in 1573. Accused by his opponents of being a secret heretic, L'Hôpital was above all a faithful servant of the crown. Realizing that doctrinal reconciliation was impossible, he saw that toleration was the only means to achieve peace and was prescient in seeing Ultra-Catholicism as the main threat to monarchical power.

See also **Catherine de Médicis; Guise Family; Toleration; Wars of Religion, French.**

BIBLIOGRAPHY

Kim, Seong-Hak. "The Chancellor's Crusade: Michel de L'Hôpital and the Parlement of Paris." *French History* 7 (1993): 1–29.

———. "Dieu nous garde la messe du chancelier: The Religious Belief and Political Opinion of Michel de L'Hôpital." *Sixteenth Century Journal* 24 (1993): 595–620.

———. *Michel de L'Hôpital: the Vision of a Reformist Chancellor during the French Religious Wars.* Kirksville, Mo., 1997.

Nugent, Donald. *Ecumenism in the Age of Reformation: The Colloquy of Poissy.* Cambridge, Mass., 1974.

Salmon, J. H. M. *Society in Crisis: France in the Sixteenth Century.* London, 1975. See the summary of L'Hôpital's policies on pp. 51–62.

Sutherland, N. M. *The Massacre of Saint Bartholomew and the European Conflict, 1559–1572.* London, 1973.

STUART CARROLL

LIBERALISM, ECONOMIC. *Economic liberalism* is an anachronistic but useful term to describe theories propounded in the seventeenth and eighteenth centuries. The term was coined by nineteenth-century thinkers to describe their own theories; rather than "economics," seventeenth- and eighteenth-century thinkers considered their inquiries "political economy," and those who defended the rights and freedoms of individuals over and against the state would not bear the appellation of liberals until the 1820s. Nevertheless, "economic liberalism" usefully describes theories of the seventeenth and eighteenth centuries that defended the individual liberty to buy, sell, work, employ, and trade without restriction or governmental interference. The general tenor of economic liberalism is succinctly captured in the French phrase of the era, *laissez-faire,* or 'leave people alone'. This theory maintained that people should be left alone because their self-interested activities in the market were self-regulating, guided by natural economic laws that were far more conducive to social well-being than the directives of state authorities. Thus, economic liberalism was the doctrine typified by seventeenth-century English, French, and Dutch pamphleteers who were critical of state restraints on trade and regulation of interests rates; by the treatises of eighteenth-century French *économistes* (retrospectively designated Physiocrats); and best exemplified by Adam Smith's 1776 *Inquiry into the Nature and Causes of the Wealth of Nations.*

MERCANTILISM BACKGROUND

Economic liberalism can be seen as a response to the wide-ranging policies of European governments from the sixteenth century onward to shape economic activity for state purposes. Such state policies are designated by historians as mercantilism. Economic liberalism manifested itself in systematic criticism of such state interference for violating natural economic laws to the detriment of society. Economic liberalism arose after a wide variety of authors who had spent decades speculating about economic processes articulated natural economic laws that produced an automatic self-regulation of economic activity most conducive to social well-being.

The enormous fiscal demands of state-building in the modern era led various European crowns in relentless efforts for new revenues. Taxation was increased and expanded, and the sale of exclusive monopolies for the production of goods and trade, domestic and foreign, also brought new revenues. Thus, in France, the seventeenth-century minister Jean-Baptiste Colbert (1619–1683) transformed the medieval system of producers' guilds into state-licensed monopolies in goods ranging from salt to lace. In England, trade monopolies were granted for trade with Russia (the Muscovy Company, 1558), the Middle East (the Levant Company, 1592), and India and southeast Asia (the East India Company, 1600). By the seventeenth century in Europe, almost any foreign goods people used were likely imported by a trade monopoly; any domestic goods, by someone operating under a monopoly patent.

European crowns also engaged in currency debasement, that is, adulterating the silver coinage with a base metal and pocketing the difference between the original silver content of the coinage and its nominal value. This had significant consequences in terms of domestic price increases and distortions of rents and real wages. It also disrupted foreign exchange rates, interest rates, and international flows of gold and silver (specie). To ameliorate such consequences, governments undertook the regulation of wages, the prices of primary consumer goods, and interest rates. Since currency debasement created incentives for holders of specie to send it out of the country (to markets where purchasing power was determined by specie value, rather than nominal values), governments were also greatly concerned about the loss of specie within their borders. The power of any state depended on its possession of specie, which allowed it to purchase mercenary troops and supplies abroad for the military struggles of European power politics. Although colonial mines served as the key source of specie for Spain, most other European powers could only obtain specie through international trade. It became an article of faith that state power was maximized by policies that produced a favorable balance of trade, that is, an influx of foreign specie in payment for domestic exports that was greater than the specie outflows to pay for foreign imports. To restrict outflows of specie, heavy import taxes restrained purchases of foreign goods and also produced revenue. To facilitate exports, and therefore specie inflows, government policy promoted the production of high-value domestic manufactures, protected by high tariffs or even prohibitions on imports of foreign manufactures.

The above mercantilist state-building objectives introduced new perspectives on economic activity. Because national power was promoted by influx of specie, international trade was seen in a new, positive light. Medieval views of merchants as exploitative were supplanted by a view of traders as national assets. From this perspective, domestic trade only transferred wealth from one group to another, but foreign trade brought in new treasure from abroad. Nevertheless, many believed that the selfish interests of merchants might run contrary to the interests of the state, and for that reason, trade needed strict regulation and the guiding hand of authorities.

MERCANTILISM AND THE DEVELOPMENT OF POLITICAL ECONOMY

By the seventeenth century, the growing role of government in control of the economy prompted extensive commentary on public affairs and public policies related to usury, prices, and the state of international trade. Such commentators, now designated mercantilists, were not mere spokesmen for the system of the same name. They frequently wrote to get the government to pursue some policy that would benefit them (for example, reduction of interest rates or prohibition of imports by competitors), but there was a wide variety of views and motives in their work, and many criticisms of government policy. Over time, the proliferation of such works resulted in a general understanding of "the economy" as a linkage of prices, money flows, interest rates, and international trade, which could be subjected to and explained by analytical theories. The analytical tools and theories developed by these writers were not terribly sophisticated, nor universally accepted or applied in anything like a systematic manner. Yet from such efforts to comprehend the intricate network of exchanges, prices, and behavior of human beings as producers and consumers, a new science emerged called political economy. Most authors now described as mercantilists showed a clear understanding, for example, of sophisticated ideas such as international trade representing a sort of barter mediated by money, and that there can be no export customers if nations do not also purchase imports from those to whom they hope to sell. Even though most recognized the need for regulated trade, virtually none proposed economic self-sufficiency. Similarly, most understood that the merchants could not simply set prices for exports; rather, prices were determined by the actions of all involved "in the common market of the world."

A pamphlet dispute in the 1620s between two early English political economists, Gerald de Maylnes (1586–1641), an official of the Royal Mint, and Edward Misselden (1608–1654), a merchant, reveals the general level of analysis. Maylnes was alarmed at specie outflows from England, and he accused merchants involved in the exchange of foreign currency of being the cause of the kingdom's loss of bullion. Since the merchants' selfish desire for gain, amounting to usury, resulted in specie outflow, Maylnes proposed government-run currency exchange at "fair rates" to keep specie in the country. Misselden, on the other hand, denied Maylnes's simplistic attribution of the problem of specie outflows to the malevolence of merchants. Specie flows, he explained, followed general levels of trade; if there was more specie flowing out of the country, it was because the balance of trade was not in England's favor. Since England imported more than it exported, specie was lost to the nation. The true solution to the problem, Misselden urged, was to restore a favorable balance of trade.

Misselden's use of the balance of trade concept illustrates a central feature of mercantilist economic theory. A favorable balance of trade provided specie for national strength, but it was also desired because plenty of money at home would stimulate domestic trade and employment. Further, since interest rates were determined by the supply of money, plenty of money would reduce interest rates and stimulate investment. Thus, the English merchant Thomas Mun's tract (written 1623; published 1664) ridiculed the idea that an exchange board could simply decree that specie stay in the country, as exchange rates were determined by supply and demand. He even expressed suspicion about any policy's capacity to maintain plenty of specie in the country: since prices were determined by the quantity of money, more specie would invariably raise prices, and thereby diminish exports. Still, Mun argued that policies restricting shipping to English carriers, sumptuary laws to limit luxury imports, and state support of exports (such as herring), would promote, as his title declared, *England's Treasure by Forraigne Trade, or the Balance of Our Forraigne Trade Is the Rule of Our Treasure.*

POLITICAL ECONOMY AND THE IDEA OF ECONOMIC LAW

The seventeenth century was a period of great intellectual ferment in which the techniques of the new natural sciences, exemplified by Galileo Galilei (1564–1642) and Isaac Newton (1642–1727), gripped the imaginations of thinkers such as Francis Bacon (1561–1626) and René Descartes (1596–1650), who boldly proclaimed that the new techniques of scientific analysis would transform the whole of human thought. Such aspirations fed the ambitions of those who sought to place human action within the descriptive bounds of similar natural laws. The notion of economic law developed out of a century's observation of the regularity of markets, of rising prices producing increased supplies, and of gluts in the market producing falling prices. Many writers believed that the cause of such regularities was economic actors responding to opportunities for personal gain. Thus, the seventeenth century saw a new regard for self-interest. On the one hand, self-interest came to be seen as a more rational, less dangerous motivation for human behavior than the passions. On the other hand, because self-interest involved rational calculation, some believed that acts of self-interest demonstrated the same kinds of regularity in human nature as was found in other scientific laws in the natural realm. The whole of human activity in buying, growing, selling, spending, and the satisfaction of human wants, without anyone's directing or even intending the result, could be explained as people pursuing their interests.

In his *Discourse of Trade* (1690) English physician Nicholas Barbon asserted that, as with all things necessary to life, everything that produced delight and pleasure, along with peace and economic development, was the product of trade, the consequence of people acting in the market for their own benefit. Such actions resulted in the nation being "well fed, clothed, and lodged" while "the richer sort are furnished with all things to promote the ease, pleasure, & pomp of life."

SEVENTEENTH-CENTURY ENGLISH ECONOMIC LIBERALS

The idea of natural economic law lay at the heart of the economic liberal critique of mercantilism. Perhaps no name is more closely associated with the concept of natural law than that of John Locke (1632–1704), the English philosopher widely accorded status as a founder of political liberalism. Although Locke's writings are concerned with both political and economic liberalism, proponents of these two fields were often at odds with one another. Locke's economic writings chiefly dealt with money and interest rates, and in both cases he utilized natural economic law to criticize government interference. In 1692, Locke published *Some Considerations of the Consequences of the Lowering of Interest and Raising the Value of Money* to oppose a legislative reduction of interest from 6 percent to 4 percent along with a scheme to reduce the silver content of England's coinage. In the case of interest rate reductions, Locke insisted that there was a "natural rate" that was the product of "the present state of trade, money, and debts," in other words, by the supply and demand for funds that could be loaned. Locke denied that interest rates could be regulated by law. The law would be flouted, as "it will be impossible by any contrivance of the law, to hinder men . . . to purchase money to be lent to them what rate soever their occasions shall make it necessary for them to have it." But all legal lending would also be reduced, since the interest reduction would reduce the supply of funds for loans, and guarantee that only the safest loans would be made. Thus, rather than making loans more available, artificial reductions of the rate of interest decreased the supply of credit. The idea of legislating interest rates, Locke says, is as absurd as legislating rents: in both cases "things must be left to find their own price." In the case of the recoinage, Locke argued that the value of a coin was determined by its silver content, and "the opinion of men consenting to it," rather than the denomination stamped on it by the mint. Since contracts and rents had been entered into based upon coins having a given silver content, to change the silver content of the coins would amount to fraud. The proponents of the scheme may call debased coins shillings, but "one may as rationally hope to lengthen a foot by dividing it into fifteen parts instead of twelve and calling them inches."

Sir Dudley North (1641–1691) was a zealous partisan of Charles II (ruled 1660–1685) and James II (ruled 1685–1688) who led the legal persecution of liberal Whigs for the crown, but he was also an economic liberal. His *Discourses upon Trade* (1692), edited and published posthumously by his brother Roger, was suffused with the "principles of the new philosophy," the "mechanical" science that alone provides "clear and evident truths." Principles derived from scientific reasoning proved that "to force men to deal in any prescribed manner, may profit such as happen to serve them; but the publick gains not, because it is taking from one subject to give to another." North, too, contested the proposal to legislate a lower rate of interest, and, like Locke, argued that the natural rate of interest was determined by the supply and demand for loans. Indeed, North observed, the reason interest rates were lower in the Netherlands—which had no interest regulations—was that the trading wealth of the Dutch meant that more money was available for loans. North argued that artificial reductions of the rate of interest would reduce the sums available for loans since "it probably will keep some money from coming abroad into trade; whereas on the contrary, high interest certainly brings it out." Nor was there any need for the government to increase the money supply by means of the recoinage that Locke had contested; in North's view, money, like any commodity, was subject to the automatic equilibrating processes of the market. As North explained, the "ebbing and flowing of money, supplies and accommodates itself, without any aids from politicians . . . when money is scarce, bullion is coyned, when bullion is scarce, money is melted." People looked in vain to the government to produce prosperity, North averred, "for no people ever yet grew rich by policies; but it is peace, industry, and freedom that brings trade and wealth, and nothing else."

Another self-conscious crafter of a new human science was the physician-politician Sir William Petty (1623–1687) who, taking a cue from Francis Bacon, sought to understand human society as a form of anatomy. (Petty also served as secretary to Thomas Hobbes, another great social anatomist.) Instead of the dissection of nerves and tissues, the scientific investigator of human society had to master quantitative data on population, tax revenues, trade and production, and all manner of social statistics. Petty called his program "political arithmetic," and, while his general view of economic policy followed predictable mercantilist lines in viewing national wealth as contingent on its share of the (fixed) world trade, he also argued that government policy had limited capacity to directly control economic events because of the immutable operation of natural economic laws. Thus he attacked legislative reduction of the rate of interest as one example of "the variety and fruitlessness of making Civil Positive Laws against the Laws of Nature."

Although Petty's contributions to social statistics and economics are today judged negligible, he had followers who pursued his program of attempting to discern and articulate economic laws. One disciple, the politician and civil servant Charles Davenant (1656–1714), illustrates how economic law came to undermine the old sureties of beneficent government direction of the economy. In the 1690s, the English East India Company began to import large quantities of cheap printed Indian cotton goods. This produced a storm of protest from writers who attacked the company for undermining the domestic production of English woolens and silks. Davenant's defense of the company (he was at this time an employee), called *Essay on the East India Trade* (1696), argued that economic regulation for the protection of a single industry ignored the systemic nature of economic life, in which all trades were linked, and injurious policies could spread their effects far beyond their intended purpose. Although he conceded that Indian imports injured English woolen manufactures, Davenant merely took this as evidence that they were akin to hothouse flowers, unable to survive without artificial aids. To force trade in this manner brought no "natural profit" and was ultimately injurious to the public. Woolen manufactures were injured only because the public benefited more from cheap Indian cottons than from woolen garments dependent upon protection for a market. "Trade is in its nature free, finds its own channel," he wrote, "and best directs its own course; and all laws to give it rules and directions, and to limit and circumscribe it, may serve the particular ends of private men, but are seldom advantageous to the public."

Five years later, Henry Martyn's *Considerations upon the East India Trade* (1701) took up the same matter and attacked the very idea of the legal monopoly of the East India Company. Cheap Indian cloth, Martyn wrote, was just one of many benefits, including from spices, silks, and wine, which foreign trade produced. While the public benefited from Indian imports, it would benefit still more, Martyn argued, if the trade were open to all, as competition between merchants would force prices and transportation costs to the minimum. Martyn also reasoned that if Indian goods could be purchased more cheaply than those produced at home, English cloth manufactures simply wasted labor. But if competition were unleashed, it might stimulate inventiveness of skill and machinery to reduce the costs of English cloth below India's. Martyn's central contention was that free competition of self-interested actors in the marketplace benefits the public by producing more at less cost.

DUTCH REPUBLICANISM AND ECONOMIC LIBERALISM

Pieter de la Court (1618–1685), polemicist for the republicans fighting the establishment of a Dutch monarchy by the House of Orange, published a very liberal tract that fused political and economic liberalism. *Political Maxims of the State of Holland* (*Aanwysing der heilsame politike Gronden en Maximen van de Republike van Holland en West-Vriesland,* 1662) attacked monarchical principles and linked the cause of crowns with standing armies, clerical mystification, and the destruction of urban commercial society. Commerce, he wrote, by "common interest wonderfully linked together" all the people of the Netherlands "from the least to the greatest" in "excellent and laudable harmony." He pleaded for religious toleration to promote Dutch economic growth since "those that deal in manufactures, fishing, traffic [and] shipping" would not come to live in a "country where they are not permitted to serve and worship God outwardly, after such a manner as they see fit." Domestic markets were integral to the prosperity of Dutch trade and shipping, he argued, and therefore he defended occupational freedom, "the liberty of gaining a livelihood without any dear-bought city freedom," since no immigrants would come to the Netherlands "if they should have no freedom of chusing and practicing such honest means of livelihood as they think best for their subsistence." Immigrants would not depress wages of native inhabitants; on the contrary, they would "lay out their skill and estate in devising new fisheries, manufactures, traffick and navigation." Immigrants were essential in a commercial society to take up those enterprises—"in Amsterdam alone there are yearly three hundred abandoned"—whose native proprietors "finding the gain uncertain, and the charge great, are apt to relinquish it." De la Court attacked monopolies and guild restrictions for violating people's "natural liberty of seeking their livelihoods." Trade should be open to "the industrious and ingenious," for monopolies—"dull, slow, unactive, and less inquisitive"—were unable to exploit even opportunities guaranteed them by law. The whaling monopoly, for example, proved unprofitable; but under competition, "everyone equips their vessel at the cheapest rate, follow[s] their fishing diligently, and manage all carefully" and whaling became profitable with fifteen times more ships involved in the industry. Monopoly did nothing more than cause the Dutch to be "bereft of the freedom of buying their necessaries at the cheapest rate they can."

ECONOMIC LIBERALISM IN FRANCE

In late seventeenth-century France, a civil servant, Pierre la Pesant, sieur de Boisguillebert (1646–1714) argued for economic laissez-faire with a sophistication that earned the respect of the great twentieth-century economist Joseph Schumpeter. In his chief work, *A Detailed Account of France* (*Le detail de la France,* 1695), Boisguillbert dismissed the mercantilist equation of money with wealth, contending that wealth lay in goods, rather than coin. Social harmony and well-being were the products of individuals acting in their self-interested pursuit of happiness. The transactions of self-interested actors in a market created order and peace, for "the pure desire of profit will be the soul of every market for buyer and seller alike; and it is with the aid of that equilibrium or balance that each partner to the transaction is equally required to listen to reason, and submit to it." The natural order produced by laissez-faire, however, could be disturbed: "nature alone can introduce that order and maintain the peace. Any other authority spoils everything by trying to interfere, no matter how well intentioned it may be." Boisguillebert claimed that good intentions gone awry were behind the French crown's efforts to diminish hunger by controlling grain prices, since price controls merely diminished cultivation of grain and exacerbated shortages. If the government would merely lift its controls on prices and grain imports, he argued, food would soon be abundant.

Boisguillebert's concern with food supplies highlights one chief difference between French and English political economy in the seventeenth and eighteenth centuries: the French focus on agriculture, rather than international trade. Liberal critics saw the persistence of a feudal land tenure system in France as responsible for backwardness in agriculture, especially in comparison with her neighbors, England and the Netherlands. Chief among these critics was the circle gathered around the physician Francois Quesnay (1694–1774). Quesnay's allies, such as Mercier de la Riviere (1720–1793) and Pierre Samuel Du Pont de Nemours (1739–1817), called themselves *les economistes,* but are now designated Physiocrats. The Physiocrats popularized the slogan, *"laissez-faire, laissez passer,"* as the essence of economic wisdom. At the heart of physiocratic doctrine was the conviction that agriculture alone was the source of all wealth, since only it provided surplus, or net product. Therefore, all restrictions on agriculture, such as price controls and barriers to internal and foreign trade, undermined national wealth. Quesnay's famous *Tableau economique* (1759) drew upon insights developed by an Irish banker living in Paris, Richard Cantillon (d. 1734) in his *Essai sur la nature du commerce,* which explained the circular flow of income produced by markets. Quesnay's intricate chart purported to demonstrate the circulation of net product throughout the entire society, which was as perpetual and self-regulating as the circulation of blood. In the eyes of the Physiocrats, the countless restrictions on free commerce imposed by the government were as socially beneficial as blood clots in human circulation.

One of Quesnay's associates, Vincent de Gournay (1712–1759) a wealthy merchant and royal administrator, spent years in the Netherlands and admired de la Courts's *Maxims*. He also commended Cantillon's work to Quesnay, and although he never wrote economic tracts, he had a profound influence as tutor and advisor to Finance Minister Anne-Robert-Jacques Turgot (1727–1781). Turgot, in a eulogy to Gournay, praised him for grasping the fundamental principle of economic policy, which was that every individual knew his or her own interest best, and that with individuals left free to pursue their interests, "it would be impossible for the aggregate individual interests not to concur with the general interest." Competition in the market, which was the consequence of the pursuit of interest, produced innovation in manufacturing, and the lowest prices for consumers. Rather than the plethora of regulations covering every aspect of economic life, or monopoly privileges, Gournay favored the "natural liberty" to buy and sell as the guarantor of production, and of consumers obtaining goods at the best price. Short of providing justice, and bestowing honors on inventors and artists, government best served the economy by removing obstacles it had erected.

Turgot's turbulent years as finance minister to Louis XVI (ruled 1774–1792) saw an effort to create the system of freedom articulated by French liberals over previous decades. His chief objective was to remove all barriers to agricultural and international trade. The farmer was "the only one who suffers from monopoly as buyer and at the same time as seller. There is only he who cannot buy freely from foreigners the things which he has need; there is only he who cannot sell to foreigners the commodity he produces." Domestic and international laissez-faire, a "general liberty of buying as selling is . . . the only means to insure on one side to the seller a price sufficient to encourage production; on the other side to the consumer the best merchandise at the lowest price." Turgot's management of the economy amounted to not interfering with natural economic law, because "in order to direct it without deranging it, and without injuring ourselves, it would be necessary for us to be able to follow all the changes in the needs, the interests, and the industry of mankind . . . Even if we had in all these particulars that mass of knowledge impossible to be gathered, the result would only be to let things go precisely as they would have gone of themselves, by a simple action of men's interests, influenced by the balance of a free competition."

ADAM SMITH'S *WEALTH OF NATIONS*

Adam Smith (1723–1791), professor of moral philosophy at the University of Glasgow, published his great contribution to economic liberalism, *Inquiry into the Nature and Causes of the Wealth of Nations* in 1776, a significant date in the history of political liberalism. Deeply affected by the example of Isaac Newton's scientific system, which explained the orbits of the planets from the operation of basic laws of motion and mass, Smith sought to explicate how basic economic laws produced the regular operation of markets he called "the system of natural liberty." As the title of the book intimates, Smith's central concern was with economic development and growth, the means to secure "universal opulence which extends itself to the lowest ranks of the people." Opulence was a matter of the material well-being of the people, which consisted of cheap and plentiful goods. The key was productivity, the secret of which Smith identified as the "division of labor." Since the degree of specialization was determined by the extent of the market, the more extensive the market, the more productive human activity would be and the wealthier people would become. Smith was scornful of all the policies that were designed over centuries to secure a favorable balance of trade. Trade itself reflects the fact that different regions, different countries, have certain "natural advantages" in producing goods; and so if "a foreign country can supply us with a commodity cheaper than we ourselves can make it, better buy it of them."

Just as Newton described the motion of the heavens in terms of simple concepts of mass, motion, and the force of gravity, Smith's "simple system" operated from little more than self-interest, competition, and enforcement of basic rules of justice. Smith's previous book, *The Theory of Moral*

Sentiments (1759), explained how people's desire to be loved led them to conform to moral rules, but this principle, so effective at the level of family, friends, and neighbors, was too weak to account for relations between strangers. Rather, the extensive transactions that characterized markets were based on mutual gains from trade. "It is not from the benevolence of the butcher, the brewer, or the baker that we expect our dinner, but from their regard to their own interest." Because the public interest is for people to live in opulence, individuals led by self-interest to employ their labor and capital to make the society more productive, and satisfy human wants, are "led by an invisible hand to promote an end which was no part of [their] intention." Smith was acutely aware of the dangers presented by self-interest, however: "People of the same trade seldom meet together, even for merriment and diversion, but the conversation ends in a conspiracy against the public, or in some contrivance to raise prices." It was for this reason that the force of competition was vital to the operation of his system. Contrivances to replace "the natural price, or the price of free competition" ranging from outright monopoly privileges, to bounties, to restrictive tarries, to restrictions on free movement of labor—there were myriad ways governments could protect some person or group against competition, and thus allow private interest to take precedence over the public good. The elimination of all schemes to insulate people against competition was vital. "All systems either of preference or restraint, therefore, being completely taken away, the obvious and simple system of natural liberty establishes itself of its own accord. Every man, as long as he does not violate the laws of justice, is left perfectly free to pursue his own interest his own way, and to bring both his industry and capital into competition with any other man, or order of men."

Economic liberalism as an influence on seventeenth- and eighteenth-century policy was limited at best. Turgot's reforms were abandoned, and Smith's myriad recommendations for overhauling Britain's policies, while admired by prime ministers, were too radical to be undertaken in an age of war and revolution. In the nineteenth century economic liberalism acquired not only its name, but the status of scientific orthodoxy, with the establishment of professorships in the new academic discipline of political economy in universities throughout Europe. The nineteenth century also saw the implementation of such iconic economic liberal policies as free trade in Britain.

See also **Bacon, Francis; Capitalism; Democracy; Hobbes, Thomas; Locke, John; Mercantilism; Money and Coinage; Petty, William; Physiocrats and Physiocracy; Smith, Adam.**

BIBLIOGRAPHY

Primary Sources

All citations from primary sources in this article are from microfilms of the catalog of the Kress-Goldsmith Library of Economic Literature, available at many large research libraries.

Barbon, Nicholas. *Discourse of Trade.* London, 1690.

Boisguillebert, Pierre de Pesant. *Le detail de la France, sous le regne present.* n.p., 1695.

Bramsted, E. K., and K. J. Melhuish, eds. *Western Liberalism: A History in Documents from Locke to Croce.* London and New York, 1978. Has selections from Turgot and Smith, especially valuable for nineteenth-century economic liberalism.

Cantillon, Richard. *Essay on the General Nature of Commerce.* Edited and translated by Henry Higgs. New York, 1931. Translation of 1757 *Essai sur la nature du commerce en general.*

Clark, Henry C. ed. *Commerce, Culture, and Liberty: Readings on Capitalism before Adam Smith.* Indianapolis, 2003. A superb collection of previously inaccessible writings, including most cited in this article.

Court, Pieter de la. *Aanwysing der heilsame politike Gronden en Maximens van de Republike van Holland en West-Vriesland.* Leiden, 1669. English translation, *Political Maxims of the State of Holland.* London, 1702.

Davenant, Charles. *Essay on the East India Trade.* London, 1696.

Locke, John. *Some Considerations of the Consequences of the Lowering of Interest and Raising the Value of Money.* London, 1692.

Martyn, Henry. *Considerations on the East India Trade.* London, 1701.

Meek, Ronald. *The Economics of Physiocracy: Essays and Translations.* Cambridge, Mass., 1963. Translated selections from Quesnay, DuPont, and others.

Mun, Thomas. *England's Treasure by Forraigne Trade.* London, 1664.

North, Sir Dudley. *Discourses upon Trade.* London, 1692.

Smith, Adam. *Inquiry into the Nature and Causes of the Wealth of Nations.* Edited by Edwin Cannan. New York, 1937. (1776) Many editions. Cannan's marginal annotations make it ideal for students.

Secondary Sources

Appleby, Joyce Oldham. *Economic Thought and Ideology in Seventeenth-Century England.* Princeton, 1978.

Brewer, Antony. *Richard Cantillon: Pioneer of Economic Theory.* London, 1992.

Cole, Charles Woolsey. *French Mercantilism, 1683–1700.* New York, 1943. Covers both policy and the political economists' discussions.

Eatwell, John, Murray Milgate, and Peter Newman, eds. *The New Palgrave: A Dictionary of Economics.* 4 vols. London and New York, 1987. Articles on most authors cited.

Heckscher, Eli. *Mercantilism.* 2 vols. 2nd rev. ed. New York, 1955.

Hirschman, Albert O. *The Passions and the Interests.* 2nd ed. Princeton, 1997.

Hutchison, T. W. *Before Adam Smith: The Emergence of Political Economy, 1662–1776.* Oxford, 1988.

Letwin, William. *The Origins of Scientific Economics.* New York, 1966.

Muller, Jerry Z. *Adam Smith in His Time and Ours.* Princeton, 1993.

Schumpeter, Joseph. *History of Economic Analysis.* New York, 1954. Encyclopedic, deeply learned, somewhat inaccessible.

RICK VERNIER

LIBERTINISM. *See* **Atheism.**

LIBERTY. While it possessed important connotations in philosophical and theological discourses, the term *liberty* (and its frequent cognate, *freedom*) conveyed primarily social and political overtones in early modern Europe. Liberty formed a central organizing principle around which myriad transformations of communal life occurred, culminating in the program of the French Revolutionaries, who placed the demand for civil and legal freedom at the forefront of their movement.

Early modern Europe inherited several different ideas of liberty that were revised, refined, and sometimes rejected entirely. The ancient republicans of Rome prized liberty as a collective good, which betokened both freedom from foreign domination and the absence of internal oppression in the form of a king. Liberty was thus connected with civic self-rule of a populist (if not quite popular) character. This republican ideal was widely disseminated among, and often endorsed by, early modern thinkers.

Christianity contributed the doctrines of freedom of the will and evangelical liberty that added a personal dimension to human freedom. Created in God's image, humanity possessed a capacity to choose between good and evil and hence to accept or to turn away from the divine will. Of course, the objects between which one chooses are not of equal worth. Rejecting God by preferring one's own desires yields dissatisfaction and unhappiness in one's earthly life as well as the misery of eternal damnation. By contrast, submitting to God properly expresses one's divinely granted freedom; it is the correct use of the will with which human begins have been endowed. At the same time, the possibility of freely renouncing self-will in favor of embracing God's law—in sum, a conversional experience—remains always open up to the very moment of one's death.

Finally, medieval Europe added a legal dimension to liberty that, in a sense, synthesized the public and the private meanings conveyed by republicanism and Christianity respectively. Under the terms of feudal law, the person designated to hold a prerogative or privilege (such as the ability to exercise forms of justice or to collect certain types of revenues) was said to possess "a liberty." Feudal liberty, in this sense, was an exclusive, independent, and nonusurpable right to the application of power over people and property, granted under fixed conditions from a superior who was deemed to be its ultimate source and guarantor. In short, liberty reflected a sphere of authority within which no one could directly intercede or interfere with the exercise of specified rights. Yet it was not wholly private. The possessor of a liberty could protect it from erosion by appeal for assistance to the lord who granted it. Someone who claimed a liberty could also be charged with its misapplication by those subjected to it, and could even be challenged to demonstrate the warrant on the basis of which it was exercised.

RELIGION

Although these inherited concepts of liberty continued to circulate in early modern Europe, the language of freedom proliferated and diversified in the context of the vast cultural changes that marked the period. Crucial to this development was religion. The Reformation brought not only a challenge in practice to the unity of the Christian Church, but also transformation of important theological categories. Martin Luther (1483–1546) insisted upon the unique presence of God alone in the conscience of believers, with the implication that the faithful Christian is responsible directly and immediately to God. The consequence of this teaching—while perhaps recognized only fleetingly by Luther and his followers—was that salvation did not depend upon submission to the authority of the priesthood or the church. Nor did it fall to the secular power, to whom pertained the control of bodies and behavior, to discipline the souls of subjects. Thus, whether intentionally or not, Luther opened the door to claims of public respect for "liberty of conscience," and eventually freedom of worship.

In the generation after Luther, inferences about freedom of religion were drawn out by reforming thinkers. Sébastien Castellion (1515–1563) published pseudonymously a treatise entitled *De Haereticis, an sint Persequendi* (1554), in response to John Calvin's (1509–1564) organization of the burning of a fellow Christian theologian for heresy at Geneva. Castellion argued that coercion is an inappropriate tool for effecting a change of religious views since Christian belief must be held with sincere conviction. Hence, clerics and magistrates must refrain from persecution of convinced Christians who cling to doctrines that do not coincide with official teachings. While Castellion does not go so far as to license broad dissemination of heterodox theology, he maintains that a Christian's duties extend to forbearance of the free and honest faith of his fellows even in the face of disagreements of understanding and interpretation.

In the seventeenth century, the theme of religious liberty became more pronounced. For instance, the Levellers in England during the 1640s made freedom to dissent from the established religion a central plank of their political program. Major figures in European philosophy weighed in on the side of freedom of religion. Baruch Spinoza (1632–1677) claimed a broad application for a right to liberty of thought and belief without inference from a sovereign power's (or a church's) determination of the truth or falsity of one's ideas. Pierre Bayle (1647–1706) boldly asserted that all forms of persecution (innocuous as well as harsh) of religious diversity encouraged hypocrisy and eroded social order. An erring conscience, if it be held in good faith, deserves as much protection as a correct one—a principle that Bayle extended even to atheists. John Locke (1632–1704) was unwilling to include atheism and other religious attitudes that he deemed dangerous to social trust and political obedience, but he, too, proposed liberty of conscience as justified in the case of most Christian (and perhaps some non Christian) rites. The role of the magistrate, according to Locke, should be confined to the maintenance of public tranquillity and the defense of individual rights, rather than the care of the soul.

Pragmatic as well as principled considerations led to the acceptance of some measure of freedom of religion throughout much of Europe over the course of the early modern period. Wars of religion undermined peace and sapped public enthusiasm for persecution. The free practice of differing confessions (usually limited to Christianity, and sometimes only to reformed Christianity) became an enshrined feature of many European states by the late eighteenth century. Where this did not occur (with certain exceptions, such as in Spain and parts of the Italian peninsula), it posed a continuing source of conflict into later times, as Johannes Althusius (1557–1638) predicted it would in his *Politica Methodice Digesta* (1603; 3rd ed., 1614). Thus, freedom of religion constituted one of the main changes sought in France during the Revolution, as expressed in the "Declaration of the Rights of Man and of the Citizen."

REPUBLICANISM AND LIBERALISM

The evolving acceptance of liberty of confession paralleled changes in other European cultural, social, and political practices and attitudes. The invention of the printing press and movable type immeasurably enhanced the ability of individuals to disseminate their ideas and for a larger public to have access to the written word. Demands were heard for freedom of the press (literally and figuratively) from censorship by clerical and secular authorities alike.

Of course, the tradition of republican liberty, inspired by the Romans, had not disappeared from the intellectual landscape. From Niccolò Machiavelli (1469–1527) and the more conventional humanists of Renaissance Italy through the thinkers and practitioners of Dutch republicanism like Hugo Grotius (1583–1645) to advocates of republican rule in England such as James Harrington (1611–1677) and Algernon Sidney (1623–1683), the praise of liberty as a distinctive feature of republican government was voiced. In the cities of Italy and of Holland, commercial vitality and strong civic loyalty, not to mention considerations of scale, rendered collective self-government a feasible option. Political practice could approach, even if never quite attain, the heights of theory.

In larger territorial states, such communally based republican liberty resonated less clearly. Indeed, republicans who spoke of their version of liberty too loudly found themselves at odds with authorities, hence Sidney's execution in England for espousal of and action upon his republican proclivities. Political liberty in more geographically extensive regimes with monarchic institutions tended to be conceived in terms of individual freedom rather than civic populism. Hence, it is at this time and place that we locate the origins of the doctrines that came to be labeled liberalism.

Thomas Hobbes (1588–1679) is generally identified as the most important direct antecedent of the modern individualist theory of liberty. In his *Leviathan* (1651), Hobbes ascribes to all human beings natural liberty (as well as equality) on the basis of which they are licensed to undertake whatever actions are necessary in order to preserve themselves from their fellow creatures. Hobbes believed that the exercise of such natural liberty logically leads to unceasing conflict and unremitting fear, so long as no single sovereign ruler exists to maintain peace. The exchange of chaotic natural freedom for government-imposed order requires renunciation of all freedoms that humans possess by nature (except, of course, for the sake of self-preservation itself) and voluntary submission to any dictate imposed by the sovereign. Yet, even under the terms of Hobbes's absolute sovereignty, the subject is deemed to remain at liberty to choose for himself concerning any and all matters about which the ruler has not explicitly legislated.

Locke begins his mature political theory in the *Second Treatise of Government* (1690) with the postulation of the divinely granted liberty of all individuals, understood in terms of the absolute right to preserve one's life and to claim the goods one requires for survival. Arguing against the patriarchal doctrine of Sir Robert Filmer (1588–1653), Locke insists that no natural basis—neither paternity nor descent—justifies the submission of one man to another. In contrast with Hobbes, Locke maintains that the condition of liberty does not represent a state of war, but instead can be maintained tranquilly because human beings are deemed sufficiently rational that they can and do generally constrain their free action under the terms of the laws of nature. Hence, should people choose to enter into formal bonds of civil society and to authorize a government in order to avoid the "inconveniences" and inefficiency of the precivil world, the only rulership worthy of consent is that which strictly upholds and protects the liberty possessed by nature. According to Locke, any government that systematically denies to its subjects the exercise of their God-given liberty (as Hobbes's sovereign would do) is tyrannical and cannot expect obedience.

While Hobbesian and Lockean lines of thought persisted into the eighteenth century alongside republican doctrines, occasional attempts were made to transcend, or at any rate to synthesize, the lessons of republicanism and nascent liberalism concerning liberty. The writings of Jean-Jacques Rousseau (1712–1778) afford an illustration of this. On the one hand, Rousseau held that Hobbes and Locke each captured an important facet of human liberty. Hobbes realized that the only way to create a truly sovereign authority—one capable of commanding the obedience of those subject to it—was the renunciation of all the liberty that one enjoyed by nature. Locke recognized that the sole reason any free person would consent to enter into a formalized social arrangement would be to protect his liberty. Hence, Rousseau concludes, the surrender of one's natural liberty must be matched by the return to each person of an amount of civil liberty (which he terms "moral liberty") that is greater than what has been given up. In other words, in a properly organized political system, every citizen enjoys more freedom than if he had remained in a precivil condition with his natural liberty intact.

From this marriage of Hobbesian and Lockean conceptions of liberty issues a set of republican conclusions. For Rousseau, sovereignty cannot be exercised by any authority external to the body of citizens whose liberty is at stake. Hence, no matter what constitutional form of government is appointed—and he contends that kingship, aristocracy, and democracy may each be appropriate, depending on the scale of the territory to be governed—it remains only the executive of the general will of the community. Freedom reposes strictly and exclusively in the communal order in which the moral liberty of each person assumes the equal moral liberty of every person, guaranteed under the terms of the law and protected by the magistrates. Hence, Rousseau's free state is guided by the collective determinations of the people about how they wish to live—a clear statement of a system of popular sovereignty.

NATURAL LIBERTY

The concept of natural liberty is also one that came to the fore in the economic doctrines of the eighteenth century. Adam Smith (1723–1790) founded his principal doctrines upon the notion of natural liberty, by which he meant simply that if every person acts freely as he sees fit in his own interests, then the welfare of the whole society will be served best. For Smith, the system of natural liberty constitutes a sort of automatic or homeostatic mechanism of self-adjustment (which he sometimes calls the "invisible hand"), so that any attempt (on the part of government or some other agent) to interfere in its operation will lead to greater inefficiency and hence less total welfare. The sources for Smith's insight about maximized individual liberty, unconstrained by coercive externalities, have been debated. Certainly, the French economic theorists known collectively as the Physiocrats may have played a role in the formulation of this idea, as may have the political theorists whose views have already been surveyed. Smith applied this discovery, however, not only to the operation of the marketplace but to all aspects of society, including its educational, religious, and judicial institutions. He narrowly confines the role of government to those functions consistent with natural liberty: foreign defense, regulation of criminal activity, and provision of "public goods" too expensive for any single segment of the private economy to undertake.

By the end of the eighteenth century, the concept of liberty had pervaded the religious, social, political, cultural, and economic dimensions of European life. Yet it remained a controversial idea for (and against) which people would continue to fight and die. Moreover, the application of principles of freedom remained in many ways incomplete. Slavery had been by no means entirely eradicated from the regions over which European nations exercised control, even if it was largely passé within Europe itself. Women occupied almost exactly the same social, political, and economic position in 1789 as in 1450, and the extent of their personal and group liberty was largely determined by their class status. Despite occasional agitation for universal manhood suffrage, such as occurred during the earliest stages of the English Civil War, the unpropertied also experienced little improvement in their effective freedom between the fifteenth and the eighteenth centuries. Finally, the diffusion of ideas and practices of religious liberty was limited almost entirely to Christian sects, although deists and advocates of natural religion seem generally to have been left alone; freedom to worship occupied a far more precarious position for Jews and members of other non-Christian confessions (for example, Turks) who made their way to Europe.

See also **Bayle, Pierre; Calvin, John; English Civil War and Interregnum; Grotius, Hugo; Hobbes, Thomas; Liberalism, Economic; Locke, John; Luther, Martin; Physiocrats and Physiocracy; Revolutions, Age of; Republicanism; Rousseau, Jean-Jacques; Smith, Adam; Sovereignty, Theory of; Spinoza, Baruch.**

BIBLIOGRAPHY

Primary Sources

Hobbes, Thomas. *Leviathan.* Edited by Edwin Curley. Indianapolis, 1994.

Locke, John. *A Letter concerning Toleration, in Focus.* Edited by John P. Horton and Susan Mendus. London, 1991.

———. *Two Treatises of Government.* Edited by Peter Laslett. Cambridge, U.K., 1988.

Luther, Martin, and John Calvin. *Luther and Calvin on Secular Authority.* Edited and translated by Harro Höpfl. Cambridge, U.K., 1991.

Rousseau, Jean-Jacques. *Basic Political Writings.* Edited and translated by Donald A. Cress. Indianapolis, 1987.

Secondary Sources

Davis, R. W. *The Origins of Modern Freedom in the West.* Stanford, 1995.

Fitzgibbons, Athol. *Adam Smith's System of Liberty, Wealth, and Virtue: The Moral and Political Foundations of* The Wealth of Nations. Oxford, 1995.

Laursen, John Christian, and Cary J. Nederman, eds. *Beyond the Persecuting Society: Religious Toleration before the Enlightenment.* Philadelphia, 1998.

Pelczynski, Zbigniew A., and John Gray, eds. *Conceptions of Liberty in Political Philosophy.* London, 1984.

Skinner, Quentin. *Visions of Politics.* 3 vols. Cambridge, U.K., 2002.

Van Gelderen, Martin, and Quentin Skinner, eds. *Republicanism: A Shared European Heritage.* 2 vols. Cambridge, U.K., 2002

CARY J. NEDERMAN

LIBRARIES. The period 1450–1789 witnessed an unprecedented expansion in the publication, circulation, and readership of books. Such dramatic changes in patterns of literacy and book use are amply reflected in the history of libraries in the period.

MEDIEVAL INHERITANCE

By the late thirteenth century the scriptoria and companion book collections of the early medieval period had been eclipsed in importance by the rise of college libraries, particularly in Paris and Oxford. The most famous of these was the Sorbonne library in Paris, founded in 1287. Its 1290 catalogue lists over 1,000 manuscripts, and the library would expand to more than 2,500 volumes by the end of the fifteenth century. Equally important were the libraries of the *studia* (study houses) of the monastic orders. Over time, a body of regulations governing college and conventual libraries evolved. Many of these libraries employed sophisticated cataloguing and classification systems. While there was no single model of classification, most conformed to a recognizably Scholastic pattern, descending from theology, through philosophy and the other two university faculties of law and medicine, to logic, rhetoric, and grammar, with appropriate subdivisions where warranted by the quantity of books.

The expansion of private libraries in the late medieval period was closely related to the institutional libraries of the university colleges and study houses. Members of the three professions—churchmen, lawyers, and physicians—responded to changing patterns of literacy and professionalization that demanded increased textual expertise with ever-expanding collections of professional textual materials.

RENAISSANCE AND REFORMATION

This milieu fostered the bibliophilia of the first major humanist book collector, Francesco Petrarch (1304–1374). Petrarch's library was not only large for the age (some two hundred volumes), but unusual in that it contained not the canonical texts and core manuals of the professions, but the works of classical authors and the church fathers. In early-fourteenth-century Florence, Coluccio Salutati (1331–1406) and Niccolò de'Niccoli (c. 1346–1437), key figures of Florentine humanism, built up collections of around eight hundred volumes. Niccoli was one of the first systematic collectors of older manuscripts, which he knew to be more accurate than later copies. Both before and after the fall of Constantinople, Greek émigrés such as Manuel Chrysoloras (c. 1353–1415) in Florence introduced many important Greek texts previously unknown to Western libraries. The library of Cardinal Bessarion (1403–1472) was the most important such collection for the transmission of Greek texts to the West. Bessarion's library contained over 1,000 volumes and was bequeathed to the Venetian republic after his death. From Venice, they were copied and recopied to furnish Western libraries with Greek manuscript texts. Important institutional Renaissance libraries were established in Florence, with the 1444 San Marco library, and in Rome, with the Vatican library first of Nicholas V (c. 1450) and, subsequently and more permanently, Sixtus IV (1471–1484).

The religious conflicts of the sixteenth century had a major impact upon libraries, both positive and negative, in Protestant and Catholic Europe. Most dramatic was the dissolution of the monasteries in England in the 1540s and the dispersal and loss of thousands of medieval manuscripts. The college libraries of Oxford and Cambridge suffered similar, if less systematic, loss. In Germany the holdings of many monastic libraries were absorbed by existing town and court libraries. In the last half of the

Libraries. The Sistine Hall of the Vatican Library, built 1587–1589 to accommodate the Vatican's rapidly growing collection. ©MICHAEL MASLAN HISTORIC PHOTOGRAPHS/CORBIS

century the French Wars of Religion resulted in the destruction of many important ecclesiastical libraries. It is no coincidence that this period witnessed the first postmedieval renaissance of systematic bibliography, with the efforts of Conrad Gessner (*Bibliotheca Universalis,* 1545) in the Swiss confederation, John Bale (*Illustrium Maioris Britanniæ Scriptorum,* 1548) in England, and Flacius Illyricus (*Catalogus Testium Veritatis Basle,* 1556) in Germany.

The upheaval of the first half of the sixteenth century was countered by a considerable consolidation of library collections in the second half. This period witnessed the consolidation and foundation of important collections across Catholic Europe: the Escorial in Spain (1575), the Imperial Library in Vienna (reorganized in 1576), the new Vatican library of Sixtus V (1589), the Hofbibliothek in Munich (1558), and the Ambrosiana in Milan (1609). This chain of Catholic libraries presented a wall of orthodoxy across Europe, a self-conscious effort at intellectual containment of Protestant gains. In Protestant Europe a number of important collections emerged: the ducal library at Wolfenbüttel (1572) and the Bodleian Library at Oxford (1602) were the most important. These libraries marked a watershed in establishing permanent institutional locations for the medieval manuscript heritage and in amassing unprecedented quantities of printed books. The Ambrosiana, for example, amassed a collection of some 15,000 manuscripts and 30,000 printed books in the decades after its foundation. By 1666, the ducal library at Wolfenbüttel held over

55,000 printed books. Most had established, if highly restricted, hours of opening. Access was equally restricted to members of established circles of scholars. Private collections also grew in size, frequently providing the nucleus of both local and far-flung networks of learning. Such was the case with the libraries of Claude Dupuy (1545–1594) in Paris and Gian Vincenzo Pinelli (1535–1601) in Padua. Pinelli, whose library and collections housed the young Galileo while he was composing his Padua lectures, could boast of over 6,000 printed books and 700 manuscripts, making it one of the largest private libraries of the period.

SEVENTEENTH AND EIGHTEENTH CENTURIES

This period saw continued consolidation and expansion of major collections and witnessed a growth in the political importance of libraries. Quasi-public libraries such as those of the de Thou family in Paris or Sir Robert Cotton (1571–1631) in London constituted loci of parliamentary intellectual activity and housed documents of great legal and historical importance. Their libraries were mirrored in the collections of legal and political élites across Europe. Conversely, Cardinal Mazarin's (1602–1661) formidable library in Paris (1643) became a powerful emblem of ministerial and royal authority: it was dispersed—forbidden to be sold intact to a single buyer—during the Fronde of 1651. The reorganization of the French Royal Library (1661) under Jean-Baptiste Colbert (1619–1683) transformed that library into a formidable political symbol of the French monarchy and, through Colbert's patronage, into a unique locus of learning in Europe.

As a result of the new cultural importance of libraries in the late sixteenth and seventeenth centuries and in response to the growing pressures of the print revolution, a recognizable discipline of library organization and classification developed. Gabriel Naudé (1600–1653) in his 1627 *Advis pour dresser une bibliothèque* (Advice for establishing a library) sought to establish universal principles for library organization and cataloguing sensitive to both the enormous growth of print and the intellectual needs of members of the republic of letters. The real home of library science during the Enlightenment would be Germany, where the subject of library organization was taught in the universities and where both professorial and university libraries were organized on a loose arrangement much indebted to both Naudé and Francis Bacon (1561–1626). This development reached its culmination in 1734, with the library at the University of Göttingen, the first modern university "research" library.

The major development of the eighteenth century was the expansion of vernacular book collections. These libraries favored romances and novels in addition to the traditional vernacular genres of religion and history. The new genres provided the backbone of the lending libraries and popular reading rooms, important new features on the European library scene in the eighteenth century. More books were increasingly available to more people, and levels of personal ownership of books increased across the social spectrum. Many of the older institutional libraries rushed to embrace the new ideal of the public library (though many had long functioned as quasi-public institutions): for example, the French Royal Library in 1720 and the Imperial Library in Vienna in 1726 both opened their doors as public libraries. In 1753, Britain finally had an institution to match its continental rivals with the establishment of the British Library. But it was the nationalization of the French Royal Library at the Revolution and its confiscation of former monastic holdings that would set the standard for the large national continental libraries of the nineteenth century.

See also **Dissemination of Knowledge; Education; Humanists and Humanism; Literacy and Reading; Printing and Publishing; Universities.**

BIBLIOGRAPHY

Dadson, Trevor J. *Libros, lectores y lecturas. Estudios sobre bibliotecas particulares españolas del Siglo de Oro.* Madrid, 1998.

Fabian, Bernhard, ed. *Handbuch der historischen Buchbestände in Deutschland.* Hildesheim, 1992.

Fehrenbach, R. J., and E. S. Leedham-Green, eds. *Private Libraries in Renaissance England: A Collection and Catalogue of Tudor and Early Stuart Book-lists.* Medieval and Renaissance Texts and Studies. 5 vols. Binghamton, N.Y., 1992–1998.

Grendler, Marcella. "A Greek Collection in Padua: The Library of Gian Vincenzo Pinelli (1535–1601)." *Renaissance Quarterly* 33 (1980): 386–416.

A History of Libraries in Britain and Ireland. 4 vols. Cambridge, U.K., forthcoming.

Hobson, Anthony. *Great Libraries.* London, 1970. A magnificently illustrated survey, with bibliography, of major Renaissance collections.

Nelles, Paul. "The Library as an Instrument of Discovery: Gabriel Naudé and the Uses of History." In *History and the Disciplines: The Reclassification of Knowledge in Early Modern Europe,* ed. D. R. Kelley, pp. 41–57. Rochester, N.Y., 1997.

Nolhac, Pierre de. *La bibliothèque de Fulvio Orsini.* Paris, 1887. Reprint Geneva, 1976.

Robathan, Dorothy M. "Libraries of the Italian Renaissance." In *The Medieval Library,* edited by James Westfall Thompson, pp. 509–588. New York, 1957.

Serrai, Alfredo. *Storia della bibliografia.* 11 vols. Rome, 1988–2001.

Sherman, William H. *John Dee: The Politics of Reading and Writing in the English Renaissance.* Amherst, Mass., 1995.

Stam, David H., ed. *International Dictionary of Library Histories.* 2 vols. Chicago, 2001.

Ullman, Berthold L., and Philip A. Stadter. *The Public Library of Renaissance Florence: Niccolò Niccoli, Cosimo de' Medici and the Library of San Marco.* Padua, 1972.

Vernet, André, ed. *Histoire des bibliothèques françaises.* 4 vols. Paris, 1988–1992.

PAUL NELLES

LIFE CYCLE. *See* **Childhood and Childrearing; Death and Dying; Family; Marriage; Motherhood and Childbearing; Old Age; Youth.**

LIFE EXPECTANCY. *See* **Death and Dying; Old Age.**

LIMA. Lima, the capital city of the Viceroyalty of Peru in early modern times, lies on the southern bank of the Rímac River, west of the Andes Mountains, and eight miles inland from the western coast of South America. Conquistador Francisco Pizarro founded the city on 18 January 1535 following the Spanish defeat of the native Incan empire. Possibly to account for Lima's title as "The City of the Kings," some scholars claim that the founding date was 6 January 1535, the Catholic celebration of Epiphany, when the Magi are believed to have visited the Christ child. Pizarro chose Lima, a Spanish misunderstanding for the native word *Rímac,* over the Incan capital of Cuzco, which was further inland and nestled in the Andean highlands, because Lima had a milder climate and was better located in terms of ocean access and defense.

Symbolic of Spanish dominance and bureaucratic opulence, the city quickly became the crown's administrative, ecclesiastical, and economic hub in South America. The crown-appointed viceroy, whose short tenure was designed to preserve Spanish control from across the ocean, sat atop a highly structured and hierarchical regional government. Like other Spanish American cities, Lima was laid out in a grid design of east-west and north-south streets organized around a central plaza, a form later codified in the Laws of the Indies. As the capital city of Spanish holdings in South America, Lima was the first American city in which the Inquisition was established and the region's principal treasury office. Lima was also the conduit, via the nearby port city of Callao, for all incoming and outgoing trade with Europe. Most important were the precious metals that were mined and produced by Spanish-controlled Indian labor in the viceroyalty—most notably the silver mines at Potosí. Peru's silver mines were central to the European economy until the ore became depleted and a fiscal crisis seized Europe and Spanish America in the late seventeenth century. Lima did not recover from this decline until the eighteenth century, when Spain's new Bourbon rulers sought to streamline government and improve the colony's and the crown's economic positions. Despite Bourbon reforms, Lima's importance outside of Peru waned after this period.

The city's population increased only slowly, restrained in part by frequent and recurring earthquakes (most notably those in 1687 and 1746). Whereas in 1613 there were a little over 25,000 inhabitants, it took almost two centuries for that to double to almost 53,000 people (1796). As with other Spanish colonies, Lima's population at the time of the conquest was composed of a few Spaniards and numerous natives. Over time the populace became increasingly mixed as more Spaniards and other Europeans arrived, the indigenous population declined, and slaves were brought in from Africa. At least in theory, Lima's social structure was as ordered as the city's administration, with legal and geographical divisions among classes and ethnicities. Nevertheless, cultural and sexual exchange among the city's residents, the steady influx of exotic goods, and the continual influence of people and ideas arriving on visiting ships ensured that Lima would become a culturally diverse center for the viceroyalty.

See also **Pizarro Brothers; Spanish Colonies: Peru.**

BIBLIOGRAPHY

Andrien, Kenneth J. *Crisis and Decline: The Viceroyalty of Peru in the Seventeenth Century.* Albuquerque, N.M., 1985.

Bromley, Juan. *La Fundacion de la Ciudad de los Reyes.* Lima, 1935.

Dobyns, Henry F., and Paul L. Doughty. *Peru: A Cultural History. Latin American Histories.* New York, 1976.

Klarén, Peter Flindell. *Peru: Society and Nationhood in the Andes. Latin American Histories.* New York, 2000.

Lockhart, James. *Spanish Peru, 1532–1560: A Colonial Society.* Madison, Wis., 1968.

Montero, Maria Antonia Durán. *Lima en el Siglo XVII: Arquitectura, Urbanismo y vida Cotidiana. Sección Historia "Nuestra América"* 1. Seville, 1994.

Oliver-Smith, Anthony. "Lima, Peru: Underdevelopment and Vulnerability to Hazards in the City of the Kings." In *Crucibles of Hazard: Mega-Cities and Disasters in Transition.* Edited by James K. Mitchell. Tokyo, 1999.

JAMIE STEPHENSON

LINNAEUS, CARL (Carl von Linné; 1707–1778; ennobled 1761), Swedish naturalist and explorer. Linnaeus was born on 23 May 1707. His father was a curator in Råshult, a small parish in Småland (southern Sweden). After attending school in nearby Växjö, he studied medicine at the universities of Lund (1727) and Uppsala (1728–1732). Coming from a low-income family, he could only afford to attend a few lectures, but patronage from Olaus Rudbeck, Jr. (1660–1740) and Olof Celsius (1670–1756) at Uppsala University, and subsidies he received from teaching botany (1730–1732), allowed him to study natural history on his own. In 1732 the Uppsala Academy of Sciences sent Linnaeus to Lapland to do research. After his return, he gave private lectures in mineral assaying, and made another research trip to Dalecarlia (a region in central Sweden) in 1734. At this early stage, the foundation for all of his later work was laid down in manuscripts. Occasion for their publication would come when Linnaeus went to Holland in 1735 to acquire a medical degree. This journey was financed by the governor of Dalecarlia, the father of Sara Elisabeth Moraea, who was promised to Linnaeus.

Skillfully seeking the patronage of leading Dutch naturalists like Jan Fredrik Gronovius (1690–1762), senator of Leiden, and Herman Boerhaave (1668–1738), only a few months after his arrival Linnaeus successfully published his first work, the *Systema Naturae* (The system of nature), a folio volume of only eleven pages that presented a classification of the three kingdoms of nature. Success was immediate, and there followed a whole series of further publications, among them the *Fundamenta Botanica* (The foundations of botany, 1735) and the *Genera Plantarum* (Genera of plants, 1737). Linnaeus extended his stay in Holland until 1738 to catalog the extensive botanical collections of George Clifford, former director of the Dutch East India Company, who also paid him for two short trips to Paris and Oxford. On his return to Sweden in 1738, he married Sara Elisabeth and settled in Stockholm as a physician. He was among those who founded the Royal Academy of Sciences in 1739.

In 1741 Linnaeus accepted the chair of medicine and botany at Uppsala University. His career was characterized by two different aspects: On the one hand, he used the contacts he had made while in Holland to establish an international network of correspondents, including such leading naturalists as Albrecht von Haller (1708–1777) and Antoine-Laurent de Jussieu (1748–1836), that would supply him with seeds and specimens from all over the world. Incorporating this material into the botanical garden at Uppsala, Linnaeus created a continuously growing empirical basis for revised and enlarged editions of his major taxonomic works. There were twelve authorized editions of the *Systema Naturae,* as well as numerous pirated editions, translations, and popular versions that appeared in Europe.

On the other hand, Linnaeus actively supported the cameralist theory that a nation's welfare depended on science-based administration. He promoted the creation of chairs in economics at Swedish universities, organized public botanical excursions around Uppsala, undertook research travels within Sweden to identify domestic products that could replace imports, and sent some twenty students on travels around the globe to find exotic plants for acclimatization in Sweden. The results of these "patriotic" projects were published in the *Flora Suecica* (Swedish plants, 1745), the *Fauna Suecica* (Swedish animals, 1746), and four volumes of reports on journeys made to various provinces of Sweden (*Öländska and Gothländska Resa,* [Travel to Öland and Gotland], 1741, *Västgötha Resa* [Travel to Western Gothia], 1747, and *Skånska Resa* [Travel to Scania], 1751).

Linnaeus and his wife Sara Elisabeth, who managed the three farm estates of the family, had five children. His only son, Carolus, Jr., succeeded him at the University of Uppsala after his death in 1778, but died only a few years later.

The significance of Linnaeus's scientific achievements in natural history is twofold. His major taxonomic works, but especially the *Species Plantarum* (1753), a catalog of all plant species known at the time, provided systematic access to earlier literature in natural history, while the *Philosophia Botanica* (Philosophy of botany, 1751) laid down rules for classifying and naming organisms that would inform all future taxonomic practice. His main innovation in this respect was the introduction of binomial nomenclature, proposed for the first time in the *Philosophia Botanica* and for the first time consistently applied in the *Species Plantarum.* The latter work and zoological part of the tenth edition of the *Systema Naturae* (1756) form the basis of all subsequent botanical and zoological nomenclature, in conjunction with Linnaeus's extensive collections of botanical and zoological specimens, today preserved by the Linnaean Society in London.

Other fields in which Linnaeus is of historical importance include plant sexuality (*Sponsalia Plantarum* [The sex of plants], 1746), ecology (*Oeconomia Naturae* [The economy of nature], 1749), and the classification of diseases (*Genera Morborum* [Genera of diseases], 1763).

See also **Academies, Learned; Biology; Boerhaave, Herman; Botany; Haller, Albrecht von; Scientific Revolution; Zoology.**

BIBLIOGRAPHY

Blunt, Wilfrid, with William T. Stearn. *The Compleat Naturalist: A Life of Linnaeus.* London, 1971.

Frängsmyr, Tore, ed. *Linnaeus: The Man and His Work.* Berkeley, 1983.

Koerner, Lisbet. *Linnaeus: Nature and Nation.* Cambridge, Mass., 1999.

Larson, James L. *Reason and Experience: The Representation of Natural Order in the Work of Carl Linnaeus.* Berkeley, 1971.

Müller-Wille, Staffan. *Botanik und weltweiter Handel: zur Begründung eines natürlichen Systems der Pflanzen durch Carl von Linné (1707–1778).* Berlin, 1999.

Soulsby, B. H. *A Catalogue of the Works of Linnaeus (and Publications More Immediately Relating Thereto) Preserved in the Libraries of the British Museum (Bloomsbury) and the British Museum (Natural History) (South Kensington).* 2nd ed. London, 1933.

STAFFAN MÜLLER-WILLE

LIPSIUS, JUSTUS (Joest Lips; 1547–1606), Dutch humanist and philosopher. Justus Lipsius was the most widely published humanist of the end of the sixteenth century. With Joseph Scaliger (1540–1609) and Isaac Casaubon (1559–1614) he formed the famous triumvirate of learning that dominated the late Renaissance. The father of the Tacitist political tradition, he also led the Neostoic movement based on the works of Seneca, which Wilhelm Dilthey (1833–1911) regarded as one of the origins of modern individualism. Lipsius's work illustrates how a pragmatic politics, ethics, and religion grew out of the convergence of classical humanism and the wars that wracked Europe during the Counter-Reformation.

Born to a well-to-do family in Overyssche near Brussels, Lipsius began his studies as a novice in the Jesuit College of Cologne, where he was recognized as a prodigy due to his extraordinary memory and voracious intellectual appetite. He first achieved renown at the age of nineteen for *Variæ Lectiones,* a work of Ciceronian Latin prose commentaries on the ancients, which he dedicated to Cardinal Antoine Perrenot de Granvelle (1517–1586), who was a minister of Philip II of Spain. Although in later life Lipsius repudiated this work for its flowery style, it caught the eye of Granvelle, who invited Lipsius to Rome as his Latin secretary. It was in Italy, between

1568 and 1570, that Lipsius blossomed as a scholar, visiting great libraries and working with famous humanists such as Paolo Manuzio (1512–1574) and Girolamo Mercuriale (1530–1606).

Lipsius's meeting with the French poet and humanist Marc-Antoine Muret (1526–1585), however, led to a defining intellectual epiphany. Lecturing in Rome, Muret was a pioneering scholar who was working on a set of commentaries on Tacitus's works. Lipsius now repudiated Ciceronian Latin eloquence and advocated Tacitus's concise, sententious style, effectively creating a second humanist rhetorical movement. In 1572 Lipsius accepted a chair at the Lutheran University of Jena in Germany, where he began his famed critical edition of the works of Tacitus, which was published in 1674. This work stands as one of the greatest monuments of Latin humanism. Mixing his own brilliant emendations with those of other scholars, Lipsius used his considerable philological skills to clear Tacitus's text of its medieval inaccuracies, differentiating the *Annals* from the *Histories,* and restoring the work closer to its original state. In 1581 he added historical and political commentaries and highlighted maxims with the aim of making Tacitus's work useful for practical life. Scaliger considered this his most important work and indeed, it became an international bestseller, elevating Tacitus to the status of a secular saint of practical politics and an acceptable stand-in for Machiavelli.

Of his many works, Lipsius considered *De Constantia* (1584; On constancy) and the *Politicorum Libri Sex* (1589; Six books of politics) to be his most important achievements. *De Constantia* explained the basic tenets of his Stoic philosophy that sought to transform contemplation and study into the basis for worldly action. Traumatized by the Spanish atrocities during the Dutch Wars and by the St. Bartholomew's Day Massacre (24 August 1572), Lipsius formulated a philosophy of personal discipline, ethics, and rational judgment in response to the chaos that engulfed Counter-Reformation Europe. The following work, *Politicorum Libri Sex,* was an exercise in Stoic practicality. Harnessing maxims from the ancients, in particular from Tacitus, he hoped to create a collection, or *cento,* of political maxims to be used as a tool by monarchs to control and stabilize their kingdoms. His theory of "mixed prudence" was an attempt to translate Machiavellian practical prudence into an acceptable tool of politics regulated by the ethics of public utility. This theory later formed the basis of Libertine political philosophy and was central to the works of Pierre Charron (1541–1603) and Gabriel Naudé (1600–1653).

Lipsius lived his life according to the Stoic principle of accommodation and rejected the religious fanaticism of his day. He was a member of the secretive, proto-Deist Family of Love movement that stressed peace and unity above denominational loyalty. A true accommodator, he went from Lutheran Jena to Calvinist Leiden in 1572, and in 1591 he returned to Louvain, where he again embraced Jesuit Catholicism and lived out the rest of his days. He supported the interests of Protestant provinces, but he also counseled the emperor on the way to a peaceful settlement of the religious strife that wracked Holland. His numerous works also include a manual of letter-writing, *Epistolica Institutio* (1580); a history of classical libraries, *De Amphiteatro Liber* (1584); *De Militia Romana* (1595), which inspired many of the military reforms of his day; and finally his masterwork of Senecan Stoicism, *Manuductionis ad Stoicam Philosophiam* (1604). His works remained popular into the seventeenth century.

See also **Humanists and Humanism.**

BIBLIOGRAPHY

Oestreich, Gerhard. *Neostoicism and the Early Modern State.* Edited by Brigitta Oestreich and H. G. Koenigsberger. Translated by David McKlintock. Cambridge, U.K., 1982.

Ruysschaert, José. *Juste Lipse et les Annales de Tacite: Une méthode de critique textuelle au XVIe siècle.* Turnhout, Belgium, 1949.

Saunders, Jason Lewis. *Justus Lipsius: The Philosophy of Renaissance Stoicism.* New York, 1955.

Wasznik, Jan. "Inventio in the Politica: Commonplace-Books and the Shape of Political Theory." In *Lipsius in Leiden: Studies in the Life and Works of a Great Humanist,* edited by K. Enenkel and C. Heesakkers, pp. 141–162. Voorthuizen, 1997.

JACOB SOLL

LISBON. Portugal's capital stood as the key city for exploration of the south Atlantic and Indian

Oceans as well as one of Europe's most important ports. Lisbon was also the center of Portugal's domestic economy. During the rise of Portugal's maritime empire, its large and strategic harbor became a major entrepôt for slaves, ivory, spices, silk, sugar, salt, and other commodities. By 1550 its population had risen to 100,000, making Lisbon one of Europe's largest cities. Thereafter, the decline in Portugal's Asian empire, together with the union with Spain, slowed Lisbon's demographic and economic growth. After 1705, Brazilian gold and diamonds revitalized the city's economic and political importance, and by 1750, Lisbon held at least 250,000 people, or approximately one tenth of Portugal's total population. All growth stopped, however, with the 1755 earthquake and its the subsequent fire, which destroyed much of the city. Rebuilding slowed with the end of the Brazilian gold rush, and Lisbon never regained its former prominence. By 1800, its population stood at less than 170,000.

The early sixteenth century saw the creation of a particularly Portuguese architectural style called Manueline, whose motifs reflected Portugal's overseas successes and whose monuments are prominent in Lisbon. The building activity brought about by the empire's wealth substantially diminished during Portugal's union with Spain (1580–1640), which coincided with economic difficulties that affected much of Europe. Vernacular architecture particularly declined as the court and much of Portugal's social and economic elite moved to Madrid. That decline continued after independence in the late seventeenth century. Both the crown and the nobility had become too impoverished to construct palaces or large public buildings. Building activities renewed during John V's reign (João, 1706–1750), when wealth from the Brazilian gold rush created an economic boom that led to the construction of new palaces, an opera house, and the Lisbon aqueduct.

Lisbon retained its medieval and Renaissance character throughout the early modern era. Its major commercial, religious, and political structures remained inside city walls. Towering over the skyline rose the castelo São Jorge, the Carmo monastery, and the Royal Hospital of All Saints, while the Royal Palace (Paço de Ribeira), the dockyards with its customhouses, and the two great squares—the Rossio and Terreiro do Paço—dominated its foreground. On Lisbon's nearly 370 streets stood twenty thousand houses and over two thousand stores, interspersed with over a hundred churches, monasteries, and convents.

From a distance, travelers in the early eighteenth century described Lisbon as one of the world's most beautiful cities. The city stood on a series of hills within what appeared to be a naturally formed amphitheater. Such impressions changed on arrival, however. John V placed absolutism above economic and urban development. Thus, despite the wealth from Brazil, Lisbon's infrastructure and its commercial facilities had badly deteriorated by the mid-eighteenth century. Poor-quality mortar caused old building walls to collapse on unwary pedestrians. Steep, ill-maintained streets were too narrow for coaches and created health hazards from waste flowing downward toward the city's center. Lisbon was also one of Europe's most dangerous cities. Astonishingly, despite the importance of commerce, the city had neither a permanent bourse nor a separate structure for its municipal council. Instead, merchants, brokers, and contractors conducted their dealings around Businessmen's Square, while the municipal council usually met in Saint Anthony's Church.

The November 1755 earthquake caused catastrophic mortality (it is estimated that from ten to thirty thousand lives were lost), and unprecedented destruction. The earthquake and the subsequent fire and tidal wave destroyed approximately seventeen thousand houses, the city center and docks, and countless cultural treasures. The appalling scale of the destruction initiated an international debate over the concepts of optimism and evil. Politically, the disaster precipitated the marquis de Pombal's rise to power as Portugal's strongman for the next two decades.

Pombal (1699–1782) sought to rebuild Lisbon symbolically as well as physically. He envisioned an imperial capital reflecting a reformed and commercially centered Portugal. Because lack of funds and resources prohibited rebuilding the entire city, construction efforts focused on the lower section. Central Lisbon was reestablished on a grid pattern of wide streets and avenues featuring two large squares. Pombal mandated that all new structures conform to certain rules regarding size and architectural style. The enormous Praça do Comércio,

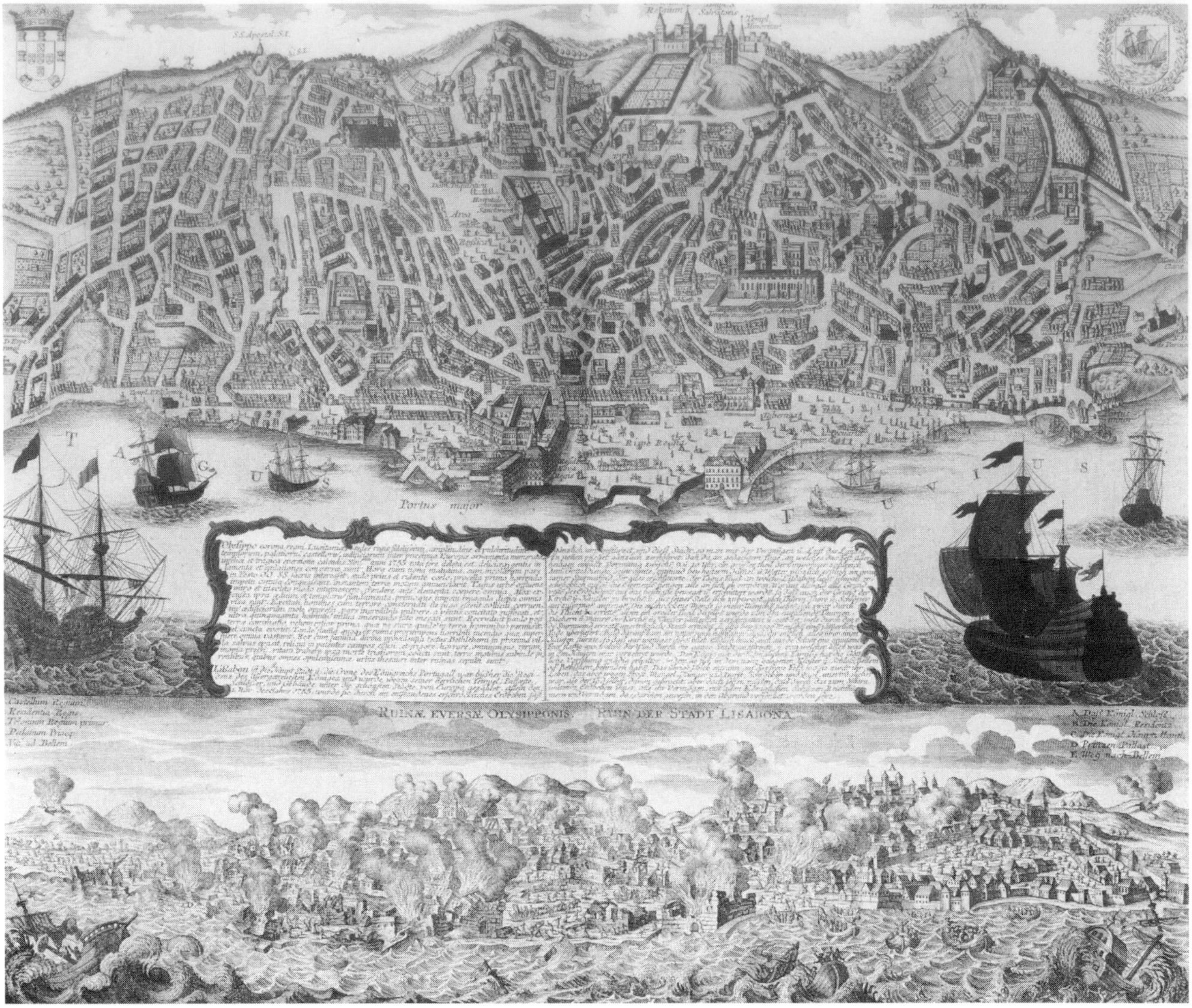

Lisbon. Aerial view of Lisbon, 1756, with a depiction of the fire that consumed much of the city in 1755. THE ART ARCHIVE/BRITISH LIBRARY

which occupied the area where the royal palace and its surrounding ground had stood, most visibly represented Pombal's commercial focus. Colonial taxes largely underwrote the enormous cost of construction.

After 1760 the rapid decline in Brazilian gold production impeded rebuilding, and travelers still spoke of ruined structures in the early nineteenth century. The French 1807 invasion, followed by Brazilian independence, heavily damaged Portugal's entire economy. Whereas Lisbon remained one of Europe's most important port cities, it never again approached its previous economic prominence.

See also **Portugal; Portuguese Colonies: Brazil.**

BIBLIOGRAPHY

Castelo-Branco, Fernando. *Lisboa Seiscentista.* 3rd rev. ed. Lisbon, 1969.

Costa, Padre António Carvalho da. *Corografia Portuguesa e descripçno topográfica do famoso reino de Portugal.* 3 vols. Lisbon, 1706–1712.

França, José-Augusto. *Lisboa pombalina e o iluminismo.* Rev. ed. Lisbon, 1977.

Freire de Oliveira, Eduardo. *Elementos para a História do Municipio de Lisboa.* 17 vols. Lisbon, 1882–1911.

Levenson, Jay. *The Age of the Baroque in Portugal.* New Haven, 1993.

WILLIAM DONOVAN

LITERACY AND READING. In the Renaissance, Europe experienced the beginnings of a profound transformation from restricted to mass literacy. In 1500 very few people could read and write, but by 1800 a majority of adults in northwestern Europe were literate. This entry outlines the special nature of early modern literacy; it charts the changing social and geographical distribution of literacy in early modern Europe; and it offers explanations and an assessment of the importance of this complex development.

THE SKILLS OF LITERACY

Early modern literacy was made up of several skills, which are best seen as bands in a spectrum of communication rather than discrete categories. Reading of print or writing was possible at two levels. Some people could decipher texts, read them aloud, and memorize them in a mechanical or ritual way—although their personal understanding may have been questionable. We should not exaggerate the understanding and facility of those who possessed this intermediate or semiliteracy. Those with better education and a deeper immersion in printed and written culture could comprehend the text with greater precision, reading and thinking silently to themselves. They could understand new texts as well as familiar ones. However, "reading" was not restricted to written or printed words alone. People could gather information and ideas from looking: interpreting pictures and prints in broadsheets and "chapbooks" (pamphlets) or watching and participating in plays and processions. Gesture remained a subtle and important form of nonverbal communication.

If they wanted to transmit their own thoughts other than through speech, people had to learn to write, or rather compose—an advanced skill that required considerable training and practice and that effectively marked "full" literacy for most people. The other, more common, level of writing was in fact copying: writing without necessarily understanding. It was at this stage that people learned to sign their names on documents, and this ability is commonly used as an indicator that someone could read and understand printed and written texts in the vernacular, the language of everyday life. In other words, he or she was well along the road to "full" literacy. A small minority of men and a handful of women could also copy or compose in Latin, the international language of learning throughout the Middle Ages, the Renaissance, and the early modern period, or in another pan-European language like French. Even those who had none of these skills were not culturally isolated, for they could listen—hear a priest's sermons or a friend reading aloud, participate actively or passively in discussions with their peers. The way to understand literacy in early modern Europe is to assess the access that people had to the different bands in the spectrum and the ways they used them.

The ability to read and write was a function of access to schooling, demand for basic learning, and prevailing social and cultural attitudes to literacy. Commercial, religious, administrative, and intellectual "revolutions" of the fifteenth century onward enhanced the supply of education and fueled a growing demand for instruction. The chances of being educated and of acquiring literacy depended on a wide variety of factors in historic Europe. Wealth, sex, inheritance laws, projected job opportunities, employment for children, even the language a person spoke in everyday life—all played their part. Thus literacy grew because of "push" and "pull" factors. For example, there was the push of religiously inspired educational campaigns (Lutheran, Calvinist, and Catholic). There was the pull of personal religious needs and economic incentives such as a desire for social or geographical mobility. Book production also grew dramatically. Perhaps 150 to 200 million copies were turned out during the sixteenth century, and 1,500 million copies were printed in the eighteenth century. This outpouring fed on and was nourished by growing literacy. More schools were provided and more were demanded. Schools were important to learning, but nowhere were they compulsory and, because of costs, many children received only a very brief and basic education. In Sweden, mass reading ability was achieved almost entirely by learning at home.

THE IMPACT OF RELIGION

The Swedish literacy campaign that began in the late seventeenth century was designed to consolidate the Lutheran Reformation there, and many of the advances in reading and writing stemmed from the religious battles of the early modern period. It is commonly asserted that Protestantism is the "religion of the Book." Indeed, Protestant countries tended to be more literate than Catholic, and where the faiths coexisted, as in France, Ireland, and the Low Countries, Calvinists tended to be more accomplished than Catholics. However, on closer inspection the picture is less clear-cut. Dynamic Counter-Reformation Catholicism could produce results comparable with the Lutheran heartland. Just 40 percent of accused adults examined by Spanish inquisitions knew the Ten Commandments well in the 1560s and 1570s, compared with 80 percent by the 1590s, while the proportions felt to be crassly ignorant fell from 50 percent to under 10 percent. Importantly, this was pure memorization rather than reading. Indeed, the distinction between the faiths was often more subtle than crude literacy rates—but no less important. Qualitative differences in the uses and importance of literacy distinguished Protestants from Catholics. Reading Scriptures was central to the Reformed faith. Religious books were probably read more frequently among Protestants, and the very status of reading was special. Protestants tended to own more books on a wider variety of religious topics than their Catholic neighbors and to use them differently. Protestants accepted the overwhelming authority of what they knew or thought was in a religious book.

As well as successes in inculcating religious knowledge in ("Christianizing") their peoples, Catholic countries could boast some excellent educational facilities. At the elementary level there were, for example, Italian Schools of Christian Doctrine, which from the mid-sixteenth century taught religion and basic reading and writing to urban children. At the postelementary level there were the famous schools of the Jesuits and other religious orders. Nor should we ignore the contribution of second- and third-generation Reformations, Protestant and Catholic alike. In Denmark and Prussia it was not the Lutheran Reformation of the sixteenth century that brought about widespread literacy, but the early-eighteenth-century campaign waged by the Pietists with the help of the new "absolutist" rulers. In France female religious orders provided the impetus behind the rapid advance in women's literacy after c. 1740.

LITERACY AMONG MEN AND WOMEN

Outcomes (the social and geographical distribution of literacy) are relatively easy to demonstrate using the universal, standard, and direct measure of ability to sign one's name in full on a document such as a court deposition, a contract, or a marriage certificate. Male achievements were superior to female, those of the rich to those of the poor; urban dwellers were almost invariably better able to write than were peasants. In the east, south, and far north of Europe, the ability to write was less than in the heartland of the continent, but reading may have been as widespread (maybe more so) in Scandinavia. For all the apparent simplicity of these patterns, they become more complex and nuanced on closer investigation—and more so still when we move away from the quantitative measures to a qualitative analysis of meanings and uses.

Around 1500 even basic literacy was restricted to less than 10 percent of men. Judged by the rather advanced skill of signing, the most pronounced early expansion occurred among the middling and upper classes, among men, and in towns. In northern England the illiteracy of the gentry fell from about 30 percent in 1530 to almost nil in 1600, but that of day laborers stayed well above 90 percent throughout the period. Male achievements were almost always superior to female. For example, one bridegroom in three could not sign Amsterdam's marriage register in 1630, compared with two-thirds of brides. Until the eighteenth century the rate of improvement for men generally exceeded that for women. The literacy of townspeople also grew more quickly than that of rural dwellers. By the mid-eighteenth century London and Paris had literacy levels not achieved nationally until the late nineteenth century. In eastern Europe almost the only literate people were townspeople.

PATTERNS OF CHANGE

Change was halting and irregular. Different groups reached "ceilings" or "plateaus" at different times, from which it might take decades to move. For men at least, Castile in the sixteenth century was on a par with France and England until the second quarter of the seventeenth century. Between c. 1620 and c. 1740 it failed to develop at the same rate. The literacy of Castilian women crept up only marginally from 1500 to 1740. The second half of the eighteenth century was better for women everywhere in western Europe. Female literacy grew much more rapidly than male in northern France in the two generations before the Revolution. In parts of northwestern Germany girls began to receive instruction in arithmetic for the first time. However, the current of change ebbed as well as flowed. For centuries the leaders in raising literacy, some early industrial towns of Britain and the southern Low Countries in the late eighteenth century saw falling levels as population growth swamped the social infrastructure and child employment created a disincentive for education.

The extent of divisions between social groups varied over both space and time. In the sixteenth century, when literacy was limited, virtually all those who could read and write came from the landlord, mercantile, or professional classes. Beneath them lay a yawning chasm of illiteracy. This stark differentiation was tempered over time as more members of the middling and lower orders—artisans and farmers, for example—picked up the skills of the book and the pen. In England, lowland Scotland, the Netherlands, northern Germany, and northeastern France, an expansion of literacy for the middling ranks had occurred by the end of the seventeenth century. Southern Italy and Poland (and, to an even greater extent, Russia) had very limited literacy deep into the nineteenth century.

READING

Much research into literacy has focused on the ability to write. However, there are many reasons to believe that reading was a more widespread skill. Children of the lower social classes, who made up 50 to 90 percent of European people, generally received no more than three to four years of education, meaning they learned only to read. For adults, reading had more religious and recreational value than writing, which was by no means essential to everyday life. Indeed, it may be that in countries like Italy and France two or three women could read for every one who could write during the eighteenth century. The campaign to promote religious literacy in Scandinavia produced remarkable results. As late as the mid-seventeenth century a third of adults were able to pass the church's tests of reading, but a century later more than four out of five men and women could read.

Tacitly or overtly, studies showing apparently extensive reading suggest that the breadth of cultural access was much broader than the figures for signing imply. Yet reading might actually mean memorization, and without practice, the reading skills of many ordinary people ill equipped them for exploring the new literature of the Renaissance and Enlightenment. As late as 1750 critical reading ability in the German lands was confined to just 10 percent of the population, a figure that applies equally well to the rest of northwestern Europe. Print and writing may therefore have had a limited impact on ordinary people who were ostensibly "readers." Nevertheless, we must be alert to the possibility that reading was more widespread than writing, especially among poorer men and among women as a whole. After all, women of the *haute bourgeoisie* or the landed classes (and especially unmarried ones, it seems) read periodicals and novels. They used circulating libraries, joined reading societies, attended the theater and concerts, collected prints, and bought paintings. Women seem to have been a crucial component of the anticipated audience for Enlightenment literature.

Yet such women were not typical. The existence of social forms, which provided visual, spoken, and sung communication (such as the French *veillée* or evening gathering and the German *Spinnstube* or spinning circle) and which were dominated by ordinary women, suggests that their cultural lives continued to be cast in an oral/aural and visual framework. Males were educated to participate in the public sphere, women in the private or domestic one. This usually meant that girls gained religious knowledge, learned to read, and were given practical instruction in gendered skills like "housewifery." In the Mediterranean lands where gender roles were most firmly delineated, it was long held to be unnecessary to train girls in more than the rudiments of religious morality. In the deep south of Italy and in parts of eastern Europe such as Hungary, reading and writing were uncommon for either sex. The people of these regions actively preferred oral forms.

LATIN AND THE VERNACULAR

The spread of literacy across western Europe made communication easier. What people did with their ability to communicate using letters depended on what tongue(s) they knew. Until the second half of the seventeenth century, the majority of printed books were in Latin. Those with Latin (perhaps 1 or 2 per cent of the population) were part of a pan-European culture in the age of the Renaissance, but theirs was a circle from which were excluded the *illiterati*—the medieval term for those unable to speak, read, and write Latin. Latin remained important as a core subject in postelementary education throughout the early modern period. During the eighteenth century, speaking, reading, and writing French came to replace Latin for cultural and intellectual purposes—at least for the elites of Catholic and perhaps Orthodox Europe. French became the new Latin. Throughout the early modern period Church Slavonic was the language of learning and literacy in Russia, but it was alien to everyday speech and was taught to a tiny number.

Indeed Latin versus vernacular was only one of many linguistic oppositions in early modern Europe. The vernacular was increasingly used in education, print, government, and administration—but which vernacular? For even within small countries many tongues could be spoken, with important implications for literacy. Seven out of ten of the inhabitants of Wales knew no English and could speak only Welsh in 1800. France was a linguistic Tower of Babel. In 1790 French *(langue d'oïl)* was the dominant language in just fifteen of eighty-nine *départements;* six million French could not understand French at all; a further six million could understand it but spoke it only imperfectly; thirty patois were spoken, plus foreign languages like Flemish or German or Basque; only three million could speak French "properly." The linguistic map of Europe resembles that of literacy: in areas where the language of everyday life was not that of education, contact with outside authority, or printed literature, literacy tended to remain low.

For all the obstacles, dead ends, and inconsistencies in the development of reading and writing, literacy certainly expanded between 1500 and 1800. What, in conclusion, can be said about its uses? Reading tastes changed, notably from the practical to the recreational. New value was placed on originality and novelty in writing. The real growth area in reading material was not the staple texts, which people perused closely, but the more varied, ephemeral, and entertaining fare that was becoming available. Readers ranged more extensively among literary forms, where previously they had focused on a few texts. Between 1700 and 1789 there were published 1,200 French-language periodicals of at least one year's duration. History and travel books became more popular. While literacy was, by all measures, on the rise in the eighteenth century, it may be that for reasons of cost and availability, or because of limited education, not everyone could enjoy its products. The fully literate indulged themselves in its novelties; the semiliterate remained within their traditional mental world. In his autobiography, Johann Wolfgang von Goethe (1749–1832) recounted childhood memories of enjoying a chapbook literature of magic, chivalry, and saints, which had changed little for centuries. Europe was well on the way to mass basic literacy by 1800, but there were still pronounced divisions in access to and uses of literacy's products.

BIBLIOGRAPHY

Houston, Robert A. *Literacy in Early Modern Europe: Culture and Education, 1500–1800.* 2nd ed. London, 2001. Unrivaled geographical coverage in a comprehensive and readable overview. Contains an extensive bibliography of further reading.

R. A. HOUSTON

LITHUANIA, GRAND DUCHY OF, TO 1569. The dates 1385 and 1569 mark important turning points in Polish historiography concerning the Grand Duchy of Lithuania and the Polish-Lithuanian Commonwealth, a governing myth of which is that of state creation by marriages and free unions. In 1385 the Act of Union signed in Krėva (Krewo) marked the beginning of a federation between the Grand Duchy and the Polish crown that was to last until the third partition of Poland-Lithuania in 1795. Grand Duke Jogaila (Polish, Jagiełło; after baptism, Władysław Jagiełło) agreed to marry the twelve-year-old queen of Poland, Jadwiga of Anjou. The ceremony occurred 14 February 1386 in Cracow.

Interpretation of the Act of Union hinges on the term *applicare* used in the document: Did Jagiełło agree to an incorporation of the Grand Duchy into the Polish state (as Polish historiography once argued), or did he envisage a federation of two more or less equal states (as Lithuanian historians have insisted)? Polish historiography sees the union as a foundational moment and emphasizes the importance, for the history of early modern Lithuania, of Jogaila's acceptance of Western Christianity and his baptism of Lithuania (Aukštaitija, the eastern "highlands" around Vilnius, in 1387; Samogitia, or Žemaitija, the western central "lowlands," in 1417). It also highlights the increasingly strong ties with Poland. Lithuanian scholarship sees the long reign of Jogaila's still pagan grandfather Gediminas (ruled 1316–1341) as the foundational moment and focuses on attempts to strengthen Lithuanian autonomies after 1385, especially during the reign of Jogaila's cousin Vytautas (Polish, Witold; ruled 1401–1430) as grand duke of Lithuania. In short, the period 1385–1569, as viewed from the Polish side, was a direct progression from the personal union, through a period of strengthening ties between the two states (during which time a single member of the Jagiellonian house most often ruled both), to the writing into law of a Commonwealth of the Two Nations at the Union of Lublin in 1569. The view from the Lithuanian side is one of lost opportunities for state formation; it focuses on moments of Lithuanian separateness and sees the union as the eventual forced marriage of two very unequal partners.

A mutual enemy helped bring the two states together. The Order of the Teutonic Knights had posed a threat to both Christian Poland and pagan Lithuania since its arrival in Mazovia and on the Baltic in 1226. A decisive victory of Lithuanian and Polish forces over the Order at Grunwald at Tannenberg in 1410 prepared the way for an ultimate subordination of what would become Ducal Prussia to the Polish crown. Lithuanian historiography views the fifteenth century as a missed opportunity, as the decline of a Gediminian concept of Lithuanian statehood and identity after the death of Vytautas in 1430 and its supplanting with a Polish-oriented Jagiellonian dynasty of Lithuanian origin. Polish historiography has emphasized a willing adoption of Polish political and cultural norms. In 1413 at a renewal of the union at Horodło, forty-seven Lithuanian noble families were "adopted" by, and took on the coats of arms of, forty-seven Polish lines. This marked the beginning of a gradual Polonization of the Lithuanian elites that reached

Grand Duchy of Lithuania to 1569

Lithuania's burghers by the early seventeenth century.

The Lithuanian state was multiethnic from the preconversion period. Large territories of Kievan Rus' (destroyed by the Mongolian Tatar invasion of 1240) gradually came under Lithuanian rule, and the Ruthenian element contributed to Lithuanian identity in later periods. Some individual conversions among the Lithuanian elite were to Orthodoxy, and many underwent a Ruthenianization before submitting to Polonization. Ruthenian became the language of the Lithuanian chancery. Lack of full legal rights for Orthodox Ruthenian nobles (fully granted only in 1563) helped speed the Polonization of Lithuanian (and Ruthenian) society.

The period immediately following the conversion of Lithuania witnessed the first settlements of Tatars and Karaim (around Vilnius and Trakai, among other settlements), to which continuing immigrations were later added those of Poles and Jews. Grand Duke Alexander (ruled 1492–1506; king of Poland from 1501) banished the Jews from the Grand Duchy in 1495 but allowed them to return in 1503. In the fifteenth and sixteenth centuries, Jews were most numerous in Brest, Hrodna (Grodno), and Pinsk, which first comprised the Vaad or Council of the Chief Lithuanian Jewish

Communities. (Vilnius joined only in 1652.) German merchants, engaged in Baltic trade and with contacts to Riga, Königsberg, and Gdańsk, were present in Vilnius before 1386, and their numbers and significance increased here and in other cities of ethnic Lithuania, such as Kaunas, throughout the early modern period. One estimate sees a Grand Duchy of the mid-sixteenth century with a population of about 3 million, of which one-third was Lithuanian and one-half Ruthenian.

The move to formalize the personal union between Poland and Lithuania that culminated in the Union of Lublin on 1 July 1569 gathered momentum as it became clear that the last Jagiellonian king, Sigismund II Augustus (ruled 1548–1572), would indeed die without a male heir. It was again a mutual enemy—now an ascending Muscovy—that helped facilitate the marriage. The middling Lithuanian gentry was now in favor of the union and saw it as a defense of the state against Muscovy. They also saw in the union and the extension of Polish views on the legal equality of the entire *szlachta* ('gentry,' or 'nobles') a strengthening of their own position vis-à-vis the Lithuanian magnates. The latter, a group of unusually wealthy and powerful families, led in this instance by the Calvinist Mikołaj Radziwiłł the Red, then palatine of Vilnius and chancellor of the Grand Duchy, attempted to block the union. In response to Lithuanian recalcitrance, Sigismund II removed the palatinates of Volhynia, Podlachia, Podolia, Bratslav, and Kiev from the Grand Duchy and subordinated them directly to the Polish crown.

Consequently a much smaller and weaker Grand Duchy of Lithuania entered into the Commonwealth of the Two Nations, forming a federation of two quite unequal partners, with one common, elected ruler, one parliament, and one foreign policy. The Grand Duchy would retain a limited sovereignty with a separate administration, army, treasury, judiciary, and legal system (based on the Third Lithuanian Statute of 1588). Other elements of Lithuanian difference—such as the use of chancery Ruthenian, which was abandoned only in 1697—remained a part of Lithuanian identity for the increasingly Polonized elite after the union. The union would bring Lithuanian causes more directly into the center of Polish politics, especially eastern questions, such as the struggles with the Tatars, the Ottoman Empire, and Muscovy. Population in the Grand Duchy declined sharply in the wars of 1648–1667 (by 46 percent according to one estimate). The growth that began in the 1730s brought numbers back to their prewar peak only by 1790. The Grand Duchy disappeared with the third partition of Poland in 1795.

See also **Lublin, Union of (1569); Poland-Lithuania, Commonwealth of, 1569–1795; Poland to 1569; Teutonic Knights; Władysław II Jagiełło (Poland).**

BIBLIOGRAPHY

Błaszczyk, Grzegorz. *Litwa na przełomie średniowiecza i nowożytności, 1492–1569.* Poznań, Poland, 2002.

Davies, Norman. *God's Playground: A History of Poland.* Vol. 1, *The Origins to 1795.* New York, 1982.

Kiaupa, Zigmantas, Jūratė Kiaupienė, and Albinas Kuncevičius. *The History of Lithuania before 1795.* Vilnius, 2000.

Ochmański, Jerzy. *Historia Litwy.* 3rd ed. Wrocław, Poland, 1990.

Stone, Daniel. *The Polish-Lithuanian State, 1386–1795.* Seattle, 2001.

DAVID FRICK

LITHUANIAN LITERATURE AND LANGUAGE. In the early modern period large portions of the societies of the Grand Duchy of Lithuania underwent Polonization. Polish began to function as a language of culture, politics, commerce, and some daily conversation (even if with a regional accent) for magnates, gentry, and burghers, and there was likely a growing bilingualism among all but rural speakers of the other represented languages. These included above all Lithuanian and Ruthenian *(ruskii),* an East Slavic language that would eventually be claimed as the progenitor of modern Belarusian and Ukrainian. Both Lithuanian and Ruthenian were used for certain cultural purposes in this period, and this entry will focus on them.

Speakers of other languages were also present. Lithuanian Jews spoke Yiddish and wrote in Hebrew, Aramaic, and Yiddish. The first Hebrew presses in the Grand Duchy were established at Shklov (1783) and Hrodna (1788). German-speaking merchants were present in cities like Vilnius and

Kaunas. Lithuanian Tatars originally spoke a Kipchak Turkic language, but numbers of them quickly assimilated linguistically and used forms of Belarusian or Polish in their *kitabs* (manuscript books of religious stories, legends, fairy tales, and prayers), which they wrote down in the Arabic alphabet. Courland and Livonia were incorporated into the Commonwealth in 1561, and the first book in Latvian, a Catholic catechism, was printed in Vilnius in 1585.

LITHUANIAN

Lithuanian elites of the Grand Duchy quickly became Ruthenianized and Polonized, so that the Lithuanian language came to have a highly circumscribed area of use, and monolingual speakers in the later part of the period were peasants. By the early seventeenth century, gentry and burghers of all ethnicities and confessions spoke Polish. The chancery language of the Grand Duchy of Lithuania was Ruthenian until 1697, when it was supplanted by Polish and Latin.

The situation was quite different in Lithuania Minor. After the Peace of Toruń of 1466, a defeated Order of Teutonic Knights established a new capital at Königsberg. Lithuanian speakers were the largest non-German ethnic group in a much diminished Ducal Prussia. With the secularization of the order in 1525 and the introduction of Lutheranism as the state religion, Königsberg became a center for Protestant learning and propaganda, drawing students and professors from neighboring states, including Poland and Lithuania. Lithuanian had higher status in the public life of Ducal Prussia than in the Grand Duchy, finding use in a broader range of institutions (some schools and a large Lithuanian parish in Königsberg).

The oldest printed book in Lithuanian, the Lutheran catechism of Martynas Mažvydas, was printed at Königsberg in 1547. Mažvydas (c. 1520–1563) also produced two volumes of hymns (1566 and 1570). In 1579 Baltramiejus Vilentas (1525–1587) published in one volume Luther's small catechism *(Enchiridion)* and a translation of the Gospels and Epistles. The Lutheran clergyman Jonas Bretkunas (1536–1602) published a hymnal and a prayer book (1589) and a two-volume collection of sermons (1591), and he worked on an unpublished Bible translation.

The union with Brandenburg in 1618 and the decline of Ducal Prussia from the 1620s led to a lowering of the status of Lithuanian in Prussian society. Nonetheless, these early works of Lutheran church literature provided a basis for the development of written Lithuanian in the Grand Duchy and an impetus for Catholic authorities to respond in kind. In the Grand Duchy, two competing forms of written Lithuanian emerged, a variant based on the central dialects of Samogitia and a second that favored the eastern variant of historic Lithuania with its seat around Vilnius. The canon of the episcopal college of the Samogitia diocese Mikalojus Daukša (d. 1613) produced the first Lithuanian book printed in the Grand Duchy; it was a translation of the Spanish Jesuit Diego de Ledesma's Catholic catechism (1595). In 1599 he produced a translation of the Polish Jesuit Jakub Wujek's monumental postil, which he prefaced with a Polish language defense of the Lithuanian language. These two works quickly drew a Calvinist response. Merkelis Petkevičius, a clerk at the Vilnius court and supreme tribunal, published a catechism and small hymnal in 1598, and Jokūbas Morkūnas published a translation of the Calvinist Mikołaj Rej's Polish postil in 1600. These were all works in the central dialects that would play a leading role in the nineteenth-century revival.

The eastern dialect was employed in a second translation of Ledesma's Catholic catechism (1605) and by the Jesuit Konstantinas Širvydas (Szyrwid) in his Latin-Polish-Lithuanian dictionary (*Dictionarium Trium Linguarum*, before 1620, 1631, 1642, 1677, 1713, and 1718) and in his bilingual (Polish and Lithuanian) collection of sermons published in Vilnius (vol. 1, 1629; vol. 2, 1644). Public use of Lithuanian declined dramatically in the second half of the seventeenth and throughout the eighteenth centuries, a result of the increasing Polonization of all but peasant societies in the Grand Duchy.

RUTHENIAN

Historians of Belarusian language and literature lay claim to a portion of early modern Ruthenian *(ruskii)*. This was a language at only the earliest stages of normalization, spoken and written by the Orthodox and Uniates of the Polish-Lithuanian Commonwealth and, by the mid-seventeenth century, showing the beginnings of differentiation from Ukrainian variants. In this genetic schema, the language is sometimes called "Middle Belarusian." Texts manifesting Ukrainian and Belarusian features were all labeled Ruthenian. They circulated and were read throughout the Ruthenian lands; moreover, some writers from Ukrainian lands, whose texts contained Ukrainian features, were active and printed their works in centers more closely connected with Belarus (e.g., Vilnius).

Ruthenian chronicles brought the history of Rus' into the period of its incorporation into the Grand Duchy of Lithuania, telling of the events of the fifteenth to the seventeenth centuries (the *Chronicle of the Grand Dukes of Lithuania*, the *First, Second, and Third Belarusian Chronicles*). The pioneer printer Frantsishak Skaryna employed a version of the language in the forty-nine exegetical prefaces to the books of his Church Slavonic Bible (1517–1525). The Protestant minister Szymon Budny published a Ruthenian catechism at Niasvizh in 1562, and the Antitrinitarian Vasil' Cjapinski published fragments of a Ruthenian New Testament in the 1570s. Ruthenian served as a medium for testaments and much state, diplomatic, and private correspondence, as well as all chancery and legal functions in the Grand Duchy of Lithuania until the Union of Lublin (1569), which ushered in an accelerating Polonization. Lithuanian elites, who had first Ruthenianized, now—along with Ruthenian elites—made increasingly broad use of Polish. Ruthenian nonetheless remained the chancery language of the Grand Duchy until 1697, when it was officially replaced by the Polish that had been making steady gains in practical employment throughout the seventeenth century. In addition to the use of Ruthenian in the record books of the Grand Duchy's courts and chancery, we may note the three versions of the Lithuanian Statute, which were printed in Ruthenian in 1529, 1566, and 1588. We also have memoirs (Fiodar Ieŭlasheŭski, 1546–1604; Afanasii Filipovich, c. 1597–1648) and a few sermons (Laontsii Karpovich, c. 1580–1620) and polemical works from the period immediately following the Union of Brest (1596). Simeon Polotskii (1629–1680) was the leading practitioner of syllabic verse (based on Polish models) in Belarusian. This variant of Ruthenian declined in public use and social status with the shift of Ruthenian cultural centers to Ukrainian cities (Lviv, then Kiev) and with the increasing Polonization of Belarusian elites.

See also **Belarus; Polish Literature and Language; Reformations in Eastern Europe: Protestant, Catholic, and Orthodox; Ukrainian Literature and Language.**

BIBLIOGRAPHY

Primary Source

Rothe, Hans, ed. *Die älteste ostslawische Kunstdichtung, 1575–1647.* Bausteine zur Geschichte der Literatur bei den Slawen, vol. 7. Giessen, Germany, 1976–1977.

Secondary Sources

Martel, Antoine. *La langue polonaise dans les pays Ruthènes: Ukraine et Russie Blanche, 1569–1657.* Lille, France, 1938.

McMillin, Arnold B. *Die Literatur der Weissrussen: A History of Byelorussian Literature: From Its Origins to the Present Day.* Bausteine zur Geschichte der Literatur bei den Slawen, vol. 6. Giessen, Germany, 1977.

Zinkevičius, Zigmas. *The History of the Lithuanian Language.* Vilnius, 1996.

DAVID FRICK

LIVONIAN WAR (1558–1583). In 1558 Tsar Ivan IV the Terrible began over twenty years of war for a Baltic foothold by invading eastern Estonia, an area made vulnerable by factional divisions within the Livonian Order (the Order of the Brothers of the Sword) and political conflict among the order, the archbishopric of Riga, and the increasingly Protestant population of the towns. Moscow's potential rivals—Sweden and Poland—were preoccupied with other concerns; Muscovy therefore enjoyed early success. By 1560 Narva and Dorpat and most of the Livonian interior as far as Courland was under Muscovite occupation. But this provoked the Danes, Sweden, and Poland into entering the war.

The second phase of the Livonian War (1563–1571) saw Muscovite armies invade Lithuania; Polotsk, Ozerishche, and other towns along the Western Dvina quickly fell to them. The tsar planned to install Duke Magnus, brother of Denmark's King Frederick II, as vassal king of Livonia to secure a Danish alliance to drive the Swedes out of Riga and Pernau (Pärnu), which they had seized in 1560. Muscovite occupation of northeastern Lithuania finally convinced the Lithuanian nobility to accept closer administrative union with Poland in a

Commonwealth (in the Union of Lublin, 1569), which considerably increased the military resources available to the Polish crown. Frederick II not only withheld the support Duke Magnus needed to expel the Swedes but signed a treaty with the Swedes at Stettin in 1570. The deposition of King Erik XIV brought to the Swedish throne John III Vasa (ruled 1568–1592), who was the son-in-law of King Sigismund II Augustus of Poland and was inclined to view Muscovy as a greater threat than Poland to Swedish interests in Livonia. The military stalemate in Lithuania and Livonia had meanwhile left Muscovy's southern frontier undermanned, with the result that Khan Devlet Girei took a large Crimean Tatar army deep into central Muscovy, sacking and burning Moscow itself in 1571.

In the third phase of the war (1572–1577) Ivan IV exploited the interregnum following the death of Sigismund II to mount another major offensive in Livonia. But the Muscovites were still unable to capture Reval (Tallinn) or Riga. Meanwhile the Commonwealth's newly elected king Stephen Báthory (ruled 1576–1586) was able to achieve rapprochement with the Ottomans and Crimeans, to convince the Sejm to raise taxes for a much larger army of 56,000 men, and to negotiate an alliance with the Swedes. By contrast Ivan IV was finding it harder to maintain large Muscovite forces in the field, for years of heavy taxation and manpower mobilization from the western Muscovite provinces (particularly Novgorod and Pskov) had left these districts devastated.

In 1578 Polish and Swedish armies combined to deal the Muscovites a crushing defeat at Wenden (Cēsis). This marked the war's final phase, which was catastrophic for the Muscovites. Over the next three years they were pushed out of Livonia altogether. Stephen Báthory recaptured Polotsk and the other towns of the Western Dvina region in 1579–1580 and carried the war into western Muscovy, placing Pskov under protracted siege in 1581. By the end of 1581 the Muscovite garrisons at Narva, Ivangorod, Yama (Kingisepp), and Kopor'e had fallen to the Swedish general Pontus De la Gardie. Ivan IV was compelled to sign a ten years' armistice with the Commonwealth at Iam Zapol'skii in January 1582 and a three years' armistice with Sweden at Pliuss in 1583. The tsar thereby forfeited all the lands his armies had occupied along the Baltic coast. Central and southwestern Livonia came under Commonwealth control; the Swedes took Estonia and the territory along the Gulf of Finland.

See also **Ivan IV, "the Terrible" (Russia); Lublin, Union of (1569); Northern Wars; Poland-Lithuania, Commonwealth of, 1569–1795; Sigismund II Augustus (Poland, Lithuania); Stephen Báthory; Sweden; Vasa Dynasty (Sweden).**

BIBLIOGRAPHY

Frost, Robert I. *The Northern Wars: War, State, and Society in Northeastern Europe, 1558–1721.* Harlow, U.K., and New York, 2000.

Koroliuk, V. D. *Livonskaia voina: Iz istorii vneshnei politiki russkogo tsentralizovannogo gosudarstva vo vtoroi polovinie XVI v.* Moscow, 1954.

Roberts, Michael. *The Early Vasas: A History of Sweden, 1523–1611.* Cambridge, U.K., and London, 1968.

BRIAN DAVIES

LOCAL GOVERNMENT. *See* **Cities and Urban Life; City-State; Intendants; Provincial Government; State and Bureaucracy.**

LOCKE, JOHN (1632–1704), English philosopher, political and educational theorist, political economist, scholar, statesman, and sometime physician. John Locke, one of the leading figures in the history of English letters, was born on 29 August 1632 in the village of Wrington, Somerset, and was immediately surrounded by the political and religious controversies that were always to be at the center of his life. His parents were Puritans, and his father later fought on the Parliamentary side in the Civil War. Locke attended Westminster School from 1646 to 1652, when he was elected to a studentship at Christ Church, Oxford, from which he graduated in 1656. During this period, he wrote but did not publish a pair of essays criticizing the extensive conceptions of religious indifference and toleration advocated by Edward Bagshawe's *The Great Question concerning Things Indifferent in Religious Worship* (1660), and he delivered a series of lectures on natural law.

At Oxford, Locke was a friend of the scientist Robert Boyle and other original members of the

John Locke. Undated portrait engraving. ©BETTMANN/CORBIS

Royal Society, to which Locke himself was elected in 1668. Rather than take religious orders, he changed his studies to medicine and was trained and influenced by the physician Thomas Sydenham. On a diplomatic mission to Cleves in Brandenburg in 1665, Locke experienced an unanticipated degree of toleration, which seems to have had a major impact on his philosophical and political thinking. In 1666 he had met Anthony Ashley Cooper, subsequently the Earl of Shaftesbury, into whose household he moved in 1667 as the earl's personal physician and advisor, political aide, and author of political documents.

Shaftesbury, who fell into and out of grace with the king, was at the center of Restoration politics, and Locke was invariably at his side. For Shaftesbury Locke wrote a tract defending toleration in 1667, a draft constitution for the Carolina colony of which Shaftesbury was a proprietor, a defense of the king's prerogative power to issue a declaration of religious toleration in 1669, and—most important—the *Two Treatises of Government.* It was also while he was a member of the Shaftesbury household that Locke's interest in philosophy deepened, and he completed various drafts of his *Essay concerning Human Understanding.*

Locke returned to Oxford in 1675, but like Shaftesbury he later went into political exile in the Netherlands, where he remained until 1689. There he enjoyed the friendship and support of Jean Leclerc, to whose *Bibliothèque universelle et historique* (1686–1693) he made several contributions, and Phillip Limborch, to whom he would dedicate the *Epistola de tolerantia,* published anonymously in the Netherlands in 1689 and translated into English (also anonymously) the next year as the *Letter concerning Toleration.* During his exile, Locke completed much of the final version of the *Essay,* an abstract of which was published by Leclerc in 1688.

While in the Netherlands, Locke presumably was involved in Monmouth's Rebellion in 1685 and in the politics of the Glorious Revolution of 1688, which brought the Dutch sovereign William of Orange and his wife Mary, daughter of James II, to the English throne. Locke himself returned to England in 1689 and began his public literary career, publishing the works that would establish his status in the pantheon of western philosophy and political theory. The *Essay concerning Human Understanding* appeared in December 1689 (dated 1690), and the *Two Treatises* were published anonymously in 1690.

The *Essay* is regarded as one of the foundational works of modern empirical, or rather "experiential," philosophy. It opens with an extensive attack on the notion that some ideas are "innate," arguing, on the contrary, that the human mind at birth is a "blank slate" *(tabula rasa)* but has the capacity to perceive and reason. Locke went on to claim that all ideas and knowledge are acquired from experience, which can be either sensationalist or rational, and that they bear direct relationships to a real, external world. The *Essay* also deals with language, its relationship to ideas, and its imperfections and abuses, and with reason and its role in the acquisition and assessment of knowledge. This "rationalism," albeit less extreme than that of René Descartes (1596–1650), is sometimes seen as conflicting with the rest of the *Essay,* but the apparent contradiction between the two positions can be found throughout the work. In a move that would be anathema to modern empiricists, Locke occasionally sidestepped difficult philosophical issues by referring to their resolution in the ultimately unknowable mind of God, for faith, as the acceptance of revelation, was one of the cardinal supports of Locke's entire system.

The *Two Treatises* are equally foundational for subsequent political philosophy as is the *Essay* for empirical philosophy, and their reliance upon divine will is even more overt. Written in the early 1680s as part of Shaftesbury's exclusion campaign, the work was not published until 1690, when it was issued as a theoretical support of the successful Glorious Revolution. The *Two Treatises* were directed against the patriarchal theory of Sir Robert Filmer (c. 1588–1653); the *First Treatise*, in particular, was a detailed and sometimes page-by-page attack on patriarchalism. In the *Second Treatise* Locke developed his own political theory, which was also an implicit assault on Thomas Hobbes (1588–1679), whom Locke never identified. Locke replaced Filmer's divine right sovereignty, derived from the paternity of Adam, with a conception of government and politics based on vaguely articulated notions of natural law and natural rights. He posited a pre-political state of nature characterized by human equality and freedom, the ownership of the world in common by God's grant, and legitimacy based on consent. Personal property was acquired by the mixing of one's labor with that which was common.

The most important part of Locke's criticism of Filmer was his insistence that fatherhood and political government are distinct forms of authority. Filmer had asserted their identity. Locke, however, was at pains to argue that while political or civil society had emerged historically and anthropologically from the household, paternal and political dominion were altogether distinct. The act of consent transformed fatherhood into government and undergirded all subsequent legitimacy.

The *Two Treatises* are perhaps best known for their theories of property and revolution. Government, according to Locke, is a human contrivance made necessary by the growing complexities of the state of nature and especially by the increasing insecurity of personal property. Locke had two conceptions of "property." In the state of nature (through chapter V of the *Second Treatise*), "property" meant land and goods, including money; in civil society, however, it almost always meant "life, liberty, and estate," which was the more widely accepted meaning in seventeenth-century England. Locke's initial reliance upon the former definition—and the subsequent importance of the *Two Treatises*—undoubtedly played a large role in popularizing that narrower understanding among modern English speakers, but his shift back to the more conventional and broader meaning was the source of some ambiguities in his political theory.

The purpose of government according to Locke is to protect property, and it is in return for that protection that people agree to transfer to the government their individual rights to interpret and enforce the law of nature. When the government no longer provides that protection, or if it becomes an enemy to property, the duty to obey is superseded by a right of revolution, whereby the power and authority conveyed to the government revert to the people (or their representatives) who may then establish a new government.

The *Letter concerning Toleration* is a specific application of the principles of the *Two Treatises.* What was innovative and radical about the *Letter* was the argument that religious imposition went so far beyond the legitimate competence of the magistrate as to be a ground for resistance. Locke drew a firm distinction between the secular ends of magistracy and the religious ends of churches. In doing so, he made a bolder move toward genuine religious liberty than had any of his contemporaries. But Locke excluded Roman Catholics from this toleration, alleging, like many of his contemporaries, that they owed their primary political loyalty to the pope rather than to civil rulers. He was confident, however, that Protestant Christians could live at peace within one civil society despite their diverse religious beliefs.

Locke spent the rest of life in public service and writing. He was a member of the Board of Trade and published revisions of the *Essay,* replies to criticisms of the *Letter concerning Toleration,* and tracts on education, religion, and money, some of which were published after his death. Locke died on 28 October 1704 at Oates, Essex, at the home of Sir Francis and Lady Masham (the daughter of the

Cambridge Platonist Ralph Cudworth), where he had been living since 1691. He is buried in High Laver Church in Essex. Much of his massive collection of personal manuscripts—including journals, diaries, letters he received, and copies of those he sent—and a substantial part of his library have survived and are now in the Bodleian Library at Oxford.

See also **Constitutionalism; Empiricism; Epistemology; Glorious Revolution (Britain); Natural Law; Philosophy; Political Philosophy; Rights, Natural; Toleration.**

BIBLIOGRAPHY

Primary Sources

Locke, John. *An Essay concerning Human Understanding.* Edited by Peter Niddich. Oxford, 1975.

———. *Two Treatises of Government.* Edited by Peter Laslett. 2nd edition. Cambridge, U.K., 1988.

Secondary Sources

Ayers, Michael. *Locke.* New York, 1991.

Franklin, Julian H. *John Locke and the Theory of Sovereignty: Mixed Monarchy and the Right of Resistance in the Political Thought of the English Revolution.* Cambridge, U.K., and New York, 1978.

Marshall, John. *John Locke: Resistance, Religion, and Responsibility.* Cambridge, U.K., and New York, 1994.

Yolton, John W. *Locke: An Introduction.* Oxford and New York, 1985.

———. *Locke and French Materialism.* Oxford and New York, 1991.

GORDON SCHOCHET

LOGIC. Recent research on the seemingly staid subject of logic has revealed not only that certain topics in logic explained how inductive reasoning came about, but also that logic itself learned to create its own history in which logic arose from simple beginnings, but over time developed ever better ways of thinking, eventually becoming a progressive force in the history of thought. Furthermore, by the eighteenth century, the history of logic served as the structure for the history of philosophy, as well as an encyclopedia of knowledge known as *historia literaria.*

Although the importance of inductive reasoning to natural philosophy has been acknowledged, other research has shown that the tradition of inductive logic, which historians of the scientific revolution have identified as new, was actually developed by Aristotelian philosophers. The best known of these is the Paduan philosopher Jacobo Zabarella. His logic developed in part as a criticism of Florentine Neoplatonism and the medieval Scotist philosophy. This tradition of logic was taught not only in Italy but also in England, where logic texts by Zabarella have been found to have been used as school texts. Further, in Germany there remain today ninety-seven copies of Zabarella's *Opera Logicae.* This logic was then adopted by Bartholomew Keckerman for more elementary teaching and finally adopted again during the second half of the seventeenth century in Finland and Scandinavia after the Ramus vogue had run its course. Finally, at Jena, texts by Zabarella and the Coimbra commentators from Portugal were seen to be the beginning of a tradition of logic that led to the philosophy of John Locke (1632–1704) and Robert Boyle (1627–1691).

The best way to explain the difference between the Neoplatonic and Scotist approaches to knowledge and logic is to follow the debate around what is now considered a guiding logical and philosophical question between 1500 and 1750: What was the first thing thought? Was it the pure concept of an object or idea as defined by the Neoplatonists and some Scotists, that is, an idea conceived in the mind without recourse to the unreliable senses? Was it being, or *ens,* as Thomas Aquinas wrote? Or was it a fuzzy notion of a whole object or concept that needed to be examined, carefully defined and refined, and finally, when more was known about it, completely reexamined?

The great innovators of logic in the seventeenth century—Francis Bacon (1561–1626), Pierre Gassendi (1592–1655), Robert Boyle, and John Locke—continued and transformed this anti-Platonic, anti-Scotist tradition. These anti-Platonic philosophers held that there were two types of knowledge, divine and human, each with its own method. Divine knowledge was accessed through inspiration; human knowledge, or artificial knowledge, had to be learned through the senses. The anti-Platonists often quoted Aristotle as saying, "There is nothing in the mind that is not in the senses."

Many philosophers did work on inductive reasoning, beginning with the sixteenth-century Aristotelians Benedito Pereira in Rome and Zabarella in Padua. Their work was drawn upon and transformed by Bacon, Boyle, and Locke in England, Gassendi and his followers in France, and members of a new German school of philosophy known as eclecticism. The eclectics, like their counterparts in England and France, were both anti-Platonic and anti-Cartesian. They gave their tradition a historical dimension, writing that since no human being could know everything, philosophers should examine the reasoning of past philosophers, criticize or accept the methods they had used to reach their conclusions, and finally judge the validity of the original concepts. Using improved logic, each philosopher would then add new information to explain his findings. Eclecticism also referred to a Neoplatonic philosophy that tried to unify all knowledge under one idea by such early church fathers as Clement of Alexandria. Although it had the same name, this was very different from German eclecticism.

How is it possible to classify Gassendi, Bacon, and Locke together? Here one can realize the pitfalls of assigning one name to logical schools. For example, Gassendi did write a treatise attacking scholastic logic, *Adversus Aristoteleos* as he called it. This treatise was really attacking the self-referential syllogistic reasoning of dialectic, and often criticizes the Scotist philosopher Eustachius St. Paul, teacher of Descartes, and quotes Benedito Pereira, the anti-Platonic and anti-Scotist Aristotelian at the Collegio Romano. Gassendi dismissed Eustachius as Scholastic or Aristotelian, while he was developing his own version of the anti-Platonic logic of the sixteenth century that he reworked with his own recreation of Epicurean logic.

A further discussion of logic can be reduced to five points: 1) the use of rhetoric as a tool of persuasion by logicians; 2) the transformation of logic by anti-Platonic Aristotelian philosophers and their development of the question, *De primo cognito?*, 'What was the first thing thought?'; 3) this orientation of logic leads to the very specific criticism of the Neoplatonic myth of the *prisca philosophiae*, the 'first philosophers'; 4) the development of a technical vocabulary for natural philosophy that was a direct result of inductive logic: as myth and metaphor were rejected for biblical commentary, so Platonic myth and metaphor was to be shunned for inductive reasoning; 5) the hermeneutic of language for logic, which was then applied to the writings of logicians in the past and provided a tool for judging past thought. Thus the history of philosophy was born, and its midwife was logic.

RHETORIC AND LOGICAL REASONING

The scholarship of Letizia Panizza and Heikki Micheli has made it quite clear that, as Micheli writes, "there is no justification for separating rhetoric from logic." The model of the correct logical proof changed dramatically when techniques of rhetoric were used. As Panizza explains, medieval philosophers "who learned their dialectic mainly from Boethius commentaries on Cicero and manuals of logic did not pay attention to Aristotle and Cicero on the close rapport of dialectic and rhetoric" (Cicero's *De Oratore*, a work only known after 1421). Panizza also explains that by the end of the fifteenth century, "Aristotle is held up as a model for an orator who wants to unite not only eloquence with philosophy in general, but rhetoric with dialectic."

She goes on to explain that logic was the instrument for philosophical thought, while rhetoric was the technique used to convince the reader. The philosophers adopted the persona of the orator, which was about the only technique used by Renaissance historians. By the time Zabarella (1532–1589) published *De Methodis* in 1578, rhetoric was being used to convince the reader of his method. Zabarella began each book of his treatises with a summary statement of method in which he declared his objectivity about his topic and his modesty towards knowledge, just as historians before him had done. After declaring his objectivity, he stated why his method of logic was superior to all others.

But the philosopher's use of the first person, in imitation of the speech of an orator, really developed in France with René Descartes's (1596–1650) *Discourse on Method* and Gassendi's persuasive voice in the *Syntagma*. In his work, Descartes declared the originality of his thoughts. He tended to assert the truth of his logical statements with rhetorically styled sincerity rather than engage in argument. Regius, a fellow philosopher, was so annoyed at the Cartesian use of persuasion rather than logic for proof that he wrote to Descartes, "any mad man can claim he is right." Descartes declared, "I think therefore I am." On the contrary, the first thing thought by Gassendi was not an a priori judgment; to him, thought had a history. He studied what past philosophers had thought, and he judged and critically examined the logic of the position. This led him to write a history of logic, the first comprehensive history up to that time.

ANTI-PLATONIC PHILOSOPHERS

Charles Schmitt wrote that Zabarella's logic set the stage for the logic used in the seventeenth century. Logic texts quoted Zabarella's attack on a priori reasoning and praised his logical method of setting out information not only in the seventeenth century but into the eighteenth. Johann Syrbius of Jena began his 1715 logic text with a critical history of the attack against a priori reasoning. He begins with a short historical discourse on the proposition that species originated in the mind, beginning with a quote from a commentary on Aristotle's *De anima* by the Portuguese Coimbra philosopher and Zabarella and ending by having linked the earlier traditions with the contemporary philosophy of John Locke and Robert Boyle. He also criticized Descartes, who believed that the species originated in the mind.

NEOPLATONISM

Not only was a priori reasoning rejected by specific philosophers, but the same anti-Platonic argument was used against the nonhistorical view that the *prisci philosophiae* or *prisci sapientes* could have known all of human knowledge without having learned it. For the Neoplatonists there was one truth that could be found in different forms in different religions around the world. This universal truth was proposed in the fifteenth century by Marsilio Ficino and was still of interest in the seventeenth to the Jesuit polymath Athanasius Kircher. Kircher's magnificently illustrated book of Noah's Ark, in which all of the knowledge known intuitively by early man is set out among the rooms, is a delightful visualization of universal knowledge.

There was an encyclopedia based on the other view. Zabarella said that as unlearned men, the *prisci* only knew what was in their nature. As the first thing thought was only hazily understood and had to be observed, identified, and then named, human civilization followed the same pattern. Initially humans knew nothing and had to understand the world through trial and error. A clever person appeared and made improvements, then others asked to become apprentices so that they could learn the logic of that person's way of working. Finally, all of this knowledge was written down. Adam, Moses, and Hermes Trimegistus are not part of this world: they all had only natural knowledge.

Just as there was not only one universal truth, there was not only one logical method for all disciplines. The greatest and most comprehensive history of disciplines was set out in 1708 in the *Polyhistor* by Georg Morhof (1639–1691). He articulated the difference between the disciplines as a logician articulates the difference between different sense impressions in inductive reasoning. Once the field of learning was identified, then the early and unclear beginnings of thought could be described and its history told as the history of the progress of the logic of that field of knowledge.

THE VOCABULARY OF NATURAL PHILOSOPHY

If logic could control the organization of knowledge, it also dictated correct vocabulary. Research has shown that this hermeneutics of language was used as a weapon against Platonic philosophers. Perhaps no one was criticized for his vocabulary more than Paracelsus (c. 1493–1541), the innovative medical philosopher who developed a vocabulary for spells to use in medicinal cures. Medical doctors like the Swiss Thomas Erastus (1524–1583) attacked the Paracelsian language of spells for its attempt to be universal. Erastus said that no word is universal, but is particular to the civilization in which it is found. Spells and magic tried to unite heaven and earth into a chain of being that did not exist, Erastus complained. He asserted that there was a separation between the realms.

If natural philosophy and medical science were to improve, logic had to be used. Logic must order sense perceptions in such a way that what is known is recorded and what is unknown discovered. To do this, a precise vocabulary had to be devised. There was such interest in identifying the correct type of vocabulary for inductive reasoning and identifying Platonic or Scotist definitions that at the turn of the seventeenth century Goclenius's *Lexicon* was published, which set out the different types of words for different types of logic.

APPLICATION OF LOGIC TO THE PHILOSOPHY OF THE PAST

Not long after Zabarella's attack on the logic of *prisci sapientes,* the various types of logic of the various philosophers came under scrutiny. Anthony Grafton pointed out that Isaac Casaubon discovered that the Neoplatonic texts by Hermes Trismegistus were third-century forgeries. This discovery paved the way for a reassessment of Egyptian civilization. When the logic of earlier philosophers was identified, examined, and judged, an important change occurred: the critical characterization of the logic of past philosophers, the identification of philosophers not chronologically but by the success of their logic, changed the way people viewed past philosophy.

Pierre Gassendi wrote the first history of logic. His little-known work *De Logicae Origine et Varietate,* published in 1648 as a preface to the *Syntagma,* took the reader on an intellectual trip from the logic of Adam to the logic of Descartes. Adam, wrote Gassendi, did not have logic when he argued with the snake: "He was merely quibbling." He also argued that none of the patriarchs in the Bible were capable of logic either. Logic began with the Greeks and Zeno. Gassendi then criticized Plato's logic because it depended on a priori thinking and "was too much like theology." Although he admitted there was much to admire in Aristotle's logic, Gassendi wrote that it had been spoiled by his followers.

Gassendi admired the logic of the ancient philosopher Epicurus, based on inductive reasoning. Gassendi constructed a believable Epicurean logic in this text that appeared in student logic texts until the mid-eighteenth century. Jean le Clerc, friend of both Robert Boyle and John Locke, wrote perhaps the most widely used of these logic texts. From Epicurus, Gassendi passed over the Middle Ages, cramming one thousand years into two paragraphs, then began in the early modern period with Francis Bacon and the establishment of inductive reasoning. Bacon, wrote Gassendi, went the "heroic way." Gassendi made Bacon as the hero of contemporary thought. There is a great deal of rhetoric in this history of logic.

Finally, the complete triumph of logic as the history of logic came with the work of the German historian of philosophy Jacob Brucker (1696–1770). At Jena, Brucker was a student of Johan Jacob Syrbius, who had linked contemporary English inductive reasoning with the earlier logic of the Coimbra commentaries and Zabarella's *De Methodis.* In 1723, Brucker wrote a history of logic called *Historia Philosophia Doctrinae de Ideis.* In this work he attacked the *prisca philosophiae* in the person of Zoroaster. Following Gassendi, whose history of logic he knew, Brucker judged each philosopher by whether he used inductive reasoning. He praised Epicurus among the ancient philosophers and dismissed Renaissance philosophers like Valla and Vives, while praising John Locke and Robert Boyle.

Although the early modern period saw many breaks with past tradition, it did not usher in a new logic all at once. Rather, it was a period in conversation with past philosophy: sometimes it agreed, sometimes it disagreed, and sometimes the philosopher transformed his sources beyond recognition. As the *De primo cognito?* question was reworked by the anti-Platonic philosophers, the concept of intellectual (as opposed to chronological) progress developed in the sixteenth and seventeenth centuries. Nowhere can the concept of progress be seen more clearly than in the history of logic.

See also **Aristotelianism; Bacon, Francis; Boyle, Robert; Cartesianism; Descartes, René; Gassendi, Pierre; Locke, John; Natural Philosophy; Neoplatonism; Philosophy.**

BIBLIOGRAPHY

Primary Sources

Brucker, Jacob. *Historia Philosophia Doctrinae de Ideis.* Augsburg, 1723.

———. "De Reformatione Philosophiae Rationalis Recentiori Aetate Tentata." In *Historia Critica Philosophiae.* 2nd ed. Leipzig, 1754. Reprint with English translations of Brucker's Praefatio and definitions of Eclecticism and Syncretism, edited by Constance Blackwell. Bristol. Forthcoming.

Gassendi, Pierre. "De Logicae Origine et Varietate." In *Opera Omnia,* vol. 1, pp. 35–66. Leiden, 1658. Reprint, Stuttgart-Bad, 1994. The English translation, *Pierre Gassendi's "Instutio Logica" (1658): A Critical Edition and Introduction* by Howard Jones (Assen, 1981) does not include a translation of Gassendi's history of logic.

Syrbius, J. J. *Institutiones Philosophiae Primae Novae et Eclecticae.* Jena, 1720.

———. *Institutiones Philosophiae Rationalis Eclectica, in Praefatione Historia Logicae Succincte Delineatur.* Jena, 1717.

Toletus, Francescus. *Commentaria Una cum Questionibus in Octo Libros Aristotelis de Physica Auscultatione.* First edition, Cologne, 1574; last edition, Venice, 1615. Reprint, Hildesheim, 1985.

———. *Commentaria Una cum Questionibus in Universam Aristotelis Logicam.* First edition, Rome, 1572; last edition, Cologne 1615. Reprint, Hildesheim, 1985.

Zabarella, Jacobo. *Opera Logica.* Frankfurt, 1608 and 1966.

Secondary Sources

Blackwell, Constance. "Epicurus and Boyle, Le Clerc and Locke: Ideas and Their Redefinition in Jacob Brucker's *Historia Philosophica Doctrinae de Ideis* 1723." In *Il vocabolario della République des Lettres: Terminologia filosofica e storia della filosofia, problemi di metodo, in memoriam di Paul Dibon,* edited by Marta Fattori. Naples, 1997.

———. "The Logic of the History of Philosophy: Morhof's 'De Variis Methodis' and the *Polyhistor Philosophicus.*" In *Mapping the World of Learning: The Polyhistor of Daniel Georg Morhof,* edited by Françoise Waquet, pp. 35–50. Wiesbaden, 2000.

———. "Vocabulary as a Critique of Knowledge: Zabarella and Keckermann—Erastus and Conring." In *Philologie und Erkenntnis: Beiträge zu Begriff und Problem Frühneuzeitlicher "Philologie,"* edited by Ralph Häfner. Tübingen, 2002.

Mikkeli, Heiki. *An Aristotelian Response to Renaissance Humanism: Jacopo Zabarella on the Nature of the Arts and Sciences.* Helsinki, 1992.

Panizza, Letizia. "Ermolao Barbaro e Pico della Mirandola tra retorica e dialettica." *De genere dicendi philosophorum del 1484, Ermolao Barbaro (1454–1493) Congress,* edited by Michela Marangoni. Venice, 1996.

Constance Blackwell

LONDON. The most salient feature of London's experience in the early modern period was the enormous growth of its population. From approximately 70,000 inhabitants in 1500, it grew to 200,000 by 1600, to 400,000 by 1650, to 575,000 by 1700, and had reached 900,000 by 1800. Its position in the tables of European urban centers rose from sixth place in 1500 to third in 1600 (after Naples and Paris), and it outstripped Paris to reach the top position soon after 1650. Whereas it contained about 2 percent of the English population in 1500, by 1700 it had reached around 10 percent, and this level was sustained through the eighteenth century. Mortality levels were extremely high in London: indeed they deteriorated after the disappearance of plague in the later seventeenth century because the capital acted as a reservoir of infections. For much of the eighteenth century tuberculosis, typhus, and smallpox were major killers. It was only from the 1760s that mortality conditions began to improve. This meant that the city's growth could only be sustained by a constant flow of migrants who came from every corner of England and Wales (and increasingly from Scotland and Ireland and the European mainland, too). By 1700 London needed probably about 8,000 newcomers a year. Only something between 20 and 30 percent of Londoners had been born in the city. And because London acted as a revolving door, not only receiving people, but sending them back to the provinces, as many as one in six of the national population had experience of London life by 1700.

ECONOMIC CHANGE

The cities that grew most rapidly in early modern Europe were capitals or ports. London was both. In the early sixteenth century London already accounted for 75 percent of the country's international trade, but it was dangerously dependent on the export of the key staple of woolen cloth to the Antwerp entrepôt in return for luxury goods. By 1600 the pattern of trade was already diversifying, as the disruptions to trade with the Low Countries encouraged London merchants to seek direct access to goods they had previously obtained there. The merchants of London returned to the Mediterranean in the 1570s, began voyaging to the East Indies in 1600, and began to develop trade with the Americas in the early seventeenth century. London entered a new phase of import-led growth, and reexports, particularly of colonial products like tobacco, became increasingly important. By 1700 London handled 80 percent of the nation's imports, 65 percent of its exports, and 85 percent of its reexports.

As a capital city London benefited from the increasing centralization of government. As the royal court became more sedentary and also asserted its monopoly of patronage, the landed elites came to

London. View of the city c. 1560. O'SHEA GALLERY, LONDON, U.K./BRIDGEMAN ART LIBRARY

see a London residence as essential to the maintenance of their power and influence, contributing to the beginning of the London winter season from 1600 onward. Likewise, the huge increase in the volume of litigation in the central law courts brought more people to the capital on legal business. This in turn contributed to the concentration of the professions in the capital: by 1730 London contained at least a quarter of the country's solicitors and attorneys. The development of the fiscal military state from the 1690s onward brought about both an increase in the size of the government apparatus (as well as annual Parliaments) and a huge expansion in the financial services sector as London acquired the key banking and insurance institutions.

London's role as capital city and port contributed to its role as center of manufacturing and shopping. The residence of the elites brought an immense demand for luxury goods in its wake, while the import trades spawned spin-off industries like sugar refining and silk weaving. Whereas in 1500 the economy had been dangerously dependent on the state of the cloth trade, the broadening of the manufacturing base contributed to the long-term resilience of the city economy. London's manufactures became increasingly heavily capitalized, entailing a diminution in the role of the self-employed artisan and a growth in larger enterprises. London was not, however, to be the cradle of the industrial revolution, and in the later eighteenth century the proving ground of industrial innovation lay in the provinces. The high labor costs associated with the capital meant that London came to concentrate on the finishing of industrial goods and on the luxury trades, but it remained the largest manufacturing center in Europe at the end of the eighteenth century. Likewise, the enormous demand represented by the concentration of people in London encouraged the precocious development of specialist retailing facilities. Already in the 1490s foreign travelers marveled at the wealth of the goldsmiths' shops in Cheapside; in the early sixteenth century moralists bemoaned the proliferation of haberdashers' shops selling fripperies; in 1568 London acquired its first shopping mall in the galleried arcades of Sir Thomas Gresham's Royal Exchange, a model for other purpose-built retailing emporia in the West End in the seventeenth century.

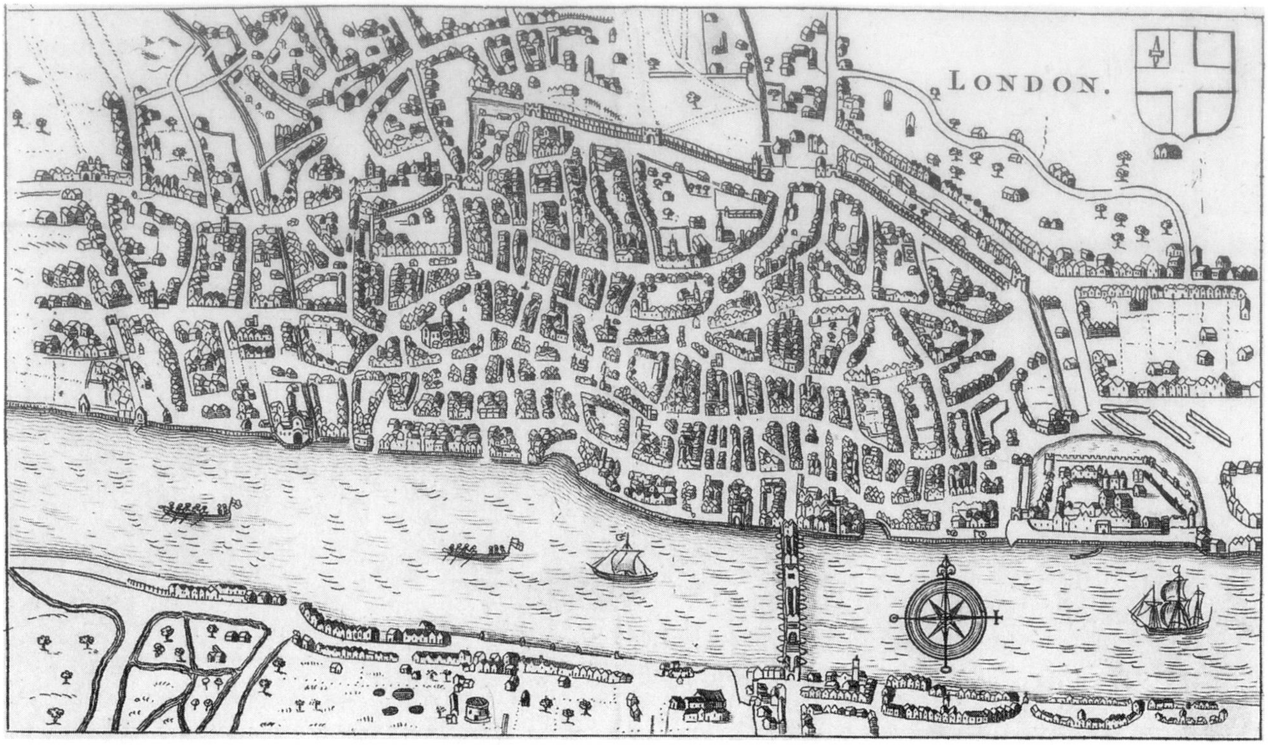

London. Based on older maps, this small sketch plan depicts London circa 1563, at a time when the population of the city was rapidly expanding. London was gradually extending west toward the City of Westminster, which was taking shape around the court. The less-developed area of Southwark, south of the Thames across London Bridge, served as an entertainment district with its theatres and bull and bear-baiting rings. MAP COLLECTION, STERLING MEMORIAL LIBRARY, YALE UNIVERSITY

The concentration of the social elites in the capital for the London season contributed to the proliferation of entertainments and the increasing commercialization of leisure. One of the earliest manifestations of this was the amphitheater playhouses (three were built in 1576–1577) with capacities of upwards of 1,500. Although subject to the constant strictures of the moralists and the fitful regulation of a nervous government, the theaters became an established feature of the London social scene. Commercial concerts began in the 1670s; although aristocratic patronage was critical in attracting high-class composers and vocal and instrumental performers, there was enormous public interest in the performances, the rehearsal for Handel's *Music for the Royal Fireworks* (1749) having an audience of twelve thousand. Citizens had long found recreation in the fields about the city, but physical expansion meant that it was necessary to create designated recreational promenades, beginning with Moorfields in 1608, but soon supplemented by the more fashionable Lincoln's Inn Fields and St. James' Park. By the eighteenth century the metropolitan area was studded with a variety of pleasure gardens, their differential pricing ensuring that the classes would not have to mingle too much. Much cultural and social exchange, of course, continued to take place in the city's drinking establishments: by the 1730s London boasted at least 200 inns, 500 taverns, 6,000 alehouses, and 550 coffeehouses.

SOCIETY AND GOVERNMENT

The two foci of court and port affected the social geography of the city. The City proper, the area under the jurisdiction of the Lord Mayor and aldermen covering what is now known as the "square mile," was, although not socially uniform in character, increasingly dominated by the commercial elites. This process was reinforced after the Great Fire of 1666, which destroyed 87 parish churches, 13,200 houses, and many public buildings. Although it proved impossible to realize the ambitions for a comprehensive redesign of the city's layout, the post-Fire rebuilding changed its face, as brick replaced timber and lath, and many overcrowded

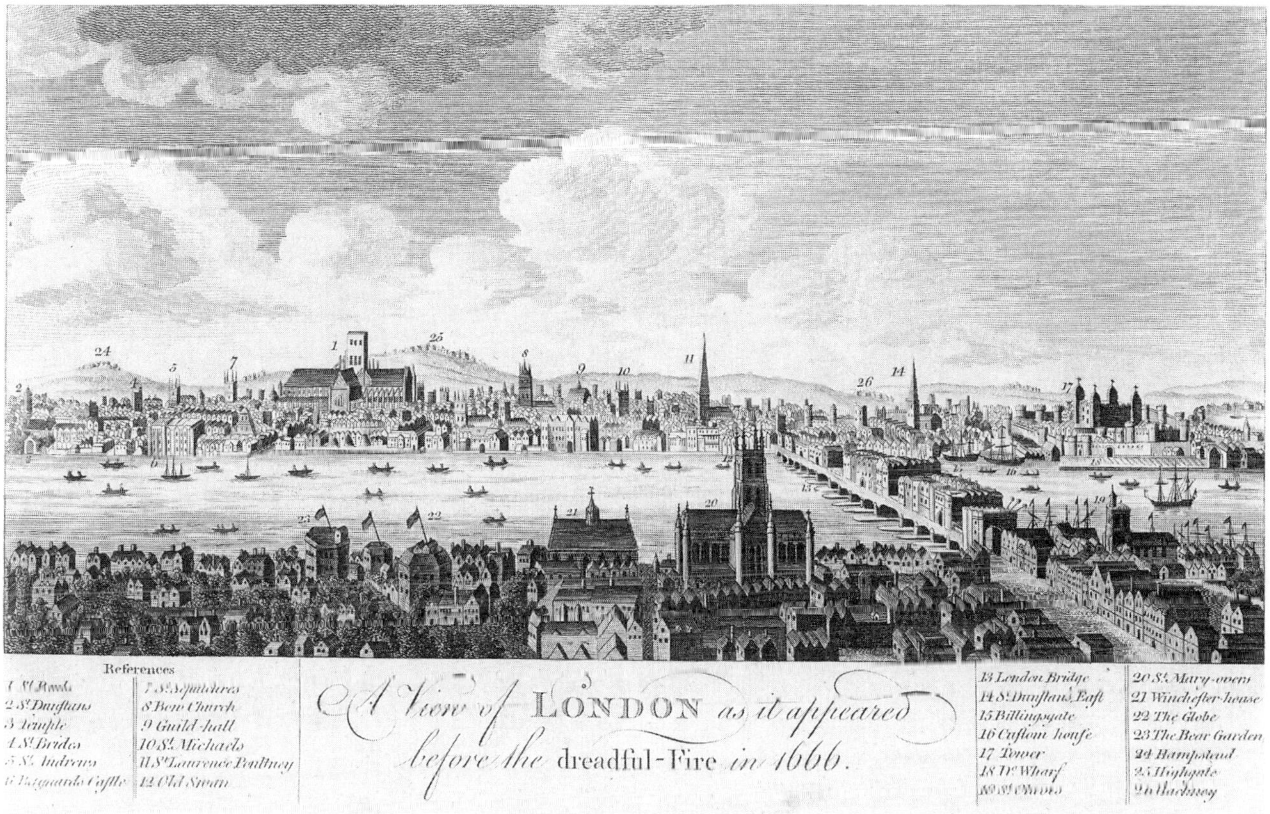

London. An engraved view from Walter Harrison's *New and Universal History, Description and Survey of the Cities of London and Westminster* published in 1776. The area depicted, looking north across the Thames, was largely destroyed by the Great Fire of 1666. The far skyline is dominated by "Old" St. Paul's Cathedral, destroyed in the fire but later replaced by the present cathedral designed by Christopher Wren. MAP COLLECTION, STERLING MEMORIAL LIBRARY, YALE UNIVERSITY

tenements were not rebuilt. Meanwhile the landed elites, many of whom had maintained residences in the City in the later Middle Ages, migrated westward toward Westminster, which constituted a separate focus for growth. The West End was characterized by a large number of speculative housing developments, usually regular terrace rows in wide streets and squares, many of them sponsored by the aristocracy themselves. By contrast, the eastern suburbs were dominated by the port, the miles of dockyards generating a huge demand for casual (and often seasonally unemployed) labor, and a variety of industrial activity, including shipbuilding, as well as the processing of imported raw materials. The northern and eastern suburbs were markedly poorer (with large numbers of subdivided properties and a high level of multiple occupancy) than the City and the West End, though it would be wrong to draw the distinctions too strongly. The presence of the elites in the West End generated an enormous demand for services and manufactures, meaning that within a few yards of the fashionable squares dominated by the aristocracy and gentry were alleys teeming with the poor. In the City the commercial core was centered on the key shopping thoroughfares like Cheapside and places of mercantile association like the Royal Exchange, but there were areas of marked poverty, particularly in the insalubrious riverside parishes.

The scale of growth meant that the traditional City was soon engulfed by the expanding suburbs. By the later seventeenth century three-quarters of the capital's population resided in areas beyond the control of the Lord Mayor and aldermen. Unlike Paris, where there was a much stronger match between topographical and administrative boundaries, there was no attempt to integrate the suburbs with the governmental structures of the City. The suburbs, all of which experienced in various degrees the social problems of poverty and petty crime atten-

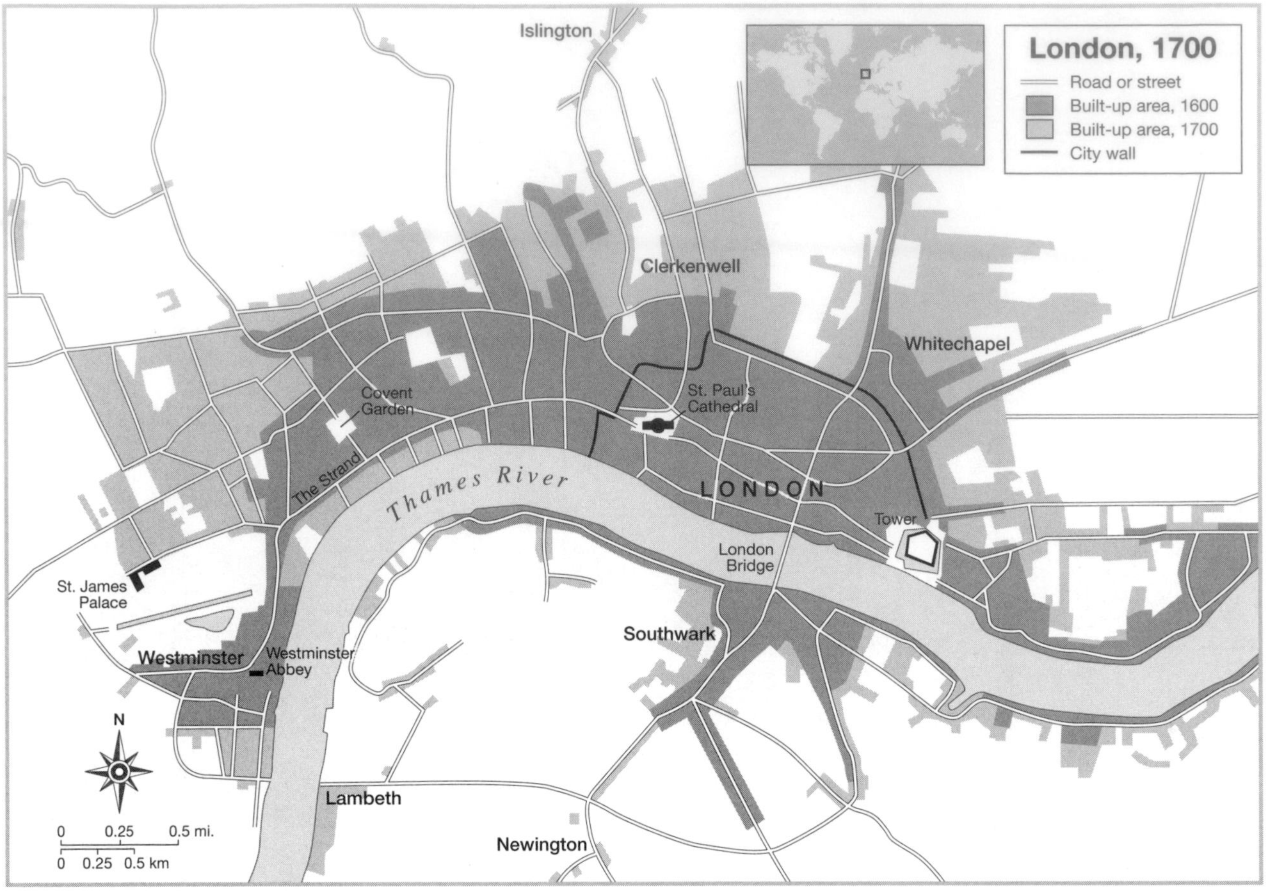

dant on population growth, were governed by overlapping manorial and parochial authorities. Nevertheless the breakdown in order was by no means as great as one might think. London was a relatively well policed capital. From Recorder William Fleetwood in the Elizabethan period to Henry Fielding in the 1750s, chosen magistrates worked closely with the central government to coordinate suburban policing. Parish vestries, particularly in the western suburbs, elaborated the poor law into a bureaucratic mechanism for controlling the poor. Local communities increasingly turned to Parliament for the powers they needed to address local problems. From 1700 there was a proliferation of improvement commissions responsible for street improvement, lighting, and sewerage. A host of voluntary organizations supplemented the work of parish vestries in the relief and schooling of the poor.

Throughout the period London evoked contrasting responses from contemporaries. Protestants might celebrate it as a model godly commonwealth when contrasting the piety of its citizens with the state of rural religion, but they would alternately condemn it as a model of Babylonian depravity when considering its social problems and the greed of its leading citizens. Economic commentators might marvel at the wealth of the City and its increasing dominance over its Continental rivals, but they might also claim that it was strangling the provincial centers. The reality, however, seems to have been that London handled the problems of urban growth more successfully than comparable centers and developed a positive economic and cultural relationship with its hinterland.

See also **Britain, Architecture in; Cities and Urban Life; England; English Literature and Language; Jones, Inigo; Shops and Shopkeeping; Wren, Christopher.**

BIBLIOGRAPHY

Archer, Ian W. *The Pursuit of Stability: Social Relations in Elizabethan London.* Cambridge, U.K., and New York, 1991.

London. A late-eighteenth-century engraving shows Blackfriars Bridge with St. Paul's Cathedral in the background. THE ART ARCHIVE/HISTORISCHES MUSEUM (MUSEUM DER STADT WEIN) VIENNA/DAGLI ORTI

Clark, Peter, and Raymond Gillespie, eds. *Two Capitals: London and Dublin, 1500–1840.* Oxford and New York, 2001.

George, M. Dorothy. *London Life in the Eighteenth Century.* Harmondsworth, U.K., 1966.

Griffiths, Paul, and Mark S. R. Jenner, eds. *Londinopolis: Essays in the Cultural and Social History of Early Modern London.* Manchester, U.K., and New York, 2000.

Inwood, Stephen. *A History of London.* London, 1998.

Merritt, J. F., ed. *Imagining Early Modern London: Perceptions and Portrayals of the City from Stow to Strype, 1598–1720.* Cambridge, U.K., and New York, 2001.

Porter, Roy. *London: A Social History.* London, 1994.

Rappaport, Steve. *Worlds within Worlds: The Structures of Life in Sixteenth Century London.* Cambridge, U.K., and New York, 1988.

Spence, Craig. *London in the 1690s: A Social Atlas.* London, 2000.

Thrupp, Sylvia. *The Merchant Class of Medieval London, 1300–1500.* Chicago, 1948.

IAN W. ARCHER

LORRAINE, DUCHY OF. Nestled between France and the Holy Roman Empire, the Duchy of Lorraine experienced a turbulent existence during the early modern period. Lorraine was an irrational patchwork of different sovereignties and jurisdictions. The duke's two largest territories were the Duchies of Bar and Lorraine; however, in the heart of ducal lands lay three sovereign bishoprics: Metz, Toul, and Verdun. Like other small states, Lorraine was vulnerable to outside forces and thus could not escape involvement in international affairs. Trade was a positive aspect of this involvement. Straddling the Meuse and Moselle rivers, and stretching from the Vosges Mountains to Luxembourg, Lorraine sat astride two major trading axes, east to west and north to south, and thus goods, people, and ideas constantly flowed through the duchy. However, Lorraine lacked the power to keep larger rivals out of its affairs and its territories. This weakness led to Lorraine's loss of independence.

The duchy's approximately 800,000 inhabitants in 1600 occupied an overwhelmingly rural territory. Lorraine's population was dominated by its natural environment, which ranged from mountains toward the southeast to rolling plains in the west. Dense forests blanketed the region. The largest urban center of the area, the sovereign bishopric of Metz, boasted a population of around 19,000. In contrast, at the beginning of the seventeenth century, the most important city under ducal control, the capital Nancy, only had about 8,000 residents. Agriculture formed the foundation of the duchy's economy, with the majority of peasants engaged in the growing of various cereal crops. A crucial aspect of Lorraine's economy was its industrial production, especially glass manufacturing and salt mining. These products as well as agricultural surpluses were sold throughout Europe and helped the duchy prosper in the sixteenth century. Although the ducal economy was devastated by mid-seventeenth-century crises, the eighteenth century witnessed gradual economic recovery.

At the beginning of the 1500s, Lorraine held the political status of an imperial fief. This situation changed in the mid-sixteenth century with two events that would define the parameters of Lorraine's geopolitical situation until the 1730s. In August 1542, Duke Antoine (ruled 1508–1544) and Emperor Charles V (ruled 1519–1556) approved the Treaty of Nuremberg, which recognized Lorraine's independence in exchange for the duke's continuing liability for certain imperial taxes. Ten years later, French King Henry II (ruled 1547–1559), as part of his dynastic wars with the Habsburgs, occupied the three bishoprics. Henry placed them under French "protection" until 1648, when the Holy Roman Empire ceded complete sovereignty over the cities. From the 1550s onward, France enjoyed a physical presence in the middle of ducal lands, and exerted increasing pressure upon the dukes.

Despite the arrival of the French, the next seventy-five years saw relative peace and prosperity for Lorraine. Lorraine's larger neighbors left the duchy alone because of their own internal crises. Close personal connections to France marked the reigns of Dukes Charles III (ruled 1545–1608) and his son Henry II (ruled 1608–1624). Lorraine elites, such as the Guise family, moved easily into positions of power within France. The period witnessed an artistic flowering, producing artists like Jacques Callot and Georges de la Tour. Because of its brilliance in comparison with what followed, the period has been called "Lorraine's renaissance."

Rebirth turned into chaos with the ascension of Charles IV (ruled 1624–1675) to the ducal throne. A strident Catholic like many of his countrymen, and more a warrior than a statesman, Charles actively opposed Cardinal Richelieu's pro-Protestant policies during the Thirty Years' War (1618–1648). This stance resulted in French occupation of Lorraine and ducal exile. Excepting the 1660s, French occupation lasted from 1634 until 1697. The dukes became imperial generals, fighting the French and the Ottoman Turks. Their greatest moment came in 1683, when Charles V (ruled 1675–1690) successfully defended Vienna against the Ottomans. Lorraine itself suffered terribly during these years. In addition to the horrors of military occupation, there was an epidemic of plague in 1635. As a consequence of these disasters, Lorraine lost nearly half of its prewar population.

In 1697, Louis XIV of France (1643–1715) restored Lorraine to its ruling dynasty. Upon his return, Duke Leopold I (ruled 1690–1729) found that although his lands were devastated, his personal power had been increased. Traditional limitations on ducal power had been eliminated; war and occupation had decimated Lorraine's elites, and the French had destroyed institutions that previously limited sovereign power. Although Leopold's predecessors had aspired to absolutism, he was able to institute it to a great extent and used his power to forward a program of internal reconstruction. Externally, he attempted to maintain good relations with both France and the Holy Roman Empire, attaining recognition of Lorraine's neutrality in the 1720s.

However, less than a decade after Leopold's death in 1729, the duchy lost its independence. In 1731 Duke Francis III (ruled 1729–1737) married Maria Theresa of Austria, the heiress to the Holy Roman Empire. The French viewed this marriage as a threat because of the potential reunion of Lorraine with the empire. After lengthy negotiations, Francis agreed in 1737 to give Lorraine to Louis XV's father-in-law Stanislaus Leszczynski, the deposed king of Poland, effectively ending Lorraine's independence. Francis attained the imperial crown in 1745. Stanislaus ruled until his death in 1766, after which the duchy was incorporated into France. Interested more in Enlightenment culture than politics, he let a French chancellor run Lorraine and concentrated upon patronizing the arts and sciences and the founding of charitable institutions. In the process, Stanislaus became extremely popular and effectively prepared Lorraine for the transition from independent state to French province.

See also **France; Guise Family; Thirty Years' War (1618–1648).**

BIBLIOGRAPHY

Briggs, Robin. *Communities of Belief: Cultural and Social Tension in Early Modern France.* Oxford, 1989.

Parisot, Robert. *Histoire de Lorraine (Duché de Lorraine, duché de Bar, Trois-Évêchés).* 4 vols. Paris, 1919–1924.

Parisse, Michel, ed. *Histoire de Lorraine.* Toulouse, 1977.

CHARLES LIPP

LOTTERY. Although lotteries had been utilized as a means of redistributing goods and wealth since Roman times, they began to develop on a large scale in fifteenth-century Europe, where they were used by governments as a means of raising revenue. The first recorded lottery was held in 1420 in Burgundy, with the proceeds going toward the fortification of the town. The state of Germany established a national lottery in 1521; between 1520 and 1539, the French *loterie,* created by Francis I, enriched some individuals as well as the nation; and Florence's *La Lotto de Firenze* was the first public lottery to pay money for prizes in 1528. In Britain, Queen Elizabeth I chartered a general lottery in 1569 to raise money for the building of harbors and other good works, and in 1612, its role was extended when the money it raised enabled the Virginia Company to establish the New World colony of Jamestown. Such funds were a lifeline to the struggling company and accounted for half its annual income by 1621. The utility of lotteries to emergent nation-states, most of which struggled to have sufficient revenues, was immense, and from the fifteenth century on, lotteries were enthusiastically exploited by the monarchs and politicians of Europe. These institutions played a crucial role in the creation of young states' domestic and foreign policy, raising funds for public projects as well as financing their imperial adventures abroad.

Lotteries were also hugely popular throughout the population, although motivation to participate varied according to social position. While the poor were attracted by the chance of huge prizes for relatively small stakes, the wealthy regarded lotteries as a means of demonstrating patriotism and supporting the national cause by purchasing tickets.

However, like other forms of gambling, the position of lotteries became increasingly tenuous throughout the seventeenth century. Although attractive as a way of generating revenue, they were also regarded with suspicion by those who thought them antithetical to the Protestant work ethic. At the same time, practical problems involved in the running of lotteries began to emerge. Private operators intervened in drawings, buying tickets in bulk for excessive markups, and also offering side bets, or "insurance," on the main lottery—practices that the state did not derive revenue from. Allegations of fraud and dishonesty were rife, and criticism that lotteries encouraged mass gambling, idleness, and greed in the populace increased.

On top of this, by the late seventeenth century, with the increasing development of their economic infrastructures and tax bases, the economic utility of lotteries to governments began to decline. Accordingly, legislation was drafted that began to limit participation in lotteries—at least for the poor. In 1710, ticket prices in Britain were increased to an expensive £10, and, in 1721, private lotteries, which had been popular because of their smaller stakes, were banned. Although many continued to operate illegally, such moves effectively outlawed the lottery for all but the wealthiest in society, destroying their popular base and ultimately demonstrating the patrician nature of legislation that had from the start been driven by political and economic expediency.

See also **Gambling.**

BIBLIOGRAPHY

Ashton, John. *The History of Gambling in England.* Montclair, N.J., 1969. Originally published London, 1898.

Reith, Gerda. *The Age of Chance: Gambling in Western Culture.* London and New York, 1999.

Sullivan, George. *By Chance a Winner.* New York, 1972.

GERDA REITH

LOUIS XII (FRANCE) (born 1462–1515; ruled 1498–1515), king of France. The only son of Charles of Orléans and Mary of Cleves, Louis was the great-grandson of Charles VI (ruled 1380–1422). As a youth, Louis did not expect to gain the throne since he was several degrees of blood distant from the ruling family. Louis XI (ruled 1461–1483) coerced him into marrying his deformed daughter Jeanne, who was probably incapable of bearing children. He spent his early adulthood seeking an annulment for the marriage. When Louis XI's son became Charles VIII in 1483, Louis competed with Charles's older sister Anne of Beaujeu to become regent for the underage king. His purpose was largely to gain a position of authority from which to secure an annulment. When the Estates-General of 1484 refused him the office, he led the "Fools' War" against the monarchy. Defeated at the Battle of St-Aubin in Brittany in 1488, he was imprisoned for three years. He was released in time to join Charles in the first French invasion of Italy (1494), to make good the French claim to the kingdom of Naples.

Because Charles's only child died at age three, Louis gained the throne when Charles died in April 1498. Those who had opposed him in the Fools' War were fearful that he would exact revenge on them now that he was king, but Louis soothed them with his famous remark: "It is not honorable for the king of France to avenge the quarrels of a duke of Orléans." After loading Pope Alexander VI's (reigned 1492–1503) son Cesare Borgia with French titles and gold, he received an annulment from Jeanne of France and married Charles's widow, Anne of Brittany, in January 1499. With her he had two daughters, Claude and Renée. Theologians of the University of Paris bitterly criticized the annulment, and when it led to unrest among the students, Louis cracked down on the university in 1499 and severely reduced its autonomy.

Louis had a claim to the duchy of Milan through his grandmother Valentina Visconti, and he sought to make good his Italian rights in the second French invasion of Italy (1499). Concentrating on winning Milan, which he achieved in 1500, he agreed to divide Naples with Ferdinand of Aragon (ruled 1468–1516), but Ferdinand expelled the French from the entire realm in 1503. For the next several years France was largely at peace. Louis dramatically reduced taxes, which, along with the era's broad prosperity, prompted the Estates-General to name him "Father of the People" in 1506. Louis's most prominent advisor was Cardinal Georges d'Amboise, whose influence and place in government were so vast that the saying "Let George do it!" is said to have referred to d'Amboise.

Although his tastes still were largely those of the Middle Ages, Louis took an interest in Renaissance culture, which he saw on several trips to Italy. He patronized the Italian humanists Lescaris and Aleandro, who taught Greek in France, and supported the classics advocate and humanist Guillaume Budé at the beginning of his career. In 1499 Louis brought Italian architects and artists to France to rebuild the château of Blois, although the principal architect was probably the French mason Colin de Briart. The rebuilt château introduced the concept that a king need not live in a gloomy, fortified stronghold but in a beautiful place with open spaces and pleasant gardens for gracious living.

Louis allowed Pope Julius II (reigned 1503–1513) to persuade him to join an anti-Venetian league, bringing him back into the thick of Italian politics. After defeating the Venetians at Agnadello in May 1509, he found that Julius had organized a league to drive him out of Italy. Louis attempted to counter Julius by convoking the schismatic Council of Pisa in 1511, but it drew only four cardinals and a few French bishops. After Louis's nephew Gaston de Foix defeated the papal-Spanish army at Ravenna in March 1512, the cardinals at Pisa declared Julius deposed and convoked the college of cardinals to elect a successor. De Foix's death prevented the French army from marching on Rome to effect Julius's deposition. The pope excommunicated Louis and promised parts of France to the Swiss, Aragón, England, and the Holy Roman Empire, which had joined his alliance. Ferdinand of Aragón seized southern Navarre, and Henry VIII invaded northern France. The French army retreated back to France, leaving Milan to the Swiss. The death of Julius in 1513 allowed Louis to make peace with the new pope, the Medici Leo X (reigned 1513–1521). When Anne died in January 1514, he secured peace with Henry VIII by marrying his sister Mary. The excitement of the wedding and his young bride probably hastened his death on 1 January 1515. His first cousin, Francis of Angoulême, who had married his daughter Claude in 1514, succeeded him as Francis I.

See also **Cambrai, League of (1508); Charles VIII (France); France; Julius II (pope).**

BIBLIOGRAPHY

Baumgartner, Frederic J. *Louis XII.* New York, 1994. A recent scholarly biography.

Bridge, John. *A History of France from the Death of Louis XI.* 5 vols. Oxford, 1921–1936. A detailed history of France for the era of Louis's reign, it is especially strong on the French wars in Italy.

Quilliet, Bernard. *Louis XII: pere du peuple.* Paris, 1986. Especially good on the cultural developments of Louis's reign.

FREDERIC J. BAUMGARTNER

LOUIS XIII (FRANCE) (1601–1643; ruled 1610–1643), king of France. The historical reputation of Louis XIII has been overshadowed by two figures close to him—his chief minister, Cardinal Richelieu (1585–1642), and his son and successor, Louis XIV (ruled 1643–1715). Cardinal Richelieu stands as the personification of seventeenth-century statecraft, and his steely brilliance is generally credited for bringing France from its sorry state following the Wars of Religion to the verge of greatness. And history has enshrined Louis XIV as the French king par excellence, the very embodiment of royalty in all its grandeur and power. In comparison, the stammering Louis XIII—sickly, dependent on a series of favorites, beleaguered by a quarrelsome family and a factious court—seems a ruler of diminished stature indeed. This second of the Bourbon kings, however, deserves a more exalted place in history, if only because his reign witnessed the decisive consolidation of monarchical power and France's rise to European prominence.

RISE TO POWER

Louis's reign formally began upon the assassination of his father Henry IV (ruled 1589–1610) in 1610, but the government remained in the hands of his mother, Marie de Médicis (1573–1642), who ruled as regent until 1617. The regency was a turbulent time, marred by noble conspiracies and revolts, the ascendancy of Concino Concini, Marie's Italian favorite, over the court, and the calling of the Estates-General in 1614. In 1617 Louis took power in a veritable coup d'état that ended with the ignominious execution of Concini and his wife. Historians looking to credit Louis with more initiative and political savvy than he is usually accorded have pointed to this decisive act by a fifteen-year-old. And in general it should be noted that Louis faced a series of daunting challenges, both at home and abroad, including near-permanent opposition, often rebellion, from his mother and brother and the growing crisis of the Thirty Years' War (1618–1648), while still a teenager and a young man in his twenties.

LOUIS AND RICHELIEU

The coup d'état of 1617 was the first in a series of acts that served as turning points in Louis's reign, demonstrating his deep and precocious appreciation of the craft of kingship. In fact, despite his sometime obsessive predilection for the hunt, Louis was, like his son, a dutiful ruler, fully cognizant of the demands of his position. His initiative was next displayed in 1624, when he appointed Richelieu to the royal council. This was a move fraught with potential difficulties, for Richelieu was his mother's man, a figure of formidable and widely recognized talents yet still identified with the *dévot* ('devout') position that saw alliance with the Habsburgs as France's proper course. The choice, however, turned out to be a brilliant stroke of talent spotting. Richelieu

Louis XIII (France). Portrait by Justus van Egmont. THE ART ARCHIVE/MUSÉE DU CHATEAU DE VERSAILLES

brought discipline, intellectual rigor, and an enormous capacity for work to the royal cabinet. He also made himself a student of Louis's personality, taking pains to learn how to balance the delicate task of both coaxing and respecting his king's will. Together they managed to concentrate royal power in a partnership that many great noblemen and especially the queen mother and the king's brother Gaston (duc d'Orléans; 1608–1660) deeply resented. But it was a partnership that soon bore fruit in the successful siege of the Huguenot stronghold La Rochelle in 1627–1628, which not only demonstrated the royal resolve in the face of a Calvinist threat but also freed France to pursue an anti-Habsburg policy in Europe.

Despite the success of La Rochelle, the partnership of Louis and Richelieu and the foreign policy course they had set upon nearly foundered the following year. The so-called Day of Dupes was another crisis that illustrated Louis's ability to act on his own. On the night of 10–11 November 1630 the queen mother demanded that Louis dismiss his minister, a move that would have altered both the king's authority and France's European alignments. To everyone's surprise, including Marie's, the king chose to keep Richelieu as his chief minister. Soon Marie de Médicis was in exile in Brussels, not to return to the realm for the rest of her life. Louis and Richelieu were free to pursue their anti-Habsburg foreign policy. In 1635 France formally entered the Thirty Years' War.

Even before that, Louis was preoccupied with martial matters. He had to face down a series of revolts, rebellions, and conspiracies—from his mother, brother, great noblemen like Henry II de Montmorency, Huguenots, peasants, and even court favorites. Backed by Richelieu, he responded in most cases with what many considered as shocking severity: his reign was the most costly in terms of noble heads lost to the executioner's axe. The notorious duelist François-Henri de Montmorency-Bouteville ended up on the block in 1627, as did his rebellious cousin Henri II de Montmorency in 1632, despite their family's long history of royal service, their personal popularity and charm, and the pleas for clemency from the highest ranks of society. Louis's last favorite, Henri Coeffier-Ruzé d'Effiat, marquis de Cinq-Mars, along with his supposed coconspirator François-Auguste de Thou, also died on the scaffold in 1642 for plotting with the Spanish. In war Louis displayed the same resolve. Well before France's formal entry into the Thirty Years' War, he engaged the Spanish and Habsburgs on several fronts, especially in northern Italy. He saw himself as a warrior-king, frequently exposing himself to great danger by personally leading his armies into battle.

Louis's martial bent contrasted with other aspects of his personality. He was constantly ill and several times at death's door. He abhorred ceremony and indeed cut a poor figure in public. He suffered from neglect, even abuse, as a child and received a poor education at court. (His childhood and youth were documented in extraordinary detail in a journal kept by his personal physician Jean Héroard, providing a remarkable, unequaled view of the upbringing of an early modern ruler.) Unlike his mother and Richelieu, Louis displayed little interest in the arts outside of the dance. He was a sincere Catholic, modeling himself on his saintly predecessor Louis IX (ruled 1226–1270), and in 1638 he placed himself under the personal protection of the Virgin. His marriage to Anne of Austria in 1615 took four years to consummate, and their married life was marked by long periods of estrangement. Louis, however, seems to have remained faithful to his wife, despite a series of attachments to male and female courtiers alike. The birth of the dauphin in 1638, after years of inactivity in the marriage bed, was considered a minor miracle. Only five years later—and a year after the death of his cardinal-minister—Louis died at the age of forty-two. His legacy was a mixed one: on the one hand, a stronger France and a refurbished monarchy; on the other, deepening involvement in a costly European war that only fueled discontent at home.

See also **Absolutism; Anne of Austria; France; La Rochelle; Louis XIV (France); Marie de Médicis; Richelieu, Armand-Jean Du Plessis, cardinal; Thirty Years' War (1618–1648).**

BIBLIOGRAPHY

Chevallier, Pierre. *Louis XIII, roi cornélien.* Paris, 1979.

Marvick, Elizabeth Wirth. *Louis XIII: The Making of a King.* New Haven, 1986.

Moote, A. Lloyd. *Louis XIII, the Just.* Berkeley, 1989.

Robert A. Schneider

Louis XIV (France). Equestrian portrait by Charles Le Brun. ©Archivo Iconografico S.A./Corbis

LOUIS XIV (FRANCE)

LOUIS XIV (FRANCE) (1638–1715; ruled 1643–1715), king of France. Hailed as *le Dieudonné,* 'the God-given', Louis XIV was the first child of Louis XIII (1601–1643) and Anne of Austria (1601–1661), born twenty-three years into their marriage.

THE EARLY YEARS (1638–1661)

Ascending the throne at the age of four, Louis XIV was educated under the tutelage of his godfather and chief minister, Jules Cardinal Mazarin (1602–1661), and under the day-to-day watch of his governor, Nicolas de Neufville, first marshal-duke de Villeroi (1644–1730). The young king received not a scholarly education in the classics, but a practical education in history, diplomacy, war, and the arts, while his preceptor Hardouin de Péréfixe guided his spiritual development under the direction of the Queen Mother Anne, imbuing in Louis a distaste for heterodoxy, and associated disorder, of any kind. His formative experiences came during the Fronde (1648–1653), when he was directly awakened to the potential instability lurking in the kingdom as other forces sought to share in the crown's sovereign powers and remove Mazarin from the government and the kingdom. The events of these years, and Louis's exposure to the wider social and economic problems of France during his military progresses, taught him to mistrust the ambitions of peers and of senior princes of the blood and bred an awareness in him of the need for far tighter regulation of the leading institutions of the kingdom. The declaration of the young king's majority, two days after his thirteenth birthday on 7 September 1651, produced some rallying of support for the crown. But it was not until 1654, the year of the coronation (7 June), that the government reestablished military control over France. For the rest of the 1650s Mazarin led the government, while Henri de La Tour d'Auvergne, marshal-vîcomte de Turenne (1611–1675), trained the king in the art of war. In these years Mazarin did not involve Louis in the details of administration but did seek to keep him informed of developments, particularly on diplomatic and strategic issues, while encouraging him to establish his chivalric leadership of the kingdom.

THE REFORM OF GOVERNMENT AND FINANCES

By the time of Mazarin's death on 9 March 1661, Louis XIV had already shown himself to be an astute military commander, a skill that he would retain all the way up to his last personal campaign in 1693. He was also regarded as an excellent horseman, a noted conversationalist with an extraordinary memory for people, and, in the cultural sphere, a good musician and one of the very best dancers at court. Furthermore, he had been married to the Infanta Marie-Thérèse of Spain since June 1660 as part of the peace settlement of the Pyrenees, and she was now one month pregnant with the future dauphin (1661–1711). But Louis had little experience of governing, and it was expected that Mazarin would be succeeded as minister-favorite, most probably by Michel Le Tellier (1603–1685). What nobody anticipated was Louis's decision to assume control of the reins of government himself and his determination to maintain a grip on affairs (albeit a fluctuating grip) for the rest of his reign. Between March and September 1661 there was a minor revolution in French government during which the person of the king assumed center stage: the inner council *(conseil d'en haut)* was reduced in size to include only a handful of senior ministers whose advice was given candidly and accepted with almost perennial good grace. After the fall of Nicolas Fouquet (1615–1680), the *surintendant* of finances, there was greater transparency in financial transactions, with the king reserving to himself the right to approve every financial decision of the central government, even if successive controllers general of finance continued to dominate financial business.

Louis XIV did not favor major overhauls of the system of government that would unsettle the kingdom, but he was willing to entertain considerable administrative reforms insofar as they diminished disorder, encouraged stability, and enhanced his own regal power. Indeed, it is fair to say that some very dramatic changes occurred during his reign not through any increase in state bureaucracy but through changes in regulations and financial arrangements. Using the provincial intendants as a tool for preventing abuses and malpractice by the venal officeholders, Jean-Baptiste Colbert (1619–1683), as senior intendant of finances from September 1661 and then controller general from 1665 until his death in 1683, managed to bring the chaotic fiscal system of taxation and borrowing to its optimum efficacy. However, when the demands of war grew in the 1690s and 1700s and net revenue as a proportion of gross revenue declined once again to the dismal levels of the 1640s, two major reforms had to be introduced that did challenge the social basis of the country, undermining the entire system of lay privileged exemption from direct taxation. In 1695–1698 the capitation imposed a graduated poll tax upon all French subjects from the dauphin down, and this was reintroduced permanently in 1701. And then in 1710 the *dixième,* a tax of one-tenth of personal income regardless of status, was brought in, lasting until 1721.

THE ARMED FORCES

In spite of setbacks in the 1700s, the reforms of finance in an era of economic stagnation enabled the crown to sustain stronger and larger armed forces than ever before during Louis XIV's "personal rule." France had almost no navy to speak of in 1661 (ten warships and twelve frigates), but Colbert was immediately given the task of working with the grand master of navigation, the duke de Beaufort, to increase the number of vessels; and by the end of 1663 he had brought the galley fleet in the Mediterranean within his own orbit. The great leap forward in the size of the fleet and in administrative and port infrastructure came in the years 1669 to 1673, and in spite of the belief that Louis XIV lacked personal interest in the navy, he gave considerable support both to Colbert and then his son Seignelay in their efforts to create and maintain by 1689 the largest battle fleet in Europe. Only during the final years of the War of the League of Augsburg (1688–1697) after 1695, and during the War of the Spanish Succession (1701–1714) after 1705, did it prove impossible to sustain such a navy. The crown was consequently forced to rely much more on privateering at sea.

Louis took a far stronger interest in the reforms of the army. With the king's close involvement, Michel Le Tellier and particularly his son, the marquis de Louvois, gradually overhauled a highly complex system of regulations and financial structures to equip France with an army that, by 1693, stood at around 330,000 men. Their sheer attention to detail prevented on occasion what would otherwise have been a series of logistical breakdowns. That the extreme difficulties of the War of the Spanish Succession did not produce a military collapse can be attributed to the earlier structural and administrative reforms that had transformed the ramshackle forces of Louis's minority into, for all its defects, the most admired and feared army on the Continent.

FOREIGN POLICY

The developing army and navy of France were there essentially to enhance the interests of the Bourbon dynasty internationally, and French foreign policy was very much the king's own, albeit based on advice from his inner ministers. Throughout his reign Louis XIV aimed at securing for himself the most senior status among European princes in an age when the concept of an equality of sovereign states did not exist, and when most rulers pushed claims that others found outrageous at one time or another. In the first part of the "personal rule," between 1661 and 1674, Louis pursued a foreign policy of single-minded vainglory in a determined effort to facilitate further dismemberment of the Spanish Habsburg empire and, after 1668, reduce the United Provinces of the Netherlands to humble submission. But the failure to conquer the United Provinces, the entry of Emperor Leopold I (ruled 1658–1705) into the Dutch War in August 1673, a difficult winter in the Rhineland, and the subsequent French retreat into the southern Netherlands seems to have been a sobering experience for Louis, who after 1673–1674 sought to consolidate and strengthen his hold in and around Alsace while rebuilding and constructing anew a chain of fortifications on his northern and northeastern frontiers to defend against invasion. Such apparently defensive concerns were, however, not satisfied by the Treaty of Nijmegen in 1678, precipitating Louis over the following six years into highly aggressive seizures of strategically vital territory based on dubious legal title—the *réunions*—that antagonized German princes and drove them to seek support against France from the imperial Habsburg court in Vienna.

The growing influence of the Austrian Habsburgs within the Holy Roman Empire, both in Germany and northern Italy, in turn compelled Louis to engage from the early 1680s in heavy-handed political manipulation at smaller European courts to secure Bourbon influence and indirectly to protect the gains he had made and the status he now enjoyed as head of Europe's leading dynasty. Failing to entrench his territorial gains in the brief War of the Réunions (1683–1684), Louis, encouraged by Louvois, became increasingly anxious about growing Habsburg strength. In a desperate attempt to secure greater security for Alsace, in September 1688 Louis seized the key Rhine fortress of Philippsburg in the hope that this would force the empire to negotiate a definitive settlement of Rhineland territorial issues. Instead it precipitated the greatest conflict of the reign thus far. Having subsequently forced the Dutch Republic, Spain, and Great Britain also to declare war upon him between November 1688 and May 1689, Louis's insensitive attack on the interests of the duke of Savoy, Victor Amadeus II, a year later earned him another theater of operations he could ill afford. The pressure of the war by June 1693 forced Louis, under the influence of increasingly moderate and chastened advisors, to abandon his excessive demands and to consider returning most of the *réunion* territories to their owners; to negotiate with William III about his succession in Great Britain after the Glorious Revolution; and to make huge concessions to Savoy in order to neutralize Italy. Even so, over three more years of demanding and exhausting war were required, in the context of a catastrophic famine that pushed the French population down by perhaps 10 percent, before Savoy could be bought off in the Treaty of Turin (June 1696) and a general peace signed with France's other enemies at Ryswick (September and October 1697).

All this left France ill equipped to deal with the looming issue of the Spanish succession, as the ailing Charles II moved toward his death in November 1700. To try to avert war, Louis XIV and William III signed two successive partition treaties for the Spanish empire in October 1698 and March 1700, but Charles II himself wanted instead to maintain the unity of his territories, so the dying Spanish king willed them all to the one power that might be able to hold them together: France, in the person of Philippe, duke d'Anjou, second grandson of Louis XIV. A conflict with the Austrian Habsburgs was inevitable, but the decisions to seize fortresses in the Spanish Netherlands and exclude the British from the lucrative Spanish slave trade in the early spring of 1701 ensured that any war would once again include Britain and the United Provinces among the anti-French belligerents. France was pushed out of southern Germany and lost her Bavarian ally in 1704, and Philip V of Spain faced allied campaigning on the Iberian mainland from that year on. The Bourbons were expelled from northern Italy and Naples in 1706–1707 and from the southern Netherlands in 1708, while in 1709–1710 another somewhat less disastrous but still severe famine struck France. But the tide turned in 1710–1711 with Bourbon successes in Spain, and with changes of regime in Britain and Austria that affected the geostrategic considerations of the various powers. The War of the Spanish Succession consequently ended in 1713–1714 with France securing Spain itself and her overseas colonies for Philip V, while the Austrians received most of the rest of the Spanish European possessions, and Savoy was temporarily awarded Sicily.

Territorially, France emerged considerably larger and more secure from Louis XIV's reign, acquiring most notably Roussillon (1659), Franche-Comté (1674), and Alsace (1648 and 1678), as well as establishing serious colonies and trading posts in the Americas and western Africa. It is true that Louis XIV's foreign policies had brought hundreds of thousands of deaths, but this cannot be put down to a callous disregard for the fate of his own or foreign subjects. In fact, Louis was genuinely anxious to minimize casualties in warfare. But he was the most assertive and best-resourced individual in an international and cultural system that had an inbuilt tendency to resolve differences through arms, and in which its sovereign players could not afford to show too much understanding for the legitimate economic or dynastic interests of their rivals.

THE REGULATION OF A STATUS-BASED SOCIETY

A similar problem afflicted domestic state management during the mid- to late-seventeenth century. The rivalries of families and the personal ambitions of individuals, articulated in social and legal terms at all levels of the propertied hierarchy, militated against an easy resolution of disputes. Colbert's determined campaign in the 1660s to emphasize that all privileges and rights stemmed from the will of the king (and could be just as easily revoked) certainly helped to encourage a sense of strong royal authority in the legal sphere. This was aided by the 1665 *Grands Jours* investigations into lawless nobles and bandits in the Auvergne in tandem with the Parlement of Paris, and it was carried forward after 1679 by repeated edicts against dueling and in favor of litigation before royal officials to settle disputes. But Louis XIV had come to realize full well by 1661 that the instability of France was rooted primarily in her political culture. The Fronde was not the last gasp of a feudal noble class but a struggle for political and military precedence within the upper noble elites who, in the context of a breakdown in state finances during a royal minority, had no other choice but to assert their own status claims—backed up, if necessary, by military force.

Removing the exposed figure of a chief minister after 1661 was but a partial solution to the difficulties. Louis remained well aware that his ministers had their own private interests to further, and this was as much the case with court appointments, or military commands, as it was with architectural projects, so the active balancing of ministers and great nobility required considerable effort that this king was prepared to make. Far more likely to entrench political quiescence in the long run was a remodeling of the system of patronage and clientage and a concerted effort to break the automatic link between service and expectation of reward. Even if he still relied on other people's recommendations, by 1672 Louis insisted that virtually all military, naval, and ecclesiastical commissions come from his own person. Furthermore, by maintaining multiple channels of access to his person at court for different groups, families, and individuals, he ensured that no one faction or person (including ministers) could dominate his decisions over patronage. On top of this, he expanded the amount of largesse, both monetary and honorific, disbursed by the crown, while widening the pool of potential recipients. All this contributed to a serious dilution of the patronage power of individual grandees. With the partial exception of his own brother Orléans, for the most part the dukes, peers, and senior military officers now became patronage brokers for the crown rather than direct providers of opportunities for the lesser nobility. Always concerned for the future of the monarchy, Louis allied this policy of supervising patronage distribution with closely managing the upbringing of his offspring and descendants to an extreme extent in controlling their households. And if he made extensive military use of illegitimate princes (of his own body and those of his ancestors), he was loath to trust the erstwhile Frondeur branches of the Bourbon, the Condé and Conti, whose interests he encouraged only so far as was commensurate with the interests of the wider Bourbon dynasty. The aim in all this was to prevent another Fronde from ever happening again. Only at the very end of the reign, in 1714, when he had lost his son, two of his three grandsons (the dukes of Burgundy and Berry), and one of his great-grandsons to smallpox, did Louis XIV depart from the established dynastic rules when he wrote the bastard lines of the House of France into the succession. Although there was some sense in trying to avoid future succession wars by laying down an order of precedence in the event of the disappearance of all the legitimate Bourbon branches, this was bitterly resented by the great nobility and was overturned by the regent Philippe II, duc d'Orléans, in 1717.

HIGH CULTURE AND THE ARTS

The royal urge to preserve and impose order in the political field was also manifested in the arena of high culture. The growing presence of royal patronage in the arts and sciences after 1661 is better attributed to Colbert than the king himself, with the most notable advances being the foundation of the Academy of Inscriptions and Belle Lettres in 1663 and the reform of the Academy of Painting and Sculpture the same year, followed by the foundation of the Academy of Sciences in 1666, and three years later that of the Royal Academy of Music. Moreover, between 1667 and 1672 Colbert oversaw the building of the Paris Observatory. Yet, if Colbert was the driving instrument who encouraged intellectuals and artists to view the crown as the foremost patron, it was Louis who set the tone and the taste and was the leading collector of objets d'art of his age. The king also took a very close interest in architectural projects, in particular the transformation of Versailles after 1669 from a relatively small hunting retreat to the largest palace complex in Europe by the mid-1680s. By and large Louis favored the classical over the baroque, in sculpture, architecture, and garden design, and in spite of the growing vogue for portraits of all manner of people, the king himself set great store by religious art.

RELIGION AND PUBLIC MORALITY

Louis XIV's preference for religious art was hardly surprising, for he was a devout Catholic, in spite of his several mistresses (most notably Louise de La Vallière [1644–1710] and Françoise, marquise de Montespan [1641–1707]) and the numerous bastards he fathered before 1680. Louis was sincere about protecting his subjects' souls and throughout his reign encouraged charitable giving. In 1693–1694, at the height of the famine, Pontchartrain, the controller general of finance, was ordered to organize grain imports from abroad and facilitate food transport within the country on a scale never previously attempted by France. But Louis was not just a charitable Christian prince. He was also instinctively hostile to anything that smacked of the heterodox, in particular Jansenism, which, under strong Jesuit influence, he equated with rebellion. By the early 1680s the king's increasingly devout attitude to personal morality and worship, encouraged by his second wife, Françoise d'Aubigné, marquise de Maintenon (1635–1719), whom he married in 1683, had become allied to his fear of religious disorder as manifested by Jansenism and the Huguenots. This combination of attitudes flowed together with a desire to live up to his title of "Eldest Son of the Church" at a time when Emperor Leopold I was pushing the Turks back in the Balkans and when relations between France and the papacy were in tatters over the *régale* dispute (when Louis extended the royal right to gather the revenues of vacant episcopal sees to areas of the kingdom that had previously been immune). Despite attempts by Colbert and Louvois to restrain persecution of Protestants by some intendants, Louis became increasingly convinced that forced conversions were effectual, an approach that culminated in the Edict of Fontainebleau in September 1685, which revoked all rights for Huguenots. Even when it became clear to ministers and generals by 1689 that this revocation had created a potentially dangerous fifth column inside France (which erupted in the vicious revolt of the Camisards in 1702–1705), the king's religious conscience would not allow him to restore Huguenot rights. Thus far, Louis XIV's religious policies were coherently Catholic and Gallican, zealous in defense of the temporal independence of the French church from Rome. But the repair of relations with the papacy in the 1690s, plus the resurfacing of the Jansenist controversy after

1703, pushed him into accepting ultramontane, pro-papal positions held by the Sorbonne. Eventually he solicited and accepted the 1713 papal bull *Unigenitus,* which condemned Jansenism but simultaneously mounted a full-scale attack on Gallican liberties, a move that did immense long-term damage to the Bourbon monarchy's image as the defender of France and French interests.

If order could be consciously pursued through state policies, Louis XIV was nevertheless also the beneficiary of changing attitudes to social and political life in the mid-seventeenth century, and in particular a growing distaste for personal violence. The need to display *honnête* behavior was not merely restricted to domestic social situations, but applied equally to public social behavior. The need for restraint, politeness, and self-discipline in deportment as well as language was emerging as the cornerstone of an ethical order to which one simply had to subscribe if one wished to remain a sociable being. What is more, the disorderly and chaotic Fronde, erupting just as such ideals were entering French cultural life, had the effect of reinforcing enthusiasm for obedience and decorum in both the social and the political fields. Louis XIV personally encouraged stronger discipline and self-control at court, in his armies and fleets, and in the church, so that such nostrums percolated through noble society and contributed to growing domestic stability in this period.

CONCLUSION

Throughout his reign, Louis XIV had placed the Bourbon dynasty, the Catholic faith, and the royal court at the center of his existence, and he had been highly mindful of the interests and outlooks of his propertied subjects. Nevertheless, compromise and cooperation had its limits, and it would be a misleading oversimplification to see this as a monarchy engaged in the revivification of feudalism in conjunction with a landed noble "class." In the first instance, the French nobility was in no sense a coherent class, and society as a whole was pervaded by myriad corporate and familial loyalties and interests. Moreover, for all the king's skill in trying to harmonize his own interests with those of his propertied subjects, Louis's reign was marked with a highly authoritarian stamp that pressed the imposition of firmer discipline in the armed forces, the curtailment of judicial independence and privileges, and a demand for religious conformity and subordination that aroused hostility across Europe. On his death, on 1 September 1715, Louis XIV left a kingdom in an unprecedented state of domestic tranquillity that was to last throughout the regency for his five-year-old great-grandson, Louis XV; this can in large part be attributed to firm royal control of the military, more sophisticated poor relief strategies, and a general ethos of political obedience. But the destabilization of the credit markets wrought by the previous thirty years of unprecedented military mobilization, the unresolved issue of tax privileges, the example of baroque kingship that Louis XIV brought to its apogee as a model for rule, and the legacy of Jansenism were to bedevil his successors' governments for the rest of the eighteenth century.

See also **Bourbon Dynasty (France); Camisard Revolt; Colbert, Jean-Baptiste; France; Fronde; Gallicanism; Habsburg Dynasty; Jansenism; League of Augsburg, War of the; Louvois, François-Michel Le Tellier, marquis de; Mazarin, Jules; Poisons, Affair of the; Spanish Succession, War of the; Versailles.**

BIBLIOGRAPHY

Black, Jeremy. *From Louis XIV to Napoleon: The Fate of a Great Power.* London, 1999. Chapter 2 gives a clear and accurate survey of French foreign policy in this period.

Bluche, François. *Louis XIV.* Oxford, 1990. Translated by Mark Greengrass. A highly conservative biographical interpretation by a French scholar.

Sturdy, David J. *Louis XIV.* New York, 1998. A clear, thematic survey of the reign and of the problems faced by the king.

Wolf, John B. *Louis XIV.* New York, 1968. The best biography in any language.

Guy Rowlands

LOUIS XV (FRANCE) (1710–1774; ruled 1715–1774), king of France. Louis, duc d'Anjou, was the second surviving son of Louis, duke of Burgundy, and Marie-Adelaïde, daughter of Duke Victor-Amadeus II of Savoy, and great-grandson of Louis XIV (ruled 1643–1715). When Louis XIV's eldest son Louis (the Grand Dauphin) died in 1711, the little duc d'Anjou's father became heir to the throne. But less than a year later his father, mother, and elder brother were killed by smallpox, leaving him the sole direct descendant and heir to the old

Sun King. During Louis's boyhood, France was ruled in practice by his distant cousin the regent, Philippe, duke of Orléans, even after the boy came officially of age in 1723. When Orléans died unexpectedly later that year, the unpopular duke of Bourbon took over as principal minister, to be succeeded by Louis's tutor, Cardinal André Hercule de Fleury, in 1726. Louis can hardly be said to have been in command during the turbulent first decade of his reign, which was marked by two bankruptcies and the dizzying stock-market and currency bubble of John Law, but his strong loyalty and affection for his tutor were the reasons the cardinal got power and kept it for so long. Louis only began to take a significant independent role in the early 1740s, when he was already in his thirties, at which time he became known as *le bien-aimé,* 'the well-beloved'.

Fleury had taken over as tutor when Louis was six years old, and he supervised the king's education by a splendid team of instructors, including some of the most learned men of letters, scientists, and mathematicians of the day. The king developed a special interest in geography, the natural sciences, and medicine, which he kept all his life. For hobbies, he enjoyed learning to operate a printing press and a lathe. Hunting was his first obsession; women came later. From the age of ten, Louis sat on the Regency council, as his great-grandfather had prescribed in his will, and he seems to have taken an active interest in proceedings; Orléans and the successive prime ministers tutored him in the political issues of the day. But, deprived of parents from an early age, Louis was secretive and often incommunicative. These traits remained with him through his life. He could play the royal part, but he did not revel in public life like the Sun King, and he lacked his great-grandfather's self-confidence.

Overturning an ephemeral engagement to the four-year-old daughter of Philip V of Spain, the duc de Bourbon persuaded Louis to marry Marie, the 22-year-old daughter of Stanislas Lesczynski, the ousted king of Poland. By 1737 the queen had borne Louis an heir, the Old Dauphin (father of Louis XVI), a second son who died in childhood, and eight daughters. Marie's social limitations and colorless personality eventually took their toll. In 1733, Louis began a series of affairs with the three aristocratic Nesle sisters, Madame de Mailly, Madame de Vintimille, and Madame de la Tournelle, countess of Châteauroux. Then, around 1743, he began a more lasting liaison with Madame de Pompadour, the wife of a tax-farmer; the physical relationship ended by 1750, but she remained the official mistress until her death in 1764. Louis prized her because she understood him and could put him at ease. His more basic needs were taken care of by several dispensable young women whom she provided for the purpose, and then, after the death of the queen (1768), by a permanent relationship with Jeanne Bécu. Bécu, who became the comtesse du Barry (1743–1793), was said to be the most beautiful woman of the eighteenth century, but she had a dubious background. Madame de Pompadour is the only woman who played a significant political role in Louis's life, principally as dispenser of royal largesse and jobs, a task in which, unfortunately, she seldom excelled.

In foreign policy, Louis was successful until the Peace of Aix-la-Chapelle (1748), when his diplomats were unable to parlay military wins in the Low Countries into territorial gains. France played a reactive rather than active role in the Diplomatic Revolution of 1756, when she lost her Prussian ally and aligned with Austria, and in the start of the Seven Years' War on the Continent. There was little choice here, but the decision to commit further to the Austrian cause in 1757, when the effort should have been concentrated on the maritime war against Britain, was a choice—a bad one. France's disastrous losses at the Treaty of Paris of 1763 (Canada, most of India, etc.) are well known. Louis did not make the same mistake again in 1770, when he restrained his bellicose foreign secretary, Étienne François, the duke of Choiseul (1719–1785) from taking an unprepared country to war with Britain to defend Spanish rights in the Falkland Islands.

Domestic policy was to a large extent conditioned by these outcomes: the end of each war in this period caused a domestic crisis because the state had to raise new revenue or carry over some wartime taxes into peacetime, in order to retire unpaid war debts. In 1748–1749, controller general Jean-Baptiste de Machault d'Arnouville (1701–1794) attempted this with a vast reform program, including a new peacetime income tax, the *vingtième,* a package of laissez-faire economic reforms, the expansion of the money market, and attempts to limit "unproductive" church acquisition of land. This

Louis XV (France). Portrait by Charles van Loo, c. 1748. GETTY IMAGES

program touched off violent conflicts with privileged groups, notably the church and the remaining provincial estates; the church and the parlements seized on the perceived weakness of the crown to fight their own wars over Jansenism and clerical control of lay society and crown control over taxation. As French rulers commonly did, Louis sought an equilibrium between the contending groups in society and within his own ministry, but through the 1740s and 1750s he came down on balance against the conservative forces to which Fleury had previously appealed—the church hierarchy, which was firmly anti-Jansenist, and the landed elites, who hated land taxes—and he tried hard to mollify the parlements, the Jansenists, and the men of letters. These tensions formed the background to a failed assassination attempt on the king in 1757 by Damiens, a domestic servant obsessed by the current religious quarrels. Louis stuck with his policy, however, going so far as to permit the suppression of the Jesuit order in 1764 and to appoint several leading members of the Parlement of Paris to ministries in order to neutralize the powerful court. After the defeat of 1763, the controllers general, Henri Léonard Jean-Baptiste Bertin (1720–1792) and Clément Charles François de Laverdy de Nizeret (1724–1793), resorted to a version of the 1749 program to solve the post-war financial crisis, but they did so in dire financial straits, without the confidence that a diplomatic victory would have inspired in the investing classes. The result was seven years of bankruptcy on the installment plan. Choiseul's position had been weakened by the death of his ally Madame de Pompadour in 1764 and his failure to quell the notorious Brittany Affair, an interminable quarrel between the Parlement of Brittany and the duc d'Aiguillon, the military commander in that province. So, in late 1770, when Choiseul pushed recklessly for war with Britain in defense of Spain's claim to the Falkland Islands, Louis dismissed him and allowed his chancellor, René Nicolas de Maupeou, to virtually destroy the parlements' powers of remonstrance and to restructure the judicial system, and his controller-general, Abbé Terray, to complete the partial bankruptcy that had begun in 1759. It was a total political reversal of the policy and personnel of the previous period. The reforms of 1770–1774 gave the monarchy a new lease on life but also created much antagonism; if Louis had lived longer, perhaps he would have ridden out the storm, but he was suddenly carried off by smallpox on 10 May 1774. Louis XV was a ruler with considerable natural gifts who had to rule in difficult times; his choices in 1749 and again in 1770 showed the lucidity and the necessary ruthlessness that are the marks of a leader, but his belated start in personally ruling the country, his indolence, and the introversion he inherited from his lonely childhood prevented him from developing into a first-rate politician.

See also **Austrian Succession, War of the (1740–1748); Bourbon Dynasty (France); France; Louis XIV (France); Polish Succession, War of the (1733–1738); Pompadour, Jeanne-Antoinette Poisson; Seven Years' War (1756–1763).**

BIBLIOGRAPHY

Primary Sources

Argenson, René-Louis de Voyer, marquis d'. *Journal et mémoires du marquis d'Argenson.* Edited by E. J. B. Rathery. Paris, 1859–1867.

Barbier, Edmond Jean François. *Journal historique et anecdotique du règne de Louis XV.* Paris, 1847–1856.

Croÿ, Emmanuel, duc de. *Journal inédit, 1718–1785.* Paris, 1906–1907.

Luynes, Charles Philippe d'Albert, duc de. *Mémoires du duc de Luynes sur la cour de Louis XV (1735–1758)* Paris, 1860–1865.

Secondary Sources

Antoine, Michel. *Le dur métier de Roi: Études sur la civilisation politique de la France d'ancien régime.* Paris, 1986.

———. *Le gouvernement et l'administration sous Louis XV: Dictionnaire biographique.* Paris, 1978.

———. *Louis XV.* Paris, 1989. Best recent treatment; good bibliography.

Bernier, Olivier. *Louis the Beloved: The Life of Louis XV.* Garden City, N.Y., 1984.

Bluche, François. *Louis XV.* Paris, 2000.

Butler, Rohan. *Choiseul.* Vol. I, *Father and Son, 1719–1754.* Oxford, 1980.

Campbell, Peter R. *Power and Politics in Old Regime France, 1720–1745.* London, 1996.

Egret, Jean. *Louis XV et l'opposition parlementaire, 1715–1774.* Paris, 1970.

Gooch, G. P. *Louis XV: The Monarchy in Decline.* London, 1956.

Jones, Colin. *Madame de Pompadour: Images of a Mistress.* London, 2002.

Meyer, J. *La Chalotais: Affaires de femmes et affaires d'état sous l'ancien régime.* Paris, 1995

Mitford, Nancy. *Madame de Pompadour.* London, 1968.

Nolhac, Pierre de. *Madame de Pompadour et la politique.* Paris, 1928.

Rogister, John. *Louis XV and the Parlement of Paris, 1737–1754.* Cambridge, U.K., 1995.

Shennan, J. H. *Philippe, Duke of Orléans: Regent of France, 1715–1723.* London, 1979.

Swann, Julian. *Politics and the Parlement of Paris under Louis XV, 1754–1774.* Cambridge, U.K., 1995.

Van Kley, Dale K. *The Damiens Affair and the Unraveling of the Ancien Regime, 1750–1770.* Princeton, 1984.

———. *The Jansenists and the Expulsion of the Jesuits from France, 1757–1765.* New Haven, 1975.

T. J. A. LE GOFF

LOUIS XVI (FRANCE) (1754–1793; ruled 1774–1792), king of France. Louis-Auguste, duc de Berry was the second surviving son of the heir to the throne (dauphin) Louis-Ferdinand and his second wife, Marie-Thérèse-Antoinette-Raphaëlle, daughter of Augustus III, elector of Saxony and king of Poland. Louis's elder brother, the duc de Bourgogne, died in 1761, so when their father died in 1765, he became eldest male heir to his grandfather, Louis XV. Once thought a dull child, recent research has shown that he was a well-taught, reflective, and intelligent student, particularly interested in the sciences (mathematics, physics, geography) and history. He was raised and remained a convinced, but intellectually curious, Catholic; he had a taste for empirical facts, and brevity in expressing them, which, together with natural taciturnity and the secretiveness he inherited from his grandfather, often made him frustrating to work with. His political principles, which became settled in his adolescence, combined the moral politics of François de Salignac de La Mothe Fénelon with a firm belief in his traditional rights as an absolute king. In 1770, he married Marie-Antoinette, youngest daughter of Maria Theresa, the ruler of Austria, but it was not until 1776 that the marriage was consummated; Derek Beales has conclusively demonstrated that the delay was caused not by a physical impediment but rather by sexual ignorance, finally rectified by advice from the queen's brother, Emperor Joseph II, who subsequently received heartfelt written thanks from the royal pair.

Louis's marriage had been designed to cement the alliance with Austria that had been concluded in 1756 and was supported by the dominant party at Louis XV's court, led by the duke of Choiseul and Madame de Pompadour. The young dauphin approved Louis XV's decision to drop Choiseul, as well as his reassertion of royal authority against the parlements in 1771, so when the old king died in 1774, it was thought that the new ruler would continue on this course. But, worried by his own youth and inexperience, he chose as close advisor and informal prime minister Jean Frédéric Phélypeaux, count of Maurepas, a veteran minister who had been disgraced in 1749 but was close to the royal family. Maurepas wanted to rebuild confidence in the monarchy, whose image had suffered from the coup of 1770–1771. He persuaded Louis to recall the old parlements, impose restrictions on their rights of judicial review of legislation through remonstrance, and choose a ministry that included the fashionable liberals Chrétien de Malesherbes and Anne Robert Jacques Turgot. The new ministry proved politically inept (for example, in their insistence on bringing back free trade in foodstuffs during the crisis year 1774–1775). Maurepas and Louis replaced them with a team that included, by late 1776, the Genevan banker and reputed financial wizard Jacques Necker as financial counsellor and the veteran diplomat Charles Gravier, the count of Vergennes, as foreign secretary.

Louis XVI, along with a large body of public opinion, enthusiastically supported France's alliance with the rebellious American colonists against Britain; he and Vergennes managed to keep the other European powers out of the conflict and avoid engagement on Austria's side in Joseph II's various adventures. The outcome in 1783 was diplomatic and military success: freedom of the seas and the restoration of France's position in Europe, although trade with the new republic did not develop as quickly as expected. Necker had hoped to finance the war on life-annuity loans serviced by economies and recovered revenue as earlier state loans were amortised, but the war went on too long, taxes had to be increased, and the usual flood of postwar claims on the government created a potential crisis. In the meantime, the political scene had changed.

Louis XVI. Coronation portrait by Joseph-Siffrède Duplessis. THE ART ARCHIVE/MUSÉE CARNAVALET PARIS/DAGLI ORTI

During the reign, two principal factions fought for control within the ministry—the remains of Choiseul's friends, grouped around Queen Marie-Antoinette and the Austrian alliance, and the so-called "king's party," which hankered after the methods of 1770–1774 and distrusted Austria. Maurepas successfully played them off against each other, but he died in 1781. Necker himself resigned that year.

Henceforward, Louis was more directly involved in politics, generally coming down on the side of the "king's party," represented in the ministry by Vergennes and Charles Alexandre de Calonne. Louis agreed with these two on the need for root-and-branch reform of the tax system to eliminate privilege and establish fiscal uniformity; with them he arranged to call an Assembly of Notables in 1787, to create a tide of public opinion to force these and other reforms through the Parlement of Paris. But Vergennes died just before the Notables met, leaving Louis and Calonne alone. They did not manage the assembly well, and Calonne, whose reforms threatened them and their like through the country, got caught in a stock-market scandal, and had to be dismissed; he was replaced by Étienne Charles Loménie de Brienne, a partisan of Necker. John Hardman has argued that this constituted a turning point in Louis's life, leading to prolonged bouts of depression, cynicism, and dependency that dogged his behavior thereafter. Brienne attempted to ram reforms somewhat similar to Calonne's through the notables and, when that failed, through the Parlement of Paris; finally he tried to rule without them. But Louis was forced by a credit crisis to drop Brienne and bring back Necker in 1788, and, in 1789, to call the Estates-General.

Though willing to admit constitutional reform, Louis and Necker proved indecisive over the method of representation in the Estates, thus setting the stage for the successful refusal by the deputies of the Third Estate, when they met in Versailles in May 1789, to meet except as a National Assembly with one vote for each deputy. Louis's instincts told him to go along with the Third Estate in the ensuing crisis, but, pressured by his advisors, he tried to slow or reverse the process of change. He put his wide-ranging reform plans, too late, to the *Séance Royale* (Royal Session) on 23 June as if nothing had happened. He consented to bring up troops to maintain order in Paris, but dismissed Necker, thus provoking the Parisian revolt in which the Bastille was stormed on 14 July; and he refused to withdraw from Versailles before the Parisian women and the national guard captured the royal family and forced them to return to Paris. Confined to the Tuileries, the king became in effect a prisoner and politically little more than a figurehead; he now secretly sent a message to his cousin Charles IV of Spain, disavowing any future actions he might take as being under duress. When matters settled down, however, he appears to have been willing to make an accommodation with the Revolution as long as the monarchy could play an active role in initiating legislation; Louis rightly refused to be a martyr to the diehard policies of the reactionary nobility, Marie-Antoinette, and his émigré brothers, the counts of Provençe and Artois. That was the nub of his program in the Royal Session, and also of the manifesto he left behind when he fled eastward and was captured at Varennes with his family on 20–25

June 1791. The king seems to have viewed his flight not as a plan to invade France with the help of foreign troops, but as a demonstration of force to make the Constituent Assembly renegotiate his place in the monarchy. Forced to return, Louis made a deal with the assembly, who were frightened to dismiss him, fearing to open the way to a democratic republic. Basically, Louis intended to bide his time until the contradictions inherent in the new regime brought about its downfall, a policy of passive resistance well-suited to his character. He sanctioned the declaration of war against Austria and Prussia in April 1792, the better to demonstrate these contradictions. This strategy was clever—there was much royalist support in the country and even in Paris—but he never thought through how to translate it into constitutional change. In the meantime, popular militants in Paris and radical volunteers from the provincial National Guards stormed the Tuileries palace in a coup d'état on 10 August 1792, driving the royal family to take refuge in the Legislative Assembly. As in the crises of 1789, Louis once again drew back from using his troops in a way that would cause major bloodshed. The rump of the assembly, from which the moderate deputies had fled, convoked a new Constitutional Convention; the Convention proclaimed a democratic Republic on 22 September, put the king on trial, and found him guilty of "conspiracy against public freedom and attacks on general state security." Louis died bravely on 21 January 1793.

See also **American Independence, War of (1775–1783); Bourbon Dynasty (France); Estates-General, French; France; Louis XV (France); Marie-Antoinette; Revolutions, Age of.**

BIBLIOGRAPHY

Primary Sources

Bombelles, Marc, marquis de. *Journal.* Geneva, 1977–.

Louis XVI. *Louis XVI and the comte de Vergennes: Correspondence, 1774–1787.* Edited and with an introduction by John Hardman and Munro Price. Oxford, 1998.

Maria Theresa. *Marie-Antoinette: Correspondance secrète entre Marie-Thérèse et le comte de Mercy-Argenteau.* Edited by Alfred d'Arneth. Paris, 1874–1875.

Mercy-Argenteau, Florimond de. *Correspondance secrète du comte de Mercy-Argenteau avec l'empereur Joseph II et le prince de Kaunitz.* Edited by Alfred d'Arneth and Jules Flammermont. Paris, 1889–1891.

Véri, Joseph Alphonse de. *Journal de l'abbé de Véri.* Paris, 1933.

Secondary Sources

Beales, Derek. *Joseph II.* Vol. 1, *In the Shadow of Maria Theresa.* Cambridge, U.K., 1987.

Girault de Coursac, Pierette. *L'éducation d'un roi: Louis XVI.* Paris, 1972.

Hardman, John. *French Politics from the Accession of Louis XVI to the Bastille.* London, 1995.

———. *Louis XVI.* New Haven, 1993.

Jordan, David P. *The King's Trial: The French Revolution vs. Louis XVI.* Berkeley and Los Angeles, 1979.

Lever, Evelyne. *Louis XVI.* Paris, 1985.

Lewis-Beck, M. S., A. Hildreth, and A. Spitzer. "Was There a Girondist Faction in the National Convention, 1792–1793?" *French Historical Studies* 15, no. 3 (1988): 519–536. Analyzes voting in Louis XVI's trial.

Murphy, Orville T. *Charles Gravier Comte de Vergennes, French Diplomacy in the Age of Revolution, 1719–1787.* Albany, N.Y., 1982.

Price, Munro. *Preserving the Monarchy: The Comte de Vergennes, 1774–1787.* Cambridge, U.K., 1995.

———. *The Road from Versailles: Louis XVI, Marie Antoinette and the Fall of the French Monarchy.* New York, 2002.

T. J. A. Le Goff

LOUVOIS, FRANÇOIS LE TELLIER, MARQUIS DE (1641–1691), secretary of state for war under Louis XIV of France. Louvois was the third and eldest surviving son of Michel Le Tellier, who was intendant of the French army of Italy at the time of Louvois's birth, and subsequently became secretary of state for war between 1643 and 1677, and then chancellor of France until his death in 1685. Louvois was educated at the Jesuit-run Collège de Clermont in Paris, and was brought into the War Ministry by his father in 1658 to prepare him for eventual management of the king's armies. Louvois had already been guaranteed the succession to his father as secretary of state for war back in 1655, but had to wait until 1664 for his father to secure for him joint control of the War Ministry. He assumed sole control of its direction in 1677. In addition, Louvois picked up a number of other offices that he also held until his death, most notably superintendent general of the Post from 1668, and superintendent of Arts, Buildings, and Manufactures from 1683, on the death of Jean-Baptiste Colbert. These and other posts brought an accumulation of responsibilities never to be exceeded by another secretary of state during the *ancien régime*. Indeed, by virtue of this set of responsibilities and through his allies, between 1683 and 1689 Louvois dominated government, though Louis XIV never allowed him to exercise a monopoly of patronage or to control access to his person.

Louvois's reputation rests upon his work as secretary of state for war, where he presided over a massive expansion of the peacetime standing army from around 55,000 men to 150,000, while even larger increases in the forces were generated during wartime. By the time of his death, the French army stood at around 300,000 men (allowing for inaccurate figures, fraud, and desertion). From the surviving documentation it is difficult to apportion credit accurately for the many improvements not only in the size of the army but also in its quality, as Louvois surrounded himself with a highly efficient group of administrators whom he had largely inherited from his father. But under Louvois's stewardship, complex financial and disciplinary rules evolved that made it far more worthwhile for the French nobility to enlist as army officers. By the 1680s the officers could sustain themselves in service for far longer than in the pre-1659 era, and collapses in morale and logistical support in the armies had become far less likely. Indeed, one of Louvois's greatest achievements was to establish more closely integrated systems for paying and feeding the expanding armies. Furthermore, he gave considerable support to the engineer Sébastien Le Prestre de Vauban's (1633–1707) fortification program to defend the frontiers, and many such fortresses became central to Louvois's logistical system.

In large part Louvois's success in equipping France with such a well-ordered army by contemporary standards can be attributed to his extraordinary grasp of the minutiae of military administration and to his remarkable stamina for business. In particular he paid unusual attention to the labyrinthine accounts of treasurers and entrepreneurs who supplied the logistical needs of the armies. He was also a strict disciplinarian who imprisoned two of his own sons, who were serving in the army, for insubordination, and he had a firm belief in the need to encourage godly behavior by officers. Louvois's power, however, also rested upon the support of the monarch. Louis XIV appreciated the need to integrate the Le Tellier family into the court and the upper reaches of French society if they were to be able to deal successfully with the great nobility and the high command. Through promoting a succession of prestigious marriages from 1660, and by endowing Louvois's cousins and sons with offices in the royal household, Louis XIV gave the family social respectability. By the time of his death on 16 July 1691 from a heart attack, Louvois had succeeded in entrenching his family at the apex of French society, and for another ten years they also held on to the War Ministry: he was succeeded as secretary of state for war by his twenty-three-year-old third son, Louis-François-Marie, marquis de Barbezieux, whom he had been preparing for the role since November 1685.

Marquis de Louvois. Portrait engraving by Pieter Louis van Schuppen. ©Réunion des Musées Nationaux/Art Resource, NY

Louvois was possibly the most divisive figure of Louis XIV's reign and still remains controversial, not least for presiding over the persecution of Protestants and the 1689 devastation of the Palatinate. He was highly partisan, driving good officers out of service on grounds of divergent personal interests, and depriving people of the full exercise of their offices. His reputation for ill-mannered brusqueness, and even occasional insolence to the king, was well established. He also encouraged Louis XIV in the pursuit of an aggressive foreign policy and, fatally for the king, he personally found it difficult to appreciate the interests of other powers, especially German princes and the duke of Savoy. Moreover, Louvois had a relatively weak grasp of grand strategy, and his operational directions to commanders were sometimes sufficiently out of touch as to provoke open protests to the king from the generals in the field. In 1691 he was even sidelined by the king from operational discussions during the siege of Mons. Yet, for all this, Louvois was fiercely loyal to the ideal of a strong monarchy, and he was immensely efficient at transacting state business. Just as important, Louvois was highly successful in the one thing that united all ministers and nobles of this era—securing the elevation of his dynasty.

See also **Colbert, Jean-Baptiste; France; Louis XIV (France).**

BIBLIOGRAPHY

Corvisier, André. *Louvois.* Paris, 1983. Easily the best biography.

Rousset, Camille. *Histoire de Louvois et de son administration politiques et militaire.* 4 vols. Paris, 1862–1864. Exhaustive, but hagiographic.

Rowlands, Guy. *The Dynastic State and the Army under Louis XIV: Royal Service and Private Interest, 1661–1701.* Cambridge, U.K., and New York, 2002. See Part One.

GUY ROWLANDS

LOYOLA, IGNATIUS. *See* Ignatius of Loyola.

LÜBECK.

With a population of 25,000 at the end of the Middle Ages, Lübeck was one of the great cities of northern Germany, located at the crossroads between the Baltic and the North Sea. It lived from international trade, and its central position had brought it leadership of the Hanseatic League. By the end of the eighteenth century, its population was still at the same level, its international trade was dwarfed by foreign competition, and its regional position was overshadowed by Hamburg. Lübeck's decline was comparatively gentle. At times, its merchants reached the Mediterranean, the Iberian Peninsula, and the eastern Baltic, particularly in the later sixteenth and seventeenth centuries. Lübeck's decline was accompanied by the slow dissolution of the Hansa itself as contrasting commercial interests drove a wedge between its members, and the once favorable trading conditions offered to Hanseatic merchants by foreign rulers were withdrawn. Meetings of the Hansetag still took place frequently in the city, and its burghers occupied many of the organization's most senior posts.

The Reformation came comparatively late to the city, in 1531. From then on, Lübeck was strictly Lutheran. Religious change was accompanied by political upheaval in the early 1530s, when a reform group, led by Jürgen Wullenwever, responded to Lübeck's growing political and economic weakness by unsuccessfully making war on Denmark in order to restore the city's former position.

The importance of long-distance trade throughout the period was reflected in the strong presence of seagoing merchants among the city's elite. Sharing power first with a small group of landowners and later with lawyers and other professionals, they ran the city's affairs, occupied the central quarter around the Rathaus (Town Hall), St. Mary's Church, and the marketplace, and maintained a close-knit network of relatives and business associates around the shores of the Baltic. Among the most famous of mercantile aristocrats was Thomas Fredenhagen (1627–1709), whose ships sailed into the Mediterranean and the West Indies. Commercial decline in the sixteenth century was accompanied by artistic decline. Lübeck's earlier reputation as a printing center was sustained during the Reformation but faded as Low German became less popular. A strong tradition of painting and wood carving (especially of altarpieces) made famous by Berndt Notke (1435–1509) also lost its wider importance. There was little continuing patronage of foreign artists. Only the organ music of Dieterich Buxtehude (1637–1707) and Franz Tunder (1614–1667) reached a wider audience.

Lübeck retained its medieval street plan. There was little rebuilding of town houses and public buildings until the eighteenth century, with the noted exception of the Rathaus, which was given a new Renaissance facade incorporating an impressive outside staircase during the sixteenth century. Instead, the appearance of the city was transformed from the outside. New and more extensive fortifications were constructed during the sixteenth and seventeenth centuries in response to the increase in military threats. These included the renewal and redecoration of Lübeck's main gates. While financial constraints prevented a complete overhaul of the city's fortifications, they proved to be a major deterrent to passing armies. Lübeck paid a high price for its neutrality during the Thirty Years' War, however. Gustavus II Adolphus levied a large sum of money as his price for leaving the city alone.

The ideas of the Enlightenment were first brought to eighteenth-century Lübeck from the universities of Jena and Göttingen. The literary society established in 1788 went on to develop into an organization for reform, bringing together men of many different interests and backgrounds.

See also **Buxtehude, Dieterich; Hamburg; Hansa.**

BIBLIOGRAPHY

Cowan, Alexander Francis. *The Urban Patriciate: Lübeck and Venice, 1580–1700.* Cologne and Vienna, 1986.

Grassmann, Antjekathrin, ed. *Lübeckische Geschichte.* 2nd ed. Lübeck, 1989.

ALEXANDER COWAN

LUBLIN, UNION OF (1569). Poland's union with the Grand Duchy of Lithuania, signed in Lublin on 1 July 1569, was the final stage of the process begun at Krewo on 14 August 1385, by which the grand duke of Lithuania, Jogaila (who became King Władysław II Jagiełło of Poland), pledged to associate (*applicare* in Latin) the territories of Lithuania and Ruthenia with the Polish Kingdom in a permanent union. Until the Union of Lublin, two conflicting conceptions of the union existed: the Polish side strove for a full incorporation of the Grand Duchy, while the Lithuanians wanted to retain their statehood in a looser union. The act of union was renewed and amended several times, the most important being the treaty signed at Horodło on 2 October 1413, which preserved the position of grand duke in Lithuania, envisaged joint Polish-Lithuanian congresses, and gave Lithuanian Catholics the same rights to land ownership as the Polish nobility. The forty-seven most important Lithuanian clans were also allowed to use the coats of arms of the Polish noble families.

Stormy debates over the union began in Lublin in January 1569; the Polish side tried to force through the incorporation of Lithuania into Poland, while the Lithuanians sought a federation in which Lithuania would retain separate central authorities and a separate parliament. As no agreement was reached, the Lithuanian negotiators left Lublin, and the Polish side, taking advantage of their absence, announced the incorporation of Lithuania's Ruthenian territories (Podlasia, Volhynia, the Kiev region, and the eastern part of Podolia) into Poland. Under pressure from the Lithuanian nobility, the Lithuanian magnates returned to Lublin, and a compromise act of union was signed on 1 July 1569.

Lithuania retained her political identity within the Commonwealth. The king and the grand duke would always be jointly elected, and parliament was to be held jointly. Lithuanian dignitaries holding posts that entitled their Polish counterparts to sit in the Senate became senators for life. The Chamber of Deputies was to include Lithuanians elected at twenty-four district diets *(sejmiki)*. The Grand Duchy retained its own armed forces, currency, treasury, and laws. The Union guaranteed freedom of settlement and land ownership throughout the Commonwealth. It created a federation of the two states, called the Commonwealth of Both Nations. A far-reaching cultural Polonization of the nobility of the Grand Duchy followed, but the Lithuanian noblemen preserved a consciousness of distinct political identity and retained their laws and traditions, as expressed in the Third Lithuanian Statute (1588; in force until 1840). A supplement to the Constitution of 3 May, adopted on 20 October 1791, stressed the federal character of the Commonwealth and the Grand Duchy's equal status with the Polish kingdom.

See also **Jadwiga (Poland); Jagiellon Dynasty (Poland-Lithuania); Lithuania, Grand Duchy of, to 1569; Poland to 1569; Poland-Lithuania, Commonwealth**

Union of Lublin. The signing of the treaty, 1569, engraving after the painting by Jan Matejko. ©BETTMANN/CORBIS

of, 1569–1795; Sigismund II Augustus (Poland, Lithuania); 3 May Constitution; Władysław II Jagiełło.

BIBLIOGRAPHY

Bardach, Juliusz. *O Rzeczypospolitej Obojga Narodów: Dzieje związku Polski z Litwą do schyłku XVIII wieku.* Warsaw, 1998.

Lulewicz, Henryk. *Gniewów o unię ciąg dalszy: Stosunki polsko-litewskie w latach 1569–1588.* Warsaw, 2002.

MARCIN KAMLER

LULLY, JEAN-BAPTISTE (1632–1687),

French composer and founder of the French operatic tradition. Lully was born Giovanni Battista Lulli in Florence, the son of a miller. Despite his humble origins, he was selected at the age of thirteen to teach Italian in Paris to Louis XIV's cousin Anne-Marie-Louise d'Orléans, known as the "Grande Mademoiselle," and he completed his education while serving in her household, mastering harpsichord, violin, and dancing. Lully became familiar with the ballet style of the royal court and by 1652 had so risen in musical status that he composed some of the music for a ballet that was given in the Grande Mademoiselle's palace. She became a partisan of the Fronde (a rebellion against the authority of the monarchy) later in the same year and was banished from Paris, freeing Lully to accept a post in 1653 as composer of instrumental music at the court of Louis XIV, functioning at first as both dancer and composer. The king, six years younger than Lully, befriended the composer, and the stage was set for Lully's extraordinary rise to musical power in France. By 1656 he had his own royal orchestra (the "*petits violons*") and began to compose all of the music for ballets, rather than collaborating with other composers. In the early 1660s he was understood to be the principal composer of ballets at court.

At this time, opera was understood to be exclusively an Italian phenomenon, and the considerable Italian presence at the court of Louis XIV (his first minister, Cardinal Jules Mazarin, was Italian) resulted in the importation of much opera. In 1664, Lully began to move in the direction of dramatic music in French, first by collaborating with Molière (1622–1673) in *comédies-ballets* (plays with much dance music). Louis XIV was in the process of extending his power in all aspects of French life, and in 1669 he added an Académie Royale de Musique to the "academies" he had established to control the artistic and intellectual life of the country; the new academy's stated purpose was to promote operas in French. Lully soon saw his opportunity and became its director in 1672, a position he held and aggrandized until his death, at the age of fifty-four. According to one contemporary source (Jean-Laurant Le Cerf de La Viéville), he died of gangrene after banging his foot while conducting with a cane.

Lully and librettist Philippe Quinault (1635–1688) created a noble new genre that signaled the beginning of a French style of opera. It was first termed simply *tragédie,* then *tragédie en musique;* later, the genre was labeled *tragédie lyrique.* Lully completed thirteen of these, approximately one a year, eleven to librettos by Quinault and two to librettos by Pierre Corneille (1606–1684): *Cadmus et Hermione* (1673), *Alceste* (1674), *Thésée* (1675), *Atys* (1676), *Isis* (1677), *Psyché* (1678, libretto by Corneille), *Bellérophon* (1679, Corneille), *Prosperpine* (1680), *Persée* (1682), *Phaéton* (1683), *Amadis* (1684), *Roland* (1685), and *Armide* (1686). Because Lully held royal privileges that gave him a complete monopoly on musical stage works, his operas dominated the musical life of the court and of Paris, and they held the stage well into the eighteenth century. Stylistically, they eschewed the rapid speechlike declamation typical of Italian recitatives. Rather, Lully created a fluid and expressive style of melodic line based on the declamation used in spoken French drama. Airs are usually dance-songs, and there are many dances interspersed with the vocal music, including full-fledged divertissements (entertainments that interrupt the plot). The five-act structure of the *tragédie en musique* was adopted from the spoken dramas of Corneille, and the prologue that either directly or allegorically praises Louis XIV came from the ballet tradition. Lully established a form for his overtures that was widely imitated elsewhere in Europe, and came to be known as the "French overture," consisting of a stately chordal section characterized by dotted-note rhythms, followed by a lively contrapuntal section.

Lully also composed a small but influential body of church music, particularly *grands motets* and *petits motets.* While he did not compose much independent instrumental music, the large amount of dance music in his stage works circulated separately, was gathered into suites, and was transcribed for other instruments. There is, for example, more harpsichord music derived from Lully's operatic dances than original music by any seventeenth-century French harpsichordist. Outside France, his influence was particularly strong in the Netherlands and Germany, and also in England. After the middle of the eighteenth century, his music was regarded for the most part as historical artifact until a revival of *Atys* in 1987 generated a new wave of appreciation for his operas.

Jean-Baptiste Lully. Getty Images

See also **Corneille, Pierre; Dance; Louis XIV (France); Mazarin, Jules; Molière; Music; Opera.**

BIBLIOGRAPHY

Heyer, John Hajdu, ed. *Jean-Baptiste Lully and the Music of the French Baroque: Essays in Honor of James R. Anthony.* Cambridge, U.K., and New York, 1989.

Isherwood, Robert. *Music in the Service of the King: France in the Seventeenth Century.* Ithaca, N.Y., 1973.

La Gorce, Jérôme de, and Herbert Schneider, eds. *Jean-Baptiste Lully: Actes du colloque = Kongressbericht: Saint-Germain-en-Laye and Heidelberg, 1987.* Laaber, 1990.

BRUCE GUSTAFSON

LUTHER, MARTIN (1483–1546), German theologian and author. Martin Luther came to be easily the most well-known public figure—and the most published author—of his time. He was born on 10 November 1483 to Hans and Margarethe Luther in the town of Eisleben and went to school in Mansfeld and Magdeburg and then in Eisenach. His father was in the copper mining business, and wanted Martin to become a lawyer. He entered the University of Erfurt in 1501 and completed the studies necessary for a master's degree four years later. By that time, however, he was suffering from doubts about the meaning of his life and from fears of death, and in the summer of 1505, against his father's wishes, he became a friar of the Observant Augustinians at Erfurt; he took monastic vows in 1506 and was ordained a priest in 1507. On a trip to Rome for the order in 1510–1511, he was disturbed by the corruption he found there, typified by the sale of indulgences to raise money for the rebuilding of St. Peter's. He returned to Saxony, earned his doctorate in 1512, and became professor of biblical exegesis at the University of Wittenberg, a post he held until 1546; he was also the preacher at the church in Wittenberg.

In his lectures on the Psalms and on Paul's Epistles, Luther began to preach the doctrine of salvation by faith rather than by works. Meanwhile, the popular Dominican preacher and papal fund-raiser Johann Tetzel appeared in the area to proclaim that the pope had authorized the sale of St. Peter's indulgences; Luther was infuriated to the point of composing a letter of protest to the archbishop of Mainz and posting his *Ninety-Five Theses on the Sale of Indulgences* on the church door at Wittenberg on 31 October 1517. By the end of the year, the theses had been printed and, a short while later, translated into German and spread throughout the Holy Roman Empire. The archbishop sent the theses to Pope Leo X, who summoned Luther to Rome to answer charges of heresy in 1518. Frederick III (Frederick the Wise; ruled 1486–1525) of Saxony intervened and arranged for Luther to have a formal hearing at Augsburg before the papal legate Cajetan rather than being sent to Rome. Luther refused to retract the views expressed in his theses, maintaining that there was no biblical justification for indulgences, and appealed to a papal council. There followed in 1519 a widely publicized debate at Leipzig between Luther and Johann Eck, a professor from Ingolstadt, on the subject of church authority. Luther's publication of three treatises in 1520 that called for revolutionary changes in late medieval German political, social, and religious life led to a papal bull excommunicating him in 1521; Luther publicly burnt the bull along with a copy of canon law and was called to the Diet of Worms for the purpose of recanting his teachings. He refused and was placed under the ban of the empire, which designated him an "outlaw" whom anyone could kill without legally committing murder.

His protector Frederick III of Saxony sent his soldiers to take Luther to the castle at Wartburg, where he spent a year writing pamphlets, preparing sermons on the Epistles and the Gospels, and translating the New Testament from Greek into German. He returned to Wittenberg in 1522 and resumed teaching and preaching. He urged the establishment of schools for all children (including girls), opposed the German Peasants' War, began the organization of the Saxon church, wrote hymns, a Small Catechism, and a Large Catechism, as well as numerous commentaries and treatises.

In 1525 Luther married Katharina von Bora, a former Cistercian nun who had fled her convent two years earlier under the influence of the Reformation. The couple moved into the former Augustinian monastery where Luther had lived as a monk; they had six children, three boys and three girls, and they also took in the six children of Luther's sister after her death; visitors reported that their home was always filled with students, guests, and boarders. Luther died at Eisleben on 18 February 1546 and was buried in the castle church at Wittenberg. In his funeral oration to faculty and students at Wittenberg, his long-time colleague and friend Philipp Melanchthon observed that in Luther "God gave this last age a sharp physician on account of its great sickness."

Martin Luther. Portrait by Lucas Cranach the Elder, 1533. ©BETTMANN/CORBIS

Luther was in his own time and remains now an object of passionate approval and disapproval, whom even supposedly scholarly accounts praised (and praise) for whatever their authors find praiseworthy in their own time while condemning him for all that they might judge as repugnant in their worlds. On the other hand, praising and condemning the reformer for all the "right" reasons and in just the "right" measures according to one's own time and culture amounts to thin porridge. The truest story is far more profound: Luther was at the same time quintessentially medieval and the single person who did most to put in motion the events that moved the clock of Western civilization into early modern times.

The notion that Luther was "medieval" refers to his motivating concerns rather than to any religious views that are no longer fashionable in polite circles, such as taking the figure of Satan or the Antichrist literally. Instead, Luther's life displays a consistent, driven search for assurance that he and those he taught and to whom he preached should be assured of their salvation both in the here and now and in the world to come. His fundamental concern was for the "care of souls," first his own and then the souls of those he served. In and of itself, this single-minded focus marks him as a premodern religious figure.

By the same token, the essential consequences of Luther's life and career are that, willy-nilly, the content of his personal spiritual quest, and the one he taught his students, changed dramatically. This change was so fundamental that, in combination with the circumstances of the early sixteenth century, it affected both the internal and public lives of many others. They too, unintentionally and perhaps even unconsciously, found themselves leaving the Middle Ages and moving into the early modern period.

The special indulgence sale of 1517, to which Luther objected in the *Theses,* has generally made indulgences the best known of the religious practices of the time. In fact, for the average believer, the sacrament of confession and penance was a far more common encounter with the medieval confrontation of sin, death, guilt, and wounded consciences. Above all, ever since the Fourth Lateran Council (1215) the faithful were obligated to go to confession at least annually, and most commonly during Lent or in preparation for partaking of Holy Communion at Easter. By contrast, going on a pilgrimage, venerating relics, and the like were all further and optional ways of strengthening and demonstrating one's faith.

For his part, Luther confessed his sins to another person and frequently on a more than daily basis. It remains impossible, of course, to learn exactly what happened within the confines of the confessional. The late medieval manuals suggest a certain rigor. Frequently enough, for example, someone would come and be unable to think of any particular sin that he or she had committed. At this point, the confessor had recourse to a printed list of questions that might be asked, such as, "Have you ever had sexual relations with your spouse for reasons other than procreation?" "Did you or your spouse enjoy the encounter?" Answering yes to either of both questions produced two sins for which penance must be done. Being first a novice and then a friar of the Observant Augustinians in Erfurt, the questions that Luther was asked and was taught to ask himself naturally turned to the internal status of his soul and in particular to the strength and commitment of his personal faith. From the posting of the theses forward, he never ceased in fact to inveigh against this practice of "inquiring about secret sins."

In the preface to the Latin works, which he completed in 1545, one year before his death, Luther eloquently and accurately described the changes that overcame his thinking, indeed his personal faith. There, he detailed rejecting the theology he had been taught, that the righteousness of God was a divine quality with which God judged humanity, and how he realized that it was rather the gift that God bestowed for Christ's sake on unrighteous people, and to which they cleaved in this life by faith alone. The basics of his more developed position appeared publicly in the Theses for the Heidelberg Disputation (spring 1518), in his lecture hall at the University of Wittenberg (1515–1519), and definitively in *Von der Freiheit eines Christenmenschen* (1520; On the freedom of a Christian). They lay beneath his insistence at Leipzig (1519) that "a simple layman armed with the Scriptures is mightier than pope and councils without them." Their consequences for Christianity and for Christendom became undeniable in *An den christlichen Adel deutscher Nation* (Address to the Christian nobility) and *De captivitate Babylonica ecclesiae praeludium* (On the Babylonian captivity of the church), both of 1520.

Each struck fundamental and telling blows against the medieval ideal of Latin Christendom. Each had politically, institutionally, and religiously revolutionary consequences. Many at the time regarded the *Address* as a call to arms against everything Roman, a call that—to the likes of Ulrich von Hutten, for example—included the political arrangements of the Holy Roman Empire. Luther cast his treatise as an appeal to the "*Christian* nobility" (or "ruling class" as some prefer to translate), the *Christlichen Adel,* to proceed with the reforms that the papacy refused to consider. The problem he faced was that common opinion held overwhelmingly that actually reforming the church was far beyond the competence of secular rulers, no matter how very Christian and upstanding they might be. Only those who had been ordained as priests, at a minimum, had the right to intervene in the affairs of the church in favor of or against any of its practices. There were many places in which local practice decreed that, if there were a property dispute between a clerical and a civil foundation, the case would be heard in an ecclesiastical court, and its outcome would be in little doubt.

This public and sanctioned conviction Luther called "the first wall" behind which papal prerogative protected itself. It was also the first one that he attacked. He did it with his famous teaching on the "priesthood of all believers," which grew directly from the proclamation that all Christians lived by the same grace through faith in the same Christ without distinctions between them. The only differences turned on the principal office or calling that a particular person had, regardless of whether he or she served in the temporal or spiritual spheres. Any baptized Christian was eligible to be called by the believers to preach, to baptize, and to administer the sacrament of the Lord's Supper on either a short- or long-term basis. With one stroke, Luther at least theoretically destroyed the very social class that helped constitute the social and political—as well as religious—reality of late medieval Christendom.

Luther's treatise *The Babylonian Captivity of the Church* performed much the same function with respect to specifically religious activities. Erasmus thought this the most radical of his treatises, for in a few pages, published initially in Latin, Luther attacked the medieval sacramental system at its core, reducing the number of sacraments from seven to first three and then (on the final pages) two. Two consequences followed. In the first place, if one accepted Luther's argument, then the Church of Rome no longer had anything to offer the laity that was essential to salvation. As then constituted, its raison d'être had ceased to exist. From pope to priest, they were all useless.

But there was an even more important aspect to what Luther had wrought. As he was working his way through one sacrament after another, he developed a consistent standard for what constituted a sacrament. It required biblical evidence that Christ had founded the practice and that it consisted of a promise added to a physical object.

Thus, the central sacrament—confession and penance—disappeared and with it went any semblance of religious authority that the clergy might hold over the laity as a matter of principle.

Yet, Luther should not be called a "reformer" without qualification. He made no effort to replace what he tore down with a "better" edifice. Instead, he and his colleagues proceeded to construct a new institution chiefly through ad hoc measures such as visitations that had the sole objective of securing the preaching of the Word of forgiveness through Christ and in the sacraments of baptism and the Lord's Supper. All else they relegated to the world in which Christians carried out their vocations. Thus, to understand Luther requires grasping the contradictory theses with which he began *On the Freedom of a Christian,* published in 1520: "A Christian is a perfectly free lord of all, subject to none. A Christian is a perfectly dutiful servant of all, subject to all." As time passed and the cause fell to less perceptive figures, this distinction metamorphosed into what became the dichotomy between church and state. In this regard and with these changes, the transition from the medieval world of Latin Christendom into early modern Europe was complete, whereas by contrast the old tensions, polarities, and rivalries persisted in France, Italy, Spain, and Catholic portions of the Holy Roman Empire until the French Revolution.

See also **Bible: Translations and Editions; German Literature and Language; Lutheranism; Melanchthon, Philipp; Peasants' War, German; Reformation, Protestant; Saxony.**

BIBLIOGRAPHY

Primary Sources

Luther, Martin. *D. Martin Luthers Werke: Kritische Gesamtausgabe.* Weimar, 1883–. The standard critical edition, the unsurpassed work of generations of scholars, which now consists of more than 100 volumes. Comprises Luther's published works, correspondence, the German Bible, and table talks. Commonly referred to as "the Weimar edition" or simply "WA."

———. *Luther's Works.* Translated and edited by Jaroslav Pelikan, Helmut Lehmann, et al. 55 vols. St. Louis and Philadelphia, 1955–1986. The standard English translation, which is not completely reliable for a number of reasons.

Secondary Sources

Brecht, Martin. *Martin Luther.* Translated by James Schaaf. 3 vols. Philadelphia and Minneapolis, 1985–1993. With three large volumes, thorough attention to detail, and the German apparatus by and large intact, these are the volumes for the serious beginner.

Edwards, Mark U. *Printing, Propaganda, and Martin Luther.* Berkeley, 1994.

Kittelson, James M. *Luther the Reformer: The Story of the Man and His Career.* Minneapolis, 1986.

Kolb, Robert. *Martin Luther as Prophet, Teacher, Hero: Images of the Reformer, 1520–1620.* Grand Rapids, Mich., 1999.

McGrath, Alister E. *Luther's Theology of the Cross: Martin Luther's Theological Breakthrough.* Oxford, 1985.

Oberman, Heiko. *Luther: Man between God and the Devil.* Translated by Eileen Walliser-Schwarzbart. New Haven, 1989.

JAMES M. KITTELSON

LUTHERANISM. Among all the major individual varieties of Latin Christianity to emerge from the Reformation, Lutheranism stands alone for two reasons. In the first place, it bears the name of an individual. Secondly, its hallmark, more vital even than the reference to Martin Luther (1483–1546), consists of its formal, agreed-upon confessions of faith, in particular the Unaltered Augsburg Confession (1530), but also (save in Scandinavia) the Formula of Concord (1577) and the other documents contained in the Book of Concord (1580), which claim faithfulness to both the Scriptures and Luther's teachings. To answer the question, "What is Lutheranism?" therefore requires, at least in principle, no more than a careful reading of these theological sources with the understanding that conduct flowed from conviction. It can be no surprise, then, that Lutherans have traditionally relegated all other religious matters—liturgy, polity, hymnody, spirituality, and the like—to the realm of *adiaphora* or "things indifferent." The teachings were at the time of the Reformation, and remain now, the heartbeat of Lutheranism.

By contrast, even the finest of Lutheran scholarship has little to say about its distinctive characteristics, if any, with respect to its political, social, intellectual, artistic, and cultural preferences over time. Thus, even its hymnody and its vibrant traditions in choral music were put in service to its teachings. For the unengaged student, Lutheranism presents the unavoidable impression that all matters which make it a distinct variety of Christianity have rightly had a theological, as well as musical, standard applied to them. To the uninitiated and the veteran alike, it may well appear that once one has gotten the teachings of the Lutherans correct and arranged them in their proper relationships to one another, one has grasped all that is essential when it comes to understanding Lutheranism in almost any place and time. One is reminded of nothing so much as the words on the back of a coin struck in Württemberg on the fiftieth anniversary of the posting of the Ninety-Five Theses: "God's Word and Luther's Teachings are Never to be Forgotten!"

Luther had been in his grave for more than twenty years when this medal was struck. The Formula of Concord, to say nothing of the period of Lutheran Orthodoxy, did not yet exist. But the conviction that true doctrine was the equivalent of true religion did. Indeed, this very characteristic is not a caricature and, no matter how obvious it is, it must be underlined whenever one seeks to penetrate to the core of Lutheranism. Luther himself reportedly declared, "Others before me have contested practice, but to contest doctrine, that is to grab the goose by the neck!"

Even when one rightly approaches the core of Lutheranism by way of its teachings, there remain more and less enlightening ways to do so. One can, as noted above, and rather in the manner of Lutheran Orthodoxy in the seventeenth and eighteenth centuries, turn the exercise into an utterly misleading game of theological pick-up sticks. If, however, the objective is to render an image of Lutheranism that encompasses its whole as well as its many parts, one further and rather subtler characteristic must be given its due. Luther was indeed a theologian, and Lutheranism does indeed remain a highly theological version of even Latin Christianity. But, both Luther and the movement that sprang from him had almost no inclinations to systematic theology in a manner that might be recognized by, for example, Thomas Aquinas.

Neither Luther nor Lutherans in general have sought to create a *Summa Theologica* in which everything from the creation *ex nihilo* to human procreation has its own perfectly consistent theological understanding. This is not to say that Lutheran religious thought consisted merely of random insights on one unrelated topic after another in the manner of some types of mysticism. Instead, the consistency or univocality of Lutheran theology derived from its genesis over time from a single, unitary point of departure. Thus it began, by Luther's own testimony, with his personal search for a gracious God. He had been taught that the righteousness of God was a quality of God against which this divine judge measured all humans and found them wanting. On the bases of his lectures and writings from late 1518 through mid-1519, it is now a matter of nearly absolute certainty that he consciously rejected what he had been taught and then gradually came to understand God's righteousness as a gift that God bestowed on humanity and by which he reconciled mankind to himself. Thus, the famous passage, "The righteous (*iustus,* 'made righteous') shall live by faith" applied directly not only to the theology he taught as a professor at Wittenberg but also to his personal religious life. "Faith" itself was no longer an attribute that played a role in moving the sinner toward salvation but the central, unwilled response to having been made righteous by the benefits of Christ. By comparison with *sola gratia,* Luther did not even use the terms *sola fide* and *sola scriptura* with much frequency. They did not do more than indicate the principal source for and the manner by which the Christian received and held grace.

The theology that marked Lutheranism was therefore intensely practical and rarely, before Kant, speculative or philosophical in the least. Two examples will illustrate the point. The first concerns the subject of predestination, which came under dispute during the 1560s in a few places that were, for the most part, south of the Main River and along the Rhine—most notably in Strasbourg. Those who introduced the issue were commonly Italian converts to Calvinism such as Girolamo Zanchi (1516–1590) and Peter Martyr Vermigli (1500–1562). The issue, certainly related theologically to Luther's position in *De servo arbitrio* (1525; On the bondage of the will), nonetheless never caught fire among the German Lutherans. In its eleventh article, the Formula of Concord observed that the subject had not been an issue "among the theologians of the Augsburg Confession" and then addressed it anyway. Taking the approach and even borrowing some of the language that was used at Strasbourg in

1561–1563, the formulators declared that there were good biblical grounds in support of both the doctrine of election and the assertion that Christ came for all. But, because God's predestining belonged to his hidden will and Christ's coming for all to his revealed will, Lutherans would henceforth ignore predestination and preach only what God had revealed to all. For the most part, Lutherans to this day have carefully observed this self-denying ordinance. They were single-minded about the original insight regarding justification and remained tenaciously within it.

A second illustration from Luther himself may also be revealing. It concerns the subject of "hiddenness" and a similar, related principle of self-denial in general. Luther observed, for example, that everyone of sound mind could know that God existed, that he created all things, that he was omnipotent, and so forth. What humans could not know were God's intentions toward them because God had hidden and continued to hide this knowledge in the folly of Christ. Moreover, this keen awareness of what God has revealed and what he has hidden guided even Luther's exegetical practices. Consequently, his biblical lectures often contained the declaration regarding a particular passage, "It is too dark there. I cannot go there because all is hidden." Indeed, his first reaction to Johann Agricola of Eisleben's (c. 1494–1566) insistence that the Law should not be preached to the saved (the fundamental issue at stake in Lutheranism's first Antinomian Controversy, which involved the notion that a saved Christian was free from the dictates of the Law) was not to press on to the truth of the matter but—in part because he was one of Luther's favorite students—that Agricola should stop talking about the matter.

Nonetheless, little more than a generation had passed before Luther's followers had fallen into so many internecine theological quarrels that Jakob Andreae of Württemberg (1528–1590) and others took up the work that led to the Formula of Concord. In addition to predestination, Andreae and his colleagues addressed ten such controversies that threatened to undo the unity implied in the name "theologians of the Augsburg Confession." To modern ears, some of these issues were truly frivolous and may have derived more from some individuals' vanity than serious theological considerations. Georg Major's (1469–1550) tactic of expressing Luther's views of the place of works in the economy of salvation may be a case in point. Somehow, his declaration that "Good works are dangerous to salvation" seems intended more to enrage than to enlighten. It is easy to understand Philipp Melanchthon's (1497–1560) giving thanks at the point of death for at last being released from the *rabies theologorum* ('the madness of the theologians').

With this much granted to the merely human, the emphasis should fall here on two related practical, political realities that forced theological reflection. The first was Emperor Charles V's (ruled 1519–1556) victory over the Schmalkaldic League in 1547–1548 and his determination to establish religious peace within the empire by force if necessary. Thus, the Augsburg Interim required of the Lutheran rulers that they reinstitute the Mass in their territories, provide for an unmarried clergy, and cease secularizing religious foundations, among other, more local, arrangements. In addition, by putting the free imperial city of Constance under siege, the emperor demonstrated that he was more than willing to employ force during this interim before the calling of a general council. Consequently, in order to meet these terms, Strasbourg found itself compelled to negotiate a treaty with its long-time non-resident bishop, while Magdeburg to the northeast resisted imperial pressure successfully by holding firm behind its outlying marshes to defend its choice of resistance. At the same time, Maurice, called on account of his political behavior the "Judas of Meissen," now enjoying the title elector of Saxony (1547–1553), found so much resistance to the new order in his territories that he felt compelled to negotiate a somewhat milder version, called the Leipzig Interim, whose intent was to defend Lutheran doctrine, albeit without much regard for contrary practices, in the face of these temporary practical concessions.

A genuine theological problem lay at what became an internecine pamphlet war among the theologians of the Augsburg Confession. Mathias Flaccius Illyricus (1520–1575) led the defenders of Magdeburg's policy on the grounds that the Leipzig Interim violated the spirit, if not the letter, of true Lutheranism. In this instance, there was no authoritative text to which the parties could turn, if only because the Augsburg Confession's seventh article was silent with respect to any of the specifics regarding what actions (or lack thereof) fell under the umbrella of "things indifferent." According to the Magdeburgers with Matthias Flaccius Illyricus, the "Genesio" or Original Lutherans (as they were now called) insisted that while some practices, such as the celebration of the Mass, might be indifferent in themselves, they were intolerable in a Lutheran territory, because they in fact promoted a false gospel. The outrage was so great that there are present-day Lutherans who still call themselves Genesios. During the late 1570s, its simple existence forced the inclusion of Section X in the Formula of Concord, which basically endorsed the Genesios' position.

The decade from the mid-1540s to the mid-1550s also called for greater theological precision in imperial politics. The Religious Peace of Augsburg (1555) inserted the Augsburg Confession (1530) into the imperial constitution by declaring that adherents to it would be guaranteed a modicum of religious freedom, depending on the confession of the town or principality that was their home. This is the famous provision that is summarized with the anachronistic term *cuius regio eius religio,* according to which the ruler's confession determined the religion of the town or principality. Some try incorrectly to draw from this provision the beginnings of state-dominated religion. Instead, this provision merely stated that the prevailing religion in any territory or city was to be the one that existed there before the Schmalkaldic War.

There was a problem, however, lurking beneath the easy reference to the Augsburg Confession as the imperial confessional standard. Which Augsburg Confession? In 1540 Melanchthon had been given the task of revising the version that was submitted at Augsburg in 1530 in light of the Wittenberg Concord of 1536. Specifically, he had used the language, approved expressly by Luther, *cum pane et vino* ('with bread and wine') rather than *in pane et vino* ('in bread and wine') as a way to describe just how the consecrated elements in the Lord's Supper were presented as the body and blood of Christ. One change of preposition provided certain Reformed theologians, notably those active at the court of the elector palatine, just enough room to assert that their understanding of the spiritual presence of the body and the blood came under the umbrella of "the Augsburg Confession" and therefore of the Peace of Augsburg.

At last an assembly of evangelical princes, meeting at the request of the elector palatine at Naumburg in January 1561, declared that the standard was the *invariata* (the version of 1530), but that the *variata* (Melanchthon's version of 1540) might be used to explain its teaching on contentious issues. No sooner had they returned home than they were confronted with a round-robin inquiry from Emperor Ferdinand I (ruled 1558–1564), in which he asked whether the elector palatine was or was not in harmony with the Unaltered Augsburg Confession of 1530. They replied that, while perhaps technically he was not, the emperor should not presume to take any actions against him.

These festering disagreements and Reformed aggressiveness in northern Germany go much of the way to explaining why, about seventy-five years later, in the aftermath of the Battle of White Mountain, the Lutheran princes decided to sit on their hands when General Albrecht Wenzel Eusebius von Wallenstein attacked the Electoral Palatinate, deposed the elector, reduced parts of Heidelberg to ashes, shipped the contents of the university library, the Palatinum, off to the pope as a gift, and inaugurated the Thirty Years' War (1618–1648). Certain developments within Lutheranism contributed to this decision not to intervene in defense of a generous interpretation of the Peace of Augsburg. Perhaps it was the price the Reformed were called upon to pay for their aggressive attempts over the past seventy years to convert Lutheran princes. In the event, it was Germany, and in particular northern, Lutheran Germany that paid the price by becoming the playground for armies from all over Europe, while the south had the burden of paying for it all.

The reference above to "certain developments within Lutheranism" points to the two paths between which Lutherans chose beginning in the early seventeenth century and continuing on through the mid-eighteenth century. They persist to this day under the terms "Pietism" and "Lutheran Orthodoxy." Both had deep roots. As should be evident, Orthodoxy can claim parentage in the heavily doctrinal character of Lutheranism from the outset, through the Genesio Lutherans, the Formula of Concord, Martin Chemnitz with his monumental

Examination of the Council of Trent (1565–1573), and into the professorial life of seventeenth-century Lutheran theological faculties. Pietism, on the other hand, can claim its origins with Martin Bucer (1491–1551) of Strasbourg and a tradition that produced such luminaries in the movement toward a more "heartfelt" religion, as evident in two later products of Strasbourg, Johannes Arndt (1555–1621) and his *Vier Bücher vom wahren Christentum* (1606; Four books on true Christianity), and Philipp Jakob Spener (1635–1705), the *collegia pietatis,* and his *Pia Desideria* (1675), which is still read and cherished by many. That the two parties did not think well of one another is evident from the story about Johann Sebastian Bach (1685–1750), who was frustrated by a powerful Pietist preacher at the Church of St. Thomas in Leipzig. It was said that whenever he encountered the preacher on the street, Bach would "compose and throw another fugue" at him.

One may legitimately wonder whether Voltaire's Dr. Pangloss, despite the evident reference to followers of Gottfried Wilhelm von Leibniz, was a parody of Lutheran theologians he had met. Research has only begun on these theologians, but two matters are presently apparent. In the first place, they were indeed extremely learned men who brought to their tasks Aristotle, both of the *Metaphysics* and the *Posterior Analytics,* the ancient authority whose very dominance of Wittenberg's theological faculty Luther once celebrated. Secondly, it was the Orthodox who turned the substance of Lutheranism into a laundry list of virtually self-standing doctrines that the theologian needed only to memorize. While so doing, they no longer studied Luther himself nor did they cite him in their general histories of doctrine or their works on specific theological topics. Finally, their influence lasted long past the eighteenth century and can be said to have peaked in the nineteenth century. This is not to say that no one read Luther any longer. The Finnish "Luther Readers" both in Finland and in the Upper Peninsula of Michigan read him regularly, but more for the sake of spiritual enrichment than of theological learning. It was left to the Swedish Luther Renaissance of the late nineteenth and twentieth centuries to return to a genuinely theological-critical study of Luther himself.

Save in a few synodical groupings and a handful of individuals, notably in North America, Lutheran Orthodoxy is no longer particularly influential. Pietism in both vibrant and decadent forms is a different matter. Beginning with Bucer, who was truthfully more a religious thinker and churchman than a theologian, those with Pietist proclivities have downplayed the theological character of Lutheranism as a distortion that drew the believer's attention away from the inclination of the heart, moral behavior, and the amendment of life that must follow the hearing of the Gospel.

To take but two examples, one at the beginning and the other near the end of the story, in the mid-1530s Bucer wrote a book called *The True Care of Souls.* In it (among other concerns) he listed Christians by type according to the extent to which they approximated the ideal and then prescribed different forms of pastoral care that would help them advance on the classification table. He did bow toward the central teaching from Luther that a Christian remained *simul iustus et peccator* ('at the same time righteous and a sinner'). But this was for him merely a background principle to the main task of creating more genuine believers and moral members of the church on earth. Still, Bucer's list of exercises remained some distance from Luther's insistence that true pastoral care occurred in the preaching of God's Word, which did all that could be done to create true people of God.

Spener differed from Bucer first in that he openly criticized the theologians and churchmen of his day for their self-serving lack of attention to improving the tenor of Christian life. Secondly, he favored the establishment where possible of *collegia pietatis* ('colleges of piety') in which the truly repentant and committed would withdraw to increase their search for true piety and their willingness to perform good works. Bucer, too, had engaged himself in similar work, known as the *Christliche Gemeinschaften* or *ecclesiolae in ecclesia* ('little churches within the church'), shortly before being forced as a condition of the Interim to leave Strasbourg for England while under a storm of criticism from both the government and many of his fellow pastors for the tendencies of these small fellowships to split the existing parishes and churches. It should be noted that these efforts were not strictly anti-dogmatic but simply did not evidence much interest in public teachings. The Pietist movement reached its apogee in August Hermann Francke (1663–1727) with his school and later university at Halle, institutions that came to specialize in the training of servants for the Prussian bureaucracy.

Lutheranism in the main experienced the same fate as most other branches of Christianity during the early modern period. By the end of the eighteenth century, true religion had retreated from the public sphere into the private. Whereas the "two kingdoms" through which God ruled his creation—the world of daily affairs in politics, society, and business, and the world of faith—had once served one another, by the end of early modern times, the kingdom of the world had come to dominate. Lutheranism in both its Orthodox and Pietist forms thus abandoned the public sphere to a heretofore-unknown realm of religious indeterminacy, and it did so well before the First Amendment to the United States Constitution. By their own doing, Lutherans turned true religion into a private matter that was by and large excluded from the "real world" of politics, business, and society. Christendom had died. Europe was born.

See also **Luther, Martin; Melanchthon, Philipp; Pietism; Reformation, Protestant; Schmalkaldic War.**

BIBLIOGRAPHY

Primary Sources

The Book of Concord: The Confessions of the Evangelical Lutheran Church. Translated by Charles Arand, et al. Edited by Robert Kolb and Timothy J. Wengert. Minneapolis, 2000.

Luther, Martin. *D. Martin Luthers Werke: Kritische Gesamtausgabe.* Weimar, 1883–. Comprises Luther's published works, correspondence, the German Bible, and table talks. Commonly referred to as "the Weimar edition" or simply "WA."

———. *Luther's Works.* Translated and edited by Jaroslav Pelikan, Helmut Lehmann, et al. 55 vols. St. Louis and Philadelphia, 1955–1986.

———. *Sources and Contexts of The Book of Concord.* Edited by Robert Kolb and James A. Nestingen. Minneapolis, 2001.

Secondary Sources

Brecht, Martin. *Martin Luther.* Translated by James Schaaf. 3 vols. Philadelphia and Minneapolis, 1985–1993.

Elert, Werner. *The Structure of Lutheranism.* Vol. 1, *The Theology and Philosophy of Life of Lutheranism Especially in the Sixteenth and Seventeenth Centuries.* Translated by Walter A. Hansen. St. Louis, 1962. Informative but filtered through a neo-Kantian framework.

Kittelson, James M. *Luther the Reformer: The Story of the Man and His Career.* Minneapolis, 1986.

———. *Toward an Established Church: Strasbourg from 1500 to the Dawn of the Seventeenth Century.* Veröffentlichungen des Instituts für Europäische Geschichte Mainz 182. Mainz, 2000.

Maurer, Wilhelm. *Historical Commentary on the Augsburg Confession.* Translated by H. G. Anderson. Philadelphia, 1986.

Nischan, Bodo. *Princes, People and Confession: The Second Reformation in Brandenburg.* Philadelphia, 1994.

JAMES M. KITTELSON

LVIV (Polish, Lwów; German, Lemberg; Russian, Lvov; Latin, Leopolis). First mentioned in 1256, Lviv arose at the intersection of important trade routes linking the Baltic with the Black Sea and Cracow with Kiev. It was named for Leo, son of Daniel, prince of Galician-Volhynian Rus', who founded the city in the mid-thirteenth century. In 1349 the principality was incorporated into the Polish crown under Casimir III the Great. Lviv became the capital of the Ruthenian palatinate in 1434.

Casimir granted the city the Magdeburg law for municipal self-government in 1356, opening the door to considerable immigration, especially from German-speaking lands. Lviv was thus highly mixed from the beginnings of the Polish period. In addition to the autochthonous Ruthenians (ancestors of Ukrainians) there were numbers of Polish, German, Armenian, and Jewish immigrants. A Roman Catholic archbishopric was established in 1412, an Orthodox bishopric in 1539 (it received the Union of Brest with Rome in 1700), and an Armenian bishopric from 1626. The burghers were largely German until the beginning of the sixteenth century, from which point they and the Armenians underwent Polonization. Rights of citizenship in Lviv under the Magdeburg law applied only to Catholics. The Orthodox Ruthenian commonality found itself in social and confessional conflicts with the Polish or Polonized nobility, patriciate, and burghers.

Lviv was a cultural center. It was home to Catholic poets working in neo-Latin and Polish—Szymon Szymonowic (Simon Simonides, 1558–1629, son of the city councillor Szymon of

Brzeziny) and the brothers Zimorowic, Szymon (c. 1609–1629) and Józef Bartłomiej (1597–1677), who served several times as Lviv's burgomaster—all of whom reflected local Ruthenian realia in their works. The Lviv Orthodox Dormition Brotherhood was an important Orthodox cultural center (its right of stauropegion, whereby it was placed directly under the patriarch's control and made independent of the local bishop, was granted by the patriarch of Antioch, Joachim V, in 1586). It established a school (1585) and printing house (first printing 1591), and it played an important role in the lives of local Ruthenians, serving also, with Vilnius, as an early center for a broader Orthodox revival in the late fifteenth and early sixteenth centuries before yielding that role to Kiev in the 1630s. The city's first printing house was that of the Belarusian printer Ivan Fedorov, recently expelled from Moscow, who issued Lviv's first Church Slavonic book in 1574. Latin and Polish printings began to appear in 1581.

By the early seventeenth century, over five hundred craftsmen worked in some thirty guilds, among which producers of metalware, jewelry, and weapons enjoyed respect abroad. Lviv's artisans and architects joined western and eastern styles. Armenian artisans produced belts, caparisons, weapons, jewelry, and embroidery. Lviv's Jews and Armenians played important roles in trade between western Europe and the Orient and offered competition to the rest of Lviv's merchants and artisans.

The first Jews may have arrived from Byzantium, but the greatest immigration came after 1349 from Germany and Bohemia. The newcomers established two Ashkenazic settlements, an older, extramural congregation (in 1550, 559 Jews lived in 52 houses) and a newer, intramural congregation (352 Jews in 29 houses), with separate synagogues, *mikva'ot,* and charitable institutions, but one common cemetery.

Lviv declined together with the Polish-Lithuanian Commonwealth, beginning in the middle of the seventeenth century. It was under frequent attack: by Bohdan Khmelnytsky's Cossack armies in 1648 and 1655 and by Turkish and Tatar forces in 1672, 1675, 1691, and 1695. The greatest depredations came at the hands of the Swedes in 1704 during the Great Northern War. Incorporated by the Habsburgs after the first partition of Poland in 1772, Lviv became the administrative capital of the Austrian Kingdom of Galicia and Lodomeria.

See also **Orthodoxy, Russian; Poland-Lithuania, Commonwealth of, 1569–1795; Poland to 1569; Polish Literature and Language; Ukraine.**

BIBLIOGRAPHY

Aleksandrovych, Volodymyr et al. *L'viv: Istorichnyi narysy.* Lviv, 1996.

Bałaban, Majer. *Żydzi lwowscy na przełomie XVI i XVII wieku.* Lviv, 1909.

Czaplicka, John, ed. *Lviv: A City in the Crosscurrents of Culture.* Vol. 24. *Harvard Ukrainian Studies.* Cambridge, Mass., 2000.

David Frick

LYON. Founded by the Romans as a provincial capital, Lyon maintained its prominence during the medieval period as the seat of a bishopric and an important law court (the *Sénéchaussée*). Its location at the confluence of two important rivers (the Rhône and the Saône) made it a commercial center as well, allowing it to act as a transportation and financial hub between the Renaissance Italian cities to the south and the French and Flemish cities to the north. From the sixteenth century, silk and other textile production combined with banking to propel the city's economy, and its four annual trade fairs emerged as among the most important in Europe. Merchant dynasties (both French and Italian) came to dominate the city's governing council, or consulate, and continued to rule the city up to the Revolution.

The Reformation came to Lyon from nearby Geneva in the sixteenth century, and religious conflict temporarily damaged the city's economic dominance. Largely an elite phenomenon, Protestantism faded during the seventeenth century although economic and family contacts with Geneva continued. Prompted in part by Genevan and Italian models, Lyonnais merchants developed several new forms of poor relief during this period, including a publicly owned general hospital that took in foundlings and orphans, training them for work in the textile trades and supplying dowries to young women. The city's governing elite also created public institutions to supply food during grain shortages, including an urban administration to purchase grain at city expense, public ovens to bake bread, and an organized rationing system. Lyon thus served as a model in France for poor relief and administrative innovation in times of famine.

While textile production (especially silks) continued to expand through the seventeenth and eighteenth centuries, the four fairs became principally important as financial markets. Their regularity, and the supervision over them by a powerful judicial court (the *Conservation des foires*) made them attractive to merchants from Italy, Switzerland, and France who wished to make, pay, and exchange loans while minimizing the dangerous transfer of coin. During the latter years of the reign of Louis XIV, royal bankers such as Samuel Bernard manipulated these markets, burdening them with the royal debt and nearly bankrupting them. Though the fairs contracted and became less internationally important as a result, they survived and continued to function on a smaller scale for the remainder of the eighteenth century. Unlike other cities, Lyon maintained a remarkable degree of independence from other royal exactions because the merchants of Lyon successfully manipulated royal patronage and the system of venal offices to preserve a degree of autonomy. As France's "second" city, Lyon enjoyed a tradition of independence and resistance to central authority that continued through the Revolution and into the modern era.

See also **France.**

BIBLIOGRAPHY

Davis, Natalie Zemon. *Society and Culture in Early Modern France.* Stanford, 1975.

Gascon, Richard. *Grand commerce et vie urbaine au XVIe siècle: Lyon et ses marchands.* 2 vols. Paris, 1971.

Monahan, W. Gregory. *Year of Sorrows: The Great Famine of 1709 in Lyon.* Columbus, Ohio, 1993.

W. GREGORY MONAHAN

30°W
20°W
10°W
0°
10°E
60°N
50°N
40°N
ICELAND
(Denmark)
Faroe Islands
Shetland Islands
Orkney Islands
NORWAY
(Denmark)
Christiania
Scotland
Firth of Forth
Edinburgh
North Sea
DENMARK
Copenhagen
Bann
Shannon
Isle of Man
Dublin
Ireland
GREAT BRITAIN
Trent
Wales
Severn
England
Bristol
Thames
London
Amsterdam
NETHERLANDS
Hanover
Elbe
Cologne
Brussels
Austrian Netherlands
Rhine
Weser
Saale
Saxon
Frankfurt
Main
ATLANTIC OCEAN
Aisne
Seine
Paris
Meuse
Neckar
HOLY ROMAN EMPIRE
Danube
Bavaria
Munich
Loire
SWISS CONFED.
FRANCE
Lyon
ALPS
Milan
VENICE
Venice
Turin
MILAN
Po
SARDINIA
PARMA
Genoa
MODENA
GENOA
Rhône
Garonne
Arno
Appennines
Marseille
LUCCA
TUSCANY
Tiber
Pyrenees
ANDORRA
Douro
Ebro
PAPAL STATES
Corsica (France)
Rome
PORTUGAL
Madrid
Barcelona
Tagus
Naples
SPAIN
Balearic Islands
Minorca (Great Britain)
SARDINIA
Lisbon
Majorca (Spain)
Iviza (Spain)
Seville
Mediterranean Sea
Sicily
AFRICA
Malta

AMERICAN NEWSPAPERS
1821 - 1936

A UNION LIST OF FILES AVAILABLE IN THE UNITED STATES AND CANADA

EDITED BY
WINIFRED GREGORY

UNDER THE AUSPICES OF THE
BIBLIOGRAPHICAL SOCIETY OF AMERICA

COMMITTEE
James Thayer Gerould
Harry Miller Lydenberg   Henry Spaulding Parsons

NEW YORK

1937

Reprinted with the permission of the Bibliographical Society of America
KRAUS REPRINT CORPORATION
New York
1967

PRINTED IN THE UNITED STATES OF AMERICA

Printed in U.S.A.

PREFACE

The Union List of Newspaper Files is the third in a series of projects designed to render more effective the resources of American libraries. The Union List of Serials, the List of Serial Publications of Foreign Governments, and now this List of Newspaper Files, have increased enormously the usefulness of the collections made by libraries and have stimulated their development. More and more we are coming to realize that education and scholarship are national, as well as local, problems, and that only by coordinating our resources can we hope to attack them.

The student and the scholar must know not only what are the publications which contain the information for which he is seeking, but where they are. Through our system of inter-library loans, and increasingly through the development of film technique, we are able to bring to the scholar's desk a wide range of materials hitherto available to him only after a time-wasting search and expensive travel.

The compilation of these publications has been made possible primarily by generous grants from the Laura Spelman Rockefeller Memorial and the Rockefeller Foundation; and to their Trustees the Committee makes grateful acknowledgment.

Upon the libraries which have cooperated in furnishing the material upon which the lists have been based the burden has been heavy, but it has been assumed cheerfully, and with a realization that the labor and expense involved was an investment, certain to pay large dividends later in the saving of time and in effective service.

The Committee is sincerely grateful to Dr. Herbert Putnam for his courtesy in providing office space for Miss Gregory's staff and for granting to her the free use of the various facilities of the Library of Congress.

The List of Newspaper Files would have been an impossible task had we not been able to enlist the aid, in each state and in the provinces of Canada, of individuals who have a sufficient acquaintance with the local libraries to know where the files are to be found and persistance enough to secure the record. To all of the men and women, whose names are listed on another page, and to the hundreds of other librarians and historical scholars who have assisted them, the Committee returns its sincere thanks.

Dr. Luther H. Evans, the National Supervisor of the Historical Records Survey of the W.P.A. has been of the greatest assistance, in many of the states, by supplementing the efforts of the agents of the Committee in bringing into the record, and ensuring the preservation, of a large number of files which otherwise would have been unrecorded.

Finally the Committee wishes to thank Daniel C. Haskell and Karl Brown, of the New York Public Library, for their contribution of the Bibliography of local lists of newspaper files, which we print as an appendix.

James Thayer Gerould

Cooperating with the Committee

Alabama. Mrs. Marie B. Owen, Dept. of Archives and History, Montgomery

Arizona. Estelle Lutrell, Univ. of Arizona, Tucson

Arkansas. Miss Jim P. Matthews, Univ. of Arkansas, Fayetteville

California. Mabel R. Gillis, California State Library, Sacramento
Southern: Blanche E. McKown, Public Library, Los Angeles
Central: Harold L. Leupp, Univ. of California, Berkeley

Canada. Chairman: W. S. Wallace, Univ. of Toronto, Toronto
D. E. Cameron, Univ. of Alberta, Edmonton
W. J. Healy, Provincial Library, Winnipeg
W. Kaye Lamb, Provincial Library, Victoria
Grace Lewis, Dominion Bureau of Statistics, Ottawa
G. R. Lomer, McGill Univ., Montreal
Angus Mowat, Public Library, Saskatoon
John Ridington, Univ. of British Columbia, Vancouver

Colorado. Malcolm J. Wyer, Public Library, Denver

Connecticut. Fremont Rider, Wesleyan Univ., Middletown

Delaware. Arthur L. Bailey, Wilmington Institute, Wilmington Free Library

District of Columbia. Roma K. Kauffman, Library of Congress, Washington

Florida. Elmer J. Emig, Univ. of Florida, Gainesville

Georgia. Duncan Burnet, Univ. of Georgia, Athens

Idaho. M. Belle Sweet, Univ. of Idaho, Moscow

Illinois. P. L. Windsor, Univ. of Illinois, Urbana
Chicago District: A. F. Kuhlman, Vanderbilt Univ., Nashville, Tenn.
Springfield District: Paul M. Angle, Illinois State Historical Library, Springfield

Indiana. Louis J. Bailey, Indiana State Library, Indianapolis

Iowa. Mary B. Humphrey, State Univ. of Iowa, Iowa City

Kansas. Charles M. Baker, Univ. of Kansas, Lawrence

Kentucky. T. D. Clark, Univ. of Kentucky, Lexington

Louisiana. James A. McMillen, Louisiana State Univ., Baton Rouge
New Orleans: Helmer L. Webb, Union College, Schenectady, N. Y.

Maine. G. G. Wilder, Bowdoin College, Brunswick

Maryland. J. L. Wheeler, Enoch Pratt Free Library, Baltimore

Massachusetts. E. H. Redstone, Public Library, Boston

Michigan. W. W. Bishop, Univ. of Michigan, Ann Arbor

Minnesota. Gertrude Krausnick, Minnesota Historical Society, St. Paul

Mississippi. Nannie H. Rice, Mississippi State College, State College

Missouri. Floyd C. Shoemaker, State Historical Society, Columbia

Montana. Mrs. Anne McDonnell, Historical Society of Montana, Helena

Nebraska, Gilbert H. Doane, Univ. of Wisconsin, Madison, Wisc.

Nevada. Thea C. Thompson, Univ. of Nevada, Reno

New Hampshire. Harold G. Rugg, Dartmouth College, Hanover

New Jersey. J. T. Gerould, Princeton Univ., Princeton

New Mexico. Wilma L. Shelton, Univ. of New Mexico, Albuquerque

New York. A. H. Shearer, Grosvenor Library, Buffalo
District Chairmen:
Fannie Borden, Vassar College, Poughkeepsie
Julian P. Boyd, Historical Society of Pennsylvania, Philadelphia
James Brewster, Connecticut State Library, Hartford, Conn.
Louis H. Fox, N. Y. Public Library, New York City
Donald B. Gilchrist, Univ. of Rochester, Rochester
J. D. Ibbotson, Hamilton College, Clinton
Otto Kinkeldey, Cornell Univ., Ithaca
Wharton Miller, Syracuse Univ., Syracuse
C. W. Spencer, Colgate Univ., Hamilton

North Carolina. William K. Boyd, Duke Univ., Durham

North Dakota. William H. Carlson, Univ. of North Dakota, Grand Forks

Ohio. Harlow Lindley, Ohio State Archeological and Historical Society, Columbus

Oklahoma. J. J. Hill, Univ. of Oklahoma, Norman

Oregon. E. Ruth Rockwood, Library Assoc. of Portland, Portland

Pennsylvania. Frances Dorrance, Wyoming Historical and Geological Society, Wilkes-Barre
Curtis W. Garrison, State Library and Museum, Harrisburg

Rhode Island. Herbert O. Brigham, State Library, Providence
H. B. VanHoesen, Brown Univ., Providence

South Carolina. M. G. Burnside, Columbia

South Dakota. Lawrence K. Fox, State Historical Society, Pierre

Tennessee, F. K. W. Drury, Public Library, Nashville

Texas. Julia Ideson, Public Library, Houston

Utah. Joanna H. Sprague, Public Library, Salt Lake City

Vermont. Harold G. Rugg, Dartmouth College, Hanover, N. H.

Virginia. Lester J. Cappon, Univ. of Virginia, Charlottesville

Washington. Charles W. Smith, Univ. of Washington, Seattle

West Virginia. L. D. Arnett, West Virginia Univ., Morgantown

Wisconsin. Joseph Schafer, Historical Society of Wisconsin, Madison

Wyoming. Margaret Burke, Wyoming State Library, Cheyenne

INTRODUCTION

"Great is journalism. Is not every editor a ruler of the world, being a persuader of it?"
—CARLYLE

A list showing the location of newspaper files has, for many years, been insistently demanded by historical scholars, genealogists, lawyers and economists, political scientists and newspaper men. Such lists as we now have, as for example, of the newspapers in the Library of Congress (1901), Wisconsin State Historical Society (1911), Illinois University (1910), Yale University (1915), the New York Public Library (1914), Virginia State Library (1912), Duke University (1932+), and a few other institutions, cover, in each case, only their own holdings, and record only a fraction of existing files. Most of these lists are seriously out of date.

The value of the information which these papers contain can hardly be overestimated. They are a primary source for national and local history and for a study of the evolution of economic and political opinion. Cases at law are frequently determined by citations from the press. In the advertising pages and commercial columns are found the record of our industrial and business history.

The increasing cost of binding and storage, and the deterioration of the paper on which the newspapers are printed, have discouraged collection, and in some cases, have been responsible for the scrapping of files which should somewhere be preserved.

The list presents, in a geographical arrangement of places of publication, files of newspapers from 1821 to date (1936) found in the libraries of the United States and Canada, and as far as possible, those that are preserved in county courthouses, in newspaper offices, and in private collections.

Selection of titles:

There are no definitions sufficiently clear to guide in the selection of titles in that narrow field between newspapers and periodicals. Selection for this list has been based on content whenever the information was available, rather than on periodicity or form. In general we have attempted to eliminate all titles already appearing in the previous union lists in this series, also those confined to news items of chief interest to a narrow group. Thus organs of labor unions, religious denominations, fraternal lodges, etc. have been omitted. Records of such papers have been sent to the H. W. Wilson Company, for possible use in later editions of the Union list of serials.

Our original plan called for the inclusion of newspapers published abroad which are held in our libraries. Examination of the material sent in proved that, while the number of titles was extensive, in most cases the files were so fragmentary as to be of little use. For hundreds of them only one or two issues were reported. It was the opinion of the Committee that the value of the information assembled did not justify the cost of printing. However, we have attempted to indicate the outstanding collections, on later pages. The original slips have been deposited in the Union Catalog at the Library of Congress where information on specific titles is available.

Method:

Bibliographical aids for the determination of the history and terminal dates of American newspapers are very few and in many cases those available are not entirely trustworthy. County histories are numerous but of varying value. Many of the articles are written by pioneers long after the events they chronicle, and in their accounting for the newspapers bristle with such phrases as "early in the '80's"—"between 1870 and 1875"—"soon after the failure of the Star, the News was begun," etc., etc.

The greatest single help in establishing the history of papers has been the trade directories. A file of Rowell's American newspaper directory, 1869-79 and Ayer's Directory of newspapers and periodicals 1880 to date has been part of our office equipment for the past three years. Every paper whose history was not reported to us otherwise, has been traced through these volumes. Before 1868 there is no similar list for the papers of the country as a whole. For this reason we have been unable to give even approximate ending dates for papers printed in that period. In using the trade bibliographies we have assumed that the paper ended the year before its last listing. Since this is not always true, we have used a question mark to indicate that we have no conclusive proof.

Arrangement:

The arrangement is alphabetical by state or province, and city. Under each city the papers are arranged alphabetically by the first important word, disregarding the name of the town, names of the days of the week, and such words as indicate periodicity as daily, weekly, etc. The key word is capitalized to facilitate quick identification.

Acknowledgment:

It is obvious that a large share of the credit for the list belongs to the State chairmen whose names appear on the opposite page. Without their active aid, so detailed a piece of work could not have been completed within the time and the money at our disposal. The completeness of the record of holdings, as well as the bibliographical information varies greatly in the various states and provinces. It is in exact proportion to the interest, the resourcefulness, and the energy of the State chairman, plus the amount of cooperation he was able to inspire. In some states the chairman himself has done most of the work, in others the organization being outlined, the actual work has been delegated. A list of all of those who have contributed would run to hundreds of names. It is impossible to include them all, but to all the Editor returns her grateful thanks.

We wish particularly to acknowledge the fine organization in Alabama, worked out by Thomas M. Owen, Jr., now at the National Archives in Washington. In few states was so careful an examination made of resources of county courthouses. Mr. Burnet's plans for Georgia were carried out by Miss Louise Fant of the University of Georgia. Mr. Glenn R. Maynard of the University of Illinois has supplemented the work of the state chairman. In Iowa, Dr. B. F. Shambaugh furnished a record for the extensive collection in the State Historical Society of Iowa, of which he is Secretary. One of the most exhaustive lists for any library was prepared by Nyle H. Miller of the Kansas Historical Society. Miss Mary N. Barton sent us the items for Maryland in such completeness that further search for information was unnecessary. In Massachusetts our thanks are due to Mr. Clarence S. Brigham, of the American Antiquarian Society, whose bibliography on early American newspapers has given us the history of papers still in existence when his list ends and ours begins; to R. W. G. Vail for organizing a staff to catalogue the thousands of titles owned by the society, and to Miss Cecile Barsky for the accurate and generous inclusion of bibliographical information which accompanied the record of holdings. We are indebted to Mr. V. M. Henderson, late librarian of the State Library, Carson City, Nevada, for a detailed list of the holdings of that library. Miss Allene Ramage has been of the greatest help to us, by her accurate detail of papers owned by Duke University. We are indebted to Laurence H. Bartlett, newspaper librarian of the State Historical and Archaeological Society of Ohio for his help. Miss Dorothy Spofford is credited by the state chairmen of Rhode Island as "having done all the work." In Texas, Miss Louise Franklin at the Public Library in Houston, and E. W. Winkler at the University of Texas have worked with us. Miss Lesley M. Heathcote, University of Washington, sent in the first completed list, and set a very high standard for those to follow.

We appreciate very much the cooperation of hundreds of newspaper editors in supplying and in allowing us to print a record of their office files. Some few have feared that if their files were known, the demands for their examination would be excessive. Since it is a primary function of the library, rather than the newspaper office to answer such requests, only the record of a unique file would invite inspection. If the file is unique, we have ventured to suggest the importance of safeguarding it by transfer to a fireproof depository, where its examination would be supervised.

In a problem of this kind, one compiler steals shamelessly from all predecessors. We owe much to all those who have published their own state lists; to Douglas C. McMurtrie for his work on papers of the pioneer periods in various sections of the country; to Edward Larocque Tinker for permission to examine his records of titles found since the publication of his Bibliography of the French newspapers and periodicals in Louisiana; to Elrie Robinson, Editor of the St. Francisville (La.) Democrat, who has furnished much information on the papers of the South, in his extensive library.

Agents of the W.P.A. working under the direction of Luther Evans, of the Historical Records Survey, have reported scores of collections unknown to our state chairmen, notably in Louisiana, Mississippi, West Virginia, Florida, Massachusetts and Pennsylvania. We are particularly indebted to Kelsey Ballou Sweatt for reports on Massachusetts libraries.

Miss Roma Kaye Kauffman has worked on the list from the beginning. She has transcribed the records of the Library of Congress, done extensive research on incomplete and elusive entries, edited whole sections of the list, and carried on a considerable part of the correspondence. To her, and to Miss Mary Bair, who prepared much of the copy for the printer, and proof-read the entire list, we owe a very considerable debt.

W. G.

Abbreviations and Symbols

Ja	January	N	November	ir	published irregularly
F	February	D	December	ed	edition
Mr	March	d	daily	+	to date
Ap	April	sw	semi-weekly	?	information incomplete
My	May	tw	tri-weekly	||	publication ended
Je	June	w	weekly	[ ]	incomplete dates
Jl	July	m	monthly	–	from the former to and including the latter
Ag	August	sm	semi-monthly		
S	September	tm	tri-monthly		
O	October				

pub when used in the list of holdings, indicates the publisher

A star (*) preceeding an entry indicates that this title is in "Bibliography of American newspapers, 1690-1820" compiled by C. S. Brigham and published in the Proceedings of the American Antiquarian Society. Holdings before 1821 are not repeated in this list.

Symbols used to Designate Cooperating Institutions

The symbols are, as nearly as possible, the same as those used in previous lists. Additional symbols are made up in the same way, i.e., the symbol for a library is a combination of letters arbitrarily assigned to state, city and individual library. The state symbol alone always indicates the State library; followed by Hi, the State historical library, followed by U, the State university library. The state symbol, followed by a city designation, indicates the public library; this followed by other letters shows certain libraries in that city; e.g. I, indicates Illinois state library; IHi, the State historical library; IU, the State university; IC, the Chicago public library; ICJ, the John Crerar library; ICU, the University of Chicago library, etc.

SYMBOLS

Alabama

A	Dept. of archives and history, Montgomery
AAC	Henry county court house, Abbeville
AAnC	Covington county court house, Andalusia
AAnnC	Calhoun county court house, Anniston
AAsC	Clay county court house, Ashland
AAtC	Limestone county court house, Athens
AAvC	Collector of taxes, Ashville
AB	Public library, Birmingham
ABC	Jefferson county court house, Birmingham
ABH	Howard college, Birmingham
ABmC	Baldwin county court house, Bay Minette
ABrC	Escambia county court house, Brewton
ABuC	Choctaw county court house, Butler
ACC	Wilcox county court house, Camden
ACaC	Pickens county court house, Carrollton
ACeC	Cherokee county court house, Center
ACenC	Bibb county court house, Centerville
AChC	Washington county court house, Chatom
AClC	Barbour county court house, Clayton
ACnC	Chilton county court house, Clanton
ACoC	Shelby county court house, Columbiana
ACuC	Cullman county court house, Cullman
ADC	Tallapoosa county court house, Dadeville
ADeC	Morgan county court house, Decatur
ADoC	Houston county court house, Dothan
ADsC	Winston county court house, Double Springs
AEC	Coffee county court house, Elba
AEnC	Coffee county court house, Enterprise
AEuC	Barbour county court house, Eufaula
AEvC	Conecuh county court house, Evergreen
AEwC	Greene county court house, Eutaw
AFC	Fayette county court house, Fayette
AFlC	Lauderdale county court house, Florence
AFpC	De Kalb county court house, Fort Payne
AGC	Etowah county court house, Gadsden
AGeC	Geneva county court house, Geneva
AGnC	Butler county court house, Greenville
AGrC	Hale county court house, Greensboro
AGuC	Marshall county court house, Guntersville
AGvC	Clarke county court house, Grove Hill
AHA	Advertiser-journal, Haleyville
AHS	Haleyville spotlight, Haleyville
AHaC	Lowndes county court house, Hayneville
AHeC	Cleburne county court house, Heflin
AHmC	Marion county court house, Hamilton
AHuC	Madison county court house, Huntsville
AJC	Walker county court house, Jasper
ALC	Chambers county court house, Lafayette
ALiC	Marengo county court house, Linden
ALnC	Sumter county court house, Livingston
ALuC	Crenshaw county court house, Luverne
AM	Free public library, Mobile
AMC	Mobile county court house, Mobile
AMP	Mobile press, Mobile
AMaC	Perry county court house, Marion
AMaJ	Judson college, Marion
AMaT	Marion times-standard office, Marion
AMnC	Monroe county court house, Monroeville
AMoC	Montgomery county court house, Montgomery
AMtC	Lawrence county court house, Moulton
AOC	Blount county court house, Oneonta
AOS	Southern democrat, Oneonta
AOpC	Lee county court house, Opelika
AOzC	Dale county court house, Ozark
AOzS	Southern star, Ozark
APC	St. Clair county court house, Pell City
APrC	Autauga county court house, Prattville
ARC	Coosa county court house, Rockford
ARuC	Franklin county court house, Russellville
ASC	Jackson county court house, Scottsboro
ASeC	Russell county court house, Seale
ASlC	Dallas county court house, Selma
ASlT	Times-journal, Selma
ATC	Talladega county court house, Talladega
ATkC	Macon county court house, Tuskegee
ATrC	Pike county court house, Troy
ATsC	Colbert county court house, Tuscumbia
ATuC	Tuscaloosa county court house, Tuscaloosa
AU	University of Alabama, University
AUsC	Bullock county court house, Union Springs
AVC	Lamar county court house, Vernon
AWC	Randolph county court house, Wedowee
AWeC	Elmore county court house, Wetumpka

Alaska

AlHi	Alaska historical library and museum, Juneau
AlPP	Petersburg press, Petersburg

Arkansas

ArAH	Henderson state teachers college, Arkadelphia
ArBA	Arkansas college, Batesville
ArBeB	Benton county record and democrat, Bentonville
ArBlC	Blytheville courier-news, Blytheville
ArCH	Hendrix college, Conway
ArDB	De Queen bee, De Queen
ArFD	Fayetteville democrat, Fayetteville
ArFP	Progressive star, Fayetteville
ArFs	Carnegie City library, Fort Smith
ArFsT	Times record, Fort Smith
ArHL	Ashley county leader, Hamburg
ArHe	Public library, Helena
ArHi	History commission, Little Rock
ArHuM	Madison county record, Huntsville
ArL	Public library, Little Rock
ArMA	Agricultural and mechanical college, Magnolia
ArMB	Banner-news, Magnolia
ArMoA	Agricultural college, Monticello
ArP	Public library, Pine Bluff
ArSJ	John Brown college, Siloam Springs
ArSuN	New Subiaco Abbey, Subiaco
ArT	Public library, Texarkana
ArU	University of Arkansas, Fayetteville

Arizona

Az	Arizona state law and legislative reference library, Phoenix
AzDD	Douglas daily dispatch, Douglas
AzHH	Lloyd C. Henning, Holbrook
AzMJ	Mesa journal-tribune, Mesa
AzPM	Estate of Col. J. H. McClintock, Phoenix
AzPMe	Messenger, Phoenix
AzPR	Arizona republic, Phoenix
AzPrG	Museum, Old Governor's Mansion, Prescott
AzPrJ	A. A. Johns, Prescott
AzSH	St. Johns herald, Saint Johns
AzScS	Star, Somerton
AzTC	Tucson citizen, Tucson
AzTP	Arizona pioneers historical society, Tucson
AzU	University of Arizona, Tucson

California

C	California state library, Sacramento
C-S	California state library, Sutro Branch, San Francisco
CA	Free library, Alameda
CAl	Public library, Alhambra
CAlt	Modoc county free public library, Alturas
CAn	Public library, Anaheim
CAnB	Anaheim bulletin, Anaheim
CAr	Free public library, Arcadia
CAz	Public library, Azusa
CAzH	Azusa herald and pomotropic office, Azusa
CB	Kern county free library, Bakersfield
CBC	Bakersfield Californian, Bakersfield
CBe	Free public library, Berkeley
CBeA	Armstrong college, Berkeley
CBh	Public library, Beverly Hills
CBpN	Buena Park news, Buena Park
CBr	Public library, Brawley
CBu	Public library, Burlingame
CC	Ralph Chandler Harrison memorial library, Carmel
CCa	Camarillo Branch, Ventura county free library, Camarillo
CCh	Public library, Chula Vista
CClP	Pomona college, Claremont
CCo	Colusa county free library, Colusa
CCol	Public library, Colton
CCor	Public library, Coronado Beach
CCoro	Public library, Corona
CCov	Public library, Covina
CCrD	Del Norte triplicate office, Crescent City
CCuS	Culver City star-news, Culver City
CE	El Segundo Branch, Los Angeles country free library, El Segundo
CEc	Free public library, El Centro
CEcI	Imperial county free library, El Centro
CEs	Public library, Escondido
CEsT	Escondido times-advocate, Escondido
CEu	Humboldt county free library, Eureka
CF	Solano county free library, Fairfield
CFaE	Fall Brook enterprise office, Fall Brook
CFi	Fillmore Branch, Ventura county free library, Fillmore
CFr	Fresno county free library, Fresno
CFrB	Fresno bee and republican, Fresno
CG	Free public library, Glendale
CGN	Glendale news-press, Glendale
CGlP	Glendora press-gleaner, Glendora
CHe	Free public library, Hemet
CHo	San Benito county free library, Hollister
CI	Inyo county free library, Independence
CK	Public library, King City
CL	Public library, Los Angeles
CLC	California Jewish voice, Los Angeles
CLH	Highland Park news-herald, Los Angeles
CLJ	Los Angeles junior college, Los Angeles
CLL	Los Angeles county law library, Los Angeles
CLM	Los Angeles museum library, Los Angeles
CLMe	Metropolitan news-press, Los Angeles
CLMo	Monk library of Arizoniana, Los Angeles
CLN	North Hollywood sun-record, Las Angeles
CLO	Occidental college, Los Angeles
CLSM	Southwestern museum, Los Angeles
CLSU	University of Southern California, Los Angeles
CLSp	San Pedro news-pilot, Los Angeles
CLSz	California staats-zeitung, Los Angeles
CLU	University of California at Los Angeles
CLW	Westward Hills press, Los Angeles
CLaS	South Coast news, Laguna Beach
CLb	Public library, Long Beach
CLbP	Press-telegram, Long Beach
CLo	Public library, Lodi
CLom	Free public library, Lompoc
CLv	Bonita Union high school, LaVerne
CM	Madera county free library, Madera
CMa	Marysville City library, Marysville
CMaA	Appeal-democrat office, Marysville
CMaC	Yuba county auditor's office, Marysville
CMe	Merced county free library, Merced
CMlC	Mills college, Mills College
CMo	Stanislaus county free library, Modesto
CMoB	Modesto bee, Modesto
CMoM	McHenry public library, Modesto
CMon	Public library, Monrovia
CMont	Monterey public library, Monterey
CMoor	Moorpark Branch, Ventura county free library, Moorpark
CMp	Monterey Park Branch, Los Angeles county free library, Monterey Park
CMv	Public library, Mountain View
CN	Public library, National City
CNpN	News office, Newport Beach
CO	Oakland free library, Oakland
COc	Public library, Oceanside
COcB	Oceanside blade-tribune, Oceanside
COcC	Carlsbad Union high school, Oceanside
COn	Chaffey library, Ontario
COr	Public library, Oroville
COx	Oxnard Branch, Ventura county free library, Oxnard

CALIFORNIA—*Continued*

CP	Public library, Pasadena
CPS	Pasadena star-news, Pasadena
CPa	Public library, Palo Alto
CPe	Public library, Petaluma
CPg	Public library, Pacific Grove
CPI	Piru Branch, Ventura county free library, Piru
CPo	Public library, Pomona
CPoP	Progress-bulletin, Pomona
CQ	Plumas county free library, Quincy
CRb	Tehama county free library, Red Bluff
CRe	Redondo Beach Branch, Los Angeles county free library, Redondo Beach
CRed	A. K. Smiley public library, Redlands
CRedU	University of Redlands, Redlands
CRI	Public library, Richmond
CRIbN	Riverbank news, Riverbank
CRiv	Public library, Riverside
CRivC	Chemawa Jr. high school, Riverside
CSa	Monterey county free library, Salinas
CSan	Public library, Santa Ana
CSanO	Orange county free library, Santa Ana
CSb	Free public library, Santa Barbara
CSbe	Free public library, San Bernardino
CSbeS	San Bernardino county free library, San Bernardino
CSd	Public library, San Diego
CSdT	State teachers college, San Diego
CSeP	Seal Beach post and wave, Seal Beach
CSeII	Selma irrigator and enterprise, Selma
CSf	Public library, San Francisco
CSfP	Pacific union club, San Francisco
CSI	Public library, Sierra Madre
CSj	Free public library, San Jose
CSl	Free public library, San Luis Obispo
CSIT	San Luis Obispo telegram tribune, San Luis Obispo
CSle	Free public library, San Leandro
CSm	Public library, San Marino
CSmH	Henry E. Huntington library, San Marino
CSma	Public library, San Mateo
CSmar	Public library, Santa Maria
CSmo	Public library, Santa Monica
CSp	Public library, South Pasadena
CSpa	Santa Paula Branch, Ventura county free library, Santa Paula
CSpaD	Dean Hobbs Blanchard memorial library, Santa Paula
CSr	Public library, San Rafael
CSro	Free public library, Santa Rosa
CSs	Public library, South San Francisco
CSt	Stanford university, Stanford University
CSt-H	Hoover war library, Stanford University
CSto	Free public library, Stockton
CStoI	Stockton independent, Stockton
CSu	Lassen county free library, Susanville
CSun	Free public library, Sunnyvale
CTeN	Tehachapi news, Tehachapi
CU	University of California, Berkeley
CU-B	Bancroft library, University of California, Berkeley
CU-L	University of California law library, Berkeley
CU-P	Bureau of public administration library, and Library of economic research, University of California, Berkeley
CUp	Public library, Upland
CVe	Ventura county free library, Ventura
CVeS	Ventura county star, Ventura
CVeV	Ventura Branch, Ventura county free library, Ventura
CWh	Public library, Whittier
CWhW	Whittier college, Whittier
CWIN	Willits news, Willits
CY	Siskiyou county free library, Yreka
CYC	Siskiyou county court house, Yreka

Colorado

Co	Colorado state library, Denver
CoAT	Adams state teachers college, Alamosa
CoAuP	Ault progress, Ault
CoBoC	Daily camera, Boulder
CoC	Public library, Colorado Springs
CoCC	Colorado college, Colorado Springs
CoCa	Public library, Canon City
CoCaG	Mr. W. G. Green, Canon City
CoCcT	Times-record, Cripple Creek
CoCrE	Empire-courier, Craig
CoD	Denver public library, Denver
CoDR	Rocky Mountain news, Denver
CoDU	University of Denver, Denver
CoDV	Mr. John Van Male, Denver
CoDeT	Deertrail tribune, Deertrail
CoDelP	Prospector, Del Norte
CoDu	Public library, Durango
CoEN	National Park library, Estes Park
CoEpT	Estes Park trail, Estes Park
CoF	Public library, Florence
CoFc	Public library, Fort Collins
CoFl	Public library, Fort Lupton
CoG	Public library, Greeley
CoGS	State college of education, Greeley
CoGJ	Carnegie public library, Grand Junction
CoGuN	News-champion and republican, Gunnison
CoGuW	Western state college, Gunnison
CoHI	Colorado state historical society, Denver
CoHoE	Holyoke enterprise, Holyoke
CoL	Public library, Longmont
CoLT	Longmont daily times-call, Longmont
CoLeH	Herald-democrat, Leadville
CoLiI	Littleton independent, Littleton
CoLJ	Woodruff memorial library, La Junta
CoLo	Public library, Loveland
CoMG	Mead gazette, Mead
CoMoJ	Monte Vista journal, Monte Vista
CoP	McClelland public library, Pueblo
CoPS	Star-journal, Pueblo
CoPU	L'Unione, Pueblo
CoPV	La Voce del popolo, Pueblo
CoRT	Rifle telegram, Rifle
CoS	Public library, Salida
CoU	University of Colorado, Boulder

Connecticut

Ct	Connecticut state library, Hartford
CtAn	Public library, Ansonia
CtB	Public library, Bridgeport
CtBe	Free public library, Bethel
CtBrl	Public library, Bristol
CtD	Danbury library, Danbury
CtDe	Derby public library, Derby
CtE	Public library, East Hartford
CtEh	Public library, East Hampton
CtGr	Greenwich library, Greenwich
CtH	Public library, Hartford
CtHC	Case library, Theological Seminary, Hartford
CtHCo	Courant, Hartford
CtHT	Trinity college, Hartford
CtHTI	Times, Hartford
CtHWe	Martin Welles, Hartford
CtHI	Connecticut historical society, Hartford
CtLL	John H. Lancaster, Litchfield
CtLW	Wolcott and Litchfield circulating library, Litchfield
CtMHI	Middlesex county historical society, Middletown
CtMR	Russell library, Middletown
CtMY	Mystic and Noank library, Mystic
CtN	Howard Whittemore memorial library, Naugatuck
CtNb	New Britain public library, New Britain
CtNbH	Herald, New Britain
CtNbI	New Britain institute, New Britain
CtNc	New Canaan library, New Canaan
CtNcH	J. E. Hersam, New Canaan
CtNh	Free public library, New Haven
CtNIC	Connecticut college, New London
CtNm	Public library, New Milford
CtNmT	New Milford times, New Milford
CtNw	Otis library, Norwich
CtNwC	Mrs. A. H. Chase, Norwich
CtNwP	Peck library, Norwich
CtPIS	Agnes L. Smith, Plantsville
CtRo	Public library, Rockville
CtS	Scoville memorial library, Salisbury
CtSe	Public library, Seymour
CtShe	Plumb memorial library, Shelton
CtSm	South Manchester library, South Manchester
CtSo	Public library, Southington
CtSp	Pequot library, Southport
CtSta	Ferguson library, Stamford
CtStr	Stratford library association, Stafford Springs
CtT	Thompson library, Thompson
CtTo	Torrington library, Torrington
CtW	Wesleyan university, Middletown
CtWa	Wallingford public library, Wallingford
CtWb	Silas Bronson library, Waterbury
CtWg	Gunn memorial library, Washington
CtWn	Beardsley library, Winsted
CtWnG	Gilbert school, Winsted
CtWp	Public library, Westport
CtWr	Free library, Windsor
CtWt	Watertown library association, Watertown
CtY	Yale university, New Haven

District of Columbia

DA	Department of agriculture
DC	Department of commerce
DCE	Carnegie endowment for international peace
DCHI	Columbia historical society
DCU	Catholic university of America
DGU	Georgetown university
DHU-M	Moorland foundation, Howard university
DIC	Interstate commerce commission
DK	Dr. G. C. Keidel
DL	Department of labor
DLC	Library of Congress
DPU	Pan-American union
DSG	Surgeon general's office
DTJ	Takoma journal, Takoma Park, D.C.
DW	Public library of the District of Columbia

Delaware

DeHI	Historical society of Delaware, Wilmington
DeST	Smyrna times, Smyrna
DeU	University of Delaware, Newark
DeWI	Wilmington institute free library, Wilmington
DeWN	News journal, Wilmington

Florida

F	Florida state library, Tallahassee
FArA	Arcadian, Arcadia
FBC	County commissioner, Bradenton
FBoC	Holmes county court house, Bonifay
FC	Public library, Clearwater
FCg	Public library, Coral Gables
FCIC	Clerk of circuit court, Clermont
FCo	Public library, Coconut Grove
FDaF	T. E. Fitzgerald, Daytona Beach
FDaN	Daytona Beach news-journal, Daytona Beach
FDe	Free public library, De Land
FDeS	Stetson university, De Land
FFD	Mrs. W. A. Davis, Fernandina
FFL	H. D. Loham, Fernandina
FFI	Public library, Fort Lauderdale
FGS	Florida state museum, Gainesville
FGcC	Clerk of the court, Green Cove Springs
FHI	Florida historical society, Jacksonville
FJ	Free public library, Jacksonville
FJJ	Jacksonville journal, Jacksonville
FJR	W. H. Rowton, Jacksonville
FKC	Monroe county court house, Key West
FKS	Sisters of the Holy Name, Key West
FKIC	Osceola county court house, Kissimmee
FL	Public library, Lakeland
FLbC	Clerk of circuit court, Lake Butler
FMH	Miami herald, Miami
FMaE	Enterprise-recorder, Madison
FMaS	Carlton Smith, Madison
FMarC	Jackson county court house, Marianna
FMbT	Miami Beach times, Miami Beach
FMIC	Santa Rosa county court house, Milton
FMnW	Women's club, Mantee
FMoC	Jefferson county court house, Monticello
FO	Albertson public library, Orlando
FOG	J. G. Glass, Orlando
FPC	Escambia county court house, Pensacola
FPY	J. C. Yonge, Pensacola
FPaC	Putnam county court house, Palatka
FPeC	Taylor county court house, Perry
FS	Public library, Sanford
FSaC	St. Johns county court house, Saint Augustine
FSaHi	St. Augustine historical society, Saint Augustine
FSrB	Miss Anne Biggs, Sarasota
FSrR	L. D. Reagin, Sarasota
FSrW	Mrs. C. V. S. Wilson, Sarasota
FStaC	Bradford county court house, Starke
FStuN	Stuart daily news, Stuart
FTS	State college for women, Tallahassee
FTW	Walker memorial library, Tallahassee
FTa	Public library, Tampa
FTaM	Tampa Bay museum, Municipal auditorium, Tampa
FTaP	Miss Carrie Pelot, Tampa
FTaT	Tampa daily times, Tampa
FTIC	Brevard county court house, Titusville
FTvC	Clerk of circuit court, Tavares
FU	University of Florida, Gainesville
FWb	Memorial library, West Palm Beach
FWpR	Rollins college, Winter Park

SYMBOLS

Georgia

G	Georgia state library, Atlanta
GA	Carnegie library, Atlanta
GAA	Atlanta university, Atlanta
GAC	Clark university, Atlanta
GAO	Ordinary, Atlanta
GAlC	Clerk, Alma
GAlO	Ordinary, Alma
GAsC	Clerk, Ashburn
GAtC	Clerk, Athens
GAtCo	E. M. Coulter, Athens
GAtMa	Dan Magill, Athens
GAtS	Stone printing company, Athens
GAuO	Ordinary, Augusta
GBaW	E. A. Wimberley, Bainbridge
GBar	Carnegie library, Barnesville
GBlC	Clerk, Blakeley
GBrC	Clerk, Brunswick
GBrCa	Mrs. G. V. Cate, Brunswick
GBrO	Ordinary, Brunswick
GBuC	Clerk, Buchanan
GBueC	Clerk, Buena Vista
GBufA	Buford advertiser, Buford
GCC	Clerk, Columbus
GCaC	Clerk, Carnesville
GCalC	Gordon county court house, Calhoun
GCamO	Ordinary, Camilla
GCeC	Clerk, Cedartown
GCeO	Ordinary, Cedartown
GCeS	Sheriff, Cedartown
GClC	Clerk, Claxton
GClO	Ordinary, Claxton
GClaC	Clerk, Clarkesville
GClaO	Ordinary, Clarkesville
GClayC	Clerk, Clayton
GCo	Public library, Covington
GCoC	Clerk, Covington
GCoO	Ordinary, Covington
GCocC	Clerk, Cochran
GCocO	Ordinary, Cochran
GCocS	Sheriff, Cochran
GColS	South Georgia teachers college, Collegeboro
GColqC	Clerk, Colquitt
GColqO	Ordinary, Colquitt
GColqS	Sheriff, Colquitt
GCorB	J. W. Bivins, Cordele
GCorD	Dispatch, Cordele
GCorO	Ordinary, Cordele
GCu	Carnegie library, Cuthbert
GD	Public library, Decatur
GDC	Clerk, Decatur
GDE	Emory university, Decatur
GDaC	Clerk, Dallas
GDahN	North Georgia college, Dahlonega
GDahoO	Ordinary, Dahlonega
GDalM	T. F. Miller, Dalton
GDalO	Ordinary, Dalton
GDalP	Kate Phillips, Dalton
GDalW	Miss Willie S. White, Dalton
GDarM	R. S. Martin, Darien
GDoC	Clerk, Donaldsville
GDouC	Clerk, Douglas
GDu	Carnegie library, Dublin
GDuC	Clerk, Dublin
GDuCo	Courier-herald, Dublin
GDuO	Ordinary, Dublin
GEC	Clerk, Eatonton
GEO	Ordinary, Eatonton
GElC	Clerk, Elberton
GElO	Ordinary, Elberton
GEllC	Clerk, Ellaville
GF	Carnegie library, Fitzgerald
GFO	Ordinary, Fitzgerald
GFoB	W. R. Branham, Fort Valley
GFoO	Ordinary, Fort Valley
GFolC	Clerk, Folkston
GForB	Bessie Tift library, Forsyth
GForO	Ordinary, Forsyth
GFrC	Clerk, Franklin
GFrO	Ordinary, Franklin
GGO	Ordinary, Gainesville
GGrC	Clerk, Greensboro
GGrO	Ordinary, Greensboro
GGreC	Clerk, Greenville
GGrlO	Ordinary, Griffin
GHaC	Clerk, Hartwell
GHi	Georgia historical society, Savannah
GHlO	Ordinary, Hinesville
GHoC	Banks county court house, Homer
GLN	News-herald, Lawrenceville
GLO	Ordinary, Lawrenceville
GLaC	Clerk, Lafayette
GLav	Carnegie library, Lavonia
GLeC	Clerk, Lexington
GLeO	Ordinary, Lexington
GLoO	Ordinary, Louisville
GMC	Clerk, Macon
GMM	Washington memorial library, Macon
GMW	Wesleyan college, Macon
GMadO	Ordinary, Madison
GMarO	Ordinary, Marietta
GMeA	Advertiser, Metter
GMiC	Clerk, Milledgeville
GMiF	Mrs. David Ferguson, Milledgeville
GMiG	Georgia state college for women, Milledgeville
GMiH	T. M. Hall, Milledgevill
GMiO	Ordinary, Milledgeville
GNO	Ordinary, Nahunta
GNaC	Clerk, Nashville
GOC	Clerk, Ocilla
GPeO	Ordinary, Pearson
GQ	Brooks county library association, Quitman
GQO	Ordinary, Quitman
GR	Carnegie library, Rome
GRC	Floyd county court house, Rome
GRN	Rome news-tribune, Rome
GS	Public library, Savannah
GSC	Chatham county court house, Savannah
GSD	De Renne library, Savannah
GSaC	Clerk, Sandersville
GSaO	Ordinary, Sandersville
GStB	Bulloch times, Statesboro
GTC	Upson county court house, Thomaston
GThC	Clerk, Thomson
GToC	Clerk, Toccoa
GToP	Public school, Toccoa
GTrC	Clerk, Trenton
GU	University of Georgia, Athens
GVC	Clerk, Valdosta
GVCu	Fannie Curry, Valdosta
GVG	Georgia state womans college, Valdosta
GVIW	Ernest Whitchard, Vidalia
GWaC	Clerk, Watkinsville
GWoC	Clerk, Woodbine
GWoO	Ordinary, Woodbine

Hawaii

H	Public archives, Territory of Hawaii, Honolulu
HB	Bernice P. Bishop museum, Honolulu
HH	Library of Hawaii
HHi	Hawaiian historical society, Honolulu

Illinois

I	Illinois state library, Springfield
IA	Public library, Aurora
IAC	Aurora college, Aurora
IAb	John Mosser public library, Abingdon
IAl	Jennie D. Hayner memorial library, Alton
IAlS	Shurtleff college, Alton
IAlT	Alton evening telegraph, Alton
IAle	Mercer township free public library, Aledo
IAmN	Amboy news, Amboy
IAsG	Ashton gazette, Ashton
IAt	Public library, Atlanta
IB	Withers public library, Bloomington
IBHi	McLean county historical society, Bloomington
IBa	Batavia public library, Batavia
IBe	Public library, Belleville
IBeaS	Illinoian-star, Beardstown
IBel	Ida public library, Belvidere
IBenN	Evening news, Benton
IBrL	Byron R. Lewis, Bridgeport
IBu	Mason memorial public library, Buda
IC	Chicago public library, Chicago
ICHi	Chicago historical society, Chicago
ICJ	John Crerar library, Chicago
ICM	McCormick historical association, Chicago
ICMc	Douglas C. McMurtrie, Chicago
ICN	Newberry library, Chicago
ICU	University of Chicago, Chicago
ICa	Public library, Cairo
ICan	Parlin public library, Canton
ICarC	Carthage college, Carthage
ICarR	Carthage republican, Carthage
ICarr	Public library, Carrollton
ICe	Public library and reading room, Centralia
ICeS	Centralia evening sentinel, Centralia
ICh	Public library, Champaign
ICha	Free Carnegie library, Charleston
IChi	Township free public library, Chillicothe
ICl	Vespasian Warner public library, Clinton
ID	Public library, Decatur
IDH	Decatur herald and review, Decatur
IDa	Public library, Danville
IDe	Public library, De Kalb
IDi	Public library, Dixon
IEN	Northwestern university, Evanston
IEN-C	School of commerce, Northwestern university, Evanston
IEa	Public library, East Saint Louis
IEaS	St. Clair county record, East Saint Louis
IEd	Public library, Edwardsville
IElC	Elmhurst college, Elmhurst
IElL	Elmhurst leader, Elmhurst
IEldJ	Eldorado journal, Eldorado
IElmG	Elmwood gazette, Elmwood
IEuC	Eureka college, Eureka
IF	Public library, Freeport
IFaR	Wayne county record, Fairfield
IFaW	Wayne county press, Fairfield
IG	Free public library, Galesburg
IGK	Knox college, Galesburg
IGa	Galva township public library, Galva
IGe	Public library, Geneva
IGeB	Mrs. Charles Wilber Bailey, Geneva
IGeR	Geneva republican, Geneva
IGeW	Mrs. Joel Niles Wheeler, Geneva
IGlG	Glenview publishing co., Inc., Glenview
IGr	Public library, Granite City
IH	Public library, Hillsboro
IHM	Montgomery news Hillsboro
IHa	Mitchell-Carnegie public library, Harrisburg
IHaC	Louis E. Coffee, Harrisburg
IHaM	Jacob W. Myers, Harrisburg
IHe	Public library, Herrin
IHeyS	Heyworth star, Heyworth
IHi	State historical society, Springfield
IHig	Louis Latzer memorial public library, Highland
IHigN	Highland news-leader, Highland
IHigh	Public library, Highland Park
IHo	Public library, Hoopeston
IIT	Ipava tribune, Ipava
IJ	Public library, Jacksonville
IJoH	Joliet herald-news, Joliet
IK	Public library, Kewanee
IKK	Kewanee star-courier, Kewanee
IKa	Public library, Kankakee
ILP	Daily post-tribune, La Salle
ILa	Lawrence township public library, Lawrenceville
ILeM	McKendree college, Lebanon
ILer	Crumbaugh library, LeRoy
ILfC	Lake Forest college, Lake Forest
ILiS	St. Procopius college, Lisle
ILib	Cook memorial library, Libertyville
ILin	Public library, Lincoln
ILoT	London times, London Mills
ILoc	Public library, Lockport
IM	Public library, Moline
IMD	Moline daily dispatch, Moline
IMa	Macomb City free public library, Macomb
IMaW	Western Illinois state teachers college, Macomb
IMacT	McLeansboro times-leader, McLeansboro
IMad	Public library, Madison
IMar	Carnegie library, Marion
IMarP	Marion evening post, Marion
IMat	Public library, Mattoon
IMatJ	Daily journal-gazette and commercial star, Mattoon
IMeH	Metamora herald, Metamora
IMeM	Melvin motor, Melvin
IMi	Milford township public library, Milford
IMilE	Millstadt enterprise, Millstadt
IMin	Filger library, Minonk
IMinN	News-dispatch, Minonk
IMo	Warren county public library, Monmouth
IMoR	Monmouth daily review atlas, Monmouth
IMokN	News-bulletin, Mokena
IMon	Allerton public library, Monticello
IMtCR	Mt. Carmel daily republican-register, Mt. Carmel
INa	Nicholas library, Naperville
IO	Reddick's library, Ottawa
IOR	Daily republican-times, Ottawa
IOd	Public library, Odell
IOlM	Olney mail, Olney
IOr	Oregon township public library, Oregon
IP	Public library, Peoria
IPC	Peoria county court house, County clerks office, Peoria
IPJ	Peoria journal-transcript, Peoria
IPa	Carnegie-Schuyler library, Pana
IParB	Beacon-news, Paris
IPeV	Peotone vedette, Peotone
IPiP	Pike county democrat, Pittsfield
IPo	Public library, Pontiac

ILLINOIS—*Continued*

IPoL	Pontiac daily leader, Pontiac
IPol	Buffalo township public library, Polo
IPolT	Tri-county press, Polo
IPrE	Prophetstown echo, Prophetstown
IPri	Matson public library, Princeton
IQ	Free public library and reading room, Quincy
IQN	Herald-whig, Quincy
IR	Public library, Rock Island
IRA	Rock Island argus, Rock Island
IRaR	Raritan reporter, Raritan
IRo	Flagg township library, Rochelle
IRoR	Rochelle news, Rochelle
IRob	Robinson township Carnegie library, Robinson
IRoc	Public library, Rockford
IRuT	Rushville times, Rushville
ISa	Public library, Savanna
ISal	Bryan-Bennet library, Salem
ISeG	Gallatin democrat, Shawneetown
ISh	Sheldon township public library, Sheldon
ISp	Lincoln library, Springfield
ISpaN	Sparta news-plaindealer, Sparta
IStC	Public library, Saint Charles
ISte	Public library, Sterling
IStr	Public library Streator
ISy	Public library, Sycamore
ITeW	Teutopolis press, Teutopolis
IU	University of Illinois, Urbana
IUr	Free library, Urbana
IWaH	Mrs. Minnie Herrod, Warrensburg
IWat	Public library, Watseka
IWavJ	Waverly journal, Waverly
IWo	Public library, Woodstock

Iowa

IaA	Public library, Ames
IaAS	Iowa state college of Ames, Ames
IaAd	Public library, Adel
IaAdD	Dallas county news, Adel
IaAl	Public library, Alden
IaAlt	Public library, Alta
IaAltA	Alta advertiser, Alta
IaAnT	Anita tribune, Anita
IaAt	Free public library, Atlantic
IaAvJ	Avoca journal-herald, Avoca
IaB	Public library, Belmond
IaBl	Belmond independent, Belmond
IaBlD	Davis county republican, Bloomfield
IaBo	Ericson public library, Boone
IaBu	Free public library, Burlington
IaBuH	Burlington hawk-eye gazette, Burlington
IaC	Public library, Carroll
IaCb	Free public library, Council Bluffs
IaCe	Drake free public library, Centerville
IaCf	Public library, Cedar Falls
IaCfT	Iowa state teachers college, Cedar Falls
IaCh	Free public library, Charles City
IaChe	Public library, Cherokee
IaCl	Morgan Evarts-Clarion public library, Clarion
IaClaH	Clarinda herald-journal, Clarinda
IaClayR	Clayton county register, Elkader
IaCle	Carnegie public library, Clear Lake
IaCli	Free public library, Clinton
IaCo	Free public library, Corning
IaCoA	Adams county free press, Corning
IaCor	Carnegie public library, Corydon
IaCr	Free public library, Cedar Rapids
IaCrC	Coe college, Cedar Rapids
IaCrM	Iowa Masonic library, Cedar Rapids
IaCre	Public library, Cresco
IaD	Public library, Des Moines
IaDG	Grand View college, Des Moines
IaDH	Historical, memorial and art department of Iowa, Des Moines
IaDR	Des Moines register, Des Moines
IaDa	Public library, Davenport
IaDaP	Davenport public museum, Davenport
IaDeL	Luther college, Decorah
IaDeP	Decorah posten, Decorah
IaDu	Carnegie-Stout free public library, Dubuque
IaDuC	Columbia college, Dubuque
IaDun	Public library, Dunlap
IaE	Public library, Eagle Grove
IaElE	Elgin echo, Elgin
IaElkC	Clayton county register, Elkader
IaEsV	Vindicator and republican, Estherville
IaFP	Parsons college, Fairfield
IaFcS	Forest City summit, Forest City
IaFd	Free public library, Fort Dodge
IaFm	Cattermole memorial library, Fort Madison
IaG	Stewart public library, Grinnell
IaGG	Grinnell college, Grinnell
IaGc	Free public library, Grundy Center
IaGl	Public library, Glenwood
IaGlO	Glenwood opinion-tribune, Glenwood
IaGoG	Goldfield gazette, Goldfield
IaH	Free public library, Hampton
IaHa	Public library, Harlan
IaHamR	Hamburg reporter, Hamburg
IaHaw	Public library, Hawarden
IaHi	Iowa state historical society, Iowa City
IaHu	Free public library, Humboldt
IaHulS	Sioux county index, Hull
IaHum	Public library, Humeston
IaI	Public library, Indianola
IaIdP	Ida county pioneer-record, Ida Grove
IaIf	Carnegie-Ellsworth library, Iowa Falls
IaInB	Bulletin-journal, Independence
IaJB	Jefferson bee, Jefferson
IaK	Public library, Keokuk
IaKC	Keokuk citizen, Keokuk
IaKeE	Keota eagle, Keota
IaKn	Public library, Knoxville
IaLG	Graceland college, Lamoni
IaLa	Public library, Laurens
IaLanA	Allamakee journal, Lansing
IaLe	Public library, Le Mars
IaLeU	Western Union college, Le Mars
IaLnJ	Leon journal-reporter, Leon
IaM	Free public library, Malvern
IaMa	Free public library, Marengo
IaMars	Public library, Marshalltown
IaMc	Public library, Mason City
IaMeN	Mediapolis new era-news, Mediapolis
IaMgN	North Iowa times, McGregor
IaMo	Public library, Monticello
IaMoE	Monticello express, Monticello
IaMou	Public library, Mount Ayr
IaMp	Free public library, Mount Pleasant
IaMt	Cornell college, Mount Vernon
IaMtH	Hawkeye-record, Mount Vernon
IaMu	P. M. Musser public library, Muscatine
IaN	Free public library, Newton
IaNaR	Nashua reporter, Nashua
IaNh	Free public library, New Hampton
IaNhT	New Hampton tribune-gazette, New Hampton
IaNoA	Northwood anchor and index, Northwood
IaOn	Public library, Onawa
IaOs	Free public library, Osceola
IaOsaM	Mitchell county press, Osage
IaOt	Public library, Ottumwa
IaP	Carnegie-Viersen public library, Pella
IaPP	Pella chronicle, Pella
IaPeC	Perry daily chief, Perry
IaS	Nissen library, Saint Ansgar
IaSM	Mr. Martin Moe, Saint Ansgar
IaSa	Public library, Sanborn
IaSacS	Sac sun, Sac City
IaSc	Public library, Sioux City
IaScJ	Sioux City journal, Sioux City
IaSh	Public library, Sheldon
IaShe	Public library, Shenandoah
IaSiC	County auditor's office, Sibley
IaSidA	Sidney argus-herald, Sidney
IaSl	Public library, Storm Lake
IaSlB	Buena Vista college, Storm Lake
IaSlP	Storm Lake pilot-tribune, Storm Lake
IaT	Free public library, Tipton
IaTaB	Tabor beacon, Tabor
IaTo	Public library, Toledo
IaU	State university of Iowa, Iowa City
IaV	Free public library, Vinton
IaWC	Waterloo daily courier, Waterloo
IaWa	Public library, Washington
IaWapR	Wapello republican, Wapello
IaWau	Public library, Waukon
IaWc	Kendall Young library, Webster City
IaWcJ	Webster City freeman-journal, Webster City
IaWb	Enlow public library, West Branch
IaWeN	News-world, Wesley
IaWh	Public library, Whiting
IaWi	Public library, Winterset
IaWl	Free public library, West Liberty
IaWo	Free public library, Woodbine

Idaho

IdB	Carnegie public library, Boise
IdBlB	Daily bulletin, Blackfoot
IdCP	Coeur d'Alene press, Coeur d'Alene
IdFC	Camas county courier, Fairfield
IdIf	Public library, Idaho Falls
IdIfP	Post-register, Idaho Falls
IdJJ	Jerome county journal, Jerome
IdLC	City hall, Lewiston
IdPT	Tribune, Pocatello
IdRM	Minidoka county news, Rupert
IdSL	Lincoln county journal, Shoshone
IdSpB	Sandpoint daily bulletin, Sandpoint
IdU	University of Idaho, Moscow
IdU-S	Southern Branch, University of Idaho, Pocatello
IdWM	Miner, Wallace

Indiana

In	Indiana state library, Indianapolis
InA	Carnegie public library, Anderson
InAK	Carnegie library, Akron
InAl	Public library, Albion
InAle	Public library Alexandria
InAm	Public library, Amboy
InAn	Carnegie public library, Angola
InAt	Public library, Attica
InAu	Eckhart public library, Auburn
InAur	Public library, Aurora
InB	Public library, Bedford
InBM	Bedford mail, Bedford
InBl	Carnegie public library, Bloomfield
InBoS	Boonville standard, Boonville
InBr	Public library, Brazil
InBro	Public library, Brook
InBrok	Public library, Brookville
InBrokF	Franklin county recorder, Brookville
InBrow	Public library, Brownsburg
InBrwB	Brownstown banner, Brownstown
InBu	Carnegie public library, Butler
InC	Public library, Cambridge City
InCa	Public library, Carlisle
InCanP	Perry county recorder, Cannelton
InCar	Henry Henley public library, Carthage
InCe	Centerville and Center township library, Centerville
InCl	Carnegie public library, Clinton
InCo	Public library, Colfax
InCoc	Peabody free library, Columbia City
InCocHi	Whitley county historical society, Columbia City
InCocP	Columbia City post, Columbia City
InCocW	Whitley county recorder, Columbia City
InCol	Bartholomew county library, Columbus
InCon	Public library, Connersville
InConN	Connersville news-examiner, Connersville
InCp	Public library, Crown Point
InCr	Carnegie public library, Crawfordsville
InCrM	Montgomery county recorder, Crawfordsville
InCuC	Culver citizen, Culver
InDG	Danville gazette, Danville
InDH	Hendricks county recorder, Danville
InDeA	Adams county recorder, Decatur
InDeD	Decatur daily democrat, Decatur
InDelC	Delphi citizen, Delphi
InDenT	Denver tribune, Denver
InEc	Public library, East Chicago
InEd	Wright-Hageman public library, Edinburg
InEl	Carnegie public library, Elkhart
InElT	Elkhart daily truth, Elkhart
InElw	Public library, Elwood
InEv	Public and Vanderburgh county library, Evansville
InEva	Willard library, Evansville
InF	Public library, Fairmount
InFo	Fowler-Benton county public library, Fowler
InFr	Public library, Frankfort
InFw	Public library of Fort Wayne and Allen county, Fort Wayne
InFwHi	Allen county-Ft. Wayne historical society, Fort Wayne
InFwN	News-sentinel, Fort Wayne
InG	Public library, Gary
InGL	Gary land company, Gary
InGc	Carnegie public library, Greencastle
InGcD	DePauw university, Greencastle
InGoD	Goshen democrat, Goshen
InGoHi	Elkhart county historical society, Goshen
InGoE	Elkhart county recorder, Goshen
InGr	Public library, Greenfield
InGsD	Decatur county recorder, Greensburg
InGsN	Daily news, Greensburg
InGuM	Grand View monitor, Grand View
InH	Hagerstown and Jefferson township library, Hagerstown
InHa	Public library, Hammond
InHc	Public library, Hartford City
InHu	City free library, Huntington
InHuH	Huntington herald-press, Huntington
InHuR	Huntington county recorder, Huntington
InI	Indianapolis public library, Indianapolis
InIB	Butler university, Indianapolis
InIS	Indianapolis star, Indianapolis

INDIANA—*Continued*

InJ	Jasonville library, Jasonville
InK	Public library, Kendallville
InKe	Public library, Kentland
InKeN	Newton county recorder, Kentland
InKi	Public library, Kirklin
InKn	Public library, Knightstown
InKo	Carnegie public library, Kokomo
InKot	Kokomo tribune, Kokomo
InL	Albert A. Wells memorial library, La Fayette
InLHi	Tippecanoe county historical society, La Fayette
InLP	Purdue university, La Fayette
InLa	Public library, La Grange
InLap	Public library, La Porte
InLaw	Public library, Lawrenceburg
InLbHi	Union county historical society, Liberty
InLeB	Boone county recorder, Lebanon
InLi	Public library, Ligonier
InLo	Public library, Logansport
InLoHi	Logansport historical society, Logansport
InLwT	Lowell tribune, Lowell
InM	Public library, Madison
InMC	Drusilla L. Cravens, Madison
InMa	Public library, Marion
InMaP	Post office, Marion
InMar	Public library, Martinsville
InMe	Public library, Mentone
InMi	Public library, Middletown
InMil	Public library, Milford
InMit	Public library, Mitchell
InMo	Public library, Monon
InMon	Public library, Monticello
InMonW	Recorder's office for White county, Monticello
InMor	Public library, Mooresville
InMorS	Mrs. W. H. Sage, Mooresville
InMov	Free public library, Mount Vernon
InMovHi	Historical society, Mount Vernon
InMu	Public library, Muncie
InMuB	Ball state teachers college, Muncie
InN	Public library, Nappanee
InNa	Nashville-Brown county public library, Nashville
InNcC	Courier-times, Newcastle
InNcHi	Henry county historical society, Newcastle
InNe	Public library, New Albany
InNh	Workingmen's institute library, New Harmony
InNJ	North Judson library, North Judson
InNo	Public library, Noblesville
InNoR	Hamilton county recorder, Noblesville
InNp	Public library, Newport
InNv	Jennings county public library, North Vernon
InO	Public library, Oakland City
InOs	Public library, Osgood
InOt	Public library, Otterbein
InOw	Carnegie library, Owensville
InOx	Public library, Oxford
InOxL	Fred Lawson, Oxford
InP	Public library, Pendleton
InPe	Public library, Peru
InPeHi	Miami county historical society, Peru
InPeR	Miami county recorder, Peru
InPet	Public library, Petersburg
InPetM	M. McStoops private museum, Petersburg
InPi	Public library, Pierceton
InPl	Public library, Plainfield
InPmM	Marshall county recorder, Plymouth
InPmP	Plymouth pilot, Plymouth
InPoJ	Jay county recorder, Portland
InPr	Public library, Princeton
InR	Morris-Reeves library, Richmond
InRE	Earlham college, Richmond
InRP	Richmond palladium, Richmond
InRe	Public library, Rensselaer
InRIO	Ohio county recorder, Rising Sun
InRIR	Rising Sun recorder (paper) Rising Sun
InRicW	Nannie Wyttenbach, Richland
InRid	Public library, Ridgeville
InRo	Public library, Roachdale
InRoc	Public library, Rockport
InRochN	Rochester news, Rochester
InRov	Public library, Rockville
InRovP	Parke county recorder, Rockville
InRuR	Rush county recorder, Rushville
InS	Carnegie library, Salem
InSHi	Washington county historical society, Salem
InSb	Public library, South Bend
InSbN	South Bend news-times, South Bend
InSc	Scott county public library, Scottsburg
InSmA	Abbey library, St. Meinrad
InSo	Public library, South Whitley
InSp	Public library, Spencer
InSpW	Spencer evening world, Spencer
InSw	Public library, Swayzee
InSy	Public library, Syracuse
InT	Emeline Fairbanks memorial library, Terre Haute
InTI	Indiana state teachers college, Terre Haute
InTS	Terre Haute star, Terre Haute
InTe	Public library, Tell City
InTh	Public library, Thorntown
InTi	Public library, Tipton
InTiT	Tipton tribune, Tipton
InU	Indiana university, Bloomington
InUpT	Taylor university, Upland
InV	Public library, Valparaiso
InVe	Public library, Versailles
InVeM	Versailles memorial museum, Versailles
InVeR	Ripley county recorder, Versailles
InVev	Switzerland county public library, Vevay
InVevHi	Switzerland county historical society, Vevay
InVi	Public library, Vincennes
InVnJ	Jennings county recorder, Vernon
InW	Public library of Warsaw and Wayne township, Warsaw
InWa	Carnegie public library, Washington
InWaC	Daviess county circuit court, Washington
InWav	Waveland-Brown township library, Waveland
InWbHi	Wabash county historical society, Wabash
InWe	Public library, Westville
InWh	Public library, Whiting
InWi	Public library, Winchester
InWiR	Randolph county recorder, Winchester
InWlW	Warren county recorder, Williamsport
InWnP	Pulaski county democrat, Winamac
InWo	Public library, Worthington

Kansas

KA	Public library, Atchison
KAb	Abilene publishing company, Abilene
KAbR	Reflector, Abilene
KArM	Mrs. C. M. McIntire, Arkansas City
KEB	Baker university, Baldwin
KBsC	Bonner Springs chieftain, Bonner Springs
KCoA	Columbus advocate, Columbus
KCg	Free public library, Council Grove
KD	Public library, Dodge City
KDB	Beeson museum, Dodge City
KDoN	News and times, Downs
KE	Free library, Eldorado
KET	Eldorado times, Eldorado
KEm	Free public library, Emporia
KEmG	Emporia gazette, Emporia
KEmT	Kansas state teachers college, Emporia
KGC	County clerk, Goodland
KGaT	Galena times, Galena
KGcT	Garden City telegram, Garden City
KH	Free public library, Hays
KHK	Fort Hays Kansas state teachers college, Hays
KHN	News, Hays
KHa	Morrill free public library, Hiawatha
KHeT	Herington times-sun, Herington
KHi	Kansas historical society, Topeka
KHoH	Horton headlight, Horton
KHu	Public library, Hutchinson
KHuN	Hutchinson news, Hutchinson
KK	Public library, Kansas City
KKaN	Kiowa news-review-record, Kiowa
KKi	Public library, Kirwin
KL	Free public library, Lawrence
KLJ	Journal-world, Lawrence
KLcC	La Crosse chieftain, La Crosse
KLeT	Leavenworth times, Leavenworth
KLiB	Bethany college, Lindsborg
KLiBe	Dr. Alfred Bergin, Lindsborg
KM	Carnegie free public library, Manhattan
KMC	Chronicle and mercury, Manhattan
KMeB	Barber county index, Medicine Lodge
KMuN	Mulvane news, Mulvane
KNeH	Ness county historical society, Ness City
KNoT	Norton daily telegram, Norton
KOH	Ottawa herald, Ottawa
KObH	Oberlin herald, Oberlin
KOlM	Olathe mirror, Olathe
KOs	Carnegie library, Osawatomie
KOsb	Carnegie public library, Osborne
KOwI	Oswego independent, Oswego
KP	Public library, Pittsburg
KPC	Pittsburg City hall, Pittsburg
KPT	Kansas state teachers college, Pittsburg
KPa	Free public library, Paola
KPe	Public library, Peabody
KPrT	Pratt tribune, Pratt
KR	Rae Hobson memorial library, Republic
KS	Public library, Saint Marys
KSS	Saint Marys star, Saint Marys
KSeC	Courier-tribune, Seneca
KSm	Public library, Smith Center
KSmC	Smith county court house, Smith Center
KTC	Topeka daily capitol, Topeka
KTrC	Greeley county clerk's office, Tribune
KU	University of Kansas, Lawrence
KWC	Winfield courier, Winfield
KWHi	Cowley county historical society, Winfield
KWeR	Westmoreland recorder, Westmoreland
KWi	City library, Wichita
KWiB	Wichita beacon, Wichita
KWiE	Wichita eagle, Wichita
KWiF	Friends university, Wichita
KWIF	Franklin county journal, Williamsburg

Kentucky

Ky	Kentucky state library, Frankfort
KyBN	Nazareth literary and benevolent institution, Bardstown
KyBoW	Western Kentucky state teachers' college, Bowling Green
KyC	Public library of Covington and Kenton county, Covington
KyClH	Hickman county gazette, Clinton
KyFM	S. I. M. Major, Frankfort
KyG	Public library, Georgetown
KyGC	Georgetown college, Georgetown
KyH	Public library, Henderson
KyHa	Public library, Harrodsburg
KyHarO	Ohio county news, Hartford
KyHi	Kentucky state historical society, Frankfort
KyHo	Public library, Hopkinsville
KyHoL	Miss Frances Lender, Hopkinsville
KyL	Public library, Lexington
KyLT	Transylvania college, Lexington
KyLo	Louisville free public library, Louisville
KyLoF	Filson club, Louisville
KyM	Public library, Madisonville
KyMoU	Union county advocate, Morganfield
KyO	Carnegie free library, Owensboro
KyOG	Green River art museum, Owensboro
KyP	Carnegie library, Paducah
KyPrL	Leader, Princeton
KyU	University of Kentucky, Lexington

Louisiana

LA	Public library, Alexandria
LBE	East Baton Rouge public library, Baton Rouge
LBL	Louisiana library commission, State Capitol, Baton Rouge
LBP	Parish school board, Baton Rouge
LBS	State times, Baton Rouge
LHi	Louisiana historical society, New Orleans
LLS	Southwestern Louisiana institute, Lafayette
LN	Public library, New Orleans
LNA	City archives, City Hall, New Orleans
LNC	Confederate museum, New Orleans
LNH	Howard memorial library, New Orleans
LNM	Louisiana state museum (Cabildo), New Orleans
LNP	Times-picayune, New Orleans
LNT-M	Department of Middle American research, Tulane Univ., N. O.
LNaS	Louisiana state normal college, Natchitoches
LSfD	Democrat, St. Francisville
LU	Louisiana state university, Baton Rouge

Massachusetts

M	State library of Massachusetts, Boston
MA	Russell memorial library, Amherst
MAJ	Jones library, Amherst
MAS	Massachusetts agricultural college, Amherst
MAd	Free library, Adams
MAm	Public library, Amesbury
MAn	Memorial Hall library, Andover
MAr	Robbins library, Arlington
MAt	Public library, Athol
MAtN	Athol daily news and transcript, Athol
MAtt	Public library, Attleboro
MAy	Public library, Ayer

MASSACHUSETTS—*Continued*

MB Public library of the City of Boston, Boston
MB-B Brighton public library
MB-C Charleston public library
MB-D Dorchester public library
MB-E East Boston public library
MB-K Kirstein branch public library
MB-S South Boston public library
MBAt Boston athenaeum, Boston
MBB Bostonian society, Old State House, Boston
MBC Congregational library, Boston
MBHe Boston herald, Boston
MBNHi New England historic and genealogical society, Boston
MBa Town library, Barre
MBar Sturgis library, Barnstable
MBe Public library, Beverly
MBeHi Beverly historical society, Beverly
MBel Clapp memorial library, Belchertown
MBelHi Belchertown historical society, Belchertown
MBelm Public library, Belmont
MBelmHi Belmont historical society, Belmont
MBer Free public library, Berlin
MBo Ingalls memorial library, Boxford
MBr Public library, Brookline
MBrC Brookline chronicle, Brookline
MBra Thayer public library, Braintree
MBraT Braintree town hall, Braintree
MBro Public library, Brockton
MBroT Brockton enterprise, Brockton
MC Free public library, Concord
MCa Public library, Canton
MCam Public library, Cambridge
MCh Public library, Chelsea
MChe Adams library, Chelmsford
MCheHi Chelmsford historical society, Chelmsford
MChi Public library, Chicopee
MCl Bigelow free public library, Clinton
MD Public library, Dedham
MDHi Dedham historical society, Dedham
MDT Dedham transcript, Dedham
MDa Peabody institute library, Danvers
MDeHi Pocumtuck Valley memorial association, Deerfield
ME Frederick E. Parlin memorial library, Everett
MES Shute memorial library, Everett
MEa Public library association, Easthampton
MEd Free public library, Edgartown
MEdHi Dukes county historical society, Edgartown
MEdV Vineyard gazette, Edgartown
MF Free public library, Falmouth
MFa Public library, Fall River
MFaH Fall River herald news, Fall River
MFh Millicent library, Fairhaven
MFi Public library, Fitchburg
MFiHi Fitchburg historical society, Fitchburg
MFiS Fitchburg sentinel, Fitchburg
MFo Boydon public library, Foxboro
MFr Town library, Framingham
MFra Public library, Franklin
MGa Levi Heywood memorial library, Gardner
MGb Mason library, Great Barrington
MGlHi Cape Ann historical society, Gloucester
MGlT Gloucester daily times, Gloucester
MGr Public library, Greenfield
MGrR Recorder-gazette, Greenfield
MGro Public library, Groton
MH Harvard university, Cambridge
MH-BA Graduate school of business administration, Harvard univ., Cambridge
MHa Public library, Haverhill
MHaR Sunday record, Haverhill
MHi Massachusetts historical society, Boston
MHin Public library, Hingham
MHinHi Hingham historical society, Hingham
MHo Public library, Holbrook
MHol Public library, Holyoke
MHu Free public library, Hubbardston
MHy Public library, Hyde Park
MHyHi Hyde Park historical society, Hyde Park
MI Public library, Ipswich
ML City library, Lowell
MLG Greenholge grammar school, Lowell
MLHi Lowell historical society, Lowell
MLT Tribune, Lowell
MLa Free public library, Lawrence
MLan Town library, Lancaster
MLeHi Lexington historical society, Lexington
MLeM Lexington minute-man, Lexington
MLee Lee library association, Lee
MLei Public library, Leicester
MLeo Public library, Leominster
MLy Public library, Lynn
MLyI Lynn item, Lynn
MMaC Manchester cricket, Manchester
MMal Public library, Malden
MMar Abbot public library, Marblehead
MMarHi Marblehead historical society, Marblehead
MMe Public library, Medford
MMed Public library Medway
MMel Public library, Melrose
MMenHi Mendon historical society, Mendon
MMer Public library, Merrimac
MMet Nevins memorial library, Methuen
MMi Public library, Middleboro
MMil Town library, Milford
MMilJ Milford journal, Milford
MMilt Public library, Milton
MMiltHi Milton historical society, Milton
MN Lilly library, Northampton
MNF Forbes library, Northampton
MNS Smith college, Northampton
MNaHi South Natick natural history and library society, Natick
MNaM Morse institute, Natick
MNb Free public library, New Bedford
MNbHi Old Dartmouth historical society, New Bedford
MNd Free public library, Needham
MNdT Town Hall, Needham
MNe Free library, Newton
MNeC Newton City Hall, Newton
MNo Public library, North Adams
MNob Free public library, North Brookfield
MNor Stevens memorial library, North Andover
MNort Free library, Northboro
MNp Public library, Newburyport
MNpN Newburyport news, Newburyport
MNr Morrill memorial library, Norwood
MOb Public library, Oak Bluffs
MOx Charles Larned memorial library, Oxford
MPR Palmer journal-register, Palmer
MPe Peabody institute library, Peabody
MPep Lawrence library, Pepperell
MPi Berkshire athenaeum, Pittsfield
MQ Thomas Crane public library, Quincy
MR Public library, Reading
MRa Turner library, Randolph
MReC Revere City Hall, Revere
MRo Memorial library, Rockland
MS City library association, Springfield
MSaE Essex institute, Salem
MSanHi Sandwich historical society, Sandwich
MSau Free public library, Saugus
MSc Allen memorial library, Scituate
MScT Scituate Town Hall, Scituate
MSh Public library, Sharon
MShr Free public library, Shrewsbury
MShrHi Shrewsbury historical society, Shrewsbury
MSo Public library, Somerville
MSob Public library, Southbridge
MSp Richard Sugden library, Spencer
MSpL Spencer leader, Spencer
MSt Public library, Stoneham
MStI Stoneham independent, Stoneham
MSte Public library, Sterling
MSto Public library, Stow
MStoR Randall memorial library, Stow
MStou Public library, Stoughton
MTHi Topsfield historical society, Topsfield
MTa Public library, Taunton
MTaHi Old Colony historical society, Taunton
MTo Public library, Townsend
MTu Carnegie public library, Turners Falls
MUx Free public library, Uxbridge
MW Free public library, Worcester
MWA American antiquarian society, Worcester
MWHi Worcester historical society, Worcester
MWS Svea, Worcester
MWa Public library, Waltham
MWaN Waltham news-tribune, Waltham
MWak Lucius Beebe memorial library, Wakefield
MWal Public library, Wales
MWalp Public library, Walpole
MWat Free public library, Watertown
MWbHi Old Bridgewater historical society, West Bridgewater
MWe Tufts library, Weymouth
MWeb Chester C. Corbin public library, Webster
MWel Free library, Wellesley
MWes Westborough public library, Westboro
MWf Westfield athenaeum, Westfield
MWfo J. V. Fletcher library, Westford
MWh Public library, Whitman
MWhT Whitman times, Whitman
MWiC Williams college, Williamstown
MWin Public library, Winchester
MWinc Beals memorial library, Winchendon
MWint Public library, Winthrop
MWmB H. A. Bullard, West Medway
MWo Public library, Woburn
MWs Public library, West Springfield
MY Public library, Yarmouth Port
MYa Public library, Yarmouth

Maryland

Md Maryland state library, Annapolis
MdAC Evening capital, Annapolis
MdBB Baltimore equitable society, Baltimore
MdBE Enoch Pratt free library, Baltimore
MdBG Goucher college, Baltimore
MdBJ Johns Hopkins university, Baltimore
MdBL Loyola college, Baltimore
MdBLe Legislative reference department, City Hall, Baltimore
MdBN Baltimore news and the Baltimore post, Baltimore
MdBP Peabody institute, Baltimore
MdBSa Mount St. Agnes school, Baltimore
MdBSt Saint Mary's seminary, Baltimore
MdBoT Times, Boonsboro
MdC Free public library, Cumberland
MdCK Charles R. Kayser, Cumberland
MdCN Cumberland daily news, Cumberland
MdCT Cumberland evening times, Cumberland
MdCaB Mrs. Shepherd Bayly, Cambridge
MdCaH W. Laird Henry, Cambridge
MdChW Washington college, Chesterton
MdCaV E. P. Vinton, Cambridge
MdCeK T. J. Keating, Centerville
MdCeO Centerville observer, Centerville
MdCeR Queen Anne's record-observer, Centerville
MdChB Morris K. Barroll, Chestertown
MdChK Kent news, Chestertown
MdCrT Crisfield times, Crisfield
MdCtS Robert C. Seip, Catonsville
MdEJ F. G. Jump, Jr., Easton
MdET. Talbott county free library, Easton
MdEkC Joshua Clayton, Elkton
MdEkP J. W. Perkins, Elkton
MdEkW Cecil whig, Elkton
MdElS M. J. Sullivan, Ellicott City
MdEmJ St. Josephs college, Emmitsburg
MdFF Burr Artz free library, Frederick
MdFN News, Frederick
MdFS G. T. Schroeder, Frederick
MdFrN Maryland state teachers college, Frostburg
MdHE Mrs. Amos Eves, Hagerstown
MdHF Mrs. David Flory, Hagerstown
MdHK Edward Knodle, Hagerstown
MdHL Miss Bird Little, Hagerstown
MdHS Ira Stover, Hagerstown
MdHW Washington county free library, Hagerstown
MdHZ H. P. Zeigler, Hagerstown
MdHi Maryland historical society, Baltimore
MdHi-H Harford county historical society, Baltimore
MdLL Leader, Laurel
MdMV Valley register, Middletown
MdPW Worcester democrat and the ledger-enterprise, Pocomoke City
MdPsM Marylander and herald, Princess Anne
MdSW Mrs. S. King White, Salisbury
MdTJ Jeffersonian, Towson
MdU University of Maryland, College Park
MdUE Enquirer-gazette, Upper Marlboro
MdWA Democratic advocate, Westminster
MdWJ J. Leland Jordan, Westminster

Maine

Me Maine state library, Augusta
MeAdS C. H. Small, Addison
MeAlC York county court house, Alfred
MeAu Public library, Auburn
MeAuC Androscoggin county court house, Auburn
MeB Captain John Curtis library, Brunswick
MeBB Bowdoin college, Brunswick
MeBHi Pejepscot historical society, Brunswick
MeBa Public library, Bangor
MeBaHi Bangor historical society, Bangor
MeBe Free library, Belfast
MeBeR Belfast republican journal, Belfast
MeBh Jesup memorial library, Bar Harbor
MeBi Public library, Biddeford
MeBt Patten free library, Bath
MeBtC Sagadahoc county court house, Bath
MeBtT Bath daily times, Bath
MeCm Public library, Camden
MeDB Mr. G. A. Bailey, Dexter
MeDW Mr. G. F. Westgate, Dexter

MAINE—*Continued*

MeDo	Thompson free library, Dover-Foxcroft
MeDoC	Piscataquis county court house, Dover-Foxcroft
MeE	City library, Ellsworth
MeEC	Hancock county court house, Ellsworth
MeEa	Public library, Eastport
MeF	Cutler memorial library, Farmington
MeFC	Franklin county court house, Farmington
MeFr	B. F. Bartol library, Freeport
MeG	Public library, Gardiner
MeHa	Hubbard free library, Hallowell
MeHar	Free library, Hartland
MeHi	Maine historical society, Portland
MeHo	Cary library, Houlton
MeHoC	Aroostook county court house, Houlton
MeK	Free library, Kennebunk
MeL	Public library, Lewiston
MeLB	Bates college, Lewiston
MeMC	Washington county court house, Machias
MeMN	Machias Valley news-observer, Machias
MeMa	Public library, Madison
MeN	Public library, Norway
MeNA	Norway advertiser-democrat, Norway
MeO	Public library, Old Town
MeP	Public library, Portland
MeR	Public library, Rockland
MeRC	Knox county court house, Rockland
MeSY	York institute, Saco
MeSoC	Oxford county court house, South Paris
MeU	University of Maine, Orono
MeW	Free public library, Waterville
MeWC	Colby college, Waterville
MeWHi	Waterville historical society, Waterville
MeWe	Conarroe memorial library, Wells

Michigan

Mi	Michigan state library, Lansing
MiAC	Alma college, Alma
MiAd	Public library, Adrian
MiAdT	Adrian daily telegram, Adrian
MiAgG	Allegan gazette, Allegan
MiAlH	Almont herald, Almont
MiAlp	Public library, Alpena
MiBcS	Battle Creek public school, Battle Creek
MiBhN	Benton Harbor news-palladium, Benton Harbor
MiBy	Public library, Bay City
MiC	Public library of the Calumet and Hecla Con. Copper Company, Calumet
MiCarA	Tuscola county advertiser, Caro
MiCh	Public library, Charlotte
MiCl	Public library, Coldwater
MiCo	Subscription library, Corunna
MiConA	Advertiser-record, Constantine
MiD	Detroit public library, Detroit
MiD-B	Burton historical collection, Detroit public library, Detroit
MiDN	Detroit news, Detroit
MiDoN	Dowagiac daily news, Dowagiac
MiE	Carnegie public library, Escanaba
MiEIS	Michigan state college, East Lansing
MiErJ	Eaton Rapids journal, Eaton Rapids
MiF	Public library, Flint
MiFJ	Flint journal, Flint
MiFN	Flint news-advertiser, Flint
MiFrN	Frankenmuth news, Frankenmuth
MiG	Public library, Grand Rapids
MiGh	Public library, Grand Haven
MiGr	School public library, Greenville
MiH	Mitchell public library, Hillsdale
MiHcR	Howard City record, Howard City
MiHo	Public library, Houghton
MiHoM	Michigan college of mining and technology, Houghton
MiHu	Public library, Hudson
MiHw	Carnegie library, Howell
MiHwC	A. R. Crittenden, Howell
MiI	Public library, Imlay City
MiIm	Carnegie public library, Iron Mountain
MiIr	Carnegie library, Ironwood
MiJ	Jonesville library association, Jonesville
MiK	Public library, Kalamazoo
MiLS	Public school library, Lansing
MiLaS	L'Anse sentinel, L'Anse
MiLiH	Alcona county herald, Lincoln
MiLo	Public library, Lowell
MiLu	Public library, Ludington
MiLuN	Ludington daily news, Ludington
MiMD	Dorsch memorial library, Monroe
MiMN	Monroe evening news, Monroe
MiMa	Public and school library, Manistee
MiMan	Manistique library, Manistique
MiManP	Pioneer-tribune, Manistique
MiMar	Peter White public library, Marquette
MiMars	Public library, Marshall
MiMasN	Ingham county news, Mason
MiMoR	Midland republican, Midland
MiMe	Spies public library of Menominee county, Menominee
MiMen	Township free public library, Mendon
MiMn	Munising township library, Munising
MiMu	Hackley public library, Muskegon
MiN	Public library, Niles
MiNeN	Newberry news, Newberry
MiOC	Olivet college, Olivet
MiOs	Public library, Oscoda
MiOtU	Otsego union, Otsego
MiOw	Public library, Owosso
MiP	Public library, Petoskey
MiPaC	Courier-northerner, Paw Paw
MiPh	Public library, Port Huron
MiPo	City library, Pontiac
MiPoHi	Oakland county historical society, Pontiac
MiPor	Public library, Portland
MiQ	Free public library, Quincy
MiRH	Reading hustler, Reading
MiRo	Public library, Royal Oak
MiS	Public library, Saginaw
MiSa	Public library, St. Joseph
MiSJR	Clinton county republican-news, St. Johns
MiSoT	South Haven tribune, South Haven
MiSp	Carnegie public library, Sparta
MiSt	Carnegie free public library, Sturgis
MiT	Public library, Tecumseh
MiTh	Free public library, Three Rivers
MiU	University of Michigan, Ann Arbor
MiU-C	William L. Clements library, University of Michigan, Ann Arbor
MiUtF	C. M. Foster, Utica
MiW	Public library, Wyandotte
MiY	Public library, Ypsilanti
MiYM	Michigan state normal college, Ypsilanti

Minnesota

MnA	Free public library, Alexandria
MnAC	Alexandria citizen-news, Alexandria
MnAil	Aitkin independent age Aitkin
MnAlT	Evening tribune, Albert Lea
MnAnA	Advocate-post, Annandale
MnAtR	Republican-press, Atwater
MnAu	Carnegie public library, Austin
MnB	Carnegie public library Bemidji
MnBl	Etta C. Ross memorial library, Blue Earth
MnBrG	Gazette-telegram, Breckenridge
MnBvV	Valley news, Browns Valley
MnC	Free public library, Caledonia
MnCh	Public library, Chisholm
MnCl	Public library, Cloquet
MnCoN	News-herald, Cook
MnCr	Carnegie public library, Crookston
MnCroC	Crosby courier, Crosby
MnD	Public library, Duluth
MnEgR	Record, East Grand Forks
MnElM	Elgin monitor, Elgin
MnEyC	St. Louis county court house, Ely
MnFC	Martin county court house, Fairmont
MnFa	Public library, Faribault
MnFaC	Rice county court house, Faribault
MnFf	Carnegie public library, Fergus Falls
MnG	Public library, Grand Rapids
MnGrN	Granite Falls news, Granite Falls
MnHb	Public library, Hibbing
MnHbT	Hibbing tribune, Hibbing
MnHi	Minnesota historical society, St. Paul
MnHo	Public library, Hopkins
MnHu	Free public library, Hutchinson
MnHuC	W. S. Clay, Hutchinson
MnJHi	Jackson county historical society, Jackson
MnK	Public library, Kasson
MnLaS	Lakefield standard, Lakefield
MnLcL	Le Center leader, Le Center
MnLf	Carnegie City library, Little Falls
MnLi	Public library, Litchfield
MnLu	Public library, Luverne
MnM	Minneapolis public library, Minneapolis
MnMa	Free public library, Mankato
MnMaHi	Blue Earth historical society, Mankato
MnMd	Carnegie public library, Madison
MnMdHi	Lyon county historical society, Madison
MnMoC	Stevens county court house, Morris
MnMoHi	Stevens county historical society, Morris
MnMr	Carnegie public library, Marshall
MnMrM	Marshall daily messenger, Marshall
MnMt	Public library, Mountain Iron
MnN	Public library, Northfield
MnNC	Carleton college, Northfield
MnNS	St. Olaf college, Northfield
MnNpT	New Prague times, New Prague
MnNuH	Mrs. August Hummel, New Ulm
MnPHi	Pipestone county historical society, Pipestone
MnPlN	Plainview news, Plainview
MnRP	Post-bulletin, Rochester
MnRe	Carnegie-Lawther library, Red Wing
MnS	Public library, St. Paul
MnSL	Luther seminary, St. Paul
MnSS	St. Paul seminary, St. Paul
MnScS	St. Cloud sentinel, St. Cloud
MnScT	Times, St. Cloud
MnSk	Bryant library, Sauk Center
MnSl	Dyckman free library Sleepy Eye
MnSp	Public library, St. Peter
MnSpH	St. Peter herald, St. Peter
MnSt	Carnegie public library, Stillwater
MnStG	Stillwater gazette, Stillwater
MnSteM	Stephen messenger, Stephen
MnTr	Carnegie public library, Thief River Falls
MnTraH	Tracy headlight-herald, Tracy
MnU	University of Minnesota, Minneapolis
MnU-A	Department of Agriculture, University of Minn., Minneapolis
MnW	Public library, Wabasha
MnWa	Public library, Warren
MnWadP	Wadena pioneer-journal, Wadena
MnWhG	Wheaton gazette, Wheaton
MnWi	Public library, Willmar
MnWn	Free public library, Winona
MnWnR	Republican-herald, Winona
MnWoG	Worthington globe, Worthington

Missouri

Mo	Missouri state library, Jefferson City
MoBeT	Harrison county times, Bethany
MoBoH	Boonville high school, Boonville
MoBoM	E. J. Melton, Boonville
MoBr	Carnegie library, Brookfield
MoC	Public library, Canton
MoCC	Culver-Stockton college, Canton
MoCaT	Southeast state teachers college, Cape Girardeau
MoCamN	Cameron news-observer, Cameron
MoCar	Public library, Carthage
MoCarrD	Carrollton democrat, Carrollton
MoCaru	Public library, Caruthersville
MoCaruD	Democrat-argus, Caruthersville
MoChE	Enterprise-courier Charleston
MoClI	Independent courier, Clarence
MoCoB	Bible college of Missouri, Columbia
MoCon	Conception college, Conception
MoCrT	Craig tribune, Craig
MoDP	Doniphan prospect-news, Doniphan
MoF	Public library, Farmington
MoFaC	Central college, Fayette
MoFuB	Ovid Bell, Fulton
MoFuW	Westminster college, Fulton
MoG	Lewis memorial library, Glasgow
MoGaT	Ozark county times, Gainesville
MoGr	Worth county library association, Grant City
MoGrT	Times-tribune, Grant City
MoH	Public library of Hamilton, Hamilton
MoHa	Free public library, Hannibal
MoHeA	Advertiser-courier, Hermann
MoHerI	Index, Hermitage
MoHi	State historical society of Missouri, Columbia
MoHuM	Munger securities company, Hunter
MoI	Public library, Independence
MoIN	News, Independence
MoJ	Free public library, Jefferson City
MoJo	Free public library, Joplin
MoK	Kansas City public library, Kansas City
MoKJ	Journal-post, Kansas City
MoKe	Public library, Kennett
MoKeD	Dunklin democrat, Kennett
MoKiT	Northeast Missouri state teachers' college, Kirksville
MoKinN	Tri-county news, King City
MoKirM	Kirkwood messenger, Kirkwood
MoL	Public library, Lee's Summit
MoLe	Public library and historical association, Lexington
MoLiW	William Jewell college, Liberty
MoLo	Public library, Louisiana
MoLozF	B. Ray Franklin, Lake Ozark
MoM	Carnegie library, Marceline
MoMaD	Democrat-news, Marshall
MoMaM	Missouri Valley college, Marshall
MoMar	Marshfield library, Marshfield
MoMaryF	Maryville daily forum, Maryville

MISSOURI—*Continued*

MoMaryT	Northwest Missouri state teacher's college, Maryville
MoMdT	Madison times, Madison
MoMeT	Metz times, Metz
MoMgJ	Mountain Grove journal, Mountain Grove
MoMoM	Monitor-index and democrat, Moberly
MoMon	Public library, Monett
MoMontL	Lewis county journal, Monticello
MoOR	Gasconade county republican, Owensville
MoP	Park college, Parkville
MoPlJ	Wayne county journal banner, Piedmont
MoPinH	Pineville herald, Pineville
MoPlL	Landmark, Platte City
MoPoM	Southeast Missourian, Portageville
MoRG	Ravenwood gazette, Ravenwood
MoS	Public library of the City of St. Louis, St. Louis
MoSC	Central bureau library, St. Louis
MoSG	Globe-democrat, St. Louis
MoSHi	Missouri historical society, St. Louis
MoSHo	G. A. Hoehn, St. Louis
MoSM	St. Louis mercantile library association, St. Louis
MoSP	The Principia library, St. Louis
MoSPo	Post-dispatch, St. Louis
MoSU	St. Louis university, St. Louis
MoSW	Washington university, St. Louis
MoSa	Public library, Savannah
MoSaR	Savannah reporter, Savannah
MoSalP	Salem post, Salem
MoSc	Public library, St. Charles
MoScR	St. Charles rectory, St. Charles
MoSe	Public library, Sedalia
MoSeD	Sedalia democrat, Sedalia
MoSJ	Public library, St. Joseph
MoSl	Public library, Slater
MoSp	Public library, Springfield
MoSpD	Drury college, Springfield
MoU	University of Missouri, Columbia
MoVC	Current local, Van Buren
MoW	Public library, Washington
MoWe	Public library, Webster Groves
MoWeW	Webster college, Webster Groves
MoWyH	Mrs. Hazel Hume, Wyaconda

Mississippi

MsAbC	Monroe county court house, Aberdeen
MsAbE	Dr. W. A. Evans, Aberdeen
MsAsC	Benton county court house, Ashland
MsBC	Humphreys county court house, Belzoni
MsBaC	Panola county court house, Batesville
MsBayC	Hancock county court house, Bay St. Louis
MsBoC	Circuit court clerk's office, Boonville
MsBrC	Lincoln county court house, Brookhaven
MsBraC	Rankin county court house, Brandon
MsCC	Tallahatchie county court house, Charleston
MsCaC	Madison county court house, Canton
MsCarC	Leake county court house, Carthage
MsClR	County register, Clarksdale
MsCoC	Marion county court house, Columbia
MsColC	Lowndes county court house, Columbus
MsCorC	Alcorn county court house, Corinth
MsDC	Kemper county court house, De Kalb
MsEC	Jones county court house, Ellisville
MsFC	Jefferson county court house, Fayette
MsGD	Democrat-times, Greenville
MsGrC	Grenada county court house, Grenada
MsGuC	Harrison county court house, Gulfport
MsHA	Hattiesburg American, Hattiesburg
MsHC	Forest county court house, Hattiesburg
MsHaC	Copiah county court house, Hazlehurst
MsHi	Mississippi department of archives and history, Jackson
MsHoC	Marshall county court house, Holly Springs
MsHouC	Chickasaw county court house, Houston
MsIC	Tishomingo county court house, Iuka
MsJC	Hinds county court house, Jackson
MsKoC	Attala county court house, Kosciusko
MsLE	Eastman memorial foundation, Laurel
MsLeC	Greene county court house, Leakesville
MsLIC	Amite county court house, Liberty
MsLuC	George county court house, Lucedale
MsMC	Issaquena county court house, Mayersville
MsMaC	Franklin county court house, Meadville
MsMaF	Franklin advocate, Meadville
MsMacC	Noxubee county court house, Macon
MsMagC	Pike county court house, Magnolia
MsMarC	Quitman county court house, Marks
MsMeC	Simpson county court house, Mendenhall
MsMerC	Lauderdale county court house, Meridian
MsMoC	Lawrence county court house, Monticello
MsMpC	Jackson county court house, Moss Point
MsNCC	Adams county court house, Natchez
MsNF	Fisk memorial library, Natchez
MsNH	Mrs. Kate Hootsell, Natchez
MsNK	Mrs. Florence Kelly, Natchez
MsNaC	Union county court house, New Albany
MsNaS	Sheriff's office, New Albany
MsNagC	Perry county court house, New Augusta
MsOC	Chickasaw county court house, Okolona
MsOM	Okolona messenger, Okolona
MsOcC	Jackson county court house, Ocean Springs
MsOxC	Lafayette county court house, Oxford
MsP	Public library, Picayune
MsPaC	Jackson county court house, Pascagoula
MsPaS	Superintendent of Education, Pascagoula
MsPgC	Claiborne county court house, Port Gibson
MsPhC	Neshoba county court house, Philadelphia
MsPoC	Pontotoc county court house, Pontotoc
MsPrC	Jefferson Davis county court house, Prentiss
MsPu	Lamar county court house, Purvis
MsQC	Clarke county court house, Quitman
MsRR	Ruleville record, Ruleville
MsRaC	Hinds county court house, Raymond
MsRicD	Richton dispatch, Richton
MsRipC	Tippah county court house, Ripley
MsSM	Mississippi state college, State College
MsSaC	Panola county court house, Sardis
MsStC	Oktibbeha county court house, Starkville
MsTC	Lee county court house, Tupelo
MsTuC	Tunica county court house, Tunica
MsU	University of Mississippi, Oxford
MsV	Public library, Vicksburg
MsVJ	Vicksburg jail, Vicksburg
MsWaC	Yalobusha county court house, Water Valley
MsWayC	Wayne county court house, Waynesboro
MsWeC	Clay county court house, West Point
MsWgC	Stone county court house, Wiggins
MsWiC	Montgomery county court house, Winona
MsWoC	Wilkinson county court house, Woodville
MsYC	Yazoo county court house, Yazoo City

Montana

MtB	Parmly Billings memorial library, Billings
MtBo	Free library, Bozeman
MtBoS	Montana state college, Bozeman
MtBu	Free public library, Butte
MtBuL	Alexander Leggat, Butte
MtD	Public library, Dillon
MtDS	State normal college, Dillon
MtDe	William K. Kohr's memorial library, Deer Lodge
MtDeS	Silver State post, Deer Lodge
MtF	Rosebud county library, Forsyth
MtFp	Fort Peck press, Fort Peck
MtGD	Dawson county review, Glendive
MtGf	Great Falls public library, Great Falls
MtH	Public library, Helena
MtHK	L. C. Keim, Helena
MtHa	Big Horn county free library, Hardin
MtHamR	Ravalli republican, Hamilton
MtHamW	Western news, Hamilton
MtHav	Public library, Havre
MtHi	Historical society of Montana, Helena
MtJT	Jordan tribune, Jordan
MtK	Carnegie public library, Kalispell
MtL	Carnegie public library, Livingston
MtLe	Carnegie public library, Lewiston
MtM	Missoula county free library, Missoula
MtMl	Carnegie public library, Miles City
MtRC	Carbon county news, Red Lodge
MtRP	Picket-journal, Red Lodge
MtRoR	Roundup record-tribune, Roundup
MtU	University of Montana, Missoula
MtU-J	University of Montana, School of journalism, Missoula
MtVM	Madisonian, Virginia City

NEW YORK

N	New York state library, Albany
NAlU	Alfred university, Alfred
NAmeB	Guy Bailey, Amenia
NAmsB	E. O. Bartlett, Amsterdam
NAn	Free library, Andover
NAnnS	St. Stephen's college, Annandale-on-Hudson
NAnt	Crosby public library, Antwerp
NAr	Free library, Arcade
NAuW	Wells college, Aurora
NAub	Seymour library, Auburn
NAubC	Citizen-advertiser, Auburn
NAubHi	Cayuga county historical society, Auburn
NAubT	Auburn theological seminary, Auburn
NAubW	G. K. Weeden, Auburn
NB	Public library, Brooklyn
NBHi	Long Island historical society, Brooklyn
NBP	Pratt institute, Brooklyn
NBa	Davenport library, Bath
NBaS	Steuben farmers' advocate, Bath
NBarR	Barker register, Barker
NBat	Richmond memorial library, Batavia
NBe	Bartlett memorial library, Belfast
NBi	Public library, Binghampton
NBo	Free library, Bolivar
NBrM	J. E. Milton, Brewerton
NBro	Public library, Bronxville
NBu	Buffalo public library, Buffalo
NBuC	Courier-express, Buffalo
NBuG	Grosvenor public library, Buffalo
NBuHi	Buffalo historical society, Buffalo
NC	Kirkland Town library, Clinton
NCH	Hamilton college, Clinton
NCam	Camillus library, Camillus
NCan	Wood library association, Canandaigua
NCanHi	Ontario county historical society, Canandaigua
NCana	Public library, Canastota
NCandC	Dr. Amos Canfield, Candor
NCanJ	Canajoharie library, Canajoharie
NCanJB	Harry V. Bush, Canajoharie
NCanJJ	Canajoharie courier, Canajoharie
NCar	Reed memorial library, Carmel
NCatHi	Greene county historical society, Catskill
NCaz	Public library, Cazenovia
NChM	Hugh McLellan, Champlain
NChaF	F. W. Ferrell, Chateaugay
NChau	Smith memorial library, Chautauqua
NChe	Memorial library, Cherry Valley
NChiH	High school library, Chittenango
NChiM	Madison county times, Chittenango
NCinB	Mrs. L. D. Blanchard, Cincinnatus
NCinS	Mrs. B. L. Smith, Cincinnatus
NClM	E. P. McKinley, Clayton
NCli	Kirkland Town library, Clinton
NCob	Public library, Cobleskill
NCohC	Cohocton Valley times and index, Cohocton
NCoo	Cooperstown Village club and library, Cooperstown
NCor	Public library, Corning
NCorL	Corning leader, Corning
NCort	Free library, Cortland
NCortHi	Cortland county historical society, Cortland
NCortS	R. L. Stilwell, Cortland
NCox	Heermance memorial library, Coxsackie
NCpHi	Historical club, Cape Vincent
ND	Public library, Dansville
NDG	Genesee country express, Dansville
NDe	Cannon free library, Delhi
NDr	Southworth library association, Dryden
NDu	Free library, Dunkirk
NEh	Free library, East Hampton
NElB	Mrs. G. L. Brown, Elizabethtown
NElP	L. S. Pond, Elizabethtown
NEm	Steele memorial library, Elmira
NEmS	Star-gazette, Elmira
NEnC	Charles T. Carluci, Endicott
NEnT	Endicott times, Endicott
NF	Free library, Fayetteville
NFe	Free library, Fort Edward
NFeH	W. H. Hill, Fort Edward
NFJ	Fort Johnson library, Fort Johnson
NFoM	Mohawk Valley democrat, Fonda
NFpH	Fairport herald-mail, Fairport
NFplM	L. B. Moore, Fort Plain
NFr	Memorial library, Freeport
NFre	Darwin R. Barker library, Fredonia
NFu	Public library, Fulton
NGL	Locust ledge museum, Gallatin
NGc	Public library, Glen Cove
NGe	Wadsworth library, Geneseo
NGen	Free library, Geneva
NGenH	Hobart college, Geneva
NGf	Crandall free library, Glens Falls
NGfP	Post-star, Glens Falls
NGl	Free library, Gloversville
NGlL	Leader-republican, Gloversville
NGo	Free library, Gowanda

SYMBOLS

NEW YORK—*Continued*

NGr Moore memorial library, Greene
NH Public library, Hamilton
NHC Colgate university, Hamilton
NHa Public library, Hammondsport
NHaK Keuka grape belt and herald, Hammondsport
NHarC Westchester county court house, Harrison
NHe Hempstead library, Hempstead
NHerHi Herkimer county historical society, Herkimer
NHf Hudson Falls free library association, Hudson Falls
NHfH F. A. Howland, Hudson Falls
NHfP High school library, Hudson Falls
NHfS J. E. Sawyer, Hudson Falls
NHi New York state historical association, Ticonderoga
NHlH Harbinger, Hillsdale
NHoS Holley standard, Holley
NHom Phillips free library, Homer
NHor Public library, Hornell
NHorT Tribune-times, Hornell
NHsS Hoosick Falls standard press, Hoosick Falls
NHuHi Huntington historical society, Huntington, L. I.
NHudS Hudson daily star, Hudson
NI Cornell library association, Ithaca
NIC Cornell university, Ithaca
NIJ Journal news, Ithaca
NIl Free public library, Ilion
NIlS Ilion sentinel, Ilion
NIr Irvington public library, Guiteau foundation, Irvington
NJ James Prendergast free library, Jamestown
NJS P. K. Shankland, Jamestown
NJo Public library, Johnstown
NKen Public library, Kenmore
NKenHi Kenmore historical society, Kenmore
NKiJ Kingston freeman, Kingston
NLaE Enterprise-times, Lancaster
NLar Public library, Larchmont
NLeC Mrs. Irving Crandall, Leonardsville
NLer Public library, Le Roy
NLg Caldwell-Lake George public library, Lake George
NLi Public library, Lisle
NLiT F. E. Terwilligen, Lisle
NLit Public library, Little Falls
NLitJ Journal and courier, Little Falls
NLiv Public library, Livonia
NLivG Livonia gazette, Livonia
NLo Public library, Lockport
NLoC Niagara county clerk's office, Lockport
NLow Free library, Lowville
NLyR Republican, Lyons
NMa Wead library, Malone
NMac Lamont memorial free library, McGraw
NMam Free library, Mamaroneck
NMar Free library, Marcellus
NMas Public library, Massena
NMeT Medina tribune, Medina
NMi Thrall library, Middletown
NMil Free library, Millbrook
NMk Public library, Mount Kisco
NMkF W. L. Fanning, Mount Kisco
NMm Mount Morris library, Mount Morris
NMmE Mount Morris enterprise, Mount Morris
NMmP Picket line post, Mount Morris
NMn Memorial library, Montour Falls
NMoQ F. H. Quick, Montgomery
NMoR Powers free library, Moravia
NN New York public library, New York
NN-J Jackson Square branch, New York public library
NN-M Muhlenburg branch, New York Public library
NNC Columbia university, New York
NNC-B School of business, Columbia univ.
NNCC College of the City of New York
NNCU Cooper Union library, New York
NNCom Commissioner of records, County of New York, New York
NNFo Council on foreign relations, New York
NNGe Genealogical and philosophical society, New York
NNHi New York historical society, New York
NNHu Huntington free library, New York
NNIHi American Irish historical society, New York
NNJ Jewish theological seminary, New York
NNJHi American Jewish historical society, New York
NNJaL Long Island daily press, Jamaica
NNMC Museum of the City of New York, New York
NNMT General society of mechanics and tradesmen, New York
NNMu New York municipal reference library, New York
NNPr Institute of Pacific relations, New York
NNPro Il Progresso italo-americano, New York
NNQ Queens public library, New York
NNRa Rand school of social science, New York
NNRo Roosevelt House, New York
NNS New York society, New York
NNSh Staats-herald corporation, New York
NNSt Standard statistics company, New York
NNT Mr E. L. Tinker, New York
NNUT Union theological seminary, New York
NNUnC University club, New York
NNW Woodrow Wilson memorial library, New York
NNY-H New York university, New York
NNaR Naples record, Naples
NNbG Gazette, New Berlin
NNe Free public library, Newark
NNeU Union-gazette, Newark
NNev Tappan-Spaulding memorial library, Newark Valley
NNewHi Town historian, New Baltimore
NNiU Niagara university, Niagara Falls
NNo Guernsey memorial library, Norwich
NNoS Mrs. F. J. Stanton, Norwich
NNr Public library, New Rochelle
NNrS Morgan H. Seacord, New Rochelle
NNt Public library, North Tonawanda
NOHi Madison county historical society, Oneida
NOg Public library, Ogdensburg
NOl Public library, Olean
NOlT Times-herald, Olean
NOn Huntington memorial library, Oneonta
NOrHi Augusta historical society, Oriskany Falls
NOs Gerrit Smith public library, Oswego
NOsC City Hall, Oswego
NOsP Oswego palladium-times, Oswego
NOvG Gazette and independent, Ovid
NOw Coburn free library, Owego
NOwHi Tioga county historical society, Owego
NOx Oxford memorial library, Oxford
NP Adriance memorial library, Poughkeepsie
NPA Harry Arnold, Poughkeepsie
NPS Star and enterprise, Poughkeepsie
NPV Vassar college, Poughkeepsie
NPa Public library, Patchogue
NPalC Courier-journal, Palmyra
NPawM W. B. Meloney, Pawling
NPc Public library, Port Chester
NPe Public library, Perry
NPhN North country advance, Philadelphia
NPj Free library, Port Jervis
NPjU Union-gazette, Port Jervis
NPo Free library, Portsville
NPoo Public library, Poolville
NPrH W. T. Howe, Prattsburg
NPuD Pulaski democrat, Pulaski
NPw Public library, Port Washington
NPy Public library, Penn Yan
NPyC Penn Yan chronicle-express, Penn Yan
NPyCl County clerk's office, Penn Yan
NPyD Penn Yan democrat, Penn Yan
NPyF William Foshay, Penn Yan
NR Public library, Rochester
NRJ Rochester journal, Rochester
NRT Rochester times-union, Rochester
NRU Rochester university, Rochester
NRaN Ravena news-herald, Ravena
NRc Public library, Rockville Center
NRcN Nassau daily review, Rockville Center
NReHi Town historian, Rensselaerville
NRiHi Suffolk county historical society, Riverhead
NRo Roxbury library, Roxbury
NRom Jervis library association, Rome
NRosM Alan Mackenzie, Rosendale
NRy Free reading room, Rye
NSD William T. Davis, Staten Island
NSHi Staten Island historical society, Staten Island
NSM Staten Island public museum, Staten Island
NSW Wagner college, Staten Island
NSa Margaret Reaney memorial library, St. Johnsville
NSaE Enterprise and news, St. Johnsville
NSal Bancroft public library, Salem
NSalC Robert Cruickshank, Salem
NSau Public library, Saugerties
NSbC St. Bonaventure college, St. Bonaventure
NSc Annie Porter Ainsworth memorial library, Sandy Creek
NSch Free public library, Schenectady
NSchHi Schenectady historical society, Schenectady
NSchS Union-star, Schenectady
NSchU Union college, Schenectady
NSh John Jermain memorial library, Sag Harbor
NShe Public library, Sherburne
NShem Minerva free library, Sherman
NSher Sherrill-Kenwood public library, Sherrill
NShi Public library, Shelter Island
NSi Public library, Sidney
NSk Library association, Skaneateles
NSkP Skaneateles press, Skaneateles
NSm Smithtown library, Smithtown Branch
NSo Rogers memorial library, Southampton
NSp Public library, Springville
NSt Public library Stamford
NStM Stamford mirror-recorder, Stamford
NStV Stamford Village library, Stamford
NSyC Court of appeals, Syracuse
NSyHi Onondaga historical society, Syracuse
NSyU Syracuse university, Syracuse
NT Public library, Troy
NTO Troy observer-budget, Troy
NTR Rensselaer polytechnic institute, Troy
NU Public library, Utica
NUHi Oneida historical society, Utica
NUO Observer-dispatch, Utica
NVe Van Etten high school, Van Etten
NWa Public library, Walton
NWal Josephine-Louise public library, Walden
NWar Richards library, Warrensburg
NWat Waterloo library and historical society, Waterloo
NWatrP A. B. Parker, Watertown
NWav Waverly high school, Waverly
NWavS Sun-recorder, Waverly
NWavSm Miss C. A. Smith, Waverly
NWe Patterson library, Westfield
NWel David A. Howe public library, Wellsville
NWh Free library, Whitehall
NWhi Durham public library, Whiteboro
NWp Public library, White Plains
NWpG Good Counsel college, White Plains
NWpL G. T. Long, White Plains
NWpM Charles E. Moore White Plains
NWy Village library, Wyoming
NY Public library, Yonkers
NYW Westchester county publisher, Yonkers

Nebraska

Nb Nebraska state library, Lincoln
NbA Township library, Alma
NbAdG Adams globe, Adams
NbArH Mrs. A. E. Harvey, Arapahoe
NbArP Public mirror, Arapahoe
NbBb Carnegie library, Broken Bow
NbBf Public library, Bloomfield
NbBl Public library, Blair
NbBlP Pilot-tribune, Blair
NbBloA Advocate-tribune, Bloomington
NbBr Public library, Bruning
NbBrB Bruning banner-Belvidere news, Bruning
NbCR Chappell register, Chappell
NbCaB J. H. Bryant, Carleton
NbCc Public library, Central City
NbCeN Ceresco news, Ceresco
NbClP Mrs. W. L. Palmer, Clay Center
NbCcC Platte county court house, Columbus
NbCrN Northwest Nebraska news, Crawford
NbCrT Crawford tribune, Crawford
NbCre Public library, Crete
NbCreN Crete news, Crete
NbFN Fairbury news, Fairbury
NbFaA Auxiliary, Fairfield
NbFrP Perkins printing company, Fremont
NbFuN Nance county journal, Fullerton
NbGi Township library, Gibbon
NbHM Hastings museum, Hastings
NbHaS Harrison sun, Harrison
NbHar Public library, Hartington
NbHarC Cedar county news, Hartington
NbHav Public library, Harvard
NbHi Nebraska state historical society, Lincoln
NbHo Public library, Holdrege
NbHsN Hay Springs news, Hay Springs
NbIR Imperial republican, Imperial
NbK Public library, Kearney
NbLeD Dawson county pioneer, Lexington
NbLeiW Leigh world, Leigh
NbLo Township library, Loup City
NbM Brenizer public library, Merna
NbMa Public library, Madison
NbMaB Mrs. Philip Bauch, Madison
NbMaS Star-mail, Madison
NbMcB Blue Valley journal, McCool Junction

NEBRASKA—*Continued*

NbMi Public library, Minden
NbMuG Dr. G. H. Gilmore, Murray
NbN Public library, Nelson
NbNbE North Bend eagle, North Bend
NbNeN Nebraska news-press, Nebraska City
NbNo Public library, Norfolk
NbO Public library, Omaha
NbOB Bee-news, Omaha
NbOT Tägliche Omaha tribüne, Omaha
NbOaC G. S. Clingman, Oakdale
NbOnF Frontier, O'Neill
NbOnH Holt county independent, O'Neill
NbOrQ Ord quiz, Ord
NbPR Pender republic, Pender
NbPaJ Palmer journal, Palmer
NbR Public library, Randolph
NbRa Public library, Ravenna
NbRcC Commercial advertiser, Red Cloud
NbSS Star-herald, Scottsbluff
NbSc Township library, Silver Creek
NbStR Stanton register, Stanton
NbTeC Tecumseh chieftain, Tecumseh
NbVD Miss Catherine Donaher, Valentine
NbWC Wayne county court house, Wayne
NbWa Lincoln township library, Wausa
NbWiH Wilcox herald, Wilcox
NbWnH Wayne herald, Wayne
NbWyA Arbor state, Wymore

North Carolina

Nc North Carolina state library, Raleigh
NcAl Stanly county public library, Albemarle
NcAlP Stanly news and press, Albemarle
NcAs Pack memorial public library, Asheville
NcAsS Sondley library, Asheville
NcBL Lees-McRae college, Banners Elk
NcBeR Benson review, Benson
NcD Duke university, Durham
NcDu Public library, Durham
NcEloC Elon college, Elon College
NcGr Greensboro public library, Greensboro
NcGrW Woman's college library of the University of North Carolina, Greensboro
NcGreE East Carolina teachers college, Greenville
NcGuC Guilford college, Guilford College
NcHe H. Leslie Perry memorial library, Henderson
NcHen Public library, Hendersonville
NcHi North Carolina historical commission, Raleigh
NcHic Worth-Elliott Carnegie library, Hickory
NcHpC High Point college, High Point
NcL Caldwell county library, Lenoir
NcLN Lenoir new-topic, Lenoir
NcMor Public library, Morganton
NcMorN News herald, Morganton
NcNwP Journal-patriot, North Wilkesboro
NcRS North Carolina state college, Raleigh
NcRoP Rockingham post-dispatch, Rockingham
NcSC Catawba college, Salisbury
NcSp Public library, Spray
NcU University of North Carolina, Chapel Hill
NcWaC Wake Forest college, Wake Forest
NcWdL Bertie ledger-advance, Windsor
NcWe Public library, Weldon
NcWi Public library, Wilmington
NcWiS Wilmington morning star, Wilmington
NcWin Carnegie public library, Winston-Salem

North Dakota

NdB Public library, Bismarck
NdCR Cando record, Cando
NdD Public library, Dickinson
NdFA North Dakota agricultural college, Fargo
NdFC Cass county court house, Fargo
NdFF Fargo forum, Fargo
NdFeW Wells county news, Fessenden
NdFIT North Dakota times, Finley
NdFoC Sargent county court house, Forman
NdG Public library, Grand Forks
NdGH Grand Forks herald, Grand Forks
NdGP City police department, Grand Forks
NdGrH Granville herald, Granville
NdHi State historical society, Bismarck
NdJ Alfred Dickey free library, Jamestown
NdJC Stutsman county court house, Jamestown
NdLA Lakota American, Lakota
NdLiF Lisbon free press, Lisbon
NdM Free public library, Minot
NdMC Ward county court house, Minot
NdMN Minot daily news, Minot
NdMcG McClusky gazette, McClusky
NdNC Chronotype-express, Neche
NdU State university of North Dakota, Grand Forks
NdV Public library, Valley City
NdVS Valley City state teachers' college, Valley City
NdWaM McKenzie county farmer, Watford City

New Hampshire

Nh New Hampshire state library, Concord
NhA Town library, Amherst
NhBr Minot-Sleeper library, Bristol
NhC Fiske free library, Claremont
NhCa Town library, Canaan
NhCe Center Sandwich free library, Center Sandwich
NhCo Public library, Colebrook
NhCon Public library, Concord
NhConw Public library, Conway
NhD Dartmouth College, Hanover
NhDe Public library, Derry
NhDuP Durham print shop, Durham
NhE Public library, Exeter
NhER Rockingham county record, Exeter
NhEn Free public library, Enfield
NhF Goodwin public library, Farmington
NhFi Town library, Fitzwilliam
NhFr Public library, Franklin
NhFrJ Journal-transcript, Franklin
NhG Public library, Gorham
NhH Howe memorial library, Hanover
NhHa Haverhill library association, Haverhill
NhHi New Hampshire historical society, Concord
NhHil Fuller public library, Hillsboro
NhHin Public library, Hinsdale
NhK Public library, Keene
NhL Weeks memorial library, Lancaster
NhLa Public library, Laconia
NhLe Public library, Lebanon
NhLi Public library, Littleton
NhLit Littleton town hall, Littleton
NhM City library, Manchester
NhMA Association Canado-Americaine, Manchester
NhMe Public library, Meredith
NhMi Free library, Milford
NhNa Public library, Nashua
NhNe Richards free library, Newport
NhNeB Ella W. Barton, Newport
NhO Public library, Ossipee
NhP Town library, Petersboro
NhPi Carpenter public library, Pittsfield
NhPo Public library, Portsmouth
NhPoH Portsmouth herald, Portsmouth
NhR Public library, Rochester
NhSF Sandwich historical society, Sandwich
NhSHi Somersworth free press, Somersworth
NhU University of New Hampshire, Durham
NhW Town library, Walpole
NhWh Public library, Whitefield
NhWo Public library, Wolfeboro Falls

New Jersey

NJ New Jersey state library, Trenton
NJAs Public library, Asbury Park
NJAt Public library, Atlantic Highlands
NJBa Free public library, Bayonne
NJBb Memorial library, Boundbrook
NJBeN Belleville news, Belleville
NJBerB Breeze, Berlin
NJBl Free public library, Bloomfield
NJBlI Independent-press, Bloomfield
NJBrC Cumberland county court house, Bridgeton
NJBrHi Bridgeton historical society, Bridgeton
NJCHi Camden historical society, Camden
NJCaP Caldwell progress, Caldwell
NJClL Clifton leader, Clifton
NJCrC Cranford citizen and chronicle, Cranford
NJD Free public library, Dover
NJDa Dover advance, Dover
NJE Free public library, Elizabeth
NJElT Elmer times, Elmer
NJEnP Englewood press, Englewood
NJEo Free public library, East Orange
NJFHi Monmouth county historical association, Freehold
NJFlC Hunterdon county court house, Flemington
NJH Free public library, Hoboken
NJHi New Jersey historical society, Newark
NJHp Highland Park press, Highland Park
NJJ Free public library, Jersey City
NJL Free public library, Linden
NJM Morris county free library, Morristown
NJMW Washington headquarters, Morristown
NJMa Free public library, Maplewood
NJMo Free public library, Montclair
NJMoT Montclair trust company, Montclair
NJN Public library, Newark
NJN-B Newark business branch, Newark
NJNb Free public library, New Brunswick
NJNu Free public library, Nutley
NJO Free library, Orange
NJOgT Ocean Grove times, Ocean Grove
NJP Princeton university, Princeton
NJPa Free public library, Paterson
NJPe Public library, Perth Amboy
NJPg Carney Point public library, Penns Grove
NJPl Free public library, Plainfield
NJR Rutgers university, New Brunswick
NJRp Free public library, Ridgefield Park
NJSS Salem standard and Jerseyman, Salem
NJSoM Somerset messenger-gazette, Somerville
NJT Free public library, Trenton
NJTT Times, Trenton
NJU Free public library, Union City
NJV Public library, Ventnor
NJVe Free public library, Verona
NJVi Vineland historical and antiquarian society, Vineland
NJW Public library, Wildwood
NJWT Tribune-jounal, Wildwood
NJWdHi Gloucester county historical society, Woodbury
NJWdN News, Woodbury
NJWdS Frank H. Stewart, Woodbury

New Mexico

NmA Public library, Albuquerque
NmAC Bernalillo county court house, Albuquerque
NmAH Health City sun, Albuquerque
NmArA Advocate, Artesia
NmAzC San Juan county court house, Aztec
NmAzI Independent review, Aztec
NmCC Union county court house, Clayton
NmCN News, Clayton
NmDC Luna county court house, Deming
NmFP Post office, Farley
NmGC McKinley county court house, Gallup
NmHC Sierra county court house, Hillsboro
NmHi Historical society of New Mexico, Santa Fe
NmHsS Sierra county advocate, Hot Springs
NmLS State college, Las Cruces
NmLv Carnegie public library, Las Vegas
NmMN News, Magdalena
NmPC Roosevelt county court house, Portales
NmPD Portales daily, Portales
NmRC Colfax county court house, Raton
NmRoC Chaves county court house, Roswell
NmSA New Mexico college of agriculture and the mechanic arts, State College
NmTC Quay county court house, Tucumcari
NmU University of New Mexico, Albuquerque

Nevada

Nv Nevada state library, Carson City
NvAC County recorder, Austin
NvCH Caliente herald, Caliente
NvEI Elko independent, Elko
NvFE Fallon eagle, Fallon
NvLR Lovelock review-miner, Lovelock
NvPC Lincoln county court house, Pioche
NvR Washoe county library, Reno
NvRW Washoe county recorder, Reno
NvT Free public library, Tonopah
NvU University of Nevada, Reno
NvV Miners' Union library, Virginia
NvWC Humboldt county recorder, Winnemucca
NvWH Humboldt star, Winnemucca

Ohio

OAU Ohio university, Athens
OAk Public library, Akron
OAkU Akron university, Akron
OAl Carnegie free library, Alliance
OAlMU Mt. Union college, Alliance
OAsh Public library, Ashland
OAshT Ashland times-gazette, Ashland
OB Bluffton college, Bluffton
OBr Public library, Bryan
OBrC Williams county court house, Bryan
OC Public library of Cincinnati, Cincinnati

OHIO—*Continued*

OCH	Hebrew Union college, Cincinnati
OCHi	Historical and philosophical society, Cincinnati
OCU	University of Cincinnati, Cincinnati
OCX	St. Francis Xavier college, Cincinnati
OCa	Public library, Canton
OCfD	Mahoning dispatch, Canfield
OchN	Dard Hunter, Chillicothe
OChN	Chillicothe news-advertiser, Chillicothe
OCl	Cleveland public library, Cleveland
OClJ	Jewish review and observer, Cleveland
OClWHi	Western reserve historical society, Cleveland
OCo	Public library, Columbus
OCoC	Capital university, Columbus
OCon	Carnegie public library, Conneaut
OCwT	Winchester times, Canal Winchester
ODW	Ohio Wesleyan university, Delaware
ODa	Public library, Dayton
OEly	Elyria library, Elyria
OElyC	Elyria chronicle-telegram, Elyria
OF	Birchard library, Fremont
OFIR	Republican-courier, Findlay
OG	Public library, Galion
OGI	Galion inquirer, Galion
OGal	Public library, Gallipolis
OGe	Public library, Geneva
OGrD	Denison university, Granville
OH	Lane public library, Hamilton
OHi	Ohio state archeological and historical society, Columbus
OHiH	Hiram college, Hiram
OIB	Briggs library, Ironton
OJS	Jackson sun-journal, Jackson
OKC	Courier-tribune, Kent
OL	Public library, Lorain
OLiC	Columbiana county court house, Lisbon
OMM	Marietta college, Marietta
OMMu	Campus Martius state museum, Marietta
OMauA	Maumee advance-era, Maumee
OMauM	Maumee Valley news, Maumee
OMcD	McArthur democrat-enquirer, McArthur
OMgU	Union register, Mt. Gilead
OMi	Free public library, Middletown
OMia	School district public library, Miamisburg
OMiIT	Township library, Milan
OMv	Public library, Mt. Vernon
ON	McKinley memorial library, Niles
ONo	Norwalk City school district public library, Norwalk
ONoF	Firelands museum, Norwalk
ONs	Public library, New Straitsville
OO	Oberlin college, Oberlin
OOxM	Miami university, Oxford
OOxW	Western college for women, Oxford
OPA	County auditor, Paulding
OPe	Way library, Perrysburg
OPi	Flesh public library, Piqua
OSHi	Clark county historical society, Springfield
OSa	Public library, Salem
OT	Public library, Toledo
OTr	Public library, Troy
OU	Ohio state university, Columbus
OW	Public library, Warren
OWT	Tribune-chonicle, Warren
OXG	Greene county district library, Xenia
OY	Youngstown public library, Youngstown
OYsA	Antioch college, Yellow Springs

Oklahoma

OkAdB	Ada bulletin, Ada
OkAl	Public library, Altus
OkAlT	Altus times-democrat, Altus
OkAnN	Anadarko news, Anadarko
OkBfH	Harper county democrat, Buffalo
OkBl	Public library, Blackwell
OkBlT	Blackwell tribune, Blackwell
OkBoN	Boise City news, Boise City
OkCO	Oklahoma college for women, Chickasha
OkCaR	Canton record, Canton
OkChL	Lincoln county republican, Chandler
OkCtH	Choteau herald, Choteau
OkDS	Southeastern state teachers college, Durant
OkE	Carnegie public library, Enid
OkEdB	Edmond booster, Edmond
OkEdC	Central state teachers college, Edmond
OkEr	Carnegie library, El Reno
OkErA	El Reno weekly American, El Reno
OkErT	El Reno daily tribune, El Reno
OkFP	Frederick press, Frederick
OkFaC	Fairfax chief, Fairfax
OkG	Carnegie library, Guthrie
OkGuP	Panhandle herald, Guymon
OkHi	Oklahoma historical society, Oklahoma City
OkHiN	Holdenville news, Holdenville
OkHn	Public library, Henryetta
OkHnN	Henryetta news, Henryetta
OkHo	Public library, Hobart
OkJV	Jet visitor, Jet
OkKT	Kingfisher times, Kingfisher
OkL	Carnegie public library, Lawton
OkLvL	Leader-tribune, Laverne
OkM	Public library, Muskogee
OkMP	Muskogee phoenix, Muskogee
OkMT	Muskogee times-democrat, Muskogee
OkMcD	McAlester democrat, McAlester
OkNT	Norman transcript, Norman
OkOOk	Oklahoma publishing company, Oklahoma City
OkOR	E. C. Routh, Oklahoma City
OkOk	Public library, Okemah
OkOm	Public library, Okmulgee
OkOmT	Okmulgee daily times, Okmulgee
OkP	Carnegie library, Ponca City
OkPN	Ponca City news, Ponca City
OkPeJ	Perry journal, Perry
OkPrJ	Pryor Jeffersonian, Pryor
OkPw	Public library, Pawhuska
OkPwJ	Daily journal-capital, Pawhuska
OkRE	Ringling eagle, Ringling
OkScN	Sasakwa news, Sasakwa
OkSeP	Seminole producer, Seminole
OkShO	Oklahoma Baptist university, Shawnee
OkSlD	Democrat-American, Sallisaw
OkSpH	Sapulpa herald, Sapulpa
OkSt	Free public library, Stillwater
OkStO	Oklahoma agricultural and mechanical college, Stillwater
OkSuT	Sulphur times-democrat, Sulphur
OkT	Public library, Tulsa
OkTE	R. S. Ellison, Tulsa
OkTT	Tulsa tribune, Tulsa
OkTa	Carnegie library, Tahlequah
OkTaC	Cherokee county democrat-star, Tahlequah
OkTaN	Northeastern state teachers college, Tahlequah
OkU	University of Oklahoma, Norman
OkWcW	Welch watchman, Welch
OkWeS	Southwestern state teachers college, Weatherford
OkWl	Public library, Walters
OkWoN	Woodward news-bulletin, Woodward
OkWoW	Woodward county republican, Woodward
OkWtF	Mrs. T. B. Ferguson, Watonga
OkWyW	Woods county enterprise, Waynoka
OkY	Public library, Yale

Oregon

Or	Oregon state library, Salem
OrA	Public library, Albany
OrAs	Free public library, Ashland
OrAt	Free public library, Astoria
OrB	Public library, Baker
OrBR	Record-courier, Baker
OrBd	Deschutes county library, Bend
OrBeE	Enterprise, Beaverton
OrC	Public library, Corvallis
OrCA	Oregon state agricultural college, Corvallis
OrCaB	Blue Mountain eagle, Canyon City
OrCoG	Globe-times, Condon
OrCqV	Coquille Valley sentinel, Coquille
OrDP	Polk county itemizer-observer, Dallas
OrE	Public library, Eugene
OrER	Register-guard, Eugene
OrEcC	W. H. Crary, Echo
OrEcN	Echo news, Echo
OrFS	Siuslaw oar, Florence
OrGC	Grants Pass courier, Grants Pass
OrHbA	Hillsboro argus, Hillsboro
OrHi	Oregon historical society, Portland
OrHrN	Hood River news, Hood River
OrK	Klamath county library, Klamath Falls
OrKN	Klamath news, Klamath Falls
OrL	Public library, La Grande
OrM	Public library, Marshfield
OrMe	Jackson county library, Medford
OrMnH	Monmouth herald, Monmouth
OrMoS	Sherman county journal, Moro
OrO	Malheur county library, Ontario
OrOr	Public library, Oregon City
OrP	Library association of Portland, Portland
OrPM	L. A. McArthur, Portland
OrPN	Nachrichten, Portland
OrPe	Umatilla county library, Portland
OrPrC	Central Oregonian, Prineville
OrRN	News-review, Roseburg
OrSB	A. N. Bush, Salem
OrShA	City auditor, St. Helens
OrT	Public library, Tillamook
OrU	University of Oregon, Eugene
OrWT	Waldport tribune, Waldport

PENNSYLVANIA

P	Pennsylvania state library, Harrisburg
P-M	Pennsylvania state library miscellaneous collection, Harrisburg
PA	B. F. Jones memorial library, Aliquippa
PAg	Carnegie free library of Allegheny, Pittsburgh
PAlC	Allentown call, Allentown
PAlCh	Allentown chronicle and news, Allentown
PAlHi	Lehigh county historical society, Allentown
PAltHi	Blair county historical society, Altoona
PAmC	Ambridge daily citizen, Ambridge
PAmL	Laughlin memorial library, Ambridge
PAmbG	Ambler gazette, Ambler
PArdL	Lower Merion junior high school, Ardmore
PArdM	Main line daily times, Ardmore
PAtM	Tioga Point museum, Athens
PB	Public library, Bethlehem
PBG	Globe-times, Bethlehem
PBL	Lehigh university, Bethlehem
PBaS	Barnesboro star, Barnesboro
PBeC	Beaver county court house, Beaver
PBeT	Beaver daily times, Beaver
PBedI	Inquirer, Bedford
PBelB	Mrs. S. C. Behers, Bellefonte
PBelC	Centre county court house, Bellefonte
PBerH	Robert L. Harder, Berwick
PBerR	C. A. Rasley, Berwick
PBf	Carnegie free library, Beaver Falls
PBfG	Geneva college, Beaver Falls
PBfT	Beaver trust company, Beaver Falls
PBl	Public library, Blairsville
PBlD	Blairsville dispatch, Blairsville
PBlaG	Mrs. J. R. Geary, Black Lick
PBlo	Public library, Bloomsburg
PBloE	G. E. Elwell, Bloomsburg
PBloHi	Columbia county historical society, Bloomsburg
PBloM	Morning press, Bloomsburg
PBlosH	Blossburg herald, Blossburg
PBlosM	Mrs. J. Mooers, Blossburg
PBmC	Bryn Mawr college, Bryn Mawr
PBoT	Boyertown times, Boyertown
PBr	Carnegie public library, Bradford
PBrS	Bradford evening star, Bradford
PBra	Carnegie free library, Braddock
PBriC	Bristol courier, Bristol
PBro	Free public library, Brownsville
PBuE	Dr. W. S. Erdman, Buckingham
PCC	Crozer theological seminary, Chester
PCHi	Delaware county historical society, Chester
PCT	Chester times, Chester
PCanB	Mrs. M. E. Berry, Canonsburg
PCanN	Canonsburg daily notes, Canonsburg
PCanP	Potts Brothers real estate office, Canonsburg
PCar	Public library, Carbondale
PCarlB	C. G. Beetem, Carlisle
PCarlHi	Hamilton library and Cumberland county historical society, Carlisle
PCarn	Andrew Carnegie free library, Carnegie
PCat	Public library, Catasauqua
PCatD	Catasauqua dispatch, Catasauqua
PCatH	Catasauqua high school, Catasauqua
PCataV	H. R. Von Dorster, Catawissa
PCh	Coyle free library, Chambersburg
PChP	Public opinion, Chambersburg
PChaW	Carl Wertz, Charleroi
PChalP	F. K. Pitson, Chalfont
PChalS	William Swartzlander, Chalfont
PClK	M. M. Kaufman, Clarion
PClaP	Clairton progress, Clairton
PCo	Carnegie free library, Connellsville
PCoaC	Mrs. F. L. Campbell, Coatesville
PCoaH	Lewis Holton, Coatesville
PCoaW	Harry Woodward, Coatesville
PCoN	Columbia news, Columbia
PConE	Mrs. John Evans, Conyngham
PCt	Free library, Coudersport
PCtA	Mrs. C. O. Armstrong, Coudersport
PCtC	Julius Colcord, Coudersport
PCtHi	Potter county historical society, Coudersport
PCtT	Mrs. E. D. Thompson, Coudersport
PD	Thomas Beaver free library, Danville
PDA	Mrs. Theodore Angle, Danville
PDC	Montour county court house, Danville
PDM	William Moore, Danville
PDN	Morning news, Danville

SYMBOLS

PENNSYLVANIA—*Continued*

PDaH	W. F. Hallstead, Dalton
PDoC	Bucks county court house, Doylestown
PDoHi	Bucks county historical society, Doylestown
PDowN	Downingtown news, Downingtown
PDu	Carnegie free library, Duquesne
PE	Public library, Easton
PEC	Northampton county court house, Easton
PEHi	Northampton county historical society, Easton
PEL	Lafayette college, Easton
PEaK	P. W. Kimmel, East Berlin
PEbC	Cambria county court house, Ebensburg
PEbCo	Commissioners' office, Ebensburg
PEbHi	Cambria county historical society, Ebensburg
PEbM	Mountaineer-herald, Ebensburg
PElJ	Elkland journal, Elkland
PEr	Public library, Erie
PErC	Cathedral of St. Paul, Erie
PErW	J. A. Wurzbach, Erie
PEsS	Morning sun, East Stroudsburg
PFgR	Ralph Rockafellow, Forrest Grove
PFr	Public library, Franklin
PFraM	Mrs. Mengal, Frackville
PFreB	W. F. Brown printing company, Freeburg
PFrlF	W. R. Flad, Freeland
PFrlJ	W. E. Joyce, Freeland
PGC	Adams county court house, Gettysburg
PGCo	Commissioners' office, Gettysburg
PGS	Star and sentinel, Gettysburg
PGT	Gettysburg times, Gettysburg
PGcR	Reporter-herald, Grove City
PGrL	R. B. Laird, Greensburg
PGrT	Tribune and review, Greensburg
PHHi	Dauphin county historical society, Harrisburg
PHT	Harrisburg telegraph, Harrisburg
PHaC	Haverford college, Haverford
PHam	Public library, Hamburg
PHawB	Hawley Bank, Hawley
PHaz	Public library, Hazelton
PHazL	L. G. Lubrecht, Hazleton
PHazM	Leon Maue, Hazleton
PHazS	Slovensky obcan, Hazelton
PHazSs	Standard-sentinel, Hazleton
PHeN	Herndon news, Herndon
PHi	Historical society of Pennsylvania, Philadelphia
PHnM	Mrs. Charles Martin, Honey Brook
PHoHi	Blair county historical society, Hollidaysburg
PHoR	Hollidaysburg register, Hollidaysburg
PHolP	Henry D. Paxon, Holicong
PHom	Carnegie free library, Homestead
PHsHi	Wayne county historical society, Honesdale
PHsS	Sheriff's vault, Wayne county court house, Honesdale
PHsT	Treasurer's vault, Wayne county court house, Honesdale
PHsWi	Wayne independent, Honesdale
PHuJ	Juniata college, Huntingdon
PHwR	S. I. Reber, Howard
PIC	Indiana county court house, Indiana
PIP	Indiana progress, Indiana
PIT	Caroline Taylor, Indiana
PIW	George F. Walker, Indiana
PIWa	Mrs. J. C. Walker, Indiana
PJ	Cambria free library, Swank collection, Johnstown
PJR	Dwight Roberts, Johnstown
PJT	Johnstown tribune, Johnstown
PJeL	A. F. Landis printing company, Jeannette
PJsJ	Jersey Shore herald, Jersey Shore
PJsK	Mrs. J. H. Krom, Jersey Shore
PJsS	Mrs. W. N. Shuman, Jersey Shore
PK	Bayard Taylor memorial library, Kennett Square
PKM	George Mitchell, Kennett Square
PKY	William Young, Kennett Square
PKiF	Mrs. James Foulis, Kittanning
PKiHa	Lavina B. Hankey, Kittanning
PKiK	J. W. King, Kittanning
PKiL	Leader-times, Kittanning
PKiR	Miss Rene Reynolds, Kittanning
PLaF	Franklin and Marshall college, Lancaster
PLaHi	Lancaster county historical society, Lancaster
PLaL	Landis Valley museum, Lancaster
PLaN	Lancaster newspapers, Inc., Lancaster
PLanA	Advance publishing company, Langhorne
PLansN	North Penn reporter, Lansdale
PLatS	St. Vincent college, Latrobe
PLeHi	Lebanon county historical society, Lebanon
PLewB	Bucknell university, Lewisburg
PLewC	Union county court house, Lewisburg
PLewJ	Lewisburg journal, Lewisburg
PLewL	Linn collection, Lewisburg
PLewT	Mrs. L. E. Theiss, Lewisburg
PLewW	W. C. Walls, Lewisburg
PLfH	Lansford high school, Lansford
PLhT	R. H. Thompson, Lock Haven
PLiA	W. S. Allen, Littlestown
PLoK	Mrs. J. L. Kemmerer, Loganton
PMK	Carnegie free library, McKeesport
PMN•	Daily news, McKeesport
PMa	Free public library, Mansfield
PMaT	Mansfield state teachers college, Mansfield
PMacK	O. P. Knauss, Macungie
PMarH	J. Thompson Henry, Martha Furnace
PMc	Dimmick memorial library, Mauch Chunk
PMcC	Carbon county court house, Mauch Chunk
PMcT	Times-news, Mauch Chunk
PMe	Public library, Meadville
PMeA	Allegheny college, Meadville
PMeR	John Reynolds, Meadville
PMeT	Tribune-republican, Meadville
PMecL	Local news, Mechanicsburg
PMedD	Delaware county Institute of Science, Media
PMerD	Mercer dispatch and republican, Mercer
PMiC	Snyder county court house, Middleburg
PMiCo	Commissioners' office, Middleburg
PMiHi	Snyder county historical society, Middleburg
PMiP	Middleburg post, Middleburg
PMiR	Snyder county recorder's vault, Middleburg
PMilA	Mrs. C. O. Armstrong, Milford
PMilC	Pike county court house, Milford
PMilD	Milford dispatch, Milford
PMilHi	Pike county historical society, Milford
PMilaS	Mrs. M. L. Skinner, Milanville
PMillH	C. H. Herrold, Millersburg
PMiltS	Standard, Milton
PMoN	Monessen news-call, Monessen
PMonR	Henry Rockwell, Monroeton
PNaK	Anna Kratz, Nace's Corner
PNar	Community library, Narberth
PNarD	Frank J. Dwyer, Narberth
PNazHi	Moravian historical society, Nazareth
PNc	Free public library, New Castle
PNcC	Lawrence county court house, New Castle
PNeB	Edward R. Barnsley, Newtown
PNeBr	Mrs. Edward Briggs, Newtown
PNewT	Times-star, Newville
PNhE	Margaret Ely, New Hope
PNhF	Richard Foulke, New Hope
PNo	Norristown library company, Norristown
PNoHi	Historical society of Montgomery county, Norristown
PNoT	Norristown times herald, Norristown
PNorG	C. W. Gutelius, Northumberland
PNuL	Lewis Lee, Numidia
POD	Dr. F. Davis, Oil City
POlG	Olyphant gazette, Olyphant
PP	Free library of Philadelphia, Philadelphia
PPAp	Apprentices' free library, Philadelphia
PPCHi	American Catholic historical society, Philadelphia
PPCo	Commercial museum, Philadelphia
PPDe	Philadelphia democrat-gazette, Philadelphia
PPF	Franklin institute, Philadelphia
PPFfHi	Frankford historical society, Philadelphia
PPG	German society of Pennsylvania, Philadelphia
PPGr	G.A.R. Memorial Hall, Philadelphia
PPJ	Jewish daily forward, Philadelphia
PPL	Library company of Philadelphia
PPM	Mercantile library, Philadelphia
PPN	Philadelphia news bureau, Philadelphia
PPPHi	Presbyterian historical society, Philadelphia
PPR	Philadelphia record, Philadelphia
PPT	C. O. F. Treisher, Philadelphia
PPaS	Harry W. Saylor, Parkesburg
PPeS	Schwenkfelder historical society, Pennsburg
PPeT	Town and country, Pennsburg
PPhA	H. S. Ashcraft, Philipsburg
PPhJ	Philipsburg journal, Philipsburg
PPhoF	Farmers' and mechanics' national bank, Phoenixsville
PPhoN	Julius Neuman, Phoenixsville
PPi	Carnegie library of Pittsburgh
PPiHi	Historical society of Western Pennsylvania, Pittsburgh
PPiU-D	Darlington collection of the Univ. of Pittsburgh, in Historical building
PPiW	Western theological seminary, Pittsburgh
PPitE	Pitcairn express, Pitcairn
PPoC	Commissioner's storage room, Schuylkill county court house, Pottsville
PPoHi	Schuylkill county historical society, Pottsville
PPoR	Pottsville republican, Pottsville
PPoU	C. W. Unger, Pottsville
PPot	Public library, Pottstown
PPotB	Pottstown blade, Pottstown
PPotM	Pottstown mercury and news, Pottstown
PPotW	George F. P. Wanger, Pottstown
PQF	Quakertown free press, Quakertown
PQZ	James Zuck, Quakertown
PR	Public library, Reading
PRE	Eagle, Reading
PRHi	Berks county historical society, Reading
PRN	J. Bennet Nolan, Reading
PRT	Reading times, Reading
PReK	P. A. Kinsley, Renovo
PSC	Swarthmore college, Swarthmore
PSF	Friends historical library, Swarthmore
PSaS	Mrs. Ellen Sigmund, Salona
PSanB	Sandy Lake breeze, Sandy Lake
PScI	Independent-observer, Scottdale
PScr	Albright library, Scranton
PScrC	Chamber of commerce, Scranton
PScrG	G.A.R. Memorial Hall, Scranton
PScrHi	Lackawanna historical society, Scranton
PScrT	Scranton times, Scranton
PScrW	Wagner printing company, Scranton
PScrWi	W. A. Wilcox, Scranton
PSeHi	Snyder county historical society, Selinsgrove
PSew	Public library, Sewickley
PShH	Mrs. K. C. Heffelfinger, Shamokin
PShN	Shamokin news-dispatch, Shamokin
PSheN	News budget, Shenandoah
PShiN	News-chronicle, Shippensburg
PSoP	Alfred Preston, Solebury
PSpF	Harry H. Funk, Springtown
PSprI	Interborough press, Spring City
PStP	Pennsylvania state college, State College
PStrR	Stroudsburg record, Stroudsburg
PSuD	Sunbury daily, Sunbury
PSuE	William H. Engle, Sunbury
PSuHi	Northumberland county historical society, Sunbury
PSuS	T. J. Silvius, Sunbury
PSuY	Caroline V. Youngman, Sunbury
PSugM	Frank Miller, Sugar Grove
PSugW	George Woodside, Sugar Grove
PSulR	Sullivan review, Sullivan
PTC	Evening courier, Tamaqua
PTaV	Valley daily news, Tarentum
PTiA	Argus, Tioga
PTioC	Commissioners' office, Tionesta
PTioF	Forest republican, Tionesta
PTioH	Mrs. R. L. Hazlet, Tionesta
PToF	A. C. Fanning, Towanda
PToHi	Bradford county historical society, Towanda
PToR	Towanda review, Towanda
PTowW	West Schuylkill herald, Tower City
PTuM	Harry Metcalf, Tunkhannock
PU	University of Pennsylvania, Philadelphia
PUn	Free public library, Uniontown
PUnC	Fayette county court house, Uniontown
PUnN	News-standard, Uniontown
PUnR	Recorder's office, Uniontown
PW	Warren library association, Warren
PWC	Warren county court house, Warren
PWCl	Frank and Alice Clemons, Warren
PWS	Asa Sigworth, Warren
PWaC	Washington county court house, Washington
PWaHi	Washington county historical society, Washington
PWatF	Clyde Fosnot, Watsontown
PWay	Public library, Waynesburg
PWayC	Commissioners' office, Waynesburg
PWayHi	Greene county historical society, Waynesburg
PWayW	Waynesburg college, Waynesburg
PWaynR	Record herald, Waynesboro
PWbN	Evening news, Wilkes-Barre
PWbT	Times-leader, Wilkes-Barre
PWbW	Wyoming historical and geological society, Wilkes-Barre
PWcHi	Chester county historical society, West Chester
PWcL	Daily local news, West Chester
PWcLa	Law library, West Chester
PWcM	Charles Miner, West Chester
PWcP	Maurice B. Pratt, West Chester

PENNSYLVANIA—*Continued*

PWcT	State normal school, West Chester
PWe	Green free library, Wellsboro
PWeA	Agitator, Wellsboro
PWeG	Wellsboro gazette, Wellsboro
PWeM	Mrs. E. R. Mulford, Wellsboro
PWeT	Tioga county treasurer's office, Wellsboro
PWfF	Westfield free press, Westfield
PWfR	J. F. Rugaber, Westfield
PWi	Public library, Wilkinsburg
PWp	James V. Brown library, Williamsport
PWpCo	F. W. Coleman collection, Williamsport
PWpHi	Lycoming county historical society, Williamsport
PWpP	Prothonotary's office, Williamsport
PWpS	Williamsport sun, Williamsport
PWyW	C. E. Woodmansee, Wycombe
PYD	Evening dispatch, York
PYG	Gazette and daily, York
PYHi	York county historical society, York

Rhode Island

RA	Free library, Apponaug
RBrC	Town clerk, Bristol
RBrP	Phoenix, Bristol
RC	Free public library, Central Falls
RChT	Town Hall, Chepachet
REdH	William H. Hall free library, Edgewood
REg	East Greenwich free library association, East Greenwich
RHi	Rhode Island historical society, Providence
RNHi	Newport historical society, Newport
RNR	Redwood library and athenaeum, Newport
RP	Public library, Providence
RPA	Providence Athenaeum, Providence
RPB	Brown university, Providence
RPC	Providence college, Providence
RPJ	News-tribune, Providence
RPNt	John Hay library, Providence
RPS	Colonel George L. Shepley, Providence
RPV	Providence visitor, Providence
RPa	Deborah Cook Sayles public library, Pawtucket
RPas	Free public library, Pascoag
RPd	Narragansett library association, Peace Dale
RPo	Free public library, Portsmouth
RW	Public library, Westerly
RWa	George Hail free library, Warren
RWaC	Town clerk, Warren
RWaT	Warren Town Hall, Warren
RWi	North Kingstown free library, Wickford
RWo	Harris institute library, Woonsocket
RWoI	L'Independant, Woonsocket

South Carolina

ScAG	Mrs. W. P. Greener, Abbeville
ScAR	Mrs. Grace H. Rogers, Abbeville
ScAP	Press and banner, Abbeville
ScC	Charleston free library, Charleston
ScCC	College of Charleston, Charleston
ScCCi	The Citadel, Charleston
ScCL	Charleston library society, Charleston
ScCN	News and courier, Charleston
ScCa	Public library, Camden
ScCh	Free library, Chester
ScChN	Chester news, Chester
ScClC	Clemson college, Clemson College
ScClP	Presbyterian college of South Carolina, Clinton
ScCo	Columbia public library, Columbia
ScCoA	John K. Aull, Columbia
ScCoC	Columbia collge, Columbia
ScCoCR	Confederate relic room, Columbia
ScCoCS	Columbia state, Columbia
ScD	Public library, Darlington
ScE	Tompkins memorial library, Edgefield
ScGF	Furman university, Greenville
ScGK	David Kohn, Greenville
ScGa	Carnegie free library, Gaffney
ScGrI	Index-journal, Greenwood
ScHC	Coker college, Hartsville
ScKC	County record, Kingstree
ScM	Public library, Marion
ScN	Public library, Newberry
ScNC	Newberry college, Newberry
ScNH	Herald and news, Newberry
ScOC	Claflin university, Orangeburg
ScRW	Winthrop college, Rock Hill
ScS	Kennedy free library, Spartanburg
ScSJ	Spartanburg journal, Spartanburg
ScSW	Wofford college, Spartanburg
ScSuI	Sumter daily item, Sumter
ScU	University of South Carolina, Columbia
ScUn	Carnegie library, Union
ScYE	Yorkville enquirer, York

South Dakota

SdA	Alexander Mitchell library, Aberdeen
SdBgG	Buffalo Gap gazette, Buffalo Gap
SdEL	Leader-courier, Elk Point
SdGN	Garretson news, Garretson
SdHN	Hill City news, Hill City
SdHi	South Dakota historical society, Pierre
SdIT	Ipswich tribune, Ipswich
SdOW	Onida watchman, Onida

Tennessee

T	Tennessee state library, Nashville
TBC	Hardeman county court house, Bolivar
TBrK	King college, Bristol
TC	Public library, Chattanooga
TCN	Chattanooga news, Chattanooga
TCU	University of Chattanooga, Chattanooga
TCaC	Carthage courier, Carthage
TCl	Public library, Cleveland
TClaL	Leaf-chronicle, Clarksville
TDrE	Dresden enterprise, Dresden
TFW	Williamson county news, Franklin
TH	Public library, Hartsville
THV	Vidette, Hartsville
THi	Tennessee historical society, Nashville
TJT	State teachers college, Johnson City
TJeD	Dandridge banner, Jefferson City
TKL	Lawson-McGhee library, Knoxville
TM	Cossitt library, Memphis
TMC	Commercial appeal, Memphis
TMG	Goodwyn institute library, Memphis
TMP	Press-simitar, Memphis
TMS	Shelby county court house, Memphis
TMa	Harper memorial library, Maryville
TMaM	Maryville college, Maryville
TMuT	State teachers college, Murfreesboro
TN	Carnegie library, Nashville
TNB	Nashville banner, Nashville
TNF	Fisk university, Nashville
TNP	George Peabody college for teachers, Nashville
TNV	Vanderbilt university, Nashville
TNY	Y.M.C.A. graduate school, Nashville
TR	Hughes free public library, Rugby
TSE	Sparta expositor, Sparta
TSS	University of the South, Sewanee
TSo	Fayette county free library, Somerville
TSpH	Springfield herald-news, Springfield
TTH	Herald-democrat, Trenton
TU	University of Tennessee, Knoxville
TU-J	University of Tennessee junior college, Martin

Texas

Tx	Texas state library, Austin
TxAM	McMurry college, Abilene
TxAS	Simmons university, Abilene
TxB	Tyrrel public library, Beaumont
TxBe	Carnegie library, Belton
TxBroH	Howard Payne college, Brownwood
TxCA	Texas state agricultural and mechanical college, College Station
TxCeC	Celeste courier, Celeste
TxCl	Carnegie library, Cleburne
TxCoE	East Texas state teachers college, Commerce
TxCor	Public library, Corsicana
TxD	Public library, Dallas
TxDM	Southern Methodist university, Dallas
TxDN	Dallas morning news, Dallas
TxDT	Daily times-herald, Dallas
TxDa	Dallam county free library, Dalhart
TxDeN	North Texas state teachers college, Denton
TxDoN	News-advocate, Donna
TxE	Public library, El Paso
TxEB	R. F. Burges, El Paso
TxEH	Herald-post, El Paso
TxET	Times, El Paso
TxF	Carnegie public library, Fort Worth
TxFS	Fort Worth star-telegram, Fort Worth
TxGR	Rosenberg library, Galveston
TxGa	Cooke county free library, Gainesville
TxGaR	Gainesville register, Gainesville
TxH	Public library, Houston
TxHR	Rice institute, Houston
TxHe	Deaf Smith county library, Hereford
TxHoA	Hondo anvil herald, Hondo
TxHuS	Sam Houston state teachers college, Huntsville
TxJ	Public library, Jacksonville
TxJJ	Jacksonville journal, Jacksonville
TxK	Public library, Kingsville
TxKC	Kleburg county court house, Kingsville
TxKT	Texas college of arts and industries, Kingsville
TxLT	Texas technological college, Lubbock
TxLoP	Lockhart post-register, Lockhart
TxM	Midland county free library, Midland
TxMR	Midland reporter-telegram, Midland
TxMi	Public library, Mission
TxNS	Stephen F. Austin state teachers college, Nacogdoches
TxOgO	Orange Grove observer, Orange Grove
TxPa	Gates memorial library, Port Arthur
TxPnB	Panhandle Bank, Panhandle
TxS	Carnegie library, San Antonio
TxSE	San Antonio express, San Antonio
TxSI	Incarnate Word college, San Antonio
TxSO	Our Lady of the Lake college, San Antonio
TxSa	Tom Green county library, San Angelo
TxSaM	Mrs. J. T. Murphy, San Angelo
TxSdF	Duval county facts, San Diego
TxSh	Public library, Sherman
TxStE	Empire-tribune, Stephenville
TxStJ	John Tarleton agricultural and mechanical college, Stephenville
TxSwP	A. N. Prince, Sweetwater
TxT	Carnegie public library, Tyler
TxTJ	Tyler journal, Tyler
TxU	University of Texas, Austin
TxVT	Vernon times, Vernon
TxW	Public library, Waco
TxWB	Baylor university, Waco
TxWM	Texas Masonic grand lodge, Waco
TxWf	Kemp public library, Wichita Falls
TxWi	Carnegie library, Winnsboro
TxWx	Nicholas P. Sims library, Waxahatchie

Utah

UHi	Utah state historical society, Salt Lake City
ULA	Utah agricultural college, Logan
UO	Carnegie free library, Ogden
UP	Public library, Provo
UPB	Brigham Young university, Provo
US	Public library, Salt Lake City
UST	Salt Lake tribune, Salt Lake City
USpP	Spanish Fork press, Spanish Fork
UU	University of Utah, Salt Lake City

Virginia

V	Virginia state library, Richmond
VAA	City auditor, Alexandria
VAM	City manager, Alexandria
VAbS	L. P. Summers, Abingdon
VAlJ	Alta Vista journal, Alta Vista
VAmN	New era-progress, Amherst
VAsH	Herald-progress, Ashland
VAsR	Randolph-Macon college, Ashland
VBP	Virginia polytechnic institute, Blacksburg
VBeD	Bedford democrat, Bedford
VBoB	R. H. Bryson, Boydton
VBrH	Herald-courier, Bristol
VBrS	Sullins college, Bristol
VBrgC	Bridgewater college, Bridgewater
VChC	Albemarle county court house, Charlottesville
VChP	Charlottesville progress, Charlottesville
VChm	Public library, Chatham
VCoP	Potomac interest, Colonial Beach
VD	Public library, Danville
VF	Wallace library, Fredericksburg
VFE	A. T. Embrey, Fredericksburg
VFF	Free lance-star, Fredericksburg
VFT	State teachers college, Fredericksburg
VFaC	Prince Edward county court house, Farmville
VFaH	Farmville herald, Farmville
VFaT	State teachers college, Farmville
VFcI	Independent record, Fairfax Court House
VHH	Hollins college, Hollins
VHaH	Hampton normal and agricultural institute, Hampton
VHarN	Daily news-record, Harrisonburg
VHarT	State teachers college, Harrisonburg
VHi	Virginia historical society, Richmond
VHo	Public library, Hopewell
VHsC	Hampden-Sydney college, Hampden-Sydney
VLC	Rockbridge county court house, Lexington
VLW	Washington and Lee university, Lexington
VLa	Brunswick county library, Lawrenceville
VLe	Thomas Balch library, Leesburg
VLoC	Central Virginian, Louisa

VIRGINIA—*Continued*

VLy	Jones memorial library, Lynchburg
VLyR	Randolph-Macon woman's college, Lynchburg
VMH	Mrs. E. H. Hibbs, Manassas
VMJ	Manassas journal, Manassas
VMaM	Madison county eagle, Madison
VN	Public library, Newport News
VNT	Times-herald, Newport News
VNo	Norfolk public library, Norfolk
VNoL	Ledger-dispatch, Norfolk
VOnE	Eastern Shore news, Onancock
VP	William R. McKenney free library, Petersburg
VPC	Virginia state college for negroes, Petersburg
VPP	Progress-index, Petersburg
VPu	Blue Ridge reading room, Purcellville
VRB	Virginia Baptist historical society, Richmond
VRC	Confederate library and museum, Richmond
VRN	Richmond news leader, Richmond
VRU	Union theological seminary, Richmond
VRV	Virginia union university, Richmond
VRaT	State teachers college, East Radford
VRo	Public library, Roanoke
VRoW	World-news, Roanoke
VS	Public library, Staunton
VSC	Augusta county court house, Staunton
VSMb	Mary Baldwin college, Staunton
VSN	News-leader, Staunton
VSaR	Roanoke college, Salem
VSaT	Times-register and sentinel, Salem
VSbC	Sweet Briar college, Sweet Briar
VSo	Public library, South Boston
VStN	Northern Virginia daily, Strasburg
VSuN	News-herald, Suffolk
VTC	Essex county court house, Tappahannock
VU	University of Virginia, University
VUr	Public library, Urbanna
VV	Public library, Victoria
VWW	College of William and Mary, Williamsburg
VWa	Warrenton library, Warrenton
VWbN	Waynesboro news-Virginian, Waynesboro
VWn	Handley library, Winchester
VWy	Public library, Wytheville

Vermont

Vt	Vermont state library, Montpelier
VtBO	Orleans county monitor, Barton
VtBa	Aldrich public library, Barre
VtBeC	Bennington county court house, Bennington
VtBeM	Bennington historical museum, Bennington
VtBf	Rockingham free public library, Bellows Falls
VtBfT	Bellows Falls times, Bellows Falls
VtBn	Free public library, Brandon
VtBr	Public library, Brattleboro
VtBrR	Brattleboro reformer, Brattleboro
VtBrl	Bristol public library, Bristol
VtBu	Lawrence memorial library, Burlington
VtBuF	Burlington free press, Burlington
VtCC	Orange county court house, Chelsea
VtCh	Whiting library, Chester
VtFM	John Metcalfe, Fairhaven
VtHi	Vermont historical society, Montpelier
VtHpC	Lamoille county court house, Hyde Park
VtHpM	B. N. McVarland, Hyde Park
VtLW	Dorothy C. Walter, Lyndonville
VtLu	Fletcher memorial library, Ludlow
VtLuT	Vermont tribune, Ludlow
VtM	Mark Skinner library, Manchester
VtMiC	Addison county court house, Middlebury
VtMiM	Middlebury college, Middlebury
VtMiS	Sheldon art museum, Middlebury
VtMo	Free public library, Montpelier
VtMoC	Washington county court house, Montpelier
VtMor	Morrisville centennial library, Morrisville
VtMorM	Morrisville messenger, Morrisville
VtNN	Northfield news, Northfield
VtNU	Norwich university, Northfield
VtNe	Tenny memorial library, Newbury
VtNf	Moore free library, Newfane
VtNp	Goodrich library, Newport
VtNpE	Express and standard, Newport
VtPJ	Journal press, Poultney
VtR	Free library, Rutland
VtRC	Rutland county court house, Rutland
VtRa	Kimball public library, Randolph
VtRi	A. A. Brown library, Richford
VtS	Town library, Springfield
VtSa	Free library, St. Albans
VtSj	St. Johnsbury athenaeum, St. Johnsbury
VtSlM	Mrs. L. J. McAllister, South Londonderry
VtSr	Royalton memorial library, South Royalton
VtU	University of Vermont, Burlington
VtV	Bixby memorial free library, Vergennes
VtW	Public library, Waterbury
VtWi	Windsor library association, Windsor
VtWil	Pettee memorial library, Wilmington
VtWo	Norman Williams public library, Woodstock
VtWoC	Windsor county court house, Woodstock

Wisconsin

WA	Free public library, Appleton
WAL	Samuel Appleton library, Lawrence college, Appleton
WAP	Appleton post-crescent, Appleton
WAbT	Abbottsford tribune, Abbottsford
WAlR	Algoma record-herald, Algoma
WAn	Public library, Antigo
WAr	Free public library, Arcadia
WB	Public library, Baraboo
WBN	Baraboo news, Baraboo
WBa	Public library, Barron
WBdA	Beaver Dam argus, Beaver Dam
WBel	Public library, Beloit
WBf	Carnegie library, Bayfield
WBl	Public library, Bloomer
WBr	Public library, Brodhead
WBu	Public library, Burlington
WCh	Public library, Chippewa Falls
WChH	Chippewa herald-telegram, Chippewa Falls
WChiT	Chilton times-journal, Chilton
WClT	Clinton times-observer, Clinton
WCor	Public library, Cornell
WCu	Public library, Cumberland
WDp	Public library, De Pere
WDu	Free library, Durand
WE	Public library, Eau Claire
WEl	Matheson memorial library, Elkhorn
WErV	Vilas county news-review, Eagle River
WF	Public library, Fond du Lac
WFo	Public library, Fox Lake
WGR	Galesville republican, Galesville
WGb	Kellogg public library, Green Bay
WGr	Public library, Greenwood
WHT	Times-press, Hartford
WHi	State historical society of Wisconsin, Madison
WJeB	Jefferson banner, Jefferson
WK	Gilbert M. Simmons library, Kenosha
WKN	Kenosha news, Kenosha
WKi	Public library, Kiel
WLa	L. D. Fargo public library, Lake Mills
WLao	Public library, Laona
WLc	Public library, La Crosse
WLoE	Lodi enterprise, Lodi
WM	Milwaukee public library, Milwaukee
WMJ	Milwaukee journal, Milwaukee
WMa	Public library, Manitowoc
WMaB	Brandt printing and binding company, Manitowoc
WMaM	Herald-times, Manitowoc
WMan	Stephenson public library, Marinette
WManE	Marinette eagle-star, Marinette
WMar	Free library, Marshfield
WMayB	Arnold Bachhuber, Mayville
WMayF	Mrs. Ottilie Forkmann, Mayville
WMe	Free public library, Medford
WMen	Elisha D. Smith library, Menasha
WMeno	Monroe evening times, Monroe
WMoT	Tainter memorial free library, Menomonie
WNgP	New Glarus post, New Glarus
WNlP	New London press-republican, New London
WO	Public library, Oshkosh
WOc	Public library, Oconomowoc
WOcF	Oconomowoc free press, Oconomowoc
WOsS	Osceola sun, Osceola
WP	Free public library, Portage
WPa	Powers memorial library, Palmyra
WPh	Public library, Phillips
WPlW	Platteville witness, Platteville
WR	Public library, Racine
WRD	Racine day, Racine
WRJ	Racine journal-times, Racine
WReF	Reedsburg free press, Reedsburg
WRh	Free public library, Rhinelander
WRl	Free public library, Rice Lake
WRlC	Rice Lake chronotype, Rice Lake
WRip	Public library, Ripon
WS	Public library, Superior
WSh	Public library, Sheboygan
WSha	Brisham memorial library, Sharon
WSp	Free library, Sparta
WSt	Public library, Stanley
WSteJ	Stevens Point journal, Stevens Point
WSv	Public library, Spring Valley
WSvS	Sun, Spring Valley
WTo	Public library, Tomahawk
WVV	Vernon county censor, Viroqua
WViN	Viola news, Viola
WWa	Free public library, Watertown
WWaG	Watertown gazette, Watertown
WWaK	Public library, Waukesha
WWap	Free public library, Waupaca
WWau	Public library, Waupun
WWb	Public library, West Bend
WWd	Public library, Wisconsin Dells
WWe	Public library, West Allis
WWr	T. B. Scott free public library, Wisconsin Rapids
WWrT	Wisconsin Rapids tribune, Wisconsin Rapids

Washington

Wa	Washington state library, Seatttle
WaA	Public library, Aberdeen
WaAW	Aberdeen daily world, Aberdeen
WaAu	Public library, Auburn
WaAuG	Globe-republican, Auburn
WaB	Public library, Bremerton
WaBu	Public library, Burlington
WaC	Free public library, Chehalis
WaCa	Public library, Camas
WaCoG	Colfax gazette-commoner, Colfax
WaColE	Colville examiner, Colville
WaDT	Davenport times-tribune, Davenport
WaE	Public library, Everett
WaEl	Carnegie public library, Ellensburg
WaElR	Ellensburg evening record, Ellensburg
WaEn	Public library, Enumclaw
WaEnC	Courier-herald, Enumclaw
WaH	Public library, Hoquiam
WaHi	Washington state historical society, Tacoma
WaK	Free public library, Kent
WaKeC	Courier-reporter, Kennewick
WaL	Public library, Longview
WaLC	Cowlitz county court house, Longview
WaM	Public library, Monroe
WaPS	State college of Washington, Pullman
WaPa	Public library, Pasco
WaPo	Public library, Port Angeles
WaS	Public library, Seattle
WaSJ	Jewish transcript, Seattle
WaSS	Washington staatszeitung, Seattle
WaSp	Public library, Spokane
WaSpG	Gonzaga university, Spokane
WaSpS	Spokesman-review, Spokane
WaT	Public library, Tacoma
WaTS	T. Sandegrin, Tacoma
WaTW	Charles B. Welch, Tacoma
WaU	University of Washington, Seattle
WaUW	Wickersham collection of Alaska papers, University of Washington, Seattle
WaV	Public library, Vancouver
WaVD	Lloyd Dubois, Vancouver
WaW	Free public library, Walla Walla
WaWW	Whitman college, Walla Walla
WaWe	Carnegie public library, Wenatchee
WaY	Public library, Yakima

West Virginia

Wv	West Virginia state library, Charleston
WvAC	Concord state normal school, Athens
WvBelC	Central-State news, Belington
WvBerM	Messenger, Berkeley Springs
WvBl	Public library, Bluefield
WvC	Public library, Charleston
WvCl	Public library, Clarksburg
WvEK	Kanawha news, Elizabeth
WvGS	Boyd B. Stutler, Grantsville
WvM	Waitman Barbe public library, Morgantown
WvMa	Public library, Martinsburg
WvMaC	Berkeley county court house, Martinsburg
WvMoE	Moundsville daily echo, Moundsville
WvP	Carnegie public library, Parkersburg
WvPS	Parkersburg daily sentinel, Parkersburg
WvRC	Jackson county court house, Ripley
WvSR	Roane county reporter, Spencer
WvU	West Virginia university, Morgantown
WvW	Public library, Wheeling

SYMBOLS

Wyoming

WyC	Natrona county public library, Casper
WyGbS	Greybull standard-tribune, Greybull
WyHi	Wyoming state historical department, Cheyenne
WyR	Carbon county public library, Rawlins
WyRiR	Riverton review-chronicle, Riverton
WySS	Saratoga sun, Saratoga
WyToT	Torrington telegram, Torrington
WyU	University of Wyoming, Laramie
WyW	Platt county public library, Wheatland

CANADA

Alberta

CaA	Alberta provincial library, Edmonton
CaAAS	Acme sentinel, Acme
CaAC	Public library, Calgary
CaADM	Drumheller mail, Drumheller
CaAE	Public library, Edmonton
CaAEO	Mr. J. Oliver, Edmonton
CaAL	Public library, Lethbridge
CaALS	Mr. F. H. Schooley, Lethbridge
CaAMG	Macleod gazette, Macleod
CaAPR	Peace River record, Peace River

British Columbia

CaB	Provincial library, Victoria
CaBN	Public library, New Westminster
CaBNH	Judge F. W. Howay, New Westminster
CaBU	University of British Columbia, Vancouver
CaBV	Public library, Vancouver
CaBVR	R. L. Reid, Vancouver
CaBVi	Public library, Victoria

Manitoba

CaM	Provincial library, Winnipeg
CaMB	Public library, Brandon
CaMP	Public library, Portage la Prairie
CaMW	Public library, Winnipeg
CaMWD	Dahl publishing company, Winnipeg
CaMWP	Free press, Winnipeg
CaMWT	Tribune, Winnipeg

New Brunswick

CaN	Legislative library, Fredericton
CaNM	Public library, Moncton
CaNS	Free public library, St. John
CaNSa	Mount Allison college library, Sackville
CaNU	University of New Brunswick, Fredericton
CaNW	L. B. Fisher memorial library, Woodstock
CaNWA	Miss Kate Appleby, Woodstock
CaNWC	Victoria-Carleton county court house, Woodstock

Nova Scotia

CaNs	Legislative library, Halifax
CaNsAS	St. Francis Xavier university, Antigonish
CaNsBrH	Mrs. E. F. Hurlburt, Brooklyn
CaNsHD	Dalhousie university, Halifax
CaNsTN	News, Truro
CaNsWa	Acadia university, Wolfville
CaNsY	Public library and museum, Yarmouth
CaNsYH	Yarmouth herald, Yarmouth

Ontario

CaO	Library of Parliament, Ottawa
CaOB	Public library, Barrie
CaOBkR	Brockville recorder, Brockville
CaOBr	Public library, Brantford
CaOC	Public library, Chatham
CaOCN	Chatham daily news, Chatham
CaOCb	Public library, Cobourg
CaOCo	Public library, Collingwood
CaOD	Public library, Dundas
CaOFw	Public library, Fort William
CaOG	Public library, Guelph
CaOGA	Ontario agricultural college, Guelph
CaOH	Public library, Hamilton
CaOHU	McMaster university, Hamilton
CaOHW	W. P. Witton, Esq., Hamilton
CaOKU	Queen's university, Kingston
CaOKe	Public library, Kenora
CaOKi	Public library, Kitchener
CaOL	Public library, London
CaOLU	University of Western Ontario, London
CaOLi	Public library, Lindsay
CaON	Public library, Niagara Falls
CaONHi	Niagara historical society, Niagara-on-the-Lake
CaONb	Public library, North Bay
CaOO	Public library, Ottawa
CaOOA	Public archives, Ottawa
CaOOR	National research council library, Ottawa
CaOOU	University of Ottawa, Ottawa
CaOOs	Public library, Oshawa
CaOOsT	Oshawa daily times, Oshawa
CaOS	Public library, Stratford
CaOSB	Stratford beacon-herald, Stratford
CaOSc	Public library, St. Catharines
CaOSm	Public library, Sault Ste. Marie
CaOSt	Public library, St. Thomas
CaOT	Toronto public library, Toronto
CaOTA	Ontario archives, Toronto
CaOTL	Legislative library, Toronto
CaOTU	University of Toronto, Toronto
CaOTV	Victoria university, Toronto
CaOWi	Public library, Windsor
CaOWo	Public library, Woodstock

Prince Edward Island

CaP	Legislative and public library, Charlottestown

Quebec

CaQ	Library of the legislature, Quebec
CaQEE	L'Eclaireur, Ltd., Beauceville
CaQGC	Grande Ligne college, Grande Ligne
CaQHC	Canadian weekly newspapers association, Huntingdon
CaQM	Montreal public library, Montreal
CaQMA	Advocates' library, Montreal
CaQME	Bibliothèque de l'Ecole des hautes études commerciales, Montreal
CaQMF	Fraser institute, Montreal
CaQMG	C. Gordonsmith, Esq., Montreal
CaQMH	Montreal daily herald, Montreal
CaQML	M. LaBruère, Montreal
CaQMM	McGill university, Montreal
CaQMMo	Monitor, Montreal
CaQMR	Royal Bank of Canada, Montreal
CaQMS	Bibliothique Saint-Sulpice, Montreal
CaQMSm	Collège Ste. Marie, Montreal
CaQMW	Witness and Canadian homestead, Montreal
CaQQF	Bulletin de la Ferme, Quebec
CaQQH	Literary and historical society of Quebec, Quebec
CaQQL	Laval university, Quebec
CaQRS	Seminaire de Rimouski, Rimouski
CaQRi	Haskell free public library, Rock Island
CaQSaC	Collège de Ste. Anne, Ste. Anne de la Pocatière
CaQShR	Sherbrooke record, Sherbrooke
CaQShS	Seminaire Saint-Charles Borromée, Sherbrooke
CaQSIC	Le Courrier de St. Hyacinthe, St. Hyacinthe
CaQSD	Le Clairon, St. Hyacinthe
CaQTS	St. Joseph's seminary, Three Rivers
CaQVP	Verdun printing and publishing company, Verdun

Saskatchewan

CaSE	Public library, Esterhazy
CaSMW	World-spectator, Moosomin
CaSMuS	St. Peter's college, Muenster
CaSR	Public library, Regina
CaSRK	King's printer, Regina
CaSRL	Leader-post, Regina
CaSRR	Regina college, Regina
CaSS	Public library, Saskatoon
CaSSS	Saskatoon star-phoenix, Saskatoon
CaSScA	Advocate publishing company, Swift Current
CaSU	University of Saskatchewan, Saskatoon

Union List of Newspapers

ALABAMA

ABBEVILLE

Abbeville ADVERTISER. w
A Mr 17 1859

Abbeville DEMOCRAT. w 1894-95||?
AAC Je 29 1894-Ja 4 1895

HENRY county register. *See* Abbeville times

Abbeville HERALD. w 1918+
A N 1921-Je 1927;Jl 1934+
AAC 1919—

Abbeville NEWS. w 1900-16||?
AAC 1901-D 21 1916

SOUTHEAST Alabamian. w 1914-18||?
AAC 1916-17

SPIRIT of the age. w 1885-90||?
AAC 1887;89

Abbeville TIMES. w My 19 1866-1911||?
1866-Ap 1? 1883 as Henry county register
A Je 22 1867;Ap 26 1878
AAC 1866-Ja 5,My 18 1867-N 20 1869;70-D 15 1871;Ja 12 1872-D 12 1873;74-D 20 1878;83-98; 1903-Ag 12 1909
NN [1873-78]
NNHi F 7 1873

UNITED south. w
A Mr 2 1861

ALABAMA CITY

DWIGHT journal. w Mr 31- 1900||?
AGC Ap 21-Ag 18 1900

ETOWAH observer. w Ja 12 1928+
Ja-Je 7 1928 as Gadsden observer (Gadsden)
A 1933+
AGC 1928+

Daily OBSERVER. d
AGC Mr 31-Ap 23 1932

ALBANY

Papers published in Albany are listed under Decatur

ALBERTVILLE

Albertville BANNER. *See* Sand Mountain banner

Albertville HERALD. w Ja 15 1934+
AGuC 1934+

Albertville JOURNAL. w Ag 3 1893-96||?
1893- My 21 1896 as Marshall county news
AGuC 1893-96

MARSHALL banner. *See* Sand Mountain banner

MARSHALL county news. *See* Albertville journal

SAND MOUNTAIN banner. w Je 17 1897+
1897-Mr 3 1910 as Marshall banner; Mr 10 1913-Mr 20 1919 Albertville banner
A Je 1899-Ja 1907;N 21 1918-Mr 14 1919;N 1921-28;33+
AGuC 1897+

ALDRICH

ALABAMA time piece. w Mr 11-D 9? 1898||
ACoC Mr-D 9 1898

ALEXANDER CITY

Weekly DISPATCH. w Ja 1888-D 24 1891||
1888-Ap 1890 as Vidette
ADC My 17 1888-Ap 17,Je-N 1890;91

Alexander City NEWS. w Je 5 1914-Ag 31 1917||
A N 1914-17
ADC complete

Alexander City OUTLOOK. w,sw Ja 12 1892+
sw Je 7 1921-Ja 4 1922
A 1914-28;35+
ADC N 11-D 1892;94+

SIFTINGS. w Ja 14-Ag 12 1910||?
ADC Ja-Ag 12 1910

VIDETTE. *See* Weekly dispatch

ANDALUSIA

COVINGTON crescent. w Ag 27 1897-F 4 1899||
AAnC complete

COVINGTON expositor. *See* Andalusia news

COVINGTON news. 1900-04 *See* Andalusia news

COVINGTON news. w 1922+
A Jl 1931-O,D 1934;Jl 1935+
AAnC F 15 1924+

COVINGTON times. w 1884-97||?
AAnC My 4 1889-N 26 1897

NEW ERA. *See* Andalusia star

Andalusia NEWS. w 1897-1909||
1897-99 as Covington expositor; 1900-Ap 4 1904 Covington news
AAnC Ap 4 1898-D 6 1899;1900-My 20 1909

PEOPLE'S gazette. w Je 10 1902-04||
AAnC 1902-Ag 27 1904

Andalusia STANDARD. w Ja 7 1914-17||?
A S 1914-Ap 1917
AAnC 1914-16

Andalusia STAR. w,sw,d N 11 1904+
1904-05 as New era; 1906-08 Andalusia times
w 1904-13;d 1924-26
A Ap 1909-S 1919;N 1926-28;O 1935+
AAnC 1904-D 9 1905;Ja 10 1906-Je 19 1908;Ap 1909+
ASIT My 11 1923

Andalusia TIMES. *See* Andalusia star

ANNISTON

Daily HOT BLAST. w,d 1882-Je 1912||?
1882-87 as Hot blast. United with Anniston evening star to form Anniston evening star and daily hot blast, later Anniston star
w 1882-87
A My 4 1892;Je 11 1893;My 9 1895;1901-03;D 9-10 1908
AAnnC 1883-Ja 9 1890;91
—w ed 1889-1912 *See* Anniston times

LITTLE watchman. *See* Evening news

Evening NEWS. d Mr 1885-93||?
1885-89? as Little watchman
—w ed *See* News-watchman

NEWS-WATCHMAN. w 1884-90||?
1884-88? as Watchman
AAnnC Ja 15 1885-D 12 1889

Anniston REPUBLIC and times. w,sw Ja 21 1837-1913||?
1837-D 29 1894 as Jacksonville republican (Jacksonville) 1895-98? Anniston republican; 1899?-1912? Anniston republic
w 1837-1908?
A Ja 28 1837-38;My 22 1840-D 16 1851;Mr 9 1852-D 20 1864;69-S 15 1885;88-93
AAnnC 1858-Ag 8 1861;68-N 13 1869;F 19 1870-73;Ja-S 19 1878;80-82;85-89;91-94;96;99-1903;05-07
DLC [F 11 1846-Ap 4 1848] My 23 1861
ICHi Mr 14 1861
NcD Mr 13 1875;Mr 8,Ap 5,My 3 1879

Anniston REPUBLICAN. *See* Anniston republic and times

Anniston STAR. d 1889+
1889-Je 1912? as Anniston evening star; Jl 1912?-D 31 1919 Anniston evening star and daily hot blast
A Jl 1901-Je 20 1903;04-Je 1912;Ag 29 1915;Ap 6 1917;Ja 27 1914;Ap-D 1918;D 1 1926;27-S 1930;Jl 29 1932-S 1935
AAnnC Mr 1913+
ASIT My 13 1923
NcD N 13 1908

Anniston TIMES. w 1889-1912||?
United with Anniston republic to form Anniston republic and times
AAnnC 1889-92;94-95;98-1901;03-07;09-12
—d ed *See* Daily hot blast

Anniston TIMES. w 1932+
A Jl 1932-Mr 1933;O 1935+
AAnnC 1933+

WATCHMAN. *See* News-watchman

ARITON

Ariton ADVERTISER. w Ap 29 1913-14||
A 1914
AOzC 1913-Je 23 1914

ASHFORD

Ashford MIRROR. w F 26 1910-15||?
ADoC 1910;F 15 1911-N 21 1912

Ashford TRIBUNE. w 1916-18||?
ADoC F 17-D 21 1917

ASHLAND

CLAY county advance. w Ja 6 1888-97||
Followed by Standard, later Ashland progress
AAsC 1888-S 3 1897

CLAY county watchman. *See under* Lineville

MOUNTAIN picket. w F 18- 1881||?
AAsC F-Jl 15 1881

Ashland NEWS. w Mr 15 1873-80||?
AAsC Mr-N 1878;My 30 1879-Je 4 1880

PEOPLE'S party advocate. w Ja 1894-1900||?
A Ap 14 1899
AAsC Ja 19,Ap 13,27 1894-O[D 1898-F 16 1899]-Mr 1 1900

Ashland PROGRESS. w My 19 1898+
Follows Clay county advance. 1898-Jl 30 1909 as Standard
A N 1921-28;33+
AAsC 1898-Ja,Mr 14 1901-N 1903;Mr 18 1904+

STANDARD. *See* Ashland progress

Ashland TIMES. w 1869-75||?
NNHi Mr 13 1873

ASHVILLE

Ashville ADVANCE. *See* St. Clair advance (Springville)

DEMOCRAT farmer. w
A Ag 31 1848

ST. CLAIR county eagle. w 1868?-70||?
A N 21 1868;Ja 23,Mr 27 My 29-Je 5,Jl 10 1869

SOUTHERN aegis. w Ja 1 1873+
A D 2 1885;D 12 1895;S 9-16,O-N 4 1897;Ag 1898-1912;15-28
AAvC 1875-76;78-80;83;85-1912;14+

SOUTHERN alliance. w,tw 1893-1900||?
Merged with Southern aegis
w 1893-1900?
AAvC 1899

ATHENS

ALABAMA courier. w Ja 7 1880+
A [Mr 1892-S 1893]Mr 1900-28;Ja 1933;Jl-O 1934;35+
AAtC 1880-[91-93]-[1900-01]-[08]10-13;16+
NcD Ag 17,S 21,D 3 1882;My 2 1895

ALABAMA farmer. *See under* Huntsville

ALLIANCE banner. w Ja 13 1888-89||?
AAtC Ja-Je 7 1888

ATHENIAN. w 1828?-
A Ja 3,Mr 13 1828
OOxM Mr 5 1829

Athens DEMOCRAT. w N 12 1886-89||?
AAtC 1886-[89]
GAtCo Mr 11 1887

Athens HERALD. w
TxU D 5 1856

Athens HERALD. w O 4 1889-
AAtC [1889-F 1890]

LIMESTONE advertiser. w F 20-S 1891||
United with Elkmont enterprise (Elkmont) to form Limestone enterprise (Athens)
AAtC [1891]

LIMESTONE democrat. w N 25 1891+
Follows Limestone enterprise?
A S 1899-Je 1911;N 1926-28;33+
AAtC 1891[94-95]-[1901]-[03-04]+

LIMESTONE enterprise. w Mr 28-N? 1891||
Mr-S 8? 1891 as Elkmont enterprise. Followed by Limestone democrat?
Mr-O 20? 1891 pub in Elkmont
AAtC [1891]

LIMESTONE news. w F 8 1871-79||?
AAtC 1871-76;Mr 16,27-Ap 3 1877
NNHi O 3 1873

Athens POST. w 1865-84||
1865-71 as Athens weekly post
A D 26 1865-D 12 1868
AAtC Ja 2-9,D 19 1868;69-My 1882[84]
NNHi Mr 14 1873

SOUTHERN patriot. w Ja 8 1847-
OCHi My 14 1847

ALABAMA (*Continued*)

ATMORE

Atmore ADVANCE. w 1927+
A O 1927-28;33+

ESCAMBIA record. w S 3 1903-28||?
1903-My 2 1912? as Atmore spectrum; My 9 1912?-22? Atmore record
A S 18 1903-S 9 1904;D 1906-My 1912;22-N 1928
ABrC 1903-S 8 1910;My 9 1912-My 20 1915; 20-22

Atmore RECORD. *See* Escambia record

Atmore SPECTRUM. *See* Escambia record

ATTALLA

Attalla ADVERTISER. w Ap 27 1933-
AGC 1933

Attalla BEACON. w 1895-98||?
Merged with Attalla mirror
AGC D 30 1897-D 16 1898

COMET. *See* Attalla courier

Attalla COURIER. w 1885-91||?
1885? as Pick and shovel; 1886?-My 1889 New age; Je 1889-Jl 2 1890 New age-herald Jl 9?-D? 1890 Comet. Followed by Attalla herald?
AGC Je 1889-[90]

Attalla HERALD. w O 10 1888?-My 1889||
United with New age to form New age-herald, later Attalla courier
AGC O 10 1888-89

Attalla HERALD. w 1891-96||?
Follows Attalla courier? Merged with Attalla mirror
AGC 1891-95

Attalla HERALD. w,sw 1908-23||?
Suspended from 1919-23?
sw 1911?-14?
A S 1908-F 1919;O 1921-N 1923
AGC D 31 1908-N 1919;Ja 18-N 1923

HOT SHOTS. w
AGC Mr 13 1897-1900

Attalla JOURNAL. w F 4- 1898||?
AGC 1898

Attalla MIRROR. w 1891-1908||?
A S 1899-1905;D 1906-S 1908
AGC Jl 29 1892-93;D 31 1896-1908

NEW age. *See* Attalla courier

Attalla daily NEWS. d 1921-22||?
A S-O 1921
AGC Mr 8 1921-22

PICK and shovel. *See* Attalla courier

BANGOR

BLOUNT county herald. w 1875-81||?
NcD Ap 4 1879

BARBOURVILLE

ALABAMA herald. w
A N 21 1840

BAY MINETTE

BALDWIN times. w My 26 1890+
1890-Ap 4 1895 as Daphne times (Daphne) pub 1890+
A My 1899;D 1906-My 1928;Ap 3 1929;33+
ABmC 1890-My 14 1896;My 16 1901-F 1910;Mr 1911-Ja 1925;F 11 1926+

BELGREEN

FRANKLIN county news. *See* Times and news

FRANKLIN democrat. w S 1885-88||?
ARuC S 11 1888

Belgreen NEWS. *See* Times and news

TIMES and news. w 1879-90||?
1879-82? as Belgreen news; 1883?-89? Franklin county news
ARuC S 30 1881;F-D 1882;F-Jl 11 1884;Ap 24 1886;My 27 1887-Ag 23 1888;Je-Jl 8 1890

BELLEFONTE

JACKSON county democrat. w Ap 1 1841-
DLC Ap 1 1841

BENTON

Weekly NEWS. w 1859-
AHaC Ap 12-D 6 1860

BERRY

Weekly RECORDER. w F 10 1899-1901||?
AFC Mr 1899-1900

BESSEMER

Bessemer ADVERTISER. *See* Bessemer tribune-advertiser

Daily BESSEMER. d 1891||?
A [Je-O 1891]

BESSEMER. w *See* Bessemer tribune-advertiser

Bessemer JOURNAL. w 1888-1908||?
A D 20 1888-My 1894;Ag 1895-Jl 1908

Bessemer TRIBUNE-ADVERTISER. w,sw Je 3 1887+
1887-Je? 1920 as Bessemer; Jl? 1920-29? Bessemer advertiser
sw 1930?-31?
A 1887-Je 1911;Ap 1916-Je,Ag 1920-N 1923;27-28;33-Mr,My 10,25 1935;Jl 1936+
—d ed *See* Daily Bessemer

Bessemer WORKMAN. w 1899-1910||
A D 1899-1909

BIRMINGHAM

Birmingham AGE. d 1881-N 7? 1888||
Title varies slightly. United with Daily herald to form Birmingham age-herald
A O 26 1884;Ag 29,N 6,18,20,24,28,D 1,4,13,15,18,22 1885;Ja 1,5-6,8,16,20,23,F 5,9,18,23,25-26,Ap 29 1886
NcD Ap 29 1886
TxGR O 19 1884;Ja 11 1885
—w ed *See* Iron age

Weekly AGE-HERALD. w 1887-1920||?
1887-N 1888 as Weekly herald; 1895?-O 1897 Weekly state herald
A O 19 1895-N 4 1896;Mr 1915-Mr 1917

Birmingham AGE-HERALD. d Jl? 1887+
1887-N 7? 1888 as Daily herald; 1895?-O 1 1897 State herald
Sunday issues as News-age-herald
Je 18 1913 is silver jubilee ed
A 1887-95;My 1896+
ASIT Ap 4,7,My 13 1923
DLC Jl 1894-[1907]-18;Mr 1919-F 1928
M [Je 10-Jl 22 1932]
MWA Je 18 1913
NcD Ag 21 1898;My 17,19 1903;Je 1 1907;Ja 24 1926;D 7,11 1927
OClWHi Mr 13 1907
TKL N 9 1887
TxGR Je 18 1913
VU My 23-24 1917;S 27-29,O 1-2,6 1934
WHi N 29 1914+
—evening ed *See* Birmingham news

ALABAMA herald. w Ja 1926+
1926-My 1934 as Jefferson county herald
A 1933+

ALABAMIAN. w 1902-03||?
A Ja 16 1902-Ja 23 1903

Weekly CALL. w 1917+
A Ja 3 1920;D 1926-28

Sunday CHRONICLE. w 1883-90||
1883? as Sunday morning chronicle. Merged with Birmingham news
A N 25 1884;85-86

Birmingham COURIER. w 1893-1912||?
F ? 1902 is jubiläums ausgabe
In German
A Ag 1899-S 1903
NN F ? 1902

ENSLEY enterprise. w 1898-1928||?
A Je 24,N 18 1899;Jl 1915-O 1922

ENSLEY herald. w 1899-1907||?
A Mr 1901-Mr 1906

HERALD. *See* Age-herald

HOWLES iconoclast. *See* Searchlight

Weekly INDEPENDENT. w 1872-82||?
1872-78? as Jefferson independent
A 1879-81

INDEPENDENT. w 1889-99||?
A 1889-90;Ag 16 1894;Mr 12 1898

INDUSTRIAL record. w 1915-18||?
A Jl 1915-Ag 1918

IRON age. w 1874-87||
United with Weekly herald to form Weekly age-herald
A F 12 1874-N 20 1878;79;81;83-87
—d ed *See* Birmingham age

JEFFERSON county herald. *See* Alabama herald

JEFFERSON independent. *See* Weekly independent

JONES VALLEY times. [Elyton] w
A Ap 1 1854-Ja 25 1855

JONES VALLEY times. w 1904-08||?
A O 1904-Ap 1908

Birmingham LEDGER. w Ag 20 1892-99||?
A Ag-D 10 1892[99]

Birmingham LEDGER. d 1896-Ap 1920||
Merged with Birmingham news
A F-Je 1898;1900-Ap 1920
NcD D 17 1907;Ap 12 1911;Mr 7 1914
TxGR Jl 6 1916
WHi 1912

Birmingham MESSENGER. w 1930+
A 1933+

Daily NEWS. d 1873-75||?
A Ag 27 1874

Birmingham NEWS. d Mr 14 1888+
Sunday issues as News-age-herald
A Mr 4 1891-Mr 1893;Jl 29 1895;S 1898-1900;F 1901+
ASIT My 13 1923
DLC [1898]Mr 1929+
MWA Ap 9 1916
NcD Ag 25 1929
OClWHi D 11 1889
VU O 5 1934
WHi Mr 14 1899
—morning ed *See* Birmingham age-herald

Sunday OBSERVER. w 1880-82||
1880-81? as Observer. Merged with Birmingham age
A 1880-81

PEOPLES weekly tribune. w 1894-97||?
A N 8 1894;S 2 1897
AEvC Mr 19-26,My 14,28-Je,Ag 20,S 10,24-O 1 1896
NN My 14-Ag 6,20 1896-F 18 1897

Birmingham POST. d 1921+
A N 1926-O 1929

Birmingham REGISTER. w 1908-10||?
A Jl 18 1908;F-Ap 1910
CoU Jl 1909-My 1910

Birmingham REPORTER. w 1902+
Negro
A 1915-18;20-28;Ja 1934

SEARCHLIGHT. w 1910-14||?
1910-12? as Howles iconoclast
A N 1910-12;My 1913-14

SPECTATOR. w 1913-19||?
A D 1914-Ag 1918

STATE. w Ap 18? 1895-
A Jl 4-D 8 1895

STATE herald. *See* Age-herald

Birmingham TIMES. w 1894-1912||?
A Ap 19,Je 28 1899;Mr 1901-S 1905;N 1906-Je 1912
AEvC My 27 1896

VOICE of the people. w 1913-24||?
Negro
A Je 1916-19; Ja 7-19 1922

WIDE AWAKE. w 1888-1900||?
Title varies: Wide-awake bulletin
Negro
A Je 17 1898
DLC Ja 24 1900

BLADON SPRINGS

Bladon Springs HERALD. *See* Choctaw herald (Butler)

BLOCTON

Blocton COURIER. w 1891-Je 1894||
United with Bibb county news (Centerville) to form News and courier, later Centerville press (Centerville)
ACenC Ja 1,D 30 1892;94

Blocton JOURNAL. w 1894-95||?
ACenC Je 28-D 1894

Blocton NEWS-HERALD. w 1897-98||?
ACenC N 27 1897[98]

BLOSSBURG

Blossburg STAR. w 1901-02||?
A Ja-S 1901

BLOUNTSVILLE

BLOUNT county dispatch. w 1887?-89||?
United with Blount county news to form Blount county news-dispatch (Oneonta)
AOC Je-Jl 1887;88-89

BLOUNT county news. *See* Blount county news-dispatch (Oneonta)

BOAZ

Boaz ENTERPRISE. w 1903-04||?
AGuC O 16 1903-Ag 1904

Boaz LEADER. w Ja 6 1915+
A Ap 1919-F 1923; Jl 1934+
AGuC N 19 1915-21; O 19 1922+

SAND MOUNTAIN record. w 1906-12||?
AGuC 1907-N 23 1911

SAND MOUNTAIN signal. w D 1894-1900||?
AGuC 1895-Jl 1900

BRANTLEY

Brantley REPORTER. w 1911-12||?
ALuC Ap 1911-12

BREWTON

Brewton BANNER. w 1883-Ja 7 1888||
Merged with Standard guage, later Brewton standard
A Je 1883-86;Jl 7 1887
ABrC 1884-88

Brewton BLADE. w 1881-82||?
ABrC Jl 2-D 3 1881

ESCAMBIA and Baldwin times. w 1885-88||?
1885 as Escambia times
ABrC D 16 1885-Jl 11 1888

LABORER'S BANNER. w 1900-02||?
A Mr 15-22,Ap 5,19-My 17 [Jl 18 1901-Je 26 1902]

Brewton LEADER. w 1892-94||?
A Jl 1892-Ja 3 1894
ABrC My 24 1892-Mr 6 1893

PINE BELT news. w F 27 1894-N 1917||
Merged with Brewton standard
A complete
ABrC F 22 1895-N 16 1916

ALABAMA (*Continued*)

BREWTON—*Continued*

Brewton STANDARD. w 1886+
1886-Je 1906 as Standard guage pub 1920+
A Ja 21 1888-F 1908;Jl 21 1914;Jl 24 1924;N 1926-28;O 1935+
ABrC 1888-Je 1892;Jl 1894+

BRIDGEPORT

CAMP illuminator. w 1864?-
OCl Ap 18 1865

Bridgeport HERALD. *See* Bridgeport news-herald

Bridgeport NEWS. w S 18 1890-98||?
ASC 1890-98

Bridgeport NEWS. 1908-26 *See* Bridgeport news-herald

Bridgeport NEWS-HERALD. w 1908+
1908-26? as Bridgeport news; 1927? Bridgeport herald
A F 14 1908-N 4 1909;14-D 2 1929

BRUNDIDGE

Brundidge NEWS. w,sw 1893-1925||?
sw 1899?
A My 1896-Je 1911;My 1913-O 1919;20-22;24-N 1925
ATrC N 20 1893-S 12 1896;My 23 1900-F 8 1906[07]F 1909-24

Brundidge RECORD. w 1907-08||
ATrC S 13 1907-D 23 1908

Brundidge SENTINEL. w 1928-30||
ATrC F 22 1928-D 18 1930

BUTLER

ALABAMA standard. w Ja 13 1851-
NcD F 17 1851
OHi F 24 1851

CHOCTAW advocate. w Je 11 1890+
A S 1901-My 1911;N 1926-28;33+
ABuC 1890[91]-[1930]+

CHOCTAW county news. w Jl 21 1876-D 31 1881||
Follows Choctaw herald. 1876-Ja 5 1878 as Butler news
ABuC complete

CHOCTAW county reporter. w 1850-
NcD Ag 15 1850

CHOCTAW herald. w S 5 1868-Ja 22 1876||
Mr 29 1871-Ja 9 1874 as Bladon Springs herald (Bladon Springs) Followed by Butler news, later Choctaw county news
ABuC complete

CHOCTAW herald. w Ja 21 1884-Ap 23 1903||
ABuC 1884-Ja 5,Ap 23 1903

Butler NEWS. *See* Choctaw county news

SOUTHERN democrat. w
A Ag 8 1859;D 24 1860

CAHAWBA

ALABAMA republican. w D 17? 1831-
MiU Ja 30 1832

ALABAMA state gazette. w 1820?-
DLC D 4 1824
MWA Ap 28,My 12 1825

AMERICAN whig. w N 1825-
Ct Ja 7 1826

DALLAS gazette. *See* Cahawba gazette

Cahawba DEMOCRAT. w 1836?-
A F 1 1840
GAtCo D 29 1838;Ja 5,Ap 6 1839

Cahawba GAZETTE. w 1843-60||?
1843-59? as Dallas gazette
A 1854-59;Jl 13, 27 1860
NcD Ja 14-My 6,20-S,O 28-D 23 1853;Ja 6, 20-F 10,Mr 3-24,Ap 7-14,28-Je,Jl 14-S,O 13-D 15,26 1854;Mr 14-Ap 4,18-My 23,Je 13-O, N 14-D 1856

***Cahawba PRESS and Alabama state intelligencer.** w,sw Je 12 1819-Jl 22 1826||
1819-20? as Cahawba press and Alabama intelligencer. Followed by Selma courier (Selma)
sw D 3-17 1821;D 6-20 1823
DLC [1821]-[23-25]26
MWA F 7,Mr 20,Ap 17,My 1,S 25,N 22,D 4 1824;Mr 19,My 14 1825
T N 12-D 3,10 1821-Ja 4 1822;D 24(extra) 1821

Cahawba SLAVE-HOLDER and bulletin. ir 1860-
OCHi F 2 1861

CALERA

Calera INDEPENDENT. w My 29 1930-
ACoC My-N 20 1930

Calera JOURNAL. w O 30 1891-92||?
ACoC 1891-D 21 1892

SHELBY county review. w F 7 1913-14||?
A 1913-D 4 1914
ACoC 1913

SHELBY news. w Ja 1 1891-94||?
ACoC 1891-92

SHELBY sentinel. *See* Sentinel (Montevallo)

CAMDEN

GAZETTE. w Ap 1 1882-Ap 13 1887||
1882-Mr 5? 1884 as Pine Apple gazette; Mr 12 1884-Je 10 1885 Huston appeal; Je 17 1885-F 10? 1886 Pine Apple enterprise. Followed by Wilcox progress, later Wilcox progressive era
1882-Mr 5? 1884; Mr 26 1885-F 10? 1886 pub in Pine Apple
ACC complete

HOME ruler. w 1881-87||?
ACC N 23 1881-Mr 19 1884

HUSTON appeal. *See* Gazette

Camden JOURNAL. w 1917-18||?
ACC N 15 1917-S 12 1918

Camden NEWS. w
ACC Mr 8 1913-My 9 1914

Camden PHENIX. w
ACC D 15 1851-D 13 1852

Camden REPUBLIC. w
A Jl 19 1860

WILCOX banner. w
ACC O 10 1873-O 6 1875

WILCOX banner. w 1878-S 5 1879||
A Je 13 1878
ACC F 1878-S 5 1879

WILCOX banner. w My 1903-My 1914||?
Merged with Wilcox progressive era
A 1903-S 1913
ACC 1903-04;Mr 1905-08;10-11;Ja-O 2 1913

WILCOX county news. *See* Wilcox news and pacificator

WILCOX farmer vindicator. *See* Wilcox vindicator

WILCOX new era. w 1889-1900||
United with Wilcox progress to form Wilcox progressive era
ACC 1897-O 10 1900

WILCOX news and pacificator. w Jl 12 1865-83||?
1865-N 1868 as Wilcox county news
A N 30 1877
ACC Ag 16 1867-Jl 6 1883
MWA Mr 25 1876

WILCOX progress. *See* Wilcox progressive era

WILCOX progressive era. w My 4 1887+
Follows Gazette. 1887-1900 as Wilcox progress
A Jl 7 1897;O 12 1898;Mr 1901-28;32+
ACC My 1888-Ap 4 1889;94;98-1908;10;12+

WILCOX vindicator. w,sw O 8 1865-73||?
1873 as Wilcox farmer vindicator
sw 1865-D 15 1868
ACC 1867-O 3 1873;O 13 1875-O 3 1877

CAMP HILL

Camp Hill NEWS. *See* Tallapoosa news

Camp Hill STAR. w S 4 1924-D 24 1930||
A N 1926-28
ADC complete

TALLAPOOSA news. w 1900+
1900-Ag 2 1907 as Camp Hill times; Ag 9 1907-Je 5 1914 Camp Hill news
A Jl 1900-Jl 1907;Jl 1934+
ADC 1903+

Camp Hill TIMES. *See* Tallapoosa news

CARBON HILL

Carbon Hill CHRONICLE. w 1897-98||?
AJC D 11 1897-Ja 1898

Weekly DISPATCH. w 1889-90||?
AJC Ap-D 1890

ENTERPRISE democrat. w 1898-1906||?
1898 -My 6 1904 as Carbon Hill enterprise
AJC Ap 1903-S 6 1906

Carbon Hill INDEX. w 1924-25||?
AJC F 1924-Ja 1925

Carbon Hill JOURNAL. w 1913-23||?
A N 1914-18;20-My 1923
AJC S 18 1913-18;Jl 29 1920-22

MOUNTAIN news. w
AJC Jl 14 1892-Mr 1894

Carbon Hill NEWS. w 1926+
A 1933+
AJC 1927+

Carbon Hill STAR. w
AJC 1900-08

Carbon Hill WEEKLY. w 1908||?
AJC Ja 8-Ag 27 1908

CARROLLTON

ALABAMA alliance news. *See* Pickens county news

ALABAMIAN herald. *See* West Alabamian

PICKENS county herald. w S 13 1904-D 27 1905||
United with West Alabamian to form Alabamian herald, later West Alabamian
ACaC complete

PICKENS county herald and West Alabamian. sw,w 1910+
1910-F 1918 as Pickens county herald
sw 1910-15?
A 1913-28;33+
ACaC F 1914+

PICKENS county news. w 1891-1902||?
1894?-99? as Alabama alliance news
A My 11 1897
ACaC N 24 1891-1901

PICKENS county press. w 1882-83||?
1882-Ja 14? 1883 as Riverside press
A F 10 1882-Ag 14 1883

PICKENS county republican. w Mr 29? 1845-
MBAt My 3,17 1845

RIVERSIDE press. *See* Pickens county press

WEST ALABAMIAN. w Ap 1849-F 11 1918||
Ja 3 1906-Ag 5 1908 as Alabamian herald. United with Pickens county herald to form Pickens county herald and West Alabamian
A 1855-D 23 1861;My 28 1866-87;89-91;Mr 1895-1918
ACaC 1865-1918
NcD Mr 19 1879
TxU 1870-Ap 1877

CEDAR BLUFF

Cedar Bluff CHEROKEEN. w Jl 3 1913-16||?
ACeC Ap 1914-D 28 1916

GLADIATOR. w N 8 1843-
DLC N 15 1843;Ja 31 1844

CENTER

TO 1912? as Centre

CHEROKEE advertiser. w 1866-92||?
ACeC Ap 19 1867-N 11 1869;71-72;75-79;82-N 20 1884;Mr 1885-D 17 1891

CHEROKEE harmonizer. w 1893-1923||?
1893-Ag 24 1899 as Cherokee sentinel
A S 1899-N 1906;15-23
ACeC 1896-Ag 1899

CHEROKEE sentinel. *See* Cherokee harmonizer

COOSA RIVER news. w 1878+
A 1933+
ACeC 1895-99;1901-02;11-12;14-16;19-23;26+

CENTERVILLE

BIBB county news. *See* Centerville press

BIBB county press. *See* Centerville press

CENTRAL enquirer. w 1861?-
MWA D 17 1863

NEWS and courier. *See* Centerville press

Centerville PRESS. w Ja 1 1879+
1879-91? as Bibb blade (1890? Blade-enterprise) 1892?-Jl 5 1894 Bibb county news; Jl 12 1894-F 14? 1895 News and courier; F 21 1895-Ap? 1898 Bibb county press
1879-90? pub in Six Mile
A D 24 1879-N 20 1891;Ag 1899-Ag 1912;33+
ACenC Ja 1 1879;D 31 1883-Ja 4 1884;D 10 1885;D 30 1886-[87;89-91]Je 4-D 7 1894;F 21 1895-Ja 2 1896[97-98]-1914;16-20;23+

CENTRE. *See* CENTER

CHATOM

WASHINGTON county news. w 1892+
1892-1906? pub in St. Stephens pub Jl 31 1924+
A 1918-28;32+
AChC S 1897-Jl 1924

CHEROKEE

WEST COLBERT news. w 1915-16||?
ATsC Je 11 1915-D 15 1916

CITRONELLE

Citronelle CALL. w 1896+
A Ag 1899-1905;14-28;33+

Citronelle TIMES. w 1897-1903||?
A 1900-Ja 1903

CLAIBORNE

Claiborne GAZETTE. w Je 10? 1824-
MWA Mr 19 1825

Claiborne HERALD. w 1828-
DLC F 27,D 5 1829

MONROE eagle. w 1868-71||?
AMrC Je 18-D 1871

SOUTHERN champion.
A Ap 26 1861

Claiborne SOUTHERNER.
AMrC [1861;68-69]

CLANTON

Clanton BANNER. *See* Union-banner

CHILTON county call. w 1897-
ACnC Ap 23-D 31 1897

CHILTON county courier. w Je 9 1876-77||?
ACnC Ja-S 1877
DLC S 15 1876

CHILTON county news. w 1921+
A Ap-D 1932;S 1935+
ARC Ja 21 1926

CHILTON view. w N 10 1881-99||?
ACnC 1881-[84-85]-[89]-[96-98]99

ALABAMA (*Continued*)

CLANTON—*Continued*

Clanton PRESS. w 1910-19||?
A Ap 1910-Jl 1918
ACnC 1910-[12]-18

UNION. w Ap 2 1903-Ap 4 1912||
United with Clanton banner to form Union-banner
ACnC [1903]-12

UNION-BANNER. w O 27 1892+
1892-Ap 4 1912 as Clanton banner; Ap 11 1912-18? Union and banner
A 1899-N 1912;N 1914-28;Ja-Mr 1933
ACnC 1892-[94]-[96]-[99]-[1902]+

CLAYTON

Clayton BANNER. w 1851-69||?
AClC My 31 1860-Ap 25 1861

BARBOUR herald.
AClC My 5-D 17 1898

BARBOUR journal. w 1897||?
AClC Ap 30-S 17 1897

Clayton COURIER. *See* Clayton record

LOUISIANA journal.
AClC Ap 8-D 17 1898

Clayton RECORD. w 1870+
1870-D 12 1896 as Clayton courier
A Jl 26 1879;Mr 2 1889;D 1 1894;Jl 27 1895;Ag 1899-N 1911;D 1926-28;33+
AClC Ag 14 1880+

CLIO

Clio FREE PRESS. w My 18 1906-20||?
A N 1906-My 1919
AClC Je 15 1906-10;15;17-Ag 15 1918

COLLINSVILLE

Collinsville COURIER. w 1922-27||?
A 1922-Ap 1927
AFpC 1925-27

MILLS VALLEY post. w -1882||?
A Ag 9 1879

Collinsville NEW ERA. w Je 23 1927+
A 1933+
AFpC 1927+

COLUMBIA

Columbia BREEZE. w Ag 25 1892-1912||?
AAC 1892-O 6 1898;F 1899-1901
ADoC F 1903-Ja 27 1911

Columbia ENTERPRISE. *See* Columbia recorder

Columbia OBSERVER. w 1883-84||?
AAC O 25 1883-Ag 27 1884

Columbia RECORDER. w 1879-92||?
1879-Mr 27 1890 as Columbia enterprise
AAC 1883-91
AOzC O 29 1891

COLUMBIANA

CHRONICLE. *See* Shelby county sun

PEOPLE'S advocate. w Je 2 1892-1924||
A F 18 1904
ACoC 1892-Jl 1924

Columbiana SENTINEL. *See* Shelby county sun

SHELBY chronicle. *See* Shelby county sun

SHELBY county democrat. w Ap 21 1932+
ACoC 1932+

SHELBY county guide. *See* Sentinel (Montevallo)

SHELBY county reporter. w Ja 18 1923+
A Ap 19 1924;N 1926-28;33+
ACoC 1923+

SHELBY county sun. w N 29 1883-N 17 1921||?
1883-N 30 1892 as Shelby chronicle; D 8? 1892-Ap 7 1904 Chronicle; Ap 14? 1904-09? Columbiana sentinel
A Mr 30 1892;O 6,20 1904;D 15 1911
ACoC 1883-[1916]N 17 1921

SHELBY sentinel. *See* Sentinel (Montevallo)

CORDOVA

Cordova HERALD. w Jl 19 1911-14||?
AJC 1911-O 1 1914

Cordova NEWS. w 1905?-06||?
AJC S 13 1905-Je 6 1906

WALKER county tribune. w
AJC Ja 21-Je 2 1932

COTTONDALE

OUR COUNTRY and its future. w
A Ap 8-N 1899

COURTLAND

Courtland ENTERPRISE. *See* Lawrence county news

FRIEND of the labourer. w 1876?-80||?
AMtC My 30-D 5 1878;Ja 23-D 18 1879;Ja 8-Jl 9 1880
NcD F 27,Mr 27-Ap 10,Jl 3 1879

Courtland HERALD. w 1824?-
CSmH Ag 20 1830
MWA O 3 1828

LAWRENCE county news. w 1894-D 1902||
1894-1901 as Courtland enterprise
A Ag 1 1901
AMtC F 15-D 13 1894;95-96;My 14-N 19 1897; F 11 1898-Ag 8 1902

LAWRENCE county times. w 1924-25||?
A 1924-O 1925

Courtland NEWS. *See* Decatur news (Decatur)

PATRIOT. w 1878-
NcD D 14 1878;Ja 18,F 15,Mr 1-8,22,Ap 5, 19 1879

Courtland RECORDER. w My 10 1877-78||?
AMtC 1877;My 3-16 1878

WIDE-AWAKE sentinel. w Mr 1881-82||?
ADeC Mr 31 1881-Mr 1882
AMtC Mr-N 2 1882
NcD Je 22,Ag 17 1882

CROSS PLAINS. *See* PIEDMONT

CUBA

Cuba ADVERTISER. w 1910-13||?
ALnC 1910-S 5 1913

CULLMAN

ALABAMA tribune. *See* Cullman tribune

Cullman DEMOCRAT. w 1900?+
A S 1900-28;Jl 1934+
ACuC Je 13 1901+

MOUNTAIN CITY gazette. w D 7 1894-O? 1898||
United with Cullman tribune to form Tribune-gazette, later Cullman tribune
ACuC F 16 1895-S 3 1898

PEOPLE'S protest. w Ap 21 1893-D 22 1899||
ACuC complete

Cullman PROGRESS. w Jl 17 1884-86||?
ACuC 1884;Ja-D 2 1886

SOUTHERN immigrant. w 1876-1880||
United with Alabama tribune to form Southern immigrant and Alabama tribune, later Cullman tribune
A Jl 4 1879
ACuC Ja 24-D 1878

Cullman TRIBUNE. w 1874+
1874-D 19 1895 as Alabama tribune (N 1 1880-82? Southern immigrant and Alabama tribune) O 20 1898-1902 Tribune-gazette
A Ag 1899-Je 1911;N 1914-28;33+
ACuC Ja 18 1880;Ja-O 6 1882;87-89;91+
NcD Mr 13 1879
VU Ap 18 1929

DADEVILLE

Dadeville BANNER and times. w 1859-
1859-61? as Dadeville banner
ADC [Ja-Je 7 1861]F 4 1864

EAST ALABAMA headlight. w 1873-79||?
ADC Ag 21 1873

EAST ALABAMIAN. w Mr 6? 1868-
MBAt Ag 7 1868

FREE PRESS. w S 12 1901-Ag 28 1902||
A complete
ADC complete

Dadeville HERALD. w Je 19 1890-D 21 1900||
1890-Ja 18 1894 as Tallapoosa voice; Ja 5-Ap 27 1900 Herald-new era
ADC 1890-97;99-1900

MESSENGER. w 1866-
MWA Je 13 1867

Dadeville RECORD. w F 25 1898+
1898-Ap 7 1932 as Dadeville spot cash
A N 1914-28;33+
ADC 1898+

Dadeville SPOT CASH. *See* Dadeville record

TALLAPOOSA courier. w Mr 16 1905-Je 8 1911||
ADC complete

TALLAPOOSA new era. w N 2 1886-D 22 1899||
Merged with Dadeville herald to form Herald-new era, later Dadeville herald
ADC complete

TALLAPOOSA voice. *See* Dadeville herald

DAPHNE

GULF breeze. w N 24 1894-96||?
ABmC 1894-N 16 1895

Daphne STANDARD. *See* Onlooker (Foley)

Daphne TIMES. *See* Baldwin times (Bay Minette)

DECATUR

ALABAMA republican. w 1867-72||
A D 2 1867

ALBANY advertiser. w S 1889-1920||?
1891-S 1916 as New Decatur advertiser
A Ag 1899-Mr 4 1920
ADeC 1889-95;98-1900;02-19

ALBANY news review. w Mr-D 1922||
ADeC complete

ALBANY-DECATUR daily. *See* Decatur daily

Decatur DAILY. d 1912+
1918-26 as Albany-Decatur daily pub 1912+
A 1919;F 1920-21;F 1922-S 1930
ADeC 1912+

Decatur FREE LANCE. w Ap 23 1887-88||?
GAtCo My 21 1887
MWA Je 4 1887

GUARDIAN. m Mr 15 1910-17||
Negro
A D 1914-Ja 1917

INVESTIGATOR. w Ap 16 1834-
DLC Ap 16,Jl 4 1834

MORGAN advertiser. w
TxU S 24 1849

MORGAN county herald. *See* Decatur vitascope

MORGAN county times. sw 1906-13||?
ADeC 1906-Je 1913

NEW DECATUR advertiser. *See* Albany advertiser

Decatur NEWS. w N 30 1870-D 1919||
1870-72? as Courtland news (Courtland); 1873?-O 1918 Decatur weekly news
A Ag 26 1892;O 1899-My 1904;15-My 1918
ADeC 1875-77;80-82;84;87-95;97;99-1909;13-19
NcD My 3 1873;Ap 5,My 3,N 22 1879;Ja 13-20, F 17,Mr 3,Ap 7-21,My,Je 30,Jl 7,28,D 29 1882;S 30 1892
TKL O 29 1881

NORTH ALABAMA times. w
A Ag 6 1859

TENNESSEE Valley. w Ap 1885-88||
ADeC complete
GAtCo Mr 10 1887

TWIN CITY herald. [New Decatur] d 1908||
A Mr-O 1908
ADeC [1908]

TWIN CITY daily telegram. d 1909-Ag 1913||?
A Ja 28 1910
ADeC 1910-Ag 1913

Decatur VITASCOPE. w Mr 21 1895-Jl 1901||
1895-Ag 1898 as Morgan county herald
ADeC complete

DEMOPOLIS

BIGBEE news. *See* Marengo news

Morning HERALD. d? 1860?-
IU Ap 26 1865

MARENGO gazette. w Mr 28- 1838||?
DLC Ap 4 1838

MARENGO news. w 1872-92||?
1872-73? as Bigbee news; 1874?-85? Marengo news-journal
A F 21 1874;Mr 25,Je 3,Jl 1 1875;Mr 27 1879

MARENGO patriot. w Mr 4 1840-
DLC Mr 4 1840

Demopolis NEW ERA. w Ap 6 1866-69||?
MWA My 18 1866

SOUTHERN republican. w 1869-71||?
A F 10 1869-F 9 1871

Demopolis TIMES. w 1905+
A O 13 1910;N 20 1919;My 20,Je 17 1920;N 1926-28;33+
ALiC 1913[14]-[23-24]-30
ASlT My 10 1923

DOTHAN

Dothan weekly EAGLE. w 1903-27||?
1903-05 as Houston eagle
ADoC 1906-Je 26 1927

Dothan EAGLE. d 1908+
A S 1915-S 1930

Dothan HOME JOURNAL. w 1899-1920||?
A 1915-18
AAC Mr 29 1899-1900;Ap 1901-02
ADoC F 10 1903-Je 15 1916;17;Ja-O 2 1919; Ja-Je 1920

HOUSTON eagle. *See* Dothan weekly eagle

HOUSTON herald. w Ja 2 1931+
ADoC 1931+

Dothan LIGHT. w 1888-90||?
AAC Mr 2 1889-My 21 1890

Weekly SENTINEL. w 1890-91||?
A Je 4 1890
AAC Ag 9 1890-Jl 1891

Dothan daily SIFTINGS. *See* Wiregrass siftings

WIREGRASS journal. w Ja 10 1923+
A Jl-S 1934;Ja-S 1935
ADoC Ja 10 1923+

WIRE-GRASS siftings. w 1890-1910||?
A S 1899-Je 1910
AAC Ja 8 1891-98;1900-02
ADoC Ja 13 1905-Jl 1 1910
AOzC S 3 1891

WIREGRASS siftings. d Mr 17 1903-09||?
1903-07? as Dothan daily siftings
ADoC D 15 1904-07

ALABAMA (*Continued*)

DOUBLE SPRINGS

ANCHOR. w
AChC Mr-Ag 1900

NEW ERA. *See* Winston new era

NEW ERA-HERALD. *See* Winston herald

OBSERVER. w 1892-98||
AChC N 1892-D 10 1896
AJC Mr 23 1893-Ja 11 1894;95-D 5 1898

WINSTON herald. w 1881+
1906-My 21 1909 as New era-herald pub 1933+
A Ja 4,18 1924
AChC N 17 1892-99;F 1901-N 7 1902;06+
AJC S 18 1884-87[94-95]-98;1908-09
AHA 1924+

WINSTON new era. w Ap 28 1899-1905||
1899-1905 as New era. United with Winston herald to form New era-herald, later Winston herald
AChC complete
AJC 1900-01

ECLECTIC

Eclectic ENTERPRISE. w 1929+
AWeC Ja 10 1930-My 15 1931

EDWARDSVILLE

CLEBURNE county news. w 1887-Jl 25 1889||
United with Edwardsville standard to form Standard-news
AHeC Ja 13-D 1888

CLEBURNE plowboy. w 1890-1900||?
AHeC [1890]-94;96[97]99

Edwardsville ENTERPRISE. w 1898-1906||
1898-O 1905 as Fruithurst weekly enterprise (Fruithurst)
A F 1901-02
AHeC 1898;1900-[04]-D 21 1906

NATIONAL megaphone. w -Ag 13 1908||
Merged with Union herald
AHeC Ap 16-Ag 1908

STANDARD-NEWS. w 1881-S 29 1905||
1881-Je 1889 as Edwardsville standard
A O 9 1884
AHeC 1883[84]-[90]-D 24 1896;98-[1904]05

UNION herald. w 1907-11||?
AHeC Jl 26 1907-08;10-Mr 10 1911

ELBA

Elba CLIPPER. w,sw Je 17 1897+
sw Jl 18 1905-25?
A My 1901-F 1912;N 1921-28;33+
AEC Ja 12 1899-1916;29+

PEOPLE'S tribune. w 1922-26||?
A S 1922-Ag 1925

ELKMONT

Elkmont ENTERPRISE. *See* Limestone enterprise (Athens)

LIMESTONE enterprise. *See under* Athens

ELMORE

Elmore BANNER. w
AWeC Ja 22-Ag 6 1903

Elmore NEWS. w 1901?-02||?
AWeC Ag 29-N 21 1901

Elmore STANDARD.
A My 8-D 20 1867

ELYTON

Papers published in Elyton are listed under Birmingham

ENSLEY

Papers published in Ensley are listed under Birmingham

ENTERPRISE

Weekly ENTERPRISE. *See* Enterprise ledger

Enterprise LEDGER. w,sw 1898+
1898-Ap 1906 as Weekly enterprise; Ap 1906-19? People's ledger
sw 1913?-14?;18?-19?;21?
A Ag 1900-10

PEOPLE'S ledger. *See* Enterprise ledger

EPES

SUMTER county call. w D 16 1905-12||?
A 1905-Ap 1912
ALnC 1905-D 20 1906;F 20-D 1908;F 10 1910-D 21 1911

ERIE

GREENE county gazette. w My 3 1830-
AEwC 1830-31
CSmH Jl 15 1830
NcD F 14-21 1831

EUFAULA

To 1840? as Irwinton

BARBOUR county times and news. w 1868?-1930||?
1868?-Ap? 1872 as Bluff City times; My? 1872-76? Eufaula times; 1877?-1919? Eufaula times and news; 1920?-26? Eufaula times news
A Ap 15 1868-Ap 1873;S 9 1880-98;Ag 1900-Jl 1925
ACIC 1881-Ag 8 1882;Jl 14 1885-Ja 19 1888; 90-Ja 15 1891;Ja 21 1892-D 21 1893
AEuC 1884-1910
—d ed *See* Eufaula daily citizen

BLUFF CITY times. *See* Barbour county times and news

Eufaula weekly BULLETIN. w Mr 5 1881-84||
A Mr 5 1881;Mr 8 1882
ACIC 1881-Ag 13 1884

Eufaula daily CITIZEN. tw,d 1872?-1929||?
1872-76? as Eufaula times; 1877?-82? Eufaula times and news; 1883?-1909? Eufaula daily times. Merged with Eufaula tribune?
A Ap 27 1872-Ap 27 1873;Mr 5 1881;N 25 1882-83;Ja-Je 1885;Jl 1886-O 1889;90-Je 1894; 95-98;Ap 1916-29
ACIC Mr 10 1921-Je 1925;Ja 29 1926-S 12 1927
—w ed *See* Barbour county times and news

Eufaula DEMOCRAT. *See* Eufaula news

Eufaula EXPRESS. w
A Jl 11 1864

Eufaula daily MAIL. d 1885-D 30 1886||
ACIC D 3 1885-86

NEPENTHES. w Jl 13 1839-40||?
DLC Jl 20 1839
IHi Je 20 1840

Eufaula NEWS, w,d,tw Je 25 1845-N 1876||
1845-Je 1851? as Eufaula democrat; Jl 1851?-Je? 1865 Spirit of the south. United with Eufaula times to form Eufaula times and news, later Eufaula daily citizen
w 1845-Je? 1865;d Jl? 1865-67?
A Je 8 1846-Je 2 1851;My 8,Je 5,Jl 31,O 9-23,N-D 1,18 1855;Ja 22-29,F 12,26,Mr 11 1856; O 13 1858;Jl 12 1859;Jl 24 1860;Ag 27,S 10 1861
DLC D 5 1848;Jl 22 1862
ICHi O 14 1865
MWA F 11 1868
OHi S 19 1865

Eufaula NEWS. w 1869-76||?
United with Eufaula times to form Eufaula times and news, later Barbour county times and news
A Mr 26 1874

SOUTHERN shield. w 1841?-
DLC O 23 1851

SPIRIT of the south. *See* Eufaula news

Eufaula TIMES. d *See* Eufaula daily citizen

Eufaula TIMES. w *See* Barbour county times and news

Eufaula TRIBUNE. d 1929+
A Ja-Je 1930

EUTAW

ALABAMA whig. *See* Eutaw whig and observer

GREENE county democrat. w Ap 22 1879+
1879-1901 as Eutaw mirror
A My 27,S 2-16,30,O 14,N 4-11,25-D 9 1884;O 12 1904;D 1914-Jl 1922;Mr 13 1924;33+
AEwC 1879+
ICM Mr 15 1881

INDEPENDENT observer. w -1861||?
United with Alabama whig to form Eutaw whig and observer
A Ja 11,My 17 1861

Eutaw MIRROR. *See* Greene county democrat

Eutaw WHIG and observer. w F 20 1840-1917||
1840-51? as Eutaw whig and public advertiser; 1852?-61? Alabama whig
A Ja 22 1847;Ja 19 1854;Jl 24-31 1878;O 25 1894;My 13 1897;Ag 1899-1917
AEwC 1859;72-1916
DLC F 20,N 7 1840
ICM My 5 1881
NcD My 28-Je 4 1842;S 29 1853;My 17,Je 7-14,Jl 19 1855;Je 11-16 1857;F 3 1859;D 27 1860; F 9,Mr 9-16 1865;F 27 1879
NcU Jl 4 1861

EVERGREEN

CONECUH record. w 1868-Je 21 1927||
1868-Mr 8 1894? as Evergreen star (Jl 17 1879-F 16 1888 Conecuh-Escambia star; F 23 1888-S 17 1892 Star) 1894? Star and record. Merged with Evergreen courant
A Mr 1895-1907
AEvC Mr 1879-F 1881;N 23 1882-Ag 6 1891;Ja 21 1892-[95]-[1910]-[12]D 11 1913-27

CONECUH-ESCAMBIA star. *See* Conecuh record

Evergreen COURANT. w S 10 1895+
A N 1926-28;33+
AEvC 1895+;extra F 25 1914

Evergreen ENTERPRISE. w Ap 5 1918-19||?
AEvC 1918-Ag 1919

Evergreen STAR. *See* Conecuh record

FAIRHOPE

Fairhope COURIER. m,sm,w Ag 15 1894+
m Ag-N 1894;sm D 1894-D 15 1904
A 1901;Ag 1910-28;Ap 3 1930;Ap,O-D 1933;Ap-S 1934;S 1935+
AEmC 1911-Jl 12 1928
ICJ S 1894[95]-My 1896;Ja,Ap-Je 1897;Ja-F, Ap,Je-Jl,N 1898;99-Jl 1931
NNR S 11 1930-Ap 19 1931
WHi F 14 1908-14

FALKVILLE

Falkville CHRONICLE. w 189?-1902||?
ADeC 1897-1902

Falkville NEWS. w Ja 1915-My 1916||?
ADeC 1915-My 1916

FAYETTE

To 1876? as Fayette Court House

Fayette BANNER. w 1900+
A Ag 1900-Mr 1918;O 1921-[25]-28;O 1932+
AFC Ag 9 1900-[03-08]-[10]+

FAYETTE county times. w F 19 1914-16||?
A D 1914-Ja 1916
AFC F 26 1914-Je 9 1916

Fayette GAZETTE. w 1852?-81||?
1852?-75? as Watchman. Followed by Fayette sentinel, later Fayette tribune?
A My 9-23,Je 8-Jl 4 1876

NORTHWEST Alabamian. w Mr 4 1925+
A 1925-28;33+
AFC 1925+

Fayette SENTINEL. *See* Fayette tribune

Fayette TRIBUNE. w 1881-O 13 1900||
Follows Fayette gazette? 1881-98? as Fayette sentinel. Merged with Fayette banner
A O 26 1894;Ap 2,O 1 1897
AFC 1898-1900

WATCHMAN. *See* Fayette gazette

FAYETTE COURT HOUSE. *See* FAYETTE

FLOMATON

Flomaton ENTERPRISE. w 1908-09||?
ABrC Jl-D 1908

FLORALA

Florala DEMOCRAT. w 1909-13||?
United with Florala news to form Florala news-democrat, later Florala news
A 1913

INTER-STATE appeal. w
AAnC S 18 1897-Ap 16 1898

Florala NEWS. w F 6 1902+
1913?-18 as Florala news-democrat
A Je 26 1917;N 1926-28;33—
AAnC Jl 10 1903-Ag 8 1912;My 29 1913+

Florala TRIBUNE. w 1931-
AAnC F 12-S 10 1931

FLORENCE

ALABAMA progress. *See* North star

AMERICAN democrat. w 1856-
MWA D 5 1856
T [1856]

Florence APPEAL. w Jl 25-Ag 29 1896||
AFlC complete

Florence BANNER. *See* Florence gazette 1883-97

Florence evening BULLETIN and times. d
AFlC 1901-02

Florence DEMOCRAT. w 1893-99||?
AFlC 1898-99

Florence ENQUIRER. w Mr 16 1840-
A Ag 22 1840
DLC Mr 23,Ap 18,N 28 1840
MBAt Ag 22,S 19 1840;Jl 10 1841
NcD S 9 1842

*Florence GAZETTE. w 1820-63||?
A O 1858-Ap 9,D 10-24 1862;Ja 1863
DLC Ag 19,O 21 1824;Ap 21 1825;D 2 1830;Ja 6 1831;O 10 1844;My 19 1849-My 24 1851
N S 20 1833
NcD My 30 1846
TKL F 12 1835

Florence GAZETTE. w 1871-89||?
1871-O 1872? as Lauderdale times; N 1872?-74? Florence times-journal
AFlC 1877;79-81;83;85-N 11 1887

Florence GAZETTE. w 1883-97||?
1883-92? as Florence banner
A 1892-97
AFlC 1883-84;86-92

Florence HERALD. sw,w Ja 4 1884+
1884-89? as Florence wave
sw 1884-90?
A Ap 27,Je 29,S 7-14,28-O 12 1893;S 2-9 1897; Ag 1899-Jl 1912;N 1914-28;33-S 1935;36+
AFlC 1886;Ag 20 1887-1901;03-04;07;11-14;16; 19-20;22+

ALABAMA (*Continued*)

FLORENCE—*Continued*

Florence JOURNAL. w S 27 1865?-O 1872||?
United with Lauderdale times to form Florence times-journal, later Florence gazette
Suspended from O-D 2 1867?
AFlC 1866
DLC Ap 29-My,Je 17-Jl,Ag 19-O 14,28-D 1869
ICHi N 1 1865

LAUDERDALE gazette. w Mr 15- 1892||
AFlC Mr-Je 22 1892

LAUDERDALE journal. w O 14-D 25 1896||
AFlC complete

LAUDERDALE news. *See* North star

LAUDERDALE times. *See* Florence gazette 1871-89

LITERARY index. w 1865-69||?
Merged with Florence journal
AFlC 1867-68

MUSCLE SHOALS Sunday news. w 1923-25||?
A Mr 1924-Ag 1925
—d eds *See* Florence daily news; Tri-cities daily (Sheffield)

Florence daily NEWS. d 1919-Je 1926||?
United with Florence times to form Florence times-news, later Florence times
A Ap 1919-N 1924;25
ASlT My 29 1923
—Sunday ed *See* Muscle Shoals Sunday news

NORTH STAR. w N 25 1879-D 25 1884||
1879-N 15 1883? as Lauderdale news; N 22 1883-Ja 1884 Alabama progress
AFlC 1881-84
NcD Jl 5,Ag 9,D 13-20 1882

Florence TIMES. w Jl 4 1889-1926||?
A Jl 4 1890;Ap 22,S 2 1893;S 1899-1928
AFlC 1890-93;1904;06-12;14;16-17;19-24
NcD N 2 1895;Je 22,Ag 17-24 1900
TxU S 30-O 7 1904;Ja 20-27,Mr 7,Jl 7-21,Ag 18-S 15 1905

Florence TIMES. d S 17 1923+
Jl 1926?-31? as Florence times-news
A S 1899-1928;O-D 1935
AFlC 1923-24;28+

Florence TIMES-JOURNAL. *See* Florence gazette 1871-89

Florence TRIBUNE. w 1931+
A My 18-Je 22 1933
AFlC 1933

Florence WAVE. *See* Florence herald

FOLEY

BALDWIN county news. w 1922-28||?
ABmC S 1923-Jl 12 1928

ONLOOKER. w Mr 15 1901+
1901-F 28 1908 as Daphne standard (Daphne)
A 1901-F 1908;D 4-11 1912;Mr 1916-28;33+
ABmC O 25 1901-Jl 19 1928

FORKLAND

Forkland PROGRESS. w Ap 1889-90||?
AEwC 1890

FORT DEPOSIT

LOWNDES signal. w 1920+
A Jl 1934-S 1935
AAtC Ap 16 1925+

Fort Deposit MAIL. w 1900-
AHaC [1900]

REFLECTOR. w 1900-05||?
AHaC Mr 26 1905

Fort Deposit VINDICATOR. w 1897-1900||?
Negro
AHaC N 25 1898-Je 1 1900

FORT PAYNE

DEKALB county herald. w Jl 22 1921-28||?
Merged with Fort Payne journal
A Mr 1922-Ag 1923;26-F,My 1927-N 1928
AFpC 1921-26

DEKALB county republican. w Ap 26 1923-26||?
A Ja 24 1924
AFpC [1923-25]

DEKALB times. w 1930+
AFpC 1932+

Fort Payne JOURNAL. w N 12 1878+
A Ap 25 1886;Ag 1899-Je 1908;Mr 1927-28;33+
AFpC Ap 1890-91;Je 1892-98;1900-16;23+

Fort Payne TRIBUNE. w My 12 1927-31||
A 1927-N 1928
AFpC complete

FRUITDALE

Fruitdale HERALD. w 1897-1912||?
AChC 1900-06

FRUITHURST

Fruithurst weekly ENTERPRISE. *See* Edwardsville enterprise (Edwardsville)

Fruithurst REPORTER. w,sm 1895-97||?
w 1895-96?
AHeC O 22-D 1895;F 11 1896-F 9 1897

Fruithurst VINEYARDIST. w 1899-1903||?
A Mr 1899-My 1903

GADSDEN

Weekly BEE. w 1888-89||?
AGC Mr 16-N 23 1889

ETOWAH herald. w Ja 29 1879-80||?
AGC F-D 1879

Gadsden HERALD. w
A Ja 24 1851

Gadsden evening JOURNAL. d 1900-24||
1901-03? Daily journal-tribune. Merged with Gadsden daily times-news, later Gadsden times
A 1907-Jl 1924
AGC 1902;F 16 1904-O 1905;06-Je 1907;08-23

JOURNAL-TRIBUNE. sw 1899-1902||?
1899-N 1901 as Semi-weekly journal
AGC 1901-02

Gadsden LEADER. w D 1889-93||?
AGC Ja 11 1890-F 10 1893

Gadsden NEWS. w 1881-Ja 1887||
United with Gadsden weekly times to form Gadsden times-news

Gadsden OBSERVER. *See* Etowah observer (Alabama City)

PEOPLE'S voice. w Ja 12 1899-1900||?
AGC 1899-1900

RADICAL reformer. ir,w D 4 1852-
1852-Ja 21 1854 as Stiff's radical reformer
MWA 1852-Ja 7,21,F 25-Mr 11 1854

Gadsden evening STAR. d D 1925-27||
Merged with Gadsden times
AGC 1926-Mr 7 1927

STIFF'S radical reformer. *See* Radical reformer

Gadsden TIMES. d Ap 5 1906+
1906-D 31 1924 as Gadsden daily times-news
A Ap 27,Je 23,N 1,28-29,D 22 1906;N 7,12 1907;Je 23 1908;D 31 1909;Ap 5 1910;Mr 20 1911;O 26 1918-Je 1920;22-23;Ap 1924-Je 1930
AGC Ap 6 1906-Jl 19 1924;Ja-Je 1925;27+

Gadsden TIMES-news. w,sw 1867-1914||?
1867-84 as Gadsden times; 1885-Ja 1887 Gadsden weekly times
w 1867-92?
A Ja 4,25,F 26,Jl 3 1867;O 1899-Mr,S 1900; My 31,Ag 1901
AGC N 9 1867-95;97-1909;11;14

Gadsden TRIBUNE. w,sw F 24 1893-N 14 1901||
United with Semi-weekly journal to form Journal-tribune
sw 1900
AGC complete

GAINESVILLE

ALABAMA reporter. w Ja 1837?-
GAtCo N 17 1837
MWA D 8 1837

ARMY argus and crisis. w Je 4 1864-
1864-Ap? 1865 pub in Mobile
A Jl 9 1864
DLC F 25 1865
LNC Mr 4 1865
MBAt Ag 13,D 3,17 1864-Ap 8 1865
MoHi N 26 1864
NNHi Ja 14-21,F 4,Mr 11-18,Ap 1 1865
PHi Je-D 17 1864
TxU O 1 1864

Daily ARMY argus and crisis. d
PHi My 8 1865

Gainesville DISPATCH. w 1875-79||
ALnC My 1875-D 21 1877;78-D 2 1879

INDEPENDENT. w 1854-68||?
A N 18 1854-Jl,O 1858-S 23 1868
MWA N 29 1856;Jl 10 1858
NcD My 10 1856

Gainesville MESSENGER. w 1880-91||?
1880-85 as Gainesville reporter. Merged with Sumter county sun (Livingston)
ALnC Ja 18 1880-D 13 1882;Ja 10 1884-S 15 1885;Ja 29 1886-D 19 1891

NEWS. w 1868-72||?
A Ja 29 1870

GAINESVILLE REPORTER. *See* Gainesville messenger

REPUBLICAN pilot. w 1840?-
NhD My 22 1841
OClWHi O 11 1845

SUMTER county whig. w
A Ap 22 1851-Ap 16 1856;O 1858-S 23 1865
NcD Mr 25 1851

Gainesville TIMES. *See* Geiger times (Geiger)

GEIGER

Geiger TIMES. w 1909-18||?
1909-10? as Gainesville times (Gainesville)
ALnC D 9-31 1909;11-Ap 22 1918

GENEVA

Geneva CITIZEN. w 1895-96||?
A 1895-Jl 1896

GENEVA county reaper. w Jl 3 1901+
1901-14? as Geneva reaper
A 1901-28;33+
AGeC My 16 1907-My 15 1908;My 21 1909-My 19 1911;Je 1913-My 11 1917;Je 1919-My 1928; Mr 22 1929+

Geneva JOURNAL. w 1898-1901||?
AGeC O 1898-1900

Geneva REAPER. *See* Geneva county reaper

GEORGIANA

BUTLER county news. w 1911+
A Mr 10-Ap 1932;Je 15-27 1933;Jl 1934+
AGnC D 12 1918 +

GIRARD

ALABAMA state register and Girard and Columbus advertiser. w Jl 1 1840-
DLC Jl 22,S 22 1840

Phenix-Girard JOURNAL. *See under* Phenix City

GOOD WATER

COOSA county enterprise. *See* Good Water enterprise

Good Water ENTERPRISE. w Ja 12 1906+
1931-32 as Coosa county enterprise
A My 1908-Ag 1910;Mr-Ap 21 1932;My 25 1933;My 1936+
ARC 1914[15]-[17-Mr 12]-D 1920;F 11-D 1921; F 17-N 17 1922;Ja 5,F 16 1923[24]Ja-N 1925; Jl 14,S 1 1926 [27-29]+

GORDO

Gordo ENTERPRISE. w 1899?-1911||?
A N 1899-F 1911

GRAND BAY

Grand Bay NEWS. w 1915-21||?
A O 1915-21

GREENSBORO

Early years as Greensborough

ALABAMA beacon. w Jl 23 1835-1911||?
1835? as Beacon of liberty; My 11- 1839? Republican and Alabama beacon; 1839-40? Alabama republican
A My 1843-Mr 1847;My 1848-55;57-Jl 1864;65-O 1881;82-Ag 1884;85-F 1911
AGrC O 24 1868-[98]-[1904]-My 12 1911
DLC Jl 23 1835;My 11 1839
GDE S 9 1835
MHi Ja 26 1850
NcD Ja 31 1839;Ja 18 1840;N 13 1841;O 19 1844;My 3 1845;Ja 12,My 11-18 1850;O 7 1853;My 11-18,Je 1-8,29-Jl 6,20 1855;S 5,D 12 1856;Je 12-19,D 4 1857;Je 4 1858;Mr 23, My 3 1860;Je 9-16,30,D 8-15 1865;O 5 1867; Ap 11,My 9 1868;Mr 15 1879
WHi Ja 18 1840

ALABAMA republican. *See* Alabama beacon

ALABAMA sentinel. w 1833?-
1833?-34? as Greene county sentinel?
A Ap 9 1836
NcD Ag 9-16,30 1834

AMERICAN eagle. w
A N 2-8,22-D 13 1855

BEACON of liberty. *See* Alabama beacon

GREENE county patriot. w 1825-
A Jl 6 1828
NcD Jl 20,Ag 31 1825

GREENE county sentinel. *See* Alabama sentinel

***HALCYON.** w 1815-
1815-Ap 17? 1823 as Halcyon and Tombeckbe public advertiser (St. Stephens)
DLC [1821-N 2 1822]Ap 24-My 1,14-Jl,Ag 21-28,S 11-O 23,N 1,D 20 1823;F 21 1824

Greensboro RECORD. w O 10 1902-Ag 28 1918||?
A 1902-Jl 1916;17-Ag 1918
AGrC 1902-[04]-[07]-09-10]-[14]-Ag 1918

REPUBLICAN and Alabama beacon. *See* Alabama beacon

SOUTHERN watchman. *See* Greensboro watchman

Greensboro WATCHMAN. w 1876+
1876-S 9 1886 as Southern watchman
A Jl 30 1879;Mr 1899-1918;20-28;33+
AGrC Mr 28 1877-[90]-[1905]+
NcD Ap 9,30 1879;N 3 1881

GREENVILLE

Greenville ADVOCATE. tw,w,sw 1865+
w 1870?-1915?; sw 1916?-25?
A Ap 9 1884;Je 24,N 25 1885;Ag 1899-Ja 1912; N 1914-22;24-28;Ap 1933+
AGnC D 20 1866-Ag 18 1868;73-99;1903-20;24+
MWA Ap 20 1876

Weekly ECHO. w N 8 1879-82||?
1879-My? 1880 as Spirit of the times
AGnC 1879-My 8,Jl 29 1880-Ja 7 1882

ALABAMA (*Continued*)

GREENVILLE—*Continued*

LIVING truth. w 1891-1914||
A Je 1899-S 1914
AEvC Je 25-Jl 2,S 24 1896
AGrC 1893-1912

Greenville MOUNTAINEER.
A Je 1829-44

Greenville weekly OBSERVER. w
MWA Ap 22(extra)1865
WHi Ap 22(extra)1865

Greenville REPUBLICAN.
A Jl 1826-Jl 1827

SOUTH ALABAMIAN. w 1847-62||?
A Ap-D 22 1860

SOUTH ALABAMIAN. w Ap 24 1869-Ag 1876||?
AGnC My 1869-Ap 1871
MBAt My 15-29 1869

SOUTHERN messenger. w?
A Mr-D 19 1860;F 20-Mr 12,Ap 3-17,My 1,Je 1,Jl 3 1861

SPIRIT of the times. *See* Weekly echo

GROVE HILL

To 1840? as Macon

CLARKE county democrat. w Ja 1856+
N 13 1862-N 15 1866 as Clarke county journal (title varies: Journal)
A 1856-S 11 1862;63-97;Ag 1898-1928;33+
AGvC Mr 8 1860-[69]-[74]-[82]-[91-92]-[96-98]+
MWA Mr 23 1865
NcD Mr 16 1865

CLARKE county journal. *See* Clarke county democrat

Grove Hill HERALD. w 1846-56||
1846-49? as Southern recorder
A Ap 7,Jl 14,Ag 15 1847;F 23,Ap 12,N 8 1848;F 7,S 19 1849;Ag 7,O 23,N 13 1850;Ag 15,N 4 1852;O 11 1854

JOURNAL. *See* Clarke county democrat

MACON banner. w Ap 25 1836-46||?
1836-40? as Clarke county post (Suggsville)
A My 9 1836-Ag 18 1837;Ap 18,Ag 4,O 1 1846

SOUTHERN recorder. *See* Grove Hill herald

GUIN

GAZETTE appeal. w 1897-99||?
-Jl 30 1897 as Guin gazette
AHmC 1897-98

GUNTERSVILLE

Guntersville ADVERTISER and democrat. w Je 2 1911+
1914-Mr 28 1928 as Guntersville advertiser
A N 1914-28;Ap 1933+
AGuC 1914+

ALLIANCE news. w S 12 1891-S 14 1892||
AGuC complete

Guntersville DEMOCRAT. w Ja 1880-Mr 27 1928||
United with Guntersville advertiser to form Guntersville advertiser and democrat
A Mr 1899-1928
AGuC S 1881-89;93-1928
NcD My 21 1896

MARSHALL eagle. w
A Ja 5 1852;N 4-11 1853;Je 9 1854;Ja 5,Mr 2,Je 22 1855

Guntersville POST. w S 23 1869-70||?
AGuC [O 14 1869-F 15 1870]

TENNESSEE VALLEY. w
A Jl 1,O 14 1856

GURLEY

Gurley HERALD. w 1894-1917||?
A Ag 1899-Ag 1910
AHuC [1896]-[98-99;1901]-[03-04]-[06-11]-[14-My 1916]
NcD N 17 1898;Mr 21,D 19 1901;O 19 1905;Ja 11 1906;Mr 11 1909;Ap 6 1911

HACKLEBURG

Hackleburg NEWS. w 1929-30||?
AHmC 1929-30

Hackleburg SENTINEL. w 1928+
A Ag 1934+
AHS 1932-33
AHmC 1929+

HALEYVILLE

Haleyville ADVERTISER. w Jl 13 1922-N 6 1924||
United with Haleyville journal to form Haleyville advertiser-journal
AChC complete
AHA complete

Haleyville ADVERTISER-JOURNAL. w 1911+
1911-N 6 1924 as Haleyville journal
pub F 1917+
A My 27 1920;N 1926-28;O 1935+
AChC 1912-O 1924;26+

BUSY bee. w 1900||?
AChC Ap 19-N 1900

Haleyville ENTERPRISE. w 1903-04||
AChC Ja 22 1903-Ja 22 1904

Haleyville JOURNAL. *See* Haleyville advertiser-journal

Haleyville SPOTLIGHT. w Je 2 1926+
pub 1926[27-28]+
A 1932+
AChC 1931+

WINSTON county news. w 1908-11||?
AChC My 1908-D 16 1909

HAMILTON

Hamilton APPEAL.
AHmC 1895

Hamilton FREE PRESS. w 1893-D 1894||
United with Marion county news to form Marion county news and free press; later Marion county news
A O 4,25 1894
AHmC complete

MARION county democrat. w 1899-1904||?
Merged with Marion county news
AHmC 1900-04

MARION county herald. *See* Hamilton times

MARION county news. w 1894+
D 1894-Ja 3 1895 as Marion county news and free press; Ja 10-D 1895? News-press
A O 3,24 1894;Ap 15,Jl 22,S 30 1897;Ag 1899-1928;33+

MARION county republican. w 1908||?
AHmC 1908

MARION herald. *See* Hamilton times

NEWS-PRESS. *See* Marion county news

Hamilton TIMES. w Mr 3 1887-94||?
1887-88? as Marion herald; 1889? Marion county herald. Merged with Marion county news
AHmC 1887-[90]-93

HANCEVILLE

Hanceville HUSTLER. w 1896-1908||?
ACuC Jl 20 1901-O 31 1908

HARTFORD

Hartford NEWS-HERALD. w 1903+
1906?-1?? as Hartford times-herald
A 1913-My 1914;Mr 1917-S 1918;Ag 1934+

Hartford TIMES. w 1900-05||?
United with Hartford news-herald to form Hartford times-herald, later Hartford news-herald
A Ag 1905-05

Hartford TIMES-HERALD. *See* Hartford news-herald

HARTSELLE

ALABAMA inquirer. w,sw 1884-My 1906||
1884-My 1887 as Morgan county news (Somerville)
w 1884-1905
ADeC 1887-90;93;95-98;1901-06

Hartselle ENQUIRER. w 1933+
A F 1935+
ADeC 1933+

Hartselle ENTERPRISE. w Ja 1908-33||?
A Ja 31 1924;Ag 17 1933
ADeC 1908+

Hartselle weekly HERALD. S 1923-D 1924||
A Jl 31 1924
ADeC complete

Hartselle INDEX. w 1879-88||
1879- 1882 as Somerville weekly critic (Somerville); 1882-83 Hartselle investigator
ADeC complete
NcD O 29,N 26 1881

Hartselle INVESTIGATOR. *See* Hartselle index

HAYNEVILLE

ALABAMIAN. *See* Hayneville chronicle

Hayneville CHRONICLE. w F 1835-69||?
1835-36 as Spirit of the times; 1836-My 20 1837 Spirit of the times and Hayneville observer; My 27 1837-38? Lowndes county observer and spirit of the times; 18??-Jl 4? 1840 South-Alabamian and Lowndes county advertiser; Jl 18?-O 1840? Alabamian; Ap 1851- Lowndes county chronicle; -My 3? 1860 Chronicle
DLC S 5 1840
MWA O 14,N 18 1852
NcD 1835-Ja 2,N 19,D 17 1836-Jl 11 1838;F 8-Jl 4,15-S 12,26-O 1840;D 29 1849-51;Ap 12-D 20 1860
NcU S 3 1842

CITIZEN-EXAMINER. w 1868-1924||?
1868-8? as Hayneville examiner. Merged with Lowndes signal (Fort Deposit)
A S 21 1870;My 15 1872;D 18 1879;F 24,Mr 30 1881;N 1914-19
AHaC D 1880-Ja 2 1884;N 1898-[1904]-[21]
NcD Ja 8 1880;Ja 11 1882

Hayneville EXAMINER. *See* Citizen-examiner

Weekly HERALD. w
A N 10 1859

LOWNDES county chronicle. *See* Hayneville chronicle

LOWNDES county observer. . . *See* Hayneville chronicle

LOWNDES news. w O 21 1893-1903||?
1898? as Weekly news
AHaC N 18-D 23 1893;1900-Jl 16 1903

Weekly NEWS. *See* Lowndes news

SOUTH-ALABAMIAN. . . *See* Hayneville chronicle

SPIRIT of the times. *See* Hayneville chronicle

TRUE citizen. w 1886-89||?
United with Hayneville examiner to form Citizen-examiner

WATCHMAN. w 1851?-
A O 12 1855
NcD Ap-D 21 1860

HEADLAND

HENRY county news. w 1899||?
AAC My 11-N 24 1899

HENRY county standard. *See* Wiregrass farmer

Headland NEWS. w
AAC Mr 29 1888-Ja 10 1889

Headland POST. w 1902-10||?
AAC 1902;04-N 7 1907

Headland PROGRESS. w 1884-87||?
AAC F 18 1885-Mr 9 1887

Headland SUN. w 1895-97||?
AAC Ja 24 1895-Ja 1897

WIREGRASS farmer. w S 1 1909+
1909-Ja 25 1917 as Henry county standard
A Ja-Mr 18,Ap 22-Je 10 1915;O 1933-S,O 24 1935;Je 11 1936
AAC 1909-14;16+

HEFLIN

CLEBURNE county news. *See* Cleburne news

CLEBURNE new era. w O 30 1890-D 28 1912||
Merged with Cleburne county news, later Cleburne news
AHeC 1892-[97-98]-N 1912

CLEBURNE news. w 1911+
1911-15? as Cleburne county news
A Ja 24 1924;Jl 1934+
AHeC S 13 1911+

HUNTSVILLE

ADVOCATE. *See* Weekly mercury

ALABAMA farmer. w 1888-89||?
1888-Ja 30 1889 pub in Athens
AAtC 1888-Ja 30 1889

*ALABAMA republican. w Ag? 1816-Ap 29 1825||
1816-F 3 1818 as Huntsville republican. United with Alabamian to form Southern advocate and Huntsville advertiser, later Southern advocate
A 1821-S 13 1822
DLC [1821-25]

ALABAMIAN. w 1822-Ap 29 1825||
United with Alabama republican to form Southern advocate and Huntsville advertiser, later Southern advocate
DLC Jl 15 1824
NNHi Je 2,Jl 5,S 6,27 1822

Huntsville AMERICAN independent. w D 12? 1855-
MWA Ap 26 1856

Weekly ARGUS. w My 12 1892-96||?
AHuC 1892-N 5 1896

Evening BANNER. d 1906-N 20? 1908||
United with Morning mercury to form Mercury-banner, later Huntsville telegram
A 1907-08
AHuC 1907

Weekly COMMUNITY builder. w Ja 20 1922+
A N 1926-28
AHuC 1922-25;D 23 1926;Ja 13 1927-28;32+

Huntsville CONFEDERATE. d 1863-
NNHi Ap 16 1863
OCl Jl 2 1863

Huntsville weekly DEMOCRAT. w O 8 1823-1919||
1823-53? as Democrat
A O 14 1823-O 9 1856;D 17-24 1881;Ja 7,F 4-11 Mr 18,Ap 1-8 1882;Mr 1883-84;F 1899-1909;13-19
AHuC 1875 - [85]-87;89[1900-01]-[09-11]-[15] -[17]-Ja 15 1919
DLC Ag 22,N 28 1828;F 6,Je 26 1829-Ja 15,D 2-16 1830;Ja 14 1831;Ag 17 1839;D 17 1842;My 4 1843;D 11 1844;Mr 12,26,Ap 16,S 24,O 15-22 1845[46-Mr 1848]Mr-D 1853
MWA Jl 31,S 4,18,O 2,16-23,N 20,D 11-25 1829;N 28 1850;O 21-N 4 1852
N O 3 1833
NcD Ja 16 1861;My 7 1879;Jl 21-Ag 4 1880;Ap 20,N 9-16,1881;Ja 18,Mr 22,Jl 12,D 12 1882;My 9 1883;My 27 1896;N 16 1898;N 7 1900;Mr 8,Ap 19,S 13,N 22-29 1905;Ap 18,My 30 1906;F 13,Ap 10,My 15,Jl 31 1907;Mr 3-10,My 19,Ag 4-11,S 8 1909;O 26 1910;Mr 15-22,Ap 12-19,S 6 1911;F 7,Ap 24 1912;N 5 1913;F 11,Mr 11,Ag 19 1914
NhD My 29 1841
PPL [Je 23-S 22 1826]

ALABAMA (*Continued*)

HUNTSVILLE—*Continued*

Huntsville GAZETTE. w N 22 1879-D 29 1894||
Negro
A My 28,Je 11-18,Jl 30-Ag 13,N 12,D 3 1881;D 23 1882;Ja 30 1883
AHuC 1879-86[Mr-D 1889]-[91]-94
DLC Je 18 1881-D 24 1888;89-94

Huntsville INDEPENDENT. w 1854-92||?
A D 1886-My 1887
AHuC 1875-[87;90-My 1892]
CSmH D 17 1859;O 24 1868
ICHi S 30-O 7 1865
NcD My 1 1879;Jl 8,Ag 19 1880;Jl 6-13,Ag 10, S 28,D 28 1882

Huntsville daily INDEPENDENT. d Ja? 1866-71||?
A Ja 16-Je 1866
MWA Jl 11,Ag 16 1867
NcD S 11 1866

Huntsville daily INDEPENDENT. d
A Jl-N 1887

JOURNAL. w Ja 5 1895-1912||?
1895-96 as Huntsville journal
Negro
A Ag 1899-F 1912
AHuC 1895-[1903]-08;10[11]

Weekly MERCURY. w,sw,tw Jl 5 1865-1919||
1865-84 as Advocate (title varies slightly)
sw 1865-69?; tw 1870?-79?
A O 27 1870;N 8 1877;S 3 1902
AHuC Jl 1866-[73-75]-87;89-[97-98]-[1900-01]-[05]-[10]-[17]-Ja 8 1919
DLC [Jl 12 1865-Ag 8 1866;68]
MBAt Mr 24,Ap 11 1866;N 26 1869
MWA My 28,Ag 23-27 1867
NcD Ap 2,23,My 7 1879;D 22 1880;Ja 5-19,F 2,23,Mr 30,Ap 20-27,N 9,D 14-21 1881;Ja 4, Ap 26,Je 28,Jl 12,Ag 2,30,O 11,D 27 1882;N 22 1905;Mr 10 1909;Ag 31 1910

Morning MERCURY. *See* Huntsville telegram

NEW SOUTH. w Ja 10 1885-87||?
AHuC 1885

NEW SOUTH. w Ja 1895?-
AHuC 1896

Huntsville NEWS. w 1917?-23||?
Negro
A Ja-Ag 1923
AHuC O 30-D 1922

Weekly NEWS. w
AHuC D 1931-Ja 13 1933

NORTH ALABAMA reporter. w 1871-75||?
AHuC Ap-D 1875

Huntsville daily POST. d 1899-1900||?
Title varies slightly
A F-D 1900

Huntsville daily REGISTER. d 1931-33||
AHuC [1932-33]

Huntsville REPUBLICAN. 1816-18 *See* Alabama republican

REPUBLICAN. w S 1899-1905||?
A 1899-Je 1905
AHuC 1900-[04]-Jl 14 1905

SOUTHERN advocate. w My 6 1825-
Formed by the union of Alabamian and Alabama republican, My 6 1825-Ag 11 1826 as Southern advocate and Huntsville advertiser
A 1825-Ja 17 1837;F 28,Mr 28,Ap 24,Jl 25 1839;Ja 4 1840;Ap 26 1844-Ap 23,My 21 1847-Je 1861
CtY Ag 29 1828
DLC 1825-[28-34]-37;D 10 1840[49;51]52
MWA Ap 3,N 20 1829;Jl 28 1841
NN Ja 9 1829-Ja 14 1832
NNHi Jl 2 1831
NSchU My 11,25-Je 1,15 1842
WHi Je 23-Jl 14 1832

SOUTHERN mercury. sw Je 29? 1833-
DLC Jl 6 1833

Huntsville STAR. w Ja 26 1900-
Negro
DLC Ja 26 1900

TENNESSEE VALLEY news. tw 1929-
AHuC [1930]-Ja 1931

Huntsville TELEGRAM. d 1885-1922||?
1885-N 20? 1908 as Morning mercury (title varies slightly) N 21? 1908-09? Mercury-banner; 1910?-15? Huntsville mercury-banner; 1916?-Ap 1919? Huntsville mercury; My? 1919-20? Huntsville telegram and mercury
A Ag 1899-1910;Jl 1911-18;My 1919-Je,Ag 1921-S 1922
AHuC My 1919-O 1922
NcD N 23-24 1905;N 22,24,29,D 2 1910;F 11 1911;My 6,Je 4 1912;Ap 2 1914
—w ed *See* Weekly mercury

Huntsville weekly TIMES. w 1910-32||?
AHuC 1911-[16]-[18]-[20]-[24-28]-32

Huntsville TIMES. d Mr 23 1910+
Title varies slightly
A My 7 1910-O 1921;22-Ap,N 14,16 1930
NcD D 11 1927

Huntsville evening TRIBUNE. d Mr 7 1894-1910||?
Merged with Huntsville mercury-banner, later Huntsville telegram
N 29 1900 is Monument ed
A S 3 1902;Ja 5 1903-Ag 9 1904
MWA N 29 1900;S 20 1902

Weekly TRIBUNE. w 1894-1910||?
United with Weekly mercury
AHuC 1895-[97]-[99-1902]-[05;08-10]
NcD D 17 1901

HURTSBORO

Hurtsboro PRESS. w
A Jl 1936+

Hurtsboro TRIBUNE. w Ja 17 1913-20||?
A N 1914-Ja 2,24 1920
ASeC D 3,24 1915;Mr 3,Ap 28 1916;Mr 15,Ap 19,Jl 12 1918

IRWINTON. *See* EUFAULA

JACKSON

SOUTH ALABAMIAN. w S 3 1887+
A S 1899-S 1918
AGrC 1887-D 19 1903

JACKSONVILLE

AMERICAN eagle. w 1855-59||?
1855- 1859 pub in Wedowee
A Ja 10-My,Je 12,Jl 10 1856

CALHOUN county democrat. w 1896-99||?
AAnnC 1897

PEOPLE'S journal. w Mr 1895-1900||?
AAnnC Mr 21-D 14 1895;97;99;F-D 13 1900

Jacksonville RECORD. w 1906-19||?
AAnnC Mr 1906-13;F 1914-Ja 1917;18

Jacksonville RECORD. w 1930?+
A Ag 1934+
AAnnC 1932+

Jacksonville REPUBLICAN. *See* Anniston republic and times (Anniston)

SUNNY SOUTH. w 1850?-
A My 27,S 16 1851;My 4,Ag 31,N 16 1852;Je 21,D 20 1853;Mr 14 1854;Je 28 1858
ICHi N 2 1852

JASPER

Jasper ADVERTISER. w 1925+
A D 1926-28;Je 2 1932;33+
AJC 1927+

ALABAMA bugle. w 1901||?
AJC Ja-Jl 1901

Jasper HEADLIGHT. w 1887?-91||?
AJC Je 21-N 8 1887;90-91

MOUNTAIN eagle. w 1872+
A S 1900-20;22-28
AJC D 1886-[87]-1906;09-14;16+

PROTECTIONIST. w 1887-89||?
AJC N 29 1887-Mr 1889

TRUE citizen. w 1884-87||?
AJC My 26 1884-[86]-Jl 1887

UNION news. w 1934+
AJC Ag 23 1934+

WALKER county news. sw,w 1906-13||?
sw 1906-12?
A D 1906-12
AJC S 20 1906-11

WALKER county record. w
AJC S 23 1893-94;98

KENNEDY

Kennedy NEWS. w N 7 1890-My 12 1892||
AVC N 14 1890-92

LAFAYETTE

CHAMBERS tribune. w 1843?-69||?
MWA D 9 1853
TxU Jl 5 1850

EAST ALABAMIAN. w
A O 21 1842;Jl 8,29,Ag 11-19,S 9,23,N 4,D 2, 16 1843

Lafayette SUN. w 1880+
A S 1,22 1897;Ag 1900-28;33+
ALC 1881-86;88-S 11 1889;90;92-97;99-1910;12;14+
ASlT My 10 1923

LANETT

CHATTAHOOCHEE VALLEY times. w 1914+
A O 1918-28;33+

LEEDS

Leeds ENTERPRISE. w 1924-26||?
A N 1924-25

LEIGHTON

Leighton NEWS. w 1892-1916||?
A S 1899-1916
ATsC F 1894-[99-1900]-F 17 1916

LINDEN

DEMOCRAT-REPORTER. w 1892+
1892 as Reform democrat; 1893-Ja 1910 Marengo democrat
A My 27 1920;Ja 10 1924;N 1926-28;33+
ALiC F 1911[12-13]-26;28-30;32+

Linden JEFFERSONIAN. w -1868||?
A Jl 4 1860

MARENGO democrat. *See* Democrat-reporter

MARENGO recorder. w
A S 5 1866

REFORM democrat. *See* Democrat-reporter

Linden REPORTER. w 1879-Ja 1910||
United with Marengo democrat to form Democrat-reporter
A Je 10 1881
ALiC O 1892-93

LINEVILLE

CENTRAL democrat. w Ap 18- 1889||?
AAsC Ap-O 1889

CLAY county free press. w 1888?-
AAsC Ja 3-10,F 14 1889

CLAY county watchman. w F 8 1884-89||
1884-88 pub in Ashland
AAsC 1884-Ja 16,Ap-D 1885;O 8 1886;Je 24 1887;88;Mr 21-O 24 1889

Lineville HEADLIGHT. *See* Lineville tribune

Lineville TRIBUNE. w Ap 1904+
1904-My 11 1933 as Lineville headlight
A Mr 1905-17;N 14-21 1919;20-28;33+
AAsC N 11 1904+

LIVINGSTON

Livingston JOURNAL. *See* Our southern home

Weekly MESSENGER. w -1861||?
A My 13,Je 24 1857

Livingston MESSENGER. w 1867?-80||?
MBAt Je 13 1867

OUR southern home. w,sw 1865+
1865-O 1895 as Livingston journal (1883-F 4 1886 Semi-weekly journal)
Suspended from 1869-72; from 1901-02
sw 1883-F 4 1886
A Je 2 1880;S 2 1881;N 16 1894;Mr 5,19 1896;S 23 1897;Ag 1898-My 1911;Jl 1913-28
ALnC Ja 12-D 1867;73-D 17 1880;F 1881-95; 97-D 6 1900;03-14;21;23-Je 1929;30;33+

SUMTER county sun. w Mr 1889-Je 26 1913||
A Mr 5 1896;S 23 1897;Ag 1899-My 1911
ALnC 1892-D 5 1895;97-1903;05-13

SUMTER democrat. w 1851-59||?
ALnC My 3 1851-Ap 22 1854

SUMTER gazette. w
GDE My 24 1836

VOICE of Sumter. w Mr 29 1836-
ALnC 1836-Mr 20 1838
MWA Mr 7 1840
NcD N 13 1838

LUVERNE

CRENSHAW county critic. w Jl 10 1902-07||?
A 1902-My 1907
ALuC 1902-07

CRENSHAW county democrat. w 1932+
ALuC S 8 1932+

CRENSHAW county news. w D 5 1907-D 30 1926||
United with Luverne journal to form Luverne journal and news
ALuC complete

Luverne ENTERPRISE. w 1884-93||?
ALuC 1888-N 1889;92-Ja 13 1893

Luverne JOURNAL and news. w Ja 2 1896+
1896-D 30 1926 as Luverne journal
A Je 29 1899;N 1914-18;22-28;33+
ALuC 1896-1902;S 10 1903-Mr 1908;09+

MACON. *See* GROVE HILL

MARION

Marion COMMONWEALTH. w 1849?-85||
A D 10 1856;Ag 2 1861;Jl 12 1866;F 7,21,Ap 4 1867;F 27 1868;Ap 8 1869;My 1871-74;Ja 21 1875-82;84
AMaC S 28,O 12 1860;S 6 1866;80-F 1 1883;D 31 1884-Mr 1885
AMaJ My 2,O 3 1867;My 20,Jl 10 1869
AMaT Ap 27 1871-74;79-F 1880
KHi Je 24 1859
NNHi Jl 17 1863

Marion DEMOCRAT. w 1898-1907||
A 1898;N 11 1899
AMaC [1898-1901]-S 4 1907
AMaJ O 1 1898;F 14 1903;Je 20 1904;Je 20 1906

Marion HERALD. w Jl 13? 1839-
Follows Southern herald?
A Ja 16 1845
DLC S 21 1839;O 7,D 1 1841
NcD F 1,My 2 1840
NcU My 16 1840;S 21 1842

Marion JOURNAL. w 1909-10||
A 1910
AMaC D 30 1909-Jl 1910

PERRY eagle. w Je 26 1840-
DLC Jl 31 1840

SOUTHERN herald. w N 16? 1837-
Followed by Marion herald?
MWA S 22 1838

SOUTHERN standard. *See* Marion standard

ALABAMA (*Continued*)

MARION—*Continued*

Marion STANDARD. w 1880-1916||
1880 as Southern standard. United with Marion times to form Marion times-standard
A 1880-90;92-Ja 1904;06-16
AMaC 1881-[84-90;92-96]F 1897-1916
AMaJ My,D 7 1881;S 6 1882;My 11 1887;D 12 1895;F 18 1897;My 15 1910[11-15]
AMaT 1890-F 7 1891;1906

Marion TIMES-STANDARD. w F 27 1911+
1911-16 as Marion times
A F 1917-S 1928;Je 24 1930;33+
AMaC Mr 1911-18;20;24-26;29+
AMaJ [1911-15]My 31 1917;My 27,Je 8 1919;N 8 1923;F 23 1924;Ap 11 1929;F 20,Mr 27,N 16 1930

TRUE democrat. w 1883-84||
A 1883
AMaJ O 17 1883;Je 11,S 10 1884

MIDLAND CITY

Midland City CLIPPER. w Ag 27? 1891-
AOzC N 19,D 10 1891-Mr 17,Ap 7-14 1892

DALE county enterprise. *See* Midland City enterprise

Midland City ENTERPRISE. w D 13 1907-14||?
1909 as Dale county enterprise
A 1908-14
AOzC 1907-09;13-F 1914

Midland City PROGRESS. w Mr 19 1914-15||?
Followed by Midland City sun?
AOzC Mr-S 17 1914

Midland City SUN. w Ja 7 1916-19||?
Follows Midland City progress? Merged with Southern star (Ozark)
A Mr 1916-17
AOzC 1916[17]-Ag 15 1918

MILLPORT

Millport MESSENGER. w 1931||
AVC My-D 20 1931

MOBILE

Mobile ADVERTISER (for the country). w,sw N 10 1823-My 1861||?
Follows Mobile argus (for the country) 1823-O 1839? as Mobile mercantile advertiser (for the country) N 1839?-Mr 1843? Mobile advertiser and chronicle (for the country) United with Mobile weekly register to form Weekly advertiser and register, later Mobile weekly register
1823-39? w four months of each year
A Jl 13,N 2 1842
AMP [S 18 1844-Je 1846]
DLC [N 10/13 1823-D 15/18 1824;F 28 1850-N 16 1851]
MWA Jl 15 1824;D 13 1833;D 16 1834;D 18,22 1853;Ja 5,29 1836;My 4 1842

Mobile daily ADVERTISER. d,tw O 7 1833-My 1861||
Follows Mobile argus. 1833-O 1839? as Mobile mercantile advertiser; N 1839?-Mr 30? 1843 Mobile daily advertiser and chronicle. United with Mobile daily register to form Mobile advertiser and register, later Mobile register
1833-39? tw during summer each year; tw Je 18-S 28 1850
A O 9 1833;My 31 1845;Ap 1,S 27,D 11 1847; Jl 2 1851
AMP N 7 1833-Mr 28,O 14 1834-O 6 1836;Mr 8-S 23,O 9 1837-O 1839;My 1840-43;Jl 1845-51;Ap 8-My 25,Jl 3-D 22 1852;Ja-[N-D]1853-Je 20 1854;Jl 1855-Je 1857;Ja-N 1859
ArHi My 26 1850
Ct Ja 14 1834
DLC O 7 1833;Mr 27 1849[50]-57;59-60
MBAt Jl 14,O 8,D 9 1840;Ap 16 1861
MWA Mr 21 1834;F 14 1846;Jl 22 1852
N O 7 1833
NcD Mr 1 1842;N 13 1843;Mr 13 1845

ADVERTISER and chronicle prices current and shipping list. w 1839?-
MWA My 20 1840

ADVERTISER and register. *See* Register

ALABAMA planter. w D 7 1846-54||?
A N 2,20 1848;Ja 29,Mr 19 1849
DLC Jl 9 1849
NNHi 1846-N 1854
—d ed *See* Mobile daily tribune

ALABAMA staats zeitung. w Ja 21 1897-1917||?
In German
A 1901-F 1917

ALABAMA tribune. *See* Mobile daily tribune

Mobile ARGUS. sw,w N 28 1822-O 1823||
Followed by Mobile mercantile advertiser, later Mobile daily advertiser
w during summer
DLC [D 5 1822-O 21 1823]

Mobile ARGUS. For the country. w 1822?-N 6 1823||?
Followed by Mobile mercantile advertiser (for the country), later Mobile advertiser (for the country)
DLC O 28/31-N 4/6 1823

ARMY argus and crisis. *See under* Gainesville

BANNER of reform. w My 4 1840-
A Je 20,Jl 20 1840
DLC Ag 10 1840
NN My 4 1840

Mobile CHRONICLE. d? 1836?-O 1839||?
United with Mobile mercantile advertiser to form Mobile daily advertiser and chronicle, later Mobile daily advertiser
A O 18,N 9 1836

Mobile CHRONICLE. d Ja 18- 1882||?
AMP Ja 21-Ap 9 1882

Mobile CHRONICLE for the country. w 1836-O 1839||?
United with Mobile mercantile advertiser (for the country) to form Mobile advertiser and chronicle (for the country), later Mobile advertiser (for the country)
NcU Ja 7,Jl 2,16,Ag 27-S 10,24,N 26,D 24 1838

CLAY banner. w F 26- 1844||?
Campaign paper
GDE [1844]
MBAt [F-O 1844]
MoSM Je 29 1844

Mobile COMMERCIAL. m 1872-
NbHi F 1873

COMMERCIAL register. *See* Register

COTTON prices current. w
MWA Ja 17 1849;D 4-11,24 1850;Ja 21 1851

Mobile COURIER. tw Ja 17 1835-
DLC Ja 31 1835

CYCLE. w D 18 1875-77||?
MH D 18 1875;Ja 15,Mr 18,Ap 26,My 27,Je 10 1876
MsHi 1875-O 7 1876

Mobile daily EXAMINER. d 1837?-
Ct [1837]
NcD Ap 13 1838
NcU O 11,13,18,N 14 1838
—country ed *See* Journal and Mobile daily examiner (country ed)

Mobile FORUM. w 1918-28||?
United with Mobile press to form Mobile press-forum
Negro

***Mobile GAZETTE and general advertiser.** w,sw 1812?-23||
1817-Jl 20 1820 as Mobile gazette and commercial advertiser. Merged with Mobile commercial register, later Mobile weekly register
Suspended from S 22-O 27 1819
1819-20? w in summer
DLC [Ja-F 9 1821]

GULF CITY. w 1877-78||?
A F 21 1878

GULF CITY home journal. w
TM F 15,Ag 10,S 5 1863

Morning HERALD. d Ja? 1842-45||?
United with Alabama tribune to form Herald and tribune, later Mobile daily tribune
A F 3 1843
MWA F 21 1842

Mobile HERALD. w Ag 7 1871-72||?
DLC Ag 7 1871
MH [1871-Je 4 1872]

Mobile daily HERALD. d 1893-1908||?
A N 1896-1908

HERALD and tribune. *See* Mobile daily tribune

Mobile ITEM. See Mobile news item

JOURNAL and Mobile daily examiner. (country ed) w
DLC Ag 3/8 1839
—city ed *See* Mobile daily examiner

Mobile JOURNAL of commerce letter-sheet price current. w O 14 1840-
Title varies slightly
MWA N 11 1840;N 13 1844;Mr 4,25 1846;Je 7-14,D 19 1848-Ja 3,30-F 6,20,Mr 6,20-27,Ap 24 1849;D 3 1853;N 18 1854

Mobile daily LEDGER. d D 5? 1841-
NcD D 11 1841

Mobile MAGNET. sw 1881-82||?
N N 8 1881

MERCANTILE advertiser. *See* Advertiser

MERCHANTS and planters journal w N 15 1838-N 1841||
United with Mobile daily commercial register and patriot to form Mobile register and journal, later Mobile register
AM [1838-39]
AMP N 11 1840-N 13 1841
ICHi Mr 7 1839
MWA My 12 1840
NcD Mr 23 1841

MERCHANTS' and planters' price-current. w 1838?-
Title varies slightly
MHi [Je-N 1860]
MWA D 7,21 1839;Ja 4,F 8,N 20-D 5 1840;Ja 16 1841;Ja 21-28,F 11,25,N 18-D 2,16 1843;D 28 1844;N 29,D 13-27 1845;D 5,19,28 1846-Ap 1847;Ja-F,Ap-My,N 18 1848;Ja 13,F 3,17-24,Mr 10,31-Ap 7,My 5-12,N 17 1849-Mr 23,Ap 20-27,My 18,N 16 1850[51]Ja 3,Mr 13,Ap-My 1,22-29,S 25,O 9-16,30,N 27,D 11 1852-[Ja-Jl 21]O 29,N 26 1853-[Ja-Jl 11]O 7,28,D 9 1854;Mr 31,Ap 14-21,My,Ag 25,O 13,27,N 17 1855
NcD D 17 1842
PP F 21,Mr 7 1846

Weekly MERCURY. w 1857-
Title varies slightly
MBAt Ag 4 1861
MWA N 10 1860

NATIONALIST. w D 14 1865-69||?
DLC [1868]
ICHi Jl 9 1868
KHi D 28 1865-N 1 1868
MBAt D 14 1865;F 15,Mr 8-15,Ap 5-12,My 3,17,Je,Jl 19,Ag 2-9,23,S 27 1866;Ja 17,D 19 1867;Ja 2-9,O 18,N 30 1868
MWA Je 21 1866;O 25-N 1 1868
NcD Ja 25 1866
NhD Mr 22,Ap 6,My 17,Je 7,O 25 1866;Mr 17,Ap 23,O 1 1869

Mobile Sunday NEWS. w Ap 15 1865-
MBAt Ap 15-23 1865
MWA My 7 1865
OClWHi Ap 15 1865

Mobile daily NEWS. d 1877-81||?
A D 17 1878;Mr 29-30 1879
NcD Ap 2,9,20,My 1,3 1879;Jl 27 1880

Mobile NEWS. w 1877-81||?
A N 10 1877

Mobile daily NEWS. d 1889-1900||?
A 1893-1900

Mobile NEWS. w 1915+
1915-23? as Mobile times-news
A 1922-Ag 1930;O 1935+

Mobile evening NEWS. *See* Mobile daily register

Mobile morning NEWS. *See* Mobile daily times

Mobile NEWS item. d 1897-1931||?
1897-Mr 1917 as Mobile item
A Ja 23 1900-S 1901;Ap-D 1902;Ja-D 3 1904; 05-Ja,O 1907-D 3 1908;09-S 1927;28-Ag 1930
AMP 1903;Ag 1908;My 1909;Ag 1917-My,Jl 1918-Mr,N 1919-F 1921;Ap-O 1922;O 1923;Ap-My,S 1924;Je-S 1926;Je 1927
WaPS O 26-29,N 1-4 1913;S 27 1914

Mobile PATRIOT. tw,w O 1830?-O 1832||
United with Mobile commercial register to form Mobile commercial register and patriot, later Mobile register
w Jl-O of each yr
Ct O 13 1830

PATRIOT. sw 1821?-O 1832||
United with Mobile commercial register (for the country) to form Mobile commercial register and patriot (for the country), later Mobile register and journal for the country
MWA My 10/13 1831

Mobile POST. w 1926+
A 1933+

Mobile PRESS. d 1929+
F 1932+ Sunday issues as Mobile press-register
pub Jl-S 1929;31+
A Ap 1929+
TxGR Ag 28 1932

Mobile weekly PRESS-FORUM. w 1894+
1894-1928? as Mobile press (title varies slightly)
Negro
A Ja 10,F 21,Ag 1 1914;N 1921-28;Ap 1929-Je 1930[33-S 1934]

Mobile PRESS-REGISTER. *See* Mobile register
Mobile press

PRICES current and shipping list of the commercial chronicle. w O? 1838-
MWA D 29 1838

Mobile weekly REGISTER. w,sw D 10 1821-Ap 30 1910||
1821-O? 1832 as Mobile commercial register; N? 1832-N 1841 Mobile commercial register and patriot; D 1841 Mobile register and journal; Je 1861-77? Weekly advertiser and register
1821-32 w four months and sw 8 months of each year
A F 13 1827;Ap 7-14,31,D 21 1832;F 10 1862; Je 27,Jl 18,Ag 1,22,S 26,O 17,N 21,D 5,19 1863-Ja 2,23,F 27,Mr 19 1864;S 24 1865-66;Ag 29 1868;D 25 1869;Mr 7 1874;Jl 31 1875;N 17,D 8-15 1877;Ja,F 9,23-Mr 9,23-My 11,Je 1 1878; S 20 1879;Ag 28 1880;Jl 9-16,O 1 1881;Jl 25 1885
AMP F 1868-81;83-99;1904-10
DLC [Ap 13-O 5 1824;25]26;28[29-30]55;Ja-My 2 1857;Je 14 1858;Je 27 1863
ICHi S 13,D 6 1825;Ag 4 1827
IaDH Ag 1861-F 1862[D 1866-Jl 1868]
MBAt F 25-28,Ap 15,My 6 1822;F 20 1864;Je 13 1868;69-[71]-75
MHi D 17-20 1821;D 26 1823
MWA Mr 28,S 26 1822;Ag 17 1824;Je 23,Jl 3,15-17,28,Ag 11,S 4,O 16,20,D 11,23 1829;N 25,D 11,16,23 1830;My 27 1871
N O 22 1833
NcD N 11 1876
OHi Ap 17,O 29 1864;Jl 25-O 10 1865
Tx Ag 1 1868;Ja 23(supp)S 18(supp)N 20 1869;Ja 1(supp)Mr 12(supp)S 17(supp)O 8(supp)N 12(supp)1870;Ap 15,My 27,Je 24,29,Ag 12,S 2,16-23,O 28-N 11 D 2 1871;Ja 6,Mr 2-16,30,Ap 6,20,Je 22 1872
TxU Mr 13 1871

Mobile REGISTER. tw,d D 1? 1821+
1821-O 1832 as Mobile commercial register; O 6 1832-N 1841 Mobile daily commercial register and patriot (title varies slightly) D 1 1841-Ja 15 1851 Mobile register and journal; Ja 17 1851-My 1861 Mobile daily register; Je 1861-Je 8 1863 Mobile advertiser and register; Je 9 1863-N 16 1864 Mobile daily advertiser and register; 1864-Ja 1868? Advertiser and register; F 1868?-D 22 1877 Mobile daily register; D 23 1877-My 24 1903 Daily register
F 1932+ Sunday issues as Mobile press-register
1821-48? tw during summer of each year

ALABAMA (*Continued*)

MOBILE—*Continued*

Mobile REGISTER. tw,d 1821+—*Continued*
A N 17 1827-D 3,26 1828-F 5,O 9 1830-S 19,O 6 1836-37;Mr 21 1843;Ap 1 1847;Ja-O 1849;F 1859-Ja 4 1860;Je-D 1861;Ja 18-D 25 1862; Ja-Je,O 1863-My,Je 14 1864;Mr 19,Jl 16-D 1865;67;Ja 18 1871;Mr 12 1872;D 24 1874;Mr 17,Ap 13 1875;Ag 26,O 29 1876;79-Je 1896;97-Mr 1926
AM D 15 1827-Mr 1828;Je-N 3 1833;S 13 1857-F 1858[59]1911-20
AMP Je-N 13 1830;Je 1831-My 1833;Je-N 1834;Je-N 1835;Je-N 1836;Je 1837-My,D 1840-My 1844;D 1845-N 1846;Je 1847-My 1848;N 1849-Ap,N 1850-Jl 21,N 4 1851-[53]-Ap,S 1854-Ag 1856;Mr-Ag 1857;Ja 10-Je 1860;Ja 18 1862-Je,O 4 1863-My 28 1864;Ag 22 1865-Je 8,Jl 3 1866-79;81-99;Jl 1900-O 1905;06-30;Ap-O 1931;Ja-Je,O 1933+
CSmH Jl 20 1830;Mr 25 1842;Jl 4(supp)1869
CSt [1888-89;95-98]
CoU 1902;04-05;S 1906-My 1910
Ct Mr 15 1833[35-37]
CtHT Je 27 1863
CtY Ap 1 1851;My 18 1864
DLC [1833-34]-[36-45]-48[57-59;S 5 1862-64]Ja 5,24,Mr 17,Jl 18 1865;69+
GDE O 25 1848
IC Ja 31-Je 27 1873
ICHi F 22 1882;F 7 1883
LNC D 15 1863
MBAt Ja 28 1862;F 1863-[65-69]
MH Ag 2,N 3,16,18,23,D 1,7-9 1864;Ja 15,17-19,21,24 1865
MWA S 7 1839;Mr 20,S 6,25,N 10,14,18,25,28,D 1,15,19,31 1845[46-47]-Ap 4 1848;O 23,N 2 1852;Je 16,Jl 10 1862;My 6,S 15,N 19 1863[F-S 1864]My 7,9-10 1876;S 1 1886;S 1 1887
MsHi Ag 9-D 5 1863
MsSM [D 13-31 1912]Ja 1913
NN My 10-11 1862;Ag 9 1863
NNHi My 23,Je 26,Jl 12,Ag 16 1863;Ja 22,Je 2,N 16 1864
NcD F 3 1842;Mr 8-10,22,26 1865;F 7 1883;N 15 1904;F 5 1906
OClWHi Mr 11 1860;Ap 26 1863;F 18-Ap 21, Ag 17 1864;Ja-Ap 9 1865
PHi O 1,8 1863
TxGR F 6,Ap 12,S 3 1862;S 11,16 1863;Ag 26,S 6,16,O 8 1864;Jl 22 1865;Mr 2 1881;Ag 30 1931
V O 12,15 1862;D 22 1867
VRC Ja 4 1863
VU N 26 1832
WHi Mr 19 1864;Ja 31 1895

Mobile daily REGISTER. [evening ed] d 1850?-94‖?
1850?-Je? 1869 as Mobile evening news (title varies slightly)
A F 18 1861;Ap 10,S 5 1862;Mr 20 1865
AMP Jl 1868-Je 1871;73-74;76;78-79;81-82;Ja-Je 1885;86-88;Ap 1889
DLC [Je 15-Jl 24 1863]S 26,N 23-24,D 5-6 1864;Ja 6,Je 15,18 1865;O 7 1872[81-My 4 1884;Ag 16-O 4 1886]
LNC Jl 20 1863;D 28 1864
MBAt Mr 28,Ap 21,Ag 29,S 14,18,30,O 5,9,12,N 3-5,23,30,D 26 1863[64]Ja 3,16,23,30,F 6-7,13-14,Mr 6,11,13,20,27,Ap 3,D 6,16,18,30 1865;Ja 3,10 1866
MH Ag 2 1864
MWA Jl 2,10,15-16,18 1862;Ag 20 1863;My 28, Je 10,Ag 12,O 8,22 1864
MsHi S 28-29,D 18,21 1863-Jl 11,15 1864;65
NN My 9 1862
NNHi Ap 16,18 1863
NSyU My 21 1861
NcD [Jl 8 1861-Ja 24 1862]
TxGR Ag 10 1863
V O 9,21 1862
WHi Ap 16 1864

Mobile REGISTER and journal for the country. sw,tw,w D 10 1821-44‖?
1821-O 1832 as Mobile commercial register (for the country) N 1832-N? 1841 Mobile commercial register and patriot
1821-32 w in summer and sw in winter; 1832-44? tw in winter and sw in summer
CSmH F 28 1842
Ct [1827-28]
DLC Ap 2-16 1824;S 11 1830;N 26 1834;Jl 21, Ag 11,S 1,N 8,25 1837;Mr 24,Ap 21,Jl 28,Ag 11-18 1838;Ja 12,Ap 27,My 18,S 7 1839;Je 13 1840;Jl 20 1844
MWA Ap 3,N 22/26 1823;N 24 1827;N 1 1828; Mr 27 1829;My 12-26,D 7 1832-[Ja-Ap 5]D 11,21 1833[Ja-Je]Jl 18,25,Ag 1,15,29[O 10-D] 1834;Ja 24,F 7-14,Mr 4-14,21 1835
NN My 20-27,Je 3-10 1840
NcD Je 29 1833
WHi Je 23-Jl 28 1832

REGISTER shipping list and prices current. w
MWA F 22 1840;F 6 1841

Mobile REPUBLICAN. d 1870-71‖?
A O 20 1870

Mobile REPUBLICAN. w 1870-72‖?
DLC Ag 12 1871;F 3,Ag 24 1872

Mobile SHIPPING and commercial list. w 1832?-
CSmH Ja 27 1838
MWA Ja 11 1834;Ja 20,Ag 17 1838

Mobile evening TELEGRAPH. d 1862?-Mr 1865‖?
Followed by Mobile evening tribune
DLC Ag 6 1864
ICN Jl 21 1863
MBAt S 15,24,O 1,27,D 7 1863;F 16,Mr 28,My 2,9,Ag 24,26-27,30-S 1,O 19 1864;Mr 7 1865
MWA Jl 2 1862;Je 8,N 17 1864
MsHi S 10,D 1862;S 29,D 18,21 1863
NcD Mr 23-25 1865
OClWHi Jl 14 1863;Ag 19 1864
V O 23-24 1862
—morning ed *See* Mobile daily tribune

Mobile daily TIMES. d Ap 13 1865-Ja 1868‖?
1865-Mr 1866 as Mobile morning news. Merged with Advertiser and register, later Mobile register
LNH [1866-67]
MB [1865]-Je 1866
MBAt [O 1865-Ag 1866;F 1867-Ja 1868]Ap 20 (extra) 1865
MCheHi Ap 11,19 1865
MWA My 27,N 21 1865
OClWHi Ap 13,20,Jl 20-N 14 1865
TxGR My 8 1865

Mobile Sunday TIMES. w 1865-Je 1869‖?
LNH [1866-68]
N Jl 14 1867

Mobile TIMES-NEWS. *See* Mobile news 1915+

Mobile daily TRIBUNE. d O 5 1842-72‖?
1842-49 as Alabama tribune (1845?-48? Herald and tribune)
A My-O 1845;My-O,N 19 1846;D 1847-My 1848; 49-Ap,O 5 1850-Mr 1851;F 7 1856;S 29 1862;Mr 26 1864;F 6 1865
DLC [Mr 18-O 7 1849]F 9 1859;N 13 1862;F 3, Mr 5,11,N 22-23,26 1864
LNC Ag 1 1863
MBAt [Ag 27 1863-N 10 1865]Ja 23-25,28,F 2, 10-14 1866;O 21 1868
MH Ja 18 1865
MHi Je 25 1863
MWA Ja 31 1846;Mr 8 1861;Je 29,Jl 8,10 1862;N 7 1863;Je 5,Jl 13,Ag 7,14,17,21,23,O 23,N 16 1864;Ap 7,10 1868
N Jl 14,18 1867;Mr 25 1872
NN Ja 17 1865
NNHi My 23 1863;Ag 21,O 2 1864;Ja 10,12,14 1865
NcD S 3 1852;S 20 1853;Mr 3 1855;Jl 11 1858;F 11 1864;Mr 17,25 1865
OClWHi Je 25 1863;Mr 14-Ap 22,Je 7,Jl 17-O 8 1864;Ja 24 25,Ap 2 1865
OHi Je 24 1863
PPiHi Ja 23 1859
TxGR Ap 20 1861;Ap 10 1862;Je 28 1863;Jl 19 1864
V O 9,11-12 1862;Jl 14 1864
VRC N 29 1863
WHi Mr 16,26,Ap 21-22,Ag 6,11,17,20-21,27-28, S 25 1864
—evening ed 1862-65 *See* Mobile evening telegraph
—w ed *See* Alabama planter

Mobile evening TRIBUNE. d Jl? 1865-72‖?
Follows Mobile evening telegraph
A Je 4,8,S 21 1868
MBAt D 4,6,11,16-18,20,30 1865;Ja 3,10 1866

Weekly TRIBUNE. w -1872‖?
NNHi O 3 1864

Mobile TRIBUNE. d 1874-79‖?
A O 20 1874-76;Ja 9 1877

MONROEVILLE

Monroe JOURNAL. w 1866+
A Ap 1878-1928;33+
AMnC [1869+]

MONTEVALLO

Montevallo ADVERTISER. w 1915-D 25 1919‖?
A Ag 1915-N 1918
ACoC 1916-D 13 1919

Montevallo NEWS. w Ap 4 1895-99‖?
A D 8 1898
ACoC [1896]-My 5 1898

Weekly REVIEW. w S 30 1910-12‖?
ACoC 1910-My 3 1912

SENTINEL. w Ap 30 1868-Mr 17 1904‖?
1868-S 2 1875 as Shelby county guide; S 9 1875-Ja 11 1900? Shelby sentinel
1868-83? pub in Columbiana; 1884?-Ja 11 1900? in Calera
Suspended from 1887?-92?
A 1868-Je 8 1882;Ag 1893-1900
ACoC 1868-Ag 11 1881;Ag 30 1883-Mr 17 1904

Montevallo TIMES. w 1932+
A F 27 1936+

MONTGOMERY

ADVANCE. w 1871-72‖?
A Jl,O 23 1871;N 4-11 1872
NNHi Jl 31 1871

ADVANCE. w 1877-82‖?
Negro
A S 11 1880;S 3 1881

Montgomery weekly ADVERTISER. w,sw D 29 1829-1905‖?
1829-Ag 1833? as Planters' gazette; S 1833?-35? Planters' gazette and Montgomery advertiser; 1836?-Ja 1? 1847 Montgomery advertiser; Ja 8? 1847-S 1849 Weekly flag and advertiser; S 1849-52? Advertiser and state gazette; 1872?-78? Weekly advertiser and mail
Suspended from Ap 1865-My 1 1866?
sw 1894?-95?
A Je 20,Jl 21,Ag 3 1848;My 31 1854-Ap 9 1856;S 14 1859;Ap 16,Jl 11,25 1860;Mr 20-Ap 10,24 1861;O 1862-S 21 1864;My 30 1867;Ap 14 1868-Mr 8 1870;75-Jl 1876;N 29 1881;Ja 17,F 7,Mr 14,28,Ap 11,My 2 1882;Ja-Je 1885
AMoC My 1866-F 1867;N 1874-76;80;82-84;88-91;93
CSmH Ag 24 1830
DLC D 29 1829;F 26,Mr 26-Ap 2,My 14-Je 18,Jl 16-30,N 9 1847;Mr 23-Ap 20,My 4-18 1849
KHi N 11 1851;Ap 3 1861
MWA Ap 27 1830;Ja 3 1832;Je 4,18 1847;N 24 1852;Ja 8-S 1862;O 1863-S 2 1864
NSchU F 4,Ap 8 1842
NcD My 23,N 14,28 1860;Je 17 1863;Je 6 1882; Ja 2 1883;S 16 1884
PEL Jl 25 1831
V My 6 1863
WHi Ag 21 1840;Ap 24(extra)1865

Montgomery ADVERTISER. d 1850?+
1850?-71? as Montgomery daily advertiser; 1872?-80? Montgomery advertiser and mail
Suspended from Ap-Jl 18? 1865
Mr 15 1828 is 100th anniversary ed
A S 4 1859;F 19,Mr 9,12,15,18-21,23,25-27,30, Ap 4-6,8-9,13,15,17-19,23-26 1861;Ja 5,Ap 15, 17,20,My 10,23,D 18 1862;F 18 1863;Je 4,9, 11,13-14 1864;Jl 21,S 21-30 1865;Mr 1866-72; Ap 25 1873-N 14,D 15 1875;My 19,N 11,D 12 1876;77-Je 1881;Jl 1882-85;Mr 30,Ap 14, 18,20,24,29-30,My 14,Jl 1886-N 1887;F 10,Je 28,Jl 1888-Je 1889;90+
AMoC N 1874-93;Jl 1895+
AOzC 1889;Ja-S 6 1901
DLC Ja 28(extra)My 9,11 1861[My 20 1862-Mr 29 1865]My 6,20,D 24 1886;Mr 18,Ap 3 1887;O 28 1888;Mr 20 1889;My 11 1901+
GDE Mr 16 1867
GU S 10 1861
ICHi O 26,N 2 1865
MBAt Ap 2,D 17 1863;F 20,Mr 9,16-20,22-23, 25-27,29-Ap 3,5-8,20-21,23,Jl 19-24,30,Ag 2,5 1864;Ja 24 1865;F 9 1868
MWA F 20 1858;Jl 9 1862;F 18,24,Mr 1,16 1864;D 21 1875;Ap 27 1877;N 27 1879;F 25 1897;Ja 14 1904;Mr 15 1928;My 27 1932
NNHi My 24 1863;S 20 1864
NSyU Ag 14(extra)N 13,16 1860;Ap 24-25,27 1861
NbHi S 8,10,15,17 1907
NcD N 20 1863;Ja 29,F 22,26,Mr 2,7-8,12,15-16,20,30,Ap 2-5,10,12,20,My 1-8,31,Jl 2 1879; Je 20,22,29,Ag 10,22,28 1880;My 28 1881;Ap 26 1882;Ja 13 1883; Ap 29,My 1 1886;Ap 9 1897;Ag 27,D 11 1898;N 22,26,29,D 17 1905; Ag 19 1906;O 27 1907;N 22 1908;N 26-27,D 4 1910;Ja 17 1911
NcGrW Jl 25 1867
OCHi [Ap 23-Jl 23 1861]
OHi Ag 6,S 9 1865
PHi Ag 16 1863
TKL Ap 29 1863;Je 30 1885
V My 8,10 1863;Je 19,25,30-Jl 3,6-7 1864
WHi 1916-Ap 16 1920

ADVERTISER and state gazette. tw Ja 12 1847-
1847-S 1849? as Tri-weekly flag and advertiser
A Je 20 1850;N 11 1851;D 14 1854;Ap 1,17, My 30,S 20 1855;Ja 9,16,23,30,F 6,13,20-24, Mr 5,D 17 1856;Ja 14,28,Mr 11,25,Ap 22,My 6,13,27,Je 10,17,24,Jl 1,8,22,Ag 12,19,26,S 23 1857;Ja 13,20,27,F 3,Mr 10,31,My 5,12,19,N 17 1858;Ja 19,26,Ap 13,20,My 14 1859
DLC [1847-Ap 5 1849]
MWA Ja 12[F 13 1847-Ap 1 1848]O 19,28-N 4,27 1852
WHi F 18 1847

ALABAMA journal. w Ja 6 1821-
1821-O 7? 1825 as Montgomery republican
Suspended from Ag-N? 1827
A N 3 1826-O 27,N 7,D 29 1828;Je 28 1851;N 20,D 4-18 1852;F 19,Jl 2,Ag 27,D 10 1853[54-57]
CSmH Ag 27 1830
Ct My 5 1826;D 10 1830
DLC O 7 1824;D 9 1825-Ja 13,F 3-10,24-Jl 7 1826;N 28 1828;Jl,S 4,25,N 13,D 25 1829;Ja 1,15,N 12,D 10 1830;Je 11-N 9,23,D 7-21 1850
MBAt Ag 22 1828
MWA Je 16 1823;Ja 24,Mr 20 1824;F 18,Ap 15,29,My 20 1825;Ja 12,Mr 9,Je 29,D 7 1827
NNHi Ap 19-My 3,Je 7-21,Jl 5-12,26-Ag 9,30-S 6,20-O 4,N 22 1822
NcU My 27 1840;N 22 1843
TxU S 20 1847

Daily ALABAMA journal. d,tw 1846?-
tw Je-S of each year as Tri-weekly Alabama journal
A Ag 8 1848;O 23 1849
DLC Ap 14 1849;51[52-53]

ALABAMA journal and the times. d 1888+
1888-99 as Evening journal; 1900-23 Montgomery journal; 1924-Mr 1927 Alabama journal
A F 11,20,Jl 1,30,O 1890-94;Jl 25-26 1895;Ag 30 1896;Jl 17,D 1898-Mr,Ag 10 1901+
AMoC 1900-S 1914;Ap-Je 1914;Ap 1915-Je,O-D 1916;Ap 1917-26;Ap 1927+

ALABAMA outlook. w 1904-15‖?
A Ap 1905-O 1911

ALABAMA state gazette. w 1848-Ag 1849‖
United with Weekly flag and advertiser to form Advertiser and state gazette, later Montgomery weekly advertiser
NcD Ag 1 1849

ALABAMA state journal. w 1867-77‖
WHi Ap-Jl 9 1875

ALABAMA state journal. d S 16 1868-77‖?
A 1868-Je 1873;Ja-N 14 1874
DLC [1869-71]-76
MBAt S 16-17,21,23,25-26,28-O 2,6,17,21-23,26-N 5,10-12,14-23 1868;D 11,15,17,21-22 1869
MWA Jl 11 1874-75
NNHi Jl 19 1869

ALABAMA state news. w 1927-28‖?
A N 1927-O 1928

ALABAMA state sentinel. w 1860?-
MBAt My 25-N 1867
—d ed *See* Daily state sentinel

ALABAMA (*Continued*)

MONTGOMERY—*Continued*

ALABAMA times. w 1906-28||?
A Ap 1915-O 1919;N 1923-Mr 1928
NcD Ap 30-Je 4 1918
—d ed *See* Montgomery daily times

ALLIANCE herald. w 1889-94||?
A My 14,Jl 16,N 19 1891;My 4,Jl 7 1893;Ap 26-My 15 1894

ATLAS. *See* New south

Evening BULLETIN. d
A Ap 19-20 1876

CAPITAL CITY record. w Ag 1868-69||?
A Ap 16 1869

COLORED Alabamian. w 1907-16||?
Negro
A O 1907-Ja 1916

Daily CONFEDERATION. d Ja 18 1858-61||?
A Je 11-Jl 27 1858;Ap 7 1860-Ag 16 1861
CSmH Ag 8,13 1861
CtY F 9 1861
DLC Ja 18-My 1858-Jl 17 1860

Weekly Montgomery CONFEDERATION. w 1858?-61||?
A D 10 1859;Je 8-15,Jl 6,27,Ag 17-S 21,O 12-D 21 1860;Ja 11,Mr 15,Ap 19-26 1861
KHi Ag 24-31 1860

Montgomery DISPATCH. d 1885-89||?
Title varies slightly
A D 19 1885;Mr 3,5,28,Ap 24,29,Je 5,9,12-13,27,Jl 19,S 13,O 6,D 29 1885;F 10,Je 18,Jl 12-13 1887
DLC N 22-23 1886;Ap 3,O 20 1887;Ja 27,Ag 4,N 14 1888
IU Ap 28 1886
KHi O 20 1887
NcD Ap 22 1886

Weekly DISPATCH. w 1886-89||?
A O 26 1888;Ag 11 1889
DLC Ja 7 1888

EMANCIPATOR. w 1917-20||?
Negro
A O 1917-Ag 1920

Montgomery ENTERPRISE. w 1898-1900||?
Negro
DLC Ja 23 1900

FLAG and advertiser. *See* Advertiser

JOURNAL. *See* Alabama journal and the times

Daily Montgomery LEDGER. d Ag 7 1865-My 1866||?
A Ag 7 1865

Montgomery daily MAIL. d 1854-71||?
United with Montgomery daily advertiser to form Montgomery advertiser and mail, later Montgomery advertiser
A 1860;F 11-12,Je 24-25,Jl 23 1861;S 6,O 2 1864;Je 5,S 22-30 1865;F 21,Ag 22,S 6 1868
DLC Ja 31 1861;Je 16,Jl 16,Ag 2,16,21,S 30 1863[64]Ap 26 1865;Ja 25 1867
ICHi S 23,O 4 1865
MBAt [Mr 9-S 1864]Ja 25,28-29 1865;Ag 11 1868
MH Ja 13,20-21,24-25,27,F 1,3-5 1865
MWA Ap 22 1861
NNHi O 2 1861;Mr 7 1863;Mr 23,Jl 19 1864;My 10 1865
NcD Ag 2 1858;My 12 1863;S 27 1864
OClWHi Ag 2,23 1864
OHi Ag 26 1865
PHi O 1,N 17 1863
V O 26 1862;Jl 14 1864
WHi F 12 1861[Ap 21-My 9 1865]

Montgomery weekly MAIL. w 1854?-71||?
United with Montgomery weekly advertiser to form Weekly advertiser and mail, later Montgomery weekly advertiser
A My 1860-Ap 1861;Ap 21 1863-Ap 1864;Mr 18 1867-N 15 1870;Mr 1 1871
AMoC My 1860-Ap 22 1861
DLC F 1,22-My 17,Je 7 1861
NN My 10 1862
NNHi Mr 4 1863
NcD O 26,N 30 1860;F 14 1862
NjR F 8 1861

MEMPHIS daily appeal. *See* Memphis appeal-avalanche (Memphis, Tenn.)

Montgomery daily MESSENGER. d 1856?-58||
Merged with Daily confederation
A O 29 1856-My 1857

NEW SOUTH. w D 1849-52||?
1849-51? as Atlas
A Ja 16 1850;My 21 1851

Weekly NEWS. w
A N 15 1854

Montgomery NEWS. w
A N 1933

Daily PICAYUNE. d Je 11?- 1868||?
A Je 11-N 27 1868
MBAt Je 18,23-24 1868

PLANTERS' gazette and Montgomery advertiser. *See* Montgomery weekly advertiser

Daily POST. d Ap 3 1860-61||
A 1860-O 4 1861
WHi F 11-12,18 1861

Montgomery weekly POST. w Jl 4? 1860-Jl 17 1861||?
A Jl 18 1860-Jl 17 1861
DLC My 1,15 1861
TxU Jl 18 1860-Jl 17 1861

Montgomery REPUBLICAN. *See* Alabama journal

SOUTHERN military gazette. w D 1 1854-57||
A D 5 1854;F 20,Ap 21 1855

SOUTHERN times. w Mr 24 1855-
MH Mr-S 1,15-N 17,D 8,25 1855

Montgomery daily STATE. d 1907||?
A My 26-Ag 1907

STATE register. tw N 22 1850-52||
A Je 27 1851;Ja 31,Je 5,Jl 3 1852

Daily STATE sentinel. d 1863?-
A My 18 1867-Ap 18 1868
MBAt Ag 22-24,26-31,S 2-18,20-26,28-O 10,12-26 1867
MWA D 5(extra)1867
—w ed *See* Alabama state sentinel

Daily SUN. d
A F 7 1878

Montgomery daily TIMES. d S 26 1903-Mr 1927||
United with Alabama journal to form Alabama journal and the times
A 1903-Je 1913;14-27
AMoC N 1903-Je 1904;Jl 1905-06;Jl 1908-Je 1909;Jl 1914-27
ASIT Ag 8 1923
—w ed *See* Alabama times

TRUE SOUTH. w
A Je 26 1852
MHi Jl 3 1852

Montgomery WEEKLY. w Ja 1 1930+
A 1930+
AMoC 1930+

WORKINGMAN'S advocate. w 1878-79||?
A Mr 2 1879

MOULTON

Moulton ADVERTISER. w 1828+
1828-1926 as Advertiser (1851-65? Moulton democrat; 1866?-1922 Moulton advertiser; 1924 Moulton advertiser and Lawrence county times)
A Ja 25 1855-D 24 1858;F 9 1867-89;Ap 13 1893;D 1898-1923;Mr 10-Ap 1932;33+
AMtC F 9-S 21 1867;F 28 1868-Ja,Ap-D 16 1870;Ja-S 2 1871;72-89;91-95;97-1905;07-11;13-N 12 1919;F 4 1920-N 22 1922;Ja 26 1923-O 11 1924;28+
NcD Mr 6-13,Ap 10,My 8,O 9 1879;F 5,Ap 7 1880;D 21-28 1882

Moulton BANNER and Lawrence enquirer. w Ja? 1839-
DLC Ag 21,S 4 1839;Ag 8 1840

Moulton DEMOCRAT. *See* Moulton advertiser

UNION. w
AMtC S 16 1867-F 4 1868

Moulton WHIG. w N 23 1832-
DLC Ja 11 1833

MOUNDVILLE

HALE county news. w Ag 21 1924+
1924-F 6 1930 as Moundville news
A 1933+
AGrC [1924-26]+

Moundville NEWS. w N 10 1911-18||?
A 1913-F 1918
AGrC 1911-[15-16]-D 21 1917

Moundville NEWS. 1924-30 *See* Hale county news

MOUNT STERLING

CHOCTAW messenger and journal. 1849-
NcD Jl 31 1849

MUSCLE SHOALS

Muscle Shoals BULLETIN. ir
MWA D 1932

Muscle Shoals Sunday NEWS. *See under* Florence

NEW DECATUR

Papers published in New Decatur are listed under Decatur

NEWBERN

Newbern NEWS. w D 1892-93||?
AGrC Mr 17-D 15 1893

NEWTON

DALE county standard. w Ag 3 1893-94||?
A 1893
AOzC Ag 17,O 12,N 23-30 1893

HARMONIZER. w Mr 30 1901-04||?
A 1902-03
AOzC 1901-03

Newton MESSENGER. w 1885-90||?
AOzC Ja 21 1888-90

Newton NEWS. w Ap 11 1896-
AOzC Ap 18-O 1896

Newton PROGRESS. w 1905-07||?
AOzC Mr-N 14 1907

SOUTHERN star. *See under* Ozark

NEWVILLE

Newville ADVERTISER. w 1919?-24||?
AAC Je 26 1919-D 18 1920;Ja 29-D 8 1921;Ja 13-D 7 1922;23-24

NORTHPORT

Northport HERALD. w Ja 5 1910-12||?
ATuC 1910-12

SPECTATOR. w N 3 1871-
ATuC 1872;74
DLC 1871-Ja 6,20-Mr 3,17-Ap 21,My 12-Je,Jl 14-S 12,26-O 17 1874

WEST ALABAMA breeze. *See under* Tuscaloosa

OAKMAN

Oakman NEWS. w 1894-1901||?
AJC 1895-97;99-Je 1901

ONEONTA

AMERICAN weekly. w Ja 31 1921-
AOC 1921

BLOUNT chronicle. w
AOC Ja 8 1891-Mr 31 1892

BLOUNT county herald. w
AOC Jl 8 1880-Mr 11,Ap 15 1881

BLOUNT county journal. w My 7 1909-Ag 1918||
A complete
AOC 1909-16;18
AOS 1917-18

BLOUNT county news-dispatch. w 1877-1904||?
1877-89? as Blount county news (Blountsville)
AOC Mr 19 1879-D 15 1881;Ja 26 1882-Mr 1892; 93-Ag 1901;02-Ja 28 1904

SOUTHERN democrat. w O 18 1894+
pub 1894+
A 1916-23;Ap 3 1930
AOC Ja 9 1896+

OPELIKA

ALABAMA monitor. *See* East Alabama signal

Opelika DEMOCRAT. w,sw S 22 1887-90||?
w 1887-89?
AOpC 1887-N 22 1888;89

EAST ALABAMA monitor. *See* East Alabama signal

EAST ALABAMA signal. w 1868-73||?
1868? as Alabama monitor; Ja?-N 8? 1869 East Alabama monitor; N 15? 1869-Ja 8? 1870 Opelika new era; Ja 15? 1870-72? Weekly era and whig
A N 21 1868;Ja 8-15,Jl 2,N 8-13,D 4 1869;Ja 8,F 7,D 9,23 1870;Ja 13-Mr 17,31,Jl 1,S 8-D 22 1871

Tri-weekly ERA and whig. tw
-S 15 1870? as Tri-weekly new era
A S 6-17,O-N 19 1870

Weekly ERA and whig. *See* East Alabama signal

Opelika INDUSTRIAL news. w 1890-1904||
A S 1899-S 1904
AOpC Mr 31 1892-94;1900
—d ed *See* Opelika daily news

Opelika LOCOMOTIVE. tw,sw 1869?-73||?
Title varies slightly. United with Opelika observer to form Observer and locomotive, later Opelika observer
tw 1869?
A Ja 2,N 8,17 1869;Mr 9,Ap 2,S 3,14,28 1870;O 14-17 1871

Opelika NEW ERA. *See* East Alabama signal

Tri-weekly NEW ERA. *See* Tri-weekly era and whig

Opelika daily NEWS. d 1904+
A My-D 1904;08-10;O 1917-N 1921;22-S 1924; 25-Je 1930
AOpC 1906;Ap-D 1908
—w ed *See* Opelika industrial news

Opelika OBSERVER. w 1872-82||?
1874?-78? as Observer and locomotive
A Ja 2-D 14 1879

Opelika morning POST. w,d S 28 1894-1909||?
1894-Je? 1908 as Opelika post(w)
A Mr 1899-1909
AOpC 1894-1900;06;Ja 17-My 1908

PROGRESSIVE age. w
A S 13-D 1872

SOUTHERN era.
A Ja 1-D 21 1861

Opelika TIMES. w 1874-89||?
Suspended from Ja 14-F 6 1886
AOpC 1885;My 10-D 1886
NcD Mr 7,My 2,20 1879

TRUE union. w
A S 13,O 14 1871

Opelika UNION.
pub by 95th Illinois regiment
WH Je 1 1865

UNION republican.
A S 8,O 16 1869

ALABAMA (*Continued*)

OPP

Opp HOMESPUN. w 1905-D 29 1906||
Followed by Opp messenger
AAnC Mr 31-D 1906

Opp HUSTLER. w 1903-05||?
AAnC Ag 14 1903-Mr 3 1906

Opp MESSENGER. w 1907-S 21 1921||
Follows Opp homespun. Followed by Opp weekly news
AAnC Ag 13 1909-21

Opp weekly NEWS. w O 20 1921+
Follows Opp messenger
A N 1926-28;33+
AAnC 1921+

OXFORD

Oxford ECHO. w My 1887-90||?
AAnnC 1887-D 27 1890

Oxford NEWS. w Mr 1883-Jl 1886||
AAnnC Mr 22-D 18 1883;85-86

Oxford TRIBUNE. w 1875-79||?
A Mr 10 1876

Oxford TRIBUNE. w 1916-Ap 16 1919||
A Ap 1916-Mr 1919
AAnnC My 1916-19

OZARK

Ozark ADVERTISER. w 1893?-Ja 1895||
United with Ozark banner to form Ozark banner-advertiser
A 1893-94

Ozark BANNER-ADVERTISER. w My 17 1892-97||?
1892-Ja 23 1895 as Ozark banner
A 1893;95-96
AOzC Jl 14 1892-Ap 1897

DALE county news. w 1897-1906||?
1897-S 25 1901 as Ozark times
A 1901;03
AOzC 1901-03;Ja-S 15 1906
AOzS F-D 1905

FREE PRESS. w S 17 1896-1903||?
A 1896-1900;03
AOzC S 24,O 8-N 12,26 1896-D 13 1900

Ozark HERALD. w S 9 1902-17||?
1902-Ag 12 1913 as Ozark tribune
A 1902-12;14-17
AOzC 1902-04;06-16
AOzS 1905

SOUTHERN star. w 1867+
1867-69 pub in Newton
pub F 8 1905;Ja-Ag 24 1927
A 1889-90;92-93;95-99;1901-03;06-Mr 1909;11;15-16;18-28;33+
AOzC S 10,N 26 1884-93;96-1903;05-06;10-14;16;18+

Ozark TIMES. *See* Dale county news

Ozark TRIBUNE. *See* Ozark herald

PARRISH

Parrish NEWS. w 1925?+
AJC Jl 1925-29;31-[33]+

PELL CITY

Pell City GLOBE. w 1889-90||?
1889-N? 1890 as St. Clair echo
AAvC Ja 12 1889-N 23 1890

Pell City NEWS. w Mr 7 1908+
1908-Ag 1911 as Progress; S 1911-19? Pell City progress
A 1913-Ag 1919;Jl 1921-25;33+
AAvC 1910-11;14;16-19
APC 1922[Jl 10 1929+]

PROGRESS. *See* Pell City news

ST. CLAIR county times. w My 7 1935+
APC 1935+

ST. CLAIR echo. *See* Pell City globe

ST. CLAIR herald. w 1902-07||?
APC 1906

Pell City TIMES. w 1906?-07||?
AAvC 1906

PHENIX CITY

Phenix-Girard JOURNAL. w 1908+
Also dated in Girard
1908-28 pub in Girard
A Ap 1915-19;N 1926-28;33+
ASeC 1913;15-16;18;25-26;29-31;34+

PHIL CAMPBELL

Phil Campbell NEWS.
ARuC O 1920-21

PICKENSVILLE

Pickensville COURIER.
A Mr 30 1860

Pickensville JOURNAL.
A Ag 24 1860

Pickensville REGISTER.
A Mr 1841-N 5 1843

Pickensville REPUBLICAN.
A Je 12 1849;Ja 23 1855;O,N 12,26,D 31 1857;F 4,18-25,Mr 18 1858;60;Ja 21,31,Mr 28,Ap 25, My 30,O 3 1861

SOUTH ALABAMIAN. w? Je 8 1839-
DLC Je 8 1839

PIEDMONT

To 1888? as Cross Plains

CROSS PLAINS post. *See* Piedmont post

Piedmont INQUIRER. w 1890-S 1902||
AAnnC 1891-96;98-S 5 1902

Piedmont JOURNAL. w 1907+
A Jl 1934+
AAnnC Mr 16 1907-08;10;13;15-[17]20-25;27-28; D 30 1932+

Piedmont NEWS. w Ja 1903-Ag 27 1905||
AAnnC complete

Piedmont POST. w Mr 1883-91||?
1883-88? as Cross Plains post
AAnnC 1883-88

PINCKARD

Pinckard PILOT. w D 2 1897-98||?
AOzC D 9 1897-S 1898

PINE APPLE

Pine Apple ENTERPRISE. *See* Gazette (Camden)

Pine Apple GAZETTE. *See* Gazette (Camden)

Pine Apple NEWS. w 1906-09||?
ACC S 1906-Ap 1909

PRATTVILLE

AUTAUGA citizen. w F 7 1853-82||?
A Jl 2 1874
APrC 1853-67;O 7 1869;O 27,D 1-15 1870;Mr 9,Je 15,22 1871;75-D 15 1881
DLC D 3 1857

Prattville PROGRESS. w O 1886+
Follows Southern signal
A 1886-1928;33+
APrC 1887-D 10 1897;N 4 1898+
WHi O 15 1925

SOUTHERN signal. w O 24 1877-86||?
Followed by Prattville progress
A Ag 12 1881;Ja 8 1886
APrC 1877-D 18 1885

SOUTHERN statesman. w
A D 20 1854;N 12 1859
APrC Ap 1860-61

RAGLAND

Ragland ADVERTISER. w 1913-14||?
A Je 1913-S 1914

ST. CLAIR county news. w 1908-12||?
AAvC 1910-11

ST. CLAIR county news. w 1914?-16||?
A Jl 30 1915
AAvC 1915-16

RED BAY

Red Bay EAGLE. w 1908-09||?
ARuC Jl 31 1908-D 11 1909

FRANKLIN county progress. w My 6 1927+
A Mr 17-Ap 1932
ARuC 1927-30;Ap 30 1931+

FRANKLIN democrat. w 1913-18||?
A Ag 1913-S 1918
ARuC 1913-S 14 1918

Red Bay weekly GAZETTE. w Ag 1908-14||?
ARuC Ag 25-D 1908;Ja-N 1910;11-Jl 17 1914

Red Bay HEADLIGHT. w
ARuC Je 29-D 1912

ROANOKE

Roanoke HERALD. w 1876-99||?
1876-87? as Randolph county news
A Jl 24 1879
AWC Ja-D 17 1897;F 11 1898-Ja 27 1899
NcD My 29 1879

Roanoke LEADER. w S 14 1892+
1892-1900 as Randolph leader
A D 1898-F 1900;Mr 1905-My 1912;15-19;My 12 1920;N 1926-28;33+
AWC D 30 1896-S 19,D 19 1900-S 17 1902;Mr 20-O 7,N 11 1903+

Roanoke PRESS. w F 10 1909-
AWC 1909-Ag 10 1910

RANDOLPH county news. *See* Roanoke herald

RANDOLPH leader. *See* Roanoke leader

ROBERTSDALE

Robertsdale AMERICAN. w 1921+
ABmC Ap 10 1926-N 14 1928

ROCKFORD

CHRONICLE. w Ja 2 1906+
A 1908;12-N 1919;20;Ap 29 1921;26-28;33+
ARC 1913-14;Ag 20-27 1915;16[17-18]-Mr 4,D 30 1921;My 25 1922;23+

COOSA argus. w 1900-09||?
A Jl 1901-09

ROGERSVILLE

Rogersville NEWS. w 1917?-20||?
AFlC 1917;20

RUSSELLVILLE

ALABAMA leader. w Ap 1897-98||?
ARuC 1897-Jl 28 1898

FRANKLIN banner. w 1924||?
Merged with Franklin county times?
ARuC 1924

FRANKLIN county times. w S 25 1896+
Formed by the union of Hustler and Southern idea. 1896-1913? as Franklin times
A D 1899-1919;33+
ARuC 1896+

HUSTLER. w Mr 1892-S 1896||
United with Southern idea to form Franklin times, later Franklin county times
ARuC 1894-96

Russellville NEWS. w
ARuC Ja 20-D 16 1898;99

SOUTHERN idea. w 1886-S 1896||
United with Hustler to form Franklin times, later Franklin county times
ARuC N-D 20 1889;90-96

RUTLEDGE

Rutledge ENTERPRISE. w 1884-89||?
ALuC 1888-N 1889

GLEANER. w 1894?-1900||?
ALuC Ap 12 1895-1900

Rutledge WAVE. w 1890-95||?
ALuC F 10 1892-Ag 1 1895

ST. STEPHENS

HALCYON. . . *See under* Greensboro

WASHINGTON county news. *See under* Chatom

SAMSON

Samson LEDGER. w Ap 11 1906+
A 1917-18;N 1926-28;33+
AGeC Mr 31 1912+

SCOTTSBORO

ALABAMA herald. w Ap 30 1868-D 29 1886||
Ap-N 1868 as Jackson county herald; D 1868-S 9 1869 Southern industrial herald; S 16 1869-71 Scottsboro industrial herald. Followed by Progressive age
A O 22 1868;D 1905-Ag 1908
ASC Ap-N 19,D 10 1868-Ap 20 1871;Ja 11 1872-86
NcD Mr 6 1879;Jl 22 1880

Scottsboro CITIZEN. w 1877-1919||?
1877-78? as Fellow citizen
ASC S 13 1878-83;86-92;94-1909;14-16;Ja 14,Je 10 1919
NcD Ap 4 1879;Jl 23,Ag 27 1880;Ja 12,O 5,D 14,28 1882

FELLOW citizen. *See* Scottsboro citizen

Scottsboro INDUSTRIAL herald. *See* Alabama herald

JACKSON county herald. *See* Alabama herald

JACKSON county sentinel. w Mr 21 1929+
A My 18,Je 8-22 1933;Jl 1934+
ASC 1929+
NcD S 25 1929

JACKSON union news. w Ja 23 1907-My 5 1909||
Merged with Progressive age
ASC complete

PROGRESSIVE age. D 29 1886+
Follows Alabama herald
A Ag 24 1899-1912;N 1926-28;33+
ASC 1886+

SOUTHERN industrial herald. *See* Alabama herald

SEALE

ALABAMA examiner. w?
A Ap 1872-My 1873

RUSSELL register. w Ag 5 1875+
A 1875-F 4 1893;My 21 1897-1907;Ap 23 1909;11-13;15-25;33+
ASeC [1915]-[17-18]-[21]-27;29-30;Ap 13 1934+

ALABAMA (*Continued*)

SELMA

ALABAMA state sentinel. w F 1853-
A Mr 30-Ap 6,27 1859;O 10-24,N 7-21,D 5-9 1860;Mr 13 1861
CSmH Ag 6 1862
DLC Ja 17,31-F 8,Mr-N 7,D 5-12,26 1855
NcD Jl 27,Ag 10,S 28,O 12,N 16 1859;Ap 11,Jl 4,Ag 22,S 5-19,O 10 1860
—d ed *See* Daily state sentinel

ALABAMA state sentinel. tw F? 1853-
DLC [Ja 6-N 13 1855]

CHATTANOOGA daily rebel. *See under* Chattanooga, Tenn.

Selma COURIER. w N 2 1827-33||?
Follows Cahawba press (Cahawba). Followed by Selma free press, later Selma reporter?
A [N 29 1827-S 3 1829]
CSmH S 4 1830
Ct Ap 24 1828
MWA Ap 3,N 27-D 4 1828

DALLAS county news. w My 31 1932+
A My 5 1933
ASIC 1932+

Selma morning DISPATCH. d 1863-65||?
DLC N 20,23 1864;Ja 4,12,F 18 1865
ICN My 25 1864;Mr 12 1865
MBAt My 7 1864;Ja 24 1865
MH Ja 18,24 1865
NNHi D 20 1864;Ja 7-8,10-13,F 10 1865
PHi N 6 1863

Selma evening DISPATCH. d 1863?-65||?
A My 24,Ag 23,N 6,18,D 20 1863;Ja 10,17,Jl 27 1864
DLC N 22 1864;F 22,25,Mr 13 1865
MBAt Mr 25,Ap 1,My 10 1864
MH Ja 16,23,25 1865
NNHi S 14 1864;Ja 13 1865
OClWHi My 12 1864

DOLLAR times. *See* Selma morning times

Daily ECHO. d 1874?-75||?
A Jl 23 1875

FEDERAL union. d Ap? 1865-
DLC Je 28 1865
ICN Je 7,22 1865
IU My 3 1865
OHi My 4 1865

Selma FREE PRESS. *See* Selma reporter

ISSUE. w
A O 17 1860-F 27,Mr 13 1861

JACKSON Mississippian. *See under* Jackson, Miss.

Selma JOURNAL. d Jl 17 1890-Mr 1920||?
United with Selma times to form Selma times-journal
A Ag 1900-S 5 1911[19-20]
NcD Je 20-27 1906

Selma evening MAIL. d 1881-87||?
United with Selma morning times to form Selma times and mail, later Selma times-journal

Sunday morning MAIL. w 1881-87||?
United with Times-argus to form Times and mail, later Selma morning times

Selma daily MESSENGER. d 1866?-68||?
United with Daily Selma times to form Daily times and messenger, later Selma times-journal
A F 21 1866-Je 29 1868

Selma weekly MESSENGER. w 1866?-68||?
United with Selma weekly times to form Weekly times and messenger, later Selma morning times
A N 10 1866-N 23 1867

Selma MIRROR. w 1888-1922||?
Je 28 1911 is industrial ed
A 1915-My 1917
WHi Je 28 1911

Daily MISSISSIPPIAN. *See under* Jackson, Miss.

Selma PRESS. w Ja 16 1869-71||?
ASIT 1869-Jl 8 1871
MBAt Ja 23 1869

Selma REPORTER. w Jl 25 1833-65||
Follows Selma courier? 1833-48? as Selma free press. Followed by Selma weekly times, later Selma morning times
A Ag 8 1835-Jl 17 1841;Ag 13 1856;Ag 1 1860
DLC F 6 1834
MWA Mr 22 1834

Tri-weekly REPORTER. tw 1854?-
MWA D 3 1856;Ja 14 1857

Selma REPORTER. [Evening ed] d 1858-64||?
Title varies slightly. Followed by Daily Selma times, later Selma times-journal
DLC Mr 24,29,N 21-25,28 1864
ICN Jl 26 1859;Je 17 1862;Mr 19 1864
MBAt Mr 26,31 1864
PHi N 3 1863
VRC Je 30 1862

Selma morning REPORTER. d 1859-65||?
A Ap 4 1861-64;F 7 1865
AMaJ F 9 1863
DLC S 21 1863
ICN Ag 16,D 30 1862;Mr 9 1864
IU Mr 23 1865
MWA N 14 1862
NcD S 8 1864

REPUBLICAN union advocate. w? Ap 27 1867-
MBAt Ap 27 1867

SOUTHERN argus. w Je 16 1869-Ja 1882||
United with Selma weekly times to form Times-argus, later Selma morning times
A D 29 1871;O 16 1874;S 3 1875;F 18,Je 9,S 22 1878;Ag 9 1879;Mr 18 1880
ASIT 1869-73;Ap 9 1875-78
NcD S 1 1871;My 2 1879
NcU Ag 26 1881

SOUTHERN observer. w
GU S 23 1864

STATE index. w 1880-83||?
A N 22,D 9 1880;Ja 1,S 24,O 8,22-D 10 1881;Ja 21,Mr 4,Ap 1,My 20-27,N 17-24,D 8 1882;Ja 12 1883

Daily STATE sentinel. d 1856?-65||?
A F 16,23,Mr 20,My 11 1862;Mr 8 1863
ICN Jl 26-27 1859
—w ed *See* Alabama state sentinel

Selma morning TIMES. w,sw 1865-1913||?
Follows Selma reporter. 1865-Ja 20 1882 as Selma weekly times (1868? Weekly times and messenger; 1874?-81? Dollar times) Ja 27 1882-87? Times-argus; 1888? Times and mail; 1889?-92? Times-mail sw 1875-1900?
pub D 27 1869-72;Mr-D 1873;82-85
A F 18 1871;Mr 13,S 11,25,O 9,D 11 1885
MWA Mr 21 1868

Selma TIMES-JOURNAL. d Jl 4 1865+
Follows Selma reporter. 1865-67? as Daily Selma times; 1868? Daily times and messenger; 1869?-1915? Selma morning times (1888? Selma times and mail 1889?-92? Selma times-mail) 1916?-Mr 1920? Selma times
pub Jl 1876-Je 1882;D 1892+
A 1865-F 6 1896;S 1902-Je 1910;Mr 12 1914;N 1915-Je 1930
ICHi S 18,21 1865
MBAt Jl 26 1866
MWA Jl 14 1878
NcD Ap 9,30,My 3,31 1879

Weekly VISITOR. w
AMaJ Mr 31 1866

SHEFFIELD

CLARION. *See* Sheffield enterprise

Sheffield ENTERPRISE. w,sw Ap 18 1885-Je 15 1893||
1885-My 28 1887 as Clarion
1885-86? dated also in Tuscumbia
sw 1887?
ATsC complete

Sheffield REAPER. w Mr 9 1891-1918||?
1891-1904 as Reaper
A S 1899-Je 1911
ATsC 1891-92;95-1909

Sheffield RECORD. w Ja 1- 1898||?
ATsC Ja-D 10 1898

Sheffield STANDARD. w N 11 1893+
A 1915-16;18-28;33+
ATsC 1893+

TRI-CITIES daily. d 1907+
A N 1926-Je 1930
ATsC Jl 1927-Je 1930
—Sunday ed *See* Muscle Shoals Sunday news (Florence)

SIX MILE

BIBB blade. *See* Centerville press (Centerville)

BIBB county blade.
A Mr 16 1859-D 19 1860

BLADE-ENTERPRISE. *See* Centerville press (Centerville)

SLOCOMB

Slocomb NEWS. w 1905-F 7 1929||
United with Slocomb observer to form Slocomb news and observer, later Slocomb observer
AGeC My 1906-[07-27]-29

Slocomb OBSERVER. w My 1913+
F 7 1929-Je 19 1930 as Slocomb news and observer
A N 1914-25;Jl-D 1934
AGeC O 27 1927+

SOMERVILLE

Somerville weekly CRITIC. *See* Hartselle index (Hartselle)

MORGAN county news. *See* Alabama inquirer (Hartselle)

SPRINGVILLE

Springville ITEM. w 1901-10||?
APC 1902-03;10

Springville NEWS. w 1897-1901||?
APC 1897-99

ST. CLAIR advance. w D 1888-D 1890
1888-S 1889 as Ashville advance (Ashville)
AAvC 1888-90

ST. CLAIR democrat. w 1911-12||?
APC 1911

STEVENSON

Stevenson CHRONICLE. w Ja 18 1887-1914||?
A 1900-F 1903
ASC 1887-1909;Ja-S 10 1914

JACKSON county news. w
CtY Je 10 1865

SUGGSVILLE

CLARKE county post. *See* Macon banner (Grove Hill)

SULLIGENT

EAGLE-EYE. *See* Lightning

Sulligent ENTERPRISE. w N 12 1909-D 31 1910||
AVC D 16 1909-10

LIGHTNING. w S 24 1894-D 21 1899||
1894-N 20 1895 as Eagle-eye
A O 3,24 1894;S 15-22 1897
AVC O 17 1894-D 15 1898

Sulligent NEWS. w 1928||?
Merged with Lamar democrat (Vernon)
AVC Ja 1 1928

Sulligent NEWS. w 1930+
AVC Ja 10 1931+

SYLACAUGA

Sylacauga ADVANCE. w F 3 1907+
Follows Sylacauga progress
A 1918-24;F 1925-28;Ap 1932+
ATC 1918;23[24-25]+

Sylacauga NEWS. w 1917+
A Mr 1917-28;Ap 1932+
ATC 1918;21;23[24-26]+

Sylacauga PROGRESS. w 1902-D 1906||?
Followed by Sylacauga advance
ATC 1905-06

TALLADEGA

ALABAMA reporter. *See* Talladega reporter

DEMOCRATIC watchtower. *See* Watchtower

Talladega daily HOME. d My 17 1909+
A O 26 1929;N 10 1930;O 6 1931
ATC [1909]-[11-18]-[20-21]-[24]-[30]+
—w ed *See* Our mountain home

NEWS-REPORTER. *See* Talladega reporter

OUR mountain home. w 1867+
A 1874 77-87;S 1899-1928;33+
ATC 1872-73;88-96;99-1906;09-17;19+
—d ed *See* Talladega daily home

PATRIOT. *See* Southerner

Talladega REPORTER. w My 16 1843-D 27 1923||
1843-72? as Alabama reporter; 1873?-88? Reporter and watchtower; 1891?-Ap 1904 News-reporter
A 1860-87;1900-F 1918
ATC [Ag 27 1863-O 3 1867]88-1923
MWA O 3 1844

SOUTHERN register and Talladega advertiser. *See* Southerner

SOUTHERNER. w Jl 17 1835-Ja 1843||
1835-Ag? 1839 as Southern register and Talladega advertiser; S 1839-42 Patriot
A My 3,Jl 1 1840;D 1-8 1841
DLC Jl 24 1835;Mr 25,Ap 15 1840
GAtCo Jl 31 1839

Talladega SUN. w 1869-71||?
A F 10 1869-Jl 1871

WATCHTOWER. w 1838-72||?
1838-S 1867 as Democratic watchtower. United with Alabama reporter to form Reporter and watchtower, later Talladega reporter
A 1860-Je 1867[Ap 19 1871-N 1872]
MWA O 27 1852
NhD My 26 1841

TALLASSEE

Tallassee TIMES. w 1911-D 31 1915||
AWeC S 28 1911-N 20 1914;My 21-D 1915

Tallassee TRIBUNE. w 1919+
A Mr 11,Ap 8-22 1932
AWeC 1929-31

TRI-COUNTY weekly. w 1900-O 24 1908||
A Mr 1901-08
AWeC Ag 31 1901-N 29 1902;Ja 10 1903-08

THOMASVILLE

Thomasville ARGUS. w 1896-99||?
Followed by Thomasville echo
AGvC D 24 1896-D 29 1898

Thomasville ECHO. w 1900-18||?
Follows Thomasville argus
A Mr 1901-S 1918
AGvC O 1903-S 22 1904

Thomasville TIMES. w 1921+
A N 1926-28;Ap 1932+

ALABAMA (*Continued*)

TROY

ADVOCATE and American. w 1860?-
1860?-Je 1861? as States rights advocate
A F 28,Je 20,Jl 18,Ag 8,S 9-12,O 24,D 15 1861; Ja 2,30,F 13 1862
NcD N 22 1860;Ja 3 1861

CITIZENS journal. w 1892-1902||
1892-Ag 7 1896 as Troy democrat
A 1893-1901
ATrC F 13 1892-Ap 11 1902

Troy DEMOCRAT. *See* Citizens journal

Troy ECHO. w 1899-1900||
A Ag-N 1899;Ja-Ag 1900
ATrC My 20 1899-Ag 1900

Troy ENQUIRER. w 1875-92||?
A Mr 1875-78;Ap 1879-O 1883;84-90
ATrC F 13 1875-77;81-Ja 16 1892

Daily GAZETTE. d 1893||?
ATrC Ap 26-Ag 19 1893

Troy HERALD. w,sw 1904+
sw 1912?-29?
A 1906;26-My 1928;Ap 1932+
ATrC Jl 9 1904+

INDEPENDENT American. w -Je 1861||?
United with States rights advocate to form Advocate and American
A Je 20 1855-My 23 1860;Mr 13,27,My 1,22-29 1861

JEFFERSONIAN. w 1893-94||
A N 17 1893-O 1894
ATrC N 17 1893-O 1894

Troy MESSENGER. w 1866-1926||
1866-68? as Southern messenger; 1869?-71? Messenger and advertiser
A D 6,20 1866;Mr 11,25-Ap 1,My 27,Je 10-17, Ag 12,O 15,S 2,23,D 16 1867;68-1923;Ja 7-14 1926
ATrC 1871-83;Ap 1884-89;91-95;97-1926
TxU Jl 28 1870

Troy daily MESSENGER. d 1892+
A S 2 1893-99;My 7 1931;Je 20,Jl-S 1933
ATrC 1927+

SOUTHERN advertiser. w 1859-68||?
United with Southern messenger to form Messenger and advertiser, later Troy messenger
A D 7 1860[61-67]F 18-25 1868
NcD N 23 1860

SOUTHERN messenger. *See* Troy messenger

Troy STANDARD. w,sw 1896-1901||?
sw 1896-99?
A 1900-Ag 1901
ATrC O 1896-D 15 1900

STATES rights advocate. *See* Advocate and American

TUSCALOOSA

ALABAMA intelligencer and state rights expositor. w Ap 10 1829-D 12 1835||?
1829-33? as Alabama state intelligencer
A 1829-Je 4,Jl 2 1830
CSmH Ag 20 1830
DLC 1831;S 29,O 27 1832;Je 1 1833
MBAt D 12 1835
MWA D 18 1830;Ja 26 1831;D 5 1835
N S 28 1833
WHi Mr 2 1833[Jl 18-D 5 1835]

ALABAMA sentinel. w D 9? 1825-
A Mr 10-Jl 15 1826
DLC D 30 1825;F 2 1826;Mr 21,Je 13-27,Jl 11 1829

ALABAMA state intelligencer. *See* Alabama intelligencer and state rights expositor

Tuscaloosa AMERICAN. w Ja 6 1898-99||?
ATuC 1898

AMERICAN mirror. *See* Tuscaloosa chronicle

Tuscaloosa BLADE. *See* Tuscaloosa gazette

*Tuscaloosa CHRONICLE. w 1819-
1819-20? as Tuscaloosa republican; 1820?-Ja 17 1827? American mirror
A F 14 1827
DLC 1824;Ja 8-15,29-F 5,19-26 1825;Ja 31,F 21,D 1 1827;Jl 6,20,Ag 10 1829
MBAt D 8 1821
MWA O 20-27 1827

Tuscaloosa CHRONICLE. w Ja 7 1896-99||?
Negro
A D 17 1898-Ja,F 11-18 1899
ATuC 1896;98

CHRYSTAL fount. w Ag 3 1849-53||?
A Je 1851-My 1852;F 14 1853

CLARION. w Ja 9 1879-82||?
A Mr 1880-82
ATuC O 1881-82

DEMOCRATIC gazette. w D 21 1843-
DLC D 28 1843;Ja 10 1844

FLAG of the union. *See* State journal and flag

Tuscaloosa GAZETTE. w Ja 17 1872-1901||
1872-75? as Tuscaloosa blade. United with Tuscaloosa times to form Times-gazette
A S 1872-O 1875;F 8 1878-F 5,O 28 1880-83;Je 30 1892-D 12 1895;F 1896-1900
ASIT 1884-85
ATuC 1874;76-79;81-1901
MWA O 17 1878
NcD My 1 1879

Tuscaloosa GAZETTE. d 1887-1901||?
United with Evening times to form Tuscaloosa times-gazette

INDEPENDENT monitor. w 1837-Ja 1872||
United with Tuscaloosa observer to form Tuscaloosa times, later Times-gazette
Suspended from 1861?-66
A Ag 11,D 15,29 1841;Ap 27 1842;F 1,Je 21 1843;F 14 1844;D 24 1845;Ap 8 1846;Ap 13 1847-Mr 22 1849;S 2 1852;Jl 15 1853;D 14 1854;N 22 1855;Ap 9 1857-Ap 14 1860;My 15,O 9 1867-71
ATuC S-D 1868
DLC D 1 1838;Ja 7,N 20 1840;Ap 30,Je 11 1841;D 11 1844-46;F 11 1858;Ja 15 1859-My 10 1861
MBAt [1838;40-44]
NcD Ja 11 1841;S 12 1849;Jl 14 1851(broadside)

Tuscaloosa INQUIRER.
A D 8 1831

Tuscaloosa JOURNAL. w Mr 29 1894-96||?
A O 10,24 1894;Jl 24 1895
ATuC Ap 1894-96

Tuscaloosa JOURNAL. w 1927-29||?
ATuC O 1927-28

Tuscaloosa NEWS. d 1910+
1915?-28? as Tuscaloosa news and times-gazette
A Jl-D 1911;Jl 1912-Je,O 1923-S 1930
ATuC Ag 1910-[15]21-[31]+
WHi My 29 1916
—w ed *See* West Alabama breeze

Tuscaloosa OBSERVER. *See* Times-gazette

RECONSTRUCTIONIST. w
A Je 6 1868

Weekly RECORD. w N 25 1907-
ATuC 1908

Tuscaloosa REPUBLICAN. *See* Tuscaloosa chronicle

REPUBLICAN banner. w S 4 1868-
ATuC S-O 1868

SPIRIT of the age. *See* State rights expositor and spirit of the age

STATE journal and flag. w Jl 4 1833-D 25 1846||
1833-N 2? 1843 as Flag of the union. United with Montgomery advertiser to form Weekly flag and advertiser, later Montgomery weekly advertiser (Montgomery)
A D 18 1833;F 12-19 1834;My 21,Je 18,27,Jl 11 1835-Jl 23 1836;Jl 25 1838;Ja 9-D 1846
CtY Jl 18,S 12 1833
DLC Jl 11 1833;Mr 26 1834;Ja 23 1836;broadside extra 1840;Mr 20,Je 19,Ag 21,O-N 20,D 1846
GAtCo O 16 1839
MBAt Ja 15 1834;F 24,D 6 1837;Jl 20,N 16 1842[43]Ja 5 1844
MWA Ja 2 1836
NcD Ja 18 1843

STATE rights expositor and spirit of the age. w O 7 1829-34||
1829-D 1? 1832 as Spirit of the age
A D 22 1832
DLC O 7 1829;Ja 12 1833
MWA My 23 1832;S 14 1833
PEL D 15 1832-Mr 8 1834

Sunday SUN. w 1900-01||?
ATuC Mr 1900-01

TIMES-GAZETTE. w Ja 1 1847-1908||?
1847-Ja 1872 as Tuscaloosa observer; F? 1872-96? Tuscaloosa times; 1897?-1901? Sunday times
A Ap 16 1847;N 1873-S 1887;Ap 21 1899-1903; 06-Je 1908
ATuC N 1868-72;74-79;81-1908
KHi S 23 1850
NcD F 14 1853;Mr 8-15 1865;Je 17 1871;Jl 31 1872;N 1908

Tuscaloosa TIMES-GAZETTE. d 1888-1914||?
1888?-1901? as Evening times. United with Tuscaloosa news to form Tuscaloosa news and times-gazette, later Tuscaloosa news
A Ja 11,14,19,Mr 25 1889;O 27 1894;Je 30 1898; 1903-Je 1912
ATuC Mr 1903[04-05]-[08]-[10]-[13]14

Tuscaloosa VINDICATOR. w D 2 1892-93||?
ATuC 1892-O 1893

WEST ALABAMA breeze. w Ap 5 1889-1929||?
1889-1907? pub in Northport
A F 20 1890;O 27 1898;Ag 1899-O 1911;13-Jl 1918
ATuC 1889-1921
—d ed *See* Tuscaloosa news

Tuscaloosa WHIG. w
DLC Ja 21 1840

YOUNG American. w
A Ja 1 1855

TUSCUMBIA

ALABAMIAN-DISPATCH. *See* Tuscumbia times 1831+

AMERICAN star. sm 1901-19||?
Negro
A 1901-12

CLARION. *See* Sheffield enterprise (Sheffield)

COLBERT county banner. w Mr 1 1895-96||?
ATsC 1895-Je 13 1896

COLBERT county reporter. w S 14 1911+
A 1915-28;33+
ATsC 1911+

Tuscumbia DEMOCRAT. w Ap 6 1878-F 1883||
ATsC 1878-81
NcD Mr 22,My 3 1879;Jl 24-31 1880

Tuscumbia DISPATCH. w 1886-Jl 1907||
1886-F 13 1902 as Weekly dispatch. United with North Alabamian to form Alabamian-dispatch, later Tuscumbia times
A Ag 1899-Mr 1907
ATsC N 1886-Je 20 1907

Tuscumbia ENQUIRER. w 1839?-
A My 17 1854
DLC Ja 10,F 14-21,Mr 21-Jl 18,Ag 1-15,29-S 19,O 3-17 1855
MWA O 27-N 3 1852

FRANKLIN chronicle. w Ap 9 1829-
DLC Ap 9,Jl 16 1829

FRANKLIN democrat. w O 9 1840-
DLC O 9 1840
P-M N 13 1845

FRANKLIN enquirer. w Mr 13? 1824-
A Mr 24-Je 9 1824
DLC Mr 27,Ap 14 1824

NORTH ALABAMIAN. *See* Tuscumbia times 1831+

Tuscumbia PATRIOT. w F 10? 1827-My 1828||?
United with Tuscumbia telegraph to form Telegraph and patriot?
A Ap 7 1827
Ct [1827]
DLC Ag 11-18 1827

STATES rights democrat.
A Je 1-D 21 1860

TELEGRAPH and patriot. w
-My 31 1828 as Tuscumbia telegraph
A O 31 1827-My 21,31-Jl 19 1828

Tuscumbia TIMES. w 1831+
1831-Jl 1907 as North Alabamian (1866?-Ja 1875 North Alabamian and times) Ag 1907-Ag 5 1924 Alabamian-dispatch
A Ag 30 1834;D 1836-Jl 7 1838;Ag 8 1840-Ap 1842;Jl 12 1844-Je 1848;Je-D 1860;My 11 1866; S 4 1873;75-78;O 1904-19;N 1926-28;Ap 1932+
ATsC O 1870-Mr 1872;Ap 27 1876+
Ct [1833;35]
CtY Ap 20 1839
GAtCo Ap 6 1839
ICHi S 29 1865
MBAt S 1 1865
MWA O 29 1847
NcD Jl 23,Ag 27 1880;O 28 1881;Je 23,Jl 14,S 22,D 29 1882
NcU My 9 1840
OCHi F 8 1861
WHi N 17 1865;F 28,D 7 1866

Tuscumba TIMES. w 1865||?
United with North Alabamian to form North Alabamian and times, later Tuscumbia times

TUSCUMBIAN. w Ag 25 1824-
DLC Jl 26,Ag 30 1826

TUSKEGEE

Weekly GAZETTE. w D 12 1885-S 23 1887||
ATkC Ja 8-S 1887

MACON county democrat. *See* Tuskegee reporter

MACON mail. w Mr 15 1876-Ag 20 1884||?
United with Tuskegee weekly news to form News and mail, later Tuskegee news
A F 1881-Je 1884
ATkC Ap 1876-Ag 20 1884
NcD Jl 21 1880;D 13 1882

MACON republican. w 1845-61||?
Title varies: Tuskegee republican
A N 8 1849-O 2,D 1856-D 8 1859
P-M D 23 1858

Tuskegee NEWS. w Mr 1? 1865+
Ag 1884-87? as News and mail
A S 27 1866;Mr 27 1873-Ap 13 1882;N 26 1891; Ag 1899-Ag 1914;Ag 1917;D 1919-Ja 1924;D 1925;Ap 1932+
ATkC S 27-D 13 1866;Ja-Ap 1867[68-74]-[86]+
NcD Mr 20,Ap 3 1879
WHi O 6 1887

Tuskegee REPORTER. w Ap 14 1892-O 21 1898||
Ap-N 4 1892 as Macon county democrat
ATkC 1892-My 11 1894;98

Tuskegee REPUBLICAN. *See* Macon republican

UNION SPRINGS

BULLOCK county breeze. w Mr 4 1902-18||?
A Mr 1902-11
AUsC 1902-11;13-D 3 1918

BULLOCK county guide. w 1876-
NcD My 5 1879

BULLOCK county reporter. w Jl 29 1887-89||?
ACeC 1887-89
AUsC D 23 1887-D 20 1889

Union Springs HERALD. w O 1? 1869+
F 1871-91 as Union Springs herald and times
A F 22,Mr 26,My 14 1884;Je 15 1887;Ap 11 1894;O 1900-17;N 20 1919;20-28;S 1929+
AUsC 1871-84;87-1905;07+

SOUTHERN home journal. w
A N 6 1861

Union Springs TIMES w F 21 1866-Ja 25 1871||
United with Union Springs herald to form Union Springs herald and times, later Union Springs herald
A complete
AUsC F 27 1867-71
MWA F 20 1867

ALABAMA (*Continued*)

UNIONTOWN

CANEBRAKE herald. w 1886?-1914||?
A 1886;88-94;96-98;Ap 1900-14
AMaC [D 3 1886-Ja 20 1887]F 19 1892-[94]-[96]-[99-1901]-10;F 19 1911-12

CANEBRAKE news. w 1878-86||?
1878-85? as Uniontown press
A 1879-83;85-86
AMaC 1885[Ja-My 1886]

NEGRO leader. w 1909-16||?
Negro
A Ja-N 1915
AMaC 1912-13

Uniontown PRESS. *See* Canebrake news

SOUTHERN republican. w?
A F 10 1869;F 10 1870-Mr 15 1871

VERNON

Vernon CLIPPER. w 1879-80||?
AVC Jl 11 1879-D 17 1880

Vernon COURIER. w Je 6 1886-S 29 1904||
Merged with Lamar democrat
A Jl 1899-1904
AVC complete

LAMAR democrat. w Jl 10 1896+
A 1915-22;33+
AVC 1896-1924;26+

LAMAR news. w N 8 1883-Jl 21 1887||
AVC complete

Vernon PIONEER. w Ja 1 1875-78||?
AVC My 27 1875-O 11 1878

WARRIOR

To 1889? as Warrior Station

Weekly ADVANCE and guide. w 1884-86||?
1884-85? as Weekly advance
A Ja 11-D 6 1885

BREEZE. w 1888-1907||?
A N 1896-Ag 1899

Warrior ENTERPRISE.
A Ja-Ap 4 1885

MINERAL age. w 1884-87||?
AOC Ap 21,My 26,Je 30,Jl 7,S 15 1885;Ja 31,F 8,My 18 1886

WARRIOR STATION. *See* WARRIOR

WATERLOO

Waterloo RECORD. w
AFlC 1889-90

Waterloo TRIBUNE. w 1896-97||?
AFlC 1897

WEDOWEE

AMERICAN eagle. *See under* Jacksonville

NEWS JOURNAL. w 1892-Mr 28 1902||
1892-97? as Toiler; 1898?-99 Randolph toiler. Followed by Randolph star, later Randolph press?
A O 1895-98
AWC F 26 1897-N 18,D 9 1898-1902

RANDOLPH press. w Ap 11 1902+
Follows News journal? 1902-Ap 3 1926? as Randolph star
A Jl 1934+
AWC 1902-Ap 10,O 1915-My,O 1916-My,S 19 1917-Ja 3,D 7 1924-D 18 1925;26+

RANDOLPH star. *See* Randolph press

RANDOLPH toiler. *See* News journal

TOILER. *See* News journal

WEST BLOCTON

Blocton ENTERPRISE. w 1906+
A Ag 1906-28;Ag 1933

WETUMPKA

ALABAMA constitution. w My 13 1870-Ap 2 1875||
1870-D 11 1874 as Elmore republican
AWeC complete

ALABAMA times. w Je 5 1840-
Follows Wetumpka courier
A Ag 21-28,S 11-18,O-N 13,D 4-18 1840;Ja 1,F 19-26,Mr 19,Ap 2-16,30,My 14,28,Je 16,30 1841
DLC Je 26,N 27 1840

ALABAMIAN. *See* Wetumpka times-democrat

Wetumpka ARGUS. w 1836?-67||
1839? as Wetumpka argus and sentinel; 1839?-F 5 1840 Wetumpka argus and commercial advertiser; Ja 5? 1847-57 State guard
A My 15 1839-Mr,Ap 10,24 1844;S 10 1852
DLC My 16 1841;My 11-Je,Jl 13-Ag 17,S 14-21,O 5 1847;Mr 21-My,Je 13-Ag 1,15-S 5,O 3 1848
GDE N 12 1852
MBAt Mr 26 1839;F 16 1842;Ja 18-25 1843
NcD N 1,15,D 20 1840;F 28,Ap 24 1844
TxU My 13 1851
—d, sw ed *See* State guard

CENTRAL Alabamian. *See* Wetumpka times-democrat

Wetumpka COURIER. w My 8 1839-F? 1840||
Followed by Alabama times
A F 28 1840
MBAt Jl 10 1839

Wetumpka DEMOCRAT. *See* Wetumpka herald

Wetumpka DISPATCH. w
-Jl 10 1857? as Dorsey's dispatch
A S 22-O 13 1854;S 1856-N 13 1857

DORSEY'S dispatch. *See* Wetumpka dispatch

ELMORE democrat. w F 7 1885-N 14 1889||
1885-Je 27 1889 as Elmore express. United with Wetumpka times to form Wetumpka times-democrat
AWeC complete

ELMORE despatch. w
AWeC O 1899-Ag 3 1900

ELMORE express. *See* Elmore democrat

ELMORE republican. *See* Alabama constitution

Wetumpka GAZETTE. w 1869||?
A Ja 26 1869

HARRY of the West. w Ap 10- 1844||?
Campaign paper
DLC Ap 24 1844

Wetumpka HERALD. w Ja 1895+
1895-Ag 25 1898 as Wetumpka democrat; 1898-Ag 4 1927 Weekly herald
A O 1918-28;32+
AWeC 1895+

PEOPLE'S banner. *See* Wetumpka times-democrat

REFORM advocate. w S 29 1892-S 1 1898||
United with Wetumpka democrat to form Weekly herald, later Wetumpka herald
AWeC complete

Wetumpka SENTINEL and advertiser. w 1837-38||
United with Wetumpka argus to form Wetumpka argus and sentinel, later Wetumpka argus
GAtCo Je 8 1838
MBAt D 7 1838

SOUTHERN dial, and African monitor. w 1858?-
CSmH D 1 1858

Wetumpka SPECTATOR. w 1856?-
A O 3,N 14 1856-O 6 1857;Je 2 1861
MWA F 8 1859

Daily STATE guard. d
A 1849

Semi-weekly STATE guard. sw
A F 3-6,Ap 24 1851;S 10 1852

STATE guard. w *See* Wetumpka argus

Wetumpka TIMES-DEMOCRAT. w Mr 27 1875-93||?
1875-O 1877 as People's banner; N 1877-80? Central Alabamian; 1881? Times and Alabamian; 1882?-N 1889 Wetumpka times
A Jl 24 1875;Ja-S 7 1880
AWeC 1875-80;82-85;S 20 1888-93

Wetumpka WHIG. w
A N 13 1846;Ja 15 1847

WINFIELD

Winfield ENTERPRISE. w? 1899-
AHmC 1899

Winfield JOURNAL. w 1926+
A Ag 28-S 4 1930[34]+
AHmC 1927;29+

Winfield NEWS. w 1929-31||?
AHmC 1929-31

Winfield WATCHMAN. 1914||?
AHmC 1914

YORK

Early years as York Station

York HERALD. w 1910-13||?
ALnC Je 16-D 23 1910;Ja-D 14 1911

York NEWS. w Jl 1887-90||?
ALnC F 14 1888-90

York weekly PRESS. w 1913-18||?
ALnC F 21 1913-16;Mr 30 1917-Mr 1918

SUMTER county journal. w 1884?+
A N 1922-28;Ap 1932+
ALnC Mr-D 1921;23;27-30;32+

York TIMES. w 1890-D 19 1891||
ALnC 1891

YORK STATION. *See* YORK

ALASKA

ANCHORAGE

ALASKA labor news. w S 30 1916-Jl 14 1917||
Merged with Anchorage times
AlHi O 1916-Je 1917
WaUW S 30-O 7 1916

Weekly ALASKAN. w D 4 1915-Jl 1917||
DLC F 19 1916
WaUW 1915-My 6 1916

Anchorage ALASKAN. w Ag 5? 1920-
AlHi Ag 12-O 1920

Anchorage weekly ALASKAN. w N 11 1923-25||?
AlHi 1923-F 1925

Anchorage daily ALASKAN. d 1923?-25||?
AlHi F 5,Mr 27,29 1924-F 1925

COOK INLET pioneer. *See* Anchorage times

Anchorage weekly DEMOCRAT. w D 14 1915-Mr? 1917||
1915-F 26 1917 as Forty-ninth star
1915-My 13 1916 pub at Valdez
DLC Ja 22,F 5-19,Mr 5-19,Ap 1,22-My 13 1916
WaUW 1915-F 1917

FORTY-NINTH star. *See* Anchorage weekly democrat

Anchorage TIMES. w O 16 1914+
1914-My 1915 as Knik news (Knik) Je 5 1915-Je 3 1916 Cook Inlet pioneer
pub 1915+
AlHi Mr 27 1915-33
DL Ap 1922+
WaUW [1915-Je 17 1916]

Anchorage daily TIMES. d O 1 1915+
1915-My 23 1916 as Cook Inlet pioneer; My 24-31? 1916 Anchorage daily times and Cook Inlet pioneer
pub 1915+
AlHi My 1-3,7-23,25-28,31-Je 2,4-13,20 1916+
IU F 13-S 2 1919
NN [Ja-My 1922;Ja-Mr 1926]+
WaU [Je 12-Ag 1934]+
WaUW [O 23 1915-Ap 10 1917]

CHENA

TANANA miner. w,sw Ag 1 1906-Jl 26 1909||
Title varies with frequency. United with Fairbanks daily news to form Fairbanks daily news-miner
1906-Ap? 1907 pub in Fairbanks; D? 1908 in Ridgetop
sw Ag-S? 1906
AlHi S 21,O 12 1906-Ap,Je 16 1907-Ja 11 1909
WaUW [Je 23 1907-09]
—d ed *See* Tanana daily miner (Fairbanks)

CHITINA

Chitina LEADER. w S 24 1910-28||?
AlHi 1910-N 1928

CORDOVA

Weekly ALASKA times. *See* Cordova times

Cordova ALASKAN. *See* Cordova daily times Alaskan

Cordova Sunday HERALD. d,w Jl 1 1918-Ap 13 1919||
1918-Ap 6 1919 as Cordova daily herald (d)
AlHi Ag 8 1918-19

NORTH star. d Ap 24 1909-Ja 22 1911||
AlHi Ag 25-26,S 30 1909;Ja 7-Jl 28 1910

Cordova TIMES. w My 4 1913-1932||?
1913-26 as Weekly Alaska times
AlHi 1913-D 16 1916
WaUW [My-N 9 1913;Ag 22 1914-My 13 1916]

Cordova daily TIMES. d 1914+
AlHi Jl 3 1919+
WaU My 10 1934+

Cordova daily TIMES ALASKAN. w,d Je 16 1906-My 31 1915||
1906-O 1908 as Cordova Alaskan (w)
NN Ag 17 1911-Ja 1912
WaUW [Ja 23-O 1906]O 26 1908-Ja,Je[Ag-D 1909;F 1910-15]

COUNCIL CITY

Council City NEWS. w Mr 15 1902-Ja 5 1907||
AlHi complete

DOUGLAS

ALASKA sourdough. w S 1-D 26 1911||
AlHi S 1-15,29-D 1911
NN O 2,D 5 1911

DOUGLAS ISLAND news. *See* Alaska daily press (Juneau)

ALASKA (*Continued*)

FAIRBANKS

Weekly ALASKA citizen. w Mr 6 1910-Ja 26 1920||
AlHi Ap 9 1910-Ja 20 1919
IU F 10 1919-20
WaUW Jl 23 1910[Ap 1912-N 3 1913]Ag 17-O 19 1914[Ja 18 1915-F 1917]

Daily ALASKA citizen. d 1917?-Ja 30 1920||
AlHi Jl 1919-20

ALASKA socialist. sm S 29 1913-F 24 1915||
WaUW [1913-F 1914]

Fairbanks HERALD. w Jl 4-Ag 8 1915||
WaUW complete

MINERS' union bulletin. w Ja 20 1907-10||?
WHi D 21 1908-Ag 8 1910
WaUW Ja 20[D 1907-F 22]Ag 30-S 1909;F 21 1910

Weekly Fairbanks NEWS. w S 19 1903-F 24 1909||
WaUW complete
—d ed *See* Fairbanks daily news-miner

Fairbanks daily NEWS-MINER. d S 19 1903+
1903-Jl 1909 as Fairbanks daily news (Jl- 1909? Fairbanks daily news-miner and Tanana tribune)
AlHi Ag 18 1911+
InNcHi D 21 1904
PP [1930]+
WHi N 29 1917;Jl 9-S 13 1923;S 30-O 6 1927[Ja 20 1928-Mr 6 1929]
WaU Ag 1934+
WaUW [Jl 18 1905-F 24 1909;Jl 24 1909-D 15 1916]F 24 1917
—w ed *See* Weekly Fairbanks news

NORTHERN light. *See* Tanana tribune

SOCIALIST press. w Je 20 1914-S 18 1915||
WaUW [Je-O 1914;Ja 23-My 22]S 18 1915

Fairbanks daily STAR. d Jl 1-Ag 8 1910||
AlHi Jl 29-Ag 7 1910

TANANA daily miner. d Ag? 1906-
WaUW S 30 1906
—w,sw ed *See* Tanana miner (Chena)

TANANA tribune. w S 8 1906-Jl 22 1909||
1906-S 14 1907 as Northern light. United with Fairbanks daily news-miner to form Fairbanks daily news-miner and Tanana tribune, later Fairbanks daily news-miner
AlHi S 29 1906-S 7 1907;Ja 18-N 6 1908
WaUW [N 1906-S 14 1907]-09

Fairbanks weekly TIMES. w S 3? 1905-N 1 1916||
1905-Je? 1906 as Fairbanks Sunday times
AlHi Jl 14 1906-O 2 1916
NN O 16 1911; N 17 1913-O 2 1916
WaUW S 17,N 5 1905[S-N 11 1912]Ag-O 19[N 1914-D 20 1915]Ja-O 2 1916

Fairbanks daily TIMES. d My 23 1906-N 1 1916||
Sunday issues as Fairbanks Sunday times
AlHi My 25 1906-S 1916
WaUW [Jl 8 1906-Ja 1916]

FORT ADAMS

Yukon press. ir Ja 1 1894-Ap 20 1899||
Issued as follows: Ja 1,My 1 1894;Je 1 1895;Ja 1,Je 1896;Ap 1897;Mr 1898 (typewritten) Ja 15,F 28,Mr 17,22,Ap 1,20 1899
DLC Ja 1 1894(photostat)
MWA My 1 1894

FORT WRANGELL. *See* WRANGELL

HAINES

Haines PIONEER press. w My 17 1909-Jl 19 1913||
AlHi 1909-Je,Jl 19 1913
WaUW [D 17 1909-O 1911;Ap 13 1912-13]

HOT SPRINGS

Hot Springs ECHO and Tanana citizen. w Jl 20 1909-Je 8 1913||
Followed by Tanana news (Tanana)
AlHi Jl-N 14,D 19 1909;Ja 8-F,Mr 12-Ap,My 21,Je 1910-Mr 4,Ap 29-Je 3,17-Jl 4,18 1911-13
NN N 11 1911
WaUW [Je 1911-13]

Hot Springs POST. w O 1 1908-My 15 1909||
AlHi complete

HYDER

Hyder ALASKA miner. *See* Hyder weekly miner

Hyder weekly HERALD. w S 8 1924-D 23 1933||
AlHi complete

Hyder weekly MINER. w O 24 1919-Ap 7 1924||
1919-Ja? 1923 as Hyder Alaska miner
AlHi O 24,N 1919-Ja 3,O 27,D 1923-24

IDITAROD

Iditarod NUGGET. w S 3 1910-Ag 30 1911||
AlHi 1910-Ja 18,F-My 24,Je-Jl 12,Ag 16-30 1911
WaUW complete

Iditarod PIONEER. w Jl 10 1910-S 27 1919||
AlHi 1910-14
WaUW 1910-S 1,N 1917-Je 1918

JUNEAU

Early years as Juneau City

ALASKA capital. w D 1 1909-Je 15 1910||
WaUW 1909-Je 8 1910

ALASKA daily capital. *See* Juneau daily capital

Daily ALASKA dispatch. d,w My 1 1899-S 27 1919||
Sunday issues as Sunday Alaska dispatch. Followed by Alaska dispatch, later Alaska weekly (Seattle)
w My 4-S 1919
AlHi [Ap 1901-Mr 14]-D 1903;O 1906-19
DLC Ja 20 1900-19
WaUW [Jl 29 1899-1915]-Je 1 1919

Weekly ALASKA dispatch. w 1915?-18||?
MnHi Mr 9 1918
WaUW Ja 3 1915;Ap 1916-Je 15 1918

Daily ALASKA empire. d N 2 1912+
1912-D 7 1926 as Alaska daily empire
Mr 10 1935 is Progress ed
AlHi 1912+
DLC [Ja 17 1913-O 1914;Mr 25-D 1915;Mr 13-S 1916]Ap 2 1917+
NN S 1922+
TxGR Mr 10 1935
WHi F 8-9,Ap 23 1926;27+
WaUW [1912]+

ALASKA free press. w 1887-91||?
KHi Ja 26 1889-F 1891

ALASKA journal. w Mr-O 14 1893||
AlHi Ap-O 1893
CU-B Ag 19 1893

ALASKA miner. w 1896-Mr 3 1900||
AlHi O 23 1897-98
DLC F 10-17,Mr 3 1900

ALASKA mining record. *See* Alaska record-miner

ALASKA news. w O 1893-97||
Merged with Alaska miner
DLC Ja 25 1894
WaS [Ap 30-Je 23 1896]
WaUW [My 10 1894-My 7 1896]

ALASKA Sunday morning post. w F 1 1914-D 5 1915||
Suspended Ag 2-O 18 1914
AlHi My 31 1914-15
WaUW [My 17-Je]D 13 1914[Ja 31-N 1915]

ALASKA daily press. w,d Je 8 1898+
Je-N 1898 as Fort Wrangell news; N 23 1898-Je 24 1921 Douglas Island news; Jl 1 1921-Mr 3 1933 Stroller's weekly and Douglas Island news; Mr 10 1933-Jl 19 1935 Alaska press
Je-N 1898 pub in Fort Wrangell; N 23 1898-Je 24 1921 in Douglas and Treadwell
w 1898-Jl 1935
AlHi N 23 1898-1902;05;07-17;19+
DLC Ja 24,F 14,28 1900;Jl 31 1901[Mr 25-D 1903]Mr 9-Je 8,23-Jl 1904
IU Ja 31 1919-Je 3 1921
OrU 1930[31-32]
WaUW 1898-Je 1917

ALASKA daily record. d F 1899-My 8 1911||
1899-1900? as Daily evening record and weekly Mining record; 1901-05? as Daily record-miner; 1906?-S 2 1907 Alaska record-miner
AlHi Jl-D 1902;N 28 1903-Je 28 1905;Ja 6-Mr 30,S 4 1907-Ap 8,My 24 1910-Ap 2 1911
DLC [F 23-D 1903;Ap 2-Jl 1904;S-D 1906]-[09]-11
WaUW [O 16 1902-N 1905;F 3-O 12 1906]Ag 12,D 21 1908[My 17 1909-11]

ALASKA record-miner. w,sw Ap 5 1888-1902||?
1888-Je 1894 as Juneau City mining record; Mr 1-Jl 19 1899 Weekly mining record
Jl 26 1899-F 1900? Alaska mining record
AlHi O 25 1888;F 14,Je 6,Jl 11,N 1889-F 13 1890
CSmH Ja 1898
DLC Ja 27-F 3 1894;Ja 18-F 8,Mr 1,22-D 27 1899
NN [Mr 10 1900-Mr 22 1902]
WHi Mr 26 1891
WaUW O 24 1899[Ja 22 1891-D 15 1892;Mr 1893-Je 2,Jl 30 1894-Jl 8 1895;Ja-N 1897]Ag 17 1898

ALASKA searchlight. w D 17 1894-F 28 1898||
AlHi 1894-D 4 1897
WaS [F-Je 6 1896]
WaUW [1894-N 23 1895;Je 27-O 10 1896]O 9-23 1897

ALASKA transcript. w,d D? 1903-11||
My 6-S 9 1909 as Juneau daily transcript (d)
AlHi O 13 1906-O 1907;Ja 11 1908-My 1 1909
WaUW Ja 14 1904[Ja 28-O 14 1905]Ja 13-20 1906;O 3 1908[Je 10-S 9 1909]

ALASKA truth. w 1899-1902||?
NN [Mr-O 1900]

ALL-ALASKA review. m My 1915-
1915-16 pub in Seward
Suspended D 1916-F 1917
Ag-S 1915 a combined issue
AlHi 1915-S 1917

Juneau daily CAPITAL. d,w Mr 5 1920-Jl 29 1923||
Mr 5-D 20 1920 as Alaska daily capital
Sunday issues as Juneau Sunday capital
d 1920-My 27 1921
WaUW Mr,Je 30-O 1920[Jl-Ag 1921]

GLEAM. w O 8 1916-S 14 1919||
Suspended from D 7 1916-Mr 16 1919
AlHi Mr 16-S 1919
WaUW O-N 5,D 3-17 1916

Weekly MINING record. *See* Alaska record-miner

Daily RECORD-MINER. *See* Alaska daily record

Juneau SPIRIT. w Mr 19 1921-F 23 1922||
not pub F 10 1922
AlHi 1921-Ja,F 17-23 1922

STROLLER'S weekly and Douglas Island news. *See* Alaska daily press

Juneau daily TRANSCRIPT. *See* Alaska transcript

KATALLA

Katalla HERALD. w Ag 10 1907-Jl 24 1909||
AlHi 1908-09
WaUW 1907-Ag 1 1908

KETCHIKAN

Ketchikan ALASKA chronicle. d Jl 9 1919+
Sunday issues as Ketchikan Sunday chronicle
AlHi 1919+

Ketchikan Sunday CHRONICLE. *See* Ketchikan Alaska chronicle

FIRST CITY news. w O 2? 1925-Jl 2 1926||
AlHi N 27 1925-26

Ketchikan weekly JOURNAL. w Jl 3? 1919-Ap 1 1920||
AlHi Jl 17 1919-20

Ketchikan morning MAIL. *See* Ketchikan times

Ketchikan daily MINER. d D 28 1905-D 2 1913||
AlHi 1906-Ja 23 1908;My 4-6,S 29 1909

Ketchikan MINER. w F 1 1907-S 16 1915||
AlHi F 1? 1907-Ap 17 1909;N 10 1911-15

Ketchikan MINING journal. w Ja 5 1901-Mr 9 1907||
Merged with Ketchikan miner
AlHi Ja-Ap 6,20-Ag 3,17-N,D 14 1901-Ja 23,F-Ap 19,My 8-Je 16,30-S 10,24-O 1,15-N,D 10 1904-Ja,F 11-My 23,Je 8,22 1905-Ag 19,S 22,O 7,20-D 8,22 1906-07
DLC O 5 1901

Ketchikan daily NEWS. d Mr 6 1922-Je 8 1923||
Suspended from Ag 9-D 8 1922
AlHi complete
WaPS [1922]

PROGRESSIVE. w Ja 18 1913-Ag 15 1917||?
1913-S 26 1914 pub in Petersburg
Suspended from S 26-O 24 1914
AlHi 1914
WaUW [Ja-N 15 1913;F 28-S]O 24-N 1914[F-Jl 24 1915]

Daily PROGRESSIVE-MINER. *See* Ketchikan times

Ketchikan TIMES. d Jl 1913-My 8 1920||
1913-S 21 1915 as Ketchikan morning mail; S 22 1915-Ap 30 1919 Daily progressive-miner
AlHi S 23 1915-20
IU 1919-20
WaUW [S 22-N 20 1913;D 1915-S 20 1916]

Ketchikan TRIBUNE. w O 24 1930-Jl 3 1931||
Merged with Ketchikan Alaska chronicle
AlHi complete

KNIK

Knik NEWS. *See* Anchorage times w (Anchorage)

McCARTHY

AVALANCH. w Ag 5-O 28 1916||
WaUW complete

COPPER bee. w F 19 1916-
WaUW F-Mr 4 1916

McCarthy weekly NEWS. w S 17 1918-Ap 30 1927||
AlHi 1919-27
DLC [S 29 1923-27]

McGRATH

KUSKO times. *See under* Takatna

METLAKAHTLA

METLAKAHTLAN. ir N 1888-D 1891||
CaB Mr 1889

NENANA

Nenana NEWS. w,d,tw O 1 1916-Ag 2 1923||
Ap 1 1918-N 16 1920 as Nenana daily news
w 1916-Mr 30 1918;d Ap 1 1918-N 16 1920
AlHi D 1916-17;Ap 1918-23
WaPS [1919-20]

NOME

ARCTIC weekly sun. w -Ag 11 1900||
Merged with Nome daily chronicle, later Nome chronicle
CLM Jl 29 1900

Nome daily BULLETIN. d
NNC Je 12,18,Ag 12,S 23,28-30,O 8-9,15,21 1925
—w ed *See* Nome nugget

ALASKA (*Continued*)

NOME—*Continued*

Nome CHRONICLE. d,w,bw Ag 11 1900-Je 18 1901||
Ag 11-S 29 1900 as Nome daily chronicle (d) O 1900-Ap 1901 Nome weekly chronicle (w)
AlHi Ag 15-S 25,N 14 1900-01
CLM O 20,S 11 1900
NN S 13-14,20 1900

Nome daily GOLD digger. w,d O 25 1899-Jl 27 1910||
1899-Jl 22 1905 as Nome gold digger (w)
AlHi O 25 1899;Jl 4 1900-My 30,S-O 27,N 21-D 26 1906;Ja 31-Je 25 1910
CaQMM Jl 4 1900
DLC Jl 24 1901
MWA S 10,O 1 1902;F 24 1909
NN Je 6 1900
WHi Jl 22 1903
WaUW S 19-26 1900;Ag 7,D 25 1901;S 30,N 18 1903[N 16-D 14 1904;F 8-D 6 1905]Jl-Ag 1906;Ag 3-12 1908

Weekly Nome INDUSTRIAL worker. d,tw,w 1907?-Je 28 1919||
1907?-Ap 30 1918 as Daily Nome industrial worker (d) My-N 1918 Tri-weekly Nome industrial worker (tw)
AlHi D 7 1915-Je 1918

Nome NEWS. w,d,sw O 9 1899-Je 1 1906||
Merged with Nome nugget
w 1899-My 26 1900;d Je 26-S 29 1900
1901-06? d in summer, sw in winter
AlHi F 10-My 26,Je 28-N 17 1900;01-My 25 1905
CaQMM [1900]
DLC Jl 5,13,20,24,27,Ag 1,7,10,14,24,S 2,5 1901
NN S 15 1900
WHi Ap 5 1904
WaUW [1899-1902]

Nome NUGGET. sw,tw,w,d My 18 1901+
Title varies slightly
Suspended N 8 1934-Ja 1935
sw 1901-Je 1 1906;tw My 1918-O 29 1919;w N 1 1919-N 8 1934
AlHi Jl 9 1901-[05-Je 11 1906]Je 17 1910+
DLC Jl 23-Ag 6,16-S 6,O 30 1901;Jl 16 1902;Jl 18 1903;N 14 1912-[24]+
MWA F 24 1909
NN Ag 16-21,24,28-S 16,19 1911
NNC Ag 29,S 12 1925
WaUW [Jl 9 1901-Jl 24 1916]
—d ed 1925 *See* Nome daily bulletin

PETERSBURG

ALASKAN. w Jl 16? 1926-S 30 1932||
AlHi Jl 16 1926-32

Petersburg HERALD. w D 5 1914-Je 25 1926||
1914-F 29 1924 as Petersburg weekly report
Suspended from F 25-My 19 1926
AlHi complete
AlPP 1914-D 10 1920
IU [1919]-[22-23]-F[Mr 14-N 7 1924]
WaUW [1914-F 20,S 11 1915-Je 17]D 9-16 1916;Mr 2 1917

Petersburg PRESS. w Ag 27 1926+
pub 1926+
AlHi 1926+

PROGRESSIVE. *See under* Ketchikan

Petersburg weekly REPORT. *See* Petersburg herald

RAMPART

ALASKA forum. w S 27 1900-Ag 4 1906||
AlHi S 27,N 1900-F 14,Mr 7-14,Ap 11-Ag 22,S 12-O 5,N 23-30,D 9-21 1901;Ja 8,F 19 1902-My 6,20-Jl 2,O 22,D 10,24 1904-Ja,F 11-18,Ap 5-19,My-Jl 1,Ag 12-19,S 9-O 7 1905;Je-Ag 1906

YUKON VALLEY news. *See under* Tanana

RIDGETOP

TANANA miner. *See under* Chena

RUBY

Ruby CITIZEN. w O 1 1911-F 1912||
United with Ruby record to form Ruby record-citizen
AlHi 1912

Ruby RECORD-CITIZEN. w O 7 1911-Ag 3 1918||
1911-F 1912 as Ruby record
Suspended O 1917-Mr 9 1918
AlHi F-Mr 2,21 1912-18
WaUW complete

SELDOVIA

Seldovia HERALD. w D 13 1930-Je 17 1933||
AlHi complete

SEWARD

ALASKA evening post. d S 1 1915-Ja 31 1917||
United with Seward gateway to form Seward gateway and the Alaska evening post, later Seward gateway
AlHi 1915-16
WaUW [1915-17]

ALASKA weekly post. w S 9 1915-23||?
AlHi 1915-19
NN N 1919-N 20 1920
—d ed 1919-23 *See* Seward gateway

ALL-ALASKA review. *See under* Juneau

Seward GATEWAY. w,tw,d Ag 19 1904+
F 1 1917-N 27 1920 as Seward gateway and the Alaska evening post (title varies slightly)
d 1904-F 25?, D? 1921-S 18? 1933;
w F 26-N 1921
AlHi 1904+
DLC 1915-[Jl 1920-24]-[30]+
IU Mr 3 1919-20
MWA My 1 1914
NN N 18 1911[F-Mr 1917;S-D 1919]-[22-23]+
—d ed 1919-23 *See* Alaska weekly post

GATEWAY. w Ag 24 1904+
Title varies: Seward weekly gateway
Suspended 1919-23? and replaced by Alaska weekly post
AlHi S 1905-11
WaU My 19 1934+
WaUW [Ag 17 1907-F 5 1916]

Seward TRIBUNE. w My 9-O 3 1914||
WaUW complete

SITKA

ALASKA herald. w Je 27 1892-Je 9 1897||
Merged with Alaskan
AlHi complete
DLC Ja 8-15,Mr 26-My 5,26,Je 9-30,Jl 21-Ag 11,S 15 1894
MWA Jl 21 1894

ALASKA times. w,sm Ap 23 1869-S 13 1870||
Followed by Alaska times, later Territorial dispatch and Alaska times (Seattle)
sm Jl 23-S 13 1870
not pub My 28 1869;Jl 6 1870
CU-B 1869[70]
CtY My 28 1870
DLC 1869-Jl 2 1870
MB [My 21-O 16 1869]
MH [N 1869-Ja 1870]
MWA N 6,D 11-25 1869
OrHi O 23 1869

ALASKAN. w N 7 1885-1908||?
AlHi 1885-1905
C Jl 14 1888-Jl 20 1889;Ag 15 1891-93
CU-B D 9 1885-F 20,Mr 20-Jl,S-D 4,18 1886;Ja 29-F 5,19-26,Ap 23 1887
DLC Ap 17-My 8,Jl 25-O 23,N 27-D 4 1886;Jl 26-F 10 1894;Ag 21 1897-S 21 1907
KHi F 23 1889-O 27 1894
MB Jl 17 1886
MWA Ag 7 1886;Ag 11 1888;Ag 5? 1893
MiU [1903]
NN Je 14 1891
PPCHi Je 21 1899
WHi N 28 1885-F 13 1886;F 29 1896-Ag 17 1907
WaUW [Mr 17 1894-N 11 1905]

ARROWHEAD. Ap 7 1934-
AlHi 1934-Je 22 1935

Sitka CABLEGRAM. w F 2 1905-Je 1906||
WHi Je 8 1905

Sitka POST. sm O 20 1876-Je 5 1877||
Not pub Mr 5,My 20 1877
DLC N 1876-77
MWA Ap 20 1877
Wa O 20 1876

Sitka PROGRESS. w D 25 1925-27||?
AlHi 1925-Ag 19 1927

Sitka SUN. w,ir,m O 30 1920-Mr 30 1928||
w 1920;m Ja 1 1921-Mr 25? 1922
AlHi 1920-Mr,N 30 1927-28

Sitka TIMES. ir S 19-N 7 1868||?
CU-B S 19,O 19-N 7 1868
DLC S 19 1868(photostat)

Sitka TRIBUNE. w My 12 1922-D 18 1925||
Suspended from D 12 1924-My 1925
not pub S 10 1925
AlHi 1922-D 3 1925

Sitka WEEKLY. w Ja 18? 1929-
AlHi Ja 25-My 3 1929

SKAGWAY

ALASKA daily guide. d 1900-Ap 30 1905||
AlHi 1905

Daily ALASKAN. d F 1 1898-Jl 31 1924||
AlHi Ap 9-D 1901;Ja 5-Ag 28 1905;S 4 1906-Je,S 16 1907-24
DLC [F 24-D 1903;Mr-Jl 1904]
IU [1919]-Jl 26 1924
WaPS [1921]
WaUW [Je 1898-N 28 1900]Ja 17 1901-N 1920;Je 1921-24

Skagway ALASKAN. tw Je 1-Ag 31 1927||
AlHi complete

INTERLOPER. w My 5-D 26 1908||
AlHi complete

Skagway NEWS. w O 15 1897-1903||
AlHi F 18,Je 17-[Ag-N]1898-Ap 21 1899
MWA Ap 5(extra)1898

TAKATNA

KUSKO times. sw Ag 1 1920-D 24 1932||
1920-Je 9? 1921 pub in McGrath
Suspended Ap 23-D 10 1927?
AlHi Jl 16 1921-Ap 23,D 10 1927-32

TANANA

Tanana LEADER. w F 1 1909-Ag 25 1910||
Merged with Yukon Valley news
AlHi Jl 11 1909-10

Tanana NEWS. w Je 14-O 25 1913||
Follows Hot Springs echo and Tanana citizen (Hot Springs)
AlHi complete

YUKON VALLEY news. w Ag 3 1904-Ag 7 1917||
1904-Ag 7 1910 pub in Rampart
Suspended from Ag 7-S 22 1910
AlHi 1904-Ag 7 1907;S 22,O 1,22-D 1910
InNcHi O 19-26 1904
WaUW Mr 22[Ag 16 1905-Mr 13 1907]Mr 30,O 28,D 16 1911[Ap-Ag 10 1912]

TELLER

Teller NEWS. w Ap 1 1901-Ap 1 1902||?
DLC Jl 25 1901
MWA Ap 11 1901

PIONEER scout. bw 1921-Jl 19 1924||
AlHi Jl 28,O 20 1923-24

VALDEZ

ALASKA prospector. *See* Valdez weekly prospector

Valdez COMMONER. w Mr 8 1913-Je 26 1915||
DLC [1913-14]15
WaUW complete

FORTY-NINTH star. *See* Anchorage weekly democrat (Anchorage)

Valdez MINER. d,w Mr 3 1911+
Mr-S 21 1911 as Valdez daily miner; Ag 4-25 1912 Valdez miner and weekly prospector; Je 15-Jl 6 1918 Valdez weekly miner
d Mr-S? 1911
AlHi N 26 1911+
DLC [1911]+
WaU [1933-Mr 1934]+
WaUW [Ap 21-D 15 1912]Mr 2,23 1913

Valdez NEWS. w Mr 9 1901-Je 1907||
Merged with Valdez weekly prospector
AlHi 1901-Mr 23 1907
DLC F-Mr 7,21-Ag 8,22-O 10,31,N 14,D 12 1903

Valdez weekly PROSPECTOR. w F 13 1902-Ag 1 1912||
1902-Ag 13 1908 as Alaska prospector.
United with Valdez miner to form Valdez miner and weekly prospector, later Valdez miner
AlHi 1902-Mr 1903;Ja 12-D 14 1905;N 15 1906-S 1908;F-O 1 1909
DLC 1902-04;Ja 7,Ag 24 1905-12

Valdez daily PROSPECTOR. d 1905-My 7 1918||
AlHi My 15 1916-18
WaUW O 23 1909;O 6 1911[Ap 16 1912-S 19 1913]D 2 1914;Jl 15,D 3 1915[Mr 10-S 1916]

WRANGELL

Early years as Fort Wrangell?

ALASKA sentinel. *See* Wrangell sentinel

FORT WRANGELL news. *See* Alaska daily press (Juneau)

Wrangell SENTINEL. w N 20 1902+
1902-My 13 1909 as Alaska sentinel
pub S 1916+
AlHi 1902-Ap 9 1903;Ja 12 1905-F 11,Je 3 1909+
WaUW Ap 9 1914-15[S 9 1916-Mr 1917]

STICKEEN RIVER journal. w Ja 2? 1898-N 11 1899||
AlHi Ja 22 1898-99

ARIZONA

AJO

Ajo COPPER news. w Ap 29 1916-Mr 7 1935||
Az Complete
AzTP D 1932-35

ARIZOLA

OASIS. *See under* Nogales

ARIZONA CITY. *See* YUMA

BENSON

Benson BREEZE. *See* San Pedro Valley news

Benson weekly HERALD, w 1883-84||
MWA D 20 1884

Benson NEWS. *See* San Pedro Valley news

OASIS. *See under* Nogales

Benson PRESS. *See* San Pedro Valley news

SAN PEDRO Valley news w 1899+
1899-1900? as Benson breeze; 1901-14? Benson press; 1915-21 Benson signal; 1922-Je 1928 Benson news
pub 1903;Ag 1928+

ARIZONA (*Continued*)

BENSON—*Continued*

SAN PEDRO Valley news—*Continued*
Az Jl 10 1915-19;29+
AzTP Jl 21 1926-27;S 19 1930+
AzU F 14 1920;O 10 1925-Je 5 1926;Ap 12-26 1929

Benson SIGNAL. *See* San Pedro Valley news

BISBEE

ARIZONA daily lyre. *See* Bisbee daily review

ARIZONA daily orb. *See* Bisbee daily review

BREWERY gulch gazette. w Jl 6? 1931+
Az N 1934+
AzTP Jl 31 1931;My 26,Jl 21 1933;Ag 3,17,31 1934
NN D 29 1933

COCHISE review and Arizona daily orb. *See* Bisbee daily review

Bisbee evening MINER. d 1902-Ag 1911||
Az Ap 9 1906-F 1911
AzU N 1909-F 1910

Weekly ORB. w 1896-1900||?
AzU [Ap 10 1898-S 24 1899]

Bisbee evening ORE. d Ag 1914+
1914-Ag 31 1927 as Bisbee ore
Az Jl 1915+
AzTP anniversary ed 1916
AzU 1915-Mr 1916;18[19-28]

Bisbee daily REVIEW. d 1897+
1897 as Arizona daily lyre; 1898-Ap 30 1900 Arizona daily orb; My 3-D 29 1900 Cochise review and Arizona daily orb
pub [1903-06]+
Az Jl 17 1899-1900;My 3 1905+
AzTP S 1907+
AzU S 14 1898;Ja 22 1899[D 4 1901-03]-N 1918

Daily SQUARE dealer. d F?-Je? 1917||
Az My 9-Je 16 1917

BOWIE

Bowie ENTERPRISE. w 1913-20||?
Az Jl 1915-20

SAN SIMON Valley oil news. *See* San Simon Valley tribune

SAN SIMON Valley tribune. w 1911+
1911-S 13 1918 as Artesian belt; S 20 1918-F 24 1928 San Simon Valley news; Mr 2 1928-S 12 1930 San Simon Valley oil news
1911-Ag ? 1921 pub in San Simon
Az Jl 1915-[18]+
AzTP S 26 1930+

BUCKEYE

Buckeye Valley NEWS. w F 1912-23||?
Az My 1912-Je 1918

Buckeye Valley NEWS. w Ag 3 1933+
pub 1933+

Buckeye REVIEW. w D 25 1926-My 3 1935||
1925-N 1930 as Buckeye Valley review
Az 1931-35
AzTP S 26 1930-35

CAMP VERDE

VERDE news. m,sw Ap 1916-Jl 1 1917||
m Ap 1916-Ja 1917
Az Complete

CASA GRANDE

BULLETIN. w S 11 1913-Mr 2 1928||
United with Casa Grande Valley dispatch to form Casa Grande Valley dispatch and the bulletin. For Jl 6 1917-Mr 1 1918 *See* Casa Grande dispatch
Az D 1915-27
AzU O 18 1913;Ap 20 1918[19-20]-[26]-28

Casa Grande DISPATCH. w Ja 5 1912+
1912-Ja 2 1914 as Casa Grande times; Ja 9 1914-Je 29 1917 Casa Grande Valley dispatch and Casa Grande times; Jl 6 1917-Mr 1 1918,Mr 9 1928-Ja 18 1929 Casa Grande Valley dispatch and the bulletin
Az Ap 1912+
AzTP [1914-15;17-18;25-27]Jl 22 1932+
AzU F 9 1912-Ja 2,Ap 17 1914-18[30-34]

Casa Grande TIMES. *See* Casa Grande dispatch

VOICE of Arizona. w 1885-86||?
AzTP Jl 24 1886

CHANDLER

Chandler ARIZONAN. w 1912+
Resource eds Mr 22 1928;Mr 21 1929
Az Jl 1915+
AzTP Mr 22 1928;Mr 21 1929;Jl 19 1930-Ja 1932
CU-B Ag 20-27,O 1,N 5,19,D 1915-Mr 3,31-Jl 7 1916
KHi S 22 1927
WHi N 15 1912-Ap 14 1916

CHLORIDE

Chloride HERALD and Chloride mining review. w 1916-17||
1916-Ap 12 1917 as Chloride herald
Az D 1916-D 6 1917

Chloride MINING review. w 1916-Ap 12? 1917||
United with Chloride herald to form Chloride herald and Chloride mining review

CLIFTON

Clifton CLARION. w F 1883-Je 1889||
Merged with Valley bulletin (Solomonville), later Arizona bulletin (Safford)
AzTP 1885-[88-89]
CU-B Ag 1,22-29,S 26,O 10-17 1883

COPPER era; Consolidated with Duncan Valley news and Morenci leader. w Ap 24 1899+
1899-Ag 1911 as Copper era; S 1 1911-S 14 1929 Copper era and Morenci leader
Az Ag 31 1899-1900;05+
AzTP Jl 19 1930+
AzU S 15 1911-[26-34]+

MINING journal and Duncan Arizonian. w 1913-S 1919||
1913 as Mining journal. Merged with Copper era. . .
Az Jl 1915-S 4 1919

COOLIDGE

Coolidge EXAMINER. w Mr 7 1930+
Az 1930+

Coolidge NEWS. q,w Ap 14 1928+
q F 1932-Je 1933
Az 1928+
AzTP 1928+

COTTONWOOD

VERDE Valley times. Combined with Camp Verde enterprise. w F-S 1931||?
AzTP S 4 1931

COURTLAND

Courtland ARIZONAN. w F 13 1909-D 25 1920||
Az Jl 1915-20
AzTP Complete
AzU Jl 22 1911-20

DOS CABEZAS

COOPERATION. *See* Southwestern progress

COPPER review. *See* Southwestern progress

SOUTHWESTERN progress. m 1925-28||?
1925-27 as Copper review; Ja 1928 Cooperation
AzTP Je,Ag,O-N 1925;F,Ap-Je,S-O,D 1926;F 1927;Ja,Ap 1928

DOUGLAS

Douglas daily DISPATCH. w,d Mr 15 1902+
1902-Mr 1903 as Douglas dispatch (w)
pub 1902+
Az 1905-N 1906;F 1907-11;Jl 1915-O 1916;S 1923+
AzU [1913-20]

Douglas EXAMINER. w F 8 1907-
CoHi Ap 19 1907
WHi Je 9,11 (extra) 1907

Douglas daily INTERNATIONAL. d 1902-Mr 31 1925||
F 1902-Jl? 1903 as International; Ag? 1903-08 International-American
Az Jl 12-S 1912;Mr 1914-25
AzDD [My 23 1904-08]-12;14-25
AzTP D 26 1903;My 1914-S 1916;Ag 1923-25
AzU S 24 1911-[16-25]
MoHi Ja 1912(special ed)

INTERNATIONAL-American. *See* Douglas daily international

DUNCAN

Duncan ARIZONIAN. w 1908-13||
United with Mining journal (Clifton) to form Mining journal and Duncan Arizonian (Clifton)
Az Ap 1911-N 5 1913

DUNCAN Valley news. w 1914-S 21 1929||
1914-20 as Duncan news. United with Copper era and Morenci leader to form Copper era, consolidated with Duncan Valley news and Morenci leader
Suspended 1921-27?
Az Jl 1915-20

Duncan NEWS. *See* Duncan Valley news

FLAGSTAFF

ARIZONA champion. *See* Coconino sun

COCONINO sun. w S 1882+
1882-My 16 1891 as Arizona champion; My 23 1891-N? 1896 Coconino sun; D 3 1896-97 Flagstaff sun-democrat
1882-Ja 26 1883 pub in Peach Springs
N 25 1927 is 45th anniversary pioneer ed
pub 1891+
Az Ja-S 1897;F 1898+
AzTP Ja 5,O 1883-O 1885;86-87;89-92;Jl 1893-95;Ja-O 1896; N 25 1927;33+
AzU Je 4,18 1898[1901]-16;N 25 1927
CL N 25 1927
CLM N 25 1927
CU-B Ap 6,Je 29,S 28 1889;F 8 1890

Flagstaff DEMOCRAT. w 1888-N 26 1896||
Merged with Coconino sun to form Flagstaff sun-democrat, later Coconino sun
AzTP F 16 1895-96
CU-B Je 28,Jl 12,S 20 1889;Ja 31,F 14-21 1890

Flagstaff GEM. w 1898-1911||?
Az Ja 27 1898-My 16 1901

Flagstaff JOURNAL. w 1932+
Az My 22 1934+

NORTHERN Arizona leader. d,sw My 2 1916-Ap 21 1921||
d My 22 1917-19
Az Complete

Flagstaff SUN-DEMOCRAT. *See* Coconino sun

FLORENCE

ALTA. w S 20 1889-90||
CU-B O 18,N 22,D 20-27 1889; Ja 11,25 1890

ARIZONA blade. w 1900-01||
United with Florence tribune to form Arizona blade-tribune
AzTP Ag 10-18 1900;Jl 19 1901

ARIZONA blade-tribune. w 1902+
Formed by the union of Arizona blade and Florence tribune
My 1928 is Coolidge dam ed. pub by the Arizona blade-tribune and Casa Grande dispatch
Az S 1903+
AzTP [1918]22-[28]Jl 18 1930+
AzU 1902-05;19-20

ARIZONA citizen. *See under* Tucson

ARIZONA weekly enterprise. *See* Arizona enterprise (Tucson)

Florence TRIBUNE. w 1892-D 28 1901||
United with Arizona blade to form Arizona blade-tribune
Az My 1897-Ja 1901
AzTP Ag 25 1892;Je 14 1895;F 15 1896;Ap 5 1899
AzU Mr 26-My,S 1898-1901
CLM N 17 1894

Daily evening TRIBUNE. d D 14 1893-
AzTP D 16 1893

FORT WHIPPLE

ARIZONA miner. *See* Weekly journal-miner (Prescott)

GADSDEN

YUMA Valley news. w Jl 1923-24||?
1923-Mr? 1924 pub in Yuma
Az Jl 27 1923;Ja 25,Mr 7 1924
AzU Je 7,Ag 15,S 12 1924

GILBERT

Gilbert ENTERPRISE. w Jl 12 1929+
Az 1929+
AzTP S 12 1930+

Gilbert SUN. w O 2 1919-
KHi 1919-N 11 1920

GLENDALE

Glendale NEWS. sw,w 1912+
Jl 1925-O 3 1927 as Northside news
sw 1919-Ja 1930
Az Jl 1915+
AzTP S 18 1930+
AzU [1919-F 9 1923]

NORTHSIDE news. *See* Glendale news

GLOBE

ARIZONA record. d,sw F 1913+
1913-My 8 1914 as Arizona record and Globe republican
d 1913-Jl 19 1931
Az [Mr 1913-14]-[19]+
AzTP Jl 16 1930+
AzU [N 28 1913-S 1918;26]

ARIZONA silver belt. *See under* Miami

ARIZONA register. w 1904-05||?
AzU O 21-28 1905

Globe CHRONICLE. w 1880-D 29 1883||
AzTP S 1882-83

Globe DEMOCRAT. d Ag 24-N 15? 1911||

Daily GLOBE. d 1909-Ja 5 1912||
AzU My 4,Je 25,Ag 11-S 24 1911;Ja 5 1912
AzU Ag-N 15 1911

Globe LEADER. w Ja 29-Je 18? 1915||
Az My-Je 18 1915

Globe MINER. w O 20-D 8? 1907||
AzU D 8 1907

Weekly RECORD. w Ag 1-D 1908||?
AzU S 26 1908

Globe REPUBLICAN. w Jl 13? 1907-F 1913||
Followed by Arizona record and Globe republican, later Arizona record
AzU My 4,Je 1 1908;O 25,N 15 1909;Ap 11-18 1910;S 4 1911;D 23 1912;F 3 1913

Globe TIMES. w O 21 1898-1901||?
Az O 28 1898-My 16 1901

ARIZONA (*Continued*)

HOLBROOK

APACHE county critic. w My 1886-S 1887||?
AzSH D 30 1886-S 10 1887

Holbrook ARGUS. w D 12 1895-F 4 1913||
Az 1897-1904[07]-13
AzHH D 12 1895;96-1913
AzU S 8-O 20,D 17 1900-13

Holbrook NEWS. *See* Holbrook tribune-news

Holbrook TIMES. w My 17-? 1884||
AzHH My 17 1884

Holbrook TRIBUNE. w 1918-F 9 1923||
United with Holbrook news to form Holbrook tribune-news
Az O 10 1918-23
AzU O 17 1918-23

Holbrook TRIBUNE-NEWS. w Ap 1909+
1909-F 9 1923 as Holbrook news
Az Jl 1915-22;F 16 1923+
AzHH D 31 1909-23
AzTP Jl 25 1930+
AzU [1918]F 16 1923-[26-O 14 1927]

JEROME

ARIZONA mining news. *See* Jerome news and copper belt

Jerome SUN. w, tw,d D 4 1916-Ap 9 1918||
AzTP Mr-Je 1 1895

COPPER belt. w 1907-Ag 17? 1912||
United with Jerome mining news to form Jerome news and copper belt

Jerome MINING news. *See* Jerome news and copper belt

Jerome NEWS and copper belt. w S 12 1895-1924||
1895-O 23 1897 as Arizona mining news; O 30 1897-Ag 17 1912 Jerome mining news. Merged with Verde copper news
Az O 23 1897-99;1903-Je 1918
AzU [S 15 1900-02]-Je 1914

Jerome REPORTER. w 1897-1902||?
1897 as Yavapai county reporter
Az 1900-01
AzU D 25 1899

Jerome SUN. w, tw,d D 4 1916-Ap 9 1918||
w 1916-Mr 29 1917;tw Ap 5-24 1917
Az Complete
AzU [Ja 18-Ap 1918]

VERDE copper news. d,sw,w My 1 1917-F 1 1935||
d 1917-Ap 2 1921;sw Ap 8 1921-D 9 1932
Az [1917-19]-35
AzTP Je 22 1930-35
AzU [Je 5-O 1918]19-[24-26;34]

VERDE truth. w S 7- ? 1918||
Az S 21-28 1918

YAVAPAI county reporter. *See* Jerome reporter

KINGMAN

MOHAVE county miner. w 1882+
1919-31 as Mohave county miner and Our mineral wealth
1882-Ja 16 1887 pub in Mineral Park
Az 1897—
AzTP Ja 28 1884-88;Ap 27 1889-[92]-96;My 1929+
AzU Mr 1901-12;N 1919-N 16 1923
CU-B [1888]-Je 1890

MOHAVE daily miner. d Mr 1 1916-Ag 10? 1917||
Az Mr 3 1916-Ag 10 1917

OUR mineral wealth. w 1893-1919||
United with Mohave county miner to form Mohave county miner and Our mineral wealth, later Mohave county miner
Az S 1903-Ap 22 1904;Jl-D 1915

MAYER

Weekly REFLEX. w N 24-D 22? 1898||
AzPrG D 22 1898

MESA

Weekly FREE press. w 1892-1913||
1892-96 as Mesa free press
AzMJ Jl 20 1901-02
AzTP Jl 6 1893-96

Mesa evening FREE press. *See* Mesa journal-tribune

Mesa JOURNAL. sw D 10 1925-Ja 14 1926||
United with Mesa tribune to form Mesa journal-tribune
Az D 21 1925-26
AzMJ Complete

Mesa JOURNAL-TRIBUNE. d,sw,w F 1901+
1901-D 12 1913 as Mesa evening free press; D 15 1913-My 19 1923 Mesa daily tribune; My 24 1923-D 3 1925 Mesa tribune; Ap 23-Jl 7 1928 Mesa evening journal
d 1901-Je 3,D 19 1921-My 19 1923,Ap 23-Jl 7 1928; sw Je 7-D 17 1921,Ja 21 1926-Ap 19 1928
pub Jl 17 1902-04;26+
Az [Ap-My 1901;14-16]+
AzTP S 10 1930+
AzU Ag 22 1912-S 1918;My 10-Jl 7 1928
KHi D 21 1911;D 20 1912;F 5 1914;Mr 20-24,Ap 15-17,Jl 5-8 1915

SOUTHSIDE union. d D? 1919-21||?
Az Ja 23 1920-Mr 3 1921

Mesa TRIBUNE. *See* Mesa journal-tribune

MESILLA

Mesilla TIMES. w O 18 1860-1862||?
AzU O 18 1860 (photostat)
CU-B O 18 1860
NN My 11 1861
Tx Jl 27 1861

MIAMI

ARIZONA silver belt. w My 2 1878-1922;Jl 24 1931+
1878-Mr 29 1913 pub in Globe
Az 1897-N 1899;1900-Je 1901;S 1903-06;Jl 24 1931+
AzTP 1879-[89-92]Jl 1893-96;1931+
AzU Mr 27 1901-13;O-N 1931
CU-B My 9-16,Je 13-20,O 10 1878-Je 1880;Mr 25,Ap 29-Jl 22 1882;Jl 12 1884;F 1885[Ja-Je 1888]-Mr 1892
DLC Jl 10 1880

Daily ARIZONA silver belt. d O 1906-Jl 18 1931||
1906-Mr 1913 pub in Globe
Az 1907-31
AzTP F 13 1930-31
AzU D 1911-12[14-26]

Miami BULLETIN. d,w F 1920+
1920-Jl 18 1931 as Miami evening bulletin (d)
Az Mr 1920+
AzU [1922]-My 1928

Miami FREE press. sw Jl 8-S 30? 1915||?
Az Jl 15-S 1915

Miami ITEM. w Mr 30-Je 22 1917||
Az complete
AzU Je 8 1917

MESSENGER. w S 30 1909-Ag 1913||
AzU My 26 1911

Miami NEWS. w My 27 1911-13||
Az 1912-Ap 1913
AzU My 27 1911

MINERAL PARK

ALTA Arizona. w O 15 1881-83||?
AzTP 1881-Ag 5 1882

MOHAVE county miner. *See under* Kingman

MORENCI

Morenci LEADER. w 1904-Ag 1911||
United with Copper era (Clifton) to form Copper era; Consolidated with Duncan Valley news and Morenci leader
Az Je 17 1905-Je 1911

NOGALES

BORDER vidette. w 1894-Jl 7 1934||
Az My 16 1897-1934
AzTP My 9 1914-34
AzU 1903-F 11 1905

Nogales morning DEMOCRAT. d O 5 1921-23||
Az complete

Nogales FRONTIER. w 1885||
CLM Ap 4 1885

Nogales Sunday HERALD. w 1888-D 31 1893||
AzTP S-D 1889;O-D 1893

Evening daily Nogales HERALD. d 1914+
1914-Ap 8 1918 as Nogales daily herald
Az Ag 13 1915-S 1919;20-[25]+
AzU O 1917-S 1918[19-22;26]-Mr 1927
Ct Jl 7 1916

INTERNATIONAL. w,sw My 25 1925+
w 1925-Ja 1928
Az 1925+

El MONITOR. w 1886-95||?
1886-89? as El Monitor fronterizo
In Spanish
CSmH S 5 1890

OASIS. w My 11 1893-O 9 1920||
1893-My 17 1894 pub in Arizola; My 24-D 6 1894 in Benson
Az 1893-My 18 1901;S 1903-04;O 1906-10;12-Je 1918
AzTP Jl 6 1893-96;Je 22 1907-20
AzU O 27 1900-20
DLC 1893-Ja 10 1895
KHi Jl 10 1920
MB [Je 1893-D 13 1894]

Daily morning OASIS. d D 1917-O 1920||
Az complete
Ct [Jl-N 1920]
M [Jl-O 1920]
WHi Jl-O 1,21 1920

Nogales morning TIMES. d F 8-Ap 24? 1917||
In English and Spanish
Az Mr 8-Ap 24 1917

OATMAN

Oatman MINER. *See* Oatman mining news

Oatman MINING news. w O 21 1915-26||?
1915-Mr 1 1916 as Oatman miner; Mr 8 1916-17 Oatman news
Az 1915-21
MWA D 23 1915;Ap 12 1916

Oatman NEWS. *See* Oatman mining news

PARADISE

Paradise RECORD. w 1906-11||
AzTP My 28 1909

PARKER

Parker POST. w 1910-18||?
Az [Jl 1911-Jl 1918]
AzU [Je 20 1914-N 9 1918]

PATAGONIA

SANTA Cruz Patagonian. w 1912-Ag 2 1929||
Az Jl 1915-29
AzTP Ap 18 1914-D 3 1915
AzU [F 26-D 1926]

PEACH SPRINGS

ARIZONA champion. *See* Coconino sun (Flagstaff)

PEORIA

Peoria ENTERPRISE. w N ? 1917-20||
AzTP 1917-S 1919;20

PHOENIX

ARIZONA weekly arrow. w Ap 5-? 1884||
AzPMe Ap 12 1884

ARIZONA beacon. *See* Arizona democrat

ARIZONA democrat. d 1901-D 22 1913||
Merged with Arizona gazette, later Phoenix evening gazette
Az Ap 1902-Ag 1903;07-Ag,O 1910-13
AzPE 1911-Je 1912
KHi 1912(48th star ed)

ARIZONA democrat. d 1930-31||
AzPE O 18-N 20 1931

ARIZONA democrat. w Ap 1 1933+
1933-Ag 3 1934 as Arizona beacon; Ag 10 1934-O 17 1935 Beacon
Az Ap 1 1933+

ARIZONA fax. w Ja 15 1932+
Az 1932+

ARIZONA gazette. d *See* Phoenix evening gazette

ARIZONA weekly gazette. w N 8 1880+
1880-85 as Arizona gazette; Ag 31 1895-D 26 1896 Arizona stock journal
Ag 1 1893 is World's fair ed
pub 1880-85;92-93;N 13 1897-1900;N 1910-O 1912;13-[18]Je 30 1928+
Az 1897-1900;Mr 14 1931+
AzTP 1882-85;Ag 31 1895-96
AzU Mr 16 1901-Je 1902
CU-B N 29 1880;Mr 16,30,My 18,Je 8,22-29, Jl 13 1882
CtY Ag 1 1893
MWA Ag 1 1893
NN Ag 1 1893
d ed *See* Phoenix evening gazette

ARIZONA miner. w F 24-Je 9 1917||?
Az Mr 31-Je 9 1917

ARIZONA mining journal. w,sw Ag 1909-10||
w Ag-O 1909?
AzU S 22,N 26 1909-Ap 1910

ARIZONA mining press. bw Ap 29-D 28 1901||?
CLMo My 20,Jl,N 1,D 28 1901

ARIZONA mining report. w F 1 1892-
AzTP F 1 1892
AzU F 1 1892

ARIZONA outlook. w 1886||?
AzPM Ja 1886

ARIZONA populist. *See* Prospect (Prescott)

ARIZONA republic. d My 19 1890+
1890-N 3 1930 as Arizona republican
pub 1890-93;1900-[14]-[28]+
Az 1897+
AzTP 1890+
AzU 1910+
CL D 25 1927;D 30 1928;N 15 1931
CLM N 17-19 1890;Ap 21 1891;Mr 25 1892
CU-B Jl 22,24,S 27,D 12 1890;My 12 1892;My 10 1893
DLC S 7 1897-[1901]+
KHi Ap 28,Je 9 1909;Ag 20 1912
N D 30 1928
OClWHi Mr 31 1899;Je 7 1905
TxGR D 27 1925
WHi N 20 1932

ARIZONA republican. *See* Arizona republic

ARIZONA screamer. w O 19 1929-30||?
AzTP [1929-N 1930]

ARIZONA state herald. w Ap 30 1915-16||
Ap-D 1915 as Five Points herald. United with Superior sun to form Superior sun and state herald, later Superior sun (Superior)
Az complete

ARIZONA state news. w O 14 1927-My 14 1928||
United with Five Points star to form Five Points star and Arizona state news, later Star news
Az complete

ARIZONA stock journal. *See* Arizona weekly gazette

Daily ARIZONAN. d 1885-89||
AzPMe O 17 1887
CLM F 9 1889
CU-B Ap 6,8,11,Jl 17-18 1889

ARIZONIAN. m 1894?-96||?
CLMo Ap-My 1896

ARIZONA (*Continued*)

PHOENIX—*Continued*

BEACON. *See* Arizona democrat

BEE messenger. w Ap 25-O 31 1932||
Ap-My 31 as Phoenix bee
Az complete
AzPR complete

DUNBAR'S weekly. w Ja 17 1914+
Az 1914+

Phoenix ENTERPRISE. d My 2 1898-1906||
1898-Ap 8 1902 as Daily enterprise. Merged with Arizona democrat
Az [Ag 1898-1900]-[04]-06
AzPR 1898-1903

Phoenix ENTERPRISE. w F 4 1898-1906||
Az F 4-11,Ap 8 1898

Phoenix EXAMINER. d S 27 1933-Ja 9 1935||
S-N 29 1933 as Phoenix morning examiner
Az complete

Phoenix EXPRESS. w N 11-D 30 1895||?
AzTP N-D 1895

FIVE Points herald. *See* Arizona state herald

FIVE Points star. *See* Star news

El FRONTERIZO. w Ap 6 1934+
Follows El Fronterizo (Tucson)
In Spanish
Az Ap 20 1934+

Phoenix evening GAZETTE. d O 28 1880+
1880-N 16 1928 as Arizona gazette (Ap 22 1926-S 1927 Irrigated empire pub as supp to Thursday ed)
pub 1880-85;F 1886-87;My 1892-Je,O 1893-94; F 21-Ap 23 1895;Mr 1896-S 1897;Ap 1898-[26]+
Az 1897-S 1906;07-13;F 1914+
AzTP Ap 1889-96;1911-15
AzU 1907;20-22[26-29]
CU-B N 1-2,5,27,29,D 6 1880;F 20 1882;Je 12,14 1888
IaDH Mr 27 1905-14
MoHi F 14 1912
—w ed. *See* Arizona gazette

Phoenix daily HERALD. d O 1 1879-1900||
1879-O 9 1882 as Phoenix herald. Merged with Arizona republican, later Arizona republic
Az 1897-S 1900
AzPR 1879-O 1,D 6 1884-S 25 1885;Je 1886-Je 1894;95-97
AzTP S 22 1881;Ap 13 1889-[91]F 1892-96
CU-B [1879]-[Ja-Je 1881]-Ag 4,25 1882;86-87; Ja-Je 1889;90-O,D 21 1891;My 22-O 20,D 21 1893
CLM O 6,21 1893
DLC Jl 1898-Je 1899

Weekly Phoenix HERALD. w,sw Ja 26 1878-1900||
Ja 1-Mr 1 1879 as Salt River herald. Merged with Weekly republican
w Ja 26-D 1878,O 4 1879-1900
AzPR F 23-D 1878;Mr 1879-97
AzTP 1878-S 1887;Mr-D 1888;Ap 1889-92;Jl 1893-96
CU-B F 23,Mr 16,Ap 6,My 1878-S 1879
DLC [1879]-[83]-92

INDEPENDENT. w 1892-94||?
AzTP O 1893-S 1894

IRRIGATED empire. *See note under* Phoenix evening gazette

JUMPING cactus. w Mr 3 1932+
Az 1932-33;Ja 30 1935
AzTP [Jl 22 1932-33]

MARICOPA county democrat. w Jl 15-S 2? 1882||
AzPMe S 2 1882

El MENSAJERO. w 1900-Ap 15 1916;Ap 22 1925+
In Spanish
AzU D 9 1933
—English ed. *See* Phoenix messenger

Phoenix MESSENGER. w Ap 22 1916+
Follows El Mensajero, 1st series
Az 1916+
AzTP N 18 1933+
AzU [Jl 1919-21]
Ct Mr 22 1919

OBSERVADOR mexicano. w 1894-98||?
In Spanish
Az O 1897-Mr 1898

OCASIONAL. w 1897?-99||?
In Spanish
Az Ja 28-Jl 15 1899

PINACATE. w O 22-N 5? 1882||
AzPMe N 5 1882

Saturday evening PRESS. w Ja 23 1897-Mr 19 1898||?
Az F 1897-Mr 19 1898

El PROGRESSO del valle. w Ap 2 1887-
In Spanish
CU-B Ap 9 1887

Weekly REPUBLICAN. w My 29 1890-D 7 1910||?
pub 1890-93;1901-08
Az Ag 24 1899-Ap 18 1903
AzU 1901-05
WHi Ja 26 1895;96-Ja 16 1902
—d ed *See* Arizona republic

Saturday REVIEW. w F 24 1894-Ag 24 1895||
Merged with Arizona weekly gazette to form Arizona stock journal, later Arizona weekly gazette
AzTP Mr 1894-95

Saturday REVIEW. w 1902-09||?
Az 1904
AzPR Ap 1905-06

RIATA. sw 1895-96||?
AzU F 23 1896

SALT River herald. *See* Weekly Phoenix herald

SOUTHWESTERN democrat. w Ag 5-26 1915||?
Az Ag 1915
MWA Ag 5 1915

STAR news. w N 4 1924-30||
1924-My 2 1928 as Five Points star; My 18 1928-Mr? 1929 Five Points star and Arizona state news
Az 1925-Jl 12,D 27 1929-S 1930
AzU Ja 20 1926;Ag 17,D 7-21 1928;Ja,Mr 29 1929

TERRITORIAL expositor. w 1878-My 6 1881||
1878-My 1879 pub in Yuma
AzTP My 9 1879-81
CU-B My 9,Je 13,Jl 11 1879;F 20-Ap 16,30-Ag 20,S 3-10,24,O 8-15,29-N,D 10 1880

Phoenix weekly TRIBUNE. w Ja 26-Je? 1889||
AzTP Ap 20 1889
CU-B Mr 9-16,Ap 6,27 1889

Phoenix daily TRIBUNE. d Je 11-Jl 10 1889||?
AzTP Je-Jl 10 1889

Phoenix TRIBUNE. w,m 1918+
w 1918-25
Negro
AzU 1920-[23-Je 1928]

PIMA

GILA Valley farmer. *See under* Safford

PINAL CITY

Pinal DRILL. w My 15 1880-84||?
AzTP S 11 1880-Ap 5 1884
CU-B 1880-Je 1882

PINAL county record. w S 11 1885-O 22 1886||
AzTP complete

PRESCOTT

ARIZONA courier-journal. d Ap 17 1934+
Ap 17-20 1934 as Prescott courier-journal
Az 1934+

Daily ARIZONA democrat. d 1880-My 1883||
AzTP Mr 9 1881
CU-B Ja 19,O 4 1880

ARIZONA weekly democrat. *See* Arizona weekly journal

ARIZONA enterprise. *See* Arizonian

ARIZONA gazette. sw,w 1866?-Jl 1867||
CU-B Jl 18,31 1867

ARIZONA weekly journal. w Ja 23 1880-Ag 1885||
Ja-Je 1880,Ja-My 4 1883 as Arizona weekly democrat; Jl 9 1880-82? Arizona democrat. United with Weekly Arizona miner to form Weekly journal-miner
AzTP 1880-81;83-84;Je 17-24,Ag 5-12 1885
DLC Ja 28 1881

ARIZONA daily journal-miner. *See* Prescott journal-miner

ARIZONA weekly journal-miner. *See* Weekly journal miner

ARIZONA daily miner. d
Issued during session of legislature
Az O 8-N 7 1866
AzTP S 7-O 8 1867
CSmH O 3 1867
CU-B O 30 1866[O 1874-Ja 1875;Mr 30 1878-79]-81
N D 1 1873

Weekly ARIZONA miner. *See* Weekly journal-miner

Daily ARIZONIAN. d 1877-Ja 6 1880||
1877-Jl 1879 as Arizona enterprise
AzTP Ja 11 1879
CU-B [N 25-D 1879]Ja 1,6 1880

ARIZONIAN. sw,w 1877-D 26 1879||
1877-Jl 5 1879 as Arizona enterprise
AzTP Ag 11 1877;78
CU-B Mr 21,31,Jl 25-N 10 1877;Mr 13-D 1878; Ja 11-D 1879

Prescott evening COURIER. d F 1882-My 21 1910; Ag 1920-Je 30 1934||
1882-F 18 1909 as Prescott morning courier
Az 1897-Jl 14,O 1900-My 21 1910;O 1920-34
AzTP 1886-87;89-96;Je 1928-34
CLM O 16 1889;Ja 4 1890
CU-B [1887-91]

Prescott weekly COURIER. w F 4 1882+
Az 1897-1908;20+
AzTP Mr 1882-96;1919-22;Je 1923-27
AzU F 15 1901-[03]-[22-26;28+]
CoU 1901-06

Prescott COURIER-JOURNAL. *See* Arizona courier-journal

Prescott daily HERALD. d D 1902-05||
Merged with Prescott journal miner
Az Ja-S 1 1903

HOWLER. d Je-Jl? 1900||
AzPrG Jl 14 1900

Weekly JOURNAL-MINER. bw,w Mr 9 1864-Ap 1934||
1864-Ag 1885 title varies: Arizona miner; Weekly Arizona miner; Arizona weekly miner; S 1885-S 23 1908 title varies: Arizona weekly journal-miner; Weekly Arizona journal-miner
Mr 9-My 26 1864 pub in Fort Whipple
bw 1864-Ag 3 1867
Az 1864;Mr 31-Je 9 1917
AzPrJ Ag 10 1866-71
AzTP [1869-71;74-76]Je 1877-80;F 27-Ag 14,S 9 1885-S 24 1890
AzU Mr 9,Je 22 (photostat) 1864;Mr 1901-O 1926
C D 12 1868
CU-B Je 22 1864;F 15,N 22 1865;D 29 1866; F 1868-[82]Jl 4,25,D 5 1884;Ja 23-F 13,Mr 27,Ap 10,Je 5 1885;86[87]F 8,S 5,N 7-14 1888; Mr 20,Ap 10,Jl 17,Ag 28 1889
DLC Mr 18 1871[72-73]-78
ICHi Mr 9 1864;N 23,D 14 1867;Ja 25 1873
KHi 1901-Jl 10 1929
MBAt Ag 10 1864
N Ag 24,N 23 1864;O 4 1865;Je 13 1866[My 1867-F 6 1874]
NN Ap 11 1879
NNHi Mr 9 1864;F 22 1873
OClWHi Ap 12 1873

Prescott JOURNAL-MINER. d S 1885-Ap 15 1934||
1885-97,1903-12 title varies: Arizona journal-miner; Arizona daily journal-miner
Az 1897-Jl 14,23 1900-34
AzTP 1886-87;Ap 1889-96
AzU [1913-16]
CU-B N 21-22,27 1889
KHi Jl 1929-F 7 1933

PICK and drill. *See* Prospect

PROSPECT. w 1894-1905||?
1894-96 as Arizona populist (Phoenix); 1897-S 1899 Pick and drill
Az Jl 1897-S 2,O 22 1899-My 1901
AzTP Je 20 1896
AzU 1901-02;S 15-D 1905

SOUTHERN Arizonian. *See* Weekly Arizonan (Tucson)

QUIJOTOA

PROSPECTOR. w F 16- 1884||
AzTP F 16 1884

RAY

ARIZONA copper camp. w 1910?-D 25 1920||
Az Ag 20 1915-20
AzTP [S 8 1917-Ap 13 1918]Jl 12 1919

SAFFORD

ARIZONA bulletin. w F 7 1889-Je 1918||
1889-Je 13 1890 as Valley bulletin; Je 20 1890-D 10 1897 Graham county bulletin. Merged with Gila Valley farmer
1889-Ja 7 1916 pub in Solomonville
Az F 21 1889-1901;03-08;10-18
AzTP Ap 12 1890-96
AzU S 14 1900-N 1917
CU-B D 20 1889-Ja 17 1890

ARIZONIAN. w Mr 17 1898-1900||
Az 1898-F 2 1900
AzTP Ag 11-18 1900

GILA Valley farmer. w 1916-Ap 20 1923||
United with the Graham county guardian to form Graham county guardian and Gila Valley farmer
1916-D 25 1919 pub in Pima
Az Jl 1920-22
AzU [Mr 20-D 1919]-23

GRAHAM county bulletin. *See* Arizona bulletin

GRAHAM county guardian and Gila Valley farmer. w,sw 1895+
1895-Ap 17 1923 as Graham guardian
sw F 3-Mr 21 1922
Az 1897-1901;03+
AzTP Ap 10-D 1896;Ag 8 1930+
AzU S 1900-26;29+

GRAHAM county news. w Jl 15-D 30 1882||
AzTP Ag 26-D 1882

GRAHAM guardian. *See* Graham county guardian and Gila Valley farmer

VALLEY bulletin. *See* Arizona bulletin

ST. JOHNS

APACHE chief. w Ja 10-D 5 1884||?
AzTP Mr 28-D 5 1884

APACHE review. w My 30 1888-Ja 9 1889||
AzSH complete

St. Johns HERALD. w Ja 15 1885+
1903-04? as Snips and St. Johns herald; 1905?-Mr 22 1917 St. Johns herald and Apache news
pub Jl 16 1885+
Az 1897-My 18 1901;06+
AzTP F 12-D 3 1885[89-92]Jl 1893-96;Jl 24 1930+
AzU [Ap-O 14 1899]1926
CU-B N 28-D 19 1889
DLC D 1889-[90]-94

St. Johns OBSERVER. w S 24 1910+
pub O 29 1910+
Az 1923+
AzU [N 1912-15;18]

SNIPS. w S 12 1901-02||
Merged with the St. Johns herald to form Snips and St. Johns herald, later St. Johns herald
In English and Spanish
AzSH 1901-S 4 1902

SALOME

Salome BONANZA. w Ja 6- 1917||
Az Ja-Jl 7 1917

ARIZONA (*Continued*)

SAN SIMON

ARTESIAN belt. *See* San Simon Valley tribune (Bowie)

SAN SIMON Valley news. *See* San Simon Valley tribune (Bowie)

SNOWFLAKE

Snowflake HERALD. w 1913+
Az Jl 23 1915-Je 1917
AzTP Ja,S 27 1930+

SOLOMONVILLE

GRAHAM county bulletin. *See* Arizona bulletin (Safford)

VALLEY bulletin. *See* Arizona bulletin (Safford)

SOMERTON

STAR. w N 16 1917+
1917-Mr 24 1933 as Somerton star; Mr 31 1933-N 2 1934 Star and Yuma county record
pub 1917+
Az 1918+
AzTP Mr 31 1933+

Somerton TRIBUNE and Yuma county farmer. w Jl 3 1931-32||
Az complete
AzU Jl 17-24,Ag 21 1931

SPRINGERVILLE

ROUND Valley press. w 1924+
1924-My 1 1931 as Tourzona
Az Ja 21 1927-30
AzTP S 12 1930+
AzU My 31 1934+

TOURZONA. *See* Round Valley press

SUPERIOR

Superior SUN. w 1914+
1917-Mr 22 1918 as Superior sun and State herald
Az F 1917+
AzTP S 1917-Mr 2 1918

TEMPE

Tempe NEWS. w 1885-N 25 1933||
1885-87 as Salt River Valley news
Az 1893-1933
AzPM Ap 30-My 1887
AzTP My 1890-96
AzU O 26-N 9 1900;Mr 1901-33
CU-B Mr 2-16,Jl 6,S 7-14 1889;Ag 16 1890

Tempe NEWS. d 1892+
1892-N 1933 as Tempe daily news
Saturday ed used as w D 1933+
Az My-D 1902;My 1903-Ap 1904;D 1934+

SALT River Valley news. *See* Tempe news

THATCHER

ADVOCATE. w S 28 1904-05||?
AzU N 23,D 30 1904[Ja-Ag 4 1905]

TOMBSTONE

ARIZONA kicker. ir, w 1892-1913||?
1893-94 as Wednesday ed of Tombstone prospector
ir 1895-1913
AzTP Ja 3,F-Ap,My 16,Ag 1-15,N 14 1894;D 5 1895;Ag 1909;Ap 16 1913
AzU Ag 1909

COCHISE daily record. d 1884-Jl? 1885||
United with Daily Tombstone epitaph to form Daily Tombstone epitaph and Cochise county record, later Tombstone daily epitaph
AzTP O 18 1884

Tombstone DEMOCRAT. d Ja 8-N? 1886||?
AzTP Ja 9 1886

Tombstone EPITAPH. w My 1 1880+
1893-Mr 1924 as Sunday ed of the Tombstone prospector
O 15 1929 is 50th anniversary ed
Az Ap-Je 1893;97-[1914]+
AzTP [Ja-F,D 1881]82;Ag 1887-88;D 1889-Ag 2 1890;O 11 1893[F 11-Ag 12 1894]1904[05-07]-22[Ap-My]Je 1923+
AzU [1900]Je 1901+
CL O 15 1929
CSmH O 15 1929
CU-B My 1-8,Je-D 13 1880;Ja 10-17 1881
DLC Jl 31 1880;My 30 1881
M [Ag 20 1931-O 6 1932]
MWA O 11 1931

Tombstone daily EPITAPH. d Jl 1880-N 30 1890||
1880-83 as Tombstone epitaph; Ap 1884-Jl? 1885 Tombstone daily epitaph and republican; Ag-D 1885 Daily record-epitaph; 1886-87 Daily Tombstone epitaph and Cochise county record
Suspended D 1 1889-Jl 1890
AzTP [Ja 1881;82]Ap 25,27,29 1884;Ap 18-N 17 1885;Ja-Je 10 1886;Ja-Jl 1887;Ag 24-S 17 1888;Ja-D 1 1889;Ag 5-N 1890
CU-B Jl 29-D 17 1880[81-Jl 1890]
DLC O 9 1880;Je 4 1881

Tombstone weekly NUGGET. w O 2 1879-82||?
AzTP O 2 1879;My 5 1882
CU-B [Mr 18-O 7 1880]
ICM O 2 1879

Tombstone daily NUGGET. d S 1880-82||?
AzTP Je 8-D 4 1881
CU-B [O 7-D 18 1880;O-D 18 1881;Ja-My 1882]

Tombstone PROSPECTOR. d Mr 7 1887-Mr 7 1924||
Az 1887-89;Ap-Je 1893;97-[1914]-23
AzTP [Mr-My,O 1887]Je[O 1888-F]S 21 1889-96[1901-10]-12;F 1913-[14]-[18-F 1924]
CLM N 17 1890
CU-B F 4 1890
—w ed *See* Tombstone epitaph, Arizona kicker

Daily RECORD-EPITAPH. *See* Tombstone daily epitaph

Tombstone daily REPUBLICAN. d 1882-Ap 1884||
United with Tombstone daily epitaph to form Tombstone daily epitaph and republican, later Tombstone daily epitaph
AzTP Ja 15-30 1883

Tombstone REPUBLICAN. w Je 1882-Ap 1884||
Merged with Tombstone epitaph
AzTP [1883-Mr 1884]

Daily TOMBSTONE. w 1882-86||
Merged with Daily Tombstone epitaph
AzTP F 23 1883;Mr 21 1885-D 7 1886
CU-B D 31 1885[86]

TUBAC

Weekly ARIZONIAN. *See under* Tucson

TUCSON

Daily ARIZONA citizen. *See* Tucson daily citizen

ARIZONA citizen and weekly tribune. w O 15 1870-1912||?
1870-79?,1902?-Mr 1910 as Arizona citizen; 1880?-1901? Arizona weekly citizen
N 9 1877-S 6 1879 pub in Florence
pub 1870-Jl 3 1875;N 30 1877-79;F 1882-Mr 8 1884;92-94;1904-05;10-12
Az Ja-Je 1893;Ja 2 1896;Ja 9-Ap 1897
AzTP [F-D 1871]-[75]-77;My 3 1878[85-92] Ag 1893-96
AzU 1870-O 1877;Mr 10-D 22 1911
CU-B N 19 1870;Mr 25,O 1871-80[86]04 1890
DLC O 15 1870(reprint);Ja-Ag,S 9-23,O 7 1871;Jl 1874-91; broadside Je 11 1881
N O 29 1870;F 15,Ap 15-22,Ag 19,S 2,16,O 14, N 18 1871;Mr 2,Je 1,N 9 1872;Je 7 1873;D 12 1874;supps Ja 9,F 13,Jl 3,Ag 28 1875
NNHi Ja 11 1873
OCIWHi Ap 19 1873;Mr 15 1884
—d ed *See* Tucson daily citizen

ARIZONA enterprise. w Ap 2 1881-94||
1881-91 as Arizona weekly enterprise (Florence)
AzTC 1881-Mr 1889
AzTP Ag 6,O 22 1881-[83-87]Je,N 10 1888-[89-92]Jl 1893-Ap 19 1894
CLM O 20,D 8 1888
CU-B Ap 30 1881[Ja-Jl 1882;86;Jl-D 1887]F 25-Je 1888[89]-F 14,Ap 4 1891

ARIZONA journal. d 1880?-Ja 21 1882||
CU-B N 30 1881

ARIZONA mining index. w Je 9 1883-D 18 1886||
AzTP Ag 11 1883-86

ARIZONA star. d,tw Mr 1-Jl 26? 1877||
Mr 1-28 1877 as Daily bulletin
AzTP Mr 2-25 1877
CU-B My 3,Je 16,21-23 1877

ARIZONA weekly star. w Je 28 1877-1907||
Je-Jl 1877 as Thursday ed of Arizona star
AzTP 1877[78]80-81;92-93
AzU Je-N 1877[78]-[80]-[84]-[86]-[88]91[92] 94-95;97-99
CLM Ag 5 1886
CU-B Jl 26-O 4,N 29 1877;Ap 4-18,Ag 8,S 19,N 21 1878[79]80;F 16,Je 8 1882;Ja 5 1888
CoU 1898-Ap 1903
ICM Je 26,N 6-13,D 4-18 1879;Ja 8 1880

ARIZONA daily star. d Ja 12 1879+
Az 1897-S 1906;07-S 1920;21+
AzTP 1882-Je 1883;84-[88-89]-99;Ag 10,15,19, S 4-5 1900;01;04+
AzU [Ja-F 9,Je 26 1879-Mr 7 1880]82-Je 1883;86-87;Jl 1888-[90-95;97]N 1901+
CLM [1881-92]
CU-B Jl 6,30[Ag 1879-80]
ICM Jl 1,3,27,29-30,N 7 1879
MWA Ag 15 1915

Weekly ARIZONAN. w,ir Mr 3 1859-Ap 29 1871||
Ag-D ? 1867 as Southern Arizonian
Mr-Jl 1859 pub in Tubac, Ag 31 1867 in Prescott
Suspended Jl 1860-Ja 1861;Ag 17 1861-My 1867?
ir Je-Jl 1867
AzPM Je 30 1859
AzTC Ja 24 1869-71
AzTP Ja 26,My 10 1860;N 17 1867;69-71
AzU (photostats) Je 2,30,Jl 14,Ag 18,S 15,29-O 6,20-N 17 1859;Ap 12 1860;Ag 31 1867;Mr 21 1869;F 19-D 24-1870
CSmH O 13 1867
CU-B Ag 31 1867;Mr 21 1869-71
DLC Jl 14,Ag 18,S 15,29-O 6,20-N 17 1859;F 19-Mr 12,26-Ap 9,30-My,Je 11-18,Jl 2,16-30,S 3,24,O 15,N 19-D 3,17-24 1870

ICHi Ja 4 1868
MWA Je 2,30,O 27 1859;Ap 12 1860
MnHi N 21 1868
N O 17 1868

Daily BULLETIN. *See* Arizona star

Tucson daily CITIZEN. d F 1879+
1879-Mr 15 1884 as Daily Arizona citizen; Mr 18 1884-D 14 1901 Arizona daily citizen; D 15 1901-28 Tucson citizen
pub 1882;Ja 16 1885-88;Jl 1889-My 1896;97+
Az 1897+
AzTP S 26 1881[Ja 9-Je 3 1884;Je 18-Ag 25 1885]Ap 12 1889-96;My 14-Ag 17 1900;My 1901;Ag 1911+
AzU 1901+
CLM Mr 15,Ap 15 1884;Ja 1 1890;Je 2 1891
CU-B Mr 6,10-11,13,15,17-20,27,29,31 1879-80; D 2 1881;86;F-D 1887[F-Je 1]S 1888-91
DLC S 10 1880;My 24 1881 Ja 19 1889;Ja 1,Mr 27,Ap 1,My 2 1890;Jl 11 1891-[1919]+
ICM Jl 1-2,26,28-29 1879
OCIWHi S 26 1881
w ed *See* Arizona citizen and weekly tribune

La COLONIA Mexicana. w D 8 1883-84||?
In Spanish
CLM Ja 20 1884

Tucson weekly FLASHES. w 1886||?
CLM My 23 1886

El FRONTERIZO. w 1878-1929||?
Followed by El Fronterizo (Phoenix)
sw 1922-26?, D 1928-29;w 1927-N 1928
In Spanish
AzTP N 23 1883-N 1884[Jl 1890-D 17 1892]
AzU [Je 23-Jl,S 1926;Jl 1927-Ja 1929]
CLM D 9 1881
CU-B Ap 13-20,My 11-18,D 21 1879 - [80-81] Ja 20-27 1882;Ap 4-11 1884;Jl 20,Ag 10 1889
DLC Jl 4 1880;F 26 1891

Tucson daily INDEPENDENT. d 1925-28||?
Az 1928
AzU Jl 19-S 16 1926[Ja-Mr 1927]
WaPS [Jl 1926]

MINER and stockman. bw 1903-Ja 1 1914||
AzTP My 1907-13
AzU Ag 1904;Je 1907-14

OLD pueblo. *See* Tucson signal

PIMA county record. w D 6 1879-80||?
AzTP D 6 1879
—d ed *See* Tucson daily record

Tucson POST. w Je 1901-Je 6 1920||
O 3 1911-N 14 1914 as Progress and Tucson post; N 21 1914-Ap 28 1917 Tucson post and progress
Az N-D 1907;09-Je 1917
AzTC Ja 14-D 1905
AzTP 1903-04;06-07[16-18]19
AzU 1902-My 1920

Tucson daily POST. d O 9-N 5 1902||
AzU complete

PROGRESS and Tucson post. *See* Tucson post

Tucson daily RECORD. d 1880||
CU-B [My-Je]Jl 3 1880
—w ed *See* Pima county record

Las dos REPÚBLICAS. w My 1877-79||
In Spanish
CU-B Mr 13,Jl 22,Ag 5,19-D 9 1877;Ja 20,F 2-9,Mr 16,My 18-Je 15,Jl 6-13,27-O 19 1878;F 8 1879

Tucson SIGNAL. w Ja 16 1916-Je ? 1917||
Ja-Ap 17? 1916 as Old pueblo
Az Ap 27 1916-Je 14 1917
AzTP Mr 13-D 1916
AzU Mr 27,Ap 10 1916

La SONORA. w 1879-
In Spanish
CU-B N-D 7 1879;My 1,15-Je 5,19-Jl 3,17 1880

SOUTHERN Arizonian. *See* Weekly Arizonan

SUNSHINE and silver. w S 14 1884-Ja 4 1885||?
AzTP 1884-Ja 4 1885

Tucson TIMES. w S 15-O 6 1933||?
AzU S-O 6 1933

Weekly TRIBUNE. w Ag 1 1908-Mr 19 1910||
United with Arizona citizen to form Arizona citizen and weekly tribune
AzTP complete
AzU Ag 15 1908-F 12 1910

El TRUENO. w N 17 1895-Ja 5 1896||?
In Spanish
AzTP 1895-Ja 5 1896

TUCSONENSE. w,tw Mr 17 1915+
tw Ap 1 1919-Ja 1933
In Spanish
Az 1934+
AzTP 1915-Mr 1926;Ag 1930+
AzU Ap 1933+

Tucson WEEK-ENDER. w F 17 1933+
Suspended during summer months
AzTP 1933+

WICKENBURG

ARIZONA state miner. w 1919-26||?
Follows Golden state miner (Randsburg, Calif.)
Az My 1919-20;23-24;My 1925-26
AzTP Jl 1923-N 13 1926
AzU [Ag 1919-26]

GRAPHIC. w 1929+
AzTP S 18 1930-N 4 1932

HASSAYAMPA miner. *See* Wickenburg miner

HERALD. w 1901||
United with News to form News-herald

ARIZONA (*Continued*)

WICKENBURG—*Continued*

Wickenburg MINER. w Ja 5 1904-18‖
1916-Je 1917 as Hassayampa miner
Az Jl 1915-Jl 1918

NEWS-HERALD. w Jl 1901-07‖
Jl- ? 1901 as News. Merged with Wickenburg miner
Az 1902-Ap 1904

WILLCOX

ARIZONA range news. w 1884+
1884-96 as Sulphur Valley news
Az 1897-My 1901;S 1903-20;S 20 1929+
AzTP 1894-96;1906;08-Ag 1918;Ag 24 1928+
AzU Mr 29 1901-[18;33-34]

SULPHUR Valley news. *See* Arizona range news

WILLIAMS

Williams NEWS. w 1891+
pub Jl 1901+
Az S 1903+
AzTP Jl 25 1930+

Williams TIMES. w D 1 1916-17‖?
Az 1916-O 19 1917

WINKELMAN

Winkelman TIMES. w Je 17? 1913-15‖?
Az Ja 21-O 3 1914

WINSLOW

Winslow MAIL. w,sw,d 1893+
1927-Jl 30 1932 as Winslow daily mail
sw Ap 28-D 1925; d 1927-Jl 30 1932
Az 1897-1900;N 10 1906+
AzTP My-D 1896;My 24 1928+
AzU 1931+

YUMA

To F 15 1873 as Arizona City

ARIZONA free press. w O 1871-F 1872‖
AzTP F 10 1872

Yuma ARIZONA sentinel. d 1928-D 1 1935‖
United with Yuma morning sun to form Yuma daily sun and Yuma Arizona sentinel
Az D 31 1931-35

ARIZONA sentinel. w *See* Yuma examiner

Yuma BEE. w 1895-96‖?
CLMo [1895]

Yuma EXAMINER. w,sw Mr 10 1872-N 1935‖
1872-Je 1911 as Arizona sentinel; Jl 1911-Je 3 1915 Arizona sentinel and Yuma weekly examiner; Je 10 1915-Je 22 1916 Arizona sentinel and Yuma southwest; Je 29 1916-S 14 1920? Arizona sentinel; S 21 1920-S 1924 Yuma examiner and Arizona sentinel; O 1924-Ag 29 1925 Examiner sentinel news; S 1925-Je 22 1926 Yuma examiner; Jl 1926-D 24 1927 Yuma examiner and Arizona sentinel. United with Yuma weekly sun to form Yuma weekly sun and weekly examiner
sw S 21 1920-21
Az O 18 1873-Je,O 1911-Mr 7 1918;S 21 1920-35
AzTP D 30 1876;Je 2 1877;78-[82-85]-87[My 1889-92]Jl 1893-96[98]Ja 7,21 1899;Ag 14 1907-Je 1911
CLM D 14 1889;Ag 29 1891
CU-B [Ap 27-D 1872]-F 1,My-O 18 1873;D 5-12,26 1874;Ja 16-30 1875;Mr 4,Je 3-17,D 2-23 1876;F 3,17,Ap 14-28,Jl 14 1877-Ap 18,Jl-Ag 23,O 4-11 1879[My-Je,S 1880-81]-Jl 22 1882;86;Ja 14-21 1888;89-90;Jl 23 1892
DLC Jl 3 1880
ICM Jl 26,O 25 1879
N My 25-Je 1,S 29 1872;My 31 1873
OClWHi Ap 26 1873

Yuma EXAMINER and Arizona sentinel. d 1906-S 18 1920‖
1906-My 8 1918 as Yuma examiner
Az Ja 28 1912-20

Yuma EXAMINER sentinel news. *See* Yuma examiner

EXPOSITOR. w Jl 18 1878-
CU-B Ag 1,15 1878

Yuma evening HERALD. w,d My 21 1924-27‖?
1924-Ja 30 1925 as Yuma herald
w 1924-Ja 30 1925
Az My 23 1924-25
AzU [1926-My 15 1927]

Yuma REPUBLICAN. w S 2 1884-85‖
AzTP Ja-O 2 1885

Yuma weekly SUN and weekly examiner. w 1896+
1896-N 1935 as Yuma weekly sun
Az Jl 23 1897-Je 24 1904;N 1935+
AzU [D 1897-S 1899;Mr 1901-02]-[04;Ag 23-D 1907]-[09-11]-[13-14]-[17-S 6 1918]

Yuma daily SUN and Yuma Arizona sentinel. d N 1905+
1905-F 15 1928 as Morning sun; F 16 1928-D 1 1935 Yuma morning sun
pub 1916+
Az F 1909-27
AzTP Ap 7 1906;Ja 17 1929-33;Jl 1934+
AzU [Mr 19 1912-15]-[Jl 1918-19;26-32]

TERRITORIAL expositor. *See under* Phoenix

Yuma TIMES. w 1890-95‖?
CLMo Je 1890[95]

YUMA county record. w Jl 1 1927-Mr 24 1933‖
United with Somerton star (Somerton) to form Star and Yuma county record (Somerton)
AzSoS complete
AzTP [N-D 1930]-Mr 16 1933

YUMA Valley news. *See under* Gadsden

ARKANSAS

ARGENTA. *See* NORTH LITTLE ROCK

ARKADELPHIA

HERALD. w 1886-95‖?
United with Siftings to form Siftings herald

SIFTINGS HERALD. sw,w 1891-1926‖?
1891-95? as Siftings
sw 1891-92?

SIFTINGS HERALD. d 1921+
pub 1921+
ArAH 1927+
ArU 1930-Jl 1932;35+

SOUTHERN standard. w Ja 12? 1868+
pub 1869+
ArHi 1869-1914

Arkadelphia TRIBUNE. w Je 19 1869-71‖?
MBAt Jl 23 1869

ARKANSAS POST

ARKANSAS gazette. *See under* Little Rock

ATKINS

Atkins CHRONICLE. w N 30 1894+
pub 1894+

POPE county mail. w 1887-93‖?
TxCeC N 1892-N 1893

BATESVILLE

DEMOCRATIC sentinel. w 1859-61‖
ArHi F 1859-Ja 1860

FORTY-ACRE boy. 1844‖?
MoSM Ag 12 1844

Batesville GUARD. w,sw Ja 1877-Ap 1932‖
w 1877-1925?
pub 1879;81[83-1928]
ArBA 1877-84

Batesville daily GUARD. d 1905+
Suspended from 1925?-29?
pub [1905-Mr 1932]+
ArBA O 1907-Je 1909
ArU 1930-Mr 1934;35+

INDEPENDENCE balance. w 1856-My 1862‖
ArBA Ap 1856-Ap 1859

Batesville NEWS. *See* North Arkansas

NORTH ARKANSAS. w My 10 1838-
1838-Jl 26 1843 as Batesville news
DLC My 24 1838[Mr 19 1840-Ap,Ag 1843-44]
MWA N 5 1840
TxU S 10 1840

NORTH ARKANSAS times. w 1866-Mr 1877‖
ArBA Ap 1866-Ap 1870

Batesville RECORD. w 1911+
pub 1911+
ArU Jl 1932-Mr 1934

BEEBE

Beebe NEWS. *See* Beebe sentinel

Beebe SENTINEL. w Jl 1918+
1918-30 as Beebe news
pub 1930+

WHITE county news. w 1893-1915‖?
TxU O 12 1912

BENTON

Benton COURIER. w 1892+
1892-97 as Saline county times; 1898-1902? Saline county times-courier; 1903?-12? Times-courier
pub 1914+
ArU O 1930-Je 1932

Benton REVIEW. w My 24 1877-N 1885‖
1877-81 as Saline county digest
OCHi O 11 1877

SALINE county digest. *See* Benton review

SALINE county times. *See* Benton courier

SALINE courier. w S 1882-97‖
United with Saline county times to form Saline county times-courier, later Benton courier

TIMES-COURIER. *See* Benton courier

BENTONVILLE

BENTON county record. w 1916-Jl 1927‖
United with Bentonville democrat to form Benton county record and democrat

BENTON county record and democrat. w 1885+
1885-Jl 1927 as Bentonville democrat
pub 1887-1906;20+
ArU O 1930-Jl 14 1932

BENTON county sun. w 1891-1921‖
Merged with Benton county record
ArBeB 1891-97

Bentonville DEMOCRAT. *See* Benton county record and democrat

TRAVELER. w My 21? 1869-70‖?
MWA Je 11 1869

BERRYVILLE

CARROLL intelligencer. *See* Carroll progress

CARROLL progress. w 1879-1916‖
1879-84? as Carroll intelligencer. United with North Arkansas star to form North Arkansas star and Carroll progress, later Star-progress
TxCeC Ja-Jl 1894

NORTH Arkansas star. *See* Star-progress

STAR-PROGRESS. w Mr 4 1905+
1905-30? as North Arkansas star (1916-21? North Arkansas star and Carroll progress)
pub 1905+
ArU Ap 1932-33

Berryville VINDICATOR. w 1894-95‖?
TxCeC O 1894-Je 1895

BLYTHEVILLE

Blytheville COURIER. w 1903-28‖
pub 1906-08;Mr 16 1911-17;F 28-O 1918;20-Mr 3 1921;Mr 1923-S 11 1924

Blytheville COURIER NEWS. d 1923+
1923-25 as Blytheville courier
pub 1923+
ArU S 20 1931-Mr 1934;35+

Blytheville HERALD-NEWS. w 1900-25‖
1900-15 as Blytheville herald. United with Blytheville courier to form Blytheville courier news
ArBlC F 23-D 14 1911;F 12-D 1913;F 19 1914-F 7 1918;F 6 1919-25

Blytheville NEWS. w 1909-15‖
United with Blytheville herald to form Blytheville herald-news

BOONEVILLE

Booneville DEMOCRAT. w 1899+
ArU O 1930-S 1933

ENTERPRISE. w Jl 1875-90‖?
Suspended from 1877-84?
ArHi 1875-Jl 5 1877

Booneville PROGRESS. w 1906-34‖
ArU O 1930-33

BRINKLEY

ARGUS. w My 5 1883+
pub [1886-1904]+

MONROE county citizen. w 1893+
1893-1900 as Brinkley times
pub 1901+
ArU O 1930-Mr 1934

Brinkley TIMES. *See* Monroe county citizen

CAMDEN

Weekly BULLETIN. w 1868-71‖
ArHi N 28 1868

Camden HERALD. *See* Ouachita herald

Camden NEWS. d Ap 20 1920+
pub [1920-23]+
ArU F 1935+
—w ed *See* Camden times

OUACHITA herald. w 1842-69‖
1842-44? as Camden herald
suspended during the Civil War
DLC O 2 1856;Mr 5 1857
MHi My 22-29 1856;Ja 8,22 1857
MWA Mr 30 1861
NcD Ap 19 1850

STATE rights eagle. w 1858-67‖
suspended during the Civil war
WHi Jl 17 1858

Camden TIMES. w My 1929+
pub 1929+
ArU Jl 16 1931-33
—d ed *See* Camden news

ARKANSAS (*Continued*)

CANE HILL

ARKANSAS traveler. 1862?-
KHi Ja 1 1863

BUCK and ball. D 6 1862-
KHi D 6 1862

CARLISLE

Carlisle INDEPENDENT. w 1905+
ArU O 1930-Mr 1934

CHARLESTON

Charleston EXPRESS. w 1901+
pub 1930+
ArU O 1930-33

CLARKSVILLE

ARKANSAS standard. w 1867-69||?
MBAt F 25,Mr 24-31 1868

Clarksville DEMOCRAT. *See* Herald-democrat

Clarksville HERALD. *See* Johnson county herald

HERALD-DEMOCRAT. w 1909+
1909-17? as Clarksville democrat
pub 1917+
ArU Jl 1931-Mr 1934;35+
KHi Ja 13 1923

HERALD-JOURNAL. *See* Johnson county herald

JOHNSON county herald. w 1879-1917||?
1879-88 as Clarksville herald; 1888-93? Herald-journal. United with Clarksville democrat to form Herald-democrat

WESTERN journal. w 1887-88||
United with Clarksville herald to form Herald-journal, later Johnson county herald

CLINTON

VAN BUREN county democrat. w Ap 1909+
ArU O 1930-Je 1933

CONWAY

ARKANSAW traveler. w D 1875-80||?
MWA Ag 24 1876
OCHi S 20-O 4 1877

Conway DEMOCRAT. w 1887-1901||
United with Conway log cabin to form Log cabin democrat

HOME exponent. w 1930-32||
ArCH 1931-32
ArU O 1930-My,S 1931-Je 1932

LOG CABIN democrat. w 1879+
1879-S 1901 as Conway log cabin
ArCH S 1904-Ag 1905; S 1907+
ICM Ag 11 1888
TxU Mr 29-Je 21 1923

LOG CABIN democrat. d 1908+
ArCH 1908+
ArU O 1930-Mr 1934;35+
KHi Ag 17 1926

Conway NEWS. w 1920+
pub 1920+
ArCH 1920+

Conway TIMES. w 1918-27||
ArCH complete
KHi Ap 6 1923

COTTER

Cotter RECORD. w 1919+
pub 1919+

COTTON PLANT

WOODRUFF county democrat. w Mr 13 1915+
pub 1915+
ArU Ja-Je 1932

COVE CREEK

MISSOURI army argus. *See under* Corinth, Miss.

DANVILLE

Danville DEMOCRAT. w 1899+
pub 1929+

DARDANELLE

Dardanelle DISPATCH. w 1893-Je? 1897||
United with Dardanelle post to form Dardanelle post-dispatch

Dardanelle POST-DISPATCH. w 1876-1929||?
1876-80 as Western immigrant; 1881-Je 1897 Dardanelle post
MWA Je 3 1886

WESTERN immigrant. *See* Dardanelle post-dispatch

DECATUR

Decatur HERALD. w 1910+
pub 1910+

DE QUEEN

De Queen BEE. w Je 4 1897+
pub 1897+
ArU [O 1930-Je]Ag 1932-Mr 1934;35+

CITIZEN. w d 1928-33||
1928-30? as Sevier county citizen (w) Merged with De Queen bee
ArDB complete

SEVIER county citizen. *See* Citizen

DERMOTT

Dermott NEWS. w 1910+
pub [1910-13]+
ArU 1931-Ap 1932

DES ARC

CITIZEN. *See* White county citizen (Searcy)

WHITE RIVER journal. w 1907+
pub 1907+

DE VALLS BLUFF

DEMOCRAT. w 1910+
pub F 1913+
ArU O 1930-Mr 1934

PRAIRIE county democrat. *See* Lonoke democrat (Lonoke)

DE WITT

De Witt ENTERPRISE. *See* De Witt era-enterprise

De Witt ERA-ENTERPRISE. w 1916+
1916-29 as De Witt enterprise
pub 1916+
ArU S 1930-33

De Witt GAZETTE. *See* New era

NEW era. w 1884-1929||
1884-91? as De Witt gazette. United with De Witt enterprise to form De Witt era-enterprise

EARLE

Earle ENTERPRISE. w 1907+
ArU O 1930-Mr 1934

EL DORADO

SOUTH ARKANSAS progress. w Ja 1928+
1928-29 as Union county progress
pub 1928+
ArU O 1930-Mr 1934

UNION county progress. *See* South Arkansas progress

EUDORA

Eudora ENTERPRISE. w N 28 1934+
pub 1934+
ArU F 1935+

EUREKA SPRINGS

CARROLL courier. w Ap 26 1929+
pub 1929+
ArU F 1935+

ECHO. w S 5 1883-90||?
United with Times to form Times-echo, later Times

Eureka Springs FLASHLIGHT. w Ja 1897+
pub Ap 1931+
—d ed *See* Times-echo

Eureka Springs weekly HERALD. w 1879-Ja 1883||
ICM Je 4-11 1882

Eureka Springs semi-weekly HERALD. sw 1880?-82||?
ICM Je 8,15 1882

Eureka Springs daily HERALD. d 1881?-82||?
ICM My 13,16 1882

RAINBOW. m N 1 1891-1903||
KHi Ag 20 1892

TIMES. w 1881-1913||?
1891?-1900? as Times-echo
MoHi Ap 4 1885

Daily TIMES-ECHO. d 1889+
1889-90? as Daily times
pub Ap 1931+
ArU 1935+
KHi My 9 1925;O 13,N 10 1927
—w ed 1914+ *See* Eureka Springs flashlight

EVENING SHADE

SHARP county record. w 1877+
pub [1877-1906]+
ArU Jl 1931-Ag 1932

FAYETTEVILLE

ARKANSAN. w 1859-61||
ArHi Mr 1859-Mr 15 1861

ARKANSAS blade. *See* Fayetteville times

ARKANSAS countryman. w 1919-34||
ArFP complete
ArU O 1930-Mr 1934

ARKANSAS sentinel. 1875-1922||
Merged with Arkansas countryman
ArFP complete

Fayetteville DAILY. *See* Fayetteville democrat d

Fayetteville DEMOCRAT. w Ag 10 1860-61||
ArFD [1861]

Fayetteville DEMOCRAT. w Jl 4 1868-1919||?
pub [1868-1915]-19
ArHi 1868-Jl 3 1891
DLC My 28 1870

Fayetteville DEMOCRAT. d 1894+
1894-1915 as Fayetteville daily
pub [1894-1915]+
ArU S 1914-Jl 1915;Jl 1917-18;Jl 1920+

Fayetteville daily LEADER. d 1928-31||
ArFF complete
ArU 1930-Ja 1931

MOUNTAIN echo. w 1867-Ja 1 1873||
1867? as Radical
DLC Je 7,Ag 2,N 29 1871

PROGRESSIVE star. w D 5 1934+
pub 1935+

RADICAL. *See* Mountain echo

Fayetteville REPUBLIC. w 1885-My 26 1932||
1885-1912 as Fayetteville republican. Merged with Fayetteville democrat
ArFD [1885-1932]
ArU O 1930-Jl 1931

Fayetteville REPUBLICAN. *See* Fayetteville republic

Fayetteville TIMES. w N 17? 1881-82||
1881- 1882 as Arkansas blade
MWA D 15 1881

WITNESS. w My 9 1840-41||?
DLC My 16 1840;F 6-13,Mr 6,20-Ap 3,17-My 8,Je 19 1841

FORDYCE

Fordyce ADVOCATE. w 1891+
1891-95? as Tri-county chronicle; 1896?-1903? Chronicle-enterprise; 1904?-30 Tri-county advocate
pub O 1925+
ArU Jl 1931-32;35+

CHRONICLE-ENTERPRISE. *See* Fordyce advocate

DALLAS county news. *See* Fordyce news

Fordyce ENTERPRISE. w F 7 1884-95||?
United with Tri-county chronicle to form Chronicle-enterprise, later Fordyce advocate

Fordyce NEWS. w 1914+
1914-23? as Dallas county news
ArU O 1930-31

TRI-COUNTY advocate. *See* Fordyce advocate

TRI-COUNTY chronicle. *See* Fordyce advocate

FOREMAN

NEW ROCKY sun. *See* Foreman sun

Foreman SUN. w 1899+
1899-1912? as New Rocky sun
pub 1918+
KHi Mr 25 1927

FORREST CITY

CROWLEY RIDGE chronicle. w 1905+
ArU Jl 1931-33

Forrest City FREE press. w Jl 1868-74||
DLC Ja 22,Ap 3,O 22 1870: F 11 1871

FORT SMITH

Fort Smith tri-weekly BULLETIN. tw
TxU F 27 1862

Evening CALL. d 1890-92||?
TxU Ja 16-F 1891

Fort Smith DEMOCRAT. d 1895||?
United with Fort Smith times to form Times-democrat, later Fort Smith times record

Fort Smith ELEVATOR. w N 1 1878-My 1909||
Followed by Southwest farmer (not in this list)
ArFs 1878-1902
OkHi 1898-[1901-04]
TxU N-D 3 1879;N 1880-1904;06;08-09

Fort Smith HERALD. w Je 23 1847-62||
TxU [D 22 1847-F 21 1852;Mr 1856-58]

Fort Smith HERALD. tw Ag 1865-1873||?
TxU D 7 1865-Ag 29 1867;S 20 1870-Mr 20 1873

Fort Smith HERALD. w 1867-83||
TxU [Jl 1867-81]

Fort Smith daily HERALD. d 1878-83||?
Suspended 1880?
TxU 1878-Ja 1879;Ag 19-N 1881

INDEPENDENT-TRUE DEMOCRAT. *See* Fort Smith tribune

Fort Smith NEW era. w O 8 1863-85||
Title varies: Weekly new era; Fort Smith weekly new era
DLC Ag 19,S 9 1865[69-72]-84
KHi D 26 1863;N 26 1864;S 9 1865
MBAt Ap 1 1865
MH My 28 1864
MWA F 20 1864;Mr 23,Jl 6 1870
OClWHi Mr 25 1865
TxU [1863-N 11 1865]S 16,N 13 1867;Mr 1874-Ap 3 1878[N 24 1880-S 3 1885]
WHi Je 4 1864

ARKANSAS (*Continued*)

FORT SMITH—*Continued*

Fort Smith NEW era. tw 1871?-72||?
TxU Ap 3-7,14,21,S 27 1871[Mr 20-D 16 1872]

Evening NEWS. d
TxU [My 22-Je 25 1884]

Fort Smith NEWS RECORD. d 1893-Ja 1908||
United with Fort Smith times to form Fort Smith times record
ArFsT [Je 1894-1908]

SOUTHWEST American. d 1906+
Sunday issues as Southwest-times record
pub 1907+
ArU 1932;35+

Daily SUN. d 1897||?
United with Fort Smith times to form Times-sun, later Fort Smith times record

THIRTY-FIFTH parallel. w O 4 1859-61||?
DLC S 28,O 26 1860
MWA Jl 24,S 14 1860

Fort Smith TIMES. w Ja 1858-S 1860||
Followed by Fort Smith times-herald
TxU [Ap 21 1858-Ag 1860]

Fort Smith daily TIMES. 1884-1909. *See* Fort Smith times-record

Fort Smith TIMES-HERALD. d Mr 1861-Ap? 1862||
Follows Fort Smith times (1858-60)
TxU [Ap 5-O 1861]

Fort Smith TIMES RECORD. d D 1 1884+
1884-Je 1909 as Fort Smith times (1896?-97? Times-democrat; 1898? Times-sun)
Sunday issues as Southwest-times record
pub Je 8-21 1894;Ag 1-21 1895;Mr 1896-97; F-N 1898;99;Jl 1900-My,Jl 1901-N 1905;06-Ap 1907;08+
ArFs 1908+
ArU O-N 1903;33
TxU Jl 16-F 28 1891

Fort Smith TRIBUNE. w D 1871-88||?
1871-O 23 1878 as Western independent; O 30 1878-Je 6 1883 Wheeler's independent; Je 13 1883-F 1885? Independent-true democrat
TxU 1872-[O 30 1878-F 17 1885]

Daily Fort Smith TRIBUNE. d Ja 1884-88||?
TxU [Ja 22 1884-My 1885;My 3-S 29 1887]

Fort Smith UNION. w 1863||
KHi S 10 1863

WESTERN independent. *See* Fort Smith tribune

WHEELER'S independent. *See* Fort Smith tribune

FORT WASHITA

CHICKASAW intelligencer. w O 1854?-
MWA Ap 21 1855

GENTRY

JOURNAL-ADVANCE. w 1894+
1894-96? as Journal
pub 1920+
ArU O 1930-Mr 1933

GILLHAM

Gillham MINER. w 1900-08||
TxU S 27,O 18,D 20 1905;Ja 2,17,Ap 11 1906

GLENWOOD

Glenwood HERALD. w 1925+
pub 1925+
ArU O 1935+

GRAVETTE

BENTON county gazette. w 1908-09||?
NcD O 21 1909

Gravette NEWS HERALD. w S 22 1894+
pub 1909-25;34+
NcD O 22 1909

GREENWOOD

Greenwood DEMOCRAT. w 1883+
pub 1923+
ArU O 1930-Mr 1934

GURDON

Gurdon TIMES. w 1894+
pub [1894-1920]+
ArU O 1930-31

HAMBURG

ASHLEY county eagle. w 1889-Jl 1922||
Merged with Ashley county leader
ArHL D 1889-1922

ASHLEY county leader. w 1912+
1912-20 as Hamburg budget
pub F 16 1912+
ArU O 1930-Je 1931;33

Hamburg BUDGET. *See* Ashley county leader

HAMPTON

ARKANSAS plaindealer. w Ag 17 1889+
early years pub in Woodberry
ArU Jl 1931-Mr 1934

HARDY

Hardy HERALD. w 1891+
ArU 1932

HARRISBURG

MODERN news. w 1888+
pub N 1891+

HARRISON

BOONE county advocate. *See* Harrison times

BOONE county headlight. w 1896+
1896-1916 as Harrison republican
pub 1923+
ArU O 1930-Mr 1934

BOONE county highlander. *See* Harrison times

Harrison HIGHLANDER. *See* Harrison times

Harrison REPUBLICAN. *See* Boone county headlight

Harrison TIMES. w Jl 1870+
1870-72 as Boone county advocate; 1873? Boone county highlander; 1874?-Je 1876 Harrison highlander
pub [1870-95]+

Harrison daily TIMES. d 1919+
pub 1919+
ArU N 1935+
KHi S 5 1927;Mr 16 1928

HAVANA

MT. MAGAZINE rural record. w 1924+
1924-29? as Rural record
pub [1924-30]+

RURAL record. *See* Mt. Magazine rural record

HEBER. *See* HEBER SPRINGS

HEBER SPRINGS
To 1910? as Heber

CLEBURNE county times. w 1923-26||?
United with Jacksonian-headlight to form Times-headlight

Heber Springs HEADLIGHT. *See* Times-headlight

JACKSONIAN. w 1888-1918||?
United with Heber Springs headlight to form Jacksonian-headlight, later Times-headlight
KHi N 27 1890-O 18 1906

Daily JACKSONIAN. d Ag 12 1891-
KHi Ag 12-28 1891

JACKSONIAN-HEADLIGHT. *See* Times-headlight

TIMES-headlight. w 1907+
1907-1918? as Heber Springs headlight; 1919?-26 Jacksonian-headlight
ArU O 1930-32

HELENA

ARKANSAS state democrat. *See* Southern sentinel

CLARION. w Ap 1 1865-75||?
1865? as Western clarion
My 2 1864 an advance number
DLC My 2 1864;Ap,Je 24-Jl 8,22,Ag 19-S,O 14-D 16 1865
ArHe Ap 1870-Ap 15 1871;Mr 22-D 20 1873
MWA Mr 24 1866

CONSTITUTIONAL journal. w Mr 8 1836-
DLC Mr-Jl 14,28-Ag 11,25,S 14-D 1,22,1836;Ja 12,26-F 9,23-Mr 23,Ap 6,20-27,My 11,N 9,D 14-21 1837

DEMOCRATIC star. w F 1853-D 20 1855||
DLC Mr 1854-55

Daily INDEPENDENT. d 1874||?
DLC [Jl 22-D 1874]

INDEPENDENT southron. *See* Helena weekly note-book

Helena weekly NOTE-BOOK. w O 1858-63||?
1858- 1859 as Independent southron
DLC S 27,O 4,18 1860
MBAt Ja 9 1862

SOUTHERN sentinel. w 1832?-41||
1832?-F 1841? title varies: Arkansas state democrat; Arkansas state democrat and Helena commercial advertiser
DLC F 14,My 15-22,Je-S,O 9-D 11,24 1840;Ja-F 12 1841

SOUTHERN shield. w,ir F 8 1840-74||?
suspended during the Civil war
w 1840-63?
DLC Mr 1840[41-42]Ja 24,F 7 1843[49-53]
MWA Jl 23 1841;Ja 3 1852

Helena SPY. w Mr 10 1838-
DLC Mr 10-17,31-Ag 7,S 10-24 1838
MWA Ap 14 1838

STATE rights democrat. w Mr 20 1856-65||
DLC [1856-Jl 1857]

WESTERN clarion. *See* Clarion

Helena WORLD. d 1871+
pub 1919+
ArHe 1917+
ArHi 1871+
ArU D 1930-Mr 1934
KHi Mr 8 1928

Weekly WORLD. w N 29 1871-1912||
ArHe 1895-1902
MH N 29 1871

HOPE

Hope PRESS. d 1927-29||?
United with Star of hope (d) to form Star and press, later Hope star

Hope STAR. d 1919+
1919-29 as Star of Hope; 1930-31? Star and press
ArU S 1930-Je 1931;35+
KHi D 29 1926

STAR of Hope. w,sw 1899-1929||?
sw 1904?-18?
pub complete
—d ed *See* Hope star

HOT SPRINGS. *See* HOT SPRINGS NATIONAL PARK

HOT SPRINGS NATIONAL PARK
To 1922? as Hot Springs

HOT SPRINGS

Hot Springs COURIER. w Je 25 1869-Ja 20 1874||
NNHi N 16 1871;Ja 2 1873

Daily HORSE SHOE. *See* Hot Springs daily news

Hot Springs NEW era. d 1906+
ArU Jl 1930-Ag 1932
KHi O 19 1920;Ag 5 1922

Hot Springs daily NEWS. d Ag 1882-1913||?
1882-N? 1883 as Daily horse shoe; D? 1883-Mr? 1885 People's hornet-horse shoe
MWA Ap 26 1885;D 22 1887

OUACHITA observer. w 1930+
pub 1930+
ArU Jl 1932-Mr 1934

PEOPLE'S hornet-horse shoe. *See* Hot Springs daily news

Hot Springs daily TELEGRAPH. d 1874-80||?
NNHi Ag 4 1876

HUNTSVILLE

Huntsville DEMOCRAT. *See* Madison county record

MADISON county democrat. *See* Madison county record

MADISON county record. w O 1885+
1885-1918? as Madison county democrat (title varies: Huntsville democrat)
pub [1925]+
ArU O 1930-S 1933

HUTTIG

Huttig NEWS. w 1906+
pub 1906+

JACKSONPORT

REVEILLE. Ap?-My 3 1864||
MWA My 3 1864

STARS and stripes. w D 1 1863-
pub by Union army
MWA D 1 1863(photostat)
NN D 1 1863(photostat)
WHi D 8 1863

JASPER

NEWTON county times. w 1908+
1908-14? as Jasper times
ArU 1933

Jasper TIMES. *See* Newton county times

JONESBORO

CRAIGHEAD county journal. w 1922+
pub 1922+
ArU O 1930-Mr 1932

CRAIGHEAD county sun. *See* Jonesboro weekly sun

Jonesboro weekly SUN. w 1888+
1888-1902 as Craighead county sun
pub 1888+

Jonesboro evening SUN. d 1902+
pub 1902+
ArU 1935+

JUDSONIA

Judsonia ADVANCE. *See* White county record

WHITE county record. w 1878+
1878-1921? as Judsonia advance
KHi S 29 1927

LAKE VILLAGE

CHICOT spectator. w 1907+
pub 1907+

LEPANTO

NEWS. *See* Lepanto press

Lepanto PRESS. w 1924+
1924-28 as News
pub 1924+
ArU O 1930-N 1931

ARKANSAS (*Continued*)

LEWISVILLE

Lewisville HERALD. w O 1917+
pub 1917+
ArU 1931-33

LINCOLN

Lincoln SUN. w 1918+
pub 1926+

LITTLE ROCK

AEGIS. *See* Unconditional union

AMERICAN guide. w 1889-
Negro
DLC Ja 27 1900

ARKANSAS advocate. w Mr 31 1830-Ap 20 1837||
United with Arkansas weekly times to form Arkansas times and advocate
ArHi complete
CSmH Ag 4 1830
DLC complete
MH Ja 19 1831
TxU complete
WHi 1830-D 14 1831;S 19 1832;33-My 22 1835

ARKANSAS banner. *See* Arkansas true democrat

ARKANSAS campaign gazette. w D 20 1867-Mr 13 1868||
DLC complete
w ed *See* Arkansas gazette

ARKANSAS democrat. 1846 *See* Arkansas state democrat

ARKANSAS democrat. d O 2 1871+
1871-Ap 9 1878 as Evening star
pub 1905+
ArAH 1927+
ArHi 1871-S 30 1878;79-91
ArL 1910+
ArU 1931-Mr 1934;35+
DLC 1898-[1906]+
ICM F 2 1883
WHi N 6 1921

ARKANSAS democratic banner. *See* Arkansas true democrat

ARKANSAS echo. w D 31 1891-Ag 1932||
In German
ArSuN complete

ARKANSAS freeman. w Ag 24? 1869-71||?
Negro
OClWHi O 5 1869

*ARKANSAS gazette. w,sw N 20 1819+
O 11 1836-F 1 1850 Arkansas state gazette; F 8 1850-54? Arkansas state gazette and democrat; 1855?-1911? Arkansas weekly gazette
w 1819-1911?
1819-N 1821 pub in Arkansas Post
suspended Ja 28-F 4 1822;Ja 17-F 1 1850; Mr-Ap 1854; from S 10 1863-My 6 1865 (for these years *See* National democrat)
pub 1821—
ArHi 1821-23;F 1826+
ArU [1828-33;35-43;45;48-49;51;56;71;1904;06]
CSmH Ag 4 1830
CoU My 1899-Ja 1903
DLC 1821-[61-63]-N 17 1868
ICM Jl 23 1885
IaDH Mr 29 1843
LNC D 21 1860
MWA [1821]-[23]-[25]-[27]-38;N 13 1839;40-[44-45]-[48-49]Ja 12 1861;N 18-D 2,16-30 1865
MiU-C [1846-48;1919]
NhD My 21 1873
TM D 17 1859;F 11,Mr 10,Ap 14-21 1860
TxU 1821-D 7 1842[74]
WHi [1821-32]O 24 1838;D 9 1840[42-45]F 8 1850-55;1922+
—campaign ed *See* Arkansas campaign gazette

ARKANSAS gazette. d My 10 1865+
My-Jl 5 1865 Arkansas state gazette; Jl 6 1865-Ag 29 1866 Little Rock daily gazette; Ag 30 1866-F 2 1889 Daily Arkansas gazette
N 20 1919 is centennial ed
pub 1865+
ArAH 1927+
ArCH Ap-My 1902;O 1908+
ArHi 1865+
ArL 1910+
ArMA Jl 1928-N 1930;31+
ArMoA 1934+
ArP D 1929;Ap 1930+
ArT 1928+
ArU [1870-77;79-81;83-85;91;99-1901;03-08;10-14]19+
DLC 1865-[76]-[79]+
KHi F 22,S 6 1917
M N 20 1919;Je 5 1929
MWA Je 11,Jl 6 1873;Mr 8 1908;N 20(supp) 1919
T [1929]
WHi Ap 15,21 1887;Jl 20 1895;1917-21

ARKANSAS mansion. *See* Arkansaw dispatch

ARKANSAS patriot. w O 1862?- S 10 1863||
Followed by Daily pantagraph, later Weekly pantagraph
KHi Ap 11,Jl 21 1863
TxU [1862-S 1 1863]

ARKANSAS press. w 1889-95||?
DLC Jl 23,Ag 18,S 1,15-22,O 6,20-D 1889;Mr 16-Ap 6 1890;Ap 11 1890-Ap 2 1892
—d ed *See* Daily press

ARKANSAS weekly republican. w Ap 17 1867-75||?
ArHi D 1867-Je 1872;Jl-S 1874
DLC Je 12,26-Jl,Ag 21-S 11,25-O 16,30,N 20-D 11,25 1867
MBAt Je 10-Jl 1,22-Ag 12,S 2-23,O 28 1868[69]
MWA O 14 1868
—d ed *See* Little Rock daily republican

ARKANSAS staats-zeitung. w 1877-1917||?
In German
KHi S 22 1888

ARKANSAS star. w Jl 28 1839-
suspended from Je 6-29 1840
DLC S 7 1839;F 13,Mr 5,My 7-14,Jl 30-Ag 6,O 21-D 17,31 1840;Ja 7,21-F 4,18 1841
MWA Mr 5 1840;Ja 28 1841

ARKANSAS state democrat. w My 21 1846-F 1 1850||
My-O 23 1846 as Arkansas democrat. United with Arkansas state gazette to form Arkansas state gazette and democrat, later Arkansas gazette
ArU Ja 25,D 24 1847
DLC complete
N [1846-49]
WHi complete

ARKANSAS state gazette. *See* Arkansas gazette

ARKANSAS times and advocate. w F 1834-44||?
1834-Ja 13? 1835 as Political intelligencer; Ja 20 1835-Ag 1 1836 Times; Ag 8 1836-Ap 24 1837 Arkansas weekly times; My 1 1837-My 17 1841 Arkansas times and advocate; My 24-Jl 19 1841 Times and advocate
Ct D 11 1834[1835-36]Ja 23 1837
DLC [1835-44]
IaDH Ja 6 1840
MWA My 16,Jl 4-11,Ag 8,N 2 1835[F 8-Jl 18 1836]My 1,Jl 31,Ag 21-28,O 18,D 18 1837[38]Jl 15 1839[Ap 12 1841-Jl 1843]Mr 11 1844
WHi My 7,Jl 23 1838

ARKANSAS true democrat. w S 16 1843-S 1863||?
1843-Mr 4 1851 as Arkansas banner; Mr 11 1851-Ag 31 1852 Arkansas democratic banner; S 7 1852-Je 2 1857 True democrat
Suspended from F 28-Ap 4 1854
ArHi F 18 1854-O 6 1858
DLC S-N,D 23 1843-D 10 1845[46-60]Je 13 1861
MBAt F 18 1863
MWA Ap 11-O 11 1854;O 12 1859-S 1860;Je 12 1862
NNHi D 22 1860
TM Ag 4 1858;S 21 1859;F 15 1860
TxU S 23 1843-D 17 1845;S 16 1846-S 1860

ARKANSAS whig. w My 22 1851-55||
DLC 1851-[53-Ag 1854]F 8,My 10,24 1855
MWA [1851-52]-Mr 3,17-24,Ap 21,D 1-8,29 1853;Ja 5,19 1854
MiU-C S 9 1852
TxU Je 19 1851-Je 12 1852

ARKANSAW dispatch. w 1880-96||?
1880-86? as Arkansas mansion
Negro
KHi Je 30 1883-Ap 19 1884
TxGR Je 23 1883

Daily evening ARKANSIAN. d F 17- 1873||?
MoHi F 17-18,24-27,Mr 1,3-4,7-8,10,15,19,21,24, Ap 4,7 1873

CHRONICLE. w O 11-D 13 1855||
DLC N 1,15,D 13 1855

Daily CONSERVATIVE. d S 1866-68||?
Follows Weekly pantagraph
TxU S 26 1866-Je 1867

Little Rock daily GAZETTE. *See* Arkansas gazette

NATIONAL democrat. w S 29 1863-My 6 1865||
pub by Union Army during suspension of Arkansas gazette
DLC O 20,D 26 1863;Ja 16,F Mr 12,26-Ap 2,16-23,My-Je 11,Jl 2,16-23,Ag 13,27-S 17,O 1864-65
MWA Ap 9 1864
WHi [O 8 1864-Ap 22 1865]

Daily NATIONAL democrat. d 1864?-My? 1865||
DLC O 4,N 9,30,D 5-6,28-29 1864;Ja 9,Mr 21-22 1865
IaGG Mr 9 1864

Little Rock daily NEWS. d 1817-27||?
KHi N 24 1922;Je 22 1927

OLD-LINE democrat. w 1859-61||
TxU S 1859-Ja 3 1861

Weekly PANTAGRAPH. d,w O? 1863-S 1866||
Follows Arkansas patriot.
1863-Mr 24 1866 as Daily pantagraph (d)
Followed by Daily conservative
TxU [Ap 17 1865-Mr 24]Je 7-14,Ag 16-23,S 6-13 1866

POLITICAL intelligencer. *See* Arkansas times and advocate

Daily PRESS. d 1887-95||?
Suspended from 1888?-94?
ArBA D 1887-Ap 4 1888
—w ed See Arkansas press

Evening PUBLIC ledger. d F? 1868-
MBAt Ap 14 1868

PULASKIAN. w 1915-29||?
ArHi 1915-Ja 5 1922

Little Rock daily REPUBLICAN. d Ap 10 1867-76||?
Title varies slightly
DLC [My 24 1867-Je 3 1874]
ICHi O 24 1871
MBAt D 6,8,10,13,15-18,21-24,30 1869
MoHi F 25 1873
—w ed *See* Arkansas weekly republican

Evening STAR. *See* Arkansas democrat 1871+

Daily STATE journal. d O 31 1861-
DLC O-D 22 1861;Ja 6-F 5 1862
TxU [N 1861-F 7 1862]

TRUE democrat. 1852-57 *See* Arkansas true democrat

TRUE democrat. w 1881-My 1883||
United with Wheeler's independent (Fort Smith) to form Independent-true democrat, later Fort Smith tribune

UNCONDITIONAL union. w Ja 23 1864-
Early numbers as Aegis
Suspended N 10 1864-Mr 23 1865
DLC 1864-65
MWA My 21,Ag 25 1864
WHi [Mr-N 3 1864]

Daily UNCONDITIONAL union. d My 9 1864-
DLC My 11,17 1864
WHi My 17,24 1864

LONOKE

Lonoke DEMOCRAT. w Ag 4 1871+
1871? as Prairie county democrat (De Valls Bluff)
pub 1879+
ArU O 1930-33

McCRORY

ARKANSAS central leader. w 1923+
pub 1923+
ArU O 1930-Mr 1934

McGEHEE

McGehee TIMES. sw,w 1925+
1925-28 as McGehee semi-weekly times (sw)
pub [1925]+
ArU O 1930-Mr 1934

MAGNOLIA

BANNER-NEWS. w Mr 17 1928+
Formed by the union of Columbia banner and Magnolia news
pub 1928+
ArMA 1931+
ArU 1931-33;35+

COLUMBIA banner. w,sw 1878-Mr 1928||
United with Magnolia news to form Banner-news
w 1878-1925?
ArMB 1878-95;1909-28
KHi D 2 1926

Magnolia NEWS. w 1901-Mr 1928||
United with Columbia banner to form Banner-news

Magnolia TIMES. w 1929+
pub 1929+

MALVERN

ARKANSAS meteor. w 1878-1932||
1878-Ag 1883 as Malvern meteor. United with Times-journal to form Meteor-journal
ArHi 1900-12
ArU 1930-31

ARKANSAS state journal. w 1888-92||?
United with Arkansaw times to form Times-journal, later Meteor-journal

ARKANSAW times. *See* Meteor-journal

Malvern METEOR. *See* Arkansas meteor

METEOR-JOURNAL. w 1882+
1882-92 as Arkansaw times; 1892-1932 Times-journal

Malvern daily RECORD. d 1916+
KHi Mr 17 1925

TIMES-JOURNAL. *See* Meteor-journal

MAMMOTH SPRING

DEMOCRAT. w Je 1890+
suspended from Jl 1914-Je 1920
pub 1920+

MARIANNA

COURIER-INDEX. w 1874+
1874-1918 as Marianna index
pub 1917+
ArU O 1930-Mr 1934

LEE county courier. w 1890-1918||
United with Marianna index to form Courier-index

MARKED TREE

Marked Tree GAZETTE. *See* Marked Tree tribune

Marked Tree TRIBUNE. w 1905+
1905-17 as Marked Tree gazette
pub 1905+
ArU O 1930-Mr 1934
KHi Ja 20,Jl 13 1928

MARSHALL

MOUNTAIN wave. w 1893+
pub 1892+
ArU O 1930-Mr 1934

Marshall REPUBLICAN. w 1890+
pub 1890+
ArU O 1930-My 1933
KHi Ja 19 1923

ARKANSAS (*Continued*)

MELBOURNE

Melbourne TIMES. w 1896+
pub [1911-31]+
ArU S 19 1930-Ap 1933

MENA

POLK county democrat. w 1896-1915||?
KHi O 28 1915

Mena weekly STAR. w Ag 18 1896+
pub 1896+
ArU 1935+
KHi Ap 24-My 1 1913

Mena evening STAR. d Mr 4 1899+
pub 1899+
ArU S 1930-Jl 1932;35+

MONTICELLO

ADVANCE-MONTICELLONIAN. w 1892+
1892-93? as Drew county advance; 1894?-1920 Advance
pub 1894+
ArU Jl 14 1931-33

DREW county advance. *See* Advance-Monticellonian

MONTICELLONIAN. w 1870-1920||
United with Advance to form Advance-Monticellonian

MORRILTON

ARKANSAS unit. *See* Morrilton headlight

CONWAY county unit. *See* Morrilton headlight

Morrilton DEMOCRAT. w 1896+
pub [1909-28]+
ArM 1930+
ArU S 1930-Mr 1934;35+
KHi Jl 12 1928

Morrilton HEADLIGHT. w 1874-1919||?
NcU N 3 1882

Morrilton HEADLIGHT. sw,w 1916+
1916-23? as Conway county unit; 1924?-Mr 1931 Arkansas unit
sw 1916-25?
pub Mr 20 1931
ArU O 1930-Mr 1931

MOUNT IDA

HERALD. w 1925+
1925-30? as Montgomery county herald
ArU Ag 1931-Mr 1933

MONTGOMERY county herald. *See* Herald

MOUNTAIN HOME

BAXTER bulletin. w 1902+
pub 1902+
ArU O 1930-1933
NN D 30 1904

BAXTER county citizen. w 1880+
pub 1880+

MOUNTAIN VIEW

Mountain View HERALD. w My 20 1932+
pub 1932+

STONE county record. w 1910+
pub 1910+

MURFREESBORO

PIKE county courier. w 1898+
KHi My 23 1919

NAPOLEON

Napoleon JOURNAL. w Ap 17 1839-S? 1840||
Followed by Messenger
DLC Ag 24 1839;S 5 1840

MESSENGER. w O 24? 1840-
Follows Napoleon journal
DLC N 14 1840

Napoleon STANDARD and commercial advertiser. w Ap 1841-
DLC My 22,Je 5 1841

NASHVILLE

Nashville NEWS. w,sw F 1884+
w 1884-95?
pub 1913+
ArU D 1930-Mr 1934

NEWARK

Newark JOURNAL. w N 29 1901+
pub 1901+

NEWPORT

Newport daily INDEPENDENT. d 1901+
pub 1901+

Newport weekly INDEPENDENT. w 1901+
pub 1901+
ArU O 1930-Mr 1934

NORTH LITTLE ROCK

To 1917 as Argenta

ARGENTA incident. w 1885-89||?
WHi O 3 1885

ARGENTA times. *See* North Little Rock times

PULASKI county times. *See* North Little Rock times

North Little Rock TIMES. w 1890+
1890-91 as Argenta times; 1892-1917 Pulaski county times
Suspended from 1917-22
pub 1896+

OSCEOLA

Osceola TIMES. w S 1 1870+
pub 1870+
ArU O 1930-Mr 1934
ICU F 24,Je 16 1883

OZARK

DEMOCRAT-ENTERPRISE. w 1887+
1887-Je 1909 as Ozark democrat
suspended from F 14 1926-Ja 13 1927
pub 1927+
ArU O 1930-33

Ozark ENTERPRISE. w 1900-Je 1909||
1900-04? as Franklin county enterprise. United with Ozark democrat to form Democrat-enterprise

FRANKLIN county enterprise. *See* Ozark enterprise

SPECTATOR. sw Ag 1911+
pub 1911+
ArU Ja 26-Je 7 1932

PARAGOULD

GREENE county events. w,sw 1882-95||?
United with Soliphone to form Soliphone-events, later Soliphone
w 1882-94?

PRESS. d 1911+
pub 1911+
ArU 1935+
—w,tw,sw ed *See* Soliphone

SOLIPHONE. w,sw,tw Ja 1 1893+
1896?-99? as Soliphone-events
w 1893-1918?;tw 1919?-30?
pub 1893+
ArU O 1930-Mr 1934
—d ed *See* Press

PARIS

Paris EXPRESS. w Mr 28 1880+
pub 1900+

Paris PROGRESS. w,sw 1910+
sw 1914?-24?
pub 1910+
ArU O 1930-Mr 1934

PERRYVILLE

Perryville NEWS. *See* Perry county news

PERRY county news. w 1884+
1884-1909? as Perryville news
pub N 1926+
ArU O 1930-1933

PIGGOTT

Piggott BANNER w. 1892+
pub 1892+
ArU Jl 1931-Mr 1934
WaPS F 7,28 1919;Ag 20 1920;Ag 5 1921

CRITIC. w 1912-18||?
1912-15 pub in Hayti, Mo.
MoHi Ja-F 19,Mr 5,My 7,Je 11 1915

PINE BLUFF

Pine Bluff COMMERCIAL. d 1887+
pub 1902+
ArP 1929+
ArU O 1930-32

Pine Bluff DISPATCH. *See* Pine Bluff republican

Pine Bluff EAGLE. w F 1880-O 1881||
United with Pine Bluff press to form Press eagle

Pine Bluff GRAPHIC. w 1886+
1910+ Sunday issues of d used as w
pub 1886+

Pine Bluff daily GRAPHIC. d 1893+
pub 1893+
ArP 1930+

Pine Bluff weekly HERALD. w Ja 13 1900-07||?
Negro
DLC Ja 27 1900

PRESS EAGLE. w Ja 1869-1916||?
1869-O 1881 as Pine Bluff press
ArP Ja 8 1883-Ja 24 1891

Pine Bluff REPUBLICAN. w S 8 1865-68||?
1865-F? 1868 as Pine Bluff dispatch
ICHi S 22 1865
TxU O 27 1866-F 1868

TRUE Southron.
NNHi Mr 2,30 1861
NcD extra Mr 1861

POCAHONTAS

COURIER and express. w D 1869-73||?
1869-72? as Randolph county courier
OClWHi F 18 1871

NEWS-HERALD. w 1881-1908||?
1881 as Scalpel; 1882-1902? Randolph herald. United with Pocahontas star to form Pocahontas star herald

RANDOLPH county courier. *See* Courier and express

RANDOLPH county express. w Jl 1868-72||?
United with Randolph county courier to form Courier and express

RANDOLPH herald. *See* News-herald

SCALPEL. *See* News-herald

Pocahontas STAR HERALD. w 1903+
1903-08? as Pocahontas star
pub 1903+
ArU O 1930-31;35+

PRESCOTT

Prescott DISPATCH. w 1876-83||?
KHi F 20 1878

NEVADA county picayune. w F 14 1878+
pub 1906+
ArU O 1930-Je 1931;33

NEVADA news. w O 8 1905+
pub 1905+
ArU O 1930-Ap 1932
KHi F 5 1925
—d ed *See* Prescott daily news

Prescott daily NEWS. d Ap 8 1907+
pub 1907+
—w ed *See* Nevada news

RECTOR

CLAY county democrat. w Mr 22 1934+
pub 1934+

RISON

CLEVELAND county herald. w 1888+
pub [1895-1922]+
ArU Jl 1931-33

ROGERS

Rogers DEMOCRAT. w 1881+
1881-90? as New era
pub 1919+
ArU O 1930-Je 1933

NEW era. *See* Rogers democrat

RUSSELLVILLE

COURIER-DEMOCRAT. w Ja 1875+
1875-99 as Russellville democrat
pub 1875+
ArU Jl 1931-33

Daily COURIER-DEMOCRAT. d 1924+
pub 1924+
ArU 1935+

Russellville DEMOCRAT. *See* Courier-democrat

ST. PAUL

MOUNTAIN air. w 1894-F 1933||
Merged with Madison county record (Huntsville)
ArHuM complete

SALEM

Salem HEADLIGHT. w 1924+
pub 1924+
ArU Jl 1931-33

SEARCY

CITIZEN. d 1890+
pub 1890+
—w ed *See* White county citizen

WHITE county citizen. w S 1854+
1854-Ja 1890 as Citizen (Des Arc)
suspended during the civil war
pub 1890+
ArU O 1930-33
—d ed *See* Citizen

SHERIDAN

Sheridan HEADLIGHT. w 1881+
ArU O 1930-33

SILOAM SPRINGS

DEMOCRAT. w 1895-1902||
United with Herald to form Herald and democrat

HERALD and democrat. w 1879+
1879-1902 as Herald
pub 1912+

HERALD and democrat. d 1934+
pub 1934+

INTER-STATE American. w 1921+
1924-28 as Sulphur Springs American (Sulphur Springs)
pub 1921+
ArSJ 1921+
ArU O 1930-Je 1931

ARKANSAS (*Continued*)

SPRINGDALE

Springdale NEWS. w,sw 1887+
w 1887-1909?
pub 1887+
ArU Ja-Jl 1931;35+
KHi Je 22 1923

STAMPS

LAFAYETTE county democrat. w S 1905+
pub 1905+

STAR CITY

LINCOLN lance. *See* Lincoln ledger

LINCOLN ledger. w 1878+
1878-87? as Lincoln lance
pub 1924+
ArU S 1930-Je 1931

STUTTGART

ARKANSAS county leader. w 1889-1928||
1889-1923? as Free press. United with Grand Prairie news to form Grand Prairie leader
KHi Ja 18 1923

Stuttgart ARKANSAWYER. d Ja 19 1920+
pub 1920+
ArU S 1930-Mr 1934;35+

FREE press. *See* Arkansas county leader

GRAND PRAIRIE leader. w 1916+
1916-28 as Grand Prairie news
pub 1916+
ArU O-D 1930;Jl 1931-33

GRAND Prairie news. *See* Grand Prairie leader

SULPHUR SPRINGS

Sulphur Springs AMERICAN. *See* Inter-state American (Siloam Springs)

TEXARKANA

Morning COURIER. *See* Texarkana gazette

FOUR states press. *See* Texarkana gazette

Texarkana GAZETTE. d 1898+
1898-1910? as Morning courier; 1911-18? Four states press and courier; 1919-25? Four states press
Also dated in Texarkana, Texas
pub 1909+
ArMA [1931]
ArT 1928+
ArU O 1930-Mr 1934
TxGR Jl 15 1926

Texarkana daily NEWS. d Mr 1926+
pub 1926+
ArT Jl 1934+

TUCKERMAN

Tuckerman RECORD. w 1919+
pub 1919+

VAN BUREN

ARGUS. *See* Press-argus

ARKANSAS intelligencer. w 1842-60||?
CSmH My 16 1846
CtY Ap 8 1843
DLC [1845-47;57-58]
MWA My 10,D 20 1845;Ja 17,F 28,Ap 25,My 16-23,Je 20,Jl 25,Ag 15,S 5,19-26,O 10,24 1846

Van Buren evening NEWS. d
TxU [Ja 15-Ap 11 1923]

Van Buren PRESS. w Jl 6 1859-1914||
United with Van Buren argus to form Van Buren press-argus
ArHi 1863-68;70;72-78;94;97-1914
TxU 1859-Ja 23 1862;F 1866-O 17 1891[93-S 7 1912]

Van Buren PRESS-ARGUS. w D 25 1875+
1875-1914 as Van Buren argus
pub 1900+
ArU S 1930-Mr 1934
KHi N 18 1927
TxU Ja-Mr 6 1909

Van Buren daily PRESS-ARGUS. d 1897-1918||?
1897-1914 as Van Buren daily argus
TxU [My 1904-N 10 1908;Mr-Ap 25 1913]

WESTERN frontier whig. w 1842-46||
WHi Ap 29 1845

WALDRON

ADVANCE REPORTER. w 1904+
1904-06 as Waldron advance
ArU O 1930-33

Waldron REPORTER. w 1878-1906||
United with Waldron advance to form Advance reporter

WALNUT RIDGE

TIMES DISPATCH. w 1910+
pub 1910+
ArU O 1930-32

WARREN

BRADLEY county democrat. *See* Democrat news

BRADLEY county eagle. *See* Eagle democrat

DEMOCRAT NEWS. w 1892-1918||
1892-96 as Bradley county democrat. United with Bradley county eagle to form Eagle democrat

EAGLE DEMOCRAT. w 1913+
1913-18 as Bradley county eagle
ArU O 1930-Mr 1934

Warren NEWS. w 1886-96||
United with Bradley county democrat to form Democrat news

WASHINGTON

Washington PRESS. *See* Washington telegraph

SOUTHWESTERN press. *See* Washington telegraph

Washington TELEGRAPH. w D 19 1840+
1876?-Ja? 1883 as Southwestern press; F? 1883-N 1891 Washington press
pub [1842-1900]+
ArBA O 21 1877-Ja,Ap 1883-D 11 1886
ArHi Ja 15 1862-65
DLC [N 1841-S 1842;F 1849-56]Ja 1857
MBAt Ap 5-12,My 10 1865
TxU O 22 1845

WEST MEMPHIS

CRITTENDEN county times. w Ja 9 1931+
pub 1931+
ArU Mr-Ag 19,O 1932-Mr 1934

WILMOT

Wilmot WEEKLY. w 1912-33||
Merged with Ashley county leader (Hamburg)
ArHL S 22 1916-O 13 1933

WOODBERRY

ARKANSAS plaindealer. *See under* Hampton

WYNNE

CROSS county democrat. *See* Wynne star

Wynne PROGRESS. w 1904—
pub 1905-06;F 1935+

Wynne STAR. w,d 1895-1929||
1895-1926? as Cross county democrat (w)
United with Wynne progress to form Daily star-progress

Daily STAR-PROGRESS. d 1929+
pub F 1935+
ArU O 1930-Je 1931;Jl 1932-33

YELLVILLE

MOUNTAIN echo. w Mr 5 1886+
pub 1914+
ArU Jl 1931-33

CALIFORNIA

ACTON

Acton BOOSTER. m 1891-1920||?
1891-1915? as Acton rooster
C N 15 1900-Ja 15 1913

Acton ROOSTER. *See* Acton booster

ADIN

Weekly Adin ARGUS. w Ag 1881+
1881-Ap 1887 as Adin argus
pub [1883-1904]+
C Ag 1887-98
CAlt Ja 1935+
CU-B [1883]-[91-92]

Adin HAWKEYE. w S 1878-80||
CU-B Ag 8 1879-N 19 1880

ALAMEDA

ARGUS. w,sw,d D 6 1877-S 30 1912||
w 1877-Ag 1881;sw Ag 1881-91
Merged with Alameda times-star
CA D 1879-[84]-[96;1900]-12
CSmH [1877-N 1880]
CU-B O 10 1878-Ja 9,Je 19,Jl-Ag 14,S 4,18-25,O 9,23 1879-80;D 30 1881;Ap 29 1882;Ja 20 1883;87;N 5 1890;Ja 7 1899;Jl 29,Ag 21 1905-12
KHi [Jl 28-N 3 1888]

O COLONIA portuguesa. *See* Jornal português (Oakland)

ENCINAL. w,sw,d S 16 1869-N 10 1906||
Title varies: Encinal of Alameda; Daily evening encinal; Daily encinal. Merged with Argus
CA 1869-[96]-[98-99]-1906
CU-B D 11 1869;Mr 26 1870-Mr,S 23 1871-80;S 14 1881-Ag 23,S 6 1882-S 15 1894;Jl 28 [Ag 10 1903-Ap 28 1906]
KHi [Mr 21 1888-F 12 1889]
MWA S 16 1876 (supp)

JORNAL de noticias. *See under* Oakland

JORNAL português. *See under* Oakland

Alameda MESSENGER. w Mr 15-Ap 19 1877||?
CU-B Ap 19 1877

Alameda NEWS. w,sw 1880-83||
1880-F 1882 as West End news
w 1880-S 5,O 20 1881-Ja 25,Mr 15-O 1883
CU-B Mr 30 1881-[82-O 4 1883]

POST. tm
CA S 21,N 1 1869
CU-B O 1,20,N 1 1869

Alameda TIMES-STAR. d 1909+
1909-Ap 17? 1921 as Evening times-star
C F 1911+
CA 1909+
CU-B O 1912-Ja 6 1919

WEST End news. *See* Alameda news

ALBANY

Albany ENTERPRISE. w 1908+
CU-B Ja 10 1923;Mr 25 1931;Ag 31 1932

ALFA

Alfa ADVANCE. w 1888-92||?
CU-B Mr 7-Ap 4 1889

ALHAMBRA

ADVOCATE. w *See* Alhambra post-advocate

ALHAMBRA. w 1887-94||?
CLM Jl 6 1889;Ag 4 1894

ALHAMBRAN advocate. *See* Alhambra post-advocate

Alhambra FEDERATED news. w Ag 1 1918-22||?
CAl Jl 1919-Jl 7 1922

Alhambra NEWS. w D 13 1912-Jl 4 1922||
CAl complete

Alhambra POST-ADVOCATE. w,d O 8 1898+
1898-Ag 12 1908 as Advocate; Ag 21 1908-F 4 1924 Alhambran advocate
w 1898-F 4? 1924
pub Ap 11 1924+
CAl 1898-Jl 1917;Ap 11 1924+

Alhambra REVIEW. w N 15 1889-90||?
CLM Ap 11 1890
CU-B D 27 1889-Ja 17,Ag 1-15,29-S 5 1890

ALTADENA

Altadena PRESS. w N 21 1929+
pub 1929+

ALTRURIA

ALTRURIAN. w D 23 1894-95||?
ICN F 25-Ag 24 1895

ALTURAS

To Jl 1876 as Dorris' Bridge

Alturas HERALD. w Je 8 1890-96||?
CU-B Jl-D 1891

Weekly MODOC. w 1874-91||
1874-Ag 28 1890 as Modoc independent. Merged with New era
CU-B Ag 14 1875-[76-80]Ag 31 1882;O 18 1883-Je 25,S 10 1885[88]-Ja 1 1891

MODOC county times. w 1928-D 27 1934||
United with Alturas plaindealer to form Alturas plaindealer & Modoc county times
C Mr 26 1931-34

MODOC independent. *See* Weekly Modoc

NEW ERA. w 1888-Ag 12 1925||
1889?-Jl 30 1915 as New era-chronicle
C F 8 1901-25
CAlt 1908-24
CU-B Ag 31-S 14,O 26-D 7,28 1889-F 1,Ag 23,O-N 1 1890

Alturas PLAINDEALER and Modoc county times. w 1895+
1895-D 26 1934 as Alturas plaindealer
C S 19 1913+
CAlt 1910+

Modoc REPUBLICAN. w 1904-Jl 30 1915||
United with New era chronicle to form New era
C 1913-N 20 1914

ANAHEIM

Anaheim BULLETIN. d Ag 15 1923+
Formed by the union of Anaheim herald and Anaheim plain dealer
pub 1923+
CAn [1923+]
CL N 23 1927

CALIFORNIA (*Continued*)

ANAHEIM—*Continued*

Anaheim **GAZETTE.** w O 29 1870+
F 3 1872-O 17 1874 as Southern Californian
pub 1870+
C 1891+
CAn 1932+
CLM S 1 1877;Je 19 1886;Je 25 1891;N 3 1898
CU-B Jl 8 1871;F 3,Je 15-22,Jl 6 1872-76;F 1877-Ag 3 1878;F 12-N 21 1879;Je 17-N 1880; My 28 1881;Mr 4,Je 3,Jl 1,15 1882;Ja 27 1883[87]My 4 1893;Jl 1 1909-Ag 4 1910;My 30-S 12 1912;Ag 12 1920-Ag 25,S 22-29,O 13,N 3,17 1921-[34+]
KHi S 13 1888-N 1 1894

Anaheim **HERALD.** d N 1913-Ag 8 1923||
United with Anaheim plain dealer to form Anaheim bulletin
CAnB 1918-23

Anaheim **INDEPENDENT.** w 1894-98||?
CU-B Je 6 1896

NEW ERA. w 1888-89||?
CU-B Ap 6-27 1889

Anaheim **PLAIN DEALER.** w 1898-1923||
United with Anaheim herald to form Anaheim bulletin
CAnB 1913-23

Anaheim **REVIEW.** w F 10-D 8 1877||?
CU-B [F-D 1877]

SOUTHERN Californian. *See* Anaheim gazette

ANDERSON

Anderson **ENTERPRISE.** *See* Anderson Valley news

Anderson **VALLEY** news. w Je 1882+
1882-92? as Anderson enterprise
pub 1913+
C 1919+
CLM [1890]
CU-B Mr 7-14,Ap 11-18,My 2-9,23-30,Jl 4-11, Ag 29-S 5, O 17 1889
KHi [N 22 1888-F 14 1889]

ANGELES MESA

Papers pub in Angeles Mesa are listed under Los Angeles

ANGELS

CALAVERAS democrat. w Ag 16 1890-91||
CU-B Ag 16 1890;F 7 1891

CALAVERAS mountaineer. sw Ag 1872-Mr 1873||?
CU-B D 11 1872-Ja 1,Mr 26 1873

COUNTY record. w 1887-90||
CU-B Mr 12-Ap 16,30,My 14,Je 11,25-Jl 9,30, Ag 13-20,S 3,17,O 8-15,N,D 3-24 1889;Ja 7-14 1890

ANGELS CAMP

MONITOR. w *See* Mountain echo

MOUNTAIN echo. w 1879-1906||?
Je 20-Ag 1 1889 as Weekly monitor
CU-B Ja 20-27,Mr 2,16-23[Je-D]1880;Mr 28-Ap 12 1882; Ja 17,F 7-14 1883;88-89

Angel's Camp **RECORD.** w 1899-1918||?
C F 29-Ja 2 1908;D 31 1910-S 5 1918

ANTIOCH

Antioch **LEDGER.** w,tw Mr 26 1870+
w 1870-O 1929
C Ap 19 1890+
CU-B Ap 1870-[72]-[76]-F 9,Ap 27-D 1878 [80]My 20 1882;D 13 1884;F 21 1885[87]S 7,N 16 1889;S 30 1893[F 17-D 1906]-[11-13]+

ARBUCKLE

Arbuckle **AMERICAN.** w 1905+
1905-09 as Planter
pub 1927+
CCo N 1916+
CU-B S 25,O 9-16,N 25-D 4,24 1909;Ja 15-F, Mr 12-Ap 9,Je 4-11 1910

PLANTER. *See* Arbuckle American

ARCADIA

Arcadia **NEWS.** w Ja 2 1925+
CAr [1934]

Arcadia **TRIBUNE.** w Je 1930+
pub Ja 1931+
CAr [1934]

ARCATA

Arcata **LEADER.** w Ag 2 1879-81||
CU-B [1879]-O 23,D 18 1880-Ja 1 1881

UNION. 1854 *See* Humboldt times (Eureka)

Arcata **UNION.** w 1886+
pub 1886+
C 1913-16
CU-B 1888-91;O 7 1893;My 1909-Ap 1910;Ja 18 1923-Mr 12,S 17 1931+

ARLINGTON

Arlington **TIMES.** w S 24 1908+
CRiv 1911-25;28+

ARMONA

KINGS county news. w F 16 1925+
pub 1925+

ARROYO GRANDE

HERALD recorder. w 1887+
1887-1910 as Herald
CU-B Ja 11,Jl 12 1890;My 3-10 1919;O 13 1933+

RECORDER. w 1904-10||
United with Herald to form Herald-recorder

ARTESIA

Artesia **NEWS.** w 1906+
pub Mr 1931+

ATASCADERO

Atascadero **NEWS.** w Ja 22 1916+
pub 1916+
C 1916+
CSl 1916-My 24 1918
CU-B Ap 29 1921-Ja 1 1932
KHi [Ag 28 1924-My 14 1926]
MWA Je 10 1916

Atascadero **TIMES.** w 1912-Je 23 1921||
1912-S 27 1920 as Templeton times (Templeton); O 4 1920-My 5 1921 Eaglet times (Eaglet)
C Mr 1913-My 5,Je 23 1921

ATWATER

Atwater **SIGNAL.** w My 5 1911+
pub 1911+
CMe 1911-Ag 23 1918;Ja 28 1927+

AUBURN

Auburn **JOURNAL** and Placer county republican. d,w Jl 13 1914+
1914-N 9 1918 as Auburn daily journal
d 1914-N 9 1918
C 1914+
CU-B My-Je 19 1919;Ag 11 1927+

PLACER argus. w 1872-My 1898||
United with Placer county republican to form Republican argus, later Placer county republican
C My 25 1878;S 20 1879;Ag 1889-97
CU-B 1873-[75]-[77-80]Ja 18 1883[86]

PLACER county leader. w My 4 1898-Jl 30 1903||
Continues numbering of Placer argus. United with Republican argus to form Placer county republican
C complete

PLACER county republican. w 1884-O 1918||
1884-Ap 29 1898 as Placer county republican; My 6 1898-Jl 30 1903 Republican argus. United with Auburn daily journal to form Auburn journal and Placer county republican
C Jl 7 1893-1918
CU-B Ag 12 1909-Ap 14,Je,Jl 14-Ag 11 1910
KHi Ag 29 1888-Ja 2 1889

PLACER herald. w S 11 1852+
pub 1852+
C 1852-S 11 1886;S 17 1887+
CSmH Ap 16 1870-75
CU-B 1869-[My 15-D 1886;Ja 21 1888-My 25 1895;Ag 8 1896-Ja 25 1902]S 6 1924
DLC Je 7,28,N 22 1856;Mr 26 1859
MH Ja 21-D 23 1899
MWA Mr 12 1853

PLACER press. w Je 2 1855-
Follows Whig
C Je 2 1855-S 4 1858
CSmH My 31 1856-My 23 1857
NNHi F 2 1856

REPUBLICAN argus. *See* Placer county republican

STARS and stripes. w 1863-N 28 1872||
C O 29 1868;Ag 8 1872
CU-B My 13 1865-72

UNION advocate. w 1860?-63||?
CU-B Ag 18 1863

WHIG. w O 18 1854-My 26 1855||
Followed by Placer press

AVALON

CATALINA islander. w 1913+
1913-S 1918 as Islander
pub [1913+]
C S 1934+
CLM [1917]-Ja 15,F 19,O 1-8 1918;F 18-D 16 1919;Ja 20-Jl 6 1920[21]S 8,29-O 20,D 1 1926;My 18,Je 8 1927
CLSU Je 29 1920-My 24 1921;F 1926-Ag 10 1932
CU-B O 30 1917+
DLC [1917-20]Ja 11-Ap,My 24,Je 1921,F 8-Ap 5,19-O 4 1922
NNHu S 25 1929

Avalon **CRUSOE.** w My 21 1893-
CLM [Je-S 1893]

ISLANDER. *See* Catalina islander

WIRELESS. d Mr 25 1903-
CPo Mr 25 1903
MWA Mr 25 1903

AZUSA

Azusa **HERALD** and pomotropic. w N 10 1885+
1885-D 20 1929 as Azusa herald
pub 1887-88;91+
CAz 1926+

Azusa **JOURNAL.** w 1924-30||
Merged with Azusa herald and pomotropic
CAzH complete

Azusa **NEWS.** *See* Azusa Valley news

POMOTROPIC. w Ag 1889-D 20 1929||
Follows Glendora signal (Glendora). United with Azusa herald to form Azusa herald and pomotropic
C Je 1900-F 20 1914
CAz Ag 23 1923-My 3 1929
CAzH 1891-1929
CLM F 6,Ap 10 1890;Jl 30,S 24,O 1,N 5,19,D 17 1891;Ja 14,F 4 1892;F 6 1895
CU-B Jl 12,Ag 1900;Ag 4,S 8,O 13,27 1904;F 16,Ap 13,My 4-11,Ag 24,S 7,21,O 19,N 16-23,D 7-14 1905;F 9,Mr 23,Ap 5,27-My 4,Je,Jl 6,20,Ag 10,31-S 14,28-N 2,16[D 7 1906-F 20 1914]My 9,23 1919

Azusa **VALLEY** news. w 1885-95||?
1885-94? as Azusa news
In English and Spanish
CLM Mr 10 1888
CU-B Mr 2,16,Jl 6,Ag 31,S 14,O 16,N 23,30,D 28 1889;Ja 25,Ag 16,O 11 1890;Mr 9-13,Ap 24,My 15 1894

BAKERSFIELD

Bakersfield **CALIFORNIAN.** w Ag 18 1866-1909||?
Ag-S 1866 as Weekly courier; O 1866-D 15 1869 Havilah weekly courier; D 22 1869-My 15 1875 Kern county weekly courier; My 22 1875-D 11 1879 Southern Californian and Kern county weekly courier; D 18 1879-Ja 31 1897 Kern county Californian
1861-71 pub in Havilah
pub 1866-Mr 1891
C O 20 1868;Je 1870-74
CB D 22 1869-75[80-N 1883]-My 1888
CU-B [1866-D 14]22 1869-Jl 25,Ag 8,23 1870-Je,Jl 12-Ag 9,23 1873-D 12,26 1874-[81]-Ag 1882;Jl 1888-[89]-[91]
KHi Ag 29 1888-Ja 2 1889

Bakersfield **CALIFORNIAN.** d Ap 1 1891+
1891-F 6 1897 as Daily Californian
pub 1891+
C Mr 17 1928+
CB Jl 1902+
CU-B Je 9 1908-[10]F 7 1911-Mr 1922;Jl 9 1927+

Bakersfield **COURIER** and Bakersfield morning echo. d Mr 20-Mr 30 1928||
Follows Bakersfield echo. Merged with Bakersfield Californian
CB complete
CBC complete

DEMOCRAT. w 1890-95||?
C Jl 13 1893-O 10 1895

EAST side news. w Ag 31 1933+
CB 1933+

Bakersfield morning **ECHO.** d Ag 1886-Mr 18 1928||
1886-F 17 1918 as Morning echo. Followed by Bakersfield courier and Bakersfield morning echo
C 1900-1928
CB 1902-1928
CLM My 11-12 1901
CU-B Ag 10 1909-Ap 19[My 7-Je 24]1910

KERN county Californian. *See* Bakersfield Californian

KERN county weekly courier. *See* Bakersfield Californian

KERN county democrat. w Ap 27-Jl 27 1877||
CB complete

KERN county gazette. w 1874-99||?
C O 20 1877-S 4 1880;83-O 4 1884;My 17 1890-99
CU-B O 30,N 13 1875-76;Ja 27-Ap 14 1877[85-86]

KERN county weekly record. *See* Kern weekly record

KERN weekly record. w My 26 1881-Ap 20 1883||
1881-Ap 27 1882 as Kern county weekly record
CU-B 1881[82]83

SOUTHERN Californian and Kern county weekly courier. *See* Bakersfield Californian

BALBOA

Balboa **BULLETIN.** w Ja 1922-Mr 1928||
Merged with Balboa times
CNpN Mr 1926-28

HARBOR outlook. w Ag 3 1934+
pub 1934+

Balboa **TIMES.** w 1924+
pub 1924+

BALDWIN PARK

Baldwin Park **BULLETIN.** w N 7 1913+
pub 1917+
C D 1913-Je 22 1917

CALIFORNIA (*Continued*)

BANNING

HERALD of Banning. w Ag 18 1888-95||
CL Ag 18 1888-N 1894
CLM [1891-93]
CU-B S 21 1893
KHi D 8 1888;Ja 5,Mr 2 1889;Ja 11 1894

Banning RECORD. w Ja 23 1908+
CRiv 1911-17 20-22
CU-B My 8 1919

BARHAM

PLAIN truth. w,sm Jl 1884?-91||?
w 1884-86
C [1885-86]-Jl 16 1891

BARSTOW

PRINTER. w 1910+
CLM Je 30 1911

BARTLE

MCCLOUD River pioneer. w 1889-93||?
CU-B Ja 2 1892

BEAUMONT

GATEWAY gazette. *See* Beaumont gazette

Beaumont GAZETTE. w 1908+
1908-Ap 12 1928 as Gateway gazette
CBea 1927-31
CRiv 1911-21;F 1928+
CU-B Jl 1909-Jl 7 1910

Beaumont (San Gorgonia) LEADER. w 1909-25||?
1909-O 9 1925 as San Gorgonia leader. Merged with Gateway gazette, later Beaumont gazette
CRiv [1911]-25

Beaumont SENTINEL. w O 20 1887-92||
CLM [1888-92]
CPo O 20 1887
CU-B S 7-21,O 12,N 16-D 14 1889;Ja 11-18,Ag 30 1890;Jl 8 1892

BELL

Bell HERALD and Maywood review. w 1914+
1914-22? as Laguna-Bell herald
WaPS [1925]Ja 21-Jl 1926

INDUSTRIAL post. w Jl 10 1924+
pub Jl 17 1924+

LAGUNA-Bell herald. *See* Bell herald

RUFF-nek news. w Ag 10? 1929-
DLC S 25 1929

BELLFLOWER

Bellflower HERALD-ENTERPRISE. w 1912+
pub Je 1925+

BELVEDERE

Belvedere CITIZEN. w Ap 27 1934+
pub 1934+

BENICIA

CALIFORNIA gazette. w Mr 22 1851-
CSmH Mr 22 1851
CU-B N 22 1851
DLC 1851-F 21 1852
MWA Ap 12 1851
NNHi Mr 22 1851

CHRONICLE. w 1877-79||?
CU-B Ag 10 1878-[Ja-Je 1879]

Benicia HERALD. w 1898-1914||?
United with New era to form Benicia herald-new era
CU-B Ag 13 1909-Ap 8,29-Ag 12 1910;Je 14-S 13 1912

Benicia HERALD-NEW era. w D 22 1877+
1877-1914? as New era
pub 1897+
CU-B D 29 1877-D 21 1878;Jl 12 1879-80[O 29 1881-Jl 1 1882]Ja 13-20,F 3 1883;Je 27 1885[86] D 28 1889;Ja 30,F 3,Mr 26 1892;S 13 1907-[09-10]-Jl 28 1911

NEW ERA. *See* Benicia herald-new era

SOLANO county herald. *See* Solano republican (Fairfield)

Benicia TRIBUNE. w My 10? 1873-74||?
CU-B O 25 1873-O 31 1874

BENTON

BENTONIAN. tw,sw,w Ag 14? 1879-80||?
tw 1879;sw Ja 1880
CU-B Ag 16-21 1879;Ja 22,F 14,28,Ap 19-26,S 29 1880

MONO weekly messenger. w F 1 1879-
CU-B F-Ap 19 1879

BERKELEY

Berkeley ADVANCE. w F 2 1905-06||?
CU-B 1905-Ag 1906

ADVOCATE. w,tw,d Mr 10 1877-O 20 1897||
United with World, to form World-advocate, later World
w 1877-Ap 14 1892;tw,Ja 19-My 22 1897
CBe [D 1892-97]
CU-B Mr-O 8,22 1887-Ap 14,19 1892-97

Berkeley BEACON. w Je 3 1882-
CU-B Je-S 14 1882

Berkeley COURIER w,sw S 24 1904+
sw Mr 11-Ap 8 1905
CU-B 1904-S 15 1906;Mr 23 1913-S 4 1926;Mr 7-Ag 1931;Mr 1932+

Evening DISPATCH. d Ap 15 1895-96||?
CU-B Ap-My 29,Je-Jl 1,5-14,16-Ag 1 1895

Berkeley daily GAZETTE. d N 20 1894+
1894-Jl 11 1898 as Berkeley gazette; Jl 12 1898-D 27 1899 Berkeley world-gazette
CBe [My 1895-1917]+
CU-B 1894-Je 1905;06+

Berkeley HERALD. d,tw,sw,w Mr 3 1886-98||
d Ap 5-D 10 1892;tw,Ja 5-Jl 27 1893;sw F 8? 1897-My 12? 1898
CU-B Mr-O 14,28 1886-87;Ja 12-O 18,N 1888-Mr 1892;Ap 5-My 21,24-Je 4,7,9-18,21 1892-O 5,N 17 1893-O 25 1894;Mr 12 1895-D 19 1896;97-Jl 9,Ag 27,S 3,O 1,15,29 1898

Berkeley HERALD. d Mr 5-D 3 1894||?
CU-B Mr 5-15,17,20,23-24,27-D 3 1894

Berkeley HERALD. d Je 5-28 1897||
CU-B complete

Berkeley INDEPENDENT. d D 31 1906-My 31 1913||
CBe [1907-13]
CU-B complete

Berkeley REPORTER. sm,w,d Ap 16 1904-D 28 1909||
Merged with Independent
sm Ap 16-Je 18 1904;w Je 25 1904-N 26 1905
CBe [N 20 1905-09]
CU Ap 18-30 1906
CU-B N 13 1906;08-Ap 1909

Berkeley STANDARD. w N 18 1882-
CU-B 1882-D 15 1883

Berkeley STANDARD. d Mr 2-Jl 6 1903||
CU-B complete

Berkeley SUN-LETTER. w,d 1901 21||
1901-S 27 1902 as Berkeley sun
CU-B Mr 29 1902-O 8 1904[05]-Mr 19 1921

Berkeley daily TIMES. w,d 1913-Ja 16 1922||
Title varies: Berkeley times
w 1913-My 9 1919
C S 1920-22
CU-B Mr 16 1917-Ap 19,S 25 1920-22

WEST Berkeley news. w 1890-N 2 1895||
CU-B S 8,D 29 1892;Ag 18,S 1894-95

WESTERN national. w F 6 1897-
CU-B F-Jl 17 1897

WORLD. d Je 12 1897-Jl 11 1898||
O 21-26 1897 as World-advocate. United with Berkeley gazette to form Berkeley world-gazette, later Berkeley daily gazette
CU-B 1897;Ja 3-22,25,My 28,31,Jl 11 1898

WORLD-ADVOCATE. *See* World

Berkeley WORLD-GAZETTE. *See* Berkeley daily gazette

BEVERLY HILLS

Beverly Hills CITIZEN. w My 9 1923+
pub 1923+
CBh Ap 18 1926+

Beverly Hills SHOPPING news. sw 1930+
pub 1930+

TOWN topics. w Ap 12 1933+
pub 1933+

BIDWELL

BUTTE record. *See* Chico record (Chico)

BIEBER

BIG VALLEY gazette. w Je 29 1893+
C 1893+
CSu 1922+

MOUNTAIN tribune. w My 6 1881-D 31 1892||
C complete
CU-B [1888]-Je 1889;Ja,F,Je 12-30,O 18,N 8-D 1890-D 8 1891]Jl 23 1892

NORTHWESTERN news. w O 15 1931+
C 1931+

BIG PINE

Big Pine CITIZEN. w D 11 1913-Je 24 1933||
United with Owens Valley progress (Lone Pine) to form Owens Valley progress-citizen
CI [1914-15]-[29]-[33]

BIG TREE GROVE. *See* MURPHY

BIGGS

BUTTE county register. *See* Oroville register (Oroville)

Biggs weekly NEWS. w N 22 1924-D 13 1930||
C complete
CU-B Ag 16,30,S 20-O 11 1925

Biggs RECORDER. w Mr 5 1880-82||?
CU-B Mr 12-Ap 9,Je 4 1880

BISHOP

INYO register. w Ap 4 1885+
C S 23 1909+
CI [1914-15]+
CLM [1891-1904]
CU-B F 28,Mr 7-14,Ag 29,S 12,O 31-N 14 1889;O 2 1890;Jl 22-D 23 1909;Ja-Jl 7 1910;Je-S 12 1912

OWENS Valley herald. w Ag 28 1908-D 21 1927||
CI [1914-15]-[19-20]-[23-24]-[27]
CU-B Ap 16,30-My 21,Je 4-11 1909

BISHOP CREEK

Bishop Creek TIMES. w N 1 1881-
CU-B 1881-Je 3 1882

BLOOMINGTON

Bloomington NEWS. w 1923+
CU-B O 9 1925

BLUE LAKE

Blue Lake ADVOCATE. w My 1 1888+
1888-N 30 1889 as Northern advocate
pub 1888+
CU-B My 1-15 1888;N 16-30 1889;Ja 4-18,F 1-8 1890; Jl 17 1909-Jl 23 1910;Ap 6-S 14 1912
NNHi My 1-15 1888

NORTHERN advocate. *See* Blue Lake advocate

BLYTHE

Blythe HERALD. *See* Riverside county gazette and the Blythe herald

PALO Verde Valley herald. *See* Riverside county gazette and the Blythe herald

PALO Verde Valley review. w O 26 1916-Je ? 1922||
CRiv 1916-Ag 23 1920

PALO Verde Valley times. w 1925+
pub 1925+

RIVERSIDE county gazette and the Blythe herald. w Ja 19 1911-28||?
1911-13 as Palo Verde Valley herald; 1914-O 6 1927 Blythe herald
CRiv 1911-[13]-25[27]

BODIE

Bodie CHRONICLE. w,d 1864-O 23 1880||
1864-N 1878 as Alpine chronicle; D 1878-My 3 1879. Mono-alpine chronicle. United with Bridgeport union to form Bridgeport chronicle-union (Bridgeport)
1864-Ag 1867 pub at Markleville; S 1867-N 23 1878 at Silver Mountain
C O 24 1868;Ap 23 1870-D 21 1872
CU-B Je 16[O 13 1866-67]-Ag 7,S 25,O 1875-Ja 1;15,F 5-Ap 8,29,My 6,20 1876-Ja 1877;Ja-O 19,D 1878;F 15-22,Mr 8,My 3-10,O 25-N 8 22 1879-F 21,Ap 24-My 15,Je 5-O 23 1880

FREE PRESS. tw,d N 3 1879-85||?
Earlier numbers published as an advertising sheet, gratuitously distributed
CU-B 1879-Ap 22 1883;Ja 23 1884

MONO-ALPINE chronicle. *See* Bodie chronicle

Bodie morning NEWS. d Mr 8 1879-Jl 20 1880||
United with Daily Bodie standard to form Bodie standard-news
CU-B [1879-80]

Bodie NEWS. w D 14 1879-Jl 1880||
United with Bodie standard to form Bodie standard-news
CU-B D 21 1879

Bodie STANDARD-NEWS. w O 10? 1877-82||?
1877-Jl 1880 as Bodie standard
CU-B N 1877-Ap 5 1879;S-O 9,D 22-29 1880;Mr 16,30-My 4,18,Je 8-Jl,Ag 10 1881-Ag 2 1882

Bodie STANDARD-NEWS. d N 1877-Jl 10 1881||?
1877-Jl 20 1880 as Daily Bodie standard
Suspended D 11 1880-Je 1 1881
CU-B D 10-30 1878[Ja 20-F 27]Mr 14,24,My 24,Je 12-13,24,27-Jl 10,12-19,24[Ag 1879-Jl 20 1880]-D 11 1880;Je 6-7,9-10 1881

BOULDER CREEK

SANTA Cruz mountain echo. w O 24 1896-1918||?
CU-B 1896-[1906]-[15-16]

BRAWLEY

IMPERIAL Valley news. *See* Brawley news

Brawley NEWS. w,tw,d S 1903+
1903-Ag 1904 as Imperial Valley news
w 1903-My 10 1912; tw My 12? 1912-13
CBr S 1932+
CEc 1910+
CU-B Ja 7-21,Je-D 1909;F-Jl 15 1910;My 10-S 13 1912;Ja 16 1923+
WaPS S 14 1917;Je 22,Jl 2 1918;Jl 3 1919

BREA

HABRA Valley progress. *See* Brea progress

Brea PROGRESS. w 1913+
1913-16? as Habra Valley progress
pub 1929+

CALIFORNIA (*Continued*)

BRENTWOOD HEIGHTS

Papers published in Brentwood Heights are listed under Los Angeles

BRIDGEPORT

Bridgeport CHRONICLE-UNION. w Jl 3 1880+
Jl-N 1 1880 as Bridgeport union
C Jl 12 1890+
CU-B Jl 3,10,24 1880-D 17 1881;Mr 11 1882 [Ja 20-Mr 1883]Jl 5 1884;F 28-Mr 7 1885; N 6 1886;Jl 7 1888-Mr 23,Ag 31,S 7-14 1889; Ja 4-18 1890;My 14 1892;O 1933+

Bridgeport UNION. *See* Bridgeport chronicle-union

BRODERICK

YOLO independent. *See* Independent-leader (Sacramento)

BROOKLYN

Papers published in Brooklyn are listed under Oakland

BUENA PARK

Buena Park NEWS. w S 20 1922+
pub 1922+

BURBANK

Burbank REVIEW. d Jl 9 1908+
pub 1914+

Burbank TIMES. w 1887-90||
CU-B Mr 30-Ap,N 6,16,30,D 28 1889;Ja 11-18,F 1,Jl-D 1890

BURLINGAME

Burlingame ADVANCE-STAR. w,d 1905+
1905-25 as Advance
CBu 1929+
OHi Ag 3-12 1923

Burlingame STAR. w 1923-25||
United with Advance to form Burlingame advance-star

BYRON

Byron TIMES. w 1906+
C Ja 7 1910+
CU-B F 2-9,My 31,Je 7-S 13 1912;My 13 1919;Ja 19 1923-27;F 24 1928+

CALEXICO

Calexico CHRONICLE. w,sw,tw,d Jl 1904+
w 1904-14;sw 1915?; tw 1916?
CEc My 1910-[13]-[18-20]+
CLM F 9 1905
CU-B My 21 1931

CALICO

Calico PRINT. w O 21 1882-86||?
1885? pub at Dagget
CLM O 10 1886
CU-B O 21 1882[F 8-Jl 19 1885]

CALIPATRIA

Calipatria HERALD. w S 1914+
CEc 1920+

CALISTOGA

Weekly CALISTOGAN. w Ap 6 1876+
D 26 1877-96? as Independent Calistogian
pub 1877+
CU-B Ap 22-Ag 2[S-D 1876]D 26 1877[Ap 30-D 17 1879;My 5-D 20 1880]Ag 28,S 11-18 1889

Calistoga FREE PRESS. w Ap 18 1874-75||
CU-B 1874-O 16 1875

INDEPENDENT Calistogian. *See* Weekly Calistogan

Calistoga TRIBUNE. w Je 15 1871-Ja 1 1874||?
Suspended from O 24-D 19 1872
CU-B Je,Jl 6,S 28-O 5 1871;72-Ja 1 1874

CAMARILLO

Camarillo NEWS w O 15 1926+
pub N 26 1926+
CCa 1926+

CAMBRIA

CAMBRIAN. w S 1931+
pub 1931+

CAMPBELL

Campbell INTERURBAN press. w 1895+
NN D 24 1904

CANOGA PARK

Papers published in Canoga Park are listed under Los Angeles

CARLSBAD

Carlsbad JOURNAL. w Ja 1 1925+
pub 1928+

CARLTON

Carlton CHRONICLE. w F 25 1888-89||?
CLM F 25 1888

CARMEL

CARMELITE. w,ir F 15 1928-D 29 1932||
ir Je 1 1931-D 31 1931
CC complete
CSa complete
CSt complete

CYMBAL. w My 11 1926-S 28 1927||
CC 1926-Je 1927
CSa 1926-S 21 1927

PINE cone. w F 3 1915+
C F 7 1918+
CC 1915+
CSa F 10 1915+
CSt F 10 1915+
CU-B Mr 3 1923;O 13 1933+

SUN. w F 2 1933+
CC 1933+

CARPINTERIA

Carpinteria CHRONICLE. w 1933+
CSmH Mr 1 1934

Carpinteria HERALD. w D 11 1911+
1911-O 1 1920 as Carpinteria Valley news
pub 1911+

Carpinteria VALLEY news. *See* Carpinteria herald

CASTROVILLE

Castroville ARGUS. w Mr 27 1869-80||?
CU-B 1869-[74]-80

Castroville weekly ENTERPRISE. w Ap 3 1891-1907||?
C My 30 1906-Mr 20 1907
CU-B O 16 1891

Castroville GAZETTE. w Ag 28 1888-
CSa Ja 10 1889

Castroville NEWS. w Mr 5 1931+
CSa 1931+

Castroville RECORD. w Je 22? 1889-90||
CU-B D 28 1889;Ja 4 1890

CEDARVILLE

SURPRISE Valley record. w 1892+
CAlt 1908+

CERES

Ceres COURIER. w 1911+
C 1921+

CHATSWORTH

Papers published in Chatsworth are listed under Los Angeles

CHICO

BUTTE county press. w Jl 30 1867-
CU-B Ag 20 1867-Ag 4 1868

BUTTE record. d Jl-S 1873||?
CU-B Ag 5,7-S 9 1873

BUTTE record. d 1876-87||
1876-83? as Evening record. United with Morning record to form Chronicle-record
CU-B [Je 18-D 1878]-80;Jl 26 1882

CALIFORNIA Caucasian. w S 23 1868-69||?
C O 24 1868
CU-B 1868-F 20 1869

Chico CHRONICLE. w 1884-S 29 1887||
United with Weekly Butte record to form Chico weekly chronicle-record, later Chico record
CU-B Ja-Mr,Ap 8-Je 17,Ag-D 16,30 1886-Mr, Ap 14,My 5-19,Je 2-9,23-Ag,S 8-29 1887

CHRONICLE-record. d 1880-1906||
1880-87 as Morning record

Chico weekly CHRONICLE-RECORD. *See* Chico record

Chico COURANT. w N 11 1865-Ap 2 1869||
1865-O 1868 as Chico weekly courant
CU-B N,D 9-16 1865;Jl 5 1867;68-69
DLC complete

Chico ENTERPRISE. w,sw Ap 17 1869-1907||?
1869-My 28 1872 as Northern enterprise
sw My 28 1880-85?
CU-B 1869-[72]-80[86]D 9 1887;Je 25,26 1889; 90

Chico ENTERPRISE. d 1881+
pub Ag 1908+
CU-B 1888-[90]91;S 10 1907+

Chico INDEX. w F 14 1863-
CU-B F 21 1863

NORTHERN enterprise. *See* Chico enterprise. w

Morning RECORD. *See* Chronicle-record

Chico RECORD. w,tw,d N 12 1853+
1853-S 15 1858 as Butte record; S 18 1858-Je 23 1864 Weekly Butte record; Je 23 1864-Mr 17 1866 Oroville union record; Mr 24 1866-O 1 1887 Weekly Butte record; O 8 1887-97? Chico weekly chronicle-record; 1898?-D 28 1906 Chico semi-weekly record
1853-Jl 12? 1856 pub in Bidwell; Jl 19 1856-Jl 4? 1874 in Oroville
d Jl 14 1856-S 10 1857; tw F-S 1858
pub Ap 1897+
C 1853-N 5 1859;64-[Mr 24 1866-O 17 1874]-91;1900+
CP My 14 1857;Mr 21 1868
CU-B Je 19 1857;Jl 8 1858;Ap 15 1865;Je 9 1866;Jl 6 1867[68]-[73-74]-[81]-[83]-N 22 1884;O 8-D 1887;Ap 6-21,24-30 1888;Ap 10 1889;Mr 4,20 1896
KHi Je 16 1888-F 16 1889

Chico REVIEW. w,sw O 11? 1871-72||
w 1871
CU-B N 22 1871-My 28 1872

CHINO

Chino CHAMPION. w N 11 1887+
1887-Ap 27 1906 as Chino Valley champion
CLM [1888-92]
CPo 1887-1918
CSmH 1887-O 1890;N 1891-O 23 1896
CU-B 1903-N 18 1904
KHi My 25,Je 1 1888;N 27 1891;Ap 21-D 22 1893

Chino VALLEY champion. *See* Chino champion

CHOWCHILLA

Chowchilla NEWS. w My 22 1913+
pub F 1932+
C O 8 1914+

CHULA VISTA

Chula Vista STAR. w F 18 1918+
pub 1918+
CCh N 1929+

CLAREMONT

Claremont COURIER. w S 1908+
pub 1918+
C S 1912-Mr 1913

CLOVERDALE

Cloverdale BEE. *See* Lake county bee (Lakeport)

Cloverdale NEWS. w 1876-79||
CU-B Ag 17 1878-My 24 1879

Cloverdale REVEILLE. w O 16? 1879+
pub 1880+
CU-B N 20,D 4 1879[80]-Ag 5 1882;Mr 16,O 12 1889;Ja 11 1890;Mr 7-28,Ap 11-25 1896
KHi N 10 1888-F 2 1889

CLOVIS

Clovis INDEPENDENT. w Mr 1919+
pub 1932+

Clovis TRIBUNE. w Mr 14 1905+
pub 1906+
CFr 1915-17;19-25

COACHELLA

Coachella VALLEY news. *See* Coachella valley submarine

Coachella VALLEY submarine. w 1904+
1904-14 as Coachella Valley news
CRiv 1911-14[17]-26;28+

COALINGA

Coalinga OIL record. w 1904-20||?
pub 1909-20

Coalinga daily RECORD. d 1916+
pub 1916+
CU-B O 24 1924

COLFAX

Colfax ENTERPRISE. w N 1 1876-77||?
CU-B D 20 1876-Ja 10,24-Ap 18,Ag 1 1877

Colfax SENTINEL. w 1891-D 10 1907||
C Jl 7 1893-1907

COLOMA

EMPIRE county argus. w N 19 1853-Jl 23 1857||
Followed by Tri-weekly argus, later Tri-weekly index (Placerville)
C 1853-N 8 1856
DLC Mr 18-Ap 15,29-Je 24,Jl 15-Ag 19,S 16, 30-O 7,21 1854-Mr 24,Ap 7-My 12 1855
MWA Mr 18-25 1854

MINERS' advocate. w O 1 1852-
MWA F 19,Mr 26,My 21,Je 11,25,Ag 6 1853
NNHi Ja 22 1853

COLTON

Colton ADVOCATE. w O 28-D 16 1876||?
CU-B N 4-11,D 16 1876

CALIFORNIA (*Continued*)

COLTON—*Continued*

Colton CHRONICLE. w,sw Ja 6 1877-1911‖?
1877-88? as Colton semi-tropic
w 1877-1905?
CLM [1891-1905]
CU-B [Ja 20 1877-78]-D 18 1880
KHi N 13 1888
MB [1878-O 1880]
NN Jl 10 1897

Colton daily COURIER. d Mr 5 1912+
CCol 1912+

Colton SEMI-TROPIC. *See* Colton chronicle

COLUMBIA

Columbia CITIZEN. w Jl 2 1866-67‖?
CU-B Jl 28 1866-Jl 20 1867

Weekly COLUMBIAN. w Je 20 1856-
MWA Mr 7 1857

Columbia GAZETTE, and southern mines advertiser. w,sw O 1852-58‖?
1852-55? as Columbia gazette; Jl 11 1854 as Clipper and gazette extra; issued jointly by the Clipper and Gazette offices
sw N 1855-Je 1856?
CSmH Mr 15 1856
MWA Mr 5,26,N 5-12 1853;Jl 11 1854;Ap 15, Ag 23-S 17,27,O 18-N,D 20-27 1856;Ja 24-F 7,21,Ap 25 1857
NNHi Mr 5-Ap 16 1856

Columbia TIMES. w 1860-61‖?
CU-B O 3 1861

TUOLUMNE courier. *See under* Sonora

COLUSA

Colusa weekly GAZETTE. w 1886-1903‖?
CU-B Jl 27 1893;Ja 16 1896

Colusa daily GAZETTE. d 1889-1903‖?
C Ja-Je 1891
CU-B O 1-2 1890

Colusa HERALD. tw,d 1886-Ja 1 1933‖
United with Colusa daily sun to form Colusa sun-herald
tw 1886-Ag 12 1929
CCo 1917-33

Colusa INDEPENDENT. w 1873-77‖
CU-B Mr 19,Ag 6 1875-F 3 1877

Colusa SUN. sw Ja 2 1895-Mr 1901‖
C complete

Colusa SUN-HERALD. w,tw,d 1862+
1862-Mr 30 1901 as Weekly Colusa sun; Ap 4 1901-Je 1919 Colusa sun; Jl 1 1919-D 31 1932 Colusa daily sun
w 1862-Mr 1901;tw Ap 1901-Je 1919
C D 19 1868;Jl 28 1877;Ap 19 1890+
CCo D 1916+
CLM D 15 1891
CMa My 29 1869-71
CP Mr 23 1867
CU-B O 3 1862;Mr 18,Ap 8 1865-78;Jl 1879-D 18 1880[86-88]-91;My 6,N 5 1901;Je 8 1908-O 21 1916
KHi Jl 7 1888
WHi S 26 1863-65

Colusa daily TIMES. d Ja 17 1933+
CCo 1933+

COMPTON

CLIPPER. w O 15? 1891-92‖
CU-B Ag 13-S 3 1892

Compton INDEPENDENT. w 1888-89‖?
CLM Ag 18 1888;D 7 1889

Compton NEWS-TRIBUNE. sw 1921+
1921-25? as Compton tribune
pub 1921+

Compton TRIBUNE. *See* Compton news-tribune

CONCORD

Concord SUN. w F 25 1882-96‖?
CU-B Mr 18-Je 24,Jl 8-15 1882;Mr 17 1894

COPPER CITY

Copper City PIONEER. w Ap 23- 1864‖?
CU-B My 21 1864

COPPEROPOLIS

Copperopolis COURIER. w Ap 15 1865-67‖?
CU-B [1865-S 14 1867]

CORNING

NEW ERA. w 1898-1920‖?
CU-B Jl 17 1909-Ag 20 1910;Ag 16-23, S 6 1913;Jl 25-S 5 1914;F 27 1915-[17]-Je 29,Jl 13, Ag 3 1918;Jl 17-O 2,16,30-N 6 1920

Corning OBSERVER. w,d S 21? 1887+
w 1887-Ap 25 1918
pub 1906+
C Ja 9 1919+
CRb [1927]+
CU-B Je 29-Jl 13,D 28 1889;S 4 1913+

REPUBLICAN of Tehama county. w Ag 19 1926+
Title varies: Corning republican
pub 1926+
CRb [1927]+

CORONA

Corona COURIER. w Ja 1886+
pub 1886+
CCoro F 1904-N 19 1914
CRiv My 1911-23;25;27-[30-31]+

Corona INDEPENDENT. w.sw,w,d Ap 2"? 1906+
w 1906-S 20 1908; Je 8 1910-F 5 1914; sw S 20 1908-Je 8 1910
pub S 1906+
C 1906-F 1918
CCoro 1905+
CRiv 1920-[24]-26[28]+

Corona MESSENGER. w 1908-Je 30 1910‖
CCoro 1909-10

PRESS and horticulturist. *See under* Riverside

CORONADO

Coronado JOURNAL. w My 24 1912+
1912-23? as Strand; 1924 Saturday night
pub 1912+
CCor 1910—

Coronado evening MERCURY. d My 16 1887-89‖?
CPo My 16 1887

MERCURY. w S 3 1888-93‖?
CLM S 3 1889
CU-B F 26-Mr 5,Jl 23,Ag 6,S 10-17 1889;Ag 16-23,O 18 1890;Jl 30,Ag 13 1892;Ag 31 1893

SATURDAY night. *See* Coronado journal

STRAND. *See* Coronado journal

COSTA MESA

Costa Mesa HERALD. 1923+
pub 1923+

COTTONWOOD

Cottonwood REGISTER. w 1886-93‖?
CU-B Jl 11-18 1889;S 4 1890
KHi [Ag 30 1888-Ja 1889]

COVINA

Covina ARGUS. w 1889+
pub 1894+
CCov Ja 18 1902+

Covina CITIZEN. w N 16 1916+
pub 1916+
CCov N 23 1916+

Covina JOURNAL. w My 4? 1889-
CU-B Jl 13 1889

CRESCENT CITY

Crescent City AMERICAN. w N 16 1926+
pub 1926—

COAST times. w -1911‖
United with Crescent City news and Del Norte record to form Del Norte triplicate

Crescent City COURIER. w S 12 1872-F 9 1881‖
Merged with Del Norte record
CU-B S 12,N 7 1872-Mr 13 1875[F 26 1876-77]-[80-81]

DEL NORTE record. m,w Ap 19 1879-D 30 1911‖
United with Crescent City news and Coast times to form Del Norte triplicate
m Ap-My 1879
C 1891-1911
CCrD complete
CU-B My 8 1880-Ag 1884;87-Ja 2 1892;N 19 1910

DEL NORTE triplicate. w Ja 1912+
Formed by the union of Crescent City news, Coast times and Del Norte record
pub 1912+
C 1912+
CU-B [O 12 1917-18]-[25]-[31]-Jl 8 1932

Crescent City HERALD. w Je 10 1854-Je 8 1861‖
CCrD [1854-61]
MWA N 1,29 1854;Mr 17-31, My 12-19,Je 2,Jl 21,Ag 11,25 1858;Ap 6,My 11-25,Je 29,Jl 6,20-Ag 3 1859
NNHi Mr 5-12 1856
OrHi Je 6 1860
VtBr Ap 22 1857

Crescent City NEWS. w 1883-D 21 1911‖
United with Del Norte record and Coast times to form Del Norte triplicate
C Jl 26 1906-11

CUCAMONGA

LIFE. w 1893‖?
CLM N 25, D 7 1893

CULVER CITY

CITIZEN. w 1922+
pub 1926+

Culver City daily NEWS. d Ja 11 1926-S 30 1927‖
United with Culver City star to form Culver City star-news
CCuS complete

Culver City evening STAR-NEWS. d 1923+
1923-S 1927 as Culver City star
pub O 30 1927+

CYPRESS

Cypress ENTERPRISE. w Je 20 1926+
pub 1926+

DAGGET

CALICO print. *See under* Calico

DARWIN

COSO mining news. w N 6 1875-
CU-B N 6-13 1875
MWA My 27,Je 3 1876

DAVIS

Davis ENTERPRISE. w 1898+
pub 1898+
CU-B Je 23 1906-N 14 1919;20+

DAVISVILLE

Davisville ADVERTISER. w D 4 1869-70‖
CU-B 1869-My 7 1870

DELANO

Delano COURIER. w 1888-96‖?
CU-B Je 21-Jl 5,Ag 30-S 13,O 25,N 1,22-29,D 27 1889;Ja 3,17-31 1890

Delano RECORD. w 1908+
CB Ja 25 1912-Jl 20 1917;1922+
KHi F 23 1917

DELHI

Delhi NEWS.
Mimeographed
CU-B [F 1922-Jl 12 1923]

Delhi RECORD. w 1924+
CMe Ja 1927+
CU-B Je 11,Ag 6 1925;Ja 28,Mr 11 1926;Je 7,O 25 1929 [Mr 28 1930-Ag 1931]Ja 15,Mr 11 1932

DE SAND

De Sand weekly NEWS. w
KHi My 20 1893

DIAMOND SPRINGS

ELDORADO county journal. w Ja 1 1856-
NNHi Ja 29 1856

DINUBA

Dinuba SENTINEL. w,sw,d 1902+
1905-08 as Dinuba tribune
w 1905-11;sw 1912-14
CU-B O 10 1933+

Dinuba TRIBUNE. *See* Dinuba sentinel

DIXON

Dixon TRIBUNE. w N 14 1874+
pub 1883+
C Ja 13 1883-Mr 1 1884;89+
CU-B N 21 1874-[75-76]-[78]-80;Ap 29 1882; Ja 31 1885 [87]Ja 4,Mr 2,S 7-14,N 9-16,D 28 1889;Ja 11 1890

DORRIS

Dorris BOOSTER. w 1909-12‖
CYC complete

BUTTE Valley star. w Oct 22 1926+
pub 1926+
CYC 1931+

Dorris TIMES. w 1915-19‖
CYC complete

DORRIS' BRIDGE. *See* ALTURAS

DOS PALOS

Dos Palos STAR. w Ag 2 1895+
pub Jl 20 1907+
CMe 1911+
CU-B Mr 31-Ap. 14,Je 9,30-Jl 7,Ag 4,S 22,O 27 1906;F 2,Je 8 1907-S 14 1923;Ap 11 1924-F, Je 27 1930+

DOUGLAS CITY

TRINITY gazette. w 1861-62‖?
CU-B F 19 1862

DOWNEY

Downey CHAMPION. w Jl 28 1888+
pub 1916+
CLM N 14 1891-Jl 17 1897;98-1901
CU-B Jl 13,N 16 1889-Ja 4,18-25,Jl 12,Ag 23,S 6,25 1890[92]Mr 6,20-Je 17,Jl 8-29 1893
KHi [S 8 1888-Jl 22 1893]

COURIER. *See* Los Nietos valley courier

Downey DISPATCH. w 1902-Je 5 1908‖
CU-B Ag 16 1907-08

Downey LIVE WIRE. w F 24 1924+
pub 1924+

LOS NIETOS valley courier. w Mr 13 1875-80‖?
1875-Mr 11 1876 as Courier
CU-B Je 19,N 27 1875-S 2[N-D 1876;F 24-O 13 1877]Ap 10 1880

CALIFORNIA (*Continued*)

DOWNIEVILLE

Downieville DEMOCRAT. w My 12 1870-71||?
C My 26 1870-My 4 1871
CU-B Jl 21 1870;Mr 2 1871

MOUNTAIN echo. w Je 19 1852-54||?
Followed by Sierra citizen
CSmH 1852-Je 11 1853
CU-B F 19 1853

MOUNTAIN messenger. w,sm,d N 19 1853+
1853-Ap 1854 as Gibsonville herald; My 1854- Gibsonville trumpet; -My 1863 California mountain messenger
1853-Ag? 1855 pub in Gibsonville; S 1855-Ja 1864 in La Porte
C D 19 1868[Mr 15 1873-D 21 1889]My 17 1890+
CP D 12 1863
CQ Ag 21 1926+
CSt [1868;70;77]81-1932
CU-B [S 20-D 1862]-[64]-[93-94]-[97]-[1905]-[09]-[11]-[14-15]-[19-20]+
MWA Ja 13 1866

SIERRA advocate. w Ja 13 1866-67||?
C 1866-My 25 1867
CU-B Ag-D 22 1866;Ja-Ap 13,My 4-Jl 20,Ag 31 1867

SIERRA age. sw,w My 10- 1871||
Merged with Mountain messenger
C My-Ag 8 1871
CU-B Je 24 1871

SIERRA citizen. w F 11 1854-62||
Follows Mountain echo
CSt Mr 20 1858-Ag 20 1859
CU-B N 18 1854;Ag 15 1857;Mr 19 1859
DLC Ap 15,Je 3,17-Jl 1, 15-29,Ag 26-S 2,23-O 7 1854
MWA My 17,Jl 5 1856
P-M Ap 14,Mr 24 1855

SIERRA county enterprise. w Ja 21 1896-99||?
CU-B Ap 1 1896

SIERRA county news. w Mr 29-S 20 1862||
CU-B complete

SIERRA county news. w Ap 1 1934+
pub 1934+

SIERRA county tribune. w 1881-85||
CU-B N 21 1884

SIERRA democrat. w Je 21 1856-F 27 1864||?
1856-S 1857 pub in Forest City
CU-B F 27 1864

Downieville STANDARD. sw 1863-64||?
CU-B My 25 1864

DUARTE

Duarte VISTA. w 1889-
CLM Jl 5 1889

DUNSMUIR

Dunsmuir DISPATCH. w 1909-12||
CYC complete

Dunsmuir HERALD. w 1897-98||
CYC complete

Dunsmuir NEWS. w My 17 1890+
pub [O 26 1901-Mr 5 1920]+
CYC 1890;92-1912;14+

Dunsmuir PLAIN-DEALER. w 1911-12||
CYC complete

Dunsmuir TRIBUNE. w Mr 1926-D 1927||
CYC complete

DUTCH FLAT

Dutch Flat ENQUIRER. w,sw 1861+
sw N 7 1866-N 9 1867
C S 17 1864;Ag 25 1866;O 19 1867
CU-B [My 13 1864-65]-S 5 1868

FORUM. *See* Placer times

PLACER times. w 1875-84||?
1875-80 as Forum
C Ja 13 1881-84
CU-B [O 28-D 1875-76]-[78]-Ja 23,Je 26 1879-Je 26,Jl 17,Ag 28 1880[My 19-D 1881]-Ja 21 1882

EAGLE ROCK

Papers published in Eagle Rock are listed under Los Angeles

EAGLET

Eaglet TIMES. *See* Atascadero times (Atascadero)

EAST LOS ANGELES

Papers published in East Los Angeles are listed under Los Angeles

EAST OAKLAND

Papers published in East Oakland are listed under Oakland

EAST SAN DIEGO

Papers published in East San Diego are listed under San Diego

EASTBERNE

SOUTHERN Californian. w 1887-
KHi Jl 28,Ag 18 1888

EASTYARD. *See* RICHMOND

EL CAJON

El Cajon STAR. w 1881-89||?
CLM Ag 31, S 14, N 30-D 6 1889
CU-B N 16 1889

El Cajon VALLEY news. w 1891+
pub 1912+
C O 21 1927+
KHi Ag 26 1893

EL CENTRO

IMPERIAL Valley farmer. *See* Post

IMPERIAL Valley press and El Centro progress. w,d Mr 3 1906+
Follows Imperial press (Imperial). 1906-Ja 9 1922 as Imperial Valley press
w 1906-S 23 1911
C O 24 1908-[20-21]+
CEc Mr 1910-[11]+
CEcI S 1930+
CU-B S 30 1911-S 11,23 1916-[19-21]-Ja 27, Mr 29 1922+

POST. d,w,sw 1917+
1917-Mr 30 1933 as Imperial Valley farmer; Ap 1933-O 2 1934 Valley farmer
w 1917-Ap 17 1923,Ja 11 1924-Ag 30 1933; sw Ap? 1923-Ja? 1924
pub 1933+
CEc N 19 1920+
CEcI Mr 1934+
CU-B 1922[23]-[32]+

El Centro PROGRESS. w,d Ja 1912-Ja 15 1922||
United with Imperial Valley press to form Imperial Valley press and El Centro progress
w Ja-S 1912
C O 1913-22
CEc F-D 1912;My 18-O 3,N 1913-22
CU-B My 1919

El Centro morning STAR. d O 15 1908-
C [O 15-N 20 1908]

VALLEY farmer. *See* Post

ZANJERO. 1918-20||?
CU-B Ap 29 1919

EL MODENA

El Modena RECORD. w Ag? 1888-
KHi O 12 1888

EL MONTE

El Monte GAZETTE. *See* El Monte herald

El Monte HERALD. w Je 10 1905+
1905-Jl 6 1923 as El Monte gazette
pub 1905-Ap 19 1906;09;14-15;18-19;Jl 13 1923+
CU-B Mr 23 1923

ELK GROVE

Elk Grove CITIZEN. w 1909+
CU-B My-Je 19 1919

EL SEGUNDO

El Segundo HERALD. w 1911+
pub F 1917+
CE D 1933+

ELSINORE

LAKE Elsinore Valley press. *See* Elsinore leader-press

Elsinore LEADER. w S 16 1925-My 20 1926||
United with Lake Elsinore Valley press to form Elsinore leader-press
CRiv F-My 1926

Elsinore LEADER-PRESS. w 1887+
1887-1912 as Elsinore press; 1913-25 Lake Elsinore valley press
CLM [1890-92]
CRiv D 30 1910-26;28;30-31
CU-B Mr 8 1914;Mr 14-Ap 25,My 9,23,Jl 24-N 6,20-D 25 1924;Ja 8-S 10,24-O 8,22-N 12, 26-D 10,24-31 1925[My 27-D 1926]-[29]-Ag 28 1930

Elsinore NEWS. w 1885-88||?
CU-B Je 16 1886
KHi N 10,D 15 1888

Elsinore TRANSCRIPT. w 1888-89||
CU-B Mr 7 1889

EL VERANO

SONOMA Valley republican. w Jl 19 1890-
CU-B O 11-N 1 1890

VITIGRAPH. w 1889||?
CLM N 16 1889

EMERYVILLE

Early years as Klinkerville; Golden Gate

GOLDEN Gate gazette. w S 27 1890-
CU-B S-D 6,20 1890-Ja 3 1891

ENCINITAS

Encinitas COAST dispatch. w F 12 1925+
pub 1925+
C O 1926+
CU-B [F 1927-N 1 1929]30+

COAST vidette. w 1888-90||?
CLM D 14 1889
CU-B Ja 11 1890

Encinitas JOURNAL. w 1887-91||?
CLM Ag 29 1889

PROGRESS. w Mr 7 1931+
pub 1931+

ESCALON

Escalon TIMES. w F 19 1926+
C 1926+

ESCONDIDO

Escondido ADVOCATE. w 1891-1908||
United with Escondido times to form Escondido times-advocate
CEsT [1886-1900]
KHi Ap 13-My 11 1894

Escondido TIMES-ADVOCATE. w 1886+
1886-1908 as Escondido times
pub [1886-1907]+
C Ag 10 1893+
CLM [1890]
CU-B [Ja 14-D 1909]Ag 12 1910

Daily TIMES-ADVOCATE. d Ag 22 1912+
pub 1912+
CEs 1912+

ESPARTO

Esparto EXPONENT. w 1913-33||
CU-B Ap 10 1927

ETNA

SCOTT Valley advance. w 1897-1916||
CYC 1897-1902;05-12;14-16

Etna STANDARD. w 1898|
CYC complete

WESTERN sentinel. w 1918+
CYC 1918+

EUREKA

DEMOCRATIC standard. *See* Humboldt standard w

Evening HERALD. d Ap 9 1879-
CU-B Ap-My 2,8 1879

Eureka HERALD. d 1902-14||?
CU-B Ag 9 1909-[Ja-Ag 18 1910]

HUMBOLDT Bay journal. w 1865-66||?
CU-B N 22 1866

HUMBOLDT mail. w 1887-90||?
CU-B N 9 1889

HUMBOLDT standard. w,sw Je 1875-1905||?
S 29 1877-83? as Democratic standard. Title varies: Weekly standard; Semi-weekly standard
w 1875-82
pub 1875-1905
C [Je 16 1877-N 1883]-S 20 1905
CU-B [1875]-Ap 1876;Ag 1878-Ja 1,15,F 5,19-My 28 1881[82-83]Ap 3,My 12,O 18,N 8 1884;Ja 12-F 2,My 2,O 24 1885;F 12 1887; Mr 7-9,Ag 28,N 13 1889;Je 2-26,S 15-19, 30-O 2 1890
KHi Ag 29 1889
N D 5 1885

HUMBOLDT standard. d 1890?+
pub 1890+
C 1911+
CU-B [Ap 16-D 1906]-18

HUMBOLDT times, w,m S 2 1854-O 28 1909||
- as Union
1854-Ag 21 1858 pub in Arcata and in Union
pub complete
C Mr 22 1856-O 17 1857;O 17 1868;O 5 1905-09
CSmH Ag 12 1876-Ag 11 1877
CU-B Jl 26 1862[63-66]-[75]-[81]-D 23 1882; Ja-Je 1887[Ja 9-Ag 21 1890;Ja-N 24 1892]
KHi [Je 28-D 6 1888]
MWA Mr 13,My 22,Jl 24,Ag 28 1858;F 5,Je 4,18,Jl 9-16,Ag 6 1859

HUMBOLDT times. d Ja 1 1874+
D 31 1885-My 1886 as Times-telephone
pub 1874+
C D 9 1909+
CU-B [1874-79;F-D 1880 D 31 1885-86]88-Mr 31,Jl 2 1889-91
KHi N 28,D 2 1888

NATIONAL index. w My 28 1867-Ja 30 1868||
CU-B Ja 11 1867;Ja 30 1868

NORTHERN Californian. w -Jl 14 1860||
Merged with Humboldt times

NORTHERN weekly independent. w Jl 22 1869-Ag 15 1872||
C Ag 1870-Jl 11 1872
CU-B complete

Daily evening SIGNAL. d O 7 1876-80||?
CU-B D 1876-D 16 1878;Ja 6-8,28,F 10-11, 16-18,23-25,Mr 11,16,18,23,25,29-31,N 1879-Mr 16 1880
—w ed *See* West Coast signal

STANDARD. *See* Humboldt standard

CALIFORNIA (*Continued*)

EUREKA—*Continued*

Evening STAR. d 1876-Ap 18 1878||
CU-B [S 14 1877-78]

TIMES-TELEPHONE. *See* Humboldt times

WEST Coast signal. w F 15 1871-Mr 17 1880||
C Ap 15 1874-F 2 1876
CU-B [1871-72]-[78-79]80
MWA Ag 23 1876
—d ed *See* Daily evening signal

WESTERN watchman. w 1884-98||
C S 18 1886-Ag 13 1898
CU-B Mr 2,Ag 31-S 7,D 28 1889
KHi Jl 14-O 20 1888

EXETER

Exeter SUN. w 1902+
CU-B My 26 1905-[Ja-N 1906]My 1919;F 28 1924-Jl 16,N 1931+

FAIR OAKS

Fair Oaks PROGRESS. sw,w 1917-F 12 1931||
United with Tribune (North Sacramento) to form Tribune-progress
C Ja 13 1927-31

FAIRFAX

Fairfax GAZETTE. w Ag 1927+
pub 1927+

FAIRFIELD

Fairfield ENTERPRISE. w 1908-23||
Merged with Solano republican
CF [1915-23]

SOLANO republican. w N 5 1855+
1855-N 30 1869 as Solano county herald 1855-57? pub in Benicia; 1858?-1923? in Suisun
pub 1855+
C N 9 1861-O 1863;Je 25 1909-20;23+
CF 1915+
CU-B Je 14 1856;N 8 1862-[72-73]-78;My 1, Jl-D 4 1879;F 20-D 24 1880;My 12 1882;F 9 1883;86[87]N 8-D 6,20 1889-Ja 3,17-31,F 14 1890

FAIRVIEW

Fairview REGISTER. w My 1888-Ap 20 1889||?
CLM Ja 12-Ap 20 1889

FALL RIVER MILLS

ADVOCATE. w Mr 1 1889-
CU-B Mr 8 1889

TIDINGS. w 1894+
CU-B Je 27 1919

FALLBROOK

Fallbrook ENTERPRISE. w Mr 1910+
pub Mr 24 1911+

Fallbrook OBSERVER. w 1891-1903||?
CFaE O 27 1893-Ap 20 1894

Fallbrook REVIEW. w Je 4 1885-1907||?
CFaE D 29 1905-07
CU-B Ag 20 1885;Mr 8,22-29,Jl 5-12,S 6-13,N 22,D 6,27 1889;Ja 3 1890

Fallbrook UNION. w 1891-93||?
CFaE Ja 6-Ag 4 1893

FELLOWS

Fellows COURIER. *See* Fellows driller

Fellows DRILLER. w 1912-29||?
1913-F 23 1915 as Fellows courier; Mr 2 1915-16? Fellows driller and courier
CU-B Ja 23 1914-15

FERNDALE

Ferndale ENTERPRISE. w My 4 1878+
pub 1878+
CEu 1913+
CU-B [1878]-D 23 1880;D 2 1881;My 12,26,Je 9,Jl 7-14 1882;N 22-29 1889

FILLMORE

Fillmore AMERICAN. sw D 1925+
CFi 1925+

Fillmore HERALD. w S 27 1907+
pub 1907+
CFi 1916+

Fillmore SUN. w 1916-19||?
C 1917-O 10 1918

Fillmore daily SUN. d Jl 1917-S 1 1919||
Merged with Fillmore herald
CFi complete

FOLSOM

Folsom HASTATE. w O 2 1880-
CU-B O 30 1880-Ja 1 1881

Folsom TELEGRAPH. w 1856+
1856- as Journal (Granite)
pub 1889+
C O 24 1868;Ag 24 1889+

CU-B O 3 1862;My 13 1865-[66]-[69]-[74-75]-[77;87]
MWA My 7 1864

FONTANA

Fontana HERALD. w 1923+
CU-B O 30-N 1931

FOREST CITY

SIERRA county tribune. *See* Sierra tribune (Sierra City)

SIERRA democrat. *See* Downieville democrat 1856-64 (Downieville)

FOREST HILL

PLACER weekly courier. w 1857?-
CU-B Jl 25 1863

FORT BRAGG

Fort Bragg ADVOCATE and news. w 1889+
CU-B O 1890-S 7 1892;Mr 17,Ap 21,My 12,Je 16-Jl 14,28Ag 11-S 15,O 13 1926-[29]+

FORT JONES

COUNTY reporter. w 1895-98||
CYC complete

FARMER and miner. *See* Siskiyou standard

SCOTT Valley news. w 1878-95||?
CU-B S 5,O 17 1878-[79-80]My 6-13 1882;F 27 1886;Mr 2,30-Ap 6,My 25,Je 29,Jl 6-13,O 26 1889-Ja 4,F 22,Mr 1,Je 7,Jl 12,Ag 9,23-S 6,20,O 18 1890[92]Ja 7,21-F 4 1893;Je 2,16-30, Ag 18-25,S 8,29,O 20-N,D 8,22-29 1894;Ja 12, 26,F 2,Mr 2-9,23-Ap,20,My 4-25 1895
CYC 1878-O 18 1882;O 1884-91;93-95

SISKIYOU standard. w 1902-22||
1902-F 16 1917 as Farmer and miner
C F 23 1917-N 24 1922
CYC 1903-S 1917;18-22

FORTUNA

HUMBOLDT beacon. w 1902+
C N 1907+
CU-B Ap 22 1932;O 13 1933+

FOWLER

Fowler ENSIGN. w O 20 1894+
pub 1894-1916;23+
C 1907+
CFr O 25 1913+
CU-B Jl 17 1909-Mr 19,Ap 2,30-My 28,Je 11,25-Ag 6 1910;Je 8-S 14 1912;Jl-D 1920

FRESNO

ASBAREZ. Arena. sw,tw,w Ag 14 1908+
sw 1908-N 14 1923;tw N 18 1923-Je 7 1924
In Armenian
C 1908+
CU-B F 14-My,Je 27 1922-Ja 5,My 3 1924+
IU D 1917-S 14 1923

Fresno BEE and Fresno republican. d O 17 1922+
1922-Mr 30 1932 as Fresno bee
pub 1922+
C 1922+
CFr 1925+
CU-B Je 16,S 8-22,O 6 1923+

CALIFORNIA post. w 1914-28||?
1914-18 as Deutsche presse
CLSz 1915-18
WaPS N 20-D 4,18-25 1924

COOPERATIVE Californian. w Ja 15 1921-Ja 17 1924||
S 6 1923-Ja 17 1924 as Fresno herald-cooperative, Californian section; a section of Fresno herald
C complete
CFr 1921-23
CU-B Jl 14-Ag 4,25,S 22,O 6,N 10 1922;Ja 19, F 16,Mr 16,Ap 27,My 4-18,Je 15,29,Jl 20-Ag 16 1923

Fresno daily DEMOCRAT. d 1888-
KHi [S 15-O 5 1888]

Fresno DEMOCRAT. w 1895-1904||
CU-B Ap 24 1901-Ap 15,My 27-N 7 1903;F 13-My 21 1904

DEUTSCHE presse. *See* California post

Fresno EXPOSITOR. w,sw Ap 27 1870-S 10 1898||
1870-Ap 15 1874 as Expositor (Millerton)
w 1874-Ag 10 1896
C My 1870-Ap 5 1882;F 1889-Je 1892;94-98
CFr 1870-Mr 1880;Ap 27 1881-Ap 22 1896
CU-B 1870-[72]-[74]Ag 4 1875-[76]-Je 13,O 24 1877-80;Ag 17 1881;Je 21-28 1882;F 21 1883 [86-87]Ja-Je 25 1890
KHi [Ag-N 1888]

Fresno daily evening EXPOSITOR. d Ap 3 1882-S 1 1898||
C Jl 1892-Je 1898
CFr complete
CU-B [Ja-Ag,S 12 1888-D 1 1891]
FU Ja 1 1890
KHi Ag 3,15 1888

Fresno GUIDE. w 1897-1907||?
CLM [1904-05]

Fresno HERALD. d 1895-1924||?
1909-12 as Fresno herald and democrat
CU-B Ag 10 1909-Ap 20,My 6-Ag 19 1910;S 14-D 7 1912;Jl 27 1922;S 6 1923-Ja 17 1924

Fresno HERALD-cooperative. *See* Cooperative Californian

Fresno INQUIRER. w 1883-90||
CU-B Ap 12,Jl 12,Ag 9,N 15-22, D 13 1889; Je 27 1890

Sunday MIRROR. w 1898-1920||?
CLM [1904-05]

MUSHAG. sw Ja 1 1925+
In Armenian
pub 1925+
CU-B Ja 11 1929+

NOR giank aror. *See* Nor or

NOR or. tw,sw,w 1902+
1902?-Mr 1920 as Nor giank; Mr 17 1920-23? Nor Giank-siswan (title varies slightly)
tw 1915-Mr 13 1923; sw Mr 16 1923-Jl 22 1927
In Armenian
pub 1902+
CtY [1931]+
CU-B F 22-O 7 1921
IU D 15 1917-Mr 22, Je 11 1919-Mr 17 1920

Weekly REPUBLICAN. w S 23 1876-Mr 1932||
1887-1932 Thursday ed of Fresno morning republican
CCIP F-D 1918
CSt F-D 1918
CU-B F 10 1877-78;Jl 5 1879-[80;Mr 29-My 24 1886;Ja-My 2 1901]Je 16-Ag 4 1904
KHi [Ag-N 1888]
WaPS [1918]D 22 1922;Ap 26 1923;Ap 20 1924

Fresno morning REPUBLICAN. d 1887-Mr 21 1932||
Title varies: Fresno republican; Daily republican. United with Fresno bee to form Fresno bee and republican
C 1901-32
CFr 1903-32
CFrB complete
CLM D 2 1890
CU-B Ja-My 3 1901;Jl 1904-21;My 1922-N 3 1926
KHi [Ag 1888-Ja 27 1889]

SISWAN. w 1918-Mr 1920||
United with Nor giank to form Nor giank-siswan, later Nor or
In Armenian

Fresno TIMES. Ja 28-Ap 5 1865||
CFr complete

Fresno TRIBUNE. d Mr 22 1932-Ja 15 1933||
Replaced Fresno republican when that paper united with Fresno bee
Sunday issues as Fresno bee and the tribune
C complete
CFr complete
CU-B Mr 27 1932

FRUITVALE

BAY side news. w Jl 8 1906-
CU-B Ja 14-Je 8 1907

Fruitvale NEWS. w N 24 1893-94||
CU-B Je 30,Jl 21 1894

Fruitvale PROGRESS. *See* Oakland progress (Oakland)

FULLERTON

Fullerton JOURNAL. w 1891-92||
CLM [1891-92]
KHi Mr 3 1892

Daily NEWS-TRIBUNE. w,sw,d 1902+
1902-24? as Fullerton news
w 1902-19?; sw 1920?-21?
pub 1925+

ORANGE county tribune. w 1888-1919||?
1888-1908? as Fullerton tribune

ORANGE county tribune. d *See* Fullerton tribune

Fullerton STAR. w 1889||?
CLM S 6 1889

Fullerton TRIBUNE. d 1914-24||?
1919? as Orange county tribune. United with Fullerton news to form Daily news-tribune

Fullerton TRIBUNE. w *See* Orange county tribune

GALT

Galt GAZETTE. w 1881-1915||?
C [Ag 1882-My 6 1911]
CU-B S 18 1886;Je 23 1888;Ja 25 1890

Galt HERALD. w,sw 1901+
1901-Ap 1914 as Weekly witness
sw My 2-Je 3? 1914
C 1912+
CU-B Je 21 1906-[10]-N 18 1921

Weekly WITNESS. *See* Galt herald

GARDEN GROVE

Garden Grove NEWS. w 1907—
pub 1920+

GARDENA

Papers published in Gardena are listed under Los Angeles

CALIFORNIA (*Continued*)

GARVANZA

Papers published in Garvanza are listed under Los Angeles

GEORGETOWN

Georgetown GAZETTE. w Ap 9 1880+
Suspended from My 8 1924-D 7 1933
C 1880-S 14 1922;Je 21 1923+
CU-B D 21 1883[84;Jl 15 1909-Je 23 1910;D 21 1911-S 12 1912]

GERBER

Gerber STAR. w Mr 12 1923+
C Je 26 1924+
CRb D 1926+
CU-B Ag 13-S 10,24,O 1 1925

GEYSERVILLE

Geyserville GAZETTE. w 1899-1919||?
C Ap 10 1913-D 19 1913

GIBSONVILLE

Gibsonville HERALD. *See* Mountain messenger (Downieville)

Gibsonville TRUMPET. *See* Mountain messenger (Downieville)

GILROY

Gilroy ADVOCATE. w S 12 1868+
C My 26 1906+
CU-B 1868-[70]-[72]-[79]80;Jl 9-23,O 22-29 1881;Ja 7-14,28-Ap 22,My 13-Ag 5,S 16 1882; Ja 20-F 10,24,Mr 31-Ap 14,My 12-Je 2 1883; My 17 1884;F 7,N 14 1885;Jl 31 1886;Mr 2,16, S 28,O 19,N 23,D 7 1889;Ja 4,18-25 1890[F 17-D 1906]+
KHi [Jl 28 1888-F 16 1889]

CALIFORNIA leader. w F 19-N 26 1875||?
Merged with Gilroy advocate
CU-B [F 26-N 1875]

Gilroy CRESCENT. w 1888-90||
CU-B F 26-Mr 19,S 17,O 1,N 12-D 3,24 1889; Ja,Ag 12,S 2-16,O 7-14,28 1890
KHi O 30-N 1888

Gilroy GAZETTE. w 1880-1929||?
CU-B N 8-D 1887;Ap 11 1889;O 1907-10

Gilroy INDEPENDENT. w S 16 1876-
CU-B S 30-O 28,N 11,25-D 1876

Gilroy TELEGRAM. w My 31? 1871-72||?
CU-B O 18,D 6,20-27 1871;Ja 10-24,Mr 7 1872

Gilroy UNION. w Mr 23 1872-
CU-B My 11,25-Je 20 1872

VALLEY record. w; sw My 6 1881-87||
CU-B My 6 1881-Ag 5 1882;D 31 1886-N 1 1887

GLADSTONE

Gladstone weekly EXPONENT. w 1885-
KHi [D 22 1887-My 1888]

GLENDALE

Glendale ENCINAL. w 1888-90||
CU-B Mr 14-21,Ap 4,N 7-28 1889;Ja 1890
KHi Jl 26-Ag 2 1888

Glendale NEWS. w Ja 4 1908-Ag 22 1913||
CG complete

Glendale NEWS-PRESS. d 1905+
1905-F 15 1928 as Glendale evening news
pub Ap 1916+
CG Ag 23 1913+
CU-B My 2 1925

Glendale daily PRESS. d Mr 1921-F 15 1928||
United with Glendale evening news to form Glendale news-press
CGN complete

VALLEY news. w Ap 7 1894-
CU-B My 5 1894

GLENDORA

Glendora ECHO. w 1892-93||
CU-B O 6-13 1893

Glendora GLEANER. *See* Glendora press-gleaner

Glendora PRESS. w 1926-33||
United with Glendora gleaner to form Glendora press-gleaner
CAz F 15 1929-33
CGlP complete

Glendora PRESS-gleaner. w 1901+
1901-33 as Glendora gleaner
pub 1910+
CAz Ag 23 1923-Jl 15 1932
CU-B My 2-30 1919

Glendora SIGNAL. w O 20 1887-Ag 8 1889||
Followed by Azusa pomotropic (Azusa)
C [1887-89]
CAzH 1887-O 1888[89]
CLM Mr 8 1888
CPo O 20,D 29 1887
CU-B 1887[88]Ja 10-17,Ap 4,Je 27-Jl 4,Ag 1889

GOLDEN GATE. *See* EMERYVILLE

GONZALES

Gonzales TRIBUNE. w 1891+
CU-B My 1-8 1919

GOSHEN

Goshen HERALD. w Ja 15-Jl 16 1887||?
C Ja-Jl 16 1887

GRAHAM

Papers published in Graham are listed under Los Angeles

GRAHAM FIRESTONE PARK

Papers published in Graham Firestone Park are listed under Los Angeles

GRANITE

JOURNAL. *See* Folsom telegraph (Folsom)

GRASS VALLEY

FOOTHILL weekly tidings-telegraph. w Ja 10 1874-1904||?
1874-Jl 19 1890 as Foothill weekly tidings (title varies slightly); Jl 26 1890-N 10 1898 Weekly telegraph
C 1877-Jl 1881;O 18 1890-Mr 1904
CU-B 1874-80;S 24 1881-Ap 8 1882[86-87]Jl 1888-89;Ag-D 1890
—d ed *See* Evening tidings

FREE LANCE. *See* Tidings

Grass Valley INTELLIGENCER. *See* Grass Valley national

Grass Valley NATIONAL. w,tw,d S 22 1853-Mr 31 1870||
1853-Jl 31 1858 as Grass Valley telegraph (-1856 Grass Valley intelligencer); Ag 1858- Nevada national. United with Nevada daily gazette (Nevada City) to form Daily national gazette (Nevada City)
w 1853-Ag 3 1861?; tw Ag 10 1861-Jl 1864
C 1853-Jl 17 1858;Ja 8 1859-Jl 21 1860;Ag 10 1861-My 27 1865;O 29 1868
CSmH extra O 5 1853
CU-B My 28 1866;Jl 1[Ag 1867-68]-70
DLC N 10-17 1853;Ja 19,F 16,Mr 30-Ap 6,My 11,Je 22,Jl 20 1854;Ja 16,Mr 20,Ap 3 1855; Ap 4 1857
NNHi D 18 1855;My 27 1856
PW O 15 1856

NEVADA national. *See* Grass Valley national

Grass Valley REPUBLICAN. d N 9 1871-Ap 9 1872||
Followed by Truckee republican, later Sierra sun and Truckee republican (Truckee)
CU-B [1871]-72

Grass Valley TELEGRAPH. *See* Grass Valley national

Evening TELEGRAPH. *See* Evening tidings

Weekly TELEGRAPH. *See* Foothill weekly tidings-telegraph

TIDINGS. d Ag 21 1880-98||
Ag-O 21 1880 as Nevada county free lance (Nevada City); O 22 1880-Jl 30 1881 Free lance; Ag 1881-82? Tidings and free lance. United with Evening telegraph to form Evening tidings-telegraph, later Evening tidings
CU-B [1880-N 2 1881]

Evening TIDINGS. d O 1 1889-1913||?
1889-N 10? 1898 as Evening telegraph; N 11 1898-1904? Evening tidings-telegraph
C My 21-S 26 1890
CU-B O 1886;My 21 1889;Ag 4,6,8 1890;91
—w ed *See* Foothill weekly tidings-telegraph

Morning UNION. d O 28 1864+
Title varies: Grass Valley daily union; Daily morning union; Morning daily union and the herald
pub 1866+
C Ap 14 1865;O 28 1868;O 1890+
CU-B [1865-67]-77;Mr-D 1878;Ap 26 1879-80; 87;Ag 7-D 24 1932
MWA Ja 27 1876

GREENVILLE

Greenville BULLETIN. *See* Plumas county bulletin (Quincy)

INDIAN Valley record. w 1930+
pub O 1931+
CQ 1931+

PLUMAS county bulletin. *See under* Quincy

PLUMAS star. w 1905-12||
CQ [1907-S 2 1912]

GREENWATER

DEATH Valley chuck walla. sm,m Ja-Je 1907||?
CSmH Ap 1907
CU-B Ja-Je 1 1907

GRIDLEY

Gridley daily GLOBE. d 1906+
C Ap 16 1935+

Gridley HERALD. w,sw O 22 1880+
w 1880-My 6 1908
pub 1880-85; 1901+
C Ap 1934+
CU-B 1880;Mr 24 1882;Mr 22-29,Ap 12-26,My 31 1883[88-89]-Je 1890;91-Ja 7 1892;Ja 19 1906-[12-Ap 12 1913]

GROVELAND

TUOLUMNE prospector. w 1901-20||?
CU-B [1906]-My 20 1916
MWA Jl 7 1906

GUADALUPE

Guadalupe ADVANCE. w F 24 1920-21||?
CU-B Je 16,Jl 8 1920

GURNEVILLE

RUSSIAN River advertiser. w 1901-12||?
CU-B Jl 31 1909-Ap 9,30-Jl 2 1910

Guerneville TIMES. w 1902+
pub 1918+

GUSTINE

Gustine STANDARD. w 1910+
CMe Ja 1911+
CU-B Jl 12,Ag 16,S 13,N 29,D 31 1929;Ap 3,My 8,Je 5-12,26 1930;Ap 9 1931

HALF MOON BAY

COAST advocate. w 1890-1906||?
CSt [1880;93;95]

Half Moon Bay NEWS. w My 6 1922+
C 1922+

HANCOCK PARK

Papers published in Hancock Park are listed under Los Angeles

HANFORD

Hanford JOURNAL. w 1881-82||
CU-B Je 23 1882

Hanford JOURNAL. sw 1891-1920||?
CU-B S-D 1907

Hanford JOURNAL. d 1895+
C 1913+

MUSSEL Slough delta. w Ja 7? 1881-83||?
CU-B D 2,16-30 1881;Ja 27,F 3-10,24,Mr 16-Je 2,23-Jl 14,Ag 4,18-25 1882

PUBLIC good. w Ag 28-S 17 1878||?
CU-B S 10-17 1878

Hanford SENTINEL. d 1886+
C S 29 1919+
CU-B Ja 5 1898;S 10 1907-Jl 1918

Hanford SENTINEL. w 1886-S 25 1919||
C 1901-19
CU-B [1889]Ja 5 1898

HAVILAH

Havilah COURIER. *See* Bakersfield Californian (Bakersfield)

KERN county weekly courier. *See* Bakersfield Californian (Bakersfield)

Havilah MINER. w Je 1 1872-74||
C Ag 17 1872-My 1874
CU-B [Je 29 1872-My 16 1874]

HAWTHORNE

Hawthorne-Lennox ADVERTISER. w Ja 1920+
pub Ag 1920+

HAYWARD

ALAMEDA county advocate. w D 10 1870-Je 27 1874||?
CU-B 1870[71]-[73]-Je 27 1874

Hayward JOURNAL. w 1877+
CU-B S-D 8,29 1877;Je,Jl 20-D 1878;N 8 1879-80;F 12-D 1881;Ja 21-Je 17,Jl 15 1882;Ja 24 1885

Hayward NEWS. d 1924-26||?
CU-B Mr 11 1926

PLAIN-DEALER. w Je 6-O 28 1874||?
CU-B O 17,31,N 14,28 1874

Twice-a-week REVIEW. w,sw 1880+
1880-My 6 1910 as Hayward review
w 1880-My 6 1910
CU-B Jl 16-23,Ag 1909-Jl 1910;Je 18-S 17 1912

Hayward REVIEW. d 1909+
CU-B N 19 1931

HEALDSBURG

Healdsburg ADVERTISER. w 1864-65||?
CU-B Je 2 1865

DEMOCRAT Standard. w O 4 1865-O 31 1868||?
C O 24 1868
CU-B D 27 1865-O 31 1868

CALIFORNIA (*Continued*)

HEALDSBURG—*Continued*

Healdsburg ENTERPRISE. w My 27 1876+
CU-B 1876-80;N 24,D 8 1881-[82]Ap 12,O 4-11,N 29 1883;87-[90-91]F 6,My 28,Ag 13-27,S 10-O 8 1892;Jl 1909-[Jl-D 1910]Je 8,22,Jl-S 14 1912
KHi Ja 16 1887;My 26 1894

Healdsburg REVIEW. w 1861-62||?
CU-B Jl 4 1862

RUSSIAN River flag. w N 19 1868-D 29 1886||
Merged with Healdsburg enterprise
C D 24 1868
CU-B 1868-78;My 22 1879-My 15 1884;86

SONOMA county tribune. *See* Healdsburg tribune

SOTOYOME scimitar. w,sw 1898+
1898-1907 as Sotoyome sun
sw N 3 1925-Ap 15 1927
pub Mr 1906+
C 1927+
CU-B [Mr-O 1908]F 14,O 3,N 21 1918;Ja 2,16-Mr 13 1919;Mr 19 1920-Ja 26,Ap 16,23,Ag 20,O 19 1926;Ja 11,Mr 11,18 1927+

SOTOYOME sun. *See* Sotoyome scimitar

Healdsburg TRIBUNE. w Mr 21 1888-1928||?
1888-93 as Sonoma county tribune
CU-B N 24 1888[Mr-D 1889]-F 1,15,Ag 21,S 4,O 9-16,30 1890[92-My 18 1893]Ag 13 1909-Jl 20 1910;My 23-S 12 1912
KHi Je 13 1888-Ja 15 1891

HEBER

Herber HERALD. w 1904-10||?
CLM O 13,N 26 1904;Ja 28-F 4 1905

HELIX

SPRING Valley herald. m? S 1887-
CU-B S 1887

HEMET

Hemet NEWS. w D 9 1893+
pub 1893+
C S 19 1913+
CHe Ja 1907
CRiv 1912-26;28+
CU-B Jl 16 1909-Jl 8 1910
KHi O 19 1894

HERMOSA BEACH

Hermosa Beach REVIEW. w 1907+
pub 1923+
CRe F 1911-F 1915

HESPERIA

Hesperia HERALD. w 1887-88||?
CLM D 24 1887;F 4 1888

HIGHLAND PARK

Papers published in Highland Park are listed under Los Angeles

HILMAR

Hilmar ENTERPRISE. w 1919+
CMe 1923+
CU-B [Jl 23 1920-Jl 1921]-Je 10 1927;Mr 1928+

HOLLISTER

Hollister ADVANCE. w,sw,tw,d Je 17 1872+
1872-My 2 1874 as Advance; My 9 1874-S 29 1920 San Benito advance; O 1 1920-F 12? 1923 Morning daily advance and San Benito advance; F 14 1923-My 20 1925 San Benito advance and morning daily advance; Mr 23 1925-Mr 1926 Hollister advance and San Benito advance
w 1872-S 1920; sw F 14 1923-Jl 1924; tw Ag 1924-33
pub 1880+
C My 16 1890+
CHo 1924+
CU-B 1872-My,O 17,31-D 1878;Jl-Ag,S 11,N 13,27-D 11,25 1879;Jl 22 1880;My 14 1881-Ag 4 1882;86[88-89]-Je 6,20-27 1890[91]-F 5 1892;Jl 21 1909-Jl 20 1910

Morning daily ADVANCE. d Ag 20 1919-S 29? 1920||
United with San Benito advance to form Morning daily advance and San Benito advance, later Hollister advance
C Ag 23 1919-20

Hollister BEE. w 1896-Ag 1917||
Follows West Coast alliance. United with Hollister free lance (w) to form San Benito county news
CU-B Ja 29 1909

CENTRAL Californian. F 6 1869-Ag 1871||?
Followed by Salinas City index, later Weekly nidex (Salinas)
1869-Ap 1870? pub at San Juan
CU-B My 6,O 28 1869;S 1870-F 8,22-Je 7,Jl-Ag 16 1871

DEMOCRAT. *See* Hollister free lance

Hollister ENTERPRISE. *See* Hollister free lance

Hollister FREE LANCE. w O 18 1873-Ag 1917||?
1873-Ja 29? 1881 as Hollister enterprise; F 5-N 25? 1881 Pacific coast; D 2 1881-1884 Democrat. United with Hollister bee to form San Benito county news
CU-B [1873-S 23 1876]Jl 12 1879;F-Mr 19,Ap,My 14-N 13,D 1881-Ap 21,My 5 1882;F 9-Mr 23 1883

Hollister evening FREE LANCE. d 1909+
Title varies slightly
C D 15 1926+
CHo 1924-Mr,S 22 1930+
CU-B My 7-31 1919;Je 30 1927+

Hollister OBSERVER. d N 22 1922-D 19 1925||
CHo 1924-25

PACIFIC coast. *See* Hollister free lance

SAN BENITO advance. *See* Hollister advance

SAN BENITO county news. w 1917-19||?
Formed by the union of Hollister bee and Hollister free lance

SAN JUAN echo. w S 17? 1870-Mr 14 1871||?
CU-B N 26-D 24 1870;Ja 14-Mr 14 1871

Hollister TELEGRAPH. w Ag 1875-Ja 29 1881||
United with Hollister enterprise to form Pacific coast, later Hollister free lance
CU-B S 28 1876-Ja 18[F 1877-O 1878]

WEST Coast alliance. Ag 1892-95||?
Followed by Hollister bee

HOLLYWOOD

Papers published in Hollywood are listed under Los Angeles

HOLTVILLE

Holtville TRIBUNE. w F 27 1905+
CEc My 1910
CU-B F-Jl 3 1908
PPiHi D 5 1912

HORSETOWN

NORTHERN argus. w 1861-63||?
CU-B O 24 1863

HOT SPRINGS

FREE LANCE. S 1889-91||?
1889-90 pub in Genoa, Nevada
Nv 1889-Ag 1891

HUENEME

Hueneme HERALD. w 1888-1905||?
CU-B Mr-Ap 4,25-My 2 1889

HUNTINGTON PARK

Huntington Park SIGNAL. d 1905+
pub Ag 5 1925+
CU-B D 5,19 1908;Ja 2,16-F 6,27,Mr 13-Ap 10,Je 19-26 1909

SOUTHWEST advertiser. w S 1 1932+
pub 1932+

IMPERIAL

Imperial ENTERPRISE. w 1907+
CEc F 1912+

Imperial PRESS. d Ap 20 1901-Mr 1 1906||
Followed by Imperial press (El Centro)
CU-B Ja 18-Je 7 1902;Ja 3 1903

Imperial STANDARD. d 1904-S 29 1911||
Merged with Imperial Valley press (El Centro)
CU-B Ap 13 1908-[10]11

INDEPENDENCE

INYO independent. w Jl 9 1870+
C 1870-Je 14 1884;1901+
CI [1914-16]+
CLM [1889-1900]
CU-B Jl 16-N 21,D 26 1870;F 18 1871-Mr,My 20,Je 10,Jl 29 1882;My 3 1884[87]-Jl,O 13 1888-[90]91;Jl 16 1909-Jl 22 1910;Je-S 13 1912; Ja 20 1923-Ja 7 1933

INYO index. w 1887-96||?
C 1891-93

INDIO

DATE palm. w Mr 6 1912+
1912-F 25 1916 as Indio date palm
CRiv 1912-[23]-[26]

INGLEWOOD

Inglewood CALIFORNIAN. w F 1922+
pub 1922+

Inglewood daily NEWS. d 1904+
pub 1904+

IONE CITY

AMADOR times. w Ja 3 1877-79||?
Ja 3 1877-O 19 1878 as Ione news
CU-B N 1878-D 20 1879

Ione CHRONICLE. w My 14- 1863||?
CU-B O 29 1863

Ione NEWS. *See* Amador times

Ione VALLEY echo. w 1883+
Mr 3 1933-Ap 14 1934 as Ione Valley echo and Sutter creek news
CU-B Jl 4 1884;O 10 1885[86]Ag 21 1909-Ag 6 1910;My 11,25-S 1912;Ag 14 1920+
DLC Ja 12-19,F 9,Mr 2-9,S 21-N 2,16 1895-Ja 11,25-F 1,15-Ap 11,My 9-S 12,26-D 19 1896;Ja,F 13-Je 5,19-Jl 24,Ag-N 13,27-D 18 1897;98
KHi Ag 1888-Ja 12 1889

IOWA HILL

Iowa Hill NEWS. w S 1855-N 1857||
Followed by North San Juan star, later Hydraulic press (North San Juan)
C O 24 1857

Weekly PATRIOT. w Ja 15 1859-
C Ja 15 1859-Ja 7 1860

IRVINGTON

To 1874? as Washington

ALAMEDA county express. w 1888-89||?
CU-B Mr 2-16 1889

ALAMEDA county independent. *See* Alameda county reporter

ALAMEDA county reporter. w Je 5 1875-86||?
1875-F 22 1879 as Alameda county independent
CU-B 1875-76;Jl 1877-[79]80 My 7 1881;F 25,Mr 11,Ap 1,Je 3-10 1882

WASHINGTON press. w 1891-
CSmH S 1898

ISLETON

DELTA news. w 1928+
C F 1929+
CU-B O 31 1932

Isleton JOURNAL. w N 1923+
pub 1923+

HORNITOS

MARIPOSA democrat. w Jl 8 1856-
1856-Je 4 1857 pub at Mariposa
CP Ag 5 1856
CU-B Ag 5 1856;Jl 23 1857
NNHi Ap 1857-Ap 1 1858

JACKSON

AMADOR dispatch. w 1858+
Suspended for a time during Civil War
1858 pub at Lancha Plana
C O 24 1868;Ap 30 1870-Mr 1875;Je 1878-Mr 9 1889; My 17 1890+
CU-B D 17 1864-F 4,Mr-My 6 1865;D 29 1866-Ja 5,19,Jl 20,D 14 1867;Ja 11 1868-[69-71]-[79]-Jl 1882;Ja 20 1883;83;Ja-Jl,Ag 25,S 8-22,D 29 1888;89-91
MWA My 27 1876

AMADOR ledger and Amador record. w O 27 1855+
1855-Ap 1857 as Weekly ledger (Volcano); Ap 1857-Ag 1921 Amador weekly ledger
C Ja 2 1869;Jl 20 1872;1900-O 4 1918;S 1921+
CSmH Jl-D 1863
CU-B [Ap 1863-67]-O 1869[My 1870-71]-79; Ap 9 1881[82]Ja 13 1883[Mr-D 1889]-Ja 11,25-F 1 1890;Jl 23-30,Ag 20 1909-[F-Ag 1910] Ja 18 1923+

AMADOR republican. w 1894-98||
C Jl 31 1896-98

AMADOR sentinel. w 1853?-
MWA Ag 16 1856

AMADOR sentinel. w Je 25 1879-88||?
CU-B Jl 30 1879-[80-82]83

Daily AMADOR sentinel. d S 8 1879-
CU-B S 9-11,13 1879
MWA S 8 1879
NNHi S 9-10 1879

JAMESTOWN

MOTHER lode magnet. w 1897-F? 1935||
Followed by Sonora news and Mother lode magnet (Sonora)

JULIAN

Julian SENTINEL. w 1887-94||?
CLM My 9-16 1890;Jl 23-D 1891;Ja-Ag 3 1893; My 12-D 1894
CU-B Jl 5-12 1889
KHi Ja 4 1889

KELSEYVILLE

Kelseyville SUN. w Mr 1902+
pub 1928+
CU-B O 12 1933-[34]+

KING CITY

King City HERALD. w,sw O 31 1914+
1914-S 10 1915 as King City Saturday herald
w 1914-Ap 16 1929
C 1914+
CSa [1915-17]-[21-27]+
CU-B Ag 9,S 9-O 7,14-18,O 25 1932

CALIFORNIA (*Continued*)

KING CITY—*Continued*

RUSTLER. w,sw My 3 1901+
1912-17 as Salinas Valley rustler
sw O 15 1929-F 12 1932
CK [1922-Ap 5 1934]
CSa S 23 1921+

SALINAS Valley rustler. *See* Rustler

SALINAS Valley settler. *See* King City settler

King City SATURDAY herald. *See* King City herald

King City SETTLER. w 1888-1905||?
1888-Je 20? 1889 as Salinas Valley settler
CU-B Je 27-Jl 11,S 5,19-O 4,17,31-N 7,21-D 5,26 1889-Ja 18,F 1,Ag 16,O 11-18 1890

KINGSBURG

Kingsburg HERALD. w 1887-89||
KHi [Jl 21 1888-Ja 5 1889]

Kingsburg RECORDER. w N 1904+
CFr 1916+
CU-B F 29-Mr 7,Ap 1924-[25]-27

KLINKERVILLE. *See* EMERYVILLE

KNIGHT'S FERRY

STANISLAUS index. w 1860-61||?
CU-B O 5 1861

KNIGHT'S LANDING

Knight's Landing NEWS. w 1856?-64||?
CU-B Mr 19 1864

Knights Landing RIVER news. w Mr 1928+
pub 1932+

LA FAYETTE

DEMOCRATIC sentinel. w Ja 26- 1866||?
CU-B Mr 16 1866

LAGUNA BEACH

Laguna Beach LIFE. w 1915-Ag 1928||
1915-27 as Laguna life. Merged with South coast news
CLM 1922-My 16 1924;O 22-29 1926
CLaS 1917;21-23

SOUTH coast news. w 1927+
pub 1928+
CLM Ag 25,S 18,D 15 1933
VU S 4 1934

LA HABRA

La Habra STAR. w Jl 13 1916+
pub 1916+

LA JOLLA

La Jolla BREAKERS. w Ap 5- 1906||
C Ap-Jl 27 1906

La Jolla JOURNAL. w 1912+
pub [1912-19]+

La Jolla LIGHT. sw,w Ap 7 1922+
sw 1922-Je 27? 1932
CU-B F 5-8,22-26,Mr-Ap 5,Je 18,S 6 1929+

LAKE ELSINORE. *See* ELSINORE

LAKEPORT

Lakeport AVALANCHE. w Mr 4-O 21 1871||?
CU-B Mr-Ag 5,19-S 9,23-O 21 1871

BEE-DEMOCRAT. *See* Lake county bee

CLEAR Lake courier. w D 8 1866-71||
C D 5 1868;My 28 1870-Ja 1871
CU-B D 15 1866-[67-Ja 21 1871]

CLEAR Lake journal. w S 13 1865-66||?
CU-B 1865-F 1 1866

CLEAR Lake press. w 1886-1923||
1886-96? as Lake county avalanche. Followed by Lakeport press and record
C My 15 1890-Ag 1 1895
CU-B Ja 21 1892;Ag 31 1893
KHi Jl 11 1889

CLEAR Lake times. w 1864-66||?
CU-B Ag 24 1865;F 22,Mr 29,Ap 19,28 1866

DEMOCRAT. *See* Lake county bee

LAKE county avalanche. *See* Clear Lake press

LAKE county bee. w Je 29 1872+
1872-F 22 1873 as Cloverdale bee (Cloverdale); Mr 8 1873-S 2 1880 Lake county bee; S 11 1880-85? Bee democrat; 1885?-94? Democrat
C S 1895-97;99+
CLM Je 7 1905
CU-B 1872-Je 1875;Je 15 1876;77-Je,D 26 1878; F 1879-80;F 10-Je 23,Jl 1882[86-87]-[90]91; Ag 12 1909-Ap 7,My-Je 1910;N 30,D 14,28 1911;Ja 11-S 12 1912;Ja 18 1923+

LAKE county democrat. w My 9- 1866||?
CU-B My 9-Je 20,Jl 4-25,Ag 18-25 1866

LAKE democrat. w Jl 10 1875-S 4 1880||
United with Lake county bee to form Bee-democrat, later Lake county bee
CU-B [Jl 17-D 1875]-S 6,20 1879-80

Lakeport PRESS and record. w Je 1924+
Follows Clear Lake press
pub 1924+

LAKESIDE

Lakeside BOOSTER. *See* Lakeside journal

Lakeside JOURNAL. w 1919-O 13 1933||
1919-22? as Lakeside booster
C O 14 1927-33

LA MESA

La Mesa SCOUT. w Mr 3 1907+
pub 1915+
C O 21 1927+

LANCASTER

ANTELOPE Valley gazette. *See* Antelope Valley ledger gazette

ANTELOPE Valley ledger. w 1906-13||
United with Antelope Valley gazette to form Antelope Valley ledger gazette

ANTELOPE Valley ledger-gazette. w Mr 1887+
1887-95? as Lancaster gazette; 1896?-1913 Antelope Valley gazette
pub 1887+
CLM Ja 4 1889;F 1 1890;Ag-D 1891;Ja-Jl 8, 22,Ag 5-12,26,S 2-23,O-N 11,25,D 16-23 1892; My 11 1894;S 27 1895
CU-B [1906]-Ag 18,O 6 1911
KHi [Ag 30 1888-S 9 1892]

ANTELOPE Valley times. w 1890-92||?
CLM Mr 16,27 1890;Je 11,25,S 10,24-O, 1,N 19, D 17 1891-Ja 7,28,F 18-My 5,19-26 1892
KHi [Ag 1889-O 1890]

Lancaster GAZETTE. *See* Antelope Valley ledger-gazette

Lancaster NEWS. w 1885-86||?
CLM D 26 1885
CU-B Mr 27 1886

LANCHA PLANA

AMADOR dispatch. *See under* Jackson

LA PORTE

To 1857 as Rabbit Creek

MOUNTAIN messenger. *See under* Downieville

La Porte UNION. w D 12 1868-Ag 21 1869||?
C D 12 1868;My 3 1869
CU-B 1868-Ag 21 1869

LARKSPUR

Larkspur-Corte Madera NEWS. w Ap 1927+
pub 1927+

LATON

Laton ARGUS. w 1901-17||?
CU-B My 8-D 4 1909;Ap 2,My 7,Je 18[Jl-D 1910]-Mr 23 1912

LA VERNE

La Verne LEADER, w My 9 1910+
pub 1910+
CLM Ag 25 1921
CU-B My 15 1919

La Verne NEWS. w Mr 15-My 3 1888||?
CPo Mr 15,29,My 3 1888

SOUTHERN Californian. w Mr 6- 1890||?
CPo Mr 6 1890

LE GRAND

Le Grand ADVANCE. w
CU-B Ag 29 1901

Le Grand ADVOCATE. w 1906+
pub S 1908+
CMe N 12 1910+

LEMOORE

Lemoore ADVANCE. w 1915+
pub 1915+

LENNOX

HAWTHORNE-Lennox advertiser. *See under* Hawthorne

LINCOLN

Lincoln GAZETTE. *See* News-messenger

NEWS-messenger. w 1889+
1889-91? as Lincoln gazette; 1892?-96? Placer news-messenger
pub Ap 15 1926+
C S 19 1913+
CU-B Ja 7,Jl 15 1909-Ag 5 1910[My 10-S 13 1912]27-[30]+

PLACER news-messenger. *See* News-messenger

LINDSAY

Lindsay GAZETTE. sw,w 1901+
sw O 1912-Mr 1913
C 1904-S 6 1907;31+
CLM [D 1903-F 1905]
CU-B S 13 1907-Ap 1918;Mr 18 1932

Tuesday NEWS. w O 13 1931+
C 1931+

LIVE OAK

Live Oak ADVANCE. w 1932+
CU-B O 12 1933-Ja 18,F-My 3,17,31 1934+

LIVERMORE

Livermore ECHO. w 1882-1918||?
CU-B Ag 29-S 5,19,O 17,N 21-D 5 1889;Ja-F 13,27,O 9 1890;Jl 22-Ag 5,26 1909-Mr 24,Ap 7,28-Jl 7 1910; My 9,30-S 12 1912

Livermore ENTERPRISE. w My 16 1874-D 16 1876||?
CU-B My 16-Jl 4 1874;Mr 27-D 16 1876
MWA Jl 1 1876

Livermore HERALD. w Ja 31 1877+
CU-B Mr 28,Ap 11-18 1877;Jl 2 1879;Ap 8-15, My 27,Je 10,Jl-Ag 5,19-S 16,O 14-21,D 16-30 1880;My 26,Ag-O 20,D 1881-My 18,Je 1,15-Ag 3 1882;Ja 25 1896;Je 4,18 1898
KHi Ag 30 1888

LIVINGSTON

Livingston CHRONICLE. w O 1909+
pub Ap 1915+
CMe 1911+

LLANO

Llano COLONIST. w 1916-19||?
MH Je 30-N 3 1917
WHi S 30 1916-N 3 1917

LODI

Lodi BUDGET. w 1892-94||
United with Valley review to form Lodi review-budget

Lodi CYCLONE. *See* Lodi review-budget

Lodi weekly NEWS. w 1885-88||?
C 1887-Jl 5 1888

Lodi REVIEW-BUDGET. w 1878-99||?
1878-Mr 1894 as Valley review, (1885-87 Lodi cyclone)
C Jl 23 1881-Jl 9 1884;S 24 1885-S 15 1887;O 25 1888-93
CSto Mr 17[Ap 1894-F 1895]
CU-B [F 1879-Ag 1884]Jl 25,O 31-N 7,21-D 5,19-26 1889[90]Mr 12 1891[92]Ja 12-19,F 2,16 1893
KHi F 14 1889

SAN JOAQUIN journal. *See* California zeitung and San Joaquin journal (Oakland)

Lodi SENTINEL. w,tw Jl 9 1881+
w 1881-1901?
pub 1881+
CLo 1928+
CU-B [1883]-Ja 12 1884;Je 27 1885;Jl 29 1893
KHi [Jl 28-N 10 1888]

VALLEY review. *See* Lodi review-budget

LOMITA

Lomita NEWS. *See* Torrance herald-Lomita news (Torrance)

LOMPOC

Lompoc JOURNAL. w My 1887-O 25 1918||
CLom 1908-18

Lompoc RECORD. sw,w Ap 10 1875+
sw S 23-D 16 1924
pub 1875-85;1908+
CLom 1875+
CSmH 1875-Ap 1 1876
CU-B Ap 10 1875[Ja-Jl 1876;F-Ag 1877]F 14 1880-[Ja-Je 1881;Mr-Ag 1882]Ja 13 1883;My 9 1919
KHi Ja 3 1891

LONE PINE

MT. WHITNEY observer. w 1924-D 25 1931||
CI [1924-26]

OWENS Valley progress-citizen. w 1932+
1932-Ag 24 1933 as Owens Valley progress
CI 1932+

LONG BEACH

Long Beach AMERICAN. w F 3-S 1 1933||
CLb complete

Long Beach ARGUS. w 1924+
CLb Ag 31 1931+

BELNAMOS. w O 19 1933+
CLb O 19 1933+

Long Beach BREAKER. *See* Long Beach press-telegram

EAST Long Beach news. w 1920-23||
CLb 1920-21

EAST Long Beach star-progress. *See* Long Beach star-progress

Long Beach JOURNAL. *See* Long Beach press-telegram

Long Beach NEWS. w Je 6 1891-
KHi Je 6 1891

NEWS. w 1901?-05||?
CLb [D 24 1904-05]

CALIFORNIA (*Continued*)

LONG BEACH—*Continued*

PACIFIC weekly tribune. sw,w Ap 22 1898-Je 30 1905||
1898-Ag 25 1899 as Semi-weekly tribune; O 6 1899-O 4 1901 Pacific tribune sw 1899-O 4 1901
CLb complete

Long Beach **PRESS-TELEGRAM.** w,sw,d 1888+
1888-90? as Long Beach journal; 1891?-S 10 1897 Long Beach breaker; S 17 1897-Ag 31 1924 Long Beach press
pub S 17 1897+
CL D 31 1927
CLM F 7-Je 20,Ag 15 1891-O 22 1892;Mr 25 1902
CLb Ja 22-Jl 2 1901;02+
CU-B O 25 1890
KHi Ag 31 1888;Ja 31 1891;My 29 1923

PROGRESSIVE review. w F 2 1933+
CLb F 21 1933+

Long Beach **REPORTER.** w Ag 29 1933+
pub 1933+
CLb 1933+

SPOKESMAN. w 1932+
CLb 1932+

Long Beach **STAR-PROGRESS.** w 1920+
1920-Ag 1933 as East Long Beach star-progress
pub 1920+
CLb 1932+

Long Beach **SUN.** d Ap 1 1923+
pub 1923+
CLb 1929+

Long Beach **TELEGRAM.** d D 26 1904-Ag 31 1924||
United with Long Beach press to form Long Beach press-telegram
CLb complete
CLbP complete
CU-B My 6-17 1919
KHi N 16 1914

Long Beach **TRIBUNE.** d 1898-1907||
1898-D 3 1906 as Long Beach evening tribune
CLb [1900]-07

Semi-weekly **TRIBUNE.** *See* Pacific weekly tribune

LORDSBURG

Lordsburg **EAGLE.** w S 15 1887-88||?
CPo S 15 1887;F 23 1888

SOUTHERN Californian. w Mr 6 1890-92||?
CLM O 9 1890;Ja 15 1891;N 8 1892

LOS ALAMITOS

Los Alamitos **PRESS.** w Jl 13 1926+
CBpN 1925+

LOS ALAMOS

Los Alamos **CENTRAL.** w D 4 1891-1900||?
CU-B Ja 23-30 1892

Los Aeamos **PROGRESS.** w 1888-90||
CU-B O 19 1889-F 1890;Je 7,S 6-13,O 4,25,N 1 1890

LOS ANGELES

ADVOCATE and Los Angeles and San Pedro shipping gazette. w O 6 1883-Ag 21 1886||?
Title varies: Advocate
CLM Ap 17-Je 5,Jl 31,Ag 21 1886
CSmH 1883-Ap 1884;Ap 24 1886

El **AGNACERO.** w 1878-
In Spanish
CLM Mr 24-31 1878

El **AMIGO** del pueblo. w 1861-
In Spanish
CLM N 30 1861

ANGELES Mesa news. w N 17 1920+
pub 1920+

ANGELUS news. w 1933+
CLC 1933+

BOULEVARD record. w S 11 1920+
pub 1920+

BRENTWOOD Heights press. w 1929+
pub 1929+
CLW 1929+

BULLETIN. sw Ja 6 1933+
pub 1933+

CACTUS; an illustrated weekly journal of the angels. w F 11 1888-Ja 1 1889||
CL F 11-D 15 1888
CLM Ap 21-28,Ag 18,S 15,O 13,31,N 24,D 15, 25 1888

CALIFORNIA. w 1891||?
CLM Jl 4-O 10,17-D 26 1891

CALIFORNIA democrat. w Ap 23 1923-24||?
CU-B D 17 1923-Ja 14,F 4,21-28,Mr 13-Ap 24,Je 9,16 1924

CALIFORNIA eagle. w Mr 3 1879+
- as Eagle
Negro
pub 1910+
CL D 23 1927
CLM S 5 1903;D 15 1906
CU-B Ja 31 Je 20[Ag 22 1914-N 1919;21-Mr 1922]F 14 1924;Ja 1-8,My 7 1926;F 4-11,O 14, D 23 1927; Je 22,Jl 13 1928;F 22,Mr 8-15,Ap 5,My 3,S 27-O 4 1929;Mr 14-21 1920

CALIFORNIA Jewish star. w,d 1919?-
1919?-Ja? 1924 title varies: Los Angeles daily zeit; Jewish daily zeit; Daily Jewish times; Jewish times; California Jewish times
In English and Yiddish
NN Jl 15 1921-My 22 1924

CALIFORNIA Jewish times. *See* California Jewish star

CALIFORNIA Jewish voice. w 1922+
In Yiddish
pub 1927+

CALIFORNIA nationalist. w F 8- 1890||?
ICJ F 8-15,Mr 8-My 3 1890

CALIFORNIA nationalist. w 1931||
CLM F 8-22,Mr 1-8,22-29,My 10 1931

CALIFORNIA staats-zeitung. w 1919+
pub 1919+

CALIFORNIA tribune. w My 31-D 27 1923||?
CLSU 1923+

CALIFORNIA veckoblad. w Ag 5 1910+
In Swedish
pub 1910+
IRA [1912+]
IU D 1917+
MnHi Mr 8 1912-Ag 1920;My 1926+

CALIFORNIA vikingen. w 1924-25||?
In Norwegian
IaDeL Ja 15-22,F 11-Ap 23 1925

CALIFORNIAI magyarsag (California Hungarian People). w
In Hungarian
PPiHi [D 29 1928-Je 5 1931]

CANOGA Park herald. w D 7 1912+
1912-F 28 1931 as Owensmouth gazette
pub 1912+

CAPITAL. w 1895-1903||
CLM [1895-1903]

CENTRAL avenue news. w Je 17 1910-11||?
C N 1910-My 19 1911

CHALLENGER. w 1900-
KHi Ja 23-O 12 1901

CHATSWORTH herald. w Ja 1926+
pub 1933+

Weekly **CITIZEN.** (East Los Angeles) w Ap 12 1890-93||?
CLM S 1890-Ap 1892;My 13-Je 17 1893
CU-B O 11 1890
KHi My 23-S 1891

CITIZEN. w 1898-
CLM Ja 1898

Los Angeles **CITIZEN.** w Mr 1 1907+
pub 1907+
C My 1916-18
CU-B My-Ag,S 8,22-D 1911;My-S 8,22 1916+
WHi 1907-Ap 1916

CITIZEN'S advocate. w 1916-23||?
CU-B D 11-18 1920;Ja-F 19,My 21,Je 18-Jl 2,16,30 1921

CIVIC review. w 1889-99||?
CLM Mr 30 1895;Ja-O 17 1896

El **CLAMOR** publico. w Je 19 1855-
Follows La Estrella de Los Angeles (Spanish section of Los Angeles star)
In Spanish
CLM D 27 1856
CSmH Je 19,Jl 10,24 1855;Jl 5,Ag 16-23,S 6 1856;Ja 24,Jl 25,Ag 22,S 5 1857;F 26,Ap 30,Jl 23,Ag 6 1859

Daily **COMMERCIAL.** d 1879-84||?
CLM Ag 13 1879;Mr 6-S 5,7,1880;Mr 6,8,S 16 1881;Mr 7-S 5 1882

COMMERCIAL news. w My 15 1920+
Follows National Jeffersonian
pub 1922+
CLSU 1925:31+

Le **COURRIER** francais. w O 17 1917+
In French
pub 1917+
CU-B Mr 17 1923

CRITIC. w 1887-89||?
CLM D 15 1888-F 2 1889

CRITIQUE. w 1893||?
CLM N 25 1893

La **CRONICA.** sw,w My 4 1872-Jl 27 1892||?
In Spanish
CLM [1873-88]
CSmH S 12 1874
CU-B 1872-D 4 1875;F 26 1876-N 3 1877;S 18,O 26 1878[Ap 1883-84]Ja 1885;Jl 20-27 1889
KHi Jl 28 1888
MnHi D 26 1885-My 8 1886

Los Angeles **DEMOCRAT.** w
CLM Ag 16-23,S 13,O 1884;S 20-O 13 1900

El **DEMOCRATA.** sw 1882||?
In Spanish
CLM O 14-25,N 1-4 1882

DEUTSCHE presse. w F 19 1915-
CU-B F 26 1915

EAGLE. *See* California eagle

EAGLE Rock advertiser. w My 1 1928+
pub 1929+

EAGLE Rock sentinel. w 1909+
pub 1920+

EAST Los Angeles exponent. w 1888-90||?
CLM [F 9,Jl 20-O 5 1889]
CU-B D 28 1889-Ja 11 1890
KHi Jl 20 1889

EAST Los Angeles gazette. sw Ag 31 1922+
pub 1932+

EAST Los Angeles tribune. w Ja 1930+
pub Ag 1932+

EAST Side champion. w 1887-89||?
CLM S 22 1888;F 27,Ap 3,S 7,N 23-30 1889
CU-B My 16 1888-Ja 11 1890
KHi Jl 6 1889

EAST Side news. *See* Los Angeles sentinel

El **ECO** de la patria. w 1878-
In Spanish
CLM F 14-21 1878

El **ECO** mexicano. d O 1-30 1885||?
In Spanish
CLM O 29 1885
CSmH O 30 1885

Los Angeles **ENTERPRISE.** w 1901+
1901-04 as Pacific veteran and enterprise; 1905-28? Sawtelle veteran-enterprise; 1928?-29? West Los Angeles enterprise
pub 1930+
CLM [Ag 30 1904-F 18 1905]
KHi Jl 10 1925

EPIC news. w Je 26? 1934+
Je? 1934-My 27 1935 as Upton Sinclair's epic news; Je 3 1935-Ja 20 1936 Upton Sinclair's national epic news
CLM Ag 24,29,N 5,19 1934
CSt Ag 14 1934+

EQUIFRILIBRICUM news service. *See* Filipino nation

ESCUALDUN gazeta. ir D 24 1885-
In Basque
CLM D 24 1885;Ja 16 1886

La **ESTRELLA** de Los Angeles. *See note under* Los Angeles star

Los Angeles **EXAMINER.** d D 12 1903+
pub 1903+
CL 1903+
CLM [1909-10]
CP Ap 21 1906
CSmH O 9,N 11 1918
CU-B 1903-N,D 27 1904-Jl 16 1918
ICM F 14 1914
KHi Ap 28 1906;Ap 1920
MWA D 25 1913;Ja 2 1924
PToF My 1-Je 10 1904
WHi D 1 1913-Ja 31 1918;Jl 30 1932

Los Angeles evening **EXPRESS.** d Mr 27 1871-D 9 1931||
1871-My 2 1916 as Los Angeles express; My 3 1916-F 28 1919 Evening express. United with Los Angeles evening herald to form Los Angeles evening herald and express
C 1911-31
CL 1873-78;Je 21,Jl 29 1893;F 19 1894;Mr 1899-1931
CLM Ag 4 1873;Ja 2,Ap-O 1875;Ja-F 1876;79-Je,C 1882-N 1883;Ag 1891-[92-97]
CPo [1893]
CSmH Ap 15,Ag 15 1871;Ja 5 1872;Mr 14 1873;Je 24,Jl 30 1875;Je 22 1877;Ja 30 1883;Ja 14 1883;N 11 1918
CU-B [1871-72]-75;Je-Jl,S 1876-[Ag 1877-78] Mr 25 S 1879-Ap,Je-D 1880[D 1883-N 1884]Ja 7 1885;Ap 12 1890;N 9 1892;Ap-Jl 18 1919
DLC Ag 6 1873;98
IaDH Mr 13 1905-14
KHi S 5 1891-My 3 1894
WHi D 1907-D 14 1913

Los Angeles **EXPRESS.** w Mr 21 1872-99||?
CU-B [Je 27 1872-75]-Jl 5 1879;Ja-O 9,23-N 6,20-D 1880;Ap 12 1890;N 5 1892

La **FE** en la democrácia. sw 1884||?
In Spanish
CLM O 25-29 1884

FILIPINO nation. w 1926-33||
1926-F 1928 as Equifrilibricum news service
pub F 1928-33

FLORENCE messenger. w Ja 18 1924+
pub S 1929+

FOOL killer. sw S 10-24 1892||?
CLM S 14,24 1892
KHi S 10-21 1892

Le **FRANÇAIS.** w 1896-1900||?
In French
CLM O 3 1896;Ja 6 1900

Morning **FREIHEIT.** d Ap 2 1922+
pub 1928+

La **GACETA** de los estados unidos. w,tw,m Mr 9? 1918-24||?
In Spanish
w Mr-Ag 24 1918
CU-B Ag 24 1918;O 5,N 10 1918;Ap 30,My 10,O 30-N,D 20 1919-Mr 10 1920

GARDENA Valley news. w Jl 26 1903+
pub Ag 1928+

GARVANZA gazette. w Je 1888-89||?
CLM F 1,22 1889
CU-B My 1-15 1889

La **GAULOIS.** w 1888-91||?
KHi [Ja 23 1889-S 2 1891]

GERMANIA. w,d 1889-Ap 30 1918||
w 1889-Ag 15 1914
In English and German
CL Jl 1915-18
CLM Mr 4 1891;D 4 1896
CLSz 1892-1915
CU-B F 21 1913-18
—w ed. *See* Germania sonntags-post

GERMANIA sonntags-post. w Ja 24-Mr 21 1915||
—d ec. *See* Germania

CALIFORNIA (*Continued*)

LOS ANGELES—*Continued*

Daily GLOBE. d Ag 22 1894-
CSmH Ag 26 1894

GLOBE. w 1904||
CLM Ja 30,Ap 16 1904

GOLDEN southwest. w 1890||?
CLM O 28 1890

GRAHAM Firestone Park news. *See* Graham news

GRAHAM news. w 1926+
1926-28 as Graham Firestone Park news
pub D 1932+

GRAPHIC. w,tm 1895-1918||
tm Ja 1-O 10 1918
CU-B F-My 1907;Je 1911-Jl 20,Ag 10-S 20,O 10-24 1918

GREATER Los Angeles. w
CLM [1896-97]

HANCOCK Park press. w 1924-Ja 12 1934||
United with other papers to form Metropolitan news press
CL O 23-D 1930;Ja 29-Mr 19,Ap 2,23,Je 12-19 1931

Los Angeles HERALD. w 1873-1918||
CU-B [1874-91]Ag 31 1905-Jl 17 1918
NcD F 24 1877

Los Angeles evening HERALD and express. d O 2 1873+
1873-Mr 22 1890 as Los Angeles daily herald; Mr 23 1890-N 1 1911 Los Angeles herald; N 2 1911-D 9 1931 Los Angeles evening herald
C Ap 9 1874-Mr 26 1876;86+
CL 1873-Je 1876;O 1884-S 1885;Ap 1889+
CLM Mr 12 1874-Mr 26 1876[77]79;Jl 1880-Ja, Je,N 1882-[84-1910]
CP S 20 1901
CPo [1892-93]
CSf 1912-Jl 1918
CSmH Ja 1 1889;S 8 1906;N 11 1918
CSt O 10-14 1893;Mr 31,Je 2 1895
CU-B 1880[81-82]Ja 2,7,9,11,13,Mr 22,Ap 3 1883;86-91;Ja 22 1892;My 15 1893;Ag 31,S 26, 29-O 8,10-18,N 1905-Jl 17 1918
DLC 1898
KHi Je 14-S 15 1893
NNHi My 16 1887
NcD Mr 6 1877
OHi 1919-F 1923
TJT S 23 1900;Ag 13 1905
WHi D 28 1907-O 1913

El HERALDO de Mexico. sw,tw,d S 15 1915+
sw 1915-D 7 1918;tw D 10 1918-Je 1919
In Spanish
pub 1915+
CU-B Ap 22-My 10 1916[O 17 1919-My 19 1920;Ag 28-D 1921;Ja 1923]
IU D 9 1917-My 12 1929
—English ed *See* Mexican herald

HIGHLAND Park news. w 1919-24||
United with Highland Park herald to form Highland Park news-herald
CLH complete

HIGHLAND Park news-herald. w Je 1905+
1905-24 as Highland Park herald
pub 1905+

HOLLYWOOD citizen-news. w,d 1905+
1905-32 as Hollywood citizen
w 1905-S 1921
pub 1905+
CU-B [1911]O 4,12 1922;N 17,D 28 1923

HOLLYWOOD clipper. w Ap 7 1932+
pub Ap 7 1932+

HOLLYWOOD news journal. sw Je 1923-Ja 11 1935||
Hollywood edition of Los Angeles news journal. Merged with Metropolitan news-press
CLMe S 1932-35

HOLLYWOOD sentinel. w 1898-1911||?
CLM F 6-27 1904

Los Angeles HOME. sw Je 6 1932+
pub 1932+

INDEPENDENT review. w S 7 1933+
pub 1933+

L'ITALO-Americano. w 1908+
In Italian
pub 1908+
CU-B O 4,N 8-22,D 27 1919;Ja 31,Mr 13-20,Ap 3-10,24,My 15 1920

JAPAN California daily news. d N 5 1931+
CL 1931+

JAPANESE American news. d
CL F 5-O 13 1932

Los Angeles JAPANESE daily news. Rafu Shimpo. d 1903+
In Japanese
pub 1914+
NN 1908+
WHi [S 28 1907-Ja 8 1908]

JEWISH daily forward. d Ja 1897+
pub 1927+

JEWISH daily press. *See* Teglache presse

JEWISH times. *See* California Jewish star

JEWISH daily zeit. *See* California Jewish star

Los Angeles daily JOURNAL. d Je 1879+
Titles varies slightly
C O 1916+
CL Mr 1891-Ap 1892;1912+
CLJ N 1932-[33]+
CLL 1879+
CLM S 14 1879;90-98;1900-[05]26+
CSmo F 21 1934+
CU-B [1879]-Ag 5 1880;Ja 13 1897
CU-L Ap 6 1888+

El JOVEN. sw 1877-78||
• In Spanish
CLM S 18 1877;Ap 12 1878

KOSMOS Greek newspaper. w F 18 1931+
In Greek
pub 1931+

LANKERSHIM laconic. *See* North Hollywood press

LANKERSHIM press. *See* North Hollywood press

Los Angeles LIFE. w 1889-91||?
CLM F 9 1889-F 7,Mr 7-21,Je 13 1891

LINCOLN Heights review. w 1934+
pub 1934+

METROPOLITAN news-press. w Jl 12 1934+
A consolidation of Hancock Park press, New era eagle, Metropolitan shopping news, Hollywood news journal, Los Angeles uptown journal, Los Angeles news journal and Midtown news
pub 1934+

MEXICAN herald. w S 15 1915+
pub 1915+
—Spanish ed. *See* El Heraldo de Mexico

Weekly MIRROR. w F 1 1873-Ag 29 1891||
United with Saturday times to form Saturday times and weekly mirror, later Saturday times and California mirror
CLM N 8-15 1884;Ap 25 1885;Mr 22 1890
CSmH [1873-Ja 1875]
CU-B [My-Ag 1873]S 4,O 30,N 13-D 11,25 1875-N 10 1877;N 29,D 20 1879[F-D 1880]My 19 1883;Ap 12,O 1884-91

El MONITOR. w 1898||
In Spanish
CLM [Jl-O 1898]

El MONITOR Mexicano. *See* La Union

Los Angeles MUNICIPAL news. w Ap 17 1912-Ap 9 1913||
C complete
CL complete
CLM Ag 28 1912-13
CO 1912-Mr 1913
CU-B [1912]13
Ct complete
MH complete
NN Ap-My,Jl 24-Ag 7,21-S 4,18 1912
NhD [1912]Ja 15,F 12-Mr 1913
WHi complete
WaU N 1912-13

NATIONAL Jeffersonian. w 1912-My 1920||
Followed by Commercial news
CLSU Mr 18 1816-Mr 1 1919

NATIONAL Townsend weekly. w Ja 21 1935+
CSt 1935+

Weekly NATIONALIST. w 1890||
CLM My 31-Je 14,28-Jl 26,S,O 11-N 15 1890
WHi My 24,Je 21,Jl 26 1890

NEW AGE dispatch. w 1904+
1904-25? as New age
Negro
pub 1934+
CU-B Ag 28 1914-[15]-Mr 10 1916;Ag 2 1918;My 23 1919;My 14,N 5-19 1920[21]Ja 6 1922

NEWS. tw,sw,w 1858-72||?
tw 1858-N 10? 1865;sw N 14 1865-68
CU-B O 9 1863;64-[66]-N 1872

Los Angeles daily NEWS. sw,tw,d Ja 18 1860-73||
1860-O 3 1862 as Los Angeles semi-weekly southern news; O 8 1862-Ja 11 1863 as Los Angeles semi-weekly news; Ja 12 1863-68 Los Angeles tri-weekly news
sw 1862-Ja 11 1863,N 17 1865-68;tw Ja 12 1863-N 14 1865
C Jl 18 1860-Jl 17 1861;O 20 1868;Ap 13 1870-N 1872
CL 1860-67;69-Je 11 1870;71-N 27 1872
CP Ja 3 1863;Jl 9 1869
CSmH S 8 1869;Ag 15 1871
CU-B O 2 1861
MnHi 1860-N 14 1865

Los Angeles NEWS. d Ja 1 1869-72||?
CU-B 1869;Mr-Jl 3 1870[O-D 1870]-N 1872

Daily NEWS. d Jl 25- 1887||
CPo Jl 25 1887

Evening NEWS. d O 2 1905-Ap 28 1908||
CL complete

Los Angeles NEWS. d 1913+
pub Ap 1926+
CL 1928-F 1931;S 1913+
CLL Ap 1926+
CU-L Ap 1929+
WaPS Ja 30-Ap 11 1929

Illustrated daily NEWS. d S 3 1923+
pub 1923+
CL 1923-Ag 1927

NEWS service. sm 1925-28||?
CU-B O 1 1926
MH [Je 15 1926-Ja 15 1928]

NORTH Hollywood press. sw,w F 25 1909+
F 25 1909-23 as Lankershim Laconic; 1923-28 Lankershim press
pub 1911+

NORTH Hollywood record. w 1927-O 22 1933||
United with North Hollywood sun to form North Hollywood sun-record
CLN complete

NORTH Hollywood sun-record. w 1927+
1927-O 22 1933 as North Hollywood sun
pub 1927+

NORTH Los Angeles herald. w Ja 1926+
pub 1926+

NORTHWEST leader. 1930+
pub 1930+

NOVAΓA zarΓa. *See under* San Francisco

A NYUGAT (The west). w
In Hungarian
PPiHi [My 8 1930-Mr 26 1931]

OBSERVER. w Jl 7-O 20 1888||?
CLM O 20 1888
KHi O 13 1888

La OPINION. d S 16 1926+
In Spanish
pub 1926+
CU-B My 21 1931;F 23,Ap 10,30 1932
CU-P 1930+
WaPS [Ja-Ag 1931]

OWENSMOUTH gazette. *See* Canoga Park herald

PACIFIC defender. w 1924+
CU-B O 22 1925

PACIFIC opinion. w 1888||?
CLM [My-N 1888]

PACIFIC veteran and enterprise. *See* Los Angeles enterprise

PALISADIAN. w My 4 1928+
pub 1928+

PARKSIDE press. sw Ap 24 1932+
pub 1932+

La PAROLA degli italiani in America. N 1 1921+
In Italian
pub S 18 1924+

PICO news. w 1934+
pub 1934+

PICO post. w S 1928+
pub 1928+

PORCUPINE. w 1877-99||?
CLM Je 20,Ag 22,O 31 1885[Ja-N 1886;Mr 1887-N 3 1888]Jl 27 1889;F 22,Je 21 1890;Mr 28 1891;D 1 1894;F 8 1897
CU-B [Ja-F 18 1888]
KHi Ag 1888-Ja 1893

Los Angeles evening POST. d 1890||?
CLM S 22-N 18 1890
CU-B N 3 1890

POST-RECORD. d Mr 4 1895+
1895-N 1 1933 as Record
pub Je 1896-[1922]+
C 1895-1905
CL 1912+
CLM Mr 4,19 1895;Ag 2 1902[04-07]
CU-B Ap 8 1895

La PRENSA. w 1912-24||?
In Spanish
CU-B N 1919-Ja 17 1920
CtY Ap 17 1915
IU D 8 1917-S 21 1918;Mr 8 1919-Ja 19 1922

Teglache PRESSE. Jewish daily press. d F 22-My 1 1934||
In Yiddish
NN complete
NNJHi complete

Le PROGRÈS. w 1884-99||?
In French
CLM Ja 26 1889;Ap 13-Ag,S 21 1892-D 21 1893;94[95-O 1896]
CU-B [1892-My 4 1893]
KHi [D 22 1888-F 16 1889]

RAFU Shimpo. *See* Los Angeles Japanese daily news

RECORD. *See* Post-record

La REFORMA. sw 1877-78||
In Spanish
CLM My 16 1878

Los Angeles weekly REPUBLICAN. w Je 1 1867-Ja 1879||
C Mr 4 1869
CSmH S 9 1869
CU-B Jl 13 1867-[69]-Ag 4 1870;Jl 6 1878-Ja 6 1879

Evening REPUBLICAN. d 1876-78||
Title varies: Morning republican; Daily republican; Los Angeles republican
CLM Ja 10-Jl 8 1876;Ag 29 1877;F 5 1878
CSmH supp F 4,11 1878
CU-B [S 25 1878-Ag 23 1877]F 4,My 11-31,Ag 1-20 1878
NcD F 11 1878

REPUBLICAN advocate. S 8 1888-89||
CLM F 16 1889
KHi O 6 1888

Los dos REPUBLICAS. w 1892-98||?
In Spanish
CLM Mr 15 1892;F 25-Mr 4,1893;F 24-Mr 3, 1894;F 2,Mr 9,1895;F 15,Mr 7 1896;F 6,My 22,S 15,O 23,N 6-13,27,D 18 1897;Ja 29,Mr 5,19,My 14,28,Jl 23,S 3 1898

REVISTA hispano-americano. Spanish American review. w N 3 1889-94||?
In Spanish and English
CLM D 1 1889;Mr 2 1890;Jl 30 1891;92;My-O 1893
CU-B D 8-15 1889;Ap 10,Ag 29,N 24 1892

REVISTA Latino-americano. w 1892-93||?
In Spanish and English
CLM N 10,D 17-24 1892;Mr-My 8 1893

ROSCOE herald. w Ja 1926+
pub 1926+

CALIFORNIA (*Continued*)

LOS ANGELES—*Continued*

ROSCOE register. w Je 13 1930+
pub 1930+

SAN PEDRO harbor advocate. w 1887-N 30 1889||
CLM Ja 26,F 9,23-Mr 23,Ag 31,N 30 1889
CU-B N 15-30 1889

SAN PEDRO news. w 1885-1900||?
CLM Ag 10,31,S 1900

SAN PEDRO news-pilot. d 1901+
1901-Mr 6 1928 as San Pedro news
pub [1901-Mr 6 1928]
CL N-D 1926
CU-B [S-D 1903]-Mr 16 1904[18-F 1919]

SAN PEDRO pilot. sw,d Ap 17 1909-Mr 6 1928||
United with San Pedro news to form San Pedro news-pilot
sw 1909-14
CL [F 10-D 1919;Mr 1920-27]
CLSp complete

SAN PEDRO record. w 1884||?
CLM S 25 1884

SAN PEDRO times. w 1890-1909||?
CLM [S 1891-S 18 1897] O 2,16,D 4 1897;Ja 15 1898

SATURDAY night. w 1920+
Jl 12 1924-Mr 28 1925 merged with Argonaut (San Francisco)
CRiv [1925]-[33]
CSmH [1922-26]

SAWTELLE veteran-enterprise. *See* Los Angeles enterprise

SEARCH-LIGHT. w 1893-1908||?
Negro
CLM Ag 11-S 1 1894

Los Angeles SENTINEL. w My 18 1933+
My 18-Ag 20 1933 as Eastside news
pub 1933+

Daily SHIPPING guide. d N 1 1921+
pub 1921+

SOUTHERN California guide. w Ja 16 1892-95||?
KHi Ja 16-23 1892

SOUTHERN Californian. w Jl 18 1854-Ja 1856||?
CSmH Mr 28 1855
CU-B Ap 25[Je-D 5 1855]
MB [Ap 25-Jl 18 1855]
NNHi O 31 1855

Los Angeles semi-weekly SOUTHERN news. *See* Los Angeles daily news (1860-73)

SOUTHWEST broadcaster. w F 1922+
pub 1930+

SOUTHWEST news. w 1891-97||?
KHi [Ja 8 1892-Jl 21 1894]

SOUTHWEST news-press. w Ag 1923+
pub Mr 1926+

SOUTHWEST sun. w,sw Jl 1927+
1927-Jl 24 1934 as Western sun
pub 1927—

SOUTHWEST topics. sw Mr 1920+
pub 1920—

SOUTHWEST wave. sw Ap 1 1920+
pub S 1 1921+
—Southern ed. 1920-F 5 1935||
pub Je 1924-35

SPANISH American review. *See* Revista hispano-americano

Los Angeles daily STAR. w,d My 17 1851-79||
1851-My 1870 as Los Angeles star
Suspended O 12 1864-My 9 1868;D 5-31 1878
1851-55 in English and Spanish
w 1851-My 1870
C Ag 21 1875
CL 1870-My 1871;73-74;Ja-Je 1876
CSmH Mr 1,Ag 15,O 7 1871;Ap 9 1872;Ap 9 1876:supp Ja 7 1878
CU-B [S 9-D 1870;Ap 4-D 1871]-D 17 1873; F 12 1874[Ap-D 1874]-My,N-D 1877[F-D 4 1878]
DLC [N 12 1898-My 27 1879]
MWA My 17,Ag 23 1851;O 23 1852;My 6 1854; F 11 1860

Los Angeles STAR. w My 17 1851-My 24 1879||
Suspended O 8 1864-My 9 1868. Spanish section: La Estrella de Los Angeles followed by El Clamor publico
C D 26 1863
CL My 17 1851;59-[63]
CLM My 17,D 13 1851[52-55]S 8 1860[My 16 1868-My 7]Je 1 1870;Je 30 1877;Jl 29 1877
CSmH My 17,Jl 12 (photostats) D 13 1851;F 28,Jl 17-31,Ag 14,28,S 18,O 16-N 13,27 1852 [53-54]Jl 28,S 29 1855;Ap 19,My 10,D 13 1856;Ag 8 1863;Mr 12,1864;Ag 8 1868;O 28 1871;Je 22 1872;supp Ap 3 1852
CU-B Jl 2 1853;Ap 24 1858;D 3 1859;My 1868-[72]-F 2 1878;Ap 19-My 1879
CtY My 17 1851
DLC My 17 (photostat) Jl 12,Ag 9-23,N 8 1851;Je 19-26,Jl 10-17,Ag 7-14,S 18,O 16-N 13 1852
NN My 17 1851 (facsimile)
NNHi My 17-24 1851
OClWHi D 23 1871-Ja,Ap 20-27,My 18 1872-O 1873;Ap 11 1874-Je 1876

SUBURBAN home and Watts news. w 1914-25||?
1914-My 2 1918 as Suburban home
CU-B My 9-Jl 25 1919

SÜD-CALIFORNIA post. w Jl 25 1874-1914||
1874-80 as Süd-Californische post. Merged with Germania
CLM [D 11 1889-Ap 19 1895]
CLSz 1874-75
CU-B Ap 10-S 1876;N 20-D 25 1880;Jl 15 1909-Jl 8 1910;Je 14-S 13 1912;F 18 1913-Ag 5 1914
KHi [Jl 16 1888-Jl 20 1889]

Der SÜD CALIFORNIER. w 1891-94||
CLM Ap 27 My 4,11,18 1894

SÜD CALIFORNISCHE post. *See* Süd-California post

Los Angeles SUN. d 1887-88||?
CLM D 3,19,23 1887;Ja 6,F 3 1888

Los Angeles morning SUN. d 1910-21||?
In Japanese
IU S 5 1917-My 11 1921

Los Angeles evening TELEGRAM. d Ag 19-S 18 1882||
CL complete

Los Angeles TELEGRAM. d 1887-93||?
CLM Jl 25,D 12 1887;Mr 3,13,Ap 10 1888;S 13-N 24,D 28 1893

Los Angeles TELEPHONE. w 1888||?
CLM Ap 21 1888

Los Angeles TIMES. d D 4 1881+
D 4 1931 is 50th anniversary ed
pub 1881-82;Mr 1883-My 1885;Je 4-O 23 1886; My,Jl-Ag,O-N 1894;Ja-Ap,Je 1895-N 1897;98-Ag,O 1904-Ap,Je 1910-Ap,Je-N 1911;Ja-Ap,O 1912+
C My 1888-My 1 1889;91+
CClP 1900+
CL S-D 1884;D 12 1885-Mr 13 1886;Ap 1889+
CLM [1881-91]-[1901-06]Ja 1 1908
CLU 1917-19;30+
CP D 4 1881(facsimile) Ap 19-21 1906;Je 1927+
CPo [1892-93]95+
CRed O 1904+
CSmH D 4 1881;Ja 21,26,30 1883;Je 5 1884;F 10 1893;S 12 1894;N 11 1918
CSt S 1904-[12;15]-[17]21-Ja 1922
CU-B O 14 1884-[91]Jl 20,D 13 1893;Je 4,Jl 30,Ag 5,D 7 1894;Ap 18-29,My 2-3,5,8,10 1906;Mr 19 1930+
DLC D 4 1881(facsimile) Je 26 1893;F 14 1900+
GDE D 1926
ICN D 11 1917-Ja 12,Mr-S,N 1920-Mr,My-D 1921
ICU Je 22-Jl 3 1931;35+
IHi D 4 1881
IaSc Last 6 months
KHi [O 12 1888-1921;25-Ja 2 1929]
M Ja 2 1930;Ja 26 1931
MWA D 4 1881(facsimile);Ap 25 1898;Ja 1 1898;Ap 28 1900;O 17 1901;Ap 17 1906;O 2 1910;Ja 1 1916;D 4 1921;Ja 1 1924;27;D 4 1931
MiU [1906]-[08]
NKenHi D 4 1881
NN D 4 1931
NNHi Ja 1 1887
NcD D 29 1881
NvR [1932]+
OHi 1923-Ja,Ap-Jl 1931
PP O 21 1892[1927]+
TJT Jl 23 1900;Jl 21 1901;Mr 5 1905;Ag 31 1919
TxGR D 28 1926;Ja 2,D 4 1931
WHi D 4 1881;My 30 1903;D 8 1907-Ja 1909[D 4 1921-O 17 1934]
WaPS Mr 1913-33

Saturday TIMES and California mirror. w S 5 1891-1912||?
1891-F 5 1898 as Saturday times and weekly mirror
CU-B 1891-[1904]-S 23 1905
OCHi D 31 1892
PP D 31 1892

Los Angeles TIMES Sunday magazine. w D 5 1897+
1915-My 19 1917 as Los Angeles times illustrated weekly; My 26 1917-Je 8 1924 Times illustrated magazine; Je 15-S 21 1924 Illustrated magazine
CL 1915+

Los Angeles TOPICS. w 1898||
CLM Ag 20 1898

Los Angeles TRIBUNE. d O 17 1886-D 5 1890||
CL Ap 1889-D 5 1890
CLM O 1886-Ap 1888[89-90]
CU-B O 8 1886-Ja 1,Mr 22 1887;Ja 1 1888;Mr 3,Je 22-24,Ag 27-29,O 11-13,D 30 1889;Ap 12 1890
KHi Ag 4-20,S 22 1888
MWA Ja 1 1888

Los Angeles TRIBUNE. d Jl 4 1911-Jl 4 1918||
1911-My 22 1912 as Tribune; My 23 1912-Mr 25 1914 Daily tribune; Mr 26 1914-My 4 1916 Los Angeles tribune; My 5 1916-Je 30 1918 Morning tribune
C complete
CL complete
CSt 1913[16]
CU-B Ja-Jl,N 7,17,D 6 1912-Ap 26 1916

TRIPLE alliance. w 1898||
CLM O 15 1898

TUJUNGA free press. w 1930+
pub [1931-34]+

TUJUNGA record-ledger of the Verdugo Hills. w S 11 1920+
pub 1920—

TUJUNGA Valley herald. w 1922+
pub 1922—

La UNION. w 1889-1912||?
1889-95? as El monitor Mexicano
CLM O 25 1895;My 15 1897
CU-B D 14 1907

L'UNION nouvelle. w 1879+
In French
pub 1913+
CClP Mr 1904-Mr 1906
CLM [My-D 1892]Ja-My,D 28 1895;My,Je 13-O 1896;Jl 16 1898;Mr 10,24-Ap 21,My, Je 30 1900-Je 1902
CLO S 24 1932+
CU-B Ag 28 1897-F,Je 1908-Mr 1916
IU D 1917-Jl 13 1918
KHi [S 15-D 22 1888]

UPTON Sinclair's epic news. *See* Epic news

UPTOWN journal. w 1922-Je 9 1933||
United with other papers to form Metropolitan news-press
CLMe complete

UTOPIAN news. w Je 23 1934+
C 1934+
CLM N 15,D 6 1934
CU-B Jl 9,23 1934+

VALLEY democrat. w 1886||?
CLM F 15 1886

VAN NUYS news. w My 1911+
pub 1912+

VAN NUYS tribune w Ag 10 1926+
pub 1930+

VARIANT. w Mr 1928+
pub 1928+

VENICE vanguard. d 1904?+
An edition of Culver City star-news
pub 1914-My,Jl 1916-Jl,S 1922-S,D 1925+
C 1921+
CU-B Ag 25-Jl 1,17 1919

Semi-weekly VINEYARD. sw 1858-
CLM Ja 9,Jl 18 1859
WHi Ap 19 1859

WATTS advertiser-review. w 1908+
1908-Ap 12 1928 as Watts advertiser
pub 1929+

WATTS news. w 1906-My 3 1918||
United with Suburban home to form Suburban home and Watts news
CU-B Ag 23 1917-18

WEST ADAMS tribune. w Ja 1924+
pub N 1933+

WEST Los Angeles enterprise. *See* Los Angeles enterprise

WEST Los Angeles independent. w F 1929+
pub Mr 27 1929+

WESTERN dispatch. w O 6 1921-
Negro
CU-B O 6,27,N 17,D 8,29 1921

WESTERN news. w 1889||?
CLM N-D 1889

WESTERN sun. *See* Southwest sun

WESTLAKE post. w F 1933+
pub 1933+

WESTWOOD Hills news. w My 13 1927+
pub 1927+

WESTWOOD Hills press. w 1929+
pub 1930+

WILMINGTON enterprise. w Ap 2 1874-75||?
CSmH Ag 27,D 24 1874
CU-B [Je 11 1874-S 23 1875]

WILMINGTON journal. w,d 1864+
w 1864-Je 1923
pub Mr 1865-Ag 15 1866;Jl 1923+
CLM Mr 25,Je 1,13 1867
CU-B [Ja 14 1865-Ag 1867]
MBAt Jl 15,S 2 1865

WILMINGTON press. d F 1925+
pub 1925+

WORLD. w 1886-1900||?
Title varies: Sunday social world; Los Angeles world; Sunday world
CLM [1886-89]D 16 1894
CU-B D 29 1889

Los Angeles daily ZEIT. *See* California Jewish star

LOS BANOS

Los Banos ENTERPRISE. w 1888+
pub 1915+
CMe 1911+
CU-B [S 15-D 1917]-[30]—

LOS GATOS

Los Gatos MAIL-NEWS. w 1883+
1883-1916 as Los Gatos mail
C Mr 1928+
CU-B [Je-N 1885]D 10,31 1886[Mr-D 1889]Ja, O 7 1890[92-94]-Ja 3,31,Mr 7-14,28,Ap 11-18 1895;D 21 1905-Ap 8 1915
KHi [My 18-Ag 10 1888]
MnHi [F 8-Jl 1894]

Los Gatos MOUNTAIN realty. m 1903-D 1927||
Title varies: Realty; Skyland realty; Skyland mountain realty. Merged with Los Gatos mail-news
1903-Ja 1919 pub in Skyland
C Je 1906-12

Los Gatos NEWS. w 1881-1916||
United with Los Gatos mail to form Los Gatos mail-news
CU-B [Jl-D 1881]-Je 24,Jl 21,Ag 4 1882
KHi My 4-Ag 17 1888

Los Gatos STAR. w Mr 8 1923-30||?
CU-B My 24 1923;My 21 1925

CALIFORNIA (*Continued*)

LOS MOLINOS

Los Molinos NEWS-HERALD. w F 10 1932+
CRb 1932+
CU-B Je 30 1932+

RIVER rambler. bw 1911-Mr 14 1930||
CU-B [F 1913-My 8 1915]Jl 4,28,Ag 11,S 8 1917;Je 26 1920-30

LOST HILLS

COALINGS reporter and Lost Hills gusher. w 1914-
1914-26? as Lost Hills gusher
CU-B Ap 22-My 13,Je 1919

Lost Hills GUSHER. *See* Coalings reporter

LOWER LAKE

Lower Lake BULLETIN. w Ag 21 1869-1919||?
CU-B 1869-S 2 1871;S-D 15 1877;D 26 1878-[79]-Ag 5 1882[Mr 9-My 25,O 12 1889-Ja 11 1890]

CLEAR Lake press. w 1886-90||?
CU-B O 19-N 2 1889;Ja 4 1890
KHi O 20 1888

CLEAR Lake sentinel. w D 18- 1866||?
CU-B D 18 1866

LAKE county observer. w
CU-B S 29 1866

LOYALTON

SIERRA Valley news. w 1912+
pub 1925+
CQ Ag 19 1926+
CU-B 1927[28-32]+

LUGONIA

CITROGRAPH. *See under* Redlands

SOUTHERN Californian. w S 3 1887-88||
CLM 1887-Mr,Ap 21 1888
KHi 1887-Mr 1888

LUNDY

HOMER mining index. w Je 12 1880-90||?
CU-B 1880-[My 21,Ag 20 1881-Jl 29 1882]
MWA N 1 1884;F 1,Mr 1 1890

McCLOUD

McCloud RIVER pioneer. w Ag 24 1889-93||
CYC complete

McFARLAND

McFarland HERALD. w 1914-19||?
1914-15 as McFarland messenger
CB O 9 1914-15

McFarland MESSENGER. *See* McFarland herald

McFarland NEWS. w 1928+
C N 8 1928+
CB 1930+

SAN JOAQUIN valley tribune. *See* McFarland tribune

McFarland TRIBUNE. w 1920+
1920-Je 28 1923 as San Joaquin Valley tribune
CB 1923-31

MADERA

Madera MERCURY. w,sw,d Mr 21 1885-Jl 31 1925||
United with Madera tribune to form Madera daily tribune and mercury
w 1885-O 1918;N 18 1920-Ap 1921;sw Mr-Ap 14 1925
C Ap 1901-O 25 1918;Ag 25 1919-O 1925
CM 1914-25
CU-B Je 9 1888;Jl 17 1909-Jl 9 1910;Ap 13-S 14 1912

Madera TIMES. w 1899-1906||?
CLM [1904]

Madera TRIBUNE. w Mr 31 1892-1920||?
CU-B Je 24 1909-Ag 11 1910;My 23-S 12 1912

Madera daily TRIBUNE and mercury. d 1903+
1903-S 1925 as Madera daily tribune
pub 1919+
C N 1925+
CM Mr 1913+
CU-B Ap 1,Je 17 1927+

MAMMOTH CITY

HERALD. sw,w Je 25 1879-81||?
w 1879-Jl 1880
CU-B [Jl-D 1879]-F 12 1881

LAKE mining review. *See* Mammoth City times

Mammoth City TIMES. w,sw My 24 1879-80||?
My-S 1879 as Lake mining review
CU-B My 31,Ag 16-30,S 13-20,O 18 1879-[Ja-Mr 3 1880]

MAMMOUTH TREE GROVE. *See* MURPHY

MANHATTAN BEACH

Manhattan Beach NEWS. w 1911+
pub 1911+

MANTECA

Manteca BULLETIN. w 1911+
pub 1911+
CU-B F 26 1931

MARE ISLAND

Weekly ADVERTISER. ir 1859||?
CSmH Ap 16 1859
CU-B Ja 15 1859

MARICOPA

Maricopa OIL news. w 1908-Ag 15 1924||
Followed by West Side tribune and Maricopa oil news (Taft)
CB 1912-24

Maricopa OIL review. w Ap 8 1925-F 24 1928||
Followed by West Side chronicle and Maricopa oil review
CB My 20 1925-28

WEST Side chronicle and Maricopa oil review. w Mr 2-My 18 1928||?
Follows Maricopa oil review
CB Mr-My 18 1928

MARIPOSA

Mariposa DEMOCRAT. *See under* Hornitos

Mariposa FREE PRESS. w 1863-66||?
CU-B Jl 28 1866

Mariposa FREE PRESS. w Ap 29 1870-71||
C My 13 1870-O 13 1871
CU-B Ja 6,Mr 24 1871

Mariposa GAZETTE. w 1854+
My-Jl 1866 as Mariposa gazette-herald; D 14 1901-N 11 1905 Gazette Mariposan
C [O 29 1864-My 24 1890]+
CMe Ag 13 1926+
CP Jl 14 1858
CU-B Je 26 1857;64-[72]-[76]-O 13 1883[86-89]-[92-94]Ja 26,Mr 16-23 1895[Mr 11-D 1905]-Ag 24 1923
KHi S 8 1888

Mariposa MAIL. w 1866-
C D 18 1868
CU-B Jl 6 1867;68-Ap 9,Je 18-S 10 1869

Mariposa MINER. w S 1934+
CMe 1934+

MARKLEVILLE

ALPINE chronicle. *See* Bodie chronicle (Bodie)

ALPINE signal. w Jl 3 1878-79||?
CU-B [Jl 17-D 1878]-Ja 1,15-Ag 22 1879

MARTINEZ

CALIFORNIA express. w Ap 18 1868-70||?
C O 24 1868
CU-B 1868-Ag 8 1870

CARQUINEZ enterprise. w Ap 8-15 1871||?
CU-B Ap 15 1871

CONTRA Costa democrat. w D 20 1889-95||?
CU-B Ja 11 1890

CONTRA Costa gazette. sw,w S 18 1858-S 11 1926||
United with Daily Gazette to form Contra Costa gazette and daily gazette, later Contra Costa gazette and Martinez standard
1858-N 15 1873 pub in Pacheco
sw 1888-92
C O 24 1868;Ap 23 1870-Ap 1878;S 1894-98; 1901-26
CP F 1 1868
CU-B Jl 23 1864-75;Jl 1876-[79]-Ap 21 1917; Ja 20 1923-26
KHi O 31 1888;S 30 1893
MWA Jl 8 1876
MnU Je 17 1893-F 22 1908

CONTRA Costa gazette and Martinez standard. d 1900+
1900-S 11? 1926 as Daily gazette; S 18 1926-N 10 1930 Contra Costa gazette and daily gazette
C S 18 1926+
CU-B S 18 1926+

CONTRA Costa news. w O 14 1875-85||?
1875-O 19 1877 pub at Pacheco
CU-B O 14-21,N 18,D 16,30 1875;76-O 24,N 28,D 5 1879;Mr 5-19, S 25-D 25 1880

CONTRA Costa standard. w,d 1874+
Title varies 1874-Ja 6 1897: Argus; Democrat; Item; News. Ja 13 1898-Ap 19 1906 as County paper
My 15 1911-N 8 1930 *See* Martinez daily standard
C Ja 13 1898-My 13 1911;N 22 1930+
CU-B [My-Ag 2 1888]D 23-26 1889;D 17 1903-Ap 7 1904

COUNTY paper. *See* Contra Costa standard

Daily GAZETTE. *See* Contra Costa gazette and Martinez standard

Martinez daily STANDARD. d My 15 1911-N 8 1930||
Takes the place of Contra Costa standard. United with Contra Costa gazette and daily gazette to form Contra Costa gazette and Martinez standard
C complete
CU-B Ap 26-Jl 3 1919

MARYSVILLE

Marysville APPEAL. w,sw Je 5 1860-Jl 1 1920||
1860-Ag 19? 1895 as Marysville weekly appeal
w 1860-Ag 19? 1895
C Ja 2 1869;F 11 1871-Je 1920
KHi Ag 10-S 14 1888
MWA Ja 26,F 23,Ap 6 1861

APPEAL-DEMOCRAT. d Ja 23 1860+
1860-Je 1905 as Marysville daily appeal; Jl 1905-Je 1911 Daily appeal; Jl 6 1911-Ag 31 1927 Marysville appeal
pub 1860+
C O 28 1868;1922+
CMa 1860-64;66-Je 1869;70-77;My 8 1898+
CMaC O 1862-1923
CP O 30 1863
CU-B 1860-Je 14,24,Jl 20,Ag 1871-N 1876; Mr 1877-78;Ja 26-My,Jl-O 1879;80;D 20 1881-Ag 4 1882[F 10-D 1886]-91;Je 13 1908-Jl 16 1918;Jl 18 1932+
DLC My 28 1862-64;Ap 12 1865;70[71-73]-82; 89-94;supps Ag 13,27,S 2 1862;Ja 8,S 2 1863; S 18,O 9 1864;N 12 1873;Ja 31,F 7,D 9 1874; S 22,D 10 1875;D 6 1877
MWA Ag 8-9 1873;Ag 15 1876;O 16 1881
OrHi Jl 24 1861

Daily CALIFORNIA express. tw,d N 3 1851-66||
1851-52? as California express
tw 1851-52?
CMa Ja-Je 1858;59-Je 1860;Ja-Je 1861;62-Ja 14 1865
CMaC O 1862-S 1864
CP Ag 25 1852
DLC D 3 1851;Jl 28 1853
NNHi F 1 1856

Weekly CALIFORNIA express. *See under* Sacramento

Marysville DEMOCRAT. w
CSmH D 16 1852

Marysville DEMOCRAT. d O 6 1884-Ag 30 1927||
1884-1906 as Marysville daily democrat; 1907-08 Evening democrat; 1909-Mr 12 1919 Marysville evening democrat. United with Marysville appeal to form Appeal-democrat
C Jl 1890-Ag 21 1927
CMa My 1898-1923
CMaA 1884-Jl 5 1886;88-Je 1927
CMaC Jl 1893-Je 1922;23-24
CU-B Ap 29-Ag 8 1912
KHi Ag 4 1888

FORTY niner. w
WaPS D 3,17 1930;Ja 15,O 15 1931

Marysville HERALD. sw,tw,d Ag 6 1850-Ja 1 1858||
Ag 8 1853-Ja 8 1854 as Daily evening herald; Ja 9 1854-My 22? 1854 Daily herald (Morning); My 24 1854-58 Tri-weekly herald
sw Ag-S 1850;tw O 1850-Ag 5? 1853, My 24 1854-58;d Ag 8 1853-My 22? 1854
C N 19 1850;Ag 12 1852;Ja 27 1853;D 9 1854
CMa 1850-Jl 17 1851;Ag 7 1855-Ag 8 1857
CMaA Ag 8 1854-Ag 4 1855
CP Ag 28 1852
CSmH My 20 1851
CU-B Ag 23 1850;S 11 1852;O 10 1853
DLC My 13 1851
NNHi Je 9 1854;F 1 1856

Marysville HERALD. w Je 9 1852-57||?
Title varies: Weekly herald; Weekly Marysville herald
CSmH Ag 7 1852
MWA Ag 10 1852
NNHi Jl 21-Ag 4 1856;O 5-12,N 2 1857

Marysville HERALD. d S-N 1875||?
CU-B O 11,19-22,26-N 5,9-11,15 1875

Marysville LEDGER. d My 5? 1880-
CU-B My 10-17,19-27,29-Je 1,3-25,28-Jl 1,3,6-Ag 6,9,13-S 18 1880

Daily NATIONAL democrat. d Ag 12 1858-O 27 1861||
Follows Marysville daily news. Merged with Marysville daily appeal, later Appeal-democrat
CMaA complete
CU-B Ag 27,29 1858
MWA S 17 1859;Ja 7 1860

Marysville daily NEWS. d Ja 9 1856-Ag 9 1858||
Followed by Daily national democrat
CSmH F 24 1856

NORTH Californian. d D 17 1866-Je 22 1867||
CMa complete
CU-B Ja 21,My 16-Je 1867

Daily NORTHERN statesman. d Je 25-Jl 13 1867||
CMa complete
CU-B Je-Jl 9,12-13 1867

PEOPLE'S cause. sw,w 1907-10||?
C Ja 9 1909-Ap 1910

SPOKESMAN. d My 26-N 19 1912||
C complete

Marysville daily STANDARD. d My 16 1870-S 14? 1872||
C Je 23 1870-Ag 27 1872
CMa 1870-S 14 1872
CU-B My 17 1870-F 25,D 4 1871-S 13 1872

Evening TELEGRAPH. d Ag 6? 1867-68||?
CU-B [Ag 13-N 26,D 10 1867-F 8 1868]

Marysville daily UNION. d Jl 1-D 31 1869||
CMa complete

YUBA county democrat. w
KHi [S 7 1888-Ja 4 1889]

CALIFORNIA (*Continued*)

MAXWELL

Maxwell MERCURY. w Jl 14 1888-93||?
CLM O 25 1888;89-My 1890
CU-B [F 28 1889-My 6 1893]
KHi O 6-N 15 1888

Maxwell TRIBUNE. w F 2 1917+
CCo 1917+

MAYFIELD

Mayfield ENTERPRISE. w Mr 5 1870-71||
CU-B [1870-My 13 1871]

Mayfield NEWS. *See* Palo Alto news (Palo Alto)

PALO ALTO. *See* Palo Alto news (Palo Alto)

Mayfield REPUBLICAN. *See* Palo Alto news (Palo Alto)

MAYWOOD

Maywood JOURNAL. w 1924+
pub 1927+

MEADOW LAKE

Meadow Lake SUN. d,sw,w Je 6 1866-67||?
Title varies with periodicity
d Je-Jl 7 1866;sw Jl 9?-N 1866
C Je 6,D 8 1866
CU-B [1866-67]

MENDOCINO

Mendocino BEACON. w O 6 1877+
C 1878+
CU-B 1877-Jl 1882;Ap 7,Ag 11 1883-[85-My 15 1886;88-89]-91;My 27 1893;Ja 1,Je 1909-Jl 9 1910;Ag 24-S 14 1912

INDEPENDENT dispatch. *See* Ukiah dispatch-democrat (Ukiah)

WEST Coast star. w Ja 3? 1874-77||
CU-B [Mr-D 1874]-[76-My 12 1877]

MENLO PARK

Menlo Park RECORDER. w 1923+
CPa Current two years

MERCED

Merced EXPRESS. w Ja 23 1875+
pub 1875+
C My 17 1890+
CMe F 1875-Mr 3 1877;N 29 1910-16;O 1920+
CU-B [1875]-S 23 1876;F 3,Ag 25 1877-80;Mr 12,Jl 30 1881[88-91]Ag 14 1909-Jl 9 1910;My 25-S 14 1912;Jl 10 1920-[30]+
KHi [Ag 14 1888-Ja 5 1889]

Merced HERALD. w 1888-89||
CU-B F 21,Mr 13-27,Ap 10-My 13 1889

MERCED county sun. w Ag 28 1869-1923||?
1869-N 15 1890 as San Joaquin Valley argus 1869-Mr 29 1873 pub at Snelling
Suspended D 1874-Mr 1875;Mr-D 1877
C F 26 1870-N 13 1875
CLM Ja 1 1892
CMe 1869-Ag 1880;S 1883-Ag 22 1885;S 17 1887-N 15 1890;1914-O 13 1922
CU-B 1869-[81-82]-[85-86;Mr 1889-Ag 1890] Jl 16 1909-Jl 8 1910;Ag 9-S 13 1912
KHi [Jl 14-O 6 1888]

Merced PEOPLE. w Mr 23-Je 22 1872||?
C Mr 30-Je 22 1872
CU-B Ap 13-20,My-Je 15 1872

SAN JOAQUIN Valley argus. *See* Merced county sun

Merced STAR. w,d 1880-Ap 30 1925||
United with Merced evening sun to form Merced sun-star
w 1880-Mr 1921
CMe Je 1886-My 24 1888;Je 1891-Je 3 1897; 1921-24
CU-B Ag 12 1909-Jl 7 1910;My 30-S 19 1912; Jl 29 1920-25
KHi S 6 1888

Merced evening SUN. *See* Merced sun-star

Merced SUN-STAR. d 1884+
1884-D 31 1924 as Merced evening sun
pub My 1925+
C D 20 1926+
CMe F 5 1891-My 16 1892;1900-03;05-Je 1907; 08;Jl 1909+
CU-B Je 11-D 1908;Ja-Ag 22 1917[O 5 1925-F 17 1926]Ja 20-23 1931

Merced TRIBUNE. w Ap 20 1872-75||?
CMe 1872-74
CU-B [D 1872-Ja 16 1875]

MERIDIAN

Meridian INDEX. w D 11 1930+
pub 1930+

MIDDLETOWN

Middletown INDEPENDENT. w 1888-1918||?
CU-B Ag 31,S 14,D 28 1889-Mr 1,Jl 12-[N-D 1890]Ja 2-Je 4,Ag 20 1892-O 14 1893;F 17 1894-N 29 1897

MILL VALLEY

Mill Valley-Tiburon-Belvedere RECORD. w 1901+
1901-14 as Record enterprise; 1915-30 Mill Valley record
CU-B S 3 1907;08-N 8 1912

RECORD-enterprise. *See* Mill Valley-Tiburon-Belvedere record

MILLERTON

EXPOSITOR. *See* Fresno expositor (Fresno)

MILLVILLE

SHASTA county democrat. *See under* Redding

SHASTA county record. w Mr 9 1878-80||?
CU-B Ap 6-13,Ag 10,24-31,S,O 19-D 1878;Jl 19-26,Ag 30-S 6,20-N 22,D 6 1879 Ap 3 1880

MODESTO

Modesto BEE and news-herald. d Ja 1884+
1884-Jl 25 1933 as Modesto bee
pub 1884+
C Jl 26 1933+
CMo 1933+
CU-B Jl 26 1933+

Modesta HERALD. w F 4 1875-1915||?
CU-B F 11,18 1875[Ap 6 1876-D 26 1878] O 17 1889

Modesto morning HERALD. d 1903-Mr 31 1925||
1903-D 29? 1924 as Modesto herald. United with Modesto news to form Modesto news-herald
C N 12 1909-25
CMoM 1911-25
CU-B [Ap 25-Jl 3 1919]

Modesto NEWS-HERALD. d 1884-Jl 25 1933||
1884-Mr 30 1925 as Modesto evening news. United with Modesto bee to form Modesto bee and news-herald
C Ja 27 1911-33
CMo O 1926-33
CMoB 1884-Mr 1925
CMoM Ap-S 1925
CU-B 1888-91;1908-Ap 19,Jl 26 1920-33
KHi O 11 1888

SAN JOAQUIN Valley mirror. *See* Valley mirror

STANISLAUS county news. w F 28 1868-1913||?
1868-N 1870 as Tuolumne City news (Tuolumne)
C Ja 1 1869;Ap 29 1870-N 17 1882 90-My 1912
CU-B 1868-[70-71]-[78]80;F 25,O 21 1881;S 15 1882[86]Mr 1,D 27 1889;Jl 16 1909-Je 17 1910
KHi [Jl 6 1888-Mr 8 1889]

STANISLAUS farmer's journal. tw 1881-82||?
MWA My 13 1882
N Ag 17 1882

VALLEY mirror. w Ag 2 1873-Jl 4 1874||?
1873-Je 13 1874 as San Joaquin Valley mirror
CU-B [O 9 1873-Jl 4 1874]

MOJAVE

Mojave PRESS. w Ag 14 1914-19||?
CB 1914-Mr 21 1919
CTeN O 12 1917-S 1918

Mojave-Randsburg RECORD-TIMES. w My 23 1924-D 29 1932||
1924-Je 14 1929 as Mojave record; Je 21-S 18 1929 Mojave record-times. United with Tehachapi news (Tehachapi) to form Tehachapi news and Mojave-Randsburg record-times (Tehachapi)
C complete
CB F 1927-32
CTeN complete

Mojave TOMAHAWK. *See* Tehachapi news (Tehachapi)

MOKELUMNE HILL

Weekly CALAVERAS chronicle. w O 9 1851-1908||?
C N 7 1868;Ap 16 1870-S 1905;Mr-Ag 15 1908
CU-B D 27 1851; Mr 19 1853[Mr-D 1866]-[68-71]Je 15 1872-[81]-Jl 1882[87-89]Jl 1890-91
NEh O 25 1851
NNHi Jl 17 1852;N 3 1855
NcD My 27,N 25-D 2 1899

MONITOR

ALPINE miner. w Je 4 1864-74||?
CP Je 27 1868
CSmH O 20 1866[F 9-O 19 1867;Ja-N 1868] Ja 16 1869
CU-B 1864-73;My 2-Jl 4,S 19 1874

Monitor GAZETTE. *See* Alpine miner

MONROVIA

Monrovia JOURNAL. tw,sw My 1 1914+
pub My 1932+

Monrovia LEADER. w 1887-88||?
CLM Ap 4 1888

Monrovia MESSENGER. w Jl 26 1888-1929||?
CLM [My 14 1891-92]-Ag 11 1893
CU-B [F 28 1889-O 1890;Ja 28-Je 2 1892]
KHi Jl-S 20 1888

Monrovia NEWS-POST. d Ja 5 1907+
1907-28? as Monrovia news
pub Mr 1929+
CMon 1907+

Monrovia PLANET. w 1886-
KHi D 24 1887-Jl 21 1888

MONTAGUE

Montague MESSENGER. *See* Siskiyou county messenger

SISKIYOU county messenger. w 1909+
1909-33 as Montague messenger
CU-B Ap-Je 16,Jl 21-Ag 4,25-S 15,O 26 1917-[18]
CYC 1909-12;14-16;18-19;24+

MONTEBELLO

Montebello NEWS. w F 14 1914+
pub 1914+

MONTEREY

AMERICAN. d Ag 1 1911-O 30? 1917||
United with Monterey cypress to form Monterey daily cypress and Monterey American
CMont 1913-16
CSa Ap 26 1916

ARGUS. w My 16 1876-89||?
1876-81 as Californian
CSa S 27 1884
CU-B My 23-Je 20 1876;D 1877[78-O 1881]Jl 15-Ag 1882;Ja 13,F 10 1883[86]
MSaE Ag 15 1846

Monterey BEACON. w S 1 1934+
CU-B N 24 1934+

CALIFORNIAN. 1846-48 *See under* San Francisco

CALIFORNIAN. 1876-81 *See* Argus

Monterey CYPRESS. w Ja 5 1889-1907||?
C 1889-D 14 1901
CU-B O 27 1894

Monterey daily CYPRESS and Monterey American. d 1904-Ja 1923||
1904-O 30 1917 as Monterey daily cypress. Merged with Peninsula herald
C O 1913-Mr,Je 1915-O 1917
CMont 1907-22
CU-B My 3-10,13 1919

Monterey DEMOCRAT. *See* Salinas democrat (Salinas)

Monterey ENTERPRISE. w O 30 1890-
KHi D 4-11 1890

Monterey GAZETTE. d D 11 1863-69||?
C O 15 1868
CU-B [1863-67]-O 7 1869
N D 9 1864

Monterey HERALD. w My 23 1874-76||?
CU-B My 30,D 26 1874-Ap 1 1876

NEW ERA. w N 1 1890-1911||?
CLM Ap 7 1892
CMont 1891-93;95-1909
CU-B Jl 28 1894

Monterey PENINSULA herald. d Je 21 1922+
F 1 1923-F 1927 as Peninsula daily herald and Monterey daily cypress and Monterey American; Mr 1 1927-Je 23? 1929 Peninsula daily herald
CMont 1922+
CSa 1922+

Monterey REPUBLICAN. w D 9 1869-71||
CU-B 1869-O 27,N 10 1870-O 5 1871

Monterey SENTINEL. w Je 3 1855-Je 7 1856||
Followed by Pacific sentinel, later Santa Cruz sentinel (Santa Cruz)
C F 23 1856

Monterey TRADER. w F 9 1933+
C 1933+

MONTEREY PARK

Monterey Park COURIER. w Je 14 1934+
pub 1934+

Monterey Park PROGRESS. w Ap 5 1918+
pub 1918+
CMp Ap 1929

MONTROSE

CRESCENTA Valley herald. w 1923+
pub 1923+

CRESCENTA Valley ledger. w S 13 1922+
pub 1922+

MOORPARK

Moorpark ENTERPRISE. w Ag 12 1912+
pub 1912+
CMoor D 30 1915-33

MORO BAY

SUN. w Ag 1931+
pub Je 1932+

MOTT

NORTH star. w Jl 16 1887-Jl 1890||
CU-B [Mr-D 1889]Ja 4 1890
CYC complete

CALIFORNIA (*Continued*)

MOUNT SHASTA

To 1922 as Sisson

Mount Shasta **HERALD.** w S 13 1887-S 7 1892||
C 1887-91
CU-B Ag 27,S 17,O 15,N 5-D 10,24,1889-Ja 14,F 25 1890
CYC complete

Mount Shasta **HERALD.** w S 15 1904+
1904-Je 29 1922 as Sisson headlight
pub 1913+
CU-B N 30-D 14 1918
CYC 1904+

SISSON headlight. *See* Mount Shasta herald

SISSON mascot. w My 28 1891-My 9 1894||
CYC [1894]

SISSON mirror. w Ag 13 1896-Mr 24 1904||
CYC complete

MOUNTAIN VIEW

Mountain View **LEADER.** w N 25 1903-10||
United with Mountain View register to form Mountain View register-leader

Mountain View **REGISTER-LEADER.** s,sw 1888+
1888-Jl 13 1910 as Mountain View register
sw Jl 13-N 12 1910
C Ag 1906+
CMv 1912+
CSu My 28 1915
CU-B Mr 2,Je 22 1889;Jl 12,Ag 16-S 6,20-O 11 1890[1909-Jl 1910]My 24-Ag 23,S 6-13 1912

MURPHY

BIG Tree bulletin and Murphy's advertiser. sw My 4- 1858||
My-Je 1858 pub at Mammouth (or Big Tree) Grove
DLC My 7,21 1858

MURRIETA

Murrieta **TRANSCRIPT.** w 1887-89||
CU-B F 28 1889;Mr 7-2 1889

NAPA

Napa **ECHO.** *See* Pacific echo

Daily morning **GAZETTE.** d Mr 1 1870-
MWA Mr 11 1870

Napa **JOURNAL.** w Ap 3 1884-1932||?
Title varies slightly
C 1885-90;93-96
CU-B [1889-N 7 1890;92-O 20 1893;F 23 1894-O 13 1899]Je 17 1909;My 7,Ag 13 1920-[21-23]-[25-26]
MWA 1884-Mr 1905

Napa **JOURNAL.** d 1889+
Title varies: Napa daily journal
C S 1913-[24]+
CU-B D 1-5,9-31 1891;Jl 24 1920-[24-26]-F 20 1931

NAPA county reporter. w Jl 4 1856-D 22 1890||?
Title varies: Napa weekly reporter
C Je 1862-F 5,Jl 1870-Je 23 1882;F 1883-F,Jl 1884-Ap 20,Ag 31 1889-90
CSmH Je 13 1857
CU-B Ag 29 1857;S 6 1862[Ag 1866-67]-Ap,N 1877-Je 1880
MWA Jl 19,N 23 1856;Ja 3,17,F,Mr 14-21,Ap 11-Je,Jl 11-O,N 28,D 19-26 1857;Ja,F 13-27, Mr 20-Je,Jl 17-31,Ag 21,S 11,25,O 16 1858-Jl 5 1862;Jl 29-Ag 19,S 2,23,O 7 1865-Je,Jl 14,S 8,22 1866-68;Jl 1872-Je 23 1882
OHi O 4 1873

PACIFIC echo. w Jl 20 1861-65||
Title varies: Napa echo
C Je 14 1862-Je 6 1863
CU-B D 24 1864
MWA 1861-Jl 12 1862

Napa **REGISTER.** w Ag 10 1863-D 7 1921||
1863 as Napa Valley register
C [Ag 1864-Ja 1874]-F 1878;F 1880-F 1881;F 1882-F 1884;85-96
CU-B 1864-[69]-78;Mr 15 1879-[81]-Ag 5 1882; 87-Je 1888[Ag 25-D 1905]-21
DLC 1863-Je 15 1867
MWA Ap 10 1875
OHi Je 7 1873

Napa daily **REGISTER.** d N 25 1872+
pub 1872+
C D 14 1926+
CU-B [D 1872-N 1873]Ap 1874-[79]-Ag 4 1882;88-90;F-D 1891
MWA D 31 1888
NNHi Jl 5 1876

Napa **REPORTER.** d 1866-Jl 1867||
Followed by Evening chronicle (Vallejo)
CU-B [Je 7-Jl 26 1867]

Napa daily **REPORTER.** d S 11 1880-91||?
CU-B S 11-D 1880;F 11,Jl 18 1882[86]
MWA 1882-83

SOLANO county advertiser. w 1867-
C D 19 1868

Napa **VALLEY** register. *See* Napa register

NATIONAL CITY

National City **NEWS.** w S 28 1882+
pub 1882+
CN 1919+

National City **RECORD.** w S 28 1882-1902||?
CLM S 28 1882;S 5,N 28 1889;90-95
CU-B Ja 31 1889;Ja 26 1893
MB [1882-D 16 1884]

National City **REPORTER.** w Je 15 1933+
pub 1933+

WESTERN world. w 1888-89||?
CU-B Jl 6 1889

NEEDLES

BOOTH'S bazoo. *See* Needle's eye

NEEDLE'S eye. w 1888-1914||?
1888-90 as Booth's bazoo
CLM [1889-93]
CU-B 1906-My 9 1914

NEIGHBORS POST OFFICE

PALO Verde valley news. w Jl 1908-15||
CRiv 1908[09-10]-[14]

NEVADA CITY

Nevada **DEMOCRAT.** w S 14 1853-63||
1853-Ja 1854 as Young America
C complete
CU-B Mr 5 1863
MWA D 30 1857;D 22 1858;D 14,28 1859;Mr 14,My 2 1860
NN extra Ag 24 1861
NNHi D 19 1855

Nevada daily **GAZETTE.** d Mr 9 1864-Ap 1 1870||
United with Grass Valley national (Grass Valley) to form Daily national gazette
C O 27 1868
CU-B Mr 10 1864-70

Weekly **GAZETTE.** w 1867-70 *See* National gazette

GAZETTE. w Mr 10 1876-78||?
CU-B Ag 25 1877-Je 1878

Nevada City **HERALD.** tw,d My 6? 1878-1901||?
tw 1878-Ag? 1886
CU-B My 21 1878-Je 1880;F 8,N 3,27 1883;Ja 17 1884;Ja,S-O 1886

Nevada **JOURNAL.** sw,w,tw Ap 19 1851-63||?
sw 1851-Ap 22 1852;w Ap 25 1852-O 18 1861
CU-B Ap 19,S 13 1851-N 17 1854;55-O 18 1861;N 4 1863
MWA Mr 13,S 18 1857;Jl 18(extra)S 16 1859
NNHi N 23-30 1855
WHi D 23 1853

MINER-transcript. *See* Transcript

NATIONAL gazette. w D 23 1867-72||?
1867-Ap 2 1870 as Weekly gazette
CU-B [1867-70]F 3,My 11-S 21,O 12-19 1872

Daily **NATIONAL** gazette. d Ap 4 1870-D 30 1871||
Formed by the union of Nevada daily gazette and Grass Valley national (Grass Valley)
C Ap 14 1870-71
CSmH 1870-Ap 1 1871
CU-B complete

NEVADA county free lance. *See* Tidings (Grass Valley)

Nevada City daily **TRANSCRIPT.** d S 6 1860-1913||?
Title varies: Morning transcript; Nevada daily transcript; Miner-transcript
C 1860-Ag 1861;O 25 1868;S 9 1882-Ja 1884
CU-B O 5-15 1861;O 17,24 1862;F 1866-[77]-F 8,S 25-D 1881;Ja 22-Ag 5 1882[88]-[91]
MWA Ja 8 1874

YOUNG America. *See* Nevada democrat

NEW REPUBLIC

JOURNAL. w Mr 23-Ag 21 1872||
Some numbers have added title: Nueva republica journal
CSa Ag 7 1872
CU-B Mr 30-Ag 1872

NEWARK

Newark **ENTERPRISE.** w F 27 1880-
CU-B Je 12 1880

NEWCASTLE

Newcastle **NEWS.** w N 30 1887-F 28 1923||
C complete
CU-B Jl 3 1889

NEWHALL

Newhall **SIGNAL** and Saugus enterprise. w F 1 1919+
pub Je 1925+

NEWMAN

WEST Side index. w Ja 1 1890+
pub [1904+]

NEWPORT BEACH

Newport **NEWS.** w 1909+
pub 1909+
CU-B My 9 1919

NIPOMO

Nipomo **NEWS.** w 1887-89||?
CLM Ag 31 1889
CU-B [Mr-D 7 1889]

NORDHOFF

OJAI. *See under* Ojai

OJAI recurrent. w 1887-90||?
1887-Ag? 1890 as Ojai Valley view
CU-B Mr 2-9,Ap 6-13,Jl 6-20,S 7,O 19-26,N 9,D 7,28 1889;Ag 12-19 1890
KHi Jl 29 1890

OJAI Valley view. *See* Ojai recurrent

NORTH HOLLYWOOD

Papers published in North Hollywood are listed under Los Angeles

NORTH LOS ANGELES

Papers published in North Los Angeles are listed under Los Angeles

NORTH SACRAMENTO

Papers published in North Sacramento are listed under Sacramento

NORTH SAN JUAN

HYDRAULIC press. w N? 1857-63||?
Follows Iowa Hills news (Iowa Hills). 1857-Ag 14 1858 as North San Juan star
CU-B Ag 21 1858-Ag 17 1861;O 25 1863

INDEPENDENT. w Ap 13 1878-79||?
CU-B D 21 1878;Ag 16 1879

North San Juan **STAR.** *See* Hydraulic press

North San Juan **TIMES.** w 1873-Mr 16 1878||
C [Mr 28 1874-78]
CU-B [Ap 11-D 1874]-[77]-78

North San Juan **TIMES.** w Je 5 1880-88||?
CU-B Je-Jl 3,17-S 11 1880;F 25,Mr 18,Ap 2 1882;Ja 20 1883;Je 28 1884

WAR club. sw Jl-Ag 1872||?
CU-B Ag 6-7 1872

NORWALK

Norwalk **CALL.** w 1892+
pub 1922+
CU-B [1906]-S 1916

NUEVO. *See* RAMONA

OAK PARK

Oak Park **LEDGER.** w 1896-My 18 1917||
1896-Jl 29 1904 as Sacramento county ledger
C 1901-17
CU-B F 1907-[09]-Ap 22 1910;Je 13 1913-F 9,23,My 11 1917

SACRAMENTO county ledger. *See* Oak Park ledger

OAKDALE

ENTERPRISE. sw 1932+
CU-B O 10 1933+

Oakdale **GRAPHIC.** w,sw 1883-Je 25 1918||
United with Oakdale leader to form Oakdale leader and Oakdale graphic
sw Mr 3 1914-Mr 3 1916
C O 10 1906-18
CU-B [F 27 1889-O 1890]

Oakdale **LEADER** and Oakdale graphic. w 1888+
1888-Je 25 1918 as Oakdale leader
C 1911+

OAKLAND

ALAMEDA county express. w
P-M My 13 1854

ALAMEDA county gazette. *See* Oakland transcript and Alameda county gazette

ALAMEDA county herald. w Jl 27 1859-
CSmH Jl 25 1860-Je 1861
MWA Je 27 1860
NPV 1859-Jl 18 1860

ALAMEDA democrat. w Je 11-Jl 30 1868||?
Je 1868 as Alameda democrat and directory
CU-B Je,Jl 9-30 1868

ALAMEDA democrat. d F 5 1869-
CU-B [F-Ap 1869]

AMERICAN sentinel. w Ja 1886-90||
CLM [1890]
CtW Jl 10 1889
KHi 1886-D 25 1889

O ARAUTO. *See* Jornal de noticias

Evening **ARGUS.** d Mr 6-18 1876||?
CU-B Mr 6-18 1876

BROADMOOR community news. *See* San Leandro news (San Leandro)

BROOKLYN home journal. *See* Oakland home journal

BROOKLYN independent. *See* Oakland home journal

CALIFORNIA voice. w 1919+
Negro
CU-B O 1 1921;Ja 7 1922;D 18 1925;Ag 6 1926;Mr 4,My 6 1927;Ja 25,F 15 1929;Ap 18, My 23,Jl 4 1930

CALIFORNIA (*Continued*)

OAKLAND—*Continued*

CALIFORNIA zeitung. 1904-14||
United with San Joaquin (Lodi) to form California zeitung und San Joaquin journal
Also dated in San Francisco
CU-B My 11 1906

CALIFORNIA zeitung und San Joaquin journal. w 1886-1915||
1886-N 1914 as San Joaquin journal
1886-1914 pub in Lodi
CU-B [Mr 15 1913-14]-Ja 23 1915

CHERRY City news. *See* San Leandro news (San Leandro)

CHUNG sai yat po. *See under* San Francisco

CITIZEN. d 1893-94||
CU-B D 13-30 1893;F 28,Mr 2-7,9-15,21-23,27 1894

CITY itemizer. w O 25 1879-
CU-B N 15 1879

A COLÓNIA portuguesa. *See* Jornal português

CONTRA costa. w
P-M N 10 1854

CO-OPERATIVE world. m Ja 30-Je 1 1931||
Merged with Elmhurst herald to form the Herald, later Herald of cooperation
CU-P complete

Evening DEMOCRAT. d Je 24 1876-O 3 1877||?
CU-B [S 2-O 27 1876]O 3 1877

DOMINION press. w My 30-Je 13 1878||?
CU-B Je 13 1878

EAST Oakland gazette. m,sm,w Mr 1 1911-1916||?
Suspended S 25-O 30 1915
C 1911-N 19 1915

EAST Oakland mail. w S 15 1896-1901||?
CL 1896-Mr 13 1897

ELMHURST herald. *See* Herald of cooperation

ENQUIRER. sw,d 1885-D 31 1921||
United with Oakland daily post to form Post-enquirer
sw 1885
C Mr 1891-1921
CLM Jl 2 1893
CMiC Ap 18-My 8 1906
CO Jl 1892-1921
CSmH Ja 1887;Ja,Jl 1888; extra Ap 18 1906
CU-B Jl 12 1886-My 22,Jl 7 1919-21
Ct Ja 2 1904
DLC Jl-D 1898
KHi Ja 23,O 12 1889;Jl 2 1893;Ap 23 1894
MWA Ja 1887;Ag 29 1891
NNR Ap 19-Je 1906
OClWHi Jl 3 1893;Ap 19 1906
TJT Ja 6 1899
TxGR Ja 29,F 12 1921
Wa My 19 1906
WHi Ja 29 1921

Morning ENQUIRER and Oakland times. d Ag 18 1913-23||?
Follows Oakland times
C 1913-My 22 1919
CO 1913-18

FREE PRESS. w 1914+
C Ag 26 1924+

Saturday GLOBE review. w 1893-95||?
CtY Jl 26 1895
MB Mr 31-N 1894

HERALD. d Ja 5- 1874||?
CU-B Ja 5-7 1874

HERALD. d Mr 31 1903-N 16 1907||
CMiC Ap 18-My 8 1906
CO complete
C-S [Ap 1906]
CU-B 1903-My,Jl-Ag,O 1907
NNR Ap 18-Je 1906
OClWHi Ap 19 1906

HERALD of co-operation. w F 24 1924+
1924-Je 26 1931 as Elmhurst herald; Jl 3 1931-Ap 14 1932 Herald
CO F 1933+
CU-B Mr 16,Je 29,Jl 20 1933
CU-P My 9 1930+

Oakland HOME journal and Alameda county advertiser. w Je 11 1870-74||
1870-Jl 1 1871 as Brooklyn independent; Jl 8 1871-D 27 1873 Brooklyn home journal and Alameda advertiser
C [Ag 1870-Ja 10 1874]
CU-B Jl 8 1871-F 1874

Oakland INDEPENDENT. w Ag 10 1929+
Follows Western American
Negro
CU-B O 19,D 14 1929;Mr 15,My 10-17 1930

INTER-CITY express. d 1907+
CO D 1929+
CU-B Ag 31 1925

JEWISH voice. w 1928-
CU-B S 7,28 O 1928

JORNAL de notícias. w Mr 11 1899-Je 22 1932||
1899-S 14 1917? as O'Arauto. Merged with Jornal português
S 21 1917?-Mr 25 1930 pub in San Francisco
In Portuguese
CU-B Ap 15 1904-06;08-Ja 1917;Jl 9 1930-My 18 1932
IU S 21 1917-32
MH [1899-1906]

JORNAL português. w F 25 1924+
1924-Je 1932 as O Colónia portuguesa
In Portuguese
CU-B Ap 8 1924-O 1930;Mr 30-Ap 6,27,My 25 1934+
IU Jl 1932+

JOURNAL. d O 2-D 15 1867||?
CU-B O 2-3,5-7,9-D 15 1867

JOURNAL. d 1871-74||
CU-B D 17,24,27 1873;Ja 2 1874

JOURNAL. w 1875-1914||
Merged with California zeitung
In German
CU-B Ja 7 1880;Mr 16,Ap 6,D 28 1889-Ja 18 1890

LEADER. w
P-M N 11 1854

MIRROR. w F 23-Ag 10 1878||?
CU-B My 11,Je 8,Ag 10 1878

Oakland NEWS. w,d S 1863-76||?
w 1863-Ja 1868?
C O 27 1868
CO Ja 9-F 1869;Mr 9-10 1870;Mr 10,My 1871-D 4 1876
CU-B Je 10 1865;Jl 12 1866-[75-N 1876]
MWA F 3 1866

Oakland OBSERVER. w Ag 5 1911+
CU-B 1911+

OUR paper. w Je 7 1879-
CU-B Je 14,Ag 9-16 1879

PACIFIC Skandinav. *See under* San Francisco

A PATRIA. w 1892-99||?
In Portuguese
CLM O 19 1892

PEOPLE'S champion. w O 30 1880-
CU-B N 13-D 5 1880

Oakland daily POST. d Ja 29 1917-D 31 1921||
United with Enquirer to form Post-enquirer
CO Jl 1917-21

POST-ENQUIRER. d Ja 2 1922+
Formed by the union of Oakland enquirer and Oakland daily post
C 1922+
CO 1922+

Oakland PRESS. w Ja-My 28 1863||?
CU-B My 28 1863

Oakland PRESS. w Mr 24 1874-82||?
1874-76? as Oakland semi-tropic press
CU-B Mr 28,Ap 11-18,My 2-16 1874;Jl 13 1878-O 4,25,N 15-D 1879;Ja 10-31 F 21-28,Mr 20-Ap 17,My 1-22,Je 5,19,Jl 10,31 1880;Je 10 1882

Saturday PRESS. w 1892+
CU-B D 29 1906;Mr 2 1907;Jl 24 1909-Jl 9 1910;Ap 20-27,My 11,25-S 14 1912;Jl 17 1920-31

Oakland PROGRESS. w 1902-26||?
1902-15 as Fruitvale progress (Fruitvale)
CU-B [1906]-Ag,N-D 1918

Morning RECORD. d 1924-O 24 1925||
1924-Ag? 1925 as Daily record
CO S-O 1925
CU-B O 22,30 1924-25

Oakland REVIEW. w Ap 7 1900-My 1909||
Merged with Oakland times
CSmH Ap 7,21-My 5,Je 9 1900

SATURDAY night. w N 16 1895-1906||?
CU-B 1895-1902;Jl 1905-Ap 14 1906

Oakland SEMI-TROPIC press. *See* Oakland press

SOCIALIST voice. *See* World

SUNSHINE. w 1897-1922||
Negro
CU-B D 21 1907;D 27 1913[Mr 20-D 18 1915] Mr 25,Jl 22,D 30 1916;D 18 1920;F 25 1922

Oakland TELEGRAM. d
CU-B [Je-N 19 1897]

TERMINI. d My 1? 1870-Ap 12 1872||?
CU-B My 17-O 29,N 18 1870;Jl 3,Ag 24,S 1-2, 19-22,O 12-19,31-N 2,4-6,25,28,D 12 1871;Ap 12 1872

Weekly TIMES. w 1855-95||
C Jl 1893-O 1895
CU-B Ja 18,F 22-Mr 1[Ag 1878-Je 18 1880;86] My 5,Je 23 1887;Mr 3,Ap 7,Mr 5,Ag 11,S 15,N 24-D 8,22-29 1892[93;F 22-D 1894]
MWA F-Mr 1 1878

Oakland TIMES. d Ja 8 1878-Ag 17 1913||
Follows Oakland daily transcript. Title varies: Oakland daily times; Morning times; etc. Followed by Morning enquirer and Oakland times
C [1878-82]Jl 1882-1913
CO complete
CU-B 1878-S 1888;Ap 1889-Ja,Mr 1892-Je 1898;99-1905;Jl 1906-07;Ag 12 1909-Ap 23,My 7-Ag 19 1910
ICM O 11 1880
KHi F 19,Jl 16 1889
MWA Mr 8-10,14-Ap 3 1878[Ja 8-N 24 1880]

Oakland TIMES. w? S 29 1923-
Negro
CU-B S 29 1923

TIMES. d O 22 1925-Mr 25 1928||
O 22 1925-Ja 1928 as supp to San Francisco examiner
CO complete

TIMES democrat. w F 11 1934+
CO 1934—

Evening TORCHLIGHT. d N 1872-N 1873||?
CU-B D 24 1872;Ap 9,14-15,17,19,21-22,24-26, 28,30-My 1,3,O 21,N 22 1873

Oakland daily TRANSCRIPT. d Ap 1 1868-Ja 6 1878||
Followed by Oakland times
C O 1868-69;Ap 12 1870-77
CO Ja-F 1869;Mr 9,12,14 1870;Ap 1871-78
CU-B Ap 3 1868-78

Oakland TRANSCRIPT and Alameda county gazette. w Ag 15 1856-Ja 4 1878||
1856-76 as Alameda county gazette
1856-Ja? 1873 pub in San Leandro
C Ag 30 1856-Je 14 1862;Je 25 1864-75
CU-B Ag 15 1857;Je 23 1860;S 6 1862;My 13 1865;S 1866-72
DLC Ag 27 1864
OHi Je 25 1864

Oakland TRIBUNE. d F 21 1874+
Title varies: Oakland daily tribune; Oakland evening tribune Oakland daily evening tribune
C F 23-N 20 1875;F 14-My 1876;Ja-Ag,O 3 1877+
CLM Ag 14 1891
CMiC Ap 20-My 2 1906
CO N 1874+
CSf 1909-13
CSmH Ja 1888
CSt Ap 19 1906
CU-B Ag 25-D 1874;Jl 8 1875-[76-78]Ja 6,F,Ap 2 1879+
KHi [Mr 1878-F 23 1916]
NNR Ap 18-Je 1906
OClWHi Ap 27 1906;Ja 29 1916
OrHi [S 1881;Ja-F 1882]
TxGR Ja 1914;Ja,F 21 1916

Oakland TRIBUNE. w Ag 16 1879-1919||?
CU-B [1879]-Je 1880
WHi Ag 30 1902
Wa Ap 19 1906
WaPS [1917]

A UNIÃO portuguesa. w 1884+
In Portuguese
IU O 8 1917+

VÄSTRA häroldén. w 1898||
IRA complete

Weekly VIDETTE. w 1876-84||?
CU-B D 18-D 6,20-27 1878;Ja 3,F-Mr 7,28,Ap 25-My 2,23 1879[Ap 22-D 1882]

Daily evening VIDETTE. d Ja 16-Je 21 1884||?
CO Ja-Je 21 1884

WEST Oakland herald. w Jl 27 1888-
KHi N 9 1888

WEST Oakland star. w 1889-93||?
CU-B O 4-11 1890

WESTERN American. w My 28 1926-Ag 3? 1929||
Followed by Oakland independent
Negro
CU-B [My 28,Je 25,Jl 30 1926-Ag 19,D 1927-Ap 6,Jl 13-D 14 1928;Ja 4 1929

WESTERN outlook. w 1894-1928||
Negro
CU-B [N 1914-Jl 22 1916]O 22 1921;Mr 25,Ap 22 1922;F 20,My 15,Je 12,Ag 21,D 18 1926;Ja 1-8,F 12,Je 11,D 10,24 1927;Ja 21,F 4,18-25, Mr 10-17,Ap 14-My 1928

Daily WINDBAG. d Jl 16-29 1901||?
CSmH Jl 16-22,25-29 1901

OCEAN BEACH

Ocean Beach NEWS. w N 1922+
pub 1922+

OCEANSIDE

Oceanside BLADE. w,sw Ja 10 1889-O 7 1929||
1889-O 20? 1892 as Oceanside herald
w 1889-Jl 5 1927
CLM S 5 1889
COc O 27 1892-1929
COcB complete
CU-B [1889-F 1890;Jl 1909-Jl 1910]

Daily BLADE-TRIBUNE. d 1927+
1927-O 7 1929 as Oceanside tribune
pub 1927+
COc O 7 1929+
COcC S 10 1933+

Oceanside HERALD. *See* Oceanside blade

Oceanside NEWS. w Je 15 1922+
pub 1925+
COc Jl 23 1925+

OLIVE leaf. w O 22 1896-My 20 1897||
COc complete

Oceanside RECORD. w My 8 1913-Mr 26 1914||
COc complete

Oceanside REGISTER. w Ja 14 1915-D 29 1916||
COc complete

SOUTH Oceanside diamond. w Mr 9 1888-O 31 1891||
COc [1888-S 13 1889]Mr 21-O 1891
CPo Mr 9 1888

STAR journal. w 1881-88||
KHi N 3 1888

Oceanside TRIBUNE. *See* Daily blade-tribune

Oceanside VIDETTE. w Mr 22- 1890||
CLM Mr 22 1890

OJAI

OJAI. w 1891+
1891-1917? pub at Nordhoff
pub 1891+
COx 1898-99;1904-18;21+
CU-B [N 1904-12]
CtY My,O 1896

ONTARIO

CHAFFEY united press. w 1931+
CSmH Mr 16 1933
CU-B O 12 1933+

CALIFORNIA (*Continued*)

ONTARIO—*Continued*

Ontario OBSERVER. w 1880-Ap 20 1901||
Merged with Ontario record to form Ontario record-observer, later Ontario record
CLM [1880-99]
CPo [1892;94]
KHi Ja 11 1889;My 13,Ag 26 1893

Ontario RECORD. w,sw 1885+
My 3 1901-S 5 1902 as Ontario record-observer
sw Je 3 1903-F 27 1904
CLM [1889-1905]
CPo [1892;1900]My 1901-02[05-06]
CU-B Mr 6 1889;F 5 1890;Ja 20,F 10 1892
KHi N 30 1887-My 1 1895

Daily REPORT. d 1910+
C 1917-Jl 13 1918
COn 1914+
CSmH My 21 1931

ORANGE

Orange NEWS. w D 19 1888-1929||?
CLM [1891-92]
CU-B S 25 1889;Ja 13 1892
KHi D 19 1888

Orange daily NEWS. d 1908+
pub 1912+

Orange POST. w,sw 1885+
1885-My 18? 1915 as Orange post; My 25 1915-S 29 1916 Semi-weekly post; O 6 1916-18? Orange post; 1919-O 7 1921 Orange post and Orange news; O 14 1921-Jl 20 1922? Orange post and star
sw My 25 1915-S 29 1916
C O 9 1913-16;Ag 1919-Jl 20 1922
CLM Ag 31-S 7,D 28 1889-N 1 1890
CU-B Ag 24,S 7-14,O 12,26,N 9-D 21 1889;Ja-F 1,My 17 1890;Ag 12 1909-Jl 7 1910
KHi Jl 1893-D 1 1894

Orange STAR. sw,tw -O 1921||
United with Orange post to form Orange post and star, later Orange post
sw -Mr 19 1918
C 1917-Mr 1921

Orange TRIBUNE. w 1885-89||
CU-B Mr 9,Jl 13 1889
KHi F 11 1888-Ja 5 1889

ORLAND

Orland GAZETTE. w Mr 31 1887-
CU-B Mr 31 1887

Orland NEWS. *See* Orland register

Orland REGISTER. w,sw 1887+
1887-97 as Orland news
w 1887-1912?
CU-B Mr 2,16-23 1889;Ap 1917-Mr 1919
KHi Ja 5 1889

UNIT. sw 1911+
CU-B Ap 13-My 11,Jl-N 27 1917[18]Ja 14-17, Mr 11 1919

ORLEANS

KLAMATH news. w 1865-66||?
CU-B Ag 25 1866

NORTHERN record and Klamath county advertiser. w Jl 2 1870-72||?
C Ag 13 1870-My 11 1872
CU-B 1870-My 4 1872

OROVILLE

Morning ADVERTISER. d Ap 1858-
Follows North Californian

BUTTE county register. *See* Oroville register

BUTTE democrat. w O 13? 1859-Ap 21 1860||?
CU-B Ap 21 1860

BUTTE record. w *See* Chico record (Chico)

Oroville MERCURY. w Jl 17 1873-1920||?
C D 31 1875
CU-B [1873]-[77]-[81-My 12 1882]Ja 19 1883; Ap 11-My,16,Je 27-Jl 18,Ag 8-22,S 26-O 3,17, 31,D 25 1884;D 23 1887[Ja-Je 1888]
DLC 1873-Ag 7 1874

Oroville MERCURY. d Mr 4 1883+
1883-S 30 1927 as Daily mercury; O 1 1927-Jl 21 1930 Oroville mercury register
C D 22-23 1887;Mr 22 1908+
COr 1911+
CU-B 1887[88]-[90]91;Ag 28 1922;O-D 24 1927
KHi My 18 1888

NORTH Californian. w,tw,d N 17 1855-S 8 1857||?
Followed by Morning advertiser
w 1855-Mr? 1857;d Ap?-Ag 8? 1857
C [1855-Ap 10 1857]
CP S 8 1857

Oroville PRESS. w Jl 16 1928+
pub 1928+

Oroville REGISTER. w 1877-1913||?
1877-87? as Butte county register
1877?-N 21 1879 pub at Biggs
CU-B [1879-Je 1880]S 22 1887
MWA D 27 1888

Oroville REGISTER. sw,d 1895-S 30 1927||
Merged with Oroville mercury to form Oroville mercury-register, later Oroville mercury
C 1908-27
COr 1911-27
CU-B Jl 27 1909-Jl 14 1910;Ag-S 17 1912;Ap 29 1916;Ja 27 1923-27

Oroville weekly UNION. w Jl 25 1862-Je 23 1864||
Merged with Weekly Butte record to form Oroville union record, later Chico record (Chico)
C [Mr 21 1863-Ja 16 1864]

Oroville UNION-RECORD. *See* Chico record (Chico)

OTAY

Otay PRESS. w 1888-98||?
CU-B [F 1889-F]Ag 18 1892

OWENSMOUTH

Papers published in Owensmouth are listed under Los Angeles

OXNARD

Oxnard COURIER. w Ja 7 1899+
pub 1899+
C Mr 1903-Ag 13 1909
CLM D 4 1903[04]Ja 13-20,F 17 1905
COx 1906-21
CU-B Je 1907-Jl 8,Ag 19 1910;My-S 13 1912;Jl 9 1920-N 9 1928;29+

Oxnard daily COURIER and the Oxnard daily news. d Je 30 1909+
1909-Jl 1918 as Oxnard courier
pub 1909+
C Jl 1909+
COx 1916+
CU-B 1909-N 14 1912;Ap 15 1921+

Oxnard daily NEWS. d 1913-Ag 2 1918||
United with Oxnard daily courier to form Oxnard daily courier and the Oxnard daily news
COx 1916-18

Oxnard REVIEW. w 1908-D 28 1911||
COx 1910-11

Oxnard daily TRIBUNE. d 1924-My 14 1927||
COx complete

PACHECO

CONTRA Costa gazette. *See under* Martinez
CONTRA Costa news. *See under* Martinez

PACIFIC BEACH

NORTH shores sentinel and the San Diegan. w
pub 1927+

Pacific Beach PRESS. w 1888-
CLM Ja 3,17 1889

PACIFIC GROVE

GROVE at high tide. *See* Pacific Grove tribune

Daily REVIEW. *See* Pacific Grove tribune

Pacific Grove TRIBUNE. w,sw,d S 1888+
1888-1929 as Daily review; 1929-Ja 5 1932 Grove at high tide
sw 1929-Ja 5 1932
CPg [My 17 1929+]
CSa [Jl 1913]
CU-B D 20 1890;N 12 1892
KHi D 20 1890

PACIFIC PALISADES

Papers published in Pacific Palisades are listed under Los Angeles

PALERMO

Palermo PROGRESS. w 1890-95||?
CU-B F 6 1891

PALM SPRINGS

Palm Springs LIMELIGHT. w D 31 1933+
pub 1933+

PALMDALE

SOUTH Antelope Valley press. w Je 17 1924+
pub 1924+

PALO ALTO

CITIZEN. w F 27 1904-N 19 1915||
Ja 2-Ag 21 1915 as Citizen and Los Altos news. Merged with Stanford Palo Alto news
CPa complete

LIVE OAK. w,m,ir O 26 1896-Je 1903||
Je 25 1900-Mr 1901 merged with Palo Alto times
w 1896-Je 25 1900;m Mr-Ag 1901; thereafter O 1901;Ja,Ap 1902;Je 1903
no 9,Jl 1902? never issued?
CPa 1896-Ap 1902;Je 1903
CSt 1896-Jl 1901;Je 1903
CU-B N 25,D 30 1896

MAYFIELD news. *See* Palo Alto news

MAYFIELD republican. *See* Palo Alto news

Palo Alto NEWS. w,d,sw 1887+
1887-F 25 1898 as Weekly Palo Alto; Mr 4 1898-D 26 1909 Mayfield republican; Ja 6 1910-Je 24 1925 Mayfield news
Mr 4 1898-Je 24 1925 pub in Mayfield
w 1887-Jl 1930;d Je 20-Jl 5 1932
C 1926+
CPa S-D 1892;D 14 1893[99-1909]+
CU-B S 19 1892-My 19,Ag 31[S-D 8 1893;94]S 4-D 16 1896;Ja 6-My 11,S-D 9 1897[98-99]Ja 12-My 11,S 7-D 11 1900;Ja 10-My 17 1901;Ag 29-D 21 1905;Ja 9-Ap 21,Ag 28-D 14 1906[Ja 8-My 10]Ag 28-D 13 1907;Ja 7-My 5,S-D 11 1908;Ag 29-S 1 1916;Mr 22 1935+

PALO ALTAN. *See* Stanford Palo Alto news

Daily PALO ALTO. *See* Stanford daily (Stanford University)

Weekly PALO ALTO. *See* Palo Alto news

PRESS. *See* Stanford Palo Alto news

SHELTER news. sw Ja-Ag 5 1933||?
CPa F 2-Ag 5 1933

STANFORD Palo Alto news. w F 20 1901-O 26 1917||
1901-02 as Press; 1903-O 22 1915 Palo Altan (My 6-Jl 22 1910 Palo Altan tribune and the Palo Altan on masthead)
C F 1904-17
CPa complete
CSt [Ap 1904-O 22 1915]-Je 23 1916
CU-B [1916]17

Palo Alto SUN. w,sw N 10 1933+
sw Ja-F 1935
C N 24 1933+
CPa 1933+
CSt 1933+
CU-B 1933+

Palo Alto TIMES. w,sw,d 1892+
w 1892-Ag 21 1903, Ag 1904-S 1906; sw Ag 28 1903-Jl 1904
C 1901-N 23 1905;S 17 1918+
CPa 1893+
CSt 1893-94;96-[1906]-08;10-[17]+

Palo Alto TRIBUNE. w,d Mr 16 1906-My 1910||
Merged with Palo Altan, later Stanford Palo Alto news
w 1906-S 1908
CPa [1906-My 2 1910]

PANAMINT

Panamint NEWS. tw,w 1874-75||
CU-B F 23-Mr,O 21 1875

PARLIER

Parlier PROGRESS. w Ja 1911-Jl 14 1932||
Merged with Selma irrigator and enterprise (Selma)
CFr complete

PASADENA

Pasadena CHRONICLE. *See* Pasadena weekly union

Pasadena CRITIC. w My 5 1888-
KHi S 1-8 1888

CROWN vista. w 1891-95||?
CLM O 13 1894

Pasadena FREE PRESS. w Mr 3-24 1932||
CP complete

Pasadena INDEPENDENT. sw F 23 1933+
CP 1933+

Pasadena daily NEWS. d 1894-F 29 1916||
United with Pasadena daily evening star to form Pasadena star-news
C 1901-16
CL 1912-13
CLM Ap 8 1895;Jl 3 1897;Mr 6 1902;F 19-24 1903
CP 1898-1916
CPS complete
CU-B [Ag-D 1909;Mr-D 1911]-16
Tx Je 1911-12

Pasadena POST. d S 1 1919+
1919-Ja 1929 as Pasadena evening post
pub 1919+
C 1919-Ja 18 1921;Mr 1932+
CP 1919+
—Alhambra ed. *See* Alhambra post-advocate (Alhambra)

Weekly STAR and the union. w Ap 21 1886-1905||?
1886-Ag 28 1889 as Pasadena star
CLM Je 17 1891-N 1 1893
CP Ap-My 19 1886;S 4-11,25-O 2 1889
CSmH D 5 1894
CU-B Mr 6,27-My 8 1889;Ja 29,F 19-My,Je 11 1890-91
KHi [Ap 26-S 20 1893]
TJT Ap 20 1898

Pasadena STAR-NEWS. d Ap 21 1886+
1886-S 1 1889; 1891-1906 as Pasadena daily evening star; S 2 1889-D 31 1890 Pasadena daily evening star and union
Je 15 1936 is 50th anniversary number
pub [1886-F 1916]+
C Mr 1916+
CLM F 9,My 30,D 22 1888;Ja 7,F 10,12,Ap 8,Je 11,N 19 1890;D 24 1891;S 4 1893;O 29 1900
CP S 1889+
CU-B Mr 21,27,Je 27,Jl 1,3,S 6 1889;D 19 1891;Jl 26 1893[Ag 10-D 1909]-Ap 16,My 7-Ag 17 1910
KHi D 15 1921;Ag 30 1922;Ja 1,Je 14 1924
MWA Je 15 1936

Pasadena morning SUN. d N 23 1925-O 6 1928||
CP complete

CALIFORNIA (*Continued*)

PASADENA—*Continued*

Pasadena weekly UNION. w Ag 16 1883-Ag 31 1889||
1883-Ja 31 1884 as Pasadena chronicle; F 1884-Ag 23 1886 Pasadena and valley union. United with Pasadena star to form Weekly star and the union
CLM [Ja-Ag 1889]
CP 1883-[84;86-89]
CU-B N 1 1883;F 6-20,Mr,S 11,D 4-18 1885 [87]Jl-D 1888

Pasadena daily UNION. d S 5 1887-Ag 31 1889||
Merged with Pasadena daily star to form Pasadena daily evening star and daily union, later Pasadena star-news
CLM D 28-29 1888;Ag 27 1889
CP complete
CU-B F 27 1889
KHi Jl 13 1888

PASO ROBLES

Paso Robles LEADER. w 1886-1919||?
CLM Ag 31,D 14 1889
CU-B O 22 1887;O 19-26 1889;Ja 18,Jl 23,Ag 6-13 1890;O 2,D 4,18 1907[08-10]Mr 8 1911
KHi D 22 1888;92

MOON. *See* Paso Robles record

Paso Robles PRESS. w 1887+
pub 1910+
KHi D 31 1924;Ja 12 1925

Paso Robles RECORD. w 1887-1917||?
1887-95? as Moon
CU-B S 5,19-26,O 10-17,N 14-28,D 28 1889;O 14 1890;Je 12-19,Jl 1909-[Ja-Jl 1910]

Paso Robles STAR. sw,d,w 1919-S 25 1925||
sw 1919-N 1922; d D 1922-Ap 18 1925
C 1920-25
CU-B 1923-24

PATTERSON

Patterson IRRIGATOR. w Ag 31 1911+
pub 1911+

PERRIS

NEW ERA. w 1890-1900||?
CLM [1891-96]
CU-B Ag 11-S 15 1892
KHi Ap 19,Je 14 1894

Perris PROGRESS. w My 12 1901+
CRiv 1911-26[28]+
CU-B Jl 22-Ag 5,19-S,O 21,N 18-D 9 1909

Perris VALLEY leader. w 1887-89||
CU-B Mr 2-9 1889

PETALUMA

Petaluma weekly ARGUS. w F 12 1861-1919||?
1861-F 17 1864 as Petaluma argus; F 25 1864-Ja 31 1873 Petaluma journal and argus
C D 17 1868
CPe 1861-Ja 19 1889
CU-B D 23 1863;F 25 1864-[Jl-D 1876]F 1877-Ag 4 1882;86;Jl 26-Ag 23 1890[92-96]Mr 6 1897
MWA Ja 11 1866;Mr 17 1876
OrHi N 22 1862

Petaluma ARGUS. d
Title varies. Pub during District fair only
CPe F 7-Ag,O 6-17 1873
CU-B [Ag 19-D 1872]-Ag 4,S 14-17 1874

Petaluma ARGUS-COURIER. d Ja 2 1899+
1899-Jl 9 1928 title varies; Petaluma daily argus; Petaluma argus
C Mr 23-Ap 21 1920
CPe 1899+

Petaluma COURIER. w O 5 1876-1920||?
CPe 1876-S 17 1890
CU-B N 30,D 21 1876-[77]78;80[81-82]Jl 20,S 3 1890
KHi My 7-14 1890

Petaluma COURIER. d 1884-Jl 8 1928||
United with Petaluma argus to form Petaluma argus-courier
C 1911-20
CPe 1899-1928
CU-B [Ja-Ag 1912]

Petaluma CRESCENT. d S 10? 1870-72||?
CU-B [S 25 1870-N 7 1872]

Petaluma IMPRINT. d 1884-95||?
CU-B O 7,9,11,N 12-14,D 28,30 1889;Ja 1 1890

Petaluma JOURNAL and argus. *See* Petaluma weekly argus

Petaluma weekly JOURNAL and Sonoma county advertiser. *See* Sonoma county journal

Petaluma REPUBLICAN. w Je 12-Jl 17 1860||
CPe Je 12-26 1860

SONOMA county journal. w Ag 18 1855-F 19 1864||
1855-Ag 16 1856 as Petaluma weekly journal and Sonoma county advertiser. United with Petaluma argus to form Petaluma journal and argus, later Petaluma weekly argus
CP O 16 1863
CPe complete
CU-B D 17 1858;O 3 1862;S 11 1863;Ja,F 12-19 1864

PIEDMONT

Piedmont HIGHLANDER. w
WaPS [1930-31]

PIRU

Piru NEWS. w Ja 1927+
pub 1927+
CPi F 1927-32

PISMO BEACH

Pismo TIMES. w Ja 30 1931+
pub 1931+

PLACENTIA

Placentia COURIER. w Ag 21 1911—
pub 1911+

PLACERVILLE

Placerville AMERICAN. w Jl 6? 1855-
NNHi F 2,Jl 19 1856

Tri-weekly ARGUS. *See* Tri-weekly index

Placerville COURIER. w Je 9? 1866-67||?
CU-B Jl 28,O 13 1866-Ag 31 1867

EL DORADO county republican. *See* El Dorado republican (1871-1924)

EL DORADO news. w 1852-
MWA F 19-26,Mr 12,26,My 21 1853

EL DORADO republican. w Je 1853-F 1854||
Merged with Mountain democrat
MWA Ag 6 1853

EL DORADO republican. w Je 22 1871-1924||
1871-91 as El Dorado county republican; My 7 1909-18? El Dorado republican and weekly nugget. Followed by Placerville republican
C 1901-23
CU-B Je 22,Ag 3-10,24,S 5-14,28 1871-78;Mr-Jl 24,Ag 7,21-O 16,30 1879-80;Je 13,Jl 25,Ag 1 1889[90-91]S 19-O,N 14-21,D 5-12 1907

Placerville HERALD. w Ap 30-N 5 1853||
C complete
MWA My 21,Je 25,Ag 6-13 1853

Tri-weekly INDEX. tw Ag 13 1857-
Follows Empire county argus (Coloma). 1857-F 6 1858 as Tri-weekly argus

Weekly MIRROR. w Je 3 1865-66||?
CU-B Jl 29 1865;Mr 10 1866
MWA Ja 27 1866

MOUNTAIN democrat. sw,w F 17 1854+
Title varies: Weekly mountain democrat, etc.
sw Ag 22-D 29 1860
Ja 6 1928 is 75th anniversary ed
pub 1861-[65-80]+
C F 25 1854-68;Ap 30 1870-S 6 1884;Ja 25 1890-97
CL Ja 6 1928
CSm Ja 6 1928
CU-B 1864-Je 1880;86-F 1,N 1 1890;Mr 3 1923;F 6 1925;Ag 3 1934
DLC Ja 3 1857;Ap 27 1861;D 17 1864
P-M My 27 1854

Placerville NEWS. d,tw 1860?-Ja 6 1865||?
1860?-N 24 1864 as Daily news
d 1860-N 24 1864
CSmH My 21-N 24 1864
CU-B Ja 6 1865

Placerville NUGGET. d 1895-D 31 1908||
C 1901-08

Weekly NUGGET. w 1896-Ap 30 1909||
United with El Dorado republican to form El Dorado republican and weekly nugget, later El Dorado republican
C 1909

Placerville RECORDER. w Ag 9? 1865-S 26 1866||?
CU-B O 18 1865;Ag 1,15-S 1866

Placerville REPUBLICAN. tw,d My 7 1909+
tw 1909-Jl 1924
C 1924+
CU-B Je 23 1927+

Placerville REPUBLICAN. w 1926+
Follows El Dorado republican

PLANADA

Planada ENTERPRISE. w 1912-18||
CMe 1912-Mr 1918

PLEASANTON

Pleasanton BULLETIN. w 1897-98||
United with Pleasanton times to form Pleasanton times-bulletin, later Pleasanton times

Pleasanton STAR. w 1882-89||
CU-B Jl 6-13 1889

Pleasanton TIMES. w 1889+
1899? as Pleasanton times-bulletin
CU-B O 18 1890;Jl 10 1909-Jl 2 1910

POINT ARENA

Point Arena NEWS. w 1877-78||?
CU-B [Mr 15-S 13 1878]

Point Arena RECORD. w 1888-1930||?
CU-B Jl 9 1920-Je 1927;Ja 18[My 11-O 5 1928]

POINT REYES STATION

WEST Marin star. w F 1928+
pub 1928+

POINT RICHMOND. *See* RICHMOND

POMONA

Saturday BEACON. *See* Pomona review

Pomona BULLETIN. d,w,sw O 3 1910-Ap 3 1927||
Follows Pomona times (1882-1910) 1910-12 as Pomona morning times; 1913-Ja 19 1915 Pomona weekly times. United with Pomona progress to form Pomona progress-bulletin
w 1913-Ja 19 1915;sw Ja 26 1915-Ja 28 1916
CPo complete
CPoP complete
CU-B My 7-23,25-27,29-31 1919

Pomona weekly COURIER. w D 15 1883-Mr 29 1884||
United with Pomona times to form Pomona times-courier, later Pomona times
CPo 1883-Mr 22 1884

Saturday POST. w Ap 15 1895-
CPo My 6,Je 8-Jl 6,Ag 17 1895

Pomona PROGRESS. m,w Ja 21 1885-N 22 1919||
m Ja-F 1885
C O 17 1912-19
CLM [1887-1904]
CPo 1885-[87;89-92]94-95[1903]10
CPoP complete
CU-B 1887;F 28,Mr 14,N 14,28-D 5 1889[1906]-19
KHi D 6 1888

Pomona PROGRESS-BULLETIN. d Ap 1 1898+
1898-O 4 1909 as Daily progress; O 5 1909-Ap 2 1927 Pomona progress
pub 1898+
CPo [1901]-[03]+
CU-B N 13 1923;Ap 24,N 7 1924;Je 1925

Pomona REGISTER. w Mr 5 1889-92||
CLM N 27-D 4,18 1889;N 19 1890;Ag-O,D 30 1891-92
CPo Mr 6,Jl 3,24-31 1889;Jl 27-Ag 3 1892

REPUBLICAN message. w My 1-Ag 7 1894||?
CPo Je 26,Jl 3-10,Ag 7 1894

Pomona REVIEW. w Je 7 1893-O 31 1903||
1893-Je 15? 1899 as Saturday beacon (Title varies: Weekly beacon; Pomona beacon; Beacon)
CLM Ap 3 1897
CPo C 14 1893-[99;1902-03]
CPoP complete

Pomona daily REVIEW. d Jl 14 1902-Mr 31 1916||
Merged with Pomona progress, later Pomona progress-bulletin
CPo [1902]-16
CPoP Je 1904-16

Thursday's TELEGRAM. w S 18 1884-85||?
CPo S 10-D 1885

Pomana TIMES. w O 7 1882-O 3 1910||
Ap 5 1884-Jl 25 1891 as Pomona times-courier.
Followed by Pomona morning times, later Pomona bulletin
CLM Je 13 1891-[S-O 1893;Mr-My,Jl 1894]
CPo 1882-[84-91]-1910
CPoP complete
CU-B O 30 1886;Ag 9 1894;Jl 21 1909-Jl 6 1910
KHi S 15 1888

Pomona TIMES. d Ap 26 1887-My 8 1891||
CLM Ap 29 1887;O 5 1889
CPo complete
CPoP complete
KHi S 21-22,N 3 1888

Pomona TIMES-COURIER. *See* Pomona times w

PORTERVILLE

Porterville ENTERPRISE. w 1888-1917||?
CLM F 17 1905

Porterville RECORDER. d 1907+
CU-B [N 20 1909-Ag 18 1910]N 13 1924

PORTOLA

Portola REPORTER. w Ap 14 1927+
CQ 1927+
CU-B My 12 1927-[29-30]+

Portola SENTINEL. w Je 24 1916-O 20 1917||
C [Jl 1916-17]
CQ [1916-17]

PUENTE

La Puente VALLEY journal. w 1910+
pub 1918-19;23;25+

QUINCY

FEATHER River bulletin. w,sw Ag 11 1866+
1866-My 12 1892 as Plumas national; My 19 1892-Ap 30 1931 Plumas national bulletin
sw Ja 26 1905-Jl 8? 1912
C O 15,D 12 1868;S 13 1870-My 18 1872;Jl 16 1881;D 13 1890+
CQ S 30 1871+
CSmH S 10 1868-S 23 1871
CU-B 1866-[68]-[71-72]-[79-My 8 1880]86[88]-91;D 31 1931;F 4 1932;O 12 1933+

CALIFORNIA (*Continued*)

QUINCY—*Continued*

PLUMAS county bulletin. w S 29 1880-My 12? 1892||
1880-Jl 8 1891 as Greenville bulletin. United with Plumas national to form Plumas national bulletin, later Feather River bulletin
1880-N 18 1891 pub at Greenville
CQ 1880-My 12 1892
CU-B O-D 1880;S 12 1883-[85-My 5]D 29 1886[88]-91
KHi Jl 18-Ag 15 1888
NNHi Jl 1885-Ag 18 1886

PLUMAS democrat. w Ag 26 1856-
MWA S 23 1856

PLUMAS independent. w 1892+
CQ F 23 1916+

PLUMAS national. *See* Feather River bulletin

PLUMAS standard. w 1859-62||?
CU-B O 18 1862

PROSPECTOR. Mr 3 1855-
CSmH Mr-N 17 1855

Quincy UNION. w 1863-D 1868||
CU-B 1864-[66-67]-O 1868
MWA Ap 8 1865

RABBIT CREEK. *See* LA PORTE

RAMONA

To Ag 1898 as Nuevo

Ramona SENTINEL. w 1887+
1887-Ag 1898 as Sentinel
C 1893-Ap 1 1904;O 21 1927+
CLM F 17 1905
KHi Ap 19 1894

RANDSBURG

GOLDEN state miner. w 1896-1918||
1896-1916 as Randsburg miner.
Followed by Arizona state miner (Wickenburg, Arizona)
CB Ap 28 1900-07;F 1912-15

Randsburg MINER. *See* Golden state miner

Randsburg TIMES. w My 23 1924-My 24 1929||
United with Mojave record to form Mojave-Randsburg record-times (Mojave)
CB 1925-27
CTeN complete

RED BLUFF

Red Bluff BEACON. w,sw Mr 25 1857-
w 1857-D 10 1862
C 1857-Mr 16 1859;O 10 1860-F 3 1864
CU-B Ag 19 1857;O 24,31 1863

Red Bluff DEMOCRAT. d 1884-85||
CU-B Ja 15 1885

Red Bluff INDEPENDENT. *See* Tehama county people's cause

Red Bluff NEWS. w 1885-O 12 1928||?
D 14 1923-D 9 1927 as Red Bluff sentinel and weekly news
C Jl 1890-D 22 1891;My 14-Mr 3 1892;93-O 12 1928
KHi S 22 1888-F 2 1889

Red Bluff daily NEWS and times-sentinel. d N 1 1885+
1885-Ap 30 1931 as Red Bulff daily news
C D 14 1926+
CRb [1926-27]+
CU-B Ja 24,Ag 11 1909-Ap 17,My 7-Je 15,23-Ag 16,D 8 1910;Mr 25 1913;O 11 1914+

PEOPLE'S cause. d *See* Tehama county republican

PEOPLE'S cause. w *See* Tehama county people's cause

Red Bluff SENTINEL. w Mr 9 1867-D 1923||
United with Red Bluff news to form Red Bluff sentinel and weekly news, later Red Bluff news
C Ap 27 1867;O 3,24 1868;My 1870-F 1882
CLM Ap 29 1882
CU-B Jl 13,Ag 17 1867-[68-69]-80;Ja 8,N 26 1881;My 20,Je 24,Jl 1-8,S 26 1882[86]

Evening SENTINEL. d 1880-Ap 1931||
United with Red Bluff daily news to form Red Bluff news and times-sentinel
CU-B O 24,28,N 3-6,11,14,16,20,24,29-D 1,7-8 1882;F 25,Mr 5,Ag 6 1889;Ja 25 1890

Red Bluff SENTINEL and weekly news. *See* Red Bluff news

TEHAMA county democrat. sw,d,w Ag 12 1875-85||
1875-F 2 1884 as Tocsin (S 26-28? 1883 Evening tocsin)
1875-82? pub in Tehama
sw 1881?-S 22 1883;d S 26-28? 1883
CU-B Ag 12,S 23,N 1875-S 1876;F 22-N 1877; 78-80[83]-N 1884;Ja 17-31,F 21,Ap 4 1885

TEHAMA county people's cause. tw,sw,w Ag 14 1860-1918||?
1860-F 1872 as Independent; Mr 1872-O 3 1874 Tehama independent; O 10 1874-1917? Red Bluff people's cause
Mr 1872-O 3 1874 pub in Tehama
C 1860-N 7 1862;D 15 1863;D 24 1868;O 10 1874-77
CU-B S 21 1860;Ag 1865-Ap 7 1877;Jl 1878-[79]80;Mr 18 1882;F 28 1885[87-Ja 21 1888] Ag 9-23 1890
DLC Ag 1861-Jl 1865
MWA Je 26,S 25 1875;Ja 8 1876;Je 23,Jl 14,D 22 1877-[78]-Ja 11,Mr 8 1879;Je 12 1880;O 1,D 10 1881[Mr-D 1884]Ja 2,Mr 6,Jl 3,Ag 7,21,O 16-23,D 4-11 1886
MiU-C O 12 1878
N O 12 1878
TJT F 18 1899

TEHAMA county republican. d Mr 18 1878-1918||?
1878-1917? as People's cause
CU-B Mr-Ap 26,My 24-D 1878;Mr 1879-80;O 6 1881;Mr 13 1882;Ap 12 1884;S 12 1887[88-89-[91]
MWA Mr 22 1878;S 28 1880;Ag 15 1883;Ja 1,Je 4 1884;Ap 27 1891
NcD O 12 1878

TEHAMA observer. w O? 1865-67||?
CU-B Jl 21 1866;Ja 5 1867

Red Bluff morning TIMES and sentinel. d Je 1 1927-Ap 30 1931||
Title varies: Morning times and Red Bluff sentinel. United with Red Bluff daily news to form Red Bluff daily news and times-sentinel
C F 16 1928-31
CRb [1927]-31
CU-B [1928]-31

TOCSIN. *See* Tehama county democrat

REDDING

COURIER-free press. d 1895+
1895-Mr 5 1906 as Free press
C 1901+
CU-B [1906]-O 23 1915[23]+
TxGR Ja 25 1919
w ed *See* Shasta courier

FREE PRESS. d *See* Courier-free press

FREE PRESS. w 1883-1906||
1883-Ap 14 1888 as Republican-free press
CU-B [1888-91]

Redding INDEPENDENT. w 1877-83||?
CU-B Jl 18 1878-80;D 8 1882;Ja 12 1883

REPUBLICAN-free press. *See* Free press

SEARCHLIGHT. d 1897+
WHi Mr 18 1903

SHASTA county democrat. w S 4 1880-1903||?
1880-81? pub in Millville
CU-B S 11-D 1880;S 20 1882;S 17 1884

SHASTA courier. w,sw Mr 12 1852+
suspended Ja-Mr 1853
1852-1906? pub at Shasta
sw 1907?-21?
C Ag 7 1852;D 29 1855;Je 17 1865;D 19 1868; Ja 25 1870-My 18 1872
CU-B [1864]-80;My 30 1885[86-87]Jl 1888-[90]Jl-D 19 1891;O 26 1915-[18]S 24 1920
DLC My 29,Je 26,Jl 17 1852;N 19 1870
MWA Mr 20 1852;D 24 1853;Ja 21 1854
NNHi O 10 1857
OClWHi Jl 20 1872;Ap 5 1873

REDLANDS

CITROGRAPH. w Jl 16 1887-N 14 1908||
1887 pub in Lugonia
C complete
CLM [1889-1908]
CPo [1887-91]1907
CRed complete
CU-B complete
MB [Jl 18 1891-92]

Redlands FACTS. w O 23 1890-F 17 1893||
CRed complete

Redlands daily FACTS. d O 23 1892+
Title varies slightly
C Jl 29 1919+
CLM [1892-93]
CRed 1892-[1922]+
CRedU Je 1928+
CU-B Ag 2 1893;Ja 13-Mr 5 1906;F 13,Ap 24 1924
KHi Je 12 1891-S 1892

Redlands REVIEW. d N 26 1901-Ja 31 1919||
1901-17 as Redlands daily review. Merged with Redlands daily facts
C 1913-19
CRed complete
CRedU 1901-Je 1918
CU-B Ag 11 1909-[10]

SOUTHERN Californian. w S 3 1887-S 15 1888||
CRed complete

REDONDO BEACH

ADVANCE. w Mr 11 1924-D 25 1928||
Supplement of Redondo reflex
CRe complete

Redondo BREEZE. *See* South Bay breeze

Redondo Beach COMPASS. w 1890-93||?
CLM My 1892-[Ja,Mr 25-O 18 1893]
CU-B S 10 1892
KHi S 25 1891

Redondo REFLEX. w Ag 18 1905+
pub 1905+
CRe F 1909+
—**Supplement.** *See* Advance

SOUTH Bay breeze. w,d Ap 24 1909+
1909-D 15 1922 as Redondo breeze (w)
CLM Ja 30-F 20 1904
CRe 1909+

REDWOOD CITY

Redwood City DEMOCRAT. *See* Redwood City standard

SAN MATEO county gazette. *See* Times-gazette

SAN MATEO county journal. w 1879-84||
C My 1880-O 23 1884
CU-B 1880;Mr 16-23,My 4 1882

SAN MATEO county times and gazette. *See* Times-gazette

Redwood City STANDARD. w 1886-O 27 1931||
1886-Ja 30 1919 as Redwood City democrat; F 6 1919-O 6 1921 Redwood City standard and Redwood City democrat. United with Redwood City tribune to form Redwood City tribune-standard
C Mr 15 1890-1931
CU-B [Mr 1889-S 4 1890]My 8-9 1919;O 29 1929-31

TIMES-GAZETTE. w Ap 9 1859-1930||?
1859-Ja 29 1876 as San Mateo county gazette; F 5 1876-My 22 1886 Times and gazette; My 29 1886-Jl 17 1909 San Mateo county times and gazette
C Ja 2 1869;Ap 16 1870-Mr 1872;Ap 1903-30
CSmH D 18 1875
CU-B O 29 1859;O 25 1862;64-80;Je 9 1883; My 3 1884;Ja 24 1885[86;Ja-Je 1888;Jl-D 1889; 91]Jl 24 1909-Ag 6 1910;23-O 1931;32+
KHi N 3 1888
TJT Ap 22 1899

Redwood City TRIBUNE-STANDARD. d 1923+
1923-O 1931 as Redwood City tribune
C D 15 1926+

REEDLEY

Reedley EXPONENT. w Mr 26 1891+
CFr Ag 31 1916-Ag 10 1933
CU-B My 3 1894;Jl 29 1909-Ap 7,My-Jl 7 1910;S 1934+

Reedley LEDGER. w 1905-21||?
CFr 1916

RIALTO

ORANGE grower. w 1888-95||?
CLM S 6 1889
CU-B Mr,Ap 19,S 6-13,27,N 8-22,D 13 1889;Ja 3,17-F 14,28 1890

RICHMOND

To Jl 7 1902? as Eastyard; Jl 7 1902- as Point Richmond

Richmond INDEPENDENT. d Je 7 1910+
C Je 28 1910+
CRi 1910+

Richmond NEWS. d,w Ja 25 1914-Ag 29 1920||
Merged with Richmond record-herald
w Mr 17-D 1916
C 1914-My 3 1917
CRi complete

Richmond PROGRESS. w F 10 1933+
CRi 1933+

Richmond RECORD. w 1900-07||?

Richmond RECORD-HERALD. d 1902+
CRi [1913]+
CU-B [1902-03]-Ap 6 1904

SANTA Fe times. w Mr 27 1902-Mr 19 1903||
CRi complete

Richmond TERMINAL. w 1903-O 3 1930||
Merged with Richmond independent
C [Je 1906-11]-30
CRi 1911-[15-17]-[20-21]-[29]30
CU-B Mr 19 1904-Ag 1930

RIO VISTA

BANNER of the delta. w -Mr 28 1930||
-S 27 1926 as Rio Vista banner. Merged with River news
sw F-Je 1927
C S 1926-Mr 1930

Rio Vista ENTERPRISE. w S 22 1877-My 30 1879||?
CU-B 1877-My 1879

Rio Vista GLEANER. w 1877-79||?
CU-B Jl 20 1878-Ja 4 1879

Rio Vista NEWS. *See* River news

Rio Vista NEWS-BANNER. *See* River news

RIVER news. w F 1890+
Title varies: Sacramento River news; Rio Vista news; River news-banner
pub 1890+
C Ap 1897+
CU-B Jl 16 1909-Jl 8 1910

SACRAMENTO River news. *See* River news

RIPON

IRRIGATION bulletin. w 1910-12||
CU-B D 15,29 1911-[12]

Ripon RECORD. w Ap 15 1912+
pub 1912+

RIVERBANK

Riverbank NEWS. w 1915+
Follows Riverbank review
pub [1915-19]+
C Ap 23 1920+

Riverbank REVIEW. w Mr 1913-15||
Followed by Riverbank news
CRibN complete

CALIFORNIA (*Continued*)

RIVERDALE

Riverdale FREE PRESS. w Mr 11 1915+
1915-F 24 1921 as Riverdale observer
CFr 1915+

Riverdale OBSERVER. *See* Riverdale free press

RIVERSIDE

Riverside ENTERPRISE. w Je 25 1890-1907‖?
CRiv 1890-Je 1892

Riverside ENTERPRISE. d Mr 3 1891+
Title varies: Riverside morning enterprise; Riverside daily enterprise. Jl 11 1909-Ap 9 1910 as Morning mission and Riverside enterprise
CLM [1891-94]
CRiv 1891-[99]+
CRivC [O 16 1931+]
CU-B Ag 20,S 3,O 1 1890[Ja 5-Ap 17 1892]Jl 1927-Mr 1928

Riverside FACTS. ir N 10 1928-F 7 1929‖?
N 10 1928-Ja 11 1929? as Riverside news
CRiv [1928-Ja 11]23-F 7 1929

HAYDEN'S weekly. w F 9 1933+
F-D 21 1933 as El Monitor
CRiv 1933-[34]

MAGNOLIA weekly news. w D 18 1930+
CRiv Je 11 1931+
CU-B Ap 16-23,My 21,Je 11-25 1931

Morning MISSION and Riverside enterprise. *See* Riverside enterprise. d

El MONITOR. *See* Hayden's weekly

Riverside weekly NEWS. w 1875-My 1878‖
Followed by Press and horticulturist
CRiv N 27 1875-Jl 22 1876
CU-B [D 16 1876-My 12 1877]

PHOENIX. w Je 1 1889-92‖
CLM [1890-92]
CU-B Je 22-29,Jl 13-20,O 19,N 30 1889;D 19 1891

Riverside daily PRESS. d Je 10 1886+
Follows Press and horticulturist (tw)
C N 1913+
CLM [1891-1904]
CRiv 1886;S 1889-91;Ja-Mr,N-D 1896;O 1897+
CU-B Jl 16 1886;Je 23 1888[89]D 6 1894;Ja 20 1900;Je 1908-F 12 1918;O 9 1933+

PRESS and horticulturist. w Je 29 1878-Ag 24 1906‖
Follows Riverside weekly news. 1878-Ja 24 1880 as Riverside press; Je-D 1897 Press and horticulturist and Riverside county reflex. Merged with Corona independent (Corona)
Ap 27-Ag 24 1906 pub in Corona
C My 22 1897-1906
CLM [1899-92]
CRiv 1880-[96]97
CSbe Ja-My 17 1884
CU-B Ap 14-D 25 1880;Ja 5,Mr 29,N 15 1884; Ja 24,Mr 14,Ag 18 1885;87[Jl 1888-89]-91
TJT My 1 1886

PRESS and horticulturist. tw Je 9 1885-Je 8 1886‖
Followed by Riverside daily press
CRiv complete

RIVERSIDE county reflex. w My 7 1892-My 1897‖
1892-95? as Riverside reflex. United with Press and horticulturist to form Press and horticulturist and Riverside county reflex, later Press and horticulturist
CL 1892-Ap 1893
CLM [1892-97]

SOUTH Riverside bee. w 1887-95‖?
CLM [1888-92]
CU-B F 28-Mr 7,Ag 30,S 13,O 25,N 8,29,D 9-13 1889;Ja,F 14,28,My 16,Je 20,Jl 4-11,Ag 12,22,O,N 21 1890;Jl 9 1892
KHi F 1888-Jl 4 1889

VALLEY echo. w 1883-88‖
CRiv Ja-N 1888
KHi Je 21-O 4 1888

ROHNERVILLE

Rohnerville HERALD. *See* Home herald

HOME herald. w 1881-97‖?
1881-92? as Rohnerville herald; 1893?-94? Home journal and herald
CU-B O 19,N 2 1887;88-91

HOME journal and herald. *See* Home herald

ROSAMOND

ANTELOPE Valley news. w 1886-87‖?
CLM Ap 16 1887

ROSCOE

Papers published in Roscoe are listed under Los Angeles

ROSEVILLE

Roseville PRESS. w 1929+
C S 13 1934+

Roseville REGISTER. w 1906-D 23 1923‖
United with Roseville tribune to form Roseville tribune and register
C F 1907-23

Roseville TRIBUNE and register. sw Je 1908+
1908-23 as Roseville tribune
pub Je 1919+

SACRAMENTO

Sacramento AGE. d D 6 1855-Mr 27 1858‖
1855-Ag 2 1856 as Spirit of the age
C 1855-Ap 18,O 1 1857-58
CSmH Mr 6-My 3 1856
CU-B 1855-My 3,19,S 22 1856
NNHi Ja 11 1856
OrHi [1856-57]

Sacramento BEE. d F 3 1857+
Title varies: Bee; Daily bee; Sacramento evening bee; etc
pub 1857+
C 1857-Ag 2 1860;76-84;Jl-D 1885;Jl 1886-Je 1887;88+
CCIP 1926+
CLM Ja 9 1880;Je 5 1886;Ap 14 1887;N 29 1890;Ja 2,Mr 8 1891;S 9,12,19 1892;Mr 21 1905
CMiC Ap 19 1906
CP D 12 1860
CS Jl 1891+
CSt S 24 1858;D 24 1880;S 9 1884;Ag 12 1886
CSto Ja 1914
CU S 1932-33;S 11 1934+
CU-B F 4 1858;S 17 1861;O 29 1863;Jl 28 1866; Jl 1 1867;F 14,Je 29-30,Jl 2 1868-[70]71;Ja 2-4,F 10-S 18,O 15,1872-80;Mr 29,Ap 9,D 24 1881;Mr 18,Ag 4 1882;N 22 1884;Je 1 1886;O 17 1891;D 1 1894;Je 24,S 10 1895;1901-[02] Ap 13 1903-O 1 1918;O 9 1933+
CtY Jl 3 1869
DLC 1898
KHi O 9 1888;Je 30 1902;My 22-30 1922;Je 30 1925
MWA F 17 1870;Mr 14 1917
N Mr 1,Jl 21 1864;N 15 1867;Ag 11,D 11 1868; My 20 1869
NvR [1932]+
TJT Ap 13,21,D 10 1898

Sacramento BEE. sw,w 1867?-76‖?
sw 1867?-73?
CU-B Je 15 1868;D 1874-F 20 1875
OrHi O 26 1876

Sacramento BEE. w S 8 1877+
Ap 12 1889-Ap 25 1900? as Pacific bee
1900+ Saturday ed of d
CU-B 1877-[84-S 17 1886]89-Ap 1900
KHi Mr 25 1891
OrHi Je 15 1878

Daily CALIFORNIA American. d Ja 8 1855-
1855-Je 1 1856 as Daily state tribune
C Jl 1855-Je 1 1856
CP D 6 1856
CU-B Ap 15 1855;D 11 1856
NNHi My 31,Ag 18-S,O 2-3,6,20-21,23-25,27-28,30,N 1-18 1855

CALIFORNIA express. w N 3 1851-Jl 1867‖
1851-66 pub in Marysville
C My 25 1867
CP S 18 1858
CU-B S 10 1852;Mr 13,Ag 27 1858;S 15 1860;S 30 1865;Jl 28 1866;My 3 1867
DLC Ag 5 1852;N 1857-[58]-My 7,21-Ag 13,S 17,O 1859
—Steamer California express. sm
DLC My 1 1855;F 20 1856

CALIFORNIA free press. sw 1871-72‖
CU-B F 25,Mr 3 1872

CALIFORNIA republican. d 1850?-63‖?
CU-B Mr 7 1863

Weekly CALIFORNIA statesman. w F 5 1852-Je 24 1858‖
1852-Mr 3 1855 as Weekly democratic state journal; Mr 8 1855-Ap 1858 Weekly state journal
C Jl 24 1852;F 4 1854;Je 23 1855;Jl 21,Ag 11,25 1855
CS S 30 1854
CU-B Ag 21 1852
DLC Mr 10 1855;Ap 10 1858
MWA Mr 12,Jl 2-9,23-30,Ag 13 1853
NNHi F 13 1858

CALIFORNIA statesman. d N 13 1854-Mr 1 1855;My 1-Je 24 1858‖
Revived My 1-Je 24 1858 to follow Democratic state journal (d)
C complete
DLC My-Je 4 1858

Daily CALIFORNIA times. d Ag 15 1856-Ja 24 1857‖
C N 9 1856
NNHi N 20-D 3 1856

Daily CALIFORNIAN. d N 17 1852-Jl 30 1853‖
Merged with Democratic state journal
CP F 3 1853
CS N-D 1852
DLC My 27 1853
OHi F 9 1853

Weekly CALIFORNIAN. w Jl 2-Ag 13 1853‖?
Merged with Democratic state journal
DLC Ag 13 1853

La CAPITALE. w 1907+
In Italian
pub 1930+
IU D 8 1917+

Daily morning CHRONICLE. d
CtY Jl 16 1869

Sacramento daily DEMOCRAT. d Mr 13- 1854‖
C Ap 1 1854

Sacramento daily DEMOCRAT. d Ag-N ? 1860‖
C S 15,22,O 1,N 3,5 1860

Sacramento DEMOCRAT. d Ag 3-S 5 1871‖
C complete

DEMOCRATIC standard. d,w F 26 1859-N ? 1860‖
1859-Je 2 1860 as Daily democratic standard
d 1859-Je 2 1860
C S 19 1859;Ap 28-Je 2 1860
DLC My 25 1859

DEMOCRATIC state journal. d F 5 1852-Ap 8 1858‖
Suspended Je 29-Jl ? 1857.
Followed by California statesman
C N 8 1852-N 1854;55-Je 1857
CP Ap 27 1852;Je 13 1854
CS N 8 1852-Je 1857
CSmH D 1 1852 (letter sheet for the steamer); D 20 1856; extra N 12 1852
CSt Mr 12 1857
CU-B F 16,Ag 28,D 23 1852;S 28 1853;Mr 8 1854;Ja 14,Mr 25,Je 20 1856
DLC Ag 26[O 1853-Ag 1854;55-58]
MWA Mr 12,26,My 20,Je 25,Ag 9 1853;Mr 7 1857
NNHi N 29 1855;My 5-15 1856;O 3,5 1857
—Steamer democratic state journal. bw
For foreign circulation
MWA Jl 31,O 14 1854

Weekly DEMOCRATIC state journal. *See* Weekly California statesman

Sacramento ENTERPRISE. w S 8-O 31 1875‖?
CU-B S 19-O 1875

Sacramento EXPOSITOR. d Jl-Ag 1867‖?
CU-B Ag 1 1867

FREE PRESS of Sacramento. w D 3 1910-O 25 1912‖
C complete

Evening HERALD. d Mr 7?-My 22 1875‖?
CU-B Mr 11,16-18,20-Ap 8,10-30,My 3-22 1875

Sacramento HOME news. w Ag 31 1933+
Ag-S 14 1933 as Sacramento news shopper
C 1933+

O IMPARCIAL. w 1915?-32‖
Merged with Jornal português (Oakland)
In Portuguese
CU-B My 8 1919
IU S 1917-Ja 5 1922

INDEPENDENT leader. w 1901-D 15 1932‖
1901-Ja 1922 as Yolo independent (Broderick). United with Tribune-progress to form Tribune-progress and the independent leader
C 1911-My 13 1932

Daily INDEX. d D 23 1850-Mr 17 1851‖
Early issues as Evening index
CSmH D 26 1850
CU-B F 6 1851
DLC F 20,Mr 4,15 1851
MWA F 20,Mr 15 1851
NNHi D 30 1850;Ja 24,29 F 1,4-5,7,10-13,17-21,24-25,Mr 8,10-11 1851
—Steamer index.
DLC F 15 1851

Sacramento JOURNAL. tw,sw Je 6 1868-89‖
Title varies: Semi-weekly Sacramento journal. United with Nord-California herold to form Nord-California herold und Sacramento journal
tw 1868-70?
In German
C Je 11 1868
CU-B Mr 21 1872;Ap 8-My 10,24-31,Je 14-21, 28,Jl 5,12,19,23,Ag 9,16,23,S 6,20 1876

Sacramento JOURNAL. sw 1905-09‖
C [My 26 1906-Jl 17 1909]

Sacramento LEADER. w S 22 1873-76‖?
Title varies: Weekly leader; Stockton leader
1873-N 3 1875 pub at Stockton
C [N 29 1873-Jl 1874]
CU-B Ap 11 1874;Ja 22-Mr 4,18-Ap 22,My 6,27-Jl 15,Ag 5 1876

Daily evening LEADER. d My 1 1874-76‖?
1874-N 3 1875 pub at Stockton
C [1874-Je 1875]
CU-B [1874-75]Ja 3-4,6-F 17,19-29 1876

Sacramento LEADER. 1879 *See* Sunday leader and North Sacramento leader

Sunday LEADER and North Sacramento leader. w O 1879-Ja 1922‖
1879- as Sacramento leader; -Ag 27 1916 Sunday leader. United with Yolo independent (Broderick) to form Independent leader (Sacramento)
C 1906-22
CLM Ja 11 1880
CU-B Ja 25 1880;Je 1-15,29 1919

Sacramento NEWS. d 1859-61‖?
CU-B O 12 1861

Evening NEWS. d Mr 26-My 16 1870‖?
CU-B [Mr-My 16 1870]

Daily evening NEWS. 1890-93 *See* Sunday news

Sunday NEWS. d,w D 22 1890-1921‖
1890-S 12 1893 as Daily evening news
C 1890-S 12 1893;1910-F 27 1921
CLM S 10 1892
CS 1890-S 12 1893

Sacramento daily NEWS. d 1907+
In Japanese
C F 1909-Ap 23 1916
IU D 5 1917-S 19 1925

Sacramento NEWS shopper. *See* Sacramento home news

NORD-CALIFORNIA herold und Sacramento journal. w 1885-1920‖?
1885-89 as Nord-California herold
In German
CU-B Ag 14 1909-Je 1910

CALIFORNIA (*Continued*)

SACRAMENTO—*Continued*

NORTH Sacramento journal. w Jl 1923+
pub 1923-Je 1926
C Ap 11 1924+

NORTH Sacramento leader. w F 11-Ag 25 1916||
United with Sunday leader to form Sunday leader and North Sacramento leader
C complete

PACIFIC banner. w O 16 1852-53||?
CP Ag 25 1853
CU-B D 11 1852;Mr 3 1853

PACIFIC bee. *See* Sacramento bee

PHOENIX. w Ag 30 1857-F 14 1858||
Followed by Ubiquitous
C complete
CSmH complete
CU-B complete
DLC complete

PICTORIAL union. *See under* Sacramento union

Daily Sacramento **PLACER** times. w,tw,d Ap 28 1849-Je 15 1851||
1849-Ap 20 1850 as Placer times; Ap 22-Je 5 1850 Tri-weekly placer times; Je 10 1850-Mr 5? 1851 Daily placer times; Mr 6?-Ap 22 1851 Sacramento daily times. United with Sacramento transcript to form Daily placer times and transcript (San Francisco)
w 1849-Ap 20 1850;tw Ap 22-Je 5 1850
C 1849-Je 7 1850
CP F 5 1852
CSt Jl 18 1850
CU-B Mr 30,Ap 24,Je 29,O 22 1850;F 26,Ap 9 1851
DLC O 20 1849;N 15-16 1850[51]
MWA Mr 17,Ap 28 1851;Ja 4-15,F 1-8,29-Mr 7,21-28 1852
NNHi D 15 1849[My 1850-F]My 15,31 1851
—Steamer ed.
DLC Mr 29 1851
IU F 15 1851
MWA S 15,O 26,N 15,30,D 21 1851
NNHi My 1851

Weekly **PLACER** times. w Je 22 1850-
CSmH Je 29 1850
NNHi N 23 1850

Wednesday **PRESS.** w 1902-07||?
CU-B Ja 24,F 21-Mr 14,Ap 18-Ag 1,15 1906-Je 19 1907

Sacramento daily **RECORD.** d F 9 1867-F 20 1875||
United with Sacramento daily union to form Sacramento record union, later Sacramento daily union
A Jl 1873-Jl 1874
C D 28 1868;D 5 1871-75
CLM D 1873-Ap 13 1874
CMa F 22 1874-75
CU-B Ap 18,Jl 2,N 2,D 10 1867;Ap 15 1868-[69-70]-75
DLC [Ja-Je 1873]
MWA My 30 1870;F 24 1872
N S 11,N 15 1867;F 26-27,My 7,Je 4 1868
NbHi O 17 1860
WHi Ja 1 1873

Sacramento **RECORD-UNION.** *See* Sacramento daily union

Daily **RECORDER.** d Je 27 1911+
pub Ja 28 1912+
C 1911+

Sacramento **REPORTER.** w,d Ja 12 1868-Jl 30 1872||
1868-Ap 9 1870 as State capitol reporter; Ap 12-Jl 30 1872 Weekly state capitol reporter (w)
C complete
CLM Ap 16 1870-My 5 1872
CP Ap 7 1868
CS 1870-My 7 1872
CSto Ap 7 1870-72
CU-B Ja-My 10,Je 2,Ag 24,O 1868-Mr 13,22, Ap 8,13,My 22[S-D 1869]-My 7,Jl 22 1872

SETTLERS and miners tribune. d,w O 30-D ? 1850||
d O 30-N ? 1850
C N 14-28 1850
DLC N 14,21-28 1850
MWA O 30 1850

SOCIALIST. w Ag 18 1899-
CU-B Ag 18-S 23 1899

SPIRIT of the age. *See* Sacramento age

Sacramento **STAR.** d My-Je 1864||?
CU-B Je 8 1864

Sacramento **STAR.** d N 21 1904-F 7 1925||
Merged with Sacramento bee
C D 1904-25
CClP 1904-S,N 21 1911-24
CS [1904-25]

STATE capitol reporter. *See* Sacramento reporter

STATE democrat. d F 22-O 29 1880||?
C F 22-O 1880

Weekly **STATE** journal. *See* Weekly California statesman

STATE sentinel. d Jl 27 1857-58||?
CU-B 1857-Ja 5 1858
OrHi Ag 11 1857

Daily **STATE** tribune. *See* Daily California American

STEAMER democratic state journal. *See under* Democratic state journal

STEAMER index. *See under* Daily index

Sacramento **STEAMER** union. *See under* Sacramento weekly union

Sacramento **SUN.** w Mr 20-Ag 17 1878||?
C Ap-Ag 17 1878

Daily **SUN.** d Mr 20-Ag 18 1878||?
CU-B Mr 20-Ag 18 1878

THEMIS. w F 24 1889-94||
CS 1889-Jl 7 1894
CSmH 1889-F 15 1890
CU-B D 14 1889;F 6,Mr 19-26,Ag 27 1892;Je 10,Ag 12,26 1893
DLC 1889-Je 24 1894

Sacramento daily **TIMES.** 1851. *See* Daily Sacramento placer times

Daily evening **TIMES.** d D 24 1855-Mr 1856||
CSmH 1855-Ja 26,29-F 5 1856

Sacramento daily **TIMES.** d Ag 15 1856-57||?
CU-B 1856-Ja 24 1857

Sacramento weekly **TIMES.** w Ag 23 1856-57||?
CU-B 1856-Ja 24 1857

Sacramento **TRANSCRIPT.** tw,d Ap 1 1850-Je 15 1851||
United with Daily Sacramento placer times to form Daily placer times and transcript (San Francisco)
tw Ap-My 1850
C 1850-Mr 1851
CSmH Ap 3,My 16 1850;Ja 11,Mr 5 1851
CU-B Jl 3,26,D 25 1850
DLC 1850-Je 5 1851
MH 1850-Je 5 1851
MWA O 15-17,N,D 30 1850;Ja-F 15,Mr 5-My 14 1851
MiU-C O 15-17 1850
NNHi [1850-My 1851]
—Steamer Sacramento transcript. sm Ap 26 1850-
MWA Ap 26-Je 29,Ag 30-O 14,N 14,29 1850; Ja 14-Mr 14,My 15-Je 15 1851
NNHi Ap 26,My 29,Je 29,Jl 30 1850

TRAVELERS guide. sw,w 1868-69||?
C My 24 1869
CU-B S 21-O 22 1868

TRIBUNE-Progress and the independent leader. w My 5 1928+
1928-F 19 1931 as Tribune; F 26 1931-D 8 1932 Tribune-progress
pub 1928+
C My 19 1928+

TWICE-A-WEEK. sw 1867-72||?
CU-B Mr 9,27-My 22 1872

UBIQUITOUS. w F 21-Je 20 1858||
Follows Phoenix
C Mr 28 1858
CU-B complete
DLC complete

Sacramento daily **UNION.** d Mr 19 1851+
1851-F 20 1875 as Daily union; F 22 1875-Je 13 1903 Sacramento record-union
C 1851+
C-S [Mr 19 1858-S 17 1859;Mr 19-D 1860]-[Ja-F 20 1875]
CL F-D 1864;O 1878-Mr 5 1879
CLM Ja 22,27 1880[86-92]
CMa 1857-83;Jl 1885-86;88-90;Jl 1892-Je 1893; 94-95
CO Je 1879-1906
CP Ap 8 1854;D 30 1858;O 17 1862
CS Jl 1856+
CSmH Ap 1 1853;D 28-29 1855;S 10 1857;D 25 1858;Ap 29,My 18,Ag 8 1859;S 19 1860-S 18 1861;Jl 1863-67
CSma Ap 8-Jl 18 1862
CSt S 1855-[59-60]-Je 1883;Jl 13 1885;Jl 1886-[88-89]Jl 1892-N 1923
CSto [1861-69]Ja 8-Mr 1895
CU-B N 25 1851;Mr 20,Je 2,N 6-8 1852;Je 2,S 13 1853;Jl 15,N 1854-Ag 22,D 1905-N 1918;Mr 23,Ap 6,13,27-Jl 1 1919;20-23;Ja 10,My 22, 26,N 11 1924;My 15,S 11 1925
CaB Ja 14 1853
DLC O 13 1851;Je 6 1853;Mr 29 1854;59-Je 1863;Ja-Je 1864;Ja-Je 1865;Jl 1867-Je 1869;F 1870-73;Jl 1874-98;My 1899+
InRE F 9 1878
KHi Mr 19 1851[Je 25 1888-Ap 1894]
MH 1859-[61]64-[66]-[69]
MHi 1864
MWA Ap 28 1851;Mr 12,My 4,21,Je 25 1853; Mr 29 1854;Mr 7,Je 19,30-D 1857;D 8 1860;Ja 1 1861;Jl 1862-Ja 1,Je 25,O 5,31,D 1 1863;Ja 2,S 13,O 11,N 3-4,D 22-23 1865;Ja 3-4 1866; Ag 13 1872;Ja 1 1873;Ja 1,F 22 1875-76
N My 9,D 20 1864;F 17,Ap 17,20,Ag 14,O 14 1865;Ja 6,F 5,26,Mr 7,My 16,D 13 1866[67] F 26,My 7,Je 3,9,Ag 12,O 28,N 26 1868;Ja 16,F 4,O 1 1869
NNHi [N 6 1855-F 19 1856]O 2,5,10,12,15 1857;F 12,Ap 9 1858
NjR My 14 1860
OClWHi Ja 8-My 21 1861
OrHi [1859-76]
PP Je 25 1863
TJT Mr 5 1905
WHi Mr 20 1854-S 18 1860;S 18 1861-Mr 18 1870

Sacramento weekly **UNION.** w Ja 10 1852-My 1 1880||
Title varies: Sacramento union; Weekly union
C 1852-F 11 1854;Mr 29 1856-Ja 1868
CLM 1880
CP Jl 1861-Je 1862
CSmH Ja 29 1853;S 28 1861
CStoI Ja-My 1 1880
CU-B Ap 2 1853;Jl 29 1854;66-68;70
DLC Ja 21,Mr 11,25,Ap 8-22,Jl 22,O 28,N 11,D 2 1854;F 17 1855;S 20-27 1856;S 27,O 11(supp) 1862;Ja 5 1867;Ag 3 1872
KHi O 6-N 17 1888
MB 1857-Jl 1860
MHi N 13 1858-64
MWA Mr 26,My 14 1853;O 2 1858;O 26 1861;S 19 1863;O 5 1872;O 11,D 13(supp)27 1873
N Jl 9 1864;F 11 1865
NNHi F 13 1858;Mr 9,30,My 11,S 28 1861;Ja 4-11,S 21 1862
NcD Ag 15 1909
OClWHi Jl 2 1864
OHi S 13,27-O 4,D 20 1873
OrHi [1859-60;62]S 23 1865;Ap 3 1869
—Pictorial union. Ap 1852-Ja 1855||
pub three times a yr: Ja,Ap,Jl
C complete
CSmH Ja 1855
DLC Jl 1852;54
MWA Ja 1855
NN Ja 1853
—Sacramento steamer union. sm Mr 29 1851-58||?
C My 1852-Ag 15 1854
CL Je 5 1856
CSmH O 15 1852;F 28 1855
DLC O 31,D 3,15 1851;Ja 15-Mr 1,Ap 15,My 1,Je 1-15,Ag 14,O 15-31 1852;Mr 31-Ap 15 1853
MWA O 15 1852;Mr 15,My 31,Je 30-Ag 15 1853;F 20 1856
NN Ag 15 1854
NNHi Ap 14,D 20 1855;Ap 5 1858
OHi Ap 21 1856
P-M Mr 1 1854

Sunday **UNION.** w My 19 1889-My 17 1891||
1889-Ja 4 1891 as Sacramento Sunday union
CSmH D 29 1889
CU-B complete
DLC complete

ST. HELENA

St. Helena **NEWS.** d 1888-89||
CU-B Mr 9,13-14,22,30,Ap 11,Je 25-27,Jl 1 1889

St Helena **STAR.** w S 25 1874+
1874-Je 12 1885 pub a mid-week issue as Junior
pub S 25 1934+
C 1874-S 19 1875;F 1879-F 20 1880;Mr 16 1885+
CU-B O 1874-[75]-[77]-[81-Ag 4 1882]F 6-13, 23,Mr 20-27 1883;Ja-Je 25,D 31 1886;1906-Ja 11 1918;Jl 16 1920+
KHi [D 9 1887-N 23 1888]

SALINAS

Salinas **DEMOCRAT.** w N 22 1867-D 26 1896||
1867-89? as Monterey democrat
1867-72 pub in Monterey
C Ja 2 1869;Ap 16 1870-Ag 3 1872;My 24 1890-96
CSa S 23 1876;F 24 1877;D 20 1884;Je 30 1888
CU-B F 15 1868-80;My 13 1882;F 24,My 26,Ag 18 1883;Ja 26 1884;Je 30 1888;Mr 2 1889;Jl 12-19 1890
KHi [S 15 1888-F 16 1889]

Morning **DEMOCRAT.** d 1894-Ag 8 1914||?
CSa 1897-99;1910-14
—w ed. *See* Monterey county democrat

Salinas **DEMOCRAT.** w 1932 *See* Independent

INDEPENDENT. w O 22 1932+
O 22-N 12 1932 as Salinas democrat
CSa [1933]+

Weekly **INDEX.** w Mr 7 1872-Je 30 1932||
Follows Central Californian (Hollister) 1872-82? as Salinas city index.
CSa Je 21,Ag 23,S 20,O 4,N 1 1877;F 28,My 9-16,O 17,N 14-28,D 12-26 1878;Ja 23,F 6-13 1879;O 13,D 1 1892;1915-32
CU-B [1872]-[74]-[76-77]Jl-D 1878;Ag 21 1879-[82]Je 5 1884;Ag 26-O 7,21-N 4,18-D 2,16,30 1886;Ja 27 1887[88-91]Jl 22 1909-Jl 7 1910;My 15 1919
KHi O 11-N 8 1888
NcD Mr 1 1877
TJT Ja 5 1888

Salinas **INDEX-JOURNAL.** d 1896+
1896-Je 30 1928 as Salinas daily index
C Mr 1905+
CSa Ap 4,6 1901;Je 8,D 30 1909;Ja 1, 20 1910;Jl 1932+
NNHi My 11 1901
TJT Mr 14 1897;Ap 14 1898

Salinas weekly **JOURNAL.** w 1867-Ag 21 1918||
C 1897-1918
CU-B Jl 17 1909-Jl 9 1910

Daily **JOURNAL.** d 1889-Je 30 1928||
United with Salinas daily index to form Salinas index-journal
CSa My 4 1897;Ja 11 1908;My 23 1909[13-15]-[17-18]-28
CU-B Ag 1,S 1890

MONTEREY county democrat. w 1897-1914||
CSa 1903-06
—d ed. *See* Morning democrat

MONTEREY county post. *See* Salinas daily post

MONTEREY democrat. *See* Salinas democrat

OWL. d D 19 1894-S 1897||
CSa complete

PHILIPPINES mail. w,ir 1930?+
In English
CSt [1933-34]
CU-P F 1933+

Salinas daily **POST.** sw,tw,d Je 28 1929+
1929-D 15 1933 as Monterey county post
sw 1929-N 11 1932; tw N 11 1932-D 15 1933
C 1929+
CSa 1929+
CU-B O 10 1933-Ja 3 1934

Salinas **RECORDER.** d O ? 1875-My 24 1876||?
CU-B D 21 1875-[Ja-My 1876]

CALIFORNIA (*Continued*)

SALINAS—*Continued*

Salinas RECORDER. w F 23-My 18 1876||?
CU-B Mr 16,Ap 27-My 18 1876

Salinas STANDARD. w D 11 1869-F 10 1872||?
CU-B 1869-F 10 1872

SAN ANDREAS

CALAVERAS advertiser. w Ag 7 1869-81||
CU-B Ag 21 1879-F 1881

CALAVERAS citizen. w My 6 1871-Ag 1926||
United with Calaveras prospect to form Calaveras prospect and citizen
CU-B My 6-13,Ag,S 9,23 1871;72-Ag 14,O 1875-80;F 19,N 26,D 24 1881;Ja 7,F 25-Mr 4,Ap 22-My 6,20 1882;S 12 1885;87-Je 1888; Ja,Mr-S 14,O 19,N-D 21 1889;90[91]

CALAVERAS prospect and citizen. w Ja 1 1881+
1881-S 4 1926 as Calaveras prospect
C 1893+
CStoI Ja 10 1881-My 1883
CU-B Je 10-17,Jl 1 1881;Ja 20 1882;F 16 1883;Mr 3 1888;N 23 1889-[90]Je 4 1892;N 24 1923;Jl 1927-[30-32]+

CALAVERAS times. w My 30-Je 6 1863||?
CU-B Je 6 1863

FOOTHILL democrat. w F 4? 1875-Mr 30 1876||?
CU-B [Ag 1875-Mr 1876]

San Andreas INDEPENDENT. w S 24 1856-S 15 1860||?
Followed by Stockton daily independent, later Stockton morning independent (Stockton)
CStoI 1856-S 15 1860
MWA D 26 1857

MOUNTAIN news. w O 24 1867-68||?
CU-B 1867-Ja 1868

San Andreas REGISTER. w 1863-68||
C Je 13 1868
CU-B 1864-Ag 15 1868

SAN ANSELMO

MARIN herald. w 1911+
pub 1911+
C D 14 1933+

MARIN news-digest. w 1932?-D 14 1933||
Merged with Marin herald

SAN BERNARDINO

San Bernardino ARGUS. d 1873-78||?
Title varies: Morning argus; Daily argus, etc.
CU-B Ag 1,19,22-26,29-S 2,7-9,13-22,26,30,O 4,N 1,21,D 19 1876

San Bernardino ARGUS. w 1873-77||?
O 1-D 24 1876 as Sunday argus
CU-B Ap 3,Jl 10,Ag 19 1873;Ag 17,31-O 12,D 21 1874-[75;Ja 17,Mr 13,Jl 1876-Ap 18 1877]

San Bernardino daily COURIER. d 1886-94||
C 1891-Je 1894
CLM [1888-94]
CU-B [F 26 1889-N 7 1890;Ja 21-Je 5,Ag 1892-O 24,D 23-24 1893;F 4,20-Je 1894]
KHi [Ag 15 1888-D 11 1892]

San Bernardino COURIER. w 1886-94||
CU-B [Mr 1889-90;92-Ag 1893]
KHi [Je 23 1888-F 18 1893]

FREE PRESS. *See* San Bernardino news

GUARDIAN. w,sw Ja 17 1867-S 16 1876||?
w 1867-Jl 22 1876
C D 19 1868
CU-B Jl 1867-[75-S 1876]
MWA Jl 29 1876

San Bernardino morning HOUR. d 1884-85||?
CLM S 15 1885

San Bernardino evening INDEX. *See* San Bernardino evening telegram

Weekly INDEX. w 1878-87||
1878-81 as Valley index. United with San Bernardino times to form Weekly times-index
CU-B Ja 30,F 27[Je-D]1880
KHi [Ag 28 1886-D 14 1892]

INDEX and news. *See* San Bernardino evening telegram

KALEIDOSCOPE. w 1889-95||
CLM Je 13 1891-94;Ja 12,26 1895

San Bernardino NEWS. d 1897-1918||?
1897-1911 as Free press; 1912-14 News and free press. United with Evening index to form Index and news, later San Bernardino evening telegram
CSbe Ja-Mr 1912;13-S 1918
CU-B O 31-D 2,4-7,10-20,23-27,30 1918
MWA My 23 1911

NEWS and free press. *See* San Bernardino news

San Bernardino Saturday REVIEW. w 1889-96||?
CLM [1895-96]

El SOL de San Bernardino. w 1926-31||?
In Spanish
CCIP My 1930-S 1931

San Bernardino daily SUN. d S 1 1894+
CSbe 1905-S 1916;21+
CSbeS Je 1918-31;Jl 1932+
CU-B My 7,9-10,12,14 1919;Ja 20 1923-Ap 1927
OClWHi Je 1 1901;Je 19 1903
WHi Ja 21 1900

Weekly SUN. w 1894-1908||?
CLM S 19-26 1896;Ja-Ap 17 1897

San Bernardino evening TELEGRAM. d Mr 16 1875+
1875-87 as San Bernardino times; 1888-1907? Times-index; 1908?-Mr 31 1921 San Bernardino evening index (Title varies: Index; Index and news)
C F 24 1910+
CLM O 15 1884[85-86;89-1904]
CSbe S 9 1887-F,N 20 1888-Ja 1889;90-99;D 1900;F,Ap,Je-Jl 1901[02]-Je 1903:04-[06]-D 1917;Ap 1921+
CU-B [O 1875-78]F 1879-Ja 1880[My-Je 1888; Ja 11-30,Jl 1890[Ag-N 1909]Ap 24,Jl 17 1919; S 18 1923

San Bernardino TIMES. d *See* San Bernardino evening telegram

San Bernardino TIMES. w *See* Weekly times-index

Weekly TIMES-INDEX. w Mr 1875-1906||?
1875-87 as San Bernardino times
CSbe Jl 1890-99;1905-S 1906
CU-B [S 25-D 1875]-Mr 10,D 25 1877-[79-80] Je 3,Jl 1 1882;Ja 20,F 17 1883;D 13 1884[86-87]
KHi [O 27 1888-Ja 5 1889]
OCHi Mr 18 1892
OClWHi Ja 23 1892

San Bernardino evening TRANSCRIPT. d My 6 1898-D 1902||
Merged with Times-index, later San Bernardino evening telegram
CSbe Mr-D 1902

VALLEY index. *See* Weekly index

SAN BRUNO

San Bruno HERALD. w 1915+
CU-B Ap 30 1921-22;Mr 1923-D 9 1927

SUBURBAN news. w Mr 5 1904-
CU-B Ap 30 1904

SAN BUENAVENTURA. *See* VENTURA

SAN DIEGO

San Diego ADVERTISER. w 1891-92||
CU-B Ja 7,28-F 4 1892

San Diego BEACON. w 1889||?
CLM Ag 10 1889

San Diego daily BEE. d Mr? 1887-D 28 1888||
United with San Diego union to form San Diego union and daily bee, later San Diego union
C My 16-O 1887
CLM D 23 1888
CSd [O 1887-N 1888]
CU-B O 13 1887;N 7,18,20,D 28 1888
KHi Jl 29 1888

San Diego BULLETIN. w Ag 21 1869-Jl 20 1872||
Followed by Weekly world
C Ag 20 1870-72
CSd [1869-72]
CSmH [S 1869-D 2 1871]
CU-B S 1869-[72]
MWA F 12 1870

Daily morning BULLETIN. d F 13-Jl 23 1872||
F-Mr 4? 1872 as San Diego bulletin
C complete
CSd complete
CSmH F-Je 4 1872
CU-B complete
MWA Ap 6-9,11-17,23,25 1872

CALIFORNIAN. d Ap 18? 1885-
CU-B Ap 21 1885

EAST San Diego press. w Mr 1 1915+
pub 1915+
KHi Jl 27 1928

San Diego EXAMINER. w 1912-17||?
CSd [Ag 23 1912-14]

San Diego FREE PRESS. tw 1888||?
CLM F 2,Mr 3 1888

San Diego GUIDE. d 1890||
CLM O 25 1890

San Diego HERALD. w My 29 1851-Ap 7 1860||
CP Mr 13 1858
CSd [1851-Ag 7,D 1852-Ap 7,My 21 1852-Ap 1854;Ap 21 1855-Ja 1860]
CSmH Je 24 1851
CU-B Je 26-Jl,S 4,18 1851;Ja 17-F 3,14-21 1852;D 3 1853
DLC S 13 1851;Ja 24,F 7-21 1852;Ap 17 1858
MWA My 21 1853(extra)
NNHi Je 5-19 1851;S-D 1853;Ja 14,28-F 10,Mr 1854-Mr 3 1855;Ag 9 1856

San Diego HERALD. w 1906?-33||?
CU-B N 9,30,D 21 1922;Ja 18[My 24-N]1923; Mr 13,27,My 15,O 9 1924[25]-[27]-[29]-Ja 5 1933

El HISPANO americano. d,tw 1914+
In Spanish
CU-B Ap 15 1931
CU-P [F 15-Je 1930]

San Diego INDEPENDENT. d Ag 1 1925-Ja 28 1928||
Merged with San Diego union
CSd complete

NEWS. w Ja? 1875-82||
CU-B S 26 1877;Ja 18 1878;Jl 6 1879;Mr 18 1882

NEWS. d Ap 9 1877-82||?
CU-B Ap 10 1877-Mr 27,D 7-10 1878[F 19-N 20 1879]

San Diego NEWS. w 1891-1931||?
CU-B S 19 1907-O 1918;D 11 1919;Ja 8,29,F 19,Mr 11-D 1920

San Diego PROGRESS-drift. w Mr 11- 1897||?
CLM Mr-Ag 1897

Daily SAN DIEGAN. d Ap 27 1885-N 12 1892||
Merged with San Diego daily sun to form San Diegan sun, later San Diego sun
C S 23 1890-92
CLM [1889-92]
CSd [S 16 1886-Ap 1890]
CU-B My 11 1886;Mr 2 1889;S 29,O 1 1890

Weekly SAN DIEGAN. w Ap 1885-N 1892||
CSd [Je 1888-Ag 1891]

SAN DIEGAN-SUN. w Jl 27 1881-1905||?
1881-98? as Weekly sun
C 1893-98
CSd [Ap 23 1887-94]
DLC 1898
KHi D 19 1885
OClWHi D 24 1891;Mr 29 1894

SAN DIEGAN-SUN. d *See* San Diego sun

SAN DIEGO county reporter. w O 14 1889-90||
CLM O 1889-F 1890

SÜD-CALIFORNIA deutsche zeitung. w 1887+
In German
CLM Ap 18 1890
CU-B Mr 1889;Ag 1890;Jl 30 1909-Jl 8,D 2 1910;Ag 13-20,S 17 1920-[Jl 15-N 11 1921]-Jl 13 1923
KHi S 28 1888

San Diego SUN. d Jl 19 1881+
1881-N 14 1892 as San Diego daily sun; N 15? 1892-My 8? 1895 San Diegan sun; My 9 1895-Mr 9 1897 San Diego sun and Daily San Diegan
pub 1881+
C [O 26 1881-N 14 1892]-1908
CLM [1889-1908]Ap 4 1917
CSd [1888-My 1894]
CU-B Jl 30,Ag 7 1886;Mr 18-19,My 4,Je 3 1887;O 17-18,21 1889;My 2,D 24 1891;F 19,Mr 26 1892;S 17 1896;F 13 1911-F,Ap 5 1913-[14-15]-Jl 1918
DLC 1898
KHi N 10 1885
NN Ja 26 1899

Weekly SUN. *See* San Diegan-sun

San Diego evening TRIBUNE. d D 2 1895+
pub 1895+
C Jl 1897-Jl 13 1918
CU-B Ag 21-23,26-31,S 2-16 1901;Je 7,11,Ag 10 1909-Ap 18,My 5-Je 15,22-Ag 18 1910
OClWHi N 1 1904

San Diego UNION. d O 10 1868+
Ja-Ag 1889 as San Diego union and daily bee
pub 1868-88
C [Mr 20 1871-Jl 15 1883]Jl 1894-96;Ap 1904+
CL Ja 2 1928;Ja 1 1929
CLM [1889-1905]Ap 3,6-7 1917
CN 1919+
CSd Mr 20 1871+
CSdT 1889+
CSmH My 26 1869;Ja 20,F 19 1876
CU-B Mr 20 1871-80;D 31 1885[86-Je,Ag 1888-89]-N,D 9,30 1890-N 13,29,D 1891;S 18 1907-Ja 20,D 1918-My 1919;S 7 1927+
DLC Jl 6-11 1873;Jl-D 1898;Ja-F 1919
KHi D 20 1885;Jl 15 1888;Ja 1 1892;S 28 1894[95-1904;14]Ja 1 1922
MWA Ap 5-6,10,12-18,23-24 1872;Jl 6 1876;Ja 1 1920
N F 23 1876
OClWHi O 26,N 5,D 5 1876;Ag 5 1877;Je 5 1881;S 12 1882;Mr 20 1884;D 24 1885
TJT Ja 1 1899
TxGR Ja 1 1920

San Diego UNION. w O 10 1868-My 21 1924||
C [O 17 1868-Ap 11 1878;Je 22 1893-Mr 1895]
CLM D 30 1869[70-72;75-95]
CSd [1868-My 22 1873]
CU-B O 17 1868-Mr 10,S 29-O 5 1871;Ja 11, Mr 14-My 2,N 7,D 19 1872-Ja 16,F 27-Ag,S 25 1873-N,D 30 1875-77;Jl-D 1879;Ap,N 25 1880;D 16 1883;Ja-Je[Ag-D]1886;Ap 21,D 1-8,22 1887;Ja 12-My 10 1888;Jl 19 1894
MWA Mr 31 1870
TJT My 4 1905

San Diego VIDETTE. w,d 1892-
d 1894
CLM [1896-99]
KHi Mr 17 1894

WORLD. d Jl 25 1872-77||?
1872-Ap 1874 as Daily San Diego world
C [1872-Mr 16 1877]
CLM S 28 1873;Ja 8,Mr 22,27 1874;S 1,N 29 1875
CSd [1872-My 1874]
CSt-H [D 7 1872-Ag 1875]Ja 19 1876
CU-B 1872-Ap 7 1877
DLC S 9-10 1873
MWA Je 28,D 9 1876
N F 1 1875

Weekly WORLD. w Jl 27 1872-77||?
Follows San Diego bulletin
C [1872-Ap 1875]
CU-B [Jl-D 1872]-F 2 1877

SAN DIMAS

San Dimas EAGLE. *See* San Dimas press

San Dimas PRESS. w 1904+
1904-S 1911 as San Dimas eagle
pub N 1911+
CLv [1927]-[34]
CU-B My 8,22-29 1919

CALIFORNIA (*Continued*)

SAN FERNANDO

San Fernando EXAMINER. w 1893||
CLM My 20-27,Je 10-Jl 15,Ag 5 1893

San Fernando SUN. sw Ap 6 1904+
Ap 8 1929 is 25th anniversary ed
pub 1904+
CL Ap 8 1929

San Fernando TIMES. w Mr 9 1889-
CU-B Mr 23 1889

SAN FRANCISCO

To 1847 as Yerba Bueno

San Francisco ABEND post. d 1860-1904||?
In German
C N 10 1868
CU-B Ja 30 1861-O 10 1892;95-S,D 1897-Ja, Mr 1898-Je 1900;01-Ja 18 1902;Ja 18-D 2 1903
IHi Ap 17 1865
KHi Jl 12 1888
—w ed *See* California journal und sonntags-post

ALASKA appeal. sm Mr 6 1879-Ap 15 1880||
CU-B Mr-My 6,Je 17 1879-80
DLC Mr 6,Ap 6,22,Jl 30,Ag 15,O 15,N 15-D 1879;F 29, Mr 30,Ap 15 1880
KHi complete

ALASKA herald. Svoboda. sm Mr 1 1868-Mr 20 1876||
In English and Russian
C Mr 1869-Ap 19 1872;Ap 24 1873-76
CU-B 1868-N 1872;73-76
DLC [1868-69;72-75]
MB Jl 9 1873
MH [1868-O 1873]
MHi Jl 9 1873;My 13-Jl 13 1874
MnHi [1868]
NN 1868
NNHi S 1873
NbHi Ja 24,F 12 1874

ALASKA tribune. sm Ap 15 1873-
CaB Ap-Je 1 1873

ALTA California. w,tw,d Ja 4 1849-Je 18 1891||
Follows California star and Californian. Title varies
w Ja-D 1849;tw D 10 1849-Ja 20? 1850
A 1854-67;Ja-Je 1871;72-78
C 1849;Ja 24-D 1852
CL My 1859-My 9 1863;F 26 1870
CLM Ja 10 1860;D 11,25 1861[Ja-S 1862]Ja 19,21-22,26,F 20,25 1863;My 7 1871;F 23 1872; Ja 1 1887;Mr 25,Ap 18,29 1888;F 19-23,Mr 30,Ap 9 1890
CPa [Jl 1872-Ap 13 1886]
CSf 1861-Ag 1890
CSmH [Jl 23 1853-Ja 1874]
CSt [1851]53[54-55;57]59;74[89]
CU 1879-Jl 1889
CtY O 1 1849
DLC Ja 25,Mr 15,26,28,O 1850-Ag,O 1852-54 [Ja,Mr-My,N 1855-Ap,O-N 1856]F 1857-68;F 1869-My 1891
ICHi D 19 1865;My 12 1870;Je 24 1871
IHi Ag 5 1859;Ap 16-21 1865
IU My 1 1850
MH Mr 15 1849[My 18 1850-Ap 1851]Ag 6 1859
MWA My 17,Ag 16 1849;Ja 13,My 18-20,31,Je 4,Jl 9 Ag 23 1854;Ap 10,13 1855;F 28,Ap 5,O 22 1857;F 4 1858;O 1 1864;Je 1865-Jl 20 1867; My 15 1869-Ap 9 1887;Jl 1889-Je 1890;Ja-My 23 1891
MiU-C F 12 1870
MsHi Ag 12 1851
N Jl 21 1856
NN Jl 23 1863
NNHi O 19 1850
OClWHi Ap 10 1858;Jl 10 1869
OrHi F 25 1860;F 8 1862
WA Ag 1 1868
—Steamer ed. sm,ir Ag 2 1849-My 8 1869||
CSmH [1849-69]
DLC [1849-69]
MBAt My 1 1852
MWA [1849-69]
NNHi Mr 16,Je 1,16,Jl 16,S 20,O 20,N 5,D 5,20 1855;Ja 5,F 5,20,Mr 5,Ap 5,21,Ag 20,S 20 1856;O 5 1857;Ja 5,N 5 1858

Weekly AMERICAN flag. w N 27? 1861-65||?
1861-F? 1864 pub at Sonora
C Ja 23 1862
CU-B D 24 1863;F 11 1864
DLC Jl 22 1865
MBAt My 20 1865
MWA Ap 29,My 13,Jl 22,Ag 12 1865
N O 1 1864

Daily AMERICAN flag. d Ap 18? 1864-S 7 1867||
CLM My 13 1865
CP Ag 3 1865
CU-B Ap 23 1864;Ap 25,N 10 1866[Ap 18-S 7 1867]
DLC D 1864-O 10 1866
MWA Jl 10,Ag 1,O 18 1865;Ap 19 1867
N My 8,Jl 20,O 7,19 1864;Ja 16,S 6 1866

AMERICAN independent. w D 18 1915-17||?
CU-B 1915-Ja 1,15-F 19,Mr 5-11,26-Ap 8,30, My 13-Je 4,Jl 2,16-30,O,N 12-D 17 1916;F 4 1917

AMERICAN standard. w S 17 1888-91||?
CLM Ag 10 1889
CU-B Mr 16 1889-Ap 12 1891
KHi S 24-O 8 1888

AMERICAN union. w 1876-77||?
CU-B Ag 30 1877

ANGLO-Spanish merchant. sm Ag 14? 1880-83||?
In Spanish
CU-B S 17 1880

San Francisco daily ARGUS. d N 4- 1857||
CU-B N 5 1857
DLC D 1,3-4 1857

San Francisco ARGUS. w 1863-64||?
CU-B S 10 1864

Daily BALANCE. (Casserley) d D 7 1850-Mr 2 1851||
D 7 1850 as Daily public balance; D 8 1850-Ja 21 1851 Public balance. Followed by Daily true standard
C 1850-F 23 1851
CSmH D 27 1850;Ja 22 1851
MSaE D 14 1850
NNHi D 24 1850-Ja 18,22-F 16,20-27,Mr 1 1851
—Steamer ed.
CSmH F 1 1851
NNHi D 14 1850

BANNER of progress. w Ja 12 1867-O 25 1868||
C O 25 1868
CU-B Jl 6,O 12 1867-68
MWA Ja 25-F 1 1868

BIEN. Bee. w Ap 22 1882+
In Danish and Norwegian
CU-B Ag 13 1909-Ag 5 1910
IaDeL 1882-90[96-1902]

San Francisco BULLETIN. d O 8 1855-Ag 28 1929||
1855-My 18 1895 as Daily evening bulletin; My 20 1895-S 19 1928 Bulletin. United with San Francisco call to form Call-bulletin
A O 23 1877-Je 1879
C 1855-O 7,N 1869-1929
C-S 1856[63-64;Je-D 1865]-[75-76]81-[83]84[Je-D 1885]-88;97-[99-1908;Je 1911-Ap 1912]
CMa O 8 1869-Ap 7 1870;Ap 8 1871-Ap 6,O 8 1872-Ap 7 1873
CO Jl 1878-90;S 1912-Ja 17,N-D 1915;Ja 17 1916-F 1919
CP Jl 19 1856;Ja 28,D 28 1857;F 3,24,Mr 3,Ap 19,23,My 20-21,S 18,O 23 1858;My 5,O 20 1859;Je 9 1860;S 22,29,O 4,8,N 11 1862;Ja 26 1864
CSf 1855-1900;My 1906-29
CSmH [O 9 1855-Ap 5]O 13 1859-Ap 2 1860; Mr 6 1869;Mr 13 1880;Ja 11 1883
CSt 1855-[79-80]82-[87]-89[91-98;1903]-[05]-Mr 1911
CSt-H [1914]
CU-B 1855-Ap 13,Ag 1925-D 9 1927;Ja 2-Ag 6,S 4,17,O 1928-29
CaB 1855-58;Ja 30 1860;O 1 1873
CaOTA Jl 29 1870
CoHi N 2 1869
CtY 1855-O 7 1856
DLC 1855-O 6 1860;Ag 22 1861-Je 1884;Je 1887-88;93-94;98
KHi D 20 1903;Ja 4[Ap-Je 21 1919]
MB [Mr 22-D 13 1879]F 4-N 3 1880
MH O 30 1855-O 7 1856
MWA Ja 5,My 3,20,Je 19,O 8 1856-O 9 1857; Ap 9 1858-O 7 1859;S 10 1860;Ap 10-O 7 1861; Ap 9 1862-Ap 7,Ag 2,N 4 1865;Ap 9-O 6 1866;Ap 8-O 7 1867;Ap 8 1869-O 9 1870;Ap 8 1871-Ap 6 1872;Ap 8 1873-Ap 8 1874;Mr 18 1876;Mr 6,10,18,Ag 27,S 8,O 13,N 25,D 3,23 1885[Ja 12-D 16 1886]Ja 6,Mr 31,Je 1,7,Jl 5, Ag 5-18 1887;My 4 1889;1909-S 1911
MiU Jl-D 1874;Ja-Je 1879
MnU [1918-20]
N Jl 20,O 18 1864;F 8 1866;Mr 6,Je 6,S 26,N 4,13 1867;Ja 15 1869;Je 11 1882
NN O 9 1855-O 8 1885;O 9 1886-Ap 7,O 8 1887-Ap 3 1888;O 11 1890-Ap 6 1891;Ap 8-O 7 1892;Ap 8-O 7 1895;Ap 9-O 7 1896;My 1906-S 1911;F 1912-Jl 13 1918
NNHi My 8 1856;Jl 28,Ag 1-3 1857;N 4 1858; Jl 1 1859;Ap 20(extra)1860;Ja 18,21,23,F 3-4,12,14,Ap 14 1862;Jl 5 1876
NNR Ap 24-Je 1906
NcD F 19 1877
OClWHi Ja 3,6-F 20 1863
OrHi [1860-63;65-66]F 7 1867-Ap 8 1868;Jl-S 1870[79-81]
TJT Ap 30 1898;O 4 1909
TxU 1855-Mr 1857
WHi 1855-91
Wa [1861-63]S 24 1864[Mr 7-Je 12 1865;Mr 9-O 1867;68-69;F 4-Ag 17 1870]Mr 12 1875
—Steamer bulletin. sm D 1855?-
CSmH Je-Jl 5 1858;Ja 5,F 19,O,D 1859;Ja 20,Mr-My 21,N 21 1860;F 21-Ap 1,My 21 1861;N 1 1862;Ja 13 1864
CtY Jl 5 1856
DLC F 20,Mr 20-Jl 20,S 5 1856;F 5,Ap 20-My 5 1857;Mr 20,Ap 20,My 20 1859-O 1 1860;Jl 11,Ag 1 1861
MWA My 5,Je-N 5 1856;Ja-My 20,Jl 20,S 21-N 20 1857;Ja-F 5,Mr 20-Ap 20,S 6,D 6 1858; Ja-Mr 5,Ap 20,My 5,Je-Jl 20,Ag 20,S 5,O-D 5 1859;Ja-F 6,Mr-My 21,Je 20-Jl 11,Ag 11 1860-Ap 11,My-Jl 1 1861;Mr 11,S 11 1862;Ja 10,Mr 1863;Je 17,Jl-D 1865;Ja 10,30,F 10-Jl,S 10,N 30-D 10 1866;F 9,My 30,Je 10,29 1867
MiU-C O 1865
N My 5 1860
NN D 20 1858;S 20 1859
NNHi Ap 5,My 20,Ag 20,S 20 1856;Je 5 1858
OClWHi My 20 1856;O 10 1866
P-M D 3 1863

Weekly BULLETIN. w Mr 1 1856-98||?
C N 14 1868
CL My 1859-My 11 1861
CU-B Ag 22 1857;Ja 4 1860;Jl 1,6 1867;Ag 7,S 4,O 2 1868;Je 29 1881
DLC 1856-F 20 1858;59-O 6 1860;Ja 26,Mr 16-N 2 1867
MH Mr 22 1856-F 20 1858
MWA F 28,Ap 4 1857;Ap 9 1859;Jl 2 1869;Mr 17,28-Ap,My 9 1873;O 6 1880;Ag 24 1887-92
MnHi Je 28 1862
NN D 11 1858
NcD Ja 13 1871
NhD Ag 21,S 4 1879
OClWHi O 28 1870;N 23 1876;Ag 14 1879
OrHi My 24 1856;N 6 1858;Ag 27 1859;Ag 9, O 18 1862[70-71;79-81]
TJT Mr 15,29 1898
WHi 1864-65
Wa My 9 1863

BUSINESS guide and commercial advertiser. w My 31 1861-
CU-B Je 28 1862

BUYERS and sellers' exchange. d O 1869-79||?
CU-B N 3,D 27 1869-Ja 25,27,Mr 15,Ap 20 1870;D 28,30 1879

CALIFORNIA. w 1907+
In Greek
CU-B 1908[09]-Ap 1 1911;Ag 24 1912-Je,S 26 1918

CALIFORNIA China mail and flying dragon. ir Ja 1 1867-76||?
"Issued every China steamer day"
CU-B Ja-D 4 1867
MWA Ja 1 1867

Daily CALIFORNIA chronicle. d N 21 1853-My 12 1858||
C 1853-Je 1856
CP Ja 7,Jl 20,Ag 21 1854;Ja 9,13,27 1855
CSmH [D 14 1853-O 26 1857]
CSt 1853-Je 1857
CU-B 1853-My 11 1858
CaB F 2 1854-Ag 22 1856
CtY N 22 1853-N 20 1856
DLC D 3 1853-Je 1854[Ja]My 26,N 29,D 4-8, 10 1855[Ja-My 1856]
MH Ap 3,6,10,12-14,17,19-22,24-25,28-29,My 1, 3-5,8,10,12,16,19-20 1854
MWA Ja 1,3-4,N 20,D 9,11,13,15 1856;Ja 30, Mr 7,23,31,My 9,N 20 1857;F 20,My 5 1858
NNHi Mr 20,22,25,27-Ap 1,O 17-24 1854;Je 19-22,25-28,S 6-20,N 20-D 25 1855;Ja 7-9,12-18,F 5,20,Ap 5,Ag 6-20,23,26,28,30,S 2-5,O 7-14,16-20 1856;Jl 29,Ag 1 1857
OCHi O 16 1854
P-M Jl 18 1854
—Steamer ed.
C Ag 5,20 1856
CP Mr 16 1854
CSmH [Ja 30 1854-Mr 5 1856]
DLC Ja 15-F,Ap 15,Ag-S,N 16-D 16 1854;Ja 1,F 16,Je 16,Ag 18,S 5-20,N 20,D 5 1855;Ja 5,Je 5 1856
MWA F 27,Ap 15,S 16 1854;Mr 16,31 1855; Ap 20,My 5,S 5,O 20 1857
NN Mr 31,My 1-16,Je 16,Ag 1,O 20,N 5,D 20 1855
NNHi Ja 30,Ag 16 1854;Ap 1,O 5,N 5,D 20 1855;F 5,Ap 5,Je 20 1856

CALIFORNIA chronicle. w 1856-58||?
CU-B D 1856-Mr 6 1858

CALIFORNIA chronik. *See* California demokrat. w

Daily CALIFORNIA courier. d Jl 1 1850-54||?
1856- as Pacific courier. Title varies: California daily courier; California courier
C D 24 1853;Ja 7,28 1854
CP Ja 16 1851
CSmH [Jl-D 6 1850]Ja 6 1854
CU-B 1850-Ja 1,3-Mr 8,11-Ap 16,19-24,O 8, 29 1851
DLC Jl 1,10-11,23,26,Ag 11,N 16 1850-Ap 4,Je 4-Jl 15 1851
MWA D 14 1850;Je 4 1851;D 10,26 1853
NN Jl 1 1851
NNHi Jl 2-14,16-S 12,19,24,O 3,9,12,23,26,31, N 6-8,25,D 9,11 1850;Ja-F 27,Mr 1-25,27-Ap 10,12-15,17-My 3,Je 4-30,Ag 16-30,S 1,29,O 2-8,10-14,N 1-28,D 1851-Ja 1,3,5 1852;supp Jl 1 1850

CALIFORNIA weekly courier. w Jl 1 1850-
DLC Jl 1,Ag 15,S 30,D 1,13 1850
MSaE N 15 1850
NNHi Jl 1 1850;Mr 15 1851
NhD S 23-O 14,N 15,D 13 1850
—Steamer ed.
CSmH O 5 1850
DLC Ja 15,F 15,My 1,Jl 1,15 1851

CALIFORNIA demokrat. w 1852-1918||
Sunday ed of California demokrat. 1852-82? as California chronik; 1883?-86? Sonntagsblatt des California demokrat
CU-B Ap 28-N 3 1866

CALIFORNIA demokrat. d,w S 1853+
d 1863-94; 1909-18
In German
C N 5 1868
CU-B S 12 1863;Ag 24 1865;Ap 15,19,24,D 11 1866-Mr 8,Jl 2 1867;Ag 1 1868;Jl 5,7 1869;Ap 22 1870;Ja 13,Ap 26,My 3-Je 25,Ag 29-S,N 1871-Ja 24,Mr 31,Ap-My 19 1872;Je 9 1874; Je 10-11 1894;N 11 1906-08;Ag 23 1909-My 12 1918;Ag 20 1922+
MWA Ag 21 1876
—w ed *See* California staats-zeitung
—Sunday ed *See* California demokrat. w

CALIFORNIA Sunday dispatch. w Jl 13 1851-52||?
Jl-N 9 1851 as Sunday dispatch
CP Ja 18 1852
CU-B Jl-Ag 10,31,S 21,N 9 1851
DLC Jl-O 5 1851

CALIFORNIA independent. w 1876-80||
CU-B O 18 1879;F 19,Mr 6,My 8 1880

CALIFORNIA weekly journal. w F 3? 1853-
CP Jl 28 1853

CALIFORNIA journal. w Jl 4 1919+
C S 19 1919+

Das CALIFORNIA journal und sonntags-post. w 1870-1904||?
1870-Ja 14 1872 as Sonntags-post
CU-B My 14-21,S 17,O 1[N 1871-72]-[77]-N 17 1878[F-My 19 1879]
—d ed *See* Abend post

CALIFORNIA leader. w Jl 15 1865-66||?
C F 7 1866
CU-B N 4 1865;Ag 26 1866
N Ag 12 1865;Ja 6 1866
NhD Ja 13 1866

CALIFORNIA (*Continued*)

SAN FRANCISCO—*Continued*

CALIFORNIA ledger. w N 12 1864-65||?
CU-B N 12 1864
OrHi Ap 1-8 1865

CALIFORNIA mail. w O 30 1854-
DLC N 27 1854;My 12,Je 9,Jl 7-14 1855
NNHi S 22 1855

CALIFORNIA maverick. w 1884?-86
CU-B F 13 1886

CALIFORNIA pathfinder and post. d S? 1856-
CP N 13 1856

CALIFORNIA police gazette. w Ja 16 1859-73||?
C O 17 1868
CP Mr 30 1861
CSmH Je 25-Jl 15 1859
CU-B S 17 1859;Ag 19-S 16,O-N 4,18-D 2,23 1865;Ja 13-27,Mr 24-Je,Jl 14,28 1866-Ja 5,26, F 9,23-Jl 6,27-Ag 17,31 1867-F 15,29,Mr 14-S 12,26-O 10,31,N 14 1868-F 20,Ap 17-My 8,22-S 11,25 1869
DLC 1859-Ja,S 20-30 1862
OrHi Ap 17 1859
P-M Jl 1859

CALIFORNIA political record. *See* Political record

CALIFORNIA posten. w D 30? 1875-77||?
In Swedish
CU-B Ap 22 1875

CALIFORNIA public balance. (Buckerlew) d Ja 20-My 7 1851||?
CSmH My 7 1851
DLC Ap 22 1851
NNHi Ja 20,22-31,F 2-16,18-21,23-Mr 24,26-My 4,6-7 1851

CALIFORNIA public balance. w Ja 26-F 9 1851||?
NNHi Ja 26-F 9 1851
—Steamer ed sm
DLC F 1 1851

CALIFORNIA register. d My 20-23 1857||
CU-B complete

CALIFORNIA reporter. w Ag 22? 1873-75||?
CU-B Jl 18,Ag 8-15 1874
MWA Jl-D 19 1874;Ja 2,16-F,Mr 20-My 1 1875

CALIFORNIA republican. sw Je 16 1857-
CU-B Je 16 1857

CALIFORNIA republican. d Ap 4 1872-
CU-B Ap-Je 20[Jl 15-Ag]O 8-N 15 1872

CALIFORNIA rural home journal. sm F 15 1865-66||?
CU-B F-S 1,N 1865-Mr 15 1866

CALIFORNIA-Scandinav. sm My? 1873-74||
In Swedish
CU-B Je 1 1874

CALIFORNIA spirit of the times and underwriters' journal. w Jl 25 1857-93||?
1857-Ja 1859 as California spirit of the times; F 1859-S 3 1870 California spirit of the times and fireman's journal
C F 12 1859-Mr 24 1860;75-80;O 1882-93
CLM Ja 1887;Mr 17,N 10 1888
CP Ag 7 1858
CSmH My 14,28 1859;Jl 4 1876(supp)D 25 1879
CSt Jl 4 1876;D 25 1877;D 21 1878;My 21 1887
CU-B N 30 1861;67-[My 1871-74]Mr 13,My 8 1875]Ja-My 20,Je 3,Jl-S 9,23-D 16 1876;77-[79]Ag 13,O 1 1881;O 14 1882;My 10,24-Jl 5,Ag 2 1890[91]-Ap 9,23-My 14 1892
CtY Ja 2,D 25 1875
DLC Ap 24 1858;D 24 1870;F 18 1871;D 11 1874;D 25 1875
MWA Ag 22 1868;D 25 1875
N Mr 2,My 26 1866

CALIFORNIA staats-zeitung. w 1852-1918||?
CSmH F 15 1853
CU-B S 20 1853;Ja 19 1871;Jl 8 1886;Je 23 1910-My 9 1918
KHi Je 28 1888-Mr 21 1889
—d ed *See* California demokrat

CALIFORNIA star and Californian. w Ja 9 1847-D 23 1848||
1847-Je 10 1848 as California star
Followed by Alta California
Suspended from Je 10-N 18 1848.
C 1847-Je 10,N 18-D 1848
CLSM Ap 1 1848(facsimile)
CP Ap 1 1848
CSmH 1847-Je 10 1848
CU-B 1847-Je 10,D 2,23 1848
MHi Ap 1 1848
NN F 6(photostat)27 1847;Ap 1 1848(reprint)

CALIFORNIA state journal. w Je 6 1931+
C 1931+

CALIFORNIAN. w Ag 15 1846-N 11 1848||
First paper in California. United with California star to form California star and Californian
1846-My 6 1847 pub in Monterey
Suspended Je 2-Jl 15 1848
C complete
CLM Mr 15 1848
CLSM Mr 15 1848(facsimile)
CP [1846-Ap 1847]
CSmH complete
CU-B S 12,N 7 1846;F 13,Mr 27,Jl 31,O 27-N 10,D 15 1847-Ja 19,Mr 15,Ap 5,19,My 24-Ag 14,S 9-30,O 14-N 4 1848
CaB D 19 1846;Mr 15 1848
CtY S 17 1846
DLC Ag-S 5,19(supp)-N 14,28-D 19 1846;Ja-F 6,20-Mr 13,27-Ap 17,30-My 6 1847;extras: S 5 1846;Ja 28 My 22-29,Jl 10,31,Ag 14 1847; O 14 1848
GU S 19 1846(photostat)
ICHi Ap 19 1848
IHi Mr 15 1848
InLHi Ag 14 1848
MSaE Ag 15 1846
MWA Ag 15 1846(photostat) Mr 15 1848
NN Ag-My 6 1846;1847(photostat) Mr 15 1848(facsimile)
NNHi Je 5 1847

CALIFORNIAN. w 1864-68||?
CU-B F 8-N 21 1868
IHi Ap 29 1865
N O 1,N 26 1864;Ag 12,S 16,O 21 1865;Ja 13, My 12,O 13 1866

Le CALIFORNIEN. w Ja 17 1850-
In French
NNHi Ja 31 1850

CALL. w 1856-1913||?
C O 22 1868
CU-B N 14,D 12 1900;Ap 3-17,My-Je,Jl 17-O 9,23-N 6,D 4 1901;Ja 8,22-29,D 17-24 1902; Ap 15-My 13,Jl 22 1903;Jl 20 1904
KHi Ja 3,Ag 1 1889
SdHi N 1907-Mr 1908

Morning CALL. *See* Call-bulletin

San Francisco CALL and post. *See* Call-bulletin

CALL-BULLETIN. d D 1 1856+
1856-Mr 4 1895 as Morning call; Mr 5 1895-D 6 1913 San Francisco call; D 9 1913-Ag 28 1929 San Francisco call and post
A Ap 1901-02
C Ja-Je 1877;78-89;Ap 1890-Je,O 1892-Ag 28, S 2 1929+
C-S [1863-66;Jl-D 1867]-[76;79]81-84[Je-D 1885]-87[My-Ag 1888;Ja-F 1889;92-96]-[99; 1901;05-09]
CL 1856-Ag 13 1865;Ag 1895[F-Ag 1898]F 1 1908;D 1912-Ja 1922
CLM Je-N 1857;Jl 24 1885;Je 3 1886[Ja-Mr 8 1900]
CMiC Ap 17,24-My 3 1906
CO Ap-Je 1906;11-F 1919
CP Ap 10 1858;N 19 1859;O 18,29 1863
CPo F 10 1893
CSf D 1877+
CSmH 1856-My 1857;F 25 1863;N 10 1879;Ag 29 1884;Ag 4 1886;S 9 1903;Ap 20 1906
CSt My 16 1863[74-76]-[1903]06[07]-Ag 17 1913[19]
CU-B D 3 1856;O 30 1857;Ja 16 1859;Jl 14 1860; Ag 28,N 26,28,D 1-5,8-9,11-12,15-19,23-24 1863[64]-88-93]Ag 24,S 9-10,O 30 1894[95]-[1903-05]-23
CoU 1905;07-Je 1909
CtY N 7,13 1897
DLC D 19 1858;Ja 25,F 21-23 1872[Je-Ag 1873] 75-Ag 1913
ICM S 2 1893
IHi F 7,12-13 1909
InTI My 1911-Ag 1913;Ap 1914-18
KHi Ag 2-9,1886;D 19 1897;O 11 1899;S 4-14 1904[F 22-Ag 7 1919]
MB [Je 1891-92]Jl 1899-S 1913
MWA Mr 3 1864;F 2 1865;F 20,Je 4,S 3 1876; F 11,O 11 1877;S 26 1881;D 19 1897;Ja 23,25 1898
MiU 1903-[06]-[08]
NNR Ap 26-Je 1906
NcD Ja 13 1908
NvR [1932]+
OClWHi My,Je 1,3,10,28,Ag 17,O 29,N 14 1872;Ja 1 1873; Ap 12, 1874;Mr 28,Ag 15 1875; Ap 3,My 17-19,28,Ag 26 1879;N 23 1880;Ap 11 1886
OrHi Ap 12 1887;Je 22-26, Jl 22,Ag 6,S 16 1888;Ap 30 1889
TJT F 22 1883;Ap 13,17,27 1898;Jl 22,27,Ag 26,S 23, 30,O 7,14,N 18,25,D 2,9,16,23,25,27,30 1900;Mr 2,5,O 5,7 1902;Ap 16 1905;S 5 1919
TxGR Ap 27 1885
Wa My 20 1906

CALL-CHRONICLE-EXAMINER. Ap 19 1906||
A joint ed issued the day after the earthquake
C complete
CLM complete
CSmH complete
DLC complete
MWA complete
MnU complete
NcD complete

CALUMET. bw,w 1867-
bw 1867-Ap 1869?
C O 14 1868
CP Je 24 1868
CU-B Ja 6,Ap 15-D 23 1868;Ja 20,F 3,17,Ap 14-28 1869;S 17 1870

CENTRO America. w F 20 1921-
CU-B F 20-26,Mr 12-Ap 16,30-Ag 13,25 1921

CHANGE. w Mr 12 1887-
CU-B Mr 12 1887

San Francisco CHINA news. 1874-75||?
In Chinese
CLM My 1 1875

CHINESE nationalist daily. *See* Kuo min yat po

CHINESE republic journal. d 1914?-26||?
In Chinese
CU-B My 17 1920

CHINESE times. d 1924+
In Chinese
DLC current year only
NNC S 1932+

CHINESE world. d 1891+
In Chinese
CSt S 30 1934+
DLC current year only
NNC S 1932+

Weekly CHRONICLE. w D 9 1854-57||?
CL My 1855-My 16 1857
MWA D 9 1854;F 28 1856
NNHi My 12,O 6 1855
Tx Ap 6 1857

San Francisco CHRONICLE. d Ja 16 1865+
1865-Ag 30 1868 as Daily dramatic chronicle
C Ap 19 1870-Ja 15,D 7 1871-Mr 1872;Jl 27 1877-Ap 13,Jl 1887+
C-S [Jl-D 1866]-90[Ap-D 1891]-[Ja-Ag 1913]
CL S 16 1889-N 1890;F-Je,Ag 1902-Mr,My, Jl 1903-O,D 1910-Ja,Mr 1912+
CLM S 29 1881[83-1903]Ap 15-My 14 1906; Ap 22 1934
CMiC Ap 23-My 1906;S 1924+
CO Jl 1883+
CP Jl 23 1868[82;93]
CPa current two years only
CPo [Ap]My 17-Je 1906;Ja-Jl 1915;16-S 1919; 20-Jl 1928
CSf 1865+
CSmH O 20-21 1869;Ja 26 1876;Ag 28 1884;O 23 1899;Ap 22 1906
CSt [1874-92]-[94]-[98]-[1901-02]-[05]+
CU-B Je 29 1866;67-[73-74]-[83-84]-[93]-Je 11,30,O 13,20,27 1895;F 16[Mr-D 1896]+
CaB 1931+
CoU 1901;05;07-Je 1910
CtY [1934]
DLC Je 26,29-30,Jl 16,20 1873;Jl 16 1874-Je 1875;D 3 1876;Mr 7 1877-Je 1879;81-82;84-Jl,S 1926-F,Ap 1927+
FU Ja 3 1921
ICM Mr 6,Jl 14 1889;Mr 1,Ag 17,S 2 1893
IHi Je 28-Jl 4 1920
IU Jl 26,Ag 2 1896
KHi Ag 9 1885;Ag 2,6 1886[My 1887-99]S 4-10 1904;Ag 3 1923;Mr 16 1927
MB S 1913+
MH 1869-70[1907]-[11-12]-23
MWA Je 7,14 1870;My 20 1875;Ap 3,My 31,S 18 1876;S 5 1878;Ap 24 1880[Ap 10 1885-87;Ag 10-D 11 1888]Ja 1[O 11-D 30 1889]F 24 1897; Jl 1899-Je,Jl 21,Ag 23,S 22,O 13,D 3,8,16 1902[Mr 1903-05;Ap 14-27]My 1906-Mr,My 1912-13;Ja 16 1915;1916-Je 1918;20-Mr 1926
MiU 1926+
MnU [1890]-1912[20]
N My 20 1869
NN Ja 15-31 1897;Mr 1898;Ap 16-17,20-23 1908;Jl 16 1909-Ag 16,O 25 1910-Ag 1911;Mr 1912+
NNR Ap 23-Je 1906
NhD Ap 22,My 1,4 1906
NvR [1932]+
OC Ap 1-18 1906
OClWHi Ap 19 1879;S 27 1881;F 12,Mr 4 1884; Ag 2-3,10 1886;Je 7 1891;Ja 1,16,My 24 1892; Ap 23 1893;D 30 1894;Jl 5-7,9-11 1897
OrCA [1928+]
OrHi D 3 1876;Mr 29 1879;Ap 24 1880;Jl 3,S 20-25 1881;Jl 1 1882;My 14-15 1884;Jl 23,Ag 9 1885;Ag 8 1886
P Jl 1890-Je 1917
PP Ap 22 1906;Je 2 1927;34+
TJT Je 19 1898;Jl 21 1901;Mr 5 1905
TxU Je 1916-F 8 1919
VU Jl 4-29,Ag 19 1934
WHi Ja 1,D 29 1889+
WaPS [1885]Ja 13 1890;Ja 2 1917;Ja 21 1923; Je 22-Ag 17 1924;D 10 1928;Ap 7 1929;Ap 23 1932
WaS 1907+

San Francisco weekly CHRONICLE. w Ja 1 1874+
1913+ as Sunday ed of Chronicle
CL S 16 1889-N 1901;F-Je,Ag 1902-Ja,Mr,My, Jl 1903-O,D 1910-Ja,Mr 1912-Je 1931
CU-B O 25-D 13 1900;Ja-Je,Ag 29 1901
KHi Ap 30 1888;F 14 1895
MH Mr 16 1893-Mr 15 1894
MWA N 29 1874;S 2 1875;Ap 2,S 28 1876;Mr 1,N 28 1877;Ag 9 1885;D 31 1893
MnHi Jl 3 1879
Tx 1912-15

CHRONOS: the Greek times. w 1914-18||
CU-B S 18 1915-My 12 1918

CHUNG sai yat po. d F 16 1900+
Jl 2 1906-Mr 28 1908 pub at Oakland
In Chinese
CSmH F 16,23,Je 22 1900
CU-B 1900-F 24,Mr 14 1903-Jl 1905;Ja 30-Ap 17,Jl 1906-D 21 1923;Ja 3 1924+
ICHi My 15 1902
IU D 5 1917+
MiG My 27 1910
NNC S 1932+
Tx N 23 1901

San Francisco daily CITIZEN. d My 25-O 10 1855||
C Je 27,Jl 2,10(supp)1855
CP O 2 1855

CITY argus. w D 14 1878-1906||?
CU-B F 22 1879;Ap 24,Je 5 1880;Jl 2 1881
NN 1878-79

CITY front gazette. w 1883-88||?
CLM Jl 2 1887
KHi Jl 12-D 22 1888

Sunday morning CLARION. w Mr 9- 1851||?
CP Ap 27 1851

La COLONIA svizzera. sw 1879+
In Swiss-Italian
CU-B O 10 1933+
IU D 1917+

San Francisco COMMERCIAL advertiser. d My 31 1852-S 27 1854||
1852-F 1853 as San Francisco daily whig; Mr-S 1853 San Francisco daily whig and commercial advertiser
C Je-D 1852;F 11,Mr 29,Je 11[D 23 1853-Mr 27]Je 15 1854
CP Je 11,Jl 28-29,D 8-9 1853
CSmH Jl 13,D 29 1853

CALIFORNIA (*Continued*)

SAN FRANCISCO—*Continued*

San Francisco COMMERCIAL advertiser. d 1852-54—*Continued*
CU-B Mr-Je 1853
DLC My 31,O 17,D 1-15 1852[Ag 1853-Ja 1854]
NNHi D 7-10,16-24,27-31 1852;Mr 16-19,22-31,Jl 1 1853

COMMERCIAL advertiser. w
CU-B F 23 1867

COMMERCIAL advertiser. w D 4 1868-F 6 1869||?
CU-B F 6 1869

COMMERCIAL advocate. w N 17 1876-D 21 1878||?
CU-B D 1 1876[Je 1877-D 21 1878]

COMMERCIAL herald and market review. ir,w Jl 10 1867-1911||?
1867-My 28 1869 pub on every steamer day
C Ja 11 1868-Ja 14 1869;70-Ja 14 1875
CLM Ja 28 1892
CSmH Ja 13 1876
CSt Ja 13 1881
CU-B 1867-71;Ja 12,Ap 12-My 3 1872[74]Jl 13 1876-77;Ja 17,Jl 1878-[80-Mr]Jl 7-14 1881; Ja 26 1882
CtY My 22 1868
DLC N 9 1867;Ja 18-F,Jl 1868-88
MHi F 18,29,My 14 1868;Ja 14 1869;Ja 14 1875;Ja 13 1876;Je 6-Jl 11 1878;Ja 15 1880;Ja 13 1881;Ja 26 1882
MWA Ja 14 1869;Ja 13 1871;Ja 17 1873;Ja 13 1876
NNHi O 30 1867-My 18 1869
WHi Ja 26 1882
See also San Francisco market review

Daily COMMERCIAL news. d Jl 1 1875+
1875-1906 as Daily commercial news and shipping list
CSf 1878-79
CU-B N 19,D 7-11,13-14,16-22 1875;N 9 1878; Mr 6,Ap 13 1880;Je 27 1882;Je 19 1914+
DA 1903+
DLC 1884-88;90+
MWA F 19 1876

COMMERCIAL record. tw 1865-69||?
C O 14 1868
CP Jl 1868
CU-B F 18,Jl 5 1867;Ja 31-Mr 4,18-My 4,Je 8-10,17-24,29-Jl 20,Ag 5,S 7 1868;Ja 25,29,F 22,26,Mr 8,My 5-12,Je 30-Jl 26 1869

COMMERCIAL record. w Mr 4 1886-98||?
CLM Mr 27 1888
CPo My 1 1892
CSmH D 6 1887
CU-B Ap 15,O 14-22,N 11-25,D 9 1886;Ap 14,Je 23 1887;Ja 26,My 1,D 13 1888;Ja 10,N 21 1889;Je 19,S 4 1890;Jl 30,O 1 1891;F 4 1892
KHi S 20 1887-Mr 1889

CONSTITUTION. d Ag 13? 1860-
MWA S 19 1860

La CORRESPONDENCIA. w 1885-87||?
In Spanish
CLM F 5-19,Mr 5,26 1887

Il CORRIERE del popolo. sw,w 1911+
sw 1911-Mr 1925
In Italian
IU D 1917+
NNRa [1928-29]

Le COURRIER de San Francisco. *See* Le Courrier du Pacifique

Le COURRIER du Pacifique. d 1852+
1852-85? Le Courrier de San Francisco; 1886?-D 31 1926 Le Franco-Californien
In French
C N 13-14 1868
CU-B F 7,Jl 2-3,10,Ap 23,Jl 1868-Ap 24 1872: Jl 10 1874;D 7 1875;Je 15 1876;N 26 1882; 1927+
IU D 7 1917+
KHi Ja 20 1889

Daily CRITIC. d S 23 1867-68||?
C-S N 25 1867-My 22 1868
CU-B 1867;Ap-My 23 1868

La CRONICA. tw Ag 1854-O 1855||
In Spanish
CP Je 1 1855
CSmH D 15 1854;F 28,Ap 11 1855

La CRONICA. 1914-17 *See* Hispano America

CRONICA italiana. *See note under* Le Phare

La CRONISTA. w Ap 2 1884-My 9 1885||
In Spanish
CU-B [1884-85]

DEMOCRATIC guard. w My 24 1894-96||?
CU-B Je 28 1894

DEMOCRATIC press. d 1863-Je 16 1864||?
CU-B Ja 18,Je 16 1864

Weekly DEMOCRATIC press. w
Or F 6 1864-F 4 1865

Der DEUTSCHE republikaner. *See note under* Star of empire

Evening DISPATCH. 1865. *See* Flag's evening dispatch

Daily DISPATCH. 1867-68. *See* Daily independent dispatch

Weekly DISPATCH and vanguard. w 1866?-68||?
C N 14 1868
CU-B Mr 28,Je 20,N 28-D 5 1868

EL DORADO. w F 27 1869-
C Ap 10 1869
CU-B [F-My 22 1869]

Daily DRAMATIC chronicle. *See* San Francisco chronicle

EAGLE of freedom. w 1856-
CP O 25 1856

San Francisco ECHO. d 1876-77||?
CU-B D 29 1877

L'ECHO de l'ouest. d 1908-D 30 1926||
United with Le Franco-Californien to form Le Courrier du Pacifique
In French
CU-B Jl 24-N 1914;Je 1915-26
IU S 1917-26

L'ECHO du Pacifique. tw,d Je 1 1852-60||?
Continues the French columns in Daily evening picayune. Followed by El Eco del Pacifico. 1852-55, p 4 as El Eco del Pacifico
In French and Spanish
tw 1852-55
C Je 10,12 1853;F 22 1854;Ap 29 1856
CSmH Ag 7 1852;Mr 23 1864
CU-B My 19 1854;Jl 5,21 1856;S 29 1860
CaB Ja 20 1858
DLC Jl 5 1856
NNHi O 1 1854

L'ECO de la razza latina. sw 1877-78||?
In Italian
CU-B Ja 9 1878

EL ECO del Pacifico. d Ja 1 1856-
1852-55 as page 4 of L'Echo du Pacifique
In Spanish
CSmH Ap 9 1857

L'ECO della patria. sw 1859-72||?
Merged with La Voce del popolo
In Italian
CU-B Jl 3 1867;F 8 1868;Ap 13,Jl 23 1870

EL DORADO republican. w
P-M F 4 1854

ELEVATOR. w N 6 1864-
CU-B Ja 16 1865

ELEVATOR. w Ap 6 1865-
C O 30 1868
CU-B Jl 5,Ag 16 1867-[69-70]D 29 1871[Ap 27-D 1872]-74;D 3 1881;My 2 1885;S 11 1886;O 11-18 1890;Je 18 1892;Je 11 1898
KHi S 8 1888
MWA My 4 1865;Ja 11,Je 21 1867
N O 13 1865

L'ELVEZIA. w 1879-96||?
In Italian
KHi [S 8 1888-Mr 1889]

San Francisco ENTERPRISE. w 1886-88||
KHi Jl 21-Ag 4 1888

San Francisco ENTERPRISE. w My 9 1892-
CU-B My 16 1892

ENTERPRISE and co-operation. w 1871-72||?
CU-B Mr 30,Je 29,S 23 1872

San Francisco EXAMINER. d Ja 16 1865+
Title varies: Daily examiner; Examiner; Evening examiner
1865-O 3? 1880 is an evening paper
A Jl 1879-Je 1894
C Je 12 1865-Je 1866;Jl 13 1867-Je 18 1868; Jl 1870+
C-S [My-Jl 1867;My-Jl 1873;F 1874;Ap 1875] 81-84[Je-D 1885]-88;97-[99-1908]
CL Mr 23,Jl,Ag 23,S 4,29,O 18,N 19,26,D 10, 25 1891;Ja-F,Mr 3-10 1892
CLM [1872-98]
CMiC Ap 20-My 6 1906
CO Ap-Je 1906;10+
CPa current 5 years only
CPo [1882;91-93]
CSmH Ja 28,Ag 22 1894
CSt [1867-68]S 1876+
CSt-H [1914-15]
CU-B Ag 13-O,N 4-9,14-23,27 1867-Mr 2,7,27-Ap 8,15-My 23,Je 25,D 21 1872[Ja-Je,S 1877-N 2 1878]Ja 6,Mr 1879-Je 1881;82;Ja-Je,Ag-S,N-D 1886;My 1-4,8,11-Jl 24,30 1887-[88]+
CtY Ap 28 1889
DLC N 29 1878+
ICM Ja 7 1889;Ja 20 1893
InU 1897-S 1898;O 1931+
KHi [Jl 1888-Jl 13 1889;D 25 1894-O 12 1899]Ja 12,Ag 10 1919;O 14,N 15 1923;N 25 1925
MWA O 20 1889;Jl 25 1912-F,Mr 2,My 2-N 1921
MoHi Je 27 1885;My 24,Je 8 1892
NNR Ap 20-Je 1906
NcD Ja 14 1882
Nv Je-Jl 1894
NvR [1932]+
OClWHi Je 4 1893;D 25 1894;Jl 8-11 1897;Ag 25 1899
OHi 1912-Ja,Jl 1915-N 1928;F-S 1929;Jl-O 1930
P S 4 1887-S 1888
WaPS S 4 1912;Ja 3 1919[30]

Weekly EXAMINER. w 1865-1914||?
CSmH Mr 24 1892
CU-B Jl 6 1867;N 19 1874
DLC My 11,Jl 20 1876
KHi [1889-Ag 18 1892]
MWA Je 4 1893
NNHi Ja 16 1873
OClWHi Mr 24 1892
TxU [F-N 22 1911]
Wa Ap 20 1906
WaPS [1892-98]Mr 12 1903
—Oakland ed *See* Times (Oakland)

FAIR play. w Ja 7 1893-
KHi F 18,N 11 1893

FITZGERALD'S home newspapers and educational journal. w Mr 17 1877-My 11 1878||
CSt Ap 28,My 12 1877
CU-B Mr 17,Ap 14-S 15,29-D 22 1877;Ja-F 2,16-Ap 20,My 4-11 1878

FLAG'S evening dispatch. d Ap 10 1865-
C Ap 10,16 1865
CP Ap 12 1865
DLC Ap 13-14 1865

Le FRANCO-Californien. *See* Le Courrier du Pacifique

FREE PRESS. w My 2-O 3 1868||
My 2-30 1868 as Free press and Alaska herald
CU-B complete
DLC My 2-16 1868
NNHi complete

Weekly GAZETTE. w O 6 1860-
MWA O 27 1860

San Francisco GAZETTE. d 1864-71||?
CU-B Ag 26,S 2 1871

Daily GAZETTE and telegram. d O 1858-60||?
1858-F 1859 as Lyceum gazette; Mr 1859-Je 1860 Gazette and telegram
CP N 28 1860
CU-B Je 20,Jl 20 1860

Daily GLOBE. d Mr 13 1856-Ag 14 1858||
Some numbers as Morning globe. Followed by Daily national
C Ag 14,O 4 1856
CP Ap 27 1857
CU-B O 2 1856;S 9 1857
DLC complete
MH Jl 4 1857-58
MWA S 13-N 19 1856;Mr 7,Ap 20,My 5,Je 20,O 7-11,N 18 1857;F 5-Ag 1858
NNHi Mr 18,20,Ap 5 1856;Ag 1 1857
NcD Jl 4 1858
—Steamer Globe.
DLC Ja 4 1857

Weekly GLOBE. w Jl 11 1857-
DLC O 10,N 7 1857;Ja 2 1858

GLOBE. w
CU-B My 7,16,Jl 12,S 17 1880;Jl 27 1883

San Francisco GLOBE. d Jl 21 1908-Je 30 1909||
Merged with Evening post
C 1909
CSf complete
CU-B complete

GOLDEN Gate gazette. w S 28 1881-
CU-B O 26 1881

GOLDEN Gate gazette. w S 27 1890-Ja 3 1891||
CU-B S-D 6,20 1890-91

GOLDEN Hill news. ? Ap? 1854-
In Chinese
CLM Ap? 1854

GOLDEN Hills' news. w Ap 28 1851-
In Chinese and English
CU-B Je 10 1904
DLC Jl 8 1851

San Francisco GRAPHIC. d,w S 20 1880-81||
d 1880-Ja 12 1881
CU-B S-O,N 4-5,8-24,26-30,D 1880;Ja 3-12,22-29,F 5 1881

GREEK times. *See* Chronos

GUIDE. tw 1863-80||?
CLM Je 2 1871
CP My 27 1868
CU-B D 7 1865[68-72]

GUIDE.
CU-B Jl 1,D 20 1900
KHi Ag 18 1888

HAYES valley advertiser. w 1878-99||?
CU-B Jl 26 1879
KHi O 20 1888

San Francisco daily HERALD. 1850-62 *See* Daily herald and mirror

San Francisco weekly HERALD. w Mr 20 1852-
C Ag 9 1860
CSmH Ag 7 1852
DLC Ap 21 1853;Je 22 1855;Mr 14 1856;Ap 12-N 2 1860;F-Je 20 1862
MWA Mr 20 1852;Ap 19,My 3,17,Je 14,28,Ag 16,S 27,N 9-16,30-D 7,21-28 1860;Ja 4,18,F 8,Mr 29,Ap 12,My 10-17,31-Je 7,28 1861
NN Ap 19 1860
NNHi Mr 20,Ap 3 1852;Ag 11 1854

San Francisco daily HERALD. d Ja 19 1869-
C Ja-O 6 1869
CU-B Ja-O 7 1869
DLC Ja-Je,Ag 6-O 1869

San Francisco morning HERALD. d Ap 24 1879-
CU-B Ap 25,My 2-3,18 1879

Daily HERALD and mirror. d Je 1 1850-Jl 14 1863||
1850-Ja 28 1862 as San Francisco daily herald
C N 22 1850;Je 3 1851;52-My 1862
CP S 15,O 8 1851;O 5 1852;Ap 13 1854;S 1 1855
CSd [S 21 1851-Mr 1852]
CSmH [Ag 9 1850-Ja 19 1859]
CSt N 1853-[55]56
CU-B Jl 2,19,Ag 16,S 4,D 13-14,18-31 1850[51]-S 1852;Ap 1853-Ja 1862;Ja 14,My 15 1863
CaB Je 30 1851-Je 1856
CtY S 21 1851-52;N 17 1853-Je 1854
DLC S 17 1850[Ap-Je 7]O 1851-Je 1862
ICHi Ja-O 21 1853
MH [1851]-[Jl 1852-54]
MWA O 6 1851-Jl 10,O 1852-Mr,My 16(supp) 17 1854-My 18 1856;Ap 5,Jl 17,S 17 1857;Jl 4,Ag 5 1858[59]Ja 20,F 5-6,20,Mr 5,20,Ap 5,20,Je 30 1860-Je 1861
MnHi N 28 1853
NN D 21 1850;Jl 28,Ag 2 1851[Ja-My 1852] Ja 19,F 22 1853;Ap 15,S 10,N 25 1855;O 2 1857
NNHi Je 4, 1850-Ja,D 5 1851;Ja 29,Mr 20, 26,Ap 5,D 7 1852;Je 27,S 1 1853;Ja 25,27-28, 30-F 1,16-23,25-26,Mr 10-16,My 1,Je 1,S 20, N 20,23,D 20 1855;Ja 5,Ap 5,My 19,Je 20,Ag 5,S 5 1856;N 5 1857

CALIFORNIA (*Continued*)

SAN FRANCISCO—*Continued*

Daily HERALD and mirror—*Continued*
NcD Ja 1-16,18-19,22-F 13,15-18,21-25,27-Mr 3, 5,7-9,11-13,15-31,Ag 16-O 1853;Mr 15-16,Je 1 1854;Ag 21,31,S 11,21,O 1,11,20,27-D 21 1860; Ap 30 1861
NhD D 15 1852
OClWHi F 7 1851
OrHi My 19 1854;O 16 1857;Mr 11 1859;N 12 1860
PPL O 1 1850;Mr 2 1852
—**Steamer ed.** sm F 1 1851-Ap 4 1860||?
CSmH [Ag 1850-Je 1855]
DLC My 15,O 13 1851-F 18 1852;F 1,My 7,Je 24-Jl 1,N-D 1853;F 16-Je,Jl 16 1854;Ja 16 1855;Ja 20-Je 6,Jl-S 5,O 1859-Ja,F 20-Ap 4 1860
KHi F 14 1851
MWA My 28 1852;Je 8 1853;Ap 5,D 20 1856; F-Je 1857;D 5 1858;Ja-F 5,Mr 5,Ap 5,My,Jl, S-N 5,D 5 1859;Ja-F 6,Mr 1860
NN N 20 1858;Ap 4 1860
NNHi My,Ag 15,S 15,O 15-N 1 1851;F-Mr 15,My 3,Je 1 1852;F 15-Mr 16,Ap 9-My 7,Je 8,N 16 1853;D 9 1854;Ja 5,Ap 5,My 19,Je 20, Ag 5,S 5 1856;N 5 1858

HERALD of trade and finance. w 1881-99||?
CU-B S 5-12 1889;Jl 8,N 25 1892

HISPANO America. w,sw Ap 18 1914+
1914-Ap 8 1917 as La Cronica
sw Jl 27 1918-Mr 5? 1919
In Spanish
CU-B Ap 25 1914-F 10 1934
TxGR [Ag 13 1932-F 10 1934]

ILLUSTRATED California news. sm S 1-D 1 1850||
CSmH complete
NNHi S 1-15 1850

ILLUSTRATED daily herald. (Oakland ed) d D 10 1923-My 5 1926||
CBe complete
CO 1923-S 15 1924
CSf complete
CU-B My 3 1924

ILLUSTRATED San Francisco news. d,w Jl 29-O 9 1869||?
d Jl-Ag 4 1869
C Jl 29 1869
CU-B Jl 29,31,Ag 2,4,14-S 4,18-O 9 1869

El IMPARCIAL. w 1926+
In Spanish
CU-B N 20 1931;D 9 1932;D 1934+

L'IMPARTIAL Californien. w 1897-1905||?
In French
CU-B Jl 8 1899

L'INDEPENDENT. w
In French
CU-B My 29 1865

INDEPENDENT defender. w Ag 23-N 15 1873||?
CU-B N 15 1873

Daily INDEPENDENT dispatch. d F 8 1867-N 5 1868||
1867-F 7 1868 as Daily dispatch
C O 20 1868
CU-B complete

San Francisco INDEX. w Jl 31-Ag 28 1879||?
CU-B Ag 28 1879

INDUSTRIAL reformer. w Ap 15-Jl 8 1871||?
CU-B My 13,Je 17,Jl 1-8 1871

INGLESIDE. w 1883-85||
CU-B Je 28 1884;Mr 28,Je 6,D 26 1885

IRISH news. sm,w 1860-76||?
C N 14 1868
CU-B O 14 1865;Ag 17,31,S 14,O 12,26,N 9 1867;Ja 18-Jl 11,Ag 8-N 1868;F 27-My 8 1869;Mr 1872

IRISH people. w 1865-
C Ja 27 1866

L'ITALIA. d 1886+
In Italian
CU-B Ap 28,My 30,Ag 3-4,S 27 1906;Ap 18, Jl 4,S 11 1907;Ap 18,Je 3 1908-Ja 2 1919;Je 30 1920+
KHi Ja 28-F 10 1889

JAPANESE American news. d 1899+
In Japanese
C 1919-25
IU S 2 1917+

JEWISH progress. w 1875-1900||?
CU-B D 3,12,26 1880;Je 3-10 1881;Ag 11 1882;My 2,D 5 1884;Jl 30 1886;Ag 15 1890
KHi [Jl 27 1888-F 15 1889]

JORNAL de noticias. *See under* Oakland

San Francisco evening JOURNAL. d My 25 1852-Mr 27? 1856||
1852-F 28 1853 as Daily evening journal
C D 6, 22 1852; F 11,D 31 1853;Ja 14,F 10,Mr 9 1854
CP S 24 1852;F 10 1854
CSmH [My 31 1852-Mr 1854]
CU-B S 1 1852;Ja 3,Jl 6 1853;N 27 1855;My 27 1856
CaB 1852-Je 1854
DLC [1852-My 13 1854]
MWA F 22,Ag 15 1853
NN N 18 1852;Ag 11 1853
NNHi N 15 1852;Mr 27,29 1855;Mr 7-8,11-15, 17-19 1856

San Francisco weekly JOURNAL. w 1852?-Mr 15 1856||?
CSmH N 17 1855
MWA Ja 5 1856
NNHi Je 1,S 29-O 20,N 17-D 1 1855;Mr 8-15 1856
—**Steamer journal.**
NNHi O 5 1855

San Francisco JOURNAL. d F 20 1855-O? 1857||
In German
DLC F-Ag 19 1855

Evening JOURNAL. d 1860-64||?
CP Ap 11 1862
CSmH Ag 9 1862
CU-B Je 11 1861;Ap 30,D 15 1863;Mr 5,Ap 7 1864

San Francisco JOURNAL. d 1867?-71||?
CU-B Ag 31 1871

San Francisco JOURNAL and daily journal of commerce. d Ja 23 1872-Je 21 1924||
1872-S 21? 1920 as Daily journal of commerce. Merged with San Francisco bulletin
C Jl 2 1906-Ja 12 1909;12-24
CMiC S 1921-24
CSf Ap 1912-24
CSt 1903-[06]-[11;22]-24
CU-B S 13,24,N 10,18,D 23 1880;Ap 27,My 27, Jl 8,Ag 5-6,8 1881;N 10,16 1882;Ja 8-9,11-12,O 31,N 7,D 14 1883;O 9,11,14-17 1884;Mr 24-25, 28,30,Ap 10 1885;O 7 1886;S 27,29-O 2 1890;Je 2 1908-Mr 23,Ap 8,My 18 1921-24
WaPS Ja 20 1921-24

Le JOURNAL du Lundi. w 1868-
In French
C N 16 1868

Daily JOURNAL of commerce. d Ja 23 1850-F 1 1851||
Suspended Je 15-Jl 24 1850
CSmH F 27,Mr 15,Ap 26(extra)My 4,Je 14,N 15(extra)1850
CU-B Jl 29,Ag 16 1850
CaB S 13 1850
DLC Mr 15,18,My 15,O 10,25,D 16-17 1850
IU Ap 26 1850
NNHi [Mr-D 1850]51
P-M Ap 30 1850
—**Steamer ed**
CSmH Mr 1,My 15 1850
NNHi My 1 1850

Daily JOURNAL of commerce. 1872-1920 *See* San Francisco journal and daily journal of commerce

JOURNAL of commerce. m,w 1872-1907||?
Title varies: Journal of commerce and mercantile directory; Journal of commerce; Journal of commerce and weekly price current
m 1872-My 1874
C Je 1874-Je 1876;80-82
CU-B My-O 1873;Ja,F,Je 3,17,Jl 8 1874;Ja 27 1875-Je 6,S 12 1877;Ap 25,My 8 1878;Ja 22 1879;Ja 21,D 16 1880;Jl 1881;Ja 28,Mr 30, My 11-N 8 1882;O 4 1883;Ja 31 1884;My 14 1885;S 9 1886;Ja 20-27,Ag 25,D 22 1887;F 9, Ag 9 1888;F 7 1891
DLC 1878-85
KHi N 1887;O 18 1888
MWA F 1888
NN Jl 5 1876
NjHi My 1874
VU Ja 22 1879
WHi Je 22 1898

KLONDYKE miner. w Mr 2 1898-
CSt Mr 2 1898

KUO min yat po. Chinese nationalist daily. d 1927+
In Chinese
CSt N 18 1931+
MH [Ag 10 1927-F 1928]
NNC S 1932+

San Francisco LEADER. w N 3-D 29 1877||?
CU-B N 24-D 1877

LEADER. w 1902+
C Je 1908+
CU-B Je 13 1908+
PPCHi Ja 4 1902[08]-[33]

LEDGER. d Ap-My 9 1857||?
CU-B My 9 1857

LEDGER. d Ag 20-N 8 1875||?
CU-B Ag 20-21,23,25-26,S 6,17,O 9,N 5,8 1875

Sunday LEDGER. w Ag 22-S 26 1875||?
CU-B Ag-S 5,26 1875

LIBERATOR. w O 11 1898-
KHi N 15 1898

LIBERATOR. w D 12 1908-10||?
CU-B 1908-Je 4 1910

Saturday LOCAL. w Jl 7 1877-83||?
1877-O 12 1878 as Mission local
CU-B Jl-Ag,N 10 1877-D 20 1879[80]-N 1881; Mr 25 1882

LUCHA obrera. w 1933+
In Spanish
CU-P [1934-35]+

LYCEUM gazette. *See* Daily gazette and telegram

San Francisco MAIL. d 1877-?
C F 13-D 1877
CU-B Ja 7,F 17,Mr 4,Ag 20,S 1 1877

MANUAL. w Ap 8 1871-My 4 1872||?
CU-B Ap 8-15,29,My 13,Jl 1-15,Ag 19 S 2 23 1871;Mr 30-My 4 1872

San Francisco MARKET review. w F 23 1867-
Letter sheet. Issued simultaneously with Commercial herald and market review "especially for transmission abroad"
CSmH [1872-74]
MHi [1867-71]F 16-23 1872;Jl 16,D 31 1874;Mr 18-25 1875[76]
MWA Mr 9,19,Ap 18,My 18,Je 18,Jl 10,Ag 30,O 19,D 10 1867;Ja 30,F 10-18,Mr 10,30-Ap 6,22,My 6,14,Je 22-Ag 6,29,S 14-O 14 1868

MEFISTÓFELES. w 1916-18||
Merged with Hispano America
In Spanish
CU-B Mr 23,Je 22-Jl 20 1918

MERCANTILE agency notification sheet. w
CU-B Je 20-27,Jl 21,S 24,N 5-19,D 3,17,31 1870;Ja 21-F 11,Mr 4-11,Ap 8-22,My 6 1871 [My 11 1874-75]Ja 3-17,Mr-Ap 3 1876

MERCANTILE gazette and prices current, shipping list and register. sm,tm,w Je 19 1856-O 18 1867||?
1856-My 4 1859 as Mercantile gazette and shipping register
sm 1856-Mr 19 1857; four times a month Ap 4 1857-Je 1860;tm on steamer day Jl 1860-My 2 1865;sm on steamer day My 17-S 16 1865;tm O 2 1865-67?
C 1856-60
CLM Ap 1 1864
CSmH 1856-O 12,N 22 1863-Ja 2,22-Ag 2,S 1864-65;Ja 18-29,Mr 9-Jl 9,28-D 1866
CU-B 1857-58;60;Ja 19-My,Je 20,29,Jl 19-Ag,S 10,O 10-31,D 10,20 1861[62]-O 9 1867
DLC Ap 14 1857;58-60;Je 30 1862;O 1863-O 18 1867
MHi Je 19,Ag 19,S 19,O 4 1856;Je 4 1857;Jl 3 1858[59]-[64-67]
MWA Jl 27-Ag 4 1858;Ja 4,19,Ap 19,Jl 10,20, Ag 20 1860;Ja 10,Ag 30,N 9 1861;Ja 10,F 10,20,Mr 10,31,Ag 30,S 10,O 10,N 10,D 10,19, 31 1862;Ja 9,F 10-Mr 21,Ap 22,Jl 19,Ag 1, 21-N 12 1863;Ja 22,F 12-20,Mr 11,Je 11,Jl 22,N 12,22,D 12 1864;Ja 3,12 1865;Ja 9,18,F 8 1867
NNHi Ap 1863-O 18 1867

MERCHANTS' exchange prices current. *See* Sloat's San Francisco prices current

San Francisco MERCURY. *See* San Francisco pioneer

Saturday evening MERCURY. *See* San Francisco pioneer

Sunday MERCURY. *See* San Francisco pioneer

MID-WINTER appeal and journal of forty-nine. w Ja 7-Je 30 1894||?
CSmH Ja-Je 1894
KHi Ja 27,Ap 7 1894

Daily MIRROR. d Jl 9 1860-Ja 29? 1862||
Early numbers as Evening mirror. United with Daily herald to form Daily herald and mirror
C Jl 9, 1860;Jl 12 1861
CSmH Ag 29 1861(supp)
CU-B S 3-O 2,N 17-D 22 1860
OrHi S 28 1861

MIRROR of the times. w 1857-58||
Negro
C D 12 1857

MISSION journal. w 1880-1906||?
CU-B Ap 30,My 21 1881;Je 3 1882;Jl 1,15,N 11 1882;Ja 6,27,Ap 7,O 13 1883;D 6-13 1884; Ap 23 1887

MISSION local. *See* Saturday local

MISSION mirror. w My 26 1877-D 27 1879||?
CU-B Je 23,O 13,D 1,22 1877;Ja 5,F 16,Mr 9-16,S 28-O 5,26,D 14 1878;Ja 25,Mr 8-15,Ap 19,Je 7-14,Jl-Ag 16,S 6,O 25,N 1,22,D 6-13, 27 1879

MONITOR. w Mr 6 1858+
Suspended Jl 3-O 16 1858
C O 17 1868
CLM S 26 1883
CU-B Mr 20 1858;Jl 6 1867[68]-Jl 2 1870;Jl 1 1871;Mr 30-My 11 1872;D 7 1881;F 8,N 29 1882;F 14-21 1883;My 1907-My 13 1916;Ag 7 1920
KHi Ag 22 1888-F 13 1889
NN [1901-05;07-09]
PPCHi [1884;86;89]-[94-95]-[1916]

NATION. d Ag 15 1860-
Title varies: Daily nation
C Ag 15,S 29,O 11,15 1860

Daily NATIONAL. d Ag 16 1858-60||?
Follows Daily globe
CP Mr 19 1860
CSmH Mr 4 1859
CU-B My 30 1859
DLC 1858-D 20 1859
MH 1858-My 1859
MWA S 20-21 1858

Weekly NATIONAL. w S 2 1858-
MH S 9 1858-Ag 1859

Le NATIONAL. w Mr 7 1864-70||?
In French
C N 13 1868
CU-B 1864-O 17 1870

NATIONAL republican. d Je 20 1868-
CU-B Je-Ag 1 1868

NEW world daily news. *See* New world-sun

NEW world-sun. d 1897+
1897-Je 20 1935 as New world daily news
In Japanese
C Ap 28 1912+
CLM Ag 5,7 1919
CU-B O 28 1899-1900;Mr 1908-O 1931;O 31 1932+
IU S 2 1917-Je 1918
WHi Ag 1 1919

San Francisco NEWS. d,w My 17 1859-
d My 17-S 10 1859
C My-S 10 1859

San Francisco daily NEWS. d Ap 15-22 1878||?
CU-B Ap 22 1878

San Francisco NEWS. d Mr 19 1884-
CU-B Mr 19 1884

CALIFORNIA (*Continued*)

SAN FRANCISCO—*Continued*

NEWS. d Mr 21 1903+
1903-Jl 6 1927 as Daily news
C S 24 1930+
CSf O 1906+
CU S 28 1934+
CU-B S 9 1910-[17]-20;Ap 8 1924;S 16-19 1929;Mr 27 1931;O 9 1933[34+]
DLC Ap 18 1906(extra)

San Francisco daily evening **NEWS** and picayune. d N 1 1853-My 20 1856||
1853-Ja 20 1854 as San Francisco daily evening news
C N 21 1853
CSmH Ap 29 1854
CU-B complete
CtY 1855-Ap 1856
DLC Je 30,D 20 1854;Ja-Je 1855
NNHi Je 24 1854;My 6-11,13-17,19-20 1856
Tx Mr 29 1864
—Steamer ed. sm
DLC Mr 16,Jl 1,O 16 1854

San Francisco **NEWS** letter. sm,w Je 20 1856-Ag 25 1928||
Subtitle varies. Merged with Wasp (not in this list)
sm 1856-58?
CP Ja 20 1860
CSf Mr 9 1861[62;75]-[78-79]81-84[86-87]1906-[09]-[14-15]-17[19-21]
CSmH Ap 5 1858;O 16 1869;Jl 21 1906;S 11 1875;D 25(supp)1887
CSt D 25 1886;D 25 1892;O 20 1906;Ja-Mr 1907
CU [1877;81;1904-06]-[09-10]-[12]-[14;16-17;19-21;23]-Ag 1928
CU-B Je 20,D 5 1856;Ja 20,My 20,Je 20 1857; O 17 1863[Ap 23 1864-Ag 17 1867]F 22 1868-[72]-[74-77]-Ap 6,Jl 20 1878-D 4 1880;Ap 16,Ag 6-13,S 24,D 17 1881;D 22 1883[84]My 8-Ag 7 1886;D 25 1889;Je 21, O 4,D 25 1890; Ap 4,Jl 18-25,Ag 15,O 24,D 25 1891[92]D 25 1893;Je 30 1894;Je 1 1895;Jl 10 1897;O 22 1898;N 18-25,D 16 1899;Ja 6,F 24,Ap 14,28,N 10,D 22 1900;Je 1,Jl 13,S 21 1901;My 31-Je 14 1902;Ja 16,F 13,Mr 12 1904;F 25,Jl 22 1905 [F 17-D 1907]D 25 1908-Ag 1 1914;Jl 31-S 11,O 2 1915;16-My 5,S 8 1917-Je,N 2 1918
DLC Mr 4 1876;D 22 1877;D 25 1891;Jl 1892-94; Ja 12 1895;D 23 1899;D 29 1900-Ja,Jl 1905-Jl 21 1906;Je 15,Ag 17-24 1912;Jl 26,Ag 16 1913; Mr 21 1914;16-28
MWA S 19 1859;Mr 11 1871;F 27 1875;F 5 1876
N S 15,O 7,21,N 18 1865; Ja 13 1866;N 20 1869
NNHi My 7 1870

NEWSPAPER union. w 1882-96||?
Title varies: San Francisco union
CU-B [S 22 1883-86]Ja 1 1887;Mr 2 1889;N 7 1896

NON-PARTISAN. w O 22-N 5 1898||
C complete

NOVAÍA zarîa. d 1928+
also dated in Los Angeles, Seattle, Chicago
In Russian
CSt-H Mr 28 1929+
DLC Je 1935+

El **NUEVO** mundo. sw 1864-67||?
In Spanish
CSmH Ap 17,My 5,D 10 1865;F 5 1866
CU-B Je 29-Jl 3 1867

San Francisco **OBSERVER.** w D 18 1915-
1915-Je 24 1916 in magazine form
CU-B 1915-S 9 1916

ORIENTAL; or Tung-ngai san-luk. tw,w,m Ja 4 1855-F? 1857||
In Chinese and English
C Jl 1856
CU-B Ja 4,25-Mr 1 1855
DLC My 26 1855;Mr 1856
MWA Ap 28,Ag 1855
MnHi Ja 11 1855
NN Ja 11,F 1-8 1855;Ag-O 1856
NNHi Jl 1855;My 1856
NjHi Jl 1855

ORIENTAL. d 1886-1904||?
In Chinese
MLei Mr 24 1903
MWA Jl 27 1894
WHi F 18 1887;Ap 27 1888

PACIFIC advertiser. w Ag 3 1872-73||?
CU-B [1872]-F 1 1873

PACIFIC appeal. w 1862-79||?
C Jl 11 1863
CU-B Mr 21,My 30 1863;Je 24 1865;Jl 6[Ag 10-D 1867]Ja 25-F 1,20,Mr 7,Ap 11,My 2,Je 6,Ag 1,29 1868;Ja 7[S-D 1870]Ap 15,My 13, 27-Je 3,Jl 1,22,Ag 12,26-S 2,23-O 7,N 4,18-25,D 9-16 1871;72-Jl 5 1879

PACIFIC chronicle. m My 1867-
CU-B Jl 15 1867

PACIFIC Coast advertiser. m Mr? 1871-74||?
CU-B S-N 1871

PACIFIC Coast commercial record. w D 5 1887-92||?
Ja 1 1892 is Hawaiian number
CPo My 1 1892
CSmH D 5 1887
CU-B My 1 1888
HB Ja 1 1892
KHi S 20 1887-Ag 20,N 20 1888

PACIFIC courier. 1850 *See* Daily California courier

PACIFIC courier. w Jl 18-S 12 1857||?
CU-B S 12 1857

PACIFIC greenbacker. w Je 19 1880-82||?
CU-B Je 26,O 9 1880

PACIFIC investigator. w D 1 1889-
CU-B D 15 1889;Ja 12 1890

PACIFIC ledger. m Ag 1871-72||
CU-B Ag-S 1871;Ja 1872

PACIFIC metropolis. w Je 12 1880-
CU-B Je 12 1880

Daily **PACIFIC** news. tw,d Ag 25 1849-My? 1851||?
1849-Mr 3 1850 as Pacific news
tw 1849-Ap 26 1850
Suspended S 18-30 1850
C Ja 21 1851
CSmH Ag 25,S 8,N-D 11 1849;50-Mr 1851
CU-B S 15,18-20,25-27,O 2-9,13-20,25-27,N 3 1849[50]Ja 1,3-F 15,18-26,28-Mr,Ap 2-24 1851; Extras[N-D 1849];supp[N 1849-Ja 5 1850]
CaB D 22 1849-Ja 24 1850
DLC 1849[50-My 15 1851]
MWA D 8,31(supp)1849;Ja 29,F 5,19,Mr 4,7,D 2,9 1850;Ja 13-15,Mr 10-13,17-22,25-Ap 1,4, 7-8,10,12-14, 1851
NEh Je 15 1850
NN D 31(supp)1849
NNHi Ag 25,S 25,N 1,15-20,24-D 1,8,25 1849 [50]-Ja 22,24-Mr 13,15-25,27-Ap 15,17-My 4, 6-7,9-15,17-26 1851;My 20(extra)1850

Weekly **PACIFIC** news. w S 1 1849-
Title varies slightly
CU-B S 8,22 1849
DLC N 14,D 31 1849;Ja 14 1850
NNHi O 30,N 14,D 31 1850;Ja 14,31,F 1,Mr 1851
NjHi Ja 8 1850
TxGR Mr 1 1850
—Steamer ed. sm,ir
Title varies slightly
CSmH S 29 1849;Ja 31 1850
CU-B Ap 1 1851
DLC D 31 1849;Ja 31,Mr 1,Ap 1,My 15-Je, Ag 15-S 1,N 15 1850;Ja 15-My 1851
MWA D 31 1849;Mr 1,Ag 15 1850;My 15 1851
NN Mr 3 1851
NNHi Ap 1,20,My 15,20,Je 1,Jl 1 1850

PACIFIC pilote. w 1880-93||?
In German
KHi Je 30 1888-Mr 30 1889

PACIFIC posten. w S 15 1904-Ap 12 1906||
In Swedish
IaDeL complete
WHi S 15 1904;My 11 1905

PACIFIC Skandinav. w S 11 1886-1901||
Also dated in Oakland
In Norwegian and Danish
IaDeL S 11 1896-D 12 1899[1900]

PACIFIC standard. w
—Steamer ed. sm
NNHi Ap 15 1851

PACIFIC star. w
—Steamer ed.
C Jl 15 1851
CSmH Jl 15 1851

PACIFIC states enterprise. w S 22 1871-Mr 16 1872||?
CU-B F 24-Mr 16 1872

PACIFIC statesman. w Mr 30 1853-
DLC Mr 30,S 2 1853
NNHi Mr 30 1853

PACIFIC whalemen's list.
—Steamer ed.
NNHi D 19 1855

Daily evening **PATHFINDER.** d
N O 27 1856
NPV O 22 1856

PEACE; a weekly newspaper devoted to the interests of Japanese and things Japanese on the Pacific Coast. w O 25 1902?-03||?
In Japanese
CMiC Mr 22 1903

PEOPLE'S journal. w Ja 21 1871-
CU-B [Ja-Jl 1871]

PEOPLE'S press. w Je 4 1892-96||?
CU-B Ag 27,S 10,O 1 1892

Le **PETIT** Californian. w 1887-97||?
In French
KHi Ag-D 23 1888

Le **PETIT** journal. w 1871-85||?
In French
CU-B My 14 1873;Ag 31 1874

Le **PHARE:** Journal Franco Californien. sw,d Jl 22 1855-63||?
Contains a separately numbered section called Cronica italiana
sw 1855?
C Jl 4 1856
CU-B Ja 23 1863
NNHi Ja 3,7-9,14,16-19,21 1856

Daily evening **PICAYUNE.** d Ag 3 1850-Ja 20? 1854||
United with San Francisco daily evening news to form San Francisco daily evening news and picayune
Suspended My 5-23 1851;Ap 17 1852-D 12? 1853
For My 24-N 14 1851 *See* Morning post
In English and French
C Ja 27[S 16 1851-Mr 26 1852]Ja 13,17 1854
CP Ag 26,D 27 1851;Mr 11 1852
CSmH [Ag-O 7 1850]Ja 17,23,F 4,18,Mr 3,21, Ap 21,Je 7,15,Jl 26,31,Ag 11,18-S 9,16-D 26, 30 1851;Ja 6[21-Ap 14]1852;D 22 1853
CU-B Ag 3-14,16-O 3,5,8,10-25,28-N 20,22-D 27,30 1850-F 8,12-Ap 5,8-9,11-23,30,Jl 1-3,5-Ag 11,13-30,S-O 9,11 1851-Ap 17 1852
CaB Jl 2 1851-Ap 17 1852
DLC S 20 1851-[Ja-Ap]-D 1852
MWA Ag 13,O 7 1850;S 20-O 1,6-31,N 14,17, 24,D 1-4 1851
NN Mr 18,Ap 9 1852
NNHi Ag 3-17,20,22-29,31,S 2-10,12-16,19-20, 24,26-O 9,11-12,17-N 6,8-13,15-19,21-23,27,D 2-3,5-16,18-24,26 1850-Ja 9,11-15,17-30,F 1-13, 15-26,28-Mr 22,27,Ap 1,3-8,12-14,16-17,19,21, 24,28,My 1,Je 2-20,26,Ag 15-30;O 15-N 25,27-29,D 1-13,16-31 1851;Ja 2-15 1852
—French section is followed by L'Echo du Pacifique
—Steamer ed.
DLC D 15,31 1851
NNHi D 15,31 1851;Ja 1 1852

PICTORIAL town talk. *See* San Francisco daily times

San Francisco **PIONEER.** w,sm O 6 1867-O 15 1873||?
1867-Ja 17 1869 as San Francisco mercury; Ja 24-My 1 1869 Sunday mercury; My 8-N 6 1869 Saturday evening mercury
w 1867-Ag 1873
C O 18 1868
CU-B O 20 1867;68-[70]-[72]-O 15 1873

Daily **PLACER** times and transcript. d Je 16 1851-D 17 1855||
Formed by the union of Daily Sacramento placer times and Sacramento transcript. Title varies slightly. Merged with Alta California
1851-Je 1852 pub in Sacramento
C Jl 28,Ag 11,13-14 1852;Mr 9 1853-D 15 1855
CP Mr 7 1854;N 13 1855
CSmH F 23,Ap 26,Jl 29-30,Ag 30,S 23 1850;Jl 26,D 30 1852[53]Jl 2-D 15 1855
CU-B S 24 1851;My 9 1852;Je 27,O 5 1853
DLC Je 28-[S-O]1852-[Ja]-[Je 1853-54]-D 4 1855
MWA Ag 31 1853;Mr 16,Ap 17,19,25,Ag 16,O 17,N 9,D 1,7-8,11-30 1854
NNHi Ag 14,D 7,9,15-18,20-28,30-31 1852[53] Ja 19 1854;Ja 25-F 1,17,19-26,Ap 10-17,25-My 1,16,Je 1,S 20,N 5,20 1855
P-M Jl 15 1854
PPFfHi O 30 1852
PYHi [1851]
—Steamer ed.
Title varies: Steamer placer times and transcript; Weekly placer times and transcript
CSmH Ja 31,F 15,Mr 15 1853;Je 1 1854
DLC Ag 14,S 25,N 20 1852;S-O,D 1853[54-S 5 1855]
MWA Jl 30,O-N 15 1853
NNHi S,O 15,N 15,D 15 1852;Ja,Mr 15,Ap 1-9, 23-30,My 31-Je 1853;My 16,Je 1,S 20,O 20,N 5,19 1855

Weekly **PLACER** times and transcript. *See* Daily placer times and transcript. Steamer ed

San Francisco **PLAINDEALER.** d O 17-D 10 1857||?
CU-B D 10 1857

PLEBEIAN. d Jl 24-Ag 16 1871||?
CU-B Jl 24-Ag 16 1871

POLITICAL record. w,tm,bw Ja 7 1882-1905||?
1882-Ja 1888 as California political record
w 1881-Jl 1892;tm Ag 1892-Je 1895
C Ag 1882-97
CLM [1887-92]
CU-B Ja 7-Jl 1,15,Ag 19,N 4 1882[83-86]-97
KHi [Ag 1888-Mr 9 1889]

POPULIST. w My 9 1896-
CU-B My-O 15 1896

PORTICO. w O 26 1877-
CU-B O-D 22 1877

Morning **POST.** d My 24-N 14 1851||
Follows and is followed by Daily evening picayune
C S 29,N 12 1851
CSmH My 24,O 3 1851
CU-B Jl 28,Ag 25,S 1 1851
DLC My 24,27,30,Jl 14,Ag 25[O-N 1851]
NNHi My 24-28,30-Je 1,5-16,18-20,22,26-30,Jl 16-Ag 15,S 2-O 6,8-31 1851
—Steamer ed.
DLC Jl 1,S 1,15,O 1,15 1851

Evening **POST.** d D 4 1871-D 6 1913||
United with San Francisco call to form San Francisco call and post, later Call-bulletin
C Ag 20 1872-85;87-1913
C-S 1871-[Ja-Mr 1880]81-84[Je-D 1885]-88 [96]-[Ja-O 1899;Jl-D 1901]-[Ja-Ap 1911]
CLM Ap 30 1884;Je 23 1886;S 13 1890
CSf 1894-Je 1895;Ag 1906-13
CSmH Jl 1 1873;F 1 1880;Ja 11 1883;Ag 27-28 1884
CSt Jl 1909-10
CU-B 1871-[83-84]-[88-91]N 29 1892;S 14 1893; My 14,Je 8,16,S 8 1894;Je 22 1895;N 3 1897;Jl 25 1898;S 1 1900;Ap 4,S 26,D 16 1901;Ja 3 1902; Ap 1903-Ag 1905[Ag-D 1906;Mr 1907-08]-13
KHi My 3 1887-My 1 1895
MWA [F 6-D 1875]-[Ja 19 1877;Ja 16 1878
N S 10 1880
Nv Je-Jl 1894

Weekly **POST.** w 1875-1909||?
CU-B F 24-Ap 13,27-Ag 1876
CtY Ja 30,F 6-13,27 1879;Ag 5 1880
KHi F 28 1878-My 1 1895
MH [1877-79]-[82]-[86]-[89]

La **PRESA** mexicana.
CLM Je 20 1868

PRESENT and the future. Le present et l'avenir. d Je 16-Jl 1853||
Followed by Daily public ledger
In English and French
C Je 20 1853
DLC Je 16-17,21-22,30,Jl 2 1853

Le **PRESENT** et l'avenir. *See* Present and the future

CALIFORNIA (*Continued*)

SAN FRANCISCO—*Continued*

PRICES current and shipping list. sm,w F 17 1852-Ap 27? 1859||
F 17 1852 as San Francisco shipping list and prices current; Mr 1-O 30 1852 San Francisco prices current and shipping list. United with Mercantile gazette and shipping register to form Mercantile gazette and prices current, shipping list and register
sm F-Je 1852
C D 30 1854-57
CLM Ja 19 1858
CSmH Ag 31 1852;Ja 31 1853
CU-B Mr 15,D 9,24 1852-56;Ja 4 1858
DLC 1852-[57-D 5 1858]
MH-BA S 30 1852[53]O 14 1854;Mr 15 1855
MHi [1850-73]
MWA Jl 14,30,D 15 1852[53-56]My 19 1857; Ag 4 1858;Mr 19,Ap 19 1859
NNHi Mr 15,N 30,D 31 1852;Ja 3 1856
OrHi Je 15 1852;D 30 1853;S 12 1855

El PROGRESO. Ja 4 1871-
In Spanish
CU-B Ja 4 1871

PUBLIC balance. (Casserley) *See* Daily balance

Daily **PUBLIC** ledger. d Ag 1 1853-Mr 1 1854||
Follows Present and the future
C Ja 11-12,14,16,26,30-31 1854
DLC Ag 1 1853

PUBLIC opinion. w D 4 1880-1901||?
CLM [1887-90]
CU-B D 4,25 1880;Ja 8-22,Jl 23,N 19 1881;D 2 1882;F 11 1893;Ap 16 1898-Ja 7 1899
KHi [O 20 1888-F 9 1889]

San Francisco **RECORD.** w
CU-B Ag 14 1865

REGISTER. d F-D 21 1868||?
CU-B [Mr 30-D 21 1868]

San Francisco **REGISTER.** d Mr 5 1872-76||?
CU-B [1872-My 1876]

San Francisco **REPORT.** w 1862-99||?
1862-N? 1882 as Stock report and California street journal
CU-B Mr 1-8,Jl 26-Ag 2,O 11 1872;O 17 1873;Jl 2 1874;S 14 1877-[80-N 8 1883]
MHi N 25-D 2 1870[71]Mr 26-Ap 3,Jl 31 1874
MWA D 23 1870-Ja 20,F 4,17-Mr 3,17,31 1871; Je 25-Jl 2,16 1875

San Francisco **REPORT.** d 1863-1900||?
1863-N 1882 as Daily stock report and California street journal (title varies); D 2 1882-Mr 6 1899 San Francisco daily report; Mr 7-Ap 19 1899 San Francisco report and San Francisco daily report
C Ja 12 1875-N 1899
C-S 1881-84[Je-D 1885]-88[Ja,My 1890;Ap,Ag-D 1891]-[Ja-O 1900]
CSf 1865-Ag 1892;94-Je 1895
CSt [1889;91-93;98-99]
CU-B [My 13-D 26 1872]O 20 1873;Jl 1,7 1874-O 4,15,20,24,N-D 1877;F-Mr,My 10,Je-D 1878;Mr 6,10 1879-[82-83]Mr 8 1884-Je 1889; Mr 31,O 5,7 1891;Jl 23,Ag 18,N 5 1892;N 3 1897;O 3 1898
MHi [My 1875]
MWA Je 1,3-10,12-16,21-29,Jl 1-2,6,26 1875; Ja 19 1898

REPUBLIC. d Jl?-S 1 1863||?
CU-B S 1 1863

REPUBLIC. w My 31 1879-
CU-B My-Ag 1879

La **REPUBLICA.** w 1879-97||?
In Spanish
CLM Mr 10 1888
CU-B S 1-8,N 21 1883-Ja 2 1884
KHi [Je 23 1888-F 23 1889]

REPUBLICAN bell-ringer. d Ag 20 1871-
CU-B Ag-S 1,4-5 1871

El **REPUBLICANO.** sw Ag 20? 1868-69||?
CU-B Ag 22-29 1868;Ja 5 1869

San Francisco **REVIEW.** bw 1888?-90||?
CU-B Mr 18 1890

REVOLT. w 1910-15||?
CU-B [Jl 22-D 1911]Ja 13,F 17,Ap 27,My 11 1912

RICHMOND banner. w 1893+
CU-B Je 27 1919

RICHMOND record. w 1912+
C N 15 1913+
CU-B Ap 26,My 3,24-31,Je 14,28 1919;S 25 1931

RUSSKAIA gazeta. Russian gazette. w Mr 23 1921-
In Russian
DLC Mr-Ap 16,My 7-14,S 21,O 5,26 1921

RUSSKAIA zhizn. Russian life. w Ap 22 1922+
In Russian
CSt-H [1931-32]
CU-B Ag 19 1922-24
DLC 1922—

SERBIAN herald. 1909+
In Serbian
CU-B Jl 23 1932

San Francisco **SHIPPING** list and prices current. *See* Prices current and shipping list

SHOP and senate. w Je 7-D 6 1873||?
CU-B Ag 9,23,D 6 1873

SLOAT'S San Francisco prices current and shipping list. sm O 31 1850-My 31 1852||
1850-Mr 31 1851 as Merchants' exchange prices current and shipping list. Merged with San Francisco prices current and shipping list, later Prices current and shipping list
CSmH My 12 1852
CU-B O-D 14 1850;Ja 14,F 14-Ap 14,My 14,Je 13,Jl 14 1851-52
NNHi Ja 22,N 14 1851;Mr 17 1852

La **SOCIEDAD.** sw,w D 8? 1869-95||?
In Spanish
CLM O 27 1877;O 21,N 18 1882
CU-B D 15 1869-Ja 19,F 12,Mr 8-19,30,Ap 6-My 4,Je 1-18,25-Jl 13,20-27,Ag-S 17 1870;Jl 25 1874
KHi D 8 1888

SONNTAGSBLATT des California demokrat. *See* California democrat. w

SONNTAGS-post. *See* Das California journal und sonntags-post

SPARK. w Ap 28-Jl 28 1877||?
CU-B Jl 28 1877

SPECTATOR. d Mr 5 1865-
CU-B Mr 6 1865

SPOKESMAN. w
C Ja 13 1933+

STAR. d N 10-19 1856||?
CU-B N 19 1856

Morning **STAR.** d My 12- 1863||?
CU-B My 12 1863

STAR. w 1872-77||?
CU-B Jl 30,N 19 1875;F 9,Ja 29,Je 8 1877

STAR. d,w,m Jl 5 1884-Ja 1921||
d Jl-O 1884;w N? 1884-Ap 1 1916
CSf Jl 1906-21
CSt My 1899-Je 1905
CU Jl 16 1887
CU-B O 26 1886;Ja-Je 1910;Ja 14-F,Je 1911-21
CaB Jl 23 1887

STAR of empire. w S 17-N 12 1856||
Back page in German as Der Deutsche republikaner
MWA S 24,O 8 1856

STEAMER bulletin. *See under* Bulletin

STEAMER Pacific news. *See under* Weekly Pacific news

STEAMER Placer times. *See under* Daily placer times and transcript

San Francisco weekly **STOCK** circular. w 1864?-70||?
MHi Ap 6,Jl 20 1867[58-70]
MWA F 27-Ap 3,17-Je 5,Jl 17,31-Ag 7,21,S 4,18-O 2 23-D 18,31 1869-F 5,Mr 12-Ap 16,N 12 1870

STOCK exchange. d 1875-77||
CU-B 1876-My 31 1877

STOCK exchange. w O 5 1876-77||
CU-B O 5-26 1876

STOCK report. *See* San Francisco report

SUN. d My 9 1853-S 5? 1857||
C Je 8 14-15 1853;Ja 2,14,20,27-28,30,F 7-8 1854
CP My 19,Je 7,Ag 26 1853;S 11 1855
CSmH 1854-My 17 1855
CtY 1854-Je 1856
DLC 1853[Ja-F 1854]Ag 21 1856-F 5 1857
MWA Je 18,S 17,D 7,10 1853
NN My 25,Je-Ag 1[S-N]D 1853
NNHi F 23,Ap 28,Jl 8 1854;Je 2-12,Ag 6-17,S 18,20-26 28-29,O 2-3,N 7-15,17-20,D 10-11,20 1855;Ja 7-8,F 20,Ap 5,My 5-21,Ag 22-28,S 20 1856
OrHi Jl 29 1853
—Steamer ed.
C Ag 4,19 1856;S 5 1857
NNHi Ja 16 1854

SUN. d D 18 1873-74||?
C 1873-Jl 20 1874
CU-B D 18,22,29,31 1873;Ja 3,6-9,Je 16 1874

SUN. w N 22 1873-74||?
CU-B N 29 1873

Daily **SUN.** d Jl 28-O 31 1879||?
CSt Jl-O 31 1879

San Francisco **SUN.** d S 3-N 29 1910||
C complete
CSf complete
CU-B S-O 4,6-15,17-N 1910

SUNDAY. . . *See* next important work: i.e. Sunday dispatch is alphabeted under Dispatch

SVOBODA. *See* Alaska herald

San Francisco **TAGEBLATT.** w 1893-1906||?
CSt Ap 1895-1905
ICJ 1898-1902
WHi 1903-Ja 12 1906
—Sunday ed *See* Vorwärts

San Francisco **TATTLER.** *See* Western weekly

El **TECOLOTE.** d 1875-79||?
In Spanish
CU-B My 4 1876

Evening **TELEGRAM.** d O 1 1858-Je 1860||
United with Daily gazette to form Daily gazette and telegram
CP Ja 11,F 16,21 1859;Ja 5 1860
CSmH N 6 1858
CU-B F 7-8 1859;Mr 29 1860

Weekly **THUNDERBOLT.** w 1886-
CU-B Ja 28 1887;N 4 1892
KHi F 9 1889

El **TIEMPO.** w 1868-69||
In Spanish
CU-B F 9 1869

San Francisco daily **TIMES** d Ap 18 1852-
CSmH Ap 20 1852
CU-B Ap 19-23 1852
DLC Ap 20-22,24 1852

San Francisco daily **TIMES.** d N 12 1854-O 30 1869||
1854-My 29 1856 as Town talk; My 30?-My 9 1857 Pictorial town talk; My 10?-S 13 1857 Times and town talk
C Jl 30,O 13 1855;Ja 17,My 21,25,29,N 9 1856-My 9 1857;My 13 1859-My 10 1861;Jl 21 1867;N 23 1868-69
CMa N 5 1866-69
CP N 25 1854;S 16 1858;Je 9 1860
CSmH My 20 1856-My 9 1857
CU-B My 10 1857-My 12 1860;N 5 1866-69
CtY My 10 1855-N 8 1856
DLC My 11-N 3 1855;Ap-My 18,21,Je 5 1856; Ap 21-N 8 1857;S 4 1868
MWA Ag 30 1855;Je 5 1857;Mr 12,Ap 5 1859
N F 1,Mr 6,Ap 6,27,Je 6,S 10 1867;My 6,Je 3,25,Ag 10,O 27 1868;F 2 1869
NNH D 20 1855;Ja 29 1856
—Steamer ed.
Title varies: Pictorial town talk. Steamer ed. San Francisco steamer times; etc.
C Je 5-Jl 5 1856
CSmH Je 5 1856;S 20 1859
MWA Jl 5 1856;D 1 1866;Mr 30 1867

Weekly **TIMES.** w 1856?-58||?
CU-B D 25 1858
NNHi N 6 1858

TIMES and town talk. 1857 *See* San Francisco daily times

TOWN talk. d *See* San Francisco daily times

TOWN talk. w 1892-1920||?
CU-B Ja 2,30 1904;S 16 1905;Je 9 1906-Ap 5 1919

TRADE and transportation. w S 30 1893-
CU-B O 21 1893
KHi N 18 1893

TRADE herald. m Ap 1878-
CU-B Ag 1878;Ag 24 1880

La **TRIBUNA.** w 1903-O 1 1920||
Merged with L'Unione
In Italian
IU My 19 1917-20

San Francisco evening **TRIBUNE.** d Je 28 1866-70||?
C Je-Jl 27 1866
CU-B Jl 5 1866;D 21 1869;Ja 25 1870

TRIBUNE. w N 12 1875-83||?
Mr 16 1878-Ja 25 1879 as Tribune and visitor
CU-B Ja 29,Jl 1876-O 20 1877;Mr 16-My 11, 25-Je 1,Ag,S 28-O 5,N 2-9 1878;Ja 25,Je 14-21,D 6 1879;Ap 24,Je 12-31,Ag 7-14,28,S 11, 25-O 9 1880;S 22-29, N 3-10 1883

Daily **TRUE** Californian. d My 26 1856-My 31 1857||
Suspended from S 7-25 1856
C [1856-57]
CSmH Ag 4 1856
CU-B My 28,N 7 1856;Ja 29 1857
CaB Ag 31 1856
DLC My-D 8 1856
MWA Je 19 1856
NNHi Je 21-Jl 3,22-Ag 5 1856
—Steamer ed. sm Je 20 1856-
NNHi Je 20,Ag 5 1856

Daily **TRUE** standard. d Mr 3-My 4 1851||
Follows Daily balance (Casserley)
CP Ap 21 1851
CSmH Mr 6 1851
NNHi Mr 3-4,6-9,11-23,27-Ap 15,17,19-20,22-My 3 1851

A **UNIAO** portugueza. w Ag 1887-1906||?
In Portuguese
KHi Jl 5 1888

San Francisco **UNION.** *See* Newspaper union

L'**UNION** nationale. L'Unione nazionale. d 1864-70||?
In French and Italian
CU-B N 8-29,D 2-4 1870

L'**UNIONE.** w 1919+
In Italian
IU O 8-D 3 1920

L'**UNIONE** nazionale. *See* L'Union nationale

VAN COUVER'S Island and British Columbia news. Including San Francisco news letter.
N My 20 1859

Weekly **VARIETIES.** w My 18 1856-65||
1856-58 as Sunday varieties
CP F 21 1858;Ag 20 1864
CSfP N 1858-My 1 1859
CU-B Je 1,S 7 1856;Ja 23 1859;S 30 1865
N Ja 7 1865
OrHi My 2 1858

Sunday **VARIETIES.** *See* Weekly varieties

VESTKUSTEN. w 1886+
In Swedish
IRA [1918-23]
IU D 13 1917+
KHi D 22 1888;Ja 26,F 9 1889

VINDICATOR. w 1884-1906||?
Negro
CU-B My 2,16,Je 11,25,Jl 30,Ag 30 1887
KHi N 17 1888;F 9-16 1889

VISITOR. w Ag 2? 1872-7?||?
CU-B F 15 1873-77

CALIFORNIA (*Continued*)

SAN FRANCISCO—*Continued*

La VOCE del popolo. w,sw,d D 26? 1867+
w 1867-90?;sw 1880-89?
In Italian
CU-B [1868-70;90]Mr 29,Ap 1916-30;Ap 29 1931
IU D 7 1917-D 8 1919

VOICE of Israel. w,sw O 7 1870-N 18 1874||?
CU-B 1870-Je 1871;Ap 19 1872;N 18 1874

VORWÄRTS. w 1893||?
In German. Sunday ed of San Francisco tageblatt
NN Mr 5 1893

La VOZ de Chile. . . *See* La Voz del nuevo mundo

La VOZ de Méjico. tw Ap 9? 1862-Ap 29 1865||?
In Spanish
CSmH Ap 19 1862;Ja 17-24,29-31,F 5-10,14-19, 24-Mr 17,21-26,Ap 11-14,18 1863;Ja 19-F 20, 27,Mr 24,Ap 2 1864
CU-B Ap 29 1865

La VOZ del nuevo mundo. sw,w 1864-
1864-My 26 1868 La Voz de Chile; My 28 1868-70? La Voz de Chile y el nuevo mundo
sw 1862-83?
In Spanish
CLM N 20,27,D 4-8 1874;Ja 11-25 1876
CU-B Je 28,O 11-N 1,29 1867-F 18,25-28,Mr 6-10,17-20,27,Ap 3-7,14,28-My 12,19-Jl,Ag 4-7, 14-28,S 4 1868;S 26 1873;F 24,My 22,Je 9-16, Jl 17,28,S 24-29,O 20,N 10,17,D 21 1874;Mr 9,Jl 23,27,N 30,D 31 1875-Ja 4,14,F 1,18,Mr 7,Ap 7,18-28,Je 23,S 3,12 1876;Ag 21 1877;Ja 8 1878;Mr 11 1879;F 24 1880;My 14 1881-My 12 1883

A VOZ portugueza. w Ag 5 1880-88||
DLC Ag 5 1880
KHi Ag 4 1888

WALL Street journal: Pacific coast edition. d O 21 1929+
C 1931+
CP Ag 1930+
CSmo N 12 1929+
CSt [1926-33]
CU [Ja 31 1931-Je 1932]+
NvR [1933]+

Daily WESTERN American. d Ja 15 1852-
CP F 11 1852
CSmH Mr 1 1852
DLC Ja 26-Mr 1 1852
NNHi Ja 29-31,F 2-6,Mr 1 1852

WESTERN appeal. sm 1918+
Negro
CU-B O 14 1920;Je,Ag 17 1921-Ja 4,F,Mr 8, Ap,My 3,Je 6,S 20 1922;D 16 1925;F 3,Ag 20,O 1,D 17 1926;Ja 21,F 25,Mr 18,Ap 1,My 6 1927

WESTERN herald. w Jl 12 1884-
CU-B Jl 26,O 11,25 1884

WESTERN standard. w F 23 1855-
NN F 23 1856

WESTERN weekly. w N 25 1911-
1911 as San Francisco tattler
CU-B 1911-Je 8 1912

San Francisco daily WHIG. *See* San Francisco commercial advertiser

San Francisco weekly WHIG and commercial advertiser. w 1852-53||
MWA Je 15 1853
—Steamer ed.
DLC Ja 15 1853
NNHi S 1,O 15,D 1,16 1852;Ja 1 1853

WIDE west. w Mr 17 1854-Jl 4 1858||
C S 30 1854[My 31 1857-58]
C-S [Ap 16 1854-58]
CLM Ap 15,Jl 4,Ag 16,D 1 1854;Ja 7 1855
CP [Mr 19 1854-F 10 1856]
CU-B O 14,Jl 4 1855;My,O 1856;Ja 1,N 29,D 13,27 1857;58
CtY Mr 19 1854-Mr 9 1856
DLC Ja 1,Je 22,Jl 4 1856
KHi My 7 1854
MB Jl 1 1854
MWA Je 17,N 18 1855;Ja 27,O 1856;Mr 1 1857; Ja 3 1858
NNHi holiday ed 1854;Jl 4,D 9 1855;My 11,Je 20 1856
—Steamer ed.
C My 20,Ag 20 1856;Ap 1857
CP Mr 1,Ag 1 1855
CSmH Mr 1,Ag 1 1855
DLC Ap 15,Je 16,Ag 1 1854;F,My 5,Jl 20 1856
MWA Ap 1 1854;Ap 5 1856

San Francisco WORLD. w Mr 27-Je 13 1869||?
CU-B Ap 3-10,Je 13 1869

Sunday WORLD. w Ja 17 1886-.
CU-B Ja 24 1886

SAN GABRIEL

EAST San Gabriel herald. w Ja 12 1889-
CLM Ja 19,F 9,S 28 1889

San Gabriel SUN. w 1912+
pub Ap 26 1917+

San Gabriel VALLEY press. w 1924+
pub 1928+

SAN JACINTO

San Jacinto REGISTER. *See* San Jacinto Valley register

San Jacinto VALLEY register. w N 1884+
1884-Jl 19 1923 as San Jacinto register
CLM [1891-1904]F 28 1907
CRiv 1913-26;28+
CU-B O 31-N 21,D 5,19 1889-F 13,Ag 14-S 4,O 16-30 1890[F 1906-Ag 1907]

SAN JOSE

Saturday ADVERTISER. w 1866-69||
CU-B Jl 13 1867;F 1[Je-O]1868-Ja 9,23-F 13 1869

San Jose ADVERTISER. d Je ?-D 1875||?
CU-B [S 13-D 4 1875]

San Jose ADVERTISER. w Ag 6-N 26 1875||?
CU-B Ag 20-S 10,N 1875

San Jose daily ARGUS. d Ja 6-F 13? 1851||
CSmH Ja 10 1851
DLC Ja 10 1851
MWA Ja 29 1851
NNHi Ja 7 1851

Weekly ARGUS. w Ja 6 1866-Ag 31 1878||
1866-Ja 10 1874 as Santa Clara argus. United with San Jose herald to form San Jose weekly herald argus, later San Jose herald
C 1868;F 1870-My 18 1872
CSt 1866-[69]-71;73-77
CU-B Jl 28 1866[Jl 1867-Ag]-D 1868;Ag 14-S 7 1869;70-Ag 1878

Daily ARGUS. d Ag 10-Mr 9 1878||
C O 28 1868
CSt Ag 10-N 7 1868

BETTER times. *See* Phoenix

CALIFORNIA state journal. sw,d D 14 1850-Mr 26? 1851||
Ja 1851 as California daily state journal (d)
C F 15 1851
CSmH Mr 15,19,26 1851
DLC Mr 15,19,26 1851
NNHi Ja 8-9,16,Mr 19 1851

San Jose CITIZEN. w
CU-B [Mr 18 1922-D 22 1923]Ja 12,26 1924

San Jose COURIER. d Mr-Jl 1865||?
CU-B F 13,Jl 8 1865

COURIER. w 1876-83||?
In German
CU-B Mr 17 1877

FORUM. w Mr 1908-
C Mr 21-My 30 1908

San Jose GUIDE. d 1871-72||?
CU-B [S 26 1871-Ja 1872]

San Jose HERALD. w S 16 1863-99||?
1863-76? as San Jose patriot; S 13 1878-84? San Jose weekly herald-argus
C 1863-O 4 1872
CU-B Jl 1866-O,D 1870;Jl 12 1872-D 11 1874;S 13,27-D 1878

San Jose HERALD. d Ja 1866-N 1 1913||
1866-S 2 1876 as San Jose daily patriot. United with San Jose daily mercury to form San Jose mercury herald
C Mr 1866-Je 1869;70;73-S 4 1875;O 17 1883-1900
CLM D 1904
CU-B My 26,Jl 5 1866-D 9,12,21 1876;77-80[D 1889]1901-13

San Jose HERALD-ARGUS. *See* San Jose herald w

San Jose INDEPENDENT. d My 17 1870-S 24 1871||?
CU-B [My-D 1870]-S 24 1871

San Jose LETTER. w 1894?-96||
CSt D 7 1895-N 28 1896
CU-B Ja 25 1896

San Jose weekly MERCURY. w Je 20 1851-1903||?
1851-Je 4 1852 as Weekly visitor; Ag 19 1852-O 20 1853 Santa Clara register; N 3 1853-Ag 7 1855 San Jose telegraph and Santa Clara register; Ag 14 1855- 1860 Telegraph and mercury
C My 26 1853-Ag 8 1860;My 15 1862-My 5,S 22 1864-My 5 1870
CLM N 13,D 25 1884;Ja 1 1887[Ja 10-S 5 1891]
CU-B Je 20 1851-Je 4,S 2 1852;O 20 1853-Ag 14 1855;Jl 22 1856;O 10 1861[O-D 1863]-Jl,D 1 1881;Ja 1 1887;Ja 4-11 1890;Ja 9 1892
DLC D 27 1860-Ja 3,Ag-S 19,N 7-21,D 1861;F 13-Mr 20,My 15-N 1862;My 12 1864-F 9,My 11 1865-Ap 26 1866;My 27-S 16 1869
MWA Ja 18 1866;Je 27 1891
N Je 30 1864

San Jose MERCURY-HERALD. d Ag 6 1869+
1869-D 24 1884 as Daily mercury; D 25 1884-Je 30 1885 Daily mercury and times (title varies slightly); Jl 1 1885-O 27 1913 San Jose daily mercury
Suspended from Ap 30 1870-Mr 12 1872
Sunday ed as Sunday mercury and herald
C Mr 13 1880+
CPa current two years only
CSj 1889+
CSt [1906]Mr 1912+
CU-B 1869-Ja,Ap 1874-Je,Ag 1877-80[Ja-S 1882;Je-D 1883]-Jl 1885;Ja-F,Mr 14-Ap,Je 20-Ag,O-[D 1886-F]Mr,My,Je,S 1888-91;D 17 1893;Ja 7,Ap 27 1894;Je 23 1895;My 10 1901; N 2 1913;Je 18,21,24-N 1915;16+
OClWHi Je 28 1888;Ja 1 1892

San Jose NEWS. d 1883+
Title varies: San Jose evening news
C 1896
CU-B My 19-21 1885;My 8-12 1919

San Jose PATRIOT. *See* San Jose herald

PHOENIX. d 1885-92||?
1885-90? as Better times
C O 13 1891-N 28 1892

San Jose POST. w,d 1910-32||?
w 1910-Ap 23 1931
C N 8 1928-Ap 23 1931

San Jose daily RECORD. d O 1? 1890-95||?
C O 22 1890-S 1891[Ap 1 1892-Ap 1 1893]

San Jose morning REPORTER. d Ja 1860-
C Ja 17-Ag 6 1860

Sunday REPUBLIC. w My 19-30 1878||?
CU-B My 19,Je 2,23-30 1878

San Jose REPUBLIC. d Mr? 1885-
CU-B My 19-22 1885

SANTA CLARA argus. *See* Weekly argus

SANTA CLARA register. *See* San Jose weekly mercury

TELEGRAPH and mercury. *See* San Jose weekly mercury

San Jose TELEGRAPH and Santa Clara county register. *See* San Jose weekly mercury

Daily morning TIMES. d Jl 15 1879-Mr 6 1890||?
D 25 1884-Je 30 1885 united with Daily mercury to form Daily mercury and times, later San Jose mercury-herald
C O 13 1882-Je 1883;84;S 7 1886-Ag 1888;S 6 1889-Mr 6 1890
CU-B [Jl 20 1879-80]Mr 10,24-25,Ap 13,My 20,26,28 1882;Ap 26,Je 8 1883

San Jose TIMES. w Ja 5 1884-
CU-B Ja 19-F 2 1884

San Jose TIMES-star. d 1906-My 19 1914||
1906-N 2 1913 as San Jose times
CU-B S 21 1913-14

San Jose weekly TRIBUNE. sw,w Jl 4 1854-D 27 1862||?
1854 as San Jose tribune (sw)
C 1854-Je 25 1858;Jl 8 1859-62
CP Je 29 1860
CU-B My 22 1857;S 11 1863

Weekly VISITOR. *See* San Jose weekly mercury

SAN JUAN

CENTRAL Californian. *See under* Hollister

MONTEREY county journal. w O 8 1864-
CU-B O 15 1864

SAN JUAN BAUTISTA

San Juan MISSION news. w 1913+
C F 9 1918+
CHo 1927+

SAN JUAN CAPISTRANO

COASTLINE dispatch. w Ag 1923+
pub [1923-S 23 1932]

SAN LEANDRO

ALAMEDA county gazette. *See* Oakland transcript (Oakland)

ALAMEDA democrat. w Je 6 1868-Ap 3 1869||?
CU-B Je 13 1868-Ja 23,Mr 6,13,Ap 3 1869

CALIFORNIA news. *See* San Leandro news

San Leandro NEWS. m,w O 1923+
1923-My 1924 as Broadmoor community news; My 22 1924-F 8 1928 Cherry City news; F 1928-My 7 1931 California news
m 1923-My 1924
1923-My 1925 pub in Oakland
CSle My 22 1924+

San Leandro PLAINDEALER. w Ap 23 1874-
CU-B Ap 23-S 10 1874

San Leandro RECORD w. Je 5 1875-
CU-B Ag 7-O 9 1875

San Leandro REPORTER. w My 17 1879+
C S 1913+
CSle 1906+
CU-B Ag 23,O 11-N,D 27 1879[80]Mr 24,My 5,19,Je 2,23-30 1882;Ja 26-F 2,Mr 2-9,23,Ap 20 1883;O 24,D 5 1885;Jl 10,Ag-O,N 13-D 1886[1906]+

STANDARD-OBSERVER. w 1892+
1892-1917? as Standard?
CSle [1913-16]

SAN LUIS OBISPO

San Luis Obispo BREEZE. d 1894-1910||?
CLM My 23 1901
CSl Jl 1896-1901
CU-B S 9-24,26-O 1907

San Luis Obispo semi-weekly BREEZE. w,sw Mr 7 1896-1909||?
Mr-N 6 1896 as San Luis Obispo weekly breeze (w)
C 1900-My 4 1909
CSl 1896-1901

DEMOCRATIC standard. w F 12 1870-72||?
C Jl 1870-Ja 1872
CU-B [F 12 1870-O 22 1870]Jl 8 1871-F 15 1872

Morning HERALD. d 1923-O 17 1925||
United with San Luis Obispo daily tribune to form Morning tribune and morning herald, later Morning tribune
CSlT complete

Semi-weekly HERALD-telegram and San Luis Obispo tribune. sw O 23-N 1925||
Follows San Luis Obispo tribune
C complete

San Luis Obispo weekly MIRROR. w O 12 1880-90||?
CSl O 9 1884-O 1 1885
CU-B Je 8-Jl 1881;Mr 15,My 17 1882;Mr 19,Jl 17-S 1884;N 14-28 1889
KHi Ja 17 1889

CALIFORNIA (*Continued*)

SAN LUIS OBISPO—*Continued*

Daily MIRROR. d 1888-
KHi O 4 1888

San Luis Obispo weekly PIONEER. w Ja 4 1868-69||?
C D 19 1868
CSl 1868
CU-B 1868-[Ja-N 20 1869]

San Luis Obispo daily REPUBLIC. d 1883-D 30 1890||
CLM My 15 1889
CSl My 19 1884-90
CU-B Je 21,25,Jl 23,30-31,S 3,O 11-12,N 30-D 5 1889
KHi [Ag 23-O 4 1888]

SOUTH coast. w Mr 20 1878-
CU-B [My 22 1878-Jl 16 1879]

SOUTHERN California advocate. w Ag 2 1879-80||
CU-B [Ag 2 1879-Jl 3 1880]

San Luis Obispo STANDARD. w Jl 15 1885-
CU-B S 2 1885;Jl 14-N 17 1886

San Luis Obispo daily TELEGRAM. d 1905+
pub 1910+
C N 1925+
CSl Ja-N 18 1916;N 30 1918+
CU-B My 7-8 1919;O 7 1922

Morning TRIBUNE. d Ag 7 1869+
1869-O 17 1925 as San Luis Obispo daily tribune; O 14 1925-Je 11 1926? Morning tribune and morning herald
pub 1890+
C O 23 1925-Je 11 1926
CSl 1869-Je 3 1925
CU-B My 1-13 1919

San Luis Obispo TRIBUNE. w Ag 7 1869-O 17 1925||
Followed by Semi-weekly herald-telegram and San Luis Obispo tribune
C Jl 11 1890-1925
CU-B 1869-S 1 1882;N 21 1884[87-91]
KHi S-D 7 1888

SAN MARCOS

PLAIN truth. sm 1884-95||?
CLM Mr 4,S 1,N 16 1889
CU-B S 1-16 1889;Ja 10-25,F 25 1890

SAN MARINO

San Marino NEWS. w S 1 1929-My 22 1931||
United with San Marino tribune to form San Marino tribune and San Marino news
CSm [S 26 1929-31]

San Marino TOWN crier. w Ja 23-My 13 1932||
CSm complete

San Marino TRIBUNE and San Marino news. w Mr 16 1928+
1928-Je 5 1931 as San Marino tribune
pub 1928+
CSm [1928-29]+
CSmH Mr 2 1934
CSp 1931[32]+

SAN MATEO

San Mateo LEADER. w My 25 1889-D 1918||
United with San Mateo county news to form San Mateo news-leader
C My 23 1906-18
CSma 1902-13

San Mateo NEWS-LEADER. d Ja 5 1914-Ja 21 1926||
1914-18 as San Mateo county news. United with San Mateo daily times to form San Mateo times and daily news-leader
C complete
CSma complete

San Mateo NEWS-LEADER. w Ja 2-S 25 1919||
C complete

SAN MATEO county news. *See* San Mateo news-leader

San Mateo TIMES. w Jl 25 1874-Ja 29? 1876||
United with San Mateo county gazette (Redwood City) to form Times-gazette (Redwood City)
CU-B 1874[75]-Ja 22 1876

San Mateo TIMES and daily news-leader. w.d Ap 4 1901+
1901-My 31 1924 as San Mateo times; Je 21 1924-Ja 20 1926 San Mateo daily times
w 1901-My 1924
C 1902+
CSma 1921-24;26+
CSs 1934+

SAN MIGUEL

CENTRAL California. *See* San Miguel messenger

San Miguel COURIER. w 1889-95||?
CU-B Ag 14 1890

San Miguel MESSENGER. w 1886-1903||
1886-96 as Central California
CU-B Ap 13-27,Je 8,29,Ag 10,31,O 5,14-21,N 2-9,D 7 1894;F 1-22,Mr 29-Ap 5,19,My 31-Je 14,28,Jl 12-19,Ag 9,D 13 1895;Ja 17,Ap 10,S 18,O 2 1896
KHi S 14 1888-Jl 12 1889

SAN PEDRO

Papers published in San Pedro are listed under Los Angeles

SAN RAFAEL

San Rafael HERALD. w Jl 30 1874-79||
CU-B [Jl 30-N 5 1874;Ap 8 1875]-Ap 19 1879

San Rafael INDEPENDENT. w,d 1886+
w 1886-1929
pub D 11 1903+
CSr 1905+
CU-B Ja 31 1923+

MARIN county journal. w,sw Mr 23 1861+
w 1861-N 9 1933
pub 1861+
C 1899+
CSr [1871-Mr 1873;Ap 1894-Ap 1899]
CU-B [Mr 23-D 1861]-[83]-[85-87]Ja 19 1888; Mr 7-14,Je 27-Jl 11,D 26 1889[Jl 27 1899-F] My 9,31,Je 20-27 1901[S 1903-Ja 1904;Ag 1908-09]-O 1918
KHi O 25-N 1 1888
MnHi 1898-Jl 20 1899

MARIN county news. w Jl 1-N 4 1871||?
CU-B [Mr 4,Ag 5-N 4 1871]

MARIN county tocsin. w Jl 5 1879-Jl 13 1918||
C Je 7 1890-Jl 13 1918
CSr Jl 8 1905-[F 1908-09]-12;14;Ap 1915-17
CU-B Jl 12 1879-D 25 1880

MARIN news digest. w Ag 15 1931-S 21 1933||
C complete

SAN YSIDRO

San Ysidro BORDER press. w O 24 1930+
pub 1930+

SANGER

Sanger HERALD. w 1889+
pub N 1920+
CFr O 1924+

SANTA ANA

Santa Ana BLADE. w 1886-1914||?
1886-Jl 1889 as Pacific weekly blade
CU-B F 6 1890
KHi [Jl 12-O 18 1888]

Daily evening BLADE. d 1887-Mr 16 1918||
Merged with Santa Ana register
C 1911-18
CLM [1888-94]F 7,Jl 19 1901
CSan Jl 1903-18

Santa Ana BULLETIN. w Je 10 1899+
CLM [1899-1907]
CU-B Jl 16 1909-Ap 8,29-Je 17 1910

Santa Ana morning DISPATCH. w,sw,d Ja 21 1882-1904||?
1882-Jl 12 1901 as Santa Ana standard; Jl 19 1901-03 Santa Ana leader
sw Ja-F 24 1882;w Mr 1882-1903
C 1891-97;1900-03
CLM [1883-98;1904]
CU-B Ja-Jl 21 1882;Ja 11,25 1890
KHi [My 19-O 20 1888]

FREE press. d 1889-91||?
CLM N 5 1889-N 1 1891

FREE press. w 1889-91||?
CLM N 1890-O 10 1891

Santa Ana HERALD. *See* Orange county herald

Santa Ana JOURNAL. d My 1 1935+
C My 6 1935+

Santa Ana LEADER. *See* Santa Ana morning dispatch

ORANGE county herald. w 1878-1903||?
1878-Jl 28 1890 as Santa Ana herald
CLM O 1,D 31 1881;Ja 7,Mr 4-11,25-Ap 1,My 6,N 18 1882;Mr 31,O 20 1883;Ja-N 22,D 16 1890
CU-B Ja 2,18,Ag 9,23-30 1890;Jl 2 1892

PACIFIC weekly blade. *See* Santa Ana blade

Santa Ana REGISTER. d 1905+
pub 1905+
CL S 25 1928
CSan Mr 1918+
CSanO 1905+
CU-B My 21 1923-D 9 1929

Santa Ana STANDARD. *See* Santa Ana morning dispatch

SANTA BARBARA

Santa Barbara ADVERTISER. w 1877-78||?
CU-B O 12 1878

El BARBARENO. w D 14 1895-Jl 31 1897||
In Spanish
CSb complete
CLM Ap 25 1896

DEMOCRAT. *See* Santa Barbara daily news

La GACETA. w 1880-81||?
In Spanish
CLM Ap 10,17,My 15,Ag 21,O 16 1880;Jl 23 1881
CSmH My 12 1881

Santa Barbara GAZETTE. w 1855-58||
CLM Mr 18 1858
CSb My 24 1855-My 14 1857
NNHi Jl 23 1857;F 11 1858

Santa Barbara HERALD. w 1885-1907||
CU-B [Je 22-N 23 1907]

Daily INDEPENDENT. *See* Santa Barbara daily news

Weekly INDEPENDENT. w,sw Ag 3 1878-1900||?
sw S 1880-81?
C Jl 1890-97
CU-B [Ap-D 1878]-80;Ap 29-Jl 8,22-29,Ag 12,S 2 1882[86-87]N 16 1889
KHi [N 29 1890-Je 16 1894]

Santa Barbara INDEX. w Ag 31 1872-D 1 1877||?
CU-B S 7 1872-[77]

Santa Barbara INDEX. d O 4-D 6 1877||?
CU-B O 18-D 6 1877

Santa Barbara daily NEWS. w,sw,d Ja 19 1878+
1878-79 as Democrat; 1880-1912 Daily independent
w Ja-F 1878;sw Mr-Je ? 1878
pub [1878-1910]+
CLM D 12 1886[90-96]
CSb 1893+
CU-B [Ag 1875-My 19 1876;F 16-Je 2 1878]Ap 18,My 3 1884;Mr 30 1885;Ap 1,11,19, 1887[Mr-D 1889]Ja 2-3,6,My 20 1890;Ja 4,Jl 19-20,22-23,27-29,Ag 1,3,6,9-10,N 3 1892;Ag 11 1909-Mr 15 1913;Mr 21 1919;Ap 30 1923+
KHi [Ag 2-S 1 1888]
MWA Je 29 1926

Santa Barbara POST. *See* Santa Barbara press

Morning PRESS. d 1863+
Title varies: Santa Barbara daily press; Morning press; Santa Barbara press; Santa Barbara morning press
pub 1910+
C 1913+
CLM J 1876;Ag 24 1881[8?-1901]
CSb N 1887;92+
CSmH Mr 2 1877
CU-B [O 25 1872-74]-My,S-D 1880;F 24 1881; F 2? Mr 7,Ap 7,My 5,Je 1,6,20-22,24,S 14 1882;F 1 1883[88]-[90]91;O 16 1892;Je 6 1907; Ag 1909-Jl 1910;My 1919 Ag 8,O 16,28 1932
ICM Ap 28 1894
MWA N 1887
OClWHi Je 18 1885
OOxM Jl 23 1878

Santa Barbara PRESS. w My 30 1868-1912||?
1868-Je 10 1869 as Santa Barbara post
C D 19 1868;Jl 23 1870-Jl 5 1879;Ap 1901-O 10 1912
CU-B Jl 18,Ag 15 1868-[My-D 1880]Je 4 1882; My 5 1888
KHi S 27 1873
MB [Je 24 1871-Ag 19 1876;80-O 15 1881]
MH 1871-73
MWA S 10? 1875
NcD S 1875
OClWHi S 27 1873

Morning REPUBLICAN. d Jl-Ag 1875||?
CU-B Jl 1,19-Ag 14 1875

Santa Barbara TIMES. w,sw F 1 1870-74||?
CLM D 16 1871
CSmH Ap 11 1874
CU-B 1870-Je 27 1874

Santa Barbara TIMES. d Jl 10 1873-Je 28 1874||?
CU-B [Jl 10 1873-Je 28 1874]

SANTA CLARA

Santa Clara ECHO. w N 7 1873-O 4 1879||
Followed by Santa Clara Journal
CSmH Jl 15 1876
CU-B [1874]-[76-Je 1877;Ag 10 1878-79]
MWA Jl 15,Ag 12,O 21 1876

Santa Clara INDEX. w Ag 13 1870-72||?
CU-B 1870-N 25 1871

Santa Clara JOURNAL. w,sw O 11 1879+
Follows Santa Clara echo
C Je 1913-O 2 1918
CLM F 2-9 1887
CU-B 1879-80;Je-N 18 1882;86;Je 26-Jl 3,Ag 28 1889;Ja 18 1890[92]
KHi S 5 1888

Santa Clara NEWS. w My 11 1867+
C 1903+
CU-B [My 11 1867-Je 1871]Mr 9-Ap 20,Ag 17-O 19 1872[Je 8 1909-F 1 1910]

SANTA CRUZ

Santa Cruz COURIER-ITEM. w My 26 1876-89||
1876-Ap 1880 as Santa Cruz weekly courier. Title varies: Santa Cruz courier and local item; Courier and local item; etc
CU-B [1876]-My 23 1879;My-D 1880;Mr 16-23,Ag 11,25-S 8,22,O 1881-Ag 10,24 1882;Jl 23,Ag 13,O 22,N 5-19 1885;Mr 9 1889
MWA O 27 1876

EAST Santa Cruz herald. w 1889-90||?
CU-B N 16-D 14 1889;Ja 11,Ag 23 1890

Santa Cruz ENTERPRISE. w D 4 1873-Mr 26 1875||?
CU-B F 13 1874-Mr 26 1875
MWA Mr 6 1874

Santa Cruz JOURNAL. w S 2 1868-69||
C D 22 1868
CU-B [S 9-D 1868]-Ja 27 1869

LOCAL item. w Ap 16 1875-Mr 3 1880||
United with Santa Cruz weekly courier to form Santa Cruz weekly courier-item
CU-B [1875]-F 1880

NEW charter. w N 21 1893-95||?
KHi Ja 10 1894-Mr 22 1895

Santa Cruz evening NEWS. d 1907+
C O 24 1908+

CALIFORNIA (*Continued*)

SANTA CRUZ—*Continued*

PACIFIC sentinel. *See* Santa Cruz sentinel

SANTA CRUZ county times. *See* Santa Cruz times

Santa Cruz SENTINEL. w,sw Je 13 1856-1914||?
Follows Monterey sentinel (Monterey).
1856- as Pacific sentinel
w 1856-O 24 1891
C O 24 1868;Jl 23 1870
CU-B Jl 25 1857;64-D 2 1882[86-Je 23 1888] 89-[91]
KHi [Jl 28 1888-Ja 12 1889]
MWA Je 21-28,Jl 19-26 1856;D 16 1876

Santa Cruz SENTINEL. d 1884+
CU-B Ja,Mr-Ap,S-O 1888[89-O 1890;Ja-Je, Ag 1892-O,D 1893;F 20 1894-Ja 19 1895]S 22 1925

Santa Cruz SURF. w 1875-O 3 1918||
C 1890-1918

Santa Cruz SURF. d 1883-My 29 1919||?
C O 4-D 26 1918
CU-B O 11,16,N 14-15,D 28-31 1889;Ag 18 1890[Ag 1905-06]-My 29 1919
KHi [Ag 8 1888-Ja 1889]

Santa Cruz TIMES. w,sw Ap 25 1863-Jl 4 1871||?
1863-Ap 15 1865 as Pajaro times; Ap 22 1865-O 20 1866 Pajaro Valley times; O 27 1866-F 16 1867 Santa Cruz and Pajaro times; F 23 1867-O 22 1870 Santa Cruz county times
1863-O 20 1866 pub at Watsonville
C O 31 1868
CU-B 1863-Jl 4 1871
KHi S 14 1867
MWA Ja 26,F 9-Mr 9,Ap 13,My-Je 22,Jl 6, 20-O 12,N 30,D 7,21 1867-Ja 16 1869
N O 6 1866
NNHi O 19-26,N 16 1867
PJR N 28 1863

SANTA MARGARITA

Santa Margarita TIMES. w 1889-90||
CU-B Ja,F 15,Mr 1-8 1890

SANTA MARIA

GRAPHIC. w D 24 1889-1921||?
CU-B Ja 16-30,F 27,Mr 6,Jl 17,Ag 14-21,S 4-11,O 2,30 1890

TIMES. w,sw Ap 22 1882-1931||
Title varies: Santa Maria semi-weekly times; etc.
CU-B S 7 1889;D 17 1904
KHi S 22 1888

Santa Maria VALLEY vidette. w 1911+
pub 1930+

Santa Maria daily TIMES. d 1918+
pub 1918+
CSmar [Jl-S 1928]-[30-31]-[Ap 1932-Je 1933]+
CU-B Ja 22 1923-Ag 1930

SANTA MONICA

Santa Monica OUTLOOK. w O 13 1875-96||
Suspended 1879-86
pub complete
CL O 13 1875(facsimile)
CLM N 26 1890
CSmH My 10-17 1876
CSmo 1875-93
CU-B O 27-D 22 1875;Ja 19[Jl 1876-F 21 1877]O 15 1890;O 1,D 17 1892;F 22 1896
KHi Jl 10 1889;Je 10 1893
MWA Je 14 1876;S 26 1877;Mr 11 1890

Evening OUTLOOK. d 1896+
Title varies slightly: Santa Monica outlook; Santa Monica evening outlook
pub 1896+
CSmo 1922+

Santa Monica PRESS. w 1929+
CLW 1929+

SANTA PAULA

Santa Paula CHRONICLE. w 1888+
pub 1907+
C 1914+
CSpa 1918+
CSpaD 1910+
CU-B [Mr-D 6 1889]Ja,F 28,Ag 15 1890[1906]-S 3 1915
KHi Ja 12 1894

Santa Paula CHRONICLE. d O 1 1923+
pub 1923+
CSpa 1923+
CSpaD 1923+

Santa Paula REVIEW. w,sw,d S 3 1926+
Title varies: Santa Paula morning review; Santa Paula daily review
CSpa 1926-S 1930
CSpaD S 1929-[30-33]+

VOZ de la colonia. w 1924-32||
In Spanish
CSpa 1927-32

SANTA ROSA

Santa Rosa daily DEMOCRAT. *See* Santa Rosa press-democrat

INDEPENDENT. w N 27 1930+
pub 1930+

Santa Rosa NEWS. w Je 5 1879-
CU-B Je 12-Ag 8 1879

Santa Rosa PRESS. w My 8- 1874||
Followed by Santa Rosa times, later Santa Rosa republican
CU-B My-S 18 1874

Santa Rosa PRESS-DEMOCRAT. w,sw O 22 1857-1923||?
1857-O 2 1897 as Sonoma democrat (w)
C Ja 2 1869;My 21 1870-97
CSro 1857[58-Ag 1860]61-[80]-90
CU-B Mr 13 1862;Mr 31 1866;67-Ap 15 1882;Jl 26-Ag 2 1884;Ja 2 1885[86]D 31 1892;Ag 5,S 16 1893;Mr 17,My 12,Jl 7,21,S 8,N 3 1894[95] Ja 11,F 8,Mr 7-21,Ap 18,Ag 8 1896;F 27,Je 19,Jl 3,24,Ag 28,S 25 1897

Santa Rosa PRESS-DEMOCRAT. d Jl 1875+
1875-S 26 1896 as Santa Rosa daily democrat
pub 1875+
C O 9 1897+
Cl Ap 19 1906
CSro [Jl-D 1883]Ja-Je 1886;Jl-D 1887;Jl-D 1889;Jl-D 1890[F 19-Je 1904]-[Ja-Je 1906] 07+
CSt S 9 1885
CU-B S 26 1896;O 9,13 1897;My 8-11,13,15,Je 7 1919
TJT O 7 1897;Ag 8 1905

Santa Rosa REPUBLICAN. w Ja 14 1875-1926||?
Follows Santa Rosa press. 1875-D 25 1879 as Santa Rosa times
C Ja 21 1875-77;79
CU-B Ja 21 1875-[76]-Ja,Mr 1876-[77]-[79-80]O 1 1885;Ja 6 1886[87]Mr 30 1893;Ag 22 1905-Ap 17 1906[Ap 1921-Ag 1923]

Santa Rosa REPUBLICAN. d S 22 1879+
1879 as Santa Rosa times
pub 1905+
C 1881-82;84+
CSro [Mr-D 1904]-[Ap-D 1906]+
CU-B S 22 1879-[80]O 1-23,27-30 1886;Mr 12 1888;O 7 1889;S 1890;D 1891;Mr 28 1906;S 13 1907-16[Mr 5 1921-Ja 24 1924]
TJT Ap 15 1899

SONOMA county herald. w 1900+
pub 1912+

Santa Rosa TIMES. *See* Santa Rosa republican

SANTA YNEZ

Santa Ynez ARGUS. *See* Santa Ynez Valley argus

SANTA YNEZ Valley argus. w 1888-1923||?
1888-1920? as Santa Ynez argus
CLM N 28 1889;Mr 30 1893
CU-B N 14-21 1889
KHi [Je-S 1888]

SARATOGA

Saratoga SENTINEL. w S 20 1890-94||?
CU-B O 11 1890

Saratoga STAR. w 1917-29||?
CU-B D 15 1922;Je 28-Jl 5 1923

SAUSALITO

Sausalito HERALD. w 1872-74||?
CU-B Mr 8 1873

Sausalito NEWS. w F 12 1885+
C Jl 24 1909+
CU-B O 25,N 8,22-D 13 1889;Ja 17,Jl 25,Ag 22 1890;O 14 1892;Ap 26-Je 1919;My 20 1932

SAWTELLE

Papers published in Sawtelle are listed under Los Angeles

SEAL BEACH

Seal Beach POST and wave. w My 1916+
1916-O 1921 as Seal Beach post
pub 1916+

Seal Beach WAVE. w Je 1917-O 1921||
United with Seal Beach post to form Seal Beach post and wave
CSeP complete

SEBASTOPOL

Sebastopol TIMES. w 1889+
pub 1914+
CU-B O 13 1933+

SELMA

Selma ENTERPRISE. w Ja 7 1888-Ja 1929||
1888-1917? as Fresno county enterprise. United with Selma irrigator to form Selma irrigator and enterprise
CFr S 19 1924-S 16 1928
CSelI [1888-1928]
CU-B N 2 1889;O 31 1891;Mr 16-Ap 6,Jl 13-Ag 24,O 1905-F 8,Mr 1,22-My 24,Je 7 1906; Ap 15-Je 10,Jl 15-O 7,21 1909-Ap 7,28-Je 23 1910

FRESNO county enterprise. *See* Selma enterprise

Selma IRRIGATOR. d 1888-96||?
CU-B Je-Jl,Ag 5-12,14-28,S 1-6,9-N 29 1890

Selma IRRIGATOR and enterprise. sw,w Ap 3 1886+
1886-Ja 1929 as Selma irrigator
sw 1911?-27?
pub 1886+
CU-B 1888-89;Jl 1890-91;Je 9 1906;Jl 24 1909-Ja 8,22-29,F 12 1910;Je 30 1920+

SEPULVEDA

Sepulveda HERALD. w Ja 1926+
pub 1933+

SHAFTER

Shafter PROGRESS. w 1921+
CB 1929+

SHASTA

Shasta COURIER. *See under* Redding

Shasta REPUBLICAN. w O 20 1855-57||?
CU-B S 20 1856
KHi F 6 1858
NNHi O 10 1857

SIERRA CITY

SIERRA tribune. w D 7 1881-90||
1881-82? as Sierra county tribune (Forest City)
CU-B Mr 23,My 25-Jl 13,Ag 17-S 7 1882;D 30 1887[88-D 5 1890]

SIERRA MADRE

Sierra Madre NEWS. w 1906+
CSi 1928+

Sierra Madre VISTA. w Mr 23? 1888-
CLM Je 28,Jl 12-26,Ag 16,30,S 6 1889
KHi Ja 26 1889

SIERRA VALLEY

Sierra Valley LEADER. w 1882-94||?
CU-B [1888]Ja 11-Mr 8,Ap 12-D 13,27 1889-My 16,Ag 22-S 19,O 3,31 1890;Ja 8-Je 3,S 2, 23,30,O 14,N 11-25,D 9 1892-Ja 6 1893

MOUNTAIN mirror. w S 10 1890-92||?
CU-B S 10,O 29 1890

SIGNAL HILL

Signal Hill TRIBUNE. w D 21 1933+
pub [1933-My 1934]+

SILVER MOUNTAIN

ALPINE chronicle. *See* Bodie chronicle (Bodie)

Silver Mountain BULLETIN. w 1865-67||?
CU-B O 13,D 22 1866;Ja-My 18 1867

SILVER miner. w Ap 25-Je 20 1868||?
CSmH Je 20,1868

SISSON. *See* MT. SHASTA

SNELLING

MERCED banner. w 1862-63||?
CU-B N 21 1863

MERCED herald. w My 13 1865-Ag 14 1869||
Followed by San Joaquin Valley argus, later Merced county sun (Merced)
Suspended from Ja 11-Ag 22 1868
C Ja 2 1869
CMe complete
CU-B Mr 9-Jl 6,20,Ag-O,D 14 1867-69

SAN JOAQUIN Valley argus. *See* Merced county sun (Merced)

SOLEDAD

BEE. w O 10 1909+
CSa 1919+

SOLVANG

SANTA YNEZ Valley news. w 1925+
pub 1925+

SONOMA

Sonoma EXPOSITOR-forum. *See* Sonoma Valley moon

Sonoma INDEX-TRIBUNE. w 1878+
1878-84 as Sonoma index
pub [1885+]
C N 1915-O 19 1918;Ap 1930+
CU-B D 25 1879-Ja 15 1881;N 24 1882;F 10-24,Ap 7-14,28,My 26-Je 9,23,Jl 21,Ag 11-S 8,22-O 1883;Mr 29,Ap 5,Je 7 1884[Ja-Mr 10 1888;89]-[Jl 4,S 26-D 1891]Jl 9-16,Ag 6 1892; Jl-S,O 23 1909-Mr 12,26,Ap 2,30-Jl 9 1910

SONOMA Valley moon. w 1899-Ag 26 1927||
1899-1925 as Sonoma expositor-forum.
Merged with Sonoma index-tribune
C S 25 1919-27

SONORA

AMERICAN eagle. w Mr 5-Ag 20 1864||?
CU-B Ag 20 1864

AMERICAN flag. *See under* San Francisco

Sonora BANNER. w 1885+
1885-1900? as Democratic banner; 1900?-08? Mother lode banner
CU-B N 22-29 1889;Je 24 1892
KHi [D 28 1888-Mr 22 1889]

DEMOCRATIC age. w 1860-
CSmH Ap 28 1860

DEMOCRATIC banner. *See* Sonora banner

CALIFORNIA (*Continued*)

SONORA—*Continued*

Sonora HERALD. w Jl 4 1850-57||?
CSmH Jl 4-13,27,D 28 1850-F 1 1851;Je 12 1852;Jl 14 1855;Mr 1 1856
DLC Ag 24 1850;O 16 1852
KHi Jl 20-O 5 1850
MWA S 25 1852;Mr 8?,D 13 1856;My 9,30 1857
NNHi Jl 13,Ag 24 1850;Je 24 1854
—Steamer ed.
NNHi Je 1 1853

Sonora HERALD. w O 28 1865-67||?
CStoI D 23 1865-Je 15 1867
CU-B Jl 28 1866;Jl 6,S 21 1867

Sonora HERALD. d Ag 15 1867-
CU-B Ag 15-S 1 1867

MOTHER lode banner. *See* Sonora banner

Sonora NEWS and mother lode magnet. sw Mr 1 1935+
Follows Mother lode magnet (Jamestown)
pub 1935+

TUOLUMNE courier. w Je 20 1857-66||?
1857-65? pub in Columbia
C Jl 11 1863
CU-B O 10 1863;D 24 1864;Je 16 1866
DLC Ap 9-16 1859
MWA [F 1863-64]Ja 1865;Ja 20 1866

TUOLUMNE independent. w Ap 1872+
pub 1872+
CSmH Mr 19 1876
CU-B Je 15,29-Jl 13,Ag 24 1872-80;F 10 1883; 86-90;Jl 21 1927+
MWA Mr 4,Ap 1-8 1876

UNION democrat. w Jl 1 1854+
C D 19 1868;Je 1870-O 6 1877;My 17 1890+
CSmH Je 2 1860
CSo 1922+
CU-B Ag 30 1856;Jl 28,N 17 1866;Jl 6,O 19-N 2 1867;F 15,Je 6,20,Ag 8,22,O 3,17,D 19 1868; Ja-Ag,O 2,23 1869-71;My 1872-80;O 12,26 1889;Ja 11-18,Ag 16 1890
MWA F 28 1857;F 11 1860

SOUTH OCEANSIDE

Papers published in South Oceanside are listed under Oceanside

SOUTH PASADENA

South Pasadena BELL. w Mr 2- 1888||?
IU Ap 6 1888
KHi S 21 1888

South Pasadena COURIER. w 1913-D 13 1927||
CSp Jl 1917-D 23 1924[Ap 12-Je 1921]26-27

FEDERATED news. *See* South Pasadena news

South Pasadena FOOTHILL review. w Je 8 1893+
1893-Je 25 1908 as South Pasadenan; Jl 2 1908-D 30 1927 South Pasadena record
pub 1893+
CSp 1893-N 1894[O 10-D 1895]-N 1896;Ja-N 14 1906;F 1908-24[Ja-Je 1926]F 18-D 1927; Ja 10 1930+

South Pasadena NEWS. w My 1916+
1916-28 as Federated news
CSp [O 18-D 1918]-[Ja-N 4 1921]24-[Ja-Ap 23 1926]Ja 17-D 1930[32]+

South Pasadena RECORD. *See* South Pasadena foothill review

SOUTH Pasadenan. *See* South Pasadena foothill review

SOUTH RIVERSIDE

Papers published in South Riverside are listed under Riverside

SOUTH SAN FRANCISCO

ENTERPRISE and South San Francisco journal. w 1895+
1895-Ja 1927 as Enterprise
C 1907+
CSs [1895]-1916[25-32]+
CU-B Ag 14 1909-Ja 22 1910;S 5-12,O 24-N 13,D 5 1914;Ja 23-30,F 20-Ap 10,24,My 8 Je 19 1915-Jl 5 1918

South San Francisco NEWS. w 1892-95||?
KHi Ap 26 1895

SPRECKELS

COURIER-ENTERPRISE. w 1907-14||?
1907-My 24 1913 as Spreckels courier
C Ag 1909-My 1914
CSa Ja 17 1914
CU-B Ja 11,Jl,Ag 16,30-S,O 11,N 8,29-D 20 1913

ENTERPRISE. w Ja 7 1910-My 1913||
United with Spreckles courier to form Courier-enterprise

STANFORD UNIVERSITY

STANFORD daily. d S 19 1892+
1892-Ag 20 1926 as Daily Palo Alto. The Stanford Daily, altho a student paper, is the local newspaper of the community
Suspended during vacations
C 1892+
CSt 1892+
NbHi [C 1900;Mr 1901-My 2 1902]

STANFORD press. w S 5 1908-10||?
C 1908-My 23 1910

STOCKTON

Stockton daily ARGUS. d Je 7 1854-S 1862||
Follows Stockton journal
C 1857-O,D 1860-S 16 1862
CSmH F 19 1852
CU-B Ja 26 1858
MWA Mr 10 1857
NNHi F 19 1856
OClWHi N 29 1855

Stockton BANNER. w 1877-99||?
In German and English
CU-B O 22,N 5-12,26 1881-Ja 14,28,Mr 11 1882;Ja 27-Mr 10,24 1883;Ja 4 1890

Stockton BEACON. d 1862-64||?
CU-B Je 18 1864

CALIFORNIA courier. w
CU-B D 22 1906-Mr 20 1909

CENTRAL California record. w,sw 1875-1918||?
1875-1904 as Stockton record
w 1875-1904?
CU-B Mr 11 1893

Stockton COMMERCIAL record. w 1875-89|
CU-B Mr,Jl 1889
KHi F 9 1889

Stockton DEMOCRAT. w D 6 1857-S 20 1862|
C complete
CU-B S 19 1858

Stockton DEMOCRAT. d D 24 1885-Mr 23 1886||
CSto complete

Stockton EXPRESS. d Ag 6 1888-Mr 1 1889||
CSto S 13 1888-89

FORUM. w Je 23 1921+
C 1921+
CSt 1921+

Stockton daily GAZETTE. d Ag 19 1867-Ag 18 1869||
Merged with Daily evening herald, later Stockton daily evening herald
C O 21 1868
CSto complete
CU-B O 21-N,D 6,11-12,14,24-25 1867;68-69

Stockton weekly GAZETTE. w Ag 31 1867-D 12 1874||
Replaces Stockton weekly herald
CU-B D 21 1867;D 10-31 1870;N 18 1871;My-N 16,D 20 1872;Ja 10-Mr 7,21,Je 20-Jl 11,Ag 1-9,29,O 17,31 1873;Ja 9 1874

Stockton daily evening HERALD. d Jl 3 1865-Ap 2 1885||
1865-Ja 31 1883 as Daily evening herald; F 1 1883-S 13 1884 Stockton daily herald
C 1865-D 14 1874
C-S 1878-[Ja-Je 1884]
CSto Je 15 1870-D 12 1874;Jl 17 1876-85
CU-B Jl 27 1866;Ja 22,Jl 2 1867[Ap 18 1868-69]-[72-73]-O,D 1875[76]Ja 4,9,O 19 1877-Je 13,O 25 1878;Ja 10 1879;80;Ja 8 1883;Mr 10 1884

Stockton weekly HERALD. w 1867-84||?
Replaced 1869-74 by Stockton gazette
CU-B F 10,D 15 1883

Stockton weekly INDEPENDENT. w 1856-1915||?
CU-B Mr 12-Jl,O 22 1864-[75]-Je 1880
MWA Ja 1871

Stockton morning INDEPENDENT. d Ag 1 1861+
Follows San Andreas independent (San Andreas). 1861-N 29? 1934 as Stockton daily independent; N 30 1934-F 14 1935 Stockton evening news
pub 1861+
C F 3 1871-Ap 24 1887;O 19 1868
CLM D 7 1889
CPo S 13 1861
CSto 1861-Jl 1874;F 1875-Jl 1884;F 1885-1901; Jl-D 1902;Je 1903-S 1914;15+
CU-B S 11 1861;63-[81]Ja 1-15,17-18 1885;Je 20 1885;86-[88]-[90]-N 1891;D 11 1892;My 31 1893;N 1921-Je 1922;O 10 1933-Jl 20 1934
CtY Jl 10 1869
DLC Jl 14 1865;My 7 1874
KHi Jl 11-12 1888
MWA Ap 27 1868

Stockton JOURNAL. sw,d Je 19 1850-Je 6? 1854||
Followed by Stockton daily argus
CSto Je 11-D 1852
CU-B Ap 9 1851;O 29,D 17 1852
DLC F 15 1854
NNHi Ag 24,N 6,20 1850;Ja 4,15-18,25-F 1,15, 22-26,Mr 5,15,22,Je 7 1851
—Steamer ed. sm
MWA Jl 1852

Stockton LEADER. w *See* Sacramento leader (Sacramento)

Evening MAIL. d F 10 1880-O 24 1917||
1880-My 8 1883 as Stockton daily evening mail; My 9 1883-N 29 1884 Stockton mail; D 1 1884-Ap 14 1892 Mail. Merged with Stockton daily evening record
C F 12 1883-O 13 1887;My 12 1890-1917
CLM F 27 1886
CSto 1880-Ag 9 1906;07-17
CU-B S 25 1882;Ja 30,F 8 1883;Jl 15 1886;S 2 1889;S 1890;Ja 3,Ag 5 1891;Ja 20,F 13 1893;D 24 1894;O 6 1896;Ja 9-Mr 14,Je 6 1903-F 9,Ag 10 1904-17
DLC 1898

Weekly MAIL. w Ag 7 1880-Mr 25 1916||
CSto Ag 1885-Jl 24 1886;Ag 8 1891-Jl 1892;Ag 1895-Jl 1909;Ag 8 1914-Jl 3 1915
CU-B Jl 9 1892
TJT D 7,17 1898

Stockton evening NEWS. *See* Stockton morning independent

PHILIPPINE examiner. sm 1932+
In Filipino and English
pub 1932+

Stockton RECORD. d Ja-My 1865||?
CU-B My 18 1865

Stockton RECORD. w 1875-1904 *See* Central California record

Stockton daily evening RECORD. d Ap 8 1895+
Ap-Je 22 1895 as Evening record; Je 24 1895-Mr 1 1904 Daily record
pub 1895+
C 1911+
CSto 1895+
CU-B O 25 1900-N 5 1902;Ja 10-Mr 14,Je 4 1903-04;Ja 4,25-28 1905;O 26-31 1917;Ap 25-Jl 18 1919;O 25-D 1921;Jl 15,22,29,Ag 5 1922; Ja 15 1923+

Stockton daily REPUBLICAN. d S 7 1890-F 3 1891||
CSto Ja 27 1891||

SAN JOAQUIN herald. w My 23? 1867-68||?
CU-B My 9,Jl 4 1868

SAN JOAQUIN journal. *See* California zeitung (Oakland)

SAN JOAQUIN daily republican. sw,tw,d My 14 1851-74||?
Follows Stockton times. Title varies: Daily San Joaquin republican
Suspended 1863-N 22? 1869
sw 1851-Je 11 1853;tw Je 14-D 24 1853,Jl 19-D 25 1854
C Je 30 1853;N 23 1869-My 22 1872
CSto 1851-D 13 1862
CU-B S 17,O 1 1851;N 18 1857;N 15 1859;S 10 1861;S 1-14 1870;71-Ja 1,Ap 2-My 24,O 15 1872-F 1 1873
DLC Je 4 1856-Ag 1 1857;D 23-30 1858;[Ja-Ag O 1859]
MWA D 3 1851;Jl 14 1852;F 3 1853;Mr 10 1857

SAN JOAQUIN republican. w N 25 1854-74||?
Follows Stockton times
Suspended from D 13 1862-N 23 1869
C [1858-My 3 1862]
CSto 1855;Ja 12-Mr 15,29-My 3,17-Je 21,Jl-N 1,15 1856
CU-B O 17 1857;S 7 1861;D 1869-My 21 1870;N 18 1871
DLC O 27 1855-S,N 24-D 8 1860
MWA Ja 29 1859
OClWHi N 17 1855

SAN JOAQUIN Valley beacon. w 1863-64||?
CU-B N 26 1864

STOCKTONIAN. w N 26 1892-
CU-B N 26 1892

Stockton TIMES. w,sw Mr 16 1850-Ap 27 1851||
My 16-D 28 1850 as Stockton times and Tuolumne City intelligencer. Followed by San Joaquin republican
w 1850
CSmH My 18 1850
CSto complete
NN Mr 16 1850(reprint)

Stockton TIMES. sw My 2 1912+
In Japanese
pub 1912+

SUISUN

SOLANO county courier. w 1895+
CU-B Jl 8-Ag 5,19-O 14,28 1909-Mr 24,Ap 28,My 5-Jl 28,Ag 12 1910;My 22 1919
CF 1915+

SOLANO county democrat. *See* People's independent. (Vallejo)

SOLANO county herald. *See* Solano republican (Fairfield)

SOLANO press. w My 31 1862-N 17 1869||
United with Solano county herald to form Solano republican (Fairfield)
C D 23 1868
CU-B O 4 1862;Ja 24,Je 27 1863;Jl 25 1866[67]-69
DLC 1862-S 5 1863

SOLANO republican. *See* under Fairfax

SOLANO sentinel. *See* People's independent (Vallejo)

SUMMERLAND

SUMMERLAND. w 1889-
KHi N 12 1891

SUMNER

KERN county gazette. w 1874-77||?
CU-B Ja 6-13 1876

SUNNYVALE

Sunnyvale STANDARD. w Ja 1905+
CU-B Ap 12,D 13,27 1912;Ja 3,24-F 7,My 2,Jl 11,25,Ag 8,O 24-31 1913
CSun D 15 1914;15-18

SUSANVILLE

LASSEN advocate. w,d Jl 1 1865+
1865-Ag 29 1868 as Sage brush; S 5 1868-D 25 1872 Lassen sage brush
pub 1875+
C D 19 1868;1909+
CSu 1916+
CU-B F 22 1868-[69]-71;F 10-D 21 1872;73-80;S 20 1883-[85-Ap 1886]-Ja 5,Jl 12-D 1888; Je 27 1889-[90]91;Je 18 1909-Jl 8 1910

LASSEN county journal. w O 21 1874-75||?
CU-B F 4,Ag 5-O 14 1875

CALIFORNIA (*Continued*)

SUSANVILLE—*Continued*

LASSEN mail. w 1885+
CSu 1916+
CU-B F 23 1912-[14]+

LASSEN sage brush. *See* Lassen advocate

SAGE brush. *See* Lassen advocate

SUTTER CREEK

AMADOR record. w Ja 5 1892-1921||
CU-B Jl 15-O 7,21-N 25,D 9 1909-F 3,17,24,Mr 10-24,Ap 7,28-Jl 21 1910
DLC Ja 5,Mr 17 1892-[94-98]

Sutter Creek INDEPENDENT. d,sw Ag 19? 1873-74||?
d 1873-Mr 21 1874
CU-B S 5 1873-Je 23 1874

SWASEY

FALL River mail. w 1886-93||?
CU-B Mr,Je 21,S 13-20,N 15-D 13 1889;Ja 3-17,Ag 16,O 4-18 1890

TAFT

Daily MIDWAY driller. d 1912+
pub 1912+
CB 1912+

MIDWAY driller and midway oil courier. w 1910-Ja 28 1914||
CB F 1912-14

OILFIELDS dispatch. w Ap 20 1928+
CB Je 1 1928+

WEST side tribune and Maricopa oil news. w Ag 22 1924-27||?
Follows Maricopa oil news (Maricopa)
CB 1924-S 9 1927

TAHOE

Tahoe TATTLER. d Jl 9 1881-Jl 15 1882||?
CSmH [Jl 9 1881-F 18]Jl 15 1882

TEHACHAPI

Tehachapi NEWS and Mojave-Randsburg record-times. w O 13 1900+
Follows Summit sun. 1900-Je 6 1919 as Tomahawk (Ja-Jl 1901 as Mojave tomahawk (Mojave)
pub 1900-[19-20]Ap 16 1921+
C Mr 16 1928+
CB 1912-F 19 1921;23+

SUMMIT sun. w O 1891-1900||?
Followed by Tomahawk, later Tehachapi news. . .
CTeN Ap 19-Jl 12 1895

TOMAHAWK. *See* Tehachapi news. . .

TEHAMA

Tehama COUNSELLER. w S 9 1882-
NNHi S 9,23-30,O 14-N 18 1882

Tehama INDEPENDENT. *See* Tehama county people's cause (Red Bluff)

TOCSIN. *See* Tehama county democrat (Red Bluff)

TEMPLETON

Templeton ADVANCE. w Jl 6 1889+
CU-B N 30-D 7 1889;Ap 5,Ag 2-16,S 27-O 18 1890;Ja 23,F 6 1892;Je-Jl 4,18 1906[F-D 1907]-N 1908

Templeton TIMES. w 1886-90||
CU-B D 10 1887;Ja-F 15,Mr 1 1890
KHi Je 23 1888

Templeton TIMES. 1912-20 *See* Atascadero times (Atascadero)

THALHEIM

Thalheim TIMES. w Ag 6 1914-15||?
C 1914-S 7 1915

TORRANCE

Torrance HERALD-Lomita news. w Ja 1 1914+
CMp [1914-19]23+

TRACY

Tracy PRESS. w,sw 1898+
w 1898-1908
CU-B Ja 20,F 17,Mr 3-10,Ap 7,21,O 13 1906

TRAVER

Traver ADVOCATE. w 1887-96||
CU-B Mr,Je 22,Ag 31,O 19,D 7 1889;Ja 11,Ag 7-21 1890;Je 29 1893
KHi [Jl-N 10 1888]

TRUCKEE

Truckee REPUBLICAN. *See* Sierra sun and Truckee republican

SIERRA sun and Truckee republican. tw,sw,w Ap 30 1872+
Follows Grass Valley republican (Grass Valley). 1872-Jl 1933 as Truckee republican tw 1872-N 1874;sw D 1874-1910?
pub 1926+
C [1901-23]
CSto D 1874-D 4 1875
CU-B D 1874-[75-76]-[78]80;Ap 26 1882-Mr 12,Ap 19,Ag 30 1884;N 25 1885[86-Je 20 1888]
KHi Ja 16 1889

Truckee TRIBUNE. w,sw S 19 1868-70||?
sw My 1869-Ja 1870
C D 19 1868
CU-B 1868-Mr 19 1870

TUJUNGA

Papers published in Tujunga are listed under Los Angeles

TULARE

Tulare ADVANCE. d 1911-25||?
United with Evening register to form Tulare daily advance-register
C S 2 1913-Ja 18 1914
CU-B Ag 15,S 15,O 15,D 15 1922;Ja 14,Ap 15,My 1923

Tulare daily ADVANCE-REGISTER. d 1887+
1887-1925? as Evening register; S 14- 1932 Tulare daily times and Tulare register
C O 8 1932+
CU-B 1889-Ap,Je-D 1891;My 6-31 1919

Tulare DEMOCRAT free press. w 1885-88||?
CLM Ja 28 1888
CU-B [1886]

Tulare REGISTER. w 1883-1920||?
CLM [1903-05]
CU-B [1887-88]Ag 30 1889;O 10 1890;Ag 13 1909-Ap 8 1915
KHi D 28 1888

Evening REGISTER. *See* Tulare daily advance-register

Tulare STANDARD. w O 22 1887-
CU-B O 22 1887

Tulare daily TIMES. d 1929+
For S 14- 1932 *See note under* Tulare daily advance register
C Ja-O 8 1932

Tulare VALLEY citizen. w 1891-97||?
C 1895-N 25 1897

TUOLUMNE

Tuolumne City NEWS. *See* Stanislaus county news (Modesto)

Tuolumne PROSPECTOR. w 1902+
pub 1902+

TURLOCK

Farmer's daily JOURNAL. *See* Turlock daily journal

Turlock weekly JOURNAL. w N 11 1904-18||?
pub 1904-10
CU-B Jl 23 1909-Ap 8,29-Jl 8 1910

Turlock daily JOURNAL. d 1911+
1911-F 1921 as Turlock journal; Mr 1921-Ap 1923 Farmer's daily journal
pub 1911-F 1921;My 1923+
C 1913+
CU-B Je 30 1920+

Turlock PIONEER. w 1887-89||
CU-B F 27,Mr 6-13,Jl 10-17 1889

Turlock TRIBUNE. tw,d,w Je 1910+
tw 1910-My 1928;d Je-S 8? 1928
pub 1910+
C Je 1919+

TUSTIN

Tustin NEWS. w N 1922+
pub 1922+
CU-B [O 13 1933+]

UKIAH

CONSTITUTIONAL democrat. w Jl 9-O 8 1863||?
CU-B O 8 1863

DEMOCRATIC dispatch. *See* Ukiah dispatch-democrat

Ukiah DISPATCH-DEMOCRAT. w 1869+
1869-S 1873 as Independent dispatch; O 1873-80? Democratic dispatch; 1881?-99? Mendocino dispatch and democrat
1869-S 1873 pub at Mendocino
CU-B [Ja 20 1870-73]-Je 1877;78-80;Je 9-16 1882;F 2,16 1883;Ja-O,D 1887[88-91]My 18 1906;Ag 13 1909-Jl 8 1910
KHi [N 23-D 1888]

INDEPENDENT dispatch. *See* Ukiah dispatch-democrat

MENDOCINO county press. w Ag 5 1871-72||
CU-B Ag 5 1871-F 29 1872

MENDOCINO county republican. w 1887-89||
United with Ukiah city press to form Ukiah republican press
KHi Ja 30 1889

MENDOCINO democrat. w 1864-81||?
United with Democratic dispatch to form Mendocino dispatch and democrat, later Ukiah dispatch-democrat
C D 18 1868;Ap 22 1870-Jl 1872
CU-B Mr 16 1866[Jl-D 1867]-D 17 1869;Je 17 1870-My 19,S 1877-[80]-Mr 5 1881

MENDOCINO dispatch and democrat. *See* Ukiah dispatch-democrat

MENDOCINO herald. w 1861-70||
C O 23 1868
CU-B Jl 21[O 27-D 1865]-F 11 1870

Ukiah PRESS. *See* Ukiah republican-press

REDWOOD journal. sw Ap 19 1929+
pub 1929+
TxGR Ap 9 1930

Ukiah REPUBLICAN-PRESS. w Jl 4 1876+
1876-89? as Ukiah city press
pub 1876+
C Ja 20 1911+
CU-B Je 6 1879-Ja,F 20-Ap,My 14-28 1880;F 11-Jl 8,29-D 2,16 1881-Ja,F 10-Ap 14,My-Ag 4 1882;Jl 24-31,Ag 14 1890;O 18 1901;Mr 7,Jl 18 1902

UNION

HUMBOLDT times. *See under* Eureka

NORTHERN Californian. w D 15 1858-Jl 4 1860||
Merged with Humboldt times (Eureka)
CSmH complete
CSt-H complete
MWA Ja 26,Ap 27,My 11,Je 8,22,Jl 6,Ag 3 1859

UPLAND

Upland NEWS. sw 1894+
CUp My 1913+

VACAVILLE

Vacaville REPORTER. w 1883+
pub 1883+
CU-B [1888]-Ja 10,24,Mr 21,N 15 1889;Ag 13 1909-Jl 15 1910;O 13 1933+
DLC Je 20 1903

VACA Valley enterprise. w 1889-90||
CU-B Ja-D 20 1890

VALLEJO

Vallejo evening CHRONICLE. d Je 1867+
Follows Daily reporter (Napa)
pub 1867+
C D 23 1868;Ap 21(extra)1906
CU-B [N 9 1868-69]-Ag,N 1879;F-D 1880;Ja 13,Mr 5,O 18 1881;Ja 28,Ap 19,Jl 20 1882;Jl 3,N 10 1884;87;Jl 5-N 1888;Ja 4,6-7 1890;D 1891;N 5 1894;My 26 1919
KHi Jl 27 1888

Weekly CHRONICLE. w Je 29 1867-1916||?
CU-B [1867]-69;Je 1870-[75-76]-[79]-80;Mr 11-18,Je 24-N 18 1882;Mr 14-21,Ap 18,S 5,N 7-14 1884;86;Ja-Je 1888;89-91
KHi Jl 20,O 12 1888

Daily INDEPENDENT. d Ja 6 1872-D 19 1873;F 17 1874-S 26 1875||
1872-73 as Vallejo daily independent; F-Ag 1874 Daily people's independent
CU-B Ja 11 1872-75

Vallejo evening NEWS. d 1895+
pub D 1934+
C Jl 17 1914+
CU-B O 9 1933-F 9 1934

Daily PEOPLE'S independent. *See* Daily independent

PEOPLE'S independent. w Ap 30 1868-N 7? 1874||
1868-Jl 29 1869 as Solano sentinel; Ag 7-N 27 1869 Solano county democrat; D 5 1869-D 20 1873 Solano democrat
1868-N 1869 pub at Suisun
C Ap 16 1870-D 21 1872
CU-B Jl 1868-73

Semi-weekly RECORDER. w,s-w F 23 1867-72||?
w 1867-S 29 1868
CU-B [F 23 1867-Ag 19 1870]
DLC N 30 1867

Vallejo RECORDER. d Je 1867-72||
CU-B Jl 1 1867;Ag 23 1870-Mr,My 1871-My 18 1872
DLC Ja 15,S 16 1871

SOLANO county advertiser. w Ap 23 1868-69||
C Jl 10 1869
CU-B Ap 23-My 14[Ag 13 1868-F 20 1869]

SOLANO democrat. *See* People's independent

SOLANO times. d *See* Vallejo times-herald

SOLANO times. w *See* Vallejo times

Vallejo TIMES. w 1876-1903||?
1876-90 as Solano times
CU-B Mr 24 1877-D 14 1878;Jl 12 1879-[80]O 22-29 1881;D 28 1889;Ag 23 1890

Vallejo TIMES-HERALD. d S 29 1875+
1875-90 as Solano times; 1890-1922 Vallejo times
CU-B [O-D 1875]-Jl 7 1877[D 16 1879-80]Ap 7 1881;Je 29,S 6 1887;N 19-20,27,D 25,27,29,31 1889;Ja 1,3,Ag 15,19-20,22,26 1890
KHi Jl 31 1888

VAN NUYS

Papers published in Van Nuys are listed under Los Angeles

VENICE

Papers published in Venice are listed under Los Angeles

CALIFORNIA (*Continued*)

VENTURA
To 1898? as San Buenaventura

Ventura DEMOCRAT. *See* Ventura post and democrat

Ventura FREE press. w,sw N 14 1875-D 1924‖?
Je 1889-Mr 15 1890 as Ventura vidette
sw Ag 15-S 8 1877
pub 1885-86
C 1891-Ag 13 1920
CLM Jl 27 1878;F 15 1879;Ag 31,N 16-23 1889[90-93]Jl 28 1899
CU-B S 30-O,N 25,D 23 1876-S,O 19,N 16,30-D 21 1878[79]80;Je 4 1881;Mr 1 1882;F 23 1884;F 6 O 23 1885;Ja-Je 1888[89]F 1,15,Mr-D 19 1890;91;S-N 1905;Ja-Mr 9,My 11 1905-Ja 16,Ag 13 1920-N 4 1921;Ja 13 1922-My 1 1925
CVe 1875-My 6 1882;83;87-88;91-95;98-1918;20-24
CVeV 1875-My 6 1882;83;87-88;Je 1889-95;98-1918,20-24
KHi Jl 21-28 1888;Jl 20 1889
MH [Ja 12 1883-Mr 6 1885]

Ventura FREE press. d Ja 4 1887+
Je 1889-Mr 15 1890 as Vidette
pub 1887+
CU-B Je 27-29 1889;Ja 3,6,8-9,F 1-13,15-28,Je 2-Jl 12,15-O 1890
CVe 1887-N 1889;D 1890-Je 27 1891;F 8-D 1892;F-Je 1902;F 3 1903-Jl 1914;F 1915-20;F 1921+
KHi N 10 1888;My 9 1891

Ventura INDEPENDENT. w 1889-Je 25 1903‖?
C 1898-Je 1903
CLM Ap-My 1901
CU-B O 14 1897
CVeV Ja 2,D 25 1902

Ventura OBSERVER. w Ag 7 1891-93‖?
CLM Ag 13 1891;Jl 20 1892-My 17 1893
CU-B Ag 2 1893
CVeV 1891-Je 1892

PEOPLES advocate. w 1891-94‖
CLM N 1893-Je 7 1894

Ventura weekly POST and democrat. w N 17 1883-1926‖
1883-D 31 1915 as Ventura weekly democrat
CL 1883-O 1885
CLM Jl 29 1886;Ag 29 1889
CU-B F 28 1889;Ag 13 1909-Ap 1,29-Jl 8 1910
CVeS N 27 1884-Ag 1894
CVeV 1902-21
KHi D 20 1888

Ventura daily POST and democrat. d Ag 1901-Ag 15 1926‖
1901-My 1915 as Ventura daily democrat.
United with Ventura county star to form Ventura county star and Ventura daily post
CVeS 1901-My 1915
CVeV D 31 1915-26

Ventura REPUBLICAN. w O 14 1887-88‖
CU-B Ja 14-Mr 10,24,Ap 14-My 12 1888

Ventura REPUBLICAN. w F 11 1904-D 28 1905‖
C F 18 1904-05
CVeV complete

Ventura SIGNAL. d 1871-86‖?
CLM My 10 1873;Jl 27 1878;F 12 1881;F 10 1883;F 16,O 25 1884

Ventura SIGNAL. w Ap 22 1871-84‖?
CSmH 1871-Je 7 1873;Ap 5 1879
CU-B Ag 1871-[72-73]-[76-79]80;Mr 29-Ap 12, Jl 26,N 8 1884

VENTURA county news. w Ap 1928+
CVe 1928+

VENTURA county star and the Ventura daily post. d Ap 1 1925+
1925-Ag 15? 1926 as Ventura county star
pub 1925+
C D 27 1926+
CVe 1925+
CVeV Je 15 1925+

VIDETTE. *See* Ventura free press

VICTORVILLE

VICTOR Valley news-herald. w 1913+
CU-B N 26,D 10 1915-F 1916

VISALIA

Visalia morning COURIER. d S 12 1905-
C 1905-My 1906;Ja-Mr,Jl-Ag 2 1907

Visalia DELTA. w Je 25 1859-F 28 1919‖?
Je-O 1 1859 as Tulare county record; O 8 1859-? Visalia weekly delta; N 8 1917-F 28 1919? as Thursday ed of Visalia delta (d)
C 1859-Je 17 1875;Je 22 1876-96;Ag 11 1898-99; Mr 21 1901-Jl 24 1902;09-16;Jl 1917-F 1919
CU-B O 3 1861;Ja-My 19,N 23-30,D 21 1864; 65-80;D 16-23 1881;Ja 27,F 10,Mr 10,Je 16-Ag, S 8 1882;Ag 2 1883;Ap 23 1885;D 15 1887;Ja-Je 1888;89[90]91;Ag,O-N 3 1892
KHi Jl 19 1888

Visalia DELTA. d 1892-F 29 1928‖
United with Visalia times to form Visalia times-delta
C F 22 1892-1907;Mr 1908-28
CU-B Ap 26-30,My 3-16,20-24,27-Je 5,7-Jl 4, 18 1919;Je 29 1927-28

EQUAL rights expositor. w 1862-63‖?
C Ag 30 1862-Mr 5 1863
CU-B F 6 1863

IRON age. w O 11 1876-78‖
CU-B 1876-Mr,D 13 1877-F 21 1878

Visalia SUN. w S 5 1860-
C S 5-D 27 1860

Visalia TIMES. d Ja-Ap 1876‖?
CU-B [Mr-Ap 1876]

Visalia TIMES. w *See* Tulare county times

Visalia TIMES-DELTA. d 1892+
1892-F 29 1928 as Visalia times
C Mr 1928—
CU-B Je 14 1906;Ja 5 1924;Mr 1928+

TULARE county news. w 1895-1905‖?
C Ja 16 1896-Ja 6 1897

TULARE county record. *See* Visalia delta. w

TULARE county times. w 1864-F 1 1917‖
Title varies: Visalia times; Tulare weekly times
C O 24 1868;My 14 1870-Ag 23 1873;90-1916
CU-B D 1 1866;Jl 13,27-D 21 1867;1868-Jl 27,S 4,18-N 6,20-D 11,25 1875-[78]-80;Ap 30 1881;Ap 9-16 1885;D 26 1889;Ja 2-16 1890;Ap 30,S 24 1891;Jl 22 1909-Ap 7,28-My,Je 16-Jl 21 1910

TULARE index. w My 28 1879-
CU-B [My 28-S 10 1879]

VISTA

Vista PRESS. w S 1926+
pub 1926—

VOLCANO

Weekly LEDGER. *See* Amador ledger (Amador)

WALNUT CREEK

CONTRA Costa courier. w 1911+
CU-B Ap 25-Je 27 1919

Walnut Creek SENTINEL. w Mr 9 1894-
CU-B Je 22 1894

WASCO

Wasco NEWS. w 1911+
1911-15? as Wasco news and San Joaquin Valley colonist
CB 1916-26;30+

WASHINGTON (Alameda county) *See* IRVINGTON

WASHINGTON (Yola county)

YOLO independent.
CU-B Je 22 1906;My 23 1919

WATERFORD

Waterford NEWS. w 1917+
CU-B [F-D 1921]-D 2 1923;Mr 14,My 2-9,Je 12,N 24,D 19 1924;Ja 23,F 13,27,Mr 27,Ap 10, 24,Jl 10,Ag 28,S 11-18 1925;Ja 29 1926

Waterford-Hickman NEWS. w S 24 1914-S 7 1915‖?
C 1914-S 7 1915

WATSONVILLE

CALIFORNIA transcript. *See* Watsonville transcript 1879-

PAJARO times. *See* Santa Cruz times (Santa Cruz)

PAJARO Valley times. *See* Santa Cruz times (Santa Cruz)

PAJARONIAN. w Mr 5 1868-1913‖?
C D 24 1868
CU-B 1868-[72]-[75-76]-78;My 1879-[81-Ag 3 1882]86;89-91

Evening PAJARONIAN. d Ap 7 1903+
C 1903-05;30
CU-B S 13 1906;Ag 11 1909-Jl 21 1910;Ap 28,My 9,22 1919;Ap 22 1927
WaPS F 15,Ag 1 1924[26]

Watsonville REGISTER. d 1893+
CU-B Ag 14 1909-Ap 9,My 3-Je 16,23-Ag 19 1910

RUSTLER. w 1888-96‖?
CU-B D 25 1891;Ja 22-F 5 1892

Watsonville TRANSCRIPT. w Jl 24 1876-79‖
CU-B [Mr 17 1877-79]
NN [Ag 26 1876-Mr 24 1877]

Watsonville TRANSCRIPT. w O 8 1879-
1879-F? 1880 as California transcript
CU-B 1880-O 26 1881;My 9 1883;Je 3 1885;Ap 20 1889;O 18 1890
KHi Ag 25,D 29 1888;Mr 23 1889

WATTS

Papers published in Watts are listed under Los Angeles

WEAVERVILLE

Weekly TRINITY journal. w F 1856 +
C D 19 1868;Jl 1890+
CLM O 16 1858
CStM Ap 12 1856
CU-B 1854-[68]-Jl 10 1872;F 8 1873-[75]-My 20 1876 My 7 1887[88-89]-91;Jl 1927+
KHi Ag 18 1888

TRINITY press. w O 11 1870-Je 27 1871‖?
CU-B N 29 1870;Je 27 1871

TRINITY times. w 1855-
MWA D 22 1855

WEED

Weed PRESS. w Mr 1926+
CYC 1926+

SUMMIT lookout. w 1912-Mr 1914‖?
CYC 1913-Mr 1914

WEST BERKELEY

Papers published in West Berkeley are listed under Berkeley

WEST LOS ANGELES

Papers published in West Los Angeles are listed under Los Angeles

WEST OAKLAND

Papers published in West Oakland are listed under Oakland

WESTMINSTER

Westminster GAZETTE. w My 5 1927+
1927-28 as Westminster news
pub 1927-[29-30]My 10 1934+

Westminster NEWS. *See* Westminster gazette

Westminster TRIBUNE. w Ja 25 1890-91‖?
CLM Ag 8 1891
CU-B Ja 25,Mr 15 1890

WESTWOOD

Westwood SUGAR pine. w Jl 11 1916+
pub 1916+
CSu Ap 1929-Mr 1933

WHEATLAND

BEAR River news. w D? 1880-81‖
CU-B N 26-D 10,24 1881

FOUR corners. *See* Wheatland herald

FREE press. w Ap 25 1874-77‖?
CU-B Je 13 1874-[75]-Ap 21 1877

GRAPHIC. w 1882-89‖
CU-B Ja 27-Je 9,23,Jl 14-21,Ag 4-11,S 8-O 13,D 1 1883;O 31 1885;Ja-Je 19,Ag 7-S 11,25-N 20,D 4-18 1886;Mr 30,Jl 6, 20 1889

Wheatland HERALD. w 1888+
1888-1923 as Four corners
CU-B Je 22 1889

Wheatland RECORDER. w D 21 1877-Ag 27 1878‖?
CU-B 1877-Je 28,Jl 12-Ag 23,S 6-13,27 1878

WHITTIER

Whittier CALIFORNIAN. w 1926+
CWh Ap 1929-1904

Whittier HERALD. w Jl 15 1909-N 7 1910‖?
CWh 1909-Ja 20,N 7 1910

Whittier HERALD. d 1910-
CWh Ja 21 1910-Ja 19 1911

Whittier NEWS. w Mr 24 1900-O 28 1910‖
pub complete
CLM Jl 23,S 17-O,N 12-19,D 10 1904;Ja 7,F 11 1905;Ja 7 1906
CWh Ap 1902-10

Whittier NEWS. d Mr 14 1904+
pub 1904+
C N 12 1913-F 24 1923
CU-B N 3 1906[Ag 11 1909-Ag 17 1910]
CWh 1904+
CWhW [Je 2 1909-Ag]O 1910+

Whittier POINTER. w My 25 1889-92‖?
CLM [Jl 27 1889-My 23]-Jl,S 26,O 24 1891;Ja 2 1892
CU-B O 11 1890
KHi Jl 27 1889

Whittier REGISTER. w Ja 28 1892-1910‖
CU-B Ag 12-N 4 1909
CWh 1892-96;98-1910
CWhW Ja-Mr 1892;F 10,Je 23 1893-N 13 1903 05-Je 1906

WILLIAMS

Williams FARMER. w 188?+
C [Jl-N 13 1909]
CCo O 1916+
CU-B Mr 30,Ap 13-20,Je 29,Jl 13,Ag 31-S 7,O 12-26 1889;Ap 3,17,My 29-Je 5,10,24,Ag 14-28,O 16,N 6-13 1909
KHi [Ag 1888-Ja 12 1889]

WILLIAMS review. w O 26 1882-
CU-B F 9-Ap 13 1883

WILLITS

LITTLE Lake herald. w 1901-N 26 1910‖
Merged with Willits news
CWiN O 8 1902-10

Willits NEWS. w 1903+
pub 1903+

CALIFORNIA (*Continued*)

WILLOWS

COLUSA county democrat. w 1886-89||
CU-B Mr 1-8,22 1889

GLENN transcript. sw;tw;w 1902+
sw 1902-F 12 1927;tw F 14 1927-Ap 29 1931
pub 1902+
CU-B Ag 11 1909-Jl 16 1910[18-Mr 1 1919] Jl 24 1920[27-31]+

Willows semi-weekly JOURNAL. w,sw 1877-F 1928||
1877-96? as Willows journal (w)
C O 12 1916-Jl 1920;My 9 1921-29
CU-B D 8 1877-Ja 19,F 2 1878;Jl 1879-80[88-89]-Je 1890[My 9-D 1891]Jl 28 1894;Ag 13 1909-Jl 1910[Jl 30 1917-D 5 1918]

Willows JOURNAL. d 1887+
pub [1892-1920]+
C O 12 1916-Jl 26 1920;My 9 1921+
CU-B Ag 31,S 3,5 1889[Ap 4 1917-D 20 1918]

Willows REVIEW. w 1890-Ag 13 1915||
C 1901-15
CU-B [Ja 19-D 1906]-15

WILMAR

Wilmar CHRONICLE. w Jl 1 1923+
pub 1923+

SAN GABRIEL Valley press. w 1924+
pub 1928+

WILMINGTON

Papers published in Wilmington are listed under Los Angeles

WINDSOR

Windsor HERALD. w 1899-1906||
CU-B Ja 27-F 3,17-24,Mr 3,24-31,Ap 14,28, My 12-19 1906

WINTERS

Winters ADVOCATE. w N 4 1875-79||
CU-B [My 27 1876-Ap 7,D 1 1877-Je 7 1879]

Winters EXPRESS. w 1883+
pub F 1907+
C My 14 1887+
CU-B Ag 20-O 8,22,N 5-19,D 1909-Ap 1,29-My 20,Je-Jl 8 1910

YOLO county record. w Jl 10 1891-O 14 1930||
1891-Ja 10 1929 as Home alliance (Woodland)
C 1917-30
CU-B Mr 15 1917-30

WOODBRIDGE

Woodbridge MESSENGER. w Ag 25 1865-69||
CU-B S 29,N-D 22 1865;Ja 5-19,F 2-12,Mr 2,Je 15,29,Jl 20-27,Ag,S 28,O 20-N 3,17,D 8 1866-Ja 12,26-F 9,23-Mr 16,30-My,Je 8-29,Jl 13-20,Ag,S 14-21,N 2-16,30-D 7 1867;Ja 4,F 15-Ap 18,My 2,30 1868-Ja 16,30-Ap 1869

WOODLAND

Woodland daily DEMOCRAT. d Je 1877+
pub 1877+
C Je 24 1877;91+
CU-B Ja 21,30,Jl 26-D 1878;F 1879-80;86;D 1887-88;Mr 1891

HOME alliance. *See* Yolo county record (Winters)

MAIL of Woodland. d Ag 3 1881+
Title varies: Daily morning mail
pub 1881+
C Ag 1920+
CSmH Ag 3-O 15 1881
CU-B O 22,N 4-5,12-15 1885;Ag 22 1888;Ag 21-31 1890;Ag 11 1909-Ap 12,My 4-Ag 19 1910;Je 23 1920-S 26 1925;Ap 13 1928+

Woodland NEWS. w 1854?-67||?
CU-B D 10 1864[Ap 21-D 1866]-N 16 1867

Woodland REPUBLICAN. w F 28 1880-
CU-B F 28-Je 26 1880

Woodland STANDARD. w Je 28 1879-
CU-B Je 28-D 27 1879

YOLO county democrat. *See* Yolo democrat

YOLO democrat. w N 23 1867-1918||?
1867-N 27 1869 as Yolo county democrat
C O 31 1868;Ap 23 1870-S 5 1873
CU-B 1867-Je 1878;79-Ja 6 1881;Je 1 1882
MWA Jl 11 1876

YOLO independent. *See* Independent leader (Sacramento)

YOLO mail. w,sw O 1 1868-1918||?
w 1868-95?
pub complete
C N 26 1868
CLM Ja 1 1892

YORBA LINDA

Yorba Linda STAR. w 1917+
pub 1917+

YREKA

Yreka JOURNAL. sw,w 1853+
1853-N 15? 1864 as Yreka semi-weekly journal
sw 1853-N 15? 1864;My 29 1880-Jl 20 1887
C N 6 1868;1902+
CU-B F 15,Ap 12 1867-[73]-[75-76]-77;N 1879-80;Mr 18,Je 17 1882[86-90]91;F 3 1892;F 14,Mr 28-D 1917;F 20,28,Mr 13 1918-Je 4 1919;O 12 1933+
CYC 1862-1910;14-17;20+
MWA Ag 2 1876

MOUNTAIN herald. *See* Yreka union

Daily REPORTER. w 1896-99||
CYC S 1898-99

SISKIYOU chronicle. w 1856-
DLC Je 25 1857;F 18 1858

SISKIYOU news. w,sw 1877+
w 1877-My 1933
pub 1901;S 13 1923-27;29;32+
CU-B [Je 1895-N 14 1896]Ja 9 1897;Jl 15 1909-Jl 21 1910;F 7,Mr 29 1917-Mr 6,Ag 21,S 4,18,D 4,18 1924-O 1 1925;Ja 21,F 1926+
CY 1929+
CYC 1895-1901;03-12;14-29

SISKIYOU weekly telegram. w Je 7 1890-92||
CU-B O 18-N 1 1890
CYC complete

SISKIYOU times. sw 1927-30||
Merged with Siskiyou news
CYC 1930

Weekly TRIBUNE. w 1852-83||?
CU-B Ap 21,N 3 1881;F-My 4,O 19-26,N 9 1882
CYC Je-D 1880;Ap 13 1882-Je 1883

Yreka UNION. w,sw Je 1852-97||
1852-54 as Mountain herald
sw 1864-Ja 7 1865
C Je 18 1853;Ap 29 1854;D 26 1868;My 27 1870-Ag 24 1872
CU-B N 24 1855[64-67]-77;Jl 6-13,27-N 9,23,D 1878-Ap 3 1880
CYC My 1864-73;75-80;85-97
DLC Mr 3 1859
KHi [Ag 9 1888-F 21 1889]
NNHi Je 3 1854
OrHi Je 30-Ag 1860

YUBA CITY

INDEPENDENT-farmer. w,sw Ap 22 1881+
1881-Mr 12 1935 as Sutter county farmer (w)
pub 1881+
C Jl 1890+
CU-B [1888]-91;Ja 26 1923+
CYu Mr 1918-Mr 1925;Je 25 1926+
IU N 22 1889
KHi S 22 1893

Yuba City JOURNAL. w Ja 21 1880-
CU-B Ap 22 1880

SUTTER banner. w Ap 8 1867-80||?
C D 19 1868[My 1870-My 4 1872]
CU-B 1867-[72]-[75]-Je 1879;80

SUTTER county farmer. *See* Independent farmer

SUTTER county sentinel. w Ap 27 1867-68||?
CU-B [My 25-D 1867]-F 8 1868

SUTTER independent. w Mr 1886-Mr 15 1935||
United with Sutter county farmer to form Independent-farmer
pub complete
C complete
C 1900-35
CLM [1903-05]
CMa N 27 1924-O 22 1925
CU-B Je 1934-35
CYu My 1919-Ap 1925;Jl 1929-35

CANAL ZONE

ANCON

AMERICAN. w Je 13? 1908-
DLC Ja 25,F 1,My 31,Jl 19,Ag 11,S 6-13,O 4,18-N 1,15,D 13,27 1909-Ja 3 1910

PANAMA times. *See under* Panama City (Panama)

BALBOA HEIGHTS

CANAL record. *See* Panama Canal record

PANAMA CANAL record. w S 4 1907+
1907-Ag 16 1916 as Canal record
DLC 1907+
NN 1907+
PJR F 23 1916

COLORADO

AKRON

Akron NEWS-REPORTER. w,sw 1910+
1910-F 28 1929 as Akron news
sw Ja-F 1929
CoHi O 13 1910+

Akron PIONEER-PRESS. w N 1 1885-1925||?
CU-B Ja 3 1890
CoHi Jl 23 1897-Je 29 1906;11-N 9 1923

Akron REPORTER. w 1916-F 1929||
United with Akron news to form Akron news-reporter

WASHINGTON county leader. w 1897-1914||?
CoHi 1899-1907;10-My 24 1912

ALAMOSA

Alamosa AERIAL. w
CoAT [O 17 1927-My 3 1928]

COLORADO independent. *See* Alamosa journal 1875-1932

Alamosa COURIER. w F 20 1889-1931||
1889-99? as San Luis Valley courier. Title varies: Alamosa courier and leader; etc.
CoAT [1925]-31
CoHi 1889-F 12 1890;1910-Ap 26 1928

Daily COURIER. d 1928+
CoAT 1928+
CoHi O 31 1932-33

Alamosa EMPIRE. w 1909-26||
CoAT [1925-26]
CoHi 1911-23;Ja-Jl 1926

EXPOSITOR. w S 27 1883-
CU-B D 6 1883

INDEPENDENT. *See* Alamosa journal (1875-1932)

INDEPENDENT-JOURNAL. *See* Alamosa journal (1875-1932)

Alamosa JOURNAL. w,sw 1875-Jl 29 1932||
1875-83? as Colorado independent; 1884? Independent; 1885-Ap 17 1914 Independent journal
CU-B Jl 18-Ag 8 1889
CoAT 1925-32
CoHi F 13 1902-05;F 11 1910-15

Alamosa JOURNAL. w F 7 1884-85||
United with Independent to form Independent-journal, later Alamosa journal
CoHi 1884-Ja 29 1885
KHi Jl 31 1884

SAN LUIS Valley courier. *See* Alamosa courier

SENTINEL. w Jl 3 1886-
CU-B Ag 7 1886
KHi Jl 3 1886

ALMA

MOUNT LINCOLN news. w My? 1875-78||?
ICHi Jl 8,S 2 1876

PARK county bulletin. w 1884-1913||?
CoHi 1899-1910

ANIMAS FORKS

Animas Forks PIONEER. w Je 17 1882-86||
CoD [Je 24 1882-O 2 1886]
KHi Jl 8 1882

ANTONITO

La AURORA. w 1911-24||?
In Spanish
IU [D 7 1917-Ag 8 1919]

Antonito LEDGER-NEWS. w 1892+
1892-1927? as Antonito ledger
CoHi 1910-My 15 1924
KHi My 29 1920

ARLINGTON

BLIZZARD. w O 9 1890-93||?
CU-B Ja 9-16,26,30 1890

COLORADO (*Continued*)

ARRIBA

Arriba MIRROR. Mr 9 1889-
CoHi Mr 16,30-My 4 1889

Arriba RECORD. w 1907+
pub 1914+

ARVADA

Arvada ENTERPRISE. w 1908+
pub [1911-22]+

Arvada SUN. w 1903-N 14 1919||
Followed by Jefferson county republican (Golden)
CoHi 1911-19

ASHCROFT

Ashcroft HERALD. ir
CoHi S 15 1883;Ap 5,My 17,Je 28,Ag 16 1884

ASPEN

Daily CHRONICLE. d Jl 5 1888-92||?
Title varies slightly
CoHi 1888-90;Jl-D 31 1892

Aspen weekly CHRONICLE. w Ja 7 1889-
CoHi 1889-F 17 1890

Aspen DEMOCRAT. w O 16 1885-
KHi O 30-N 7 1885;Ja 2,Jl 1 1886

Aspen DEMOCRAT-TIMES. d 1900-26||
1900-Je 5 1909 as Aspen democrat
CoHi F 11 1902-26

Aspen daily LEADER. d F 1 1892-93||?
CoU 1893

Aspen daily PRESS. d My 17? 1885-86||?
KHi My 21 1885;Je 18,Jl 15 1886

ROCKY MOUNTAIN sun. w 1881-99||
CoHi Jl 9 1881-99
CoU [Ja 31 1885-D 12 1891]
KHi Ja 24 1885

Aspen morning SUN. d 1895-97||?
CoHi Mr 25-Ag 8 1895

Aspen TIMES. w 1880-D 12 1930||
CoHi 1923-30
CoU 1885-[89-91]93
KHi Jl 14 1883;Ap 19 1884

Aspen TIMES. d Ap 1885-1909||?
United with Aspen democrat to form Aspen democrat-times
CU-B Ap 21 1889
CoHi Ja 13 1897-O 22 1899
CoU S 1885-96
KHi Mr 13,My 28,Jl 4,23 1885

Aspen TRIBUNE. d Ag 13 1895-1901||
CoHi 1895-96;Je 29 1897-Jl 2 1901

UNION era. w Ag 13 1891-
CoHi 1891-99

ATWOOD

LOGAN county advocate. *See* Republican-advocate (Sterling)

AULT

Ault ADVERTISER. *See* Ault booster

Ault BOOSTER. w 1897+
1897-S 24 1920 as Ault advertiser
CoAuP N 21 1904-14;26-35
CoHi 1911+

Ault PROGRESS. w
pub 1936+

BACHELOR

TELLER topics. w Jl 22 1892-94||?
CoHi Jl-O 1 1892

BASALT

Basalt JOURNAL. w 1897-1909||?
CoHi 1899-D 14 1907

BAYFIELD

Bayfield BLADE. w Jl 8 1909-26||
United with Ignacio chieftain (Ignacio) to form Ignacio chieftain and Bayfield blade, later Ignacio chieftain (Ignacio)
CoHi 1909-D 21 1917

BELLVUE

CRYSTAL HILL pilot. w Je 9 1883-
KHi Je 9,23 1883

BERTHOUD

Berthoud BEACON. w Jl 10 1886-
KHi S 11 1886

Berthoud BULLETIN. w 1890+
pub [1891-1902]+
CoHi Jl 1897-My 25 1923

BLACK HAWK

Tri-weekly COLORADO mining journal. tw F 10-15 1864||
CoHi complete

Weekly COLORADO mining journal. *See* Weekly mining journal

Daily COLORADO times. *See under* Central City

Weekly COLORADO times. *See under* Central City

Daily Black Hawk JOURNAL. d Mr 28? 1872-O 4 1873||
NNHi Je 3 1873

Weekly Black Hawk JOURNAL. w 1872-73||

Black Hawk MINING journal. d N 30 1863-D 1 1866||
CoD My 2,Je 9,21,Jl 11,20,29,N 1865;Ap 7,23,Je 22-23,26,28-29 1866
CoHi complete
MWA Je 15 1864;Je 10 1865

Weekly MINING journal. w D 2 1863?-66||
1863-64 as Weekly Colorado mining journal
CoD S 6 1864;Ja 3,24,Je 13 1865
MWA N 20 1866

POST. w S 9? 1876-80||?
CoU My 31 1879

Black Hawk TIMES. *See* Gilpin observer (Central City)

BLANCA

To 1910? as Fort Garland

SAN LUIS Valley news. w N 2 1907+
pub 1907+

BONANZA

Bonanza daily ENTERPRISE. d,w 1881-84||?
d 1881-82?
CSmH Ag 1882

BOSTON

BACA county journal. w 1887-90||
CU-B Ja 10,24 1890

BOULDER

BOULDER county bee. w Ap-N? 1875||
Formed by the union of Rocky Mountain eagle and Longmont inter-ocean (Longmont)

BOULDER county courier. w My 29 1875-N 8 1878||
1875-Jl 27 1878 as Sunshine courier (Sunshine) Merged with Boulder county news to form News and courier, later Boulder news-herald
CoHi My 25-N 8 1878
ICHi Jl 22 1876

BOULDER county herald. w 1880-1904||
CoHi Jl 1899-Je 30 1904

BOULDER county herald. d *See* Boulder daily herald

BOULDER county miner and farmer. w 1901+
1901-20 as Boulder county miner
CoBoC Jl 20 1916
CoD Je 11,25-Jl,S 3-10,O 8,22-29,N 26-D 10,31 1931-Ja 7 1932
CoHi Ap 1902-S 2 1904;Je 8 1905-23
CoU S 10 1889;Jl 1 1904;F 7 1907;D 9 1909;Mr 19,My 23,Jl 4 1918

BOULDER county news. *See* Boulder news-herald

BOULDER county times. w,sw 1897-1907||
1897-F 12 1903 as Colorado representative; 1903?-04 Semi-weekly times
sw 1903?-04
CoBoC Ja 12 1905
CoHi Je 30 1898-F 14 1907

Boulder daily CAMERA. d 1889+
1889-My 1913 as Boulder camera
pub 1891+
CoHi Jl 1897+
CoU My 29 1892;My 31,O 15 1895;D 15,29 1899; Ja 15 1900;F 22,Ap 3 1907;N 24 1909;Ja 8 1910

COLORADO banner. w S 30 1875-83||?
United with Boulder news and courier to form News and banner, later Boulder news-herald
CoBoC My 8 1879;My 31 1881;Ap 17 1883
CoU 1875-My 18 1878
ICHi Jl 6,S 21 1876

COLORADO representative. *See* Boulder county times

Boulder daily HERALD. d 1880-1916||
1880-87 as Boulder herald; 1887-Je 1903 Boulder county herald; Jl 1903-F 10 1913 Boulder herald. United with Boulder news and banner to form Boulder news-herald
CoHi N 1898-F 12 1916

Boulder NEWS-HERALD. w,d O 12 1869-1932||
1869-78 as Boulder county news. Title varies: News and courier; Boulder news and banner; Boulder news
Suspended D 6 1870-Ja 18 1871
w 1869-My 9 1917
CoBoC 1872-77;S 10 1880;Je 15,Ag 3 1882
CoHi Ap 1871-Mr 21,My 23 1873-Ap 1875;N 17 1876-N 2 1877;F 16 1916-Ap 1925
CoU 1869-N 20 1874;Ja 1,N 12-26 1875;Ja 7,N 10-17,D 29 1876;Ag 1886-1922
ICHi O 6 1876
KHi Ja 14,Mr 18 1881
NNHi Mr 28 1873
OCHi S 7 1877

PROGRESSIVE citizen. w 1917-
CoU Mr 23-Ap 2 1917

ROCKY MOUNTAIN eagle. w S 1873-Mr 1875||?
United with Longmont inter-ocean (Longmont) to form Boulder county bee
CoBoC F 4 1875
CoU O 1 1873;Ja 1-7,Mr 26,Ag 27 1874

Boulder SENTINEL. w 1884-89||
CoHi Ap 24 1885
CoU S 1886-89

Semi-weekly TIMES. *See* Boulder county times

Boulder TRIBUNE. w 1888-1920||?
CoBoC 1894-D 1920?
CoHi 1910-17
CoU S 1907-18

Boulder VALLEY news. w Ap 3 1867-68||
Follows Valmont bulletin (Valmont)

BRANDON

Brandon BELL. *See* Brandon news and westland

Brandon NEWS and westland. w 1909-23||?
1909-15 as Brandon bell; 1916-17 Brandon westland
CoHi Jl 1912-Jl 21 1921

Brandon WESTLAND. *See* Brandon news and westland

BRECKENRIDGE

Breckenridge BULLETIN. w 1898-1909||
Merged with Summit county journal
CoHi S 22 1899-My 1906

Daily JOURNAL. d Jl 22 1880-87||?
CoHi Jl 22 1880
KHi D 31 1881;My 18 1882

SUMMIT county journal. w 1884+
Title varies slightly
CU-B Jl 6-13 1889;Ja 11 1890
CoHi D 11 1897+
KHi Jl 31 1886

SUMMIT county leader. w 1880-92||?
CoHi Ja 1 1881

BRIGHTON

ADAMS county republican. w My 1924+
pub 1924+

Brighton BLADE. w,sw 1903+
Title varies slightly
w 1903-Je 1918
pub 1903+
CoHi 1903+

Brighton REGISTER. w 1886-1932||?
CU-B Ja 11-25 1890;Ag 13-27 1892
CoHi My 25 1900-S 1914

BRIGHTSIDE

CHAMPION. w F 2 1901-
KHi 1901-O 25 1902

BRUSH

Brush LARIAT. w My 10 1884-
KHi [My-S 20 1884]

MORGAN county republican. *See* Brush news

Brush NEWS. w 1900+
1900-25? as Morgan county republican
CoHi N 22 1912-20

Brush TRIBUNE. w,sw 1894+
CoHi F 1899-1924;Ap 17 1928

BUENO VISTA

CHAFFEE county republican. w 1881+
CoHi Mr 23 1924+

CHAFFEE county times. w 1880-86||
CoHi Ja 1 1881
KHi D 30 1881;F 3 1882;F 2 1883;F 1 1884;Ag 26 1886

COLORADO democrat. w 1881-95||?
1881-91? as Buena Vista democrat
CU-B Ja 9 1890
KHi Ag 14 1884

Buena Vista DEMOCRAT. *See* Colorado democrat

Buena Vista HERALD. w 1881-1900||?
CU-B D 27 1889-Ja 3,24-31 1890
KHi Ag 2 1884

WASP. d Ag 21 1883-85||
KHi Ag 21 1883;My 5,Je 30 1885

BURLINGTON

Burlington BLADE. w 1887-89||
CU-B D 27 1889

KIT CARSON county record. *See* Burlington record

Burlington RECORD. w 1901+
1901-20? as Kit Carson county record; 1921-30? Republican and record
CoHi 1910-Jl 7 1921

Burlington REPUBLICAN. w 1890-1913||?
United with Kit Carson record to form Republican and record, later Burlington record
CoHi Mr 1907-11

REPUBLICAN and record *See* Burlington record

COLORADO (*Continued*)

CANON CITY

ADVANCE. w Mr 4 1884-
KHi Ap 1 1884

Canon City **AVALANCHE.** *See* Canon City record

CANNON. w,sw 1888-1912||?
1888-1905 as Canon City clipper
sw 1895-1905?
CoHi Je 29 1897-1905

Canon City **CLIPPER.** *See* Cannon

Daily **EXPRESS.** d Ja? 1882-
KHi [F 26-Ap 20 1882]

Weekly **EXPRESS.** w My 13 1882-
KHi O 7 1882

Canon City **FREE PRESS.** m Jl-S 1874||?
CoD S 1874

FREMONT county leader. w 1910-20||?
CoHi O 19 1911-N 9 1917

FREMONT county record. *See* Canon City record

GATE CITY. m Je 1885-
CU-B N 1885
KHi Jl 1885

Canon City **MERCURY.** w My 9 1884-85||
CU-B Ag 22-29 1884
KHi Ag 1,N 28 1884;Jl 3 1885

MINING gazette. w 1879-82||?
KHi My 31 1882[Ja 31-N 18 1883]

Canon City **RECORD.** w F 18 1875+
1875-78 as Canon City avalanche; 1878-83 Fremont county record
pub 1893+
CoCa Ag 1882-Ja 6 1883;84-Ap 5 1900
CoD Ap 12-O 4 1934
CoHi My-Je 1880;F 1881-Je,Ag 1882-Jl 14 1883;Jl 1897-1920
ICHi F 10 1876
KHi Mr 19 1881;F 10,Je 9 1883;Ag 2 1884

Canon City daily **RECORD.** d 1906+
pub 1907+
CoD Mr 1 1928
CoHi O 1921+

REPORTER. w 1880-87||?
CU-B S 25 1884

Canon **TIMES.** w,sw S 8 1860-O 7 1861||?
sw My 9-Ag 19 1861
CoCaG S 8-15,D 29 1860
CoU S 29-O 13,27-N 10,D 15-22 1860;Ja-Mr 23,Ap 6,20-My 4,9,16-Jl,Ag 5-12,19,29-S 19,O 7 1861
NN D 22 1860(photostat)
NNHi D 22 1860

Canon City **TIMES.** w Mr 7 1872-My 3 1877||
Followed by Ouray times (Ouray)
CoCa complete
ICHi Ap 6 1876
NNHi Mr 13 1873

Canon City **TIMES.** w 1898-O 19 1911||
CoCa Mr 23 1899-Ja 3 1907;10-11
CoHi My 11 1899-1911

CARBONDALE

AVALANCHE. w 1889-Mr 11 1891||
United with Echo (Glenwood Springs) to form Avalanche-echo (Glenwood Springs)
CoHi Jl 13 1889-91

Carbondale **ITEM.** w 1898-1923||?
CoHi Ja 12 1911-F 24 1921

CASTLE ROCK

DOUGLAS county news. *See* Castle Rock independent

Castle Rock **INDEPENDENT.** w Ag 16 1873-81||?
1873-89 as Douglas county news
1873-My? 1874 pub in Frankstown
CoHi Ag 16 1873
ICHi Jl 8-15 1876

Castle Rock **JOURNAL.** w Mr? 1880-D 29 1911||
United with Castle Rock record to form Castle Rock record-journal
CU-B Ja 1-8,29 1890
CoHi Jl 13 1881-1911
KHi Mr 9 1881

NEWS letter. w 1874-79||
CoHi Ja 14 1879

Castle Rock **RECORD-JOURNAL.** w F 7 1908+
1908-11 as Castle Rock record
CoHi 1908+

CEDAREDGE

SURFACE Creek champion. w Je 16 1904+
pub 1904+
CoHi 1911-Je 1921

CENTER

Center **DISPATCH.** *See* Center post-dispatch

Center **POST.** w 1910-11||
United with Center dispatch to form Center post-dispatch
CoHi D 8 1910-Mr 9 1911

Center **POST-DISPATCH.** w 1901+
1901-11 as Center dispatch
CoAT N 1932+
CoHi My 31 1901-Mr 16 1916

CENTRAL CITY

Evening **CALL.** d 1877?-My 1878||
United with Daily Central City register to form Central City register-call

CAMPAIGN herald. w Ag 13 1870-
CoHi S 3-10 1870

COACH. w N 9 1872-O? 1873||
DLC My 24 1873

COLORADO herald. d Ja 1 1868-73||?
Follows Daily Colorado times
CU-B Ja 25-30 1869
CoD Je 18 1868
CoU Ja 6-D 1868
NNHi F 24 1873

Weekly **COLORADO** herald. w Ja 1 1868-73||?
N 20-27 1872 never pub
C D 16 1868
CU-B N 13-D 11,25 1872-Ja,Mr 5,19-26,Ap 9, My 7-14,28,Je 11,Jl 2 1873
CoHi My 6 1868
CoU 1868
NNHi Ja 22 1873

Daily **COLORADO** times. d D 1 1866-67||
Followed by Colorado herald
1866-Mr? 1867 pub in Black Hawk
CU-B O 17 1867
CoD D 19 1866;Ap 1-2,My 1,S 4,7-9,14 1867
CoDV My 20-24 1867
CoHi My 21-24 1867
MnU Je 21,24,Jl 2 1867

Weekly **COLORADO** times. w D 11 1866-
1866- pub in Black Hawk
CU-B O 29 1867
MWA Ap 2,23,My 14,18,Je 18,Jl 16 1867

Daily **GILPIN** graphic. d
CoHi O 14,18-19 1882

GILPIN miner. w 1898-1901||
CoU F 22-Ag 30 1901

GILPIN observer. w 1886-1921||?
1886-Jl 20 1887 as Black Hawk times (Black Hawk); Jl 27 1887-97? Gilpin county observer
CoBoC N? 1899
CoD S 16,N? 1897;D 11 1902
CoHi D 28 1898-1920
CoU [Je 1887-O 12 1895;Je 16 1898-S 6 1900;F 22-Ag 1901;Ag 18 1904-O 1910;Ag 31 1911-Mr 4,Ag 12 1915-N 16 1916]
MWA D 6 1900;Je 11 1903

Weekly **LEDGER.** w N 10 1883-
KHi N 10-17 1883

MINER'S register. tw,d *See* Central City register-call

MINING life. tw D 23 1862-
CoD D 23 1862

Central City **POST.** w Mr 2 1863-
CoHi Je 18-D 1863;N 1867-Ja 28 1868

Central City **POST.** w 1876-83||
CoHi Mr 18 1882-Mr 17 1883
KHi F 3 1883

Central City **REGISTER-CALL.** tw,d Jl 28 1862-90||?
1862-Ag 20 1863 as Tri-weekly miner's register; Ag 21 1863-Jl 25 1868 Daily miner's register; Jl 26 1868-My 1878 Daily Central City register
tw 1862-Ag 20 1863
C Ja 7 1869
CoD Ag 6,8-11,15,20,24-25,O 3,18-19 1865;My 29,N 14,16 1866;My 23,26,Ag 3,N 24,27 1867
CoDV My 16,N 19 1867
CoHi 1862-Jl 1873;79-81;D 30 1882
CtY My 24 1875
DLC Ja 16-N 26 1863;68-69;F 10 1870-72
ICHi S 29 1876
MWA Je 15-16 1864
MnU Je 19 1867
NEh Ap 25 1863
NNHi Ap 9 1873

Central City **REGISTER-CALL.** w Jl 22 1863+
1864-Jl 23 1868 as Weekly miners' register (title varies slightly); Jl 1868-Je 15 1878 Weekly Central City register
CSmH Ja 4 1865
CU-B 1868;Ja 14,F 25-Mr,Ap 8,22,My 13 1869
CoD Jl 3,S 11 1872;Ja 8,F 26 1873;Jl 15 1932
CoHi N 1867-Ja 1868;O 4 1869;Ap 24 1875;Je 8 1878-80;89-D 19 1890;Jl 1898+
CoU 1886;Jl 29 1890-Mr 1913
ICHi S 27 1876
KHi D 5 1878;O 22 1886;Je 30 1916
MWA N 24 1882
NN Ag 21 1864
NNHi Ap 10 1872;F 12 1873

ROCKY Mountain gold reporter and Mountain City herald. w Ag 6 1869-
CoD Ag 6,20,S 3-17 1869

CHEYENNE WELLS

CHEYENNE county news. w 1889+
1889-Ag 22 1913 as Cheyenne republican
CoHi 1910+

EASTERN Colorado times. w 1905-14||?
CoHi Mr 29 1912 Mr 28 1913

Cheyenne Wells **GAZETTE.** w Je 4 1887-89||
CoHi 1887-Mr 16 1889

Weekly **HERALD.** w 1889-90||
CoHi Ap 26 1890

Cheyenne **RECORD.** w 1912+
CoHi Ap 14 1913-Mr 3 1921

Cheyenne **REPUBLICAN.** *See* Cheyenne county news

CHIVINGTON

CHIEF. w 1887-95||?
CU-B Ja 17-F 7 1890

COAL CREEK

Coal Creek **ENTERPRISE.** w 1882-97||?
1887?-91? as Growler
KHi S 25 1886

GROWLER. *See* Coal Creek enterprise

COLFAX

WEST side citizen. w 1889-99||?
KHi N 20-D 25 1896

COLLBRAN

Collbran **ORACLE.** w 1899-1902||?
CoHi S 15 1900-Ap 6 1901

PLATEAU Valley voice. w 1895+
CoHi 1911-N 1924

COLORADO CITY

Papers published in Colorado City are listed under Colorado Springs

COLORADO SPRINGS

COLORADO City independent. *See* Colorado Springs independent

COLORADO City iris. w 1888-1915||
CoHi 1910-My 21 1915

COLORADO City journal. w Ag 1 1861-Ja 1862||
CoHi N 28 1861
CoU Ag 1 1861

COLORADO mountaineer. w S 3? 1873-Ap 1882||
Merged with Republic
CoCC Ag 30 1876-S 21 1877
ICHi Jl 26 1876
MB N 29 1876-S 19 1877;O 23,D 11-18 1878;Ja 15,Mr 5-19,Ap 30,My 28,Je 11 1879

COLORADO state republic. d *See* Republic

COLORADO state republic. w *See* El Paso county republic

EL PASO county democrat. *See* Colorado Springs farm news

EL PASO county republic. w 1872-89||?
1872-85? as Colorado state republic
CU-B O 21-28 1886;Jl 4 1889
CoCC Ja-My 1891
KHi Ja 5-12,My 17,Jl 19 1882;Ja 23,F 7 1883;O 15 1885[86-O 1888]

Colorado Springs **FARM NEWS.** w 1889+
1889-D 29 1922 as El Paso county democrat
pub Je 1905-Ag 11 1906;10+
CoCC [1894]+
CoHi 1910-17

Weekly **GAZETTE.** w Mr 23 1872+
1872 as Out west; 1873-Ap 1878 Colorado Springs gazette and El Paso county news
Mr 30 My 2,Ag 29,O 24,D 19 1872 never pub
CU-B O 4 1884
CoCC 1872-79;81-91;93-1906;24-34
CoD Jl 1873
CoHi Ja 22 1876;Jl 9-S 1905;1907-08
DLC 1876-My 1896
ICHi S 16 1876
MWA F 7 1874;F 5,Mr 18,S 16 1876
NbHi D 6 1907

Colorado Springs **GAZETTE.** d My 1 1878+
Sunday ed as Sunday gazette and telegraph
S 20 1906 is Pike's Peak centennial ed
CU-B O 4,7,10-11,20 1884;Ja 1 1888;Ja 1 1889
Co S-O 1911
CoC S 1897;99[1900]+
CoCC 1873+
CoHi D 31 1882;1897-S 1903;04+
DLC Je 1896-Je 1897;Jl 1898+
KHi Ja 28,31 1883;O 24 1884;Mr 18,Jl 2,24,26 1885;Ja 1 1891;Jl 23 1899
MWA Mr 4 1902
OOxM O 24 1882
WHi Ja 1 1897;S 20 1906

Evening **HERALD.** d N 1 1909-Jl 30 1910||
United with Evening telegraph to form Herald-telegraph, later Colorado Springs evening-telegraph
CoCC complete

HERALD-TELEGRAPH. *See* Colorado Springs evening telegraph

HOUR. w Ap 4? 1885-86||
KHi Jl 25 1885[My-O 23 1886]

Colorado Springs **INDEPENDENT.** w 1884+
CoHi Ja 21-D 1917
KHi Je 28 1917

Colorado Springs **INDEPENDENT.** w 1888-
1888-Je 4 1917 as Colorado City independent
CoHi Ag 21 1914-Je 4 1917

Colorado Springs **LABOR** news. w 1902+
pub 1928+
CoHi S 8 1904-17

Saturday **MAIL.** w 1888-
KHi Mr 22-Ap 19 1890

OUT west. *See* Weekly gazette

PIKE'S PEAK herald. *See* Weekly telegraph

PUBLIC opinion. w 1905+
pub 1928+

COLORADO (*Continued*)

COLORADO SPRINGS—*Continued*

REPUBLIC. tw,d S 3 1881-Je 30 1891||
Title varies: Colorado state republic; Daily republic; Evening republic. Merged with Evening telegraph to form Republic and telegraph, later Colorado Springs evening telegraph
tw 1885-87
CoCC 1881-Ag 1883;88;Jl 1889-90
CU-B D 31 1883;O 2-4,9 1884
KHi D 5 1883

REPUBLIC. w *See* El Paso county republic

REPUBLIC and telegraph. d *See* Colorado Springs evening telegraph

SUN. w 1890-
KHi 1891-N 4 1893

Weekly **TELEGRAPH.** w O 1 1887-1900||?
1887-Mr 9 1893 as Pike's Peak herald
CoCC 1887-91;93-96
MWA Ja 3 1891

Colorado Springs evening **TELEGRAPH.** d F 5 1891+
Jl 1891-F 28 1893 as Republic and telegraph; Jl 1910-12? Herald telegraph
CLM D 22 1908
CoC 1906+
CoCC Jl 1891-92;My 1893+
CoHi 1897-Jl 3 1905;13-Ap 1923
KHi My 12,D 31 1892
WaPS N 24 1920[21]

Daily **TIMES.** d 1884-85||
CU-B O 3,8 1884
KHi Mr 12-13 1885

Weekly **TIMES.** w F 5 1885-
KHi Mr 12-13 1885

WESTERN enterprise. w 1896-1912||
Negro
DLC Ja 6,27 1900

COMO

Como **HEADLIGHT.** w 1883-85||?
KHi Ja 7,F 4 1885

Como **RECORD.** w 1889-1906||?
CoHi Mr 2 1899

COPPER ROCK

Copper Rock **CHAMPION.** w Je 4 1892-
CoU Je 4 1892

CORTEZ

MONTEZUMA Valley journal. w 1889+
CoHi Ag 1897-1917

CRAIG

Craig **COURIER.** *See* Craig empire-courier

EMPIRE. w Ja 28 1911-29||
United with Moffat county courier to form Craig empire-courier
CoCrE complete
CoHi 1911-Mr 1923

Craig **EMPIRE-COURIER.** w 1891+
1891-94? as Pantagraph; 1895?-Ja 1899 Craig courier; F 1899-Mr 2 1911 Routt county courier; Mr 9 1911-29 Moffat county courier
pub 1891+
CoHi F 18 1899+

MOFFAT county courier. *See* Craig empire-courier

PANTAGRAPH. *See* Craig empire-courier

ROUTT county courier. *See* Craig empire-courier

CREEDE

Daily Creede **CANDLE.** d
CoHi N 1-6 1892;Ap 3,N 1-7 1893;N 1-6 1894

Creede **CANDLE.** w Ja 7 1892-1930||
CoDelP complete
CoHi 1892-N 1894; Ja 30 1904-D 27 1930

CRESTED BUTTE

ELK MOUNTAIN pilot. w Je 7 1880+
1880-My 3? 1884 pub in Irwin
pub 1880+
CoHi Ja 19 1899-O 25 1917
KHi [Je 14 1880-Ap 16 1885]

Crested Butte **GAZETTE.** w O 6 1883-85||?
KHi O 6 1883;D 6 1884

Daily **GAZETTE.** d D 18 1884-85||?
KHi D 18,22 1884

Crested Butte **REPUBLICAN.** w O 5 1881-S 26 1883||
KHi [1881-83]

CRIPPLE CREEK

Cripple Creek **CITIZEN.** d 1897-99||
United with Morning times to form Morning times-citizen, later Cripple Creek times-record
CoHi Jl 13 1897-Jl 7 1899

Cripple Creek **CRUSHER.** w 1891-94||?
CoCC D 9 1892-Je 29,Jl 13 1894

Cripple Creek **GUIDE.** w Ap 25 1896-
CoCC Ap-My 2,Jl? 1896-Mr 20,Ap 22-S 16 1897

Morning **JOURNAL.** d 1893-95||
KHi S 29 1894-My 14 1895

Weekly **JOURNAL.** w 1893-96||
KHi My 18 1895-Ap 4 1896

Cripple Creek **MAIL.** w 1895-98||
CoCC Ag 17 1895-Ap 30 1898
CoHi Ap 25 1896-Jl 9 1898
CoP complete

Weekly **MINER.** w 1893-95||
CoCC O 13 1894-Ag 24 1895

Daily **PRESS.** d Je 27 1899-1903||
Je 27-D 7 1899 pub at Victor
CoHi Mr 16 1900-01
WHi 1899-Mr 1903

Cripple Creek evening **STAR.** d 1898-1904||?
CoCcT 1900-01;Jl-D 1904
CoHi 1900-01;Jl-D 1904

Cripple Creek **TIMES-RECORD.** w 1892—
1892-Mr 1913 as Cripple Creek times. Title varies: Cripple Creek times and Victor record; etc.
CoCC D 17 1892;D 31 1893-Ja 14,F 11-18, Mr 11-Ap 15,My 6-13,Je-Jl 15,29,Ag 12 1894; Je 16 1898-Ja 8 1899
CoHi Ag 11 1897-1918
KHi F 22 1927

Cripple Creek **TIMES-RECORD.** d 1894+
1894-F 18 1900 as Morning times; F 20 1900-Mr 30 1902 Morning times-citizen; Ap 1 1902-12? Cripple Creek morning times; 1912-20? Cripple Creek times and Victor record
pub D 1895-Mr 15,Ap 16 1913+
CoHi D 1895-Ap 1 1913;Ap 16 1916-18
KHi Ja 1 1899

Weekly **TRIBUNE.** w 1896-1900||
CoCC My 13 1899-Ja 20 1900

CRITCHELL

ROCKY Mountain reveille. w Mr 31 1899-1900||
KHi [1899-S 21 1900]

CRYSTAL

Crystal River **CURRENT.** w O 2 1886-92||?
KHi O 2 1886

DEBEQUE

BUGLE. *See* Debeque news

NEW ERA. *See* Debeque news

Debeque **NEWS.** w 1898-(1930/33)
1898-99? as Debeque post; 1899?-1900? Bugle; 1910?-17 New era; 1918-21 Debeque shale and oil news
CoHi Jl 24 1909-23

Debeque **POST.** *See* Debeque news

Debeque **SHALE and oil news.** *See* Debeque news

DEER TRAIL

Deer Trail **TRIBUNE.** w 1913+
pub N 1920+

DEL NORTE

Del Norte **PROSPECTOR.** w F 7 1874+
1874-1923 as San Juan prospector
pub 1874+
CU-B My 15,S 4 1886;Jl 6,27 1889
CoHi Ja 1 1881;1884-91;Jl 16 1898+
ICHi Ag 26 1876
ICN O 15 1887
KHi [D 1878-81]Ja 28,D 30 1882;Je 2 1883; Mr 14 1885

SAN JUAN prospector. *See* Del Norte prospector

DELPHI

WALL Street gold miner. w 1897-1900||?
CoU O 23 1897

DELTA

Delta **CHIEF.** *See* Delta independent

DELTA county advertiser. w O 13 1885-
Merged with Delta independent
KHi O 13,N 3 1885

DELTA county laborer. *See* Delta county tribune

DELTA county tribune. w 1890+
1890-1911 as Delta county laborer
CoHi F 1897-Ja 5 1917

FREE PRESS. sm Ag 1930-
CoHi N 12 1930-S 6 1934

Delta **INDEPENDENT.** w Mr 7 1883+
1883-84? as Delta chief
CoHi Ag 3 1883;1897—
KHi Mr 18,Ap 15 1885;My 19 1916

DENVER

ALTRURIAN. w Ja 1895-
KHi 1895-S 1896

Denver **BEE.** w 1891-92||?
CU-B Ja 1,15 1892

BRIGHTSIDE. w 1894-
KHi N 1897-My 1900

BULLETIN and supplement to the Rocky Mountain news. *See under* Rocky Mountain news

La **CAPITALE.** w 1907-26||?
In Italian
IU [D 29 1917-O 27 1923]

CAPITOL HILL news. w F 23 1935+
CoD My 17 1935

CHERRY Creek pioneer. w Ap 23 1859||
Dated Denver City, Kansas. Merged with Rocky Mountain news
CoHi complete
MWA complete
MnHi complete

Daily **CITY item.** ir Ag 1 1870-Ap 20 1872||
1870- 1871 as Lorgnette. Followed by Denver times

COLORADO. w 1923+
pub 1923+

COLORADO courier. w 1882-88||?
In German
WHi Mr 16 1884

COLORADO exchange journal. w 1887-91||?
O 1889 industrial ed
CoD [D 29 1888-Ap 1891]
CtY O 1889
KHi O 1889
TxGR S 8 1888

COLORADO graphic. w S 4 1886+
CoHi 1886-17;Ap 17 1928;35+
KHi S-N 6 1886

COLORADO herold. w My 11? 1872+
1872-1902 as Colorado journal
In German
pub 1872+
CoD Ja-Je 1896
CoHi 1918+
ICHi O 28 1876
KHi [S 15-D 22 1888]

COLORADO herold. d 1902-O 1918||
In German
pub complete
CoHi Ja-Je 1918
IU S 1917-Je 1918

COLORADO journal. *See* Colorado herold

COLORADO monthly. m Jl 1871-73||?
DLC Ag-D 1871;Mr 1872

COLORADO post. bw Jl 16 1879-
CoHi 1879-Jl 10 1880

COLORADO posten. w 1883-85||?
1883-84 as Nya Colorado posten. Merged with Svenska härolden
IRA 1883-84

Daily **COLORADO republican and Rocky Mountain herald.** *See* Daily commonwealth

Weekly **COLORADO republican and Rocky Mountain herald.** *See* Weekly commonwealth

COLORADO statesman. w 1894+
Negro
CoHi Ja;O 29 1904+
DLC Ja 27 1900

COLORADO evening sun. d Mr 8 1891-Je 30 1894||
1891-Mr 12 1893 as Colorado sun. United with Denver times to form Denver times-sun, later Denver times
CoD complete
CoHi 1891-D 7 1892;Mr 13 1893-94
CtW My 20 1893
KHi [D 13 1891-92]
MWA Mr 9 1891-92
NN Jl 1891-94

COLORADO weekly sun. *See* Colorado times

COLORADO times. w 1893-1902||
1893-96 as Colorado weekly sun; 1896-1900? Times-sun
CoD Mr 16 1898-Mr 14 1900;Mr 27 1901-Mr 19 1902
CoBoC Ap 20,My 2,7,8 1895
CoDU [1893]-[96]
CoHi O-D 1894[1899-1902]
CoU Ja-Je 1893;Mr 20 1895-Mr 11 1896;Ja-Mr 1900;Ap-Je 1901
NbHi Ag 30 1893;D 18 1901

COLORADO times. d,tw 1918+
d 1918-Ja 5 1921
In Japanese
IU Mr 6 1918+

Daily **COLORADO transcript.** d Mr 15- 1875||
CoHi Mr 16-My 20 1875

COLORADO tribune. *See* Denver tribune

Denver **COMMERCIAL.** w 1909-26||?
WHi F 4 1915;Ja 3 1918-My 18 1922

Weekly **COMMONWEALTH.** w My 5 1860-Je 22 1864||
1860-My 18 1861 as Rocky Mountain herald; My 25 1861-Je 26 1862 Weekly Colorado republican and Rocky Mountain herald; Jl 3 1862-Ag 20 1863 Weekly commonwealth and republican
CoD Je 30 1860;My 25 1864
CoHi 1860;My 25 1861-Je,Jl 10 1862-63;My 25-Je 1864
DLC My 25,Ag 24,O 5,N 23 D 5 1861;Ap 10, My 29,Ag 8,S 18 1862;Je 15-22 1864
KHi My 11 1861

Daily **COMMONWEALTH and republican.** d My 1 1860-Je 11? 1864||
1860-My 22? 1861 as Daily herald and Rocky Mountain advertiser; My 23 1861-Je 1862 Daily Colorado republican and Rocky Mountain herald
CoBoC My 1 1860
CoD Je 15-Jl 1861;N 5-7,10,13,21,D 11 1863
CoHi My 1 1860;Jl 18-N 1861[N 1863-My 1864]
DLC S 1-13,O 15,N 9-13 1861;Ja 15,23-24, 29-30,F 3,15,17,Mr 15-24,27-Ap 7,15-18,22-23, 29-My 5,8,12,15-23,28,31-Je 13,19-20 1862
MWA Je 11 1864

COLORADO (*Continued*)

DENVER—*Continued*

Tri-weekly COMMONWEALTH and republican. tw
DLC Jl 21,25-Ag 1,13 1862

CRIPPLE CREEK gold pan. w? Mr 20 1892-
CU-B Mr 20 1892

Denver Daily. *See* Denver daily tribune

Denver daily DEMOCRAT. *See* Denver republican

Weekly DEMOCRAT. w 1876-79 *See* Weekly republican

Denver DEMOCRAT. w 1896+
CoHi 1902-17;Ap 14 1928
KHi Je 22 1918

ELITE. w
KHi N 14 1885;Ja-Ap 3 1886

Denver EXPRESS. d Ap 26 1906-N 20 1926||
United with Denver daily times to form Denver evening news
CoD Ja-Ap 1911;12-16
CoDR 1906-07;F 1908-26
CoHi Ja-Je 1907[15-23]-26

Denver EYE. *See* South Denver eye and bulletin

Daily Denver GAZETTE. d My 15? 1865-Je 5 1869||
Title varies slightly: Ap-Je 1869 as Daily gazette and commercial advertiser
CoD [My 17 1865-69]
CoDV [Ja 10 1866-Ap 5 1869]
CoHi [My 26 1865-My 5 1869]
DLC My 16,19-20,25-28,31-Je 1,4-5,7,9-17,19, 21-23,25-27,29,Jl 2-3,10-11,15-17,20 1865;F 17 1866

Weekly Denver GAZETTE. w My 31 1865-Je? 1869||
CoBoC O 18 1865;Ja 2 1867
CoD Ag 2,S 20,N 22 1865;Ja 3-10,F 7 1866; Ag 21, N 27 1867;Je 24-Jl 1,Ag 26,S 30,N 11 1868;Ap 14 1869
CoDV Ja 24,My 2,Jl 18 1866;Ja 2,Ap 24 1867; My 11 1868
CoHi Jl 26,Ag 30 1865;Ja 3-10,24,Ap 25,My 2,16,Je 27,Jl 18 1866;Ja 2,23,Ap 17,My 8,Je 26,S 4,18,N 13,D 25 1867;F 28,Mr 11,O 14-21 1868;Mr 3 1869

Sunday GRAPHIC. w
CoHi N 4-D 8 1888

GREAT divide. w 1902-27||?
w ed of Denver post
CoHi F 11 1920-21
IU Ag 22 1917-O 13 1920;N 22,D 25 1922;Ja 3, 31,F 14,28,Mr 28,N 7,D 12 1923-Ja 9,Ap 30, Jl 16,D 3 1924
KHi [F 22-Je 1915;19-S 21 1927]

GREAT West. w 1880-82||
CoHi D 25 1880
KHi N 14 1880[81]Mr 18,My 13 1882
TxU O 2 1880

Daily HERALD and Rocky Mountain advertiser. *See* Daily commonwealth and republican

Denver HEROLD. w 1884-99||
In German
KHi [S 22 1888-F 16 1889]

HIGHLAND chief. w 1889+
pub 1925+
CoHi S 10 1897-1921

HOME journal. w 1881-87||
CoHi Ap 2-Jl 9 1887

INTERMOUNTAIN Jewish news. w 1915+
1915-29? as Denver Jewish news
pub 1929+
CoHi O 24 1918-33
NN 1915+

INTER-OCEAN. w 1880?-83||?
KHi Ja 15 1881[My 27-S 9 1882]Je 30,D 22 1883

Denver JEWISH news. *See* Intermountain Jewish news

Denver daily JOURNAL. d 1897-
CoHi My 24 1897-Je 27 1910;Ja 3-N 29 1911; My 22-N 21 1922;Ja 2-N 1923;Ap 14-16,18 1928

Denver JOURNAL of commerce. w Jl 16 1881-94||?
CU-B O 18 1884
CtY O 22 1881
KHi D 24 1881;Jl 21 1883;F 11 1886

LORGNETTE. *See* Daily city item

Denver MERCURY. w Jl 15 1882-
KHi Jl 15,29 1882

Daily MINING and financial record. d 1889-1929||?
1889-1913 as Daily mining record
CoHi O 1897-1909
IU 1915-Je 7 1918
NN 1911-21
NcD O 26 1906
WHi Mr 28 1906;Mr 20 1907

Daily MINING record. *See* Daily mining and financial record

Denver MINING record. w 1905?+
1905- as Daily mining and financial record. Saturday ed
pub 1905+
CoD N 30 1929-My,Je 14-Jl,Ag 16-D 6,20 1930;Ja 17-Jl 18,Ag 1931-Jl 15,Ag 5,19-26, S 9,23,O 14,N 11-D 1933
CoHi 1935+
IU My 11 1912-14
WaPS O 26 1918-F 7 1920

Denver MIRROR. w Je 8 1873-79||
CU-B N 11 1876
CoHi Je 22 1873-My 1874
ICHi 1873-Mr 9 1878
MWA Ap 9-16,Ag 20,S 3-10,O 1-8,N 4 1876; Ja 6 1877

Denver MIRROR. w My 20 1932-
CoHi My 20 1932

Daily Denver MOUNTAINEER. d Ag 25 1860-My 15 1861||
CoD Mr 12,15,24,My 7,15 1861
CoHi S 20-21 1860;Mr 31 1861

Denver weekly MOUNTAINEER. w S 3 1860-S 3 1860 dated "Denver, Jefferson Territory"
CoD S 3 1860

NEW road. w 1887-98||?
1887-95? as Road
CU-B D 28 1889;Ap 19-26,My 17-24 1890
NbHi Ag 15 1891;D 21 1895;F 29-Mr 7, Ap 4-18,My 2 1896

Denver daily NEWS. d
KHi [D 12 1880-Ja 18 1881]Jl 1883;N 7 1884; D 5 1899[Jl 9 1908-Jl 27 1922]
NbLeD N 28 1906

Denver evening NEWS. d N 23 1926-O 31 1928||
Formed by the union of Denver express and Denver daily times.
CoD complete
CoHi complete
KHi Jl 13 1928

NYA Colorado posten. *See* Colorado posten

OPINION. w Mr 23 1884-86||
CU-B O 25 1884
CoD N 22 1884
DLC Mr-Jl 5,19-26,Ag 30,N 15 1884-Je 13,Jl 4, 18,Ag-N 14,28 1885-Mr 13 1886
KHi [Ap 26-D 6 1884]F 7,Ag 15-22 1885; My 29 1886

POMEROY'S democrat. w 1881-83||
KHi Ja 13 1883

Denver POST. d Ag 8 1892+
Title varies: Evening post; Denver evening post; etc.
Co N-D 1907
CoAT [1929+]
CoBoC My 12 1898;My 31 1900;Ja 6 1901; Ag 12 1908;Ap 22 1914;Jl 4 1915
CoD 1895+
CoDR Ja-S 1901;02-O 1904;Ja-O 1905;06-F, Ap 1908-My,Jl 1913+
CoDU 1901-Mr 1902
CoHi Jl 1896;1897-[1926]+
ICN Ja 31-Ap 22 1898
IU [S 16 1924-Je 25 1925]
KHi S 25 1896;Jl 8 1908;D 31 1911;Ap 26 1914;My 18 1926
MWA 1898;D 31 1925
MnU [1918-21]
NvR [1932]+
OHi Ap 1898-Ap 18 1901;Ap 1921-O 1922
—w ed *See* Great divide

Denver morning POST. d Ja 3 1927-N 5 1928||
CoD complete

Denver evening PRESS. d Jl 4 1881-
KHi Jl 4 1881

Denver PRESS. w
CU-B Jl 12,26,Ag 9 1889
KHi Ap 26 1889-99

PROGRESS. w D 8 1892-95||?
KHi Ja 27 1893

Denver RECORD-STOCKMAN. d 1880+
1880-99? as Denver daily stockman
pub 1920+
CoD F 11 1916-19;Jl 22,S 19 1931;Ja 5 1932; Ja 3 1935
CoHi D 6 1897-N 1 1899;1901-Je 1903;04-11; 13-20;22-24;Ap 13,17 1928

Denver REPORTER. d 1879-86||?
KHi Jl 11 1885

Denver REPUBLICAN. d S 11 1876-O 26 1913||
1876-Je 3 1879 as Denver daily democrat: Je 4-D 22 1879 Denver daily republican; Ag 12 1884-86 Denver tribune republican
A Jl 1900-02
CLM Ja 1 1892;Mr 23 1906
CU-B Ja 23 1882[84;86-87]-90;Mr,My 1891;Ag 19,26 1901
Co O-D 1886;95-Je 1898;O 1898-O 1908;09-F 1913
CoBoC Ja 5 1890
CoD 1881-1913
CoDR 1888-Je 1890;Mr 1891-Mr,Jl 1893-Je, O 1894-Je,S 1896-1900;Ap 1901-F,My 1902-Ag, N 1903-Ap,Jl 1905-F,My-Ag 1907;Ja-S 1908; Ja-Ag,O 1909-10;F 1911-O 1913;My-Je 1915
CoDU [1891]-Mr 1894;95-[1902]
CoHi 1881-Ag 1913
CoU Mr 27 1886;92-Ap 1902
CtW My 20 1893
CtY Jl 4 1886
DLC Mr 20 1879-1913
IP Ja 1 1894
KHi [D 10 1880-S 14 1883]Ja 1[Je 7-Ag 2] 1884;Ja 1,N 24 1887-My 25 1905
MWA 1896-Ag 1913
MiU 1903-My 1908
NcD 1898;O 1909
OOxM O 24-25 1882
P Jl 1890-S 1 1913
TxU N 11 1885;D 15-17,19 1897

Weekly REPUBLICAN. w S 11? 1876-O 1913||
1876-My ? 1879 as Weekly democrat; 1884-Ja 1 1887 Weekly tribune-republican
CU-B S 16-D 1886
CoD 1882-93
CoHi 1882-1912
CoU Ja-S 1891;Ja-S 1892;93-Mr 1894;Ja-S 1895;Ja-S 1899;1900-O 1901;Ja-Ap 1902
IaDH 1908-13
KHi N 5 1884[Je-O 15 1885]
NbHi S 8 1887;Ja 1 1888;Ja 1 1891;D 10 1894; Je 25 1899;Ag 31 1907
WHi 1899-1912

REPUBLICAN journal. w O 21 1882-
KHi O 28 1882

Il RISVEGLIO. w 1905+
In Italian
pub 1905+
CoHi Je 14 1906

ROAD. *See* New road

ROCKY MOUNTAIN celt and Globeville chronicle. w 1881-93||?
CU-B Ag 13-27 1892
KHi N 17 1883;Jl 4,N 14 1885;Ag 21 1886
PPCHi [1893]

ROCKY MOUNTAIN globe. w 1893-1901||
CoHi S 26-O 10 1895;Jl 16 1896-Mr 9 1901

ROCKY MOUNTAIN herald. w 1860-61. *See* Weekly commonwealth

ROCKY MOUNTAIN herald. w F 1 1868+
pub F 1 1868
CU-B [Mr 1868-Jl 1871]Ap 13 1873[74-My 19] O 6 1877;Ja 25,Mr 11,Ag 23 1879
CoAT 1928+
CoD Jl 16 1870;Je 24 1871;D 26 1903
CoHi 1897-1918[20-23]+
DLC F,Mr 14-21,Ap 4,18,My 9-Je 20,Jl 4,18, S 5,O 30,N 13,27-D 11,25 1868
IHi [1913-31]
KHi Ap 19 1884;Ag 8,S 19 1885;F 27,O 23 1886;Je 8 1912+
MB N 2 1872[Ag 22-D 5 1874;F 16-S 4 1875] Mr 4 1876
MHi [1912-20]
NN D 14 1912+
NNHi Ja 11 1873;Jl 24 1874;Jl 24 1875
NbHi N 16 1912-N 21 1925;26-Ag,D 31 1927; Mr 1928-Ap 20 1929
PP [S 19-N 7 1914]S 29,O 13,N 3,D 1 1917[18-19]-34+
VHi [My 1914-Jl 1915]

ROCKY MOUNTAIN illustrated weekly. w
CoHi 1895-Mr 1908
TJT F 6 1901

ROCKY MOUNTAIN leader. w D ? 1872-Ag 1873||?
NNHi My 10 1873

ROCKY MOUNTAIN news. w Ap 23 1859+
Title varies slightly
1929+ Sunday ed of d used as w
pub 1861-Je 1879;80-Je,O 1882-83;Ap 1884-Mr, O 1886-Mr,Jl 1887-S 1897;98+
CSmH Ag 20 1859;Ag 3 1864;Mr 31 1875
CU-B [D 1866]Ja 2,D 4 1867[68-F 17 1869] Je 6 1895
CoD Ap 23,Je 11,Ag 20,D 14 1859;F 8 1860; O 30 1862;Ja 8 1863;Ag 3-10 1864;Ap 19 1865-[81]-88;90-1902;Je-D 1920
CoHi 1859-Ap 16 1863;My 18 1864-78;D 25 1882-Ja 1 1883
CoU Ap 23 1859;Ap 1865-My 1871;D 25 1882-Ja 1 1883;Ap 1895-S 1897;98-My,Jl-S 1899; Ja-Ag 1900;Mr-Ag,N 1901-Je 1902;Ja-F 1904
DLC Ap 23 1859(facsimile)[Ag 28-D 1861; F-D 1862;Mr 1863-D 1864]Mr 15,29 1865 [66;68-71]Ja 6 1875;82+
IC Ap 30 1889
IaHi Ap 8-O 1897
MBAt O 5-12 1864
MWA Ag 29 1860;N 2 1913
N Ap 23 1859
NN Ag 13 1859(photostat)
NNHi D 4 1872
OrHi Ap 19 1865
P-M O 24 1885;N 1913-O 1917
WHi F 13 1896-Ja,Mr 1902-14

Denver ROCKY MOUNTAIN news. d Ag 27 1860+
Title varies slightly
My 20-Je 26 1864 never pub
pub 1861-Je 1879;80-Je,O 1882-83;Ap 1884-Mr, Jl 1887-S 1897;98+
CSmH Mr 31 1875
CU-B Jl 2 1867;Ja 22 1868;Mr 12 1869-[70]-Ap 18 1871;My 9,S 26,O 5,17,20,N 6,D 3 1884;N 24 1889;My 13 1890;My 30 1901
Co Jl 24,S 26 1885;O 13 1892;My 30 1895; Mr 5 1897;Ag 13 1899
CoAT 1929+
CoBoC Ag 2 1876
CoCC 1875;78-79
CoD Ag 27 1860;Mr 1,Jl 31 1861;Mr 9 1863; Je 27[Ag 24 1864-Ag 25 1865]-[73]+
CoDU O 1894-[97]-[99-1902]
CoDV Ap 20 1867
CoGS O 1913-[27]+
CoHi 1860-Ag 1862;64-Je 1878;Jl 1879-Ap 1887; 88[89]+
CoU Ap 1865-My 1871;Ap 1895-S 1897;98-S 1899;Ja-Ag 1900;Ja-Ag,N 1901-Je 1902;Ja-F 1904
CtW My 20-21 1893
DLC S 10 1861-S 5 1863;Jl 21-N 1864;65-O 1866;Jl 30 1868;Mr 21,Ap 25-26,My 6,Jl 29, O 25,31 1871;73+
ICHi O 25 1876
ICU 1935+
IaDH N 1913-14
IaSc current six months
InRE S 17,O 24,29-30,N 1,6 1880

COLORADO (*Continued*)

DENVER—*Continued*

Denver ROCKY MOUNTAIN news—*Continued*
KHi S 29-O 5 1864;My 4,Ag 1 1877[F 13 1878-Ja 1 1896]
MWA Mr 20 1863;N 1 1865;76-77;Je 1 1888; S 22 1917-25;Ap 22 1934
N S 21 1875
NbHi F 11 1882;Mr 25,S 24 1893-F,Jl 8,21 1894;O 7,N 1-8 1896;N 4-11 1900
NcD Je 30-Jl 6 1935
OHi Mr 10 1915-Ja 1921;23+
OOxM O 23-25 1882
P N 1913-O 1917
Tx Jl 1904-20
TxU Ag 25,28 1901
WHi Je 7 1862;S 9-D 10 1896;1915+
WaPS Ap-My 1 1929
—BULLETIN and supplement to the Rocky Mountain news. w My 2 1860-
CoHi My 1860;Ja 25-Jl 5 1862

ROCKY MOUNTAIN post. w Ja 1896-
KHi Ap 3 1896

ROCKY MOUNTAIN sentinel. w 1887-1930||?
CoHi 1897-My 13 1916
NbHi Ja 26 1901

Il ROMA. w 1892-1920||
In Italian
IU D 8 1917-Jl 17 1920

SILVER age. w 1891-93||?
CU-B Ap 2 1892

SILVER state. w Jl 15 1882-
KHi Ag 26 1882

SOUTH DENVER bulletin. w 1901-04||
United with Denver eye to form South Denver eye and bulletin

SOUTH DENVER eye and bulletin. w 1882-1930||?
1882-1904 as Denver eye
CoHi Ja 15 1910-21

Denver STAR. w 1889-1930||?
1889-N 15 1912 as Statesman
Negro
CoHi 1905-O 1918
DLC Ja 27 1900

STATESMAN. *See* Denver star

La STELLA. w O 3 1885-
In Italian
CoD O-N 21 1885
CoHi O-N 21 1885

Denver daily STOCKMAN. *See* Denver record-stockman

SVENSK-AMERIKANSKA westen. *See* Westerns nyheter

SVENSKA korrespondenten. *See* Westerns nyheter

Daily Denver TIMES. d Ja 1869-
CoD Ja 8,14,16,20,29-30,F 4,17 1869
MWA Ja 13 1869

Denver TIMES. d Ap 1 1872-N 22 1926||
Follows Daily city item.
Title varies: Daily Denver times; Evening times; Denver evening times; Times-sun; etc. United with Denver express to form Denver news
C Jl 1889-93
CU-B Ap 20,My 6 1876;Ja 14 1879;O 16,N 5 1884
Co Ja-F 1913
CoD [Je 24-D 1872]-1926
CoDR Jl-D 1890;Jl-S 1891;Ja-Mr,Jl-S 1892;Jl 1893-Mr,Je 1894-99;Ap 1900-26
CoDU Ap-Je 1892[93]Ja-Mr 1900;Mr-Je 1901
CoHi Ap 23 1872-85;Jl 1886-1926
CoU [Je-D 1872]-75;Ja-Je 1893;Ja-Mr 1900; Ap-Je 1901
DLC 1919-Ap 1925
ICHi O 10 1876
KHi N 19 1877;D 28 1880;Mr 18 1881;Jl 29 1882;D 3 1883;My 5 1884;Mr 25,Ap 6,Ag 3,D 31 1885;D 25 1894;D 31 1895;D 31 1896;O 1 1919;Ag 3 1923;Ja 30 1926
MB [My 25-D 1889;Jl-D 24 1890]
MWA Ap 27 1876;My 25 1889-Ja 5 1891
NN O 1894-S 1896
NNHi Je 13 1873
OOxM O 24 1882
Tx S 1911-13
WHi My 6 1891

Weekly Denver TIMES. w F 19 1873-89||?
Title varies: Denver weekly times
CoD 1873-[87]
CoDU [1873-82]
CoHi 1880-86;89
CoU [1873-75]
ICHi Ag 23 1876
KHi S 7,D 27 1881
MWA O 11 1876
NNHi Jl 2 1873
NbHi N 3 1898;Ja 14,F 8,Mr 21 1899

TIMES-SUN. d *See* Denver times

TIMES-SUN. w *See* Colorado times

Denver daily TRIBUNE. d F 5 1867-Ag 11 1884||
F-My 14 1867 as Denver daily; My 15 1867-Ja 19 1871 Daily Colorado tribune. Merged with Denver republican to form Tribune republican, later Weekly republican
Both F 5 and F 6 1867 are numbered 1
CU-B Jl 29-30 1868;S 26 1879-80;O 9 1881
CoBoC N 17 1870
CoD F 6 1867-71;Jl 1872-Je 1873;Je 26-D 1876;Jl 1877-Je 1878
CoDV O 19 1867;F 9 1868;Mr 18 1870
CoHi 1867-N 22 1868;Ja-Je 1869;Ja-Je 1870;Jl-D 1872;Jl 1873-Je 1874;75-Je 1876;Ja-Je 1877; Ap 30,Jl 1878-Je 1879;80-Je 1884
CoU [My 15 1867-Ja 19 1871]My 22 1872
DLC O 5 1878
ICHi O 8 1876
KHi Ag 28 1877;Je 9 1878[80-84]
MWA My 29 1876
NNHi Ap 3 1873
OClWHi Ja 3 1871;S 20-21 1881;Ja 1 1882
OOxM O 25 1882

Denver TRIBUNE. w My 15 1867-84||
1867-Ja 25 1871 as Colorado tribune. United with Weekly republican to form Weekly tribune-republican, later Weekly republican
CoD 1867-Ja 3 1872
CoHi 1867-70;73;Ja 1 1881;Ja 1883
CoU My 22 1872
ICHi Ag 2 1876
MWA Ap 28,My 29 1876;Jl 11 1879,Ja 1,Jl 1 1881;Ja 1 1882
NNHi Ja 15 1873

TRIBUNE-REPUBLICAN. *See* Republican

TRUMPET. La Tromba. w Mr 15 1935—
In Italian
CoHi 1935+

Denver VECKOELAD. *See* Westerns nyheter

WESTERNS nyheter. w 1888+
1888-N 2 1889 as Denver veckoblad; N 9 1889-1901 Svenska korrespondenten; 1901-N 25 1928 Svensk-Amerikanska westen
In Swedish
CoHi 1918-20
IRA 1890-1928
MnHi Ja 25 1906-D 6 1928

Denver evening WORLD. d 1882-83||?
KHi Jl 12,Ag 24 1882;Ja 30-F 1883
NbHi Mr 14 1882

Denver WORLD. w F 5 1882-83||?
CoHi Ja 5 1883
KHi Ap 2,Je 4 1882

DILLON

BLUE VALLEY times. w 1911-14||?
CoD D 26 1913

Dillon ENTERPRISE. w 1882-1901||?
CoHi Jl 10 1896
KHi My 28 1886

DOLORES

Dolores STAR. w 1897+
CoHi S 23 1904-S 20 1918

DUBOIS

Dubois CHRONICLE. w Ap 14 1894-
KHi [Ap-D 22 1894]

DURANGO

Durango DEMOCRAT. w 1893-1930||?
CoHi 1901

Durango DEMOCRAT. d 1897-1927||?
United with Durango evening herald to form Durango evening herald-democrat
CoDu D 1908-27?
CoHi Mr 31 1899-1909
KHi Ap 30 1919

Durango HERALD. w,sw 1881+
1881-91? as Durango herald; 1892?-95? Solid Muldoon
w 1881-1918?
CoHi 1898-N 15 1917

Durango evening HERALD-DEMOCRAT. d 1886+
Title varies: Durango morning herald; Durango evening herald
CoDu Ag 7 1907+
CoHi S 1904
KHi D 29 1881;Mr 31,Ap 21 1882;F 5 1883;Ja 1 1888

IDEA. w Ag? 1884-89||?
CoDu Jl 19 1884-86
KHi Ag 1 1885;My 8 1886

Durango NEWS. w 1930+
pub My 1930+

Durango RECORD. d D 29 1880-82||
IC 1880-Jl 19 1881
KHi [Ag 5 1881-Ja 14]Ap 8 1882

SOLID Muldoon. *See* Durango herald

Daily SOUTHWEST. d 1880-83||?
KHi Ag 7 1881;Je 2 1883

SOUTHWEST. w O 6 1882-Jl 1884||
CoDu complete
KHi F 3 1883

TOP o' the world. w
CoAT [1931-32]

Durango WAGE-EARNER. w
CoHi Jl 8 1897-N 9 1911
CoDu 1910

EADS

COLORADO farm and ranch. w 1896-1917||
CoHi Mr 27 1914-D 23 1917

KIOWA county press. w 1887+
pub 1903+
CoHi D 27 1901-Ja 1918;My 1920+

EAGLE

Eagle VALLEY enterprise. w 1896+
CoHi My 24 1901-O 10 1924;Ap 1925+

EASTONVILLE

Eastonville WORLD. w 1889-1901||?
CU-B Ag 13,27,S 10-17 1892

EATON

Eaton HERALD. sw,w Je 1894+
sw 1929-30
pub 1894+
CoHi Jl 8 1898-1918

ELBERT

ELBERT county news. w 1922-24||
CoHi S 22 1922-S 1924

ELBERT county tribune. *See under* Elizabeth

WESTERN recorder. w
CoHi F 17-Jl 28 1898

ELIZABETH

ELBERT county banner. w 1888-1919||
United with Elbert county tribune to form Elbert county tribune banner, later Elbert county tribune
CoHi Ag 13 1897-1911

ELBERT county tribune. w 1884-1925||?
1922-23? as Elbert county tribune banner
1884-1918 pub in Elbert
CU-B Ja 2-23,F 6 1890;Ag 18-25 1892
CoHi F 17 1898-Jl 12 1900;S 26 1901-D 2 1921

EL MORO

DISPATCH. w 1888-90||
CU-B Ja 4 1890

ENTERPRISE and chronicle. *See under* Trinidad

EMPIRE

Empire TRUE fissure. w Jl 3 1901-
CoD Jl-Ag 23,S 13-O 4 1901

ENGLEWOOD

ARAPAHOE democrat. w 1906-19||?
1906-15? as Englewood tribune
CoDeT [1916-17]

Englewood MONITOR. w 1924+
pub 1932+

Englewood TRIBUNE. *See* Arapahoe democrat

ESTES PARK

ROCKY MOUNTAIN mountaineer. w Ja 4 1908-
CoEpT Ja-Ag 27 1908

Estes Park TRAIL. w Ap 15 1921+
pub 1921+
CoHi 1921+
CoLo 1924-33

EVANS

Evans COURIER and messenger. w Jl 1 1871-1917||?
1871-89 as Evans journal; 1890-1914? Evans courier
CU-B S 21 1901
CoD Jl 30,Ag 3,17 1872;Mr 29 1873
CoHi Jl 13 1872;Jl 9 1898-Ag 31 1917
ICHi Jl 6,Ag 17 1876
KHi Ja 18 1883;Jl 31 1884
NN Jl 27,Ag 17-31,S 21 1872-Ja 4,Ap 5,19-26, My 9,23-Jl 4,18 1873
NNHi Ja 11 1873

Evans JOURNAL. *See* Evans courier and messenger

FAIRPLAY

Fairplay FLUME. *See* Park county republican and Fairplay flume

MOUNT Lincoln sentinel. w Mr ? 1873-Ag 1878||
ICHi Ap 6 1876

PARK county republican. w 1912-19||?
United with Fairplay flume to form Fairplay flume-Park county republican, later Park county republican and Fairplay flume

PARK county republican and Fairplay flume. w F 20 1879+
1879-1919? as Fairplay flume; 1920?-21? Fairplay flume-Park county republican
CU-B Ja 9-16 1890
CoD Ja 18 1883
CoHi O 20 1899-1918;Jl 1921+
KHi Mr-Ag 5 1886

FALCON

Falcon HERALD. w 1888-90||
CU-B Ja 18 1890

FLAGLER

Flagler NEWS. w 1913+
pub 1915+
CoHi Ap 12 1928;1935+

Flagler REGISTER. w 1888-90||
CU-B Ja 2-16,F 6,20-27 1890

FLEMING

Fleming HERALD. w 1888-90||
CU-B D 28 1889;Ja 11-18 1890

COLORADO (*Continued*)

FLORENCE

Florence daily CITIZEN. d 1909+
pub 1910+
CoF 1918+
CoHi S 21 1921-23;Ap 16-17 1928
KHi Ap 17 1928

Florence CITIZEN-DEMOCRAT. w 1898-1924||?
1898-1915? as Florence citizen
pub 1909
CoHi O 1912-18

EX PARTE. *See* Fremont democrat

FREMONT democrat. w,sw 1887-1915||?
1887-96? as Oil refiner; 1896?-1901? Refiner; 1902?-13? Ex parte
sw 1897-1901?
CU-B Ja 9-16,30,F 20 1890;F 14,Mr 7-14,28-Ap 18,My 16 1894

Florence daily HERALD. *See* Florence daily tribune

OIL refiner. *See* Fremont democrat

REFINER. *See* Fremont democrat

Florence daily TRIBUNE. d 1896-1909||?
1896-F 1898 as Florence daily herald
CoD My 22 1897
CoHi 1897-[1900]-My 11 1909

FORT COLLINS

Fort Collins ARGUS. *See* Larimer county democrat

Evening COURIER. d Je 1882-Ag 1923||
United with Fort Collins morning express to form Express-courier
CoF [1902-23]
CoFc My 30 1882-Je 4 1883;S 9 1902-14;Ag 1916-Ap,Jl 1919-23
KHi Jl 8,17 1882;Ja 30 1883

Fort Collins COURIER. w *See* Larimer county independent

Fort Collins EXPRESS. w Ap 25 1873-1921||
1873-81 as Larimer county express (title varies slightly) United with Fort Collins courier to form Larimer county independent
CoFc Mr 12 1880-[86]-D 3 1892;Ap 1893-1908; 10-18;Jl 1920-S 9 1921
CoHi Jl 1898-1918
ICHi Ag 4 1876
WaPS N 28,D 4 1919

EXPRESS-COURIER. d 1873+
1873-Ag 31 1923 as Fort Collins morning express
CoF S 1923+
CoFc S 5 1881-Mr 29 1882;Ja-My 15 1884;My 28 1907-35
CoHi N 25 1917-18;22+
KHi My 18 1882;Ja 23 1883;D 9 1925

LARIMER bee. w O 3 1885-86||?
KHi N 14 1885[Mr 13-Jl 17 1886]

LARIMER county democrat. w 1895-1908||
1895-Mr 12 1904 as Fort Collins argus
CoHi Mr 19 1904-F 19 1908

LARIMER county democrat. w 1916-19||
CoFc F 3-Jl 3,20-O,D 1916-D 4 1919

LARIMER county express. *See* Fort Collins express

LARIMER county independent. w Je 29 1878-1930||?
1878-1920? as Fort Collins courier
CoFc 1878-Je 14 1900;Je 20 1901-Je 11 1902;Je 17 1903-18;Jl 1921-28
CoHi D 11 1890-94;Je 18 1896-Ag 1924
KHi Ja 5,19,Mr 16 1882;Ag 9 1883;F 26 1885

Fort Collins LEADER. w 1929+
pub 1929+
CoD Je 8 1934
CoFc 1929+
CoHi S 1923-D 14 1926

MOUNTAIN and plains weekly. w 1919+
CoFc 1930-D 1 1933

Fort Collins STANDARD. w Mr 11 1874-76||
CoFc Mr 11-N 18 1874
ICHi Je 28-Jl 5 1876

FORT GARLAND. *See* BLANCA

FORT LUPTON

Fort Lupton PRESS. w 1898+
CoFl 1925+
CoHi F 8 1907-18;D 15 1922-N 14 1924

FORT MORGAN

MORGAN county herald. w 1888+
CoHi Ja 15 1897-Jl 4 1918

Fort Morgan TIMES. w S 4 1884-1928||?
CoHi 1884-Ag 1891;Jl 1897-Ag 1921;O 25 1923-Ja 1924;Ja-Ap 1925;Ja-Mr 1926
KHi S 18 1884;Mr 12,Je 18 1885

Fort Morgan evening TIMES. d 1908+
CoHi O 1921+

FOUNTAIN

Fountain HERALD. w 1899+
CoHi Ag 1921-Jl 16 1924

FOWLER

Fowler TRIBUNE. w S 17 1897+
pub S 1902-S 1904;D 10 1909+
CoHi S 17 1897-1911

FRANKSTOWN

DOUGLAS county news. *See* Castle Rock independent (Castle Rock)

FRUITA

MESA county mail. *See* Fruita times

Fruita STAR. w Jl 3 1889-90||
KHi S 25 1889-O 16 1890

Fruita TIMES. w 1893+
1893-1927 as Mesa county mail
pub 1915+
CoHi F 14 1908-D 6 1923

FULFORD

Fulford SIGNAL. w Ap 14 1893-
KHi Ap-N 10 1893

GENOA

Genoa SENTINEL. w Ag 12 1912+
pub 1912+

GEORGETOWN

CLEAR Creek topics. w Ja 1902-03||?
CoD Ja-O 1 1903

COLORADO miner. w My 30 1867-N 1888||
CoD Jl 11 1867;Ja 12 1878
CoDV D 16 1869;Ja 20-27,F 10,Ap 28,My 12-19,Je 2-9,23-Jl 1870;Ap 17 1873
CoHi Ag 5,S 1876-S 14,O 12 1878-83;D 19 1885;86;87
CoU S 1869-D 20 1884;85-87
ICMc S 2 1869;My 26 1870
KHi D 31 1881;Ja 14,My 20 1882;Ap 2,O 18 1884
MWA S 18,27 1869

Daily COLORADO miner. d Jl 1-O 1869;S 8 1872-Mr 11 1874||
CoHi S 12 1872-74
CoU [1869-74]
ICMc Jl 16 1869

Georgetown COURIER. w My 24 1877+
CoD 1877-1933
CoHi 1877-1933
CoU Jl 31 1909-S 24 1921
KHi Ja 13,Mr 17 1881

Georgetown HERALD. w 1899-1902||
CoD S 22-N 17,D 1899-Ja 1902

GLENWOOD SPRINGS

Glenwood Springs ADVOCATE. w Ag 11- 1886||
KHi Ag 11 1886

AVALANCHE. d My 6 1891-1918||?
1891? as In it daily
CoHi My-N 25 1891;Je 11 1893-My 5 1897;My 10-N 3 1899

AVALANCHE-ECHO. w 1887-1928||?
1887-Mr 11 1891 as Glenwood echo
CU-B Ja 1890
CoHi Mr 18-S 4 1891;Jl 1897-S 14 1916
KHi O 27 1886

Glenwood ECHO. *See* Avalanche-echo

IN it daily. *See* Avalanche

NEW empire. d 1888-89||?
Formed by the union of News and Ute chief
CU-B Ap 17,20-21 1889

NEWS. w 1887-88||
United with Ute chief to form New empire

PEOPLE'S herald. w 1885-95||?
Title varies: People's herald and Glenwood Springs republican
CU-B [Ja-S 1893;F 1894-Ag 1895]

Glenwood POST. w 1892+
pub 1898+
CoHi Ja 14 1899+

REPUBLICAN. w 1881-92||
Merged with People's herald to form People's herald and Glenwood Springs republican, later People's herald
CU-B [1892]

UTE chief. w 1885-88||
United with News to form New empire
CU-B Mr 3 1888
KHi My 8-Ag 16 1886

GOLD RUN

Gold Run SILVERTIP. w Je 17 1893-
CoHi Je 17-My 16 1894

GOLDEN

COLORADO central. w Jl 27 1878-
KHi S 7 1878

COLORADO transcript. w N 1866+
pub 1866+
CoBoC Je 1 1868
CoD D 19 1866;Ag 14-21,D 11 1867;68-71;F 17 1892
CoHi D 19 1866-D 11 1867;68-N,D 17 1873-N 17,D 8 1875-N 1,D 12 1877-1918
CoU Ja 18 1871-N 1905
ICHi S 13 1876
KHi Ja 12,Mr 2 1881;S 1 1886
MWA Mr 17,N 3,D 29 1875
MnU Jl 3 1867

Golden GLOBE. w 1872-1919||?
CU-B D 28 1889-Ja 18 1890
CoHi 1909-My 1917
ICHi Jl 8,29 1876
InRE N 6 1880
KHi My 20 1872;D 31 1881;Ja 21,Jl 15 1882
NNHi My 24 1873

JEFFERSON county graphic. w 1906-08||?
CoHi S 8 1906-08

JEFFERSON county republican. w N 20 1919+
Follows Arvada sun (Arvada). 1919-N 8 1923 as Jefferson county republican and Arvada sun
pub 1919+
CoHi 1919-N 13 1924;26+

WESTERN mountaineer. w D 7 1859-D 20 1860||
Follows Rocky Mountain gold reporter (Mountain City)
CSmH S 27 1860
CoD D 7 1859;Je 28-D 1860
CoHi D 7 1859
DLC D 14 1859
NN Ja 11 1860(photostat)

GOTHIC

ELK MOUNTAIN bonanza. w Je 12 1880-
KHi [Jl 10 1880-Mr 26 1881]

Gothic MINER. w Ja 15 1881-
KHi [Ap-N 5 1881]

SILVER record. w Je 24 1882-
CU-B Ag 16 1884
KHi Je-Jl 22 1882

GRANADA

Granada JOURNAL. w O 1927+
pub 1927+

SENTINEL. w 1888-
KHi [My 9-Ap 18 1890]

Granada TIMES. w 1898-1913||?
CoHi S 6 1900-Je 16 1911

GRAND JUNCTION

Grand Junction DEMOCRAT. w Mr 30 1883-84||?
Followed by Mesa county democrat
KHi S 21,N 9 1883

GRAND Valley star. *See* Grand Junction star

Grand Junction HERALD. w 1903-10||?
CoHi S 10 1904-Jl 14 1910

MESA county democrat. w S 5? 1884-88||?
Follows Grand Junction democrat
KHi Ag 8 1885

Grand Junction NEWS. w O 28 1882-1924||
CU-B Jl 13 1889
CoHi O 28 1882;1897-Je 1918;Jl 19 1921-Je 7 1924
CoGj 1882-1905
KHi [1882]-Ja 6,D 29 1883;Ja 19 1884-F 14 1885;Je 29 1918

Daily NEWS. d 1906-24||
CoGj 1908
CoHi Jl 6-D 1918;Jl 19 1921-Je 1924

Grand Junction daily SENTINEL. d N 20 1893+
pub 1893+
CoHi 1897-N 18 1910;N 20 1911+
KHi N 21 1893

Grand Junction weekly SENTINEL. w 1894+
CoHi 1897-S 27 1918

Grand Junction STAR. w 1889-99||?
1889-94? as Grand Valley star; 1895?-96? Grand Valley star-times; 1897?-98? Grand Junction star times
CU-B Ja 16,F 27,Mr 6 1890
KHi 1890-Jl 3 1897

GRAND LAKE

Grand Lake PROSPECTOR. w 1882-87||?
CoEN N 9 1882-85
CoHi Ja 6 1883

GRAND VALLEY

Grand Valley NEWS. w 1905+
CoHi Mr 13 1907-11

Grand Valley STAR. *See under* Grand Junction

GREELEY

Greeley BOOSTER. w 1910+
1910-33 as Weld county news
pub 1910+
CoHi O 25 1918-Ap 1920;Mr 1922+

COLORADO advocate. m Ag 1886-
KHi Ag 1886

COLORADO sun. *See* Greeley sun

Greeley COLORADOAN. w
CoBoC Mr 17 1932

HOWITZER. w 1882-88||?
1882-85 as Rocky Mountain howitzer
KHi F 2,N 16 1883;Ag 1 1884;Mr 13 1885;My 21,Ag 20 1886
WHi D 3-10 1886

ROCKY MOUNTAIN howitzer. *See* Howitzer

COLORADO (*Continued*)

GREELEY—*Continued*

Greeley SUN. w N 9 1872-1909||
1872-83? as Colorado sun
CoG [1872-91]-N 12 1898;My 20 1899-O 13 1908
CoHi Ap 21 1894-Je 1909
ICHi Ag 26 1876
KHi Mr 7,Je 12,Ag 1 1886
MWA N 8 1873;Jl 11,O 17,D 19 1874;My 8,Ag 31,N 27 1875;Ja 15,Jl 29 1876;My 7 1881

Greeley TIMES. w 1893-97||?
CoHi Jl-S 18 1897

Greeley TRIBUNE. d
1871 as Evening tribune
OClWHi D 6,13 1871;N 20 1872

Greeley TRIBUNE and republican. d 1908+
1908-Ja 1913 as Greeley daily tribune
pub Je 29 1908+
CoG Ag 29 1908+
CoGS F 1913+
CoHi F 1913-Je 3 1915
KHi Je 22 1910

Greeley TRIBUNE and Weld county republican. w N 16 1870+
1870-F 1 1913 as Greeley tribune
pub 1870+
CSmH Ja 2? 1873
CU-B S 29 1886;Jl 3-24 1889
CoD Ja 18,Jl 5,Ag 23,O 18 1871;Ap 3,My 1 1872;My 28 1873
CoG 1870-78;81-88;91-1900;02-11
CoGS [1874-85;87-88;90-92;95-1900]09-F 1 1913
CoHi 1897-Je 3 1915
KHi Mr 13 1872;Ja 11,Mr 1 1882;Mr 26,Jl 23 1884;Je 3,Jl 8 1885[Ap 28-O 1886]O 24-31 1912
MWA My 1 1872;Je 21 1876;Ag 4 1880
NNHi D 25 1872
OClWHi N 20,D 6-13 1872

WELD county news. *See* Greeley booster

WELD county republican. w 1887-Ja 1913||
United with Greeley tribune to form Greeley tribune and Weld county republican
CoHi S 25 1897-1910

GREEN MOUNTAIN FALLS

Green Mountain Falls ECHO. w 1888-
KHi [Ap-Jl 1 1891]

GROVER

PAWNEE press. w 1908+
KHi Ja 10 1924

GUNNISON

Gunnison ADVERTISER. sm D 20 1881-
KHi [1881-N 1882]

Gunnison DEMOCRAT. w Ag 4 1880-Je 1881||
United with Gunnison news to form Gunnison news-democrat, later Gunnison news-champion and republican
KHi [Ag 1880-My 11 1881]

Gunnison FREE PRESS. sw S 7 1881-Jl 29 1882||
United with Gunnison review to form Gunnison review-press
CoHi complete
KHi complete

Gunnison NEWS-CHAMPION and republican. w Ap 17 1880+
1880-81?, 91?-Ja 11 1901 as Gunnison news; 1881?-90? Gunnison news-democrat; Ja 18 1901-S 21 1918 Gunnison news-champion (title varies: Gunnison news and people's champion; Gunnison news-champion and tribune)
pub O 17 1891-Ap 1893;99+
CoGuW 1931+
CoHi S 25 1897+
KHi Ap 24 1880-Je 11 1881;Jl 8 1904+

Gunnison daily NEWS-DEMOCRAT. d Je 17 1881-84||?
1881 as Gunnison daily news
KHi 1881-Ag 1 1882

PEOPLE'S champion. w 1894-Ja 10 1901||
United with Gunnison news to form Gunnison news-champion, later Gunnison news-champion and republican
CoGuN 1900
CoHi 1897-1901

Gunnison REPUBLICAN. w D 4 1884-85||?
KHi 1884[F 12-My 21 1885]

Gunnison REPUBLICAN. w Ja 3 1901-S 21 1918||
United with Gunnison news-champion to form Gunnison news-champion and republican
CoHi complete

Gunnison REVIEW. w *See* Gunnison tribune

Gunnison daily REVIEW. d *See* Gunnison daily review-press

Gunnison daily REVIEW-PRESS. d,tw O 11 1881-D 1890||
1881-Jl 28 1882 as Gunnison daily review d 1881-N 22 1886
CU-B Ja 1 1883;Ag 31,S 7,14 1889;Ja 18,F 1,8 1890
CoGuW [1881-90]
CoHi Ag 1882-90
KHi 1881-85

Gunnison REVIEW-PRESS. w *See* Gunnison tribune

SUN. w S 29 1893-Jl 26 1894||?
CU-B 1893-Jl 26 1894
KHi 1893-Jl 19 1894

Gunnison TRIBUNE. w My 15 1880-Jl 1 1904||
1880-Jl 29 1882 as Gunnison review; Ag 5 1882-Ja 10 1891 Gunnison review-press
CU-B Ja 1 1883
CoGuN 1893-1904
CoGuW Je 1880-Jl 1882;91-1904
CoHi 1880-My 7 1881;Mr 11,S 2 1882;Ja-Je 1886;Mr 16 1891-1902
KHi complete

Gunnison TRIBUNE. d Ja 29 1891-
KHi Ja 31 1891

HAXTUN

Haxtun HARVEST. w Mr 13 1919+
pub 1919+

HAYDEN

ROUTT county republican. w 1903+
CoHi Ja 31 1908-My 20 1921

HOLLY

ARKANSAS Valley call. w 1909-14||?
KHi Jl 3 1914

Holly CHIEFTAIN. w 1897+
CoHi F 12 1897-My 8 1924

HOLYOKE

Holyoke ENTERPRISE. w,sw Jl 1 1901+
sw O 1927-S 1931
pub 1901+
CoHi Ag 1921-Je 12 1924;My 1925-27;S 13 1928+

PHILLIPS county herald. w S 7 1887-1927||
1887-1921? as Holyoke state herald
CU-B Ja 22,F 12 1892
CoHi 1887-Je 1889;Mr 1897-1913;S 29 1916-S 19 1919
CoHoE 1889-1927

Holyoke STATE herald. *See* Phillips county herald

HOOPER

HOOPER-MOSCA tribune. w 1891-1921||?
1891-Ja 30 1914 as Hooper tribune
CoD Ag 8 1911
CoHi O 8 1897-Mr 21 1914

Hooper TRIBUNE. *See* Hooper-Mosca tribune

HOT SULPHUR SPRINGS

MIDDLE Park times and Kremmling register. w 1881+
1881-D 23 1926 as Middle Park times (title varies slightly)
CoHi Ja 31 1908+

HOTCHKISS

Hotchkiss HERALD. w 1905+
CoHi O 1912-S 19 1918
KHi F 5 1925

NORTH Fork times. w 1897-1926||?
CoHi Ap 28 1905-My 13 1920

HUGO

EASTERN Colorado plainsman. w 1912+
1912-28 as Lincoln county democrat
pub 1912+

LINCOLN county democrat. *See* Eastern Colorado plainsman

RANGE ledger. w 1889+
pub 1889+
CoHi 1899+

HYDE

COLORADO topics. w Ap 9 1886-88||?
KHi [Ap 30-S 24 1886]

IDAHO SPRINGS

Idaho Springs ADVANCE. *See* Idaho Springs mining gazette

CLEAR Creek miner. w Jl 30 1910-12||?
CoD Ag 20 1910-Je 7 1913

CLEAR Creek mining journal-gazette. w 1924+
1924-S 16 1927 as Clear Creek mining journal
CoD 1927-31

CLEAR Creek reporter. sw Ja 27 1892-
Ja-Mr 16 1892 as Idaho Springs iris
CoD Ja 27,F 20,24-27,Mr 5-23,Je 16,30-S 8 1892

COLORADO mining gazette. *See* Idaho Springs mining gazette

Idaho Springs IRIS. *See* Clear Creek reporter

Idaho Springs MINING gazette. w 1881-1927||
1881-S 9 1882 as Idaho Springs advance; S 16 1882-N 9 1901 as Colorado mining gazette. United with Clear Creek mining journal to form Clear Creek mining journal-gazette
CU-B Ag 6 1892
CoD [Mr 30-N 1882]-S 16 1927
CoU D 30 1899

Idaho Springs NEWS. w 1883-My 27 1905||
United with Idaho Springs siftings to form Idaho Springs siftings-news
CoD [My 11 1883-84]-1905
CoHi F 1888-O 13 1899
KHi S 11 1891-My 20 1905
OkHi [1893-95;98]-1900

Idaho Springs SIFTINGS-NEWS. w D 21 1900-22||?
1900-My 27 1905 as Idaho Springs siftings
CoD 1900-D 4 1921
CoHi Ja 12 1901-My 16 1919

IGNACIO

Ignacio CHIEFTAIN. w Jl 21 1910+
1926-32 as Ignacio chieftain and Bayfield blade
CoD 1927-32
CoHi Jl 21 1910-Jl 11 1924;My 1926+

IRONTON

RED MOUNTAIN review. w 1883-
KHi S 13 1884

IRWIN

ELK Mountain pilot. *See under* Crested Butte

JOHNSTOWN

Johnstown BREEZE. w Ap 21 1905+
pub 1905+
CoHi D 31 1908-D 22 1910; D 26 1912-D 17 1914; D 21 1916-D 12 1918

JULESBURG

Julesburg ADVOCATE. w 1895-N 10 1899||
United with Julesburg grit to form Julesburg grit-advocate
CoHi Ja 12-N 1899

Julesburg GRIT-ADVOCATE. w 1893+
1893-N 9 1899 as Julesburg grit
CoHi Ag 1898-Jl 20 1906;O 1907+

KEOTA

Keota NEWS. *See* Pawnee herald

PAWNEE herald. w My 26 1911-25||?
1911-24? as Keota news
CoHi 1911-My 14 1915;My 19 1916-N 1918

KIM

DRY land record. *See* Kim county record

KIM county record. w 1912+
1912-21 as Dry land record
pub My 1918+

KIOWA

COUNTY seat news-tribune. w 1923+
CoHi Mr 12 1926+

DIVIDE review. w 1899+
pub Je 1920+

KIT CARSON

Kit Carson HERALD. w 1911+
pub 1911+

KOKOMO

SUMMIT county times. w 1879-81||?
CoHi Ja 1 1881
KHi Ag 13 1881

KREMMLING

Kremmling NEWS. w 1905-23||?
CoHi N 1 1912;Je 16 1916-My 28 1920

LAFAYETTE

Lafayette LEADER. w 1905+
1912-17? as Lafayette leader and news-free press (title varies slightly)
CoHi F 28 1907-F 2 1917

Lafayette NEWS-FREE PRESS. w 1898-1911||?
1898-Ap 7 1906 as Lafayette news. Merged with Lafayette leader to form Lafayette leader and news-free press, later Lafayette leader
CoHi Je 1902-N 4 1910

LA JARA

La Jara CHRONICLE. w 1900-14||?
CoHi O 14 1904-D 22 1911

La Jara GAZETTE. w 1916+
pub 1916+
CoHi Ap 12 1928;1935+

LA JUNTA

La Junta daily DEMOCRAT. d 1897+
CoHi Ag 16 1897-Ja 20 1900;Ag 1921+

OTERO county republican. w S 11 1889-91||
KHi 1889-Je[Jl 11 1890-F 13 1891]

COLORADO (*Continued*)

LA JUNTA—*Continued*

La Junta TRIBUNE. sw,w 1880+
Jl 3 1895-Ap 18 1896 as Semi-weekly tribune
CoD Jl 16 1926
CoHi 1898-1917;Ap 13 1928
CoLj Ap 29 1886-1921

LAKE CITY

HINSDALE phonograph. *See* Lake City phonograph

Lake City MINING register. w My 21 1880-85||
CoHi 1880-Ap 24 1885

Lake City PHONOGRAPH. w O 5 1888-1911||?
1888-90? as Hinsdale phonograph
CoHi S 18 1897-1911
KHi 1888-Ja 11 1890

Lake City SILVER world. w Je 19 1875+
Je 28 1917-Je 19 1919 as Silver world and Lake City times
CoHi 1875-78;80-Je 2 1883;Je 28 1917+
KHi [O 14 1876-Mr 1888]

Lake City TIMES. w Ja 15 1891-Je 28 1917||
United with Lake City silver world to form Silver world and Lake City times, later Lake City silver world
CoHi Ag 1897-1917

LAMAR

Lamar daily NEWS. d Ag 5 1907+
pub 1907+
CoHi 1922+

PROWERS county news. w 1901-20||
CoHi O 28 1904-F 5 1920
WHi Ag 25 1905-D 4 1914

Lamar REGISTER. w 1886+
CoHi S 5 1900-My 23 1923

Lamar SPARKS. w,d 1887+
Mr 14 1901-D 28 1911 as Lamar sparks and Lamar leader
w 1887-1930?
CoHi D 24 1896-1923

Lamar daily TIMES. d
pub 1930-Je 1932
CoHi 1930-Je 1932

LAS ANIMAS

BENT county democrat. w 1886+
pub Jl 17 1916+
CoHi Jl 14 1898+

Las Animas LEADER. w My 23 1873+
Follows Pleasant Hill leader (Pleasant Hill, Mo.)
pub 1921+
CoHi 1873-Je 13 1879;My 21 1880-Ap 24 1885; F 18 1898-My 15 1924
CoU Ja 16 1874-Ja 5 1883
CtY F 24 1888;My 24 1889
ICHi Jl 28 1876
MWA Jl 21 1882
NNHi Je 23 1873
OHi Jl 4 1879

LA VETA

La Veta ADVERTISER. w 1895+
pub 1895+
CoHi Jl 1898-Ap 9 1920

LEADVILLE

Leadville CARBONATE chronicle. w Ja 29 1879+
pub 1879+
CU-B N 15 1879;Ja 3 1880;Jl 19,Ag-S 20 1884
CoD F 26 1894
CoHi Ja 1 1881;89;O 16 1899+
MWA Ja 7 1929
OOxM Ap 3 1882
WHi Ja 1 1881

Evening CHRONICLE. d Ja 29 1879-D 27 1913||
pub 1879-1922
CU-B O 11 1879
CoD Ja-Jl 1879
CoHi 1888-89;1902-05;08-10;12-13
CoLeH complete
KHi My 6 1884

Leadville weekly DEMOCRAT. w 1879-84||
United with Weekly herald to form Herald-democrat
CU-B Ja 1,D 31 1881;Jl 1 1883;Ja 1 1884
CoHi Ja-Mr,Jl-S 1880;Ja 1 1881

Leadville DEMOCRAT. d Ja 1 1880-86||
United with Leadville herald to form Leadville herald-democrat
CoHi Ja-Je 1880;Jl-D 1884
CoLeH complete

Leadville DISPATCH. w S 4 1886-92||
KHi S 4 1886

Leadville HERALD-DEMOCRAT. d O 21 1879+
1879-86 as Leadville herald
pub O 1879+
CU-B Ja 1 1882;Ja 1,S 26 1884
CoD Ja 1 1881;My 3 1885;Ja 1 1886;Ja 1 1893;Mr 4,15,Ap 1,15,D 23 1894;D 22 1895;S 21-22,D 11 1896;Ja 19-20,29,F 7 1897;Ja 1 1899;Ja 1 1900;Ja 1 1903;Ja 1 1906;Ja 1 1912;Ja 1 1935
CoHi O 21 1880-Ap 23,O 21 1881-Ap 20,O 21 1883-O 21 1884;Jl 1891-Je 1896;97-S 21,O 15 1901-S 1 1903;04-34
CtY Ja 1 1888
DLC Jl-D 1898
IU Ja 1 1889
KHi D 25 1880;Ja 1,15,Mr 19,Jl 15 1882;Ja 1,26,N 6 1883;My 1 1884;Ag 19 1886
MWA Ja 1 1889;S 28 1933;F 9 1934;Mr 5-12 1935

HERALD-DEMOCRAT. w 1879-94||
1879-85 as Weekly herald
CoHi N 8 1879-O 23 1880;Ja 6 1883
KHi Jl 4 1885;D 23 1894
NbHi My 7 1881(supp)

Leadville daily JOURNAL. d 1885-87||?
KHi S 23 1886

LAKE county reveille. w F 23 1878-
N Ap 6 1878

Leadville LEAFLET. m Ja 5 1881-
KHi Ja 5 1881

Leadville evening NEWS-DISPATCH. d 1895-1903||
1895-1901 as Leadville news-reporter
CoHi F 1899-Je 1903

Leadville NEWS-REPORTER. *See* Leadville evening news-dispatch

LESLIE

Leslie REPUBLICAN. w 1888-91||?
CU-B Ja 4,25 1890

LIMON

EASTERN Colorado leader. w 1912+
1912-22? as Limon express
pub 1925+
CoHi Ap 13 1928

Limon EXPRESS. *See* Eastern Colorado leader

LITTLETON

ARAPAHOE herald. w 1902-Ja 2 1915||
United with Littleton independent to form Littleton independent and Arapahoe herald, later Littleton independent
CoHi Je 13 1903-Ja 2 1915
CoLiI 1908-15

Littleton INDEPENDENT. w 1888+
1888 as Littleton gazette. Title varies: Littleton independent and herald; Littleton independent and Arapahoe herald
pub 1888-91;Jl 1892+
CoHi Ag 1897+
CoLiI 1888

Littleton REPUBLICAN. w
CoLiI Ja-Je 1892

LONGMONT

Longmont CALL. w 1898-My 29 1931||
United with Longmont times to form Longmont times-call
CoHi O 14 1899-Ag 1918
CoL Ap 1927-31
CoLT [1898-1931]

COLORADO press. *See* Longmont press

Longmont INTER-OCEAN. w S 1873-Mr 1875||?
United with Rocky Mountain eagle (Boulder) to form Boulder county bee (Boulder)
CoL Mr 21 1875

Longmont LEDGER. w,sw S 12 1879+
Follows Valley home and farm
sw 1929-S 22 1932
CU-B Jl 26 1889;Ja 10 1890
CoHi Ja 15 1897-1911;S 10 1920-S 14 1923
CoL 1879+

Longmont PRESS. w Ag 23 1871-87||?
1871-Ag 21 1872 as Colorado press
CoD Ag 21 1872
CoHi Mr 20 1872
CoL S 1-9 1875
CoU S 30 1886
ICHi Jl 27 1876
NN F 21-Ap 10,24,My 8,22-Je 5,19,Jl 3,24,Ag 28-S 18,O 9-23,N 6 1872
WHi S 11 1880

Longmont TIMES. w 1888+
CU-B Ja 9-16 1890

Longmont TIMES-CALL. d 1896+
1896-My 29 1931 as Longmont times
pub 1896+
CoHi Jl 16 1921-D 12 1922;35+
CoL Mr 28 1927+

VALLEY home and farm. w 1879||
Followed by Longmont ledger
WHi Mr 20 1879

LOVELAND

Loveland HERALD. w 1906-15||?
CoHi F 1908-11

Loveland HERALD. d *See* Loveland reporter-herald

Loveland LEADER. w Ja 1 1892-93||
CoHi 1892-Ag 1893

Loveland REGISTER. w D 20 1894-1906||
CoHi 1894-Ja 1897; Jl 13 1898-Ja 1906

Loveland REPORTER. w 1880+
CoHi 1891-1911

Loveland REPORTER-HERALD. d 1908+
1908-21 as Loveland herald
pub [1908-Ag 1922]+
CoHi O 23 1914-N 22 1915;Ag 1917-21;23-24;35+
CoLo 1925-33

LYONS

Lyons RECORDER. w 1899+
CoHi Jl 10 1902-11;18-My 18 1922
CoMG 1914-My 18 1918

MANCOS

Mancos TIMES-TRIBUNE. w 1892+
1892-1905 as Mancos times
CoHi Ag 15 1897-Mr 1920;Ap 1926+

Mancos TRIBUNE. w 1902-05||
United with Mancos times to form Mancos times-tribune

MANITOU

Manitou Springs JOURNAL. w Mr 14 1882+
CoHi 1905-19
KHi Ap 11,Ag 22 1885
NbHi Je 1 1893

PIKE'S Peak daily news. d 1891+
KHi S 8 1893
MWA S 25 1891;S 13 1904
NN Jl 21 1929
OClWHi Je 6 1891

MANZANOLA

Manzanola SUN. w 1901+
CoHi Ap 24 1908-Mr 21 1919

MAYSVILLE

Maysville MINER. w 1880-
KHi F 4,Ap 1 1882

SOUTH Arkansas miner. w 1880-
KHi Ap 30 1881

MEAD

Mead GAZETTE. w 1931+
pub Jl 1935+

Mead MESSENGER. w 1916-27||
CoHi My 8 1919-Ap 6 1923
CoMG 1918-27

MEEKER

Meeker HERALD. w 1885+
pub 1895+
CoHi Ag 22 1885-Ag 4 1894;Ag 10 1895+

RIO BLANCO news. w Ag 16 1889-92||
CoHi 1889-Jl 16 1892

WHITE River review. w 1902+
CoHi Jl 1902-11;18-F 18 1922

MILLIKEN

Milliken MAIL. w 1909+
pub N 1909+
CoHi D 1918-N 13 1924

MINNEAPOLIS

CHICO. w 1887-90||
CU-B Ja 3-10,31 1890

MONTE VISTA

Monte Vista GRAPHIC-REPORTER. w 1884-1921||?
1884-1919 as San Luis Valley graphic
CU-B Ag 10 1892
CoMoJ [1884-1915]

Monte Vista JOURNAL. w 1888+
pub 1888+
CoHi My 29 1897-1911;S 24 1921-24

SAN LUIS Valley graphic. *See* Monte Vista graphic-reporter

Monte Vista TRIBUNE. w 1913+
CoHi 1918-F 4 1922
CoMoJ [1913-35]

MONTEZUMA

Montezuma MILLRUN. w Jl 1882-87||?
CoD N 17 1883
CoHi My 12 1883

MONTROSE

Montrose ENQUIRER. w F 22 1884-85||
KHi Ap-My 3 1884;Mr 21 1885

Montrose ENTERPRISE. w,sw,d 1888+
1924?-25? as Montrose enterprise-press
sw 1904?-19?;d 1920?-23?
CU-B Ja 11,25-F 1,Mr 1,S 6,O 4,25-N 1 1890
CoHi My 29 1897-Je 1906;O 1921-F 1923

Montrose MESSENGER. w My 25 1882-90||
CU-B Jl 11-Ag 22,S 12 1889
CoHi S 20 1922
KHi [My 25-N 23 1882]Jl 12 1888

Montrose PRESS. w 1882-1920||
United with Montrose enterprise to form Montrose enterprise-press, later Montrose enterprise
pub 1901-20
CoHi S 8 1898-Jl 5 1911;12-Jl 7 1913;Jl 1914-Jl 1917;18-20
KHi My 8,29 1885;Jl 6,O 26 1886

COLORADO (*Continued*)

MONTROSE—*Continued*

Montrose daily PRESS. d 1908+
pub 1908+
CoHi 1910+
KHi Mr 25 1924

Montrose REGISTER. w My 8 1885-
KHi My 8,29 1885

Montrose REPUBLICAN. w 1885-
KHi Jl 6,O 26 1886

MORRISON

BUD. w 1888-1900||?
CU-B Ja 11,25 1890

JEFFERSON county graphic. w 1900-06||
CoHi Mr 10 1900-Ag 24 1906

Morrison MONITOR. w 1914-17||?
CoHi F 19 1914-Ja 25 1917

MOSCA

Mosca HERALD. w 1891-1907||
CoD Je 8 1900
CoHi Jl 2 1897-1901;04-Mr 1907

MOUNTAIN CITY

ROCKY MOUNTAIN gold reporter. Ag 6-O 1859||
Followed by Western mountaineer (Golden)
CoD Ag 6,20,S 3-17 1859
CoHi Ag 6 1859

NATHROP

CHAFFEE county press. w O 9 1880-
KHi N 13 1880

NATURITA

ALTRURIAN. w 1894-
KHi O 1896-Ap 1897

NEW CASTLE

GARFIELD county democrat. w 1901-22||?
CoHi 1918-O 8 1920

NEW RAYMER

Raymer ENTERPRISE. w 1910+
pub My 1913+

NIWOT

Niwot TRIBUNE. w Ag 19 1921+
pub 1921+

NORWOOD

Norwood POST-INDEPENDENT. w 1912+
1912-28? as Norwood post
CoHi Ap 1926-30

NUNN

Nunn NEWS. w 1907+
pub N 12 1907+

OLATHE

WESTERN slope criterion. w 1905+
pub 1905+
CoHi D 1905

ORDWAY

Ordway CALL. *See* Crowley county leader

CROWLEY county leader. w 1910-28||?
1910-15? as Ordway call
CoHi 1918-N 18 1927;28

Ordway NEW era. w Mr 1902+
pub 1902+
CoHi 1910-15;18+

OTIS

COLORADO clipper. w N 4 1887-88||
CoHi N 18,D 2-9 1887;Ja 13,27,F 10-17 1888

Otis INDEPENDENT. w 1911+
pub 1911+

OURAY

Morning BUDGET. w Jl 6 1886-88||
Followed by Ouray plain-dealer
KHi Jl 6-7 1886

Ouray HERALD and plaindealer. w 1880+
1880-1911 as Ouray herald
CoHi Ap 1896+
KHi N 17 1921

Ouray PLAIN-DEALER. w 1888-1911||
Follows morning budget. 1893?-1901 as Silverite plaindealer. United with Ouray herald to form Ouray herald and plain-dealer
CoHi 1896;Ag 13 1897-My,Ag 1904-11

SAN JUAN silverite. w 1891-92||?
United with Ouray plain dealer to form Silverite plain-dealer, later Ouray plain dealer

SIERRA journal. w
CoHi 1884-S 24 1885

SILVERITE plain-dealer. *See* Ouray plain-dealer

SOLID Muldoon. w 1879-91||
Followed by Solid Muldoon (Durango) later Durango herald
CoHi D 29 1882-Ag 8 1884
KHi My 27,Jl 1 1881;Mr 13 1885

Ouray TIMES. w Je 23 1877-85||?
Follows Canon City times (Canon City)
CoHi 1877-Je 12 1880;Je 18 1881-Je 10 1882
KHi D 31 1881;F 4,My 27 1882;F 3 1883;Ap 26 1884

OVID

Ovid RECORD. w 1925+
pub Je 30 1932+
CoMG 1927-Je 1932

PAGOSA SPRINGS

Pagosa HERALD. w
CoHi Jl 4 1889;Mr 6,My 29 1896

Pagosa JOURNAL. w 1916+
CoHi Ja 24 1918-30

Pagosa Springs NEW ERA. w 1905-15||?
CoHi Mr 17 1905;N 16 1906

Pagosa Springs NEWS. w Ap 10 1890-1903||?
CoHi 1890-95;97-98;Ag 11 1899-1900

Pagosa Springs OBSERVER. w 1903-05||?
United with Weekly times to form Times-observer

Pagosa Springs SUN. w D 3 1909+
CoHi D 3 1909;Ap 13 1928

TIMES-OBSERVER. w 1899-1911||?
1899-1905? as Weekly times
CoHi Jl 25 1901;Mr 23 1906

PALISADE

Palisade TRIBUNE. w 1903+
CoHi D 8 1905;Ag 4,D 15,29 1906;1909-11

PAONIA

Paonia BOOSTER. *See* Paonian

PAONIAN. w Je 1904+
1904-Je 1912 as Paonia booster
pub 1904+
CoHi O 6 1905-11

Paonia PROGRESSIVE weekly and newspaper. w 1904-12||?
1904-My 19 1911 as Paonia newspaper
CoHi O 1905-11

PARKER

Parker NEWS. w 1923+
CoHi Ap 12 1928

PEETZ

GAZETTE. w F 16 1917+
pub 1917+

PENROSE

Penrose PRESS. w 1910+
pub Ja 7 1910-Ja 3 1919;22+
CoHi 1918-Ja 1919;20-21

PINON

ALTRURIAN. m,w Ja 1895-
m 1895-96
KHi My 1897-Ap 1901

PITKIN

Pitkin BULLETIN. Ja 6 1893-
CoHi Ja-N 4 1893

Pitkin INDEPENDENT. w Jl 17 1880-83||?
KHi [Jl 31 1880-D 1 1883]

Pitkin MINING news. w O 7 1881-86||?
KHi [O 21 1881-Ap 11 1885]

PLATTEVILLE

Platteville HERALD. w 1907+
KHi Je 23 1911

PONCHA SPRINGS

Poncha HERALD. w 1881-82||
KHi [Ap-Ag 1882]

PUEBLO

ABRUZZO-MOLISE. w 1917-D 31 1926||
1917-23 as Marsica nuova
F 19-D 31 1926 pub at Rochester, N.Y.
In Italian
CU-B [Ap 15 1922-25]
CoPU 1918-26
CoPV 1924-26
IU Ap 30 1922-26

ARKANSAS Valley review. *See* Pueblo post

Pueblo CHIEFTAIN. d My 1872+
1872-86? as Daily Colorado chieftain
CoHi Ja 1 1881;98+
CoP 1904+
CoPS Ap 1873+
CoU [Jl 9 1868-F 16 1890]
KHi N 21 1880;Jl 23 1884;Mr 12 1885[91-N 23 1928]Je 24 1930
MWA Ap 15,20 1876;Mr 25 1879
WHi 1917-Ja 1 1920

Pueblo CHIEFTAIN. w *See* Colorado chieftain

CHIEFTAIN and people. *See* Colorado chieftain

COLORADO chieftain. w Je 1 1868+
Title varies: Pueblo chieftain; Chieftain and people; etc.
CU-B S 30 1884;86-Je 1887
CoD Mr 10 1870;N 23 1871;F 1,22 1872;Ja 9,F 6 1873
CoHi Mr 17 1914-17;19-24;S-D 1926;O 1927+
CoPS 1868+
CoU [Jl 9 1868-F 16 1890]
ICHi S 7,O 20 1876
KHi F 8,N 6 1883
NNHi D 26 1872

COLORADO tribune. w Je 1 1933+
pub 1933+
CoD O 5 1934
WHi O 19 1933-Ja 12 1934

Pueblo COMMERCIAL standard. w Je 1882-Mr 21 1885||
United with Stock review to form Stock review and commercial standard, later Review and farmer (not in this list)
CU-B S 27 1884
CoHi complete
KHi Je,O 14 1882

FLAG of freedom. w
PHi [1847-48]

GREAT west. w 1870-
CoU O 1870

INDEPENDENT reform press. *See* Pueblo post

Pueblo INDICATOR. w 1890+
pub 1890+
CoHi Ja 26 1913-Ja 19 1924

INDIVIDUAL. w 1896-98||?
CtY F 6 1896

Evening JOURNAL. d 1900-Je 1901||
United with Pueblo evening star to form Pueblo evening star-journal

LEADER. d 1911-13||?
CoP Je-N 1911;12-Mr 1913

MARSICA nuova. *See* Abruzzo-molise

Daily evening NEWS. d 1882-
KHi Jl 13 1882[F 5-D 17 1885]

Saturday OPINION. *See* Pueblo times

Sunday OPINION. *See* Pueblo times

PEOPLE. w 1871-F 1875||
United with Pueblo chieftain to form Chieftain and people, later Colorado chieftain
MB [S 14 1872-F 6 1875]

Daily PEOPLE. d Je-N 1873||
MB Je 10 1873

Pueblo POST. w 1895-1910||?
1895-1900? as Independent reform press; 1901?-02? Arkansas Valley review
OkHi [1895;98]99

Daily Pueblo PRESS. d My 1886-88||?
KHi Je 1,Ag 10 1886

PUBLIC opinion. *See* Pueblo times

Pueblo REPUBLICAN. sw O 25? 1875-76||?
ICHi Ag 10 1876

Daily REPUBLICAN. d Mr? 1882-
KHi My 18 1882

RISING sun. *See* Western ideal

Pueblo evening STAR. d 1883-Je 29 1901||
United with evening journal to form Pueblo star-journal
CU-B D 30 1889;Ja 2 1890
CoHi O 1899-1901
DLC Jl 16-N 1892
KHi My 7,Ag 18 1886

Pueblo STAR-JOURNAL. d Jl 1 1901+
Formed by union of evening journal and Pueblo star
pub 1901+
CoHi 1901-Ap 1910;S 1911-Ag 1915
CoP 1903-15

Pueblo SUN. d S 1 1906-10||
CoHi 1906-D 3 1910

Pueblo TIMES. w Je 1882+
1882-S 1885 as Saturday opinion; O 1885-1922? Sunday opinion; 1893?-1925? Public opinion
CU-B Jl 14-21,Ag 4 1889;Mr 16,30 1895
CoHi 1918-21
KHi S 5 1886

L'UNIONE. w N 1897+
In Italian
pub 1897+
CoHi 1935+
CoPV 1897+
IU 1918-N 12 1920;Mr 11-Je 3 1921;Ap 15 1927-D 12 1930
PP Ap 15,17 1925;My 20 1927+

Il VINDICE. w 1908+
In Italian and English
IU [D 22 1917-Feb 16]Ap 27 1918-S 10 1921

La VOCE del popolo. w 1926+
In Italian
pub D 1926+
PP Ja 14-28,O 20-27 1936

COLORADO (*Continued*)

PUEBLO—*Continued*

Daily VOX populi. d N? 1881-
In Italian
KHi Ja 5,7,10,28 1882

Pueblo WELCOME. w Mr 16 1882-
KHi Mr 30 1882

WESTERN ideal. w 1919+
1919-23? as Rising sun
Negro
pub Mr 23 1921+

RED CLIFF

COMET. w 1881-92||?
1881-89? as Eagle River shaft
CoHi Ap 5 1884

EAGLE county blade. w 1894-1911||?
CoHi 1899-N 17 1911

EAGLE county times. w S 4 1886-1910||?
1886-88? as Times
CoD D 31 1892
CoHi N 5 1887;Ag 13 1898-Je 1906
KHi S 4 1886

EAGLE River shaft. *See* Comet

HOLY CROSS trail. w 1911+
CoAT 1929+
CoHi 1923+
MWA S 20 1930

TIMES. *See* Eagle county times

RED MOUNTAIN CITY

Red Mountain PILOT. w Ja 11 1883-
CoD F 22-Jl 21 1883

Red Mountain REVIEW. w Ja 20 1883-84||
CoD Mr-D 1883
KHi Mr 1 1884

RICO

DOLORES news. *See* Rico news

DOVE-CREEK news. w 1879+
1879-1933 as Rico item
CoDU 1921+
CoHi D 14 1918+

Rico ITEM. *See* Dove-Creek news

Rico NEWS. w 1879-1908||?
1879-85 as Dolores news. Title varies: Rico news; Rico news-record; Rico news-sun
CoHi 1897-D 5 1908
KHi D 10 1881;Mr 11,Jl 15 1882;N 10 1883;My 10 1884;Mr 14 1885;Jl 10-17 1886

Rico RECORD. w 1883-84||
United with Dolores news to form Rico news-record, later Rico news
KHi O 4,N 8-15 1883;Ap 10,My 1 1884

RIFLE

Rifle REVEILLE. w 1889-1914||?
United with Rifle telegram to form Telegram-reveille, later Rifle telegram
CoRT S 6 1889-1913

Rifle TELEGRAM. w 1891+
pub [Ja 23 1903-30]+
CoHi Mr 27 1903-16;35+

ROBINSON

Robinson TRIBUNE. w D 1880-83||?
KHi Jl 14 1881

ROCKY FORD

Rocky Ford ENTERPRISE. w Je 1 1887+
pub 1887+
CoHi Ag 31 1893-1901;04-1916

Rocky Ford GAZETTE-TOPIC. w 1895+
1895-99? as Rocky Ford times-republican; 1900?-01 Rocky Ford republican; 1901-09 Rocky Ford gazette
CoHi F 1897-Mr 14,O 17 1901-O 8;Mr 6-D 18 1909;F 19 1910-16

Rocky Ford REPUBLICAN. *See* Rocky Ford gazette-topic

Rocky Ford TIMES-REPUBLICAN. *See* Rocky Ford gazette-topic

Rocky Ford TRIBUNE. w 1897+
pub [My 18 1900+]
CoHi Mr 1900-16

ROSITA

Rosita INDEX. w S 1875-87||
1881-85 as Sierra journal
CoD O 15 1885
CoHi [1881-N 1886]-Mr 18 1887
ICHi Je 29 1876
KHi Ag 26 1886

SIERRA journal. *See* Rosita index

SAGUACHE

Saguache ADVANCE. *See* Saguache crescent

Saguache CHRONICLE. w O 10 1874-86||
CoHi Ap 15 1876-Ja 1 1881
ICHi S 2 1876
KHi D 30 1881;Ja 6,20 1882;Mr 13 1885
OCHi Jl 8,D 9 1876

Saguache CRESCENT. w 1882+
1882-84? as Saguache advance; 1885?-89? Saguache democrat
CoHi S 9 1897-Jl 14 1921;22+
KHi Mr 16,Jl 27 1882;Jl 31,Ag 1 1884;N 12-26 1885

Saguache DEMOCRAT. *See* Saguache crescent

SENTINEL. w 1888-90||
CU-B Ja 2 1890

ST. ELMO

St. Elmo MOUNTAINEER. w 1881-85||
KHi Ja 31,Mr 7,Ap 25,S 26 1885

SALIDA

CHAFFEE county record. *See* Salida record

Salida MAIL. sw Je 5 1880+
1880-84 as Mountain mail
CU-B D 31 1889-Ja 10 1890
CoHi 1897-1916;35+
CoS 1909+
KHi 1880-Ap 21 1905

Salida daily MOUNTAIN mail. d 1882-84||
KHi My 20 1882;F 3,N 16 1883;Ag 1 1884

MOUNTAIN mail. w *See* Salida mail

Salida daily NEWS. d S? 1883-90||?
KHi N 15,19 1883;Mr 3,My 5 1884
TxH N 4 1885

Salida RECORD. w,d,sw 1893+
1893-99? as Chaffee county record
w 1893-1924?;d 1924?-26?
CoHi Ag 12 1898-1916;Ap 17 1928
CoS 1909-33

Salida daily SENTINEL. d Je 1882-
KHi [Jl 10-29 1882]Ja 31 1883

Salida daily TIMES. d 1883-
KHi N 8 1884

SAN LUIS

El HERALDO del valle. sw
CoAT 1931+

SAN MIGUEL

San Miguel JOURNAL. *See* Telluride journal (Telluride)

SEDGWICK

Sedgwick INDEPENDENT. w 1910+
1910-25? as Sedgwick sun
pub Ap 1926+

Sedgwick SUN. *See* Sedgwick independent

SEIBERT

FREE PRESS. w 1887-90||
CU-B Ja 10,31-F 7 1890

SILVER CLIFF

Silver Cliff daily HERALD. d 1882-
CoHi [1882]
KHi Jl 12-15 1882

Silver Cliff weekly HERALD. w 1882-
CoHi [1882]

Weekly MINER. w 1878-81||
Title varies: Silver Cliff miner
CoHi Ja 7 1880
KHi D 3 1880;Mr 18 1881
MWA Ag 22,S 19,O 10 1879

Daily MINER. d 1879-80||?
MWA F 27,Mr 16,18,Ap 26 1880

Silver Cliff daily PROSPECTER. d 1879-81||?
CoHi Ja 1 1881
KHi Ja 6 1881
MWA Mr 16,30 1880

Silver Cliff weekly PROSPECTER. w 1880-81||?
KHi Jl 15 1881

Silver Cliff RUSTLER. w 1885-1911||?
CoD Ag 4,O 27 1897;Ja 5,Mr 10,Je 15,Ag 3,S 21,N 30,D 21 1898-Ja 4,F 8,Jl 19,Ag 30,O 11,N 8,29,D 20-27 1899
CoHi 1886-D 16 1908

SILVER PLUME

COLORADO jack rabbit. w Ag 22 1885-
KHi Ag 22,S 12 1885

Silver Plume COLORADOAN. w O 8 1881-84||
CoD 1881-Je 21,Jl-S 13,27-N 15 1884
CoHi N 8 1884

SILVER standard. w S 19 1885-D 28 1907||
CoD S-N 21,D 12 1885-1907
CoHi Jl 16 1898-1907
KHi S 19,N 7 1885

SILVERTON

Silverton DEMOCRAT. w Ap 28 1883-87||
Ag 4-11 1885 as Democrat-herald; Ap 18-O 31 1885 Silverton democrat-herald. United with San Juan to form San Juan-democrat
CoD My 1883-D 24 1887
KHi N 8 1884;Mr 7 1885

Daily DEMOCRAT-HERALD. d 1885-
NcD Je 30 1885

DEMOCRAT-HERALD. w *See* Silverton democrat

LA PLATA miner. *See* Silverton miner

Silverton MINER. w Jl 10 1875-1921||?
1875-86? as La Plata miner. Title varies slightly
CU-B Ja 25-F 8,Mr 1 1890
CoD [1879-85]
CoHi D 30 1882;97-1916
ICHi Jl 27 1876
KHi Jl 8 1882;Mr 12 1887
MWA My 7 1881
OCHi Ja 31 1878

SAN JUAN-democrat. w O 14 1886-88||
1886-87 as San Juan. Merged with Silverton miner
CoD 1886-D 22 1887

SAN JUAN herald. w Je 23 1881-Mr 1885||
United with Silverton democrat to form Democrat herald, later Silverton democrat
CoD Je 30 1881-[Ja-Mr 1885]
KHi Ag 11 1881;Ja 12 1882;Je 7 1883

Silverton STANDARD. w N 2 1889+
pub 1889+
CoHi N 2-9 1889;Jl 16 1898-1916

SOUTH DENVER

Papers published in South Denver are listed under Denver

SPRINGFIELD

BACA county democrat. w 1912-19||?
United with Springfield herald to form Springfield democrat-herald

BACA county republican. w 1920+
CoHi My 24 1935-Ja 3 1936

Springfield DEMOCRAT-HERALD. w 1887+
1887-1919? as Springfield herald
CoHi 1897+

Springfield HERALD. *See* Springfield democrat-herald

Springfield REPUBLICAN. w 1889-90||
CU-B Ja 3,24 1890

STEAMBOAT SPRINGS

INTER mountain. w 1889-95||?
CU-B F 6,20-27 1890
CoHi Ap 17 1890

Steamboat PILOT. w 1885+
CoBoC O 2 1889
CoD Je 18 1924
CoHi Ag 18 1897+

ROUTT county sentinel. w 1900-27||?
CoHi 1918-O 3 1924

STERLING

Sterling DEMOCRAT. *See* Sterling farm journal

Sterling FARM journal. w Ag 17 1895+
1895-O 31 1929 as Sterling democrat
pub [1895-O 1929]+
CoHi Ag 1898+

LOGAN county advocate. *See* Republican-advocate

LOGAN county democrat. w My 13 1882-
1882-83? as Sterling record; 1884?-86 Sterling news
KHi My 27 1882

Sterling NEWS. *See* Logan county democrat

Sterling RECORD. *See* Logan county democrat

REPUBLICAN-ADVOCATE. w O 3 1885-1929||?
1885-1907? as Logan county advocate
1885-87 pub in Atwood
CoHi Jl 21 1898-N 17 1909;O 27 1918-S 16 1920; S 28 1922-S 1924
KHi N 21 1885

SUGAR CITY

Sugar City GAZETTE. w 1900+
1900-1916 as Sugar City saccharine gazette
pub 1900+
CoHi Ag 8 1902-16

Sugar City SACCHARINE gazette. *See* Sugar City gazette

SUMMITVILLE

Summitville NUGGET. w My 12 1883-
KHi S 8 1883

SUNSHINE

Sunshine COURIER. *See* Boulder county courier (Boulder)

TARRYALL MINES

MINER'S record. w Jl 4-S 14 1861||
CoHi complete

TELLURIDE

Telluride JOURNAL. w Jl 1881+
1881-82? as San Miguel journal (San Miguel)
CU-B Jl 6-20 1889
CoHi 1897-Ag 5 1916;Ag 1921+
KHi F 4 1882;S 19 1885;My 1 1886

COLORADO (*Continued*)

TELLURIDE—*Continued*

Telluride daily JOURNAL. d 1894-1929||
Title varies slightly
CoHi 1897-1902;Jl 1903-Ag 4 1916;Ag 6 1921-Ag 1929

MINING news. w S 9? 1884-85||
KHi Mr 18 1885

Evening NEWS. d My 1884-
KHi [Jl 21-D 1884]

Telluride NEWS. d Ag 1885-
KHi O 14 1885

SAN MIGUEL examiner. w Jl 3 1886-1928||?
1886-96? as Telluride republican; 1896?-Ag 21? 1897 San Miguel democrat
CoHi Ag 28 1897-1902;06-1916
KHi Jl-Ag 21 1886

SAN MIGUEL journal. *See* Telluride journal

THURMAN

Thurman TIMES. w 1888-94||?
CU-B Ja 16 1890;Ag 19,S 30 1892

TIN CUP

GARFIELD banner. *See* Tin Cup miner

Tin Cup MINER. w S 10 1881-84||?
1881-82 as Garfield banner
CoHi S 24 1881
KHi 1881-Jl 1882;O 25 1884

NEW democrat. w F 7 1885-
KHi Mr 21 1885

TOMICHI

HERALD. w 1882-
KHi N 1884-F 14 1885

TRINIDAD

Trinidad weekly ADVERTISER. w 1882-1900||?
1885-87 as Cattlemen's weekly advertiser
CU-B Ag 29,S 12 1889
CoU [D 29 1884;87;Ap 19 1888-F 1891]
KHi Je 9 1884
—Spanish ed *See* El Anunciador

Trinidad ADVERTISER. d Je 24 1882-1917||?
1882 as Trinidad daily democrat; 1883-My 1898 Trinidad daily advertiser; Je 1898-99 Trinidad advertiser-sentinel
CoHi S 24 1897-1910
CoU 1882;83-Ap 3,Ag-D 1886;Ap 30 1887-F 1891;D 28 1893;Ap-Je,O-D 1903

ADVERTISER-MONITOR. w,sw 1892-1918||?
1892-N? 1900 as People's monitor; D 1900-12? Trinidad monitor
CoHi Jl 22 1898-1916
CoU Jl 30 1897-Ag 12 1899;Ag 1900-Jl 1903

Trinidad ADVERTISER-SENTINEL. d *See* Trinidad advertiser

El ANUNCIADOR. w 1904+
pub F 1906+
CoHi 1935+
IU Ap 1918-N 18 1922
—English ed *See* Trinidad advertiser

CATTLEMEN'S weekly advertiser. *See* Trinidad weekly advertiser

CHRONICLE. d 1889-Mr 1899||
Title varies: Evening chronicle; Morning chronicle. United with Daily news to form Trinidad chronicle-news
CoU Ag 4 1890-Je 1895;Jl 8 1897-Jl 1898

Trinidad CHRONICLE NEWS. w 1878+
1878-Mr 6 1899 as Trinidad weekly news
CoU [N 1880-O 1883;Ap 30 1885-S 1889]Jl 1914-Jl 2 1915
KHi Jl 21 1881;O 23 1885

Trinidad CHRONICLE-NEWS. d Jl 1881+
1881-Mr 3 1899 as Daily news (title varies slightly)
CoHi [O 18-D 1899]Je 29-Ag 10 1900;Je 20 1901-Ag 1909;10-N 21 1924;25+
CoU Jl 31-S 1881;Ja 31-S 1882[Ja-N 1883;84] D 1887-Mr,Je 1893-N 4 1896;D 11 1897-1900;F-Mr 1904;06-Jl 1907-Ap 3 1908;Jl 1914-Jl 2 1915
KHi O 29 1925

Trinidad CITIZEN. d 1887-90||
CU-B D 28 1889;Ja 7-9 1890
CoU O 17 1887-F 25 1890

COLORADO chronicle. w D 5 1873-Mr 21 1875||
United with Trinidad enterprise to form Enterprise and chronicle
KHi Ja 31 1874

COLORADO pioneer. w F 6? 1876-78||?
In English and Spanish
ICHi My 11 1876

CORRIERE di Trinidad. w 1903+
In Italian
CoHi 1918-21;35+

Trinidad daily DEMOCRAT. *See* Trinidad advertiser

Trinidad ENTERPRISE. w S 1870-Mr 21 1875||?
United with Colorado chronicle to form Enterprise and chronicle
CoD F 16 1872

ENTERPRISE and chronicle. w Mr 28 1875-77||?
Formed by the union of Trinidad enterprise and Colorado chronicle
Also dated at Elmoro
OCHi Ja 31 F 14-28,Mr 28-Ap 11,Ag 16-23,S 13 1877

El EXPLORADOR. w 1874?-77||?
In Spanish
ICHi Je 29 1876

El FARO. (Lighthouse) w Ja 1912+
In Spanish
pub 1912+

FORSYTH'S chips.
MbHi S 7 1899;Jl 5-12,S 6,20-O 11,25 1900

MONITOR. *See* Advertiser-monitor

Trinidad NEWS. *See* Trinidad chronicle-news

PEOPLE'S monitor. *See* Advertiser-monitor

Evening PICKETWIRE. d 1915-27||?
CoHi Jl 1921-Ag 1923
KHi Ag 16 1924

Trinidad PICKETWIRE. w 1915-29||?
CoHi Jl 5 1921-Ag 31 1923

Trinidad REPUBLICAN. w S 17 1880-
CoU S 17 1880-Je 2 1882

Trinidad REVIEW. w D 1 1883-86||
CoU [1883-Ap 3 1886]

Trinidad daily TIMES. d 1881-
CoU [Je 1881-Ja 1882]

TURRET

GOLD belt. w 1899-1910||?
CoHi S 14 1904-09

TWIN LAKES

Twin Lakes MINER. w 1901-14||?
CoHi O 7 1905-D 9 1911

VALMONT

Valmont BULLETIN. w Ja 1 1866-Mr 1867||
Followed by Boulder Valley news (Boulder)

VICTOR

Daily PRESS. *See under* Cripple Creek

Victor RECORD. d 1895-Mr 1913||
United with Cripple Creek times to form Cripple Creek times-record (Cripple Creek)
CoHi 1897-S 1909
KHi F 3-Mr 4 1903

Victor weekly RECORD. w 1899-Mr 1913||
United with Cripple Creek times to form Cripple Creek times-record (Cripple Creek)
CoHi 1899-1902;Ag 1908-D 1 1911

Victor TIMES. d 1897-1902||
CoHi Jl 16 1898-D 29 1902

VILLA PARK

WEST side citizen. w 1889-96||?
KHi O 17 1890-F 8 1895;N 20-D 25 1896

VIRGINIA CITY

TIN CUP record. w My 14 1881-
KHi My 28 1881-Jl 22 1882

WALDEN

JACKSON county star. w 1913+
CoHi Mr 1935+

Walden NEW ERA. w 1906-14||?
CoHi F 7 1907-11

WALSENBURG

Walsenburg CACTUS. *See* Walsenburg yucca

HUERFANO cactus. *See* Walsenburg yucca

HUERFANO independent. w D 11 1875-76||?
In English and Spanish
ICHi Jl 22 1876

Walsenburg INDEPENDENT. w 1908-30||
United with Walsenburg world to form Walsenburg world-independent.
CoHi Ag 1921-30

Walsenburg WORLD-INDEPENDENT. w,d 1887+
1887-My 12 1930 as Walsenburg world
w 1887-Ap 1933
CoHi Jl 1898-1916;18-20;23+

Walsenburg YUCCA. w D 19? 1883-1904||?
1883-88? as Huerfano cactus; 1889?-98? Walsenburg cactus
KHi My 10 1884

WALSH

Walsh TAB. w Je 21 1928+
pub 1928+

WARD

Ward MINER. w 1893-1901||?
CoU F 4 1898

WELDONA

WELDEN Valley news. w 1907-17||?
CoHi F 4 1908-11

WELLINGTON

Wellington SUN. w Je 1905+
1905-Ja 30 1909 as Wellington
pub 1905+
CoHi 1906-Je 1914

WELLINGTON. *See* Wellington sun

WESTCLIFFE

WET Mountain tribune. w 1883+
CoHi 1899-1917;Ap 13 1928;35+

WHITE PINE

White Pine CONE. w Ap 13 1883-D 30 1892||
CU-B Ja 3,17 1890
CoGuW complete
KHi complete
OClWHi F 27 1891

White Pine JOURNAL. w My 19 1881-
KHi My-Je 1881

WHITEHORN

Whitehorn NEWS. w S 10 1897-1912||?
CoHi 1897-Ja 4 1907

WINDSOR

POUDRE Valley. w 1898+
pub 1902+
CoHi 1908-09;1935+

WRAY

Wray GAZETTE. w 1901+
CoHi F 26 1904-16

Wray RATTLER. w 1886+
CU-B Ja 4-11 1890
CoHi Je 16 1898-1921;35+

Wray TIMES. w Je 25 1898-1901||
CoHi 1898-S 1 1901

YAMPA

Yampa LEADER. w 1903-26||?
CoHi F 15 1908-16;Mr 15-29 Je-Jl 1918;22;24

YUMA

Yuma PIONEER. w D 25 1886+
CoHi Ag 1898-1916

REPUBLICAN news. w N 29 1899-1902||?
1899? as Spooktown fixer
CoHi D 12,21 1899-Mr 15 1900

SPOOKTOWN fixer. *See* Republican news

CONNECTICUT

ANSONIA

Daily ADVERTISER. *See under* Derby

Ansonia JOURNAL. w My 23-Jl 31 1885||?
Ct Je 13,Jl 3-10,31 1885

NAUGATUCK Valley sentinel. *See* Ansonia weekly sentinel

Ansonia weekly SENTINEL. w N 9 1871-1902||
1871-89 as Naugatuck Valley sentinel
Ct Je 1872-Je 1880
CtAn Jl 10 1873
CtDe Je 13 1872;S 17 1874;Ap 11 1878;Mr 31-Ap 14 1880 My 25 1881[My 1882-83]Ja 30,O 22 1884[85-86]F 23 1887[88]Ja 23 1889;Ja 1 1890;Ja 28 1891;D 14-21 1892;Ja 18 Ap 25 My 17 1893

Evening SENTINEL. d Ja 16 1884+
Ct N 1921+
CtAn Ag 18 1896+
CtDe Mr 29 1884[85-Mr 26 1887;1888]Ja 23,D 7 1889;Ja 12,F 25 1890;Ja 28 1891[D 1892-93] Ap 2,O 25 1894;My 29 1895[Mr 1896]Ag 3 1898;Ap 14-15 1899[Je 1900-02]F 1903+

BALTIC

Baltic weekly NEWS. w 1869-
CtHWe Mr 25 1869

BERLIN

Berlin NEWS. w 1891-1908||
Ct N 30 1893;Ja 20 1898

CONNECTICUT (*Continued*)

BETHEL

HERALD of freedom. w 1831-
Ct Jl 17 1833
MWA Je 6 1832

Bethel LEDGER. w 1875-96||?
1875-My 1879 as Bethel press
Ct Je 1876-Jl 1896
MWA S 23 1876

Bethel PRESS. *See* Bethel ledger

BIRMINGHAM. *See* DERBY

BRANFORD

Branford GLEANER. w 1878-80||
Ct Mr 1878-F 1880
CtHWe Ap 3,My 29 1878

Branford REVIEW and East Haven news. w Ap 13 1928+
Ct Ag 3 1933+

BRIDGEPORT

Daily ADVERTISER and farmer. d S 1856-
CtHWe Mr 25,27 1857;Jl 30 1859
NN S 29,O 16,N 1856

Bridgeport ADVOCATE. w Ag 8 1896-1913||?
Ct Ag 22 1896
WHi O 10 1903

BRIDGEPORT. w 1914+
In Hungarian
pub 1915-18;20+

*CONNECTICUT courier. w N 10 1813-
Ct Mr 20 1822;F 15,Mr 1,15 1826
CtB Ja 9-S 1822
CtY N 13,27 1822;Jl 23 1823;My 12 1824;Ja 12,F 9 1825
DLC N 20,D 11 1822;Jl 9-23 1823
MWA My 7 1823
NN O 31,N 14,D 19 1821;Ja-F 6,Ap 10,My 8,Jl 3-17,Ag 21,O 16,N 6-13,27 1822[23-24]

CONNECTICUT patriot. w Ag 30 1826-
Ct O 4 1826;F 14 1827
CtB [Mr 26-D 17 1828]
CtY F 7,Jl 4 1827

Bridgeport Sunday EAGLE. w D 5 1880-82||
Ct 1880-Jl 22 1882

Bridgeport evening FARMER. *See* Times-star

Sunday HERALD. w 1890+
Ja 10-D 1926 as Bridgeport-Waterbury herald
Ct Ap 1890-Mr 1893;Mr 21-D 1901;09+

Bridgeport evening HERALD. *See* Bridgeport star

Bridgeport INDEPENDENT-LEADER. m,sm,w Ap 1890-1904||?
m S 1890-My 1892; sm Je 1892-Ja 1893
Ct S 1890-S 1901

JOURNAL. sw D 1875-78||?
MWA Ap 29 1876

Bridgeport LEADER. w Mr 25 1854-
Ct Mr 25-Jl 1 1854

LEADER. sw,d F 3 1872-F 13 1883||
sw 1872-Ja 1882
Ct 1872-Ja 1883
CtB N 1872-F 5 1881
CtY D 21 1872
MWA O 7 1876

Bridgeport LIFE. w Ap 3 1915+
pub Ap 3 1915+
Ct Jl 10-16 1915[18-21]+

Bridgeport MESSENGER. w N 26 1831-N 21 1832||
Ct [1831-32]
CtB complete
CtHWe O 24 1832
MWA Ja 7,O 3 1832

Evening NEWS. d O 27 1879-98||
1879-D 3 1892 as Bridgeport morning news
Ct 1880-Jl 1898
CtB Ap 1882-84;Jl 1885-91
CtY Ja-Je 1885

Bridgeport POST. d F 7 1883+
Title varies: Evening post; etc.
N 1908 as 25th anniversary number
Ct 1885-F 1893;Mr 31 1923;Jl 10 1925;Mr 8 1927
CtB Je 1893+
CtSp N 1908
DLC 1898
WHi N 1908

Bridgeport REPUBLICAN. w Ja 1830-Ag 5? 1839||
Followed by Republican standard
CtSp F 25,D 23 1835;Ap 26,D 13 1837;D 5-12 1838
CtY [1836]
MWA Ag 29 1838
NN Je 17 1835

*REPUBLICAN farmer. w Ap 25 1810-1920||?
Follows Republican farmer (Danbury) (not in this list)
CSmH Ag 25 1830
Ct F 15-22 1826;Ag 22 1827;D 16,30 1829;D 5-12 1832;Ja 9 1833;Je 7 1837
CtB 1848-49
CtSp N 14 1821;My 22 1822;D 19 1832
CtY Ap 14 1824;Ag 24 1825;Ag 16 1826;Ag 8 1827;D 19 1832;F 6 1874
DLC 1857-60
MSaE Ag 6 1823
MWA Jl 2 1828;Jl 24 1839;F 1 1842;Ag 10 1852;D 18 1863;My 27 1864
N O 16 1833
NN Jl 17 1839;S 7 1866
NNHi Ap 15 1845;Ja 10 1873
NSyU Jl 19-26,Ag 23 1861
OClWHi Ag 8 1862

REPUBLICAN standard. w Ag 21 1839-1912||?
Follows Bridgeport republican
Ct O 12 1852;O 19 1861;Je 9 1871;O 24 1890
CtB [Ag 12-N 20 1839;F-S 16]30 1840-Ag 9 1842;Ag 1845-52
CtHWe Ap 2 1844;Ag 12 1864
CtSp [1841;43]Jl 9 1844[45-46;65-66]Je 19 1868 [70;87-91;94-95]
CtY Ja 8,F 26,Je 7 1840
MWA N 7 1873;S 15 1876
N D 4 1839
NN Ja 25 1842;Ja 3 1857
NNHi S 16 1840;67[68]-Je 1871;Jl 1872-F 1873; extras:Jl 24 1868;Ag 6 1869
NjR Je 9 1860
OClWHi Ag 20-S,O 8,22 1859

SENTINELLA. w 1913+
In Italian
Ct [1920]22+

SPIRIT of the times. w O 6 1830-
CtB 1830-S 26 1832
DLC N 7 1832
MWA D 29 1830

Bridgeport STANDARD. d *See* Bridgeport standard American

Tri-weekly STANDARD. tw Ja 4 1850-
Ct 1850-Jl 1854
MWA Ag 23 1852

Bridgeport STANDARD American. d 1854-1918||
1854-Jl 17 1917 as Bridgeport standard (title varies slightly). Merged with Bridgeport post
Ct O 1 1869;F 1872-Ag 1917;Ag 3 1918
CtB 1861-1918
CtHi 1873-74;Jl-D 1875
CtSp N 12 1900;Ja 15 1902;My 4 1911
CtY F 5,Ap 18 1877
DLC 1869-70
MWA S 23,O 11 1876

Bridgeport STAR. w My 6? 1876-
MWA O 7 1876

Bridgeport STAR. d Mr 1919-O 1926||
1919-Je 1920 as Bridgeport evening herald. Title varies: Evening star; Bridgeport evening star. United with Bridgeport evening farmer to form Times-star
Ct Ap 1919-26

Morning TELEGRAM. d 1891+
F 11 1901-Je 1906 as Morning telegram-union
Ct D 17 1895[96-F 10 1901]-Ag 1907;Ja-Mr 1908;F 11,Mr 6 1909;Mr 25 1936+
CtB F 11 1901-Je 1909;S 1915+
DLC 1898

TIMES-STAR. d 1857+
1857-D 31 1917 as Bridgeport evening farmer
Ct O 1890-Mr 1908;My 1910+
CtB My 1866-Ap 1869;Ap 1871-73;Jl 1874-O 1878;79;Jl 1880+
CtSp Mr 17 1888
CtY D 2,12 1872;My 12,Je 13 1873;S 15,O 16-30 1882;Jl 23 1887

TRIBUNA del Connecticut. w Mr 3 1906-D 9 1908||
In Italian
Ct 1906-08

Morning UNION. d Ag 1 1891-F 9 1901||
United with Morning telegram to form Morning telegram-union, later Morning telegram
Ct [Ag-O 1891]Ap 1892-1901
CtB Jl 1895-1901

Bridgeporter ZEITUNG. w 1873-79||?
In German
MWA Ag 23 1876

BRIDGEWATER

FIRESIDE journal. w Je 8 1872-
NcD O 12 1872

BRISTOL

FARMINGTON Valley herald. w 1889+
1889-1901 pub in Hartford
Suspended from Ap 13 1901-08
Ct Mr 23-Ap 13 1901;08+

Bristol HERALD. w 1885-1901||?
CtHWe Ag 4 1892
CtNbH 1892-1900
—d ed *See* New Britain herald (New Britain)

Bristol PRESS. w,sw,d Mr 9 1871+
w 1871-1909; sw 1910-O 23 1916
Ct 1903+
CtBri 1871+
CtHWe D 1 1871
OClWHi Je 1 1922;Ja 10-14,F 12,21,Mr 1923-31

BROOKLYN

HARRISONIAN. w Ja 1 1840-
CtY [Ja 22-D 16 1840]
MWA Ja 1 1840

INDEPENDENT observer and county advertiser. w Jl 1 1820-26||
CtHWe Jl 30 1821[22]Ja 6 1823;Mr 29 1824
MH S 3 1821
MWA S 10,D 24 1821
NjR O 8 1821

Brooklyn JOURNAL. *See* Windham county advertiser

Weekly PENNANT. w 1842-
DLC Ap 26 1843

UNIONIST. w Ag 1 1833-
CtW Ag 8 1833
MWA S 5 1833
NNHi Ag 8 1833

WINDHAM county advertiser. w Ag 15 1826-35||
1826-D 29 1828 as Brooklyn journal and Windham county advertiser
Ct Ap 25 1833
CtHWe Ja 8 1828;Je 8 1831
CtT Ja 25 1832
CtY Ap 8,S 9,D 2-9 1828;F 3 1830;N 9 1831;Jl 18 1833
DLC D 4 1827
MWA S 12 1826;My 22 1827;My 21 1828;My 26 1830;Ag 2 1831;Ap 11 1832;My 9 1833
NcD My 22 1827

WINDHAM county gazette. w 1835-
MWA N 22 1837

CANAAN

CONNECTICUT western news. w 1871+
Ct Je 1877-F 1893;1921+

CLINTON

Clinton ADVERTISER. m
DLC Mr 1861-F 1863

Clinton RECORDER. w 1895+
1895-1901 as Shore recorder
pub 1895+
Ct D 12 1918-Mr 13 1919

SHORE recorder. *See* Clinton recorder

COLCHESTER

Colchester ADVOCATE. w S 16 1887-96||
Ct S 16 1887-O 9 1896

COLLINSVILLE

Collinsville RECORD—for Collinsville, Burlington, Canton, Grandby. w Ja 11 1906-08||
Ct Mr 1 1906-Ja 1908

RISING star. *See* Collinsville star

Collinsville STAR. w My 27 1858-
My-Jl? 1858 as Rising star
CtHWe My 27 1858
MWA Ag 26 1858;Ja 26,F 23,My 11 1859

DANBURY

Danbury CHRONICLE and Fairfield county democrat. w My 18 1836-
Ct Ag 3 1836
CtD O 26 1836

Danbury DEMOCRAT. w 1877-88||
Ct Je 9 1877-F 1888
CtY Mr 12 1887

Danbury GAZETTE. w Ja 9 1833-
Ct N 20 1833;Ap 2,O 15 1834
CtD Ja 16,Mr 13 1833
CtY Ja 2 1835
DLC F 12 1834

Danbury GLOBE. w 1873-82||
Ct S 1875-82

INDEPENDENT whig and people's advocate. w Jl 3 1848-
MWA Jl-O 2 1848

JEFFERSONIAN. w Mr 11 1860-Mr 5 1870||
United with Danbury times to form Danbury news, later Danbury news-times
CtD [1861]-70
DLC Mr 14 1860
NN Mr 11 1860

Danbury NEWS-TIMES. w Mr 17 1870+
Formed by the union of Jeffersonian and Danbury times
CaOT F 28 1874-[75]-F 17 1877
Ct Mr 17 1926-32
CtD 1870-1933
CtHWe [1875-Mr 1878]
MB Ja 9-30 1875;F 1 1882
MWA Ap 30,Je 11,Ag 13-27,S 10,24,O 15 1873; My(supp)Ag 1-8 1874;Mr 11,Ap 5,Je 3 1876
NjR [1873;75]

Danbury NEWS-TIMES. d 1883+
1883-Ja 28 1933 as Danbury evening news
1906+ Wednesday issue used as weekly
Ct Jl 30 1918;My 6 1922;Ag 3 1923;Ag 5 1924; Mr 16 1926+
CtBe F 1933+
CtD 1883-F 1890;1904+

Danbury RECORDER. w F 28 1826-
CSmH Jl 14 1830
Ct Mr 7,Je 13,O 17 1826;Je 5 1827
CtD F 15 1832
CtHWe 1826-F 20 1827;Jl 14 1830
CtY Ag 27-S 3 1828

Danbury REPUBLICAN. w Mr 29 1879-84||
Ct 1879-84
CtY [1879]

Danbury TIMES. w 1837-Mr 10 1870||
United with Jeffersonian to form Danbury news, later Danbury news-times
CtD complete
NN F 24 1859;D 4 1862

DANIELSONVILLE

Weekly HERALD. w Mr 31 1870-75||?
InRE Ag 11-18 1870
MWA Ag 18 1870

CONNECTICUT (*Continued*)

DANIELSONVILLE—*Continued*

WINDHAM county transcript. w Mr 8 1848+
1848-54 as Windham county telegraph (West Killingly)
1855-75 also dated at Putnam
Ct My 7 1863-Ap 11 1878[S 1883]Mr 27,My 8 1889;S 11 1902;N 3 1904;Jl 2-9 1908;D 12 1918+
CtT D 20 1860[65]F 1,Je 7 1866;My 14 1868
CtY 1848-O 1854
DLC 1864
MWA 1848;S 12 1850;Mr 24 1853;F 14 1856 Ja 10,F 7,S 19,O 24,N 21-D 5 1861;Ja 9,F 27,Mr 27-Ap 3,Jl 3 1862;Ja 7 1864;Ag 18,D 15 1870;F 24,O 12 1876;Ag 14 1879;Je 13 1888; My 10 1899;S 26 1901
OClWHi Jl 23 1863
P-M Ag 3 1854

DARIEN

Darien REVIEW. w 1896+
Ct Mr 16 1901+

DEEP RIVER

Deep River NEW ERA. w My 1874+
Ag 28 1936 contains Chester centennial supplement
pub 1874+
Ct Ja 30 1891;D 29 1893;N 3 1899(supp);Mr 15-N 1901;Mr 27 1936+
CtW Ag 1 1884;Mr 10 1888(supp);Mr 8 1895
MWA Ag 28 1936
OClWHi Jl 19 1929-Mr 7 1930

DERBY

To 1893 as Birmingham

Daily ADVERTISER. d 1886-
Also dated in Shelton and Ansonia
CtDe Ap 28 1887

Derby JOURNAL. w D 25 1846-58||?
N 1855-57 as Valley messenger
Ct D 25 1846[47-49]Ap 4,Ag 6 1850;D 18 1851; F 21 1857
CtDe 1847-50;Ja 15 1852[Ap 1853-O 11,N 10 1855-58]
CtHi [1847-57]
CtY Ja 18,Mr 8 1849;Ag 9 1855
MnHi 1846-50

Daily Derby JOURNAL. d Ja 1 1850-F 14 1851||
CtDe complete

Derby JOURNAL. w Jl 26 1881-84||
Ct Ag-S 20 1881
CtY Mr 28 1884

Derby weekly NEWS. w My 18 1858-
CtDe My 25,Je 15 1858

Derby NEWS. w
Ct Je 8-Jl 1901

Weekly TRANSCRIPT. w S 14 1867-97||?
1867-90 as Derby transcript
Ct S 14 1878;Je 8 1892
CtDe N 1868-[90]Jl 13,Ag 31,S 14 1892
CtY 1867-O 28 1875
MWA Ap 14 1882

Evening TRANSCRIPT. d D 1 1888-98||?
Also dated at Birmingham and Shelton
Ct N 7 1890
CtDe 1888-[90;92]F 16 1893
CtW Mr 28 1889

VALLEY messenger. *See* Derby journal

EAST HADDAM

East Haddam JOURNAL. w Ap 9 1859-
CtHWe Mr 3,N 15 1860;S 28 1861
CtHi 1859-Ap 6 1861
CtW F 23 1861

EAST HAMPTON

East Hampton NEWS. w Ag 12 1887-88||
Ct Ag 17 1888
CtEh Ag 12 1887
CtW O 14 1887

East Hampton NEWS. w Jl 1 1932+
Ct Mr 27 1936+
CtW 1932+

EAST HARTFORD

AMERICAN enterprise. *See* Greater Hartford

ELM leaf. m,sm,w My 18 1863-78||?
m 1863; sm 1864-65?
Ct Je 15-Ag 11 1863;Ja-F 3,Mr 16-Je 15,Jl-Ag 17,D 7-21 1864;Ap 19-Je,S 28 1865[D 1870-Mr 8 1873]
CtE My-O 1863;64-Je 1865
CtHWe [1864]My 3,17 1865;Ap 22 1871;Ap 15 1876
CtHi 1863-S 1865;F-Jl 22 1871
MWA S 17,O 17 1863;Jl 20 1864

Weekly GAZETTE. w O 2 1885+
Scattered numbers dated also in Glastonbury and South Windsor
pub 1885+
Ct D 28 1888;Ja 29 1892;Mr 8,N 29(supp) 1901;D 19 1902[O 1920-22]+
CtE 1885-S 1888

GREATER Hartford. w 1888+
1888-1930? as American enterprise
Ct Ap 25 1902

ESSEX

SAYBROOK minor. w 1849-
DLC Mr 14 1850

FAIRFIELD

Fairfield NEWS. w Jl 1 1922+
pub 1922+
Ct Ap 3 1936+
CtSp 1922+

Fairfield RECORD. w Ap 29 1897-99||
CtSp complete

Fairfield REVIEW. w F 26 1913-17||?
F 26-Mr 5 1913 as Fairfield review and the times
CtSp 1913-[15]

Weekly TIMES. w Mr 31 1905-Ja 12 1906||
CtSp complete

Fairfield TRIBUNE. w Mr 15 1934+
Ct Mr 15-My 17 1934

FARMINGTON

FAITHFUL and fearless chronicle monthly. m O 1834-
Ct N 1 1834[35]

GLASTONBURY

Weekly GAZETTE. *See under* East Hartford

GREENWICH

Greenwich GRAPHIC. *See* Daily news-graphic

Greenwich NEWS. w F 2 1888-1914||
United with Greenwich graphic to form Greenwich news and graphic, later Daily news-graphic
Ct 1888-Ja 1893

Daily NEWS-GRAPHIC. w,sw,d D 3 1881+
1881-1914 as Greenwich graphic; 1915-Ap 29 1932 Greenwich news and graphic
w 1881-My 1928; sw Je 1928-Ap 1932
Ct 1882-Ag 1887;S 30 1921+
CtGr 1881+

Greenwich OBSERVER. w 1874-83||
Ct S 26 1878-Ja 1883
CtGr N 15 1877-82

Greenwich PRESS. w 1910+
N 25 1931 is 21st anniversary number
pub 1912;20+
Ct 1920+
CtGr 1911+
MWA N 25 1931
OClWHi Mr 15 1928-32

GROTON

Weekly REVIEW. w 1888-1901||?
Ct O 1-8 1891;D 29 1893;Ja 12 1894

GUILFORD

SHORE line times. w Mr 8 1877+
1877-96? pub in New Haven
Ct My 28 1903+
CtY 1923+

HARTFORD

AMERICAN dispatch. w Jl 7 1855
CtHWe Jl 14-21 1855

***AMERICAN mercury.** w Jl 12 1784-Je 25 1833||
Followed by Independent press
CSmH S 13 1830
Ct [1820-28]S 20 1830;O 24 1831[32]
CtHWe 1821-22;Ag 19 1823;24-27;29-30;32-Ap 1833
CtHi 1821-29;Jl 1830-33
CtY Je 7,21,Jl 5-19,Ag 2-23,S 6,20-27 1830;Ja 3-17,31-F 14,28-Mr 21,Ap 4-18,My 16-30 1831; 32
DLC 1821-Ja 12,26,My 30,Je 2,Jl 14-28,Ag 11,S 1,15-22,N 17 1829
MWA Ja 16 1821[My-D 1822]-[24]Mr 1,Ap 26-My 3,Ag 2,S 27,N 29,D 27 1825;Ja 24,F 14 1826;F 13-20,D 25 1827-[29-30]-Je 11 1833
MiU-C [1822-24;29;31-32]
NNHi 1821-22
NcD F 18-25,Mr 25-Ap 1,My 6,Je 3,17,Jl 1,22, Ag 19-O 21,N 4-11,25-D 1823;F 5,19,Mr 11,Ap 8,29,My 13-20,Je 10,Jl 1,22,Ag 5,S 2,16-O 7,21-28,N 18-D 9 1828;Ja 10-17,31-Mr,Ap 11-Je 6, 27,Jl 11,25-Ag 1,22-29,S 26-O 10,N 14-D 1831
PDoHi D 7 1824;My 24 1825
T N 26-D 3 1821

AMERICAN protector. w My 24 1841-
MWA My 24 1841
NNHi My 24,Je 5,19,Jl 3,17,31,Ag 14,28,S 11, 25,O 9,23,N 6,20,D 4,18 1841;Ja 1,15,29,F 12, 26,Mr 12,26,Ap 2,16,30 1842

BATTERY. bw 1847-
CtHWe Mr 3,17,Ap 23,Je 18 1848

CHARTER oak. m,w F 28 1838-48||
1843-45 as Christian freeman. Followed by Republican m 1838-42
Ct 1843-45
CtHWe Ap,Je,D 1838-39;F-Ap 1840;Ag,N-D 1842;Ap 7,O 26 1843;47-48
CtSp [My]S 1838[39]Mr 1840;Je 24 1847
CtY [1843]-45

DLC My 1,Je,Jl 1,S 1,D 1 1838;Ja 1,Mr 1,Ap 1 1839;F 17 1848;Je 8,S 7 1848
IU Jl 17 1845
MHi N 9 1848
MWA Ja 8 1846;Ag 17,S 28 1848
NBHi [1846-48]
NNHi 1838-40
NhD O 19-26 1843

CHRISTIAN freeman. *See* Charter oak

COLUMBIAN. *See* New England weekly review (1844-47)

COMET. w Ja 6 1859-
NN Mr 17 1860

COMMONWEALTH. w Mr 19 1875-D 8 1876
1875-Je 9 1876 pub in New Haven
MWA N 26,D 24 1875;Ja-My,Je 9-D 1876

CONNECTICUT bank note list and City of Hartford monthly advertiser. m 1848?-
MWA Ja 1 1856
PPL Ja 4 1851

***CONNECTICUT courant.** w,sw N 26 1764-O 29 1914||
A prospectus was issued O 29 1764. Je 7 1774-F 10 1778 as Connecticut courant and Hartford weekly intelligencer; F 24 1778-Mr 14 1791 Connecticut courant and weekly intelligencer
w 1764-1894
CSmH S 7 1830
Ct 1821-[23-26-28;Ja 29-F 3,Ap 21 1829;Ja 12, Jl 6,S 4 1830[31-33]-[36]37;Ap 7 1838;N 20,D 18 1841;42-1843[44]Je 1854-80;1883;N 4 1886; Jl 7-D 29 1887;Ag 15 1889;N 6 1890;Ja 8 1891;Ag 18 1892[93]Ag 2,N 29 1894;F 6 1896
CtAn F 1 1825;Ag 9 1831;Ja 31 1832;Mr 3 1834
CtHC 1821-26
CtHCo 1821-1914
CtHTi 1821-1914
CtHWe 1821-[24-25]F 4 1826[27-34]-[37]S 26 1840;Mr 6 (extra)1841;Ja 8 1842[43-44]-46
CtHi 1821-41;61
CtMHi 1821-36
CtSm Je 3 1823
CtY Ja 2-9,Mr 27-N 1847;48-54;57[65-66]-[72; 84;88]
DLC 1821-26;Ja 15 1827;28;Ag 18 1829;Ja 18, N 15 1831;Mr 27,N 6,D 13(extra)1832;Jl 14 1834;F 13 1835;O 20 1838;O 25,29 1839;S 19,D 2 1840;Ap 16,24,Je 12-D 1841;N 7 1842;Ag 14 1844;F 23,Mr-D 1850;Jl 2 1859;My 13-D 23 1865;Mr 2 1867;Je 27-Jl 18 1868;73-77
ICHi D 3 1864
MB Ap 13 1824;N 26 1827[F 23 1835-39]
MBAt 1821-[23]Ja 4 1831
MHi My 8,Jl 3 1821;Jl 1 1823;Ag 23 1825;F 12-19 1827;Ja 26,Je 22-29 1867;F 15 1868;Ag 14,N 6 1869
MNaHi S 10,O 22 1822;O 28 1823;F 22 1825;D 3 1842;Ap 5 1846;N 27 1847;My 13,S 13 1848; Ag 6 1864
MWA 1821-87;My 31 1888;Je 22 1893
MiU-C [22-24;26-27;29-33;37-43;45;47;49;54-62; 66;76]
N F 14,Je 12,Jl 31,Ag 28,S 4,O 9 1826;O 28 1833
NBHi 1821-25;38-46
NN 1821-[28;30-31]-39;Ap 10 1841;O 29 1864; Je 19 1869
NNHi 1822-[29-35]-[48-49]D 30 1861;O 29 1864; Mr 1 1873;Jl 16 1842(extra);Mr 25 1848;Ap 13(supp)Je 8,29 1830;My 13 1837
NcD [1822]Mr 1829-F,Ap 1831-F 1832[34;37-38;40;42-43;45-46;48;50-58;64-68]
NhD 1821-26;Ap 10-Je 12,26-D 1832
OClWHi 1821;D 2 1843;O 4 1855;O 15 1864;Ap 8 1871;Jl 5 1894
P-M My 20,Ag 12,S 16 1837;O 4 1845
PU [1902]
TxU 1847-48
WHi 1821-Ja 7,Mr 11 1823;Mr-D 1824;Ap 19 1825;Mr 19 1827;Mr 18 1828
—d ed *See* Hartford courant
—**Supplements.** bw 1825-88||
CSmH My 5 1849-50
Ct 1825-55;57-60;62-64;66-70;73-75;F 17 1876; 77-79;S 29 1887
CtE S 3 1827
CtHCo 1825;29;32;35;38;40-41;44-48;50;52;58-69; 73-81;83-88
CtHWe 1825-71;74-76;78;80;82-83
MWA O 18 1825-37;O 26,N 9,30,D 14,28 1839; 40-42
MiU-C [1840-42;44-55]
NN My 14 1833;Ja 12 1835-D 9 1837;My 9 1840;Ag 19 1848;N 5 1864
WHi Mr 10 1829-D 23 1837;40-43;47-48;Mr 11 1854-Ag 24 1861;Ja 14 1865-D 21 1867

***CONNECTICUT mirror.** w Jl 10 1809-D 15 1832||
Merged with American mercury
CSmH D 31 1827
Ct 1821-[29]Ja 2,Ag 28 1830;Jl 30,D 3 1831
CtHWe [1821-22]-Ja 14 1828 F 21 1829;Mr 12 1831
CtHi [1821-32]
CtSp D 18 1826
CtY 1821-30;Je 25 1831
DLC Ag 27 1821;Ap 22-D 1822;Ja 20-Ap 7,Jl-S 1 1823;F 9-Ag 23 1824;Ag 27 1827;Ja 21 1828; Jl 11,S 5 1829;Ja 2,16,Ag 14-21,D 25 1830;Ja 22 1831
ICU Je 4,Jl 2,S 2,O 29 1821;Jl 15,O 7 1822
MHi My 28 1821;My 30 1825
MBAt D 6-13 1824;Ap 30 1827;Ja 10,F 14,Je 20 1829
MWA 1821-32
MiU-C [1822-23;32]
NcD Ja 27,Mr 3,Je 14,O 4-11 D 20 1824;My 16 1825
OHi 1821-F 11 1822;F 24,Mr 10,24-31 1823
PHi 1820-22
PPL [Jl 17-O 23 1826]
WHi Ap 15 1822-Ag 20 1827;29-O 16 1830

CONNECTICUT organ. w S 16 1854-
Ct S 30,O 28,N 18 1854
CtHWe D 2 1854

CONNECTICUT (*Continued*)

HARTFORD—*Continued*

CONNECTICUT observer. w Ja 4 1825-Je 1840||
United with New Haven record to form Congregational record (not in this list)
CSmH Jl 5 1830
CtY 1825-36[40]
DLC 1825-Ag 1831;Ap 23 1832;D 7 1835[Ja-S 1836]
ICN D 12 1831
MBAt S 5 1831[39]
MWA 1825-[30]-[32;35]O 15 1836;S 9,O 14-21, N 25,D 16,30 1837;Ja 27,My 12 1838;Ag 31 1839;Ja 4 1840
MiU-C [1826-29]
NCanHi Je 5 1826
NN Ja 9,Ap 2-9,O 29 1836;Jl 15,S 2-9,O 21,N 4-11 1837;Ja 27-F 3,Mr 10,Ag 25,S 8,29,O 27, N 17-24,D 8,20 1838;Ja 5-19,F 2 1839
NNHi [1826-28]Jl 1830-[31]S 9 1833;Ja 6-13, Je 2 1834
P-M My 13 1832

CONNECTICUT post. w Je 5 1858-1903||?
1858-Ap 25 1866 as Hartford weekly post
Ct [1860]65;O 30 1875;S 22 1877;Ja 19 1878;F 17 1883;Ja 19,O 24 1885
CtHi 1858-My 1863;64;66-1903
MWA 1858-59;F 17 1866;D 1 1883;S 22 1888; Je 20,O 3 1889
NN My 18,Je 29,Ag 17 1861;Mr 14 1863
OClWHi Mr 28 1863
—Supplement.
Ct [1871]Ja 13 1876;Ja 12 1878;Ja 10 1880;Ja 21 1882;Ja 9 1884;S 25 1886;Ja 5 1887
CtTo Ja 15 1881
MWA S 22 1888
—d ed *See* Hartford evening post

CONNECTICUT press. w Mr 8 1856-Ap 28? 1866||
United with Hartford weekly post to form Connecticut post
Ct Mr 5 1864-1866
CtHCo 1856-66
CtHWe Mr 8 1856;S 25 1858;Ag 31 1861;Mr 15 1862
CtSp N 10 1860
CtY D 12 1857
DLC N 23 1861;Ap 15-29 1865
MHi Ja 27,My 5,S 29 1866
MWA Mr 8,22,O(extra)1856;Ja 17 1857;Ja 19 1861;D 12 1863;F 17 1866
—d ed *See* Hartford evening press

CONNECTICUT real estate register and commercial advertiser. w
CtY Je 24 1871
MWA Ag 19 1871

CONNECTICUT weekly review. *See* England weekly review (1844-47)

CONNECTICUT staats-zeitung. w 1908+
Also dated in Holyoke, Mass.
In German
CtY My 31-D 1934
IU Mr 1918+

CONNECTICUT union. w 1842-
CtHWe Ja 12,26,My 4 1854

CONNECTICUT whig. d N 1847-49||
Merged with Connecticut courant
CtHWe N 20 1847-Mr 4 1848
MWA Je 19 1847
NN Ag 19 1848

Hartford COURANT. d S 12 1837+
1837-Jl 8 1887 as Hartford daily courant
O 25 1914 is 150th anniversary number
pub 1837+
CLM Ja 1 1890
CPo S 17 1879
CU-B O 25 1914
Ct My 7,17,D 13 1838;Mr 1840-Mr 10,12-22,24-Ap 2,4,6-16,18-My 24,26-Jl 16,18-29,31-Ag 18, 20-N 26,28-D 1841;44;S 26 1846;My 20 1850; Jl 28 1851;My 17 1852[55]N 18 1856;My 15 1857;58;O 13 1859;O 12 1860;D 19 1861;N 4 1862;Mr 25 1864;Ap 15 1865;Ja[Ag-S]1866[67] Ja 31 1868[69]-+
CtDe Mr 26 1880
CtH 1932+
CtHTi 1837+
CtHi S 12 1837-Ap,D 1838-48;Ag 1851+
CtMHi S 26 1881;Mr 15 1888;My 7 1896;O 11 1900;S 9,13,19 1901;O 6 1908;N 8,13 1909;S 7 1911;O 25 1914;N 11 1918;My 12 1930
CtPlS Mr 27 1878
CtSm S 30 1923
CtW Mr 17 1887;D 31 1888[89-90]F 21 1891;S 7-8 1892;S 8-9 1893
CtY S 13 1837-62;D 21 1863;D 7,14 1866;My 6 1872-95;1915+
DLC Mr 21 1849-My 5 1853;Jl 22 1861-67;F 1868-72;Jl 9 1874-1907
MBAt Ap 20 1865
MHi Je 24 1867[68-76]F 23 1878;Mr 15 1879
MWA Ap 29,Jl 23 1840;Je 28 1843;O 11 1844; Mr 5,My 8-9 1845;Ag 19 1848;Mr 22 1851;F 20 1852;Jl 21,D 4 1854;Jl 1856(extra)My 8[O-N]1860[61]-[66]Mr 4,Je 10,N 19,D 4 1867;Ap 7,O 21,N 5,D 8,10 1868[69]-98;Ja-F 1909;10+
MiU-C [1862;70-72;74-76;85-86]O 25 1914
N O 25 1842
NN Ap 19 1875
NNHi My 13,15,N 17,D 4 1840;Mr 31 1868;My 29 1873;S 8 1886
NcD F 5,My 4 1838;Jl 14 1842(extra);Jl 4-Ag 20 1881
OClWHi Ag 14 1844;D 25 1852;Mr 26 1863;My 4,Jl 22 1865;N 2 1867;O 2 1876;My 25 1886; Jl 25-26 1904
WHi O 25 1914
—w ed *See* Connecticut courant

Hartford daily COURIER. d My 1 1839-
1839- as Hartford evening courier
CtY My 24 1839
MWA My 24 1839
P-M Mr 15 1842;S 30 1845

Hartford COURIER. w
CtHi Mr 1847-F 1848
NNHi D 3 1846

DEMOCRAT. w Mr 4 1841-
MWA Mr 4 1841

Weekly EXAMINER. *See under* Waterbury

FARMINGTON Valley herald. *See under* Bristol

FREE elector. w
MB [Jl 22 1834-My 19 1835
NN Je 10,N 25,D 30 1834;Ja 27-F 1835

FREE soil advocate. w Jl 15 1848-
Campaign paper
CtHWe Ag 5 1848
CtY Jl 15-N 18 1848
NNHi Jl 22,Ag 12,O 7 1848

Hartford GLOBE. (Sunday) 1876-N 16 1919||
Ct Je 21 1891;1904-19
CtHCo 1909-18
CtHi 1879
CtSp F 24 1889

INDEPENDENT press. w Jl 1 1833-
Follows American mercury
CtHWe 1833-O 20 1834
MWA Jl 1833-Ja 6,My 5,26,Je 16-23,Jl 7-14, Ag 11,S 15-22(extra)1834
NcD Ja 6 1834

JEFFERSONIAN. w Je 1 1832-
Ct Mr 23,Ap 6,20 1833
CtHi 1832-My 11 1833
CtHWe My 11 1833
MWA Je 8,Jl 27 1832
NN D 21 1832

JEWISH ledger. w 1929+
Jl 26 1935 is Tercentenary issue
M S 30 1929;O 28 1932
MWA Jl 26 1935

Hartford evening JOURNAL. d N 1 1843-
CtHi 1843-Ja 1845
CtMHi F 22 1844(extra)
DLC N 1,13 1843
NN F 22 1844

Hartford weekly JOURNAL. w D 2 1843-
CtHWe 1843-Ja 25 1845
OClWHi Ap 30 1844
P-M Ja 18 1845

Hartford Sunday JOURNAL. w 1867-1919||?
1867-Mr 1874 as Hartford journal?
Ct Ap 1881-88;Ap 1889-My 24 1903
CtMHi S 14 1901
MWA O 1-8 1876;Ja 20 1878;Mr 4 1883

NEW ENGLAND examiner. sm F 1 1834-
Ct [1834]
CtHWe Ap 12,Jl 19,N 22 1834
MWA Mr 15,Ap 12 1834

NEW ENGLAND weekly gazette. w Mr 4 1848-
CtHWe Mr 4,25,S 23 1848
CtHi 1848-Mr 9 1850
DLC Ap 21 1849

NEW ENGLAND weekly review. w Mr 17 1828-Mr 11 1843||
Je 30 1834-S 14 1839 as New England review (F 20 1836-38 Review and telegraph)
CSmH Jl 26 1830
Ct Jl 21 1828;Jl 27 1829;Jl 4 1831;Jl 14 1834-36;Jl 8 1837
CtAn Ap 2 1835(extra)
CtHWe [1828-31]O 8 1832[33]35[36-37;39-41]Ja 28 1843
CtHi 1828-O 1832
CtT N 7 1835
CtY 1828-Ap 1830;N 19 1836;My 27 1837;S 24,N 5 1842
DLC Mr 17,Ag 18,S 15,N 10,D 8,22 1828;Ja 26,Je 8,S 7-14,28,O 12,N 16-30,D 7,28 1829-Ja 18,Mr 8,Ap 19,Ag 30,N 1,D 6,20 1830;Ja 3-10 1831;N 12 1832;Ja 5 1835;39-43
MBAt N 16,D 14,28 1829-[32]Mr 9 1839
MSaE [1828]29[30]Ja 3,17,My 16 1831
MWA Ap 14,28,My 19,Ag 4 1828;Mr 23,Ap 27,N 23 1829;Je-Ag,N 8 1830;F 14,Je 27 1831;My 7 1832;My 20 1833;Ja 13,Mr 24,Ap 7,Je 16 1834; N 7 1835;Ag 25 1838;Ap 27,Ag 17,D 28 1839; Ja 25,Ap 18,My 2 1840;Jl 1841-[42]Ja 7,21,F, Mr 11 1843
MiU Ja 7,S 1833-34;D 24 1836-[37-38]
N 1828-Mr,N 30,D 9 1829;O 4,D 6 1830
NN Ap 28 1834;Je 10 1837;N 13 1841
NNHi N 16 1829;My 1830-O 1 1832
NSchU My 28 1842
NcD Mr 16 1829
P-M Jl 13 1829;Mr 9 1839
PEF Ag 29 1831
PEL Ag 29 1831
TxU O 6-13 1828;Ap 25 1831

NEW ENGLAND daily review. d 1833-
Ct Ag 22 1833
CtT My 18 1833
NcD Je 25 1833

NEW ENGLAND weekly review. w Ja 6 1844-N 6 1847||
1844 as Columbian; 1845 Hartford Columbian; Ja-N 7 1846 Connecticut weekly review. Merged with Connecticut whig
CtHWe [1844-45]Mr 14 1846-N 6 1847
CtHi 1844
MWA Ja 6,Mr 2-9,Je 8,22,D 28 1844;S 20,N 8 1845;F 7 1846
NN S 20 1845
NhD F 3 1844
P-M Ja 25 1845;N 6 1846

NEWS and advertiser. w O 17 1839-
CtHWe N 14 1839
NcD N 14,D 5 1839
P-M F 13 1840

NORTHERN courier. *See* Republican courier

PATRIOT and democrat. *See* Patriot and eagle

PATRIOT and eagle. w Mr 7 1835-
1835-Mr 13? 1841 as Patriot and democrat; Mr 20 1841 as Hartford patriot and state eagle
Ct Mr 7 1835;Mr 19 1836;Ja 16 1841
CtHWe 1835-[41]
CtHi 1835-F 20 1841
CtY Ap 16 1836
DLC 1835-40;Ja-Mr 11,25-Ap 1,My 13-Je 3,Jl 8 1843;Je 1 1844
MWA Ag 1,D 19 1835;Mr 19 1836[37]-[40]F 20,Mr 20,My 1,O 9 1841;Ap 29 1843
MiU-C [1838;40]
NN Je 27 1835
NNHi Jl 8 1837;Mr 31,S 1,O 27 1838[39-41]D 2 1843
NcD Mr 12 1836
P-M My 21 1836;Mr 11 1837
WHi D 5 1835;Ja 23-F 6,27-Mr 5,19,Ap 9,D 17 1836

Hartford PATRIOT and state eagle. *See* Patriot and eagle

Hartford evening POST. d Ap 10 1858-O 6 1920||
1858-66 as Hartford daily post
Ct Ag 17 1860[Mr 1862]Mr 25 1864;Jl 4 1865-F 1866;68-71;Jl 19 1872;Jl 10,O 16 1875[76]Ja 3 1877;Ja 9,D 25 1878[79]-91;D 31 1900-20
CtDe Ja 7 1880
CtHCo F 1868-1913
CtHTi Jl-D 1900;18-Mr 1919
CtHi 1858-Je 1900;01-03
CtMHi Je 14,23 1888
CtSp Ja 9,D 25 1879;Mr 17,N 3,D 25 1880;F 18-20 1889;My 23 1892
CtW O 13 1888[89-O 22 1890]Ja 7 1891
CtY S 7 1872;Ag 16 1894
DLC Mr 26 1868
MBAt Ap 18-20 1865
MH [N 26 1894-My 6 1895]
MWA S(supp)1866;N 4 1868;D 25(supp)1872; Je 24,O 9,13,17 1876;Ja 31,S 16-17 1879;Ap 3,Je 26,N 3,6 1880;Ja 28 1881;Mr 1,Je 3 1882; Ap 8 1884;S 29 1885;My 4,O 23(supp)1886;Mr 14,Je 14,O 13(supp)N 22 1888;Ja 9(supp)1889; Ja 3 1890
NN Ap 18,Ag 4,6-11 1859
NSyU Jl 26 1861
OClWHi Ap 19 1887
P-M Ag 28 1860
PWbW Ja 1879

Hartford Sunday POST. w N 20 1908-17||?
Ct 1908-S 20 1917

Hartford weekly POST. *See* Connecticut post

Hartford evening PRESS. d F 27 1856-Ja 1868||
United with Hartford daily post to form Hartford evening post
Ct N 1856-F 1857;O 17 1860;61-[67-68]
CtHCo 1856-Je 1867
CtHi complete
MBAt Ap 20 1865
MHi [1866-67]-Ja 18 1868
MSaE Ap 5 1859
MWA Ag 3,O 24 1857[O 17-D 11 1860]Ja 7,F 15,Mr 8 1861;Jl 24,D 3 1862;Ap 23 1866
NNHi My 13,Jl 30 1862
OClWHi O 25 1860;Je 9,Jl 10 1865
—w ed *See* Connecticut press

PROGRESSIVE democrat. w Jl 15 1848-
CtHWe Jl 15 1848

Hartford morning RECORD. d Ag 20 1888-
CtSp Ag 21 1888

REPUBLICAN. w 1849-56||
Follows Charter Oak. Merged with Hartford evening press
CtHWe Jl 17 1851
CtHi 1849-51
CtY Jl 25-O 10 1850
MWA My 2 1850;F 5 1852;D 14 1855
NNHi My 10 1849[55]
P-M Jl 7,N 4 1854
WHi Ag 30 1849-My 1 1851

REPUBLICAN courier. w Mr 17 1836-
1836-39? as Northern courier
Ct Mr 30 1837
CtHWe [1837]Ap 5 1838;Ja 17,Mr 21-28 1839; O 5 1843
CtHi 1836-Ag 1838
DLC Je 16 1836-Ja 19,My 25 1837;F 8 1844
MWA Mr 17 1836;S 8 1842;F 23,N 9 1843
N Mr 1,Ap 5 1838
NNHi 1836-Mr 7,O 12 1839
NhD O 19 1843;N 14 1844

Daily morning REVIEW. d
DLC Ja 22 1834

Daily REVIEW. d D 3? 1838-
MWA Ja 5 1839
OClWHi D 5 1838

REVIEW and telegraph. *See* New England weekly review (1828-43)

Hartforder STADT-BOTE. w Jl 30 1881-
In German
Ct O 22 1881

STATE eagle. w Ja 3 1840-Mr 13? 1841||
United with Patriot and democrat to form Patriot and eagle
DLC D 12 1840
MWA Je 27 1840

Hartford TELEGRAM. d N 1 1883-1906||
Mr 8 1889-90 as Telegram-record
Ct 1883-90;Jl 1891-1906
CtHi 1883-O 1887
CtMHi My 5-6 1884;S 14 1901
CtW [1889]

TELEGRAM-record. *See* Hartford telegram

THISTLE. w Ag 5 1840-
Campaign paper
CtHWe S 9 1840
DLC Ag 12 1840
NNHi Ag 19 1840

CONNECTICUT (*Continued*)

HARTFORD—*Continued*

*Hartford TIMES. w,sw Ja 1 1817-Jl 1 1920||
1817-N 9 1818 as Times; N 16 1819-My 12 1828 Times and weekly advertiser (title varies slightly)
w 1817-95
pub 1821-1920
CSmH S 6 1830
CoD D 28 1829
Ct [1822]Je 3 1823[24]Mr 24 1825;Ap 25 1826;33[34]-37;My 31 1856;Ja 11 1862;Ag 6,N 26 1864;Jl 15 1865[66-69]Mr 5,Ap 2 1870;Ag 26,S 30 1871[72-76]N 1880;N 17 1887;Jl 28 1892;Ag 23 1894;Mr 29,Jl 26 1897
CtHCo O 26 1844-57;61-95
CtHT [1835-39]
CtHWe Jl 9 1822[23-24]My 3 1825[26-28]-[30-34]-[37-43]44;Mr 29 1845[46-48;50-51;58]Ap 5 1862
CtHi 1821-N 10 1834
CtSp S 26 1826;Ja 12 1829;Mr 27(extra)1834
CtW N 3 1892
CtY F 19 1822;Mr 11 1823;Je 30,D 1 1828;Ag 3 1829;35-4;Je 29 1893
DLC D 20 1825;26-27;Mr 24 1828;Mr 2,23-Ag 3,31,S 14,28,N 16-30,D 14,28 1829;30-31[33-Je 1834]D 16 1837;F 24 1838-40;Mr 15 1845-46;N 14 1857-60
MHi My 30,Je 27 1825
MWA Jl 24 1821[Ap 1822-23]24;My 23-Je 6,S 19,N 7,28 1826;Mr 26,Je 11,Jl 23,Ag 20,S 24,O 1,D 10-17 1827;Jl 27-Ag 3,S 28,N 16-23 1829;Ja 4,25,Ag 23-30 1830[31]F 6,Mr 5,My 21,Je 11,Jl 9,Ag 6-13 1832;Mr 25,Jl 22,Ag 12,D 9 1833;F 24 1834;Mr 3,Je 23,Jl 28,D 22 1834;35[36]Je 17,D 23 1837[38]-[41-42]N 25 1843[Mr-Jl 1844;Je 1845-46]N 11 1854;Ja 27 1855;Mr 31 1860;Ap 18,S 12 1868;O 2 1884[1906-07]
MiU-C Je 24 1823;Mr 26 1827[31-32;40]
MnHi Mr 25 1843
NBHi 1821-25;Jl 15 1901-Ag 10 1903
NN Mr 6 1821;N 7 1831;Ap 30 1832;Ag 7 1852;Ap 2 1853;Jl 28 1860
NNHi Mr 28 1831-Ap 1836;S 5 1840
NcD Ag 23 1830;My 13 1833;Ja 26 1835;O 3 1840
NjR D 10 1832;Ag 12 1848
OClWHi My 10 1845;Ag 1 1863;Jl 22 1905;F 27 1919-20
OHi Ja 10 1821
P Jl 23 1836;Je 2 1855
PEF Ja 10 1831
PEL Ja 10 1831
PU [1901-02]
TxU Jl 16 1822;Ag 24 1850
WHi Ag 16-O 25 1830;My 1832-My 1833
WaPS F 24 1866;D 25 1869[70]Mr 18 1871[72] Ja 11,Ap 19 1873[74-75]My 3,Je 7 1877
—Supplements.
Ct Ag 19,S 30 1871[72-73;78-83]Ap 1884;Mr 15 1888
CtHCo My 17-D 27 1883
CtSp My 12 1881;Mr 30 1882
MWA O 15 1832;Mr 31 1860;D 25 1871
NN My 4 1844
OClWHi F 14 1889
WaPS D 25 1869[70-75]F 12 1876

Hartford TIMES. sw My 10 1833-
1833-O 18 1834 as Times and Hartford advertiser; O 25 1834-N 29 1837 Times
CtHi Je 10 1835-S 22 1838
DLC 1833-S 22 1838
MWA Mr 8,Ap 26,Je 14 1834;D 5 1835;Mr 19 1836;Ap 15 1837;Ja 17 1838
N O 19 1833
NcD Ap 16 1834
WHi 1833-D 31 1836

Daily TIMES. d Ja 14-Ap 13 1839||
pub complete
CtHi complete

Hartford TIMES. tw Ja 22 1840-
CtHi 1840-F 1 1841
CtSp Je 15 1840
MWA F 10,N 2,D 23 1840

Hartford TIMES. d Mr 2 1841+
1841-Ap 12 1846 as Daily times; Ap 13 1846-Jl 2 1883 Hartford daily times
pub 1841+
Ct [Je 26-O 1841]S 23 1843[44-45;47]My 17 1851;My 14 1852;My 17 1853;Je 6-7 1854;61-[63]N 16 1869;Jl 28 1870;N 1871-[77]Jl 19 1878;N 28 1885[86;96]98;Ap 7 1900[01]+
CtHCo 1855+
CtHi 1841-48;Jl-D 1851;F 17-S 9 1852[My 3 1853-54]-65;68+
CtMHi Mr 12-14 1888;S 9,16 1901;Ap 18-19 1906;Ap 22,O 29 1913
CtSp Mr 26 1878;My 23 1892
CtW 1868[89-93]
CtY O 31 1843
DLC O 16 1893+
ICHi D 4 1861;Ja 2 1862
MBAt Ap 15 1865
MWA [Mr-D 1841]Mr 29(extra)31 1842;Ap 13 1843;Ja 7[Jl 5-O 15]1845;Jl 20 1846;Ag 31,N 1 1852;D 19 1859[O 17-N 22 1860]Ap 25 1866;My 12 1874;S 23 1876;Ja 31 1879;Jl 9 1881;Jl 7 1894;Mr 6,D 4 1920
NN F 9-D 1843;Mr 14 1844;Jl 5 1876
NNHi Ja 3,9,13,28,Mr 5,12,18,S 30 1845;S 11 1846;D 15 1849;D 16 1850;Je 17,21 1869;Je 2 1873

TIMES and Hartford advertiser. sw F 11 1825-
DLC D 8 1825
MWA N 17 1825
WHi Je 16 1825

Daily evening WHIG. d My 2 1848-
CtHi 1848-Ja 22 1849

Hartford morning WORLD. d S 28 1880-
CtSp S 28-29 1880

Saturday WORLD. w Ap 23 1892-
CtSp Je 18 1892

JEWETT CITY

Jewett City PRESS. w 1883+
Ct Ja 25 1895
MHi Je 5 1913

LAKEVILLE

Lakeville JOURNAL. w 1897+
Ct N 19 1898;Mr 26 1935+
CtS 1897-[1913]+

LITCHFIELD

AMERICAN eagle. w S 9 1822-
Ct F 13 1826
CtHWe O 17 1825
MWA S 1 1823;Ap 19-26,Ag 30,O 4,N 22 1824
WHi N 22 1824

DEMOCRAT. w N 2 1833-
N N 2 1833

DEMOCRATIC watchman. w Ja 20 1844-
CtTo Ja 20 1844

Litchfield ENQUIRER. w Je 20 1826+
1826-Ja 22 1829 as Litchfield county post
Ct Ag 8 1826;Je 7 1827;Mr 15 1832;D 1 1853;S 18 1856-Ag 1857;Ag 15 1862(extra)Ag 24 1911[Ap 24-D 18 1919]20+
CtHWe Je 5,O 17 1839;S 7 1843[45-46]
CtHi [1829-54]
CtLL 1826+
CtLW 1892+
CtTo Mr 11 1841;Jl 12 1849;Ap 25 1850;Ap 7,O 27 1853;Jl 27,Ag 10 1854
CtWg 1857-63;66-73;75-90
CtY 1828-D 19 1833;S 22 1842;Ap 2,My 6 1847;Ag 1 1849;My 3,Mr 8-15 1860;Ag 1865;D 6 1866;Ap 9 1896;N 10 1899;N 7 1901;D 11 1902;Mr 3 1905;F 11 1909;Mr 23 1911;Ag 4 1920
DLC Mr 20 1828;Jl 23,O 22 1829;Ja 7 1830
MWA [1826]-My 22,Je 19,Jl 3,Ag 1828-[37]-[43]-Ja 2,Jl 24-Ag 7 1845;Mr 4,D 30 1847;50[51]F 17,Mr 1853-Ag 1856;O 22 1857;Ja 28,Mr 4,Ag 12 1858[59-60]Ja 24,S 10,D 26 1861[62]Ja 8,My 21,Ag 20 1863;Ja 7,F 25,Mr 24,My 5,19,S 1-8 1864;Ja 5,Mr 16,N 9 1865[66-69]O 7 1875;Ja 20,F 10 1876;Mr 6,My 22 1879;Mr 4,S 2-9,N 4 1880;Je 2,Jl 14,S 29 1881;F 1,Mr 8 1883;Ja 8,Je 25 1885;Jl 7,Ag 18,D 22 1887;Ap 26 1888;Je 6 1889;90-1900[06]F 4,N 4 1909;Ag 24 1911;N 5-12 1914
N O 17-24 1838
NN Je 18 1835;My 28 1840;Ap 8,S 2,N 18 1841
NNHi Mr 14 1844;My 12 1870;Ja 30 1873
NSyU O 26 1848
NcD Ap 28,S 29,O 13,D 8 1853;Ja 19,F 9 Ap 20-27,My,Ag 24 1854;Jl 26 1855
OClWHi Jl 3 1862;Mr 2,24 1865
PW Ja 17 1828
WHi Je 20 1826

LITCHFIELD county post. *See* Litchfield enquirer

MERCURY. w Ja 15 1840-
IU S 10 1840
MWA Ag 12 1841

*Litchfield REPUBLICAN. w My 12 1819-
CtHWe Ja 22 1821
CtTo D 8 1847;D 26 1850;Ag 14 1851;F 12 1852
CtWg Je 1854-Je 14 1855
DLC O 28 1847;Ja 7,My 17 1855;Ja 11 1856
MWA Je 26-N 11 1847;Ja 6,O 5,D 7 1848[Ja 11-Jl 12 1849]Ag 18 1853;Ja 26-F 2,D 14 1854;My 1855-[Ja-Je 13 1856]

Litchfield SENTINEL. w F 10 1865-75||
CtHi [1865-75]
CtTo F 10 1865
MWA 1865-Ja 1870;Ja,Ag 4 1871;Mr 22 1872;S 1874-F,Ap 9 1875
OClWHi Mr 17 1865;S 23 1866

SUN. w F 7 1835-
Ct F 20,Ap 2 1836;F 3 1838
CtTo O 24 1835
CtW Ja 28 1837
CtY Jl 22 1837
DLC 1835-S 1837
MWA S 23-30,N 18,D 2 1837[38]Ja 26,Mr-Ap 20 1839

MADISON

Madison JOURNAL. w Ap 30 1915-17||?
Ct [S 1915-F 2 1917]

MANCHESTER

Manchester Saturday HERALD. w O 1 1881-96||?
Ct [1882]Mr 14 1885;Mr 23 1889;D 13 1890;S 26,O 10 1891 Ap 2 1892
MWA O 11 1884

Half-weekly HERALD. sw 1894-1917||
Ct S 15 1908
CtSm Je 13 1914

Manchester evening HERALD. d O 1 1914+
Ct Ap 21-O 3 1919;D 9 1920;Mr 16 1926+

MERIDEN

CALL and citizen. sw 1871-
Ct Je 22 1875-Ja 1877
MWA O 4 1876

Meriden CHRONICLE. w N 29 1856-
Ct Je 26 1858
MWA N 29 1856

CONNECTICUT organ. w Ag 16 1851-
CtHWe N 22 1851;Ap 24 1852
MWA Ag 28 1852

CONNECTICUT whig. w 1852-
CtHWe [Je 23 1853-My 11 1854]

Meriden daily HERALD. d Ap? 1876-
MWA Ag 10,12 1876

Meriden daily JOURNAL. d Ap 17 1886+
pub 1886+
Ct 1905+
CtW Mr 2 1891
MWA Ap 17 1926
OClWHi Mr 30 1892

Meriden weekly MERCURY. w Ap 28 1849-
CtHWe Je 23 1849

NEW ENGLAND ledger. sm N 13 1875-
NjHi N 13 1875

Meriden PRESS-RECORDER. d D 19 1881-83||
1881-N 25 1882 as Meriden evening press
MWA D 19,22,29 1881;82-S 1 1883

Meriden RECORD. d 1868+
1868-98 as Meriden daily republican; 1899-1900? Meriden morning record and republican
Ct N 1921+
CtY Ap 5-10 1869
MWA S 2 1869;O 14 1876;F 4 1882

Meriden morning RECORD. d 1892-98||
United with Meriden daily republican to form Meriden morning record and republican, later Meriden record
Ct D 17 1897
DLC Jl-D 1898

Meriden weekly REPUBLICAN. w Ja 7 1871-1917||?
Ct Je 4,Jl 2 1891;N 17 1892

Meriden daily REPUBLICAN. *See* Meriden record

MIDDLETOWN

AMERICAN sentinel. *See* Sentinel and witness

CASTIGATOR. w Ag 28 1840-
MWA S 18,O 23 1840
OClWHi S 4 1840

CENTENNIAL sentinel. *See* Sentinel and witness

CONSTITUTION. w Ja 3 1838-90||
Ct [1838-43]-[50-69]71;My 12 1875;Jl 5 1881
CtHWe [1838]S 13 1843[44-45]D 30 1846;F 17 1847;My 31,O 25 1848;Ap 7 1852;Jl 5 1854[58] Jl 16 1862
CtMHi 1838-72[76-78]79;Ja 17,N 7,28 1882;Mr 4,Jl 15,Ag 12 1884;O 5 1886[87]Je 26 1888;My 18-Je 1 1889
CtMR [1842-44]-N 8 1871;72[73-75]My 1877-84;86-90
CtW [1838;47]Ap 20 1853;Ap 6 1864;68[69]Mr 9 1870;Ag 23 1871;Mr 13,O 16 1872[O 22 1873-75]My 24,Ag 3 1876;Ag 21,O 9 1877;Mr 23 1880;Jl 15 1882;O 26 1886;Mr 1,20,My 24 1887;Je 15 1889;Jl 5 1890
CtY 1838-42;S 6 1843;D 16 1846;O 24 1849;Mr 20,Ap 24 Je 12,Jl 31,D 4 1850;Ag 27 1862
DLC Ja 3,O 10 1838;My 22 1839;Je 9 1841;Ja 11 1843
MWA Jl 10 1844;Je 9 1852;S 30 1879;F 3,My 18 1880
N F 25 1846
NN Ap 18,D 5,19 1838
OClWHi Ag 24 1842

Daily CONSTITUTION. d Jl 10 1872-75||
CtMHi 1873-75
CtMR [Jl 10-D 1872]-[74]-Je 30 1875
CtW Jl 31 1873

Middletown DEMOCRAT. bm Ja-Mr 1861||
Follows Middlesex county democrat
CtHWe complete
CtHi complete

ELEPHANT. w Jl 4 1849-
CtHWe Jl 4 1849

Middletown HERALD. d O 19 1883-96||
Title varies slightly
Ct Mr 16 1888
CtMHi [1884-85]Mr 5 1886;S 17,29,O 8 1887;Ja 9,17,My 2 1888[89]F 10 1890[91-92]S 25 1893
CtMR [Ag 24-N 9 1888]S 2,7 1889[Jl 29-O 24 1892]My 8,11 1893[95-Ap 11 1896]
CtW Ja 2,16,Jl 25 1884[85]Ag 20,O 30 1886;S 9 1887;Ag 16 1888[Je 5 1889-My 11 1891]N 7-17 1892[93]F 20 1895
MWA O 16 1884

Saturday evening HERALD. w 1883-84||?
MWA O 4 1884

Evening JOURNAL. d D 10 1887-88||
Ct Mr 12,14-15 1888
CtMHi D 20 1887[Ja-Je 1888]
CtW [1887-Jl 16 1888]

MIDDLESEX county argus. w 1851-
CtHWe F 27,Mr 20 1857
CtMHi S 25 1857

MIDDLESEX county democrat. sm,w Ja 26 1850-N 10 1860||
1850-D 25 1852 as Middletown oasis (sm); Ja 15 1853-Ag 1860 Rainbow. Followed by Middletown democrat
Ct 1850-[57-60]
CtHWe 1851-57;Ja 30,My 1,28 1858[59-60]
CtHi 1850-[57-60]
CtMHi S 22,O 20 1860
CtW Mr 6 Ap 17 1852
DLC Je 7 1851
NNHi F 28,Mr 14,28,Jl 4,18,Ag 8,S 19,N 21 1857;Ja 30,My 1,22 1858;Mr 12,Ap,Je 1859-My,Jl-Ag,N 10 1860

MIDDLESEX explorer. w Ag 14 1856-
Campaign paper
CtMHi N 20 1856

CONNECTICUT (*Continued*)

MIDDLETOWN—*Continued*

***MIDDLESEX gazette.** w N 8 1785-1834||
N 5 1787-F 24 1792 as Middlesex gazette, or Federal adviser
CSmH Ag 25 1830
Ct [1821-25]-[27-33]Ja 23 1834
CtHWe Ap 5 1821;My 22 1822[24-34]
CtHi 1821-My 1 1834
CtMHi Ja 4 1821;Ag 22-O 24 1822;Ja 9 1823; Mr 24 1824;Ja 5,O 19,N 23 1825;Jl 12,S 27, O 18 1826;S 12 1827
CtMR Ag 11-18 1824[26]27;Jl 16 1828;29-[33; Ja 9-Mr 20 1834]
CtW [1823]Mr 1824-[28;30-33]Ja 9 1834
CtY Je 25,S 17,D 3-10 1828;Ja 6,O 14-21,N 4, 18,D 23-30 1829;Ja 6,20-27,F 3-10,24,Mr 3,17, 31-Ap 14 1830;My 4,Jl 27,S 7 1831;F 29,My 2,Jl 11-18 1832;Jl 3,Ag-D 1833
DLC Ja 31,Jl 11 1822;Ja 28,My 26,S 15 1824; Ap 13,S 21,N 30-D 14 1825;Ja 18,F 8 1826; Mr 26,Ap 9,23-30 1828;S 30,N 25,D 30 1829; Ja 13,27,Ag 11 1830;Ja 5,Jl 13 1831;N 7 1832
MSaE O 6 1824
MWA Mr 29 1821;Ja 10-D 5 1822;Mr 27-N 1823;24;F-Mr 2,My 18,Je 1,22,O 5-12,N 23 1825;My 10,31,Je 14,Ag 16,O 18 1826;Ja 23, Je 11-25,Ag 20-27,S 10-24,O 8,22,N 5 1828;Ja 6 1829;Ap 28,D 29 1830
NN Je 27 1832
NcD My 5 1824
PPL Ag 30,S 27-O 11 1826
WHi [Ap 25 1822-D 19 1827]

MIDDLESEX republican. w Ja 29 1857-
Ct Ja-O 15 1857
CtW Ag 13 1857

NEW ENGLAND advocate. w Jl 30 1834-36||
Ct F 25,My 20,D 16 1835
CtW S 17 1834-Mr 2 1836
CtY 1834-Jl 20 1836
DLC Ag 6 1834
MWA Mr 23 1836

Morning NEWS. d O? 1850-
Title varies
CtHi F 24-O 2 1851
CtMHi N 14,D 7 1850;Je 15 1855

Middletown NEWS. w Ja 4 1851-
Title varies: News and advertiser
CtHWe Ag 3 1855
CtMR 1851-54
CtW S 29 1854
MWA Ag 14 1852;Ag 13,N 11 1853
NNHi Ag 28 1852

Middletown NEWS. w Ap 3 1881-
Ct Ap 3,24-S 24 1881

Middletown OASIS. *See* Middlesex county democrat

OUR country. *See* Sentinel and witness

Daily PATRIOT. d D 9 1861-
Ct D 12 1861

PENNY press. *See* Middletown press

Middletown PRESS. d S 29 1884+
1884-Mr 12 1918 as Penny press; Mr 13 1918-My 31 1919 Evening press
O 29 1935 is 50th anniversary number
Ct Mr 12 1888;O 3 1889;Ag 26 1908;O 29 1921+
CtEh N 14 1898
CtMR My 24 1897;S 16-19 1901;18+
CtW [O 29-D 22 1884]Ap 30,Je 16,D 22 1885 [86-88]My 2-3,Je 15,N 19 1889;F 20[S-N 6 1890;91]Ja 25,N 8-17 1892;Ja 13[My]1893;D 4, 12 1895;Ja 31 1896;Jl 21 1897;1906+
MWA O 29 1935

RAINBOW. *See* Middlesex county democrat

Middletown daily SENTINEL. d Ja 3-Je 10 1876||?
CtMR Ja 3-Je 10 1876

SENTINEL and witness. w Ja 1 1823-98||?
1823-Ag 7 1833 as American sentinel; Je 1867-S 19 1868 Our country; Jl 4 1876 Centennial sentinel
CSmH Ag 25 1830
Ct Ag 1833-[34]-[37-38]-40;Ja 27,S 1 1841;F 11 1846;Je 24 1851;Mr 2 1852;Ag 19-S 2 1856; S 1-8 1857;N 29 1859;O 8 1861;Je 29 1864;F 25,Jl 7 1876;D 13 1879;D 18 1880;D 17 1881
CtHWe 1823;O 13 1824;Je 8 1825;O 25 1826;F 20 1828;O 28 1829;My 8,Je 19 1833;Ag 20 1834;O 25 1843;D 1 1847;Jl 5,O 25 1848[49]N 25 1856;D 9 1863
CtMHi O 1 1823;Ap 21 1824;My 6 1835;Ja 11 1837;F 3-10 1841;Ap 3 1849;My 7,Je 18 1850; Jl 29 1856; My 5,D 29 1857[58]F 22 1859;Ja 29 1861;Mr 26 1862;Mr 25 1863;O 4 1865;D 2 1870;N 17 1871;S 19 1873;O 20 1875;Jl 4,7 1876[77-78]Ja 25 1879;O 29 1881;O 7 1882; S 15,O 27 1883;Jl 19,O 11 1884;S 19 1885[86]-90
CtMR 1823-26;Ag 14 1849;Ap 17,Je 1867-86; Je,D 1887-Jl 14 1894
CtW F 18 1824;Ag 3,S 28,D 21 1825;Ja 23 1828[29-30]-Ja 12,S 7 1831[Ag 29-D 1832]-[34-36]Ag 23 1837; Ja 10,Je 27 1838[39-41]Mr 2,16,My 18 1842;Ap 26 1843;N 20 1844;Ag 20 1845;D 2 1846;F 10,S 7,O 5 1852;Mr 15,O 18-25 1853;S 19-26 1854[55-59]My 8 1860[61-65]F 28 1866[68-73]Ap 17,My 8 1874[75-79] My 8 1880[81-87]Je 9,S 1 1888[89;91-92]Ja 7 1893; F 7,My 16 1895[O 21 1897-F 24 1898]
CtY F 6 1828-Ag 7 1833;My 17 1843;Ag 26 1856;S 1 1857;Ag 31 1858;Ag 30 1859;Ag 28 1860;Ag 20 1861
DLC Mr 31-Ap 7,My 5,26 1824;Mr 30,O 5,N 3,17,D 21 1825;Mr 26,Ap 30,N 26 1828;Mr 4, My 6,S 30 1829;Ja 27 1830;S 3 1834;D 9 1840; Mr 26 1850
ICHi Jl 4 1876
MBAt Ag 6 1828
MWA S 2 1823;My 5,Je 30,Jl 21-Ag 4,S-O 6,27-N 17,D 22 1824;Ja 5,Mr 30,Je 1,N 9-23 1825;Ja 4-18,F 22-Mr,Ap 19,O 4,D 27 1826;N 28 1827;Ja 2 1828;29-31;Je 20,O 24 1832;Mr 16 1836; Mr 16 1852;Ag 18 1857;Ag 14 1860;D 2 1863;O 13 1876;N 4 1882
NNHi N 9 1852;F 14 1873
NbHi My 17 1878
NcD Mr 15 1826
NhD N 9 1825;Jl 13 1852
OClWHi Jl 26 1843;Mr 6 1844;Jl 19 1884
P-M S 19 1832;Ja 16 1855
WHi [1823-D 12 1827]

Middletown SUN. d My 16 1908-Ap 30 1914||
Merged with Middletown times
CtW complete

Middletown TIMES. d
CtW O 1 1914-Ja 5 1915

Middletown TRIBUNE. d Ap 24 1893-1906||
CtMHi 1893-O 9 1896;F 1897-Jl 1903;Mr 11 1904;F-Jl 1905[06]
CtMR S 20 1901
CtW [1893;F 8-Mr 2 1898]

WATCHMAN. D 20 1834||
CtHWe complete

WITNESS. w Ja 3-Ag 7 1833||
United with American sentinel to form Sentinel and witness
Ct Ja 3-17,31-F 14 1833
CtW Mr 28,Ap 11-18,Jl 4 1833

MILFORD

Milford CITIZEN. w My 25 1894+
pub 1925+
Ct 1894-Ap 1895;Mr 1898-Mr 1902;N 27 1919+

Milford NEWS. w Mr 17 1928+
pub 1928+

Milford SENTINEL. w 1873-76||
CtY Ja 20-O 21 1876

MOHEGAN

MOHEGAN.
CtNwP Je 16 1842(extra)

MOODUS

CONNECTICUT Valley advertiser. w 1869-1929||
Ct 1877-Mr 1904;Ap 27 1906-Jl 11 1929
CtEh N 16 1923
CtW F 8,Ap 5 1873;S 2 1876;Mr 10 1877;N 15(supp)1879; My 6 1882;O 11,D 20 1884[85] Ja 9 1886[87-89]S 27 1890[91-92]Ap 8 1893 [94-95]Je 26 1896[97-99]Ja 12 1900[06]S 20 1907[08]
KHi Ap 1892-D 13 1901
NSyU O 26 1900
OClWHi 1914-Jl 11 1929

MOOSUP

Moosup JOURNAL. w Ja 7 1882+
pub 1882+
Ct N 24 1921+

MYSTIC

Mystic JOURNAL. w Mr 12 1859-1917||?
1859-Ja? 1869 as Mystic pioneer
Ct Ja 12,O 19 1861;Mr 8 1862
CtHi 1859-Mr 3 1860
CtMy 1859-72
CtNlC O 10 1863
ICHi N 16 1861;Ja 4,Ap 5-12,S 13 1862
MWA Mr 26 1859
NCor D 1861-Ap 4 1868
OClWHi My 23 1863
RW Ap 20 1861;Je 18,Jl 2 1870

Mystic PIONEER. *See* Mystic journal

Mystic PRESS. w F 7 1873-1902||?
Ct Ap 17 1890;Mr 19 1891;Ja 7,F 4 1892;94-F 1897
CtMy 1873-83

NAUGATUCK

Naugatuck CITIZEN. w 1879-96||?
Ct O 10 1891

Daily CITIZEN. d 1895-96||?
CtN Ag 12 1895

Naugatuck ENTERPRISE. w 1877-1930||?
Ct Mr 18 1881;S 16 1921-[27]
CtW Ag 29 1879

Naugatuck NEWS. w,d O 31 1894+
w 1894-Ag 9 1895
Ct Ja 24-O 1895;D 21 1899;O 1921
CtN Ag 12 1895;S 27 1900;D 24 1909;Jl 19 1913;My 30,D 16 1914;D 17 1915;Mr 16 1918; O 11 1929+

Naugatuck REVIEW. w 1880-90||
Ct Mr 3 1881;Ap 13 1883;Ap 18 1890

Naugatuck Sunday TIMES. w 1908-10||?
CtN My 22 1908

NEW BEDFORD

New Bedford REGISTER. w 1840-
MnHi Ja 6 1841

NEW BRITAIN

New Britain weekly HERALD. sw,w 1880-88||?
sw 1880-82?
pub 1880-82
CtNb Ap 1880-F,D 26 1884-Ja 22 1886
MWA Ja 20 1882

New Britain HERALD. d D 2 1882+
Title varies: New Britain daily herald; Evening herald
pub 1886+
Ct N 1921+
CtNb 1882-Ja 1886

INDEPENDENT. w 1886-1901||?
PPCHi [1891-92;94-96]

New Britain JOURNAL. w My 17 1872-
CtNbI 1872

Il MESSAGGERO del New England. ir
In Italian
Ct [Je-S 1931]

NORTH and South. *See* New Britain times

New Britain OBSERVER. w 1876-87||
Title varies slightly
CtNb Mr 7 1876-O 7 1887

OSTERNS härold. w 1892-1912||?
In Swedish
MnHi 1900-Jl 1908

New Britain RECORD. w 1850-Jl 23 1932||
Merged with New Britain herald
1902-32 Thursday ed of daily used as weekly
CtNb 1869-71

New Britain RECORD. d 1892-Jl 23 1932||
Merged with New Britain herald
Ct O 16 1929-32
CtNb 1894

New Britain TIMES. w My 8 1858-
1858-S 1859 as North and South
Ct [1858-Ap 7 1860]
CtHWe Ap 9,Je 11 1859
DLC D 18-25 1858
MH [1858-S 1859]
MWA Je 19,Jl 10 1858

TRUE citizen. w Ja 18 1862-
Ct Mr 15 1862
CtHWe Ag 23 1862;Je 5 1863;S 1 1865
MSaE S 16 1864

NEW CANAAN

New Canaan ADVERTISER. m S 1870-
CtNcH S 1870

New Canaan ADVERTISER. w Jl 25 1908+
pub 1908+
Ct [1918]+
CtNc Jl 10 1913-S 19 1918;F 27 1919+

New Canaan ERA. w O 3 1868-76||?
Followed by New Canaan messenger
CtNc 1868-Ap 22 1871

New Canaan GAZETTE. w Ag 2 1932-Jl 31 1934||
Ct complete
CtNc complete

New Canaan MESSENGER. w Ja 13? 1877-1913||
Follows New Canaan era
Ct Je 1877-Ja 1880
CtNc Ja 20 1877-78;Ag 9 1879-84;86-O 19 1913

NEW HARTFORD

New Hartford TRIBUNE. w 1880-1910||?
Ct Ja 30 1891

NEW HAVEN

New Haven ADVERTISER. sw My 1 1829-
CSmH Ag 27 1830
CtY My 1 1829-Ap 27,O 26 1832
DLC O 2 1832
MBAt S 25 1829
MWA My 29,S 25 1829;Ja 27,S 4 1832
NjR My 1 1829;Ap 27 1830

ADVOCATE and examiner. w 1852-
CtHWe Ap 17 1856

AMERICAN eagle. w
CtY My 4 1826(supp)

BROADWAY news. w
Ct [1917-18]F 15 1919

New Haven CHRONICLE. w Mr 3 1827-
Ct My 19 1827
CtHWe [1828-29]
CtY 1827-30
MWA F 9,Ag 30 1828;N 27 1829;Je 24 1831
NN Ag 25 1827;Mr 22,Ap 26,N 29 1828

Saturday CHRONICLE. w 1902-Ap 27 1918||
Ct Ag 23 1902;07;S 5 1908;13;15-18
CtDe O 23 1915-Ap 20 1918
CtNh Jl 1903-18
CtY F 8 1902-My 1906

New Haven CITY gazette. w Ap 3 1830-
Ct N 13 1830-My 7 1831
DLC D 11 1830;F 5 1831
MWA S 4 1830

COLUMBIAN register. tw *See* New Haven evening register

***COLUMBIAN weekly register.** w D 1 1812-D 28 1911||
1812-55 as Columbian register
Ct F 11-25, Mr 18 1826;Ag 12 1828;D 3 1831;D 8-15 1832;Je 11,Jl 5,D 24 1836;Ap 22,Je 24 1837;My 22 1838;Mr 23 1839[42-43]Jl 29 1848;O 19 1850[52]Ap 2 1853[54-55]My 10 1856;Mr 1860-68;My 15 1869-[83]
CtDe S 3 1825;Jl 12 1879
CtHT 1821-Ap,My 11-O,N 9 1822-Ap 19,My, Je 21-Jl 19,22,26-S 6 1823
CtHWe 1821[22]My 14 1825;Jl 10 1827[30-31]O 13,D 8 1832;Je 4 1836;S 23 1837[39]Ja 30,Ap 10 1841;Ap 29 1843[44-45]My 16,S 19 1846;Ag 4,D 1 1849[51]53-54;O 4,N 29 1862
CtHi [N 28 1835-O 15 1842]

CONNECTICUT (*Continued*)

NEW HAVEN—*Continued*

COLUMBIAN weekly register—*Continued*
CtMHi Ag 26 1826
CtNh 1821-24
CtSo My 14 1836;S 1 1849
CtSp My 27 1837
CtW F 15 1843
CtY 1821-44;45-1911
DLC 1821-26;Ap 14 1827-D 2 1828;Je 20,Jl 11 1829;30-My 15 1841;Je 14 1842;O 17-24,N 21 1846-Ag 5 1849;Ap 12 1856-60
MWA [1822]F 18,My 3,Ag 30 1823;My 1-8,Je 12,Jl 10,N 13 1824;F 5,D 24 1825;D 29 1827;Ja 16,D 18 1830;Ap 23 1831-[32-33] Ap 4 1835;36-37;Ja 13-27 1838;Je 1 1839;My 8,D 25 1847;O 13 1849[50-51]Ja 31,F 14,Mr 6,Je 12,Jl 3,S 11,D 4 1852;Ja 15,Jl 9,23,O 1 1853[54-56]Mr 14,Je 6,Jl 4,D 12 1857[58]-O 1861[62]-92
MiU-C [1824;49;52;56;59-72;75;79;82;84-87;92]
N O 19 1833
NN My 7,Jl 30 1825-Ja 7,Ap-Jl,O 1826-Jl 14, S-O 13 1827;Ap 21 1832
NcD S 24,O 1 1881;D 2 1882
NhD D 15 1821
OClWHi Jl 13 1835;D 21 1839;Mr 25 1865
P-M Je 2 1832
WHi Ap 13 1822-D 8 1827;Jl 4 1829
—d ed *See* New Haven register

COMMONWEALTH. *See under* Hartford

***CONNECTICUT herald and journal.** w N 1 1803-1912||?
Title varies: Connecticut herald; Connecticut herald; Connecticut herald and weekly advertiser; Connecticut herald and weekly courier; Connecticut journal and herald and weekly courier
Ct Ja 31,Mr 7,N 28 1826;O 3,N 17,D 19 1837; O 5 1844;S 21 1861
CtHWe Je 12 1847;Ja 1,Jl 8 1848;D 10 1853;Ap 22 1865
CtHi [D 1824-S 18 1832]
CtY 1821-Ap 21 1835;My 16,30 1837;Je 19 1841;Ja 14 1843;S 3 1853;Ja 14,F 10,25,Mr 25 1854;My 12 1855;F 9 1856;Ag 7 1858;F 25,Ap 2,Je 4,O 22,N 26 1859;Ap 28,Jl 21,D 15 1860; Ja 12,Mr 2,16,S 14,D 28 1861;F 22,S 27 1862;Je 13 1863;F 21,My 26,Je 23 1866;My 23,Ag 1 1868;Ja 30 1869;Ja 28 1871;Ja 4 1873;Ag 1 1874;Je 19 1875
DLC O 2,N 6,20-27,D 18 1821-Mr,Je 4,Jl 16,O 1 1822;My 6,20,Je 7,Jl 8,O-D 1823;Je 14 1831
ICN Ag 16 1831;65
IU My 3 1831
MBAt O 28 1828;Je 9 1829
MHi Je 12 1821;My 11 1824;Ap 18 1826
MWA [1821]-30;Je 21 1831;O 8,N 12 1833[34-37]-F 13 1838;O 7 1848;Ag 17 1850;Jl 24 1852
N [1821-N 1823]F 22-Mr 8 1825;Ja 3-10 1826;S 25 1827;My 20 1828;D 1 1829;O 29 1833;Je 3 1834
NN My 22 1832;N 5 1833;Jl 14,S 8,N 3-10 1835; F 16,Mr 15,29,O 4 1836;Ap 4,My 9 1837;Ja 16,Mr 27 1838
NNHi Jl 13 1824;Je 19 1827;D 21 1830
NhD [1822-23]My 31,Jl 27 1824;Je 14-Jl 12 1825;O 24-31,N 14-28 1826;F 20,Ap 3 1827;F 26,My 13 1828;Mr 24,Ap 28 1829;S 4 1832
OClWHi F 19 1842;Jl 17 1858;Mr 3,O 24 1863; Je 4 1864;Mr 3 1866
WHi Je 28 1825

CONNECTICUT Jewish times. w S 1 1893-94||?
IU S 1 1893

***CONNECTICUT journal.** w O 23 1767-Ap? 1835||?
Title varies: Connecticut journal and New Haven post-boy; Connecticut journal and weekly advertiser; Connecticut journal and advertiser. United with Connecticut herald to form Connecticut herald and weekly journal (various changes of title. In this list as Connecticut herald)
Ct D 6 1825;Mr 14,Je 13 1826
CtHC Ag 21 1821-S 24 1822
CtWHe [1821]Ap 9,Jl 9 1822[23]N 6 1827[28-29]My 4 1830;D 6 1831;S 11 1832;My 13,O 21 1834;Ja 27 1835
CtHi 1821-23[25]27
CtSo Ja 14 1823;Jl 11 1826
DLC Ja 23,Jl 3 1821;22-25;Mr 14 1826-30;N 6 1832;Ja 7-14,28-F 4,18-25,Mr 11,25-Ap 15,29, My 13,Ag 5,26 1834;Ja 13 1835
MBAt Ja 9-16,F 6,20 1821
MHi My 9 1826
MSaE O 5 1824
MWA [1822-23]Ja 27,Mr 30,Ap 27,Jl 6,27,O 5 1824[25]Mr 28,My 9,N 14 1826;Jl 24-O 9, N 1827-Ap,My 26-Je,N 3-10,24-D 8,22 1829 [30-32]Ja 13,F 3 1835
MiU [1830]
N S 28,O 12 1824[Ja 29 1828-Mr 23 1830]O 8 1833
NN D 30 1823;N 1,D 6 1831;My 7,O 22 1833
NNHi Je 17 1828
NcD Je 11,D 10-24 1822;Ja 7,F 18-25 1823;S 18 1827;F 5,Mr 25,My 27,N 11 1828;Ap 27, My 11,Jl 20-27 1830
OClWHi My 20 1823
P-M My 31 1825
WHi Ap 23 1822-D 18 1827

CONNECTICUT journal and herald and weekly courier. *See* Connecticut herald and journal

CONNECTICUT times. w Ap 17 1920-27||?
Ct [1920]D 7 1921

CONNECTICUT volksblatt. w 1884-90||?
In German
CtY Mr 16 1889

CORRIERE del Connecticut. w 1897+
In Italiana
Ct 1901+
IU D 8 1917

Daily morning **COURIER.** d 1843-F? 1848||?
United with New Haven morning journal to form Morning journal and courier, later New Haven journal-courier
CtDe D 21 1843;Je 16 1845
CtSo Ap 3 1844
CtY Je 3 1843-Je 1847
MWA Mr 7 1844
NN Je 12 1843
OClWHi Jl 11 1843

New Haven **DEMOCRAT.** tw Ap 22 1845-
Ap-S 19 1845 as Democrat
CtHWe Ap 22 1846-Ap 20 1847
CtY Ap 21 1845-Ap 20 1847
MWA My 5 1845
P-M Ag 6 1845

New Haven **DEMOCRAT.** w 1845-
CtHWe Ag 23 1845
CtY My 1 1845-O 31,N 14 1846-Mr 20,Ap 3-24 1847

New Haven **DEMOCRATIC lever.** w N 3 1871-
Ct F 1872-O 1873

DOLLAR courier. w N 1 1844-
CtHWe S 13 1845
MWA Ap 12 1845

ELM CITY daily press. *See* New Haven daily press

New Haven **EXAMINER and watchtower of freedom.** w O 20 1832-
1832? as Watchtower of freedom
Ct O 20,N 24 1832;F 22,Mr 29 1834
CtY O 20 1832;Jl 27 1833;Ap 19 1844
MnHi N 24 1832
NNHi O 20 1832

New Haven daily **HERALD.** d N 1832-48||?
1832-40 as Daily herald
Ct 1836
CtHWe Mr 9 1837;Mr 21 1838;F 20 1840;My 24 1844;My 22 1846
CtHi N 29 1833-My 24 1834;37
CtT My 16 1838
CtY N 26 1832-46;Jl 22,Ag 11,16-18,20,S 7,N 4,24,D 2,8 1847;Ja 20,F 25 1848
DLC Jl 13 1833;S 30 1835;Ap 13 1836;My 8, 20,Ag 23 1839;O 27,N 13,D 4 1840;Ap 1,Ag 17 1841;Ag 19,O 3,D 6-7 1842;F 9,My 2 1844; Ag 17 1844
IU D 8 1842
MWA F 2 1833;Mr 12 1836;Jl 6,11,Ag 29,31,S 6 1837;My 21 1838;39-40;43;Ja-Je 29 1846
NN Je 24,28,Jl 6 1842;My 20,Je 22 1843
NNHi [1833]Mr 12-Ag 17 1835;F 10 1836;38; S 2 1845
P-M Ag 16 1838;D 11 1845
WHi 1835-39;42;44-45

ILLUSTRATED current news. tw
Ct N 18 1921+

JEFFERSONIAN democrat. w Je 7 1834-
CtY Je 7,28,Jl 12 1834
DLC Jl 5 1834

New Haven **JOURNAL.** w 1836-
CtHWe Je 3-O 7 1837
MWA Je 24 1837

Evening **JOURNAL.** d S 9? 1874-
CtY S 23,D 17 1874;Ja 30 1875
MWA S 23 1874

Morning **JOURNAL and courier.** *See* New Haven journal-courier and New Haven times

New Haven **JOURNAL-COURIER.** d F? 1847+
1847-F? 1848? as New Haven morning journal; Mr 1848-F 23 1913 Morning journal and courier
CClP Je 28-Jl 1,3-4 1876;Jl 5 1879;Je 24 1880
Ct Mr 28 1850[My-Je 1854]65-72;74;My 2 1888; S-D 1898;S 6 1924;Ag 4 1925;Mr 31 1936+
CtDe Ap 13 1880
CtNh 1908-Mr,My-Ag,S 1910+
CtSp Je 18 1887
CtY Je 1843-Jl 1844;Jl 28 1845-Je 11 1846; Je 19,Ag 17 1848;Je 13 1849;50+
DLC Ap-D 1861;63-65;Ja-O 3 1867;73-81;D 6 1882-94;Jl 1916+
ICHi O 7,13,18,N 9 1865
ICN [My 8-D 1863;65]
MHi Ap 25 1861
MWA Jl 27 1847;Mr 22-23,27 1850;My 27,O 28 1852;Jl 7,O 18-19,23-30,N 9,12,15,19-22 1860; F 20 1861;Jl 25 1862;F 20 1863;Ag 26,S 19-20 1864;Ap 16-17,My 18,22,Je 6,14,Ag 9,14,17 1865;Ja 6,F 21,24,Ap 5,12-13 1866;Jl 18-20,22 1867;Jl 21,24,O 1,30,N 19-20,25,28 1868;My 1 1869;S 29 1873;Ap 22,Jl 9-D 1874;N 19,21,D 2 1879;Jl 4,8 1881;Je 28 1882;O 2 1926
MiU 1875-Je 1879
NN Mr 1-2,27,My 20,Ag 15 1848;My 26,Je 4 1852;My 14 1859
NNHi My 29 1850;D 31 1851;Ja 20 1854;My 1 1873
NcD Ag 15 1850
OClWHi Mr 1 1866
OHi My 26 1868

Evening **LEADER.** *See* New Haven times-union

Daily **LEVER.** d 1869-70||?
Ct [1870]

NATIONAL pilot. *See* Pilot

NATIONAL republican. w Jl 23 1831-
CtHWe Ja 27 1832
ICN O 29,N 12 1831
MWA D 31 1831

Daily **NEW HAVENER.** d 1833-
CtStr O 9 1833

New Haven daily **NEWS.** d 1858-
1858-O? 1859 as New Haven morning news
CtY My 10 1858;Ja-Je 1859;Mr 30 1860
MWA S 19 O 10,13 1859;N 22 1860

New Haven daily **NEWS.** d 1870-73||
Ct F 1872-Ja 1873

Morning **NEWS.** d O 12 1882-D 31 1898||
O 12-D 2 1882 as Observer;D 4 1882-Ap 8 1891 Morning news; Ap 9 1891-My 1 1893 New Haven news
CtDe N 28 1883
CtHWe O 12 1882
CtNh D 4 1882-98
CtY complete
IC Ap 30 1889
MWA S 29 1884

OBSERVER. *See* New Haven morning news

New Haven **PALLADIUM.** w N 7 1829-1910||?
1832-O 24 1835 as Palladium and republican
CSmH S 6 1830
Ct F 29 1840;O 9 1841;44-46;Je 24 1854;Ja 1 1863
CtHWe [1837]Ja 19 1839;40[41-42]-[44]-Jl 1846;Jl 1848;S 29 1849;Ja 19 1852;S 10 1853; Mr 25 1854[55]
CtHi [D 1836-37]
CtNh 1829-O 15 1842
CtSo Jl 9 1859;Jl 9 1863;F 16 1865
CtStr Ag 27 1842
CtY Ag 7 1841;Je 17 1848;F 17 1855
DLC O 13 1832
ICN 1864
MSaE Ja 16,F 13 1836;N 30 1839
MWA Ap 24 1830;Ja 23,Je 4 1836;F 3,Ap 28 1838;D 14 1839;Ap 25 1840;F 6 1841;Ag 24 1844;S 18 1847;My 27 1848;S 18 1852;S 26 1857;My 15 1883;O 2 1884
NN F 13 1830;Jl 14 1832;S 21 1833;My 31,Ag 2,N 29 1834;Ja 24-31,F 14,Je 27,S 12,26-O 3,31 1835;D 10,31 1836;D 11 1852;N 12 1853;F 3-10,24,Mr 17-31 1855;Ja 21 1875;Ja 10 1878
NNHi [Mr-O 1854] Mr 31,O 20 1855;Mr 15-29 1856;F 27,Mr 20,My 1,N 27 1858;Ag 27-S 3 1859;F 25,My 19,Je 16,N 3 1860[61-62]Mr 12,Je 17,S 3-10,24-N 19 1863;F 18-Mr 17,Ap 14,28 My 19,S 29-O 13 1864;Ag 27 1867;Mr 6, Je 3 1873
NcD D 12 1857
NhD Ja 6 1860
OClWHi D 29 1864
P-M D 20 1845;Ap 16 1853

New Haven **PALLADIUM.** tw,d O 2 1839-Ag 19 1911||
Title varies: New Haven daily palladium; Evening palladium; etc.
tw 1839-F 22 1841
Ct [My-Je 1854]F 26,My 30 1856;57-64;72-Ag 1874;75-Ja 1893
CtAn O 26 1867
CtDe Mr 2,30 1880
CtHWe Ap 5 1841
CtNh 1839-64;66-1911
CtW [1867]68;Ag 27 1881;Je 22 1889;S 6,12-13,16-22,O 6,17-21 1890;Ja 30,Mr 20,26 1891
CtY N 7 1829-F 8 1831;N 9 1833-56;Ap 30 1864;Jl 12 1865;70-91;Mr 8 1892;N 7 1861;94
DLC O 23 1839;O 30 1840;Ag 21 1841-My 6 1843[F-S 1850]Ja 29 1851-Ag 11 1853;63-65;S 24 1867;77;82
ICN [1864]
MWA S 27,O 29,N 2 1841;Jl 1 1842;My 25 1852;Je 17 1856;Jl 27 1859;O 19-31,N 9-22 1860[62-63]My 11-12,Je 6 1864;Ag 17 1865;Ap 4 1866;Ap 30,My 1,Je 14,Jl 6 1867;S 9 1868 [Mr 29-My 28 1869]My 23 1870(supp);Ja 13 1873;O 11-22,N 19-22,26,D 2 1879;Jl 3-10,S 21 1881;Ja 10,My 15,Je 28-29,N 14 1882;N 17 1883;Je 11 1886;Je 10 1893
MiU-C D 29 1884;D 15 1894
N Mr 5 1841
NN My 29,Je 1,14 1843
NNHi My 23 1840;Ap 29 1845;S 30,D 29,31 1851;Mr 27 1862
NSchU Je 14-15 1842
NSyU Ja 13 1840
OCHi Ap 3 1843
OClWHi Ja 2 1865
TxU O 16 1850
WHi O 7 1839-N 14 1851;Mr 19-D 1856

PILOT. w S 20 1821-
1821-Mr 13 1823 as National pilot
CtY S 6 1821-S 11 1824
DLC My 2,16,30 1822;My 8,Jl 10,Ag 14 1824
MSaE Jl 10 1824
MWA D 27,1821;Jl 4 1822;My 1,D 11 1823
NN Ja 22,31-F 7,O 31-N 7,D 5 1822;Mr 20, My 1,22,Je 19-26,Jl 24-31,Ag 14-N 13 1823; Ja 15,Mr 4,18-25,Ap 24,My 8-15,Je 13,26-Jl 17 1824
NNHi O 22 1822

New Haven daily **PRESS.** d 1869-74||?
1869-72? as Elm City daily press
CtY Je 9 1871

New Haven **RECORD.** w F 26 1839-Je 27 1840||
United with Connecticut observer to form Congregational observer (not in this list)
CtHWe My 18-Je 1 1839;D 1839-Ja 18 1840
CtY complete
MWA Mr 30,Ap 20-27,Je 1-15,Jl 6,20-27,Ag 17,S 21-28,N 23,D 7 1839;Ja 18-25,F 15,Mr 28,Je 20 1840
NN Ap 20,My 11,Je 8,29,Jl 13 1839;Ja 18, My 23 1840

New Haven weekly **RECORD.** w 1881-95||
Ct 1890-Ja 1895

New Haven **REGISTER.** tw,d 1840+
1840-45 as Columbian register; Ja 1-My 2 1845 New Haven register; My 5 1846-Ap 30 1864 New Haven daily register; My 2-Jl 1864 New Haven morning register; Jl 11 1864-D 31 1869 New Haven evening register; Ja 3 1870-O 10 1874 Evening register
tw 1840-My 2 1846
Ct [My-Je 1854]F 10 1859;S 1883-84;N 28 1888;Ja 28 1889;Ap 23 1898;1903+
CtDe Mr 30 1880;My 1 1895
CtHWe N 12 1847[48-49]F 28 1851;Ap 15 1852[53-58]Ja 15 1861
CtNh 1908-S,N 1909+
CtSp O 25 1880
CtW S 12 1890

CONNECTICUT (*Continued*)

NEW HAVEN—*Continued*

New Haven REGISTER—*Continued*
CtY Ag 10 1840+
DLC O 23 1878-1907
MWA My 24,N 27 1852;Ap 2-3,16 1869;O 9,13-14 1876;My 4,Ag 10 1878; Jl 5 1881;F 5 1883; S 14,O 16-23,28-30 1886;O 23 1901;F 13 1920
MiU-C Jl 7 1882;My 12,14 1887;Ap 13 1892
NNHi 1844
NcD Ag 28,S 18,25 1881;Mr 7 1882;D 30 1885
OClWHi My 19 1853;Mr 28 1865
—w ed *See* Columbian weekly register

New Haven Sunday REGISTER. w 1877+
Ct O 29 1882;Ap 24 1898;Mr 1903-Mr 10 1912; 13-17;Jl 1921+
CtDe F 1 1880
MWA F 18,Jl 29 1883

SEA world. w 1879-80||
MB S 24,N 24 1879-F 23 1880

SHORE line times. *See under* Guilford

STELLA d'Italia. w 1892-1907||?
In Italian
CtY Mr 17-24 1894

New Haven TIMES-LEADER. *See* New Haven times-union

New Haven TIMES-UNION. d Ap 9 1892-Ag 7 1927||
1892-Ja 2 1910 as Evening leader; Ja 3 1910-Ap 19 1925 New Haven times-leader
Ct S 10 1902;Ap 2,D 29 1919
CtNh 1892-S,N 1910-26

TOWN talk. w 1890-91||
CtY Mr 27 1890;Mr 5 1891

New Haven UNION. d Jl 1 1873-Ap 19 1927||
Title varies: Evening union; Daily evening union; etc. United with New Haven times-leader to form New Haven times-union
Ct [Jl 29-Ag 12 1918]Ap 21-Je 24 1919
CtDe Mr 30 1880
CtNh 1908-09;F-Mr 1910;Mr 1911-26
CtY Ag 2,5 1873;Je 8,25,Ag 16 1874;Mr 4, Je 27 1875;F 16 1882;S 26 1886;My 2 1890
MWA O 13 1876;Je 29 1882
MoHi Ap 7 1908

WATCHTOWER of freedom. *See* New Haven examiner and watchtower of freedom

NEW LONDON

ADVERTISER. sm Je 1 1856-
Ct Jl 14 1856
CtY Mr 8 1858

New London daiily CHRONICLE. d 1848-67||?
Ct Je 27 1856;Jl 1859;Ap 3,18,Je 29,Jl 29 1861; Jl 11 1866-Mr 14 1867
MWA Ag 12 1853;My 9 1857
RW Jl 24 1855;S 5 1863

New London CHRONICLE. w My 3 1848-68||?
Ct 1850-Jl 2 1851;Ag 8 1861;O 26 1865[66]
CtHWe My 3,S 20,O 18 1848;My 7 1857
CtY D 7 1854
MWA Ag 16 1860

CONNECTICUT centinel. w 1818-
CtHWe Je 10 1829
CtHi D 17 1828-Jl 7 1830
MWA N 25 1829

CONNECTICUT gazette. 1773-1823 *See* New London gazette

CONNECTICUT gazette. w 1873-84||?
MWA Je 11 1875;O 13 1876

New London DAY. d Jl 2 1881+
S 7 1931 is Sesquicentennial ed, Battle of Groton Heights
pub 1881+
Ct N 23 1882;1907+
CtSp Ap 26 1893
CtY Jl 2 1881
M S 7 1931
MHi S 7 1931
MWA O 31 1882;Jl 6,S 7 1931
WHi My 6 1896;S 7 1931

DAY. w 1881-1909||?
1881-98? as Week
Ct F 8 1883;Jl 16 1885

New London DEMOCRAT. w Mr 22 1845-
Title varies: Democrat; Weekly democrat
Ct Je 21 1845;D 5 1846;S 25,O 2 1847
CtHWe My 18 1867
DLC Ja 20 1855-F 14 1857
MWA 1845-48
P-M D 6 1845;Mr 5,Ap 9 1853

***New London GAZETTE.** w N 18 1763-My 29 1844||
A prospectus was issued O 12 1763. 1763-D 10 1773 as New London gazette; D 17 1773-F 26 1823 Connecticut gazette (subtitle varies)
CSmH Jl 7 1830
Ct D 29 1824; N 2 1836
CtHWe [1827] O 22 1828; My 26 1830[31-40] Ap 20 1842;My 29 1844
CtHi 1821-Ja 3 1838
CtNlC Je 6 1821
CtY My 21 1823-D 10 1828;Je 26 1836
DLC My 2,D 5-19 1821;Ja 23 1822;Mr 3,My 26-Je 9 1824;D 3 1828;Mr 25-Ap 8,29-O,N 11,D 2-16 1829;Ja 6 1830;Ja 29,O 7 1840
IC N 24 1830
ICHi Ag 19 1829
M S 15 1824
MHi Je 7 1820
MSaE Ag 6 1823
MWA F 7,Ap 25-N 14,D 5 1821;F 13-20,My 8,O 2-9 1822;F 16,N 16-30 1825; Jl 16,O 8 1828;My 20 1829;O 7 1835;Mr 31(extra)1838; Ap 4(extra)1840
MiU-C N 5 1823
NN Ap 30,O 8 1828;Ja 24,D 16-23 1829;F 3-10,Mr 3-10, Ag 18,N 24 1830;Mr 9,Ap 20-27 1831;F 29,Mr 14 1832;Ja 9-16,Ap 3-10,My 1,Je 26,Jl 3,24 1833;F 25, Je 24,D 2 1835;Ap 13 1836;Jl 12,S 20,N 1, 1837;Ja 10 1838
P-M Mr 9 1831
RW O 16 1822;Mr 31 1835;My 22 1844

New London daily GLOBE. d 1890+
Ct Ag 24 1918;N 1921-Ap 6 1934

Morning NEWS. d 1844-
Ct [F 20 1845-47]
CtY [1846]
MWA F 12,S 8 1847

PENNY press. d 1881-82||
RW D 31 1881; Ja 3,6,9,20,23,24,F 8, Mr 25 1882

PEOPLE. w
CtY Ap 18 1821

PEOPLE'S advocate and New London county republican. w Ag 26 1840-
CtHWe [S 16 1840-41]Ag 24 1842[45]Ja 11, Mr 8 1848
DLC Ag 26,S 30 1840;F 25 1846
MBAt Ap 7 1841
MWA F 1 1843;S 3 1845
RW Ja 19 1842;S 10-24 1845

PIONEER. w 1848-
DLC Ag 16 1848

POLITICAL observer and working man's friend. w My 4 1831-
CtHWe D 7 1831; Mr 28 1832

REPOSITORY. w F 24 1858-
CtHWe 1858-F 14 1861

***REPUBLICAN advocate.** w F 1818-
Ct Ag 22 1821;Mr 12,My 7 1823;Jl 20,O 12 1825[26-28]
CtNw 1825-27
CtY My 30-Je 13,Jl 25-D 1821;Ap 9 1823
DLC 1821-23;Ja 14-F 11,Mr-Ag 18,N 1824-26; Ag 15 1827
MWA F 1821-F 2,Je 1 1825;F 28-Ap 1827;Ja 9 1828
MiU-C Je 14 1820;N 12 1823
NN Ap 4,My 17-23 1821

New London daily STAR. d 1846-72||?
Titles varies slightly
CSmH My 29 1865
Ct N 28(extra)1846;Jl 22 1865[66]Ap 18 1868
CtHWe Jl 9 1853;F 16 1855;Ap 10 1865
DLC [Ja-My 1857;My-S 1858] Ap 15-D 1859 [My-Ag 1860]Ja 2 1861
MWA N 30 1846;D 23 1848;Mr 7,17 1849;Je 26, Jl 31,N 8 1852;F 23 1870
OClWHi Mr 30 1863;S 15 1865

New London TELEGRAM. d 1874?-84||
Ct My 23 1879;N 24 1880;Ja-Je 1883
MWA O 14 1876;S 6 1881
RW N 8 1884
—w ed *See* New London gazette

Morning TELEGRAPH. d 1885-1921||?
CtTo Ag 8 1885
DLC 1898
RW My 28 1892

WEEK. *See* Day

NEW MILFORD

New Milford GAZETTE. w 1872-Mr 11 1920||?
1872-D 1874 as New Milford journal; D 1874-N 25 1882 Housatonic ray; D 21 1882-Mr 30 1883 New Milford ray and gazette
Ct Ap 1877-Mr 1884;F 21 1919
CtNm 1874-Mr 11 1920
CtNmT 1881-90;93-96;1905-06;08-20
CtY [1879]
MWA N 3 1905;My 3-10,O 11 1907;Mr 15 1912
NEh Je 19 1875

HOUSATONIC rays. *See* New Milford gazette

New Milford JOURNAL. *See* New Milford gazette

New Milford RAY and gazette. *See* New Milford gazette

New Milford REPUBLICAN. w D 5 1845-
CtHWe Ja 16,Ap 17 1846
CtTo D 5 1845

New Milford TIMES. w Ja 3 1914+
pub 1914+
Ct Ap 15-29,Je 1920+
CtNm 1914+
CtWg 1921+

NEWTOWN

Newtown BEE. w Je 28 1877+
pub [1877-91]+
Ct 1877-1900;D 29 1918[Ja-F]Ap 25 1919+
CtY Mr 9,Je 1,22-Jl 6,20,Ag 17-24 1923

Newtown CHRONICLE. w 1880-82||
Ap-Je 12 1880 as Chronicle
Ct Ap 1880-Ap 1882

NORFOLK

Norfolk TOWER. w 1888-94||?
Ct O 1888-Ag 1890;N 6 1890

NORTH CANAAN

CONNECTICUT western news. w 1871+
pub 1871+
M [Ap 16-Je 18 1931]

NORTH MANCHESTER

Papers published in North Manchester are listed under Manchester

NORWALK

Norwalk EAGLE. w D 20 1876-79||
Ct 1876-F 1879

FAIRFIELD county democrat. w 1851-
MWA O 30-N 6 1852
NNHi D 30 1845-D 14 1847

***Norwalk GAZETTE.** w My 6 1818-1900||?
CSmH Ag 31 1830
Ct [1826]S 16 1828[31]Ag 1840;D 28 1893;My 11 1894-Ja 18 1895
CtHWe D 21-28 1858[59]
CtY Mr 1 1821-F 24 1824;F 2 1830;My 21 1861;Ap 20 1880
DLC S 1,15-22,O 6 1829;Mr 19,Jl 23-30,Ag 20 1845
MBAt S 9 1828;O 16 1832
MWA Ja 17 1821;My 4 1824;My 13 1828;Je 23 1829;O 2,D 18 1832;Ja 12-19,F 2-9 1836;D 24 1845;N 18 1846;Jl 26 1848[66-75]
NBuG S 14 1869
NN Ja 23-F 13 1839;Mr 29 1859
NNHi S 23 1834;D 12 1839;D 24 1845-F 18 1846;My 19,Je 16,Jl 15,28 1863;S 15,29,O 20 1868-Ja 12,26-F 9,23-Mr 2,Je 8 1869;N 1 1870; Ap 16 1872;Ja 7,Je 17 1873;Ja 27,F 10 1874
NjR Je 10 1873
WHi Ag 2 1831;My 22 1832

Norwalk HOUR. w 1871-1922||?
1871-72 as Hour
1871- also dated at Westport
CtHWe Ag 10-17,S 7 1872
MWA Ja 5,O 4 1884;Je 25 1892

Norwalk HOUR. d 1895+
Ct Mr 31 1936+
OClWHi Mr 29 1911

Norwalk RECORD. w My 7 1887-90||
Ct My 1887-90

NORWICH

Norwich daily ADVERTISER. d 1867-74||
CtNw 1867-74
CtY Je 22 1874

AMERICAN patriot. w 1847-
DLC S 25-O 16,D 4,25 1847;Ja 29,F 26,Ap 8, 29,Je 3 1848

Daily ARGUS. d
MWA Mr 4 1876

Norwich AURORA. w My 20 1835-N 26 1878||
1835-Ag 1838 as Aurora
CSmH Jl 28 1860
Ct Mr 16-30 1836;Jl 28 1841;44-46;Je 16 1847; 48-[68-69]My 18 1877
CtHWe D 10(extra)1835;My 18 1836;D 27 1837; My 6 1840;My 17 1843;My 8 1844;O 16 1850;F 11,Jl 28 1852;F 26,Mr 26 1859
CtHi [My 15 1839-My 12 1841]-Ap 1851;My 1855-58;60-61;63
CtNw 1874-78
CtNwC Mr 20 1842;F 17,My 5 1847;Ap 20 1861
CtY Jl 22-29 1835
DLC [Ja-S 5 1838]Ap 17-Je 5 1839;Mr 6,S 2 1840;F 17-Je 23 1841;Jl 16 1842;My 19 1876
MWA Jl 8 1835;Ap 4 1838;Ag 12 1840;Ap 7 1841;Ap 24,D 25 1844;Mr 5 1845;Ap 22 1865;Je 9 1869;Ja 25,Je 28 1871;S 26 1874;S 29 1876
NN Ap 4 1838
NNHi Mr 7 1844
OClWHi Ag 7 1844;Mr 26 1864

Norwich daily AURORA. d 1860-
CSmH Ag 4 1860
MWA D 13 1860

Norwich BULLETIN. d D 15 1858+
1858-1901 as Norwich morning bulletin
Ct D 15 1858;N 22 1864;Ap 2 1866;O 27 1868; Jl 10 1869;Ag 1877-O 1880;My 1882-Ja,Mr 1 1883;Ja 7,22 1885[86]N 12 1887;N 15 1889;Ag 23 1894[Mr 1901]+
CtNw 1877;O 1912-O 1934
CtNwP Mr 6 1900[Ag 31-S 7 1901]Ja 11 1905; Jl 3-7 1909
CtW My 30 1889
DLC D 15 1858;Ap 15(extra)1865;F 26 1869;Je 30 1870
IHi Ap 15(extra)1865
MBAt Ap 17-20 1865
MWA D 15 1858;D 15 1859[O 16-N 23 1860] Ja 24,Ap 1,19,23 1861;Ja 22,F 18,Ap 9,14, 28,My 2,S 1,D 3 1862;Ja 5,26,My 2,Jl 14,S 24,O 2(supp)1863;My 6,9,11-12,14,19,Je 3-4, 11,14,D 26 1864[Ja-O 1865]Mr 29 1867;S 3 1870;Ja22,My 15 1874;Mr 12,Je 14,Jl 6,Ag 18, S 27,O 11 1876;N 17,21,D 16,20,22-25,27 1879; Ja 6,9,17,N 18 1880;Jl 2(extra)1881;Ag 27,O 1,15 1884;Ag 11 1931
MiU-C Ap 17 1865
NNHi O 12 1859
OClWHi Ap 10 1863
RW D 15 1858;Mr 22-23,Ap 11,13 1861
WHi Jl 3 1909

CANAL of intelligence. w Je 2 1826-
Ct [1828]Ag 5 1829
CtNw 1828
CtT Ag 26,D 3-10 1829
CtY 1826-My 21 1828;My 27-N 18 1829
DLC Ag 22,D 5 1827
MWA Je 6,Ag 29 1827;Ag 27 1828;Jl 22 1829
NN N 12,26,D 3 1828

CHELSEA courier. *See* Norwich courier, sw,w

COOLEY'S weekly. w 1876-1927||?
Merged with Norwich courier
CtNw 1876-84;94-97
CtW My 31 1889
CtY S 10 1881
MWA O 14 1876;N 15 1879;Ja 10,S 11 1880
RW S 24 1881
—d ed *See* Norwich evening record

CONNECTICUT (*Continued*)

NORWICH—*Continued*

Norwich COURIER. d,tw 1842-60||?
Title varies slightly
tw Jl 19 1856-Mr 23 1858
CSmH Jl 21-Ag 7 1860
Ct Jl 19 1856-Mr 23,D 1858-Ag 2 1859
DLC My-D 23 1851;Je 4 1868;N 12 1872
MWA O 4,25 1842;O 17-N 3,10-22 1860
RPB Jl 1 1842

***Norwich COURIER.** w,sw N 30 1796-1930||
1796-My 24 1798 as Chelsea courier. Title varies: Courier; Norwich weekly courier; Norwich semi-weekly courier; Norwich courier-Cooley's weekly
sw Jl 20 1859-61; 1902-N 1 1927
CSmH S 3 1830
Ct Mr 29 1826;Jl 22,Ag 5 1829[30-31]Ap 11,Jl 4 1832;O 9 1833[34-36]Mr 20 1839-Mr 3 1847 [50]59;62-63;Ag 11 1880;D 1881-94;Mr 29 1895; 1902-O 31 1930
CtHWe [1822]Ag 20 1823[24-26]Mr 28 1827;O 29 1828;Je 23 1830;Mr 30 1831[32;34]Ag 19 1835[36]S 20 1843;My 22 1844;Jl 23 1845;Ja 21 1846[48;51]O 27 1858;S 10 1859
CtNwP Jl 7 1824;S 14 1825;Ap 22 1829;Jl 17 1850;Ap 20 1865
CtY N 17 1824;Jl 5 1826;D 3 1828;D 16 1829; Ag 13-14 1844;N 7 1849;Ag 28 1850;Ag 6 1851;S 6 1854;Jl-D 1864;O 26-D 7 1865
DLC [1824-25 27-30;41-46;50-61;63-73]
IHi Je 12 1822
MHi N 25 1835
MSaE Ag 6 1823
MWA O 3,N 14-21 1821;Ap 10-D 18 1822;23-S,N 9 1825[Ap 18-D 1827]Ja 2-9 1828;N 25 1829;S 26 1832;My 28 1834-Ja 7,21-28,F 11, 25,N 25 1835;Ja 27,Ap 1836-Mr 15 1837[Ap 1838-39]-F 19,Ap 15-D 15 1840[Ap-D 1841] Ja 5,F 2-23,Mr 2-16,30 1842;Jl 7 1847;Ap 28 (supp)1850;F 20(supp)Mr 5(supp)19(supp) 1856;S 10-24,N 12 1859;S 14 1859;F 15,Ag 16 1860;Jl 9,D 3 1863;Mr 3,Ap 28 1864;Ap 20 1865; Jl 12 1866;Jl 5,Ag 16 1876
MiU-C N 12 1823
NIC Ag 5(supp)1846
NN 1821-Ja 14,F 25-Mr 1824;Ja 11,25-F 8, Mr 8-15,Ap 5,Je 21 1826;S 29(supp)1847;Mr 29 1848;S 10 1859;Ja 16 1868
NNHi D 29 1830
NcD Mr 16 1825;Ap 20 1865
NhD N 3 1824
NjR Mr 31 1847
OClWHi Je 19 1822;S 9,N 3 1824;Je 6,Ag 15,S 12 1827;Ja 8 1840;Je 4 1853;F 8 1882
P-M Ag 30 1854
—Supplements. sm
CtHWe My 13 1846-My 1856

EXAMINER. w O 23? 1852-
Ct Je 1 1855
CtHWe D 24 1853;S 21,N 16 1855
CtY Ag 20 1853
MWA Ag 20-27,S 10-17 1853;Mr 4(extra) [Ag-D 1854]Ja 12-F 2,Mr 9,30-Ap 6 1855
NNHi D 3 24-31 1853;Ja 14,Mr 4-11,Ap 1, 22,Je 3,24,Ag 12,26,S 29-O 13,N 10,24-D 1, 15,29 1854;Ja 12,Ap 13,27,Je 15-22,S 14 1855
P-M N 26 1853
RW D 3 1853

Norwich FREE PRESS. w F 4 1830-
Ct Ap 1 1830
CtY [Ap 14 1830]

FREE soil pioneer. w Jl 22 1848-
Campaign paper
CtY Ag 4 1848
MWA Ag 19 1848

HERALD of peace. w O 31 1830-
Ct [N-D 1831]-Ap 1832
CtNwC Ja 3 1831

MECHANICS, operatives and laborers advocate. w Ag 22 1836-
Ct N 28 1836;Ja 16 1837
CtHWe 1836-My 15 1837

Norwich NEWS. w Ap 28 1841-
Title varies slightly
CtHWe My 26,Ag 28 1841;Mr 16,O 19 1843
CtNwC N 21 1844
DLC Mr 2 1844
MWA O 16 1841
NEh Je 22 1842
PPiHi F 9 1842
RPB Jl 6 1842

Norwich evening RECORD. d 1888+
CtNw 1916-O 1934;Jl 28 1936+
CtNwP Ag 31-S 6 1901
MWA Jl 31 1931
—w ed *See* Cooley's weekly

Weekly REPORTER. w My 10 1845-
CtHWe Ja 9 1847
CtY Jl 5,19,S 13 1845
MWA D 13 1845;F 21 1846

Norwich REPUBLICAN. w O 1 1828-
Ct [1828-Ap 1836]
CtHWe Ap 29 1829;Ag 1 1832;My 7 1834
CtNw 1828-30
CtNwP S 16 1835
CtY Ag 26 1829;Je 25 1833-Ap 1 1835
MHi N 21 1835
MWA D 29 1830;Mr 30 1831
N O 16 1833
NNHi Je 12,O 16,N 6 1830
P-M S 12 1832

Weekly REVEILLE. w O 1 1858-
Ct [1858-Ag 19 1859]
CtHWe O 1 1858
MWA D 31 1858

Norwich SPECTATOR. w N 29 1829-
Ct D 15 1829
CtHWe 1829-Ja 19 1830
MWA D 15 1829(photostat)
OClWHi D 29 1829

SPECTATOR. w 1842-
1842-Mr? 1844 as Norwich spectator
CtNwC Je 5 1844
MWA Mr 13,Jl 17,S 4 1844

TELEGRAPH. w
DLC Jl 8,15 1829

Norwich TRIBUNE. w Ja 12 1852?-
MWA Ap 6 1853

UNCAS monument. (1492/1842)
"Published once in 350 years"
CtNwP Jl 1842
NcD Jl 1842

YANKEE whig. w? F 20? 1844-
Campaign paper
CSmH Mr 20 1844
CtNwC Mr 6 1844
MWA Mr 6 1844

PORTLAND

MIDDLESEX county record. w Jl 2- 1885-95||?
Ct O 17 1885;Ap 8 1887;F 20,Je 12 1891;Ja 29 1892
CtMHi O 29 1886;Je 28 1889
CtW Jl 24 1885;My 21,S 10 1886;Ap 15 1887;Mr 29,Ap 26 1889;Ja 31 1890

PUTNAM

Putnam PATRIOT. w D 5 1872+
pub 1880+
Ct N 9 1883[84]O 29 1886;My 13 1887-O 1889 [Jl-D 1890]Ja 23 1891-[93]O 12 1894-[97-1903]-Jl 14 1905;Ag 28 1908;13+
CtY [1930]+
MWA My 9 1873;Ap 16 1875;Ap 28,O 13 1876;O 3 1884;Ja 13-My,Je 15 1888
NNHi S 10-24,N 12 1886;F 7 1873
NbHi Je 14 1878

WINDHAM county news. w 1875-76||
MWA O 6 1876

WINDHAM county observer. w My 30 1882+
1882-84 as Windham county sunbeam; 1885-97? Windham county standard
Ct My 25 1887;O 30,N 27 1889[90]Ap 15 1891;N 28 1901;Mr 26,Ap 23 1919+
MWA O 3 1883;S 24 1884;S 26 1901

WINDHAM county standard. *See* Windham county observer

WINDHAM county sunbeam. *See* Windham county observer

WINDHAM county transcript. *See under* Danielson

RIDGEFIELD

Ridgefield PRESS. w Ja 13 1875+
pub 1900
Ct Mr 1876-S,D 1881-Je 1888;Ja 30 1891;Ja 29 1892
MWA N 6 1878
NN F 12 1886
OClWHi S 16 1919

ROCKVILLE

Rockville JOURNAL. w F 7 1867+
1867-83 as Tolland county journal
Ct Je 1872-78;N 28-D 5,19 1889;Ja 2,F 27,Mr 6 1890;N 5 1891;Mr 19(supp)1908;N 3 1910;Ap 24 1919+
CtRo 1867-99;1911+
MWA O 6 1876

Rockville LEADER. w,sw F 1879+
Follows Tolland county gleaner. 1879-F 17 1898 as Tolland county leader
pub 1894+
Ct Ja 15 1885;Ja 12,Mr 1 1888;D 19 1889[90]
CtRo 1918+
MWA O 2 1884

Rockville REPUBLICAN. w 1857-
1857-59 as Tolland county republican
CtY Ap 12 1859;Ap 11 1860

TOLLAND county gazette. w Ap 20 1854-
CtHWe Jl 13-Ag 24 1854
P-M My 10 1855

TOLLAND county gleaner. w My 9 1875-Ja 1879||
Followed by Tolland county leader, later Rockville leader
MWA O 6 1876

TOLLAND county herald. w 1864-
OClWHi Ap 6 1865

TOLLAND county journal. *See* Rockville journal

TOLLAND county leader. *See* Rockville leader

TOLLAND county record. w O 23 1861-
Ct N 20 1861

TOLLAND county republican. *See* Rockville republican

ROCKY HILL

AMERICAN enterprise. *See under* Wethersfield

SAUGATUCK

FAIRFIELD county republican. w Mr 24 1830-
CSmH Jl 14 1830

SEYMOUR

Seymour NEWS. w Mr 19 1902-
Ct [1902]

Seymour RECORD. w My 1 1871+
Ct 1871+
CtHWe Je 1 1872[73]
CtSe 1871+
CtSp [1912]
CtY 1871-[72-75]-[77]-[79]-[82-83]-[89]-[99]-[1918]-[20-22]-[25-28]+
KHi Ag 1896-S 11 1924]
OClWHi N 12 1896

SHELTON

Shelton weekly ADVANCE. w My 6 1893-
Ct Jl 15 1893

Daily ADVERTISER. *See under* Derby

Shelton BOOSTER. *See* Shelton times

Shelton TIMES. D 1908-D 26 1914||
1908-N 12 1910 as Shelton booster
CtShe O 1909-14

Evening TRANSCRIPT. *See under* Derby

SOUTH MANCHESTER

Manchester daily NEWS. w,d 1893-1924||
1893-My 19 1923 as South Manchester news(w)
Ct [1901]-[24]

SOUTH NORWALK

CONNECTICUT republican. w O 9 1880-89||
Ct N 1880-Ag 1889

NORWALKI hirlap. (Norwalk herald). w
In Hungarian
PPiHi [Mr 1928-Jl 10 1931]

South Norwalk SENTINEL. w d N 17 1870+
w 1870-86
Ct Mr 1872-85;D 1887-F 1893;My 7 1920
CtY O 5 1878
MWA N 17 1870;N 7 1872;Mr 8 1873;N 4 1875; Ag 26 1876

SOUTH WINDSOR

Weekly GAZETTE. *See under* East Hartford

SOUTHINGTON

CHESHIRE courier. w Je 8 1877-
CtSo S 21 1877

Weekly ECHO. w Ja 6 1893-
CtSo Ja 6 1893

Southington MIRROR. w O 30 1863-Je 9 1865||
CtSo complete

Southington NEWS. w O 2 1873+
1873-Ag 25 1876 as Southington reporter; S 1 1876-1911 Southington weekly phoenix
Ct O 2-9 1885;Je 17 1887;D 7 1888;Mr 29 1889; Ap 18 1890;Ja 30 1891[1919];Mr 27 1936+
CtSo N 6 1873;D 24 1875;79-[84-86]-92;D 16 1897;Mr 2,16 1899;N 24 1933;N 9 1934
MWA O 6 1876
WHi 1898-Ag 10 1899

Southington weekly PHOENIX. *See* Southington news

Southington PRESS. w Ap 4 1859-
CtSo Ap 4 1859

Southington REPORTER. *See* Southington news

SOUTHPORT

ADVERTISER. w Ap 24 1884-My 2 1890||
1884-S 1886 as Fairfield advertiser
Ct complete
CtSp complete

Southport CHRONICLE. m,bm,w N 1867-77||?
m 1867-N 1868;bm D 1868-N 1869
Ct 1872-Je 1877
CtSp 1867-[72-75]Jl 5 1876;My 2 1877

CHRONICLE. w,sw Ja 2 1891-Mr 31 1904||
w 1891-Ja 1892
Ct O 22 1891-Je 1903
CtSp complete

FAIRFIELD advertiser. *See* Advertiser

FAIRFIELD county times. *See* Southport times

Southport TIMES. w N 20 1878-81||
1878-Mr? 1879 as Fairfield county times
Ct Mr 27,Jl 31 1879-81
CtSp My 29 1879[80]Ap 8,Jl 29 1881

STAFFORD SPRINGS

Stafford NEWS letter. w 1859-
MWA Ja 21 1865
RP F 8 1862

PRESS. w Ap 1 1858+
1858-63 as Tolland county press
pub 1858+
Ct My 4 1871;O 25 1877;Jl 18 1878;O 2 1879; D 26 1889;Ja 16,F 20 1890;Je 22,Jl 13 1893; Je 21,O 11 1894;D 3 1896;N 10 1898;D 4 1902;Ap 7-14 1904;Mr 27 1907;Ap 24 1919+
MWA Ag 24,O 12 1876;Je 21 1877

TOLLAND county press. *See* Press

STAMFORD

Stamford ADVOCATE. w 1829+
1829-F 1830 as Stamford intelligencer; F 16 1830-F 1838 Stamford sentinel; Mr 1838-F 1840 Democratic sentinel; Mr 1840-Mr 6 1842 Farmer's advocate; Mr 23-Ap 1842 Farmer's and mechanic's advocate

CONNECTICUT (*Continued*)

STAMFORD—*Continued*

Stamford ADVOCATE. w 1829+—*Continued*
pub Ag 8,D 8 1829;D 17 1830;O 4 1831;Ap 7,D 8 1834;Mr 21 1836;Mr 19 1838;Ja 28,F 4-11 1840;Jl 1,22,D 29 1840[49-59]+
CSmH Jl 13 1830
Ct Mr 13 1832;Jl 14-28 1834;Mr 16 1835;Ag 8 1836;Mr 1926+
CtHWe Je 30 1834
CtSta [Je 22 1830-31]34[35]-[38-43]-46[60]62-67;83-87;90+
CtY Ag 9 1872
DLC Je 23 1834;S 23 1840
MWA Je 9 1876
NN Mr 1830-O 4 1831
NNHi Jl 3 1863;F 7 1873
P-M Ap 22 1845;My 23 1854

Stamford ADVOCATE. d 1892+
Thursday ed used as weekly
pub 1892+
Ct Mr 1926+
CtSta 1892+

DEMOCRATIC sentinel. *See* Stamford advocate

FARMER'S advocate. *See* Stamford advocate

FARMER'S and mechanic's advocate. *See* Stamford advocate

Stamford HERALD. w 1875-93||?
Ct Ag 1876-F 1893
CtSta 1883-86;89-90

Stamford INTELLIGENCER. *See* Stamford advocate

Stamford NEWS. w Ja 16 1886-92||
Title varies: Stamford Saturday news; Stamford weekly news
Ct 1886-Jl 1892
CtSta O 8 1887-F 22 1890

Stamford PRESS. w 1928-F 15 1929||
CtSta complete

Daily REPUBLICAN. d My 15 1899-1900||
Ct 1899-F 1900
CtSta [My 29 1899-Ap 11 1900]

Stamford SENTINEL. d 1923-25||
CtSta Mr 1923-Ap 1925

Stamford SENTINEL. w *See* Stamford advocate

Stamford TELEGRAM. d 1897-1901||
Ct [Mr-N 1901]
CtSta Ag 19 1897-N 16 1901

STONINGTON

ADVERTISER. w 1853-
MWA S 23 1854

ADVOCATE. w
RW Ap 8 1854

LUX mundi. w
RW O 29 1849

Stonington MIRROR. w,sw 1869+
sw 1896?-1910?
Ct Je 27 1872-Mr 1887;Mr 27 1936+
CtNw Ja 6 1911
CtY Ag 27,N 12,16 1897
MWA S 3 1870;O 12 1876;O 11 1884;S 9 1910
RW D 18 1869;F-N 19 1870;O 9 1879

Stonington PHENIX. w Ag 11 1830-
CSmH S 1 1830
RW Ja 5,19,Ag 24 1831

Stonington SPECTATOR. w
CtY Jl 30 1834

Stonington TELEGRAPH. w Jl 28 1824-
1824-My? 1827 as Yankee
Ct Mr 22 1826
CtHWe Jl 12 1826
DLC O 13 1824;D 21 1825;Mr 18 1829
MWA F 16-23,Mr 16-Ap,Je 8,22 1825;S 12 1827;O 15 1828
NN N 24 1824;F 16 1825
RW [1824-Jl 1825]Mr 8,S 20 1826;F 21,Ap 25,My 9-30 1827

YANKEE. *See* Stonington telegraph

STRATFORD

Stratford TIMES. w 1912?-29||?
CtDe N 11 1921

THOMASTON

Thomaston EXPRESS. w 1880+
pub 1880-1900;05+
Ct Ja 30 1891;1922+

THOMPSON

WINDHAM county gazette. w Ag 14 1835-
CtT Ja 21 1836
MWA O 9 1835

THOMPSONVILLE

Thompsonville PRESS. w 1880+
Ct Mr 14 1901+

TOLLAND

NATIONAL examiner. w Mr 16 1830-
CSmH Ag 24 1830

PEOPLE'S advocate. w Ap 3 1830-
CSmH Jl 17 1830
Ct My 15 1830;Ap 13 1831
DLC My 15 1830
MWA Je 26 1830;Ag 29 1832
NNHi Ag 1830-N 21 1832

TORRINGTON

To 1887 as Wolcottville

Evening NEWS. d Ap 17 1916-Ap 1 1918||
1916-Mr 29 1918 as Torrington news
CtTo complete

Torrington weekly REGISTER. w Ag 8 1874-D 1926||
1874-Ag 9 1881 as Wolcottville register
pub complete
Ct Mr 1878-Ag 1880;Ja 19 1884;Ja 10 1886
CtW D 9 1882

Torrington REGISTER. d S 30 1889+
Title varies: Torrington daily register; Evening register
S 18 1935 is Connecticut tercentenary ed
pub 1889+
Ct O 27 1899;1901+
CtTo 1898+
MWA S 18 1935

Torrington TELEGRAM. w S 10 1891-
CtTo S 10 1891

WOLCOTTVILLE register. *See* Torrington weekly register

WALLINGFORD

Wallingford TIMES. d,tw
d D 1891-Ja 1892
Ct Ja 29,Je 4,D 31 1891;Ja 9,18 1892;S 19,N 23,D 16 1893;Ja 7,F 18 1897

Wallingford TIMES. w 1886-97||?
1886-87 as Wallingford witness
CtWa [Au 20 1886-Je 3 1887]

Wallingford WITNESS. *See* Wallingford times

WASHINGTON

POLITICAL register. w
Ct Mr 25, and supp 1833

WATERBURY

ADVOCATE of the union. w Ag 19 1856-
CtHWe S 2, 16,N 12 1856

Waterbury AMERICAN. w,sw D 7 1844+
w 1844-99
Ct Mr 5 1852;O 27,D 22 1854[55]Mr 28,My 30 1856;Jl 25 1862;Ap 17 1863
CtDe D 3 1852;F 25 1853
CtHWe N 8,29,D 13 1845;Jl 4 1846;Jl 11 1851;F 17 1854;Je 9 1856
CtSp Ap 9 1858
CtTo Ap 28 1854;Ja 8 1858;F 7 1879
CtWb 1844-65;My 23 1866+
CtY 1852-59
MWA Ag 6 1852;My 27 1853
NNHi Je 19 1863;F 14 1873
OClWHi Ap 14 1865

Waterbury AMERICAN. d My 2 1866+
Title varies: Waterbury daily American
Ct 1882-87;97;99-1915;19+
CtN N 30 1909;My 30 1914;N 24 1915
CtTo F 28 1879;D 8,15 1882
CtY My 22 1866
MWA My 4 1867;O 11 1876
NN Ag 12 1881;F 3 1902
OClWHi Je 8 1866

Waterbury BEOBACHTER. w 1899-1917||
In German
Ct Je 1909-[13]-[17]

Waterbury DEMOCRAT. d 1887+
Ct 1913+
CtWb D 6 1887-92;Jl 1893-1900;26+

Weekly EXAMINER. w 1881-1909||
1881-1900? pub in Hartford
Ct Mr-Ag 1901
CtW Je 29 1889
WHi Jl 4 1885

Waterbury HERALD. (Sunday) F 19 1888-Ja 3 1926||
Followed by Bridgeport-Waterbury herald, later Sunday herald (Bridgeport)
Ct 1888-Mr 1891;1901-26

Waterbury INDEX. w Je 18 1869-79||
1869-Ag 2 1878 as Valley index
Ct F 23 1872-My 14 1879
CtY Je 30 1869

Waterbury JOURNAL. w 1857-
CtY Jl 14 1857
MWA Ja 26 1858

Waterbury MONITOR. w Ap 3 1880-
CtTo Ap 3 1880

NAUGATUCK VALLEY democrat. w O 2 1852-
CtY O 16 1852;Ap 19-26,Mr 24,Ag 23,S 6 1853
MWA O 23,N 6 1852

Il PROGRESSO del New England. w 1905+
In Italian
IU [N 24 1917-Ag 28 1920]

Waterbury REPUBLICAN. d 1884+
Ct 1906+
CtW N 14 1892
CtWb 1884-1900;18+

VALLEY index. *See* Waterbury index

WATERTOWN

FREEMAN'S advocate. w
NhD Ag 13,27 1824

Watertown NEWS. m,w 1914-S 27 1929||
m 1914-19
Ct Jl 1923-29
CtWt 1913-Mr 1 1919

WEST HARTFORD

West Hartford NEWS. w F 27 1931-32||
Ct F 27 1931-Ja 1932

POST. w F 25 1932-
Ct My 27-Jl 8 1932

WEST HAVEN

West Haven ADVERTISER. *See* Evening herald

West Haven BUDGET. w Je 27 1885-94||
Ct 1891-S 1894
CtY Jl 25-Ag 1,S 5,N 28 1885;Mr 4 1891

Evening HERALD. w 1905-16||
1905-14 as West Haven advertiser
CtY Je 17,Jl 8,22 1915-My 11 1916

West Haven JOURNAL. sm 1873-
CtY O 1 1873-S 15,O 1 1874-S 1 1875

Weekly TIMES. w Ja 6 1894-1903||?
Ct Ja 6 1894

TOWN crier. w 1930+
CtY N 27 1930

WEST KILLINGLY

Weekly ARENA. w F 19? 1844-
1844-47? as New England arena
CtT Ap 22,S 23 1846;Ap 28,Jl 14,Ag 4 1847
DLC Ja 2 1849
MWA O 29 1845
P-M N 19 1845

NEW ENGLAND arena. *See* Weekly arena

TRUE democrat. w D 7 1850-
MWA D 7 1850

VOICE of freedom. Mr 29 1849-
NNHi Mr 29 1849

WINDHAM county telegraph. *See* Windham county transcript (Danielson)

WEST MERIDEN. *See* MERIDEN

WEST WINSTED

Winsted ADVERTISER. w F 24 1853-
CtHWe F 24 1853

WESTPORT

HOUR. *See* Norwalk hour (Norwalk)

NORWALK hour. *See under* Norwalk

Westport STANDARD. sw,tw,w Mr 15 1923-25||?
CtWp 1923-D 18 1925

WESTPORTER-HERALD. w,sw 1876+
1876-98 as Westporter
w 1876-Mr 13 1928
Ct 1876-98;Mr 12-Ap 12 1901;My 12 1936+
CtSp Ja-Je 1903
CtWp My 1908-[10]S 17 1915[16]-[18]+
OClWHi N 24 1894

WETHERSFIELD

AMERICAN enterprise. w 1888-95||?
Also dated at Rocky Hill
Ct Ap 19 1890
CtW Je 22 1889

Wethersfield weekly FARMER. w D 11 1886-92||?
D 11 1886 as Wethersfield farmer
Ct 1886-D 3 1887
CtHi 1886-87
CtSp 1886-D 3 1887
MHi My 17,31-Je 14 1888
MWA [Mr-O 1887]
NN S 10 1891
NNHi F 12-26 1887

WILLIMANTIC

Willimantic weekly CHRONICLE. w Ja 4 1877-D 26 1894||
1877-N 25 1879 as Willimantic weekly enterprise
pub complete
MWA Ja 24-31,O 17 1883;Mr 5 1884

Willimantic daily CHRONICLE. d D 29 1891+
pub 1891+
Ct D 3,13,18 1907;My 20-21 1908;Jl 22 1909;D 6 1918;S 24 1921+

Willimantic weekly ENTERPRISE. *See* Willimantic weekly chronicle

Willimantic JOURNAL. w 1848-1910||
Ct 1861-63;Ja 5-12,Ag 10 1865[O-N 1866]72-1910
CtHWe Ja 20 1862;S 18 1863
CtSp 1892[93]
DLC O 10 1862;O 1865-D 13 1866
MWA My 27 1859;Ag 15 1862;F 8 1866;O 13 1876;S 19 1884
NN O 17,N 7 1862

PUBLIC medium. w 1848-
CtHWe D 8 1855

WILLINGTON

HOME messenger. w 1879-
CtHWe S 19 1882

WINDSOR

Windsor HERALD. m Ja 1 1886-
CtHWe Ja-Mr,My 1886

Windsor HERALD. w 1926+
CtWr 1934+

CONNECTICUT (*Continued*)

WINDSOR LOCKS

Windsor Locks JOURNAL. w Ap 30 1880+
pub 1888+
Ct Ap 30 1880-[81-82]D 1921+

WINSTED

Winsted evening CITIZEN. d 1889+
Ct 1901+
CtWn 1889+

Winsted HERALD. w My 14 1853+
1853-Ap 30 1858 as Mountain county herald
Ct D 16 1864;My 26 1865;S 18 1868;F 12 1875; S 27 1889;Mr 13 1901+
CtHWe O 11 1878
CtHi My 1858-Ja 2 1863
CtTo Je 18 1853;Ag 12 1854;Jl 28-Ag 4,25 1865;N 23 1866
CtW S 4 1855
CtWn 1853+
CtWnG My 1861-My 1 1901
DLC Mr 4(extra)1861
MWA Mr 27 1863;Mr 24,D 29 1865;F 9 1866; Ap 5,My 24,Je 14,Ag 16 1867;Ja 17,F 7,Mr 13 1868;Je 30 1876
N Ag 8 1862;Mr 4 1864
NN Mr 3 1855
NNHi Ja 5 1873;O 29 1880
OClWHi Mr 13 1863;Mr 18,Jl 5 1864;F 24 1865;N 8 1867;Je 25 1875
P-M Jl 8 1854
WHi My 21 1853-D 7 1866

LITCHFIELD county leader. w 1888+
Ct 1901-02;1904+

MOUNTAIN county herald. *See* Winsted herald

Winsted NEWS. w Jl 1875-79||?
Ct My 27 1876
MWA D 7 1876

WOLCOTTVILLE. *See* TORRINGTON

WOODBURY

Woodbury REPORTER. w 1877+
pub 1877+
Ct Ag 1878-N 1882;Je 1883-Ja 1884;Ja 28 1891;F 27 1892;F 15-22,Mr 8 1893;1912+

DELAWARE

CHESTER

Weekly VISITOR; or, Delaware county gazette. w Mr 21 1828-
NjHi Je 6 1828;F 6,Mr 6-13,O 30 1829

CLAYMONT

NEW CASTLE county herald. w Ag 27-D 4 1931||
DeWI Ag-O 22,N 20,D 1931

CLAYTON

Clayton HERALD. w My 1867-69||
DeHi Ap 25 1868[69]
DeWI Jl 13 1868

DOVER

*DELAWARE intelligencer. w 1820-22||?
1820-Mr? 1821 as National recorder
MWA F 8-15,Mr 22,Ap 12,My 3,Jl 19 1821

DELAWARE republican. w O 1907+
pub 1907+
DeWI My 1923+

DELAWARE sentinel. *See* Dollar sentinel

DELAWARE state news. w 1901+
DeWI N 20 1919;My 1923+

DELAWARE state reporter. w,sw Mr 1 1853-59||?
sw 1853-N 12 1856
DLC Je 17 1853;54-[56-Je 12 1857]-[Ja-O 14 1859]
DeU N 21 1854;N 11 1856
MWA 1853-Je 1857

DELAWAREAN. w,sw My 7 1859-Mr 25 1927||
sw 1898-Ag 1900
DLC Mr 24-My 5,Je 1860-My,Je 15,Jl 20,Ag 3 1861;D 19 1863-Ja 2 1864;Ja 12 1878-Je 1880
DeHi Ap 21 1860;N 4,D 9 1865;O 31 1874;My 18 1895
DeU My 21 1859-60;My 17 1862[64-65]-Ap 24 1886;87[88-90]-[92-1905]Ap 18 1914[16-19]-[21-26]
DeWI Ag 11 1860;Ja 17 1863;O 22 1881;O 14, 28 1882
NNHi Ja 4 1872

DOLLAR sentinel. w 1855-56||?
1855? as Delaware sentinel
DLC D 19 1856
DeWI My 4 1855

INDEX. w Jl 21 1887+
pub 1887+

NATIONAL recorder. *See* Delaware intelligencer

POLITICAL primer; or, a horn book for the Jacksonites. sw Ap 12-S 29 1828||
Campaign paper
DLC complete
DeWI complete

STATE sentinel. w My 15 1874+
DeHi Ja 29 1876
DeWI Ap 27 1889;F 24 1894;Jl 26 1933;Ja 17 1934+

GEORGETOWN

AMERICAN republican. O 1840-My 1841||
United with Democratic free press and farmers', manufacturers' and mechanics' advocate (Wilmington) to form Delaware, republican and farmers' manufacturers' and mechanics' advocate, later Delaware republican (Wilmington)
DLC N 12 1840

DELAWARE democrat. w Ja 7 1882-1905||?
United with Sussex journal to form Sussex journal and Delaware democrat, later Sussex journal
DeHi S 23 1882;Mr 23,My 18 1895
DeWI Jl 1 1882

DELAWARE inquirer. w 1878-82||
Merged with Delaware democrat
DeWI N 27 1880

MESSENGER. w F 1858-
DLC F 18-Mr 4 1863
DeU D 30 1858[59-63]Mr 16 1864

NATIONAL republican and peninsula advertiser. w 1831-
DLC O 12 1832

SUSSEX countian. w 1888+
1888-S 1933 as Sussex republican
pub 1929+
DeWI N 12 1932+

SUSSEX journal. w Ag 9 1867-1931||?
1906?-16? as Sussex journal and Delaware democrat
DeWI F 20,Mr 6,Jl 31 1874

SUSSEX luminary and peninsula advertiser. w
MWA S 27 1833

SUSSEX news. w
DeWI Je 8 1853

SUSSEX republican. *See* Sussex countian

UNION. w S 11 1863-66||?
DLC Mr 9-D 22 1865
DeHi [1863]Ja 1 1864
DeU [1863-64]
MWA D 4 1863;Je 3 1864;F 23 1866
MiU-C O 9 1863

GRUBBS

BRANDYWINE HUNDRED news. m Ap,Je 1928||
DeWI complete

LAUREL

STATE register. w 1885+
1885-1904 as Sussex countian
pub 1920+
DeWI N 3 1894

SUSSEX countian. *See* State register

LEWES

BREAKWATER light. w Ag 12 1871-90||?
Followed by Delaware pilot
DLC F 3 1877
DeWI [1875-79]

DELAWARE pilot. w 1891-1920||?
Follows Breakwater light
DeHi Ag 3 1895

LINCOLN

Lincoln HERALD. w O 18? 1865-
MWA N 29 1865;Je 13 1866
WHi D 15 1856

MIDDLETOWN

Middletown TRANSCRIPT. w Ja 4 1868+
pub 1868+
DeHi [1871]
DeWI F 17-24 1894;S 16 1899;N 24 1932+

MILFORD

Milford ARGUS. *See* Our mutual friend

Milford BEACON. *See* Diamond state and Milford beacon

Milford CHRONICLE. w O 4 1878+
pub 1920+
DeWI Je 22 1883;Ja 30 1914;O 28 1932+
MWA S 3 1886

DIAMOND state and Milford beacon. w S 30 1848-59||
1848-54? as Milford beacon
DeHi Jl 20 1855
DeWI Ja 17 1851;D 5 1855
PDoHi Ap 29 1852

OUR mutual friend. w F 1867-71||
Replaces Peninsular news and advertiser.
1867-68 as Milford argus
DeWI Mr 23 1867;Ap 24 1869;Mr 12 1870

PENINSULAR news and advertiser. w 1857-1904||
Merged with Milford chronicle
Suspended from 1864?-72
DLC Ag 1861-F 13 1863
DeWI S 2 1859;N 21 1873
MWA Ja 29 1864
See also Our mutual friend

NEW CASTLE

New-Castle GAZETTE. w 1835-37||?
DLC Jl 20 1835

NEWARK

DELAWARE ledger. w F 11 1876-D 21 1934||?
F-M-? 1876 as Saturday visitor; Ap?-D? 1876 Record; Ja?-Jl? 1877 Journal; Ag? 1877-81 Newark ledger
DeWI My 1923-D 21 1934

JOURNAL. *See* Delaware ledger

Newark LEDGER. *See* Delaware ledger

Newark POST. w Ja 26 1910+
pub 1910+
DeWI My 1923+

RECORD. *See* Delaware ledger

Saturday VISITOR. *See* Delaware ledger

ODESSA

Odessa HERALD. *See* Odessa leader

Odessa LEADER. w 1888-94||?
1888-91? as Odessa herald
DeWI N 3 1888;Mr 2 1889;My 2 1891;S 21 1892

REHOBOTH BEACH

DELAWARE COAST news. w Ap 1 1928+
pub 1928+
DeWI Je 1928+

SEAFORD

Seaford ENTERPRISE. *See* Seaford item

Seaford ITEM. w 1877-85||?
1877-84 as Seaford enterprise (1878-81 Sussex county index)
DeWI [1879]Ja 3 1880

LEADER. w Je 13 1930+
pub Ap 20 1934+

NEWS. w 1891+
pub 1891+

SUSSEX county index. *See* Seaford item

SMYRNA

DELAWARE herald. *See* Herald and advocate

HERALD and advocate. w 1847?-Je 1854||
Follows Smyrna telegraph. Title varies: Delaware herald; Delaware herald and peninsular advocate. Followed by Smyrna times
DeHi My 28 1851
DeST Mr 22-Je 1854
PPL N 28 1850

Smyrna TELEGRAPH. w 1839-46||?
Followed by Delaware herald and peninsular advocate, later Herald and advocate

Smyrna TIMES. w Jl 5 1854+
Follows Herald and advocate
pub 1854+
DLC Ja 14-21,My 26,Je 9,23-30,S 8,O 13,D 8,22 1864;Mr 2-16,Ag,S 13-20,O-N 8,22,D 1865;N 8 1871[72]Je 11,Jl 16,O 17-24 1873
DeHi My 23 1861;Ag 28 1852;Mr 19 1863;Ap 3 1867[69]Ap 27 1887;Jl 6 1904
DeWI Jl 6 1904

WILMINGTON

ADVANCE. w 1899-1901||?
Negro
DeWI S 22 1900

Wilmington ADVERTISER. w Mr 18 1870-Mr 9 1880||
DeHi [1879-80]
DeWI N 29-D 6,27 1879;Ja 17 1880

Wilmington ADVERTISER. w O 31 1932-Je 9 1933||
DeWI complete

AMERICAN watchman. *See* Delaware patriot and American watchman

Wilmington ARGUS. w 1877-80||?
DeHi Ja 14 1880

BLUE hen's chicken. w Ag 22 1845-54||
Merged with Statesman
DeHi [1848-49]
DeWI Ag 20 1847-Ag 11 1848[52-53]
OClWHi D 13 1850
PCHi Ag 20 1847
PPM [Ag 18 1848-Ag 10 1849]
PWcHi Je 18 1847

BLUE hen's chicken. w 1862-63 *See* Commonwealth

DELAWARE (*Continued*)

WILMINGTON—*Continued*

BLUE hen's chicken and commonwealth. sw
MH My 7,14-17 1862;Jl 22 1863

BRANDYWINE free press. w Ag 28 1934+
DeWI 1934+

BRANDYWINE news. w Jl 19 1931+
DeWI 1931+

Wilmington daily COMMERCIAL. d O 1 1866-Mr 31 1877||
United with Every evening to form Every evening and commercial, later Every evening
DLC Ag 19 1867-77
DeHi 1867-71
DeWI complete
DeWN 1866-68;70-73
MBAt [1866]-71;73-76
MWA Mr 5-6 1868;Je 25-D 1875;Je 9 1876
—w ed *See* Delaware tribune

COMMONWEALTH. w 1855-66||?
1855-Ap? 1858 as Delaware democrat; 1862-Ag? 1863 Blue hen's chicken
DeHi [1857]Ag 14 1858;Mr 12 1859;My 21,O 1 1862;S 30 1863
DeWI Ap 6 1865
MH S 9 1863
—sw ed *See* Blue hen's chicken and commonwealth

CRITIQUE. w F 1871-
DeHi [1872]

DELAWARE advertiser and farmer's journal. w 1827-31||?
1827-S 11 1828 as Delaware weekly advertiser and farmer's journal. Merged with Delaware gazette and American watchman, later Delaware gazette and state journal
DLC Ja 31-F 14,Mr 20-My 8,22-Jl 10,24-31, Ag 14-N 20,D 4-19 1828;Jl 30,Ag 13,O 29,D 3 1829;Ja 6-14 1830;Ja 20 1831
DeHi Mr 12,Jl 30 1829;O 20 1831
DeWI My 8 1829
MWA D 11 1828

DELAWARE blue. w 1840||
DeHi S 19 1840

DELAWARE blue; or, whig looking-glass. sw 1840||?
DeHi Ag 12-20 1840

DELAWARE democrat. *See* Commonwealth

DELAWARE free press. w Ja 2 1830-
DeHi 1830-31;O 4 1856
DeWI F-D 1830;Ap 21 1832;O 4 1856
MWA Ja 21 1832-Je 22 1833
NNHi 1830-31
PSF D 29 1832[33]

*DELAWARE gazette and state journal. w,sw Ap 19 1814-1902||
1814-Je 1884? as Delaware gazette (N 10 1814-F 19 1820 Delaware gazette and peninsular advertiser; D 12 1828-37 Delaware gazette and American watchman)
sw 1814-Je 8 1841;S 1843-Mr 1872
CSmH Je 22 1830
Ct [1826-36]
DLC F 26 1821-24;F 1825-[26]D 12,28 1828; Ja 13 1829-[31]-Ag 1843[44]Ja 14 1845-N 1855;56-Mr 5 1861;Ja-N 15 1867
DeHi My 20,Je 31 1831;Mr 6,Jl 13,D 14 1832; F 7 1873[80-82]
DeU O 10 1862
DeWI 1821-F 1824;Mr 1825-F 11 1831;Jl 25 1834;Ja 1 1885
DeWN Ag 6 1822-Mr 17 1837;D 1829-48;54-59; 61;63-68;F 1869-72;74-79;Jl 10 1884-1902
MHi Ja 4 1822;F 13 1824
MWA Mr 6,S 7,21,D 11 1821;Mr 15,O 4 1822; Ja 17,28,Ap 8,My 6,13,Je 20,Jl 15,Ag 8 1823; F 20,O 8 1824;Mr 6,Je 30,Jl 7-14,21-24,31-Ag 14,S 11,29-O 5,30-N 3,24,D 4,22 1829-Ja 8, 15,26-29,Ag 31,D 7 1830;Ja 7 1831;Mr 6 1832; Ja 10,20,D 1 1840;Mr 9 1849;My 14 1852
MiU-C [1823-24]
MoS My-S 1861
NNHi [Mr-Ap]-[Jl]1822-Ap 15 1823;F 21 1873
PP Ag 20-24 1847;N 2 1849;Mr 8 1850;Ap 25 1856
T N 20,D 7 1821;S 10-17 1834
TxU Jl 7,Ag 4 1854
—d ed *See* Every evening

DELAWARE inquirer. w Ap 30 1859-60||?
DeWN My 1859-Ap 1860

Daily DELAWARE inquirer. d 1860-65||?
DeU My 6 1861

DELAWARE intelligencer. w Ap 5 1821-
DeHi Ap 26 1821

DELAWARE journal. *See* Delaware state journal

DELAWARE morning news weekly. w 1882-1902||?
pub 1884-93
—d ed *See* Wilmington morning news

*DELAWARE patriot and American watchman. sw Ag 2 1809-D 5 1828||
1809-13 as American watchman and Delaware republican; 1814-Mr 12 1822 American watchman; Mr 15 1822-Ja 15 1828 American watchman and Delaware advertiser. United with Delaware gazette to form Delaware gazette and American watchman, later Delaware gazette and state journal
Ct Je 1 1827[28]
DLC 1821-28
DeHi [1821]-[23]-28
MBAt Ap 5 1822
MWA [1822]O 10 1823[24]-[27]Ja 8,F 1,12,22, Mr 18,Jl 29,Ag 12 1828
NcD Ja 6 1828
PDoHi Ap 20 1827
PHi 1821
REdH Ag 21 1827
WHi Ap 22 1825;Ag 28-31 1827

DELAWARE post. O 20,N 3 1933||
DeWI complete

DELAWARE republican. tw,sw My 1841-Je 1874||?
Formed by the union of Democratic free press and farmers, manufacturers, and mechanics advocate and American republican (Georgetown) 1841? as Delaware republican and farmers, manufacturers and mechanics advocate (tw)
DLC [My-Ag 1841]My 30 1844;Ja 26 1846[49-50]-[56]Ja 12 1857-My 2,16,23,Je 3,Jl 15 1861
DeHi S 16 1842;Ag 28 1843;Ap 30 1847;N 10 1848;N 1 1849;Jl 18 1850;My 17 1852;D 13 1855[56-72]
DeU N 25 1842;O 18,N 18 1852;Mr 24 1853
DeWI O 8 1841;F 24 1843;58;60-Je 1874
MWA Ag 24 1876

DELAWARE weekly republican. w 1841?-1906||?
DeU S 1 1864
DeWI Je 19 1862
MWA Ag 24 1876

DELAWARE sentinel and farmers' and mechanics' advocate. *See* Democratic free press and farmers', manufacturers' and mechanics' advocate

DELAWARE state journal. w,sw,d Ap 24 1827-Je 1884||?
1827-31 as Delaware journal; 1832-N 1833 Delaware state journal, advertiser and star; 1855-70? Weekly Delaware state journal and statesman; 1871?-72? State journal and statesman. United with Delaware gazette to form Delaware gazette and state journal
sw 1827-Mr 1872;d Ap 1872
DLC Ap 27 1827-[31;33]Ja 14 1834-[Ja-My 5 1843]Mr 12 1844;F 1847-52;Je 4,Jl 16 1861-65
DeHi Ap 22 1828-Ap 17 1829;Ap 19 1831-[32] My 5 1835[37;48]49;My 6,Jl 11 1856;N 5 1858; N 1 1861;Mr 24 1868[69]Ap 10,O 18 1870[71-72]
DeU Jl 5 1832
DeWI S 5 1828;O 31,D 12 1834;N 3 1837[38-39] Jl 31,D 18 1840;Ja 8 1841;My 11-14 1847; Jl 30 1860;Ja 9 1863;Ap 7,21 1865;N 28 1871
DeWN D 1838-47;50-53;55-[57]-59;62-67[72]-[74]-[80-81]-84
MWA Je 5,12,S 4,28-N 6 1827[28-O 2 1829]Ja 5-15,D 17-21 1830;Ja 7,18,21,Jl 6 1831;D 1 1840;Je 25 1850;F 26 1867
MiU-C N 6,27 1827
N F 28 1837
NcD Jl 21 1829;Ja 29 1830
NjR S 12 1838
OClWHi My 28 1841
WHi Je 24,O 3 1828
—d ed *See* Every evening

*DELAWARE straight-out truth-teller. 1872||?
DeHi O ? 1872

DELAWARE tribune. w 1866-79||?
DeHi [1874-76]
DeWN 1867-D 3 1869;70
—d ed *See* Wilmington daily commercial

DELMARVIA leader. *See* Delmarvia monthly review

DELMARVIA monthly review. w,m 1880+
1880-Ap 19 1924 as Delmarvia leader (w)
In English and German
DeWI My 1923+

DELMARVIA star. *See* Sunday morning star

DEMOCRATIC free press and farmers', manufacturers' and mechanics' advocate. tw 1839-My 1 1841||
1839-40 as Delaware sentinel and farmers' and mechanics' advocate. United with American republican (Georgetown) to form Delaware republican and farmers', manufacturers' and mechanics' advocate, later Delaware republican (Wilmington)
DLC D 1 1840;Ja 7,Ap 3-6,10 1841

DEMOCRATIC free press and farmers', manufacturers' and mechanics' advocate. w 1840?-My 1 1841||?
DLC My 1 1841

Il DEMOCRATICO. w O 29-N 5 1932||
In Italian
DeWI complete

Daily ENTERPRISE. d Ap 3-23? 1858||
DeHi Ap 3 1858
DeWI Ap 23 1858

EVERY EVENING. d S 4 1871-D 31 1932||
Ap 2 1877-Mr 1878 as Every evening and commercial; Ap 1878-Jl 14 1928 Every evening (Wilmington daily commercial) United with Evening journal, to form Evening journal every evening, later Journal-every evening
DLC Ap 2 1877-1932
DeHi 1871-73;S 1874-86;88-1915;29-32
DeU Jl 1883-1900;02[04-10]12;15-20
DeWI S 4 1871;N 29 1873;F 23 1875[76]Ap 1877-1932
DeWN complete
LU S 1 1917
MB [1877]Ja 11,F 15,Je 3,14,21 1878;Ap 1,My 20,D 6 1879
MiU 1878-81
NN 1890-92
—w ed *See* Delaware tribune; Delaware state journal; Delaware gazette and state journal

Il FUOCO. bw 1928+
In Italian
DeWI Je 14 1930+

Daily GAZETTE. d Ap 1 1872-D 10 1883||
1872-Ag 20 1874 as Wilmington daily gazette. Merged with Every evening (Wilmington daily commercial) later Every evening
DLC Jl 1875-D 7 1883
DeWI [1872-73]75-79;My 8 1880[82-83]
DeWN Ap 13 1872-74;Jl 1875-81

Morning HERALD. d Ag 23 1875-F 23 1880||
Followed by Morning news, later Wilmington morning news
DeHi Ag 24,D 7-8 1875;Jl 1 1876;D 31 1878; Ap 11 1879
DeWI Ag 23,D 7-8 1875[76]Ap 3 1877[78]Ap 11,Je 19 1879
MWA Je 10 1876

INDEPENDENT Delawarian. w?
DeWI N 29 1848

JOURNAL-EVERY EVENING. d 1886+
1886-1932 as Evening journal (N 25 1905-My 24 1906 Evening journal and the daily republican) 1933-Ag 28 1934 Evening journal every evening
pub 1888+
DLC My-Je 16,D 1905-Ag 1918;19-N 9 1931; 32+
DeWI My 21 1888-1902;Mr 26 1904;Jl 1907+
NN 1889-91;Jl 1892-Je 1902
PDoHi S 14,17 1901

JUSTICE. w 1888-1903||?
1888-95 pub in Philadelphia
KHi N 1895-My 1902
MWA Ja 25,Mr 22 1890
WHi My 5 1888;F 3 1889;F 1,Mr 15 1890[F 24 1894-Jl 1895]Ap-N 7 1896[1900-S 3 1902]

Wilmington morning NEWS. d Mr 1 1880+
Follows Morning herald. 1880-Mr 9 1913 as Morning news
pub 1882+
DLC 1898-1927
DeHi 1880-Je,Jl 19 1881
DeWI My 7-8,10 1880;Ja 13 1881[82]Ap 18,My 19 1884;Mr 1885-[1914]+
IC My 1 1889
—w ed *See* Delaware morning news weekly

PATRIOTIC politician. w Ag? 1852-
MWA O 27-N 3 1852

Daily REPUBLICAN. d 1874-N 24? 1905||
D 25 1890-Ap 8 1902 as Wilmington daily republican; Ap 9-O 3 1902 Evening daily republican. United with Evening journal to form Evening journal and the daily republican, later Journal-every evening
DLC O 23 1878-1902
DeHi Jl 27 1874;Jl 31 1875;Ap 3,13,O 8 1877;Je 3,25-26 1878;Jl 2 1881;Mr 17,D 22 1883;Ja 1 1885;Jl 6 1886
DeU Jl 12 1881;Ja 12 1882
DeWI Ap 16 1877;Je 25-26 1878;My 8 1880[81] D 22 1883;Mr 9 1885;S 28 1886;F 22 1888;Jl 1889-Je 1900;01-02

Wilmington SPECTATOR. w 1823-
DLC Ap 1,My 20 1824

Sunday morning STAR. w Mr 6 1881+
Title varies: Delmarvia star
pub 1881+
DLC Je 1885-Ja 8 1893
DeWI 1881-[83]-[85]-[87]-[89-91]+

STATE journal and statesman. *See* Delaware state journal

STATESMAN. w 1854-55||
United with Delaware state journal to form Delaware state journal and statesman, later Delaware state journal

SUN. d,w 1897-1909||?
d 1897-S 1904
DeWI O 25 1897-1901;Jl-D 1902
DeWN 1897-1901

SZTANDAR. *See* Tygodnik polonia

Weekly TIMES. w O 1886-Mr 1887||?
DeHi O 16-23 1886;Mr 19 1887

TYGODNIK polonia. w 1915-27||?
1915-19 as Sztandar
In Polish
DeWI [1925]

WILMINGTONIAN and Delaware advertiser. w 1823-
DLC 1826-S 13 1827
DeHi Jl 1 1824;D 29 1825;Mr 22 1827

WILMINGTONIAN-DEMOCRAT. w Ap 1 1882-90||?
1882-89? as Wilmingtonian
DeHi [1882-88]
DeWI Ja 31-F 7 1885

DISTRICT OF COLUMBIA

ALEXANDRIA

This city formed a part of the District of Columbia from the time of the establishment of the District in 1791 until restored to Virginia in 1846. Papers published in Alexandria, D.C. are listed under Alexandria, Va.

GEORGETOWN

Papers published in Georgetown are listed under Washington

WASHINGTON

Daily ADVERTISER. (Georgetown) d O 15 1835-
DLC O 15 1835

Daily ADVERTISER. d Ag? 1858-
DLC O 28 1858

Daily evening ADVOCATE. d My 14 1860-
DLC My 14,19 1860

Daily AMERICAN. tw,d Ja 12-Jl 24 1847||
Ja-Je 12 1847 as American(tw)
DLC complete

Weekly AMERICAN. w 1854?-
NcD D 29 1855;My 17 1856

Weekly AMERICAN. sw,w Jl 31 1857-Je 12 1858||
1857 as American(sw)
DLC complete
MWA Ag 15 1857

Washington AMERICAN. w Ja 1909?-
Negro
DLC Mr 11,My 27,Ag 12-19,S 9 1911

AMERICAN argus. sw Ja 15? 1830-
DLC Ja 22 1830

AMERICAN auditor. w My 20 1826-
DLC My 20 1826

AMERICAN cotton plant. w Jl 1? 1852-
1852-56 title varies: Cotton plant. Southern advertiser and European price current; Cotton plant and southern advertiser
Also dated in Baltimore
DLC Jl 29 1852
MWA S 2-23 1852;Ja-Ap 21 1853;S 8 1855;56 [Ja-Je 1857]
TxU [Jl 8 1852-Ag 4 1853]

AMERICAN flag. w Ja 1? 1887-
DLC Mr 12,26,Ap 2,16 1887

AMERICAN loyalist. w 1865-66||?
MHi [1865-66]

Daily AMERICAN organ. d N 13 1854-N 14 1856||
DLC complete
DW Ap 14,29 1856
MWA 1854-[56]
MiU-C Mr 1 1855
N D 1 1855
NcD N 13,D 27 1854;My 10,O 11-12,29 1855

Weekly AMERICAN organ. w N 20 1854-My 28 1857||
Ja 1 1857 as American weekly organ
N 22-D 13 1856 used as country ed
DLC Jl 1856-57
MWA F 13,Mr 19,O 13,N 17,D 15 1855;My 10 1856
NcD N 20 1854;F 12,O 27 1855;Mr 15,Ap 5,Je 28,Ag 23 1856;Ap 2 1857
P-M Mr 26 1855

Weekly AMERICAN organ. (city ed) w D 4-11 1856||
Specimen number N 26 1856; undated prospectus
DLC complete

AMERICAN spectator and Washington City chronicle. *See* Washington City chronicle

AMERICAN statesman. d,sw Ag 28 1830-
d during sessions of Congress
Suspended from Ag 28-S 11 1830?
DLC Ag,S 11 1830

AMERICAN statesman. w Ag 28 1830-
MWA Ag 28-O 2,23 1830

Daily AMERICAN telegraph. d Mr 24 1851-N 18 1852||
Mr-D 20 1851 as American telegraph
DLC 1851[52]D 2(extra)1851
DW Ag 18,O 10-11 1851
In S 28 1852
MWA complete
MiU-C Mr 4,Jl 3,O 30 1852
N Ja 12-13 1852
TxU 1851

AMERICAN union. d
In Ap 26 1851

ANDERSON zouave. (Tenleytown) w Mr 8 1862-
OClWHi Mr 8 1862

Täglicher Washingtoner ANZEIGER. d 1871-Mr 29 1873||
United with Columbia to form Washingtoner journal, later Washington journal
In German
DLC Ja 8 1872;73

APPEAL. sw F-Ap 18 1835||
Merged with Sun
DLC Ap 4-15 1835
MWA F 21-Mr 4,14,28,Ap 1835

ARMORY SQUARE hospital gazette. w 1863?-
DLC Ja 27,F 10,Mr 26-Ap 16,30-My 14,28-Je 18,Jl-Ag 20,S-D 10,24 1864-Mr 4,18-Ap 8, 22-29,My 13-Je 10 1865
MBAt D 10 1864
MHi Ag 21 1865
MiG Mr 11 1865

BALANCE. w My 20 1865-
DLC My 27-Je 17 1865

BATTERY. w Jl 6 1848-Ja 25 1849||
Suspended from N 2-16, from N 16 1848-Ja 25 1849
Campaign paper
CSmH prospectus
DLC complete
KyLo complete
MHi [1848-49]
MWA Jl 6,O 26 1848
NNHi Jl-N 2 1848
PPiHi O 19-26 1848

Daily BEE. d Ag 19-S 16 1845||
DLC complete

Washington BEE. w Je 3 1882-Ja 21 1922||
1882-Jl 1884 as Bee
Suspended from Ja 14-28 1893; from F-Ap 1895
Negro
DLC Je 10,24,D 23 1882-[93-96]-[1905]-22
NNHi D 16 1882;Ja 13,27 1883
NcD N 26-D 2,16 1893

Weekly BEE and model advertiser. w My 3 1856-
My-Jl 26 1856 as Washington bee
Suspended from Jl 26-Ag 9 1856
DLC My 10-Je,Jl 12-Ag 9,S 27-O 11,25-N 8, 22-D 6 1856

Evening BULLETIN. tw,d My 1-Je 5 1858||
tw My 1-22 1858
DLC complete
NcD My 15 1858

BUSY-BODY. w S 25? 1830-
DLC N 20 1830

CAMP kettle. ir
MHi [1861]

CAMPAIGN. w My 31 1848-Ap 11 1849||
Suspended from N 1 1848-Ap 11 1849
Campaign paper
DLC complete
ICN complete
ICU complete
InI complete
MB complete
MWA O 20-25 1848
N complete
NN complete
NNHi complete
NcD complete
NcU My-Je 21,Ag 2-9,30,O 13-20 1848
NjCHi Je 21 1848
PCarlHi complete
VHi My-N 1 1848
WHi complete

CAMPAIGN. w Je 12 1852-Ap 9 1853||
Campaign paper
Suspended from O 30 1852-Ap 9 1853
DLC complete
MWA Ag 21 1852
NN complete
PNoHi Je 12-19 1852

CAMPAIGN constitution. w 1860||?
Campaign paper
DLC O 18 1860
TxU O 11 1860
Vt O 4 1860
See also Constitution. 1859-61

Sunday CAPITAL. w Mr 12 1871-Ja 26 1890||
1871?-88? as Capital
DLC 1871-75;Ap 9,Jl 30-Ag 6,D 3-17 1876;F 1877-S 21 1879[80]-Ja 2,16-F 20 1881;Ja 14, My 27 1883;Mr 2,Ag 17 1884;Ja 1 1888;90
ICM Ag 26 1877;Mr 23 1879
KHi [F 9 1873-80]
MB 1871-Jl 1872[73]
MH [Ap 1871-74]-[81-82]
MWA Mr 26 1872;S 28 1873;F 27 1875;F 18-25, Mr 11-18 1877;F 16 1879;Mr 16 1884
N My 28 1871;Mr 4 1873;D 27 1885
NNHi S 3 1871;My 18 1873;O 2,N 6 1881
NbHi Mr 4 1877
NcD Ap 16 1871;Ja 21 1872;My 25,Ap 31,S 14 1873-Ja 11,25-Mr 1,My 3,24 1874;Ja 9,D 3 1876;F 16-Mr 2,16-Ap 6 1879;Ap 4,My 2,Je 6 1880;F 13,Ag 21 1881
NcU My 9,Je 27,D 5 1875;O 15 1876;Jl 3-17,31-Ag 7,21-S 4,18-25 1881;My 7-21,Jl 2-9,23,S 17 1882
WHi [Mr 11 1877-Ap 9 1882]

CAPITAL. d *See* Critic-record

CAPITOL. *See* Democratic capitol

Washington City CHRONICLE. w Jl 5 1828-Jl 27 1833||
Jl-N 1 1828 as Washington chronicle; Jl-D 1829 Washington City chronicle and literary repository; 1830-Jl 14 1832 American spectator and Washington City chronicle
CtNwC My 2 1833
CtY Ja 2-16,F 13,My 22,Jl 17,31 1830;Ag 13 1831;D 22 1832
DLC complete
DW Ag 27 1831
MHi My 7 1831
MWA My 7,N 19 1831
MiU-C N 19 1831
N [Mr 20 1830-My 5]Ag-D 1 1832;Ja 26-F 2, Mr 9 1833
NcD [1829]-Je,Jl 17,31 1830;Ja 22 1831;Je 16-30 1832
NjR Ag 21 1830
P My 23 1829-Je 19 1830
RPB Jl 12 1828-O 1829

Washington CHRONICLE. tw,sw Ja 25 1838-Ja 3 1839||
tw during sessions of Congress
DLC complete
GAtCo Je 30 1838
MiU complete
N Mr 6 1838
NcD [F-D 1838]
NcU Ag 10,N 27 1838
Tx O 9 1838
WHi Ap 3,14,My 8,12,24 1838

Washington CHRONICLE. w Mr 31 1861-1911||?
1861-D 15 1872 as Sunday morning chronicle (S 6 1863-My 22 1864 Sunday chronicle) D 22 1872-D 28 1873 Forney's Sunday morning chronicle; Ja 4 1874-Ag 28 1881 Forney's Sunday chronicle
CSt [1861-64]-[72-73;77-78;81-82]87
DCHi Ap 9 1865
DLC 1861-[80]-1902
extras:My 11 1862;Mr 4,Jl 17,23 1885;My 12, 13 1887;Mr 3,O 13 1889;S 19,21 1892;Mr 4,5 1893
ICN [Ap-N 1864;65]
ICU Jl-D 13 1863;Ja 8-22,Ap 6,23-30,Je 4 1865; Ap 1866-68;Ja-Je 1870[71-72]Ja 1-8,29,F 19-26,Mr 12-26 1882
IF Ap 16 1865
IU Ap 1,My 20 1888
In Je 30 1889
MBAt Ap 26,My 10,Ag 2 1863[68]-74
MMarHi Ap 22 1865
MWA Jl 7,28,S 29,O 13 1861;F 23,Ap 1862-Mr 22,N 22,D 27 1863;Ja 10-My 8,22 1864;F 26-Mr 5,Ap 2,16,30,O 8 1865;Ap 14,Jl 14,O 27 1867;Ja-Jl,D 6-20 1868;Mr 21 1869;N 20 1870; My 12 1872;O 22 1876;Mr 4,25 1877
MiU-C Ag 10,31 1862
NcD [Ap-Je]-D 1861;D 17 1865;S 2 1888
NcU Ag 8 1869;D 29 1871;Mr 15 1874;F 6,20, My 15,Jl-O,N 27 1881[82]N 30,D 28 1884;Ag 16 1885
NhD Ap 16,My 14-21 1865
OCHi N 10 1861;Mr 3(supp)1867
OClWHi D 21 1862;Mr 27 1864-Ja 5,My 3 1868
OHi Ja 22 1883
P Ap 22 1865
PMe My 6 1865
PPL Ja 28 1883
TxGR Ag 28 1864
V My 1861-N 2 1865
WHi F 9,23,Mr 9 1862;Ap 15,30,Mr 5 1865

Washington CHRONICLE. d N 3 1862-Ja 1877||?
1862-Ja 5 1874 as Daily morning chronicle
CSt 1862-Je 1874
CoHi Jl 1 1864;Ap 14-15,17-18 1865
CtNlC Ap 20 1865
CtY N 1865-F 1872
DLC 1862-Ja 22 1877
extras:Je 15 1863;Jl 13 1864;D 3 1867;Mr 4 1869;My 15 1871
DW Ja 6 1872
GU Jl 25,27,D 25 1872;F 11,19,Mr 5,Je 18,Ag 26 1873
ICHi O 13 1864;Ap 10,15,19 1865;Mr 4 1869;O 9 1872
ICN [1864]65
ICU 1862-O 1867;F 7-Ap 1868;69-Ja 22 1877
IF Ap 17,19 1865
IHi [Ap 15-Je 1865]
In My 20 1863;O 21 1865;My 29,Ap 2 1866;D 16 1872
MB Ap 7 1865
MBAt [1863-64]-[77]
MWA Ja 14-Ap 18,My 19,Je 18 1863;Ja-Ap, Je 16 D 19 1864;Ja 14,Mr 22,31,Ap 3,10,15,17, 22,My 24-26,Jl 4-6,11,17,28,Ag,N 1865-My 5 1866;67-[69]-O 1870;Ja-Je,N 1871-Ap 1872;Ap 12 1874;Ja 25,My 23 1876;extra Mr 3 1865
MiG Mr 4(extra)1869
MiU 1874-76
MnHi F 8 1864;F 1-3 1865;S 7 1867-Mr 8 1869
N Ja 24,Mr 2,Ap 5 1863;Ja 28 1864;Ja 27,My 18,23-26 1865;F 23,S 9 1865;Ja 1 1867;Jl 1 1869
NN Ap 14,18,20,24,27,My 1-3,6 1865[Ja-Ag 1866]
NNHi My-O 1864;Ja 26[Ap]1867;Ja 9,My 17 1868;Mr 4,Jl 1 1869[Mr-Ag 1870]Jl 22 1873;D 11 1868
NbHi Mr 10,Ap 4,Je 15,29 1863
NcD [Ap-Je 1861]-64;Ap 15,My 1865-Je,Jl 20 1872;Ja-Jl 1 1873;Ag 22 1874;N 10 1876;Ja 1877
NcU Ap 26,O 28,D 6,20 1865;D 21-22 1866;F 18,22,Mr 15,Ap 11,O 10 1867;S 3 1868;My 1, Ag 7 1869;O 3 1870;D 16,20 1871;Ja 11,20,23 1872
OClWHi Ja 9,20 1863;My 16 19-20,24,Jl 13,Ag 19 1864;Mr 7,Ap 15,20-21,My 23-24,O 6,9 1865; Ja 25 1870
OHi Jl 13 1864-75
PP N 25 1865-Je 25 1868
PPL N 21 1867-S 5 1870
TKL Mr 30,Ap 7,9,14,16-17,20,My 4,12,14-15,27 1868;D 1 1873
Tx F 23,F 18 1866
TxU 1863;My 2-O 29 1864;Ja 5-O 1865;My 2-O 1870;Jl 1871-73;76
WHi N 1864-Ap,My 26,N 1865-O 1872

Washington CHRONICLE. w My 7 1864-76||?
1864-75 as Washington weekly chronicle
CLM Ap 22 1865
CtY Ap 22 1865
DLC Ap 22,My 20 1865;My 12 1866-My 7 1870; Ja 26-F 23 1872;Ja 17-F 21,Mr-My 9,30 1873; Mr 6 1876
DW Ap 22 1865
ICHi Ap 22 1865

DISTRICT OF COLUMBIA (*Continued*)

WASHINGTON—*Continued*

Washington CHRONICLE. w My 7 1864-76||?
—*Continued*
ICM Jl 1 1865
ICN [Ap 13-D 1865]
IHi Ap 22,My 6 1865
MWA Ap 22,My 27 1865;70-74
MiG Ap 22 1865
N My 6 1874
NN My 13 1865-My 4 1867;My 14 1870-Ap 8 1871
NNHi My 11 1867;F 1 1868;Mr 19,My 14-D 1870;Ja 17-28,F 11-Ap 8 1871;Mr 28 1873
NcD N 16 1867-[Ja-Ap 18 1868]69-My 7 1870; Ja 5-12,S 16,O 28-N 11,24 1871-72;Ja 24-F 7 1873
NcU O 23,D 29 1871;D 15 1874;F 3-16 1875;N 1 1876
NhD Ap 29 1865
OClWHi Jl 16,30 1864;Ap 22,Jl 15 1865
Tx Ap 22 1865
TxU S 15 1866
VU Mr 19 1876
WHi 1864-My 5 1866

CITIZEN. d S 30-N 7 1871||
DLC O 2-16,18-25,27-N 7 1871
NcU O 23 1871

CITIZENS' compiler. w Jl? 1841-
DLC D 11,21 1841

CITY item. sw
DLC S 26 1874

COLORED American. w 1893-1904||?
Negro
DLC Mr 12 1898-N 12 1904

COLUMBIA. w O 17 1863-Mr 24 1873||
United with Täglicher Washingtoner anzeiger to form Washingtoner journal, later Washington journal
In German
DLC 1863-Mr 20 1869

COLUMBIAN fountain. *See* Daily fountain

COLUMBIAN gazette. (Georgetown) sw,tw N 16 1826-
1826 as Columbian; Ja-F 1827 Columbian and District advertiser; Mr-Jl 11 1828 Georgetown Columbian, and District advertiser; Jl 13? 1828-Je? 1829 Georgetown Columbian, District advertiser and commercial gazette
tw Jl 2 1829-Mr 30 1833
CSmH Ag 3 1830
Ct [1827]
DLC [1826-27]Jl 11,N 21 1828;Jl 1829-Mr;Jl 16,O 29,N 1 1833;Ag 22 1834
DW Jl 24 1827;My 20,Jl 11 1828
MWA N 21,28,D 1-8,22,29 1826-Jl,O 10 1828; Ja 2,30,Mr 20,Ap 10,Je 2,19,Jl-D 1829;Je 9 1831;Ja 2-16,20-27,F 11 1835
NcD [Jl 1829-Ja 1830]Ag 21,O 6,13,D 11 1832
WHi Jl 1829-Mr 1833

COLUMBIAN observer. w N 28 1821-
DLC N 28 1821
MBAt N 28 1821

Washington COMMERCIAL. w D 7 1878-
DLC D 7 1878

COMMERCIAL herald, and general advertiser. w Ja 1837-
DLC F 4 1839
PBL Ag 1 1842

COMMON sense, the workingman's advocate. w O 2 1847-
DLC O 2 1847

COMMONER. w S 4 1875-
MWA S 4,N-D 18 1875

CONFEDERATION. d Ja 29 1861-
DLC Ja-F 17,19-Mr 2 1861
NcD Ja 31 1861

Tuesday's CONGRESSIONAL globe. w D 5 1854-Ap 28 1857||
DLC complete
MWA 1854-Ja 16,30-F 13,Ap 3 1855
PWcHi Ja 16-23 1855
—d ed *See* Daily globe

CONGRESSIONAL intelligencer. w 1845-46||
MWA My 6 1846

CONGRESSIONAL supplement. *See under* Weekly union

CONSTITUTION. 1844-45 *See under* Baltimore

CONSTITUTION. d Ap 13 1859-Ja 31 1861||
Follows Washington union
DLC complete
ICU Ap-Je 1859;S 20,D 29 1860
In S 29 1860
MB [1859-O 25 1860]Ja 12 1861
MWA complete
MiU 1859-60
NcU [1859-60]
OClWHi Jl 1859-60
PHi 1860-61
PPi Jl 16 1859-61
WHi complete
See also Campaign constitution

Weekly CONSTITUTION. w Ap? 1859-Ja 1861||?
Follows Weekly union?
CtHi 1859-N 1860
DLC F 14,Mr 24 1860
MB Ja 12 1861
MWA Mr 10,N 10 1860
NcD Ap 30 1859
Tx D 20(extra)1860
TxU Ap 14,O 6 1860
WHi Je 11 1859-Ja 19 1861

Semi-weekly CONSTITUTION. sw Ap? 1859-F 1861||?
Follows Semi-weekly union
NcD D 24 1859;Ja 11-Ap 18,S 15,O 24 1860-F 1 1861
OHi Jl 1869-60
PP Ja 18 1860

Weekly CONSTITUTIONAL union. w Je 21 1862-70||?
1862-Mr 21? 1863 pub in Philadelphia, Pa.
CtY Ag 9 1862
DLC F 20 1864;Ap 22 1865
MB Je 26 1863
MWA [1862-Ja]Mr 28-S 1863
OClWHi Jl 13 1867
PWcHi N 8 1862;Ja 10,My 2 1863
WHi N 29 1862

Daily CONSTITUTIONAL union. *See* Evening union

COTTON plant. *See* American cotton plant

CRITIC-RECORD. d 1868-My 14 1896||
1868-O 16 1872 as Critic; O 17 1872-Je 11 1881 Daily critic; Je 13 1881-My 6 1885 Evening critic; My 7 1885-O 13 1888 Washington critic; O 15 1888-Ja 5 1889 Evening post; Ja 7-Jl 3 1889 Washington critic; Jl 5-8 1889 Capital and critic; Jl 9-12 1889 Evening capital and critic; Jl 13 1889-Ja 26 1890 Evening capital; Ja 27-My 24 1890 Washington critic; My 26-D 12 1890 Daily critic; D 13 1890-Mr 25 1891 Critic; Mr 26-Ap 25 1891 Critic and record
DLC D 1-2 1868;Ja 11 1869-Ag 1878;N 1 1879; My 22,Je 28,Jl 3 1880;Je 1881-Je 1883;84-My 14 1891
extras:N 10 1872;Ag 9,13,D 4,7,13 1875;Mr 4 1877;Ag 28,S 18 1881;N 25 1885;Ag 17 1887;Je 19,20,22,23,25 1888;Mr 30,Ap 24,29,30,My 1,2, 3,4,17 1889;F 24 1890
IC Ap 30 1889
In S 15 1872;Mr 4 1873
MWA Mr 16 1872;Mr 23,26-27 1877;Ap 9 1880; F 25,O 28 1881;Je 30 1882
MiU Jl-D 1886;Ja-Je 1889;90
NN Jl 23 1885
NNHi Jl 5 1873;D 6 1886
NcD F 25,Mr 16,Ap 25,My 9,Je 22-23 1870;Ag 17 1871;My 22,Je 24-25,D 17 1872;F 1,Ap 9, 11,My 12 1873;Je 18 1874;F 25 1875;O 11 1876; Je 13-S 1881;Je 30 1882;My 27 1887
NcU Ap 4 1871;O 10 1874;N 23 1877[Jl-S 1881]
PWpHi Jl 5 1881
TJT D 12 1875

DE BOW'S weekly press. w Ja 16 1858-
DLC Ja-Ap 3 1858
MsHi Ja 16,30 1858
NcU F 20 1858
Tx Ja 16,Mr 13 1858

DEMOCRATIC capitol. d My 12 1843-
1843-F 16? 1844 as Capitol
DLC My 9-D 24 1843;Ja 18,F 1-6,8-12,14-15,28 1844
MWA Jl 22,D 28 1843

DEMOCRATIC expositor and United States journal for the country.
TxU O 18 1845
See also Daily times 1845-46

DEMOCRATIC flag-ship. w Je 1- 1852||?
Campaign paper
DLC Je 1 1852

Daily evening DISPATCH. d Ap 29-My 6 1867||
DLC complete

DISTRICT news. d N 5-24 1838||
DLC complete
NcD N 22-23 1838

DOLLAR globe. ir Je 8 1844-F 13 1845||
DLC complete
ICN complete
PRHi [1844-45]
TxU complete

DRAGOON. (Camp Barker) Mr 5 1862-
DW Mr 5 1862

EAST WASHINGTON press. w Ap? 1880-82||
DLC Jl 3 1880

EXAMINER. tw 1832-
CtY S 12 1832

Washington EXAMINER. w,sw Jl 4 1833-
1833? as Examiner (w)
DLC Ag 22,S 5 1833;Ja 8-22,29-F 15 1834
N O 10 1833
NcD Ja 25 1834
PEL Jl 11 1833

Washington EXAMINER. w Mr 19 1859-
DLC Mr 19,Ap 9,30-My 7 1859

Washington EXPOSITOR; and independent political and literary gazette. w Ag 21? 1830-
DLC S 4 1830

Washington EXPRESS. d Je 10 1867-S 18 1869||
1867-Mr 20 1869 as Evening express. United with Daily national intelligencer to form Daily national intelligencer and Washington express, later Daily national intelligencer
DLC complete;F 23(extra)1868
MB Jl 5,8,Ag 28,O 28,30,N 4,24-25 1867;F 23, Mr 8,My 26-31,Je 26 1869
NcD N-D 1867;N 3 1868
NcU O 9 1867
OHi My 16 1868
RPB Je-N 16 1867
TKL Ap 14 1868

EXTRA globe. w My 10-N 10? 1832||
Campaign paper
Ct [1832]
MWA My-N 10 1832
MiU-C [1832]
NcD Jl 2 1832
NhD My-N 10 1832
—*See also* Globe

FORNEY'S Sunday morning chronicle. *See* Washington chronicle w 1861-1911

Daily FOUNTAIN. tw,d N 4 1845-
1845-N 13 1846 as Columbian fountain (Ag 13 1846 Fountain)
tw 1845-Ja 24 1846
DLC 1845-Ja 1847;extra:D 8 1846
NcD Mr 3 1846

Weekly FOUNTAIN. w Ja 31 1846-
DLC Mr 7 1846

***Washington GAZETTE.** w,d N 25 1815-F 4 1826||
1815-O 18 1817 as Washington City weekly gazette; O 27? 1817-F 14 1821 City of Washington gazette. Followed by United State telegraph
w 1815-O 18 1817
CtY [Ja-F 1821]
DLC 1821-26;extras:Ja 1 1821;D 7 1824
GU [1824-25]
ICU [1821-22]24-25
MBAt [1821-22]N 29 1823;Ap 12 1824;F 14,26, Mr 1 1825
MHi My 6,N 9 1822;Ja 16,Mr 25,Ap 28,My 24, N 19 1823;Ap 12,29,S 14 1824;F 8,14,Mr 12, Ap 13,23,N 3 1825;Ja 7,31 1826
MWA Ap 3 1821[24-Je 1825]Ja 7 1826
MeBt 1823-26
MiU 1821-22;24[25-26]
N Ja 29-Je 17 1822;O 28,N 11 1823;S 17 1824; Mr 16,21,24,Ag 4,S 27-28 1825
NNHi Ja 5,24,F 10 1821;Ja 17 1822
NjR [1821;23-25]

***Washington GAZETTE (for the country).** tw O 27 1817-Ja 1826||
DLC [My 1821-S 1822;Je 1823-24]F 12/14, 26/28,N 5/7,D 20/21 1825
ICU D 7 1821-Ap 26,Ag 9,S 30,O 9 1822;S 21 1825
MBAt [1821;24-25]
MWA Ag 13 1821;Jl 24 1822;F 20,Ag 14 1823; Ja 19,31,F 4-9,28,My 3 1825
NN My 2 1821;Ap 2-5 1824
NNHi [1821]Jl 7/8,Jl 5/7,D 11/12,20/22 1823;S 29/O 1 1824;Ja 29/31,D 2/3 1825
NcD F 26 1825

Sunday GAZETTE. w 1868-91||?
Title varies: Sunday morning gazette; Gazette
CSmH F 21 1885
DLC Ag 29,N 28 1869;Ja 23 1870;F 5,Ap 23 1871;S 21 1873;O 11 1874;Ja 31 1875;My 7 1876;My 12,N 24,D 22 1878;S 21 1879;Jl 4 1880;Jl 24 1887
MWA Ja 15 1871;Ag 19 1877;D 30 1883;F 22 1885
~~Tx F 27 1870~~
VRC Ap 6 1870

GEORGETOWN advocate. sw,tw,d Ap 21 1835-1841||
1835-Jl 17 1837 as Metropolitan; Jl 19 1837-Ap 15 1839 Potomac advocate and metropolitan intelligencer (Ja 1-F 12 1838 Potomac advocate) Ap-O 25 1839 Potomac advocate and Georgetown intelligencer; O 28-N 1 1839 Georgetown daily advocate
sw Ap-D 2 1835;d O 28-N 1 1839
Ct [1835]Mr 26 1836[37]
DLC 1835-Ja 18,F 12-13 1841
DGU 1835-Mr 15 1837
InI N 30 1824
MWA [1835]-O 4 1837;O 17,N 7 1838;Ja 2,S 8 1840
MiU-C [1835-37]
WHi Je 19 1835

GEORGETOWN advocate. tw My 1 1841-
DGU 1847-49
DLC My 4,N 23 1841[Ja 24 1843-44]-[54-55]Ag 9,S 16 1856;broadside:S 16 1846
DW F 2 1841;Ag 22 1850
MWA [1841-42]D 21 1843[Ja-Je 1846;47]50[51-52]-F 15 1853;Ag 12 1854
NhD O 7 1841

GEORGETOWN citizen and semi-weekly register. sw 1869-
MWA My 19 1869

GEORGETOWN Columbian. . . *See* Columbian gazette

GEORGETOWN courier. w N 18 1865-My 6 1876||
DLC complete
MiU N 18 1865;O 30,N 13 1869-N 1 1873
NcD F 18,Ap 1,15 1871;My 25 1872

GEORGETOWN gazette. sw O 20 1823-
DLC Mr 23,Ap 13 1824

GEORGETOWN gazette. (for the country) w
DLC Ap 20/23 1824

GEORGETOWN reporter. tw Ap 1851-
DLC My 15,O 16 1851;S 20 1852

GLOBE. sw D 7 1830-Ap 30 1845||
Followed by Semi-weekly union
Ct 1831-[34]-37
CtHi 1830-N 6 1831;F 24 1836-D 6 1841
CtY Ja 19 1831-Ap 26 1834
DLC 1830[31-32]F 2,Mr 2,23,Ap 6,17,My 22 1833;34-45
GAtCo Mr 17 1832
ICU 1830-Je 11 1831;Ap 17 1833[34-42]Mr 13, My 11,Ag 28 1843;44;Ja 20,F 13 1845
IHi [1841-45]
IU D 6 1841;Je 6(supp)1844
IaHi 1840-42
IaU complete
In 1832-45

DISTRICT OF COLUMBIA (*Continued*)

WASHINGTON—*Continued*

GLOBE. sw D 7 1830-Ap 30 1845||—*Continued*
MB Ap 20 1831;Je 27 1832;Jl 13-D 1836[Mr 22 1837-38]Ja 21,31,F 11,Mr 18,My 30,Ag 29 1839;42-45
MBAt Ja 18 Jl 11 1832[35]-[45]
MHi [1833-45]
MSaE S 1834-[37]-Jl 14 1838
MWA My 7,28,Je 4,Jl 2,Ag 27 1831-O 1832;D 11 1833-[41]-Mr 3,My 16,Jl 28,Ag 29 1842;D 26 1843;Mr 21,Jl 3,Ag 15,O 31,N 7 1844;45
MdFS D 5 1832-Mr 15 1833
MdHi Jl 8-N 1844
MiG Jl 20 1838-42;D 4 1843-N 1844
MiU-C [1832-36;39]
MnHi D 17 1831;Ja 23,Ap 2 1836;Ja 11-14,F 15,Mr 4 1841
N Mr 26 1831-N 1833;O 1-14 1835;Ap 4,Jl 30, S 10,D 7,21-24 1836;Ja 18-25,F 11,18-22,Mr 8,Je 2 1837;Jl 10 1840
NCH Ja-Je 21 1834
NNHi Mr 5 1831-42;extra:Ag 27 1832
NPV [Ap 1831-Ap 4 1832]
NR Ap 1831-N 25 1835;D 1836-D 2 1839
NSchU D 7 1833-[34]
NcD Jl 14,Ag 29 1832[33-37]-[39-40]N 1,22 1841;F 3 1842;Ja 1,Jl 15 1843;Ja 1,My 6,Je 10,Jl 15,Ag 29,S 2,19 1844[45]
NjT Mr 1838-45
OAU D 1835-N 1836
ODW N 8 1834;Ja 17-28,O 10-N 25 1835;S 4 1838;Jl 9 1840
OHi N 8 1831-45
PBL 1831-O 1832;My 1833-D 6 1834
PEL D 21 1831-Jl 6 1833
PWCl Ja 29,F 8,N 26,D 17 1834[35;40-42]
Tx S 10,O 29 1834;Ja 10,31-Mr 7,D 2-5 1835; 36-[38]-40
WHi Je 30-Jl 1832;Je 21 1834;F 14,Mr 21-25, Jl 4-D 23 1835;Ja 9 1836;Jl 3 1839
WaPS N 1839-45

GLOBE. w D 1830-Ap 30? 1845||
Followed by Weekly union
DLC D 8-22 1831;32-O 23 1834;Ag-S,O 8 1835-[36-N 1837]
GAtCo Mr 17 1832
ICU My 14 1835
MHi [1842-44]
MWA N 29 1832;F 23-D 7 1837
MiU My 6 1844
NNHi My 24,Je 18,Jl,Ag 13,27-S 17 1832
NSchU D 7 1833-[F 1834-N 1835]
PHi F 1831-45
WHi 1843

Daily GLOBE. d Je 13 1831-Ap 30 1845||
1831-D 30 1843 as Globe. Followed by Daily union, later Washington union
CaB 1845
Ct 1832-F 1845
CtHi N 29 1831-Je 1838;39[40-41]-45
CtY [1831-32]My 4 1833-45
DLC complete
extras:My 10,D 4 1832;F 28 1833
DW Jl 20 1837
GAtCo Ja 8 1838
GU [Ja-Je 1832;N 1833-34]
ICHi Jl 27 Ag 31,S 7,19,N 9,D 1,24 1831;Ap 12, Je 1,6,8 1832;D 17 1838;O 7 1839
ICN S-D 1841
ICU complete
IU 1834-40;N 13 1844
In 1832-45
InRE Ja 6,29,F 4,6,Mr 29,Je 21 1834
InU Mr-D 1834;36;38-39;Jl 1840-Je 1842
LNH Mr 26 1844-45
MB Jl 12 1831[Ag 19-N 25 1834;36-Ja 10 1845]
MBAt Jl 11(supp)1832[35-36;38]Ag 5 1840
MHi D 24 1831;S 1 1832;Ja 17,23 1835[36-39] Ja 8 1845
MMarHi Mr 6 1837
MSaE [1839]
MWA complete
MiU-C [1831-41]
MnHi D 12 1835;Ja 18,F 4 1841;D 18 1843
MsHi 1837;39-45
N My 17 1832
NIC O 1832-Je 1835;Ap 1836-Je 1837;Ja-Je,O-D 1838;O-D 1839;Ap-S 1840;Ja-F,Jl 1842-Mr 1843
NN Ap-S 1833;Mr 21 1834;36-Mr 1837[My-O 1838]40-41;Ja-Mr 1843;45
NNHi 1831;Ap 12,Je 30 1832;My 9,Je 11 1833-O 1834;N 20 1837-S 1839;Mr 1,D 28 1844;F 18 1845
NNY-H F 7-Je 5 1833
NSchU N 22 1831-N 22 1832;Ap 29,My 12 1834;Ja 20,F 23,Je 22 1835
NT 1837-45
NcD 1831[32]-[34]-45
NcU [1838-43]
NjHi F 24,Mr 8,16,25,Ap 7,25 1836
OCHi My 19 1835;Jl 1844-45
OT S 9 1841-Ap 29 1843
OrU [D 1833]
PBL D 8 1834-Je 10,D 12 1836-N 26 1841;Ja 10,13,Ap 5,7,17 1843
PHi complete
PLewL Ap 5 1832
PP [1832]-[34]-36;38[39]-45
PPL 1832-36;38-45
PPM Ap 14 1832-Je 12 1833;Je 12 1834-Je 12 1838
PPiHi F 11 1833
PWCl [1841]
PYHi D 1840-44
Tx Jl 8 1840;41-45
TxU [1831-45]
VU Je 9,D 28 1832;Ja 25,F 19 1833;Ja 29 1841
WHi 1831-Je 11 1832;33-45
—*See also* Dollar globe; Tuesday's congressional globe; Extra globe

Daily GLOBE. d D 5 1848-My 2 1873||
Suspended during recesses of Congress except in 1854 and 1856
Ct [1850;56]58-60;D 1862-Je 1864;Ja-My 1866; Ja-Ap 1872
CtY [1850;54;56-57]F 10 1858;59[60-62]-[63-68]-[70]D 1872-Mr 13 1873
DLC complete
extras:Ja 20,Ag 23 1849;Ag 23 1851;Ja 17,30, F 13,Mr 6 1854;Ag 16,21 1860;My 7,S 5 1861; Ap 18 1865
GU Mr 11-12 1873
IC D 3-21 1872;Ja 7-Mr 13 1873
ICHi F 1 1858;My 24 1864
ICU 1850[52]54[55]-[57]-70;D 1871-Je 19 1872; Ja-Mr 13 1873
extras:Ap 28 1859;Ap 18 1863
supp:Jl 18 1865
IHi Mr 11 1858
IU D 9 1853
InIB D 3 1872-Mr 11 1873
MB D 31 1852[55-Je 23 1856]Je 16,Jl 11 1860; F 26,Mr 6,D 1861[62-My 26 1864]F 20 1869; Je 14 1870;Mr 13 1873
MHi Mr 10,13 1860[1865]D 1867
MSaE D 16 1853;54[Ja-Mr 1855]
MWA D 5,16,21-23,27-28 1848;Ja 3-24,F 6-7, 23,D 4 1849-Mr,Je 25,Ag 15,S 6,19,D 1850-Mr 17,D 1851-S 23,D 7 1852-Mr 26,Ap 2,9,14,Je 4,D 1853-D 4 1854;Ja-Ap 4 1855;Ja-Mr,D 1857-Jl 7,22(extra)D 7 1858-Mr 25,D 1859-Jl 16,D 6,13 1860[Ja-Mr]D 1861-Jl 21,Ag 26 (extra)D 1862-F 1863;Mr 5,7,17,28,Ap 7,My 4, 5(supp)6,D 1864-Mr 20,D 19 1865;Ja 12,F 22, Ap 5,10,My 8,15,25,D 4 1866-Ap 6,Jl 4-20,N 22 1867-Jl,N,D 8-22 1868;Ja 6-My 6,D 7-23,30 1869;Ja 11-Jl 17,26,D 6-24 1870;Ja-My 6,D 5-22 1871;Ja 9-Je 22,D 3-21 1872;Ja 7-Mr 13 1873
MiU-C [1850;52;54;57]
MnHi My 4 1854;D 8 1863;Ap 22-23,27,Je 16 1864;Mr 18 1865;Ja 25 1866;My 4-5,13,Je 11, Jl 23 1868
MoHi My 14 1860
NIC D 1861-Jl 1862
NN 1848-Mr 1849;D 6,28,30 1859-Jl 15 1860; My 6 1863;Jl 6 1864;Ja 19,F 22,Jl 11,D 14,19 1866;Mr 27,Ap 6,10,16 1867
extras:Ag 16,20 1860
NNHi F 10 1863;F 27 1864;Ja 31 1866;Ja 14 1873
NSyU My 5 1854
NcD D 5,13 1848;F 9,Mr 3 1849;Ap 10,Je 13,S 3,D 7 1850;Ja 16,F 13-14,Mr 17 1851;D 16 1852;Ja 13,D 7-9,12 1853-[54-My 1856;58]D 6 1859-[60]Ja 1,18,23,F 9,13,16,22-23,Mr 15-16,26 1861;D 5 1865-Jl 22,N 22 1867-Mr 2 1869;Je 6 1871
NcGrW Ja 14,F 19 1873
NcU My 4,Ag 23,26 1854;Jl 31 1868
NjT D 1857-Je 1858
NjWdHi Ja 17 1865
OCHi N 30 1867-Jl 1868
ODW D 14 1854-Ap 28 1859
OHi D 1861-Jl 21 1862
OOxM Je 7 1872;F 23 1873
P D 1861-Je 1862
PHi 1848-Mr 17 1851;D 7 1857-Jl 22 1858;68
PP My 27 1854;Je 7-8,26-30,Jl 5-6,11,16 1860
PPL F 14 1852;My 27 1854[60]
PShH Je 1 1852
PWcHi F 13 1854
RW Mr 21 1861;F 6,Je 29 1870;Mr 5,7-8,Ap 1-2,4,D 21 1871
TKL Mr 23(supp)1860
TU Ag 1 1854;Ja 14 1856
Tx Mr 9 1859;F 15 1871
TxU [Jl 1850-Mr 12 1851;54;D 7 1857-Mr 13 1873]
V Ja 27 1864
WHi D 2 1862-Mr 25 1863

Weekly GLOBE. w D 12 1848-Mr 4 1851||
DLC complete
ICU O 15,N 26 1854
MWA N 13 1849

Sunday Washington GLOBE. w My 5 1901-02||?
Title varies slightly
DLC 1901-Je 1902

GRAFT. *See* Washington truth

GRIT. w D 21 1883-84||?
Negro
KHi [1883-O 18 1884]

GUARDIAN. w Je 8 1867-
DLC Je 15 1867

HATCHET. w D 1 1883-
DLC 1883-Jl 19 1884;Ag 29-My 13,27,Je 10-24, Jl 8,29,Ag 19-S 2,16 1900
In N 27 1886
MWA Ja 19,F 16 1884;F 18 1888
MeBa F 1 1885
NcD Mr 21 1886
WHi Ja 24 1886

Washington HERALD. d O 8 1906+
Sunday issues 1922-23 as Washington times-herald
Ag 28 1915 is "Washington in 1915" ed
pub 1922+
CSt My 1920-Je 21 1921
DLC 1906+
DW 1906+
IC Ag 28 1915
ICU Ja 11 1907-My 1908
IHi Ag 28 1915
M Mr 5 1929
MWA Ag 28 1915;N 11 1918;F 3 1924
MoS Ag 28 1915
NcD F 12 1914;D 11 1919;D 9,30 1924;Ja 12, 14-15,17,19,21,30 1925;F 21 1932
PWbW Mr 5 1929
PWcHi Mr 21 1926
PWp Ag 28 1915
TxGR S 18 1908;Ag 28 1915
VU Jl 13 1909;N 10 1922
WaPS [1921]

HERALD and Georgetown advocate. (Georgetown) w
-Ap? 1858 as Potomac herald
DLC Ja 20 1857(broadside)Ap 6,20 1858
DW Je 15 1858

Sunday HERALD and weekly national intelligencer. w Ap 1 1866-96||?
1866-Ja 30 1887 as Sunday herald
DLC Ap 1,Ag 5 1866;S 22,N-D 1867;My 31,Je 28,Jl 12 1868;Je 27,Ag 29,O 24,N 7-14 1869;F 1870-Mr 18 1877;Mr 21 1880-Mr 13 1881;Mr 19 1882-Mr 18 1883;Mr 22 1885-Mr 20 1887;Mr 23 1890-91;My 17-24,Je 7-13,28-Jl 5 1898;Mr 4(extra)1877
MWA Je 16 1867;Ap 22 1871;Ag 19 1877;N 3 1889;F 22 1891
NcU S 4 1881
—Army and navy ed w
DLC Mr 26 1876-Mr 18 1887;N 3 1878;Mr 21 1880-Mr 13 1881;Mr 19 1882-Mr 18 1883
TKL Mr 20 1881

HICKORY tree. sw Je 27 1844-
DLC Je 27 1844
NNHi N 13 1844

HOME gazette. w Ja 20- 1866||?
Suspended from F 3-17 1866
DLC Ja-F 17 1866
MWA Ja 20 1866

INDEPENDENT. sw D 14 1841-
DLC 1841-Je 24 1842
NcU D 31 1841;Ja 4,F 22 Mr 11,25,Ap 1,My 10-17,27 1842

INDEPENDENT. (Georgetown) tw 1853-
DLC F 25 1854

INDEX. tw,sw,d Ap 21 1841-Ag 27 1842||?
Suspended Ag 13-26 1842
1841-Ap 26 1842 pub in Alexandria
sw Ag-N 1841; tw D 1841-Ag 12 1842 (d Je 2-Jl 15 1842)
DLC 1841-Ag 27 1842
V Je 28 1842

Washingtoner INTELLIGENZBLATT. w Ap 2 1859-
In German
DLC 1859-Ag 11 1860

Washington JOURNAL. d,tw,w Mr 31 1873+
Formed by the union of Columbia and Täglicher Washingtoner anzeiger. 1873-Mr 31 1888 as Washingtoner journal
d 1873-Mr 31 1885; tw Ap 2 1885-Mr 1 1888
In German
DLC 1873-Je 1874;O 10 1876;Jl 9 1877-78;Ap 7 1888-D 15 1894;98+
MWA Ag 24 1876
PScrHi O 7 1914

Evening LEADER. d F 14-Ap 11 1867||
Prospectus N 26 1866
DLC complete;Ap 11(extra)1867
MWA Mr 7 1867
NNHi F 26 1867

LEADER. w Ja 1888-1902||?
1888-S 28 1889 as National leader; 1894?-98? Leader and clipper
1890?-1900? pub in Alexandria, Va.
Negro
DLC D 8,22 1888-Mr 9,23-My 4,18-Je 22,Jl 13-20,Ag,S 7-14,28 1889

Dos Washingtoner LEBEN. *See* Washington life

LE DROIT advertiser.
MHi Jl 1 1875

Washington LIFE (Dos Washingtoner leben). w S 15? 1911-F 23 1912||
In Yiddish
DLC complete
NN complete

LOAFERS' weekly gazette. w Ag 22 1839-
DLC Ag 22-29 1839

MADISONIAN. tw,sw Ag 16 1837-Ap 1845||
Followed by United States journal, later Semi-weekly times
Suspended from Ap 16-30 1840
tw during sessions of Congress
CSt 1837-39
CtHi S 16 1837-Ag 18 1840
CtY Ja 16 1841;Jl 26 1844
DLC 1837-[Ag 1842]Ja 24,Mr 20,Je 12,15,22, 26,Jl 10,17-20,Ag 17,21,N 13,30 1843;Ja 15,F 7,Mr 8,15,26,Ap 16,My 4,Jl 5,N 26 1844;Ja 30,F 11,18,Mr 18,25 1845;extras:Mr 4,Je 1 1842
IU Je 24 1841
KHi O 12 1837-S 21 1841
KMC O 12 1837-S 21 1841
LU 1837-40
MBAt [1838]
MWA Ag 16 1837[F 25 1840-41]F 12-Ap 1842; Ja 15 1844
MdBJ Jl 23-O 22 1842
MdHi Ja 21 1840-Mr 27 1843;F 16-N 1844
MsHi 1840-My 24 1844
N 1837-Jl 18 1838;D 7 1839-S 1841
NIC 1837-Ag 7 1839
NN [N 1839-F 1842]
NNHi 1837-S 21 1839;Ja 23 1841;Jl 15,Ag 9 1844
NNS D 7 1839-45
NcD Je 9-16,21-23,28,Jl 11,14,18-21,26-28,Ag 25,D 18 1838[40]Mr 6,N 27 1841;Ap 20 1843
NhD Ag 5,10,24,S 4,14 1841;F 10,Jl 14,29,O 28, D 2 1842;Ja 4 1843
NjR Je 17 1843
OCHi Ap 10 1841
PEL 1837-Ag 14 1839
PP [1838-39]
PShH Ja 19,F 4,13 1841
RW N 24,D 1 1840
TNV S 16-19,O 14-31,N 7,21-30,D 7,14-16 1837; F 6 17-24,Mr 3,13-27,Ap-Ag 15 1838;Ap 6-My 1,8-D 5,N 9,16,27 1839[40]Ja 7-14,F 9-16,20, 27,Mr 4,Jl 24 1841;Ja-Je,Jl 8 1843-45
WHi Je-D 1841[O 18 1842-44]

DISTRICT OF COLUMBIA (*Continued*)

WASHINGTON—*Continued*

MADISONIAN. w 1837-Ap? 1845‖
Followed by United States journal, later Weekly times
IHi Ja 18 1840
MWA D 8 1838-Mr 2,Ap 20 1839;Ap 4,Je 13, O 3,31 1840;41-F 26 1842;Je 17,Jl 15,29,Ag 12-19 1843
MiU-C Jl 15 1843
NSchU Je 11 1842
NcU Ja 2-16,F 6-20,Mr 6 1841
NjWdHi F 15 1840
OClWHi D 14 1839-Ja 1,29 1842
OHi S 15 1837-Mr 1845

Daily MADISONIAN. d D 15 1841-Ap 29 1845‖
Followed by United States journal, later Daily times
CSt 1841-Ap 28 1845
DLC complete
IU D 27 1843;F 13 1844
MB [1842-43]45
MWA D 15 1841;O 13-14,17-19 1843;F 5,Ap 9 1844-Ja 17 1845
MiU Ap 2,My 10,14 1844
N My 8 1844
NN 1841-43;Jl 1844-Mr 1845
NcD Ja-Je 1843;Ja 19 1844
OClWHi Jl 20,O 8 1844
PBL Ap 21 1842;Ja 14,Ap 1,6,17,My 1 1843
TxU My 14,20 1844
WHi 1843-Je 1844

MADISONIAN. (For the country) w
DLC Ja 8,O 14 1842;My 11,Je 1,27 1844;Ja 18 1845
NN Ap 17 1841

Evening MAIL. d 1874-
DLC Ja 8 1875

MERCHANTS' journal and ladies' guide for shopping. w D 7 1850-51‖
DLC 1850-Ja 18,F 1,Mr 1 1851

Saturday MERCURY. w O 18?- 1856‖?
MWA N 1 1856

MESSENGER. *See* National messenger

Tägliche METROPOLE. w,d 1859-Ja 7 1861‖
1859-S? 1860 as Metropole (w)
In German
DLC Ag 25,S 1-8,O 1860-61

Washington METROPOLIS. tw,w N 29 1838-Ap 11 1840‖
1838-F 8 1840 as Metropolis
tw 1838-Ja 21 1840
DLC complete
NcD [D 1838-39;Mr 1840]
NjR F 5 1839
P F 26 1839-F 1 1840

METROPOLITAN. (Georgetown) 1820-26 *See* Metropolitan and Georgetown commercial gazette

METROPOLITAN. (Georgetown) 1835-37 *See* Georgetown advocate

Weekly METROPOLITAN. w Jl 12 1851-
1851-Jl 9 1853 as Metropolitan
DLC 1851-Jl 22 1854
In 1851-Ja 1856
InRE [1853-55]
MWA 1851-Jl 2 1854[F 10-D 22 1855]
NcD O 13 1855
NjWdHi Jl 17 1852

***METROPOLITAN and Georgetown.. commercial gazette.** (Georgetown) tw,sw,w Ja 26 1820-27‖?
tw 1820-Mr 11 1823; sw Mr 14 1823-Ja 11 1826
Ct [1826]
DLC 1821-[23-26]Jl 12(extra)1826
DW Jl 15 1826
MBAt D 3 1822
MHi Ja 20 1824
MWA [1821-22]Jl 29 1823;24[25-26]
NcD Ag 10 1824;N 4-18,D 9,18 1826;Ja 6 1827

Washington MIRROR. w,sw Ag 9 1834-N 5 1836‖
w 1834-Ag 6 1836
DLC complete
MB Ja 16,Ag 10-N 1836
MWA N 29,D 20 1834;Ja 31,F 28,Mr 21-28,Jl 11 1835;Ap 2,16 1836
NNHi D 19-26 1835;Ja 16-Mr 12,26-Ap 2 1836
NcD [F 1835-Ja 1836]
OCHi S 3 1836
OClWHi F 20,Ap 30,My 14,28,Je 4 1836

MODERATOR. w O 10 1833-
CtY O 10 1833
DLC Ja 11-25,F 8-22 1834
MWA O 10 1833
NN O 10,N 9-16 1833
PEL Ja 4,F 1-15 1834
NcD F 8 1834

Weekly MONITOR. w -N 30 1867‖?
DLC N 1867
TxU Jl 27 1867

MRS. COLVIN'S weekly messenger. w Je 15 1822-Mr 29 1828‖?
1822-Ag 18 1827 as Mrs. A. S. Colvin's weekly messenger
Suspended from S 1822?-Jl 22 1826
DLC Je-S 15 1822;Jl 22 1826-Mr 1828
DW [Mr 31-Ag 18 1827]
GMM [F-Ag 18 1827]
MWA Jl 22 1826-Mr 17 1827
PHi F 17 1827
PLewL Mr 24 1827

Daily NATION. d 1876-O 15 1877‖
Merged with National union
DLC Jl 9-O 1877
MWA D 2 1876;Mr 26 1877

NATIONAL. w Ja 1 1836-
DLC F 12-My 20 1836
MWA Ja-Jl 8 1836
N Ap 8 1836

—d ed *See* Daily national intelligencer

NATIONAL citizen soldier. w 1875-Ja 1881‖?
United with Washington world to form Weekly Washington world and citizen-soldier?
In Ja 5 1881

NATIONAL democrat. w S 5 1889-95‖?
MB 1889-Ag 1890
MHi 1889-Ag 1890
MWA 1889-S 13 1890
MnU 1889-Je 6 1891;Mr-Ap 23 1892
NNHi 1889-Ag 1890
NcD O 5 1889;Ag 30 1890
PMilC S 5 1889
PWcHi Ag 5 1894
TJT Ap 9 1892
TxU S 14 1889-Ag 1890

NATIONAL democrat. w N 11 1916-
DLC N 25-D 1916;Ja 27-Mr 10 1917

Der NATIONAL demokrat. w My 6 1847-
In German
DLC N 11 1847

Der NATIONAL demokrat. w Jl 9 1853-
Undated prospectus. Suspended from Jl 9-23 1853?
In German
DLC Jl 9,23 1853
MWA prospectus;Jl 9 1853

NATIONAL demokrat. sw
In German
MiG Jl 31 1856

NATIONAL era. w Ja 7 1847-Mr 22 1860‖
CLM Je 20 1853
CSt 1848
CtY 1847-58
DHU-M 1847-52
DLC complete
I 1854-55
IA [1853;55]
ICHi 1847-55;Ja 10-Jl 24,Ag 7,28,O 9-N 6,20 1856-Ja 1,S 24 1857-[58-59]Ja 12-Mr 1,15 1860
ICU 1847-53;Ja-S 1856
IEN 1847-51
IU Mr 29 1849;Je 5 1850;54-Je 1855;Ag 20 1857;D 2 1858
IaK 1847-54
InI F 1848-Ja 1851;Jl 17 1856;O 2 1858
InU [1847-50;52-60]
KHi [1847-59]
MB complete
MH complete
MHi Ap 1848-49;Ap 4 1850;My 29 1856
MSaE 1848-59
MWA complete
MdBJ 1847
MiD-B [1855]
MiG N 23 1848
MiU Ja 3,My 22-28,Jl 18 1850
MnHi 1847-[55-56]-[58]
N [1847-50;53-54;56;59-60]
NBHi 1847-53
NBu 1851-53
NCanHi D 1847-49
NIC complete
NN [1847-51]
NNHi 1847-55;D 1856-F 12,26-Ap 16,Jl 16 1857;My 13-Ag 12,S-N 4,18-D 2,16 1858-[59]60
NPe 1854
NSyU F 25 1847;Ja 20 1848;Ja 6 1853;O 19 1854
NbHi Ag 12,O 21,D 1847-[49]-F 19,Mr-D 10 1857[Ja-Ag 1858]-60
NcD S 30-D 1847;Ja 27,O 12 1848;49-55;57-58
NjR 1850-55
NjVi [1849-50]
OCHi 1847-Mr 15 1860
OHi complete
OMM D 1847-Ja 5,Ag 17 1854-Mr 1856
OMv 1847-[60]
P My 24 1855
PAtM S 22 1853
PHi 1847-48
PNoHi 1847;Je 1851-Ja 1852
PP 1847-Je 22 1848[49-59]
PPL 1847-48
PPiHi Je 1849-50
PSF 1847-[52]-60
PToHi F 10-N 16 1848
PWaHi Jl 19,D 14 1848;S 5,27 1849;O 12 1850;F 6 1851;Jl 17 1852;D 1,22 1853;F 2 1854
PWaHi-C 1848-49
RP complete
RPB 1847-59
TC Ja-N 6,30 1851
Tx 1848-49;Mr,Je 27,S 5,19 1850[53]Ja 26,F 16,Mr 2,16-Ap 6,My 18,Je 1 1854
TxU 1847-56
WHi 1847-59

Daily NATIONAL era. d Ja 2-Ag 5 1854‖
DLC complete
MB complete
MH complete
MSaE [1854]
MiU-C My 3 1854
NCanHi complete
OCHi [My 27-Ag 1854]
OMM Ja 5-Ag 1854

NATIONAL forum. w Ap 1910-
Negro
DLC My 28-Je 4,Jl 9-30,Ag 20-27,S 10-O 22,N 5-12 1910

NATIONAL graft. *See* Washington truth

***NATIONAL intelligencer.** tw,sw O 31 1800-69‖?
1800-N 24? 1810 as National intelligencer and Washington advertiser
tw during sessions of congress sw during recess My 12 1819-Jl 15 1824;Jl 4 1829-44; sw only Jl 30 1827-Je 1829; tw only at all other periods
CSmH 1823;25-[31-37;39-40]-[50-52]-[54-55]-[57]Ja 20 1861;F 17,Mr 21 1863
CSt [1821-30]
CoHi Ja 12 1826
Ct S 27 1825;Mr 8 1827;Ja 17 1828;Ja 20 1835;N 17 1864
CtHT [1821;27-28]supp Ja 17 1828
CtHi 1821-25[Je 28 1827-29]O 28 1835-59
DLC 1821-[33]-[44]-[Ja-Mr 1852]54[55]-58;61;F 4 1862;Ap 11,18,Ag 1-6,D 5-10 1863;F 6-11 1864
extras: F 26,D 5 1821;F 5,Mr 4 1825;Mr 27,28 1826;D 2 1828;D 8 1829;Mr 26 1835
GAtCo Mr 26 1840
GDE [1849;52]53
GMiG [1825-30]
GU [1821-Ag 30 1824]
IC D 23 1837-39;O 13,N 3 1840;41-48
ICHi Ja 6,13,30,Mr 3,13,S 29 1821;Je 7 1830;Je 28 1834;D 15 1835[36]F 13 1838;39-49;N 16 1859;Ag 21 1860;S 26-28 1865
ICM Mr 3 1866
ICN Ap-D 1830;32-34;37-38;46;60
ICU 1821-[33-35]-[60-63]
IEN D 1822-61
IElC F 11 1832;Mr 1 1834;N 18,25,D 2 1835
IG 1838-39
IHi [D 1835-Jl 1865]
IU Ja 6-7,23-27,F 8,24,Mr 1-3 1821[22;25]-[27-41]-[43-47]My 8 1848[49;58]Ja 27,F 26,Mr 3,10,24,Ap 23,N 3 1859;60;Ja 29 1861;63-64;My 29 1865[68]
IaDH D 1821-23;25-54
IaK 1852-D 3 1854
In My 27-O 8 1824;N 16 1826-29;35;S 28 1837-39;Jl 21 1840-57
InI D 25 1832-Ag 1 1857
KU 1821-[47]-[68]
LNH [S 1827-Jl 1828]
LNM Jl 24 1822-My 11 1824
M Ja 15 1831-38;Jl 21 1840-Je 24 1869
MBAt 1821-[68]
MBC 1821-39
MH 1821[22-23]30-[59-64]
MHi 1821-23;26;D 6 1831;S 20,D 13 1832;F 2,14,25,Mr 2 1833;Ja 7,21,Mr 27,O 1,N 29 1834[35-69]
MNF D 1827-D 9 1834
MWA 1821-Je 24 1869
Md 1822-25;27-42;44-56;49;Ja-N 8 1852
MdBSt 1821-41
MdEmM Mr 1855-56
MdFF Jl 30 1831;Jl 30-S 6 1832;My 19 1835;Ap 16 1836;N 9-D 7 1837;Mr 8 1838;Ja-Je 15 1852;My 21 1853-60;62-63
MeB Ja 20-31,F 21,Mr 25,Ap 8,20,30,My 1,Je 10 1824
MeBC Ja 20-31,F 21,Mr 25,Ap 8,20,My 1,Je 10 1824
MeBa Jl 18 1826;My 5-10 1827
MeBt 1821-26
MeP Ja-N 6 1822;24;F-D 1826;F 6-D 1828;43-54
MeU F 24 1829;Je 4 1834
MiG Ap 13-N 1841;42-My 1845;F 26 1848
MiU-C [1821-34;36-38;40;42-52;54-57;59-65]
MnU Mr 8 1834-Je 2 1835;45-46
MoHi F 7 1846-S 7 1852
MsHi Ap-Jl 1825;37-41;46-48
MsNc D 7 1826-D 1 1827;Mr 16 1843-54
MsWJ [Ag 1846-Ja 1853]
N [1822-65]
NAubHi Ja-O 1821
NBuHi 1834-N 12 1868
NCH 1821-24;Ja-Ap 1828
NN 1821-Je 28,Jl 19,26,O 4,11,N 11,29,D 9,20 1823;24-O 16 1839[40]-42;D 16 1847;F 24,Mr 14,Jl 6 1848;F 10-Ag 28,D 25 1849-51;54-60;S 16 1865-N 1867
NNHi [1821;23-24]-D 1 1825;Je 1,Jl 20,S 12,21,D 1826-[32]D 1833[34]S 26-D 22 1835;Jl 21-D 3 1836;Je-Ag 1837;Ja 24 1846;Ag 18 1849;S 6-9,27,O 23 1851;Ja 22-27,Mr 18,Jl 13 1852;Ja 1-6,Ap 16,My 9-16,26-30,Je 13-18,27-30 1863;66
supp D 22 1825;F 22 1834
extras:D 3 1822;F 5,Mr 4 1825;D 6 1831
NSchU D 5 1827-Je 4 1833[Mr-S 1842]
NT 1821-F 1835
NcAsS D 12,21,28 1844[45-50]
NcD 1821[22]23;Ja 10,O 14,N 27,D 4 1824;25[26]D 1 1827;Mr 4 1828[29-34]-[36]-[39]-[41-45]-[47]-[51-61]F 26 1863;O 6 1865[S 1866-Je 1869]D 3(extra)1866
NcGrW My 28,Je 11,18,Ag 6 1867
NcU [1822-23]-[26-29]-[33-36]-[39]-[42-43]-58;O 6 1860;Ja 12,F 2,14,21,Mr 2,9,14 1861
NhD 1821-[43-51]
extras:Mr 1 1823;F 5 1825;Mr 27 1826;D 2 1828
NjHi Ap 1827-28
NjP D 20 1861-Ap 4 1862
NjR [1821-25;27;29-31;45]
NjVi Ja 14 1823-Jl 10 1824
NjWdHi [1850-51]Ja 15 1852;Je 17 1860;Ja 27 1863
OC 1821-34;Ag 8 1835;Mr 15 1836-My 9 1840;41-48;52-53
OCHi 1821-Jl 7 1840;F 25 1841-65;Ja 12 1867-N 12 1868
OCl Ag 19 1824;Ja 4,Mr 3,Je 28 1825;N 6 1839;Je-D 1840
OClWHi Ap 15 1824;F 7 1826;Jl 29,Ag 19 1835;Je 13 1840;O 2 1841;S 10 1844;Mr 20 1845;My 5 1846;O 16 1860;Mr 21 1861;O 25 1866;Jl 13 1867
OCo Ja 20 1825-52
OCoC O 3 1840;Ap 24 1841;Mr 8,Je 7-9 1842;F 22 1844-46
ODW Mr 25 1828-33;Ap 26-My 21 1836;48-N 1852
OHi 1821-22;D 1823-32;Jl 1833-N 5 1836
OOxM Ja 16,27,F 8,Mr 8 1827-28[30]-[32-Jl 1834]
P 1836-Jl 10 1838
PAg S 1832-Ag 1836;41-48
PBL Je 30 1829;D 6 1831;My 24,D 1 1832;O 31-N 1 1833[34]My 11 1837;Je 18 1845;Ja 12-14,24 1848
PCarlHi Ag 8,29-S 1 1821;Je 5 1832;Mr 23 1833
PEr [1821-50]
PHHi N 25 1824-Je 11,Ag 28 1825-Ap 8 1826
PHi 1821-Je 6 1826
PLaF [1857-60]-[62]63
PPL 1821-22;41-46;Ja 16 1858;Ja 16 1863

DISTRICT OF COLUMBIA (*Continued*)

WASHINGTON—*Continued*

*NATIONAL intelligencer. tw,sw O 31 1800-69||?—*Continued*
PPM Ap 20-D 4 1841
PPi N 1829-53
PPiHi Ag 31 1826[Mr 17 1827-Ap 16 1829]F 4,Mr 10 1836;My 29 1841-42[45-50]
PPiU-D [1822-25;32]-My 14 1833
PToHi My 20 1843-Ja 14 1845;Ja-My 1847;Ja-D 5 1848
PWbW 1839-44;Ag-S 1857
RPB 1821-[25]-[27-28]-My 18 1829[32]
THi 1821-24;40;47-48
TNY Ja-O 9 1822
TU [1826;58-61;66-69]
Tx 1838
TxGR F 28,Mr 13-29 1856;My 11 1861
TxU [1822-24]26;28-29;36-59
V 1821-59
VU [1821-23;25-Ap 1827]29-31;34;Mr 17 1836; 38-[42]-51;S 19 1854-60
Vt Ja-N 1821;D 1823-S 16,D 7 1824-Ap,D 6 1825-Ag 4 1826;Ap 1827-My,D 1828-Jl 11 1829; 30;32-N 1834;37-[41-44;46]Ja 14-N 1847;48;D 1850-51;Ja-S 26,D 1853-N 1855;56-N 1859
WF N 1821-Ap 24 1823
WHi 1821-My 11,D 31 1822-23;25-31;33-36;Mr 1837-[46-47]-54;Ja 30 1855-[62-63]-[66-Je 19 1869]
WaPS 1827-49

*Daily NATIONAL intelligencer. d Ja 1 1813-Je 24 1869||
Ag 30-S 22 1814 as National intelligencer. United with Washington express to form Daily national express and Washington intelligencer, later Daily national intelligencer
Suspended from Ag 24-30 1814
CL Mr 12 1864
CSmH [1821-Mr 4 1823]Ag 31 1830;Ap 26 1831; F 15 1833;D 15-16,27 1834[Ja 23 1837-Mr 1 1845]Mr 3 1848[D 25 1850-59]
CSt 1821-[43]-[51]-[57]-[67-68]
CtHi 1832-44
CtW Ag 15 1844;62-63;Jl 6 (extra)1863
CtY Ja 19 1822;Ja 25,F 14 1828;Mr 17 1829;Ag 28,D 31 1830-[31]F 11 1832-43;F 8,S 12 1844; Ja 11,Je 10,Jl 22,S 1845-Ap 1846;47[48-49]-O 22 1850;F 3,7,25,28 1851;Ja-Ag 1852[53]Ja 25, Ap 8,My 27 1854;Mr 9,S 6 1855;56;My 18,N 13-14,D 15 1857;Ja 4,12,28 1858;D 17,24,29 1860-Jl 1 1861;My 26-27,Je 13 1862;Mr 21-Jl 13 1863;Jl 15 1867
DGU 1828-48
DLC 1821-69
extras:Mr 1 1823;F 5,D 6 1825;Mr 27,28,D 5 1826;D 6 1831;D 4 1832;D 3 1833;Mr 4,Je 1 1841;Ja 18 1854;Ja 20,27,F 3,9,16,23,Mr 2,9,16, 23,30,Ap 6,13,My 19 1866;Ja 3,7,21,28,F 4,7,11, 13,18,20,25,27,Mr 4,11,18 1857;Ja 9,16,23,30,F 6,13,20,27,Mr 6,13,20,27 1858;Jl 6 1863;Ap 15, 16 1865
DW 1821-69
DeWI [1823-41]-[43;45]-[47]-[49]58-[62]-[64]-68
GMiG [Jl-D 1831]
GU Ag 30 1824-27;29-34[36-39]
ICN [1824]-Je 1826;Ja-Je 1827;Ja 10-My 1828; Ja-Je 1829;Jl-D 1830;Ja 24-D 1832;Jl-D 1833; 35;Jl-D 1836;Jl 1837-45;Ja-Je 1848
ICU D 1822[23-24]-Je 1825;26-[35]D 1836-N 1837;Jl 24 1841[47]48;N 23 1852;Mr 30,Je 29,Jl 6,23,Ag 1-2,9,12-13 1853;Jl-D 1855[Je-D 1856] 61-Je 1867;Ja-Ag 1868;69
IU N 2 1822;23-24;O 6 1830;Ap 15,D 13 1831;Jl 31,S 12,O 13,N 13 1832;Mr 11 1833[36-41;43] Jl 1846-[47]-56;Je 11 1857;N 1 1862;D 3 1863; 65-[66]
KyLo 1822-O 24 1835;D 1845-55
LNH 1845-Jl 19 1847
LSfD [1831-47]O 13 1860
LU D 1837-N 27 1839[43]-59[69]
M Jl 1861-Je 1866
MB [Mr 10-N 10 1828;Mr-D 1829;48-59;61-Je 1865;66-69]
MBAt [1821-25;27-29]Je 15 1840;Ag 21,31 1841; Ap 18-19,22,27,My 4 1865
MH 1821-23;32-49;My-S 5 1850[51-57]
MHi 1821-69
MNS [1821-65]
MSaE 1821-[58-61]
MWA Ja 10-Mr 3,Jl 24 1821[22]-34;36-[65-66] Ja 23,N 28,D 14,17 1867;My 7,Je 9 1868
MdBJ 1825
MdBP 1832-Je 1838
MdBSj D 1832-35;S 1836-My 26 1837
MdHi 1821-24;26;32-65
MiU 1821-27;29-31;33-37;40;42;49-55;57-60[64-65]-67
MiU-C [1824-51;54-58;61-67]
MoSU 1857-59
MoSW [1846-49]
N 1822;26;D 1827-My,D 1828;31-45;47-54;57[Je 1862-67]
NBHi Jl 1844-45;My 19 1848;My 5 1854;Je 20 1857
NBu Ag 4-D 1847;Jl-O 1850;F 1851-69
NIC 1821-27;31-32;35-39;50-N 24 1852;Ja-Je 1854;Ja-Je 1855;56-57
NN 1821-My,D 7(extra)1824;28-31;Ja 10,My 22,Je 22-23,Jl 12,D 6-7,11,25,27 1832;33-Mr 26 1841;Mr 12,D 16,23,30 1843-53;Ja-Je 1856;58-Je 22 1869
NNHi Ja 20 1821;My 8 1834[D 1835]-Jl 4 1836;Ja 18,Jl 15 1837-38[44]F 21,S 19-20,22 1845;My 27-28 1846[47]50;52-Je 1854;S 25-26, 28-30,O 2,N 7 1857;F 12-20,Ap 15-16 1858;60-61;Ap 9-10,29-30,Je 14[D]1862;Je 5,Ag 1[O 1863;64;Jl 1865;66]extra F 13,19,20 1858
NNS N 27 1821-31
NR Mr 5-S 1846;47
NT F 25 1835-Je 1855
NcD F 23,N 19-20 1821;22-[31]-Je 1833;34-[47]-62;Jl 1863-Ag 19,O 5-6,N 29 1864;65-69
NcU [1821]-[23-24]-[26-27]-[34]-[37]-[39-40]-[47]-[49]-[57]-Je 1863;O 22,31,N 5 1866;F 19, Mr 15,Ap 27 1867;Jl 29 1868
NhD [1845]My 29 1865
Nj 1853-57
NjR [1821-22;26;33-34;41;43;49;53-54;56-57;61; 65]
OC D 8 1829-S 1 1830;Jl 27 1832-Mr 1833;49; 55-60;65
OCHi Ja-Je D 1829-My 1833;34-42;45-54;Ja-Je 1861;63;Jl-D 1864
OClWHi 1821-69
OHi N 8 1826-69
OOxM Ja-Mr 2,D 4-11 1827;Mr 16-17 1828;D 8 1831
OT 1850-54
P D 5 1831-Ap 12 1847
PCarlHi D 1832-Ap 1833
PDoHi [1821-Ap 15 1828]
PHi 1821-Je 1863
PP Ap 17 1839[46]N 17 1864[Ap 1865]
PPL 1823-36;Mr 30 1850-65
PPM D 7 1821-Mr 24,My 27-30 1822[29]-38;40-Ja,N 25-D 1841;46-48[57]-60;Jl 1862-S 21 1869
PPi F 12 1835-37;O 1840-Mr 1867
RPB D 6 1841-57;Jl-D 1860;63-65
ScCa 1821-42
ScHi 1821-29;31-59
ScNC Ag 1840-Ap 1842
TKL Ag 29 1850;Mr 15 1851;My 22 1852;Mr 5,30,Je 15 1861;Mr 5 1867;Mr 9,Ap 2,7,11,14-15,18,24,28,My 2,5,9,12-14,16 1868;D 24 1846 supp
TxDM [1846]
TxGR Mr 8 1856
TxU 1831-37[Mr 17 1840-42]45-46[49-53;55-68]
VHi Mr-N 1831;My 14 1835[Ja-My 1842]Mr-D 1845;48-Ag 1857[Ja-O 1859]
VP Ag-D 1835;Je 1853-60;68-69
VRB Mr 16 1850-D 2 1852;55-My 6 1856
WHi 1821-Je 1828;29-Je 1830;31-41;43-68
WvMaC [1821-64]
—w ed 1836 *See* National

Weekly NATIONAL intelligencer. w Je 5 1841-S 12 1869||
Merged with Sunday herald, later Sunday herald and weekly national intelligencer
CSmH F 19,My 28,Je 11-18 1842;Je 15,N 23,D 7-14 1850[51]D 17 1853;Jl 5 1856;S 26 1857;F 6 1858;N 5,19 1859
CtY Je 5,Jl 17,31-Ag 7,S 4 1841;Ja 29 1842;Ja 9,Mr 20,Ap 3,My 8-15,Je 12-19,Jl 3,24-S 18,O 1858-Ja 15 1859;O 27,D 1-15 1860;Ap 13 1861
DLC Jl 1 1843;Ap 27,My 18-25 1844;Ja 18 1845-Mr 13,Jl 1847-48;Jl 3 1852 My 12,Ag 4 1860;63-64
IG 1844-47
In 1835-36;S 1837-39;51-52;55-Ja 1857
MHi Je 26 1841[66-67]Mr 4 1869
MWA Je-D 1841;S 2 1843;Ap 27 1844;Ap 4,D 19 1846;Jl 1847-62;Jl 23-Ag 20 1863;64
MWiC D 1847-54
MdBJ [Ap 23 1842-D 9 1843]F 17 1844-Ag,N 1846-49
MiU Ag 28,N 31 1841;N 13 1844
MiU-C [1841;47-56;62]
MnD Ag 27 1853-54
N [1846-Jl 1848]
NN [F-D 1842;Ag 1848-49]-Ap 19 1851
NNHi 1841-S 1 1849
NcD S 18 1841;My 26,Je 9-Jl 7,21 1849;Ja 19, Mr 9,O 19 1850;Ja 24 1852;56-F 14 1857;Mr 9,30 1861;N 29 1866;Ag 20,O 1-8 1868;Ja 7,21,F 25,Mr 11,25,My 13-20 1869
NcGrW [Ap 1868-Mr 1869]supps Ap 2,16,My 7 1868
NcU Ag 14,O 20,N 17,D 22 1849[50]-55;Ap 21 1859
NhD Ag 12 1843;47-54
OClWHi F 26 1848;Je 4 1853;Mr 5 1859
OCo Mr 1848-My 5 1855
OT 1848-49
PMe 1849
PToHi Ja-N 8 1856
PUn Ag 20,S 17 1863;O 13 1864
TU [1850-51;58;60-61;67-69]
VU D 9 1848-Mr 10,D 1-8,29 1849[50]-Je 1851; D 10,31 1853-S 16 1854;S 24-O 22,N 6 1868
WHi [Ja 24 1846-49]-Ag 18 1855

NATIONAL intelligencer. d S 20 1869-Ja 10 1870||
Formed by the union of Washington express and Daily national intelligencer. S-D 1 1869 as Daily national intelligencer and Washington express; D 3-25 1869 Daily national intelligencer and express
DLC 1869-Ja 8 1870
ICU D 1 1869
PPM S 20-21 1869

NATIONAL intelligencer. w 1898-
DLC My 17-24,Je 7-13,28-Jl 5 1898

Daily NATIONAL intelligencer and Sunday herald. d 1853-96||?
DW Jl 1 1895

NATIONAL Jewish ledger. w S 26 1930+
pub 1930+
PPiHi Mr 11 1932+

NATIONAL journal. sw,tw N 12 1823-Ja 22 1832||
Prospectus Ag 1823
sw 1823-Jl 14 1824;Je 1-N 26 1830;Mr 8-N 29 1831
CtHi Mr 10 1825-Ag 1831
CtY Ja 28,F 25,Ap 6,27 1826
DGU Ap 23 1825-27
DLC 1823-[30-31]
extras:D 7 1824;D 6 1825;Mr 18,D 5 1826;D 4 1827;D 2 1828
DW Jl 20 1825
GU Jl 20,31,Ag 5 1824
ICHi Jl 14,31 1824
ICU 1823-[26-28]Mr 5,Je 11,S 19,O 1,N 26 1829;Ja 30,Mr 9-11,Ag 13,O 24-31 1830
IEIC [Ag-D 1827]
KyLo Ag 1826-My 12 1827;28-29;Je 29 1830-N 1831
LU Jl 27 1824-Ja 16 1827
MB 1826-28;Je 1829-30
MBAt [My 1824-25]N 13,D 11 1828;F 12 1829 [30]Jl 20(extras)1831
MHi Ap 21 1825;Je 18 1829;Ja 15 1831
MSaE 1823-30
MWA 1823-[30]-Ja 21 1832
MeB D 25 1824-26
MiU 1823-Ag 8 1824
MiU-C [1823-31]
NN Ap 28,My 29,N 13 1827
NNHi F 21,Mr 6(extra)N 13 1824-[28]-Ag 1830
NbHi D 22,28 1824-Ja 6 1825
NcD 1824[26-27]
NcU [1824-28]
NhD Ja 31 1824;S 20 1825[26-30]Ja 11,Mr 29, Jl 12 1831;Ja 19 1832
NjHi Ja 26 1830;Ja 7-10,21 1832
ODW Jl 14 1824-Ag 25 1829
OOxM [Jl 1824-Jl 1825]Mr 25,Ap 18-20 1826;Jl 17,N 6 1827[28-Jl 1829]
PBL F 3,D 26-28 1825;Ja 3 1826
PDoHi Mr 18,25,O 7-9,14,23 1824;N 6 1827
PHH N 25 1824-Je 2 1825
PLewL Ap 24 1827
PWcHi [1824-25;28]
TxU 1828
V Mr 1829-Mr 4 1830
WHi Je 9-D 18 1824;25-30

Daily NATIONAL journal. d Ag 9 1824-Ja 23 1832||
My 17-Je 6 1831 as National journal
CSmH Jl 26 1827
CSt 1824-28
Ct [1824-25]
DLC 1824-31;Jl 30(extra)1831
GAtCo Ja 3 1827
GU [1824;26;28]
ICU 1824-30;Jl-D 1831
IU [Ja-Ap,D 1831]
MBAt D 10 1825;S 5,O 11-12 1827[28-29]F 22 1830;Ja 4,F 24-25 1831
MH D 7 1825-Je 9,D 8 1826-27
MHi [1826-27]Jl 2,27,O 11 1831
MWA Ag 9 1824-30;Ja 5,F 7,My 17,21 1831
MiU 1824[25]-[27]30
MiU-C [1824-31]
NChM S 3 1825
NN Ja 20 1826[27-Je 1828;Ja-Jl 1830;Ja-Jl 1831]
NcD D 16 1824;Ja 21,26,28,31,F 14,D 1825-N 1827
NcU Jl 13 1826
NhD [1826-27]O 19-24,26-31 1829;Ja 1,4-5 1830
OCHi O 26 1824
OOxM [F 8-My 20 1826]D 3 1827;My 9 1828;F 10 1829
PLewL Ap 24 1827
PPL [1829]-F 18 1830
TxU 1824-30
VU Ja-Je 1828

NATIONAL leader. *See* Leader

*NATIONAL messenger. (Georgetown) sw,tw Ap 17 1816-My 21 1821||
1816-O 24 1817 as Messenger. Merged with Metropolitan, later Metropolitan and Georgetown commercial gazette
sw Ap-D 16 1816
DLC 1821
NcD [1821]

NATIONAL observer. w Ja 10 1822-
DLC Ja 10,19,F 9,Mr 2-16 1822
MBAt Mr 2 1822
N Ja 10 1822

NATIONAL palladium and congressional register. w N 6 1823-
N 6-20? 1823 as National palladium
DLC N 20 1823
MBAt N 27 1823

NATIONAL radical. w Mr 26- 1868||
Campaign paper
MWA Mr 26,Ag 27 1868

NATIONAL republican. d N 26 1860-Je 11 1888||
Title varies slightly
CtY Ja 3-Je 27 1862;63-83
DLC complete
extras:Mr 4 1869;S 20 1881
DW Mr 24 1864;Jl 4,6 1876 Ap 1,5 1878;O 5 1883
GU Ap 17,Ag 14,S 14 1872;F 19,Mr 5,Je 18,21, 27,Jl 25,29 1873;S 20 1881
ICHi Ap 12,14-15,S 23 1865
ICM Mr 1 1882;O 25 1883;S 24 1885
ICU Jl 1861-Je 1864;Je-D 1865;Jl-D 1866;Jl 1868-79;Jl 1880-Je 1881;Ja-Je,O 1882-[87]Ap-Je 1888
KHi [Je 1865-Jl 1885]
MBAt 1862-63;Ap 20,25-27,My 4,Jl 6,N 10 1865 [Ap 12 1866-F 10 1868]
MSaE O 19 1875
MWA D 28 1860;My 10,16,21,27,Je 5,Ag 1861-Je 1862[Ja-Je 1863]-[Ja-My]Ag 27-D 6 1864[65-66]Mr 30-My,Ag 12,17,N-D 1867;N 21 1868[69-70]-Je,Jl 25 1876[Ja-Je 1877]78-[80;82-83]84; Ja 10 1885[86]
MiU [1861-63]-[65]-[88]
MnHi N 5 1872[84-85]F 20 1886
NN Jl-D 1871;Jl 25,Ag 9 1885
NNHi My 7 1864;D 2 1865;Ja 18 1869;Mr 10, 23 1870;Je 4 1873;N 1 1886
NbHi Mr 1,Je 22 1863;Mr 13,20,22 1877;F 21 1885;My 24 1887
NcD Ja-Je 28 1864;O 11 1865[Ap 1866-67]-Mr 2 1869;Jl 22 1874;Ap 5,Je 7,9 1882
NcU Ja 2 1862;Ap 3 1866;Ag 13 1868[70-77]D 12 1878;Ja 28,30,F 11,14,My 22-23,Je 2 1879 [81-84]Ag 9 1885
NhD Ap 27 1865
OCHi S 30 1886
OClWHi Jl 31 1861;My 20,S 15-D 1862;Ja 1-3, Jl 1863-Je 1865;Ap 21 1870 Mr 20 1874;Je 21 1877;Mr 5 1881
OOxM Ja 29-31 1885
PPot Mr 4-5 1881;Mr 3-5 1885
RW F 13 1869
Tx Je 14 1870
Vt O 10 1861;F 28 1882
WHi Ap 15,My 4 1865;Ap 6 1871-74

DISTRICT OF COLUMBIA (*Continued*)

WASHINGTON—*Continued*

Weekly NATIONAL republican. w D 1860-77||?
DLC D 1863-My 5 1865;Mr 2,Ag 24 1866;Je 3-10 1871
In Ap 13 1866;Ja 5 1869
MB S 20,O 4,18,N 8,D 20 1861;My 2-9,Ag 29,O 3,N 14-21 1862[63-65]Je 8-15,Ag 24,O 12 1866
MWA S 6 1861;N 20(supp)1863;F 17,My 5,O 13,D 15 1865;Je 8 1876
NNHi Ja 11 1872
NbHi Ap 13 1866;S 11 1869;Ag 19 1871;D 21 1872;Ja 17 1874
NcD Ap 27 1866
OClWHi Jl 10 1864;Ag 24 1866
WHi [Je 24 1864-O 1865]

NATIONAL republican. w Ja 1882-92||?
CtY Ja 19-D 1882
ICU [1882]
In D 21 1880;D 25 1886
NcD Jl 30,S 14 1882;Ap 14,My 19 1887
VU My 26 1887
WHi Ag 9 1885[D 30 1886-Ag 18]O 1888-S 19 1889

NATIONAL republican. (Foreign and consular ed) w O 1885-
DLC N 17 1885;Je 27 1889

NATIONAL republican. w 1914-Mr 7 1925||
Followed by National republic (not in this list)
DLC 1919-25
GU [1924]
In My 11 1918-24
InU 1915-[21]Ja 1 1922[23-24]
M S 1923-25
MHi F 12 1921
MiG S 24 1921-24
MnU Mr 1919-25
NN My 11-Jl 13 1918;Jl 12 1919-25
OClWHi Je 1 1920;O 7 1922
OHi My 18 1918-25
TJT Mr 13-Ap 10,My-Je 1920
VU N 13 1920

NATIONAL union. sw My 1 1832-
Prospectus Ap 11 1832
DLC Ap 11,My 1,25,Je 1-5,26,Jl 3 1832
MWA My-Jl 10 1832
OCHi My 1 1832

NATIONAL union. d O 3 1877-Ap 13 1878||
United with Washington post to form Washington post and union, later Washington post
DLC complete
DW O 3 1877;Ap 3 1878
MiU [1877-78]

NATIONAL union. w N 1 1877-78||?
NbHi N 1,15 1877

NATIONAL view. w 1879-95||?
DLC Ja 29,F 19,Jl 16,Ag 6,20-27,O-D 3,17-31 1887;Jl 30,O 29 1892
IU Ap 14 1888
In 1888-Je 1894
KHi Mr 15-22 1884
MWA D 17 1881
NcD F 12,O 29 1881;Mr 18 1882;F 12 1887
NcU Ag 6 1881
OClWHi F 18 1893
WHi Je 19 1880-Mr 19 1881;N 10 1883;Mr 8 1884;Jl 15 1893

NATIONAL watchman. w 1892-Mr 1896||?
United with Silver knight to form Silver knight-watchman, later National watchman
Also dated in Alexandria, Va.
KHi [1892-96]
NcD My 21,Jl 23,Ag 6,S 14 1892;Je 15,Ag 25,O 6 1893;My 3 1895;F 27-Mr 7 1896
OkHi [1893]-[95]

NATIONAL watchman. w 1895-Ag 8 1901||
1895-Mr 1896? as Silver knight; Ap 1896?-98? Silver knight-watchman
DLC 1898;1900-01
ICM N 9 1899
KHi [1895-1901]

NATIONAL whig. w Ap 28? 1838-
DLC My 12-Jl 14 1838
P-M Ag 11 1838

Daily NATIONAL whig. d Ap 7 1847-Je 20 1849||
Ap-Ag 7 1847 as National whig
Suspended S 30-O 7 1847
DLC [1847-Ja 8 1848]49
DW F 10 1849

NATIONAL zeitung. w My? 1843-
In German
DLC O 11 1843
PPeS F 25-Ap 1 1847

NATIVE American. w Ag 10 1837-
Suspended from Ag 8-25 1840
DLC Ag-S 9,23-O 14,D 1837-N 1840
MWA Ja 5,26,Mr 30,Ag 10,24-31 1839
NcD D 9-16 1837;S 5 1840

NEW ERA. d Ap 12 1864-My 14 1865||
DLC Ap 12-21,26-My 1865

Weekly NEW ERA. w 1864-65||?
NcU My 11 1864

NEW ERA. 1870 See New national era and citizen

NEW national era and citizen. w Ja 13 1870-75||
1870 as New era; 1871-73? New national era
DLC Ja 12 1871-Ja 4,18-25 1872;Ja 15 1874
MWA Ja 13,F 24 1870;Mr 19 1874
N S 12,O 24-31,N 14,D 12 1872
NNHi D 22 1870-S 7 1871[Ja-Ag 1873]-O 1874

Washington NEWS. w,sw Jl 18 1846-Mr 13 1858||
1846-Ap 8 1848 as Saturday evening news and district general advertiser; Ap 15-Jl 1 1848 Saturday news; Ag 13 1852-Ag 16 1854 Washington semi-weekly news
sw Ag 18 1852-Je 9 1855
DLC complete
MWA O 16,D 24 1852;Ag 22 1857
NcD O 14 1848;Ag 25,S 11,N 10 1852;Ag 17 1853-Ag 16 1854
OCHi My 17 1854

Morning NEWS. d S 18 1869-72||
DLC 1869-F 15 1870
NcD Ja 28 1870

Daily NEWS. d 1875-77||?
Title varies slightly
DLC My 11,18,Ag 3 1876

Washington NEWS. d D 17 1892-F 27 1896||
1892-F 28 1894 as Evening news
DLC 1892-Mr 1895
MiU 1892-[95]
NcD Ap-Je 1893;94

Weekly NEWS. (Anacostia) w 1909-
DLC Ag 7-21,S 4-18,O 9,N-D 11 1909

Washington daily NEWS. d N 8 1921+
pub 1921+
DLC 1921+
DW 1922+
NcD D 1-2,4,16 1924;Ja 22 1925
WaPS [1929]

NORTH AMERICAN. w,sw Ap 12 1834-F 11 1835||
Suspended from Jl 12-O 1,D 31 1834-Ja 14 1835
w 1834
DLC Ap-Je,O 1,29-N 5,19-D 3,17,31 1834;Ja 14-F 1835

L'OPINION publique. w 1868||
In French
MWA F 20 1868

Daily PATRIOT. d N 14 1870-N 11 1872||
DLC complete
MB N-D 5 1870;Ja 1-17,O 28 1872
NNHi Ja 23,My 16 1871-72
NcD Mr 28-O 10,D 16 1871-72
WHi My-N 1872

Weekly PATRIOT. w 1870-72||?
NcD [My 1871-Ap 1872]

PENNSYLVANIA thirteenth. (Camp Tennally)
PPiHi Ja 4,F 15 1862

POLITICAL reformer. *See under* Richmond, Va.

Washington POST. d D 6 1877+
Ap 15-29 1878 Washington post and union
D 6 1927 is 50th anniversary ed
pub D 6 1877;Ja-My,Jl 1878+
A 1898-Mr 1899;Ap 1901-Jl 1910;Jl 1912+
CClP S 1904-Je,S 1905-20
CL F 3,22 1924;D 6 1927
CLM S 19,25 1892
CSt S 1901-Ag 1902
CU Jl 1929-Ag,O-N 1931;My 28 1932-F 1933
Ct Jl 1921+
CtY Ap 9 1898-S 28 1899
DLC 1877+
DW 1882-84;Jl-D 1886;1906+
GA Mr 4 1929
GU Je 1 1880
ICM Jl 13 1878;Ap 2,My 25 1883;Mr 7-8,Ap 7 1894;Mr 29 1896;Mr 21 1903;F 19 1912;O 24,26 1913;F 22 1914
ICU [S 1883-84]S 13 1885[92;96;1902;05]-[07-08]
IEN 1895
IHi F 12 1909;Mr 4 1929
IaDH [1892-94]
In Ag 25 1889;D 19 1890;Mr 4 1929
InU Mr 4 1929
KHi [Mr 1893-S 1915]
M Mr 1914+
MBAt Mr 4 1929
MHi Mr 4 1929
MWA My-D 1880;Mr 4(supp)O 8,N 17,D 31 1889;O 1 1902;D 31 1906;D 6 1927;Mr 4 1929
MiU 1878-[82]-[86]-[88]-[91-98]-[1901-02]-[12] 13;26+
MiU-C S 21 1892;O 16 1931
MoHi D 29 1908
MsU [Ja 1888]
NBuG Mr 4 1929
NNHi [1886]
NcD Ja 1,4,F 14,Mr 27,D 7 1882;Mr 19,25,27, Ap 1,8-10,13 1892[97]Ap 23 1898;My 16,D 1899-My,N 13,24,27,D 22 1900[02]Ja 1,S 19 1903;N 21 1907;F 11 1912;Mr 3-5 1913;F 4,Ap 6,Je 9,D 6,27 1914;Mr 30-31,Ap 9,My 30 1915; N 5,9,21 1916;Je 19,Jl 16,25,O 11 1918;N 17, 26,D 26-27,29 1919;Ag 2,4-5,7-10,S 15,18-25 1921;D 2,6,9,12 1924;Ja 15-17,23,Ap 1,Jl 3 1925
NcU Ag 22,O 11,N 13 1878;Jl 2 1881;Je 29 1883;Ap 19 1885;My 29 1890[92;94-96]D 22 1901[02]-[05]-[09-10]My 14 1916;Mr 4 1929
NjWdHi N 19-20 1879
OClWHi Ja 7 1883;Mr 3 1889;Ja 18 1891;Mr 3,5 1897;O 16 1903;F 14-15,Ap 3 1920
OOxM Ja 29-31 1885
P Mr 1905-17
PJ My 11 1894
PP [1927]+
PPiHi Mr 5 1897
PWbW Mr 5 1929
TKL S 19-21 1892;F 11 1894
TU My 16 1879
Tx My 1904-Ja,Mr,My,Jl,N 1924;25-Je,Ag 1930+
TxAS S 12 1925+
VHi Ag 8 1897
VU Ja 6 1887;S 27 1908;F 2,Ag 26-27,S 29-30,O 2-3,7-8 1934
VtMS [1885-1901]
WHi S 9 1883;92+
WaPS [1917]25[26-27]-33

Washington weekly POST. w 1878-1916||?
ICM Jl 5 1882;Ag 1 1883;F 4 1885
MWA Jl 1889-90;92
NcD Ja 9,My 7,21,Jl 23,D 24-31 1884;F 25 1885;Mr 24 1886;D 19-26 1893;My 1 1894;Ag 3 1897

Evening POST. 1888-89 *See* Critic-record

POTOMAC advocate and metropolitan intelligencer. (Georgetown) *See* Georgetown advocate (1835-41)

POTOMAC herald. (Georgetown) *See* Herald and Georgetown advocate

Washington PRESS. d D 3 1888-Ja 15 1890||
DLC complete
MWA Mr 15 1889

PRICE current and commercial advertiser. w N 1865-
DLC My 5 1866

PUBLIC voice. Ap 10 1871-
DLC Ap 10 1871

RECONSTRUCTION. w D 14 1865-66||?
MH D 14 1865
MnHi Mr 10,24 1866

REFORMER. d F 22-Ap 29 1837||
Follows United States telegraph. Followed by Merchant (Baltimore, Md.)
DLC complete
N F 22 1837
NN F 22-24,28,Mr 1,3,7-18,21-31 1837

REFORMER. (country ed) sw,tw F 25 1837-
Follows United States telegraph
tw during sessions of Congress
ICU F-Mr 1,8,15-25 1837
MWA [Mr 8-S 6 1837]
NcD Ap 15,Jl 12,S 20,27,O 21,25,N 1 1837
WHi Jl 19,Ag 9,23,S 23,O 25 1837
See also Merchant (Baltimore, Md)

Daily REPUBLIC. d Je 13 1847-Ag 27 1853||
1849-Je 1853 as Republic
Suspended from Jl 1-5 1853
CtY Ag 26,S 7,21 1852
DLC complete
ICU 1849;F 1850-[51]-53
MB [Jl 3 1849-My 1853]
MHi complete
MWA complete
MiU [1849]-[53]
MiU-C N 1,4 1852
N Jl 26 1850
NBuHi 1850-52
NN Jl 4,Ag 8-10,24 1849-Je 1850;51;Ja-Je 1853
NcD D 6 1849;Mr 7-14,Ap 5 1850
NhD [1849-53]
OCHi My 13,15 1850;Ag 30 1851
OClWHi D 3 1849;Mr 29,Jl 4 1850;F 5 1851
OHi 1849-Mr 15 1852
PAg Ag 1849-N 1850
PHi 1849-Je 1853
WHi 1849-Je 13 1850

REPUBLIC. tw Je 1849-Je 30 1853||
DLC Jl 4 1850;Ap 3,Ag 21,S 14,D 4-7 1852
ICU O 9 1851;Je 15,Jl 15,Ag 19,26 1852;Ja 6 1853
MB Ja 28 1850;Mr 25 1851
MHi [1849]
MWA Je 28,Jl 10,19,Ag 5 1851
MsHi F 11-Je 1853
NN Je 14-Jl 26,28-Ag 7,11-23 1849
NNHi Jl 10 1849-[Je 1850]
NjR F 16 1850

REPUBLIC. w Je 1849-53||?
DLC Ap 8 1852
MHi Jl 1849-Jl 1851
MWA Ag 16 1849
MeU Jl 18 1850
MiU [1849-50]
MiU-C [1850-52]
MsHi 1851-Je 1853
N Ag 30 1849-S 5 1850;Mr 9 1852
OCl Je 20 1850
TxU Ap 14 1853

REPUBLIC. sw S 22 1857-
CtY 1857-S 17 1858
MWA D 15 1857-58
OHi Jl 31 1858-S 17 1859

REPUBLIC. w S 26? 1857-
DLC D 19 1857;F 27,Ag 28 1858
MWA F 11 1860
NjR D 10 1859
P-M O 2 1857
TxU Ap 17 1858

Weekly REPUBLIC. w 1878||?
DLC Je 5 1878(broadside)
MWA Je 5,15 1878

Washington REPUBLICAN. w 1839?-
NcU S 30 1840

Washington REPUBLICAN and congressional examiner. sw,tw,d Ag 7 1822-Jl 10 1824||
Merged with National journal
sw 1822-Jl 9 1823;d D 1 1823-My 26 1824
Ct [D 31 1823-24]
DLC 1822;Mr 1823-24
ICU 1822[Mr 8-Jl 9]D 1823-Jl 8 1824
MBAt [1822-23]
MHi Ag 28,31,S 4-7,18 1822;D 27 1823;Ja 14, Ap 20,28 1824
MWA Ag 7,S 7,O 23,D 4 1822[Jl 1823-Jl 10 1824]prospectus(photostat)
MiU 1822-23
NNHi Ja 22-24,F 7,14-27 1824
NcU [1822]Mr 22,Je 18,Jl 9,Ag 12,N 4,29 1823
NhD [1822]Ja 8-15,F 26 1823
PDoHi Je 24 1824
PNoHi My 18 1824
PWcHi Ag 31-N 27 1822;Mr 12-D 24 1823;My 29-Jl 1924
PWcT [1822-24]
WHi D 23 1822-23;Ja 28 1824

Washington REPUBLICAN and congressional examiner. d D 2 1822-Mr 3 1823||
DLC complete
ICU 1822-[F]Mr 1,3 1823

DISTRICT OF COLUMBIA (*Continued*)

WASHINGTON—*Continued*

Washington REPUBLICAN and congressional examiner. (For the country) tw D 1822-My 1824||
Suspended from F-D 1823
DLC [1822-24]
ICU D 23/24,30/31 1822;Ja 28/29,D 1823;Ja 2/3,23/24,F 11/12,23/24,Mr 15/16,Ap 12/13, 19/20,30/My 1,7/8,26/27 1824
MWA Ja 18,F 1,N 13-22,D 1/2,15/16 1823;Ja 12/13,Mr 26/27,Ap 7/8-12/13,19/20,26/27,My 3/4 1824
NcU [1824]
PDoHi Mr 18,Ap 12,My 10/11 1824
PPot F 11 1824

REPUBLICAN herald.
NbHi Mr 8 1834

REVEILLE. (U.S.General Hospital) w?
PMilC Jl 15 1865

ROLL CALL. tw
NN Mr 12 1864

Washington SENTINEL. d S 24 1853-Mr 25 1855||
DLC complete;O 22(extra)1854
ICU O 18 3-55
KHi [1855]
MB [1853-F 1854]
MWA O 1853-Mr 24 1855
MiU complete
NNHi [1853]Ja 20,Mr 19,Ap 30 1854

Washington SENTINEL. tw S 1853-Ag 19 1856||?
DLC Mr 27 1855-Ag 19 1856
DW My 29 1855;Jl 26 1856
ICU O 24 1854;Mr 27-D 1855;F 5 1856
KHi [Mr-Ap 14 1855]
MB O 8 1853-O 5 1854
MWA O 8 1853;Mr 27,Ag 30 1855;Mr 1 1856
MiU 1853-Ag 16 1856
NcD [D 1853-Ag 1856]
TxU [O 4 1853-O 10 1854]

Washington SENTINEL. w O 1853-56||?
MWA O 21 1853
NB 1853-Ag 1856
NcD S 8,N 10,D 15 1854[Ja-O 1855]Mr 21,Jl 18-25 1856

Washington SENTINEL. w Jl 4 1873-1910||?
DLC 1873-Je 16 1894;Jl 27,N 9 1895;Mr 7,Ap 4,My 2,Ag 1 1896[98]-Je 1901
extras:Mr 4,11,18,25,Ap 1,8,15,22,29,My 6,13, 20,27 1874
ICU S 24 1881
NcD Ag 23 1876;Jl 3 1880
NcU F 8 1879

SIGNAL. w Jl 1 1852-Mr 1853||
Suspended from O 30 1852-Mr 1853
Campaign paper
DLC complete
MHi [1852]
MWA Jl 1,S 11-O 2 1852
NN Jl-O 1852

SILVER knight. *See* National watchman. 1895-1901

SOUTHERN citizen. w 1857-
DLC Jl 2,30 1859
NNHi My 21 1859
OCHi Ap 2,Je 4 1859

SOUTHERN press. d Je 17 1850-Ag 9 1852
A Ag 9 1851-F 17,Jl 24 1852
DLC complete
In Je 24-25 1850
MWA Je 17-18,N 4 1850
KyLo 1850-Je 1851
MWA Je 17-18,N 4 1850
MiU Jl 1851-52
MsHi F 1851-Jl 1852
NcD Jl 11,15-Ag 10,13-S 17 1850
OHi Jl 19 1850-Je 1852
Tx Jl 23 1850

SOUTHERN press. tw,sw Je 25 1850-Ag 14 1852||
tw during sessions of Congress
DLC Je 25 1850[Ap 9 1851-52]
GU Mr 26,Ap 26-My 3 1851
MWA D 14 1850;Mr 29,S 5 1851
MsHi F 27 1851-Jl 1852
NcD [Jl 16 1850-Jl 19 1852]
NcU [1850-51]F 28 1852
WHi F 11,19,My 10,O 8 1851

SOUTHERN press. w Je 1850-Ag 1852||
DLC Ag 30 O 11-18,N 1,29,D 20 1851;Mr 20, My 29 1852
MWA Ap 10 1852
NcD O 26-N 2,30 1850;Jl 12,Ag 16-23,O 1,25 1851;Mr 6 1852
TxU [Ag 13 1850-Ag 14 1852]

SPECTATOR. w 1842-44 *See* Young hickory

SPECTATOR. d,sw N 28 1843-O 4 1844||
Followed by Constitution (Baltimore)
d N 28 1843-Je 22 1844
DLC [1843-44]
MWA N 29 1843;Ap 30-My 1,Jl 30 1844
NcD My 15(extra)1844
NcU F 10,My 7,24,Je 13,Jl 23,S 13 1844

SPECTATOR. w Je 9? 1855-
DGU N 23 1865-Ap 14 1866
DLC Jl 21 1855
PPCHi [1865-66]

Washington STAR. w S 3 1841-
DLC S 3 1841

Evening STAR. d D 16 1852+
1852-O 7 1854 title varies slightly
pub Jl 1853+
C 1919-23
CLM D 13 1852
CtY S 14,16 1901;Je 30-Jl 6 1934
DCHi S 20 1881;Je 30 1882
DLC D 16(facsimile)1852;Mr 5,Jl 1853-[67]+
extras: D 5 1853;Ja 16,O 21,D 4 1854;Jl 13,22 1861;D 14 1862;My 8 1864;N 25 1867
DW Jl 1855-Je 1856;Jl 1857-Je 1863;64+
GU N 19 1922
ICN 1864-65
IF Ap 15 1865
IHi F 12 1909
IaDH 1905-14
In Mr 5 1856;Mr 4 1869;Ap 16 1891
InRE Je 10 1899
MBAt Ap 3,15,17,Jl 7 1865
MWA 1852-[55]-57;D 1 10,28 1858;59-65;F 8 1868;O 25,28 1869;O 26 1872;N 17 1873;Ap 13 1874;My 24,Jl 22,27,O 20 1876;Mr 5,26 1877;Ja 25 1878;F 1,N 8 1881;82-[1904]-[06;08-09]-[17]+
MdBJ Mr 4-5 1889
MdBLe Jl 1854-Jl 3 1855;F-Je 1856;Jl-D 1858
MiU 1882-Je 1885;86-93[97;1902]-[04]-[06]-13
MiU-C [1862;64;82;1901;05]
MsU [1887]
N 1914+
NNHi 1860-63;My 3 1873
NbHi Mr 20 1877;F 21 1885;F 21 1885;Mr 5 1887;Ap 14,D 7 1888;Mr 5,O 7,26,N 15,D 7 1889;F 1,Ap 25-26,N 29,D 6,20 1890;Jl 18,Ag 18,O 3,5,19,24,N 14 1891;Ja 2,9,16,23,30,F 3,13, Mr 12,Ap 2,Jl 2,5,9,Ag 9,S 19-24,O 1,N 5 1892;Ap 15,My 20,27,Je 24,Jl 1,Ag 5,S 16,21, 23,30,O 7,15 1893;N 5-10 1900
NcD My 19 1864;Ap 4 1865;S 1867-F 25 1869; Je 4,15,Ag 13 1883;F 24,My 27 1887;S 21 1892; F 6 1897;Ja 4 1894;Jl 11 1904;Je 1 1918;D 6-7 1924;Ja 13,18,25,30,F 1,7,24 1925
NcU F 20 1871;Ag 26,O 5 1872;O 29 1873;Mr 24,Ap 4 1874;My 31 1875;Ap 16 1877;Jl 25,Ag 19-20,22 1878;My 14 1879[81]Mr 27,N 16 1883; Ap 1 1884;Ag 8,S 12 1885;Ag 9-10,12,14,24-25 1886[1904]-[07]-My 1908;Mr 13 1927
NhD Ag 23-24 1880;F 2 1884
OCHi Ag 17 1861;Ap 3 1862;F 21 1885
OCl D 16 1852
OClWHi Ja 9 1863;My 20 1864;My 24,O 7 1865;Mr 4 1881;F 2 1889;S 19-24 1892;Mr 4 1897;Ap 13 1907;O 1908
OHi 1912+
OOxM Ja 29-30 1885
PScrHi Ap 29 1922;Ap 21 1925
PWbW Mr 4 1929
TJT Ja 27 1888;Ja 23 1890;Ap 22,Ag 10 1905; My 27,Je 10,17,24,Jl 15,22,29,S 16,O 14,N 4,D 9,23 1906;Ja 13,20,27 1907;F 11 1912
TKL Mr 23 1868
TxGR D 31 1898
TxU D 20 1855;Mr 14 1859
VHi F 21,24,26,Mr 3,5 1885
VU [Ag-D 1918]Ja 5,8-9,F 2,8-11,14-16,Mr 9 1919
VtMS [1888-97]
WHi [Jl-D 1856]Ap 15,Jl 7 1865;Mr 6,F 26 1873;O 15 1903;Mr 21 1917
WaPS [1923-24]

Weekly STAR. w S 1853-91||?
CLM Ja 10 1889
CSmH Je 2 1855
DLC Ap 23 1856-N 17 1860;Ja 13,F 24 1871;Je 30,Ag 18 1876;Ap 19 1878;82;86;88-90
ICN 1864-65
MWA S 6 1872;O 6 1876
NNHi F 26 1860;Ja 21 1873
TxU Je 16 1860
WHi Jl 19 1861

Washington morning STAR, and district chronicle of the times. d S 15 1834-
DLC S 15 1834

STATES and union. d Ap 17 1857-Ap 20 1861||
1857-N 8 1859 as States
CSmH My 15 1857
DLC complete; Ag 17(extra)1860
MB N 9 1859;Mr 28,Je 9,12 1860[F 6-Ap 19 1861]
MWA O 20 1857;Ja 21,Je 22,26 1858;Mr 30,My 7,19,Je 28,Ag 22,S 7,14,16-17,O 31-N 1,9,16-19 1859;My 28 1860
NcD O 2,7,N 10,17,30 1857-Ja 1,4,7,Je 7 1858; My 21,D 14 1859;Ja 24 1861
NcU O 12,31 1860;Ja 22 1861
TU Jl 18 1860
V N 22-D 4 1858;Ja 6-S 12 1859;Ja-D 13 1860

STATES and union. w Ap 1857-Ap 1861|
1857-N 5 1859 as States
DLC D 3 1859
In Ag 22 1857;O 2,30 1858
LNC S 5 1860
NcD O 24 1857
NcU N 26 1859
TxU F 27 1858
WHi My 26 1860;Mr 4 1861

STATES and union. sw
PToHi Ap 4-N 24 1860

SUBURBAN citizen. w Ja 1891-1902||?
DLC [F-D 1893]Ag 28 1897-1902

SUN. sw,w F 21 1835-Ag 1837||?
Suspended from My 18?-Jl 30? 1835
sw 1835-Mr 1837
DLC 1835-My 18,Jl 30-N 12 1836;Ja 14,F 25, Mr 1,My 1,Je 5,26-Jl 17 1837
In [Ag 1836-Ag 7 1837]
MWA F-Mr 25,Ap 1-4,18-Jl,Ag 12-S 19,26-O 17,N 4-14,21-D 12,19 1835;Ja 2,16-F 10,17-Mr 5,12,19-Ap 20,My 7-18 1836
NjHi F 24 1836
PBL Mr 11-18 1835
TKL Mr 14,My 9,18 1835

SUN. w 1877?-
DW Mr 10 1878

Washington SUN. w 1914-
Negro
DLC D 25 1914-Jl 23 1915

Washington daily SUN. d Mr 24-My 5 1933||
DLC complete

TÄGLICH. . . *See under* next important word: e.g., Täglicher Washingtoner anzeiger is alphabeted under Anzeiger

TAKOMA journal. (Takoma Park) w F 17 1928+
pub 1928+
MdBE Je 8 1934+

TAKOMA news. (Takoma Park) F 23 1923-Ag 19 1927||
Followed by Maryland news (Silver Spring, Md.)
DTJ complete

Evening TELEGRAM. d Ag 1870-
DLC Ag 27,29 1870

Daily TELEGRAM. d,ir My 22 1875-F 4 1880||
Title varies slightly
Suspended from Ag 30?-O 2 1875;Ag 28-S 2 1876;Jl 6-Ag 31 1878;Ja 1-6 1879
d 1875-My 22 1877;S 1-D 31 1878
DLC complete
GU O 11 1875;Mr 25 1876
MWA Mr 5 1877
MeU Mr 2 1877
NcU [1876-80]
OCHi Mr 6,8 1877
OClWHi Mr 12 1877

Washington TELEPHONE. w S 18 1880-81||?
1880-F 1881 as Telephone
DLC S 18,N 27,D 11 1880-Ja 8,F 26-Mr 5,17, 31-Ap 7 1881

Daily TIMES. d My 1 1845-Mr 24 1846||
Follows Daily Madisonian. 1845-Ja 31 1846 as United States journal
DLC 1845-Mr 23 1846
ICU Ja 1846
IU My-Ag 12 1845
NcD 1845
OClWHi Je 17,D 12 1845
—country ed *See* Democratic expositor and United States journal for the country

Semi-weekly TIMES. sw My 3 1845-Mr 24 1846||
Follows Madisonian. 1845-Ja 1846 as United States journal
DLC Mr 24 1846
In My-O 1845
MWA My 3,9-13,23,Je 3,24,N 8 1845;Ja 17 1846
MiU-C My 3 1846
OClWHi Mr 3 1846
WHi 1845-Ja 27 1846

Weekly TIMES. w My 3 1845-Mr 1846||?
Follows Madisonian. 1845-Ja 1846? as United States journal
DLC Jl 5 1845;F 28-Mr 21 1846
MWA Mr 7-14 1846
NcU O 24 1845

TIMES. w Ja 15- 1848||?
Campaign paper
MWA Ja 15 1848
N Ja 15 1848

Daily TIMES. (Georgetown) w,d F 22 1863-
1863-Mr 6 1864 as Sunday times(w)
1863-Je 19 1866 pub in Washington
Suspended from Mr 6-15 1864
DLC 1862-[65]-Jl 21 1866
ICHi S 16,D 14 1873
NcD N 10 1864
VRC Ag 9 1862

TIMES. w N 29? 1868-
DLC My 22,Ag 19,S 4-11 O 2-9,30,N 13,D 4 1869;D 31 1871

Washington TIMES. (Morning ed) Mr 18 1894-N 29 1902||
Jl 4 1895-Mr 11 1897 as Morning times; Mr 12 1897-Je 29 1901 Times
DLC 1894-O 1902
WHi Ap-D 1896

Washington TIMES. d Ag 5 1895+
1895-N 29 1902 as Evening times. Sunday issues 1922-23 as Washington times-herald
pub Ap 1897+
CL 1920-21
DLC 1895+
DW 1905+
KHi [Jl 1918]
MWA N 7 1918
MiU Jl 1902-My 1908
NcD F 20-25 1932
OClWHi Mr 4 1897
PArL Mr 4 1933
PWbW Mr 4 1929
TJT F 7 1915
VU S 22 1905
WHi Ap-D 1896

Washington TIMES-HERALD. *See* Washington herald; Washington times 1895+

Washington TRIBUNE. w My 14 1921+
Negro
DLC 1921+

TRUE whig. w D 11 1841-F 4 1843||?
DLC 1841-42
InNcHi Mr 19 1842
InU Ap-D 1842
MWA D 18 1841;Je 11,Jl-S 3,O 1-22,N 12,D 3-17 1842
NSchU Ap 23 1842
NcD O 15 1842
PBL 1842
TC Ag 13 1842

TRUE whig. d D 13-23 1842||
DLC complete

TRUTH. Jl 4 1853-
DLC Jl 4 1853

Washington TRUTH. w S 3 1905-
S 3-O 1 1905 as Graft; O 8-29 1905 National graft
DLC S 3,17-N 1905

DISTRICT OF COLUMBIA (*Continued*)

WASHINGTON—*Continued*

Washington UNION. d My 1 1845-Ap 10 1859‖ Follows Daily globe. 1845-Ap 15 1857 as Daily union. Followed by Constitution
A Ja 14 1846-48
CSmH 1845-F 23 1847
CSt [1845]-[57]
Ct Mr 8 1850
CtHi 1845-58
CtY 1845-Ap 1846;Jl 30,Ag 25,S 20,O 2 1850;F 4,16,27,Ag 19 1851;S 18,29-O 2,5,7,19,23 1852
DGU Ag 16 1845-Ap 1849
DLC complete;extras:N 23 1845;D 2 1851
DeU Jl 1 1852
IC Ja-Ap 26 1856
ICM Ag 9 1856
ICU [1845]-Je 1849;50-59
IU Jl 18 1846
InRE Jl 27 1850
InU 1851;O-D 1852;Ja-Je 1854;S 1855-Je 1856
KHi [Ag 1854-57]
LNH 1845-Jl 16 1847
MB S 29 1845;Jl 13 1846-Mr 27 1847[N 21 1852-O 5 1854]Ja 9 1855;57-59
MHi Ap 20,28,My 4 1846;S 27 1849;Jl 18 1852; S 13 1854;F 16 1855
MWA complete
Md Ja-S 1849
MiU Jl 1845-59
MsHi 1845-49;Jl 16-17 1852
NBu [Ag-D 1847]-[51]-Jl,S 1853-O,D 1854-N 1855;56-[58]
NNHi N 29 1845;My 22,25 1846;F 12,14 1848;Jl-D 1852;N 8 1855
NR O 13 1845-47
NT 1845-Je 1855
NcD [1845-47]F 8,18,Mr 13,Je 21,Ag 11 1848 [49-51]D 29 1852;Ja 4,6,26,F 8,22,Mr 26,Ap 28, Ag 28 1853;Ja 27-28? My 13,N 1 1854[Ja-Mr] My 29 1855;My 7,20 1856;Ja 24,Mr 21 1857; F 26,Ap 11,24-25,Je 27,Jl 11,16,Ag 12,D 1858-59;Ja 28(extra)1845
NcU Jl-D 1846;Ag 21 1847;Jl 1852-[56-59]
Nj 1853-57
NjHi 1846-47
NjR F 11,O 26,D 29-30 1849
NjWdHi Jl 28 1852
OClWHi Je 16,18,21,Jl 10,25 1845;50-Mr 4 1851;Ap 14 1858-59
OHi complete
PBL Mr 23 1846;S 25-N 12 1847;Ja 13,17,22,F 12,Mr 24 1848
PHi Jl 1845-59
PPL Ap 14 1846;Mr 27 1852[54]55
PPM S 20 1848
PPi Jl 30 1845-Ap 1846;Mr 8 1847-Ag 19 1848;My 15 1849-Mr 4 1853;Je 18 1858-59
PToHi D 20 1852-Mr 13 1853
RPB [Ja-Je 1858]
RW Ap 3 1850
THi 1851-52
TNV 1846-Je 1849;50-58
TxU complete
V 1846-57
VHi Jl 1845-F 1850
WHi complete

Semi-weekly UNION. sw,tw My 5 1845-Ap 1859‖ Follows Globe (sw). Followed by Semi-weekly constitution
tw during sessions of congress, as Union
A Je-N 1851;D 1852-My 24,31,Ag 2 1853
CtY My 5 1845;46-My 1 1849
DLC 1845-46[48-My 4]D 4 1849-Jl 1,22,Ag 5,O 14,21-24,31,N 7,14,18,D 11 1857-[52-53]-[55]-My 5 1858
GMM 1845-Jl 22 1848
ICU O 22 1847;Ja 1,Ap 1 1848
IHi [1845-Mr 1857]
IU Ag 22 1848;Ja 2-6 1849
IaHi 1845-46
In N 1847-57
InI My 1846-Ap 23 1847;My 1848-My 1 1849; My 1850-Ap 11 1851
MB [1845-48;D 1850;Je 1851-Ja 19 1856]
MBAt [1845]
MHi [1845-54]
MWA 1845-[53-F 1856]
MdEmM My-D 1855
MiU-C [1847-49]
MsHi 1845-54
NcD 1845-[48-53]Ja 24,28 1854;My 23-26,N 7,D 18-20 1855[56]Ja 8,F 3,Ag 15,S 2 1857
NcU Jl 17-21,D 29 1845;F 26,Mr 21,Je 16-18,D 8,15 1846;F 2,Ap 13,My 28,Je 11,Jl 20,Ag 27,N 26,D 23 1847[48]-Ja 4 1849;50[51]-[53-54]
NjR Ja 29 1848
NjT 1845-46
OClWHi D 8 1845-Je 9 1846;47-Ap 1858
ODW My 4 1849
PToHi Mr 17 1853-O 25 1856;Mr 14 1857-S 1 1858
Tx 1845-[50]Mr 1,D 2 1851[Mr-D 1853;Mr-D 1854]-Mr 3 1855
TxU [Jl 1845-Mr 4 1851]
V 1845-Je,D 1846-Ap 18 1851;Ja 22-D 6 1856
Vt 1846
WHi 1846-F 17 1849[Mr 9 1850-F 26 1853]

Weekly UNION. w My 10 1845-Ap 1859‖ Follows Globe. Followed by Weekly constitution
CaB Ja-Jl 1846
DLC My 24 1845-D 8 1849[Ja-N 2 1850]Ap 26 1851-Jl 16 1853;55-56;D 19(extra)1846
ICN D 12 1846-Ap 17 1852;N 26-D 10 1853;Ap 22 1854-Ap 24 1856
InI Je 21 1845
MB Ja 23,Ag 7 1847;Je 24,Ag 8 1857
MHi [1845-46]Ap 6,Ag 17 1850
MSaE 1849-54
MWA 1845-[47-49]-[54]Je 25 1857
MeBa 1845-46
MiU D 12 1846-D 4 1847
MiU-C [1845-46;49-51]
MnHi Jl 24 1856-Ag 1 1857
MoHi D 8 1849
N D 12 1846-Mr 11 1848
NB 1845-Ap,D 1846-53
NN 1845
NNHi N 29,D 20 1845-[46]Ja 9-16 1847;N 3 1848[D 1854-Ag 1855]extra:N 20,D 19 1846
NcD D 12,26 1846-Ja 23,F 6,27,Mr 13 1847;Ap 22 1848;D 1,29 1849;Mr 16,30,Jl 13,Ag 3,O 12 1850;Ja 3-17 1852;Ag 23 1855;S 18-25,O 16,N 20,D 11-18 1856;Ja 29,S 26-O 3,N 28-D 1857
NcU N 1854-55
OCHi Mr 11-Je 3 1848
OCX O 25 1845-Ap 1846
OClWHi D 12 1846-Ja 1848;Ap 23 1853;O 16 1856;F 19,Mr 26 1857
OkHi [1848]
OrHi Jl 4 1846
P-M D 4 1852
Tx O 30 1847;N 22 1855-O 23 1856
V My-Ag 6 1846
VNo Ap 27 1854;F 15 1855;Mr 27,S 18,N 27 1856;Mr 5,19 1857
VRC Jl 17 1856
—Congressional supplement. ir D 6 1848-
DLC 1848-Mr 3 1849
NNHi 1848-F 16,Mr 3 1849
PJR Ja 4 1849

Evening UNION. d 1862-
1862-Ja? 1867 as Daily constitutional union 1862-Mr 1863? pub in Philadelphia, Pa.
DLC S 8,O 14 1862;63-[66]My 1867-Je 1868;F 22(extra)1864
DW My 16 1865;O 19 1866
MB [Je 9-N 11 1863]
MWA Jl 23 1864;Jl 13 1867
OCHi Ag 3 1867
OClWHi Mr 9,Jl 7 1864;Jl 8,13 1867
—Georgetown ed
DLC Jl 9,11 1867
—w ed *See* Weekly constitutional union

UNION. d D 7 1876-Mr 3 1877‖
DLC complete
MH complete
MHi complete
OCHi Ja 9 1877
WHi complete

UNION democrat. w O 19 1841-
DLC N 2,D 28 1841;Ja 11 1842
PWCl N-D 14 1841;F 1,15-Mr 8,22,Ap 5,19-My 10 1842

UNION guard. w Jl 12- 1860‖
Campaign paper
CSmH O 11 1860
DLC Jl-S 1860
TU Jl 12,Ag 9-23,S-O 18 1860

UNITED American. w,ir Ag 11 1894-N 28 1896‖
Suspended frequently for short periods w 1894-My 5 1895
DLC complete
MWA Ja 15 1895
OCHi Ja 23 1895

UNITED STATES daily. *See* United States news

UNITED STATES democrat. w Mr? 1884-
DLC Ag 16 1885
GAtCo Mr 7-14 1885
VU Mr 21 1885

UNITED STATES journal. *See* Times 1845-46

UNITED STATES news. d,w Mr 4 1926+
1926-My 13 1933 as United States daily
Suspended from Mr 6-18 1933
d 1926-Mr 6 1933
pub 1926+
A Mr 1929-Ag 1930
ArP 1931+
ArU Mr 1930-33;Jl-D 1934
C 1926-Mr 3,My 20 1933+
CBeA Ag 1928-Mr 3 1932
CClP 1926-Mr 13,My 13 1933+
CL 1926-My 13 1933
CLJ [N 1929]My 13 1933+
CLO F 10 1927-32
CLSU Ap 4 1926+
CLU 1926+
CLb [1926]My 13 1933+
CMiC 1926+
CO 1926+
CP 1926+
CPa Mr 31 1926-Mr 3,My 1933+
CRed 1926+
CRiv 1926+
CSdT S 26 1926+
CSfB My 1933+
CSmH 1926-Mr 3 1928
CSt 1926-Mr 3,My 1933+
CU 1926+
CU-B 1927-O 9 1933
CU-L 1933+
CU-P 1926+
CaB 1926-S 1932
CaQMR D 1931+
CoAT 1926-33
CoD 1926-33
Ct 1926+
CtHT 1926+
CtNlP 1926+
CtW 1926-[29]+
CtY 1926+
DA 1926+
DCE 1926+
DIC 1926+
DL 1926+
DLC 1926+
DW 1926+
DeWI 1926-Ap 22,My 13-20 1933
FO 1933+
FTS 1926+
FTa Je 28 1927+
FU 1926+
FWpR Mr 1932+
GA 1926+
GDE [1926]+
I 1926+
IAC [O 28 1931-33]
IAlS 1926+
IC 1926-32
ICJ 1926+
ICN 1926+
ICU 1926+
ICarC Ja-Je 6,S 19 1930-Je 2,S 15-D 1 1931
IEN 1926-Mr 3,My 1933+
IEN-C 1926+
IElC 1926+
IEuC 1926+
IF current year only
IG 1926+
ILfC 1926+
IMaW current 2 months
INaN 1926+
IU 1926+
IWW 1928-34
IaCfT 1926-Je 1930;current year
IaD Mr 1927+
IaDa current year only
IaFm current 6 months
IaHi 1926+
IaMu current year only
IaSc 1933+
IaU 1926-Mr 3,D 1929+
IaU-L F 12 1927+
IdIf 1926-My 20 1933
IdU 1926-My 20 1933
IdU-S My 20 1933+
In 1926-32
InCr 1927-28
InEv 1927+
InI 1926+
InLP 1926-Mr 6 1933
InSb 1926+
InTI 1926+
InU 1926+
K 1926+
KHi [1926-28]
KPT 1926+
KU 1926+
KWi [1926]+
LBL 1926+
LNH My-Je,Ag 1928-S 1932
LSC [1926-27]+
LU O 1929-32
M 1926+
MB 1926-Mr 3 1933
MH-BA 1926+
MHi 1926-Je 1930;Ag 1935
MNS Mr 1927-Je 1930;31-34
MWA 1926-Ag 25 1932
Md S 1926+
MdBE 1926+
MdBJ 1926+
MdBLe 1926+
MdU 1926+
MeAu Je 1932+
MeBa 1926+
MeU Je-O,D 1929-F 1933
MiAC [1926-29;32]
MiElS 1926+
MiU 1926+
MiYM 1926-Ap 1934
MnD 1926+
MnHi 1926+
MnM Jl 1926-Mr 6 1933
MnS 1926-33
MnU 1926+
MoB S 1933+
MoF 1932-33
MoFuW D 16 1930-Mr 25 1931
MoK 1926+
MoKiT [O 4 1926-Mr 3 1927]+
MoMaryT 1926+
MoP 1926-29
MoS [Mr,My,Jl 1926]Mr 4 1927+
MoSW 1926+
MoSp D 1934+
MoU 1926-My 13 1933
MoWe 1933+
MsLE Ja 18 1927+
MsSM 1926+
MsU [1928]-Mr 1933
N 1926+
NBP 1926+
NBu 1926-34
NBuG 1926+
NCH 1926+
NHe Mr 1931+
NIC 1926+
NMam Ag 27 1931+
NN 1926+
NNC 1926+
NNCC 1932+
NNQ Mr 1927+
NNRa 1933+
NNUT O 4 1928-O 12 1932
NNW Jl 1929+
NPV 1926+
NRU 1926+
NSyC 1926+
NSyU 1926+
NWhi Je 1934+
NWpG Mr 21 1930-Ap 16 1932
NcD Mr-N 1926[27-28]Jl 1930+
NcRS 1926+
NcU 1926-33
NdU 1926+
NhD 1926+
NjJ Mr 8 1927-My 2 1928
NjM Ap 1926-My 1932
NjN 1926+
NjP 1926+
NmSA S 1926+
NmU 1929+
Nv Ag-N 1930
OAU 1926+
OAkU 1926+
OC 1926+
OCU 1926-O 1929[30-32]
OCl 1926+
OClWHi Mr 4,6,8-10 1926;Jl 16-O 15 1927;O 17,19,22-25 1928
ODW 1926+
OGrD My 13 1933+
OHi Mr 1927-32
OOxM 1926-O 1931;33+
OOxW 1931+
OY 1926-32
OYsA 1926+
OkL 1927+
OkOOk 1926+
OkStO 1926+
OkU [1926]-[28]+
OkWeS 1928+
OrCA 1926+
OrU 1926+

DISTRICT OF COLUMBIA (*Continued*)

WASHINGTON—*Continued*

UNITED STATES news. d,w Mr 4 1926+ —*Continued*
P 1926+
PA [1928+]
PBL 1926+
PEr 1926—
PHi [1927]29[30]
PLaF Jl 1926+
PMeA 1926-Ja 22 1934
PP 1926+
PPR [1926-27]
PStP 1932[33]
PU 1926+
PUn D 29 1932-N 4 1933
PWp Mr 4 1927+
REdH F 1927+
RPB 1926+
TMG Mr 4 1927+
TNV [1926-27]+
TU [1926]+
Tx O 1930-Je,O 1932+
TxAS N 1929+
TxDM 1926+
TxDeN S 1926+
TxF 1926+
TxGR 1926+
TxH Ja 13 1927+
TxHR 1926+
TxHuS Ag 1926+
TxLT 1926+
TxPa Ap 24 1928+
TxU 1926-32
UPB 1926+
US 1926-31
UU 1926+
V 1926+
VHaH 1926+
VHi [Jl-O 1927]
WAL 1926-My 13 1933;My 14-D 1934
WHi 1926-Mr 3 1933
WLc 1926+
WM 1926+
WMJ 1926-O 7 1933
WO 1928+
Wa Je 1927-Jl 1932;S 1933+
WaPS [1926]S 14 1927;D 21 1929-My 6 1933
WaS 1926+
WaSp 1926+
WaU 1926+
WaWW 1929+
WyU 1926+

UNITED STATES telegraph. d F 6 1826-F 21 1837||
Follows Washington gazette. F-N 20 1826 as United States' telegraph; N 21 1826-Mr 6 1827 United States' telegraph and commercial herald. Followed by Reformer
A 1829-31
CLM S 11 1834
CSmH Ag 7 1827
CSt 1828;30
DLC complete;D 8(extra)1829
DW O 7 1831;F 11,Je 23,S 7 1832;Mr 6 1833;S 28 1835
GA Mr 15 1828-F 24 1829
GU Ja-Je 1827[Ja-Je 1831]
ICHi Jl 28 1827;F 20,Ap 26,My 25 1830
ICN N 17-20,22 1830[31]
ICU [1826]-[28]Ja 6-N 12 1829;30;Jl-D 1831; Je-D 1832;Jl 1833-[34]-[36]
In Ja 11,14,18,24-25,28 1834
KyLo Ap 5 1828;Ja 29,F 9,22,Ap 2,N 1,11,26, 29,D 3,10,12,14,17,28,31 1833;Ja 9,16,18,23,25, 30,F 1,4,13,15,18,20,24,Mr 4,6,8,13,My 22 1834
MBAt [1827-30]
MH Ja-Je 1827;Je-N 1830;Jl 1832-33
MWA [1826-27]-My 5,16[Je-D 1828]-[33]-Jl 2, Ag 18 1834[Je-D 1835]36
MdFF 1830
MiU 1826-28;30-[33-34]-[36]
MiU-C [1828-31]
NN 1826-D 3 1829;30-34;Jl 1835-F 21 1837
NNHi [N-D 1827]-[32-34]
NcD [1826]Je 2 1829[30]Ja 3 1831;Ap 26 1832; Ja 9,18,24 1834;My 5,O 29,D 14 1836
NjR Ap 11 1827
OCHi Ja 12 1836
PCarlHi Ja 15 1829
PEL D 17 1831-D 11 1833;F-N 1834
PHi Ja-Jl 1827;29-30;34-Je 1835
PPL [Ja-Je 1827]Ap 17-N 28 1829
RPB Ja-Je 29 1833
TxU [D 28 1829-Je 1832]
WHi [F 23 1827-My 1828;Ap 4 1829-31]-[Jl 3-N 9 1832]Ja-Je 29 1833[34]-Je 1835[Ja-Je 29 1836]

UNITED STATES' telegraph. w Je 13 1827-
Ct [1826-28]
DLC Je 20-27,O 24,N 7,21-D 12 1827;Ja-Je 11,25,Jl 9-O 15,29-N 5,19-26 1828;Ja 14(extra) 1828
MB [1828]
MHi Mr 11,Ag 10 1827
NN S 12,O 24 1827;Ag 9(extra)1828
PToHi Je 28 1828
Vt Ag 1827-[28]

UNITED STATES' telegraph—extra. w Mr 1 1828-Ja 24 1829||
Campaign paper
DLC complete
ICHi complete

UNITED STATES telegraph. tw,sw 1826-F 21 1837||
Follows Washington gazette. (for the country) 1826 as United States telegraph; Ja-Ap? 1827 United States telegraph and commercial herald. Followed by Reformer (country ed)
tw during sessions of Congress and 1828
DLC Mr 18/20,25/27,My 20/22,Je 22/23,29/30 1826[Je 1827-33]Je 26,30 1834;S 5 1835;N 9-26,D 7,10,17 1836;Ja 14,F 11,18 1837
DW F 9 1836
ICU Ag 18,S 1 1827;Je 30 1828-Ja 1834;D 1836-37
MWA Mr 31/Ap 2-3/4,Jl 10,S 8,N 3,D 8-18 1827;Mr 11-13,My 1,Je 18,23,Jl 14-16,21,28,D 27 1828;Ja 3-10 1829[F 27-Jl 16]S 17 1830;Je 3 1831[Ag 1832-33]Ja 4,9,16-23,Jl 8 1834-[35] 36;Ja 4-11,18 1837
N Jl 21-F 1827;My 31 1828-S 4 1829;Ap 4 1831;O 18 1833
NN My 29,Je 5,17-19,O 11-N 20,30 1826[27]Ja 1828
NcD Ja 3,8-12,31-F 5,18 1833;Jl 15,Ag 26 1835
NcU [1829]-[32;34]35;D 7-21 1836;37
NhD F 2,27,D 18,21 1830;Ja 3,Mr 29,O 18 1831; Ja 30,Ap 21,24,28 1832;Ja 8,F 22,My 3,O 18-25,N 22 1833;Ja 4,9,26,28,F 11-13,22,Mr 1-4, 11,Ap 5,22-24,Je 12,15-16,24,Jl 8,S 9,30,O 17, 21,N 11 1834
NjR [1827-32]
OHi Ap 14 1829-37
OOxM F 5-My 26,D 2-5,11-31 1828;Ja 3-Mr 3 1829[D 1831-33]-Je 17 1834
PBL My 17 1828;N 11-D 1831;Ja 3-5,My 19 1832;Mr 19 1833;Ap 25,My 23-Je 11 1834
PCarlHi Ag 21,D 18 1827-30
PHi [1827 29-30;34;35]
PP [1827;29]
WHi [Je 4 1827-29]30[S 1831-O 12 1832;33-N 26 1836]

Saturday evening VISITOR. w Jl 3 1869-70||?
DLC 1869-Je 4 1870
MWA Jl 3 1869

Der VOLKS-TRIBUN. w 1875-1902||?
In German
DLC Jl 29 1876;Jl 10 1880;Je 18 1881
MWA Ag 26 1876

VOX populi. w 1868?-
NcU N 7 1868

WASHINGTONIAN. w Je 7-S 27 1845||
DLC complete

WASHINGTONIAN: and farmers, mechanics and merchants gazette. d,w My 26 1836-
My-O 22 1836 as Washingtonian(d)
Suspended from O 22-D 3 1836
DLC My-D 1836;F 10(extra)1837
MWA D 10 1836
N Mr 1 1837

"WE the people". w Mr 1-N 1828||?
DLC Mr-N 22 1828;O 28(extra)1828
ICM Ap 12 1828
MBAt S 13,O 25,N 1-8 1828
MWA Mr 29-O 11,25-N 1,15 1828
MeU Ap 26 1828
NNHi My 10,Je 7,21 1828
NcD Ap 26-My 10,Je 14-Jl 19,S 6-20,O 4-11,N 1 1828
OOxM Ap 5,26,S 6 1828

Washington WHIG. w 1840?-D 21 1842||
1840? as Washington whig and republican gazette
DLC F 23-D 21 1842
NcD Jl 29 1840;My 5 1841;N 30 1842

WHIG standard. d N 6 1843-N 16 1844||
CSmH Ag 19 1844
CtY My 16 1844
DLC complete
MWA My 23,Jl 27 1844

WORKINGMAN'S national advocate. w Ap 23-Je 11 1853||
DLC complete
NcD Ap-Je 4 1853

Weekly Washington WORLD. And citizen-soldier. w 1879-83||?
1879-Ja 1881? as Washington world
DLC S 2 1880;F 19-26,Mr 26 1881
MWA N 6 1880
NbHi D 14 1879
NcD F 18 1882
NcU My 3 1879
NhD Mr 5 1881
OClWH 1882-Mr 1883
TJT F 2 1884

YOUNG Hickory. w Je 11 1842-44||?
1842-Je 11 1844 as Spectator
DLC Je 1842-[Ja-S 1843]
MB S 21,O 26-N 2,16-30 1844
MWA Mr 30,Ap 27,My 25 1844
NcU My 4 1844
PBL Jl 20,S 7 1844
WHi Je 18 1842-O 1844
—d,sw ed *See* Spectator

Der ZUSCHAUER am Potomac. w Ja 10 1850-
In German and English
DLC Ja 10 1850
MWA Ja 10 1850
NhD Ja 28,Mr 23,Jl 17,Ag 18,S 29,N 21,D 19 1850;Ja 2 1851

FLORIDA

ALLIGATOR

COLUMBIA democrat. w Ja 9 1858-
FGS My 16 1858
FPY F 11,Mr 4-11,20-Ap 10,My 1,15 1858
FU My 15 1858

APALACHICOLA

APALACHICOLIAN. w,sw Jl 25 1840-Mr 27 1841||
Jl-D 15 1840 as Commercial advertiser
w during summer season
DLC D 26 1840
F Ag 1,15-29,S 12-O 3,17-24,N 7,28,D 16 1840; Ja 16-23,F 13,Mr 1841
GAtCo Ag 1 1840
MWA Ag 1,S 12 1840

COMMERCIAL advertiser. 1840 *See* Apalachicolian

COMMERCIAL advertiser. w F 4 1843-
DLC 1844;F 14,Mr 7,21-Jl 7,21,Ag 4-18,31,D 26 1846-F 13,27-Mr 6,Ap 10,My 15,Je 22-29, Jl 17,Ag 7-O 2,14-N 18 1847;F 3-My 18,Je 1-17,Jl 1-29,Ag 12-19,S 9-16,D 10 1848;Ja,F 8-Mr 15 1849
F [1843-Mr 1846]
MWA D 25 1843;Ja 8,22,F 26 1844
NcD Mr 5 1856
WHi Je 25 1851

Apalachicola COURIER. w Ap 24 1839-Ja 1840||?
DLC Ap-My 8 1839
FPY Ag 20 1839
NhD O 15 1839

FLORIDA journal. w Mr 10 1836-F 19 1844||?
1836-O 31 1840 as Apalachicola gazette; N 18 1840-Ap 22 1843 Florida journal; Ag 12-O 28 1843 Watchman of the gulf
Suspended O 31-N 18 1840;Ap 22-Ag 12 1843;O 28 1843-Ja 4 1844?
DLC D 23 1840;Ag 12 1843;Ja 25 1844
F Ja 13-20,Mr 1 1838;Ja 4,18-Mr 1,Ap 4-17,Je 23,Ag 15,S 12-19,O 31 1840;Mr 17,My 1 1841; Ja 7,F 19,Mr 5,Ap 2,My 14-Je 11,Jl 15-Ag 19,S 23-30,N 12 1842-Ja 21,F-Mr 4,Ap-Ag 19, S 9 1843
FPY Mr-My,Jl 27-O 8,19 1836-My 13,Je-O 4, N 11 1837-D 1838;Ja 12-19,30-F 6,16-S 18,O 2-16,30-N 23,D 7,21 1839;F 1 1840
GAtCo F 16 1839;Mr 7 1840

Apalachicola GAZETTE. *See* Florida journal

Apalachicola HERALD. w 1884||?
United with Apalachicola tribune to form Apalachicola times

STAR of the west. w Ag 2- 1848||
DLC Ag 16,S 13,O 26 1848
MWA S 13 1848

Apalachicola TIMES. w 1885+
Formed by the union of Apalachicola tribune and Apalachicola herald
N 2 1935 is golden anniversary and Gorrie Bridge ed
NcD N 2 1935

Apalachicola TRIBUNE. w 1881-84||?
United with Apalachicola herald to form Apalachicola times

WATCHMAN of the gulf. *See* Florida journal

APOPKA

ADVERTISER. w 1888-91||?
KHi Mr 11,Ap 15,Je 3 1890

Apopka CHIEF. *See* Orange county chief

Apopka NEWS-BUDGET and South Florida citizen. w Ap 9 1879-86||?
1879-83? as South Florida citizen
NcD F 20 1886

ORANGE county chief. w,sw Ap 20 1923+
1923-Mr 13 1933 as Apopka chief (w)
pub Ap 20 1933+
FU [1924]+

SOUTH FLORIDA citizen. *See* Apopka news-budget and South Florida citizen

ARCADIA

ARCADIAN. w,sw O 1 1924+
Formed by the union of De Soto county news and Arcadia enterprise
sw F 23- 1926
pub 1924+
FU Jl 15 1925-[Ja-Ag 1926;31]+

Arcadia CHAMPION. w Ja 1898-1910||
FArA 1906-10

DE SOTO county news. w 1898-S 1924||
United with Arcadia enterprise to form Arcadian
FArA 1912-16

Arcadia ENTERPRISE. w 1894-S 1924||
United with De Soto county news to form Arcadian
FArA 1913;16;18-24

AUBURNDALE

Auburndale TIMES. *See* Tri-city times (Winter Haven

FLORIDA (*Continued*)

AVON PARK

HIGHLANDS county pilot. w 1919+
FU 1934+

SCENIC Highlands sun. w 1925+
1925-33? as Twin cities sun
FU 1934+

Avon Park TIMES. w F 15 1929+
pub 1929+

TWIN CITIES sun. *See* Scenic highlands sun

BARTOW

ADVANCE courier. w 1886-88||?
United with Informant to form Courier-informant
F Mr 30 1887-Jl 18 1888

COURIER-INFORMANT. w,tw 1881-O 31 1919||
1881-88? as Informant. Merged with Polk county record
tw 1917?
F Je 9 1881-My 1884;My 10 1893-My 18 1918
P-M Mr 6 1886

INFORMANT. *See* Courier-informant

POLK county record. w,sw,d 1902+
w 1902-O 1919;sw N 1919-N 24 1925
FU [Ag 1918-Je 1926;O 1929-30]-Mr,Ag 29,N 1932+

BONIFAY

HOLMES county advertiser. w 1892+
FBoC [1914+]

Bonifay TIMES. w 1891||?
NbHi Ap 4 1891

BRADENTON

GULF COAST progress. w 1881-85||?
NcD N 8 1884

Bradenton HERALD. d 1921+
1921-Ja 1926 as Evening herald
pub S 15 1922+
FBC Ja-N 1932
FU Ja 26 1924;O 11 1925;Ja 18-19,Ag 6,S 23 1926-Je 15 1927;My 6,O 23 1928-My,S 19 1931-My,Ag 15 1932-Ag 19,O 4 1934+
—w ed *See* Manatee River journal-herald

MANATEE RIVER journal-herald. w 1888-1931||
1888-Ag 1922 as Manatee River journal; S 7 1922-S 30 1924 Manatee River journal and Bradenton herald
pub S 1922-31
FBC Ag 1919-31
FSrB My 21 1909
FU [Jl 25 1918-19]-Ap 15 1926
—d ed *See* Bradenton herald

BRISTOL

Bristol FREE press. w 1887+
Title varies slightly
FU [Ag 9 1918-20]-22;F 10-17,Mr 10,My 19,Je 9,23-30 1923;N 29 1924;D 15 1928;Ja 7,Ag 27-S 17,O 22 1931-[33]+

BRONSON

LEVY county journal. w My 1 1928+
pub 1929+

LEVY county news. w Ag 2 1923-28||?
1927? pub in Williston
FU S 13 1923-[24-25]

LEVY times-democrat. w 1883-1924||?
1883-89? as Levy county times
FU Ag 28-S 11,O-D 1919;Mr 1920-[21-23]

BROOKSVILLE

Brooksville JOURNAL. w 1928+
FU Ja 3,My-D 1929;F 6-20,Mr 6,27-My 1 1930;D 1934+

CALLAHAN

Callahan NEWS. w S 1930+
pub 1930+

CANAL POINT

EVERGLADES news. w 1924+
F N 27,D 25 1925;Ja 8,S 24,O 8,D 17 1926;Mr 15 1929
FWb 1928-30

CLEARWATER

Clearwater HERALD. w,d 1894-1926||?
1894-1909? as West Hillsboro press; 1910-25 Clearwater news. Merged with Clearwater sun
w 1894-1919?, and during Je-O 1919-25?
FC 1913-17

Clearwater NEWS. *See* Clearwater herald

Clearwater SUN. d My 1 1914+
pub 1928+
FU Je 28 1931+

WEST HILLSBORO press. *See* Clearwater herald

WEST HILLSBOROUGH times. *See* St. Petersburg times (St. Petersburg)

CLERMONT

Clermont CLARION. *See* Clermont press

Clermont PRESS. w D 15 1914+
1914-21 as Clermont clarion; 1921-22 South Lake press
pub 1914+
FClC 1916+
FU O 1925-[31]+

SOUTH LAKE press. *See* Clermont press

COCOA

FLORIDA star. *See* Indian River star

INDIAN River star. w Jl 1914-20||
1914-O 1917 as Florida star
FTiC F 28-O 24 1913;F 6,Je 24 1914;N 23 1917; F 8-D 6 1918;Ap 1-15 1919;Mr 5 1920

STAR. w 1916-O 26 1917||
United with Florida star to form Indian River star
FTiC N 10,D 1 1916;Ja 6,Mr 2-9,O 26 1917

Cocoa TRIBUNE. w Mr 1917+
pub 1917+
FU My 21 1926;Jl 25 1929-[31]+

CRESCENT CITY

Crescent City JOURNAL. w 1924+
FPaC 1925+

CROSS CITY

Cross City NEWS. w O 1934+
pub 1934+

DADE CITY

Dade City BANNER. w 1904+
FU [F-Ag 1925]S 16-30,N 1932+

DAYTONA

GAZETTE-NEWS. w 1889-1922||?
1898? as Gazette-news and commonwealth
FDaF 1900-02

HALIFAX journal. *See* Daytona-Halifax journal

Daytona-Halifax JOURNAL. w 1882-1923||?
1882-1914? as Halifax journal
Ja 1890 trade ed
NcD Ja 1890
—d ed *See* Daytona Beach news-journal

DAYTONA BEACH

Daytona Beach JOURNAL. d 1915-26||
United with Daytona daily news to form Daytona Beach news-journal
FDaN N 1915-Ap,O-D 1916;Ap-S 1918;Ja-Mr, O 1919-26

Daytona Beach NEWS-JOURNAL. w,d 1903+
1903-26 as Daytona daily news
w during My-N,1903-16
pub 1926+
FDaF 1903-26
FU [Ap-My 1928]S 27 1929+
VU F 1-4 1924

OBSERVER. w D 7 1934+
pub 1934+

Daytona Beach SUN record. d 1931+
FU Ja 27 1932+

DE FUNIAK SPRINGS

BREEZE. w,d F 1892+
d during F-Mr 1901-04?
pub [1899]+

De Funiak HERALD. w 1893+
FU D 17 1908;N 24 1932+

DELAND

Deland NEWS. w 1887-1927||?
FU Ag 6 1919;Mr 26,My 21 1924

Deland daily NEWS. *See* Deland sun-news

Deland daily SUN. w,d 1922-O 19 1929||
1922-Ap 20? 1928 as Deland sun (w)
United with Deland daily news to form Deland sun-news
FDe 1925-29

Deland SUN-NEWS. d 1914+
1914-O 19 1929 as Deland daily news
FDe My 1925+
FDeS 1929+
FU Ja 21,Mr 1,29-31,Ap 25 1921;F 24,O 16 1924;Jl 28 1925[28]-D 19 1929;O 5 1930-Jl,Ag 21 1931+
KHi Ja 23 1926

VOLUSIA county record. w 1888-Ag 27 1921||
Merged with Deland news
ICU [Ap 25 1903-05]

DUNEDIN

Dunedin TIMES. w F 1924+
pub 1924+

WEST HILLSBOROUGH times. *See* St. Petersburg times (St. Petersburg)

DUNNELLON

Leroy and Dunnellon NEWS. *See* Leroy news (Leroy)

ESTERO

AMERICAN eagle. w 1906+
pub 1906+
FWpR My 1933+
NN Je 1906-Je 2 1910

EUSTIS

Eustis LAKE region. w O 20 1884+
pub [1884+]
FTvC Jl 27 1887+
NcD D 11 1884

SEMI-TROPICAL. w
FTvC O 1887-Mr 1889

EVERGLADES

COLLIER county news. w Ag 24 1923+
FE My 31 1924-Jl 16 1925;Jl 28 1927+

FERNANDINA

Fernandina COURIER. w Ap 25? 1866-
FFD O 3 1866
MBAt My 9-16 1866;Ja 2 1867

Weekly EAST FLORIDIAN. w N 3 1838-
1838-52? as News; 1853;-My 19 1859 Florida news; My 26 1859-My 1860 East Floridian
1838-45? pub in St. Augustine; 1845?-57 pub in Jacksonville
CtY Ja 9-16 1846
DLC 1838-D 21 1844;Ja 11-F 15,Mr 8,29-Ap 12,26-My 3,17-24,Je 7-14,28,Ag 30-S 6 1845; Ja 23 1846-Ja 5,19,F 2-Ap 6,20-My 18,Je 8, 22-Ag 3,17-S 14 1850;Ja 4,Mr 1-8,Ap 19-D 27 1851;Ja 1 1853-D 13 1856;Ja 3,17-F 21,Mr 7-My 9,30,Jl 18-Ag 7,S 26,O 10,D 12-25 1857; F 10 1858-D 19 1860
F My 10,31,Je 14-28,Jl 12-S 13,O 4,25,N 8-15, D 12-19 1845;Ja 2,16,30,F 13-27 1846
FJ Ag 7 1850;Ap 24,My 15,Je 26,Jl 10-17,D 6 1853-Ja 1,22-29,F 19,Mr 12-19 1854;O 13 1855
FPY 1838-Ap 26,My 10,31-Je 7,28-Jl 26 1845; Mr 1,15-29,Ap 12-26 1860
FSaC Ag 18 1849
FSaHi Je 15 1839
ICHi O 30 1852
MBAt Mr 5,Ag 20-27 1868
MWA N 3,17 1838;F 23,Ap 13-20,My 11,Je 15,S 27,N 1 1839;O 30 1840;Ja 22-F 19 1842;F 19-26,My 20,Jl 8 1848;Jl 3 1852
NNHi My 4 1873
NcD Ap 16 1841
NcU Ja 8 1841

FLORIDA mirror. w,tw,sw S 1877-1900||?
Merged with Nassau county star
w 1877-89?;tw 1890-92?
DLC Jl 1882-Jl 1886;Mr 30 1889-N 22 1893
F N 30 1878
FTaT Ag 21 1880
P-M Mr 13 1886

FLORIDA news. *See* Weekly East Floridian

ISLAND CITY. w 1869-71||?
FFL Ja 12 1871
FHi Je 30,S 20 1870

NASSAU county star. w 1897-1906||?

OBSERVER. w 1871-76||?
FHi S 5 1874;Je 5-12,S 4,O 2 1875;Ja 29,F 12 1876
NNHi Ja 18 1873

PENINSULA. *See under* Jacksonville

FORT LAUDERDALE

Fort Lauderdale daily NEWS and sentinel. d 1925+
1925-27? as Fort Lauderdale daily news
FFl 1926+
FU O 16 1930+

Fort Lauderdale SENTINEL. w 1910-27||?
United with Fort Lauderdale daily news to form Fort Lauderdale daily news and sentinel

FORT MEADE

Fort Meade LEADER. w 1909+
FU F 1933+

FORT MYERS

Fort Myers NEWS-PRESS. sw,d 1920+
1920-My 1931 as Fort Myers tropical news; Je-Jl 1931 Fort Myers press and tropical news
sw 1920-F 15 1922
pub 1931+
FU [My-D 1920]-[22]-Je 4 1924;Ja 30-Je 8 1926;Je 4,8-12 1927;Jl 28,Ag 16 1928;Ap 1929+

Fort Myers PRESS. w 1885-1930||?
KHi S 21 1925

Fort Myers PRESS. d 1911-My 1931||
United with Fort Myers tropical news to form Fort Myers press and tropical news, later Fort Myers news-press
FU N 22 1919-[26-27]Ja 12,F 24,30,Je 23,Jl 3,Ag 4 1928;Ja 22,Je 15 1929

Fort Myers TROPICAL news. *See* Fort Myers news-press

FORT PIERCE

Fort Pierce NEWS-TRIBUNE. w,sw,d 1903+
1903-20 as Fort Pierce news; D 1922-Mr 3 1923 Daily news-tribune
w 1909-N 19 1925 (sw(d during season) 1920-S 1925)
FU O 9,24-N 13 1919[20-F 1923]-[Ag-D 1925]-[Mr-Ap 1931]-O 1932;33+

FLORIDA (*Continued*)

FORT PIERCE—*Continued*

ST. LUCIE county tribune. w,sw 1905-Mr? 1920||
United with Fort Pierce news to form Fort Pierce news-tribune
FU [Jl 23 1918-19]-Mr 16 1920

GAINESVILLE

Gainesville ADVOCATE. d 1884-Ap 2? 1890||
1884-88? as Daily advocate. United with Daily morning record to form Gainesville daily sun
FGS Ag 26 1887
FU Je 26,Jl 27 1888;F 15 1890

ALACHUA county news. w 1919+
FU Ag 23 1934+
—d ed *See* Evening news

ALACHUA gazette. w F 5- 1891||?
FU Jl 2 1891

COTTON states. w D 1860-
1860-61? pub in Micanopy
FPY S 28 1861
NN Je 21 1862
OClWHi Ap 16 1864
V Mr 19,My 7,21-Je 18 1864
WHi Ap 16 1864

Daily LEADER. d 1892?-
FU S 14 1892

NEW era. w Jl 8 1865-74||?
FGS Jl 8 1865-N 23 1866;O 5 1867;Ag 30 1873
FPY My 18 1867
FU 1865-N 23 1866;O 5 1867;Ag 30 1873
NNHi Mr 22 1873

Gainesville NEWS. d 1885||?
MWA Ap 1,4 1885

Evening NEWS. d Ag 1919-Ag 10 1934||
1919-23? as Gainesville daily news
FU [S-N 1919]-[23]D 17 1925;F 27 1926;Ap 12,Jl 5,S 30,O 10,17,N 7,29,D 20 1927;Ja 23,Ap 16,S 13,O 16 1928;Ag 13,S 25,O 9 1929;S 5 1931;F 17-Ag 1934
—w ed *See* Alachua county news

Daily morning RECORD. d 1887-Ap 2? 1890||
United with Gainesville advocate to form Gainesville daily sun
FU O 2 1888

Gainesville daily SUN. d Ap 3 1890+
Formed by the union of Daily morning record and Gainesville advocate
pub 1903+
FTS [1931-33]+
FU Ap 29,My 30 1891;Ja 21,S 14 1892;F 11,14, 18 1907[08]-[10]-[18]-[20-22]-[25-26]-[32]+

GREEN COVE SPRINGS

CLAY county crescent. w S 4 1919?+
FGcC F 14 1928+

CLAY county times. w 1898-1923||?
FGcC [Je 14 1898-Je 1917;Je 1921-Ag 2 1929]
FU [Ag 15 1918-19]-Ap 1920

Green Cove SPRING. w 1880-1905||?
FGcC Ap 1,21 1888;Jl 13 1889;My 2,24-31 1890

GROVELAND

Groveland GRAPHIC. w 1922+
FTvC 1922+

HAINES CITY

Haines City HERALD. w 1916+
FU Ap 23-30,My 28 1921;Ja 12 1922;Ap 30 1925;O 26 1933+

HALIFAX RIVER

HALIFAX settler. w F 1875-
FGS F 1875(no day)
FU F 1875(no day)

HASTINGS

Hastings HERALD. w 1914+
Suspended from D 24 1920-F 11 1921
FU S 1918-F,Mr 11-18,Ap 15,My 20-27,Ag 12, 26 1921;Ag 18 1922

HIALEAH

COMMUNITY review and Dade county courier. w 1925+
pub Je 1929+
FU Ja 20,F 3,24 1933+

Hialeah HERALD. w 1921+
FMbT 1927+

HOMESTEAD

Homestead ENTERPRISE. w 1912-O 1931||
United with Homestead leader to form Leader-enterprise
FU Jl 1 1920;Ag 3 1922;Ap 27,Je 22 1928;Ap 22 1929[D 1930-O 16 1931]

LEADER-ENTERPRISE. w,sw,d,tw 1923+
1923-O 1931 as Homestead leader
d D 10 1925-26?; tw 1927?; sw 1928?-O 5? 1929
FU [Je 14-O 1923]-[26;N 1928-O 1931]+

HOMOSASSA

Homosassa HERALD. d,ir D 16 1925-
MWA D 16 1925;Ag 26 1926;Mr 19,N 23 1927

HOWEY

Howey TRIBUNE. w 1916-29||?
KHi [F 1927-Je 1929]

INVERNESS

PHOSPHATE field. w 1890-93||?
NcD S 11 1891

JACKSONVILLE

Daily evening CHRONICLE. d 1877-
FJ N 1 1877

Jacksonville COURIER. w Ja 1 1835-Ag 1839||?
Followed by East Florida advocate
Suspended three times for short periods
DLC Ja 29 1835(facsimile)
FJ Ag 3-17 1837
FPY Ja 29,Mr 26-Ap 2,Jl-O 22,N 26 1835-Ja 14,F 4-11 1836
ICHi O 24 1835
MDeHi F 26-Mr 5,Ap 30-My 21,Je 8,D 17-31 1835
MWA Ja 1,F 12,26,Mr 26 1835

DIXIE. w D 1910-17||?
Follows Sun
FJ 1910-N 21 1914
MWA D 11 1915

EAST FLORIDA advocate. w S 7 1839-Ja 1841||?
Follows Jacksonville courier
DLC S 7,20,O 12 1839;Ap 21,S 1 1840
FPY S 21 1839
MWA My 12 1840

FINANCIAL news. d 1915+
FJ Jl 1924-Mr,Je-O 1926;Ap-Jl 1927;28-32

Daily FLORIDA citizen. d 1893-97||
United with Florida times-union to form Florida times-union and citizen, later Florida times-union
F My 19 1897
FJ Je 22 1895
FPY Ap-Je 8 1897
KHi D 20 1894

FLORIDA commercial. w 1929-30||?
Ct My 24 1929-F 12 1930

FLORIDA dispatch. w 1875-92||?
Merged with Florida farmer and fruit grower (not in this list)
FJ Mr 11-18 1882
FU Je 20 1877-Je 11 1879;D 1,29 1880;Je 15 1881-Mr 13,Ap 3,17 1882
KHi F 11 1884-92
MHi N 5-12,D 17-24 1883;Ja 7,28-F 11 1884

FLORIDA journal. sw,w 1880-85||?
sw 1880-84?
MB My 29-Ag 28 1884

FLORIDA metropolis. *See* Jacksonville journal

FLORIDA news. *See* Weekly East Floridian (Fernandina)

FLORIDA republican. 1848-57 *See* St. John's mirror

FLORIDA republican. w 1871-73||?
NNHi F 5 1873

FLORIDA republican. w 1889-93||?
NcD O 1 1892

FLORIDA sentinel. 1887+
1887-1912? pub in Pensacola
Negro
DLC Ja 26 1900;Ap 19 1919

Daily FLORIDA standard. d 1890-92||?
FJ Mr 25 1891
FU O 10-D 1891

FLORIDA sun. 1876-77 *See* Daily sun and press

Daily FLORIDA sun. w,d 1902-04||?
Ja-Mr 5 1904 as Florida sun and labor journal; Mr 12-N 14 1904 Florida sun
w Ja-S 1904
FHi Ja 9-D 19 1904

FLORIDA daily times. d 1881-F 3 1883||
United with Daily Florida union to form Florida times-union
DLC Ja 30-F 1883

FLORIDA times-union. d 1875+
1875-F 3 1883 as Daily Florida union; S 9 1897-Ja 20 1903 Florida times-union and citizen
D 31 1914 is state ed
pub 1880+
A N 1878-N 1879;Jl 1901-O 1910
CL D 31 1914
CoU S 1906-Je 1908
DLC 1876-My 13 1877;N 20 1881+
F D 19 1897[1928-29]+
FDe Jl 1931+
FDeS 1929+
FHi O 1885;D 19 1897;F 1898;My 7 1905;D 16 1906;17-18
FJ Je 17,N 11 1879;S 1-5 1886;Ja 1 1895;Ap 1901+
FJU 1919+
FMaS [1884]
FO 1932+
FPY Je 1906-My 1919;21+
FTS [O 1928-S 1929;My 1930-31;Mr-N 1932; My-S 1933;Mr-Ap 1934]
FU Mr 19 1887;Ja 1890;D 19 1897;F 23 1902;N 1907+
FWpR S 1931-My 1932
IC My 6,D 31 1914
KHi Mr 24 1899-Ag 6 1918;Je 10-Jl 4 1920;D 26,28 1924
MWA F 6,S 20-21 1881
NbHi S 26 1907;My 6,D 31 1914
NcD F 14 1886;Je 14 1901
NcU Ag 24 1881;F 1885
OClWHi My 7 1905
OHi Ap 26 1923-Ap 1925;26+
P Mr 14 1886
PEr My 6,D 31 1914
PPL F 12 1884
PPeS 1885-86
PWp My 6 1914
TM D 31 1914
Tx F 12 1884
TxGR My 6,D 31 1914
VRC Mr 19 1887
—w,sw ed *See* Florida union; Semi-weekly times-union

FLORIDA union. w,sw Ag 1864-Ja 1883||
Title varies slightly
sw Ap 15-My 25 1868
DLC D 31 1864;F 11-18,Mr 11-Ap 8,22,My 6, 27-Je 3,17-Jl 1,15-Ag 5,19-S 16,30-N 18,D 1865;F 3,My 5-12,26-Je 23,Jl 1866;F 22-D 1868
FJ My 8(supp)1875
MBAt Ap 19 1865[67-69]
MWA N 16 1871;Je 17 1875;S 16 1876
N Mr 21 1868
NNHi Ja 23,Ap 15 1873
NcU S 1 1881
OClWHi Ag 18 1866

Daily FLORIDA union. *See* Florida times-union

FLORIDIAN. w,sw,d O 7 1828+
Ag 25 1829-O 3 1831 Floridian and advocate; Ja 6 1849-64? Floridian and journal] 1865?-99? Weekly Floridian (Ap 6-Je 7 1891 Daily Floridian)
sw Jl 2 1880-Mr 1891;d Ap 6-Je 7 1891
1828-98 pub in Tallahassee
pub [1901-02;04;07-10;12;15;17-18;23-25]+
DLC N 18 1828;S 1829-S,O 24 1831-Ja 5,19-My 11,Je 1-8,N 1833-Ja 15,F 19,Ap 2 1842;N 1,22-D 20 1845;Ja 10 1846-60;My 15 1877-N 1893
supps:N 11,25 1854
extras:Jl 2,30,S 17,O 22 1854;O 1 1860
FFL Ap 3 1877
FJ 1922-Ja,Ag 1925-26
FPY Ja-Jl,Ag 9-S 6,20-O 18,N 8,29-D 6,20 1851-Jl 24 1852;N 21 1861;Jl 26 1862;S 26,O 24,27,N 3-D 5,12-19,26 1865;Ja 5,9,16,26-Mr 2,9-27,Ap 13-Je 15,21-Ag 6,16-S 21,28-O 19, 30-N 16,23,30-D 25 1866;Ja-Jl 2,9-N 5,12 1867-Jl 13,Ag 10-N 1869;Ja 25-Mr 1,15,29 1870-D 19 1871;Ja 2-9,23 1872-O 5,19-N 30,D 14 1875-Ja 18,F 8-Mr 7,21-My 16,30-Jl 4,18,Ag 8-N 21,D 5 1876-Ja 1 1889
FTW F 12-Ap 16,23-Je 25,Jl 2, 9-S 6 1867;Ag 11-N 10,24-D 29 1868;Ja 3-10,24-F 28,Ap 4-Ag 22,S 5-O 3,17-D 12,26 1871;Ag 13-N 12,D 3-31 1873;Ja 20-Mr 10,24,Ap 7,My 5,19-Je 30,Ag 4,25,S 8-15,O 6-20,N 3-29 1874;Ja 12-F 16,Mr 2-9,23-My 25,Je 15,29-Jl 20,Ag 3-10,31 1875
FU Ap 6-Je 7 1891
GAtCe My 11 1839;My 9 1840
ICHi O 30 1852
MWA S 15-22,O 20,N 17,D 15 1829;Ap 14 1831; Je 1 1833;Mr 14-21,My 16 1846;Ja 9-16,30-F 13,Mr 6-20,Ap 3-17,My 8-15,29,Ag 21,S 18-25,O 30 1847;F 5,19-Mr,Ap 8-22,My 20,Je-Jl 1,22-Ag 19,S 30,O 21,N,D 9,30 1848-Ja 13,27-F 10,24,Mr 3 1849;Je 19 1852;Ja-F 3,17-Ag 18,S 1-8,29-N 17,D 15-22 1855;My 18 1866;F 4 1868;Mr 21 1871
NBuG N 1 1837
NN N 18 1828(facsimile) Je 7 1862
NNHi Jl 9 1864
NcD Ja 31 1846
NcU Ja 19-26,Mr 9-16,Je 29,Ag 17-24 1861;Ja 11 1862;Ag 15 1882
NhD Mr 28 1840
OClWHi Mr 5 1864
P-M N 1 1834;Mr 4,11 1886
WHi Mr 25 1848;F 24 1849

Jacksonville HERALD. w 1861-
FPY S 15 1865
MBAt Ag 24-31,S 22,O 13 1865
OHi S 15 1865

Jacksonville JOURNAL. d 1887+
1887-Je 5 1922 as Florida metropolis
pub My 1901+
F Ap 16 1926
FFL F 22 1894
FJ Je 1905-Jl,S 1929+
FU O 10,14,25 1918;Ap 1,N 17-18,26,D 6,8,23 1919[20]-[23]F 16,Ap 22,O 24,N 23-24 1925;F 8,Ap 26,Je 17,Jl 6 1926;My 21,O 29 1927[28]-Ja 2,F 9 1931+
KHi D 31 1913

Jacksonville MERCURY and Floridian. w S 14? 1867-69||?
1867-68? as Jacksonville mercury
MWA Ja 18 1868
N N 16 1867

NEW south. w,sw Ja 1851?-
w Ja 1851?
FPY Ja 18-25,F 15-My,Jl 19-Ag 25,N 1851-Ja 10,31,F 28,Mr 13 1852

NEW South. w 1874-75||?
DLC My-Je 23 1875

NEW South. sw Ap 1874-75||?
DLC Jl 15 1874-Ap 17 1875
OClWHi Ap 17 1875

NEWS. *See* Weekly East Floridian (Fernandina)

PENINSULA. w Ap 23 1863-
1863? pub in Fernandina
Ct Ap 30 1863
MBAt O 15 1863;Ap 7 1864
MH Je 4,O 29,N 12 1863;Ja 14 1864
MHi Je 4,Ag 13-20,S 17-24,O 15-29,D 24 1863; Mr 24-Ap 14 1864
MWA Jl 2,S 3 1863
NNHi My 14-21 1863
OClWHi Ap 21 1864
PDoHi Ja 7 1864
PPGr Je 25 1863
PWcHi O 15-D 24 1863;F 11 1864

FLORIDA (*Continued*)

JACKSONVILLE—*Continued*

Semi-weekly PRESS. sw 1875-77||?
United with Sun to form Daily sun and press

RECHERCHE.
OClWHi D 31 1865

Semi-weekly REPUBLICAN. *See* St. John's mirror

ST. JOHN'S mirror. w,sw Jl 6 1848-
1848-57? as Florida republican (Ap 28-Je 5 1856 Semi-weekly republican)
Suspended from Ap-Je 8 1854; from Je 5-Jl 9 1856
sw Ap 28-Je 5 1856
DLC Jl 20,Ag 3,S 28,N 30,D 14-21 1848;Ja 4-18,F 1-15,Mr 1-15,My 3,17,31,Je 14,Jl 26,Ag 9,30-S 13,D 6-13 1849;50-Ap 1 1857
ICHi N 4 1852
MWA Mr 6,Ap 10-My 1,15-Je 26,Jl 17,31,Ag 14-21,S 4,O 23-30,N 13 1851;Ja 1,15,29,F 19-26,Ap 8,Je 17,Jl 1-29,Ag 12-O 7,21,N 4-11,25, D 2,16,30 1852;Ja 13-27,F 10,24-Mr 24,Ap 7-My 5,19-Je 16 1853;Ap 5 1855;My 7,Jl 17(extra)1861
WHi S 4 1851

Jacksonville STANDARD. w 1858-
DLC F 24-Mr,Ap 21,My 5-12 1859
FJR Ag 18 1858

Jacksonville tri-weekly STANDARD. tw 1869||?
MBAt Je 8 1869

SUN. w 1905-N 1910||?
Followed by Dixie
F My 12 1906
FJ 1905-08

Daily SUN and press. tw,d 1876-80||?
1876-Ja 1877 as Florida sun; F 6-D 1877 Sun
tw 1876-Ja 1877
FHi Ja 22-Jl 20 1876
FPY Ja 16-F 25 1877
MWA Ag 22 1876;Jl 26 1879

Semi-weekly TIMES-UNION. w,sw O 5 1865-1909||?
1865-88? as Florida weekly times; 1889-94? Weekly times-union; S 1897-Ja 1903 Florida times-union and citizen
w 1865-94?
DLC O 5-12,D 7-14,28 1865;Ja 25,My 3-24,Je 14-Jl 1866
FMaS [1884]
FU F 22,Jl 12-16,Ag 9-13,23,O 4 1901;Mr 4, 11,18,Ap 8-15,N 4-11,D 26 1902;F 12-19 1907
KHi Ag 7 1890
MBAt N 23,D 7-14,28 1865-Ja 11,F 1-8 1866
NcD Jl 17 1884;S 30 1886;D 4,18 1890;N 12 1891;Ja 28,Je 16,Jl 7,N 10,D 1 1892;F 2,N 2,D 7 1893;Jl 19,O 18,N 22 1895;Jl 17,Ag 28,S 4 1896;Jl 6 1897;Ap 15 1898;Je 22 1900;Ja 25,S 24,D 6 1901;Ja 2,My 3 1903;Ja 8 1904
—d ed *See* Florida daily times; Florida times-union

TROPICAL paradise. w 1883-89||?
NcD My 31 1884
NcU Mr 17 1883

Tri-weekly UNION. tw 1864-75||?
MWA Mr 7 1874
—w,sw ed *See* Semi-weekly times-union

JUNO

TROPICAL sun. w 1887-94||?
WHi Ja 21 1892-Ap 6 1893

KEY WEST

Key West CITIZEN. w,d 1904+
1904 as Citizen (w)
pub 1922+
FU F 18-Ag 16 1926;Je 4-6,8,10 1927;S 28 1932+

Key West DISPATCH. w 1867-80||?
MWA Jl 13 1872;Mr 6 1880
NNHi Ja 4 1873

ENQUIRER. *See* Key West inquirer

Key West GAZETTE. w Mr 21 1831-S 5 1832||?
FKC Mr 21,Ap 20-Ag 1,22 1831-S 5 1832

Key West GAZETTE. w Mr 16 1844-
1844-F? 1845 as Light of the reef
DLC D 6-13 1845

Key West GUARDIAN. w 1870-74||?
NNHi Ja 18 1873

Key West HERALD. d 1894-99||
Followed by Inter-ocean
KHi O 23 1895

Key West INQUIRER. w O 15 1834-S 17 1836||?
1834-D 12 1835 as Enquirer
FKC 1834-Mr,Ap 11 1835-S 17 1836

INTER-OCEAN. d 1899-1904||
Follows Key West herald. Merged with Citizen, later Key West citizen

KEY of the gulf. w 1874-87||
MWA Jl 1-8 1876

LIGHT of the reef. *See* Key West gazette 1844

NEW era. w 1862-63||
CLM S 13 1862
FKS F 14 1863
MBAt My 17-23,O 4,N 8 1862
MWA Ag 16,S 6-20 1862
NHuHi S 6 1862
NNHi S 6 1862
RP S 6 1862

Key West OVERSEA Sunday star. w Jl 7 1929+
pub 1929-Jl 7 1930;Ag 1935+

Key West REGISTER and commercial advertiser. w Ja 8- 1829||?
DLC F 12-Ap 9,30-My 14,28-Jl 2,16-30,Ag 13-S 3 1829

SOUTH FLORIDIAN. w Je 30 1838-40||?
DLC N 10 1838

KISSIMMEE

FLORIDA. w 1881?-
MWA S 9 1882

KISSIMMEE VALLEY gazette. w 1894+
1894-97? as Kissimmee Valley
FKiC 1894+

OSCEOLA gazette. w 1891-97||?
United with Kissimmee Valley to form Kissimmee Valley gazette

LAKE BUTLER

BRADFORD county times. *See* Union county times

UNION county times. w 1912+
1912-20? as Bradford county times
FLbC [1922-35]
FU [Mr 24 1922-Ag 3 1923]

LAKE CITY

COLUMBIAN. w 1862?-
FJ My 18 1864
MWA Mr 22 1865
VRC N 20 1862;S 23,O 21 1863

FLORIDA index. w 1899-1918||?
F Je 16 1899-Ag 10 1906;Je 28 1907-Je 5 1909

INDEPENDENT press. *See* Lake City press

Lake City PRESS. w 1859-72||?
Early years as Independent press
TC F 29 1860

Lake City REPORTER. w 1874+
FU N 28 1919;Ag 24 1923;My 14 1926;Ja 6 1928;My 10 1929;Mr 18-Je 1932
MB Ag 14-O 2,N 3-10,24-D 8 1875

LAKE WORTH

Lake Worth LEADER. d 1922+
FU Mr 18, Je 19-20,27,Ag 21 1931-[32]+

LAKELAND

FLORIDA cracker. w 1884-88||?
FSaHi Mr 3 1888

Lakeland evening LEDGER and star-telegram. d 1924+
1924-Ja 10 1928 as Lakeland evening ledger
FL 1929+
FU S 24 1924+
TxGR N 1 1925
VU Ja 12 1930

Lakeland NEWS. w My 1931+
1931? as Polk county news
pub 1931+
FL 1932+

POLK county journal. w 1925-30||?
1925-Ja 22 1926 as Polk county labor journal
FU N 27 1925-[26-Jl 1927]

POLK county labor journal. *See* Polk county journal

POLK county news. *See* Lakeland news

Lakeland STAR-TELEGRAM. d 1916-Ja 10 1928||
1916-Ja 15 1921 as Lakeland star; Ja 16 1921-Ag 1922 Lakeland morning star. United with Lakeland evening ledger to form Lakeland evening ledger and star-telegram
FU [1918-19]-[23]S 27 1924-28
TxGR Ag 16 1925
VU F 2-3 1924

Lakeland evening STAR-TELEGRAM. d 1924||?
FU S 26-D 27 1924

Lakeland evening TELEGRAM. d 1911-Ag 1922||
United with Lakeland morning star to form Lakeland star-telegram
FU O 22,D 6 1918;D 23 1921[Je-Ag 1922]

LARGO

Largo SENTINEL. w 1912+
Suspended from Ja 11-Mr 8 1923
FU S 28 1922-[31]+

LEESBURG

Leesburg COMMERCIAL. w 1884+
FTvC Jl 27 1887+
PBlosM N 17 1887

Leesburg LEDGER. w 1928+
FTvC 1928+

Weekly LEESBURGER. w
FTvC 1889-91

Leesburg NEWS. w 1882-85||?
1883? as Leesburg news-advance
NcU Ap 11 1883

LEROY

FLORIDA news. *See* Leroy news

Leroy NEWS. w 1890-97||?
1890-Ap 1891 as Leroy and Dunnellon news (Dunnellon) Ap 15 1891- Florida news
MWA Ap 15 1891
OClWHi D 4 1891;Jl 27 1892

LIVE OAK

FLORIDA crescent. w 1903?-
F Je 30,D 8 1903;Je 14 1904;Mr 14 1905

SUWANNEE citizen. w 1907-28||?
FU Je 10,O 1927-Ap 1928

SUWANNEE democrat. w 1884+
FU O 24 1918;N 13-D 4,14 1919;Ja 1 1920;Ap 10-17,O 23 1924;F 19,Jl 2 1925;Je 24,S 22 1926;O 1927+

TIMES. w 1871-76||?
NNHi Mr 22 1873

LIVERPOOL

SOUTH FLORIDA orange grove. m 1884-89||?
DLC Je 1 1884

MACCLENNY

BAKER county press. w Ap 12 1929+
pub 1929+

MADISON

CHERRY LAKE pioneer. w? Ag- 1935||
FMaE Ag 1935

ENTERPRISE-RECORDER. w S 5 1901+
1901-Je 18 1908 as New enterprise
pub 1906+
F My 1 1903

FLORIDA intelligencer. w 1870-71||?
FMaS F 26 1870

NEW enterprise. *See* Enterprise-recorder

NEW era. w 1882-85||?
FMaS Ag 7 1884

Madison NEWS.
FMaS S 30 1876

Madison NEWS. w? Mr-D? 1914||?
FMaE [1914]

Madison RECORDER. w 1865-Je 18 1908||
United with New Enterprise to form Enterprise-recorder
F Ja 7 1882
FMaS N 5 1880;N 4 1882;Ag 9 1884;Ag 28 1885;D 3-7,21-28 1888;My 17-D 1889;D 3-7, 21-28 1890;My 8 1891;Mr 10 1893;Jl 24-S 18 1896;Ja-My 14 1897

SOUTHERN messenger. w 1854-71||?
FMaS D 25 1858
V Ap 20-27 1866

MAGNOLIA

Magnolia ADVERTISER. w D 12 1828-
DLC D 19 1828

MANATEE

Manatee BANNER. w 1917-19||?
FMnW Ap 1917-Mr 1918

MANATEE county advocate. *See* Sarasota county times (Sarasota)

MANATEE RIVER advocate. *See* Sarasota county times (Sarasota)

MARIANNA

COURIER. *See* West Florida courier

FLORIDA whig. w S 18 1847-
DLC D 31 1847;F 2-9,23-Ap 12,26-My 10,24, Je 17-Jl 1,15,29-Ag 12,D 16,30 1848;Ja 20,F 24-Mr 3 1849;extra Ap 27 1848
FPY [1847-O 6 1849]
MWA D 29 1847;Je 19 1852
NcU Mr 24 1849

Marianna FLORIDAN. *See* Jackson county Floridan

JACKSON county Floridan. w Je 11 1927+
1927-S 4 1934 as Marianna Floridan
pub 1927+
FU Ja 25,N 22-D 6,27 1929[30]Ja 9,F 13-20,Ag 28 1931+

JACKSON county times. *See* Times-courier

TIMES-COURIER. w 1883+
1883-84? as Times; 1885-86? Jackson county times
FMarC O 14 1909-D 9 1920
FU My 9,D 12 1929-[30-34]+

WEST FLORIDA courier. w 1866-86||?
1866-82? as Courier. United with Jackson county times to form Times-courier
NNHi Mr 13 1873

FLORIDA (*Continued*)

MELBOURNE

BREVARD advertiser. w Je 12 1930+
pub 1930+
FTiC 1932–

Melbourne JOURNAL. tw 1926||
United with Melbourne times to form Melbourne times-journal, later Melbourne times
FU D 17 1926

Melbourne SENTINEL. w 1927-
Merged with Melbourne times. journal, later Melbourne times
FTiC F 15 1929-Ap 26 1930
FU S 28,O 12-26 1928

Melbourne TIMES. w,sw 1894+
1927-Ap 1930 Melbourne times-journal
sw Jl 8 1925-D? 1926
pub 1926+
FTiC 1915-26 33+
FU O 31 1923-[26]Je 10 1927;Ag 19-26 1932; Ja 13 1933

MELROSE

WALLACK'S Melrose daylight. sw Mr- 1886||?
FU Mr 27 1886
MWA D 18 1886

MERRITT

ROCKLEDGE press and Merritt Island peninsula times. w
FTiC Jl 27-O 26 1929

MIAMI

CUBAN news. sm? Mr 7? 1935-
MWA Mr 7,Ap 4 1935

ILLUSTRATED daily tab. d Ja 12- 1925||?
MWA Ja 12 1925

Miami HERALD. d 1910+
Follows Morning news-record
S 18-24 1926 are cyclone eds
pub S 1910+
CL S 18,21-24 1926
FCg 1932+
FTS Je 2,11,13,30 1930;Ja 1,Ap 14,16 1931;Mr 1,My 1 1932–
FU N 29 1918;S 6,O 25 1919;Ja 27-30,Mr 9,13, 23,25,Ap 7 1920;F 5,N 30 1921;Jl 1-10,15,20,S 13,D 14,26 1922;Ja 6,10,26,F 12,21,Mr 22,Jl 6, O 27 1923;Ap 26,My 7-8,21 1924-N 22 1926;Ja 3,20,25,My 28,31,Je 5,9,Jl 6,Ag 2,4,21 1927;Mr 10,Jl 1928+
InU 1926+
KHi Jl 28 1929

Miami LIFE. w Ja 26? 1924-29||?
MWA F 16 1924

Miami METROPOLIS. *See* Miami daily news

Miami daily NEWS. w,d My 15 1896+
1896-D 11 1903? as Miami metropolis; D 12 1903?-Je 3 1923 Miami daily metropolis; Je 4 1923-Ap 9 1924 Miami news-metropolis; 1924-25? Miami daily news and metropolis
w 1896-D 11 1903
pub 1896+
FMH 1912–
FU Jl 13 1913;Ap 29,S 30 1915;Ja-Ag 1916; O 14,25,N 1 1918;Ja 27 1919-Mr 24,My 12 1922-F 14,Je 20 1928-Je 8,N 1932+
IU Jl 26 1925
KHi N 2 1912
MWA Je 28 1924
NjR Jl 26 1925

Miami NEWS. w -1908||?
United with Miami evening record to form Morning news-record?
FHi Mr 27 1904

Morning NEWS-RECORD. d S 15 1903-10||?
1903-08? as Miami evening record. Followed by Miami herald

Miami POST. w 1922+
pub 1924+

Miami evening RECORD. *See* Morning news-record

Miami TRIBUNE. d Mr 1924-F 28 1927||
Mr-Je 29 1924 as Daily tribune
FU [1924]-[26]27

MIAMI BEACH

Miami Beach SUN. w 1925+
FU O 1931+

Daily TAB. d 1925||?
FCo My 3,15 1925

Miami Beach TIMES. w 1928+
pub 1928+

Miami Beach TRIBUNE. d Ja 6 1934+
MWA Ja 6 1934

MICANOPY

COTTON states. *See under* Gainesville

MILTON

Milton GAZETTE. w,sw 1910+
sw 1918-Mr 7? 1931
FMIC 1928+
FU [Jl 23 1918-24]-[26]+

MONTICELLO

Monticello ADVERTISER. w 1869-74||?
FMaS Mr 10-D 1871;Mr 20,Je 12-Jl 3,Ag 14, 28-S 18 1874

Weekly CONSTITUTION. w 1874-1902||?
FMaS S 10 1875
NcD D 19 1901

FAMILY friend. w F 22 1859-
FHi 1859-D 21 1861

Monticello NEWS. w 1903+
FHi F 22 1907
FMoC 1906+
FU N 20 1925-[31]+
TJT Ag 27 1926

MOOREHAVEN

GLADES county democrat. w 1922+
FWpR Jl 1931-Jl 1932

MOUNT DORA

Mount Dora TOPIC. w Mr 1916+
pub 1927+
FTvC 1916–

MULBERRY

Mulberry PRESS. w F 1925+
pub 1932+

NEW PORT RICHEY

Port Richey PRESS. w 1918+
OClWHi N 13 1919;Mr 11,Je 24 1920
PP N 18 1927;O 5 1928

NEW SMYRNA

New Smyrna NEWS. w Je 1 1913-My 30 1930||
Ag 31 1928 is historical ed
pub complete
CSmH Ag 31 1928
FTW Ag 31 1928
MHi [1928-29]
OClWHi Ag 31 1928

New Smyrna daily NEWS. d N 2 1925+
1925-Je 1 1930 as New Smyrna news
pub 1925+
F Ag 31 1928

NEWNANSVILLE

FLORIDA dispatch. w
FGS My 11 1860;My 11 1867;Ja 11 1873
FU My 11 1860

NEWPORT

Newport GAZETTE. w S 15 1846-
DLC D 15-22 1846;Ja 5,19-26,F 16-23,Jl 20, Ag 31,S 14-O 12,26 1847

WAKULLA times. w 1849?-
FMaS F 9 1859
MWA Je 16 1852;Mr 31 1858

OCALA

Ocala ARGUS. w Ag 1847-
DLC Ja 29,F 26,Mr 25,My 25,Je 8 1848
FOG D 13 1849;O 19 1850

Ocala BANNER. w 1866+
1866-81? as East Florida banner
pub 1882+
CLM D 19 1874
FTaP Jl 1903-O 9 1925
FU Jl 3 1880;Mr 9 1906[Ag-D 1918]-[20]-[31]+
NNHi Mr 1 1873

Ocala BANNER. d 1902+
Title varies slightly
pub 1902+
FU S 5,19 1931;Ja 10,Mr 16,N 17,D 8,18 1932

CONSERVATOR. w Ag 13 1851-52||?
Followed by Florida mirror
DLC O 22 1851
FOG Jl 21 1852
MWA Je 23 1852
NcD N 19 1851;F 11,Mr 24;Ap 21 1852

EAST FLORIDA banner. *See* Ocala banner w

FLORIDA home companion. w 1857-
FPY [F-Je 8 1858]
NcD Ja 10 1860

FLORIDA mirror. w Ap 1 1853-
Follows Conservator
NcD Jl 8,Ag 19,O 14,D 9,30 1853

MARION star. w 1851-
NcD Jl 2 1851

NEW capitol. d 1890-94||?
FU Je 10 1891

Ocala evening STAR. d 1895+
pub 1895+
FU Ag 11,S 1,10 1919;Je 2 1928;Mr 8,S 11,O 1 1932;Ja 26,F 14 1933

Ocala weekly STAR. w 1897+
pub 1897+
FU Ag 30,S 19-26 1919;Ap 25,Jl 11,S 12 1924; My 8,22,S 4,D 4-11 1925;Jl 16,O 22 1926;S 23 1927;N 16 1928;Mr 8,Jl 12,Ag 9 1929

OKEECHOBEE

Okeechobee NEWS. w 1915+
FU Ja 8 1926;S 28 1928;O 4,N 8 1929;Ja 17 1930;Ag 31,S 21 1934+

ORANGE CITY

SOUTH FLORIDA times. *See* Times

TIMES. w 1880-98||?
1880-87? as South Florida times
NN O 29 1881
NcD Mr 19-26 1887

ORLANDO

ORANGE county reporter. w 1878-98||?
FO Ja 17 1884
KHi Ap 10 1890
MWA Ag 23,S 6-O 4,18 1883-Ja 10 1884

Orlando REPORTER. d 1892-1903||?
United with Evening star to form Evening reporter-star

Evening REPORTER-STAR. d 1903+
1903? as Evening star; N 12 1920-Ap 20 1921 Daily reporter-star
Sunday ed as Sentinel-reporter-star
pub 1903-10
FO 1911+
FTS [Ja-My 1931]
FU [Jl-D 1918]-Je 7,Ag 11 1926;N 20 1927-Jl 18,O 3 1928-My 26 1931
FWpR S 1930+

Orlando morning SENTINEL. d 1912+
Sunday ed as Sentinel-reporter-star
pub 1912-13
FO 1914+
FU O 22,25 1919-My 1931;Je 1933+
FWpR S 30 1930+
—w ed *See* South Florida sentinel

SENTINEL-REPORTER-STAR. *See* Orlando morning sentinel; Evening reporter-star

SOUTH FLORIDA sentinel. w 1885-1918||?
NcD Mr 30 1887
—d ed *See* Orlando morning sentinel

Evening STAR. *See* Evening reporter-star

PALATKA

ADVERTISER. *See* Palatka news

EASTERN herald. *See* Times-herald

Palatka daily NEWS. d F 28 1884-Mr 4 1888||
FU F-Ag 27 1884;F 28 1885-Ag 28 1886;Mr 11 1887-88
MWA N 21 1885

Palatka NEWS. w 1896-1928||?
1896-1901? as Advertiser; 1902-04? News and advertiser
FU [Ag 16-D 1918]-F 13 1920

Palatka daily NEWS. d 1919+
pub 1919+
FU Ap 7 1926;Je 4,9-11 1927;Je 13,25,Jl 2-3,21, 23,27,Ag 6,8,13,N 13,15,21 1928;F 4,Ap 10,Je 14,Jl 27 1929;F 10,17,26,Ap 2,My 6 1930;Ap 7 1931+

PUTNAM county journal. sw 1880-83||?
MWA Ap 13 1882;Ja 28 1884

Palatka TIMES. w 1889-91||?
United with Eastern herald to form Times-herald

TIMES-HERALD. w 1869+
1869-91? as Eastern herald
FPY Ap 18 1874
FPaC 1917+
NNHi Ap 5 1873

WHIG banner. w Je 21 1846-
DLC Je 21,Jl 7-14,28,D 22 1846;Ja 26 1847

PALM BEACH

Palm Beach LIFE. w 1906+
pub 1906+

Palm Beach daily NEWS. d 1894+
pub only D 20-Mr 31 each year
pub 1896+
FU F 13 1931+

Palm Beach POST. *See under* West Palm Beach

Palm Beach TIMES. *See under* West Palm Beach

PALMETTO

HERALD. w
VRC Jl 18 1864

Palmetto NEWS. w 1894+
FBC O 3-17 1930[31-32]
FSrB Je 4 1903

PANAMA CITY

BAY county beacon-tribune. w,sw 1916-26||?
1916-18? as Bay county beacon
sw F-Ag 1926
FU [N 15 1918-O 10 1919]O 22,D 31 1920;Ja 14-21,Ap 15,Ag 26,S 16,D 30 1921;Ag 17 1923; Ja 18,S 26 1924-[26]

BAY county herald. *See* Panama City herald

Panama City HERALD. w Ag 1931+
1931-S 30 1935 as Bay county herald
pub 1931+
FU 1932+

Panama City PILOT. w 1907+
pub 1907+
FU Ag 29 1919-[20]-[22]-D 4 1930;Ja 29-F 19,Je 4-11,Ag 20 1931+

FLORIDA (*Continued*)

PENSACOLA

Daily COMMERCIAL. w,sw,d F 14 1882-89‖?
1882-F 16 1887 as Weekly commercial w F-Ap 1882;sw Ap 11 1882-F 16 1887
DLC N 13 1886;N 8 1888
F Ja 17,F 14 1885
FPY 1882-My 23 1889

FLORIDA argus and Pensacola literary, agricultural and commercial register. Je 17-N 18 1828‖
ICN complete

FLORIDA democrat, and mechanic's and workingman's advocate. w 1845-
1845-Jl 22 1846 as Florida democrat
DLC Ja 23-30,F 13-27,Mr 25-Ap 22,My 6,20-27,Jl 1,15-22 1846;Jl 13-20,Ag 10-24 1848;Ja 18,F 22,Mr 15,29 1849
F Ja 30,F 13-27,Mr 6,N 28,D 19 1845;Ja 16 1846
MWA Ag 10 1848;Mr 20,Ap 3 1856

FLORIDA express. w 1870-75‖?
FPY S 2-9 1871;Ap 20 1872;Ag 28 1875

FLORIDA sentinel. *See under* Jacksonville

FLORIDIAN. *See* Pensacola gazette

Pensacola GAZETTE. w Ag 18 1821-
1821-Mr 8 1824 as Floridian; Mr 15 1824-Mr 14 1828 Pensacola gazette and West Florida advertiser; Mr 21 1828-S 18 1830 Pensacola gazette and Florida advertiser
Suspended for short periods in 1833
CSmH Ag 14 1830
DLC 1821-Ag 17 1822;Mr-D 20 1823;Mr 13 1824-O 1828[29]30;Ja 11,O 22 1831[33]Je 13 1835;36-[43-49]-O 8 1853;F 28,Je 6,27,O 10 1857
F 1824-Jl 1829;Jl 23 1836;F 1 1845
FJ Ja 2 1835;O 9 1841
FPC 1841;43;46-48;51-56
FPY Je 21,S 13,D 13 1823;Ja 12,Ag 14,O 23 1824;F 9,23,N 16,D 17 1827;My 2,S 23,N 7-14 1828;Mr 12 1834-Ap 1 1843;Mr 30-Ap 20,Je-Jl 13,27-Ag 3,17-31,S 14-O 19,N 9 1844-Mr 24, Ap-Je 16,30,Jl 21,Ag,S 8-N,D 8-15,29 1849; Ja 12-Mr 9,23-Ap 20,My 4-11,25-Je 1,15,29,Jl 20-Ag,S 14 1850-Mr 1858;S 28 1860
MBAt Ap 13-20 1822;Ja 7 1843
MWA S 1,O 8 1821;Ap 13 1822;Je 26,S 13(extra),O 9 1824;Je 18 1825;My 18,O 26 1827;Mr 10,Je 9-23,Jl 21-28,O 13,S 8,D 19 1829;Ja 2,D 4 1830;O 17 1840;Ja 9 1847;My 13 1848;Mr 9,29 1856
N O 2 1833
NN Mr 20 1824(facsimile)
NNHi My 18-Je 22,Jl 27-Ag 10 1822
PHi Ja 31 1835

Pensacola JOURNAL. d 1898+
DLC 1905+
F D 9 1923-[25-26]-[29]-30
FHi S 23(D 16 1906
FJ Ja 1 1904
FPY 1906+
FTS [My 1930-F 1934]+
FU N 19,23-25,D 4 1909;Ag 11 1910-Ap 26,O 2 1920-Ap 1,23-24,Je 4-10,Jl 21 1924;Ap 13,Jl 3,Ag 30,S 12,O 11,18,20 1925;Ag 12,26,S 5,8,N 21 1926;Ja 4,Mr 17,Je 5,9-12,17,O 15 1927;D 26 1928;Ja 30,F 6,Ag 31,S 1-2 1929;S 4-5 1931

LIVE OAK. sw Ag-O 13 1847‖?
Suspended S 22-O 6 1847
DLC S 22,O 13 1847;O 8(extra)1847

NEUTRAL. w D 28 1847-
In English and French
DLC F 15-Ap 11,My 2-23 1848

Pensacola daily NEWS. d 1889+
1898-Ap 1902 as Daily news
A 1901-02
DLC 1898-1912
F D 24 1892;Ja 13 1924-[25-N 1929]
FPY 1889-[98;1900-05;07]-Mr 1909
FHi F 1890
FU N 15 1892-My 15 1894
NcD Je 15 1894

Pensacola weekly NEWS. w 1889-1909‖?
FPY Mr 1891-[96]-Mr 1898;Ap 1902-[03]04

OBSERVER. w 1840-70‖?
FPY Ag 18 1870

Pensacola OBSERVER. tw 1866-70‖?
1866? as Tri-weekly observer
MBAt [Je-D 1868]
OClWHi Ag 4 1866

Weekly PENSACOLIAN. w D 15 1883-89‖?
FPY 1883-Ag 16 1889

WEST FLORIDA commercial. tw,w N 1867-71‖?
tw 1867-69?
FPY O 12 1868;F 25 1871
MBAt N 25,D 13,20 1867[68-69]

WEST-FLORIDA times. w D 2 1856-
DLC Ja 6,20,F 17,Mr 17 1857

PERRY

Perry HERALD. w,sw 1896?-1933‖
1905-25? as Taylor county herald. Merged with Taylor county news
sw 1927?
FPeC [1915-33]
FU Ag 30-S 6,N 22,D 12 1918-Mr,My 1919-Ap 9,30-My 7,21 1920

TAYLOR county herald. *See* Herald

TAYLOR county news. w 1929+
FU N 27 1930;Ag 27-S 17,O 15 1931+

PLANT CITY

Plant City COURIER. w,sw,d S 24 1884+
1884-91? as South Florida courier
w 1883-1913?;d N 1925-Mr 14? 1927;F 3-6 1931
pub 1911+
FTaT 1886-88
FU [Jl 23-S 1918]-[20-22]-Je,Ag 1923-[27]-[33]+
NcD Ap 23,My 14,Jl 23,D 1887;Ja 7,F 18 1888
NcU Je 12 1886;Ap 24 1896-F 11 1898

Plant City ENTERPRISE. sw,w 1926+
sw 1926-30?
FU Ja 20,Ag 5 1927-[28-Mr 1929]S 25 1931+

SOUTH FLORIDA courier. *See* Plant City courier

PUNTA GORDA

Punta Gorda HERALD. w 1893+
pub 1902+

QUINCY

Quincy COMMONWEALTH. sw 1865-
NNHi Je 5 1866

Quincy semi-weekly DISPATCH. sw 1859?-
FPY Mr 15 1865
MWA Mr 15 1865

GADSDEN county times. w 1901+
FU D 12 1918;F 12 1920;S 20,N 1923-[31]+

JOURNAL. w 1868-76‖?
1868-70? as Quincy monitor
NNHi Ja 31 1873

Quincy MONITOR. *See* Journal

Quincy REPUBLIC. w 1858-
NcD Ap 6 1861

Quincy SENTINEL. w N 15 1839-F 19 1841‖
Followed by Florida sentinel, later Tallahassee sentinel (Tallahassee)
DLC N 15 1839
F Mr 20-27,My 16,Jl 24,Ag 14,S 11-25,O 9-N 20 1840
FPY Jl 10 1840-41
MWA N 15,D 20 1839

Quincy TIMES. w 1847-
DLC My 13-20 1848

RIVER JUNCTION

River Junction TRIBUNE. w 1929+
FU D 1929[30]Ja 9 1931;D 30 1932-Je 15 1934

RUSKIN

FLORIDA beacon. w 1911-13‖?
KHi F 21-Je 13 1913

ST. ANDREWS

St. Andrews BAY news. w 1915+
FU S 9 1919-[21]-[23]-[26]-[31]+

ST. AUGUSTINE

ANCIENT city. w Ja 5 1850-
DLC Je 24 1854
FJ F 28,Mr 6-20 1852
FPY Ja 5-12,26,F 9-Ap 13,27-My 18,Je 1-29,Jl 13-Ag 31,S 14-28,N 16,30,D 21 1850;Ja 4,Je 14,Jl 5-O 18,N 1,15,D 6-13,27 1851-Ap,My 8-D 11 1852;Ja 8-D 17 1854;Ja 14,My 20,N 18,D 9 1854
FSaHi Mr 24 1855
MHi F 17 1855

EAST FLORIDA herald. *See* Florida herald and southern democrat

St. Augustine EXAMINER. w 1858-76‖?
DLC Ja 5-12,Mr 9,23 1867;Ap 11-18 1868;F 20 1869
FJ N 18 1871
FPY O 29,N 12,26-Ja 21,F 4-Je 9,23-Jl 21,Ag 4-11,25-D 29 1860;Ja 19-F 16,Mr 2-My 18,Je 8-29 1861;S 8-N 24,D 15,29 1866;Ja 5-Je 15,29 1867-Je 20,Jl 4-D 12,26 1868;Ja 16-F 27,Mr 13-Ap 10,My 8,22,Je 5-Ag 21,S 4-N 13,27-D 11 1869;D 16 1871;Ja 11,O 4 1873;My 23 1874
FSaHi S 21 1867
MBAt Ap 9-My 8 1862
MWA Ap 28 1860
NNHi My 11 1867;Ja 11 1873

FLORIDA examiner.
pub by Fourth New Hampshire regiment
NNHi Ap 16,My 1,8 1862

FLORIDA gazette. w Jl 14 1821-
DLC Jl 14,Ag 4,S 1-15,O 20,N 24-D 22 1821
MWA Ag 4,D 10 1821
NN Jl 28 1821(facsimile)

FLORIDA herald and southern democrat. w,ir Ag 31 1822-
1822-Mr 18 1829 as East Florida herald; Mr 25 1829-O 1838 Florida herald
Suspended from Ja-Ap 1835
ir 1832;48
CSmH Jl 21 1830
DLC 1823-26;N 7 1827;Mr 25 1829-D 1 1830; Ja-F,Mr 15,29-Ap 5,27,My 17,Je,Jl 12,Ag 9,S 6-13,O 11-N 1,29-D 6,27 1832;Ja 10 1833-D 3 1834;Ja 10-17,Ap-O 1835;Ja 6-20,F 6,Mr 9,25, Ap 16-23,My 11-18,Je 25,Jl 2-9,Ag 17-31,S 22, O 27,N 17-D 9,29 1836-Ja,F 16,Mr-Ap 12,26, My 3,17-Je 1,15-Jl 21,Ag 10,25,S 6-13,D 31 1837-Ja 6,F 15,Mr 9,22,Ap 5,20,My-Je 2,16-O 13,25,N 8-1838-D 10 1844;Ja 14,28,F 18-25,Mr 18,Ap 15-My 6,20,Je 3-10,24,D 2-23 1845;Ja 27-My 5,26-Ag 18,S 1-8,N 3,D 22 1846-F 23, Mr 23-Ap 6,My 11-18,Jl 6-20,Ag 3,17,S 21-28, O 13,26-N 16 1847;F 1;Mr 28,Ap 11,21-Je 13, 27,Jl 20,Ag 9,23,S 7,21,N 2-D 14 1848;Ja 24,F 16-23 1849
F O 10 1839;Ja 9-30,Mr 26,Je 12,Jl 10,Ag 28, D 31 1840;Ja 15,F 5,Ap 2 1841;Ag 1-15,S 26 1842;Ag 7 1843;Jl 15-22 1845
FJ Je 22 1837
FPY F 13 1828;S 5 1833;Ja 10,My 9,23-Jl 18, Ag 15-O,N 14 1839;F 13-O 9,N 6-D 1840;Ja 15-Mr 5,Ap D 1841;F 18 1842;Ja 9-F 13,Mr 13-20,Ap 10-Jl 3,17-N 13,27-D 3 1843;Ja 1,F 5,20-Jl 2,16-S 10,O-D 17 1844;D 28 1847;D 21 1848;Mr 10 1849
FSaHi D 8 1836;Ap 20,S 1 1838
MH D 4 1843
MWA Je 17-24,Jl 8-15,Ag 26,S 16,N 18,D 16 1829;D 1 1830;Je 2,23,Jl 14-Ag 18,S 8,22,O 6-13,25,N 1,15,D 27 1838;Ja 3-17,31-F 7,28-My 16,30,Je 6-Jl 5,18-O 25,N 14-D 12 1839;Ja 22-15,30-Mr 26,Jl 17,N 6,D 11 1840;Ja 15,F 26, Mr 12,Ap 2-16,30,My 14 Je 25,Jl 23,N 5,26,D 10 1841;F 11,25-Mr 11,25-Ap 1,22,My 6-13,Je 3-10,24-Jl 8,25-Ag 8,O 24,N 7-14,28,D 26 1842; Ja 19 1847
N Je 13 1833
NGl D 21 1845
NN Ja 4 1823(facsimile)
NhD D 25 1840
PHi N 27 1834
WHi Ag 4 1838;My 2,Ag 15 1839

FLORIDA weekly press. *See* St. Augustine press

NEWS. *See* Weekly East Floridian (Fernandina)

St. Augustine PRESS. w 1870-99‖?
1870-81? as Florida weekly press; 1882-83? Press-pathfinder
FJ S 24 1881
FSaHi Mr 3 1888
MWA Mr 4 1876
NNHi F 1 1873
NhD Mr 18 1871

St. Augustine evening RECORD. d 1894+
FSaHi O 2 1900
FU 1908-Je,S 1915-O 7 1916;Ag 21 1919-[21-26]O 15,26 1928;O 7 1929+

ST. JOHN'S county weekly and St. Augustine chronicle. w F 28 1879-88‖?
FSaHi My 16 1879
FU Mr 12 1887
P-M Mr 27 1886

ST. CLOUD

St. Cloud TRIBUNE. w S 9 1909+
pub 1909+
FKiC 1909+
FU D 1933+
FWpR Jl 1932+
KHi S-N 6 1919
MWA S 16-23,O-N,D 9 1909-Mr 24,Ap 7-14,Je 17-24 1910

ST. JOSEPH

St. Joseph TIMES. w N 1836-S 1841‖?
DLC 1839-40
F Jl 18,Ag 1-22,S 5-26,O 24 1838;S 24 1839; Jl 14,Ag 4,S 4,19-O 5,N 7-14 1840;Ja 23,F 20 1841
ICHi F 23 1839;My 5 1840
NN Mr 23 1839(facsimile)

ST. PETERSBURG

St. Petersburg ADVOCATE. w 1927+
FU Ag 21-S 4,24-O 9 1931[Mr 8-D 1934]+
FWpR My 1931+

St. Petersburg INDEPENDENT. w 1906-23‖?
pub 1913-17

Evening INDEPENDENT. d N 4 1907+
pub 1907+
MWA N 15 1924

St. Petersburg TIMES. w,sw,d Jl 25 1884+
1884-S 1892 as West Hillsborough times
1884 pub in Dunedin; 1885-S 1892 pub in Clearwater
w 1884-Mr 1901;sw Ap 1901-Ja 1912
pub 1904+
M Mr 30 1930
FTaT Mr 1886-N 1887
FU F 26,Mr 4,9-26,31-Ap 1,3,23-25,27,My 20-Je 4 1915;16+

SAN ANTONIO

San Antonio HERALD. w 1892‖?
PPCHi [1892]

San Antonio NEWS. sm Ag 25 1887-91‖?
FU Ag 25 1887

SANFORD

ARGUS-ALLIANCE. tw,w 1884-90‖?
1884-89? as South Florida argus; 1888? Florida argus-alliance
tw 1884-89?
IU F 23 1888
MB F 26 1885-Mr 1887
P-M F 24 1886

Sanford CHRONICLE. w 1891-1908‖?
1895-1901? as Gate City chronicle
Ct F 5 1897

FLORIDA argus-alliance. *See* Argus-alliance

GATE CITY chronicle. *See* Sanford chronicle

Sanford HERALD. w,sw 1908-33‖?
sw 1911?-18?
FU Jl 23,Ag 6-S 3 1918;Ja 31-Je 1923;O 19 1924;O 21 1931-Ap 1932

FLORIDA (*Continued*)

SANFORD—*Continued*

Sanford HERALD. d 1920+
pub 1920+
FS 1920+
FU Ag 6 1928[31-32]+

Sanford JOURNAL. w 1874-93||?
1874-82? as South Florida journal
FS My 16 1874
MB S 14 1882-N 6 1884
MWA Ap 26,My 10,31 1883-N 20 1884

Sanford daily JOURNAL. d 1886-89||?
MWA Ja 23,F 1 1889

SOUTH FLORIDA argus. *See* Argus-alliance

SOUTH FLORIDA journal. *See* Sanford journal

SARASOTA

Sarasota HERALD. d 1925+
FU F 18-Jl 8,O 16 1927;Je 2,Ag 2 1928;O 6 1929+

SARASOTA county times. w Mr 20 1886-1929||
1886-87? as Manatee River advocate; 1888?-My 1899 Manatee county advocate; Je 1 1899-1923? Sarasota times. Merged with Sarasota herald
1886-My 1899 pub in Manatee
FSrR [Mr 27-D 1886]Ja-O 1890;Mr 10-D 22 1898
FSrW 1911-22
FU Ag 21-28 1919;Mr 11 1920;F 17 1921
—d ed *See* Sarasota daily times

Sarasota daily TIMES. d 1924-29||
Merged with Sarasota herald
FU Ap 14 1924;S 15,D 28-29 1926;27-D 9 1929
MWA Je 15 1926
—w ed *See* Sarasota county times

Sarasota TRIBUNE. w,sw,d 1925+
w 1925-33?sw 1933-Ap 1934
pub Ap 9 1934+
FU O 1934+

SEBRING

Sebring daily AMERICAN. d 1925+
FU Mr 31,Ag 21 1931+
KHi Ja 26 1926

Sebring WHITE way. w 1914-26||?
FU Je 11 1920;Je 10-17,Ag 12,26,S 9-16 1921; Je 16 1922-Ap 30,N 1923-My 7 1926

STARKE

BRADFORD county telegraph. w 1877+
1877-86? as Weekly Florida telegraph; 1887?-88? Starke telegraph
pub 1887+
FStaC Ap 13 1887+
P-M Mr 6 1886

Weekly FLORIDA telegraph. *See* Bradford county telegraph

STARKE telegraph. *See* Bradford county telegraph

STUART

Stuart MESSENGER. w 1915-Ja 1925||
Followed by Stuart daily news
FStuN 1916-25
KHi N 17 1916;My 23 1918

Stuart daily NEWS. d Ja 11 1925+
Follows Stuart messenger
pub 1925+
FU F 15-26,Jl 21,Ag 21 1931-S 11 1933;N 1934+

Stuart NEWS. w 1933+
Follows South Florida developer
pub 1933+

SOUTH FLORIDA developer. w 1921-33||
Followed by Stuart news (w)
1922 pub in West Palm Beach
F Ja 13 1928
FStuN 1921-32
InU Jl 1921-My 1922
KHi Ag 6 1926

Stuart TIMES. w 1913-16||?
FStuN 1915

TALLAHASSEE

Daily CAPITAL. *See* Morning sun

Daily DEMOCRAT. d 1915+
pub 1915+
FTS [Je-N 1916;Je-O 1917;Ap 1918-S 1919; Ja-O 1920;Ag 1921] Ag 12 1922;F 21,S 21 1923 [Jl-Ag 1924;Mr-My 1926;S 1928-31] Ag 14,S 4,9,N 18,20,D 14,16 1932[33]+
FU 1916-Je 3 1917;Ap 1919[20;22-23]My 17 1924;Je 3,6,10-11,O 4 1927;Ag 1,4,26,29,S 5-6,8 1929;Mr 5 1930;F 18,Mr 29 1931+
—Morning ed *See* Florida morning state

DEMOCRAT. w *See* Smith's weekly

Tallahassee DISPATCH. w N 12 1923-
FTS N 12,30,D 28 1923;F 8,Ap 25,My 16-23, Je 20 1924

FLORIDA advocate. w F 1827-Ag 8? 1829||
Follows Florida intelligencer. United with Floridian to form Floridian and advocate, later Floridian (Jacksonville)
DLC D 16 1827;N 11-25,D 24 1828;Ja 3, F 7-21, Mr-Ap 4,25,Je 13-Ag 8 1829
FPY My 12-19,S 29 1827
MWA S 23,N 11 1828;Je 20,Ag 1 1829
NcD Jl 4 1829

FLORIDA courier. w D 1830-O 1831||?
DLC Ap 21 1831

FLORIDA democrat and weekly record. *See* Smith's weekly

FLORIDA intelligencer. w F 19 1825-26||?
Followed by Florida advocate
DLC F 24-Mr,Ap 14,18-My 5,19,Jl 22,S 1-8, 29-O 13,28,N 24,D 8 1826

FLORIDA morning state. d 1925-28||
FTS Ap 14,18,My 6,Jl 30,Ag 8,11 1926;Ja 19, My 16,18 1928
—evening ed *See* Daily democrat
—w ed *See* Smith's weekly

FLORIDA sentinel. *See* Tallahassee sentinel

FLORIDA state news. d 1927-30||?
FDE Ap-S 1930

FLORIDA watchman. . . *See* Star of Florida

FLORIDIAN. *See under* Jacksonville

LAND of flowers. *See* Weekly Tallahasseean

Tallahassee SENTINEL. w,sw F 1841-D 30 1876||?
Follows Quincy sentinel (Quincy) 1841-N 17 1866? as Florida sentinel
sw 1866-68?
DLC My 21-Je 4,18-Ag 20,S,O 15-D 10,31 1841;Ja 14-D 23 1842;Ja-F 17,Mr-Ap 18 1843; N 4,D 1845-Jl 21,Ag 4-17,S 8 1846;47-Ja,F 13-Mr 1849;50-D 21 1852;Ja-Mr 22 1853;S 17 1861;My 13 1876
F S 2,D 1 1842;Mr 17,D 5 1843;Ja 22,O 29 1844;Ja 28,F 25,Mr 4-11,Ap 15,29,My 13-Je 3,24-Jl 15,29-Ag 12,S 6,23,O 7-21 N 18,D 23 1845-Ja 6,27,Mr 10 1846;F 1-12,Mr 19,Ap 2,16, 30,My 3,21,31-Je 6,13,Jl 8,22,29,Ag 8-15,S 2, 19,26-O 7 1867
FMaS [My-O 1860]
FPY Je 1843-Je 4 1844;My 30 1854-F 20,Mr-D 1855;Ja-Jl 15,29,Ag 5,19 1862-N 6 1866;67-O 1 1868;70-Ja 4 1873[74-75]76
FTW F 4,Mr 11,25-Ap 15,My 13-27,Je 10-24, Jl 1-8,Ag 12-19,S 2,23-O 21,N 18 1-Ja,F 19-26,Mr 25-Ap 8,29 My 13-N 4,18-D 2,16-30 1876
MBAt D 21 1866;Je 25-Jl 23,O 1,22-29,D 10-24 1868;Ja 20-F 13,27-Mr 13,27-Ap 3,24-My 1,15-22,Je 19,Jl 1869
MWA Jl 30 1844;Mr 17 1846;S 2 1867;N 18 1871;S 16 1876
N Jl 6 1868
NNHi Je 5 1866;F 22 1873

SMITH'S weekly. w,sw 1905-29||
1905-11 as Weekly true democrat; 1912-13 Semi-weekly true democrat; 1914-18 Democrat; 1919-22 Democrat and Florida record; 1923-24 Florida democrat and weekly record
sw 1912-13
F My 18 1906
FTS Ag 18 1916;O 31,N 14 1924;Ja 1 1926;Ja 6, N 11,25,D 30 1927;D 16 1928
FU Jl 30 1909-N 7 1913;14-S 15 1916;N 22 1918;F 14 1919
—morning ed *See* Florida morning state
—evening ed *See* Daily democrat

SOUTHERN journal. w Ja 13 1846-Ja 1 1849||
United with Floridian to form Floridian and journal, later Floridian (Jacksonville)
DLC complete
F Ja 13,F 10 1846
MWA My 12 1846

Tallahassee STAR. *See* Star of Florida

STAR of Florida. w N 1836-
1836-F 12 1838 as Florida watchman and Tallahassee literary gazette; F 19 1838-F 1839 Florida watchman; Mr 6 1839-40? Tallahassee star
DLC F 17,Ap 21-My 5,19,S 8,N 3 1838;Mr 13 1839;My 21 1840;Jl 14-28,Ag 11-O 6,20-27,N 10,24,D 9 1841-Ja,F 9-16,Mr-Ap 20,My-Jl 6, Ag 11-18,S 1 1843;F 23,Mr 8,22-29,Ap 19-26, My 17-24,Je 28,Jl 19,Ag 9-S 6,N 22,D 6-13, 27 1844-Ja 17,31-F 14,28,Mr 14,28-Ap 4,18-My 2,16-30,Je 13-27,Ag 1-8,29,S 12,26,O 10-17,31-N 22,D 5,19 1845
F Ja 6 1837
GAtCo Ap 8 1840
MBAt S 8 1843

SUN. w 1905-08||?
F Ag 1 1908
FHi N 30 1907-Ja 18,F 23,Mr 2-Ap 20,My 4-Je 15,Ag 31,S 21,O 5 1908

Morning SUN. d 1901-07||?
1901-06? as Daily capital
F My 15,O 21 1904;Mr 10 1905
FBC Ap-Je 1 1907

Weekly TALLAHASSEEAN. m,w,sw,ir Ap 5 1881-1905||?
1881-85 as Land of flowers
m 1881-Ja 1882;sw 1884;ir 1885
F D 1892;Ag 3 1893;N 5 1896;Mr 11 1897;Je 19 1903
FPY [1881-82]-Ag 16 1889
FTS Je 5 1903

Weekly TRUE democrat. *See* Smith's weekly

TAMPA

Tampa BULLETIN. w My 1914+
Negro
pub 1914+

FLORIDA peninsular. w Mr 1854-74||?
FPY Jl 5,Ag 23 1856;F 27-Ap 3,24-My 1,Je 19 1858
FTa Ja,F 11,25,Mr 31-Ap,My 26-Je,Jl 21,31, Ag 18-S 15,29-O 6,20-27,N 10-17,D 1 1860;Ja 19-26,Mr 16 1861
FTaT 1855-71

La GACETA. d 1922+
In Spanish
FU [Ag 21-D 1929]-[33]+

Tampa GUARDIAN. w My 1874-86||?
FTaT Jl-Ag 1878;My 1879-Ag,O-D 1880;86

Tampa HERALD. w? Ja 1854-
FPY O 25 1854
FTaT [1855]56

El HERALDO dominical. w 1914+
In Spanish
IU [F-S 1 1918]

Tampa JOURNAL. w D 1885-92||?
FTaT D 1886-Jl 1891
KHi Mr 27 1890

Tampa daily JOURNAL. d 1886-91||?
FTaT Ja 10-My 2 1890

Tampa evening NEWS. d
FTaT Mr 26-Jl 1908

SUNLAND tribune. *See* Tampa tribune

Tampa morning TELEGRAPH. d 1925-26||?
FTa Mr 3,8,My 18,29,31,Je 8-9,24 1926
FU O 22 1925-Mr,Ap 9 1926

Tampa daily TIMES. d 1893+
Ja 28 1915 is "Tampa and the Tampa territory" ed. Ap 30 1930 is historical ed
pub 1893+
CL Ja 28 1915
FTa Ap 21 1915;S 11-13,25-27,O 1,16 1917[F-N 1918]Mr 1919+
FTaM My 12 1899;Ap 30 1930
FU D 27 1911;Je 9 1914[Mr-My]Je 1-4,Jl 1 1915;16-Jl 13 1918;D 10,15 1919[20;22-24]+
KHi O 24 1895;O 16 1924
NbHi Ja 28 1915
MoS Ja 28 1915
PP D 29 1931
TM Ja 28 1915
VU F 4-5 1924;Ag 24-25,S 27,29,O 1,4 1934

Tampa weekly TIMES. w 1893+
pub 1893-1910

Tampa morning TIMES. d My 1-31 1898||
pub complete

Tampa TRIBUNE. w,sw F 1875-1905||?
1875-82 as Sunland tribune
sw 1886-Je 1891
FTaT 1877-Je 1891

Tampa TRIBUNE. tw 1890-91||
FTaT 1890

Tampa morning TRIBUNE. d Ja 1 1894+
pub 1894+
FTS [1929-34]+
FTa Ap 22,Je 30,Jl 26 1921;22+
FTaT 1924+
FU Ja 31,F 5,7-10,12-17,19-20 1907;Mr 1910-14;[16-25]-Ag 8 1928;My 3,Jl 6 1929+
KHi O 26 1895
MWA Ja 1 1933
VU F 3 1924;Ja 11 1930

TRUE southerner. w O 22 1868-69||?
MBAt O-D 10 1868

TARPON SPRINGS

Tarpon Springs LEADER. w,d,tw,sw 1914+
d 1914-19?;tw 1920-21?;sw 1922-Mr 1933
FU O 18 1929-[31]+

TITUSVILLE

Titusville STAR-ADVOCATE. w,sw 1890+
1890-99? as Indian River advocate; 1900-19? East Coast advocate
w 1890-1925?
pub 1890+

UMATILLA

EXPONENT of Umatilla. *See* Umatilla tribune and exponent

Umatilla TRIBUNE and exponent. w 1921+
1921-24? as Exponent of Umatilla
FTvC 1921+

VERO BEACH

Vero weekly BULLETIN. w 1913-
IU F 7,Mr 3,14 1917-My 10,Ag 9 1918

Vero Beach PRESS-JOURNAL. w,sw S 13 1919+
1919-26? as Vero Beach press
sw 1927-31?
pub 1919+

WAUCHULA

FLORIDA advocate. w Mr 15 1901+
pub 1901+
FU O 21 1932+

WEST PALM BEACH

Palm Beach POST. d 1908+
Also dated at Palm Beach
pub 1909+
FU 1918-Jl 1928;29+
PP 1926[27]D 20 1928-[30]-[34]

SOUTH FLORIDA developer. *See under* Stuart

Palm Beach TIMES. d 1922+
Also dated at Palm Beach
pub 1921+
FU N 9 1922;Ap 1,N 11,D 16 1923;N 18 1926; My 3,Je 4-6,8,10-12,N 13,D 28 1927;Ja 22 1928;Ag 30-31 1929

TROPICAL sun. w 1887+
FU [Ag 1918-21]-Mr,Ap 9-23,My 7-14,O 8 1926

FLORIDA (*Continued*)

WILLISTON

LEVY county news. *See under* Bronson

Williston PROGRESS. w 1918-Jl 28 1922‖
FU Ag 23 1918[19]-[22]

Williston SUN. w Jl 21 1922+
FU Jl-S 1 1922;Ag 31,N 23,D 7 1923;Ja 4,N 21,D 12 1924;F 27,Mr 20,S 3-10 1925

WINTER HAVEN

Winter Haven daily CHIEF. d 1911+
FU Jl 21,Ag 21 1931+
KHi Je 30 1927

Winter Haven HERALD. w My 1930+
Follows Tri-city times
pub 1930+

TRI-CITY times. w S 1925-29‖?
1925-27? as Auburndale times (Auburndale) Followed by Winter Haven herald
NcD N 18 1925

WINTER PARK

FLORIDA post. w,d 1915-22‖?
1915-F 14 1922 as Winter Park post
w 1915-F 14 1922
FU D 25 1919[20]-[Ja-Jl 18 1922]

Winter Park HERALD. w 1922+
Suspended from 1929?-My 1930
FU Ag 12 1927;O 1929-[31]+
FWpR F 1929+

Winter Park POST. *See* Florida post

ZEPHYRHILLS

Zephyrhills COLONIST. *See* Zephyrhills news

Zephyrhills NEWS. w 1910+
1910-24? as Zephyrhills colonist
FU 1933+
OClWHi Ja 16 1913

GEORGIA

ABBEVILLE

Abbeville CHRONICLE. w 1896+
pub 1902+

ADAIRSVILLE

Adairsville LEDGER. w 1890-
GU Ag 21,S 11 1890

ADEL

Adel NEWS. w 1890+
pub N 1902+

ALAPAHA

BERRIEN county news. w 1875-86‖?
GAA Jl 2 1881

ALBANY

Albany ADVERTISER. *See* News and advertiser

CENTRAL city. w 1871-74‖?
Ct N 14 1874

Albany COURIER. w Mr 14? 1843-
DLC N 21 1843

Albany HERALD. d 1891+
O 11 1928 is Randolph county centennial ed
pub 1891+
GCu O 11 1928

Albany NEWS. w,sw 1844-80‖
United with Advertiser to form News and advertiser
CLM S 30 1870
DLC Ja 26 1869
ICU F 7 1871

NEWS and advertiser. w 1877-94‖?
1877-79 as Albany advertiser
GAA S 27 1891

Albay daily NEWS and advertiser. d 1880-94‖?
GAA D 16 1890

Albany PATRIOT. w Ap 16 1845-65‖?
DLC Jl 15-22 1846;My 13,D 9 1848-Ja 20,F 3-17 1849
GMM 1845-Mr 21 1861
MWA Je 18 1852;Mr 16 1865
NN Je 2 1864
NcD Jl 6,D 13 1860

ALMA

Alma TIMES. w 1913+
GAlC 1915+
GAlO 1915+

AMERICUS

Americus weekly POST. w 1854-62‖?
1854-My 1861 as Southwestern news
NcD Ag 6 1856

Americus RECORDER. *See* Americus times-recorder

SOUTHWESTERN news. *See* Americus weekly post

SUMTER republican. w 1854-89‖?
Suspended for one month in 1865
GAA Jl 4 1877;My 18 1883
GBueC 1870-75
GEllC 1857-85
NN Jl 6 1867

Americus daily TIMES. d 1890‖
United with Americus daily recorder to form Americus times-recorder
GAA N 22 1890

Americus TIMES-RECORDER. d 1879+
1879-90 as Americus daily recorder
pub 1879+
GAA O 29 1890
NcD Jl 13 1915

Americus TIMES-RECORDER. w 1879+
1879-90 as Americus recorder
pub 1879+
GAA My 12 1889
GU Ag 26 1887
NcU Ag 3 1881

WHITE man's paper. w? Mr 11? 1868-
MBAt Mr 18 1868

ASHBURN

WIREGRASS farmer and stockman. w 1902+
pub [1902-14]+
GAsC 1906+

ATHENS

ATHENIAN. w D 28 1826-32‖?
GU [Ja 19-D 14 1827]28-Mr 13 1832
MWA N 2 1827;Mr 14,Ap 25,Je 10,Ag 5,N 18,D 9 1828

Weekly BANNER. w 1831+
1831?-72 as Southern banner; 1873-75 North east Georgian; 1875-77 Athens Georgian (other slight changes in title) Je 16 1901 is centennial ed
Ct [1833-37]
CtY Jl 27 1833
DLC My 29 1845;O 21-N 4 1852;Ja 18 1865
GAA Je 18,Ag 13 1889;My 30 1917;O 11 1929
GAtC [1852]-[55]Mr 24 1875-Ja 1877[78-80]-[89]92-94;96+
GAtCo Mr 5 1841;D 12 1893
GAtS Jl 3 1894
GSD [My 29 1861-Je 1864]
GU Mr 23 1833-S 8 1846;My-D 1851;Ja 16-22 1852;Jl 4 1873;Je 17 1896;Je 16 1901;Je 17 1903;D 21 1906;Ap 26 1912;O 18 1917;O 16 1918;N 25 1923;Ap 26 1926;Ap 27 1927[28]Je 1931+
ICHi N 15-22 1865
MBAt N 15 1865
MWA Je 17 1852;Jl 5 1855;Ja 4 1865;Mr 13 1868
NNHi D 11 1861
NcD Mr 26 1835-Mr 18 1837;Mr 20 1840-S 8 1846;Mr 8 1849;O 27 1853;D 30 1863;My 16 1866;My 2 1876;Ag 14 1877;My 4 1878;S 2 1879;Je 15 1900;O 18 1904
NhD My 28 1841
NjP Mr 13 1861-Ag 9 1865
OClWHi Je 24 1858;My 3 1865

Athens BANNER-HERALD. d 1879+
Title varies: Athens daily banner; Athens banner-watchman; Athens daily banner
GU N 25 1923;Ap 24 1926;Ap 24,Ag 17 1927+
M Jl 4 1932
NcD N 11,D 14,16 1881;Je 22 1882;My 20,N 13 1884;F 17 1887;O 19 1890;N 13 1892;Ag 13 1898;N 4 1899
TxU [D 21 1912-D 12 1914]

BANNER-WATCHMAN. *See* Athens banner-herald

Athens BLADE. w 1879-80‖?
Negro
NN O 31 1879;Ja 16,F 6,20-27,Ap 23 1880

Athens CHRONICLE. w 1878-90‖?
Title varies: Athens weekly chronicle
GAtC [1889]90
GAtS F 1 1879
NcD Ag 3 1878;D 24 1881;My 27 1882;O 25 1885;My 19 1888

COLUMBIAN centinel. w 1825-
DLC O 20 1826
MWA Ap 7,My 5,Je 30,D 8 1826

Weekly COMMERCIAL reporter. w Jl 22 1877-
NcD S 2 1877

GEORGIA democrat. *See* Athens daily times

Athens GEORGIAN. *See* Weekly banner

HARRISONIAN. w Jl 15 1840-
Campaign paper
DLC Jl 15 1840

Athens HERALD. d 1912-24‖
United with Athens banner-watchman to form Banner-herald
GU 1914-Je 1916

NORTHEAST Georgian. *See* Weekly banner

SENTINEL. w
NcD Je 6 1901;F 6 1902

SOUTHERN banner. *See* Weekly banner

SOUTHERN herald. w
MWA Je 17 1852

SOUTHERN watchman. w 1854-Ap 6 1882‖
United with Athens daily banner to form Banner watchman, later Banner-herald
DLC Ja 18 1865
GAtC 1855-[58]-[65]-[75]F 16-Ap 6 1882
GSD [Ag 19 1863-Ag 17 1864;Ja 9 1867-O 1868]
GU D 6 1860;D 3-10 1862;F 22 1865;S,O 19,N 2,16,30-D 21 1870;My 29,Je 12 1872;Ja 28 1874
MWA Mr 22 1865
NNHi S 2 1868;Mr 5 1873
NcD Ja 5 1864;S 20 1865;F 14,Mr 21,My 16,30 1866;Mr-D 1868;My 12,Je 9 1869;O 25-N 8 1871;Mr 6-13 1872;Je 16 1875;Jl 4 1876;N 18 1879

SOUTHERN whig. w 1833-49‖?
CtY F 14 1840
DLC Ap 30 1841;Je 28,Jl 12-S 27,O 11-N 29, D 13-20 1849
MWA Ag 20-27,S 10-O 22,N 5,D 3-17 1841;Mr 3 1843
NcU Je 20,Ag 11 1838
ScGK Ap 23 O 29,N 26,D 10 1835;Je 11,D 24 1836-Ja 14,28-F 4,N 18 1837;Ja 6,F 10-17,Je 23-Jl 7,Ag 4,18,D 22-29 1838;Ja 16,F 23 1839

Athens daily TIMES. d S 28 1933+
1933-Mr 23 1934 as Georgia democrat
pub 1933+
GAtMa 1933-Mr 23 1934
GU 1933+

Athens daily TRIBUNE. d
GU Ja 14 1912

ATLANTA

To D 26 1845 as Marthasville

ADAIR'S Georgia-land register. O 1 1867-
NNHi O 1 1867

Atlanta ADVANCE.
GU F 14 1891

Atlanta AGE. w 1898-1908‖?
Negro
DLC Ja 13 1900

Sunday AMERICAN. *See* note under Atlanta Georgian

Atlanta COMMERCIAL bulletin. d Mr 22 1866-
GAA Ap 3 1866
MBAt Mr 23-25,27-Ap 13 1866

COMMONWEALTH. d Mr 1861-62‖?
CSmH Jl 3 1862
GSD Ag 16 1862
MBAt [Ap-D 1861]O 28-29,31-N 8,10-12,14-D 8,13 1862
MsHi S 6 1862
OHi Je 12 1863
WHi My 2,4 1861

Atlanta COMMONWEALTH. d 1874-75‖?
GA D 1874-Je 1875

Atlanta CONSTITUTION. d Je 18 1868+
1868-S 3 1875 as Atlanta daily constitution; S 4 1875-O 19 1876 Constitution; O 20 1876-S 14 1881 Daily constitution
S 26 1917 is golden jubilee ed; Ap 24 1933 is Georgia bicentennial ed
pub 1868+
A My 1884-Mr 1897;Mr 1899-1908
C F 4 1887-F 23 1889;Jl 4-D 1890
CClP S 1903-17
CLM Je 18 1872;Ag 7,14 1883
Ct S 2-3 1886
DLC Je 16 1871-72;F 1873-Jl,S 1899+
G 1873-[78-79]-[82]-[1907]+
GA 1869-Je 1883;84+
GAA [1868-78]O 10,23,29 1890;1907-18;S 26 1917
GAC 1930[31]-[33-34]
GAO 1871+
GAtCo Ag 3 1878;My 9 1880;Jl 20,O 27,N 17,20 1881;F 1,Mr 9,My 25,28,31,Je 3,22-23 1882;Ja 9-31 1889;Ja 3,Ag-S 1891;Ja-F,Ap-Jl 1892[Mr-D 1894]Mr 1-15 1895;Ap 20 1897;N 6-7,9,20,24,D 1,12 1899;Ja 24,Mr 6 1900;Ja 22,25 1901;D 28,31 1903;Ja 16-17 1909;Ja 15,Je 7,11,15,D 12 1910[12;Ja-S 1915]S 19 1916;Ap 21 1917;Ja 21,25 1919[22]-[26-Je 1929]S 1931-[32]+
GDE [1875-88]-[90-92]-[94]-[96]1925+
GSD Ap 7,15,22 1877;Mr 4 1883;D 7 1889
GU D 1928+
ICM D 8 1881;My 14 1885
ICN D 9 1917-18;F 9 1919-Ap 7 1920
ICU 1935+
IaDH My 18 1905-14
KHi [O 1919-Ja 1925]
M Ap 24 1933
MB 1895+
MBAt D 13,15-18,22-24,27-31 1869
MHi O 24 1880
MWA Mr 27,Jl 15 1871;Ap 21 1906;Je 12 1921;N 20 1933
MiU 1903-[08;22]26+
MnU 1890-93;Ap 17-S,D 1918-Mr,D 1919-Ja 1920;F-N 1921
MsU [1887-88]
NN Ja 9 1856;Je 4 1913
NcD Je 28 1868;D 31 1871;S 10,O 18 1872;My 21 1878;Ag 19,O 7 1879;My 9 1880[81]F 20,S 23,O 21 1882[83]Mr 30 1884;Mr 2,S 22 1885;Mr 29,My 31,S 2,O 5 1886[87-88]Jl 21,N 1 1889;Jl 6 1890;O 21 1891;D 7,26 1893;Ap 24,29,Je 2 1894;Ap 6,Jl 14 1895;Je 6,Ag 7,26 1897;O 16,D 2,15 1898;Mr 15,Jl 15 1899[1900]S 7 1901;Je 1,O 11,31 1902-Ja 1,4 1903;O 10 1904;Ag 5-6 1906;Mr 14 1907;Je 30 1912;N 12-14,17 1918;F 10-11,13-15 1920;S 1930+

GEORGIA (*Continued*)

ATLANTA—*Continued*

Atlanta CONSTITUTION. d Je 18 1868+—*Cont.*
NcU Ag 19 1879;Jl 23 1881
OHi 1912-Jl 1931
OOxM My 20-21 1885
P Jl 1890-N 1917
PP My 21 1899[1927]+
TJT N 30 1912
TSS Jl 1880-Je 1882;Jl 1897-Ap,S-O 1899
Tx Jl 1904-20
TxGR Je 21 1868(facsimile)S 9,12 1899;S 26 1917
VU N 12 1879
WHi 1896+
WaPS F 1913-F 17 1917[18-19]-Ja 13 1922[29]

Atlanta CONSTITUTION. w,tw 1868+
w 1868-1905
CClP 1918-Je 1924
DLC Mr 30,Ap 13,27 1886
FU [1887-89]Jl 1-15 1890;Ap 7 1891
GAtCo Jl 31-Ag 7,21 1877;Je 9 1891;Mr 18 1895
KHi N 29 1887-N 1888
M S 20 1928
N Jl 1873-F 1875
NNHi S 29 1874
NcD Ja 2 1872;Ja 14,F 11,Jl 1,S 30-N 1873; Ja 6 1874;Ap 27,Je 8 1875;Mr 25 1880[82] Mr 31,Ag 18,D 1,29 1885[86]Ap 3,N 8-15 1887[88]Ja 1,15-29,Jl 2 1889;D 23-30 1890;Mr 31-Ap 7,Je 23,D 15 1891;Ag 2,16,O 25,N 29 1892[93-99]F 12,Mr 5-12,26-Ap 9,Je 12 1900; Ja 7,S 16,D 16 1901;Ap 14,Jl 28,S 8,N 10,D 22 1902[03]O 11 1907;Jl 27,O 3,N 12 1918
NcU Je 6 1882;F 24 1885;Ap 6,My 18,D 7 1886;My 2,23,Je 27-Jl 11,Ag 15,29,S 12 1898
VU Mr 5 1889;F 4 1890;O 20 1891;F 18 1895; O 26,N 23 1903;Ag 15-S 14,19-O 7 1916;My 4,Je 25-Jl 23 1918;S 28-30,O 26-30,N 6-11 1920

Weekly DEFIANCE. w 1881-89‖
Negro
NN O 8,22-29 1881
NNHi O 24 1882;F 24 1883

Daily DISPATCH. d
VU N 12 1879

Atlanta daily EXAMINER. d 1854?-68‖
Merged with Daily intelligencer
GA Jl 18 1857-Mr 9 1858

Atlanta weekly EXAMINER. w 1854-56‖?
NcD D 20 1855

GATE CITY guardian. d F 12-Mr 3 1861‖
Followed by Southern confederacy
DLC complete
GA complete

Atlanta daily GAZETTE. d Ag 10? 1863-
GDE S 12 1863
MBAt Ag 28,S 2-4,8 1863
ODW Ag 25 1863

GEORGIA advertiser. d 1818-21‖?
T S 12,D 8,12 1821

GEORGIA courier. w
TKL Ag 8 1834

GEORGIA weekly opinion. w
GAA Ag 21,S 17,O 1,15,29,N 12,D 31 1867
GAO [1867]
—d ed *See* Daily opinion

GEORGIA progressive. ir
GU Ag 31,O 14,31 1914

GEORGIA record. w
G Jl 1899-Je 1900

GEORGIA weekly. w S 15 1860-
NjR S 15 1860

Atlanta GEORGIAN. d Ap 25 1906+
F 2-Ap 12 1912 Atlanta Georgian and news
Sunday ed as Sunday American; Hearst's Sunday American; etc
CL F 15 1912-N 1921
DLC Jl 1924-27
GA 1906+
GAA D 24 1909;Mr 19 1933
GAO 1906+
GAtCo S 8 1917;S 2 1918
GU O 25-26 1920;Je 26 1921;O 8,N 22 1922;F 22 1925;Ap 24,N 10 1926;F 20 1927;S 19 1928
NcD Je 3 1907;Mr 7,O 17 1912;F 12 1914;F 12 1916

GEORGIAN'S weekly news-briefs. w 1909-Ja 26 1912‖
Merged with Atlanta Georgian
NcD Jl 21,O 21,N 24 1911;Ja 4 1912

HEARST'S Sunday American. *See* note under Atlanta Georgian

Atlanta daily HERALD. d 1872-76‖
G My-O 1873;74-F 1876
GA Ag 22-D 1875
GAA Ja 5,F 16 1875
GU Ja 23-25 1873;F 21,26 1874;My 21 1875;Jl 19,30 1872

Atlanta weekly HERALD. w 1872-76‖
NcD D 3 1873
OClWHi F 9 1873

Atlanta INDEPENDENT. w 1903+
Negro
GAA 1904-28
WHi My 9,N 7 1914-My 22 1916

Daily INTELLIGENCER. d 1854-71‖
Title varies slightly
CtHT Je 28 1863
DLC Je 19 1863;Mr 17-18,20,22,24,26,31,Ap 2 1864;Ap 2[Je-D 1865]66-67
G Ja-Je 1869
GA 1869-Ap 1871
GAA S 13 1862;Ja 16,F 13,Mr 5,Je 10 1863;My 11 1864;Ag 10,13,15,29,S 5,7,9,14,N 7 1865;Ja 7,10,13,18-20,Je 7,17,Jl 10,O 4,D 1-2 1866;Ja 1,23,F 10,Je 2 1867[Ja 7-F 7 1868]
GAO Ja 11 1867-Mr 3 1871
GDE Je 2 1864
GSD [Ag-N 1863]F 28 1864
GU My 11 1864;Ja 10 1871
ICHi My 28,O 1,7 1865
MBAt Ap 24,My 18 1860[Ap-D 1861]O 28-N 4,6-8,11,14,16-21,25-26,29-D 9 1862;Je 3 1863; Mr 19,22 1864[65-Je 1866]Mr 23 1867
MH Ja 27-28,31,F 2-5,7 1865
MWA D 11 1856;Ja 9,20,Je 4 1857;Ja 5-6 1865
NNHi D 27 1861;Ja 3 1862;Mr 14,S 3 1863;Mr 18,Je 24 1864[Ja-Mr]Ag 19,O 8,24-25 1868[Ja-Jl 1869]
NcD Je 27,D 19 1862;Mr 12 1863;Ap 3,My 10 1864;Mr 19,My 11,Je 18 1865;Ja 31,Mr 2 1866
OCHi N 6 1862
OClWHi O 7 1858-S 19 1859;60-64;Ja 25-27,My 10,12 1865
OHi S 10,22-23,26,30,O 5 1865
TU Ag 7 1862;Ap 11,My 29,Je 17-20,23-25,27-28,Jl 1-2,4,Ag 12 1863;S 11 1867
V My 21 1864
VU My 11 1864
WHi Jl 9 1863;Ja 20,Mr 18 1864

Weekly Atlanta INTELLIGENCER. w 1858-71‖
G O 14 1858-O 6 1859
GAA [Je-D 1865]-[My-Jl]-[S-D 1866]Mr 20 1867
GMiG N 28 1866
MBAt F 20-My 22,Je 5-12,Jl,Ag 21,S-O 9 1861
NN Ag 4 1859
NcD Je 19,Jl 3,Ag 17-21,S 18-25 1861;Ja 22 1862

JEFFERSONIAN. *See under* Thomson

Atlanta JOURNAL. d F 24 1883+
Title varies: Evening journal; etc.
F 19 1933 is fiftieth anniversary ed and Georgia bicentennial
pub 1883+
A Ap 1897-Ag 1910
CLM Jl 30 1886;Ja 16 1909
DLC 1898+
G 1895-[1905]+
GA F 24 1883-Je 1884;97+
GAA D 1,20 1890;N 22 1892;Ag 25 1894;Mr 30 1901;Jl 1915-Je 1918
GAO 1893+
GAtCo Ja 15 1909;S 11 1913
GDE [1890;1927]-[32]+
GDahN Ag 2 1889
GMiG Jl 1930+
GSD N 23 1891
GU S 4 1890;N 3,23-24 1891,Ag 16,18 1894;Jl 13,28,Ag 24,O 1,N 19,D 1 1896;Ja 13,Jl 20,S 8,D 11 1897;Ap 21,Jl 11,O 29 1898;Ja 21,Je 15 1901;D 4 1904;Mr 6 1905;Ap 15-17,19,22 1912; Je 22 1915;Je 2,Ag 9,D 10 1916;S 28,D 23 1919;My 27,Je 8 1920;Ag 19 1923;My 23 1927; My 19 1929;O 12,D 1930+
IC My 1 1889
KHi O 19-26 1924
NcD Mr 14 1888;D 7 1889;My 29 1890;Ja 21 1891[92;94-95;97-99;1903]
NjR Ap-Je 1900
TKL F 16 1895;Ap 25 1898
TxU F 18-Je 2 1898
VU [Jl-S 1934]

Atlanta JOURNAL. w,sw,tw 1885-1930‖?
Title varies slightly
w 1885-98; sw 1899-1920
GU Je 12 1928
NcD N 3 1891;My 5,N 14 1899;F 23,Mr 2,13,23 1900;D 3-14 1903;O 10 1904

MEMPHIS daily appeal. *See* Memphis appeal-avalanche (Memphis, Tenn.)

NATIONAL. w 1882-
TJT N 26 1891

NATIONAL American. tw,d 1858-F 1861‖
Merged with Gate City guardian
NcD N 24 1860

Atlanta daily NEW ERA. d Jl? 1865-71‖
DLC O 27 1867;68-D 24 1869;Ag 1870-71
GA [O 1866-Je 1867]Ja-Je 1868;69-71
GAA [Ag 1867-68;F,Je 1869]
GAO Mr 20 1869-70
GAtCo Je 4 1868
ICHi S 23 1865
MBAt O 3 1865[68-Ap 1869]
MWA S 27 1868;Ag 30 1870
NNHi S 25,D 10,12-13,18 1867[68-70]
OHi S 5 1865

Weekly Atlanta NEW ERA. w 1866-71‖
GAA Mr 26,Ap 2,16,Je 4,Jl 9 1868
GAtCo S 10 1868
MWA Jl 9 1867;Ja 23-F 6,27,Ap 2-16,My 7-14, 28,Je 18 1868
NNHi Ag 27 1867;Ja 16,Mr 28,Je 11 1868

Daily NEWS. d Jl 5 1874-My 25 1875‖
G Ag 23-O 24 1874
GA complete
GAA Jl 5 1874

Atlanta daily NEWS. d 1900-01‖
GA 1900-O 1901
GAA My 25 1901
GAO complete

Atlanta NEWS. d Ag 4 1902-12‖
Merged with Atlanta Georgian
GA 1902-F 1 1907
GAO 1902-08
GU Ag 19 1904;S 24 1906
NcD O 14,D 26 1902;Ja 10 1903;Mr 7 1905
Tx 1908-10

Daily OPINION. d 1866-68‖?
GAA Ag 18 1887
GU Ja 9,31,F 28,Mr 9 1868
—w ed *See* Georgia weekly opinion

PEOPLE'S party paper. w 1891-98‖
DLC N 26 1891-S 14 1894
G My 28 1897
GAtCo D 17 1891
GU D 15 1893;Ag 10,31,N 9,O 5-12 1894;Mr 8 1895;My 29,S 25,O 9,N 13 1896;S 2,16 1898
NcD [1892-98]
WHi D 29 1893-Ja 1 1897

Sunday PHONOGRAPH. w 1878-82‖?
GAtCo My 28-Je 4 1882
NcD O 13 1881

Atlanta weekly POST. w 1878-81‖
GDahN Je 2 1881

Atlanta POST-APPEAL. d 1878-84‖?
1878-79? as Atlanta daily post
G N 1-16 1882
GAtCo Mr 22 1879
GU F 10 1882

Daily PRESS. d
GU Ja 20 1869
MBAt Ap 12-15 1864

Daily PRESS. d 1894-
GU Ag 16,28,S 17,19,N 2,O 2 23,26,29 1894
NcD Ag 6,O 1,29 1894

Daily Atlanta REGISTER. d 1862-
NNHi Ja 16,20,My 7,12,13,17,20,27,Je 2 1864
OClWHi Ja 28-31,F 4,Mr 18-Ap 8,My 10 1864
WHi Mr 19,23,Ap 3,S 16,29,O 1,4,5,10 1864

REPUBLICAN. w 1874-86‖?
GU May 15 1880

Weekly REPUBLICAN and discipline. w 1851-1851-52? as Atlanta republican
MWA Je 17 1852
NcD Mr 28,Ap 11-My 2,Je 6-13 1856

Atlanta daily REVEILLE. d Ap 16 1864-
MBAt Ap 16 1864

SOLDIERS' friend. ir Ja 10 1863-
PCA Ja 10,My 2,Je 18,Jl 9 1863

SOUTHERN advance. w 1874-82‖?
NcD D 21 1882

SOUTHERN confederacy. w F 1859-65‖
DLC F 26 1862-S 2 1863
GAA O 8 1862
GDE [1861-62]
GU S 15 1861
MWA N 11 1859
NNHi Ja 29 1862;Ja 3 1863;Ja 1,17 1865
NcD N 9 1860;Ap 28,My 2 1861
TKL Ap 29,My 11,Jl 3 1863
TxU D 2 1862
VRC N 27 1863
WHi Ag 15 1863

SOUTHERN confederacy. d Mr 4 1861-65‖
Follows Gate City guardian
DLC Mr 4 1861-My 26,Je 25 1863;Mr 9,23,Ap 22,S 1(extra)1864
GA 1861-My 23 1863
GSD [Ag 1861-Jl 9 1864]
MBAt [1862]Ag 1,7,O 24,28,30-N 2,5-7,11-20, 25-26,28-D 9 1862;D 3 1863[Ja-Jl]S 18 1864; Ja 27 1865
MH Ap 6,9 1861;D 14-15 1864;Ja 20,22,24,26-27,F 3 5,7-8 1865
MWA Mr 13,Jl 8,Ag 28 1862
NcD Mr 1,19,22 1863
OCHi Mr 7[Ap 19 1862-Ap]Je 4,Jl 17 1863
PHi Ag 15 1863
TU O 27 1863
Tx F 13 1863
V My 9 1863;My 20,Je 21-25 1864

Atlanta daily SUN. d 1870-Je 24 1873‖
Merged with Atlanta constitution
DLC Ag 23 1871-72
GA My 18 1870-72
GAtCo Mr 20,Je 24 1873
GU Mr 29,Ag 21,O 26 1872;Ap 1 1873
NNHi D 12 1872
NcD My 23,31,S 10,28,O 27 1872
NjR Ap 20 1873

Weekly SUN. w 1872-Je 1873‖
GAtCo Ja-Je 3 1873
N complete
NcD F 21-Mr 6,Ap 3-10 1872
TxU O 9,N 6-13 1872

Atlanta TELEGRAM. d
G Ja 20-26 1877

Atlanta TIMES. d
G D 3-14 1876

Atlanta daily TRIBUNE. d
G Ja-Mr 1875

Daily TRUE Georgian. d
GA Je 28-D 24 1870

WATSON'S weekly Jeffersonian. *See* Jeffersonian (Thomson)

Atlanta WHIG.
GU S 12 1872
NNHi S 12 1872

Atlanta WORLD. w,sw,tw,d Ag 1928+
w 1928-Ap? 1930; sw My? 1930-Ap 1931; tw Ap 20 1931-Mr 1932
Negro
GAA D 1931+
GAC 1933+

AUGUSTA

Augusta ADVERTISER. w N 3 1877-
NcD N 10 1877

*Augusta CHRONICLE. d 1785+
Title varies: Daily chronicle; Daily chronicle and sentinel; Daily chronicle and constitutionalist
pub 1916+
CoU 1901;03-04;S 1906-My 1910
CtY D 29 1833;Ap 11 1845;S 22 1863;O 14 1864-F 3 1865

GEORGIA (*Continued*)

AUGUSTA—*Continued*

Augusta CHRONICLE. d 1785+—*Continued*
DLC N 30 1840;Mr 23 1849-54;58-60;F 26 1861;Mr 13,Je 16,S 22 1862[My 1863-Ap]My 24-D 1865;Mr 13,Je-N 2 1866;98+
G Ja 15 1916
GAtCo My 1885
GAuO Ag 6 1868-1903;Jl 1904+
GDE Jl 31 1862
GGrO Je 28 1935
GSD 1861-85;Ja 16 1887;My 21 1888
GU S 16 1861;D 23 1862;My 7 1863;My 9,Jl 12 1864;Ja 18,F 26,Je 27,Jl 3-4,6,26,29,Ag 1,O 16 1867;S 8 1870;Ap 27,Je 22 1873;S 4 1874;O 7 1885;O 10 1886;Je 25,O 1 1887;My 13 1888;Je 29 1889;N 22 1894;S 11 1896
ICM F 17 1874[S]D 20 1881;Ja 19,F 7,Mr 1 [S]1882;Mr 4 1883;Ap 9[Jl-D]1885;Ja 29 1886
KHi My 21 1895
LNH My 16,Jl 10,Ag 15,N 9,15,D 7-9 1860[F 23 1862-Jl 24 1863]Je 7,Ag 3,N 17 1864;F 25 1866;Je 22 1869
MBAt Mr 2 1861[My 1862-63]-[65-F 1867]Ja 8 1869
MHi Mr 6,Ap 12 1865
MWA My 19,21 1840;Jl 1 1852;D 11 1856;Ja 17,Je 3 1857;D 7 1861;Je 17 1862;Mr 21 1863;Mr 18,23,O 18-25,27-N 15 1864;Mr 24 1865;F 6 1866;Ag 15,S 5,O 5 1877;My 1885;D 12 1889;D 28(supp)1915
MnHi Ap 5 1863
N N 5 1881
NBHi O 28-N 8,23-24,27,D 3 1863
NN My 12 1865
NNHi D 24 1861;N 11,19 1862[Ja-Jl 1863;Mr-Jl 1864]
NcD S 4,O 30,N 6,13,28,D 4,11,18,24 1830;Ja-F,S 1840-S 1841;Je 13-14,Jl 7 1842;Jl 21 1843;Jl-D 1845;Jl-D 1846;Jl-D 1847;Jl-D 1848;50;S 6-9,26,D 25 1851;Ja-Je 1856;F 21,Je 5,Jl 22 1860;O 30 1861;O 17 1862[63-66]My 4,Ag 19 1869;O 29 1870;Mr 25 1871;Ja 4,11,N 8 1872;F 7,Je 18 1873;D 25 1874[77-79]Ja 2,28,Mr 13-14,N 27 1880;S 27,N 26 1881[82-85]S 3 1886;Ag 1 1887;S 12,O 29 1888;D 28 1889;Mr 26 1890;S 2 1893;S 23 1894;Je 11,Jl 23,Ag 22 1897;F 22,26 1899;Mr 1,10,25 1900;Ja 29 1902;D 27 1925
NcU Ap-My,Jl 9,17,26,30-Ag 26,N-D 13,22 1862-Ja 28,Mr 2-31,Je 30,O,D 5-31 1863;Mr 12,My-Je 1864;F,Mr 15-16,24-25,Je 3-Jl 29,D 1865[Ja-Je 1 1866]S 26-27,O 18,N 12,16,23-24,26 1879;Ja 24,29,Jl 28 1880
NhD Je 2,8 1841
OCHi Jl 1 1859
OClWHi 1855;57;O 11 1861[Ja 15-D 13 1862]F 5,27,Ap-D 1863;Ja 7,Mr 11-N 15 1864;Ja 7-My 20,Ag 1865-Ja 14,Jl 23 1866;Mr 9,My 2,Je 30,O 10 1867;Ja 5,Mr 19,28,Jl 4,D 8,15 1868
OHi Je 27,Jl 16-17,21,Ag 9 1865
OOxM Ap 17 1880
P-M Ag 21 1863
TxU 1840;Jl-D 1841;43;Jl 1845-Je 1847;48-Je 1850;Jl-D 1851;Ja-Je 1853;54;56-57;Jl-D 1859;Ja-Je 1869;Ja-Je 1870[72-Je 1874]Ja-Je 1875;Ja-Mr 1876;79-80;85-Je 1887;Jl-D 1890;93-94;Jl 4 1896-98;Jl-D 1899
V Jl 23 1864
VHi Ap 6 1864
VRC Ap 3 1864
VU N 12 1918
WHi N 5 1861-Ap 29,O 29 1862[Mr 18-N 15 1864]Ap 22 1865

***Augusta CHRONICLE.** w S 30 1786-1910‖?
1786-Ap 4 1789 as Georgia state gazette or independent register; Ap 11 1789-1803 Georgia. The Augusta chronicle and gazette of the state. 1804+ subtitle varies: . . . and Georgia advertiser; . . . and state rights' sentinel; . . . and sentinel; . . . and constitutionalist; etc
D 20 1816-30? pub irregularly tw or sw
A 1862-S 1863
CLM S 1 1886
CSmH Ag 28 1830
Ct F 1 1828;Ja 29,F 19 1831;S 1,3-4 1886
DLC 1821-30;My 9 1832;F 26,My 29 1861;F 3,28,Mr 16-30,My 18,Je 1,22,O 12,S 28,D 21 1864;Ap 19,My 3 1865
GGrO 1868
GHi [O 15 1821-Ap 11 1822]
GHirC 1832[33]-36;N 21 1860;N 25 1862[64]F 1 1866;S 11 1870;F 24 1871
GMiG Ja 29 1857;N 14,D 5-26 1866
GU [1821-22]-[26]-29;D 28 1831-32
IC Ap 6 1864
MBAt D 3 1821;N 23 1864;Ja 10-17,F 8,My 23,Ag 15 1866;Mr 23 1916
MWA Mr 31,My 15,22,O 16 1824;Je 27,Jl 1-11,22,Ag 8,S 19-30,N 25,D 23 1829;Ja 2-6,23 1830;Mr 26 1831;N 7 1839;Je 30 1852;Mr 21 1860;Mr 27 1861;Ap 15 1868
NNHi F 10 1865;Ja 22,Mr 20,Ap 1 1873
NcD F 5,Ag 20,S 3 1846;F 3 1847;D 29 1852;Mr 9-16,Ap 20,Ag 24 1853;Ja 4,F 15 1854;O 3 1860;Mr 20,My 1 1861;Je 10,S 9-23,O,N 11,25-D 2,16-23 1862;Ja 6,27-Mr 24,Ap-My 12 1863;My 11,Ag 24-31 1864;Ap 5-12 1865;F 12 1868;Je 14,30 1869;Mr 4,Je 3 1874;Je 20 1877;Ap 3 1878;Ja 29 1879;My 25,Je 15,Jl 27,Ag 10 1881;My 3 1882;Ap 18,Jl 18,Ag 29 1883;Je 9,Jl 21,O 27 1886;Ja 18,Ap 13,My 18,Je 8,22 1887;Ja 11 1888;Ag 28,N 13,Ja 11,Ap 12-My 3,Ag 16,S 27 1893
NcU N 10 1832;My 21,Je 18,Jl 2 1840;N 24 1842
OClWHi Ag 12,N 21 1829
ScGK Ja 11 1834;Ja 6,20,Mr 3,N 23,D 21 1837;F 16 1838;Ap 19 1839
TKL Ap 21 1842;My 3 1847;Ap 12 1848
TU [1848-53]-[56;58-60]
TxU [1822;24-S 13 1826]Ag 29 1835-36;44;87-88;90-91;93-94[97]99
WHi Jl 11 1829

Tri-weekly CHRONICLE. tw 1837-82‖?
Title varies: Tri-weekly chronicle and sentinel; Tri-weekly chronicle and constitutionalist
CtY Je 2 1850
DLC D 15,24 1858;Ja 16 1859
GU 1837-41
MWA Ag 3 1843
NcD [1845;51]Ag 16 1870;Ja 21,F 11 1871;Jl 8,10 1873;Ja 31,F 2,28 1877[79-82]
OClWHi Ap 13,O 5 1859

COLORED American. w D 16 1865-
Negro
DLC D 21 1865
MBAt D 30 1865;Ja 6 1866
MWA D 30 1865
NNHi Ja 13 1866

Tri-weekly CONSTITUTIONALIST. tw 1823?-1877‖
MBAt O 9,14-18,25,D 13 1863;Ja 17,F 5,12,28,Mr 6,20,27,My 18 1864
NNHi Je 19 1863;F 5 1873
NcD Jl 23,Ag 8,O 2 1851;Ag 1,10 1855;Jl 22 1860[61-76]F 14 1877
OClWHi Ja 24 1864;Mr 17 1865
OHi Jl 22 1866;My 3 1868
ScCoCR D 8 1858;Ap 12 1861
TxU My 19 1837;42;44-46
VRC S 15 1861

Augusta CONSTITUTIONALIST. sw,d Jl 1 1823-Mr 8 1877‖
Title varies: Georgia constitutionalist; Daily constitutionalist; Daily constitutionalist and republic. Merged with Augusta chronicle
sw 1823-S 1835
CSmH Jl 13 1830;Jl 10 1861
CtY F 26 1830;Ag 14 1835;D 3 1839;F 6 1844
DLC Jl 27 1824;D 27 1833;D 1 1840;56-60;F 26,Mr 6 1861;Je 19,24,Jl 15,D 18,25 1863;F 11,14,18,28,My 1,15,Jl 30,Ag 2,21,S 27-30,O 2,4,N 18 1864;Ja-My 26 1867;Ja-My 24 1873;Ja-Jl 1875
GAA My 24,29,Je 2 1864
GAuO Ag 6 1868-76
GSD [Je 12 1861-D 20 1865]
GU My 2,Je 2 1826[Ja 19 1827-D 23 1828;30-31]-41;Ja 7-Jl 15,22 1857;Je 24 1867;Ja 4,S 3 1868;Je 30 1869;D 18 1870;Ap 27,Mr 22 1873
ICHi Jl 18,O 25 1865
ICM F 12 1874
LNC Mr 2 1865
LNH Je 10-11,13-14,16,21,24,27-28 1862;Je 10-14,17 1863
MBAt S 15 1861;Je 11,Ag 7-8 1862[Ja-N 1863;64;F-N 1865;66]S 7 1867
MH D 2 1864;Ja 25,S 8 1865
MWA Jl 17 1838;My 14 1840;Ja 31 1846;Jl 1 1852;Jl 31,O 6 1860;Mr 23(extra)1861;Ag 27 (supp)O 17 1865;Ap 19,Ag 25 1876
N O 8 1833;O 21 1868;Jl 8-9 1871
NN Ja 9 1856
NNHi O 7 1856;Mr 17,N 3-4,6 1860;Ja 25 1861;Ja 19,F 27 1862;Je 19,29,Jl 7,Ag 7,S 6 1863;Ap 10,24,Jl 22,Ag 4,O 1,12-16,N 15,D 20,25 1864[Ja,Jl 1865-66;Jl 1867-N 1868;Ja-Mr 1869;Ja,O 1870-O 1871;Ja-F,My,O 1872;Ja-My,Jl,S,N 1873-F,Jl-D 1874;Ap,S,D 1875-F 1876]O 20 1882
NSchU My 31,Je 2,4,7,9,11 1842
NcD Ag 28 1827;Jl-D 1847;Ag 1849-50;Ag 3,S 3,N 27,D 25 1851;Jl 10 1853;My 10 1859;Mr 22-24,Jl 10,Ag 9,S 6,N 1,3 1861[62-65]Jl 6,N 4 1866;Jl 20,Ag 27,29-30,S 22,D 27 1867;Ja 3,31,Ap 12,D 27 1868;Ja 3,F 13,Mr 10,Ag 10,N 21,D 25 1869;Ja 11,My 26,Jl 6,O 27,N 13,D 8,25,28 1870;Mr 26,Jl 4,N 3,19,D 27 1871[72-77]
NcU D 6 1862
NhD N 26 1846
NjHi [1867]
NjR S 2 1860
OC N 13 1860-69
OClWHi Ap 19,Jl 1859-Je 26 1861;Ap-S,D 1862-Jl 25,O 4,8,10,15,17 1863;Mr 17-S 21,N 9,11,26,29 1864;Ap 28,Ag 6-D 1865;Ja 10,21,30,F 1,16,Mr 1,Ap 10,20,24,26,S 13,D 21 1866;S 30 1867;Je 24 1869
OHi Ja-Je 1864;Jl 1865-67
ScCoCR Jl 14 1863
TxU Jl 3 1827-Je 17 1831;O 1835-Mr 1836;S-D 1840;43;S 1846-Je 1847;48-49;Jl-D 1851;Jl-D 1852;Ja-Je 1853;Ja-Je 1854;Jl-D 1856;Ja-Je 1860;66-Je 1867;Ja-Je 1868[69-Je 1870]Ja-Je 1871;Jl-D 1872;Ja-Je 1875
V [Je 19 1832-Je 17 1834]
WHi [Mr,Jl,S 1864]Mr 14 1866

Weekly CONSTITUTIONALIST. w 1823-77‖
Title varies: Georgia constitutionalist; Weekly Georgia constitutionalist and weekly republic; etc.
Ct [1833-38]
DLC S 26,O 31-N 7 1860;Ja 20-27,F 10-Mr 2 1864
G S 20 1854
GMiG D 9 1863;Ap 28 1864
ICHi Mr 27 1847
MBAt Ja 9,Mr 20,My 29,Je 12,Jl 17,Ag 14-S 11,O 16,30-D 4 1861;Ja 1 1862;S 14,O 12-19,D 21 1864;F 1 1865
MWA Je 2,30 1852
NNHi S 1 1858;Ap 27,N 23 1859;Ja 8-15,F 19,Je 15,Jl 2-9,23-Ag 6,S 3,17-O 1 1862;Mr 8-Ap 11,My 3,24-31 1865
NcD D 24 1840;Je 14 1848;S 3 1851;Ja 9,Mr 16,Jl 6,27,S 28 1853;N 1 1854;F 20 1856[57-64]-Ja 23 1865;F 14,Mr 15 1866;Ag 23,S 6 1871;Je 19 1872;Ja 28,Jl 1 1874
OClWHi Je 28 1868
OHi Je 17 1865
ScGK O 18,N 22 1834;N 29 1838
TxU 1849-50;D 31 1856-57;D 29 1858-59;65-66;68-71

DEMOCRATIC champion.
NcD S 21 1894

Augusta evening DISPATCH. d Ja? 1857-61‖?
GAuO Ja-Je 1859
GHi 1857
GSD Ap 13,My 3,6,14,17,24-25,Je 3,6 1861
LNH [My 30-Ag 1860;F,Ap-My 1861]
MWA Je 1 1857
NcD Ja 12,N 30 1860
NcU O 29 1858
OClWHi [Mr 31-Ap,Je]Ag 17,N 14-D 8 1860;Ja 23-25,31,F 15 1861

Daily GAZETTE. d
NNHi Je 17 1865

GEORGIA. The Augusta chronicle and gazette of the state. *See* Augusta chronicle

***GEORGIA advertiser.** tw,sw Mr 1819-22‖?
Merged with Augusta chronicle
GU Ag 28 1822

GEORGIA constitutionalist. sw,d *See* Augusta constitutionalist

GEORGIA constitutionalist. w *See* Weekly constitutionalist

GEORGIA courier. sw,d 1825-37‖?
sw 1825-36
CSmH S 13 1830
Ct My 16,O 6 1831;Ja 29,F 3,20 1837
DLC Ag 20 1827;Mr 20 1828;Mr 19,Je 29-Jl 6,16,23,30-Ag 3,10-13,S 3-7,14-21,O 22,N 16,D 27 1829;Ja 21,Ap 1,Jl 22,D 2 1830;Je 6 1831;O 4 1833
GMiG My 6 1830-36
GSD Je 27 1827-28
MHi S 7 1832
MWA Ag 9,N 12 1827;Je 11 1829;N 1 1830
ScGK Ag 1833;Ag 1 1834;Jl 22 1836;Ap 8 1837
TxU Je 19 1826

GEORGIA home gazette. w O 20 1851-
MWA D 22 1851;Je 16 1852

GEORGIA republican. w 1869-71‖
DLC Ja 29 1870
MWA Jl 2 1870
NNHi Ja 8 1870;N 4 1871

GEORGIA weekly. w
OClWHi Jl 18 1864

***Augusta HERALD.** w,sw Jl 17 1799-1822‖?
w 1799-1816
GU 1821
TxU 1821-Je 1822

Augusta HERALD. d 1892+
CoU 1903;S 1906-My 1910
DLC Ja-Je 1898;Ja-Ap 1905
GAuO Jl 1902-Je 1904;08+
GU N 30 1916
NcD Ja 13 1894;Mr 3 1900;Jl 27 1914

Weekly JEFFERSONIAN. *See* Jeffersonian (Thomson)

LOYAL Georgian. w Ja 13 1866-68‖
GU Ag 10,24 1867
MBAt Ja 20-F 3,17,Mr 3-17,My 5 1866;Ap 10,My 9-16,Jl 6 1867
MWA O 13 1866
NcD F 24 1866;F 15 1868

Daily LOYAL Georgian. d 1867-
NcD [Je-Jl 1867]

Augusta MIRROR. w
GMiG My 11,25,Je 29,Jl 13,27,Ag 10 1839

NATIONAL republican. d 1867-D 31 1868‖
Follows and is followed by Daily press
DLC 1868
GAuO Jl-D 1868
MBAt O 10 1868
MWA My 12,S 10,O 15,17,31 1868
TxU [Ja 28 1867-Je 1868]
WHi D 25 1868

Daily NEWS. d Ag 12 1839-
DLC Ag 12 1839

Augusta evening NEWS. d 1878-95‖?
DLC Jl 11 1878
GU S 12 1880;F 1 1882
ICM My 25[Ag-D]1885
LNC Ap 26 1879
MWA D 11 1889
NNHi F 28,Je 23 1883
NcD N 20 1877-N 19,D 9 1878;My 21 1879;Jl 2,N 18 1881;O 16 1884;My 6 1885;S 1 1886;S 10,13 1888;Mr 18 1889;Je 30 1893
NcU S 1,N 5 1879
ScCoCR O 20 1884
TxU Mr-Ag 1886

PACIFICATOR. w O 8 1864-65‖?
NNHi F 4 1865
NcD O 8-22 1864

PEOPLE'S defense. w 1882-83‖?
NNHi Ja 13 1883

PEOPLE'S press. 1837-38‖?
GAtCo Jl 27 1838
ScGK My 23,S 25,O 19,N 16 1838

Daily PRESS. d Ja 1? 1866-Ap 18 1869‖
1867-D 31 1868 replaced by National republican
DLC Ja 21 1866-Jl 27 1867;Ja 2-Ap 18 1869
GAuO Ja-Ap 18 1869
GSD Ap 28,Je 16 1867
MBAt F 19,24,26,28,Mr 6,10,12-19,21-24,29,Ap 2-4,7,11,17,23-24 1867
OClWHi Mr 28 1866;Jl 19 1867
TxU Jl 2-27 1867

Augusta PROGRESS. w F 11 1888-90‖?
NcD F 11 1888

Weekly REGISTER. w
MiU-C Jl 16 1850

GEORGIA (*Continued*)

AUGUSTA—*Continued*

Daily REGISTER. d 1861-65||?
DLC S 6,O 4 1864
MBAt O 5 1864
MH N 20,24,26,Ja 27-28,31,F 6 1864
MWA O 4,10 1864
NNHi Ja 19,20,F 1 1865
OClWHi [S-O 10 1864]
WHi S 16,29,O 1,4-5,10 1864

Tri-weekly REPUBLIC. tw 1848-Jl 1851||
Merged with Augusta constitutionalist
NcD Jl 12 1851
TxU 1848-Je,Ag 1849-Je 1851

Weekly REPUBLIC. w
GU N 19 1850

SENTINEL. sw
NcD S 23 1836
OHi S 23 1836

Evening SENTINEL. d 1878-79||?
NcD O 2 1878;Ap 26 1879

SOUTHERN republic. d 1861||?
Follows Daily true democrat. Merged with Augusta constitutionalist
GSD My 6,10,28,30,Je 3 1861
GU Je 5 1861

SOUTHERN spy. w My 26 1829-
DLC My 26,Je 23-30,Jl 28,Ag 4,25-S 1,O 13-20,N 10,D 15.29 1829;Ja 5 1830

SOUTHERNER. w Je 6 1840-
NcD Je 13 1840

STATE right's sentinel. sw,w Ja 9 1834-D 28 1836||
Merged with Augusta chronicle
sw: 1834-35
DLC F 3-10 1834
GDE [1834]-[36]
ScGK F 20,Mr 27,Je 9,30,Ag 28,O 2 1834;Je 19,Jl 3,Ag 7,21,S 4,25 1835;D 16 1836
TxU [1834-36]

Augusta daily TRANSCRIPT. d 1865-66||
Title varies: Daily morning transcript; Augusta evening transcript
ICHi S 20,N 2 1865
MBAt Jl 13,Ag 2,15,18-19,22,O 9,14,16,19-20, 23-24,31,N 3-4,6-7,15-16 1865
NNHi Ja 23 1865; Ja 23 1866
OHi Je 29,Jl 21,24,Ag 10-12,S 21 1865

Daily TRUE DEMOCRAT. d 1860||?
Followed by Southern republic
NcD N 17-20,25,D 16 1860

Augusta UNION. w 1889-1904||?
Negro
DLC Ja 27 1900

AURARIA

WESTERN herald. *See under* Dahlonega

BAINBRIDGE

Bainbridge ARGUS. w 1856-70||?
GBaW 1856-1859
NNHi O 25 1860

Bainbridge POST-SEARCHLIGHT. w 1915+
Mr 28 1929 is 105th anniversary of Decatur county
GAA Mr 28 1929

SOUTHERN spy. w My 26 1829-30||?
CSmH Je 1 1830
DLC My 26-Je 2,23-30,Jl 28-Ag 4,25-S 1, O 13-20,N 10,D 15 1829

BARNESVILLE

Barnesville weekly GAZETTE. *See* Barnesville news-gazette

Barnesville NEWS-GAZETTE. w 1868+
1868-1900? as Barnesville weekly gazette
GAA N 28 1929
GBar 1932
NNHi o F 18 1869;F 18 1873

BAXLEY

Baxley BANNER. *See* Baxley news-banner

Baxley NEWS-BANNER. w 1885+
1885-1903* as Baxley banner

BLAKELY

EARLY county news. w 1859+
pub 1931+
GBlC 1873+

BLUE RIDGE

FANNIN county times. w Ap 1931+
pub 1931+

Blue Ridge POST. *See* Blue Ridge summit-post

SOUTHERN world. w 1898-1906||?
NcD Mr 30 1899

Blue Ridge SUMMIT. w 1910-18||
United with Blue Ridge post to form Blue Ridge summit-post

Blue Ridge SUMMIT-POST. w 1888+
1888-1918 as Blue Ridge post

BOSTON

Boston WORLD. w 1888-93||?
NcD My 31 1890

BOWDON

Bowdon BULLETIN. w S 9 1913+
pub 1913+

BREMEN

GATEWAY. w Ja 1902+
pub 1902+

BRUNSWICK

Brunswick ADVERTISER. w 1875-93||
1881?-88? as Brunswick advertiser-appeal
GBrCa complete

Brunswick ADVOCATE. w Je 8 1837-
DLC F 22 1838
GAtCo F 15 1838
GBrCa 1837-39
MWA Je 8 1837;Ja 3 1839

Brunswick BREEZE. *See* Brunswick times-call

GAZETTE and land bulletin. *See under* Waycross

Brunswick NEWS. d 1901+
GBrC 1901+
GBrO 1903-13;30

Brunswick PILOT. w Jl 26 1926+
pub 1926+
GAA My 17 1929

Brunswick SEAPORT appeal. w 1869-80||?
United with Brunswick advertiser to form Brunswick advertiser-appeal, later Brunswick advertiser
MBAt N,D 17 1869
NcD My 23 1869
OClWHi O 21 1876;Ja 7 1880

Brunswick TIMES-CALL. d 1884-1902||
1884-97? as Brunswick breeze; 1898?-1900 Brunswick times (Title varies: Brunswick times-advertiser; etc)
GBrC 1898-1900
GBrO 1897-1902

BUCHANAN

HARALSON county tribune. w 1897+
1897-1919 as Buchanan tribune
GBuC 1897

Buchanan TRIBUNE. *See* Haralson county tribune

BUENA VISTA

Buena Vista ARGUS. *See* Marion county patriot

MARION county argus. *See* Marion county patriot

MARION county patriot. w 1875+
1875-81? as Buena Vista argus; 1882?-83? Marion county argus; 1884-85? Marion county sentinel
pub 1925+
GBueC 1875+

MARION county sentinel. *See* Marion county patriot

BUFORD

ADVERTISER. w 1916+
pub 1920+

BUTLER

Butler HERALD. w 1874+
pub [1876-1928]+

CAIRO

Cairo MESSENGER. w Ja 15 1904+
pub 1904+

CALHOUN

SOUTHERN statesman. w Ja 18 1855-
MWA Ap 5 1855

Calhoun TIMES. w Ag 14 1870+
GCalC 1870+

CAMILLA

ENTERPRISE. w 1902+
pub 1904+
GCamO 1909+

CANON

AMERICAN union. *See* Union

FREE press. w 1892-97||?
NcD Mr 23 1894;Ag 14 1896;Ap 2,Jl 30 1897

UNION. w Ja 3 1885-1905||?
1885-1901? as American union
1885-92? pub in West Bowersville
GAtCo F 1 1896
NcD Ja 3,Je 27 1885;Jl 31,Ag 7-14 1886;Ja 25,Mr 29 1890;My 26 1894;Ja 12 1895;My 9 1896;D 23 1899

CANTON

CHEROKEE advance. w 1880+
NcD O 16 1891
NcU F 17 1893

CARNESVILLE

FRANKLIN county register. w 1875-88||
1875-82 as West Bowersville register (West Bowersville). Followed by Weekly tribune, later Free press-organ
NcD Je 24 1882;Ja 5 1884;Ap 3,17 1888

FREE press-organ. w 1889-99||
Follows Franklin county register. 1889-98 as Weekly tribune
NcD S 17 1890

HERALD. w 1916+
pub 1916+
GCaC 1930+

Weekly TRIBUNE. *See* Free press-organ

CARROLLTON

Carrolton ADVOCATE. w 1860-
NcD O 5,26,N 16,D 7 1860;F 15 1861

CARROLL county times. w Ja 1871+
pub [1871-1925]+
GAA O 13 1927
NcD Je 21 1895

Carroll FREE press. w N 23 1883+
pub S 10 1912+
GAA O 13 1927

CARTERSVILLE

Cartersville AMERICAN. *See* Cartersville news

BARTOW herald. w 1929+
pub 1929+

BARTOW tribune. *See* Cartersville tribune-news

Cartersville COURANT. w 1885-86||?
United with Cartersville American to form Courant-American, later Cartersville news
GU F 12-My 21,Ag 20-O 1885
NcD Jl 23-Ag 13,S 3,O 1-8 1885

COURANT-AMERICAN. *See* Cartersville news

Cartersville EXPRESS. w
1871?-75? as Standard and express
Suspended for a time in 1864
GU Mr 28,Ap 11 1872;F 27,My 15,Ag 21 1873;F 5 1874;Ag 3-10 1876
NNHi Ap 28 1869;Mr 6 1873

FREE press. w 1878-83||
GU Ag 22,N 21 1878;O 28,N 25 1880;F 9,Ap 13,Ag 10,O 19 1882;N 22 1883
NcD My 18 1882

Cartersville NEWS. w 1882-1916||
1882-86? as Cartersville American; 1886?-1901? Courant-American; 1902?-05? News and courant. United with Bartow tribune to form Tribune-news
GU S 19 1882;Ag 26 1885;O 17,31 1889;My 14, Jl 30 1896;D 29 1898
NcD Ap 21 1885

Cartersville NEWS. sw 1895-1901||?
United with Courant-American to form News and courant, later Cartersville news
GU Jl 28 1896;Ja 26 1897

NEWS and courant. *See* Cartersville news 1882-1916

Cartersville STANDARD. w 1870||
United with Cartersville express to form Standard and express, later Cartersville express

STANDARD and express. *See* Cartersville express

Cartersville TRIBUNE-NEWS. w 1910+
1910-16 as Bartow tribune
pub 1929+
GAA Je 27 1929
GU Ap 4 1911;N 7 1912;Mr 15 1923;Mr 19-Ap 2 1925

VOICE of the people. w
GU S 16 1892

CASSVILLE

Georgia PIONEER. w 1836?-45||?
Title varies: Georgia pioneer and retrenchment banner, etc.
CSmH Ap 29 1842
DLC Ag 30 1844;My 30-Je 6,20,Ag 8,S 12,26-O 3 1845
NcU Je 4 1840;Ap 2 1841
NhD My 28 1841
ScGK S 2 1837;Ja 4,F 17,Mr 10,My 2,19,Je 30,Ag 11,O 2 1838;N 6 1839

Cassville STANDARD. w 1849?-
GHi [F 9-D 6 1855]
MWA Je 17 1852

CEDARTOWN

ADVANCE-courier. *See* Cedartown courier

Cedartown ADVERTISER. *See* Cedartown standard

Cedartown COURIER. w S 13 1894-1905||?
1894-1903? as Advance-courier
GU S 20 1894
NcD D 14 1899

Cedartown EXPRESS. w 1874-Ja 1879||
Followed by Cedartown advertiser, later Cedartown standard
GCeC F 1877-79
GCeO F 1877-79

GUARDIAN. w 1888-
NcD N 8 1888

GEORGIA (*Continued*)

CEDARTOWN—*Continued*

IRON city news. w
GU S 3 1890

Cedartown RECORD. w Jl 1874-Ja 1877||
GCeC complete
GCeO complete

Cedartown STANDARD. w,sw Ja 6 1879+
Follows Cedartown express. 1879-Ap 1888 as Cedartown advertiser
pub 1900+
GAA Ag 22 1929
GCeC 1879-Ap 1888
GCeO 1879-Ap 1888
GCeS 1900+
NcD O 15 1891

CLARKESVILLE

AEGIS. w
DLC O 14 1847-Ap 19 1849

JOURNAL. w Ja 14? 1859-
MWA Ja 14 1860

NORTH-EAST Georgian. w 1857-
NcD D 23 1857

TRI-COUNTY advertiser. w 1879+
pub 1910+
GClaC 1921+
GClaO [1925-26]+

CLAXTON

Claxton ENTERPRISE. w D 4 1912+
pub 1912+
GClC 1915+
GClO 1915+

CLAYTON

Clayton TRIBUNE. w 1895+
pub 1924+
GClayC 1925+

CLEVELAND

Cleveland ADVERTISER. w Ja 9 1880-
MWA Ap 3 1880

Cleveland COURIER. w 1899+
pub 1899+

COCHRAN

Cochran JOURNAL. w 1907+
pub 1912+
GCocC 1913+
GCocO 1913+
GCocS 1913+

COLQUITT

MILLER COUNTY liberal. w 1897+
GColqC 1897+
GColqO 1897+
GColqS 1897+

COLUMBUS

Columbus CHRONICLE. w 1895-1900||
Negro
DLC Ja 27 1900

DEMOCRAT. w O 16 1830-32||?
GMM 1830-O 6 1832

Columbus ENQUIRER. tw 1855-
NcD Jl 18,28 1857

Columbus daily ENQUIRER. d 1858+
1858-79 as Daily Columbus enquirer. Title varies: Daily enquirer-sun; etc.
pub 1858+
DLC Ja 12 1876;Ja-Je 1898;Ja-Je 1900
GAA F 27 1927;Ap 22 1928
GDE [1873]+
GMiG O 22 1850
GSD O 26 1863
GU Ja 7 1832-41;F 22 1882;Mr 24 1886;S 22 1922;O 5,14-15,D 1 1924
ICHi O 1,27,N 9 1865
MWA Ap 30 1861;S 6 1865
NN Je 14 1863
NcD Ag 8 1860;F 19 1864;Je 22,O 29,N 9 1871; Je 15-16,Ag 23,O 16,23 1872;Ap 14 1877[F-My 1883]
NcU Jl 17,30,S 1 1881
OClWHi Mr 11-Ap 23 1864;Mr 4 1869
OHi Jl 3,11,29,Ag 21,S 20,O 5 1865
—Sunday ed *See* Ledger-enquirer

Columbus ENQUIRER-SUN. w My 31 1828-1930||
1828-73 as Columbus enquirer
pub complete
CSmH Ag 27 1830
CtY Jl 15,Ag 5,19 1851
DLC Je 21 1828;Ja 15 1831;N 11,25 1840[Ap 1841-45]-47;D 24 1861
GAtCo Ja 1 1840
GDE [1838-40]41
M O 25 1928
MBAt S 11 1844
MWA Jl 19 1828;Jl 2 1830;My 13 1840;O 27 1841;Je 22,N 23 1852
NN Jl 5 1834;N 12 1845
NcD Ja 5 1837;My 27 1840;Ja 7 1846;Ag 19 1856
ScGK N 1 1834

GEORGIA argus. w 1838-41||?
DLC S 5 1839
GDE [1838]-[41]
NcU My 20 1840

Columbus LEDGER. d 1886+
pub 1886+
NcD S 23 1893
—Sunday ed *See* Ledger-enquirer

LEDGER-ENQUIRER. w 1930+
Sunday ed of Columbus ledger and Columbus enquirer
pub 1930+
GAA Jl 16 1931

MUSCOGEE democrat and mercantile advertiser. w 1844?-
DLC O 9 1846(extra)
GDE Jl 13 1848
IU N 29 1849

REPUBLICAN herald. w
NN F 10 1857

Columbus SENTINEL and herald. w 1832?-F 3 1841||
Followed by Columbus times
GU Ja 4 1838;F 3 1841
NcD Je 22 1837

SOUTHERN sentinel. w 1850-
DLC O 28 1852
GDE 1850-52
MWA Je 18 1852

Daily SUN. d Jl 30 1855-D 31 1873||
O 1 1865- as Daily sun and times. United with Columbus enquirer to form Columbus enquirer-sun
Suspended from Ap 17-Ag 31 1865
ArHi Jl 16,31 1856
CtY Jl 11 1863
DLC F 1 1864[O-N 1865]
GCC Ja 24-Jl 29 1856;Ap 1858-Jl 1860;Mr 19-N 22 1861;Jl 10 1862-My 27 1863;Ag 31 1865-Je 27,S 1870-Ag 1872;Mr-D 1873
GDE complete
MBAt Mr 18,29,Ap 3 1864[65-Ap 1866]
MWA Ap 5 1856;Ap 19 1862;Ap 2-4 1868
NN Je 14 1863
NNHi F 25,N 24 1864;Mr 10 1869;F 1 1873
NcD F 23 1864;Mr 5,17,21,23,25-26,28,Ap 7,11 1865
OClWHi Mr 15-Ap 9 1864;Ja 25-27 1865
V My 11 1863

Weekly SUN. w 1855?-D 30 1873||
United with Columbus enquirer to form Columbus enquirer-sun
GCC Jl 16 1861-My 26 1863;F 11-D 1873
GDE [1859]-[73]
OClWHi F 23 1864

Columbus TIMES. w F 11 1841-70||?
Follows Columbus sentinel and herald. 1841?-58 as Columbus times and sentinel
DLC Ap 22 1841;My 1845-My 2 1848;Ja-F 6,20, Ap 10,My 8,Je 5 1849;N 2 1852
GBueC 1844-70
GCC 1853;55-61
GDE 1845-[47]-51
GU F 18-D 1841
ICHi Ja 6 1842
MBAt S 22 1842;Je 22 1852;Ja 13 1857
NNHi Ap 9 1860
NcD Jl 24 1844
NhD Ap 22 1841

Columbus TIMES. tw,d 1851-65||
1853-58 as Columbus times and sentinel. United with Daily sun to form Daily sun and times, later Daily sun
tw 1851-58
DLC N 30 1860;Jl 30 1862;F 16,Mr 18,29-30,Ap 2,11 1864
GCC 1864-Ap 1 1865
GDE 1853-61;64[65]
MBAt Mr 10-11,15-Ap 2,5-8,25 1864;Ja 25,27,30 1865
MH N 18,D 10,13-14,20-21,24,26-28 1864;F 3-4 1865
MWA Je 16 1852;Mr 18 1865
NN Je 15 1863
NcD Ap 23 1861;Ap 13 1864
V Jl 25-27 1864

Daily TIMES. d 1875-85||
GCC 1875-Ap 1 1885
NcD [Ap-Je 1883]
NcU Jl 28 1881

Sunday TIMES. w 1875-85||
GCC Mr 1879-Mr 1885

Columbus TIMES and sentinel. *See* Columbus times.

COMMERCE

Commerce OBSERVER. w 1909-23||?
NN Mr 9 1916

CONYERS

SOLID South. w 1883-90||?
NcD Ag 18 1883

CORDELE

Cordele DISPATCH. sw,w,d 1908+
sw Mr 4 1914-D 22 1915 My 1916-N 13 1917;w Mr 1-Ap 1916
pub Je 4 1913;Mr 1914-D 22 1915;Mr 1916+
GCorO Je 1920+

Cordele RAMBLER. w 1907-16||?
GCorO 1913-F 21 1914

Cordele SENTINEL. w 1913-Ap 1920||
Merged with Cordele dispatch
GCorB F 4,N 4,O 14 1910
GCorD Ja 13 1920
GCorO Je 5 1914;16-20

COVINGTON

EXAMINER. w 1865-70||?
WHi My 2 1866

GEORGIA enterprise. *See* Covington news

Covington NEWS. w 1864+
1864-1910 as Georgia enterprise
pub 1927+
GCo 1900+
GCoC 1870+
GCoO 1868+
GDE D 11 1874
GU O 21 1927
NcD Ap 2 1875;Je 24,Jl 21 1881
WHi Ap 27,My 11,Jl 6 1866

TYPE of the times. w 1857-
MWA Mr 18 1858

CRAWFORDVILLE

ADVOCATE-democrat. w 1876+
1876-94? as Crawfordville democrat
NcD Ja 3-18,Mr 14,Ag 8,N 28 1879;Mr 17 1880; N 19 1881

Crawfordville DEMOCRAT. *See* Advocate-democrat

PEOPLE'S advocate. w 1892-94||
United with Crawfordville democrat to form Advocate-democrat

CUTHBERT

Tri-weekly GEORGIA times. w 1864-65||?
MH Ja 24 1865

Cuthbert LEADER. w 1891+
pub 1891+

DAHLONEGA

Dahlonega ECHO. w 1915-20||?
GMiG My 10 1917;S 4 1919

MOUNTAIN signal. *See* Dahlonega signal

Dahlonega NUGGET. w 1892+
GDahN [1933+]
GMiG D 23 1910;Mr 21 1913;My 15,O 16,N 13 1914;O 29 1915;Mr 10-17 1916;Mr 1 1918; Jl 4,Ag 22,O 24 1919;Jl 9-16,30,Ag 27 1920;Mr 25,My 27,O 7 1921;Ja 26,N 30 1923;Ja 25,F 22,Mr 21,Ap 18,Je 13,S 19,O-N 14 1924;Ja 16,Ap 10,My 15 1925;My 28 1926;Ja 21 1927

Dahlonega SIGNAL. w 1839-1909||?
1839-83? as Mountain signal (1877? as Signal advertiser)
DLC O 30 1852
GDahN F 21 1869
GDahO 1873-89
GMiG Jl 3,O 23-30,N 13 1858;Ja 22-29,F 26,Ap 16,Jl 9,Ag 20-27,O 29 1859;Jl 31 1875;O 27 1876;Ja 28 1881;Mr 10,Ap 28,Je 30 1882;O 25 1883
MWA Je 12,D 4,18 1852
Tx Mr 26 1864

WESTERN herald. w 1834-35||?
1834 pub at Auraria
ScGK F 21-28 1834;Ap 4 1835

DALLAS

NEW ERA. w 1882+
GDaC 1929+

DALTON

CHEROKEE Georgian. w O 1865-66||?
GDalW Ja 20,Mr 16,Ap 6 1866

Dalton CITIZEN. w 1847+
1847-N? 1862 as Mountain eagle; D 1862-67? North Georgia times; 1868-1919 North Georgia citizen
pub 1869-D 22 1870;1883;O 4 1894+
GAA O 16 1930[O 26 1933-My 1934]
GDalP D 13 1862
GU Ag 5 1932
KHi Jl 14,Ag 18 1881
MWA Je 17 1852
NcD Ap 15 1869

Dalton ENTERPRISE. w 1874-77||?
GDalM D 19 1876

MOUNTAIN eagle. *See* Dalton citizen

Dalton NEWS. w 1927+
pub 1934+
GAA My 30,O 10 1929
GDalO 1927+

NORTH Georgia citizen. *See* Dalton citizen

NORTH Georgia republican. w S 27 1867-
MBAt O 4 1867

NORTH Georgia times. *See* Dalton citizen

DANIELSVILLE

Weekly MONITOR. w Mr 3 1882+
pub 1895+
NcD Je 2-16 1882;N 9 1883;Ag 17 1888

DARIEN

Darien GAZETTE. w 1818-
CtY Jl 22,Ag 12,S 2 1828
DLC Jl 20 1824
G 1824-Ap 12 1825
MWA Ap 25,My 16,Je 6,27-Jl 11,25,Ag 17-24,S 14-O 10,31-D 5 1822;My 18 1824

Darien GAZETTE. w 1874+
1874-93? as Darien timber gazette
Suspended from 1920-Ap 1933
pub Ap 1933+
GAA S 29,O 13 1888

GEORGIA (*Continued*)

DARIEN—*Continued*

MCINTOSH county herald. w Ja 22 1839-
DLC Ja 22 1839
MWA F 5 1839

MCINTOSH county herald. w S 1920-Ag 1934||
GDarM complete

Darien PHENIX. w Ja 22 1829-
DLC Ja 22 1829

DAWSON

Dawson NEWS. w 1883+
pub 1908+

DAWSONVILLE

DAWSON county advertiser. w 1876?+
pub 1925+

DECATUR

DEKALB chronicle. w 1876-89||?
1876-85? as DeKalb news
NcD Jl 14,Ag 4-11 1887

DEKALB new era. w 1885+
pub 1885;87;97;1911+
GD 1927+
GDC 1897+

DEKALB news. *See* DeKalb chronicle

DONALSVILLE

Donalsville NEWS. w 1916+
GDoC 1931+

DOUGLAS

Douglas BREEZE. *See* Douglas enterprise

COFFEE county progress. w 1912+
GDouC [1913]21-25;27;29;31

Douglas ENTERPRISE. w 1888+
1888-96 as Douglas breeze
pub 1920+
GDouC 1917-[22-23]-26;28;30;32

DOUGLASVILLE

DOUGLAS county sentinel. w 1905+
pub 1927+

Weekly VIEW. w 1887-
WHi Ap 18,My 16,Jl 4 1887

DUBLIN

Dublin COURIER-HERALD and dispatch and post. w,sw 1878-Je 25 1929||
1878-94 as Dublin post; 1894-99 Dublin courier; 1900-Ag 14 1913 Dublin courier-dispatch
w 1878-98?
pub N 1913-Je 21 1929
GDuC D 1910-12;Ag 19 1913-Je 21 1929
GDuO Je 20 1878-Je 15 1887;1901-03;06;10-12; Ag 19 1913-Ja 1 1914;15-N 17 1916
GU Mr 8,Je 17-24,Ag 12,S 30,O 21 1926
NcD Jl 7 1898

Dublin COURIER-HERALD, dispatch and press. d 1913+
Title varies slightly
pub N 1913—
GDu [Jl 21 1929+]
GDuC [Jl 21 1929+]

Dublin DISPATCH. w 1894-99||
United with Dublin courier to form Dublin courier-dispatch, later Dublin courier-herald and dispatch and post
GDuCo S 21 1898-S 7 1899

LAURENS citizen. w Ag 13 1930+
pub 1930+

LAURENS county herald. w Mr 1910-Ag 14 1913||
United with Dublin courier-dispatch to form Dublin courier-herald and dispatch, later Dublin courier-herald and dispatch and post
GDuC Je-Ag 1913
GDuO Je-Ag 1913

Dublin MESSENGER. *See* Dublin press

Dublin POST. *See* Dublin courier-herald and dispatch and post

Dublin PRESS. w 1923-Je 25 1929||
1923-27? as Dublin messenger. United with Dublin courier-herald and dispatch to form Dublin courier-herald dispatch and press
GDuC F-Je 21 1929
GDuCo Ja 14 1927-29

Dublin TIMES. sw Ap 18 1903-09||
GDuCo 1907-09
GDuO 1904-05;08-09

EAST POINT

ATLANTA'S suburban reporter. w 1921+
pub 1927+

EATONTON

COUNTRYMAN. w Mr 4 1862-My 8 1866||
Suspended from Je 27 1865-Ja 30 1866
DLC S 29-D 16 1862
GDE 1862-[Je-Je 1864]-[Ja-Je]-D 1865;Mr 20,Ap 10 1866

MESSENGER. w 1874+
GEC [1874-75;89]-98;1901-06;30+
GEO 1893-1904;18+

EDDYVILLE

Daily CITY item. d
MSaE My 23 1866

ELBERTON

GAZETTE. w 1859-81||
DLC Mr 19 1873;Jl 14,Ag 4,S 29 1875;Ap 5, My 10,24 1876
GU Jl 14 1866;78-81
NcD Je 25 1869[73-77]F 18 1880
OHi N 5 1873;Ag 14 1875

GAZETTE. w 1881-92||?
1881-84 as New South
GU 1881-D 19 1888
NcD Mr 1 1882;Mr 14-Ap 4,Jl 4,Ag 1,29 1883; Mr 5,My 21,Je 11 1884;F 25 1885

NEW South. *See* Gazette (1881-92)

Elberton STAR. w,sw 1888+
w 1888-1904?
GElC 1889+
GElO 1889+
GU 1891
NcD My 6 1892;Je 2 1904

ELLAVILLE

SCHLEY county news. w 1885+
pub [1910+]
GEllC 1885+

FAIRBURN

CAMPBELL county news-letter. *See* Campbell news

CAMPBELL news. w 1881+
1881-84? as Campbell county news-letter
pub 1932+
GAA Je 26 1884;1901-28

Fairburn SENTINEL. w 1871-72||
GAA My 5,Je 30,Jl 14-21,S 1,O 27-N 3,D 15 1871;F 23-Mr 1 1872

Fairburn STAR. w 1877-78||
GAA F 8 1878

Fairburn WAIF. w
GAA Je 14,Jl 12-19 1872

FAYETTEVILLE

Fayetteville ADVERTISER. w
GDE Ag 9 1845
GHi O 10 1846

FITZGERALD

Fitzgerald CITIZEN. w D 24 1896-1906||?
1896-99 as Colony citizen; 1900-01 Citizen-leader; 1902-03 Irwin county citizen
GF D 24-31 1896;Ag 19 1897;My 7,S 24 1903

COLONY citizen. *See* Fitzgerald citizen

Fitzgerald ENTERPRISE. *See* Fitzgerald leader-enterprise and press

Fitzgerald HERALD. sw N 30 1916+
pub 1916+
GF 1916+
GFO 1920+

IRWIN county citizen. *See* Fitzgerald citizen

Fitzgerald LEADER. w 1896-98||
United with Fitzgerald enterprise to form Leader-enterprise and press
GF Ja 21 1897;F 3 1898
GOC Mr 25 1897-98

LEADER-ENTERPRISE and press. w,tw 1895+
1895-1912? as Fitzgerald enterprise
w 1895-1903?
pub 1911+
GF Ja 15 1897;F 4 1898[99-1900]-08;10[11+]
GOC F 14-N 7 1901
OClWHi Ja 13 1913

FLORENCE

GEORGIA mirror. w Ap 2 1838-40||?
GMM 1838-Ap 11 1840

FOLKSTON

CHARLTON county herald. w 1898+
pub [1898]+
GFolC 1929+

FORSYTH

BEE. w 1848||?
GForB Ag 12 1848

ENTERPRISE. w Ag 8 1843-
KHi S 12 1843

LITTLE Georgian. w
GDE Je 5 1846

MONROE advertiser. w 1854+
Suspended for a short time in 1865
pub 1916+
GAA O 24 1929
GForB My 11 1875;1930+
GForO 1876+

FORT GAINES

MODERATOR. w Jl 5 1842-
DLC Jl 5,S 6 1842

Fort Gaines WHIG. w 1840-41||?
DLC Je 1 1841

FORT HAWKINS

GEORGIA messenger. *See* Georgia journal and messenger (Macon)

FORT VALLEY

Fort Valley BANNER. w
GFoB 1884-85

LEADER-tribune. w 1888+
1888-1911 as Fort Valley leader
pub 1920+
GFoB [1888+]
GFoO 1925+

FRANKLIN

BANNER. w 1889-O 1892||
United with Franklin news to form News and banner
NcD D 1 1891

NEWS and banner. w Mr 1876—
1876-O 1892 as Franklin news
pub F 15 1929+
GAA Je 8 1928
GFrC 1894+
GFrO 1894+

GAINESVILLE

Gainesville EAGLE. w 1860+
pub 1830+
GGO 1931-32;35+
NcD Ap 19 1923

FARMERS' outlook. w 1894-97||?
NcD Ag 24,S 7 1894

GEORGIA cracker. *See* Gainesville news

Gainesville NEWS. w 1889+
1889-1902? as Georgia cracker
pub 1889+
GGO 1928-30;33+

PIEDMONT press. w 1883-84||
Merged with Gainesville eagle
GMiG My 28,Ag 20 1884

GIBSON

Gibson RECORD. w 1891+
NcD Ja 19 1894

GREENSBORO

BEACON. w
DLC S 28 1844

GEORGIA home journal. w 1873-86||
United with Greensboro herald to form Herald and journal, later Herald journal
NcD Je 22 1877[1883-84]

Greensboro HERALD. w 1866-86||
United with Georgia home journal to form Herald and journal, later Herald journal
GGrO 1867;69;75-86
NcD [1871,73-77,80-81;84-86]
OHi F 9 1877

HERALD-JOURNAL. w 1887+
Formed by the union of Greensboro herald and Georgia home journal. 1887-90 as Herald and journal
pub 1917+
GGrC 1921+
GGrO 1887+
NcD Jl 22 1887;O 17 1890;F 24-Mr 3,My 12-19,N 17 1894;Ag 4,D 1 1905

GREENVILLE

GEORGIA weekly. w F 6-O 1861||?
DLC O 23 1861
OClWHi F 6-20,Mr 6,My 1 1861

MERIWETHER county vindicator. *See* Meriwether vindicator

MERIWETHER vindicator. w 1872+
Title varies: Greenville vindicator; Meriwether county vindicator
pub 1872+
GGreC 1872+
NcD My 16 1879;Ag 27 1880 Ja 6 1882

Greenville VINDICATOR. *See* Meriwether vindicator

GRIFFIN

AMERICAN union. *See under* Macon

AMERICAN whig. w 1846-
MWA Mr 5 1847

Daily CHATTANOOGA rebel. *See under* Chattanooga, Tenn.

CONFEDERATE states. w?
P-M My 16 1861

EMPIRE state. w Je? 1855-
GU [1856]Ap 1857;Ja ? Jl 20 1859

EMPIRE State. w Ap 2 1870-
DLC Jl 16 1870
NNHi Jl 2 1870

GEORGIA (*Continued*)

GRIFFIN—*Continued*

GEORGIA Jeffersonian and Griffin gazette. w 1840?-
GU [1853-54]
MWA Je 17 1852
NcD Jl 9 1842

Griffin daily NEWS. d 1871+
1888-1925 as Griffin news and sun
pub 1875+
GAA Ag 1 1929
GGriO 1871+
NcD S 10,18 1889

Griffin NEWS. w,sw 1871+
1888-1925 as Griffin news and sun
w 1871-1925
pub 1875+
GAA N 11 1876
GGriO 1871+
NcD Mr 2 1876

SOUTHERN herald. w
GGriO 1866-69

SOUTHERN union. w
GSD Je 14 1861;My 1 1863

Griffin STAR. tw,sw O 28 1865-73||?
Title varies: Griffin tri-weekly star; Griffin semi-weekly star
tw 1865?-68
GAA Jl 25 1866;F 9,Je 1,Jl 9,S 23,O 3,15,N 9-16 1867;Ja 2,Mr 25,Ap 24,My 15-18,Je 24,D 4,18 1868;Ja 8,F 9,Je 29,Jl 30 1869;Ag 12,30,S 6,13,O 4,N 8,22 1870;Jl 2 1872
ICHi O 28,N 2 1865
NNHi Ja 28-30,F 18,22 1868;Ja 29,F 2,19,26, Mr 2 1869;F 14 1873

Griffin SUN. w 1877-88||
United with Griffin news to form Griffin news and sun, later Griffin news

HAMILTON

HARRIS county enterprise. w
P-M Jl 4 1861

HARRIS county journal. w,sw 1872+
1872-1920 as Hamilton journal
Suspended for a time during the Civil War
GAA N 18 1927;Ap 12,26,My 17,Jl 19,N 22 1929
NcD My 31 1887

Hamilton JOURNAL. *See* Harris county journal

HAPEVILLE

FULTON county review. w 1927+
GAA O 4 1929

HARLEM

COLUMBIA news. w 1918+
pub 1926+

COLUMBIAN sentinel. *See under* Thomson

HARTWELL

Hartwell SUN. w 1876+
pub 1908+
GHaC 1876+
NcD N 12,D 24 1879;O 13 1883;N 8 1884;Ja 27,F 10 1905

HAWKINSVILLE

Hawkinsville DISPATCH and news. w 1866+
1866-89 as Hawkinsville dispatch
GAA My 6 1926
GOC Mr 23-Je 1893
GU [Ap]My 6 1926

Hawkinsville NEWS. w 1881-89||
United with Hawkinsville dispatch to form Hawkinsville dispatch and news

HIAWASSEE

TOWNS county herald. w N 10 1928+
pub 1928+

HINESVILLE

Hinesville GAZETTE. *See* Liberty county herald

LIBERTY county herald. w 1871+
1871-93? as Hinesville gazette
GHiO 1871+

HOMER

BANKS county gazette. w 1890-97||
GAA Je 3,Jl 8 1891

BANKS county journal. w 1890+
GHoC 1890+

HOMERVILLE

CLINCH county news. w 1894+
1933? as Ed Rivers weekly
GAA 1926

ED RIVERS weekly. *See* Clinch county news

IRWINVILLE

IRWIN county courier. w Ja 1 1903-Ag 23 1907||
Followed by Ocilla star (Ocilla)
GOC complete

STAR of San Marino. w F 18 1843-
DLC Ap 1 1843

JACKSON

Jackson ARGUS. *See* Progress argus

BUTTS county progress. w 1882-1915||
United with Jackson argus to form Progress-argus

MIDDLE Georgia argus. *See* Progress argus

PROGRESS-argus. w 1873+
1873-1915 as Jackson argus (Title varies: Middle Georgia argus)
pub N 1908+

JEFFERSON

FOREST news. *See* Jackson herald

JACKSON herald. w Je 1875+
1875-Ja 1881 as Forest news
pub 1875+
GAA Je 26 1891

TWIGGS county new era. w N 1928+
pub 1928+

JESUP

Jesup SENTINEL. w 1865+
GAA Ag 15 1929
GU N 11 1897

JONESBORO

CLAYTON county news. w 1919+
pub 1928+

KINGSLAND

SOUTHEAST Georgian. w 1903+
pub N 24 1911+
GWoC 1929+
GWoO 1921+

KINGSTON

Kingston TIMES. w 1908-12||?
GU F 11 1910

KNOXVILLE

CRAWFORD county herald. w 1890-
GAA S 26,O 3,N 21 1890

CRAWFORD county news. w
pub 1926+

LAFAYETTE

WALKER county messenger. w Jl 27 1877+
pub 1892+
GAA Jl 29 1927
GLaC 1883+

LA GRANGE

La Grange BULLETIN. w,d 1863-Je 1864||
Merged with LaGrange reporter
NcD Mr 28 1864

GRAPHIC. w 1888-1929||?
GU Ja 1 1920

La Grange HERALD. *See* La Grange reporter. w

La Grange NEWS. d 1918+
1918-29? as La Grange reporter

La Grange REPORTER. d *See* La Grange news

La Grange REPORTER. w S 7 1843-1930||?
1843-44? as La Grange herald
DLC S 7,28 1843;F 14 1844;Mr 3,17 1865
ICHi S 29-O 6 1865
LSfD D 12 1889
MBAt S 22-29,O 13,N 3-10,D 1-22 1865;Ja 5, 19,F 9-16 1866
MWA Mr 31 1865
NNHi Mr 24-31 1865;Mr 14 1873
NcD N 30 1860;O 17 1862;Mr 24 1865;Je 14 1888;Je 13 1890
OClWHi Mr 24-31 1864

LAKELAND

To 1922 as Milltown

LANIER county news. w N 1 1914+
1914-19 as Milltown advocate
pub 1922+

MILLTOWN advocate. *See* Lanier county news

LAKEMONT

'MOUNTAIN star. w 1924-27||?
Jl 5 1924 is Historical ed
GU Jl 5 1924

LAVONIA

Lavonia TIMES. w Jl 28 1905+
F 23 1934 is Historical ed
pub 1908+
GAA Ja 19,F 23,Mr 16 1934
GLav F 23 1934

LAWRENCEVILLE

GWINNETT atlas. *See* Gwinnett herald

GWINNETT herald. w Mr 1871-97||
1871-72 as Gwinnett atlas. United with Lawrenceville news to form News-herald
G My 14 1879
GAA Ag 27 1879
GLN complete
GLO complete

GWINNETT journal. w 1902+
pub 1902+

Lawrenceville NEWS. 1893-97 *See* News-herald

NEWS-HERALD. w 1893+
1893-97 as Lawrenceville news
pub 1893+
GLO 1893+

LEARY

CALHOUN county courier. w 1882-90||?
GAA Je 15 1883

LEXINGTON

OGLETHORPE echo. w 1873+
pub 1880+
GLeC 1915+
GLeO 1879+
NcD Ag 3,O 4 1878;My 16,30,Jl 4,Ag 8,S 12 1879;Ja 5 1882

LINCOLNTON

LINCOLN home journal. *See* Lincoln journal

LINCOLN journal. w 1893+
1893-1909? as Lincoln home journal
GU N 2,23-30 1922;Ap 5,Jl 5,26-Ag 2,S 6,N 22,D 13-20 1923;Mr 13-20,Je 5,Jl 24,Ag 21-S 4,O 16 1924
NcD Mr 15 1900

LOUISVILLE

*AMERICAN advocate. w F 15 1816-
G Ja-O 27 1821

Louisville INDUSTRIAL and commercial gazette. w F 1 1860-
1860-61? as Louisville gazette
GAA O 30 1869
MWA Mr 22,Ap 5,Jl 24 1860;Ja 9 1861

JEFFERSON news and farmer. *See* News and farmer

NEWS and farmer. w 1871+
1871-Jl 1875 as Jefferson news and farmer
pub 1871+
GLoO 1871+
NcD [1874-78]
OHi Ag 9,O 11 1877

LUMPKIN

Lumpkin INDEPENDENT. *See* Stewart-Webster journal (Richland)

STEWART-Webster journal. *See under* Richland

McDONOUGH

McDonough ADVERTISER. w 1922-O 1 1934||
Merged with Henry county weekly
pub complete

HENRY County weekly. w 1875+

MACON

Macon ADVERTISER and agricultural intelligencer. sw Ap 19 1831-D 28 1832||
Title varies slightly
DLC N 8 1832
GDE [1831-32]
GMM complete

AMERICAN democrat. w My 17 1843-44||?
GMM 1843-Ag 14 1844
MWA My 17 1843

AMERICAN republic. w O-D 1859||?
GSD D 10 1859

AMERICAN union. w 1848-73||
1848-My 13 1867 pub in Griffin
DLC Mr 2,D 14 1871
GAA Ja 29 1869
GGriO 1854-66
KHi Ag 16 1867-Ja 2 1872
MWA Je 24 1852;My 28,Je 4,Ag 13 1869
NcD My 30 1872

ARMY and navy herald. sm S 24 1863-65||
DLC Ja 5,Mr 16-30 1865
MWA N 1 1864;Mr 30 1865
NNHi N 1 1863;Mr 16-Ap 13 1865
NcD F 9,Mr 16-Ap 6 1865
OClWHi F 23 1865

Daily CITIZEN. d Ap 1857-
NcD My 7,Je 11,Jl 7,S 7,15,21,24,28,O 3 1857

Macon daily CONFEDERATE. d F 9 1863-S 19 1864||
Merged with Macon daily telegraph
DLC Jl 20 1863;Mr 10,15,17,19,21-26,28,Ap 1-2,7 1864
GDE Ap 29,My 5 1864
MBAt Mr 15-Ap 8,12 1864
NNHi Mr 11 1863
P-M Ja 30,Mr 11,Ap 12-13,17,My 12 1864
V Jl 22-24,27 1864

Macon daily ENTERPRISE. d 1872-73||?
GMM S 16 1872-[Ap 12-D 1873]
NcD Ag 1,23,O 17 1872;Ja 20 1873

GEORGIA (*Continued*)

MACON—*Continued*

Macon daily **GAZETTE.** d
P-M Ag 10 1865

GEORGIA weekly **citizen.** w Mr 21 1850-61||?
Title varies slightly
GMM 1850-Mr 22,29(supp)1860
MWA Je 19 1852;D 9 1853
NcD O 18 1856;Ag 14,S 25 1857;S 10 1858;Jl 20 1860
NhD D 23 1853
P-M Ag 9 1859
PPL D 7 1850
WHi Jl 19 1856

Daily **GEORGIA citizen.** d Ag 1859-S 24 1861||
Merged with Macon telegraph
NcD S 3 1859

Daily **GEORGIA citizen.** d Mr 5 1866-
MBAt Mr 5,7,20,22,Ap 3 1866

GEORGIA journal and messenger. w Mr 16 1823-N 1869||
Mr-D 3 1823 as Messenger; D 10 1823-49? Georgia messenger. Merged with Macon telegraph
1823-24 pub in Fort Hawkins
CSmH S 25 1845
Ct Ag 7 1827
CtY Je 14,Ag 9,30,O 18 1828;Jl 20 1843;Je 4 1844
DLC O 20,N 10,D 15 1824[25-Mr 1832]D 10 1840
GDE [1826-27;30]-[47;51;]-[57-58]-[60]
GHi [Ap 8 1847-Mr 1849]
GMM Mr 21 1823-Mr 16 1825;26;29;Mr 13 1830-61
GMiG Ap 1852-Mr 1853;54-55
GU My 19 1845;N 13 1850;Ap 23-30 1851[Je-N 1856]D 15 1865[Ja-F,Je-Jl 1866]Ja 12 1868
GViW [1859-61]-[63]
MWA F 19 1831;O 20 1842;Ag 28 1845;Je 23 1852;Je 3 1857
N Ja 4 1826
OClWHi Mr 5,O 1 1851;Ja-Ag 1856;S 1857-Ja 6,My 26,Je 9,23,S-D 1858;67-68;Ap 20-27,Je 15,Jl 6,27,O 5 1869
P S 12 1860-S 1865
P-M Ag 8 1839;My-D 1860;Ja 13 1864;65
ScGK Mr 13 1834;Ap 30,My 21,Jl 2,O 29 1835;Ja 19 1837;N 22 1838;My 9,Je 13,S 5,O 24,N 21 1839

GEORGIA messenger. *See* Georgia journal and messenger

GEORGIA telegraph. *See* Macon telegraph

Macon daily **HERALD.** d
DLC My 13 1865
GMM My 8 1865
KHi My 8 1865
OHi Je 11 1865

HOLLIDAY herald.
GMM D 5,25 1877

Daily **INTELLIGENCER.** d 1855?-
NcD S 3 1864
OClWHi O 2 1864

Macon daily **JOURNAL and messenger.** d
DLC N 17-18 1867
ICHi Jl 1,S 26 1865
MBAt Mr 28 1868
N O 23-24 1866
NNHi N 17 1865;Mr 1 1869
OClWHi Jl 24,S 14 1866;Mr 18,25-26,S 8 1868
OHi S 2,20 1865

MERCANTILE mirror and railroad guide. w Ag 5 1865-
OHi S 16 1865

MESSENGER. *See* Georgia journal and messenger

Daily evening **MIRROR.** d
GHi Ja 13-My 25 1866
NcD Ja 19,22 1860

Daily evening **NEWS.** d Ap 20-My 11 1865||
pub in office of Macon telegraph while that paper was suspended
GMM My 4 1865
ICHi Ap 26 1865

Macon **NEWS.** d 1884+
Title varies: Evening news My 6 1923 is Centennial ed; Jl 10 1929 Macon history ed
pub 1884+
DLC 1898
GAA Jl 10 1929
GMM S 3-8,10-11 1906[O 1908-09]My 23,25,28 1910;Ap,Jl 7-8,10,13-15 1911[Ja-Ag 1912;F-D 1913]Ap 4,11,27-28,My 1-2,Je 20,22-23,27,Jl 7 1914;Ja 14 1916;Jl 10 1929
MWA My 6 1923
NcD Je 20 1888;Ap 29,Je 3,12,Jl 3,O 29 1890;F 17,Mr 11 1891;F 3 1892;F 1,Je 13-14 1894;F 22 1895;F 11-12,My 14 1904;Jl 10 1929
—morning ed *See* Macon telegraph

REPUBLIC. w O 10 1844-Ap 16 1845||
United with Georgia telegraph to form Georgia telegraph and republic, later Macon telegraph
GMM complete

Macon **SENTINEL.** w 1899-1900||?
Negro
DLC Ja 27 1900

SOUTHERN museum. w D 2 1848-Ja 5 1850||
Followed by Southern tribune
DLC F 3 1849
GMM complete

SOUTHERN tribune. w Ja 12 1850-F 22 1851||?
Follows Southern museum
GMM 1850-F 22 1851

STATE press. w O 22 1857-59||?
GMM 1857-O 22 1859

Macon **TELEGRAPH.** d,w,sw N 1 1826-1906||
1826-O 2 1832 as Macon telegraph; O 3 1832-Ap 25? 1845 Georgia telegraph; Ap 28 1845-S 18? 1858 Georgia telegraph and republic; S 21 1858-Ja 1860 Georgia telegraph; F 1860-S 12? 1864, My 11 1865-N 1869 Macon telegraph; S 19 1864-Ap 20 1865 Macon telegraph and confederate; N 1869-84 Telegraph and messenger
Suspended from Ap 20-My 11 1865. For this period *See* Daily evening news
d O 17 1831-S 1832; sw O 3 1832-S 1858; w O 1858-98?
pub complete
CSmH Ag 28 1830
Ct [1826-27]
CtY Jl 13 1841
DLC N 17 1827;Je 20-27,Jl 11,Ag 1,29-S 5,19-26,O 17,D 18 1829;Ja 2-16 1830;Ja 1 1831;Mr 20 1849;Ag 31 1852;Jl 18,Ag 1-2 1862;Mr 10,15,17,19,20-26,28,Ap 1-2 1864;F 3 1880
GAtCo Mr 20 1877
GDE [1826-27;30]-[35-37]Ag 24 1860;74[75]
GMiG Ap 17 1852-Ap 9 1853;Ja 10 1854-55;S 22 1876
GU 1832-35;D 22-29 1840;Ap 29 1845-Ap 13 1847
MWA D 11 1827;My 14 1835;My 13 1840;Je 22 1852;My 12,Je 2,D 29 1857
NN N 21 1826
NcD Jl 20 1858;My 4 1886;N 23,D 14 1893
NhD My 18 1841
OClWHi 1855;D 10 1869
P-M S 11,Jl 24 1863
TxU N 1 1826;N 4 1851;N 2 1876;N 1 1901;N 1 1926

Macon **TELEGRAPH.** d F 1 1860+
1860-N 1869 as Macon daily telegraph (S 19 1864-Ap 20 1865 Macon daily telegraph and confederate) N 1869-84 Daily telegraph and messenger
Suspended from Ap 20-My 11 1865. For this period *See* Daily evening news
N 25 1926 is Centennial ed
pub 1860+
G Jl 1913-Je 1916;18[19]+
GAA N 1 1926
GForB Je 12 1864
GMC 1876+
GMW Ja-Mr 1919;N 1926+
GSD N 22 1860;Ja 31,F 7,21,Ap 3,My 1,24,Je 21,Ag 5,23,O 11,N 15,D 20 1861 F 21,28,Je 13,S 19,O 24 1882;Ja 23,30 1863
GU D 24 1830[Mr]Ap 15 1861;O 25 1863;Ja 7 1866;Mr 14,24,Ag 29,O 6,14 1867;Mr 7 1869;D 15 1871;F 21-22,My 9 1872;Jl 13,S 19-20 1882;Je 29 1883;F 10,Mr 17,My 1,Je 3,15,Jl 8,26,D 12 1886;Mr 7,Jl 31 1887;Jl 6 1899 F 22 1903;Ag 19 1906;My 27,N 3 1911;F 24 1913 S 6 1916;S 17 1918;N 1 1926;Ag 15,21 1927;O 20 1928+
IC Ag 10 1915
ICHi O 1,N 10 1865
MBAt S 23,N 30 1863;Ja 28 1865;Ja 25,F 6,Jl 1,13 1866;Je 23 1868
MH Ja 24,26,30,F 1,6-8 1865
MWA O 4 1866;O 21 1875;Ag 25 1876;Ja 18 1881
MiU N 25 1926
MoS Ag 10 1915
N O 24 1866
NNHi Jl 27,O 4,N 19 1861;Ja 29 1863;Ap 13,15 1864;Mr 9,My 14 1865;F 2,19,26 1868;F 12,17,Mr 5 1869;F 5,Ap 14 1870;Ag 3 1872;My 20 1873
NcD Mr 25 1865;Je 11 1868;O 23 1872;F 13 1873;Jl 31 1881;Je 3 1882;F 14,28,Mr 3 6,13,Ap 1,5,10,My 19,22,27,30-31 1883;Ap 20 S 25,O 25 1886;My 1 1888;F 23,Mr 21,D 7,9-12 1889;F 12,Ap 21,S 16,27 1890;Ja 30,Jl 30 1891;N 18 1892;Ja 30 1894;Jl 2,D 19 1896;Ja 28-31,Mr 3,6,D 19 1897;Ap 20 1898;Mr 15 1899;Ja 24,D 15 1900;My 22,29,Je 3,11 1904;N 12 1905;My 24 1908;My 6-9 1912;Ag 10 1915;N 5,12 1918;N 25 1926
NcU Mr 1 1923
OCHi Jl 19 1884
OClWHi F 15,21 1860[1874]Jl-O 1,D 3,31 1875;F 5,Mr 11,24-25 1876
OHi Ag 14,25,25,S 12,28,30 1865
P [My 9 1860-O 25 1865]
P-M [1864-65]
Tx My 14 1835
TxGR N 25 1926
WHi Je 3 1864;Ap 1 1866

UNION banner. ir Ag 1-N 12 1851||
GDE [1851]
GMM complete

McRAE

TELFAIR enterprise. w 1887+
pub Je 1902-19;20+

MADISON

Madison **FAMILY visitor.** w 1847-64||?
DLC Ag 19 1848
GHi [Ja-D 6 1856]
MWA Ja 15 1848;Je 17 1852

MADISONIAN. w 1870+
pub 1912-Ja 1 1934
GMadO 1912—

SOUTHERN miscellany. w Ap 5 1842-
DLC D 8 1843
GMM 1842-Mr 22 1844

MARIETTA

Marietta **ADVOCATE.** w 1843?-52||?
CtY F 26 1852
DLC O 26 1852
MWA Je 17 1852

CHATTANOOGA daily rebel. *See under* Chattanooga, Tenn.

COBB county times. w O 24 1916+
pub 1916+
GAA S 1931-S 1 1932
GMarO O 1919+

CONSTITUTIONAL union. w 1844?-
MWA Je 17 1852

Marietta **JOURNAL.** w 1866+
pub 1900;03+
GAA Ap 26 1928;My 9 1929
GMarC [1870-1900]+
NcD My 9 1929

MARTHASVILLE. *See* ATLANTA

METTER

Metter **ADVERTISER.** w 1912+
pub N 1912+

Metter **NEWS.** w My 1933+
GMeA 1933+

MILLEDGEVILLE

CONFEDERATE union. *See* Federal union

EVERY Saturday. w 1873-76||?
GMiG My 9 1874;My 1 1875

FEDERAL review. w
NhD D 22 1840

FEDERAL union. w Jl 10 1830-Ag 28 1872||
Follows Statesman and patriot. 1830-Ja 22 1861 as Federal union; Ja 29 1861-S 16 1862 Southern federal union; S 23 1862-My 4 1865 Confederate union. United with Southern recorder to form Union recorder
CL Ap 26 1864
Ct My 19-26 1831
CtSp Ag 1 1837
CtY Mr 3 1840
DLC Ja-Je 13,Jl 18 1843;Ja 2,F 27,Mr 19-Ap 9,23,My 7,28,Je 11,Jl 2,23-O 1,N 5,26,D 10 1844-45;47-49;O 26 1852;My 7,Ag 13 1861;S 16 1862;Jl 10-17 1866
GDE 1832-37
GMM 1830-My 22 1860
GMiF N 21 1863
GMiG S 6 1842;Ag 22 1848;N 1859-Ja 20 1863;Ag 1866-Jl 1870
GSD complete
GU [1855]Ja-O 12 1858
KHi My 7 1844
MBAt My 31,Je 21 1864
MWA Je 22 1852;O 29 1857
NNHi D 9 1862
NcD Jl 16,S 21 1844;Mr 4 1845;F 2 1847;S 4,25 1855;S 14 1858;D 18-25 1860;Mr 14 1865;Jl 3 1872
OClWHi F 2 1869
P-M Ap 28 1863

Daily **FEDERAL union.** d
pub during sessions of the legislature
GSD N 7-D 15 1861
NcD N 4-D 17 1859

*__GEORGIA journal.__ w,sw O 31 1809-Mr 10 1847||
United with Georgia messenger (Macon) to form Georgia journal and messenger (Macon)
sw during sessions of the legislature
CSmH Ag 21 1830
Ct [1826]S 22 1835[38]
CtY My 31 1832
DLC 1821-28;Je 22,Jl 11-Ag 1,S 26,O 17-24,N 14,28,D 16-23 1829;30-31;D 8 1840;41-[43]F 27 1844-45
GAA Ag 14 1827
GAtCo O 30 1838
GDE 1821-[23;32]-[35;37]
GForB Je 14 1825
GMM O 1835-S 1836
GMiG Mr 13,Ag 14-21 1821;N 22 1825-Ja 10,Ap 11-Jl 18 1826[27-30;32]-Ja 17 1833;S 24-D 1839;Ag 24-31 1841;O 1842-S 1843;S 30 1845-47
GSD [1821-S 23 1823;26-S 1827]
GU 1821-[29-31]-39
MBAt N 27 1821;Ja 28 1823[28]S 12,N 7 1829;F 13,Mr 27,Jl 24 1830
MHi N 11,23,D 16 1823-Ja 6,27,Mr 4,Ap 13,My 25,S 30,O 26 1824;Mr 22,Ap 12,My 24,Je 14 1825;F 28,N 14,D 19 1826
MWA O 23 1821;Je 25,Jl 2,16-23,Ag 13-20,S 24,O 1-8,N 19 1822;Mr 11-18,Jl 1,N 11,D 23 1823;Mr 9,Ap 13,My 4-11,Jl 27,D 14 1824;Mr 29,Ap 26,D 27 1825;D 26 1826;Ja 2-9,Jl 5,O 29,S 17 1827;Mr 17,Jl 14,S 5 1828;Ja 2-9,23,O 23,N 6-13,D 1-15 1830;F 3,Ap 7,Je 16 1831;Ja 19,Mr 3 1832;F 12 1834
N O 9 1833
NN Mr 3 1831
NcD F 17 1835;My 10 1836
NcU My 26,Je 16 1840
NhD Ag 30 1832
ScGK O 20,D 11 1835;N 1 1836;Ja 24 1837;F 5,My 1,Je 5-12,Je 26,Ag 7 1838;Ja 1,22,F 12,Mr 2-16,My 7,28,Je 18,S 3-10,O 22-29,N 12,21 1839
TC Mr 1824-N 1827
WHi Ja 19-Je 26 1836

Georgia **patriot.** w N 5 1822-26||?
United with Georgia statesman to form Statesman and patriot
DLC [1823-24]Ja 25 1825
GHi [1824]
MWA 1822-Jl 8,Ag-D 1823;My 11 1824
N N 4 1823
NcD N,D 10 1822[26]

GEORGIA statesman. *See* Statesman and patriot

GEORGIA times and states rights advocate. w,sw Ja 15 1833-35||?
Ja-Mr 18 1833 as Times and states rights advocate
sw during sessions of the legislature
Ct Ag 12 1834
GDE N 18 1834
GMM Ja-Mr 18 1833;N 18 1834
NcD [1833]
ScGK Jl 30,O 4 1834;Mr 17 1835

GEORGIA (*Continued*)

MILLEDGEVILLE—*Continued*

NEWS. w 1901-25||?
GMiC 1913-14;17-18
GMiO 1913-14

SOUTHERN federal union. *See* Federal union

*****SOUTHERN** recorder. w,d 1819-73||
United with Milledgeville union to form Union and recorder, later Union recorder 1859-73 d during sessions of the legislature
CSmH Ag 28 1830
CtY Ag 9,N 22 1828
DLC Ap 9 1822-F 8 1825;Ag 20 1827;Je 27,Jl 4,Ag 1,S 26,O 24-31,N 21-28,D 19-26 1829;Ja 23 1830;Ja 15 1831;36-47;51-52;57-60;My 14,Je 11-18,Jl 30,Ag 20-27,S 10 1861;Ja 21,F 18,Mr 4,18,Jl 29,Ag 5,26,S 9,23,O 28,N 4-11,25-D 9,23 1862;D 15 1865(extra)N 17 1868;Ap 6 1869
G 1822-27;29-34;36-37
GDE [1821-22]24[32;34-35;37;52]
GHi N 18 1823;F 17,Mr 9 1824;My 24-31,Je 14-21,Ag 9,S 27 1825[S 12-D 1826]-[42]-44
GMiF [1857]
GMiG Ag 28 1830-F 3 1831[32-33]-Ja 17 1837;43-45[47-48]-[51]-Ja 4(supp)1853[Ag 1854-58]-60;My 21 1861[63]66
GSD 1861-[63-S 1865]
GU 1822-27;29-34;36-37
MB Ja 22-Mr 1861;Ap 30 1867
MBAt F 13 1821;N 14-D 19 1865;Ja 2,23,F 6 1866
MWA N 5 1834;Mr 15 1836;Ag 20 1844;Je 15 1852;My 6 1856;Mr 21 1865
MiU-C N 20 1830
N O 9 1833
NNHi Mr 1,Ap 5 1864;Ja 26,Mr 2-9 1869
NcD Ap 14,Jl 21,D 15 1831;Mr 15 1832;N 12 1834;O 9 1838;Mr 29,Jl 12 1842;Je 21 1853;Je 5(supp)1855;N 17,21 1860;Mr 14 1865;F 20 1866
NcU F 28 1837;My 19 1840
NjR Mr 20 1849
OClWHi D 26 1843;S 18 1866;Je 22 1869
ScGK Ja 22,F 12-26,My 21,Jl 9,30,Ag 20,S 3-10,O 1 1834;Ap 14,28-My 12,Jl 21,Ag 4,D 11 1835;Ja 17,Mr 7 1837;Ja 2-9,23,F 13,Mr 27,My 8,22,Je 19-26,Jl 17,S 4,N 27,O 16 1838;Ap 16,Jl 2-9,30,Ag 20,S 3,24,O 15-29 1839
Tx D 15 1860
WHi 1864-Jl 1872

SOUTHRON. w F 15 1828-
Ct [1828-Ja 17 1829]
CtY Ag 16,N 26 1828
DLC Ja 24 1829
GDE Ag 9 1828
MBAt Ap 5 1828
MWA F 23,Mr 15,Ap 5 1828

SPIRIT of the South. w
GMiG O 5-19,N 2-16 1875

STANDARD of union. w Ja 18 1834-41||?
Title varies: Standard of union and free trade advocate
Ct Mr 14 1835
DLC Ap 26 1834;Ja-F,Mr 12,Ap 2-9,My 14-28,Jl 2,Ag 20 1841
GDE Mr 5 1841
GMiH N 3 1840
NhD Je 4 1841

STATESMAN and patriot. w D 20 1825-Jl 3 1830||
1825-Je 11 1827 as Georgia statesman. Followed by Federal union
DLC F 7,21-N 14 1826;F 19 1827;Je 27-Jl 11,25-Ag 8,S 26,O 24,N 14-D 5,19-26 1829;Ja 9,23 1830
GMM complete
GMiF Ja 16 1827-28
GSD 1825-Je 1827
KHi My 1 1830
MHi F 14,My 2 1826
MWA N 12,D 24 1827
PDoHi Ag 30 1828

Milledgeville **TIMES.** w 1900+
pub O 1933+
GMiG Ja 16 1931+

TIMES and states rights advocate. *See* Georgia times and states rights advocate

UNION and recorder. *See* Union recorder

UNION recorder. w Ag 28 1872+
Formed by the union of Southern recorder and Federal union. 1873- as Union and recorder
Ag 18 1927 is Centennial ed
pub 1872+
CLM F 14 1888
G Ag 18 1927
GMiC 1891-93;1901+
GMiG [1873-82]-[85]86;D 10 1931+
GMiO 1887-90;94-95;97-1901;05-12;15-16
GSD 1872-Jl 22 1879
GU Je 13 1935

MILLEN

Millen **NEWS.** w 1903+
pub 1923+

MILLTOWN. *See* LAKELAND

MONROE

SOUTHERN witness. w Ja 15 1870-
NcD Ja 15 1870

Monroe-Walton **TRIBUNE.** w 1900+
GAA O 18 1929

MOULTRIE

OBSERVER. d 1894+
GU My 23 1922

MOUNT ZION

HANCOCK advertiser. w O 13 1826-32||?
GMiG S 25 1827;N 17,D 22 1832
GSD 1826[27-28]-[30]

*****MISSIONARY.** w My 1819-
"Contains news"
GMiG Je 16 1823-Je 20 1825
GU F 2 1821-O 10 1825
MWA My 9 1825

NAHUNTA

BANNER. *See* Brantley enterprise

BRANTLEY countian. *See* Brantley enterprise

BRANTLEY enterprise. w Ag 1 1919+
1919-25 as Banner; 1926 Brantley countian
pub 1929+
GNO 1924+

NASHVILLE

Nashville **HERALD.** w 1905+
pub 1905+
GNaC 1912+

NEW ECHOTA

CHEROKEE phoenix and Indians' advocate. w F 21 1828-O 1835||
1828-F 4 1829 as Cherokee phoenix
Not pub My 1 1828; My 6-20 1829; Ja 13, F 5 1830; Jl 8 1831
In English and Cherokee
CSmH Mr 13 1828-My 1834
Ct Mr 12 1831
DGU 1828-My 1834
DLC Mr 1828-N 3 1832
GHi Mr 13 1828
GSD F 11 1829;Ap 24-Jl 1830;Jl 9-N 12 1831
ICHi [1828-My 17 1834]
ICN Ja 21,Ag 19,S 9 1829
MBAt [1828]-[32]
MHi Jl 8 1829
MSaE 1828-34
MWA F 21 1828-[32-33]F 8,22,Mr 1-15,29-Ap 5,My 1834
MiU-C [1830-31]
N Ag 27,S 17,O 15,N 19,D 10 1828;Ja 14 1829-F 2 1833
NN Je 4,25 1828;F 11-Mr 11,S 2,N 18 1829;F 17,Ap 21,My 15-22,Je 5,Jl 24-31,Ag 14,S 11-18,O 9,23-N 6,20-D 11 1830;Ja 22,F 12,Mr 19-Ap 2,16,30,My 14,28-Je 11,S 10 1831;Jl 21,S 1,15 1832;Ag 17,O 19 1833;F 8 1834
NNHi Mr 12 1831
OCHi Ja 8 1831
OkHi [1828-29]-[32-34]
OkU [1828-29]
PHi Ag 10 1833-My 10 1834
WHi [1828-Ap 19 1834]

NEWNAN

COWETA advertiser. w 1883-87||
United with Newnan herald to form Newnan herald and advertiser, later Newnan herald
NcD Ja 21 1887

GEORGIA banner and sentinel. w
-1852? as Georgia banner
GDE N 26 1852
MWA Je 18 1852;S 18,N 6 1857;Mr 12 1858;N 16 1860

Newnan **HERALD.** w S 9 1865+
1887-1914 as Newnan herald and advertiser
pub O 1903+
GAA [1867-69;1924-28]
ICHi S 16,30 1865
MWA Ag 25 1871
NN S 25 1865
NcD Ag 27 1869;O 17 1873;Jl 24 1874;Ag 9 1877;D 23 1879;Ja 25 1883;My 27,D 9 1884

Newnan **INDEPENDENT** blade. w 1855-
GAA Ag 3 1860
MWA S 18 1857

PALLADIUM.
Ct S 19 1835

PEOPLE'S defender. w 1869-73||?
MWA S 6 1871
NNHi Ap 14 1869

WINCHESTER daily bulletin. d F? 1863-
OClWHi N 4 1863

NORCROSS

NORCROSS news. w 1929+
GBufA 1929-34

OCILLA

Ocilla **DISPATCH.** w 1896-1905||?
GOC F 1899-Ja 1901

Ocilla **STAR.** w S 13 1907+
Follows Irwin county courier (Irwinville)
GOC 1907+

OGLETHORPE

SOUTHERN democrat. w 1851-53||?
DLC O 22 1852
KHi My 20 1853
MWA Je 5 1852

SOUTH-WEST Georgian. w
GDE Je 11 1852

PALMETTO

GAZETTE. w 1871-72||
GAA My 20,N 4 1871;Mr 2 1872

Palmetto **SHIELD.** w 1872-73||
GAA F-Ap 2,24,My 8,22,Jl 25,Ag-S 5 1873

PAVO

Pavo weekly **NEWS.** w 1921+
GAA Je 15 1933-Je 7 1934

PEARSON

TRIBUNE. w 1915+
GPeO 1919+

PERRY

HOME journal. w 1870+
1890-1900? as Houston home journal
pub 1870+

HOUSTON home journal. *See* Home journal

QUITMAN

Quitman **ADVERTISER.** w 1898+
pub 1898+
GQ 1898;1906;12-18;23-24;30+
GQO 1909-11;14-15

Quitman **BANNER.** w 1866-73||
GQO complete

FREE PRESS. w 1877+
pub 1877+
G Ja 26 1934
GQ 1894-1902;04;06;12-[15-17]+
GQO S 22 1877-D 22 1883;F 1889-92;94-Jl 1895;My 30 1896-1903;06-08;12+

GALLAHER'S independent. *See* Quitman independent

Quitman **INDEPENDENT.** w 1873-75||
Title varies: Gallaher's independent
GQO complete

Quitman **REPORTER.** w 1874-77||?
GQO F 26-N 19 1874;76-D 13 1877

REIDSVILLE

TATTNALL journal. w 1891+
pub 1908-09;12+

RICHLAND

NEWS. w 1907-25||?
United with Lumpkin independent (Lumpkin) to form Stewart-Webster journal
GU My 21 1915

STEWART-Walker journal. w 1872+
1872-1924? as Lumpkin independent (Lumpkin)
PErW Mr 2 1878

RINGGOLD

CATOOSA courier. w 1872-90||?
NcD D 11 1879

Ringgold **EXPRESS.** w 1858-59||?
DLC F 11 1859

ROCKMART

Rockmart **REPORTER.** w 1871-74||
GCeC My 16 1872-O 2 1874

ROME

Rome daily **BULLETIN.** d 1869-87||?
1869-71? as Rome daily
GAA O 15 1884

Rome weekly **BULLETIN.** w 1870-87||?
1870-71? as Rome weekly

Rome **COMMERCIAL.** w 1865-76||
1865-70? as Southerner and commercial. Merged with Rome courier
NNHi F 19 1869;Ja 16 1870;Mr 6 1873

Rome daily **COMMERCIAL.** d 1868-76||
Merged with Rome daily courier
CLM F 20 1874
GU S 4 1872

COOSA River journal. *See* Rome weekly courier

Rome weekly **COURIER.** w 1843-87||?
1843-49 as Coosa River journal
Suspended from My 17 1864-Ag 31 1865
DLC N 14 1862
GR 1860-63;Ag 31 1865-S 20 1867
GRC O 17,N 14,D 12 1850-O 1851;Ja 9-S 23 1852;59-71
ICHi S 21-O 12,26,N 10 1865
MWA Je 10 1852;N 21 1854
NcD [Ap-Jl 1868;Ja-Ag 1869]My 27 1874

Rome daily **COURIER.** tw,d 1861-87||?
1861-79? as Rome tri-weekly courier
GAA [Ja 17-N 20 1860]N 16 1872-73[F 14-D 1874]
GCeC Ja 15 1870-Mr 13 1873
GR 1862-Ap 1864
GRC D 30 1865-N 1 1866[68-71]76;79
GU Je 15 1880;O 7 1885

GEORGIA (*Continued*)

ROME—*Continued*

Rome daily COURIER. tw,d 1861-87||—*Continued*
MBAt Ja 27 1866
NNHi Ap 29 1869
NcD Ag 27 1868[F-D 1875]Jl 19-20,Ag 31,S 5 1882;D 3 1883
NcU Jl 27 1881

Rome tri-weekly COURIER. *See* Rome daily courier

Rome DAILY. *See* Rome daily bulletin

Rome GEORGIAN. w 1895-99||?
NNHi Jl 31 1897

Rome daily HERALD. d 1904-09||?
United with Rome daily tribune to form Rome tribune-herald

HUSTLER of Rome. d 1891-98||?
GRC [1894-98]

Rome NEWS-TRIBUNE. d S 19 1919+
1919-Je 29 1923 as Rome news
pub 1919+
GAr S 21 1930
GR 1923+
GRC 1922+
GU 1920-O 23 1921

REPUBLICAN sentinel. w 1843-44||?
GSD Mr 23 1844

SOUTHERN and commercial advertiser. w
GU N 4 1858

SOUTHERN argus. w 1893-99||?
GU Jl 20 1899

SOUTHERNER. w 1849-52||?
GU N 14 1850
ICHi O 28 1852
MWA Je 17 1852

SOUTHERNER and commercial. *See* Rome commercial

TRIBUNE of Rome. *See* Rome tribune-herald w

Rome TRIBUNE-HERALD. d 1887-Je 30 1923||
1887-1907 as Rome daily tribune. United with Rome news to form Rome news-tribune
GR Jl 17 1921-23
GRC My 1883-1923
GRN complete
GU Ag 17 1890;Ag 14 1894;My 12 1896

Rome TRIBUNE-HERALD. w 1887-1923||?
1887-1907 as Tribune of Rome
GRC N 8,D 29 1887;Ja 19-Ap 5,19-26,My 31, Je 28,Jl 12,Ag 16-30 1888

Semi-weekly TRUE flag. sw 1860-
NcD D 12 1860

Rome WEEKLY. *See* Rome weekly bulletin

WESTERN Georgian. w Ja 1838-
CtY F 9 1839
GAtCo S 11 1838

ROYSTON

RECORD. w 1905+
pub 1920+

SANDERSVILLE

CENTRAL Georgian. *See* Sandersville herald

Sandersville HERALD. w 1841-1908||
1841-79 as Central Georgian; 1879-99 Herald and Georgian. Merged with Sandersville progress
GAA S 11 1902
GMiG N 10 1852;54-55[58-69]
GSaO 1852-53;55-63;66-70;73-89;91-1903;06-08
GU Ap 27 1852-Ja 1853;O-D 22 1858;69-D 21 1870
MBAt N 16 1864
MWA Je 22 1852
NcD Mr 13 1861;Mr 22 1865;Je 27,Ag 1,15-29,S 12 1866
NcU Ag 25 1881

HERALD and Georgian. *See* Sandersville herald

MERCURY. w 1880-90||?
GSaO 1880-87

MIDDLE Georgia progress. *See* Sandersville progress

Sandersville PROGRESS. w 1887+
1887-99 as Middle Georgia progress
pub current year only
GAA Ap 3 1901
GSaC 1887+
GSaO 1887-94;96-1909;18+
NcD Ap 23 1901

Sandersville TELESCOPE. w
DLC O 27 1843

SANFORD

Sanford JOURNAL. w 1874?-
NcU Ag 23 1883

SAVANNAH

Savannah ABEND zeitung. w 1871-87||?
In German
GHi F 21-S 1872

Savannah daily ADVERTISER. d N 3 1868-75||
Je 1873-74 as Advertiser-republican. Merged with Savannah morning news
DLC Jl 22-Ag 12 S 8 1874-Je 1875
GHi [1868;Je-D 1870]-S 19 1875
MBAt N 29 1865[66]N 3-4,6-21,24-30,D 2,7-8,10,12,16-24,30-31 1868[69]
MWA D 8 1868;Ja 5 1869;O 2-D 1870;Ap 1871-Mr 1872;Ap-Je 29 1873;Ja-Ag 11 1874

Savannah weekly ADVERTISER. w 1872-75||
GHi O 19 1872-[Ja-N 19 1874]
MBAt [1873]-[75]

ARGUS. w My 30 1828-29||?
DLC S 24 1829
GMM 1828-O 1829
MWA My 30,Je 14 1828

COLUMBIAN museum. *See* Savannah museum

Savannah COURIER. d 1852-
GDE S 14,O 26,N 9,25 1852;F 22,Mr 27,Ap 3 1853
NNHi Mr 15,21 1853
WHi N 28 1852

Daily DISPATCH. d 1894-
GSD [Je 12-23 1894]

Savannah weekly ECHO. w 1879-84||
Negro
NNHi Ag 26-D 2 1883;Ja 13-20,F 3-10 1884

Savannah FREE PRESS. tw Ap 17? 1835-
MWA My 6 1835

FREEMAN'S standard. w,d F 15 1868-
w F 15-Ap 2 1868
MBAt Ap 14-15 1868
MWA F 15,Mr 7,Ap 4,9 1868
NNHi F 15-Ap 8 1868

FRIEND of the family. w Mr 1 1849-51||?
GMM 1849-Mr 1 1851

GEORGIA messenger. w 1823?-41||?
GU D 31 1831-41

GEORGIA republican. *See* Savannah daily republican

***Savannah daily GEORGIAN.** tw,d N 25 1818-56||?
Title varies: Georgian; Daily Georgian; Savannah Georgian; Savannah daily Georgian and journal; etc.
tw Je 1-O 19 1819
A My 26-N 24 1821;Jl-D 1854
CSmH Ag 14 1830
CtY Ag 14 1839
DLC O 10,12 1822;My 10,24,S 2,4,O 25,28,N 18,20,24,D 6,10-13,15-16,18-20,22-24,27,30 1823 [Ja-Mr 1824]25-N 10,29,D 1 1828;Jl 6,16,31,S 12,17,19,22,26,29 (O-D 1829)30;Mr 30,Je 18,Jl 24 1831;N 6 1832;33-40(Ja-Ag 1841)N 22 1843; Mr 25,Je 24 1844;Mr 12 1846-Ag 11 1849;N 23 1852;Ap 20 1853-Ap 6,My 10-D 1 1856
GHi 1821-[40]-Je 1854
GSC 1852
GSD Ja 4,Jl 7 1825;33-Ap 1836;O 25 1844
ICHi Ap 2 1834
MBAt My 7 1822;D 6 1827;Ap 3,5 1828;Jl 17 1839
MHi N 6 1821;N 21 1826
MWA N 26 1821-N 23 1822;Mr 29,Je 12,N 15 1823-Ja 1 1833;Jl 22,Ag 5 1834;My 25 1835;N 29 1840;D 20 1841;F 14 1843;F 13 1844;Ap 24, Ag 8 1845;F 1851-Je 1852
NN F 15 1826;Ag 18 1831
NcD F 23 1824
OClWHi D 17 1849

Evening GUN. tw S 19 1840-
DLC O 3,13 1840

HAWKEYE. w 1915-31||
GU Ag 23 1927

Savannah daily HERALD. d Ja 11 1865-
United with Savannah morning news to form Daily news and herald, later Savannah morning news
CtHT Ja 16-19,28,F 23,My 1-6 1865
GHi My 20,Je 2-3,6,10,14-15,17-22,25,Jl 1,Ag 16,S 2,11,O 6,9,11,13,24 1865
GSD F 27 1865
IU [Mr-My 1865]
MBAt [Ap 13-D 1865]Ja 23,Mr 8,21-22 1866
MWA Mr 19,Ap 28,O 11,D 11(supp)28-29 1865; Ja 1,4,20 1866
NBHi Mr 11,Ap 12 1865
NN Ap 29 1865
NNHi Ja 25,F 11,13,Jl 15,D 27 1865
OClWHi Ja 12,16-18,23,28,30,Mr 6,Jl 15 1865
OHi My 31,Ag 1-2,11,15-16,18,S 16 1865
PDoHi [Ja 19-Ap 9 1865]
PHi F 25,27,Ap 21-25 1865
WHi Ap 23 1865

Savannah JOURNAL. w F 14 1872-73||
GD D 28 1872
MWA Ag 1 1872(and extra)
NNHi F 14-21 1872;F 8 1873

Savannah daily JOURNAL and courier. d 1851-
1851-53? as Savannah evening journal
GHi [1852]-N 1853;Jl-D 1855;Ja 8-Je 1865
MWA Je 22 1852

Savannah daily LOYAL Georgian. d D 24-28 1864||
Merged with Savannah republican
CL D 27 1864
DLC D 26 1864
IC D 24 1864
MWA D 28 1864
MiHi D 26 1864
NNHi D 26 1864
OClWHi D 28 1864
P D 28 1864

Savannah MERCANTILE index. 1865?-
MBAt My 12 1866

Savannah MERCURY. tw,d Je? 1828-29||?
tw during summer months
DLC Ag 6,N 18,D 1,3 1828;S 11,21,25,30 1829
MWA Ag 15 1828

***Savannah MUSEUM.** sw,tw,d Mr 4 1796-O 3 1822||?
1796-Ja 1817 as Columbian museum and Savannah advertiser; F 3 1817-21? Columbian museum and Savannah advertiser; etc.
GHi [Ja-O 3 1822]
GU Je 23 1821
MWA [Ja-O 3 1822]

Savannah NATIONAL republican. *See* Savannah republican

Savannah morning NEWS. d Ja 15 1850+
Title varies: Daily morning news; Daily news and herald; Morning daily news; etc.
pub 1850+
CtHT N 9-10 1864
DLC Ja-Je,Ag 22,S 3 1862;Ag 14 1863;F 15, Mr 17-18,29,N 9 1864;70;Ja 12 1876+
GAA O 31 1929
GHi F-Je 1851;Ja-Jl 1852[61-63]Je 22,25,27-30, Jl 2 1866;Mr 7 1867;Ag 1870-1911
GS 1919+
GSC 1876-Je 1901;O 1910-16
GSD Ag 9,13,N 27 1861;Mr 21 1891;Ag 28 1892; O 3 1897;Jl 27 1902;F 26 1905
GU My 30 1861;D 13 1870;Ap 10,24,My 15,18, 22,Ag 27 1872;My 13,15,19,Je 23 1873;Ja 12 1877
GVCu Je 23 1862
ICM Je 27 1903
IU D 24 1853;F 18 1854
M [Jl-D 1930]
MBAt Ja 5,25 1861;Ap 21,24 1862[F 1863-N 1864]Ap 2,18,24,Je 7,S 4,15,24-25,N 8,D 14 1866;Ja 26,Mr 5-6,Ap 30 1867
MWA Jl 8 1852;Ap 24,D 9 1856;Je 2-3 1857; Ja 17,Jl 7,S 6,11,18,25-27,O 11,13,23-31,D 8 1862;Mr 21 1867;Je 13,O 20,22,N 12,18,20,24, 26,D 1-15 1868;Ag 7 1871 Mr 29 1872;F 14 1883;Je 29,Jl 25 1886;F 13 1889
N Ap 20 1870
NN Je 5 1862;F 13 1883
NNHi S 28,D 18 1860;Ja 29[N 19 1861-Mr 7 1862]Je 10 1863;N 5,23 1864 Je 13 1873
NcD N 16 1860;S 30 1863;Jl 29 1868;O 31 1870; D 25 1878;Je 12,Jl 1,14 1879;F 14 1883;S 7 1886;Ja 24 1889;D 9 1891;F 15 1893;My 5 1895;N 11,D 3 1918
NcU Jl 26 1875;Jl 28 1881;Je 27 1916
NjWdHi Ap 25 1860
OClWHi Ap 23,Jl 4,D 8 1862;Ag 27 1877;My 7 1885;Je 3 1905
OOxM Ap 20-21 1880
P-M Je 21 1862;Ja 18 1863
T Ja 18 1930
TJT O 1902
V Jl 16,18-19,21-23,25 1864
VRC Ja 17,Jl 24 1862

Savannah weekly NEWS. w 1850-1920||
FU Ja 14-F 18,Mr 11-Ap 22 1882
GAA O 17 1888
GColS 1872-75;78-85[90-98]
GHi My 31 1862
MB Mr 1876-Je 1877
NcD O 4 1879;Mr 1,Ap 26,Jl 19 1890;S 17 1893
NcU Jl 30 1881
TJT Ja 10 1898
MWA Mr 29 1873;F 17 1883,Jl 10,24,1886

OBSERVER. sw 1907-08||?
GSD Ap 25 1908

Savannah evening PRESS. d N 19 1891+
1891-1930 as Savannah press
pub 1891 Ap 15-N 18 1892;My 19-N 20 1893; Je 1894-1902;Jl 1903+
GSC Jl 1901-S 1903;04-Mr,Jl 1907-10;17-S 1920; 21+
GSD Je 19 1905
GU Ap 23 1933
NcD D 1891;Mr 31 1900;N 11(extra)12,14 1918
NcU Ja 19 1915

REASON. w Ap 23 1898-
GSD Ap-Jl 11 1898

Savannah daily evening RECORDER. d 1878-83||?
GHi 1879-Ag 16 1880

***Savannah REPUBLICAN.** w,sw,tw,d Ag 21 1802-My 31 1873||
1802-05 as Georgia republican and state intelligencer; 1806-Mr 7? 1807 Georgia republican; Mr 10 1807-Je 15? 1816 Republican and Savannah evening ledger; Je 18 1816-73 Savannah republican; Daily Savannah republican; Savannah national republican; etc. United with Savannah daily advertiser to form Advertiser-republican, later Savannah daily advertiser
w Ag-O 16 1802, sw O 23 1802-O 10? 1817; tw Jl 8-O 16 1819
A 1850-52 Jl-D 1865
CL Ja 6 1865
CSmH D 26 1829;Ag 30 1853;extra 1865
Ct [1826;33;35-37]
CtHT N 9-10 1864;Ja 28,F 22 1865
CtSp Mr 16 1833
CtY Mr 4 1847;Ag 20 1851
DLC Jl 3 1821-My 12,Jl 2-D 18 1860;Jl 1861-Je 28,O 20,N 21 1862;63-S,D 29 1864-65;Jl 2 1866-72
GHi [1825;40]41;Ag-Jl 17 1847;F 1851-Je 1852; D 27,29,31 1860[61-65]Ag 3 1870-Ja 1,My 31 1873
GSD N 21 1838;My 18,Ag 19-20 S 28,O 28,N 1, 20,D 31 1861;Ja 13,My 2 1862;Mr 13,Ap 10,Je 27,Jl 19,S 9,27,O 16,N 5,D 7-8,20 1863;Ja 16, Mr 7,15 Je 24,Jl 14,22,26,Ag 3,5,8,18,S 4,8-9, O 3,9,12,17,N 1-2,6-7,9 1864;Ja 3 1865;Ag 28 1869
GU [1821]-[30-31]-33
ICHi Ja 18,F 5,Ap 18,O 26 1865
IP Ap 16 1865
IU Ja 7,F 18 1854
KHi Je 29 1861
MB Ja 3-Ap 26 1865;F 2 1867;D 1 1870
MBAt My 7 1822;Ja 14,22,O 10 1861[62-69] My 27 1871
MDeHi Je 5 1865
MHi Je 13 1821;D 11 1823;N 7,18 1824;Mr 4, My 25 1825;F 13 1844;F 16 1846[64-67]
MSaE Je 23 1868

GEORGIA (*Continued*)

SAVANNAH—*Continued*

Savannah REPUBLICAN. w,sw,tw,d 1802-73‖
—*Continued*
MWA Ag 8 1822;O 16,D 7,21,23 1824;D 19 1827;My 23 1835;D 4 1840;Ja 4-7,12,17 1843; Je 24 1844;Ap 1,17,Ag 7 1845[Ag-D 1849]N 27 1852;My 13,S 10 1861[Mr-My,O,D 1862-63] F 15,D 29-31 1864;Ja 5,F 27,Ap 6,11-12,17,27, My 16(extra),Jl 3,Ag 24,N 11,D 27(supp)-30 1865;Ja 1-6,10-11,F 26,Jl 13 1866-67;Ja 2-28, Jl 20,D 13 1868;F 16,Mr 28 1872
MnHi Je 3 1865
N N 8 1824;Mr 11 1826;O 14 1833
NN Je 5,11,19 1862;Mr 25,27 1863;Jl 10 1864; F 11,Mr 3,My 17 1865
NNHi [Jl 1861-Ap 1862;F,Ag 1863-Ag,O 1864-Ap,Je,S 1865-Mr 1867]Ja 26 1870
NbHi S 11,14 1863
NcD Je 20 1848;Ag 12 1863;Je 16,Ag 4 1864; Ja 9 1865;F 26 1870
NjP [1860-65]
OClWHi Je 5 1834;O 5 1861;Mr 27,Ag 11,17-18 1863;Mr 15-Je 28,Ag 6-29,O 12-20 1864;Ja 18,23,26,28,F 5,Ap 25,Jl 28 1865;Ja 30-F 12 1870
OHi Jl 27,31,Ag 16,18 1865
P Mr 31 1863
PHi Ap 23,25,My 13 1865
PPL N 4 1850
WHi Mr 11 1825;Ap 1 1845;Mr 16,20,Ap 21-22 1864;Ap 24 1865

Weekly Savannah REPUBLICAN. w 1854-73‖
DLC Ja 24,F 7-21,Mr-Je 6,27 1863
MBAt Ja-Mr 6,20-Je 19,Jl 3-10,24-S 11,25 1869-[73]
MWA S 8 1861
NcD Jl 25 1863
OCHi Ap 23-Jl 25 1863
OClWHi S 21-O 26 1867;Ja 11-Mr 28 1868
PHi Jl 25 1863
VRC Jl 3 1862

Savannah REPUBLICAN. tw D 26? 1864-
CaOTA Ja 6 1865
NBHi D 30 1864;F 26-Ap 12 1865
NUHi Ap 3 1865
NjR Ja 16 1865
ODW Ja 2 1865

Savannah REPUBLICAN prices current. w 1841-
MHi [1860-61]
MWA O 28,N 18,D 2,16-23 1842;Ja 27-F 3,24, Ap 14,Jl 14-28,Ag 25,S 22-O 20,N 17,D 1,15-22 1843;Je 28,Ag 2,31,N 23,D 29 1844-Ja 3,17, Mr 7,Ap 25,My 16,Ag 1,S 1,12,26,N 28 1845;Ja 9,S 1,18-25 1846;Ja 14,O 1,22-29,N 19,D 10-18,31 1847;Ja 10,28,F 11,25,Mr 17,Ap 7,26,My 31,Je 7,S 1,O 18-N 1,22,D 13 1848;Ja 31-F 14,Je 27 1849;Ja 16,Mr 20,My 22,Jl 31,N 20-27 1850;Ap 11,Je 6,O 10,D 5 1851;Mr 5 1852;O 21-28 1853

REPUBLICAN standard. sw Ag? 1868-
MBAt Ag 29 1868

SEARCHLIGHT. w Ap 28 1906-
GSD Ap-Je 9 1906

Savannah SHIPPING and commercial list. w 1834?-
MHi O 1 1836
MWA O 11,N 22,D 13,20 1839,Ja 3,24,F 7,21, Mr 20,Ap 10,O 9,1840,O 16,1841

SUN. d O 16 1843-
DLC O 18 1843

Sunday morning TELEGRAM. w
GHi Je 25 1882
MWA S 2 1883
NcD Mr 16 1879
NcU My 29 1881

Daily TELEGRAPH. d
DLC My 20,S 28 1840

TIMES. w,sw Je 18 1823-
GSD Jl 2,16 1823
MWA Jl 23 1823;Ja 28 1824

Savannah daily TIMES. d 1882-90‖?
GSD D 24 1884-My 1885

Savannah TRIBUNE. 1875+
Suspended 1878?-85
Negro
pub 1886+

TRUTH. w My 27 1917-19‖?
GSD My 27 1917

SOPERTON

Soperton NEWS. w 1914+
DLC Mr 31 1933
G Mr 31 1933

SPARKS

BERRIEN county pioneer. *See* Tifton gazette (Tifton)

SPARTA

GEORGIA reporter and Christian gazette. w Ap 3-O 2 1826‖?
GSD My 8-O 2 1826
GU Ap 10-O 1826

HANCOCK weekly journal. w 1868-70‖
GMiG [Je 1869-O 13 1870]

Sparta ISHMAELITE. w Mr 12 1878+
Follows Sparta times and planter. Title varies slightly
pub 1878+
GMiG [1878]83-[85;89]

STANDARD of union. w Ja 12 1833-
KHi My 4 1833

Sparta TIMES and planter. w 1869-77‖
Followed by Sparta Ishmaelite
GMiG [1874;77]

STATESBORO

BULLOCH county banner. w 1884-94‖
1884-91 as Statesboro eagle
GStO F 28,Ap 18,My 23,Ag 22 1889;Ja 2,27,O 2,D 18 1890-Ja 5,Mr 19 1891;Mr 2,30 1893;Mr 8 1894

BULLOCH herald. w 1899-1900‖?
GStO S 28,D 8 1899

BULLOCH times and news. w Jl 1892+
1892-Ja 1917 as Bulloch times; F-D 1917 Bulloch times and Statesboro news
pub Mr 23 1905+
CStO [1893-98]1913[14-15]-[17;19;24-26]+

Statesboro EAGLE. *See* Bulloch county banner

Statesboro NEWS. sw Mr 1901-Ja 1917‖
United with Bulloch times to form Bulloch times and Statesboro news, later Bulloch times and news
GStB complete
GStO Je 12 1908

Statesboro STAR. w 1893-1900‖?
GStO Mr 30 1894

SUMMERVILLE

Summerville GAZETTE. w 1874-89‖?
GAA Je 9 1881

SYCAMORE

IRWIN county news. w 1890-97‖
GOC F 24 1893-Ap 1897

SYLVANIA

Sylvania TELEPHONE. w 1879+
GColS [1879-81]
NcD D 2 1886;Mr 1,15 1888

TALBOTTON

GEORGIA register and standard. w 1877-83‖?
1877-81 as Georgia standard
NcU Ag 9 1881

Talbotton STANDARD. w 1869-80‖?
United with Georgia register to form Georgia register and standard

TALLAPOOSA

Tallapoosa JOURNAL. w Ja 1 1886+
pub 1886+

TENNILLE

Tennille NEWS. sw 1899-1903‖
NcD Mr 12 1902

THOMASTON

BACKWOODSMAN and Upson yeoman.
ScGK Jl 30 1834

GEORGIA herald. *See* Thomaston herald

Thomaston HERALD. w 1869-78‖?
1869-70? as Georgia herald
MWA O 22 1870

HICKORY nut and Upson vigil. w Ap 17? 1833-34‖?
N O 2 1833
ScGK Mr 5,19 1834

Thomaston TIMES. w N 1858+
1858-91 as Upson county pilot (Title varies slightly)
pub 1930+
GAA F 1 1929
GTC 1858+
NNHi Ap 28 1860;My 11,D 7 1861

THOMASVILLE

GEORGIA watchman. *See* Wiregrass reporter

SOUTHERN enterprise. w Je 12 1855-88‖
United with Thomasville times to form Times-enterprise (w)
CSmH [Ap 1860-D 20 1866]

TIMES-enterprise. sw,w 1873+
1873-88 as Thomasville times
MWA S 18 1880

Thomasville TIMES-enterprise. d My 1889+
IU Je 4 1889

WIREGRASS reporter. w 1831?-59‖?
1831?-S 8 1857 as Georgia watchman
GDE F 2 1859(supp)

THOMSON

Thomson ADVERTISER. w 1866-74‖?
NcD Ja 1,30,F 27,O 9,D 1,18 1869;Ja 22,Ap 30,O 15 1870;F 11,Mr 27 1871

COLUMBIAN sentinel. w 1882-1924‖?
1882-1918 pub in Harlem
GU S 26,O 31 1919;Ap 5-12,My-Je 21,S 20,N 1,D 27 1920;Ap 4 1921;S 11,O 2,23 1922;F 19,Jl 23 1923;Ja 14 1924
NcD Mr 1 1906[20-23]
T Ap 25 1921

Semi-weekly ENTERPRISE. w,sw 1893-1900‖
1893-My 18? 1899 as McDuffie enterprise w 1893-My 18? 1899
NcD F 2,Ap 20,Je 1,Ag 31,S 21-28 1893[94]D 19 1895;Ja 23 1896[97]Ja 6-13,Ap 14,O 27,N 17 1898[99]Ja 30,F 23 1900

Thomson GUARD. w 1914-17‖?
NcD S 20 1917

JEFFERSONIAN. w N 1906-17‖?
1906-Mr 28 1907 as Weekly Jeffersonian; Ap 4-N 28 1907 Watson's weekly Jeffersonian
1906-07 pub in Augusta; 1908-10 in Atlanta
DLC 1909-14
G S 1915-Jl 23 1917
GU N 28 1912;Jl 23,Ag 13-20,D 17 1914;Ag 19 1915;O 5 1916
KHi My 27 1915
NN Mr 14-28 1907;S 12,26-D 19 1908;09-Ja 4 1912
NcD [1906-17]

McDUFFIE enterprise. *See* Semi-weekly enterprise

McDUFFIE weekly journal. w 1871-1909‖?
GAtCo [Ja 17 1877-S 1878]D 1-8,22 1880;Ap ? 1881;Ja-Mr,My 17-Je 7,26,Jl 12,26 1882
NcD Ja 1 1871[72]-[75-76]F 7,Mr 14,Je 27,Ag 29-S 5 1877[78-81]Mr 29,Ag 9,S 20 1882[83-85]Je 8,S 7,N 30 1887;F 22,N 2-23 1888;Mr 21 1890;My 13,Jl 29,O 7 1892;Je 2,S 15,29-O 6,27 1893;Ap 27,D 7 1894;Je 12,Jl 10 1897;Jl 11,Ap 15-22,S 12,O 21,N 7-14 1898;S 12,N 7 1899;Ja 2,Mr 23,Ap 6,Jl 6,N 30-D 7 1900;Ja 4 1901;S 13,N 15 1902
OHi O 16 1872-D 18 1874

McDUFFIE progress. w 1901+
GThC 1909+
NcD Ja 3,F 2,N 28 1902;Mr 13,D 25 1903;Ag 24 1906;Jl 29 1921

PROGRESSIVE democrat. w 1911-12‖?
NcD O 14,28 1911;F 3 1912

WATCHMAN. w 1903-
NcD Mr 20 1903

TIFTON

Tifton GAZETTE. w 1889+
1889-90? as Berrien county pioneer (Sparks)
pub Ja 22 1892+

Tifton daily GAZETTE. d S 14 1914+
pub 1914+

TOCCOA

Toccoa RECORD. w 1891+
1891-1900? as Southern record
GToC F 1906+
GToP Ag 29 1929[31-32]+

SOUTHERN record. *See* Toccoa record

TRENTON

DADE county sentinel. *See* Dade county times

DADE county times. w 1901+
1901-08 as Dade county sentinel
pub 1928+
GTrC 1926+

TURNWOLD

COUNTRYMAN. w Mr 4 1862-66‖?
GAtCo S 29-O 13,N-D 15 1862
GU S 29-O 13,N,D 18 1862;Jl 7 1863;My 3-10, Je 7,S 13 1864;Ja 3-10,31-F 7,28-Mr 7 1865
GVG S 29-O 13,N-D 15 1862
MBAt Ag 18 1863;F 6,20-Mr 13 1866
NNC [1862-Ap 10 1866]photostat
NcD S 29 1862-[63]My 24-Je 14,Ag 16-23 1864; Ja 10,Ap 4 1865
OClWHi Ja 12 1864-Mr 21 1865

UNION CITY

CAMPBELL-Fulton merger news.
GAA D 18 1930;Ja 29 1931

VALDOSTA

SOUTH Georgia times. *See* Valdosta times

Valdosta TIMES. w 1867+
1867-74? as South Georgia times
pub 1876+
GAA N 11 1928
GVC 1885+

Valdosta daily TIMES. d 1905+
pub 1905+

VILLA RICA

Villa Rica BREEZE. w Ja 1926+
pub 1926+

WALKINSVILLE

OCONEE enterprise. w 1887+
pub 1925+
GWaC 1925+

WARRENTON

Warrenton CLIPPER. w 1852?+
1852?-75? as Georgia clipper
NNHi F 10 1869;My 15 1873
NcD Je 9 1899

GEORGIA clipper. *See* Warrenton clipper

RURAL cabinet. w My 31 1828-
GMM 1828-Je 26 1830

GEORGIA (*Continued*)

WASHINGTON

Washington CHRONICLE. w 1885-1905||
United with Washington gazette to form Washington gazette-chronicle
GSD N 18 1895
NcD S 21 1886;Ag 7,O 16,D 11,25 1889;Mr 26 1890;Je 29,S 14 1891;Je 4 1900

Washington GAZETTE. w 1849-
MWA Je 28 1852

Washington GAZETTE. 1866-1905 *See* Washington gazette-chronicle

Washington GAZETTE-CHRONICLE. w Ap 27 1866-1912||?
1866-1905 as Washington gazette
GSD S 3,N 18 1869
GU Ag 14 1874
MBAt Jl 6 1866
NcD [My 25 1866-80;82-85]My 11-18 1887;Mr 8,Ap 5,20 1888;N 23,D 7,21 1889;N 23,D 7,21 1889[90]My 2-8,S 18 1891;Ja 29 1892;Mr 30-Ap 6,20,Jl 6-20 1907
OHi Ap 4,D 12 1873;Mr 2 1877

Washington INDEPENDENT. w 1854?-
MWA Ap 5 1861
NcD D 20 1861

INDEPENDENT press. w Jl 22 1840-
DLC Jl 22 1840
NcD Ag 12 1840

*NEWS and planters' gazette. w Ja 19 1816-44||?
1816-Je 1840? as Washington news
CSmH Ag 24 1830
DLC O 1 1840
GA Jl 23 1840-Ag 17,S 14 1843-O 17,D 5 1844
GSD Mr 29 1838
GU Ja 4 1822;Je 26 1823[24]Ja 1,Je 23,Ag 26,D 24 1825;D 20 1827;Mr 27 1828;Ja 27,Mr 10,My 19,O 30 1829;F 26 1831;S 19 1832;Ap 25 1833;D 25 1834;F 5,Je 18 1835
MHi D 7 1821
NN D 1 1829
NNHi Je 15 1821
NcD [1830-31]Ap 9 1840;Jl 11 1844
NcU My 7-14,Je 4,18 1840

Washington NEWS-REPORTER. w 1895+
GAr O 25 1929
OClWHi F 25 1927

SOUTHERN spy. w S 6 1834-
DLC S 13 1834

WILKES county forum. w 1922+
GU Ja 29 1924

WILKES republican. w
NcD Je 19,Jl 3 1857

WAYCROSS

Waycross evening HERALD. d 1892-1913||
United with Waycross journal to form Waycross journal-herald

Waycross JOURNAL-herald. w 1895+
1895-1913 as Waycross journal
pub 1901+
GAA 1933

Waycross JOURNAL-herald. d 1897+
1897-1913 as Waycross journal
pub 1901+

WAYNESBORO

Waynesboro EXPOSITOR. w 1870-80||?
GColS [1874-75]

INDEPENDENT south. w Mr? 1860-
OClWHi N 14 1860

Waynesboro NEWS.
NNHi Ag 27 1861

TRUE citizen. w 1881+
GAA D 6 1890

WEST BOWERSVILLE

AMERICAN union. *See* Union (Canon)

West Bowersville REGISTER. *See* Franklin county register (Carnesville)

WEST POINT

West Point ADVOCATE. w 1851-
DLC O 28 1852
MWA Je 17,N 25 1852

GEORGIA Jeffersonian. w S 4 1839-40||?
DLC S 4,O 9 1839
NcD Mr 18,Jl 8 1840

West Point NEWS. w 1897+
pub 1921+

West Point SHIELD. w 1869-70||
MWA N 11 1870

SOUTHERN alliance. w 1888||?
NcD O 26 1888

WILLACOOCHEE

SUN-TIMES. w 1919+
1919-31 as Willacoochee times

TIMES. *See* Sun-times

WINDER

Winder NEWS. w Ap 1893+
pub Ap 1919+
GAA Ap 11 1929

WRIGHTSVILLE

Wrightsville HEADLIGHT. w 1880+
pub 1880+

ZEBULON

PIKE county journal. w 1888+
1903-22 as Pike county times-journal

PIKE county times-journal. *See* Pike county journal

HAWAII

HILO

HAWAII herald. w 1896-1922||?
United with Hilo tribune to form Hilo tribune-herald
DLC 1902-05
HHi 1903-05
MWA D 29 1898

Ka HOKU o Hawaii. Star of Hawaii. w 1906+
In Hawaiian
HB [1906-29]
HHi Ap 19 1909-18

Ke OLA O Hawaii. w 1915-19||
In Hawaiian
HB D 28 1916-F 21,Mr 14 1918-F 13 1919

STAR of Hawaii. *See* Ka Hoku o Hawaii

Hilo TRIBUNE-HERALD. w 1895+
1895-1922? as Hilo tribune
DLC 1903-05
HHi 1896-1905
NN N 1904-O 1905;O 27 1908-O 18 1910

HONOLULU

Honolulu ADVERTISER. d My 1 1882+
1882-Mr 30 1921 as Pacific commercial advertiser Jl 2 1906 is Fiftieth anniversary number 1856/1906
C D 1918;O 15 1919+
CSt Ap 1,3-5,N 25,D 28 1893;Ja 27,29-30,F 2,6,Mr 9,14,15,23 1894;Ja 10,S 6 1895
CU-B Jl 12,17,19,Ag 14,23-25,27-28,30-S 1,20,24-25 1909
CtW My 27 1893
DLC My 25-Je 2 1893;N 1901+
H 1882+
HB [Mr,Je,Ag 1884;85-86;89;91-92]-Je 1894[95-96;98;1902-03]Jl 2 1906
HH 1882-85;88+
ICHi Je 28 1898
KHi Jl 20 1894;Je 28,S 1,3 1898;D 16 1904
MWA Jl 27 1888;Ag 2 1889 Ja 18,F 1 1893;Mr 26,Ap 26 1894;Jl 10 1896;Ja 28,F 10 1897;Ag 13 1898;Ja 3,Jl 4 1903;Jl 2 1906;Mr 16,D 14 1907;Mr 12 1922
MiU [1883-88]-[92]-[94]-98[1902]-Je 1905
N Ap 2 1885
NbHi Jl 13 1898
P O 1898-Ja 1913
WHi N 19 1892;Ap 24 1893;Mr 4,6,Ap 30,Je 8-10 1919;Ap 5 1936
—w ed *See* Pacific commercial advertiser

Ka ALAKAI o Hawaii. w
In Hawaiian
HB Ag 31-S 12,O 22 1887;Ja 7,Mr 29,Ap 30,Ag 2,10 1888

Ke ALAKAI o Hawaii. w 1914+
In Hawaiian
HB [F 12-O 8 1919]Ja 28,Ap 7,21-28,My 12-26,O 6 1920;S 6,My 17 1928;Ja 31-My 23,Je-Jl 4,Ag 22 1929;My 8-22,Je 12,Jl 3,17 1930[31]D 8 1932;Ap 20 1933

Ke ALOHA Aina. Love of country. w,d My 25 1895-1922||?
d 1897?-99?
In Hawaiian
H 1897-1907
HB 1895-F 1,15 1896-[97-99;1901-20]
HHi Ag 7 1909-Je 6 1912

Ke ALOHA Aina, Ka Nupepa Puka La. d
In Hawaiian
HB S 30 1893-Je 1894

Ka ALOHA Aina Oiaio. w 1896-
In Hawaiian
HB [1896]

Weekly ARGUS. w Ja 14 1852-S 18 1853||
Followed by New era and weekly argus
DLC Jl 20 1853
HB [1852]53
HHi Ja 14-Jl 21 1852;My 4 1853
MWA Mr 24-Je 16,Jl 7-21 1852

Ka AU Hou: Ke Kilohana o Hawaii. w 1910-
In Hawaiian
HB [1910]-F 1912

Ke AU Okoa. w Ap 1865-
HB 1865-Mr 1873
MWA D 31 1866;Ja 21 1867;D 22 1870

AUSTIN'S Hawaiian weekly. w Je 17 1899-
HB Je 24 1899

BENNETT'S own. w S 15 1869-S 6 1870||
Merged with Hawaiian times
H complete
HHi complete

Evening BULLETIN. d F 1 1882-Je 30 1912||
1882-My 16 1895 as Daily bulletin. United with Hawaiian star to form Honolulu star-bulletin
CPc [1886;91;93]
CSt N 24 1893;Ja 27,29,31 1894
DLC My 23-Je 2 1893;Mr 1904-Ap 1907
H 1882-Ja 1885;86-Mr 1910
HB 1882-Je 1893
HH 1882-My 15,Jl 1895-1912
KHi S-N 5 1898
MWA F 11 1886;Ag 2 1889;F 9 1897;F 9 1904
WHi F 1911(special ed);F 12(supp)1912

Weekly BULLETIN. w Ja 6 1891-
CPc [1891-93]

COMMERCIAL advertiser. sw 1872-
HB [S 1872-Ja 1873]

CONVENTION. d Jl 14-Ag 31 1864||
In English and Hawaiian
HB complete
HHi complete
ICN Jl 14 1864
MWA Ag 13,17-18,23 1864
NN Jl 27 1864

DEMOCRAT. d O 25 1910-
DLC O 25-N 8 1910

Ka ELELE E. w 1846?-
HB My 17-Ag 22 1855

Ka ELELE Hawaii. Hawaiian messenger. ir,sm Ap 1845-
In Hawaiian
DLC [S 14 1849-D 21 1855]
HB 1845-[50-55]
HHi [1845-46;53-54]
M Ap 1,My 6 1845

Ka HAE Hawaii. Hawaiian flag. w Mr 5 1856-D 25 1861||
In Hawaiian
DLC 1856-Mr 24,Ap 14,28,My 12,26-Je 9 1858
H Mr 1857-61
HB [1856-60]
MH [1856]
MiU 1856-58

Kuu HAE Hawaii. My Hawaiian flag.
In Hawaiian
HB Ap 19-Jl 4 1913

HAWAII Hochi. d 1912+
In Japanese and English
PP N 27 1930;31+

HAWAII Holomua. Hawaii progress. w 1892-94||
In Hawaiian
CPo [1892-93]
CSt N 24,D 19-20,22-27 1893;Ja 23 1894
DLC Jl 9-10 1894
HB D 10 1892-Je 30 1894
MWA D 28 1892

HAWAII Holomua. 1912-14 *See* Ka Holomua

HAWAII pae Aina. w Ja 1878-
CU-B F 24 1883
HB [1878-91]
MWA S 11 1880;Je 2 1883

HAWAII Ponoi. w 1873-
In Hawaiian
HB Je 1873-Je 1874

HAWAII progress. *See* Hawaii Holomua

HAWAII shinpo. d 1890-1930||?
In Japanese and English
KHi S 11 1911
WHi Mr 28 1909

HAWAIIAN. w Ja 15 1852-
HHi Ja 15-N 15 1852

Daily HAWAIIAN. d My 1 1884-Mr 2 1885||
HB complete
HHi complete

HAWAIIAN. w Ja? 1898-
HB My-N 1898

HAWAIIAN Chinese news. w
In Chinese and English
CCIP 1926-27
WHi My 12,Je 2 1883

HAWAIIAN flag. *See* Ka Hae Hawaii

HAWAIIAN gazette. w,sw Ja 21 1865-N 29 1918||
w 1865-93
C Ag 1901-03;Je 1904-18
CPo [1887]91-[93]
CSt Ja 8 1895
DLC Ja 20 1866-75;F 3 1891;F 1895-1906
H 1865-1913;15-16
HB 1865-96;Jl 1897-1906;08-09
HHi 1865-98
KHi Ag 26 1898-Mr 22 1912
MWA N 4 1865;N 30,D 28 1870[71]-F 21 1872;Jl 5 1876;Ag 22 1877;S 4-25 1878[Je 11 1879-N 10 1880]F 2 1881;F 1-8[S-D 1887]-Ap 10 1896;N 13 1900;D 24 1902-[03]-Ap 15 1904
MiU [1865]-76;82
MnHi Ja 20-F 24 1891
NFre Ap 13 1917
NN Ja 14(supp)1880;Ja 18 1893
OHi S 26 1877;Jl 30 1879;Ja 19,O 5,12 1881;Ag 26 1882
P Jl 1898-1913

HAWAII (*Continued*)

HONOLULU—*Continued*

HAWAIIAN gazette. w,sw 1865-1918||—*Cont.*
PPCHi Jl 5 1895
PPot Ja 23,F 2 1894
WHi N 29 1892;Mr 28 1893
WaPS [1916]

HAWAIIAN gazette. d Ag 3 1887-My 26 1888||
H complete

HAWAIIAN government gazette. Kukala Pili Aupuni. w F 1887-
In Hawaiian and English
HB F-Je 1887

Daily HAWAIIAN herald. d S 4-D 21 1866||
H complete
HB complete
HHi complete

HAWAIIAN news. *See* Ka Nuhou Hawaii

HAWAIIAN observer. *See* Ka Puuhonua

HAWAIIAN star. w 1893-98||
HB Mr 28 1893-Je 1894;O 12 1897;My 13 1898
MWA Ja 25,F 6,Mr 1 1897

HAWAIIAN star. d Mr 28 1893-Jl 1 1912||
United with Evening bulletin to form Honolulu star-bulletin
CPo Mr 28,My 8-9 1893
CSt Ap 1,3,My 9-11,15-17,23-24,Je 9,Jl 20-21, 26,N 15,24,D 18-19,22 1893;Ja 8,23,F 6-7 1894; Ja 31 1895
DLC My 24-25,27,29-Je 2 1893;Ap 3-D 1902;D 7-8,10-11,17-18 1906
H Ap-N 1893;Ap 1894-95;Jl 1896-Mr,Jl-D 1903
HH complete
MiU Ja-Je 1895

HAWAIIAN star. sw *See* Honolulu star-bulletin

HAWAIIAN times. sw S 13-D 13 1870||
H complete
HHi S 30-D 1870

Daily HERALD. d S 1 1886-Jl 30 1887||
HB complete
MWA Ja 26 1887

Ka HOKU Loa. Morning star. m Jl 1859-D 1864||?
In Hawaiian
DLC S 1859-Je 1862
HB Jl,S,N-D 1859;Mr 1860-[63]
MH [1859]64
MiU [1859]-62

Ka HOKU Loa o Hawaii.
In Hawaiian
HB [Je 2 1856]

HOKU o ka Pakipika. Star of the Pacific. w S 26 1861-
In Hawaiian
HHi [1861-My 14 1863]

Ka HOKU o ke Kai. Star of the sea. m Ja 1883-84||
In Hawaiian
HB Ag-S 1883;Ja,Mr-Ap 1884
HHi Ja-Mr,Je 1883-84

Ka HOLOMUA. The progressive. w Mr 1912-19||?
1912-14? as Hawaii Holomua. Hawaii progressive
In Hawaiian
HB 1912[15;19]

HOME Rula Repubalika. Home rule republican. N 2 1901-12||?
In Hawaiian and English
HB 1901-Mr 15 1902

INDEPENDENT. w 1861-1911 *See* Ka Nupepa Kuokoa

INDEPENDENT. d My 1 1895-O 31 1905||
DLC D 17-30 1896;Ja 2,4-5,7 1897
H 1895-Je 1904
HB 1895-Je 1897
KHi N 4 1898

INDEPENDENT home rule. *See* Kuokoa home rula

ISLANDER. w Mr 5-O 29 1875||
CU-B complete
DLC [1875]
H complete
HHi complete
ICN complete
MB complete
MH complete
MiU complete
NN complete
OO [1875]

Ke KOO O Hawaii. sm Ag 1883-
In Hawaiian
HB Ag-O 1883

KUKALA Pili Aupuni. *See* Hawaiian government gazette

Ke KUMU Hawaii. ir N 12 1834-
In Hawaiian
DLC 1834-My 22 1839
WHi N 26 1834

KUOKOA home rula. Independent home rule. w 1902-12||
In Hawaiian
HB [1907-11]
HHi Ja 10 1908-12

Ka LAHUI Hawaii. w Ja 1875-
In Hawaiian
HB 1875-77

Ka LAHUI Hawaii. d Ja 1899-1904||?
In Hawaiian
HB [1899;1901-02]

Ka LANIKILA. Liberty. w Jl 1909-
In Hawaiian
HB [Jl-S 1909]

Ka LEI Momi. d Je 1893-
In Hawaiian
HB Je-S 1893

Ka LEI Momi. w Ag 1893-
In Hawaiian
HB Ag-D 1893

Ka LEI Rose o Hawaii. sm
In Hawaiian
HB [1898]

Ka LEO O Ka Lahui. Voice of the Nation. d 1889-
In Hawaiian and English
CPo [1891-92]
DLC N 28-D 2,5-8,12-16,19-23,27-30 1892;Ja 3-6,9-10 1893
H [Ja-Je,S 1892-Ja 1893]D 17-19 1894
HB Jl 1893-Je 1894
MiU N 19 1894

LIBERTY. *See* Ka Lanikila

Na LIMA Hana. Working hands. m Ap 1883-
In Hawaiian
HB 1883-Ja 1884

Ka LOEA Kalaiaina. w O 1897-1901||?
In Hawaiian
HB [1897-1900]

LOVE of country. *See* Ke Aloha Aina

O LUSO. w 1885-1921||?
In Portuguese
HHi Ag 15 1885-86;Mr 5 1910-17

Ka MAKAAINANA. w Ja 1894-99||
In Hawaiian
HB [1894-97]
KHi O 31 1898

Ka MANAWA. w N 1870-
In Hawaiian
HB 1870

Ka MOMI O Hawaii. w Ja 1913-
In Hawaiian
HB Ja-Ap 1913

MY Hawaiian flag. *See* Kuu Hae Hawaii

Ka NA'I Aupuni. d N 1905-
In Hawaiian
HB 1905-S 1906

NEW ERA and weekly argus. w O 22 1853-Je 28 1855||
Follows Weekly argus
DLC Jl 27-Ag,O 26,N 2,23 1854
HB complete
MSaE F 16 1854
MWA 1853-S 7,N 2 1854;Ap 19-My 3 1855

NEW FREEDOM. w 1913+
WHi Mr 12,19 1914

NEWS. *See* Ka Nu Hou

Ka NONANONA. (The ant) w Jl 6 1841-45||
In Hawaiian
HHi 1841-Mr 18 1845
M F-Mr 4 1845
MH [1841-45]

Ka NU Hou. The news. w?
In Hawaiian
HB Ap 26 1854

NUHOU. 1873 *See* Ka Nuhou Hawaii

Ka NUHOU Hawaii. sw,w F 25 1873-Ap 28 1874||
F-O 24 1873 as Nuhou. Hawaiian news(sw)
In Hawaiian and English
CU-B F 28 1873-Ap 7 1874
HB complete
HHi complete

Ka NUPEPA Elele. w?
In Hawaiian
HB [1887;89]

Ka NUPEPA Elele Poakolu. w Ag? 1880-
In Hawaiian
HB S 1880;83;Ap 1885

NUPEPA ka Oiaio. Truth. w
In Hawaiian
HHi 1894-Je 2 1898

Ka NUPEPA Kuokoa. (The independent) m,w O 3 1861-D 25 1927||
In Hawaiian
CSmH Mr 22,Ap 12 1862
CU-B 1865-67
DLC Ap 3-10,My 1 1875
H 1861-62
HB 1861-[72-73]-[77]-[92]-[94-95]-[1900-01]-[06-07]-[09-10]-[14-22]-[24-26]
HHi [1861-1911]
IU D 21 1917-Ja 3 1919
KHi Je 24 1898
MiU [1861-62]
NN Ap 21 1877

Ka NUPEPA Kuokoa Puka La. d
In Hawaiian
HB [1893;1919]

OFFICIAL and commercial record. sw Mr 2 1903-N 29 1907||
H complete

PACIFIC commercial advertiser. w Jl 2 1856-My 21 1888||
C O 24 1868
CSt [1856-63]
CU-B Ag-S 10,N 19,D 10 1863-[64-66]-Mr 1869 [Ja-O 1 1870]F 25,N 1871-[73]-My,Ag 28 1875;Ja 1 1876;Jl 21 1877-D 20 1879
CaB S 23 1858
DLC 1856-60[Ja-Mr 1871]
H complete
HB 1856-Je 1868;Jl 1875-Je 1876[77-78;82-83]
HH 1856-Je 1878;Jl 1879-85
ICN Jl 9 1864
KHi Jl 2 1856;Mr 19 1863
MB Jl 1874-F 19 1876
MBAt Jl 2 1856(reprint)
MWA Jl 2 1856-[67]-[Ja-Jl 10]O 2,D 25 1869; Ja 29,Je 8 1870;Mr 25,S 30,O 14 1871;My 13 1876;Ag 18 1877;Ap 19,My 10,Jl 26-D 6 1879; Ja 3,Ap 10,S 4-O 9,D 11 1880
supp S 30 1871;Ap 26,My 17,Je 28,Jl 19 1879; Ja 3,17,24,31,F 28,Mr 13,Ap 10,My 15,Je 19 1880
MiU [1865]-67;70[72-73]83;88
N F 28 1874
NN D 27 1873;F 14,Je 27,N 14 1874;Mr 18,Je 10,24 1876
NSyU Mr 7 1861
NjHi Jl 24 1856
OHi N 24 1877;Mr 23 1878;Mr 25 1882
WHi F 12,O 1,15 1857;Ja 28,O 14 1858;S 4-11 1869
—d ed *See* Honolulu advertiser

PACIFIC commercial advertiser. d *See* Honolulu advertiser

POLYNESIAN. w Je 6 1840-D 11 1841;My 18 1844-Ap 25 1863||
CSmH Je 6 1840-My 12 1849
CSt [1849-57]
CU-B O 2 1844;My 10 1856-Ap 25 1863
CaB Je 15 1844-Ja 25 1845
CtY 1840-Je 5,S 25-D 1841;Ja 12,N 8 1845-My 6 1846
DLC 1840-My 12 1849;Ja 26,Ag 17 1850;Ja 18,O 18 1851;My 8-15,Je 5,Jl 24,O 16-30,N 20 1852;F 5,Ap 16,My 14,Je 11,Jl 2-9,30,Ag 20,S 3-10,D 26 1853[54-My 1858]Je 23 1860;F 1, Jl 5 1862
H complete
HB 1840-Je 5 1841;44-63
HHi complete
ICHi Je 12-Ag 1841;S 19 1846
ICN My 18 1844-My 8 1852;My 10 1856-My 2 1857
MH 1840-41;44-53
MHi My 18 1844-My 15 1847[48-54]D 5 1863
MSaE Ap 21 1849;Ap 7 1855
MWA 1840-D 4 1841;My 18 1844-48;Ja 20,Ap 28,My 19 1849-My 7 1852;My 14 1853-63
MiU [1840-41;44]-[47]-[50;52-53]
N My 22 1847-Ag 25 1849;My 10 1851
NN 1840-O 16 1841;Je 29,Jl 27,Ag 10,31,S 28, N 23 1844-My 3 1845;Ja 10-Jl 11,Ag 22-D 1846
NbHi F 2 1850
NcD [Je 20-D 1840]-Je 5 1841[Jl 1844-45]F 14,S 12-O 3 1846[47]Ja 29-F 5,26-Mr 4,My 6 1848[My-D 1857]
OrHi O 28 1848
P Jl 28 1840-D 4 1841
WHi [1846]Mr-N 1856;N 1857-S 1858

Saturday PRESS. w S 4 1880-Ag 29 1885||
Followed by Daily Honolulu press
CU-B 1880-S 2 1882;F 14,Mr 7-14,Jl 4,Ag 29 1885
H 1880-Ag 1882
HB 1880-84;Mr 14 1885
HHi complete
MWA Je 2 1883;N 29-D 20 1884;Ja 3-10 1885
MiU [1880-81]
OHi S 4,N 20 1880;O 8 1881;My 31 1884

Daily Honolulu PRESS. d S 1 1885-
Follows Saturday press
HB 1885-F 27 1886
HHi 1885-Je 3 1886

PROGRESSIVE. *See* Ka Holumua

PUNCHBOWL. q Jl 1869-O 1870||
HHi complete

Ka PUUHONUA. Hawaiian observer. w 1914-18||
In Hawaiian
HB [1916-18]

REPUBLICAN. d Je 14 1900-02||
H 1900-Je,Jl 14-S 28,O 1-D 1901
HHi Je 15 1900-Ja 1 1902
MWA O 27 1901

SANDWICH ISLAND gazette and journal of commerce. w Jl 30 1836-Jl 27 1839||
Followed by Sandwich Island mirror and commercial gazette
C Ag 1837-39
CSmH 1836-Jl 22 1837
CaB complete
DLC complete
H complete
HB complete
HHi complete
MH complete
MSaE F 11,Jl 8 1837
N complete
NN 1836-Jl 22 1837
NNHi 1836-Jl 22 1837
OHi Ag 1837-39
PHi complete

SANDWICH ISLAND mirror and commercial gazette. m Ag 15 1839-Jl 15 1840||
Follows Sandwich Island gazette

SANDWICH ISLAND news. w S 2 1846-Ap 14 1849||
Suspended from Ag 25-N 4 1847
DLC 1846-N 1847;Je 15-D 21 1848
H complete
HB N 1847-O 26 1848
HHi 1846-O 26 1848
ICN 1846-Ag 1847
MSaE Mr 29 1849
MeBB 1846-Ag 1847
MiU [1846-47]
NcD Mr 10,Je 16-Jl,Ag 11-25 1847;Jl-Ag 3 1848

Weekly STAR. w Ja 15 1894-
MWA Ja 29 1894

Morning STAR. *See* Ka Hoku Loa

STAR of the Pacific. *See* Hoku o ka Pakipika

STAR of the sea. *See* Ka Hoku o ke Kai

Honolulu STAR-BULLETIN. sw 1898-1925||?
1898-My 24 1912 as Semi-weekly star; My 31-Je 28 1912 Hawaiian star
CLS Ja 16 1922
DLC 1900-S 18 1925
HB Mr 7-8,13 1899;F 9 1901;F 11 1902;Mr 16, Ag 26 1903
KHi N 8 1908

HAWAII (*Continued*)

HONOLULU—*Continued*

Honolulu STAR-BULLETIN. d Jl 1 1912+
Formed by the union of Hawaiian star and Evening bulletin
Ap 12 1920 is Centenary number 1820/1920
CCIP D 13 1922-Ja 3 1923
DLC Jl 1912+
H 1914-20;Ap 1921+
HB Ap 1920;O 10 1921
HH 1912+
NN 1911+
WHi O 13 1913;Ap 12,Je 7 1919;Ag 14,O 13, 19,25 1920;Je 6-12,14-16,S 24 1921;Ja 11 1926; Mr 28 1927;N 22,23 1935

TIME. w 1895-96||?
HHi Ap 27 1895-Ja 4 1896

Honolulu TIMES. w Ja 8 1849-Jl 1851||
DLC N 8,14 1849
HB N 1849-F 1851
HHi 1849-O 1850
MWA D 27 1849(extra)

Honolulu daily TIMES. d Ja 1890-
DLC F 1,3,5 1890
MiU [1890]

TROPIC topics. w 1912-14||
HHi O 1912-Ja 3 1914

TRUTH. *See* Nupepa ka Oiaio

VOICE of the nation. *See* Ka Leo o Ka Lahui

Sunday VOLCANO. w 1899-1901||?
HHi F 12 1899-D 15 1901

WHALEMEN'S shipping list of arrivals at the ports of the Sandwich Islands.
MWA Ap 28 1853;D 30 1854

WORKING hands. *See* Na Lima Hana

LAHAINALUNA

Ka LAMA Hawaii. m F 14 1834-
First newspaper printed in these Islands
In Hawaiian
MiU Ja 1 1841

WAILUKU

MAUI news. sw 1900+
KHi D 4 1926

Wailuku TIMES. w 1911-21||?
MWA O 12 1921

IDAHO

ABERDEEN

Aberdeen GAZETTE. w Ag 12 1909-10||?
KHi [Ag 12-O 7 1909]

Aberdeen TIMES. w 1911+
IdBlB [1918-20]

ALBION

CASSIA county times. w 1886-1909||?
1895?-1905? as Albion times
CU-B Ja 22 1892

Albion TIMES. *See* Cassia county times

AMERICAN FALLS

American Falls PRESS. w 1902+
pub 1902+
KHi Ag 21 1909-Ag 1912

ARCO

ADVERTISER. w Mr 9 1909+
pub 1909+

ASHTON

Ashton ENTERPRISE. *See* Ashton herald

Ashton HERALD. w Ap 26 1919+
1919-Ja 1922 as Ashton enterprise
pub 1919+

BANNOCK CITY

BOISE news. w 1863-
DLC O 20 1863(facsimile)

BELLEVUE

Bellevue PRESS. w F 2? 1889-
CU-B Je 29,Ag 3,31-S 14 1889

WOOD river news. *See* Wood river news-miner (Hailey)

BLACKFOOT

BINGHAM county news. d,w 1909-30||?
1920-21 as Bingham county daily news d 1920-21
IdBlB 1915-23

Daily BULLETIN. d 1917+
pub 1927+

IDAHO Falls register. *See* Idaho register (Idaho Falls)

IDAHO republican. w 1904-32||?
IdBlB 1904-32

Blackfoot twice-a-week OPTIMIST. w,sw 1907-19||
1907-10? as Blackfoot optimist
w 1907-10?
IdBlB 1911-17

Blackfoot REGISTER. w 1880-83||?
DLC Jl 31 1880;F 12 1881

BOISE

CAPITAL chronicle. sw Jl 1869-70||
CU-B [Ag 4 1869-D 14 1870]

Boise CAPITAL news. d 1901+
pub 1901+
DLC 1913—
OrHi Ag 2-27 1908

Boise DEMOCRAT. sw N 29 1868-Je 1869||
C Mr 3 1869
CU-B Ja 15,Ap 4,My 6 1868-[Ja-F]Mr 20,24 1869

IDAHO democrat. sw D 21 1870-71||
CU-B [D 24 1870-Jl 8 1871]

IDAHO herald. tw O 14?1871-Ap 5 1872||
CU-B N 8,17 1871[Ja-Ap 5 1872]

IDAHO daily statesman. tw,d Jl 26 1864+
1864-Ja 10 1888 as Idaho tri-weekly statesman
tw 1864-Ja 7 1888
pub 1864+
C O 10 1868
CSmH N 3 1864
CU-B S 6[N 17 1864-65]-My 30,Jl 7-9,O 1,N 5,10,17,29,D 1-3,8-10 1868;69;Ja 15, 19,F 8, Je 10 1876-[78]-Je 29 1880;87;Ja-My,Je 29, Jl-D 1888[89-91]
DLC Jl 3 1880;Ag 26 1890+
IdB 1875-[77]-[80]-83
IdIf Ja 1 1925
OClWHi S 20 1881
OrHi O 18 1866;Ap 27 1867
WHi 1917-Ja 2 1922

IDAHO weekly statesman. w Ag 6 1865-1908||?
CU-B 1865-[67]-[69]-[76-79]80;86
DLC Ag 28 1875-Jl 1891

Boise City NEWS. sw Mr 24? 1870-
CU-B Mr 26 1870

Boise City NEWS. w Ag 5? 1870-71||
CU-B Mr 4 1871

Boise City REPUBLICAN. w Mr 1 1879-87||?
CU-B Ag 16-23,D 20 1884-[85-Je 11 1887]
DLC Jl 3 1880

BONANZA CITY

YANKEE Fork herald. w Jl 24 1879-82||?
CU-B [1879-80]-Mr 5,Ag 18,N 3-10,D 15-22 1881;F 9-16 1882

BONNERS FERRY

HERALD. w Jl 1 1891+
pub 1891+

KOOTENAI Valley daily sentinel. w,d My 5 1932+
My-D 29 1932 as Kootenai Valley sentinel
w My-D 29 1932
pub 1932+

BRUNEAU

OWYHEE nugget. w 1889+
pub 1889+

BURLEY

Burley BULLETIN. w My 1 1905+
pub 1905+
MWA Mr 30 1906

CALDWELL

Caldwell NEWS. w,sw 1893-Mr 1928||
United with Caldwell tribune to form Caldwell news-mirror

Caldwell NEWS-TRIBUNE. w,sw,d 1883+
1883-Mr 1928 as Caldwell tribune
w 1883-1928;sw 1929-Je 1933
pub 1883-[1915-17]+
CU-B Ja 18,O 1890

SOCIALIST. *See* Workingman's paper (Seattle, Wash)

Caldwell TRIBUNE. *See* Caldwell news-tribune

CAMBRIDGE

NEWS reporter. w 1890+
1890-O 1923 as Cambridge news
pub 1891+

CHALLIS

IDAHO messenger. w 1881-90||
Followed by Silver messenger, later Challis messenger
CU-B Ap 21 1885;Jl,O 8 1889;Ja 7-14 1890
KHi Jl 10 1888-Jl 16 1889

Challis MESSENGER. w 1889+
Follows Idaho messenger. 1889-1912 as Silver messenger
pub 1896+

SILVER messenger. *See* Challis messenger

COEUR d'ALENE

Coeur d'Alene AMERICAN. d 1922-26||?
IdCP 1922-26

Couer d'Alene PRESS. w,d F 17 1891+
w 1891-1906
pub 1891-92;94+
WaPS O 17 1929[31-33]

Coeur d'Alene TIMES. w 1888-91||
CU-B O 3 1889

COUNCIL

ADAMS county leader. w F 1900+
1900-12 as Council leader
pub 1910+

Council LEADER. *See* Adams county leader

CRAIGMONT

LEWIS county register. w 1908+
OrWT 1910-12

DRIGGS

TETON valley news. w 1909+
pub [1909+]
WaPS [1925-26]

EAGLE ROCK

IDAHO register. w 1880-90||
CU-B Mr 2-23,Jl 6-13,27 1889;Ja 4 1890

EMMETT

INDEX. w 1893+
pub 1893+

FAIRFIELD

CAMAS county courier. w O 27 1905+
1905-17 as Camas prairie courier
pub 1905+

CAMAS prairie courier. *See* Camas county courier

Fairfield SUN. w 1911-14||
IdFC 1912-14

FERDINAND

ENTERPRISE. w 1912+
OrWT 1915-26

FILER

TWIN FALLS county citizen record. w 1906?+
pub 1906+

GENESEE

Genesee NEWS. w 1888+
WaPS [Je 1928]

GLENNS FERRY

Glenns Ferry GAZETTE. w S 1908+
pub 1908-10;13+

GOODING

GOODING county times. w
IdJJ Ap 20 1934+

Gooding LEADER. w D 25 1908+
pub 1908+

GRANGEVILLE

IDAHO county free press. w Je 18 1886+
pub 1886+
NcD Ag 12 1887;F 8,22,O 18 1889

HAILEY

Hailey TIMES. w 1881+
1881-1919 as Wood River times; 1920-22 Wood River times news-miner; 1923-28 Hailey times news-miner
CU-B [F 17-D 1886]Jl-D 1887;F 24 1888;Ag 27 1889

IDAHO (*Continued*)

HAILEY—*Continued*

WOOD River news-miner. w My 7 1881-1919||
1881-82 as Wood River news (Bellevue). United with Wood River times to form Wood River times news-miner, later Hailey times
CU-B [1881-Ap 1882;87-Je 1888]89;Jl 11 1890-91

WOOD River daily news-miner. d Ag 31 1881-1919||
1881-82? as Wood River news (Bellevue) United with Wood River times to form Wood River times news-miner
CU-B Ag,S 1-13,15-17 1881;S 15 1887[Ja-F]Mr 24,30,Ap-Je 3,26,S,D 1888;F,Jl 19,Ag,O 13, 15,19,D 28,31 1889-Mr[Je]S 28,30,O[D]1890

WOOD River times. *See* Hailey times

WOOD River times news-miner. *See* Hailey times

HARRISON

Harrison SEARCHLIGHT. w My 11 1893+
1893-My 2? 1900 as Fog horn

HOMEDALE

OWYHEE chronicle. w Ap 30 1931+
pub 1931+

IDAHO CITY

IDAHO commoner. w Ap 28 1932+
IdIf [1932-33]+

IDAHO news. *See* Idaho world

IDAHO register. sw,d Jl 1880-S 14 1920||
United with Idaho Falls times to form Times-register, later Post-register
1880-84? pub in Blackfoot
IdIf My 24-Jl 7 1901;17-20
IdIfP complete

IDAHO world. w,sw S 29 1863-1919||?
1863-O 1864 as Idaho news
w 1863-Ap 1867
C D 24 1868
CU-B My 21 1864 [F 1865-77;79-83;86-87;89-O 1890]
DLC Jl 2,9 1880
MH O 20 1870

Idaho Falls POST. d 1903-O 31 1931||
United with Times-register to form Post-register
IdIf Mr 31 1916-31

POST-REGISTER. d N 1 1931+
Formed by the union of Idaho Falls post and Idaho times-register
pub 1931+
IdIf Ja 1 1932

Idaho Falls TIMES. w 1890-S 16 1920||
United with Idaho register to form Times-register, later Post-register
IdIf Jl 9 1891-1920

TIMES-REGISTER. d,sw S 17 1920-O 30 1931||
Formed by the union of Idaho Falls times and Idaho register. United with Idaho Falls post to form Post-register
sw 1920-29
IdIf Complete
IdIfP complete

JEROME

EDEN eagle. *See* Jerome county journal

JEROME county journal. w 1898+
1898-1913 as Meadows eagle; 1913-22 Eden eagle
pub 1931+

MEADOWS eagle. *See* Jerome county journal

NORTH Side news. w N 12 1908+
pub 1908+

JULIAETTA

GEM. w 1889-90||
CU-B Ag 9 1890

KAMIAH

Kamiah PROGRESS. w 1905+
pub [1905+]
WaPS [1916]-[18-26]

KELLOGG

Kellogg-Wardner NEWS. w 1886+
1886-1912 as Wardner news (Wardner)
pub [1886-1906]+

Kellogg evening NEWS. d 1924+
pub 1924+

KENDRICK

Kendrick GAZETTE. w 1890+
WaPS Ag 15,O 17-D 5 1919;Ag 22 1924

KETCHUM

KEYSTONE. w 1882-89||?
CU-B Jl 13 1889

KOOSKIA

IDAHO mountaineer. *See* Kooskia mountaineer

Kooskia MOUNTAINEER. w 1899+
1899-1916 as Idaho mountaineer
pub 1908+
WaPS [1917-21]

KUNA

Kuna HERALD. w 1914+
pub 1914+

LEWISTON

GOLDEN age. sw Ag 2 1862-Ja 1865||
CU-B Mr 12 1864
MH N 19 1864

IDAHO signal. w 1872-74||
CU-B Ja 3[Mr 15-D 1873]-S 5 1874

Lewiston JOURNAL. w Ja 17 1867-F 1872||
Followed by Lewiston signal
DLC Ja 13 1872

Lewiston NEWS. w F 1909+
pub 1924+
WaPS [1932-33]

NEZ Perce news. w S 3 1880-88||
CU-B N 5-19,D 3-24 1880;Ja 21-28 1881; Ag 23 1887;Ja 3,17-F 21,Mr 6-Ap 24,My 1 1888

NORTHERNER. w S 12 1874-75||?
Follows Lewiston signal. Followed by Teller, later Lewiston teller
CU-B 1874-Je 5 1875

OUR stars and bars. w 1888-89||
NcD F 6-13 1889

Lewiston SIGNAL. w Mr 9 1872-74||
Follows Lewiston journal. Followed by Northerner
DLC Ag 10 1872
IdLC 1872-S 12 1874

Lewiston TELLER. w O 21 1876-1910||
CU-B Je 23-N 1877[86-Je 1888;89]-91
DLC My 12 1877;D 19 1879;Ap 21 1881
IdLC O 28 1876-S 19 1895
NcD N 3 1887;Ja 31-F 7 1889
OrHi Mr 21 1879

Lewiston morning TRIBUNE. w,sw,d S 1 1892+
w 1892-S 28 1895;sw O 1895-My 9 1898
pub [1892-93]O 1895+
CSmH Mr 3 1918
WaPS N 10 1904;D 27,29 1918;Ag 1 1919[22-25]Ja 19 1929;N 6 1930+

Lewiston TRIBUNE. w Ja 1 1896-Je 25 1931||
pub complete

McCALL

PAYETTE Lake star. w 1917+
pub 1918+

MACKAY

Mackay MINER. w F 1906+
pub 1906+

Mackay TELEGRAPH. w 1901-05||
IdBlB 1902-05

MALAD CITY

IDAHO enterprise. w 1874+
CU-B Mr 2,23-30,O 16 1889;Ja 1-15 1890

MERIDIAN

Meridian TIMES. w 1909+
pub 1909+
WaPS [1918]

MIDDLETON

BOISE Valley herald. w 1906+
1906-Je 7 1928 as Middleton herald
pub 1912+

Middleton HERALD. *See* Boise Valley herald

MOSCOW

IDAHO post. w 1907+
pub 1910+
—d ed *See* Daily star mirror

LATAH county advocate. w 1922+
pub My 1931+

Moscow MIRROR. w 1882-1906||
United with North Idaho star to form Moscow star-mirror
CU-B [Jl 19 1889-90;92-S 14 1894]
NcD F 1-15 1889

NORTH Idaho star. *See* Moscow star-mirror

STAR of Idaho. *See* Moscow star-mirror

Moscow STAR-MIRROR. w 1887-1918||?
1887-89 as Star of Idaho; 1889-1906 North Idaho star
CU-B Mr 29,Jl 12,S 6 1889
NcD F 15 1889

Daily STAR-MIRROR. d 1910+
pub 1910+
IdU 1910+
WaPS [1917-18]Jl 9 1919;Ap 20 1920;My 20 1921[22]-30;Jl 1931-33
w ed 1919?+ *See* Idaho post

MURRAY

COEUR d'ALENE record. *See* Coeur d'Alene sun

COEUR D'ALENE sun. w 1884-1913||?
1884-89 as Coeur d'Alene record
CU-B Mr 1889
DLC Jl 27 1888
KHi [D 1888-F 17 1889]

NAMPA

Nampa HERALD and times. w 1902-05||
United with Idaho leader to form Nampa leader-herald

IDAHO leader. *See* Nampa leader-herald

Nampa LEADER-HERALD. w,d 1891+
pub 1900+
M Mr 7 1930
MnHi My 4 1918-D 18 1920
WaPS Jl 12 1918[19]

Nampa PROGRESS. w 1888-98||?
CU-B S 14,O 19,D 28 1889;Ja 11-F 1,Mr 1,Jl 5,27,Ag 9,23,S 13,O 4,18-N 1 1890

Nampa RECORD. sw,w 1904-23||?
WaPS [1919]

NEZPERCE

Nezperce HERALD. w 1898+
WaPS My 8 1919[25]-[27-30]-33

OXFORD

IDAHO enterprise. w Je 5 1879-82||?
CU-B [Jl 31-D 1879]80[Je 15-S 6 1882]
DLC Ag 21 1879-Je 1 1882

PARIS

SOUTHERN Idaho independent. w 1886-92||?
CU-B O 11 1889

PARMA

Parma REVIEW. w D 15 1909+
pub 1912+

PAYETTE

Payette INDEPENDENT. w Mr 1891+
pub [1891-1900]+

PIERCE

Pierce City MINER. w Mr 20 1903-Mr 6 1908||
pub complete

POCATELLO

IDAHO herald. w Ap 12? 1889-96||?
CU-B S 27-O 11 1889

IDAHO state journal. d 1922+
IdPT 1922+

Pocatello TRIBUNE. d 1892+
pub 1893+
CoU S 1906-My 1910
NcD D 26-31 1924

POST FALLS

Post Falls ADVANCE. w 1901+
pub 1915+

PRIEST RIVER

Priest River TIMES. w Ap 16 1914+
pub 1914+

RATHDRUM

Rathdrum COURIER. w 1881-92||?
1881-89? as Kootenai courier
CU-B Mr 9-23,Je 29,Jl 6-13,Ag 3,31-S 14,O 19,D 14-21 1889;Ja 4,18-F 8,22,Je 7,21,Jl 12,S 7 1890

KOOTENAI courier. *See* Rathdrum courier

SILVER blade. *See* Rathdrum tribune

Rathdrum TRIBUNE. w 1895+
1895-1903? as Silver blade
pub Je 1895-[96-97]+
WaPS [1922-23]

REXBURG

Rexburg CURRENT journal. *See* Rexburg journal

FREMONT county journal. *See* Rexburg journal

FREMONT current journal. *See* Rexburg journal

FREMONT journal. *See* Rexburg journal

Rexburg JOURNAL. w 1897+
1897-1902? as Fremont county journal; 1903?-04? Fremont journal; 1905? Fremont current journal; 1906?-15? Rexburg current journal
pub 1906+

SNAKE River current. w 1899?-1904||?
United with Fremont journal to form Fremont current journal, later Fremont journal

IDAHO (*Continued*)

RICHFIELD

Richfield RECORDER. w 1909+
Richfield ed of Lincoln county journal (Shoshone)
IdSL 1909-Ag 1931

RIGBY

Rigby STAR. w 1903+
pub 1905+

RUBY CITY

OWYHEE daily avalanche. *See* Idaho daily avalanche (Silver City)

RUPERT

MINIDOKA county news. w 1914+
pub 1914+

Rupert PIONEER. w 1905-08||
United with Rupert record to form Pioneer-record
IdRM complete

PIONEER-RECORD. w 1905-24||
1905-08 as Rupert record. Merged with Minidoka county news
IdRM 1905:21

Rupert RECORD. *See* Pioneer-record

SAINT ANTHONY

TETON Peak-chronicle. w 1899+
pub 1899—

SALMON CITY

Salmon City HERALD. w 1901-27||
United with Idaho recorder to form Recorder-herald

IDAHO recorder. *See* Recorder-herald

RECORDER-HERALD. w 1886+
1886-1927 as Idaho recorder
CU-B S 5-12,N 28,D 12-19 1889;Ja 1-8,F 12,Mr 8 1890;D 30 1891-Ja 6,20-27,F 17-24,Mr 2,Ap 6,27-My 4 1892

SALUBRIA

IDAHO citizen. w 1889-99||?
CU-B Ag 22-29 1890;Ja 1 1892

SANDPOINT

Sandpoint daily BULLETIN. d 1924+
pub 1927+

PEND d'OREILLE review. w O 1 1905-My 1933||
IdSpB complete
IdU S 1916-33

SHELBY

Shelby PIONEER. w 1916+
IdBlB [1918-20]

SHOSHONE

Shoshone JOURNAL. *See* Lincoln county journal

LINCOLN county journal. w 1883+
1883-1931 as Shoshone journal
pub 1891+
KHi D 21-28 1906;Je 5 1908
—Richfield ed *See* Richfield recorder

SILVER CITY

IDAHO daily avalanche. d O 17 1874-Ap 26 1876||
CU-B O 17,19 1874;S 18,N 20,D 31 1875;76
WHi complete

IDAHO avalanche. w *See* Owyhee avalanche

OWYHEE avalanche. w Ag 19 1865+
S 1875-Ag 1897 as Idaho avalanche
1865-Ag 4? 1866 pub in Ruby City
C D 19 1868
CU-B [Ap 21-Ag 18 1866]-S 9 1882;87-Ja 10 1891;O 23 1893[F 17-N 9 1894]
DLC D 24 1870;Ja 7,D 30 1871-S 1874;S 11,O 16 1880;Ja 25 1890
WHi 1865-N 7 1868:F 26 1870-Ap 17,S 18 1875-Jl 1904

OWYHEE daily avalanche. *See* Idaho daily avalanche

OWYHEE bullion. w N 14?1866-67||?
CU-B Ap 18 1867

OWYHEE tidal wave. sw D 11? 1868-70||
Title varies: Tidal wave. Merged with Idaho avalanche, later Owyhee avalanche
C D 29 1868
CU-B Ja 15-19 1869
WHi D 15 1868-F 10 1870

TROY

LATAH county press. w 1933+
pub D 1933+

TWIN FALLS

IDAHO citizen. w,sw
WaFS [1927]-F 28 1930

IDAHO evening times. w,tw,d 1905+
1905-24 as Twin Falls times
w 1905-12;tw 1913-17
pub Mr 23 1905+

Twin Falls NEWS. w O 28 1904+
pub 1904+
KHi O 28 1904

WALLACE

COEUR D'ALENE miner. w Je 1 1890-Ag 10 1895||
IdWM [1890-96]

Wallace FREE press. *See* Wallace press

IDAHO press. w *See* Wallace press-times mining review

Wallace MINER. w 1906+
pub F 21 1907+

Wallace PRESS. w Jl 2 1887-92||?
1887-Jl 1 1889 as Wallace free press
CU-B O 1,11-25 1890
IdWM 1887-Jl 1 1889

Wallace PRESS-TIMES. d 1906+
1906-11 as Idaho press
WaPS S 25 1925-[26-30]

Wallace PRESS-TIMES mining review. w 1894+
1894-1904 as Wallace press; 1905-11 Idaho press
OrHi O 16 1921-Mr 7 1926

WARDNER

Wardner NEWS. *See* Kellogg-Wardner news (Kellogg)

WEISER

Weiser SIGNAL. w Ag 5 1882+
pub 1882+
CU-B My 18-Je 15 1893

WENDELL

Wendell IRRIGATIONIST. w Ap 15 1909+
pub 1909+

WINCHESTER

Winchester REPORTER. w Ag 24 1922+
pub O 1926+

YANKEE FORK

Yankee Fork herald. *See under* Bonanza City

ILLINOIS

ABINGDON

KODAK. sw 1897+
IAb 1922+

ADAIR

Adair weekly BEACON. w 1909+
pub Jl 1934+
IU Ap 1918-33

ALBANY

Albany REVIEW. w 1899+
IU O 16 1914-[16]-F 1 1923

ALBION

Albion JOURNAL-REGISTER. w 1869+
1869-72 as Albion pioneer; 1873-1919 Albion journal
pub 1926+
IHi [N 23 1899-My 17 1900]
IU 1884-Mr 15 1900
MWA My 6 1871

Albion PIONEER. *See* Albion journal-register

PRAIRIE hen. w? N 2 1844-
IHi N 2 1844
MWA N 2 1844

Albion REGISTER. w 1907-19||
United with Albion journal to form Albion journal-register

ALEDO

Aledo BANNER. w 1869-81||
1869-73 as Democratic banner. Merged with Aledo democrat, later Mercer county news and Aledo democrat
IGK My 18,Ag 5,15,29,S 12 1879

Aledo DEMOCRAT. *See* Mercer county news and Aledo democrat

DEMOCRATIC banner. *See* Aledo banner

DEMOCRATIC press. w O 15 1879-
IGK F 19 1880

MERCER county news and the Aledo democrat. w 1880-D 28 1927||
1880-S 6 1927 as Aledo democrat. Merged with Times record
IU 1918-27

MERCER county press. w O 11 1866-69||
IHi [1866-Mr 1867]

Aledo weekly NEWS. w My 3 1879-
IGK Ag 16,30 1879

Aledo RECORD. w Jl 14 1857-94||
United with Aledo times to form Aledo times-record
IAle 1857-Je 10 1885
NbHi My 9 1877

Aledo weekly REGISTER. w
KHi Ja 17,31 1894
NNHi Je 30,Ag 4 1863

Aledo TIMES-RECORD. w 1884+
1884-94 as Aledo times
pub 1894+
IU O 15 1914+
KHi S 12 1895;Mr 5 1896

ALEXIS

Alexis ARGUS. w 1884+
IU D 1917-N 5 1931

Alexis JOURNAL. w 1874-77||
MWA F 8 1877

ALTAMONT

Altamont NEWS. w 1881+
pub 1885+
IU D 19 1917+

ALTON

ALTONIAN. w Mr 13-27 1838||
IHi Mr 13 1838

Alton AMERICAN. w N 8 1833-34||
ICHi N 22,D 6-13,27 1833-Ja 3,17,30,Mr 17,Ap 14-21,My 12,Je 2 1834
IHi N 8 1833

Alton BANNER. w 1866-1913||?
In German
MWA Ag 26 1876

Alton COMMERCIAL gazette. w F 8-D 25 1839||
DLC complete
IU F,Mr 19-Je 4,18,Jl 9-23,Ag 21-S,O 9,30-D 4,25 1839

Alton daily COURIER. d My 29 1852-My 31 1859||
Title varies: Alton daily morning courier
IAl 1855
ICHi 1852-My 1854;Je 1858-59
IHi [Je 1854-59]
IU 1852-My 1854;Je 1858-59
MWA N 24 1852;Ja 12 1858

Alton weekly COURIER. w Je 1852-61||
IAlT 1852-My 1858
ICHi 1852-My 1853
IU Je 1854-My 22 1856;Je 1857-My 1858
MWA D 23 1853

Alton daily DEMOCRAT. d Jl 10 1860-69||
1860-Jl 10 1861 as Alton daily evening democrat
IAl 1860-Jl 10 1863
ICHi S 27,30 1865
IP N 26 1862-F 24 1864
InLHi Mr 17 1866-Mr 16 1869
MWA N 30 1868
OClWHi Ap 3 1866

Alton DEMOCRAT. 1875-88 *See* Alton sentinel-democrat

Alton DEMOCRATIC union. w S 5 1845-46||?
IGK Ap 4 1846
IU F 14 1846

GOLDEN era. *See under* St. Louis, Mo.

MADISON county sentinel. w 1879-88||
United with Alton democrat to form Alton sentinel-democrat
IU O 11 1882-Je 27 1888

Alton OBSERVER. w S 8 1836-Ap 19 1838||
Suspended from Ag 17-D 28 1837
CtY Ja 12,Je 15 1837
IAlS Ja 15,Ap 9 1838
ICHi 1836-Ap 12 1838
IHi [1836-38]
MB Mr 30 1837
OOxM S,O 27,N 27-D 1,15 1836-Jl,Ag 17 1837

PEOPLE'S miscellany and Illinois herald. w Jl 27 1842-
DLC Jl 27 1842

Alton morning SENTINEL. d 1885-88||
United with Alton daily democrat to form Alton daily sentinel-democrat
ICHi [My-D 1886]-Jl 1 1888

Alton SENTINEL-DEMOCRAT. w 1875-1911||
1875-Ja 29 1888 as Alton democrat
ICHi Jl 1888-S 1889
IHi [Je 10 1897-N 17 1910]
IU 1881-96;99-1905

ILLINOIS (*Continued*)

ALTON—*Continued*

Alton daily SENTINEL-DEMOCRAT. d 1876-1911||
1876-88 as Alton daily democrat
ICHi F 22 1878-Je 1884;Mr 25 1887
IHi [1878-Je 1888]
IU S 6 1876-Je 21,S 25 1877-D 6 1879;80;97-98;1901-05
OHi Ja 31,Ap 11,Ag 8 1879

Alton SPECTATOR. w 1832-39||
CSmH My 14 1835
Ct [1837]
ICHi Ja 27-F,Mr 16-30,Ap 27-My 18,Je 8,Ag 28,O 23 1832;Ja 1-8,22-F 19,Mr 5,19,Ap 2,16-23,My 7-21,Je 11-25,Jl 9,23-30,N 23 1833-Ja 11,25-F 18,Mr 18-25,Ap-My 1,29,Je 5,24,Jl 1-15,Ag 12-S 2 1834;My 21,O 8,22,N-D 1835;Ja 21-Ap 1,15-22 1836;O 19 1837;D 13 1838;Ja 3 1839
IHi [My 25 1832-S 15 1838]
IU Ap 9-Jl 2,11-20,N 23-D 7,21 1833-Ja 4,18,F 1,11-Mr 18,N 5 1834
MWA F 17 1832;Jl 16,30-Ag 6 1835
MoSM Je 1 1832

Alton TELEGRAPH. w Ja 20 1836-1919||?
1836-Mr 1841 as Telegraph; Ap 1841-52 Alton telegraph and democratic review; 1853-55 Alton telegraph and Madison county record. 1855-60 merged with Alton weekly courier
pub 1839-50;Mr 1861-62;S 1863-68;71-75;77-80;83-86;88-90;96-1900;02;09-10
DLC Ja 21 1843;Jl 19-Ag,S 20-27,O 18 1850-54;Ag 30 1861
ICHi Ja 1836-50
ICU F 11,S 2 1843
IHi [Ja 17 1838-42]
IU Ag 27 1842;43-52;Mr 13 1861-F 20 1863;75;Ja 18-D 1877
MWA O 5 1839;N 27 1846;D 30 1853
MoSM Mr 9 1836-52
N Ja 24 1838
NN D 18 1846
P-M F 28 1855

Tri-weekly TELEGRAPH. tw Ja 1-My 22 1852||
ICHi complete

Alton daily TELEGRAPH. d My 22 1852+
Title varies: Alton evening telegraph; Daily Alton telegraph; etc.
Ja 15 1936 is Centennial ed
pub 1853-55;Mr 1861-62;S 1863-Mr 1866;68;78-Je 1896;97+
DLC 1898
IAl 1853
ICHi My 1852-My 17 1855;O 29 1886-S 1889
IU 1878;1935+
MWA Ja 15 1936

Alton daily TIMES. d 1909-24||?
ICHi N 8 1921

UPPER Alton herald. w Ja 13 1887-89||
ICHi F 24 1887-[88]-S 1889

ALTONA

Altona JOURNAL. w 1878-90||?
IGK F 21,Jl 4,25,Ag 29 1879

Altona MIRROR. w Mr 19 1868-70||
MWA Ap 23 1868

AMBOY

Amboy JOURNAL. w 1854-S 1913||
1854-56 as Lee county times; 1856-66 Amboy times; 1866-S 1870 Lee county journal. Merged with Amboy news
IAmN [Ap 10 1856-80]-1913
ICHi O 13 1859
MWA Je 24 1858
OrU 1881-Ja 2 1889

LEE county journal. *See* Amboy journal

LEE county times. *See* Amboy journal

Amboy NEWS. w 1878+
pub 1878+

Amboy TIMES. *See* Amboy journal

ANDERSONTON

WESTERN athenaeum. w O 17 1840-
DLC O 17 1840

ANNA

DEMOCRAT. w 1890+
1890-92 as Union democrat
Suspended 1893-F 1897
pub Mr 1897+
IU Je 1925-Jl 6 1934

TALK. w 1883+
pub [1883+]

UNION democrat. *See* Democrat

ANTIOCH

Antioch NEWS. w 1886+
pub 1895+

ARCOLA

Arcola HERALD. w 1883-My 1905||
United with Arcola record to form Arcola record-herald

Arcola RECORD-HERALD. w N 1866+
1866-My 1905 as Arcola record
pub 1899+
ICHi F 26 1876
IU O 8 1914+
NbHi Mr 3 1883

ARENZVILLE

Arenzville ADVOCATE. w D 25 1885-86||
IHi Ja 1 1886

Arenzville ENQUIRER. w My 31 1922-25||?
Follows Virginia enquirer (Virginia)
IHi [1922]

Arenzville INDEPENDENT. w 1898-1918||?
1898-1905? as Arenzville times
IHi Jl 8 1899

Arenzville TIMES. *See* Arenzville independent

ARGENTA

Argenta REGISTER. w 1916+
IU 1918-D 8 1921;Mr 22 1923+

ARGO

DESPLAINES Valley news. w Je 1913+
pub O 1915+

ARLINGTON HEIGHTS

COOK county herald. w 1872+
IU [My 29 1928-N 1930]

ARTHUR

CLARION. w My 26-O 1905||
United with Graphic to form Arthur graphic-clarion

Arthur GRAPHIC-CLARION. w My 6 1887+
1887-O 1905 as Graphic
pub [1905-24]+

ASHKUM

Ashkum JOURNAL. w 1898+
IU Jl 6 1917+

ASHLAND

Ashland weekly EAGLE. w Mr 2-Ag 10 1876||
IHi [Mr-Ag 1876]

ASHTON

Ashton GAZETTE. w F 28 1895+
pub 1895+

Ashton NEWS. w
IAsG [1873]

Ashton NEWS. w O 19 1889-91||?
An edition of Rochelle register (Rochelle)
IU O 26 1889

Ashton SENTINEL. w 1878-81||
IAsG [1879-81]

Ashton TIMES. w 1901-04||?
IAsG [1901-02]

ATHENS

Athens CYCLONE. w Ja 17 1885-88||
Followed by Athens free press
pub complete

Athens FREE PRESS. w 1888+
Follows Athens cyclone
pub 1888+
IU N 1917+

ATLANTA

Atlanta ARGUS. w My 7 1869+
pub 1869+
IAt 1870-1900;29-32
IHi Mr 31 1905-16;S 1918+

AUBURN

Auburn CITIZEN. w Ap 30 1874+
pub 1874+
IU D 28 1917+

AUGUSTA

Augusta weekly BANNER. w D 1864-67||
1864-65? as Home banner
IGK Je 8-22,O 26,N 16,D 7 1866
MWA F 22 1867

Augusta EAGLE. w 1884+
IU D 13 1917+
KHi Jl 20 1893

Augusta HERALD. w Ag 1878-80||
IGK Je 5,19,Jl 24,S 11 1879

HOME banner. *See* Augusta weekly banner

Augusta TIMES. w Ag 15 1856-57||
IGK Ag 29-S 11,26,N 7,21,D 12-19 1856;Ja 9, F 27,Mr 13-20,Ap 10,24 1857

AURORA

Aurora BEACON. w,sw Je 1847-1906||?
Jl-Ag 1857 united with Aurora guardian to form Republican union, later Aurora weekly republican
w 1847-90?
IA Ap 6,18,28 1857;F 15 1864;Ap 26 1866-67;Ja-S 6 1871;72-75
ICHi F 15 1864
IU S 20-1890
MWA F 21 1867
N My 31,O 5 1855;My 3-10,Je 14 1866

Aurora daily BEACON-NEWS. sw,d 1875+
1875-1911 as Aurora beacon
sw 1875-Mr 1891
IA 1875[76]77[85]86;88;Ja-O 1898;99-1900;My 1901+
ICHi S 3 1910
IHi Ag 1 1917;20-34
IU D 16 1917+

Aurora BLADE. w 1881-98||?
IA Ag 15 1882-N 11 1884

Aurora DEMOCRAT. w Ag 6 1846-
IA Ag 6-27 1846

Aurora daily DEMOCRAT. d 1888-92||?
IA [Ja 8-Mr 31 1892]

Aurora EXPRESS. d 1882-1903||
IA Ag 21 1882-Je 1883;84-Je,S 1885-91;Mr-Ag 1892;93-1901

FOX River leader. w 1903+
IA F 1920-Ap 6 1922

Aurora GUARDIAN. w N 3 1852-Jl 1857||
United with Aurora beacon to form Republican union, later Aurora weekly republican
IA 1852-O 1855[56-57]

Aurora HERALD-EXPRESS. w 1866-1903||
1866-86 as Aurora herald
IA Ag 12 1878-79;Je 24-D 1880;S 8 1881-S 8 1882;85-92;94-97;99-1901
MWA Jl 22 1876
N O 13 1866;S 13 1873
NbHi O 26 1877
WHi Je 22 1869

Aurora daily JOURNAL. d
IA O 28-D 13 1920

Aurora daily NEWS. d 1872-1911||
United with Aurora daily beacon to form Aurora daily beacon-news
IA N-D 1876;N 1877-Mr,Jl 1886-N 9 1887;Ja-Jl 1888;Ja-Ap,S 1889-Mr,O-D 1890;Ja-My 27, N 11 1892-O 31 1911

Aurora evening POST. d 1878-97||
IA Ja-O 1884;Ja-F 1885

Aurora weekly REPUBLICAN. w Jl 1857-N 5 1858||
1857 as Republican union (formed by the union of Aurora beacon and Aurora guardian)
IA Jl-N 5 1858
N Ja 8 1858

Aurora SENTINEL. w
IA [Ap 5-S 20 1912]

Aurora daily STAR. d 1921-24||
IA Ap 16 1921-23

SUN. w 1886-1905||?
IA S 16-D 1886

Aurora daily TIMES. d 1888-93||?
IA [Mr 26-Ap 20 1892]

Aurora VOLKSFREUND. w 1868-1929||?
In German
IU Mr 1921-Je 16 1922

Aurora VOLKSFREUND. d My 27 1895-1921||
In German
IU Jl 1917-F 25 1921

AVA

Ava CITIZEN. w 1900+
IU D 21 1917-[21-D 1 1922]25+

AVON

Avon SENTINEL. w 1879+
pub 1880+
IGK Jl 3,31 1879
IHi Ja 18 1917-O 3 1918
ILoT D 31 1885-87
IU 1918+

BARDOLPH

Bardolph NEWS. w Ag 30 1893+
pub 1893-Ap 18 1930

BARRY

Barry RECORD. w 1905-Jl 28 1920||
IU D 12 1917-20

BATAVIA

Batavia HERALD. w D 1 1892+
pub 1892+

Batavia weekly NEWS. w 1869-D 1908||
IA Ag 13 1880;Ag 6 1885

BAYLIS

Baylis GUIDE. w 1892+
IU N 20 1914-O 22 1930;My 1932+

BEARDSTOWN

CASS county democrat. w 1875-83||
1875-79 as Cass county messenger. United with Central Illinoian to form Illinois democrat, later Illinoian star
IGK Ja 4,F 22,S 6-13 1879
IHi [Ja-O 1877]

CASS county messenger. *See* Cass county democrat

CENTRAL Illinoian. d 1858-61||
IHi F 7 1859

ILLINOIS (*Continued*)

BEARDSTOWN—*Continued*

CENTRAL Illinoian. w *See* Illinoian star

Beardstown CHAMPION. w S 25 1875-76||?
IHi S 25,N 20,D 18 1876

Beardstown CHRONICLE and Illinois military bounty land advertiser. w Je 18 1833-34||
Ct S 28 1833
ICU N 22,D 6,20-27 1834
IHi Mr 8-22 Ap 5-19 1834
IOr N 1 1834
IU N 1,22,D 27 1834
MWA O 12 1833

Beardstown DEMOCRAT. w Mr 12 1858-65||
IHi Je 13,Ag 22 1861

Beardstown ENTERPRISE. w 1879-1925||
IHi [S 22 1883-Mr 16 1895;Jl 1899-Je 19 1900]

Beardstown GAZETTE. *See* Illinoian star

Beardstown ILLINOIAN. *See* Illinoian star

ILLINOIAN democrat. *See* Illinoian star

ILLINOIAN star. w,sw Ag 15 1845-1914||
1845-D 2 1852 as Beardstown gazette; D 9 1852-54 Beardstown and Petersburg gazette; 1854-83 Central Illinoian; 1884-85 Illinoian democrat; 1886-Ap 28 1899 Beardstown Illinoian
IBeaS Je 14 1866-S 1868
IGK N 14 1845;Ag 21 1846
IHi [F 12 1847-Ag 1852]Mr 14,28-Ap 4,D 5-19 1867;Ja 2,O 22 1868;Ap 1 1869;S 1 1870;Ap 30 1886
MWA Je 15 1852
WHi My 19 1864

ILLINOIAN-STAR. d My 31 1891+
1891-99 as Evening star
pub [1891-1926]+
IHi D 16 1903

Evening STAR. *See* Illinoian-star. d

STAR of the west. w,sw 1888-Ap 28 1899||
United with Beardstown Illinoian to form Illinoian-star
IHi [F-O 1888]

BEECHER

Beecher HERALD. w Ag 1907+
pub 1907+
IU Mr 21 1918+

BELLEVILLE

Belleville ADVOCATE. w,sw Ap 4 1840-1916||
Follows Representative and gazette
pub 1840-60;66-1916
DLC Ap 11,N 28 1840
IBe 1840-69;72-1901
ICHi Jl 11 1844;S 24 1846;Je 9 1882
IHi Je 20 1850-Ag 21 1851[S 1881-1915]
IU Ja 20,F 5,Mr 10,Je 30-Jl 7,D 15,29 1842;Ja 26,F 16-Mr 9,30-Ap 6,Je 15 1843;F 3,17-24 1848;O 11 1849;Ag 8 1862
MWA D 4 1863;F 9 1866
WHi N 8 1854

Belleville daily ADVOCATE. d 1880+
1880-Ja 20 1935 as Daily advocate
pub 1880+
IBe 1901+
IHi [1916-Ap 1934]
IU O 13 1915+

Belleville weekly DEMOCRAT. *See* News-democrat. w

DEUTSCHER demokrat. w 1856-57||
In German
IBe Jl-D 1856

FARMERS' and mechanics' repository. w S 3 1842-Jl? 1843||
DLC S 10 1842
IU Jl 15,29 1843

Der FREIHEITSBOTE für Illinois und Missouri. w 1840||
In German
IU My 6-O 28 1840

GREAT western. w My 11 1839-41||
DLC My 25 1839

ILLINOIS beobachter. w Mr 21 1844-Ap 10 1845||
1845 pub in Quincy
In German
DLC My 25 1844
IHi complete

ILLINOIS republican. w Ja 31 1849-52||
Follows Belleville times. Merged with Belleville advocate
ICHi Ja 9 1850
ICU 1849-Ja 22 1851
IU S 26 1849

ILLINOIS republikaner. d Jl 20 1872-73||
Merged with Belleviller zeitung, later Belleviller zeitung und stern
In German
IHi [1872-N 29 1873]

MESSENGER. w 1907+
IU 1918+

NEWS-DEMOCRAT. w F 3 1858-1928||?
1857-82 as Belleville weekly democrat
IBe 1858-70
ICHi Mr 10,15,My 1-8,22,Je 5,19-26,Jl 10-17,Ag 7,O 9,30,D 4,25 1858-Ja 1,Mr 19,S 3,N 26 1859;Ja 14,28-F 11,25,Ap 14-28
IHi F 18 1910;My 13 1916
IU Ag 27 1859
OClWHi My 20 1869

Belleville NEWS-DEMOCRAT. d 1882+
pub 1901+
DLC N 9 1901
ICHi D 8 1905
IHi Ag 16 1930
IU O 5 1914-18

POLITICIAN. ir Ap 13-Je 8 1844||
IHi Ap 13,20,Je 8 1844

Belleviller POST und zeitung. d Ag 27 1884-1919||?
1884-93 as Belleviller post
In German
IHi 1884-Mr 10 1917

Belleviller POST und zeitung. w 1884-1923||
1884-93 as Belleviller post
In German
IHi D 18 1884-Ja 12,S 1893-Ag 1916
IU O 22 1914-Je 1917

REPRESENTATIVE and gazette. w 1837-39||
1837-D 22? 1838 as Representative and Belleville news. Followed by Belleville advocate
ICHi Ja 20,D 22 1838
ICU D 22 1838

ST. CLAIR banner. w Ag 1 1843-46||?
DLC Ja 16 1844(extra)
IBe 1844-46
IHi 1843-Ja 23 1844

ST. CLAIR tribune. w 1854-58||
Merged with Belleville advocate
IBe 1856-57

STAR of Egypt. w Jl 9 1858-59||
Campaign paper
IU O 15 1858

Der STERN. w N 4 1877-81||
United with Belleviller zeitung to form Belleviller zeitung und Stern
In German
IHi 1877-O 25 1879

Der Tägliche STERN. d Ja 8 1878-O 8 1881||
United with Belleviller zeitung to form Belleviller zeitung und stern
In German
IHi [Ja 9 1878-81]

STERN des Westens. w 1860-77||
Merged with Belleviller zeitung
IBe Jl 19 1865-Jl 16 1867
IHi [Jl 23 1867-Jl 10 1877]

STERN des Westens. d 1865-O 20 1877||
United with Belleviller zeitung to form Belleviller zeitung und Stern
In German
IHi [Jl 4 1868-77]

Belleviller TAGEBLATT und arbeiterzeitung. d 1884-1912||
In German
NNC [Ja 20 1903-10]

Belleville TIMES. w D 23 1847-Ja 24? 1849||
Followed by Illinois republican
IU F 4,25-Mr 10,Ap 14,Jl 28-Ag 4 1848

TREU-BUND. w 1873-75||
In German
IHi O 16 1874-O 8 1875

VOLKSBLATT. w 1856-Mr 13 1858||
Merged with Belleviller zeitung
In German
IBe F 23 1856-S 12 1857
IHi [O 1857-58]

Belleviller ZEITUNG und Stern. w 1848-93||
1848-77 as Belleviller zeitung; 1878-79 Belleviller zeitung und Stern des Westens. United with Belleviller post to form Belleviller post und zeitung
IBe 1849-69
IHi [Mr 18 1858-Ja 12 1893]
MWA Je 24,Ag 26 1852

Belleviller ZEITUNG und Stern. d 1856-93||
1856-77 as Belleviller zeitung; 1878-79 Belleviller zeitung und Stern des Westens. United with Belleviller post to form Belleviller post und zeitung
IHi [Jl 2 1856-Ja 14 1893]

BELLFLOWER

Bellflower NEWS. w Ap 2 1915-Ag 18 1921||
IU 1915[16-17]-21

BELVIDERE

Belvidere NORTHWESTERN. *See* Belvidere republican-northwestern

Belvidere daily REPUBLICAN. d 1892—
pub 1900?+
IBel Ap 1917+

Belvidere REPUBLICAN-NORTHWESTERN. w 1866+
1866-1905? as Belvidere northwestern
MWA O 16,D 18 1868

Belvidere STANDARD. w O 21 1851-Mr 18 1896||
IBel complete

BEMENT

Bement REGISTER. w 1888+
pub Ja 10 1890-[1923-25]+
IU O 15 1914+

Bement UNION. w F 7-D 26 1861||
OHi F-Mr,Ap 18,D 26 1861

BENLD

Benld ENTERPRISE. w 1906+
pub Ag 24 1923+

BENTON

Benton evening NEWS. d Ja 1 1921+
pub 1921+
IU Je 6 1921+

Benton REPUBLICAN. w 1879-F 28 1924||
IBenN [1893-1920]
IU Ap 21 1921-24

Benton STANDARD. w 1849+
pub 1900+

BERWYN

Berwyn BEACON. w Ag 31 1925+
pub 1923+

Berwyn LIFE. w 1926+
pub 1926+

BETHANY

Bethany ECHO. w Ap 14 1887—
pub Mr 14 1898+

BIGGSVILLE

Biggsville CLIPPER. w 1875-1919||?
IGK My 24,Jl 26,Ag 16,30 1879

BLOOMINGTON

APPEAL. w 1875-76||
IHi Ap 8 1876

Daily BULLETIN. d 1881-O 1927||
Merged with Daily pantagraph
IC My 1 1889
ICHi F 9-Jl 23 1881
IU Mr 12,14,16-17,19,Je 5,N 13 1916;S 2 1917-N 22 1918
WHi O 28 1888;S 1 1897

Bloomington DEMOCRAT. w Ap 1868-73||
Ap-Jl? 1868 as McLean county democrat
IHi Jl 16 1868;F 9 1871
WHi Ag 15 1868

ILLINOIS central times. *See* Bloomington times

ILLINOIS state bulletin. *See* Bloomington times

ILLINOIS statesman. w Je 9 1858-63||?
Follows Weekly national flag
IHi [O 1858-My 8 1863]
TxU Je 23 1858-My 25 1859

INTELLIGENCER. *See* Weekly pantagraph

JOURNAL. *See* Weekly leader

Weekly LEADER. w 1868-My 1899||
-N 8 1868 as Journal
IB N 15 1868-Ag 1897
IHi Je 30 1882
NcU F 18 1869
OClWHi Ja 15,Ap 30,Ag 20-27 1873

LEADER. d F 22 1869-My 1899||
IB 1869-Ag 1898
IHi N 29 1871
KHi My 24 1881
OClWHi Jl 4 1881

McLEAN county democrat. *See* Bloomington democrat

McLEAN county Deutsche presse. w Mr 1870-92||?
In German
MWA Ag 19 1876

Weekly NATIONAL flag. w 1855-58||
Followed by Illinois statesman
IBHi 1855

Bloomington OBSERVER. w Ja 14 1837-39||
Title varies slightly
IB Ja 13 1838
ICU D 22 1838

Daily PANTAGRAPH. d 1846+
DLC 1898
IB 1926+
IBHi [1857-65]+
IHi [Ag 5 1863-1934]
IU My 1909+
MWA Ja 6 1869
OClWHi Je 2 1879

Weekly PANTAGRAPH. w 1846-1918||?
1846-51 as Western whig; 1852-53 Intelligencer
IA [1850]
IB S 22 1849-N 19 1851;Ja 14 1852-N 9 1853
IBHi [1852-54]-57
IHi [D 11 1847-Ag 1851;52-Ja 19 1853;Ap 1854-Je 5 1861]
IU 1904-Jl 23 1909
MWA Ag 22 1860
NNHi Je 10 1863
OClWHi Ag 29 1865;D 29 1871;Mr 19 1875;N 9 1877;O 11 1878;Jl 8 1881

Bloomington TIMES. w My 1850-Ag 1862||
1850-53 as Illinois state bulletin; 1853-O 1855 Illinois central times
DLC O 23 1852;F 23 1861
IHi F 10 1854

WESTERN whig. *See* Weekly pantagraph

BLUE ISLAND

Weekly REVIEW. *See under* Chicago

Blue Island STANDARD. *See* Blue Island sun-standard

SUBURBAN star. *See* Blue Island sun-standard

Blue Island SUN. w 1891-1918||
United with Blue Island standard to form Suburban star, later Blue Island sun-standard

Blue Island SUN-STANDARD. w 1876+
1876-1918 as Blue Island standard; 1918-30 Suburban star
pub 1918-27;31+

ILLINOIS (*Continued*)

BLUE MOUND

Blue Mound LEADER. w 1887+
IHi [My 11-D 1916]
IU S 12 1918+

BLUFFS

Bluffs TIMES. w Ja 6 1899+
1899-Ja 1935 as Bluffs weekly times
pub 1899;1901-05;07-09;15+

BOWEN

Bowen CHRONICLE. w 1889+
pub [1898-1915]+
IU O 8 1914-My 4 1933

BRADLEY

Bradley ADVOCATE. w Ja 29 1914-Je 7 1918||
ITeW complete
IU 1915-Ja 19 1917

BREESE

Breese JOURNAL. w 1921+
pub 1921+

BRIDGEPORT

Bridgeport LEADER. w 1900+
pub [1908]+
IBrL Je 1913+

BRIGHTON

Brighton ADVANCE. w 1871-80||
IGK O 31 1878;Jl 24,Ag 14,28,S 11 1879;Ja 22 1880

Brighton NEWS. w O 20 1880+
pub S 12 1908+
IU Ag 15 1912+

BRIMFIELD

Brimfield GAZETTE. *See* Elmwood gazette (Elmwood)

BROADLANDS

Broadlands NEWS. w 1911+
pub Ap 18 1919+

BROCTON

Brocton weekly REVIEW. w 1892+
IU O 1914+

BROOKPORT

Brookport INDEPENDENT. w D 6 1923+
pub 1923+

BUCKLEY

Buckley CHRONICLE. w 1895-1924||
Issued as a supplement to Onarga leader and review (Onarga) Ja 1922-D 1924
pub Ag 20 1895-Ag 2 1907;Ag 21 1908-Ag 6 1915;Ag 23 1918-Je 4 1920
IU Jl 13 1923-24

Buckley INQUIRER. w 1876-86||?
IGK Ag 2,S 20 1879

BUDA

Buda PLAIN-DEALER. w Ja 1 1887+
pub Jl 1929+
IBu 1887-Je 1929
IHi [My 21 1915-16]Ag 30 1918-34
IU D 1917+

BUFFALO

Tri-city REGISTER. w 1913+
pub 1913+

BUNKER HILL

Bunker Hill GAZETTE-NEWS. w Ja 19 1866+
1866-79 as Union gazette; 1879-1905 Bunker Hill gazette
pub 1866+
IU Mr 25 1932+

Bunker Hill NEWS. w 1886-1905||
United with Bunker Hill gazette to form Bunker Hill gazette-news

UNION gazette. *See* Bunker Hill gazette-news

BUSHNELL

JOURNAL of information. w Mr 23 1872-
CSmH Mr 23 1872

McDONOUGH democrat. w 1884+
pub Jl 4 1884+

Bushnell RECORD. w 1864+
1864-68? as Union press
pub Jl 1880+
IGK D 6 1878;Ag 1 1879
IU Ja 18 1918+
MWA F 21 1867

UNION press. *See* Bushnell record

BYRON

Byron EXPRESS. w Jl 21 1882+
IU [Jl 28 1882-86]-[89]-[92]-[94]-[1900-My 1901]D 1917+

Byron NEWS. w N 21 1874-N 13 1877||
IU 1874-S 8 1877

Byron TIMES. w Mr 2 1876-80||
IU [1876]Mr 9-N 2 1877[Je 14-D 1878]-[Ja-O 29 1880]

CAIRO

Cairo daily ARGUS. d 1878-D 1907||
ICa S 27 1899;1904-07

ARGUS-JOURNAL. w 1876-O 1907||
Follows Mound City journal (Mound City)
ICa N 8 1879

Cairo BULLETIN. d 1868-S 15 1928||
United with Cairo evening citizen to form Cairo evening citizen and Cairo bulletin
ICa D 21 1868-84;1904-28
IHi 1916-Ap 1928
IU Jl 24 1875;O 6 1914-Je 1918;D 13 1925;Je 23 1927
InRE D 24 1870

Cairo CITIZEN. w O 1 1885-1916||?
ICa 1885-Mr 1905

Cairo evening CITIZEN and Cairo bulletin. d 1899+
1899?-S 16 1928 as Cairo evening citizen
ICa Ap 1905+
IHi S 1920-29;35+
IU Ap 8 1918+

Cairo weekly DELTA. w Ap 13 1848-N 21 1855||
United with Cairo City times and Cairo weekly to form Cairo weekly times and delta, later Cairo times
ICa 1848-S 20 1849;N 21 1855

Cairo daily DEMOCRAT. d Ag 3 1863-68||
ICHi S 29,O 4 1865
ICa Ap 17,O 3 1865-Ag 29 1868
IHi [F 22 1865-Jl 11 1866]
MWA D 21 1865
MnHi Ap 16 1865

Cairo DEMOCRAT. w 1863-68||
ICa Jl 30-Ag 29 1868

EGYPTIAN. *See* Cairo City gazette

Cairo City GAZETTE. w F 23 1857-64||
1857 as Egyptian
IHi [F-Je 1857]Je 27 1861
IU Jl 8 1859

Cairo HERALD. d 1915-19||?
IHi [Ag 1915-Jl 13 1919]
IU Je 9-10,15 1916

Cairo City ITEM. w S 30 1865-66||
ICa S 30 1865

Cairo JOURNAL. w S 19 1857-My 6 1858||
In German
ICa complete

Monday LEADER. w Mr 20 1865-
ICa Ap 17-24 1865
N Ap 17 1865

Cairo morning NEWS. ir 1863-65||?
ICa Ap 16 1865

Cairo SUN. w 1851-52||
ICa Ap 10 1851-Ap 8 1852

Cairo evening SUN. d 1869-80||
ICa S 2-N 1878

Cairo daily TELEGRAM. d 1887-1906||?
ICa Mr 29-Ap 19 1905

Cairo TIMES. w My 31 1854-D 31 1868||
1854-N 14 1855 as Cairo City times and Cairo weekly; N 28 1855-59? Cairo weekly times and delta
DLC F 14 1855
ICa 1854-56;F 25 1857-[Jl 14 1858-Jl 8 1859];D 2-31 1868

WAR eagle. Daily evening extra. d N 15? 1864-65||?
ICa N 18 1864-Ap 21 1865

CAMBRIDGE

Cambridge CHRONICLE. w D 1858+
1858-79? as Henry county chronicle
pub [1858-80]+

HENRY county chronicle. *See* Cambridge chronicle

CAMP DEFIANCE

Camp register.
NNHi Je 13 1861

CAMP POINT

Camp Point ENTERPRISE. w 1866-71||?
MWA F 22 1867

Camp Point JOURNAL. w F 1873+
IGK My 23-30 1879
IHi 1904+
IU O 8 1914-Jl 2 1931

CANTON

FULTON advertiser. w 1877-79||
IGK Jl 31,S 4 1879

FULTON banner. w 1843-46||?
DLC Ap 24-My 1,29-Je 5 1846
IGK Ja 30 1846

FULTON county ledger. w 1849-1912||
1849-52 as Illinois public ledger; 1853-54 Fulton ledger
1849-54 pub in Lewiston
DLC N 13 1852
IHi [N 18 1856-O 24 1912]
MWA D 31 1853

FULTON telegraph. w 1840-
1840-Mr 1841 as Western telegraph
DLC Ag 28 1841

Canton HERALD. w 1837-38||
Ct Mr 3 1838

Canton daily LEDGER. d O 3 1912+
pub 1919
ICan 1927+
IHi 1912+
IU O 1914+

Canton weekly REGISTER. w 1849-1918||?
ICan 1869-71
IGK My 12 1904
IHi [1852-Ap 1915]
MWA Ja 5 1853
NNHi Ag 12 1862;S 26 1864

Canton daily REGISTER. d Je 7 1890-D 31 1925||
Merged with Canton daily ledger
IHi complete

WESTERN telegraph. *See* Fulton telegraph

CAPRON

BOONE county courier. w My 13 1921+
1921-Je 1930 as Nutshell
pub 1921+

NUTSHELL. *See* Boone county courier

CARBONDALE

Carbondale FREE PRESS. w 1877-1923||?
CLM Mr 8 1890
IU O 21 1914-Jl 3 1918

Carbondale FREE PRESS. d 1903+
IU S 23 1918-Ag 23 1921;35+
NN Ap 9 1923

Carbondale HERALD. w 1892+
1892-Ap 6 1922 as Southern Illinois herald
IU D 13 1917-Ap 6,27 1922-D 23 1932

NEW ERA. w 1863-72||
Follows Weekly Carbondale times
IHi Ap 27 1872

SOUTHERN Illinois herald. *See* Carbondale herald

Weekly Carbondale TIMES. w 1859-62||
Followed by New era
IHi Mr 14-21 1861

CARLINVILLE

Carlinville DEMOCRAT. w S 1856+
1856-Ap? 1865 as Carlinville free democrat
pub 1856-Ag 1857;61+
DLC D 13 1860
IU Ja 16-23 1868;O 10 1889

Carlinville FREE democrat. *See* Carlinville democrat

MACOUPIN county enquirer. w 1872+
Follows Macoupin times
IU Mr 27 1918-[23]+

MACOUPIN county spectator. w 1855-68||
Follows Macoupin statesman. Followed by Macoupin times
IU My 18 1860(supp)

MACOUPIN statesman. w Mr 4 1852-55||
Followed by Macoupin county spectator

MACOUPIN times. w Je 4 1868-71||
Follows Macoupin county spectator. Followed by Macoupin county enquirer
IHi 1868-My 26 1870

CARLYLE

CALUMET of peace. w Mr 17 1855-59||
Followed by Reveille
ICHi Jl 4 1857
IHi [1855-O 9 1858]

CLINTON county pioneer. w F 4 1874-Ap 1878||
In German
IHi 1874-Ja 1875

CLINTON vindicator. w S 7 1867-My 19 1868||
Merged with Constitution and union, later Carlyle constitution
IHi complete

Carlyle CONSTITUTION. w Jl 18 1863-1928||
1863-95 as Constitution and union
CSmH D 14 1867;Ja 4 1868
ICHi O 3 1867
IHi [1873-Jl 21 1881]

CONSTITUTION and union. *See* Carlyle constitution

REVEILLE. w 1859-63||
Follows Calumet of peace. Followed by Carlyle union banner

Carlyle UNION banner. w 1863+
Follows Reveille. Title varies: Weekly union banner; Union banner; etc.
IHi [Ag 1865-S 5 1878]
IU O 9 1914-20

CARMI

Carmi DEMOCRAT-TRIBUNE. w 1872+
1872-1911 as Carmi times; 1912-30 Carmi tribune-times
pub 1872+

Carmi TIMES. *See* Carmi democrat-tribune

ILLINOIS (*Continued*)

CARMI—*Continued*

Carmi TRIBUNE-TIMES. *See* Carmi democrat-tribune

WHITE county democrat. w 1858-1930||
United with Carmi tribune-times to form Carmi democrat-tribune
IHi [Ja 18-Jl 18 1912]
IU O 1914-Je 1921

WHITE county tribune. w 1909-11||
United with Carmi times to form Carmi tribune-times, later Carmi democrat-tribune

CARROLLTON

Backwoodsman. *See under* Jerseyville

Carrollton GAZETTE. w Je 26 1846+
pub 1846+
ICHi Je 11 1847;Je 28 1862
MWA F 16 1861

PATRIOT. w My 1864+
pub 1875+
ICarr 1895-1929
IHi [Mr 1904-34]

PEOPLE'S advocate. w F 5 1842-44||?
ICU F 19 1842;Mr 4,Jl 1 1843
IU Mr 4,Jl 1 1843;F 19 1844
NNHi Mr 5 1842

CARTERVILLE

Carterville HERALD. w 1889+
IU D 21 1917+

CARTHAGE

CARTHAGENIAN. w Jl 30 1836-37||
IGK O 15-22 1836

Carthage GAZETTE. w Je 29 1865+
ICarC F 11-D 1916;Ja 11 1918-S 23 1921
ICarR 1925+
IU Ja 13 1923+
MWA Jl 6 1865
NN Ag 30 1866;Ap 2,O 8,22,N 5,D 31 1868[69-71]-Je 13,27,Jl 11-Ag 8,22-O 10,24-N,D 12 1872;73-F 1,Mr-My 17,31-Jl 12,26-Ag 16,31-N 8,22 1876-F 10,24-My 12,26,Je 30-Jl 14,Ag 11,25-O 13,27-N 10,24-D 1 1882;Je 29,Ag 24,S 14,O 5-12,N 9 1883;F-Je 13,27,Jl 11-O 17,31,N 14-21,D 5,26 1884-Mr 12,26-S 17 1886;Jl 1 1887

HANCOCK county journal. w 1886+
pub 1886+
ICarC F 18 1916+
NN My 27 1886

Carthage REPUBLICAN. w 1853+
pub 1853+
ICarC Mr 29-D 1916
IGK Ja 31 1854
IU O 1914+
NN O 11 1866;Je 17 1869;S 14 1871;Ja-Ap 15,29-Jl 22 Ag 5,19-S 2,23-N 18,D 2-9,23 1874-Mr 1,15-Ap 12,26,My 10-17,31-Je 21,Jl 5,19,Ag 2-9,S 13-20,O 4-18 1876;Je 4 1879;Je 9,Jl 14 1880;Je 18 1884;Ag 26 1885;Je 16,Ag 25 1886

CASEY

Casey BANNER. w 1879-97||
United with Casey times to form Casey banner-times

Casey BANNER-TIMES. w Ag 1872+
1872-97 as Casey times

Casey COMMERCIAL. w 1887-1918||
Merged with Casey banner-times
IU N 1914-18

Casey TIMES. *See* Casey banner-times

CENTRALIA

Centralia DEMOCRAT. w N 30 1867-1913||?
ICeS 1867-68 85;87
IUr 1867-N 5 1869

EGYPTIAN republican. w N 10 1859-61||
ICeS N 17 1859-Jl 6 1861

Centralia SENTINEL. w My 28 1863-D 1916||
pub My 28 1863-My 18 1871;My 29 1873-My 13 1875;82;Mr 1 1884-1916
ICe Je 1863-My 15 1873
MWA Mr 2 1876
NNHi D 10 1863

Centralia evening SENTINEL. d Mr 11 1884+
1884-1905 as Centralia daily sentinel
pub 1884+
ICe 1927+
IHi Je 29 1916-N 1919;Ag 28 1934
IU Ap 1918+

CERRO GORDO

Cerro Gordo NEWS. w S 24 1908+
pub 1908+

CHAMPAIGN

CENTRAL Illinois gazette. *See* Champaign county gazette

CHAMPAIGN county democrat. w 1898-1900||?
IU D 1,15 1899-Ja 6 1900

CHAMPAIGN county gazette. w Mr 1858-1909||
1858-61 as Central Illinois gazette; 1862-Ap 5 1866 Champaign county union and gazette; Ap 13 1866-F 19 1868 Union and gazette; F 26 1868-F 24 1869 Gazette and union
DLC Ap 24,Je 19 1861
IHi Mr 21 1867
IU Mr 10 1858-F 1862;O 14 1864-Ag 1901;02-05;F 1906-D 11 1907
IUr N 18,D 1864-[66]-Ja 11,F-Mr 1,15-My 22 Je-Jl 24,Ag-N 13 1867;Mr-Ap 22,My-Jl 1,15-29,Ag 12-S,O 14-D 9,23 1868-Ap 13,27-My 11 25-Je,Jl 13-O 19 1870
MWA D 3 1868

CHAMPAIGN county news. w,sw F 21 1891-Je 30 1917||
w 1891-D 23 1916
IU complete

Champaign and Urbana CITIZEN. w Ja 15? 1920+
1920-O 16 1929 as Twin City review; O 23 1929-Mr 11 1931 Mid-West farmer
IU N 19 1920+

DADS Illini. w 1871+
1871-F 10 1934 as Illini weekly
IU Ja 15 1923+

Champaign daily GAZETTE. d N 5 1883-D 11 1919||
United with the Champaign daily news to form Champaign news-gazette
IU complete

GAZETTE and union. *See* Champaign county gazette

Champaign evening HERALD. d Ja 1-Mr 26 1923||?
IU Ja-Mr 26 1923

ILLINI weekly. *See* Dads Illini

LIBERAL democrat. *See* Times

MID-WEST farmer. *See* Champaign and Urbana citizen

Champaign daily NEWS. d Jl 29 1895-D 13 1919||
United with Champaign daily gazette to form Champaign news-gazette
IU complete

Champaign-Urbana NEWS-GAZETTE. d D 14 1919+
Formed by the union of Champaign daily news and Champaign daily gazette. 1919-Jl 28 1934 as Champaign news-gazette
IU 1919+

TIMES. w Ag 1872-1914||
Ag-? 1872 as Liberal democrat
IU N 15 1884;D 24-31 1898;D 30 1899;F 6-12 Mr 6,Jl 24,Ag 1914

TWIN CITY review. *See* Champaign and Urbana citizen

UNION and gazette. *See* Champaign county gazette

CHANDLERVILLE

CASS county journal. *See* Chandlerville times

SANGAMON Valley times. *See* Chandlerville times

Chandlerville TIMES. w Ag 5 1876+
1876-Ag 1878 as Cass county journal; Ag 3 1878-82 Independent; 1882-87 Sangamon Valley times
pub 1880+
IHi Je 30 1899;Ag 5 1876[Ag 10 1878-D 2 1880]

CHARLESTON

Charleston COURIER. w Ap 3 1841-1915||
DLC Je 19,Jl 3,D 4-11 1841
ICHi F 4 1857
IHi Jl 10 1841;Ja 11 1843;Mr 31 1849;Ap 2 1856;F 17,Je 2 1858;Mr 21 1867;My 28 1896

Charleston daily COURIER. d Je 1 1894+
pub 1894+
ICHa [1918;20-21;27-Jl 16 1929;30]Jl 1931-[32]+
IU Jl 1916-Ap 7 1917

ILLINOIS globe w 1846-49||?
DLC Mr 6,Ap 3,24,My 22-Je 5,19,Jl,Ag 14-21,S 4,18-35,O 9-N 6,21-D 1847;Ja 6,Je 16,Jl 7-14, 28-S 23,O 13-20,N 3,17-D 22 1849

Charleston weekly NEWS. w 1892-1918||?
ICHi S 18 1908
IHi [N 25 1899-My 12 1900;S 1905-N 1906;08; Ja-N 19 1910;F 13 1914-My 1915]

Charleston daily NEWS. d 1892+

CHEBANSE

Chebanse HERALD. w 1868+
NbHi F 2 1878

CHENOA

Chenoa CLIPPER-TIMES. w 1893+
1893-1917 as Chenoa clipper
pub 1915+
IU D 1917+

Chenoa GAZETTE. w 1876-1900||?
N Je 8 1889

Chenoa TIMES. w 1867-1917||
United with Chenoa clipper to form Chenoa clipper-times

CHESTER

EGYPTIAN picket guard. d
OCIWHi Ag 5 1863

Chester HERALD-TRIBUNE. sw,w 1896+
1893-1922 as Chester herald
pub 1900+
IU Ja 17-F 7,21,Mr 7-14,Ap 4-11,Ag 9,S 1935+

RANDOLPH county democrat. w 1857-78||
ICHi Ap 16,Jl 9 1859;My 3,17 1862

SOUTHERN Illinois advocate. w Ap 4 1839-40||
DLC Ap 4 1839

Chester TRIBUNE. w 1872-1922||
United with Chester herald to form Chester herald-tribune
IHi Ag 2 1917

CHICAGO

ABEND presse. d Ja 1 1883-1913||?
1883-O 23 1889 as Chicagoer freie presse. Mittags-blatt; O 24 1889-Mr 15 1891 Neue Chicagoer freie presse. Abendblatt; Mr 22 1891-N 1896 Neue Chicagoer freie presse und Chicagoer hausfreund-vereinigtes abendblatt
In German
ICN 1883-84;O 29 1885-N 1889;90-My 1898
IU 1890-My 1898

ABENDBLATT. d 1891-Jl 27 1899||
1891-O 23 1894 as Illinois staats-zeitung. Abendblatt Evening ed of Illinois staats-zeitung
In German
IC Mr 27 1893-99
ICN Mr 27 1893-99

ABENDPOST. d S 2 1889+
In German
pub 1889+
IC Jl 1890+
ICHi Mr 28 1907
IEN S 1894-[Jl 1918]
IU Je 17 1906;O 1914+
—Sunday ed *See* Sonntagpost

AFTON-BLADET Skandia. w 1890-91||
In Swedish
IRA 1890-91

AGE. w D 15 1894-95||?
Ap 13 1895 as Age and Chicago search-light
ICHi D 22-29 1894
KHi Ap-My 18 1895
WHi Ap 13-27 1895

ALBANY PARK times. w N 16 1925+
pub 1925+

Chicago daily AMERICAN. w,d Je 8 1835-O 18 1842||
1835-Ap 9 1839 as Chicago American (w)
Ct Je 11 1836
DLC O 14 1837;O 30 1840
IC Jl 1,15,29-Ag 5,26,O 28-N 4 1837[Je 1841]
ICHi My 8 1835-Je 3,O 14 1837;Ap-N 1839;Ap 1840-42
ICN [1839-42]
MWA [Mr 11-D 1837]-Ja 20 1838;N 11 1839; My 3 1840
NBi Je 11 1836-Je 3 1837
NSchU Je 1 1842
P-M Mr 27 1840
VtBr Jl 10-N 13,27 1840-Ja 15,F 5,19-My 7,21-28,Je 11-N 5,24-D 22 1841;Ja 19-26,F 23-Mr 16,30,Ap 13-27,My 18,Je 8,Jl 6,20-Ag 24 1842
WHi Ag 30,S 27 1839;Ja 3,24,F 7,Jl 18 1840;Jl 30 1841;Ap 6,Ag 2,10,17 1842

Chicago AMERICAN. d Jl 4 1900+
Title varies: Chicago evening American
pub 1900+
CL [1903]-[05]-[07]-[11]-[14]-[20]-22
CoU 1905-My 1910
IC Ag 4 1901+
KHi S 21-N 1900
WHi S 3 1902

AMERIKA. w Ag 13-D? 1872||
Merged with Skandinaven
In Norwegian-Danish
IaDeL Ag 20,S 11-O 28 1872

AMERIKA. w 1884-96 *See under* Madison, Wis.

AMERIKAN. w,sw Mr 3 1875+
1875-81 as w ed of Svornost
w 1875-1906
In Bohemian
pub 1875+

AMERIKANSKI slovenec. w,d S 3 1891+
Je 20 1924-Ag 26 1925 as Amerikanski slovenec and Edinost
w 1891-Je 13 1924
In Slovenian
pub 1891+

Chicagoer ARBEITER-ZEITUNG. tw,d 1876-1920||
tw 1876-78
In German
IC My 1894-1910
ICJ O 1886-Ap 1920
ICN My 1879-84;Jl 1886-Je,Ag 1887-89
IU [Ja 1917-18]-Je 4,Ag 20 1922;Ja 21 1923;Ja 9,My 4-O 12 1924
WHi O 24 1887-Mr 1888;1903-S 12 1920
—w ed *See* Vorbote
—Sunday ed *See* Die Fäckel

ARBEJDEREN. w 1896-1902||?
In Norwegian-Danish
IaDeL Ja-S 16 1897;Ap 14 1898-Ap 17 1900
WHi O 1898-Ap 7 1900

ATHENA. w,sw 1905-13||?
In Greek
ICHi S 17 1906

AUBURN PARK spotlight. *See* Auburn Parker

ILLINOIS (*Continued*)

CHICAGO—*Continued*

AUBURN PARKER. w O 22 1931+
1931 as Auburn Park spotlight
pub 1931+

AUSTINITE. w 1885+
IU O 16 1914+

AZ IRAS (Hungarian news weekly). w
In Hungarian
PPiHi [Ap 1928-N 1931]

BALKAN world. *See* Jugoslavia

De BATAVIER in America. w 1863-
In Dutch
MWA O 11 1864

Chicago BEE. w 1909-31||
Negro
TNY Ja 12-My,Ag 1,24,S 28 1930-Ja 4 1931

BELLETRISTISCHE zeitung. w 1866-76||
1866-74? as Westliche unterhaltungs-blätter
Sunday ed of Die Chicago union
In German

BELORUSSKAfA tribuna. bw
CSt-H [1931-32]

BEOBACHTER. *See* Bürgerzeitung und Illinois staats-zeitung

BEZZADONIKH. . . (Saloniki) w 1912-F 3 1934||
In Greek
IC 1917-F 8 1919
IU 1917-Ja 1,Ap 1921-34

Saturday BLADE. w 1887-1924||?
IHi S 5 1896
KHi Ja 7 1893[Je 1898-Mr 19 1901]
MWA My 20 1899;Je 14 1913
PDoHi F 15 1890
PLaL Mr 15 1892
PPiHi My 22 1915
WHi 1894-96

BOYCE'S weekly. w Ja 1-S 2 1903||
Merged with Saturday blade
WHi complete

BRITISH American. w O 8 1864-
ICHi D 3 1864

BRITISH American. w 1888+
CaM 1913-18

BROADAX. w 1895-1919||?
Negro
DLC Ja 27 1900

BÜRGERZEITUNG und Illinois staats-zeitung. w,sw 1877-1924||?
1877-1906 as Beobachter; 1906-14 Beobachter und post; 1914-Ap 3 1920 Das Echo, post und beobachter; Ap 10 1920-Jl 7 1922 D.A. Bürgerzeitung
w 1877-Jl 7 1922;sw Jl 12 1922-24
(Thursday ed used as a w)
IU 1918-[Ja-Jl 7 1922]-My 5 1923

Daily CALUMET. d 1881+
1881-83 as Tribune of Hyde Park village
pub 1884+
ICHi Mr 23,Ap 2-3 1885
IU 1918-19

CALUMET index. w Ag 2 1906+
1906-Mr 21 1907 as Index; Mr 28 1907-Jl 27 1907 Weekly index; Ag 3 1907 Weekly index, South end telegram; Ag 10 1907-F 8 1908 Weekly index with which is consolidated the South end telegram; Ja 23 1909-Ap 11 1913 Calumet weekly index
pub 1906+

CALUMET record. w Ja 15 1898+
pub 1901+

CHICAGOER. . . *See under* next important word: i.e. Chicagoer freie presse is alphabeted as Freie presse. . . ; etc.

CHINESE news. w N 4 1896-97||?
In Chinese
ICHi N 11 1896

Chicago CHRONICLE. w O 2 1880-1900||?
ICHi O 16 1880

Chicago CHRONICLE. d My 28 1895-My 31 1907||
CoU 1902;04;S 1906-Ap 1907
DLC 1898-1902
IC 1895-F,My 1902-07
ICHi 1895-S,N 1902-07
IHi Jl 1904-07
IU Mr 13 1898;Ag 17 1902;My 24 1904;Jl 16 1905
InMovHi S 19 1901
KHi Jl 1896-N 1900
WHi S 3-4 1896;F 18 1904

Chicago CITIZEN. w Ja 14 1882-1926||?
Mr 21 1919-Ap 28 1922 as Irish news and Chicago citizen
DLC F 25 1893-D 6 1896
ICHi Ja 14 1882;1883-Ap 18 1914
IU Ag 24 1917-26
PPCHi [1883;86-1900;12]

CITIZEN'S league. w D 14 1878-Jl 5 1879||
ICHi complete

Chicago daily COIN. d Je 1 1895-
KHi [Je 1-11 1895]

Daily COLUMBIAN. d My 1-O 31 1893||
Official bulletin of the World's Columbian Exposition, combining various Chicago newspapers
DLC complete
IC complete
ICHi complete
ICN complete
KHi My 1 1893
MWA complete
NAubHi complete
NN My 1-26,28-O 1892

COMING city. bw Je 27 1900-01||?
IHi 1900-Ja 23 1901
KHi D 12 1900

COMMERCIAL advertiser. w O 11 1836-37||
ICHi N 22 1836;F 6,Je 6 1837

COMMERCIAL advertiser. w F 3 1847-53||
1847-Ja 1 1851 as Chicago commercial advertiser
DLC Ap 1849-51
ICHi S 15 1847;S 6 1848;My 16,Je 13,S 5,26,O 3,24,D 19 1849;Mr 27,Ap 3,31,My 29,Je 19,Ag 17 1850
ICN Mr 1848
MWA Jl 20 1850;Ag 21,S 11 1852

Chicago daily COMMERCIAL advertiser. d 1849-53||
DLC My 28 1852-Ja 6 1853
MWA My 28,Je 29[Ag 10 1852-Ja 1 1853]
MiU-C O 18 1852
WHi My 22,S 7,10,O 18,D 7 1852

Chicago daily COMMERCIAL report. d 1866-
1866-76? as Daily commercial report and market review
ICHi S 1877-S 30 1882
PMcT [1875]

CORREO Mexicano. d S 4 1926-
In Spanish
CU-B 1926-Mr 4 1927

Chicago COURIER. w Je 9 1855-
MWA Je 9 1855

Chicago morning COURIER. d Ja 1 1874-77||?
DLC Ja 4 1875
ICHi Ja 1 1874;Ja 20 1876
MWA N 10 1876

COURRIER-CANADIEN. *See* Courrier franco-américain

Le COURRIER de l'Ouest. w Ja 2 1857-58||
1857 as Le Journal de l'Illinois
In French
MWA My 1 1857
WHi Ja 8-Ag 27 1858

COURRIER franco-américain. w Jl 31 1903-31||?
Formed by the union of Le Courrier de l'Ouest (Chicago), La Voix du peuple (Minneapolis) and Canadien (St. Paul).
1903-04 as Courrier-canadien
IHi [1905-16]
IU [Ag 24-D 7 1917]
MnHi 1903-D 14 1917
NdHi My 31 1907-13
WHi 1903-D 7 1917

Weekly CURRENT. w 1883-91||?
NbHi O 5,D 7-21 1885;Ja-My,S 20,N 8 1886;Ja-My 2,16-Je 6,N-D 1887;Ja 5,F 23,Mr 9,23-My 11,25 1891

D.A. BURGERZEITUNG. *See* Bürgerzeitung und Illinois staats-zeitung

DAHEIM. *See* Chicagoer sonntagsbote

DANSK tidende og revyen. w Ap 20 1895+
1895-S 24 1921 as Revyen
In Danish-Norwegian
pub 1895-Ja 1907;09+
ICJ 1903+
NNC 1903+

DAY book. d 1911-16||?
MWA Mr 27 1916

Chicago DEFENDER. w 1905+
Negro
PP D 30 1933-Ja 6 1934

Chicago DEMOCRAT. w N 26 1833-Je 23 1861||
Title varies: Weekly Chicago democrat.
Merged with Chicago daily tribune
Suspended Ja-My 20 1835(except for Ja 21,Mr 25)
Ct Ap 5,S 6 1837
DLC O-D 15 1846;Ja 5-12,F 23-N 2 1847
ICHi 1833-N 11 1854;55-61
ICN O 21,N 4 1845;Mr 31,Ap 14,O 6-13,N 24 1846[47]F 1,22Mr 14-Ap 4 1848;Ap 15-29,My 13 1854[58]
ICU N 21 1838
IGK My 1853
IHi N 26 1833(facsimile); Mr 4 1854
IU D 7 1836;Jl 6 1847
MHi N 26 1833
MWA N 26 1833;S 13,N 1-22,D 13 1837-Ja 3,17 1838;S 24 1845
MiU Ag 4 1841
NN Ag 28 1844
OClWHi D 6 1843
PWCl Je 1 1842
WHi Je 4 1835;Ja 15,F 26,Jl 1 1840;Ja 20,My 5,S 1,22,O 6 1841;Ap 13,My 11 1842;Ap 25,Jl 12,Ag 23,O 25 1843;Jl 16 1845;F 9 1850;Ja 22,Je 11 1853;Ja 16,F 6 1858;S 29 1860

Chicago DEMOCRAT. d F 24 1840-Jl 24 1861||
Title varies: Chicago daily democrat; Daily democrat. Merged with Chicago daily tribune
DLC Jl 7 1851-N 12 1853;Ag 11 1860
IC [Jl-N 1856]Mr 16,My 10,13,Je 2,12 1858
ICHi Mr 21,23,30,Ap 10,13,Je 9,Jl 17,Ag 8,13 1840;S 11,14-15,17 1841;Je 30 1847-D 20 1852;F 26 1856-61
ICU F 26 1841

Sunday DEMOCRAT. w Je 5-Jl 3 1870||
ICHi Je 19,Jl 3 1870

Chicago DEMOCRAT. w 1870-91||?
DLC Ap 8 1876
ICHi My 9-O 3 1889;Ja 22-Ag 6 1891

Chicago DEMOCRAT. d O 22 1881-98||?
United with Chicago dispatch to form Chicago democrat and dispatch, later Chicago democrat
ICHi Jl 14,S 22 1888

Chicago DEMOCRAT. d O 19 1892-1901||?
1892-Ag 1898 as Chicago dispatch; S 1898-Ja 22 1899 Chicago democrat and dispatch
IC 1892-Jl 5 1900
ICHi D 31 1892;Jl 8 1894;Ag 31-S 1 1898
KHi Jl 7-11 1896

DEMOCRAT. w,m
In English-Greek
NN Jl 3,S 27,O 11,25 1924;Ja 1,F 1,Mr 11,Ap 1-N 1 1925;Ja 1-Jl 1,O 23,30,D 1 1926;Ja-Mr,Je-D 1927;F-O 1928;Ja,Je,Ag,O 1929;Ja,Mr-My,O 1930
PP [1927-28]Ja 1929

DEMOCRATIC bugle. w Ag 21 1856-
IGK Ag 2-9 1856

Daily DEMOCRATIC press. *See* Chicago daily press

Weekly DEMOCRATIC press. w O 1 1852-Jl 1858||
United with Chicago tribune to form Chicago press and tribune, later Chicago weekly tribune
IGK Ap 30,My 14,Je 4,Jl 30,S 17,O 22 1853;F 18,Mr 18,My 6-13,S 30-O 14,D 23 1854;Mr 3,My 13-26,Je 23,Jl 7,S 15,O 20-27,D 8-15 1855;Ja 5,F 2,Mr 1,15-22,Ap 12,26,My 10,Je 28,S 13,27,O 11,D 6 1856;Ja-F 21,Mr 7 1857
MWA O 20 1855
WHi Mr 1854-58

DENNÍ hlasatel. Czechoslovak daily herald. w My 1 1891+
In Bohemian
pub 1891+
IU O 14 1909-Je 14 1910;F 9-Jl 21,O 19 1915+

DETROITSKÉ listy. w 1924+
In Bohemian
pub 1924+

DEUTSCHE warte. w,sw 1877-1915||?
w 1877-88
In German
KHi [Je 14 1888-My 16 1889]

Chicagoer DEUTSCHE zeitung, wochenausgabe der Illinois staats-zeitung. w
In German
IU Ja 10,Ag 1925-My 22 1926

Chicago DISPATCH. d 1892-98. *See* Chicago democrat. d 1892-1901

Chicago weekly DISPATCH. w Jl 13 1895-1901||?
IU F 11 1898
KHi Jl 13-27 1895

Chicago DOLLAR post. w Ja 1861-
ICHi Jl 25 1861

Chicago DOLLAR tribune. w
KHi [Je 11-O 1884]
MoHi S 11,25,O 2 1884

DOMACNOST. sw Mr 3 1879+
1879-Ja 1 1931 pub in Milwaukee, Wis.
In Bohemian
pub 1931+

DUCH casu. w Je 25 1885+
In Bohemian
pub 1885+

DZIENNIK chicagoski. d D 15 1890+
In Polish
pub 1890+
IU S 1917-Jl 2,O 21 1921+
PPCHi [1890;92]

DZIENNIK-LUDOVY. d Mr 16 1907-Ap 21 1925||
In Polish
IU S 1917-Ap 20 1925
WHi complete

DZIENNIK związkowy. d Ja 9 1908+
In Polish
IU S 1917+
MiG 1917+
NN 1908+

Chicago EAGLE. w 1889+
Negro
ICHi S 17 1892
IHi F 14 1925+
IU D 8 1917+

Das ECHO, post und beobachter. *See* Bürgerzeitung und Illinois staats-zeitung

EDGEWATER news. w Je 11 1924+
Je 11-O 14 1924 as Edgewater ed of Howard news
pub 1924+

EDINOST. sw 1914-Je 1924||
Merged with Amerikanski slovenec
In Slovenian

EDISON-NORWOOD times. w Ja 1 1930+
pub 1930+

ENGLEWOOD times. w 1886-1928||?
Title varies: Sullivan's Englewood times; etc.
IU D 14 1917-D 28 1928

ERITASSARD hayastan. *See under* New York City

Chicago EXAMINER. d 1900-My 1 1918||
United with Chicago record-herald to form Chicago herald and examiner
CL D 14 1903-Ja,Mr 1907-Ag,O 1911-Je,S 1914-Jl,S 1917-My 1 1918
IC 1908-18
ICHi D 5 1902;F 7 1909;My 8 1914
KHi [Je 19-Ag 8 1912]

Chicago EXPRESS. d O 24 1842-Ap 20 1844||
Followed by Chicago journal
ICHi Je 16,27,Jl 1,O 7,11-12,19,30 1843
ICN complete

Chicago daily EXPRESS. d
DLC N 18,20 1871
ICHi N 4 1871(advance sheet)

ILLINOIS (*Continued*)

CHICAGO—*Continued*

Chicago EXPRESS. w 1879-99||?
1882-83 as Saturday express
DLC Ap 17-D 18 1886
ICHi Jl 12 1881-86;Ja-My,Je 13 1891-Ja 1892
KHi F-D 1 1898
MWA Mr 23,D 14 1880-Ap,My 24,Je 7,21 1881; Je 10 1882
NbHi N 26,D 24-31 1879;Je 15,S 28,O 26 1880; Ja 11 1881
NcU O 29 1879
WHi S 20 1880-Ag 12 1882[Mr 15 1883-F 2 1896]

EXPRESS. w My 26 1933+
In Yiddish and English
NN 1933+

Die FACKEL. w My 11 1879-1924||?
Sunday ed of Chicagoer arbeiter zeitung
IC My 19 1889-1910
ICJ [1883-85]-Ja 11,My 29 1891-O 12 1910
ICN 1879
ICU F 10 1901-F 2 1902
NN Je 6,20-27,Jl 11-18,Ag 8-S 5,19,O 3-10 1886;Jl 1 1888;Je 7 1891;D 17 1893
WHi Ap 1903-O 12 1919

FACKLAN. *See* Ny tid (New York City)

FÄDERNESLANDET. w 1878-80||
Merged with Svenska tribunen-nyheter
In Swedish
IRA 1879-80

FIELD piece. w Je 14-N 1 1848||
Campaign paper
ICN complete

FOLKEBLADET. w S 22-O 29 1860||
In Swedish
MnSL complete

Chicagoer FRAUEN-zeitung. w D 3 1893-98||?
A Sunday publication of Chicagoer freie presse
ICN 1893-98

FREE soil banner. w Ap-N 1848||
Campaign paper
IHi S 28 1848

Chicagoer FREIE PRESSE. (Morgenblatt) d Jl 1871-1919||?
1871-Je 1874 as Freie presse; Jl-D 13 1874 Chicagoer freie presse; D 14 1874-82 Chicagoer neue freie presse. Merged with Illinois staats-zeitung
In German
IC F 5-My 1872;Ja 6-Je,Ag-S 1873;91-1901
ICN Mr 11-Jl 25 1872;Ja 22,27-29,31,Mr 1873-74;76-82;My 1883-O 27 1898
MWA N 24 1876
—**Evening ed** *See* Abend presse
—**Noon ed** *See* note under Abend presse
—**Sunday ed** *See* Chicagoer frauen-zeitung; Chicagoer sonntagsbote
—**Weekly ed** *See* Wochen-ausgabe

FREMAD. w 1868-1871||
1868? pub in Milwaukee, Wis.
In Norwegian
IaDeL [1869-71]

FRIHEDSBANNERET. w O 4 1852-My 7 1853||
In Norwegian
IaDeL 1852-Ja 8,22-My 7 1853

El GALLITO. w Mr 26 1927-
In Spanish
CU-B Ap 23,My 8,21 1927

Det GAMLA och det nya hemlandet. w Ja 7 1855-S 24 1914||
Merged with Svenska Amerikanaren
1855-58 pub in Galesburg
In Swedish
IRA complete
MWA Ag 26 1873
MnHi Ja 3 1855[Je 8 1864-1907]-14
NbHi Ap 10,Ag 14 1913
TxU 1859-65
WHi O 1898-1914

GARFIELDIAN. w 1913-16||
IU O 9 1914-D 17 1915[F 11-Ap 28 1916]

GARFIELDIAN. w 1919+
pub Ap 1933+

GAZETA polska. *See* Nowy swiat

GEM of the prairie. w My 29 1844-52||
Merged with Chicago daily tribune
CSmH Jl 13 1844
ICHi 1844-My,O 11 1845;D 11 1847-My 24 1851
ICN Mr 25,S 30,N 25,D 9,30 1848
IU O 7 1848
MWA O 5 1844;Ag 10,N 30 1850

GLAS svobode. (Voice of liberty) w,sw 1902-31||?
In Slovenian
IU Ag 28 1917-Ap 12 1927
WHi My 25 1905

Chicago GLOBE. d 1887-93||?
IC Ap 9 1888-D 17 1893
ICHi F 8 1889
MWA S 2 1888

Chicago GLOBE transcript. w 1898-
ICHi O 7 1899-Ja 25,F 8-Mr 1,22-Ap 5,26 1900

GLOS Polski. w N 1925+
In Polish
MiG Jl 11 1926-29

GOLOS truzhenika. (Toilers voice) w D 8 1918-My 17 1922||
In Russian
CSt-H complete
MnHi D 27 1919-24
NN [1918]-20

GREAT campaign. w Jl 13-N 14 1876||
Greenback paper
WHi complete

GREEK star. w Ja 18 1904+
Greek and English. Greek title: Hellenikos aster
pub 1904+
IU 1909+
WHi 1915+

HARD CIDER press. w Je 6-O 24 1840||
Campaign paper
ICHi complete
MWA Ag 22 1840

HEIMATBOTE. (Home herald) w 1920+
Also dated at Winona, Minn.
In German
MnHi Jl 15 1926-N 1928

HEJMDAL. w O 3 1874-76||?
In Scandinavian
IC O 17 1874-Jl 17 1875;76

HELLENIKOS aster. *See* Greek star

HEMLANDET. *See* Det Gamla och det nya hemlandet

Weekly HERALD. w Ja 3 1857-
IGK Ja 3 1857

Daily Chicago HERALD. d My 1858-Jl 30 1860||
1858-Mr 15 1860 as Chicago daily herald. United with Daily Chicago times to form Daily times and herald, later Chicago times
DLC Ja 21-Jl 30 1860
IHi [Mr-O 21 1859]

Chicago daily HERALD. d Ag 16-D 23 1873||
ICHi Ag 16 1873
ICU complete

Chicago Sunday HERALD. w O 29 1876-94||
IC Ja 11 1885-Je 27 1886
ICHi O 29 1876;O 16 1881;Jl 8 1894
MWA Je 20 1886;Ag 9 1891-Mr 6,Ap 24 1892

Chicago morning HERALD. d Mr 17 1879-S 1881||?
ICHi Mr 17,My 10 1879
IU S 20 1881
MiGh S 20 1881

Chicago HERALD. d 1881-95 *See* Chicago herald and examiner

Chicago HERALD and examiner. d My 10 1881+
Follows Chicago daily telegraph. 1881-My 3 1895 as Chicago herald; My 4 1895-Mr 26 1901 Chicago times-herald; Mr 28 1901-My 7 1914 Chicago record-herald; My 8-Je 13 1914 Chicago record-herald and Inter-ocean; Je 14 1914-My 1 1918 Chicago record-herald
A 1896;98;Ja-Ag 1900
CL My 2 1918-Ja 1922
CLM Ja 26 1892;N 18 1896
CSt 1898[99]-1918
CSt-H [1914-16]-[19]
CoU 1900;02;S 1906-My 1910
CtY O 9 1893
DLC Jl 29 1881-83;S 26 1885;87-Je 1893;Jl 1894-95;My-Ag 1896;97+
GU S 16-17,23,25 1893;D 29 1894
I 1914-21
IA [Ja,Ap-My 1886]Jl 1906-Mr 1918
IC 1886-F 28,My 2 1918+
ICan 1926+
ICHi Mr 21,Jl-D 1881;88-89;F 21 1890;O 22 1892;My 2 1893; Mr 1896-Ap 1898;1901-S 1916
ICN My-O 1893;94-Ja,Mr 1918-O 20 1919
ICU N 1895-1909;D 1917-F 1920
IEN 1891-95;Ap 1896-Mr,Jl 1898-Je,N 1900;Ap 1901-Ja,Je 1903-N 1907;08-Ap,D 1911-Mr,My 1912-My 2 1918
IF My 1898-1900; current year only
IHi Ap 9 1898-Mr 1899;Ap 1908-32
IP 1892-Mr 1896
IU My 10 1886;O 8 1897;1900-Ap 1902;Ap 15, My 20,Je 17,24,Jl 1 1906;N 17 1908-Ap,Je 1910;Jl 1911+
IaDH Mr 1895-1914
IM&W current two months
In Ap 1906-08;14-18
InU 1897-Ap 1918
KHi [Jl-D 1893]-[Ag 1896-99;Jl 28-S 29 1907] Ag 6-8 1912
MB 1914+
MNS 1899-1914
MWA Ag 4 1885;Mr 5 1889;Ag 5 1891-Mr 7 1892;Ja 23 1895;My 10-12 1902
MiG Ja 1 1892;Ap 30-O 1893
MiGh Mr 5-6,Ap 27 1897[Mr 29-Ag 1898]
MiHoM Je 1896-My 1897
MiU [1900]-[02]26+
MnU [1898-99]
NNC 1913-17
NcD O 10-N,D 13 1902-Ja 2 1903[F-O 1919]S 26 1985(humorous ed)
OCl 1904-[16]-Ap 1918
OClWHi O 21-22,N 5 1892
ODW 1908-S 1918
OHi 1912-31
OOxM Ap 22-S 24 1898;1909-18
PPi N 5 1895-1900
TM N 25 1892
TMuT O 1900-O 1901
Tx F 6 1891;Jl 1904-Ag,N 1915-16
TxU [S 1898-Mr 1901]-My 9 1902[Ap 1905-13]; N 1926-Je 1929
VtMS [S 1886-Ja 1890]
WHi Mr 4 1895+
WaL 1901-04;Ap 1905-S 1907;08-Je,O 1914-Mr 1916;17-Je,S 1918
WaPS [1911-F 1914]

El HERALDO. w Je 23 1927-
In Spanish
CU-B Je 30 1927;F 13,Ap 7-28,My 12 1928

El HERALDO de las Americas. w N 1 1924-
In Spanish
CU-B N 1,15-22 1924

Chicago HEROLD. w Ja 4 1929-
In German
MnHi Jl 5-D 1929

HLASATEL. sw Je 1 1892+
In Bohemian
pub 1892+
IU Ja-Ap 23 1920

HOWARD news. bw,w D 15 1923+
bw O 30 1928-Ja 28 1930
pub 1923+
—**Edgewater ed** *See* Edgewater news

HRVATSKA. w 1905+ *See under* Calumet, Michigan

HRVATSKA zastava. d 1901-N 1 1917||
United with Hrvatski svijet and Slovenski svet to form Jugoslovenski svijet (New York City)
In Croatian
IU S-N 1917

HRVATSKI glasnik. w 1909-32||?
1909-21 printed in Pittsburgh, Pa.
In Croatian
IU D 1,22 1917-S 1 1921

HUMORISTEN. *See* Svenska nyheter

HYDE PARK herald. w Ap 10 1881+
pub 1881-[84-1927]+
ICHi Ap 29 1882;O 4,N 22 1884;85-Mr 1889

ILLINOIS staats-zeitung. w Ap 21 1848-1922||
In German
ICHi Je 26,Jl 10,S 11,O 16-N 13,D 4-11 1876; Ja 1 1877
ICN Ja 9 1862-65;Ja 23 1866-Jl 19,O 24 1871-84;86-99
KHi Je 16 1888-S 1 1891
PPiHi O 10-17,N 14-D 19 1887
—**Evening ed** *See* Abendblatt
—**Sunday ed** *See* Der Westen

ILLINOIS staats-zeitung. d 1851-1922||
United with D. A. Bürgerzeitung to form Bürgerzeitung und Illinois staats-zeitung
Ap 21 1898 is Golden jubilee no.
In German
DLC S 1873-80
ICHi Mr 2 1867;Ja-O 1871;72-Mr,Jl 1898-1916; Mr-D 1917
ICN 1861-Je 7,30 1862-Ag 3,O 8-N 18,D 16-31 1864;Ja-Mr,My-S 1866;67-Ap,Je 22-27 1868; Ja-F 20,Mr 31-My 8 1869;My 11,Jl 22 1870-Je,Ag 9 1885-Ap 1 1901
IEN Je 1-8 1901
IU Ja 15,Mr 1 1894;Je 14 1906;13;N 1915-Je 26,O 10 1918-Mr 26,D 5-14 1921
MWA My 17(extra)O 16-19,22-N 3,8-14,16-17, 20-21 1860;N 28 1876
NN Ap 21 1898

ILLINOIS Swede. *See* Svenska tribunen-nyheter

ILLINOISER volkszeitung. w
In German
WHi Ap 22-My 27 1893

ILLUSTRATED Chicago news. w Ap 24 1868-
ICHi Ap 24-Je 13 1868
MWA My 29-Je 6 1868
WHi My 29 1868

ILLUSTRATED graphic news. w 1878-95||?
ICHi Mr 1886-S 24 1887;Ja 11,28,F 25,Mr 24, My 15-Jl,Ag 30 1888;Mr 8 1890-91

ILLUSTRATED news. w My 8 1881-
ICHi My 8 1881

ILLUSTRERET ugeblad. *See* Det Danske ugeblad (Tyler, Minn.)

INDEX. *See* Calumet index

INTER-OCEAN. d Mr 25 1872-My 10 1914||
Follows Chicago republican. United with Chicago record-herald to form Chicago record-herald and Inter-ocean, later Chicago herald and examiner
C F 4 1887-F 1889;Jl 1890-96
CLM Mr 12 1888;Mr 25 1893
CoU 1889-1909
DLC 1872-My 7 1914
I Ja-My 9 1914
IA My 11-N 7 1872[S 2 1874-My,Jl 1879-Ap,N 1881-Ja 1889]-94
IC 1873-1914
ICHi Mr-N 16 1872;O-D 1877 N 1879-88;Mr-Ap 1892;My-O 1893;1902-Ap,Ag 1906-Ap,Jl 1909-F 1914
ICN Ap 1874-1914
ICU [1879]-Mr 1882
IGK D 3 1875
IH 1893
IHi [My 4 1874-My 9 1914]
IU 1873;1909-Jl 10 1910;My 20 1911-14
IaDH 1878-Mr,Je 1894-Je 6 1905
KHi S 26 1874;Ja 16 1875;F 7 1876;F 23 1878[S 19 1881-Ap 25 1899]-Mr 5 1905
MB J. 1874-Je 1879;80-Je 1887;My 1895-1914
MWA S 7,13,O 8 1872;F 16 1874-Ag 1875;Ag 11,N 11 1876;Ag 3 1878;Je 7,Jl 31 1880;Jl 16 1883;Mr 22 1884;Ag 10 1885;D 31 1887;F 6,Jl 7,31,Ag 13,N 9,D 26-27 1888;Ja 21,Mr 1,7,Jl 1,26 1889;Mr 13 1890;N 21 1891;Ap 27 1892;Mr 25,Je 23,O 9-10,N 1 1893;O 8 1896
MiG Jl 4 1876
MiU Jl-D 1893
MnU 1890-Ag 1898
MoHi Je 17 1898
NIC 1880-Ag 1897
NNHi Je 20 1874
OHi S 1894-O 1895
P My 19 1880-Jl 1903
PBf Ja 28 1881
PScrHi Jl 24 1885
VtMS [S 1883-92]96
WHi 1873-N 1876;Ja-S 29 1877;My 1879-[80-Jl 1882;Ja-Jl]O 1886-Mr,Jl,Ag 24 1891-F 1894;95-96

Semi-weekly INTER-OCEAN. sw 1872-96||?
DLC Ja 22 1880
IaDH Ap-D 1880;Ag 1881-82
KHi Ap 15 1880;F 4[D 15 1896-Mr 1899]
MWA Je 17,Ag 5 1880

ILLINOIS (*Continued*)

CHICAGO—*Continued*

Weekly INTER-OCEAN. w Mr 25 1872-S 4 1914||
Follows Chicago republican
DLC Jl 30 1874
ICHi Jl 20 1876-83
ISal My 13 1875
IU Ja 23,Mr 27,Ap 3,17-Jl 17,Ag 14-S 4 1914
InRE Jl 3 1894
MWA S 28 1876;Ag 5,D 2 1880;Jl 7 1886
NbHi O 3 1877;F 19,Jl 1,15-Ag 5,26,S 30 1880; Jl 7 1881;Ja 8 1885;S 17 1901
TJT D 9 1902
WHi 1892-Ja 3,My 1893-94

IRISH news and Chicago citizen. *See* Chicago citizen

IRISH voice and American echo. w 1915-19||?
NN D 18 1915-Mr 4,17 1916

L'ITALIA. The Italian news. ir Ap 28 1886+
w 1886-Jl 13 1912;tw Jl 15 1912-Ag 29 1920;4 times a week Ag 31 1920+
In Italian
pub 1886+
ICHi O 25 1886-1915
IU S 1917+

JEFFERSON PARK times. w Ja 1 1930+
pub 1930+

Daily JEWISH call. w F 10 1901-
In Yiddish. Yiddish title as Der Täglicher jüdischer kol
NN F 10-Jl 19 1901

Daily JEWISH courier. d D 4 1887+
In Yiddish and English. Yiddish title: Der täglicher jüdischer courier. Suspended Mr 20-My 19 1933
pub 1900+
ICU [Je-S]1933+
IU [N 1917-Ap 1921]+
NN 1910+

Sunday JEWISH courier. w D 4 1887+
Sunday ed of Daily Jewish courier
pub 1900+

Daily JEWISH press. d 1888+
In Yiddish
ICHi Ap 1 1910

JEWISH record. . . Der Jüdischer record. w 1910-My 5 1922||
In Yiddish
IU Ag 31 1917-Jl 12,S 1918-22
NN My 24 1912-22

Chicago JOURNAL. d Ap 22 1844-Ag 21 1929||
Follows Chicago express. 1844-Ap 22 1861 as Chicago daily journal; Ap 23 1861-O 31 1871 Chicago evening journal. Merged with Chicago daily news
DLC 1851[63-65]-[68;70;75]98
IC [O 1871]Jl 1873-1929
ICHi Jl 27,Ag 14,17,S 26,D 11-12 1844[Ja-My 1845]My 1847-52;Ag 3 1853;Ag 14 1854;Mr 19 1858;S 1,18,22,O 5 1860;Ap 20,My 29 1861;My 2 1862;[Ap-D 1863;My-N 1864;65]N 13 1866; Ag 26 1867[68-S 1871]-[Ja-Mr 1873]Ag 1 1874;Ap 13 1875;76-Ap,Ag 1885-Ag 1886;89-Je 1895;97-98;F 12 1909;Ap 22 1914;Ag 22 1924
ICN Ag 31 1844-Ap,O 6 1845-Mr,N 1851-Mr 1852;53-Je,O 1854-Mr 1855;Ja-Mr,O 1856-Je 1857;58-65;Ap 1866-S 1867;Jl 1868-70;Jl 1871-Ag,O 1873-N 1905;06-29
ICU Jl 23,S 5,26 1862;S 21,N 13,27,D 2,5,18,31 1863;[Ja-My 1864]O 13 1871
IF Ja 11 1853;F 9 1863;Je 3 1865;S 7 1866;D 18 1868
IGK Jl 24 1855;My 22-29,My 21-Je 2,4-21,N 7-20,22-D 12,16-18 1862[Ja 10-Je 13 1863]My 29 1866;Ag 5 1869
IHi [Ag 27 1856-Ap 22 1924]
IU Mr 25 1862;Mr 12 1888
InI O 14 1871
KHi D 19 1877;Ap 8 1878;Jl 20 1895-S 5 1896
MWA My 27,N 16 1852;D 2 1858;Ja 4,Ap 14 1864;Ag 16 1866;O 9(extra)12,14 1871;S 16 1872;N 7,17 1876;Ap 23 1894;Ja 25,Je 6,13,27, Jl 3,11,18,25,Ag 1,8,15,22,29,S 5,12,19,26,O 3, 10 1896;Ap 22 1919
MnHi My 7 1846;My 16-19 1860;My 8 1861-D 12 1862;Jl 2 1863-F 21 1865
NN O 24 1865
NNHi [O-N 1871]Je 2 1873;extra O 9 1871; supp N 11 1871
OClWHi Ag 10 1859;Ja 21 1861;My 18,O 3 1864;D 22 1866
Tx N 10 1869
VtMS [Ag 1886-F 1890]
WHi Mr 28 1846;O 26 1847;My 16 1860;S 23,N 12 1864;Mr 30,Ap 15,21-22,My 1,5,9 1865;Mr 6,N 13,16 1869;S 17 1896-Ap 1897

Chicago weekly JOURNAL. w 1844-96||?
ICN 1847-50;52-53;63-72;Ap 1873-Ap 14,Ag 25 1875-94
IGK Ap 16 1849;O 21 1864
IU Je 14 1856
KHi D 26 1877
MWA Ag 16 1847
MnHi Ap 21 1845[46-50;58]
OClWHi Ja 20-26 1865

Le JOURNAL de l'Illinois. *See* Le courrier de l'Ouest

Chicago JOURNAL of commerce and La Salle street journal. d O 14 1920+
1920-22 as Chicago daily journal and daily financial times
pub 1920+
CSt 1922+
I [Jl 1923-24]+
IC 1920+
ICU Mr 3,6-27,31-S 4,6 1921+
IEN Je 6 1930+
IEN-C 1922+
IU N 14 1922+
IaD Je 1930+
IaDa current 6 months
MiD Mr 1924-[33]+
MnHi Jl 2,Ag 5-8,10,S 1931-My,O 1932-[34]+
MoS [Mr 1930+]
OCl 1930+
WM 1924+

JUGOSLAVIA. w 1912+
1912-Mr 6 1919 as Balkan world
In Croatian, Serbian and Slovenian
IU S 1917-Mr 11 1922

KURRE. *See* Svenska kuriren

Chicago LEADER. w 1881-84||?
ICHi Ap 8 1882;Ag 16,S 6 1884

Chicago LEDGER. w 1872-1924||?
ICHi Ap 10-Jl 17,31-N 27 1880;F 7 1885;Ja 8 1890
KHi F 11 1899-Ja 19 1901
VU Jl 17 1875
WHi 1894-96

LIBERTY bell. *See* South side news

LOGAN SQUARE herald. w Ja 1 1910+
IU 1918+

LOXIAS. w Je 17 1908-1921||?
ICHi 1908-18
IU Ag 29 1917-Ap 25 1919

MAGYAR tribune. w Ap 13 1915+
In Hungarian
pub 1915+
PPiHi [F 10 1922-Je 19 1931]

Chicago morning MAIL. d 1846-47||
ICHi Ja 14 1847

Chicago evening MAIL. d Ag 18 1870-Ja 10 1874||
United with Chicago evening post to form Chicago post and mail; later Chicago post
DLC O 11-12,18-19,21,D 18 1871;N 12 1872
IC O 11-12 1871;72
ICHi complete
IG O 12 1871

Chicago evening MAIL. d 1884-95||
Title varies slightly
FTa O 21 1892
IC S 1886;F,Jl-S 1888
ICHi Jl-S 1885;Ja-Ag,O 1886-Jl 1887;Jl 3,O 21 1893;Jl 7,9,16 1894
ICN Jl 1885-Ag,O 1886-Ja,S 1888-Jl 1894;Ja-Je 14 1895

MAYFAIR times. w N 16 1925+
pub 1925+

Il MESSAGGIERE. sw Je 21 1888-89||?
In Italian and English
ICHi Jl 5,13-24 1888

Il MESSAGGIERE italiano dell'ouest. w Ag 6 1867-69||
1867-N 11 1868 as L'Unione italiana
DLC O 1-16,30 1867-D 23 1868;Ja,F 10 1869

MEXICO. *See* El Nacional

El NACIONAL. w Ja 18 1924+
1924-D 18 1930 as Mexico
In Spanish
pub 1925+
CU-B Ja 18 1924;Ja 24-F 7,Mr 7,21,Ap 4-11 1925;My 15,Je 5[Ag 1926-D 12 1931]

NÅD och sanning. *See* Vårt land och folk

NÁROD. d F 8 1894+
In Bohemian
pub 1894+
ILiS [1933]+
IU S 13 1917+

NATIONAL democrat. w 1897-1900||?
WHi Jl 7,28,Ag 25-N 3 1900

NATIONAL demokrat. d Je 29-D 12 1876||?
In German
ICN [Jl 27-D 12 1876]
MWA Ag 29 1876

Daily NATIONAL union. d Mr 16 1858-
MWA [Mr-My 23 1858]

NATIONAL zeitung. w S 14 1891-92||?
In German
IC 1891-Mr 1892

Weekly NATIVE citizen. w N 8? 1855-56||?
IGK Mr 1 1856
IHi S 6 1856

NAUJIENOS. The Lithuanian daily news. d F 9 1914+
In Lithuanian
pub 1914+
IU O 23 1917+

NEDELNI svornost. w
Sunday ed of Svornost
In Bohemian
IU D 4 1932+

NEUE Chicagoer freie presse. *See* Chicagoer freie presse

Chicago weekly NEWS. w 1866-93||?
IC 1881-92
ICHi Jl 11 1878-90;93
ICU 1881-88
KHi N 13 1884-My 7 1885
MWA D 15-29 1881
NN Ap 3,17,My 22,Je 5 1879
NcD S 30 1880
VU Ag 18,S-O 13,27-N 3,17,D 8 1892-Ja 12, 26-My 6,27-Je 10,24,Ag 12,26-S 2,16,30,O 28 1893
WHi 1892

Chicago daily NEWS. d Mr 7 1872-
ICHi Mr 7-8 1872
WHi Je 24-O 4 1872

Chicago daily NEWS. d Ja 2 1876+
A specimen number was issued D 23 1875
Ja 5 1926 is 50th anniversary number
pub Jl 1878+
CCIP D 1921-N 1927;Ja-Je 1928
CLM F 11 1886;Ag 5 1893
DLC 1898;My 1900+
I current year only
IA Ja,Mr-S 1886
ICHi D 23 1875;Ja-Jl,O 1877-N 1880;81-F,My 1883-Je,Ag 1889-Mr,Je 1890-91;Mr 1892-Mr, My 1899-S,N 1900+
ICN My-Je,O 1877-Je,Ag 1895-My 15,Je 16 1900-O 15 1901
ICU O-D 1883;D 1 1885;D 1888;97-Jl 15,Ag-D 1902;D 1917;Ja-O,D 1918-F,Ap-Je,Ag-O 1919;F 1920;Ja 5 1926
IF My 1898-99
IGK Je 5,N 6 1879;S 17 1886
IGa current 6 months
IHi Ap 1911-34
IMaW current 2 months
IMi 1933+
IU O 31 1888;Ag 6 1909;Mr 31-Ap 2 1910;Ap 17-19 1913; Mr 20 1916;Je 12 1926
KHi [Jl 1896-Ag 1912]
MWA Je 2 1894
MdBJ Je 17,24,Jl 1,8 1929
MdBSa My 27 1933
MiAC [1930-31;33]34
MiG N 12 1887;Je 5,13,26-27,Jl 3 1889;Ja 5 1926
MoS Ap 26 1893-Ja 18 1894
NBHi [1924]
NN [My 10-Jl 26 1893]
NcD Ag 3 1887;Ap 30 1889;Je 17,24,Jl 1,8 1929
NjPa Je 17,24,Jl 1,8 1929
NjR Je 17-Jl 1929;Je 13 1934(supp)
OClWHi Je 5,7 1880;Jl 23 1885;O 1886-Ap 1891
OHi Ag 1927+
PEL [1929]
T Je 17-Jl 8 1929
TxGR Ja 5 1926
VtMS [N 1884-Ja 1891]
WaPS O 1-11 1923;N 5-9 1928

Chicago morning NEWS. d 1881-82 *See* Chicago record

Chicago daily NEWS-RECORD. *See* Chicago record

NORDEN. w O 13 1874-O 2? 1897||
United with Amerika to form Amerika og Norden (Madison, Wis.) later Amerika
In Norwegian
IaDeL O 22 1874-[92-94]96-Ag 28 1897
MWA O 1891-Ja 2 1894
MnSL 1874-79
WHi D 31 1879-Mr 22 1892;94-O 2 1897

NORSKE Amerikaner. bw My 25 1866-
In Norwegian
MnSL My-S 7 1866

NORTH LOOP news. bm S 11 1930+
pub 1930+

NORTH SHORE news. w 1890+
1890-92 as Rogers Park news; 1893-1903 as Rogers Park news-herald
pub 1890+
IHi 1892[95-1901;S 1902-Jl 7 1911]

NORTH SIDE reporter. w Jl 20 1878-80||
ICHi N 23 1878;O 4 1879;Ja 31,Je 5 1880

NORTH TOWN news and the West Rogers Park news. w Mr 1928+
Mr-Jl 1928 as West Rogers Park news
pub 1928+

NORTHCENTER news. w D 10 1925+
pub 1925+

La NOTICIA mundial. w Ag 7 1927-
In Spanish
CU-B 1927-F 12 1928

NOVAÏA zarîa. *See under* San Francisco, Cal.

NOVÉ časy. New times. w Mr 1 1918+
In Slovak
pub 1918+

NOWY swiat. (New world) w,sw O 1873-Jl 23 1921||
1873-Ja 20 1917 as Gazeta polska (title varies). Merged with Cepy (not in this list)
sw 1915
In Polish
IU O 8 1914-Ja 20 1917
MiG 1906-21

La NUEVO solidaridad. w N 30 1918-19||?
In Spanish
MnHi 1918-Ap 28 1919
PP My 31,Je 28 1919

NY tid. *See under* New York City

NYA Svenska amerikanaren. S 8 1866-76||
1866-Mr 1873 as Svenska amerikanaren. Merged with Svenska tribunen, later Svenska tribunen-nyheter
In Swedish
IRA complete

NYA världen. *See* Svenska tribunen-nyheter

OSADNÉ hlasy. Slovak-parish-news. w S 1 1928+
In Slovak
pub 1928+

OTTHON. At home. m,w Ag 1 1908+
m 1908-N 1911
In Hungarian
pub 1914+
PPiHi [1924;30-31]

Weekly PANTAGRAPH. w
IRA F 17-24 1858

La PAROLA del popolo. w 1908+
In Italian
IU D 1921-Mr 3 1923

PEOPLE'S paper. w Jl 26-Ag 16 1873||
ICHi Jl 26,Ag 16 1873

PEOPLE'S press. w
KHi [Mr 18 1911-Je 27 1912]
PP O 24-31 1936

Le PETIT journal de Chicago. d 1901-03||
In French
IHi Jl 8-10 1903
WHi Je 22-Jl 24 1903

ILLINOIS (*Continued*)

CHICAGO—*Continued*

POKROK. w 1868-
In Czechoslovakian
MWA Je 26 1868

POLONIA. w 1906+
In Polish
pub 1916+
IU 1918+

POMEROY'S illustrated democrat. w 1869-80||?
1869-Ja 1878 as Pomeroy's democrat
1869-75 pub in New York City
DLC 1870-78
GAA Ap 12 1871
ICHi 1876-Ap 3 1880
KHi [1874-F 1875]Jl 8 1876
MWA Mr 3 1869;Jl 6,Ag 24 1870;F 15,Jl 29,S 9-23,O 7-28,N 18-D 2,16,30 1871;Ja 6,20,F 10, Mr 9-16,N 9 1872;Jl 1,22,S 23 1876
N My 3,24,Jl 8,9(supp)15,16(supp)22(supp)23 (supp),Jl 29,30(supp)1871
NN D 17 1870;Ja 6-My 5 1871
NNHi Ap 27 1870
NbHi Ap 6 D 14 1870;Ap 6 1878
NcD F 17 1869
PPiHi Ag 24 1870
WHi D 25 1875-D 21 1878;Ja 11-18,F 8-15 1879

PORTAGE PARK times. w Ja 1 1930+
pub 1930+

Chicago POST. d D 23 1860-Ag 1865||
1860-63 as Chicago morning post. Merged with Chicago republican
DLC 1860-Mr 1861;Ap 5,Je 3,S 14 1864
ICHi O 13 1861;S 1862-Ap,My 8,15,22,Je 12 1864
ICN 1860-Mr 1861;Jl 1862-64
MBAt Ap 17-19 1865
MWA O 6,9,11 1862
MnHi F 2,Ag 9 1862
NjR Je 4 1863

Chicago POST. d S 4 1865-Ag 1878||
1865-Ja 1866 as Daily Chicago post; F 3 1866-Ja 10 1874 Chicago evening post; Ja 12 1874-Ag 6 1876 Chicago post and mail. Merged with Chicago daily news O 6 1871 is "Fire extra"
pub Jl 31 1872-Ja 10,Jl-S 1874;Je 1875-Je 1878
DLC My 30 1868;O 18 1871
IC Jl-S 1874,75-Je 1876;Ja-Je 1878
ICHi O 24-D 14,17-31 1866;F 20 1867-77;F 14-15,17-Jl 1 1878
IG O 10-11 1871
IHi Ap 17 1866;My 23-24 1872
MWA O 10(extra)17,D 5 1871;S 28,N 24 1876
N O 6,N 11,20,25,28 1871;My 2 1873
NCanHi O 18 1871
NCort O 18 1871
NbHi S 21 1875
WHi O 10(extra)16,18-19,21-23,28 1871

Chicago weekly POST. w 1865-78||
DLC O 26 1871
IC O 26 1871
ICHi O 26 1871;Ja 18 1872
IHi N 18,D 2,16 1869;Ap 7,Ag 18,S 1-9 1870;O 26 1871

Chicago evening POST. d Ap 29 1890-O 29 1932||
Merged with Chicago daily news
O 8 1921 is 50th anniversary Chicago fire ed
pub complete
A 1911
DLC 1898;Ap 1911-27
ICHi 1890-S 1904;05-S 1906;08-S 1912;Ap 1913-30
ICN Je 15 1894;Ap 29 1915;O 8 1921
IEN 1890-Mr 1896;97-1903;Jl-D 1904;O-D 1905; O 1906-07,My 1909-Je 1910;Je-Ag 1911-20; N 1921-22;Ag 1923;Je,D 1924;F 1925;26-32
IEN-C Mr 1925-32
IU S 1908-Ap 28,My 1-25 1914;Jl 1-27,D 14,31 1916;D 8 1917-Jl 27,S 17,20,N 27,D 31 1918-My 1920;Jl 1921-Ag 9 1926
KHi Jl 1896-N 1899
MWA O 8 1921
MiU Jl 1890-[1914-15]
NN [My 2-O 1893]N 26 1898;N 28 1896
NcD Mr 4 1913
OHi 1901
WHi N 11 1903-S 22 1905;S 30 1916
WaPS [1911-12]-Ja 17 1913[17]Ja 18 1918

Chicago POSTEN. w 1881-1929||
1918-29 pub in Minneapolis, Minn. but dated also at Chicago
In Danish
IaDeL S 17 1896;Je 3 1897;D 28 1899;N 22,D 16-20 1900[Ja 31 1901-F 1902]
MnHi Je 21 1917-Ap 4 1929
WHi 1899-S 1919

Chicago daily PRESS. d S 16 1852-Je 30 1858||
1852-My 1857 as Daily democratic press; My 8-Je 1857 Chicago daily democratic press. United with Chicago daily tribune to form Chicago press and tribune, later Chicago daily tribune
DLC 1854-56;F 20 1857
IC S 16 1854-[57-58]
ICHi complete
IGK Jl 23 1855;Jl 7,O 21 1856;Jl 18,Ag 1,22,S 19,D 12 1857;Ja 30,F 13,Mr 6,Ap 3-17,My 15-22 1858
IHi [Mr 4-D 1853]
KHi O 18 1858
MWA N 25 1852;N 2 1853;F 13 1854;F 12 1857
MnHi D 11 1856;D 14,24 1857;Ja 4,7 1858
NhD [1856-S 1857]
OClWHi O 30 1857
PEHi Je 3 1856
WHi Ja 7 1856-58

Chicago PRESS and tribune. d *See* Chicago daily tribune

Chicago PRESS and tribune. w *See* Chicago weekly tribune

PROLETAREC. w Ja 1906+
In Slovenian
pub 1906+
NN 1929-33
WHi F 1906;N 16 1909+

Chicago PUBLIC ledger. w 1898-1900||?
ICHi 1899-Ap 26 1900

QUID nunc. d Jl 12-Ag 16 1842||
First one cent daily pub west of the Alleghenies
DLC Jl 12,18 1842

RAIL splitter. w Je 23-O 27 1860||
Campaign paper
ICHi Jl 21,Ag 18-O 13,27 1860
PMe O 13 1860

RASSVET. d 1916+
1916-My 14 1926 as Russkiĭ vestnik; My 21-N 1926 Russkiĭ vestnik-rassvet
In Russian
CSt-H [1924-26]29-33
DLC N 12 1923+

La RAZA. w Ap 7 1928-
In Spanish
CU-B Ap 28 1928

Chicago daily RECORD. d 1857?-
MWA S 12 1867

Chicago RECORD. d Mr 21 1881-Mr 27 1901||
1881-Jl 20 1882 as Chicago morning news; Jl 24 1882-My 7 1892 Chicago daily news. Morning ed; My 9 1892-Mr 11 1893 Chicago daily news-record. United with Chicago times-herald to form Chicago record-herald, later Chicago herald and examiner
DLC 1881-82;85-Ja,Mr 1886-Ja,Mr 1887-F,My-Je 1888;Ap 1896-Ap 1897;Ja-Ap,S 1898-1901
—**Saturday ed.** *See* Chicago Saturday record
IC Mr 21-My 7 1881;82-1901
ICHi complete
ICN My-N 1893
ICU 1881-88;O 1884-O 1888;Ja-Ag,N 1889-Je,S-O 1891;My 1892-1901
IEN F 21,Mr 21-Ap 3,5-Ag 1898
IHi Ap 11 1894;Mr 15,N 11,19,D 5 1895;D 30 1897
IU O 10 1893;S 20 1897;Ja 15,Ap 22 1898
IaDH S 1898-1901
MWA O 3,N 1,6 1856
MiGh Ap 27,My 2,13 1898
MiU Jl 1896-Je 1900
OClWHi Ja 15 1861
WAL 1899-1900
WHi 1895-Je,O 1899-1901

Chicago Saturday RECORD. w 1892-D 28 1895||*
IC 1894-D 21 1895
ICHi 1894-D 21 1895
WHi Ap 8 1893-95

Chicago RECORD-HERALD. *See* Chicago herald and examiner

Weekly REPORTER. w 1893-F 6 1925||
Merged with South end reporter
IC D 14 1917-25

Chicago REPOSITORY. d O 29 1932||
Chicago repository published to fill in intervening day in merger of Chicago evening post and Chicago daily news in order to retain Associated Press membership
MWA complete

Chicago REPUBLICAN. d My 30 1865-Mr 22 1872||
1865 as Chicago daily republican. Followed by Inter-ocean
DLC Je 9,15 1865;Ja-S 1866;Jl 23 1867-69;O 13,15-16 1871
IA Ja 15 1866-68
IC O 12 1871
ICHi N 25 1865-S 1870;F 20,Mr 28,Je 1,3,Ag 7,S 15,O 7 12,13-18 1871;Ja 22-Mr 22 1872
ICN complete
IGK D 23 1865;D 10 1866;Mr 18 1867;D 19 1870
IHi N 1 1863;Ja 9 1867
MB F 18,Jl 27 1868;Je 6,20-21 1869;N 14 1870
MBAt 1865-Ja 12 1871
MWA D 10 1865;O 6 1866;Ag 6 1867;My 25,D 29 1870
NNHi N 1865-Ja 1 1867;Mr 20 1869;O 17,N 30, D 4-5 1871
OOxM S 29 1871
WHi [O 3 1867-69]O 5[14-D 15]1870

Tri-weekly REPUBLICAN. tw
ICHi N 22 1865
NNHi D 4 1865

Chicago REPUBLICAN. w 1865-Mr 1872|
Followed by Weekly inter-ocean
DLC Mr 12-19 1868
IU O 23 1865
NbHi O 22 1868
NcD S 4 1867;F 29-Mr 7,21-Je 22 1868

REPUBLICAN. w D 25 1916-21||?
ICHi 1917-D 13 1919
IU Je 9,Jl 1917-D 13 1919;Ja-My 7 1921
WHi N 17 1917

Saturday evening REVIEW. w N 5 1859-
ICHi D 17 1859

Chicago daily REVIEW. d
IaDH Ja 12-O 23 1905

Weekly REVIEW. w 1905+
Ap 15 1921-Ap 6 1923 pub in Blue Island
IU Ap 15 1921-Mr 4 1932

REVYEN. *See* Dansk tidende og revyen

ROVNOST Ľudu. Slovak daily newspaper. w,sw d O 6 1906—
w 1906-My 1 1920;sw My 1920-My 1 1926
In Slovak
pub 1906+
IU Ag 29 1917-Jl 19 1926
WHi N 24 1909-Jl 17 1926

RUSSIAN review. *See* Russkoe obozrenie

RUSSKIĬ vestnik. *See* Rassvet

RUSSKOE obozrenie. Russian review. w S 1 1927+
In Russian and English
pub 1927+
CSt-H 1929+

SALONIKI. *See* Bezzadonikh

SAN MIN morning paper. d
In Chinese
IU Ja 22 1935+

SATURDAY express. *See* Chicago express

SCANDIA. Norwegian weekly. w O 1888+
1888-99? pub in Superior, Wis. and Duluth, Minn.
In Norwegian
pub 1910+
IU S 1917+
IaDeL [S 10 1896-Ag 1897;S 22 1900-D 14 1901;F 14 1920-22]+
MnHi Jl 4 1890;Ja 9 1891-[99]N 30 1907-My 25 1917

Chicago SEARCHLIGHT. w Je 7 1894-Ap 6 1895||
United with Age to form Age and Chicago searchlight, later Age
KHi 1894-Mr 1895
WHi 1894-Mr 1895

SENTINEL. w 1878-1904||?
ICHi N 15 1883-O 1884
MWA S 23 1880
NbHi Ag 21-28,S 11-25 1879 Mr 6,Ap 24 1884

SKANDINAVEN. w,tw,sw My 2 1866+
Suspended O 9-14 1871
In Norwegian
pub [1871]+
ICHi Jl 4 1877
IU Ag 27 1909+
IaSc current 6 months
MWA O 25 1881
MnHi [1868-74]-76;78[79]-83-88;90-92;94;96-1900;02-06;17;27]29+
MnSLS 1870-79
MnU 1926+
NdHi D 10 1926-34
WHi O 11 1866;Mr 30 1870-72;74-76;F 1878-1911;Ap 1930+
WaPS S 17 1915-[17-20]
—**Minneapolis ed** *See under* Minneapolis, Minn.

SKANDINAVEN. d 1870-My 1930||
In Norwegian
IaDeL [1901]-03;Ap-Je 1904 Ja-Je,O 1905-30
MnHi [1905-07]-[09-10]-[12]-[14-15]-[27]
WHi O 3 1895-98;Mr 28 1900-Mr 1930
—**Minneapolis ed.** *See under* Minneapolis, Minn

SLAVIE. w O 30 1861+
Follows Slovan amerikansky (Racine, Wis.) 1861-Je 18 1912 pub at Racine, Wis.
In Bohemian
pub 1918+
IU Ag 28 1917-Jl 8 1918
WHi 1861-Ap 1862[Ja 12-S 13 1865]74-Jl 5 1918

SLOVAK American news. . . Slovensko-Ameriky zabavnik. w 1904+
In Slovak and English
pub 1930+

SLOVENSKO-AMERIKY zabavnik. *See* Slovak American news

SOCIAL-DEMOKRATEN. w 1911-18||?
In Danish and Norwegian
NN Ag 1911-18

SOCIALIST. w S 14 1878-Ag 16 1879||
ICHi complete
MB complete

Chicago daily SOCIALIST. d F 23 1901-Ap 27 1912||
1901-Mr 1 1902 as Workers call; Mr 8 1902-F 28 1903 Chicago socialist. Followed by Evening world
CtY Jl 25,S 9,23,N 1 1911
DLC S 1909-Ja,My-O 1910;F 1911-Je 1912
ICHi My 4 1912
ICJ My 1907-Ap 27 1912
ICN N 1907-(Ap-Ag) 1912
ICU Mr 8 1902-F 1903;My 1905-O 1909;N 1910-Ap 1911
NNRa [1908]
TxU N 4 1907-Ja 1909
WM 1901-Mr 1907;My-O 1908;My-O 1909;N 1911-12

SÖNDERJYDSK tidende. w 1895-
In Danish
WHi [O 15 1895-Ag 18 1896]

SONNTAGPOST. w Mr 5 1899+
Sunday ed of Abendpost
In German
pub 1899+
IU O 11 1914+

Chicagoer SONNTAGSBOTE. w 1871-1913||?
1871-S 1882 as Daheim; O 1882-O 20 1889 Chicagoer daheim; O 27 1889-Jl 24 1898 Daheim
Sunday ed of Chicagoer freie presse
In German
IC F 11-My 1872;91-1901
ICHi Jl 3 1881;My 16 1886
ICN Mr 10-31,My 5,26-Jl 21 1872;Mr 1873-74; 76-Je,S 13,N 1885-Jl 11,S 5 1886-96
KHi S 2,16 1888;My 23 1893

Chicago SONNTAGS-ZEITUNG. *See* Der Westen

SOUTH END reporter and weekly reporter combined. w 1893+
IU Mr 5 1925-Je 25 1925

SOUTH SIDE news. w S 13 1924+
1924-Ag 25 1932 as Liberty bell
pub [1924-34]+

ILLINOIS (*Continued*)

CHICAGO—*Continued*

SOUTHTOWN economist. sw F 14 1924+
pub 1924+

SPRAVEDLNOST. d,w Mr 1905+
d Jl 4 1905-N 1930
In Bohemian
pub 1905+
IU O 18 1917+
WHi Mr 28,Ap 4,My 30,Je 20,Jl 4,O 11 1903
—sm ed *See* Zájmy lidu

STAATS-HEROLD. w 1906+
In German
IU [Ap-S 1932]

STANDARD opinion. w S 1896+
pub 1896-Ja 1933;S 1934+

Chicago evening STAR. d Ag? 1861-
ICHi S 25,O 2 1861

Chicago daily STAR. d 1882-87‖?
ICHi Mr 16-My 16 1887

Chicago Sunday SUN. w
ICHi Ja 19 1908-Mr 21 1909

SVENSKA amerikanaren. w 1866-73. *See* Nya Svenska amerikanaren

SVENSKA amerikanaren. w 1876+
1876-S 1877 as Svenska posten; O 1 1914-26 Svenska Amerikanaren hemlandet
In Swedish
ICHi D 8 1887
IRA 1876+
IU O 15 1914+
KHi Ap 28 1885-S 26 1918;Ag 12-My 3 1923
MiG O 1914+
MnHi 1891+

SVENSKA kuriren. w 1884-O 3 1929‖
1884-87 as Kurre. Merged with Svenska amerikanaren
In Swedish
IRA 1889-1929
IU Ag 30 1917-29
MnHi [D 20 1892-1908]-29
WHi Ap 14-Ag 18 1896;O 1898-Ja 1899

SVENSKA nyheter. m,w 1891-Je 1906‖
1891-1903 as Humoristen. United with Svenska tribunen to form Svenska tribunen-nyheter
In Swedish
IRA 1902-05
WHi O 1901-O 21 1902

SVENSKA posten. *See* Svenska amerikanaren.

SVENSKA socialisten. *See* Ny tid (New York City)

SVENSKA tribunen-nyheter. w Ja 4 1869+
Ja-N 1869 as Illinois Swede; D 1869-76 Nya världen; 1876-Je 1906 Svenska tribunen
1869-70 pub in Galva
In Swedish and English
pub 1876+
CLM F 12 1891
CtY Jl 15 1885
IRA 1870-Ja 5 1874;77-1933
IU O 9 1917+
KHi Ja 31-Mr 2 1923
MWA N 4 1876
MnHi [1879-S 20 1905]Mr 3,Je 23 1908+

SVENSKA världen. w 1904-08‖
Merged with Svenska Amerikanaren
In Swedish
IRA complete
MnHi [Ag 1907-F 28 1908]

SVOBODNAÎA rossîîa. w 1917-23‖?
In Russian
CSt-H [1922-23]
DLC F-Ag 19 1918;Jl 19 1922-N 10 1923

SVORNOST. d O 8 1875+
In Bohemian
pub 1875+
IU N 28 1932+
MWA Ap 22 1895
—Sunday ed *See* Nedelni svornost
—w ed *See* Amerikan

TABLET. w My 8 1880-81‖?
ICHi My 8 1880

Evening TELEGRAM. d O 15 1882-86‖
ICHi O 16 1882;Ja 9-13,15,17-20,22,24,F 21,S 20,O 11-13,15-16 1883;Ag 19 1884;Mr 17 1886
MWA Ag 10 1883
NbHi Jl 5 1884

Chicago evening TELEGRAPH. d Ja 5 1876-
DLC Je 20 1876
IC Ja 5-Ag 5 1876
ICHi Ja 5 1876
WHi Jl 8 1876

Chicago daily TELEGRAPH. d Mr 26 1878-My 9 1881‖
Followed by Chicago herald
ICHi complete
WHi My 31-Jl 7 1879

Chicago Sunday TEMPEST. w S 9 1894-
ICHi S 16 1894

Daily TIMES. d,tw Je 12 1852-O 18 1853‖
MWA Jl 14 1852

Chicago TIMES. d Ag 30 1854-Mr 3 1895‖
1854-Jl 30 1860 as Chicago daily times; Jl 31-N 26 1860 Daily times and herald; N 27 1860-Je 21 1861 Daily Chicago times. United with Chicago herald to form Chicago times-herald, later Chicago herald and examiner
pub Ag 9 1861-95
C F 2 1887-F 22 1889
CaM 1889-92
Ct Ag 18-19 1880
CtY O 9 1872
DLC Jl 3 1855;56;58[60;63-66;71]72[74]Ag 1876-[77-78]91-Ag 1894
IA Ag 7 1868-Ap 1873[S 2 1874-Ap,N 1881-Ag 1889]
ICHi Ap 3,My 2 1856;Ja 13 1857[58]S 23 1859; Mr 15,My 24,S 10,17,24 1860;Je 8,11-19,O 15 1861[62-72]Ap 13,S 26,D 14 1873;Jl 15-16, O 8 1874;75-Jl 1888;N 2 1893
ICN Ag 20 1857-Je,O-D 1858;Ap 1859-Mr 1860; Ja-Je 1864;O 1866-67;Jl-D 1868;Ap 1869-Je 1871;72-Je 1891;My-O 1893;94
ICU [Ja-Ap 1855]Jl 22 1862;Mr 22[S 1863-Mr 1865]74;Jl 1875-Je 1876[78-79]-Ja 3,5-17,20,Ap 1880-Je 1882
IGK F 11 1865;Ag 9 1867;O 6,27 1868;F 4,Je 18,N 19 1870;My 24,Ag 6 1873;O 19 1876
IHi [1860-65]
ILeM My 2-Ag 28 1868
IP 1883-Mr 1884;O 1890-91
IU O 15.20,23,N 2,13 1866[67-N 1868;Mr-Ag 1869;F-S 1870]F 9,Mr 10-13,17,20,Ap 7,19,My 5 1871;Je 6-8 1880;S 20 1881;Jl 1(supp)1882; S 12 1884;Ag 5 1885
IaDH Jl 1894-F 1895
IaGG D 13 1860
InI O 18 1871
InRE Je 15 1872[S,D 1873-Ap 1874]
KHi Mr 12 1891-[F 8 1893-Ag 7 1894]
LNH N 30 1863
MWA Jl 19 1860;Jl 7,O 8,11 1862;N 11 1863;Je 21 1870;Ja 12,O 18 1871;F 14,16 1872;My 16 1874;My 8,Je 15,N 7 1876;My 30 1881;N 2 1893
MiG D 31 1861;Ja 11,Jl 23,O 21,D 27 1862;N 30,D 25 1863;My 27,Ag 30 1864;F 21,Ap 8,Jl 7,S 18 1865;D 3,28 1867;Mr 21,D 17 1868;D 22 1870;Ja 4,18 1871;S 20 1881;Jl 1(supp)1882
MnHi My 10,Ag 18 1861[62]Ap 15 1865
N Je 26 1859;N 3 1861;F 23 1863;Mr 17,20 1864; Jl 16 1867;O 18 1871
NN Ja-Ag 16,N 26 1873;Ag 25 1874;F 5,Je 19-23,28 1876
NNHi Ja 11 1864;Mr 30,Ap 6,13 1870[O-N 1871]My 1 1873
NSyU Ag 14 1862;Ag 30-S 1 1864
NbHi Je 9,Ag 16,N 11 1880;Je 18,Jl 4,S 21,23-24,N 19 1881;D 13,15-16 1882;Ag 14 1884;My 31 1890;F 26 1892;O 9 1893;Ag 16-21 1894;S 4-14,16-O 4,7-16,19-N 16,18-23,25-27,29-30 1894
NcD [1871-72;77]
NcU Ja-Mr,Jl-S 1877
NhD S 6-7 1866;Mr 26 1867
ODW F 2 1869;F 15,17,Ap 4 1870
OOxM S 29 1871;Mr 15,O 23-25 1873
P My 19-D 1880
PDoHi S 7 1866
Tx D 16 1862;Ja 24-26 1867;Je 18 1868;F 11 1870;D 25 1894
VU Je 22 1870
VtMS [O 1884-89]
WHi Ag 27-S 13 1861;My 13 1863;F 20 1864;O 1866-95

Chicago TIMES. w Ag 31 1854-93‖?
1866-70 as Times
IA S 14 1854;Ap 10 1856;Ag 25 1862;S 25 1866
IC O 16 1856;S 25 1866-90
ICN Mr 1882-F 1883
ICU Mr 29-Ap 19,My 3-17,31-Jl,Ag 9,30-S 20,O 4,18-D 6 1855;Ja 10-17,31,F 28-My 15,Je-Jl 3 1856
IGK N 11 1858
IU [Ap-D 1856]-Mr 5,19,Ag-D 10,24 1857-[58]-F 17,Mr-Ap 21,O 13-27,N 17 1859;Ja 12,F 2-16,Mr 22 1860;Ja 10,F 21,Mr 14-28,My 23,S 3, N 19,D 10 1861;Ja 7,F 11-18,Mr 4-11,Ap 29,S 30,N 11,D 16 1862;S 29,N 10 1863;Ja 5,Ap 12 1864;My 3 1871
IaHi Jl 1889-O 1891
In 1855-93
MoHi My 2 1893
N Ap 26,D 13,27 1855;My 15,29,Jl 3 1856;Ap 2 1857;S 15 1863;O 25 1864;Ja,My 8,29,Ag 7-21, S 11-25,O 9-16,N 20,D 4 1866;Ja 8,22 1867
OClWHi Je 16,Jl 7,28-Ag 4,25,S 1-8,O 13 1863; Ja 19,Mr 1,15-22,My 10,Je 14,28,Ag 30,N 8,29 1864;Je 30 1865;S 14 1867;Ja 30 1868;O 18-23 1871;S 4 1873;Je 9 1880;F 21 1883;D 28 1884
OHi N 10 1863;N 14 1866;Mr 2 1868;Ja 4,9 1869;N 1 1873;S 30 1876
WHi Ja 13 1859;D 27 1864

Sunday TIMES. w 1866-
MWA My 16,30,O 10 1869;S 29 1872;F 16 1873; My 22 1881
OOxM O 26 1873

Daily illustrated TIMES. d S 3 1929+
pub 1929+
IC 1929+

Sunday TIMES. w Mr 20 1932+
pub 1932+

Chicago TIMES-HERALD. *See* Chicago herald and examiner

TOWN of Lake Eye. w 1878-1906‖?
ICHi Mr 10 1883-Ap 26 1884

La TRIBUNA Italiana trans-Atlantica. w 1898+
In Italian
IU Jl 23 1910;Ap 15-22,D 2 1911;Mr 22 1913;O 17 1914-Jl 9 1932
PPCHi [1898]

TRIBUNE. w Ap 4 1840-Ag 21 1841‖
Followed by Milwaukee journal (Milwaukee, Wis)
CSmH Jl 18 1840
DLC Ap 11 1840,Ap 24 1841
ICHi complete

Chicago daily TRIBUNE. d Je 10 1847+
1847-Je 1858 as Chicago daily tribune; Jl 1858-O 24 1860 Chicago press and tribune; O 25 1860-O 6 1872 Chicago tribune Mr 23-24 1849,O 9-10 1871 never published. Section 2, D 25 1933 "Facsimilies of sixteen historic front pages": Ap 15 1861;Ap 10, 15 1865;O 11 1871;Ap 6 1895;F 16,My 2 1898; S 7 1909;Ap 16 1912;Ap 3 1917;N 11-12 1918; Je 9 1919;My 22 1927;F 16,N 8 1933
pub 1857+
A Jl 1880-Je 1882;Jl 1884-1902
C F 3 1887-89;O 1 1915
CClP F 4 1868;O 28 1911-O 1925
CL N 1899-1914
CLM N 13 1892
CSt [1874]-[76;79]-[88;1918]-[21]
CSt-H [1914-15;17-18]
CU [1885]98;S 9 1901
CaM 1884-87
CoBoC O 11 1871
CoU 1900;02;S 1906-My 1910
CtY O 9 1872;Ja-Je 1873;F 1876-Mr 1887[1933]
DLC Je 12 1855;Ap 7,10,16,24,O 9 1868;Mr 22 1861;Jl 24 1862;Ja 15,29,F 12,Je 3 1863-Jl, 1866;F 18-Je 1867;Ja 15,Jl 1,25 1868;Je 23-24 1869;Mr 16,27,Ap 17,29-Jl 16,D 5-26 1870;Ja-Mr,My 30,Je 11,25,Jl 4,S 3,O 18,20,D 1871+
I Mr 9-D 1888;1914-Ja 1922;current year only
IA [S 2 1874-My,Jl 1879-Ap,N 1881-F,My-D 1882;O 1884-Ag 1889]Jl 1906-Ap 1921
IAC [Mr 2 1935+]
IB current 5 years
IC 1861-Ap 29 1870;My 6-Jl 14,O 2 1871-Ja 1872
ICHi Ap 23 1849;D 28 1850;Ja 4,O 4 1851;Jl 11-12 1854;Jl 1858-[66-67]-1913;Jl 29 1914-19; F 1920-Jl,O-D 1921;25+
ICN [1861-66;68-69]+
ICU O 21,N 1,D 30 1863[Ja-Je 1864]O 1872-74; Jl-D 1875;Ap-My,Ag 1876-S 1891;92-S 1901; 14-F,My 1920+
ICan 1926+
IEN D 17 1892-99;Mr-Ap,Jl-Ag,N 1900-F,S 1905-F,Jl 1911-F,My 1913+
IEuC current 3 months
IF 1918-29[32+]
IG 1874+
IGK Jl 13 1855;Jl 15 1856;Ap 26,My 1-17,20-24,S 8-13,15-O 5,8-9,18-19,24,N 6,11 1861;Ja 8, 15,28,Mr 12,14-15,18-Ap 4,6-8,10-18,25-28,My 3 1862;D 2 1869;Ja 12,F 23,Mr 9,S 7,28-N 16,30 1870;Ja 4-11,25-F 1,Mr 8,22,Je 29 1871;My 22,O 1 1874;Ag 16,S 25 1875
IGr current 6 months
IHi Ja 21,27 1854;Ag 23,S 9,17-18,22,O 6,9,15, 18 1858[Ap 1861-67]Ja 23,30 1868;Ap 13,Jl 4 1870;Ja 12,Ag 12,O 11 1871[Mr-D 1872;Je-Ag 1873]Je 18 1874;Ap 5 1878;Jl 3,S 20-30,O 1-2, 5-6 1881;Ag 9 1885;O 22 1892;Ap 30 1893+
ILfC Ag 1905-O 1906
IMaW current 2 months
IP 1864-F 1865;Jl-O 1867;F-S 1868;O-D 1870; 72-74;Mr 1875-F,Je 1876-Ap,Jl 1882-1906;08+
IU Jl 1858-62;Ja-My,Jl 1865-Ja 1873;74-Ja 1, My 1880+
IaCfT current year only
IaDH Jl-Ag,O-D 1898;My 21 1905-14
IaDa current 6 months
IaFm current 6 months
IaGG current year only
IaHi Ja-S 1854;Ja 11-Je 1855;Ap 1897-1903
IaMu current 3 months
IaSc current 6 months
In Mr 1863-N 1865;Je 1873-N 1893;O 1918-23
InI Ap 1876-Ja 1878;87-95
InLHi D 6 1870
InRE Ag 4 1869;F 28 1879
InTI Ap 1911-Je 1925
InU 1921+
KHi Jl 11 1862-O 26 1863[Je 1874-Ag 1912]+
LNaS 1930+
MB D 27 1855-S 20 1856;D 13 1861;My 29 1863; Ap 20 1865;O 25,N 2,8 1879;S 20 1881
MBAt 1861-76
MHi Ap 29 1861
MWA Ap 21 1852;D 23 1853;My 15 1855;Mr 11 1856[My-D 1869]My 17-18 1860[My-D 1861]Jl 15,D 10 1862;Ja 11 1864;F 1,My 2-4,31-N 1865;66;Ja 21 1867-[69]-[O 12-D 1871]-98;Jl 1899-1904;Ap 1905-06;N 17,D 25 1933
MWo O 9 1858
MiElS 1906-[21-23]
MiGh O 9 1893
MiU [1891]-[93]95+
MiU-C [1874-76;80;93;1900]
MnHi Ja 8 1861-My 1865;O 9 1872;78-1912
MnU [1862-66;1917-20;22-23]+
MoS Ja 28,Ap 26 1893-Ja 15,26-27 1894;1928-32
MsU N 1928+
N My 15-16,18-19 1860;Ag 24,S 2,N 2 1861;Je 27 1862;My 6,15,Jl 15 1867;Ag 6 1868;Ja-Je 1911;12-22
NIC S 1897-98;N 18-22,24-25 1919;Mr-O 1920; 21+
NN Mr 5 1862;Ag 2 1866;N 12 1871;D 7,9 1872; Ja 26,F 15,18,Ap 19 1873-[Je 1874]-[Jl 1875]-Je,Jl 8 1876;Ap 30-[Jl]-[S-O]1893;Ja-Je 1894; Je 10 1897
NNC 1918-19
NNHi [O-D 1871]F 15,O 9 1872;Je 3 1873
NbHi [Je,O 1873;Ja 1874]Jl 24 1885;Mr 12 1886-88[N 15 1890-My 6 1891]S 4,6 1892;Ja 27,S 26,O 9-10 1893;Ja 14 1894;My 14,29 1895; My 24,Jl 11,S 1,18,N 3-8 1896;Je 10 1897;Ap 12,Jl 21 1898;Je 9 1912;Ag 30 1914;F 28,Mr 7 1915
NcD Ap 22 1876;Mr 10 1891;Je 19 1892[1906]-My 1908
NvR [1933]+
OCl My 1918+
OClWHi My 25,Jl 27[Ag-N 1864]Ja 16,F 13,Ap 4,10 1865;Je 14 1866;Mr 5,16 1868;Mr 1870-My 1873;Ap 24,Jl 1 1875;F-N 1878;Je 3-5,11 1880; S 20 1881;Ja 2,Je 17,S 9-10 1886;My 10 1887; Je 20-25 1888;O 9-10 1893;Je 14-20 1897;S 22 1901
OHi Je 17 1859;My 1887-Je 1889;92-93;1917+
OOxM O 22-27 1873;My 4 1878;1919+
OrU [1878]
P My 19-D 27 1880
PBf F 5 1861;O 26 1878;Ja 28 1881
PLaF F 16 1933+
PP O 18 1893[1927]+
PPM 1863-67
Tx O 19 1860
TxF O 1908+
TxGR S 21 1912+
TxHuS D 25 1933+
TxU My 5 1884-85;N 1920-Ag 1921;25-S 1926
VU N 1-25,27-28 1933;Jl 11,S 27-28,O 1-3,6 1934
VtMS [N 1884-1901]
WAL Ag 1918-S 1919
WHi My 11-D 1857;Jl 1 1858;60-My 5,Je 1870+

ILLINOIS (*Continued*)

CHICAGO—*Continued*

Chicago daily TRIBUNE. d Je 10 1847+—*Cont.*
WM N 1883-O 1884
WMar 1914-Ap 1919
WMJ current 10 months
WO current 3 months
WaPS [1913]-[16-20]-[22-26]-[29-30]-33
WaS 1907-F 1923

Chicago weekly TRIBUNE. w Jl 10 1847-87||?
1847-58 Chicago weekly tribune; 1860-72 Chicago press and tribune
DLC Jl-D 1873
IGK Jl 10,S 30-O 7,21,N 18-25 1858
IHi D 9 1858;Mr 21,Ap-Je 20,Jl-N 7 1861;D 4 1862
IU Ag 26-D 1858
MBAt 1861[62]
MHi F 13,17 1868
MWA F 11,S 16,O 21 1854;Ja 19 1855;O 31 1856
NNHi O 29 1851;F 14 1861;Ja 8 1864;Ap 8-9, My 9 1865;Mr 19 1873
NbHi Je 30-Jl 7,28 1880;O 9 1882
NhD Ag 10,O 5,19,N 23-D 7,21 1865;Ja 4-11,Mr 1,Ap 26,Jl 12,Ag 9 1866
OClWHi F 27 1878;Jl 20 1881;Ap 4 1883
OHi 1873
WHi Jl 10 1858-Ja 1860;F 28,Ap 25 1861;O 5 1865

Chicago TRIBUNE (Paris ed) *See under* Paris

TRIBUNE of Hyde Park Village. *See* Daily calumet

UKRAINIA. w
In Ukrainian
PP N 20 1931;Mr 4 1932
PPiHi D 1931-Mr 4 1932

Die Chicago UNION. d 1855-76||?
In German
IC [Ja-Je 1873]
—Sunday ed *See* Belletristische zeitung

L'UNIONE italiana. *See* Il Messaggiere italiano dell' ouest

VÅRT land och folk. w Ap 11 1879-N 9 1888||
1879-O 20 1886 as Nåd och sanning
In Swedish
IRA 1877;81-82;84-88

VĚK rozumu. w
In Bohemian
IU Ap 27 1933+

La VERDAD. w Je 5 1927-
In Spanish
CU-B Jl 3 24 1927

VERDENS gang. w 1878-1919||?
In Norwegian
IU 1917-D 26 1919
IaDeL [1897]99-[1902]-[04-18]

VOICE of liberty. *See* Glas svobode

VOICE of the fair. w,d Ap 27-Je 24 1865||
w Ap-My 1865
ICHi complete
MBAt My-Je 1865
MnHi Ap 27 1865
NNHi complete
NjP Ap-Je 16 1865
WHi complete

VOICE of the people. w Je 29 1838-Ag 1838||
Campaign paper
DLC Je 29 1838

Chicago VOLKSFREUND. w 1845-48||
In German
IU F 12 1848

VOLKSFREUND. d Jl 1 1878-79||?
Je 19 1878 is "probe nummer"
In German
ICN Je 19,Jl 2,4-6,8-16,18-22,24-25,27-31,Ag 2,5-6,8-13,15-21,23-S 1,4-6,8 1878;Ag 8,14,28 1879

Chicagoer VOLKS-ZEITUNG. d F 18 1877-
In German
ICN [F 19-My 10 1877]

VORBOTE. [Wochenblatt der "Chicagoer arbeiterzeitung"] w F 14 1874-1924||
IC 1874-[76]-D 23 1885
ICJ [1884-1902]
IU O 10 1917-Ap 30 1924
KHi Jl 25-Ag 1 1888
NN 1874-1907
NNC Jl 1910-Ap 30 1924
NNRa [1885]-[88]

Die WESER-NACHRICHTEN. bw 1896-1926||?
In German
IU [S-D 1917]-Je 7 1919

WEST END advocate. w 1870-1906||?
IC D 14,28 1878;S 11 1880;S 5 1885

WEST Rogers Park news. *See* North town news

Der WESTEN. w 1854-1914||?
1854-67 as Chicago sonntags-zeitung; 1909-11 Westen und daheim
Sunday ed of Illinois staats-zeitung
In German
CtY O 31 1880
IC Ag 24-S,D 1862;F 1863-66;Jl 1881-Je 1885; 87-88
ICHi Ap 5 1891;O 15 1911
ICN My-Ag 1861;My 1862-Je 14,Ag 16-O 5 1863;Ja 17 1864-Je 11,Ag 1865-Jl 22,O 31 1869-O 5,D 1871;73;Jl 1874-79;81-1900
IU Ag 1,29,S 12 1909-D 10 1911;13
KHi My 1868-F 7 1889
MWA N 4-11 1860

WESTERN British American. w 1888-1922||?
IU Ja 21 1905-N 9 1907

WESTLICHE unterhaltungs-blätter. *See* Belletristische zeitung

Chicago WHIP. w Je 3 1919-32||?
Negro
ICHi Je 24 1919-22

WOCHEN-AUSGABE. w 1871-98||?
w ed of Chicagoer freie presse
In German
ICN 1879-Mr,Jl 12 1881-N 1884;F 3,Mr 31,Ap 14,My 12,26,Je 2-9,23-30 1885;Jl 6 1886[90-N 2 1898]

Chicago WORKER. *See* Daily worker (New York City)

WORKERS call. d *See* Chicago daily socialist

Chicago WORLD. w 1891-97||?
MWA My 17 1894
WHi 1894-95

Chicago WORLD. w Ja 20 1900-
Negro
DLC Ja 27 1900

Evening WORLD. d My 3-D 4 1912||
Follows Chicago daily socialist
ICHi My 4 1912
KHi Ag 7 1912
NN My 27-D 1912
WHi My 27-D 1912

ZÁJMY lidu. sm 1898-1930||
sm ed of Spravedlnost
In Bohemian
IU O 23 1917-O 17 1930

CHICAGO HEIGHTS

Chicago Heights SIGNAL. w 1888-1926||?
IHi Jl 13 1911-D 19 1913

Chicago Heights STAR. w,sw Mr 1901+
w 1901-F 19 1926
IU D 13 1917+

CHICAGO PARK

Chicago Park TIMES. w 1888-
CLM F 18-25,Mr 10 1888

CHILLICOTHE

Chillicothe BULLETIN. w 1883+
IChi 1917+
IU O 9 1914+

Chillicothe ENQUIRER and Peoria county democrat. w 1891-1927||
1891-1914? as Chillicothe enquirer
IChi 1923-27

Chillicothe weekly REPORTER. w Je 3 1874-96||?
IHi Ag 5 1874;Ja 5 1876;My 30 1877;Mr 1 1882; Ja 16,My 29 1884

CHRISMAN

Chrisman COURIER. w 1878+
Title varies: Chrisman weekly courier; etc.
pub 1905+
IU O 16 1914-D 22 1916

CHRISTOPHER

Christopher PROGRESS. w 1879+
IU Je 1 1923

CICERO

Cicero LIFE. w 1926+
1926-F 1932 as Suburban leader; F-S 1932 Suburban life
pub 1926+

SUBURBAN leader. *See* Cicero life

SUBURBAN life. *See* Cicero life

CISSNA PARK

Cissna Park NEWS. w 1906+
pub [1906-28]Ap 1929+

CLAY CITY

CLAY county advocate. w 1889+
pub [1889-1916]19+

CLAYTON

Clayton ENTERPRISE. w 1879+
pub 1880+
IGK Ag 20 1879
IU O 8 1914+

Clayton STANDARD. w 1865-68||?
ICHi N 3 1868

CLIFTON

Clifton ADVOCATE. w 1893+
1893-1902 as Comet
pub 1893+

COMET. *See* Clifton advocate

CLINTON

DE WITT county democrat. w Mr 13 1858-
InDG Mr 13-My 22 1858

DE WITT register. *See* Clinton register

Clinton JOURNAL and public d 1908+
1908-27 as Clinton morning journal
IU Ja 9 1909; D 6 1917-Je 10 1920;N 24 1925; Ja 6 1926

Clinton daily PUBLIC. d 1895-1927||
United with Clinton journal to form Clinton journal and public
IHi Ag 1 1917
IU Ja 14 1902;Jl 12 1919-26

Clinton REGISTER. w 1868-1927||?
1868-70? as DeWitt register
ICl Ag 9 1895-S 24 1915

COAL CITY

Coal City COURANT. w 1900+
IU D 1917-[18-19]+

COBDEN

Cobden SENTINEL. w 1886-1918||?
IU O 15 1914-Dec 21 1916

COLETA

Coleta JOURNAL. w Ap 14 1892-O 26 1893||
Issued as a section of the Milledgeville free press (Milledgeville)
IU 1892-Je 23,Ag 11 1892-93

COLLINSVILLE

Collinsville HERALD. w S 15 1879+
pub S 1924+

COLUMBIA

Columbia STAR. w My 1906+
pub 1906+
IU D 27 1917+

CORNELL

Cornell JOURNAL. w Jl 10 1890+
IU O 23 1914+

COULTERVILLE

REPUBLICAN. w F 1885+
pub S 1911+
IU Ap 19 1918+

COWDEN

Cowden REFLECTOR. w Mr 1892+
pub 1892+

CREAL SPRINGS

Creal Springs NEWS. w 1899-1918||?
IU F 22-Mr 8,22-D 27 1918

CRESTON

MORRIS' Creston times. w Mr 2 1872-87||?
1872-Jl 21 1881 as Creston times
IU [Je,S 1872-Ja 4,O 18-D 1873]-[76-Ag 11 1881]

Creston OBSERVER. w Ap 27 1887-1916||?
IU [1887-89]-[92-94]-Ja 2,30,Je 12-S 18,N 6 1897;Je 25-S 3,N 5,19 1898;My 20-Je 3,Jl 22-Ag 19 1899;Ja 13,Mr-Ap 14,Je 30-Jl,D 22 1900;Ja 1901

Creston TIMES. *See* Morris' Creston times

CRYSTAL LAKE

To 1908 as Nunda

Crystal Lake HERALD. w O 1 1875+
1875-84? as Nunda advertiser; 1885?-1908 Nunda herald
pub 1875+

NUNDA advertiser. *See* Crystal Lake herald

NUNDA herald. *See* Crystal Lake herald

CUBA

Cuba JOURNAL. w Ag 29 1884—
pub 1891+

CULLOM

CHRONICLE-headlight. w 1893+
1893-My 26 1932 as Cullom chronicle
IU Ap 14 1921+

DAHLGREN

Dahlgren ECHO. w 1899—
IU O 8 1914-[27]

DALLAS CITY

Dallas City ENTERPRISE. w 1899+
IU O 15 1914-O 17 1918

Dallas City NEWS. w 1878-79||
IGK Ag 2,30-S 6 1879

Dallas City REVIEW. w S 7 1887+
pub 1887-Ag 1897;S 1898+
IU D 11 1917+

DANVERS

Danvers INDEPENDENT. w 1912+
pub 1912+

ILLINOIS (*Continued*)

DANVILLE

Danville ARGUS. w 1871-74||
IDa 1871-73

Danville CHRONOTYPE. w Mr 31 1860-
IU Ap-My 12,Je-Jl 21,Ag 11,S 8-N 3 1860

Danville COMMERCIAL-NEWS. w,sw Ap 1866-1909||
1866-98 as Danville commercial (title varies slightly: 1868-Mr 1870 Weekly commercial and plaindealer); 1899-1903 Twice-a-week commercial (sw)
IDa 1866-Jl 1883;84-O 1887;99
IGK D 16 1928
IU Ap 18 1867;Ap 9-16 1868;Ap 7 1870;Ap 6 1871;F 1-8 1872;Ap 23 1874;N 7 1878;F 6 1896
NjR D 16 1928

Danville COMMERCIAL-NEWS. d S 1878+
1878-1903 as Daily commercial (title varies: Evening commercial; etc.)
IDa 1878-Ja 1887;Ja-Je 1888;89-93;Ja-Je 1895; 97-Je 1898;Jl-D 1899;1904+
IHi S 30 1878;F 20 1879;1920+
IU F 24 1897;Ap 1918-Ap 26,Je 29 1920-Jl,D 6 1922+

Danville daily DEMOCRAT. d 1897-1908||
United with Danville morning press to form Danville press-democrat, later Danville morning press
IDa S 1898-F 1908

Danville weekly DEMOCRAT. w D 1897-1904||?
IDa 1897-1901

DEUTSCHE zeitung. w 1877-1912||
United with Danviller herold to form Danviller herold und zeitung
In German
IHi S 13 1907-My 1912

Danville weekly GLOBE. w Ap 30 1863-
IU My 7-14,28,Je 25,Ag 20,O 29 1863

Danviller HEROLD und zeitung. w 1906-19||
1906-12 as Danviller herold
In German
IU Jl 1917-Jl 13 1919

ILLINOIS citizen. w S 5 1849-56||?
IU S 12,O 3-10,24,N 21,D 12 1849-Ja 2,16-Ap 3,24-Jl 17,Ag-S 18,O 2-16 1850;Je 30,Jl 14 1852

ILLINOIS herald. w 1850-
NcD Jl 23 1850

INDEPENDENT. w F 14 1856-58||?
DLC F 28-Mr 6,Ap 10,My 1,15-22,Je 5-12,Ag 7-14,28;S 11,N 27-D 4,18-25 1856;Ja 8-15,F 12-19,Mr 26,Ag 27,S 24 1857;Ja 20,Ap 21,Jl 28 1858
IU My 15,Je 26-Jl 3,N 6 1856;Ja 1,Ap 23-My 21,Je-Jl,Ag 13-S 3,24,O 8-15 1857;F 10,Mr 3-17 1858
MWA F 28 1856

Danville JOURNAL. w
IDa O-D 1865

Danville LEADER. w 1878-87||?
IU Ap 27 1883

Sunday LEDGER. w 1883-85||
IHi F 8 1885

NATIONAL era. Ag 1878-79||
IDa 1878-Mr 1879

Danville weekly NEWS. w O 1873-My 1903||
United with Danville commercial to form Danville commercial-news
IDa 1873-Jl,O 1877-87;89;91-1903
IU Ap 25 1877;Ap 22 1881

Danville daily NEWS. d 1876-1903||
United with Daily commercial to form Danville commercial news
IDa O 1876-Je 1885;86-87;Ag 1888-90;Jl 1891-Je 1902;Ja-My 1903
IU Ap 23 1880

Saturday OPINION. w 1881-82||
IDa Je 1881-N 1882

Danville PATRIOT. w Ap 12? 1844-47||?
IU Ag 16,S 1844;Je 12,Jl 10,31-Ag 7 1845;My 1,15,29,Jl 17,S 4,18 1846

Danville PLAINDEALER. w 1862-D 1867||
1862-Ap? 1866 as Vermilion county plaindealer. United with Danville commercial to form Weekly commercial and plaindealer, later Danville commercial-news
ICHi O 24 1863
IDa 1865-67
IU Ap 13 1865

Danville POST. w 1878-81||?
IDa 1878

Danville weekly PRESS. w 1878-1905||?
IDa Ag 1887-1902

Danville morning PRESS. d 1886-1926||?
1908?-14 as Danville press-democrat
IDa Jl-S 1908;09-25;Je 1926-S 1927
IU F 7,28 1909;Jl 17,19 1910;O 15 1911;S 17,28, N 7 1915
WaPS D 2,4-6,8-9,12 1923

Daily REPUBLICAN. d S 25? 1860-
IU O 4,8,11,15-16,23,N 8,15 1860

Danville REPUBLICAN. w *See* Republican press

REPUBLICAN and chronotype. w F 1861-
IDa F-Mr 1861

REPUBLICAN press. w Ja 26 1860-62||?
1860-Ag? 1861 as Danville republican
IDa 1860-61
IU [1860]Ja 10-24,Ag 15,29,O 2,23,N 20 1861;Ja 8,F 26,Mr 19-Ap 2 1862

Danville TIMES. w Ja 1868-My 1879||
IDa 1868-75;S 1877-79
IU Ap 26 1873

Danville daily TIMES. d 1875-78||?
IHi O 26 1877;O 1 1878

VERMILION chronicle. w
IDa My 1872-73

VERMILION county plaindealer. *See* Danville plaindealer

VERMILION county press. w Ap 1 1857-Mr 27 1861||
DLC Ap 22,Je 24,D 30 1857;Ja 20,My 12 1858
IDa Je 1858-61
IU Ap 1,22,Jl 15-29,Ag 5,19 1857;Ja 27,O 6 1858;Mr 9,Ap 13-27,My 11,Jl 27,Ag 17,S 7,O 26-N 9,D 14 1859-Ja,F 8-15,29,Mr 14,28,Ap, My 16,Je 6-13,S 5,26,D 12-26 1860;F 20,Mr 20-27 1861

VERMILION county star. w Je 16 1923+
pub 1923+

DAVIS

Davis LEADER. w My 11 1911+
pub 1911+

DAVIS JUNCTION

Davis Junction ENTERPRISE. w Ja 1-O 20? 1876||
IU F 4,25,Mr 10,24-My 19,Je 2-23,Jl 21-29,Ag 12-19,S 29,O 20 1876

MONROE Center leader. *See under* Monroe Center

DECATUR

Decatur daily DISPATCH. d Jl 4 1889-Ag? 1890||
United with Morning herald to form Morning herald-despatch, later Decatur herald
ID 1889-F 1890

GAZETTE and chronicle. w Jl 2 1851-71||
1851-Je 1865 as Decatur weekly gazette (some issues as Shoaff's family gazette)
ICHi Ag 13 1855
IHi Ag 13 1851;Ag 5 1853
IU Ag 13 1851
MWA Ap 18 1860
OHi Mr 12-Ap 1856;O 28-D 1857;Ja 20-Ag 1858

Decatur HERALD. w,sw 1879-1907||
1879-89 as Saturday herald; 1890-99 Herald-dispatch
w 1879-95?
pub O 1880-Ag 1890

Decatur HERALD. d O 1880+
1880-Ag 1890 as Morning herald; S 1890-99 Morning herald-dispatch
pub 1880-O 1883;84-Je,O 1903-Je,O 1906-Je,O 1907+
ID 1894+
IHi 1897-98;1900-34
WHi F 7 1909

Decatur evening HERALD. d
pub 1927-Ag 1931

HERALD-DISPATCH. w *See* Decatur herald

ILLINOIS state chronicle. w 1855-65||
United with Decatur weekly gazette to form Gazette and chronicle
Suspended 1862-63
ICHi D 24 1857;F 18,O 7-14 1858

LOCAL review. *See* Twice-a-week review

Decatur REPUBLICAN. w Ag 1 1867-99||
ID 1867-Jl 18 1872
IDH Jl 1868-Ag 6 1896
NbHi Ja 6,Ap 28 1881

Daily REPUBLICAN. d Ap 1 1872-Ag 26 1899||
ID complete
IHi [1894-98]

Twice-a-week REVIEW. w,sw Ap 1872-1907||
1872-79 as Local review; 1880-94? Weekly review
pub 1873-93;95-1907

Decatur daily REVIEW. d 1878+
Title varies: Daily review; Decatur review
pub 1879+
ID 1894+
IHi [1893-Je 1920]
IU Jl-D 23 1903;Ja 3-Je 22,Jl-D 15 1904;Ja-Mr,Ap 4-Je 1907;13-Mr,Jl 1918-Je 1920

SHOAFF'S family gazette. *See* Gazette and chronicle

DEERFIELD

Deerfield NEWS. w Ja 1 1923+
pub Mr 10 1930-31;Ag 1932-Je 1933;34+

DEKALB

DeKalb daily ADVERTISER. d 1908-14||
IDe Je 1909-Apr 1914

DeKalb daily CHRONICLE. w,sw,d Mr 8 1879+
w 1879-84;sw 1885-Ap 1897
pub 1879-1907;09+
IDe Jl-Ag 3 1907;Je 1909-F,Jl 1924-Mr,My-Je 1927;Ag 1928+
IHi S 10 1934
IU O 6 1914+

DEKALB county news. w Mr 6 1867-83||?
IHi 1867-My 1869
ISy 1867-F 1869

DeKalb REVIEW. w
NcD Jl 23 1850

DeKalb REVIEW. w 1883-1924||?
IDe Mr 1911-[20-D 20 1923]
IHi [Ag 29 1918-My 1919]
IU F 14 1918-22
MWA Ag 31 1899
VHi Ag 19 1915

TAX-GATHERER. w Ja 16 1886-
ICHi Ap 24 1886

DE LAND

De Land TRIBUNE. w 1897?+
IU D 14 1917+

DELAVAN

Delavan ADVERTISER. w 1868-Jl 1918||
United with Delavan tri-county times to form Delavan advertiser-times, later Delavan times
MWA Ap 17 1869

Delavan TIMES. w S 5 1874+
1874-Jl 25 1918 as Delavan tri-county times; Ag 11-D 26 1918 Delavan advertiser-times
pub 1874+
IGK My 22 1879
IU O 14 1914-18

TRI-COUNTY times. *See* Delavan times

DES PLAINES

Des Plaines SUBURBAN times. w 1887+
Title varies slightly
IU S 1917-Ap 9 1926

DIETERICH

SPECIAL-GAZETTE. w 1897+
1897-1904? as Dieterich gazette
pub 1905+

DIXON

Dixon weekly CITIZEN. w 1908-15||?
ICHi Je 11 1914-S 2 1915
IHi [Ag 20 1914-Ag 26 1915]

FREMONTER. ir Jl-N 1856||
DLC S 5 1856
MWA Ag 22-S 12 1856

Dixon weekly HERALD. w F 12 1868-N 17 1869||
United with Dixon telegraph to form Telegraph and herald, later Dixon telegraph
IHi complete

Dixon evening LEADER. d Mr 12 1914-Mr 1919||
Title varies: Dixon daily leader; Dixon morning leader. Merged with Dixon evening telegraph
IDi 1914-15;Ja-Ag 1917;My 1918-19
IU My 8 1914-Mr 8 1919

LEE county democrat. *See* Dixon sun

Dixon daily NEWS. d 1908-Je 19 1915||
Merged with Dixon evening leader
IDi 1912-Je 1915
IU Ja 8-Je 1915

REPUBLICAN. w 1857-59||
Merged with Dixon telegraph
MWA Ja 15,F 5 1857

REPUBLICAN and telegraph. *See* Dixon telegraph

Dixon STAR. tw 1889-1905||
IDi Ap 1901-05
IU Ag 22 1899

Dixon STAR. d 1904-11||
IDi complete

Dixon SUN. w,sw 1868-1910||?
1868-F 26 1872? as Lee county democrat. Title varies slightly: Dixon weekly sun; Dixon semi-weekly sun
w 1868-99
IDi 1874-89;91-Je 1896;97-98;1903
IF Ja 10 1872
IHi D 25 1868;O 1 1869;Ja 14,Ag 19 1870;Mr 10 1871;Jl 12 1876
IU N 8 1876;F 23 1881;N 26 1884;My 2 1888

Dixon daily SUN. d 1894-1909||
IDi Ja-Je 1898;99-Je 1900;Ap 1901-09

Dixon TELEGRAPH. w 1851-1918||?
Title varies: Dixon telegraph; Republican and telegraph; Telegraph and herald; etc.
ICHi F 27,My 8 1873
IDi 1851-61;70-71;76-N 1883;84-85
IHi O 25 1866;My 21,Je 25 1868;My 20,Jl 1,S 16,O 21 1869;Mr 4,Ap 29 1880;Ag 18 1881
MWA F 7 1852;Jl 4,N 21-D 8,22 1855;Ja 5 1856;Ap 4 1857;N 4 1858;F 11 1864;Mr 2 1876

TELEGRAPH and herald. *See* Dixon telegraph

Dixon evening TELEGRAPH. d 1883+
ICHi S 17 1930
IDi Ja-Je 1888;90-99;Mr-O 1901;02+
IHi S 17 1930
IU My 13,Je 17 1886;F 16,Ag 23 1888;Jl 14 1898;S 16-18,24,27,O 6,9,11-12,N 1,6,D 30 1915; Ja 17,O 27,N 1,6,8,20,23,29 1916;17+

DONOVON

Donovon ECHO. w 1921+
pub 1924+

DUQUOIN

DuQuoin evening CALL. d 1895+
IHi [Jl 23-D 1931]

ILLINOIS (*Continued*)

DUQUOIN—*Continued*

DuQuoin RECORDER. w 1864-67||
1864-65 as Stars and stripes. United with DuQuoin tribune to form Tribune and recorder, later DuQuoin tribune
MWA Ja 12 1866

DuQuoin REPUBLICAN. w,sw My 13 1871-73||
w My ?-N 28 1871
IHi [My-? 12 1871]

STARS and stripes. *See* DuQuoin recorder

DuQuoin TRIBUNE. w 1863-Je 19 1925||
- 1867 as Tribune and recorder
IHi complete

DURAND

Durand GAZETTE. w Mr 28 1907+
pub 1907+

DWIGHT

Dwight HERALD. w 1878-91||
United with Dwight star to form Dwight star and herald

Dwight STAR and herald. w My 5 1868+
1868-93 as Dwight star (title varies slightly)
pub [1868]-4+

EARLVILLE

Earlville LEADER. w 1880+
pub N 19?—
IU O 8 19?+

EAST DUBUQUE

East Dubuque REGISTER. w Mr 20 1893+
pub 1893+

EAST GALESBURG

East Galesburg TRIBUNE. w 1892-1903||?
IGK 1900-?;Ja-S 12 1903

EAST MOLINE

East Moline ENTERPRISE. *See* East Moline herald

East Moline HERALD. w,sw D 4 1903+
1903-O ? 1907 as East Moline enterprise
Suspended from Jl 6 1918-Ap 2 1925
sw O 23 1907-32
pub 1903+

EAST PEORIA

EAST side news. w 1902+
1902-S ? 1924 as East Peoria post; S 1? 1924-Mr 19 1926 Illinois Valley herald
IU F 1918-? 23 1926

ILLINOIS Valley herald. *See* East side news

East Peoria POST. *See* East side news

EAST ST. LOUIS

GAZETTE. w 1866-1914||?
IEa 1866-8?;89-90;92-93;1912

Sunday HERALD. w My 1865-
IEa 1865

East St. Louis daily JOURNAL. d 1888+
pub 1888+
IEa 1890+
IHi [Ja 16 1920-34]
IU O 28 19?-Ja 12 1933
MWA D 2? 1919

Weekly JOURNAL. w 1889-
IEa 1889

East St. Louis MAIL-REVIEW. *See* East St. Louis news-review

East St. Louis NEWS-REVIEW. w,d 1913-28||?
1913-25? as East St. Louis mail-review
w 1913-25?
IEaS 1920-?

PEOPLE'S gazette. *See* Weekly press

Weekly PRESS. w 1871-77||
1871-72 as People's gazette. Merged with Gazette
IEa complete

ST. CLAIR county record. w S 1925+
pub 1925+

ST. CLAIR tribune. w F 1875-78||
IEa complete

Weekly SIGNAL. w 1882-93||?
IEa 1882-86

EDINBURG

Edinburg HERALD. w Je 14 1882+
pub 1883-87 1925+

EDWARDSVILLE

CRISIS. ir Ap 14 1930-F 1931||
Followed by Illinois advocate (Vandalia)
CSmH My ? 1830
Ct [1830]
ICHi S 9 1830
IHi Jl 13 18? (extra)
IU S 9,O 2? 1830
N D 15 1830

ILLINOIS advocate. *See under* Vandalia

ILLINOIS corrector. w 1827-28||
ICHi Ag 25 1828
MWA N 14,D 12 1827

ILLINOIS republican. w 1823-Jl 28 1824||
IHi Jl 14 1824
InI Je 18 1824
MWA Je 28 1823
MoSM Jl 21 1824

Edwardsville INTELLIGENCER. w sw,tw,d N 13 1862+
w 1862-89?;sw 1890-1903;tw 1904-07
pub 1862+
ICHi My 26,Je 9-23,Jl 14-28,S 22-D 8,22 1886-[87-88]-Ap 10,24-My 1,15-Je 12,26-S 1889
IEd current 2 years
IGr current 6 months
IHi F 3 1885;S 14-21 1912
IHig My 1929+
IU Ag 31,S 26 1912+

Weekly MADISON advertiser. w 1856-O 5? 1865||
Followed by Madison county courier
IHi D 26 1861

MADISON county anzeiger. w My ? 1875-79||
In German
MWA Ag 25 1876

MADISON county bote. w 1869-73||
Follows Der Highland böte (Highland)
In German

MADISON county courier. w O 12 1865-O 5 1869||
Follows Weekly Madison advertiser
IHi N 23 1865

MADISON county news. w Jl 1 1869+
1869-F 1933 as Edwardsville republican
pub 1869+
IEd current 2 years only

Edwardsville REPUBLICAN. *See* Madison county news

*Edwardsville SPECTATOR. w My 29 1819-O 20 1826||
DLC 1821-26
ICHi 1821-Ja 15,F 5,My 25-Je 8,Jl 20-Ag 3, 31,S 14-N 1822;Jl 12,Ag 9,30-S 20,O 4,18-N 8,22-29, D 13-20 1823;Ja 13-27,S 28-O 12,26-31 1824;Ja 1-8 1825
IHi Jl 18 1820
IU 1821[22]Ja 18-Ap,My 10-Ag 16,S 13 1823-24;Ja 11-F 15,Mr 1-15,Ap-Je 14,Jl 30,Ag 13-S 10-24-D 10 1825; Ja-Ap 15,29-Jl 14,28-Ag 4, 25-S 8,29-O 1826
MWA Mr 15,N 29 1823;Mr 16-Ap 13,27-My 4, Jl 6,O 19-26 1824
MoSM complete
NNHi Ap,Je 8,22,Ag 3,17-24,S 7,21 1822

EFFINGHAM

COUNTY review. w Ja 27 1915+
pub 1915+
IU Mr 1918+

Effingham DEMOCRAT. w 1856+
1856-Ap 1861 as Pioneer; My? 1861-62 Unionist; 1862-65 Gazette; 1865-68 Effingham county democrat
1856-60 pub at Ewington
IU Ja 16 1919-O 5 1922

EFFINGHAM county democrat. *See* Effingham democrat

Effingham GAZETTE. w Ap 1860-Ap 1861||
United with Pioneer to form Unionist, later Effingham democrat

GAZETTE. 1862-65 *See* Effingham democrat

PIONEER. *See* Effingham democrat

Effingham RECORD. d 1902+
IU Mr 3-D 1919;Jl 29 1926

Effingham REGISTER. w N 1864-O 1872||
OClWHi Mr 22 1866

Effingham REPUBLICAN. w 1872+
IHi Ag 2 1917

UNIONIST. *See* Effingham democrat

ELBURN

Elburn HERALD. w Ap 1907+
pub 1912+

ELDORADO

Eldorado daily JOURNAL. w,sw,d S 29 1911—
1911-F 1921 as Eldorado journal
w 1911-19;sw 1920-F 1921
pub [1916-17]+

SALINE county republican. w Ap 1889-Mr 20 1918||
IEldJ N 1906-[14-18]

ELGIN

Elgin ADVOCATE. w 1847-1917||
Merged with Elgin daily news
DLC O 3 1874
ICHi D 22 1883

Elgin COURIER-NEWS. d 1878+
1878-1925 as Elgin daily courier
Je 15 1935 is Centennial ed
IU Ja 2-16 1926;Ja 24 1935+
MWA Je 15 1935
MiG Je 15 1935
TxGR Je 15 1935
WHi Mr 27 1926;Je 15 1935

FOX River courier. w 1851-52||
WHi [Jl 7 1852]

Elgin GAZETTE. w 1850-My 30 1874||
Merged with Elgin advocate
DLC Jl 19 1851;Mr 25 1871-N 22 1873
ICHi Ja 18,F 8 1851
MWA Je 17 1871

Elgin HEROLD. *See* Illinois wochenblatt

ILLINOIS palladium. *See* Kane county journal

ILLINOIS wochenblatt. w 1891-O 14 1921||
1891-O 8 1920 as Elgin herold
Dated also at Springfield and Winona, Minn.
In German
IU Ag 3,31 1917-O 1919;O 15 1920-21
MnHi Mr 26 1920-21

KANE county journal. w 1853-56||
1853-55 as Illinois palladium
MWA Ja 24 1856
WHi My 31 1855

Elgin daily NEWS. d 1871-D 31 1925||
United with Elgin daily courier to form Elgin courier-news
IU D 5 1917-25

ELIZABETH

Elizabeth weekly NEWS. w 1892+
pub 1916+

ELIZABETHTOWN

HARDIN county independent w 1882+
1882-1915? as Elizabethtown independent (title varies slightly)
pub N 22 1933+

Elizabethtown INDEPENDENT. *See* Hardin county independent

ELKVILLE

Elkville JOURNAL. w My 5 1922+
pub 1922+

ELMHURST

Elmhurst LEADER. w N 9 1926+
pub 1926+

Elmhurst PRESS. w 1893+
IU Ja-Jl 12 1918;F 28 1919-D 1 1922;Mr 5 1926

ELMWOOD

Elmwood GAZETTE. w 1872+
1872-Jl 3? 1879 as Brimfield gazette (Brimfield)
pub [1872-78]+
IHi Mr 24 1904-Jl 16 1913

Elmwood MESSENGER. w Mr 6 1874-Ag 28 1902||
ICHi Je 26-Jl 1874;Jl 13-20 1877;Jl 23-Ag 6 1880

EL PASO

El Paso JOURNAL. w Ap 5 1865+
IU 1918+

EMINGTON

Emington JOKER. w 1902+
pub 1910+

ENFIELD

Enfield EXPRESS. w 1893-1923||
IU O 15 1914-16;F 1917-21;Mr 23 1922-S 20 1923

ENGLEWOOD

Papers published in Englewood are listed under Chicago

EQUALITY

Daily PROGRESS. w
IHa Jl 23 1884

ERIE

Erie INDEPENDENT. w Ap 1 1877+
pub 1896+

EUREKA

WOODFORD county journal. w 1868+
Title varies slightly
IHi Ag 2 1917

EVANSTON

Evanston INDEX. w Je 8 1872-1915||
United with Lake Shore news to form Evanston news-index
ICHi Ja 15 1876;F 13 1909
IEN 1872-1914
IHi F 13 1909
IU My 20-27,S 9-16,O 14-21,N,D 23 1911;Mr-Ap 20,My 4-11,25-Je 1,15-29,Jl 13,S 21-28, O 12 N 2-9 1912;Jl 12 1913

LAKE SHORE news. *See* Evanston news-index

Evanston NEWS-INDEX. d N 1909+
1909-My 1911 as Evanston news; Je 1911-15 Lake Shore news
ICHi Ag 30 1923
IEN 1909-F 1914;My-Ag 1923;Mr 1925-Ja 1926
IU Jl 1917-Ja 23 1926

ILLINOIS (*Continued*)

EVANSVILLE

Evansville ENTERPRISE. w F 1 1895+
pub 1900+
IU 1918+

EWINGTON

PIONEER. *See* Effingham democrat (Effingham)

EXETER

BATTLE axe. *See under* Winchester

FAIRBURY

Fairbury BLADE. w Ap 14 1871+
1871-76 as Independent; 1877-83 Independent blade
pub 1884+
IU O 29 1915-Je,S 20 1918+

INDEPENDENT. *See* Fairbury blade

INDEPENDENT blade. *See* Fairbury blade

Fairbury JOURNAL. w Ap 15 1866-72||
Merged with Independent, later Fairbury blade
NhD Jl 9 1868

LIVINGSTON county blade. w N 6-D 30? 1876||
United with Independent to form Independent-blade later Fairbury blade

FAIRFIELD

DEMOCRAT. w Jl 3 1868-81||
Merged with Wayne county record
IFaR complete

REGISTER. *See* Wayne county record

Fairfield REPUBLICAN. w 1890-1910||
IFaW [1900-10]

WAR democrat. w Ja 1864-65||
Followed by Wayne county press

WAYNE county press. w Ja 1 1866+
Follows War democrat
pub [1866-72]+
IHi Ag 2 1917

WAYNE county record. w S 1879+
S-D 1879 as Register
pub 1879+
IHi F 16 1911-34
IU Jl 30 1914-18

FAIRVIEW

Fairview GRAPHIC. w N 16 1933+
pub 1933+
ILoT 1933+

FARINA

Farina NEWS. w 1882+
pub 1915+

FARMER CITY

Farmer City JOURNAL and Mansfield express. w N 1872+
1872-1934 as Farmer City journal
IU 1935+
NNHi Ja 9 1872

Farmer City REPORTER. w 1878-Ag 1880||
OClWHi Je 26,Jl 31 1879

FARMERSVILLE

Farmersville POST. w 1902+
pub Mr 1933+

FARMINGTON

Farmington BUGLE. w 1881+

Farmington HOME visitor. w 1882-D 7 1928||
Merged with Farmington bugle
IU 1918-28

Farmington NEWS. sw 1874-79||
IGK Ag 21 1879

FISHER

Fisher REPORTER. w 1890+
pub 1899+
IHi Ja 5 1900
IU Ap 1917+

FITHIAN

Fithian HERALD and Oakwood township news. w 1908+
IU Ja 15-22,Mr 5,26,Ap 16,Je 18-Ag 6,S-O 22,N 5,19-D 10,24 1925;Ja 7,21-F 11 1926

FLANAGAN

HOME times. w D 26 1885+
pub 1885+
IU D 21 1917+

FLORA

Flora JOURNAL-RECORD. sw 1912+
1912-20 as Southern Illinois record

SOUTHERN Illinois journal. w 1870-D 30 1920||
United with Southern Illinois record to form Flora journal-record
IHi F 22 1907-D 4 1908;Ag 3 1917
IU O 16 1914-20
MWA D 24 1875

SOUTHERN Illinois record. *See* Flora journal-record

FOREST PARK

Forest Park EAGLE. w Ja 14 1910-18||?
1910-N 15 1912 as Weekly eagle
IU Ag 1910-Ja 2 1915

FORREST

CORN belt news. w 1883+
1883-1924 as Forrest rambler
IU D 1917-My 21 1920

FORREST rambler. *See* Corn belt news

FORRESTON

Forreston HERALD. w My 1 1875-1901||
United with Ogle county review to form Ogle county review-herald
IPolT My 17 1877-My 1878
IU 1875-[82-83]-[85]-[88-96]-[1900]-Je 1 1901

Forreston HUSTLER. *See* Ogle county review-herald

Forreston JOURNAL. w Ap 1867+
Title varies slightly
Suspended 1875-1910?
pub 1922+
IHi [Je 1871-D 20 1873]
IU Ap 15 1871-O 18 1873;74-Ja 2 1875;Ja 13 1915-Jl 17 1918

OGLE county review-herald. w D 1897-1909||
1897-Ag? 1899 as Forreston hustler; S? 1899-1901 Ogle county review
IU Mr 16-23,Jl 13,Ag 17 1898;Mr 1899-Ja,Mr-Ap 6,Je 29,Ag 10 1900-My 17 1901

FOX LAKE

LOTUS news. w My 4 1933+
pub 1933+

FRANKLIN

Franklin TIMES. w 1886+
pub My 1915+

FRANKLIN GROVE

ELECTRIC light. w 1881-85||?
IU Jl 14 1883

Franklin REPORTER. w Ag 16 1869+
pub 1915+
IU Ja 18 1889;Jl 17 1896;Jl 15 1898;Mr 2-23, Jl 13 1900;D 27 1917-Jl 11 1918;Mr 6,Ap 3, 17 1919-My 27 1920

FREMONT

TAZEWELL county whig. w My 17 1844-
OClWHi Ag 9 1844

FREEPORT

Freeport ARGUS. w Ag 15 1914-
KHi Ag 29 1914

Freeport BANNER. w 1879-1904||
In German
IF My-N 15,29 1890-92;95-97;99-1904
—Sonntagsblatt. w 1882-1904||
IF My-D 1890;Ja 25-D 1891;Ja 1 1893;1900-Ja 6,20-Ap 21,My-N 10,21-D 1901;Ja 12-F 16,30-Mr 15,29-Ag,S 14-D 7,21 1902-04

Freeport BUDGET. w 1870-83||
Merged with Freeport journal
IF Je 22 1878;My 28-Ag 27 1881
NbHi My 10 1879

Freeport BULLETIN. w 1847-1919||?
1847-53 as Prairie democrat
IF Ja 26 1848;Ja 27,Mr 17,Ap 7 1853;Ja 17, S 3,O 22 1857;58-F 16,Mr 3-10,30-My 12,26-S 1,22 1859-Ap,My 9,23,Jl 18-25,S 26,O 17, 31,N 21-28,D 19 1862-Ja 7,21-Mr 10 1864; F 29-Jl 5,19-S 13,Ag 29-S 19,O-N 1,22 1867-Je 11,Ag 20,S 24,O 22,D 24 1868;Ja 21-28, Mr 18-Jl 1;18,Ag-S 16,30-O 14,D 30 1869; Mr 1870-F 8,Ap-Je 20,Ag-D 1872;Jl 17,Ag 14-S 18,O 23 1873-F 4,My 27-Ag 19,S 2,16 1875-Ap 1876;Ja 18,F 15-Mr 22,Ap 12,My 10-17,Jl 12,Ag 30,D 13 1877;F-Ap,My 13-N, D 12 1878-79;82;92;97;1900-02;04;06
MH F 9 1854-Jl 10-1856
MWA Ap 9 1863;O 3 1872
WHi My 6 1852;My 5 1853;Ja 25 1868-D 2 1869

Freeport BULLETIN. d 1877-1919||
IF S 18 1877-S 20 1919
IU Mr-S 19 1919

Freeport daily DEMOCRAT. *See* Freeport evening standard

Freeport DEMOCRAT. w 1883-1904||?
IF Jl,Ag 13-S 10,24-O 14,28-N 14,D 1887-O, N 24 1893-1902

DEUTSCHER anzeiger. w 1853-1917||
In German
IF Ap 30 1890-92;96-97;99-Mr 22,Ap-N,D 13 1911;12-My 5,Je-Jl,S 8-29,O 27-D 22 1915;16-17
—Sonntagsblatt.
IF 1899
—Sonntagspost. Jl 3 1897-D 31 1910||
IF complete

ILLINOIS monitor. w Ja 10 1874-77||
IF Ap 18,My 2,Je 27,Jl 18-25,S 5-12,N 21 1874;S 11 1875-F 12,26,Ap 8-Jl 22 1876;Mr 17 1877
WHi Je 17 1874-My 29 1875

INDEPENDENT. w Mr 4 1869-
IF My 13,Ag 26-S 2 1869

Freeport JOURNAL. w N 29 1848-F 5 1913||?
IF 1848[49]-F 19,Mr-Jl 9,23-N 22,D 1850;Ja 10-F 21,Mr-Ap 4,18-25,My 9,Je 13,Jl 1,25, Ag 15,S 12,O 1851-[52]53;F-Je 1,Jl 6,20-S 14, 29-O 12,26,N 16,D 7 1854[55]Ap 24 1856;Ja-Mr 11,25,Ap 15-My 13,27-O 14,N 4-18 1858; F 10-17,Mr 3,Ap 14,28,My 5,26-Je 16,Jl 7,21-28 Ag 11,S 29-O 6,20-27 1859;My 23-30,Ag 8 1860;My 15 1861;Ap 27 1864-F 14,Ap 25-My 16,31-Ag,S 12 1866-S 4,18,O 1867-F 19,Mr 1873-Mr 1882;89
IHi Mr 9 1904-12
MWA My 14 1852;Ag 16 1876
NNHi My 20 1863
WHi My 8 1856-57;N 17 1859-N 14 1860;Ap 25 1866-Mr 1880;Ap 1882-Mr 1886;Mr 30 1887-F 5 1913

Daily JOURNAL. d My 14 1856-57||
IF My-N 12,14-S 24,26-O 15,17-26,28-N 5,7 1856-F 12,14-25,27-Mr 5,7-Jl 8,12-S 24,26-N 7 1857
MH My 15-N 13 1856
WHi My-N 12 1856

Freeport daily JOURNAL. d D 10 1866-67||
IF 1866-Mr 27,29-My 10,12-14,16,18-24,26-S 14 1867
WHi 1866-Ap 16 1867

Freeport daily JOURNAL. 1879-1913 *See* Freeport journal-standard

Freeport daily JOURNAL. O 1-N 13 1880||
Campaign paper
MWA O 21-22 1880
WHi complete

Freeport JOURNAL-STANDARD. d Je 1 1879+
1879-O 18 1913 as Freeport daily journal (title varies: Freeport daily journal and Chicago telegraph; Daily journal and republican; etc.)
ICHi Ag 27 1929
IF My 4-7,9-Ag 13,15-D 21,23 1883-Je 1885;86-O 18 1913;14-[22]-[24]+
IHi Ag 1 1917
IU Je 21 1882;My 1891;Ag 19 1896;Je 1,8,10 1909+
WHi Je-Jl 7 1879;Ag 27 1908;17-19;Ag 27 1929

Daily NORTH-WEST. d S 26 1865-66||
Merged with Freeport journal
OClWHi S 26 1865

NORTHWEST. w Ag 17 1865-66||
Merged with Freeport journal
IF 1865-66;Ja 10-31 1867
WHi Mr-My 10 1866

PRAIRIE democrat. *See* Freeport bulletin

Freeport REPUBLICAN. w 1870-83||
Merged with Freeport journal
IF S 1881-Ap 21 1883

Freeport weekly STANDARD. w 1883-1910||
IF Ja 6,20-Ap 7,21-Jl 14 1905;08-S 3,24-O 22, N 6,19 1909-Ag 5,19-S 9,30-D 2,16-30 1910

Freeport evening STANDARD. d S 5 1887-1913||
1887-D 13 1904 as Freeport daily democrat. United with Freeport daily journal to form Freeport journal-standard
IF 1887-Ja 1903;04-13
IU Mr 15 1888;O 19 1895;S 1 1899;S 28,D 3,5, 10-13,15,17,19-23 1904;Ja 13,24,F 23,Ap 1 1905

Freeport WIDE AWAKE. w
WHi Ag 6-N 17 1860

FULTON

Fulton City ADVERTISER. *See* Fulton journal

Fulton weekly COURIER. *See* Fulton journal

Fulton JOURNAL. w,sw Mr 1 1854+
1854-55? as Whiteside investigator; 1855-59 Fulton City advertiser; 1859-63 Fulton weekly courier
sw 1882-My 1 1933
pub Mr 15 1854;87+
IU O 13 1914+

WHITESIDE investigator. *See* Fulton journal

GALENA

Galena daily ADVERTISER. *See* Galena daily gazette

Galena ADVERTISER. w Jl 20 1829-Je 1830||
Merged with Northwestern gazette, later Galena weekly gazette
DLC S 7,O 5-12,26,N 9,30-D 21 1829
ICHi 1829-My 24 1830
IU S 7,O 5-12,26,N 9,30-S 21 1829
MWA Ag 24 1829

Galena semi-weekly ADVERTISER. sw
ICHi Mr 16,Je 15 1847
WHi S 12,30 1845

Galena BUDGET. w My 12 1841-
DLC Je 16 1841

ILLINOIS (*Continued*)

GALENA—*Continued*

Galena COMMERCIAL advertiser. *See* Industrial press

Galena weekly COURIER. w 1855-62||
MWA D 1 1861

Galena daily COURIER. d Ja 1856-
ICHi F 8 1856

Galena DEMOCRAT. tw 1836-
WHi D 6 1838;S 12 1840

Galena DEMOCRAT. w 1839-
Follows Miners' free press (Mineral Point, Wis.)
ICHi My 31 1840

Galena DEMOCRAT. w D 1862-68||
IC D 22 1862

GALENIAN. w My 2 1832-36||
Follows Miner's journal. Followed by Belmont gazette (Belmont, Wis.)
Ct [1835-36]
DLC 1833-34;My 24 1836
ICHi 1832-Je 2 1833
IHi Jl 3 1832;N 3 1833
MoSM My 1 1832
N S 15,O 6 1834
WHi [Je 1 1834-S 20 1835]

Galena weekly GAZETTE. sw,w N 29 1834+
1834-43? as Northwestern gazette and Galena advertiser; 1844?-64 Weekly Northwestern gazette
sw 1834-
pub 1834+
DLC D 21 1834;Ja 13 1838;Mr 21 1849-52
ICHi Je 18 1842;Ja 13 1843;N 2 1852;N 23 1869;Mr 27 1874;Ag 26 1881
IHi My 4 1
IU My 14 1880
IaDH Ap 8 1837
MWA D 26 1835;Ja 9-16 1836;D 8 1843;Ag 27 1847;F 29 1848;S 9-16 1851;O 18 1853;My 1 1855;Mr 31,Ap 21,Jl 21-28 1876
N Ap 3 184
OHi Ap 15 1861
WHi 1834-Ag 2 1848

Galena daily GAZETTE. d Ja 1 1848+
1848-61? as Galena daily advertiser
pub 1848+
DLC S 21 1861;67
ICHi Ap 15 1835;Ap 21 1870
IHi 1914-19
IU Ap 3 1918+
MWA Ag 1/19 1852;S 2 1861
MiD-B Je 1849
N S 27 18
WHi O 20 1852

INDUSTRIAL press. w 1864-84||
1864-Ja 1 74 as Galena commercial advertiser
MWA Ag 1-S 23 1875

Galena JEFFERSONIAN. w,sw 1845-55||
DLC Ag 24 1849
ICHi Mr 25 1848
WHi O 27 1845-Ja 1 1847

MINER'S journal. w Ag 15 1828-Ap 1832||
Followed by Galenian
Ct [1828-30]
DLC N 15,D 27 1828;F 21,Je-Jl 4,Ag 15, O 3-10,27-N 3,24-D 22 1829;Ja 9,Jl 10 1830
ICHi Jl 22 1828-S 19 1829;Je 12 1830
IU N 15,D 1826;F 21,Je-Jl 4,Ag 15,O 3-10, 27-N 3,24-D 22 1829;Ja 9,Jl 10 1830
MBAt Mr 7 1829;F 13 1830
MWA S 13 1828;Mr 14-28 1829;Ja 2 1830
MoSM Jl 30 1831
WHi S 26 1829-D 4 1830

NORTHWESTERN gazette. *See* Galena weekly gazette

REGISTER of news. w Ja 1 1841-
DLC Ja 1 1841

Galena REPUBLICAN. w 1893-94||?
ICHi D 16-2 1893;Ja 6-13,F 3 1894

Galena SENTINEL. sw 1841-46||
DLC F 24 1844
IU My 25 1844
MiD-B Ja 1 1844
NhD F 14 1844
PWCl Je 4 1842
WHi S 2 1843-N 23,D 7-14 1844

Galena VOLKSFREUND. w 1868-92||?
In German
KHi Mr 23 1877

GALESBURG

EAST Galesburg tribune. *See* Galesburg tribune

Daily FREE democrat. d Mr 17 1857-
IGK Mr 17-Ag 15 1857

Galesburg FREE democrat. w *See* Galesburg press and people

Galesburg FREE press. *See* Galesburg press and people

Galesburg GAZETTE. w 1891-1905||
IGK 1903;Ja-S 29 1905

ILLINOIS democrat. w 1892-1930||?
1892-1901 as Galesburg spectator
IGK 1893-98;Je 22 1900-01;Ja 20-N 10 1905; 06-Je 19,Jl-D 1908

Daily morning JOURNAL. d Mr 27 1897-
IGK Mr 27-Ap 3 1897

KNOX county news-letter. *See* Galesburg news-letter

Galesburg evening MAIL. d My 1891-Mr 31 1927||
United with Galesburg republican register to form Daily register-mail
IG 1902-27
IGK Ap 17 1896
IHi 1920-27
IU O 12,17 1914-27

Galesburg weekly MAIL. w 1892-1911||?
IGK 1893-98;1900-01;05-08

Galesburg NEWS-LETTER. w Ag 1 1850-53||
Title varies: Galesburg news-letter and Henry county news; Knox county news-letter; etc.
IG O 10 1850;Ja 23 1851;O 29 1852
IGK F 22 1853
IHi O 10 1850

NORTHWESTERN gazeteer. w 1849-50||?
IG O 4 1849

NORTH-WESTERN intelligencer. w 1848-50||
IU D 7 1849

Galesburg PLAINDEALER. sw,w 1873-1906||
1873-75 as Republic (sw)
IGK 1897;1900-01;03;05-O 12 1906

Galesburg POST. w Jl 6 1928+
pub 1928+

Galesburg PRESS and people. w 1854-94||
1854-65 as Galesburg free democrat;1865-76 Galesburg free press; 1876-82 Galesburg press
IG F 20 1858;My 29,N 20 1860;Ap 10 1862; F 19 1863;Ag 4 1864;65-68;70
IGK 1854-57;S 1858-60[64]Ja-Ap 6 1894
MWA Je 18,Jl 9 1868
P-B Mr 23,Je 22 1854

Galesburg REGISTER. d *See* Daily register-mail

Galesburg REGISTER. w *See* Galesburg republican-register

Daily REGISTER-mail. d 1870+
1870-72? as Galesburg register; 1872?-Mr 1927 Galesburg republican-register
IG Ja 27,30,F 3,Mr 24,My 5,Ag 15,D 24 1877; Ap 2,13,16,20 1878;Ja 25,Mr 29,S 30 1879; Mr 18 1882;Mr 2,Je 12 1886;1902+
IGK N 1892-1922
IHi Jl 30,Ag 2,N 16 1917;Ap 1927+
IU My 8 1897;Ap 1927-F 8 1928
T 1908

REPUBLIC. *See* Galesburg plaindealer

Galesburg REPUBLICAN. w 1870-72||?
United with Galesburg register to form Galesburg republican-register

Galesburg REPUBLICAN-register. d *See* Daily register-mail

Galesburg REPUBLICAN-REGISTER. w 1866-1919||?
1866-72? as Galesburg register
IG F 4 1869;80-1906
IGK 1893-96;1900-01;03-06;D 27 1907-08
IHi F 28,Mr 28-Ap 4,My 16-23,S 12,O 31 1867

Galesburg SPECTATOR. *See* Illinois democrat

Galesburg TRIBUNE. w 1892-1903||
1893-99 as East Galesburg tribune
IGK 1900-01;Ja-S 12 1903

GALVA

ILLINOIS Swede. *See* Svenska tribunen-nyheter (Chicago)

Galva NEWS. w O 1879+
IGa 1910+

NYA världen. *See* Svenska tribunen-nyheter (Chicago)

Galva REPUBLICAN. w D 1862-70||
1862-S 1867 as Galva union
IGa Je 1865-My 24 1866
MWA F 21 1867

Galva STANDARD. w 1850-
NbHi S 2 1846

Galva STANDARD. w 1881-1915||
IGa 1910-12;14-15

Galva UNION. *See* Galva republican

GENESEO

DEMOCRATIC standard. w Ag 30 1855-58||
ICHi N 1 1855

Geneseo REPUBLIC. w 1856-1922||?
IGa Jl 1910-Je,Ag 1912-Ja 1917
MWA Je 3 1864

GENEVA

KANE county advertiser. *See* Geneva republican

KANE county republican. *See* Geneva republican

PATROL. w,sw 1884-1910||
IGeB 1890-1910
IGeW 1884-90

TWICE a week republican. *See* Geneva republican

Geneva REPUBLICAN. w,sw Ja 7 1847+
1847-59? as Kane county advertiser; 1860?-80 Kane county republican; 1899-1917 Twice-a-week republican
sw 1899-1917
pub Mr 1893+
IA O 20 1859
ICHi D 16-23 1893;Ja 6-13,F 3 1894
IGe 1900+
IHi [F 20 1904-Ag 1905]
NNHi N 20 1856;Mr 22 1873;Ap 13 1878-Ap 1879

GENOA

Genoa JOURNAL. w Je 1 1900-S 1904||
United with Genoa republican to form Genoa republican-journal, later Genoa republican
IGeR 1900-Je 20 1902

Genoa REPUBLICAN. w My 16 1902+
1902-S 9 1904 as Genoa republican; S 16 1904-My 19 1919 Genoa republican-journal
pub Mr 18 1894-96;My 23 1902+
NN O 16 1914

Genoa REPUBLICAN-JOURNAL. *See* Genoa republican

GEORGETOWN

Georgetown NEWS. w 1898+
pub 1929+
IU Je 29 1917+

Georgetown X. w 1892-93||?
KHi O 21 1893

GIBSON CITY

Gibson COURIER and Gibson City enterprise. w 1872+
1872-73 as Gibson City enterprise; 1873-My 10 1934 Gibson courier
pub 1875+
IU O 16 1914+

Gibson City ENTERPRISE. 1872-73 *See* Gibson courier and Gibson City enterprise

Gibson City ENTERPRISE. w 1883-My 12 1934||
United with Gibson City courier to form Gibson courier and Gibson City enterprise

TIMES. w O 17 1935+
pub 1935+

GILLESPIE

Gillespie NEWS. w 1905+
IU D 12 1917+

PROGRESSIVE miner. w 1932+
NNRa D 29 1933+
WHi S 16 1932+

GILMAN

Gilman STAR. w 1868+
pub Mr 1923+
IU D 13 1917-Jl 18 1918;Ap 14 1921+

GLASFORD

Glasford GAZETTE. w Ja 1 1899+
pub 1899+
IU O 8 1914+

Hanna City-Trivoli INDEX. *See under* Hanna City

GLEN ELLYN

Glen Ellyn NEWS. w My 12 1922+
Title varies: Glen Ellyan
pub 1922+

GLENVIEW

Glenview VIEW. w Ja 1 1923+
pub Mr 10 1930-31;Ag 1932-Je 1933;34+

GOLCONDA

Golconda ENTERPRISE. w 1887-89||
United with Golconda herald to form Herald-enterprise

HERALD-ENTERPRISE. w Ag 8 1858+
1858-89 as Golconda herald
pub My 1887+
IU D 13 1917-Ja 22,Jl 22 1920+

POPE county transcript. w 1863-
MWA D 26 1865

GRAFTON

BACKWOODSMAN. *See under* Jerseyville

Grafton PHOENIX. w 1842-43||?
DLC Ap 20 1843
ICU Ag 3 1843

GRAND DETOUR

ROCK RIVER register. w Ja 1 1842-Ag? 1843||
Ja-S 16 1842 pub at Mt. Morris
DLC Mr 10 1843
IOr Ap 2,16-27,Jl 6,20,N 11 1842;Ap 7,Ag 4 1843

GRANITE CITY

NARODEN glas. (National herald) sw 1907+
In Bulgarian
IU Ag 25 1917-Jl 13 1926
KHi F 29 1908

Granite City POST. sw 1919-27||
IGr 1920-27

ILLINOIS (*Continued*)

GRANITE CITY—*Continued*

Granite City PRESS-RECORD. w,sw 1903+
1903-08 as Granite City press; 1909-13? Granite City press and herald
w 1903-13?
IGr 1916+
IHi [Jl 31 1914-N 1918]

Granite City TRIBUNE. sw
IGr Je 16 1930-Jl 22 1933

GRANT PARK

ANCHOR. w 1899+
pub [1899-1924]+

GRAYVILLE

Grayville weekly HERALD. w 1853-59||
1853-54 as Grayville news
ICHi S 12 1857

Grayville INDEPENDENT. w 1859-Jl 1919||
United with Grayville mercury to form Grayville mercury-independent
MWA Ap 10 1863;Ap 10 1868-Mr 6 1874

Grayville MERCURY-independent. w 1886+
1886-Jl 31 1919 as Grayville mercury
IHi [Ja 13 1904-19]+
IU D 1917+

Grayville NEWS. *See* Grayville weekly herald

GREENVILLE

Greenville ADVOCATE. w,sw F 11 1858+
w 1858-Mr 1911
pub 1858-91;93-99;1901+
IHi S 27 1915

ILLINOIS chronicle. w F 3 1848-
IU Mr 24-31 1848

GRIGGSVILLE

Griggsville INDEPENDENT-press. w Jl 3 1869+
1869-S? 1879 as Griggsville independent
pub My 11 1887+
IHi Jl 10 1869

PIKE county free press. *See* Pike county republican. (Pittsfield)

PIKE county union. w My 2 1855-57||?
Follows Pittsfield union (Pittsfield)
Followed by Pike county democrat (Pittsfield)
DLC 1855-Je 9 1856

Griggsville REFLECTOR. w 1871-82||?
IHi Jl 12 1879-Jl 13 1882

HAMILTON

ELVASTON press. w
IU Je 23-D 1 1916;N 1918-Mr 5 1925

Hamilton PRESS. w 1885+
IU O 9,D 1914-[16]-Mr 5 1925

HANNA CITY

Hanna City-Trivoli INDEX. w 1925+
pub Ag 17 1928+
IU Je 12 1930+

HARDIN

CALHOUN news. w Ap 1 1915+
pub 1915+

HARRISBURG

Harrisburg CHRONICLE. w N 2 1859-69||
IHaC N 2-9,30-D 7 1859;My 30-Je 6 1860;N 6 1861;Ja 10-17,My 2,Jl 18-25 1863;Mr 5,My 3,O 4,N 1 1864;O 11 1865
MWA Ap 4,Je 27,N 28 1863

Evening CHRONICLE. d 1914-23||?
IHi Jl 7 1916

Daily REGISTER. d Je 28 1915+
pub 1915+
IHaM 1915+
IU Ja 17 1935+

HARVARD

Harvard HERALD and independent. w D 23 1887+
1887-O 1924 as Harvard herald
pub 1887+
IU F 14 1896;S 21 1899;D 27 1928+

Harvard INDEPENDENT. w 1866-1924||
United with Harvard herald to form Harvard herald and independent

HARVEY

Harvey TRIBUNE. w 1891+
pub 1930+
IU Ja 18 1918+

HAVANA

MASON county democrat. w 1849+
IGK My 30,Jl 18 1879

Havana VOTER. w 1864-
Campaign paper
MWA F 12 1864

HEBRON

Hebron TIMES. w Ag 1 1928+
pub [1928+]

HENNEPIN

Hennepin JOURNAL. w My 4 1837-D 22 1838||
ICHi O 12,26 1837;Ja 27,Mr 3,D 22 1838
ICU D 22 1838
IHi S 28,D 7 1837,Jl 14,Ag 11,25,D 22 1838
IU D 22 1838

PUTNAM record. w Je 25 1868-1928||?
IU O 14 1914-S 15 1926

HENRY

Henry COURIER. *See* Henry news-republican

Henry CURRENT-news. sw,w 1886-Je 2 1921||
1886-N 25 1920 as Henry times. United with Henry republican to form Henry news-republican
sw 1886-S 18 1904
IHi F 26 1904-21

Henry NEWS-REPUBLICAN. w 1852+
1852-Je 1866 as Henry courier; Jl 1866-Je 2 1921 Henry republican
IHi Je 9 1921+
MWA Ja 2 1879
NbHi Ap 29 1880

Henry REPUBLICAN. *See* Henry news-republican

Henry TIMES. *See* Henry current-news

HERRICK

Herrick BULLETIN. w Ja 1932+
pub F 1932+
IU Ap 1932+

Herrick REPORTER. w O 12 1926-31||
IU 1927-My 13 1931

HERRIN

Herrin daily JOURNAL. d F 11 1913+
pub 1913+
IHe Ap-Je 1923;Je 1931-33

Herrin NEWS. w Ja 1 1899+
pub 1899+
IHe S 1925-Mr,Jl 1931-34
IHi Je 1911-13
IU My 28 1909-Ag 19 1920

HERSCHER

Herscher PILOT. w 1896+
IU D 20 1917; Ja 24 1918-S 23 1920

HEYWORTH

Heyworth NATURAL gas. *See* Heyworth star

Heyworth REPORTER. *See* Heyworth star

Weekly STANDARD. w 1881-88||?
IHeyS [1882]

Heyworth STAR. w 1892+
1892-98? as Heyworth reporter; 1899-1925 Heyworth natural gas
pub 1914+

HIGHLAND

Der Highland BÖTE. w 1859-N 1869||
Followed by Madison county bote (Edwardsville)
In German
IHigN complete
MWA F 1 1867
NN Ag 2 1861;D 23 1864

Highland JOURNAL. w Ja 3 1894+
pub 1894+
IHig My 1929+
IU D 13 1917+

Highland LEADER. *See* Highland news leader

Highland NEWS. w 1920-Ag 9 1921||
United with Highland leader to form Highland news-leader

Highland NEWS-LEADER. w 1900+
1900-Ag 9 1921 as Highland leader
pub 1900+
IHig My 1929+
IU D 11 1917+

Highland TELEPHONE. w 1883-86||
IHigN complete

Die Highland UNION. w O 24 1863-1913||
In German
IHigN complete

HIGHLAND PARK

Highland Park NEWS. m Ap 1874-My 1875||
IHigh complete

NORTH SHORE news-letter. w 1892?-1911||
1892?-F 1899 as Highland Park news; F 1899-N 1904 Sheridan Road news-letter; D 1904-07 Highland Park news-letter
IHigh 1896-1911

Highland Park PRESS. w Mr 1 1911+
pub 1911+
IHigh 1911+
IU O 15 1914+

HILLSBORO

Hillsboro ANTI-MONOPOLIST. *See* Hillsboro journal

Hillsboro BLADE. *See* Hillsboro journal

Hillsboro DEMOCRAT. *See* Hillsboro journal

ILLINOIS free press. w 1860-62||?
MWA Ap 4 1861

Hillsboro JOURNAL. w,sw 1850+
1850-56 as Prairie mirror; 1856-68 Montgomery county herald; 1868-Ap 22 1874 Hillsboro democrat; Ap 29-N 18 1874 Hillsboro anti-monopolist; 1875?-77 Hillsboro blade
w 1850-1914?
pub 1870+
ICHi Jl 3 1858
IH 1900+
IHi Ag 3 1917
IU O 1914+
MWA D 4 1863

Hillsboro JOURNAL. 1870-75 *See* Montgomery news

MONTGOMERY county herald. *See* Hillsboro journal

MONTGOMERY news. w,sw 1869+
1869-74? as Hillsboro news-letter; 1874?-75 Hillsboro journal
w 1869-D 9 1913
pub 1870-F,Ap 1872-N 18 1874;Jl 21 1882-Jl 10 1885;92+
IH Jl 1876-Jl 1880;1900+
IHi Mr 11 1904-Je 1917
IU O 9 1914+

Hillsboro NEWS-LETTER. *See* Montgomery news

PRAIRIE beacon. w 1838-39||
NN D 1 1838

PRAIRIE mirror. *See* Hillsboro journal

HINDSBORO

Hindsboro NEWS. w Mr 4 1896+
pub Mr 4 1896;1907+

HINSDALE

Hinsdale DOINGS. w O 5 1895+
pub 1895+

HOMER

Homer ENTERPRISE. w 1877+
pub D 16 1912+

HOOPESTON

CHRONICLE-HERALD. w Ja 4 1872-1927||
1872-Ap 14 1921 as Hoopeston chronicle
pub 1872-Ap 14 1921
IDa 1873-79
IHo Jl 1882-1908;10-14
IU My 1918-My 5 1921
MWA D 24 1874

CHRONICLE-HERALD. d 1881+
1881-Ap 14 1921 as Hoopeston chronicle
pub Ap 1921+
IHo 1914+

Hoopeston HERALD. w 1889-Ap 1921||
United with Hoopeston chronicle to form Chronicle-herald

Hoopeston evening HERALD. d 1903-Ap 1921||
United with Hoopeston chronicle to form Chronicle-herald

HOPEDALE

Hopedale REVIEW. *See* Hopedale times-review

Hopedale TIMES. w 1903-05||?
United with Hopedale review to form Hopedale times-review

Hopedale TIMES-REVIEW. w 1887+
1887-1905- as Hopedale review
pub N 1928+

HULL

Hull ENTERPRISE. w 1906+
pub 1906+

HUME

Hume RECORD. w N 1890+
pub 1890+

HUTSONVILLE

Hutsonville weekly JOURNAL. w Je 5 1852-
1852-53 as Wabash sentinel
ICHi Je 12 1852
MWA Je 26 1852

WABASH sentinel. *See* Hutsonville weekly journal

ILLIOPOLIS

Illiopolis SENTINEL. w 1929+
pub O 1933+

INA

Ina OBSERVER. w My 1909+
pub 1909+

ILLINOIS (*Continued*)

INDUSTRY

Industry PRESS. w Mr 23 1916+
pub 1916+

IPAVA

Ipava INDEPENDENT. w 1890-1912||
IIT 1896-98

Ipava weekly TRIBUNE. w Ag 19 1926+
pub 1926+

IRVING

Irving GAZETTE. w Jl 13-D 21 1872||?
IHi [Jl-D 21 1872]

JACKSONVILLE

Jacksonville BANNER. w Ap 24 1832-33||?
DLC D 4 1833
N O 16 1833

Jacksonville CONSTITUTIONALIST. w Ap 1852-56||?
DLC Ap 13-Je 1,15-Jl 6,20,Ag 10-D 14 1853
IHi Je 12-26,N 6-13 1852;Jl 27,N 2 1853

Daily CONSTITUTIONIST. d 1854-55||?
IHi Je 13,15 1854
IU Ja 23 1855

Jacksonville COURIER. tw,d 1876+
1876-1912 as Daily Illinois courier tw 1876-82
IHi F 6,11-13 1909[1920-34]

ENTERPRISE. w 1874-76||
United with Illinois sentinel to form Illinois courier

ILLINOIS courier. w F 2 1855-
1855-Ja 30 1857 as Illinois sentinel; F 6 1857-76 Jacksonville sentinel
ICHi D 23 1889
IHi 1855-Mr 5 1868
KHi Mr 27 1857

Daily ILLINOIS courier. *See* Jacksonville courier

ILLINOIS democrat. w My 20 1840-42||
DLC My 27-Je 3,Jl 1,O 15 1840
ICHi Je 3 1840

ILLINOIS patriot. *See* Illinoisan

ILLINOIS sentinel. *See* Illinois courier

ILLINOIS standard. w Mr 10-D 29 1838||
Merged with Spirit of the west
DLC Mr 17-Ap 7,21-My 5,19-26,D 22-29 1838
IU Mr 17-My 5,19-26,D 22-29 1838

ILLINOIS state gazette and Jacksonville news. w O 1834-37||?
1834 as Illinois state gazette
DLC Ja 17 1835-37
ICU D 23 1835
NN O 24 1835

ILLINOIS state journal. w
ICHi Mr 13 1861

ILLINOIS statesman. w Ap 29 1843-My 27 1844||
ICHi Ap 29,My 29-Je 12,26,Jl 10-17,31,Ag 14, 26-S 4,18-N 6,20-D 18 1843;Ja-Mr,Ap 22-29, My 13 1844
IHi complete
IJ complete

ILLINOIAN. w D 20 1831-Ap 9 1844||
1831-36 as Illinois patriot
DLC D 22 1832;N 17 1838;O 31,N 21 1840;F 27,Mr 13,27-Ap 3,17-Jl 3,17-Ag 21,S 4,18-O 16, 30,N 13-27,D 18-25 1841
ICHi O 21 1831;Ap 11 1840;F 13 1841;N 17 1843; Mr 22,Ap 9 1844
ICU O 19 1833;Ap 23 1842
IGK O 19 1833;Ap 27 1837
IHi N 2 1833
IJ Ja-Ag 24 1839
IU O 31,N 21 1840;F 27,Mr 13,27-Ap 3,17-24, My-Jl 3,17-Ag 21,S 4,18-O 16,30,N 13-27,D 18-25 1841
IaBu O 27 1832-N 1833
MWA D 26 1835;Ap 25 1840
MoSM Ap 12 1832

JACKSON standard. w S 10 1845-
IGK Mr 12 1846

Jacksonville JOURNAL. w 1845-1920||?
1845-58 as Morgan journal
ICHi Jl 21 1849;D 25 1889
IGK F 6,Mr 5 1846;D 27 1851;Ja 17 1852;Je 15 1854
IHi Ja 29,Ap 17-24,Je 26,Jl 10-24,Ag 14 1847; Jl 21 1849; Je 22,S 28-O 5, N 16 1850;Mr 1, 22-29,Ap 12 1851;Ja 10-17,Ap 10,My 15,Je-Jl 17,31-Ag 7,N 20 1852;Ja 29,Ap 9,28,My 12,Je 2,23-30,Jl 28-Ag 4,18,S 8,29,O 20,D 22 1853; Ja 26,F 16,Je 15,Jl-Ag 10,O 26,N 4,9 1854;F 1 1855;F 21,My 29,Je 19-Jl 3,D 11-18 1856; Ja 22,O 22 1857;F 3 1859;Jl 4 1861;Mr 3 1862; Ja 18-F 8,Mr 1,My 3 1866;Ja 24,F 21 1867;Mr 5,N 5 1868;S 2,D 16 1869
IJ My 31 1882-1917
IU Je 22 1854;F 8 1866;Ja 24 1867;Mr 1 1882
NN F 12 1847

Daily Jacksonville JOURNAL. d Ap 14 1866+
DLC Je 25 1867
IC Ap 30-My 1 1889
ICHi Ja 23 1868;Je 2 1880;Ag 3-4 1881;D 22 1889
IHi N 9,D 31 1866;Ja 25-26,31-F 1,4-5,D 25 1867[68-Je 1869]D 21,23,29-30 1870;Ja 6,29,My 13 1871;Ja 10 1879;F 13,Jl 24 1885;Jl 19 1892;Jl 24 1885;F 12 1909+
IJ Ja 12 1880+
IU Ja 28 1868;O 4 1914-My 20,Je 30 1915-Jl 1918
MWA S 21 1866;Je 25 1868
NbHi S 20 1881;Ag 9 1885;O 16 1903

MORGAN bee. w Jl 25 1845-
IHi Ag 8 1845

MORGAN journal. *See* Jacksonville journal

Jacksonville NEWS. 1834|
United with Illinois state gazette to form Illinois state gazette and Jacksonville news

PRAIRIE argus. w D 24 1846-
OClWHi D 31 1846

Tri-weekly Jacksonville PRESS. tw O-N 1852||
IHi O 29,N 8,10,17 1852

Jacksonville SENTINEL. *See* Illinois courier

SPIRIT of the west and Illinois standard. ir,w 1837-39||
1838 as Spirit of the west
Ja-Je? 1837 pub in Naples
IHi Ap 21,Jl 14 1838

WESTERN observer. w My 1830-
CSmH Ag 14 1830
MWA Ja 15 1831

JERSEYVILLE

BACKWOODSMAN and Jersey and Green counties' advertiser. w 1837-42||
Title varies slightly. Followed by Newspaper
1837-40? pub at Grafton; 1841? at Carrollton
DLC My 9 1839
ICHi F 29 1840
IHi Je 21 1838;Ja 15 1841
IU N 21 1837;Je 11-18 1841

DEMOCRATIC union. *See* Jersey county democrat

JERSEY county democrat. w 1854+
Follows Newspaper. 1854-65 as Democratic union
IHi O 1870-O 20 1871
IU My 25 1916+

JERSEY county news. w Ja 1 1863+
1863-1927 as Jerseyville republican
pub 1885+
IHi [1904-26]+

NEWSPAPER. w 1842-56||
Follows Backwoodsman. Followed by Democratic union, later Jersey county democrat

Jerseyville PRAIRIE state. w 1850-64||?
MWA Ja 19,Ap 6 1861

Jerseyville REPUBLICAN. *See* Jersey county news

JOHNSTON CITY

PROGRESS. w Mr 2 1897+
pub 1905+

JOLIET

Joliet COURIER. w 1839-Je? 1843||
Followed by Signal
ICU F 2 1842

GENERAL-ANZEIGER. w F 14 1896+
In German
pub 1896+
IU 1896-F 13 1897;S 8,O 13 1917+

Joliet evening HERALD. *See* Joliet evening herald-news

Joliet evening HERALD-NEWS. d 1904+
1904-Je 1915 as Joliet evening herald
pub 1904+
IHi [Ap 6 1917-Je 1919]
IJoH N 18 1904-Je 1915
IU D 11 1917-D 22 1919

Joliet daily NEWS. d Ap 1877-Je 1915||
United with Joliet evening herald to form Joliet evening herald-news
pub 1904-15
Ct N 12 1908
IHi [Mr 20 1912-My 15 1914]
MoHi N 28 1911

Joliet NEWS. w 1877-1915||
IHi [F 17 1893-1911]

REPUBLIC. *See* Joliet Republican

Joliet REPUBLICAN. w 1847-1906||?
1847-62 as True democrat; 1862-69 Joliet republican; 1869-82 Republic; 1882-O 17 1885 Joliet republic and sun
DLC Ap 2 1864;O 28 1865
ICHi Je 8 1861;Mr 7 1863;Mr 21 1874,S 6 1888
NCH My 25 1848;F 8,22 Ap 19,Jl 26 1849

SIGNAL. w Je 14 1843-99||?
Follows Joliet courier
ICHi D 27 1843-Ja 3 1844
MWA D 20 1853

Joliet SUN. d 1874-83||
United with Republic to form Joliet Republic and sun, later Joliet republican
ICHi O 6 1879

TRUE democrat. *See* Joliet republican

JONESBORO

Jonesboro weekly GAZETTE. w 1849+
pub 1849+
DLC D 31 1859-S 15 1860
IU My 24,Je 14-21,Jl 5,Ag 9,23-30,S 27,O 18 1854;F 28 Ap 4,Ag 8-15,29,S 19-O 10,24-31,N 17-28 1855[Ja-S 1856;57-58]-[61-63]D 3 1864;N 17 1865;O 20,N 3 1866[67-72]Mr 27,My 6,22,Je 19,Ag 21 1875;F 12,Jl 29,N 4 1876[Mr 1878-O 1885]Ja 16,F 20,Mr 20 1886;F 11,Ag 11 1888;D 26 1913+
MWA Mr 4 1876

KANKAKEE

Evening DEMOCRAT. d 1892-O 13 1919||
United with Kankakee daily gazette to form Daily gazette and democrat, later Kankakee daily news
IKa [1892-1919]
IU Jl-O 1919

Kankakee daily GAZETTE. *See* Kankakee daily news

Kankakee weekly GAZETTE. *See* Kankakee weekly news

Daily GAZETTE and democrat. *See* Kankakee daily news

Weekly GAZETTE and news. *See* Kankakee weekly news

Kankakee HERALD. w 1872-83||
ICHi Ap 26 1873
IKa [1872-83]

Le JOURNAL de l'Illinois. *See* Le courrier de l'Ouest (Chicago)

Kankakee weekly NEWS. w 1853-My 29 1931||
1853-O 13 1919 as Kankakee weekly gazette; O 20 1919-Ap 1920 Weekly gazette and democrat
IKa 1868-[95-1931]
N Ap 1 1855
PDoHi S 6 1866

Kankakee daily NEWS. d 1896-My 29 1931||
1896-O 13 1919 as Kankakee daily gazette; O 14 1919-Ap 30 1920 Daily gazette and democrat. United with Kankakee daily republican to form Kankakee republican-news
IKa [1896-1921]-31
IU Ap 1918-31

Kankakee weekly REPUBLICAN. w 1868-1925||
1868-99? as Kankakee weekly times
IKa [1878-1925]

Kankakee REPUBLICAN-NEWS. d 1884+
1884-1902? as Kankakee daily times; 1903?-My 1931 Kankakee daily republican
IKa [1884-1919]+
IU F 1928+

Kankakee daily TIMES. *See* Kankakee republican-news

Kankakee weekly TIMES. *See* Kankakee weekly republican

KANSAS

Kansas JOURNAL. w 1878?+
pub [1891-1935]+

KASKASKIA

Kaskaskia DEMOCRAT. w Ag 19 1829-31||
1829 as Western democrat
DLC S 19,O 10,D 22 1829;Ja 2,13,N 27 1830
IHi Je 30 1830
MoSM Jl 26 1831

ILLINOIS intelligencer. *See under* Vandalia

ILLINOIS reporter. w 1826-29||?
DLC O 25 1826

Kaskaskia REPUBLICAN. w F 27 1822-25||
1822-Mr 2 1824 as Republican advocate
DLC Mr 30,Ap 20,My 11,25 1824
IHi Mr 31 1825
IU Ag 21 1823;Mr 30,Ap 20,My 11,25 1824
N My 4-11,N 6,D 7-14 1824;Ja 4,F 1-8,Mr 15, 31,Ap 28 1825

Kaskaskia REPUBLICAN. w Je 1840-49||
DLC Je 24 1841
ICHi Mr 2 1844
ICU Jl 8,Ag 7,21 1841;F 12 1842
IHi Ag 28 1841

REPUBLICAN-ADVOCATE. *See* Kaskaskia republican. 1822-25

WESTERN democrat. *See* Kaskaskia democrat

WESTERN intelligencer. *See* Illinois intelligencer (Vandalia)

KEITHSBURG

MERCER county democrat. w Ap 23 1856-59||
1856-58 as Keithsburg observer
IGK 1856-Ag 1 1857
OClWHi My 29 1858

Keithsburg NEWS. w Ap 1874+
IGK Ag 14,S 4 1879
IU O 22 1914-Ag 1920

Keithsburg OBSERVER. 1856-58 *See* Mercer county democrat

Keithsburg OBSERVER. w D 12 1861-70||
IHi 1861-Ag 24 1854

OQUAWKA spectator. *See under* Oquawka

KENNEY

GAZETTE-HERALD. w Mr 25 1881+
1881-1910 as Kenney gazette
pub 1881-93;97+

KEWANEE

Kewanee ADVERTISER. w F 1856-63||?
IK 1857-63

ADVERTISER. 1870-71 *See* Kewanee independent

Kewanee daily COURIER. *See* Kewanee star-courier

Kewanee COURIER. w *See* Kewanee weekly star-courier

HENRY county dial. *See* Kewanee radical

ILLINOIS (*Continued*)

KEWANEE—*Continued*

Kewanee INDEPENDENT. w Jl 1870-96||
1870-71 as Advertiser
IK D 8 1870-96
WMA Ap 13,S 20 1876

Kewanee RADICAL. w 1855-70||
1855-68 as Henry county dial
IGK Ag 14 1856
MWA Je 25 1857;Je 19 1861

Kewanee STAR. w 1889-Ap 1898||
United with Kewanee courier to form Kewanee weekly star-courier
IKK Ja 18 1891-98

Evening STAR. d 1895-My 1898||
United with Kewanee daily courier to form Kewanee star-courier
IKK My 15 1896-98

Kewanee weekly STAR-COURIER. w 1876-1928||
1876-Ap 1898 as Kewanee courier
pub complete
IGK My 28,Ag 20 1879
IHi [Mr 16 1904-09]
IK Mr 1878-My 14 1902
MWA Ap 12,S 20 1876

Kewanee STAR-COURIER. d My 11 1896+
1896-My 1 1898 as Kewanee daily courier
pub 1896+
IGa current 6 months
IK 1896-98;1913-21;26+
IU 1918+

KINMUNDY

Kinmundy EXPRESS. w 1883+
F 6 1918-Ja 15 1920 as Marion county express
IU O 15 1914+

MARION county express. *See* Kinmundy express

KIRKLAND

Kirkland ENTERPRISE. w 1900+
IGeR N 1932+

KIRKWOOD

Kirkwood ENTERPRISE. w 1877-79||
IGK Jl 24 1879

KNOXVILLE

CAMPAIGN republican. w
KHi S 24 1858

Knoxville JOURNAL. w O 5 1849-56||
IGK 1849-F,O 19 1852-Ja 18,F 1853-Mr 21 1855
MWA Ja 3 1854

KNOX county republican. w O 8 1856+
1856- as Knox republican
IG F 17 1869;D 25 1876
IGK 1856-Ap 3 1861;Ap 12 1876-Ag 1895;Ap 28,D 15 1897;Ja 12,26-Ag,S 14,28 1898-Mr 15 1899;S 22 1900-S 14 1901;Ag 6,D 17 1903;O 12 1909-F 1912
IU O 1914-[18-19]-21
MWA D 17,31 1856;O 7,21,D 30 1857

KNOX republican. *See* Knox county republican

LACON

Lacon HERALD. *See* Lacon home journal

Lacon HOME journal. sw,w D 13 1837+
1837-My 7? 1840 as Lacon herald; My 14 1840-My 1841 Ninawah gazette (Peru); Je 1841-Je 13 1866 Illinois gazette
Je-O 1841 pub in Peru
pub [1869-1935]+
DLC F 10 1838;My 23 1840;Ja 14 1843;Ag 9 1928
ICHi Mr 18 1840(extra)
ICU F 13 1841
IHi 1837-[40-95]
MWA F 8 1882

Lacon HOME journal. d Je 15 1891-
IHi Je 15,S 9-10 1891

ILLINOIS gazette. *See* Lacon home journal

ILLINOIS statesman. w Ap 6 1867-73||
ICHi Ag 3 1867;Jl 30,D 24 1869;Ag 9 1870;F 28 1871

LA GRANGE

La Grange CITIZEN. w Je 1905+
pub 1905+
IU O 16 1914-My 21 1920

LA HARPE

La HARPER. w 1874-1931||?
IGK My 16,30,Jl 25-Ag 1,O 31 1879

LAKE FOREST

LAKE FORESTER. w 1895+
pub 1895+
IU D 22 1917+

LAKE VIEW

Lake View RECORD. w 1888-89||?
ICHi Ap 6 1889

LANARK

CARROLL county gazette. *See* Lanark gazette

Lanark GAZETTE. w 1868+
1868-79? as Carroll county gazette
IHi [Jl 30 1870-78]
IU Ap 9 1880;Ap 20 1887;O 14 1914+

Lanark daily GAZETTE. d Ag 1? 1883-
IU Ag 17 1883

LANE. *See* ROCHELLE

LANSING

Lansing JOURNAL. w Jl 16 1931+
pub 1931+

LA ROSE

La Rose VIDETTE. w
Printed as an ed of Lacon home journal (Lacon)
IHi N 8 1882;D 26 1883

LA SALLE

La Salle DEMOCRAT. w 1876-83||
United with La Salle county press to form La Salle democrat-press

La Salle DEMOCRAT-PRESS. w 1856-93||?
Follows La Salle watchman. 1856-82 as La Salle county press
MWA Ap 6 1861

LA SALLE county press *See* La Salle democrat-press

Daily POST-TRIBUNE. d 1894+
1894-Ag 1926 as Daily post
pub 1903-17;S 1926+

La Salle STANDARD. w 1851-52||
MWA My 8 1852

La Salle daily TRIBUNE. d 1890-Ag 1926||
United with Daily post to form Daily post-tribune
ILP Jl 1892-1926

TWIN City journal. d 1880-93||?
dated also at Peru
IO S 1892-Je 30 1893

La Salle WATCHMAN. w O 16 1852-55||
Followed by La Salle county press, later La Salle democrat-press
MWA N 20 1852;D 24 1853;Jl 16 1855

LAWRENCEVILLE

LAWRENCE county news. w 1894+
pub 1898+
IBrL 1913+
ILa 1922+
IU O 1914-16;Mr 4 1925

Daily RECORD. d 1922+
IU [Ap 20 1927-Ja 16 1929]Ja 18 1935+

Lawrenceville REPUBLICAN. w 1873-D 27 1928||
1873-91? as Rural republican
IBrL 1913-22
ILa 1922-28
IU O 1917-[18]-[22]-28

RURAL republican. *See* Lawrenceville republican

LEAF RIVER

Leaf River ENTERPRISE. w O 29 1881-86||
IU D 10-24 1881;F 4,My 27,N 4,25-D 16 1882 [83]Ja 5,F 23-D 20 1884;Ja 17 1885-Je 19,S 11,O 30[N-D]1886

Leaf River MIRROR w Ja 19 1891+
IU Ja 16,Je 12 1891[92-1900]-Je 6 1901;O 30 1914+

LEE

Lee GAZETTE. w
Issued as a part of the Shabbona express
IU D 13 1917-O 30 1919

LENA

Weekly INDEPENDENT. w Ja 31 1901-05||
Ja-F 9? 1901 as Lena independent
IU Ja 31-F 7,My 9 1901

Lena STAR. w Ja 4 1867+
Title varies: Lena weekly star
pub 1867+
IF Je 4,Jl 23 1869
IU S 23 1881[Je 8-D 1916]+
MWA F 22 1867

LERNA

Lerna weekly EAGLE. w Je 15 1894+
pub 1918+
IU Mr 8 1918+

LEROY

Leroy JOURNAL. w 1888+
ILer 1926-Mr 1933;S 1934+
IU D 1917+

Leroy NEWS. w 1894-Mr 4 1917||
Merged with Leroy journal

LEWISTOWN

Lewistown DEMOCRAT. *See* Fulton democrat

FULTON advocate. w Je 4 1842-
ICU Je 25 1842

FULTON democrat. w Jl 1855+
Jl-O? 1855 as Lewistown democrat
pub 1855+
ICHi O 22 1869;Jl 12 1922
IHi [D 1897-Mr 2 1898]Jl 22 1922
IU N 1914+

FULTON ledger. *See* Fulton county ledger (Canton)

FULTON republican. w 1847-
ICU Ap 7 1848
MWA D 15 1853

ILLINOIS public ledger. *See* Fulton county ledger (Canton)

Lewiston REPUBLICAN. w Mr 19 1844-54||
DLC Mr 19,Ap 2 1844

LEXINGTON

McLEAN county journal. w 1901-06||?
United with Lexington unit to form Lexington unit-journal

Lexington UNIT-JOURNAL. w 1881+
1881-1906? as Lexington unit
pub 1881+
IU D 20 1917+

LIBERTY

Liberty BEE. w O 10 1912+
pub 1912+

LIBERTYVILLE

INDEPENDENT register. w 1892+
1892-1916 as Lake county independent; 1917-29 Libertyville independent and Lake county independent
ILib 1912+

LAKE county independent. *See* Independent register

LAKE county register. sw 1917?-29||
United with Libertyville independent to form Independent register
ILib 1917-29

LINCOLN

Lincoln BEOBACHTER. w Ja 5 1917-18||?
In German
IU 1917-Ap 26 1918

Lincoln COURIER. w,sw 1890-N 1902||
United with Lincoln times to form Lincoln times-courier, later Lincoln courier-herald
w 1890-1900
ILin 1895-O 9 1900;01-02

Lincoln evening COURIER and Lincoln herald. d 1887+
1887-Ja 28 1915 as Lincoln evening courier; Ja 29 1915-Jl 23 1921 Lincoln courier-herald
pub 1893+
IHi Ag 1 1917
ILin 1895-1909;Jl 1918-21;Jl 1922+
IU 1918-Ap 1922;Mr 1928+

Lincoln COURIER-HERALD. w,sw 1872-1922||?
1872-S 1900? as Lincoln times; O? 1900-11? Lincoln times-courier; 1912?-14? Lincoln times-herald
sw O? 1900-11?
ILin 1896;D 1902-Je 1903;04-06;08-09

Lincoln HERALD. w 1856-1911||?
United with Lincoln times-courier to form Lincoln times-herald, later Lincoln courier-herald
ILin Ap 1859-My 1863;66-O 25 1906

LOGAN county courier. w 1856-64||
1856-62 as Logan county democrat
MWA D 3 1863

LOGAN county democrat. *See* Logan county courier

LOGAN county volksblatt. *See* Volksblatt-rundschau

Lincoln NEWS. d *See* Lincoln daily news-herald

Lincoln NEWS. sw Ap 18 1899-1900||
ILin 1899-My 29 1900

Lincoln daily NEWS-HERALD. d O 20 1890-1915||?
1894-S 8 1900? as Lincoln news. United with Lincoln evening courier to form Lincoln courier-herald, later Lincoln evening courier and Lincoln herald
ILin 1890-Jl 2 1892;Je 1894-Je 1895;Ja-Je 1898;99-Ja 1900;Ap-D 1901

POPULAR review. sw,tw
IU S 18 1918-My 12 1920

Lincoln daily STAR. d My 3 1911-O 1 1927||
1911-Je 24 1923 as Lincoln evening star; Je 26 1923-Ag 6 1927 Star. Merged with Lincoln evening courier
IU O 13 1914-27
NN S 12 1925

Lincoln TIMES. *See* Lincoln courier-herald

Lincoln TIMES-COURIER. *See* Lincoln courier-herald

Lincoln TIMES-HERALD. *See* Lincoln courier-herald

ILLINOIS (*Continued*)

LINCOLN—*Continued*

VOLKSBLATT-rundschau. w My 25 1874-Ap 24 1918||
1874-87 as Logan county volksblatt; 1888-98? Lincoln volksblatt. Merged with Elgin herald, later Illinois wochenblatt (Elgin)
My 25 1899 is 25th anniversary ed
In German
IU Jl 1917-18
NN My 25 1899

LISLE

Lisle COURANT. w Je 1 1934+
IElL 1934+

LITCHFIELD

Litchfield ADVOCATE. w N 1874-Mr 8 1888||
1874-81 as Montgomery county democrat
IHM N 10 1887-88

Litchfield HERALD. d 1890-Ap 1913||
United with Litchfield daily news to form Litchfield news-herald

Litchfield MONITOR. w 1863-1918||?
1863-Mr? 1868 as Republican monitor; Ap? 1868-79? Union monitor
IHM D 6 1867

MONTGOMERY county democrat. *See* Litchfield advocate

Litchfield NEWS. w N 2 1865-N 22 1867||
IHM My 18 1866-67

Litchfield NEWS-HERALD. d 1886+
1886-Ap 1913 as Litchfield daily news
IHi [1917-19]
IU N 17 1914-Je 1918

Litchfield daily REPUBLICAN and clipper. d Mr 1892-96||?
IHM Ap 7 1892-My 2 1896

REPUBLICAN monitor. *See* Monitor

UNION monitor. *See* Monitor

LITTLE FORT

LAKE county visitor. w Ap 20 1847-
ICHi My 4,Je 1,15,Jl 6,20,Ag 7,24,28,S 4,18-O 2 1847

Little Fort PORCUPINE and democratic banner. w Mr 4 1845-Mr 23 1847||?
ICHi [1845-Mr 23 1847]

LOCKPORT

Lockport COURIER. *See* Will county courier

Lockport HERALD. w N 17 1933+
ILoc [1933-My 1935]

Lockport LEADER. w My 3 1929+
ILoc My 10 1929-Mr[Ap 28 1933-Je 1934]

Lockport PHOENIX-ADVERTISER. w 1875-S 26 1918||
1875-1901 as Lockport phoenix
IHi [1905-Mr 1916]
IU D 9 1909;Ja 20 1910;Ja 5,Ap 27,N 23,D 21 1911;My 23,N 14 1912;F 22,Mr 22,Ap 12 1917-18

Lockport TELEGRAPH. sw Ap 22 1850-
Follows Will county telegraph
ICHi S 6 1856
ICN My 6-8,15,22,Je 26,Jl 10,17,31,Ag 14,S 4,O 4,16,23,30,N 6 1850
ILoc Ag 6 1851

WILL county advertiser. w 1878-1901||
United with Lockport phoenix to form Lockport phoenix-advertiser

WILL county courier. w 1873-74||
Title varies:Lockport courier
ILoc [My 13-D 23 1874]

WILL county telegraph. w Ja 6 1849-Ap 15? 1850||
Followed by Lockport telegraph
ICHi Mr 22 1849

LODA

GARDEN state. w My 14 1856-60||
MWA Jl 23 1856;Jl 15 1857

Loda TIMES. w
Issued as an ed. of Paxton record
IU Ja 8 1915+

LOMAX

Lomax HERALD. w 1912-16||?
IHi Ag 22 1913
KHi Ap 25-My 3 1913

LOMBARD

Lombard SPECTATOR. w Je 16 1927+
pub 1927+
M Ja 23-F 6 1930

LONDON MILLS

London TIMES. w F 1 1888+
pub 1888-Mr 1890;91+

LOVINGTON

MOULTRIE county press. *See* Piatt county press (Monticello)

Lovington REPORTER. w Jl 31 1891+
pub 1891+

McCONNELL

McConnell NEWS. w 1915-16||?
Issued as an ed. of Lena weekly star
IU D 23 1915-Jl 20 1916

McHENRY

McHenry PLAINDEALER. w Ag 11 1875+
pub 1875+
KHi O 20 1897

MACKINAW

Mackinaw ENTERPRISE-GAZETTE. w 1886+
1886-1902 as Mackinaw enterprise
pub [1886-1927]+
IU 1918+

McLEAN

McLean LENS. w 1880+
pub 1880+

McLEANSBORO

McLeansboro LEADER. w 1882-Je 1933||
United with McLeansboro times to form Times-leader
IMacT [1882-1933]

TIMES-LEADER. w 1868+
1868-Je 1933 as McLeansboro times
pub 1900+

MACOMB

Macomb daily BY-STANDER. d 1904-25||
IMa O 1919-Jl 1925

Macomb EAGLE. w 1856-1919||
ICHi D 21 1861
ICU My 23 1874
KHi N 7 1874
MoHi Ap 4 1863

Macomb INDEPENDENT. w 1873-79||
IGK Mr 11,Je 24 1879

Macomb JOURNAL. w 1855-1923||?
IGK Ap 2 1876;My 29 1879

Macomb daily JOURNAL. d 1894+
IHi Ag 1 1917
IMaW current 2 months
IU O 12 1914-Jl 23,Ag 14 1918+

MCDONOUGH democrat. w 1851-57||
1851-S 7 1855 as McDonough independent
MoHi Mr 5 1852

MCDONOUGH independent. *See* McDonough democrat

MADISON

Madison REPUBLIC. w 1905+
IMad current numbers only

MAHOMET

Mahomet SUCKER state. w 1879+
IU Jl 6 1895

MALTA

Morris' Malta MAIL. w 1876-86||
IU N 11 1880

MANSFIELD

Mansfield EXPRESS. w 1881-D 28 1934||
United with Farmer City journal to form Farmer City journal and Mansfield express (Farmer City)
IU D 28 1917-[25-26]-34

Daily Mansfield EXPRESS. d Ag 7 1895-
IU Ag 8 1895

MAQUON

Maquon CHRONICLE. *See* Maquon tomahawk

Maquon TOMAHAWK. w 1899-1929||
1899-1908 as Maquon chronicle
IHi Ag 13 1907

MARENGO

Marengo NEWS. w 1892-1905||
United with Marengo republican to form Marengo republican-news

Marengo REPUBLICAN-NEWS. w 1867+
1867-1905 as Marengo republican
pub 1910+
MWA Mr 31 1877

MARION

EGYPTIAN press. sw 1875-F 1928||
Merged with Marion evening post
IMarP Je 21 1883-1928

Marion weekly LEADER. sw,w Mr 17 1887+
O 9 1914?-Ja 30 1925 as Marion semi-weekly leader
pub Mr 1913—
IMar 1887-1900
IU O 9 1914+

Marion MONITOR. w 1866-85||?
1866-74 as Our flag
IMar Jl 1874-Ap 9,17 1879-Ja 1 1882

OUR flag. *See* Marion monitor

Marion evening POST. d 1902+
pub 1902+
IMar [1921-28]+

Marion daily REPUBLICAN. d 1908+
pub Mr 19 1913+
IMar [1921-28]+

MARSEILLES

Marseilles CHRONICLE. d 1903-05||
United with Marseilles register to form Marseilles register-chronicle

ECLIPSE. d Ja 17 1891-
IU Ja 17 1891

Marseilles HERALD. *See* Marseilles register-chronicle

Marseilles daily NEWS. d 1887-90||
IU My 2,19,21,26 1887;My 27,Je 1 1889;Mr 29,O 30 1890

Marseilles PLAINDEALER. m,sm,w D 1876-1918||
Title varies: Plaindealer; Weekly plaindealer
m 1876-O 1879;sm N 1879-N 1882
IHi 1912-16
IU Ja-Ap,Jl-N 1877;F,Ap-Ag,O 1878-F 15,My 1,Je-S 1,N 15-D 1 1880;Ja 1-15,Ap 15,My 15-Je 15,Ag 15,S 15-O 1,N 1,D 1-15 1881;My 1-15,Je 15,Jl 15,N 1 1882;F 5,Mr 5[My 7 1886-93]-[95]-S 13 1918

Daily PLAINDEALER. d Mr 21 1887-
IU Mr 21 1887

Marseilles daily PRESS. d D 16 1921+
pub 1921+

Marseilles REGISTER-CHRONICLE. w 1874-1917||?
1874-79 as Marseilles herald; 1879-1905? Marseilles register
IU My 10 1884;Mr 19,Je 1 1887;My 11-18,Je 1-15,29,S 13 1889;Ag-O,N 11-D 9,23 1893-Mr 1894
KHi Ag 5 1876

MARSHALL

ACORN. *See* Marshall republican

CLARK county acorn. *See* Marshall republican

CLARK county democrat. w 1853+
1853-83? as Eastern Illinoisan
ICHi Ap 15,Je 24 1854;My 10 1856;Ap 3,Ag 7 1858;Ag 27 1880;Jl 1 1882
IHi Ap 26 1856;Ap 3 1858;Je 18 1859;Ap 20 1860;Jl 19 1861;Je 20 1862 Jl 17 1863;Ap 15 1864
IU D 12 1917+

CLARK county herald. *See* Marshall herald

CLARK county telegraph. *See* Marshall telegraph

EASTERN Illinoisan. *See* Clark county democrat

Marshall HERALD. w Ag 21 1868+
1868-1911 as Clark county herald
pub 1868
ICHi N 13,D 4 1868;F 19,My 7 1869;O 14 1870; Jl 21 1871;Ag 18,O 13-20,D 8-15 1875;F 2,Ap 12,My 17,Jl 26 1876;O 28 1879
IHi S 11 1868;My 14,Jl 30 1869;Ap 28,N 17 1871;Ag 5,O 7 1879;N 11 1896;O 26 1904
OClWHi Mr 4 1874;D 15 1875;Mr 29 1876;Ag 6 1878;Ap 27 1880
TxU [Ag 19 1870-Jl 1 1874]

HORNET. w O 11 1859-60||
ICHi N 1,D 6 1859;Ja 3-10,Mr 29,Ap 12-My 3,Je 7,28,Ag 2 1860
IHi N 15-22,D 13 1859;Ja 24,F 21-28,Mr 22,Jl 12,Ap 16-23,S 27 1860

ILLINOIS state democrat. w F 10 1849-52||
CSmH Ap 3 1852
ICHi S 21 1850
IHi Ja 4 1851;My 1 1852
IU Mr 24 1849

Marshall MESSENGER. w Ap 28 1865-94||?
Merged with Clark county democrat
ICHi Je 1 1866;My 13 1869;My 1 1871;N 5 1874;Ja 6,Ap 6-13, S 7 1876 Ja 30 1884
IHi Ap 28,Jl 21 1865;Ja 5,Ap 20 1866;Ap 1-8 1869;Ag 7 1878

Marshall REPUBLICAN. w 1881-Jl 15 1910||
1881-99 as Acorn; 1900-07 Clark county acorn. Merged with Marshall herald
IHi My 12 1899
IU Ag 16 1907;N 13 1908-My 7,Jl 9 1909-10

Marshall TELEGRAPH. w Jl 3 1852-58||
Title varies: Clark county telegraph
ICHi S 25-O 2,16,N 27 1852;Ja 29,Jl 2-9 1853; Ja 2 1854;Mr 31,My 21 1855;Jl 26 1856
IHi S 4,O 30,D 18 1852;F 5,Ap 9,23,Ag 20,N 12 1853;My 3,16 1856;Ap 29 1857

MASCOUTAH

Mascoutah HERALD. w Ja 1 1885+
pub 1885+

Mascoutah TIMES. w 1899-1903||
IMilE 1899-F 18 1903

ILLINOIS (*Continued*)

MASON CITY

Mason City BANNER. w 1891-1918||
United with Mason City times to form Mason City banner-times

Mason City BANNER-TIMES. w 1867+
1867-71 as Mason City news; 1871-98 Mason City independent; 1899-1918 Mason City times
pub 1902-17;20+
IGK Je 27 1879
IHi D 14 1893

Mason City INDEPENDENT. *See* Mason City banner-times

Mason City NEWS. *See* Mason City banner-times

Mason City times. *See* Mason City banner-times

MATHERVILLE

Matherville NEWS. w 1914-25||?
IU 1918-O 25 1922

MATTOON

Mattoon COMMERCIAL-STAR. d 1872-F 1919||
1872-1911 as Mattoon commercial. United with Daily journal-gazette to form Daily journal-gazette and commercial-star
IHi Ja 26 1899;My 19,23 1917
IMat Jl 1874-1919
MWA S 1887(special ed)

Weekly GAZETTE. w Je 7 1856-D 1904||
United with Mattoon weekly journal to form Mattoon journal-gazette
IMatJ 1860-64;75-1904
OClWHi Ag 1 1873

Mattoon JOURNAL-GAZETTE. w N 1865-1919||?
1865-1904 as Mattoon weekly journal
IMatJ 1902-12
KHi Ap 18 1868

Daily JOURNAL-GAZETTE and commercial-star. d 1874+
1874-1904 as Daily journal; 1906-20? Daily journal gazette
pub 1905+
IHi Ag 14 1928
IMat 1905+

Mattoon RADICAL republican. w 1867-71||
MWA N 19 1870

Morning STAR. d 1897-1910||
United with Mattoon commercial to form Mottoon commercial-star
IMat 1904-10

MAYWOOD

Maywood HERALD. w 1894+
1903-Jl 7 1922 Maywood herald-recorder
IU O 23 1914+

MAYWOODIAN. w 1924-29||
IU Ap 23,My 7-14,28,Je 18-Jl 9,Ag 13,S 3-10,D 31 1926;Ja 14,Je 10,O 14 1927;My 25,Jl 13,Ag 10-N,D 14 1928-Jl 5,19-26,S-N 1,15-22 1929

SUBURBAN advertiser. w Jl 28 1924+
pub 1924+

MAZON

GRUNDY county register. w F 1892-N 25 1921||
IU D 14 1917-21

MEDIA

Media RECORD. w 1894-1917||
IRaR Jl 16 1916-S 6 1917

Media RECORD. w 1927-28||?
IRaR My 12 1927-S 1 1928

MEDORA

Medora MESSENGER. w 1895-F 12 1926||
Merged with Jerseyville republican, later Jersey county news (Jerseyville)
IHi [Jl 15 1904-26]
IU D 1917-Jl,O 1918-26

MELVIN

Melvin MOTOR. w O 1908+
pub 1908+

Melvin TRANSCRIPT. w 1893-1908||
IMeM 1894-98

MENDON

Mendon DISPATCH-Times and Quincy times. w O 2 1878+
1878-S 1933 as Mendon dispatch; O 1933-Mr 7 1934 Mendon dispatch-times
pub 1872+
IGK Je 19 1879
IHi 1904-Ag 1907

MENDOTA

Mendota BULLETIN. *See* Mendota sun-bulletin

Mendota REPORTER and sun-bulletin. w 1878+
1878-1927 as Mendota reporter

Mendota SUN-BULLETIN. w 1862-1927||
1862-96? as Mendota bulletin. United with Mendota reporter to form Mendota reporter and sun-bulletin
ICHi D 17 1892

METAMORA

Metamora HERALD. w D 20 1889+
Follows Woodford sentinel
pub 1889+
IHi Ag 26 1921

Metamora SENTINEL. *See* Woodford sentinel

WOODFORD county argus. *See* Woodford sentinel

WOODFORD sentinel. w My 1854-D 13 1889||
My-Jl? 1854 as Woodford county argus; Ag? 1854-58? Metamora sentinel. Followed by Metamora herald
IMeH Je 4 1858

METROPOLIS

Metropolis DEMOCRAT. *See* Metropolis herald

Metropolis GAZETTE. w 1898+
Title varies: Metropolis weekly gazette
IU D 12 1913-[18]-22[Mr 9 1923-Ap 22]My 13 1927+

Metropolis HERALD. w 1878-1918||
1878-98 as Metropolis democrat. United with Massac journal-republican to form Republican-herald
IHi My 31 1911
MWA D 11 1879

MASSAC journal. *See* Republican-herald

MASSAC journal-republican. *See* Republican-herald

PROMULGATOR. *See* Republican-herald

REPUBLICAN-HERALD. w 1865+
1865-69 as Promulgator; 1870-92? Massac journal; 1893-1918 Massac journal-republican
IHi Ag 1 1917
IU O 8 1914-16;F 1918+

MIDDLEPORT

IROQUOIS county herald. *See under* Watseka

IROQUOIS county press. *See* Weekly press

IROQUOIS journal. *See* Weekly press

IROQUOIS republican. *See* Watseka republican (Watseka)

Weekly PRESS. w F 19 1851-65||
1851-Ap 1 1854 as Iroquois journal; Ap 8 1854-55 Iroquois county press
MWA D 21 1853

MIDDLETOWN

Middletown LEDGER. w N 20 1905+
pub 1905+
IU 1918-Mr 1924

MIDLOTHIAN

Midlothian MESSENGER. w F 1930+
pub 1930+

MILAN

Milan INDEPENDENT. w Ap 1902+
pub 1926+
IU D 1917-F 8 1923

MILFORD

Milford HERALD. w Jl 1876-1928||
United with Milford news to form Milford herald-news
ICHi Ja 1 1903
IHi My 21 1903
IMi 1905-13
IU 1915-17

Milford HERALD-NEWS. w 1919+
1919-28 as Milford news
IMi 1927-30;Ap 1932+

Milford NEWS. *See* Milford herald-news

MILLEDGEVILLE

Milledgeville FREE PRESS. w D 11 1885+
D 13 1900-Je 6 1901? as Tri-county free press
IU 1885[86]-[89]-Je 23,Ag 11 1893-O 1894[95]-[97]-[99]-Ap 5,Je 28 1900-Je 6 1901

TRI-COUNTY free press. *See* Milledgeville free press

MILLSTADT

Millstadt ENTERPRISE. w My 14 1896+
pub 1896+

MILTON

Milton BEACON. w 1875-86||?
IGK Jl 11,Ag 15,29 1879

BEACON. w Ja 1906+
pub 1906+

MINONK

Minonk BLADE. *See* Minonk news-dispatch

Minonk DISPATCH. *See* Minonk news-dispatch

Minonk LOCAL times. 1872-73||
Followed by Minonk blade, later Minonk news-dispatch

Minonk NEWS. w 1878-O 1913||
United with Minonk dispatch to form Minonk news-dispatch
IMinN 1887-88

Minonk NEWS-DISPATCH. w Je 18 1874+
Follows Minonk local times. 1874-96? as Minonk blade; 1897?-1905? Minonk register; 1906?-O 1913 Minonk dispatch
pub 1903+
IMin 1916+
IU D 13 1917+

Minonk REGISTER. *See* Minonk news-dispatch

MOKENA

NEWS-BULLETIN. w 1919+
pub 1919+

MOLINE

Moline daily DISPATCH. d Jl 31 1878+
Title varies: Daily evening dispatch; etc.
pub Jl-D 1894;F 1895-96;98;Jl 1899-Je 1900;01-Je 1903;04;10;My-Ag 1911;12+
IHi 1926-34
IM Ja-Je 1894;Jl 1900-Je 1901;Jl-D 1903;05-Je 1909;Jl 1910-Je 1913;Ja-Ag 1914;15+
IU Jl-N 1878;Ja-F 27 1879;O 19 1914-Jl 14 1915;Ap 2 1918-My 1920;Ja 21 1935+
MWA Jl 31 1928

GAZETTE van Moline. w N 1907+
In Flemish
pub 1907+
IU Mr 20 1914-Ja 1927;Ag 17 1933+

Moline INDEPENDENT. w Ag 21 1854-O 1862||
1854-F 18 1857 as Moline workman
MWA Ag 21 1854;F 7-21,Ap 18,Jl 11,25-Ag 1 1855
OClWHi Ap 3 1861

Daily JOURNAL. d 1883-1907||
1883-90? as Daily republican; 1891-98 Daily republican-journal. United with Evening mail to form Moline mail and journal
IM Jl 1901-Je 1902;Jl-D 1904
IMD Ja-Je 1886;1897;Ja-Je 1904
WHi D 22 1901

Moline weekly JOURNAL. w
IM Jl 1903-04;06

Moline MAIL. d 1893-1915||
1893-1907 as Evening mail and journal
IM Mr 11 1900-02;07-Je 1914;Jl-S 4 1915
IMD O 23 1909-Ap 1910;Je-D 1911

Sunday MAIL. w 1893-1902||
IM 1899-1900;S 12 1901-Ag 14 1902

NEUE volks-zeitung. *See under* Rock Island

Daily REPUBLICAN. *See* Daily journal

Daily REPUBLICAN-JOURNAL. *See* Daily journal

Moline REVIEW-DISPATCH. w N 26 1870-1911||
1870-S 9 1880 as Moline review
ICHi Ja 10 1880
IHi N 24 1899-My 11 1900;05-06
IM 1890-92;1905;07;10
IMD 1873-76;78-86;89
IU N 16 1877-F 22 1878
IaDH D 1870-S 3 1880

SCHIBBOLETH. w 1878-
In Swedish
IRA [1878-79]

SKANDIA. w D 29 1876-My 27 1878||
Merged with Svenska tribunen, later Svenska tribunen-nyheter (Chicago)
In Swedish
IRA complete
MnHi 1877-78

Daily TIMES. *See under* Davenport, Iowa

TRIBUNEN. w 1903-15||
In Swedish
IRA 1910-15
MnHi [Mr 1912-Ja 1915]

VIKINGEN. *See under* Omaha, Neb.

Moline WORKMAN. *See* Moline independent

MOMENCE

Momence PRESS. w 1887-97||?
United with Momence reporter to form Momence press-reporter

Momence PRESS-REPORTER. w Ag 3 1870+
1870-97 as Momence reporter
pub 1891-96;1911-12;14+

Momence PROGRESS. w 1901+
IU D 7 1917+

Momence REPORTER. *See* Momence press-reporter

MONEE

Monee REVIEW. w 1905?-S 24 1931||
Merged with Peotone vedette(Peotone)
IHi [My 16-Ag 1 1913]
IU D 20 1917-31

MONMOUTH

ADVANCE. w 1889-92||
United with Monmouth atlas to form Republican atlas-advance, later Republican-atlas

Monmouth daily ATLAS. d 1904-Jl 20 1924||
United with Monmouth review to form Monmouth review atlas
IHi [O 30 1911-N 26 1912]Ag 8 1919-24
IMo complete
IMoR complete

ILLINOIS (*Continued*)

MONMOUTH—*Continued*

Monmouth ATLAS. w *See* Republican-atlas

Monmouth ATLAS-ADVANCE. *See* Republican-atlas

REPUBLICAN-ATLAS. w O 30 1846-1913||
1846-92 as Monmouth atlas; 1892-96? Republican atlas-advance
ICU F 5 1847
IGK Ag 22-29,S 12 1879
IMo complete
IMoR 1889-1913
IU N 9 1856
MWA D 30 1853

Monmouth REVIEW. sw,w D 28 1855-1912||
sw 1887-1905
IHi Je 25,Jl 2,30 1869;Mr 25 1887
IMo complete

Monmouth daily REVIEW, *See* Monmouth review-atlas

Monmouth REVIEW-ATLAS. d Ag 1888+
1888-Jl 20 1924 as Monmouth daily review
D 28 1915 is 60th anniversay no
pub 1888+
IHi D 28 1915;Jl 21 1924+
IMo 1888+
IU My 7 1917-Ag 3 1918

MONROE CENTER

Monroe Center LEADER. w D 3 1896-97||
O 8-29 1897 pub at Davis Junction
IU My-O 29 1897

Monroe Center NEWS. w Mr 25 1898-1900||?
IU Ap 1[My-D 1898]-Jl 14,S-O 20,N 17,D 1 1899-Ja 12,F 23,Mr 9-23,Ap 6,Je 29,Ag 3,24-31 1900

MONTICELLO

Monticello BULLETIN. w 1876+
IMon O 1897-1905;07+

PIATT county herald. w 1874-91||?
ICHi Ja 30 1889

PIATT county pilot. w 1896-1908||?
IMon O 1897-My 1904

PIATT county press. w 1883-84||
1883-Je? 1884 as Moultrie county press (Lovington)
MWA F 13 Ap 30,My 21,Jl 18-25,Ag 15,29-S 19 1884

PIATT county republican. w My 1896+
pub 1896+
IHi [1908-16]Ag 2 1917
IMon O 1897-1905;07+
IU Ag 1916+

PIATT independent. *See* Piatt republican

PIATT republican. w 1865-75||?
1865-73? as Piatt independent
OHi F 12-Jl 15 1868;Ap 14,My 12 1869

MORRIS

Morris ADVERTISER. w 1865-66||
United with Grundy county herald to form Herald and advertiser, later Morris herald
ICHi Ag 4 1866

GRUNDY county herald. *See* Morris herald

Morris HERALD. w 1854-1923||
Follows Morris yeoman. 1854-66 as Grundy county herald; 1866-74? Herald and advertiser
ICHi F 8 1865;D 27 1873;S 17 1875
IU F 27 1882

Morris daily HERALD. d 1878+
IU Ap 3 1918+

HERALD and advertiser. *See* Morris herald

Morris YEOMAN. w 1852-54||
Followed by Grundy county herald, later Morris herald
MWA D 14 1853

MORRISON

WHITESIDE county farmer. *See* Whiteside county news

WHITESIDE county news. w Ag 21 1921+
1921-F 5 1931 as Whiteside county farmer
pub Ag 21 1921+

WHITESIDE sentinel. w,tw Jl 23 1857+
w 1857-1909?
pub 1857+
IU N 1914-Jl 15 1918;F 28 1919+

MORRISONVILLE

Morrisonville TIMES. w Ag 1 1874+
pub 1874+
IU Ag 27,S 10,O 1914+

MORTON

Morton NEWS. w 1887+
pub Ja 21 1909+

MOUND CITY

Mound City EMPORIUM. w 1856-59||
1856-57 as National emporium
ICHi O 9 1856
ICa 1857-D 22 1859
IHi F 12-26 Ap,My 14-28 1857

Mound City JOURNAL. w 1864-74||
United with Argus (Cairo) to form Argus-journal (Cairo)
ICHi S 28 1865

NATIONAL emporium. *See* Mound City emporium

MOUNDS

Mounds INDEPENDENT. w D 11 1924+
pub 1924+

Mounds NEWS. w 1887-1925||?
IU F 21 1919-N 2[D]1923

MT. AUBURN

Mt. Auburn TRIBUNE. w Jl 17 1901+
pub 1901+

MOUNT CARMEL

Mount Carmel evening REGISTER. *See* Mount Carmel daily republican-register

Mount Carmel REGISTER. w *See* Mount Carmel republican-register

REPUBLICAN. d 1899-1918||
United with Mt. Carmel evening register to form Mount Carmel republican-register
IMtCR 1900-18

REPUBLICAN. w 1875-1919||
United with Mount Carmel register to form Mount Carmel republican-register
IMtCR 1875-1918

Mount Carmel REPUBLICAN REGISTER. w Je 11 1839-1924||
1839-N 1918 as Mount Carmel register
DLC Je 11 1839;D 4 1841;Ja 28 1843
IMtCR [1850-67]-1919
IU Ap 23 1842

Mount Carmel daily REPUBLICAN-REGISTER. d 1901+
1901-N 25 1918 as Mount Carmel evening register
pub 1901+
IU 1918+

Mount Carmel SENTINEL and Wabash advocate. w O 15 1834-39||
ICU N 19 1834
IU N 19 1834

MOUNT CARROLL

CARROLL county herald. w Ap 6 1876-D 26 1890||
United with Carroll county mirror to form Carroll county mirror and herald
IHi complete
IU Jl 7 1882

CARROLL county mirror. w,sw,tw 1858-O 1919||
Je 19 1891-D 18 1892 as Carroll county mirror and herald. United with Semi-weekly democrat to form Carroll county mirror-democrat
w 1858-D 13? 1892;sw D 20 1892-1911?
IHi [D 12 1860-Je 12 1891]-[1893-My 23 1895]
IU N 28 1884

CARROLL county mirror-democrat. sw,w My 13 1890+
1890-O 1919 as Semi-weekly democrat
sw 1890-D 4? 1933
pub Jl 1930+

CARROLL county republican. w D 29? 1898-99||?
IU F 24 1899

Mount Carroll DEMOCRAT. *See* Daily mirror-democrat

Semi-weekly DEMOCRAT. *See* Carroll county mirror-democrat

Mount Carroll MIRROR. d 1899-1910||?
United with Mount Carroll democrat to form Daily mirror-democrat

Daily MIRROR-DEMOCRAT. d 1893-D 1933||
1893-S 1919 as Mount Carroll democrat
pub Jl 1930-33

MOUNT MORRIS

Mount Morris GAZETTE. w My 10 1850-Je 23 1853||
IOr S 27 1850;Ja 3-23,F 6,27-Mr 6,20-Ap 3,My 1(extra),15,29-Jl 24,Ag,S 11-D 1851;My 13-Je 3,17,Jl 1,22,Ag 5 1852;Mr 10-Ap 7,Je 23 1853

Mount Morris INDEPENDENT. w Jl 27 1876-77||
IU [1876-My 17 1877]

INDEPENDENT watchman. w O 2 1856-61||
1856-57 as North-western republican
IHi Ag 25 1858;N 5 1859
IOr D 18 1856-Ja 22,F 5-19,Mr 5-19,Ap 16,Je 13,27,Jl 18-Ag 15,29-S 5 1857
MWA Je 15 1859

Mount Morris INDEX. w Ag 1 1890+
pub 1898+
DLC O 27 1933
IHi D 13 1905
IU 1890-[92]-[94]-Ap 11,Je 13,Jl 5,Ag 1,S 5,26 O 24,D 12-19 1900;Ap 17,My 22 1901

Mount Morris NEWS. w Ap 28 1896-F 20 1901||
Merged with Mount Morris index
IU Ap 28,My 19 1896-[97-98]-Ja,Mr 14-Ap 4,Je 27 1900-01

NORTH-WESTERN republican. *See* Independent watchman

OGLE county democrat. w My 31 1877-Mr 22 1888;Ap 25-Jl 4 1890||
Mr 22 1888-Ap 18 1890 merged with Oregon independent (Oregon) to form Independent-democrat (Oregon)
IU Je 1877-[83]-Mr 22 1888;Ap 25,My 9,23,Je 13,Jl 4 1890

Mount Morris REGISTER. w Ap 13 1889-90||?
IU My 18 1889

ROCK RIVER press. w Ap 4 1860-
IHi My 2,Je 13 1860

ROCK RIVER register. *See under* Grand Detour

MOUNT PULASKI

Mount Pulaski NEWS. w 1884-1932||
United with Mount Pulaski times to form Mount Pulaski times-news

Mount Pulaski REPUBLICAN. w 1884-86||?
ICHi O 9 1886

Mount Pulaski TIMES-NEWS. w 1903+
1903-Jl 1931 as Mount Pulaski times
pub Ag 1932+
IHi F 10 1909

MOUNT STERLING

BROWN county democrat. *See* Democrat-message

DEMOCRAT-MESSAGE. w,sw 1872+
1872-Jl 1886 as Brown county democrat
w 1872-98?
pub 1874+
IGK Ag 23,S 13 1879
IU Ap 12,My 6 1911;Ap 10 1912;Jl 13 1917-My 4 1918;Mr 1919+
NbHi Ap 26 1879

ILLINOIS weekly message. w 1872-86||
United with Brown county democrat to form Democrat-message
IGK My 16 1879
IHi Jl 19 1878

MOUNT VERNON

Mount Vernon ADVOCATE. 1851-58||
1851-56 as Mount Vernon Jeffersonian; 1856-Mr? 1857 Mount Vernon sentinel; Ap?-D 9? 1857 Egyptian torchlight. Followed by Mount Vernon star
IGK N 18 1853
MWA Je 18 1852

EGPTIAN torchlight. *See* Mount Vernon advocate

Mount Vernon FREE PRESS. w 1865-F 1880||
Merged with Mount Vernon news
DLC F 22 1867

Mount Vernon daily HERALD. d 1921-29||
IU Ja 14,16,18,31 1928-Jl 17 1929

Mount Vernon JEFFERSONIAN. *See* Mount Vernon advocate

Mount Vernon NEWS. w S 2 1871-S 21 1920||
United with Mount Vernon register to form Mount Vernon register-news
IHi F 19 1879[Mr 9 1904-S 1 1920]

Mount Vernon daily NEWS. d 1892-S 27? 1920||
United with Mount Vernon daily register to form Mount Vernon register-news
IU D 6 1917-S 4 1920

Mount Vernon REGISTER-News. w 1876+
1876-S 21 1920 as Mount Vernon register
IGK My 27 1929
IHi S 28 1920+
IU F 13 1889

Mount Vernon REGISTER-NEWS. d 1892+
1892-S 1920 as Mount Vernon daily register
IHi Ag 1 1917
IU S 28 1920-Ap 1930
WHi My 27 1929

Mount Vernon SENTINEL. *See* Mount Vernon advocate

Mount Vernon STAR. w 1858-65||
Follows Mount Vernon advocate
OClWHi My 7 1861

MOWEAQUA

Moweaqua NEWS. w 1882+
IU O 14 1914+

MURPHYSBORO

Murphysboro ARGUS. w 1868-73||
IHi Je 14,O 18 1871

Murphysboro INDEPENDENT. w 1873-1922||
IHi My 7,Jl 30 1874;Ap 17 1875[1910-16]

Daily INDEPENDENT. d 1891+
pub 1925+
IU D 5 1917,Jl 24,D 4,12,31 1918;Ja 7 1919;Ag 1-20 1925

JACKSON county era. w 1873-1901||
United with Murphysboro republican to form Republican era
IHi Ag 15 1874

Daily REPUBLICAN-ERA. d 1898-Jl 30 1925||
1898-1902 as Daily republican. Merged with Daily independent
IU Ap 1918-Je 1920;21-25
OClWHi Mr 28,Ap 4 1924

REPUBLICAN-ERA. w 1898-1924||
1898-1902 as Murphysboro republican

ILLINOIS (*Continued*)

NAPERVILLE

Naperville CLARION. w 1863+
1863-68 as DuPage county press
pub 1905+
IHi [Ap 1911-34]
INa 1898+
IU D 12 1917-Ag 7,O 1918-S 22 1920

DUPAGE county press. *See* Naperville clarion

Naperville SENTINEL. w Jl 1 1858-62||
IHi 1858-Je 20 1861

NAPLES

Naples OBSERVER. w 1849-50||?
IHi F 15 1850

SPIRIT of the west and Illinois standard. *See under* Jacksonville

NASHVILLE

Nashville DEMOCRAT. w 1851-1926||?
1851-53 as New era; 1853-56 Monitor
IU D 13 1917-Je 1924
MWA D 17 1853

Nashville JOURNAL. w Ja 23 1863+
pub 1880+
ICHi Je 11 1880
IHi [F 13 1863-70]

MONITOR. *See* Nashville democrat

NEW ERA. *See* Nashville democrat

NATIONAL STOCK YARDS

ST. LOUIS daily live stock reporter. d 1889+
DA [Jl 1906-23]+
DLC 1898;Mr 1910-27
LU Je-N 1932
MoCaT F 23 1898
MoHi D 1 1905;D 27 1907
MoU Ag 1901-Jl 1928
MsSM O 5 1933+
WaPS [N 24 1915-Ag 1916]

NAUVOO

Nauvoo EXPOSITOR. w Je 7 1844||
IHi complete
NN complete
WHi Je 7 1844(photostat)

HANCOCK eagle. w 1845-46||
Follows Nauvoo neighbor. Followed by Nauvoo news citizen
ICHi Ap 3-24,My 8-15,29-Je 12 1846
IGK Jl 17 1846
NN Ap 10-17,My 29-Je,Jl 10-24,Ag 14-28 1846

Nauvoo INDEPENDENT and rustler. w N 14 1873+
1873-O 1924 as Nauvoo independent
N 14 1923 is Golden jubilee ed
pub 1873+
IHi N 14 1923
NN Ap 26,O 25-N 1 1878;Jl 25-Ag 22 1884

Nauvoo NEIGHBOR. w My 3 1843-O 29 1845||
Follows Wasp. Followed by Hancock eagle
CSmH Jl 24 1844
ICHi Je 7,28 1843;Ja 10,31,Mr 27,Ap 10,Je 26, Jl 10,Ag 7,28-O 2,23-30 1844;Ja-F,Mr 26,Ap 23-30,My 14-Je 18,Jl 2,16,Ag 13-S 3,17-O 1845
MB [1844]
MWA Jl 3 1844
NN D 27 1843;Mr 6,27-Ap 10,24-My 8,Je 19,Jl 17,31 1844;Ja 9-F 5,19-26,Mr 12,26-Ap 2,30, My 21,Jl 9,S 24-O 1 1845

Nauvoo NEW citizen. w 1846-47||
Follows Hancock eagle
ICHi F 24,Mr 10 1847
NN D 23 1846

POPULAR tribune. Ja 16 1851-53||?
IGK Ja 16,F 15 1851

Nauvoo RUSTLER. w 1890-1925||
United with Nauvoo independent to form Nauvoo independent and rustler
NN My 13 1890-F 16 1892

TIMES and seasons. w 1839-46||
CSmH My-Ag 16 1841;S 1 1843
IaK 1844-Ja 1 1845

WASP. w Ap 16 1842-Ap 26 1843||
Followed by Nauvoo neighbor
MWA Ag 27 1842
NN Jl 2 1842

NEBO

Nebo BANNER. w 1900?-25||
IU D 27 1917-Jl 29 1925

NEOGA

Neoga NEWS. w 1867+
MWA F 1 1870

NEW ATHENS

New Athens JOURNAL. w 1894+
IU Ja 11 1918+

NEWMAN

Newman INDEPENDENT. w 1875+
pub 1883+

NEWTON

MENTOR-DEMOCRAT. w 1882+
IU Mr 23 1922+

Newton PRESS. w,sw Jl 1866+
w 1866-99?
pub [1871-Ap 1882]+

NILES CENTER

Niles Center PRESS. w 1924+
IGlG Mr 10 1930-31;Ag 1932-Je,Ag 25 1933;34+

NOKOMIS

DEUTSCH-AMERIKANER. w 1880-S 17 1913||
In German
IHi Mr 1909-13
MoSC D 12 1888-D 4 1889;D 1896-N 1899;N 28 1906-N 18 1908[N 27 1912-13]

FREE PRESS-progress. w 1877+
1877-Mr 1878 as Free press; Mr 1878-My 31 1918 Free press-gazette
IHi F 19 1909-16
IU O 9 1914-Jl 18 1918

Nokomis GAZETTE. w 1872-78||
United with Free press to form Free press gazette
IHi F 15 1873-74

Nokomis PROGRESS. w 1895?-My 30 1918||
United with Free press-gazette to form Free press-progress
IU O 8 1914-18

NORTH CHICAGO

North Chicago TRIBUNE. sw F 1 1928+
pub 1928+

NORTHBROOK

Northbrook NEWS. w Ja 1 1923+
IGlG Mr 10 1930-31;Ag 1932-Je 1933;34+

NUNDA. *See* CRYSTAL LAKE

OAK PARK

OAK leaves. w 1880+
ICHi D 20 1919;Ja 31,F 28,Jl 10-17 1920
IU Ap 29,O 17 1914-Je 1924;Jl 1925-Mr,Jl-S 1927;O 1928+

The OAK Parker. w 1884+
IU 1923+

OAKLAND

COLES county ledger. w S 6 1877+
1877-1919 as Oakland ledger
pub My 10 1916+

Oakland LEDGER. *See* Coles county ledger

The Oakland MESSENGER. w 1883+
IU O 8 1914-Ag 1920

OBLONG

Oblong ORACLE. w 1894+
pub 1935+
IHi [F 24 1911-34]
IU N 13 1914+

ODELL

Odell weekly NEWS. w 1915+
IOd current issues only
IU Ap 1927+

O'FALLON

O'Fallon PROGRESS. w F 1894+
pub 1897+

OGDEN

Ogden COURIER. w 1892+
IU 1918+

OHIO

Ohio HERALD. w 1891+
pub N 1898-N 1899;N 1901-N 1902;N 1904-N 1905;1918+

OKAWVILLE

Okawville TIMES. w D 1 1893+
pub 1893+

OLNEY

Olney ADVOCATE. w 1883+
IHi [F 19-D 1909]
IU D 24 1914-F 18 1915;D 13 1917+

Olney LEDGER. *See* Olney republican

Olney daily MAIL. d Ap 15 1898+
pub 1898+
IU Ja 21 1935+

Olney REPUBLICAN. w,sw 1872-
1872-78? as Olney ledger; 1879?-84? Richland county republican
sw 1901?-09
IOlM 1872-95

RICHLAND county republican. *See* Olney republican

Olney weekly TIMES. w Ap 10 1856+
DLC My 1872-Mr 1876
ICHi N 19 1858;My 18,Jl 6 1860;Mr 1 1861;Je 1 1881
IOlm 1856-F 20 1857

ONARGA

CENTRAL Illinois review. *See* Onarga leader and review

Onarga LEADER. w 1885-91||?
United with Central Illinois review to form Onarga leader and review

Onarga LEADER and review. w 1872+
1872-80? as Onarga review; 1880?-91 Central Illinois review
pub Mr 1892-Ag 10 1906;07-Ag 8 1919;20-22;F 23 1923-Ja 4 1924;26;My 1929+
IU D 14 1917-Ja 15 1926

Onarga TIMES. *See* Iroquois county times (Watseka)

ONEIDA

Oneida NEWS. w 1877-79||
IGK Jl 18,Ag 1,29 1879

OQUAWKA

HENDERSON county journal. w 1878-79||
IGK My 8,Ag 28-S 4 1879

Oquawka PLAIN DEALER. w
MWA Ja 25 1866

Oquawka SPECTATOR. w F 12 1848-Ja 22 1908||
ICN 1848;F-D 1851
IGK 1848-Ja 1 1908
IU [1860-61]-76
MWA Ap 21 1852;N 10 1864;Ap 20 1885

ORANGEVILLE

Orangeville COURIER. w 1884+
pub Mr 1888+

OREGON

ADVOCATE. w O 28 1891-F 1893||
United with Ogle county local to form Local-advocate, later Ogle county republican
IU Ja 7,21 1893

CONSTITUTION-DEMOCRAT. w S 14 1900-My 31 1901||?
S 14-28 1900 as Ogle county constitution; O 4-D 27 1900 Ogle county constitution and independent democrat
IU 1900;Ja 10-My 31 1901

OREGON courier. *See* Independent-democrat

OREGON independent. *See* Independent-democrat

INDEPENDENT-DEMOCRAT. w Je 13 1866-S 28 1900||
1866-My 7 1873 as Oregon national guard; My 14 1873-My 1875 Ogle county grange; Je 1875-F 1881 Oregon courier; Mr 1881-Mr 21 1888 Oregon independent. United with Ogle county constitution to form Constitution-democrat
IGK My 14 1879
IOr Mr 1881-84
IU [1866-67]-D 16 1868;Jl 21,Ag 25-S 8 1869; Ap 11[My 30-N 7]1870;F 11[My 10-D]1871-[76]-[83]-[86]-My 9,Jl 25 1894;Je 26 1895;F 5,S 2,16-23 1896

INDEX. w N 5 1892-
IU N 5 1892

LOCAL advocate. *See* Ogle county republican

OGLE county constitution. *See* Constitution-democrat

Oregon NATIONAL guard. *See* Independent-democrat

OGLE county grange. *See* Independent-democrat

OGLE county local. *See* Ogle county republican

OGLE county reporter. w Je 11 1851+
Je-O 22 1851? as Ogle county gazette
CSmH O 29 1851;S 16 1852
IHi [N 23 1853-Jl 7 1886]
IOr Jl 8,22-29,Ag 12,S 23,D 4 1852[53]-[Ja-N 1855]56;Ja 2,Ap-Jl 3,17-O 15,29,N 19 1857;D 12 1860;D 4 1861;Ja-S,O 22-N,D 10-31 1862;Ja 28 1863;Je 22,Jl 6-13 1864;S 27 1866;Ap 9 1868-S 16,O 1869-Mr 9 1871;Je 7 1905;S 23 1908+
IU [Je 14,28 1866-D 10 1868]Ag 5-12,O 28 1869;Je-S 8,O 20 1870;My 10,27 1871-Je 15,Ag 10 1892-N 14 1894[F-D 1895]-Ap 11,Je 13[Jl-D 1900]-My 22 1901
MWA Jl 6 1864
P-B N 1 1854

OGLE county republican. w N 17 1888+
1888-Ja 1893 as Ogle county local; F-D 1893 Local advocate
pub 1894-Ap 2 1897;F 10 1898+
IOr 1909+
IU 1888[F 16-D 1889]-Je,Ag 1892-[Ja-N 2 1894;F-D 1895]-Ap 5,Je 28,O 11 1900-Je 6 1901;O 15 1914-D 21 1916

Daily OREGON. d O 2 1895-96||?
IU [O 3 1895-Mr 11,23 1896-My 2]11,15,Je 17, 19,27,Jl 6,16 1896

Semi-weekly OREGON. *See* Silver advocate

SILVER advocate. sw My 6? 1896-
My 6?-Ag 29 1896 as Semi-weekly Oregon
IU My 23-Je 3,20-S 5 1896

ILLINOIS (*Continued*)

ORION

Orion TIMES. w 1877+
pub 1880+

ORLAND PARK

Orland Park HERALD. w 1930+
IMokN 1930+

OTTAWA

CENTRAL Illinois wochenblatt. w 1868-1925||
In German
IU Je 1,8,Jl 13 1917-S 25 1925

CONSTITUTIONALIST. *See* Ottawa republican times

Ottawa FAIR DEALER. w 1892-1920||
United with Free trader journal to form Free trader journal and fair dealer
IO Je 28 1902-F 3,D 8 1911-Mr 5 1920
IU O 9 1914-D 26 1919

Ottawa FREE-TRADER. w Je 1840-1918||
1840-My 20 1842 as Illinois free trader; Je 3 1842-S 29 1843 Illinois free trader and LaSalle county commercial advertiser
DLC Jl 30 1841
ICU Mr 12 1841
IHi Ja 1 1857
IO My 23 1840-90
IU Je 19 1880.D 18 1881;Ja 17 1891;Ja 2,F 20 1892
MWA O 4,D 27 1844;My 17 1851;Je 26 1852
N Je 6 1845
WHi F 28 1895

FREE TRADER-JOURNAL and fair dealer. d 1887-D 1926||
1887-1916? as Free trader; 1917-18 Free trader-journal. Merged with Daily republican-times
IO 1891-96;1901-26
IU Jl 2 1917-Je 29 1918

ILLINOIS free trader. *See* Ottawa free-trader

Ottawa JOURNAL. d 1880-1917||
1880-Mr 1881 as Evening journal. United with Free trader to form Free trader-journal
IO Ja 20 1880-S 2 1881;87-1916
IU Je 16 1891;Mr 21,29 1893;O 10,24,N 21 1894

LA SALLE county journal. w 1883-1917||
IHi D 1913-O 7 1915
IO 1896;99-1916
IU S-N,D 1894-Ja 2,16,30-Ap 17,Jl 17 1895;Jl 21-N 10,24 1897-My 18,Je 1-8 1898

LA SALLE county record. w 1907-16||
1907-N 13 1913 as Ottawa tidende; N 20-27 1913 La Salle county times
IHi [1911-N 13]-27 1913
IaDeL S 27 1900-F 1902

LA SALLE county times. *See* La Salle county record

Daily REPUBLICAN-TIMES. d S 1 1890+
pub Je 2 1903+
IO 1915+
IU Mr 8 1895;Ja 23 1935+

Ottawa REPUBLICAN-TIMES. w,sw 1844-1918||
1844-Je 12 1852 as Constitutionalist; Je 19 1852-Ag 28 1890 as Ottawa republican
IHi Je 17 1855
IO Ja 12 1850-1914
IOR Je 19 1852-Je 14 1860;Je 13 1867-1916
IU My 20 1887;Ap 12 1889
MWA My 12-19 1860
N Ja 19,My 4,Jl 27,Ag 24 1861
WHi S 5 1878

Ottawa STATESMAN. w D 14? 1868-69||?
ICHi Mr 23 1869
WHi N 9 1869

Ottawa TIDENDE. *See* La Salle county record

Ottawa weekly TIMES. w 1879-89||
United with Ottawa republican to form Ottawa republican-times
IU Ja 23 1889

PANA

Weekly DEMOCRATIC herald. w D 23 1857-67||
IHi Ja 18 1859

Pana GAZETTE. w Jl 27 1865-91||
IPa 1865-72;75-86

Pana NEWS. sw,w O 1932+
w 1932-Ag 1933
pub O 20 1932+

Pana PALLADIUM. d 1869+
pub 1879+
IPa 1879-1912;26-32
IU Ap 1918+

PARIS

Paris BEACON. w 1848-1909||
1848-64 as Prairie beacon; 1864-80? Prairie beacon and Valley blade
DLC Jl 19 1861
IHi Je 19 1863
IParB N 30 1849-My 18,Ag 25 1853-Ag 17 1860;D 31 1880-1909
MWA N 28 1863
PP N 22 1850

Paris BEACON-NEWS. d 1888+
1888-N 1927 as Paris beacon
pub 1888+

ILLINOIS statesman. w Mr-N 1838||?
ICHi N 9 1838

ILLINOIS statesman. w Ja 17? 1840-
DLC My 1 1840
ICHi Ja 31 1840

Paris NEWS. d 1908-28||?
United with Paris beacon to form Paris beacon-news

PRAIRIE beacon. *See* Paris beacon

VALLEY blade. w 1853-64||
United with Prairie beacon to form Prairie beacon and Valley blade, later Paris beacon
KHi Ag 6 1856

PARK RIDGE

Park Ridge WEEKLY. w 1923-29||
IU Mr-N 29 1929

PATOKA

Patoka ENTERPRISE. w 1881-95||?
ICeS O 15 1885-87

Patoka REGISTER. w N 1 1907+
pub 1907+

PAW PAW

LEE county times. w Mr 21 1878+
pub Ap-D 1882;86+

PAWNEE

Pawnee HERALD. w 1901+
IU D 27 1917+

PAXTON

Paxton APPEAL. *See* Eastern Illinois register

EASTERN Illinois register. w N 1879-1928||
1879-80 as Paxton appeal
IU N 5 1914-D 27 1928.

Paxton RECORD. w F 9 1865-
pub 1865+
IU D 20 1917+
MWA My 15 1869;Jl 20 1876

Paxton daily RECORD. d S 1 1897+
pub 1897+

PEARL CITY

Pearl City NEWS. w F 22 1889+
pub Mr 10 1910+

PECATONICA

Pecatonica NEWS. w D 22 1872+
pub 1872+

PEKIN

Pekin FREE PRESS. w Je 1876-D 6 1934||
1876-Ap 25 1918 as Pekiner freie presse
1876-Ap 25 1918 in German
IU O 11 1917-34

Pekiner FREIE PRESSE. *See* Pekin free press

Pekin REPUBLICAN-POST. w 1860-99||?
1860-85? as Tazewell county republican
MWA Ap 2 1869

TAZEWELL county republican. *See* Pekin republican-post

TAZEWELL mirror. w 1848-54||
DLC Mr 3-10,24-Ap 7,21,My 5,Je 2,Ag 18-S 1,O 6,D 19 1849
IU Ap 30 1852
MWA Je 25 1852;D 30 1853

TAZEWELL register. w 1856-73||
Followed by Pekin weekly times
IHi F 19 1861

TAZEWELL reporter. w 1840-41||
DLC Mr 23 1841
ICU Je 9,23 1841

Pekin weekly TIMES. w 1873-74||?
Follows Tazewell register
IP O 24 1873-O 23 1874

Pekin daily TIMES. d 1881+
pub 1924+
IHi Ag 1 1917
IU O 3 1914-16;Ja 3-6,9-F 15,17 1927

PEORIA

Peoria AMERICAN. w Jl 1845-Ja 1850||

Saturday evening CALL and mirror. w Ap 7 1877-99||?
1877-96? as Saturday evening call
ICHi Ap 5-9,30,S 27,O 1879-F 19,Mr 5,26,O 1-8,22,N 26,D 24 1881-Ap 1,15-29,My 27-Jl 1,15-Ag 19,S 16-O 14 1882
IP 1881-86
KHi Ap 7 1877
MWA N 3 1877

Peoria DEMOCRAT. w
Vt Ap 7 1841-Ag 28 1850

Peoria weekly DEMOCRATIC press. w F 20 1840-57||
CSmH D 28 1842
DLC Je 10 1846;Ja 13-20 1847;Ja 19,F 9,Mr, Ap 12,My 10-24,Je,Jl 12-Ag 9,23-S 6,20-D 5, 20 1848;O 13 1852

Peoria DEMOCRATIC press. d
IP 1854-55

Peoria DEMOCRATIC union. d F 27 1857-S 1862||
DLC 1859
IP F-Ag 29 1857;Je 1860-62
KHi Ag 14 1861
NjR Je 1 1857

Täglicher DEMOKRAT. d Ag 18 1860-1915||
In German
IP 1898-1915

EMERY'S daily Peorian. d
IP Ja-Ag 1881

Peoria evening FREEMAN-POST. d 1879-O 1887||?
1879-85? as Peoria freeman; 1886 Peoria evening penny freeman
IP 1881-Je 1886;F-O 1887

Peoria daily HERALD. d Mr 1889-D 29 1898||
1889-Mr 4 1898 as Peoria herald. United with Peoria daily transcript to form Peoria herald-transcript, later Peoria transcript
DLC 1898
IP complete

Peoria HERALD. w 1889-98||
United with Peoria weekly transcript to form Peoria herald-transcript

Peoria HERALD-TRANSCRIPT. d *See* Peoria transcript

Peoria HERALD-TRANSCRIPT. w Ja 1 1856-1905||?
1856-98 as Peoria weekly transcript
IP O 1857-92
OClWHi My 21 1858;F 8 1866

ILLINOIS champion and Peoria republican. w Mr 22 1834-37||
1834-Mr 31 1836 as Illinois champion and Peoria herald. Followed by Peoria register and North-western gazetteer
DLC Mr 29,S 27 1834;F 28 1835
ICU N 15 1834
IPC Mr 29 1834;D 16 1835
IU N 15 1834

Peoria JOURNAL. d D 1 1877+
pub O 1881-Mr,O 1885-Je 1896;97-S 1908;F-My 1909;Jl 1920+
IC Ap 30-My 1 1889
IHi 1920-34
IP 1881+
MWA D 23 1928

Peoria weekly JOURNAL. w 1880-1906||?
IPJ 1902-04

Peoria morning MAIL. d
IP O 1862-Je 1864

Peoria MIRROR. w 1892-96||?
United with Saturday evening call to form Saturday evening call and mirror

Peoria daily NATIONAL democrat. d S 1865-87||?
ICHi O 26,N 5 1865
IHi Ja 8,11 1868
IP 1865-Je 1886
IPJ S 1870-Ag 1871
InRE Ap 30 1871
NNHi Ap 17 1878
OClWHi Je 20 1866

Peoria weekly NATIONAL democrat. w S 1865-87||?
IP 1865-66
IU Ag 19 1869
N S 27,O 11 1866
OClWHi Je 21 1866

Peoria morning NEWS. d My 26 1852-58||
DLC N 3 1852
IP D 1854-My 1858

Peoria NEWS. d O 1883-D 1884||
IP complete

Peoria evening PENNY freeman. *See* Peoria evening freeman-post

Peoria tri-weekly PRESS. tw Ja 1853-Ja 1854||
IP complete

Peoria daily RECORD. d Mr 11 1925+
pub 1925+

Peoria REGISTER and North-western gazetteer. w Ap 1 1837-Ja 26 1850||
Follows Illinois champion and Peoria republican
DLC D 2 1837;Ap 14,Je 30 1838;D 4 1840;Je 11 1841-N 1842
ICHi 1837-N 16 1839;Ap 4 1840
ICU N 24,D 15 1838;Ja 12 1839;Ap 2 1841;Mr 11 1842
IHi Ag 28,O 10,30 1840-F 19 1841;Ja 14,My 27, Je 10,24,Ag 12,26-S 2,O 21-28,N 25-D 16 1842; F 10-17 1843
IP Ap 1840-Mr 1843
IPC N 18 1837
IU Je 11-Ag 6,20,S 1841-F 4,18-Jl 8,22-29,Ag 12,O 7,28-N 1842
MWA D 2 1837;Ap 1840-Mr 1843
N S 16 1842
NN N 17 1838
WHi [S 1837-Ap 1838]

Peoria weekly REPUBLICAN. w Je 1 1850-Jl 1857||
IP 1852-57
MWA D 23 1853

Peoria daily evening REPUBLICAN. d Je 17? 1866-
OClWHi Je 22 1866

Peoria evening REVIEW. d 1873-84||
IP 1875-O 1884

Peoria SOCIALIST. w Ap 2 1903-N 16 1907||
Followed by Indiana socialist (Indianapolis, Ind.)
WHi Ap 2,16,My 7,21 1903;My 11-N 16 1907

ILLINOIS (*Continued*)

PEORIA—*Continued*

Peoria evening STAR. d S 27 1897+
pub 1897+
IHi S 28 1925
IP 1897+

Peoria TRANSCRIPT. d D 17 1855+
1855-D 29 1898 as Peoria daily transcript; D 30 1898-Ag 1914 Peoria herald-transcript
pub S 1904-Ap,S 1906-Ag 1908;09-Ap,S 1912-13;My 1914-Ap 1916;20+
DLC 1898;Ja-Ag 1900
IGK My 18-Je 8,12,15,18-25,29 1861
IP 1855-1914
IU My 14 1917-Ag 1918
MWA Ag 24-25 1858;Ja 13 1869;S 26 1925
WHi 1917-19

Peoria tri-weekly TRANSCRIPT. tw 1856-81||?
OClWHi F 13 1866

Peoria weekly TRANSCRIPT. *See* Peoria herald-transcript

PEOTONE

ADVANCE. w 1881-85||
InT O 27 1885

Peotone EAGLE. ir 1877-88||
IPeV O 1877-87

Peotone VEDETTE. w F 2 1894+
pub 1894+
IHi [Jl 22 1904-34]
IU O 8 1914+

PERRY

Perry CITIZEN. w 1903-D 19 1929||
IU D 28 1917-29

PERU

Peru daily CHRONICLE. d Ja 2 1853-My 20 1854||
IO complete

ILLINOIS gazette. *See* Lacon home journal (Lacon)

LA SALLE county sentinel. w
PJsJ S 4 1857

Daily NEWS-HERALD. d 1886+
pub 1928+
IU D 5 1917-19;Mr 1 1920

NINAWAH gazette. *See* Lacon home journal (Lacon)

Twin City journal. *See under* La Salle

PETERSBURG

Semi-weekly AXIS. *See* Petersburg democrat

Petersburg DEMOCRAT. sw,w N 1 1859+
1859-60? as Semi-weekly axis; 1861?-Ag 29 1868 Menard county axis
IHi 1859-N 3 1860[My 1861-O 1868]-[Mr 1869-73]-[F-S 1876]Ja 13 1877;My 11,Je 29,Jl 6,Ag 17,O 26,N 2 1878
IU Jl 20 1917+

Petersburg EXPRESS. *See* Menard index

MENARD county axis. *See* Petersburg democrat

MENARD index. w 1854-63||
1854-55 as Petersburg express
DLC F 28-Mr 14 1861
IHi Ag 4 1855;F 6 1858;F 2,23,Mr 8 1860;D 26 1861;N 13,27,D 18-25 1862

Petersburg OBSERVER. w Mr 1 1874+
1874-77? as Tallula observer (Tallula)
pub 1874+
NN S 23,O 7,21-N 18,D 1876-Mr 17,Ap 21 1877

PINCKNEYVILLE

Pinckneyville DEMOCRAT. w 1875+
1875-78 as Pinckneyville independent
pub 1880+
IU D 20 1917-Je,S 12 1918-19

Pinckneyville INDEPENDENT. *See* Pinckneyville democrat

PERRY county banner. w My 27 1869-71||
IHi My-Ag 20,S-N 19,D 3-10,24 1869;Ja 7,21-F,Mr 11-Ap 8,22-29 1870;Mr 31,Ap 14-21,My 12-S 15,O 6,20-N 24 1871

PERRY county times. w S 5 1856-
IGK O 10 1856

PIPER CITY

Piper City ADVERTISER. w 1876-83||?
MWA Mr 9 1878

Piper City JOURNAL. w 1897+
pub My 1900+
IU D 27 1917+

PITTSFIELD

OLD flag. *See* Pike county republican

PIKE county democrat. w 1857+
Follows Pike county union (Griggsville)
pub O 1860+
DLC Jl 16,N 12,D 2 1868
MWA My 29 1873

PIKE county free press. *See* Pike county republican

PIKE county journal. *See* Pike county republican

PIKE county republican. w Je 1 1842+
1842-Ap 6 1846 as Sucker and farmer's record; Ap 13 1846-58 Pike county free press; 1858-61 Pike county journal; 1862-63 Old flag
1846?-58? issued also at Griggsville
pub 1842;95;Mr 1901+
DLC Je 1 1842;52-56;My 5 1859;Mr 15 1860
ICU F 23,Jl 20 1843;F 8-15 1844
IHi My 1 1856;Ja 24 1861;F 25 1864;S 2 1868; Je 22 1921+
IU F 23 1843;N 11 1847;N 21 1861;F 1928+
MWA Ja 13 1876

Weekly RADICAL. w
DLC My 13 1859

SUCKER and farmer's record. *See* Pike county republican

Pittsfield UNION. w 1848-Ap 25 1855||
1848-52 as Union. Followed by Pike county union (Griggsville)
DLC S 11 1850;Je 11 1851;Je 21 1852-55
IPiP 1848
MWA Je 16 1852

PLAINFIELD

ENTERPRISE. w Ag 8 1888+
pub 1888+

PLANO

KENDALL county news. w 1872+
1872-80 as Plano news
pub Je 9 1877+

Plano NEWS. *See* Kendall county news

PLEASANT PLAINS

Pleasant Plains weekly PRESS. w 1899-1923||
IHi S 6 1912

PLYMOUTH

Plymouth PHONOGRAPH. w 1879-81||?
IGK Ag 14,D 25 1879

POLO

Weekly ADVERTISER. *See* Tri-county press

Polo weekly BULLETIN. w D 16 1910-F 14 1913||
Follows Polo semi-weekly visitor
IHi 1911-12
IPolT complete

CHAMPION of freedom. w Ja-Je 1857||?
IHi Ja,Je 16 1857

Polo CLIPPER. *See* Polo semi-weekly visitor

OGLE county banner. w Ap 14 1858-60||
IHi My 5,D 1 1858;Jl 25,Ag 1 1860

OGLE county press. *See* Tri-county press

Polo PRESS. *See* Tri-county press

Polo TRANSCRIPT. w Je 10 1857-Ap 1858||
IHi F 11 1858

TRI-COUNTY press. w My 6 1858+
1858-F 1863 as Weekly advertiser; Mr 1863-66 Polo press; 1866-Je 29 1901 Ogle county press
pub Jl 1901+
ICHi [1871-73]-[75-76]-[78-79]-N 17,D 1,15-22 1883;84-Ap 11,My 9-N 21,D 1885-Ap 18,My-O 17,N 7-21,D 5-12,26 1896-1901
IHi [1858-Ag 21 1862]My 16,Ag 1-22,O 31,N 28 1863;F 1865-Je 1901
IOr [My 13 1858-N 22 1860]
IPol N 11 1871+
IU [F 11-D 9 1865]F 17,Mr 31,Ap 21-28,My 26,O 27-N 3,D 1-8 1866;Je 8,Jl 6,Ag 3-17 1867[Ja-O 1868;F 13-D 1869]-[71-76]-Je 1901; Ag 1917-Mr 19 1931
WHi F 11 1871-Je 1901

Polo semi-weekly VISITOR. sw F 16 1881-D 9 1910||
1881-Ap 16 1890 as Polo clipper. Followed by Polo weekly bulletin
IHi Je 29 1881;Je 20 1906-N 11 1908;Ag-D 13 1910
IPolT Mr 30 1889-1905;Jl-D 1910
IU F 15 1882-Ap 7,Je 12[Jl 3,24-D]1886-Jl 6, Ag 6 1892-[94]-Ap 11,Je 6[Jl-D]1900-Je 8 1901

PONTIAC

FREE trader and observer. w 1869-1907||
1869-82 as Free trader
IPoL 1869-71;76-79;81-1906

Pontiac daily LEADER. d S 14 1896+
pub 1896+
IPo 1916-20
IU O 14 1914+

Pontiac SENTINEL. w 1857-1911||
Title varies: Sentinel and press; etc.
CU O 20,N 10-24 1863
IPoL 1871-78;80-81;84-95;97-98
KHi My 4 1865
MWA Ja 11 1866
OHi Je 14 1859

PORT BYRON

Port Byron GLOBE. w 1880+
IU D 20 1917-O 18 1928

POTOMAC

Potomac RECORD. w 1898+
1898-1905 as Potomac republican
IU Ja 2,16-Je 18,Jl 9,23,Ag 27,1920

Potomac REPUBLICAN. *See* Potomac record

PRAIRIE CITY

Prairie City HERALD. w 1870-81||?
IGK S 20,1878;My 2,Ag 29-S 5,1879

PRAIRIE DU ROCHER

DEMOCRAT. *See* Prairie du Rocher sun

Prairie du Rocher SUN. w 1899?+
1899?-1920? as Democrat
pub 1901-Je 1 1914;Je 10 1921+

PRINCETON

BUREAU county democrat. w 1856-63||
Followed by Bureau county patriot, later Bureau county herald
IA [1856]
MWA Je 26 1860

BUREAU county herald. w Ap 21 1862-76||
1862-My 2 1871 as Bureau county patriot
ICHi D 13 1864
ICU Ap 21 1863-My 2 1871
IPri My 1863-My 1872

BUREAU county news. w 1881-95||
IPri 1881-87

BUREAU county patriot. *See* Bureau county herald

BUREAU county record. w 1895+
1895-1900? as Princeton record
pub 1902+
IPri 1916+

BUREAU county republican. w Ja 14 1858+
pub 1858+
ICHi D 26 1861;Ja 30,F 27,O 30 1862;Mr 10 1864
ICU 1858-66;68-76
IPri 1862-91;1914+
IU F 20 1896

BUREAU county tribune. w Ap 1 1872+
pub 1872+
IPri 1873-91;1916+
WHi D 27 1889

Princeton HERALD. w 1845?-
OClWHi D 17 1847

Princeton RECORD. *See* Bureau county record

PRINCEVILLE

Princeville TELEPHONE. w 1876+
pub My 1906-My 6 1909;Je 1911+

PROPHETSTOWN

Prophetstown ECHO. w 1892+
1892-94 as Rock River Valley echo
pub 1893-94;96+
IU 1915+

ROCK River Valley echo. *See* Prophetstown echo

Prophetstown SPIKE. w 1871-94||
Merged with Rock River Valley echo, later Prophetstown echo
IPrE 1893-94

QUINCY

Quincy ARGUS. *See* Quincy herald

Evening CALL. d 1870-75||
Title varies slightly
IHi [S 5 1870-Je 1872;Jl 1873-Je 6 1874]
IQ [O 26-N 17 1870]-71

Quincy COMMERCIAL review. *See* Saturday review

Daily morning COURIER. d S 12 1845-
ICHi S 22 1845

Quincy daily DEMOCRAT. d S 1858-
ICHi N 2 1858

GERMANIA. d 1874-1918||?
In German
MWA Ag 25-26 1876

GERMANIA. sw,w N 9 1874-1922||
Formed by the union of Westliche presse and Quincy wöchentliche tribüne
In German
IHi [Ag 9 1907-S 8 1922]

Quincy HERALD. w Ap 17 1835-1909||?
1835-N? 1838 as Illinois bounty land register; D 1838-S 1841 Quincy argus
CLS D 8,22 1848;Ja 5-19,F 2,23,Mr 2-16 1849; Ag 2,16,30 1850
Ct [1837-38]
DLC My 1 1835;S 26 1840;O 27 1843;54
ICHi Ap 17 1835;O 16 1846;S 5 1862;Jl 18,N 28 1863
ICU Ja 1(extra)1836;D 1,29 1838;F 13,27 1841; Mr 3 1842;F 9 1844
IGK Jl 31 1835;My 18,Jl 6 1849;N 14 1853;Ag 21,S 1,21 1854;My 26,Je 9,S 15,29,N 24,D 22 1856
IHi Jl 24 1841;O 13 1848-[N 23 1849-S 13 1850]
IQN Ap-Jl 1840;O 1841-Ap 7,S 22 1842-48
MoHi Jl 21,D 15 1856;D 21 1857;F 1 1858
NNHi D 1 1838
OClWHi Ag 11 1848;Jl 31 1865
PWCl Jl 1 1835
WHi F 13 1841

ILLINOIS (*Continued*)

QUINCY—*Continued*

Quincy HERALD-WHIG. d 1849+
1849-My 31 1926 as Quincy daily
pub Je 1926+
CtY [1888]
DLC Je 28-D 1867
IGK My 23 1871;Ap 4 1875;O 21 1879
IHi [1920-My 1926]-34
IQ 1889;Jl-D 1891;Jl-D 1892;94-95;Jl 1896-Je, S-O 1897;My 1898-Je 1901;02-03;S-D 1904;Je 1905-Je 1907;11-Je 1913;15+
IQN 1849+
MWA Ag 25 1876
OClWHi Ag 3 1865;Jl 16 1878

ILLINOIS beobachter. *See under* Belleville

ILLINOIS bounty land register. *See* Quincy herald

Quincy evening JOURNAL. w 1867-71||
IQ O 1868-Ap,O 1869-Ap,O 1870-Mr 1871

Quincy JOURNAL. d S 11 1883-Mr 1920||
United with Quincy whig to form Quincy Whig-journal
DLC 1898
IHi Mr 12 1917-S 10 1919
IQ 1891-Je 1892;Ja-Je 1893;94;96-Je 1897;Jl-D 1898;1901-Je 1905;Jl 1906-09;11-13;Ap 1914-15;My,O-N 1916;F-My,O-N 1917;18-Je,O 1919-20
IU O 2 1914-Jl 1918

JOURNAL of industry. w 1884-1923||
IU Ja 31,Mr 21 1901-[04-05]-[07]-[09]10;F 16 1911-F 1 1923

MODERN argo. w 1878-82||
InRE D 27 1879

Quincy daily NEWS. d 1877-88||?
ICHi Ag 7 1877

OLD statesman. w Jl 4-N 1840||
DLC Jl 4 1840

Quincy OPTIC. w 1885-1915||?
IQ 1893;97-98;1901-04;09;Je-D 1910;12-Je 1913

Quincy RECORD. w,m 1898-1920||?
w 1898-1914?
IQ 1904-08;11-12

Quincy daily REPUBLICAN. d 1855-58||
IGK F 9 1856

Quincy weekly REPUBLICAN. w Ja 7 1856-
IGK Ja 12 1856;Ja 10 1857

Saturday REVIEW. w 1872-1905||?
1872-86? as Quincy commercial review
IGK Mr 29,My 17 1879
IQ 1898;1902-03
MWA D 19 1874
NNHi O 30 1875

Quincy wöchentliche TRIBÜNE. w 1852-N 1874||
United with Westliche presse to form Germania
In German
IQ 1870-71;Ag-S 1872

Quincy TRIBUNE and free soil banner. w S 13 1848-
Campaign paper
ICHi S 13 1848

WESTERN patriot. w 1853-
IGK F 9,Ag 24,O 11-N 2 1854;N 22-D 13 1855
MWA Jl 12 1855
N Ap 24 1856

WESTLICHE presse. w Ag 11-N 7 1874||
United with Quincy wöchentliche tribüne to form Germania

Quincy WHIG. sw,w My 5 1838-1915||
1838-57 as Quincy whig; 1858-My 2 1868 Quincy whig-republican
sw O 23 1845-Ap 16 1846
DLC My 5 1838;Ja 3-17 1863
ICHi My 26 1838;O 1 1845;S 16-23,N 4-11,D 2 1846;F 6 1854
ICU 1843-O 11 1844;Ap 1850-Mr 17 1855;Mr 22 1856-Mr 14 1857;Mr 31 1860-Mr 1863;Ap 11 1868-Mr 11 1871
IGK Mr 18 1846;Jl 1,29 1851;My 5,S 8 1855;F 2,Ag 23,O 1-11 1856;Ap 24 1890
IHi [My 12 1838-1915]
IQN complete
MHi Ag 2 1856
MWA Ap 18 1840;Ja 27 1866
MoHi Jl 3 1854

Tri-weekly WHIG. tw O 25 1845-Ap 21 1846||
ICU complete

Quincy WHIG-JOURNAL. d Mr 22 1852-My 31 1926||
1852-57 as Quincy whig; 1858-My 3 1868 Daily whig and republican; My 4 1868-Mr 1920 Quincy whig. United with Quincy daily herald to form Quincy herald-whig
DLC 1863;Ja-Je 1898
ICHi Mr 9 1855;O 22 1858;Jl 30 1859;My 13 1861;Ap 28,S 8,O 1 1866;My-Ag 8 1868;D 12 1877
ICU Mr 1,4,25,Ap 1868;F 1870-72;74-76;Jl-D 1877
IGK Jl 1 1861;Ag 10,O 7,29,N 2,4,7,14,17-18,25, 30,D 8 1864;Ja 4,My 2 1865
IHi [1916-S 1919;D 1921-26]
IQ 1899;1901;03-06;My-Jl 1907;08-Je 1909;12-19;Je-S 1920;Ja-Je 1921;Ja-Mr,Jl 1922-S 1923; Ja-Je 1924
IQN 1852-My 30 1926
IU N 5 1909-Ja 1,28,F 1,Mr 3-8,Ap 6-26,Je 1,4,10-18 1910;O 13 1914-15
NNHi Mr 1,My 29 1873;D 20 1875
PLhT [1884]
WHi N 7 1863;S 5 1864

RALEIGH

Raleigh FLAG. w Ap 25 1856-
IHaC Je 20 1856

RANKIN

Rankin INDEPENDENT. w 1887+
1887-98 as Reveille
pub 1887+

REVEILLE. *See* Rankin independent

RANTOUL

Rantoul weekly NEWS. w 1889-D 13 1918||
IU Ap 28 1916-18

Rantoul PRESS and Chanute Field news. w 1875+
1875-1926 as Rantoul press
pub 1901+
IU S 10 1909,Jl 1917+

RARITAN

Raritan BULLETIN. w 1876-Jl 1884||
IGK My 29 1879

Raritan REPORTER. w O 29 1884+
pub 1884+

RAYMOND

Raymond INDEPENDENT. w Je 9 1881+
pub 1881+

RED BUD

Red Bud PILGRIM. w 1897+
IU O 8 1914-[22-23]+

REDDICK

Reddick COURIER. w 1906+
pub 1921+

REYNOLDS

Reynolds PRESS. w Ja 24 1896+
pub 1896+
IHi [F 1897-1934]
IU D 14 1917+

RICHMOND

Richmond GAZETTE. w 1876+
MWA My 17 1877

Richmond daily WHIG. d
ICHi S 6 1848

RIDGE FARM

Ridge Farm REPUBLICAN. w 1887—
pub 1920+

RIVER FOREST

River Forest LEAVES. w 1906+
1906-O 24 1924 as Forest leaves
pub 1912-15;Je 1924+
IU Je 27 1924-D 18 1925

RIVERDALE

POINTER. w 1907+
IU D 14 1917+

RIVERSIDE

Riverside GAZETTE. m My 1871-
ICHi My 1871

Riverside HERALD. *See* Riverside news

Riverside NEWS. w 1889+
1889-1908 as Riverside herald
pub 1909+

ROANOKE

Roanoke CALL. *See* Roanoke post

Roanoke POST. w 1891+
1891-1912 as Roanoke call
pub Ag 1891-[99]+

ROBERTS

Roberts HERALD. w N 4 1898+
pub 1898+
IU D 19 1917+

ROBINSON

Robinson ARGUS. w D 1863+
1863-73? as Crawford county argus
pub 1868+
IHi O 30 1895;My 21 1925-34
IRob 1910-21;23;30+
IU S 15-N 10 1864;D 12 1917+

Robinson CONSTITUTION. w 1863+
ICHi Ja 3 1883
IHi 1917-18
IRob 1910;12-13
IU D 12 1917-O 1929

CRAWFORD county argus. *See* Robinson argus

Robinson daily NEWS. d Je 16 1919+
pub 1919+

ROCHELLE

To 1865 as Lane

Rochelle FREE LANCE. *See* Tri-county courier

Rochelle HERALD. w Ag 25 1881-Mr 9 1932||
1881-Jl 5 1883 as Morris' Rochelle herald
IRo N 12 1913-32
IU 1881-[83]-[92]-D 12 1894;F 1895-Ap 4,Je 13 1900-Je 20 1901;Jl 25 1917-32

Rochelle HOME journal. *See* Rochelle leader

Rochelle INDEPENDENT. w S 4 1872-73||?
IU S 11 1872-Jl 3 1873

Rochelle INDEPENDENT-REGISTER. w D 16 1897-Ag 9 1928||
1897-Je 17 1926 as Rochelle independent. Merged with Rochelle news
IRo N 27 1913-28
IU D 23 1897-[98]-Ja,Mr-Ap 5,Jl 1900-Je 13 1901 Je 24-N 1926;Ja-O 13 1927;F-Ag 1928

LANE leader. w O 13? 1858-61||
IHi [F 1859-F 2 1861]

Rochelle LEADER. w N 1 1928+
1928-F 2 1933 as Rochelle home journal;F 9 1933-Jl 12 1934 Northern Illinois democrat
pub 1928+
IRo D 27 1928-Jl 1933
IU Mr 14 1929+

MORRIS' Rochelle herald. *See* Rochelle herald

NATIONAL greenbacker. *See* Rapalee's greenbacker

Rochelle NEWS. w N 1 1921+
pub 1921+
IRo Ja 19 1922+

NORTHERN Illinois democrat. *See* Rochelle leader

RAPALEE'S greenbacker. w Ag 2 1878-My 9 1879||
1878 as National greenbacker
IU complete
WHi D 20 1878

Rochelle REGISTER. sw,w Jl 25 1863-Je 15 1926||
Title varies: Semi-weekly Rochelle register; etc. Merged with Rochelle independent to form Rochelle independent-register
IHi Je 20 1902
IRo D 1913-26
IRoR [1864-1926]
IU Ap 3 1869;My[Je-D]1871-Je 19,Ag 7 1875; Ap 22,My 1876-[83]-[86-89]-Ap 6,Je 29 1900-My 1901;O 29-D 1915;19-26
OClWHi S 13 1865

Rochelle TELEPHONE. w Jl 12 1879-Jl 23 1881||
IU complete

TRI-COUNTY courier. w D 5 1896-S 3 1897||?
1896-Ag 6 1897 as Rochelle free lance
IU 1896-Ag 13,S 3 1897

ROCK FALLS

Rock Falls NEWS. w 1882-1915||
IU Ag 8 1896

ROCK ISLAND

Rock Island ADVERTISER. w N 1845-58||
1847-57 as Northwestern advertiser
IGK O 15 1850
IHi Ag 15 1848
MWA Je 23 1852

Tri-weekly ADVERTISER. tw Ja 21 1852-D 31 1856||
IR complete
MWA My 18 1854

Daily ADVERTISER. d S 13 1855-58||
IR S 2 1856-F 12 1857

Rock Island weekly ARGUS. w O 18 1851-1915||
1851-Jl 24 1854 as Rock Island republican
pub [1855-58]
DLC O 20 1852; N 4 1863
IR 1851-Jl 1854
IRA 1851-Jl 1854
MWA Je 23 1852;D 7 1853-Mr 7 1855;S 28 1906
NbHi Ja 25 1873

Rock Island ARGUS. d Jl 31 1854+
Mr 25 1920-My 4 1923 as Rock Island argus and daily union
pub 1858+
IHi Ap 1920-34
IR 1854-D 15 1855
IRA 1854-55
IU Ap 1 1913;Mr 25-Ap 8 1920
MWA O 31 1862
VU Je 27 1882

Rock Island BANNER and Stephenson gazette. w Ag 1839-40||
MWA D 12 1840

Rock Island daily COMMERCIAL. d Jl 5 1858-F 3 1859||
IR complete

NEUE volks-zeitung. sw Ag 30 1875-Ag 24 1915||
Also dated in Moline
In German
IR complete
MWA Ag 26 1876

NORTHWESTERN advertiser. *See* Rock Island advertiser

Rock Island REGISTER. tw F 5 1859-Ag 27 1862||
United with Moline independent to form Rock Island weekly union
IR complete

ILLINOIS (*Continued*)

ROCK ISLAND—*Continued*

Rock Island REPUBLICAN. *See* Rock Island weekly argus

ROCK ISLANDER. w S 14 1854-S 6 1857||
Title varies slightly
IR complete

ROCK ISLANDER. w Ja 5 1878-D 31 1892||
DLC My 24 1884
IR complete
WHi O 29 1887

Daily TIMES. *See under* Davanport, Iowa

Rock Island daily UNION. d N 5 1862-Mr 24 1920||
United with Rock Island argus to form Rock Island argus and daily union, later Rock Island argus
IHi [1920]
IR Jl 1867-Mr 7 1920
IRA Jl-D 1867;Jl 1868-Je 1877;78-Je 1879;80; 90;Ja-Je 1893;Ja-Je 1897;1904-19
IU Mr 27-Ap,Je,Ag,O-N 11 1877;O 16 1914-20
OClWHi My 29 1865

Rock Island weekly UNION. w N 5 1862-Mr 7 1920||
Formed by the union of Rock Island register and Moline independent
IHi [1863]
IR complete
NNHi My 20 1863;F 15 1873
OClWHi My 31 1865

UPPER Mississippian. w O 21 1840-D 1846||
Dated also at Davenport, Iowa
DLC N 5 1840;F 18,Ap 1 1841
ICU Mr 31-Ap 7 1842;Ap 25 1843
MWA O 22,N 19 1840;Ja 14,My 6 1841;Jl 21 1846(extra)
NN My 25-Je 1 1844

WHIG banner. w
MnHi Jl 25,O 5 1844

ROCKFORD

Rockfords ALLEHANDA. w 1884-Ap 10 1886||?
In Swedish
IRA [1884]-Ap 10 1886

FOLKETS nyheter. w 1913-
In Swedish
IRA [1913-14]

Rockford FORUM. w F 24 1843-D 1854||
1843-F 1844 as Winnebago forum. Followed by Rockford republican
DLC F 24 1843
IRoc 1843-44;Ja 15 1845-53
MWA My 19 1852
MnHi [1843-47]
NNHi Je 24 1846

FRAMTIDEN. w 1892-94||?
In Swedish
IRA [1892-94]

Rockford weekly GAZETTE. w N 1866-90||
United with Rockford weekly register to form Rockford weekly register-gazette
ICU Mr 27-D 1878;85
IHi [Ap-N 1872]
IRoc N 22 1866-72;75-77;79-87
KHi O 22 1879-My 11 1881

Rockford semi-weekly GAZETTE. sw 1878-90||?
ICU F 23-Mr 20 1878
IRoc 1879

Rockford daily GAZETTE. d Ag 1879-Je 1891||
United with Rockford register to form Rockford register-gazette, later Rockford register-republic
ICU 1885
IRoc complete

HORNET. *See* Times

Rockford JOURNAL-HERALD. w N 1866-Mr 1888||
1866-Jl 1867 as Winnebago chief; Jl 1867-68 Winnebago county chief; 1868-82 Rockford journal
IHi [N 19 1881-F 18 1882]
IRoc 1873-82

Rockford daily NEWS. w F 1859-60||
IRoc F 8 1859-O 1 1860

Rockford POSTEN. *See* Svenska posten

Semi-weekly REGISTER. sw 1884-94||
IHi Ap 15 1889;My 12,Jl 7,S 8 1891;S 12 1893;My 1 1894

Rockford weekly REGISTER-GAZETTE. w F 15 1855-1918||?
1855-90 as Rockford weekly register
DLC S 10,O 1,15 1859
ICHi D 29 1876
IHi Mr 22,Jl 5,19,Ag 23-S 6,20,N-D 1862;Ja 10-31,N 28 1863[64]Ja 12,Je 29,Ag 10-17 1867; F 15 1868;S 6 1873;N 14-21,D 12-19 1874;75 [76-91]93-94
IRoc 1855-79
IU Ap 18-25 1884;S 17 1886;S 7 1888
MWA Ap 11 1857;S 3 1859;Jl 26,N 29 1862;Jl 22 1865
WHi Jl 19 1856;Jl 20 1861

Rockford REGISTER-REPUBLIC. d 1873+
1873-90 as Rockford register; 1891-S 29 1930 Rockford register-gazette
pub S 29 1930+
IC Ap 30 1889
IHi O 4 1873;D 14 1895;Ag 17 1896;Ja 16 1920+
IRoc Ja 6 1873-F 10 1874;O 1877+
IU O 4 1930-My 8,Jl 10 1931+
WHi My 1917-19

Rockford REPUBLICAN. w Ja 1855-62||
Follows Rockford forum. Merged with Rockford register, later Rockford weekly register-gazette
IRoc 1855-Jl 24 1862
IU My 13,Ag 12 1858
MWA My 17 1854;Ap 18 1855
WHi Mr 19 1856

Rockford daily REPUBLIC. d Ap 10 1890-S 27 1930||
1890-S 2 1925 as Rockford republic. United with Rockford register-gazette to form Rockford register-republic
IF My 15 1894
IRoc complete
IU Je 17 1916;D 5 1917-30
MB [Mr 13-S 20 1922]

ROCK RIVER democrat. w Je 8 1852-Je 1865||
IRoc complete
MWA Je 22 1852

ROCK RIVER express. w My 5 1840-My 22 1841||
IRoc complete
MWA Ag 11 1840
MnHi [1840]

Rockford semi-weekly STAR. sw 1888-1923||
1899?-1923 Tuesday and Friday editions of the d used as sw
IU Ja 24 1901

Rockford morning STAR. d Mr 20 1888+
pub 1901+
IF current year only
IHi Ag 23 1924
IRoc Jl 1888+
IU 1918;Ag 5 1931+

SVENSKA journalen. w 1912-
In Swedish
IRA 1912-13

SVENSKA posten. w 1889-1920||
1889-S 21 1911 as Rockford posten
In Swedish
IRA 1889-1918
IU Ag 31 1917-19
MnHi [D 1889-1920]

TIMES. w 1874-76||
1874-F 24 1875 as Hornet
IRoc F 24 1875-F 16 1876

WINNEBAGO chief. *See* Rockford journal

WINNEBAGO county chief. *See* Rockford journal

WINNEBAGO forum. *See* Rockford forum

ROCKTON

Rockton HERALD. w 1875+
pub [1882-1912]+
IU N 6 1885;Ja 17 1918-D 16 1920[Je-D 1922]+
WHi My 21 1903-Ja 1913

ROGERS PARK

Papers published in Rogers Park are listed under Chicago

ROODHOUSE

HARPER'S weekly herald. w N 10 1877-78||
IHi N 10,D 28 1877

Roodhouse RECORD. w S 1 1898+
pub 1917+
IU D 1917+

ROSEVILLE

Roseville TIMES. w 1876-83||?
IGK Jl 25,Ag 15,S 12 1879

ROSSVILLE

Rossville OBSERVER. w 1873-77||
IDa complete

Rossville PRESS. w 1879+
pub O 10 1883+
IHi [1909-34]
IU O 8 1914-D 12 1918;Ag 18 1921-D 11 1924

RUSHVILLE

ILLINOIS republican. *See* Whig

Rushville JOURNAL. *See* Test

JOURNAL and military tract advertiser. *See* Test

Rushville PHOENIX. w D 20 1838-
ICU D 20 1838

POLITICAL examiner. *See* Whig

PRAIRIE telegraph. *See* Rushville times

SCHUYLER advocate. *See* Test

SCHUYLER citizen. w Jl 6 1856-1926||?
IGK Ag 22,N 27,D 12 1856;Ag 18 1858;Je 24, S 23 1880
IRuT Jl 14 1858-Je,Jl 13 1859-Jl 4 1860

TEST. w My 1835-D 6 1838||
1835-36 as Journal and military tract advertiser; 1836-My 20? 1837 Rushville journal; My 27 1837-F 1838 Schuyler advocate
ICHi D 6 1838
ICU D 16 1837;D 6 1838
IGK Je 27,O 2-17,N 14 1835;F 6,Mr 5 1836

Rushville TIMES. w Jl 3 1848+
1848-My 24 1856 as Prairie telegraph
pub 1856-My 1858;66+
IGK Jl 7,D 7 1849;Mr 21,Je 27 1856
IHi F 21 1860;Jl 11 1928
IU 1918+
MWA F 11 1864

WHIG. w D 14 1839-44||
1839-Ap 2? 1840 as Illinois republican; Ap 9? 1840-S 1843 Political examiner
DLC Ja 23 1840
ICHi Ja 2,F 3(extra)1840;N 12 1842
ICU Ja 30 1841

RUTLAND

Rutland RECORD. w My 26 1894+
pub 1894+

ST. CHARLES

AGE. w Je 30 1843-
DLC Jl 21 1843

St. Charles CHRONICLE. w 1881+
1881-99? as Valley Chronicle
ICHi Ag 27 1886
IStC O 31 1929+
IU D 20 1917+

DEMOCRATIC platform. *See* Kane county democrat

KANE county democrat. w 1849-55||
1849 as People's platform; 1849-50 Democratic platform
MWA Je 23,N 24 1852

PEOPLE'S platform. *See* Kane county democrat

PRAIRIE messenger. w 1846-47||
WHi Jl 16 1846

VALLEY chronicle. *See* St. Charles chronicle

ST. JOSEPH

St. Joseph RECORD. w S 8 1893+
pub D 1893+
IU 1918-Mr 10 1922;F 17 1928+

SALEM

Salem ADVOCATE. *See* Salem herald-advocate

Salem HERALD-ADVOCATE. w Ja 1 1858-1924||
1858-S 12 1880 as Salem advocate
CSmH 1858-Ag 10 1865
IHi [F 10 1905-16]
ISal N 19 1880-My 19 1882
IU Ja 25-Jl 5,S-O 18,D 27 1918-Jl 23,S 3-10, N 19[D]1920-Ap 1 1921

MARION county democrat. w 1889+
ISal 1922+

MARION county herald. w 1876-N 12 1880||
United with Salem advocate to form Salem herald-advocate
ISal My 30 1879-80

MARION county republican. *See* Salem republican

Salem REPUBLICAN. w O 1879+
1879-98? as Marion County republican
IHi [S 22 1904-F 18 1915]
ISal 1923+

SANDWICH

Sandwich ARGUS. w 1878-1918||?
IHi [Mr 1904-16]Jl 11-25 1917

Sandwich GAZETTE. w,sw 1864-90||?
sw 1880-82?; 90?
N Je 23 1866

PEOPLE'S press. w S 10 1857-58||
N S 17,O 1 1857

SAVANNA

Savanna INDEPENDENT. w 1884-85||?
IU My 14 1885

Savanna JOURNAL. w 1885-S 1917||
United with Savanna times to form Savanna times-journal
ISa 1904-O 1917

Savanna REGISTER. w 1853||
WHi O 11 1853

Savanna TIMES-JOURNAL. w,tw 1875-1921||
1875-S 1917 as Savanna times
IU D 7 1900;Ja 7,D 12 1917-Jl 17 1918;Mr 5, 19 1919-F 2 1921

Savanna TIMES-JOURNAL. d 1895+
ISa O 1917+

SENECA

BUMBLE bee. w 1893-95||
IU Jl 8,S 9-D 16,30 1893-Je 16,Jl 14-S 15, O 20-N 17,D 8,18 1894-F 15,Mr 2-9,23,Ap 6-13 1895

Seneca MESSENGER. w Ja 29 1887-88||?
IU F 5 1887

Seneca daily MESSENGER. d Ap 11? 1887-
IU Ap 19 1887

Seneca NEWS. w 1893-1901||
United with Seneca record to form Seneca record and news
IU Je 15-Jl 6,20-N 9,23-30 1895

Seneca RECORD and news. w 1878-1918||?
1878-N 29 1901? as Seneca record
IU Ag 24 1883;Mr 6 1885;Jl 6 1888;D 20 1889;S 13 1895-N 1901;S 22 1905;O 2 1908

ILLINOIS (Continued)

SESSER

Sesser HERALD. w 1909-Ap 13 1933||
Merged with Christopher progress (Christopher)
IU 1918-33

SHABBONA

DE KALB county express. w 1874+
1874-1926? as Shabbona express
pub D 1928+
ICHi My 3 1912
IU D 13 1917-Mr 1925

Shabbona EXPRESS. *See* De Kalb county express

SHANNON

Shannon EXPRESS. w 1879-99||?
IU N 12 1886;My 5,Je 16,Ag 5,19,S 16 1897;Jl 7 1898;Je 15 1899

Weekly REPORTER. w Ag 11 1897+
IU Ag 18 1897

SHAWNEETOWN

GALLATIN democrat. w 1887+
pub Jl 1888+
ICHi O 7 1893
IHa My 18 1888;F 14 1890
IU Ja-Ag 1918;Ja 16 1919+

HOME news. *See* News-gleaner

ILLINOIS advertiser. w 1836-N 4 1837||
DLC Ja 21,F 8,25-Mr 4,Ap 8-15,My 13,27-Je 10,Jl 1-15,Ag 12,25,S 9-O 14,28-N 4 1837

ILLINOIS emigrant. *See* Illinois gazette

***ILLINOIS gazette.** w Je 13 1818-D 18 1830||
1818-S 18 1819 as Illinois emigrant
Suspended from Je 23-Ag 24 1819
CSmH Jl 3 1830
DLC 1821-26;O 6 1827;F 9 1828-30
ICHi F 2 1822;Ap 17 1824
IHi F 16 1822-F 18 1826
IU [1821-26;28-30]
InI Ja 15,29,Mr 12-19,Je 25 1825
MBAt Mr 2 1822
MWA Ja 24,My 22 1824;F 26 1825;F 16,Mr 8,Je 21-28 1828;Ja 16,D 11 1830
MoSM Ag 3 1822;F 14 1826;Jl 2 1831
NN Je 8 1822

ILLINOIS journal. w My 25 1833-
IU N 23,D 7 1833;Ja 4 1834

ILLINOIS republican. w F 1841-D 23 1843||?
DLC 1842-Je 3,Jl 1 1843
ICHi N 12 1842
IU 1842-Ja 7,28-Ap 22,My 6-13,Je 3,D 23 1843
NNHi Ap 3 1841

ILLINOIS state gazette. w Ap 14 1843-47||?
IU Je 29 1843;Ag 21 1845

LOCAL record. w D 1877-92||?
IHa Ja 1-8,22-Mr 12,26-Ap 9,30-Je 18 1881;D 9,30 1882;Ja 6-20,F 3-10,Mr 24-My 19,Je 9 1883;My 8-Je 5,19,Jl 3-10,24,Ag 7-14,S 11,O 2,N 13 1886;Ja 1 1887

NEWS-GLEANER. w 1873-Ja 12 1923||
1873? as Home news; 1874-1901? Shawnee news. Merged with Gallatin democrat
ICHi Mr 3 1905
IHa O 8 1875;O 29 1887;Ap 21 1881;Ap 5 1883;Ap 14 1887;Ap 5 1888
IU S 1914-23

SHAWNEE herald. w F 11 1876-79||
IHa O 5 1877

SOUTHERN Illinois advocate. w O 5? 1848-49||
IU My 25,Jl 13 1849

SOUTHERN Illinoisan. w My 7 1852-60||
DLC O 5,N 16 1855
ICU O 29 1852;My 1 1857
IHi Jl 25 1856
ISeG 1856-59
MWA S 7 1855

WESTERN voice. w D 23 1837-40||?
Title varies: Western voice and internal improvement journal; etc.
DLC 1838;Ag 1 1840

SHEFFIELD

Sheffield TIMES. w 1886-1932||?
KHi D 22 1922

SHELBYVILLE

CENTRAL Illinois times. *See* Shelby county leader

Shelbyville DEMOCRAT. w 1873+
pub 1888+

SHELBY county leader. w S 9 1863+
1866-68 as Central Illinois times
pub 1900+
ICHi F 9 1928
IHi F 18,Ap 7,S 8,N 3 1864

SHELBY county union. w My 9 1863+
pub My 23 1863-Ap 23 1864;Mr 28 1867+
IU O 15 1914+

Shelbyville daily UNION. d Ja 1887+
pub 1887+

SHELDON

Sheldon JOURNAL. w 1879+
pub 1900+
ISh current year only

SIBLEY

Sibley JOURNAL. w 1884+
Suspended from 1924-31
pub [1884]+

SOMONAUK

Somonauk REVEILLE. w D 17 1875—
pub 1875+

SOUTH CHICAGO

Papers published in South Chicago are listed under Chicago

SOUTH WAUKEGAN

South Waukegan NEWS. w 1892-93||?
MWA Jl 21 1892;Ja 26-F 9,23,Mr 2-16,Ap 6,20-My 4,18,Jl 20 1893

SPARLAND

Sparland CHRONICLE. w 1868-96||?
IHi My 24 1882;D 5 1883

SPARTA

COLUMBUS herald. *See* Sparta herald

Sparta DEMOCRAT. w My 8 1840-43||
Follows Sparta herald
IHi My 15 1840-My 21 1841
IU N 5 1842

Sparta HERALD. 1839-My 1? 1840||
1839-40 as Columbus herald. Followed by Sparta democrat
ISpaN 1839

Sparta NEWS. w 1896-S 1901||
United with Sparta plaindealer to form Sparta news-plaindealer

Sparta NEWS-PLAINDEALER. w O 1 1863+
1863-65 as Star of the west 1865-71? Randolph plaindealer; 1872?-S 1921 Sparta plain-dealer
pub 1875+
IGK Ja 10 1890

Sparta PLAINDEALER. *See* Sparta news-plaindealer

RANDOLPH plaindealer. *See* Sparta news-plaindealer

STAR of the west. *See* Sparta news-plaindealer

SPRING VALLEY

BUREAU county democrat. w D 1 1932+
pub 1932+

SPRINGFIELD

Weekly CAPITAL enterprise. w Jl 1854-55||
IHi Jl 8,Ag 12-S 9,23,D 30 1854

CONSERVATIVE. w Ag 14-O 30 1856||?
IHi [Ag 14-O 30 1856]

Morning COURIER. d N 1 1840-
IHi [N 2 1840-F 27 1841]

EVERYBODY'S advertiser. w Ag 18 1861-
IHi S 1 1861

FORUM. w 1904-2?||
Negro
IHi [F 1906-Jl 19 1917]

ILLINOIS adler. w My 21-O? 1844||
Title varies slightly
In German
DLC My 21 1844

ILLINOIS atlas. w 1869-71||
DLC My 4 1871
IHi Je 8 1871
MWA My 4 1871

ILLINOIS herald. w O 1831-33||
ICHi Ap 13 1833
MoSM My 3 1832

ILLINOIS journal. *See* Illinois state journal

ILLINOIS organ. w Je 24 1848-51||?
IHi Mr 22 1851
IU Je 24-Jl 1,O 21,D 2 1848;Mr 31,N 17 1849;S 14-21,O-N 9 1850;Ja 18,F 1,Mr 1, Ap 5-12,26,Je 28,Jl 12-19 1851

ILLINOIS state democrat. sw,w Jl 17 1858-60||
sw 1858-59
IHi [1858-Mr 1859;Ja 12-O 10 1860]

ILLINOIS state gazette. w Je 25-O 31 1878||?
I Je-O 31 1878

ILLINOIS state journal. w N 10 1831-1917||?
1831-Ja 12 1833 as Sangamon journal; Ja 19 1832-S 16 1847 Sangamo journal; S 23 1847-Ag 6 1855 Illinois journal (title varies: Illinois weekly journal; etc.)
DLC Jl 26 1832[Mr 1841-Je 1 1843]Mr 21-28, Ap 13-My 9,23-30,Je 20,Jl 11 1844;F 6,27 1850;57;60-F 1861
ICHi Ja 23-30,F 13-Ap 16,30-Je 11,25-O 1836; N,D 9 1837-Ja 20,F-S,O 13-27 1838;S 6 1839; Mr 13,D 22 1840-F 5 1841;O 28 1842;Ap 13-20 1843;Ag 7 1844;Ja 16 1845;N 5 1846;F 25 1847;F 12 1851;Ja 28 1852
ICU N 15 1834;Mr 20-My 1 1835;Mr 11-My 20 1847[F 1857-N 10 1858]59-[65]-[76-77]-O 20 1881;83-[85-87]-[89-90]supps:S 18 1861;Ja 22-Mr 26 1862;Ap 13 1864;Ap 12 1865;Ja 10, Mr 7,Ap 18 1866;My 25 1870;D 6-13 1871; S 3,D 3 1873

IGK Ja 14 1842;F 14 1863 Ag 15 1879
IHi [1831-49]
IP Ja-Mr 21 1861
IU Ja 26,F 9,Je 18,O 15 1841;Ja 21-28,F 11, Ap 29(extra)My 13-20 1842;N 9 1843;Ap 1, 15,29 O 14,N 18,D 7(extra)9 1847-Je 15 1848; F 12 1851;Ja 28 1852;Je 15 1854;F 11 1857-[61]-[63-67]Ja 22-29,F 19 1868[Mr-D 1869; 74-76]-78;Jl,Ag 11-O 13,27 1881-[82-O 1883; 84-85]Ja 7 1886
MWA Je 28 1834,Je 24 1852;D 14 1853
MoSM Je 7 1832
NN My 31-Je 7,21-28,Jl 12-19,Ag 2,11,S 1-15 1832;Je 23 1858
NNHi N 10 1838
OHi N 26 1866
WHi My 4 1853;Mr 12 1856;My 27 1857-Mr 1863;My 19-30 1882

ILLINOIS state journal. d Je 13 1848+
1848-N 19 1851 as Illinois daily journal (Title varies: Illinois daily state journal; etc.)
N 8 1931 is Centennial number
pub 1857[59]61-Je,D 1864-66;68;Jl 1869-Je 1870;Ja-Je 1871;73-74;Ja-Je 1876;77-Je 1878; 79-Je 1880;Ap-Je 1882;Ja-Mr,O-D 1884;Ja-Mr,Jl 1886-87;My 20-D 1889;Jl-D 1892;Ap 1893+
CL N 8 1931
CtY Ag 25 1855
DLC Ap 21 1849-N 19 1851;Ja 6-F 21 1857; Mr 4 7,14-15,23,Ap 1,4,6,My 4 1861-O 1866; 67-71;Jl 2 1874;Ag 8 1877;Ja-N 21 1878
I [1853;Ja-My 28 1859]Ja 7-F 23,28,Mr 21 1861;Jl-D 11,13-21 1862[Je-D 1863]-[65]-[70-O 1871]73[74]-[76-77;Jl 1878-81;83;Jl 1884-My 18,N-D 1889;98-1900]14-F 1922
IC Ja 5-F 21 1857;Ap 30-My 1 1887
ICHi Je 11 1852;Je 9 1854;Ag 13 1855-Ap 16 1873;S 20 1881;Ja 3 1884;S 13 1887
ICU My 21 1861[Ja 9-O 12 1867]S 17 1868;S 9 1874;Ja 1,Je 5 1878;Ja 3,17,31,F 14 1889
IF Ja 8-Ap 3 1862;Ja 8-Mr 1 1867;Ja 5-Mr 23,Ap 16-20,22 1869
IGK F 6 1855
IHi [1849-1934]
IMaW current 2 months
IP Ja-Ap 1862
IU [Je 1848-50]F 12,17-18,27-Mr 1,Ap 1 1851; Ja 21 Je 8,11,22-24,26,Jl 6-7 9-10 1852;D 3, 28,30 1853 [Ja-Jl 22]Ag 24,26,O 7 1854;Je 18-19,Ag 8,O 1, D 18,20,27 1855-[56-57]F 1-27, Ap 2 1858-F,Ap,O 1-13,22-D 15,28 1859-[63-64]65;F-Mr,Ap 30-My 4 1866[67-Mr 2 1869] Ja 1 1878;Ap 23 1879;S 20 1881;My 1909+
IaDH N 8 1931
MBAt Ap 17,My 2 1865
MWA D 20 1853;Ap 5 1854;O 13,19,22,24-27, 31,N 5,9,13-16,19 1860;S 16-17 1862;Ag 9 1866; O 21 1881
N Ja 23 1861
OClWHi S 20 1850;F 17 1860;S 9 1874

ILLINOIS state register. w,sw F 11 1836-1918||?
F 11-Mr 18 1836 as Illinois state register; Mr 25-Je 17 1836 Illinois state register and Illinois advocate; Je 24 1836-Ag 17 1839 Illinois state register and people's advocate
1836-Ag 17 1839 pub in Vandalia
pub Jl-Ag 1847
Ct N 24 1837
DLC 1836-40;Ap 19 1844-46;48-57
IA 1850-55
ICHi Mr 25-Je 3,24,D 2 1836;Mr 6,Je 2 1837; F 2,Mr 25,Je 15,29,Jl 6,20,Ag,S 14,28,O 12-N 23,D 7-14,28 1838-Ja 25,F 8-22,Mr 8-29, Ap 19-Je 7,21-28,Jl 12-S 21,O 5 1839;Ja-F 21, Mr 13-Ag,S 11-18,O 1840;O 2 1846;Ja 1-8, 22,F 5,Je 17,Ag 6,O 15,D 3 1847;Ap 6 1854; Mr 27,My 22,Jl 17,S 4-11,O 9,D 4-11 1856;Ja 8,29-F 1857;Ja 16 1867
ICU [S 1837-D 7 1838;Mr 1839-42]-[44-46]-[50-52;55;My 1856-Mr 12 1857]extras:D 18-25 1839
IF Ja 28 1875
IGK Jl 17 1851
IHi [Ag 24 1839-1918]
IU 1836-56;Ap 14,Jl 16 1857;Ag 3,9 1860;79 [80-Je 1881]
MH 1851-Mr 12 1857
MWA N 13 1840;N 24 1843-D 21 1854;Jl 12 1931
NcD Mr 18 1842
WHi Je 10 1842(extra)[1851-Mr 5 1857]

ILLINOIS state register. d Ja 2 1849+
Title varies: Daily Illinois state register; etc.
pub Jl-D 1855;Jl-D 1860;Jl 1861-64;Ja-Je 1868; Ja-Je 1869;Ja-Je 1870;71-Je 1872;73;Jl 1874-77;Jl-D 1879;Jl 1881+
DLC Ag 29 1859;Ag 16 1891;98+
I Ja 9-F 25 1861[Ja-N 13 1864;Jl 1872-Je 1876; 77-80]1914-22
IC Ja 31 F 4,12,14,19,21 1857;Ap 30 1889
ICU Ja 7 1867
IGK F 27 1869
IHi [1849+]
IP Je-S 1847
ISp 1910—
IU Mr 12,22,Ap 2,S 3 1849;Ja 17,F 19 1850;N 15 1856;Ap 11,S 26,N 26 1857;Ja 9-F 25 1861; 71;My 3 1909-Ja 4,30 1921+
In Ja-Ap 1862
N S 10 1861
OClWHi Je 16 1865
P-M Ap 16 1868
WHi 1917-21

ILLINOIS unionist and statesman. w Jl 27? 1852-53||
ICHi Mr 9 1853
MWA Ag 24 1852

ILLINOIS wochenblatt. *See under* Elgin

INDEPENDENT democrat. w Mr 20 1843-
IU Mr 20 1843

LEGISLATIVE state register. tw 1842-43||?
IU D 7(extra)1842;Mr 1 1843

ILLINOIS (*Continued*)

SPRINGFIELD—*Continued*

Morning MONITOR. d 1877-1900||?
1877-Ag 29? 1880 as Sangamo daily monitor
I [Ag-N 1877]78-O 1880
InRE Mr 18 1880

Springfield evening NEWS. *See* Springfield news-record

Springfield NEWS-RECORD. d Mr 6 1879-My 5 1919||
1879-F 12? 1910 as Springfield news; F 15? 1910-Ja 9 1915 Springfield evening news
I 1914-Ap 1919
ICHi N 17 1892
IHi [Jl 1891-1919]
IU Ag 24,S 4-18 1907;Je 5 1908-Jl,S 1910-19

OLD Hickory. w F 17-N 1 1840||
IHi [F-O 19 1840]
WHi Ag 31 1840

OLD soldier. sm F 1-S 30 1840||?
DLC F 15,Ap 15-My 1,23 1840
IGK F 15-Mr 2,Ap 1,My 1,26-Jl 2,S 30 1840
IHi Mr 14,My 24,Jl 15,28,Ag 24,S 10,23 1840
IU S 23 1840
MBAt My 1 1840(photostat)
MnHi F 1 1840

OLIVE branch. w Mr 15-O 19? 1844||
IHi [Ap-O 19 1844]
MnHi Mr 15,Ap 3,Je 3 1844
MoSM My 1,15 1844

PERFECTLY independent. w
IU Ja 1,14 1860

Springfield POST-CAPITAL. d 1880-85||?
1880-84 Title varies: Daily post; Evening post
I F-Je,Ag-D 1880
IHi Jl 2 1881

Springfield RECORD. d Jl 1 1907-Ja 9 1915||
United with Springfield evening news to form Springfield news-record
I 1914-15
IHi [1907-15]

Daily REGISTER. d F 1849-50||?
IGK Ja 23,F 10 1851
IU Mr 12,22,Ap 2,S 3 1849;Ja 17,F 19 1850
MWA Mr 2,30,Ap 4,S 3 1849;Jl 15 1850

Daily Springfield REPUBLICAN. d F 9 1857-
IHi Jl 6 1857
IU F 9,My 30,Jl 6,23 1857

ROUND table. w Ja 7 1882-F 24 1883||
IHi complete

SANGAMO journal. *See* Illinois state journal

SANGAMO daily monitor. *See* Morning monitor

SANGAMO spectator. *See* Sangamon spectator

SANGAMON journal. *See* Illinois state journal

SANGAMON spectator. w F 21 1827-29||
CL O 31 1827
DLC F 28,Ag 29 1827
IHi Mr 21,My 30,Jl 11,N 7 1827;Ja 30 1828

STAATS-wochenblatt. w 1878-O 8 1920||
United with the Elgin herald to form Illinois wochenblatt (Elgin)
In German
IU Je 15 1917-20

STATE argus. w Jl 10 1879-
ICHi Jl 10 1879

STATE capital. w 1886-1910||?
Negro
DLC Ja 13 1899
IHi [Mr 28 1891-D 10 1892]

STATE register. tw Je 8-S 3 1847||
ICHi complete
IU complete
WHi Ag 19-21 1847

Evening TELEGRAM. d 1893-95||
IHi [N 1894-N 30 1895]

Springfield TIMES. w O 17 1843-45||
DLC N 8 1843

UNION herald. w Ja 1 1862-
IHi Ja 8-15 1862

STANFORD

Stanford STAR. w 1895+
pub 1932+

STAUNTON

Staunton STAR-TIMES. w Jl 12 1906+
1906-10 as Staunton star
pub 1906+
IU D 13 1917+

Staunton TIMES. w Ag 1878-1910||
United with Staunton star to form Staunton star-times

STEPHENSON

UPPER Mississippian. *See under* Rock Island

STERLING

Daily BLADE. d 1881-83||?
ICHi Ja 5 1882

GAZETTE. w 1857-Mr 13? 1858||
United with Republican to form Republican and gazette

Sterling GAZETTE. w,sw 1858-1907||
Follows Republican and gazette
w 1854-89?
ICHi S 1 1866;N 4 1871;Ja 6 1872;Ap 5,My 31, Ag 16 1873;Ap 3 1875
IU Ap 16 1881
MWA Ag 10 1861

Sterling daily GAZETTE. d 1882+
1882-1911? as Sterling evening gazette
ICHi Je 18,Ag 7,N 7,19 1913;Je 17,26,Ag 7,S 17,22,29,O 6,N 10,D 30 1914;Je 24 1915
IHi Je 14-17 1934
ISte current year only

Sterling HERALD. w 1878-1902||
IU F 20 1891

REPUBLICAN and gazette. w Jl 1856-58||
1856-Mr 13? 1858 as Republican. Followed by Sterling gazette
ICHi Je 26 1858

Sterling STANDARD. w,sw 1868-1908||?
1868-70 as Whiteside chronicle
w 1868-99?
ICHi Mr 8 1878
IU D 6 1888

Sterling daily STANDARD. d 1893-1915||?
ICHi Ag 27 1913;Je 20,N 12,21,D 11 1914;F 3, 16-17 1915
IU O 5 1914-Ja 31 1915

WHITESIDE chronicle. *See* Sterling standard

STEWARDSON

Stewardson CLIPPER. w 1886+
IHi S 22 1926+
IU 1918-My 24 1922

STILLMAN VALLEY

Stillman Valley GRAPHIC. w N 29 1889+
IU N 29 1889;Ja 10 1890-[92]-My[Jl 1894-96]-[99-Ap 6,Je 22 1900]-Je 7 1901;My 30 1918

STOCKTON

Stockton HERALD-NEWS. w 1888+
pub [1888+]

STREATOR

Streator daily FREE press. d 1880-1927||
United with Independent-times to form Streator times-press
IStr 1917-19;23
IU O 21 1914-Je 5 1916

INDEPENDENT-times. *See* Streator times-press

Streator TIMES-PRESS. d 1885+
1885-89? as Streator times; 1890?-1927 Independent-times
pub 1927+
IStr 1914+

STRONGHURST

Stronghurst GRAPHIC. w 1888+
IU S 10 1914+

SULLIVAN

Sullivan DEMOCRAT. *See* Sullivan progress

EXPRESS. *See* Sullivan progress

Sullivan HERALD. w 1898-1927||
1898-1923 as Saturday herald
IHi [Mr 19 1904-15]

MOULTRIE county news. w 1884+
pub 1884+

Sullivan PROGRESS. w 1857+
1857-66 as Express; 1866-69 Sullivan democrat
pub 1916+
OClWHi Jl 29 1875

SYCAMORE

DEKALB county republican sentinel. *See* DeKalb county sentinel

DEKALB county sentinel. w My 21 1854-My 20 1861||
1854-F 1857 as Republican sentinel; Mr 1857-58 DeKalb county republican sentinel. United with True republican to form True republican and sentinel, later True republican
ISy 1854-F 18,Mr 1857-D 20 1858;My 7 1859-61

REPUBLICAN sentinel. *See* DeKalb county sentinel

Sycamore TRIBUNE. w,sw,tw 1872+
1872-1903? as Sycamore City weekly; 1904-05? Twin City weekly
w 1872-1904; sw 1905-28
ISy S 22 1892-D 6 1901;Jl 16 1907+
IU D 11 1917-O 10 1932

TRUE republican. w,sw S 15 1857+
1861-65 as True republican and sentinel
w 1857-69
pub 1857+
ISy 1857-My 22,O 9 1861-Ja 18 1865;F 1893-1901;06+
IU O 21 1914+
N My 29 1861;My 27 1863

TWIN City weekly. *See* Sycamore tribune

Sycamore City WEEKLY. *See* Sycamore tribune

TALLULA

OBSERVER. *See* Petersburg observer (Petersburg)

Tallula STANDARD. w S 18 1929+
IU F 20 1930+

TAMAROA

PERRY county watchman. w Ja 11? 1871-72||
IHi My 17-24,Je 28-Ag 23,S 20,N 15,D 27 1871

TAYLORVILLE

Semi-weekly BREEZE. w,sw 1894-1911||
1894-1908? as Weekly breeze (w)
IHi F 12 1909

Daily BREEZE-courier. d Ap 30 1894+
1894-Ja 13 1934 as Daily breeze
pub 1894+
IHi Ag 1 1917

INDEPENDENT press. w 1858-68||
IHi N 4 1859

TEUTOPOLIS

Teutopolis PRESS. w Ap 21 1898+
pub 1898+
IU O 15 1914-Ap 1931

TINLEY PARK

Tinley Park TIMES. 1922+
IMokN 1922+

TISKILWA

Tiskilwa CHIEF. w 1887+
pub [1889-1930]+

TOLEDO

CUMBERLAND democrat. *See* Toledo democrat

Toledo DEMOCRAT. w Jl 1 1859+
1859-85 as Cumberland democrat
pub Ag 1883+
IU Ag 1914-26;Ja 20 1927

TOLONO

Tolono HERALD. w 1875+
IU F 19 1931+

TONICA

Tonica NEWS. sw,w Ap 5 1874+
sw 1874-78
pub Mr 1878+

TOULON

PRAIRIE advocate. *See* Stark county news. 1856-60

STARK county news. w Ja 4 1856-60||
1856-Mr? 1857 as Prairie advocate
IHi D 17,31 1857;Ja 14-21 1858

STARK county news. w 1863+
pub 1869+
IHi Mr 16,D 22 1865;S 7 1866;My 29,Jl 24 1868
IU Jl 24 1868;Ag 6 1924
MWA Mr 16,D 22 1865;Jl 24 1868
N Jl 24 1868
NN Jl 24 1868
NNHi Mr 16,D 22 1865;S 7 1866;Ja 31 1873
NcD Jl 24 1868

STARK county sentinel. w O 6 1880-1907||?
IHi Mr 17-24,Ap 7,21 1881

TREMONT

Tremont NEWS. w My 8 1893+
pub 1893+

TRENTON

Trenton SUN. w Jl 1880+
pub 1880+

TUSCOLA

Tuscola JOURNAL. w Ap 1864+
1864-S 26 1896 as Saturday journal; O 3 1896-S 14 1900 Tuscola journal; S 21 1900-S 25 1903 Journal republican
pub Mr 20 1876-77[95-1927]+
IHi Jl 18 1929-34
IU O 15 1914+

JOURNAL-REPUBLICAN. *See* Tuscola journal

Tuscola REVIEW. w 1874+
pub 1900+

UPPER ALTON. *See* ALTON

URBANA

CENTRAL Illinois gazette. *See* Champaign county gazette (Champaign)

CHAMPAIGN county democrat. w 1860-O 1862||
1860-Ja 1862 as Champaign Illinois democrat; F 13?-27? 1862 Champaign democrat. Followed by Champaign county patriot
IUr Ja 12-19,F 16-23,Mr 16,Ap 6,20,My 11,25, Jl 6-20,Ag 3,17-31,N 6-13 1861;Ja 9,30,F 13,27, Mr 13,27,Ap 17,Je 19,Jl 10-31,Ag 14-21,S 11,O 9,23 1862

CHAMPAIGN county gazette. *See under* Champaign

ILLINOIS (*Continued*)

URBANA—*Continued*

CHAMPAIGN county herald. w 1877-1906||?
United with Urbana weekly courier to form Urbana courier-herald
IU S 15 1880;Ag 20 1884;Ag 8 1894;S 18 1895;Ja 5,Je 9,D 22 1897;Jl 5 1899

CHAMPAIGN county patriot. w N 6 1862-65||
Follows Champaign county democrat
IUr N 6,27-D 18 1862;Ja 15,Mr 12-19,Ap 2-9,23, My 21-28,Je 11,25,Jl 2,23,Ag 6 1863

CHAMPAIGN democrat. *See* Champaign county democrat

CHAMPAIGN Illinois democrat. *See* Champaign county democrat

Urbana CLARION. w O 22 1859-60||
IUr O 29 1859;F 18-25,Mr 17,31-My 5,Je 2-16,30-Jl 7,28-Ag 11,25-S 1 1860

Evening COURIER. d 1894+
1894-Je 16 1934 as Urbana daily courier (1907-Mr 6 1915 Urbana courier-herald)
IHi [Ap 1920-34]
IU N 28 1897;S 7 1898;Ag 22 1902;My 24 1904;S 18 1905;Ja 4,6,9,Ap 8-9,29,Jl 7,18,23,25-Ag 6,10-13,25,S 1908;Mr 1909+

Urbana COURIER-HERALD. d *See* Evening courier

Urbana COURIER-HERALD. w 1894-1915||
1894-1906 as Urbana weekly courier
IU Ag 31 1894;Mr 12 1897-My 20,Ag 26,D 30 1898;Ja 18 1901

ILLINOIS democrat. w 1867-71||
IU F 25-Mr 11 1870

OUR constitution. w Jl 22 1856-59||
DLC Mr 13 1858
ICh 1856-Ag 7 1858
IUr 1856-N 1859

Urbana UNION. w 1852-62||
United with Central Illinois gazette (Champaign) to form Champaign county union and gazette, later Champaign county gazette (Champaign)
DLC O 21 1852
ICh Je 1854-Ja 4,F 22-Ag 1855
IUr Jl 21 1853-Ag 19 1858

UTICA

Utica weekly GAZETTE. w 1886-D 15 1921||
IU N 13 1908-21

VANDALIA

AGE of steam. w Ap 21 1852-55||?
1852-Ap 2 1854 as Age of steam and fire
ICHi My 20,Jl 15,Ag 26-S 9,O 21,N 11-25,D 13-20 1854;Ja 20,F-Mr 3,17-31,Ap 21,Je 23 1855
IU My 5 1852
MWA Je 22 1852

FAYETTE county democrat. w 1858-1919||
ICHi My 9 1888
IU D 12 1917-Ag 20 1919

FAYETTE county news. w F 1878-81||
ICHi Je 10 1880

FAYETTE yeoman. w Je 23 1849-51||
Early title as Fayette yeoman and railroad journal
ICHi Je 23,Ag 4,25,D 1,15-22 1849;Ap 13-20,My 25 1850;My 31 1851

Vandalia FREE PRESS and Illinois whig. w My 13 1836-41||
Follows Vandalia whig and Illinois intelligencer
1836-37 as Vandalia free press
DLC Je 24 1836;My 8 1840
IHi Ap 4 1839;Ag 28 1841
IU Ap 10 1841

FREEMAN. w Je 4 1842-
DLC Jl 23 1842

ILLINOIS advocate. w F 16 1831-Mr 18 1836||
Follows Crises (Edwardsville). United with Illinois state register to form Illinois state register and Illinois advocate, later Illinois state register (Springfield)
1831-32 pub in Edwardsville
Ct Ag 19 1831[33-35]
DLC 1833-36
ICHi F 23,Mr 23-My 6,20,Je 17,S 2,16-23,O 14-N,D 9-30 1831;Ja 13-F 3,17-24,Mr 9-23,Jl 24,Ag-N 1832
ICU N 19-26,D 31 1834
IHi [F 23 1831-Ag 2 1839]
IU Mr 23,Ap 13 1831;N 2,23-30,D 14,28(extra) 1833;S 3,N 19,D 3,31 1834;My 20,Ag 26,S 30-N 11,25-D 2,30 1835;Ja 16,27,F 10,24 1836
MWA Ja 5 1833
MnHi F 9 1833
MoSM Je 5 1832
N O 12 1833
NN D 2 1835
P-M Ap 20 1832

***ILLINOIS intelligencer.** w Ap 24 1816-Mr 3 1832||
1816-My 20 1818 as Western intelligencer. United with Vandalia whig to form Vandalia whig and Illinois intelligencer.
1816-O 14 1820 pub in Kaskaskia
CSmH My 22 1830
DLC 1821-32
ICHi N 13 1821;D 23 1822;D 2 1825;Mr 14-21, Ag 29,O 31,D 5 1829[30]Ja 22,F 5,26,My 14-21, S 2-16,30-O 7,22,D 1 1831;Ja 28 1832
IHi D 1822-Jl,Ag 9,23,S,O 11,N-D 13,27 1823; Ja 9-16,30,F 13-Mr 19,My-O,N 12 1824-Mr 16, O 28-N 11,D 16 1826;N 24 1827;F 16 1828;My 1 1829;Ap 10,Jl 10 1830
IU Ja 9-23,F-My,Je 12-19,Jl-O 2,23-N 13,27-D 4,18 1821;Ja-F 12,Mr,Ap 13-Je,Jl 13-Ag,S 15 1822-Ja 11 25-My,Je 21-S 13(extra),27-D 13 1823[24-25]-F 17,Mr-Je,Jl 28-Ag 18,S-O 20,N 1827-Ap,My 10-O 11,N 8,29-D 6,20 1828-Jl 4, 18-Ag,S 13-19,O-N 21,D 5-12,26 1829-F 20,Mr-My,Je 12-19,Jl-Ag,S 11-O 16,N 6,20 1830-Ja,F 11-Mr 1832
MBAt Ag 14 1821
MWA O 29 1824;S 7 1826;N 3,24-D 8 1827;Ag 16 1828;Je 27,Jl 18,Ag 29,S 19,O 24,N 7-21,D 5-12,26 1829;Je 9,D 11-18 1830;My 28 1831;Ja 7 1832
MoSM F 20 1821;O 12,D 7 1822;Mr 30 1826-32
N F 5 1822
OClWHi O 25,D 13 1828
WHi Ja 4,Ap 24,O 30 1821;S 21 1822;photostat copy 1821-My 31 1823

ILLINOIS sentinel. w N 8 1839-46||?
DLC N 22,D 7 1839;Mr-My 2,16-Jl,Ag 15-S 19, O-D 5 1840
IU N 22,D 7 1839;Mr-My 2,23-Jl,Ag 15-D 5 1840

ILLINOIS state register. *See under* Springfield

Vandalia LEADER. w 1889+
pub 1922+
IU My 10 1920-My 5 1921

Vandalia UNION. w Ap 1864+
ICHi Ag 10 1881;Jl 12 1888
IHi [1915-19]N 1 1928
IU N 27 1919-D 7 1922

WESTERN intelligencer. *See* Illinois intelligencer

Vandalia WHIG and Illinois intelligencer. w 1831-34||?
1831-Mr 14 1832 as Vandalia whig
Ct [1833]
DLC Mr 28 1832-D 17 1834
ICHi D 28 1832;Ag 21 1833;Ja 15-22,Ap 3,24-My 8,Je 12-19,Ag 28 1834
IHi Ag 22 1832;Ap 4 1833(extra);Ap 17,O 23, D 10 1834
MWA Jl 17 1833;My 8 1834
N O 9 1833

VERMONT

Vermont BANNER. w 1854-
IGK Jl 25 1855

Vermont UNION. w 1898?+
pub 1898+

VIENNA

Vienna TIMES. w Ag 1879+
pub 1920+

UNION courier. w 1862-
MWA Ap 4 1863

VILLA GROVE

Villa Grove NEWS. w My 7 1907+
pub 1907+
IU D 27 1917+

VILLA PARK

Villa Park ARGUS. w O 11 1924+
pub 1924+

VIOLA

Viola ENTERPRISE. w S 1892+
pub 1892+

VIRDEN

Virden RECORD. *See* Virden recorder

Virden RECORDER. w Ag 1866+
1866-Mr 25 1921 as Virden record
IU O 22 1914-16;Mr 31 1921+

Virden REPORTER. w 1879-Mr 25 1921||
United with Virden record to form Virden recorder
IU N 1914-21

VIRGINIA

Virginia ADVANCE. 1884-86||?
IHi Ap 1886

CASS county courier. w Jl 21 1866-F 16 1872||
N 1870?-O 1871 as Weekly Virginia courier. Followed by Virginia gazette
IHi Jl 21 1866;My 10,24,Je 28,Jl 19,Ag 16,30-S 6,O 3,N 22,D 1867-Ja 24,F 7-21,Mr 6-13,O 9,23 1868;Ap 30-My 7,Je 11,Jl 30,S 10 1869;My 27, N 18 1870;Ja 13-F 10,24,Je,O 6,20-N 3,17-24 1871

CASS county democrat. w 1866-68 *See* Cass county times

CASS county democrat and weekly enterprise. w 1925?-Mr 18 1926||
1925?-Ja 21 1926 as Weekly enterprise. United with Republican gazette to form Enterprise gazette, later Virginia gazette
IHi [Jl 23 1925-26]

CASS county republican. w Je 16 1916-Mr 9 1917||
United with Virginia gazette to form Republican gazette, later Virginia gazette
IHi [1916-17]

CASS county times. w My 8 1866-70||
1866-68 as Cass county democrat
IHi N 29 1866;Ja 17,31-F 7,21-28,Mr 14-Ap 4, My 2-23,Je 6,29,Jl 20,S 27,N 1,29,D 13 1867-Ja 3,31-F 7,Jl 24,Ag 28[S 24 1868-Ja 7 1870]

Weekly Virginia COURIER. *See* Cass county courier

Virginia ENQUIRER. w Jl 3 1875-My 24 1922||
Followed by Arenzville enquirer (Arenzville)
IHi [1875-1922]
IU D 12 1917-Jl 1918

Weekly ENTERPRISE. *See* Cass county democrat and weekly enterprise

ENTERPRISE-GAZETTE. *See* Virginia gazette

Virginia GAZETTE. w F 23 1872+
Follows Cass county courier. 1872-Mr 9 1917 as Virginia gazette; Mr 16 1917-Mr 19 1926 Republican gazette; Mr 26 1926-D 27 1929 Enterprise-gazette
IHi [1872-Mr 19 1926]-[30]
IU D 23 1898
KHi Jl 14 1893;My 2 1896

HARPER'S weekly herald. w My 21 1878-79||
IHi Mr 19 1879;Ap 5 1879

ILLINOIS observer. w Ap 12 1848-49||
IU Ap 13 1849

JEFFERSONIAN. w Ap 2 1870-D 26 1873||
IHi [Ap 30 1870-D 12 1873]

PEOPLE'S advocate. w Jl 31 1886-D 17 1887||
IHi complete

REPUBLICAN-gazette. *See* Virginia gazette

WALNUT

Walnut LEADER. w 1892+
pub Je 1893+

WARREN

Warren INDEPENDENT. *See* Warren sentinel-leader

Warren LEADER. w 1890-1906||
United with Sentinel to form Warren sentinel-leader

Warren REPUBLICAN. w My 28 1856-57||
IU Je 4 1856

Warren SENTINEL-LEADER. w Ja 20 1857+
1857-66 as Warren independent; 1866-1906 Sentinel
pub 1857+

WARRENSBURG

COMMUNITY citizen. w N 27 1931-Ap 8 1932||
United with Warrensburg times to form Warrensburg times-citizen, later Macon county times
IWaH complete

MACON county times. w Ja 9 1885+
1885-N 20 1931 as Warrensburg times; N 27 1931-Ja 4 1934 Warrensburg times-citizen
pub 1888;94;97;99;1907-08;N 1916-O 1918;19-20
IU O 21 1932-Ag 4 1933
IWaH 1885-87;89-93;95-96;98;1900-06;09-O 1916; N-D 1918;21-N 1931;Ap 1933+

Warrensburg TIMES. *See* Macon county times

Warrensburg TIMES-CITIZEN. *See* Macon county times

WARSAW

Warsaw BULLETIN. w Je 1 1865+
pub 1865+
IGK Ap 19 1879
IU Mr 12 1915+
NN Ap 4,My 1-8,Jl 24,Ag 14,N 1856-[57-59] Mr 15,Ap 26,My 17,31-Je 14,Jl 5,Ag 2 1860; Mr 28,O 31 1861[67-77]-[79]80;Mr 12-19,Ap-Jl 9,29,S 10 1881;My 20 1882-[83-S 1886]Jl 1 1887

Daily Warsaw BULLETIN. d
NN S 6 1882;S 5 1883

Warsaw COMMERCIAL journal. S 5 1850-53||
IGK S 5,14-21 1850;Je 12,Jl 24,Ag 14 1851; F 14-21 1852
MWA Je 19 1852

Warsaw DEMOCRAT. w F 10 1880-
IGK Je 16 1880

Warsaw EXPRESS. w 1853-56||?
IGK Jl 26 1855;Je 28 1856

HANCOCK democrat. w Mr 18-Ap 11 1844||
NN complete

HANCOCK democrat. w 1865-79||
1865-67 as Public record
MWA F 22 1867
NN O 25-N 2,30,D 28 1877-Ja,F 15,Ap 12, My 3,17,Ag 30-N 1,15-D 20 1878

HANCOCK new era. w Ap 1864-65||
NN Je 30-S 1,O 6 1864

Warsaw MESSAGE. *See* Warsaw signal

PUBLIC record. *See* Hancock democrat. 1865-79

Warsaw SIGNAL. w My 13 1840-Mr 19 1853||
1840-My 5 1841 as Warsaw western world; Ja 14 1843-F 7 1844 Warsaw message
Suspended between Ag 21-O 2,N 20-D 11 1852;Ag 25-O 13 1846
DLC Ag 12 1840
ICHi Ja 15,F 10,My 14,S 17,O 29 1845;Je 17, O 20-27,N 14 1846
ICU Mr 17 1841;Mr 19,S 3 1842;Mr 18 1843; F 10 1845;F 4 1846
IGK Ja 13 1841;F 6-20 1847;Ja 15,D 30 1848; Ag 6-13 1851;Ap 3-24,My 22,Je 5,Jl 3,O 16 1852

ILLINOIS (*Continued*)

WARSAW—*Continued*

Warsaw SIGNAL. w 1840-1853—*Continued*
IHi My 13-Je 3 1840
IU Mr 18 1843
MWA D 8 1841;N 13 1852
NN 1840-[My 1841-O 1842]43-Je 19,Jl 17 1844-Ap 12 1850;Ag 1851-53
NNHi S 3 1842;F 10 1845

Warsaw WESTERN world. *See* Warsaw signal

WASHBURN

Washburn LEADER. w 1890+
pub O 1905+
IU D 27 1917+

Washburn REVEILLE. w 1872-96||?
IHi Jl 3 1873;Ja 4 1874;Mr 8 1882;Ja 30 1884

WASHINGTON

Washington HERALD. w 1868-84||?
IGK Ag 21-28,S 11 1879

POST and news. *See* Tazewell county reporter

TAZEWELL county reporter. w 1886+
1886-1912 as Tazewell news; 1913-17 Post and news
pub 1890+

TAZEWELL news. *See* Tazewell county reporter

WATERLOO

Waterloo ADVOCATE. *See* Waterloo republican

DOLLAR advocate. *See* Waterloo republican

Waterloo REPUBLICAN. w 1858+
1858-79 as Waterloo advocate; 1880-89 Dollar advocate
pub 1890+
IHi Ap 1862-69[Mr 15 1911-34]
IU O 1914-N 20 1918

WATSEKA

BLADE. w Ja 6-D 1 1898||
IWat complete

IROQUOIS county democrat. w Mr 18 1898-Ag 1920||
United with Iroquois county times to form Iroquois county times-democrat, later Iroquois county times
IWat 1898

IROQUOIS county democrat. w Mr 3 1932+
pub 1932+

IROQUOIS county herald. w N 17 1865-69||
1865-Ja 1867? pub in Middleport
MWA F 21 1867
OClWHi Ja 20,27 1866

IROQUOIS county news. w 1895-Mr 11 1898||
ISh Je 19-26 1896
IWat 1898

IROQUOIS county times. w D 1 1870+
1870-My 4 1871 as Onarga times (Onarga); My 11? 1871-Ag 10 1876 Iroquois times; Ag 3 1900-F 25 1921 Iroquois county times-democrat
ICHi Ag 30 1879
IU D 14 1917+
IWat My 27 1871+

IROQUOIS county times-democrat. *See* Iroquois county times

IROQUOIS republican. *See* Watseka republican

IROQUOIS times. *See* Iroquois county times

Watseka REPUBLICAN. w My 8 1856+
1856-72 as Iroquois republican
1856-63 pub at Middleport
pub 1856-73;76+
CtY Ja 28 1858
ICHi Mr 15(facsimile)1860;Je 28(excerpt) 1865
ISh Jl 1 1863
IU 1918-My 1920
IWat 1875+
OClWHi Jl 25 1866

Watseka STALWART. w Je 28 1900-D 17 1903||
IWat complete

WAUKEGAN

Waukegan weekly GAZETTE. w O 12 1850-1917||
DLC Ja 29 1881
IP O 9 1852-S 10 1853
MWA O 9 1852;Je 27 1863;S 24 1881
OClWHi Ja 9 1864

Waukegan daily GAZETTE. d 1892-1918||
IU F 12 1915-D 27 1918

LAKE county chronicle. w 1847-55||
MWA Je 22 1852

Waukegan evening NEWS. d 1908-09||
ICHi F 13 1909

Waukegan NEWS-SUN. d D 7 1921+
1921-Mr 31 1930 as Waukegan news
pub 1921+
IU Ja 24 1935+

Waukegan daily SUN. d 1897?-1930||
United with Waukegan news to form Waukegan news-sun
ICHi F 13 1909
IU O 2 1914-Je 1918;Mr 17 1920

WAVERLY

Waverly GAZETTE. w Je 24 1869-F 23 1871||
IWavJ complete(typed)

Waverly JOURNAL. w 1876+
1876-79? as Morgan county journal
pub 1899+
IGK My 30 1879
IU O 9 1914-N 15 1918;F 28 1919+

MORGAN county journal. *See* Waverly journal

WAYNE CITY

Wayne City JOURNAL. w 1913-Ag 2? 1929||
Followed by Wayne City news
IHi Ap 29 1920-28
IU Ap 14 1921-My 16 1929

Wayne City NEWS. w Ag 9 1929+
Follows Wayne City journal
IU Ag 9-16,S 13-20 1929

WELDON

Weldon RECORD. w 1892+
IU D 20 1917+

WENONA

Wenona INDEX. w F 1865+
1865-Je? 1870 as News index
IU D 25 1884

NEWS index. *See* Wenona index

WEST CHICAGO

West Chicago PRESS. w 1884+
pub 1925+

WEST FRANKFORT

Daily AMERICAN. d S 1 1916+
pub 1920+
IU D 19 1931+

WEST YORK

West York ADVANCE. w Mr 28 1884-95||?
ICHi Ag 22 1884;Ag 14 1885
IHi Jl 31 1885

WESTFIELD

Westfield INTELLIGENCER. *See* Westfield review

Westfield PANTAGRAPH. w 1879-84||
ICHi Ap 28 1881

Westfield REVIEW. w 1890+
1890-99 as Westfield intelligencer
pub F 1905+
IU O 8 1914+

WESTVILLE

Westville NEWS. w
pub 1930+

WHEATON

DUPAGE county gazette. *See* DuPage gazette

DUPAGE county news. w 1907-10||
ICHi S 9 1910

DUPAGE gazette. w Ag 2 1856-My 14 1857||
1856-My 14 1857 as DuPage county gazette
IHi [1856-57]

DUPAGE tribune. *See* Wheaton progressive

Wheaton ILLINOIAN. w 1861+
1861-70 as Northern Illinoian
IU S 20 1889
MWA D 23 1868

Wheaton daily JOURNAL. d Ap 24 1933+
pub Je 6 1933+

NORTHERN Illinoian. *See* Wheaton Illinoian

Wheaton PROGRESSIVE. w,sw N 4 1910-Je 1933||
1910-S 1 1912 as DuPage tribune. United with Daily journal to form Wheaton daily journal
pub 1910-17;19-33
IU Ap 1932-33

WHITE HALL

White Hall REGISTER-REPUBLICAN. w Ag 21 1869+
1869-Jl 27 1917 as White Hall register
pub 1869+
IU N 20 1914+

WILLIAMSFIELD

Williamsfield TIMES. w 1889+
pub [1889-99]+

WILLOW HILL

Willow Hill ECHO. w 1915-18||
IU [Mr 21-O 3 1918]

WINCHESTER

BATTLE axe and political reformer. w Jl 1841-Jl? 1843||
Jl-O 16 1841 pub in Exeter
ICU F 4 1843
IGK N 20 1841
IU F 4 1843

Winchester REPUBLICAN. w D 14 1844-45||?
DLC D 28 1844
IU F 22 1845

SCOTT county herald. w 1901-22||?
IHi Ag 2 1917

SCOTT county news. w Jl 12 1860-
DLC S 6 1860

Winchester TIMES. w S 14 1865+
pub 1918-19;22+
IU D 14 1917+

WINDSOR

Windsor ADVERTISER. *See* Windsor semi-weekly gazette

Windsor semi-weekly GAZETTE. w,sw Je 1877+
1877 as Windsor advertiser; 1877-O 1922 Windsor gazette
w 1877-O 1922
pub Je 1877[78;86]94+

WOOD RIVER

Wood River JOURNAL. sw,w Ag 27 1920+
sw 1927-28
pub 1920+

WOODHULL

Woodhull DISPATCH. w 1879+
1879-83? as Woodhull gazette
MWA Ja 26 1899

WOODSTOCK

Woodstock AMERICAN. w My 31 1918-Jl 2 1926||
IWo Je 7 1918-26

ILLINOIS republican. w
NhD Jl 16 1846

Woodstock JOURNAL. d,w D 9 1929+
1929-Ja 15? 1931 as Woodstock evening journal
pub 1929+
IWo 1929+

McHENRY county democrat. *See* Woodstock republican

McHENRY county republican. *See* Woodstock republican

NEW ERA. w 1874-80||
MWA D 14 1876

Woodstock NEWS. w Ag 12 1926-D 29 1932||
IWo complete

Woodstock REPUBLICAN. w 1877-D 21 1917||
1877-O 10 1902 as McHenry county democrat; O 17 1902-O 1905 McHenry county republican
CoDL Jl 21 1883-90;O 17 1902-Ap 18 1913
IHi [Ap 15 1904-O 13 1905;06-16]
IU O 9 1914-17
IWo Mr 13 1914-17

Woodstock daily SENTINEL. w,d 1856+
1856-Jl 1 1926 as Woodstock sentinel (w)
pub 1856+
CoDL 1891-O 16 1902
IU Ap 20 1916+
IWo Mr 12 1915-Ja 2 1926
OClWHi S 20 1865

WYOMING

Wyoming HERALD. sw 1878-84||
United with Wyoming post to form Wyoming post-herald

Wyoming POST-HERALD. w Ag 9 1872+
1872-85 as Wyoming post
pub 1872+
IGK Jl 25,Ag 8-15,29 1879
IHi [1911-34]
IU O 14 1914+

YATES CITY

Yates City BANNER. w D 25 1879+
1879-89 as Industrial banner
ICHi Ap 15-My 13,27,Je 10 1881
IElmG 1925+

INDUSTRIAL banner. *See* Yates City banner

YORKVILLE

KENDALL county record. w My 1864+
pub 1864+
IU O 21 1914+
MWA Mr 8 1866

ZEIGLER

Zeigler NEWS. w Ag 1 1918+
pub 1918+

ZION

BENTON advertiser. *See* Community news

COMMUNITY news. w Ap 25 1930+
1930-Ap 1933 as Benton advertiser
pub 1930+

INDEPENDENT. w 1910-27||
Title varies: Zion City independent; Zion City independent and Winthrop Harbor news
IU D 14 1917-Ag 25 1927

INDIANA

AKRON

Akron NEWS. w 1890+
InAk 1921—

ALBANY

Albany CHRONICLE. w 1903+
pub [1924+]

ALBION

Albion NEW ERA. w 1870+
In 1932+
InAl 1934+
InU 1914-15

NOBLE county democrat. w 1881+
pub 1922+
InAl 1934+

Albion OBSERVER. w
In N 28 1850

ALEXANDRIA

Alexandria TIMES-TRIBUNE. d 1898+
InAle 1905+

AMBOY

Amboy INDEPENDENT. w 1902+
pub 1902+
In S 27 1935—
InAm 1902+

ANDERSON

Anderson daily BULLETIN. d Mr 25 1885+
In Je 1919+
InA 1917-18

Anderson DEMOCRAT. w 1869-1919||?
1883-85? as Review-democrat
In Ap 19 1872;Je 16 1893-94
MWA Jl 7 1876
NNHi Ja 5 1872

DEMOCRATIC standard. w 1855-72||?
In N 17 1859
InGoE Ja 12 1860
MWA Ap 9,D 3 1863

Anderson GAZETTE. w S 12 1850-
In S 12 1850;Ja 16 1851;N 17 1859

Anderson HERALD. w 1868-1915||?
DLC Ja 14-F 11 1869
In My 13 1870-Ja 6 1871
InNcHi O 1,N 19,D 17 1863
MWA Mr 17 1871;Je 16-23 1876

Anderson HERALD. d 1883+
pub 1903+
InA 1924+

INDIANA union. w Jl 3 1862-
In Jl 3 1862

Anderson REVIEW. w 1877-82||
United with Anderson democrat to form Review-democrat, later Anderson democrat
In Jl 15 1881;My 5 1882

REVIEW-democrat. *See* Anderson democrat

TRUE democrat. w 1848-
In F 3 1849

ANGOLA

Angola HERALD. w 1876+
In Je 1893-94;97-D 7 1898;1932+
InAn [1916-33]+

STEUBEN county journal. w 1881-Ap 9 1884||
In N 9 1881-[82]-Ap 2 1884

STEUBEN county republican. *See* Steuben republican

STEUBEN republican. w 1857+
1857-76? as Steuben county republican
In Ap 9 1884-Ja 1886;1906;14+
InAn D 1915-[17]+
InU 1915+
MWA S 7 1865;Je 28 1876

ARGOS

Argos REFLECTOR. w 1881+
pub Ag 30 1883+
In S 26 1935+
InPmM Ag 18 1892+

ASHLEY

Ashley-Hudson TIMES. w 1928+
pub [1928—]

ATTICA

FOUNTAIN ledger. *See* Attica ledger-tribune

FOUNTAIN-Warren democrat. w 1880+
In 1892-94;97+
InAt 1892+

Attica LEDGER-TRIBUNE. w 1851+
1851-66? as Fountain ledger; 1867?-1920? Attica ledger
In O 11 1866
InLHi F 6 1868;Ap 3 1879
MWA Ap 4 1861;Je 8,Jl 6 1876
NN N 19 1857
PPeS F 4 1904;Ja 7 1909

Attica LEDGER-tribune. d 1895+
Title varies: Attica ledger; Attica ledger-press
In My 1908-15;Ap 10 1923;S 1931+
InU 1914-Ag 1921
PPeS Je 29 1923

Saturday PRESS. w 1899-S 21 1911||
United with Attica ledger to form Attica ledger-press, later Attica ledger-tribune

Attica TRIBUNE. d 1911-20||?
United with Attica ledger to form Attica ledger-tribune

AUBURN

Auburn COURIER. w,sw 1871+
w 1871-1909
In Ja 20 1876;Jl 13 1893-94;97-F 13 1913

DE KALB county republican. *See* Auburn dispatch

Auburn DISPATCH. w,sw 1874+
1874-85 as DeKalb county republican
w 1874-1910?
In 1881-F 1885;My 19 1898-1902
InAu 1899
InGoE Mr 2 1876
MWA Jl 27 1876

Auburn STAR. d 1895+
pub 1929+

AURORA

Aurora BULLETIN. w 1893+
1893-99? as Saturday bulletin
In D 19 1896;O 7 1899;Ag 1935+
InU [1929-30]+

Saturday BULLETIN. *See* Aurora bulletin

Aurora COMMERCIAL. w Ja 1859-Je 25 1868||
Followed by Dearborn independent
In Ap 28 1859-60;F 21,Mr 21,N 7 1861;62-68
InVevHi Ap 7 1859;Ja 19-26,F 16-23,Mr 7,My 17 1860
MWA Ja 1 1863
NNHi 1861-64;66
WHi Ja 1 1863;S 8 1864[Mr 16-O 26 1867]

DEARBORN county democrat. w D 22 1838-
DLC Ja 23,F 19 1840
In 1838-S 24 1840

DEARBORN independent. w Jl 2 1868-1928||?
Follows Aurora commercial
In Ag-D 1868[My-N 18 1869]-[75]-[78-79]-D 13,N 17 1881;F-Ag 10,O-D 23 1882;Ja 25-F 8, 22,Mr 8,22,Je 21-Jl 5,19-O 4,25,N 29 1883-Jl,S 18 1884-[86]-F 10,24,Ap-My 1887;O 18 1888-[90-93]94;Ja 10,24-Ap 25,Ag 22,N 7 1895;Mr 19,Ap 2,16,My 7,21-Je 18,Jl 30-Ag 13,S 3,D 10 1896;Ap 29 1897;Ap 14,My 25,S 28 1899;Jl 5,19,S 13 1900
WHi [Mr 1870-D 19 1872]Jl 5,19 1900

INDEPENDENT banner. w Ag 12 1852-
In S 4,28,N 16 1853
NNHi 1852-Mr 8 1854

INDIANA signal. w
Ct Ag 26 1836
In Ag 20,S 3,N 5,19 1836

Aurora JOURNAL. w 1868+
InAur [1917+]

Aurora NEWS. w Je 4 1873-74||
In [Je 1873-Ja 7 1874]

Saturday NEWS. w O 17 1874-81||
1874-Jl 21 1876 as Saturday news; Jl 28 1876-Je 1 1877 Rising Sun news
1874-My 8 1879? pub in Rising Sun
In Ap 10 1875
OOxM 1874-81

PEOPLES advocate. w 1868-70||
In Jl 1,Ag 12,S 2,D 16 1869;Ja 20-27,Je 30,N 3,D 22 1870

REPUBLICAN leader. w Jl 15 1876-
In Jl 29-Ag 5,26,S 23,O 7 1876
MWA Jl 15 1876

SCOTT eagle. w Ag 19 1852?-
NNHi S 2 1852

Aurora SPECTATOR. w 1880-93||
In D 28 1880-Ja 4,Jl 5 Ag 9-30 1881;S 21,O,N 16-23 1882[83]S 18-N 5 1884[85]
OOxM Ja 18,Mr 1 1883

STANDARD and press. w 1851-
1851-F? 1856 as Aurora standard
In Je 12,26-Jl 3 1851;Ja 22-29,F 12,Mr 4 1852; Je 9-23,Ag 4,S 22-O 6,20-27,N 10,D 15 1853-[54;55]Ja 17,31-F 14,Ap 23-30,My 14-21,Je 4, Jl 2,16-23,Ag 6,20-27,S 10,24-O 1,N 5-12,D 17-24 1856;Ja 28 1857
MWA Mr 24 1853
P-M Jl 13 1854
WHi O 6 1853;Ag 6 1856

WESTERN commercial. w D 2 1848-
In [1848-49]Mr 16,Ap 27,Ag 22,O 30 1850
InAur 1848-51
NNHi 1850-My 1851
PPL N 14 1850
WHi N 17 1849

WESTERN republican. w Ap 1846-
In N 25 1847;Ja 1,29,F 10,Mr 2,16,30-Ap 20,Je 1,Jl 6-13,Ag 10-17,S 7-14,O 5,19,N 9 1848
NNHi D 9 1847[Ja-N 1848]

AVILLA

Avilla NEWS. w 1886+
pub [1886+]

BATESVILLE

DEMOCRATIC-herald. *See* Batesville herald-tribune

Batesville HERALD-TRIBUNE. w 1892+
1892-1919? as Democratic-herald; 1920?-F 1930 Batesville herald
pub Je 22 1893+
In Ag 31,S 7 1893;94;1932+
InVeR 1906-14;17-26;28-29;31-32

Batesville TRIBUNE. w 1887-1930||
United with Batesville herald to form Batesville herald-tribune
InOs 1915-F 13 1930
InVeR 1888;Je-D 1897;99-1901;03;06-14;17-24

BEDFORD

Bedford GAZETTE. w 1874-76||
MWA Je 15 1876

Bedford INDEPENDENT. w 1850-75||?
In Mr 27 1867

Bedford weekly MAGNET. w 1881-83||
InBM complete

Bedford weekly MAIL. w 1876-1919||
pub S 11 1884-1919
InU 1915-O 1919

Bedford MAIL. d 1892+
pub 1892+
In Ap 24,Ag 14 1896
InB Ap 6 1903[Ja-Mr 1907]Ap 28,N 10 1930;Ag 28 1931
InU N 1919-[Ja-Mr 1927]

Bedford PRESAGE. w
InVevHi D 7-21 1858;Ja 18-F 15,Mr 29,Ap 5, My 10 1859

Bedford daily TIMES. d 1892+
In F 1914+
InB N 16 1923;N 11 1930

Bedford TRANSCRIPT. w 1836-
In S 17-24 1836

WESTERN spy. w
InBM [1836]

WHITE River standard. w
In D 21 1854-D 20 1855

BERNE

Berne REVIEW. sw 1925+
pub 1925+

Berne WITNESS. tw 1896+
pub 1896+
InU 1914-17

BICKNELL

Bicknell BEACON. *See* Bicknell herald-news

Bicknell HERALD-NEWS. w 1895-
1895-99? as Bicknell beacon; 1900?-09? Bicknell news; 1910?-13? Knox county herald-news
In Je 13,27 1918

KNOX county herald-news. *See* Bicknell herald-news

Bicknell MONITOR. sw 1911-19||
pub Ap 1917-O 1 1919
In [Je-D 1918]

Bicknell NEWS. d 1919+
pub O 1919+
In D 31 1919+

Bicknell NEWS. w *See* Bicknell herald-news

BLOOMFIELD

Bloomfield DEMOCRAT. w 1863+
In 1888-94;Jl 1 1921;Je 20 1929
InBl [Mr 25 1887-F 18 1904]
InSpW Je 20 1929
InU Ap 1916-17
MWA Jl 29 1876

Bloomfield NEWS. w 1876+
pub 1876+
In Ja 29 1886;93;94;97+
InU 1914-15

BLOOMINGDALE

Bloomingdale WORLD. w 1890+
pub [Mr 1909+]
InRov 1928+

BLOOMINGTON

Bloomington COURIER. w,sw O 28 1875-1928||?
1875-94? as Saturday courier
w 1875-95?
In O 28 1875[1902]-[04]
InU 1881-92;94-1900;12-13;15-16

DEMOCRAT. w 1843-
In Jl 15 1843
InNcHi Mr 30 1844

Bloomington weekly EQUATOR. w
DLC My 8 1841

Bloomington HAWKEYE. w 1880-
InU Ja 10-Mr 3 1881

INDIANA (*Continued*)

BLOOMINGTON—*Continued*

Bloomington HERALD. w
In O 11 1845;Mr 23 1850

INDEPENDENT. ir
InU O-N 1913

INDEPENDENT whig. w Ja 2 1830-
CSmH My 14 1830
DLC Ja 9 1830;O 22 1831
InNcHi D 24 1831

***INDIANA gazette.** w N 1816-26||?
1816-S 15 1824 pub at Corydon
DLC 1821-S 15,N 1824-Ja 22 1825
In Ja 14-21,F 4,Ap 14,My 5,19,Je 9,Jl 21 1824
InI Ja 21,Mr 28,Ap 18,My 9,30,Je 27-Jl 4,18-25, Ag 8,N 13 1822;Je 25,Jl 9,30,S 24 1823;My 12, 26-Je 2,Jl 7,21-28,O 30-N,D 18 1824;Ja 1-8,F 19-26,Mr 12-19,Ap 5,9,23-30,My 14-28 1825
InNcHi Ap 1 1826
InRP Ja 15 1823
InU 1821[22]-[24]-Ja 22 1825
MBAt N 29 1821

INDIANA globe. w
In N 14 1845

INDIANA tribune and Monroe county farmer. w N 27 1847-
In 1847-Ap 20 1850

Bloomington JOURNAL. d 1914-15||
InU F 1914-S 1915

Bloomintgon NEWS-LETTER. w Ja 28 1854-
In My 26 1855
InNcHi Ja 28-F 4 1854

NORTHWESTERN gazette. w
In F 28 1853

Bloomington POST. w 1835-
DLC N 6 1840
In N 1835-37;Ja-F,My-S,N 2-9,D 7 1838;F 22, Mr 15-22,Je 14-N 15,D 29 1839[40;41]
InNcHi Je 25 1841

Bloomington PRESAGE. w
InVevHi Ag 21-S 4,18,O 9 1858

Bloomington PROGRESS. *See* Republican progress

Bloomington REPORTER. w
In N 9,D 14 1850;Ja 4 1851

Bloomington REPUBLICAN. w 1827-65||?
United with Bloomington progress to form Republican progress
In Ja 6,S 15-22,N 3 1827;Ag 28 1856;N 18 1865
InU [Ag 1858-60]

REPUBLICAN progress. w 1835-1900||
1835?-76? as Bloomington progress
InU My 1867-Je 1873;81-82;84-90;92-Mr 1900

Bloomington STAR. w 1890+
pub 1895+
InU [1896-98]1921+

Bloomington weekly TELEPHONE. w 1877-1922||
InU S 28 1878;81-84;86-95;97;O 1904-22

Bloomington daily TELEPHONE. d 1892+
InU 1923+

Bloomington WORLD. w,d 1892+
Title varies: Morning world; Evening world
w 1892-94
In Je 15 1893-94;F 11 1914+
InU D 1892-1900;03+
WaPS [1923-24]

BLUFFTON

Bluffton BANNER. w 1850-1917||?
CSmH Mr 20 1851
In Ja 16 1851;Ag 22 1862;Mr 6,Ag 21 1863;My 4-11,Ag 25 1865;Je 14 1893-94;97-Ja 3 1900; 03-Mr 8 1905
MWA Ag 18 1876

Bluffton CHRONICLE. w 1868-1918||?
MWA My 19 1876

Bluffton evening NEWS-BANNER. d 1888+
pub 1892+
In F 10 1914+
InU Mr 1918+

BOONVILLE

Boonville ENQUIRER. w 1850+
In D 13 1873;O 3 1874;F 22 1935+
InBoS 1870-1915

Boonville STANDARD. w 1875+
pub 1888+
In F 20 1914+
InU Mr 1923-O 1925

BORDEN

CLARK county sentinel. w 1893+
pub 1893+
MWA N 8,D 13-20 1895;Mr 27,Je 26 1896

BOSWELL

Boswell ENTERPRISE. w 1886+
pub 1913+

BOURBON

Bourbon MIRROR. *See* Bourbon news-mirror

Bourbon NEWS. sw 1894-99||?
United with Bourbon mirror to form Bourbon news-mirror

Bourbon NEWS-mirror. w 1871+
1871-1900? as Bourbon mirror
InPmM D 1872+
MWA My 25 1876

BOWLING GREEN

CLAY county democrat. w
InVevHi Ap 23,My 7,Je 18,Jl 30,N 26,D 16 1858;Ap 21 1859;F 8-29,Mr 28,My 16 1860

BRAZIL

CLAY county enterprise. w 1872-1926||?
InU 1914-15
MWA Jl 20 1876

Brazil DEMOCRAT. w 1880-1921||?
In Jl 1907-15

Brazil ECHO. w 1873-76||
In Jl 22 1875;Ja 13 1876

Brazil GAZETTE. w 1922+
pub 1922+
In S 27 1935+

Brazil daily NEWS. d 1888-1919||?
United with Brazil daily times to form Brazil daily times and news

Brazil daily TIMES and news. d 1888+
1888-1919? as Brazil daily times
pub Ag 5 1932+
In Jl 12 1907+
InBr S 28-O 4,16 1933

BREMEN

Bremen ENQUIRER. w 1884+
pub 1885+
InPmM Ap 24 1884+

BRISTOL

Bristol BANNER. w Ap 6 1877+
pub [1877+]
In F-Je 7,S 13 1918;F 22 1935+
InGoE 1878-79

BROOK

Brook REPORTER. w 1895+
pub 1895+
In Jl 5-12,S 27,O 18,N,D 13-27 1933
InBro [1912-25]+

BROOKVILLE

Brookville AMERICAN. w 1832+
1832-57? as Indiana American
In [Ap-D 1834]Ja 2,23-F 6 1835;Ag 5,S 2-9, 30-O,14,D,23 1836;Ja 18-25 1839;Ag 19-26 1842; D 29 1843-50;Ja 31 1851;Je 11 1852-O 23 1857; Jl 2-16 1858;O 19 1866;Je 17 1870;O 3 1878;N 11 1886;O 3 1889;Je 30 1892;1901+
InBrok 1917-19;22+
InBrokF [1834+]
InLoHi Jl 19-26,Ag-O 2,18-N 22,D 6,20 1833; Ja 3,17,F-Mr 7,21,Ap 4-11 1834
InVevHi N 5,26,D 17 1858;Ja 14,F 11,Mr 4,D 23 1859;Ja 20,Mr 2,16 1860
MWA F 15 1867;F 25 1870;Je 8 1893
PPL N 22 1850

Brookville DEMOCRAT. w 1838+
In Ap 30 1841;S 15 1848;D 23 1859;My 10,Ag 2, N 15,D 6 1861;F 6-13 1863;Je 24-Jl 1,D 23 1864;D 23-31 1869;Ap 9 1874;O 3 1889;97+
InBrok 1917-19;22+
InBrokF [1859+]
InNcHi F 12 1913
OOxM Ja 17 1895-[1900]Ja 10,O 31,N 14-28,D 26 1901[02-12]-[15-20]-[22-23]-[25-27]-[29-32]-Ag 17 1933

Brookville ENQUIRER. *See* Franklin repository

FRANKLIN democrat. w 1838-
DLC Ap 12 1844

***FRANKLIN repository.** w F 5 1819-
1819-F 18 1820 as Brookville enquirer and Indiana telegraph; Mr 1820-S 1824 Brookville enquirer; O 16-23 1824 Brookville inquirer; O 30 1824-O 4 1825 Brookville inquirer and Franklin republican
DLC 1821-26;28
IU 1821-O 4 1825
InI Ap 2,30 1822;Mr 19 1823

INDIANA American. *See* Brookville American

Brookville INQUIRER. *See* Franklin repository

NATIONAL defender. w 1862-
In My 2 1862;F 5,Je 17 1864

PEOPLE'S friend. w 1837-
In F 24 1837

VALLEY sentinel. w 1878-80||
In My 21 1880

WESTERN agriculturalist and general intelligencer. w 1829-
DLC S 5-19,O 10,N 12-24,D 16 1829;Ja 16 1830

BROWNSBURG

Brownsburg RECORD. w 1882+
InBrow 1922+

BROWNSTOWN

Brownstown BANNER. w 1869+
pub Ag 26 1869;71+
In N 12 1896;Ja 1-15,29-F 12,Ag 27 1919;20+
InU N 1870-87;91+
MWA Je 22 1876

JACKSON county advocate. w
InBrwB Je 2 1849

JACKSON county democrat. w Ap 13 1852-
MWA O 19 1852

JACKSON union. w
InBrwB O 16 1862
InVevHi N 25 1858;Mr 10,My 5-12 1859

BROWNSVILLE

FLYING roll. w F 17 1825-
DLC Mr 3 1825
IU Mr 3 1825(photostat)

BUNKER HILL

INDEPENDENT press. *See* Bunker Hill press

Bunker Hill NEWS. w 1873-75||
1873-74 as Our village news
In Je 21 1873

OUR village news. *See* Bunker Hill news

Bunker Hill PRESS. w 1875+
1875-79? as Independent press
pub 1905+
In Mr 28 1878

BURNETTSVILLE

Burnettsville NEWS. w 1907+
pub N 21 1907+

BUTLER

DEKALB county herald. *See* Record-herald

Butler RECORD. w 1877-1928||
United with DeKalb county record to form Record-herald

RECORD-HERALD. w 1869+
1869-1928 as DeKalb county herald
pub 1929+
InBu 1895-1929

CAMBRIDGE CITY

Cambridge City BULLETIN. w 1855-
InRP Mr 5,S 10,O 15 1859;Ja 5,Je 7-14 1860

Cambridge City FLAG of the free. w 1860-
InRP O 4 1860

INDIANA bulletin. w 1856-
InRP Ja 1 1856;F 12 1857

Cambridge City JOURNAL. w
InRP D 1 1865

NATIONAL road traveler. w 1908+
1908-09? as Lewisville freeman
1908-26? pub in Lewisville
pub 1931+
InNcHi Mr 26 1925
MWA Mr 8 1935

Cambridge City NEWS. w
InI Mr 30 1853
InRP D 20 1854

Cambridge REVEILLE. w 1845-
In 1847[48]Ja 6,20,F,Mr 10,Ap 7-14,My 5,O 29, N 24-D 8,22 1849-50
InI My 12 1847
InRP My 5 1849

Cambridge City REVIEW. w 1873-76||
In O 4-11,25-N 8,22 1876

Cambridge City TRIBUNE. w Ja 12 1866+
1866-68 as Western mirror
pub 1866+
In Ja 24 1867
InC 1913+
InNcHi N 8 1866;Ag 20 1868
OClWHi Ap 5 1866

WESTERN mirror. *See* Cambridge City tribune

CAMDEN

Camden EXPOSITOR. *See* Camden record-news

Camden RECORD-NEWS. w 1880+
1880-1912? as Camden expositor; 1913?-24? Camden record
In S 26 1935+

CAMPBELLSBURG

Campbellsburg GRAPHIC. w 1888-1933||
pub 1931-Ja 1933

CANNELTON

Cannelton ECONOMIST. *See* Cannelton reporter

Cannelton ENQUIRER. w 1870-1925||?
1876?-87? as Enquirer and reporter
In Jl 29 1871
MWA Jl 22 1871

ENQUIRER and reporter. *See* Cannelton enquirer

INDIANA weekly express. w
InU D 6 1851;Mr 27,Ap-Jl 17,31,Ag 21-28,S 11-O 9,23,N 6,20-D 25 1852;Ja 8-F 19,Mr-Ap 2,16 1853

Cannelton MERCURY. w
InU Ja 20-Mr 3 1855

Cannelton REPORTER. w 1849-76||?
1849-N 1851 as Cannelton economist. United with Cannelton enquirer to form Cannelton enquirer and reporter, later Cannelton enquirer
InU Ap 1849-76
InVevHi Je 19,Ag 7,S 11,O 30,N 20 1858
NN Ja 19 1850

INDIANA (*Continued*)

CANNELTON—*Continued*

REPUBLICAN banner. w
InU Ag 16-23, S 6-13 1856

Cannelton TELEPHONE. w 1891+
In Je 9 1933+
InCanP 1891+
InU 1914-32

CARLINVILLE

Carlinville SPECTATOR. w 1855-
PWpCo Ja 14 1859-My 1861

CARLISLE

Carlisle NEWS. w 1895+
InCa 1915+

CARTHAGE

Carthage CITIZEN. w 1907+
InCar My 17 1907+

Carthage RECORD. w 1888-My 25 1906||
InCar Jl 19 1895;Ja 29 1904;F 10 1905-06

CAYUGA

Cayuga HERALD. w 1890+
pub 1893+

CENTREVILLE

DOLLAR news-letter. w 1846-
In My 9,26,Je 6-13,Jl 18 1846

FREE territory sentinel. *See* Indiana true democrat

INDIANA true democrat. w Ag 16 1848-D 23 1852||
1848-D 26 1849 as Free territory sentinel
DLC S 30 1852
In 1848-D 16 1852
InI Ja 9 1850-52
InNcHi Ja 10 1849;O 11,N 15,D 5,19 1850;Mr 22,N 20 1851;S 9 1852;F 3 1853
MWA Jl 10 1850;D 23 1852

INDIANA true republican. w Je 17 1858-
In 1858-N 21 1872
InNcHi Mr 5,14 1859;F 25 1864
OClWHi Jl 1862-Je 1864
WHi Mr 31 1864

NATIONAL patriot. w Ja 1 1840-
DLC Ja 29,Ap 22,O 28 1840
In F 12,26-Mr 4,Ap 1-8,My 6,Jl 8,Ag 5,19-S 2,O 14,28,N 18-25,D 9-23 1840

OLD trails echo. w 1915+
InCe 1929—
InNcHi Mr 4 1926

PEOPLE'S advocate. w Ja 2 1835-
IU My 22 1835
In Ja 9,Mr 13-20,Ap 17,My 1,Je 5,Jl 10,31, Ag 21,S 18,O 9,N 20 1835;Ja 8,29-F 5,Mr 11, 25,Ag 27,S 30 1836
InRP S 11 1835

WAYNE county chronicle. w
In Mr 24,Je 16,S 28 1837;F 14,Ag 8 1838;S 4 1839
InNcHi Jl 14 1837

WAYNE county chronicle. w 1871-79||?
In S 5,O 17 1874;Ja 9 1875;Ag 26,S 16,30,O 21, N 11-18 1876

WAYNE county record. w D 11 1840-
In [1840-My 1848]
InNcHi N 22 1843
MWA S 15 1841

WAYNE county whig. w 1840-
In Jl 26 1846;S 13,O 11-18,N 29,D 13,27 1848-Ja 3,F 14,Mr 7 1849

WESTERN emporium. w Ap 9 1824-
DLC Ap 24,My 8-29 1824
In Ap 30 1825
InI Jl 3,D 18 1824;Ja 7-15,F 5-12,26,Mr 12-Ap 2 1825
PDoHi Jl 4 1828

WESTERN times. w Ag 21 1828-
CSmH Jl 24 1830
DLC Jl 25,Ag 8,22,S 5-12,26,O 24,D 12-17 1829;Ja 2,16,D 11-18 1830;Ja 8 1831;Je 14 1833
ICHi D 4 1830
In Ag 28-S 5 19-O 3,31,D 13-20 1828;Ja 10, 24,F 7,21-Mr 21,Ap 4-18,My 2-9,23-30,Je 13-Jl 18,Ag 8-S,N 21-D 1829;S 21 1832;Ja 3 1834
InCe O 3 1828
InNcHi Ag 3 1833
InRP N 7 1829;N 9 1832;Je 28 1833
MWA O 3 1828

CHARLESTOWN

CITIZEN-RECORD. w 1869-1919||
1869-97? as Clark county record (1888?-90? Indiana state record); 1898-Jl 1907? Hoosier democrat; Ag 1907?-N 8 1912 Hoosier record
In F 24 1853;O 9 1886;My 20 1893-94;Mr 27 1897;D 23 1898-1906;08-09;11-D 23 1915
InU 1915-O 1919

CLARK county citizen. w 1895-N 1912||?
United with Hoosier record to form Citizen-record
In O 24,N 14,D 5 1902;Ja 9,23,F 27,Jl 10 1903;N 17 1905;Je 8,Jl 6 1906;Jl 1907

CLARK county record. *See* Citizen-record

CLARK county republican. w 1894-1903||
1894-1901 as Charleston hustler
In Mr 9 1899;O 23 1902;Ja 29,F 26 1903

FARMERS and mechanics' advocate. w
DLC Ag 23 1828
In N 10,24,D 22 1827

Charlestown HERALD. w 1875-78||?
MWA Je 16,Jl 21 1876

HOOSIER democrat. *See* Citizen-record

HOOSIER record. *See* Citizen-record

Charleston HUSTLER. *See* Clark county republican

INDIANA banner. w
In N 29 1848

INDIANA intelligencer. w Jl 27 1820-
InI Ap 5,19,My 3-10,24,Je 20-27,Ag 15,O 31-N 7,D 12 1821;Ja 2,16,F 20,Ap 10-17,My 3-17,Je 5-12,Jl 24-Ag 7,23,O 23,N 6 1822;Mr 5,Je 4, 18-Jl 9,O 8 1823;My 22-29,D 4 1824;Ja 3,15-22, F 26,Mr 12-Ap 2,My 7,28-Je 18 1825

INDIANA mirror. w 1849-
In O 10 1850

INDIANA state record. *See* Citizen-record

INDIANIAN. *See* Southern Indianian

PEOPLES gazette. w 1840-
DLC Ap 3,My 27,Jl 15 1841
In My 20,Je 24,Ag 12,S 2,N 4 1841

REPUBLICAN statesman. w
DLC D 26 1829-Ja 2 1830
In Mr 21 1829

SOUTHERN Indianian. w 1836-
1836-Ag 19 1840 as Indianian
DLC Ja 22,Mr-Ap 1,15-Je 3,17-Jl 8,29-Ag 12, 26-S 2,23-30 1840;F 10,Mr 3-10,24 Ap 7,Je 30 1841
In N 6 1839;D 23 1840;Ja 22 1845

SPIRIT of progress. w 1848-
InSHi Mr 4 1850

CHESTERTON

Chesterton TRIBUNE. w 1884+
pub S 2 1884+
In 1901-Ag 5 1904;Ap 5 1934
InG 1924-31

CHURUBUSCO

Churubusco TRUTH. w 1882+
1882-99? as Saturday truth
pub Mr 15 1882;1930+

Saturday TRUTH. *See* Churubusco truth

CICERO

Cicero GAZETTE. w 1874-78||?
In F 1,Ap 26 1877
InNoR 1876-Ag 1877

NEW ERA. w 1871-75||?
InNoR N 1872-75

CLAY CITY

Clay City NEWS. w 1912+
pub Ag 8 1912+

CLINTON

Clinton Saturday ARGUS. w 1882-1922| ?
InU 1915-17

CLINTONIAN. w 1890-1918||?
InCl 1901-04

CLINTONIAN. d 1912+
In Je 12 1934+
InCl 1924+

Clinton EXPONENT. w 1874-77||?
MWA Jl 8 1876

CLOVERDALE

Cloverdale GRAPHIC. w 1894+
pub Mr 13 1896;Ja 6-13 1905;Mr 21 1913;16+

COATSVILLE

Coatsville HERALD. w 1910+
pub 1910+
InU Jl 25 1929+

COLFAX

CLINTON county review. w 1881+
1881-1916 as Clinton standard
InCo [1917+]

CLINTON standard. *See* Clinton county review

COLUMBIA CITY

Columbia City COMMERCIAL-MAIL. w 1869-1920||
1869-76 as Whitley county commercial; 1876-1904 Columbia City commercial
pub 1871-1920
In O 5 1876
InCoC Ap 1918-Je 1920

Columbia City COMMERCIAL mail. d 1889+
1889-1904 as Columbia City commercial
pub 1889+
InCocW 1905-29

Columbia City NEWS. w
InCocHi Ap 30 1861

Columbia City POST. w 1853-1928|
pub 1865-1928
In Je 23 1869;My 14-Je 11 1884
InCocHi N 25 1868
InCocW 1865-1928

Columbia City POST. d 1895+
pub 1895+
In 1928-Ap 15 1930;34+
InCoC 1917-20;22+
InCocW 1895+

WHITLEY county commercial. *See* Columbia City commercial-mail

WHITLEY county news. w
InCocP 1859-64

WHITLEY county republican. w
In Ja 30 1868
InCocHi D 14 1865
InCocW 1864-1870

WHITLEY pioneer. w
InCocHi [D 1855-D 6 1856]

COLUMBUS

Columbus ADVOCATE. w
DLC Mr 8 1839
In Mr 10 1841

BARTHOLOMEW democrat. *See* Columbus democrat

Columbus BULLETIN. w 1867-
In O 14-21 1870

Columbus DEMOCRAT. w 1870-84||?
1870-76 as Bartholomew democrat
In S 29 1871;O 25 1872;Mr 20,Je 26 1874;F 18,Mr 31,Ap 14 1876
MWA Jl 21,Ag 18 1876

Daily DEMOCRAT. d 1877-84| ?
InCol 1879-82

Columbus GAZETTE. w
In D 9 1846

Columbus HERALD. w 1881+
In O 19 1883;Je 30 1893-94;D 11 1896
InCol Je 1911-18

Columbus HERALD. d 1882+
CLM F 15 1892

INDIANA democrat. w
InVevHi O 7 1858

Columbus NEWS. w
InVevHi Mr 5-12,26-Ap 2 1859;Mr 3 1860

Columbus NEWS. w 1886-87||
InCol [F 8-Je 9 1887]

REPUBLICAN. w,sw 1872-1918|?
sw 1894?-95?
In Ap 8 1880-81;Ap 5 1883-94;97-1915
InCol Mr 28 1878-Mr 18 1880;82-Mr 22 1888;98
MWA Je 22 1876
WHi F 2 1895

Evening REPUBLICAN. d N 12 1877+
pub 1877+
In 1877-87;Jl 11 1907+
InCol 1877-89;94+
InU 1914-Jl 1918

CONNERSVILLE

ADVERTISER. w Je 10 1876-
MWA D 30 1876-Ja 13,27,F 10 1877

COURIER. w 1899-1910||
In 1909-Mr 11 1910
InConM Ag 24 1899-1901;03-10

Connersville EXAMINER. w 1857-1919||
In N 20 1877
InCon 1889-Ja 13 1898;Ap 5 1906;Je 30,S 30,O 10 1913;S 15 1914;Ja 11,Jl 22 1915-19
MWA Jl 12 1876

Connersville EXAMINER. d 1887-1919||
United with Connersville news to form Connersville news-examiner

FAYETTE and union telegraph. *See* Connersville telegraph

FAYETTE county democrat. sw Jl 1 1933+
pub 1933+
InCon Ag 17 1934+

FAYETTE observer. w 1826-
DLC My 5 1827
In Jl 29-S 9,23,O 14-N,D 9 1826;Ja 6,27,F 17,Ap 14-My 19,Je 23-30,Jl 21-S 3,O-D 1827
MWA S 1 1827
PDoHi Jl 12 1828

FREE press. d 1924-26||
InCon O 24,D 1924-Mr 17 1923

INDIANA sentinel. w
In Ag 23 1834
InI Je 2 1832
InNcHi D 29 1832
N O 12 1833

INDIANA statesman. w 1823-
DLC Ja 10 1824

INDIANA telegraph. w Je 11 1841-
DLC Je 11,Ag 6 1841
In D 10 1846;Mr 16-D 1848

Connersville NEWS-EXAMINER. d 1887+
1887-1919 as Connersville news
pub 1887-Je 8 1888;Je 10 1893-Je 8 1894
In F 7 1914-Je 1916;34+
InCon F 20,Ap 18 1907;13+

POLITICAL clarion. w My 22 1830-
DLC Ag 7,21,D 4 1830;Ja 8 1831
In Je 12,Jl 17-24,O 9,N 6 1830;Mr 19,Ap 9-16, 30,O 8 1831;Ap 7 1832

SPIRIT of the times. w
InI Ag 2 1849

INDIANA (*Continued*)

CONNERSVILLE—*Continued*

SPIRIT of the valley. w
In D 10 1846

Connersville TELEGRAPH. w 1854-
1854-Jl 13 1860 as Fayette and union telegraph
DLC Ja 6-13,F 10,24,Mr 9,23-Ap 20,Je 8,22-29, Jl 13-20,S 7 1860
In Ap 25 1856;My 20 1859;D 4 1860
InVevHi Je 18,Jl 26,O 1,N 26,D 3,17 1858;D 9 1859;F 24,Ap 13 1860
Tx N 2 1860

Connersville weekly TIMES. w 1850-1917||?
InCon O 24 1867-My 17 1871;N 1881-89;O 24 1900
InConN S 21 1854-S 11 1856;O 17 1861-Ja 1866; O 24 1867-Jl 6 1875;N 17 1881-82;87;Je 25 1888-Je 8 1893
InNcHi Jl 26 1877
MWA O 26 1865
OClWHi Ja 2 1862

VILLAGE press. w D 2 1824-
DLC D 2 1824

WATCHMAN. w My 31 1834-
In [My 31 1834-Jl 11]N 7 1835[36-Je 1837] D 6 1839
InI N 12 1836

CONVERSE

Converse JOURNAL. w 1883+
pub 1884+

CORYDON

Corydon DEMOCRAT. w 1856+
pub 1897+
In Ja 28 1879;S 5 1882;F 29 1887;Ja 1 1897; 1933+
InSHi Ja 1 1897
InVevHi Mr 8,Ap 5,My 10,N 22 1859;Ja 3, 24,F 7-14,Mr 6-13,Ap 17,My 15 1860
MWA Mr 9 1874

HARRISON democrat. w 1857-
In Je 23 1857
InVevHi My 11,S 7,O 5,N 9,23 1858

HARRISON gazette. w
In Ag 21 1845;O 24 1848;Ja 21 1851
PPL N 19 1850

INDIANA gazette. *See under* Bloomington

INVESTIGATOR. w S 3 1835-
DLC S 10 1835-Ja 24 1839

Corydon REPUBLICAN. w 1868+
pub [1868-85]+
In D 17 1874;97-1900;03+
MWA Je 23 1870
WaPS [1923]

SOUTHERN Indianian. w 1847-
In F 15 1848

WESTERN argus. w 1851-
In O 14,28 1851;D 13 1853

COVINGTON

FOUNTAIN democrat. w 1854-
In Ja 3 1855

Covington FRIEND. w N 1841+
1841-88? as Peoples' friend
pub 1841+
DLC Ja 1 1842;F 10-24,Mr 17,Ap 7-My 12,26-Jl 7,21,Ag 4-11,25-S,O 13-20,N 1,24 1849;Mr 15 1871
In N 7 1846;47[48]50;My 17 1851;Jl 22 1880
MWA My 12 1876

PEOPLES' friend. *See* Covington friend

PEOPLE'S paper. *See* Covington republican

Covington REPUBLICAN. w 1873+
1873-90? as Spence's people's paper; 1891?-94? People's paper
pub 1898-1913;19+
In 1932+
InU 1916-Ja 5 1917
MWA Je 29,Jl 27 1876

SPENCE'S people's paper. *See* Covington republican

WESTERN constellation. w Jl 18 1834-
In Jl 18-O 10,31-D 1834;Ja 2-F 6,My 16-Ag 22, S,N 6,20 1835-Jl 22,Ag-N 4,D 8-22 1836; Ja 12-F 2,16,Mr 2-16,Ap 6,20,My 11,Je 1-8 1837

Covington WHIG. w
In N 24,D 8 1838

CRAWFORDSVILLE

Evening ARGUS. d 1882-85||
United with Crawfordsville news to form Crawfordsville argus-news
InCr complete

Crawfordsville ARGUS-NEWS. d 1878-1900||
1878-85 as Crawfordsville news
InCr 1886-1900

Crawfordsville ARGUS-NEWS. w 1889-99||
InCr 1890-95
InCrM 1890-99

INDIANA record. w O 18 1831-
1831-33 as Record
DLC My 29 1833;N 28 1840
In O 18 1831
NN O 18 1831
MWA Ap 4 1840

Crawfordsville JOURNAL. w 1848-1918||
1848-56 as Montgomery journal; 1857-Ap 18? 1874 Crawfordsville journal; Ap 25 1874-87 Saturday evening journal
CSmH Mr 20 1862
In N 8-15 1849;N 14 1850;Jl 25 1861;Mr 19 1863;My 12 1864;Ag 1,N 28 1874;D 21 1878;Jl 2,S 24 1881;O 19 1894;Ap 1903-18
InCr Ap 16 1868-72;Ap-D 1874;77-1918
InCrM Je 8 1854-F 14,Ag 21-28,1856;Mr 12 1857-S 10 1863;S 14 1865-69;72-77;80-88;90-1917
M O 1 1881
MWA Ap 9 1863;Je 2 1864
OClWHi D 4 1856

Saturday evening JOURNAL. *See* Crawfordsville journal

Crawfordsville JOURNAL and review. d 1887+
1887-O 12? 1929 as Crawfordsville journal
In Ap 1903+
InCr 1887+
InCrM O 19 1929-31
InU 1916;18+

Crawfordsville LOCOMOTIVE. w 1851-
In O 28 1854
InCrM Je 25 1853-Ap 27 1855

Saturday MERCURY. w 1875-77||
InCrM O 1875-S 15 1877

MONTGOMERY journal. *See* Crawfordsville journal

Crawfordsville NEWS. *See* Crawfordsville argus-news

NEWS-REVIEW. *See* Crawfordsville weekly review

PEOPLE'S press. w My 11 1844-
DLC My 11-18 1844
In O 3 1845;N 12,26 1847

RECORD. *See* Indiana record

Crawfordsville weekly REVIEW. w 1841-1918||?
1899-1907 as News-review
CSmM Mr 1 1862
DLC F 28 1874
In D 28 1850;O 30 1852;Jl 7 1883
InCrM Je 18 1853-Ap 23,Jl 16-23 1859;Ap 28 1860-74;Je 1875-81;83-My 1884;85-88;90-1901; 04-07;11-18
InVevHi O 9,N 13-20,D 4 1858;Ja 1,F 19,Mr 26,D 10 1859;Ja 21,F 4,18,Mr 3,Ap 21,My 12 1860
MWA My 20 1876

Crawfordsville daily REVIEW. d 1882-1929||
United with Crawfordsville journal to form Crawfordsville journal and review
InCrM 1919-22;24-25;27-29

Crawfordsville Sunday STAR. w 1872-1903||
In Ag 4 1874
InCrM F 1872-1903
MWA Jl 27 1876

CROWN POINT

LAKE county herald. w Je 7 1876-
MWA Je 14 1876

LAKE county Jeffersonian. w
NjR S 6 1860

LAKE county star. w 1873+
In Mr 11 1881;1932+
InCp Mr 28 1908+
InG Ap 28 1882-Ap 1884;Ap-D 1887;My 24 1889-Ja 10 1890;My 24 1895-O 6 1899;1901+

Crown Point REGISTER. w 1857+
In Mr 31,S 1 1864;N 29 1888;1928-33
InCp D 25 1919+
InG N 13,27,D 11-18 1913;Ja 8-15,F 26-Mr 12,Ap 9-30,N 12 1914;F-Mr 4,25,My 6-20,Jl 15 1915;Ja 13-Mr 9,Ag 17 1916-O 11 1917;F 7 1918;N 13 1919+
MWA Jl 20 1876

CULVER

Culver CITIZEN. w 1903+
pub 1903+
In Je 1934+

Culver City HERALD. w 1896-1902||
InCuC S 24 1897;S 7 1900
InPmM complete

CYNTHIANA

Cynthiana ARGUS. w 1889+
pub [1893-94]+
In F 1935+

DALE

Dale REPORTER. w 1885+
pub S 11 1885+
InSmA O 28 1932

DANVILLE

Danville weekly ADVERTISER. w 1846-
In [Jl 15 1848-53]
WHi O 5 1850

Danville BULLETIN. w
In My 13 1857

Danville GAZETTE. w S 14 1880+
1880-99? as Hendricks county gazette
pub S 14 1880-S 6 1881;1900+
In N 27,D 11 1884;Mr 20 1890
InDH 1911+

HENDRICKS county advertiser and ledger. 1846-
InDH 1854-64

HENDRICKS county democrat. w 1878-
InDG F 19 1878-S 2 1879

HENDRICKS county gazette. *See* Danville gazette

HENDRICKS county ledger. w O 9 1857-
In O 9,D 11 1857;Ap 7,21,Je 9,S 1,N 10 1858

HENDRICKS county republican. w O 13 1881+
1893?-1910? as Danville republican
pub 1900+
In Ap 6 1882;F 28 1884;Ja 8-Mr 12,My 21,Je 4-18,Jl,Ag 13-20,S 3,17-24 1885;Ap 1 1886; 1914+
InDH 1880+
InU 1918+

HENDRICKS county union. w Ap 23 1856-83||
In F 16,Mr 30,Ap 20,Jl 27 1865;Ja 18,F 8,22, Mr 8 1866;Mr 24 1870;Jl 27, S 14,N 23-30,D 21 1871;Ap 18,S 5 1872;Ag 14-21,S 11,25,N 13-20,D 25 1873;Ja 22-29,F 12,Mr 5,My 28,Je 11, 18,Jl 16-23,S 10,O 8-15,D 10 1874;F 4,Mr 11, Je 24,Jl 15 1875;Ag 31,S 21,O 19,N 16 1876;F 22,O 4-11,D 27 1877-Ja 3,Mr 14,Ap 4,Ag 22, S 5,O 3 1878;Ap 3 1879;D 15 1881;S 6,O 4,25 1883
InDH 1861-79
MWA Je 8-15 1876

Weekly INDIANIAN. w 1871-78||?
MWA Je 1 1876

Danville PROGRESS. w
In Ag 23 1883

DARLINGTON

Darlington HERALD. w 1889+
pub 1916+

DAYTON

Dayton SQUARE dealer. w 1878-84||?
InLHi Ja 13 1883

DECATUR

ADAMS county democratic press. w 1894-96||
InDeD O 1894-Ag 20 1896

Decatur DEMOCRAT. w 1857-1917||
1857-74? as Decatur eagle
pub F 13 1857-My 6 1859;1881-82;Ag 26 1896-1917
In [1870-92]
InVevHi N 10,24,D 8,29 1858;F 9,Ap 20 1859
MWA My 10 1876
NNHi N 11 1870

Decatur DEMOCRAT. d 1903+
pub 1903+
In F 4 1914+
InU 1915-Mr 1919[N 1926-Mr 1927]

Decatur EAGLE. *See* Decatur democrat

Decatur JOURNAL. w 1879-1912||?
In Ap 9 1880

DELPHI

CARROLL county citizen. *See* Delphi citizen

CARROLL express. w 1841-
In O 30 1841;Ap 10,Je 5,O 10 1844;Mr 22,Ap 5-19,Ag 16,S 13 1845;F 24,Mr 3,31 1846;Ap 24,O 9 1847;S 16,O 1,21 1848
InIB Je 18 1842;Je 10 1843
OClWHi Mr 17 1846

Delphi CITIZEN. w 1892+
1892-95 as Carroll county citizen; 1896-1920 Carroll county citizen-times
pub 1892+
In Mr 30 1895;N 21 1896;Mr 26 1898;1932+
InU Mr 1918+

Delphi HERALD. w
In My 5,O 31,N 7 1849

Delphi JOURNAL. w 1850+
pub 1900+
In N 14 1850-Ag 25 1886;My 1 1890;D 15 1892; Jl 18 1907-09
InCr Ag 1865-66
MWA Jl 5 1876

NEWS-letter. w 1885-86||
In Ap 10 1886

Delphi ORACLE. w 1836-
In Mr 18 1837;S 8 1838;O 28,D 9,25 1843;Mr 9,23,O 18 1844;Jl 12,O 18 1845;F 14 1846
IU O 7,21,N 11,D 23 1843;Ja 6,20-27,F 10 1844

Delphi TIMES. w 1848-94||
United with Carroll county citizen to form Carroll county citizen-times, later Delphi citizen
In Ap 28-My 5,N 3-10 1849;My 2-9,Ap 20 1850;Ja 11,Ap 2,Jl 12,N 8-15 1851;F 7,28,Ap 24 1852;O 28 1853;N 3 1854;My 12 1857;O 2 1858;My 28,Je 25,O 8 1859;My 12 1860;N 2 1861;N 1,D 27 1862;Je 20 1863;Ag 18 1865;F 16,Ag 17 1866;F 15,Jl 26,Ag 23 1867;F 12-19 1869;Ag 12-19 1870;F 17 1871;Ag 16:30 1872;S 7 1877;Jl 9 1880;Je 16 1893-94
InDelC 1857-58;61-63;80-91
MWA Jl 7 1876
P-M Ja 3 1855

WESTERN banner. w
In O 22 1836

WESTERN republican. w
In D 19 1846;Mr 27,Ap 10,24 1847;O 21 1848

DEMOTTE

KANKAKEE Valley post. w 1929+
In Ag 10,O 26-D 7,28 1933

INDIANA (*Continued*)

DENVER

Denver SUN. w 1883-96||
InDenT [1890-96]

Denver TRIBUNE. w 1897+
pub [1897-1908]+

DUBLIN

Dublin TIMES. w 1875-
In My 5-19,Je 2,23-Jl 14 1875

WAYNE register. w 1875-1910||
In Ja 7,Ag 27 1876

DUNKIRK

Dunkirk NEWS. w 1899+
pub 1928+
In S 1935+

DUNRIETH

Dunrieth RECORD. w O 14 1909-
InNcHi N 12 1909

DYER

LAKE county globe-ledger. w 1929+
In Jl 13,O 26,N 16,D 14 1933+
InG D 15 1932-F 23,My 25,Je 29-D 1933

EAST CHICAGO

CALUMET news. sw 1923+
pub [1923-26]+
In Ap 20,27,My 11,25,Je 15 1934+
InEc [1924]+
InWh O 4 1929

GLOBE. w 1891-1921||?
InEc F 21-28 1919;20

INDIANA courier. *See* East Chicago press

East Chicago PRESS. d 1914-
1914-15? as Indiana courier
In N 12 1914
InG S 12-N 27 1914

SENTINEL. d
InEc Jl-S 1922

EAST GARY

Papers published in East Gary are listed under Gary

EDINBURG

Edinburg COURIER. d 1890+
InEd 1930+

INDIANA visitor. w
InVevHi Mr 26 1859

ELKHART

Elkhart DEMOCRAT. *See* Elkhart sentinel

DEMOCRATIC union. *See* Elkhart sentinel

Elkhart DEMOCRATIC-SENTINEL. *See* Elkhart sentinel

Elkhart JACKSONIAN. w Ap 10 1863-
MWA Ap 10 1863

Elkhart MONITOR. w 1882-83||
InGoE 1882-Ag 24 1883

Elkhart OBSERVER. w Ag 21 1872-Ag 25 1875||
InEl complete
InGoE complete

Elkhart PROGRESSIVE democrat. d
InU F-My 1914

Elkhart REVIEW. w,sw 1859-1910||
w 1859-96?
In Je 17 1895[1904]-09
InEl Jl 1896-1910
InElT complete
InGoE Ja 7 1860;My 23 1872-Ja 1881;82-Ap 1910
MWA Mr 26 1864

Elkhart evening REVIEW. d 1872-1920||
In [1918]
InEl 1910-18
InElT 1910-20
MWA Jl 18 1876

Elkhart SENTINEL. w -S 14 1883||
United with Elkhart democrat to form Elkhart democratic sentinel, later Elkhart sentinel
InGoE Ag 31-S 14 1883

Elkhart SENTINEL. w 1866-90||
1866-79 as Democratic union; 1880-S 14 1883 Elkhart democrat; S 21 1883-85 Elkhart democratic-sentinel
InGoE My 1872-N 14 1873;74-Mr 9,My 23 1879-Jl 23 1880;S 21-D 1883;D 19 1885-F 6 1890
MWA My 2 1873
TxU Mr 10-17,S 27 1871

Elkhart TRUTH. d 1889+
In Jl 13 1907-Je 26 1917;Je 12 1934+
InEl 1904+
InGoE F 13 1890-S 29 1910
MWA N 19-21 1890

Elkhart TRUTH. w 1889-1910||?

ELLETSVILLE

Elletsville FARM. w 1882+
1882-94? as Monroe county citizen
InSpW D 15 1932

MONROE county citizen. *See* Elletsville farm

ELWOOD

Elwood CALL leader. d 1891+
pub 1891+
In My 11,N 21 1934+
InElw Je 1904+

FREE press. w 1885-1914||?
InElw [1893-1909]

Elwood PRESS. d 1892-96||
In N 13 1892
InElw [1893-96]

Elwood RECORD. d 1892-1919||?
InElw [Je 1897-Ag 1911]

Elwood REVIEW. w 1876-85||?
In Mr 22 1878;My 15-29 1880

ENGLISH

CRAWFORD County democrat. w 1879+
In 1934+
InU Je 1920-Ja 1922

English NEWS. w 1889+
In 1900-15

EVANSVILLE

Evansville COURIER. d O 4 1865+
DLC Jl 4 1874;Jl 9-16,D 20 1876;O 7 1877
ICHi O 4-6 1865
ICM Ap 9,18,30 1880
In Jl 1871-72;Ja 8 1876;Je 10 1877;D 4-5 1887;Ap 1903+
InEv Ja 31,F 14,27[My-Je]Jl 5,N 27 1881;My 1898;My 14,28,Je 19,Jl 16,Ag 6,20,O 1,D 17 1899;My 1 1909-20;25+
InEva N 1878+
InMov My 23 1886
InMovHi S 14 1916;Ja 6 1933
InSmA O 15 1896
MWA N 14 1865;Jl 2 1916;Ja 7 1917;Ja 6 1918

Evansville COURIER. w *See* Ohio Valley courier

Evansville daily DISPATCH. d
NN Mr 6 1865

Evansville ENQUIRER. w
InEva 1855-S 1860
InVevHi O 6,N 3-10,D 22 1858;F 9,Ap 13-20, My 4,Je 15-22 1859;Ja 18,F 22 1860
WHi Ap 27 1850

Evansville GAZETTE. w 1821-25||?
DLC Ap 20 1822-Ag 13 1825
In Jl 13 1861-Ja 2 1864
InI Ap 25,My 8-22,Je 5,23-30,Jl 14,Ag 18,S 1,29 1821[22]F 19,Ap 9 1823;Je 3,O 14 1824;Ja 22,Mr 19-26,Ap 16,30,My 14,28,Je 4-11 1825
IU Ap 20,My-Ag,S 14-21,O 5-19,N 2-23 1822; 23-Ja,F 11-Jl 22,Ag 12-N 4 1824;Ja 8-Mr 5, 19-Ap 9,30-Jl,Ag 13 1825

INDIANA statesman. *See under* New Harmony

Weekly Evansville JOURNAL. w,tw 1833-84||
w 1833-69?
In O 31,1850;Mr 20 1851;Jl 15 1855;Ja 1 1856; My 23 1860;Ja 5-8 1876
InEv Je-D 1860;N 12 1872-Je 1875;76-Je 1884
InEva Ag 24 1843-Mr 25 1847;Ap 25-D 1848; 50-84
InMov My 23 1882
MWA Ag 25 1842;Ap 5 1844;Mr 5 1857
OClWHi O 26 1865
TxU Ap 5 1855

Evansville daily JOURNAL. d 1848+
1902?-19? as Evansville journal-news
DLC Ja 24 1860;Ag-O 14 1861;F 11-D 1864;69
ICHi S 26,30 1865
In F 14 1904;O 1905-S 5 1916
InEv My 1909-20
InMovHi Ja 3-6 1933
MWA O 24 1861;O 25 1865;Mr 22,Ap 3,My 3,28 1884
OOxM F 25,1875;S 23 1887
WHi F 9 1864;65

OHIO Valley courier. w N 9 1865-1906||?
1865-1904? as Evansville courier
MWA N 9 1865
—d ed *See* Evansville courier

POCKET.
InNh Ja-Jl 1898

Evansville PRESS. d 1906+
pub 1906+
InEv Ja-Mr,O 1920-22;Mr 1923+
InMovHi Mr 5 1932

PUBLIC. d 1884-95||?
DLC My 31 1887

SOUTH-WESTERN sentinel. w F 1840-
DLC Mr 6-20 1840

Das STERNENBANNER. w 1882-1910||?
In German
InSmA My 4 1900

Evening TRIBUNE. d 1877-97||?
InMovHi O 1892;Ag 30 1897

Tägliche Evansville UNION. d 1863-84||?
In German
MWA Ag 25 1876

VANDERBURGH democrat. w
In O 5 1848

FAIRMOUNT

Fairmount NEWS. w 1877+
pub 1888-93;98-1910;12-14;16-24;31+
In [1897-1900]Ja 20 1921
InF 1923+

FARMLAND

RANDOLPH county enterprise. w 1888+
pub 1889-90;92;94;96;1900-01;03-04;26+

FERDINAND

Ferdinand NEWS. w 1906+
pub 1906+

FLORA

CARROLL county press. w F 1911+
pub 1911+

HOOSIER democrat. w 1897+
pub S 1897+
In Jl 13 1935+

FORT WAYNE

DAWSON'S Fort Wayne times. *See* Fort Wayne weekly times and sentinel

Fort Wayne DEMOCRAT. w
InFw Ja 15-My 31 1866;69-N 1870

FREIE PRESSE-Staats-zeitung. w 1888-1926||?
1888-1907? as Freie presse
In German

Fort Wayne GAZETTE. w 1862-Je 1899||
In O 27 1864;Je 6 1866;N 23 1868;Ag 8-9,15-17, 19,22 O 14 1870;Ag 1,14,16-17,S 28,O 18-19,23, N 6,8-12,14,17-18,30 1871;Mr 6-8,15,19-20,22, 27-29,Ap 1-2 1872;O 4-5 1873;Ja 25,27-28,N 16-18 1876;S 15 1877;Mr 24 1882;92-94;97-98
InFw My 1864-[65]-71;73-Ja 10 1874;77-99
InIB Ag 16 1871-F 1875

Fort Wayne GAZETTE. d 1863-Je 1899||
United with Fort Wayne journal to form Fort Wayne journal-gazette
MWA D 4 1872;My 19 1891
N O 6-7 1875
OClWHi N 11 1865
WHi Ja 27-28 1876;Jl 22 1886

INDIANA staats-zeitung. w 1859-1908||?
United with Freie presse to form Freie presse-staats-zeitung
In German
MWA Je 14 1876

INDIANA staatszeitung. tw 1867-76||?
In German
In Ja 13-Je 27 1872

Fort Wayne JEFFERSONIAN.
NNHi O 1,15,N 12 1857

Fort Wayne JOURNAL. w 1856-Je 13 1899||
In S 9 1856;Mr 11 1871;N 19 1884
InFw 1895-99
InLoHi 1895
MWA Ag 12 1871;Je 17 1876

Fort Wayne JOURNAL-gazette. d 1881+
1881-Je 13 1899 as Fort Wayne journal
In N 1907+
InFw Je 14 1899+
InU Mr 1918-N 1921
NcD Jl 18 1919

LAUREL wreath. w Je 1 1852
NNHi Je 15-22,Jl 6-13 1852
WHi Je 22,Jl 27 1852

Fort Wayne NEWS. d *See* Fort Wayne news-sentinel

Fort Wayne NEWS. w 1833-Ja 1918||
pub Je 1874-1918
InFw Ja 29 1895-1917
InFwHi Ap-D 1875
InFwN 1905-08;Jl 1909-Je 1911

Fort Wayne NEWS-sentinel. d Je 1 1874+
1874-1917 as Fort Wayne news
pub 1918+
In Ja 27-28 1876;Ja 3-5,7-11 1918;Je 15 1926+
InFw 1918+
N O 6 1875
NN Je 1 1874(facsimile)

PEOPLE'S press. w -1844||
United with Fort Wayne times to form Fort Wayne times and People's press, later Fort Wayne weekly times and sentinel
DLC My 14 1844
In Jl 16,S 17 1844

Fort Wayne evening POST. *See* Fort Wayne evening times-post

Fort Wayne REPUBLICAN. w My 5 1858-
In My 5-12 1858;F 16 1860
InFw 1858-My 1860

Fort Wayne SENTINEL. w 1833-1917||
DLC Mr 22 1834;F 29 1840;Ja-F 4,25,Mr 17-Ap 14,My 5,19-Je 2,30,Jl 14 1860
In Mr 23,28 1861[Jl-D 1872]Jl 21 1875;Mr 2,N 15 1876;Ag 1 1881;Ag 21 1883 My 25 1887;Ag 15 1888;Ap 20 1914-17
InFw Mr 27 1841-My 7 1844;Jl 17 1847-Je 16 1849;Ag 14 1852-Je 18 1864;F 1871-Ja 15 1873; 74-79;81-1917
InIB F 17 1875-Jl 8 1880
InCocHi D 10 1836
MWA N 16 1839;Ja 4,Mr 14 1840;N 6 1841
NN Ja 14 1837(facsimile)

Daily Fort Wayne SENTINEL. d 1860-1917||
United with Fort Wayne news to form Fort Wayne news-sentinel
DLC D 16 1860;98
MWA D 3 1872
PWayHi O 3 1872

INDIANA (*Continued*)

FORT WAYNE—*Continued*

Fort Wayne STANDARD. w 1854-
In Jl 13-Ag 24,S 7-O 19,N 1854-My 3,Je 7,S 13 1855
InFw Jl 1854-Je 1856

Fort Wayne TAGEBLATT. d 1876-
In German
MWA Ag 26 1876

Fort Wayne weekly TIMES and sentinel. w 1841-65||
1841-44 as Fort Wayne times; 1844-Ag 1854 Fort Wayne times and people's press; S 1854-64 Dawson's Fort Wayne times
DLC N 14 1840
In Mr 7,S 5,O 10-17,N 17 1846;Mr 6,Ag 21-28, 1847;Ag 23 1849;Mr 18 1852;My 15-22,Je 20,23, D 4 1856;Ag 27-S 3 1857;Ja 7,Mr 11-18 1858; Ap 11,F 15,18 1860;Ag 24 1861;F 25 1862
InFw Ja 25 1845-60;Ag 28 1861-O 12 1864
InFwHi F-Jl 1859
InGoE Ja 11 1860
InVevHi N 12 1859
MWA S 27 1865
OClWHi S 5 1846;Ap 26 1861(extra)

Fort Wayne daily TIMES and sentinel. d 1860-65||
1860-64 as Dawson's Fort Wayne daily times
DLC Jl 7 1860
In S 6 1865
MWA S 26 1865

Fort Wayne evening TIMES-POST. d 1895-96||
1895-Je 1896? as Fort Wayne evening post?
InFw Mr-Je 1896

Fort Wayne TIMES-POST. w My 25 1895-96||
InFw My-N 1 1895

Fort Wayne VINDICATOR. F 22 1873-
NNHi F 22 1873

FORTVILLE

Fortville TRIBUNE. w 1894+
pub Ap 29 1909+

FOWLER

BENTON county democrat. *See* Benton review

BENTON county tribune. w 1914+
1914-15 as Fowler tribune
InFo 1916+
InOx 1932-33

BENTON review. w 1874+
1874-79 as Benton county democrat
In 1932+
InE My 1923-[24-25]-[28-30]+
InFo 1875-77;83-1904;08-09;12-26;28+
InOx 1932-33
InU [1874-77]1912-18

ERA. *See* Republican-leader

Fowler LEADER. w 1893-1908||
United with Fowler republican to form Republican-leader

Fowler REPUBLICAN. *See* Republican-leader

REPUBLICAN era. *See* Republican-leader

REPUBLICAN-LEADER. w,sw 1872-1914||?
1872-90? as Era; 1891-98 Republican era; 1899?-1908 Fowler republican
w 1872-1908
In F 3 1911

Fowler TRIBUNE. *See* Benton county tribune

FRANCESVILLE

Francesville TRIBUNE. w 1897+
pub 1917+
In Jl 6,O 5,19,N 9,D 14 1933;Ja 4 1934

FRANKFORT

Frankfort BANNER. *See* Frankfort news

Saturday BANNER. *See* Frankfort news

CLINTON news. w 1849-
In N 6 1849

CLINTON union banner. *See* Frankfort news

COMPILER. w 1852-
In F 21 1852

CRESCENT-NEWS. *See* Frankfort news

Frankfort CRESCENT-STANDARD. w,sw 1850-1920||
1850-1906? as Frankfort crescent (1903?-04? Old weekly crescent)
In Mr 27 1858;My 24 1861;My 20 1864;Je 19 1872;S 10 1873;N 2 1874;N 24 1875;Je 26 1878; Ja 26 1881;D 27 1882;N 14 1883;My 14 1889;S 22 1893;F 17 1914-[Ja-S 24 1918]
InFr O 8 1853-D 13 1855;79-1919
MWA Jl 5 1876

Frankfort DEMOCRAT. w 1885-87||
InFr Ja-Mr 12 1887

Frankfort NEWS. w 1863-My 1918||?
1863-65? as Clinton union banner; 1866?-79? Frankfort union banner; 1880-94? Saturday banner; 1895-1910? Frankfort banner
In Ag 10 1865;O 10 1887
InFr Mr 27,Ap 3,24,My 1 1879;81-85;87-My 1918
MWA Jl 8 1876

Frankfort NEWS. d 1887-1925||
1887-1915? as Evening news; 1916?-Je 1923 Crescent-news
InFr Je 1914-O 1915;F 1916-S 1925

Frankfort OBSERVER. w
In My 20,Jl 1 1843

OLD weekly crescent. *See* Frankfort crescent-standard

Frankfort TIMES. w 1877-1923||?
InFr 1888-92

Frankfort TIMES. d 1894+
pub 1894+
In O 11 1927+
InFr 1894-95;97-1919;25+

Frankfort UNION banner. *See* Frankfort news

FRANKLIN

Franklin DEMOCRAT. w 1859+
1859-75 as Democratic herald
pub 1879+
In Jl 30 1875;D 1876;Je 12,26 1877;Jl 11 1879-Ap 2 1886;88-94;97+
InU N 1859-Ja 1862;Jl 1879-82;Jl 1883-My 1884;1914-Ag 4 1916
InVevHi Ja 19,F 16-23,Mr 29-Ap 5 1860

DEMOCRATIC herald. *See* Franklin democrat

Franklin EXAMINER. w
InU D 1845-F 1852

Franklin JACKSONIAN. w 1883-85||
In D 8 1883;Jl 18-25 1885

Franklin JEFFERSONIAN. *See* Franklin republican

JOHNSON county press. w 1859-69||?
InU O 1865-Jl 1868
MWA F 21 1867

Franklin REPUBLICAN. w Mr 1 1852+
1852-85? as Franklin Jeffersonian
ICHi Ag 18-25 1852;S 9 1865
In Jl 25 1863
InU 1856-Ag 1857
InVevHi Ap 18 1856;Ap 24,Je 5,Ag 21-28,N 20-27 1858;F 12,My 28 1859;Mr 17-25,Ap 7 1860
MWA Ja 27 1866;Je 22 1876
OClWHi N 11 1865

Franklin STAR. d 1885+
pub 1918+
In Jl 1933+

FREMONT

Fremont EAGLE. w 1892+
pub D 1892+
In S 26 1935+

FRENCH LICK

SPRINGS Valley herald. w 1903+
pub 1904+
In Je 1934+

FULTON

Fulton LEADER. w 1901+
pub [My 1913-31]+

GALVESTON

Galveston LEADER. w 1897+
pub Mr 11 1897+

Galveston TIMES. w 1884-87||
In O 9 1884

GARRETT

Garrett CLIPPER. w,sw 1885+
w 1885-1920?
pub O 22 1885-O 20 1887;1900+
In F 21 1934+
InU Ap 1914-O 1915

Garrett HERALD. w 1877-89||
InGoE Je 13,14 1889

GARY

Gary AMERICAN. w 1927+
Negro
InG N 10 1927+

Gary COMMONWEALTH. w 1923+
InG Ja-S 1930;31-F 5,26,Mr 18,Ap 1,15,29,Je 3-10 1932;33+

EAST Gary bulletin. w
InG 1932+

EAST Gary times. w
InG Je 29 1927-D 14 1928

EAST Gary tribune. w 1907-09||
InG Jl 1909

EAST Tolleston advance. w
InG Ja 8-29,Mr 12,Ap 9,O 22 1897

GLEN Park and Gary news. w 1928-32||
1928-30? as Glen Park news
InG Ap 12 1928-Je 17 1932

GLEN Park herald. w
InG S 15-D 1933

GLEN Park times. w
InG N 18 1932

Gary JOURNAL. d
InG F 24-My 15 1927

LAKE county democrat. w 1909-10||
InG S 1909-Ja 21 1910
InGL S-D 1909

Gary LIFE. w 1927||
In My 27-Je 10 1927
InG My 13-Je 10 1927

Gary NEWS. d 1906-Mr 15 1909||
InG S 1908-09.
InGL 1908-09.

NORTHERN Indianian. w 1906-09||
In F 14,Ag 7,S 25 1908
InG S 21 1906-F 19 1909
InGL D 20 1907-F 28 1909

Gary POST-TRIBUNE. d O 1909+
1909-Ap 21 1921 as Gary post
In Ap 22,28,Je 20 1911;O 2 1915;Ap 10 1919-[20-22]+
InG 1909-Je 1912;13+
InGL 1909+

REKORD tygodniowy. w
In Polish
InG Ja 27-N 10 1929

Gary REPUBLICAN. w 1916-17||
InG Mr 25 1916-F 1917

Gary SUN. w
InG Ja 12 1923-Ap 1929

Gary TELEGRAM. w 1927||
In S 30 1927
InG S 30 1927

Gary TIMES. d 1906+
In Je 22 1911
InG S 21 1908-S 3 1927
InGL Mr 3 1908

Gary TRIBUNE. w Je 21 1907-21||
ICHi 1907-Je 12 1908
InG 1907-Jl 9 1921
InGL 1908-Ap 21 1921

Gary TRUTH. w 1927||
In Jl 1-15 1927
InG Jl-S 23 1927

GAS CITY

Gas City JOURNAL. w 1887+
pub 1903+
In 1897-98
InU My 1915-S 1916

GOODLAND

Goodland HERALD. w 1874+
1874-95? as Saturday herald
pub 1904+
In N 26 1881

Saturday HERALD. *See* Goodland herald

GOSHEN

Goshen ADVERTISER. w N 21 1844-
InGoE N 21 1844

BALANCE. w
In Jl 18 1844

Goshen DEMOCRAT. w 1837-1918||
In Jl 18 1844;Mr 16,S 4 1845;S 1 1847;Ag 2 1848;My 16 1849;S 25 1850;F 25,Ag 18 1852;S 26 1855;My 26 1859;N 11 1874;Je 28 1893-94; 97-1918
InGoD complete
InGoE complete
InGoHi 1840-80
InU 1843;1914-18
MWA N 1 1865

Goshen DEMOCRAT. d 1897-1932||
United with Goshen news-times to form Goshen news-times and democrat
In 1919-[26]-32
InGoD 1919-32
InGoE 1924-32
InU 1919-32

ELKHART county times. *See* Goshen times

Goshen EXPRESS. w Ja 28 1837-Ja 16 1840||?
Followed by Northern Indianian
InGoD 1837-38
InGoE Je 28 1837-N 17 1838
MWA F 25,Mr 18 1837

Goshen INDEPENDENT. w,sw 1877-85||
InGoE 1878-Mr 20 1885

INDIANA statesman. w
InGoD 1850-51

KINDERBOOK Dutchman. w
InGoE My-O 10 1840

Goshen NEWS-TIMES. w 1875-1917||?
1875-Je 1901 as Goshen news
InGoE 1885-Je 1901

Goshen NEWS-TIMES and democrat. d 1883+
1883-Je 1901 as Goshen news; Jl 1901-32 Goshen news-times
pub 1915+
In Jl 11 1907-Jl 1916
InGoE Jl 9 1901+

NORTHERN Indianian and Elkhart county gazette. w Ja 23 1840-
DLC Ja 23,F 13 1840
InGoE Je 25 1840-F 10,Mr 25 1842-F 16,Ap 1843-Ap 4 1844

Sunday POST. w
InGoE Ap 12-S 13 1896

Goshen TIMES. w 1856-1900||
1856-58? as Elkhart county times. United with Goshen news to form Goshen news-times
In My 26 1859
InGoD 1870-74
InGoE Mr 1859-66;Je 18-25 1868;Jl 14 1870-Mr 1884;85-86;88-1900
MWA F 22 1866;Ja 26 1871;Jl 13-20 1876
NNHi My 21-28 1863;My 8 1873
TxU Ag 20 1857

INDIANA (*Continued*)

GOSPORT

Gosport REPORTER. w 1897+
pub 1909+
In Je 13 1929

GRANDVIEW

Grandview MONITOR. w 1867+
pub 1906+
In 1934+

GREENCASTLE

Greencastle BANNER. w,d 1852+
1852-69 as Putnam republican banner. Title varies slightly: Banner-star; Banner-times; etc.
In Je 15 1853;Je 15 1854;Ja 7,D 31 1856;My 27,S 23 1857;F 10,Jl 7 1858;D 28 1859;D 6 1860;Ja 10,D 27 1866;F-Mr 14,28-My,Je 13,Jl 4-11,Ag 7,N 6-13,D 4-11 1867;Ja 15,Mr 25,Ap 8,22,My 13,Je 10,24-Jl 15,Ag 12-O 14,28 1868-[69]S 18 1873;74[75]-87;1934+
InGc [Ag 17 1853-54]+
MWA F 8 1866;Jl 13 1876

Greencastle DEMOCRAT. w 1892-1903||?
United with Greencastle star-press to form Greencastle star-democrat, later Greencastle herald-democrat
InGc F 20 1892-F 8,Ag 1896-F 6 1897

Greencastle HERALD. d 1906-31||
pub complete
In Jl 18 1907-Mr 1 1918

Greencastle HERALD-DEMOCRAT. w 1858-1928||?
1858-77? as Indiana press; 1878?-81 Greencastle press; 1881-Ag 1904 Greencastle star press; S 1904-12? Greencastle star-democrat
In S 12 1891;Jl 17 1893-94;97-1915 1895
InGc Ap 23 1892-Mr 4 1893;Ap 21 1894-Ap 6 1895
InU 1913-My 1914
OClWHi Ap 5 1871

INDIANA patriot. w
In Jl 2 1845

INDIANA press. *See* Greencastle herald-democrat

Greencastle PRESS. *See* Greencastle herald-democrat

PUTNAM county sentinel. w 1849-
In O 23 1851

PUTNAM republican banner. *See* Greencastle banner

Greencastle STAR. w 1874-81||
United with Greencastle press to form Greencastle star-press, later Greencastle herald-democrat
InGc 1880-81

Greencastle STAR-Democrat. *See* Greencastle herald-democrat

Greencastle STAR press. *See* Greencastle herald-democrat

SUN. d 1889-90||
InGc Ja 21-Ag 30 1890

Greencastle TIMES-news. w 1882+
1882-89 as Greencastle times
In F 21 1935—
InGc D 1885-N 4 1887

Greencastle VISITOR. w 1838-
In Ag 16 1840-Ag 1843;O 3 1844
MWA Jl 11 1839

WESTERN plough boy. w
In Je 23 1836

GREENFIELD

Greenfield COMMERCIAL. w 1868-71||
InNcHi O 2 1868;S 6 1871

HANCOCK democrat. w 1859+
pub 1859+
In N 28 1867;F 24 1876;Je 8 1893-94;F 1914-15
InGr 1907+
InU 1914-15

HANCOCK Jeffersonian. *See* Greenfield herald

Greenfield HERALD. w 1876-1908||?
1876-92? as Hancock Jeffersonian
In Je 29 1893-94;97-1900

REPORTER. d 1908+
pub Ap 1908+
In 1934+

Greenfield REPUBLICAN. w 1880+
pub [1883-86;94]1910+
In 1934+
MWA S 23 1881

Greenfield SENTINEL. w
InVevHi N 12 1858;N 19 1859

GREENSBURG

Greensburg CHRONICLE. *See* Greensburg standard

DECATUR county press. *See* Greensburg new era

DECATUR democrat. w
In Mr 10,My 26,Je 30,Jl 14,28-Ag 11,S 25,O 16,N 17 1858;Je 29 1859
InGsN O 28 D 16 1857
InVevHi Ja 18,Mr 7 1860

DECATUR democrat. w 1881-
In O 5,N 2 1882;Je 28 1883;Ap 5 1892

DECATUR news. *See* Greensburg new era

DECATUR republican. w 1851-
In Ap 21 1864
InGsN 1860-62

DEMOCRATIC hornet. w
In S 12 1854

Greensburg GUARD. w
In O 21 1856

Greensburg HERALD. w 1867-68||
In D 21-28 1867;Je 18,Jl 30 1868

INDIANA repository. w 1835-
InGsN My 7 1842[48;52;56;58]

Greensburg NEW ERA. w 1868-1924||?
1868-79? as Decatur county press; 1879?-Jl? 1885 Decatur news
In Jl 4 1866;O 5,19 1870;Ap 29,S 30 1871;Ap 20,My 25,Je 1 1872;F 8,My 3,17 1873;Je 12,Jl 3,S 16-23 1885;N 10 1886;Je 18,Jl 30 1890;F 24,Mr 16,Ap 30,Ag 10,D 7 1892;Mr 22,Ag 30-O 4 1893;Ja 10,F 14,Je 20,Jl 11,Ag 29,D 12 1894;N 21 1895;My 13 1896
InGsN Ja 14,My 7,Ag 26-S 9,D 30 1853;Ja 20,F 2,10,N 21 1854;Jl 6 1855

Greensburg NEWS. d 1894+
pub F-Mr 1 1914
In Jl 19 1907-15;Mr 20 1931+
InGsD 1926+

Greensburg REPOSITORY and advertiser. w
Title varies
DLC N 7,28 1840
In O 1 1836

Greensburg REVIEW. w 1879-1914||?
1879-94? as Saturday review
In My 6 1893

Saturday REVIEW. *See* Greensburg review

Greensburg STANDARD. w 1835-1925||
1835-67 as Greensburg chronicle
ICHi Mr 23 1865
In O 28 1869;Ja 13,My 19,Ag 4 1870;Je 12 1873
InGsD 1868-1925
InGsN Ag 15 1867
InU 1915-17;Mr 1918-25
InVeM Ag 21 1891
MWA Je 7 1876

Greensburg TIMES. d,w 1910+
d 1910-28?
pub Ap 16 1924+

GREENTOWN

Greentown GEM. w 1894+
In Jl 12 1935

GRIFFITH

CALUMET news. w 1930+
pub My 1930+
In Je 1,Jl 6,N 2,16-23,D 7,21-28 1933
InG 1930+
InWh Ap 13 1933

SOUTHEAST Calumet news. w
In My 30-Je 1930
InG My 1930+

HAGERSTOWN

Hagerstown EXPONENT. w 1875+
pub 1875-[1909-30]+
InH Je 1931+
InRP S 21 1881

FRIENDLY visitor. w 1873-75||
In O 7-21 1874;Ja 6-20,F 3 1875

HAMMOND

LAKE county democrat. w
InWh O 1 1930

LAKE county news. w 1890-1917||?
In Je 8 1893-94;97-1915

LAKE county times. *See* Hammond times

Hammond TIMES. d 1906+
1906-Je 1933 as Lake county times
In O 3 1911;Je 28,Jl 12,O 26[N-D]1933;Ja 2-6 1934
InEc 1925+
InHa Je 1906-S 1916;26+
InWh N 7,11 1918;Ja 6 1919;Je 28 1933

HARTFORD CITY

Hartford City GAZETTE. d 1900-04||
United with Hartford City times to form Hartford City times-gazette

Hartford City NEWS. w 1852-85||?
MWA My 5 1876

Hartford City evening NEWS. d 1895+
In N 12 1918-20;1934+
InHc 1905-31

Hartford City TELEGRAM. w 1877-1914||
In Ja 15 1893-1894;97-98;1903-14

Hartford City TIMES-GAZETTE. d 1896+
1896-1904 as Hartford City times
In 1934+
InHc 1905-31

Hartford City UNION. w 1862-
In Ag 20 1863

HEBRON

Hebron NEWS. w 1894-1916||?
In S 10 1914;S 9-16 1915

PORTER county herald. w 1929+
pub 1929+
In Jl 6-13,N,D 14,28 1933-Ja 4 1934

HILLSBORO

Hillsboro TIMES. w 1899+
pub 1916+

HOBART

Hobart GAZETTE. w 1888+
In 1887-1902;09-15;Ap 1917-N 15 1918
InU Ap 17 1891+

Hobart NEWS. w 1910-Je 5 1930||
In 1928-30
InG Ap 1910-Je 5 1930
InU Ap 1917-Mr 1918

HOPE

CHAMPION. *See* Hope journal

Hope JOURNAL. w 1883-1912||
1883-84 as Champion; 1885-1900? News-journal. United with Hope star to form Hope star-journal
pub D 13,18,20 1883;My 22 1884

NEWS-JOURNAL. *See* Hope journal

Hope STAR-JOURNAL. w Jl 13 1906-S 15 1933||
1906-S 27 1912 as Hope star
pub complete
In complete

Hope STAR-JOURNAL. d 1909-17||?
1909-S 1912 as Evening star
In My 1909-O 1912;14-Ja 6 1917

HOWE

To Je 23 1909 as Lima

LA GRANGE whig. w
In Jl 17 1850

HUNTINGBURG

Huntingburg ARGUS. w 1880+
pub 1880-1903;07+

Huntingburg INDEPENDENT. w 1885+
pub Ag 1885+
In Ag 10 1912+
InU 1915-F 24,Mr 8-Ap 1930

Huntingburg NEWS. w 1889-1904||
In 1893-94

Huntingburg SIGNAL. w 1868+
In English and German
pub 1868+
In 1932+
InSmA F 16 1911;Ja 16 1913
InU 1923-[25-32]+

HUNTINGTON

Huntington DEMOCRAT. *See* Huntington news-democrat

Huntington HERALD. w 1848-1909||
1848-85? as Indiana herald
ICHi D 20 1854;Ag 22 1855
In S 17 1851;F 18 1852;S 14 1853;S 13 1854;F 14 1855;Ag 26 1857;Ag 25 1858;Ap 18 1860;Mr 6 1861;F 5,Ap 9,Je 25,Ag 27 1862;F 18,Je 10,Ag 26 1863;Ap 26,My 10,O 25 1865;My 2,O 17,31 1866;My 22 1867;My 20,N 11-25 1868;F 3 1869;N 30 1894
InHu Jl 1848-S 7 1864;67-70;72-74;O 1875-S 19 1877;O 1879-S 1881;My 1883-Ap 1887;Ap 8 1891-1902;Jl 1903-09
InHuR Mr 31 1860-1909

Huntington HERALD-PRESS. d 1882+
1882-1929 as Huntington herald
pub 1911+
In Jl 19 1907+
InHu 1910+
InHuR 1917+
InU [1915]-[30]+

INDIANA herald. *See* Huntington herald

Huntington NEWS. d 1930+
InHu S 30 1930+

Huntington NEWS-DEMOCRAT. w 1858-1911||
1858-97 as Huntington democrat
In Ap 19 1860;S 12 1861;Ap 3 1862;Ja 1,F 19-Mr 5,Je 11 1863;F 25 1864;My 4-11,O 26 1865;My 3,O 25 1866;My 2?,N 19 1868;Mr 7 1872;Mr 1 1892;N 30 1894
InHu 1861-62;Je 21 1877-Je 14 1883;Ap 1886-88;Ap 1889-My,S 1895-96;Ap-S 1897;Ap 1898-1910
InHuR Jl 1863-Ap 1 1897;1902-11

Huntington OBSERVER. w
In Ap 26 1853;Mr 4 1854

Huntington PRESS. d F 1912-Je 1929||
United with Huntington herald to form Huntington herald-press
In F 13 1925-Mr 1926
InHu complete
InHuH 1916-29
InHuR 1918-29

Morning TIMES. d 1907-1911||
InHu 1908-11

INDIANA (*Continued*)

INDEPENDENCE

WABASH register. w
In S 21 1844

INDIANAPOLIS

Indianapolis AMERICAN. d
In N 20 1861

AMERICAN tribune. w 1880-1906||
CLM Mr 28 1890
DLC Mr 1890-Mr 22 1900
In My 23 1890;O 1897-1906
InI 1890-1905
KHi Ja 11 1889;S 25 1891-Mr 1906
OClWHi Mr 20,Ap 17,My 15,Je 5 1891;F 28,Ap 18 1895

ATLAS. d Ag 22 1859-Mr 12 1860||
Title varies slightly: Daily evening atlas
In complete
InI complete
MWA Ag 22 1859

Weekly ATLAS. w Ag 27 1859-
MWA S 3-17,O 15-N 5,19-D 10,24 1859;Ja 10 1860

Sunday morning CALL. w N 16 1879-81||
In 1879[80]
InI 1879-Ja 2 1881

CALL. w
InI N 10-D 12 1887

CAPITAL. w Mr 22 1879-80||?
1879-Ja 10 1880 as Democrat
In Mr-Ap 5,19,My 10,N 22-29,D 20 1879;Ja 17-F 7 1880
InI 1879-Ja 1880

CHAPMAN'S chanticleer. w N 17 1853-N 23 1854||
In complete
InI Ja 26-N 1854
MWA Mr 9 1854
NNHi Ap 13 1854

CHAPMAN'S coon skinner. w
In Ag 27,S 17,O 8,22 1844;Ag 12,S 2 1848
InI O 1 1844
InCr My-Ag 1843;44-45
InG Ja 1845;My 1849

Indianapolis daily CHRONICLE. d
ICHi N 26 1861;O 13,N 3,7,24,26-27,D 4,17 1862;Mr 14-15 1867

Indianapolis CITIZEN. d 1856?-
In My 24 1858;My 21 1868
InI Ap 5 1858-My 10 1859
MWA F 12 1859

Indianapolis COMMERCIAL. d 1867-72||
In 1868-71
InI N 11 1867-S 1869;F 11-Je 1872

Indianapolis COMMERCIAL. d 1895+
1895-Mr 1903 as Indianapolis reporter; Ap 1903-08? Indianapolis commercial-reporter
pub S 3 1895+
In Jl 1913+
InI Ap 1903-Je 1917

CONSTITUTION. w
In Je 3 1840

COURIER. d Ag 6 1845-
In Ag-O 18 1845

Indianapolis Saturday COURIER. w 1875-
In Ap 24,My 22,Je 13-20,Jl 18,Ag 1,29-S 5,26 1875

Indianapolis Sunday COURIER. w 1875-
In Je 20,Jl 15,Ag 1,29-S 5,26 1875

CRISIS. w Ap 4 1885-
WHi Ap 4-My 30 1885

DEMOCRAT. 1879-80. *See* Capital

Indianapolis DEMOCRAT. w
InI S-N 3 1887

DEMOCRATIC platform. w
In Jl 19,Ag 9,23-S 13,O 3 1854
InIB Jl 19-O 3 1854

FREE press. w
In S 21 1847

FREE soil banner. w
In Ag 25 1848

FREEMAN. w 1884-1926||?
Negro
DLC D 30 1899
In 1892-94;97-98
InI Jl 1888-1916
MWA D 2 1886
NN O 3-10,31 1896;F 13-20 1897;D 24 1898 [Ja-S 1902;My 1903-04]Ja 7 1905
OHi 1915-20

FREIE presse von Indiana. w 1853-
In German
In Ap 19 1854
InI Jl 1856-62;Ja 11 1865-S 19 1866
MWA F 14 1855

Indianapolis GAZETTE. 1822-29. *See* Indiana state gazette

Indianapolis GAZETTE. w 1862-
In D 29 1862-[63-67]

Indianapolis daily GAZETTE. d Mr 16 1863-Mr 8 1867||
ICHi S 26-27 1865
In [1863-67]
InI complete
PUn Ja 5 1865

Indianapolis GLOBE. d
In F 26,Ap 2,9 1875
InI Mr 30-My 15 1875

Indianapolis GLOBE. d
InI My-Je 1903

Indianapolis HERALD. d 1862-N 1865||
United with Daily state sentinel to form Indianapolis daily herald, later Indianapolis sentinel
ICHi [Jl-D 1862]N 25 1865

Indianapolis HERALD. w 1873-88||?
1873-Ja 24 1875 as Sunday herald; Ja 31 1875-87? Saturday herald
In 1875-[77]-80;F 5,Je 11 1887
InI F 8 1873-89
InNcHi S 13 1874
MWA S 27 1879;Jl 4 1885

Saturday HERALD. *See* Indianapolis herald

Sunday HERALD. *See* Indianapolis herald

HOOSIER herald. w
In N 28 1931

HOOSIER sentinel. w 1933+
In 1933+

INDEPENDENT. w 1882-1917||?
In F 9 1884;Ap 1906-13
InI 1906-12.

INDIANA American. sm
In S 10 1858-60;Ap 30 1861
InI Jl 1858-59

INDIANA American. w 1870-72||
In Ag 17 1870-My 11 1872
InI Ag 17 1870-My 25 1872

INDIANA democrat and spirit of the constitution. w,sw Ag 14 1830-My 1841||
1830-Ag 14 1840 as Indiana democrat. Followed by Indiana state sentinel, later Indianapolis sentinel
Ct [1830-31;33;35-38]
DLC S 15 1832;33-41
ICHi Ag 14 1830;F 5 1841
In 1830-Mr,Ap 14-21,S 8,29 1832;F 22,Mr 8,My 3,24 1834;Ja 30,N 25-D 1835;Ja 12,F 25 1836 [Ja-S 1837;38]-F 4,Ap 17,My 1,Jl 3,D 31 1839-F 5,18-Ap 9,30-My 1841
InI Ja 8 1836
InRP Je 20 1832
MWA Jl 4 1834
N O 12 1833
OClWHi Ja 16 1835

INDIANA deutsche zeitung. d 1874?-
In German
In O 19 1876
InI Ap 14 1875-Ap 28 1877
MWA Ag 25 1876

INDIANA forum. w 1915-17||
In O 10 1915-16.
InU O 1915-O 1917

INDIANA free democrat. w
In Je 9,Ag 11,S 15-22,O 1853-Ja,F 9,Jl 6 1854
NhD Ap 14 1853

INDIANA freeman. w
In N 23 1844
InNcHi Jl 6 1846

Daily INDIANA journal. d 1839-
OHi D 16 1841-Ja 26 1842;D 1851-Je 1852

INDIANA journal. w *See* Indiana state journal

INDIANA journal of commerce. w 1870-71||
In Mr 1870-71

INDIANA register.
In Ag 1 1856
ODW My 1 1856

INDIANA republican. w 1853-
DLC D 13 1855
ICHi D 21 1854
InI N 30 1854-55
MWA Ag 16 1855
NNHi D 28 1854

INDIANA socialist. w N 23-D 28 1907||
Follows Peoria socialist (Peoria, Ill)
WHi complete

INDIANA state gazette. w Ja 28 1822-Jl 29 1830||
1822-O 15 1829 as Indianapolis gazette. Merged with Indiana democrat
DLC Je 18,Jl 16,Ag 27,S 17,O 8-22,N 12,D 9-23 1829;Ja 14 1830
In Ja 28-Ap 10,24 1822-Ag 12,S 1823-Je 18 1824;D 1825-Ag 1,S 11 1828-30(1822-24 photostat)
InI Ja 28,Ag 17,S 14,28 1822;Ap 5,S 16,30,O 14-21 1823;My 4-18 1824
MWA Jl 12 1825

INDIANA weekly state gazette. w 1864?-
MWA Ja 9 1866

INDIANA state guard. w N 10 1860-61||
Formed by the union of Locomotive and Old line guard
DLC D 22-29 1860;Ja 12-Mr 9,30-Jl 20 1861
In N 10 1860;Mr 9 1861
InI 1860-Jl 27 1861

INDIANA state journal. w Mr 7 1823-1904||
1823-Ja 4 1825 as Western censor and emigrant's guide; Ja 18 1825-42? Indiana journal
sw during sessions of the legislature
CSmH Ag 25 1830
DLC Ja 18 1825-D 11 1829;Ja 2,6,9,14,16,20,23,27,F,Mr 3 1830;Jl 16-23 1831;O 13 1832;O 16 1835;My 23 1840;O 22 1841-F 1,16-Je 1,22-Jl 20 1842;Ap 2,23-30,My 14-21,Je 11-Jl 2,16-S,O 15,N 1849-Je 1852
ICHi D 11 1830;Ja 1 1834;S 17 1836
IU [1825]-Mr,Ap 18-My,Je 20-Ag 8,22-S 19,O 10 1826-Ap 24,My 8-22,Je-Jl 10,24,Ag-O 2,16,30-N 20,D 11 1827-Mr 3,D 25,29 1830;Jl 16-23,D 27 1831;N 6 1844
IaDH Ja 23 1835
InI Je 4,25,S 15-22 1823
InL 1831-34
InNcHi D 11 1835;D 20 1836
InRE D 22 1841;Ja 13,17,Mr 23-Ap 20,My-Je 22,Jl 6,20,Ag 3,17 1842
KHi F 20 1878-Je 8 1904
MWA N 13 1828;Je 4,D 17 1831;Ja 14 1832;My 21 1857;F 9 1860;Ja 24 1865;D 11 1878;D 26 1888
NbHi My 15,Ag 7,O 16-23,N 6 1878;Ja 8,F 19 1879
OClWHi Ja 26-F 16,Mr 16-23 1847
OHi Mr 16 1847-Mr 6 1848
OOxM Ja 8,D 10 1831-Ja 7,18-21,Ap 21-My 19,Je 9 1832
PErW My 12 1830
WHi Jl 2,9 1829;F 1,11-Ap 7,21-My 12,26,Je 30-Ag 4 1832;Jl 2-9,23,Ag 6,27-O 1836;Ja 4,7,21-Mr 4,18,Ap 8-15,My 13-Je 7 1837;Je 24,N 30 1846;O 22 1849;N 27 1856;96-99

INDIANA state sentinel. sw Je 4 1845-
tw during session of legislature
DLC 1845-Mr 6 1849
MWA Jl 12,N 15-19,D 6,23 1845[46]S 8 1847;Ja 11,18-22,F 19,Mr 15 1848
—d,w ed *See* Indianapolis sentinel

INDIANA statesman. w S 1850-Ag 11 1852||
In complete
InGoE 1850-Ag 1851
InI 1851-52
InNcHi O 2 1850;Ag 11 1852
InU 1850-Ag 1851
MWA Ag 28 1852

INDIANA tribüne. w 1878-98||
In German
InI Ag 17 1878-S 17 1881;F 26 1882-Ja,Jl 1883-98
NN F 20 1892;Ja 3 1895

INDIANA tribüne. d 1882-Je 1907||?
United with Tägliches telegraph to form Telegraph und tribüne
In German
ICJ [Ap 1898-Mr 6 1902]
InI 1905-Mr 1907

INDIANA volksblatt. w 1848-73||?
In German
In D 30 1854;N 27 1858

Indianapolis JOURNAL. w,tw My 7 1823-Je 8 1904||
tw during sessions of legislature
In F 27,Jl 3 1827;F 24,Mr 13-20,My 15-Je 12,Jl 10,Ag 7-21,O 2-9,23,N 6-13,27 1828-Ja 3,17-31,F 12 1929-Ap 21,My-D 1830;Ja 26 1833-O 17 1834;Ja 29,Ap 16, Jl 1836-N 22 1843;Mr 23 1844-[53-Mr 19 1855]Ja 24 1856-1904
InI 1823-24;Ja 11 1825-Ap 20 1851;52-1904
InIB Jl 1859-62;Jl 1863-Jl 1884;85-Mr,Jl 1897-1900;Jl 1901-02;My-S 1903;Ja-Je 1904
InLP Mr 29 1866
InLoHi My 17-20 1881;N 7 1888;Mr 5 1889
InMuB Ap 1891-Je 1898;99-Je 1903;Ja-Je 1904
InNcHi Ja 21 1837;Ja 9 1839;O 22 1846;Je 1 1850;My 12 1864;N 1872-Ja,Ag 22 1873;Ap 30 1874[Ja-Ap 20 1875]S 27 1876;Je 10 1878;N 6 1883;O 6 1888;Mr 22 1896
InRE Mr 5 1889
InRP S 20-21,27 1881
InSHi D 21 1837;Ja 16 1838
InTI Jl 1895-98
InU Mr 1844-Ag 1847;F 1850-S 1886;97-1904
WHi F 10,17,21,Mr 2 1855;Ja 5,21 1857;S 13 1858;My 20,O 7,D 10 1864;Je 18 1866;My 12 1876-F 7 1877 [Ja 7-Je 24 1882]-[1883-Ag 29 1885]-N 29 1900

Indianapolis JOURNAL. d O 7 1850-Je 8 1904||
1850?-Ag 1867 as Indianapolis daily journal. Merged with Indianapolis daily star
CoHi Ap 16 1865
CtW My 24 1893
DLC My 27-D 1854;Mr 2 1855;Je 26,Jl 2,10,13,D 11 1860;Jl 19-D 1861;64-65;67-68;Jl 10 1874-1904
IC Ja 10-Je 1873;My 1 1889
ICHi N 19 1856;N 6 1861;O 13,N 3,7,23,25-26,D 5,17 1862;S 14 1865;Mr 14-15 1867;Ja-Ap 1870;Ja-Je 1886
ICM S 5 1855;Jl 17 1877;Je 23 1884
IU Je 25 1862[Ja-O 1863]My 5,Je 1,Jl 7 1865
InI F 1872-Ag 8 1874
InIS 1859-1903
InLoHi Ja 21 1881
KHi Ja 29 1875;Jl 12 1888;Jl 19 1890;S 2-7 1893
MBAt Ap 15,17 1865
MWA Jl 31,N 19 1856;N 3 1857;Ja 21,Je 17 1858;Mr 10, My 19,Je 13 1859;Ag 2(extra) 1864;Ja 25 1865;Mr 29 1869;N 21 1872;Ag 16 1879;Mr 18 1885
MoHi Ap 13 1865
N N 7 1861;Ap 30 1865;Ag 16-23 1871
NNHi My 4 1865;F 3 1889
OClWHi Mr-Ap 1870;S 20 1881
OHi O-D 1877;Ap-Je 1878
OOxM D 15-16 1874;Mr 9 1875;Ja 26 1876;N 2-3,5-6 1877
TKL S 14 1878
WHi Jl 2-D 1873

Semi-weekly JOURNAL. *See* Semi-weekly state journal

Indianapolis LEADER. w 1879-83||?
InI Ag 30 1879-Je 1882
NNHi D 9 1882

LEGISLATIVE sentinel. w
DLC D 7 1844
In D 3,24 1844-Ja 2 1845
InI D 1844-Ja 14 1845

LIBERTY port-folio. w 1832-
DLC Ja 31 1834

LOCOMOTIVE. w Ag 16 1845-N 3 1860||
United with Old line guard to form Indiana state guard
IU D 3 1853
In Ag-S 6,20-27,O 11-N 1 1845;Ap-Je 19 1847;48-60
InI S-N 1 1845;Ap-Je 19 1847;S 1849-60
MWA F 21 1852
MoHi F 15 1851
WHi N 30 1850-Ap 10 1852

INDIANA (*Continued*)

INDIANAPOLIS—*Continued*

MACEDONIAN tribune. w
In Greek
PPiHi N 1932

Indianapolis MAIL. d 1879||
In S 18,22-24,O 4-16,25,28-30,N 1-6,15-22 1879
InI Jl 26-N 29 1879

MARION county mail. w 1902+
In 1915-Ag 1932;Jl 6-20 1934
InI 1906-27

MECHANIC and Indiana state gazette. w N 3 1838-
DLC N 3 1838

Evening MINUTE. d 1884-86||
InI D 1884-Ja 16 1886

MIRROR. d 1868-72||
In 1868-71
InI complete
InNcHi D 30 1868

NATIONAL democrat. w Mr 29 1858-
In Mr 29-D 4 1858
InVevHi O 9,23 1858

NEUE freie presse. w
In German
InI 1876-Ag. D 1877-80

Indianapolis NEWS. d D 7 1869+
pub 1869—
CoU 1900
CtW My 24 1893
DLC Ja 1 1875;My 8-9,16 1885;1904+
ICM Je 13 1894
IU My-Jl 1915
In 1869+
InCol 1905+
InEv 1925+
InFr Ap-Je 1908;O 1909-My 1914
InFw 1910+
InG F 1909-Ap 1911
InGcD Jl 1925+
InI F 10 1870+
InIB 1882;My 1903
InLoHi Ap 19 1912
InMa 1911-Ap 2 1916;32-33
InMovHi N 24 1891
InMuB 1914-12;25+
InNcHi F 23 1888
InRE Ja 6 1881;Ap 30 1889
InRP S 2 1881
InTI 1911+
InU [1875-86]97+
InV 1906-14
InWh N 11 1918;Mr 7 1933
KHi D 22 1888[F-Ag 4, 1917]
MWA N 26 1885
MiU 1926-My 5 1934
NbHi Mr 26 1873;My 22 1908-Ag 11 1916
NjP 1892-[1903-04]
OCHi Ja 26 1898
OClWHi N 5 1877;My 15 1902
OHi 1923-30
OOxM N 6 1877
WHi N 8 1905-Je 13 1906;D 18 1916+

OLD line guard. tw Jl 17-N 3 1860||
United with Locomotive to form Indiana state guard
DLC complete
In complete
InI complete
InU complete

PEOPLE. w N 12 1870-1903||?
In 1871-72 Je 15, S 14 1873;S 13-27, D 27 1874 [75-80] O 10 1885;My 25 1889;Jl 20 1895; My 25 1896
InI 1871-75;77-81
N Ag 20 1871
WHi My 20,S 9,D 20 1876

Indianapolis POST. d
In Je 5-7,23-28 1877
InI Jl 15-N 5 1877

Indianapolis POST. d 1927||
In Jl 11-Ag 19 1927
InI Jl 11-Ag 20 1927

Indianapolis PRESS. d D 13 1899-Ap 16 1901||
In complete
InI complete
InIB complete
InU 1899-Mr 1901
MH D 13-26 1899
PPiHi Mr 13 1901

RAILWAY city times. w 1854-
In My 25 1854

Indianapolis RECORDER. w 1897+
Negro
pub 1913+
In 1899-O 1906;My 1932+
InI 1899-1916

Indianapolis REGISTER. w 1906-12||
InI 1908-12

Indianapolis REPORTER. *See* Indianapolis commercial 1895+

Indianapolis REPUBLICAN. d
In F 2-3,Je 1,Ag 28 1855
InI 1855

Indianapolis REPUBLICAN. d Ap 10 1875-Mr 10 1876||
In Ap 10,21,24,27 1875;Ja 25-26,F 7,16,23,Mr 10 1876
InI complete

Indianapolis REPUBLICAN. w 1879-84||
In Ag 9,23-S 20,O 4 1879;Mr 3 1883;Ja 19 1884
InI Jl 1879-Je 1884

Indianapolis Saturday REVIEW. w 1880-84||
In O 30 1880-Jl, O 7 1882;Mr 24, My 19, Je 2, 16 1883
InI N 1880-84
InNcHi Ap 6 1884

SATURDAY. . . *See* under next important word: i.e. Indianapolis Saturday review is alphabeted as Review

Indianapolis SENTINEL. w,sw,d Jl 21 1841-F 25 1906||
Follows Indiana democrat. 1841-96? as Indiana state sentinel
d during sessions of the legislature
DLC O 5 1841;Ja 11,O 3,17,N 14-D 6, 19 1844; Ja 2,F 13, 27-My 1845;Mr 2,My 4,Je 15-29, Jl 13,Ag 3-10,S 21 1848; Mr 8,29 Ap 12,26,My 17,31,Je 28,Jl 26,S 6,D 6-13 1849;O 27 1853; Jl 1872-Ap 1874
In 1841-Je 2,Ag 30 1849;Ja 8,O 8 1850-F 6,N 3,D 1851-54;Ja 13,F 5,13,28-Mr 5,My 30-Je 2,S 12,17 1855;Jl 9 1856-F 25 1906
InFr 1841-Je 20 1844
InI complete
InIB Je 28 1842-My 1854;55-65;Ap 18 1868-Je 1903;04-06
InLoHi Mr 18 1862
InMovHi S 14 1890;S 6,19 1901
InMuB 1891-S 1902;Ap 1904-06
InNcHi Ja 19 1847;Ja 16 1878;S 21 1883
InRE Ja 5-12,Ag-D 1862;Ja 19-Mr,Ap 13-20, My-Jl 1863
InRP S 20 1881
InTI 1876;Jl 1895-Je 1896
InU 1841-Jl 1843;Jl-D 1854;Jl-D 1857;Jl 1858-71;73-80;Ag-D 1883;Ap 1884-Ag 1887;88-1906
KHi Ja 13 1862
MHi O 24 1844
MWA D 22 1841
NbHi Ag 12 1873;F 14 1878;Mr 19 1879;My 23 1886
OClWHi D 5 1850;N 18 1852
OHi Je 1847-My 1848
Tx F 21 1850
WHi Ja 18,24 1842;Jl 18-24 1844;Ag 21 1854;D 23 1857;Mr 12 1864
—sw ed *See* Indiana state sentinel

Indianapolis SENTINEL. d Ap 28 1851-F 25 1906||
Mr 14 1853-F 1855 as Daily Indiana state sentinel; Mr 1855-Mr 1857 Indianapolis daily state sentinel; Ap 1857- Indiana daily state sentinel; -N 1865 Daily state sentinel;N 1865-Je 1868 Indianapolis daily herald. Merged with Indianapolis daily star
CoU 1899-1903;Ja-Je 1905;S 1906-My 1910
DLC Mr 14 1853-Ja 1859;Jl 31-N 2 1861;64-Ag 7 1866;Ja 10 1871;Jl 2 1872-F 25 1906
ICHi [1847;Ja-Je 1871]
ICM N 14-15 1876[Ag 1877]Ja 6 1882
IHi Ag 9 1885
IU Ap 8,10-11 1862
In N 1865-Je 1868
InVevHi [Je 3 1857-Ap 28 1860]
MWA O 31,N 3 1857;Je 22,24-25 1870;Jl 22 1872;F 5-Ag 1874;D 20 1880;Je 13 1881;Ap 7 1882
MnHi Jl 19 1861
MoHi S 18 1901
N Ag 23 1871
NN S 11 1901
NNHi Ja 20 1855
OClWHi N 11 1876
OHi Ap-Je 1852
OOxM D 16-17 1874;Ja 10 1876;N 3,5-6 1877
WHi Je 4 1869;F 2,My 10 1876-F 5 1877;Jl-D 1882;Mr 23 1888

SPECTATOR. d 1844-
In O 21 1845-Ja 17 1846

SPIRIT of 76. w F 21 1840-N 15 1840||?
DLC Ap 4,My 9,Ag 1 1840
MWA Ap 25 1840

SPOTTVOGEL. w 1866-My 1918||
In German
In S 19 1869-72
InI My 14 1871-76;78-1918

Indianapolis STAR. d Je 6 1903+
pub 1903+
DLC F 1906+
IHi F 12 1911
In Je 9 1904+
InI 1903+
InIB Je-S 1903;04-Mr 1905
InLoHi Je 2 1904;Ap 20 1906;Ag 3 1907;Ag 22 1909;Ag 27 1921;Jl 9 1922
InMuB Jl 1904-Je,O 1907-Je 1910
InRE My 24 1915;N 11 1918
InTI Ap 1911-24
InU Je 6 1904+

Semi-weekly STATE journal. sw My? 1839-
1839- as Semi-weekly journal
DLC N 26 1840;Je 8-15,26-Ag 18,25,S 4,11-O 6,13-16 1841 F 23 1844
MWA O 13 1839

STATE sentinel. d. *See* Indianapolis sentinel

Extra STATE sentinel. w Mr 25 1842-
InI My 25-S 16 1842
ICHi Jl 29-Ag 12 1842

Indianapolis SUN. w S 13 1873-82||
In F 21,Ag-D 1874;Ja 23-F 6,Ap 24,My 22,Je 19,Ag 28,S 25,O 16 1875;Ja 8,29,F 12-19,Ap 22,My 13-20,Je 3-10,S 9,O 21,N 18,D 23 1876; Ja 6 1877;My 2 1878;Je 21,Jl 5 1879;N 1 1882
InI complete
InLoHi O 7 1876;My 5 1880
NbHi S 2,O 24,N 4,D 2 1876;S 28,N 2-9 1878; Ag 4 1880
NcD F 12 1876
WHi My 20 1876

Indianapolis daily SUN. d Mr 24 1878-Je? 1881||
Followed by Indianapolis times
OClWHi Mr 25 1878

Indianapolis SUN. 1888-1914. *See* Indianapolis times

Sunday. . . *See under* next important world: i.e. Sunday courier is alphabeted under Courier

Täglicher TELEGRAPH. *See* Telegraph und tribüne

TELEGRAPH und tribüne. d 1865-1918||
1865-Je 1907 as Täglicher telegraph
In German
In 1867-72;Ap 1914-Je 1918
InI Ag 21 1865-Je 12 1867;S 28 1869-My 1918
MWA Ag 26 1876

Indianapolis TIMES. d Jl 14 1881-Ag 9 1886||
Follows Indianapolis sun
ICM Je 11,Ag 31 1884
In Jl 16 1881-86
InI complete
InIB Jl 15 1881-Je,Ag 1884-86
InNcHi S 10 1884
InRE Jl 14-15 1881
InRP S 20,22,27 1881;Ja 15 1884

Indianapolis TIMES. d 1888+
1888-Jl 18 1914 as Indianapolis sun
pub 1913+
CtW My 24 1893
In O 15 1895;S 26 1899;Je 1910+
InI 1913+
InLoHi My 14 1906;Je 19,22 1911

WE, the people. w
In My 27-D 5 1856

WESTERN censor and emigrant's guide. *See* Indiana state journal

WESTERN citizen. w 1876-82||
DLC N 22 1879-82

WESTERN democratic review. w
InU 1854-F 1855

WEST-SIDE herald. w 1893-97||
InI 1894-Ap 3 1897

WEST-SIDE messenger. w
In N 23 1934-Ja,My 3,Je,Jl 12,Ag 13 1935

WHIG rifle. w F 29-N 24 1844||
DLC Mr 7 1844
In Mr 28-S,O 10-24,N 24 1844
InI complete
MWA Ag 1 1844
MoSM Ap 11 1844

Indianapolis WORLD. w 1883-1920||?
Negro
DLC Ja 27 1900

Die ZUKUNFT. w N 1867-82||?
In German
DLC D 17 1868-Ap 8,22-29 My 13,Jl 15,S 30-O 7,21-N 4 1869
TxU Jl 8 1869-O 22 1873;O 21 1875-Ja 9 1879

JAMESTOWN

Jamestown PRESS. w 1878+
pub Je 6 1885;Jl 6 1895;98—

JASONVILLE

Jasonville LEADER. w 1899+
pub 1916+
InBl F 27 1902-Ap 9 1903
InJ 1925+

JASPER

Jasper COURIER. w 1858-1922||
In Je 9 1893-94;97-1915
InU Mr 1858-My 1920

Jasper HERALD. w 1895+
pub 1895-Jl 1898;S 1899+
In Jl 27 1917;20+
InU 1915+

JAY COURT HOUSE

DEMOCRATIC review. w O 1 1863-
MWA D 3 1863

JEFFERSONVILLE

BULLETIN. d 1922-24||
InU Ja 1[O 1922-Ap 1924]

CLARK county journal. w 1854+
1854-S 1919? as National democrat
In O 20 1858;Ap 9 1868
InU D 1919-N 1923
InVevHi Mr 26,Je 23,Ag 11,N 3,24 1858; Mr 9 1859

Jeffersonville COURIER. w D 10 1836-
CSmH D 24 1836

FRENCH'S republican. w
In My 6 1859

Jeffersonville JOURNAL. w
DLC Ap 5 1839

NATIONAL democrat. *See* Clark county journal

Jeffersonville NEWS. d 1872+
Title varies: Evening news
In My 31 1898;My 15 1901;34+
InU 1925-26

Jeffersonville POST. w 1931+
In Ag 9 1935+

Jeffersonville STAR. d 1903-21||
United with Jeffersonville news to form Jeffersonville news and star, later Jeffersonville news
In [My 30 1919-21]

Jeffersonville WORLD. w 1894-96||
In [Ap 3-Ag 22 1896]

JONESBORO

Jonesboro JOURNAL. w 1916+
pub 1916+

INDIANA (*Continued*)

KENDALLVILLE

Kendallville NEWS. w 1877-1910||?
United with Kendallville standard to form Kendallville standard-news
KHi Ag 27 1903-Ja 1905

Kendallville NEWS. d 1906-10||?
United with Kendallville sun to form Kendallville news-sun

Kendallville NEWS-SUN. d 1890+
1890-1910? as Kendallville sun
pub [1890-1910]+
In My 3 1928;34+
InK 1917+
InU Ag 1914+
NN O 17 1925

NOBLE county journal. w 1860-70||?
MWA Ja 26 1866

Kendallville STANDARD-NEWS. w 1863-1920||?
1863-1910? as Kendallville standard
InGoE Mr 1 1876;Je 13,14 1889

Kendallville SUN. *See* Kendallville news-sun

KENTLAND

Kentland DEMOCRAT. w 1884+
pub 1884+

Kentland GAZETTE. *See* Newton county gazette

NEWTON county democrat. w 1868-72||?
In F 17 1870

NEWTON county enterprise. w 1865+
1865-89? as Kentland gazette
pub [1865+]
In F 5 1914+
InKe 1921-32
InKeN 1900+

NEWTON county gazette. w
In Ap 6 1867

NEWTON county news. w 1880-82||
InFo complete

KEWANNA

Kewanna HERALD. w 1883+
pub Ja 2 1896;Ag 11,25 1899;F 14 1902;F 21 1912+
In Je 20 1895;F 18 1898-1900

Kewanna POST. w
In Ja 27 1876

KINGMAN

Kingman STAR. w 1898+
pub 1901+

KIRKLIN

Kirklin JOURNAL. w 1897-1918||
Followed by Kirklin press
InKi Je 15 1916-18

Kirklin PRESS. w 1919-32||
Follows Kirklin journal
InKi 1920-32

KNIGHTSTOWN

Knightstown BANNER. w 1867+
pub My 1892+
In F 18 1876;D 22 1905;Ja 4,18 1907;Ap 24-My 8,O 9 1908
InKn [1908+]
InNcHi My-Je 7,21,Jl 5,19-Ag 2[16-N 29]D 6 1867[F-D 8 1868]Ja 1,22 1869;O 23,N 6,D 4-19 1873;Ja 2,23,O 30 1874;Ap 23 1875;N 10,25,D 9-16,30 1881;Je 30,Ag 25,N 10 1882;Ja 19 1885; Ja 8 1886;Mr 2,Je 1 1888;Mr 1 1889;Mr 25 1894;Ap 1902-08;F 21 1930;O 2-9,N 13-20 1931; Ja 20,Ap 28 1933;Ap 19 1935
InU 1915

Knightstown CITIZEN. w 1859-
InNcHi Ja 27 1860

CITY chronicle. w Ap 5 1870-75||?
InNcHi Ap 26 1870

FEDERAL union. w
DLC Ag 31 1833

INDIANA citizen. w
InI O 7 1859

INDIANA courier. *See* New Castle courier (New Castle)

INDIANA sun. w 1837-40||
Followed by Indiana courier, later New Castle courier (New Castle)
In D 5 1838
InNcHi Je 25,D 26 1840

Knightstown JOURNAL. w 1876-77||
In D 15 1876;Ja 11 1877

Knightstown SUN. *See* Tri-county journal-sun

TRI-COUNTY journal-sun. w 1885-1905||?
1885-1903? as Knightstown sun
InNcHi Ap 9,My 28 1886;Ja 31 1895;Mr 31 1898

KNOX

STARKE county democrat. w 1866+
1866-92? as Starke county ledger
In 1885;N 19 1891-Mr 1892;1919+

STARKE county enterprise. *See* Starke county republican

STARKE county ledger. *See* Starke county democrat

STARKE county republican. w 1876+
1876-86? as Starke county enterprise
pub [1895-1904]+
In Jl 10 1935+
InU 1915-17

KOKOMO

Kokomo DEMOCRAT. *See* Kokomo dispatch

Kokomo DISPATCH. w 1870-1912||?
1870-D 4? 1879 as Kokomo democrat
In Ap 13 1871;S 25,D 25 1884;Mr 24 1887;O 6 1890;Ag 14,15-21,27,S-O 16,30-D 4,8,22 1891-Ja 4,8,22,F 5 1892;Je 8 1893-94;1907-10
InKo Mr 25 1871-My 1881;My 10 1883-Ag 1888;My 1889-My 1903
MWA Je 29 1876

Kokomo DISPATCH. d 1890-1930||
InKo Ap 1907-30
InLoHi Ap 14 1925
InU Jl-O 1916

Evening GAZETTE. *See* Kokomo daily tribune

Kokomo GAZETTE-TRIBUNE. *See* Kokomo tribune

HOME journal. w
In Ap 12-19 1860

HOWARD county republican. w 1871-73||
In F 23 1872-F 14,Ag 15 1873

HOWARD tribune. *See* Kokomo tribune

Kokomo JOURNAL. w 1870-
In 1870

Kokomo LIBERAL. w
In Jl 20 1872

Morning NEWS. d 1896-1907||?
InKo S 1904-Ap 1905

RADICAL democrat. w
InKo My 18 1870-My 18 1871

Kokomo TRIBUNE. w 1851-1912||?
1851-69? as Howard tribune;1870?-74? Kokomo tribune;1875-82? Saturday tribune; 1883?-91? Kokomo gazette-tribune
pub 1860-1912
DLC My 26 1874
In O 30-N 6,20,D 3-10,24 1850-Ja 7,21-28,My 27,S 2,N 25 1851;O 3 1854;S 23 1857;Ja 18 1859;F 21,My 29 1860;Ap 9,O 9 1862;Ja-F,Mr 12-Ap 2,23,My 14-Je 4,25-Jl 2,23-30,Ag 13-D 17 1868;S 9,D 23 1869;70;Jl 23-30 1872; Je 30,O 20,N 10,D 5 1874
InNcHi F 4 1857
MWA Je 17 1876

Kokomo daily TRIBUNE. d 1879+
1879-82? as Evening gazette;1883?-91? Gazette-tribune
pub 1883+
IU Ja-D 21 1920
In 1911+
InKo Ap 1912+

Saturday TRIBUNE. *See* Kokomo tribune

LADOGA

Ladoga RURALIST. w
In My 4,25,Ap 27,Je 1-8,22-Jl 20,Ag 3-10 1860
InU My 25,Je 1-8,Jl 20,Ag 3-10 1860

LAFAYETTE

Lafayette AMERICAN. tw,d Je 27 1854-64||
In S 2,28,D 19-30 1854;My 1 1855;Ap 24-30,O 28,N 29 1856
InLHi 1854-S 12 1855

Lafayette ARGUS. w 1857-
In N 29 1860;My 5 1864
InL 1859-64
InVevHi My 27,Jl 8,O 21,N 11 1858;Ja 13 1859;Ja 12 1860

Lafayette evening CALL. d 1883-1905||
InL 1884-1905

La Fayette weekly COMMERCIAL advertiser. w 1864-
In S 28 1865
OClWHi Jl 20 1865

COMMERCIAL intelligencer. w
DLC Ja-Mr,Ap 21-My,Je 23,Jl 7-21,Ag 11,S 1-8,22,O 6,N 3,17 1838

Lafayette weekly COURIER. w 1845-1919||
In 1847-48;N 16 1849
InL [1851-1915]
InLoHi S 6 1901
MWA N 26 1847;Ag 29 1865
NbHi S 2 1879

Lafayette daily COURIER. d D 3 1849-1919||
United with Lafayette daily journal to form Lafayette journal and courier
DLC Mr 11-12,19-20,23,27,Ap 12-13,My 2,Je 26,Jl 5,11,Ag 3,23,30,O 2-3,N 2,11,14,D 1,3,21, 28 1861;98
ICHi S 27 1865
In 1850;S 27,D 10 1851;Ap 21 1852;Mr 16,Je 10 1853;Ja 4 1855;Ap 15-29,S 1 1856;Je 18 1857;O 19 1858;F 19,My 30,Je 9 1859;Ja 25,Mr 13,My 31-Je 5,Jl 9,D 4,6 1860;Ja 31,F 11,Mr 22,Ap 26,My 31[Je-Jl]S 7,10,17,N 21,23 1861;My 29,O 7,31,N 1,13 1862[My]Jl 7,11,O 26 1863;Ap 25[My-Je]O 26 1864;My 13,S 2,O 13 1865;Ja 19,My 5,Ag 16,21,S 21,O 5,8,13 1866;Ap 23,My 7,Ag 10,18,S 15,N 16 1868;F 17 1869[F]-Mr 2,4 1870;F 20[Ag]D 27 1871;F 20,Jl 19-20,Ag 13,17,19,D 28 1872;Ja 16 1873;Je 12,18 1875;S 14-15,D 18-20 1876;S 6 1878;Je 7 1879;Jl 18-19 1890;Ag 9 1892;F 28 1899;Jl 18 1907-19
InLHi D 1849-D 15 1853;Je 29 1858-Jl 1 1862; Ap 28 1868;Je 8 1869;O 16,23 1888;O 8 1904;Je 23 1916;N 11 1918

MWA D 29 1855;Ag 28 1865;N 18 1876
OClWHi Ap 15 1865
PPeS D 28 1903
TKL S 26 1881
WHi Jl 2 1860

Lafayette DEMOCRAT. w
In O 25 1864

Lafayette DEMOCRAT. d 1902-04||
InL complete

Lafayette DEMOCRAT-LEADER. w 1873+
1873-1928? as Lafayette leader
InL 1922+
InLHi N 1874-S 1878;Mr 9 1879-F 20 1881;92-93;Ap 23 1905

Lafayette DISPATCH. d Ap 1 1869-85||
In D 1 1869;F 16,22,Ag 9,17-19,22 1870;F 15, 23,28,Ag 15,17,22,28,D 28 1871;S 3 1877;N 20 1879;Jl 22 1880
InL 1871;73-85
InLHi 1869-S 1871;Mr 14 1872;N 10 1880

Lafayette DISPATCH. w 1869-85||
MWA Ag 24 1876

Lafayette FREE press. *See* Lafayette journal

Lafayette GAZETTE. w
In O 28,D 30 1854

GRAPHIC. w
InL 1880-81

INDIANA. w D 12 1838-
DLC 1839-D 21 1840

INDIANA journal. w
InL 1831-34

INDIANA state commercial and home advocate. m Ap 1 1864-
In N 1 1866
MWA Je-N 1867

INDIANA trade gazette. w 1869-
In Ag 25 1869

INDIANA union. w 1868-
In German
In S 12 1868

Lafayette JOURNAL. w S 23 1829-1914||?
1829-46 as Lafayette free press; 1846-54? Tippecanoe journal and Lafayette free press; 1855?-59? Journal and free press
DLC N 18-D 23 1829;S 30,O 27 1840;Jl 21 1841;Mr 9,Ag 3,23,N 23 1855;S 26 1856;F 5,Ap 9,O 1,N 5-D 16 1858;Ap 29,Jl 8-Ag 19,S 1859
In My 27 1836;Ja 27 1841;F 3 1843;Ja 12 1846; Ag 19,S 23 1847;Je 8 1848;My 4,N 1 1849;50-51;Mr 26,N 28 1853;Mr 4,18,My 29,31,N 3,D 20 1854;F 29,Mr 27,Ap 14,24 1856;58[59-67]F 19,My 12,Jl 18,Ag 13,18,N 4,D 11 1868[F]My 7,S 30,O 5,6,D 20 1869;F 14-18,22,24,25,Mr 1-3,Ap 18,Je 10-D 1870;F 13,14,17,23,24,27,Mr 1,20,My 23,Ag 14-18,21-25,28-30,N 4,D 27,28 1871;Ja 1,F 28,Ap 9,16,My 31-N,D 28,30 1872; My 10,Ag 27,O 20 1873;F 12,Mr 12,Ap 16,Jl 17,Ag 19 1874;F 2,5,Mr 8,Jl 12,13,S 9,15,16,D 19-21 1876;Mr 12 1877;S 6 1878;N 15 1883;Ap 27 1886;88-94;97-1914
InI D 29 1846
InL 1841-45;50;60;62-80;83-84;87;93-1914
InLHi My 19 1830;O 12 1832;Je 7 1834;S 8 1852-My 1 1854;D 29 1859;Jl 25 1873;Je 11 1875;O 18 1877;Ja 19,Ag 24 1878;Ja 27 1879; Jl 23 1885;S 20 1901;N 8 1905;Ap 25 1906;N 11 1918
InLoHi Ap 17 1865
InU [Ap 1855-O 1868]
MWA Ag 17 1848;O 20 1865

Lafayette JOURNAL and courier. d 1848+
1848-1919 as Lafayette daily journal (title varies: Morning journal;etc)
DLC S 3 1853-N 4 1859
ICHi Je 4 1864
In 1915-18;20+
InL 1915+
InMo N 28 1918
InNcHi D 2 1925
MBAt Ap 15,17,19 1865
MWA D 24 1853;D 18 1854;O 20 1865;N 20 1876
WHi S 30 1859-Mr 1861;My 25,O 26 1864

Lafayette LEADER. *See* Lafayette democrat-leader

Lafayette Sunday LEADER. w 1873-1929||
In Mr 28 1880;Mr 14 1886
InL 1883-1929

STAR City. w 1851-
In N 8 1851

Lafayette Sunday TIMES. w 1879-1914||
In O 25 1891;Ag 13 1899
InL 1879;83-1914
MWA Ja 22 1882

TIPPECANOE American. w 1855-
In F 28 1856

TIPPECANOE county democrat. w 1908-28||?
United with Lafayette leader to form Lafayette democrat-leader

TIPPECANOE journal. w 1841-46||
United with Lafayette free press to form Tippecanoe journal and Lafayette free press, later Lafayette journal
In My 30 1844;My 15,Jl 31,O 30 1845;F 5 1846
InL 1845-46
MBaT S 21 1843
OClWHi S 21 1843

TIPPECANOE journal and Lafayette free-press. *See* Lafayette journal

WABASH atlas. w
In Ag 24 1848-Ja,F 13-My 1,15-Ag 14,S 11, 25-O 2,30-N 13, 27 1849-50

WABASH mercury. w 1834-
OClWHi F 27 1836

WABASH standard. w
In S 27,O 25 1844;Ap 11-18,Je 27,Jl 18-25, Ag 1,15 1845

INDIANA (*Continued*)

LA GRANGE

Saturday CALL. w 1892-1913||
United with La Grange county democrat to form La Grange democrat-call, later La Grange news

La Grange COUNTY democrat. *See* La Grange news

La Grange DEMOCRAT. w O 17 1859-
DLC F 28 1860

La Grange DEMOCRAT. 1879-1907. *See* La Grange news

La Grange DEMOCRAT-CALL. *See* La Grange news

La Grange NEWS. w 1879+
1879-1907? as La Grange democrat; 1907?-13? La Grange county democrat; 1914?-20? La Grange democrat-call
In F 21 1935+
InLa 1917+

REGISTER. w 1874-96||?
InLa Ag 8 1879;My 30 1882;O 1,15,29 1884;Je 1 1887;Ja 8,22,F 26 1890

La Grange STANDARD. w 1857+
pub [1857+]
CSmH O 5 1859
ICHi Ap 18 1907
IHi Ap 22 1865
In F 1914+
InGoE 1860-F 1876
InLa 1917+
InU Mr 1918-Ja 16,30,D 4,18 1925;Ja-Je 1926
MWA Je 29-Jl 6 1876
OClWHi Ag 27 1864

LAGRO

LaGro EXPRESS. w
InWbHi Jl 1876-Je 1878

INDIANA eagle. w
In Jl 17 1850

LaGro LOCAL. w
InWbHi My 28-N 19 1875

LAPEL

Lapel NEWS. w 1891-1923||?
InElw Mr 14 1907

LA PORTE

La Porte ARGUS. w 1869-1924||
In Je 1893-94;97-S 11 1902;F 1912-O 21 1924
InLap Ap 15 1869-Mr 9 1893;Jl 11 1896-Jl 3 1900;15-O 18 1924
MWA Je 29 1876

La Porte ARGUS. d 1895-1924||
1900-14 as La Porte argus-bulletin. United with La Porte herald to form La Porte herald-argus
InLap Ag 1900-14

BULLETIN. d 1898-1900||
United with La Porte argus to form La Porte argus-bulletin, later La Porte argus
InLap F 1898-Je 1900

La Porte CHRONICLE. sw Jl 18 1874-81||
United with La Porte herald to form Herald-chronicle, later La Porte herald
DLC N 17 1874-Jl 18 1876
InLap 1874-Je 6 1877;79-81
MWA Jl 18 1876

La Porte DEMOCRAT. w Ag 22? 1862-
MWA F 14 1863

La Porte HERALD. w 1836-1925||
1838-S 1867 as La Porte herald; O 1867-Jl 9 1870 Union and herald; Jl 16 1870-Je 1877 La Porte herald; Jl 1877-My 1879 Saturday evening herald; 1880-Jl 1889 Herald-chronicle
In N 5-12 1836;Mr 26 1864;F 18 1865;Ap 8 1871; Ja 23 1875;O 15 1897
InLap Ag 26 1859-78;Jl 1879-Ja 1880;82-Ja 1925
MWA S 22 1838;Ap 6 1861;O 21 1865;Jl 15 1876

La Porte HERALD-argus. d 1888+
1888-S 1924 as La Porte herald
In 1934+
InLap O 1925+

INDIANA tocsin. w
In Jl 18 1845;Jl 11 1846

LA PORTE county whig. *See* La Porte union

REPUBLIC herald. d
InLap Jl 30 1888-Jl 1889

La Porte REPUBLICAN. w 1894-1906||
InLap 1896-Ja 1906

La Porte TIMES. w 1852-60||
In Ap 5,S 14 1854;Ap 25,S 12 1855;Jl 12 1856; Jl 11-S 25 1857;58-N 10 1860
InGoE Ja 14 1860
InVevHi Mr 26 1859;Ja 4,28-F 4,Ap 7,21,My 12 1860

La Porte TIMES. d 1925-26||
InLap O 1925-Ja 1926

La Porte UNION. w Je 23 1838-S 1867||
1838-S 6 1854 as La Porte county whig. United with La Porte herald to form Union and herald, later La Porte herald
DLC Jl 14 1838;Ap 22,Je 20 1840
In S 15 1838;D 3 1851;S 29 1852;N 8 1854;S 12 1855;F 15 1860;Mr 30 1864
InLap Ag 1847-Jl 1851;S 13 1854-Jl 25 1855;Jl 30 1856-Jl 21 1858;Je 27 1866-S 25 1867
InNcHi N 17 1849
MWA Jl 14 1838;Ja 24 1866
P-M My 31 1845
TKL S 13 1854
WHi My 17-Je 7 1845;D 25 1847

LAUREL

Laurel REVIEW. w 1874-1931||?
InBrok 1891-93
InBrokF 1887-88

LAWRENCEBURG

DEMOCRATIC register. *See* Lawrenceburg register

INDEPENDENT press. w O 17? 1850-64||
Followed by Union press, later Lawrenceburg press
In O 18 1850-Ag 22 1851;Ja 17-24,F 21-28 1855; Mr 12 1856
InLaw 1850-56
OOxM Jl 25-Ag 26 1851

***INDIANA oracle.** w 1819-
In O 4 1823
InI Je 9-23,Jl 7,S 29,O 13,N 3,D 22-29 1821;Ja 19,F 2,16,Mr 30,My 18,Je 1,29,Jl-Ag 3,S 14-N 9,23-D 1822;Ja 9-Ap,My 10-17,31-Jl,Ag 23-30,O 4-18,N 1 1823;Mr 20,Ap 10,My 8 1824

INDIANA palladium. w Ja 7 1825-
CSmH Jl 31 1830
Ct [1826]
DLC N 18 1825;Jl 4,Ag 1 1829;30;33-36
ICHi D 29 1832;O 26 1833
IU 1830
In 1825-Ja 1836
InI 1825;S 5 1835
InLoHi Ag 25,D 22 1832;Je 1 1833
MWA Jl 15 1825;Mr 3 1827;F 23 1833;D 10 1836
WHi 1825-D 27 1828

INDIANA register. w 1845-48||?
Merged with Democratic register, later Lawrenceburg register
InI My 15 1847-My 6 1848
MWA Jl 31 1847

INDIANA reveille. w
InI Mr 11 1857

INDIANA spectator. w
InI D 11 1824;Ja 1,Mr 26,Ap 2,15 1825
VU D 23 1825

INDIANA whig. w 1834-
Follows Western statesman
In Je 14 1834;D 21-28 1843;Ja 4-11,F 1-8,My 9 1844;F 27 1845
InLaw 1834

JOURNAL. d
In O 26,30 1849

POLITICAL beacon. w O 7 1837-
DLC Je 4 1837;My-O 7 1842
IHi [O 13 1838-O 5 1839]
In 1837-O 19 1839;Ja 11,Je 27-Jl 11,O 24-D 19 1840;Ja 16-Ap 10,Jl 2-9,Ag 6 1841;D 2,16 1842;F 3-10,Mr 3,Jl 21,O 27-N 10,D 8,21 1843-Ja 4,18-Mr 7,28,My 30-Je 13 1844;Ag 14,O 23-30 1845
InI O 1838-O 19 1839
MWA O 12 1839

Lawrenceburg PRESS. w 1864+
Follows Independent press. 1864-66 as Union press; 1866-68 Union press and Lawrenceburg press
In O 27 1864;My 31 1866;O 17 1872;Mr 2 1876;1909-Ap 19 1911;32+
InLaw 1864-78;1911+
KHi O 18 1928-O 17 1929
MWA Jl 13 1876
WHi Ag 17 1865

Lawrenceburg REGISTER. w 1837+
1837-79? as Democratic register
IU O 8 1914-S 1918
In O 25,D 27 1850;Ja 23 1852;D 29 1854;Ja 26 1855;O 24 1862;Je 5,O 2 1863;S 15 1865;Mr 10,Ap-Je 1,22,Jl 1871-Mr 7,21-My,Je 13-D 1872;Mr 6 1873;F 24 1876;Jl 5 1883;88-94;97-99;Jl 11 1907-15
InLaw 1911+
InU 1915-17
InVevHi Je 18,N 26-D 3 1858;My 6 1859;Ja 13, Mr 9 1860
MWA Je 22 1876
WHi S 19 1872

Lawrenceburg REPUBLICAN. w
In Jl 12,26 1860

REPUBLICAN banner. w
In Jl 7-14 1858

STANDARD and press. w
WHi Ag 6 1856

UNION press. *See* Lawrenceburg press

WESTERN statesman. w Mr 10 1830-34||
Followed by Indiana whig
DLC Mr 10,D 3,24 1830;Ja 7 1831
In Ag 23-30,S 11 1833
InLaw 1830-34
InLoHi Mr 8,Jl 20,Ag 24 1832-Jl 5,S 25,N 8,22 1833
MWA Ag 4 1832
OCHi S 9 1831

WESTERN times. w
InLoHi Ag 3 1832

LEAVENWORTH

Leavenworth ARENA. w 1838-
DLC Jl 30 1840
In My 17 1838-Je 3 1841

LEBANON

BOONE county pioneer. *See* Lebanon pioneer

BOONE county progressive. w 1912-14||
InLeB 1913-14

EXPOSITOR. w
InLeB 1859

Lebanon PATRIOT. w 1857-1917||?
In 1897-1901;05-10;12
InCr F 22 1866-Jl 11 1877
InLeB 1867-75;78-81;83-92;94-96;99-1915
MWA Jl 27 1876

Lebanon PIONEER. w Jl 27 1852+
1852-60? as Boone county pioneer
DLC N 2 1852
In [Ag 25 1855-Jl 5 1856]Mr 25 1860;1910-15
InLeB 1856-57;61;68-76;78-80;83+
InVevHi Jl 9,D 3,24 1858;F 2 1860
MWA O 26 1852

Lebanon REPORTER. d 1891+
In Jl 1935+
InLeB 1917+
InU N 4,11 1932

LEWISVILLE

Lewisville DEMOCRAT. w 1877-79||
InNcHi F 14,28,D 12 1878;S 4 1879

Lewisville FREEMAN. *See* National road traveler (Cambridge City)

NATIONAL road traveller. *See under* Cambridge City

LEXINGTON

Lexington ENTERPRISE. w D 17 1868-
MWA F 19 1869

LIBERTY

Liberty EXPRESS. w 1903-24||?
InU 1915-20

Liberty GAZETTE. w 1827-
In O 6 1827

Liberty HERALD. w 1851+
In My 4-11 1876;Ap 16 1914-15;Je 12,26,Jl 3-10 1919
InLbHi 1884-[87]
MWA Mr 11 1858
OClWHi F 3 1864

Liberty REPUBLICAN. w Mr 14 1834-
DLC Ap 18 1834

Liberty REVIEW. w 1886-1902||?
In N 5 1886;Mr 17 1892;Ja 4 1894

Liberty STAR and banner. w Ap 16 1836-
In Ap 16,30-My 14,Je 4,18-Jl 2,16-O 15,N 5,19 1836-Ja 7,21-28,F 11-25 1837

UNION county democrat. *See* Union county news

UNION county news. w 1882-86||?
1882-83 as Union county democrat
In S 22,O 6,N 10,24 1882
OClWHi My 7 1886

UNION times. w
In O 5,26-N 23 1876

LIGONIER

Ligonier BANNER. w My 1866+
1866-82? as National banner
pub 1918+
In My 1873-Ap 20 1876;Ap 22 1880-Ap 14 1881; Je 2 1893-94;97+
InLi [1908]+
InSbN 1866-My 1 1867
InU [1917]

Ligonier LEADER. w 1880+
pub 1880+
InLi [1908+]

NATIONAL banner. *See* Ligonier banner

NOBLE county herald. w 1860-
DLC D 7 1860

LIMA. *See* HOWE

LINTON

Linton CALL. w 1888-1920||?
InBl O 11 1889[91-98]1900-03

Linton CITIZEN. d 1900+
pub 1921+
In Je 11 1934+
InU Mr-My 1914

Linton RECORD. w 1897-1917||?
InBl Ap 5 1901;Mr 21-28,O 9 1902;Mr 20 1903; Mr 18 1904

LOGANSPORT

Logansport ADVANCE. w 1892-1906||?
In O 21 1892
InLoHi O 28 1892;Jl 22 1893;F 10 1899;D 31 1903
WHi Jl 13 1900

Logansport ADVERTISER. d 1882-84||
In Ja 19,O 6,11,N 30,D 21 1882;My 5 1883
InLoHi Jl 27 1884

Logansport BANNER. w
In Ag 26 1871-Ag 1873

CANAL telegraph. *See* Logansport telegraph

CASS county times. w
In N 16 1831-D 19 1832

Logansport CHRONICLE. w 1875-1917||
ICM Ag 25 1888
In [Ap 18 1875-81]-[99-1901]
InLoHi F 11 1882;F 25,Mr 1,Ap 4 1911;Je 23 1917

INDIANA (*Continued*)

LOGANSPORT—*Continued*

COLORED visitor. sm 1879-
In Ag 1 1879

Logansport Sunday CRITIC. w 1884-87||
In My 11 1884-Ja 18,F 15,Mr 1-15,Ap 5-12,My 10-17,31,Je 14-Jl,Ag 9 1885-Mr 6 1887

DEMOCRATIC pharos. *See* Logansport pharos-tribune. w

Logansport DEMOKRAT. w
In German
In Ja 19 1867-Mr 21 1868
WHi Ja 19,Mr 2 1867

DEUTSCHE zeitung. *See* Das Sternebanner

Logansport FREIE PRESSE. w 1894-95||
In German
In Ap 26 1894-F 8 1895

Logansport HERALD. w Ag 3 1837-41||?
DLC Mr 18-25,Ap 8,22-My 13,27,Je 10-17,Jl 8-15,Ag 5,19-23,O 7 1840
In Ag 10 1837-D 16 1840;Je 8-22,Jl 6-20 1841
InU 1837-O 1839

Logansport Sunday HERALD. w O 25 1874-
In O 25 1874

Logansport JOURNAL. w Ap 21 1849-1911||
United with Logansport tribune to form Logansport journal-tribune, later Logansport tribune
ICM Ag 24 1888
In 1849-F 1903;Ag-D 10 1907
InLo [1849-1911]
InLoHi Ag 2 1854;My 24 1862;Ja 9,Je 4,Jl 13 1864;My 6 1865;O 31 1874;D 11 1875;S 27 1881;Je 13 1883;Ja 13,25,F 5-12,My 17,Je 29,Jl 10,24,O 13,26,N 10 1876;Je 29,Jl 14,15 1877;D 7 1890;S 17 1892;My 15 1900;Je 11,S 14,20 1901;Ja 1 1904;Ap 19,20-27 1906;Jl 27,Ag 6-13,S 3,5 1907;F 20,26,28,Mr 3,Ag 9 1908[Mr] Ag 14 1910;F 1,2,3,28,Mr 9,Ap 19,Jl 9,S 16,O 5 1911
InU 1849-78
N Mr 22 1856
WHi Ap 23-D 17 1864

Logansport daily JOURNAL. *See* Logansport tribune. 1875-1920

Logansport JOURNAL-TRIBUNE. *See* Logansport tribune. 1875-1920

Logansport LEADER. w D 7 1893-94||
In D 7 1893;My 8-11,23-31,Je 19,Jl 1 1894

Sunday LOCAL. w Ag 30 1874-
In Ag 30-O 11 1874

LOGAN chief. w
In F 20,Mr-S 6,20,O 4-11 1845

Logansport NEWS. d D 8 1868-70||
In 1868-Ja 6 1869;Ja 1-5,7-10,12-15,D 19,21,23, 26-28,30-31 1870

Logansport evening NEWS. d 1877-
In Mr 5-Ap 1877[O 18-28]N 3-6,8 1882

Logansport PHAROS-REPORTER. *See* Logansport pharos-tribune

Logansport PHAROS-TRIBUNE. w,sw 1844-1925||?
1844-73 as Democratic pharos; 1873-1903 Logansport pharos; 1914-Mr 14 1920 Logansport pharos-reporter
w 1844-1909?
In Jl 24 1844-Jl 16,Ag 6,S 3,17,O 8,22-29,N 12-19,D 3-10,24 1845;46-47;F 1848-Ja 2,3,6 1906;14-Mr 14 1920
InI F 1876-Ja 1877
InLo Je 1858-My 1859;69-73;F 18-D 1874;81-93;95-1907;09;11-Je 1919
InLoHi Ja 2-9,23,F 6,Mr 6,20,My 1,22-29,Jl 10-O 1,23-30,N 27,D 18-25 1861;O 29 1865;D 26 1866;D 25 1867;Jl 24 1872;Ja 24,N 11 1876;Je 9 1886;Mr 24 1888;Ja 31 1895;F 16 1898;S 30 1903;N 9 1906;S 12,O 1,N 2,6 1912;Mr 4,28,29, My 5,Jl 3,Ag 20,S 19,N 5,26 1913;F 27,28,Mr 27,Ap 3,11-15,28,My 12,20,S 4,16,N 4,D 31 1914;Mr 4,13,My 8-12,22 1915;Ja 31,F 19,29, Mr 22,Jl 19,S 16,O 4,14,21,28,N 9 1916;F 1,Ap 18,Je 18,Jl 20,28,Ag 13,S 6,O 22,N 2 1917
InU 1849-85;91-Ap 1896;97-1902
MWA O 20 1852
WHi Ja 9 1861;Je 15 1864

Logansport PHAROS-TRIBUNE. d 1874+
1874-1913? as Logansport pharos; 1914-Mr 14 1920 Logansport pharos-reporter
In Mr 15 1920+
InLo 1920+
WHi N 1-2,8,14,16-18,20,22 1905

POTAWATTIMIE and Miami times. w
In O 10-17 1829;Ja 9,23,F 6,My 26-Je 2,Jl 2 1830;My 11,31,Jl 20,Ag 24 1831

Logansport PRESS. d 1921+
pub 1921+

Sunday RAMBLER. w O 8 1876-
In O 8-15,29 1876

Logansport REPORTER. d 1889-1913||
United with Logansport pharos to form Logansport pharos-reporter, later Logansport pharos-tribune

Logansport REPORTER. w 1889-1913||
United with Logansport pharos to form Logansport pharos-reporter, later Logansport pharos-tribune
In Ja 25 1890-D 17 1913
InLo 1889-1909;11-My 1913
InLoHi Je,D 1892;N 29 1899;Ap 19-22,24-29, My 2,Je 23,Jl 13,14,17,19,24,28[Ag]S 5,O 4,5 1911;N 2,6,30,D 7 1912;Mr 25 1913

Logansport REPUBLICAN. w My 22 1866-
In My-O 23 1866

Logansport REPUBLICAN and Indiana herald. w N 9 1831-
In N 16-23,D 1831-Ap 14,My 12-Jl,Ag 18-O 20,N 24-D 1832;F 14-21,Mr 7-21,My 9-Jl 18,Ag 8-15,29-D 19 1833

Logansport SATURDAY night. w
In Mr 25-Ag 26,S 9-16,O 28 1882

Logansport SATURDAY night review. w O 13 1894-D 1895||
In 1894-Mr 23,Ap 20-N 2,16-D 1895
InLoHi complete

Logansport STAR. w,d 1873-78||
In [F 28-N 18 1876]D 9 1876-Ap 6 1878
InLoHi N 11 1873;S 17 1875;Ja 12,My 26,O 7 1876
WHi Mr 19 1876

Das STERNEBANNER. w 1882-99||
1882-93? as Deutsche zeitung
In German
In O 1882-Je 12 1891;D 7 1894

Logansport SUN. w 1872-75||
In 1872;O 16 1873-Mr 6 1875

Logansport TELEGRAPH. w Ja 4 1834-
1834- as Canal telegraph
DLC Ja 18 1834;D 26 1840
ICHi O 29 1836
In 1834-Jl 9,Ag 1836-Mr 23,Je 8 1839-Ag 1847
InLoHi Je 6 1835
InU F 1840-Mr 1849
MWA Mr 1 1834
TxU 1845-N 11 1848
WHi F 17 1838;F 29 1840;Ja 8,My 14,Je 18-25,Ag 13,27,O 1,N 5,19-26,D 10,24 1842;Ja 14,20,F 4,10,25,Ap 8,N 11,25,D 16 1843;My 4,Jl 6,Ag 10-S 28 1844;Ja 4,F 1-22,S 6 1845

Logansport TIMES. w
In Ja 24-Je 22 1871

Logansport TIMES. w 1886-1917||
In [Ap 1896-F 1903]O 1914-15
InLoHi F 3,Jl 7,S 15-22,D 15,29 1911;Ja 12,Je 14 1912;Jl 25,S 19 1913;Ja 9,Mr 6,20-Ap 3,S 4,18 1914;Ja 1,D 31 1915;Ja 7,S 29 1916;F 9,Jl 6 1917

Logansport TRIBUNE. d 1875-Mr 14 1920||
1875-1911 as Logansport daily journal; 1912-16 as Logansport journal-tribune. United with Logansport pharos-reporter to form Logansport pharos-tribune
In 1914-Jl 1918;Ap 26 1919-20
InLo O 1912-Je 1913;15-Je 1916
InLoHi O 5,9,15,N 2,D 4,6,22 1912;Mr 26-30,Ap 1,13,Jl 4,22,O 16,D 13,24,27 1913;Ja 1,10,31,F 4,28,Mr 1,4,10[Ap]My 21,Je 25,Ag 6,11,15,20, 23,S 3,13,19,22,O 24,N 4-5,8,10,20,25 1914[15-17]
MWA Jl 14 1876
WHi Je 27,Jl 4 1883;D 12 1888

Logansport TRIBUNE. d 1907-S 1912||
United with Logansport daily journal to form Logansport journal-tribune, later Logansport tribune
InLoHi D 1 1907;D 20 1908;Jl 6,S 27 1911;Je 8,Jl 2-3,Ag 2 1912

WABASH gazette. w N 10 1842-
In N 10,24-D 15,29 1842;Ja 12,26,F 9-16,Mr 16-30,Je 8,N 8-D 6,20 1843
InLo Mr 20 1834-Ja 1835;Ap 15 1837-Ag 24 1839;S 25 1841-Ja 20 1849

LOOGOOTEE

MARTIN county tribune. w 1874+
1874-83 as Loogootee tribune
In Jl 11 1935+

Loogootee TRIBUNE. *See* Martin county tribune

LOWELL

Lowell SOUVENIR. w 1901-14||
InG Ag 3 1911;Jl 3,31-Ag 7,N 13,27,D 18 1913-Ja 8,29,Ap 9-23 1914

Lowell STAR. w 1872-78||?
InLwT 1874-75
MWA Jl 22 1876

Lowell TRIBUNE. w 1885+
pub 1897+
In S,O 2,16,30-N 6,20,D 11 1930[31-33]+
InG Jl 13 1911[13-19;22-23]D 15 1925;F 25 1926-27;Ap 27 1928-N 14 1929;Ag 28 1930+

MADISON

Madison daily BANNER. d 1848-
DLC Mr 5-N 27 1849;Ja-N 27 1851
In Je 1851-Ap 1 1853;D 29 1854
InMC Je 1848-53

Madison COURIER. w 1837-1921||
pub [1837-1921]
DLC O 26 1844
In [D 14 1839-41]-1900;Ap 2 1902;08-21
InI F 1876-87
InM 1851
InMC D 14 1839-1900
InU O 1914-Je 1916
MWA O 18 1865;Ja 31 1866
OClWHi My 15 1846
OHi 1868-70
OOxM O 23-30,N 27-D 4 1847;Ja 8,29 1848;Jl 11,Ag 29 1849;D 31 1851
WHi D 15 1858;Mr 5,Ap 30 1890

Madison daily evening COURIER. d Ap 30 1849+
pub [1920+]
DLC Ja 22-O 9 1866
In 1920+
KHi [Jl 24 1888-Ja 15 1889]
MWA O 23 1865
OOxM My 1 1849;N 16 1850;Jl 25,Ag 11-20,22-26,28 1851[Je 1852-Mr 1854]
WHi O 15 1858

Madison DEMOCRAT. w 1875-
In Ja 16,Mr 13 1875

Madison DEMOCRAT. w 1889-1903||?
In N 18,D 8,11 1896

Madison daily FREE press. d Je 4 1866-
DLC Je 12-O 8 1866

Madison FREE press. w 1866-70||
In D 14 1867;Je 20,Jl 18,O 17 1868;F 26-Mr 5, My 7,S 3,O 15-22 1870

FREE soil democrat. w
ICHi S 22,O 20 1848

Madison HERALD. w 1871-1925||?
1871-75 as Madison progress
In O 26 1871;S 23,O 10,11-19 1872;F 27,Mr 29, Ap 19,24,Je 5,D 11-18 1873;My 14,Jl 2-9,O 15-22 1874;Jl 29,S 30,D 30 1875;Ja 29,Ap 27 1876; Mr 24,Jl 21,D 15 1880;O 1,N 1,15-22 1882;Mr 28,N 21,D 19 1883;Ja 9,F 21,My 15 1884;Jl 29, S 15,24 1885;N 6 1886;S 1,7,8 1893;S 18,N 7 1896

INDIANA republican. *See* Republican banner

Daily MADISONIAN. d 1852-
DLC N 1 1852
In Ja 21,Jl 2,4-11,13-[Ag]S 5-25 1852;My 31 1854
MWA N 4 1852

Madison NEWS-letter. w
In O 17,31,N 14 1860

Madison PROGRESS. *See* Madison herald

REPUBLICAN and banner. *See* Republican banner

*REPUBLICAN banner. w D 6 1816-
1816-Ag 15 1833 as Indiana republican; Ag 22 1833- Republican and banner
DLC Mr 24,Ap 28 1825;Ag 7 1828;F 13 1834;My 12,Je 2,16,Ag 18,S 22,D 1 1841
IU Ap 28-Mr 4 1825;Ag 7 1828
In Ag 9 1821;Ag 23 1827;Jl 1830-N 16 1836;S 4 1850
InI Ag 9 1821;Je 19,S 25 1823
InMC 1821-Jl 15 1824;Ap 23 1828-Je 3 1830;Ag 22 1833-Ap 21 1836;Ap 1844-Ap 1845
InSHi O 2 1834
MWA My 20 1829
NNHi O 30 1823

Madison evening STAR. d 1876-84||
In N 16 1877-Ap,My 20-D 1878
InI F 5 1877-Ag 2 1884

Madison TIMES. d
InVevHi S 9 1859

Madison TRIBUNE. w Ap 7 1851-Ja 21 1852||
In complete
InU complete

WESTERN clarion. w 1822-
In Mr 6-My 8,29,Je 19-Jl,Ag 21-S 11 1822
InI Mr 20,Ap 3,Je 19-Jl 17,S 18 1822

MANILA

Manila TIMES. w
InLoHi Mr 28 1902

MARION

Marion CHRONICLE. w 1867-1916||?
In Ja 27 1869-Jl 20 1871;N 28 1872;Ag 28 1885; My 2,4 1892;Mr 14,15 1901;Mr 1912-16
InLoHi S 28 1907
InMa Ag 31 1870;My 9-S 12 1872;F 27-Ap 17, Ag 7-21,N 13-D 18 1873;1911-16
MWA My 11 1876

Marion CHRONICLE. d 1886+
In 1917+
InMa 1917+
Sunday ed *See* Marion Sunday chronicle-tribune

Marion Sunday CHRONICLE-TRIBUNE. w 1930+
Sunday ed of Marion chronicle, and Leader-tribune
InMa Jl 13 1930+

Marion DEMOCRAT. *See* Marion leader-tribune

Marion DEMOCRATIC herald. w 1842-
DLC S 16 1843

GRANT county democrat. w
In Je 20,Jl 25 1846

GRANT county republican. w
In Je 14 1861;F 14,Ag 22 1862

GRANT county union. w
In Ag 6 1863;Ag 11 1864;Je 1 1865

Marion JOURNAL. w 1851-
In O 30 1851;Mr 4 1852;F 14,Ag 15 1862;S 1,N 10 1865;My 11,S 7,N 9 1866

Marion LEADER-TRIBUNE. w 1870-1915||?
1870-88 as Marion democrat; 1889-1912? Marion leader
In F 17 1876;Mr 13 1888;Ap 17 1891;Ag 2 1895
InMa 1911-My 1912
Sunday ed *See* Marion Sunday chronicle-tribune

LEADER-TRIBUNE. d 1889+
1889-1912? as Marion leader
InMa 1912+

MISSISSINEWA monitor. *See* Marion weekly monitor

Marion weekly MONITOR. w 1868-75||
1868-73? as Mississinewa monitor
KHi Mr 9 1871-D 16 1875

Marion NEWS-TRIBUNE. d 1894-1912||
1894-1900? as Marion morning news
InMa 1911-Mr 16 1912

INDIANA (*Continued*)

MARION—*Continued*

Marion OBSERVER. w 1912+
pub 1912+
In D 3-10 1914,Ja 7,My 13-20,Jl 15 1915
InMaP 1912+

Marion RECORD. w 1858
In S 30-O 7 1858

MARKLE

Markle JOURNAL. w 1890+
pub 1890+

MARSHALL

NEWS and Parke county recorder. w 1896+
pub 1932+
InRov 1923+

MARTINSVILLE

Martinsville DEMOCRAT. w 1848+
1848-95 as Morgan county gazette (1876?-85? Weekly gazette)
In F 1852-Ja 1854;My 12 1855-My 10,S 20 1856;Je 1857-Je 3 1858;F 5 1876;92-94;F 13 1914-15
MWA Je 3 1876

Weekly GAZETTE. *See* Martinsville democrat

Martinsville MONITOR. w 1855-
In S 18 1856

MORGAN county clarion. w 1860-
In Ja 17 1862

MORGAN county gazette. *See* Martinsville democrat

Martinsville REPORTER. d 1891+
In Ag 9 1934+
InMar S 1908+

Martinsville REPUBLICAN. w 1870+
pub [1870-1900]
In Ag 11 1870-91

MENOQUET

KOSCIUSKO republican. w Je 25 1845-
InGoE 1845-Jl 1,15-O 14 1846

MENTONE

Mentone GAZETTE. w 1885-1925||
1890?-1918? as Tri-county gazette
InMe 1885-1915;21-24

TRI-COUNTY gazette. *See* Mentone gazette

MEXICO

Mexico HERALD. w 1896-1901||
InLoHi O 3 1901

MICHIGAN CITY

Michigan City DISPATCH. w 1879-1913||?
KHi [O 18 1888-Mr 14 1889]

Evening DISPATCH. d Ap 25 1881+
pub 1881+
In Je 30,Jl 1 1881;Je 8 1893-94
NN Ap 25 1881

Michigan City ENTERPRISE. w F 28? 1855-
DLC Ja 23 1856
ICHi S 19 1855
In D 15 1860

Michigan City GAZETTE. w Jl 8 1835-
1835-36? as Michigan City gazette and general advertiser
DLC O 21 1840
In Ja 18,N 1,D 6 1837
MWA Ag 12,N 11 1835;Jl 5 1837

Michigan City NEWS. w Mr 5 1847-
In Je 11,Jl 23-30 1847
MWA S 17 1847
NjR Mr 5 1847

Michigan City evening NEWS. d 1882+
pub 1882+

WESTERN citizen. w
NNHi Ag 10 1843

MIDDLEBURY

Middlebury INDEPENDENT. w 1887+
In F 22-N 8 1918

Middlebury RECORD. w 1878-84||?
InGoE Je 1878-80

MIDDLETOWN

Middletown COURIER. *See* Courier-times

COURIER-TIMES. d
-Jl 2 1930 as Middletown courier
InMi Jl 5 1929+

Middletown NEWS. w 1885+
pub 1886-1907;09+
InLoHi Mr 1902-09;Ap 29,Je 17-24,Jl 15,Ag 5,O 14 1932[33-34]+

Middletown TIMES. d -Jl 1 1930||
United with Middletown courier to form Middletown courier-times
InMi D 1928-30

MILAN

Milan COMMERCIAL. w S 1917-Mr 1 1926||
InOs complete
InVeR 1919-25

MILFORD

Milford MAIL. w 1888+
pub 1900+
InMil 1889-90;98-1900;04-05;07-10;12-18

Milford weekly NEWS. w F 23 1876-
MWA Jl 27 1876

MILLERSBURG

Millersburg GRIT. w 1892+
pub [1892+]
In Mr-My 9,Je 6 1918

MILROY

Milroy PRESS. w 1898+
In N 6 1930
InRuR Mr 1934-F 1935

MISHAWAKA

Mishawaka DEMOCRAT. w 1891-1910||?
In 1897-98;Jl 5,19 1907-Mr 13,My 15,29,Je 12-26,Jl 10-31,Ag 14 1908

Mishawaka ENTERPRISE. w 1854+
In Ag 8 1934+
InSb Ag 1858-S 21,O 12 1861-O 1865
MWA S 23 1865

Mishawaka TOCSIN. w
In Je 7 1844

MITCHELL

COMMERCIAL. w 1866-1921||
In Mr 23 1876;N 3 1892
InMit 1896-1921
InU 1896-1920

Mitchell DEMOCRAT. w
In Ap 19 1892

Mitchell TRIBUNE. w 1898+
In D 28 1905;Ja 7 1909;Ag 1 1912;Mr 5,23 1916;Mr 25 1920;Ja 12,Je 10 1933
InMit 1917+

MONON

Monon NEWS. w 1889+
In Ap 24,Jl 7,O 27-D 15,29 1931

MONTEZUMA

Montezuma ENTERPRISE. w 1913+
In Ja 24-S 12 1935
InRov 1928+

Montezuma ERA. w 1876-83||?
In Jl 1 1880

MONTICELLO

Monticello CHIEFTAN. w
In S 17,31-O,N 18-25,D 10 1850-Ap 1,15-My 6,20-Je 13,27-Jl 8,Ag-O 9,30,N 13-D 11 1851;Ja 8,F 5-19,Ap 15,My 13-Je 3,17-O 7,D 9-30 1852;F 10-17,Mr 10-17,31-Ap 7,21-My,Je 15-Jl 14,O 13-N 10,D 3-17,31 1853;Ja 26-F 22,Mr 23,My 25-Je 1,15-Jl 13,27-Ag 7,D 16-30 1854

CONSTITUTIONALIST. w 1866-76||
In F 10 1870;O 13 1876

Monticello DEMOCRAT. w 1865-80||
In O 8 1880

Monticello HERALD. w F 14 1862-
In Ap 4 1862;Ja 14 1863;Mr 31 1864;Ag 12,S 2 1865;Mr 7 1868;S 21 1882;D 8 1910;F 12 1914+
InMonW 1866+
MWA D 1 1863

Monticello JOURNAL. d 1896+
pub 1914+
In N 18 1918+
InMon [1914+]

POLITICAL frame. w 1856-
In Jl 31-Ag 21,O 23,D 11 1856-Ja 1,Mr 19,Ap 9-30,My 14-21,Je-Jl 4,18 1857

Monticello SPECTATOR. w 1859-
In F 15 1860
MWA Mr 29 1861

WHITE county democrat. w
In My 30 1860;O 23-30 1861;Ja 10 1863;Ag 31 1864

WHITE county democrat. w 1882+
In My 27 1892;Je 9 1893-94
InMonW 1882+
InU 1915+

WHITE county register. w 1854-
In Je 28-Ag 9,23,S 13,27 1854

MONTPELIER

Montpelier HERALD. d,sw 1895+
1895-1910? as Evening herald
d 1895-1919?
pub 1903+
InU S 1929+

MOORELAND

Mooreland MONITOR. w 1921+
InNcHi Ja 1 1926

MOORESVILLE

Mooresville ENTERPRISE. w 1872-73||?
InMor Jl 25 1872-F 27 1873

Mooresville GUIDE. *See* Mooresville times

Mooresville TIMES. w 1889+
1889-1903? as Mooresville guide
pub 1929+
In Ap 17 1914+
InMor 1914-24;26+
InMorS 1900-29
InU 1915+

MOROCCO

Morocco COURIER. w 1876+
pub 1913+
In Jl 6-13,N 30 1933

MT. SUMMIT

Mt. Summit and Springport ENTERPRISE. w Ap 24 1891-
InNcHi Ap 24 1891

MT. VERNON

Mount Vernon DEMOCRAT. w 1867-1922||
In O 27 1887;F 23 1888
InMov Ap 1879-[83]-[87]-[96-98]

Mt. Vernon DEMOCRAT. d 1891+
pub 1918+
InMovHi S 11-16 1923;My 29 1926;Jl 3 1931;S 29 1932;Ja 5,S 12-15 1933

FREE press. w
InMovHi My 29 1931

Mount Vernon NEWS. d,sw 1897-1903||?
d 1897-98?
InMov [S 27-D 4 1897]

PUBLIC. w 1904+
1904-15 as Unafraid; 1916-26 Unafraid republican
InMovHi Ja 1 1905;Jl 16,Ag 13,O 15 1916;Ja 6 1923;25-26
InU 1921-22

Mount Vernon REGISTER-NEWS. d
In My 27 1929

Mount Vernon REPUBLICAN. d 1893-1915||?
United with Unafraid to form Unafraid republican, later Public
InMov [F-Ap,Ag 1893]F 16,Je 17 1894[Jl 1895-Jl,N-D 1896]Ag 13-S 22,N 5-D 10,24 1897;Ja 21,28,F 18,25,Mr 18 1898

SUN. w 1879-1916||
In Ag 5 1892
InMov O 13 1882;Ap 20 1883;My 9 1884;D 4 1885;Ag 8 1886;Mr 18,N 27 1887;F 12,Ap 30,S 12 1888;Ag 15,D 9 1889;Je 14 1890;Ja 26,F 16 1891;My 20,N 18 1892;F 3 1893;F 15-23,Mr 9,N 16 1894;Mr 15,Jl 5,26-Ag 9,23,O 4,25 1895
InMovHi S 1 1916

UMPIRE. sw 1860-
InMov S 22 1860

UNAFRAID. *See* Public

UNAFRAID republican. *See* Public

WESTERN star. w 1877+
pub 1877+
In Ja 21,Ag 7,22 1935
InMov Ap 13 1882;S 20 1888;Mr 18,Ap 10 1890;My 5-12,Je 16,Jl 7,Ag 11,N 4,18 1892;Jl 11,O 24 1895;1918+
InMovHi Jl 2 1931;32-Ja 5 1933
InU Mr 1923-[Ja-Je 1925;Je-D 1932]
MWA Mr 10 1881

MUNCIE

Muncie COURIER-DEMOCRAT. *See* Muncie herald

DELAWARE county democrat. w 1843-
InMu O 10 1843-N 1844

DELAWARE county free press. w 1857-
InMu 1860-66

DELAWARE county telegraph. *See* Muncie herald

DELAWARE county times. w 1860-
InMu 1860-66
InNcHi Je 21 1866;S 24 1868

Muncie DEMOCRAT. *See* Muncie herald

Muncie DEMOCRAT-HERALD. *See* Muncie herald

Muncie HERALD. w 1870-1915||?
1870-72? as Delaware county telegraph; 1873-75 Muncie democrat; 1876-79? Courier-democrat; 1880-84 Muncie democrat; 1885-39 Muncie democrat-herald
In O 10 1871;F 26,Ap 8 1876;O 25 1889
InMu 1892-1906

INDIANA signal. w
FSrS O 3 1849
InMu Ap 22 1848-Ja 2 1850

INDIANA state journal. *See* National republican

Muncie JOURNAL. w 1846-
In Ja 10,31,Mr 28,Ap 18,My 2,S 5,19-26,O 24,N 7 1846;Ap 3 1847
InMu Ja 10 1846-My 22 1847

MUNCIETONIAN. w
InMu Je 1837-F 2 1838

INDIANA (*Continued*)

MUNCIE—*Continued*

NATIONAL republican. w My 15 1913-15||
1913-N 6 1914 as Indiana state journal
In 1913-N 6 1914;Ja 2,My 8 1915
InLoHi N 14 1914;Je 12 1915
InPeHi Mr 25 1916
InU 1913-N 14 1914

Muncie NEWS. w 1872-1901||
In S 14 1893
InMu 1876-77;79-1901
MWA Jl 9 1876

POST-DEMOCRAT. w 1920+
pub 1920+
In Mr 24-31,Ap 14,Je 16,Jl,Ag 18,S 8,O 13,D 1,29 1922-Ja 5,26,Mr 30,Ap 13,My 4,18,Je 8,Jl 6-13,27,O 26-N 16 1923;Mr 7-14,Ap 4,18,My 23-30,S 19,O 31,N 14,D 19 1924-[25-26]Ja,F 10-Mr 1927

Muncie PRESS. d 1905+
pub 1905+
In Jl 11 1907+
InMu 1905+

Muncie morning STAR. d 1899+
pub 1921+
In Jl 21 1907+
InMu 1900+

Muncietown TELEGRAPH. w Mr 15 1841-42||
Followed by Village herald
DLC Mr 15 1841
InMu 1841-Mr 1842

Muncie TIMES. w 1861-1913||?
In O 17 1872
InMu 1880-93;1904-05
KHi [D 1886-Jl 18 1889]
MWA Jl 27 1876
NNHi Ja 2 1872

VILLAGE herald. w 1842-
Follows Muncietown telegraph
InMu Je 25-N 5 1842

WHIG banner. w
In Ja 18 1851

Muncietown YOEMAN. w 1843-
InMu Ag-O 7 1843

NAPPANEE

Nappanee ADVANCE. w 1891-1920||
United with Nappanee news to form Nappanee advance-news
InN Ag 1916-Ag 1920

Nappanee ADVANCE-NEWS. w 1879+
1879-1920 as Nappanee news
In Mr-N 8 1918;S 26 1935+
InGoE Mr 27 1879-Mr 1880
InN Mr 25 1880-Ag 1917;S 1920-32

Nappanee NEWS. *See* Nappanee advance-news

NASHVILLE

BROWN county democrat. w 1870+
1870-82? as Jacksonian; 1883?-84? Jacksonian-democrat
In Mr 26 1914+
InNa 1922+

NEW ALBANY

ALL around the week. w Ja 18 1873-
NNHi Ja 18 1873

AMERICAN campaigner.
In S 30 1856

New-Albany ARGUS. w 1837-
DLC Ja-Mr 1840
In S 12 1839

New Albany BULLETIN. d
In Je 20 1846

CAMPAIGN tribune.
In S 15-22 1852

*New Albany CHRONICLE. w S 30 1820-
InI My 5-19,Je 30,S 15,O 27,N 17 1821
MWA N 11 1820;Ja 13,F 3,Mr 17,My 12-26,Je 16,Jl 28 1821

New Albany daily COMMERCIAL. d 1864-70||?
OClWHi O 25-26 1865

New Albany COMMERCIAL. w 1864-70||?
In [S 1865-N 1866]Ag 16 1867
InNe 1849;1867-68

CRESSET. w Mr 8 1828-
In Mr 8 1828

New Albany DEMOCRAT. w 1844-
DLC D 16 1847-48
In Jl 8 1847-S 12 1849
InU Jl-N 1847
WHi S 2 1847

New Albany GAZETTE. w N 17 1830-51||?
Followed by New Albany tribune
DLC Ja 12 1831
ICHi D 8 1830
In Ja 22-29,Mr 25-Jl 1,S 2-9,23 1836;F 3,24-Ap 14,28-My 5,19,Je 2-9,Jl 7,21,Ag 4,S 15,O 20 1837
InNe Ag 10 1838-S 15 1842
MWA S 29 1842

New Albany daily GAZETTE. d 1838-
DLC D 21 1838;F 21 1839

New Albany GAZETTE. tw My 1840-
DLC My 21,D 3 1840

HERALD. d
InU S-N 1854

HICKORY club. w
In Je 13 1840

INDIANA recorder and public advertiser. w
DLC Ja 6-13,O 23,N-D 16,30 1826
In Mr 3 1827
MWA O 13 1827

INDIANA republican. w 1883-
InSHi Mr 23 1883

New Albany daily LEDGER. d S 21 1849-1922||?
1873-81 as New Albany ledger-standard
DLC F 11 1854-S 15 1860
ICHi Ag 15 1860-Mr 23 1861
MBAt Ap 15 1865
MWA Ag 14 1876

New Albany LEDGER. w 1849+
1873-81 as New Albany ledger-standard
In S 21 1849-1922
InMov D 3 1885;My 18,N 6,22,D 26,29 1888;Mr 20,My 1-8,Je 15,O 30,D 18 1889;Ja 1,Je 14,S 27,O 30 1890;Ap 15,My 20 1891[92]F 1,20,Mr 2-8,Ap 26,My 3,Je 21-28,Ag 23,N 1 1893;Ja 31,Mr 7,28,Jl 31 1894
InNe 1849+
InSHi N 14 1876;Je 19 1880;S 14 1881
InU My 1852-Jl 1853;Ja-F,My-D 1858;Je 1859-N 1860;My 23 1864;Jl-D 1866;Jl 1871-80;Je 1881-Jl 1885
InVevHi D 31 1852[58]Ja 1,18,F 1-8,Mr 7,23,O 26 1859
MWA Jl 5 1865
NbHi N 20 1861;Je 5 1867;Jl 1 1868;Mr 9 1870;F 8 1871;My 1,D 25 1872;My 7 1873;Ap 8,29 1874
WHi O 15 1853

New Albany LEDGER-STANDARD. *See* New Albany ledger

MICROSCOPE and general advertiser. w Ap 17 1824-
Ap-O 23 1824 as Microscope
Ap-S 15 1824 pub in Louisville, Kentucky
ICU Ap-Je 5,26 1824-Mr 26,Ap 23-S 10 1825
In D 25 1824
MWA My 7 1825

New Albany PUBLIC press. w 1881-1917||
In Je 22 1881-[89]-1915
InNe 1889-1917

New-Albany REGISTER. w D 3 1840-
DLC D 31 1840

REPUBLICAN banner.
MoSM My 11 1844

New Albany STANDARD. w 1871-73||
United with New Albany ledger to form New Albany ledger-standard, later New Albany ledger

TIPPECANOE banner and spirit of democracy. w Ap 16? 1840-
CtY My 6 1840
DLC Ag 6 1840

TOCSIN of liberty. w Ap 2? 1844-
IU Ap 30 1844

New Albany TRIBUNE. w Mr 31 1852-
Follows New Albany gazette
In 1852-O 22 1860
InU 1852-Mr 1853;O 1854-Mr 1856;S 1857;F-D 1859

New Albany evening TRIBUNE. d 1888+
pub Ap 16 1888+
In 1934+

New Albany TRIBUNE. w 1888+
1925+ as Thursday ed of New Albany evening tribune
pub 1888+
In F 22 1896;97-98
InNe 1907;24+

TRUTH teller. d Ag 5 1889-90||
In Ag 5 1889;F 1 1890

WESTERN union democrat. w Ja 8? 1842-
In My 10 1844
MWA O 1,22 1842

NEW CARLISLE

CARLISLE eagle and whig advocate. w
In My 7 1844

NEW CASTLE

New Castle BANNER. w,sw 1836-
InNcHi Mr 31,O 20 1836;S-N 25,D 9-23 1853; Ja 13-F 10,Mr-Ap 21,My 12-19,Je 9,Jl 14-S 8,22-29 1854

BEECH tree. 1857-
InNcHi Jl 1857-F 1858

New Castle COURIER. w 1841-1918||?
Follows Indiana sun (Knightstown) 1841-45? Indiana courier (Knightstown)
pub F 1902;05-18
In [1853;59-60]Mr 14,28 1861;O 16,30-N 13 1862[63-66]-[68-76]Mr 30,My 25 1877;O 15-22, D 3,17,31 1880;Ap 1,Jl 29,S 30 1881;Je 9,Ag 18,S 22,O 20 1882;Jl 27,S 21,O 5,D 21 1883 [84]Mr 20,S 4,N 13 1885;Ja,F 12,Mr 2,19,My 7,Je 4,O 8,N 12 1886[87-89]F 7,My 9,D 26 1890[91-93]Ap 27-My 4 1894;Mr 20 1896;Mr 10,Ap 28 1898[1905-07]S 16 1909;Je 15 1911-15
InI F 11 1843
InNcHi O 14 1841;Je 15,N 23 1844;S 20 1845; Ja 24-31,Mr 14,My 23 1846;Ap 10,S 4-11,O 9-16 1847[48-49]Ja 4,Mr 2,Ap 25,N 20,D 13 1850[51-52;Jl 30-D 1857]Ap 8 1858;59[60-62]-[64-68]70-71;S 20 1872[73]-[77]80[81]-Ja 3 1896[97]-Mr 1898;My 1902-08;Jl 26 1909;11-15
InRP Jl 19 1845
MWA Ja 25 1866;My 19 1876

New Castle COURIER-times. d 1896+
1896-Je 28 1930 as New Castle courier
pub 1916+
In [Ja-Mr 1919]My 27,31-[Je]1930
InNcHi My 1918-S 1921;24-Je 1930

New Castle CRESCENT. w 1886-87||
InNcHi Jl 8 1886;Ag 25 1887

New Castle DEMOCRAT. w 1878-1925||
InNcC 1887-1924
InNcHi N 4 1880[Mr-D 1882]-84;1902-07;O 1912-16

DEMOCRATIC banner. w 1851-
InNcHi S 16-23,O 14,N 4,19,D 17-24 1852;Ja 21,F 4,Mr 13 1853

New Castle DEMOCRATIC times. *See* New Castle mercury

New Castle EXAMINER. w My 27 1868-70||
InNcHi Je,Jl 8,29-Ag 5,O 15-22,N 5-19 1868; Ja 8,F 11 1869,O 7 1870

HENRY county adventurer. w 1870-
InNcHi D 1 1870

HENRY county argus. w 1882-83||
InNcHi Je 2 1883

HENRY county independent. w Ap 17 1867-
InNcHi My-Je 19,Jl-S 18,O 2,N 27,D 4 1867

HENRY county republican. w Ag 4 1870-72||
InNcHi Ag 4 1870;71-Je 1872

HENRY county republican. w 1890-99||?
InNcHi Ja 2,Mr 20,N 27 1896;Ja 1,15,F 5,19,Mr 5-19,Ap 2-9 1897

HENRY county times. w O 13 1865-
InNcHi O 13,27,N 17-24,D 15-22 1865;Ja-F 2 1866

New Castle MERCURY. w Ja 1867-85||
1867-Ap 1874 as New Castle democratic times; My-D 1874 New Castle times
In My 12 1871;S 29 1879;Ap 8-22,My 6,27,Je 3-17,Jl 8 1882;Ja-F 10,24,Mr-Ap 20,Jl 6,Ag 10-24 1883;Ja 18,Jl 4,O 18 1884
InNcHi O 6,20 1871;Ja 5 1872;Ap 14,My 28 1874;Ja 7,F 18-25,Ap 1 1875[76-79;82]-Ag 1885
MWA Je 29,Jl 6 1876

NEWS-republican. w Ag 6 1931+
pub 1931+
InNcHi [1931-34]+

New Castle PRESS. d 1895-1904||
InNcHi 1899;Ja 28,Mr 27,My 30 1903-Ja 1904

PROGRESSIVE herald. sw 1914-
InNcHi Ag 4 1914

SIGNS of the times. w 1868-
InNcHi Mr 4 11 1868

New Castle STAR. d 1913-14||
InNcHi Ag 2 1913
InU Ja 27 1913-Ja 10 1914

New Castle TIMES. d 1907-Jl 2 1930||
United with New Castle courier to form New Castle courier-times
In F 1913-Je 1928;My 19 1930
InNcC 1912-30
InNcHi S 27 1916;18-[21]Mr 30 1923-30

New Castle TIMES. w *See* New Castle mercury

New Castle TRIBUNE. w 1894-1909||
In [N 1897-O 1898]Je 24,Jl-D 1904;Ja 20-Je 9 1905[Ag 17 1908-Ag 15 1909]
InNcHi [1898-1900]02-08;F 19 1909

New Castle TRIBUNE. 1905-06. *See* Henry county tribune (Spiceland)

NEW GARDEN. *See* NEWPORT

NEW HARMONY

New Harmony ADVERTISER. w
InNh Je 12 1858;Je 11 1859;Je 30 1860;Jl 20-Ag 11 1861

DISSEMINATOR. w Ja 1828?-
DLC Ap 23 1840;Mr 4 1841
MWA Je 29-D 1830;Ja 15-Mr 19,Ap-My 21,Je 1831
NNHi Jl 19 1834
OCHi My 14 1840

New Harmony and Nashoba GAZETTE; or, the free enquirer. w O 1 1825-
1825-O 22 1828 as New Harmony gazette
Ct O 15 1825-Mr 7 1827
IaDH My 10 1826;Ap 2 1828
In 1825-O 20 1832
InGcD 1825-28
InI O 8 1825-S 20 1826
InLP 1825-O 22 1828
InNcHi D 17 1828
InNh 1825-O 22 1828
MiD-B 1825-S 20 1826
N O 1 1825;Ja 25-Mr 22 1826
NN 1825-O 1828
OCHi 1825-O 22 1828
OClWHi 1825-S 20 1826
OHi N 19 1828
PLatL N 12 1828-Mr 4 1829
WHi 1825-S 20 1826

INDIANA statesman. w My 13 1842-
My-O 22 1842 pub in Evansville
In My-S,O 22 1842-45
InNh 1842-46

MORTAR. w
InNh My 1883-87

New Harmony NEWS. w
InNh N 2,D 11 1890;Mr 28 1891

New Harmony REGISTER. w 1867-O 14 1932||
In My 21 1870;Jl 1 1871;Ap 6 1872
InMov Mr 23 1877;Ap 6 1894;Jl 9 1897
InMovHi O 1899
InNh Mr 4 1867;68;70-1932

SOUTHWESTERN sentinel. w
InNh F 28 1840

TELEPHONE. w 1902-03||
InNh O 17-25,N 22,D 6,27 1902-Ja 10.F 7 1903

INDIANA (*Continued*)

NEW HARMONY—*Continued*

New Harmony TIMES. w 1892+
pub 1892+
In Mr 29 1912+
InMovHi Ag 9 1929;Mr 6 1932
InNh Ag 20 1892-Ag 1904;Ag 1905+
InU 1914—

New Harmony WESTERN atlas. w
InNh Ag 1846-Ag 5 1847

NEW HAVEN

ALLEN county times. w 1920+
1920-26? as Idea
In S 26 1935+

IDEA. *See* Allen county times

NEW LONDON

New London PIONEER. w 1848-1850‖
In Jl 4 1849;My 8,Je 26,Jl 24-31 1850
InKoT [1848-50]
InNcHi Je 26 1850

NEW WASHINGTON

New Washington COURIER. w 1896+
pub D 17 1896+
In My 24 1900

NEWBURGH

Newburgh REGISTER. w Mr 9 1917+
pub 1917+
In My 1934—

WARRICK democrat. w 1850-
DLC O 5,23 1852
MWA O 30 1852

NEWPORT

To 1845? as New Garden

ANTI-SLAVERY advocate. w
In O 5 1844

ANTI-SLAVERY chronicle and free labor advocate. *See* Free labor advocate and anti-slavery chronicle

FREE labor advocate and anti-slavery chronicle. w F 8 1841-48‖
1841-Mr 11 1847? as Anti-slavery chronicle and free labor advocate
In O 1,15,N 26,D 10 1842;Je 10 1843;O 5 1844; D 8 1845;Ja 19,F 23 1846;Je 30,Ag 25 1848
InNcHi Ap 8,Jl 16 1846;Mr 11 1847;Je 30 1848
MdBJ Jl 30,Ag 13,S 17-D 21 1842
NcD Ja 23 1846;Mr 18 1847

HOOSIER state. w Ja 23 1855+
In F 11 1914-15;Ap 22 1925;34+
InNp Jl 30 1930+
InPeHi Je 5 1858

NOBLESVILLE

Noblesville DEMOCRAT. *See* Hamilton county democrat

ENTERPRISE. w 1905-09‖
Follows Hamilton county democrat
InNoR complete

HAMILTON county democrat. w Ag 1 1876-1903‖
1876-88 as Noblesville independent; 1889-1900 Noblesville democrat. Followed by Enterprise
In Ag 1 1876
InNoR 1876-89;1901-03

HAMILTON county ledger. w,sw Ja 1871-1916‖
1871-81 as Noblesville ledger; 1881-86 Republican-ledger
pub 1882-1916
In N 7 1873
InNoR 1872-81;83-84;87;89-92;94-1909
OClWHi Jl 13 1883
—d ed *See* Noblesville ledger

HAMILTON gazette. w Jl 4 1840-
DLC Jl 4,30 1840

HOOSIER patriot. w
InVevHi D 8 1859;F 2,16-23,Ap 26 1860

Noblesville INDEPENDENT. *See* Hamilton county democrat

Noblesville INTELLIGENCER. w Ag 24 1839-
DLC Ag 31 1839

Noblesville LEDGER. 1871-80 *See* Hamilton county ledger

Noblesville LEDGER. d 1887+
pub 1889+
In 1934+
InNoR 1915+
—w ed *See* Hamilton county ledger

Noblesville REPUBLICAN. w Mr 10-D 29 1880‖
United with Noblesville ledger to form Republican-ledger, later Hamilton county ledger
InNoR complete

REPUBLICAN-LEDGER. *See* Hamilton county ledger

Noblesville TIMES. w Ap 1904+
pub 1931+
In 1931+
InNo 1915-Jl 1918;Je 1920-Jl 1930;31+
InNoR 1904-06;08;15-18

TRUE whig. w 1851-
In O 25 1851

WHITE River clipper. w 1863-68‖
InNoR Ap 19-N 12 1868

NORTH JUDSON

North Judson NEWS. w 1889+
In 1897+
InNj [1889-1900]

NORTH LIBERTY

North Liberty NEWS. w 1895+
pub Ap 1895+

NORTH MANCHESTER

North Manchester JOURNAL. w,sw 1875-1920‖?
United with North Manchester news to form North Manchester news-journal
w 1875-1915?
InSHi My 9 1878-Ap 12 1894

MANCHESTER republican. w 1865-75‖
InSHi D 26 1872-75

North Manchester NEWS-JOURNAL. w,sw 1904+
1904-20? as North Manchester news
w 1904-12?
pub 1904+
In Jl 8 1935+

NORTH VERNON

JENNINGS county news. w 1925-33‖
pub 1925-33
In 1932-33
InNv [1925-33]

PLAINDEALER. w 1864+
In Je 23 1870;Je 4 1872;Mr 1935+
InVnJ 1864+
MWA O 25 1865;Jl 22 1876

North Vernon SUN. w 1872+
In O 15 1874;My 5 1911+
InVnJ 1876—
MWA Je 29 1876

OAKLAND CITY

Oakland City JOURNAL. sw 1893+
pub 1893-1909;11+
InO 1923+
InU Mr 1918-21

OAKTOWN

Oaktown RECORD. w 1898-1921‖?
In Je 13-D 5 1918

ODON

Odon JOURNAL. w 1873+
pub 1873+

ORLEANS

Orleans EXAMINER. *See* Orleans progress-examiner

Orleans PROGRESS-EXAMINER. w 1879+
1879-99? as Orleans examiner
pub 1891+
In Mr 26 1914+
InU 1929;Ag 15 1930+

OSGOOD

Osgood JOURNAL. w 1865+
1865-94? as Ripley county journal
pub 1919+
In O 22 1868;O 21 1869;Jl 7 1870;S 7 1871;Ap 4,Jl 18,O 17,D 26 1872;D 4 1873;D 24 1874;S 14 1876;N 8 1877;Mr 27,Jl 3,N 30 1879;Je 22, Jl-Ag 10,N 16-23 1882;Mr 29,Jl 5,D 13 1883; Ja 10-17,F 14,Ap 10,Je 5 1884;F 18,N 4-11 1886;My 1,Je 19 1890;Mr 17,Ap 21 1892;Je 8 1893-94;My 7-21,Je 4,S 3 1896;97-1906;F 21 1935+
InOs 1913+
InU 1929+
InVeM Ap 18 1928
InVeR 1881-86;88-91;94;96-98;1900-03-04;06-14; 17-21;24;26-29;31+

RIPLEY county journal. *See* Osgood journal

OSSIAN

Ossian JOURNAL. w 1914+
pub 1916+

OTTERBEIN

Otterbein PRESS. w 1918-25‖?
InOt S 18 1919-My 1922

OTWELL

Otwell STAR. w 1903+
pub F 1904+

OWENSVILLE

Owensville GLEANER. w 1888-96‖?
InOw O 1888-95

NEW echo. w 1904-13‖?
United with Owensville star to form Owensville star-echo

Owensville STAR-ECHO. w 1896+
1896-1913? as Owensville star
pub 1896+

OXFORD

BENTON county tribune. *See* Oxford tribune

BENTON mail. w 1856-
In Mr 19 1857

Oxford GAZETTE. w 1908+
pub 1908+
In 1910+
InOx 1918-32

OXFORDITE. w
InOx F 7,Ap 17 1863

Oxford TRIBUNE. w 1865-1912‖
1865-70 as Benton county tribune
In S 11 1865-S 5,O 10 1867-Jl 1870;Jl 8 1874
InOxL [1866-1912]
MWA My 18 1876

PAOLI

AMERICAN eagle. w 1858-
DLC Ja 12,26-F 16,Mr 15-Ap 19,My 24-Je 7,21, Jl-S 6,O 4,18-25,D 13-20 1860

INDIANA patriot. w D 11? 1833-
DLC F 13 1834

Paoli NEWS. w 1872+
pub 1907+
In F 1934+

Paoli REPUBLICAN. w 1874+
pub 1883+
In F 25 1914+
InU 1915-16

TORCH-LIGHT. w D 1 1837-
DLC D 1 1837

PARKER

Parker City NEWS. w 1893-94‖
In Jl 1893-94

PEKIN

Pekin BANNER. w 1923+
pub 1927+

PENDLETON

Pendleton BOOSTER. w 1933+
In N 24 1933+

Pendleton DOLLAR register. w 1872-76‖
MWA Je 16 1876

Pendleton GAZETTE. w N 24 1899-Ja 30 1903‖
InP complete

Pendleton TIMES. w 1904+
pub Je 1905+
In S 6 1923
InP 1922+

PERRYSVILLE

Perrysville BANNER. w
In Ja 26 1839

Perrysville EAGLE.
IU N 24 1848

Perrysville RECORD. w 1895-1903‖?
In 1897-1902

Perrysville REPUBLICAN. w N 19 1842-
DLC D 3 1842

PERU

Peru CHRONICLE. d Je 23 1894-D 8 1926‖
United with Peru journal to form Peru journal chronicle
InPe Jl 1897-1926
InPeHi Je 29-N 27 1894;Ja-Mr 24 1913
InPeR Mr 19 1925-1926

Peru CORK-SCREW and gimlet of reform. w F 9 1844-
Title varies slightly
In F 23,Mr 8-15 1844
InPeH F 23 1844
MWA F 9 1844

Peru FREE PRESS. w Oct 28 1852-
InPeH 1852-Ag 16 1853

Peru GAZETTE. w Jl 20 1839-
In 1839-Ap 3,O 9 1841-Mr,Jl 16,Ag 6-13,S 3-10, 24,O 8 1842
InPeH Je 13,D 19 1840;F 6,N 13 1841
NN 1839-Ag 8 1840

Peru HERALD. w Dec 9 1847-
In F 11,Mr 11,My 13,Je 24,Jl 17,D 11 1847;Mr 11 1848

Peru JOURNAL-CHRONICLE d 1883-D 9 1926‖
1883-D 8 1926 as Peru journal. Merged with Peru chronicle
In [1907-27]
InPe Jl 1897-1927
InPeHi Ja-Je 1887;88-Je 1890;Ja-Je 1891;Ja-Je 1897;O 1908;Je,O 1911-Mr,Jl-D 1913;Ap-Je,O-D 1914;Ap-S 1915;My-S 1916;Ja-S 1917; Jl 1919-Mr,O-D 1920

MAYFLOWER. w F 1 1861-
InPeHi Mr 1 1861

MIAMI county record. w 1895-99‖?
In S 25 1895-[96]-Ja 21 1897

INDIANA (*Continued*)

PERU—*Continued*

MIAMI county sentinel. w,sw Je 29 1848-Mr 2 1925||
w 1848-95?
In Mr 7,Je 20,Ag 22,S 19-26 1850;Ja 23,Mr 6, Ap 3,Jl 17,N,D 25 1851;F 5,19-26,Mr 11-Ap 1, S 2,D 23 1852;Mr 17,31,Ap 14,Je 16,S 8-15 1853;My 18,S 14 1854;Ja 4,25,S 6,20 1855;F 14 1856;Ap 2,Je 4,S 10-17 1857;F 25,Mr 18,Jl 1 1858;Mr 1,Ap 12,26,Ag 9,S 27,O 25 1860;Jl 18 1861;Ag 27 1863;F 25,Mr 31,Ag 25 1864;S 21,N 2 1865;S 20 1866;O 1-15,N 26 1868;Mr 4,Ap 1-15 1869;Ap 21-28,O 13-20 1870;Ap 13-20,My 4, O 26-N 2 1871;Ap 11,25,O 24,D 5 1872;F 19, Je 18 1874;O 4 1877;Je 24 1880;N 13 1884;Mr 12 1885;91-94[97-1906]
InGoE Ja 12 1860
InPe Ag 1904-25
InPeHi 1848-61;Ap 1863-Mr 1864;Jl 20 1865;My 1869-Ap 1875;O 1879-1923
InPeR Ag 11 1881-1904;06-15
NN Je 29 1848-Je 21 1849;Je 24 1852-Je 15 1854
OHi Ag 18,S 1-8 1859
P-M Je 14 1855

Peru NEWS. w My 19 1855-
In My 19 1855,F 13 1856
InPeHi My 19 1855-Ag 30 1856

Peru OBSERVER. w Je 1 1844-
In Je,Jl 13-Ag,S 14-N 23,D 14-28 1844;Ja-Mr, Ap 12-19,My-Je 14 1845
InPeHi 1844-Je 28 1845

Peru REPUBLICAN. w O 9 1856+
pub 1868+
In F 26 1857;Mr 18,Jl 29 1858;Ap 5,My 3 1860; My 9 1861;O 1 1862;Mr 25-Ap 15,S 30 1863;Mr 30-Ap 20,My 4,S 28 1864;S 27 1865;Mr 21-28 1866;Ap 3,O 9 1867;Je 5,O 2-16 1868;Ap 2-16 1869;Ap 22-29 1870;Ap 14-My 12,N 3 1871;Ap 12,26 1872;S 2 1881;S 7 1883;Je 18 1884;Je 16 1893-94;Ag 1897+
InPeHi O 1856-O,N 12,D 10 1857;S 30 1858;F 17 1859;N 15 1860;Ap 17(extra)22(extra)1861; Ap 2 1869;Ja 20 1871;Mr 3 1876;S 14 1877-78; My 9 1879;D 24 1880;Ag 25 1882;1904-05
InPeR 1881-1904;06+
InU [F 1923-24]Ja,F 13,My 22,Jl 24-31,Ag 28-S,O 9,23,N 6,27 1925;Je 11,25,Jl 23,Ag-N 5 1926;F 11,Mr 4,18,Je 10,Ag 12,O 7,D 9-23 1927 [28-29]Ap 25,My 9,23,Je 20 1930;My 22 1931; Ap 22,My 20,Je 17,Jl 8,Ag 12-19 1932
MWA Je 2 1876
OClWHi Jl 19 1878

REPUBLICAN-ARGUS. w S 20 1854-
In S 27-O 4 1854
InPeHi S 20-D 20 1854

SENTINEL. sw
InPeR 1916-Ap 16 1925

Peru TRIBUNE. d 1921+
pub 1921+
In D 6-10 1927;Jl 7 1928+
InPe 1921+
InPeR 1928+

WABASH Valley olio. w Dec 23 1852-
In Mr 17,My 12 1854
InPeHi 1852-S 20 1854

PETERSBURG

PIKE county democrat. w 1868+
pub Mr 16 1925+
In F 20 1914+
InPet Ja 25 1884-1925
InPetM 1892-1925
MWA My 25 1876

Petersburg PRESS. w,sw 1869+
1869-72? as Republican press
w 1869-1924
InU 1915-[32]

REPUBLICAN press. *See* Petersburg press

PIERCETON

Pierceton INDEPENDENT. *See* Pierceton record

Pierceton RECORD. w 1879+
1879-84? as Pierceton independent
pub Je 28 1920+
InPi 1924+

Pierceton REVEILLE. w
InLoHi F 14 1867

PLAINFIELD

Plainfield CITIZEN. w 1874-77||
MWA Je 17 1876

FRIDAY caller. *See* Plainfield messenger

Plainfield MESSENGER. w 1880+
1880-1903 as Plainfield progress; 1904-15 Friday caller
In 1934+
InPl [1881-1903]+
InU 1916-My 1917

Plainfield PALLADIUM. w
InPl F 11 1867

Plainfield PROGRESS. *See* Plainfield messenger

PLYMOUTH

Plymouth BANNER. w Ap 16 1851-O 2 1856||
1851-F 5 1852 as Plymouth pilot. Followed by Marshall county republican, later Plymouth republican
In Mr 4,Ag 19 1852;My 17 1855;F 28 1856
InPmM Mr 1853
InPmP D 17 1851

Plymouth CHRONICLE. w 1902-11||
InPmP complete

Plymouth DEMOCRAT. d *See* Plymouth news

Plymouth DEMOCRAT. w 1855+
1855-58? as Marshall county democrat
In F 28 1856;F 16 1860;F 6 1873;S 23 1875;My 18,Jl 27 1876;Je 15 1893-94;Ag 22 1907-15
InGoE F 24 1876
InPmM N 1855+
InU 1916-Ja 1917;18-Je 1925;26-[29]+
InVevHi Ap 22,Jl 1,22,N 4,D 2,16-30 1858
d ed *See* Plymouth news

Plymouth INDEPENDENT. d *See* Plymouth news

Plymouth JOURNAL. w
In N 13 1844

MARSHALL county democrat. *See* Plymouth democrat

MARSHALL county republican. *See* Plymouth republican

Plymouth NEWS. d 1895+
1895-1909? as Plymouth independent; 1910?-32? Plymouth democrat
In 1929;32+
InPmM 1897;1900;08+
w ed *See* Plymouth democrat

Plymouth PILOT. w *See* Plymouth banner

Plymouth PILOT. d Jl 27 1922+
Follows Plymouth republican
pub 1922+
In 1922+

Plymouth REPUBLICAN. w O 9 1856-Jl 26 1922||
Follows Plymouth banner
1856-79? as Marshall county republican; 1880?-O 3 1901 Plymouth republican; O 10 1901-Ja 8 1911 Plymouth tribune
In F 2,16 1860;Mr 31 1864;My 13 1897-1915
InPmM complete
InPmP 1911-22

Plymouth TRIBUNE. *See* Plymouth republican

PORTLAND

Portland COMMERCIAL-REVIEW. w,tw 1865-1905||?
1865-1900? as Portland commercial
MWA Jl 13 1876

Portland COMMERCIAL-REVIEW. d 1894+
1894-1905? as Portland commercial
In Je 15 1895;F 7 1914-Je 1916

JAY torch-light. w 1859-
MWA Je 6 1860

Portland SUN. w 1877-1918||?
InPoJ [1888-1900]

Portland SUN. d 1908+
In My 9-10,19,21,26 1934;Ag 23-O 9 1935
InPoJ 1916+

POSEYVILLE

Poseyville NEWS. w 1882+
pub 1882+

PRINCETON

BROAD axe. w Ag 8 1874-
In Ag 8,22-S 12,26-O 3 1874

Princeton CLARION-NEWS. w 1846-1916||?
1846-72? as Princeton union-clarion; 1872?-1902? Princeton clarion
ICM Ag 17 1893
In F 16 1850-N 21 1863
MWA F 15 1866;Je 22 1876

Princeton CLARION-NEWS. d 1897+
1897-1902? as Princeton clarion
pub 1919+
In Jl 12 1907+

Princeton DEMOCRAT. w 1860-1919||
1860-65 as Union democrat
ICHi O 28 1865
In [1866-O 1868]F 27 1869;S 3,24,O 22,N 19,D 3,17 1870[Ja-Mr,Ag-D 1871]Ja 6,F 17,Ap 13, My 1872-S 6 1873;Jl 6 1878;F 22 1879;Ap 3,Ag 28 1880;F 19-26 1881;Ja 6-20,Mr 24,N 3 1883; Mr 5 1887
InPr complete
MWA Jl 17 1876

Princeton DEMOCRAT. d 1893+
In F 11 1914+
InPr 1893+
InU 1923+

GIBSON review. w
In Ja 2 1851

Evening NEWS. d 1893-1902||?
United with Princeton clarion to form Princeton clarion-news

Princeton UNION-CLARION. *See* Princeton clarion-news

UNION democrat. *See* Princeton democrat

PRINTER'S RETREAT

Weekly MESSENGER. *See* Weekly messenger and Vevay sentinel (Vevay)

REDKEY

Redkey TIMES-JOURNAL. w 1889+
1889-1921? as Redkey times
In 1934+

REMINGTON

Remington PRESS. w Jl 3 1872+
pub [1872+]

RENSSELAER

DEMOCRATIC sentinel. w 1877-1911||?
In [Je 1893-D 14 1894]
InRe Ja 18 1877-98

Rensselaer GAZETTE. w 1857-
In N 14 1860
NN Ja 9 1861

JASPER banner. w 1853-1861||
InRe D 22 1853-F 19 1858

JASPER county democrat. w,sw Ap 1898+
w 1898-1907?
pub 1899+
In 1914+
InRe 1911+

JASPER republican. *See* Rennselaer republican

Rensselaer JOURNAL. w 1891-1903||
Merged with Rensselaer republican
InRe My 20 1897-Mr 9 1903

PRAIRIE telegraph. w O 18 1865-
MWA N 15 1865;F 2 1867

Rensselaer REPUBLICAN. w 1864+
1864-74? as Jasper republican; 1875? Union and Jasper republican; 1876-79 Union
pub 1916+
In My 26 1881-84;Jl 2,S-N 5,26 1885;87-98;Ag 1899-1900;02;19;Je 1935+
InRe 1868;S 18 1874-Je 1876;Je 12 1879-1917

Rensselaer STANDARD. w 1879-
InRe Je 21-D 1879

Rensselaer UNION. w 1868-81||
InRe O 8 1868-Ag 1881
MWA Jl 27 1876

RICHMOND

Richmond BLADE. w 1918-22||?
Negro
In My 28-Je 4,18,S 17-O 15,29-N 5 1920

BROAD axe of freedom. w 1854-64||
DLC Jl 19 1862
In Jl 4 1857;Ap 17 1858;S 17 1864
InNcHi O 10 1857
InRP Ap 26 1856;O 8 1859;Mr 17,O 1860-Je 4 1864
MWA F 13 1864

Richmond DEMOCRAT. *See* Richmond sun

Richmond DEMOCRATIC herald. w 1870-72||
InR My 1871-N 21 1872
InRP N 7 1872

Richmond FREE PRESS. w,d 1874-79||
In O 3,24-31,D 12,24 1874-Ja 14,27,F 18 1875;Ja 13,F 3,25,Mr 9,17,Ap 6,8-9,11,Jl 20,28,30,Ag 1, 3,5,17,25,S 14-N 2,10 1876;O 3 1878
InR 1875-Jl 1876
InRP Ja 9,F 16,20,28,Mr 4-11,20,Ap 6,11,15,My 9,28-29,Je 9,19,27,29,Ag 27,S 19,23,25,28,O 1,24, N 6,14 1875;Ja 6,28,F 8,Ap 6,Ag 6,O 1,6,18 1876;F 1 1877;D 25 1878

HUMMING bird. *See* Richmond independent

Richmond INDEPENDENT. w My 1866-95||?
1866-O 1870 as Humming bird
IU Ap 9 1870
In My 1866-Ag 22 1868;D 24 1873-Je 1875
InNcHi D 30 1874
InR My 1866-N 9 1867
InRP Je 2,Jl-Ag 18,S-O 20,N 10 1866-F 9,23-Mr 9,23-30,Ap 13-Je 1,15-22,Jl 13-20,Ag-S 7, 21-O 5,19,N-D 21 1867;My 8-O 1869;N 1870-Ap 22 1871;Ja-Je 1874;D 1875-Je 1876;Mr 6,S 20 1881;Ja 29,F 11,Je 11,Ag 2,O 12 1882;Jl 19 1889

Richmond daily INDEPENDENT. d 1873-95||?
WHi Mr 6,S 3 1874

INDEPENDENT press. w
InI Ag 24 1861

INDIANA radical. w 1858-72||?
1858?-Je 25 1868 as Indiana radical (some issues as Julian's radical); Jl-D 31 1868 Indiana radical and true republican
InNcHi Ag 19,O 14,N 4,18 1869;Mr 30,Ag 31 1871
InR Jl 1868-N 21 1872
InRP S 9 1869;F 17-D 22 1870;Ja 5 1871
MH Mr 14 1872
OClWHi Jl 1868-N 21 1872
OHi 1870
WHi Je 27 1872

INDIANA telegram. *See* Richmond sun-telegram

INDIANA true republican. w 1864-Je 1868||
United with Indiana radical to form Indiana radical and true republican, later Indiana radical
InR Ja 12 1865-Je 25 1868
InRP Je 29 1865;Je 21,S 20,O 4 1866
OClWHi Jl 1866-68

Richmond INTELLIGENCER. w 1822-
In Mr 13-S 25 1822
InI F 2 1822

Richmond ITEM. d 1876+
Title varies: Richmond evening item
pub 1913+
In Ap 1903-D 1 1916
InNcHi S 23 1882;S 13 1884;S 28 1898
InR Ap 20 1878+
InRP Ap 7 1877;Ap 13 1878;S 20 1881;N 18 1882;Ja 13,Mr 9 1883;Ap 12 1884;Je 22,25,S 14 1885;S 10 1897

JEFFERSONIAN. w 1836-
Title varies: Jeffersonian and working men's advocate
DLC S 21 1839;Ja 11-My 2 1840;O 28 1852
IU Ag 7 1838;F 9 1854

LITTLE paper. w
InU 1915-16

INDIANA (*Continued*)

RICHMOND—*Continued*

Richmond NEWS. w 1880-82||
InRP S 18 1880-S 9 1882

Richmond morning NEWS. d 1908-12||
InR Ap 1908-F 1912

Richmond NEWS-REGISTER. w 1881-99||?
1881-89 as Sunday register; 1890-97 Richmond register
InR N 10 1889;Ag 8 1896-S 1897
InRP Ja 1 1881;Ap 27 1884-S 6 1885

Richmond PALLADIUM. w Ja 8 1831-1906||
pub Ja 8,Ap 9,Jl 23,Ag 13,D 2 1831;Je 29-D 7 1833;Mr 22,O 11 1834;Ja 7-14,28,Mr 11,Je 14 1837-Je,S 21,D 28 1839;41-D 20 1844;Ja 3,F 12 1845,F 11 1847-N 14 1850;51-75;77;79;81-82;84; 87;89-91;97-1902
CSmH Ja 18 1834
DLC N 28 1840;My 29,S 11 1841-D 17 1842;Mr 1852-O 14 1853
ICHi N 2 1865
In Ja 8 1831;Je 16 1832;34;Ja 10,F 14 1835-Ja 2,Ap 9,30 Je 4,O 15,D 24 1836;F 18,Ap 22,S 30,O 28 1837;F 3 1838;F 9,23,S 21,N 16 1839; Ja 11,Mr 14,Ap 11,My 2,Je 20,S 12,O 3,24,N 28,D 19 1840;My 14-23,Je 18,Jl 2,16 1842;O 14, 28 1843;F 1847-48;50;Ag 7,N 5 1851;Ag 26 1858;Ag 11 1859;F 16,S 6 1860;Mr 14 1874;F 2,3,5,My 8 1876;S 4 1879;89-94
InNcHi N 29 1834;Ja 23-30,F 27,Mr 20,Ap 24-Je 12,Jl-S 18,O 2,30-D 11 1863;O 20-26 1880; D 23,27,29 1882
InR N 1 1834;Ja 14 1837-Ja 5 1839;D 25 1850-D 15 1852;Ap 13 1865-O 1875
MWA Ja 8 1831(photostat)D 12-19 1840;Ja 14 1853
NNHi Ap 20 1833;Je 1 1869;Ap 26 1873
NcD Ja 8 1831(photostat)
OHi Ja 8 1831(facsimile)My 20-D 2 1837
WHi Ja 3,O 25,N 8,22,D 6,27 1834; Ja 17-F 7, Mr 7,21,Ap 4-25,My 9-30,Je 27-Jl 11,25,Ag,S 12,O 17,31 1835;F 27 1836

Richmond PALLADIUM and sun-telegram. d 1876+
1876-1906 as Richmond palladium
Ja 1 1931 is 100th anniversary ed
pub 1908+
In S 1904+
InR 1904+
InRE Ja 1 1931
InU Jl 1920+
MWA Ja 1 1931
NNC Ja 1 1931
NcD Ja 1 1931

PUBLIC ledger. w Mr 6 1824-Je 1828||
DLC 1824-D 17 1825
IU Mr-My 22,Je-Jl 17,31-Ag 7,21-D 25 1824 [25]
In Mr 27-Jl 3,24-N 6,20 1824-Ja 1,22-Mr 5,26-Ap 23,My-Ag 6,20 1825-Ap 15,29-Je 10,Jl 1, 15-29,Ag 12-D 16,30 1826-Mr 17,31,Ap 14-My 12,Je-S 22,O 6,N 17-24,D 8-15 1827;Ja 12-26,F 20-27 1828
InI D 11 1824;F 5,Mr 5,26,Ap 9 1825
InRP Mr 27-O 9 1824
MWA Mr 20,My 1,15,N 6 1824;Ag 18 1827
MiG Ag 4 1827

QUAKER City telegram. w 1862-
DLC Ag 15 1863
InNcHi Je 18 1864
InRP Jl 1862-Je 27,Ag 1,22-S 5,19,D 10,19 1863;Mr 26 1864

Richmond REGISTER. *See* Richmond news-register

Sunday REGISTER. *See* Richmond news-register

SPIRIT of old Wayne. w
In S 30 1840
InRP Jl 14,Ag 4,S 17 1840
MoSM Ag 12,S 3 1844

Richmond SUN. w 1881-97||
1881-84 as Richmond democrat. United with Richmond telegram to form Richmond sun-telegram
InR 1881-84
InRP 1891-S 1893;Ja 23-O 17 1895

Richmond SUN. d 1896-97||
United with Richmond telegram to form Richmond sun-telegram
InR Ag 7 1896-My 10 1897
InRP 1896-97

Richmond SUN-TELEGRAM. w 1862-1916||?
1862-80? as Indiana telegram;1880?-97 Richmond telegram
In S 29 1876;D 11 1885
InNcHi F 2 1882;Je 11 1885
InR Jl 1864-N 7 1889;97-Mr 1907
InRP Ap 22,Je 17,O 14,N 18 1865;S 1866-Ap 1867;N 14 1868;S 4-25,O,N 11,D 1869-Ja 14,F 2,11,25-Mr,My 20-Je 10,S 30,D 23 1870;Je 30,D 15 1876;S 1 1881;O 1885-96;Mr 8 1897-98; S 4 1901;05-F 1907
MWA D 28 1867-Ja 4,18-F 15,29-Ap,My 9-30 1868
OClWHi S 21 1867

Richmond SUN-TELEGRAM. d 1885-1906||
1885-97 as Richmond telegram. United with Richmond palladium to form Richmond palladium and sun-telegram

Richmond TELEGRAM. *See* Richmond sun-telegram

Richmond TIMES. w
InR D 14-28 1872;Ja 25-N 22 1873

RIDGEVILLE

RANDOLPH county news. w 1888+
InRid [1888+]

RISING SUN

CENTENNIAL recorder. d 1914-
In Ag 11-16 1914

Rising Sun HERALD. *See* Herald and mirror

HERALD and mirror. w Ag 24 1850-
1850-Mr 6 1851 as Rising Sun herald
OOxM 1850-Ag 21 1851

HOOSIER paper. *See* Rising Sun recorder

HOOSIER patriot. w S 18 1852-
OOxM S-O 9 1852

INDIANA blade. w Mr 25 1843-Je 10 1848||
Followed by Indiana whig, later True whig
ICHi Ap 26 1846
In D 9,23 1843-Ja 6,20-F 10,24,Mr 9,23,Je 1,15, Ag 17,N 16 1844;Ja 1,D 27 1845
InRiR F 19 1848
MWA Mr 30 1844
OOxM 1843-[46]-[Ja-Je 3 1848]
WHi 1843-Je 3 1848

INDIANA democrat. w
InVevHi S 23 1858

INDIANA oasis. w S 5 1878-
In O 3 1878
OOxM S 5 1878

INDIANA patriot. w O 10 1840-Mr 1841||
Followed by Dearborn county register (Wilmington)
DLC O 10 1840
OOxM 1840-F 1841

INDIANA republican. w Ag 30 1851-
OOxM 1851-Ap 22 1854

INDIANA weekly visitor. w My 6 1854-
InVevHi Je 6,Ag 8-15,O 24 1857;F 27,Mr 20, Je 26[Jl 1858-My 1860]
MWA Jl 17 1858
OOxM My-Je 3,Jl 15 1854-Ap 24 1858

INDIANA whig. *See* True whig

Rising Sun JOURNAL. w S 12 1838-
DLC O 20 1838
MWA Je 27 1840
OOxM 1838-S 12 1840

Rising Sun LOCAL. *See* Ohio county news

Rising Sun MIRROR. w N 24 1849-Mr 1851||
United with Rising Sun herald to form Herald and mirror
OOxM N-D 1 1849;F 2,Mr 9,Ap 27,Je 8,Jl 20, Ag 17-24 1850;Ja 2,23 1851
In N-D 22 1849;Ja-Ap,My 18 1850-Ag 21 1851

NEUTRAL pennant. w O 13 1853-
OOxM O,N 10,D 2 1853;Ja 6-13,F 3-10 1854

Weekly NEWS. w F 24 1854-
OOxM Mr 3-17,31,Ap 28-S 15,29 1854

Rising Sun NEWS. 1874-79. *See* Saturday news (Aurora)

OBSERVER and recorder. *See* Rising Sun recorder

OHIO county news. w Jl 26 1879+
1879-1912 as Rising Sun local
CLM S 12 1891
In My 15 1880;1934+
InRiO 1884-87;90+
OCHi Ap 23-My 13 1893
OOxM 1879-85

OHIO county recorder. *See* Rising Sun recorder

Rising Sun recorder. w F 20 1864+
1864-Mr 4 1865 as Hoosier paper; Mr 11 1865-Ja 5 1867 Observer and recorder; Ja 12 1867-My 31 1873 Ohio county recorder
pub 1866+
In Jl 18,O 17 1868;Mr 6 1869;F 19-26,Ap 30 1870;Je 1 1872;Ap 1914-15
InRiO 1868-83;96+
InU 1915+
OOxM [1868]-[72]73

RISING SUN. *See* Rising Sun times

SCOTT eagle. w Ag 16 1852-
CSmH O 24 1852
In S 27 1852

Rising Sun TIMES and farmers' journal. w N 16 1833-S 9 1837||
1833-My 17 1834 as Rising sun; My 17 1834-F 11 1837 Rising Sun times
In 1833-N 7 1835;F 18-Ag 12,26-S 2 1837
InRiR complete
OOxM complete

TRUE whig. w Je 17 1848-Ag 17 1850||
Follows Indiana blade
1848-Je 15 1850 as Indiana whig
In complete
OOxM complete

ROACHDALE

INDIANA statesman. *See* Roachdale news

Roachdale NEWS. w 1882+
1882-90? as Indiana statesman
pub Mr 13 1886;Ap 28 1899[Je 20 1902+]
InRo 1912+

ROANN

Roann CLARION. w 1878+
pub N 7 1890 Je 14 1895;D 24 1897;1901+

ROANOKE

Roanoke REVIEW. w 1895+
pub 1918+
In Jl 1935+

ROCHESTER

Rochester CHRONICLE. w Ap 10 1862-
Follows Rochester mercury
IaDH 1862-64
In S 6 1866;Je 6 1867
OClWHi Ap 10 1862
OHi O 12 1865

FULTON county flag. w 1853-
In Mr 1,S 13-20,N 22 1854;Ap 5,N 22 1856

FULTON county sun. w 1913-22||
InRochN [Ja 9 1913-F 2 1922]

Rochester MERCURY. w 1860-Mr 1862||
Followed by Rochester chronicle
IcDH My 1861-62
In Ap 12-19,Je 14,Jl 12 1860;Ja 17 1861

Rochester NEWS-sentinel. d 1924+
pub D 1924+
In 1934+

Rochester REPUBLICAN. d 1886-1922||?
In Ja 9 1889;Ja 4 1894

Rochester SENTINEL. w 1857-1924||
Followed by Rochester news-sentinel
IU N 1917-O 1923
In S 25,O 23 1858;59-O 20 1860;Jl 4 1863;Je 16 1893-94;F 1914-24
InRochN [1862-1924]
InU 1914-15;Mr 1918-O 1923
InVevHi O 16,30,N 13-20,D 18 1858

ROCKPORT

Rockport DEMOCRAT. w 1855+
In Mr 24 1855-Mr 1862;Jl 19 1907+
InRoc Ap 25 1857-58;S 20 1929+
InU Ap 1855-Mr 1862;My 1868-Ja 1882;85-S 1890
MWA Je 3 1876

Rockport GAZETTE. w 1877-81||
InU My 1880-Mr 1881

INDIANA herald. w 1844-
In N 1 1844
InGvM N 1 1844

Rockport JOURNAL. w 1861-74||?
United with Rockport republican to form Rockport republican-journal
InRicW Mr 23 1871-73

Rockport JOURNAL. w 1877+
In Ag 1907+
InEv F 12 1904;F 6 1914
InU My 1880-Ap 1881;D 1889-Jl 1890;1918+

Rockport REPUBLICAN-journal. w Jl 24 1872-76||?
1872-74 as Rockport republican
In 1872-Jl 21 1875

ROCKVILLE

INDIANA register. w My 1839-
DLC Je 8 1839

Rockville INTELLIGENCER. w Jl 11 1835-
DLC Jl 18 1835
In Ja 7 1837

OLIVE branch. w
DLC Ja 7 1841

PARKE county democrat. w 1864-
In O 27 1864

PARKE county republican. *See* Rockville republican

PARKE county whig. w 1847-
In My 5,Ag 4 1848;N 15 1850

Rockville REPUBLICAN. w 1854+
1854-66? as Parke county republican
In 1897+
InRov 1928+
InRovP [1860+]
InU 1915+
MWA F 21 1866

Rockville TRIBUNE. w 1870+
In Ap 1893-94;97+
InRov 1928+
InRovP 1878+

TRUE republican. w
In N 5 1857

WABASH herald. w 1830-
DLC D 8 1832
ICHi D 31 1831

ROYAL CENTRE

Royal Centre RECORD. w 1889+
pub 1889+
In S 20 1935+
InLoHi Je 30 1911

Royal Centre SENTINEL. w 1890-91||
InLoHi S 19 1891

RUSHVILLE

Rushville GAZETTE. w
InNcHi Ja 19,F 2 1833

Rushville GRAPHIC. w 1882-1907||
In Mr 5 1887
InRuR 1890-1896,1898-1907.

HOOSIER and Rushville democratic archive. 1840-44||?
Followed by Jacksonian
DLC Mr 7 1840

INDIANA herald and Rushville gazette. w 1835-
ICHi D 2 1837
In O 13 1838

INDIANA Jacksonian. *See* Rushville Jacksonian

INDIANA (*Continued*)

RUSHVILLE—*Continued*

INDIANIAN. w
In S 14 1830
InNcHi Ag 24 1830

Rushville JACKSONIAN. w 1845-1912||
Follows Hoosier and democratic archive. 1845?-52? as Indiana Jacksonian
DLC O 28 1852;Mr 21,Je 6,20-S 1860
In Jl 2 1862
InRuR 1854-63;69-71;73-81;85-90;92-1907;10-12
InVevHi My 23,O 22-N 19,D 17,31 1858;Ja 14-F 4,18-Mr 18,Ap,My 13,27-Je 3,17,Jl 1,22,Ag 5-24,S 7-14,O 5 1859;My 23 1860
MWA Mr 4 1852

Rushville JACKSONIAN. d 1895-1917||
InRuR 1914-17

Rushville REPUBLICAN. w 1846-1912||
1840?-52? as True republican
In Mr 25,D 2 1846;O 6 1847;S 17 1851;My 24 1852;N 5 1862
InLoHi My 10 1854
InRuR 1850;55-64;66-71;74;77-79;81-92;94-1912
InVevHi N,D 8-15,29 1858;Ja 12,F 9-16,29-Mr 9,23-30,Ap 20-27,N 2 1859;F 15,Ap 4,My 9 1860

Rushville REPUBLICAN. d 1904+
In My 18 1908+
InRuR 1914+

Rushville TIMES. w
InRuR 1855-56.

TRUE American. w
InNcHi N 24 1831;Ap 7 1832

TRUE republican. *See* Rushville republican

Rushville WHIG. w 1840-
In Ap 25 1840-Ap 14 1843;F 25 1846

RUSSELLVILLE

Russellville NEWS. w 1908+
pub 1923+

RUSSIAVILLE

EXAMINER. w 1875-78||
InKo Ag 16 1877-Je 1 1878

SALEM

Salem ADVOCATE. w
InSHi D 21 1865

AMERICAN true flag. w Je 10 1855-
OHi Ag 12 1855

ANNOTATOR of news, politics and literature. *See* Western annotator

Salem DEMOCRAT. w 1847+
1847-65 as Washington democrat
In 1890-94;97+
InGoE F 23 1876
InNcHi Je 9 1859
InSHi Je 1,Jl 13 1850;Ja 27 1854;Ja 26 1855;Ja 2 1857;F 14 1861;Ja 1,Mr 2 1863;F 16 1865;Ap 25 1867;Je 6 1870;F 23 1876;Je 11 1879;Mr 10, Je 9,O 6 1880;S 12 1883;Mr 4 1885;O 29 1886; Ag 28 1889;98-1907;My 14,Je 10,Jl 1,22-Ag 12, 26-S 2,16-23,O 28,D 2 1914;Ja 13 1915;My 1 1918
InU 1850-Ag 1863;Mr 1874-81;Ja-Mr 1883;O 1 1884;1914+

DEMOCRATIC banner of liberty. w 1861-62||
InSHi Ag 21 1862

DEMOCRATIC sun. w 1889-98||
InSHi S 22 1893;D 6 1895;S 1896-O 14 1898

INDEPENDENT. w N 26 1874-77||
InSHi N 26 1874;N 2 1876;Mr 22 1877
MWA My 25 1876

INDIANA farmer. w My 3 1822-26||
Follows Tocsin. Followed by Annotator, later Western annotator
DLC F 13,Mr 13-20,Ap 3,17,My 1,15 1824
In F 21 1824;Ja 13 1826
InI Je 1,Jl 19-26,Ag 30 1822;Ja 17,F 7,Je 27-Jl 4,25,S 26-O 3,31 1823
InSHi Ja 9,F 21 1824
MWA My 30 1823;N 18 1825

INDIANA monitor. w 1835-41||
Follows Western annotator
ICHi Mr 3 1836
InSHi My 10 1838
MWA Mr 22 1838

INDIANA phoenix. w 1830-33||
DLC N 1 1832
InSHi S 22 1831;O 4 1832;Ja 3,F 27,Mr 13 1833

INDIANA times. w 1830-
In S 30 1830

JOURNAL. d 1898-99||
InSHi Ag 10,S 15 1898;Ja 4-7 1899

Salem LEADER. w 1885-86||
United with True blue republican to form Republican-leader
InSHi O 16 1886

Salem LOCOMOTIVE. w 1850-
InSHi O 5,12 1850

Salem MERCURY. w 1869-
InSHi My 5 1869

Salem NEWS. w,d 1845-52||
In Ap 9-30,My 28,Je 11,Ag 6 1852
InSHi Ag 2,10,15,17,31 1847;Mr 14,Ag 2,15 1848;Ag 29 1851

NEWS. w 1893-
InSHi Ag 21 1896

PEOPLE'S advocate. w 1845-
InSHi Ag 11 1845

Salem PRESS. *See* Republican leader

REPUBLICAN leader. w 1878+
1878-84? as Salem press; 1885? True blue republican
In Jl 1907+
InS N 18 1885-1900;17+
InSHi N 14 1878;D 11 1879;Ja 8,D 30 1880;Mr 16 1882;Je 4 1885;F 4,My 20,Je 3 1886;Je 3,S 9,O 28,N 30,D 16 1887;F 10,Mr 9 1888;Mr 8, My 18,O 11 1889;Je 19 1891;Ja 22 1892;Mr 10 1893;Ap 17 1896;Jl 28,Ag 25 1905;F 23 1906;Jl 28,Ag 4-11 1922
InU Je 11-D 1932

Salem SEARCHLIGHT. w 1891-
InSHi D 29 1891

Salem SENTINEL. w 1901-02||
InSHi Jl 4 1902

Salem TIMES. w
InSHi Ag 9 1860;My 16 1861

***TOCSIN.** w 1818-21||
Followed by Indiana farmer

TOP light. w 1899-1900||
InSHi F 28 1900

TRUE blue republican. *See* Republican leader

Salem UNION advocate. w 1859-
InSHi O 29 1863;S 29, O 20 1864
MWA Je 1 1864
OClWHi N 23 1865

WASHINGTON county dispatch. w
InSHi Jl 10 1897

WASHINGTON county news. w
InSHi Ap 9, N 5 1850

WASHINGTON county republican. w
InSHi Ag 29 1838;O 17 1840;Jl 9 1847

WASHINGTON democrat. *See* Salem democrat

WESTERN annotator. w 1827-35||
Follows Indiana farmer. 1827-30? as Annotator of news, politics and literature. Followed by Indiana monitor
CSmH My 8 1830
DLC N 24 1827;Je 20 1829-31
ICHi Ag 18 1829
In My 31 1828;Ag 1,S 5-12,O 10,N 7,D 12 1829;Ja 8 1830
InSHi Mr 31 1828;Mr 20,O 1,6 1830;Ap 25,S 8,O 6-13,D 22 1832;Mr 2 1833
MWA O 6 1829

SCOTTSBURG

Scottsburg CHRONICLE. w 1880+
pub 1880+

SCOTT county journal. w 1882+
pub Ag 26 1909+
In Mr 25 1914-15;S 4,19 1934+
InSc 1923+
InU 1914-29

SELLERSBURG

CLARK county mirror. w 1927+
In Jl 12 1935+

SEYMOUR

Seymour DEMOCRAT. w 1857-1919||?
In D 30 1875;Ap 5,Mr 2 1876

Seymour JOURNAL. w 1881-97||?
In German and English
In S 5 1895

Seymour LEVER. d 1877-82||
In Mr 31 1882

Seymour NEWS. w 1895-1900||?
In N 19 1896;Ap 29 1897

Seymour REPUBLICAN. w 1879+
pub 1900+
In Je 17 1913-Ag 7 1920
—d ed *See* Seymour tribune

Seymour REPUBLICAN. d. *See* Seymour tribune

Seymour TIMES. w 1857-82||?
InMov F 4 1880
MWA Jl 26 1879

Seymour TRIBUNE. d 1879+
1879-1919? as Seymour republican
pub 1900+
In Ag 9 1920+
—w ed *See* Seymour republican

SHELBYVILLE

Shelbyville REPUBLICAN. d 1879+
In Jl 19 1907+
InU 1915-Ag 1916

REPUBLICAN banner. w 1854-
In N 27 1856

SHELBY democrat. w 1848?+
InI S 1878-D 9 1880

SHELBY democrat. d 1880+
pub 1880+
In 1907+
InU 1917+

SHELBY national volunteer. *See* Shelby volunteer

SHELBY republican. w,sw 1864+
sw 1895?-1909?
MWA My 11 1876
NbHi Ja 24 1878

SHELBY volunteer. w 1844-84||
1844-71? as Shelby national volunteer
In Mr 23 1882;Ja 31,Ap 10-17 1884
InGoE Ja 12 1860
InVevHi F 17 1859
OClWHi F 1 1866

SHERIDAN

Sheridan NEWS. w 1882+
pub 1900+
InU O 19-D 1928;Ja 11-F 8,22-Mr 22 1929

SHOALS

HERALD-democrat. *See* Martin county democrat

MARTIN county democrat. w 1868-88||
1868-84 as Martin county herald;1885? Herald-democrat
In N 6 1885

MARTIN county herald. *See* Martin county democrat

Shoals NEWS. w 1889+
pub 1889+
In F 1914+

REFERENDUM. w 1895-99||
In Ag 8 1895-Ag 10 1899
InU Ag 1896-Jl 1897
WHi D 22 1898

SILVER LAKE

Silver Lake RECORD. w 1893+
pub 1900+

SOMERSET

Somerset BUGLE. w
InWbHi 1883

SOUTH BEND

South Bend COURIER. w 1873-1904||?
1873-77 as Indiana courier
In German
In O 1873-S 1877;O 1879-S 1901

ENQUIRER. w
In S 16 1911-Ag 1913

South Bend FORUM. w
InSb Ap-N 10 1858

South Bend FREE press. w 1836-
In Ap 29 1843;Je 13-20,Jl 18 1844;Mr 14,28,My 30,Jl 4,Ag 7 1845
InSb Jl 9 1836-Jl 19,O 1837-O 20 1838;N 30 1839-Mr 4 1842
NN Ja 14 1842

GONIEC Polski. sw 1896+
In Polish
IU My 1918+
In 1934+

HERALD. d
InSb O 1875-N 12 1876;Ag 24-O 13 1880

INDIANA courier. *See* South Bend courier

INDIANA posten. w 1897-1900||
In Swedish
IRA [1899-1900]

MIRROR. w 1924+
pub 1924+
In 1934+
InSb 1930+

NATIONAL union. *See* South Bend union

South Bend NEWS. d 1887-1912||
United with South Bend times to form South Bend news-times
pub 1887;Ap 22 1888-Ap 14 1889;My 17 1892-Ap 1897;Je 26 1898-Ap 1902;My 1903-Mr,Ag 1911-12

South Bend NEWS-TIMES. d 1883+
1883-1912 as South Bend times
pub 1913+
In Jl 1907+

NORTHWESTERN pioneer. *See* St. Joseph beacon

Evening REGISTER. d 1875-85||
InSb N 16 1879-Je 1885

South Bend morning REPORTER. d 1896-97||
InSb O 1896-F 19 1897

ST. JOSEPH beacon. w N 23 1831-
1831-My 16 1832 as Northwestern pioneer
In 1831-Ag 24 1833
InSb 1831-[My 23-O 20 1832]

ST. JOSEPH county forum. w Ag 13 1853-
In 1853-Ag 4 1866
InSb N 28 1857-Mr,N 13 1858-S 1860

ST. JOSEPH Valley register. w S 12 1845-86||
Merged with South Bend weekly tribune
DLC Mr 25 1852-Jl 21 1853
IaDH N 1865-N 1867
In Ja-Mr 3,31,Ap 21-O 5,19-D 1848;Mr 29,My 10,Je 7,Jl 12,O 4 1849;Je 13,27,Jl 18,Ag 15-22, S 26,O 24-N 7,D 26 1850;F 13,27,Ap 24,My 8, 29,Jl 10-31,Ag 21,O 9,N 20-27,D 11 1851;Ja 22,Ap 22,Je 17,Jl 15-22,Ag 12-S 9,30-N 4,18,D 2 1852;Mr 9,Je 8,N 16 1854;My 17,N 8 1855;F 28,Ap 10,Jl 24-Ag 7,S 11,O 2 1856;Mr 9 1857; Mr 18,N 11 1858;Ap 21,O 13 1859;Ap 19 1860; Mr 31 1864
InSb S 12 1854-78;Jl-D 1879;82;84
MWA F 22,Mr 8,29,O 25 1849;D 28 1865;Je 16 1876
N S 9 1858
NNHi Jl 2 1862;Ap 17 1873
PPL D 12 1850

INDIANA (*Continued*)

SOUTH BEND—*Continued*

ST. JOSEPH Valley register. d
KHi S 4 1856

South Bend SPIRIT of the times. w Ag 29 1863-
MWA D 5 1863

South Bend TIMES. w 1876-1912||
InSb 1905-Je 1911
InSbN 1881-1912

South Bend TIMES. d *See* South Bend news-times

South Bend TRIBUNE. w,d Mr 9 1872-1909||?
pub [1872-1909]
In Mr 11,My 28 1873;Jl 13 1907-09
InSb 1872-My 26 1886;My 1891-My 1897;My 28 1898-My 1904
KHi Je 16-S 8 1888
MWA Je 8 1878

South Bend daily TRIBUNE. d My 28 1873+
Mr 10 1932 is 60th anniversary ed
pub [1873+]
CL Mr 10 1932
DLC My 28 1873;98;Ja-Je 1900
In 1910+
InSb Je 1910-F 1913[Ap 1917+]
MWA My 28 1873(facsimile)Ag 22 1876;My 7 1932
NN My 28 1873(facsimile)
P Ag 17 1898
PPiHi Ja 4 1931
WHi 1917-19

South Bend UNION. w 1866-74||?
1866-71 as National union
InSb Ag 25 1866-71

VAROSI elet (City life). w 1919+
In Hungarian
In 1934+
PPiHi [D 14 1923-N 1928]

SOUTH HANOVER

STANDARD. w
OClWHi 1835
OOxM [F-D 1835]

SOUTH WHITELY

EEL River weekly. w D 20 1934+
In 1934+

South Whitely TRIBUNE. w 1884+
InSo 1914+

SPENCER

NATIONAL guard. w
In Ap 1 1858

OWEN county democrat. w 1876+
pub 1876+
In 1892-94;F 1914+

OWEN county journal. w 1858+
InSp Jl 1873-Je 19 1879
InU 1915-16
MWA Je 15 1876

OWEN county sentinel. w 1900-01||
InSp Ag 9 1900-Mr 14 1901

Spencer OWEN leader. w 1913+
InSp D 1913+

Spencer REPUBLICAN. w 1879-86||
In N 3 1886

Spencer WORLD. d 1927+
pub Je 29 1927+

SPICELAND

Spiceland GAZETTE. w 1897-99||
InNcHi Ap 22,D 16,30 1898;S 1 1899

HENRY county tribune. w 1905-08||
1905-06? as Newcastle tribune (Newcastle)
In Jl 14-D 1905;F 2,Mr 16-D 1906;Ja 11,F 1907-My 1908

Spiceland HERALD. w Ja 28 1891-92||
InNcHi F 25,Ag 5 1891;Mr 16 1892

Spiceland REPORTER. w Je 21 1873-80||
In Ag 23,O 25,N 8,22 1873;O 1 1874;Ja 14,Jl 22,Ag 12 1875;F 17,Jl 6 1876
InNcHi 1873-Ag 10 1876;Ag 23,S 27,N 8,D 6 1877;Ja 3,24,F 7,Ap 11,My 16,Jl 26,Ag 16-S 12,O 11-N 8,22-29,D 20 1878-Ja 3 1879;Mr 5 1880
MWA Ag 10 1876

SULLIVAN

Sullivan DEMOCRAT. *See* Sullivan times-democrat

SULLIVAN county union. *See* Sullivan union

Sullivan TIMES. d 1903+
pub 1903+
In F 5 1914-Ap 9 1921;34+

Sullivan TIMES-DEMOCRAT. w 1854+
1854-1903 as Sullivan democrat
pub 1862-1903
InU 1914-15
OClWHi Ap 5 1871

Sullivan UNION. w 1866+
1866-79 as Sullivan county union
pub 1880-81;1902+
ICHi Ag 16 1868
InU 1915+

SUMMITVILLE

Summitville NEWS. w 1919+
pub [1926+]

SWAYZEE

Swayzee PRESS. w 1894+
pub 1905+
InSw D 1927+

SYRACUSE

Syracuse JOURNAL. w 1908+
pub 1909+
InSy 1909+

TELL CITY

Tell City ANZEIGER. w 1866-1911||?
In German
InTe My 9 1868;Ag 26 1871-73;Ag 19 1876-78; Ag 1881-81;Ag 1887-Jl 1890
InU S 1866-Ag 1870

Tell City COMMERCIAL. w 1873-75||?
InTe My-N 1873

Tell City JOURNAL. w 1891-1918||?
InTe F 22 1893-94

Tell City NEWS. w 1890 +
pub 1903+
In 1893-94 97+
InMovHi C 24 1930
InTe 1921+
InU 1923+

PERRY county tribune. w 1910-18||
InU 1914-Ja 11 1918

Tell City POST. w
InTe S 23-N 4 1887

TEMPLETON

Templeton TOCSIN. w
In My 13 1876

TERRE HAUTE

Terre Haute AMERICAN. w
InT My-S 13 1855

ARGO. w 1882-88||?
OClWHi O 29 1887

ATLAS. d 1861-
In My 29 1861

Saturday COURIER. w 1877-83||
1877-79 as Terre Haute courier
In Ja 11,Mr 22-29,Ap 12,My 24 1879;Ja 3,Je 19,Ag 14 1880;O 20 1883
InU Ap 1877-80

Terre Haute EXPRESS. w D 28 1841-1903||
1841-65? as Wabash express
DLC 1841-D 21 1842;Ja 18,F 1-8, Mr 8,29,Jl 5-12,Ag 16-23 1843;Mr 6,Ag 21 1844;D 23 1846-D 14,1847;Ap-D 1851;Ja-Je 1898
In D 23 1846-N 8 1848;S 4 1850;Ap 2,30,Je 4 1851;Ag 11 1852;Ja 28 1867-Ja,F 11,Mr 11,27, Jl 28-1868-Jl 1869;N 18,D 22 1870[Mr 31 1871-81]Jl 1885[S7-Jl 1891]93-98
InT [1842-My 1843]D 22 1847-N 8 1848;D 17 1851-D 8 1853;S 22 1858-S 12 1860;Ja 28 1863-1903
InU O 1870-73;F 1874-85;F-D 1887[N 1890-Jl 1900]
MWA D 2 1846;Ja 5 1853;Mr 21 1885
OClWHi S 27 1865
WHi F 21,O 31,D 25 1878;Ja 22,Jl 30 1879

Terre Haute EXPRESS. d 1851-1903||
1851-65? as Daily Wabash express. Followed by Terre Haute star
IHi F 27,D 5,26 1900;Ap 21 1901
In Ag 25-O 1851;Je 1856-Ja 8 1857;Ja 22-23, Ap 18,20,23-24,29-My 7 1858;N 7 1860;Ap 16, Ag 14-17,19-23 1861;Ja 23,Ap 19,29,My 28, Jl 21 1862-Jl 27,D 28-29 1864;Ja 17-19,23,26, 31,F 11,18,22,Mr 6,16,18.30-31,Ap 3,8,12-14,19, 27,My 3 1835
MWA Ag 23 1876;Ap 8,Je 13,15 1882;Mr 8,Ap 1 1883;S 19 1884;Mr 18-20 1885
OClWHi S 29 1865

Terre Haute GAZETTE. d 1869-1904||
United with Terre Haute tribune to form Terre Haute tribune-gazette, later Terre Haute tribune
IHi O 6 1900
In Mr 1 1872;86-87;Mr 27 1888;93-Je 1895
InT 1870-81;85-96
InU Je 1869-My 1870;Jl 1872-Je 1902;F 1904
MWA Ag 18 1879;S 19 1884;Mr 17-20,23 1885

Terre Haute weekly GAZETTE. w 1869-1904||
United with Terre Haute tribune to form Terre Haute tribune-gazette
IU S 23 1875;Ja 2 1890

Terre Haute JOURNAL. w 1848-76||?
In Ag 11 1854;Ag 8 1856;Jl 15 1859;Je 30 1860; Ag 23 1871-72
InT D 6 1850;O 8,N 3-10,D 10-17,31 1852-Jl 15 1853
MWA D 24 1852

Terre Haute daily JOURNAL. d 1855-74||?
DLC Je 15 1867;N 2 1874
InVevHi O 5,20,N 24 1858

Terre Haute JOURNAL. tw,d 1884-1913||?
tw 1884-88?
In German
InT Je 1892-94

Saturday evening LEDGER. w,sw 1877-82||
1877-79 as Ledger(w)
In Ja 4-11,F 1,Mr 22,Ap 12 1879;F 14,Je 5,26, N 6,20,D 11 1880;Mr 12,N 26 1881;Je 3 1882
InU Mr 1877-Ap 1882

Saturday evening MAIL. w 1870-99||
In D 20 1873
InT 1870-99
InU 1872-79
MWA Jl 22 1876;Ag 23 1879;Mr 21 1885;My 11 1889
N Ag 19 1871
NcD Jl 30 1887

Terre Haute NEWS. d 1880-91||
InT F 1880-F 1881;O 1889-91
InU Ag 1889-91

Terre Haute POST. d N 1906-My 1929||
Merged with Terre Haute star
InTS complete

PRAIRIE City. w
MWA Ja 4 1853

Terre Haute REPORTER. w D 11 1872-
ICHi D 25 1872

Terre Haute REPUBLICAN. d Je 17 1878-
In Ag 26 1878

Saturday SPECTATOR. w 1904+
1904-05? as Spectator
InT 1904-07;Ap 1911-32

Terre Haute STAR. d 1903+
Follows Terre Haute express
pub Ag 29 1903+
In N 12 1909-Jl 12 1918
InT 1903+
InTI 1925;Ap 1926+
InU Je 1904-12

Terre Haute TRIBUNE. d 1894+
1905-06? as Terre Haute tribune-gazette
IHi F 16,19,26,Mr 1 1901
In 1934 +
InT 1896+
InU S-D 1903;Ja-N 1906;Ja-N 1907;F-Jl 1908; Ap 1911-Mr 1913

Terre Haute TRIBUNE-GAZETTE. w 1895-1905||?
1895-1904 as Terre Haute tribune

Terre Haute TRIBUNE-GAZETTE. d *See* Terre Haute tribune

Terre Haute UNION. d 1856-
In Ja 5-6,12 1857-Ja 11,Ap 25 1858
InT Je 20 1857;Ja 11 1859

UNION democrat. d
In Ag 10 1863

WABASH courier. w Jl 21 1823-
1823-Je 1832 as Western register and Terre-Haute advertiser.
DLC Mr 31-My 13,Je 10-24,Jl 8-15,29,Ag 19,O 14,28,N 25,D 1826;Jl 31 1830;Ag 2 1832;O 31 1840;Jl 3-10,Ag 14,S 18-25,O 9-N 6,20-D 1841
ICHi D 23 1840
IU Mr 31-My 13,Je 10.24,Jl 8-15,29,O 14,28-N 2,D 27 1826
In Jl 21-28,Ag 13 1823;My 7 1825;Mr 31 1827; Mr 25,D 7 1837;Ja 11,25,Mr 8-15,Ap 5,My 31 1838;Mr 26,Jl 23 1842[48-Jl 12 1856]
InI S 24,N 5 1823;My 19-26,Je 9,Ag 11 1824
InT F 5,19-Ap 9,30,My 14-Je 4,Jl-Ag 13,S 3,N 26,D 21 1825;Je 14 1832-Jl 4 1833;Jl 24 1834-S 3 1835;Ja 12-My 11 1839[N 21 1840-43]S 1847-Ag 1848[S 1849-Ag 3 1850]Ja-Ag 20 1852[Ag 27 1853-Ja 7,Ag 26 1854-56]
MWA F 18,O 27 1836;Mr 25 1848;Ja 1 1853

WABASH enquirer. w O 20 1833-
DLC Ja 15-29,F 19-26 1840
In 1838-Ja 20 1841
MWA D 15 1838

WABASH express. *See* Terre Haute express

WESTERN register and Terre-Haute advertiser. *See* Wabash courier

THORNTON

Thornton TIMES. w 1908+
pub 1908+
InTh 1928+

TIPTON

ADVANCE. w 1874-75||
In N 21-28,D 12,26 1874-Ja 2 1875

Tipton ADVOCATE. w 1878-1911||?
InTi S 10 1878-S 8 1882;S 1894-Ag 23 1895

Tipton REPUBLICAN. w 1860-
In Ap 13 1860

Tipton REPUBLICAN. w 1876-
In S 23 1876

Tipton TIMES. w Je 1857-1912||?
In Ap 5 1869
InTiT Jl 9 1868,Je 7 1872
InVeM Mr 5 1879

Tipton daily TIMES. d 1903-24||
WaPS [1923-24]

TIPTON county argus. w 1857-
InVevHi Jl 2,23-Ag 6,N 5,D 10 1858
OClWHi My 27 1859

Tipton daily TRIBUNE. d 1895+
pub 1895+
InTi 1924+
WaPS N 27 1922[23]N 28 1928

WESTERN dominion. w
InVevHi Ag 21 1857

UNION CITY

Union City EAGLE. w 1863-1919| ?
In Ja 6 1876

Union City TIMES. w 1871-1931||
pub complete
In D 17 1874;Ja 14 1875
MWA Je 29 1876

INDIANA (*Continued*)

UNION CITY—*Continued*

Union City TIMES. d 1895+
pub 1895+
In Je 11 1934+

UPLAND

COMMUNITY courier. w 1892+
1892-1917? as Upland monitor
pub [1894+]
InUpT Ag 1929+

Upland MONITOR. *See* Community courier

VALPARAISO

Valparaiso MESSENGER. w 1871-
MWA Jl 20 1876

Valparaiso evening MESSENGER. d 1891-Je 1927||
United with Valparaiso vidette to form Valparaiso vidette-messenger
InV 1907-15

PORTER county vidette. w 1857-1918||?
In S 24,O 8 1867
InU 1915-17
InV 1874-85
MWA My 25 1876
—d ed *See* Valparaiso vidette

PRACTICAL observer. w
CSmH My 23 1853
In S 20-27 1852;S 26 1854
InV 1849-51;53-57

REPUBLIC. w
WHi N 1 1860

Valparaiso REPUBLICAN. w
In Ja 10-F 7,21-N 7,21 1867

Valparaiso VIDETTE. d 1893-Je 2 1927||
United with Valparaiso messenger to form Valparaiso vidette messenger
In Mr 9 1914-27
InV Mr 10 1894-1927

Valparaiso VIDETTE-messenger. d Jl 6 1927+
Formed by the union of Valparaiso vidette and Valparaiso evening messenger
In 1927+
InV 1927+

WESTERN ranger. w
In Jl 19 1845;Ag 9 1848
InV Ap 12 1847-Jl 1849
WHi Ja 11 1845

VAN BUREN

Van Buren NEWS-EAGLE. w 1897+
1897-1903? as Van Buren news
pub 1913+
In F 21 1935+

VEEDERSBURG

Veedersburg NEWS. w 1890+
InU 1916

Veedersburg REVIEW. w 1875-77||?
MWA Jl 19 1876

VERNON

Vernon BANNER. w 1851-90||
In Je 30 1870
InVevHi F 25 1858;Mr 5 1859
MWA Je 14 1876

VERSAILLES

DEMOCRATIC flag. w
In Jl 6 1848

Versailles DISPATCH. *See* Versailles republican

Versailles GAZETTE. *See* Versailles republican

Versailles INDEX. *See* Versailles republican

Versailles REPUBLICAN. w 1856+
1856-70 as Versailles dispatch; 1871-72? Versailles gazette; 1872-79 Ripley index; 1880 Versailles index
pub D 23 1863;D 22 1864;D 31 1868;Ja 14-21 1869;Ja 5 1871;F 22-29 1872;Ja 23,Ag 28 1873-Ag 12 1875;F-Ap 14 1881;Mr 1889+
In F 12,Jl 9,O 8 1858;Jl 12-19 1860;N 27,D 25 1862;My 19 1864;F 22,Ap 12,My 31 1866;Je 16 1897-Je 1908;F 1914+
InU Ap 18-My 9,30,Jl 18-25,O 17-24 1867;S 1919+
InVe 1913+
InVeM Ja 4,Mr 21,Ap 18-My 9,O 17 1872;S 1,15-22 1897;Ja 26,F 16-Mr 9 1898;Ag 22-29 1900;Ag 27 1902;S 12 1917;S 13 1922;Ag 27 1924;O 30,N 13 1929;30+
InVeR 1882-85;89-94;96-97;1900-04;06-14;17+
InVevHi O 22,D 1858-Ja 6,24,28 1859

RIPLEY index. *See* Versailles republican

VEVAY

BULLETIN. d
In S 12-15 1876

Vevay DEMOCRAT. *See* Switzerland democrat

Vevay ENTERPRISE. w 1916-F 1922||
United with Vevay reveille to form Vevay reveille-enterprise
In Jl 3 1919

INDEPENDENT examiner. w
InI F 15,Mr 22 1821

INDIANA palladium. w 1843-
In Jl 10,Ag 21-S 4,O 30,N 20,D 4 1847;F 5, D 9 1848;Je 30,Jl 14,28,Ag 25-S 1,D 15,29 1849-Ja 5,26,F 23,Mr 2,23,My 11,Je 15 1850-Je 10 1852
InVevHi Ja 2 1847;Mr 4 1848

*INDIANA register. w Je 17 1816-
Suspended 1818?-Ja 16 1824
DLC Ja 30,F 13,Mr 19-Ap 2,23 1824;Mr 18,Ap 29 1825
IU Ja 30,F 13,Mr 19-Ap 2 1824;Mr 18,Ap 29 1825
In Mr 11,S 2,D 2 1825
InI Je 11,O 1,15,N 5,19,D 10,24 1824;Ja 14,F 4,25,Mr 11,Ap 8,22 1825
InVev Jl 7 1826
MWA Je 10 1825
N Mr 19 1824

Weekly MESSENGER and Vevay sentinel. w S 15 1831-
1831-36 as Weekly messenger (Printer's Retreat)
In 1831-36;F 11 1837

NEWS. w
InVevHi My 28,Jl 23,Ag 6,D 9 1856;F 11-18,Mr 11,My 13-20,Je 3,17-24,Jl 22,O 21,D 9 1857;Ja 13,Mr 3,31,Ap 14,My 19,Je-D 1858;Ja 19-F 9, Ap 6,My 25-Je 15,Jl 6-13,Ag 3,24,S 7,21-28,O 19,N 1859-Ja 4,18,F 22,Ap 18,My 16 1860

OHIO valley gazette. w Je 19 1851-
DLC O 21 1852
ICHi N 4 1852
In 1851-Je 10 1852
InVev Je 17 1852-Je 9 1853
MWA O 28 1852

*Vevay REVEILLE-ENTERPRISE. w 1816+
1816-F 1922 as Vevay reveille
In Ag 31 1854;Ja 2,23 1856;O 17 1860;Ja 4 1861; Ja 14 1864-1901;Jl 18 1907+
InU 1861-63;1914-15
InVevHi Je 29 1854-Je 20,Ag 22,N 28 1855;My 6,20,Je 3,24 1857;My 7,Jl 8,O 20 1858;Mr 30,Jl 6 1859;Jl 19 1862;Je 3 1863;Ap 14 1864;Jl 6 1865;Jl 5 1866;Ap 1,D 16 1869;Jl 1 1871;F 26 1876;Jl 25 1895;F 24 1898
NNHi Je 3,25,Ag 13 1863;Mr 29 1873
OOxM O 12-19 1876

SPIRIT of the times. w 1840-
In F 11-18,Mr 4,Ag 19,S 16,D 16 1841
InVevHi Ag 5,N 11 1841

SWITZERLAND democrat. w 1868+
1868-1905? as Vevay democrat
In S 18 1879
InU 1915-My 22 1931
InVevHi My 6 1869;F 10 1870;Jl 1 1871;My 3,S 13 1877;Mr 2,O 26 1882;F 1 1883;Ja 17 1884;Ag 14,N 6 1895
MWA My 20 1876

SWITZERLAND guest. w 1826-
In My 8-22 1827

SWITZERLAND monitor. w
InLoHi N 8 1832

Vevay TIMES. w 1882-1903||?
In Je 23,N 24 1892;F 8 1894;N 12-19 1896
InVevHi [Ap 1882-Ap]My 21,Je 11,Jl 2,S 17,O 8,22,N 12,D 3 1884;Ja 7,28-F 4,Mr 18,Ap 8,22, My 13,Jl 1,22-29 1885;Ja 20,Mr 24,Ap 7 1886; F 20 1889;Je 1,Ag 31 1893;F 21,N 6 1895;Ja 16 1896

Vevay TIMES and Switzerland county weekly news. w
Title varies
DLC N 24 1838
PWCl S 24-O 8 1840

WESTERN statesman and democratic whig. w Jl 23 1840-
DLC N 26 1840

VINCENNES

Vincennes CAPITAL. d 1899-Ag 7 1920||
In Je-N 1918
InU 1901-20
InVi F 24 1899-Ag 7 1920

Vincennes COMMERCIAL. d 1882-Ja 1931||
United with Vincennes sun to form Vincennes sun-commercial
In S 13 1887;My 26,Je 7 1889;Je 5 1891;Ja 15, Mr 30,My-N 1918;Mr 6-7 1930
InMovHi F 24 1929
InU Mr 1880-Jl 1917
InVi complete

Vincennes COURANT. w
InU F 1855-Je 1856

Vincennes GAZETTE. w O 2 1830-
Title varies: Vincennes Saturday gazette
DLC Ja 8,Je 25 1831;S 14 1839;Jl 11,25-Ag 22 1840;My 17-31,Je 21-Jl 8,26-Ag 2,16-D 20 1849;Ja 1,29-F 12,26-Ag 19 1852
ICHi Mr 5,Ap 30,Je 18,Ag 27 1831;F 25,Je 9 1832;Jl 6,D 28 1833;Mr 29,O 4 1834;Ja 3,24 1835;Ja 30,F 13-20,Ap 9,30,Jl 2,D 31 1836;D 2 1837;Mr 3 1838;Ap 13,D 7 1839;Ap 3,N 20 1841;Ja 22,Ap 23,Jl 23,N 19 1842
IHi N 12 1831;D 26 1835;O 27 1853
In O 23-N 13,27-D 4,18 1830;Ja 1-15,29-F 19, Ap 16,My 21,Ag 6,S 10,O 1,15-22,N 5 1831; Ap 28-My 12,26,Jl 21-28,Ag 25,S 8-22,O 6-20 1832;Je 15 1833-My,Je 13-Ag 8,22-S 5,O 1835-Ap 16,30-My,O 1 1836;Jl 27,N 2 1839;Ja 25,Mr 7,21,Ap 18,My 2-16,30-Je 13,27,Jl 11-18,Ag 1,29,S,O 10 1840-F 13,27,My 15-Ag 14, 28-O 16,30-D 6,19 1841;Ja-Mr,Ap 23-My 7,21-28,O 29 1842;Ja 28-Ap 1,29-My 13,27,Jl 1,15, 29,S 23,O 21-N 4,18-25,D 9 1843-Ja,F 17-24, Mr 9-23,Ap 6,20-My,Je 8-29,Jl 11-18,Ag 1-15, 29,S 19-N,D 19 1844;Ja 2,23,F 20,Mr-Ap 3, My 1-8,22-Jl 3,17,Ag 7,28-S 18,O 2 1845;S 3, D 31 1846;Ja 14,Je 3,S 2 1847;Ja 20 1848-50; Ag 4 1852;Je 21 1854-Je [S 1855-F 6]Mr 1856-O 2 1858
InU My 1855-64;Ag 1866-69
InVi O 1830-D 1 1832;Je 15 1833-My 25 1848; Je 1850-My 1854
MWA Ap 30 1831;My 17 1834;Ap 18 1835[F 14 1855-S 3 1856;57;F 10-My 19 1858]
NNHi Jl 2 1831
OHi Ag 8 1844
PPL N 21 1850

*INDIANA centinel and public advertiser. w Mr 14 1817-S 8 1821||
1817-Ap 8,Ag 19,S 2 1820;F 3-Ag 25 1821 as Indiana centinel
DLC 1821
IU Ja-Je,Jl 21-S 1821
In 1821
MWA Ja 13-27,S 1-8 1821

INDIANA patriot. w
In Ja 27 1855

JONES' Vincennes sentinel. w N 16 1850-
In N 16 1850;My 10 1851

Vincennes NEWS. w 1879-88||
In Je 16 1881;S 20-27 1883;Ag 28 1884;O 27 1887;F 21,Mr 12,13 1888
InU S 1879-S 1888

NEWS of the day. w
InU F 1855-My 1856

Vincennes POST. w 1932+
InVi My 1932+

Vincennes REPORTER. w 1875-79||
In Jl 20 1878
InU D 1876-Ag 1879
MWA Je 10 1876

Vincennes SUN-commercial. d F 1879+
1879-Ja 1931 as Vincennes sun
Je 14 1936 is George Rogers Clark memorial dedication ed
In Ap 24,Ag 24 1855;D 11 1916;Mr 12 1926-S 22 1933;Jl 11 1935+
InSmA F 25 1929
InU My 1887-1910;12-26
InVi 1879-80;F 1881-Ap 1885;O 1895-1908;Jl 1909+
MWA Je 14 1936
NBuG F 25 1929

Vincennes TIMES. w 1865-79||
InU D 1865-Je 1866;D 1869-O 10 1879
InVi D 9 1865-N 1873
MWA Je 24 1876

WABASH telegraph. w My 25 1827-
In My 25 1827
InVi My 25,Je 8,22,Jl 6-13,27,S 7-14,N 12 1827;Je 20-27,Ag 1,S 12-N 21 1828
OClWHi O 31,N 21 1828

Vincennes semi-weekly WESTERN sun. sw 1856?-79||?
ICHi S 22-26,O 27 1865
MWA Jl 25-28 1876

*WESTERN sun and general advertiser. w Jl 4 1807-1925||?
Follows Indiana gazette (not in this list). Title varies; Western sun; Western sun and weekly advertiser; Weekly Vincennes western sun; etc.
CSmH My 1 1830
DLC 1821-F 2,My 4-11,Je 22 1822;Ja 4,F 2-15,Ap 19,Ag 2 1823;F 7,Ap 3,24,N 27 1824;Ja-D 16 1826;Je 28 1828;Je 20-Jl 11,25,S 26,O 24,N 21,D 5-12 1829;Ja 2,16 1830;Ja 8 1831; 37;Ja-Mr,Ap 10,My 15,29-Je 12,26-Jl 10,31-Ag 21,S 11,25-O 23,N 6,20-D 4,18 1847-F 19, Mr,Ap 15,Ag 19-26,S 9,23 1848
IU 1821-F 2,My 4-11,Je 22 1822;Ja 4,F 1-15,Ap 19,Ag 2 1823;Ap 3,24,N 27 1824[26]Je 28 1828; Je 20-Jl 11,25,S 26,O 24,N 21,D 5-12 1829;Ja 2,16,D 18 1830;Ja 8 1831
In 1821-N 8 1845;Mr 1847-O 6 1849;N 10 1860; My 10 1867;D 8 1871;S 7 1877;Ap 5,Jl 27 1878;F 6 1880;88-94;97-1915
InRP D 29 1821;F 11 1822
InU Mr 1830-N 1831;Mr 1840-N 1844;O 1856-64;Ag 1866-Je 1908;Jl 1909-Je 1915;Jl 1916-Je 1917
InVi O 6 1830;Jl 23 1831;D 8 1832;Jl 12 1834-F 14 1835;Mr 18-25 1837;Ja 11 1840-44;Ag 23 1856-Je 1915;Jl 1916-Je 1919;Jl 1921-Jl 1924
MWA S 22,O 27,D 8,22 1821;Je 22,O 12 1822; My 31,S 13,O 25-N 1,D 13 1823;Je 5,O 21 1824;Ap 16,30,Je 18,Ag 6 1825;Je 17,D 16 1826;Mr 31 1827;D 12 1857;Jl 4 1904
WHi Mr 6 1830;Jl 4 1904

WABASH

Sunday morning CALL. w 1892-93||
InWbHi complete

Wabash CITIZEN. d 1926-28||
InU Ja-Ap 7 1928

Wabash COURIER. w 1871-86||
1871-Ap 1875 as Wabash free trader
In Mr 13-27 1872
InWbHi Jl 25 1873-74;Ap 30 1875-Ap 9 1886
MWA Mr 12,26 1876

Wabash DEMOCRAT. w 1870-
In S 1-15 1870

DEMOCRATIC standard. w 1868-
In O 22-29 1868

Wabash FREE trader. *See* Wabash courier

Wabash GAZETTE. w 1847-60||
United with Wabash intelligencer to form Gazette-intelligencer
In F 27,Mr 20-27,My 16 1849;Ag 7,N 6 1850; Ja 22,Mr 26,S 10,24-O 8,D 31 1851;Ap 5,My 12-26,S 29,O 27 1852;Ja 19,Mr 23,Je 15-Jl 6,20,Ag 24,S 7,O 19 1853;S 15 1854;F 14,My 9,Je 13,Jl 4,18,Ag 8 1855; Ja 2,F 20,Jl 2 1856;F 25 1857;F 25 1858
InWbHi O 10 1849-F 11 1852

INDIANA (*Continued*)

WABASH—*Continued*

GAZETTE-intelligencer. w 1854-
1854-Ap 10 1860 as Wabash intelligencer
In Ap 26 1854-S 1855;56-S,D 30 1857-My 6,Ag 26 1858;O 20,D 22 1859;Mr 8,Ap 17,N 1,15 1860;Mr 7,Ap 25,S 19 1861;Mr 6 1862;Mr 26 1863;F 18 1864
InWbHi Ap 29 1858-Ja 1864

Wabash **INTELLIGENCER.** *See* Gazette-intelligencer

Wabash **MERCURY.** w
InL 1833-34

Wabash **PLAINDEALER.** w,d 1859-1915||?
1859-70? as Wabash republican
In D 26 1859;F 18,Ap 14,28,D 21 1860;F 1,Mr 8,Ap 1861-62;Ja 9,S 18-25 1863;F 5,S 9-16 1864;Ap 12,My 10,Je 14,S 20,O 11 1866;My 9 1867;Je 11,O 15-29 1868;Ap 29 1869;F 17,Mr 3,31,S 15 1870;Mr 9-23,Ag 6 1871;F 1-8 1872; Mr 14-28,Je 6 1873;D 5 1879;Ag 27 1880;O 12 1883;Ag 31 1888;N 1 1889;Ag 24-31 1894
InWbHi Ag 8 1859-79;My 20 1881-Je 1893
MWA Ap 15 1869

Wabash **PLAINDEALER.** d 1891+
In F 1914-Ap 5 1930;F 1934+

Wabash **REPUBLICAN.** *See* Wabash plaindealer

Wabash **STAR.** w 1896-1904||
United with Wabash times to form Wabash times-star
InWbHi Ag 27 1896-F 4 1904

Wabash **TIMES.** w 1884-1904||
In Mr 15,Ap 26,Je 21 1895;Mr 25 1898
InWbHi 1884-1900

Wabash **TIMES-STAR.** d 1895-1925||?
1895-1904 as Wabash times
InNcHi O 14 1909
InWbHi F 9 1904-D 11 1911

Wabash **TRIBUNE.** w 1865-
In O 19 1865;Ap 5-12,Je 14,O 11 1866
InWbHi F 23 1865-F 20 1868

UPPER Wabash argus. w
In Ap 4,Ag 1 S 2,D 9 1846;Ja 13,F 3-10,My 19 1847

WAKARUSA

Wakarusa **SUN.** w 1874-79||
InGoE Je 18 1874-Mr 6 1879
MWA My 25 1876

WALKERTON

Walkerton **INDEPENDENT.** w 1875+
1875-85? as Visitor; 1885?-97? St. Joseph county independent
pub 1925+

ST. JOSEPH county independent. *See* Walkerton independent

VISITOR. *See* Walkerton independent

WANATAH

Wanatah **MIRROR.** w 1895+
pub 1900+

WARREN

Warren **TRIBUNE.** w 1898+
In Ja 30 1931

WARSAW

KOSCIUSKO republican. w 1845-
In Mr 22 1849
InGoD 1845-46

LAKE city commercial. w D 1859-
DLC My 23 1860

NATIONAL union. *See* Warsaw union

NORTHERN Indianian. w 1856-1917||
Merged with Warsaw times
In F 7 1861;My 1869;Ja 27 1870;Mr 21 1872;F 12 1914-15
InGoD 1840-44
InU 1915-17
MWA Ag 11 1870;Jl 20 1876
MoS Ap 20 1865

Warsaw **TIMES.** d 1881+
1917-25? as Warsaw times and Northern Indianian
InW 1917+

Warsaw **UNION.** w 1860+
1860-1900? as National union
In D 12 1862;Ag 13 1868;Ag 13 1903-05
InW 1917+
MWA Jl 7-14 1876

WASHINGTON

DAVIESS county democrat. w 1867-1922||?
In Je 24 1893-94;97-1915
InU 1914-16;18-21
InWa 1867-74;77-93;96-99;1902-22
MWA Je 17 1876

Washington **DEMOCRAT.** d 1866+
InU 1923-33
InWa 1920+

Washington **GAZETTE.** w 1869-1924||?
InWa 1869-77;98-99
InWaC O 17 1891-92
WHi D 26 1868

Washington **HERALD.** w 1895+
In 1934+
InWa 1903+

Washington **TELEGRAPH.** w 1857-
InWa 1857-61

WATERLOO

Waterloo **PRESS.** w 1859+
pub 1869+
In 1897+
InGoE Ja 13 1860

WAVELAND

Waveland **CRICKET.** w
InWav Mr 15-22 1879

Waveland **INDEPENDENT.** w 1886+
pub 1924+
InWav 1899+

WAYNETOWN

Waynetown **DISPATCH.** w 1892+
In Jl 25 1930

WEST BADEN

West Baden **JOURNAL.** w 1894-1917||?
InSHi S 19 1916

WEST LEBANON

West Lebanon **GAZETTE.** w 1883+
pub 1883+
In 1932+
InWlW 1895-1916;18+

WESTVILLE

Westville **INDICATOR.** w 1882+
pub My 27 1882+
InU N 1923-Mr 19 1925

Westville **WEEKLY.** w
InWe D 13 1855-Je 1859

WHITING

BEN FRANKLIN news. w 1925+
1925-Ap? 1928 as Whiting news
In 1927-32;Ag 16,O 25,N 1,D 20 1933;Je 13-20 1934
InWh [Mr 21 1925-Ap 5 1928]O 24 1928+

Whiting **CALL.** w 1906-21||
1908?-09 as Whiting call-sun
InWh Je 30 1906-Mr 21,S 20 1907[09-S 20 1918;Ja-S 5 1919;20-N 25 1921]

CALUMET world press. w
InWh O 3-10 1930

Whiting **DEMOCRAT.** w 1894-97||
InWh [Je 14 1894-My 22 1897]

Whiting **HERALD.** w
InWh [Ap 11-D 19 1928]

Whiting **NEWS.** w 1891-1907||?
InWh Ap 20-Jl 13 1894;Ap 16 1904-Ag 11 1906
MWA Jl 6 1894

Whiting **STAR.** w
InWh [Mr 20 1925-Mr 25 1927]

Saturday **SUN.** w 1893-1907||
United with Whiting call to form Whiting call-sun, later Whiting call
InWh [Ja 16 1897-1907]

WILLIAMSPORT

Williamsport **PIONEER.** w 1915+
pub 1915+
In 1932+
InU Jl 1915+
InWlW 1916;18+
PPeP Ap 28 1927

REVIEW-republican. w 1854+
1854-1914 as Warren republican
In Ja 11-18,Mr 8-N 8 1865;Ag 1,15 1867;D 19 1872;S 24 1908
InU O 1922+
InWlW Jl 17 1856-N 21 1861;Mr 10 1864-Mr 2 1865;66-67;My 28 1868-1916;18+
MWA Ja 25 1866

WABASH commercial. w
In Jl 29 1851;Ap 28 1852
InWlW Ap 1853-D 6 1854

WARREN leader. w 1871-72|
In S 23 1871-S 1872

WARREN republican. *See* Review-republican

WARREN review. w 1891-1914||
United with Warren republican to form Review-republican
In Ag 7-8 1912;My 8 1913
InWlW complete

WILMINGTON

DEARBORN county register. w Mr 27 1841-
Follows Indiana patriot (Rising Sun)
DLC Mr 27 1841
In Ap 10,24-Ag 14,28 1841;S 17 1842-Ap 8,My 13 1843
OOxM Mr-Jl 3,24,Ag-S,O 9 1841

HOOSIER state. w
In Ag 31,S 14 1854

INDIANA whig. w
In O 12-N 9,23-D 14 1843

WINAMAC

Winamac **DEMOCRAT-JOURNAL.** w 1857-1917||
1857-84? as Winamac journal; 1885?-92? Winamac democratic-journal
In S 27,O 18 1862;Je 13,Ag 15-22,N 28,D 12-19 1863;Mr 26,Ag 11 1864;Ag 10,O 19,D 28 1865;Ja 18 1866;Je 24 1893-D 15 1894;Mr 27 1914-15
InU 1869[70-78]-89;91-94;S 1895-1904;06-17
MWA Je 22 1876

Winamac **DEMOCRATIC-JOURNAL.** *See* Winamac democrat-journal

GREENBACK democrat. w
InU S-D 1878;Ja-Ag 1880

Winamac **HERALD** w 1864-
In Jl 14 1864

Winamac **JOURNAL.** *See* Winamac democrat-journal

Winamac **PREFECT.** *See* Pulaski county democrat

PULASKI county democrat. w 1888+
1888-F 20 1889 as Winamac prefect
pub 1888+
In Je 22 1893-94; 1932+
InU Ag 1906-[18]-24;26-27;29+

Winamac **REPUBLICAN.** w Je 10 1867+
pub 1909+
In S 19 1935+
InU 1878-76;82;89;93-1905;13+
InWnP 1891-92;94-96;98;1905-06;10+

WINCHESTER

Winchester **DEMOCRAT.** w 1885+
pub 1914+
InU 1915-1916
MWA Mr 28 1929

Winchester **HERALD.** w 1875-1920||
United with Winchester journal to form Winchester journal-herald
In Ja 2-15 1875;F 3 1876
InWiR N 13 1878-1920
MWA My 10 1876

Winchester **JOURNAL-HERALD.** w 1858+
1858-1920 as Winchester journal
In F 11 1914-15;32+
InWi 1855-1916
InWiR 1858+

Winchester **PATRIOT.** w O 27 1843-
DLC O 27 1843
InI Ap 30 1845

RANDOLPH journal. w 1862-
InNcHi D 14 1865

WINDFALL

Windfall **NEWS.** w 1876-79||?
NbHi O 25 1877

WINSLOW

Winslow **DISPATCH.** w 1898+
pub [Mr 16 1898+]
In Ag 1935+

WOLCOTT

Wolcott **ENTERPRISE.** w 1893—
pub Ap 2 1893;O-D 1902;My 15-O 9 1903;F-D 14 1906;O 23-N 6 1908;11+

WORTHINGTON

SUN. w 1893-1906||?
InBl [1900-04]

Worthington **TIMES.** w 1853+
1853?-72? as White River Valley times
In D 27 1855-F 17 1859;D 26 1872-Ja 1 1874;92-94;97-[1904-06]
InBl [1886-1904]
InWo Mr 1915+

WHITE River gazette. w
In My 16-23,Je 6-20,Jl-O 10,N 1860-Ja 7 1864; N 9 1865-Jl 18 1866

WHITE River Valley times. *See* Worthington times

ZIONSVILLE

Zionsville **TIMES.** w 1870+
pub 1870;73-76;78-79;81;84;86-87;90,92-1906;09-12;14-16;18-21;26+

IOWA

ADAIR

Adair NEWS. w 1881+
IaDH N 1903+

ADEL

DALLAS county democrat. *See* Dallas county record

DALLAS county news. w 1872+
pub 1878+
IaAd Ag 24 1932+
IaDH Ag 1899+
IaHi 1905-06
MWA My 19 1875

DALLAS county record. w 1866-Ap 1 1929||
1866-79 as Dallas county gazette; 1880-94? Dallas county democrat. Merged with Dallas county news
IaAdD 1915-28
IaDH Jl 1893-1902;Ap 1912-28
IaHi My 25 1866-O 18 1867;Mr 6-20,Ap 10,My 1 1868

AFTON

Afton ENTERPRISE. *See* Afton star-enterprise

Afton STAR-ENTERPRISE. w 1880+
1880-97? as Afton enterprise
pub 1900+
IaDH Je 1893-96;S 1905+

Afton TRIBUNE. w 1899-1901||
IaDH My 1899-1901

ALBIA

ALBIAN union-republican. w My 20 1862+
1862-Ap 1922 as Albian union (title varies)
pub Ap 1922+
DLC My 18-Ag 17,31-S 6,28-O,N 9-D 7 1871
IaDH 1883-Ag 1886;Je 1893-Ap 1922
IaHi 1859;Ag-O 1864[65]-[69]
MWA S 7 1865;F 29 1866

Albia weekly GAZETTE. w N 10 1861-Ja 1862||
Follows Jeffersonian blade
IaHi N 10-17,D 7-14 1861

JEFFERSONIAN blade. w Ja 26 1860-O 15 1861||
Followed by Albia weekly gazette
IaHi N 27 1860-[Ja-O 9 1861]

MONROE county democrat. *See* Monroe county news

MONROE county news. w 1890+
1890-97 as Monroe county democrat
pub 1898+
IaDH 1898+

Albia REPUBLIC. w Ag 27 1868-69||
IaHi 1868-F 18 1869

Albia REPUBLICAN. w O 24 1894-Ap 1922||
United with Albian union to form Albian union-republican
IaDH 1900-Ap 1922
IaHi F 9 1905-06

SPIRIT of the west. w D 1 1869-72||?
DLC Ap 26,My 17,Je 28,Jl 19 1871

ALBION

CENTRAL journal. *See* Iowa central journal

IOWA central journal. w N 1855-O 1858||
1855-56 as Central journal. Followed by Marshall county times, later Marshalltown times-republican (Marshalltown)
IaMars D 31 1856-Ag 1858

ALDEN

Alden TIMES. w Ap 12 1878+
IaAl 1879+

ALGONA

Algona ADVANCE. *See* Kossuth county advance

Algona COURIER. w 1884-1918||
IaDH My 1893-1918

KOSSUTH county advance. w Jl 1901+
1901-O 29 1908 as Algona advance
pub N 1908+
IaDH Ag 1901-O 1908

PIONEER press. w Ap 13 1861-64||
Followed by Upper Des Moines
IaDH Ap-Ag 1861;My-O 1862

Algona REPUBLICAN. w 1872-1902||
United with Upper Des Moines to form Upper Des Moines-republican, later Algona Upper Des Moines
IaDH 1884-Je 1902

Algona UPPER Des Moines. w 1865+
Follows Pioneer press. 1865-1902 as Upper Des Moines; 1902-32 Upper Des Moines republican
pub 1865+
IaDH N 1866-1902
IaHi [1905]06
MWA S 7 1876
OClWHi My 14,Je 11,O 8 1873;Ap 21 1875

ALLERTON

Allerton NEWS. w My 1876+
pub 1880-1913;15+
IaDH 1931+

ALLISON

BUTLER county tribune. *See* Allison tribune

Allison TRIBUNE. w Jl 1881+
1881-1916? as Butler county tribune
Jl 29 1931 is 50th anniversary ed
pub 1881;83;85;96;1920+
IaDH Ap 1894+

ALTA

Alta ADVERTISER. w S 1876+
pub 1886-[90-99]-1921;23+
IaAlt 1914-34
IaDH 1886;93+

Alta ECHO. w 1895-98||?
IaAltA 1895

ALTON

Alton DEMOCRAT. w 1882+
1882-84? as Alton review
IaDH 1916+

ALTOONA

Altoona HERALD. w 1888+
IaDH 1916+

ALVORD

Alvord REGISTER. w 1892+
pub 1921+

AMES

Ames INTELLIGENCER. w,d Ap 1868-Ag 7 1913||
N 9 1911-Ap 14 1913 as Ames daily intelligencer (d). Followed by Ames tribune, later Ames daily tribune-times
IaA 1877-1913
IaAS [1894]99[1906]-10
IaDH My 1883-85;87;90-My 8 1913
IaHi Je 27-S 1912
NbHi Ap 25 1879

MILEPOST. w O 1 1928+
pub 1928+
IaA O 23 1930+

Ames evening TIMES. w,tw,d My 12 1892-Je 30 1919||
1892-Ag 28 1912 as Ames times. United with Ames tri-weekly tribune to form Ames daily tribune and Ames evening times, later Ames daily tribune-times
w 1892-Ag 1912;tw S 1912-F 9 1916
IaA 1892-F 9,19 1916-19
IaAS [1917]18
IaDH D 1915-19

Ames daily TRIBUNE-TIMES. tw,d My 15 1913+
Follows Ames Intelligencer. May 15 1913-Mr 28 1918 as Ames weekly tribune; Ap 1 1918-Je 20 1919? Ames tri-weekly tribune; Jl 1 1919-S 28 1928 Ames daily tribune and Ames evening times; S 29 1928-D 28 1929 Ames daily tribune and evening times
pub Mr 1921+
IaA Jl 1918-Je,S 1919+
IaAS 1920+
IaDH Jl 1919+

ANAMOSA

Anamosa EUREKA. w Ag 1856+
pub 1856+
IaDH 1883+
IaHi [Je 17-D 1859]61-80;87-93;1905-06
IaMoE 1863-71
KHi Ap 20 1865
MWA Ag 10 1865;F 15 1866
NNHi Mr 22,Jl 17-24 1863;Ap 24 1873

Anamosa GAZETTE. w 1856-
IaHi Mr 11-O 12 1859

Anamosa JOURNAL. w D 1872+
IaDH 1916+
N D 25 1879

Anamosa NEWS. w
P-M Ag 12 1854

ANDREW

WESTERN democrat. w N 14 1839-O 6 1852||
Followed by Jackson county press (Bellevue)
IaDH complete

ANITA

Anita RECORD. w Ja 1 1912-O 1 1931||
IaAnT complete
IaDH 1916-31

Anita REPUBLICAN. w 1885-1911||
IaDH 1893-S 13 1911

Anita TRIBUNE. w D 13 1883+
pub 1883+
IaDH N 23 1911+

ANKENY

Ankeny TIMES. w 1902+
pub 1902+

ANTHON

Anthon HERALD. w 1901+
pub Je 25 1924+

ARLINGTON

To My 15 1895 as Brush Creek

Arlington NEWS. w 1874+
1874-1904 as Brush Creek news
pub 1876+
IaDH O 1903-O 21 1909
IaHi O 22 1903-06

ARMSTRONG

Armstrong JOURNAL. w 1892+
IaDH 1916-17

ATLANTIC

BRUCE'S optimist. w F 1910-
Follows Farmer's messenger
IaDH F-D 1910

CASS county democrat. *See* Atlantic news

FARMER'S messenger. w 1864-Ja 1910||
1864-N 1903 as Messenger. Followed by Bruce's optimist
IaDH N 1903-10
NcU My 31 1879

MESSENGER. *See* Farmer's messenger

Atlantic NEWS. w 1877-1912||
1877-1906 as Cass county democrat. United with Atlantic news to form News-telgraph
IaHi 1905-06

NEWS-TELEGRAPH. d D 1879+
1879-1912 as Atlantic telegraph
IaAt [1912-34]
IaDH 1922-29
IaHi Jl-S 1912

Atlantic TELEGRAPH. d *See* News-telegraph

Atlantic TELEGRAPH. sw,w 1871-1912||
United with Atlantic news to form News-telegraph
IaAt [1901-12]
IaDH 1893-1904;Ap 1905-10
IaHi 1903-06

AUDUBON

ADVOCATE-REPUBLICAN. w 1879+
1879-My 1 1925 as Audubon advocate
pub 1900+
IaDH 1916+
IaHi 1905-06

Audubon REPUBLICAN. w 1885-My 1 1925||
1885-94? as Audubon County republican. United with Audubon advocate to form Advocate-republican
IaDH 1894-1921

Audubon TIMES. w 1879-86||
IaDH 1881;Ap 1883-84;Ja-Mr 1886

AURELIA

Aurelia SENTINEL. w Mr 1881+
pub 1891+
IaDH 1912+
IaHi F 18 1886-N 3 1887

AVOCA

Avoca DELTA. *See* Avoca mail

Avoca HERALD. w 1880-1902||
United with Avoca journal to form Avoca journal-herald

Avoca JOURNAL-HERALD. w N 6 1896+
1896-1902 as Avoca journal
pub 1896+
IaDH 1906+

Avoca MAIL. w 1871-89||?
1871-86? as Avoca delta
IaAvJ 1874-76

Avoca TRIBUNE. w 1900-08||
IaAvJ 1906-08
IaHi F 10 1905-06

BANCROFT

Bancroft REGISTER. w 1881+
pub Jl 1913+
IaDH 1916+

BARNES CITY

Barnes City NEWS. w 1915+
KHi S 13 1928

BATAVIA

Batavia NEWS. w F 1 1907+
pub 1907+
IaDH 1916+

BATTLE CREEK

Battle Creek TIMES. w Ap 1880+
IaDH Mr 1883-84;86-89;90-98;1900-29

IOWA (*Continued*)

BAXTER

Baxter NEW ERA. w 1895+
IaDH S 1915-11;13+

BAYARD

Bayard NEWS. w 1920+
1920-O 1 1934 as North Guthrie news
pub 1921+
NORTH Guthrie news. *See* Bayard news

BEDFORD

Bedford FREE PRESS. *See* Bedford times-press
IOWA south-west. w F 1 1858-
IaHi D 24 1859;F 25,Ap 14 1860
IOWA south-west. 1867-85? *See* Bedford times-press
SOUTH-WEST democrat. *See* Bedford times-press
TAYLOR county democrat. *See* Bedford times-press
TAYLOR county herald. w 1884+
1884-1931 as New Market herald (New Market)
pub 1932+
TAYLOR county republican. w Ja 5 1878-94||?
United with Bedford times to form Bedford times republican.
IaDH 1883;F-Jl 1884
TAYLOR county tribune. w Jl 20 1860-
IaHi 1860-O 17 1861
Bedford TIMES-PRESS. w 1867+
1867-85? as Iowa south-west; 1886?-89? South-west democrat; 1890?-95 Taylor county democrat; 1895-1931 Bedford free press
IaDH Je 1895-1917;Mr 1933+
Bedford TIMES-REPUBLICAN. w 1882-1931||
1882-90? as Bedford times. United with Bedford free press to form Bedford times-press
IaDH 1901-3

BELLE PLAINE

Belle Plaine INDEPENDENT. w Ja 1876-85||
IaDH 1883-85
Belle Plaine LEVER. w 1888-96||
IaDH [1895-96]
Belle Plaine TRANSCRIPT. *See* Belle Plaine union
Belle Plaine UNION. w D 13 1866+
1866-Mr 4 1869 as Belle Plaine transcript; 1917-21 Belle Plaine union and herald
pub 1914+
IaDH 1897+
IaHi 1866-Ap 22 1868;70-F 24 1876

BELLEVUE

Bellevue HERALD. w Mr 8 1887+
pub 1887+
JACKSON press. w N 16 1852-
Follows Western democrat (Andrew)
IaDH Mr 15-Jl 14 1852;53-54
MWA My 11 1853
Bellevue LEADER. w 1870+
pub 1870+
IaDH My 18[illegible]+
UNION banner. w Jl 14 1863-
IaHi 1863-Je-Ag 1864-Je 1865

BELMOND

Belmond HERALD. w 1873-1914||
1873-75? as Mirror. United with Iowa Valley press to form Herald-press
IaBI 1883-1914
HERALD-PRESS. w 1914-27||
Formed by union of Belmond herald and Iowa Valley press. Merged with Belmond independent
IaB complete
IaBI complete
IaDH 1916-27
Belmond INDEPENDENT. w N 18 1919+
pub 1919+
IaB 1919+
IOWA VALLEY press. w 1894-1914||
United with Belmond herald to form Herald-press
MIRROR. *See* Belmond herald
OBSERVER. *See* Clear Lake mirror (Clear Lake)

BENNETT

Bennett GAZETTE. w F 17 1916+
pub 1916+

BENTONSPORT. *See* BONAPARTE

BETTENDORF

Bettendorf NEWS. w Jl 5 1925+
pub 1925+
El TRABAJO. *See under* Davenport

BIRMINGHAM

Birmingham ENTERPRISE. w N 1869+
pub 1882+
IaDH D 1871-72;1905-07;21+
IaHi Je 11 1870-O 7 1871

BLAIRSTOWN

Blairstown PRESS. w 1913+
pub S 10 1919+

BLENCOE

Blencoe HERALD. w 1911-17||
IaDH 1916-17

BLOOMFIELD

DAVIS county index. w Ap 10 1857-N 6 1858||
Ap 10 1857-Ag 28 1858 as Ward's own
IaDH Jl 9 1857-58
IaHi My-N 1858
DAVIS county republican. w Ag 1863+
1863-68 as Union guard
pub 1863+
IaDH 1863-65;My 1873-Je 1876;79-88;My 1893+
IaHi S 26 1863-D 9 1865;1905-06
Bloomfield DEMOCRAT. w S 15 1869+
pub 1869+
IaDH S 1890-Ap 1892;Je 1893+
IaHi Je 23 1870-N 16 1871;F 1,O 24,D 19 1872;73-Mr 9 1876
DEMOCRATIC clarion. w Jl 1 1858-64||
IaDH 1858-O 5 1859
IaHi D 29 1858-[60-61]
IOWA flag. w My 13 1854-D 13 1856||
1854-Jl 14 1855 as Western gazette; Jl 21-N 3 1855 Western radiator; N 17 1855-Ap 12 1856 True flag (Title varies: Ober's true flag)
IaDH My 13 1854;Jl 14-21,N 3,17 1855-56
IaHi N 17 1855-[Ja-Je]Jl 26-D 1856
Bloomfield MESSENGER. w 1922-S 17 1927||
Merged with Davis county republican
IaBlD complete
IaDH complete
OBER'S true flag. *See* Iowa flag
TRUE flag. *See* Iowa flag
Bloomfield UNION and Davis county democrat. w Jl 12,24 1856||
IaDH complete
IaHi complete
UNION guard. *See* Davis county republican
WARD'S own. *See* Davis county index
WESTERN gazette. *See* Iowa flag
WESTERN radiator. *See* Iowa flag

BLOOMINGTON. *See* MUSCATINE

BODE

Bode BUGLE. w Ap 1894+
pub 1911+

BONAPARTE

To 1870 as Bentonsport

BENTONSPORT signal. w Ja 31 1866-Jl 30 1868||
IaDH Ap 23 1868
IaHi complete
Bonaparte RECORD. w 1890-1928||
United with Van Buren barometer (Keosauqua) to form Van Buren record
IaDH 1911-27
VAN BUREN record. w 1928+
Formed by union of Van Buren barometer (Keosauqua) and Bonaparte record
IaDH 1928+

BOONE

To 1872 as Boonesboro

BOONE county advocate. *See* Boone county republican
BOONE county democrat. w 1857-59||
IaBo 1858
BOONE county democrat. w 1868-1920||?
IaBo 1868-70;73-1914
IaDH F 26 1868-Ja 1890;93-1915
IaHi Mr 1905-06
BOONE county news. w 1856-60||
Followed by Boonesboro times
IaHi S 17-D 17 1858;59[60]
BOONE county republican. w 1865-S 1906||
1865-72 as Boone county advocate
IaBo 1866;69;72-75
IaDH Ag 1883-N 1891;92-1906
IaHi Je 28 1876-Ag 22 1877;F 12 1903-06
MWA S 6 1876
—d ed *See* Evening republican
BOONESBORO index. *See* Boone standard
BOONESBORO news. w 1875-76||
IaBo complete
BOONESBORO times. w 1860-65||
Follows Boone county news. Followed by Boonesboro advocate, later Boone county republican
IaBo 1862
Boone NEWS-REPUBLICAN. w 1888-1922||?
1888-S 1906 as Boone news
IaDH 1895-Ap 1899
Boone daily NEWS-republican. d 1888+
1888-S 1906 as Boone daily news
pub N 1906+
IaDH My 1899-Je,S 1906-15;My 1916+
IaHi Ja-S 1907
MWA S 11 1924
Boone STANDARD. w F 1 1865-1908||
1865-My? 1867 as Boonesboro index; S 12 1867-70? Montana standard (Montana)
IaBo 1865-69;77-1907
IaDH 1865-87;93-My 1908
IaHi F 8 1865-My 2,S 12 1867-S 17 1870

BOONESBORO. *See* BOONE

BOUTON

Bouton PRESS. w 1911-22||?
IaDH 1916-21

BRADFORD

CEDAR VALLEY news. w My 1857-
IaHi N 8-D 22 1860[Ja-Jl 1861]
WHi Ja 26,S 20,O 11 1860 D 14 1861

BREDA

Breda NEWS. w 1909+
IaDH O 14 1909-O 1911

BRIDGEWATER

Bridgewater TIMES. w 1893+
IaDH 1916-18

BRIGHTON

Brighton ENTERPRISE. w 1882+
pub 1882+
Weekly NEWS. w 1879-1906||?
OCIWHi O 23 1891;Je 10 1892
PIONEER. w 1868-70||
IaDH [Ja 28 1869-Ag 27 1870]

BRITT

Britt NEWS-TRIBUNE. w 1894+
1894-1919 as Britt news
IaDH 1895+

BROOKLYN

CENTRAL Iowa. w
OkHi [1868]
CHRONICLE. w 1875+
pub 1896+
IaDH 1887-89;Je-D 1890;95+

BRUSH CREEK. *See* ARLINGTON

BURLINGTON

Burlington weekly ARGUS. *See* Burlington gazette
Burlington GAZETTE. w,tw,d Jl 10 1837-Jl 1 1933||
Follows Belmont gazette (Belmont, Wis.) 1837-Jl 7 1838 as Wisconsin territorial gazette and Burlington advertiser; Jl 14 1838-Je 13 1840 Iowa territorial gazette and Burlington advertiser; Je 20 1840-D? 1846 Iowa territorial gazette and advertiser; Ja 2? 1847-62? Iowa state gazette (title varies slightly: Weekly Iowa state gazette) My 24 1862-N 31 1864? Burlington weekly argus; D 1864?-My 1867 Gazette and argus; Je 1867-1933 title varies: Gazette; Daily gazette; Evening gazette; etc. United with Burlington hawk-eye to form Burlington daily hawk-eye gazette
w 1837-Je 1855;w and d Jl 1855-95?;sw and d 1895?-1905?
CU Ag 18,S 29 1838
DLC Jl-S,O 26-N 2,25-D 2 1837;Ja 6,27-My 5,19,Je 9-16,30,Jl 14 1838-F 1841;Ja 1,F 26 1842;Mr 29-My 3,17-O 18,N-D 1845;Ja 10-F,Mr 14,Ap-My 16,30,Je 20,Jl 4,25-Ag 2,29,O 10-24,N 8-14 1846;47-Ap 4 1849;O 20 1852;Mr 23 1853-S 13,26-O 4,N 22 1854;Ja 17-F 14,Mr 14-21,D 5 1855;58-O 20 1859
ICHi N 9 1839;My 9 1840;Ja 23 1847;F 2 1848; Ag 31 1853
IU S 26 1840;Mr 27,S 4 1841
IaBu Jl 1852-My 23 1855
IaBuH S 1867-1933
IaDH Ag 25 1838;Ap 6,N 30 1839;Mr 28,Jl 25 1840;Jl 3 1841;Jl 6 1842;Mr 3 1852;Mr 31 1875-My,Jl 1888-89;93-1900;My 1911-Ap 1919
IaDaP My 22,Je 5 1847
IaHi My 24-N 21 1862;Jl-N 1864
MWA Ap 5,N 29 1845;Ja 2,16-23,F 6,Ap 17-24,My 15-22,Je 19,D 22 1847;Je 1 1883
PPL D 4-11 1850
WHi 1837-My 6,D 8-15 1838
Burlington daily HAWK-EYE gazette. w,sw,tw, d Je 6 1839+
Je-Ag 29 1839 as Iowa patriot; S 5 1839-Je 1843 Hawk-eye and Iowa patriot; Je 1843-Je 27 1855 Burlington hawk-eye; Jl 4 1855-Jl 26 1857 Hawk-eye and telegram; Ag 1857-Jl 1 1933 Burlington hawkeye
w and d 1839-1905?
pub 1933+
C F 6 1887-S 3 1888
CU [1895]
DLC Je 27,S 5 1839;N 6 1840;F 25-Mr 9 1843; Ja 4,18,Ag 1 1844;Ap 5 1849-Je 26 1851;Ag 7 1861-62

IOWA (*Continued*)

BURLINGTON—*Continued*

Burlington daily HAWK-EYE gazette. 1839+ —*Continued*
ICHi D 22 1842
IU O 1 1840
IaDH O 15 1840-My 27 1841;Jl 1862-N 1864;72-81;Je-D 1882;Mr 1883-Ag 1884;85-Ag 1919;Jl-S 1933
IaDaP Ja 23 1840;D 21 1843-44;My 20,Je 10-17 1847
IaGG Mr 2 1854;F 18,Je 9 1860
IaHi 1859-60;Ag 1865-N 1866;My 11 1871-73;75 [Jl 19 1877-Je 1878]Mr-D 1883;Je-Ag 1884;Ja-Ag 7 1885;95-Mr 1922
KHi S 20-21,N 17 1881-Ag 6 1885;Jl 13 1928
MWA Jl 11,Ag 1 1839;Jl 16,S 24,O 29 1840;N 4 1841;Ja 6,Ap 14 1842;Ag 19 1852;S 12 1855;Je 8,19 1863;Ag 30 1876;Mr 9 1878
N Mr 16 1858;Mr 3 1880
NNHi Mr 29 1925
NbHi Je 10 1875;N 3,29,D 13 1877;Je 12,D 21 1878
OClWHi Ag 29 1878;Mr 12,S 20 1881
P-M O 16 1845
PHHi D 31 1887
TJT D 21 1876;S 13 1900
WHi Ja 6 1864-65

IOWA patriot. *See* Burlington daily hawk-eye gazette

IOWA state gazette. *See* Burlington gazette

IOWA territorial gazette. *See* Burlington gazette

Die IOWA tribüne. *See* Volksfreund-tribüne

MISSISSIPPI posten. w 1898-
In Swedish
IRA 1898

Burlington POST. w Ag 12 1882+
1882-F 14 1925 as Burlington Saturday evening post
IGK 1882-Jl 2 1932
IaDH 1882-89;Ag 1892-1932
IaHi 1887-1906;S 20 1919+
MnHi Je 27 1914-Mr 13 1933
WHi 1913-S 24 1921

Burlington SATURDAY evening post. *See* Burlington post

Burlington daily TELEGRAPH. w,tw,d Ag 10 1850-Jl 4 1855||
1850-Je 14 1851 as Burlington telegraph. United with Burlington hawk-eye to form Hawk-eye and telegraph, later Burlington daily hawk-eye gazette
IU Ag 10 1850
IaDH Ag 2 1851
IaGG Ja 20 1853

VOLKSFREUND. w 1894-99||
United with Die Iowa tribüne to form Volksfreund-tribüne

VOLKSFREUND-TRIBÜNE. w 1861-1919||?
1861-99 as Die Iowa tribüne
In German
MWA Ag 22 1876
NN F 18 1865

WISCONSIN territorial gazette. . . *See* Burlington gazette

BURT

Burt MONITOR. w 1893+
IaDH 1916+

BUTLER CENTER

BUTLER county argus. w Ag 1860-66||?
1860-61 as Butler county Jeffersonian; 1862-Ag 1865 Stars and stripes
IaDH Ag 23 1865
IaHi S 22 1860-[61]-63

BUTLER county Jeffersonian. *See* Butler county argus

STARS and stripes. *See* Butler county argus

CALLIOPE

SIOUX county herald. w 1871-72||
OClWHi My 9 1872

SIOUX county independent. *See* Hawarden independent (Hawarden)

CANTRIL

Cantril REGISTER. w D 1930+
pub 1931+

Cantril TRIBUNE. w 1897-1917||?
IaDH 1916-17

CARROLL

Daily HERALD. w,d S 8 1868+
1868-Mr 1871 as Western herald
w 1868-N 18 1929
pub 1868+
IaC 1871+
IaDH S 1893-1920
IaHi F 1886-90;1904-06
NbHi Ap 28 1880

Carroll SENTINEL. w,sw 1876-Jl 26 1911||
1876-81? as Sentinel (Glidden)
IaDH Jl 21 1893-1911
IaHi Ap 26 1904-06

Carroll TIMES. w 1897+
pub 1897+

WESTERN herald. *See* Daily herald

CARSON

CRITERION. *See* Carson critic

Carson CRITIC. w 1881+
1881-85 as Criterion
IaDH O 1887-S 1889;1910+

CASCADE

Cascade PIONEER. w Je 23 1876+
pub 1876+
IaDH 1916+

CASEY

Casey VINDICATOR. w F 22 1878+
pub 1878-1923;25+
IaDH 1916+

CEDAR FALLS

Cedar Falls BANNER. w Jl 11 1854-D 1858||
Followed by Blackhawk courier, later Waterloo courier (Waterloo)

DANNEVIRKE. w 1880+
In Danish
pub 1880;83-86;88-95;98+
IU 1918+
IaDG [1895+]
IaDH 1916+
IaHi Ag 1902-03
KHi Jl 13-Ag 22 1888
MnHi Mr 20 1918+
WHi Je 1899+

Cedar Falls GAZETTE. w,sw Mr 16 1860-1916||
IaCf 1860-F 10 1903;N 1910-O 1912
IaDH O 1893-1908
IaHi Ja 30,Ap 3,Je 19-Jl 10,31-Ag 7,28 1863-Mr 15 1867;D 1868-[Ja-Ap,S-D 1872]-74;Ap 1875-Mr 1877;Ap-My 1880;F 19 1886-Je 1892;1903-06
MWA D 29 1865;Ap 23 1886
N F 21 1868
WHi Jl 19 1878

Cedar Falls GLOBE. w 1889-1909||
IaDH Je 21 1906-Ap 29 1909
IaHi Je 21-D 1906

Daily RECORD. d 1899+
pub 1900+
IaDH Je 1922+

CEDAR RAPIDS

CEDAR VALLEY times. *See* Cedar Rapids times

Cedar Rapids DEMOCRAT. w Je 24 1856-Je 23 1857||
IaCrM

Cedar Rapids GAZETTE. d Ja 10 1883+
Title varies: Cedar Rapids evening gazette; Cedar Rapids evening gazette and republican
IaCrC 1928+
IaCrM Jl 1885-99;Jl 1900+
IaDH Je 1893+
IaHi Ag 1902-Je 1916
IaU Ja-Ap 1931
PPiHi D 24 1886
WHi Ja 9 1904

Cedar Rapids GAZETTE. w 1883-1906||
DLC 1898
IaHi 1891-1906

IOWSKY pokrok. w 1906-15||
In Bohemian
KHi My 12-13 1915

Cedar Rapids LEADER. w 1906-16||
1906-Mr 27 1914 as Cedar Rapids optimus
IaDH Mr 16 1906-16

Cedar Rapids OBSERVER. *See* Cedar Rapids republican

Cedar Rapids OPTIMUS. *See* Cedar Rapids leader.

PROGRESSIVE era. *See* Cedar Rapids times.

Cedar Rapids REPUBLICAN. w,d S 1 1870-Ap 18 1927||
1870-Mr 9 1872 as Cedar Rapids observer. United with Evening gazette to form Cedar Rapids evening gazette and republican, later Cedar Rapids gazette
w 1870-72;w and d 1872-1904?
DLC Jl-D 1898
IHi F 7 1909
IaCr 1883-1927
IaCrM S 1871-Mr 8,S 2 1872-77;79-82;Jl 1883-89;Jl 1890-Je 1892;Jl 1900-05;Jl 1906-Ap 17 1927
IaDH Jl 1885-Mr 1927
IaHi Ag 1902-S 1907;08-17;26;Ap 1927
MWA Mr 4 1873
N Mr 31 1883
WHi D 2 1886;Ja 6 1887

SLOVAN Americky. w,sw 1869-1920||?
Title varies: Slovan amerikansky
1869-90 pub in Iowa City (w)
In Bohemian
IU D 1917-Jl 7 1919
IaHi 1870-97
NbHi D 5 1917

Cedar Rapids STANDARD. w 1865-96||
ICM S 10 1885
IaDH 1878-1885;S 1887-1888
IaHi F 25-N 1886;F 10-Je 9,S 1887-Ag 1896

Cedar Rapids TIMES. w 1851-97||
1851-54 as Progressive era; 1854-My 21 1868 Cedar Valley times
IaCr [O 1867-S 1868;O 9 1873-S 1893]
IaCrM S 1857-S 16 1858;S 22 1859-S 12 1861;O 1864-S 1865;Mr 15 1866-Jl,O 8 1874-S 7 1893
IaHi Je 11 1857-My 8 1862;My 28 1868-[77-80]-82;Ja 25-Mr 15 1883;Mr 1886-96
MWA My 6 1858

Cedar Rapids evening TIMES. d 1902-O 31 1921||
Merged with Cedar Rapids daily republican
IaCr S 1902-09
IaCrM 1905-Je 1909
KHi Ja-Je 1909

Cedar Rapids TRIBUNE. w 1903+
pub 1903+
IaDH 1909+
IaHi 1908-29

CENTERVILLE

APPANOOSE chieftain. w My 1856-63||
Followed by Loyal citizen, later Centerville citizen

APPANOOSE times. *See* Centerville times

Centerville daily CITIZEN. *See* Daily Iowegian and citizen

Centerville CITIZEN. w 1864-Je 1 1916||
Follows Appanoose chieftain. 1864-69? as Loyal citizen
IU D 9 1891
IaDH 1883-88;Ap 26 1893-99
IaHi N 5 1870-Jl 11 1873;My 12 1886-87
MWA Ag 16 1865

Centerville IOWEGIAN. w,sw Ap 7 1883-1920||
1917-19 as Semi-weekly Iowegian
pub 1903-20
IaDH 1903-15;17-19
IaHi 1905-06

Daily IOWEGIAN and citizen. d D 22 1894+
1894-My 1916 as Centerville daily citizen
pub 1894+
IaCe 1903+
IaDH 1895-99;Jl 1900+

Centerville JOURNAL. w,sw 1871-1922||
w 1871-1919
IaDH O 19 1893-1922

LOYAL citizen. *See* Centerville citizen

Centerville TIMES. w 1875-82||?
1876-81? as Appanoose times
IaHi Ap 13 1876-Ap 26 1877

CENTRAL CITY

NEWS-LETTER. w 1888+
pub 1890+

CENTRE JUNCTION

ELI Perkins in Centre Junction.
KHi Ja 25 1879

CHARITON

Chariton DEMOCRAT. w 1867-71||
Followed by Democrat-leader, later Chariton leader

Chariton DEMOCRAT-LEADER. *See* Chariton leader

Chariton HERALD-PATRIOT. w 1885+
1885-O 7 1909 as Chariton herald
IaDH 1886+
IaHi 1905-06

IOWA patriot. *See* Chariton patriot

Chariton LEADER. w Ap 27 1872+
Follows Chariton democrat. 1883-O 1886? as Democrat leader; O 1886?-Mr 1904 Democrat
ICM My 21 1884
IaDH [My 1875-82]Mr 21 1883-88;F 14 1889-My 1892;Mr 30 1894+

LUCAS county republican. w 1875-78||
Merged with Chariton patriot
IaDH Ag 31 1875;D 5,19-26 1876[77]

Chariton PATRIOT. w N 24 1858-O 7 1909||
1858-59? as Iowa patriot. United with Chariton herald to form Chariton herald-patriot
ICM My 21 1884
IaDH O 1872-77;Je 1888-S 1909
IaGG O 13 1859
IaHi Ag 1870-S 11 1872

CHARLES CITY

To S 5 1851 as St. Charles City

Charles City CITIZEN. w 1879-1901||
1879-95 as Iowa citizen
IaDH Ag 1896-My 1901

FLOYD county advocate-herald. w,sw N 20 1868-N 2 1915||
1868-1908 as Floyd county advocate. Merged with Charles City intelligencer
w 1868-99?
IaDH Ap 20 1894-1915
IaHi 1886-Ap 1890
WHi Ag 13 1878;Ja 27 1887

Charles City INTELLIGENCER. w,sw Jl 31 1856-1920||
1856-Je 1864 as Republican intelligencer
w 1856-1910?
DLC Ag 1,29-N 21,D 1861
IaDH Jl 31 1856-O 1858;59-N 1870[93-94]-1920
IaHi Mr 31 1864-O 10 1867;D 24 1868;Ja 7,F 11-18 1869;1905-06
MWA D 28 1865

Charles City daily INTELLIGENCER. d Jl 24 1906-N 2 1915||
United with Charles City press to form Charles City press and evening intelligencer, later Charles City daily press
IaDH complete

IOWA citizen. *See* Charles City citizen

Charles City twice-a-week NEWS. sw,d N 1920-F 13 1929||
Title varies: Charles City daily news; etc.
Merged with Charles City daily press
d 1920-Ap 1921
IaDH 1920-Ap 1921

IOWA (*Continued*)

CHARLES CITY—*Continued*

Charles City daily PRESS. d 1896+
N 1915-32? as Charles City press and evening intelligencer
IaCh current 6 months only
IaDH N 1915+

REPUBLICAN intelligencer. *See* Charles City intelligencer

CHARTER OAK

Charter Oak TIMES. w Je 1887+
IaDH 1919+

CHEROKEE

Cherokee CHIEF. w Ja- 1870||
Followed by Cherokee times, later Cherokee daily times

Cherokee CHIEF. sw,w 1886+
1886-Ja 1922 as Cherokee democrat
sw 1899?-1927?
pub 1886+
IaChe D 1888+
—d ed *See* Cherokee daily times

Cherokee DEMOCRAT. *See* Cherokee chief. 1886+

Cherokee HERALD. sw 1892-1902||
IaDH 1900-02

Cherokee HOME guard. w Ag 4-N 10 1893||
IaDH complete

Cherokee LEADER. w Ap 1872-S 1876||
IaChe complete

Cherokee daily TIMES. w,sw,tw,d S 18 1870+
Follows Cherokee chief. 1870-S 1928 as Cherokee times
w 1870-98?; sw 1899?-1921?; tw 1922?-S 1928
pub 1870+
IaChe O 1870-1932
IaDH 1886-88;90+

CHESTER

Chester HERALD. w 1902-05||?
United with Lime Springs sun to form Lime Springs sun-herald, later Lime Springs herald (Lime Springs)

CHURDAN

Churdan REPORTER. w 1890+
IaDH 1916-21

CLARENCE

Clarence INDEPENDENT. w 1871-72||
IaDH Ap 26,My 10-17 1872

IOWA age. *See* Clinton age (Clinton)

Clarence weekly NEWS. w O 22 1872-73||
IF Je 25 1873

Clarence SUN. w My 1 1884+
pub 1884+

CLARINDA

Clarinda HERALD. *See* Clarinda herald-journal

Clarinda HERALD-JOURNAL. w,sw,d My 27 1859+
1859-Mr 1878 as Page county herald (1864-65 Southern observer; Ap 1871-72 Republican and herald) Ap 1878-1932 Clarinda herald
w 1859-92?,1910-22?;d 1930-32
pub 1895+
IaDH Je 28 1893-My 11 1894;95-Ap 1897;98-1930;33+
IaHi 1859[60-61]1905-06

Clarinda JOURNAL. w 1890-1932||
United with Clarinda herald to form Clarinda herald-journal
IaClaH complete
IaDH 1916-30

PAGE county democrat. w Ag 1868-1926||
Merged with Clarinda herald, later Herald-journal
IaClaH 1884-1915
IaDH Ap 27 1893-1926

PAGE county herald. *See* Clarinda herald-journal

REPUBLICAN and herald. *See* Clarinda herald-journal

SOUTHERN observer. *See* Clarinda herald-journal

CLARION

Clarion CLIPPER. *See* Wright county news

WRIGHT county democrat. *See* Wright county news

WRIGHT county monitor. w Mr 1869+
pub 1869+
IaCl 1918+
IaHi Ap 20-D 1870;72;Ag 26 1873-[74]-F 4 1880

WRIGHT county news. w 1884-1924||?
1884-1905? as Wright county democrat; 1906?-Je 1920 Clarion clipper
IaDH Je 28 1893-Je 1920

CLEAR LAKE

Clear Lake INDEPENDENT. w F 10 1860-61||
IaGG Mr 9 1860

Clear Lake MIRROR. w Ap 1870+
1870-79? as Clear Lake observer
pub 1896+
IaCle 1917+
IaDH 1893-Je 1932

Clear Lake OBSERVER. *See* Clear Lake Mirror

Clear Lake REPORTER. w Ap 13 1896+
pub 1896+
IaCle 1917+

CLEARFIELD

Clearfield ENTERPRISE. w F 1 1882+
pub [D 1886-94]+
IaDH 1915+

CLERMONT

Clermont ENTERPRISE. w 1905-Ja 1 1928||
IaElE complete

IOWA state express. w 1870-79||?
1870-78? as People's paper
MWA S 7 1876
WHi Ja 31 1877

PEOPLE'S paper. *See* Iowa state express

CLINTON

Clinton ADVERTISER. w,sw,tw,d My 1873-F 28 1928||
Follows Lyons advocate. 1873-1901? as Clinton county advertiser. Merged with Clinton herald
w My 1873-85?;sw 1885?-89?;tw 1890?-1904?
IaCli Jl 1905-27
IaDH 1915-N 1919
IaHi 1905-Je,O 1918-28

Clinton AGE. w,sw Ap 23 1868-F 18 1905||
1868-N 19 1869 as Iowa age
Ap-Je 18 1868 pub in Clarence
sw S 10 1895-1901
IaCli Ap 1869-1902
IaDH My 1893-1904
IaHi 1868-Je 1877[89-90]92-1901;03-F 18 1905
PHHi Ap 1 1870

Clinton morning AGE. d 1882-F 18 1905||
1882-85? as Clinton morning news

CLINTON county advertiser. *See* Clinton advertiser

CLINTON county advocate. *See* Lyons advocate

Clinton HERALD. w D 18 1856-1907||
IaCli 1863-64
IaDH Mr 23 1895-1902
IaHi D 1858-[61]-D 5 1868;86-95;97-1903
MWA Ag 29 1857;O 15 1858;F 22 1862

Clinton HERALD. tw,d 1868+
O 31 1934 is Corn empire ed
tw 1868-71
IaCli 1904+
IaDH Ap 14 1903-Jl 1918;22+
IaHi Mr 1928+

IOWA age. *See* Clinton age

IOWA volkszeitung. w 1867-1925||
In German
IaDH 1916-25

LYONS advocate. w 1855-Ap 1873||
1855-63? as Lyons City advocate; 1864-67? Clinton county advocate. Followed by Clinton county advertiser later Clinton advertiser
IaDH S 22 1860;F 27 1867;Mr 18 1868;Mr 2,Je 29 1870
IaHi Ap 9 1859-[60]Ja 12-Je 11 1861[N 1864-66]-My 1867

LYONS weekly mirror. *See* Clinton mirror

Clinton MIRROR. w My 2 1854-S 1922||
1854-97 as Lyons weekly mirror
IaDH N 2 1861;Ap 18,F 21,O 17 1863;F 13,Ap 9,My 21,Je 3,Ag 20 1864;Ag 26 1865;S 22 1866; Ag 29 1868;93-1921
IaHi [Mr 17-D 1859]-[61]-Je 1864[71-1900;Jl 1902-06
MWA Ja 17 1863

Clinton morning NEWS. See Clinton morning age

COGGON

Coggon MONITOR. w 1889+
IaDH 1916+

COIN

Coin EAGLE. *See* Coin gazette

Coin GAZETTE. w 1881-1934||
1881-92? as Coin eagle; 1893?-94? Page county gazette
IaDH Ag 24 1893-F 1908

PAGE county gazette. *See* Coin gazette

COLFAX

Colfax CLIPPER. w 1879-1918||
IaDH 1916-17

Colfax TRIBUNE. w 1892+
pub 1912+
IaDH 1922+

COLLEGE SPRINGS

CURRENT-PRESS. w 1892+
pub Mr 1904+

COLLINS

Collins CLIPPER. *See* Collins gazette

Collins GAZETTE. w 1891+
1891-1905? as Collins clipper
IaDH 1918+

COLUMBUS CITY. *See* COLUMBUS JUNCTION

COLUMBUS JUNCTION

Columbus City ENTERPRISE. w F 26 1859-
IaHi F-Jl 28 1859

Columbus GAZETTE. w 1887+
pub 1887+
IaDH Je 8 1893-Ap 1933
NN Jl 15 1896

IOWA people. w D 16 1874-75||
IaHi D 16 1874;Ja-My 22 1875

LOUISA county safeguard. *See* Columbus safeguard

Columbus SAFEGUARD. w O 27 1870-1924||
1870-75? as Louisa county safeguard. Merged with Columbus gazette
IaDH O 1870-89;Je 1900-23
IaHi 1870-Je 22 1871
MWA Ag 31 1876

CONRAD

Conrad JOURNAL. *See* Conrad record

Conrad RECORD. w 1880+
1880-99? as Conrad journal
IaDH 1916-17

COON RAPIDS

Coon Rapids ENTERPRISE. w 1882+
pub 1882+
IaDH 1899+

CORNING

ADAMS county free press. w F 2 1883+
pub 1883+
ICM Ja 31 1889+
IaCo 1901-02;04-05;07-14;34+
IaDH My 1893+

ADAMS county union-republican. w 1874-1929||
1874-98 as Adams county union
IaCo S 13,O 4 1877;N 20 1879;S 9 1880;O 14 1897
IaCoA 1900-29
IaDH Ap 1893-96;98?-F 1929
IaHi Ap 8-D 2 1875;1905-06

Corning COURANT. w 1877-79||
IaCo Ag 31 1877;Je 17 1879

REPUBLICAN. w 1896-98||
United with Adams county union to form Adams county union-republican
IaCo Ja 1898

Corning SENTINEL. 1858-60||
IaCo [Ap 1858-Ap 1860]
IaGG D 14 1859

CORRECTIONVILLE

Correctionville NEWS. w Je 1882+
Je 1882-1909? as Sioux Valley news
pub 1882-1900;02+
IaDH 1916+

SIOUX VALLEY news. *See* Correctionville news

CORWITH

Corwith CRESCENT. *See* Corwith hustler

Corwith HUSTLER. w F 9 1888—
1888-94? as Corwith crescent
MnHi F 9 1888

CORYDON

Corydon DEMOCRAT. *See* Wayne county democrat

Corydon MONITOR. w 1863-71||
Followed by Wayne county republican
IaHi 1866-N 1867;F 8 1868-Jl 1870

SOUTH-TIER democrat. w 1858-64||?
IaHi Ja 19 1859-S 1862

TIMES-REPUBLICAN. w 1875+
1875-84? as Corydon times
pub 1906+
IaCor 1919+
IaDH My 1894+

WAYNE county democrat. w 1879-1925||
1879-84 as Corydon democrat. Merged with Times republican
IaCor 1919-25
IaDH Ap 1893-1925

WAYNE county republican. w 1872-75||?
Follows Corydon monitor

COUNCIL BLUFFS

To D 10 1852 as Kanesville

Council Bluffs BUGLE. w,sw My 1851-Jl 8 1870||
Title varies: 1851-53 as Kanesville bugle; Western bugle
sw 1854?-Ap? 1856
DLC S 29 1852;Ja 12-D 1855;F 1859-Ja 2 1861
IaCb Je 16-23,O 20 1852;S 7-21,D 21 1853[55-Ap 6 1856;Mr 1857-68]
IaHi Jl 1864-68;Je 1869-Je 1870
MWA Je 6,13,27 1854

Council Bluffs BUGLE. d
IaCb [Jl-N 1857]
P-M S 5 1854

IOWA (*Continued*)

COUNCIL BLUFFS—*Continued*

CENTRAL press. w Ja 6 1872-
IaCb Ja 6 1872

CHRONOTYPE. *See* Democratic clarion

Council Bluffs COMMERCIAL. Ja 15 1868-
MWA Ja 15 1868

Council Bluffs DEMOCRAT. d My 3-O 31 1868|| My 16-Je 27? 1868 as Democrat and sentinel on the border
IaCb [My 16-Je]-O 21 1868

DEMOCRAT and sentinel on the border. *See* Council Bluffs democrat

DEMOCRATIC clarion. w D 13 1854-Je? 1857|| 1854-Mr? 1857 as Chronotype
IaCb 1854-56;Mr 18 1857

DEMOCRATIC globe. d S 6 1888-
IaCb S-N 8 1888

Weekly Council Bluffs EAGLE. w
IaGG O 12 1859

Council Bluffs FREIE presse. *See* Freie presse und wöchentliche tribüne (Omaha, Neb.)

FRONTIER guardian and Iowa sentinel. w F 7 1849-Jl 16 1852||?
1849-Mr 11 1852 as Frontier guardian
CSmH N 14 1851
DLC My 29,Je 12 1850;Je 13,O 3 1851;F 6,Mr-Je 1852
IaCb Mr 1849-Ja 23 1850;F-Ap 3,My 1850-Ja 8 1851
MH 1849[50]-Je 18 1852
MSaE F 6,Ap 22-29,My 6 1852
MWA S 5 1849;D 25 1850;Jl 25 1851-Ja 23,F 20,Mr 11-Ap 15,My 15,Jl 16 1852
NN F 7,Ap 18 1849
UH 1849-52

Council Bluffs daily GLOBE. d 1872-97||
IaCb [O 15 1883-Je 1897]
MWA Ja 30 1889

GLOBE. w 1873-97||
IaCb [1888-96]
IaDH My 1893-97
NbHi Je 5 1890

Council Bluffs daily HERALD. d 1883-88||?
MWA D 24 1883;Ja 29 1884
NbHi S 3 1885

INDEPENDENT. w 1874-
IaCb Ag 12-O 15,N 5-D 25 1874

KANESVILLE bugle. *See* Council Bluffs bugle

Council Bluffs NONPAREIL. w My 2 1857-1910||?
pub [1858-79]
IaCb [1859-79]
IaHi D 22 1860;61;S 1864-Je 1867
MWA Ag 8 1857;Je 25 1866;N 25 1876

Daily NONPAREIL. d Ja 28 1862+
Title varies: Council Bluffs daily nonpareil; Evening nonpareil
pub 1880+
CoU 1899;S 1906-Je 1910
DLC Ap 23 1879-98
IaCb [1862-Ap 19 1865]My 10 1882+
IaDH Ap 1887+
IaHi Ag 1902-Ag 1917;Jl 1922+
MWA D 7 1873;D 14 1880;Mr 4 1884
VU O 10 1911

NORTHWESTERN republican and globe. w 1872-
IaHi Ag 15-O 17 1872

POTTAWATTAMIE journal. m
IaCb S 1905-My 1906

REPUBLICAN. w 1872-74||
IaCb [Ja 9 1873-D 25 1874]

Daily TELEGRAM. *See under* Omaha, Neb.

Council Bluffs daily TIMES. d F 26 1870-O 14 1872||
IaCb Ja 25-O 11 1872
MWA Ap 18 1872

WESTERN bugle. *See* Council Bluffs bugle

COVINGTON

PEOPLES friend. w
In 1847-50

CRESCENT CITY

Crescent City ORACLE. w 1857-58||
IaCb [1857-58]

CRESCO

HOWARD county times. w Ja 2 1867+
1867-68? as Cresco times
pub 1867+
IaCre D 15 1910
IaDH Mr 1883+
IaHi 1867-N 12 1868;1905-06

IOWA plain dealer. *See* Cresco plain dealer

Cresco PLAIN DEALER. w,sw Ag 20 1859+
1859-My 17 1867 as New Oregon plain-dealer (New Oregon) My 20 1867-Je 1899 Iowa plain dealer; Je 6 1899-Ja 31 1913 Twice-a-week plain dealer
CaOTA Ja 4 1867
IaCre F 1915+
IaDH Ap 27 1893+

Cresco PUBLIC opinion. *See* Decorah public opinion (Decorah)

Cresco TIMES. *See* Howard county times

CRESTON

Creston ADVERTISER. *See* Creston news-advertiser

ADVERTISER gazette. *See* Creston news-advertiser

Creston GAZETTE. w 1873-1903||
United with Creston advertiser to form Creston advertiser-gazette, later Creston news-advertiser
IaDH 1894-1903
IaHi 1900

INDEPENDENT American. w 1875-
NbHi Ag 13 1891

Creston NEWS. w 1927-S 8 1928||
United with Creston advertiser to form Creston news-advertiser

Creston NEWS-ADVERTISER. w Mr 27 1879+
1879-S 8 1928 as Creston advertiser (1905? Advertiser-gazette)
IaDH 1893-1921

Creston daily NEWS-ADVERTISER. d 1881+
1881-S 8 1928 as Creston daily advertiser
pub S 8 1928+
IaDH 1885-1919;Ag 1925+
KHi Jl 28 1928

TIMES. w Mr 15 1872+
1872-Ag 9 1877 as Murray record; Ag 16 1877-O 27 1933 Murray news (Murray)
pub 1880+

DAKOTA CITY

HUMBOLDT county independent. *See* Humboldt independent (Humboldt)

DAVENPORT

Davenport COMMERCIAL.
OClWHi Ap 8 1854

Davenport DEMOCRAT and leader. d O 15 1855+
1855-Ap 1856 as Daily state democrat; Ap 1856-O 1859 Daily Iowa state democrat; O 11 1859-Ap 19 1864 Daily democrat and news; Ap 20 1864-1904 Daily Davenport democrat (title varies: Morning democrat; etc.)
DLC [1855-O 1856;F-D 1857;O-N 1859]Je 25 1860;Ap 28 1889;98
IC O 27 1871
ICHi O 22 1905
IaD 1891+
IaDa Jl 4 1856+
IaDaP [Jl-D 1861]
IaGG Mr 15,Ap 18 1860
IaHi Jl 11 1864;1922+
IaMu current 6 months only
MWA Jl 30 1866
WHi O 22 1905;Ap 5 1908

Davenport DEMOCRAT and leader. w O 15 1855-1914||?
Follows Democratic banner. 1855-O 1859 Iowa state democrat; O 1859-Ap 1864 Weekly democrat and news; Ap 1864-1904 Davenport weekly democrat
DLC O 15,N 5 1852;F 10 1854-O 5 1855;Ja-F 16,Mr 1,22-Ap,My 24-Je 21,Jl-Ag 1860;Ja 10 1861
IaDa 1877-78
IaHi D 1864-O 1867;68-73
MWA Ag 2 1866
OClWHi F 20 1862

DEMOCRATIC banner. w S 1848-O 5 1855||
Title varies: Iowa democratic banner. Followed by Iowa state democrat, later Davenport democrat and leader
DLC Je 25,O 15,N 5 1852;F 10 1854-55
IaBu Ap 7-21,D 15 1854-Ja 5,19-Mr,Je 15,Ag 3 1855
IaDH 1852-53

Der DEMOKRAT. w N 22 1851-S 7 1918||
Title varies: Der wöchentliche demokrat
In German
IU O 16 1884
IaDH 1901-18
IaHi 1862-S 1912
MWA Mr 1 1866

Der DEMOKRAT. d Ja 3 1856-1918||
Title varies: Der tägliche demokrat
In German
IaHi 1913-S 1918
MWA Ag 27 1876

Davenport GAZETTE. w Ag 26 1841-Ja 30 1889||
CSmH Je 25 1846
DLC S 2 1841;Ja 13 1842;Ja 12 1843
IaBu Ap 20,D 14-21 1854[Ja-Ag 1855]
IaDH Ag 4 1842;Jl 30 1879-82
IaDa 1841-Ag 21 1845;Ag 26 1847-80
IaDaP 1841-My 15 1851;Ap 23 1855-60
IaGG O 13 1859;F 3,Ap 19 1860;Ap 17 1865
IaHi Je 11 1857-Ap,D 9 1858-Ag 23 1860[Jl 1864-66]Jl 1867-Ag 16 1871
KHi O 1877-Ap 17,S 13 1878
MWA O 18 1849;S 6 1871
WHi F 1864-D 20 1865

Davenport daily GAZETTE. d O 16 1854-Ap 1889||
Merged with Davenport democrat, later Davenport democrat and leader
DLC 1863;F, 9,21,Ag 8 1871;My 7 1881
IaDH 1878-80;Jl 4 1883-Je 1884
IaDa 1881-Ja 1889
IaHi Ap 19 1866;N 5 1868;My 12 1869
MWA Je 6 1860;Je 15 1876
OClWHi F 1 1874
WHi Ja 4 1864-65

IOWA democratic banner. *See* Democratic banner

IOWA reform. w Jl 12 1884+
In German
pub 1884+

IOWA state democrat. *See* Davenport democrat and leader

Davenport IOWA sun. w Ag 4 1838-42||
1838-Mr 7 1840 as Iowa sun and Davenport and Rock-Island news.
DLC Ag 4 1838;Mr 16 1839-D 1840;F 24-Je 5,21-Jl 10 1841
IaD [1838-42]
IaDaP S 29,D 8 1838;My 3 1839;My 8 1841;Jl 16,O 8 1842

Davenport daily JOURNAL. d My 10 1869-My 20 1870||
IaDaP My-N 6 1869

Davenport daily LEADER. d O 27 1891-1904||
Title varies slightly. United with Davenport democrat to form Davenport democrat and leader
IaDa 1891-Mr 22 1904

Daily morning NEWS. d S 1856-O 10 1859||
Merged with Daily Iowa state democrat to form Daily Davenport democrat and news, later Davenport democrat and leader
DLC Mr 17-O 1859
IaD Mr 31-D 1858

Davenport REPUBLICAN. d S 26 1895-S 30 1904||
Follows Davenport tribune. Followed by Tri-city star
IaDH 1895-F,My 1896-1904
IaDa complete
IaHi Jl 1902-O 1904

STATE democrat. *See* Davenport democrat and leader

Davenport TIMES. w Ja 1 1874-78||?
Title varies: Tri-city times
DLC Ag 1-15,29-D 1874

Davenport TIMES. d S 18 1886+
Jl 11 1936 is 50th anniversary edition
Early years dated also at Moline, Ill.
pub N 1887+
IaDH Ag 11 1907-Je 1916
IaDa current year only
IaDaP D 18-22,28-30 1886;Ap 8-10,My 12,O 29 1888
IaHi Ag 1902-S 1907;08-Ag 1916
MWA Jl 11 1936

El TRABAJO. ir Ap 4 1925-
Ap 4 1925 pub at Bettendorf
CU-B Ap-My 23,Je 11-19,Jl 10-17,31-Ag 7,28, O 17 1925

Davenport TRIBUNE. d Ag 21 1887-S 18 1895||
Followed by Davenport republican
IaDH O 18 1893-95
IaDa complete
IaDaP Jl 6 1888

TRI-CITY star. d S 17 1904-05||
Follows Davenport republican. Sometimes as Tri-city evening star.
IaDH 1904-F 14 1905

TRI-CITY times. *See* Davenport times

TRUE radical. w 1867-68||
MB Ja-Je 1868

UPPER Mississippian. *See under* Rock Island, Ill.

WESTERN soldier's friend. w 1867-69||
IaHi [1868]

WESTERN weekly. w D 9 1871-Ag 1874||
IaHi 1871-My 4 1872

DAVIS CITY

Davis City ADVANCE. w 1888-1901||
IaDH [1895-S 1901]
WHi S 17 1898

DAYTON

Dayton REVIEW. w 1878+
pub 1880+
IaDH 1895+

DECORAH

FOR hjemmet-et tidsskrift for nyttig og underholdende laesning. sm
In Norwegian
WHi Ja 15-D 31 1874

FRA fjärnt og nár. w 1869-70||
In Norwegian
IaDeL [1870]

Decorah JOURNAL. w 1864+
pub [1865-69]+
IaDH My 1894+
NbHi Je 2 1886

Decorah-POSTEN og ved arnen. w,sw 1874+
1874-1908? as Decorah posten
w 1874-1904?
In Norwegian
pub 1874+
IU Ag 27 1909-D 22 1916;18+
IaDH Ag 1905+
IaDeL 1888-[1909-Ag 6 1915]Ag 8 1916+
KHi Je 27-N 1888
MnHi [S 11 1889-1906]+
NdHi 1925-34
WHi O 15 1895+

Decorah PUBLIC opinion and Decorah republican. w F 22 1895+
F-S 1895 as Cresco public opinion (Cresco) O 1895-1928 Decorah public opinion
pub 1895+
IaDH O 11 1895+

IOWA (*Continued*)

DECORAH—*Continued*

Decorah REPUBLICAN. w Ap 12 1860-D 27 1928||
United with Decorah public opinion to form Decorah public opinion and Decorah republican
IaDH 1891;Je 1893-1914
IaDeL complete
IaGG Mr 15 1866
IaHi [Ag 25-D 1864]-[Ja-Jl 1866;67-68]-Ja 15 1869

DEEP RIVER

Deep River RECORD. w 1899+
IaDH Ag 26 1910+

DELHI

DELAWARE journal. w F 9 1859-Mr 1864||
IaHi F-My 1859

DELMAR

Delmar JOURNAL. w 1922+
Suspended 1926-28?
pub 1923-25 29+

DELTA

Delta PRESS. w 1904+
IaDH 1915+

DENISON

Denison BULLETIN. w 1873+
1873-88? as Crawford county bulletin
pub 1898+
IaDH 1894+

CRAWFORD county bulletin. *See* Denison bulletin

Denison REVIEW. w My 3 1867+
pub 1867+
IaDH Jl 23 1873-Jl 15 1874;Mr 30 1883-90;My 1893+
IaHi F 1905-06
MWA Ag 30 1876

DES MOINES

BEAVERDALE news. w Mr 11 1926+
pub 1926+

Des Moines daily BULLETIN. d Mr 11 1869-D 1870||
IaDH complete
IaHi [1869-F 1 1870]

Des Moines BULLETIN. w Mr 11 1869-70||
IaDH Jl 24 1869-Jl 23 1870
IaHi Jl 31 1869-Ja 8 1870

—Legislative supplement. Ja 10-Ap 12 1870||
IaDH complete
IaFd complete
MB complete
NBHi complete
NjHi complete
VHi complete

BYSTANDER. w 1894+
Title varies: Iowa bystander; Iowa state bystander
Negro
IaDH N 1896—

CAMPAIGN state journal. w Jl 21 1859-
IaDH Jl-S 8 1859

Des Moines CAPITAL. d S 1 1883-F 12 1927||
Merged with Des Moines evening tribune to form Des Moines tribune-capital, later Des Moines tribune. 1883-1900? as Iowa capital
IaD 1919-F 1 1927
IaDH 1883-Ag 1923;27
IaHi Ag 1902-27
KHi S 24 1921-S 1922
WHi D 15,30 1886;Ja 15,19 1887

Des Moines CHRONICLE. w 1904||
United with Des Moines democrat to form Des Moines democrat-chronicle

Tri-weekly CITIZEN. tw Ja 12-Mr 23 1858||
IaDH Ja 12,19-23,F 4-6,11,16,23,Mr 9,13,18,23 1858
IaGG Ja 19,28-F 4 1858
IaHi complete

COMMONWEALTH. w 1860-62||
Merged with Iowa state journal, later Des Moines leader
Suspended Je 28-Ag 7 1860
IaGG Ap 12 1860
IaHi [Je 14-D 4 1860]Ja 1,22,Mr 5-19,Je 18 1861

Des Moines DEMOCRAT. *See* Des Moines democrat-chronicle

Des Moines DEMOCRAT chronicle. w 1899-1908||?
1899-1904 as Des Moines democrat
IaDH 1899-[1903-04]-Jl 23 1908

Des Moines DISPATCH. w Mr 24 1933+
Mr-My 15 1933 as Post dispatch
IaD 1933+

FARMERS' tribune. w 1879-1904||
1879-92 as Iowa tribune. Followed by Farmers' tribune (Sioux City), later Farmer and breeder (Sioux Falls, S.D.)
IaDH 1883-1904
NbHi My 28 1884;D 9-16 1885;Ja 13-F 17,Mr, Ap 21-Jl,Ag 11-18,S-O,N 10-17,D 1886-Ja 5, 19-Mr 23 1887;O 10 1888
WHi S 30 1880;D 1,22 1886;Ja 5,Je 8 1887;F 20 1889;Ja 29 1890;Je 10 1891;My 30 1894-O 2 1895

FORT Des Moines argus. *See* Des Moines leader

FORT Des Moines post. w Jl 25 1918-S 20 1919||
IU complete
IaDH complete

FORT Des Moines star. *See* Des Moines leader

Des Moines GAZETTE. w 1896-1902||
IaDH 1896-Ap 1902

Des Moines GLOBE. w 1895-1910||
IaDH Jl 2 1895-Jl 14 1910

Des Moines GRAPHIC. w 1889-91||?
IaDH Je 15-D 1889

Des Moines HAWKEYE blade. w 1883-85||
IaDH Jl 28-D 1885

HERALD of liberty. w 1875-76||
MWA S 2 1876

Des Moines INDEPENDENT. w
IaDH O 6 1880-N 9 1881

IOWA bystander. *See* Bystander

IOWA capital. *See* Des Moines capital

IOWA citizen. *See* Iowa state register

IOWA forum. w N 30 1917-26||?
IaHi 1917-O 1924

IOWA journal of commerce. w 1871-86||
IaDH 1884-86
MWA Je 21 1884

IOWA new broom. sm N 25 1869-N 4 1871||
IaDH complete

IOWA weekly people. w 1876-79||
WHi D 26 1878-Ja 16,F 6,13 1879

IOWA post. w Ja 1860-
Title varies: Die wöchentliche Iowa post
In German
IaHi [Ja 26-N 17 1860]My 27,30 1861

IOWA posten. w 1904-19||
In Swedish
IRA complete
MnHi [1909-Ag 2 1918]

IOWA progress. w Jl 1872-Je 1873||
IaDH complete

IOWA review. *See* State journal. w

IOWA scout. w
IaDH S 16-O 14 1865

IOWA staats-anzeiger. w O 7 1871-1914||?
In German
IaDH 1897-1914
IaHi Je 1872-[76-78]-1914

IOWA star. *See* Des Moines leader

IOWA state bystander. *See* Bystander

IOWA state journal. w,d. 1857;60-61. *See* Des Moines leader

Tri-weekly IOWA state journal. tw Ja 13 1858-
IaDH Ja-Mr 22 1858
IaGG Ja 13,Mr 15 1858
IaHi Ja-Mr 22 1858

IOWA state leader. *See* Des Moines leader

IOWA state register. d. *See* Des Moines register

IOWA state register. w F 1856-1905||
1856-F 8 1860 as Iowa citizen. Followed by Iowa state register and farmer, later Iowa farmer and corn belt farmer (not in this list)
IaDH My 1861-66;69-70;72-76
IaHi [Ap 29-D 1857]-[F 15-D 1860]S 18 1861-66;68-73;77-85;87;93-1900;02-05
DLC Mr 18 1868
MWA Je 23 1882;O 30 1885
NNHi My 20-27,Je 14 1863;Ap 11 1873

IOWA statesman. *See* Des Moines leader

IOWA tribune. *See* Farmers' tribune

Des Moines LEADER. d 1849?-Je 1902||
Title varies: Daily Iowa state journal; Daily Iowa state leader; Des Moines daily leader
IaD 1896-1902
IaDH F 15 1858-F 5 1859;F 1860-F 1861;Jl 4 1863-N 24 1864;Ja 9-Ap 3 1866;68 N 1870;72-81;83-1902
IaGG Ja 30,F 2,8,Mr 2 1860
IaHi Ja 9-Ap 3 1860;S 1901-02
KHi D 26 1878
MWA Ag 21 1876;O 21 1880;S 7 1901
NbHi S 3 1880
WHi Jl 31 1879;Je 25 1891;My 18 1892

Des Moines LEADER. w Jl 26 18-9-Je 1902||
1849-Ap 28 1853 as Iowa star; 1854 Fort Des Moines argus; Je 15 1854-55 Fort Des Moines star; 1855-57 Iowa statesman; 1857 Iowa state journal; 1858-Ja 9 1860 Iowa statesman; Ja 16 1860-62 Weekly Iowa state journal; 1862 Times; 1862-70 Statesman; 1870-Ja 1884 Iowa state leader. United with Iowa state register to form Des Moines register and leader, later Des Moines register
IaDH [1849-54]F 1857-F 6,Jl 1858-Ap 1859
IaDR 1885-1902
IaGG Ap 9 1859;Mr 24 1860
IaHi Ag 8-D 12 1857;S 29,O 6 1859;90-1902

Des Moines Saturday MAIL. *See* Mail and times

MAIL and times. w 1879-1907||
1879-87 as Des Moines saturday mail
CtY D 18 1886
IaDH S 1883-1907
IaHi Jl 23 1904-06

Des Moines NATIONAL democrat. w 1899-1921||?
IaDH D 3 1909-13

Des Moines NEWS. w 1879-99||?
IaDH Mr 7 1879-Jl 16 1880

Des Moines daily NEWS. d N 9 1881-N 8 1924||
United with Des Moines tribune to form Tribune-news, later Des Moines tribune
DLC 1898
IaD 1896-S 1919
IaDH complete
IaHi D 1906-S 1907;Je 30-S 27 1912
WHi O 5 1889

PERSINGER'S Saturday times. w 1883-87||
United with Des Moines saturday evening mail to form Mail and times
IaDH Jl 5 1884-87

PLAIN talk. w 1870+
IaDH Ap 1882+
OClWHi Je 26 1875

POST-DISPATCH. *See* Des Moines dispatch

Des Moines RECORD. w 1895-97||
IaDH My 18 1895-Jl 10 1897

Des Moines daily RECORD. d 1904+
pub 1918+
IaD 1926+

Des Moines REGISTER. d Ja 9 1860+
1860-Je 29 1876 title varies: Daily Iowa state register; Daily state register; Iowa daily state register; etc. Jl 1 1902-Je 21 1915 Register and leader; Je 22 1915-S 30 1916 Des Moines register and leader
pub 1902+
CU My 17 1891
CoU S 1906-My 1910
DLC Ja-S 8 1866;Ap 28 1867-Ag 1869;Jl 11 1874-Je 1897;98+
ICHi F 2-Mr 10,12,19-Ap 13-22,24-Ag 4,6-D 1864
ICU Mr 14 1932-34
IaAS [1913]-[20]+
IaCfT N 1908+
IaCre current year only
IaD 1902+
IaDH 1862+
IaDa current 3 months only
IaFP current 5 years only
IaFm current 6 months only
IaGG My 1907+
IaHi 1867+
IaLeU S 1930+
IaMu current 6 months only
IaSc current 6 months only
IaWi Jl 17 1931+
KHi S 12-O 15 1922
MWA Jl 25 1865;Ag 4 1867;Ag 17 1869;S 7 1876;Mr 4 1881;D 13 1885
MnU Ag 13-D 1918
NNHi My 11 1865;Je 7 1873
OClWHi S 22 1883;Jl 11 1896
TxU Jl 30-D 1 1932
WHi Je 3 1898;Je 16 1908;O 18 1910;1917-20

Des Moines REGISTER and leader. *See* Des Moines register

Des Moines REPUBLICAN. *See* State journal. w

Des Moines Saturday REVIEW. w 1890-97||
IaDH complete

STATE journal. w D 31 1870-88||?
1870-My 25 1872 as Iowa review; My 27 1872-O 18 1873 Des Moines republican
IaDH 1870-My 1872;My 21 1877-Ap 1881

STATE journal. d My 27 1872-O 23 1875||
1872-O 18 1873 as Daily republican
IaDH complete

STATE register. d. *See* Des Moines register

STATESMAN. *See* Des Moines leader

SVITHIOD. w Jl 5 1882-1903||
Merged with Svenska folkets tidning (Minneapolis)
In Swedish
IaDH 1884-N 1903
IaHi O 18 1900-O 1903
MnHi 1889-O 29 1903

TIMES. 1862. *See* Des Moines leader

Des Moines TRIBUNE. d 1906+
N 10 1924-F 12 1927 as Tribune-news; F 19 1927-Ja 1932 Tribune and capital
pub 1906+
IaD N 1924+
IaDH Ap 1907-O 1924
IaHi Ja-Je 1927
KHi S 26-29 1922

TRIBUNE and capitol. *See* Des Moines tribune

TRIBUNE news. *See* Des Moines tribune

DE WITT

CLINTON county journal. w F 1 1859-60||
IaHi Mr 29-S 17 1859

De Witt OBSERVER. w Jl 15 1864+
Follows Signal
pub 1864[86-90]1926+
IaDH Jl 1864-[82-F 1888]-90
IaHi 1864-Mr 23 1870

SIGNAL. w 1862-63||
Follows De Witt standard. Followed by De Witt observer

De Witt STANDARD. w S 1 1858-Jl 1862||?
Followed by Signal
IaDH 1858-N 23 1859
IaHi Mr-S 1859[Ja 16-S 4 1861]
MWA D 5 1860
NhM Ja 19 1857

WIDE awake. w? 1860||
MWA S 24 1860

DIKE

Dike NEW era. w 1910+
pub 1931+

IOWA (*Continued*)

DONNELLSON

LEE county record. *See* Donnellson review

Donnellson REVIEW. w F 12 1886+
1886-97 as Lee County record
pub Je 23 1910+
IaDH 1912+

DOON

LYON county press. *See* Doon press

Doon PRESS. w 1889+
1889-1902? as Lyon county press
pub Mr 8 1934+

DOW CITY

Dow City ENTERPRISE. w F 1891-1912||?
IaHi D 8 1905-D 12 1906

Dow City INFORMER. w 1914-18||
IaDH complete

DOWS

Dows ADVOCATE. *See* Wright county reporter

WRIGHT county reporter. w Je 2 1893+
1893-1926? as Dows advocate
IaDH Ag 1 1914+

DUBUQUE

Daily AMERICAN tribune. *See* Catholic daily tribune

CATHOLIC tribune. w 1899-1934||
pub complete
IU Jl 1918-S 1919
IaDH 1916-32

CATHOLIC tribune. tw 1919-20||
IaDH 1919-Je 1920

CATHOLIC daily tribune. d 1920+
1920-Jl 1929 as Daily American tribune
pub 1920+
IaDH Jl-S 1920;21+
KHi S 19-24 1921;F 14 1925
MoSC Jl 1920-[22-25]-[Jl 1928-Je 1929]-[Jl 1930-Je]Jl 1931
OkSt [1932-33]+
PP [1928-29]-Ja 4 1930
PPCHi [1922-24]
WHi O 6 1933-34

DEMOCRAT. w S 25 1852-
DLC N 20 1852

Dubuque DEMOCRATIC herald. d N 1862-65||?
IaDuC F 11,Mr 5,11,30,Ap 22,S 30 1864
OClWHi N 7 1865

Dubuque ENTERPRISE. w O 20 1901-S 30 1905||
IaDu 1901-O 17 1903;O 22 1904-05

Daily EXPRESS and herald. *See* Telegraph-herald and times journal

EXPRESS and herald. w *See* Dubuque herald

Evening GLOBE journal. d 1891-1905||?
Title varies slightly
DLC Ja-Je 1898;1900-Je 1901

Dubuque daily HERALD. *See* Telegraph-herald and times-journal

Dubuque HERALD. w Ap 19 1851-1901||
1851-O 1854 as Dubuque herald; O 27 1854-59 Express and herald. United with Dubuque telegraph to form Dubuque telegraph-herald
ICHi Ap 24 1891
IaDH N 1854-S 1855;58;60
IaDu N 17-D 1855;My-D 1857;F 1858-59
IaDuC N 5 1865;Je 16 1869
IaGG O 30 1859
IaHi Ap 21 1858-[62-Jl 1863]My 17 1865-Ap 10 1867;My 10 1871-Jl 24 1872
MH Jl 21 1858-61
MWA N 8 1865;Mr 16 1888
NjR D 9 1857;F 3 1858
OHi Ja 21 1857

Daily INDEPENDENT. d 1887-89||
WHi N 24,30,D 7-10,12,14 1888;Ja 2-9,11-15, 17,19 1889

IOWA news. w My 11 1836-Ag 14 1841||?
1836-My 24? 1837 as Du Buque visitor. Merged with Miners' express
Suspended from O 14-N 15 1837;Mr 7-My 5 1840;Ja 26?-My 29 1841
Ct Ag 3 1836;My 17 1837
DLC Ja 18-Ap 12,26-My 17,Je 17-24,Jl 15-Ag 5,S 2,16-23,N 15-D 23 1837;Ja 13-F,Mr 10-My, Je 16-Ag,S 15,30,O 27,N 3-17,D 1-21 1838;My 18,Je-Jl 20,Ag 10,24-O 6,N 2-9,23-30 1839;Ja 11-25,F 15-N 10,24-D 9 1840;Ja 5-19,Je 19-26,Jl 10,31,Ag 14 1841
ICHi Jl 14 1840
IU Jl 6,20-27,Ag 17,O 26-N 2,D 14 1836;Ja 18,F 1,15 1837
IaDH [My 11 1836-My 1837]-Je 1838
IaDu Je 1837-Je 16 1838
MWA D 7 1839;Je 19 1841
WHi N 9 1836;Jl 8 1837;Mr 17,Ap 14,N 3 1838; Jl 27 1839

IOWA socialist. w 1902-05||
ICJ O 1902-D 17 1904

IOWA staats-zeitung. w Ja 13 1855-
In German
Tx Ja 20 1855

IOWA transcript. w My 1843-S 1845||
IaDH Jl 12,26,N 1 1844

MINERS' express. w Ag 1 1841-O 27 1854||
United with Dubuque herald to form Express and herald
DLC Jl 7 1843
IU Je 14 1844
IaDH N 8 1844;My 7 1845;S 1847-54
IaDaP Je 16 1847
IaDu [1841-51]
NN F 19 1851

MINERS' express. d Ag 19 1851-O 27 1854||
United with Dubuque daily herald to form Daily express and herald, later Telegraph-herald and times-journal
IaDH 1851-Ag 1852;Je 1853-54

Dubuque NATIONAL demokrat. w Ag 1856-Ja 5 1932||
Title varies: Wöchentlicher national demokrat
In German
IaDH N 16 1899-1930
IaHi My 17 1859;Ap 1860;My 30 1861[Ja-Je 19 1862;63-Je 1864]Ag 1865-My 1868;Ag 1902-06

Daily NEWS. d Jl 1919-F 1921||
IaDH 1920

Dubuque daily NORTH-WEST. d Ag 1856-61||?
Suspended My 27 1858-Je 1859
DLC Ap 16 1858
IaDH Jl 1857-My 1858
IaDu [1857]
NNHi Jl 21,Ag 11,S 29,D 22,29 1856;F 2,16 1857

OBSERVER. w F 1854-Jl 1855||?
IaDH N 1854-Ap 1855

Dubuque REPUBLICAN. d N 26 1855-O 20 1857||
Merged with Dubuque tribune
IaDH complete

Dubuque REPUBLICAN. w N 26 1855-O 20 1857||
Merged with Dubuque tribune
Suspended Ja 27-Je 6 1857
IaDH Je 17-O 20 1857

Dubuque morning SUN. d Je 1859-
IaDu [1859]

Dubuque daily TELEGRAPH. d Jl 6 1870-O 25 1901||
United with Dubuque daily herald to form Dubuque telegraph-herald, later Telegraph-herald and times-journal
DLC 1898-1901
IaDH My 1894-1901
MWA My 15 1872

Dubuque TELEGRAPH-DEMOCRAT. *See* Dubuque telegraph-herald

Dubuque TELEGRAPH-HERALD. w,sw 1871-1918||?
1871-98 as Dubuque telegraph
w 1871-95?
IaHi 1907-10
MWA Je 18 1850

TELEGRAPH-HERALD and times-journal. d Jl 14 1851+
1851-O 25 1901 as Dubuque daily herald (O 27 1854-59 Daily express and herald) O 26 1901-Ap 1 1927 Dubuque telegraph-herald
DLC Ag 15 1860;O 25 1878-N 24 1882;83-97; 1901-Ap,S 1902-05;Ap 1927+
ICM Jl 4 1885
IaDH [Ap 1853-My 1854]-Ap,O 1855-59;Ja-Je 1861;62-O 1901;02+
IaDu 1901+
IaDuC Jl 18 1862
IaHi My 5-D 1856;Ja-Ap 6 1858[F 6-Ag 11 1861]F 1905+
MWA N 22 1852;My 16,Ag 23 1872;Jl 6 1876

Dubuque weekly TIMES-JOURNAL. w 1857-1918||
1857-S 1906 as Dubuque weekly times
IaDH 1873;Ap 1893-1903
IaHi [N 16 1857-61]Ja 9 1862;Jl 1863-67;69-[75]-Mr 1881;S 1885-F 1886;Ap-D 1891;93-1913
MWA Jl 7,S 22 1859;F 28 1861;N 15 1865
NNHi F 3 1869;Mr 26 1873
OClWHi N 14 1865
TxGR S 27 1901

Dubuque daily TIMES-JOURNAL. d Je 15 1857-Ap 1 1927||
1857-S 1906 as Dubuque daily times. United with Dubuque telegraph-herald to form Telegraph-herald and times-journal
DLC 1869-72;Jl 10 1874-Je 1 1879;98-1901;My 1902-05
ICN [1864]65
IaDH 1857-Je 1861[66]Jl-D 1867;78-80;O 1903-Mr 1927
IaDu 1857-N 20 1858;61-1927
IaGG Ap 18-19,S 9,O 30,N 19 1859
IaHi Je 27 1857-Je 8 1858;Mr-D 1886
MBAt Ap 11,15,17 1865
MWA F 13 1864;N 15 1865;Jl 6,Ag 25 1876
N N 3 1861
OClWHi Ja-Je 1862;63

Dubuque TRIBUNE. w D 21 1846-58||?
IaDaP Ap 19 1847
IaDuC 1846-Mr 1 1850
P S 27 1854
PPL D 25 1850

Dubuque TRIBUNE. sw F 22 1848-
IaDuC F 25-Ag 22 1848

Dubuque daily TRIBUNE. d Mr 26 1851-Mr 1858||?
Suspended Mr? 1852-F 1854
IaDH [1856-Mr 1858]

Die TURNZEITUNG. w
In German
MnHi Je 21-N 1 1859

Dubuque UNION. d Ag-D 1861||
Title varies: Daily evening union; Daily union
IaDH complete

Dubuque VISITOR. *See* Iowa news

WESTERN star. w 1858||?
IaDuC F 13,Mr 3 1858

DUNLAP

Dunlap REPORTER. w Ap 20 1871+
IaDun 1916+

DURANT

Durant NEWS. w Mr 1 1925+
pub 1925+

DYERSVILLE

Dyersville COMMERCIAL. w Mr 1872+
IaDH S 1893+

Dyersville MERCURY. w N? 1857-
IaHi [Ap 1859-Mr 27 1860]

DYSART

Dysart REPORTER. w 1878+
pub 1878-[79-1914]+

EAGLE GROVE

BOONE VALLEY gazette. w 1882-1902||
United with Eagle Grove times to form Eagle Grove times-gazette
IaDH 1884-86;88-N 11 1891;93-1902
IaHi 1883-94

Eagle Grove EAGLE. w F 4 1895+
pub 1895+
IaDH 1916+
IaE 1902+

Weekly TELEPHONE. w F 10 1882-
IaHi 1882-N 8 1883

Eagle Grove TIMES-GAZETTE. w 1881-1927||
1881-1902 as Eagle Grove times. Merged with Eagle Grove eagle
IaDH 1903-17

EARLVILLE

Earlville GRAPHIC. w N? 1881-86||
MWA D 1 1882
NbHi D 8,29 1882;Mr 2-9,Ap 6,Je 1 1883

Earlville REVIEW. w Mr 1925+
pub 1925+

EAST PERU

East Peru MAIL. w 1898-1919||
IaDH 1916-19

EDDYVILLE

Eddyville ADVERTISER. w F 1869-84||?
IaHi Je 18-D 1870

COMMERCIAL. w Ag 11 1853-59||
1853-55? as Eddyville free-press
IaBu Ap 6-13,D 22 1854-[Ja-Ap 1855]

Eddyville FREE-PRESS. *See* Commercial

Eddyville STAR. w 1862-66||
IaHi Ap 12 1862-Je 24 1864;F 10-My 5 1866

Eddyville TRANSCRIPT. w 1867-68||
IaHi Ag 8 1867-Je 4 1868

Eddyville TRIBUNE. w 1886+
pub [1890-1900]05+
IaDH Ap 1893+

EDGEWOOD

Edgewood JOURNAL. w 1890-1928||?
IaDH 1915-28

ELDON

Eldon FORUM. w 1894+
IaDH 1912+

ELDORA

Eldora ENTERPRISE. w 1893?-1904||?
IaDH 1893-96

HARDIN county index. w Ja 18 1933+
pub 1933+

HARDIN county ledger. *See* Eldora herald-ledger

HARDIN county sentinel. *See* Iowa Falls sentinel (Iowa Falls)

Eldora HERALD. w,sw 1873-Mr 1931||
1873-75 as Reform herald. United with Hardin county ledger to form Eldora herald-ledger
sw 1902?-09?
IaDH [Ag 1879-82]-[88-91]93-1931
IaHi 1898-1900;03-06
MWA S 6 1876;Ag 22 1883

Eldora HERALD-LEDGER. w Ja 6 1866+
1866-1914? as Eldora ledger; 1915?-Mr 1931 Hardin county ledger
pub 1866+
DLC Ja 9 1868
IaDH 1885-97;1921-30
IaHi 1866-Mr 1872;86-Jl 9 1891

IOWA (*Continued*)

ELDORA—*Continued*

Eldora LEDGER. *See* Eldora herald-ledger
REFORM herald. *See* Eldora herald

ELGIN

Elgin ECHO. w S 1 1892+
pub 1892+
IaDH 1898+

ELK HORN

Elk Horn-Kimballton REVIEW. w 1923+
pub 1928+

ELKADER

Elkader ARGUS. w 1891-O 1907||
United with Elkader register to form Elkader register and argus, later Clayton county register
IaClayR complete
IaDH F 1901-Ag 1907

CLAYTON county journal. w My 6 1856-88||?
1856-Ap 9 1859 pub in Guttenburg; Ap 26 1859-Ap 23 1860 in Garnavillo
IaDH 1873-79;85-87
IaHi 1856-[60]-Ag 14 1862;D 27 1865-[71-74]-Ag 6 1879

CLAYTON county register. w Ja 3 1878+
1878-O 1926 as Elkader register (O 1907-18 Elkader register and argus)
pub 1878+
IaDH 1878;91-1910;21+
IaHi 1905-06
WHi D 16 1886

Elkader REGISTER. *See* Clayton county register

ELLSWORTH

Ellsworth CHRONICLE. w 1895-1902||
IaDH O 12 1899-1902

Ellsworth NEWS. w 1905+
IaDH 1923+

EMMETSBURG

Emmetsburg DEMOCRAT. w 1884+
pub 1884+
IaDH Ap 1893+
IaHi Jl 1905-06

PALO ALTO reporter. w 1874+
IaDH Ap 20 1894-[1903-05]+
MWA Ag 19 1876

PALO ALTO tribune. w 1893+
pub 1913+
IaDH Je 1909-18;20+

Emmetsburg REPORTER. *See* Palo Alto reporter

ESSEX

Essex INDEPENDENT. w 1894+
pub 1897+

ESTHERVILLE

Estherville DEMOCRAT. *See* Estherville daily news

EMMET county republican. w 1880-O 1902||
United with Northern vindicator to form Vindicator and republican
IaDH F 20 1896-1902
IaEsV complete

Estherville ENTERPRISE. w D 1901+
pub 1901+
IaDH 1902+
IaHi [1905]06

Estherville daily NEWS. w,d 1888+
1888-Ag 1 1927 as Estherville democrat 1927-O 6 1930 as Estherville news (w)
pub 1888+
IaDH O 2 1895+

NORTHERN vindicator. *See* Vindicator and republican

VINDICATOR and republican. w,sw D 14 1868+
1868-O 1902 as Northern vindicator
w 1868-1930?
pub 1868+
IaDH S 28 1893+
IaHi 1871-77;N 1904-06

EVERLY

Everly NEWS. w S 18 1887+
pub O 1901+
IaDH F 1893-Ag 1901;16+
MWA F 17 1898

EXIRA

AUDUBON county journal. w S 1884+
pub 1900+
IaDH Je 29 1893-1903;Jl 1904+

FAIRFIELD

HOME visitor. D 1 1865-68||
Merged with Fairfield ledger
IaDH [1865-Ja 3 1868]

IOWA democrat. Jl 1 1866-67||?
IaDH Ap 27 1867

IOWA sentinel. w Je 1847-Je 1857||
DLC O 13 1848;Ap 27-Je 15,29 1849;My 11 1854-D 18 1856
IaBu Ap 13-20 1854[Ja-Ap 1855;F-Mr 1857]

Fairfield JOURNAL. d 1879-My 1921||
United with Fairfield ledger and Fairfield tribune to form Fairfield ledger-journal
IaDH O 16 1880-82;Mr 19 1883-92;1913-21

Fairfield JOURNAL. w 1879-1914||
IaDH 1882;84-90;93-O 1914

Fairfield daily LEDGER. d My 1921+
Formed by the union of Fairfield ledger, Fairfield journal and Fairfield tribune
IaDH 1921+
KHi Ap 26 1927

Fairfield LEDGER-JOURNAL. w N 1849-S 1930||
1849-My 1921 as Fairfield ledger
IaBu Ap 13 1854[Ja-Ag 1855]
IaDH D 10 1851-54;62-64;80;83[84-86]-89;93-[99]-1930
IaHi [Ap 30 1857-Ag 1860]Jl 1865-D 19 1867;1905-N 1918
MWA Ja 25 1866
OClWHi My 10 1853;Ja 21 1859;F 4 1875

Fairfield TRIBUNE. w 1878-My 1921||
United with Fairfield ledger and Fairfield journal to form Fairfield ledger-journal
IaDH 1879-89
IaHi Mr 1885-94;96-99;N 1905-06

FARLEY

Farley ADVERTISER. w 1880+
IaDH 1893-1919

FARMINGTON

Farmington HERALD. *See* News-republican

Farmington NEWS. w 1894-1909||
United with Farmington herald to form the News-republican
IaDH complete

NEWS-REPUBLICAN. w 1886+
1886-1909 as Farmington herald
pub 1923+
IaDH 1909+

FAYETTE

FAYETTE county leader. w 1896+
1896-O 29 1914 as Fayette reporter
pub O 29 1914+
IaDH S 8 1910+

IOWA Postal card. w 1882-S 1 1910||
Merged with Fayette reporter
IaDH O 1901-10
WHi Ja 5 1887

Fayette REPORTER. *See* Fayette county leader

FENTON

Fenton REPORTER. w 1899+
IaDH 1899-My 1900

FONDA

Fonda JOURNAL and times. *See* Fonda times

POCAHONTAS times. *See* Fonda times

Fonda TIMES. w Ap 6 1876+
1876-94 as Pocahontas times; 1895?-Ja 9 1913 Fonda times; Ja 16 1913-16 Fonda journal and times
Ap-O 1876 pub in Old Rolfe; O 1876-My 1878 in Pocahontas Center
IaDH Mr 29 1883+

FONTANELLE

ADAIR county register. w 1862-75||
IaHi [Jl 14 1865-68]-75

ADAIR county reporter. *See under* Greenfield

Fontanelle OBSERVER. w 1879+
pub 1890+
IaDH F 28 1884-88;Jl 19 1894+

FOREST CITY

Forest City INDEPENDENT. w 1887-N 1921||
IaDH 1895-1921

Forest City SUMMIT. w Jl 14 1867+
1867-73? as Winnebago press; 1873?-1904 Winnebago summit
pub 1896+
IaDH 1872-73;75-92;My 1893+
IaHi 1898-1900;04
MWA F 24 1876

WINNEBAGO press. *See* Forest City summit

WINNEBAGO Republican. w 1901+
pub 1928+
IaHi 1904-06

WINNEBAGO summit. *See* Forest City summit

FORT DES MOINES. *See* DES MOINES

FORT DODGE

Fort Dodge CHRONICLE. d 1883-O 1918||
United with Fort Dodge messenger to form Messenger and chronicle
IaDH Je 14 1893-O 1911
IaFd Ja 27,F 8,Je 23,Ag 26 1886
IaHi Ag 1906-Je 1917

Fort Dodge CHRONICLE. w 1883-O 1918||
1883-89? as Northwest chronicle
IaFd O 29 1884-O 1887

Fort Dodge DEMOCRAT. w 1861-62||
IaFd [Jl 1861-Jl 1862]

FRONTIER sentinel. *See* Fort Dodge sentinel

Fort Dodge INDEPENDENT-ARGUS. w Je 1932+
Follows LeHigh Valley argus (Lehigh)
Je 1932-Ap 25 1935 as Fort Dodge independent and LeHigh Valley argus
IaDH 1932+

IOWA northwest. w O 17 1864-71||?
IaDH 1864-Ag 24 1871
IaFd 1864-Ag 24 1871
IaHi 1864-S 7 1871
MWA S 8 1870

Fort Dodge MESSENGER. w S 1863-O 1918||
1863-My 1877 as Fort Dodge messenger; My 1877-Webster county gazette and Fort Dodge messenger. United with Fort Dodge chronicle to form Messenger and chronicle
IaDH Je 11 1874-F 17 1876;My 11 1893-1910
IaFd My 1877-My 24 1878;1903-Ap 1916;17-Je 1918
IaHi S 14 1871-Je 1874
MWA Ag 31 1876;Ja 11 1878

Fort Dodge MESSENGER and chronicle. d 1884+
1884-O 1918 as Fort Dodge messenger
IaDH 1911-O 1918;Je 1922+
IaFd Mr 28 1888-Mr 23 1889
IaHi F 18 1886-95;97;Ag 1906+

NORTHWEST chronicle. *See* Fort Dodge chronicle

Fort Dodge REPUBLICAN. w O 31 1860-64||?
IaDH 1860-Ag 24 1864
IaFd Mr 16 1864
MWA Jl 29 1863

Fort Dodge SENTINEL. w Jl 31 1856-60||?
D 1859-F 1860 as Frontier sentinel
IaDH Jl 31,S 11 1856;Ap 23,S-N 5 1857;F 13 1858-[59-S 1860]
IaHi [Ap 30-D 1859;Ja 21-O 13 1860]

Fort Dodge TIMES. w O 1868-99||
IaDH Mr 23 1883-99
MWA Ag 22 1876

WEBSTER county gazette. w F 2-My 4 1877||
United with Fort Dodge messenger to form Webster county gazette and Fort Dodge messenger, later Fort Dodge messenger
IaFd complete

FORT MADISON

Fort Madison COURIER. *See* Plain dealer

Fort Madison weekly DEMOCRAT. w Jl 4 1869-1925||
DLC Ag 2 1871
IaDH Ag 24 1882;Ag 23,29 1883
IaFm 1887-1915
IaHi 1905-06;08;20-25

Fort Madison DEMOCRAT. d 1887+
IaDH N 6 1897-1919;Je 1922-28
IaFm My 1888-1917;19+
IaHi F 1905-S 1919;26-My 15 1929

IOWA freeman. *See* Iowa true democrat (Mount Pleasant)

IOWA statesman. *See* Plain dealer

LEE county democrat. *See* Plain dealer

LEE county republican. *See* Fort Madison republican

Fort Madison PATRIOT. w Mr 28 1838-
DLC Ap 4 1838

PLAIN DEALER. w Jl 24 1841-97||
Jl-D 1841 as Fort Madison courier; D 1841-47 Lee county democrat; 1847-52 Iowa statesman
CSmH O 19 1844
DLC Je 25-Jl 16,30 1847;F 5-12,My 6 1848
IaDH Jl 24,D 1841-Jl 13 1844;Mr 3 1849
IaHi Ag 12 1864-F 8 1866;67-72;F 1874-Ja 1876
MWA Jl 8 1869
PPL D 7 1850

Fort Madison REPUBLICAN. w 1898-1902||
IaDH Ja 23 1900-Jl 10 1902

WESTERN independent. w
IaGG My 20,Je 10 1858

GARDEN GROVE

Garden Grove EXPRESS. w 1875+
1875-80? as Iowa express
IaDH Ap 27 1893-S 1932

IOWA express. *See* Garden Grove express

GARNAVILLO

CLAYTON county herald. w Ja 28 1853-F 1858||
IaDH 1853-F 9 1855;Mr 14 1856-Ap 1857
IaMgN 1854-55

CLAYTON county journal. *See under* Elkader

GARNER

HANCOCK county democrat. *See* Leader and signal

HANCOCK signal. *See* Garner signal

Garner HERALD. w 1896-1901||
IaDH F 23 1900-Je 6 1901

IOWA (*Continued*)

GARNER—*Continued*

Garner HERALD. w O 1932+
IaDH 1932+

Garner LEADER and signal. w 1885+
1885-1920 as Hancock county democrat; 1921-29 Garner leader
IaDH 1887+

Garner SIGNAL. w 1871-1929||
1871-1902? as Hancock signal. United with Garner leader to form Leader and signal
IaDH F 28 1894-1928
MWA Ag 31 1876

GILMAN

Gilman DISPATCH. w 1876-Mr 30 1933||
1876-77 as Gilman record
IaDH 1916-18

Gilman RECORD. *See* Gilman dispatch

GLADBROOK

TAMA northern. w 1881+
pub Jl 1893+
IaDH 1916+
MWA F 24 1888

GLENWOOD

MILLS county journal. w 1873-96||?
IaDH Je 1893-O 1896
NbHi Jl 15-22,Ag-S 2 1876

MILLS county tribune. w 1891-Ap 1 1927||
United with Glenwood opinion to form Glenwood opinion-tribune
IaDH 1894-Mr 1927
IaGlO complete
IaHi 1905-06

Glenwood OPINION-TRIBUNE. w,sw Ap 16 1864+
1864-65 as Our opinion; 1865-Ap 1 1927 Glenwood opinion
w 1864-Ap 1 1927
pub 1864+
IaDH Ag 19 1897-1921;27+
IaGl Ap 1927+
IaHi [Jl 1865-S 21 1867]F 1905-06
MWA S 9 1876

OUR opinion. *See* Glenwood opinion-tribune

Glenwood PHONOGRAPH. w
IaHi F 1905-06

Glenwood WEEKLY. w 1858-
NbHi Jl 1 1858

GLIDDEN

Glidden GRAPHIC. w Mr 14 1890+
pub 1895+
IaDH F 1898+

SENTINEL. *See* Carroll sentinel (Carroll)

GOLDFIELD

Goldfield CHRONICLE. w 1882-1926||
Followed by Goldfield gazette
IaGoG complete

Goldfield GAZETTE. w 1928+
Follows Goldfield chronicle
pub 1928+

GOSHEN

DEMOCRAT. w
CU Jl 8 1841

GOWRIE

Gowrie NEWS. w 1889+
IaDH 1916+

GRAND JUNCTION

ERA-HEADLIGHT. *See* Grand Junction headlight

Grand Junction GLOBE. *See* Globe-portrait and news

GLOBE-PORTRAIT and news. sw,w 1896+
1896-1932? as Grand Junction globe
pub 1904+
IaDH 1905+
MWA O 10 1896

Grand Junction HEADLIGHT. w 1870-1909||?
1899-1900? as Era-headlight. Merged with Grand Junction globe
IaDH 1870;Je 8 1894-99
IaHi 1870-Jl 1872

NEW ERA. w 1892-98||?
United with Grand Junction headlight to form Era-headlight, later Grand Junction headlight

GRAND RIVER

Grand River LOCAL. w 1906+
pub 1914+

GRANT

Grant CHIEF. w 1911-22||?
IaDH 1916-19

GREELEY

Greeley HOME press. w 1898+
pub 1898+
IaDH 1916-23

GREENE

BUTLER county recorder. *See* Iowa recorder

IOWA recorder. w 1885+
Title varies: Butler county recorder
IaDH Mr 26 1895-1904

GREENFIELD

ADAIR county democrat. *See* Adair county free press

ADAIR county free press. w 1889+
1889-1903? as Adair county democrat; Ag 31 1916-28? Adair county free press and Greenfield transcript
pub 1889+
IaDH Je 27 1893-F 1901;16+
IaHi 1905-06

ADAIR county reporter. w Mr 15 1872-89||
Merged with Greenfield transcript
1872-Jl 2 1875 pub in Fontanelle
IaHi 1872-[Jl 10 1875-78]-82;87-89

Greenfield TRANSCRIPT. w Jl 2 1875-Ag 31 1916||
Merged with Adair county free press
IaDH 1912-15
IaHi O 15 1891-S 13 1900

GRINNELL

Grinnell GAZETTE. *See* Grinnell register

Grinnell HERALD-REGISTER. w,sw Mr 18 1868+
1868-Ag 9 1871 as Poweshiek county herald; Ag 16 1871-F 9? 1936 Grinnell herald
w 1868-F 28 1878
IaDH S 19 1893-1916;18+
IaG Ja 11 1871+
IaGG [1874-1904]-26;28-29;31+
IaHi 1903-06
MWA Je 20 1882

POWESHIEK county herald. *See* Grinnell herald

Grinnell REGISTER. sw 1898-F 9 1936||
1898-1906? as Grinnell gazette. United with Grinnell herald to form Grinnell herald-register
IaDH 1921-36
IaGG [1925-30]

GRISWOLD

Griswold ADVOCATE. *See* Griswold American

Griswold AMERICAN. w 1880+
1880-85 as Griswold advocate
pub 1880+
IaDH 1916+

GRUNDY CENTER

ARGUS. *See* Grundy county argus

GRUNDY county argus. w Ag 10 1877-89||?
1877-My 25 1882 as Argus
MWA O 26 1877;D 6 1878;Ap 11,O 9 1879; My 13,N 26,D 10 1880;Mr 3,Je 2-9,S 1-8, N 10 1881;My 18-25 1882;D 25 1883(supp); Mr 13 1884;Jl 16 1885;Je 10-Jl 1,Ag 12,S 9,23, O 21,N 18-25 1886;F 3 1887

GRUNDY county democrat. *See* Grundy county dispatch

GRUNDY county dispatch. w 1896-Ap 1923||
1896-1918 as Grundy county democrat. United with Grundy county republican to form Grundy register
IaDH 1906-23
IaHi Mr 1905-06

GRUNDY county republican. w 1877-Ap 1923||
United with Grundy county dispatch to form Grundy register
IaDH 1885-Je 1888;93-O 1909;11-23

GRUNDY county spokesman. w 1932+
IaDH 1933+

Grundy Center HERALD. w Ja 7 1887-98||
IaDH Jl 1893-98
MWA Je 24,D 25 1887

Grundy REGISTER. w Ap 1923+
Formed by the union of Grundy county dispatch and Grundy county republican
IaDH 1923+
IaGc 1923+

GUTHRIE CENTER

GUTHRIE county times. *See* Guthrie Center times

GUTHRIAN. w My 25 1872+
pub 1876+
IU Mr 10 1892
IaDH 1883-1908;19+

IOWA star. *See* Guthrie Center times

IOWA times. *See* Guthrie Center times

Guthrie Center TIMES. w 1883+
1883-86? as Iowa star; 1887-88? Guthrie county times; 1888-1903? Guthrie times
IaDH 1931+

GUTTENBERG

CLAYTON county journal. 1856-59. *See under* Elkader

CLAYTON county journal. w 1903-13||
IaDH Jl 1903-S 26 1913

MISSISSIPPI VALLEY register. w My 19 1859-61||
CaOTA N 15 1860
IaDH 1859-My 10 1861

Guttenberg PRESS. w 1897+
pub 1899+

HAMBURG

Hamburg DEMOCRAT. w Jl 20 1870-81||
United with Iowa state news to form Fremont democratic news, later Fremont democrat

FREMONT democrat. 1878-1904? *See* Hamburg republican

FREMONT democratic news. *See* Hamburg republican

IOWA state news. *See* Hamburg republican

Hamburg REPORTER. w 1893+
pub 1893+
IaDH Ag 25 1905+

Hamburg REPUBLICAN. w 1879-Jl 1928||
1879-81 as Iowa state news; 1882-87? Fremont democratic news; 1888?-1903 Fremont democrat. Merged with Hamburg reporter
IaDH Ap 28 1893-1903;16-28
IaHamR complete

HAMPTON

Hampton CHRONICLE. w 1873+
IaH 1895-97;99;N 1905-06;17+

FRANKLIN county recorder. My 1 1866-D 25 1930||
Follows Franklin record. 1866-Mr 1872 as Franklin reporter. Merged with Hampton chronicle
IaDH Ap 26 1863-1930
IaH 1891-1904;07-08;17-30
IaHi 1905-06

FRANKLIN record. w Mr 28 1859-63||
Followed by Franklin reporter, later Franklin county recorder
IaHi [Ap 1859-Mr 28 1863]

FRANKLIN reporter. *See* Franklin county recorder

Hampton FREE PRESS. w O 1 1869-Ap 3 1872||
United with Franklin reporter to form Franklin county recorder
IaHi Je 24 1870-Mr 8 1872

Hampton GLOBE. w 1891-1912||?
IaDH My 12 1893-1908;My 1910-Mr 20 1913
IaH 1895-98;1901-04;06

HARLAN

Harlan HERALD. *See* Harlan republican

Harlan REPUBLICAN. w 1874+
1874-83 as Harlan herald; 1883-1921? Shelby county republican
IaDH Ap 19 1894+
IaHa Je 19 1924+
MWA Ag 24,S 7 1876

SHELBY county republican. *See* Harlan republican

Harlan TRIBUNE. w Je 4 1879+
IaDH My 1883+
IaHa Je 18 1924+

HAWARDEN

Hawarden CHRONICLE. w S 5 1902+
pub 1902+
IaHaw [1902+]

Hawarden INDEPENDENT. w Ja 1 1878+
1878-Ja 1887 as Sioux county independent (Calliope)
pub 1878+
IaDH Mr 14 1895+
IaHaw O 1919+
IaHi [1906]

SIOUX county independent. *See* Hawarden independent

HAWKEYE

Hawkeye BEACON. w 1893+
pub 1893+
IaDH 1916+

HEDRICK

Hedrick JOURNAL. w Ag 6 1886+
pub Ag 1887+

HILLS

Hills ECHO. w O 26 1905-06||
IaHi 1905-F 22 1906

HOLSTEIN

Holstein ADVANCE. w N 1886+
pub 1893+
IaDH 1916+

IOWA (*Continued*)

HOSPERS

TRIBUNE. w D 1908+
pub 1913+

HULL

Hull INDEX. *See* Sioux county index
IOWA index. *See* Sioux county index
SIOUX county index. w F 1878+
1878-83? as Pattersonville index; 84?-1920 Hull index
1878-87? pub in Pattersonville
pub 1878+
IaDH 1914+

HUMBOLDT

HUMBOLDT county independent. *See* Humboldt independent
HUMBOLDT county republican. *See* Humboldt republican
HUMBOLDT county true democrat. *See* Humboldt kosmos
Humboldt INDEPENDENT. w Ag 2 1860+
1860-75 pub in Dakota City; 1876-95? in Dakota City and Humboldt
Suspended 1861-Je 1868
pub Jl 31 1868+
IaDH Mr 22 1883+
IaHi [Ja 14 1870-My 11 1876]
MWA N 19 1875;Jl 20,S 7 1876
Humboldt KOSMOS. w Je 1 1866-Ap 1 1893||
1866-N 1869 as Humboldt county true democrat; D 1869-73 Springvale republican. Merged with Humboldt republican
IaDH 1866-N 1869;Ag 26 1874;Ja 13 1875;80-82
IaHi 1872-73
MWA Ja 13 1875;Jl 19,Ag 16 1876;F 12 1879; S 14 1881
Humboldt REPUBLICAN. w 1888+
1888-Ap 1 1893 as Humboldt county republican
pub 1888+
IaDH F 14 1895-1905;Mr 1912+
IaHi 1890[91]92;1905[06]
IaHu Mr 9 1917+
SPRINGVALE republican. *See* Humboldt kosmos

HUMESTON

Humeston ERA. *See* Humeston new era
Humeston NEW ERA. w 1880+
1880-82? as Humeston era.
IaDH 1922+
IaHum Ag 19 1931+

IDA GROVE

Ida Grove ERA. *See* Ida Grove record-era
IDA county pioneer-record. w 1872+
1872-My 1 1927 as Ida county pioneer
pub 1872+
IaDH Mr 29 1883-85;97+
IaHi 1905-06
MAPLE Valley era. *See* Ida Grove record—era
Ida Grove RECORD-ERA. w 1877-My 1 1927||
1877-92? as Maple Valley era; 1893?-1903 Ida Grove era. United with Ida county pioneer to form Ida county pioneer-record
IaDH My 22 1884-89;95-1918;26-27
IaIdP complete

INDEPENDENCE

BUCHANAN county bulletin. *See* Bulletin-journal
BUCHANAN county guardian. w D 13 1856-Je 1866||
Title varies: Quasqueton guardian; Independent guardian. Merged with Buchanan county bulletin, later Bulletin-journal
1856-Jl 1858 pub in Quasqueton
IaDH 1856-Mr 24 1863
IaHi [S 18 1860-Ja 1864]
BUCHANAN county journal. w 1879-90||
United with Buchanan county bulletin to form Bulletin-journal
1879-82? pub in Jesup
IaInB complete
BULLETIN-JOURNAL. w Je 20 1865+
1865-90 as Buchanan county bulletin (title varies slightly: Buchanan county bulletin and guardian)
pub 1869+
CaOTA O 17,N 14-21 1873;O 20 1876
IaDH Mr 23 1883-1903;S 1904+
IaHi 1865-[Jl 1867-Ap 2 1869]1905-06
MWA Jl 2 1880
Independence CIVILIAN. *See* Independence conservative
Independence CONSERVATIVE. w My 17 1855+
1855-Mr? 1864 as Independence civilian
IaDH Mr 1883+
IaHi Mr 17 1859-[60-S 17 1861;Ap 15 1864-S 7 1866]
WHi Mr 1859-Ag 16 1861;Ja 12 1887

INDIANOLA

ADVOCATE-TRIBUNE. *See* Indianola tribune
Indianola HERALD. w Ap 2 1857+
1857-Mr 1864 as Weekly Iowa visitor Mr 1864-S 1866 Warren county banner; S 1866-Je 1868 Weekly Iowa visitor; Je 1868-74 Indianola journal
pub 1857+
IaDH My 18 1893+
IaHi Ap 17 1864-Ag 10 1865
IaI 1885-Ja 3 1895;Jl 1896-1916;22+
Weekly IOWA visitor. *See* Indianola herald
Indianola JOURNAL. *See* Indianola herald
PEOPLE'S advocate. w 1879-82||
United with Indianola tribune to form Advocate-tribune, later Indianola tribune
IaI Mr 16 1880-O 5 1881
Indianola RECORD. w 1893+
1893-F 1896 as Warren county record
pub 1920+
IaDH 1922+
IaI 1895-F 12 1896
Indianola REPUBLICAN. w Ag 27 1855-79||?
IaI Ja-Je 1879
MWA O 25 1855
Indianola TIMES. w 1892-96||
IaDH 1893-96
Indianola TRIBUNE. w O 2 1873+
1873-F 4 1875 as Warren county tribune; 1882-My 1923 Advocate-tribune
pub Jl 16 1885-Jl 7 1887;1902;04-Ap 1923;My 20 1924+
IaDH O 1873-Ag 1876;83-[99]+
IaI 1873-Ag 1876;Mr 1885-1916;22-My 1923
WARREN county banner. *See* Indianola herald
WARREN county leader. *See* Warren record
WARREN county record. *See* Indianola record
WARREN county tribune. *See* Indianola tribune
WARREN record. w Jl 1870-Ja 2 1879||
1870-Je 1874 as Warren county leader. Merged with Indianola republican
IaHi S 1870-Ap 1875
IaI complete

INWOOD

Inwood HERALD. w N 27 1890+
pub 1890+

IOWA CITY

AMERICAN union. d S 22 1856-
CL S 23 1856
ANTI-MONOPOLIST. w S 20 1873-N 26 1874||
IaHi complete
Iowa City ARGUS. w,sw Jl 31 1841-42||
Merged with Iowa capital reporter, later Iowa state reporter
w 1841
DLC Jl 31,D 4 1841;Ja 10 1842
Iowa City CITIZEN. w,tw,d 1891-O 1920||
1891-1909? as Iowa citizen. United with Iowa City press to form Iowa City press-citizen
w 1891-1903?;tw 1904?-10?
IaDH S 7 1894;D 1904-20
MWA My 22 1891
CLARION. w S 7 1905-06||
IaHi 1905-N 22 1906
Daily CRESCENT. d
IaH Ag-S 185?
DEMOCRAT. w 1901-06||
IaHi Mr 11 1904-06
Saturday HERALD. w 1891-98||
Title varies: Weekly herald; Independent herald
IaHi [1892]-Mr 26 1898
INDEPENDENT herald. *See* Saturday herald
IOWA banner. w Ag 1899-D 1900||
In German
IaHi S 15 1899-1900
IOWA daily capital reporter. *See* Daily state reporter
IOWA capitol reporter. w *See* Iowa state reporter
IOWA citizen. d. *See* Iowa City citizen
IOWA standard. *See* Iowa City standard
IOWA state journal and sunbeam. w
-Je 1854? as Iowa state journal
IaHi Jl 20-27,Ag 17,S 1 1854
IOWA state press. *See* Iowa City press
IOWA state reporter. w D 4 1841-61|?
1841-55? as Iowa capital reporter. Followed by State democratic press later Iowa City press
CU Ag 5 1843[46]F 18 1848;F 20,Ap 17 1861
DLC D 4 1841;Ja 21,F 11,Mr 4,Je 17 1846; 47-D 13 1849;O 13,N 3 1852
ICHi F 23 1852;S 13 1854
IaBu Ja 11,Ap 5-19,D 20-27 1854;Ap 4-11, Mr 28 1855
IaGG Mr 4 1860
IaDH D 30 1843;Je 8 1859;Ap 4,My 9,Jl 18,O 10 1860;Ja-O 1861
IaDaP Je 30 1847
IaHi D 11 1841-Je 3 1846,59-61
MWA Ja 20,F 3,Mr 3 1847;Mr 27 1850;S 29 1852
JOHNSON county independent. w 1912-16||
IaHi 1915-Je 1916
Iowa City JOURNAL. w
IaHi Mr 27 1879-My 14 1880
Iowa City daily NEWS. d
IaHi N 25 1906-Ja 9 1907
Iowa City POST. w 1881-1903||
In German
IaHi [1885]-[94]-1903
Iowa City PRESS. w Ag 15 1860-1910||
Follows Iowa state reporter. 1860-63 as State democratic press; 1863-1904 Iowa state press
CU [1861-62]N 4 1868
IaDH 1860-My 1862;F-N 1864;Mr 28 1883-S 1893;94-Mr 1904
IaGG Ag 21 1867
IaHi 1860-1902
IaU Ja-Ag 1900;01;03
Iowa City PRESS-CITIZEN. d 1898+
1898-O 1920 as Iowa City daily press
pub Mr 1930+
IaDH Ap 1904+
IaHi O 3 1898-Ja 11,Ap 6 1899-O 1 1903;05-Mr,O 1907-08;11-S 1912;Ja-S 1913;14+
Iowa City daily REPORTER. *See* Daily state reporter
Iowa City REPUBLICAN. w 1848-1924||
Follows Iowa City standard. Title varies slightly
Suspended 1908-Je 1916
CU F 13 1850;Ag 18-25,S 1 1858;My 25,Jl 6, D 28 1859;Ja 4,Jl 18,N 21 1860;Mr 6 1861; Jl 16 1862;My 10 1865;Je 3 1868
DLC My 1849-O 18 1854;Je 9 1858;Ap 13 1859; S 30 1885
IaDH Ap 14 1852[Ap 13 1860-O 22 1862]84-1907;Jl 1916-F 1922
IaDaP Ja 29 1842
IaGG Ja 1 1853
IaHi Je-Jl 4,31-N 12 1856;F 10 1858-N 20 1861;F 26 1862-F 23,Ag 1881-1907;17-20
MWA Mr 21,Jl 18 1866
Iowa City REPUBLICAN. d 1876-S 1922||
Title varies slightly
Suspended Jl 1917-F 1922
DLC Ag 18 1904
IaDH 1908-22
IaHi Je 1876-79;Jl 1880-Je 1892;93;Jl-S 1902; 03-Je,O 1905-16
IaU Ag 1898-1903;Ap-Je 1904
SLOVAN Americky. *See under* Cedar Rapids
Iowa City STANDARD. w Je 10 1841-48||
Follows Iowa standard (Bloomington, now Muscatine). Followed by Iowa City republican
CU [1842]F 22,Jl 25 1844;Ag 5 1846
DLC Ap 16 1841-N 16 1842;Ja 19,F 1843
IaDH Je 10-D 11 1841;Ap 27 1843;Jl 9 1845; Ja 28,Jl 8,22 1846
IaHi 1841-44;Je 1846-Je 7 1848
MWA Ja 19 1843
STATE democratic press. *See* Iowa City press
Daily STATE reporter. d
Title varies: Iowa daily capital reporter; Iowa City daily reporter, etc.
ICU Mr 26 1858
IaHi My-N 1856
Iowa City VOLKSFREUND. w 1874-82||?
In German
IaHi 1875-76

IOWA FALLS

Iowa Falls SENTINEL. w Mr 22 1856-1927||
1856-N? 1865 as Hardin county sentinel (Eldora). Merged with Hardin county citizen
CL Mr 9 1864
IaDH 1897-1921
IaHi [Ag 17 1864-Je 1871]
IaIf [1862-65]
MWA S 6 1876

IRWIN

Irwin JOURNAL. w 1890-
IaFcS 1890

JEFFERSON

Jefferson BEE. w Ap 6 1866+
1866-Mr? 1871 as Jefferson era (some issues as New era)
pub 1871-74;82-86;92+
IaDH Mr 1871-Ja 17 1874;95-[1904]+
IaHi 1866-Mr 24,My 13 1871-Mr 8 1872;F-O 12 1905;06
MWA Ap 18,Je 17-24,Jl 8-15,29,Ag 19-26,S 16 1868
Jefferson ERA. *See* Jefferson bee
Jefferson FREE lance. *See* Jefferson herald
Jefferson HERALD. w 1894+
1894-1917 as Jefferson free lance
IaDH 1915+
KHi Ag 25 1920
NEW era. *See* Jefferson bee
Jefferson SOUVENIR. w 1884-1903||
IaDH My 12 1894-Ag 1903
IaJB complete

JESUP

BUCHANAN county journal. *See* Bulletin-journal (Independence)
CITIZENS' herald. w 1900+
pub 1900—

JEWELL

Jewell RECORD. w 1884+
pub 1905+
IaDH Ap 11 1895-97;1915+
IaWc 1889-1914

IOWA (*Continued*)

KALONA

Kalona NEWS. w N 1891+
pub 1891+

KANESVILLE. *See* COUNCIL BLUFFS

KENSETT

Kensett NEWS. w 1897-1917||
United with Manly signal to form Manly signal and Kensett news, later Manly signal
IaDH S 1897-1917

KEOKUK

Die Keokuk ANZEIGER. w 1891-99||?
United with Die Keokuk post to form Die Keokuk post-anzeiger
In German

CHIEF. w 1889-S 29 1892||
Merged with Constitution-democrat
IaDH Mr 16-Je 8 1889

Keokuk CITIZEN. w O 27 1922+
pub 1922+
IaDH 1922-26
IaHi O 27 1922;23+
IaK 1922+

CONSTITUTION-DEMOCRAT. w Jl 1855-1912||?
1855-N 1857 as Weekly times; N 1857-N 1861 Keokuk weekly journal; D 1861-Mr 1888 Keokuk weekly constitution
MWA Ap 3 1861

CONSTITUTION-DEMOCRAT. d Jl 1855-Ap 3 1916||
1855-N 1857 as Daily evening times; N 1857-N 1861 Daily journal; D 1861-Mr 26 1888 Keokuk daily constitution. United with Daily Gate City to form Daily Gate City and constitution-democrat, later Daily Gate City
IaDH D 5 1866-74;Je 1875-87;91-1916
IaHi Je 25 1862-Je 1864;F 18-O 25 1886
IaK Mr 6 1862-S 9 1864;F 8 1866-1916

DEMOCRAT. d Ja 9 1883-Mr 1888||
United with Daily constitution to form Constitution-democrat
IaK Je 1883-Ag 1 1886

DES MOINES Valley whig. *See* Weekly Gate City

Keokuk DISPATCH. *See* Saturday post

Weekly GATE CITY. w Jl 1846-1904||?
1846-N 11? 1861 as Des Moines Valley whig
DLC Mr 28 1850-Ap 10 1851;Ja 22-D 16 1852;Ja-Je 21 1900
ICHi Ag 11 1886
IaDH Ap 1851-Ag 1857
IaDaP Mr 26 1847
IaHi Mr 21 1859-[60-N 11 1861]-[62-Je]-Ag 24 1864;My 10 1865-N 1872;73-74;Ag 11 1892-99
IaK D 26 1855-D 23 1861
KHi O 3 1901
NcU Jl 9 1856
OClWHi F 4 1848
OHi My 5 1848

Daily GATE CITY. d My 26 1847+
1847-Mr 1849 as Keokuk register; Mr 1849-Mr 3 1854 Valley whig and Keokuk register; Mr 1854-Mr 1855 Daily whig; Ap 1916-29? Daily Gate City and constitution-democrat
pub 1923+
DLC 1875-Je 1883;84-Ap,O 1890-92;Je 26-D 1900
ICHi Ag 11 1886
ICarC 1933-Ja 18 1934
IaDH [1847-Mr 1849]Mr 3 1854;My 9 1855+
IaGG O 17,N 8 1859
IaHi My 9 1855-My 9 1856;Jl 6 1861(extra); 1900-Je 1901
IaK F 27-Ap 10 1851;Mr 1855-1922
MWA D 25 1858
WHi D 31 1857
Ja-F 1855 as Nipantuck or Nip-and-tuck. Merged with Daily evening times, later Constitution-democrat
IaBU F 27-S 13 1855
IaK Ja-F 24,27-S 14 1855

Daily JOURNAL. *See* Constitution-democrat

Keokuk weekly JOURNAL. *See* Constitution-democrat

MORNING glory. d Ja 1-S 1855||

NIP-AND-TUCK. *See* Morning glory

PEOPLE'S dollar. w
IaDH [F-Jl 1879]

Saturday POST. w My 20 1848-60||
1848-O 1855 as Keokuk dispatch (Title varies: Keokuk telegraphic weekly dispatch; Keokuk weekly dispatch). Followed by Doniphan weekly post (Doniphan, Kansas)
DLC My 27,Je 8-Jl 6,20-Ag 12,26-S 2 1848
IaDH 1848-Je 1849[Jl 1854-Jl 1855]
IaK Jl 29 1851-S 6,N 10 1855-Ja 1858

Daily POST. d 1855-
IaDH F 13 1857;Mr 29 1859
IaK O 28 1855-Ja 21 1858
IaKC 1857-58

Die Keokuk POST-ANZEIGER. w 1869-1911||?
1869-99? as Die Keokuk post
In German
MWA Ag 24 1876

Evening PRESS. d 1897-99||
IaDH D 2 1898-Ap 29 1899
IaK Mr 19-Ag 22 1898

Keokuk REGISTER. *See* Daily Gate City

RICKEY and Allyn's real estate bulletin and commercial advertiser. w S 2 1867-
IaDH S 2 1867;S 1 1869

SHARP stick; or Campaign Keokuk dispatch. w Jl 9 1852-
MWA O 15 1852

STANDARD. w 1895-1910||
1895-1900? as Sunday standard
IaK Mr 17 1895-Mr 11 1900;O 11 1902-O 8 1910
IaKC 1897

SUNBEAM. bw,w Ja 1 1852-Je? 1854||
United with Iowa state journal to form Iowa state journal and sunbeam (Iowa City)
IaDH Jl 15 1852
IaHi Ja 16,O 1,15,N 15 1852;53;Ja 16,F 2 1854

SUNBEAM. sm,w
IaDuC Ag 1 1860
IaGG F 8 1860

Keokuk TELEGRAPHIC weekly dispatch. *See* Saturday post

Daily evening TIMES. *See* Constitution-democrat

Weekly TIMES. *See* Keokuk constitution-democrat

VALLEY whig and Keokuk register. *See* Daily Gate City

Daily WHIG. *See* Daily Gate City

KEOSAUQUA

DES MOINES news. w 1858-
Suspended Ja 10 1862-Ja 1864
IaHi [Ap 1860-O 18 1861]

DES MOINES Valley whig. *See* Weekly Gate City (Keokuk)

IOWA democrat and Des Moines River intelligencer. w Jl 20 1843-65||
OClWHi N 30 1843

Keosauqua REPUBLICAN. w S 12 1854+
DLC D 4 1873
IaDH Jl 1893+
IaHi Mr 26 1859-Je,Ag 19 1864-Mr 1870[1905]06
MWA Ag 10 1865;Ja 25 1866

KEOTA

Keota ALTA. w 1889-91||?
IaKeE Jl 1889-Je 1891

Keota EAGLE. w D 4 1875+
pub My 1876+

STATE line democrat. *See* Van Buren barometer

Keosauqua TIMES. w D 9 1844-
DLC D 9 1844

VAN BUREN barometer. w 1870-1928||?
1870-90? as Van Buren democrat; 1890?-1922? State line democrat. United with Bonaparte record to form Van Buren record (Bonaparte)
IaDH Ag 22 1878;Ag 28 1879;Mr 25 1880;D 24 1885;S 12-19 1889;Mr 1894-1927

VAN BUREN democrat. *See* Van Buren barometer

WESTERN American. Jl 5 1851-Jl 3 1852||
IaDH [1851-52]

KESWICK

Keswick LEADER. w 1911-21||
IaDH 1916-21

KIMBALLTON

Kimballton-Elk Horn RECORD. w 1912-21||
IaDH 1916-21

KNOXVILLE

DEMOCRAT standard. Je 1856-60||
IaK Ag 31 1858-N 3 1860

Knoxville EXPRESS. w S 19 1865+
1865-F 1878 as Marion county democrat; F 1878-1884 Marion county express
pub D 1884+
IaDH 1893+
IaKn current two years only

IOWA voter. *See* Knoxville journal

Knoxville JOURNAL. w O 1 1855+
1855-58 as Knoxville journal; 1858-Mr 1867 Marion county republican; Je 20 1867-Je 4 1875 Iowa voter
Suspended Mr-Je 13 1867
pub [1855-70]+
IaDH My 31 1893+
IaHi N 13-20,D 4 1860[Ja-Jl 1861]Je 20 1867-Mr 21 1872;Jl 1903-06;19+
IaKn current two years only

MARION county democrat. *See* Knoxville express

MARION county express. *See* Knoxville express

MARION county republican. *See* Knoxville journal

LACONA

Lacona LEDGER. w 1897-1932||?
IaDH 1916-32

LAFAYETTE

To Mr 2 1846 as Ottercreek

LAKE CITY

CALHOUN county journal. *See* Manson journal (Manson)

Lake City GRAPHIC and news. w 1885+
1885-1926 as Lake City graphic
IaDH Ap 1893+

Lake City JOURNAL. w 1874-77||
MWA Ag 31 1876

Lake City NEWS. w 1899-1926||
United with Lake City graphic to form Lake City graphic and news
IaDH 1921-26

LAKE MILLS

REPUBLIKANAREN. w 1899-1903||?
In Norwegian-Danish
WHi 1899-Ag 28, S 11 1903

LAKE PARK

Lake Park NEWS. w S 1 1890+
pub 1890-93;1908+
IaDH 1916+

LAKE VIEW

Lake View RESORT. w 1888+
pub 1888+

LAMONI

Lamoni CHRONICLE. w Je 28 1894+
1894-1903? as College City chronicle
IaDH S 1895+
IaHi F-D 1900;O 9 1902-06
IaLG 1894-98[1922-25]27+

COLLEGE CITY chronicle. *See* Lamoni chronicle

Lamoni GAZETTE. *See* Independent-patriot

INDEPENDENT-PATRIOT. w 1885-1910||
1885-88? as Lamoni gazette
IaDH S 1895-Ap 1910

LANSING

ALLAMAKEE journal. w My 29 1860+
1860-Ja 14? 1880 as North Iowa journal (1867-71 Chronicle) 1922-23? Allamakee journal and Lansing mirror
Dated also from Waukon
pub 1880+
IaDH Ap 9 1861[Je-D 1862]F 6 1863;My 10 1871;Ap 1893-1919
NSyU S 13-20 1864

CHRONICLE. *See* Allamakee journal

Lansing INTELLIGENCER. *See* Lansing mirror

Lansing MIRROR. w N 23 1852-1922||
1852-53 as Lansing intelligencer; 1863-66 Lansing union. Merged with Allamakee journal
Suspended from 1861-63
IaHi 1905-06
IaLanA 1866-1922
MWA F 13 1866

NORTH IOWA journal. *See* Allamakee journal

Lansing UNION. *See* Lansing mirror

LA PORTE CITY

LOCAL review. w 1879-92||?
United with La Porte progress to form La Porte progress-review

La Porte PROGRESS-REVIEW. w 1870+
1870-92? as La Porte progress
IaDH F 1897+

LARCHWOOD

Larchwood LEADER. w 1888-1932||
Followed by Lyon county leader (Rock Rapids)
IaHulS 1893-94

LAURENS

POCAHONTAS county sun. *See* Laurens sun

Laurens SUN. w Je 15 1885+
1885-1918 as Pocahontas county sun
IaDH 1916+
IaHi 1905-06
IaLa 1885

LAWLER

CHICKASAW county times. *See* Lawler times

Lawler DISPATCH. w 1884+
pub 1884+

Lawler TIMES. w Ap 9 1875-79||
1875-78? as Chickasaw county times
IaDH 1875-Ap 1876

LE CLAIRE

Le Claire REGISTER. w O 1 1859-
IaDH D 17 1859

LE GRANDE

Le Grande REPORTER. w 1909+
IaDH 1916+

IOWA (*Continued*)

LEHIGH

Lehigh VALLEY argus. w 1883-Je 1932||
Followed by Fort Dodge independent and LeHigh Valley argus, later Fort Dodge independent-argus (Fort Dodge)
IaDH Je 1900-32

LE MARS

Le Mars GLOBE-POST. sw O 1884+
1884-1902 as Le Mars globe
pub 1917+
IaDH My 1893+

Der Le Mars HEROLD. w 1884-1917||
Merged with Le Mars globe-post
In German
KHi Mr 29 1888

IOWA liberal. w Jl 17 1873-73||?
MWA Ap 3 1873;S 6 1876

LeMars semi-weekly SENTINEL. w,sw F 3 1871+
1871-89? as Le Mars sentinel (w)
pub [1871-89]+
ICM Ja 31 1878
IU Ja 20 1888;Mr 20 1891
IaDH F 1890+
IaHi 1882;Ja 20-Je 8 1888;F 1905-06

LENOX

Lenox TIME-TABLE. w 1874+
pub [1914-25]+

LEON

DECATUR county journal. *See* Leon journal-reporter

DEMOCRAT-REPORTER. *See* Leon reporter

Leon JOURNAL-REPORTER. w 1868+
1868-Mr 1930 as Decatur county journal
pub [1868-1909]+
IaDH My 1893+
IaHi 1905-06

Leon PIONEER. w F 3 1859-
IaHi [F 10-O 6 1859;Ja 19-S 10 1860;Ja 28-Ag 26 1861]

Leon PIONEER. w 1865-73||?
MWA F 22 1867

Leon REPORTER. w 1875-Mr 1930||
1875-86? as Democrat reporter. United with Decatur county journal to form Leon journal-reporter
IaDH 1894-1929
NcD Ap 5 1906

LEWIS

Lewis STANDARD. w 1880+
pub 1880+
IaDH 1916-32

LIME SPRINGS

Lime Springs HERALD. w 1887+
1887-1905? as Lime Springs sun; 1906?-33 Lime Springs sun-herald
IaDH 1916+

Lime Springs SUN. *See* Lime Springs herald

LISBON

Lisbon HERALD. w 1894-D 17 1922||
United with Mount Vernon hawkeye to form Mount Vernon hawkeye-Lisbon herald later Hawkeye-record and Lisbon herald (Mount Vernon)
IaDH 1895-1922

Lisbon SUN. w 1875-1909||?
MWA S 10 1881

LITTLE ROCK

FREE lance. w 1895+
1895-1925 as Free lance; 1925-29 as Little Rock herald
pub 1902-05;08-09;12-15;F 1929+

Little Rock HERALD. *See* Free lance

LITTLE SIOUX

HUSTLER. w Mr 14 1901+
pub 1901+

Little Sioux SENTINEL. w 1877-80||?
Follows Magnolia sun (Magnolia)
NN Ja 12-Mr 9,23-Je 15,29-Jl,Ag 10-17,S-N 2,23 1877

LOCKRIDGE

Lockridge HERALD. See Lockridge times

Lockridge TIMES. w 1909+
1909-15 as Lockridge herald
IaDH 1909-15

LOGAN

Logan NUCLEUS. w 1890-1906||?
IaDH 1897-1905

Logan OBSERVER. w 1886+
pub My 1890+
IaDH 1916+

LOHRVILLE

Lohrville ENTERPRISE. w 1889+
IaDH Ag 1894-1920

LONE TREE

Lone Tree BRANCH. *See* Lone Tree reporter

Lone Tree REPORTER. w Ap 2 1892+
1892-94? as Lone Tree branch
pub 1900+
IaHi D 15 1905-06

LORIMOR

Lorimor JOURNAL. w 1888+
pub 1888+

LOVILIA

Lovilia PRESS. w Mr 14 1907+
pub 1907+
IaDH 1916+

LYONS

Papers published in Lyons are listed under Clinton

LYTTON

Lytton STAR. w 1904-27||
IaDH 1916-27

McGREGOR

HOME journal. w Ja 1 1873-
NNHi Ja 15 1873

MILLION. w Ag 4 1870-
KHi Ag 18 1870

McGregor NEWS. w Ag 1859-1913||
1859-D 1861 as McGregor press; D 1861-63 Pocket City news. Merged with North Iowa times
IaDH My 1893-Ja 1913
KHi Ja 1,Ap 9 1870
MWA Ja 20 1863;Ja 20 1866
NNHi [Je-O 1861]My 12-Je 1862
NdU D 9 1864-Ap 7 1866

NORTH IOWA times. w O 10 1856+
pub 1856+
IaDH 1856-N 1877;79-88;97-1907;Mr 27 1913+
IaHi [My 1857-Ap 1858]Mr 16 1859;My 29 1861[Je 18 1862-My 1865]1903-06
MWA Ap 13 1859;Ag 10 1864;Jl 13 1876
N Ap 8 1863
NNHi Ag 7 1857;Je 12 1861-My,Jl 9,O 22 1862-Ja 7,F 4,Ap 1,15-22,My 20-Je 10,Jl 29 1863-Ja 20 1864;Ap 24 1873

POCKET City news. *See* McGregor news

McGregor PRESS. *See* McGregor news

MACKSBURG

Macksburg INDEPENDENT. w 1916-20||
IaDH 1916-20

MADISON

Madison COURIER. w N 22 1839-
IU F 1 1840

MADRID

Madrid REGISTER-NEWS. w 1882+
1882-94? as Madrid register
pub 1890+
IaDH My 1907+

MAGNOLIA

Magnolia SUN. w 1876||?
Followed by Little Sioux sentinel (Little Sioux)
NN Ag 18,S 8-O 6,20-D 22 1876

MALCOM

Malcom LEADER. w 1889+
IaDH 1916-26

MALLARD

Mallard LEADER. w 1908-11||
IaDH O 1909-Ja 1911

MALVERN

Malvern LEADER. w 1875+
1880-N 1883 as Republican-leader
pub 1875+
IaDH 1912+
IaM Ag 10 1916-Ag 5 1921;Ag 1923-25;Jl 28 1927-Jl 19 1928;Jl 24 1930+

REPUBLICAN-LEADER. *See* Malvern leader

MANCHESTER

DELAWARE county news. w 1895-S 30 1912||
Title varies: Manchester news
IaDH complete
IaHi 1905-06;12

DELAWARE county radio. w 1925-30||
United with Manchester democrat to form Manchester democrat-radio

DELAWARE county union. w Mr 25 1864-72||
IaDuC My 20 1864;Je 23 1865;Ap 6 1866;F 27 1868
IaHi [Jl 29 1864-66]-O 31 1872

Manchester DEMOCRAT-RADIO. w 1875+
1875-1930 as Manchester democrat
IaDH 1894-1930

Manchester NEWS. *See* Delaware county news

Manchester PRESS. w Je 16 1871+
pub 1871+
IaDH 1890;93-1913;My 1914-15
IaHi [O 20 1871-Je 20 1873]

MANILLA

Manilla TIMES. w 1899+
pub 1899+

MANLY

Manly SIGNAL. w 1916+
1918-Ja 1920 as Manly signal and Kensett news
IaDH 1918+

MANNING

Manning HERALD. w 1894-Ap 2 1919||
1894-S 27 1918 as Der Manning herold (In German). Merged with Manning monitor
IU D 7 1917-19

Manning MONITOR. w N 27 1881+
pub 1882+
IU Ap 10 1919-Ap 7 1921
IaDH 1896-F 1916

MANSON

CALHOUN county journal. *See* Manson journal

Manson DEMOCRAT. w 1891-1920||?
1891-92 as Northwest democrat. Merged with Manson journal
IaDH 1918-20

Manson JOURNAL. w 1874+
1874-83 as Calhoun county journal
1874-77 pub at Lake City 1877 at Rockwell City; Ja?-Je 1878 at Pomeroy
pub 1874+
IaDH F 20 1896+

NORTHWEST democrat. *See* Manson democrat

MAPLETON

ADVOCATE. w 1883-1901||?
1883-94? as Home advocate. United with Mapleton press to form Mapleton press-advocate, later Mapleton press
IaOn D 30 1888
WHi Ja 14 1887

HOME advocate. *See* Advocate

PEOPLE'S press. *See* Mapleton press

Mapleton PRESS. w 1870+
1870-95? as People's press
IaDH Ap 1893-94;97-1915
IaOn S 1875-78;Ag 28 1879-81

Mapleton STANDARD. w 1877-78||
Merged with People's press, later Mapleton press
IaOn N 29 1877-D 5 1878

MAQUOKETA

Maquoketa BEACON. w
IaDH [1896]

Maquoketa EXCELSIOR. w,sw Mr 18 1856-1930||
1914?-21? as Maquoketa excelsior-record. Merged with Jackson sentinel
sw 1897-1900;22
IaDH 1860-65;Mr 1866;84-[96]-F 1902;03-12,14-30
IaGG Jl 8 1856
IaHi 1859[60]-Jl 1861;Mr 22 1866-Ap 1873;Mr 1874-O 1876
MWA F 1 1866

JACKSON county record. *See* Maquoketa record

JACKSON sentinel. w,sw My 15 1854+
1854-Ap 1868 as Maquoketa sentinel
Suspended 1862-64;66-68
pub 1854+
ICHi Je 16 1904
IaDH Je 1893+
IaHi 1905-06
OClWHi Ja 11 1872;My 4 1876;S 12-19,O 3 1878

Maquoketa RECORD. w 1878-1913||
1878-81? as Jackson county record. Merged with Maquoketa excelsior
IaDH F 1897-1913
WHi D 24 1878;D 1,15 1886;Ja 19 1887

Maquoketa SENTINEL. *See* Jackson sentinel

MARCUS

Marcus NEWS. w S 1882+
IaDH S 1910+

MARENGO

Marengo DEMOCRAT. *See* Marengo pioneer

IOWA county review. w 1859-
IaHi 1863

IOWA (*Continued*)

MARENGO—*Continued*

IOWA VALLEY democrat. w Ja 18 1860-
IaHi [Mr 28 1860-Ja 15 1862]

IOWA VALLEY review. *See* Marengo pioneer-republican

IOWA weekly visitor. *See* Marengo pioneer-republican

Marengo PIONEER. w 1875-1927||
1875-1918 as Marengo democrat; 1918-22? Marengo sentinel democrat; 1922?-26 Marengo democrat. United with Marengo republican to form Marengo Pioneer-republican
IaDH 1893-1920
IaHi 1905-06
KHi F 26 1891

Marengo PIONEER-REPUBLICAN. w S 6 1856+
1856-60 as Iowa weekly visitor; 1861-S 11 1865 Iowa Valley review; S 18 1865-S 7 1871 Progressive republican; S 14 1871-S 27 1927 Marengo republican
pub 1927+
IaDH 1895-S 1927;28+
IaHi Mr 20 1857[59-Ap 11 1860]S 1871-Jl 1873;Jl 15 1874-Je 1875;Jl 12 1876-Jl 3 1878; 79-1900;04-06
IaMa Je 1896-Mr 1904;Je 1934+

PROGRESSIVE republican. *See* Marengo pioneer-republican

Marengo SENTINEL. w 1911-17||
United with Marengo democrat to form Marengo sentinel-democrat, later Marengo pioneer

MARIETTA

Marietta weekly EXPRESS. w D 17 1857-
IaHi D 9,23 1857-[59]F 1860

MARION

Marion DEMOCRAT. w O 24 1860-
Follows Marion herald
MWA Ap 11 1861

Marion HERALD. w 1857-60||
Followed by Marion democrat
IaHi Mr 17-O 13 1859;F 23,Mr 1,Ap 26,My 30 1860

LINN county patriot. *See* Marion register

LINN county pilot. *See* Marion pilot

LINN county register. *See* Marion register

Marion PILOT. w 1871-1905||
1871-83? as Linn county pilot
1871-74 pub in Mt. Vernon
IaCr Ag 23 1877-Ag 4 1881
IaDH N 1895-My 1905

PRAIRIE star. *See* Marion register

Marion REGISTER. w,tw,sw 1852-1920||
1852 as Prairie star; 1852-63 Linn county register; 1863-64 Linn county patriot
w 1852-99;tw 1900-09
IaCr 1867-74
IaDH Je 1893-Je 1920
IaGG Ag 1859;Mr 23 1861
IaHi 1859[60-63]-[S 26 1866-D 22 1869]-O 19 1871
MWA D 11 1861

Marion SENTINEL. w S 1879+
pub [1890+]
IaDH 1916+
IaMars 1917-19;27+

MARNE

Marne FREE PRESS. w F 24 1893-1920||?
KHi Ap-D 1893

MARSHALL. *See* MARSHALLTOWN

MARSHALLTOWN

CENTRAL Iowa democrat. w S 14 1933+
1933-Ag 1934 as Free lance; Ag-D 1934 Marshalltown free press
IaMars 1933-Ag 1934

FREE lance. *See* Central Iowa democrat

Marshalltown FREE press. *See* Central Iowa democrat

MARSHALL county expositor. w My 1862-64||
United with Daily times to form Union, later Marshalltown times-republican
IaHi [Jl 14 1863-Je 21 1864]

MARSHALL county reporter. w
IaHi Je 28-S 9 1864

MARSHALL county times. *See* Marshalltown times-republican. w

MARSHALL statesman. *See* Marshalltown statesman-press

Marshalltown NEWS. w,sw Je 1911+
IaLe Je 1931+

Marshalltown REFLECTOR. w 1880-1908||
Title varies: Sunday reflector
IaDH S 1901-O 1908
IaHi 1905-06

Marshalltown REPUBLICAN. w 1871-80||
United with Marshall county times to form Marshalltown times-republican

Marshalltown STATESMAN. *See* Marshalltown statesman-press

Marshalltown STATESMAN-PRESS. w 1875-99||
1875-90? as Marshall statesman; 1891-96? Marshalltown statesman
IaDH Jl 1875-Ap 1899

Daily TIMES. *See* Marshalltown times-republican

Marshalltown TIMES-REPUBLICAN. w O 13 1858-94||?
Follows Iowa central journal (Albion). 1858-80 as Marshall county times
DLC Jl 13 1867;Mr 14-Ag 15,29-S 19,O 3,17, N-D 22 1868;Ja 9-Mr,Ap 10-30,My 15-Je 12, 26-Jl 3,17,31-Ag 21 1869
IaHi Mr 9-My 18 1859[My 8-D 17 1861;62-Ap 17 1873]
IaMars 1858-N 14 1860;O 29 1861-My 5 1862;N 1863-S 14 1864
MWA D 27 1865
NBuG Ap 14 1870
NcD S 19 1860

Marshalltown TIMES-REPUBLICAN. d Ap 1875+
1875-80 as Daily times
IaDH 1893+
IaHi Ag 1902-S 1907;08+
IaMars Jl 1907+

MASON CITY

CERRO GORDO county republican. *See* Mason City republican

CERRO GORDO press. w Je 1858-60||
IaMc Jl 17-Ag 25 1859
NNHi Jl 19 1860

CERRO GORDO republican. *See* Mason City republican

Mason City EXPRESS. w D 8 1870-S 1886||
United with Cerro Gordo republican to form Express-republican, later Mason City republican
IaHi [Jl-D 1871]
IaMc D 8 1870-N 14 1885

Mason City EXPRESS. w 1895-99||?
IaMc Ag 7 1895-Ag 31 1898

EXPRESS republican. *See* Mason City republican

Saturday GAZETTE. *See* Mason City globe-gazette

Mason City GAZETTE. *See* Mason City globe-gazette

Mason City GLOBE-GAZETTE. w My 28 1887-1917||
1887-My 1888 as Saturday gazette; Je 1888-95 Mason City gazette
IaDH 1896-1917
IaMc 1887-Ag 1 1889;90-Je 4 1892

Mason City GLOBE-GAZETTE. d 1893+
1893-95 as Mason City globe
IaDH 1927+
IaMc Ja 7 1893-My 22 1895;S 18 1900-My,Jl 1911+

Daily JOURNAL. d Ag 24-S 16 1880||
IaMc Ag 4-S 4, 13-16 1880

NORTH IOWA journal. w F 28 1877-D 20 1882||
1877-80 as Western democrat. Merged with Mason City times-herald, later Mason City times
IaMc F-Mr 1877;80
WHi D 21 1878

Mason City REPUBLICAN. w F 9 1861-1910||?
1861-S 1886 as Cerro Gordo republican; O 1886-F 1893 Express republican; F 1893-1906? Cerro Gordo county republican
IaDH 1892;F 1893-1910
IaHi Ag 25 1864-Jl 1 1869
IaMc [1861-65]-[67-68;75-77;81-Ag 1883]O 7 1886-O 5 1887;Ja 4,O 10 1888;S 4 1889;93-1904; 06-08;N 22 1909-My 19 1910
MWA My 18 1876

Mason City TIMES. w 1882-S 18 1918||
1894?-1909? Mason City times-herald. Merged with Mason City globe-gazette
IaMc S 6 1885;Ja 6 1886;Mr 26,S 15 1900;D 31 1909-18

Mason City daily TIMES. d 1891-S 9 1918||
1895?-1909? as Mason City daily times-herald
IaHi O 1912-18

Mason City TIMES-HERALD. *See* Mason City times

WESTERN democrat. *See* North Iowa journal

MASSENA

Massena ECHO. w N 15 1884+
pub 1916+

MAURICE

Maurice TIMES. w 1909-19||
IaDH 1916-19

MAXWELL

Maxwell TRIBUNE. w Je 1 1883+
pub 1883+
IaDH Mr 24 1892;94+

MAYNARD

Maynard NEWS. w 1889-1929||
IaDH 1916-29

MECHANICSVILLE

Mechanicsville PIONEER-PRESS. w 1867+
1867-1904? as Mechanicsville press
MWA Je 14 1878
NbHi Ja 23 1875;Jl 26 1877;Ja 18,Ap 12 1878

Mechanicsville PRESS. *See* Mechanicsville pioneer-press

MEDIAPOLIS

Mediapolis ENTERPRISE. *See* Mediapolis new era-news

Mediapolis NEW era-news. w 1874+
1874-82 as Enterprise; 1883-1907 New era
pub 1874+
IaDH O 1909+

Mediapolis NEWS. w 1897-1907||
United with New-era to form Mediapolis new era-news
IaMeN complete

MELBOURNE

Melbourne RECORD. w 1896+
IaDH 1916+

MELROSE

Melrose BELL. w 1908-26||
IaDH 1918-26

MERRILL

Merrill RECORD. w Jl 1 1890+
pub Jl 1921+

MILFORD

Milford MAIL. w 1882+
IaDH 1886-91;93+

MILO

Milo ENTERPRISE. *See* Milo motor

Milo MOTOR. w 1882+
1921-25 as Milo enterprise
pub 1921-23;31+
IaDH 1916-19

MILTON

Milton HERALD. w 1878+
IaDH 1878+

MISSOURI VALLEY

HARRISON county news. w 1882-Ag 1931||
United with Missouri Valley times to form Missouri Valley times-news
IaDH Mr 1893-1931

Missouri Valley TIMES. w 1868-Ag 1931||
MWA Mr 4 1881

Missouri Valley TIMES-NEWS. d 1891+
1891-Ag 1931 as Missouri Valley times
IaDH 1894-[1903-04]

MITCHELL

Mitchell GAZETTE. w
IaHi My 30-O 31 1862

MITCHELL county republican. w O 25 1856-
IaHi N 1856-58;Ja 13-F 24 1859

MONDAMIN

Mondamin ENTERPRISE. w 1899+
pub O 1919+

MONONA

Monona LEADER. w Je 1,1892+
pub 1892+
IaDH Mr 1901+

MONROE

Weekly ALBIA republican. *See* Monroe county sentinel

JASPER county mirror. w S 20 1872+
1872-74 as South side transcript; 1875-1930? Monroe mirror
pub Mr 1925+
IaHi 1872-Mr 7 1874

Monroe MIRROR. *See* Jasper county mirror

MONROE county sentinel. w N 5 1857-61||
1857-D 29 1859 as Weekly Albia republican
Suspended -Ag 4 1858
IaHi 1859;N 10,16,D 7-14 1861

Monroe RECORD. w 1869-72||
IaHi [Je 11 1870-Ag 1872]

SOUTH SIDE transcript. *See* Jasper county mirror

MONTANA

Montana STANDARD. *See* Boone standard (Boone)

MONTEZUMA

Montezuma DEMOCRAT. w 1877-1903||
1877-87? as Poweshiek county democrat
IaDH 1894-S 1903

POWESHIEK county democrat. *See* Montezuma democrat

POWESHIEK county palladium. w 1895-1921||
IaDH 1916-My 1921

IOWA (*Continued*)

MONTEZUMA—*Continued*

Montezuma REPUBLICAN. w My 1856+
Title varies slightly
pub 1856;71+
IaDH 1856-59;O 1897+
IaHi [My 30-D 12 1857;58-59;Je 13-O 10 1860; 1905]06

MONTICELLO

Monticello EXPRESS. w Jl 10 1865+
pub 1865+
IaDH Ap 1897+
IaHi Mr 22 1866-Je 4 1868;Ag-Jl 1873
IaMo 1888+

JONES county liberal. w 1872-81||
IaMoE 1872-73

MONTROSE

BLUFF PARK journal. *See* Montrose journal

IOWA advocate and half breed journal. sm Ag 16 1847-
IaDH Ag 16,S 1,D 15 1847

Montrose JOURNAL. w 1885-
1885-95* as Bluff Park journal; 1896?-98 Park journal
IaDH 1916-32

PARK journal. *See* Montrose journal

Montrose VINDICATOR. w
IaDH Ag 17 1876

WESTERN adventurer and herald of the Upper Mississippi. w Je 28 1837-38||
IaDH Je 28-Jl 5,Ag 12,S 2-9,30-O 21 1837
WHi Ag 19 1837

MOULTON

Moulton INDEPENDENT. w 1869-73||?
IaHi Je 16-D 8 1870

Moulton TRIBUNE. w 1884+
IaHi F 5 1891-N 8 1901

MOUNT AYR

Mount Ayr JOURNAL. w 1873-1924||
IaDH 1894-1924

Twice-a-week NEWS. sw 1892-F 26 1907||
Title varies: Mount Ayr news. United with Ringgold record to form Mount Ayr record news
IaDH Ap 1898-1907
IaHi 1905-07
IaMou Mr 6 1894-Jl 1900

Mount Ayr RECORD news. w 1865+
1865-1907 as Ringgold record (some issues as Mount Ayr record)
IaDH O 1895+
IaHi F 1905-06

RINGGOLD record. *See* Mount Ayr record news

MOUNT PLEASANT

FREE PRESS. w Ap 1866+
1863-73 as Henry county press
pub 1900+
DLC My 12 1892
ICHi Je 18 1891
IaDH 1872-85;87-1919;28+
IaHi S 9 1868-My 4 1870;Ag 1873-74
IaMp 1872-95;99;1911-12

HENRY county press. *See* Free press

HOME journal. *See* Mount Pleasant journal

IOWA freeman. *See* Iowa true democrat

IOWA true democrat. w 1849-52||
1849-50 as Iowa freeman (Fort Madison)
IaDH Jl 10 1849[Ap-D 1850;F-Jl 1851;Ja-Mr,S-O,D 1852]
MWA N 10 1852

Mount Pleasant JOURNAL. w 1854-1914||
1854-58 as Mount Pleasant observer; 1859-69 Home journal. United with Mount Pleasant news to form News-journal, later Mount Pleasant news
IaBu Ap 6-D 1854;Ja 11-18,Mr,Ap 12-19,Jl 26 1855
IaDH My 1893-S 1914
IaGG S 8 1859
IaHi [Mr 17-D 1859]-[61]-[64-66]Ap 17 1868; Mr 19-D 3 1869;F 1905-06
IaMp 1870-98
MWA Ja 5 1866
NNHi F 15 1872

Mt. Pleasant NEWS. d 1875+
S 1914-19 as Mount Pleasant news-journal
pub 1895+
IaDH O 29 1879;S 15-N 11 1914;F 1915-27
IaMp 1894+

Mount Pleasant NEWS-JOURNAL. *See* Mount Pleasant news

Mount Pleasant OBSERVER. *See* Mount Pleasant journal

Mount Pleasant daily REPORTER. d 1877-82||?
IaDH Ag 15 1879

MOUNT VERNON

Mt. Vernon CITIZEN. w 1863-
1863-65? as Franklin record
IaHi D 5 1863-O 1864[Ag-O 26 1866]

FRANKLIN record. *See* Mt. Vernon citizen

HAWKEYE-RECORD and Lisbon herald. w Ja 1 1869+
Ja-Je 1869 as Linn county hawkeye; Jl 1869-D 17 1922 Mount Vernon hawkeye; D 24 1922-Jl 30 1925 Mount Vernon hawkeye-Lisbon herald
pub Ag 1925+
IaCf My 11 1871-S 26 1873
IaDH 1916+
IaHi D 8 1905-06
IaMt Jl 15 1869-D 17 1922;Ag 1925+

LINN county hawkeye. *See* Hawkeye-record and Lisbon herald

LINN county pilot. *See* Marion pilot (Marion)

Weekly NEWS. w Ja 1859-
IaGG N 18 1859
IaHi 1860-D 10 1862

Mount Vernon RECORD. w 1893-Ag 6 1925||
1893-Mr 1901 as Remarker. United with Mount Vernon hawkeye-Lisbon herald to form Hawkeye-record and Lisbon herald
IaMt cmoplete
IaMtH 1901-25

REMARKER *See* Mount Vernon record

MOVILLE

Moville MAIL. w 1887+
pub O 1894+
IaDH 1916+

MURRAY

Murray NEWS. *See* Times (Creston)

Murray RECORD. *See* Times (Creston)

MUSCATINE

To Je 26 1849 as Bloomington

BLOOMINGTON herald. *See* Muscatine journal

Muscatine daily COURIER. d S 20 1860-72||
1860-Je 24 1862 as Muscatine daily review
IaDH 1860-Jl 14 1861;Je 1862-N 1864
IaHi Je 26 1862-O 1863;Jl 6-Ag 29 1864

Muscatine weekly COURIER. w 1860-73||
Follows Iowa democratic enquirer. Merged with Muscatine tribune, later News-tribune
IaDH [Jl 1863-N 1864;Ag-N 1866]
IaHi O 22 1863-F 1872

DEMOCRATIC enquirer. *See* Iowa democratic enquirer

Die DEUTSCHE zeitung. *See* Muscatine herald

DEUTSCHER anzeiger. *See* Muscatine herald

Muscatine HERALD. w 1874-1932||?
1874-81? as Deutsche zeitung; 1882?-96? Wacht am Mississippi; 1897?-1906? Deutscher anzeiger; 1907?-21 Muscatine herold
1874-1921 in German
IaDH 1916-31

Muscatine HEROLD. *See* Muscatine herald

Muscatine INDEPENDENT telegram. w Jl 6 1919-21||
1919-Je 27 1920 as Muscatine telegram
IaMu Jl 13 1919-Je 23 1921

IOWA democratic enquirer. w Jl 7 1848-S 1860||
Followed by Muscatine daily review, later Muscatine daily courier. Title varies: Democratic enquirer
CU F 14 1850
IU Ag 30 1860
IaDH 1848-Jl 4 1850;N 1859-60
IaHi [Ap 1859-Ag 1860]
IaMu Jl 1850-Je 1852

IOWA messenger. w S 29 1860-
Title varies: Messenger
IaDH S 29 N 3 1860

IOWA standard. w O 23 1840-Ap 29 1841||
Followed by Iowa City standard (Iowa City)
IaDH complete
IaHi O 30 1840-Ap 16 1841
OClWHi N 20 1840
P-M Ap 9 1841

Muscatine JOURNAL. w,sw O 27 1840-1915||
1840-49 as Bloomington herald
w 1840-1901?
CU Ap 16 1841
DLC Ap 9,My 14 1847;Mr 18,Ap 29,Ag 12,26 1848
IaDH 1840-Mr,Ap 17 1846-S 2,N 1848-F 20, My 9 1849-Ja 19,Je 1850-My 1851;Je 1853-Je 1855;95-1902
IaDaP Je 10 1842;My 5,Jl 7 1843
IaHi [Ap 17 1846-S 2 1848]59-Mr 2 1879; F 1905-09
IaMu D 11 1840-1915
OClWHi Ja 26 1844

Muscatine JOURNAL and news-tribune. d Je 1855+
1855-S 1 1918 as Muscatine journal
CU Mr 20 Ap 10 1863
ICM My 21 1884
IaDH Je 27 1855-63;1903-Ag 1916;Jl 1922-Ag 1923
IaHi Ag 1863-N 1866;1905;07+
IaMu 1855+
MWA N 25 1870
NbHi Je 12 1890

Muscatine Saturday MAIL. w 1892-1904||
IaDH 1897-Ap 1904

MESSENGER. *See* Iowa messenger

MIDWEST free press. d,w D 19 1930-F 8 1934||
IaMu complete
NN D 19 1930

MUSCATINE county courier. sw 1915-19||
IaMu Mr 7-Je 18 1919

Muscatine NEWS. w 1879-Ap 1889||
United with Muscatine tribune to form News-tribune

NEWS-TRIBUNE. d 1874-Ag 1918||
1874-Ap 1889 as Muscatine daily tribune. United with Muscatine journal to form Muscatine journal and news-tribune
IaDH 1900-18
OClWH My 29 1874

NEWS-TRIBUNE. w,sw 1874-1918||
1874-Ap 1889 as Muscatine tribune
IaDH Ag 1893-99

Muscatine daily REVIEW. *See* Muscatine daily courier

Muscatine TELEGRAM. *See* Muscatine independent telegram

Muscatine TRIBUNE. *See* News-Tribune

WACHT am Mississippi. *See* Muscatine herald

NASHUA

PEOPLE'S rights. w
WHi J 4-N 29 1878

Nashua POST. w 1867-1918||
IaDH 1894-1918
IaHi F 5,My 7,O 8,D 24 1869;Ja-Je 1870; S-O 1? 1873
IaNaR 1875-99
WHi [S 24 1869-Ag 1879]D 16-30 1886;Ja 20-27 1887;My 18 1916-D 5 1918

Nashua REPORTER. w Ag 1893+
pub 1899+

NEOLA

Neola GAZETTE. w 1902-05||
United with Neola reporter to form Neola gazette-reporter

Neola GAZETTE-REPORTER. w 1879+
1879-1905 as Neola reporter
IaDH 1899+

Neola REPORTER. *See* Neola gazette-reporter

NEVADA

Nevada evening JOURNAL. tw,d 1895+
tw 1895-My 1929
IaDH Je 1926+

Nevada REPRESENTATIVE. w,sw Ja 8 1857-F 1927||
1857-My 1862 as Story county advocate; Je 1862-63 Republican reveille; 1863-Ap 1870 Story county aegis. Merged with Nevada evening journal
IaDH N 1863-Je 1868;85-90;92
IaHi Mr 16 1859-[Je 1862-O 1863]S 1866-O 1876;Jl 1877-Jl 1878
N Jl 4 1876

REPUBLICAN reveille. *See* Nevada representative

STORY county advocate. *See* Nevada representative

STORY county aegis. *See* Nevada representative

STORY county watchman. w 1874-1906||
IaDH Ap 1893-O 1906

NEW HAMPTON

New Hampton COURIER. w Ja 16 1860-N 8 1917||
Merged into New Hampton tribune, later New Hampton tribune-gazette
IaDH Jl 1901-09
IaHi [Ag 1864-O 1874]
IaNhT 1875-1915
OClWHi Ja 19,F 2,D 6 1864
WHi Ag 4-18 1862;Ag 16-23,S 13 1864;Ag 8 1865;O 2 1867;O 9 1868;O 1,22,D 17 1869;F 10,Je 10,Jl 1 1870;O 6-13 1871;F 9,Ag 9 1872;Ap 11,Jl 18,O 4 1873 Ja 14 1875;Ap 11 1878;Ja 9 1879

New Hampton ECONOMIST. w Ag 1932+
pub 1932+

New Hampton GAZETTE. w S 1893-D 31 1930||
United with New Hampton tribune to form New Hampton tribune-gazette
IaDH O 1895-[1906-07]-30
IaNh complete
IaNhT complete

New Hampton TIMES. w 1835-94||
WHi N 2 1894

New Hampton TRIBUNE-GAZETTE. w 1876+
1876-1930 as New Hampton tribune
pub 1893+
IaDH N 1876-83;Mr 1885-Ap,Je 1893+
IaHi 1905-06
IaNh 1910+
WHi Je 19 1878

NEW MARKET

New Market HERALD. *See* Taylor county herald (Bedford)

NEW OREGON

New Oregon PLAINDEALER. *See* Cresco plaindealer (Cresco)

NEW SHARON

New Sharon STAR. w 1873+
pub 1909+
IaDH 1876-78

IOWA (*Continued*)

NEW VIRGINIA

NEW VIRGINIAN. w 1895+
Title varies: Virginian
IaDH 1916+

VIRGINIAN. *See* New Virginian

NEWELL

Newell MIRROR. w 1875+
pub 1875+
MWA S 3 1876

NEWTON

Newton EXPRESS. *See* Newton journal

FREE PRESS. *See* Newton journal

Newton HERALD. w 1877-1913||?
1877-78 as Iowa national. Merged with Newton daily news
IaDH Je 1893-My 1913
IaN 1904-12

IOWA national. *See* Newton herald

IOWA state democrat. w 1881-1901||
IaDH D 1897-1901

JASPER county liberal. w Ag 24 1872-73||
IaHi 1872-Ja 3 1873

JASPER county record. w 1894+
1894-1923? as Newton record
IaDH Mr-D 1898;1916+
IaN 1905-19

JASPER free press. *See* Newton journal

Newton JOURNAL. w,d Mr 1856-D 4 1916||
1856-57? as Newton express; 1857?-Ja 1869 Jasper free press; F 1869-74? Newton free press. Merged with Newton daily news
w 1856-S 1911
IaDH Mr 21 1883-1916
IaGG Mr 1 1860
IaHi [Mr-N 3 1859]F 2 1860;F 1869-74
IaN 1877-O 1916

Newton daily NEWS. d 1902+
IaN D 1906+
KHi My 1 1926;S 10 1928
OClWHi My 25 1904
WHi Ja 6 1914

Newton RECORD. *See* Jasper county record

NORTHWOOD

Northwood ANCHOR and index. w 1885+
1885-88? as Northwood beacon; 1889-D 1 1922 Northwood anchor
pub Jl 1888+
IaDH 1921+

Northwood BEACON. *See* Northwood anchor and index

PIONEER. w S 24 1869-78||
1869-70 as Worth county pioneer
IaHi S 24 1869[Jl-D 14 1870]

WORTH county index. w D 22 1881-D 1 1922||
United with Northwood anchor to form Northwood anchor and index
IaDH Je 1893-1922
IaNoA complete

WORTH county pioneer. *See* Pioneer

OAKLAND

Oakland ACORN. w 1881+
IaDH 1916+

OAKVILLE

Oakville SENTINEL. w Je 2 1902+
pub 1902+
IaDH 1916+

O'BRIEN

O'Brien PIONEER. *See* Sanborn pioneer (Sanborn)

OCHEYDAN

Ocheydan ARROW. w 1927+
IaSiC Mr 1931+

Ocheydan PRESS. w Ag 7 1891-1926||
IaDH 1916-26

ODEBOLT

Odebolt CHRONICLE. w 1887+
IaDH Je 1893-1930

Odebolt NEWS. w 1914-27||?
IaDH 1916-18

OELWEIN

INDEPENDENT. *See* Oelwein Iowan

Oelwein IOWAN. tw 1912-23||
1912-16 as Independent. Merged with Oelwein daily register
IaDH 1916-23

Oelwein REGISTER. w Ag 1880-1922||?
IaDH Je 1893-1920

Oelwein daily REGISTER. d 1906+
pub 1906+

OGDEN

Ogden REPORTER. w 1874+
pub Je 6 1874+
IaDH 1915+
IaHi N 9 1905-06

OLD ROLFE

POCAHONTAS times. *See* Fonda times (Fonda)

OLIN

Olin "C" PRESS. *See* Olin recorder

Olin RECORDER. w 1880+
Je 1928-31? as Olin "C" press
IaDH 1916-32
OClWHi O 3 1907

ONAWA

Onawa DEMOCRAT. w F 5 1890+
1890-94? as Monona county democrat
IaOn 1905-08;10+

Onawa ENQUIRER. w Je 16 1880-
IaOn Je-Jl 28 1880

Onawa GAZETTE. *See* Monona county gazette

MONONA cordon. D 19 1860-62||?
IaOn Jl 20 1861

MONONA county democrat. *See* Onawa democrat

MONONA county gazette. w D 2 1865-F 18 1904||
Title varies: Onawa gazette
IaDH 1894-1904
IaOn Mr 30 1870-1904
MWA Ja 4 1873

Onawa SENTINEL. w Mr 1885+
IaDH My 1903+
IaOn 1905-07;10+

ORANGE CITY

Orange City JOURNAL. w 1922+
Follows Sioux County herald
pub 1934+

SIOUX county herald. w 1871-1921||
Followed by Orange City journal
IaDH 1891-1916

De VOLKSVRIEND. w S 2 1874+
In Dutch
pub 1874+
MnHi Ap 27 1922-Mr 12 1925

ORIENT

Orient AVALANCHE. w Je 26 1931+
pub 1931+

OSAGE

MITCHELL county news. *See* Osage news

MITCHELL county press and Osage news. w Mr 1 1865+
1865-Ag 1 1931 as Mitchell county press
1865-Je 1870 pub in West Mitchell
pub 1865+
IaDH 1893-1918;31+
IaHi Mr 8 1865-Mr 1872

Osage NEWS. w O 4 1868-Ag 1 1931||
1868- as Mitchell county news. United with Mitchell county press to form Mitchell county press and Osage news
IaDH 1888-91;93-Jl 1931
IaOsaM 1868-1923

NORTH IOWA standard. *See* Osage tribune

NORTH IOWAN. *See* Osage tribune

Osage TRIBUNE. w 1857-68||
1857-60 as North Iowan; 1860 St. Ansgar journal (St. Ansgar); 1860-61 North Iowan; 1861-65 North Iowa standard; 1865-68 North Iowan. Merged with Mitchell county press and Osage news
IaGG N 12 1859
IaHi Ag 20 1859-[Ja-N 10 1860]68

OSCEOLA

CLARKE COUNTY clipper. w 1898-
IaDH 1898

CLARKE COUNTY sentinel. *See* Osceola sentinel

Osceola COURIER. *See* Osceola sentinel

Osceola DEMOCRAT. *See* Osceola tribune

Osceola REPUBLICAN. w 1870-72||
IaHi Jl 1870-Ag 1872

Osceola SENTINEL. w Jl 30 1859+
1859-62 as Osceola courier; 1863-67 Union sentinel; 1867-74? Clarke county sentinel
pub [1859-82]+
IaDH 1890;93+
IaHi 1905-06
IaOs 1906+

Osceola TRIBUNE. w 1873+
1873-1918? as Osceola democrat
pub Ap 1931+
IaDH 1883-89;96+

UNION sentinel. *See* Osceola sentinel

OSKALOOSA

Saturday GLOBE. w 1881-Ja 1922||
United with Oskaloosa times to form Oskaloosa times-globe
IaDH 1889;91-1921
IaHi 1905-06
IaOT complete

Oskaloosa HERALD. w Jl 1850-1919||
Jl-N 1850 as Iowa herald. Title varies: Weekly Oskaloosa herald; Saturday herald; etc.
pub complete
DLC S 16 1869-S 7 1871;80;Ja 16 1886-90;96-97;Ja-Je 1903;04-05;07-10;15-16
IaDH 1850-Jl 1859;64-88;90;92-1919
IaHi [My 18-D 7 1860]Jl 28 1864-S 7 1871
MWA Ag 1 1856;Ja 25 1866
NbHi Ja 27 1881

Oskaloosa daily HERALD. d S 3 1887+
Title varies: Daily herald; Evening herald; Daily evening herald
DLC 1887-Mr 2 1888;Ja-S 1898;Jl 2-S 29 1900; 01;S 29-D 1902;Ja-Je 1904;05;Jl 2-S 29 1906;07-Ap 29,S 1910-17;My-Ag 1919;My-Ag 1924;Ja-Ap 1928
IaDH 1887-1919
IaHi S 1902-Je 1918

IOWA herald. *See* Oskaloosa herald

IOWA reform leader. *See* Oskaloosa standard

Oskaloosa MESSENGER. w 1878-85||
WHi O 24 1885

PROGRESSIVE conservator. *See* Oskaloosa standard

Oskaloosa REFORM leader. w Jl 13 1871-76||?
IaDH Ja-O 1876
IaHi 1871-F 15 1872

Oskaloosa STANDARD. w 1875-84||?
1866-Je 1871 as Progressive conservator; Jl 1871-O 1873 Iowa reform leader
IaDH 1876-78
IaHi 1870-Je 1871

Oskaloosa weekly TIMES. w Ja 1854-64||
IaHi Mr 17 1859-S 5 1861
OHi N 5 1857

Oskaloosa TIMES-GLOBE. w 1885-1931||?
1885-Ja 1922 as Oskaloosa times. Followed by Oskaloosa tribune
IaDH 1887-1931
IaOT complete

Oskaloosa TRIBUNE. w 1831?+
Follows Oskaloosa times globe
pub 1931+
IaDH 1932+

WATCHMAN. w 1864-
IaHi D 15 1864-F 23 1865

OSSIAN

Ossian BEE. w 1885+
pub 1885+

OTTERCREEK. *See* LAFAYETTE

OTTUMWA

COPPERHEAD. w 1844-
IU My 20 1844

COPPERHEAD. w Mr 1868-70||
Follows Copperhead (Pella). Followed by Ottumwa democrat
IaHi Je-D 1870

Ottumwa COURIER. w,tw Ag 8 1848-1918||
1848-56 as Des Moines courier
w 1848-1904
IaDH 1849-1918
IaHi Mr 17 1859-[Ja-Ag 23 1860]N 26 1868-Mr 7 1872
IaOt Ag 8 1848;71;Jl 1872-Jl 1873;74-S 1883; Ap-S 18 1901;F 1903-Je 1905;S 1906-Mr,O 1914-Mr 1918;Ap 1924-Ag 1925;Mr 1926-27; Mr 1928+
MWA Ap 2 1879

Ottumwa daily COURIER. d Ap 5 1865+
DLC Jl-D 1898
IaDH S 1868-Je 1881;82-90;Ja-Je 1892;Jl-D 1897;Je 1918+
IaHi 1903-16;F 1928+
IaOt Jl-S 1918;19-Ap,Jl 1920-Mr 1922;Ap 1924-Ag 1925;Mr 1926-27;Mr 1928+

Ottumwa DEMOCRAT. w F 1871-Ap 12 1902||
Follows Copperhead. 1878?-80? as Democrat and times
IaDH 1876;N 1878-80
IaHi 1871-F 1876
IaOt F-D 1871;73;N 1878-N 1879;S 1881-Ap, D 1882-Jl 1883;Ja-Je 1885;My-D 1891;Je 1901-02
MWA Je 8 1876

Daily DEMOCRAT. d 1881-1902||
IaDH Jl-D 1884
IaHi 1886-87;My-Ag 1891;N 1892-94;My 1896-97

DEMOCRAT and times. *See* Ottumwa democrat

DEMOCRATIC mercury. w 1858-68||
1858-61 as Ottumwa democratic statesman; 1862-63? Ottumwa democratic union
IaHi Jl 19,O 25,N 12-26,D 10,24 1860[Ja 14-Ag 8 1861]

Ottumwa DEMOCRATIC statesman. *See* Democratic mercury

Ottumwa DEMOCRATIC union. *See* Democratic mercury

DES MOINES courier. *See* Ottumwa courier

DES MOINES republic. w Je 1850-D 1852||
IaDH D 18 1851;F 26 1852

IOWA (*Continued*)

OTTUMWA—*Continued*

Ottumwa Saturday HERALD. w 1899-1912||
IaOt My 1899-Je 1912

Ottumwa INDEPENDENT. m 1889-1903||?
IaDH Je 1899-My 1903
IaHi 1899;1902

Ottumwa daily REVIEW. d Ap 1909-F 1920||
IaOt Ap-D 1909;Jl-D 1910;Jl-D 1912;Jl 1913-16;Jl-D 1917;Jl 1918-19

Ottumwa SUN. w 1890-97||
IaDH Ag 1890-96
IaHi D 1891-Jl 1897

Ottumwa SUN. d 1894-
IaDH S-D 1894

OXFORD

Oxford JOURNAL. w 1878-1900||?
IaHi 1889-99

OXFORD JUNCTION

Oxford MIRROR. w 1879+
IaDH 1921+

PACIFIC CITY

Pacific City ENTERPRISE. w Je 18 1857-
NbHi Je-N 19,D 10-24 1857;Ja 7,21-F,Mr 11-Je 10 1858

Pacific City HERALD. w Jl 1858-
IaHi [Mr 24 1859-Ag 2 1860]

PANORA

GUTHRIE county news. *See* Guthrie county vedette

GUTHRIE county vedette. w 1864+
1864-66 as Guthrie county news; 1866-89? Guthrie vedette; 1889?-92? Panora umpire vedette; 1892?-1910? Panora vedette
IaDH 1889-1910;16+
IaHi O 14 1865-S 1868
MWA F 21 1867

GUTHRIE sentinel. Ja 25 1856-57||
IaDH 1856

GUTHRIE vedette. *See* Guthrie county vedette

Panora UMPIRE vedette. *See* Guthrie county vedette

PARKERSBURG

Parkersburg ECLIPSE. w 1872+
pub 1923+

PATTERSONVILLE

Pattersonville INDEX. *See* Sioux county index (Hull)

IOWA index. *See* Sioux county index (Hull)

PELLA

Pella BLADE. *See* Pella chronicle

Pella BLADE-CHRONICLE. *See* Pella chronicle

Pella BOOSTER. *See* Pella press

BOOSTER-PRESS. *See* Pella press

Pella CHRONICLE. w F 3 1865+
1865-1900 as Pella blade; 1900-01 Pella blade-chronicle
pub 1906+
IaDH 1883-87;O 1895+
IaP 1906-31

COPPER HEAD. Ja 8 1866- F? 1868||
Followed by Copperhead (Ottumwa)
IaDH Ja 15 1868

Pella GAZETTE. F 1 1855-Mr 1860||
IaPP 1857

Pella weekly HERALD. w 1889-95||?
IaHi D 1891-93

Pella PRESS. w D 1906+
1906-14? as Booster; 1915?-Je 1 1928 Booster press
IaDH 1916+

WEEKBLAD. w Ja 1 1860+
In Dutch
pub 1899+
IaDH 1916+

PERRY

Perry ADVERTISER. w 1885-Jl 1916||
United with Perry daily chief to form Chief-advertiser, later Perry daily chief
IaDH 1886-90;92-Je 1916
IaPeC 1899-1916

Perry daily CHIEF. d 1901+
Jl 1916-20? as Chief advertiser
pub 1901+
IaDH 1911+

CHIEF-REPORTER. w S 19 1874-1910||
1874-1900? as Perry chief; 1901? Chief-pilot
pub complete
IaDH 1903-10

Perry PILOT. w 1880-85||
United with Perry chief to form Chief-pilot, later Chief-reporter
IaPeC 1883-85

Perry PRESS. w 1889-91||
IaPeC complete

Perry REPORTER. w 1892-95||?
United with Perry chief to form Chief-reporter
IaPeC 1892

PIERSON

Pierson PROGRESS. w 1908+
pub Ap 8 1926+

PILOT MOUND

Pilot Mound LEADER. w 1914-17||
IaDH 1915-17

POCAHONTAS

Pocahontas DEMOCRAT. w 1901-31||
United with Pocahontas record to form Pocahontas record-democrat
IaDH Mr 1901-31

Pocahontas RECORD-DEMOCRAT. w Ap 24 1884+
1884-1931? as Pocohontas record
IaDH 1931+
IaHi 1905-06

Pocahontas TIMES. *See* Fonda times (Fonda)

POMEROY

CALHOUN county journal. *See* Manson journal (Manson)

Pomeroy HERALD. w Mr 21 1889+
pub 1889+

POSTVILLE

Postville HERALD. w N 1 1892+
N 1 1892-Je 1 1918 as Iowa volksblatt
1892-1918 in German
pub 1892+

IOWA volksblatt. *See* Postville herald

PRAIRIE CITY

Prairie City INDEX. w 1869-72||
IaHi 1871-S 1872

Prairie City NEWS. w Ap 30 1874+
MWA My 21 1875;Jl 12 1878
NbHi Ag 16-23,S 20 1878

PRESCOTT

ADAMS county argus. *See* Prescott argus

ADVOCATE. *See* Prescott argus

Prescott ARGUS. w 1889-1921||
1889-1900? as Advocate; 1900?-05? Adams county argus
IaDH 1916-Jl 1921

Prescott CHRONICLE. w 1883-86||?
IaCo Je 26 1884

PRESTON

Preston TIMES. w 1894+
IaDH Jl 1905+

PRIMGHAR

O'BRIEN county bell. w 1886+
IaDH D 1910+
IaHi 1905-06
IaSa S 1927+

O'BRIEN pioneer. *See* Sanborn pioneer (Sanborn)

QUASQUETON

BUCHANAN county guardian. *See* Buchanan county guardian (Independence)

Quasqueton GUARDIAN. *See* Buchanan county guardian (Independence)

RAKE

Rake REGISTER. w Ag 3 1900+
pub 1900+

RANDOLPH

Randolph ENTERPRISE. w Je 28 1896+
pub 1917+

FARM bureau advocate. w My 1 1931+
pub 1931+

RED OAK

Red Oak EXPRESS. w Mr 28 1868+
pub 1868+
IaDH N 1883-89;Ag 1893-1916
IaHi 1905-06

PEOPLE'S telephone. *See* Red Oak sun

Red Oak REPUBLICAN. w 1895-1904||
IaDH Ag 1900-N 16 1904

Red Oak SUN. w 1877+
1877-84? as People's telephone
pub 1877+
IaDH 1893+

REINBECK

Reinbeck COURIER. w 1889+
1889-1901? Grundy courier
pub 1889+

GRUNDY courier. *See* Reinbeck courier

Reinbeck TIMES. w N 7 1879-84||?
MWA N 7 1879;Ap 22 1880;Ja 6,Mr 31-Ap 7, My 26,Je 9-16,30,Jl 14,Ag 4,18-25,S 15 1881; Mr 2,Je 9 1882

REMSEN

BELL enterprise. w 1887+
1887-1900 as Remsen bell
IaDH 1916+

RENWICK

Renwick TIMES. w 1884+
pub 1913+
IaDH 1895-1910

RICEVILLE

Riceville RECORDER. w 1886+
pub 1920+

RICHLAND

Richland CLARION. w 1881+
pub 1881+
IaDH 1916+

RINGSTED

Ringsted DISPATCH. w Mr 1901+
pub 1913+

RIVERSIDE

Riverside LEADER. w Ag 10 1883+
IaDH Jl 1925+

RIVERTOWN

Rivertown ADVOCATE. 1874-
NbHi Ap 13 1876

ROCHESTER

CEDAR county news-letter. w S 13 1852-N 1853||
Followed by Tipton advertiser (Tipton)

ROCK RAPIDS

LYON county leader. S 20 1932+
Follows Larchwood leader (Larchwood)
pub 1932+

LYON county reporter. w 1881+
1901?-29? as Rock Rapids reporter
IaDH 1893+
IaHi My 13 1887-Jl 8 1890

Rock Rapids REVIEW. w 1872-1929||?
IaDH 1893-1916

ROCKFORD

Rockford GAZETTE. w 1894-1901||?
IaDH Je 1894-96

Rockford REGISTER. w 1876+
1876-86? as Rockford reveille
IaDH 1903+

Rockford REVEILLE. *See* Rockford register

ROCKWELL

Rockwell PHONOGRAPH. *See* Rockwell tribune

Rockwell TRIBUNE. w 1879+
1879-1917 as Rockwell phonograph
pub Mr 1920+

ROCKWELL CITY

Rockwell City ADVOCATE. w Ja 16 1891+
1891-92? as Farmers' advocate
pub 1894+
IaDH 1891+
IaHi F 1905-06

CALHOUN county journal. *See* Manson journal (Manson)

FARMERS' advocate. *See* Rockwell City advocate

ROLAND

Roland RECORD. w F 28 1895+
pub 1895+

ROLFE

Rolfe ARROW. w My 10 1910+
pub 1910+
IaDH 1913+

POCAHONTAS times. w Ap 6 1876-
MWA Ag 31 1876

Rolfe REVEILLE. w 1888-1912||
Merged with Rolfe arrow
IaDH My 1893-1912

RUNNELLS

FOUR-COUNTY neighbor. *See* Runnells telegram

Runnells TELEGRAM. w 1887-1920||
1913-14 as Four-county neighbor
IaDH Mr 1910-14

IOWA (*Continued*)

RUTHVEN

FREE PRESS. w 1883+
pub 1917+

SABULA

Sabula GAZETTE. w 1872+
pub 1874+
IaDH S 1899+

SAC CITY

SAC county bulletin. w 1882-1924||
1882-1909? as Sac county democrat. Merged with Sac sun
IaSacS 1890-1924

SAC county democrat. *See* Sac county bulletin

SAC sun. w Jl 1871+
pub 1871+
IaDH Mr 1894+
IaHi 1905-06
MWA S 8,22 1876

ST. ANSGAR

St. Ansgar ENTERPRISE. w N 1 1878+
Follows St. Ansgar register
pub 1892+
IaS O 26 1887-D 18 1889
IaSM 1878-91

St. Ansgar JOURNAL. *See* Osage tribune (Osage)

St. Ansgar REGISTER. w 1876-Ag 1878||
Followed by St. Ansgar enterprise
IaSM My 1877-78

ST. CHARLES. *See* CHARLES CITY

ST. MARY

NEBRASKA palladium. *See under* Belleview, Neb.

SALEM

Salem NEWS. w 1884+
pub 1894+
IaDH 1916-19;My 1934+

SANBORN

Sanborn JOURNAL. w 1885-93||
IaDH O 1885-F 1893

O'BRIEN pioneer. *See* Sanborn pioneer

Sanborn PIONEER. w My 17 1872+
1872-82 as O'Brien pioneer
1872-Jl 1873 pub in O'Brien; Jl 1873-N 1879 in Primghar
pub [1900+]
IaDH 1872-93;1901+
IaHi F 1893-97
IaSa 1872-Jl,D 7 1883-1903;S 1918+

SCRANTON

Scranton JOURNAL. w 1879+
ICM Jl 27 1882
IaDH My 1900+

SERGEANT'S BLUFF

WESTERN independent. w Ag 1857-Jl 1858||
Followed by Sioux City register (Sioux City)
IaSc D 31 1857

SEYMOUR

DEMOCRAT. *See* Seymour herald

Seymour HERALD. w 1884+
1886-88? as Lone Tree press; 1889?-1906? Press; 1907?-17? Democrat
IaDH 1918-Je 1932

Seymour LEADER. sw 1891-1918||?
IaDH 1916-17

LONE TREE press. *See* Seymour herald

PRESS. *See* Seymour herald

SHARPSBURG

NORTH TAYLOR review. w 1909-19||
1909-10? as Sharpsburg review
IaDH 1916-19

Sharpsburg REVIEW. *See* North Taylor review

SHEFFIELD

Sheffield PRESS. w 1880+
pub 1880+
IaDH 1916+

SHELBY

Shelby NEWS. w Ap 1877+
pub F 1879+

SHELDON

Sheldon EAGLE. w 1889-99||?
IaDH Ag 1897-99

Sheldon MAIL. w Ja 1 1873+
IaDH S 1874-92;Je 1893-1906;16+
IaSh 1933+

Sheldon NEWS. w 1879-87||
IaDH F 1880-87

Sheldon SUN. w 1895+
pub [1895+]
IaDH 1916+
IaSh 1933+

SHELL ROCK

Shell Rock NEWS. w 1874+
IaDH O 1905+

SHENANDOAH

DEMOCRATIC world. *See* Shenandoah world

Evening SENTINEL. w,sw,tw,d N 25 1887+
1887-1904 as Shenandoah sentinel; 1904-24 Sentinel-post; 1924-26? Sentinel-world
w 1887-93?sw,tw 1894?-1919
pub 1890+
IaDH S 1908+
IaShe 1888-89;91-96;98-99;1905+

Shenandoah WORLD. sw,d 1891-1924||
1891-99? as Democratic world. United with Sentinel-post to form Sentinel-world, later Evening sentinel
IaDH N 1897-1921

SIBLEY

Sibley GAZETTE-TRIBUNE. w 1872+
1872-F 1931 as Sibley gazette
IaDH Jl 1893+
IaHi 1905-06
IaSiC 1931+

Sibley HERALD. w 1896-99||
IaDH 1898-99

OSCEOLA county tribune. w 1881-F 1931||
1881 as Sibley tribune. United with Sibley gazette to form Sibley gazette-tribune
IaDH N 1883-89;F 1895-1930

Sibley TRIBUNE. *See* Osceola county tribune

SIDNEY

AMERICAN union. *See* Fremont county sun

Sidney ARGUS. w Jl 27 1916-S 1927||
United with Fremont county herald to form Sidney argus-herald
IaSidA complete

Sidney ARGUS-HERALD. w S 1885+
1885-S 8 1927 as Fremont county herald
pub 1885-93;95+
IaDH 1916-27

DEMOCRAT. *See* Fremont county sun

FREMONT county herald. w 1858-My 14 1859||
IaHi Mr 26-My 14 1859

FREMONT county herald. 1885-1927. *See* Sidney argus-herald

FREMONT county sun. w 1862-1909||
1862-F? 1866 as American union; Mr?-1866 Democrat; 1866-85? Union; 1886?-92? Union-times
IaDH 1894-[1904-06]-My 1909
IaHi Ag 25-S 1,15,29 1864;Jl 13-Ag 24,O 5-12,N 16 1865
MWA Mr 17 1866
WHi O 23 1863;Ag 18 1864

UNION. *See* Fremont county sun

UNION-TIMES. *See* Fremont county sun

SIGOURNEY

IOWA democrat. w Ja 21 1858-62||
IaDH [1859-60]
IaHi [Mr 11-N 18 1859;F 10-N 2 1860]

KEOKUK county news. w O 13 1860+
Follows Life in the West. 1860-98? as Sigourney news
pub 1860+
IaDH My 1893+
IaHi O 20,29,N 23,D 14 1860[61]-S 1862;1905-06
NNHi Ag 5 1863;Mr 5 1873

LIFE in the west. w 1856-59||
Followed by Keokuk county news
IaDH Je 1856-Jl 1858[Ja-Ag 1859]
IaGG O 18 1859
IaHi [Ap 14-S 22 1859]

Sigourney NEWS. *See* Keokuk county news

Sigourney REVIEW. w Mr 1873+
pub Ap 1897+
IaHi Mr 15-Jl 5 1876

SIOUX CENTER

Sioux Center NEWS. w 1894+
1894-Ag 1930 as Sioux Center nieuwsblad
1894-1922? in Dutch; 1923?-Ag 1930 in Dutch and English
pub 1910+
IaHi 1905-13

Sioux Center NIEUWSBLAD. *See* Sioux Center news

SIOUX CITY

Sioux City INDUSTRIAL press. w 1877-78||
IaDH S 15,O 6 1877;Ja 12-Ap 2 1878

Sioux City IOWA eagle. w Jl 4 1857-O 15 1859||
Merged with Sioux City register
IaDH complete
IaHi Ja 8-O 8 1859
IaSc complete

IOWA times. w Mr 16-N 16 1860||
IaSc complete

IOWA weekly times. *See* Sioux City weekly times

Sioux City JOURNAL. w Ag 20 1864-1910||
IaDH 1864-Ja 1881;Mr 1886-95
IaHi O 1891-O 1892
IaSc Mr 24 1870-Ja 16 1873;Ja 22 1874-Ja 20,S 8 1887-Ja 10 1889
MWA Ag 31-S 7 1876
NbHi O 23 1879;Ap 21 1881;O 9 1890;F 23 1893

Sioux City JOURNAL. d Ap 19 1870+
pub 1870+
CLM F 16 1906
DLC My 16 1871-N 23 1872;Ja 25 1873-74;D 20 1894-99;My-Ag 1900;01+
IaDH My 1893-1933
IaHi Ag 1902-S 1907;08+
IaSc My 1892+
IaSh 1933+

Sioux City daily NEWS. d 1906-16||
IaDH Ja-Jl 1916

Sioux City ORACLE. w Mr 17 1894-Mr 16 1895||
DLC D 8 1894
IaSc complete

Sioux City REGISTER. w Jl 22 1858-71||
Follows Western independent (Sergeant's Bluff)
IaDH Jl 1858-N 1870
IaHi 1859[60]-Ap 1864
IaSc Ag 11 1858-Ag 11 1859

Sioux City REGISTER. d 1924-
IaSc Je 20-S 30 1924

REPUBLIKANEREN. w 1889-1902||
1889-Mr 1897 as Sioux City tidende
In Norwegian and Danish
IaDeL [N 1890-Ag,N 1892-N 1895]96-Je 6 1902
WHi O 12 1895-Ag 8 1896

SKANDIA. *See* Svenska tidningen och Skandia (Kansas City, Mo.)

SVEAS tidning. w O 25 1890-
In Swedish
MnHi 1890-F 28 1891

SVENSKA Amerikanska pressen. w 1891-92||
In Swedish
IRA 1891
MnHi Je 6 1891-Je 30 1892

SVENSKA monitoren. w Je 7 1895+
In Swedish
IRA 1895-1923
IaDH 1916-31
IaSc Last 6 months only
MnHi 1895+

Sioux City TIDENDE. *See* Republikaneren

Sioux City daily TIMES. d My 25 1869-Jl 1901||
Merged with Sioux City journal
Suspended from Mr 2 1872-Jl 1881
IaSc 1869-84
IaScJ 1884-1901
NjHi Ag 2 1871

Sioux City weekly TIMES. w Je 5 1869-91||
Title varies: Iowa weekly times
Suspended from F 1876-Jl 1881
IaDH 1869-F 1876;S 1882-Ja,O 1887-N 1891
IaHi My 13 1871-N 1873
IaSc Je 12 1869-My 4 1872;Je 1873-F 1876;Ag 25 1882-83
NbHi F 13,Mr 6 1875

Sioux City TRIBUNE. w Mr 24 1876-1904||?
IaDH 1876-85

Sioux City TRIBUNE. d Ja 1 1880+
F 21 1929 printed on corn-stalk stock
Je 17 1930 is 50th anniversary ed
CL F 21 1929
DLC 1898
IaDH D 19 1889;91-Jl 1918
IaHi O 1901-S 1910
IaLeU O 1930-Ag 1934
IaSc Ja-Mr,My 1893-Je,Ag 1910-Je,S 1922+
NN F 21 1929;Je 17 1930
TxGR Je 17 1930
WHi 1928

UNIONIST and public forum. w My 5 1927+
pub 1927+
IaSc current 6 months only

Sioux City VOLKSFREUND. w My 7 1885+
In German and English
IU N 29 1917-Je 1918
IaDH 1916+
IaSc current 6 months only

SLATER

Slater NEWS. w 1890+
pub 1890+

SOLDIER

Soldier SENTINEL. w 1916+
pub 1916+

SOLON

Solon ECONOMIST. w 1896+
1896-1922? as Economy
IaHi D 15 1904-06

ECONOMY. *See* Solon economist

SPENCER

CLAY county news. *See* Spencer news

CLAY county reporter. *See* Spencer reporter

Spencer HERALD. w 1891-Mr 1 1916||
United with Spencer news to form Spencer news-herald
IaDH Ap 1893-Ag 13 1915

IOWA (*Continued*)

SPENCER—*Continued*

Spencer NEWS-HERALD. w 1870+
1870-1909 as Clay county news; 1910-Mr 1 1916 Spencer news
pub 1870+
IaDH 1884-85;94-Mr 1 1916

Spencer REPORTER. w,d 1875+
1875-82 as Clay county reporter
IaDH Mr 1883+

SPIRIT LAKE

Spirit Lake BEACON. w S 6 1870+
pub N 1870+
IaDH F 1884—
IaHi F 1888-99;Jl 1903-06
MWA Ag 24 1876
NbHi Mr 28 1878

SPRINGVALE. *See* HUMBOLDT

STANHOPE

Stanhope MAIL. w 1894-1910||?
IaDH My 1894-1905

STANTON

Stanton CALL. w 1881+
IaDH 1916—

STATE CENTER

State Center ENTERPRISE. w 1871+
pub S 1916+
IaDH Ag 1901+
MWA N 8 1878
NbHi Ag 31,N 29 1878;Mr 28-Ap 4 1879

MARSHALLTOWN lance. w S 7-N 2 1934||
IaMars complete

STOCKPORT

Stockport NEWS. w 1900-24||
IaDH 1914-24

STORM LAKE

BUENA VISTA sentinel. w My 18 1877-D 30 1879||
IaSl complete

BUENA VISTA vedette. *See* Storm Lake register

Storm Lake PILOT-TRIBUNE. w O 26 1870+
1870-Ag 13 1896 as Storm Lake pilot
pub 1870+
IaDH 1870-O 1875;O 1878-90;95+
IaHi Mr 1903-06;O 1870-71
IaSl 1870+
IaSlB 1870-O 11 1876;O 17 1877-O 6 1880;O 12 1881-O 4 1883

Storm Lake REGISTER. w N 13 1885+
1885-Jl 2 1917 as Buena Vista vedette
IaDH 1895+
IaSl 1885-86;1913+

Storm Lake TRIBUNE. w Mr 26 1880-Ag 13 1896||
United with Storm Lake pilot to form Storm Lake pilot-tribune
IaDH My 1895-96
IaSl 1883-88
IaSlB Mr 22 1890-Mr 7 1891
IaSlP Ap 1880-88

STORY CITY

Story City HERALD. w 1890+
pub 1891+
IaDH 1916+

VISERGUTTEN. *See under* Canton, South Dakota

STRATFORD

Stratford COURIER. w 1891+
pub 1892+
IaDH 1916+
IaWc 1905-10

STRAWBERRY POINT

CLAYTON county press-journal. w 1874+
1874-94 as Strawberry Point press; 1895;-1915? Strawberry Point mail-press; 1916-28? Strawberry Point press
IaDH Ag 1901-19

Strawberry Point MAIL-PRESS. *See* Clayton county press-journal

Strawberry Point PRESS. *See* Clayton county press journal

STUART

Stuart HERALD. F 23 1871+
1871-O 1900 as Stuart locomotive
pub Mr 2 1871+
IaDH 1883-O 1884;94+

Stuart LOCOMOTIVE. *See* Stuart herald

Stuart NEWS. w 1887-1921||
IaDH 1916-My 1921

SUMNER

Sumner GAZETTE. w 1880+
pub 1880+

TABOR

Tabor BEACON. w 1881+
1881-86 as Tabor union
pub 1887+
IaDH Jl 1911+

NONCONFORMIST. w 1879-86||?
IaTaB Ag 5 1880
MWA D 8 1881

Tabor UNION. *See* Tabor beacon

TAMA

Tama FREE press. w 1880-1904||
IaDH Ap 1893-1904

Tama HERALD. *See* Tama news-herald

Tama NEWS-HERALD. w 1875+
1875-Jl 8 1925 as Tama herald
IaDH 1905+
IaTo Jl 31 1930+

THOMPSON

Thompson COURIER. w 1895+
1924-25 as Thompson journal
pub 1902-09;12-23[25]+

Thompson JOURNAL. *See* Thompson courier

THURMAN

Thurman TIMES. w 1906+
IaDH 1916+

TINGLEY

VINDICATOR. w 1888+
pub [1904+]
CU-B S 11 1890

TIPTON

Tipton ADVERTISER. w,sw N 12 1853+
Follows Cedar county news letter (Rochester). N 28 1853-Ja 19 1856 as Cedar county advertiser
sw O 1901-Ap 12 1907
IaDH My 1863-64;Mr 22 1883+
IaGG Ag 20 1859
IaHi D 1858-59;F 1860-[61]62;Ap-My 7,Jl 2 1863;64-[71-75]-Ag 1876;1905-06
IaT 1853+
NNHi Jl 16 1863;My 8 1873

CEDAR county advertiser. *See* Tipton advertiser

CEDAR county post. w Ag 30 1871-73||
IaHi complete

CEDAR democrat. w 1856-64||
IaHi Mr 26 1859-O 11 1860
MWA Je 13 1861

Tipton TIMES and Cedar county conservative. w Ap 6 1850-51||
DClWHi Je 1,Jl 6 1850

TITONKA

Titonka TOPIC. w Ja 26 1898+
pub 1898+
IaDH 1916+

TOLEDO

Toledo CHRONICLE. w 1867+
1867-72? as Tama county republican; S 1924-Jl 1925 Toledo chronicle-democrat
IaDH Ag 1871-80;My 1888-[90-95]Mr 1899+
IaHi Jl 1868-Je 19 1873
IaTo Jl 31 1930+

IOWA transcript. w Ap 21 1856-66||
1856-O 21 1858 as Toledo tribune
IaHi [F 1859-D 12 1861;62-66]

TAMA county democrat. *See* Tama county journal

TAMA county journal. w 1873-S 1924||
1873-O 18 1923 as Tama county democrat. United with Toledo chronicle to form Toledo chronicle-democrat, later Toledo chronicle
IaDH Ap 1878-79;Jl 1893-1924

TAMA county republican. *See* Toledo chronicle

Toledo TIMES. w 1874-81||?
IaDH 1878-80

Toledo TRIBUNE. *See* Iowa transcript

TRAER

Traer CLIPPER. *See* Traer star-clipper

Traer STAR-CLIPPER. w 1874+
1874-83 as Traer clipper
pub My 1878+
IaDH [Ap 1879-Ja 1881]82;D 1883-My 1887;88-[92-F 1896]
IaTo Ag 1930+

TREYNOR

Treynor RECORD. w 1898—
pub Jl 1913+

TRIPOLI

Tripoli LEADER. w 1894+
pub 1906+

TRURO

Truro ENTERPRISE. w 1892-1901||
IaDH [1900-01]

UNDERWOOD

Underwood TRIBUNE. w 1909-11||
IaDH O 1909-Je 1911

UTE

Ute INDEPENDENT. w Ja 24 1890+
pub 1910+

VAIL

CRAWFORD county observer. *See* Vail observer

Vail OBSERVER. w My 1 1878+
1878-1907 as Crawford county observer
pub 1878+
IaDH 1916+

VALLEY JUNCTION

BOOSTER-EXPRESS. w 1893—
1893-1929? as Valley express and booster
IaDH Jl 1904+

VALLEY express and booster. *See* Booster-express

VALPARAISO

REPUBLICAN extra. w
WHi N 18-D 2 1843

VAN HORN

BENTON county record. *See* Van Horn record

Van Horn ENTERPRISE. *See* Van Horn record

Van Horn RECORD. w 1891-1935||
1891-1902? as Van Horn enterprise; 1903?-14? Benton county record
IaDH 1917-18;Ag 1919-25

VICTOR

Victor INDEX. w 1885-1907||
IaDH Mr 1899-1907

Victor RECORD. w 1906+
IaDH 1908+

VILLISCA

Villisca weekly REVIEW. w 1871+
pub 1900+
NNHi Ja 3 1872

VINTON

BENTON county democrat. w O 2 1856-O 27 1859||
Suspended O? 1857-58
IaV complete

BENTON county herald. w 1878-85||
IaDH 1878-82;84-Je 1885

BENTON county herald. 1891-92. *See* Vinton review

Vinton EAGLE. w,sw Ja 10 1855-Mr 4 1926||
w 1855-81?
IaDH Je 1893-1926
IaGG D 13 1859
IaHi F 20 1858-[61]-Mr 1866;67-69;Mr 1870-Mr 1872;Mr 1873-74;Mr 1875-Mr 1876;77-87
IaV Ja 16 1856-Mr 15 1871

Vinton HERALD. *See* Vinton review

Vinton OBSERVER. *See* Vinton review

PEOPLE'S weekly journal. w D 19 1868-79||?
IaHi D 1869-Je 1871

Vinton REVIEW. w 1882-1919||
1882-89? as Vinton observer; 1890-94 Vinton herald (1891-92 Benton county herald)
IaHi 1898-[1909]-19

VOLGA CITY

Volga City NEWS. w 1914-D 1933||
Merged with Clayton county register (Elkader)
IaElkC complete

WALKER

Walker NEWS. w 1882+
pub [1882-99]+
IaDH 1893+

WAPELLO

Wapello INTELLIGENCER. w N 27 1850-60||
1850-53 as Louisa county times
IaBu My 31 1853-Jl 1855
IaHi My 14 1859-Ag 4 1860

LOUISA county record. 1870-94||?
United with Wapello republican to form Wapello record-republican, later Wapello republican
NbHi N 18 1880;Ja 6 1881

LOUISA county times. *See* Wapello intelligencer

Wapello RECORD-REPUBLICAN. *See* Wapello republican

IOWA (*Continued*)

WAPELLO—*Continued*

Wapello REPUBLICAN. w 1859+
1894-96? as Wapello record-republican; D 1923-24? Wapello republican and tribune
pub 1896+
IaDH [1893-96]+
IaHi [1861]Jl 8 1863-Ag 1870;1905-06

Wapello TRIBUNE. w 1898-N 1923||
United with Wapello republican to form Wapello republican and tribune, later Wapello republican
IaDH 1898-1913
IaWapR complete

WASHINGTON

ARGUS. w 1854-56||
IaWa Je 8 1854

Washington DEMOCRAT. w N 22 1860-66||?
IaHi 1860-Je 1866
IaWa Je 10 1862

Washington DEMOCRAT-INDEPENDENT. w 1878+
1878-Je? 1927 as Washington democrat
IaDH 1893-1918

Daily HUSTLER. *See* Evening journal

Evening JOURNAL. d 1893+
1893-96 as Daily hustler
pub 1893+
IaDH D 1915

Washington PRESS. *See* Washington county press

WASHINGTON county press. w Ap 9 1856-O 1918||
1856-66? as Washington press. Merged with Washington evening journal
IaDH Je 1893-1906;Ap 1910-17
IaHi 1856-[62-68]1903-07;10-18
IaWa 1863-1906;10-18
MWA Ag 8 1866
OClWHi F 22 1860

WATERLOO

BLACKHAWK courier. *See* Waterloo courier

Waterloo COURIER. w Ja 18 1859-1910||
Follows Cedar Falls banner (Cedar Falls). Ja 18-N 22 1859 as Blackhawk courier
pub complete
IaDH 1899-1909
IaHi 1859-60;D 1868-Mr 1872;1905-06
OClWHi My 30 1877

Waterloo daily COURIER. d D 13 1890+
Mr 10 1914-19? as Waterloo evening courier and daily reporter
pub 1890+
IaDH 1910-19;Jl 1922+
IaHi 1905+

Weekly IOWA state register and Waterloo herald. w D 15 1855-59||
IaHi [D 25 1858-S 19 1859]

IOWA state reporter. *See* Waterloo reporter

Waterloo REPORTER. w,sw My 13 1868-Mr 10 1914||
1868-1902 as Iowa state reporter. Merged with Waterloo courier
w 1868-98?
CSmH O 21 1868
IaDH My 1871-1902
IaHi [Ap 1869-My 1875]1902-Je 1904;05-Mr 1914
IaWC My 30 1871-F 1914
MWA N 9-16 1870
OClWHi My 30 1877

Waterloo daily REPORTER. d 1896-Mr 1914||
United with Waterloo evening courier to form Waterloo evening courier and daily reporter, later Waterloo daily courier
IaDH 1903-14
IaHi Jl 1904-06

Waterloo TIMES-TRIBUNE. *See* Waterloo tribune

Waterloo TRIBUNE. w,sw,d 1879-F 1931||
1901-22? as Waterloo times-tribune. Merged with Waterloo daily courier
IaWC 1901-31

WAUCOMA

Waucoma SENTINEL. w 1885-1932||
IaDH 1916-32

WAUKON

ALLAMAKEE herald. w F 26 1857-59||
1857? as Waukon journal
IaDH [F 26-N 25 1858]

ALLAMAKEE journal. *See under* Lansing

Waukon DEMOCRAT. w 1877+
IaDH 1901+
IaWau current 2 years only

Waukon JOURNAL. *See* Allamakee herald

NORTH IOWA journal. *See* Allamakee journal (Lansing)

Waukon REPUBLICAN and standard. w Ja 9 1868+
1868-1921 as Waukon standard
IaDH F 1884-86;89-90;S 1892-Ap 1920;21+
IaHi N 1870-S 1878;Mr 1885-1900;04-06

Waukon REPUBLICAN and standard. w 1877-1921||
1877-98? as Waukon democrat. United with Waukon standard to form Waukon republican and standard
IaDH N 1901-20

Waukon STANDARD. *See* Waukon republican and standard

WAVERLY

BREMER county argus. w Ja 1860-Ja 1861||
WHi Ag 23 1860

BREMER county independent. w 1867+
1867-70 as Democratic news; 1915-29 Independent-republican
pub 1867+
IaDH F 1893+
IaHi D 1893-1900;05-06

BREMER county phoenix. *See* Waverly republican

Waverly DEMOCRAT. w 1880+
pub 1880+
IaDH Je 1893+

DEMOCRATIC news. *See* Bremer county independent

INDEPENDENT-REPUBLICAN. *See* Bremer county independent

Waverly JOURNAL. w Je 16 1932+
pub 1932+

Waverly PHOENIX. w 1884-1923||
In German
IaDH 1916-23

Waverly REPUBLICAN. w Mr 5 1856-1914||
1856-66 as Bremer county phoenix
IaHi Ap 1868-N 1869;F 1886-87
WHi S 25 1873;O 4 1877

WAYLAND

Wayland NEWS. w 1893+
pub 1893+

WEBB

Webb RECORD. w 1900+
IaDH 1916+

WEBSTER CITY

Webster City ARGUS. w 1875-87||?
MWA Ag 29 1876

Webster City FREEMAN. d 1894-99||
United with Webster City tribune to form Webster City freeman-tribune, later Webster City freeman-journal

Webster City FREEMAN-JOURNAL. w,sw Je 29 1857+
1857-82 as Hamilton freeman; 1882-1925? Webster City freeman
Suspended S 1862-64
w 1857-1926?
pub 1885+
IaDH 1857-62[66]D 1877-Je 1879;81-Mr 1891; 92-1930
IaHi 1857-[59-61]-S 1862[My 1864-Ja 1874] 1905-06
IaWC 1857+
InRE Je 25 1873
MWA Ag 18 1866

Webster City FREEMAN-JOURNAL. d 1894+
1894-99 as Webster City tribune; 1899-Je 1917 Webster City freeman-tribune
pub Jl 1917+
IaDH N 1899+
IaWc Jl 1917+
WHi N 19 1902

Webster City FREEMAN-TRIBUNE. *See* Webster City freeman-journal

Webster City GRAPHIC. w 1884-91||
United with Webster City herald to form Graphic-herald

HAMILTON county journal. *See* Webster City journal

HAMILTON freeman. *See* Webster City freeman-journal (w,sw)

Webster City HERALD. w,d 1891-1915||
1892-1909 as Graphic herald
IaWc 1892;97;1901;08-15

Webster City JOURNAL. w 1894-1934||
1894-1902 as Hamilton county journal
IaDH My 1894-1930
IaWcJ 1896-1934

Webster City JOURNAL. d N 1902-Je 1917||
United with Webster City freeman-tribune to form Webster City freeman-journal
IaDH N 1902-06

Webster City daily NEWS. d Je 20 1920-Ja 25 1925||
IaDH 1921-24
IaWc complete

Webster City TRIBUNE. d *See* Webster City freeman-journal

Webster City TRIBUNE. w Jl 16 1886-Je 1917||
IaDH Ap 1893-1916
IaWc complete

WELLMAN

Wellman ADVANCE. w S 13 1889+
pub 1889+
IaDH 1916+

WELLSBURG

Wellsburg HERALD. w 1906+
IaDH 1931+

WESLEY

Wesley NEWS. w 1898-Je 1903||
United with Wesley world to form News world
IaWeN 1899-1903

NEWS-WORLD. w 1891+
1891-99 as Wesley reporter; 1900-Je 1903 Wesley world
pub 1911+

Wesley REPORTER. *See* News-world

Wesley WORLD. *See* News-world

WEST BEND

West Bend JOURNAL. w 1888+
pub 1915+
IaDH 1916+

WEST BRANCH

LOCAL record. *See* West Branch times

West Branch TIMES. w 1878+
1878-89 as Local record
pub O 3 1878+
IaDH 1890;93+
IaHi 1890-1900;N 1903-05
IaWb Ag 30 1928+

WEST LIBERTY

West Liberty ENTERPRISE. w Ap 4 1868-92||?
IaWl Ap 4 1868

West Liberty INDEX. w 1880+
1880-94 as Wapsie index
IaDH 1887-91;93-Ag 1894;95-1918

WAPSIE index. *See* West Liberty index

WEST MITCHELL

MITCHELL county news. *See* Osage news (Osage)

MITCHELL county press. *See* Mitchell county press and Osage news (Osage)

WEST POINT

West Point BEE. w 1893+
pub 1900+
IaDH 1916+

WEST SIDE

West Side JOURNAL. w 1891+
pub 1900+
IaDH 1916+

WEST UNION

ARGO-GAZETTE. w 1881+
1881-1910 as West Union argo
IaDH F 1901+
IaHi 1905-06
WHi D 1 1886

FAYETTE county pioneer. w O 21 1853-64||
Followed by Fayette county union
Suspended from N 8-D 6 1854
IaHi Mr 28 1859-Je 1864

AYETTE county union. w Ja 4 1866+
Follows Fayette county pioneer
IaDH 1916+
IaHi Ag 1870-79;S 1885-88
WHi D 7-21 1886

West Union GAZETTE. w 1867-1910||
1867-79? as Republican gazette. United with West Union argo to form Argo-gazette
IaDH 1868-77;Mr 1883-[94]-1909

IOWA public record. w 1863-
MWA D 20 1865

PUBLIC review. w Mr 3 1859-Mr? 1861||
Followed by Republican era
IaGG Ag 18,O 13 1859
IaHi Jl 28,Ag 11,O 6 1859;Ja 24-31,F 14-Mr 7,28 1860

REPUBLICAN era. w Ap 10 1861-62||
Follows Public review

REPUBLICAN gazette. *See* West Union gazette

WESTERN

Western GAZETTE. w 1869-74||?
IaHi S 16 1869-Ja 1870

WESTERN COLLEGE

Western College ADVOCATE. *See* Western College reporter

Western College REPORTER. m,sm Je 1858-
1858-60? as Western College advocate
m 1858-63?
IaHi 1859;Ja-F,Ap-Jl 1860;Jl,S 15,N 1,15,D 1, 15 1861-S 1863;Ag 6 1864-Ja 1 1865

WESTGATE

Westgate HERALD. w 1897-1917||
IaDH 1916-17

IOWA (*Continued*)

WHAT CHEER

What Cheer CHRONICLE. w 1888-Mr 7 1929||
United with What Cheer patriot to form What Cheer patriot-chronicle

What Cheer PATRIOT-CHRONICLE. w 1880+
1880-Mr 7 1929 as What Cheer patriot
IaDH My 1883-92;F 1893-1919
IaHi O-D 1905

What Cheer REPORTER. w 1882-1905||
IaDH 1884-1905

WHEATLAND

CLINTON county advocate. w O 1864-
Follows Wheatland times
IaHi [N 3 1864-Je 6 1867]
MWA F 21 1867

Wheatland GAZETTE. w My 1888+
pub 1888+
IaDH My 1894-F,Ag 1913+

Wheatland TIMES. w F 4 1860-64||
Followed by Clinton county advocate
IaHi [O 18 1860-Je 1864]
MHi Jl 26 1860

WHITING

Whiting ARGUS. w 1908+
IaWh [1915-20;22-30]32+

WILLIAMS

Williams ENTERPRISE. w 1897+
1897-1912? as Williams wasp
IaWc 1898-1910

Williams WASP. *See* Williams enterprise

WILLIAMSBURG

IOWA county tribune. w 1895-1903||
United with Williamsburg journal to form Williamsburg journal-tribune

Williamsburg JOURNAL-TRIBUNE. w 1884+
1884-1903 as Williamsburg journal
IaDH N 1903+

WILTON JUNCTION

Wilton ADVOCATE. w S 20 1867+
1867-76? as Wilton chronicle; 1877?-99 Wilton review; 1899-1922? Wilton advocate review
DLC O 23 1873
IaHi [1867-Ag 12 1869]

Wilton ADVOCATE. w 1893-99||?
United with Wilton review to form Wilton advocate review, later Wilton advocate

Wilton ADVOCATE review. *See* Wilton advocate

Wilton CHRONICLE. *See* Wilton advocate

Wilton REVIEW. *See* Wilton advocate

WINFIELD

Winfield BEACON. w 1881+
IaDH 1922+

WINTERSET

HAWKEYE flag. *See* Winterset Madisonian

IOWA pilot. *See* Winterset Madisonian

MADISON county reporter. *See* Winterset reporter

MADISON county review. *See* Winterset review

Winterset MADISONIAN. w N 6 1856+
1856-57 as Iowa pilot; 1857-60 Winterset Madisonian; 1860-65 Hawkeye flag
pub [1860-70]+
IaDH 1884+
IaHi [1861]Ag-D 1864;Ja 13-F 10 1865;1904-06
IaWi S 1928+
OClWHi Jl 6 1871;N 13 1880

Winterset NEWS. w S 26 1868+
1868-71 as Winterset sun
pub 1886-93;96+
IaDH 1923—
IaHi Je 21-O 18 1873
IaWi Ag 1928+

Winterset REPORTER. w 1885-
1904?-08? as Madison county reporter
IaDH My 1898-1916
IaHi F 1905-06

Winterset REVIEW. w 1891-1901||
1891-92? as Madison county review
IaDH 1894-Jl 1901

Winterset SUN. *See* Winterset news

WINTHROP

Winthrop NEWS. w 1890+
1890-1900 as Winthrop review
pub [1890+]

Winthrop REVIEW. *See* Winthrop news

WOODBINE

Woodbine TWINER. w 1879+
IaDH 1897+
IaWo 1908+

WOODWARD

Woodward ENTERPRISE. w 1889+
pub 1930+

WYOMING

Wyoming JOURNAL. w 1871—
pub 1873—
IaDH 1893+

YALE

Yale TRIBUNE. w 1897-1911||
IaDH Je 1909-My 1911
IaHulS 1908-11

YARMOUTH

Yarmouth LETTER. w F 28 1894-Ja 9 1895||
IaMeN complete

KANSAS

ABBYVILLE

Abbyville TRIBUNE. w
KHi Ag 12 1886-Mr 3 1887

ABILENE

ALLIANCE monitor. *See* Monitor-herald

Abilene CHRONICLE. w,tw 1870-1933||
1870-72 as Weekly chronicle; 1873? Chronicle-journal; 1874?-Ap 23 1886 Dickinson county chronicle
w 1870-1931?
pub [1929-D 16 1933]
KAbR [1870]-73
KHi Mr 3,Ap 21,My 12-19,S 1,15 1870;Jl 16 1875-Jl 1933
MWA F 6 1874

Abilene daily CHRONICLE. d 1896+
Suspended from 1928-Jl 1933
pub [1904-28]D 1933+
KHi S 1897-Jl 14 1928;Jl 30 1933+

Abilene DEMOCRAT. w 1880-82||?
KHi 1880-Mr 1 1882

Abilene DEMOCRAT. w 1897?-1913||?
Merged with Dickinson county news
KHi D 30 1898-Ja 9 1913

DICKINSON county chronicle. *See* Abilene chronicle

DICKINSON county news. w 1888-1918||?
KHi N 22 1888-N 1918

Abilene DISPATCH. w 1886?-95||?
KHi D 14 1893-My 23 1895

Abilene GAZETTE. w My 27 1876?-Ap 18 1889||
1876?-Ap 26 1878 as Kansas gazette
1876?-Jl 1877 pub in Enterprise
KAbR Ap 27 1876-Jl 1877;78-Je 13 1884
KHi Ap 27 1876-89

Abilene GAZETTE. d Ap 1885-88||?
KHi My 6 1885-N 25 1888

Abilene HERALD. w 1892-S 15 1893||
United with Alliance monitor to form Monitor-herald
KHi D 16 1892-93

HOME rule. w My 9 1907-08||?
KHi My 16 1907-Mr 1908
OkHi 1907[08]

Abilene JOURNAL. w 1873||
United with Weekly chronicle to form Chronicle-journal, later Abilene chronicle

KANSAS gazette. *See* Abilene gazette

MONITOR-HERALD. w 1890-98||?
1890-S 15 1893 as Alliance monitor
KHi Jl 31 1890-98

Abilene REFLECTOR. w Ag 1883+
pub 1883+
KHi S 1883-F 21 1935

Abilene REFLECTOR. d My 2 1887+
pub 1887+
KAb [1908-17;26]+
KHi My 9 1887+

ADA

Ada RECORDER. w 1909-11||?
KHi Je 1909-Ja 5 1911

ADMIRE

FREE PRESS. w 1886-88||?
KHi 1887-Ap 1888

Admire INDEPENDENT. w 1891-93||?
KHi D 11 1891-S 15 1893

Admire JOURNAL. w 1895-97||?
KHi N 1895-Jl 1897

NORTHERN star. w 1909-17||?
KHi D 12 1912-N 22 1917

AETNA

Aetna CLARION. w 1885-87||?
KHi S 1885-S 22 1887

AGRA

GRAPHIC. *See under* Kirwin

KANSAS razoo. w 1896-98||?
KHi D 1896-Je 17 1898

Agra NEWS. w 1893-95||?
KHi Jl 22 1893-S 20 1895

POLITICIAN. w 1890||?
KHi Ja 16-Je 13 1890

Agra SENTINEL. w D 1903+
KHi Ja 21 1904+

ALBERT

Albert NEWS. w 1925-Ap 26 1933||
Merged with Pawnee Rock herald (Pawnee Rock)
KHi F 1926-33

ALDEN

Alden HERALD. w 1888||?
KHi My 19-S 1888

Alden JOURNAL. w Je 8 1905-18||?
KHi Jl 27 1905-S 17 1908;O 1914-F 1918

ALEXANDER

Alexander BOOSTER. w N 24 1931-
KHi 1931-O 4 1935

ALLEN

Allen ENTERPRISE. *See* Northern Lyon county journal

Allen HERALD. w 1894-97||?
KHi N 16 1894-Jl 15 1897

Allen JOURNAL. *See* Northern Lyon county journal

NORTHERN Lyon county journal. w 1887+
F 4 1900-13? as Allen enterprise; Ja?-F 13 1914 Allen journal
KHi Ag 1897+

Allen TIDINGS. *See* Emporia times (Emporia)

ALLIANCE. *See* CHANUTE

ALLISON

Allison BREEZE. *See* Oberlin times (Oberlin)

Allison TIMES. *See* Oberlin times (Oberlin)

ALMA

Alma BLADE. w 1873?-78||?
KHi Mr 14 1877-F 20 1878

Alma ENTERPRISE. w O 11 1884+
pub 1884+
KHi 1884+

HOME weekly. *See under* Eskridge

Alma NEWS. w 1869-94||?
1869-Mr 9 1871 as Wabaunsee county herald; Mr 16-1872? Alma weekly union; 1873?-89? Wabaunsee county news
KHi Ap 1869-My 8 1872;73-Ja 4 1894

Alma SIGNAL. w S 7 1888+
pub 1888+
KHi 1889+

Alma weekly UNION. *See* Alma news

WABAUNSEE county herald. 1869-71 *See* Alma news

WABAUNSEE county herald. w Ap 1 1869-81||?
1869-Mr 2 1871 as Alma weekly union
KHi 1869-S 1881

WABAUNSEE county news. *See* Alma news

ALMENA

Almena ADVANCE. *See* Farmers' advance (Norton)

Almena ENTERPRISE. w 1894||?
KHi Ap-N 1 1894

Almena LANTERN. w 1895-1900||?
KHi O 8 1896-D 6 1900

NORTON county plaindealer. *See* Plaindealer

PLAINDEALER. w 1887+
1898?-1912? as Norton county plaindealer
KHi F 1888-N 1911;Je 30 1927+

Almena STAR. w 1885-89||?
KHi D 17 1885-Je 9,S 22 1887-F 8 1889

KANSAS (*Continued*)

ALTA VISTA

Alta Vista BUGLE. w 1889-90||?
KHi Je 1889-Ja 3 1890

Alta Vista JOURNAL. w Je 9 1899+
KHi 1899+

Alta Vista RECORD. w 1890-95||?
KHi Ap 17 1890-D 17 1895

Alta Vista REGISTER. w 1887-89||?
KHi Je 16 1887-Mr 1889

ALTAMONT

Altamont GAZETTE. w 1895||?
KHi Ja 25-O 1895

Saturday ITEM. w 1896-97||?
KHi Ag 29 1896-N 1897

Altamont JOURNAL. w 1903+
KHi F 16 1905+

PILOT. w 1902-04||?
1902? pub in Oswego
KHi F 1903-04

Altamont SENTINEL. w 1883-90||?
KHi Ap 28 1886-Jl 16 1890

WESTERN world. *See under* Parsons

WHITE banner. w 1894-1902||?
1894? pub in Wilsonton
KHi Jl 1894-Jl 1902

ALTON

To 1885 as Bull City

BULL CITY post. w 1880||?
KHi Ja 22-Je 24 1880

Alton EMPIRE. w 1880+
1880-Je 1881 as Mitchell county key (Glen Elder) Ag? 1881-Ja 11? 1883 Osborne county key; Ja 18 1883-O 30 1895 Western empire
KHi Ap 15 1880+

OSBORNE county key. *See* Alton empire

WESTERN empire. *See* Alton empire

ALTOONA

Altoona ADVOCATE. w 1886-87||?
KHi Ag 27 1886-N 4 1887

Altoona JOURNAL. w 1887-1903||
Merged with Wilson county sun (Neodesha)
KHi D 23 1887-Jl 24 1903

Altoona MIRROR. w 1905-Mr 31? 1908||
Followed by Toronto record (Toronto)
KHi Jl 27 1905-Mr 1908

Altoona TRIBUNE. w 1903+
KHi Ja 19 1905+

AMERICUS

Americus GREETING. w Ag 22? 1890+
Suspended Ap 1892-Jl 1893
KHi S 12 1890+

Americus HERALD. w
KHi D 1880-82

Americus LEDGER. w 1885-89||?
KHi Mr 14 1885-89

Americus SENTINEL. w
KHi My 25 1900-Ja 1901

AMES

Ames ADVANCE. w 1885-86||?
KHi Je 15 1885-S 17 1886

Ames BUREAU. w
KHi F 18-O 1 1887

Ames COURIER. w 1887?-88||?
KHi Mr 23-Je 1888

ANDALE

Andale GLOBE. w 1911-23||?
KHi N 15 1911-My 10 1923

Andale TIMES. w 1925+
KHi Ag 26 1927-Mr 9 1934

ANTHONY

Anthony BOOSTER. w
KHi N 1931-My 8 1933

Weekly BULLETIN. w 1884-O 1925||
1884-O 2 1891 as Harper county enterprise. United with Anthony republican to form Anthony republican-bulletin, later Anthony republican
Suspended from Mr 1899-F 1900
KHi Mr 13 1885-O 1 1925

Daily BULLETIN. d Mr 7-O 24 1904||
KHi complete

Anthony BULLETIN. d 1924-25||?
KHi Ag 21 1924-Ja 1925

Anthony FREE PRESS. d Ap 25 1887-
KHi 1887-88

Anthony FREE PRESS. w Ap 28 1887-
KHi 1887-88

HARPER county democrat. w 1886-87||?
KHi Mr 27 1886-Ap 21 1887

HARPER county enterprise. *See* Weekly bulletin

Anthony HERALD. w
KHi Ja 14-My 8 1886

Anthony JOURNAL. w 1878-84||?
KHi Ag 22 1878-Ja 24 1884

Anthony JOURNAL. d 1887-88||?
KHi Ap 16-S 12 1888

Anthony JOURNAL. w 1888-95||?
KHi Ap 27 1888-95

Anthony REPUBLICAN. w Je 6 1878+
N 1925?-32? as Anthony republican-bulletin
pub 1878+
KHi O 9 1879+

Daily REPUBLICAN. d 1886-89||
KHi My 26 1886-Je 11 1889

Anthony TIMES. d,w 1932?+
d 1932?-My 1933
KHi Jl 1932+

WESTLAND home. w
KHi N 8 1904-O 24 1905

APPLETON

Appleton ERA. w 1886-87||?
KHi 1886-87

APPOMATTOX

STANDARD. w 1887-88||?
1887? pub in Cincinnati
KHi D 24 1887-N 3 1888

ARCADIA

ARCADIAN. w 1888||?
KHi Jl 14-D 1888

CRAWFORD county times. *See* Arcadia times

Arcadia DEMOCRAT. *See* Arcadia news

Arcadia JOURNAL. w Je? 1909+
1909-N 26 1915 as Arcadia sunlight
KHi O 15 1909+

Arcadia NEWS. w 1888-98||?
1888-Ag 7 1890 as Arcadia democrat
KHi S 1888-N 3 1898

Arcadia RECORD. w 1903-04||?
KHi My 22 1903-Mr 25 1904

Arcadia REPORTER. w 1882-88||?
KHi S 21 1882-Ag 18 1888

Arcadia SUNLIGHT. *See* Arcadia journal

Arcadia TIMES. w 1882?-1909||?
1882?-1903? as Crawford county times
KHi S 10 1896-S 2 1909

ARGENTINE

Papers published in Argentine are listed under Kansas City

ARGONIA

ARGOSY. w O 9? 1913+
KHi O 23 1913+

Argonia CLIPPER. w 1884-1914||?
KHi Mr 8 1884-1914

PEOPLE'S press. *See* Milan press (Milan)

Argonia VOICE. w
KHi Mr 16 1894-F 1895

ARKALON

Arkalon NEWS. *See* Southwest daily times (Liberal)

ARKANSAS CITY

ARK light. w 1917?+
KHi S 17 1931+

ARKANSAS VALLEY democrat. w Jl 25 1879-1909||?
United with Arkansas City X-rays to form X-rays-democrat (later pub in Topeka)
CoU 1903;Ja-Jl 1905
KArM 1879-95
KHi Ag 1879-S 1909

BORDER bulletin. d
KHi Jl 27-O 1892

CANAL CITY dispatch. w 1887-98||?
KHi 1887-Ap 1898
—d ed *See* Evening dispatch

CHEROKEE STRIP guide. *See* Oklahoma state guide (Ponca City, Oklahoma)

Evening DISPATCH. d My 12? 1887-94||?
Ap 4 1888-Ap 7 1889 as Canal City dispatch
KHi My 13 1887-Ja 1894
OkHi [1893]
—w ed *See* Canal City dispatch

Arkansas City ENQUIRER. w 1898-1905||?
United with Gate City journal to form Gate City journal and enquirer, later Gate City journal
KHi Ap 1900-Ja 20 1905

FAIR play. w 1888-93||?
KHi Je 14 1888-Ja 6 1893

GATE CITY journal. w 1891-1908||?
1905?-06? as Gate City journal and enquirer
KHi Ja 20 1894-F 14 1908

Arkansas City NEWS. d 1911-23||?
KHi Ap 12 1911-Ap 26 1921

OKLAHOMA war chief. *See under* Caldwell

PEOPLE'S leader. w
KHi My 30-O 1891

Arkansas City REPORTER. d 1895||?
KHi Je 30-D 1895

Arkansas City REPUBLICAN. w 1884-Ap 2 1887||
United with Arkansas City traveler to form Weekly republican traveler
KHi F 16 1884-87

Daily REPUBLICAN. *See* Arkansas City daily traveler

Weekly REPUBLICAN traveler. w 1870-1908||
1870-Ap 2 1887 as Arkansas City traveler
KHi Ja 26 1876-Ja 2 1908
OClWHi Je 3 1887

Arkansas City SEARCHLIGHT. w 1905-07||?
KHi Mr 1906-My 3 1907

Arkansas City STAR. w 1896||?
KHi Ja 10-Je 12 1896

TRADERS exchange. w 1898-1900||?
KHi Jl 15 1898-Mr 1900

Arkansas City daily TRAVELER. d 1886+
1886-Ap 9 1887 as Daily republican; Ap 11 1887-Ja 31 1888 Daily republican-traveler
pub [1893]+
KHi Ag 14,N 22 1886+

Arkansas City TRAVELER. *See* Weekly republican traveler

Arkansas City TRIBUNE. w My? 1924+
pub 1929+
KHi Ap 11 1929+

Arkansas City X-RAYS. d Je 1? 1903-11||?
KHi Je 2 1903-Ap 11 1911

X-RAYS-DEMOCRAT. *See under* Topeka

ARLINGTON

Arlington ENTERPRISE. w 1885+
KHi Ap 1886+

ARMA

Arma RECORD. w Je 24 1915+
KHi 1915+

ARMOURDALE

Papers published in Armourdale are listed under Kansas City

ARRINGTON

Arrington TIMES and Atchison county times. w 1896-97||?
KHi My 28 1896-Mr 19 1897

ARTESIAN CITY

HORNET.
pub at Spring Lake
KHi Je 1885-N 1889

ASH GROVE

Ash Grove GAZETTE. w 1917?-
KHi Ja 17-Jl 11 1918

ASHLAND

CLARK county citizen. w
KHi N 29 1889-Ap 11 1890

CLARK county clipper. w S 18 1884+
Mr 2 1911-Je 23 1927 as Ashland clipper
pub O 1884+
KHi S 25 1884+

CLARK county republican. 1888-89 *See under* Minneola

CLARK county republican. w 1909-10||
Merged with Clark county clipper
KHi S 16 1909-Mr 1910

Ashland CLIPPER. *See* Clark county clipper

Ashland HERALD. w 1885-88||?
1885-86? as Ashland republican herald
KHi N 1885-88

Ashland JOURNAL. w 1886-97||
Merged with Clark county clipper
KHi O 8 1886-Ja 21 1897

Ashland LEADER. w 1886-89||?
KHi F 15-Ap 5 1889

Ashland LEADER. w 1907-08||?
KHi Ag 23 1907-D 24 1908

Ashland REPUBLICAN herald. *See* Ashland herald

ASSARIA

Assaria ARGUS. w 1887-90||?
KHi F 1887-My 23 1890

ATCHISON

ATCHISON county graphic. *See* Graphic

ATCHISONIAN. w 1877||?
KHi Mr 24-My 1877

KANSAS (*Continued*)

ATCHISON—*Continued*

Atchison BANNER. w 1878-79||?
In German
KHi Mr 1878-Jl 12 1879

Atchison BLADE. w 1892-94||?
KHi Jl 23 1892-Ja 20 1894

Weekly BULLETIN. w Je 20 1861-
DLC Je,Ag 8,22-29 1861
KHi Je 27-Jl 18,Ag 2-15 1861

Atchison BULLETIN. tw
KHi Je 20 1861

Sunday morning CALL. *See* Western mercury

Atchison CHAMPION. w F 3 1855-1909||?
1855-F 10 1858 as Squatter sovereign; F 20 1858-Ag 10? 1868 Freedom's champion; Ag 11 1868-73 Atchison champion and press
DLC 1855-Ap 20 1857;Mr 2,My 25,Ag 24,S 28, D 28 1861
KHi 1855-D 5 1857;F 20 1858-F 3 1861;Mr 13, Ap 6,Je 29,Ag 3,17,D 28 1861;F 14 1862-Ja 1863;Ag 15 1868-Je 25 1909
MB S 11 1858
MHi O 19 1861
MWA F 15 1866
NNHi Je 27 1863
WHi S 12 1857;F 20 1858-O 15 1870;Mr 1871-Je 16 1892

Atchison daily CHAMPION. d 1865-1917||?
1868-71? as Atchison daily champion and press
Suspended from Ag 1901-My 1907
DLC Je 30,Ag 25-26,S 28,O 30,N 26,D 13,18 1868;S 17 1880
InRE N 16 1878
KHi N 6,15,16 1873;F 10-11,28,Je 17,Jl 7,Ag 25,S 13,O 17,D 3,18 1874;Ja 1,12,31,F 2,Jl 4,6 1875;Jl 1876-Mr 15 1917
MWA Mr 22 1866;Ja 1 1873;My 24 1878
N S 17 1880
WHi Mr 22 1865-Mr 21,Ag 11 1868-Je 12 1892

Der Atchison COURIER. *See* Topeka courier (Topeka)

Sunday morning FACTS. w
KHi S 1883-F 3 1884

Atchison daily FREE PRESS. d 1864-Ag 1868||
United with Freedom's champion to form Atchison daily champion and press, later Atchison daily champion
DLC My 7 1866-My 8 1867
KHi My 8 1865-Ag 8 1868
NNHi Je 6 1865
WHi [O 3 1864-65]My 7 1866-Ag 8 1868

Weekly FREE PRESS. w 1864-Ag 8 1868||
United with Freedom's champion to form Atchison champion and press, later Atchison champion
DLC My 12 1866-My 2 1868
KHi Je 22 1865-68
WHi [Je 8 1865-My 5 1866]

FREEDOM'S champion. *See* Atchison champion

Atchison daily GLOBE. d D 1877+
1877 as Little globe
D 8 1927 is 50th anniversary ed
pub 1878+
IU F-Jl 19?;S 12-O 20 1924;N 9 1925;Ap 15 1926
KA 1928+
KHi Mr 29 1878+
MWA D 8 1927

Atchison GLOBE. w 1878-1933||?
KHi Jl 16 1908-Je 17 1926

GRAPHIC. w D 12 1887-Ja 10 1894||
1887-S 12 1891 as Effingham times; S 26 1891-S 22 1892? Atchison county graphic. Merged with New leaf (Effingham)
1887-S 22 1892 pub in Effingham
KHi complete

Atchison JOURNAL. w,d N 29? 1880-82||?
w 1880?
In German
KHi Ap 19 1881-My 20 1882

KANSAS staats anzeiger. w 1879-1915||?
1879-F? 1881 pub in Topeka;1886-Ja 1895 in Wichita
In German
KHi Ag 28 1879-F,Jl 1881-Je 20 1913

KANSAS statesman. w F 15-O 11 1901||
Merged with Atchison champion
KHi complete

KANSAS telegraph. w D 23 1880-
In German
KHi 1880-Je 18 1881

KANSAS zeitung. w Jl 15? 1857-
In German
KHi Jl 22 1857-N 6 1858
MBAt [Ag 26 1857-Jl 3 1858]

LITTLE globe. *See* Atchison daily globe

Atchison PATRIOT. w O 25 1867-96||?
DLC Ja 15 1876-N 1877
KA D 11 1875-O 14 1876
KHi S 24,N 12,D 10-17 1870;Mr 28 1874-Ap 4 1896

Daily Atchison PATRIOT. *See* Atchison morning star and daily patriot

PUBLIC ledger w 1880-81||?
KHi Ag 19,O 30 1880

SQUATTER sovereign. *See* Atchison champion

Atchison morning STAR and daily patriot. d S 7 1868-96||?
Follows Atchison real estate and insurance bulletin (not in this list) 1868-O 11 1895 as Daily Atchison patriot
KA S-O 17 1868
KHi N 17 1873;S 23,O 19 1874;Ja 11-Jl,O 21 1876-Ap 21 1877;Jl 1879-F 23 1896
—w ed *See* Atchison patriot

Atchison TIMES. w 1887-91||?
KHi F 9 1887-Ja 1891

Daily TIMES. d
KHi Jl 11 1887-N 1 1889

Atchison UNION. w Je? 1859-
DLC Mr 31 1860
KHi [Je 4 1859-Je 22 1861]

WESTERN mercury. w 1880-86||?
1880-N 1883 as Sunday morning call
KHi F 1880-Ja 1886

ATHOL

Athol NEWS. w 1888-89||?
KHi N 24 1888-89

Athol NEWS. w
KHi N 30 1905-Jl 1906

PEOPLE'S friend. w 1885-88||?
1885-86? pub in Reamsville
KHi O 27 1887-O 1888

Athol RECORD. See Smith county review (Smith Center)

Athol REVIEW. *See* Smith county review (Smith Center)

ATLANTA

Atlanta CRICKET. w
KHi O 1888-Je 1889

Atlanta JOURNAL. w 1907?-19||?
KHi O 21 1909-Ap 2 1914

Atlanta NEWS and record. w 1904||?
Early issues as Atlanta record
KHi F 18-Ag 5 1904

Atlanta RECORD. *See* Atlanta news and record

ATTICA

Attica ADVOCATE. d Mr 14 1887-
KHi Mr-Je 13 1887

Attica ADVOCATE. w *See* Harper advocate (Harper)

Attica BULLETIN. w 1886-88||?
KHi S 1886-Je 9 1888

Attica INDEPENDENT. w Ag 23 1895—
KHi 1895+

Attica TRIBUNE. w 1891-95||?
KHi D 1891-Ap 20 1895

ATWOOD

CITIZEN-PATRIOT. w S 3 1880+
1880-Ja 4 1911 as Republican citizen
KHi S 10 1880-Ja,Ap 1883+

Atwood DEMOCRAT. w 1894||?
KHi Jl 20-N 2 1894

Atwood JOURNAL. w 1884?-89||?
KHi Ap 25 1888-O 1889

Atwood JOURNAL. w
KHi 1898-Ja 7 1899

Atwood PATRIOT. w 1885-1912||
1885-Ag 30 1888 as Celia enterprise (Celia); S 6 1888-Ag 13 1891 McDonald times (McDonald); Ag 20 1891-Je 8 1894 Atwood times. United with Republican citizen to form Citizen-patriot
KHi D 12 1885-O 14 1909

Atwood PIONEER. w 1879-80||?
KHi O 23 1879-D 11 1880

RAWLINS county democrat. w 1885-94||
Merged with Atwood patriot
Suspended from O 30 1889-F 7 1890
F 8 1888-O 23 1889 pub in Blakeman
KHi S 30 1885-Je 8 1894

RAWLINS county pioneer. w
KHi Ja-Ag 23 1882

REPUBLICAN citizen. *See* Citizen-patriot

SQUARE deal. w D 22 1905-34||?
KHi 1905-[S 1923-Ag 16 1934]

Atwood TIMES. *See* Atwood patriot

AUGUSTA

Augusta ADVANCE. *See* Augusta news 1880-86

Augusta BUGLE. w 1889-1919||?
1889-Jl 31 1890 as Augusta news; Ag 7 1890-1909? Industrial advocate; 1910?-O 7 1913 Advocate; O 14 1913-F 4 1915 Butler county democrat
Ag 7 1890-F 4 1915 pub in El Dorado
KHi O 25 1889-Ja 9 1919
—d ed *See* Industrial advocate (El Dorado)

Augusta ELECTRIC light. *See* Augusta news 1880-86

Augusta GAZETTE. w Jl 15 1892-D 25 1908||
KHi complete

Augusta daily GAZETTE. d 1902+
pub D 1928+
KHi D 18 1903-Jl 1 1918;O 6 1917-Jl 17 1926; 27+

Augusta GAZETTE. sw 1918?-27||?
KHi Jl 5 1918-O 3 1919;Jl 1926-Ja 27 1927

Augusta JOURNAL. w Ap 14? 1887+
KHi S 15 1887-Mr 6 1919;Ap 29 1932+

Augusta JOURNAL. d S 17 1907-N 30 1909||
KHi complete

Augusta NEWS. w 1880-86||?
1880-F? 1883 as Augusta republican; Mr? 1883-Je? 1884 Augusta advance; Jl? 1884-Jl 1886 Augusta electric light
KHi Je 16 1880-F,Ap 25 1883-Je,Jl 24 1884-N 13 1886

Augusta NEWS. 1889-90 *See* Augusta bugle

Augusta PRESS. w 1894?-97||?
KHi 1894-N 4 1897

Augusta REPUBLICAN. w 1871?-75||?
KHi S 25 1873-75

Augusta REPUBLICAN. 1880-83 *See* Augusta news 1880-86

SOUTHERN KANSAS gazette. w 1873-Je 30 1887||
Merged with Augusta journal
KHi 1876-87

AUGUSTINE

Augustine HERALD. w 1887-91||?
KHi Ag 31 1887-Ap 1891

AURORA

Aurora BEACON. w 1847?-
N Ap 28 1853

Aurora NEWS. w 1892-94||?
KHi N 23 1892-Ja 1894

Aurora SEARCHLIGHT. w,bw Je 3 1920-35||?
w 1920-24?
KHi 1920-Ap 18 1935

AVILLA

COMANCHE county citizen. w 1885-87||?
KHi Ja 16 1885-Ja 21 1887

Avilla DEMOCRAT. w 1886-87||?
KHi O 1886-My 6 1887

AXTELL

Axtell ANCHOR. w 1883-1908||
Merged with Axtell standard
KHi O 18 1883-S 4 1908

Axtell STANDARD. w N 4? 1898+
KHi N 11 1898+

Axtell VISITOR. w 1882-84||?
KHi Ag 9 1883-Jl 1884

BALA CITY

Bala City ADVANCE. w 1890-91||?
KHi My 24 1890-F 14 1891

BALDWIN

Baldwin BEE. w 1896-98||?
KHi Ag 13 1896-Ag 18 1898

Baldwin CRITERION. *See* Baldwin ledger

Baldwin LEDGER. w N 29 1883+
1883-Ap 23 1885 as Baldwin criterion
CoU 1899-My 1910
KBB [1885-97]-[1903]-[05]-[07]-25[27]+
KHi 1883+

Baldwin REPUBLICAN. w Mr? 1901-11||
KBB [1901-09]-Mr 24 1911
KHi Ap 1901-11

Baldwin VISITOR. w 1884-Ap 24 1885||
United with Baldwin criterion to form Baldwin ledger
KHi Jl 11 1884-Ap 24 1885

YOUNG America. w
KHi 1864-Ap 24 1865

BANCROFT

Bancroft WORLD. w
KHi Je 21 1901-Je 6 1902

BANNER CITY

Banner City REGISTER. w 1887-88||?
KHi Ap 1887-S 22 1888

BARNARD

Barnard BEE. w Mr 8 1902+
KHi 1902-O 3 1918;N 29 1923+

Barnard TIMES. w 1888-92||?
KHi Ag 9 1888-My 12 1892

BARNES

Barnes CHIEF. w Mr 15 1894+
KHi 1894+

Barnes ENTERPRISE. w 1885-95||?
KHi Ag 1885-Ja 18 1895

BARTLETT

Bartlett BREEZE. w 1910-11||?
KHi S 15 1910-Ap 1911
OkWcW 1911

Bartlett NEWS. w 1915-16||?
KHi Ag 26 1915-N 23 1916

KANSAS (*Continued*)

BAXTER SPRINGS

CHEROKEE county republican. w 1893-1914||?
KHi D 16 1893-O 1 1914

CHEROKEE sentinel. w 1868-72||?
KGaT O 23 1869-Ag 1870
KHi O 30,N 27 1868;S 1871-Je 22 1872

Baxter Springs CITIZEN and herald. w 1918?+
1918?-26? as Baxter Springs citizen
KHi Ja 31 1918+

Baxter Springs DELTA. w
KHi Mr 31-D 22 1887

Baxter Springs ENTERPRISE. d Ja 26 1909-
KHi Ja-Ap 1909

Baxter Springs EXAMINER. w 1871-72||?
KHi S 14-O 1871

Baxter Springs HERALD. w
KHi F 8,22-29 1868

Baxter Springs HERALD. w F 1? 1917-26||?
United with Baxter Springs citizen to form Baxter Springs citizen and herald
KHi Mr 15 1917-Jl 1926

Baxter Springs NEWS. w 1882-1919||?
KHi F 23 1882-Jl 15 1919

Baxter Springs NEWS. w 1927-33||?
KHi Je 1928-33

Baxter Springs REPUBLICAN. *See* Cherokee county republican (Columbus)

SUNFLOWER state. w 1893||?
KHi Mr 25,O 14-D 9 1893

Baxter Springs TIMES. w 1878-80||?
KHi O 17 1878-Jl 1880

BAZINE

Bazine ADVOCATE. w Mr 4 1926+
KHi 1926+

Bazine LEADER. w 1887-89||?
1887-Ag 1888? as Bazine register
KHi F 17 1887-Ag 5 1888;F-Ag 16 1889

Bazine REGISTER. *See* Bazine leader

BEATTIE

Beattie BOOMER. w 1883-84||?
1883-Mr 15 1884 as Boomerang
KHi S 22 1883-My 22 1884

BOOMERANG. *See* Beattie boomer

Beattie EAGLE. w 1885?-1922||?
1885?-Mr 23 1894 as Williamson's Beattie eagle
KHi O 1891-D 1922

Beattie JOURNAL. w Mr 20 1919+
KHi 1919+

NORTH STAR. *See* Beattie star

Beattie PALLADIUM. w 1898-D 27 1901||
Merged with Beattie eagle
KHi N 11 1898-1901

Beattie STAR. w 1884-91||?
1884-85 as North star
KHi S 1884-Jl 3 1891

WILLIAMSON'S Beattie eagle. *See* Beattie eagle

BEAUMONT

Beaumont BUSINESS. w
KHi S 10 1886-N 5 1887

BELLAIRE

Bellaire NEWS. w 1900-01||
Merged with Smith county pioneer (Smith Center)
KHi Ja 12 1900-Je 14 1901

BELLE PLAINE

DEFENDER. w 1895-1904||
Merged with Belle Plaine news
KHi N 1895-1904

Belle Plaine HOME news. *See* Belle Plaine news

Belle Plaine NEWS. w D 6 1879+
1879-80 as Belle Plaine home news
KHi 1879+
OkHi [1893]

Belle Plaine RESIDENT. w
KHi Ap 9 1885-86

Bell Plaine VOICE. w
KHi Mr 16 1894-F 1895

BELLEFONT

TIMES-ENSIGN. w 1889-93||?
1889-92? as Western Kansas ensign (Dodge City)
KHi F 22 1889-93

BELLEVILLE

Belleville DEMOCRAT. w 1885-95||?
N 7-D 5 1890 as Democrat-press
KHi Je 18 1886-D 12 1890;O 1891-Ap 12 1895

Belleville FREEMAN. w 1879-O 14? 1909||
1879-Ja 3 1884 as Logan enterprise; Ja 10 1884-S 25 1890 Phillips county freeman; O 9 1890-99 Republic county freeman. United with Belleville telescope to form Telescope and freeman, later Belleville telescope
1879-S 25 1890 pub at Logan
KHi Ag 29 1879-O 14 1909

FREEMAN. d F 15?-D 1905||
KHi F 25-D 1905

KANSASKE noviny. w 1892||?
In Bohemian
KHi F-My 17 1892

Belleville PRESS. w O 6 1910-18||?
1910-Jl 31 1913 as Munden press (Munden) Ag 14 1913-Ja 31 1918 Narka press (Narka)
KHi 1910-O 4 1918

Belleville RECORD. w 1883-85||?
KHi O 1883-Jl 1885

Belleville REPUBLIC. *See* Scandia journal (Scandia)

REPUBLIC county democrat. w 1906-26||?
Suspended O?-D 1906
KHi S 26 1906;Ja 10 1907-Ap 1926

REPUBLIC county freeman. *See* Belleville freeman

REPUBLIC county news. w 1935?+
KHi Ja 24 1935+

REPUBLIC county press. w 1889-O 23 1890||
United with Belleville democrat to form Democrat-press, later Belleville democrat
KHi Ag 21 1889-90

Belleville SWATTER. m 1915-18||?
KHi Ja-My,N 1915-N 1916

Belleville TELESCOPE. w S 30? 1870+
O 22 1909-22? as Telescope and freeman
pub 1904+
KHi O 14 1870;N 10-24,D 8,29 1871;Ja 19 1872;Ap-O 12 1876;Ap 1877+

BELOIT

CALL. w S 27 1878+
1878-S 19 1879 as Beloit democrat; S 26 1879-N 14 1890 Western democrat (1882-83 Western nationalist); N 21 1890-My 1910? Western call
CoU 1899-My 1910
DLC D 30 1887
KHi 1878-F 19 1910;31+

Beloit CALL. d O 1 1901+
KHi 1901+

Beloit COURIER. w 1879-95||?
KHi F 27 1879-95

Beloit DEMOCRAT. *See* Call

Beloit GAZETTE. w Ap 11 1872+
KHi 1872-Ap 1873;Je 1876+

Daily GAZETTE. d N? 1907-11||
1907-Jl 31 1909 as Beloit daily times; Ag 2 1909-Mr 18 1910 Gazette-times
KHi D 27 1907-D 9 1911

MITCHELL county mirror. w 1871-72||?
KHi My 17-Je 1871

Beloit RECORD. w 1877-79||?
KHi F 20 1877-F 15 1879

Beloit TIMES. w 1895-1909||?
Merged with Beloit gazette
KHi Ag 22 1895-Jl 1909

Beloit daily TIMES. *See* Daily gazette

WESTERN call. *See* Call

WESTERN democrat. *See* Call

WESTERN nationalist. *See* Call

BELPRE

Belpre ARGOSY. w Ja 4? 1912-17||?
KHi F 22 1912-Je 20 1917

Belpre BEACON. w 1888||
Merged with Banner-graphic, later Kinsley graphic (Kinsley)
KHi Je 15-S 1888

Belpre BULLETIN. w 1905+
KHi Mr 1906+

BELVUE

Belvue DODGER. w
KHi Ja-Ag 6 1889

Belvue MIRROR. w
KHi N 18 1897-My 12 1898

BENEDICT

Benedict COURIER. w 1899-1902||?
KHi Mr 10 1899-Jl 1902

Benedict ECHO. w 1886-90||?
KHi N 11 1886-Ja 1890

BENNINGTON

HERALD and star. w 1883-91||?
1883-Ja 1889 as Bennington star
KHi Jl 13 1883-F 1884;Jl 1886-Jl 3 1891

Bennington JOURNAL. w 1885||?
KHi Ap-N 20 1885

Bennington NEWS. w 1935?+
KHi Ap 25 1935+

OTTAWA county democrat. w 1884+
1884-My 29 1891? as Solomon Valley democrat
1884-Ap 14 1893? pub in Minneapolis
KHi Jl 24 1884-My,Ag 14 1891-Ap 14 1893; O 18 1895-S 1916;Mr 26 1931+

Bennington STAR. *See* Herald and star

BENTLEY

METEOR. w
KHi S 24 1929-N 10 1931

Bentley NEWS. w 1900-10||?
KHi My 25 1900-N 11 1910

BENTON

Benton BULLETIN. w My 22 1913-19||?
KHi 1913-O 1918

Benton CALL. w 1893||?
KHi Mr-S 1893

Benton REPORTER. w 1884-85||?
KHi Mr 1884-F 1885

BERN

Bern GAZETTE. w 1889+
1889-F 1898 as Bern press
KHi My 1889-F,My 1898+

Bern PRESS. *See* Bern gazette

BERRYTON

Berryton BREEZE. w
KHi Ja 15 1926-S 1927

BEVERLY

Beverly BANNER. w Ap 3? 1930-
KHi Ag 1930-My 1932

Beverly TRIBUNE. w Jl 28 1910-28||?
KHi 1910-Jl 5 1928

BIGELOW

Bigelow GAZETTE. w
KHi O 20 1911-Je 1912

BIRD CITY

CHEYENNE county democrat. w 1886-89||?
KHi N 13 1886-Jl 13 1889

CHEYENNE county herald. w 1889-90||?
1889? pub in Saint Francis
KHi D 1889-Jl 19 1890

Bird City FRONTIERSMAN. *See* Herald of independence

HERALD of independence. w 1886-87||?
1886? as Bird City frontiersman
KHi O 13 1886-Je 1887

Bird City NEWS. *See* Kansas eagle (Saint Francis)

Bird City TIMES. w 1925+
KHi D 1927+

BISON

Bison BEE. w Ag 22 1902-18||?
KHi 1902-Ag 1918

Bison COURIER. w 1926+
KHi D 12 1930+

BLAINE

Blaine NEWS. w 1897-1901||?
KHi S 10 1897-Ag 9 1901

BLAKEMAN

RAWLINS county democrat. *See under* Atwood

Blakeman REGISTER. w 1887-94||
Merged with Atwood patriot (Atwood)
KHi N 10 1887-Ag 1894

BLOOM

Bloom BOOSTER. w F 15 1916-19||?
KHi Mr 15 1916-O 10 1918

Bloom TELEGRAM. w 1888-89||?
KHi Ap 1888-89

BLUE MOUND

FARM record. w 1890||?
KHi Ja-Je 13 1890

SEARCHLIGHT. w 1895-99||?
KHi N 1895-O 6 1899

Blue Mound SUN. w My 31 1883+
KHi 1883+

BLUE RAPIDS

Blue Rapids JOURNAL. w 1908-12||
Merged with Blue Rapids times
KHi N 1908-D 21 1912

Evening JOURNAL. d 1911-12||
KHi F 21-Ap 10 1912

LANTERN. *See under* Marysville

Blue Rapids LEADER. w 1908-09||?
KHi O 1908-Ja 1 1909

Blue Rapids LYRE. w 1886-87||?
KHi D 18 1886-Jl 16 1887

Blue Rapids MOTOR. w 1890-1901||
Merged with Blue Rapids times
KHi Jl 25 1890-Ag 2 1901

Blue Rapids TIMES. w 1871+
KHi Ja 13 1872;Ja 29 1874;Ja 27 1876+

KANSAS (*Continued*)

BLUFF CITY

Bluff City HERALD. w 1888-90||?
KHi Je 1888-89

Bluff City INDEPENDENT. w 1891-95||?
KHi N 20 1891-My 3 1895

Bluff City NEWS. w D 24 1897-1919||?
KHi 1897-S 19 1918

Bluff City NEWS. w 1930+
KHi S 1933+

Bluff City TRIBUNE. w 1886-88||?
KHi Ja 13 1886-O 1888

BOGUE

Bogue MESSENGER. w D 31 1931+
KHi 1931+

Bogue SIGNAL. w 1888-90||?
KHi N 29 1888-N 1890

BONASA. *See* LEOTI

BONNER SPRINGS

To 1887 as Tiblow

Bonner Springs CHIEFTAIN. w Ap 30 1896+
1896-1900 as Wyandotte chieftain
pub 1896+
KHi 1896+

Bonner Springs CITIZEN. w F 28?-Jl? 1890||
F-Ap 4? 1890 as Kaw Valley news
KHi F 28-Jl 11 1890

Bonner Springs ENTERPRISE. w 1935?+
KHi My 16 1935+

Bonner Springs HERALD. w 1913?-Mr 25 1920||
Merged with Bonner Springs chieftain
KBsC 1916-20
KHi Je 21 1916-20

KAW VALLEY news. *See* Bonner Springs citizen

WYANDOTTE chieftain. *See* Bonner Springs chieftain

BORDERS

BORDER rover. w 1887-89||?
KHi Ag 12 1887-F 8 1889

BRAINERD

Brainerd ENSIGN. w 1885-89||?
1885-S 1886 as Brainerd sun
KHi O 15 1885-Je 15 1889

Brainerd SUN. *See* Brainerd ensign

BREWSTER

Brewster GAZETTE. w 1888-90||
F 10-Ag 18 1888 as Hastings gazette (Hastings). Merged with Thomas county cat (Colby)
KHi F 10 1888-N 13 1890

Brewster HERALD. *See* Sherman county herald (Goodland)

Brewster HUSTLER. w 1908-09||?
KHi Ja 15-Jl 1909

Brewster RECORD. w 1907-08||?
KHi Je 28 1907-N 5 1908

Brewster TIDINGS. w 1935?+
KHi N 14 1935+

BRONSON

Bronson PILOT. 1884-96 *See* Weekly republican (Fort Scott)

Bronson PILOT. w Ja 15 1902+
KHi 1902+

Bronson RECORD. *See* Weekly republican (Fort Scott)

BROOKVILLE

Brookville EARTH. w 1890-97||?
KHi D 26 1890-97

HEADLIGHT. w 1901-17||?
KHi S 26 1902-16

Brookville INDEPENDENT. *See* Brookville transcript

Brookville NEWS. w 1918||?
KHi Ja 31-O 3 1918

Brookville TIMES. w 1887-88||?
KHi Mr 26 1887-Mr 1 1888

Brookville TRANSCRIPT. w 1879?-90||?
1879?-N 18 1880 as Brookville independent
KHi Mr 31 1880-S 19 1890

BROWNELL

Brownell COURIER. w 1908-12||?
KHi D 11 1908-S 1912

BUCKLIN

Bucklin BANNER. w 1895+
KHi My 31 1901-Mr 23 1919;Je 10 1926+

Bucklin HERALD. *See* Bucklin journal

Bucklin JOURNAL. w 1887-90||?
1887-D 1888 as Bucklin herald
KHi N 1887-Jl 19 1890

Bucklin STANDARD. w 1887-88||?
KHi Mr 31 1887-Ag 1888

BUCKNER. *See* JETMORE

BUFFALO

Buffalo ADVOCATE. w 1888-1916||?
1888-Mr 1889? as Buffalo express
KHi Mr-N 16 1888;Ap 1889-Jl 1916

Buffalo BLADE. w S 28 1916+
KHi 1916+

Buffalo CLIPPER. w 1886-87||?
KHi Jl-D 2 1887

Buffalo EXPRESS. *See* Buffalo advocate

BUFFALO PARK

Buffalo Park EXPRESS. w 1880-81||?
KHi Je 1880-Jl 23 1881

Buffalo Park PIONEER. w 1885-87||?
KHi Ap 16 1885-D 1 1887

BUHLER

Buhler HERALD. w 1913-14||?
KHi O 23 1913-Jl 1914

Buhler NEWS. w 1922-23||?
KHi Ag 17 1922-Ag 10 1923

BULL CITY. *See* ALTON

BUNKER HILL

Bunker Hill ADVERTISER. 1880-81 *See* Russell county advertiser

Bunker Hill ADVERTISER. w Ap 25 1912+
KHi 1912+

Bunker Hill BANNER. w 1881-85||?
KHi F 1881-82;My 29 1884-Ap 9 1885

Bunker Hill BANNER. w 1911-12||?
KHi Mr 30 1911-12

Bunker Hill GAZETTE. w 1888-89||?
KHi Mr 15 1888-Mr 7 1889

NEW republic. *See* Russell record (Russell)

Bunker Hill NEWS. w 1886-88||?
KHi N 26 1886-F 10 1888

RUSSELL county advertiser. w 1880-81||?
Titles varies: Bunker Hill advertiser
KHi Ap 16 1880-Ja 7 1881

BURDEN

Burden EAGLE. w 1885-89||?
KHi Ja 24 1885-Ag 24 1889

Burden EAGLE. w 1892-1908||?
KHi S 1892-F 13 1908

Burden ENTERPRISE. *See* Saturday journal

Saturday JOURNAL. w 1879-93||?
1879-Jl 1891 as Burden enterprise; Ag? 1891-N 1893 Spirit of the west
KHi Ap 29 1880-93

SPIRIT of the west. *See* Saturday journal

Burden TIMES. w Ja? 1907+
KHi Ap 11 1907+

BURDETT

Burdett BUGLE. w 1886-88||?
KHi Jl 27 1886-O 1888

Burdett NEWS. w S 1 1925-26||?
KHi 1925-Ag 1926

BURLINGAME

Burlingame BLADE. w 1892-93||?
KHi F 25-Je 3 1893

DEBTOR and workingman. *See* Fulcrum

Burlingame DEMOCRAT. w 1888-90||?
KHi N 1888-Mr 1890

Burlingame ENTERPRISE-CHRONICLE. w O 10 1895+
1895-My 29 1919 as Burlingame enterprise
KHi 1895+

FULCRUM. w 1895-96||?
1895-F 1896 as Debtor and workingman
KHi Mr 1895-O 16 1896

Burlingame HERALD. w 1881-84||?
KHi S 29 1881-F 9 1884

Burlingame INDEPENDENT. w 1886?-88||?
KHi My 13 1886-Ja 1888

OSAGE county chronicle. w 1863-My 29 1919||
1863-72? as Weekly Osage chronicle (S 14 1867-Mr 26 1870 Osage Burlingame chronicle) United with Burlingame enterprise to form Burlingame enterprise-chronicle
KHi O 17 1868-Ja 1872;S 1873-1919
KWiE S 26 1863-[S 14 1867-Mr 26 1870]-D 21 1871

OSAGE county democrat. *See under* Osage City

BURLINGTON

Burlington COURIER. w 1891-O 25 1901||
KHi Je 1891-1901

Burlington DEMOCRAT. *See* Burlington independent

Burlington INDEPENDENT. w,tw 1875-1914||
F 6 1907-Je 16 1910 as Burlington democrat Merged with Burlington republican tw 1908-10?
KHi My 27 1876-O 1914

JEFFERSONIAN. w 1892-1906||
1892-Ja? 1895 as Waverly sun (Waverly). Merged with Burlington republican
KHi Ag 1894;Ja 11,F 9 1895-Ap 2 1906

Burlington JEFFERSONIAN. d *See* Burlington republican. 1895+

KANSAS patriot. *See* Burlington patriot

LITTLE cassino. w
KHi F 15-My 15 1877

NEOSHO VALLEY register. w 1859-
DLC D 27 1859
KHi O 4 1859-N 14 1860;O 17-24 1861

Daily NEWS. d 1896-98||
Merged with Jeffersonian
KHi Ja 13 1897-N 26 1898

Burlington NONPAREIL. w 1886-93||
Merged with Burlington republican
KHi S 1886-S 8 1893

Burlington NONPAREIL. d 1887||
Merged with Burlington republican
KHi Ap 4-My 7 1887

Burlington PATRIOT. w 1864-Ap 23 1886||
1864-70 as Kansas patriot. United with Burlington republican to form Burlington republican-patriot, later Burlington republican
KHi S 1864-68[O 15 1869-D 9 1875;76-86]

Burlington REPUBLICAN. w,sw Ja 1882-O 12 1915||
Ap 30 1886-88? as Burlington republican-patriot
w 1882-1905?
KHi Ja 25 1882-1915
OkHi [1893-94]

Burlington REPUBLICAN. d 1887||
KHi Ap 16-Je 15 1887

Burlington REPUBLICAN. d 1895+
1895-Mr 31 1906 as Burlington Jeffersonian
KHi My 15 1897+

Burlington STAR. w
KHi Ja 13-F 3 1878

VOICE of the people. w
KHi S 5-N 18 1874

BURNS

Burns CITIZEN. w Jl 13 1893+
KHi 1893+

Burns MIRROR. w 1889-91||?
1889-Ag 1890 as Burns monitor
KHi N 1889-Ja 16 1891

Burns MONITOR. *See* Burns mirror

BURR OAK

CENTRAL reflex. *See* Burr Oak herald

Burr Oak HERALD. w 1879—
1879- as White Rock independent (White Rock); Ja 1 1880-83 Burr Oak reveille Ja 1 1880 issue has two sections: Central reflex; Burr Oak reveille
pub [1879]+
KHi Je 20 1879+
M F 9 1933

Burr Oak INDEPENDENT. *See* Burr Oak republican

JEWELL county independent. *See* Burr Oak republican

Burr Oak REPUBLICAN. w 1886-87||?
-1886? as Burr Oak independent; 1886 Jewell county independent
KHi D 17 1886-O 20 1887

Burr Oak REVEILLE. *See* Burr Oak herald

THINKER. w
Some issues pub at McPherson
KHi Je 30 1883-Mr 4 1884

BURRTON

Burrton BREEZE. w 1901-02||?
KHi O 18 1901-My 2 1902

Burrton FREE lance. w 1890-93||?
KHi F 22 1890-Mr 17 1893

Burrton FREE lance. w 1904-12||
1904-Mr 3 1910 as Kansas grit weekly. Merged with Burrton graphic
KHi Jl 14 1904-12

Burrton GRAPHIC. w My 20 1881+
1881-N 19 1886 as Burrton monitor
pub 1911—
KHi 1881+

KANSAS grit weekly. *See* Burrton free lance

Burrton MONITOR. *See* Burrton graphic

Burrton TELEPHONE. w S 18 1878-O 10 1881||
KHi N 1878-Ap 22 1881

Burrton TRIBUNE. w 1913-14||
Merged with Burrton graphic
KHi Mr-N 18 1914

BUSHTON

Bushton NEWS. w Ap 3 1896+
1896-N 3 1899 as Chase news (Chase)
KHi 1896+

Bushton STAR. w 1894-95||?
KHi Ag 17 1894-Mr 1 1895

KANSAS (*Continued*)

BUTLER. *See* YATES CENTER

BYERS

Byers JOURNAL. w Je 18 1915-19||?
KHi 1915-S 10 1919

CAIN

To 1889? as Cain City

Cain NEWS. w 1881-83||?
KHi Ja 12 1882-Ja 11 1883

Cain NEWS. w 1884-86||?
KHi Ag 1884-Mr 11 1885

Cain City NEWS. w
KHi Ag-D 6 1889

RAZZOOPER. w 1887-88||?
KHi Ag 18 1887-Ag 2 1888

CALDWELL

Caldwell weekly ADVANCE. w Ja 2 1879-1918||?
1879-Ap 26 1883 as Caldwell post; My 1883-F 1894 Caldwell journal
KHi 1879-S 17 1891;Ap 28 1892-Ja 16 1918

Caldwell COMMERCIAL. w 1880-83||
Merged with Caldwell journal
KHi My 6 1880-My 3 1883

FREE PRESS. w 1885-86||?
KHi S 19 1885-My 15 1886

INDUSTRIAL age. *See under* Wellington

Caldwell JOURNAL. d F 22- 1887||
KHi F-S 1887

Caldwell JOURNAL. *See* Caldwell weekly advance

Caldwell MESSENGER. w 1920-23||?
KHi My 23 1921-Ap 2 1923

Daily MESSENGER and news. d 1920?+
1923-25 as Daily messenger
pub 1923+
KHi My 23 1921+

Caldwell NEWS. w Mr 23 1887-D 31 1925||
United with Daily messenger to form Daily messenger and news
pub 1887[88]-1925
KHi 1887-1925

Caldwell NEWS. d O 7- 1887||?
KHi O-N 29 1887

OKLAHOMA war chief. w Ja 2? 1883-86||?
Ja?-Mr 9 1883 pub in Wichita; Mr 23 1883-Ap 1884? in Geuda Springs; Ap-My 3 1884 in Oklahoma Territory; My 10 1884-Je 11 1885 in Arkansas City (Je 14-Ag 7? 1884 in Rock Falls, Okla.; O 23?-D 4? 1884 in South Haven)
Suspended frequently for short periods
KHi Ja 12 1883-Ag 12 1886
OkHi [1883-86]
TxU My 31 1883

Caldwell POST. *See* Caldwell weekly advance

Caldwell STANDARD. w
KHi F-S 11 1884

Caldwell TIMES. w
KHi Je 1886-Jl 2 1887

CALIFORNIA

LANE county gazette. w 1880-82||?
KHi Ja 29 1880-Mr 23 1882

CALVERT

Calvert GAZETTE. w 1889-90||?
KHi My 9 1889-F 5 1890

CAMBRIDGE

Cambridge COMMERCIAL. w 1881||?
KHi F 19-N 19 1881

Cambridge NEWS. w 1882-90||?
KHi O 14 1882-Mr 1886;Mr 1888-Je 1890

CANADA

Canada ARCADE. w 1886-87||?
In English and German
KHi Ja-N 1 1887

CANEY

Caney ADVANCE. *See* News advance

Daily CHRONICLE. d,w Jl 24 1885+
1885-1919? as Caney chronicle (w)
KHi 1885-[My 1911-F 1913]-N 1919;Ap 9 1923+

Caney CHRONICLE. d My 18 1911-13||?
KHi [1911-F 1913]

Caney HERALD. w 1904||?
KHi Je 10-D 1904

Caney NEWS. w S 8? 1904-24||?
KHi D 1905-24

NEWS advance. d 1906-07||?
1906-Ja 4 1907 as Caney advance
KHi S 5 1906-Ja 10 1907

Caney PATRIOT. w 1899-1900||?
KHi Ap 21 1899-1900

Caney PHOENIX. w 1889-98||?
1889-Mr 5 1897 as Caney times; Mr 12-1897 Times and phoenix
KHi My 17 1889-98

Caney TIMES. *See* Caney phoenix

CANOLA. *See* GRENOLA

CANTON

Canton ARGUS. *See* Canton pilot

Canton CARRIER. w 1882-88||?
KHi Je 1885-S 6 1888

Canton CHAMPION. w 1895-98||?
KHi S 20 1895-Jl 20 1898

Canton LEADER. w
KHi D 1898-F 17 1899

Canton MONITOR. w 1880-81||?
KHi Mr 1880-Ja 21 1881

Canton NEWS. w 1887?-92||?
KHi Ja 29 1891-Ap 22 1892

Canton PILOT. w D 1 1898+
1898-F 1899 as Canton argus
KHi Mr 1899+

Canton REPUBLICAN. w 1887-90||?
KHi Ja 11 1889-D 18 1890

Canton REPUBLICAN. w 1892-95||?
KHi Ag 1892-S 13 1895

CARBONDALE

ASTONISHER and paralyzer. *See* Carbondalian

CARBONDALIAN. w 1885-1909||?
1885-Ap 16 1887 as Astonisher and paralyzer
KHi 1885-F 1909

Carbondale INDEPENDENT. w 1880-84||?
KHi F 22 1882-83

Carbondale JOURNAL. w
KHi My 29-D 4 1879

OSAGE county courier. w 1893-Jl 29 1894||?
KHi Ag 11 1893-Jl 13 1894
OkHi [1893]-Jl 29 1894

Carbondale POST. 1909-17||?
KHi Jl 1909-16

Carbondale RECORD. w 1888||?
KHi Ap-D 15 1888

Carbondale RECORD. w My 2 1923+
KHi 1923+

Carbondale REVIEW. w Jl 4 1918-20||?
KHi Jl 1918-Ap 22 1920

CARLTON

Carlton ADVOCATE. w 1886-88||?
KHi Je 17 1886-Ap 12 1888

Carlton TRIBUNE. w 1907-14||?
KHi S 11 1907-S 9 1914

CASH CITY

Cash City CASHIER. w 1886-88||?
KHi O 29 1886-Mr 23 1888

CASSODAY

MIRAGE. w 1887-89||?
KHi Je 23 1887-Mr 22 1889

STAFFORD county herald. w
KHi Ag 27 1886-Ap 1887

Cassoday TIMES. w 1907-13||?
KHi My 9 1907-13

Cassoday TIMES. w 1919?-28||?
KHi O 8 1925-Mr 1 1928

CAWKER CITY

ECHO. w 1875-78||
Followed by Cawker City free press, later Public record
KHi My 18 1876-Je 21 1878

Cawker City FREE PRESS. *See* Public record

Cawker City JOURNAL. w 1880-90||?
KHi My 12 1880-Mr 22 1890

Cawker City LEDGER. w Ja 6 1899+
KHi 1899+

Cawker City NEWS. w
KHi N 22 1934-O 10 1935

PUBLIC record. w 1878-1917||?
Follows Echo. 1878-Ap 12 1883 as Cawker City free press
KHi N 30 1878-D 27 1917

Cawker City TIMES. w 1888-94||
KHi Je 8 1888-Ag 30 1894

Cawker City TRIBUNE. w 1873-75||?
KHi 1873-74

CEDAR

To 1900? as Cedarville

Cedar ENTERPRISE. *See* Cedar headlight

Cedarville GLOBE. w 1886-91||?
KHi Jl 11 1886-N 1890

Cedar HEADLIGHT. w 1911-19||?
1911-16? as Cedar enterprise
KHi Ap 13 1911-N 21 1912;Ag 16 1917-Je 13 1918;Ap-S 9 1920

Cedarville REVIEW. w Ja 31 1884-85||?
KHi 1884-F 12 1885

Athol-Cedar-Gaylord REVIEW. *See* Smith county review (Smith Center)

SMITH county pioneer. *See under* Smith Center

Cedarville TELEPHONE. w
KHi My 17-D 1883

CEDAR BLUFFS

BEAVER VALLEY booster. w Ag 17 1910-18||?
KHi 1910-Ag 1918

CEDAR POINT

COTTONWOOD VALLEY news. w 1912-18||?
KHi O 22 1914-Ap 1916

POINTER. w 1895-96||?
KHi Mr 30 1895-S 1896

CEDAR VALE

Cedar Vale BLADE. w 1876-78||?
KHi Ag 24-D 21 1877

Cedar Vale COMMERCIAL. w Jl 20 1889-My 22 1914||
United with County liner to form County liner and Cedar Vale commercial
KHi complete

COUNTY liner and Cedar Vale commercial. w Ja 1914-O 30 1925||
F-My 22 1914 as County liner
KHi F 27 1914-My 22,Ag 14 1914-25

Cedar Vale MESSENGER. w 1921+
KHi O 14 1921+

Cedar Vale STAR. w My 9 1884-Ja 12 1894||
United with Sedan times-journal (Sedan) to form Sedan times-star (Sedan)
KHi complete

Cedar Vale TIMES. *See* Sedan times-star (Sedan)

CEDARVILLE. *See* CEDAR

CELIA

Celia ENTERPRISE. *See* Atwood patriot (Atwood)

CENTERVILLE

Centerville COURIER. w
KHi F-N 16 1905

Centerville ECHO. w 1906-07||?
KHi Mr 29 1906-My 16 1907

CENTRALIA

Centralia ENTERPRISE. *See* Centralia journal

Centralia JOURNAL. w 1883+
1883-D 19 1884 as Centralia enterprise
KHi Jl 20 1883+

Centralia TIMES. w 1893-1900||
Merged with Centralia journal
KHi F 24 1893-D 8 1899

CHANTILLY

KEARNY county coyote. *See under* Hartland

CHANUTE

Formed in 1873? by the union of Alliance, Chicago Junction, New Chicago and Tioga

ALLIANCE breeze. *See* Oberlin times (Oberlin)

ALLIANCE times. *See* Oberlin times (Oberlin)

Chanute BLADE. w Ag 9 1883-1906||
Merged with Erie sentinel (Erie)
CoU F 1899-1900
KHi 1883-Ag 17 1906

Chanute BLADE. d My 11 1903-05||?
KHi 1903-O 11 1905

Chanute CHRONICLE. w 1882-83||?
KHi My 1882-Ag 2 1883

Chanute DEMOCRAT. w 1879-82||?
KHi F 27 1879-Ap 1882

NEOSHO county chronicle. w 1894||?
KHi Je 22-O 5 1894

NEW CHICAGO times. *See* Chanute times

NEW CHICAGO transcript. w 1870-72||?
KHi S 23 1870-Ap 6 1872

Chanute NEWS and shopper. w My? 1933-
1933-Mr 7? 1934 as Chanute shopper
KHi Ag 25 1933-34

Chanute SHOPPER. *See* Chanute news and shopper

Chanute STAR. w 1916-18||?
KHi N 18 1916-F 1918

Chanute morning SUN. d 1896-1909||?
KHi N 21 1896-Je 1909

KANSAS (*Continued*)

CHANUTE—*Continued*

Chanute TIMES. w,d O 19 1872-1913||?
1872? as New Chicago times (New Chicago) Ja 16 1891-D 24 1896 Chanute vidette times
w 1872-My 30 1913
KHi O 19 1872;Ag 1874;76-Jl 19 1913

Chanute daily TIMES. d 1890||
KHi Je 14-S 13 1890

Chanute daily TIMES. d Je 3-Jl 19 1913||
Merged with Chanute daily tribune
KHi complete

TIMESETT. d 1912?-31||?
KHi Ap 1923-31

TIOGA herald. w 1871-72||?
KHi My 1? 1871-S 21 1872

Chanute TRIBUNE. d 1892+
KHi Jl 1892+

Chanute TRIBUNE. w 1904-27||?
KHi F 12 1904-S 9 1927

Chanute VIDETTE. w D 21 1887-Ja 1891||
United with Chanute times to form Chanute vidette-times, later Chanute times
KHi 1887-Ja 7 1891

Chanute VIDETTE-TIMES. *See* Chanute times

CHAPMAN

Chapman ADVERTISER. w 1887+
1887-Ap 3 1891 as Chapman courier; Ap 10 1891-D 23 1892 Chapman howitzer; D 30 1892-F 22 1901 Chapman standard
KHi 1887+
OkHi [1892-94]

Chapman BULLETIN. w
KHi O 192?-My 1931

Chapman COURIER. *See* Chapman advertiser

DICKINSONIAN. w S 1922+
KHi S 24 1923+

Chapman GAZETTE. w 1910-12||?
KHi 1910-Mr 1912

GOLDEN belt star. *See* Chapman star

Chapman HEADLIGHT. w Ap 11 1919-20||?
KHi 1919-Ag 20 1920

Chapman HOWITZER. *See* Chapman advertiser

Chapman LOOKOUT. w 1903-07||
Merged with Chapman advertiser
KHi S 1903-Ja 24 1907

Chapman NEWS. w 1899-1901||
Merged with Chapman standard, later Chapman advertiser
KHi Ap 1899-F 1 1900

Chapman STANDARD. *See* Chapman advertiser

Chapman STAR. w 1884-86||?
1884? as Golden belt star
KHi Je 19 1884-O 22 1886

CHASE

Chase BREEZE. *See* Chase register

Chase DISPATCH. w 1884-85||?
KHi Je 14 1884-D 4 1885

Chase NEWS *See* Bushton news (Bushton)

Chase RECORD. w 1886-95||?
KHi My 1886-Jl 4 1895

Chase REGISTER. w Je 12 1902+
1902-My 21 1903 as Chase breeze
KHi 1902+

CHAUTAUQUA

To 1899? as Chautauqua Springs

Chautauqua Springs EXPRESS. w 1888-89||?
KHi My 11 1888-Jl 19 1889

Chautauqua Springs GLOBE. w 1905-09||?
KHi Jl 7 1905-Ap 23 1909

Chautauqua Springs MAIL. w 1887||?
KHi Mr-O 1887

Chautauqua Springs SPY. w 1882-83||?
KHi My 1? 1882-Jl 1883

CHAUTAUQUA SPRINGS. *See* CHAUTAUQUA

CHENEY

Cheney BLADE. w 1888-90||?
KHi Ja 20 1888-O 12 1890

Cheney JOURNAL. w 1884-87||?
KHi Mr 1884-Ja 22 1887

Cheney SENTINEL. w Mr 1 1894+
KHi 1894+

CHEROKEE

Cherokee BANNER. w 1875-78||?
1875-S 1877 as Cherokee index
KHi My 26 1876-O 4 1878

Cherokee CYCLONE. w 1884-88||?
KHi O 1884-Mr 1888

Cheokee ENTERPRISE. w 1899-1900||?
KHi N 10 1899-Ag 1900

Cherokee INDEX. *See* Cherokee banner

Cherokee SENTINEL. w Mr 28 1879+
1879-82 as Sentinel on the border
KHi 1879+
WHi Mr 28 1879-Mr 19 1880

YOUNG Cherokee. w
KHi Je 10 1876-My 1877

CHERRYVALE

Cherryvale BULLETIN. w 1884-88||?
KHi Ap 12 1884-N 3 1888

Cherryvale CHAMPION. w 1887-95||?
KHi Je 1887-N 23 1895

CHERRY VALLEY torch. w 1882-85||
United with Cherryvale globe-news to form Cherryvale globe and torch
KHi Mr 1882-Ap 22 1885

Cherryvale CITIZEN. w 1928-30||?
1928-Ja 30 1930 as Montgomery county citizen
KHi Ap 1929-Mr 1930

Cherryvale weekly CLARION. *See* Cherryvale weekly journal

Daily CLARION. 1894 *See* Daily republican 1894

Cherryvale evening CLARION. 1898-1903 *See* Cherryvale daily republican

Cherryvale ECHO. w
KHi N 1923-My 2 1924

Cherryvale GLOBE and torch. w 1878-88||?
1878-82 as Cherryvale globe; 1883-85 Cherryvale globe-news
KHi Jl 26 1879-Ap 14 1882;My 1885-Jl 6 1888

Daily GLOBE and torch. d My 16 1885-Ja 12 1889||
Merged with Cherryvale republican
Suspended Je 1887-D 9 1888
KHi 1885-Ja 5 1889

Cherryvale weekly JOURNAL. w 1898-O 1903||
1898-Ap 13 1900 as Morehead searchlight (Morehead); Ap 20 1900-03 as Cherryvale weekly clarion
KHi My 13 1898-1908

Cherryvale JOURNAL. d 1905-14||?
KHi N 22 1906-D 17 1914

KANSAS commonwealth. w 1890-91||
1890-My 1891 as Southern Kansas farmer. Merged with Cherryvale republican
KHi S 11 1890-Ag 27 1891

KANSAS populist. w 1893-98||?
KHi Ag 12 1893-My 1898

KANSAS populist. d *See* Daily news

Cherryvale LEADER. w 1877-78||?
KHi Jl 9-D 14 1877

MILLS' weekly world. *See* Western world (Parsons)

MONTGOMERY county citizen. *See* Cherryvale citizen

Cherryvale NEW ERA. w 1899-1901||
United with Weekly independent to form Independent-new era, later Weekly independent (Coffeyville)
KHi Mr 23 1899-F 1 1901

Cherryvale NEWS. w 1881-D 29 1882||
United with Cherryvale globe to form Cherryvale globe-news, later Cherryvale globe and torch
KHi Ap 28 1821-82

Cherryvale NEWS. w 1893-1907||?
KHi Je 1898-F 9 1906

Daily NEWS. d Mr 28 1894-1907||?
Mr 28-Ap 8 1894 as Kansas populist; Ap 11-O 7 1894? Morning news
KHi Mr-O 7 1894;96-Jl 1 1907

PEOPLE'S party plaindealer. w 1892-93||
United with Cherryvale republican to form Republican-plaindealer, later Cherryvale republican
KHi S 14 1892-Ja 13 1893

Cherryvale REPUBLICAN. w Je 18 1886-1920||?
- 1893 as Republican-plaindealer
KHi 1886-Ap 15 1920

Daily REPUBLICAN. d Je 5-Ag 8 1894||
Jl 30-Ag 7 1894 as Daily clarion
KHi complete

Cherryvale daily REPUBLICAN. d Jl? 1898+
1898-N 7 1903 as Cherryvale evening clarion; N 9 1903-N 8 1904 Republican and clarion
KHi Ag 25 1903+

SOUTHERN Kansas farmer. *See* Kansas commonwealth

Cherryvale morning TELEGRAM. d Ja 28?-1892||?
KHi Ja 30-My 8 1892

WESTERN world. *See under* Parsons

CHETOPA

Chetopa ADVANCE-CLIPPER. w 1868+
1868-Mr 1878 as Southern Kansas advance; Ap 1878-N 28 1928 Chetopa advance
KHi Jl 8 1875;Jl 1876+

Chetopa CLIPPER. w Mr 16 1888-N 28 1928|
1888-D 25 1902 as Chetopa democrat. United with Chetopa advance to form Chetopa advance-clipper
KHi 1888-1928

Chetopa DEMOCRAT. *See* Chetopa clipper

Chetopa HERALD. w 1876-78||?
KHi Ap 8 1876-F 16 1878

SOUTHERN Kansas advance. *See* Chetopa advance-clipper

Chetopa STATESMAN. *See* Labette county times-statesman (Oswego)

CHICAGO JUNCTION. *See* CHANUTE

CHICO

Chico ADVERTISER. w
KHi Ap 17 1886-Ap 9 1887

CIMARRON

GRAY county beacon. w 1912?-13||?
KHi 1912-My 15 1913

GRAY county echo. w 1886-My 5 1888||
United with New West to form New West-echo, later New West
KHi Mr 24 1887-88

GRAY county Jacksonian. *See* Jacksonian

GRAY county republican. w 1897-99||?
KHi Ja 28 1897-Ja 6 1899

GRAY county republican. w 1902||?
KHi Mr-Jl 24 1902

GRAY county sentinel. *See* Jacksonian

GRAY county times. w 1903-04||?
KHi Ja-Ag 4 1904

Cimarron HERALD. *See* Ravanna leader (Ravanna)

JACKSONIAN. w 1885+
1885-1900? as Gray county Jacksonian; 1901?-Ja 1902? Gray county sentinel
KHi Ap 1886+

KANSAS sod house. *See* Ravanna leader (Ravanna)

NEW West. w 1879-82||?
KHi Mr 22 1879-Ja 14 1882

NEW West. w 1884-95||?
My 12 1888-F 1891 as New West-echo
KHi F 1885-My 18 1895

Cimarron OPTIC. w
KHi Jl 11-S 1879

Cimarron SIGNET. w 1880-81||?
KHi Ap 24 1880-My 7 1881

CINCINNATI

Cincinnati COMMERCIAL. w 1887?-88||
United with Ulysses tribune to form Tribune-commercial (Ulysses)
KHi Ap 1887-O 4 1888

STANDARD. *See under* Appomatox

CIRCLEVILLE

JACKSON county world. w 1900-09||?
Suspended from Jl 31 1908-Ap 23 1909
KHi D 1900-Ag 27 1909

KANSAS bazaar. w 1891-93||?
KHi Je 18 1891-Ag 3 1893

KICKER. *See* Circleville news

Circleville NEWS. w 1894-1900||?
1894-N 12 1896 as Kicker
KHi N 22 1894-N 8 1900

CLAFLIN

Claflin BANNER. w Ja 14 1897-Je 15 1899||
1897-Jl 14 1898 as Barton banner. Merged with Claflin clarion
KHi complete

BARTON banner. *See* Claflin banner

BARTON county banner. w N 6 1890-Je 28 1894||
Merged with Claflin leader, later Ellinwood leader (Ellinwood)
KHi complete

Claflin CLARION. w Mr 23 1899+
KHi 1899+

Claflin GAZETTE. w 1888||?
KHi Ja 26-Jl 1888

Claflin LEADER. *See* Ellinwood leader (Ellinwood)

CLARINDA

NESS county pioneer. *See* Sidney advance (Sidney)

WALNUT VALLEY times. *See* Ness City times (Ness)

CLAY CENTER

Clay Center ARGUS. w 1885-86||?
KHi Ag 27 1885-My 1886

CLAY county critic. w 1890?-91||?
KHi S 1890-91

CLAY county dispatch. *See* Clay Center dispatch republican

CLAY county independent. *See* Clay Center dispatch republican

CLAY county times. *See* Clay Center times

Clay Center CRESSET. w 1882-83||?
KHi O 1882-Mr 24 1883

Clay Center DEMOCRAT. w
KHi 1879-80

Clay Center DEMOCRAT. w 1884?-90||?
Jl 1888-Jl 1889 as Republican Valley democrat
KHi Jl 8 1886-Ag 29 1890

KANSAS (*Continued*)

CLAY CENTER—*Continued*

Clay Center DISPATCH. d 1903+
1903-Je 5 1914 as Daily dispatch; Je 6 1914-My 23 1930 Dispatch-republican
pub 1903+
KHi 1905+

Clay Center DISPATCH republican. w 1871-1917‖?
1871-73 as Clay county independent; 1873-81 Clay county dispatch; 1882-1914? Clay Center dispatch
pub 1893-1917
KHi O 12 1871;Ap 13 1876-My 24 1917
OClWHi Je 11 1885

Clay Center EAGLE. w 1884-86‖?
KHi F 1885-Jl 1 1886

Clay Center ECONOMIST. w 1914+
pub S 14 1915+
KHi Ag 17 1915+

Clay Center FIRE brand. w
KHi D 20 1883-N 18 1884

LOCALIST. *See* Clay Center times

Clay Center MONITOR. *See* Leonardville monitor (Leonardville)

Clay Center PROMOTER. w
KHi O 1925+

Clay Center REPUBLICAN. d D 10 1906-Je 5 1914‖
United with Daily dispatch to form Dispatch-republican, later Clay Center dispatch
KHi complete

REPUBLICAN VALLEY democrat. *See* Clay Center democrat

Clay Center SUN. w 1890-92‖?
KHi N 27 1890-Mr 3 1892

Clay Center TIMES. w 1878+
1878? as Clifton localist (Clifton) 1879-80? Localist;1881? Clay county times
pub 1884+
KHi Mr 16 1878+

Clay Center TIMES. d Ag 16 1886-88‖
KHi Ag 17 1886-S 29 1888

WESTERN record. w
KHi S 10 1892-Mr 18 1893

CLAYTON

Clayton PEP. w 1930+
KHi Ap 1930+

CLEARWATER

Clearwater COURANT. w 1902-24‖?
1902-Je 25 1908 as Clearwater echo
KHi My 15 1902-F 1924

Clearwater ECHO. w Je 17 1892-93‖?
KHi 1892-S 8 1893

Clearwater ECHO. 1902-05 *See* Clearwater courant

Clearwater GAZETTE. *See* Kansas jayhawker

KANSAS jayhawker. w Je? 1899-1900‖?
Je?-Jl? 1899 as Clearwater gazette
KHi Je 16-Jl 21[O 1899-Ap 13 1900]

Clearwater LEADER. w 1885-87‖?
KHi Ap 30 1886-87

Clearwater NEWS. w My 22 1924+
KHi 1924+

Clearwater SUN. w 1888-90‖?
KHi Je 23 1888-N 7 1890

Clearwater TIMES. w 1884-87‖?
KHi N 26 1886-Ja 21 1887

CLEBURNE

Cleburne NEWS. w 1913-16‖?
KHi F 1913-Mr 23 1916

CLEVELAND

Cleveland STAR. w
KHi Jl 20 1881-F 22 1882

CLIFTON

Clifton JOURNAL. w
KHi My 18-Je 22 1878

LOCAL news. *See* Clifton news

Clifton LOCALIST. *See* Clay Center times (Clay Center)

Clifton NEWS. w D 18 1885+
1885-D 26 1890 as Local news
KHi 1885+

Clifton REVIEW. *See* Clifton times

Clifton TIMES. w 1879-93‖?
1879-My 1892 as Clifton review
KHi F 27 1879-N 10 1893

CLIMAX

Climax CHRONICLE. w
KHi Je 26 1918-23

CLYDE

Clyde ARGUS. w 1888-96‖?
KHi 1888-Ap 10 1896

CLINE'S press. *See* Clyde mail

Clyde DEMOCRAT. w 1880-82‖?
KHi Jl 24 1880-S 6 1882

FARMERS' voice. w Ja 22 1891-My 1918‖
United with Clyde republican to form Voice-republican, later Clyde republican
KHi 1891-1918

Clyde HERALD. w 1878-1906‖
Merged with Clyde republican
KHi Je 1878-F,D 1881-Ja 1906

KANSAS sunflower. w 1894-95‖?
KHi Jl 1894-Jl 1895

Clyde MAIL. w 1883-87‖?
1883-O 1884 as Cline's press
KHi F 14 1884-87

Clyde REPUBLICAN. w 1900+
Je 1918-Mr 7 1929 as Voice-republican
KHi F 21 1901+

REPUBLICAN Valley empire. *See* Concordia empire (Concordia)

VOICE-REPUBLICAN. *See* Clyde republican

COATS

Coats COURANT. w 1904+
KHi Ag 1905+

CODELL

Codell NEWS. w 1917-18‖?
KHi Mr 22 1917-Ja 16 1918

COFFEYVILLE

AFRO-AMERICAN advocate. w 1891-93‖?
KHi S 1891-S 1 1893

AMERICAN. w
KHi Ap 23 1898-Ap 1 1899

Coffeyville BEE. d 1908-09‖?
1908-F 1909 as Coffeyville chronicle
KHi Ja 13-S 18 1909

BROAD-AXE. w 1891-Ap 29 1892‖
United with Coffeyville news to form News-broad-axe
KHi D 31 1891-92

Coffeyville CHRONICLE. *See* Coffeyville bee

Daily DAWN. w 1924-25‖?
KHi Ap 11 1924-Ja 1925

Coffeyville DEMOCRAT. w 1896-1902‖?
1896-Je 8 1900 as Montgomery county democrat
KHi My 14 1896-My 1902

Coffeyville EAGLE. w 1888-89‖?
KHi O 27 1888-89

EARTH. d 1907?-
KHi Je 23 1909-S 25 1915

GASLIGHT. w 1898-1903‖?
KHi N 1898-Ag 1903

GATE CITY enterprise. w 1884-85‖?
KHi O 17 1884-N 13 1885

GATE CITY gazette. w 1886-87‖?
KHi Ag 20 1886-Ap 15 1887

GATE CITY independent. *See* Weekly independent

Coffeyville HERALD. d 1909-11‖?
KHi Jl 7, 21 1910-My 28 1911

Weekly INDEPENDENT. w,sw 1893-1919‖?
1893-Ja 1901 as Gate City independent; F 1901-02 Independent-new era
sw 1901-07
KHi Ag 18-25 1893;Mr 8 1895-Ja 1897;F 1901-Mr 20 1919

Coffeyville INDEPENDENT. d N 26 1896-99‖?
KHi 1896-D 30 1899

Coffeyville INDEX. w
KHi O 1889-Jl 1891

Coffeyville JOURNAL. w O 30 1875-1920‖?
1889-90 as Journal and sun
pub 1875-1920
KHi 1875-Ja 8 1920

Coffeyville JOURNAL. d 1893+
pub 1893+
KHi Jl 31 1894

KANSAS blackman. w 1894‖?
- Je? 1894 pub in Topeka
Negro
KHi Ap 20-Je,Ag 17-D 1894

MONTGOMERY county democrat. *See* Coffeyville democrat

Morning NEWS. d 1919-29‖?
KHi F 22 1919-Ja 12 1929

NEWS-BROAD-AXE. w 1890-93‖?
1890-Ap 29 1892 as Coffeyville news
KHi F 1890-Mr 1893

Coffeyville RECORD. d My 11 1902-08‖?
KHi My 11 1902-Ag 4 1908

Coffeyville RECORD. w 1902-06‖?
KHi Je 1902-D 7 1906

Coffeyville STAR. *See* Star and Kansan (Independence)

Coffeyville SUN. w 1886-89‖
United with Coffeyville journal to form Journal and sun, later Coffeyville journal
KHi N 26 1886-Jl 13 1889

Coffeyville SUN. d 1911-19‖?
KHi Mr 28 1913-Ja 5 1919

TELEGRAM. d 1891?-93‖
KHi Ja 10-My 1893

VINDICATOR. w 1905-06‖?
KHi D 17 1904-N 2 1906

COLBY

Colby DEMOCRAT. w 1886-89‖?
KHi Ag 12 1886-Ap 11 1889

FREE PRESS-TRIBUNE. w Ag 29 1889+
1889-Jl 2 1925 as Free press
KHi 1889+

Colby NEWS. w 1891-93‖?
KHi My 25 1892-S 9 1893

THOMAS county cat. w Mr 12 1885-91‖?
KHi 1885-F 5 1891

THOMAS county cat. w
KHi Je 20 1923-Mr 15 1929

Colby TRIBUNE. w My 17 1888-Jl 2 1925‖
United with Free press to form Free press-tribune
KHi complete

COLDWATER

ECHO-ADVOCATE. w 1885-92‖
1885-Jl 29 1886 as Protection echo (Protection) Ag 5 1886-Ag 8 1891 Coldwater echo. Merged with Western star
KHi Ap 23 1885-S 1 1892

Coldwater ENTERPRISE. w 1886-95‖
1886-Jl 14 1888 as Nescutunga enterprise (Nescutunga). Merged with Western star
KHi Mr 20 1886-Ja 12 1895

PEOPLE'S advocate. w 1890-91‖
United with Coldwater echo to form Echo-advocate
KHi O 18 1890-Ag 1 1891

Coldwater REPUBLICAN. w 1884-87‖?
KHi Je 1885-Ja 1887

Coldwater REVIEW. w 1884-91‖
Merged with Western star
KHi N 29 1884-Mr 6 1891

Coldwater TALISMAN. w F 3 1905+
KHi 1905+

WESTERN star. w Ag 30? 1884+
KHi S 20 1884-F,Jl 1885+

COLLYER

Collyer ADVANCE. w 1916+
KHi Jl 20 1916+

COLOKAN

Colokan GRAPHIC. w 1887-88‖?
KHi N 10 1887-Jl 13 1888

COLONY

ANDERSON county advocate. w Ap 1 1926-32‖?
1926-S 12 1930 as Greeley advocate (Greeley)
KHi 1926-F 4 1932

Colony FREE PRESS. w Ja 5 1882+
KHi Ja 26 1882+

COLUMBUS

Columbus ADVOCATE. w My 5 1882+
1882-84 as Lea's Columbus advocate
pub 1882+
KHi 1882+

Columbus daily ADVOCATE. d O 1885+
Suspended from My 28 1887-My 21 1895
pub 1885+
KGaT Ap 1895-1913
KHi Je 8 1886-F 27 1904;10+

BORDER star. 1878-N 12 1886‖
United with Columbus courier to form Star-courier, later Columbus courier
Suspended from Ag 6 1880-Je 9 1882
KHi My 1878-Ag 6 1880;Je 9 1882-86

CHEROKEE county republican. w 1872-77‖
1872-76 as Baxter Springs republican (Baxter Springs). United with Columbus courier to form Republican courier, later Columbus courier
KHi Je 1876-Ja 1877

Columbus COURIER. w S 30 1874-O 2 1902‖
F 15 1877-Je 13 1878 as Republican courier; N 18 1886-Jl 9 1896 Star-courier. Merged with Columbus advocate
KCoA 1874-1901
KHi Jl 8 1875;Ja 13 1876-1902

Columbus DEMOCRAT. w 1875-76‖?
KHi Ap 14-O 1876

Columbus ENTERPRISE. w 1905-08‖?
KHi D 15 1905-08

FRANK'S news. w D 14 1882-
1882-My? 1883 as Columbus news
KHi 1882-My 3,S 29-D 6 1883

LEA'S Columbus advocate. *See* Columbus advocate

MODERN light. w Mr 5 1891+
KHi Mr 19 1891+

Columbus NEWS. *See* Frank's news

REPUBLICAN courier. *See* Columbus courier

STAR-COURIER. *See* Columbus courier

Columbus TIMES. w Ag 5 1880-86‖?
KHi 1881-Mr 1886

Columbus VIDETTE. w 1875-78‖?
KHi S 28 1877-Ap 1878

WORKINGMAN'S journal. w O 29 1869-75‖?
Also dated in Girard
KHi 1869-O 1870;Ja 19,Ap 12,Je 15 1872;Mr 1874-Mr 17 1875

KANSAS (*Continued*)

COLWICH

Colwich COURIER. w 1887-92||?
KHi Ap 2? 1887-92

SEDGWICK county reporter. w
KHi Ja 13-Je 23 1893

COMANCHE CITY

Comanche City NEWS. w 1886-88||?
KHi D 23 1886-Je 1888

CONCORDIA

ALLIANT. w 1890-Ap 4 1895||
Suspended 1894
KHi Jl 1890-95

Weekly Concordia BLADE. w 1879-My 1902||
1879-80? as Blade; 1881? Cloud county blade; 1882?-89? Kansas blade. United with Concordia empire to form Blade and empire, later Concordia empire
KHi Ap 23 1879-1902

Concordia BLADE. d D 22 1884-88||
Suspended from F 7 1885-Mr 19 1887
KHi 1884-N 3 1888

BLADE-EMPIRE. d My? 1902+
1902-Je ? 1919 as Concordia blade
KHi Jl 12 1902+

CLOUD county blade. *See* Weekly Concordia blade

CLOUD county critic. *See* Kansas kritic

Concordia DAYLIGHT. w 1885-1900||
1885-N ? 1886 as Concordia democrat. United with Concordia empire to form Empire-daylight, later Concordia empire
KHi My 188?-Ja 1900

Concordia DEMOCRAT. *See* Concordia daylight

Concordia EMPIRE. w 1870-1919||
1870-75 as Republican Valley empire; 1883-87 Republican-empire; F 1 1900-F 14 1901 Empire-daylight; My 22 1902-D 22 1904 Blade and empire
1870 pub in Clyde
KHi 1876-My 15 1919
OClWHi Jl 22 1871

Concordia EXPOSITOR. *See* Concordia republican

Concordia KANSAN. w 1881+
1881-N 1890 as Cloud county Kansan; D 6 1890-O 27 1893 New era
1881-Ap ? 1895 pub in Jamestown
KHi O 15 1881+
OkHi [1893-95]

Concordia KANSAN. d Mr 17 1905-19||?
KHi 1905-My 10 1919

KANSAS blade. *See* Weekly Concordia blade

KANSAS kritic. w 1880-88||?
1880-86? as Cloud county critic
KHi S 20 188?-88
WHi My 2 1888

Concordia NEWS. w O 2 1916-My 13 1935||
Merged with Concordia press
KHi 1916-35

Concordia PRESS. w,sw 1892+
1892-Ja 18 1901 as Miltonvale press (Miltonvale)
KHi S 16 1892-Ag 4 1893;O 23 1896+

Concordia REPUBLICAN. w 1875-83||
1875-81? Concordia expositor. United with Concordia empire to form Republican-empire, later Concordia empire
KHi Ja 18 1877-S 13 1883

REPUBLICAN-EMPIRE. *See* Concordia empire

REPUBLICAN VALLEY empire. *See* Concordia empire

Concordia daily TIMES. d D 1884-Ja 1885||
KHi complete

Concordia TIMES. w 1884-91||
Merged with Concordia empire
KHi Mr 28 1884-D 4 1891

CONDUCTOR

Conductor PUNCH. w 1887-88||?
KHi N 25 1887-F 3 1888

CONWAY SPRINGS

Conway Springs REFLECTOR. *See* Garden City reflector (Garden City)

Conway Springs STAR. w 1884+
KHi Je 12 1885+

TRUTH. w 1898-99||?
KHi Mr 17 18?-Ag 1899

COOLIDGE

BORDER ruffian. w 1886-87||?
KHi 1886-Ja 15 1887

Coolidge CITIZEN. w 1886-90||?
KHi S 17 1886-? 5 1890

Coolidge ENTERPRISE and unmuzzled truth. w 1894-98||?
1894-98? as Coolidge enterprise
KHi Je 1894-O 30 1899

HAMILTON county bulletin. w 1890?-93||?
KHi S 12 1890-? 22 1893

Coolidge INTERSTATE. w 1893||?
KHi Ja 20-O 1893

Coolidge LEADER. w 1908-09||?
KHi Ja 16 1908-09

Coolidge TIMES. w 1887-90||?
KHi N 1887-Ja 16 1890

COPELAND

Copeland CALLER. w 1929+
1929-31? as Copeland chronicle
KHi D 25 1931+

Copeland CHRONICLE. *See* Copeland caller

CORA

Cora UNION. w 1886-87||?
KHi F 11 1886-Je 9 1887

CORBIN

Corbin VOICE. w
KHi Mr 16 1894-F 1895

CORNING

Corning CHIEF. w 1884||?
KHi Ap 12-Jl 12 1884

Corning CLIPPER. w
KHi Jl 1893-94

Corning GAZETTE. w Ja 3 1895+
KHi 1895+

Corning INDEPENDENT. w
KHi Ap 18-Jl 19 1890

CORONADO

Coronado STAR. w 1886-87||?
KHi Ag 12 1886-D 8 1887

WICHITA county herald. w 1886-87||?
KHi Jl 15 1886-87

CORWIN

Corwin DISPATCH. w 1897||?
KHi Ap 23-My 21,Ag 28-S 18 1897

COTTONWOOD FALLS

CENTRAL Kansas index. w
KHi Ap 20 1870-Ja 4 1871

CHASE county banner. w 1867-70||?
KHi Ag 1867-My 1869
WHi O 5 1867

CHASE county courant. *See* Cottonwood Falls courant

CHASE county leader. w,sw,tw 1871+
sw 1916?-26?(tw 1918?-21?)
KHi F 25 1875+

Cottonwood Falls COURANT. w O 26 1874-D 9 1909||
1874-O 13 1900 as Chase county courant; O 18 1900-Ja 10 1907 Courant and reveille. United with Strong City news to form News-courant (Strong)
KHi complete
OkHi [1893]-[95]

KANSAS press. w
KHi My 30-Ag 1859

REVEILLE. w 1890-O 11 1900||
United with Chase county courant to form Courant and reveille, later Cottonwood Falls courant
KHi Ag 21 1890-1900

SCALPING knife. w
KHi S 15 1874

TRUE reformer. w
KHi N 1 1876

VALLEY echo. w
KHi O 28 1880-Ja 1881

COUNCIL GROVE

ADVERTISER. w
KHi D 25 1869-Ag 1870

ALLIANCE herald. w 1891||
United with Council Grove guard to form Alliance herald-guard, later Council Grove guard

ALLIANCE herald-guard. *See* Council Grove guard

ANTI-MONOPOLIST. *See* Jeffersonian gazette

APPEAL. w 1904-06||?
KHi O 27 1904-D 20 1906

APPEAL. d Jl? 1906-07||?
KHi S 20 1906-Je 1907

BUGLE. w 1896||?
KHi F-O 2 1896

Council Grove COURIER. w 1889-97||?
United with Council Grove guard to form Courier-guard, later Council Grove guard
KHi D 18 1891-D 10 1897

COURIER-GUARD. *See* Council Grove guard w

DEMOCRAT. w
KHi Ja 26-D 1 1866

Council Grove DEMOCRAT. w 1871-S 27 1877||
United with Morris county republican to form Republican and democrat, later Council Grove republican
KHi O 26 1871-77

Council Grove GUARD. w Ag 9 1884-1923||?
1891-92 as Alliance herald-guard; 1898?-1903? Courier-guard
KCg 1884-[90-93;1900-03]-08;15-[18]
KHi 1884-O 5 1923

Council Grove GUARD. d N 1 1915-24||?
KHi 1915-Ag 1924

KANSAS cosmos. w S 5 1879-86||
1879-O 7 1881 as Morris county times. Merged with Council Grove republican
KCg 1879-S 1 1881;Ag 29 1884-N 1886
KHi Ap 30 1880-Ja,Jl 1885-O 8 1886
NcD Ja 30-F 6 1880

KANSAS press. w
KHi S 26 1859-O 6 1865

MORRIS county advance. w 1908-10||?
KHi Ag 26 1908-D 7 1910

MORRIS county republican. *See* Council Grove republican

MORRIS county times. *See* Kansas cosmos

NEOSHO VALLEY times. w 1899-1900||?
KHi S 14 1899-N 1900

Council Grove REPUBLICAN. w,d 1872+
1872-S 29 1877 as Morris county republican; O 6 1877-Ja 4 1879 Republican and democrat
w 1872-Ag 28 1924
DLC F 5 1876
KCg 1876-[1910]12;14-[16]F 23-D 13 1917[18-24]
KHi Je 6,Jl 25 1874;76+

VIDETTE. w 1883||?
KHi My 19 1883

COURTLAND

Courtland COMET. *See* Courtland journal

Courtland ECHO. w
KHi D 1916-My 1917

Courtland JOURNAL. w F 27 1903+
1903-Ap 9 1915 as Courtland comet
KHi 1903+

Courtland REGISTER. w F 2 1889-1924||?
KHi 1889-Mr 1924

COWLAND

Cowland CHIEFTAIN. w
KHi Ap 30-O 1885

COYVILLE

Coyville PRESS. w
KHi O 1887-Ja 6 1888

Coyville STAR. w 1897-98||?
KHi My 21 1897-My 13 1898

CRESSON

Cresson DISPATCH. w 1887-88||?
KHi D 8 1887

CRISFIELD

Crisfield COURIER. w 1885-90||?
KHi O 30 1885-F 14 1890

CUBA

Cuba ADVOCATE. w 1897-1901||?
KHi O 22 1897-O 11 1901

ALLIANCE sun. w 1891-92||?
KHi My 14-O 1891

CESKY lev. w
In Bohemian
KHi My 1891-Je 1892

CONSERVATIVE Cuban. w,ir 1884-86||?
w 1884-85?
KHi Ag 22 1884-Mr 1 1886

Cuba DAYLIGHT. w 1888-D 1922||?
1888-F 1889 as Cuba union; Mr 1889-Ap 18 1890 Union pilot. Merged with Belleville telescope (Belleville)
KHi Mr 8 1889-1922

Cuba PILOT. w 1885-O? 1888||
1885-Mr 26 1887 as Republic county pilot. United with Cuba union to form Union pilot, later Cuba daylight
KHi Mr 26 1885-O 1888

REPUBLIC county pilot. *See* Cuba pilot

Cuba TRIBUNE. w N 22 1923+
KHi 1923+

Cuba UNION. *See* Cuba daylight

CULLISON

Cullison BANNER. w 1886-88||?
KHi Ap 22 1886-Mr 16 1888

LET'S go. w Ja? 1924-26||?
KHi Je 13 1924-Ja 6 1926

Cullison TIMES. w 1913-15||?
KHi Mr 14 1913-My 1915

Cullison TOMAHAWK. w 1888-90||?
KHi S 1888-Ja 3 1890

KANSAS (*Continued*)

CULVER

Culver HERALD. w Je 2? 1927+
KHi O 12 1927+

Culver RECORD. w N 6 1913-19||?
KHi 1913-D 11 1919

CUNDIFF

Cundiff JOURNAL. w 1888-89||?
KHi Mr 25 1888-Ag 3 1889

CUNNINGHAM
Early years as Ninnescah

Cunningham CHRONICLE. w 1886-94||?
1886-92 as Cunningham herald
KHi Ag 12 1886-Ja 1894

Cunningham CLIPPER. w O 17 1902+
KHi 1902+

Cunningham HERALD. *See* Cunningham chronicle

CYRUS

Cyrus GLOBE. w 1882-84||?
KHi My 20 1882-Je 9 1883

DANVILLE

Danville ARGUS and courant. w 1882-84||?
1882-83? as Danville courant
KHi N 24 1882;Mr 9 1883-Mr 1 1884

Danville COURANT. *See* Danville argus and courant

Danville EXPRESS. *See* Harper county express

HARPER county express. w 1885-86||?
1885? as Danville express
KHi Je 1885-Ag 1886

Danville NEWS. w 1899-1900||?
KHi F 11 1899-N 17 1900

Danville NEWS. w 1916?-18||?
KHi Ap 18-Je 1918

DEARING

Dearing NEWS. w
KHi N 1907-Jl 1908

Dearing SENTINEL. w
KHi Ag 13-D 1909

Dearing TIMES. w 1910-12||?
KHi Ag 18 1910-Ag 1912

DEERFIELD

ARKANSAS VALLEY builder. w
KHi S 16 1926-27

Deerfield FARMER. w 1904-05||?
KHi D 22 1904-S 7 1905

Deerfield NEWS. w 1909||?
KHi Ap 15-O 14 1909

DELAWARE

KANSAS free state. w 1856?-
MWA O 10-17 1857

DELIA

Delia NEWS. w 1915-20||?
KHi F 18 1916-20

Delia PAPER. w 1907-08||?
KHi Ap 1907-Je 8 1908

DELL RAY. *See* GLASCO

DELPHOS

Delphos CARRIER. w 1881-88||?
KHi Jl 8 1881-N 23 1888

Delphos HERALD. w 1879-81||?
KHi F 1879-Jl 17 1880

Delphos REPUBLICAN. w 1888+
KHi D 1888-O 1918;Ap 17 1924+
OkHi [1893]-[95;98]99

DENISON

Denison HERALD. w
KHi O 1902-Ja 1903

Denison JOURNAL. w
KHi N 14 1895-Jl 9 1896

Denison LEADER. w
KHi O 1900-Jl 10 1901

Denison NEWS. w 1909-10||?
KHi O 1909-Ag 1910

Denison STAR. w 1889-90||?
KHi D 20 1889-S 4 1890

DENNIS

Dennis LEADER. w 1899-1900?
KHi F 9 1899-N 15 1900

DENSMORE

Densmore DISPATCH. w 1889||?
KHi My 16-Jl 1889

Densmore NEWS. w
KHi Je 21-S 1888

DENTON

Denton JOURNAL. w 1897-98||?
KHi Mr 25 1897-Ja 16 1898

Denton WHEEL. w 1895-96||?
KHi Mr 28 1895-Je 18 1896

DERBY

Derby DISPATCH. w 1889-90||?
KHi O 26 1889-My 3 1890

MIMEOGRAM. w
KHi O 1891-My 5 1892

DERMOT

Dermot ENTERPRISE. w 1887-88||?
KHi Je 1887-N 1888

DESOTO

EAGLE eye. *See* DeSoto news

DeSoto HERALD. *See* DeSoto news

DeSoto NEWS. w O 21? 1898+
1898-N 17 1921 as Eagle eye (1910-12 DeSoto herald)
KHi N 1898+

DeSoto PIONEER. w
KHi O 29 1897-98

DETROIT

Detroit FREE PRESS. w
KHi Ap-Ag 11 1898

WESTERN news. w
KHi F 11,Jl 5 1870

DEXTER

Dexter ADVOCATE. w 1898-1907||?
KHi S 1898-N 1907

Dexter DELTA. w 1892-93||?
KHi N 10 1892-S 7 1893

Dexter DISPATCH. *See* Dexter tribune

Dexter EYE. *See* Dexter post

Dexter FREE PRESS. *See* Industrial free press (Winfield)

Dexter NEWS. w 1912-Mr? 1915||
United with Dexter dispatch to form Dexter dispatch-news, later Dexter tribune
KHi Ap 1914-15

Dexter OBSERVER. *See* Dexter tribune

Dexter POST. w 1884-88||?
1884-My 1888 as Dexter eye
KHi Mr 21 1884-N 1885;S 10 1887-Jl 14 1888

Dexter TRIBUNE. w 1905-27||?
1905-Mr 1915? as Dexter dispatch; Ap 1915 Dexter dispatch-news; My 1915-Jl? 1919 Dexter observer
Suspended from Jl 17 1921-Jl 3 1925?
KHi Ap 1905-S 1918;Ag 8 1919-Jl 17 1921;Jl 1925-27

DIGHTON

Dighton HERALD. w My 1 1885+
1885-92 as Lane county herald; 1911-16? Journal herald
pub 1885+
KHi 1885+

Dighton JOURNAL. w 1886?-92||?
KHi F 18,Mr 1886-Mr 10 1892

JOURNAL herald. *See* Dighton herald

LANE county farmer. w 1890-92||?
KHi D 1890-Jl 1 1892

LANE county herald. *See* Dighton herald

LANE county journal. w F 11 1897-1911||
United with Dighton herald to form Journal herald, later Dighton herald
KHi 1897-Ja 9 1911

Dighton NEWS. w My 1 1913-N 23 1916||
Merged with Journal herald, later Dighton herald
KHi complete

Dighton REPUBLICAN. w 1887-89||?
KHi Ja 29 1887-F 13 1889

WESTERN progress. w
KHi F-Ag 3 1880

DILLON

Dillon REPUBLICAN. w
KHi Ja 10 1895-Ap 22 1898

DODGE CITY

Dodge City ADVANCE. w
KHi My 24 1900-01

Dodge City CHAMPION. w
KHi Jl-S 1887

Dodge City CLARION. d
KHi Ap 26-Je 14 1909

Dodge City DEMOCRAT. w 1883-1905||
United with Dodge City journal to form Journal-democrat, later Dodge City journal
KHi D 29 1883-My 19,D 21 1889-1905

Dodge City DODGER. w 1919?-
KHi S 1925-My 1927

FORD county globe. *See* Dodge City globe

FORD county leader. w 1894-99||?
KHi Ag 17 1894-Mr 1899

FORD county republican. w 1886-D 18 1889||
United with Globe livestock journal to form Globe-republican, later Dodge City globe
KHi Ja 19 1887-89

Dodge City GLOBE. w Ja 1 1878-N 7 1918||?
1878-D 23 1884 as Ford county globe; D 30 1884-D 18? 1889 Globe livestock journal; D 25? 1889-D 1 1910 Globe-republican
CoU 1899-Je 1902
KD 1879[80]-[83]-[86]87[1909-11]
KDB D 25 1878-93;1910-11
KHi 1878-N 7 1918

Dodge City daily GLOBE. d D 11 1911+
pub 1911+
KD D 13 1911[12-13]-[15-18]27+
KHi Mr 7 1912+

Dodge City JOURNAL. w,d 1884+
1905-08 Journal-democrat; 1909? Dodge City Kansas journal
d O 1916?-Ja 1919?
pub 1919+
KD [1909-17]27+
KHi 1905+

Dodge City KANSAS journal. *See* Dodge City journal

Dodge City MESSENGER. w 1874||?
KHi F 26,Je 25 1874

Dodge City REPORTER. w 1899?-1901||?
KHi Ap 1899-My 24 1901

SOUTHWEST news. w 1924-27||?
KHi Ja 25 1925-F 3 1927

Dodge City SUN. w
KHi Ap 22 1886-Je 16 1887

Dodge City TIMES. w 1876-94||?
United with Western Kansas ensign to form Times-ensign (Bellefont)
KHi O 14 1876-91;S 16 1892-Je 9 1893

WESTERN central Kansas cowboy. w 1883-85||?
KHi Je 28 1884-D 5 1885

WESTERN Kansas ensign. *See* Times-ensign (Bellefont)

DONIPHAN

KANSAS constitutionalist. w
KHi Ja 7 1857

KANSAS crusader of freedom. w D 19 1857-
CSmH D 19 1857
KHi Ja 30-Mr 6 1858
WHi Mr 6 1858

Doniphan weekly NEWS. w 1882||?
KHi Mr 17-Ag 25 1882

DORRANCE

Dorrance NEWS. w 1911-13||?
KHi Ag 1911-Ag 7 1913

Dorrance NUGGET. w 1886-89||?
KHi O 28 1886-F 21 1889

Dorrance STAR. w O 9 1913-18||?
KHi 1913-O 10 1918

DOUGLASS

Douglass INDEX. w 1880-83||?
KHi Je 25 1880-D 21 1883

NEW enterprise. w 1879-80||?
KHi Ap 24 1879-Ap 15 1880

Douglass TRIBUNE. w Ja 4 1884+
KHi 1884+

DOVER

Dover HERALD. w 1911-13||?
KHi Ag 24 1911-N 6 1913

DOWNS

Downs CHIEF. w 1885-91||
Merged with Downs times
KHi N 20 1885-N 19 1891

Downs GLOBE. w 1888?-90||?
KHi Jl 28 1888-Je 1890

NEWS and times. w 1903+
1903-Ja 13 1916 as Downs news
pub 1905+
KHi Mr 1904+

Downs TIMES. w F 19 1880-Ja 6 1916||
United with Downs news to form News and times
KDoN 1905-16
KHi complete

Downs WORLD. w 1892-95||?
KHi N 1893-Ja 10 1895

DRESDEN

Dresden BEACON. w S 17 1931-
KHi 1931-Ap 13 1933

Dresden STAR. w 1890-93||?
KHi Mr 29 1890-Jl 22 1893

Dresden SUNFLOWER. w 1907?-14||?
KHi Jl 9 1908-Mr 19 1914

KANSAS (*Continued*)

DUNLAP

Dunlap CHIEF. w 1882||?
KHi Mr-Je 2 1882

Dunlap COURIER. w 1889?-91||?
KHi N 23 1889-D 12 1891

Dunlap LEADER. w 1903-06||?
KHi D 25 1903-Je 14 1906

Dunlap NEWS. w 1894||?
KHi Ap 14-Ag 1894

Dunlap REFLECTOR. w 1896-98||
Merged with White City register (White City)
KHi F 1896-Jl 15 1898

Dunlap REPORTER. w 1883-89||?
KHi Jl 20 1883[Mr 21 1884-My 10 1888]

Dunlap RUSTLER. w 1913-19||?
KHi Ap 18 1914-S 13 1919

SWEET chariot. w
KHi S-D 1887

DURHAM

Durham JOURNAL. w
KHi O 1906-Ag 1 1907

Durham TRIBUNE. w S 2 1915-20||?
KHi 1915-N 1920

DWIGHT

Dwight ADVANCE. w Je 25 1919+
KHi 1919+

Dwight INDEPENDENT. w 1887-91||?
1887-O 1? 1891 as Dwight wasp
KHi Ag 29 1887-D 11 1891

Dwight SIGNAL. w My 9? 1912-18||?
KHi Je 13 1912-Mr 1918

Dwight SPIRIT. *See* Dwight tribune

Dwight SUN. w 1896-98||?
KHi Ag 29 1896-Ag 1898

Dwight TRIBUNE. w 1905-11||?
1905-O 14 1910 as Dwight spirit
KHi N 1905-Ap 1911

Dwight WASP. *See* Dwight independent

EAGLE TAIL STATION. *See* SHARON SPRINGS

EASTON

Easton HERALD. w 1891?-1905||?
1891?-1904? as Easton light; 1905? Light and herald
KHi Jl 26 1895-Jl 1905

Easton LIGHT. *See* Easton herald

Easton TRANSCRIPT. w 1908+
KHi O 29 1908;Ja 29 1922+

EDGERTON

ENTERPRISE. *See under* Olathe

Edgerton GAZETTE. w 1895?-96||?
KHi My 10 1895-Mr 17 1896

Edgerton GLOBE. w 1899-1901||?
KHi Mr 1899-Je 7 1901

Edgerton JOURNAL. w D 21? 1906-25||?
KHi D 28 1906-Ja 1925

Edgerton JOURNAL. w Ag 29 1932+
KHi 1932-Ag 16 1935

Edgerton NEWS. w 1902-03||?
KHi My 22 1902-03

EDMOND

NEW leaf. w 1910+
KHi F 12-Ap 20 1911;Ap 16 1931+

NORTON county badger. w 1886||?
KHi F 26-Jl 1886

Edmond TIMES. w 1886-90||?
KHi Ag 1886-S 12 1890

EDNA

Edna ENTERPRISE. w 1887||?
KHi Ap 15-S 2 1887

Edna ENTERPRISE. w 1899-1905||?
KHi S 23 1899-Jl 6 1905

Edna INDEPENDENT. *See* Edna news

Edna NEWS. w 1889-94||?
1889-O 21 1893 as Edna independent
KHi Ag 23 1890-S 8 1894

Edna STAR. w 1887-88||?
KHi O 28 1887-Je 22 1888

Edna SUN. w 1894+
KHi N 24 1894-1902;My 13 1920+

EDWARDSVILLE

Edwardsville VISITOR. w 1912-13||?
KHi O 18 1912-Jl 11 1913

EFFINGHAM

ATCHISON county visitor. w 1905-07||?
KHi Mr 10 1905-Jl 13 1907

Effingham ENTERPRISE. w 1886||?
KHi Ap-Ag 7 1886

Effingham JOURNAL. w
KHi S 1892-F 1893

NEW leaf. w 1887?+
KHi Ap 13 My 25 1894+

Effingham TIMES. *See* Graphic (Atchison)

ELBING

Elbing HATCHET. w
KHi Jl 29 1893-Ja 13 1894

EL DORADO

ADVOCATE. *See* Augusta bugle (Augusta)

BUTLER county citizen. w 1880?-Ja 24 1895||?
1880?-F 16 1882? as El Dorado democrat; F 23 1882-F 9 1883 El Dorado eagle; F 16 1883?-83? Butler county democrat (1886?-S 1888 El Dorado democrat; O 1888-N 7 1889 Butler county Jeffersonian)
KHi Mr 24 1881-Ap 1891;My 18 1893-Ja 24 1895

BUTLER county democrat. 1883-93 *See* Butler county citizen

BUTLER county democrat. 1913-15 *See* Augusta bugle (Augusta)

BUTLER county Jeffersonian. *See* Butler county citizen

BUTLER county news. w,sw Je 21 1921+
1921-Je 30 1927 as Community announcer
w 1921-D 18 1934
pub 1921+
KHi 1921+

COMMUNITY announcer. *See* Butler county news

El Dorado DEMOCRAT. 1880-82 *See* Butler county citizen

El Dorado DEMOCRAT. 1896-97 *See* El Dorado news

El Dorado EAGLE. *See* Butler county citizen

ELI. *See under* Parsons

INDUSTRIAL advocate. d My 2-Je 13 1892||
KHi complete

INDUSTRIAL advocate. w *See* Augusta bugle (Augusta)

El Dorado NEWS. sw,w 1896-97||?
1896-Ap 1 1897 as El Dorado democrat sw 1896?
KHi O 9 1896-[Ap 8-N 19 1897]

El Dorado PRESS. w 1877-83||?
KHi Ap 25 1877-N 1 1883

El Dorado REPUBLICAN. w N 9 1883-1929||?
CSU F 1899-My 1900
KET 1883-N 1 1884;89-1902;05;07;09-12;14-16; S-D 7 1917
KHi 1883-Mr 1929

El Dorado REPUBLICAN. d My 5 1885-N 29 1919||
United with Walnut Valley times to form El Dorado times
Suspended from 1886-91?
KET 1885[86;95-98]1900[01-02;05-09;12;14-15]
KHi 1885-1919

El Dorado TIMES. d D 1 1919+
Formed by the union of Walnut Valley times and El Dorado republican
pub 1919+
KE My 25 1932+
KHi 1919+

WALNUT Valley times. w Mr 4 1870-N 29? 1919||
KET 1870-78;80 82;F 15 1884-F 6 1885;86;88; 90;92;94;96-98;1900;02;04;06;08;10;13-16
KHi Ap 17 1874-Ap 19 1918

WALNUT Valley times. d Mr 1 1887-N 29 1919||
United with El Dorado republican to form El Dorado times
KET 1887-1911;Jl 1913-16;19
KHi Mr 2 1887-1919

ELGIN

Elgin CLIPPER. w
KHi Mr 7-N 14 1891

DERRICK. w 1900?-15||?
1900?-13? pub in Peru
KHi F 1902-My 10 1913;Ag 14 1915

Elgin JOURNAL. w Ap 13 1916-Jl 5 1934||
United with Sedan advertiser to form Advertiser-journal (Sedan)
KHi complete

ELI

Eli GAZETTE. w
KHi Ag 18-O 7 1887

ELK CITY

COURANT. *See* Howard courant (Howard)

Elk City DEMOCRAT. w
KHi S 1885-Mr 6 1886

Elk City EAGLE. w 1886-90||?
KHi S 17 1886-Ag 8 1890

Elk City ENTERPRISE. w 1889-1905||?
United with Elk City sun to form Enterprise and sun, later Elk City sun
KHi Ag 31 1889-Jl 21 1905

ENTERPRISE and sun. *See* Elk City sun

Elk City GLOBE. w 1882-87||?
KHi Ag 9 1882-S 9 1887

Mid-week REPORTER. w 1915-
KHi D 8 1915-Ja 17 1916

Elk City STAR. w 1884-85||?
KHi Je 1884-D 19 1885

Elk City SUN. w Ag? 1903+
1905?-10? as Enterprise and sun
KHi O 1903+

ELK FALLS

ELK county ledger. *See under* Howard

Elk Falls JOURNAL. w 1903-09||?
KHi Jl 23 1903-D 23 1909

LONGTON news and Elk Falls reflector. *See under* Longton

Elk Falls REFLECTOR. w 1911-23||?
United with Longton news to form Longton and Elk Falls reflector-news, later Longton news and Elk Falls reflector (Longton)
KHi My 12 1911-Ag 17 1923

Elk Falls SIGNAL. w 1880-82||?
KHi Mr 26 1880-F 3 1882

ELKHART

Elkhart ENTERPRISE. w 1907-N? 1915||
United with Elkhart news to form Elkhart tri-state news
KHi Ap 23 1914-N 25 1915

Elkhart MESSENGER. w S 4? 1931-Ap 16 1932||
Merged with Elkhart tri-state news
KHi O 9 1931-32

MONITOR-REPUBLICAN. *See* Elkhart tri-state news

MORTON county progress. w 1920-26||?
1920-Mr 30 1923 as Rolla progress (Rolla)
KHi Je 24 1921-Ap 15 1926

Elkhart NEWS. *See* Elkhart tri-state news

Elkhart TRI-STATE news. w S 22 1888+
1888-Ap 12 1890 as Morton county monitor; Ap 26 1890-Ap 19 1895 Monitor-republican; Ap 26 1895-O 28 1898 Monitor-republic; N 4 1898-Ap 2? 1915 Richfield monitor; Ap 29-N? 1915 Elkhart news
1888-Ap 21 1890 pub in Morton; Ap 26 1890-Ap 24 1915 in Richfield
KHi 1888+

ELLINWOOD

Ellinwood ADVOCATE. w My 18 1888-Ap 14 1898||
Merged with Ellinwood leader
KHi complete

BARTON county presse. w 1901-13||?
1901?-03? pub in Great Bend
In German
KHi Ja 18 1901-My 23 1913

Ellinwood EXPRESS. w 1878-89||?
KHi Ap 13 1878-Ag 2 1888

Ellinwood LEADER. w Mr 29 1894+
1894-S 11 1896 as Claflin leader (Claflin)
KHi 1894-Ja 1917;Mr 15 1923+

ELLIS

BETTER business buckle. w
KHi S 1928-Je 1929

Ellis HEADLIGHT. w 1880-N 1890||
United with Ellis review to form Review-headlight
KHi Mr 13 1880-N 18 1890

REVIEW-HEADLIGHT. w 1886+
1886-N 28 1890 as Ellis review
KHi Jl 30 1886+

Ellis STANDARD. w
KHi S 22,O 27 1877

ELLSWORTH

CYCLONE. *See* Ellsworth messenger

Ellsworth DEMOCRAT. *See* Ellsworth messenger

ELLSWORTH county leader. w O 9 1919-
KHi 1919-N 1920

Ellsworth HERALD. *See* Ellsworth republican 1888-91

Ellsworth MESSENGER. w My 5 1881+
1881-F 28 1883 as Rural West; Mr 7 1883 Cyclone; Mr 14 1883-O 1 1885 Ellsworth news; O 8 1885-Jl 2 1891 Ellsworth democrat
1881-N 9? 1882 pub in Little River
pub O 1885+
KHi 1881+

Ellsworth NEWS. *See* Ellsworth messenger

Ellsworth POPULIST. w 1895-99||?
KHi Ag 10 1895-Ap 12 1899

Ellsworth REPORTER. w D 1871+
KHi Mr 19-26 1874;F 11 1875+
MWA Jl 20 1876

Ellsworth REPUBLICAN. w
KHi Ap 30-S 3 1880

KANSAS (*Continued*)

ELLSWORTH—*Continued*

Ellsworth REPUBLICAN. w 1888-91||?
1888?-Ap 1890 as Ellsworth herald
KHi D 29 1888-Jl 18 1891

Ellsworth TIMES. w 1879-80||?
KHi My 1879-Ap 22 1880

ELMDALE

Elmdale GAS jet. w 1909||?
KHi Mr-D 24 1909

Elmdale NEWS. w
KHi S 1921-My 15 1931

Elmdale REPORTER. w 1899-1906||?
KHi [D 15 1899-1900]-F 22 1906

ELSMORE

Elsmore EAGLE. w 1890-92||?
KHi N 1890-D 24 1892

Elsmore ENTERPRISE. w 1895-97||?
KHi O 25 1895-Mr 1897

Elsmore ENTERPRISE. w 1898-1907||?
KHi F 17 1899-F 1 1907

Elsmore LEADER. w 1907-12||?
KHi F 8 1907-Ap 4 1912

Elsmore LEADER. w F 6 1914-18||?
KHi 1914-Je 1918

ELWOOD

Elwood ADVERTISER. w
KHi Je 25 1857-58
MB O 8 1867

Elwood FREE PRESS. w 1858-
1858-Je? 1859 as Kansas weekly press
KHi Je 1858-61
MB Jl-N 1859

KANSAS weekly press. *See* Elwood free press

EMINENCE

Eminence CALL. w 1887-93||?
1887-92? as Garfield county call
KHi Jl 1887-Je 1893

GARFIELD county call. *See* Eminence call

EMMETT

Emmett CITIZEN. w 1907-12||?
KHi My 1907-F 4,Je 24 1909-S 12 1912

EMPIRE CITY

ECHO. *See* Mining echo

Empire City JOURNAL. w 1896-1903||?
KHi Jl 23 1896-My 14 1903

Empire City MINING echo. w 1877-80||?
Title varies: Echo
KHi Je 1877-D 4 1879

EMPORIA

Emporia BULLETIN. d My 16 1881-
KHi My-Jl 16 1881

Emporia CITIZEN. w
KHi Ap-N 1 1932

COLUMBIA. w 1888-91||?
In Welsh and English
KHi D 11 1890-Ag 13 1891

CONVINCER. w
KHi F-N 2 1912

Emporia DEMOCRAT. w 1882?-D? 1889||
United with Emporia news to form Emporia news-democrat
KHi 1882-D 19 1889

Emporia DEMOCRAT. d Ag 28 1886-D? 1889||
1886-Je? 1889 as Emporia globe. United with Emporia evening news to form Emporia evening news-democrat
KHi 1886-Ag 15 1887[N 1888]Jl 22-N 15 1889

Emporia DEMOCRAT. w 1898-99 *See* Democratic record

Emporia DEMOCRAT. d Mr? 1899-
KHi Ap 12 1899-My 14 1900

DEMOCRATIC record. w 1898-1900||?
1898-Ja 1899 as Emporia democrat
KHi Je 24 1898-O 4 1900

Emporia GAZETTE. d Ap 18 1890+
pub 1893+
DLC N 1912+
IU N 8 1909-Jl 1 1910
KEm Ap 1903-[05-06]+
KEmT 1891;93+
KHi 1890+
P [1927]-Ja 5 1933
WHi 1917-19

Emporia weekly GAZETTE. w Ap 23 1890+
1890-My 28 1892 as Emporia standard
pub 1893+
KHi 1890+

Emporia GLOBE. w
KHi N 18 1886-Ag 11 1887

Emporia GLOBE. d *See* Emporia democrat d 1886-89

Emporia HERALD. w 1890||?
KHi Ja 16-Ap 10 1890

Emporia JOURNAL. w 1880-82||?
KHi Ja 24 1880-Ja 12 1882

Emporia JOURNAL. w 1908?-10||?
KHi My 22 1908-D 22 1910

Emporia JOURNAL. d 1909-11||?
KHi F 8 1910-Ja 6 1911

KANSAS greenbacker. w 1878-79||?
KHi S 1878-My 9 1879

KANSAS news. *See* Emporia news-democrat

KANSAS sentinel. w 1880-82||?
KHi Mr 1880-Ag 9 1882

KANSAS state bugle. w 1918?-
KHi Ap 9 1926-F 1929

Emporia LEDGER. w Je 3 1871-82||?
InRE Ag 25-S 1 1881
KHi Jl 8 1875;76-82
N Je 10 1871

LYON county democrat. w 1892-95||
KHi Mr 1893-F 1895

LYON county news. *See* Emporia times. w

NATIONAL era. w
KHi My 16-D 1879

Emporia NEWS-DEMOCRAT. w Je 6 1857-90||?
1857-Jl 24 1858 as Kansas news; Jl 31 1858-D 19? 1889 Emporia news
DLC Ja 24 1868
KEm 1857-[63-64]-[69]-[71]-[73-74]-[81-83]
KEmT 1862-68
KHi Ag 1,N 21 1857;S 2-9 1860;D 30 1865-Ja, O 1873-90
MB Ag 22 1857
MWA Jl 4 1857
OClWHi Jl 13 1861

Emporia evening NEWS-DEMOCRAT. d N 1 1878-Ap 30 1890||
1878-D 23? 1889 as Emporia evening news. Merged with Emporia daily republican
KEmT Ja-Ap 1890
KHi complete

Daily POPULIST. *See* Emporia tidings

Emporia daily REPUBLICAN. d Ja 21 1882-1905||
KEm 1882-Je 1897
KEmG 1883-1900
KEmT [1882]-85[90]91;93-1904
KHi 1882-Je 3 1905

Emporia weekly REPUBLICAN. w 1882?-1905||?
KEm [1882]85-86;89-96
KEmG 1883-1900
KHi D 9 1886-Je 1 1905

Emporia STANDARD. *See* Emporia weekly gazette

Emporia SUN. w 1878-79||?
KHi Ap 10 1878-Ap 5 1879

Emporia TIDINGS. d Mr 18 1894-
Mr 18-24 1894 as Daily populist; Mr 26-Ap 13 1894 Populist and tidings
KHi Mr 20-N 7 1894

Emporia TIDINGS. w *See* Emporia times

Emporia TIMES. sw,w 1887+
1887-My 28 1892 as Allen tidings (Allen); Je 4 1892-F 1 1895 Emporia tidings; S 7 1922-Ap 27 1923 Lyon county news
w 1887-1931?
KHi My 1887+

Emporia TIMES. d
KHi Je-Jl 13 1905

Emporia TRIBUNE. w 1869-70||?
KHi D 29 1869-N 1870

ENGLEWOOD

Englewood CHIEF. w 1888-92||?
Suspended from Je 1889-Ag 1891
KHi Ap 1888-N 10 1892

CLARK county chief. *See* Englewood enterprise

Englewood ENTERPRISE. w 1885-89||?
1885-D 9 1887 as Clark county chief
KHi Ap 24 1885-Ap 5 1889

HOME builder. w 1906-07||?
KHi My 31 1906-Ag 18 1907

ENNIS CITY

Ennis City COURIER. *See* Obelisk (Monument)

WESTERN Kansas advocate. m
KHi Jl 1886-Ja 1 1887

ENSIGN

GRAY county record. w 1915-25||?
KHi F 1916-Ja 15 1925

Ensign RAZZOOP. w 1887-88||?
KHi N 16 1887-Ap 1888

ENTERPRISE

ANTI-MONOPOLIST. *See* Jeffersonian gazette (Lawrence)

Enterprise EAGLE. w 1900||?
KHi S-D 20 1900

Enterprise ENDEAVOR. w
KHi Jl 1924-Mr 1928

Enterprise GAZETTE. w Je 29-N? 1894||
KHi Je 29-N 1894

Enterprise HERALD. w 1903-05||?
KHi Jl 25 1903-O 14 1905

Enterprise INDEPENDENT. *See* Enterprise journal

INTEGRAL cooperator. w
KHi S 17 1891-94
WHi F 18,Mr 31 1892

Enterprise JOURNAL. w 1888-1906||
1888-Ag 14 1890 as Enterprise independent. United with Enterprise push to form Enterprise push and journal, later Enterprise journal
KHi Ja 21 1888-My 25 1906

Enterprise JOURNAL. w D 14 1905+
1905-My 25? 1906 as Enterprise push; Je 1? 1906-Mr 2 1922 Enterprise push and journal
KHi 1905+

KANSAS gazette. *See* Abilene gazette (Abilene)

Enterprise PUSH. *See* Enterprise journal 1905+

Enterprise REGISTER. *See* Jeffersonian gazette (Lawrence)

Enterprise STAR. w
KHi S 1901-Mr 19 1903

ERIE

NEOSHO county record. *See* Erie record

NEOSHO county republican. w O 26 1882-S 30 1886||
Follows Neosho Valley enterprise (Osage Mission). United with Neosho county record to form Republican record, later Erie record
KHi complete

PEOPLE'S vindicator. *See* Erie sentinel

Erie RECORD. w My 5 1876+
1876-O 1 1886 as Neosho county record; O 8 1886-D 9 1904 Republican record
KHi 1876-Je 1884;Ap 1885+

REPUBLICAN RECORD. *See* Erie record

Erie SENTINEL. w 1883-D 1912||
1883-Mr 13 1888 as Neosho county democrat (Osage Mission) Mr 20 1888-D 26 1889 People's vindicator
KHi Ja 19 1883-1912

Erie SENTINEL. d,w Jl 1 1909-23||?
1909-D 30 1916 as Erie daily sentinel (d)
KHi 1909-O 26 1923

ESBON

JEWELL county searchlight. *See* Light of liberty

Esbon LEADER. w 1892-93||?
KHi Je 30 1892-S 1893

LIGHT of liberty. w 1893-95||?
1893-N 9? 1894 as Jewell county searchlight
KHi F 1894-Ja 11 1895

Esbon TIMES. w F 3 1899+
KHi 1899+

ESKRIDGE

HOME weekly. w 1881-88||?
1881-Ja 19 1882 pub at Alma
KHi S 1881-S 13 1888

Eskridge INDEPENDENT. w 1918+
KHi F 18 1920+

LAND MARK. w 1872-83||?
Suspended from D 1874-Je 1883
KHi O 17 1873-O 5 1883

Eskridge STAR. *See* Eskridge tribune-star

Eskridge TRIBUNE. *See* Wabaunsee county tribune

Eskridge TRIBUNE-STAR. w O 19 1883-1920?
1883-F 4 1909 as Eskridge star
KHi 1883-S 1920

WABAUNSEE county democrat. w
KHi Je 11-D 3 1886

WABAUNSEE county tribune. w Ag 18 1900-F 4 1909||
1900? as Eskridge tribune. United with Eskridge star to form Eskridge tribune-star
KHi complete

ESSEX

Essex SUNBEAM. w
KHi Je 10-N 1887

EUDORA

Eudora NEWS. w My? 1886+
KHi S 8 1887+

EUREKA

Eureka BANNER. w 1912?-33||?
KHi [S 25 1925-Ap 13 1926;S 1928-My 3 1933]

Eureka CENSORIAL. w 1875-79||?
KHi Ap 12 1876-Ja 1879

DEMOCRATIC messenger. w Ja 18 1884+
Ja 18-F 15 1884 as Severy enterprise (Severy)
Suspended from F 15-My 2 1884
KHi 1884+

Eureka GRAPHIC. d 1903-04||?
KHi O 24 1903-Ja 7 1904

Eureka GRAPHIC. w *See* Greenwood county democrat

GREENWOOD county democrat. w 1879-84||?
1879-Mr? 1882 as Eureka graphic
KHi F 12 1879-Mr 2,Ap 13 1882-83

KANSAS (*Continued*)

EUREKA—*Continued*

GREENWOOD county republican. w 1879-O 5 1892||
1879-N 5 1880 as Eureka sun. United with Eureka herald to form Eureka herald and Greenwood county republican, later Eureka herald
KHi My 30 1879-92
OClWHi D 4 1885

GREENWOOD sunflower.
KHi Jl 24 1896-Je 1897

Eureka HERALD. w 1868+
1892? as Eureka herald and Greenwood county republican
KHi O 30 1868;O 15,D 24 1869;Ja 27 1876+
OClWHi O 6 1881

Eureka evening NEWS. d
KHi Ja 10-F 9 1898

Eureka REPUBLICAN. w 1899?-1900||?
KHi D 8 1899-My 11 1900

Eureka SUN. *See* Greenwood county republican

Eureka TIMES. *See* Eureka union

Eureka UNION. w 1893?-99||?
1893?-95? as Eureka times
KHi D 29 1893-D 1 1899

EUSTIS

NEW Tecumseh. w 1885?-87||?
1885?-Mr 1886 pub in Gandy; Ap-Ag 13 1886 in Leonard; Ag 20-N 5 1886 in Itasca
KHi N 9 1885-Mr 1887

SHERMAN county dark horse. *See under* Goodland

SHERMAN county democrat. *See under* Goodland

EVANSVILLE

Evansville HERALD. w
KHi O 1885-Ja 1887

EVEREST

Everest ENTERPRISE. w Mr 9 1888+
KHi 1888-[My 13 1920-Je 22 1923]+

Everest REFLECTOR. w 1884-87||?
KHi S 18 1884-Ja 1887

FAIRVIEW

Fairview COURIER. w 1893-99||?
KHi S 29 1893-O 1899

Fairview ENTERPRISE. w Mr 24 1888+
KHi 1888+

FALL RIVER

Fall River CHIEF. w
KHi Je-N 14 1891

Fall River CITIZEN. w 1892-97||?
1892-96? as Kansas advocate
KHi N 10 1892-Jl 10 1896;N 12-D 1897

Fall River COURANT. w 1886-88||?
KHi Jl 16 1886-O 19 1888

Fall River ECHO. w 1883-86||?
KHi Ap 1883-Ap 13 1886

KANSAS advocate. *See* Fall River citizen

Fall River NEWS. w 1898-1909||?
KHi N 11 1898-Jl 16 1909

Fall River STAR. w 1914+
KHi Ap 27 1917—

Saturday morning SUN. w
KHi D 8 1888-Jl 13 1889

Fall River TIMES. w 1881-91||?
KHi S 8 1881-O 1 1891

Fall River TIMES. w 1910-13||?
KHi F 1910-Jl 17 1913

FARGO SPRINGS

Fargo Springs NEWS. *See* Southwest daily times (Liberal)

PRAIRIE owl. w 1885-88||?
KHi O 8 1885-Ja 5 1888

SEWARD county democrat. w 1886-88||?
KHi Ap 30 1886-88

FARLINGTON

Farlington PLAINDEALER. w 1885-86||?
KHi O 11 1885-Je 12 1886

WESTERN gem. w
KHi S 1886-Ja 20 1887

FLORENCE

Florence BULLETIN. w F 17 1887+
KHi 1887+

Florence HERALD. w 1876-91||?
KHi O 13 1876-My 1885;Mr 1887-Ag 1891

Florence NEWS. w 1884-87||?
1884-Je 1886 as Florence tribune
KHi Jl 12 1884-Ja 1887

Florence TRIBUNE. *See* Florence news

FONDA

FORD county democrat. w 1886-88||?
1886? pub in Spearville
KHi Ap 8 1886-Ja 12 1888

FONTANA

Fontana BULLETIN. w 1896-97||?
KHi O 1896-F 1897

Fontana NEWS. w 1885-93||?
KHi Je 1885-Je 19 1890;N 3,17 1892

Fontana NEWS. w
KHi F 1908-Je 22 1909

FORD

Ford GAZETTE. w 1886-90||?
KHi Je 1886-N 21 1890

Ford PROGRESS. w O 22 1923-33||?
KHi 1922-Ap 1933

Ford PROMOTER. w 1909-18||?
KHi Mr 24 1910-S 1917

FORDHAM

Fordham REPUBLICAN. w
KHi Ap 9-O 15 1879

FORMOSO

Formoso ENTERPRISE. w
KHi Ja-Ag 1896

NEW ERA. w D 21 1900+
KHi 1900+

Formoso SPIRIT. w 1912-14||
Merged with Lovewell index (Lovewell)
KHi N 1912-Ap 9 1914

Formoso TIMES. w
KHi O-N 8 1889

FORT HARKER. *See* KANOPOLIS

FORT LEAVENWORTH

Fort Leavenworth NEWS. w 1903-14||?
KHi Jl 23 1904-N 1 1905;Je 20 1908-14

FORT RILEY

GUIDON. w 1895-1912||?
KHi F 25 1900-S 7 1912

SOLDIER'S letter. *See under* Kansas City, Mo.

FORT SCOTT

Fort Scott BANNER. *See* Tribune-monitor

BOURBON news. *See* Morning herald

Fort Scott BULLETIN. w
KHi S 6,O 4 1862

Sunday CALL. w 1889||?
KHi Ja 20-Je 1889

Fort Scott DEMOCRAT. w
KHi Ja 12,26,S 21 1861
OClWHi D 1 1860

DEUTSCHER krieger. w
In German
WHi My 20 1852

Fort Scott DISPATCH. w 1892?-94||?
KHi Je 9 1892-Jl 1894

EASTERN Kansas herald. *See* Morning herald

FAIR play. w 1898-99||?
KHi Ap 1898-Je 16 1899

Fort Scott evening GLOBE. d
KHi S 11 1888-Mr 6 1889

Fort Scott HERALD. w 1871?-85||?
1871?-Mr 1878? as Fort Scott pioneer (1875? Sentinel and pioneer); S 28 1882?-D 4 1884 Fort Scott herald and record
KHi Ja 6,27 1876-Mr 14,My 9 1878-Ag 1885

Fort Scott evening HERALD. d 1881?-85||?
KHi Je 5 1882-Ag 1885

Morning HERALD. w,d Jl 1 1921+
1921-Je 25 1925 as Bourbon news; Jl 2 1925-Ag 30 1928 Eastern Kansas herald
w 1921-Ag 30 1928
pub 1921+
KHi Ja 14 1923+

Der HEROLD. w 1880||?
In German
KHi Ap-My 1880

INDUSTRIAL union. w 1890?-91||?
KHi O 10 1890-Ap 24 1891

Fort Scott JOURNAL. w 1889-Ag 19 1893||
1889-S 3 1892 as Sunday spectator. Merged with Fort Scott lantern
KHi Ja 19 1890-93

KANSAS staats zeitung. w 1886?-88||?
In German
KHi Ja 14 1886-My 10 1888

Fort Scott LANTERN. w S 24 1890-S 19 1901||
1890-F 11 1891 as Mapleton lantern (Mapleton)
KHi complete

Fort Scott MESSENGER. w Ag 2 1917-
KHi 1917-S 13 1918

Fort Scott weekly MONITOR. w 1862-Ap 13 1904||
1863-66? as Union monitor. United with Fort Scott weekly tribune to form Tribune and monitor, later Tribune-monitor
CtY Je 17 1875
KHi Je 19 1867-70;Je 16 1876-N 12 1891;N 1892-1904

Fort Scott daily MONITOR. d 1869?-Ap 12 1904||
United with Fort Scott daily tribune to form Tribune-monitor
Suspended 1865
KHi D 16-17 1869;S 24 1871-My 25 1878;Ja 11 1880-D 8 1891;N 1892-1904
MWA Ag 26 1876
OClWHi Je 7,12,Jl 24 1870

NEW century. w
KHi 1877-Ap 1878

Fort Scott daily NEWS. d N? 1889-D 8 1890||
Merged with Fort Scott daily tribune, later Fort Scott tribune-monitor
KHi D 23 1889-90

Fort Scott NEWS. w 1889-90||?
KHi N 28 1889-Mr 1890

Fort Scott PIONEER. *See* Fort Scott herald

Fort Scott POST. d 1869-71||?
KHi O 16,D 14,29-30 1869;Ja 4 1870

Fort Scott PRESS. *See* Girard press w (Girard)

Weekly REPUBLICAN. w 1883-Ag 26 1915||
1883-N 26 1896 as Bronson pilot; D 3 1896-Ja 9 1902 Bronson record
1883-Ja 9 1902 pub in Bronson
KHi Mr 27 1884-1916

Daily REPUBLICAN. d Ja 1902-S 6 1916||
Merged with Fort Scott tribune-monitor
KHi Ja 19 1902-16

REPUBLICAN record. w 1879-S 15? 1882||
United with Fort Scott herald to form Fort Scott herald and record, later Fort Scott herald
KHi Ja 30 1879-S 15 1882

SASNAK. w Ja 5-O 7 1905||
Followed by Town and country
KHi complete

SENTINEL and pioneer. *See* Fort Scott herald

SOUTHERN argus. w
KHi O 15 1891-F 4 1892

Sunday SPECTATOR. *See* Fort Scott journal

TOWN and country. w O 20 1905-F 1 1907||
Follows Sasnak. Merged with Weekly republican
KHi complete

TRIBUNE-MONITOR. w,sw O 12 1882+
1882-O 30 1884 as Fort Scott banner; N 6 1884-Ap 13? 1904 Fort Scott weekly tribune; Ap 20? 1904-20 Tribune and monitor
sw 1905?-17?
KHi 1882+

Fort Scott TRIBUNE-MONITOR. d O 1 1884+
1884-Ap 13? 1904 as Fort Scott daily tribune; Ap 14? 1904-32? Tribune and monitor
KHi 1884+

Fort Scott UNION. w 1887-88||?
KHi O 22 1887-Mr 24 1888

UNION monitor. *See* Fort Scott weekly monitor

Fort Scott UNIONIST. w 1902-04||?
KHi D 11 1903-My 1904

FORT WALLACE

Wallace NEWS. D 27 1870-
CoHi D 27 1870
CoU D 27 1870

FOWLER

Fowler ADVOCATE. w 1886||?
KHi Ap 30-Jl 9 1886

Fowler GAZETTE. *See* Fowler news

Fowler GRAPHIC. w 1885-90||?
KHi Jl 1885-F 8 1890

Fowler HUSTLER. *See* Fowler news

Fowler NEWS. w 1906+
1906-My 10 1907 as Fowler hustler; My 17 1907-D 25 1913 Fowler gazette
KHi S 19 1906-13;Ap 1914-Je 1918;Jl 1920+

FRANKFORT

Frankfort BEE. w 1881-98||?
KHi N 18 1881-Je 18 1898

GREENBACK headlight. *See* National headlight

Frankfort INDEX. d F? 1906+
KHi Ap 27 1906+

MARSHALL county index. w 1905-06||?
KHi N 17 1905-Ap 20 1906

NATIONAL headlight. w 1879-81||?
1879-Ja 2 1880 as Greenback headlight
KHi O 24 1879-N 11 1881

Frankfort RECORD. w 1876-79||?
KHi Ag 1876-79

Frankfort REVIEW. w 1893-1910||?
Suspended N 12 1909-Je 16 1910
KHi Jl 21 1893-1910

Frankfort daily REVIEW. d My? 1909-10||?
KHi Je 12-D 1909

Frankfort SENTINEL. w 1886-92||?
KHi My 21 1886-Mr 11 1892

KANSAS (*Continued*)

FREDERICK

Frederick BULLETIN. w 1893-94||?
KHi S 28 1893-F 3 1894

Frederick FLAME. w
KHi O 14-D 1897

Frederick INDEPENDENT. w 1886?-89||?
KHi Ja 19 1888-F 21 1889

Frederick NEWS. w 1908-10||?
KHi S 1908-N 1910

Frederick REPUBLICAN. w
KHi Ag 24 1892-Ag 1893

RICE county news. w 1890-95||?
KHi Ag 28 1890-Jl 20 1895

FREDONIA

ALLIANCE herald. *See* Fredonia herald

Fredonia CHRONICLE. w
KHi S 16 1885-N 11 1888

Fredonia CITIZEN. d
KHi F 17-Ap 28 1923

Fredonia DEMOCRAT. w 1882-90||?
KHi My 25 1882-D 5 1890

Fredonia HERALD. w Mr 20 1891-1923||?
1891-1901? as Alliance herald
KHi 1891-My 18 1923

Fredonia HERALD. d Ap? 1904+
KHi Ap 29,Jl 14 1904;Ja 15 1905+

Fredonia TIMES. w 1883-85||?
KHi Jl 21 1883-Jl 1885

Fredonia TRIBUNE. w 1876-79||?
KHi Ja 31 1878-Ja 1879

WILSON county citizen. w,sw Ap 21 1870+
Ap-O 22 1870 as Guilford citizen (Guilford)
Suspended from O 22 1870-Je 6 1873
w 1870-1919?
KHi 1870+

FREEPORT

Freeport LEADER. w 1885-91||?
KHi Ag 13 1885-Ja 1 1891

Freeport NEWS. w 1914-15||?
KHi [Jl 9-D 10 1915]

Freeport TRIBUNE. w 1885-86||?
KHi Mr 11-S 1886

FREMONT

Fremont EAGLE. w 1889-90||?
KHi My 29 1889-Jl 1890

Fremont PRESS. w 1888-89||
Merged with Hill City reveille, later Hill City times (Hill City)
KHi Mr 1888-Ap 2 1889

Fremont STAR. w 1886-88||?
KHi Je 1886-F 9 1888

FRISCO

MORTON county democrat. w 1886?-F 11 1888||
United with Southwest leader to form Leader-democrat (Richfield)
KHi D 25 1886-88

Frisco PIONEER. w
KHi 1886-Mr 1887

FRONTENAC

Frontenac JOURNAL. w
KHi Ap 18-Jl 4 1896

Frontenac STAR. w 1927||?
KHi Ap 15-Je 1 1927

Frontenac VINDICATOR. w 1902||?
KHi F 8-15 1902

FULTON

Fulton GLOBE. w S 19 1912-17||?
KHi 1912-S 17 1917

Fulton INDEPENDENT. w 1884-1907||?
KHi Ag 8 1884-F 1 1907

Fulton NEWS. w 1923+
KHi My 17-Jl 19 1923;Ap 1928+

Fulton RECORD. w 1907?-12||?
KHi O 15 1909-F 1912

Fulton TIMES. w 1896-98||?
KHi O 8 1896-Ja 6 1898

GALENA

Galena BANNER. *See* Short Creek banner

Galena ECHO. w N 28 1912-20||?
KGaT 1912-18
KHi Ag 1913-Je 3 1920

Galena JOURNAL. w 1928-31||?
KHi D 21 1928-N 13 1931

Galena LEVER. d,w Ap 15- 1900||?
d Ap-Je 17? 1900
KHi Ap-Je 17,24-D 14 1900

Galena MESSENGER. w
KHi Ja 18-O 23 1879

Galena MINER. w 1877-81||?
KHi My 26 1877-O 2 1881

Galena MINER. w
KHi Je 14 1888-F 14 1889

Galena NEWS. d 1900?-
KHi F 14-Je 22 1901

Galena POST. w 1895-96||?
KHi My 16 1895-F 21 1896

Galena POST. d 1897?-
KHi Mr 29-My 28 1898

Galena REPUBLICAN. w 1881+
1881-Ja 21 1893 as Short Creek republican
KGaT 1901-04;07-08;12+
KHi Ja 19 1883+

Galena REPUBLICAN. d S 24? 1897-1900||?
KHi S 29 1897-Je 1900

Galena REPUBLICAN. d Ap 23 1906-
KHi Ap 23-Je 23 1906

SHORT CREEK banner. w 1878-79||?
Early issues as Galena banner
KHi O 12-D 1878

SHORT CREEK republican. *See* Galena republican

Galena TIMES. w D 12 1890-S 1 1899||
pub 1895-F 1896;97-99
KHi complete

Galena TIMES. d,tw,sw S 14 1896+
d 1896-Je 2 1923;tw 1926?;d 1928?
pub 1897-1904;14-26;29+
KHi 1896+

GALESBURG

Galesburg ENTERPRISE. w 1896?-1907||?
KHi Ja 15 1897-O 3 1907

Galesburg JOURNAL. w 1884-85||?
KHi Ap 22-Jl 15 1885

GALVA

Galva CLARION. w 1899-1901||?
KHi Jl 21 1899-Je 21 1901

Galva GAZETTE. w N 19 1931+
KHi 1931+

Galva TIMES. w 1888-92||?
ICHi O 11-25,N 8-15,D 6-13 1889
KHi Jl 21 1888-Ja 29 1892

GANDY

NEW Tecumseh. *See under* Eustis

GARDEN CITY

ARKANSAS VALLEY journal. w,sw 1911-14||?
w 1911-12?
KHi Ag 23 1912-Jl 14 1914

FINNEY county democrat. *See* Garden City taxpayer

Weekly HERALD. w Mr 17 1883-Mr 1 1929||
Merged with Garden City telegram
KGcT [1883-1929]
KHK 1927-28
KHi 1883-84;87-1929

Garden City HERALD. d Ap 23 1886-90||?
Suspended from O 1888-Ap 1889
KHi 1886-Ja 1890

Garden City IMPRINT. *See* Garden City daily telegram

Garden City IRRIGATOR. *See* Garden City taxpayer

Garden City LOOKOUT. w
KHi Ag 1891-O 15 1892

Garden City NEWS. w 1929+
pub 1929+
KHi Jl 25 1929+

Garden City daily NEWS. d O 1929+
pub 1929+
KHi N 12 1929-Je 16 1930

Garden City OPTIC. w 1880-81||?
KHi N 13 1880

Garden City PAPER. w
KHi Ap-O 1879

Garden City PROLOCUTOR. w 1909-11||?
KHi Ja 13 1910-Ag 17 1911
WHi Ap 16 1909-Jl 13 1911

Garden City REFLECTOR. w 1902?-07||?
1902-Je? 1905 as Conway Springs reflector (Conway Springs)
KHi F 20 1902-Je 27 1907

Garden City REFLECTOR. d S 26 1906-
KHi 1906-Je 28 1907

Garden City SENTINEL. w 1884-1909||?
Jl 1887-Ag 1888 as Sentinel and cultivator
CoU 1899-1900
KHi Jl 30 1884-D 24 1909

Garden City SENTINEL. d Ja 5 1886-88||?
KHi 1886-N 24 1888

Garden City TAXPAYER. w 1882-91||?
1882-Ja 1887 as Garden City irrigator; F 1887-F 1891 Finney county democrat
KHi Je 29 1882-Ap 1891

Garden City daily TELEGRAM. w,d Ap 20 1889+
1889-Ja 26 1912 as Garden City imprint; F 1912-N 6 1921 Garden City telegram
w 1889-N 6 1930
pub 1915+
KHK 1929
KHi 1889+

Evening TELEGRAM. d D 10 1906-12||
KHi 1906-Ja 1912

Garden City TRIBUNE. w 1892-94||?
KHi S 1892-N 10 1894

WESTERN times. *See under* Sharon Springs

GARDEN PLAIN

Garden Plain HERALD. w 1887-88||?
KHi D 29 1887-D 20 1888

Garden Plain NEWS. w
KHi S 30 1905-S 1906

Garden Plain NEWS. w Jl 7 1910-18||?
1910-My 16 1913 as Goddard gazette (Goddard)
KHi Jl 14 1910-My 2 1918

Garden Plain TRIBUNE. w 1919-29||?
KHi Ag 1920-Ap 24 1929

GARDNER

Gardner FLAG. *See* Kansas true flag

Gardner GAZETTE. w Ag 17? 1899+
KHi S 28 1899+

Gardner GRAPHIC. w 1891-93||?
KHi Ap 24 1891-Je 1893

KANSAS true flag. w 1894-95||?
Title varies: Gardner flag
KHi S 22 1894-95

GARFIELD

Garfield BOOSTER. w Ap 29? 1909-23||?
1909-Mr 31 1911 as Garfield leader
KHi My 13 1909-Ja 11 1923

Garfield LEADER. *See* Garfield booster

Garfield LETTER. w 1885-86||?
KHi Jl 23 1885-Jl 16 1886

Garfield NEWS. w 1887-88||?
KHi Je 17 1887-Je 8 1888

PAWNEE county news. w Jl 10 1924-27||?
KHi 1924-Ap 1927

Garfield REFLECTOR. w F 2?- 1923||?
KHi Mr 8-D 20 1923

GARLAND

Garland GAZETTE. w O 20 1905-F 1 1907||
Merged with Fort Scott weekly republican (Fort Scott)
KHi complete

Garland GLEANER. w 1886-87||?
KHi Ap 1886-O 1 1887

Garland GRAPHIC. w
KHi D 14 1905-Mr 22 1906

GARNETT

ANDERSON countian. w 1891+
1891-N 8 1923 as Greeley graphic (Greeley)
KHi Je 24 1892+

ANDERSON county democrat. *See* Garnett eagle

ANDERSON county republican. *See* Eagle-plaindealer

Garnett EAGLE. w Ag 4 1884-Mr 25 1904||
1884-Ja 16? 1885 as Westphalia independent; Ja 22-Je 25 1885 Westphalia democrat; Jl 3 1885-Je 25 1886 Anderson county democrat. United with Garnett plaindealer to form Eagle-plaindealer
1884 pub in Westphalia
KHi complete

EAGLE-PLAINDEALER. w 1865-My 10 1912||
1865-Mr 30 1883 as Garnett plaindealer; Ap 6 1883-My 23 1884 Anderson county republican; My 30 1884-1903 Republican-plaindealer; 1903-Mr 25 1904 Garnett plaindealer and Anderson county republican. United with Garnett journal to form Garnett journal-plaindealer
KHi Ag 26-S 2,16 1870;Ja 16,Jl 17 1874;Jl 9 1875;76-1912
MWA O 3 1873

INDEPENDENT review. w Je 7 1890-Mr 1 1907||
1890-My 19 1905 as Kansas agitator. Merged with Garnett journal, later Garnett journal-plaindealer
KHi complete
MWA Ap 19 1894

Garnett JOURNAL-PLAINDEALER. w 1873-My 17 1912||
1873-My 10 1912 as Garnett journal. Merged with Garnett review
KHi Ja 24 1874;Jl 10 1875;76-1912

KANSAS agitator. *See* Independent review

Garnett evening NEWS. d Ja 25? 1902-My 11 1912||
Suspended from S 3 1903-Jl 5 1904
KHi F 4 1902-12

Garnett PLAINDEALER. 1865-83 *See* Eagle-plaindealer

Garnett PLAINDEALER. w Ja 4-My 23 1884||
United with Anderson county republican to form Republican plaindealer, later Eagle-plaindealer
KHi complete

Garnett REPORTER. d F 28 1898-
KHi F-My 28 1898

KANSAS (*Continued*)

GARNETT—*Continued*

REPUBLICAN-PLAINDEALER. *See* Eagle-plaindealer

Garnett **REVIEW.** d,w D? 1906+
1906-S 11 1915 as Evening review (d)
KHi Ja 4 1907+

GARRISON

Garrison **STAR.** w 1914-15||?
KHi Jl 24 1914-Ag 13 1915

Garrison **TIMES.** w
KHi Jl 27-S 7 1880

GAS

To 1910? as Gas City

Gas City **GASLIGHT.** w 1901-02||
1901 as Gas City headlight. Merged with Gas City herald, later Tri-city herald
KHi F 22 1901-O 3 1902

Gas City **HEADLIGHT.** *See* Gas City gaslight

Gas City **HERALD.** *See* Tri-city herald

TRI-CITY herald. w,sw S 5 1902-30||?
1902-F 18? 1917 as Gas City herald
w 1899-1905?
KHi 1902-[10]-N 19 1915;Je 12-15,N 16 1917; Mr 19-22,S 9 1919-23

GAYLORD

Gaylord **HERALD.** w 1879-1901||
Merged with Smith county pioneer (Smith Center)
KHi S 1879-1901

Athol-Cedar-Gaylord **REVIEW.** *See* Smith county review (Smith Center)

Gaylord **SENTINEL.** w Jl 24 1902-24||?
KHi 1902-24

GEARY CITY

Geary City **ERA.** w
KHi Ag 1-15 1857

GEM

Gem **LEADER.** w 1908-11||?
KHi Ag 18 1909-Ja 19 1911

GENESEO

Geneseo **HERALD.** w Ja 13 1887?-99||?
KHi Ja 27 1887-O 1899

Geneseo **JOURNAL.** w Mr 10 1904+
KHi 1904-Ap 19 1906;My 27 1909+

Geneseo **POST.** w 1908-09||?
KHi Ag 1908-N 1909

GETTYSBURG

GRAHAM county lever. *See* Gettysburg lever

Gettysburg **LEVER.** w 1879-81||?
1879? as Graham county lever
KHi Ag 1879-Je 10 1881

TIMES. *See under* Penokee

GEUDA SPRINGS

CRANK. w 1886||?
InSHi N 6 1886
KHi S-N 1886
WHi N 6 1886

Geuda Springs **HERALD.** w 1882-95||?
KHi Ag 25 1882-95

Geuda Springs **HERALD.** w 1901-06||?
KHi Je 21 1901-My 11 1906

Geuda Springs **NEWS.** w 1884-85||?
KHi Jl 1884-85

Geuda **NEWS.** w
KHi S 16 1898-Ja 6 1899

Geuda **NEWS.** w 1912-14||?
KHi Je 21 1912-Ja 1914

Geuda Springs **NEWS.** w F 22 1924-33||?
KHi 1924-33

OKLAHOMA war chief. *See under* Caldwell

GIRARD

CRAWFORD county enterprise. w 1904-17||?
KHi 1915-Je 22 1917

CRAWFORD county news. w 1874-80||?
D 13 1878-Ap 3 1879 as Girard news
KHi Ag 1875-Ap 1880
WHi 1878-My 13 1880

GAA paa. *See* Folkets röst (Minneapolis, Minn)

Girard **HERALD.** d
KHi Ja 3-F 24 1894

Girard **HERALD.** w *See* Western herald

INDEPENDENT news. w My 18 1896-1909||?
KHi 1896-Ag 14 1909
WHi 1896-Ag 7 1909

Girard **MESSENGER.** w 1916?-24||?
KHi S 20 1923-D 18 1924

Girard **NEWS.** d D 7 1903-
KHi D 7 1903-Mr 26 1904

Girard **NEWS.** w *See* Crawford county news

PEOPLE'S vindicator. w
KHi Ag 18 1870

Girard **PRESS.** w N 4 1869+
1869 as Fort Scott press (Fort Scott)
pub 1869+
CSmH N 3(extra)1878
CoU 1899-N 1907;10
KHi Ja 6,My 19 1870;Jl 3,15,Ag 10 1871;My 28 1874+

Girard **PRESS.** d 1894-97||?
KHi S 17 1894-Ja 18 1897

Girard **TIMES.** *See* Pittsburg gunn powder (Pittsburg)

Girard **VERDICT.** w 1891?-1900||?
1891?-97 as Girard world; 1898-N? 1899 Western world
KHi 1894-Ag 10 1900

WESTERN herald. w 1878-96||?
1878-89 as Girard herald
KHi Jl 26 1878-Je 1882;Mr 1883-Ja 3 1896
WHi 1881-95

WESTERN world. *See* Girard verdict

WORKINGMAN'S journal. *See under* Columbus

Girard **WORLD.** d 1890-95||?
1890-Mr 1892 as Pittsburg star; Ap 1892-Je 1894 Pittsburg world
1890?-Je 1894 pub in Pittsburg
KHi F-[Je-D 1891]F-Mr 12,Ag 22 1892-N 9 1895

Girard **WORLD.** w *See* Girard verdict

GLADE

Glade **ECHO.** w
KHi S 10 1915-Ja 1916

GLASCO

To 1879? as Dell Ray

Glasco **BANNER.** w
KHi F 25-Jl 10 1880

Glasco **SUN.** w Ja 20 1883+
KHi 1883+

Glasco **TRIBUNE.** w 1881-82||?
KHi Ag 18 1881-Ag 24 1882

GLEN ELDER

Glen Elder **INDEPENDENT.** w 1898-1904||?
KHi Ja 28 1899-Je 4 1904

KANSAS herald. w 1885-90||?
KHi Mr-My 1885;Je 1886-O 1890

MITCHELL county key. *See* Alton empire (Alton)

PEOPLE'S sentinel. *See* Glen Elder sentinel

Glen Elder **REPUBLICAN.** w 1893-94||?
KHi O 13 1893-My 1894

Glen Elder **SENTINEL.** w Ja 1 1891+
1891-1913 as People's sentinel
KHi 1891+

GODDARD

Goddard **GAZETTE.** 1910-13 *See* Garden Plain news (Garden Plain)

Goddard **GAZETTE.** w N? 1922-25||?
KHi Ja 18-My 10 1923

Goddard **PAPER.** w
KHi D 1905-06

Goddard **REPORTER.** w 1889-90||?
KHi Ag 1889-Mr 20 1890

GOFF

Goff **ADVANCE.** w Mr 31 1892+
KHi 1892+

Goff **NEWS.** w 1887-90||?
KHi Je 16 1887-90

GOGNAC

STANTON county telegram. *See under* Johnson

GOLDEN

Golden **GAZETTE.** w 1887-89||?
KHi F 16 1887-O 1889

GOODLAND

Goodland **BANNER.** *See* Goodland news. 1898-1907

Goodland **NEWS.** w O 20 1887-96||?
KHi 1887-Jl 23 1896

Goodland **NEWS.** w 1898-My 30 1907||
1898-My 13 1899 as Goodland banner. United with Goodland republic to form Goodland news-republic, later Goodland republic
KHi 1899-1907

Goodland daily **NEWS.** d O 3 1932+
pub 1932+
KHi 1932+

Goodland **NEWS-REPUBLIC.** 1907-10 *See* Goodland republic

Goodland **NEWS-REPUBLIC.** w Je? 1916+
1916-Ap 1926 as Western Kansas news (N? 1917- Western Kansas news and Kanoradian)
pub Ap 1926+
KGC 1917-19;24+
KHK 1928-32
KHi D 22 1916+

Goodland **RECORD.** *See* Sherman county record

Goodland **REPUBLIC.** w Ag? 1886-Ap 1 1926||
1886-Ja 25 1889 as Sherman county republican; F 1 1889-O 9 1891 Goodland republican; Ap 28-D 1892 Goodland republic and Sherman county farmer; Je 7 1907-10? Goodland news-republic; 1914?-Ap 7 1916 Republic and news; Ag-D? 1917 Sherman county record and Goodland republic. United with Western Kansas news to form Goodland news-republic
Ag?-S 1886 pub in Itasca; O 1886-S 1887 in Sherman Center
KGC 1898-1926
KHi Ag 27 1886-1926

Goodland **REPUBLICAN.** *See* Goodland republic

SHERMAN county dark horse. w 1886-94||?
1886? pub in Eustis
KHi Je 10 1886-D 27 1894

SHERMAN county democrat. w 1886?-90||?
1886?-My 24 1888 pub in Eustis
KHi Ap 1887-Ja 13 1889

SHERMAN county farmer. w 1888-Ap 1892||
1888-90? as State line register (Kanorado) United with Goodland republic to form Goodland republic and Sherman county farmer, later Goodland republic
KHi O 11 1888-92

SHERMAN county herald. w 1916+
1916-N 22? 1933 as Brewster herald (Brewster)
KHi Je 24 1920+

SHERMAN county record. w Ag 9 1906-Jl 1917||?
1906-07? as Goodland record. United with Republic and news to form Sherman county record and Goodland republic, later Goodland republic
KGC 1917
KHi 1906-F 9 1917

SHERMAN county record and Goodland republic. *See* Goodland republic

SHERMAN county republican. *See* Goodland republic

WESTERN Kansas news. *See* Goodland news-republic 1916+

GOODRICH

Goodrich **GRAPHIC.** w 1889-91||?
KHi D 13 1889-N 6 1891

Goodrich **SENTINEL.** w
KHi S 19-N 14 1889

GOULD CITY. *See* SEVERY

GOVE

GAZETTE. *See* Gove county republican-gazette

GOVE county advocate. *See under* Quinter

GOVE county echo. w 1891-94||
United with Gove county gazette and republican to form Gove county gazette-echo, later Gove county republican-gazette
KHi Mr 1891-Ag 3 1894

GOVE county gazette and republican. *See* Gove county republican-gazette

GOVE county gazette-echo. *See* Gove county republican-gazette

GOVE county graphic. *See* Gove county republican

GOVE county leader. w 1894?-1901||?
KHi N 23 1894-Ja 11 1901

GOVE county republican. w 1887-90||
1887-N 23 1888 as Gove county graphic. United with Gove county gazette to form Gove county gazette and republican, later Gove county republican-gazette
KHi Jl 22 1887-Ap 25 1890

GOVE county republican. w 1889-O 15 1896||
1889-Je 4 1896 as Quinter republican (Quinter) United with Gove county gazette-echo to form Gove county republican-gazette
KHi Ap 11 1889-96

GOVE county republican-gazette. w 1886+
1886-88 as Gazette; 1888-Ag 3 1894 Gove county gazette and republican; Ag 10 1894-O 15 1896 Gove county gazette-echo
KHi Ap 9 1886+

SHORT grass advocate. *See* Gove county advocate (Quinter)

GRAINFIELD

Grainfield **ADVOCATE.** *See* Gove county advocate (Quinter)

CAP sheaf. w 1885-94||?
KHi Jl 17 1885-N 16 1894

Grainfield **CAP sheaf.** w O 14 1910—
KHi 1910—

GOLDEN belt advance. w
KHi Je 21-S 10 1881

Grainfield **REPUBLICAN.** w 1879-80||?
KHi Ja 28-D 10 1880

KANSAS (*Continued*)

GRANTVILLE

Grantville NEWS. w 1901-02||?
KHi N 21 1901-Mr 22 1902

GRASSHOPPER FALLS. *See* VALLEY FALLS

GREAT BEND

ARKANSAS VALLEY democrat. w 1877-82||?
KHi Ag 18 1877-D 9 1882
OOxM O 14 1882

BARTON county beacon. *See* Great Bend beacon

BARTON county democrat. w,d 1885-1918||?
w 1885-F 12 1915
KHi N 11 1886-Je 21 1916

BARTON county presse. *See under* Ellinwood

Great Bend BEACON. w,tw,sw 1890?-1903||?
1890-1900? as Barton county beacon
w 1890-1900?;tw 1901?
KHi S 1890-F 1903

Great Bend GRAPHIC. d 1887-88||?
KHi Mr 14 1887-Je 20 1888

INLAND tribune. *See* Great Bend tribune

Daily ITEM. *See* Great Bend daily tribune

KANSAS volksfreund. w 1878-79||?
In German
KHi S 1878-Ag 16 1879

Evening NEWS. d 1888-Ap 30 1897||
KHi F 6 1890-97

Great Bend morning NEWS. d F?-S 28 1910||
Merged with Great Bend tribune
KHi Mr 12-S 1910

Great Bend REGISTER. w 1874-1908||
United with Great Bend tribune to form Register and tribune, later Great Bend tribune
KHi Jl 1876-Jl 1908

REGISTER and tribune. *See* Great Bend tribune

Great Bend daily RUSTLER. d Mr 1 1904-Ag 22 1908||
Merged with Daily item, later Great Bend daily tribune
KHi complete

Great Bend evening STAR. d
KHi My 6-Je 27 1893

Great Bend TRIBUNE. w Ag 12 1876-Ap 9? 1915||
1876-87 as Inland tribune; 1908?-09? Register and tribune
CoU 1876-Ap 9 1915
KHi 1876-Ap 9 1915

Great Bend daily TRIBUNE. d Ag 4 1900+
1900-D 7 1908 as Daily item
CoU 1900-08
KHi 1900+
M Ag 8 1931

GREELEY

Greeley ADVOCATE. *See* Anderson county advocate (Colony)

Greeley GRAPHIC. *See* Anderson countian (Garnett)

Greeley LIGHT. w 1892-98||?
KHi Jl 1892-N 2 1898

Greeley NEWS. w 1881-95||?
Mr-Je 1892? as Greeley tribune
KHi Je 9 1881-Jl 12 1895

Greeley TRIBUNE. w 1880-81||?
KHi Ap 23 1880-Mr 25 1881

Greeley TRIBUNE. 1892 *See* Greeley news

GREEN

Green BANNER. w 1908-09||?
KHi Mr 1908-Ag 1909

CLAY county star. *See under* Morganville

Green HERALD. w 1904-06||?
KHi F 9 1905-F 22 1906

Green NEWS. w 1909?-15||?
KHi Mr 10 1910-Jl 10 1913

GREENLEAF

Greenleaf ENTERPRISE. w 1896||?
KHi Mr 20-O 9 1896

Greenleaf HERALD. w 1883-89||?
KHi S 14 1883-O 9 1889

Greenleaf INDEPENDENT. w 1882-S 7 1883||
United with Greenleaf journal to form Independent-journal, later Greenleaf journal
KHi S 15 1882-83

INDEPENDENT-JOURNAL. *See* Greenleaf journal

Greenleaf JOURNAL. w 1881-95||?
S 14 1883-S 29 1887 as Independent-journal
KHi Ja 15 1881-S 1895

SAFEGUARD. w
KHi S 22 1887-Ja 20 1888

Greenleaf SENTINEL. w Jl 13? 1894+
KHi Ag 10 1894+

GREENFIELD. *See* GRENOLA

GREENSBURG

KIOWA county independent. w 1899-1900||?
1899? pub in Haviland
KHi 1899-My 12 1900

KIOWA county opinion. w 1897-98||?
KHi Jl 30 1897-D 23 1898

KIOWA county signal. w F 19 1886-Je 19 1924||
United with Greensburg progressive to form Greensburg progressive-signal
KHi complete

KIOWA county times. w 1888-95||
Merged with Kiowa county signal
KHi Ag 17 1888-S 15 1895

Greensburg NEWS. w Jl 19 1928+
pub 1928+
KHi 1928+

Greensburg PROGRESSIVE-SIGNAL. w S? 1912+
1912-Je 19 1924 as Greensburg progressive
KHi 1913+

Greensburg REPUBLICAN. w 1887-88||?
KHi Mr 22 1887-88

Greensburg REPUBLICAN. 1890-91 *See* Republican banner

Greensburg REPUBLICAN. w 1902-11||
Merged with Kiowa county signal
KHi Ag 1902-11

REPUBLICAN banner. w 1890-95||?
1890-Ap 11? 1891 as Greensburg republican
KHi Ag 8 1890-95

Greensburg RUSTLER. w 1886-D 27 1888||
Merged with Kiowa county times
KHi Ap 15 1886-88

GRENOLA

Formed 1879 by the union of Greenfield and Canola

Grenola ARGUS. *See* Grenola chief

CANA VALLEY herald. *See* Grenola chief

Grenola CHIEF. w 1879?-1902||?
1879?-Mr 10 1882 as Grenola argus; Mr 17? 1882-Je? 1883 Cana Valley herald; O 11 1890-Je 5 1891 Crisis. United with Grenola greeting to form Grenola greeting and chief
KHi Ja 17 1880-Ap 20,Jl 1883-F 7,Jl 20 1889-1902

CRISIS. *See* Grenola chief

Grenola GAZETTE. w Mr? 1908+
1908-Ag 2 1928 as Grenola leader
KHi Je 11 1908+

Grenola GREETING and chief. w 1900-07||?
1900-02? as Grenola greeting
KHi Mr 9 1900-S 1907

HORNET. *See under* Howard

Grenola LEADER. *See* Grenola gazette

GRIDLEY

Gridley GAZETTE. *See* Waverly gazette (Waverly)

Gridley HERALD. w 1894-1901||?
KHi Mr 1894-Je 1 1900

Gridley LIGHT. w N 1907+
KHi D 20 1907+

Gridley STANDARD. w
KHi Jl 26 1889-Mr 1890

Gridley STAR. w 1902-07||?
KHi Je 11 1902-Je 13 1907

GRIGSBY

Grigsby CHRONICLE. *See* Scott City news-chronicle (Scott City)

Grigsby SCORCHER. w
KHi N 26 1886-Ap 21 1887

GRINNELL

GOLDEN belt. *See* Gove county golden belt

GOVE county golden belt. w 1885-90||?
1885-88? as Golden belt
KHi Jl 18 1885-Ap 1888;Mr 1889-Ap 12 1890

GOVE county record. w 1905-13||?
KHi Ap 20 1906-S 5 1913

RECORD-LEADER. w F 9 1917+
1917-Ap 30 1931 as Grinnell record
KHi My 1919+

GUILFORD

Guilford CITIZEN. *See* Wilson county citizen (Fredonia)

GYPSUM

Gypsum ADVOCATE. w Jl 16 1886+
1886-Ag 8 1890 as Gypsum Valley echo
KHi 1886+

Gypsum BANNER. w 1886-87||?
KHi My 1886-Ap 1 1887

GYPSUM VALLEY echo. *See* Gypsum advocate

Gypsum NEWS. w 1896-97||?
KHi Ag 21 1896-97

HADDAM

Haddam CLIPPER-LEADER. w 1883+
1883-My 2 1912 as Haddam clipper
KHi 1895+

Haddam GAZETTE. w
KHi N 22 1879

Haddam INVESTIGATOR. w 1888-89||?
KHi My 10 1888-F 7 1889

Haddam LEADER. w Ap 15 1910-My 1 1912||
United with Haddam clipper to form Haddam clipper-leader
KHi complete

NEW era. w 1886-87||?
KHi Ag 26 1886-S 8 1887

POLITICIAN. w 1888-89||?
KHi F 15-S 5 1889

HALL'S SUMMIT

Hall's Summit NEWS. w Mr 18? 1921-22||?
KHi Ap 29 1921-Ja 6 1922

HALSTEAD

Halstead CLIPPER. w 1884-86||?
KHi Ja 12 1884-Mr 5 1886

Halstead ECHO. w 1918?+
KHi N 1933+

Halstead HERALD. w 1886-88||?
KHi Ja 13 1887-D 13 1888

Halstead HERALD. d
KHi Mr 15-Ap 14 1887

Halstead INDEPENDENT. w 1880+
Ag-O 1892 as Independent-tribune
KHi 1882+

Halstead RECORD. w 1876-77||?
KHi Mr 9 1877

Halstead TRIBUNE. w 1890-Jl 29 1892||
United with Halstead independent to form Independent-tribune, later Halstead independent
KHi Mr 14 1890-92

HAMILTON

Hamilton BROAD axe. w
KHi N 8 1889-Mr 1890

Hamilton EAGLE. *See* Grit

Hamilton ENTERPRISE. *See* Hamilton post

GRIT. w 1901+
1901-Jl 10? 1903 as Hamilton eagle; Jl 17 1903-D 25 1908 Hamilton times
KHi F 14 1901-My 2 1902;Jl 17 1903+

Hamilton HERALD. w 1925?-
KHi [Jl 15 1931-Je 21 1932]-34

Hamilton POST. w 1897-99||?
1897-Jl 16? 1898 as Hamilton enterprise
KHi Jl 1897-Ag 18 1899

Hamilton TIMES. *See* Grit

HAMLIN

Hamlin NEWS gleaner. w
KHi Jl 20 1889-Mr 1890

Hamlin REPORTER. w 1912-15||?
KHi Jl 1913-D 16 1915

HAMPDEN

Hampden EXPOSITOR. w
KHi Jl 9 1864

HANOVER

Hanover DEMOCRAT. w O 25 1877+
1877-Ap 5 1878 as Washington county sun; S 1 1899-Ja 7 1927 Hanover democrat and enterprise
KHi 1877+

Hanover ENTERPRISE. w
KHi My 24 1873

Hanover ENTERPRISE. w O 9? 1896-Ag 25 1899||
United with Hanover democrat to form Hanover democrat and enterprise, later Hanover democrat
KHi N 20 1896-99

Hanover GRIT. w 1884-85||?
KHi Ag 8 1884-Ag 21 1885

Hanover HERALD. w Jl 6 1900+
KHi 1900+

WASHINGTON county sun. *See* Hanover democrat

WESTERN independent. w 1872-78||?
KHi My 18 1876-O 18 1877

HANSTON

Hanston HERALD. w Ja 3? 1927-
KHi Ja 10 1927-Je 14 1928

HARDTNER

Hardtner PRESS. w 1911+
KHi O 16 1914+

KANSAS (*Continued*)

HARLAN

Harlan ADVOCATE. w 1885-87||?
KHi Je 25 1885-Je 9 1887

Harlan CHIEF. w 1883-85||?
KHi N 29 1883-N 13 1885

Harlan ENTERPRISE. w 1887-88||?
KHi N 24 1887-N 8 1888

INDEPENDENT. *See under* Kirwin

HAROLD

Harold BOOMER. *See* Harold record

Harold RECORD. w Ap? 1887-89||?
Ap?-S 15 1887 as Harold boomer
KHi Ap 14 1887-Ag 22 1889

HARPER

Harper ADVOCATE. w 1885+
1885-D 25 1891 as Attica advocate (Attica)
KHi F 12 1885+
OkHi [1893-94]
—d ed *See* Attica advocate (Attica)

ALLIANCE bulletin. w 1890-91||
United with Harper county enterprise to form Weekly bulletin (Anthony)
KHi S 19 1890-S 25 1891

Harper GRAPHIC. w,sw 1883-92||?
Suspended from Ag 1 1888-S 6 1889?
sw 1889?
KHi Ag 14 1883-N 1892

Harper GRAPHIC. d 1885-86||?
KHi F 17-Je 1886

HARPER county times. w 1878-85||?
KHi O 24 1878-S 24 1885

Harper NEWS. w
KHi N 23 1900-Ja 1901
OkJV N 23 1900-S 1 1901

Harper PROPHET. w
KHi Je 9-N 1888

Harper REPUBLICAN. d 1888-89||?
KHi Ja-F 1889

Harper SENTINEL. w 1882-1917||?
KHi Ag 17 1882-D 6 1917

Harper SENTINEL. d 1884-88||?
KHi O 1885-F 9,My 21 1887-Ag 3 1888

HARRIS

Harris COMMERCIAL. w 1914-18||?
KHi Ap 23 1914-Ag 15 1918

Harris NEWS. w 1894||?
KHi Je 29-D 21 1894

Harris SUN. My 28 1909-Je 23 1911||
Merged with Garnett journal (Garnett)
KHi complete

HARTFORD

Hartford CALL. w 1879-91||?
KHi O 17 1879-Ap 17 1891

Hartford ENTERPRISE. w 1877-80||?
KHi Ja 10 1879-F 11 1880

NEOSHO VALLEY times. *See* Hartford times

Hartford NEWS. w 1890-98||
Merged with Neosho Valley times, later Hartford times
KHi My 8 1890-Ag 1898

Hartford TIMES. w 1874+
1894-N 28 1895 as Neosho Rapids times (Neosho Rapids) D 1895-My 11 1923 Neosho Valley times
KHi 1895+

HARTLAND

Hartland HERALD. w 1886-92||?
KHi F 27 1886-Jl 4 1891

KEARNY county coyote. w 1887?-90||?
1887? pub in Chantilly; 1888? in Omaha
KHi 1887-Mr 15 1890

Hartland STANDARD. w
KHi D 24 1888-Mr 2 1889

Hartland TIMES. w 1886-87||?
KHi Ap 1886-O 1887

HARVEYVILLE

Harveyville MONITOR. w 1903+
KHi F 1904+

HASTINGS

Hastings GAZETTE. *See* Brewster gazette (Brewster)

HATFIELD

Hatfield NEWS. w 1887-89||?
KHi Ag 18 1887-Mr 1889

HAVANA

Havana CITIZEN. w Mr? 1922-
KHi D 22 1922-Ag 14 1925

Havana HARP. w 1905-07||?
KHi O 1905-S 1907

Havana HERALD. w 1887-89||?
KHi Jl 1887-89

Havana NEWS. w 1890||?
KHi Ap 12-Ag 2 1890

Havana PRESS. *See* Havana torch

Havana RECORDER. w 1889||?
KHi Mr 8-D 6 1889

Havana TORCH. w 1891-93||?
1891-Ja 5 1893 as Havana press
KHi Je 12 1891-Je 16 1893

Havana VIDETTE. w 1885-87||?
KHi D 1885-F 11 1887

HAVEN

Haven DISPATCH. w
KHi Jl 28 1883-Ja 12 1889

Haven INDEPENDENT. w 1886-93||?
KHi Je 10 1886-Je 2 1888;Ja 19-Mr 23,D 1889-93

Haven ITEM. w 1894-95||?
KHi Mr 23 1894-95

Haven JOURNAL. w Jl 4 1896+
KHi Ag 8 1896-N 11 1909;N 14 1913+

HAVENSVILLE

Havensville INDEPENDENT. w
KHi O 27 1880-Jl 16 1881

Morning NEWS. w 1881-82||?
KHi F 18-S 2 1882

Havensville REGISTER. w 1889-90||?
KHi Jl 1889-D 11 1890

Havensville REVIEW. w 1891+
1891-Ag 1900 as Havensville torchlight
KHi N 19 1891+

Havensville TORCHLIGHT. *See* Havensville review

HAVILAND

KIOWA county independent. *See under* Greensburg

Haviland ONLOOKER. w My 16 1903-18||?
KHi 1903-18

Haviland REVIEW. w Je? 1919+
KHi D 18 1919+

Haviland TRIBUNE. w 1887-89||?
KHi N 17 1887-Ag 22 1889

HAYS

To 1898? as Hays City

ADVOCATE. *See* Hays free press

DEMOCRATIC times. w 1882-91||?
1882-My 8? 1886 as German-American advocate (in English and German) My 15? 1886-87 Hays City times
KHi O 1882-N 1884;Je 1885-91
—*See also* Hays free press

ELLIS county democrat. *See* Hays free press

ELLIS county free press. *See* Hays free press

ELLIS county news. w 1897+
1897-N 4 1899 as Ellis independent; Jl 20 1912-D 6 1914 Ellis county news and republican
KH [My 1911-15]-[17-22;24]+
KHK Jl 20 1912;13;Ja 30 1915-D 19 1929
KHi 1897+

ELLIS county star. w 1876-Ap? 1882||
United with Hays City sentinel to form Star-sentinel, later Hays sentinel
KHN Ap 1876-80
KHi Ap 1876-Je 7,D 13 1877-Mr 21 1878;Ap 24 1879-Ja 12 1882
NN [Ag 24 1876-Ag 2 1877]

ELLIS independent. *See* Ellis county news

Hays FREE PRESS. w,sw 1883?+
1883?-N 29 1884 as Advocate; D 6-27 1884 Advocate and Ellis county democrat; 1885 Ellis county democrat and advocate; Ja-My 1886 Ellis county democrat; My 1886-88 Ellis county free press and democrat; 1889-93? Hays City free press (in English and German)
sw 1887?-89?
KH [1887;Jl 1911-Je 1924]
KHK Mr 1912-Jl 1 1924
KHi N 22 1884+
—*See also* Democratic times

GERMAN-AMERICAN advocate. *See* Democratic times

KANSAS repealist. w
KHi My 1933-34

Hays daily NEWS. d N 11 1929+
KHK 1929-32
KHi 1929+
MWA N 11 1929

PUBLIC service. w 1919?-
KHi O 8 1925-Ag 15 1929

Hays RAILWAY advance. w
KHi Je 23 1868

Hays REPUBLICAN. w 1888-Jl 13 1912||
United with Ellis county news to form Ellis county news and republican, later Ellis county news
KH [1888-89]92-[1905]-[08]-[11]12
KHK F 16 1889-F 7 1891;F 13 1892-1912
KHi F 25 1888-1912

Hays SENTINEL. w 1874-95||?
My 1882-My 1887 as Star-sentinel
KHN [Mr 1876-Mr 1878]82-85
KHi Ja 26 1876-My 8 1884;My 1885-My 1886; My 12 1887-O 8 1895

STAR-SENTINEL. *See* Hays sentinel

Hays City TIMES. *See* Democratic times

HAZELTON

Hazelton BEE. w 1894||?
KHi Mr 24-S 8 1894

Hazelton EXPRESS. w 1884-98||?
Suspended O 27 1893-Ag 15 1896
KHi 1884-F 1898

Hazelton HERALD. w 1905+
KHi N 24 1906+

HEALY

Healy BANNER. w
KHi D 1903-S 1 1904

Healy HOMESTEAD. w 1929+
KHi F 14 1930-O 21 1932

HECTOR

Hector ECHO. w 1886||?
KHi Ap-Jl 1886

HEPLER

Hepler BANNER. w 1887-89||?
KHi F 1887-Jl 6 1889

Hepler ENTERPRISE. w 1904-12||?
KHi Ja 13 1905-Ja 19 1906

Hepler ENTERPRISE. w 1914-16||?
KHi S 13 1914-Ap 7 1916

Hepler HERALD. w
KHi S 28 1928-N 1 1929

Hepler LEADER. w 1883||?
KHi Ja 18-D 20 1883

Hepler LEADER. w
KHi Ja 10-Ag 6 1890

HERINGTON

Herington ADVERTISER. w 1933?+
1933?-Je 20 1934 as Mimeo news
KHi Jl 19 1933+

Herington HEADLIGHT. w 1888-89||?
KHi Mr 1888-Mr 1889

Herington JOURNAL. sm,m 1890?-95||?
1892-94? as Kansas exchange journal
m 1892?
KHi 1892-Ag 15 1894

KANSAS exchange journal. *See* Herington journal

MIMEO news. *See* Herington advertiser

Herington SIGNAL. w 1891-96||?
KHi Ja 9 1891-D 8 1892;D 28 1893-Ap 23 1896

Herington SUN. w Je 1 1903-Jl 26 1934||
United with Herington times to form Herington times-sun
KHeT complete
KHi complete

Herington TIMES-SUN. w Jl 25 1889+
1889-Jl 26 1934 as Herington times
pub 1912+
KHi 1889+

Herington TRIBUNE. w 1884-90||?
KHi D 11 1884-N 13 1890
MWA Ap 30 1885

Herington TRIBUNE. w
KHi Ap 30-O 1896

Herington VINDICATOR. w
KHi F-Jl 9 1890

HERNDON

Herndon COURANT. w 1888-90||?
KHi Mr 16 1888-90

Herndon NONPAREIL. w 1905+
KHi D 10 1908+

HESSTON

Hesston GAZETTE. *See* Harvey county news 1917+ (Newton)

Hesston RECORD. w 1932+
KHi D 1932+

HEWINS

Hewins SAYINGS. w 1907-09||?
KHi Ag 1907-Ap 15 1909

HIATTVILLE

Hiattville NEWS. w 1908-10||?
KHi F 21 1908-F 1910

Hiattville OPTIC. w
KHi Je 16 1892-My 6 1893

HIAWATHA

BROWN county advocate. *See* Kansas herald

BROWN county republican. w 1896?-Ag 7 1902||
KHa [1901]
KHi Ap 1901-02

KANSAS (*Continued*)

HIAWATHA—*Continued*

BROWN county sentinel. w Ag 20 1864-70||
1864-Ap 1868 as Union sentinel. Merged with Hiawatha dispatch, later Brown county world
KHa 1864-Ap 21 1870
KHi 1864-Ag 10 1866;S 9,D 30 1869
MWA S 22 1865

BROWN county world. w 1870+
1870-Mr 9 1882 as Hiawatha dispatch; Mr 16 1882-84 Hiawatha world
KHa Ap 30 1870-Mr 9 1882;85-1914
KHi Ap 13 1876+
—d ed *See* Hiawatha daily world

BROWN county world. d S? 1891-Ap 28 1892||
KHi D 28 1891-92

BROWN county world. d Mr 15-O 7 1899||
KHi complete

Hiawatha DISPATCH. *See* Brown county world

FREE PRESS. w Ap 1887-88||?
KHa 1887-F 1888
KHi F 17 1887-Mr 1 1888

Hiawatha HERALD. w 1904||?
KHi F 18-N 3 1904

Hiawatha JOURNAL. w My 23 1889-Je 27 1895||
Merged with Kansas democrat
KHa 1889-O 1890;91-95
KHi complete

KANSAS democrat. w,sw S 15 1883-Ap 24 1924||
Jl 15? 1909-13 Kansas news-democrat
sw 1904?
KHa Ja 26 1884-[92-94]-[1907]-24
KHi complete

KANSAS herald. w Je 25 1874-N 22 1883||
1874-O 2 1875 as Brown county advocate. Merged with Hiawatha world, later Brown county world
KHa complete
KHi O 16-23 1874;Jl 3 1875;76-83

KANSAS news-democrat. *See* Kansas democrat

KANSAS sun. *See* Hiawatha sun

Weekly MESSENGER. w D 10 1881-84||?
Merged with Kansas democrat
KHa Jl 8 1882-D 21 1883
KHi 1881-Ja 19 1884

Hiawatha NEWS. Mr 4-Jl 8? 1909||
United with Kansas democrat to form Kansas news-democrat, later Kansas democrat
KHa Mr-Je 1909
KHi Mr-Jl 8 1909

NORTH Kansan. w S 7 1878-79||
KHa complete
KHi S-N 1878;Ja 8 1879

Hiawatha SUN. w Je 7 1879-O 27 1880||
Je 7-S? 1879 as Kansas sun
KHa complete
KHi complete

UNION sentinel. *See* Brown county world

Hiawatha WORLD. *See* Brown county world

Hiawatha daily WORLD. d 1908+
KHa 1915-23;Jl 1924+
KHi 1908+

HIGHLAND

CENTRAL state. w 1880-82||?
KHi N 1880-My 26 1882

Weekly HIGHLANDER. w Ja 1 1859-
KHi Ja 1 1859
MH Ja 1-F 3,24-Mr 3 1859

Highland SENTINEL. w 1878-79||?
KHi F 13 1878-F 21 1879

Highland VIDETTE. w F 18 1892+
KHi 1892+

HILL CITY

Hill City DEMOCRAT. 1887-91||
Merged with Hill City reveille, later Hill City times
KHi Jl 21 1887-Ja 23 1891

Hill City DEMOCRAT. w
KHi O 19 1894-D 6 1895

GRAHAM county recorder. w 1897-1905||
1897-Ap 5 1901 as Graham gem. Merged with Hill City reveille, later Hill City times
KHi D 24 1897-1905

GRAHAM county times. w 1889?-91||?
KHi Ap 25 1889-O 1 1891

GRAHAM gem. *See* Graham county recorder

GRAHAM republican. w
KHi Ag 1881-Ja 7 1882

NEW ERA. w 1906-Mr? 1911||
United with People's reveille to form Reveille and new era, later Hill City times
KHi Mr 1906-Ja 5 1911

Hill City NEWS. w 1894-95||
Merged with Hill City reveille, later Hill City times
KHi O 1894-Ja 10 1895

PEOPLE'S advocate. w 1890-95||
United with Hill City reveille to form People's reveille, later Hill City times
Suspended from Mr-O 1891
KHi Ag 14 1890-Ap 4 1895

PEOPLE'S reveille. *See* Hill City times

Hill City REPUBLICAN. w Jl 9 1890-1930||?
KHi 1890-D 20 1930

Hill City REVEILLE. *See* Hill City times

Hill City STAR. w 1888-89||?
KHi Ag 1888-Ap 18 1889

Hill City SUN. w 1887-89||
Merged with Hill City reveille, later Hill City times
KHi S 20 1888-Ap 16 1889

Hill City TIMES. w Ag 8 1884+
1884-Ap 4 1895 as Hill City reveille; Ap 11 1895 Hill City reveille and people's advocate; Ap 18 1895-Mr 9 1911 People's reveille; Mr 16 1911-Mr 20 1930 Reveille and new era
pub Mr 1930+
KHi 1884+

WESTERN star. w 1879-80||?
KHi D 25 1879-Je 10 1880

HILLSBORO

Hillsboro ANZEIGER. w 1887-97||
1887-90? as Marion county anzeiger. United with Das Kansas volksblatt (Newton) to form Volksblatt und anzeiger, later Der Herold (Newton)
1887-S 7 1888 pub in Marion
In German and English
KHi Jl 15 1887-D 3 1897

FREIE PRESSE. w
In German
KHi F 21-Ag 1890

Hillsboro HERALD. w 1886-90||?
In English and German
KHi S 30 1886-Je 1889

Hillsboro INTELLIGENCER. w
KHi S 8 1881-Ap 1882

Hillsboro JOURNAL. *See* Vorwärts

KANSAS courier. w 1891-93||?
In German
KHi S 25 1891-Ag 1893

MARION county anzeiger. *See* Hillsboro anzeiger

PHONOGRAPH. w 1880-81||?
KHi Ja-Je 3 1881

Hillsboro POST. w 1898-Ja 24 1902||
United with Das Kansas volksblatt (Newton) to form Post und volksblatt, later Der Herold (Newton)
In German
KHi Mr 25 1898-1902

Hillsboro STAR. w My 2 1924+
KHi 1924+

VORWÄRTS. w 1903+
1903-09? as Hillsboro journal
In German and English
KHi 1910+
OB 1929+

HODGEMAN CENTER

Hodgeman Center AGITATOR. w 1879-80||?
KHi Mr 1879-Ja 10 1880

HODGEMAN county herald. *See* Kalvesta herald (Kalvesta)

HOISINGTON

Hoisington BLADE. w 1892-93||?
KHi Ap 14 1892-Ag 17 1893

Hoisington DISPATCH. w Mr 7 1889+
pub 1896;1901+
KHi 1889+

Hoisington ECHO. w 1887-89||?
KHi Jl 30 1887-Ja 1889

HOLLENBERG

Hollenberg RECORD. w 1888-89||?
KHi Ja 19-O 19 1889

HOLTON

Holton ARGUS. w
KHi Ap 20-O 24 1877

Holton EXPRESS and news. w 1872-Mr? 1875||
1867-74? as Holton express. United with Holton recorder to form Recorder and express, later Holton recorder
KHi Ap 12 1872-Mr 1875

HOLTONIAN. bw 1918?+
KHi N 23 1926+

INDEPENDENT tribune. w 1888-1905||
1888-Je 12 1890 as Soldier tribune (Soldier). Merged with Holton recorder
KHi Ja 26 1888-Ag 3 1905

JACKSON county federal. sw 1886-88||?
KHi S 1886-D 21 1887

JACKSON county news. *See* Holton news

JACKSON county signal. w Ja 9 1878+
1878-Jl 2 1931 as Holton signal
KHi 1878+

KANSAS sunflower. *See* Holton sunbeam

Holton NEWS. w 1867-74||?
1867-72 as Jackson county news. United with Holton express to form Holton express and news
KHi Ap 11 1872-D 11 1873

Holton RECORDER. w 1868+
Ap? 1875-77 as Recorder and express
pub Mr 1872+
CoU F 1899-1901;Je 1904-My 1910
KHi Mr 30 1875+

Holton SIGNAL. *See* Jackson county signal

Holton SUNBEAM. w,sw 1894-1904||?
1894-1903? as Kansas sunflower
sw 1894-98?
KHi D 19 1895-Ag 17 1904

HOLYROOD

Holyrood BANNER. w 1900-18||?
KHi N 1900-Jl 19 1918

Holyrood ENTERPRISE. w 1887-90||?
KHi Mr 31 1887-Jl 5 1890

Holyrood GAZETTE. w 1919+
KHi F 14 1919+

Holyrood SENTINEL. w 1891-92||?
KHi O 8 1891-Ag 12 1892

Holyrood SUN. w 1894-95||?
KHi Ag 1894-N 1895

HOME CITY

Home City JOURNAL. w 1908-17||?
1908-16 as Home City tribune
KHi N 20 1908-N 9 1917

Home City TRIBUNE. *See* Home City journal

HOPE

Hope CRESCENT. w 1893-96||?
KHi Je 22 1893-Jl 2 1896

Hope DISPATCH. w 1886+
Ja 21 1892-Mr 3 1893 as Hope dispatch-herald
KHi Mr 1886+

Hope HERALD. w 1884-Ja 21 1892||
United with Hope dispatch to form Hope dispatch-herald, later Hope dispatch
KHi F 1885-92

Hope STAR. w
KHi Ag 18 1892-Ja 13 1893

WESTERN news. w 1895-96||
Merged with Hope dispatch
KHi Ap 18 1895-96

HORACE

Horace CHAMPION. w 1888-89||?
KHi Je 29 1888-S 1889

GREELEY county gazette. *See* Horace messenger

GREELEY county journal. *See* Horace headlight

GREELEY county news. w
KHi N 1886-Ja 1888

GREELEY county tribune. *See* Greeley county republican (Tribune)

Horace HEADLIGHT. w 1890-93||?
1890-Ap 1892 as Greeley county journal
1890-91? pub in Tribune
KHi Mr 27 1890-N 9 1893

Horace MESSENGER. w 1886-89||?
1886-87? as Greeley county gazette
KHi Ap 15 1886-Jl 7 1887;F 1888-My 16 1889

HORTON

BROWN county star. w 1888-89||?
KHi Ja-Ap 23 1889

Horton COMMERCIAL. w N 8 1887-Je 8 1911||
United with Horton headlight to form Horton headlight-commercial, later Horton headlight
KHi 1887-1911
KHoH O 1890-1911

Horton GAZETTE. w
KHi Je 25 1887-My 11 1889

Horton HEADLIGHT. w,sw O 29 1886+
1901 as Horton headlight-leader; Je 15 1911-Ag 21 1933 Horton headlight-commercial
w 1886-1924?
pub O 30 1890+
KHi 1896-O 14 1897;Mr 17 1898+

Horton HEADLIGHT. d 1887-D 31 1889||?
KHi O 29 1887-89

Horton LEADER. w 1898-1901||?
United with Horton headlight to form Horton headlight-leader, later Horton headlight
KHi Ja 17 1899-Jl 4 1901

Horton NEWS. w 1912-14||?
KHi S 12 1912-Ap 9 1914

Horton RAILWAY register. d 1886?-
KHi Ap 4 1888-F 26 1890

Horton RAILWAY register w. *See* Horton telegram

Horton TELEGRAM. w 1888?-90||?
1888?-Je 19 1889 as Horton railway register (w)
KHi Ap 1888-F 1890

TRI-COUNTY news. w Mr 26 1931+
pub 1931+
KHi 1931+

KANSAS (*Continued*)

HOWARD

Howard CITIZEN. w 1878+
1878-80? as Industrial journal; 1881?-Ag 3? 1883 Howard journal; Ag 15? 1883-Ag 27 1884 Grip; S 3 1884-Jl 29 1891 Howard democrat; Ag 6? 1891-1918? Elk county citizen
KHi Jl 4,24 1878+

Howard COURANT. w 1874+
1874-75? as Courant; 1878-79? Courant-ledger
1874 pub in Elk City; 1875 in Longton
KHi Mr 17 1875+

Howard DEMOCRAT. *See* Howard citizen

ELK county citizen. *See* Howard citizen

ELK county ledger. w 1870-D 27 1877||
1870-O 28 1876 as Howard county ledger. United with Howard courant to form Howard courant-ledger, later Howard courant
1870-73 pub in Longton; 1874-O 28 1876 in Elk Falls
KHi Ja 20 1876-77

GRIP. *See* Howard citizen

HORNET. w 1884?-85||?
1884? pub in Grenola
KHi N 17 1884-85

INDUSTRIAL journal. *See* Howard citizen

Howard JOURNAL. *See* Howard citizen

KANSAS rural. w 1881||?
KHi Ja-Je 15 1881

KANSAS searchlight. *See* Howard searchlight

KANSAS traveler. w 1886-87||?
KHi N 20 1886-Je 1 1887
—d ed *See* Howard traveler

Howard SEARCHLIGHT. w
Occasional numbers as Kansas searchlight
KHi S 1900-Je 1903

Howard TRAVELER. d Mr 10- 1887||?
KHi Mr-Je 1 1887
—w ed *See* Kansas traveler

HOXIE

Hoxie DEMOCRAT. *See* Hoxie palladium

Hoxie PALLADIUM. w 1885?-1906||?
1885-Mr 12 1886 as Kenneth democrat (Kenneth) Mr 19 1886-Ag 14 1921 Hoxie democrat
KHi Ag 21 1891-O 1906

Hoxie SENTINEL. w Jl 17 1884+
1884-85 as Weekly sentinel; 1885-Mr 11 1886 Kenneth sentinel
1884-Mr 11 1886 pub at Kenneth
pub 1884+
KHi 1884+

SHERIDAN county democrat. w 1892-96||?
1892? as Hoxie times
KHi Ap 30 1892-Ap 17 1896

Hoxie TIMES. *See* Sheridan county democrat

HOYT

Hoyt BOOSTER. w 1915-16||?
KHi Jl 23 1915-Jl 6 1916

Hoyt JOURNAL. w 1896||?
KHi Jl 30-D 1896

Weekly REPORTER. w 1915?-20||?
KHi N 22 1917-20

Hoyt TIMES. w
KHi Je 9-N 10 1887

HUDSON

Hudson HERALD. w 1914+
KHi Ja 27 1915+

Hudson JOURNAL. w 1909-13||?
1909-11? as Hudson patriot
KHi N 10 1909-13

Hudson PATRIOT. *See* Hudson journal

HUGOTON

Hugo HERALD. w 1886-89||?
KHi F 13 1886-S 5 1889

HERMES. w Ag 4 1887+
Suspended from F 21 1890-D 22 1893
KHi 1887+

SOUTHWEST Kansan. w 1896-97||?
KHi Ja 11 1896-Mr 6 1897

STEVENS county sentinel. w 1893?-94||?
KHi Ap 1893-N 10 1894

Morning SUN. d,w
d -O 4 1934
KHi O 2 1934-My 17 1935

HUMBOLDT

ALLEN county herald. *See* Humboldt herald 1887-1913

Humboldt HERALD. w
KHi F 3-10,Mr 24,Ap 28-My 12,Je 2,23-30 1865

Humboldt HERALD. w,d,sw Ag 4 1887-My 21 1913||
1904?-08? as Allen county herald. Merged with Humboldt union
w 1887-1901?;d My 17 1901-Ag 3 1912
KHi complete

Humboldt INDEPENDENT press. w 1882-83||?
KHi Mr 8 1882-Ja 10 1883

Humboldt INTER-STATE. w 1877-87||?
KHi D 1877-My 5 1887

KANSAS derrick. w 1903-05||?
KHi Ja 20 1903-Ag 15 1905

Humboldt daily NEWS. d D 24 1908-My 16 1909||
Merged with Humboldt herald
KHi complete

Humboldt UNION. w 1866+
DLC My 31 1873
KHi O 9-D 11 1869;Je 1876+

HUNNEWELL

Hunnewell HERALD. w F? 1915-23||?
KHi D 1915-Mr 1923

Hunnewell REPORTER. w 1897-98||?
KHi S 1897-My 1898

Hunnewell RUSTLER. *See* South Haven rustler (South Haven)

Hunnewell STAR. w 1904-05||?
KHi Ja 14-N 1905

Hunnewell VOICE. w
KHi Mr 23 1894-F 7 1895

HUNTER

Hunter HERALD. w Ag 24 1916+
KHi 1916+

HURON

Huron GRAPHIC. w 1890-91||?
KHi Ap 1890-N 21 1891

Huron HERALD. w Ja 7 1892-Ag 9 1900||
Merged with New leaf (Effingham)
KHi complete

Huron HERALD. w Ap 12 1907-17||?
KHi 1907-N 1 1917

Huron TIMES. w 1901-03||?
KHi F 22-Je 14 1901

HUTCHINSON

ALLIANCE gazette. *See* Semi-weekly gazette

Saturday BEE. w 1895-1905||
Merged with Hutchinson independent
KHi D 21 1895-Jl 8 1905

Hutchinson daily BEE. *See* Hutchinson herald. 1902+

Hutchinson BLADE. w 1914?-22||?
Negro
KHi D 20 1919-Ap 1 1922

Hutchinson CALL. d Ap 11 1888-
KHi Ap-Je 18 1888

CLIPPER. *See* Hutchinson independent

Hutchinson DEMOCRAT. w 1882-90
1882-Ag 19 1883 as Sunday democrat; Ag 25 1883-Ja 26 1884 Dollar democrat
KHi 1883-Ag 20 1890

Hutchinson DEMOCRAT. w 1889-1902||?
1889-Mr 30 1895 as Hutchinson times (Jl 4 1890-D 4 1891 Times-republican)
KHi D 1889-My 1902

DEMOCRAT-REVIEW. *See* Labor review

DOLLAR democrat. *See* Hutchinson democrat 1882-90

Hutchinson EXAMINER. w 1875-77||?
KHi Mr 22-N 23 1876

GAS bomb. w 1927?-
KHi Mr 1931-My 1933

Semi-weekly GAZETTE. w,sw 1890-1910||
1890-94 as Alliance gazette; 1895-1902 Hutchinson gazette
w 1890-1902
KHi S 1890-1909

Hutchinson daily GAZETTE. *See* Hutchinson herald 1902+

Hutchinson HEADLIGHT. w 1889?-95||?
KHi S 29 1893-Mr 20 1895

Hutchinson weekly HERALD. w 1876-1903||
Ja 10 1885-1902? as Weekly interior herald
KHi Ap 1877-Ap 9 1887;Ja 13 1902-Je 20 1903
KHu Ja 10 1885-1903
OOxM O 14 1882

Hutchinson HERALD. d Ap 12- 1887||?
KHi Ap 12-D 1887

Hutchinson HERALD. d Mr 19 1902+
1902-Je 30 1905 as Hutchinson daily bee; Jl 1 1905-My 30 1908 Hutchinson daily independent; Je 1? 1908-Je 1 1924 Hutchinson daily gazette
KHi 1902+
KHuN 1924+

Hutchinson INDEPENDENT. w F 11 1889-1908||
1889-Ja 15 1902 as Clipper. Merged with Semi-weekly gazette
KHi 1889-My 1908

Hutchinson daily INDEPENDENT. *See* Hutchinson herald 1902+

Hutchinson INTERIOR. w Ja 18 1877-Ja 9 1885||
United with Hutchinson weekly herald to form Weekly interior herald, later Hutchinson weekly herald
KHi 1877-Ja 1 1885
KHuN complete
OOxM O 12 1882

Weekly INTERIOR herald. *See* Hutchinson weekly herald

Hutchinson KANSAN. *See* Hutchinson mail

KANSAS herold. w 1888-90||?
In German
KHi Ap 28 1888-Ap 19 1890

KANSAS observer. w 1914-20||?
KHi Mr 1915-Jl 23 1920

LABOR review. w 1925+
Je 2 1933-Mr 30 1934 as Democrat-review
KHi Jl 30 1926+

Hutchinson MAIL. w 1894-1901||?
1894-Ag 1898 as Hutchinson Kansan
KHi 1896-N 1901

NEW times. [South Hutchinson] w
KHi F 10-Ap 1887

Hutchinson NEWS. w Jl 4 1872-1933||
Jl 2 1932 has reprint of Jl 4 1872
pub complete
KHi Jl 15 1875;F 17 1876-Jl 7 1933
OOxM O 5 1882

Hutchinson NEWS. d Jl 4 1885+
pub 1885+
CoU 1901
KHK Jl 1926-Mr 1933
KHi Ag 17 1886+
KHu S 1929+

Hutchinson PATRIOT. d
KHi Jl 10-S 19 1893

Hutchinson PRISM. w
KHi My 1927-Ag 1929

RENO county independent. w 1875-76||?
KHi F 23 1876

Hutchinson REPUBLICAN. w 1889-Je 28 1890||
United with Hutchinson times to form Hutchinson times-republican, later Hutchinson democrat
KHi Mr 23 1889-90

Saturday REVIEW. [South Hutchinson] w 1887-90||?
Follows South Hutchinson leader?
KHi S 10 1887-My 24 1890

SOUTH HUTCHINSON journal. w
KHi My 11 1888-Mr 16 1889

SOUTH HUTCHINSON leader. w 1886-87||?
Followed by Saturday review?
KHi N 30 1886-Ag 1887

SOUTH HUTCHINSON record. w 1922+
KHi Ja 29 1926+

Hutchinson TIMES. 1889-95 *See* Hutchinson democrat 1889-1902

Hutchinson TIMES. w 1906-09||?
KHi N 1906-D 17 1909

Hutchinson TIMES. w S 16 1932+
KHi 1932-My 5 1933

Hutchinson TRADESMAN. w 1902-08||?
KHi N 22 1902-D 21 1907

Weekly VISITOR. w
KHi Ap-O 1900

Hutchinson WORLD. w 1889-90||?
KHi D 19 1889-Mr 20 1890

IDANA

Idana JOURNAL. w
KHi D 1886-N 4 1887

INDEPENDENCE

Evening CALL. d Mr 2 1896-
KHi Mr-Jl 8 1896

Independence COURIER. *See* Workingman's courier

Daily FREE PRESS. d 1912-26||?
Mr 23-Je 3? 1913 as Independence times
Suspended from Ap 26-Mr 23 1913
KHi F 28-Je 3 1913;O 2 1923-S 1926

ITEMIZER. w
KHi Jl 19-Ag 5 1879

Independence KANSAN. w 1873-D 24 1884||
1873-74? as Southern Kansan. United with Independence star to form Star and Kansan
KHi Ja 28 1876-84

KANSAS democrat. w 1871-74||?
KHi F 1871-74

KANSAS populist. *See* Independence times

LIVING age. w 1881||
Merged with Independence star, later Star and Kansan
KHi F-S 1881

MONTGOMERY argus. w
KHi Jl 30 1886-Ja 7 1887

Independence NEWS. d 1885-86||?
KHi Mr 23-Jl 18 1886

PEOPLES' elevator. w 1924?-31||?
1924?-27 pub in Wichita
Negro
KHi F 21 1924-Ap 1930

Independence PIONEER. w
KHi N 13 1869-Ja 1 1870

Evening REPORTER. d 1881+
Title varies slightly
KHi Ja 27-D 1882;84;86+
MWA Ap 18 1887

SOUTH Kansas tribune. w 1871+
KHi F 9 1876+
NbHi Ja 2 1878

KANSAS (*Continued*)

INDEPENDENCE—*Continued*

SOUTHERN Kansan. *See* Independence Kansan

Evening STAR. d 1900-24||?
KHi [Mr 4 1901-Mr 15 1924]

STAR and Kansan. w Ap 14 1881-1905||
Ap 14-O 5 1881 as Coffeyville star (Coffeyville); O 14 1881-84 Independence star
ICJ 1894-1902
KHi 1881-N 23 1905

Independence TIMES. w 1898?-1913||?
1898?-Mr? 1904 as Kansas populist
KHi Je 1898-F 7 1913

Independence TIMES. d *See* Daily free press

WORKINGMAN'S courier. 1874-N 19 1879||
1874-O 25 1878 as Independence courier. Merged wtih Independence Kansan
KHi Ag 28 1874-D 14 1876;79

INDUSTRY

Industry HERALD. w
KHi D 30 1886-Ag 4 1887

INGALLS

Ingalls ECHO. w
KHi O 1886-Mr 3 1887

GRAY county republican. w 1888||?
KHi Ja 12-O 4 1888

Ingalls MESSENGER. w 1889-90||?
KHi Jl 17 1889-Jl 2 1890

Ingalls UNION. w 1887-96||?
KHi O 8 1887-96

INMAN

Inman INDEPENDENT. w 1891-92||?
KHi Jl 11 1891-Ap 2 1892

Inman REVIEW. w Ja 7 1892+
KHi 1892+

IOLA

ALLEN county courant. 1867 *See* Iola register

ALLEN county courant. w S 27 1883-Ap 13 1889||
1888 as Democrat-courant. Merged with Iola register
KHi complete

ALLEN county democrat. w N 27 1886-Ja 7 1888||
United with Allen county courant to form Democrat-courant, later Allen county courant
KHi complete

ALLEN county democrat. w 1894-1901||?
United with Farmer's friend to form Farmer's friend and Allen county democrat, later Iola democrat
KHi Ag 1898-Ag 9 1901

ALLEN county herald. w 1890-93||?
United with Farmer's friend to form Friend-herald, later Iola democrat
KHi D 26 1890-Mr 16 1893

ALLEN county independent. w 1879-80||?
KHi D 17 1879-N 24 1880

ALLEN county journal. *See* Allen county news-journal

ALLEN county news-journal. w 1903+
1903-Jl 11 1929 as Allen county journal
KHi Mr 1913+

Iola CO-OPERATOR. *See* Freedom's banner

Iola DEMOCRAT. w 1890-1904||?
1890-1900? as Farmer's friend (1893?-95? Friend-herald); 1901?-F 26 1904 Farmer's friend and Allen county democrat
KHi Mr 29 1890-Je 1904

DEMOCRAT-COURANT. *See* Allen county courant

FARMER'S friend. *See* Iola democrat

FREEDOM'S banner. w 1912-14||?
1912-Jl? 1913 as Iola co-operator
KHi [My 11 1912-Jl]Ag 9 1913-N 21 1914

FRIEND-HERALD. *See* Iola democrat

Iola weekly INDEX. w F 11 1907-Jl 3 1909||
Merged with Iola daily register
KHi complete

KANSAS state register. *See* Iola register

NEOSHO VALLEY register. *See* Iola register

Iola weekly NEWS. w N 20 1896-N 4 1897||
Merged with Iola register
KHi complete

Iola evening NEWS. d N 28 1896-N 6 1897||
Merged with Iola daily register
KHi complete

Daily NEWS. d 1926-Jl 13? 1929||
United with Allen county journal to form Allen county news-journal
KHi Ja 31 1927-Jl 13 1929

Iola daily RECORD. d O? 1898-Jl 3 1909||
Merged with Iola daily register
KHi N 4 1898-1909

Iola weekly RECORD. w Je 23 1899-Mr 29 1907||
KHi complete

Iola REGISTER. w 1867-D 21 1906||
1867 as Allen county courant; 1868-74 Neosho Valley register (1870 Kansas state register)
pub complete
KHi Ja-D 8 1869;S 13 1873-D 12 1874;Ja 9 1875-1906

Iola daily REGISTER. d O 25 1897+
pub 1897+
CoU 1901-Jl 1910
KHi 1897+

WESTERN sentinel. w 1894-98||?
KHi Ag 10 1894-Jl 1898

IONIA

Ionia BOOSTER. w Je 5 1931+
KHi 1931+

Ionia INDEPENDENT. w 1917-
KHi Ap 12 1917-S 19 1918

IOWA POINT

Iowa Point DISPATCH. w 1859-
DLC My 19-Je 2 1860

IRVING

BLUE VALLEY gazette. w 1874-79||?
KHi Ap 8 1876-78

Irving CITIZEN. w 1880||?
KHi F 13-Jl 2 1880

Irving LEADER. w My 20 1886+
KHi 1886+

Irving RECORDER. w 1868-71||?
KHi D 10-31 1869

ISABEL

Isabel HERALD. w 1905-09||?
KHi F 10 1905-09

Isabel NEWS. w D 1925?+
KHi 1930+

ITASCA

NEW Tecumseh. *See under* Eustis

SHERMAN county republican. *See* Goodland republic (Goodland)

IUKA

HUSTLER. w
KHi F 24 1910-Ja 1911

Iuka INDEX. w 1911?-15||?
KHi N 21 1913-Jl 9 1915

PRATT county press. *See* Pratt republican (Pratt)

PRATT county times. *See under* Pratt

Iuka TRAVELER. w 1886-88||?
KHi O 21 1886-Ja 14 1888

Iuka TRIBUNE. w 1915-16||?
KHi D 1915-N 9 1916

IVANHOE

Ivanhoe TIMES. *See* Santa Fe times (Santa Fe)

JACKSONVILLE

NEOSHO VALLEY eagle. *See* St. Paul journal (St. Paul)

JAMESTOWN

CLOUD county Kansan. *See* Concordia Kansan (Concordia)

KANSAS optimist. w My 4 1895+
KHi 1895+

NEW ERA. *See* Concordia Kansan (Concordia)

QUILL. w 1888-90||
United with Cloud county Kansan to form New era, later Concordia Kansan (Concordia)
KHi D 1888-N 22 1890

JAQUA

Jaqua CYNOSURE. *See* Jaqua gleaner

Jaqua GLEANER. w 1887-88||?
1887? as Jaqua cynosure
KHi Ap 1887-Jl 20 1888

JENNINGS

ALLIANCE times. *See* Oberlin times (Oberlin)

Jennings ECHO. *See* Jennings gazette

Jennings GAZETTE. w 1888+
1888-O 28 1915 as Jennings echo
KHi Jl 26 1888+

Jennings REPORTER. w 1912-13||?
KHi F 22 1912-Ja 2 1913

Jennings TIMES. *See* Oberlin times (Oberlin)

JEROME

SMOKY globe. w 1887-88||?
KHi Ap 16 1887-Ap 2 1888

JETMORE

To 1881? as Buckner

BUCKNER independent. w 1879-81||?
KHi N 1879-Mr 4 1881

HODGEMAN county news. w My 19 1932-
KHi 1932-My 4 1933

HODGEMAN county scimitar. w Mr 27 1886-S 20 1889||
Followed by Wichita times (Wichita Falls, Texas)

Jetmore JOURNAL. w 1885-90||?
KHi D 11 1887-Je 22 1889

Jetmore REPUBLICAN. w 1886+
1886-Ja 17 1895 as Jetmore siftings
KHi N 11 1886-O 27 1887;Ag 9 1888+

REVEILLE. *See* Western herald

Jetmore SIFTINGS. *See* Jetmore republican

Jetmore SUNFLOWER. w 1889-95||
Merged with Jetmore republican
KHi D 18 1889-Ja 23 1895
OkHi [1883-94]

WESTERN herald. w 1882-1911||
1882-F 11 1892 as Reveille
KHi 1882-1911

JEWELL

JEWELL county clarion. *See* Jewell county diamond

JEWELL county democrat. w 1885-87||?
KHi D 11 1885-Ap 1887

JEWELL county diamond. w 1872-78||
1872-73 as Jewell county clarion. United with Jewell county monitor (Jewell Center, later Mankato) to form Jewell county monitor-diamond, later Jewell county monitor (Mankato)
KHi Ag 30 1872;Je 4 1874;76-77

JEWELL county news. w 1891-95||?
KHi O 9 1891-Mr 1895

JEWELL county record. w
KHi Ap 9-Ag 20 1897

JEWELL county republican. w N 28 1879+
pub 1879+
KHi D 19 1879+

OUR booster. w
KHi N 1918-Jl 1924

JEWELL CENTER. *See* MANKATO

JOHNSON

1885 as Veteran; 1886-1927? Johnson City

Johnson JOURNAL. w 1888-98||?
KHi Ap 1888-Mr 12 1898

Johnson JOURNAL-NEWS. w 1899-Mr 3 1916||?
1899-1913 as Stanton county journal. United with Johnson City pioneer to form Johnson City pioneer and journal-news, later Johnson pioneer
KHi Je 22 1899-Mr 3 1916

Johnson PIONEER. w Mr 19? 1914+
1914-Mr 1916? as Johnson City pioneer; Ap 1916?-27? Johnson City pioneer and journal-news
KHi Je 11 1914+

PROGRESSIVE news. w 1912-13||?
United with Stanton county journal to form Johnson journal-news
KHi Mr 22-O 4 1913

Johnson SENTINEL. w
KHi My 28-D 10 1886

STANTON county eclipse. w
KHi My 27 1887-Mr 16 1888

STANTON county journal. *See* Johnson journal-news

STANTON county new era. w
KHi N 1922-23

STANTON county republican. w 1888-91||?
KHi N 23 1889-F 7 1891

STANTON county sun. w 1891-94||?
KHi D 11 1891-Ja 12 1894

STANTON county telegram. w 1888-89||?
1888-Mr 29 1889 pub in Gognac
KHi Mr 30 1888-N 16 1889

Johnson WORLD. w 1886-88||?
KHi O 1886-N 1888

JUNCTION CITY

BLUE jay. w 1918?+
KHi Mr 1925+

Junction City COURIER. *See* Junction City union

DAVIS county republican. *See* Junction City republican

DEMOCRATIC sentinel. *See* Junction City sentinel

GEARY county critic. w Ja 16-Je? 1892||
United with Democratic sentinel to form Sentinel and critic, later Junction City sentinel
NbHi Ja-Mr 12,My-Je 18 1892

Junction City INDEPENDENT. d
KHi Je 27-S 23 1931

KANSAS frontier. w
KHi My 25,Je 15 1861

KANSAS (*Continued*)

JUNCTION CITY—*Continued*

KANSAS statesman. *See* Junction City statesman

REPUBLIC. w Ag 14 1873+
1873-Ja 17 1902 as Junction City tribune
pub [1873-1900]+
DLC 1873-Jl 11 1895
KHi 1873+
MWA Jl 28 1887-Jl 18 1889
NbHi Ap 6-13,My 4,Ag 10 1876-Jl,Ag 2,O 4-11 1877;Ja 3,Ap 4-11,My 2,Jl 4 1878;Ja 2,Ap 3-10,My 1,Jl 3,Ag 1879-Ja 9 1896;S 3 1897
NcD Ja 15 1880

Junction City REPUBLICAN. w S 13 1882-1901‖
1882-85? as Davis county republican
KHi S 22 1882-F 1 1901
NbHi My 25 1883-S 3 1886;Mr 11,25 1887-Mr 16,My 18 1888-S 8 1893

Junction SENTINEL. w
KHi My 14 1859

Junction City SENTINEL. w Mr 16 1889-1919‖?
1889-Je 1892? as Democratic sentinel; Jl?-D? 1892 Sentinel and critic
KHi 1889-Je 1919
NbHi 1889-F 8,22,Mr-Ap 1890

Daily SENTINEL. d O 1 1894-
NbHi 1894[Ja-Ap 1895;96-O 2 1905]

SMOKY HILL and republican union. *See* Junction City union

Junction City STATESMAN. w 1860+
Early issues as Kansas statesman?
DLC O 27 1860
KHi Je 30,O 13 1860

Junction City TRIBUNE. *See* Republic

Junction City UNION. w S 12 1861+
1861-63 as Smoky Hill and republican union; 1864 Junction City courier
Suspended N 1864-Ap 1865
DLC Jl 26 1873-N 5 1881
KHi 1861-Ap 1868;Je 1869-Mr 1879;My 1880+
MBAt S 12 1861
MWA O 7-14,N 4 1865;Jl 8 1882
NNHi Jl 25,N 25,D 23 1871-[72]Ja 11,F 1,15, Mr 1,Ap 12 1873;Mr 21-Ap 4 1874
NbHi My 1880-90;My 16 1891-O 8 1892;Ja-My 19 1893;My 26-Ag 4,S 1894-My 1895

Daily UNION. d 1887‖
KHi Mr 22-O 10 1887
NbHi [Mr-O 1887]

Junction City UNION. d 1896+
KHi S 1897+

KACKLEY

Kackley LEADER. w 1893-94‖?
KHi Ap 1893-Je 22 1894

WESTERN record. w
KHi Ap-S 19 1893

KALVESTA

Kalvesta HERALD. w 1886-88‖?
1886-Je 24 1887? as Hodgeman county herald (Hodgeman Center)
KHi My 14 1886-88

KANOPOLIS

To 1884 as Fort Harker

Kanopolis INDEPENDENT. w 1898-99‖?
KHi Ag 25 1898-F 1899

Kanopolis JOURNAL. w 1886-90‖?
KHi Je 17 1886-N 18 1890

Kanopolis JOURNAL. w 1907-18‖?
KHi Ap 1907-Jl 11 1918

KANSAN. w 1890-93‖?
KHi F 13 1890-Je 1893

KANORADO

KANORADIAN. w Je 8-N 17 1916‖
United with Western Kansas news (Goodland) to form Western Kansas news and Kanoradian later Goodland news-republic (Goodland)
KHi complete

Kanorado STAR. w 1928-29‖?
KHi O 18 1928-Mr 21 1929

STATE line register. *See* Sherman county farmer (Goodland)

KANSAS CITY

Kansas City ADVERTISER. w 1924-32‖?
KHi Ap 1926-O 14 1932

Kansas City ADVOCATE. w 1914-26‖?
1914-Ja 7 1916 as Kansas City independent
Negro
KHi My 26 1915-My 7 1926

Kansas City AGE. w 1890?-93‖?
1890?-91? as Riverview age (Riverview)
KHi Jl 12-S 13 1890;Ag 19 1892-Jl 12 1893

AMERICAN citizen. w 1887-1909‖?
Negro
KHi Jl 26 1889-Je 6 1890;F 20 1891-[D 15 1898-Ap 1900]-03;05-Ag 2 1907

AMERICAN citizen. d
Negro
KHi [D 15 1898-1900]

ARGENTINE advocate. w 1888‖?
KHi F 14-N 1888

ARGENTINE argus. w
KHi Ag 25-D 1 1887

ARGENTINE eagle. w 1892-94‖?
KHi Ap 8 1892-94

ARGENTINE Kansas citizen. w
KHi D 30 1894-Mr 1895

ARGENTINE republic. *See* Kansas City republic

ARGENTINE siftings. w 1885-86‖?
KHi Ja 9-My 1886

CHAMPION. w
KHi Ag 28,D 25 1897;Ja-Ap 14 1898

COMMERCIAL gazette. *See* Gazette-globe

Kansas City CONSTITUTION.
A My 1856-O 1857

CROMWELL'S Kansas mirror. [Armourdale] w 1887-97‖?
KHi D 22 1887-Je 4 1897

FACKLAN.
In Swedish
IRA 1892

Daily GAZETTE. *See* Kansas City globe. 1887-1918

GAZETTE-GLOBE. w Ag 7 1858-1917‖?
1858-69? as Commercial gazette; 1870?-87 Wyandotte gazette; 1887-1913? Weekly gazette
KHi O 20 1860;Ap 1 1865;F 17,Ap 21,Je 30,O 31 1866-O 1872;O 10 1873-O 1903;Ap-O 1909; D 1913-N 1917
—d ed *See* Wyandotte gazette

Kansas City GLOBE. d Mr 15 1887-1918‖?
1887-Ap 12 1909 as Daily gazette; Ap 13 1909-16? Gazette-globe
KHi 1887-S 1 1918

Kansas City GLOBE. d Je 19 1905-Ap 12 1909‖
United with Daily gazette to form Gazette-globe, later Kansas City globe
KHi complete

Kansas City HERALD. w 1913?-
KHi Je 21 1916-Mr 1920

Kansas City INDEPENDENT. *See* Kansas City advocate

INTER-STATE news. [Rosedale] w 1904?-22‖?
KHi Ag 23,O 18,N 8 1905;O 27-N 3 1911;Mr 1 1912

Kansas City KANSAN. w 1912?-25‖?
1912?-Jl 6? 1917 as Wyandotte news; Jl 15?- 1917? Wyandotte news and Kansan
KHi F 12 1914-S 20,N 8 1918-Je 1921

Kansas City KANSAN. d Ap 3 1916+
pub 1921+
KHi 1916+
KK 1921+

KANSAS cyclone. w 1886-88‖?
KHi Ja 15 1887-My 1888

KANSAS elevator. w 1916-18‖?
Negro
KHi F 12-N 4 1916

KANSAS globe. d 1905-Ap 12 1909‖
United with Daily gazette to form Gazette globe, later Kansas City globe
KHi Je 19 1905-09

KANSAS herold. w 1887-91‖?
In German
KHi Mr 1890-Ap 1891

KANSAS pilot. w 1878-81‖?
KHi Mr 1879-F 1881

KANSAS pionier. [Wyandotte] w 1881-89‖?
In German
KHi S 29 1883-My 4 1889

KANSAS progressive. *See* National progressive

KANSAS staatszeitung. *See* Neue Kansas staats-zeitung

KANSAS sun and globe. w 1884-86‖?
1884? as Kansas City sun
KHi My 10 1884-Ja 1886

KANSAS topics. w
KHi My 16-D 1895

KANSAS tribune. [Quindaro] w
KHi S 20 1860

KANSAS tribune. w 1894-98‖?
Title varies: Kansas City tribune
KHi Je 28 1894-Ag 1898

KAWSMOUTH pilot. *See* Wyandotte kawsmouth

LABOR record. *See* National progressive

NATIONAL progressive. w 1894?-1913‖?
1894?-O? 1911 as Labor record; O? 1911-Je 1912? Kansas progressive
KHi O 20 1911-Je 14 1912;Mr-D 1913
MNC [1903-11;Ja 19-Je 14 1912]

NEUE Kansas staats-zeitung. w 1894-1916‖?
1894-1906? as Kansas staatszeitung
In German and English
KHi Ap 18 1895-1916

Evening NEWS. d Jl 1 1889-90‖?
KHi 1889

Kansas City NEWS. w 1896-1908‖?
KHi N 1900-Jl 4 1902;D 1905-Jl 1907

PLAINDEALER. w Je 6 1899+
1899-D 25 1931 pub in Topeka
Negro
DLC Ja 26 1900
KHi 1899+

Kansas City PRESS. w Ag 10 1889+
KHi Ag 17 1889+

QUINDARO chindowan. w My 13 1857-
CSmH Je 6 1857;Je 12 1858
KHi 1857-58
MB My 13 1857;Je 5 1858
MWA Ag 22,S 26 1857;Mr 27 1858
NN Je 27 1857
WHi Ag 29 1857;F 27-Mr,Ap 10 1858

REPUBLIC. w D 8 1887-1923‖?
1887-Jl 18 1912 as Argentine republic
KHi D 8 1887-Jl 22 1923

Kansas City REPUBLICAN. w
KHi S 10 1881-Ag 1882

Kansas City REPUBLICAN. d
KHi S 13 1881-Je 14 1882

RIVERVIEW age. *See* Kansas City age

ROSEDALE bee. w 1889-94‖?
KHi [D 1889-S 18 1890]

ROSEDALE commercial. w Ag? 1895-1911‖?
Ag?-D 28 1895 as Town topics
KHi Ag 10 1895-Je 23 1902

ROSEDALE enquirer. w
KHi Ja 25-Je 14 1890

ROSEDALE era. w 1888-93‖?
1888-89? as Rosedale record; 1890? Record and era
KHi Ap 14 1888-F 8 1890

ROSEDALE record. *See* Rosedale era

ROSEDALE wasp. w
KHi [S 15 1883-N 7 1885]

Evening SPY. w 1880-82‖?
KHi D 25 1880-Mr 4 1882

Kansas City SUN. 1884 *See* Kansas sun and globe

Kansas City SUN. 1889-1932 *See* Wyandotte news 1889+

TOWN topics. *See* Rosedale commercial

Kansas City TRIBUNE. d 1896-97‖?
KHi Ag 12 1896-Jl 17 1897

Der WAECHTER. w 1892-94‖?
In German
KHi Ap 21 1892-O 1894

WESTERN argus. [Wyandotte] w My 25 1858-61‖
Follows Wyandotte citizen. Merged with Wyandotte gazette, later Gazette-globe
DLC Ja 1-8,F 12-My 7,21-Je 4,18-24,Jl 16-Ag 6,27,S 10,O 1-15,29-D 10,31 1859-F,Mr 21,Ap 7,Ag 11 1860
KHi [1858-Mr 2 1861]
N Je 17 1858

WYANDOTT CITY register. d
MB My 23 1857

WYANDOTT CITY register. w *See* Wyandotte citizen

WYANDOTTE chief. w
KHi S 12 1883-My 6 1885

WYANDOTTE chief. w -1913‖?
KHi Je 20 1912-O 1913

WYANDOTTE citizen. w My 1857-Ap? 1858‖
1857- as Wyandott City register. Followed by Western argus
KHi Jl 25 1857
—d ed *See* Wyandott City register

WYANDOTTE county record. w Mr 8 1929+
KHi [1929-Jl 4 1930]

WYANDOTTE cricket. d 1912-14‖?
KHi Jl 10 1912-N 2 1914

WYANDOTTE democrat. w
KHi My 21 1867-S 4 1868

WYANDOTTE echo. w 1928+
KHi Ap 1930+

WYANDOTTE gazette. d 1859-
WHi Ja 28-F 4 1865

WYANDOTTE gazette. w *See* Gazette-globe

WYANDOTTE herald. w 1872-1910‖?
KHi 1872-1910

WYANDOTTE kawsmouth. w 1881‖?
Title varies: Kawsmouth pilot
KHi Mr-S 3 1881

WYANDOTTE kawsmouth pilot. d 1881‖?
KHi Ap 6 1881

WYANDOTTE news. w 1889+
1889-S 23 1932 as Kansas City sun
KHi 1891-[S 30 1932-Ag 1933]+

WYANDOTTE news. 1912-17 *See* Kansas City Kansan w

WYANDOTTE sentinel. w 1931-32‖?
KHi Ja 15-N 4 1932

KELLY

Kelly BOOSTER. w 1914-15‖?
KHi Jl 23 1914-Ja 14 1915

Kelly INDEPENDENT. w
KHi Jl 18-D 1899

Kelly REPORTER. w 1902-04‖?
KHi Ap 1902-04

KENDALL

Kendall BOOMER. *See* Kendall free press

Kendall FREE PRESS. w 1886-90‖?
1886-N 1889 as Kendall boomer
KHi Mr 17 1886-My 24 1890

Kendall GAZETTE. w 1887‖?
KHi Mr 30-Ag 18 1887

KANSAS (*Continued*)

KENDALL—*Continued*

HAMILTON county republican. w
KHi My-S 9 1886

Kendall KEN. *See* Kendall signal

Kendall SIGNAL. w
1886? as Kendall ken
KHi F 12 1886-F 18 1887

KENNETH

Kenneth DEMOCRAT. *See* Hoxie democrat (Hoxie)

Kenneth SENTINEL. *See* Hoxie sentinel (Hoxie)

KENSINGTON

Kensington MIRROR. w My 10 1888+
KHi 1888+

KICKAPOO CITY

KANSAS pioneer. w N 1854-
DLC N 22-D 6 1854
WHi N 15,29-D 6 1854

KINCAID

Kincaid DISPATCH. w Ag 3 1888+
KHi 1888+

Kincaid KRONICLE. w 1886-92||?
KHi Ja 30 1886-Ap 21 1888;S 19 1889-Ag 1892

Kincaid NEWS. w 1894-96||?
KHi Ja 11-Ag 16,N 29 1895-Ja 17 1896

Kincaid NEWS. w 1900-01||?
KHi Je 29 1900-Ja 4 1901

Kincaid TATTLER. sm O 9 1914-
KHi 1914-S 1921

KINGMAN

Kingman BLADE. w Je 14 1878-80||?
1878-Ag 19 1880 as Kingman mercury
KHi 1878-D 23 1880

CITIZEN republican. w 1882-84||?
1882-Mr? 1884 as Kingman county republican
KHi Mr 1882-Ag 21 1884

Kingman COURIER. w 1884-89||
United with Kingman leader to form Leader-courier
KHi Ap 18 1884-Ap 22 1889

Kingman COURIER. d 1887-89||
KHi My 1887-89

Kingman JOURNAL. w Ja 3 1890+
Follows Voice of the people. 1890-Jl 10 1901 as Kingman weekly journal
pub 1901+
KHi 1890+

KINGMAN county citizen. w 1879-Mr? 1884||
1879-80? as Kingman citizen. United with Kingman county republican to form Citizen republican
KHi S 13 1879-Mr 13 1884

KINGMAN county democrat. w 1883-95||?
1883-85? as Southern Kansas democrat
KHi O 13 1883-Ap 11 1895

KINGMAN county republican. *See* Citizen republican

KINGMAN county telegraph. w 1906-15||?
In German
KHi S 1906-Ap 12 1912

LEADER-COURIER. w D 16 1884+
1884-N 21 1889 as Kingman leader
CoU 1899-Jl 1910
KHi 1884+

Kingman MERCURY. *See* Kingman blade

Kingman morning NEWS. d D? 1886-88||?
KHi D 16 1886-O 1887;Mr-Ap 22 1888

Kingman NEWS. w 1886-88||?
KHi D 16 1886-My 1888

SOUTHERN Kansas democrat. *See* Kingman county democrat

VOICE of the people. w 1888-89||
Followed by Kingman journal
KHi Mr 8 1888-N 22 1889

KINGSDOWN

Kingsdown CLARION. w 1912-16||?
KHi Ja 16 1913-D 21 1916

Kingsdown NEWS. w N 10? 1922-
KHi N 24 1922-My 11 1923

KINSLEY

Early years as Petersburg

BANNER-GRAPHIC. *See* Kinsley graphic

EDWARDS county banner. w 1887||
United with Kinsley graphic to form Banner-graphic, later Kinsley graphic
KHi Ja 21-S 1887

EDWARDS county leader. w 1877-80||?
KHi [Mr 29 1877-O 7 1880]

Kinsley GRAPHIC. w N 1877+
1877-Ap 20 1878 as Valley republican; 1882?83? Republican-graphic; N? 1887-89 Banner-graphic
pub 1894+
KHi 1877+

KANSAS staats-zeitung. w 1878-79||?
In German
KHi Jl 13 1878-F 15 1879

Kinsley MERCURY. w Ag 4? 1883+
pub 1909+
KHi Ag 18 1883-Ja 1891;Jl 30 1896+

Daily MERCURY. d Je? 1887-88||
KHi Jl 1887-Jl 14 1888

Kinsley REPORTER. w 1873-76||?
KHi S 21-D 21 1876

Kinsley REPUBLICAN. w 1878-D 31 1881||
United with Kinsley graphic to form Republican-graphic, later Kinsley graphic
KHi Je 1878-81

REPUBLICAN-GRAPHIC. *See* Kinsley graphic

VALLEY republican. *See* Kinsley graphic

KIOWA

ALLIANCE review. *See* Kiowa review

Kiowa HERALD. w 1884-90||?
KHi Je 19 1884-Ag 14 1890

Kiowa JOURNAL. w 1885-Jl 16 1921||
Merged with Kiowa news-record-review
KHi N 1886-1921

Kiowa daily JOURNAL. d
KHi Jl 21-N 15 1916

Kiowa KANSAN. w 1910-11||?
KHi F 15-S 1911

Kiowa NEWS-REVIEW-RECORD. w 1898+
1898-Ap 11 1902 as Kiowa news; 1902-32 Kiowa news-review
pub 1898+
KHi 1903+

Kiowa RECORD. w 1915-D 26 1932||
United with Kiowa news-review to form Kiowa news-review-record
KHi 1932
KKaN complete

Kiowa REVIEW. w Ap 1 1891-Ap 16 1902||
1891-Ap 6 1892 as Alliance review. United with Kiowa news to form Kiowa news-review, later Kiowa news-review-record
KHi complete

KIRWIN

Kirwin ARGUS. w 1904?-09||?
KHi My 10 1906-My 15 1909

Kirwin CHIEF. w 1873-91||?
KHi Ja 8 1876-Mr 13 1891

Kirwin GLOBE. w 1885?-1901||?
KHi O 9 1891-O 5 1901

Kirwin HOT shot. w 1923-
KHi O 13 1924-My 1926

ICONOCLAST. w
KHi N 13-D 4 1879

GRAPHIC. w Ja?-N 1889||?
Ja?-Jl 1889 pub in Agra
KHi Ja 26-N 14 1889

INDEPENDENT. w D 22 1879-O 25 1888||
1879-Ap 9 1880 pub in Smith Center and Harlan; Ap 16-N 19 1880 pub in Harlan
ICJ 1879-86
KHi complete

Kirwin INDEPENDENT. 1889-1902 *See* Kirwin Kansan

Kirwin KANSAN. w N 6 1889+
1889-My 8 1902 as Kirwin independent
KHi 1889+
KKi N 1889-O 1899;1903-26

Kirwin PROGRESS. w 1876-78||?
KHi Ja 11 1877-Jl 1878

Kirwin REPUBLICAN. w 1883-85||?
KHi Ag 1883-S 5 1885

SOLOMON VALLEY democrat. w 1878-79||?
KHi Ag 14-D 1878

KISMET

Kismet CLIPPER. *See* Southwest tribune (Liberal)

Kismet KLIPPER. w Ja 18 1917-24||?
KHi 1917-Jl 1924

LABETTE

Labette RECORD. w 1899-1901||?
KHi O 21 1899-S 6 1901

LACROSSE

La Crosse CHIEFTAIN. w Ja 18 1881+
pub 1893+
KHi Ja 18-Mr 22,S 26 1882-Ja 1891;Jl 1892+

La Crosse CLARION. w Jl 19 1889-Jl 30 1897||
Merged with La Crosse chieftain
KHi complete
KLcC 1889;91;94-96

La Crosse DEMOCRAT. w 1887-91||?
KHi 1887-Ja 22 1891

La Crosse EAGLE. w
KHi My 13-D 1878

KANSAS rundschau. w
In German
KHi S 17 1897-F 18 1898

La Crosse PROGRESS. w Je? 1877-79||?
Je?-N 2 1877 as Rush county progress
KHi Je 22 1877-Mr 1878

La Crosse REPUBLICAN. w F 5 1897+
KHi 1897+

RUSH county progress. *See* La Crosse progress

WESTERN economist. w 1887?-94||?
KHi Ja 29 1891-S 6 1894

LA CYGNE

La Cygne weekly JOURNAL. w 1870+
1893? as Journal clarion; N 1915-18? Journal-record
KHi 1876+
OClWHi Ap 2,S 13 1879

KANSAS standard. w 1903-06||?
KHi Ja 23 1903-O 5 1906

La Cygne LEADER. w 1886-88||?
KHi Ja 13 1887-N 8 1888

La Cygne RECORD. w 1907-O 1915||?
United with La Cygne weekly journal to form Journal-record, later La Cygne weekly journal
KHi O 1907-O 14 1915

LAFONTAINE

Lafontaine BANNER. w 1907-13||?
KHi Je 1907-Ap 13 1913

Lafontaine SPY. w 1887||?
KHi F 10-My 1887

LA HARPE

La Harpe ADVERTISER. w 1920-21||?
KHi O 8 1920-My 5 1921

ALLEN county journal. w 1904-12||?
1904-11? as La Harpe journal
KHi Ap 1904-S 1912

La Harpe ARGUS. w 1899-1900||?
KHi S 22 1899-F 2 1900

La Harpe ENTERPRISE. w 1912-17||?
KHi Ja 16 1913-Je 1917

La Harpe JOURNAL. *See* Allen county journal

KANSAS review. w,sw 1898-1905||?
1898-Ap 8 1904 as La Harpe news w 1898-1903?
KHi Mr 1898-1905

La Harpe NEWS. *See* Kansas review

LAKE CITY

Lake City BEE. w 1888-89||?
Follows Kansas prairie dog?
KHi F 24 1888-F 1 1889

KANSAS prairie dog. w 1884-88||?
Followed by Lake City bee?
KHi F 19 1885-F 9 1888

Lake City TRIBUNE. w 1919-21||?
KHi Ja 19 1919-F 4 1921

LAKIN

Lakin EAGLE. w
KHi My 20-O 10 1879

Lakin HERALD. w 1881-84||?
KHi My 13 1882-Je 1884
OOxM O 14 1882

Lakin INDEPENDENT. w 1914+
KHi Jl 22 1920+

Lakin INDEX. w 1890-98||?
KHi My 1890-Ap 22 1898

Lakin INVESTIGATOR. w 1898-1911||
Merged with Kearny county advocate
KHi Ap 13 1898-Ja 6 1911

KEARNY county advocate. w My 23 1885+
KHi 1885+

PIONEER democrat. w 1885-90||?
KHi 1886-Je 7 1890

LAMONT

Lamont LEADER. w Ag 14 1912+
KHi 1912+

LANCASTER

PRAIRIE press. w 1888-90||?
KHi My 12 1888-Mr 7 1890

LANE

Lane ADVANCE. w 1881-82||?
KHi Jl 1881-D 1 1882

Lane COMMERCIAL bulletin. w 1885-88||?
1885-Ja 1886? as Lane leader
KHi S 26 1885-O 1888

Lane GAZETTE. w Ag 6 1926-28||?
KHi 1926-28

Lane GRAPHIC. w
KHi Ja 18 1895-D 7 1900

Lane JOURNAL. w N 7 1913-19||?
KHi 1913-S 1919

KANSAS (*Continued*)

LANE—*Continued*

Lane LANDMARK. w 1904-05||?
KHi Ag 25-S 22 1904

Lane LEADER. 1885-86 *See* Lane commercial bulletin

Lane LEADER. w 1890-93||
United with Ottawa times to form Times-leader (Ottawa)
KHi Jl 3 1890-93

Lane LIGHT. w 1894||?
KHi Ag 31-N 1894

NEW leaf. w 1902-03||?
KHi My 1902-My 22 1903

Lane NEWS. w Je 18 1920-23||?
KHi 1920-Je 8 1923

LANGDON

Langdon LEADER. w N 23 1911-30||?
Suspended from O 1918-21?
KHi 1911-O 24 1918;S 8 1922-O 10 1930

LANSING

Lansing NEWS. w O 25 1895-1918||?
Suspended from Je 15 1906-N 1907
KHi 1895-Ag 1918

LARNED

Larned CHRONOSCOPE. w 1878+
Ja 1931-N 30 1933 as Larned news
pub 1907+
KHi D 11 1878;Ja 1-8,22-29,Mr 5,O 2 1879;80+
OOxM O 6-13 1882

CHRONOSCOPE. d Mr 9 1887-88||
KHi 1887-N 10 1888

Larned DEMOCRAT. w 1888-89||?
KHi O 26 1888-Ja 5 1889

Larned EAGLE. w 1884-85||
United with Larned optic to form Larned eagle-optic
KHi 1885

Larned EAGLE-OPTIC. w 1877-D 27 1901||
1877-O 22 1878 as Pawnee county herald; O 22 1878-85 Larned optic. Merged with Tiller and toiler
KHi complete
OOxM O 13 1882

Larned NEWS. *See* Larned chronoscope

Larned OPTIC. *See* Larned eagle-optic

PAWNEE county herald. *See* Larned eagle-optic

PAWNEE county republican. w
KHi Ag 1886-F 23 1887

Larned PRESS. w 1873-79||?
KHi Je 10 1873;O 20 1876-O 24 1878

TILLER and toiler. w 1890+
KHi Ap 30 1892+
WaPS [1932]

TILLER and toiler. d
KHi Ap 26-My 19 1893

LATHAM

Latham ADVERTISER. w My 9 1918-
KHi 1918-My 13 1920

Latham JOURNAL. *See* Latham signal

Latham LEADER. w My 27 1926+
KHi 1926+

Latham MIRROR. w 1901-Ja 17 1918||
KHi D 20 1901-18

Latham SIGNAL. w 1885-90||?
1885-S 6 1886 as Latham journal
KHi S 1885-F 8 1890

Latham TIMES. w 1890-93||?
KHi My 23 1890-Mr 1893

LATIMER

Latimer LEADER. w 1915-17||?
KHi Jl 15 1915-Ag 16 1916

LAWRENCE

Lawrence ADVERTISER. w D 25 1913-18||?
KHi 1913-N 1917

Lawrence DEMOCRAT. d Jl 16 1888-
KHi Jl-N 10 1888

Lawrence DEMOCRAT. d O 25 1908-11||?
KHi 1908-O 5 1910

Lawrence DEMOCRAT. w O 13 1910+
IU 1918+
KHi 1910+

DOUGLAS county republican. w Mr 4 1926+
pub 1926+
KHi 1926+

Lawrence weekly GAZETTE. w S 7 1882-Mr 30 1899||
1882-Ja 1883 as Kansas weekly gazette. United with Jeffersonian to form Jeffersonian gazette
KHi complete
KLJ S 1883-Ag 1885;92-Jl 1894

Lawrence daily GAZETTE. d O 15 1884-85||?
KHi 1884-Ja 5,S 2-O 1885
KLJ 1884-[85]

Lawrence daily GAZETTE. d 1890?-95||
Merged with Lawrence daily world
KHi Jl 2 1893-My 1895
KLJ Jl 1893-94

Lawrence GAZETTE. d F 9 1903-20||
KHi 1903-Ag 5 1920
KLJ 1903-06;Jl 1907-08;Je 1909-15

GERMANIA. w 1877-1918||?
In German
KHi S 8 1877;Ja 8 1880-Je 1881 F 1883-Ag 23 1918

HERALD-TRIBUNE. w *See* Kansas weekly tribune. 1875-90

Daily HERALD tribune. *See* Evening tribune

Lawrence JAYHAWK. w My 1918-
KHi My 1918-O 1931

JEFFERSONIAN gazette. w 1883-1920||?
1883-84 as Enterprise register; 1884-88 Antimonopolist; 1889-Mr 1899 Jeffersonian
1883-Ja 3 1888 pub in Enterprise; Ja 10 1888-F? 1889 in Council Grove; Mr? 1889-90 in Topeka
KHi D 1883-Ag 5 1920
KLJ Ap 1899-1909;13-14

JEFFERSONIAN gazette. d
KHi O-N 10 1900

Lawrence weekly JOURNAL. w F 21 1861-1909||
Follows Kansas herald of freedom. 1861-F 1869 as Kansas state journal; Mr? 1869-85 Western home journal
Suspended from Ag 21-O 1863
CSmH Mr 28 1861;D 10 1863;Mr 24 1864;O 26 1865
DLC Mr 1871-F 20 1873
IU Ap 15 1887
KHi 1861-[64-67]-Ap 3 1868;Mr 11 1869-Mr 15 1885;F 18 1886-Ap 10 1909
KL Mr 1861-Mr 1865;Mr 1868-Je 1869
KLJ 1871-76;86-88
MBAt Ag 11,O 13 1864
MWA Ap 9 1863;Mr 24 1864;Ag 26 1869
NN [1861-64]
WHi Ja 19 1865

Lawrence daily JOURNAL-WORLD d 1865+
1865-Mr 3 1869 as Daily Kansas state journal; Mr 4 1869-73? Republican daily journal; 1874?-Je 17 1879 Lawrence daily journal and the daily Kansas tribune; Je 1879-F 17 1911 Lawrence daily journal (1890? Journal-tribune)
pub 1869-73;Mr-O 1875[76]-Je 1877 Jl 1879-Jl 1881[82]-84;87-Je 1893;Jl 1894-1906,Jl-D 1907; Jl 1908-09;Jl 1911-[24]+
CoU 1901;03;S 1906-My 1910
DLC [Jl 18-D 18 1866]67;69;My 8 1870;Ap 25 1871;Ja 26 1881;98
KHi Jl-D 1868;D 5 1869;Ja-Je,S 17-18,N 13 1870;71;Jl 25 1874;Ap 21,Ag 17-18,20-21,26,S 15 1875;Mr 29,Jl 12,14 1876;Jl 1,6 1877-1911
KL Jl-D 1 1869;Jl-D 1 1870[74-79]
MWA S 8 1866

KANSAS free state. w Ja 3 1855-
CSmH S 24 1855
DLC N 19-D 3 1855;Ja 7,F 18,Mr 3,17-24,Ap 7-14,28-My 5,19 1856
KHi 1855-My 19 1856
MWA Mr 17 1855

KANSAS weekly gazette. *See* Lawrence weekly gazette

KANSAS herald. d Mr 7 1883-84||
United with Kansas daily tribune to form Herald-tribune, later Evening tribune
KHi 1883-Jl 16 1884

KANSAS herald of freedom. w O 21 1854-60||
Followed by Kansas state journal, later Lawrence weekly journal
O 21 1854 pub in Wakarusa
Suspended from O 21 1854-Ja 6 1855;from My 17-O 25 1856;from Mr 21-Ap 4 1857
CSmH [F 1855-D 3 1859]
CtY Jl 8,N 10,29-D 1,15 1855;Ja 12-My 3,N 1856-F 7,21-28,Mr 14,Ap 11-Je 1857
DLC Mr 10 1855-Ja 17,F 28,My 16,Jl 11-18,Ag 15,S 12,26-O 10,24-D 18 1857;Ja 2-9,O 13 1858; Mr 19,Ap 23,My 7,Jl 30 1859
ICHi O 21 1854;55;Ja 12-Mr 1,15-Ap,My 10,N 1,22-29,D 13,27 1856;Ja 10,31-F 7,21-28,Ap 18, Ag 22 1857-Jl 24 1858;Jl 2-9,N 26 1859
KHi complete
MB 1854-F 2,N 1856-N 14 1857;Ja-S 11 1858
MH 1854-[56]-N 1858
MHi S 8 1855
MWA O 21 1854;55-D 12 1857;Ja 2,F 6-13 1858
MiU-C [1855]
NN O 21 1854;Ja-D 22 1855[56-59]
NNHi Ja-Ap 14,D 1 1855;Mr 29-Ap 12,D 13 1856[Ja-S 1857]
NcD F 2 1856;My 16 1857
OClWHi Je 13 1857;Ja 29 1859
WHi 1854-F 2 1856;Je 20 1857;Mr,Ag 14-28 1858

KANSAS mirror. w
KHi O 20 1881-Ja 19 1882

KANSAS progress. w
KHi Je 15 1882-83

KANSAS state journal. *See* Lawrence weekly journal

Daily KANSAS state journal. *See* Lawrence daily journal-world

KANSAS tribune. 1853 *See under* Topeka

KANSAS daily tribune. d 1863-74||
United with Republican daily journal to form Republican daily journal and the daily Kansas tribune, later Lawrence daily journal-world
DLC Ag 16 1864;66;Jl 4 1867;70;Ap 25,Ag 1 1871;Jl-D 1874
KHi N 29 1863-Je,Ag 1872-74
KL Mr 1871-72;Ag 1873-Jl 7 1874
MWA Ap 3 1866
WHi Ag 24 1864

KANSAS weekly tribune. w 1863-74||
Merged with Western home journal
DLC Ag 11 1864
KHi 1863-Jl 24,O 1873-74
KL 1869-[73-74]
MWA Mr 29 1866;Jl 4 1867

KANSAS daily tribune. 1875-83 *See* Evening tribune

KANSAS weekly tribune. w 1875-90||?
1884-85 as Herald-tribune. Merged with Lawrence weekly journal
KHi 1876;My 1877-79;81-88
KL [1875]-O 16 1879

NEWS-TRIBUNE. *See* Evening tribune

NORTH LAWRENCE leader. w
KHi Ag 21 1884-F 19 1885

ONCE a week. w 1882-84||?
KHi 1883-Ag 9 1884

Weekly PEOPLE'S forum. w Mr 6- 1919||?
KHi Mr-O 6 1919

Lawrence PRESS. w 1891||?
KHi Ja 16-Jl 3 1891

PROGRESSIVE herald. w 1911-15||?
KHi O 17 1913-15

Daily RECORD. d S 12 1889-93||
Merged with Lawrence daily gazette
KHi 1889-Jl 1 1893
KLJ 1889-My 1893

Lawrence RECORD. w N 14 1889-93||?
KHi 1889-Jl 1893
KLJ Mr 1892-F 1893

Lawrence REPORTER. d F 22 1879-
KHi F-O 13 1879

Lawrence REPUBLICAN. w,d My 28 1857-F 1869||
United with Kansas state journal to form Western home journal, later Lawrence weekly journal
Suspended from Ag 21 1863-68
d during sessions of legislature
CSmH [Ag 1859-Ap 16 1863]
DLC O 27 1859;Ag-D 1861
KHi 1857-Jl 10 1862;F 21,Jl-D 1868
KLJ 1857-58
MB My 28 1857;Ag 26,S 2-9 1858
MWA Ja 21 1858;Mr 1,Je 28,O 11-25 1860; Jl 17 1862
NN [1859-63]

REPUBLICAN daily journal. *See* Lawrence daily journal-world

SPIRIT of Kansas. w 1871-84||?
KHi F 1872-[74-75]-[83-Mr 22 1884]

Evening STANDARD. *See under* Leavenworth

STATE sentinel. w 1875-76||?
Early issues pub in Leavenworth
KHi Ap 1,S 16,O 7,N 18 1875

Daily morning SUN. d 1883||?
KHi Ja 14-Je 9 1883

Lawrence evening TELEGRAM. d 1888||
Merged with Kansas daily tribune
KHi My 25-Jl 20 1888

Evening TRIBUNE. d 1875-Mr 29 1890||
1875-O? 1883 as Kansas daily tribune; N 1883-Jl 1884 News-tribune; Jl 1884-My 13 1886 Daily herald tribune. United with Lawrence daily journal to form Journal-tribune, later Lawrence daily journal-world
KHi 1876-S 1878;My 17-O 18 1879;80-90
KL O 20 1875-[76-79]
KLJ 1883;Jl 1884-My,O 1886-Je 1888;89-Mr 1890
OClWHi My 15 1880
—w ed *See* Kansas weekly tribune 1875-90

TRUE citizen. w
KHi Ag 13 1886-F 19 1887

VOX populi. w
KHi Ap 18 1873

WESTERN home journal. *See* Lawrence weekly journal

WESTERN record. w
KHi Mr 17 1883-N 6 1884

Lawrence weekly WORLD. w 1892-1909||
KHi Mr 11 1892;Mr 25 1909
KLJ 1892-1908
OkHi [1893]-[95]

Lawrence daily WORLD. d Mr 2 1892-F 19 1911||
United with Lawrence daily journal to form Lawrence daily journal-world
KHi Mr 3 1892-F 18 1911
KLJ [1892-94]-1907;Jl 1909-10

LAWSON

Lawson LEADER. w
KHi O 28 1887-Ja 20 1888

LEAVENWORTH

ADVERTISER. 1899 *See* Western life

Leavenworth ADVERTISER. w Jl 9 1931+
pub Jl 1931;Ja 1932;33+
KHi 1931+

Leavenworth ADVOCATE. w 1888-91||?
Negro
KHi Ag 18 1888-Ag 22 1891

APPEAL and tribune. d,w 1873?-80||?
1873?-S 1879? as Leavenworth appeal
d 1873?-D 8? 1877
KHi Ja 11 1876-D 8,29 1877-S 22,O 14 1879-80

KANSAS (*Continued*)

LEAVENWORTH—*Continued*

Weekly BULLETIN. w 1861-71||?
Ap-My? 1871 as Times and bulletin
KHi Je 27-Ag 15 1861;Ag 19 1868
WHi S 2 1863

Leavenworth BULLETIN. d 1862-N 10 1871||
Ap 2-My 5 1871 as Leavenworth times and bulletin. Merged with Leavenworth times
DLC Jl 20 1867-71
KHi O 1864(extra);O 3,5,20-21,28,30,N 13 1868
MWA Ja 27 1866

Evening CALL. d 1870-74||?
KHi Ja 25,Ap 8,Ag 26 1872;F 10,Mr 6,D 15 1873;Mr 17 1874

Leavenworth CHRONICLE. w
KHi N 1883-84

Weekly CHRONICLE. w 1908+
1908-25? as Labor chronicle (1912?-15? Labor chronicle and resubmissionist)
KHi F 12 1909-[29-33]+

CHRONICLE-TRIBUNE. d 1892?-Ag 23 1903||
1892?-Ap 1901 as Leavenworth chronicle. Merged with Leavenworth times
KHi D 28 1900-Mr 12 1902

Leavenworth COMMERCIAL. w 1866?-75||?
KHi Jl 25 1867

Leavenworth daily COMMERCIAL. d 1866-76||?
Merged with Leavenworth times
DLC My 28-D 17 1867
KHi Mr 3,S 20,O 11 1868;Jl 18,D 7 1869;Ap 4 1871-Mr,Ap 18 1872;N 16 1873-Je 1876
MWA Je 6 1874;Je 29 1876

Leavenworth daily CONSERVATIVE. d Ja 28 1861-S 16 1868||
Follows Daily evening dispatch. United with Leavenworth times to form Times and conservative, later Leavenworth times
DLC 1861-O 9 1862;64-Ag 10 1866;My 10 1868
KHi 1861-Ja,Je 1867-68
MWA Ap 28,Jl 17 1861;Ja 14 1862;Ap 18,N 17 1865
NNHi Je 2,Jl 21,S 6 1868
OClWHi S 20 1863
WHi Jl 27,Ag 2 1864

Leavenworth weekly CONSERVATIVE. w 1861-68||
Merged with Leavenworth weekly times
CtHT N 24 1864
DLC Ag 8,29,S 12-19,O 3-17,31-N 21,D 26 1861
KHi My 24,Je 29-Jl 2 1861;62;Ja 8,22,Mr 26 1863
WHi O 3 1867

DEMOCRATIC standard. *See* Leavenworth standard

Daily evening DISPATCH. d 1860||
Followed by Leavenworth daily conservative
DLC F 1,Ag 13-14 1860

Leavenworth DOLLAR dispatch. w 1860||?
DLC Ag 9 1860

Weekly Leavenworth HERALD. w S 15 1854-61||
1854-My 1859 as Kansas weekly herald
DLC 1854-D 19 1857;Ag 14-21 1858;Ja 8,29-F 5,19-Mr 12,26,Ap 9-My 7,28 1859-Jl 1860;Jl 20-Ag 3 1861
KHi 1854-O 1859;Mr 10 1860
MWA My 25,Jl 7 1855
WHi F 27-Mr 20 1858

Daily Leavenworth HERALD. d 1861||?
DLC My 29-Je 2,5-13,16-19,22,27 1861

Leavenworth HERALD. w 1894-99||?
KHi F 17 1894-Jl 4,D 1896-Ap 23 1898

Leavenworth INQUIRER. w
KHi My 29 1862

Leavenworth INQUIRER. d
KHi O 24,29 1862

Leavenworth weekly JOURNAL. w Jl 30? 1856-58||
Title varies slightly
CSmH Ja 21 1857(extra)
DLC Ja 22,F 5,Mr 19,My,Je 11,25-Ag 1,22-S 5,19-26,O 4,N 4,28,D 11-18 1857
KHi [Ag 13 1856-S 18 1858]
MWA My 21 1857
NN Ja 21 1857(extra)
WHi D 11 1856;Mr 12-29,Ag 12,26 1858

Daily Evening JOURNAL. d My 24- 1858||
CoD My 24 1858
KHi Ja 26 1859

JOURNAL of commerce. bw 1892-94||?
KHi S 15 1892-94

KANSAS commoner. w
KHi S 20 1884-My 1885

KANSAS freie presse. d 1868?-86||?
In German
KHi Ja 12-Ap 1876;D 1879-86

KANSAS freie presse. w 1868?-86||?
In German
KHi Je 2,D 31 1869;N 16 1870;76-My 7,Jl 12 1881-O 8 1886

KANSAS weekly herald. *See* Weekly Leavenworth herald

KANSAS daily ledger. d
KHi Ap 13 1859
—w ed *See* Leavenworth ledger

KANSAS territorial register. w Jl 7-D 22 1855||
DLC Jl 7,21,Ag 4-11,O 13-20 1855
KHi complete
MWA D 15 1855

LABOR chronicle. *See* Weekly chronicle

Leavenworth LEDGER. w
KHi My 18,S 12 1858
—d ed *See* Kansas daily ledger

LIVE wire. w 1925?-
KHi S 1928-Ap 1932

Leavenworth POST. d,w O 7 1895-97||?
d 1895-F 29 1896?
KHi 1895-F,Jl 10 1896-97

Leavenworth POST. d Ag 19 1905-Je 10 1923||
Merged with Leavenworth times
KHi 1905-Mr 1923
KLeT 1908-23

Leavenworth POST. (In German) *See* Leavenworth tribüne

Daily PRESS. d Ap 2 1877-82||?
1877-79? as Daily public press
KHi 1877-82
NNHi Ap-S 1877

Weekly PRESS. w 1877-83||?
1877-79? as Weekly public press
KHi Je 21 1877-My 24 1883
NNHi Je 21-S 1877

PUBLIC press. *See* Press

Weekly SENTINEL. *See* Tonganoxie republican (Tonganoxie)

SONNTAGS-GAST. w
In German
KHi O 23 1898-My 12 1901

Leavenworth STANDARD. w 1870-1903||?
1870-74? as Democratic standard; 1875?-76? Standard of reform; 1877?-O 13 1880 Lawrence standard; O 20? 1880-1900? Democratic standard. Merged with Leavenworth times
1870-O 13 1880 pub in Lawrence
KHi S 29,N 17,D 8-15 1870;Ap 1877-Je 30 1903

Evening STANDARD. d Ap 7 1873-Ag 23 1903||
Merged with Leavenworth times
1873-O 16 1880 pub in Lawrence
DLC O 25 1878-82;84-1900
KHi S 16 1879;Jl 24 1881-1903

STATE sentinel. *See under* Lawrence

Leavenworth SUN. d S? 1887-90||?
KHi O 4 1887-[D]1890

Leavenworth TIMES. d Mr 6 1857+
S 17 1868-70? as Times and conservative; Ap 2-My 5 1871 Times and bulletin
pub 1857+
DLC Mr 31-N 2 1867;N 24 1870(supp);Ap-My, N 12 1871-84;98+
KHi Ja 25 1859;Ap 5,Je 12,Ag 27-28,S 10,30,N 6 1862;F 14,17,Mr 14,O 25,D 1 1863;Mr 1 1864;S 17 1868-Jl,O 1878+
MB Ag 1 1857
MBAt Ap 15-16 1865
MWA S 19 1862;N 10 1867;O 9 1868;Jl 12-D 1874;O 11-12,18-19 1876
NNHi My 30[Ag 1867-Mr,Jl-Ag 1868]My 1 1873
NbHi F 15 1858;1904;S 1906-My 1910
OCHi Je 19 1877
WHi F 23 1864

Leavenworth weekly TIMES. w Mr 7 1857-1918||?
1868-70? as Times and conservative; Ap-My 1871? Times and bulletin
A 1875-81;Ja-Ag 1884
CSmH Je 20 1857
DLC Mr 19,Ap 16-23 1874
KHi Mr 14 1857;Ja 9,My 22,Je 12,Jl 10,Ag 7,S 18,O 9 1858;My 28 1859;O 24 1863;Ja 20 1876-87;96-S 5 1918
NNHi D 11-18 1867;Mr 11,Ag 5,S 16 1868;Mr 6 1873
OClWHi F 11-17,S 22 1881;Je 14 1883
PEHi Je 27 1857
WHi Mr 6,Ag 24-S 4 1858

TIMES and bulletin. *See* Bulletin; Times

Leavenworth TRIBÜNE. d D 2 1887-Ap 1901||
1887-96 as Leavenworth post; 1897? Post and tribune. United with Leavenworth chronicle to form Chronicle-tribune
In German
KHi 1887-Ag 21 1897
—English ed *See* Leavenworth post

Leavenworth TRIBÜNE. w,sw 1887-1917||?
1887-96 as Leavenworth post
sw 1896?-99?
In German
KHi My 10 1901-My 25 1917
—English ed *See* Leavenworth post

WESTERN life. w 1899-1908||?
1899? as Advertiser (in English and German)
KHi My 1899-F 6 1908

WISCONSIN volunteer. w
KHi F 6 1862

LEBANON

Lebanon ARGUS. w My 13 1898-Ap 16 1909||
Merged with Lebanon times
KHi complete

Lebanon CRITERION. *See* Lebanon times

Lebanon JOURNAL. w 1887-My 2 1903||
United with Lebanon criterion to form Lebanon times
KHi D 21 1889-1903

LEBANONIAN. w O 12 1921-
KHi 1921-My 6 1926

LIGHT of liberty. m,w 1891-95||
1891-92? pub in Smith Center
m 1891-92?
KHi S 1891-Je 28 1895

Lebanon TIMES. w,sw Je 24 1887+
1887-My 1 1903 as Lebanon criterion
sw 1916?-18?
KHi 1887+

LEBO

Lebo COURIER. w 1889-91||?
KHi Ja 11 1889-Ap 24 1891

Lebo ENTERPRISE. w 1891+
KHi My 28 1891-1905;F 10 1916;Mr 21 1918+

Lebo LEADER. w Je? 1931+
KHi N 24 1931+

Lebo LIGHT. w 1884-89||?
KHi Mr 25 1884-89

Lebo STAR. w My 1 1908-23||?
KHi 1908-Mr 16 1923

LECOMPTON

KANSAS national democrat. w Jl 30 1857-
DLC Jl-Ag 5,20,S 3,24-O 1,15-22,N-D 24 1857;Mr 25 1858;59-Mr 14 1861
KHi [1857-F 21 1861]
MWA F 21 1861

KANSAS new era. *See* New era (Valley Falls)

Lecompton LEDGER. w 1889-90||?
KHi D 13 1889-D 19 1890

Lecompton MONITOR. w
KHi Je 1885-Je 10 1886

Lecompton SUN. w Ap 23 1891+
KHi 1891-S 20 1934
OkHi [1893]-[95;98]99

Weekly Lecompton UNION. w 1856-
DLC Ap-My 9,Je 12-19 1857
KHi [Ag 30 1856-My 9 1857]

Lecompton UNION. sw
KHi F 7 1857

LENEXA

Lenexa LEADER. w 1908-09||
Merged with Olathe mirror (Olathe)
KHi O 14 1908-N 10 1909

Lenexa NEWS. *See* Olathe independent (Olathe)

LENORA

COMMON people. ir 1884?-
KHi Ag 19 1886-Ag 1887

Lenora INDEPENDENT. w 1898||?
KHi My 28-S 3 1898

KANSAS monitor. w 1884-86||?
1884-Jl 1885 as Kansas northwest
KHi Ap 9 1884-My 1886

KANSAS northwest. *See* Kansas monitor

Lenora LANTERN. w 1895-96||?
KHi Ag 29 1895-O 1 1896

Lenora LEADER. w 1882-88||?
KHi Mr 16 1882-Ag 1888

NEW ERA. w
KHi S 23 1898-Ap 1899

Lenora NEWS. w 1902+
KHi Je 27 1902+

Lenora RECORD. *See* Lenora sun

Lenora SUN. w 1887-90||?
1887-F? 1890 as Lenora record
KHi S 1887-Je 1890

Lenora TIMES. w
KHi F-Je 3 1893

LEON

Leon INDICATOR. w 1880-1911||?
My 24-D 27 1894 as Leon press
KHi Ja 31 1880-S 28 1911

Leon NEWS. w D 7 1911+
KHi 1911-My 24 1918;Je 15 1923+

Leon PRESS. *See* Leon indicator

Leon QUILL. w 1886-87||?
Merged with Leon indicator
KHi Ag 12 1886-F 3 1887

LEONA

DONIPHAN county hustler. w 1894-98||?
1894-96? as Leona sun
KHi Ja 18 1895-Ja 8 1898

DONIPHAN county hustler. w 1903-08||?
KHi Mr 20 1903-Je 19 1908

Leona SUN. *See* Doniphan county hustler 1894-98

LEONARD. *See* LEONARDVILLE

LEONARDVILLE

Early years as Leonard

Leonardville ECHO. 1885 *See* Randolph enterprise (Randolph)

Leonardville ECHO. w 1912-13||
United with Leonardville monitor to form Leonardville echo-monitor, later Leonardville monitor
KHi D 26 1912-Ag 7 1913

KANSAS (*Continued*)

LEONARDVILLE—*Continued*

Leonardville ECHO-MONITOR. *See* Leonardville monitor

Leonardville MONITOR. w 1883+
1883-Mr 15? 1884 as Clay Center monitor (Clay Center) Ag? 1913-19? Leonardville echo-monitor
KHi D 8 1883+

NEW Tecumseh. *See under* Eustis

LEOTI

Early years as Bonasa

Leoti LANCE. w 1886-87||?
KHi Ap 29-D 1886

Leoti STANDARD. w N 19 1885+
1885-89 as Wichita standard
pub N 1885+
KHi 1885-O 14 1909;Mr 15-D 1910;S 9 1915-Mr 16 1916;Mr 15 1917+

WESTERN Kansan. w 1891-96||?
KHi 1891-96

WICHITA county democrat. w 1886-87||?
KHi Jl 15 1886-87

WICHITA standard. *See* Leoti standard

LERADO

Lerado LEDGER. w 1886-88||?
KHi N 1886-Ja 12 1888

LE ROY

Le Roy EAGLE. w 1887-88||?
KHi N 11 1887-S 1888

NEOSHO VALLEY blade. w 1901-03||
Merged with LeRoy reporter
KHi S 20 1901-Ag 1903

Le Roy weekly NEWS. w D 12 1923-24||?
Merged with LeRoy reporter
KHi 1923-O 15 1924

Le Roy REPORTER. w D 12 1879+
KHi D 26 1879+

LEWIS

Lewis PRESS. w Je 24? 1904+
KHi Ag 25 1904-My 12 1905;Ag 1914-D 22 1923;F 1928+

LEXINGTON

Lexington LEADER. w 1886-88||?
KHi O 22 1886-Mr 1888

LEXINGTON county beacon. w
KHi Je-Jl 16 1886

LIBERAL

Liberal DEMOCRAT. w 1908-Jl 31 1924||
1908-Ja 4? 1911 as Liberal independent. Merged with Liberal news, later Southwest daily times
KHi F 12 1909-24

Liberal DEMOCRAT. d 1920-21||?
KHi S 6 1920-Mr 12 1921

Liberal INDEPENDENT. *See* Liberal democrat

Liberal LEADER. w 1888-90||?
KHi Ap 26 1888-Jl 1890

LIBERALIST. w
KHi Ja 13-D 1911

Liberal LYRE. w 1890-93||
Merged with Liberal news, later Southwest daily times
KHi N 21 1890-F 1893

Liberal NEWS. d
KHi O 15 1920-Mr 12 1921

Liberal NEWS. *See* Southwest daily times

SOUTHWEST chronicle. w 1888-90||?
KHi Ag 1888-My 1890

SOUTHWEST daily times. w,d 1886+
1886-Ap 19 1888 as Fargo Springs news (Fargo Springs); Ap 26 1888-D 15 1892 Arkalon news (Arkalon) D 22 1872-O 1935 Liberal news
w 1886-My 30 1929
pub 1886+
KHi Ap 22 1886+

SOUTHWEST tribune. w Ja 17 1929+
1929-Ja 25 1931 as Kismet clipper (Kismet)
KHi 1929+

LIBERTY

Liberty EXPRESS. w 1904-05||?
KHi Ap 28 1904-D 24 1905

Liberty LIGHT. w 1886||?
KHi Mr-Jl 1886

Liberty REVIEW. w 1886-92||?
KHi Ja 14 1887-N 4 1892

Liberty SENTINEL. w 1905-09||?
KHi N 23 1905-Ap 22 1909

LINCOLN

Lincoln BANNER. *See* Lincoln republican

Lincoln BEACON. w 1879-1901||
1879-81? as Lincoln county beacon
KHi Mr 25 1880-F 1 1901

LINCOLN county beacon. *See* Lincoln beacon

LINCOLN county democrat. *See* Lincoln county farmer

LINCOLN county farmer. w 1886-92||?
1886-S? 1890 as Lincoln county democrat
KHi My 1886-S,D 1890-Mr 4 1892

LINCOLN county news. 1873-75 *See* Lincoln county patriot

LINCOLN county news. w 1930+
KHi Je 1932+

LINCOLN county patriot. w 1873-75||?
1873-Ja 1875? as Lincoln county news
KHi Mr 5-D 1 1873;Jl 15 1875
MB S 1874-Ja 7 1875

LINCOLN county register. *See* Lincoln republican

Lincoln REPUBLICAN. w Je 30 1875-N 19 1925||
1875-F 21 1884 as Saline Valley register (S 1879-N 1881 Lincoln county register) F 28 1884-D 30 1886 Lincoln banner. United with Lincoln sentinel to form Lincoln sentinel-republican
KHi Ap 19 1876-1925

SALINE VALLEY register. *See* Lincoln republican

Lincoln SENTINEL-REPUBLICAN. w 1887+
1887-My 25 1894 as Sylvan Grove sentinel (Sylvan Grove) Je 1 1894-N 19 1925 Lincoln sentinel
Suspended from O 1890-Mr 1892
KHi Jl 28 1887+

LINCOLNVILLE

Lincolnville LANCE. *See* Marion county lance

MARION county lance. w Je?-D 27 1907||
Early issues as Lincolnville lance. Followed by Marion review (Marion)
KHi Je 28-D 1907

Lincolnville STAR. w
KHi Jl 16-N 19 1887

LINDSBORG

KANSAS posten. w O 4 1882-83||
Merged with Hemlandet, later Det Gamla och det nya hemlandet (Chicago)
In Swedish
IRA [1882-83]
KHi complete
KLiB 1882
MnHi 1882-S 19 1883

KANSAS staats tidning. w 1879-80||
In Swedish
IRA [1879-80]
KHi D 24 1879-F 18 1880

Lindsborg LOCALIST. w 1879-83||?
KHi My 1879-Mr 15 1883

Lindsborg NEWS and record. w S 21 1881+
1881-Jl 30 1887 as Smoky Valley news; Ag 5 1887-Mr 23 1912 Lindsborg news
IRA 1898-1902;12-18
KHi S 21 1881+
MnHi [F 21 1908-Ja 18 1918]

Lindsborg POSTEN. w 1897-D 31 1930||
Followed by Kansas conference Lutheran (not in this list)
In Swedish
IRA 1898-1930
KHi F 8 1898-1930
KLiB 1899-[1901-29]30
KLiBe [N 1904-30]
MnHi 1908-29
NdHi Mr 17 1909-D 24 1913

Lindsborg PROGRESS. w Ja 23 1930-32||?
KHi 1930-D 8 1932

Lindsborg RECORD. w 1896-Mr 1912||
United with Lindsborg news to form Lindsborg news and record
IRA 1897-1912
KHi D 25 1896-1912

SMOKY VALLEY news. *See* Lindsborg news and record

LINN

Linn DIGEST. w Jl 30? 1897-1924||?
KHi O 8 1897-F 8 1924

Linn GAZETTE. *See* Local record

LOCAL record. w 1889-91||?
1889-Jl? 1890 as Linn gazette
KHi N 1889-91

Linn-Palmer RECORD. w D 18 1903+
1903-F 8 1924 as Palmer index
1903-27? pub in Palmer
KHi 1903+

LINWOOD

Linwood LEADER. w 1883-84||?
KHi D 27 1883-Ag 14 1884

Linwood LEAF. w 1901-02||?
KHi Ag 1901-Mr 12 1902

Linwood LEDGER. w
KHi Ap 23 1898-My 20 1899

Linwood LIGHT. w 1917-19||?
KHi Ja-S 12 1918

Linwood TIMES. w
KHi S 29 1909-10

Linwood TIMES. w F 5 1925+
KHi 1925-Mr 21 1935

LITTLE RIVER

Little River COMET. w
KHi My 15-D 23 1891

Little River MONITOR. w Jl 1 1886+
KHi 1886+

Little River NEWS. w
KHi N 1880-Ja 1881

RURAL West. *See* Ellsworth messenger (Ellsworth)

LOCO

Loco MOTIVE. w
KHi D 16 1886-Mr 17 1887

LOGAN

Logan ENTERPRISE. *See* Belleville freeman (Belleville)

Logan HERALD. w 1909-11||?
KHi O 15 1909-11

PHILLIPS county freeman. *See* Belleville freeman (Belleville)

Logan REPUBLICAN. w Je 24 1886+
1912?-19? as Logan republican and Prairie View news
pub [1886-1920]+
KHi 1886-[1919-30]+

LOGAN SPRINGS

LOGAN county times. w 1886-88||?
1886-87? pub in Oakley
KHi D 23 1886-88

LONE ELM

Lone Elm LEDGER. w 1896-99||?
KHi My 1896-Ja 6 1899

LONG ISLAND

Long Island ARGUS. w 1884-85||?
KHi Ja 16-O 1885

Long Island LEADER. *See* Long Island new leaf

Long Island NEW LEAF. w 1885-1918||?
1885-My 27 1905 as Long Island leader
KHi Jl 29 1886-Jl 11 1918
WHi My 2 1903

Long Island NEWS. w 1918?-22||?
KHi Ap 22 1920-S 1922

PHILLIPS county democrat. *See* Phillips county inter-ocean

PHILLIPS county inter-ocean. w 1886-91||?
1886 as Phillips county democrat
KHi Jl 31 1886-F 21 1891

Long Island PRESS. w
KHi Ag 28 1925-Ag 11 1927

LONGFORD

Longford JOURNAL. w S 27 1923-32||?
KHi 1923-Jl 1931

Longford JOURNAL. w 1935+
Follows Longford leader?
KHi F 14 1935+

Longford LEADER. w 1910-14||?
KHi O 14 1910-14

Longford LEADER. w F 25 1915-18||?
KHi 1915-Jl 1918

Longford LEADER. w N 5 1931-Ja 1935||?
Followed by Longford journal?
KHi 1931-Ja 1935

LONGTON

COURANT. *See* Howard courant (Howard)

Longton GLEANER. w 1881-1918||?
1881-Jl 15 1892 as Longton times
KHi My 20 1881-N 22 1918

HOWARD county ledger. *See* Elk county ledger (Howard)

Longton LEADER. w 1887||?
KHi F 10-N 3 1887

Longton NEWS and Elk Falls reflector. w S 28 1898+
1925?-29? Longton and Elk Falls reflector-news; 1930?-33? News-reflector
Also dated in Elk Falls
KHi 1898+

Longton PIONEER. w 1880-81||?
KHi Mr 24 1880-Ja 13 1881

Longton SIGNAL. w 1885?-92||?
KHi F 28 1890-Mr 4 1892

Longton TIMES. *See* Longton gleaner

LOST SPRINGS

Lost Springs COURIER. w 1888-89||?
KHi Jl 12 1888-N 1 1889

Lost Springs JOURNAL. w
KHi S 17-N 1887

Lost Springs NEWS. w 1915-16||?
KHi Ag 1915-S 7 1916

Lost Springs TRAIL. w 1908-10||?
KHi N 1908-F 10 1910

KANSAS (*Continued*)

LOUISBURG

BORDER chief. *See* Border watchman

BORDER watchman. w 1879-81||?
1879-Mr 11 1881 as Border chief
KHi N 1879-Ag 1881

Louisburg HERALD. w Jl 4 1876+
pub 1901+
KHi Ag 30 1877;S 9 1887+

LOUISVILLE

Louisville COURIER. *See* Wheaton courier (Wheaton)

Louisville INDICATOR. w 1887-89||?
KHi Ap 28 1887-89

KANSAS reporter. *See under* Wamego

Louisville LYRE. *See* Saint George news (Saint George)

POTTAWATOMIE county herald. w
KHi Ja 29-Jl 2 1879

POTTAWATOMIE county times. *See* Wamego times (Wamego)

POTTAWATOMIE gazette. *See* Kansas reporter (Wamego)

Louisville REPUBLICAN. w 1881-87||?
KHi Ap 20 1882-O 8 1886
MWA O 30,N 20-27 1885

LOVEWELL

Lovewell INDEX. w Ja 30 1913-24||?
KHi 1913-[Ap 1916-Mr 2 1922]-Mr 13 1924

LOYAL

GARFIELD county journal. w 1887-89||?
KHi Jl 1887-N 17 1889

LUCAS

Lucas ADVANCE. w 1888-97||?
KHi Je 29 1888-D 2 1897

Lucas DEMON. w 1928-
KHi [1929-Ap 1 1932]

Lucas INDEPENDENT. w N 12 1908+
KHi 1908+

Lucas JOURNAL. w 1906||?
KHi Ag 24-D 1906

Lucas SENTINEL. w 1901-09||?
KHi Ap 1901-Mr 11 1909

LUDELL

Ludell GAZETTE. w 1887-93||?
KHi My 14 1887-Ag 1893

Ludell SETTLER. w 1884-87||?
KHi O 18 1884-D 10 1887

LURAY

Luray HEADLIGHT. w 1887-90||?
KHi Ag 25 1887-S 1890

Luray HERALD. w D? 1901+
KHi F 27 1902+

Luray STAR. w
KHi Ja 19-Je 8 1893

LYNDON

CURRENT remark. *See* Lyndon record

Lyndon JOURNAL. w 1882?-99||?
KHi F 9 1882-Je 1 1899
OkHi [1893-94]

KANSAS plebeian. *See under* Scranton

KANSAS times. *See* Lyndon times

Lyndon LEADER. w 1881-83||?
KHi F 1882-Ja 11 1883

OSAGE county democrat. w 1910-13||?
KHi 1910-Ja 2 1913

OSAGE county graphic. w 1888-95||?
KHi Ag 1888-Mr 21 1895

PEOPLE'S herald. w 1889+
1889-Ag 1 1890 as Quenemo leader (Quenemo)
KHi My 18 1889-N 11 1915;D 26 1918+
OkHi 1894

Lyndon RECORD. w 1895-1906||?
1895-1902 as Current remark
KHi S 19 1895-S 1906

Lyndon TIMES. w 1875-81||?
Ag 7 1879-D 30 1880? as Kansas times
KHi My 1876-81

LYONS

Weekly BULLETIN. *See* Sterling bulletin (Sterling)

CENTRAL Kansas democrat. d S 27? 1886-87||
KHi S 29 1886;Mr-N 23 1887

CENTRAL Kansas democrat. w *See* Rice county democrat

CENTRAL Kansas news-democrat. *See* Rice county democrat

Lyons NEWS. d 1906+
KHi Ja 19 1909+
—w ed *See* Rice county democrat

PROHIBITIONIST. *See* Rice county eagle

Lyons REPUBLICAN. w,sw S 11 1879-1927||?
sw 1913?-23?
KHi 1879-Ja 13 1927

Lyons REPUBLICAN. d Jl 10 1882-
KHi Jl-Ag 5 1882

Lyons REPUBLICAN. d F 18 1887-88||
KHi 1887-Je 1888

RICE county breeze. w
KHi S 24 1897-Ag 21 1898

RICE county democrat. w 1878-1918||?
1878-1905? as Central Kansas democrat; 1906?-15? Central Kansas news-democrat
Suspended from N 1887-Mr 1890
KHi My 8 1879-My 21 1881;F 21 1884-Ap 1918
—d ed *See* Central Kansas democrat; Lyons news

RICE county eagle. w 1884-1908||?
1884-89? as Prohibitionist
KHi Mr 1890-Ap 1908

SOLDIERS tribune. *See* Lyons tribune

SPOTLIGHT. sm
KHi O 12 1933+

Lyons TRIBUNE. w 1887-93||
1887-S 6 1888 as Soldiers tribune. Merged with Lyons republican
KHi D 1887-Ag 1893

McALLISTER

McAllister HERALD. w 1887-88||?
KHi Je 11 1887-Mr 3 1888

McAllister RECORD. w
KHi Je 11 1887-Mr 3 1888

McCRACKEN

McCracken ENTERPRISE. w Mr 18 1887-Ag 24 1894||
KHi complete

McCracken ENTERPRISE. w Ag 7 1896+
1902?-03? as Republican-enterprise
KHi 1896+

McCracken REPUBLICAN. w 1900-02||?
United with McCracken enterprise to form Republican-enterprise, later McCracken enterprise
KHi O 19 1900-02

REPUBLICAN-ENTERPRISE. *See* McCracken enterprise 1896+

RUSH county leader. w 1895||?
KHi My 18-N 14 1895

McCUNE

BRICK. *See under* Pittsburg

CRAWFORD county democrat. *See* McCune herald

McCune HERALD. w 1889+
1889-Je 1903 as Crawford county democrat; Jl 1903-Ap 14? 1904 Times-democrat
KHi Jl 27 1889+

McCune LEADER. w 1893||?
KHi My 18-S 7 1893

McCune REPUBLICAN. w
KHi N 9 1894-Ja 25 1895

McCune STANDARD. w
KHi Mr 12 1881-Jl 1882

McCune TIMES. w 1882-91||?
KHi S 9 1882-D 11 1891

TIMES-DEMOCRAT. *See* McCune herald

McCune TRANSCRIPT. w 1897-1902||?
KHi N 26 1897-1901

McDONALD

McDonald NEWS. w 1907-11||?
KHi O 1907-Je 15 1911

McDonald STANDARD. w S 10? 1925+
KHi O 1925+

McDonald TIMES. *See* Atwood patriot (Atwood)

MACKSVILLE

ALLIANCE herald. w 1890-92||
KHi My 29 1890-Ja 1892

Macksville ARGUS. w Mr 9 1900-Jl 8 1904||
Followed by Macksville enterprise
KHi O 1900-04

Macksville ENTERPRISE. w Jl 1904+
Follows Macksville argus
KHi Je 1905+

Macksville INDEPENDENT. w 1891-92||?
KHi Ap 23 1891-Je 1892

Macksville INDEX. w 1901-04||?
KHi Jl 18 1901-Jl 7 1904

Macksville TELEPHONE. w 1888?-89||?
KHi My 17 1888-F 18 1890

Macksville TIMES. w 1886-88||?
KHi My 1886-O 5 1888

McLOUTH

McLouth CHAMPION. w 1895-97||
Merged with McLouth times
KHi My 8 1896-Je 22 1897

McLouth TIMES. w My 5 1887+
KHi 1887-Jl 19 1918;O 1921+

McPHERSON

McPherson ADVERTISER. w 1934?+
KHi Je 29 1934+

ALLIANCE index. *See* People's advocate

McPherson ANZEIGER. w 1887-90||?
In German
KHi Ap 15 1887-Ag 1890

McPherson COMET. w 1881-82||?
KHi Ag 1881-Ja 1882

McPherson DEMOCRAT-OPINION. w O 1 1886+
1886-Ag 2 1912 as McPherson democrat
KHi 1886+
OkHi [1893]-[95]

DEUTSCHE westen. w 1907-11||?
In German
KHi Ap 11 1907-10

FARMERS' advocate. w
KHi Jl 9-S 11 1874

McPherson FREEMAN. w Ag 9? 1878-1919||?
Ag? 1891-95 as Freeman-vim
KHi Ag 16 1878-Ap 18 1918

FREEMAN. d S 13 1887-88||?
KHi S 13 1887-N 9 1888

McPherson INDEPENDENT. 1874-79 *See* McPherson republican

McPherson INDEPENDENT. 1882-84 *See* McPherson press

KANSAS American. w 1903-06||?
KHi Jl 9 1903-My 2 1906

KANSAS state register. w 1887||?
KHi Ja 27-N 3 1887

KANSAS vim. 1889-Jl? 1891||
United with McPherson freeman to form Freeman-vim, later McPherson freeman
KHi F 1889-Jl 1891

McPherson LEADER. w 1879-82||?
KHi Mr 24-Jl 14 1881

McPHERSON county champion. w 1885-87||?
KHi My 21 1885-Ja 21 1887

McPHERSON county times. w F 3-Jl 7 1883||
United with Wichita opinion (Wichita) to form McPherson opinion
KHi complete

McPherson MESSENGER. *See* McPherson republican

McPherson OPINION. w 1889-Ag 9 1912||
1889-Jl 7? 1893 as Wichita opinion (Wichita) United with McPherson democrat to form McPherson democrat-opinion
KHi Je 23 1889-S 1890;D 1891-1912

PEOPLE'S advocate. w 1888?-93||?
1888? as Alliance index
KHi 1891-Jl 1892;Ap-Ag 11 1893

McPherson PRESS. w 1882-85||
1882-Jl 30 1884 as McPherson independent. Merged with McPherson republican
KHi Ag 30 1882-S 16 1885

McPherson REPUBLICAN. w 1872+
1872-S 1874 as McPherson messenger; O 1874-S 1879 McPherson independent
pub O 1879+
CoU 1899-Jl 1910
KHi D 19 1872-73;O 28 1874;Ap-S 1876;Mr 1877+
OOxM O 12 1882

McPherson REPUBLICAN. d O 1 1886+
pub 1886+
KHi F 5 1887+

MADISON

Madison INDEX. *See* Madisonian

LIVE stock belt. *See* Madison news. 1911+

MADISONIAN. w 1893?-1908||?
1893?-S 13 1901 as Madison index
KHi N 30 1894-1908

Madison MIRROR. w O 7? 1914+
KHi O 21 1914+

Madison NEWS. w 1879-92||?
Ap?- 1886 as Madison zenith; 1886-F 17 1888? Madison times
KHi My 9 1879-Jl 1 1892

Madison NEWS. w 1900-01||?
KHi Jl 1900-S 13 1901

Madison NEWS. w 1911+
1911-14? as Live stock belt
KHi Mr 18 1915+

Madison SPIRIT. w 1907-13||?
KHi D 5 1907[My 20 1909-O 23 1913]

Madison STAR. w 1892-1900||?
KHi S 16 1892-D 7 1900

Madison TIMES. w 1877-78||?
KHi O 1877-My 4 1878

Madison TIMES. 1886-88 *See* Madison news 1879-92

Madison ZENITH. *See* Madison news 1879-92

MAHASKA

Mahaska LEADER. w S 22 1905-19||?
KHi 1905-Ag 22 1919

KANSAS (*Continued*)

MAIZE

Maize CRITIC. w
KHi S 8 1894-Jl 1896

Maize REVIEW. w Je? 1915-17||?
KHi S 17 1915-F 9 1917

MANCHESTER

Manchester MOTOR. w Mr 31 1910+
KHi 1910+

Manchester NEWS. w 1896-1906||?
KHi N 26 1896-N 22 1906

Manchester SUN. w 1887-93||?
KHi D 8 1887-Ag 1893

THINKER. *See under* Burr Oak

MANHATTAN

Manhattan BEACON. w 1872-75||?
KHi Mr 21 1872-Ja 6 1875

Morning CHRONICLE. d O 1-N 9 1916||
United with Riley county democrat to form Riley county chronicle
KM complete
KMC complete

Morning CHRONICLE. d Mr 8 1921+
pub [1921-23]+
KHi F 11 1923+
KM Mr 8 1921+
—w ed *See* Riley county chronicle; Manhattan republic
—evening ed *See* Manhattan mercury

Manhattan ENTERPRISE. *See* Manhattan republic

Manhattan EXPRESS. *See* Manhattan independent

Manhattan INDEPENDENT. w My 4 1859-S 12 1868||
My-S 10 1859 as Kansas express; S 17 1859-63 Manhattan express (S 15 1860-S 21 1861 Western Kansas express) United with Kansas radical to form Manhattan standard
DLC [1859-O 11 1862]
KHi Ag 20 1859-62;Ag 10 1863-F 1865;S 1866-68
MWA Mr 10 1860;O 28 1865
WHi Ag 20,N 26 1859;Ap 7,O 20 1860;F 9,My 11 1861

KANSAS express. *See* Manhattan independent

KANSAS radical. w Jl 14 1866-S 12 1868||
United with Manhattan independent to form Manhattan standard
KHi complete
MWA F 16 1867
WHi Jl 13 1867-68

Manhattan MERCURY. w My 9 1884-D 30 1909||
Merged with Manhattan republic
KHi complete
KM [My 1885-Ap 1888;96-1904]
KMC [1884-1909]

Manhattan MERCURY. d F 8 1909+
pub 1910+
KHi 1909+
—w ed *See* Manhattan republic
—morning ed *See* Morning chronicle

Manhattan NATIONALIST. w D 23 1870-Mr 11 1926||?
Follows Manhattan standard. Merged with Manhattan republic
KHi 1870-Mr 11 1926
KMC O 20 1871-Mr 1 1877
WHi [Ja 20 1871-72;75-O 1876] F 9 1877-D 20 1878;80-84;86-D 16 1887

Tri-weekly NATIONALIST. tw O-N 1893||
KHi N 2-7 1893

Manhattan NATIONALIST. d F 1 1909-Mr 13 1926||
Merged with Manhattan republic
KHi complete
KMC 1914-26

Manhattan REPUBLIC. w 1876+
1876-Je 9 1882 as Manhattan enterprise
KHi My 25 1876+
KMC [My 1876-Jl 18 1879;96]+
WaPS F 23,Ag 17 1922;Ag 9 1923;Jl 30 1925; F 11 1926;D 8 1927[28-29;32]Ja 4 1933
—morning ed *See* Morning chronicle
—evening ed *See* Manhattan mercury

Daily REPUBLIC. d Ap ? 1887-91||
KHi Jl 9 1887-Jl 1891

Evening REPUBLIC. d Ja 4 1904-D 30 1905||?
KHi 1904-05

RILEY county chronicle. w,sw 1909-22||?
1909-N 10 1916 as Riley county democrat w 1906-F 27 1917
KHi Ag 26 1909;F 11 1911-S 1922
KM N 10 1916-F 25 1921
KMC [N 10 1916-21]

RILEY county democrat. *See* Riley county chronicle

Manhattan SIGNAL. w 1888-91||
1888-90 as Saturday signal
KHi D 22 1888-Jl 3 1891

Manhattan STANDARD. w S 19 1868-D 9 1870||
Formed by the union of Manhattan independent and Kansas radical. Followed by Manhattan nationalist
KHi complete
KM 1868-S 4 1869
KMC Ja-D 2 1870

Manhattan TRIBUNE. w 1914+
KHi S 23 1915+
KM [1915-26]

WESTERN Kansas express. *See* Manhattan independent

MANKATO

To 1879 as Jewell Center

JACKSONIAN. w 1888-90||?
KHi F 1888-O 1890

JEWELL county advertiser. *See* Jewell county monitor

JEWELL county monitor. w 1874+
1879? as Jewell county monitor-diamond; 1904-07 Jewell county advertiser
KHi Je 5 1874;Je 30 1876+

JEWELL county review. w 1879-95||?
Mr 1883-85 as Mankato review
KHi Jl 18 1879-My 9 1895
—d ed *See* Mankato review

JEWELL county daily review. d Ag 2 1886-
KHi Ag-S 30 1886

KANSAS Jewellite. w 1882-84||?
KHi Ag 16 1882-F 14 1884

Mankato REVIEW. *See* Jewell county review

WESTERN advocate. w Jl 1890+
pub 1890+
CoU 1899-Jl 1910
KHi Ag 1890+

MANTER

CITIZEN press. w S 6 1923-28||?
KHi 1923-Ap 12 1928

MAPLE HILL

Maple Hill NEWS. w 1910-11||?
KHi D 30 1910-O 1911

MAPLETON

Mapleton DISPATCH. w 1886-95||
KHi Je 24 1889-S 6 1895

Mapleton DISPATCH. w O 20 1905-F 1 1907||
Merged with Weekly republican (Fort Scott)
KHi complete

Mapleton LANTERN. *See* Fort Scott lantern (Fort Scott)

Mapleton PRESS. w 1905-10||?
KHi D 20 1905-Jl 9 1910

Mapleton TELEPHONE. w 1886-89||?
KHi Mr 1887-Ja 17 1889

MARION

To 1881? as Marion Centre

Marion BANNER. w 1880-82||?
KHi Mr 11 1880-Mr 16 1882

CENTRAL advocate. w 1889-91||?
1889-F 4? 1891 as Marion globe
KHi Jl 23 1889-N 1891

CENTRAL Kansas telegraph. w
KHi Ap 24-N 20 1880

COTTONWOOD VALLEY times. *See* Marion headlight

Marion GLOBE. *See* Central advocate

Marion GRAPHIC. w 1882-83||?
KHi D 22 1882-N 23 1883

Marion HEADLIGHT. w 1887-1909||
1887-89? as Cottonwood Valley times; Ja?-O? 1890 Marion scimiter; N 6 1890-99 Marion times
CoU Ja-N 1899
KHi Ap 21 1887-S 19 1889;Ja 9 1890-S 1909
—d ed *See* Marion times

Marion INDEPENDENT. w 1883-84||?
1883? as Marion county democrat
KHi Mr 15 1883-84

MARION county anzeiger. *See* Hillsboro anzeiger (Hillsboro)

MARION county democrat. *See* Marion independent

MARION county record. *See* Marion record

Marion RECORD. w S 1869+
1869-71 as Western news; -Ag 1871 Western giant; S 1871-81? Marion county record
KHi Jl 23 1875+

Marion REGISTER. w 1885-88||?
KHi Ja 14 1886-Ja 12 1888

Marion REVIEW. w Ja 2 1908+
Follows Marion county lance (Lincolnville)
pub 1920+
KHi 1908+

Marion SCIMITER. *See* Marion headlight

Marion TIMES. d F 6 1888-
KHi F-S 29 1888

Marion TIMES. w *See* Marion headlight

Marion TRIBUNE. w
KHi Jl 10 1886-F 10 1887

WESTERN giant. *See* Marion record

WESTERN news. *See* Marion record

MARION CENTRE. *See* MARION

MARKLEY'S MILL. *See* MINNEAPOLIS

MARQUETTE

Marquette MONITOR. *See* Marquette tribune

Marquette TRIBUNE. w Mr 25 1887+
1887-Mr 1889 as Marquette monitor
KHi 1887+

MARVIN

Marvin MONITOR. w 1886-88||?
KHi S 1886-F 17 1888

MARYSVILLE

ADVOCATE-DEMOCRAT. w 1880+
1880-Ja 28 1898 as Marshall county democrat
Suspended from N 3 1880-D 21 1882?
CoU Ja-Mr 1899
KHi O 21-N 3 1880;D 29 1882+

BIG blue union. w Mr? 1862-
KHi Ap 5 1862-Ag 3 1863
MH Ag 30,S 13 1862
NNHi D 13 1862

BUGLE call. *See* People's advocate

Marysville COURIER. *See* Marshall county courier

Evening DEMOCRAT. d Jl 1? 1889-92||
1889-D 20? 1890 as Daily free press
KHi Jl 31,Ag 5 1889-Mr 26 1892

Marysville ENTERPRISE. w
KHi Jl 14 1866-Jl 11 1868

Daily FREE PRESS. *See* Evening democrat

KANSAS staats-zeitung. w 1878-81||?
In German
KHi Ap 12 1879-My 12 1881

LANTERN. w
- 1876 pub at Blue Rapids
KHi Ap 22-D 15 1876

LOCAL lantern. w 1898-1900||?
KHi Ja 21 1899-1900

MARSHALL county courier. w 1906-15||?
Title varies: Maryville courier
In German
KHi S 1906-Ap 12 1912

MARSHALL county democrat. *See* Advocate-democrat

MARSHALL county news. w O 5 1872+
pub 1872+
KHi 1872+

PEOPLE'S advocate. w 1885-Ja 28 1898||
1885-Ag 5 1886 as Bugle call; Ag 12 1886-Ag 14 1890 True republican. United with Marshall county democrat to form Advocate-democrat
KHi D 10 1885-98

Marysville POST. w 1881-1901||?
In German
KHi Jl 30 1881-1901

Marysville REPUBLICAN. w 1900-02||?
KHi O 1900-N 13 1902

Marysville SIGNAL. w 1881-83||?
KHi S 1881-F 8 1883

TRUE republican. *See* People's advocate

MATFIELD GREEN

Matfield Green INDEPENDENT. w
KHi Ag 20 1904-Ja 6 1905

Matfield Green MIRROR. w 1893-94||?
KHi Ja 27 1893-Ja 19 1894

Matfield Green MIRROR. w
KHi S 27 1907-Ag 5 1908

MAYETTA

Mayetta HERALD. w F 17 1910-20||?
KHi 1910-Ja 1920

Mayetta NEWS. w 1904-05||?
KHi Jl 20 1904-F 1905

MAYFIELD

Mayfield VOICE. w
KHi Mr 16 1894-F 1895

MEADE

To 1890? as Meade Center

Meade GLOBE. w Jl 9 1885-S 27 1918||
1885-1903? as Meade county globe. United with Meade county news to form Meade globe-news
KHi 1885-1918

Meade GLOBE-NEWS. w Ja 11 1900+
1900-O 3 1918 as Meade county news
KHi 1900+

MEADE county democrat. *See* Meade county nationalist

MEADE county globe. *See* Meade globe

MEADE county nationalist. w 1885-93||
1885-86 as Meade Center press; 1886-90 Meade county press-democrat; 1890-Ja 31 1891 Meade county democrat. Merged with Meade globe
KHi S 24 1885-92

MEADE county news. *See* Meade globe-news

MEADE county press. w 1931+
KHi F 1932+

KANSAS (*Continued*)

MEADE—*Continued*

MEADE county press-democrat. *See* Meade county nationalist

Meade Center PRESS. *See* Meade county nationalist

Meade REPUBLICAN. w 1887-93||
Merged with Meade globe
KHi Mr 9 1887-My 17 1893

Meade TELEGRAM. w
KHi Mr 15-S 9 1886

MEADE CENTER. *See* MEADE

MEDICINE LODGE

BARBER county democrat. w 1888||?
KHi Mr 23-Jl 6 1888

BARBER county herald. w 1890-91||?
KHi Ag 23 1890-Ja 24 1891

BARBER county index. w Je 10? 1880+
pub 1880+
KHi D 16 1880+

BARBER county mail. *See* Medicine Lodge cresset

Medicine Lodge CHIEF. w 1886-88||?
KHi Jl 1886-F 3 1888

Medicine Lodge CRESSET. w My 21 1878-1917||?
1878-Mr 6 1879 as Barber county mail; Mr 13? 1879 Medicine Lodge mail. Merged with Barber county index?
KHi Mr 20 1879-Ag 1917
KMeB 1879-1917

Medicine Lodge MAIL. *See* Medicine Lodge cresset

Medicine Lodge REPUBLICAN. w 1918-19||?
KHi My 18 1918-Jl 26 1919

MEDINA

KANSAS new era. *See* New era (Valley Falls)

NEW era. *See under* Valley Falls

MELVERN

Melvern MESSENGER. w My 4 1932-
KHi My-Ag 3 1932

Melvern RECORD. w 1883-90||?
KHi Mr 12 1884-S 4 1890

Melvern REVIEW. w 1890-S 18 1931||
United with Quenemo news to form Quenemo news-review-enterprise (Quenemo)
KHi Ja 8 1891-1931

MENLO

Menlo ENTERPRISE. w 1909-12||?
KHi Ag 27 1909-My 17 1912

Menlo LEADER. w Ap 3 1924-29||?
KHi 1924-N 14 1929

Menlo RECORD. w
KHi Je 17 1907-12

MERIDEN

ADVOCATE. *See* Farmers advocate (Topeka)

Meriden LEDGER. w Mr 30 1894-1921||?
KHi 1894-Jl 14 1921

Meriden MESSAGE. w O? 1921+
KHi D 9 1921+

Meriden REPORT. w 1885-89||?
KHi Je 27 1885-Je 1 1889

Meriden TRIBUNE. w 1890-97||?
KHi Je 1890-S 18 1897

MERRIAM

Merriam LEADER. w Ap 6 1932+
1932-F 15 1934 as Shawnee chief (Shawnee)
KHi 1932+

SUBURBAN news. w 1928||?
KHi O 16 1930+

MERTILLA

MEADE county times. w 1885-88||?
KHi Ap 1886-S 15 1888

MICHIGAN VALLEY

WOLVERINE. w 1914||?
KHi Ja 15-D 1914

MIDLOTHIAN

Midlothian SUN. w
KHi Ag 20 1885-Mr 4 1886

MILAN

Milan NEWS. w 1910-18||?
KHi Ja 19 1911-F 7 1918

Milan PRESS. w 1890-98||?
1890-92 as People's press (Argonia)
KHi 1890-Jl 14 1898

MILDRED

Mildred LEDGER. w 1909-12||?
KHi Jl 15 1910-S 1912

MILFORD

Milford MESSENGER. w Ap?- 1923||?
KHi Jl 26-N 1 1923

MILLBROOK

GRAHAM county democrat. w 1885-88||?
KHi O 22 1885-N 15 1888

Millbrook HERALD. w 1882-83||?
KHi My 16 1882-Mr 14 1883

Millbrook HERALD. w 1885-88||?
KHi S 1885-My 1888

Millbrook TIMES. w 1879-89||?
KHi Jl 11 1879-D 20 1889

MILTON

Milton CRESCENT. w 1917||?
KHi Ap 26-D 6 1917

MILTONVALE

Miltonvale ADVANCE. w 1890?-92||?
1890?-91 as Morganville advance (Morganville)
KHi Mr 25 1891-Ap 6 1892

Miltonvale CHIEFTAIN. w 1887-88||?
KHi Jl 21 1887-N 3 1888

Miltonvale ECHO. w
KHi Jl 26 1892-Ja 6 1893

FARMER'S tribune. *See* Miltonvale tribune

Miltonvale LEADER. w 1893-94||?
KHi Ag 31 1893-Ja 4 1894

Miltonvale NEWS. w 1882-91||?
KHi Ag 25 1882-S 18 1891

Miltonvale PRESS. *See* Concordia press (Concordia)

Miltonvale RECORD. w F 1 1901+
KHi 1901+

Miltonvale REVIEW. w 1889-90||?
KHi Jl 25-N 14 1889

Miltonvale STAR. w 1885-86||?
KHi Ap 14-Ag 1886

Miltonvale TRIBUNE. w 1894||?
early issues as Farmers' tribune
KHi F 16-S 6 1894

MILWAUKEE

Milwaukee BEE. *See* Stafford county bee

STAFFORD county bee. w
-O 12 1882 as Milwaukee bee
KHi Je 13 1882-Mr 9 1883

MINERAL

Mineral MAGNET. w 1897||?
KHi My-N 1897

MINNEAPOLIS

To 1870? as Markley's Mill

BETTER way. w Ag 6 1896+
KHi 1896+

Minneapolis COMMERCIAL. w 1886-92||
1886-O 26 1887 as Ottawa county commercial
KHi N 1886-Je 1891

Minneapolis INDEPENDENT. w 1871-80||?
KHi Ja 15 1876-O 9 1880

Minneapolis JOURNAL. w 1890-1903||?
1890-Ja 29 1891 as Kansas union; F 5 1891-S 4 1902 Ottawa county index
KHi O 1890-Mr 1903

KANSAS union. *See* Minneapolis journal

Minneapolis MESSENGER. w 1875+
1875-S 22 1883 as Minneapolis sentinel
DLC O 18-N 1 1883
KHi Ag 1875+

Minneapolis MESSENGER. d Ap 9 1887-
KHi Ap-Je 11 1887

OTTAWA county commercial. *See* Minneapolis commercial

OTTAWA county index. w 1880-83||?
KHi F 18 1880-S 19 1883

OTTAWA county index. 1891-1902 *See* Minneapolis journal

PROGRESSIVE current. w 1883-84||?
KHi D 1883-N 8 1884

Minneapolis REVIEW. w 1891?-1901||?
KHi O 9 1891-Jl 4 1901

Minneapolis SENTINEL. *See* Minneapolis messenger

SOLOMON VALLEY democrat. *See* Ottawa county democrat (Bennington)

MINNEOLA

CLARK county republican. w 1888?-89||?
Also dated in Ashland
KHi My 10 1888-Ag 15 1889

Minneola ERA. w 1886?-88||?
KHi Jl 28 1887-Ag 16 1888

Minneola JOURNAL. w
KHi Mr 19-S 3 1864

Minneola RECORD. w 1908+
KHi Ag 1908-O 1912;My 1929+

MITCHELL

Mitchell COURIER. w
KHi Je 8 1887-Jl 1888

MOLINE

Moline ADVANCE. w 1882+
1882-N 1 1889 as Moline mercury; N 8 1889-Je 30 1899 Moline republican; Jl 7 1899-N 8 1912 Moline review
KHi Ap 29-S 1882;Mr 27 1885+

Moline FREE PRESS. w 1883-85||
Merged with Moline mercury, later Moline advance
KHi S 7,O 19 1883-Mr 1885

Moline GAZETTE. w 1910-12||
United with Moline review to form Moline advance
KHi Jl 28 1910-12

Moline MERCURY. *See* Moline advance

Moline NEWS. w 1880||?
KHi Ap 28-O 20 1880

Moline REPUBLICAN. *See* Moline advance

Moline REVIEW. *See* Moline advance

MONTEZUMA

Montezuma CHIEF. w 1886-89||?
KHi Ag 1886-Jl 1889

Montezuma CHIEF. 1914-15 *See* Montezuma press

GRAY county republican. w 1888-89||?
KHi Mr-Jl 1889

Montezuma NEWS. w 1912-13||?
KHi Je 26-O 16 1912

Montezuma PRESS. w 1914+
1914-S? 1915 as Montezuma chief
KHi O 1915+

MONUMENT

Monument COURIER. *See* Obelisk

Monument OBELISK. w 1886-89||
1886-S 1 1887 as Ennis City courier (Ennis City) S 18? 1887-Je 1888 Monument courier
KHi Je 10 1886-N 14 1889

Monument OBSERVER. w 1890||?
Title varies: Western observer
KHi Jl-N 1890

WESTERN observer. *See* Observer

MORAN

To 1883? as Morantown

Moran HERALD. w 1883+
KHi Jl 1885+

MORANTOWN. *See* Moran

MOREHEAD

Morehead SEARCHLIGHT. *See* Cherryvale weekly journal (Cherryvale)

MORGANVILLE

Morganville ADVANCE. *See* Miltonvale advance (Miltonvale)

CLAY county argus. w 1901-02||?
KHi S 27 1901-F 7 1902

CLAY county sentinel. w 1885-91||?
KHi Ap 20 1887-Ja 8 1891

CLAY county star. w 1894-95||?
1894? pub in Green
KHi Mr 29 1894-95

Morganville ENTERPRISE. w 1894||?
KHi [Mr 16-D 14 1894]

Morganville NEWS. *See* Morganville sunflower

Morganville SUNFLOWER. w 1885-87||?
1885? as Morganville news
KHi My 20 1885-Ap 14 1887

Morganville TRIBUNE. w My 19 1904+
KHi 1904+

MORLAND

Morland ADVANCE. w 1904-07||?
KHi Ja 28 1904-Ja 10 1907

Morland INDEPENDENT. w 1901-02||?
KHi [Mr 21 1901-F 6 1902]

Morland MONITOR. w 1916+
KHi F 28 1918+

Morland PROGRESS. w
KHi S 26 1907-Ag 1908

KANSAS (*Continued*)

MORRILL

Morrill NEWS. w 1890+
KHi Ap 1890+

Morrill VINDICATOR. w 1894-96||?
KHi Ja 12 1895-Jl 24 1896

MORTON

MORTON county monitor. *See* Elkhart tri-state news (Elkhart)

MOSCOW

Moscow REVIEW. w 1887-88||?
KHi Ap-D 15 1888

MOUND CITY

BORDER sentinel. w 1864?-74||?
KHi Ap 1866-Jl 10 1874

BORDER sentinel. m,w 1886-1919||?
1886-Ja 21 1909 as Torch of liberty; Ja 28 1909-Ja 7 1916 Linn county democrat
m 1886-89
KHi S 1886-O 23 1919

LINN county clarion. w 1876-93||
United with La Cygne weekly journal to form Journal clarion, later La Cygne weekly journal (La Cygne)
KHi O 12 1876-Ag 1893

LINN county democrat. *See* Border sentinel 1886-1919

LINN county enterprise. w 1875||?
KHi Jl 15 1875

LINN county republic. *See* Mound City republic

Mound City PROGRESS. *See* Mound City republic

Mound City REPUBLIC. w Ap 18 1884+
1884-Ja 4 1895 as Mound City progress; Ja 11 1895-F 7 1896 Linn county republic
KHi 1884-Ja,Je 18 1886+

TORCH of liberty. *See* Border sentinel 1886-1919

MOUND VALLEY

Mound Valley HERALD. w Ap 6 1882-Ag 1913||?
United with Mound Valley journal to form Herald-journal, later Mound Valley times-journal
KHi Jl 16 1885-1913

HERALD-JOURNAL. *See* Mound Valley times journal

Mound Valley JOURNAL. *See* Mound Valley times-journal

Mound Valley NEWS. w
KHi Ap 29 1886-Ja 13 1887

Mound Valley TIMES. w 1881-82||?
KHi D 16 1881-Ap 1882

Mound Valley TIMES. w 1913-20||
United with Mound Valley journal to form Mound Valley times-journal

Mound Valley TIMES-JOURNAL. w S 28 1906+
1906-Mr 26 1920 as Mound Valley journal (Ag 8 1913 as Herald-journal)
KHi 1906+

MOUNDRIDGE

Moundridge JOURNAL. w 1887+
1887-Je 14 1894 as Moundridge leader
Suspended from S 27 1895-Ja 23 1896
KHi Mr 1887+

Moundridge LEADER. *See* Moundridge journal

MOUNT HOPE

Mount Hope CLARION. sw 1885+
1885-N 6 1903 as Mount Hope mentor
Suspended from Jl 22-D 9 1892
KHi S 11 1885+

Mount Hope MENTOR. *See* Mount Hope clarion

MULBERRY

Mulberry INDEPENDENT. w 1919?-27||?
KHi S 1923-Ja 7 1927

Mulberry NEWS. w N 20 1903+
KHi N 27 1903+

Mulberry SUN. w 1898||?
KHi Je 17-O 22 1898

MULLINVILLE

Mullinville MALLET. w 1886-88||?
KHi Ap 9 1886-Ag 1888

Mullinville NEWS. w 1905+
1905-F 25 1913 as Mullinville tribune
KHi Jl 27 1905-Jl 11 1918;Mr 1928+

Mullinville TELEGRAM. w 1886-87||?
KHi S 30 1886-Je 1887

Mullinville TRIBUNE. *See* Mullinville news

MULVANE

Mulvane GRAPHIC. w 1891-93||?
KHi Je 18 1891-Ja 12 1893

Mulvane HERALD. w 1880-82||?
KHi Mr 26 1880-Je 1882

Mulvane NEWS. w Jl 30 1903+
pub [1903+]
KHi 1903+

Mulvane RECORD. w 1883-1906||
Merged with Mulvane news
KHi Mr 21 1885-O 19 1906
KMuN [1887-1906]

Mulvane VOICE. w
KHi Mr 16 1894-F 1895

MUNDEN

PEOPLE'S advocate. w
KHi My 1912-Mr 1913

Munden PRESS. *See* Belleville press (Belleville)

Munden TIMES. w 1898?-99||?
KHi O 28 1898-99

MUSCOTAH

Muscotah NEWS. w
KHi Je 16 1880

Muscotah RECORD. w 1884+
Suspended from Je 24-Ag 12 1892
KHi Jl 1885-Jl 1886;F 1887+

NARKA

Narka BAZOO. w 1888||?
KHi Ap-Je 15 1888

Narka NEWS. w Je 24? 1893-1922||?
KHi S 1893-1922

Narka PRESS. *See* Belleville press (Belleville)

NASHVILLE

Nashville JOURNAL. w 1912-23||?
KHi S 26 1912-S 20 1923

Nashville NEWS. w
KHi Ap 12-Jl 12 1888

NATOMA

Natoma COURIER. w 1901-02||?
KHi N 8 1901-D 12 1902

Natoma INDEPENDENT. w F 19 1909+
KHi 1909+

NEAL

Neal NEWS. w Ap? 1916-22||?
S 12-26 as Neal news and Quincy quill
KHi Ag 30 1916-N 20 1920

NEODESHA

Neodesha CITIZEN. w 1870-72||?
KHi N 18 1870-N 1872
OClWHi My 5 1871

Neodesha daily DERRICK. *See* Neodesha sun

Neodesha FREE press. w 1873?-83||?
1873?-75? as Wilson county free press
KHi Mr 8 1875-N 16 1883

Neodesha GAZETTE. w 1881-82||?
KHi Ag 28 1881-Jl 6 1882

Neodesha INDEPENDENT. w 1887-89||?
KHi N 18 1887-Ja 11 1889

Neodesha REGISTER. w 1883+
pub S 1905+
KHi N 30 1883-Mr 1893;Mr 1894+

Evening REGISTER. d O 18 1897-98||?
KHi 1897-O 13 1898

Neodesha daily REGISTER. d N? 1902-05||?
KHi N 21 1902-S 20 1905

Neodesha SUN. d My 14 1896+
1896-S 20 1898 as Neodesha daily derrick
Suspended from D? 1898-My? 1900
pub 1900+
KHi My 27 1896+

Neodesha SUN. w *See* Wilson county sun

WILSON county free press. *See* Neodesha free press

WILSON county sun. w 1891-1905||
1891? as Neodesha sun
KHi Mr 12 1891-D 1 1905

NEOSHO FALLS

Neosho Falls ADVERTISER. *See* Woodson county post

FOUR counties paper. w Je 25 1927-28||?
KHi 1927-My 23 1928

FRONTIER democrat. *See* Woodson county post

Neosho Falls INDEPENDENT. w 1886-87||?
1886-Ja 5 1887 as Woodson county republican. United with Yates Center sun to form Independent sun (Yates Center)
KHi S 8 1886-Ag 3 1887

PEOPLE'S herald. w
KHi Ag 14-O 23 1878

Neosho Falls POST. *See* Woodson county post

Neosho Falls RECORD. w
KHi Ag 12-19,S 9 1879

WOODSON county post. w C 1869+
1869-Ja 1870? as Frontier democrat; F 1870?-72? Neosho Falls advertiser; 1883?-1933? Neosho Falls post
Also dated in Yates Center O 25 1934+
KHi S 24 1873-F 1926;Je 16 1927+

WOODSON county republican. *See* Neosho Falls independent

NEOSHO RAPIDS

NEOSHO VALLEY press. w
KHi S 16 1886-Mr 10 1887

Neosho Rapids PILOT. w 1889-91||?
KHi F 1889-Ja 8 1891

Neosho Rapids RECORD. w My 8? 1918-26||?
KHi Je 12 1918-Ap 12 1926

Neosho Rapids RECORD. w
KHi S 1931-33

Neosho Rapids TIMES. *See* Hartford times (Hartford)

Neosho VIVIFIER. w 1885-86||?
KHi O 1885-Jl 15 1886

NESCATUNGA

COMANCHE chieftain. *See* Western Kansan

Nescatunga ENTERPRISE. *See* Coldwater enterprise (Coldwater)

WESTERN Kansan. w 1884-86||?
1884-Ja 9 1885 as Comanche chieftain
KHi O 17 1884-Ja 1 1886

NESS CITY

Ness GRAPHIC. w 1886||?
KHi My-O 1886

Ness LANCE. w
KHi O 19-D 21 1892
KNeH [1892]

NESS county echo. w 1893-1915||?
KHi Mr 18 1893-1915

NESS county news. w N 22 1884+
pub 1884+
KHi 1884+
KNeH 1884+

NESS county republican. w 1894-96||?
KHi Mr 9 1894-Ag 1896

Ness City SENTINEL. w 1886-Je 24 1893||
1886-92? as Walnut Valley sentinel
KHi Jl 31 1886-93
KNeH 1886-92

SIXTEENTH amendment. w 1882-86||?
KHi Ap 11-N 17 1885

Ness City TIMES. w S 20 1879-Je 13 1891||
1879-Ja 10? 1880 as Walnut Valley times (Clarinda) Merged with Ness county news
KHi Je 24 1880-Je 4 1891
KNeH 1879-86

Ness TRUTH. w 1882-84||?
KHi Ap 21 1883-N 10 1884

WALNUT VALLEY sentinel. *See* Ness City sentinel

NETAWAKA

Netawaka CHIEF. w 1872-74||?
KHi Je 1872-Jl 16 1874

Netawaka CHIEF. w 1916||?
KHi My-N 2 1916

Netawaka HERALD. w 1896?-99||?
KHi Jl 31 1896-Je 1899

Netawaka STAR. w 1893-94||?
KHi Ap 1893-D 21 1894

Netawaka TALK. w 1907-Ja 28 1916||
Merged with Hoyt booster (Hoyt)
KHi [N 1907-16]

Netawaka TIMES. w
KHi O 15 1903-N 17 1904

Netawaka WASP. w
KHi Ja 11-O 4 1895

NEUCHATEL

L'ÉTOILE du Kansas. m
In French
KHi Ja 1873

NEW ALBANY

KANSAS x-ray. w D 10? 1897-1920||?
KHi D 31 1897-N 1 1918

NEW CAMBRIA

New Cambria TIMES. w 1914||?
KHi F 12-S 24 1914

NEW CHICAGO. *See* CHANUTE

NEW MURDOCK

New Murdock HERALD. w 1887||?
KHi Ap 8-D 23 1887

KANSAS (*Continued*)

NEWTON

Newton ANZEIGER. w 1887-92||?
In German
KHi Je 10 1887-92

ARKANSAS VALLEY democrat. *See* Newton democrat

Newton BEE. w
KHi Je-Ag 2 1879

Newton DEMOCRAT. w Mr 1883-88||?
Mr-Je 1883 as Arkansas Valley democrat. Merged with Newton journal
KHi Mr 30 1883-Je 17 1887

GOLDEN gate. w 1879-82||?
KHi Ag 13 1879-Mr 1882

HARVEY county banner. w 1896-98||
United with Newton journal to form Newton journal and Harvey county banner, later Newton journal
KHi Jl 1896-Ag 1898

HARVEY county news. 1875-79. *See* Newton republican

HARVEY county news. w 1893-95||?
KHi Je 23 1893-F 18 1895

HARVEY county news. w F 16 1917+
1917-D 8 1932 as Hesston gazette (Hesston)
KHi 1917+

HARVEY county voice. w
KHi O 15 1892-Ja 7 1893

Newton daily HERALD. d 1895-
Merged with Evening Kansan-republican
KHi Ja 9 1896-F 28 1906

Der HEROLD. w 1897+
1897-Ja 23? 1902 as Das Kansas volksblatt (1898? Volksblatt und anzeiger) Ja 30 1902-09 Post und volksblatt
In German
KHi N 26 1897-99;1902-D 23 1920;Je 15 1926+
OB 1929+

Newton JOURNAL. w,sw F 10? 1888+
F-D 14 1888 as Kansas chronicle; F 9-Je 28 1894 Journal and Kansan; S 1898?-99? Journal and Harvey county banner
sw 1894?-98?
pub 1889+
KHi F 10 1888+

Newton JOURNAL. d F 10 1902-Mr 1903||
KHi 1902-Mr 14 1903

Newton KANSAN-REPUBLICAN. w Ag 22 1872-D 29 1925||
1872-Mr 1899 as Newton Kansan
For F 9-Je 28 1894 *See* Newton journal
pub complete
CoU My 1902-My 1910
KHi 1876-1925
OOxM O 12 1882

Evening KANSAN-REPUBLICAN. d 1887+
1887-Mr 31 1899 as Evening Kansan
Suspended from S 1888-N 1891; from Ja 12 1894-Mr 11 1897
pub 1887+
KHi S 15,O 31 1887+

KANSAS chronicle. *See* Newton journal

KANSAS commoner. w 1887-90||?
KHi S 1887-90

Das KANSAS volksblatt. *See* Der Herold

MENNONITE weekly review. w S 18 1923+
KHi My 26 1925+
OB 1923+

Das NEUE Vaterland. w
In German
KHi Ja 11-Ag 16 1879

POST und volksblatt. *See* Der Herold

Newton REPUBLICAN. w 1875-Mr 31 1899||
1875-Jl 31 1879 as Harvey county news. United with Newton Kansan to form Newton Kansan-republican
KHi Mr 15 1876-99
OOxM O 11 1882

Daily REPUBLICAN. d 1884-Mr 31 1899||
United with Evening Kansan to form Evening Kansan-republican
KHi F 25 1886-99

VOLKSBLATT und anzeiger. *See* Der Herold

NICKERSON

Nickerson ARGOSY. w D 7 1878+
KHi 1878+

Nickerson INDUSTRY. *See* Nickerson register

Nickerson RECORD. w 1894-96||?
KHi Mr 1895-Je 3 1896

Nickerson REGISTER. w 1884-91||
Mr 9-Jl 6 1889 as Nickerson industry. Merged with Nickerson argosy
KHi S 1884-Ja 10 1891

Nickerson REGISTER. d Ag 2 1887-
KHi Ag-O 7 1887

NICODEMUS

Nicodemus CYCLONE. w 1886-88||?
1886-87? as Western cyclone
KHi My 13 1886-S 7 1888

Nicodemus ENTERPRISE. w
KHi Ag 17-D 23 1887

WESTERN cyclone. *See* Nicodemus cyclone

NILES

Niles RECORDER. w 1914||?
KHi Ap-S 24 1914

NINNESCAH. *See* CUNNINGHAM

NIOTAZE

Niotaze HOROSCOPE. w
KHi Ag 1893-Jl 20 1894

NONCHALANTA

Nonchalanta HERALD. w 1887-89||?
KHi My 20 1887-F 8 1889

NORCATUR

Norcatur DISPATCH. w 1909+
KHi Ag 18 1910+

Norcatur REGISTER. w 1886-1910||?
KHi Ap 30 1886-Jl 1910

NORTH TOPEKA

Papers published in North Topeka are listed under Topeka

NORTON

Norton CHAMPION. w F 28 1884+
KHi 1884+
MWA O 19 1933

Norton COURIER. w Jl 15 1880-S 8 1932||
1880-F 1 1883 as Norton county people. Merged with Norton daily telegram
KHi complete
KNoT complete

Norton DEMOCRAT. *See* New era

FARMERS' advance. w 1889-90||?
1889-My 1890 as Almena advance (Almena)
KHi Je-S 11 1890

Norton LIBERATOR. w 1892-Mr 1905||?
Merged with Norton county news
KHi F 10 1893-Mr 10 1905

NEW ERA. w Ap 18? 1886-92||?
Ap?-Je 10 1886 as Norton reporter; Je 17 1886-Je 1888 Norton democrat; Jl 1888-89? New era and weekly democrat
KHi Je 17 1886-My 7 1891

NORTON county advance. w 1878-82||?
KHi Je 1878-N 22 1882

NORTON county bee. w
KHi My 7 1877

NORTON county news. w 1904-17||?
KHi My 11 1905-N 8 1917

NORTON county people. *See* Norton courier

Norton NUGGET. w 1923-
KHi F 26 1924-Ap 1927

Norton REPORTER. *See* New era

Norton REPUBLICAN. w 1892-95||?
KHi D 16 1892-O 1895

Norton daily TELEGRAM. d F 28 1906+
pub S 15 1919+
KHi Ap 5 1907-Ap 12 1908;My 23 1911+

Norton TELEGRAM. w 1906-20||?
KHi Ap 18 1906-Jl 3 1918

NORTONVILLE

Nortonville HERALD. w 1896-S 23 1898||
United with Nortonville news to form Nortonville news-herald, later Nortonville news
KHi F 1896-98

Nortonville NEWS. w 1885+
S 30 1898-Mr 17 1899 as Nortonville news-herald
KHi My 8 1885+

Nortonville SENTINEL. w 1903||?
KHi F-D 1903

NORWICH

Norwich HERALD. w Ja 20 1899+
1928?-32? as Norwich herald and Four Corners herald
KHi 1899+

Norwich NEWS. w 1885-94||?
KHi 1886-Ag 1894

OAKHILL

Oakhill ECHO. w 1888-89||?
KHi Ap 12-O 25 1889

Oakhill GAZETTE. w My 18? 1911-18||?
KHi Jl 1911-Ag 8 1918

Oakhill HERALD. w 1888-89||?
KHi S 13 1888-D 19 1889

OAKLAND

Oakland BLADE. w 1904-15||?
KHi D 9 1904-15

Oakland NEWS. w 1890-92||?
KHi O 31 1890-Jl 23 1892

OAKLEY

Oakley GRAPHIC. w Mr 24 1888+
Mr-N 17 1888 as Saturday press; N 24 1888-N 15? 1889 News letter
KHi 1888+

LOGAN county times. *See under* Logan Springs

NEWS letter. See Oakley graphic

Oakley OPINION. w 1885-89||?
KHi O 12 1885-Jl 20 1889

Saturday PRESS. *See* Oakley graphic

Oakley REPUBLICAN. w 1887-88||?
KHi D 8 1887-S 1 1888

OBERLIN

ALLIANCE times. *See* Oberlin times

DECATUR county news. w 1883-1912||?
1883-D 22 1910 as Oberlin eye
KHi S 1883-D 5 1912
KObH [1892-93]

DECATUR dictator. w 1915?-
KHi [Ja 30 1919-My 11 1931]-Ja 22 1933

Oberlin EYE. *See* Decatur county news

Oberlin HERALD. w Je 12 1879+
pub 1879-[81]+
KHi 1879+

Oberlin OPINION. w 1886-96||?
KHi D 18 1886-96
KObH [1892-93]

Oberlin TIMES. w 1887-F 27 1930||
1887-Ja 6 1888 as Allison breeze; Ja 13-N 16 1888 Allison times; N 23 1888-S 15 1893. Alliance times. Merged with Oberlin herald
1887-N 16 1888 pub in Allison; N 23 1888-90 in Jennings
KHi S 1887-1930
KObH [1892-93]1920-30

Oberlin WORLD and democrat. w
KHi D 10 1885-Jl 1886

OFFERLE

Offerle NEWS. w F 10 1916-20||?
KHi 1916-Je 20 1919

OGDEN

Ogden COURIER. w
KHi My 14 1915-My 5 1916

OKETO

Oketa EAGLE. w Ja 2 1908+
KHi 1908-Mr 24 1910;S 17 1914+

Oketo HERALD. *See* Sun and herald

Oketo SUN. w 1887-91||?
United with Oketo herald to form Sun and herald

SUN and herald. w 1889-1903||?
1889-91? as Oketo herald
KHi N 30 1889-1903

OLATHE

Olathe ALLIANCE. *See* Republican tribune

ENTERPRISE. w
1903? pub in Edgerton
KHi N 27 1903-D 10 1904

Olathe GAZETTE. w 1879-82||
United with Mirror and news letter to form Mirror-gazette, later Olathe mirror
KHi Jl 24 1879-Ja 25 1883
KOlM D 9 1880-Jl 20 1882

Olathe weekly HERALD. w 1892-98||
United with Olathe news to form Olathe news-herald
KHi S 8 1893-98
KOlM 1892-S 1893

Olathe INDEPENDENT. w 1905-Ag 9 1916||
1905-F 2 1912 as Lenexa news (Lenexa)
KHi N 23 1906-16
KOlM 1912-13

JOHNSON county democrat. 1882-91 *See* Olathe leader 1882-93

JOHNSON county democrat. w N 25 1921+
pub 1921+
KHi 1921+

KANSAS central. w
KHi Mr 11,Ap 12-My 6,Je 17 1868

KANSAS patron. w 1878-1903||?
1878-Mr 3 1881 as Olathe leader; Mr 10-Ag 18 1881 Patron and farmer
KHi 1879-N 5 1903

Olathe LEADER. 1878-81 *See* Kansas patron

Olathe LEADER. w 1882-93||?
1882-Ag 20 1891 as Johnson county democrat
KHi My 18 1882-D 7 1893

Evening METEOR. w
KHi Ap 1879

Olathe MIRROR. w Mr 9 1861+
1875?-Ja? 1883 as Mirror and news letter; F ? 1883-Je 10 1886 Mirror-gazette; Je 17 1886-O 1894 Olathe republican-mirror
Suspended from S 6- 1862
pub My 16 1861-My 22 1862;Jl 11 1863-D 21 1865;D 9 1880-[82-83]Ja-Je 10 1886;Ja 18-O 4 1894;95;1900+
KHi Mr 15 1866-Ja 23 1868;76+
OClWHi Ja 24 1878

Olathe NEWS-HERALD. w 1892-1902||
1892-98 as Olathe news. Merged with Olathe mirror
KHi 1898-Je 19 1902

KANSAS (*Continued*)

OLATHE—*Continued*

Olathe **NEWS LETTER.** w 1870-74||?
United with Olathe mirror to form Mirror and news letter, later Olathe mirror
KHi O 30,N 13 1873;Ja 15,Jl 2,O 1 1874

PATRON and farmer. *See* Kansas patron

Olathe **REGISTER.** w N 11 1898-1928||?
KHi 1898-Ja 1910;My 11 1911-Jl 19 1928
KOlM 1913;18-19;26

Olathe **REPUBLICAN.** w 1884-Je 1886||?
United with Mirror-gazette to form Olathe republican mirror, later Olathe mirror
KHi My 8 1884-My 1885

REPUBLICAN tribune. w 1891-1907||
1891-94 as Olathe alliance; 1894-1905 Olathe tribune. Merged with Olathe register
KHi Jl 21 1893-Jl 12 1907

Olathe **REPUBLICAN-MIRROR.** *See* Olathe mirror

Olathe **TRIBUNE.** *See* Republican tribune

WESTERN progress. w 1870-80||
1870-74? as Spring Hill progress (Spring Hill) Merged with Olathe gazette
KHi Ja 28,F 11,Ap 1,N 4 1875;76-Ap 1 1880

OLCOTT

Olcott **PRESS.** w 1888-89||?
KHi Ja 11-N 1 1889

OLIVET

Olivet **ADVERTISER.** w 1910-11||?
KHi D 9 1910-Ag 4 1911

Olivet **OBSERVER.** w
KHi Mr-Ag 3 1932

OLPE

Olpe **OPTIMIST.** w Ag 23? 1906+
KHi N 22 1906+

OLSBURG

Olsburg **GAZETTE.** w 1897-1918||?
1897-F 17? 1899 as Olsburg optic
KHi N 1897-Ap 21 1898;F 24 1899-Ap 1918

Olsburg **GRAPHIC.** w 1896-97||?
KHi D 1896-97

Olsburg **MESSENGER.** w Ag 22 1918-19||?
KHi 1918-Ja 1919

Olsburg **NEWSLETTER.** w 1886-96||?
KHi F 17 1887-Mr 6 1896

Olsburg **OPTIC.** 1897-99 *See* Olsburg gazette

Olsburg **OPTIC.** w 1921-24||?
KHi N 8 1922-23

OMAHA

KEARNY county coyote. *See under* Hartland

OMIO

DEMOCRATIC mail. w
KHi My 17-S 1884

JEWELL county journal. w 1879-80||?
KHi My 29 1879-Ap 2 1880

WESTERN advocate. w
KHi F 14-S 7 1882

ONAGA

Onaga **COURIER.** w 1897-99||?
KHi Jl 1898-N 16 1899

Onaga **DEMOCRAT.** *See* Onaga herald

Onaga **HERALD.** w 1878+
1878-O 1 1885 as Onaga journal; O 8 1885-Mr 27 1890 Onaga democrat
KHi My 16 1878+

Onaga **JOURNAL.** *See* Onaga herald

Onaga **REGISTER.** w 1896-97||?
KHi Jl 16 1896-Ag 5 1897

Onaga **REPUBLICAN.** w 1900-10||?
KHi Je 1900-N 18 1910

ONEIDA

Oneida **CHIEFTAIN.** *See* Oneida dispatch

Oneida **DEMOCRAT.** *See* Oneida dispatch

Oneida **DISPATCH.** w 1883-84||?
1883-F 23 1884 as Oneida chieftain; Mr 8-Ap 17 1884 Oneida democrat
KHi Mr 31 1883-Jl 17 1884

Oneida **JOURNAL.** w 1879-82||?
KHi O 1879-My 6 1882

Oneida **MONITOR.** w 1885?-86||?
KHi Ap 17 1885-Ag 6 1886

Oneida **NEWS.** w
KHi F 24-Jl 1895

Oneida **WORLD.** w 1892||?
KHi Mr 25-D 24 1892

ORONOQUE

Oronoque **COURANT.** w
KHi Ja-Ag 8 1907

Oronoque **MAGIC.** w
KHi Je 12-N 12 1886

ORWELL

Orwell **TIMES.** w 1885-86||?
KHi Ja 14-D 23 1886

OSAGE CITY

Osage City **FREE** press. w 1871-F 23 1933||
1871-Ja 1? 1876 as Osage City shaft; Jl 1 1912-F 25 1913 Public opinion-free press. United with Osage county journal to form Osage City journal-free press
KHi [Mr 23-Ap 13,N 1872-Ap 13 1874]Jl 10 1875;Ja 8 1876-1933

Osage City **JOURNAL-FREE PRESS.** w 1927+
1927-F 23 1933 as Osage county journal
KHi 1930—

KANSAS people. d S 8 1887-90||?
KHi 1887-D 17 1890

KANSAS people. w 1887-91||?
KHi F 1887-F 1891

OSAGE county democrat. 1881-87||?
1881-Ap 30 1886 pub in Burlingame
KHi N 1881-Ja 1887

OSAGE county journal. *See* Osage City journal-free press

PUBLIC opinion. w 1892-1918||
Jl 1912-F 1913 Merged with Osage City free press
KHi O 26 1915-Ag 27 1918

Osage City **REPUBLICAN.** w 1882-83||?
KHi Je 9 1882-S 1883

Osage City **SHAFT.** *See* Osage City free press

OSAGE MISSION. *See* ST. PAUL

OSAWATOMIE

Osawatomie **ADVERTISER.** w 1888-90||?
KHi N 1888-Mr 1890

FARMERS' signal. w
KHi My 8 1890-Je 1891

Osawatomie **GASLIGHT.** w 1887-88||
Followed by Osawatomie graphic, later Osawatomie graphic-news
KHi Mr 25 1887-Mr 2 1888

Osawatomie **GLOBE.** w 1891-1912||
United with Osawatomie graphic to form Osawatomie graphic and globe, later Osawatomie graphic-news
KHi S 1891-N 15 1900;S 1905-My 1912

Osawatomie **GRAPHIC-NEWS.** w Mr 23 1888+
Follows Osawatomie gaslight. 1888-Ag 28 1930 as Osawatomie graphic (Je? 1912-15? Osawatomie graphic and globe)
pub 1894—
KHi 1888+
KOs 1925+

Osawatomie **JOURNAL.** w 1896-98||?
KHi My 15 1896-Jl 1898

Osawatomie **NEWS.** w My 28 1926-Ag 28 1930||
United with Osawatomie graphic to form Osawatomie graphic-news
KHi complete

Osawatomie **PROGRESS.** w 1902-03||?
KHi O 9 1902-D 3 1903

Osawatomie **SENTINEL.** w 1885-86||?
KHi My 23-N 21 1885;My 8-Je 1886

Osawatomie **TIMES.** w 1880-81||?
KHi Jl 22 1880-Jl 21 1881

Osawatomie **WORLD.** w Je 28 1923-24||?
KHi 1923-My 8 1924

OSAWKIE

Osawkie **CHIEF.** w
KHi D 21 1901-My 1902

Osawkie **TIMES.** w 1885-86||?
KHi D 1885-N 5 1886

OSBORNE

Osborne **JOURNAL.** w 1934+
KHi Mr 29 1934+

Osborne daily **NEWS.** d Je 10-Ag 31 1881||
KHi complete

Evening **NEWS.** d 1911-Ja 29 1915||
KHi F 25 1914-15
—w ed *See* Osborne county news

OSBORNE county farmer. w D 1874+
1874-N 1875? as Osborne weekly times
pub 1877—
KHi Ja 14 1876+
KOsb [1878]88-95;98-1910;15+

OSBORNE county journal. w 1886-89||
Merged with Osborne county farmer
KHi N 10 1886-F 1889

OSBORNE county news. w My 11 1883-Ap 8 1920||
Merged with Osborne county farmer
KHi My 18 1883-1920
KOsb 1890-1920
—d ed *See* Evening news

Osborne weekly **TIMES.** *See* Osborne county farmer

TRUTH teller. w 1879-81||?
KHi O 10 1879-F 23 1881

OSKALOOSA

Oskaloosa **INDEPENDENT.** w 1860+
pub Jl 11 1860-Jl 1892;Ag 1912+
KHi 1870-Ja,S 1876+

JEFFERSON county tribune. w 1899-1920||?
KHi Ap 21 1899-F 7 1920

KANSAS statesman. w 1868-72||?
KHi D 17,31 1869

Oskaloosa **TIMES.** w 1891-1916||?
KHi Ja 10 1891-N 1916

OSWEGO

AMERICAN crank. w
KHi N 19 1892-Mr 11 1893

Oswego **BEE.** d Mr 7 1887-88||?
KHi 1887-D 25 1888

Oswego **BEE.** w *See* Oswego courant

Oswego weekly **BLADE.** w Ja 27 1894-1909||
Ja-S 22 1894 as Union blade; S 29 1894-F 10 1897 Oswego news-blade. Merged with Oswego democrat
KHi 1894-F 4 1909

Oswego **COURANT.** w 1881-91||?
1881-86 as Oswego republican; 1887-My 18 1889 Oswego bee
KHi Ag 12 1881-F 7 1891
—d ed *See* Oswego bee; Oswego republican

Oswego **DEMOCRAT.** 1879-80 *See* Labette county democrat

Oswego **DEMOCRAT.** w O 21 1899+
pub 1899+
KHi 1899+

Oswego **INDEPENDENT.** w Je 15 1872+
pub Je 22 1872+
KHi Ja 22 1876+

Evening **JOURNAL.** d Mr? 1903-
KHi Mr 10-My 9 1903

KANSAS democrat. w
KHi My 26-N 17 1870

LABETTE county democrat. w 1879-96||?
1879-80? as Oswego democrat
KHi Ap 23 1880-96

LABETTE county statesman. *See* Labette county times-statesman

LABETTE county times. w 1891-92||
United with Labette county statesman to form Labette county times-statesman
KHi Je 18-Jl 9 1892

LABETTE county times-statesman. w Ag 6 1885-Ja 11 1900||
1885-Jl 1889 as Chetopa statesman (Chetopa) Ag 1889-Jl 1892 Labette county statesman
KHi complete

Oswego **NEWS.** d -S 22 1894||
United with Union-blade to form Oswego news-blade, later Oswego weekly blade

Oswego **NEWS-BLADE.** *See* Oswego weekly blade

PILOT. *See under* Altamont

Oswego **REGISTER.** 1868-76||?
KHi Jl 30 1869;D 6-12 1873;Jl 10 1874
KQwt 1868-Je 15 1872

Oswego **REPUBLICAN.** d Ag 9 1881-83||?
KHi 1881-Mr 6 1883

Oswego **REPUBLICAN.** w *See* Oswego courant

UNION blade. *See* Oswego weekly blade

OTIS

Otis **REPORTER.** w 1912-19||?
KHi My 31 1912-Jl 14 1916

Otis **REPORTER.** w 1921+
KHi My 20 1921+

OTTAWA

Ottawa **BEE.** d N 7 1887-
KHi 1887-88

Ottawa **BULLETIN.** w
KHi Ag 1869-Ag 1870

Ottawa **BULLETIN.** 1894 *See* Ottawa times

Ottawa **COURIER.** w 1892?-93||?
KHi Ag 26 1892-F 3 1893

Ottawa **EAGLE.** d
KHi O 5-N 5 1896

Ottawa **GAZETTE.** w
KHi Jl 12-D 20 1879

Ottawa **GUARDIAN.** w 1901-19||?
KHi F 23 1901-My 9 1919

Ottawa weekly **HERALD.** w 1881-1915||
1881-89 as Queen City herald
pub 1895[96]-1905;08-[15]
KHi Ag 19 1886-1915

Ottawa **HERALD.** d N 1896—
1896-1906 as Evening herald
pub 1896-1900;02-[05]+
KHi D 22 1896+

INDEPENDENT-JOURNAL. w D 7 1865-1906||?
1865-68 as Western home journal; 1869-Ag 23 1902 Ottawa journal (Ap 1877-97 Journal and triumph)
KHi 1865-68;D 30 1869-O 1871;O 1872-Mr,S 1873-Ag 13 1874;Ap 1877-Jl 1897;Mr 24 1898-N 1 1906
KOH [1865-68]Je 15 1871-74;77-[89;98-99]
OClWHi Jl 19 1883;Ja 15 1887
OkH [1894-95]

KANSAS (*Continued*)

OTTAWA—*Continued*

Ottawa evening JOURNAL. d
KHi O 28 1915-Ap 3 1916

Ottawa JOURNAL. w *See* Independent-journal

KANSAS home news. w 1879-80||?
KHi N 21 1879-O 22 1880

KANSAS lever. w 1887-95||?
1887-92? as Lever
KHi Ap 1887-F 6 1895

Ottawa LEADER. w 1880-83||?
Suspended F 1881-Ag 1882
KHi My 13 1880-My 12 1883

LEVER. *See* Kansas lever

LOCAL news. d 1885-88||?
KHi Ap 9,12 1886-S 4 1888

Ottawa MUSTARD seed. w
KHi My 1888-My 1889

QUEEN CITY herald. *See* Ottawa weekly herald

Ottawa RECORD. w
KHi O 9 1931-Ap 4 1933

Ottawa weekly REPUBLIC. w 1872-1906||
1872-D 15 1898 as Ottawa republican; D 22 1898-F 6 1902 Ottawa republican and weekly times
KHi O 15,30 1873;Ja 15 1874;75-S 1906
KOH [1873]-[77;79-81]-[86]-[1900]-[02-03]-06

Ottawa daily REPUBLIC. d S 29 1879-D 31 1914||
1879-F 8 1902 as Ottawa daily republican
KHi complete

Ottawa REPUBLICAN. *See* Ottawa republic

STATE press. w 1878-79||?
KHi O 26 1878-Mr 15 1879

Ottawa TIMES. w,tw 1893?-S 1899||?
O 20-D? 1893 as Ottawa times-leader; 1894? Ottawa bulletin; 1895? Tri-weekly times and bulletin. United with Ottawa republican to form Ottawa republican and weekly times, later Ottawa weekly republic
tw 1895?
KHi Ag-N 3 1893;94;F 21-N 7 1895;96-98

Ottawa TRIBUNE. w 1884?-93||?
KHi Ag 30 1889-Jl 21 1893

Ottawa TRIBUNE. d Jl 13 1889-92||?
KHi [1889-92]

Ottawa TRIUMPH. w 1869-Mr 1877||
United with Ottawa journal to form Journal and triumph, later Independent-journal
KHi D 17 1875-77

WESTERN home journal. *See* Independent-journal

Ottawa WORLD. w S 13 1917-25||?
KHi 1917-25

OVERBROOK

Overbrook CITIZEN. w Ja 14 1898+
KHi 1898+

Overbrook HERALD. w 1889-1901||
Merged with Overbrook citizen
KHi Ap 11 1889-1901

Overbrook REPORTER. w 1893-94||
Merged with Overbrook herald
KHi Ag 18 1893-D 14 1894

OVERLAND PARK

Overland Park HERALD. *See* North East Johnson county herald

NORTH EAST Johnson county herald. w Jl 17 1924+
1924-Ap 18 1929 as Overland Park herald
pub 1924+
KHi 1924+

OXFORD

Oxford BEE. w 1899-1901||?
KHi Je 8 1899-S 1 1900

Oxford INDEPENDENT. w 1876-79||?
KHi My 27 1876-O 10 1878

MOCKING bird. *See* Oxford register

Oxford PRESS. *See* Monitor-press (Wellington)

Oxford REFLEX. w 1879-80||?
KHi Ap-Ag 1880

Oxford REGISTER. w F 15 1884+
Ag 14 1888-Ag 12 1893 as Mocking bird
KHi 1884-O 7 1910;F 11 1932+

Oxford TIMES. *See* Monitor-press (Wellington)

Oxford WEEKLY. w 1880-81||?
KHi D 16 1880-Mr 11 1881

PAGE CITY

Page City MESSENGER. w 1886-90||?
KHi My 1889-Mr 1 1890

PALCO

Palco ENTERPRISE. *See* Palco news

Palco NEWS. w 1905+
1905-Mr 4 1915 as Palco enterprise
KHi Mr 16 1905+

PALERMO

Palermo LEADER. w
KHi N 19 1859

PALMER

Palmer GLOBE. w
KHi F 23-Ag 23 1884

Palmer INDEX. w D 1893-94||?
KHi Ja-Jl 1894

Palmer INDEX. 1903-24 *See* Linn-Palmer record (Linn)

Palmer PIONEER. w 1888-91||?
KHi 1888-O 1890

Linn-Palmer RECORD. *See under* Linn

PAOLA

Evening CALL. d Jl 30? 1896-
KHi Ag-S 2 1896

Paola DEMOCRAT. w 1871-72||?
KHi S 28 1871

KANSAS spirit. *See* Western spirit

MIAMI farmer. w 1882-1903||
Follows Miami talisman. 1882-84? as Paola times. Merged with Western spirit
KHi Mr 23 1882-1903

MIAMI republican. w 1866+
1866-71? as Miami county republican
pub 1866-80;82-99;1901+
CaOTA S 14 1867
InRE Mr 15 1873
KHi F 2 1867;Ap 18 1868;D 11 1869[71-76]+
KOs 1926+
KPa 1914+

MIAMI talisman. w 1881-82||
Followed by Paola times, later Miami farmer
KHi S 15 1881-Mr 9 1882

Paola RECORD. w 1904-05||?
KHi Ap 21 1904-05

REPUBLICAN citizen. w 1878-80||
Merged with Miami republican
KHi Ag 22 1878-Jl 23 1880

SOUTHERN Kansas herald. w
KHi Ap 7 1865

Paola TIMES. *See* Miami farmer

WESTERN spirit. w Je 7 1871+
Je- 1871 as Kansas spirit
pub 1871+
CoU 1899-S 1903
KHi D 26 1873;Ag 28 1874+
KOs 1926+
KPa 1914

PARADISE

Paradise FARMER. w Ap 5 1920+
KHi 1920+

PARKER

Parker MESSAGE. w Ja 2? 1896+
KHi Mr 1896+

Parker PILOT and graphic. w 1889-94||?
KHi Ap 12 1889-Ag 24 1894

Parker POINTER. *See* Kansas standard (Pleasanton)

PARKERVILLE

MORRIS county enterprise. w 1878-84||?
KHi 1878-S 9 1884

MORRIS county news. w 1898-1900||?
KHi F 11 1898-S 22 1900

Parkerville TIMES. w 1887-88||?
KHi O 8 1887-Jl 14 1888

Parkerville TRIBUNE. w 1896-98||?
KHi Ja 16 1896-F 4 1898

PARSONS

Parsons weekly BLADE. w 1892-D 27 1901||?
Negro
DLC Ja 26 1900
KHi S 4 1892-1901

BROADAXE. w
KHi D 28 1877;Ja 11 1878

Parsons CLARION. w 1888-91||?
KHi Jl 1888-Mr 13 1891

Parsons weekly ECLIPSE. w 1876-1922||?
KHi Ja 13 1876-F 20 1919
CoU 1904-My 1910

Parsons ECLIPSE. d 1878?-1921||?
KHi Jl 1881-Mr 24 1921

ELI. d O 20 1890-91||
1890-F 7? 1891 pub in El Dorado
KHi 1890-D 3 1891

Evening GLOBE. d 1898-99||?
KHi My 23 1898-O 21 1899

Parsons GLOBE. w 1899?-1900||?
KHi O 27 1899-Ag 1900

Evening HERALD. d F 11 1902-
KHi 1902-Ap 1904

Parsons INDEPENDENT. w 1894?-1908||?
KHi Mr 10 1894-Jl 24 1908

INFANT wonder. d D 24? 1878-
KHi D 26 1878-Ap 30 1880

Parsons JOURNAL. d O 1889-90||?
KHi N 6 1889-90

Parsons NEWS. d Ap 23? 1900-01||?
KHi Ap 25 1900-Mr 6 1901

OUR home visitor. w 1891-92||?
KHi My 1891-Ap 22 1892

Parsons OUTLOOK. d Ag 20 1877-
KHi 1877-Ja 31 1878

Parsons PALLADIUM. w 1883-1911||?
KHi F 24 1883-1911

Parsons REPUBLICAN. d My 10 1880-
KHi 1880-My 7 1881

Parsons REPUBLICAN. d 1916-28||?
KHi S 15 1916-My 1928

Evening STAR. d Ap 6 1881-
KHi Ap-O 19 1881

Parsons SUN. w 1871-D 25 1908||
KHi Mr-N 1876;My 1877-1908
MWA O 21 1876

Parsons SUN. d 1880+
KHi F 19 1884+

SURPRISE. w
KHi Je 13 1874-Ja 20 1875

WESTERN world. w 1888-93||?
1888-89? as Mills' weekly world
1888-91? pub in Cherryvale; 1892? in Altamont
KHi Ag 8 1888-Ag 1893

PARTRIDGE

Partridge BULLETIN. w Ag 18 1922-26||?
KHi 1922-Ja 22 1926

Partridge CRICKET. *See* Partridge press

Partridge PRESS. w 1886-87||?
1886?-Ap 28 1887 as Partridge cricket
KHi N 1886-O 20 1887

Partridge REPUBLICAN. w 1896-97||?
KHi Mr 1896-Je 1897

PAWNEE ROCK

Pawnee Rock ALLIANCE globe. w 1891-92||?
KHi S 11 1891-F 1892

Pawnee CHIEFTAIN. w 1898-99||?
KHi O 21 1898-Ag 1899

Pawnee Rock HERALD. w Jl 21 1904+
KHi 1904+

Pawnee Rock LEADER. w 1886-93||?
KHi Ap 30 1886-Ap 20 1893

PAWNEE VALLEY

Pawnee Valley DEMOCRAT. w
KHi D 31 1886-Mr 5 1887

PAXICO

Paxico COURIER. w 1888-89||?
KHi Ag 30 1888-Ag 1889

PEABODY

Peabody GAZETTE. d Ap 18-D 31 1887||?
KHi Ap-D 31 1887

Peabody GAZETTE-HERALD. w 1873+
1873-S 2 1915 as Peabody gazette
pub 1915+
KHi Ja 21 1876+
KPe 1873-1914

Peabody HERALD. w Je 8? 1911-S 2 1915||
United with Peabody gazette to form Peabody gazette-herald
KHi Je 29 1911-15
KPe 1911-14

PEACE

RICE county gazette. *See* Sterling gazette (Sterling)

PEARLETTE

Pearlette CALL. w
KHi Ap 15 1879-Mr 1880

PENALOSA

Penalosa NEWS. w 1887-88||?
KHi Ag 12 1887-Jl 20 1888

Penalosa NEWS. w 1910-14||?
KHi F 25 1910-Ag 20 1914

Penalosa TIMES. w 1914?-18||?
KHi Ag 12 1915-Jl 14 1918

Penalosa TIMES. w Ap 20 1923-25||?
KHi 1923-25

PENCE

Pence PHONOGRAPH. w 1887-89||?
KHi O 15 1887-89

PENOKEE

TIMES. w 1889-90||?
1889? pub in Gettysburg
KHi My 23 1889-Mr 1890

KANSAS (*Continued*)

PERRY

To 1875? as Perryville

JEFFERSON county journal. w 1897-98||?
KHi S 24 1897-Ap 9 1898

KAW VALLEY chief. w 1879-82||
Merged with North Topeka times (Topeka)
KHi O 10 1879-82

KAW VALLEY chief. w 1883-84||?
1883? as Perry monitor
KHi My 25 1883-Je 6 1884

Perry **MIRROR.** w Je 2 1898+
KHi 1898—

Perry **MONITOR.** *See* Kaw Valley chief 1883-84

Perry **NEWS.** w 1891?-92||?
KHi Mr 21 1891-D 17 1892

Perryville **TIMES.** *See* Kansas Valley times (Rossville)

Perry **WORLD.** w 1895-97||?
KHi Ag 1895-My 6 1897

PERRYVILLE. *See* PERRY

PERU

Peru **CALL.** w 1888-89||?
KHi F 10 1888-N 8 1889

CHAUTAUQUA county democrat. w 1900-02||?
KHi Jl 1900-Ja 10 1902

CHAUTAUQUA news. w 1875?-80||?
Suspended N 1879-O 1880
KHi Je 1876-N 13 1880

Peru **CITIZEN.** w 1909-11||?
KHi Je 1909-Ap 7 1911

DERRICK. *See under* Elgin

Peru **EAGLE.** w 1890-91||?
KHi F 1890-Ja 23 1891

FREEMAN'S lance. w
KHi F 20 1891-92

Peru **OIL gazette.** w 1904-06||?
KHi Ap 27 1904-F 16 1906

Peru **TIMES.** w 1886-87||?
KHi Jl 1886-My 5 1887

PETERSBURG. *See* KINSLEY

PHILLIPSBURG

Phillipsburg **DEMOCRAT.** w 1887-91||?
KHi Ag 11 1887-S 10 1891

Phillipsburg **DISPATCH.** 1886-N 5 1908||
United with Phillipsburg news to form Phillipsburg news-dispatch, later Phillipsburg news
KHi S 23 1886-1908

Phillipsburg **HERALD.** w F 13 1878-1905||
1878-Ag 31 1882 as Phillips county herald. Merged with Phillipsburg dispatch
KHi 1878-Ap 13 1905

LIVELY times. w
KHi My 9-16,Je 27-Jl 4 1874

Phillipsburg **NEWS.** w My 31 1899+
N 19 1908-Ap 13 1916 as Phillipsburg news-dispatch; Ja 12 1922-Je 2 1927 Phillipsburg news and Phillips county post
KHi 1899+

PHILLIPS county herald. *See* Phillipsburg herald

PHILLIPS county post. w D 4 1902-22||?
United with Phillipsburg news to form Phillipsburg news and Phillips county post, later Phillipsburg news
KHi 1902-Ja 5 1922

PHILLIPS county review. w 1921+
KHi D 27 1923+

Phillipsburg **TIMES.** w 1884-85||?
KHi Jl 1884-Ap 4 1885

PIEDMONT

JOURNAL. *See under* Severy

Piedmont **NEWS.** w
KHi 1907

Piedmont **NEWS.** w 1916-17||?
KHi F 10 1916-Ag 1917

PIERCEVILLE

Pierceville **COURIER.** w 1886-87||?
KHi My 14 1886-Ag 1887

PITTSBURG

Pittsburg **ADVANCE.** w
KHi N 18 1892-Ja 20 1893

Pittsburg **ADVERTISER.** w O 16 1930+
pub 1930+
KHi O 23 1930+
KP 1930-[32]+

Pittsburg **BOOSTER.** w 1915?+
KHi [S 26 1929+]

BRICK. w 1885-87||?
1885-86? pub in McCune
KHi Ap 10 1886-My 14 1887

CRAWFORD news. w 1902?-30||?
KHi Ja 14 1927-29

Pittsburg **DEMOCRAT.** w 1883?-86||
Merged with Pittsburg headlight
KHi S 21 1883-My 14 1886

Pittsburg **DEMOCRAT.** w 1888-89||?
KHi Jl 1888-Jl 12 1889

Pittsburg **DEMOCRAT.** 1913 *See* Pittsburg gunn powder

Pittsburg **GUNN powder.** w 1909?-14||?
1909-My 22 1913 as Girard times (Girard) My 29-N 13 1913 Pittsburg democrat
KHi S 16 1909-Ja 8 1914

Pittsburg **HEADLIGHT.** w 1885-1921||?
KHi 1893-Ap 14 1921

Pittsburg daily **HEADLIGHT.** d Jl 1 1887+
pub 1887+
KHi Jl 5 1887-S 8 1888;My 21 1891-Mr 1909; My 14 1928+
KP Ap 1913+
KPC 1914+

Pittsburg **HEROLD.** w 1890-91||?
In German
KHi Je 1890-Ag 13 1891

Pittsburg daily **JOURNAL.** d Mr 10 1902-
KHi Mr 10-My 3 1902

Pittsburgh **KANSAN.** w Jl 3 1889-1920||
KHi 1889-S 17 1920
KP [1889-Je 1916]

IL LAVORATORE italiano. w,tm,sm Mr 3 1911-30||?
w 1911-21?;tm 1922?-23?
In Italian
IU N 30 1917-22
KHi 1912-Ag 1927

Pittsburgh evening **LEADER.** d Ja 22? 1906-
KHi Ja 27-Ap 22 1906

Pittsburg **MESSENGER.** *See* Pittsburg tribune

MINERS' echo. w 1892-93||?
KHi S 23 1892-N 10 1893

PENNY post. d O 26 1892-
KHi O 26-N 17 1892

PEOPLE'S exponent. w 1880-81||?
KHi Je 16 1880-Mr 16 1881

Pittsburg **PLAINDEALER.** w
KHi Ag 1899-My 12 1900

Pittsburg **SMELTER.** w 1880-91||?
KHi Mr 26 1881-D 5 1891

Pittsburg **SMELTER.** d 1890||?
KHi Ja-D 21 1890

Pittsburg **SMELTER.** d 1895-96||?
KHi Jl 1895-Ja 11 1896

Pittsburg **SMELTER.** w 1895-1906 *See* Pittsburg tribune

Pittsburg **STAR.** *See* Girard world (Girard)

Pittsburg **SUN.** d 1915+
pub 1915+
KHi F 1917+

Pittsburg daily **TIMES.** d Ag 2? 1891-
KHi Ag 7-S 5 1891

Pittsburg **TRIBUNE.** w Mr 3 1893-1903||?
1893-Je 28 1895 as Pittsburg messenger; Jl 1895-Ja? 1906 Pittsburg smelter
KHi 1893-Ja 10,Mr 21 1896-97
WHi 1893-Je 1895

Pittsburg daily **TRIBUNE.** d 1895-1903||
KHi Je 14 1895-Mr 4,Ag 10 1898-1901
KP F 10-My 8 1897

Pittsburgh **VOLKSFREUND.** w 1901?-12||?
In German
KHi Ja 17 1901-Ap 12 1912

Pittsburg **VOLKS-ZEITUNG.** w
In German
KHi N 11 1892-Ja 6 1893

Pittsburg **WORLD.** *See* Girard world (Girard)

PLAINS

Plains **JOURNAL.** w 1905+
KHi D 21 1907-Jl 1919;Jl 1925-Ap 1927;31+

PLAINVILLE

Plainville **ECHO.** w 1884-86||?
KHi Ap 9 1884-Ja 21 1886

Plainville **GAZETTE.** w 1898-1913||
Merged with Plainville times
KHi Jl 1898-Je 1913

Plainville **NEWS.** *See* Western news (Stockton)

Plainville **PRESS.** w 1885||?
KHi F 28-D 23 1885

SOUTH SIDE gazette. w Ap 1 1920-
KHi Ap-N 11 1920

Plainville **TIMES.** w 1886-94||?
KHi Ja 28 1886-93

Plainville **TIMES.** w D 1 1904+
pub 1929+
KHi 1904-Mr 10 1927;S 19 1930+

PLEASANTON

Pleasanton **ADVERTISER.** w 1895-97||?
1895-Ja 1897? as Item
KHi Jl 26 1895-97

BORDER sentinel. w 1902||?
KHi Je 27-O 25 1902

Pleasanton **ENTERPRISE.** *See* Pleasanton observer-enterprise

Pleasanton **FREE press.** *See* Linn county weekly press

Pleasanton **HERALD.** w 1881+
KHi Ja 27 1882+

ITEM. *See* Pleasanton advertiser

KANSAS standard. w 1896-1901||
1896-F 5 1897 as Parker pointer (Parker) Merged with Pleasanton enterprise later Pleasanton observer-enterprise
KHi O 29 1896-N 8 1901

LINN county weekly press. w 1896-71||?
-O 1869 as Pleasanton free press
KHi O 1869-F 10 1871

Pleasanton **OBSERVER.** w 1871-Jl 27 1911||
United with Pleasanton enterprise to form Pleasanton observer-enterprise
KHi F 14 1874;F 12 1876-1911

Pleasanton **OBSERVER-ENTERPRISE.** w My 25 1899+
1899-Jl 26 1911 as Pleasanton enterprise
KHi 1899+

PLEVNA

TORCHLIGHT. w 1888-89||*
KHi Je 14 1888-Ag 15 1889

POMONA

Pomona **ENTERPRISE.** w 1884-1902||?
Suspended Ap 1886-S 1887
KHi Je 1884-1901

Pomona **REPUBLICAN.** w O 31 1889-90||?
KHi 1889-S 1890

Pomona **REPUBLICAN.** w D 23 1897-1928||?
KHi 1897-N 1 1928

PORTIS

Portis **INDEPENDENT.** w Je 18 1904+
KHi 1904-S 19 1918;Mr 17 1921+

Portis **PATRIOT.** *See* Portis whisperer

Portis **WHISPERER.** w 1881-90||
1881-Mr 29 1890 as Portis patriot. Merged with Downs times (Downs)
KHi D 8 1881-Jl 1890

POTTER

ATCHISON county recorder w 1900||?
KHi Je-O 26 1900

Potter **KANSAN.** w N 22 1900+
1900-D 17 1903 as Potter leaf; D 24? 1903-Mr 1908 Kansan and leaf
KHi 1900+

Potter **LEAF.** *See* Potter Kansan

Potter **PRESS.** w
KHi Mr 25 1898-S 1 1899

POTWIN

Potwin **ARGUS.** w 1906-07||?
KHi Ap 26 1906-S 20 1907

Potwin **LEDGER.** w Ja 20 1916+
KHi 1916+

Potwin **MESSENGER.** w 1888-89||?
KHi 1888-O 11 1889

POWHATTAN

Powhattan **BEE.** w 1901-24||?
KHi F 18 1910-My 23 1913

Powhattan **POST.** w 1894-95||?
KHi My 1894-Je 15 1895

Powhattan **POST.** w 1896-1901||?
KHi Jl 23 1897-Mr 22 1901

PRAIRIE CITY

FREEMEN'S champion. w
KHi Je 25 1857-S 16 1858

PRAIRIE VIEW

Prairie View **NEWS.** w 1903-12||
United with Logan republican to form Logan republican and Prairie View news, later Logan republican (Logan)
KHi Ja 15 1903-Je 13 1912

WIDEAWAKE. w My 31? 1917-20||?
KHi Je 28 1917-Ap 1 1920

PRATT

Pratt **INDEPENDENT.** w
KHi D 1913-Ag 19 1914

MIRROR. w 1912?-
KHi S 27 1912-My 29 1914;S 15 1922-My 5 1933

Pratt daily **NEWS.** d O 7? 1909-
KHi O 9-D 24 1909

PLAIN dealer. w
KHi Jl 14-U 9 1888

PRATT county citizen. w 1902-04||?
KHi O 21 1902-Ap 9 1904

PRATT county register. w 1886-90||
Merged with Pratt union
KHi O 1886-D 11 1890

KANSAS (*Continued*)

PRATT—*Continued*

PRATT county republican. *See* Pratt republican

PRATT county times. w 1881-94‖
Merged with Pratt republican
1881-Ap 11 1884 pub in Iuka
KHi O 8 1881-Ja,Ap 1886-94
KPrT 1893

PRATT county union. *See* Pratt union

Pratt REPUBLICAN. w,d 1878-1925‖?
1878-D 22 1887 as Pratt county press (Iuka) D 29? 1887-1905 Pratt county republican
d S 7 1919-D 31 1920
KHi Ag 29 1878-S 10 1925
KPrT 1889;95

Pratt daily TRIBUNE. w,d 1914+
1914-F 1917 as Pratt tribune (w)
pub Mr 1917+
KHi Ag 19 1915+

Pratt UNION. w My 29 1890+
1890-1901 as Pratt county union
KHi 1890+

PRESCOTT

Prescott EAGLE. w 1882-88‖?
KHi Ap 28 1883-Je 23 1888

Prescott ENTERPRISE. w 1888-89‖?
1888-Ja 1889 as Prescott republican
KHi Ag 1888-O 1889

Prescott REGISTER. w 1898-99‖?
KHi Ap 22 1898-Ag 18 1899

Prescott REPUBLICAN. *See* Prescott enterprise

Prescott SENTINEL. w 1899-1902‖?
KHi D 1900-Je 20 1902

Prescott SUNFLOWER. w 1893‖
KHi Mr-O 1893

PRESTON

Preston HERALD. w 1887-88‖?
KHi Ag 11 1887-Je 7 1888

Preston NEWS. w 1905+
1905-12? as Preston pilot
KHi 1905-08;S 14 1916+

Preston PILOT. *See* Preston news

Preston PLAINDEALER. w 1889-1901‖?
KHi Mr 9 1889-Ag 1901

PRETTY PRAIRIE

Pretty Prairie CHRONICLE. w 1899-1900‖?
KHi Jl 21 1899-Ja 1900

Pretty Prairie PRESS. See Turon press (Turon)

Pretty Prairie RECORD. w 1906-07‖?
KHi F 23 1906-07

Pretty Prairie TIMES. w 1910+
KHi Ja 26 1911+

PRINCETON

Princeton PROGRESS. w 1885-88‖?
KHi My 15 1885-Ag 3 1888

PROTECTION

Protection ECHO. *See* Echo-advocate (Coldwater)

KANSAS weekly ledger. w Ap? 1887-88‖?
Formed by the union of Western Kansan and Protection press?
KHi Ap 1887-Ja 3 1888

Protection LEADER. w 1888‖?
KHi Ap-N 1888

Protection POST. w 1907?+
KHi Ja 14 1909+

Protection PRESS. w My 8 1886?-Mr 1887‖?
My?-Jl 1886 as Western advocate?. United with Western Kansan to form Kansas weekly ledger?
KHi My 8 1886-Mr 1887

WESTERN advocate. *See* Protection press

WESTERN Kansan. w 1886-Mr 1887‖?
United with Protection press to form Kansas weekly ledger?
KHi N 11 1886-Mr 24 1887

QUENEMO

Quenemo LEADER. *See* People's herald (Lyndon)

Quenemo NEWS-REVIEW-ENTERPRISE. w O? 1902+
1902-S 18 1931 as Quenemo news
KHi D 1902+

OSAGE county republican. *See* Osage county sentinel

OSAGE county sentinel. w 1886-93‖?
1886-Mr 3 1892 as Osage county republican
KHi Jl 29 1886-Jl 6 1893

Quenemo REPUBLICAN. w 1892-1906‖
Merged with Quenemo news, later Quenemo news-review-enterprise
KHi Ap 1892-S 6 1906

Saturday TRIBUNE. w 1900-02‖
Merged with Quenemo republican
KHi S 15 1900-Ja 4 1902

QUINCY

Quincy QUILL. w Ja? 1916+
KHi S 13 1916+

QUINDARO

Papers published in Quindaro are listed under Kansas City

QUINTER

GOVE county advocate. w 1894+
1894-Jl 1 1905 as Short grass advocate (Gove) Jl 8 1905-Ja 25 1908 Grainfield advocate (Grainfield)
KHi D 31 1897-1901;Je 25 1904+

Quinter REPUBLICAN. *See* Gove county republican (Gove)

SETTLERS' guide. w 1886-89‖?
KHi Jl 15 1886-Ja 1889

RANDALL

Randall BEACON. w 1889-90‖?
KHi S 27 1889-D 18 1890

Randall ENTERPRISE. w Mr 24? 1921-26‖?
KHi Ap 21 1921-Ap 1926

Randall EXPONENT. w 1891-92‖?
KHi 1891-D 23 1892

Randall INDEPENDENT. w
KHi Ja 11-O 11 1895

Randall NEWS. w O? 1901-19‖?
KHi D 1901-O 17 1919

Randall REGISTER. w 1885-88‖?
KHi Ap 25 1885-N 10 1888

RURAL record. w 1924?-
KHi 1928-My 1932

RANDOLPH

Randolph ECHO. *See* Randolph enterprise

Randolph ENTERPRISE. w,sw 1882+
1882-Ap 6 1888 as Randolph echo (Ap-D 1885 Leonardville echo (Leonardville)
w 1882-1920?
pub 1890+
KHi N 22 1882+

Randolph LEADER. w 1889-90‖
Merged with Randolph enterprise
KHi O 10 1889-Ja 2 1890

SPIRIT of the Valley. w 1896‖
Merged with Randolph enterprise
KHi Mr 26-Ag 13 1896

RANSOM

Ransom JOURNAL. w 1903-04‖?
KHi Mr 20 1903-Ag 1904

Ransom RECORD. w Ja 11 1917+
KHi 1917+

RANTOUL

Rantoul CITIZEN. w 1896-98‖?
KHi N 21 1896-Jl 9 1898

RAVANNA

Ravanna CHIEFTAIN. w 1885-94‖?
KHi Ap 22 1886-N 8 1894

Ravanna ENQUIRER. w 1887-88‖?
KHi D 9 1887-S 5 1888

Ravanna LEADER. w Jl 16 1885-87‖
Jl-O 1885 as Cimarron herald; N 1885-Ap 2? 1886 Kansas Sod house
1885-Ap 2 1886 pub in Cimarron
KHi My 1886-S 9 1887

Ravanna RECORD. w 1885-89‖?
KHi Jl 15 1887-N 1 1889

RAYMOND

Raymond ADVANCE. w
WHi N 20 1885-Ap 1886

Raymond INDEPENDENT. w 1887-88‖?
KHi My 1887-My 11 1888

READING

Reading ADVANCE. *See* Reading ledger

Reading HERALD. w Je 26 1908+
KHi Je 26 1908;Mr 31,S 1913+

Reading LEDGER. w 1893-96‖?
1893-95? as Reading advance
KHi Mr 21-O 3 1896

Reading RECORD. *See* Reading recorder

Reading RECORDER. w 1898-1907‖?
1898-Ja? 1899 as Reading record
KHi F 25 1898-1907

REAMSVILLE

Reamsville DISPATCH. w 1884-86‖?
KHi F 14 1884-Ag 21 1885

PEOPLE'S friend. *See under* Athol

REDFIELD

Redfield EXPRESS. w 1894‖?
KHi Jl 12-N 1894

Redfield HERALD. w 1905-07‖?
KHi Ap 8 1905-F 1 1907

Redfield LEDGER. w My 29 1913-Ag 3 1916‖
KHi complete

REECE

Reece SUNFLOWER. w 1885-86‖?
KHi My 23 1885-O 2 1886

REEDER

COMANCHE chief. w
KHi Ja 23-Jl 10 1886

REID

GREELEY county republican. *See under* Tribune

REPUBLIC

Republic ADVERTISER. w Mr? 1883+
1883-F 21? 1935 as Republic news
pub F 28 1935+
KHi D 21 1883-Ja 17,F 28 1935+
KR Jl 13 1883-Ja 8 1897

Republic NEWS. *See* Republic advertiser

RESERVE

Reserve REPORTER. w
KHi D 19 1912-Je 19 1913

REXFORD

Rexford NEWS. w 1902+
KHi Ap 24 1903+

RICHFIELD

GREAT Southwest. w 1886-Ag 4 1887‖
United with Richfield leader to form Southwest leader, later Leader-democrat
KHi O 1886-87

LEADER-DEMOCRAT. w 1886-89‖?
1886-Ag 6 1887 as Richfield leader; Ag 13 1887-F 25 1888 Southwest leader
KHi Ja 9 1886-Ja 1889

Richfield MONITOR. *See* Elkhart tri-state news (Elkhart)

MORTON county pioneer. *See under* Rolla

MORTON county star. w 1887-O 27 1893‖
1887-D 5 1890 as Taloga star (Taloga) Merged with Monitor-republican, later Elkhart tri-state news (Elkhart)
KHi O 1887-D 5 1890;Ja 23 1891-93

Richfield NEWS. w
KHi Ag 10 1889-Ja 18 1890

Richfield REPUBLICAN. w 1886-Ap 19 1890‖
United with Morton county monitor to form Monitor-republican, later Elkhart tri-state news
KHi My 1887-90

SOUTHWEST leader. *See* Leader-democrat

RICHLAND

Richland ARGOSY. w 1893-95‖
Merged with Topeka mail, later Farmers mail and breeze (Topeka)
KHi My 11 1893-S 6 1895

Richland OBSERVER. w 1903-04‖
Merged with Mail and Breeze, later Farmers mail and breeze
KHi Jl 30 1903-04

RICHMOND

Richmond ENTERPRISE. w Ap 30? 1914+
KHi Je 25 1914+

Richmond RECORDER. w 1885-88‖?
KHi My 15 1885-Ag 3 1888

Richmond STAR. w 1901‖?
KHi F-D 1901

RILEY

Riley INDEPENDENT. w 1879-83‖?
KHi S 11 1879-F 15 1883

Riley REGENT. w Jl 5? 1889+
KHi Jl 26 1889+

Riley TIMES. w 1887-89‖?
KHi N 11 1887-S 20 1889

RIVERVIEW

Papers published in Riverview are listed under Kanses City

ROBINSON

Robinson INDEX. w 1893+
KHi Jl 28 1893+

Robinson REPORTER. w 1891-92‖?
KHi Ag 14 1891-Mr 18 1892

KANSAS (*Continued*)

ROCK

Rock REPORTER. w
KHi Ag 15 1912-O 17 1913

ROLLA

MORTON county farmer. w 1926+
KHi Ap 1926+

MORTON county pioneer. w Ja 1906-17||?
1906-12? as Pioneer
1906-Ag 10 1911 pub in Cosmos, Okla; Ag 25 1911-12? in Sid; 1912?-14 in Richfield
KHi S 1912-Ja 5 1917
OkHi [1906;08]-[12]

Rolla NEWS. w 1917-N 22 1918||
KHi 1918

Rolla PROGRESS. *See* Morton county progress (Elkhart)

ROSCOE

Roscoe TRIBUNE. w 1880-82||?
KHi Je 23 1880-Jl 1881

ROSEDALE

Papers published in Rosedale are listed under Kansas City

ROSSVILLE

Rossville CRITIC. w 1892-93||?
KHi Jl 1892-Ag 18 1893

KANSAS Valley times. w D 12 1870-82||?
1870- 1874 as Perryville times (Perryville, later Perry) 1874-Ja 25 1879 St. Marys democrat (St. Marys)
KHi F 12,Ap 1876-N 3 1882

Rossville NEWS. w 1883-84||?
KHi Jl 14 1883-O 3 1884

Rossville NEWS. 1899-1901 *See* Rossville reporter

Rossville REPORTER. w S 7 1888+
1888-N 9 1899 as Rossville times; D 1 1899-Jl 19 1901 Rossville news; Jl 26 1901-My 1905 Shawnee county news
Suspended from N 9-D 1 1899
KHi 1888+

SHAWNEE county news. *See* Rossville reporter

Rossville TIMES. *See* Rossville reporter

RUSH CENTER

To 1888? as Walnut City

Walnut City BLADE. w 1878-82||?
KHi Jl 19 1878-D 21 1880

Rush Center BREEZE. w My 23 1902-16||?
KHi 1902-N 21 1916

Walnut City DEMOCRAT. w 1886-88||
1886-87? as Rush county democrat. United with Russell review to form Russell democratic review (Russell)
KHi Ag 20 1886-My 10 1888

Rush Center GAZETTE. w 1886-90||?
1886-87? as Walnut City gazette
KHi F 10 1886-Je 20 1890

Walnut City HERALD. w
KHi My 18 1883-85

Walnut City NEWS. *See* Rush county news

RUSH county democrat. *See* Walnut City democrat

RUSH county news. d,w Je 20 1887-90||?
1887-My 1888? as Walnut City news (d)
KHi 1887-Mr 5 1890

WALNUT VALLEY standard. w 1874?-77||?
KHi D 24 1874;D 13 1876

WALNUT VALLEY standard. w 1893-1901||?
KHi Ja 13 1893-S 20 1901

RUSSELL

Russell ADVANCE. w
KHi Mr 8-O 5 1878

Russell BUGLER. w
KHi N 1922-Ap 1923

Russell DEMOCRATIC review. w 1886-88||
1886 as Saturday record; Ja-Je 25 1887 Saturday review; Je 29-Jl 27 1888? Russell review. Merged with Russell journal
KHi Ag 14 1886-Ap 1888

Russell HAWKEYE. w 1882-83||?
KHi Mr 23 1882-My 17 1883

Russell INDEPENDENT. w 1879-81||
Merged with Russell county record, later Russell record
KHi F 8 1879-Ag 11 1881

Russell INFORMER. w Ja 8 1897-1921||?
1897-S 14 1920 as Russell reformer
KHi 1897-N 3 1921

Russell JOURNAL. w 1884-98||
1884-85? as Western live stock journal; Ja?-D 29 1886 Russell stock journal. Merged with Russell record
KHi D 10 1884-Jl 1898

KANSAS plainsman. w 1872-76||?
1872-73? as Western Kansas plainsman
MWA F 26 1876

KANSAS record. *See* Russell record

Saturday RECORD. *See* Russell democratic review

Russell RECORD. w 1872+
1872-N? 1874 as New republic (Bunker Hill) N 19 1874-81? Russell county record; 1882? Kansas record
Suspended S?-O? 1875
KHi Jl 13 1876+

Russell RECORDER. w 1905-08||?
In German
KHi S 1905-My 1908

Russell REFORMER. *See* Russell informer

Saturday REVIEW. *See* Russell democratic review

RUSSELL county news. w D 18 1931+
KHi 1931+

RUSSELL county record. *See* Russell record

Russell STOCK journal. *See* Russell journal

WEST Kansas bote. w
In German
KHi Jl 21 1898-Ja 1899

WESTERN Kansas plainsman. *See* Kansas plainsman

WESTERN live stock journal. *See* Russell journal

RUSSELL SPRINGS

Russell Springs LEADER. w D 1? 1905-18||?
KHi D 29 1905-O 1918

LOGAN county banner. *See* Logan county clipper

LOGAN county clipper. w 1886-1900||?
1886-O 11 1894 as Logan county republican; O 18 1894-95? Logan county banner
KHi Mr 1888-95;Mr 19 1896-1900

LOGAN county leader. w 1887-89||?
KHi O 1887-F 1889

LOGAN county record. *See* Russell Springs record

LOGAN county republican. *See* Logan county clipper

Russell Springs RECORD. w 1887||?
Title varies: Logan county record
KHi Mr-S 22 1887

RYANSVILLE

Ryansville BOOMER. w
KHi D 18 1885-Je 1888

SABETHA

Sabetha ADVANCE. w 1874-78||?
KHi My 28-Jl,Ag 27 1874;Ap 22 1875;Ja 20 1876-D 15 1877

Sabetha COMMERCIAL. w
KHi N 30 1899-My 1900

Sabetha HERALD. w Ja 3 1884+
My 3 1893-95 as Republican-herald
pub 1900+
KHi 1884+

NEMAHA county republican. w 1876-Ap 26? 1893||
United with Sabetha herald to form Republican-herald, later Sabetha herald
KHi O 1876-93

REPUBLICAN-HERALD. *See* Sabetha herald

Sabetha STAR. w Ja 3 1896+
KHi 1896+

Sabetha STAR. d 1926-27||?
KHi Jl 1926-Jl 9 1927

SAINT FRANCIS

CHEYENNE county citizen. w 1907-10||?
KHi F 14 1909-Jl 7 1910

CHEYENNE county herald. *See under* Bird City

CHEYENNE county rustler. *See* Saint Francis herald

Saint Francis HERALD. w Jl 10 1885+
1885-1911 as Cheyenne county rustler (Ja-N 12 1911 Cheyenne county rustler-review)
1885-86 pub in Wano
pub 1885+
KHi 1885+

KANSAS eagle. w 1885-1911||
1885-Mr 28 1895 as Bird City news (Bird City) United with Cheyenne county rustler to form Saint Francis herald
KHi O 21 1886-1904

PEOPLE'S defender. w 1892-94||?
KHi Ap 1892-N 22 1894

PLAINDEALER. w 1886-89||?
1886-88? pub in Wano
KHi Ap 1887-Ap 1889

Saint Francis REVIEW. w 1889-Ja 1 1891||
United with Cheyenne county rustler to form Cheyenne county rustler-review, later Saint Francis herald
KHi D 19 1889-91

SAINT GEORGE

Saint George NEWS. w 1904+
1904-D 29 1912 as Louisville lyre (Louisville)
KHi Ag 19 1904+

SAINT JOHN

Saint John ADVANCE. w 1880-93||
Merged with Saint John weekly news
KHi Ap 10 1880-Ag 14 1885;Ap 16 1885-Je 1893

Daily CAPITAL. d 1935?+
KHi Ja 8 1935+

COUNTY capital. w Ja 21 1887+
KHi 1887+

Saint John weekly NEWS. w 1885+
1885-Jl 19 1888 as Saint John sun
KHi Ja 20 1885-Je,N 1894—

STAFFORD county republican. w Ap 24 1886-Je 7 1917||
KHi complete

STAFFORD county rustler. w 1889-90||?
KHi F 14 1889-My 22 1890

Saint John SUN. *See* Saint John weekly news

Saint John TELEGRAM. w 1886-
KHi My 1887-88

SAINT MARYS

Saint Marys DEMOCRAT. 1874-79 *See* Kansas Valley times (Rossville)

Saint Marys DEMOCRAT. w 1893-95||?
KHi Je 15 1893-F 21 1895

EAGLE-JOURNAL. w 1893?-1912||
1893-S 1908 as Saint Marys eagle
KHi Mr 14 1895-1911
KSS 1907-08

Saint Marys EXPRESS. w 1880-88||?
KHi My 21 1880-Ja 20 1888

Saint Marys GAZETTE. w 1888-91||?
KHi Mr 1888-Mr 12 1891

Saint Marys JOURNAL. w 1894-S 1908||
United with Saint Marys eagle to form Eagle-journal
KHi Je 1894-S 1908
KSS 1895-96;1907-08

POTTAWATOMIE chief. w 1878-79||?
KHi 1878-S 13 1879

Saint Marys STAR. w Mr 13 1884+
KHi 1884+
KS 1923-31
KSS 1898+

Saint Marys TIMES. w 1871-78||
KHi F 12,Ap 7 1876-Ja 1878
KSS Jl 24 1875

SAINT PAUL

To 1895 as Osage Mission

Saint Paul JOURNAL. w Ag 5 1868+
1868-94 as Osage Mission journal (1871-90 Neosho county journal) 1895-1900? Neosho county journal
KHi Ag 12 1871+

NEOSHO county democrat. *See* Erie sentinel (Erie)

NEOSHO county journal. *See* Saint Paul journal

NEOSHO VALLEY enterprise. w 1880-82||
Followed by Neosho county republican (Erie)
KHi O 1880-O 14 1882

Osage Mission TRANSCRIPT. w 1872-74||?
KHi My 1872-My 1 1874

SALEM

Salem ARGUS. w 1883-90||?
Jl 12 1888-Ja 17 1889 as Kansas labor clarion
Suspended Ja-Je 1889
KHi Mr 1883-Ag 22 1890

JEWELL county chronicle. w 1881-83||?
KHi Ap 13 1882-Ja 18 1883

KANSAS labor clarion. *See* Salem argus

PEOPLE'S friend. w 1885-87||?
KHi My 20 1885-O 13 1887

SALINA

Salina DEMOCRAT. w 1878-79||?
KHi O 31 1878-S 12 1879

Salina ENTERPRISE. w 1908-09||?
Negro
KHi N 14 1908-F 4 1909

FARMERS' advocate. *See* Farmers' news

FARMERS' news. w 1874-80||?
1874-D 12 1879 as Farmers' advocate
KHi Mr 24 1876-O 2 1880

Salina GAZETTE. d 1888?-89||
KHi Ja 9-Je 23 1889

Salina HERALD. w 1866-1909||?
KHi D 18 1869;Ja 1 1870;F 1876-Je 3 1909
MWA N 29 1879

Salina evening HERALD. d F? 1887-88||?
KHi Mr 7 1887-S 8 1888

Salina INDEPENDENT. *See* Salina republican

Salina JOURNAL. d Mr 31 1887-My 31 1888||
KHi complete

Salina evening JOURNAL. d N 18 1888+
1888-Ag 10? 1894 as Salina daily republican; Ag 11 1894-F 19 1903 Salina daily republican-journal
KHK Jl 1926-Mr 1933
KHi 1888+

KANSAS (*Continued*)

SALINA—*Continued*

Salina semi-weekly JOURNAL. *See* Western Kansas journal

KANSAS farm journal. *See* Western Kansas journal

KANSAS leader. *See* Saline county independent

Morning NEWS. d
KHi Jl 4-31 1878

Evening NEWS. d Ag 19 1889-D 28 1891||?
KHi 1889-91

Salina NEWS. w 1891||?
KHi My-D 25 1891

Evening RECORD. d Je 23 1897-
KHi Je-N 13 1897

Salina REPUBLICAN. w 1882-Mr 1893||
1882-Mr 1 1885 as Salina independent. United with Saline county journal to form Salina republican-journal, later Western Kansas journal
KHi O 21 1882-Mr 10 1893

Salina daily REPUBLICAN. *See* Salina evening journal

Salina REPUBLICAN-JOURNAL. See Western Kansas journal

RISING sun. *See* Salina sun

SALINE county independent. w 1919-27||?
1919-My 27 1926 as Kansas leader
KHi D 16 1920-Je 1927

SALINE county journal. *See* Western Kansas journal

Salina SUN. w O 14 1885+
1885-89 as Rising sun
KHi 1885+

SVENSKA härolden. w D 13 1878-84||?
In Swedish
IRA 1879-84
KHi 1878-81
MnHi [1878-Je 6 1883]

Salina TIDINGS. w 1890-93||?
KHi Ja 15 1890-Jl 19 1893

Salina UNION. w,sw 1890-1916||?
sw 1905?-13?
KHi S 26 1890-1915

Salina daily UNION. d Je 13 1898-1925||?
KHi 1898-O 12 1925

WESTERN Kansas journal. w,sw 1871-1918||
1871-Mr 10 1893 as Saline county journal; Mr 17 1893-O 3 1902 Salina republican-journal; O 10? 1902-16? Salina semi-weekly journal; 1917-Ja 1918? Kansas farm journal
w 1871-O 3 1902
pub complete
CoU 1898-F 1903
KHi Ap 1876-Ag 8 1918
—d ed *See* Salina evening journal

SANTA FE

Santa Fe CHAMPION. w 1887-88||?
KHi My 27 1887-88

HASKELL county republican. 1888 *See* Sublette monitor (Sublette)

HASKELL county republican. 1899-1913 *See* Haskell county clipper (Sublette)

HASKELL county review. w
KHi Jl 1887-F 1 1888

Santa Fe LEADER. w 1886-88||?
KHi Ap 26-D 1888

Sante Fe MONITOR. *See* Sublette monitor (Sublette)

Santa Fe TIMES. w 1885-D 1892||
1885-N 18 1892 as Ivanhoe times (Ivanhoe). Merged with Santa Fe monitor, later Sublette monitor (Sublette)
KHi D 12 1885-N 18 1892

Santa Fe TRAIL. w 1886-87||?
KHi Je 11 1886-87

Santa Fe TRAIL. w 1895-98||?
KHi Je 1895-Ja 6 1898

SARATOGA

PRATT county democrat. w 1885-86||?
KHi Jl 9 1885-N 1886

Saratoga SUN. w 1884-87||
Merged with Pratt county republican, later Pratt republican (Pratt)
KHi Mr 1885-D 21 1887

SATANTA

Satanta CHIEF. w 1917+
KHi My 13 1919+

SAUTRELLE FALLS. *See* VALLEY FALLS

SAVONBURG

Savonburg RECORD. w Ap? 1898+
KHi Je 17 1898+

SAWYER

Sawyer NEWS. w O 6 1905+
1905-N 6 1906 as Sawyer saw
KHi 1905-N 26 1920;D 25 1925+

Sawyer SAW. *See* Sawyer news

Sawyer SPARKS. w 1900-01||?
KHi D 27 1900-D 14 1901

SAXMAN

Saxman BULLETIN. w
KHi Ja 16 1911-12

SCAMMON

Scammon BOOMER. *See* Scammon echo-boomer

Scammon ECHO boomer. w Ag 10 1922-29||?
KHi 1922-O 11 1929

Scammon GLOBE. *See* Scammon miner 1892-1918

Scammon JOURNAL. w 1903-08||?
KHi [Ag 8 1903-S 18 1908]

Scammon MINER. w 1891-Je 25 1892||
United with Scammon globe to form Globe-miner, later Scammon miner
KHi Ja 29-Je 1892

Scammon MINER. w Ap 22 1892-1918||?
Ap-Je 24 1892 as Scammon globe; Jl 1892-Jl 13 1894 Globe-miner
KHi Jl 1892-Mr 1918

Scammon NEWS HERALD. w N? 1929+
KHi D 20 1929+

Scammon REGISTER. w 1891||?
KHi Ap 10-N 20 1891

SCANDIA

Scandia INDEPENDENT. w 1886-89||?
KHi D 17 1886-Ag 9 1889

Scandia JOURNAL. w F 7 1872+
1872-Ag 9 1876 as Belleville republic (Belleville) Ag 16 1876-N 21 1877 Scandia republic; N 28? 1877-82 Republic county journal
KHi F 7,28,Jl 10 1872;F 26,Ap 16,Je 4,D 10 1873;Ja 28 1874;Ap 19-D 1876;78+

Scandia REPUBLIC. *See* Scandia journal

REPUBLIC county chief. w 1884-86||?
KHi My 22 1885-N 19 1886

REPUBLIC county independent. w 1883-84||?
KHi S 13-D 13 1883

REPUBLIC county journal. *See* Scandia journal

SCHOHARIE

Schoharie GLOBE. w 1882-84||?
KHi Jl 1883-N 22 1884

SCOTT CITY

Scott City NEWS-CHRONICLE. w 1900+
1900-02 as Grigsby chronicle (Grigsby) 1903-09 Scott county chronicle
KHi Ap 20 1900-02;10+

Scott City REPUBLICAN. w 1892-96||?
KHi D 22 1892-My 21 1896

Scott City REPUBLICAN. w 1909-26||?
KHi F 16 1911-Jl 1 1926

SCOTT county chronicle. *See* Scott City news-chronicle

SCOTT county herald. w 1879?-88||
United with Scott sentinel to form Sentinel-herald, later Scott county news
KHi Ap 22 1886-D 15 1888

SCOTT county lever. *See* Scott county news 1886-1909

SCOTT county news. w D 31 1886-D 1 1892||
United with Scott county lever to form Scott county news-lever, later Scott county news
KHi complete

SCOTT county news. w 1886-1909||
1886-88 as Scott sentinel; 1889-F 12? 1891 Sentinel-herald] F 19? 1891-D 1 1892 Scott county lever; D 8? 1892-1903 Scott county news-lever. United with Scott county chronicle to form Scott City news-chronicle
KHi S 1886-1909

SCOTT county record. w D 31 1931+
KHi 1931+

SCOTT sentinel. *See* Scott county news 1886-1909

WESTERN times. See *under* Sharon Springs

SCOTTSVILLE

Scottsville ADVANCE. w 1904-18||?
KHi Je 30 1904-S 1918

Scottsville ADVANCE. w 1921?-23||?
KHi Je 1921-23

Scottsville INDEPENDENT. w 1886-89||?
KHi F 13 1886-Ja 5 1889

Scottsville NEWS. w
KHi Je-D 5 1929

Scottsville REGISTER. w 1899-1900||?
KHi Mr 9-N 9 1899

TRI-COUNTY news. w 1889-98||?
KHi Mr 15 1889-98

SCRANTON

Scranton GAZETTE. w My 2 1890+
KHi 1890+

KANSAS plebeian. w 1882||?
Early issues pub in Lyndon
KHi Jl 13-D 1882

SEDAN

Sedan ADVERTISER-JOURNAL. w My 23 1934+
My-Jl 11 1934 as Sedan advertiser
KHi 1934+

Sedan BORDER slogan. w
KHi Ag 10 1883-F 22 1884

CHAUTAUQUA county democrat. w 1884||?
KHi F 28-Jl 10 1884

CHAUTAUQUA county times. *See* Sedan times-star

CHAUTAUQUA journal. w 1875-D 26 1884||
United with Chautauqua county times to form Sedan times journal, later Sedan times-star
KHi Ap 21 1876-84

Sedan GRAPHIC. *See* Sedan republican

Sedan LANCE. w 1891?-1909||?
KHi Ag 24 1892-O 14 1909

Sedan REPUBLICAN. w 1884-92||?
1884-S 3 1890 as Sedan graphic
KHi D 24 1884-Ag 17 1892

Sedan TIMES-STAR. w My 1878+
My-D 6 1878 as Cedar Vale times (Cedar Vale) D 13 1878-D 26 1884 Chautauqua county times; Ja 2 1885-Ja 12 1894 Sedan times journal
My-D 6 1878 pub in Cedar Vale
KHi My 24 1878+

WIDE AWAKE. w 1874-75||?
KHi Jl 10 1875

SEDGWICK

Sedgwick JAYHAWKER. *See* Sedgwick pantagraph

Sedgwick PALLADIUM. *See* Sedgwick pantagraph

Sedgwick PANTAGRAPH. w Mr 20 1882+
1882-My 12 1883 as Sedgwick jayhawker; My 19 1883-Mr 7 1884 Sedgwick palladium
KHi 1882+

SELDEN

Selden INDEPENDENT. w 1901-12||?
KHi N 1901-Ag 1 1912

Selden INDEPENDENT. w F 12 1931+
KHi F 12 1931+

Selden OBSERVER. w Ap 24 1913-D 29 1932||
Merged with Selden independent
KHi complete

Selden TIMES. w My 5 1887-90||?
1887-Je 7 1888 as Sheridan times (Sheridan)
KHi 1887-D 11 1890

SELKIRK

Selkirk GRAPHIC. w 1889-91||?
KHi S 26 1889-Ap 1891

SELMA

Selma TELEPHONE. w 1895-96||?
KHi Ap 1895-Mr 1896

SENECA

Seneca CHRONICLE. *See* Nemaha county republican

Seneca COURIER-TRIBUNE. w,sw O 1 1863+
1863-71 as Nemaha courier; 1871-N 28 1884 Seneca weekly courier; D 5 1884-Jl 31 1919 Seneca courier-democrat
w 1863-N 1924
pub F 1871+
CL N 26 1880-N 18 1881
KHi O 21 1869;My 16,O 10 1873;Mr 13,My 29-Je 12 1874;Jl 9,D 3 1875+
NNHi N 14 1863-N 1864;65

INDEPENDENT press. w 1870||?
KHi Je 11 1870

NEMAHA county republican. w 1887-1903||?
1887-Je 8 1899 as Seneca news; Je 15 1889-Ap 5 1900 Seneca chronicle
KHi Ag 1890-F 20 1903

NEMAHA courier. *See* Seneca courier-tribune

NEMAHA Kansan. w 1899-D 29 1904||?
1899-D 15 1904 as Rural Kansan
KHi Je 1900-04

Seneca NEWS. *See* Nemaha county republican

RURAL Kansan. *See* Nemaha Kansan

Seneca TIMES. w N 20 1924+
KHi 1924+

Seneca TRIBUNE. w Ap 16? 1879-Jl 31 1919||
United with Seneca courier-democrat to form Seneca courier-tribune
IU Ja 22 1891
KHi My 28 1879-1919
KSeC 1885-1919

SEVERANCE

Severance ADVERTISER. w
KHi Ag 1883-My 2 1884

Severance ENTERPRISE. w 1883||?
KHi 1883

KANSAS (*Continued*)

SEVERY

To 1880? as Gould City

Severy ENTERPRISE. *See* Democratic messenger

Gould LEADER. w 1880||?
-Ap 2 1880 as Gould news
KHi F 27-My 14 1880

Severy LIBERAL. w 1884-86||?
KHi D 11 1884-Jl 1886

Gould NEWS. *See* Gould leader

JOURNAL. w 1910-11||?
1910? pub in Piedmont
KHi My 1? 1910-11

KANSAS clipper. *See* Severyite

PIONEER. w 1880-83||?
KHi 1881-My 1883

Severy RECORD. *See* Severy telegram

SEVERYITE w 1887+
1887-Ja 19 1889 as Kansas clipper
KHi D 31 1887-1920;S 9 1926+

SOUTHERN Kansas journal. w 1883-87||?
KHi D 29 1883-Ja 1887

Severy TELEGRAM. w 1887-92||?
1887-F 13 1891 as Severy record
KHi F 1887-Ag 1892

SEWARD

Seward INDEPENDENT. w 1887-90||?
KHi Ag 1? 1887-Jl 1890

SHARON

Sharon ADVOCATE. w 1903-04||?
KHi Ap 24 1903-My 4 1904

Sharon NEWS. w 1884-86||?
KHi O 22 1884-S 15 1886

SHARON VALLEY times. w 1911+
pub 1922+
KHi Ap 1? -D 2 1915;Je 1930+

Sharon SHIELD. w
KHi F 25-Ag 12 1910

SHARON SPRINGS

To 1885 as Eagle Tail Station

ALLIANCE echo. w 1890-S 25 1891||
Merged with Western times
KHi Jl 18 1890-91

COMMONWEALTH. w 1910-13||
Merged with Western times
KHi Jl 8 1910-Jl 6 1913

Sharon Springs LEADER. w 1887-91||
Merged with Western times
KHi 1887-S ? 1891

PEOPLE'S voice. w 1892-97||?
KHi My 1892-My 14 1897

ROSE of Sharon. w 1886||?
KHi Ap 28-S 9 1886

WALLACE county news. w My 1 1924-30||?
KHi 1924-My 14 1925

WESTERN times. w Ja? 1885+
Ja?-My 5? 1885 pub in Garden City; My 13? 1885-O 16 1886 in Scott City
pub 1903+
KHi Ja 30 1885+

SHAWNEE

Shawnee CHIEF. *See* Merriam leader (Merriam)

SHAWNEE BAPTIST MISSION

SIWINOWE kesibwi. (Shawnee sun)
In Shawnee
CSmH N 1841(photostat)
MBAt N 1841(photostat)

SHERIDAN

Sheridan TIMES. *See* Selden times (Selden)

SHERMAN CENTER

Sherman Center NEWS. w 1886-87||?
KHi Jl 22 1886-O 13 1887

SHERMAN county republican. *See* Goodland republic (Goodland)

SHOCKEYVILLE

Shockeyville EAGLE. w 1885-87||?
KHi Mr 16 1886-Ag 4 1887

Shockeyville INDEPENDENT. w 1887-88||?
KHi D 1887-Ja 18 1888

PLAINSMAN. *See under* Ulysses

SID

PIONEER. *See* Morton county pioneer (Rolla)

SIDNEY

Sidney ADVANCE. w 1879-83||?
1879-O 14 1880 as Ness county pioneer
1879? pub in Clarinda
KHi My 10 1879-O 14 1880;F 9 1882-Mr 10 1883
KNeH [O 21 1880-82]

NESS county pioneer. *See* Sidney advance

WESTERN Central Kansas cowboy. w
KHi S 1883-Je 14 1884

SILVER LAKE

Silver Lake MIRROR. *See* Shawnee county mirror (Topeka)

SIMPSON

Simpson NEWS. w Mr 28 1912+
KHi 1912+

Simpson RECORD. w 1905||?
KHi Ag-D 22 1905

Simpson SIFTINGS. w 1884-86||?
KHi O 11 1884-Je 17 1886

SMITH CENTER

BAZOO. *See* Smith county messenger

DEMOCRATIC messenger. *See* Smith county messenger

INDEPENDENT. *See under* Kirwin

KANSAS free press. w 1879-81||?
KHi O 1879-81

KANSAS pioneer. *See* Smith county pioneer

LIGHT of liberty. *See under* Lebanon

Smith Center PIONEER. d N 16 1887-89||
KHi 1887-Jl 20 1889
—w ed *See* Smith county pioneer

PIONEER-BULLETIN. *See* Smith county pioneer

SMITH county bulletin. w 1881-90||
1881-F 29 1884 as Smith county record. United with Kansas weekly pioneer to form Pioneer-bulletin, later Smith county pioneer
KHi F 1882-Jl 17 1890

SMITH county democrat. *See* Smith county messenger

SMITH county journal. w Ag 16 1890-1926||?
KHi 1890-Ap 1926
KSm My 29 1891-[1918;20-21]23-[26]
KSmC 1894-1902

SMITH county Kansas pioneer. *See* Smith county pioneer

SMITH county messenger. w 1885-1910||?
1885-89 as Bazoo; 1889-S 29 1899 Stewart's bazoo; O 6 1899-Ag 30 1900 Smith county democrat; S 6 1900-04? Democratic messenger
KHi F 1885-N 1910

SMITH county pioneer. w N 1872+
1878-84 as Smith county Kansas pioneer; 1885-89 Kansas pioneer; 1889-90 Kansas weekly pioneer; 1890-93 Pioneer-bulletin
1872-S 1874 pub at Cedarville
pub 1879+
KHi [1876]+
KSmC 1903+
—d ed *See* Smith Center pioneer

SMITH county record. *See* Smith county bulletin

SMITH county review. w Jl 16? 1908+
1908-S 1923? as Athol record; O 1923?-My 1930 Athol review; Je 5 1930-Je 21 1933 as Athol-Gaylord-Cedar review
1908-My 1930 pub in Athol
pub Ap 17 1924+
KHi N 12 1908-S 1923;Je 19 1930+

STEWART'S bazoo. *See* Smith county messenger

SOLDIER

Soldier CLIPPER. w Ja 15 1891+
KHi 1891+

Soldier TRIBUNE. *See* Independent tribune (Holton)

SOLOMON

Solomon SENTINEL. w 1879-99||
Merged with Solomon tribune
KHi Jl 30 1879-N 16 1899

Solomon TRIBUNE. w D 4 1896+
KHi 1896+

SOUTH HAVEN

NEW era. w F 20 1886+
KHi 1886+

South Haven NEWS. w 1885-86||?
KHi Je 22 1885-86

OKLAHOMA war chief. *See under* Caldwell

PATRICK HENRY. w 1890-92||?
KHi Ja 9 1890-Je 6 1891

South Haven RUSTLER. w 1889-92||?
1889-Mr 17 1890 as Hunnewell rustler (Hunnewell)
Suspended 1891?
KHi D 14 1889-Ag 2 1890;S 24-D 1892

South Haven VOICE. w
KHi Mr 16 1894-F 1895

SOUTH HUTCHINSON

Papers published in South Hutchinson are listed under Hutchinson

SPEARVILLE

Spearville BLADE. w 1885-92||?
Suspended 1891?
KHi Ja 31 1885-Jl 1890;Mr-My 20 1892

Spearville ENTERPRISE. w
KHi My 18-Ag 10 1878

FORD county democrat. *See under* Fonda

FORD county record. w 1885-86||?
KHi S 29 1885-F 16 1886

Spearville NEWS. w
KHi Ag 24 1878-F 21 1880

Spearville NEWS. w Ap 7 1899+
KHi 1899+

PRAIRIE home. w
KHi My 15-Je 14 1879

SPEED

CLARION. w 1908-09||?
KHi Jl 1908-Je 10 1909

Speed RECORD. w
KHi S 24 1915-Ja 1916

SPIVEY

Spivey DISPATCH. w 1887-88||?
KHi F 24 1887-O 18 1888

Spivey INDEX. w 1889-91||?
KHi 1889-N 5 1891

SPRING HILL

KANSAS register. w
KHi Ap 13-O 1878

NEW era. w N 15 1883+
KHi 1883-Ja 1885;Ag 1888+

Spring Hill PROGRESS. *See* Western progress (Olathe)

Spring Hill REVIEW. w 1881-82||?
KHi S 30 1881-O 20 1882

SPRING LAKE

HORNET. *See under* Artesian City

SPRINGFIELD

Springfield REPUBLICAN. w 1889-93||?
KHi Ja 26 1889-Ag 11 1893

SEWARD county courant. w 1887-88||?
KHi My 21 1887-My 4 1888

SOAP-BOX. w 1887-88||?
KHi My 1887-Ja 6 1888

Springfield TRANSCRIPT. w 1886-89||?
KHi S 9 1886-S 6 1889

WESTERN vidette. w
KHi Je 14-O 18 1890

SPRINGVALE

Springvale ADVOCATE. w 1888||?
KHi F 11-Jl 14 1888

STAFFORD

Stafford CITIZEN. w 1877-78||?
KHi N 30 1877-Je 1878

Stafford COURIER. w 1902+
KHi D 18 1902+

PEOPLE'S paper. w 1892-97||?
KHi Je 16 1892-97

PLAIN truth. w 1889||?
KHi Ap 10-S 1889

Stafford REPUBLICAN. *See* Stafford county republican

STAFFORD county democrat. *See* Stafford county herald

STAFFORD county herald. w 1879-90||?
N 1885-88 as Stafford county democrat
KHi Je 14 1879-Mr 14 1890

STAFFORD county leader. w 1898-1900||?
KHi F 24 1899-N 2 1900

STAFFORD county republican. w 1886-1917||?
1886-97? as Stafford republican
KHi Ap 24 1886-Je 7 1917

Stafford TELEGRAM. w 1887-88||?
KHi My-D 1887

STARK

Stark ENTERPRISE. w
KHi D 16 1898-S 1 1899

Stark FREEMAN. w 1891-92||?
KHi Je 1891-Mr 4 1892

Stark NEWS. w 1901-09||?
KHi S 28 1901-O 1909

PLAINDEALER. w
KHi Mr 20-Ag 14 1896

KANSAS (*Continued*)

STERLING

ARKANSAS VALLEY times. w 1888||?
KHi Ja-O 10 1888

Sterling BULLETIN. w My 17? 1877+
My-O 18 1877 as Weekly bulletin (Lyons) Jl 3 1891-D 30 1898 Bulletin and gazette; 1899? Sterling Kansas bulletin; 1908?-09? Kansas bulletin
KHi My 24 1877+

Sterling evening BULLETIN. d My 10 1887-88||?
KHi 1887-Jl 7 1888

Sterling CHAMPION. w 1888-94||?
KHi Jl 28 1888-Ag 17 1894

FARM journal. w 1901-12||?
1901-Mr? 1908 as Sterling journal
KHi Ap 27 1901-Ja 20 1912

Sterling GAZETTE. w Ja 20 1876-Je 27 1891||
1876-Ja 15 1880 as Rice county gazette. United with Sterling bulletin to form Bulletin and gazette, later Sterling bulletin
Ja-Ap 20 1876 pub in Peace
KHi 1876-91

Sterling JOURNAL. *See* Farm journal

Sterling KANSAS bulletin. *See* Sterling bulletin

Sterling NEWS. w 1889||?
KHi F 23-Je 1889

Sterling NEWS. w 1910-13||?
KHi O 26 1910-S 3 1913

Saturday REPUBLICAN. w 1886-88||?
1886-87? as Sterling republican
KHi Ag 1886-88

Sterling REPUBLICAN. d Mr 7 1887-
KHi Mr-Ag 25 1887

RICE county gazette. *See* Sterling gazette

STOCKTON

ALLIANCE signal. w 1891-98||?
KHi 1891-98

Stockton DEMOCRAT. *See* Rooks county democrat

Stockton EAGLE. w 1885-88||?
1885-N 5 1887 as Webster eagle (Webster)
KHi S 1885-Jl 13 1888
NcD My 11 1888

Stockton NEWS. *See* Western news

Stockton POST. w 1905||?
KHi Mr 23-O 1905

Stockton RECORD. *See* Rooks county record

Stockton REVIEW. w 1903-Ap 12 1923||
1903-Ja 31 1907 as Weekly echo; F 7 1907-F 25 1909 You all's doin's. United with Rooks county record to form Review and record, later Rooks county record
1903-09 pub in Woodston
KHi My 28 1903-23

REVIEW and record. *See* Rooks county record

ROOKS county democrat. w 1885-89||?
1885-S 24 1886 as Stockton democrat
KHi O 23 1885-[S 30 1886-Jl 2 1889]

ROOKS county record. w D 6 1879+
1879? as Stockton record; Ap 19 1923-30? Review and record
KHi 1879+

WESTERN news. w 1876-1909||?
1876-Mr 21 1883 as Stockton news (My 1881-Ap 1882 Plainville news (Plainville)
KHi Ap 20 1876-S 16 1909

STRAWN

Strawn STAR. w S? 1931+
KHi N 24 1931+

STRONG

To 1915? as Strong City

Strong City ADVANCE. w 1893-94||?
KHi S 1893-My 10 1894

CHASE county news. w My 28 1908+
1908-D 23 1909 as Strong City news; D 30 1909-My 30 1919 News-courant
pub Jl 1922+
KHi 1908-My 1918;21+

CHASE county republican. *See* Strong City herald

COTTONWOOD VALLEY news. w
KHi My 1916-Jl 19 1917

Strong City DEMOCRAT. *See* Strong City herald

Strong City DERRICK. *See* Strong City herald

Strong City HERALD. w 1881-1906||?
1881-87? as Strong City democrat; 1887?-Ap 21 1892 Chase county republican; Ap 28 1892-Ja 1905 Strong City derrick. Merged with Cottonwood Falls courant (Cottonwood Falls)
KHi O 15 1887-1906

Strong City INDEPENDENT. w 1881-88||?
KHi O 8 1881-Ja 13 1888

Strong City NEWS. *See* Chase county news

SUBLETTE

HASKELL county clipper. w 1899-1917||?
1899-1913 as Haskell county republican (Santa Fe)
KHi Ja 27 1899-D 27 1917

Sublette MONITOR. w 1886?+
1886?-My 1888 as Haskell county republican Je 1888-Jl 18 1918 Santa Fe monitor
1886?-Jl 18 1918 pub in Santa Fe
KHi F 8 1888+

SUMMERFIELD

Summerfield SUN. w F 14 1889+
KHi 1889+

SUMNER CITY

Sumner GAZETTE. w 1857?-
KHi S 12 1857-Ag 1859
MB O 17 1857
MWA My 1,Jl 24 1858
NNHi F 27,Jl 3 1858;O 29 1859

Sumner City GAZETTE. w 1871-72||?
KHi S 16,30,O 28,N 19 1871

SUN CITY

Sun City UNION. w 1884-89||?
KHi N 21 1884-Mr 1 1889

SURPRISE

Surprise POST. w
KHi Je 1886-Mr 1887

SYLVAN GROVE

Sylvan ALERT. *See* Sylvan Grove news

Sylvan Grove NEWS. w 1893+
1893-Ap 26 1900 as Sylvan alert
KHi Ap 25 1895+

Sylvan Grove SENTINEL. *See* Lincoln sentinel-republican (Lincoln)

SYLVIA

Sylvia BANNER. w 1889-95||?
KHi D 1889-My 24 1895

Sylvia CHRONICLE. w
KHi Jl 10-D 4 1896

Sylvia HERALD. w
KHi Ap-Ag 1889

Sylvia INDEPENDENT. w
KHi D 1897-My 7 1898

RENO county globe. w
KHi Je 30-D 15 1899

Sylvia SIFTINGS. w 1898-99||?
KHi Je 17 1898-F 3 1899

Sylvia SUN. w D 1 1901+
pub 1901+
KHi My 30 1902+

Sylvia TELEPHONE. w 1886-89||?
KHi My 25 1886-My 3 1889

SYRACUSE

ARKANSAS VALLEY sentinel. *See* Syracuse sentinel 1900-01

Syracuse DEMOCRAT. w 1885-87||?
KHi Ja 15-Ag 1887

DEMOCRATIC principle. w 1887-94||?
KHi O 12 1887-Je 7 1894

HAMILTON county republican. w Mr 16 1906-S 1907||
United with Syracuse news to form Hamilton county republican-news
KHi complete

HAMILTON county republican-news. w 1898-1921||?
1898-S 13 1907 as Syracuse news; S 20? 1907-15? Hamilton county republican and Syracuse news
KHi Mr 25 1898-My 20 1921

Syracuse JOURNAL. w Je 12? 1885+
KHi Jl 17 1885+

Syracuse NEWS. *See* Hamilton county republican-news

Syracuse REPUBLICAN. w 1893-1900||?
KHi S 29 1893-Ap 13 1900

Syracuse REPUBLICAN. w 1902-03||
Merged with Syracuse news, later Hamilton county republican-news
KHi Jl 31 1902-My 27 1903

Syracuse SENTINEL. w 1885-89||?
KHi D 24 1886-Mr 15 1889

Syracuse SENTINEL. w 1900?-01||?
1900? as Arkansas Valley sentinel
KHi Ap 20 1900-Mr 8 1901

Syracuse TIMES. w F 16 1921+
KHi [1922-Je 1 1934]

TALOGA

Taloga STAR. *See* Morton county star (Richfield)

TAMPA

Tampa STAR. w
KHi Ap 25-Ag 15 1912

Tampa TIMES. w 1915?-21||?
KHi D 1920-N 10 1921

TECUMSEH

KANSAS settler. w
KHi F 3,17-24,Mr 10-17,31-Ap 7 1858

NOTE book. w
KHi Ag 13-27,S 10-17,O 2 1857

TERRY

Terry ENTERPRISE. w
KHi Jl 9 1886-Ja 1887

Terry EYE. w 1887-89||?
KHi F 17 1887-N 14 1889

TESCOTT

Tescott HERALD. w 1887-91||?
KHi My 27 1887-91

Tescott NEWS. w O 2 1930+
KHi 1930+

Tescott PRESS. w Mr 31 1910-18||?
KHi Ap 14 1910-My 2 1918

Tescott TELEGRAM. w 1902||?
KHi Je 13-O 1902

THAYER

Thayer CRITERION. w
KHi Mr 6,Ap-My 12 1871

Thayer GRAPHIC. w 1894-95||?
KHi S 14 1894-O 4 1895

Thayer HEADLIGHT. w 1871-92||?
KHi Jl 26 1871-Jl 15 1892

Thayer HERALD. w 1885-86||?
KHi Ag 1885-Ag 7 1886

Thayer INDEPENDENT news. *See* Thayer news

Thayer LEADER. w 1900-01||?
KHi D 20 1900-D 5 1901

Thayer NEWS. w N 6 1891+
1891-1905 as Thayer independent news
KHi 1891+

TIBLOW. *See* BONNER SPRINGS

TIOGA. *See* CHANUTE

TIPTON

Tipton TIMES. w Ap 29 1915+
KHi 1915+

TONGANOXIE

Tonganoxie MIRROR. w My 4 1882+
KHi 1882+

Tonganoxie NEWS. w 1883?-87||?
KHi Mr 1885-Ja 1887

Tonganoxie REPUBLICAN. w 1889-1903||
1889-My 10? 1902 as Weekly sentinel
Suspended from N 1893-Je 1894
1889? pub in Leavenworth
KHi F 23 1889-S 11 1903

Weekly SENTINEL. *See* Tonganoxie republican

TOPEKA

ADVOCATE. *See* Farmers advocate

ALLIANCE tribune. *See* Topeka tribune 1889-92

Topeka AMERICAN. w 1896-98||?
1896-Ja 14 1897 as American bimetallist
KHi O 10 1896-My 13 1898

AMERICAN bimetallist. *See* Topeka American

AMERICAN citizen. w 1888-89||?
Negro
KHi F 23-D 1888

Daily Topeka ARGUS. d 1874-My 10 1876||
1874-Mr? 1876 as Topeka daily times
DLC My 9-10 1876
KHi F 26 1874-Mr 10,My 8,10 1876

Topeka BEE. w
KHi Mr 30-Ag 1890

BLADE. *See* State journal

Topeka BUDGET. w
KHi N 15 1884-Ja 5 1888

Topeka BUDGET. w 1890-94||?
O 24 1891-Jl 15? 1893 as Budget and news
KHi N 15 1890-F 17 1894

Topeka BULLETIN. d 1873-74||?
KHi F 2-7 1874

Topeka CALL. w 1891-98||?
Negro
KHi [Je 28 1891-O 1898]

Evening CALL. d
KHi My 17-Jl 8 1893

KANSAS (*Continued*)

TOPEKA—*Continued*

Topeka daily CAPITAL. d Ap 21 1879+
N 1 1883-Ap 1889 as Capital-commonwealth
Mr 13-17 1900 is Sheldon ed
pub Ap 21 1879-[80]+
CU O 1890;F 15,22 1891
CoHi Ja 29 1936
DLC S 9 1885;92-93;98-1904;19+
ICHi Ja 28,F 23 1890
IU Mr 13-17 1900
KBB 1887-[1905]-[08-10]-[17-18]+
KEmT 18—
KHK 1905-Ja,D 1920-Ap 1933
KHi 1879+
MB Ja 4-Mr 17 1900
MWA Mr 13-17 1900
MiU Mr 13-17 1900;D 1920-[24]
NN Ap 21 1879(photostat)
NcU Mr 13 1900
NjN Mr 13-17 1900
OCHi Ja 23-28 1896;Mr 13-17 1900
OCl Mr 13-17 1900
OClWHi Mr 13-17 1900
OOxM O 13 1882
OkHi [1895-95;1900]-03

Weekly CAPITAL. *See* Kansas weekly capital

Topeka CITIZEN. d Ap 11 1885-86||?
KHi 1885-[illegible] 1886

COLORED citizen. w 1878-80||?
Followed by Topeka tribune?
Negro
KHi Ap 19 1878-Ja 10 1880

COLORED citizen. w 1897-1900||?
Negro
KHi [Je 17 1897-N 16 1900]

COLORED patriot. w
Negro
KHi Ap 20-Je 22 1882

COMMERCIAL advertiser. w
KHi Mr 25-Ag 5 1877

Daily COMMONWEALTH. w My 1 1869-O 31 1888||
1869-72 as Kansas daily commonwealth. United with Topeka daily capital to form Topeka daily capital-commonwealth, later Topeka daily capital
CU S 20-22,25 1881;Jl 24-26,28,31-Ag 2,4-5 1885;Ja 30,Je 30 1886
DLC O 8,15,25,N 4,9,15-16,D 9,31 1871;Ja 3-5, 11,Mr 8,12-15,17,23,31,Ap 7,16,My 12,17,Je 4 1872;Ja-Je 1873;Ja-Je 1874;Jl 1875-76;Mr 13 1877-83;Jl-D 1884;Ja-Je 1886-187
ICHi Ap 21 1877;Ja 20,30 1886;My 25 1888
KHa Ja-Mr 1873
KHi complete
MWA Ja 1-3 1886
N Ja 12 1873
NbHi F 17 1877
OCHi Ja 30,Ag 17,24,S 4 1886
OOxM O 13 1882
WHi Jl 2-D 1872;Jl 22 1873-85;Ja 30,Jl 1886-88

Weekly COMMONWEALTH. w My 1 1869-N 1 1888||
1869-Je 1873 as Commonwealth. United with Weekly capital to form Weekly capital-commonwealth, later Kansas weekly capital
DLC My 6 1875-88
KHi [1869-70 72]Jl 1874-88
MWA D 5 1872;Mr 13 1873;Jl 20 1876

COOPERATOR and press. d 1895-97||?
1895?-96 as Topeka cooperator
KHi S 2 1895-96

COOPERATOR and press. w 1895?-96||?
KHi Mr 20-O 16 1896

COURIER. w,sw 1873?-80||?
1873?-79* as Der Atchison courier (Atchison)
sw 1875?
In German
KHi My 1870-S 2 1879
MWA Ag 24 1876

Topeka CRITIC. d Mr 5 1884-
KHi Mr-Je 23 1884

CURRENT comment. w
KHi S 15 1899-Je 22 1901

Topeka DEMOCRAT. w O 10 1881-
Ja 3-F 28* as State press
KHi 1881-F 1-10 1882

Topeka DEMOCRAT. d,ir 1892-1901||?
KHi F 20 1892-1901

DEMOCRAT news. *See* Kansas state news

DEMOCRATIC advocator. w 1935?+
KHi N 14 1935+

EQUITY. w
KHi Ap 15 1899-S 7 1901

FARMERS advocate. w Ag 10 1889-D 5 1908||
1889-91 as Advocate; 1892-Ja 10 1894 Advocate and Topeka tribune; 1897-Ap 12 1899 Advocate and news. Merged with Kansas farmer (not in this list)
1889? pub at Meriden
CoU Ap 1899-N 1901
CtY Mr 15 1893
DLC 1894-95
KHi complete

FARMERS mail and breeze. w O 20 1882-D 1919||
1882-Ap 2- 1885 as North Topeka mail; My 1 1885-S 6 1895 Topeka mail; S 13 1895-F 17 1899 Topeka mail and breeze; F 24 1899-Je 1906 Mail and breeze. Merged with Kansas farmer (not in this list)
CoHi S 12 1887
DLC 1882-O 1884;88-92
KHi complete
KTC S 1893;98-1919
WHi O 16 1885-O 20 1893

Evening HERALD. d 1882||?
KHi Jl 10-D 5 1882
OOxM O 12 1882

Topeka daily HERALD. d Jl 1 1901-07||?
KHi 1901-Jl 22 1907
NN S 10-18 1901

Topeka HERALD. d
KHi Ap 26-Je 23 1913

HERALD of Kansas. w 1880||?
Ja-F 6 1880 as Kansas herald
KHi Ja 30-Je 11 1880

Topeka INDEPENDENT. w
KHi My-N 18 1897

JEFFERSONIAN. *See* Jeffersonian gazette w (Lawrence)

Topeka daily JOURNAL. *See* Topeka state journal

KANSAS blackman. *See under* Coffeyville

KANSAS breeze. w 1894-95||
United with Topeka mail to form Topeka mail and breeze, later Farmers mail and breeze
KHi Ap 13 1894-S 6 1895

KANSAS weekly capital. w,sw 1879-Ag 30 1913||
1879-O 1888 as Weekly capital (F 9-N 15 1883 Weekly capital and farmer's journal) N 1888-Ap 1889 Weekly capital-commonwealth; My 1889-S 3 1891 Topeka weekly capital; Ap 21 1892-S 1894 Weekly capital and farm journal; O 1894-1907 Kansas semi-weekly capital. Followed by Capper's weekly (not in this list)
sw O 1894-1907
DLC N 8 1888-94;Ag 24 1897-98
ICHi Ap 6 1882
InRE O 11 1888
KHi S 14 1882;83-1913
KTC N 22 1883-[88]-[1908]-13
ME Mr 17 1889
WHi Ja 23 1896-Ja 21 1902[N 28 1912-My 1913]

KANSAS daily commonwealth. *See* Daily commonwealth

KANSAS democrat. w 1871?-82||?
KHi 1874-Ap 7 1882
WHi Ap 1876-N 23 1877

KANSAS democrat. d 1886-93 *See* Topeka press

KANSAS democrat. w 1888-93 *See* State press

KANSAS freeman. w S 19 1855-
DLC N 14 1855
KHi N 14 1855;Ja 9 1856
MWA S 26 1855;Ja 26 1856

Daily KANSAS freeman. d 1855||
KHi O 24-N 7 1855
MWA O 31 1855

KANSAS herald. *See* Herald of Kansas

KANSAS monitoren. *See* Folkets nya tidning (Omaha, Nebr.)

KANSAS news. *See* North Topeka news

KANSAS staats anzeiger. *See under* Atchison

KANSAS state journal. *See* Topeka state journal

KANSAS state ledger. w,ir 1892-1906||?
Negro
KHi Jl 22 1892-1906

KANSAS state news. w Ag 22 1922-30||?
1922-D 11 1924 as Democrat news
KHi 1922-Jl 16 1930

KANSAS state record. w O 8 1859-Ap 28 1875||
1859-Ag 1862 as State record. Merged with Commonwealth
DLC 1859-Ag 1862;Ap 12 1871-O 16 1872;Jl 1874-75
KHi O 15 1859-[63-67]-75
MWA O 13 1860;Ag 17,O 12-19 1861;Je 14 1865

KANSAS state record. d Mr 26 1861-
pub only during sessions of the legislature
KHi Mr 26-Je 1861;Ja 11-Mr 11 1862
MWA F 18 1865

KANSAS state record. d My? 1868-D 7 1871||
1868-Mr 8 1871 as Daily Kansas state record. Merged with Commonwealth
DLC My 20-N 1869;Ja 6,12-F 22 24-Mr 2,8, Ag-N 28 1871
KHi D 20 1868-D 5 1871

KANSAS telegraph. w 1881-1904||?
In German
KHi 1881-1904

KANSAS tribune. *See* Topeka tribune

KANSAS watchman. w 1903-05||?
Negro
KHi My 25-N 15 1905

Saturday evening LANCE. w 1883-96||
Merged with Topeka mail and breeze, later Farmers mail and breeze
CLM Je 27 1891
KHi Je 9 1883-Ja 11 1896

Topeka LANTERN. w 1887||?
KHi Ja 15-D 1887

Topeka LEADER. w D 9 1865-Mr 4 1869||
Merged with Weekly commonwealth
KHi complete

Topeka LEADER. w S- 1876||
Merged with Weekly commonwealth
KHi 1876

Topeka LEADER. d
KHi O-N 3 1888

LUCIFER the light-bearer. bw,w 1881-95||
1880-90? pub in Valley Falls
bw 1880-85?
CLM Mr 22 1889
KHi Ag 24 1883-D 17 1890

Topeka MAIL. *See* Farmers mail and breeze

NEW ERA. w 1892-95||?
1892-My 1893 as People
KHi Mr 25 1893-F 3 1895

Topeka NEWS. *See* North Topeka news

NORDEN. d 1913||?
In Swedish
IRA 1913

NORTH TOPEKA daily argus. *See* North Topeka daily times

NORTH TOPEKA courier. w 1887-89||?
KHi [D 16 1887-Ap 18]Jl-O 17 1888

North TOPEKA daily courier. d D 1887-88||?
KHi D 17 1887-Je 29 1888

NORTH TOPEKA mail. *See* Farmers mail and breeze

NORTH TOPEKA news. w 1885-99||?
Title varies: Kansas news; Topeka news. Merged with Advocate, later Farmers advocate
KHi O 24 1885;Mr 17 1888-92;N 18-D 2 1894; Ag 25-N 17 1897;Jl 9-S 8 1898

NORTH TOPEKA evening news. d Ja 4 1888-
KHi Ja-D 21 1888

NORTH TOPEKA news-letter. w
KHi D 1898-Mr 4 1899

NORTH TOPEKA news-letter. d Mr 17 1899-
KHi Mr-Je 23 1899

NORTH TOPEKA times. d 1871?-84||?
KHi S 1880-81

NORTH TOPEKA times. w 1871-85||
Merged with North Topeka mail, later Farmers mail and breeze
DLC Je 8 1876-F 13 1880
KHi Mr 17 1871-Mr 1873;F 1874-85
MWA D 19 1872;My 7 1875
OClWHi O 1,N 19 1874

NORTH TOPEKA daily times. d S 1 1880-81||?
S-N 6 1880 as North Topeka daily argus
KHi 1880-D 13 1881

NORTH TOPEKAN. w
KHi Ja 9 1922-N 2 1923

OBSERVER. *See under* Wichita

PEOPLE. *See* New era

PLAIN talk. w
KHi 1932-Ap 1935

PLAINDEALER. *See under* Kansas City

POPULIST. w 1892-93||?
KHi My 1892-O 13 1893

Topeka POST. d Jl 22 1880-
KHi Jl-S 21 1880

Topeka POST. w 1885-88||?
KHi Ja-S 14 1888

Topeka PRESS. d Ap 8 1886-D 31 1896||
1886-F 14 1893 as Kansas democrat. United with Cooperator to form Cooperator and press
KHi complete

Topeka REPUBLICAN. w D 28 1889-93||?
Jl?-D? 1892 as Republican topics
KHi 1889-O 1893

Topeka SENTINEL. d Jl 11 1892-
KHi 1892-F 18 1893

SHAWNEE county mirror. w 1911-20||?
1911-S 5 1918 as Silver Lake mirror (Silver Lake)
KHi 1918-Ap 22 1920

SHAWNEE county news. w 1928+
KHi My-N 7 1935

SHAWNEE independent. w 1895-96||?
KHi O 1894-Ja 18 1896

SPIRIT of Kansas. w 1871?-1919||?
KHi [S 27 1884-O 1892]

Topeka STATE journal. d Ag 1 1873+
1873-S 30 1879 as Topeka daily blade; O 1 1879-Ap 7 1884 Daily Kansas state journal; Ap 8 1884-O 30 1885 Topeka daily journal; N 1885-Jl 15 1887 Kansas state journal; Jl 16 1887-D 31 1899 Daily state journal
Suspended F-D 1874
Mr 22 1924 is scrapbook ed; Ag 18 1928 special historical ed
pub Jl 11 1878+
CoU 1904;07-My 1910
DLC [Je-O 1876]-My,S 18,N 6,17 1877;Mr 7 1878;92+
InRE N 23 1878
KEmT Jl 1889-1908;12+
KHi Ag 9 1873+
MWA Mr 22 1924;Ag 18 1928
NbHi F 16 1877
WHi O 1909+

Topeka STATE journal. w Ag 1 1873-O 5 1905||
1873-S 1879 as Topeka weekly blade; O 1879-Ag 3 1884 Weekly state journal; Ap 10 1884-Ap 25 1889 Kansas state journal; My 1889-S 8 1892 State journal
pub Mr 14 1878-S 1879;83-[89]-1904
ICHi Ja 19 1893
KHi Ap 1876-O 1885;N 1891-1905
TJT Ag 16 1900;D 10 1891

STATE press. w 1888-96||
1888-Mr 16 1893 as Kansas democrat. United with Cooperator to form Cooperator and press
KHi S 22 1892-F 13 1896

STATE press. d *See* Topeka democrat 1881-

STATE record. 1859-62 *See* Kansas state record w

KANSAS (*Continued*)

TOPEKA—*Continued*

STATE record. w,bw,ir 1899-1909‖
w 1899-1901?; bw 1902?
KHi Jl 20 1899-Ja 14 1909
WHi Jl 20 1899

Topeka daily **TIMES.** *See* Daily Topeka argus

TIMES-OBSERVER. w 1888?-92‖
Negro
KHi S 1891-S 10 1892

Topeka **TOPICS.** d O 5 1891-92‖?
United with Topeka republican to form Republican topics, later Topeka republican
KHi 1891-Jl 9 1892

Topeka **TRIBUNE.** d Mr 1853-
1853-My 1858? as Kansas daily tribune
Ja?-O? 1855 pub in Lawrence
CSmH Mr 14 1853
KHi Jl 14 1855;Mr 7-8,11,15 1856;Ja 12-Mr 1 1864;Jl 20 1866-Ag 16 1867

Topeka **TRIBUNE.** w 1855-
1855-My 1858? as Kansas tribune
Ja?-O? 1855 pub in Lawrence
CSmH N 28 1857;Ag 15 1863
DLC Ja 28,F 18,Ap 14-21,My 12,Je 23,Jl 9, 29,Ag 18-25,D 1,15-22 1856;Ja 14-Je 9 1860
KHi [Ja 24 1855-Je 1861;Jl 1866-67]
MBAt S 7 1864
MWA Ja 7,Ap 21,Je 6,D 22 1856;D 26 1857;Ja 2-23,F 20,Mr 6,27,Ap 10-17,My 1,29 1858;Ja 14 1860;S 6 1862
NbHi F 24 1859

Topeka **TRIBUNE.** w 1880-81‖?
Follows Colored citizen?
Negro
KHi Je 24 1880-O 6 1881

Topeka **TRIBUNE.** w 1889-92‖
1889-92 as Alliance tribune. United with Advocate to form Advocate and Topeka tribune, later Farmers advocate
KHi D 10 1889-Jl 21 1892

TRIBUNE-RECORDER. w 1883?-85‖?
1883? as Tribune; 1884?-My 2 1885 Western recorder
KHi Je 1883-O 21 1885

Topeka **VOLKSBLATT.** w
In German
KHi Jl 26 1898-My 10 1899

Topeka **VOLKSFREUND.** d O 14 1885-
In German
KHi 1885-N 29 1886

WEST SIDE broadcaster. w
KHi Ap 10 1931-Mr 18 1932

WESTERN recorder. *See* Tribune-recorder

X-RAYS-DEMOCRAT. w Ag 26? 1899-1917‖?
1899-1909? as Arkansas City X-rays
1899-Mr 22 1912 pub in Arkansas City
KHi Ag 26 1899-S 1 1917

TORONTO

Toronto **RECORD.** w 1908?-Je 3 1909‖
Follows Altoona mirror (Altoona) United with Toronto republican to form Republican record, later Toronto republican
KHi D 17 1908-09

Toronto **REGISTER.** w 1885-87‖?
KHi Je 12 1885;F 12,S 1886-Jl 8 1887

Toronto **REPUBLICAN.** w Ja 5 1883+
1883-Jl 27 1888 as Toronto topic; Je 10-N 18 1909 Republican record
KHi 1883+

Toronto **TOPIC.** *See* Toronto republican

TOWANDA

Towanda **ADVOCATE.** w Ap 3 1919-
KHi 1919-Ag 12 1920

Towanda **HERALD.** w 1885-93‖?
KHi Ap 9 1885-My,N 1886-Je 15 1893

Towanda **NEWS.** w Je 6? 1905-N 14 1918‖
KHi Ja 13 1905-18

Towanda **TIMES.** *See* Western Butler county times

WESTERN Butler county times. w 1921+
1921-28? as Towanda times
KHi Je 22-Ag 10 1922

TRIBUNE

GREELEY county enterprise. w 1887-89‖
Merged with Greeley county republican
KHi Jl 8 1887-Je 7 1889

GREELEY county journal. *See* Horace headlight (Horace)

GREELEY county news. w Jl 30 1930-31‖?
KHi 1930-31

GREELEY county republican. w 1886+
1886-N 9 1887 as Greeley county tribune (Horace) N 17 1887-N 8 1888 pub in Reid pub 1912+
KHi Ap 24 1886+
KTrC 1886+

Tribune **LEADER.** w 1894-96‖?
KHi O 25 1894-96

Tribune **TRAIL.** w O 12 1933-D 27 1934‖
KHi complete

TROY

Troy **BULLETIN.** w 1877-79‖?
KHi My 1877-Ja 18 1879

DONIPHAN county patriot. w
KHi Ap 11 1863

DONIPHAN county republican. w 1868-75‖?
KHi O 23,N 6 1869;Ja 1 1870;Ja 28 1871-Ag 10 1872;Ag 16,S 20 1873-Jl 2 1875

Troy weekly **INVESTIGATOR.** w Ja? 1864-
MiG Je 18 1864

Weekly **KANSAS chief.** w Je 4 1857+
Follows American republican (Germantown, Ohio) 1857-Jl 4 1872 as White Cloud Kansas chief (White Cloud)
CSmH S 25 1862
KHa Je 29 1871-Je 13 1878;Je 16 1881-My 1889;96
KHi 1857+
MB Je 11,Jl 9 1857
MWA Ap 4 1861;Ap 6 1916
MoS [S 30 1875-85]
WHi Ag 19 1858;Jl 28 1864

Troy **REPORTER.** w
KHi Ap 26 1866-Ap 11 1867

Troy **REPUBLICAN.** w 1910-11‖
Merged with Wathena times (Wathena)
KHi O 1910-Jl 1911

Troy **REPUBLICAN.** w 1923-O 1924‖?
United with Wathena times to form Wathena times and Troy republican, later Wathena times (Wathena)
KHi N 13 1923-O 1924

Troy **TIMES.** *See* Wathena times (Wathena)

TURON

Turon **HEADLIGHT.** w 1889-93‖?
KHi My 1889-S 8 1893

Turon **PRESS.** w 1894+
1894-Mr 28 1895 as Pretty Prairie press (Pretty Prairie)
KHi F 1894-Ap 1 1909;11+

Turon **REPUBLICAN.** w
KHi D 8 1893-Je 22 1894

Turon **RUSTLER.** w 1886-89‖?
KHi O 14 1886-Ja 1889

TYRO

Tyro **HERALD.** w 1906-09‖?
KHi [Ja 25 1907-My 1909]

Tyro **LIFE.** w 1905-06‖?
KHi Jl 13 1905-Ja 1906

Tyro **LIFE.** d Ag 20 1905-
KHi Ag-D 18 1905

Tyro **TELEGRAM.** w 1909-10‖?
KHi S 16 1909-S 1910

Tyro **TRUTH.** w 1915-18‖?
KHi S 29 1916-My 10 1918

UDALL

Udall **HERALD.** w 1914-21‖?
KHi Ag 14 1914-Mr 19 1915;N 3 1921

Udall **NEWS.** w 1900-10‖?
KHi D 15 1900-F 1910

Udall **RECORD.** w 1885-93‖?
Suspended Ja 10-Je 19 1891
KHi Mr 12 1886-Mr 2,D 1888-93

Udall **RECORD.** w 1926+
KHi O 1926-Ag 1930

Udall **REPORTER.** w 1894-95‖?
KHi D 13 1894-Jl 4 1895

Udall **SENTINEL.** w 1885-86‖?
KHi Je 12 1885-F 19 1886

Udall **TIMES.** w 1910-13‖?
KHi Ap 8 1910-Ap 1913

ULYSSES

GRANT county new era. w Jl 25 1929-33‖?
KHi 1930-Ja 6 1933

GRANT county register. w 1885-90‖?
KHi Jl 21 1885-F 22 1890

GRANT county republican. w Ap 30 1892+
KHi 1892+

PLAINSMAN. w 1888-90‖?
1888-Ag 10 1889 pub in Shockeyville
KHi 1889-O 18 1890

Ulysses **TRIBUNE.** w Ja 12 1887-93‖?
KHi Mr 19 1887-Ag 19 1893

UNIONTOWN

Uniontown **CICERONE.** w 1905+
KHi N 10 1911-12;Ag 16 1918+

Uniontown **HERALD.** w
KHi Jl-D 14 1883

Uniontown **NEWS.** w Ap 24 1903-F 1 1907‖
Merged with Weekly republican (Fort Scott)
KHi complete

Uniontown **SUN.** w
KHi D 13 1900-S 20 1901

Uniontown **TELEPHONE.** w 1885-87‖?
KHi O 24 1885-Ja 1887

UTICA

Utica **COURIER.** *See* Star-courier

Utica **ENTERPRISE.** w 1899-1923‖?
KHi Je 10 1899-Mr 12 1915

STAR-COURIER. w D 10 1924+
1924-Mr 12? 1915 as Utica courier
KHi 1924-D 1925;N 17 1927+

VALLEY CENTER

Valley Center **INDEX.** w 1896+
KHi Ja 15 1897-S 23 1910;O 20 1911+

Valley Center **NEWS.** w 1884-90‖?
KHi Ag 15 1885-90

VALLEY FALLS

1873? as Grasshopper Falls; 1874? Sautrelle Falls

EASTERN Kansan. w 1911-14‖?
KHi Ag 24 1911-Ja 16 1914

FAIR play. w 1888-90‖?
CLM Ja 25,My 24 1890
KHi My 19 1888-Ag 16 1890

FARMER'S vindicator. d
KHi O 2-N 6 1916

FARMER'S vindicator. w *See* Valley Falls vindicator

KANSAS Jeffersonian. w
KHi N 3 1866

LUCIFER the light-bearer. *See under* Topeka

NEW ERA. w 1865-1916‖?
1865-67? as Kansas new era (Lecompton)
1865-My 1867 pub in Lecompton; My 1867-71 in Medina
KHi Ag 28 1866-S 4 1867;S 25 1873-1916

Valley Falls **REGISTER.** w 1881-91‖?
KHi F 11 1881-S 1891

Valley Falls **REPORTER.** d Je? 1915-17‖?
KHi Jl 21 1915-Je 1917

Valley Falls **REPUBLICAN.** *See* Valley Falls vindicator

Valley Falls **VINDICATOR.** w 1889+
1889-S 16 1890 as Valley Falls republican; S 13 1890-1924? Farmer's vindicator
KHi S 1889+
—d ed *See* Farmer's vindicator

VERMILLION

Vermillion **MONITOR.** w 1896-99‖?
KHi N 20 1896-Jl 1899

Vermillion **OWL.** w 1891-96‖?
1891-Ap 24 1896 as Vermillion record
KHi My 28 1891-S 18 1896

Vermillion **RECORD.** *See* Vermillion owl

Vermillion **TIMES.** w 1900-01‖?
KHi Ap 13 1900-D 20 1901

Vermillion **TIMES.** w 1904+
KHi D 8 1904+

VETERAN. *See* JOHNSON

VICTORIA

Victoria **GLOBE.** w 1925-27‖?
KHi F 1925-Jl 14 1927

Victoria **REVIEW.** w
KHi N 26 1915-N 10 1916

VIOLA

Viola **NEWS.** w 1904‖?
KHi Ap-D 10 1904

Viola **SENTINEL.** w 1931-32‖?
KHi My 19 1931-Ja 6 1932

VIRGIL

GREENWOOD review. *See* Virgil review

Virgil **LEADER.** w 1894-1908‖?
KHi O 19 1894-1907

Virgil **REVIEW.** w 1887-92‖?
1887? as Greenwood review
KHi Jl 8 1887-Ag 12 1892

Virgil **VISITOR.** w O 1921?+
KHi N 12 1921+

VLIETS

Vliets **ECHO.** w 1899-1905‖?
KHi My 26 1899-N 10 1905

VOLTAIRE

Voltaire **ADVISER.** w 1885-86‖?
KHi D 1885-D 2 1886

SHERMAN county news. w 1886-88‖?
KHi O 1886-Ap 1888

VOORHEES

Voorhees **VINDICATOR.** w 1887-90‖?
KHi O 14 1887-90

WABAUNSEE

Wabaunsee **PATRIOT.** w
KHi S-O 19 1861

KANSAS (*Continued*)

WACONDA SPRINGS

CHIEF. w Je 1932?+
KHi Ja 16 1933-Jl 3 1934

WAKARUSA

KANSAS herald of freedom. *See under* Lawrence

Wakarusa STAR. w Jl 18 1918-20||?
KHi Jl 18 1918-Jl 3 1919

WAKEENEY

Wakeeney INDEPENDENT. *See* Wakeeney Tregonian

KANSAS leader. *See* Wakeeney leader

Wakeeney LEADER. w 1879-81||
1879-80? as Kansas leader
KHi Ag 18[illegible]-Ag 3 1881

Wakeeney NEWS. d My? 1912-13||?
KHi My 1[illegible] 1912-Ap 23 1913

Wakeeney DEMOCRAT. w 1893-95||?
KHi F 9 1[illegible]-F 2 1895

Wakeeney SUN. w
KHi N 18[illegible]-F 2 1893

TREGO county reporter. *See* Weekly Tregonian

TREGO county republican. 1887-89||
Merged with Western Kansas world
KHi My 12 1887-S 12 1889

TREGO county tribune. w N? 1885-90||?
IU D 31 1885
KHi D 10 1885-Ja 17 1890

TREGO pepto[illegible]eter. w 1923?-
KHi D 192[illegible]-Ap 23 1929

Wakeeney TREGONIAN. w D 21 1895-Je 16 1921||
1895-S 2 1909 as Wakeeney independent; S 9 1909-Ja 31 1919 Trego county reporter
KHi 1895-19[illegible];F 1919-21

WESTERN Kansas world. w Mr 8 1879+
1879-85 as Wa Keeney weekly world
pub 1881+
IU Jl 3 1886
KHi Mr 15 1879+

Wa Keeney weekly WORLD. *See* Western Kansas world

WAKEFIELD

Wakefield ADVERTISER. w 1886-99||?
KHi Mr 29 1886-F 10 1899

Wakefield NEWS. w Je 9 1904-D 30 1909||
Merged with Wakefield pointer, later Wakefield news
KHi Je 16 1904-09

Wakefield NEWS. w 1908+
1908-Je 1914 as Wakefield pointer
KHi Jl 1914—

Wakefield POINTER. *See* Wakefield news

Wakefield SEARCHLIGHT. w 1899-1901||?
KHi Ag 28 1899-D 19 1901

Wakefield WIDEAWAKE. w 1902||?
KHi Mr 12-S [illegible]1 1902

WALDO

Waldo ADVOCATE. w D 22 1910+
KHi 1910+

Waldo ENTERPRISE. w 1888-90||?
Suspended Jl 1889-Ap 1890
KHi Jl 21 1888-Ag 21 1890

NEW ERA. w [illegible] 2 1904-09||?
1904-My 4 1906 as Waldo shadows
KHi D 2 1904;My 1905-Ja 7 1909

Waldo SHADOWS. *See* New era

WALDRON

Waldron ARGUS. w 1906-13||?
KHi N 15 190[illegible]-F 6 1913

STATE line democrat. w 1911-16||?
KHi D 25 191[illegible]-D 22 1916

WALKER

Walker JOURNAL. w 1887-88||?
KHi O 1887-S [illegible]0 1888

WALLACE

Wallace HERALD. w 1888-89||?
KHi Mr 10 1888-F 23 1889

WALLACE county gazette. w
KHi Je 1890-F [illegible] 1891

WALLACE county index. w 1906||?
KHi Mr 9-Ag 3 1906

WALLACE county news. w 1886-87||?
KHi Je 12 1886-N 1887

WALLACE county register. w 1886-90||?
KHi 1886-Mr [illegible] 1890

WALNUT

Walnut ADVANCE. w Jl 12 1895-1912||
KHi 1895-Ja 5 1912

Walnut COMET. *See* Walnut journal

Walnut EAGLE. w Je 9 1894+
Suspended from O 5 1895-Mr 14 1896; from D 15 1914-N 26 1915
KHi 1894+

Walnut JOURNAL. w 1881-95||?
Ja 8-O 1892 as Walnut comet
KHi 1882-Ja 5,F 16 1894-Ja 1895

WALNUT CITY. *See* RUSH CENTER

WALTON

Walton INDEPENDENT. w 1886-88||?
KHi Ap 1886-Ja 5 1888

Walton REPORTER. w 1890-93||?
KHi My 23 1890-Ag 18 1893

Walton REPORTER. w 1913-16||?
KHi Jl 1913-F 17 1916

WAMEGO

Wamego BLADE. w 1873-77||?
KHi Je 25 1873;76-Mr 3 1877

Wamego DEMOCRAT. w
KHi N 12 1885-Ag 12 1886

KANSAS agriculturist. *See* Wamego reporter

KANSAS reporter. w Jl 1867-89||
1867-S 1870 as Pottawatomie gazette. Merged with Kansas agriculturist, later Wamego reporter
O? 1870-O 1881 pub in Louisville
Suspended from Jl 1887-Ag 1888
KHi Jl 17 1867-S 16,O 16 1870-N 8 1889

KANSAS VALLEY. w 1869-71||
KHi N 25 1869-N 15 1871

POTTAWATOMIE gazette. *See* Kansas reporter

Wamego REPORTER. w 1879+
1879-D 30 1910 as Kansas agriculturist
KHi F 22 1879+
OkHi [1883-95;99]

Wamego TIMES. w,sw 1889+
1889-D 30 1892 as Pottawatomie county times
1889-N 11 1892 pub in Louisville
sw 1929?-31?
pub N 1921+
KHi Ag 16 1889+
OkHi 1893-[95]

Wamego TIMES. d 1892||
KHi Je 7-Jl 2 1892

Wamego TRIBUNE. sm,w 1877-81||?
sm 1877?-D 31 1878
KHi S 1877-N 10 1881
OkHi [1877]-[80-81]

Daily WAMEGAN. d Ap 5 1887-89||
Merged with Kansas agriculturist, later Wamego reporter
KHi 1887-S 3 1889

Weekly WAMEGAN. w 1889||
Merged with Kansas agriculturist, later Wamego reporter
KHi Je 28-N 15 1889

WANO

CHEYENNE county rustler. *See* Saint Francis herald (Saint Francis)

PLAINDEALER. *See under* Saint Francis

WARWICK

ADVANCED leader. sm,w 1886?-88||?
1886?-Ag 1887 as Warwick leader
sm 1886?
KHi Je 17 1886-F 17 1888

Warwick LEADER. *See* Advanced leader

WASHINGTON

KANSAS magnet. *See* Washington republican

Washington KANSAS republican. w Ag 18 1870-Ja 11 1871||
United with Kansas magnet to form Republican and magnet, later Washington republican
KHi complete

KANSAS republican. d O 19-N 7 1870||
KHi complete

LITTLE blue. w 1867-70||?
1867-69? pub in Jenkins Mills, Neb.
KHi Ag 21 1869-Mr 16 1870

Washington PALLADIUM. w Ja 13 1893-F 26 1926||
Suspended from S 15 1893-N 27 1897
KHi complete

Washington POST. w 1883-Jl 13 1895||
United with Washington county register to form Post-register, later Washington county register
KHi My-D 14 1883;N 1885-95

Washington POST. d Ap 19- 1887||
KHi Ap-Ag 2 1887

POST-REGISTER. *See* Washington county register

Washington REGISTER. *See* Washington county register

Washington REPUBLIC. *See* Washington republican

Washington REPUBLICAN. w My 25 1869-F 24 1905||
1869-Ap 1870 as Western observer; My-D 1870? Kansas magnet; 1871 Republican and magnet 1872?-F 16 1894 Republican; F 23 1894-95 Washington republic. United with Washington county register to form Republican-register, later Washington county register
KHi 1869-D 2 1870;76-1905

Washington REPUBLICAN. w Ag 18 1870-Ja 1871||
United with Kansas magnet to form Republican and magnet, later Washington republican

REPUBLICAN-REGISTER. *See* Washington county register

Washington TIMES. d My 13 1887-
KHi 1887-F 15 1888

WASHINGTON county register. w 1880+
Jl 19 1895-D 4 1902 as Post-register; D 11 1902-F 23 1905 Washington register; 1905-26? Republican-register
KHi Ag 20 1881+

WASHINGTON county register. d Ag 3 1884-85||?
KHi 1884-Jl 11 1885

Washington WATCHMAN. w 1896-98||
Merged with Post-register, later Washington county register
KHi 1896-D 2 1898

WESTERN observer. *See* Washington republican

WATERVILLE

BLUE VALLEY clipper. w 1901-02||?
KHi O 24 1901-Ag 1902

BLUE VALLEY telegraph. *See* Waterville telegraph

Waterville TELEGRAPH. w 1870+
1877-80 as Blue Valley telegraph
KHi 1870-My 1873;F 1876+
OkHi [1873]-[75]-[77]

WATHENA

DONIPHAN county news. w Ja 3 1923-28||?
KHi F 14 1924-O 25 1928

Wathena GAZETTE. w 1887-92||?
KHi Jl 1889-S 11 1890

Wathena MIRROR. w 1878-79||?
KHi Mr-S 5 1878

Wathena REPORTER. w 1865-77||?
KHi Ap 18 1867-Ap 9 1868;S 18 1873-Ap 1877

Wathena REPUBLICAN. w Mr 30 1900-17||?
KHi 1900-Ja 12 1917

Wathena STAR. w 1896-1900||?
KHi My 14 1896-My 4 1900

Wathena TIMES. w 1886+
1886-N 15 1901 as Troy times (Troy) N 1924?-34? Wathena times and Troy republican
KHi S 1886+

WAVERLY

COFFEY county populist. w 1900||?
KHi Je 19-D 1900

Waverly GAZETTE. w 1887+
1887-88 as Gridley gazette (Gridley) My 28-D 31 1897 Post-gazette
KHi Mr 19 1887+

Waverly NEWS. w 1883-89||?
KHi Mr 29 1883-Mr 1884;Mr 1885-Ja 1889

Waverly POST. w 1896-My 21 1897||
United with Waverly gazette to form Post-gazette, later Waverly gazette
KHi Ap 1896-97

POST-GAZETTE. *See* Waverly gazette

Waverly RECORD. w 1898-99||?
KHi O 1898-Je 1899

Waverly SUN. *See* Jeffersonian (Burlington)

WAYNE

Wayne JOURNAL. w 1907?-10||?
KHi D 17 1909-Jl 22 1910

Wayne REGISTER. w 1885-87||?
KHi Je 1885-S 1887

WEBBER

Webber HERALD. w Mr 30?-Je 1 1894||?
Mr?-My 11 1894 as Webber times
KHi Mr 30-Je 1 1894

Webber TIMES. *See* Webber herald

WEBSTER

Webster EAGLE. *See* Stockton eagle (Stockton)

Webster ENTERPRISE. w 1888||?
KHi Mr 8-N 15 1888

MERCHANT'S journal. w
KHi N 21 1894-Ap 19 1895

KANSAS (*Continued*)

WEIR

Weir CITIZEN. w 1893-94||?
KHi S 19 1893-Ag 15 1894

Weir EAGLE. w 1887-89||?
KHi N 17 1887-My 1889

Weir JOURNAL. w 1888-1920||?
KHi My 31 1889-O 4 1895;F 25 1898-1920

Weir JOURNAL. d
KHi Mr 23-My 5 1895

LABOR tribune. *See* Weir tribune

Weir RECORD. w 1921-25||?
KHi D 16 1921-Jl 1925

Weir SPECTATOR. w 1928+
KHi O 14 1928+

Weir SUN. d F 18 1895-98||?
KHi F 18 1895-N 6 1897

Weir TELEGRAM. w 1905-07||?
KHi D 28 1905-Ja 3 1907

Weir TRIBUNE. w,sw 1883-1904||?
1883-Ja 6 1887 as Labor tribune
sw 1895?-99?
KHi Ag 14 1884-Jl 1 1904

Weir TRIBUNE. d O 1 1897-98||?
KHi 1897-S 12 1898

WELLINGTON

Wellington GAZETTE. d S 7 1889-
KHi 1889-My 3 1890

INDUSTRIAL age. w 1887-89||?
1887-88? pub at Caldwell
KHi Jl 29 1887-Ja 11 1889

Wellington JOURNAL. w
KHi Jl 30 1892-S 18 1893

Wellington JOURNAL. d D 14 1896-1917||?
1896-1900 as Evening journal
KHi 1896-N 7 1917
—w ed *See* People's voice

Daily MAIL. d N 2 1889-1909||
Merged with Wellington journal
KHi 1889-O 30 1909

Wellington MONITOR. w 1886-F? 1892||
United with Sumner county press to form Wellington monitor and Sumner county press, later Monitor-press
KHi Ja 15 1886-92

MONITOR-PRESS. w Je 22 1871+
1871-72 as Oxford times; 1872-My 1873 Oxford press; Je 1873-F 18 1892 Sumner county press; 1893? Wellington monitor and Sumner county press
1871-My 1873 pub in Oxford
KHi S 18 1873+
MH Je 22 1871
—d ed *See* Wellington daily press

Wellington NEWS. d S 2 1901+
KHi 1901-N 22 1902;Ag 1927+
—w ed *See* Sumner county news

PEOPLE'S voice. w Ag 29? 1890-1917||?
KHi S 12 1890-N 8 1917
—d ed *See* Wellington journal

POSTAL card. d Mr? 1886-87||?
KHi Ap 11 1886-Je 6 1887

POSTAL card. d Ja 1 1896-
KHi Ja-Je 17 1896

Wellington daily PRESS. d 1884?-87||
KHi F 20 1886-Je 4 1887
—w ed *See* Monitor-press

QUID NUNC. d Ja 14 1887-88||?
KHi 1887-Ag 5 1888

QUID NUNC. w 1887-88||?
KHi F 11 1887-S 1888

Wellington REPUBLICAN. w
KHi Mr 27-Ag 1886

Wellington STANDARD. d Je 7 1887-89||?
KHi 1887-Ag 24 1889
—w ed *See* Sumner county standard

SUMNER county democrat. *See* Wellingtonian

SUMNER county news. w 1901+
1906?-30? as Sumner county republican
KHi N 26 1902-Ja 21 1903;My 23 1934+
—d ed *See* Wellington news

SUMNER county press. *See* Monitor-press

SUMNER county republican. *See* Sumner county news

SUMNER county standard. w 1883-96||?
KHi S 27 1884-F 1896
—d ed *See* Wellington standard

SUMNER county star. w 1893-1909||
Merged with Monitor-press
KHi Mr 14 1895-O 1909

Wellington VIDETTE. sw
KHi My 9-D 4 1879

Wellington VOICE. d S 14- 1896||
KHi S-N 7 1896

WELLINGTONIAN. w Ag 11 1876-85||?
1876?-Ja? 1881 as Sumner county democrat
KHi Ap 25 1877-Ja 4,Mr 1881-O 1 1885
NN S 29 1876-Je 26 1878
OOxM O 12 1882

WELLINGTONIAN. d Mr? 1885-
KHi My-O 6 1885

WELLSFORD

DEMOCRAT and watchman. *See* Wellsford reformer

KIOWA county democrat. *See* Wellsford reformer

Wellsford RECORD. w
KHi Ja 8-Je 11 1914

Wellsford REFORMER. w Je 13? 1885-89||?
Je?-N 21 1885 as Wellsford register; N 28 1885-Ag 14 1886 Democrat and watchman; Ag 20 1886-F? 1887 Wellsford republican; Mr? 1887-D 22 1888 Kiowa county democrat
KHi Je 13 1885-Ag 9 1889

Wellsford REGISTER. 1885 *See* Wellsford reformer

Wellsford REGISTER. w 1890||?
KHi Ja-O 1890

Wellsford REPUBLICAN. *See* Wellsford reformer

WELLSVILLE

Wellsville EXCHANGE. w 1887-89||?
KHi Ap 28 1887-My 17 1889

Wellsville GLOBE. w S 11 1890+
KHi 1890+

Wellsville NEWS. w 1882-86||?
1882-Mr 13? 1884 as Wellsville transcript
KHi O 26 1882-S 3 1886

Wellsville TRANSCRIPT. *See* Wellsville news

WENDELL

Wendell CHAMPION. w 1885-D 31 1886||
Merged with Banner-graphic (Kinsley) later Kinsley graphic
KHi O 9 1885-86

WESKAN

WESKANSAN. w 1888-99||
Merged with Western times (Sharon Springs)
KHi D 1888-99

WEST PLAINS

West Plains DEMOCRAT. *See* West Plains mascotte

West Plains GUARDIAN. *See* West Plains mascotte

West Plains MASCOTTE. w 1886?-89||?
1886?-My 19 1887 as West Plains guardian; My 26-S 8? 1887 West Plains news; S 15? 1887-O 1888 West Plains democrat
KHi F 25 1886-89

West Plains NEWS. *See* West Plains mascotte

WEST WICHITA

Papers published in West Wichita are listed under Wichita

WESTMORELAND

ALLIANCE news. *See* Westmoreland signal

Westmoreland INDICATOR. w 1887-91||?
KHi O 9 1889-Je 17 1891

INKSLINGER'S advertiser. w
KHi Ja-My 11 1878

Westmoreland NEWS. *See* Westmoreland signal

Westmoreland PERIOD. w O 1 1882-Jl 1885||
Merged with Westmoreland recorder
KHi 1882-Jl 15 1885
KWeR complete

Westmoreland RECORDER. w My 7 1885+
Ap 1918-21? as Recorder-signal
pub 1885+
KHi 1885+
OkHi [1893]-[95]

Westmoreland SIGNAL. w 1890-Mr 1918||
1890-95 as Alliance news; - 1895 Westmoreland news. United with Westmoreland recorder to form Westmoreland recorder-signal, later Westmoreland recorder
KHi N 21 1890-Mr 7 1918
KWeR 1906-18

WESTOLA

Westola WAVE. w 1888-89||?
KHi My 25 1888-My 24 1889

WESTPHALIA

Westphalia DEMOCRAT. *See* Garnett eagle (Garnett)

Westphalia INDEPENDENT. *See* Garnett eagle (Garnett)

Westphalia TIMES. w O 22 1885+
KHi 1885+

WETMORE

Wetmore ENTERPRISE and Nemaha county spectator. *See* Wetmore spectator

NEMAHA county spectator. *See* Wetmore spectator

RURAL enterprise. w 1899-Mr 1904||?
United with Nemaha county spectator to form Wetmore enterprise and Nemaha county spectator, later Wetmore spectator?
KHi My 11 1899-Ag 2 1900

Wetmore SPECTATOR. w D 2 1882+
My 20 1887-Ap 1 1904 as Nemaha county spectator; Ap 8 1904-06 Wetmore enterprise and Nemaha county spectator
KHi 1882-Ag 1884;Ag 29-S 1885;S 1886+

WHEATON

Wheaton COURIER. w
O?-D 16 1897 as Louisville courier (Louisville)
KHi O 14 1897-Je 1898

Wheaton EXPONENT. w 1903-04||?
KHi O 1903-04

WHITE CITY

MORRIS county news. *See* White City register

White City NEWS. *See* White City register

White City REGISTER. w 1885+
1885-Ja 30 1886 as White City whig; F 6-D 11 1886 Morris county news; D 18 1886-My 31 1889 White City news
KHi S 19 1885+

White City WHIG. *See* White City register

WHITE CLOUD

White Cloud GLOBE. w Mr 25 1892-Jl 28 1921||
United with White Cloud tribune to form White Cloud globe-tribune
KHi 1892-Jl 14 1921
OkHi [1893-95]

White Cloud GLOBE-TRIBUNE. w 1919+
1919-Jl 1921 as White Cloud tribune
KHi N 20 1930+

White Cloud KANSAS chief. *See* Weekly Kansas chief (Troy)

White Cloud NEWS. w
KHi Je 15 1891-Mr 15 1892

White Cloud REVIEW. w 1880-87||?
KHi O 30 1880-S 22 1887

White Cloud REVIEW. w 1888-89||?
KHi O 12 1888-89

White Cloud TRIBUNE. *See* White Cloud globe-tribune

WHITE ROCK

White Rock INDEPENDENT. *See* Burr Oak herald (Burr Oak)

WHITEWATER

Whitewater HERALD. w Je 20 1889-96||?
1889-My 4 1893 as Whitewater ttribune
KHi 1889-O 1 1896

Whitewater INDEPENDENT. w O 8 1896+
KHi 1896+

Whitewater TRIBUNE. *See* Whitewater herald

WHITING

Whiting JOURNAL. *See* Whiting visitor

Whiting NEWS. w 1883-93||?
KHi Mr 16 1883-Mr 18 1893

Whiting SUN. w 1894-D 31 1897||?
KHi Ag 17 1894-97

Whiting TELEPHONE. w
KHi My 24-Jl 5 1878

Whiting VISITOR. w 1897+
1897-Jl 4 1925 as Whiting journal; Jl 11?-1925? Journal-visitor
KHi F 18 1898+

WICHITA

AMERICAN. w
KHi D 27 1912-My 16 1913

Wichita ARROW. w 1885-93||?
KHi Jl 1885-S 16 1893

Wichita weekly BEACON. w 1872-S 27 1907||
pub N 29 1876-Ja 1 1898;99;1903-04
ICM D 20 1882
KHi F 11,Jl 29 1874-1907
KWi D 1878-N 17 1886
WHi F 1876-Ap 18 1877

Wichita BEACON. d S 1 1884+
1888-Ag 31 1890 as Evening news-beacon
pub 1884-[87-89]-[93]-[95-96]+
IC My 1 1889
IU N 23 1911-Ag 14,O 3 1912-Jl 1916
KHi 1884+
KWi 1884[85]-Mr 1887;N 13-D 25 1911;26+
KWiE Jl-S 1922;N 1926+
OkHi [1903]

Wichita BLAZE. *See* Wichita democrat 1886+

Wichita BOOSTER. w S 8 1921+
pub Je 1923+
KHi Ap 24 1925+

Saturday evening CALL. w
KHi D 19 1885-Ap 24 1886

Wichita CALL. d F 12? 1887-
KHi F 24-S 2 1887

CITIZEN. *See* Wichita independent 1886-89

KANSAS (*Continued*)

WICHITA—*Continued*

COLORED citizen. w 1902-04||?
KHi F 21 1903-F 6 1904

Wichita COMMERCIAL. w 1887-89||?
KHi D 24 1887-F 1889

COMMERCIAL bulletin. w
KHi S 29 1888-Mr 2 1889

Wichita COMMERCIAL review. w,m 1889-1931||?
1889-Ja 1931 as Wichita price current
Suspended F 1890-My 1891
w 1889-Ja 1931
KHi Ag 15 1889-D 18 1897;Je 11 1898-F 1931

Wichita DEMOCRAT. w D? 1886+
1886-Ag 1888 as Sunday growler; S 1888-O 8 1898 Wichita mirror; O 12-D 31 1898 Wichita blaze
pub 1914+
KHi D 1886+

Wichita DEMOCRAT. w 1890||
Merged with Wichita weekly beacon
KHi Ja 23-S 1890

Wichita EAGLE. w Ap 12 1872-1919||
Title varies slightly
pub 1872-[87]-[96-97]-Ap 1899;Je 25 1907-[17]
ICM Mr 14 1878
IHi Jl 2 1911
KHi 1872-Ap,D 1873-My 1919
KWiF Ap 1877-Mr 1880;Mr 1899-1905

Wichita EAGLE. d My 20 1884+
Title varies: Wichita daily eagle
My 29 1932 is 60th anniversary number
pub 1884-[88]-[1900-01]+
CL My 29 1932
DLC Jl-D 1898;F 1934+
KHi Jl 15 1884+
KWiB Ap 1915+
KWiF 1884-S 1917;18-S 1920;Ja-Mr 1922;Jl-D 1924;26-Ag 1927;My-Je,S 1929-Je,S 1932+
OkHi [1893]-[96]-[1902]-[07;31]+
WHi 1917-19

Wichita evening EAGLE. d Mr 28 1927+
pub 1927+
KHi Mr 31 1928+
KWiF Mr 1929-Je,S 1932+

Wichita GLOBE. d
KHi 1887

Wichita GLOBE. w *See* Kansas globe

Sunday GROWLER. *See* Wichita democrat 1886+

Wichita HERALD. w
KHi D 22 1877-O 18 1879

Der HEROLD. w 1885-1922||?
In German
KHi My 1885-Jl 4 1913;S 11 1914-My 16 1919

Wichita INDEPENDENT. w Je? 1886-89||?
Je?-S 9 1886 as Citizen; S 12 1886-Mr 12 1887 Labor union; Mr 19 1887-N 10 1888 Union labor press
KHi Je 24 1886-Je 1 1889

Wichita INDEPENDENT. w 1928||?
KHi Ap 26 1932-33

Evening JOURNAL. d 1886?-N 15 1890||
Merged with Wichita beacon
KHi F 16 1887-90

Wichita JOURNAL. w 1888-90||?
KHi My 23 1888-Jl 1890

KANSAS commoner. w 1887-1913||?
KHi 1891-Mr 15 1913
WHi N 17 1904

KANSAS globe. w F? 1887-88||?
F?-O? 1887 as Wichita globe
Negro
KHi F 17-O,N 21 1887-N 1 1888
—d ed *See* Wichita globe

KANSAS grit. w
KHi Ag 24 1895-Jl 1896

KANSAS staats anzeiger. *See under* Atchison

KANSAS star. *See* Wichita star w

KANSAS state register. w 1897-1906||?
1897-Ja 1900 as Wichita register
KHi My 15 1897-N 21 1906

LABOR union. *See* Wichita independent 1886-89

Wichita LEADER. d S 27? 1881-82||?
KHi S 29 1881-My 23 1882

Wichita LEADER. w 1882?-83||?
KHi F 16 1882-83

Wichita MIRROR. *See* Wichita democrat 1886+

NATION. w 1886-87||?
KHi S 1886-My 6 1887

NATIONAL leader. w 1902||?
KHi Ja 31-Ag 2 1902

NATIONAL monitor. w 1879-80||?
KHi My 1879-N 10 1880

NATIONAL reflector. w 1895-97||?
Negro
KHi D 8 1895-97

NATIONAL reflector. w
KHi Jl 13 1912-Ap 5 1913

NEGRO star. w 1908?+
Negro
KHi My 1920+

NEW republic. w 1883-90||?
KHi F 24 1883-D 3 1887

Wichita evening NEWS. d 1885-88||
United with Wichita beacon to form Evening news-beacon, later Wichita beacon
KHi N 26 1885-F 24 1886

Evening NEWS-BEACON. *See* Wichita beacon d

NORTH END news. w 1920-31||?
KHi O 1924-Ap 10 1925

NORTH star. w O 18 1929+
KHi O 25 1929+

NORTH WICHITA times. w 1929?-
KHi Ap 1930-Mr 1932

Wichita OBSERVER. w S 19 1901-
1901-Ag? 1902 pub in Guthrie, Oklahoma; Ag 29-N 7 1902 in Topeka
KHi D 13 1902-N 7 1903
OkHi 1901-02

OKLAHOMA war chief. *See under* Caldwell

Wichita OPINION. *See* McPherson opinion (McPherson)

PEOPLE'S elevator. *See under* Independence

PEOPLE'S friend. w
KHi My 24-S 1894

PLAINDEALER. w 1919+
pub [1919-27];Ja 20 1928+
KHi O 15 1920+

Wichita PRICE current. *See* Wichita commercial review

Wichita PROTEST. w 1918-30||?
Negro
KHi Je 1919-O 19 1923

PUBLICITY. w N 20 1930+
pub 1930+
KHi 1930+

Daily RECORD. d 1882+
pub Je 14 1921[22-26]+
KHi D 1893-92

Wichita REGISTER. *See* Kansas state register

Wichita REPUBLICAN. *See* Wichita times

Evening RESIDENT. d Ap 12-D 27 1886||?
KHi Ap-D 27 1886

ROUND and round. w
KHi Je 1930-33

SEARCHLIGHT. w 1899-1913||?
Negro
KHi Je 1900-11

SEDGWICK county news. w 1922?-
KHi S 22 1927-F 7 1929

SOUTH SIDE independent w 1922+
1922-32? as South side standard
KHi 1931+

Wichita STAR. w 1887-1903||?
1887-1900? as Kansas star
OkHi [1894-95]

Wichita STAR. d Je 15 1897-98||?
KHi 1897-Je 11 1898

STERN des westens. w
In German
KHi F 21-Ag 15 1879

Wichita weekly STOCKMAN. d,w 1907-33||
1907-Ag 8 1931 as Wichita daily stockman (d)
DA 1916-33
KHi Jl 11 1910-33

Wichita daily TIMES. d 1878-84||?
1878-Je 24 1881 as Wichita republican
ICM O 8 1881
KHi Mr 18 1880-Ag 1884

Wichita TIMES. w 1878-84||?
1878-Je 1881? as Wichita republican
KHi Mr 20 1880-Je 18 1881;My 19 1883-D 6 1884

Wichita TRIBUNE. w 1871||?
KHi Mr 15-N 16 1871

Wichita TRIBUNE. w 1898-99||?
Negro
KHi Jl 23 1898-99

UNION labor press. *See* Wichita independent 1886-89

Wichita VIDETTE. 1870-72||?
KHi Ag 13 1870-Mr 11 1871
OClWHi D 29 1870;Ja 12,F 2,Mr 4,11 1871

WELSH'S weekly. w 1911||?
KHi F 10-S 8 1911

WEST WICHITA news. w 1909-13||
Merged with Wichita democrat
KHi Ap 24 1909-Je 14 1913

WILBURN

Wilburn ARGUS. w 1886-87||?
KHi Ap 16 1886-87

WILLIAMSBURG

Williamsburg EAGLE. w 1884-89||?
KHi F 27 1885-Jl 5 1889

Williamsburg ENTERPRISE. w 1889-93||?
KHi Je 22 1889-Je 10 1893

Williamsburg ENTERPRISE. w Ag 31 1923+
KHi 1923+
KWiF Ap 1926+

FRANKLIN county journal. w S 27 1930+
pub 1930+

FRANKLIN county star. *See* Williamsburg star

Williamsburg GAZETTE. w 1880-83||?
KHi Ap 23 1880-F 16 1883

Williamsburg RECORD. w 1930?-
KHi Ag 1931-My 5 1932

Williamsburg REPUBLICAN. w 1898-1902||?
KHi N 19 1898-N 15 1901

Williamsburg REVIEW. w
KHi Je-O 2 1879

Williamsburg STAR. w 1893-1923||?
1893-Mr? 1894 as Franklin county star
KHi D 1893-F 2 1922

WILLIAMSTOWN

Williamstown MAIL. w 1901-02||?
KHi O 17 1901-Je 14 1902

Williamstown NEWS. w Ja 31- 1918||?
KHi Ja-O 3 1918

WILLIS

Willis JOURNAL. w 1897-99||?
KHi Jl 8 1897-F 16 1899

WILMORE

Wilmore NEWS. w Ag 23 1912—
KHi 1912-Mr,O 31 1913+

WILSEY

Wilsey BULLETIN. w 1889-91||?
KHi Je 1889-91

Wilsey INDEPENDENT. w 1892?-95||?
1892?-Mr 23 1893 as Morris county republican; Mr 30-My 18 1893 Morris county independent
KHi 1892-My 8 1893;Mr 1894-95

MORRIS county independent. *See* Wilsey independent

MORRIS county republican. *See* Wilsey independent

Wilsey WARBLER. w Ja? 1905+
KHi My 1905-D 16 1920;S 1926+

WILSON

Wilson EAGLE. w 1888-89||?
KHi Je 1888-F 9 1889

Wilson ECHO. *See* Wilson world

Wilson HAWKEYE. w 1886-88||?
1886-S 1887 as Wilson wonder
KHi Ap 15 1886-D 19 1888

Wilson INDEX. *See* Wilson world

KANSASKÉ rozhledy. w 1906?-14||?
In Bohemian
KHi Je 13 1906-My 1914

KANSASKY pokrok. w 1906?-26||?
In Bohemian
KHi My 22 1912-My 19 1926

Wilson WONDER. *See* Wilson hawkeye

Wilson WORLD. w 1878+
1878-My 13? 1880 as Wilson index; My 20? 1880-F 24 1913 Wilson echo
KHi O 10 1878-My 22 1879;My 20 1888+

WILSONTON

Wilsonton JOURNAL. w,m 1888-1908||?
w 1888-90?
KHi My 1888-1908

WINCHESTER

Winchester ARGUS. w 1877-88||?
KHi Ag 23 1877-Ja 12 1888

Winchester HERALD. *See* Winchester star

Winchester STAR. w 1888+
1888-Ja 1893 as Winchester herald
KHi 1888-O 14 1892;F 1893+

WINDOM

Windom ENTERPRISE. w 1886-88||?
KHi My 28 1886-Ag 9 1888

Windom ENTERPRISE. w 1892-93||?
KHi My 1892-93

Windom PRESS. w 1906-07||?
KHi Ap 20 1906-S 1907

Windom RECORD. w 1884-86||?
KHi Ag 16 1884-D 6 1885

WINFIELD

Winfield COURANT. d 1879?-82||?
KHi N 1881-Je 1882
—w ed *See* Cowley county courant

Winfield COURIER. w Ja 13 1873-D 25 1919||
pub complete
KHi F 1873-D 18 1918
N N 11 1875

Winfield daily COURIER. d Ap 7 1885+
pub 1885+
KHi 1885+

COWLEY county courant. w 1881?-82||?
KHi N 17 1881-Jl 4 1882
—d ed *See* Winfield courant

COWLEY county democrat. w 1874-76||?
1874? as Plow and anvil
KHi N 19 1874;Ja 27-Ag 17 1876

COWLEY county monitor. w 1879-81||?
KHi F 1880-Je 4 1881

COWLEY county telegram. *See* Winfield telegram w

KANSAS (*Continued*)

WINFIELD—*Continued*

Daily FREE PRESS. d 1902-S 30 1924||
Title varies: Evening free press. Merged with Winfield daily courier
KHi S 17 1902-1914
KWC complete
—w ed *See* Industrial free press

Winfield INDEPENDENT RECORD. w 1885?+
KHi Jl 28 1932+

INDUSTRIAL educator. *See* Industrial free press

INDUSTRIAL free press. w 1888-1906||
1888-Ap 25 1890 as Dexter free press (Dexter) My 2? 1890 Industrial educator
KHi S 14 1888-N 8 1906
KWC 1889-1906
—d ed *See* Daily free press

Winfield MESSENGER. w 1870-72||?
KHi [Mr 15-O 18 1872]

Winfield NEWS. d
KHi F 19-My 4 1885

Winfield evening NEWS. d Mr 14 1899-
KHi Mr 14-Je 1899

Winfield ORACLE. w 1912?+
KHi S 18 1931+

PLOW and anvil. *See* Cowley county democrat

Winfield SEMI-WEEKLY. sw
KHi F 1879-Ja 1880

Winfield SENTINEL. w 1895-96||?
KHi Ja 11 1895-S 1896

SOUTHWESTERN advocate. w 1901?-02||?
WHi D 4 1902

Winfield TELEGRAM. w 1872?-91||?
1873?-S 22 1887 as Cowley county telegram
KHi Ap 21 1876-Ja,Jl 14 1882-S 1891
KWHi Ja 29-D 1879
N F 8 1883

Winfield TELEGRAM. d Ja 1 1879-O 1881||?
KHi 1879-O 1881

Winfield TELEGRAM. d 1886-88||?
KHi Mr 14 1887-S 18 1888

Winfield TRIBUNE. w 1884-1909||
1886-89 as Saturday evening tribune
KHi N 26 1884-O 1892;Je 25 1897-Ja 30 1909
KWC 1884-1907
NbHi 1884-Ag 18 1886

Winfield daily TRIBUNE. d Ja 21 1886-91||
1886-Ap 21 1889 as Winfield visitor; Ap 23-Jl 26 1889 Daily tribune visitor
KHi Ja 22 1886-Je 4 1891
KWC 1889-91

Winfield daily TRIBUNE. d S 6 1907-Ja 30 1909||
Merged with Daily free press
KHi complete
KWC complete

Winfield VISITOR. w 1886-89||
Merged with Saturday evening tribune, later Winfield tribune
KHi O 14 1887-Ap 19 1889

Winfield VISITOR. d *See* Winfield daily tribune 1886-1901

WINONA

Winona CLIPPER. w 1887-95||?
KHi D 1887-95

LOGAN county news. w O 21? 1904+
KHi D 16 1904+

Winona MESSENGER. w 1886-89||?
KHi D 10 1886-Ap 1889

WOODBINE

Woodbine JOURNAL. w Mr 12 1914-17||?
KHi 1914-D 6 1917

WOODRUFF

Woodruff BUDGET. w 1906-11||?
KHi D 20 1906-O 5 1911

Woodruff GAZETTE. w 1886-87||?
KHi S 1886-My 1887

WOODSDALE

Woodsdale DEMOCRAT. *See* Stevens county sentinel

Woodsdale SENTINEL. *See* Stevens county sentinel

STEVENS county sentinel. w 1887-94||?
Ag 26 1887-Mr 1 1889 as Woodsdale democrat; Mr 8 1889-Jl 1 1892 Woodsdale sentinel; Jl 8 1892-Ja 20 1893 Tribune sentinel
KHi Mr 11 1887-Mr 1893;N 10 1894
WHi Ag 26 1887-Ag 16 1889

STEVENS county tribune. w 1890-Je 1892||?
United with Woodsdale sentinel to form Tribune sentinel, later Stevens county sentinel
KHi Ja 29 1890-Ja 14 1892

TRIBUNE sentinel. *See* Stevens county sentinel

WOODSTON

Woodston ARGUS. w Ap 22 1909+
KHi 1909+

Weekly ECHO. *See* Stockton review (Stockton)

Woodston REGISTER. w 1886-89||?
1886-Ap 15 1887 as Woodston saw
KHi O 29 1886-Je 7 1889

Woodston SAW. *See* Woodston register

Woodston STAR. w 1901-02||?
KHi O 11 1901-02

YOU all's doin's. *See* Stockton review (Stockton)

WYANDOTTE

Papers published in Wyandotte are listed under Kansas City

YATES CENTER

To 1870? as Butler

Yates Center ARGUS. w 1882-85||?
KHi Mr 18 1882-Ja 15 1885

FARMERS advocate. *See* Woodson county advocate

INDEPENDENT sun. w 1886-88||?
1886-S 2 1887 as Yates Center sun
KHi Ag 20 1886-D 7 1888

Yates Center NEWS. w Je 8 1877+
Title varies slightly
pub 1886+
KHi 1877+

Yates Center SUN. *See* Independent sun

Yates Center TRIBUNE. w 1889-90||?
KHi Ja 19 1889-F 1 1890

Saturday TRIBUNE. w 1902||
KHi F 15-N 8 1902

WOODSON county advocate. w 1890-1928||?
1890-99 as Farmers advocate
KHi Ja 9,F 1891-Ap 1928

WOODSON county journal. w O 3 1912-34||?
KHi 1912-Mr 23 1934

WOODSON county post. *See under* Neosho Falls

WOODSON democrat. w 1884-94||?
KHi Jl 11 1884-Je 1894

WOODSON gazette. w 1894-96||?
KHi S 14 1894-F 21 1896

WOODSON republican. w
KHi N 15 1894-Ja 10 1895

ZENDA

Zenda CITIZEN. w Ag 20 1909-17||?
KHi 1909-Ja 11 1917

Zenda HEADLIGHT. w 1923+?
KHi O 1923+

ZIONVILLE

Zionville SENTINEL. w 1886-88||?
KHi Je 30 1887-O 18 1888

KENTUCKY

KENTUCKY

INDEPENDENT. w 1871-86||?
DLC N 10 1881-Je 26 1884

Ashland daily INDEPENDENT. d 1896+
M N 7 1926
MWA N 7 1926

Ashland REPUBLICAN. w 1879-95||?
MWA N 8 1888

AUBURN

Auburn ADVOCATE. w Ap 13 1895-96||?
KyBoW My 11 1895

AUGUSTA

COLONIZATIONIST and literary journal. w N 7 1838-
DLC N 14 1838

Augusta TELEGRAPH. w
VU O 5-12,N 16,D 7-14 1833

BARDSTOWN

Bardstown GAZETTE. w
Title varies: Bardstown family gazette
DLC Jl 23 1842
KyBN Ja 7,21-28,F 11-18,Mr 4,25-Ap 15,29-Jl 8,22-Ag 5,19,S 2 1857
NNHi My 5 1860

Bardstown HERALD. w D 8 1827-30||?
D 8 1827 as Bardstown western herald
CSmH S 1 1830
DLC Jl 21,Ag 18 1830
MWA D 8 1827;Ja 5 1828

Bardstown HERALD. w 1851-55||?
Ky Ap 1852-F 1855
KyBoW O 28 1852-Ag 1853
KyLo D 28 1833-Mr 15 1834
KyLoF O 28 1852;Ag 25 1853
MWA Ja 28 1854

KENTUCKY standard. w 1900+
KyBoW 1929+
KyLT My 1906-Jl 20 1911

WESTERN American. *See under* St. Louis, Mo.

Bardstown WESTERN herald. *See* Bardstown herald

BARDWELL

CARLISLE county news. w S 1894+
pub 1894+
KyBoW 1929+

BEDFORD

BANNER-DEMOCRAT. *See* Trimble democrat

TRIMBLE banner. *See* Trimble democrat

TRIMBLE democrat. w 1893+
1893-96? as Banner-democrat; 1896-1901 Trimble banner
pub S 13 1923+

BEREA

CITIZEN. w Je 21 1899+
1899-1903 as Reporter
pub 1899+

REPORTER. *See* Citizen

BERRY

LICKING Valley journal. w 1915+
pub 1918+

BOWLING GREEN

Bowling Green GAZETTE. w 1853-60||?
KyBoW [1854-55]Ja 11 1860

GREEN RIVER correspondent. w 1824||?
ICU S 25 1824

GREEN RIVER gazette. w 1832-40||?
DLC N 4 1840
ICU F 2 1833;Mr 18 1840

GREEN RIVER pantagraph. w 1872-78||
VRC Ag 28 1878

KENTUCKY standard. w 1852-54||?
KyBoW S 9 1854

LOUISVILLE daily courier. d 1861-62||?
GSD Ja 4 1862
NcD O 22,N 7,18-19,22 1861;F 3,13 1862

Bowling Green MESSENGER. w 1908-16||
Ky 1910-15
KyBoW S 5 1916

Bowling Green NEWS. *See* Park City daily news

PARK CITY daily news. d 1882+
1882-1905 as Bowling Green news. 1906+ title varies: Park City daily news and democrat; Park City daily news and messenger; Park City daily news-democrat-messenger; etc.
KyBoW D 1920+

PARK CITY times. *See* Times journal

PUBLIC advertiser. w N 24 1827-31||?
CSmH Ag 20 1830
DLC N 4 1831
MWA N 24 1827;S 19 1828

SPIRIT of the times. w N 25 1826-27||?
DLC D 23 1826
KyBoW 1826-N 17 1827

TIMES journal. d 1882+
1882-99? as Park City times
KyBoW 1929+

BRANDENBURG

MEADE county news. w 1882-92||?
CLM S 22-29 1887

BURKESVILLE

CUMBERLAND county news. w 1922+
KyBoW 1929+

BURLINGTON

BOONE county recorder. w 1875+
pub 1875+

CAMPBELLSVILLE

TAYLOR county star. w 1927+
pub 1927+

CANEYVILLE

GRAYSON county news. w 1920-25||
KHi My 8 1924

KENTUCKY (*Continued*)

CARLISLE

Carlisle MERCURY. w Ja 1867+
pub 1873-92;1911+
Ky 1910-19
KyLT Jl 4 1872;S 29 1881
KyU 1910-19

CARROLLTON

Carrollton COURIER. w
KyU 1851

SIGNS of the times. w My 2? 1861-
OClWHi D 19 1861;Ja 31 1862

CLINTON

Clinton DEMOCRAT. w,sw 1876-1906||
w 1876-1904
KyClH [1876-1906]

Twice a week GAZETTE. *See* Hickman county gazette

HICKMAN county gazette. sw,w 1902+
1902-03? as Twice a week gazette (sw)
pub [1902-20]+

CLOVERPORT

BRECKENRIDGE news. w 1876+
pub 1876+
NN S 30-O 7,21-D 1876;F 28-Mr 7,Ag 29,S 19,O 1-N 21,D 19 1877;F 20-27,Mr 27,Ap 10, My 1,22 1878

COLUMBIA

ADAIR county news. w 1896+
KyBoW 1929+

COLUMBUS

Columbus BEACON. 1881-82||?
KyClH [1881-82]

Daily CONFEDERATE news. d 1861-
OClWHi Ja 15 1862

HICKMAN county times. w 1884-85||?
KyClH [1884-85]

Columbus SENTINEL. w F 22 1878-
MWA My 17 1878

WAR eagle. w 1862-63||?
ICHi S 26 1863
IHi Je 13-27 1863
NNHi Je 27 1863

CORBIN

Corbin TIMES TRIBUNE. sw 1904+
pub 1923+

COVINGTON

Saturday ADVERTISER. w 1873-74||?
KyC Ja 25-Je 7 1873

AMERICAN sentinel. w My 2 1855-
KyLoF My 2 1855

COMMONWEALTH. w,m 1873-1913||?
w 1873-1902
KyC Jl 8 1875-Ja 1876

COMMONWEALTH. d 1877-99||?
GDE Je 28 1880
KyC S 30-D 18 1877;80-81;83;Ap-D 1884

CONCILIATOR. w
DLC Ag 24 1839

Covington COURIER. w 1902-08||
KyC S 20 1902-S 11 1903

DEMOCRATIC union. w Mr 1850-51||?
KyC O 24 1850;Ag 28 1851

Covington ENQUIRER. w 1833?-36||?
DLC Ag 12 1835;F 13 1836

Covington FREE PRESS. w 1838-39||?
KyC D 8 1838;Ja 5-12,26-F 9,23-Mr 9,23 1839

Covington JOURNAL. w 1849?-76||
Suspended Ag 30 1862-F 8 1868
KyC 1849-S 1876
NcD Jl 3 1869
OClWHi Mr 19 1849

KENT-on-bugle. w Ap 10 1840-
KyC Ap 10 1840

Covington KENTUCKIAN. w 1854-55||?
OOxM Jl 18-Ag 15 1855

KENTUCKY and Ohio journal. w Ag 3 1837-38||?
KyC [1837-Jl 1838]

Weekly KENTUCKY flag. w
DLC O 20-27 1852

KENTUCKY intelligencer. w F 14 1845-46||?
ICU My 13 1846
KyC F 14 1845

KENTUCKY post. d 1890+
DLC 1898+

LICKING Valley register. w Jl 21 1841-48||?
CSmH My 28 1842
DLC Ag 4-11,25-S 1,O 6,D 25 1841;O 29 1842
KyC 1841-Jl 23 1842;Ap 29 1843;Jl 27 1844-Jl 19 1845;46-D 22 1848
MWA F 25,Ap 22-My 27,Je 10-17 1843;My 4 1844
NbHi Jl 21 1841;Ag 6,S 10-17,O 1842-Ja 13,28-F,Mr 11-Ap 1,29-My 20,Je 3-10,24-Jl 15,29-Ag 19,S 2,16 O 1843-Mr 16,30-Je 8,22-Jl 20,Ag 31,S 1844-Jl 1845
OCHi 1841-45

NORTH Kentuckian. w 1836-37||?
KyC Ja 5,19-26,F 9-23,Mr 30-Ap 13,My,Je 8 1837

PIKE'S campaign flag. w 1850-
MWA Jl 17 1852

Daily Covington REGISTER. d Ja 1-19 1844||
NbHi Ja 1,3-6,8-19 1844

TICKET. tw,d 1871-79||?
tw 1871-76?
KyC Ap 8 1875-79

Covington UNION. w Jl 1847-49||?
ICU Ap 14 1848
KyC Jl 11,O 3 1849

WESTERN colonization. w Ja 18 1839-
KyC Mr 29-Ap 5,19,My 24,Je 7-14,Jl 19 1839

WESTERN globe. w D 1838-40||?
ICU F 26 1840
KyC Jl 26-S 20,O 11-D 6,25 1839-Ja 1,15-Ap 1,29 1840;Jl 29 1839(extra)

WESTERN visitor. w 1837-44||?
KyC Mr 28,My 2,23,S 26,O 31 1844

YANKEE Doodle. w
KyC My 15-Jl,Ag 13 1840

CYNTHIANA

Cynthiana ADVERTISER. w 1826-
MWA F 17 1827

Cynthiana DEMOCRAT. w 1868+
pub 1904+

LOG CABIN. w Ja 1 1896+
pub 1896+

Cynthiana NEWS. w 1850-86||?
KyHi Mr 10,Jl 14-O 6,20,N-D 8,22 1870;Ja-D 21 1871;Mr 11-18,Ap 1-8,29,My 27,Je 17-24,Jl 8-22,O 7-14,N 18-D 21 1875;O 5,26,N 16-22 1876;Ja-F 22,Mr 1,29,Ap 5,19-My 24 1877;Ja 31-F 7,Ag 15-22,S 19 1878

Cynthiana TIMES. w 1855?-65||?
ICHi O 25 1865

WESTERN visiter. w
DLC O 10 1839;Ap 23 1840

DANVILLE

Danville ADVERTISER. w 1825-
KyBoW Jl 4 1825-Je 1826
MWA F 17 1827

CENTRAL Kentucky gazette. w
KyHi Ag 15 1866-S 11 1867

CLARION. w Ag 21 1841-
DLC Ag 21,O 2 1841
KyHi O 6 1841

KENTUCKY advocate. w,sw,tw,d 1865+
w 1865-90; sw 1891-1901; tw 1902-10
Ky 1910-19
KyLT D 15 1899
KyLo Mr 27 1888
KyU 1910-19

KENTUCKY rifle. w Jl 25 1840-
DLC Mr 2 1841
ICU O 31 1840

KENTUCKY tribune. w Ag 18 1843-48||?
DLC Ag 18,S 22 1843
KyHi 1843-S 13 1844
KyLo Ag 25 1848

KENTUCKY tribune. 1878-80 *See* Danville tribune

Wednesday MERCURY. w
KyHi O 26-D 7 1842

Danville daily MESSENGER. sw,d My 6 1910+
1910-Ap 1919 as Danville semi-weekly messenger (sw)
pub 1910+

***OLIVE branch and western union.** w Mr 24 1820-
Follows Kentucky advertiser (Winchester) (not in this list). 1820 as Olive branch
DLC O 27 1832
ICU Ap 21,Je 23 1821;D 23 1825
KyFM Jl 14 1821

Danville TRIBUNE. w 1878-84||?
1878-80 as Kentucky tribune
KHi Ag 19 1881
OClWHi N 5-12 1880
OHi Ap 16 1880

EDDYVILLE

LYON county herald. w 1906+
Follows Tale of two cities
pub 1924+

TALE of two cities. w 1890-1905||
Followed by Lyon county herald

Eddyville TELEGRAPH. w
DLC O 22 1852

ELIZABETHTOWN

Elizabethtown DEMOCRAT. w Ja 1858-
DLC Ap 13-Ag 16 1859

HARDIN county enterprise. w S 26 1926+
pub 1926+

KENTUCKY register. w Je 1834-
DLC Jl 19 1834
KyLoF S 21 1847
MWA Je 27 1854

KENTUCKY statesman. w O 1828-
DLC N 19 1829;Mr 3-10,Ap 7,Jl 7,S 8-15,N 24 D 8 1831

Elizabethtown NEWS. w,sw Ag 7 1869+
w 1869-1905
KyLoF F 9 1871;D 13 1878

WESTERN intelligencer. w Mr 28 1826-
DLC Mr 28 1826
IU Mr 28,N 29-D 6,20 1826
MWA Ja 17 1827

ZOUAVE gazette of the 19th regiment Illinois volunteers. w O 30-N 23 1861||?
ICHi O-N 23 1861
MWA N 17 1861

EWING

Ewing ENQUIRER. w 1898+
pub My 11 1933+

FAIRVIEW

REVIEW. w 1895-1908||
T S 27 1901

FLEMINGSBURG

FARMERS' register and village chronicle. w
InI D 13 1824

FLEMING county gazette. *See* Fleming gazette

FLEMING flag. *See* Kentucky flag (Maysville)

FLEMING gazette. w 1880+
1880-85? as Fleming county gazette
MWA D 13 1893

FLEMING star. w 1860-
MWA Ja 18 1861

Flemingsburg KENTUCKIAN. w O 27 1837-
Follows Kentucky whig (1835-37)
DLC O 30 1840
MWA 1837-O 19 1838
MnHi Je 4 1842
WHi Jl 31 1840-D 16 1841

KENTUCKY intelligencer. w N 13 1829-30||?
CSmH My 29 1830

KENTUCKY whig. w 1835-O 13 1837||
Followed by Flemingsburg Kentuckian
MWA Ap 8 1836-37

KENTUCKY whig. w Ap 1 1843-
MnHi Ja 27 1844
NNHi 1843-Ap 20 1844

FRANKFORT

ALBION. w
KyHi 1836-57

***Frankfort ARGUS.** w Ja 27 1808-38||?
1808-30 as Argus of Western America; N 4 1835-D 14 1836 Argus
CSmH S 1 1830
DLC 1821-Ap 1838
ICHi Ag 11 1830;Je 15 1831 Mr 2 1836
ICU Ja 25,F 8-15,Mr 22,Ap 20,Jl 5 1821;D 26 1822;O 5 1825;F 22 1826[27-31]Ja 25 1832;F 9,Mr 2 1838
KyFM Je 9 1824-N 22 1826
KyHi D 17 1826;Jl 5,Mr 7 1827;Ja 14-F 11,Ap 8-Je 3,Ag 19 1829-Ja 13,F 3,Mr 24-Je 23,Ag-O 13,N-D 1830
KyL Mr,My 19-D 22 1824;Ja 5,19-Ap 13,Je 15-S 13,N-D 1826[27]F 20-Mr,Ap 16-30,My 14-28,Je 11 1828-Jl 8,Ag-S,O 14 1829-Mr,Jl 28 1830;Ap 4 1832
KyU D 3 1834
MBAt Mr 28 1822
MWA Ja 25 1821;O 20,N 17,D 1 1824;Ja 11,F 1,22,Mr 1,15,29,Ap 12,26,My 31,Jl 5,Ag 2,N 15,29 1826;F 28,My 30,Je 20,Ag 22,S 12,O 3,N 21,D 26 1827;Ja 2-23,F 6,Mr 19-26,Ag 6 1828; Je 10,24-Jl 8,22-29,D 2-9 1829;Ja 20,Mr 17 1830;F 1 1832;N 12 1834;Mr 2 1838
N O 9 1833
NN O 21 1829
NNHi Je 10,N 18 1829
WHi N 17 1824

CAMPAIGN. w 1840||
Campaign paper
DLC My 14-28,S 3 1840

Frankfort CAPITAL. w,d 1884-Je 1897||?
w 1884-91 (d during sessions of legislature)
Ky 1886-Je 1897
KyLT O 9 1886

***COMMENTATOR.** w,sw Ja 3 1817-Ap 24 1832||
United with Kentuckian to form Kentuckian and commentator
1826-32 issued sw during sessions of the legislature
CSmH S 7 1830
DLC 1821-N 15 1823[24]-Mr 1830;Ja 11,Mr 1-15 1831
ICHi Ja 17 1832
ICU D 13 1823;O 1824-32;D 6 1827(extra)
IU [1821-23]25-Ja 17 1827
KyHi D 22 1827;28-30;Ap 1831-My 18 1832
MBAt Mr 20 1822;D 27 1823 S 22,D 29 1827; Ap 5,S 13,O 18 1828;S 8-15 1829;Mr 2 1830; Ja 25,F 15 1831
MHi N 15,D 6-20 1823;S 11,N 13 1824;F 12 1825
MWA 1826;F 17,Mr 17,Ap,My 19,Je 9-Jl 21, Ag 18-O 6,20-D 22 1827;28;Je 23-Jl 21,O 27,D 22 1829;Mr 23,Ag 17,D 28 1830
NcD D 6 1827(extra)Ag 23 1828;Ja 5 1830
OCHi S 1831-Ja 1832
TxU Ap 8 1826-Mr 1828
WHi Ja 17 1817[My 19 1829-N 16]D 14 1830-Jl 5 1831

KENTUCKY (*Continued*)

FRANKFORT—*Continued*

Frankfort COMMONWEALTH. w,tw,sw Ap 9 1833-Ap 5 1872||
sw,tw during sessions of the legislature
DLC Ap 9,Je 25,Jl 2 1833;Ja 28 1834;S 19 1835;Mr 30,S 17,O 8 1839;Mr 9 1841-N 15 1842;Ap 10-D 1849[Jl-D 1861]63-S 1866;Ap 1867-Jl 9 1869;Ja 26-F 16 1872
ICHi O 11 1859;O 2 1860;Jl 28 1863
ICU S 2 1834;My 9,Jl 11,25,Ag 8,22-29 1835; Mr 30,Ap 20 1836;Ap 1837-Ap 3,My 21 1839; Mr 7,My 23-Je 6,N 7 1843;Je 24,S 23 1845;Ja 20 1846;Mr 11-Jl 8 1862
IU F 28 1835;O 18 1837;Ja 3 1838
Ky 1832-52;62-67;69-71
KyFM 1833-D 6 1837
KyHi 1833-Ap 4 1835;Ap 10 1839-Mr 21 1848; Ap 6 1852-Ap 6,Je 30 1856;Je 30,Jl 11 1862; Je 20,Ag 6 1864;Jl 4 1865-72
KyL Ja 19 1841
KyLo F 25 1834;D 17 1860-D 23 1861
KyLoF Ap 1844-Ap 1 1851;Mr 14 1856-F 24 1858
KyLT F 27 1849
MWA D 1838-Mr 20 1839;N 8 1842;D 2 1856; D 9 1868(extra)
N O 8 1833
NcD Ag 8 1848
NcU S 12 1848
OC Ap 25 1835-Mr 8 1837;Ap 1841-Mr 1843
OClWHi D 1 1852
OHi 1833-Mr 1837;Ap 10 1839-My 1847
TxU N 16 1841-61
WHi Ap 18 1854-60

Daily COMMONWEALTH. d
pub during sessions of legislature
ICU Ja-Mr 6 1844
Ky 1845-47
KyHi 1844-Mr 6 1845;Ja-F 12 1846;Ja-F 25 1847;Ja-Mr 2 1848;Ja-Mr 2 1849;N 6 1850-Mr 24 1851
KyLoF Mr 2 1849;Mr 10 1856
KyU N 27,D 18 1849
OC Ja-F 25 1846

CONSTITUTIONAL advocate. w O 5 1825-Mr 31 1826||
Follows Harbinger. Merged with Commentator
DLC Ja-Mr 1826
ICU O 5,19-N 2,30-D 1825;Ja 13-F 10,Mr 10, 24-31 1826
OC [1825-Mr 24 1826]

CONVENTION. w Ja 2 1847-49||?
KyHi 1847-F 2 1848
KyLoF Ja-Jl,D 21 1847;Ja 11-18,F 8,22 1848

Frankfort daily DESPATCH. d
PScrHi Ag 2 1861;F 2 1862

HARBINGER. w Mr 30-S 28 1825||
Follows American republic (not in this list) Followed by Constitutional advocate
ICU complete
OC complete

KENTUCKIAN and commentator. w Ap 10 1828-33||?
Follows Spirit of seventy-six. 1828-Ap 1832 as Kentuckian
CSmH F 26 1830
DLC 1828[29]Ja 1,D 10 1830;Ja 14 1831;O 4,N 1 1832
ICU Ap-Ag 14,28-S 11,25-O 2,16-N,D 11 1828-N 7,D 11 1829-Ja 8,22-29,F 12-My 1830;Je 21,Jl 26-Ag 9,23 1832
KyFM Ap 17 1828-Ap 2 1830
KyL My 21-Jl 3 1829
MBAt Ag 21-28,D 25 1828;Ag 13-20 1830
MWA Je 19,Jl 10,24-31,Ag 14-28,S 11-O 2,16-30,N 13-D 11 1828;Ap 27 1832
OClWHi F 3 1832
OOxM [Mr 1832-Mr 1833]
WHi F 10,24,Mr 23 1832

KENTUCKY democrat. *See* Western democrat

KENTUCKY sentinel. w 1823-
1823-28 as American sentinel
Ct F 9 1838
DLC Jl 9,S 10 1824;Jl 15 1825-[26]S 22,O 13,D 29 1827-Ag 2 1828;D 26 1829-Ja 9,23,D 18 1830;Ja 8 1831
ICU S 10-17,O 8-22 1824;Ja 26-Jl 14,28,S 1,15-N,D 8-29 1827;Ja 19-F 8,29 1828;S 3 1829
OOxM Ja 28,F 28,My 9-16,Je 13,27,Je 11,N 29 1829
WHi F 16-Mr 2,10-17 1827;Ap 11 1828

KENTUCKY state journal. d 1899+
Ky 1910-12

KENTUCKY yeoman. w,tw,d F 13 1840-85||?
Title varies: Daily session Kentucky yeoman; Daily session yeoman; Daily Kentucky yeoman; Tri-weekly Kentucky yeoman; Weekly Kentucky yeoman
tw and d during sessions of legislature
DLC Mr 5,S 10 1840;O 1846-49;51;O 15 1852; 53-55;59-61;Ja-My 22 1863
ICU Ja 8,13 1846;F 3 1860;F 18 1879
Ky 1841-50[59;61;66-69;71-77;79-83;85-86]
KyFM Mr 17 1842;Mr 9 1843
KyHi 1843-Mr 7 1844;Ja-F 25 1846;Jl 28 1849
KyL 1870-72
KyLT Ap 25 1844
KyLoF S 17 1840;F 29 1844;Mr 6-8,Ap 8,Jl 12 1851;Mr 18 1852[55-N 14 1856]Ja 22,F 19,Mr 26,S 17 1858;Mr 11,25,Jl 1,O 14,D 9 1859[60] Ja 11,15,18,Mr 8-22,My 3,Je 14,S 20 1861;F 28,Mr 14-28,Ap 18-My 2 1862
KyU F 24 1880;My 13 1882
MBAt O 24 1868
MWA O 24 1844;My 25,S 14 1848;Ap 6 1855
NSyU Ag 16 1862
TU-J My 11 1854

Frankfort NEWS-JOURNAL. d 1908-12||
1908-11 as Frankfort news
Ky 1910-12

NIXON'S phiz. ir Ja 24-Ap 28 1852||
KyFM complete

PATRIOT. w F 22-Jl 31 1826||
ICU complete
KyFM complete
KyHi Je 19 1826
KyLoF complete

Daily POST-DESPATCH. d
PScrHi F 2,Jl 31 1881

Frankfort ROUNDABOUT. w 1877-1908||?
KyHi F 15 1890

SPIRIT of '76. w Mr 10-Ag 4 1826||
Campaign paper of Old Court Party. Followed by Spirit of seventy-six
DLC complete
ICU complete
KyBoW complete
KyLoF complete
MH Mr-Jl 7 1826
MoS complete
NjP complete
WHi complete

SPIRIT of seventy-six. w D 7 1826-My 27 1828||
Followed by Kentuckian, later Kentuckian and commentator
DLC F 7 1828
ICU D 13 1826-28
KyFM complete
KyHi O 25 1827

TOCSIN. w Je 24-Ag 26 1843||?
ICU Ag 26 1843
WHi Ag 26 1843

WESTERN argus. w 1886-1902||?
KyHi S 1886-Ag 1900;O 10 1901;F 13 1902

WESTERN democrat. w O 15 1838-
O-N 8 as Kentucky democrat
DLC O 15,25,N 8,22-D 6,27 1838
ICU D 27 1838

WESTERN statesman. w My 31? 1824-
DLC Je 14,Jl 5 1824
OC My 31-Ag 10,O 28-N 10 1824

WESTERN volunteer. w Ag 25-O 20 1824||
DLC O 1824
ICU S 8 1824
OC complete

FULTON

FULTON county news. w Ja 26 1933+
pub 1933+

GEORGETOWN

AMERICAN sentinel. *See* Kentucky sentinel

Georgetown HERALD. w 1845?-56||?
DLC Ap 4 1848
KHi Mr 16 1854-F 21 1856
Ky 1851
KyLoF Je 2-16,Jl 14-21,Ag 18,O 13 1847;Mr 8,22,N 1 1848;Ap 11,25-My 2,Je 6,Ag 1,15 1849

KENTUCKY sentinel. w
MHi Jl 28 1832

Georgetown NEWS. sw,w 1887+
Ky 1918-19
KyBoW 1929+

POLITICAL examiner. w
OOxM Ag 13-O 5 1844

Georgetown TIMES. w Ja 1 1867+
pub 1867+
ICU Je 27 1894
KyL 1870-72
KyLT My 4 1898

WHIG banner. w F 10 1838-39||?
DLC F 17 1838;Je 28 1839
KyHi Ap 26 1839

GLASGOW

KENTUCKY reveille. w 1848-50||?
KyLT S 27 1850

Glasgow REPUBLICAN. w 1892+
pub 1932+
KyBoW 1894+

Glasgow TIMES. w 1865+
KyBoW 1870-1927
KyLT My 9,S 29 1898

GREENSBURG

Greensburg RECORD-HERALD. w 1894+
pub 1894+

GREENUP

Greenup GAZETTE. w 1881-1912||
KyLT Jl 22 1908

GREENVILLE

Greenville LEADER. w 1922+
pub 1926+
KyBoW 1929+
KyLT 1929+

RECORD. w F 9 1899+
pub 1899+
KyBoW [1902-03;08-09]

HARRODSBURG

AMERICAN. w N 12 1830-31||?
Ct Ja 28,Mr 11,25 1831
DLC D 24 1830
ICU Ja 28,Mr 4-11,25,My 6,Jl 8,22 1831

CENTRAL watchtower and farmer's journal. w 1827-30||?
CSmH Jl 3 1830
DLC F 9-16,Mr 15,Jl 12 1828;Je 6,20-Jl 18,Ag 29,N 21,D 12,26 1829
ICU D 29 1827;Mr 1-8,S 3,N 19 1828;Mr 20, My 16,Je 13 1829;My 22,Je 12,Je 19(extra) 1830
MWA Ja 12 1828

Harrodsburg DEMOCRAT. w 1881+
1881-33 as Harrodsburg republican
pub 1883-84;1916+
ICU Je 20 1890;Jl 18 1902
KyHa 1890-98

Harrodsburg HERALD. w S 21 1885+
1885-87? as Sayings and doings; 1888?-90 Sayings
pub 1885+
ICM D 28 1923
KyH 1887-88;90
KyHa 1887-88;1901+
KyLT S 27 1912
KyLoF Ag 10 1905;Je 17 1932
OClWHi My 12 1916

KENTUCKY republican. *See* Harrodsburg leader

Harrodsburg LEADER. w 1881-1916||
1881-1912 as Kentucky republican
Ky 1912
KyLT S 25 1912
OClWHi Jl 7,N 24 1915

Harrodsburg REPUBLICAN. *See* Harrodsburg democrat

SAYINGS. *See* Harrodsburg herald

UNION. w
DLC D 11 1830

HARTFORD

Hartford HERALD. *See* Ohio county news

OHIO county messenger. w Mr 1930+
pub 1930+

OHIO county news. w Ja 1 1875+
1875-1926 as Hartford herald
pub 1875+
KyBoW 1929+
TU-J Ag 8,N 7 1883;Ja 30 1884

Hartford REPUBLICAN. w 1888-1926||
United with Hartford herald to form Ohio county news
KyHarO complete

HAWESVILLE

PICK and plow. w F 26 1853-
KyLoF Je 11 1853

HENDERSON

COLUMBIAN. w 1823-30||?
CSmH Jl 3 1830
DLC S 11-18,O 2-16,30,N 30-D 25 1824;S 6,O 25 1828;Je 27-Jl 4,S 5,19,D 5 1829
ICU Ag 30 1828

Tri-weekly COMMERCIAL. tw Ag 4 1856-
MWA Ag 4 1856

Henderson weekly COMMERCIAL. w 1856-
MWA N 12-19 1857;Ja 22-29,Mr 12,Ap 2-9, 30,My 14-21 1858

Henderson daily JOURNAL. d 1889+
KyLo Ja 15 1905

Henderson weekly MAIL. w F 6 1860-
IU Jl 31 1860

Henderson weekly REPORTER. w 1853-84||?
NNHi My 6 1861

HICKMAN

COMMERCIAL gazette and South-western weekly democrat. w
-1844 as Hunter of Kentucky and South-western weekly democrat
MiU-C [1842-45]

Weekly COMMERCIAL standard. *See* Leigh's commercial standard

Hickman COURIER. w 1859+
pub 1869+
KyBoW 1929+
TU-J Ag 26 1871;My 25 1872;Mr 8-15,O 11 1873;Ap 7,S 1 1876;Mr 9-16 1877;F 22,Jl 5 1878;O 10 1879;F 24 1882;Mr 28,Jl 24,Ag 8,N 14,D 12 1884;Je 15 1888

HUNTER of Kentucky. *See* Commercial gazette

LEIGH'S commercial standard. w N 26 1845-
1845-Mr 4 1847 as Weekly commercial standard
DLC Ja 8 1846-N 1848
MWA D 11 1845;Ja 1 1846

HIMLERVILLE

HIMLER Marton hetilapja (Martin Himler weekly). w 1923+
In Hungarian
PPiHi O 17 1925-[29-Jl 1931]

HOPKINSVILLE

Hopkinsville GAZETTE. w Jl 9 1835-
DLC S 4 1835

GREEN River advocate. w
P-M S 13 1833

KENTUCKY (*Continued*)

HOPKINSVILLE—*Continued*

Hopkinsville KENTUCKIAN. w,sw,tw,d Ja 1879+
1879-S? 1888 as South Kentuckian
w 1879-O 1880;sw N 1880-1920;d during Spanish American and World Wars
KyHo 1888+

KENTUCKY new era. w 1870+
pub Ap 5 1872+
KHi O 12 1923

KENTUCKY new era. d 1888+
pub 1888+
KyBoW 1929+

KENTUCKY republican. w
DLC Jl 31 1824;O 25-N 22,D 13 1826;Mr 8 1828
MWA F 14 1827;F 2 1828

KENTUCKY rifle. w 1851-
KyBoW Mr 3 1855
MWA Ag 19 1852

SOUTH Kentuckian. *See* Hopkinsville Kentuckian

VIDETTE. ir
KyHoL O 28 1862(photostat)

HORSE CAVE

HART county news. w 1919+
pub 1919+

KENTUCKY intelligencer. w Ja 28 1868-
KyBoW Jl 29 1868

HYDEN

THOUSANDSTICKS. w 1911+
pub 1919+
KyLT O 7 1909

IRVINE

ESTILL herald. sw 1927+
pub 1927+

ESTILL tribune. w 1890+
pub 1917+

Irvine TIMES. w Ja 6 1920+
pub 1920+

JACKSON

Jackson HUSTLER. w 1888-1907||
ICM Ag 25 1899

JEFFERSONTOWN

JEFFERSONIAN. w Je 1907+
pub 1907+

LAGRANGE

OLDHAM era. w 1876+
pub 1910+
KyLo Mr 25 1921-Ap 1924
KyLoF Je 14 1929+

LANCASTER

CENTRAL record. w 1883+
KyBoW 1929+

LAWRENCEBURG

ANDERSON news. w 1877+
Ky 1911-19
KyLT Je 7 1888

LEBANON

CENTRAL Kentuckian. w 1858-
Follows Lebanon post
ICU Je 11 1863

Lebanon ENTERPRISE. w 1886+
pub 1915+

Lebanon POST. w 1852-57||
Followed by Central Kentuckian
Ky 1852;Ap 1853-F 1857

LEITCHFIELD

AMERICAN news. w
KyLT Je 7 1888

Leitchfield GAZETTE. w Ap 1881+
1881-86? as Leitchfield sunbeam; 1887?-1905 Grayson gazette
pub 1913+
KyBoW 1929

GRAYSON gazette. *See* Leitchfield gazette

Leitchfield SUNBEAM. *See* Leitchfield gazette

LEXINGTON

AMERICAN democrat and weekly courier. w
KyLoF [1845-46]

ANTI-JACKSON bulletin and messenger of truth. w Ag 30 1828-
DLC Ag 30,O 4-11 1828

Daily ARGONAUT. d D 15 1895-99||?
KyLT D 15 1895[96-97]
KyU S 21 1896

ARROW. w N 16 1902-04||?
KyLT N 23 1902

Daily Lexington ATLAS. d D 13? 1847-
KyLoF D 23 1847

Lexington tri-weekly ATLAS. tw
DLC Je 13,Jl 27,Ag 20 1849
KyLoF My 16,Ag 8 1849

BLUE Grass world. w N 4 1896-
KyLT N 18 1896

CENTRAL Kentucky times. w Je 27 1894-
KyLT Ag 8-S 1894

Lexington morning DEMOCRAT. d 1900-04||?
KyLT Je 11,19,21,S 27 1901;Je 9,Jl 23-24,D 13 1903;S 15 1904

Lexington ENTERPRISE. w
KyLT S 1897

FARMERS' register and western spirit of the times. w Ja 21 1840-
DLC F 11 1840

FORTUNE'S herald, or Western lottery and exchange intelligencer.
TH S 1824-O 1825

Weekly GLOBE. w 1894-99||?
KyLT Ap 17 1899

Lexington HERALD. d O 1870+
1870-94? as Lexington daily press; 1895?
Lexington daily press-transcript; 1896-1904 Morning herald
ICM N 30 1884
Ky S 1928
KyBoW Jl 11 1915
KyHi Ap 4-Mr 27 1874;1928+
KyL 1870-Ap,N 1874-94;96+
KyLT N 13-20 1887
KyLo Lexington Herald Golden Jubilee Edition 1920
KyLoF 1896+
KyU N 13 1877;S 3 1879;My 12,18,Je 9 1882;S 3,27 1892;Ap 19 1899;1904-20

Lexington INQUIRER. tw,sw,w N 1843-
tw 1843-Ap? 1844;sw My? 1844-F 1845?
KyHi S 17 1844
MWA Ja 11,Ap 9,S 6,20,O 11 1844;Mr 21-28 1845

Lexington INTELLIGENCER. w,sw,tw 1833?-43||?
DLC Ja 4 1834
ICU [Jl 1840-41]-My 1843
KyBoW Jl 22 1834(extra)
KyHi S 11 1835;Mr 16 1838;Jl 6 1841
KyL 1834-39
MHi O 20 1835
MWA Ap 12 1834;My 2 1837;My 12 1840,Je 24 1842
WHi 1834-39

Daily Lexington INTELLIGENCER. d D 7 1840-
DLC D 7 1840

*KENTUCKY gazette. w,sw Ag 11 1787-1848||
1787-Mr 7 1789 as Kentucke gazette; Mr 14 1789-Ja 11 1803 Kentucky gazette; Ja 18 1803-Ap 4 1809 Kentucky gazette and general advertiser
sw 1797,F 19-D 1806,Ap-D 1836
CSmH S 30 1830;D 10 1847
Ct [1827-37]
DLC 1821-[29]Ja 1,22,D 23 1830;Ja 13 1831;33-N 1841
ICHi Ag 27 1830
ICU [1827-28]Ja 2-9,Mr 20,Ap 3,Je 5 1829;Je 25,Ag 20 1830;My 18 1833;My 31,Ag 30 1834;Ja 30,Ap 2,1836extras:Mr 3,N 13 1825;Jl 19,Ag 2,O 23,25 1832;S 26 1836;Ja 10 1843
KyHi D 10(extra)1837
KyL 1825-26;F 23-Mr 9,30-My 18,Je 1 1827;Ap 26,Je 13 1828;Ja 8,Mr 12,Ap 2-23,Jl 9,S 10,O 14-21 1830;Ja 6,Ag 4,N 10 1831;F 18 1832;35-40
KyLoF Ap 23,Je 18 1847;N 3 1848
MWA Ag 7,N 6-13,D 25 1823-Ja 1,22,F 5-19,Mr,Ap 8-22,My 13-20,Je 17,O 14-21,N 4,D 16-23 1824;Ag 25,D 1 1826;F 16,Mr 16,Ap 6,My 11-Je 1,Jl 13,27,D 28 1827;Ja 4,Ap 4,Ag 15,D 12 1828;Mr 30,D 7-14 1844;Ag 2,D 27 1845;Mr 7-14,Ap 4 1846;Jl 30 1847;F 25,Ag 11 1848
MnHi My 5 1836
N Ag 3 1827;O 12 1833
NN F 6,O 2,16,N 6 1823
NcD S 19 1828
OC Ap 28-O,D 1831-34
OHi F 12 1824
OOxM F 29 1828;N 10 1832-Je 1834
TKL Ja 24,F 14 1835
WHi F 5-12 1824

KENTUCKY gazette. sw,d 1866-1910||?
sw 1866-
Ky 1867-72;74
KyBoW 1866-Mr 5 1868
KyLT Ag 9 1873;Ja 23 1895;N 3 1897;Mr 25 1899;S 14 1901;Ag 15,D 9 1903;N 25 1905
KyLoF Mr 5 1868
NNHi Ag 31 1867;Ja 28,My 30 1885;O 6 1886

KENTUCKY herald. w 1873-74||
Ky complete
KyHi Ap 4 1873-Mr 27 1874

KENTUCKY leader. *See* Lexington leader

KENTUCKY loyalist. w Jl 4 1863-
MWA Jl 11,D 5 1863
PLewL O 17 1863

KENTUCKY new-era. w 1850-
MWA Je 10 1853

*KENTUCKY reporter. sw,w Mr 12 1808-Ap 4 1832||
1808-S? 1817 as Reporter. United with Lexington observer to form Lexington observer and Kentucky reporter, later Lexington observer and reporter
sw during sessions of legislature 1808-12
CSmH S 1 1830
DLC [1821-25]-32
ICHi D 22 1830
ICU [1821-30;32]

KyL 1821-F 1,Mr 7-21,Ap 4 1832
MBAt Mr 18 1822;O 13,31 1827;Ap 2 1828;Ag 18 1830
MHi O 29,D 24-31 1821;N 4 1822;My 5-12,N 24,D 8-22 1823;Ja 19,S 20 O 18,N 8,22,D 13 1824;F 7-14,N 28 1825;Ag 4 1827
MWA F 16 1824;Ag 29,S 5-12 1825;Jl 10,Ag 21-28,S 11,O 2-9,N 6,D 1826-27;Ja 16-Je 4,Jl 2,16-23,Ag 6-13,S-D 1828;Mr 4,Ap 8,Je 3,Jl 1,22 S 2,23,O 21,N 25 1829;Ja 20,F 17,Ap 21, Jl 7,Ag 18,O 20 1830;Ja 12,Je 15 1831
NN N 12 1821;Ap 14 1823;S 13 1824;N 14 1825
NNHi My 21 1828;Jl 7,O 27 1830
NcD Ag 21,S 11,O 2 1826[27-28]
OCHi Ja 14 1822
OClWHi Jl 8-15 1850
OHi 1827-Ap 1828
OOxM Mr 5 1828
WHi Ap 21 1823;Jl 24-31 1826

KENTUCKY statesman. sw O 10 1849-S 24 1861; S 1862-65||?
DLC My 7-10 1851;O 19,N 2 1852;Ap 8 1853-60
ICHi Ja-Ap 11,Ag-S 26,O-N 7 1856
ICU Mr 27 1855;Ap 1 1856
KyL 1849-S,D 1850-S 1851;O 1852-My,S 1853-S 1855;S 1856-65
KyLoF O 24 1849;Ja 26,D 21,28 1850;Mr 5-8 1851;Ja 12[Ap 1855-Ag 15 1856]-61
OClWHi Je 8,26 1850
TxU Ag 19 1859

Daily KENTUCKY statesman. d S 24,28 1867||?
ICU S 24,28 1867

Tri-weekly KENTUCKY statesman. sw,tw 1867-72||
1867 as Kentucky statesman (sw)
DLC N 29 1867
ICU Ja 2,11-16,N 10 1868;F 6 1869
KyHi 1868-Mr 19 1873
KyL 1868-72
KyLoF 1868-72
MBAt [1868]69

KENTUCKY whig. w S 22 1825-S 14 1826||
Followed by North American literary and political register
DLC S 22,O 1825-Jl 13 1826
ICU S 22-N 3,D 1825-Mr 2 23-My 4,18-Je 8, 22,Jl 6-13,20(extra)1826
KyLo [1825-26]

Lexington LEADER. d My 1 1888+
1888-93? as Kentucky leader
pub 1888+
DLC 1898
KyU Ap 15 1891;Ap 30 1893;My 7 1898;Je 2 1899
WHi Ap 30 1893

LEXINGTONIAN. w Ja 23 1915-16||?
KyLT Ja 23,Mr 4 1915

MAIL bag. *See* Army mail bag (Knoxville, Tenn.)

MESSENGER weekly. w 1897-98||
KyLT S 24 1898

NATIONAL monitor. w
DLC My 7 1824

NATIONAL unionist. *See* Union standard

NORTH American literary and political register. w S 21 1826-
Follows Kentucky whig
DLC S 21-D 28 1826
ICU S 21-D 21 1826
MWA O 5,D 14 1826

Weekly OBSERVER. 1880-1907 *See* Weekly observer and tobacco growers journal

Lexington daily OBSERVER. d 1885-86||?
KyU D 30 1885

Lexington OBSERVER and reporter. w My 14 1831-73||?
1831-Ap 6 1832 as Lexington observer; Ap 13 1832-My 2 1840 Lexington observer and Kentucky reporter
DLC N 25 1831;Ja 20 1832;Mr 10,N 10-24 1841; Mr 8,30,Ap 13,My 4-18,Je 8 1842;Je 30 1858
ICU My 21,Je 11-D 1831;Ja 13-Mr 9,Ap 13-Jl 5,19 1832-34;Ag 10,S 21,N 23,D 21 1836;My 10 1837;Ap 26,Ag 2 1843:D 13 1845;Je 9 1848;S 18 1861;Je 12 1867
Ky Ap 1845-N 1851
KyHi N 21 1835;D 14 1836;O 25,28,D 13 1837; Je 16 1838;D 16,30 1840-Ja 6,Je 12 1841;Ja 5,1842;Ja 17,F 21,My 4,8,11,14,22,N 27 1844; Ja 15,Mr 22 1845
KyL My 21 1831-36;38-S 2 1840;My 1844-70
KyLoF [1852-Ag 1856]F 1863-Mr 11 1868
MWA My 14 1831;My 17-24,D 1832;Ja 3-10,F-Ap 13,N 7,20-28 1833;Ja 2,16-23,F 13,27,Mr 20(extra)25,Ap 17,My 1,Jl 9-16,Ag-S 10,24,O 8,22-29,N 19-26,D 10-31 1834;Ja 7,28-F,Mr 11,26(extra)1836
NcD Ja 16 1861
OClWHi F 11 1857;My 30 1866
OOxM Ap 26 1832-[My 1833-Jl 1834]
PPiU-D Ap 19 1832
Tx S 16 1857
WHi F 10-Je 2,27-Jl 28 1832;My 1-D 18 1833

Lexington OBSERVER and reporter. sw My 9 1832-Mr 19 1873||
1832-My 9 1840 as Observer and reporter
Suspended Je 13 1833;Ja-F 1835;Jl 19,Ag 27-O 25 1862;O 29 1864-Ja 28 1865
DLC N 7 1832;Jl 7 1852;Ja 21-24 1857;N 28 1840[41-42]My 12-16,Je 16,Jl 7 1849;Je 1863;N 17 1866
ICHi Mr 1 1854
ICU O 24,D 22 1832;D 13-31 1834[Mr 1835-N 1868]
KyL Ag 29 1838-39;My 1844-Ap 1850;55;57-58; N 20-30,D 21 1861-My 24,O 25-D 1862;N 11 1863-O 19 1864;Ja 28 1865-72
MWA Ja 16 1833;S 3 1834;Ag 5 1837;Je 5 1841; Ja 23 1869
NNHi F 22 1862;Je 13 1866
OOxM F 13,O 16 1833;Je 4 1834
PP N 20 1847

KENTUCKY (*Continued*)

LEXINGTON—*Continued*

Lexington daily OBSERVER and reporter. d Ja 1-F 1835||
ICU Ja 6,16-17 1835

OBSERVER and reporter. tw Ja 1-F 26 1835||?
ICU Ja 1-15,18-29,F 1,4-22 1835

Weekly OBSERVER and tobacco growers journal. w 1880-1908||?
1880-1907 as Weekly observer
KyLT Je 15,Jl 19,Ag 3 1901

Lexington daily PRESS. *See* Lexington herald

Lexington daily PRESS-TRANSCRIPT. *See* Lexington herald

Lexington PRESS-TRANSCRIPT. w 1871-1904||?
1871-95? as Lexington press
KyLT Ap 17 1895

PROGRESS of the age. w Je 7 1850-
ICU Je 7 1850
MWA Ap 19 1851

***Lexington PUBLIC advertiser.** sw,w Ja 5 1820-
sw 1820-22?
DLC S 20,N 15-22 1823[Ja-O 1824]
ICHi Ja 31 1824
ICU Ap 15,Je 7,Ag 2,S 6 1823
KyHi F 14,28-My 1,15,29,Je 12-Jl 3,17,Ag-S 4,N 13,27 1824
MBAt Mr 13 1822
MWA Je 12,N 2 1822;My 10,24,Je 28,S 13,N 15-22,D 13 1823;Ja 24-F 7,Mr 27,My 22 1824
OHi My 24 1823

REPORTER. *See* Kentucky reporter

SOUTHERN luminary. w
TxU Ja-O 21 1835

SPIRIT of Washington and Lexington literary journal. w S 7 1832-
DLC O 5 1832
MWA D 7 1832

Lexington STANDARD. w 1892-1912||?
Negro
DLC Ja 27 1900
KyLT Mr 1900-F 7 1903

Lexington morning TRANSCRIPT. d 1878-94||
United with Lexington daily press to form Lexington daily press-transcript, later Lexington herald
KyL 1879-94
KyLT [Ap 1879-94]
KyU Ja 12 1892

Lexington weekly TRANSCRIPT. w 1878-94||
United with Lexington press to form Lexington press-transcript
KyU Ja 20-27,F 17-24,Ap 11-25,Je 13-Jl 18, Ag 1,22-29,O 10-17 1889;Ja 12 1892

TRUE American. w Je 3 1845-O 21 1846||
Ct Jl 8 1846
CtY Jl 8 1845-O 21 1846
ICHi Ag 5-19,N 18,D 9,23 1845-Ja 13,27-F 24,Mr 10,Ap 14-My 5,26,Je 16,30,Jl 15-22,Ag 26,S 15-O 20 1846
ICU Je 10 1845-O 21 1846
IElC S 2 1846
KyLoF O 21 1845
MB Je 17 1845-46
MH complete
MHi N 4 1845
MWA Je 3,24,Jl 1-8,22,Ag 5-12,O 21-28,N 11,D 16-23 1845;Ja-O 21 1846
MiU [1845-46]
NNHi Ag 19,S 9 1846
NSyU Mr 11 1846
OCHi 1845-O 7 1846
WHi D 23 1845-O 21 1846

TRUE American and Western monitor. w Ap 16 1825-
DLC My 21 1825
PP Mr 11,Ap 1-8 1846

UNION standard. sw Ap 8 1864-66||?
1864-S 8 1865 as National unionist
DLC 1864-N 2 1866
KyL 1865-66
KyU Ag 23 1864
MBAt Jl 17-20 1866
OC 1864-Ap 4 1865

***WESTERN monitor.** w,sw Ag 3 1814-Ap 1825||
My 25 1819-20? as Western monitor and Lexington advertiser. United with True American to form True American and western monitor
w 1814-S 1822
DLC 1821-[24]Mr 12 1825
ICU [1821-Ap 1825]
MWA Jl 17,Ag 1821-Ja 15,29-S 3,17-O 1,18-22,29,N 8-12 1822;Mr 11,O 10,17,N 7,14-21,D 2,23,30 1823;Ja 6,F 3,17-20,Ap 13,My 21 1824; Ja 12 1825

WESTERN monitor. (weekly country ed) w O 1 1822-S 29 1824||
ICU [1822-24]
MWA O 8-15,N 19,D 3-10,24-31 1822;F 4,18-25, Mr 18-25,Ap 8,22-Ag 26,S 9-D 16 1823;Ja-F, Mr 9,23-My 18 1824

LONDON

MOUNTAIN echo. *See* Sentinel-echo

London SENTINEL. w 1900-18||
United with Mountain echo to form Sentinel-echo

SENTINEL-ECHO. w 1873+
1873-1917? as Mountain echo
pub 1907+
KyLT Jl 16 1908
VU Jl 20 1888

LOUISA

BIG SANDY news-recorder. w 1885+
1885-1930 as Big Sandy news
KHi S 19 1913;My 15 1914-My 7 1920;S 29 1922
KyBoW S 1 1922

LAWRENCE county recorder. w 1914-30||
United with Big Sandy news to form Big Sandy news-recorder

LOUISVILLE

Louisville ADLER. d Ag-O 1852||?
In German
ICU O 14 1852

ADVERTISER. w
OHi Je 5 1822;D 3 1823;Ap 26 1826

ADVERTISER. sw
IU O 30 1822

ADVERTISER. d
Ct [1833-35]
N O 9-10 1833

AGE. w Ja 4 1879-
ICU Ja-Je 1879

Louisville AMERICAN. w 1918+
KyLo 1922-N 2 1932

AMERICAN democrat and weekly courier. w
KyLo Mr 21-O 3 1846
KyLoF F 1,Je 1845-O 3 1846

Louisville ANZEIGER. sw,d Mr 1 1848+
sw 1848?
Mr 1 1898 Jubilee ed
In German
ICHi S 29 1865
ICU S 8 1849;Jl 23 1852;Jl 26 1853;Ja 14 1894
IU O 16 1884;My 12 1912;S 1917-Je 1918
KyLo My 1905+
MWA Ag 23 1876
NN Mr 1 1898

Louisville ANZEIGER. w 1848+
In German
IU Ja 9,30,F 20-Mr 20,Ap 3-10,My 8,22,Je 5-12,Jl 3,17 1870;Jl 1 1882;Ja 7 1906;Ja 28 1907

Louisville ARGUS. w
In German
IU D 13 1917-Je 13 1918
TxU Je 1892-94

BEOBACHTER am Ohio. w 1845-53||?
In German
ICU Jl 21 1852
MWA F 14 1853

Louisville BULLETIN. tw S 7? 1839-
DLC S 17 1839

Louisville evening BULLETIN. d 1851-62||?
CtY Jl 22 1862
ICU Ag 7 1855;O 13 1856;N 10 1862
KyLo My 11-S 29 1855;O 10 1856-Ja 16 1858
KyLoF O 29 1852;Mr 22-23,25,28,31,Je 16 1853[Ja]Mr 22,S 23,O 7 1862
MWA Ap 19,D 2 1862
Tx D 6-8 1860
WHi Ap 29 1859
—morning ed *See* Louisville daily journal

Louisville weekly BULLETIN. w 1851-
KyBoW [1852]

BULLETIN. w 1879-84||?
Negro
NcD S 24 1881

Tri-weekly CAMP journal. tw
TxU Ja 7 1862

Louisville CHRONICLE. Ja? 1849-
KyLoF F 1,Ag 11 1849

Daily CITY gazette. *See* Daily gazette and reporter

Daily CLIPPER and daily public ledger. d 1845-46||?
1845-Jl 27 1846 as Public ledger
ICU Ap 27-Ag 14 1846
MWA Ap 14 1846

Louisville COMMERCIAL. d D 27 1869-1902||
1871-73,My 18 1874-F 29 1880 as Daily Louisville commercial
A Jl 1874-77;79-81
CtW My 10-12 1893
DLC 1871-1902
ICU S 7,O 26 1884;F 4,Jl 16 1885;Je 30 1889; Mr 28 1890;My 17 1893;Ja 12,My 6,Jl 4 1894; My 13 1901
In Ap 1872-S 1873
Ky 1883-84
KyBoW Je 8,29 1880
KyL 1869-70
KyLo D 29 1869-My,Jl 1873-75;78-Je,O 1890-97
KyLoF My 14,19,Je 16,Ag 14,20 1872;My 1-2 1880;Ag 20 1882;D 1 1889;Mr 3 1892;Je 2 1893;Mr 1,Ag 19 1896
MWA O 3 1871;My 24 1874-N 1875;Ap 1,S 23 1876;O 8 1882(supp)
TKL Ap 21,26,My 11,20,29,Je 4,14,Jl 9,22, Ag 14 1873;My 29 1878
WHi Jl 1892-95

Weekly Louisville COMMERCIAL. w 1869-1902||?
DLC Mr 20,Ap 17-24 1872[73]Jl 14 1875
N Ja 22 1870

Louisville COMMERCIAL record and letter price-current
OClWHi My 11 1865

COMMERCIAL review. w 1855-
KyLo Mr 28 1856-O 16 1857
MWA N 15,30-D 14 1855

Louisville weekly COURIER. w 1843-N 11 1868||
United with Louisville weekly journal to form Weekly courier-journal
ICU N 12 1856
KyLo O 10 1846-56;D 1865-67
KyLoF [O 10 1846-54;58-O 1866]
MWA Jl 1-8,22-N 1868
OCHi Ag 3 1861(extra)

Louisville daily COURIER. d 1844-N 1 1868||
Follows Louisville daily dime. 1844-50 as Louisville morning courier. United with Louisville daily journal to form Louisville courier-journal, later Courier-journal
CSmH Ja 19 1867
CtY Je 9 1866
DLC Mr 20 1849-O 25 1852;O 4 1856;F 17 1858-60
ICU F 22,Ag 7-8 1849;Mr 24 1851(extra)[Ag 1855]O 4 1856;57-59;S 9 1861;Ap 10,My 31 1867
IU Ja 10-12,Mr 20,My 17,Je 6,Jl 30,Ag 5,15-17, 21,S 6,10-11 1861
KyBoW [1854-56;61;66-68]
KyLo Je 1844-48;Jl 1850-S 18 1861;D 4 1865-68
KyLoF Jl 17,S 17 1852;D 29 1856;Ap 16,My 3,10,Ag 11,13,S 12-14,16-18 1861;My 7,10,14, 18 1866
LNH Jl 20 1861
MWA Je 9 1847
MoS Ag 1861
NNHi Ja 3,7 1861
NcD Ag 12,S 4 1861;D 20-21 1867
OCHi O 14-D 1861
OClWHi My 5 1859;Jl 22,S 17 1861
OOxM Jl 16 1851
PBf O 19 1863
T Ja 29,F 15 1862
TH N 4 1861
Tx D 13 1860

COURIER-JOURNAL. d N 8 1868+
Formed by the union of Louisville daily courier, and Louisville daily journal. 1868 as Louisville courier-journal
Mr 25 1913 Southern prosperity ed; Mr 12 1918 George Rogers Clark centennial ed; Mr 2 1919 Marse Henry ed
A O 18 1877-78;80-Je 1881;Ja-S 1882;83-84;Ap-S 1885;86;Ap-Je 1887;O-D 1888;O-D 1890;Jl-Ag 1894;My-Je 1896;98-O 1902
ArHi Mr 8 1876;Mr 6,D 30 1889;My 30 1897; Jl 10 1898
C F 1887-My 4,Ag 29 1888-Mr,Jl 1890-96;Ja-Je 1898
CtY F 14-D 1869
DLC 1868;Jl 10 1874-95;Mr 1896+
IC My 1 1889
ICHi Je 2 1892
ICM Je 27 1878;F 23 1881;Mr 16,D 20 1882 Je 20,S 10 1883;My 14 1884;F 23 1886;Mr 11,N 6 1887;Mr 31 1888;Je 6 1931
ICU D 20 1871;D 11 1872;Jl 9 1873;74-O 1919; Ja 1920;Ap 24 1923-F,My 1924-27;F 1928-Mr, My-S 1929;30;My-Jl 1931
IHi [1917-18]
IU O 7,11,25,30-N 3,28 1918-Jl 3 1919
IaDH O 16 1877-80;Mr 7 1905-14
In [1871]Ap-Je 1875
InRE Ag 8-9 1869
InTI 1912-Je 1925
KHi S 8 1877;Mr 28-Ap 6 1890;Ag 14 1897
Ky 1868+
KyBoW 1891+
KyLo 1868-Je 1872;73-74;Jl 1875+
KyLoF Ja 29,O 2,D 17-20 1871[Ja-Ag 1872] 73-Jl,N 1875;Ag-N 1876;My-Ag 1877;Ja 18 1879[Ap 1880-Mr,N 1881;Je 1883-1900]Je 3 1902;Ap 4-5 1905;Je 16 1906;Mr 12 1918;31+
KyP Ag 23,N 19 1883;Mr 15 1885;Mr 28-29 1890;N 9 1892
KyU N 1 1875;F 16 1882;Ap 25 1886;S 4 1896;Ap 17 1898;Ag 1913+
M Mr 12 1918;Mr 2 1919;My 18 1930;My 8 1932
MWA My 5 Ag 8/9(supp)1869;Ag 25 1871;My 17,Ag 2,O 13 1876;Ag 15-16 1877;Ag 16 1879; O 17 1882;Mr 19 1887;Ag 27,O 26 1890;Jl 30 1912-Ag,O 1913-Ag,O 1914+
MBAt 1868-O 15 1869
MeBa Mr 2 1919
MiU [1887;1922]26+
MoS Mr 25 1913;Mr 12 1918
N O 18 1878
NN Jl 4-5 1876;S 1878-Ja 3 1884;Mr 2 1919
NNC Mr 12 1918;Mr 2 1919
NNHi Mr 3 1869
NcD Jl 4 1873;Ja 28 1876;O 20 1879;Mr 24 1880;S 21 1881;Ag 27 1901;Ja-S 1903;Je-Jl 11, S 1904-Mr,My 1905-My 1908;N 8 1912
NcU Ja 26 1876-Ja 1878
NjWdHi N 13 1879
OCHi F 6 1887;Ap 6 1890
OClWHi D 22 1879;S 9-15 1895;F 21 1897;Ja 13 1901;Mr 2 1919;My 23 1930
OHi Je-S 1880;Ja 28 1888-Je 1891;O 1914-19;D 1920-33
OOxM S 28-29 1869;D 14 1873;Je 11 1874
P Jl 1890-O 1917
PBL Mr 2 1919
PBf Ap 29 1869
PJR Ap 25 1898
PU [1890-91]
T My 21 1880
TKL N 11,17,28-29 1887
Tx Ag 15-16 1869;N 9 1870;My 24 1871;Jl 1904-12
TxGR Mr 12 1918;N 22 1926;O 29 1929
WHi Ap 16 1915+
WaPS [1916]N 14,16-17 1917;N 22 1926;My 7 1933

KENTUCKY (*Continued*)

LOUISVILLE—*Continued*

Weekly COURIER-JOURNAL. w N 18 1868-1917||?
Formed by the union of Louisville weekly courier, and Louisville weekly journal
Mr 2 1919 is Marse Henry ed
CLM Mr 29,Ap 7,N 10-17 1890;Ap 28 1907
CoU 1897;1900-01;S 1906-My 1910
DLC O 13-27 1875
ICM My 19 1879
ICU D 20 1871;D 11 1872
KHi F 20-D 20 1878
KyLo 1871-73;75;78
LSfD Ap 15 1885
MB 1876-Je 1877;N 27 1883
MBAt D 23 1868-75
MWA N 13 1868-F 10,24-Mr 3,Ap 7-14,28-Je, Jl 14 1869-O 5 1870
MiU-C Mr 29 1839;O 24 1844;Mr 2 1919
MoHi N 20 1872;S 18 1885;Ag 30 1901
NN 1880-83
NcD Mr 10,My 5,Ag 4,N 10,D 15,29 1875;Mr 22,Ap 12 1876;O 6,20-27,N 10,D 1,22-29 1879; F 6,My 15,D 11 1882;N 5 1883;My 19,Jl 28 1884;S 14 1885[87-88]-[92-93;96]
NcU Ja 8,F 12,Ap 16 1883
RP Mr 2 1919
TKL Mr 25 1873;Mr 11 1874;My 21,Je 4,Jl 2-9,30,Ag 13,S 17 1873
TM S 12 1878
TSS My-D 1881;O-D 1882;My-Jl 1884;Ja-Mr 1885;Ap-Je 1886;S 17-30 1887;Ja-F 1896;Ja-Mr 1897;My-Ag 1898
TU-J Mr 23 1885;S 26 1887;My 28 1888
Tx S 15 1869
TxU Mr 2,13 1870;Jl 15,N 18,D 9-16 1874;Ja 27,O 12 1875;D 29 1879-80;Ja 3,Ap 5,O 23,D 2 1881;My 6 1882;S 30 1883;Jl 20,S 7 1884
WHi Jl 1888-Jl 1889;Jl 1 1895

Twice-a-week COURIER-JOURNAL. sw
OCHi Jl 17 1897
WHi Jl 17 1897

Louisville daily DEMOCRAT. d 1843-D 31 1868||
1843?-Ja 8 1862 as Daily Louisville democrat. Merged with Courier-journal
CtY Ag 22 1851
•DLC O 28 1844;Ag 21 1845-48;S 18 1852;F 5,Je 18 1853;57-N 8 1864;67-68
ICHi Je 23 1863;S 30,O 2-3,19 1865
ICU N 27 1844;F 9 1848;Jl 10-11,18,O 4 1856; 62-64
IU F 8,12,15,19,23,27-28 1861
In Ap 1855-N 1860[62-68]
Ky 1853-Jl 1856
KyBoW [1851-62]
KyLT Jl 22,Ag 2,25,S 12,O 31,N 2 1860
KyLo Ja 13 1851-Je 29 1854;55-Ap 17 1869
KyLoF My 26 1848;Jl 1 1852[Ja-O 1854]My 23 1855;My 25 1861;Ja 2,4,S 22,O 2-3,7,16-17, 23 1862;O 1,12,D 5 1863;S 21 1864;F 19,Mr 18 1865;Mr 17-18,21,28,Ap 5,8 1866;F 21 1867
MBAt Ap 15 1865
MWA Ap 5 1848;S 2(extra)N 27 1852;Je 7 1862;Ap 4 1865
OClWHi Je 19 1864
TC S 4 1864;F 21,Mr 3 1865
Tx D 9 1860

Louisville weekly DEMOCRAT. w 1843-68||
Merged with Courier-journal
KyLo Mr 21-O 3 1846[52]
KyLoF Jl 23,Ag 27 1845;S 10 1851;My 5 1852; Ag 3-10,S 21 1853;Ja 11,25-F 1,22,Mr 1,22, Ap 5,26,My 24,Je 7,Ag 16,30,S 27,N 15-22 1854;F 14,Mr 21-Ap 4,My,Ag 8,O 10 1855;F 20,Mr 5,19-26,My 14 1856;D 16 1857;My 12 1858
MWA Ap 7 1852
OClWHi S 26 1855

Evening DEMOCRAT. d My? 1854-O 1860||?
Followed by Evening news
ICU S 18,20 1855

DEMOCRATIC banner. w Ja 12 1844-
IU Ap 6 1844

Louisville daily DIME. d Mr 11 1843-Je 1? 1844||
Followed by Louisville daily courier
KyLo F 27-Je 1 1844

Louisville daily DISPATCH. d 1897-1900||?
ArHi Je 26 1898
Ky 1899-1900
KyLoF Ap 29 1900

Weekly DOLLAR democrat. w
TxU S 22 1855

Louisville ENQUIRER. w 1837-
Ct D 30 1837
DLC Ap 28 1838

EXAMINER. w Je 19 1847-D 8 1849||
CtY complete
ICU complete
In 1841
MB [Je 26 1847-49]
MHi Je 19 1847;D 9 1848;Mr 10 1849
MWA Je 19,Jl 17,Ag 7,21-D 4,25 1847;48-49
MiU Jl 24 1847
NSyU D 16 1848;My 5 1849;Ag 1850
NcD O 28-N 4,25 1848;Je 16,S 29 1849
OClWHi Je 19-O 2 1847;Ja 6,Jl 15,O 28 1848;F 24-Jl 7 1849
WHi 1847-Mr 3 1849
TxU Je 19 1847

Louisville daily EXPRESS. d My 19? 1862-
CtY Jl 21 1862
KyLo Ap 18-30 1869
MBAt My 20 1862

Louisville evening EXPRESS. d
KyLo Ap 20-D 31 1869

FOCUS. w N 22 1826-Ja 31 1832||
1826-Mr 21 1827 as Focus of politics, commerce and literature. Merged with Louisville weekly journal
CSmH Jl 19 1827(extra)Ag 24 1830
CSt S 8 1829
DLC 1826-28;Jl 7,21-28,S 1,22,D 15 1829-Ja 5,19,D 14 1830;Ja 4-11 1831
ICU N 22 D 1826;Mr 1827-N 17 1829
MWA D 20-27 1826;F 7-21,Mr 14,Ap 25-My 2, Je 5,19,Ag 7-14,S-N 20,D 4 1827;Mr 11-18,Jl 15-Ag 12 1828;O 27 1829
NcD Ag 4,14 1827;Ag 5-12 1828
PHi D 27 1826
RPB Ag 3 1830

Louisville daily FOCUS. d Ja 28 1831-Ja 30 1832||
Merged with Louisville daily journal
DLC Je 4 1831
ICU complete
KyLo complete

Louisville GAZETTE. sw O 25 1825-26||?
Follows Morning post
Suspended F 7-Mr 17 1826
DLC [N 8 1825-My 26 1826]
ICU Je 23 1826
MWA S 15 1826

Daily GAZETTE and reporter. d My 1836-
1836-Ap 1839 as Louisville city gazette
DLC N 30 1840
ICU Ag 8 1839
MWA My 23 1840
N F 21 1837
OClWHi S 28 1837;Ja 2-3 1839;S 16-17 1841;F 12,My 9,30,Ag 10,O 31,N 1,11 1842

Daily GLOBE. d 1875||
KyLo S 1,D 3 1875

GUARDIAN. w My 1 1858-62||
CaOTA Mr 31 1860
DGU 1858-Ap 20 1861
KyBN 1858-Je 22 1861
MoS Je 1861

HALCYON. w Ag 1 1841-
DLC Ag 1 1841

Daily Louisville HERALD. d Ag 3 1832-F 28 1834||
1832-N 30 1833 as Daily Louisville herald and commercial gazette
DLC N 3 1832;S 25,D 14 1833
ICU N 28 1832-[34]
KyLo D 14 1833-F 10 1834[Ja 14-F 5 1834]
TH complete

Louisville HERALD. w 1832-F 1834||?
1832?-N 6? 1833 as Louisville herald and commercial gazette
Ct [1833]
DLC Jl 3 1833
MWA O 3,24 1832
OOxM N 28 1832-F 1834

Louisville HERALD. tw
ICU Ja 7/8 1834

Louisville HERALD. d 1905-O 1925||
United with Evening post to form Herald-post
KyLo Ja 7 1905-25
KyLoF Jl 2 1906

HERALD-POST. d N 1925+
Formed by the union of Louisville herald and Evening post
DLC 1925-27
Ky 1928
KyLo 1925+
KyLoF O 8 1925;31+

Louisville INDUSTRIAL and commercial gazette. w 1855-73||?
KyLo N 25 1865-N 24 1866
TxU My 13 1871

Louisville daily JOURNAL. d N 24 1830-N 7 1868||
United with Louisville daily courier to form Louisville courier-journal, later Courier-journal
Suspended Ag 1855-O 1856
Ct [1831]
CtSp Ag 23 1844
CtY Mr 1863-67
DLC D 13 1830;Mr 10 1831;N 1 1832;Ag 20 1833;N 2 1840;Ap 19-D 1841;Je 20 1844;Mr 26 1849-52;Je 22 1862;Je 8 1863;F 10 1864[Ap-D 1865]Ja 4-F 27 1867-N 7 1868
ICHi [S-O 1865]
ICU My 25-26 1831;Ag 7 1855;O 13 1856;N 10 1862;Mr 3 1858
IU O 12 1863
In Ap 30 1840-D 4 1841
Ky 1853-56;58-68
KyBoW [1861-64]
KyG [1831-32;37;41]
KyGC [1831-32;37]39;41
KyLo D 1840-My 22,N 24 1841-My 23 1842;N 24 1843-N 22 1845;N 25 1846-My 23,N 24 1847-My 23,N 25 1848-My 23 1849;50-Ap 24, Ag 22 1854-68
KyLoF Ap 9 1835;D 21 1836;Mr 11 1840;Ag 11 1847;N 15 1852;Ja 5 1860;Ja 10,18,22,30,F 4,7, 19,S 5,O 14 1862;Je 16 1863;O 2 1864;F 22 1867
KyU Je 10,Jl 15 1861
MB My 30-Jl 12 1862;Jl-S,D 29-31 1864;F 13 1865
MBAt S 30 1863-Je 1864;65-68
MHi My 22 1840
MWA Je 12 1835;N 29 1837;My 20 1841;Je 8 1847;Ap 28 1855;Ap 22-24,29,My 8,D 4-6 1856; My 30 1857;My 17 1860;Mr 12,D 5,12,18-19 1861;Ap 10 1862
MdS S 1861
MdSM Jl 25 1844
N O 4-5 1833;Ap 17,21-22,24 1850
NN My 10 1832
NNHi Ag 30 1845
NcD Mr 1 1866
OClWHi Je 7 1837;Ag 13 1862;D 30 1863;Ja 25,F 19,Ap 27 1864;Ap 7,My 11 1865
P-M O 16 1833
PBf O 19 1863
RW Ja 4 1861
TKL Jl 13 1863;Ap 26 1864;D 4 1867
TxHuS Ap 10 1864
TxU My 20 1836-Mr 9 1837;39-40;42-45;S 8 1865-S 8 1868
WHi My 14,S 19 1865
—Evening ed *See* Louisville evening bulletin

Louisville JOURNAL. sw N 24 1830-
ICU Je 26 1839;My 5-6 1841;My 5-6,28-31 1848
N Ag 5-11 1845
NNHi Jl 15,S 7,D 7 1831
NcD [1841-Jl 17 1845]

Louisville weekly JOURNAL. w 1831-N 1 1868||
United with Louisville democrat to form Weekly courier-journal
CSmH Je 24 1835;Ag 12 1846
CtY Mr 10-Ap 21,My 5,19 1863-Je,Jl 8 1864; 65;Je 14,O 13-20,D 1 1866
DLC O 27 1852;F 11 1857;Ap 22-Je 1862
GAtCo My 20 1840
ICHi Ag 15,29-O 10,31,N 21,D 5 1855
ICM Je 10 1857
ICU Je 26 1839;Je 23 1847;Ap 12-19,My 31,Ag 23 1848;F 12 1851
IHi My 13 1840
In My-Jl 1841;D 1842-N 1856[57]
KHi D 17 1856;Jl 22 1857;Ja 16,F 13 1861
KyBoW [1862-67]
KyLT S 27 1854
KyLo My 21 1845-S 22 1847;My 28 1849-Jl 10 1850;Ag 15 1851-My 10 1852;S 16 1853;My 24 1854[O 7 1857-S 26 1865]
KyLoF Ap 16-My 1845;F 25 1846;S-D 15 1847;S 6 1848;My 2,23-S 12 1849;Mr 6 1850;F 15-Je 7,21-Ag 23,S 13,27,N 15 1854;My-Jl 4,25-Ag 15,29,S 12-19 1855;Ja 21,F 4 1862;O 2 1866
MWA My 16-D 1844;My 14-Ag 13,S 1845-[46]-51;Ja 21-28,F 18-25,Mr 31-Ap 7,Jl 7,16,Ag 13,S 8-15,O 1 1852;My 3,S 6,O 11,N 22,D 20 1854;Ag 15 1855;F 4 1862;N 10-17,D 15 1863; My 9,23-N 7,D 12 1865-My 1,15-Jl 24,Ag 14, O 1866-Ag 18 1868
MoHi Jl 17 1844
N Ja 10 1838
NcD D 12 1855-Ap 1 1857 O 6 1868
NcU My 20,Je 17 1840;Ag 21 1844
OC O 25 1848
OCHi F 20 1850
OOxM My 16 1832-Jl 2 1834
TU Ag 3 1860
Tx Mr 19-Je 11 1861

KATHOLISCHER glaubensbote. w 1866-1923||
In German
IU Jl 31-S 11 1867;D 20 1917-N 22 1923
TxU N 19 1891-D 13 1894

Daily KENTUCKIAN. d 1842-43||?
DLC Ja 1-N 8 1843

KENTUCKIAN. w 1842-43||?
ICU Ja 3-24,F 14,Mr 18-25,Ap 8-15,My 20,Je 24,O 21 1843

***KENTUCKY herald and mercantile advertiser.** w N 18 7?-
IU Je 20 1821

KENTUCKY sun. w 1915-16||?
KyLo Ja 14-Ag 26 1915

Louisville daily LEDGER. d 1871-76||
KyBoW [1872;74]
KyLo F 16 1871-74
KyLoF F 12,Ag 19 1872;Ap 7 1874

Louisville weekly LEDGER. w 1871-76||
TU-J Ap 16,S 10,O 22 1873

Daily MESSENGER. d My 12? 1840-41||?
DLC My 15 1840
ICU Ap 9 1841

MICROSCOPE. *See* Microscope and general advertiser (New Albany, Ind.)

Louisville NATIONAL union press. *See* Louisville daily union press

Evening NEWS. d N 1860-79||
Follows Evening democrat. 1861-62? as Daily evening news. Merged with Evening post
CtY Je 11 1861;Ag 9 1862;My 11,S 16 1864
ICU Ap 15 1865
KyLo Ap 15 1865
KyLoF My 25 1861;Ja 2,4,S 22,O 2-3,7,16-17,23 1862;O 12 1863;S 21 1864

Louisville NEWS. d 1899-1902||
ICU My 13 1901

OHIO Falls express. w 1878-1904||?
Negro
ICU Jl 11 1891

Evening POST. d 1878-O 31 1925||
United with Louisville herald to form Herald-post
DLC S 21 1898-1925
ICU S 5 1884;Jl 16 1885;Je 29 1889;Je 1 1892; D 17 1898;Jl 12 1900;My 13 1901;Jl 30 1904
KyLo My 1878-Mr 1892;Ja 1893-O 1925
KyLoF Je 2 1893;Je 14 1894;N 2 1901;Je 15 1905;Je 13 1906;Ja 9 1909
MsSM Ap 1914
TJT Jl 24 1900
WaPS [1916-19]

Morning POST and commercial advertiser. w,sw F 12 1822-O? 1825||
Followed by Louisville gazette
DLC [Ja 13 1824-Ag 16 1825]
ICU F 14-18,Ag 29-S 2 1823
MBAt D 12 1823
MWA Ja 21 1825

Louisville PRICE CURRENT and commercial register. w
DLC N 10 1832
MWA Ap 25 1840

KENTUCKY (*Continued*)

LOUISVILLE—*Continued*

*Louisville PUBLIC advertiser. w,sw,tw Je 30 1818-D 31 1928||
1818-Ja 19 1819 as Public advertiser. Followed by Louisville public advertiser (d)
w 1818-Ja 19 1819;sw Ja 23 1819-S 19 1829
DLC 1821-Ja 16,Je 12,Ag 28 1830;Ja 21,D 11 1832;O 2-8 1839
ICU [1821-26;28-29]F 17 1844
IU N 28 1840
KyFM O 10 1821
KyU N 1 1828
MWA Ja 6 1827;S 15 1832
N Ag 25,S 1,O 13-N 28 1827
NcD [1821-22;28]
OClWHi Jl 3 1840

Louisville PUBLIC advertiser. tw 1819?-38||
ICU N 12-13 1832;F 8-9,22-23,Mr 15-16,25-26, Jl 8-9 1833;[Mr-N 1834]Ja 26-27,F 20-21,My 22-23 1835;Ap 6-7 1836;[F,Ap,N 1837;Ja,My, O 1838]
MWA 1821-[O-D 7 1822]Jl 2 1823;Jl 10,Ag 11, O 16,27,D 8-11 1824[Jl 1825-S 1826]F 17,Jl 11 1827-N 1828[Je-D 1829]

Louisville PUBLIC advertiser. (for the country) w,sw 1826?-Jl 9 1842||
1827 as Louisville weekly public advertiser.
w 1826-38,Ja 25 1840-42;sw 1839-Ja 25 1840
ICU Ja 28,My 20,Je 24,Jl 15,29 1826[27]F 2 1828]S 28 1833;Ap 15,Jl 1,15,N 11 1837[Ap 1838-Jl,N 1839;Ja-O 1840]N 20 1841;F 12,Je 18 1842

Louisville PUBLIC advertiser. d Ja 1 1830-Jl 9 1842||
Follows Louisville public advertiser (tw) Je 14-D 31 1830 as Daily Louisville public advertiser
CSmH Jl 12 1832
Ct [1827-28;36-37]
DLC Ja 18-D 1830;Ja 8-13,Mr 11,Ap 28,Je 17, Ag 5 1831;My 25,Ag 24,O 8 1832;Jl 8,Ag 21 1833;Jl 18,Ag 22 1835;My 1,O 2-9 1839;Ja 22, N 9,D 11 1840;Ja-My 14 1841
ICU [1830-38]40-O 1841
KyBoW Ap 16 1831
KyHi O 4 1834
KyLoF F 27,Mr 5,19,Ap 9-23,My 7-21,Je 11-18,Jl 2,Ag 27,S 3,N 26 1836;Mr 25,Ap 8,My 20-Je 3,17,Jl 1-15,S 9,23 1837;Ja 6-20,F 27 1838;Je-Jl 1839;D 19-23 1840;N 20 1841;Ap 30 1842;Ja 9 1844
KyU N 1828
MWA [Ja 1-22;Jl 3-Ag 13]-O 7,N 29-30,D 14-20,27-28 1830
WHi Ag 18 1827;Ja 19 1830

PUBLIC ledger. *See* Louisville clipper and daily public ledger

Daily STANDARD. d Mr 27 1844-
DLC Mr 29 1844

Louisville weekly SUN. w 1842-
Title varies: Weekly sun and advertiser
ICU Ag 20,N 22 1842

Daily Louisville TIMES. d F 28 1852-D 31 1856||
Followed by Paducah tri-weekly herald (Paducah)
CSmH Ag 28 1853
DLC Mr 1852-56
ICU Ag 9-11,15-18,S 20 1855
Ky 1853-54;Ja-Je 1856
KyLo Ja 1-Je 28 1856
KyLoF Ap 1,Ag 1 1855;O 17 1856
MWA Ag 10 1852;Ap 9(extra)1853;Mr 1,N 30 1854;Ja 12,30,N 28 1855

Louisville TIMES. d My 1 1884+
1884 as Evening times
A My 1906-Ja 1908
CtW My 9-11 1893
DLC Ap 24,My 15,21,30,Je 22-23 1885;98;1910+
ICU S 5 1884;Jl 16 1885;Je 29 1889;Ap 29,S 21 1891;My 31-Je 2 1892;S 14 1896;My 13 1901
KHi S 9-14 1895
KyLo 1884-89;91-Mr,Je 1900+
KyLoF Ap 29 1891;Je 2 1893;Ap 5 1905;Je 15 1906;Mr 5 1910
KyP S 19 1890
KyU Mr 10[Ap]My 4-7 1898
MHi Mr 12 1918

Louisville daily UNION press. d Ap 18 1864-D 30 1865||
Ap-? 1864 as Louisville national union press
CtY My 30,Ag 28 1865
DLC 1865
ICHi O 7,21,N 17 1865
ICU [Ap 20-Ag 1864]
KyBoW [1865]
KyHi Ja 7,Ap 10-11,15,17-29,My 1-4 1865
KyLo 1865
MBAt Ap 15,17,22 1865
MWA Ap 19 1865
OClWHi Ap 19,21,My 4,Jl 22 1865

Louisville weekly UNION press. w S 7 1864-
MBAt N 30 1864
OClWHi My 31,Jl 19 1865

UNION volunteer. w My 8-Jl 10 1863||?
DLC Jl 10 1863(facsimile)
ICHi Jl 10 1863
NbHi Jl 10 1863

Tägliches Louisville VOLKSBLATT. d 1861-82||?
In German
ICU S 5 1866
KyLo [1871]
MWA Ag 23,27 1876

Wöchentliches Louisville VOLKSBLATT. w 1861-82||?
In German
MWA Ja 31 1866

WESTERN American. *See under* St. Louis, Mo.

McKEE

JACKSON county sun. w 1922+
1922-My 3 1926 as Laurel county sun
pub 1922+

LAUREL county sun. *See* Jackson county sun

MADISONVILLE

GLENN'S graphic. sw,w 1889-1907||
KyM complete

HOPKINS county gleaner. sw 1883-85||?
KyM 1885

Madisonville HUSTLER. sw,d 1888+
Title varies: Hustler; Daily hustler d 1910-11
ICU F 24 1893
KyM 1889-98;1910-13;17

Madisonville JOURNAL. d,sw 1906-11||?
KyM Ja-My 1909

KENTUCKY times. *See* Madisonville times

Madisonville daily MESSENGER. d 1918+
pub 1925+
KyM 1925+

SOUTHERN Kentucky register. w
TxU 1860-Mr 11 1861

Madisonville TIMES. w 1868-88||?
1868-71? as Kentucky times
KyM 1885-88
Tx Mr 18 1869-My 17,31-N 15 1871

MARION

CRITTENDEN press. w 1879+
1908?-20 as Crittenden record-press
KyBoW [1915]29+

CRITTENDEN record. w 1904-08||?
United with Crittenden press to form Crittenden record-press, later Crittenden press

MAYSVILLE

Maysville BULLETIN. w 1862-1930||
KyHi [1872-79]
MHi Jl 1 1869
NcD Jl 4 1901
TxU O 13,27 1864

Daily BULLETIN. d 1882+
OClWHi S 13 1913

CAMPAIGN flag. w Mr 24-D 1 1848||?
ICU Mr 24,Ap,My 12-Jl,Ag 11-S,O 20-N 3,D 1 1848
KyP Mr 24 1848

*Maysville EAGLE. w Je 1814-87||?
1814-N 8 1826 as Eagle
CSmH Ag 24 1830
CtY Ja 18 1831;F 2 1832
DLC My 25 1825-[29]Ja 5-12 1830;Ja 5-15,D 13 1831;Ja 2 1834;N 28 1840;Mr-O 1845
ICHi Ja 19 1832
ICU My 26 1824-My 1836;My 17-31 1837;Jl 24 1839;Ja 10 1844;Mr 1845-N 3 1847
KyHi F 19-D 3 1873[75-76;78-79]
KyLo D 1886
MWA D 13 1826-[27]28;O 16 1844;Ja 14 1846
MdBJ Jl 29 1846
NcD Je 18 1828
PM Ap 16 1845
TKL Ag 12 1874

Tri-weekly Maysville EAGLE. sw,tw N 7 1835-74||?
1835-45 as Maysville eagle (sw)
DLC Je 21 1853
ICU 1835-F 24,28,My 13 1852-My 1855;O 1856-58
Ky Ag 1857-Mr 1858
KyHi Ja-Jl 1855
KyU Ag 27 1859

Maysville ENTERPRISE. w 1879-
KyHi N 1 1879

EXPRESS. w
KyLo Ja 7 1857-O 21 1859

HENRY Clay bugle. w Mr 23-O 31 1844||
DLC My 23 1844
ICU Mr 23-S 5,26-O 10,24-31 1844
MWA Mr 23,Ag 1 1844
OClWHi O 31 1844

Maysville HERALD. tw,d F 19 1847-50||?
d D 11 1848-F 17 1849
ICU [1847]-F 17 1849

KENTUCKY flag. w Ag 12 1846-
1846-N 3 1847 as Fleming flag (Flemingsburg and Mt Sterling)
ICU O 20-D 15 1847;Ja-My 3,17-Ag 9,30,S 13,27-N 22,D 6 1848
IU Ag 28 1846

Daily KENTUCKY flag. d D 10 1848-49||?
D 10-15 1848 as Daily Maysville Kentucky flag
ICU D 12-15,19-21,23-28,30-31 1848[Ja-Mr 14 1849]

KENTUCKY review. tw O 1841-
DLC O 9 1841

Maysville MONITOR. w
DLC Ja 10 1833;Ja 4 1838-S 2 1841

NEW Maysville republican. *See* Maysville republican

Daily PUBLIC ledger. d 1892+
OClWHi S 4 1913

Maysville REPUBLICAN. w 1867-90||?
Jl 8 1882-D 13 1884 as New Maysville republican
DLC F 18 1871;Ap 20 1872;Mr 29,My 24 1873; Mr 18 1882-D 27 1884
KyHi [1875-79]

SPIRIT of '44. w 1844||?
MnHi Ag 15 1844

TIPPECANOE banner and old soldiers shield.
OHi O 27 1840

VINDICATOR. w My 26 1842-
DLC My 26 1842

WESTERN star. w
DLC N 7 1843

MIDDLESBORO

Middlesboro NEWS. w 1889-90||?
CtW N 13 1890

THREE states. w 1914+
pub 1914+

MIDWAY

BLUE Grass clipper. w F 4 1875+
pub F 1922+
NNHi O 23 1890

MILLS POINT

COMMERCIAL herald. w My 6 1841-
DLC My 6,Je 10-17,Jl 15,29 1841

MONTICELLO

WAYNE county news. w O 22 1891-92||?
ICU D 10 1891;F 25 1892

WAYNE county outlook. w My 26 1904+
pub 1904+

MOREHEAD

Morehead ADVANCE. w 1895-99||
Followed by Mountaineer

MOUNTAINEER. 1902-17||?
Follows Morehead advance. Followed by Rowan county news

ROWAN county news. w 1918+
Follows Mountaineer
pub 1926+

MORGANFIELD

Morganfield SUN. w,sw 1886-1924||
KyMoU Je 1894-1924

UNION county advocate. w Ap 1 1924+
pub 1924+
KyBoW 1929+

MORGANTOWN

GREEN RIVER republican. w 1885+
pub 1885+
KyBow 1929+

MOUNT STERLING

Mount Sterling ADVOCATE. sw 1890+
pub 1890+

Mount Sterling DEMOCRAT. w 1877-83||?
United with Kentucky sentinel to form Sentinel-democrat

FLEMING flag. *See* Kentucky flag (Maysville)

SENTINEL-DEMOCRAT. w 1867+
1867-83? as Kentucky sentinel
KyLT Jl 22 1898

Mount Sterling WHIG. w 1829-30||?
CSmH Je 12 1830

MURRAY

CALLOWAY news. w 1879-83||?
KyP O 16 1879

NEW CASTLE

New Castle ADVERTISER. w 1832-
DLC Ja 5 1833;Ja 31 1834

NEWPORT

FREE South. w 1851-65||?
1851?-Ja? 1858 as Kentucky weekly news
DLC S 3 1858;Ja 7,F 11 1859[Mr-D 1865]
ICHi S 27 1865
KHi N 30 1864
MBAt Ap 19 1865
MHi My 18 1857;O 1 1858;Ag 13 1860
MWA Ja 8-22,O 29-N 12,D 31 1858-Ja 21,F-Mr 18,Ap-My 13 1859;N 2 1864;F 1 1855;Mr 14 1866

KENTUCKY journal. tw,d 1876-94||?
tw 1876-90?
NcD Je 16 1881
WHi Jl 6 1891-Ja 2 1893

KENTUCKY weekly news. *See* Free south

Daily evening LEADER. d 1859?-
MBAt Ag 10,23,31,S 13 1866

Newport and Covington daily NEWS. d Mr 7 1850-
DLC N 16 1850
KyU O 29 1850
MWA Ag 5 1856

KENTUCKY (*Continued*)

NICHOLASVILLE

Nicholasville DEMOCRAT. w My 17 1859-
MWA Ag 30 1859;Mr 14 1861
NSyU My 30 1861

JESSAMINE journal. w 1873+
KyU My 6,S 7 1877

Nicholasville NEWS. w 1883+
pub 1904+

OLIVE HILL

CARTER county herald. w Ja 1 1904+
1904-12 as Olive Hill times; 1912-14 Progressive
pub 1904+

PROGRESSIVE. *See* Carter county herald

Olive Hill TIMES. *See* Carter county herald

ONEIDA

Oneida MOUNTAINEER. w 1915?-
KHi D 15 1918

OWENSBORO

Owensboro' BULLETIN. w O 8 1842-
DLC O 8 1842

Owensboro EXAMINER. w Ja 1 1875-80||
Merged with Owensboro daily messenger
KyO 1875-78

Owensboro GAZETTE. w Ap 10 1852-54||?
Ky 1852;Ap 1853-Ap 1854

Owensboro INQUIRER. d Je 5 1884+
pub 1896+
ICU N 18 1893-F 23 1894
Ky 1918-19
KyU Jl 4 1915
VHi My 28 1896

Owensboro daily MESSENGER. tw,d 1880+
1880-82 as Messenger and examiner
pub 1880+
KyO F 4 1896-Mr 15 1901
VHi O 17 1897

Owensboro MESSENGER-INQUIRER. w 1875+
Sunday ed of Owensboro daily messenger and Owensboro inquirer
MWA Je 19 1932

Owensboro MONITOR. w Ag 13 1862-74||
Suspended fall of 1864-My 1865
KyO 1860;63;65-66
KyOG D 24 1862
MWA My 1 1867

Owensboro daily TRIBUNE. d
Ky S 1895-Ap 1896
KyO F 4 1896;Je 3 1898

OWENTON

Owen NEWS-HERALD. w 1869+
1869-1902 as Owen news
KyLT F 14 1901

PADUCAH

Paducah weekly AMERICAN. w N 7 1854-
KyLoF N 14 1854;F 14-Mr,Ap 11-18,My 2-9,Je-Jl,Ag 8-15,S 5,O 3,31 1855

Paducah daily DEMOCRAT. d
KyP [Ja-Ap 17 1854]

Paducah DEMOCRAT. w 1851-
DLC O 9 1852

Sunday EYE. w Jl 10 1887-
Ky Jl 10,Ag 28,S 18 1887

FEDERAL union. d 1864-65||?
DLC [Ja 26-Ag 11 1865]
KyP Ap 7 1865

FEDERAL union. w 1864-65||?
TxU Ag 31 1865

Paducah tri-weekly HERALD. tw Ja 1857-71||?
Follows Daily Louisville times (Louisville)
DLC 1859-Je 19 1860
KyP Ap 12,Jl 12 1870

Paducah daily HERALD. d Ap? 1866
Ky Ag 4-5 1866
MWA Jl 4 1866

Paducah weekly JOURNAL. w
KyLoF Mr 29,Jl 5-19 1855

Paducah daily KENTUCKIAN. d 1861-78||?
KyP F 14 1872-Je 21,30 1878
TKL Ap 29 1868

NEWS-DEMOCRAT. d 1872-Je 1929||
1872-1900? as Paducah daily news. United with Paducah evening sun to form Sun-democrat
KyP Je 29 1883;Ja 1,My 31,Je 26,Ag 11,15,O 17,N 1,5,10 1884;My 11,20-21 1885;F 13,15,17-18,22 1886;Ja 1,Ap 23,Je 17,23,Jl 2,O 19 1887; Ja 1,My 15 1888;Jl 1905-29

Daily REGISTER. d 1884-1909||
1884-94 as Daily standard (title varies slightly)
KyP N 24 1884;Ja 22-29 1888;Je 20 1891;Je 3 1894

REGISTER. w 1884-1909||
1884-94 as Standard
KyP Jl 1905-07

Paducah REPUBLICAN. w S 8 1887-88||?
KyP S 8 1887

Daily REPUBLICAN. d 1888||?
KyP Je 21-30 1888

SOUTH-WESTERN Kentuckian. w
DLC Mr 27 1844

STANDARD. *See* Register

SUN-DEMOCRAT. d 1896+
1896-Je 1929 as Paducah evening sun
KyP 1905+

Weekly TRUTH. w N 20 1887-
KyP N 20 1887

Sunday TRUTH. w Ja 25 1891-
KyP Ja 25-My 24 1891

Paducah UNION. w
KyP D 24 1887;Jl 1905-07

UNION picket guard. w O 2? 1861-
ICHi O 30 1861

WEST Kentuckian. w 1844-
KyLoF My 9 1849

PAINTSVILLE

Paintsville HERALD. w 1900+
KHi Ja 7 1907-Ag 13 1925
KyBoW D 20 1923

PARIS

Paris weekly ADVERTISER. w O 20 1827-
Ct O 20,N 24 1827;Mr 1,15,My 10 1828
KyHi O 20 1827-O 11 1828
MWA Ja 5 1828

BOURBON news. sw 1881+
pub 1881+

Semi-weekly BOURBON sun. sw 1880-82||?
KyLT S 16 1881

***KENTUCKIAN-citizen.** w,sw F 1808—
1808-86 as Western citizen
w 1808-93?
pub 1866+
DLC [1824-32;40;50-51;56;59;60;62;64;66]
ICHi N 16 1839
ICU 1824-31;Je 15,S 14 1832;F 14 1834;D 16 1836-Ja 6 1837;O 25 1839;Jl 31 1840;Ja 28-F 18,Mr-My 13,Je 3-24,Jl 15-22,Ag 5-S 9 1842; N 3,D 22 1843;Ja 19,Jl 19,S 27 1844;49;D 6 1850;51;Ja 2,N 12 1852;O 19 1855;56;59[60-62]63
KyHi D 16 1826;N 8 1828
KyL 1870-72
KyLT [1821-S 1826]
KyLoF My 11,Je 8,29,S 7,28 1849;Ap 16,30 1852;Jl 8,22 1853;Je 30,Jl 14,Ag 4,D 29 1854; Mr 2,30,Ap 13-My 18,Je-Jl,Ag 10,24-S 14,28-O 5 1855;Jl 7 1928;Jl 18 1934
KyU My 6 1826
MWA Mr 7 1862
NcD My 27 1893;Mr 6 1897;Je 10 1899;Mr 5 1887(extra)Mr 17 1888
OClWHi Jl 15,29 1826

KENTUCKY state flag. w 1847?-
KyLoF Je 20 1855
NcD F 4 1857

Paris TRUE Kentuckian. w F 22 1866-86||
United with Western citizen to form Kentuckian-citizen
ICU Mr 27 1872
KyHi Ja 13-20,F 10,Mr 3-10,Ap 9,21-Je 2,23, Jl-Ag 11,S-O 1875;Ja 26-Je 21,Jl 5-12,Ag 9-O 4,18,N 1 1873
KyLT Jl 4 1877;Mr 10 1880
NcD Ja 27-F 3,N 17 1869;Mr 9 1870;Ag 9 1871;N 13 1869(supp)

WESTERN citizen. *See* Kentuckian-citizen

PIKEVILLE

PIKE county news. w 1913+
pub 1923+

YOUNG mountaineer. w 1908-10||?
CHi Jl 3 1908-Ap 25 1910

PRINCETON

BANNER. w 1871-1905||
KyBoW Ag 30 1883-O 1892;Mr 20 1903
KyPrL complete

CALDWELL county times. w D 1925+
pub 1925+
KyBoW 1929+

Princeton EXAMINER. w 1838?-
DLC Jl 16 1841
N O 2 1840

Princeton twice a week LEADER. w,sw 1902+
1902-28? as Princeton leader (w)
pub [1902-13]+
KyBoW Je 26,Ag 14,S 21-25 1917

PROVIDENCE

Providence ENTERPRISE. sw 1902+
KyU Ag 20 1915

RICHMOND

CLIMAX-Madisonian. w,sw 1887-1917||?
1887-1915 as Climax
ICU D 11 1895
KyLT Ap 6 1898

CONVERSATIVE. w S 13? 1865-
ICHi O 4 1865

FARMER'S chronicle. w 1823?-40||?
CSmH Ag 18 1830
DLC Ag 11 1830;O 9 1832;O 31 1840

KENTUCKY register. *See* Richmond daily register

Richmond weekly MESSENGER. w 1852-61||?
MWA Mr 15 1861
MoHi Ag 30 1861
P Jl 25 1861

Richmond daily REGISTER. w,sw,d 1866+
1866-1916 as Kentucky register
w 1866-96;sw 97-1900?
pub 1866+
CtY Ag 28 1896
ICU Je 8-29 1894;Ag 28 1896;Ap 6 1897(extra)
KyL 1872-73

Richmond REPUBLICAN. w 1822-25||?
KyBoW O 22 1824-My 1825

RUSSELL

Russell TIMES. w 1908+
pub 1929+

RUSSELLVILLE

Russellville ADVERTISER. w N 19 1835-Ag 18 1841||
Merged with Logan herald to form Herald and advertiser, later Herald
ICU Ja 21 1836;O 27 1837;O 19 1839;S 4 1840

Russellville CALL. w 1894-96||?
KyBoW [1895]

HERALD. w D 11 1839-50||?
1839-Ag 18 1841 as Logan herald; Ag 25 1841-49 Herald and advertiser
DLC D 11 1839;Ag-S 8,22-29,O 20-27,N 10-24 1841
ICU D 8,22 1841;O 19 1842;Ja 30,Mr 11(extra) 1850

LOGAN herald. *See* Herald and advertiser

***Weekly MESSENGER.** w 181-34||?
CSmH Ag 27 1830
DLC F 3,Mr 10 1821;22-26;28;F 27,Je 26,Jl 10-24 1829
ICHi Ja 18 1834
ICU Ap 20 1822;My 5 1827;Ja 16 1829
MWA Ja 21,F 4-11,Ap 8-15,Je 17,S 16,30,O 14,N 18 1826;Ja 20,D 29 1827

SALYERSVILLE

Salyersville HERALD. w Je 17 1915-
KHi Je 24-Jl 1 1915

Salyersville INDEPENDENT. w 1921+
KHi 1921-My 1930

KENTUCKY mountaineer. w Ja 12 1912-15||?
KHi 1912-F 5 1914

SCOTTSVILLE

ALLEN county times. w 1915?-18||
United with Citizen to form Citizen-times

CITIZEN-times. w 1890+
1890-O 3 1918 as Citizen
pub 1912+

SEBREE

Sebree BANNER. w 1895+
1895-1901 as Sebree herald; 1902-S 4 1914 Green River news
pub S 11 1914+

GREEN RIVER news. *See* Sebree banner

Sebree HERALD. *See* Sebree banner

SHELBYVILLE

ADVOCATE of popular rights. w Ag 21 1833-34||?
DLC N 9 1833
ICU 1833-S 6 1834

KENTUCKY advocate. w O 19 1827-
DLC N 30 1827[Ja 11-O 17 1828]
MWA N 2 1827

POLITICAL examiner and general recorder. w
DLC Mr 23,My 11 1833
ICU My 10 1832-Je 22 1833

PUBLIC ledger. w Ja 27-Jl 14 1830||?
CSmH Jl 14 1830

SHELBY news. w 1840-57||?
DLC F 22,Mr 13,N 25 1840;My 2 1849
ICU Ja 10 1844
Ky 1852-53;57
KyLoF Mr 17,D 8 1847;Mr 7,17,Je 27 1849
PPL N 13 D 11 1850
WHi Jl 22 1846

SHELBY news. w N 10 1886+
pub 1886+
KyLoF Ja 8-Je 4 1925;Ja 14-Ap 15,O 28 1926; S 8 1927;Ap 17,My 8,Je 12-Jl,Ag 21-O 23 1930;Ja 22,F 5 1931;Ja 28,Ag 25 1932

SHELBY sentinel. w 1840+
ICU Jl 5 1888
KyBoW 1929+
KyLo Je 3 1866-My 29 1867;Je 2 1869-Je 1 1870
KyLoF [N 1923-26]+

SMITHLAND

JACKSON republican. w 1845-
DLC [Ja 17-O 10 1846]

Smithland TIMES. w N 21 1839-
DLC D 12 1839

KENTUCKY (*Continued*)

SOMERSET

Somerset DEMOCRAT. w 1853-
DLC N 21,D 5 1855

Somerset JOURNAL. w 1895+
KyBoW 1929+
TxU D 13 1929-S 23 1932

Somerset TIMES. w 1907-11||?
LNC S 28 1910

SPRINGFIELD

Springfield SUN. w O 1904+
pub 1904+

STANFORD

Stanford INTERIOR journal. sw 1872+
Ky 1910-19

TAYLORVILLE

SPENCER magnet. w 1914+
pub 1914+

TOMPKINSVILLE

Tompkinsville MONROE county. w 1888-89||
KyBoW F 14-My 2 1889

Tompkinsville NEWS. w 1903+
pub Ja 1 1929;N 21 1934+

VERSAILLES

Versailles CLARION. w 1891-94||?
KyLT F 17 1892

COMMONWEALTH. w 1824-
DLC [Mr 18-D 16 1825]

CONSTITUTIONALIST. w 1824-
DLC Jl 23 1825

WOODFORD sun. w Ja 13 1869+
1869-76 as Woodford weekly
pub 1869+
ICU S 19 1884
KyLT S 6 1889
NNHi F 8,Mr 2-9,My 18-25,Ag 31,N 9-23 1877;Mr 11,Je 1881-92

WOODFORD weekly. *See* Woodford sun

WALTON

Walton ADVERTISER. w 1914+
pub 1914+

WARSAW

GALLATIN county news. w 1926+
KyBoW 1929+

Warsaw PATRIOT and Gallatin, Owen, and Boone counties advertiser. w 1837-38||?
NCanHi Je 23 1838

WASHINGTON

***UNION.** w Ja 4 1814-
DLC Jl 28 1824

WEBSTER

DIXON journal. w 1929-32||
KyBoW complete

WEST LIBERTY

LICKING Valley courier. w 1910+
pub 1910+

WHITESBURG

MOUNTAIN eagle. w 1907+
KHi D 17 1908-D 2 1909;O 29 1914;Je 10 1921

WICKLIFFE

BALLARD yeoman. w 1891+
pub S 1928+

WILLIAMSTOWN

Williamstown COURIER. w 1879-1904||
KyBoW My 30 1901
KyLT My 30 1901

WINCHESTER

CLARK county democrat. *See* Winchester democrat

Winchester DEMOCRAT. w 1867-1920||?
1867-86? as Clark county democrat
ICU D 20 1893

LOUISIANA

ABBEVILLE

INDEPENDENT. *See* Abbeville meridional

Abbeville MERIDIONAL. Le Méridional. w 1856+
1856 as Independent. L'Indépendant 1856-91 in English and French; 1892+ in English only pub 1856+
pub 1856+

Le MESCHABÉBÉ. *See under* Lucy

Abbeville PROGRESS. w Mr 1913+
pub 1913+

REPUBLICAN idea. w 1897-1905||?
LNH My 26 1904

ALEXANDRIA

CAUCASIAN. w Mr 28 1874-Mr 27 1875||
LU Ap 1874-75

CONSTITUTIONAL. w Ag 4 1860-
LU 1860-Je 1 1861
OClWHi Ap 20,Je 15 1861

Alexandria GAZETTE and planters' intelligencer. *See* Planters' intelligencer

LOUISIANA democrat. w 1845-1918||?
DLC Je 20 1860
IaDH Mr 15 1864
LA Je 14 1865-Je 17 1868;Je 30 1869-72;Ag 23 1873-Ja 1883;F 1884-91;95-97
LU Jl 13 1859-Ap 1860;Je 14 1865-Jl 12 1871; Ag 11 1875-Ag 9 1876;Mr 20,Ap 17 1889
MWA Ja 9 1861
NbHi Mr 15 1864
NcD N 18 1863
OClWHi My 15 1861

***LOUISIANA herald.** w O 1818-
DLC 1821-O 19 1822;Ja 11 1823-Ag 31 1825
MWA Je 30 1824

LOUISIANA messenger and Alexandria advertiser. w Ja 6 1826-
DLC Ja 20,Je 23-Jl 7,Ag 11-25,S 15-29,O 20,N 10-17,D 15 1826
PHi Ja 18 1827

PICTORIAL democrat.
Ap 15 1863 printed on wall paper
CtY Ap 15 1863
DLC Ap 15 1863
LA Ap 15 1863
MDeHi Ap 15 1863
MWA Ap 15 1863
NNHi Ap 15 1863

PLANTERS' intelligencer. w 1829-
1829-30? as Alexandria gazette and planters' intelligencer
DLC Je 20,O 2-9,N 28,D 5 1829;Mr 19 1834; Ja 2-N 6 1839
LNC D 4 1830

RAPIDES gazette. w 1869-77||?
LA D 23 1871-73
TxU Ja 6 1872

RED RIVER republican. w 1838?-
DLC Ja 30 1847-48;Ja 6,20 1849;50-O 1853
LSfD My 22 1839
MWA D 18 1847
TxU N 2 1850

RED RIVER whig. w My 5 1838-
DLC Je 2 1838;O 17 1840
LNH F 6 1841
LU N 14-28 1840;Ja 23-F 6,Mr 1-15 1841
MWA Mr 9 1839;S 5 1840

SOUTHERN sentinel. w Mr 21 1863-
MHi Ap 4,O 24 1863
MWA Mr 21-28 1863
NN Je 13 1863
NcD My 16 1863

Alexandria daily TOWN TALK. d Mr 17 1883+
pub 1883+
LA O-D 1912;O 13 1914-15;Jl 1916-Mr,Ag 8 1919-S 1920;21-S 1926;Ap 1927+
LNH N 13 1906;Ja 16 1907;Jl 14 1908

Alexandria TOWN TALK. w Mr 18 1883+
pub 1883+

ALGIERS

ALGERINE newsboy. sw
LNC O 16 1861
MWA D 14 1861-Ja 11 1862
NN Ap 26 1862

Algiers HERALD. *See under* New Orleans

HOOSIER newsboy. w
PHi My 27 1862

AMITE

Amite City ADVOCATE. w 1905-06||
LNH Je 1905-My 1906

Amite City DEMOCRAT. w 1874-76||
LU Ag 21-O 2,N 6-20,D 1875;Ja 8,29-F 5,19-Mr 11,25-My,Jl 24 1876

FLORIDA parishes. *See* News-digest

FLORIDA parishes-times. *See* News-digest

Amite City INDEPENDENT. w 1874-1903||?
LU O 17,N 14 1874;N 8 1879;O 4 1884;O 5 1889

NEWS-DIGEST. w 1888+
1888-1911? as Florida parishes; 1912-21 Amite times] 1922-26 Florida parishes-times; 1927-29? Tangipahoe Parish news
pub Je 21 1935+
LU Je 8 1907;My 25 1917;Ap 16 1920;D 30 1922

TANGIPAHOE democrat. w 1872-74||
LU Jl 25-Ag 6 1872;Je 7 1873;O 3 1874

TANGIPAHOE Parish news. *See* News-digest

Amite TIMES. *See* News-digest

Daily WANDERER. d
LNC O 20,N 10 1864

Tri-weekly WANDERER. tw 1865-
LNC Ap 29 1865
NcD Ap 18 1865

Sunday WANDERER. w
LNC F 12 1865

ARABI

ST. BERNARD voice. w Ja 11 1890+
pub 1890+
LBL Mr 1929+
LNH Ja 11,Ap 5 1890;F 17 1894;D 12 1896

ARCADIA

BIENVILLE democrat. w Ap 11 1912+
pub Mr 1918+
LU Mr 10 1932

LOUISIANA advance. w 1882-96||?
LU My 17,31-Je 21,Jl 19 1889;My 20 1890

LOUISIANA forum. w Je 5-O 3 1933||
LNH Je 5-20,Jl 4,18-S 5,26-O 1933

BASTROP

MOREHOUSE clarion. w 1874-1909||
LU Ag 27 1886

BATON ROUGE

ADVOCATE. w 1842-1903||?
1842?-Je 7 1855 as Democratic advocate; Je 14 1855-Ja 1882? Weekly advocate; F 1882-Jl 1888 Weekly Capitolian advocate
DLC My 24 1848;56-57;S 23 1860(extra)
LNM Ap-S 1898
LSfD Ap 22 1860;Je 2 1861
LU Je 1847-My 17 1848;N 30 1854-N 1855;D 17 1858-N 6 1859;Ja 13 1872-Ap 1877;F 8 1878-81;F 10 1882-Jl 1888
MWA Mr 25 1846;Jl 22 1852
NN My 28,D 24 1845;My 27 1846;Jl 31 1851

Daily ADVOCATE. d,tw Ja 2 1854-1903||?
1867-Ja 1882 as Tri-weekly advocate; F 1882-Jl 1888 Daily Capitolian-advocate
DLC 1854;56-57;Ja 26 1861
ICHi Ja 26 1861
LNH Je 20 1855;Jl 10 1883
LNM Ja 19 1882-O 1903
LU Jl-D 10 1858;67;Mr 30,Ap 17,My 13 1868; Ag 1882-[85]-Ap 1887;Ja-Jl 1 1888;Je 7 1890
MBAt F 4 1862;O 25,D 27 1865;Ja 1,24,F 9,21, Mr 5,12-16 1866;Jl 24 1867
MsHi Mr 7 1857
NcD Ja 26 1861
TxU Ag 1882-Ja 17,Ag 1883-Ja 19 1884

Morning ADVOCATE. d 1925+
LBL My 1930+

CAPITOLIAN advocate. *See* Advocate

CAPITOLIAN vis-à-vis. w S 1 1852-
LU 1852-Ag 24 1853

Sunday CHRONICLE. w
LU Jl 11 1915

Daily COMET. d 1850-D 27 1856||
United with Baton Rouge gazette to form Daily gazette and comet
LU S 1852-Ag 1854;My 1855-56

Weekly morning COMET. w My 29 1853-D 21 1855||
1853-55 as Weekly comet. United with Baton Rouge gazette to form Weekly gazette and comet
LU My 29 1853;Je 10 1855-56
MWA Ag 21 1853
TxU 1856

Weekly COURIER. w S 19 1868-70||
LU Jl 30 1870
MBAt O 17 1868

DEMOCRATIC advocate. *See* Advocate

Weekly DISPATCH. w N 10 1883-84||?
LU Mr 5,Ap 2,16,My 31 1884

FILLMORE ranger. w Jl 7 1856-
campaign paper
LU Ag 18 1856
LSfD S 15 1856

Baton Rouge GAZETTE. w O 10 1892-
LNH D 15 1892

Weekly GAZETTE and comet. w F 1819-74||?
1819-D 20 1856 as Baton Rouge gazette 1819-My 13 1845 in French and English
DLC Jl 17,Ag 14 1824;F 18 1826-N 1827
ICU F 14-21 1846;Je 14 1851;Je 18 1855
LNH My 20 1838
LSfD N 2,30 1844
LU Mr 1827-F 14 1835;Je 10,Jl 1,15-29,Ag 12-17,S 2 1837;F 24,Mr 17,31,My 19,Je 23,S 29,O 20 1838;Jl 13,D 7 1839;Ja 18,Ap 25,Jl 11,S 12-19.O 17 1840;F 6 1841;Ap 2,My 12 1842; Ap 20,Jl 27-Ag 3,N 23 1844;D 27 1856-[57]-[59]-Mr 15 1862;Ag 29 1863-Je 17 1865 Ja 27 1866-Je 20 1867;Ja-Je 1868
MWA Je 21 1823;Ag 4,S 15 1827;Mr 2 1839 Mr 12 1864
MsHi 1821-23;Je 30 1860
OClWHi O 27 1866

LOUISIANA (*Continued*)

BATON ROUGE—*Continued*

Daily GAZETTE and comet. d 1852-
1852-D 27? 1856 as Baton Rouge daily gazette
LU 1856-D 10 1858;59-60
TU O 5 1854

Tri-weekly GAZETTE and comet. tw
LU Je 1855-Je 1868
MWA N 20 1866
MBAt Ag 26,31,S 5,9-26,30,O 7-14,21-24,28,N 2-14,18,25-D 5,9-12 1865

GAZETTE de Baton Rouge. *See* Gazette and comet

GRAND era. w 1870-76||?
Carpet Bag
LSfD D 23 1871

LITTLE giant. w
Campaign paper
LSfD O 10 1860

LOUISIANA capitolian. d F 8 1879-Ja 20 1882||
United with Daily advocate to form Daily Capitolian-advocate, later Daily advocate

LOUISIANA capitolian. w F 8 1879-Ja 20 1882||
United with Advocate to form weekly capitolian advocate, later advocate
LU 1879-Ja 1,F 8 1881Ja 20 1882||

Baton Rouge weekly MESSENGER. Le messager hebdomadaire et feuille d'avis de Baton Rouge. w Mr 15 1826-
In English and French
DLC [Ap-D 6 1826]
MWA D 6 1826

NEW advocate. d 1908-Ag 1913||
Merged with State times
LBE O-D 1908;Ap 1909-12;My-Jl 1931
LBS S 1908-My 1909;Mr 1910-12;Mr-Ap,Je-Ag 1913
LNH Ag 19 1912
LNaS My 13 1912-13

Daily NEWS. d Jl 25? 1862-
LNC Ag 7 1862

OBSERVER. w 1899-1900||
Negro
LNH Ja 13 1900

REPUBLIC. w,sw Mr 19 1822-
sw during sessions of legislature
DLC [Ap 3 1822-Ap 16 1823]
ICU Jl 16 1822
LU 1822-Ag 30 1823
MsHi Je 15-S 10 1822

Daily STATE. *See* State times

STATE journal. w 1871-72||
Carpet Bag
LSfD F 28 1872

STATE times. d 1905+
1905-08? as Daily state
pub Ag 1906-09;13+
LBE [Ap]-S 1909;Jl 1-14 1910;O 1913-[Je 1916-Mr 1928]O 1930
LBL My 1926+
LBP My 15 1919-My,Jl 1920-Je,O-D 1922
LNH Mr 10 1910
LNaS Je 1921-N 1922
LU Mr 1917-F,Ap-Je 1918;S 1923+

Baton Rouge TIMES. d 1904-08||?
United with Daily state to form State times
LBS Ja 1907;O-D 1908

Weekly TRUTH. w 1882-1908||?
LNC Ag 6 1892;Je 22 1900
LNH Jl 1 1882
LU S 9 1882-[85]86;Ag 4 1894

Daily TRUTH. d 1890-1908||?
Title varies: Evening truth; etc.
LNC Jl 3-4 1899
NcD My 27 1892

BAYOU SARA

FELICIANA ledger. w 1864-71||
Followed by Dunn leader later Feliciana ledger (St. Francisville)
LSfD My 19 1866;Mr 16 1867;Je 16 1809-My 6 1871

Bayou Sara LEDGER. w 1842?-62||?
DLC N 2 1852
LSfD S 13 1843;F 28 1852;Ag 20 1853;F 18 1854;My 18,Je 8,22,Ag 14,S 7,28,D 7 1861;Ja 4,Je 28 1862
OClWHi F 3 1862

PHOENIX ledger. w
N Ja 16 1858

BENTON

BOSSIER banner. w 1859+
LNH My 23 1895;Ja 24,F 14 1918
MWA F 8,My 30,Ag 1 1868

BOGALUSA

Bogalusa AMERICAN. w 1907-18||
LNH My 11 1907;Ja 10 1914

Bogalusa ENTERPRISE and American. w 1914+
1914-18 as Bogalusa enterprise
LBL Mr 1929+

BONNET CARRE. *See* LUCY

BREAUX'S BRIDGE

ATTAKAPAS sentinel. *See under* St. Martinsville

BRINGIER

Le MESSAGER. w Jl 24 1846-58||?
In French
DLC Ag 18 1849
LNH F 1?,My 26,D 8 1849;Ja 26,My 18,Je 22,Ag 10,24 1850
LNM D 4 1846
LSfD S 16 1848;S 15-22 1849;Je 15-29,Jl 27-Ag 3,S 14-21 1850;Ja 18,28-F 1,Mr 1,My 17,31,S 12 1851;Ap 23-30,My 28,Je 18,Ag 17,N 26 1852;F 4-11,Ap 29,My 13,Jl 1 1853;Ja 27-F 3,Ap 21-My 12,26,Je 16-30,Jl 21-Ag 11,25 1854;My 25-Jl 14,28-Ag 4,S 8-15 1855
NNT S 22 1849

BUNKIE

Bunkie RECORD. w 1908+
pub 1928+
LBL Mr 1929+

CAMP PARAPET

BLACK warrior. sm My 17 1864-
CSmH My 17 1864

TWENTY-SIXTH. ir
MWA Mr 29,My 28 1863

CARROLLTON

LOUISIANA state register. sw,w 1869-74||?
sw 1869-70?
TxU Ap 27 1872

RADICAL standard. w Ag 5 1868-
MBAt Ag 26-S 16 1868

Carrollton SENTINEL. *See* Jefferson sentinel (Gretna)

Carrollton STAR. w Mr 29 1851-56||
Followed by Southern star (New Iberia)
DLC Je 28,Ag 9,O 4 1851
LNA My 17 1851-F 7,Mr 27 1852-Mr 22 1854;Mr 24 1855-Mr 22 1856
LNH Mr 29 1851-Mr 20 1852;Mr 24 1855-Ap 26 1856

Carrollton TIMES. sw,w O 28 1863-71||
LNH 1863-F 25 1871

CHALMETTE

Weekly HERALD. w Ag 10 1868-
MBAt S 14-21 1868

CLINTON

AMERICAN patriot. *See* Patriot-democrat

EAST Feliciana democrat. w 1855-70||
1855-64? as Feliciana democrat. United with East Feliciana patriot to form Patriot-democrat
LNM Ap 14 1856-My 7 1859
LSfD N 11 1866;Ja 2,16,F 27,Je 26,Ag 7-14,S 4-18 1869;F 26,Ap 20-27,My 29,Je 15,Jl 6 1870
LU D 19 1864

EAST Feliciana patriot. *See* Patriot-democrat

EAST Feliciana press. Ag 25 1933-Je 1 1934||
Ag 25- 1933? as New deal
LSfD complete

EAST Feliciana republican. w
Principally reprinted from Patriot-democrat
LSfD My 6,Je 3-10,24-Ag 5,19,S 9-23 1871

FELICIANA citizen. w S 13 1935+
LSfD 1935+

FELICIANA democrat. *See* East Feliciana democrat

FELICIANA whig and peoples press. w Ja 30 1839-
DLC Ja 30 1839
LNH F 13 1841;Ap 25,My 9-O 10,24,N-D 19 1849;50-Ap 9 1851
LSfD Ap 10-17 1841
MWA S 11 1845

LOUISIANA democrat. w My 1839-
DLC My 9 1840

LOUISIANA state paper. w
LSfD Ja 7 1854

NEW deal. *See* East Feliciana press

PATRIOT-DEMOCRAT. w 1851-90||
1851- as American patriot; -1872? East Feliciana patriot
LSfD S 13 1859(extra)Ag 29 1868;Mr 13,My 15,29,Jl 3-10 1869;Ja 15-22,F 12-Ap 9,My 7,21,Je 4,18-Jl 23,Ag 13-20,O 29,D 17 1870;F 11-18,Je 24 1871;D 20 1873;Jl 10 1875;F 17-Jl 14,28-O,D 1-22 1877;Ja 12-F 9,Mr-My 11,25,Ag 17-24,S 14-21,N 2,23,D 7-14 1878;Ja 25,F 8-15,Mr 1-15,My 17,Jl 12,26-Ag 2,16-23,S 6-20,O 4,18,N 8-15 1879;Ja 3 1880;S 30 1882;F 24 1883;O 13 1884;F 5 1887;Ja-My 3 1890
MWA O 31 1863

SOUTHERN watchman. *See* Clinton watchman

Clinton WATCHMAN. w 1878+
1878-1928 as Southern watchman
LSfD Mr 23-Ap 20,My 25-Je,Jl 13-27,Ag 10-24,S-O 12,N 9-D 7,21 1878;Ja 4,F 15-22,My 3,17,31,Je 21,Jl 19,Ag 2,S 6,27,O 11,N 15,29 1879;Ja 3,My 8 1880;Ag 26 1882;D 26 1893;F 1 1900;F 13,Mr 14 1902;S 18,O 2 1908;Ag 29,S 5 1913;Ja 15,N 12,26,D 10-24 1915;Ja-Ap 7,21-Je 23 1916;Ja 5,F 9-Mr,Ap 13-My 4,18-Je,Ag 31-O 19,N 16-D 21 1917;Ja-Je 13,Jl 11-D 1919;29+
LU Ap 13,My 4 1889;O 30 1917

COLFAX

Colfax CHRONICLE. w Jl 8 1876+
Suspended Ag 4-N 12 1877
pub Jl 15 1876+
LNH Ja 26,F 16 1918

CONVENT

Le COURRIER de St. Jacques. *See* St. James courier

Le FOYER Créole. *See* Interim

La GAZETTE. w 1895-1902||?
In French and English
LNH Je 11 1898
LU S 16-N 11,25-D 9 1899 My 5 1900

INTERIM. L'Interim. w D 15 1880+
1880-S 29 1888 as Le Foyer Créole
1880-1915? in French and English; 1916?+ in English only
pub 1921+
LNH O 29 1884;My 6,Ag 19,D 5 1885;Jl 16,30,O 29 1887;Ap 23 1904
LSfD Mr 12 1884;S 15 1885;My 8 1886;D 17 1887;Ag 18,S 8 1888;My 30 1891;D 11 1897
LU Ja-N 2,23-30 1881[82-83]-S 1,29 1888-[89-92]Ap 15,My 13,N 4 1893[94-99]-S 1 1900;Ja 24,My 23-30,S 5,19,O-N 14,28 1903[04]F 11,Ap 15 29-My 6,Je, Jl 1,15-22,Ag 12-S 2 1905;S 7,O-N 9 1907;Ag 21 1909[11-14]Jl 29,N 11,D 2 1916;F 10,Ap 11,O 14,D 22 1917;Ja 26-F 2,Mr 30,Ag 10-17,S 28 1918;My 17,D 6,27 1919 Ag-S 11 1920;Ja 22,D 17 1921[22-23]F 9-D 1924
NNT [1884-87]

Le LOUISIANAIS. *See* Le Rappel louisianais

Le RAPPEL louisianais. w 1865-84||?
1865-83? as Le louisianais
DLC [1865-67;69-81]
LNH 1865-73;N 1874-81
LU Ag 12 1865-Jl 1871;Je-D 1872;F-N 1873;N 1874-[76-81]

ST. JAMES courier. Le Courrier de St. Jacques. w 1889-91||
In English and French
NNT N 21 1891

ST. JAMES voice. *See under* Lutcher

COVINGTON

LOUISIANA advocate. w 1835?-
DLC O 31 1846;O 6 1849;Ap 22-29 1854;F 17,D 29 1855;Ja 26 1856

Covington PALLADIUM. w Ja 14? 1832-
DLC Je 2 1832

ST. TAMMANY farmer. w 1874+
DLC Ap 28 1877;Ja 27 1906
LNH D 17 1887;Ja 13 1906;My 23 1908

WANDERER. w
DLC Ap 23,Jl 9 1864
LNC O 8-15 1864

CROWLEY

ACADIAN signal. w Mr 13 1886+
1886-88 as Rayne signal; 1888-1929 Crowley signal
pub 1886+
LNC D 19 1896

RAYNE signal. *See* Acadian signal

Crowley daily SIGNAL. d S 1 1898+
pub 1898+
LNH Jl 4 1899

Crowley SIGNAL. *See* Acadian signal

DENHAM SPRINGS

Denham Springs NEWS. w 1898+
pub Jl 1902+
LU N 13 1929

DERIDDER

De Ridder ENTERPRISE. w 1906+
pub 1910+

DONALDSONVILLE

L'AMI des planteurs de Donaldsonville. *See* Planters' advocate

La BOUSSOULE de l'Assomption. w 1865-
In French
LSfD O 28 1865;Je 26 1867

Donaldsonville CHIEF. w 1871+
LNH F 14 1891;O 8,22 1892;N 16 1912
LU O 25 1919;D 4 1920;F 19 1921;Ag 5,N 18 1922

Weekly DEMOCRAT. w 1905-14||?
LNH Ap 19 1913

Le DRAPEAU de l'Ascension. w 1858-Ap 1870||
In French
LSfD O 8 1859;Mr 7,My 26,Je 2 1860

La GAZETTE de La-Fourche. *See* Lafourche gazette

Le JOURNAL de la Côte. w
In French
LSfD Ag 19 1855;F 22 1857

LAFOURCHE gazette. La Gazette de La-Fourche. w Ja 8 1826-
In English and French
DLC Ja 8-28,F 11,Mr 4,25,Ap 8,29,My 20-27,Je 24,Jl 22-Ag 5,S 16 1826

LOUISIANA (*Continued*)

DONALDSONVILLE—*Continued*

LOUISIANA gazette and Acadia and Lafourche advertiser. w Ja 22 1831-
In English and French
DLC Je 25,Jl 2 1831

LOUISIANA state gazette and Creole. w O 3 1829-
CSmH My 15 1830

Le LOUISIANAIS. w
In French
LSfD Ap 12,26 1845

PLANTERS' advocate. L'Ami des planteurs de Donaldsonville. w
In English and French
InRE Ap 29-My 6 1836
LNH F 7 1841

Daily TIMES. d 1895-1909||?
LNH Mr 30 1895
LU F 1898(extra)

Le VIGILANT. sw S 28 1845-O 1858||
In French
LNH Ja 10-O 1847;Ja 17 1848-D 20 1851;Mr 1852-D 23 1854;Ja 26-D 20 1856
LNM N 6 1847-O 7 1848
LU Jl 16,O 4 1846;Ag 21-25,S 11,25,29-O 6,16 1847[F-N 1849]

EDGARD

Le MESCHACÉBÉ. *See under* Lucy

REPUBLICAN pioneer. w Ja 11 1868-72||?
MBAt F 15-Mr 21 1868
MWA Mr 28 1868

FARMERVILLE

GAZETTE. w 1878+
LNH My 15 1907

FRANKLIN

ATTAKAPAS register. w 1859-61||
1859-60? in English and French
DLC My 2 1861
MBAt Mr 5 1863
MHi [1861]
MWA Mr 21 1861
NNHi Ja 17-N 14 1861
PHi [F 14-N 7 1861]
WHi Ja 17-N 14 1861

La BANNIÈRE des habitants. *See* Planters' banner

Franklin JOURNAL. w 1856-
ICU Ap 30,My 21,D 17 1857

Weekly JUNIOR register. w D 5 1861-
1861-Ag 1862 as Junior register
My 9 1863 printed on wallpaper
DLC Ap 9 1863
LNH My 9 1863
MBAt Mr 1(extra)My 2-9 1863
MH D 26 1861;Ja 9,30-F 20,Mr 6-13,Ap 3-10, 24-My 1,15-Je 21,Jl 3-10,Ag 7,21-S 4 1862
MHi [1861-62]
MWA Ag 21 1862;F 12 1863
NNHi [1861-N 1862]Ja 3,F,My 2 1863
NcD My 8 1863
NjP Ap 2,My 2 1863
OClWHi My 22,O 9 1862
PHi [D 19 1861-S 4 1862]
WHi F 26 1863

PLANTERS' banner. La Bannière des habitants. w 1836-63||?
N? 1843-48? as Planters' banner and Louisiana agriculturist
In English and French
DLC Mr 21,O 8 1840
ICU Ag 5,S 9-16,N 25,D 16 1843;Ja 13,F-Mr 23,Ap 13,My 11,Je 22,Jl 6,N 16 1844;F 22,My 17-24,N 22-29,D 27 1845;F 14,My 21 1846;Ja 14,Ap 29 1847;Mr 23,Ap 20 1848;My 31 1849; My 9-16,D 5-12 1850;Ja 2,F 6-13,Mr 8,29,Ap 5-11,26,Je 7,21,Jl 5 1851;Ja 3-17,31,S 25,O 9, N 13-20,D 4,18 1852;F 24-Mr 3,24-Ap,My 12, Je 2,16,D 1 1853;N 30 1854;Ja 11,Mr 29 1855; My 7 1859;Ap 14 1860;Mr 9,Ap 6,20,My 4,25, Jl 13 1861
LNH F 4 1841
LU S 20,N 1,15,D 6 1845;Ja 3,Jl 9 1846;Ja 14 F 18,Ap 8-22,My-O 7,21 1847-Ja 1 1855
MBAt Mr 14,Ap 11 1863
MWA F 5 1863
NN Mr 30(extra)Ap 4 1863
NhD Mr 11 1841

Le Franklin REPUBLICAIN. w 1840-41||
In French
LNH D 19 1840;F 10 1841

ST. MARY union bell. w Ag 16? 1860-
NcD S 20 1860

FRANKLINTON

ERA-leader. w 1906+
1906-Mr 23 1910 as Washington leader
pub Mr 30 1910+

NEW era. w 1886-Mr 23 1910||
United with Washington leader to form Era-leader
LSfD My 1 1890

WASHINGTON leader. See Era-leader

GARYVILLE

Garyville SENTINEL. w Ag 3 1923-
LU Ag-D 1,29 1923;Ja 5 1924

GREENSBURG

Greensburg IMPERIAL. w S 19? 1856-
LU Ap 30 1859;O 12 1861

ST. HELENA echo. w 1856+
pub [1856-89]+
LBL Mr 22 1929+
LU Ag 24 1889;F 17 1890[Jl 1891-O 1893;Mr 1895-99]-[1905]- [07-08]- [11]-[17-18]-[20]-[25-29]O 3 1930;My 6 1932;O 27 1933

Weekly STAR and journal. w 1865-72||?
LU Ag 28 1869;Ag 3 1872

GRETNA

Gretna COURIER. *See* Jefferson democrat

JEFFERSON democrat. w 1879+
1879-96? as Gretna courier
LNH Je 9 1906

JEFFERSON sentinel. w O 4 1873-79||?
1873-D 1 1875 as Carrollton sentinel (Carrollton)
LNH 1873-S 1874;S 1875-S 1876

GUEYDAN

Gueydan NEWS. w 1898+
LNH Mr 16 1900;S 10 1909

HAHNVILLE

ST. CHARLES herald. w 1873+
LNH Ja 12,Je 30-N 17,D 1-22 1883;F 1884-Ja 8,22,F 5-12,My 7 1887

HAMMOND

Hammond LEADER. w 1889-Jl||?
LNH D 10 1890

Hammond NEWS. w 1893-95||?
LNH O 21 1893-O 9 1895

SOUTHERN vindicator. *See* Hammond vindicator

Hammond VINDICATOR. w 1892+
1892-1919 as Southern vindicator
pub 1932+
LBL Mr 1929+
LNH Ag 11 1933
LU D 6 1918

HARRISONBURG

CATAHOULA news. w 1852+
1857-72 as Independent
pub 1857+
LBL Mr 1929-[34]
LSfD [1857-59]

INDEPENDENT. *See* Catahoula news

SOUTHERN advocate and Catahoula register. w 1849-
GU Ap 24 1851
MWA Jl 15 1852

HAYNESVILLE

Haynesville NEWS. w 1910+
pub 1910+

HOMER

BLACKBURN'S phoenix Homer Iliad. w 1859-68||
Title varies: Blackburn's Homer Iliad; Homer Iliad
InI Ag 11 1866
MBAt Ag 8-29,O 3-10,24-31 1868
MWA Je 22,Ag 10-17,S 7-14,D 1867;F 1-8,22, Mr 21 1868

CLAIBORNE advocate. w 1851-
ICU Mr 22 1854;F 21,Mr 28,My 16 1855
MWA Jl 27,Ag 24,N 23 1853

CLAIBORNE advocate. 1856-74||?
NbHi My 1 1873

CLAIBORNE guardian. *See* Guardian-journal

GUARDIAN-JOURNAL. w 1876+
1876-89? as Claiborne guardian
pub [1876+]

LOUISIANA journal. w 1886-89||?
United with Claiborne guardian to form Guardian-journal

HOUMA

Houma CERES. w 1855-
TxU Ag 27,O 1 1859;O 13 1860;Ja 5 1861
WHi O 13 1860

Houma COURIER. Le Courrier de Houma. w Ja 1 1878+
1878-87? in English and French
My 3 1934 is Houma centennial ed
pub 1878+
LNH S 30 1922
LSfD My 3 1934

TERREBONNE patriot. w S 19 1868-74||?
MBAt O 31-N 7,28,D 12 1868

TERREBONNE times. w 1881-92||?
LNH Je 22 1889

Houma TIMES. w 1913+
LNH My 12 1928

JACKSON

DEMOCRATIC record. *See* Feliciana record

***FELICIANA gazette.** w D 23 1820-
DLC Ja 10,Mr 1,20,Ap 10-17 1821

FELICIANA record. w 1894-1920||?
1894-1904 as Democratic record
LSfD Je 8 1895;D 14-21 1906;Ag 10,S 14-21,O 26,N 23 1909;11-O 18 1913;O 14 1914;My 19 1915;Ap 1,22 1916;D 8-15 1917;Jl 6 1918

FELICIANA republican. w 1838-
1838-39? as Feliciana republican and literary messenger
GAtCo D 21 1839
LNH Ja 30,F 13 1841

FELICIANAS. w 1902-
LSfD Ag 30 1902

FELICIANIAN. w 1892-93||?
LSfD Jl 29,Ag 26 1893

Jackson HERALD. w Je 19 1841-
DLC Je 19,Jl 10,S 18 1841

JEANERETTE

Le PILOTE du Têche. *See* Teche pilot

TECHE pilot. Le Pilote du Têche. w 1887-89||
In English and French
DLC Mr 31 1888-D 14 1889

JEFFERSON CITY

Jefferson City NEWS. w 1862-
MWA F 14 1863

JENA

Jena TIMES. w 1906+
pub Ag 25 1927+
LBL Mr 1929-Mr 7 1934

KENTWOOD

Kentwood COMMERCIAL. w Ja 14 1895+
pub [1895+]
LU Ag 23 1912

LAFAYETTE

To 1884 as Vermilionville

Lafayette City ADVERTISER. w
LNA Ap 15-N 18 1843

Lafayette ADVERTISER. w,sw 1865-1927||?
1865-89 in English and French
LLS 1869-79
LNC S 5 1885
LNH Ag 26 1903

Daily ADVERTISER. d 1913+
pub Ap 20 1920+
LBL My 1927+
LLS 1930+

Le COTTON-BOLL de la louisiane. *See* Louisiana cotton-boll

ECHO of Lafayette. L'Echo de Lafayette. w 1854?-62||?
In English and French
MWA D 27 1862
NNT F 12 1859

Lafayette GAZETTE. w,sw 1893-1923||?
w 1893-1909?
LNH Je 20 1903

GLADIATOR. Le Gladiateur. w Jl 20 1839-
In English and French
DLC Ag 10 1839

IMPARTIAL. L'Impartial. w 1840-61||
In English and French
NNT D 26 1846-F 7 1847

LIVE oak. w
GDE S 22 1848

LOUISIANA cotton-boll. Le Cotton-boll de la louisiane. w D 17 1872-83||?
1872-80 dated also at New Iberia
In English and French
ICHi S 20 1876
LLS Ap-Ag 1873
LNC Jl 8 1880
NNHi Je 4 1873

LOUISIANA republican. w D 5 1925-28||?
DLC Mr 20 1926

LOUISIANA state republican. w,sw 1850-
ICU O 16-N 6,20-7,D 11-14,21-25 1850;Ja 1,8, 25,F 1,15,19,Mr 8 1851
MsHi 1858

LOUISIANA stateman. sw 1844?-
DLC F 7 1846
MsHi My 12 1849-My 15 1850

NEW ORLEANS daily telegraph. *See under* New Orleans

SIGNAL. sw Ap 26 1843-
DLC Ap 26 1843

SOUTHERN times. w O 7 1834-
DLC O 21 1834

Lafayette SOUTHERN traveler. w
LNA N 12 1843-N 16 1844;Ja-My 27 1848

Lafayette TELEGRAPH. w
LNA N 20-D 1844

Lafayette TRIBUNE. w 1928-32||?
LLS Mr 1931-Je 1932

VOLUNTEER. w 1863-
InSHi N 7 1863

LOUISIANA (*Continued*)

LAKE CHARLES

Lake Charles AMERICAN press. w 1885+
1885-1910 as Lake Charles American
pub 1886+
CLM O 30 1889;Ja 22,F 26,Mr 12-26,Ap 16,My 14,Je 11-18,Ag 13,S 10-17,O 15,30,D 31 1890

Lake Charles AMERICAN press. d 1897+
1897-1910 as Lake Charles American
pub 1897+

Lake Charles PRESS. w 1893-1910||
United with Lake Charles American to form Lake Charles American-press

Lake Charles PRESS. d 1895-1910||
United with Lake Charles American to form Lake Charles American-press

Lake Charles REPUBLICAN. w 1899-
LNH S 23 1899

LAKE PROVIDENCE

To 1874 as Providence

Lake Providence BANNER-DEMOCRAT. w 1888+
1888-93? as Carroll democrat
LU Ag 11-S 15,29-O 6,N 10,D 1,15 1888[89]-My 17 1890;Je 20-N 21 1891;My-Je 4 1892;F 17-Mr 17,Je 16 1894-Ja 19,F 16-Mr 1895;N 4 1905;Jl 29 1922

CARROLL banner. w 1880-93||?
United with Carroll democrat to form Lake Providence banner-democrat
NcD Je 1 1888

CARROLL conservative. w 1877-79||
LU S 15 1877;Jl 20,Ag 17,N 23-30 1878;F 1 1879

CARROLL democrat. *See* Lake Providence banner-democrat

CARROLL record. *See* Elton eagle

CARROLL republican. w 1871-73||?
LU Ap 15,Je 14-21,N 1 1873

CARROLL watchman. w 1844-
DLC F 8-22,Mr 8-Ap 5,28-My 13,Je 3,17,Jl 1,8-S 2,D 2,16 1845

CARROLL watchman. w Ap 8 1875-76||
LSfD Ja 20 1876
LU [1875-76]

EAST Carroll democrat. w 1881-86||?
LU My 24-Je 21 1884;Mr 27,Ap 10-17,My 29, Jl 10-31,Ag 14-28 1886

ELTON eagle. w 1866-71||?
1866-68? as Carroll record
LU F 8 1868-Je 5 1869

LAKE republican. w 1872-
LU Je 17,Ag 2,O 16 1873

Lake Providence SENTRY. w 1900-06||?
LU F 9-Mr 9 1906

LEESVILLE

INDUSTRIAL democrat. w Jl 1918+
pub 1918+

LUCY

L'AVANT-COUREUR de la Paroisse St. Charles. w 1853-77||
pub with Le Meschacébé
In French
LNH O 12 1861
MH S 22 1860;Mr,Ap 20,My 18 1861
NNT Ja 29 1854-Ja 20 1856;58-59[Ja-Ag 1862] O 25 1865-Je 9 1868;69;71-73;75-77

Le MESCHACÉBÉ. w 1852+
1852-78? pub in Abbeville; 1879? in Edgard; 1880?-99 in Bonnet Carré; 1900-10? in Reserve
In French and English
DLC [1879-80;85;87-89;91-92;98-1901]
ICHi Ag 12 1876
LHi Ap 23 1904;D 16 1905
LNH O 12 1861;Mr 1-22,Ap 5,N 8 1879;Ja-F 14 1880[86-88]Ja 12,Mr 2,Jl 13-20,D 28 1889; Ja 24,F 14-21,Ap 4-11,Je 13-20,S 19,O 17 1891;O 23 1897[Ja-S 1898]S 21-28 1901
LU Mr 27-Ap 3 1869[98]Mr-D 16 1899[1900-01]
MH D 22 1860;Mr,Ap 20,My 18 1861
MWA O 23 1897[98;Mr 1899-1901]
NNHi Ap 5 1873
WHi [O 23 1897-1901]

LUTCHER

ST. JAMES voice. w 1916+
1916-26? pub in Convent
LU Ag 2,D 6 1919;N 20 1920;F 12 1921;O 14, N 4 1922;Mr 24,D 15-22 1923[24-26]Mr 5,Je 11-18,Ag 6,27,O 22 1927

MANSFIELD

ADVERTISER. w 1850-
DLC F 1 1851

Mansfield DEMOCRAT-JOURNAL. *See* Mansfield journal

DESOTO democrat. w 1887-92||
United with Mansfield journal to form Democrat-journal, later Mansfield journal

Mansfield ENTERPRISE. w 1906+
pub Je 1911+

Mansfield JOURNAL. w 1891-1914||?
1893-95 as Mansfield democrat-journal
NcD N 8 1895

MARKSVILLE

Weekly NEWS. w 1903+
pub 1925+

MINDEN

BANNER of liberty. *See* Minden democrat. 1895-1910

Minden DEMOCRAT. 1864-87. *See* Signal-tribune

Minden DEMOCRAT. w 1895-Jl 1910||
1895-1901 as Banner of liberty. United with Webster signal to form Signal-democrat, later Signal-tribune

DEMOCRAT-TRIBUNE. *See* Signal-tribune

Minden HERALD. w O 11 1928+
pub 1928+

LOUISIANA eagle eye. *See* Signal-tribune

SIGNAL-TRIBUNE. w 1864+
1864-Ap 9 1887 as Minden democrat; Ap 16 1887-Jl 3 1889 Democrat-tribune; Jl 10 1889-91 Louisiana eagle eye; 1891-Jl 1910 Webster signal; Ag 1910-16 Signal-democrat; 1917-28? Webster signal
D 31 1934 is Historical edition
M S 19 1933

Minden TRIBUNE. *See* Webster tribune

WEBSTER signal. *See* Signal-tribune

WEBSTER tribune. w N 6 1878-84||
1878-82? as Minden tribune. United with Minden democrat to form Democrat-tribune, later Signal tribune

MONROE

Daily ELECTRIC letter. d S 1877-
MWA N 13 1877

INTELLIGENCER. *See* Louisiana intelligencer

LOUISIANA intelligencer. w Jl 22 1865-76||?
1865 as Intelligencer
ICHi S 2 1865
MBAt Jl 29-Ag 5,19-26,S 9 1868

Monroe NEWS-STAR. d 1892+
1892-1908? as Monroe news (some years as Monroe evening news)
Sunday ed as World-news-star
pub Ag 1899+
LBL Mr 1929+
LNH D 25 1905

Monroe OLIVE branch. w Mr 28 1840-
DLC Ap 3 1840

OUACHITTA banner. w S 13 1839-
DLC O 4 1839

OUACHITTA standard. w Mr 8 1839-
DLC Mr 29,Ap 12 1839

OUACHITA telegraph. *See* Telegraph-bulletin

REGISTER. w 1850?-
MsHi Ag 23 1860

Monroe STAR. d 1898-1908||?
United with Evening news to form Monroe news-star

TELEGRAPH-bulletin. w 1865-93||?
1865-88? as Ouachita telegraph
TxU Mr 7 1870

WASHITA gazette. w Mr 19 1825-
DLC [My 21-N 29 1825]

Monroe morning WORLD. d O 20 1929+
Sunday ed as World-news-star
pub 1929+

MORGAN CITY

Morgan City FREE press. w 1879-89||?
DLC Ap 11 1889
LNH Jl 22 1880;Ap 18 1889

Morgan City REVIEW. w,sw 1870+
DLC Ja 27 1900
LNH Jl 6 1889

NAPOLEONVILLE

ASSUMPTION pioneer. Le Pionnier de l'Assomption. w S 7 1850+
1850-85? as Assumption pioneer; 1886?-95? Pioneer of Assumption
1850-72? in French; 1873?-95? in French and English; 1896? in English only
pub [1850+]
LHi Ap 13 1858
LNH F 7,My 30,Jl 25 1891;Ap 15 1893
LSfD Mr 6 1853;Je 1 1856;Ap 6 1858
NNT [1886-1901]

Le PIONNIER de l'Assomption. *See* Assumption pioneer

NATCHITOCHES

Natchitoches CHRONICLE. w 1844-
MWA Je 5 1847
NNHi Je 16 1860

CONSTITUTIONAL advocate. w D 2 1840-
DLC D 16 1840

Natchitoches COURIER. Le Courrier des Natchitoches. w 1824-27||
In English and French
DLC F 14 1825-N 5 1827
MWA Ja 30,F 27 1827
PHi Ja 30 1827

Natchitoches ENTERPRISE. w O 1888+
pub Je 22 1933+
LBL Mr 14 1929-My 4 1933
LNaS O 1912+
LU Jl 25,Ag 8 1889;My 29 1890

Natchitoches HERALD. w 1837-
DLC Ap 10 1841

LOUISIANA populist. w 1894-99||
LU Ag 24 1894-Mr 9 1899

PEOPLES' vindicator. w 1874-81||?
LNaS Je 20 1874-O 22 1881
OClWHi Ag 15 1874

RED RIVER chronicle. w My 14 1834-
Ct Je 21 1834
DLC My 14 1834

RED RIVER herald. w 1832-
Ct My 2 1835

RED RIVER news. w 1868-74||?
N S 16,O 24 1868

Natchitoches REPORTER. w Ja 27 1841-
DLC Ja 27 1841

Natchitoches TIMES. sw,w 1859-73||?
1859-69? as Semi-weekly times (sw)
LNaS 1866-Ap 6 1867

Natchitoches TIMES. w 1903+
LNaS 1913+

Natchitoches UNION. L'Union de Natchitoches. d
In English and French
DLC Ap 1-2 1864
ICHi Ap 4 1864
MWA Ap 1 1864(extra)
NNHi Je 5,12,19 1862;Ap 16 1863
OClWHi Ap 1-2 1864

NEW IBERIA

CONFEDERACY. w Ja 1? 1865-
LU F 18 1865

CONFEDERATE states. w,ir 1858?-
LU My 13,25 1864

New Iberia ENTERPRISE. w 1885+
pub 1905+
LNH D 10 1892

INDEPENDENT observer. w 1899-1901||?
LNH Ja 13 1900

LOUISIANA cotton-boll. *See under* Lafayette

Weekly NEW IBERIAN. w Je 23? 1859-
LU Je 9 1860

SOUTHERN star. w Je 28 1856-
Follows Carrollton star (Carrollton)
LU Je 28 1856

UNCONDITIONAL S. Grant. w O 24 1863-
ICHi O 24 1863
IHi O 24 1863
MHi O 31 1863

NEW ORLEANS

L'ABEILLE de la Nouvelle Orleans. New Orleans bee. d S 1 1827-1917||?
1827 in French only; 1828-Jl 1 1872 in French and English;Ag 1872-1917 in French
CSmH Ag 10 1830
CtY My 10,Ag 3 1830
DLC Mr 5 1836;O 31 1840;Ap 22-D 27 1841; Ap 19,Je 7,Ag 19,23,31 1843;Mr 28 1849-51; Mr 3,20 1860;Je 2 1862;F 1874-N 28 1893;O 5 1901-02
GAtCo N 23 1837
ICHi O 22 1876
ICU Mr 27,Ap 1,7,9-10 1850;N 19 1857;F 18, N 9 1858;O 25 1859;Je 2 1860;F 5,My 3,20,Ag 7, 16,20,23 1861
LNA Je 1830-31;33-35;My 1836-37;40-60;Jl 1861-67;69-77;F 1878-85;Jl-D 1886;D 1887-88
LNC N 27 1827[28]Ja 27,F 11,Mr 4-28 1829; Ag 20,S 20,N 9,D 15 1861[62]Ap 14,My 20,Je 29,Ag 10 1863;Mr 9,14 1864
LNH Mr 22 1853;Ja 25-26,F 4 1861;S 23 1862;Ja 30 1863;Ja 15 1864;O 2 1865;Ag 14 1884;O 9-10,12-17,19-N 7,9-10,D 1-3 1886;D 25 1888;S 16-20,22-26 1896;Ap 2 1897;D 25 1898;Ja 8 1899;My 25 1902;S 20 1903;Ag 13 1905;Ja 27,F 10 1907;1910-[12-13]Ap,Je-Jl 19, S-O 17,N-D 1913;F 15-Mr 16,Ap 8-My,Je 17, Jl-O 1914;Ja-Ap 10,13-17,20-29,My,Jl-S,N 1915-Ap,Jl 1916;Ja,My-Je,Ag 14-D 1917
LNM S 1827-Mr 27 1917
LSfD Mr 13,Je 29 1863;Mr 15 1865
LU [1869;93-94]Ap 27 1897;S 8-9,N 3-4,D 9 1914[15]Ja 9 1916
MBAt Ap 1-3,5-24,26-30 1862;S 6-8,19-20,O 4, 6,9,11,14,19,23-26,31,N 4,18,D 2,7 1865;Ja 1, 10-11,F 12,24,26-Mr 1,3,My 7 1866;O 31-N 3, 9,14,19,21-26,28-D 1,5-7,12-15,20-24,27,31 1867 [Ja-Ap 1868]
MWA Mr 14 1828;Ap 16 1830 My 11 1840;Ja 25 1843 Ap 2,Ag 8 1862;Jl 12 1863(extra)Ja 21,23,26-F 5 1875;Ja 10 1915
N My 9 1862
NN D 6 1843
NNHi Mr 29 1873
NjR D 15 1860
MWA N 27 1827
OClWHi [Ap 1862]
SdHi S 1911-Je 1915
Tx Ap 26 1837;D 31 1860
TxU 1843
WHi [My-D 1862]

LOUISIANA (*Continued*)

NEW ORLEANS—*Continued*

L'ABEILLE de la Nouvelle Orleans. sw,w 1827-1923‖?
sw 1827?-71?
In French and English
ICHi S 2 1876
LNH S 30 1885;Ap 19,O 27-N 4 1890;S 19 1891[92]Ja-Mr 12,Ap 9-30,My 14-D 1918;D 9 1919;Ja 6,27,F 10,24,Mr 23-24,Ap 6,20,My 11,Je 1 1920;F 3-10,Jl 7-14,Ag 10,25,D 29 1921-Je 1922;Ja 11-25,F 8,22,Mr-Je 21,Jl-D 1923
NNHi S 2 1876

ADVANCE. w 1889-1903‖?
LNM Jl 2 1893
PPCHi [1891-92]

New Orleans ADVOCATE. w -1869‖
MsHi S 1869
NNHi Ja 20 1866
TxU Ja 6 1866-1868

ALGIERS herald. w 1893+
LBL Mr 1929+

New Orleans AMERICAN. d 1914-17‖
LHi Ag-O 1915;My 1916
LNH [Ja-O 1915]Ja-Jl,S,N 1-9,11-30 1916;Mr 4 1917
LNM D 1915-F 1917
MWA Ja 1 1916

AMERICAN exponent. L'Explicateur américain. w D 1854-
LNA Ja 5-Mr 1 1856
NNT O 17 1855

AMERICAN progress. w Ag 24 1933+
Ct Ag 24 1933-Ap 5[My-Ag 1934]
LNH 1933+
M [S 14-D 14 1933]

L'AMI des lois. *See* Louisianian and the friend of the laws

New Orleans ARGUS. L'Argus. *See* Louisiana whig

Daily ATLAS. d Ja 1847-
DLC F 23 1847

L'AVENIR de la Nouvelle Orléans. *See* New Orleans prospect

L'AVENIR du peuple. The Future. El Porvenir del pueblo. tw Ag 1 1840-
In French, English, and Spanish
DLC S 16 1840
LNH Ag 7-9,14,19-21,26-30,S 13,18-27,O 2-4, 9-11,25,N 4 1840

AVISPA de Nueva Orleans. tw 1843-
In Spanish
LNH Ja 18 1844

New Orleans BEE. *See* L'Abeille de la Nouvelle-Orleans

BLACK republican. w Ap 15 1865-
MBAt Ap 15-29,My 13-20 1865
MWA Ap 22 1865

Le BON sens. d Jl 1 1842-
In French
DLC Jl 1 1842
LNH Je 30,Jl 3,13,15,S 4,11,O 19 1842

BULL frog. tw F 8? 1841-
LNH F 10 1841

BULLETIN. sw
WHi Je 1849-Je 1850

New Orleans weekly BULLETIN. w 1838-
LU Ag 10 1844

New Orleans BULLETIN. d Mr 25 1874-77‖
LNA Ap 1874-N 1876
LNH My 10,13-31,Ag-D 1874;Ja 4-5,My 15,18,S 10,30,O 7 1875;Ja-N 12 1876;F 3-Je 25 1877
LNM Mr-S 1874;75-N 12 1876
LU 1874-Mr 1 1876
MWA F 6 1875
NNHi S 15 1874;S 14 1875
TxU Mr-S 1874

CALL. w Ja 1? 1877-
LNH Ja 13 1877

Le CARILLON. w S 12 1869-My 2 1875‖?
Suspended from My 1 1870-N 3 1872
In French
LNH Mr-Ap 1870;N 1872-Mr 23,Ap 20,My 11,Jl-Ag 10,24,S 7-14,O 26-N 9 1873
NNT 1869-My 2 1875

CARNIVAL bulletin.—Rex ed.
Ct F 11 1902
LU Mr 3 1908

Le CHARIVARI Louisianais. w 1842‖
The first newspaper printed by lithography in the United States
In French
LNH My 24,Jl 2-8 1842

CHOCTAW democrat. ir N 5 1933-My 7 1934‖
LNH complete

CHRONICLE. F 8 1868-
MBAt F 8 1868

New Orleans CHRONICLE. d 1883-88‖?
Title varies slightly
CLM Mr 27 1886
LNA Ag 1884-Je 1886
LNH Je 13 1883;O 23 1886;Ja 5 1888

La CHRONIQUE. w D 4 1847-49‖
In French
DLC Ja 30,F 6-13,27-Mr 5 1848
NNT 1847-My 16 1849
NcD Ap 14 1848(extra)

La CHRONIQUE. w Jl 4 1877-
In French
NNT Jl 4-D 30 1877

Daily CITY item. *See* New Orleans item

COLONIAL voice. *See* La Voce coloniale

New Orleans COMMERCIAL. d 1866-
MBAt [My-S 1866]

Daily COMMERCIAL advertiser. d 1857-
DLC Je 1 1858

New Orleans COMMERCIAL bulletin. d 1832-71‖
United with New Orleans price current to form Commercial bulletin, price current and shipping list
A 1862;O 1866-Mr 1868;Ap 1870-Je 1871
DLC Je-N 1833;O 13 1835-S 1836;Ap 25-26, My 7,Ag 1839-Ap 1840;Ja 22 1841-42;Jl-D 1844;46-48;F 26 1849-60[My-Jl 1862]O 8 1866-Mr,Jl 19 1869-O 7 1871
LNA My-Ap 1836;Ja-Je 1838;39-Je 1844;Jl 1845-Jl 1862;O 1866-67;69-70;Jl-D 1871
LNC Ag 26,O 29,N 1,13,15-16,21-22,26,29,D 1, 3,16,20,27,29 1860[61]Mr 10,Je 2,9,Ag 16 1862; Ag 23 1863;Ja 3 1867
LNH My 25 1850;Jl 31 1858
LNM Ap-Jl 17 1869
LU S 1 1851;Je 9-10,13 1868;F 15,22-23,Ap 3 1869
MBAt Ap 19-24,26-30 1862;O 8-11,13-18,20, 23-N 17,20,D 3-5,7-17,20-21,24,26,28 1866-[67-68]69
MWA D 21 1832;Ap 24 1834;Ag 10 1835;F 27 1836;Mr 12,My 12,O 28 1840;Ja 14 1842;Ja 16 1845;Je 15,18 1846;Ap 17 1848;Ap 17 1849; My 16,Jl-D 1851;Ag 3 1852;Je 16 1854;S 6, 11 1861
MiU 1850[51]
PP Mr 7 1846;O 13 1849
Tx D 25 1835;D 31 1860
TxU Ja 23-D 15 1843;Mr 14 1855

New Orleans COMMERCIAL bulletin. w,sw 1839-60‖?
w 1839-56?
DLC Mr 6 1841-D 17 1842;Jl 6-D 21 1844;O 9 1847;O 13 1849;D 12 1855;Jl 4-N 29 1856;Mr 27,Ap 10,24,Jl 3,Ag 7,D 4 1847;Ap-Ag 1857; Ja 26 1859
NNHi F 11 1860

COMMERCIAL bulletin, price current and shipping list. w,sw Jl 27 1822-Ag 29 1884‖
1822-Mr 18 1882 as New Orleans price current (title varies slightly)
w 1822-My 21 1842
A 1858-Ag 1859
CSmH D 5 1829;N 22 1834;Je 20-27,Jl 25,D 19 1835;N 11 1837
DLC S 13 1823-Jl 18 1829;N 12-D 3,17 1836;Je 27 1839-Jl 1841;D 19 1846;S 1847-Je 9 1849;S 1851-Ag 5 1854;S 1855-S 1 1859;S 1 1860;Ap 14,Ag 11,N 1866-Ag 11 1877;N 1878-84
GDE Ag 26 1848
LNA S-N 1851;Ja-My 4 1853;Ja-Je,S-D 1869
LNH Jl 30 1825-O 2 1830;O 22 1831;Mr 31 1832;36-39;S 13 1841-Ap 26,S 1 1862;S 1864-84
LNM Jl 25 1829-Jl 17 1830;Jl 20 1833-Jl 19 1834;S 1844-Ag 23 1847;S 1855-S 1856;S 1858-59;Jl 21 1865-66;S 1 1874;S 1 1876;S 1 1878
LU D 29 1838-O 1 1839;S 1845-S 1 1848;51-S 1 1852;S 1853-Ag 1861;S 1865-Ag 1867;S 1870-Ag 1873;S 8 1875-Ag 1876;S 1877-Ag 1883
MBAt O 20 1860;Ja 10,Ag 11 1866;Je 5,12,Jl 3,10,17,24-Ag 7,31-S 25,O 2-19,23-26,N 6,16, 27-30 1867;Mr 18-21 1868
MH-BA 1830-[34]-[38]-[40-42]-[50]-[61-62;64]-[73-75;78-80]-[82-84]
MHi [1823-24;38;42]S 4 1847
MSaE Ap 3 1861
MWA Ja 24,Ap 17 1824;D 29 1827;O 1,D 28 1839[Ja-Mr 14 1840;O 22-D 1842;Ja 11-My 10, N 15-D 20 1843;Ja-Mr 2]N 13-D 1844;Ja 4,25, F 22,Mr 29[O 29 1845-Ap 11,N-D 23 1846]Ja 30,Mr 31,Ap 10,O 23,N 20,24,D 1,4 1847;Ja 1, F 23,Mr 22,My 31,S 1848-S 1 1849;O 26 1850; F 15,Ap 2 1851;Mr 20,My 26,Jl 24,D 29 1852 [53-Ag 1854]-S 1 1859;O 27 1860;S 1 1862;N 24-28 1866;Mr 27 1867
MiU [1845]-[47]
N My 16 1866
NIC Mr 1844-Je 1861
NN O-N 16,30 1839-O 1 1840;S 11-O 16,30 1841-S 1 1842;S 9 1843-S 1 1848;S 15 1849-Ap 5 1862;Ag 31 1868-Ag 1875
NNHi D 1839-N 1841;O 31 1860;F 22 1873
NcD [N 1878-Ag 1879]
NcU [S 1842-44]-[46-47]-[49-52]55-56
OCHi Ag 1845-Ag 1847
P-M My 17 1845
TM Mr 24 1849
Tx Ap 6 1861
TxU S 1843-S 1 1844;S 1845-S 1 1851;52-Ag 24 1861;S 1865-S 1 1869;S 1870-S 1 1874;S 5 1876-S 1 1877;S 1878-Ag,D 31 1881-Ag 1883

COMMERCIAL comet. w 1890-93‖?
LNH Ap 1 1893

New Orleans COMMERCIAL herald. w,d 1837-
CSmH Ja 12 1838
DLC Mr 25 1837
MWA Je 23-24 1838

COMMERCIAL letter sheet prices current. sw N 1836-
MWA F 15,Ap 22 1837

New Orleans COMMERCIAL times. d,sw N? 1845-
DLC N 27 1847
LNA Jl 1846-F 1849
MWA N 17 1845,Ja 19-F 11 1846
MsHi D 13 1845-Ja 13 1849
PWCl D 12 1846
TxU [Mr 15-Jl 15 1848]

Le COMPILATEUR. tw
In French
WHi S 2 1862

Le COUP-d'oeil. w N 25? 1853-
In French
LNC Ja 8 1854

Le COURRIER de la louisiane. *See* Louisiana courier

Le COURRIER Français. d 1863?-
In French
DLC Ap 29 1864
LNC Je 23 1863;Ap 11 1864
LNH S 11 1863;F 9 1864
LSfD S 16 1864
NNT Ap 22 1864(extra)

La CRÉOLE. sw N 12 1837-
In French
LNH N 12 1837;Ja 4-7,14,25-28 1838
NNT [1837-F 1838]

Semi-weekly CREOLE. sw 1854-
IU My 6 1857
LNA O 1854-D 12 1855;56
MBAt Jl 29 1854
MWA D 16 1854;Ap 16,23 1856
MsHi D 16 1845-My 7 1856
WHi Je 10 1854

New Orleans daily CREOLE. d
CtY Ja 10 1857
DLC My 23 1857
LNA Ja-Jl 1857
TxU D 20 1856

New Orleans CRESCENT. d 1848-Ap 18 1869‖
Title varies slightly
Suspended My 13 1862-O 12 1865
DLC Mr 20-23,Je 14 1850-Ja 1 1851;D 28 1860; Ja 19,F 2,25,Jl 30 1861;F 8,Mr 27,My 5 1862; Ap 30,S 14,O 27,29-31 1866;67
GDE S 16 1848
ICU Ap 25,Ag 11,O 3,D 4 1866;Ja 18,Mr 4,8 1867
LNA Je 1849-54;Jl 1855-67;Ja-Ap 1869
LNC F 25,Je 27,Jl 29,D 9,23,30 1861;Ja 13, 20,F 3,10,17,24,Mr 17,24,31,My 12-13 1862;D 4 1865;Ja 31 1866;Ja 21 1867
LNH Mr 6-S 4 1848;Mr 5 1849-My 13 1862; O 13 1865-S,N 1867-Je,Ag 1868-Ap 18 1869
LNM Mr 5 1848-Mr 1,S 7 1851-Mr 4 1862;S-N 1867
LSfD S 3 1861
LU S 5 1848-[49]-Mr 1 1851;Mr 5 1853-[54]-[58]-[60]-Mr 5,Je-Ag 1862;O 12 1865-Ag,D 1866-[68]-Ap 18 1869
MBAt Ap 17 1861;Ap 19-21,23-25,My 10 1862; O 21-23,25,28,N 4,7-16,18-23,27,D 11,16,21 1865;Ja 4-5,10,15,20,24,F 1,16,23,Mr 5,20,31,My 5,Ag 14 1866;Mr 2,Ap 25 1867
MWA F 27 1850;Ja 13 1851;N 23 1852;Mr 19 1860;S 29,O 5,10,16,18,22-24,N 14,D 21 1861
N My 9 1862
NNHi Jl 30,S 10,17,23 1860;Je 6 1861
NcD Je 26 1848;Mr 6-S 20 1849;55;Jl-D 1856; Ap 10 1866
OClWHi F 25 1861;N 6 1866;Mr 8 1867
TNY F 7-Mr 4 1856;F 7 1857-Ag 17 1858;F 7-Mr 12,S 6 1859-F 17,Ag 17 1860-F 18 1861
Tx Ja 4 1868
TxU Mr 5 1849-S 5 1850;Mr 5-S 5 1853;Mr 7 1854-Mr 5,S 5 1859-S 3 1860;S 6 1861-Mr 5 1862;O 12 1865-Ag 1866;68-Ap 18 1869
WHi [Ja 8-My 6 1862]

New Orleans weekly CRESCENT. w 1851-69‖
ICU O 15,N 19 1853;N 20 1854;Ja 29,Ap 30, O 20,N 12,26 1855;F 18-25 1856;Mr 30 1857;F 8 1858;D 4-11 1866
MBAt N 11,D 30 1865;Mr 2 1867
MWA Jl 10 1852
NNHi Ap 13 1850
OClWHi D 8 1860

CRESCENT city. d O 1 1840-
CSmH Je 10 1841
DLC O 6,29 1840
LNH O 25-30,N 13-27,30-D 4,7-8,10-25 1841
MWA F 3,Ap 21,Je 4,Jl 11 1842
NhD My 29 1841

Weekly CRESCENT City. w Ja 24 1841-
LNH Mr 14,Ap 13,18-25,My 2,16-30 1841

CRISIS. w Ag 14 1840-
DLC Ag 14 1840
IU Ag 20 1840

Saturday CRUSADER. w 1889-98‖?
LNH Jl 19 1890
LSfD My 3 1890

Daily CRUSADER. d My? 1894-98‖?
In French and English
LNH Jl 10 1894

Daily DELTA. d O 12 1845-F 14 1863‖
Followed by Era
CSmH S 2 1846
CtY Je 20 1862
DLC Je 17 1846;Ja 18,29,Ag 18,S 6-8,12-14 1848;F 12 1856;Ja 8 1857;Ap-D 28 1860;F 15 1861;My 24 1862-F 12 1863
GDE Je 25,F 27,S 21 1848
ICU F 23 1848;Ag 9 1861
LNA 1845-F 4 1863
LNC [1861]F 28,Jl 29,O 2,D 10 1862;Ja 29 1863
LNH Je 27 1848;Je 10 1849;Je 9 1857;S 24,29 1858;Jl 22 1859;Ap 24,Jl 2,25,O 12 1860-Ap 10,20,23,My 1,25,Jl 23 1861;Mr 4,20,26,My 13, Jl 4,S 17,Ag 29 1862
LNM 1845-O 8 1848;O 12 1849;Ap 12 1857;Je 1858-O 1859;Ja 12-O 6,N 8 1860;O 1861-My 16 1862
LSfD Ap 26,My 16,Je 5,22 1861;Ap 14 1862
LU 1845[46]-Ap 11,O 12 1847-Ap 8,O 12 1849-[51]-O 10 1852;Ap 12 1854-O 11 1855;Je 1858-O 11 1859;Ja 12-O 11 1860;O 11 1861-My 16 1862
MBAt Ap 17 1861;Ap 19,22-23,My 7-8,Je 6-7, 10-11,S 23-25,27,O 7,N 19-20,27-28,D 2,5,10, 12,24-25,30 1862;Ja 1,3 1863
MH My 7,Ag 20 1862
MHi [1862-63]
MSaE N 1 1846
MWA Mr 22,S 20 1846;Je 3 1849;S 8 1852;Ag 7 1853;D 15 1854;F 7 1860;Jl 4,S 5-6,11,Ag 6,O 18,22-23,25,D 21 1861;F 11,Je 10-11,14,17, 28,Jl 1,O 22,24 1862;Ja 1 1863
MeBa Ja 6,8 1863
MsHi [O 13 1850-Ap 16 1862]
N My 9 1862

LOUISIANA (*Continued*)

NEW ORLEANS—*Continued*

Daily DELTA. d 1845-63||—*Continued*
NNHi D 29 1860;Ja 12,F 16,28,Mr 13 1861 [Jl-D 1862]
NNHu N 20 1849
NcD Ag 21 1861;Je 7,10,Jl 4 1862
NcU O 25 1846;D 2 1849
NjP O 31,D 31 1862;Ja 1,7,16,F 13 1863
OClWHi Je 20 1847;F 6 1854;My 24,Je 19, Jl 9, 1846;Jl 18,S 5,O 31 1862
TxGR Ja 10,Ap 29 1862
TxU O 13 1846-Ja 3 1847;Ap 10-O 7 1848;O 13 1849-Ap 11 1851;Ap 13-O 10 1852;Ap 12-O 1 1854;Ap-D 1855;Ja 13-O 11 1859;Ap 13-O 10 1860
VRC F 26,28,Mr 7 1862
WHi D 20 1861;Ja 29,F 1,8,Ap 26,30-My 1, 6-7,24 1862-F 7 1863

New Orleans weekly DELTA. w 1845-63||
A O 1845-S 1847;O 1850-51;O 1853-Ag 1856
CSmH Ag 31 1846
CtY Ag 18 1851
DLC O 25 1847;My 29 1848-O 1 1849
In S 1848-O 1849
LNC Mr 26 1860;F 16 1861
LNH N 11 1845-O 9 1853;Ja 12,F 2,23,N 16 1861
LNP O 1845-O 7 1850;O 13 1851-O 9 1853
LSfD F 16 1861
LU O 26 1846-O 9 1853
MWA S 25 1853;Ja 19 1861
MsHi 1851-56
NN O 16 1848-O 5 1856
NNHi N 6 1848;Ja 1,My 7 1849
NcD O 2 1848
NhM Ap 12 1857
OC [1846-48]
OCHi O 11 1847-Ja 3 1848
OClWHi Je 22,Jl 22,Ag 3,17-24,N 30 1846;Ap 17,My 1858
P D 1 1845
PRHi N 29 1847-D 18 1848
T N 23-30 1846;Ja 4,25,F 8,22,My 10,24-O 18,N 1,D 28 1847
TSS My 11 Je 15,Ag 10,31,S 14-N 2,23,D 21-28 1861;Ja 11-18,F 1,15,Mr 8,22-29,Ap 19 1862
Tx O 18-N,D 13-20 1847;Ja 3,17-F,Mr 13-My 15,29-Jl 3,17,Ag,S 11-D 18 1848;Ja 8-Mr,Ap 9-Jl 9,23-S 10,24-N 5,19 1849-F,Mr 11-25,Ap 8 1850-F 10,24-Je,Jl 14 1851-O 24,N 7 1852-Ap,My 8-Je 5,19-S 4,18 1853-Ja,F 19-Ap 16, 30-Je 11,25-S 3,17 1854-Jl,Ag 12 1855-S 7, 28-O,N 9 1856-Ja 11,25-Mr 1,22-Ap 5,19-My 3,17-Ag 23,S 13,27,O 11-17,N 21-D 5 1857; Ja 23-Mr, 5,20,Ap 3-17,My,Je 12-26,Jl 17, 31-Ag 7,21-S 11,O 2,16-23,N 13-27,D 11-18 1858;Ja 1-15,29-F,Mr 19-My 14,28,Je 18-O 8, 22-N,D 10 1859-F 4,Mr 17,31,Ap 14,28,My 12, 26-Je 2,16,30 1860-My,Je 8,22-29,Jl 13,27-O 5,26-D 1861;Ja 11-18,F 1,Ap 19 1862
TxGR D 28 1861
TxU O 20 1845-O 8 1849;O 13 1851-O 9,D 18 1853;Ag 11 1854
WHi F 8-15 1862

Sunday DELTA. w 1845?-F 8 1863||
DLC [S 28 1856-F 8 1863]
LNA Ja-Je 1856
LNC O 25 1860;Ja 20,Mr 17,My 12,Jl 14,Ag 4,S 12,15,O 13-20,N,D 8 1861;Mr 2,30,Je 8-15,Jl 6,Ag 31,S 21,O 5,N 10 1862
LNH S 5 1858;Ap 14 1861;Ap 20 1862
LNM Jl 6 1862
LSfD My 19 1861
MBAt Ap 20-27,My 11,Je 8,S 21,O 5,N 16,D 7-21 1862
MWA O 19 1856;Mr 14,Ap-Ag,S 26-O 17,N 21 1858;Ja 22,Ap 15,Jl 8 1860;Ag 4,N 24 1861;F 23 1862;S 12 1875
NN Ag 10 1862
NNHi Je 21 1857;Jl-D 1862
NjP S 1 1861;Ja 5,28,Mr 16,Je 1 1862;Ja 4,F 8 1863
OClWHi Ja 20,Je 2,Ag 4 1861;Je 29,S 7,21,N 2 1862
TSS My 12 1861
Tx S 13 1857
TxGR Ap 20 1862
TxU S 7 1862
VRC F 23,Ap 27 1862
Vt My 25 1862
WHi Ap 27,My 25 1862-63

Evening DELTA. d
CSmH N 22 1853
DLC Jl 30 1861;F 6,Ap 8,My 2,Je 18,Ag 2,5, 1862
LNC [N 12 1860-62]O 29 1862(extra)
LNH O 1 1861;F 11 1862
LNM Mr 14,Ap 22,Jl 9 1862
MBAt My 5,9,Je 2 1862;S 16-O 3 1868
MWA Jl 13 1852;S 28,30 1861;Je 4,24,Jl 5 1862
MsHi F 1 1854;Ja 11 1862
NSyU O 30 1860
NcD Ap 7 1862
OClWHi Ja 23,F 12,Jl 6 1861;Ap 29,Ag 30,S 3-6,9-10,O 31,N 10 1862
WHi F 4,17,Mr 20,Ap 28,Je 7,18,20,25,Ag 1,6,S 27 1862

New Orleans DEMOCRAT. d 1875-81||
United with New Orleans times to form Times democrat
DLC Ag 5 1876;Ap 7 1877
ICM Ap 14 1881
LHi Jl-S 1881
LNA D 1875-78;Jl-D 1879;Jl 1880-Je 1881
LNH Mr 3,Ag 5,12,D 10,22 1876;Mr 1879-Je 1880;Ja-N 1881
LNP D 19 1875-81
LU My-Ag 1876;Ja 1877-Je,O 1879-81
MWA S 1 1881
NNHi Ap 22 1877
NcU F 11 1880
OClWHi O 21 1878
OOxM D 8-13 1880
TNY Jl-D 1880
TxU Ja-Ag 1878;O 1879-Je 1881

Weekly DEMOCRAT. w 1875-81||
United with New Orleans weekly times to form Weekly times-democrat
LNP My-D 1880
LU F 17 1877-Ja,S 1878-Je 1879

New Orleans DEMOCRAT. w S 23 1933-
LNH S 23 1933

La DÉMOCRATE française. *See* Le Franco-louisianais

Der DEUTSCHE. w N 13 1839-N 1840||
In German
DLC F 8 1840
—English ed. *See* German-American

Der DEUTSCHE courier. sw Ja 8 1842-
In German
DLC Ja 15 1842
LN 1842-43;45-47

New Orleans DEUTSCHE presse. d Mr 15 1868-My 26 1869||
Merged with Wöchentliche deutsche zeitung
In German
LN Mr-Ag 1868

Tägliche DEUTSCHE zeitung. d 1847-1907||
In German
LN Jl 1848-Jl 1865
LNA Ag-D 1861;Jl 1862-Je 1864;Jl 1865-Je 1867;Jl 1869-Je 1887;Ja-Je 1888
LNH Ap,22,My 6 1864;Mr 8 1867;Ja 17 1868;O 29 1887
NNHi [Jl-D 1860]Je 11 1861;Ja-F,Ap-Jl,S 6, O,N 11 1862;D 17 1872

Wöchentliche DEUTSCHE zeitung. w 1859-1907||
Followed by Neue deutsche zeitung
In German
LN 1859-60;78;80;81-86;S 1887-1907
LNH My 7 1891;F 12,S 1 1892;Ja 9 1897;D 9 1900
NNHi Ap 24 1862;Ja 16 1873

Le DIMANCHE. w Ja 1861-
In French
DLC Ap 6 1862
LNH S 8 1861
WHi F 10 1861;Je 8-15,29-Jl 6 1862

Le DIMANCHE. w N 27 1875-76||
In French
ICHi Ja 23 1876
NNT Ja 2-Mr 19 1876

L'ECHO de la Louisiane. d,tw Ag? 1836-
In French
DLC D 25 1836
LNH O 16 1836

L'ECHO national. w Mr 21? 1847-
In French
LNM Jl 18 1847
NNT Ap 16-23 1848

Das ECHO von New Orleans.
In German
LN My-S 1870

L'ECUREUIL. sw N 19 1837-
In French
NNT N 19 1837

EMIGRANTS register. w Ap 14 1844-
DLC My 26 1844

New Orleans EMPORIUM and daily evening journal. d Ja? 1832-
DLC O 3 1832
LNA S-D 1832
MeBB Ag 30-N 28 1832

L'EPOQUE. w 1865-69||
In French
LNC O 15 1865
LNH N 19 1865;Ap 7 1867;My 23 1869
LNM Ap 18 1869
NNT D 8-22 1867,F 9 1868

L'EQUITÉ. w Ap 9-O 1871||
In French
LNH Ap 9-S 24 1871

ERA. d F 15 1863-
Follows Daily delta
CL N 11 1863
DLC Ap 26,D 17,25 1863;F 9-D 1864
LNA F 15-Je 1863;64
LNC N 15,D 13 1863;Mr 30 1864
LNH Mr 22,Ap 30,My 18,Jl 6 1863
LNM Ag-D 1863
MBAt My 6,9(extra)Ag 2 1863
MDeHi My 14,Jl 11-12,14-15,17-18 1863
MH Ja 1,F 3,Mr 8-10,12-13,16,My 17-21,Jl 26 1864
MHi [1833]
MWA F 21,Ap 9,My 10,Je 2,7,14,Jl 10,14.16,19, 23,S 24,O 8-9 1863;Mr 13,Je 29 1864
NNHi [Ap-Jl 1863;My-Ag,O-D 1864]Je 24,Jl 6 1865
NjP [1863-F 14 1864]
VRC Ja 1 1864

ERA. w Mr 28 1864-
DLC My 30 1864

El ESPANOL. w Ap 6 1829-
In Spanish
CSmH 1829-Ag 8 1830

L'ESTAFETTE du Sud. d,w Je 2 1861-
Je-O 1861 as L'Estafette
w O 6 1861-S 1862?
In French
DLC My 2(extra)Ag 7,N 16,D 22 1862
LNC S 26,N 7 1862
LNH Mr 23,Je 4,8,S 17,25 1862;Ja 21 1863
LNM D 17 1862
LSfD Ap 17 1863
WHi [My 12-D 23 1862]

L'ETOILE du sud. *See* Daily southern star

L'EXPLICATEUR américain. *See* American exponent

FACTS. w O 22 1933-
LNH O 22 N 12 1933

Le FIGARO. d 1838
Campaign paper
In French and Spanish
DLC Jl 3 1838

Sunday FIGARO. w 1891-96||*
LNH My 29 1892;N 26,D 17-24 1893;Ja 7,21-F 11,25-Mr 4,Ap 1-8,My 6,N 4 1894;Je 23-Jl 21,Ag 4,18,S 10-17,D 15-22 1895;Ja 5 1896

Le FRANC-PARLEUR. w,sw tw 1835-
In French
CtY My 19 1836
LNC F 21 1836
LNH Jl 5 1835;Ap 7 1836
NNT Jl 2 1835

Le FRANCO-AMÉRICAIN. tw,d 1846-My 24 1850||
1846-O 5 1847 pub in New York, N.Y.
Merged with Le Moniteur du Sud
In French
DLC Je 8 1846-O 5 1847;Mr 21-23,25-28,30-Ap 1,4-5 1848
N Ag 11 1846
NcD [My-O 1847;Mr-Je 1848]
OCHi Ag 4,10,12,27,S 2,5-6,15-16 1848
OCX Mr 12 1847-Je 21 1848

Le FRANCO-italien. w Je 19 1859-
In French
NNT Jl 24 1859

Le FRANCO-LOUISIANAIS. m,w Ap 1880-96||
1880-Ap 26 1884 as La Démocrate française
In French
LNH D 15 1881;82-84;Ja 22 1886;My 9-Je 6 1891;Jl-Ag 20,S 17-N 1892;Ap 15 1893;Ja 20, F 3-10,24-Mr 17,31-Ap,S 8 1894;F 16-23,Mr-Ap,My 11-Je 15,Jl 1895-Mr 1896

Sunday FREE press. w 1892-97||?
LNH F 5,Mr 19,Ap 2-23,My 7-14,Je 1,25-Jl 2,30 1893;Ag 26,S 5,D 19-26 1896;Ja 2,16,30 1897

FREE South. sw F 1 1868-
MWA F 15 1868

FRIEND of the laws. *See* Louisianian and the friend of the laws

FUTURE. *See* L'Avenir du peuple

La GAZETTE de la louisiane. *See* Louisiana gazette

La GAZETTE d'état de la louisiane. *See* Louisiana state gazette for the country

GERMAN-American. w My 13 1840-
English ed of Der Deutsche
DLC J 15 1840

GOLDEN Rule pilot. ir 1878-
pub on board Steamer Golden Rule plying between Cincinnati and New Orleans
MsHi D 24 1878-Mr 9 1879

GREAT western. w D 8 1839-
DLC D 8 1839
NcU My 21 1840
NhD D 12 1840

Le GRELOT. sw Jl 5? 1846-
In French
LNH Jl 30 1846
NNT Jl 16 1846

La GUÊPE. w O 11 1920+
In French
LNH O 11-18,N 1 1902;Ja 31 1903;N 3 1904;N 11 1905;My 8 1909;Mr 12 1910;O 14 1922;S 21 1929

HALCYON. w D 22 1826-
CSmH F 3 1827

New Orleans HERALD. My 4 1873-
ICM My 4 1873
KyLo O 10 1873
LNH Jl 6,D 31 1873
LNM My-D 15 1873

Morning HERALD and Jeffersonian. d 1841-
DLC D 7,13 1842
LNH Ja 15 1843
TxU Je 14 1844

L'INDÉPENDENT. tw 1834-
In French
LNH My 26 1835
LNM O 17 1835

New Orleans daily INDEPENDENT. d
LSfD Mr 15 1865
NNHi Ja 22,F 22,Mr 11-12,14,16,18,25 1865

INDEPENDENT. w 1880-82||?
LSfD S 22 1881

El INDICATOR. w 1866-
In Spanish
LNC Ja 18 1868

Morning INTELLIGENCER. d N 23? 1840-
DLC N 27,D 15 1840

El IRIS de paz. sw Jl 8 1841-
In Spanish
DLC Jl 25 1841

ISSUE. w 1890-1905||?
LNH Ag 1 1891;Je 3,D 10-17,31 1892;Ja 14,Ap 8,D 29 1893;Je 23-Jl,Ag 18-N 3 1894;Jl 6-Ag 10 1895;Jl 14 1900

L'ITALO-americano. w 1884-1921||?
IU S 22 1917-O 19 1918
LNH Je 10 1898;N 19 1921
LNM 1902;06

LOUISIANA (*Continued*)

NEW ORLEANS—*Continued*

New Orleans ITEM. d Je 11 1877+
Title varies: Daily city item; Daily item
Sunday ed as Item-tribune.
pub 1877+
DLC N 23 1897-Je 1898;Jl 1933+
LBL My 10 1932+
LHi 1901-03;My-Ag,D 1912-Mr,My-Je 1913;Ja 1914;D 1916-O,D 1917-Ja,My,Jl-O,D 1918-Mr, D 1922-Ja,Mr-Je,S-N 1924;Ja-O,D 1925-Je 1933
LNA S 1890-94;My 1903-Jl 8 1909;Je 1920-O 1926
LNH Jl 12-13,16-17,N 15-16,21-22,D 1-2 1879; Je 4 1880;Ap 29,N 30 1882;Mr 11,Ap 10,O 19 1886;D 18 1887;S 28 1889;Mr 12 1893;Jl 21 1895;D 8 1896;Ja 3 1897;1900+
LNM O 22 1886
LNP Je-D 1883;D 1892-Ja 25 1893;Je-D 1896; Je 1911-Mr,Jl 12 1912-Je 1914;D 1915-N 1916; F-S,N 1917-Je,Ag 1919-Ag,N 1920-F 1925
LU Ja-Ap 1894;Ap 1917-Je 1918
TxGR D 12 1886
TxU Ag 13 1889

New Orleans semi-weekly ITEM. sw
LNP Jl-D 1896

JEFFERSONIAN. w
MnHi My 30 1842

JEFFERSONIAN. d N 15 1845-
Follows Jeffersonian republican
DLC N 20-22,25-29,D 1-4,12-13,15-16,18-21 1845; 46
LNA 1845-Je,Jl 20 1846-F 1847
MWA N 15,25,D 18-19,30 1845;Ja 1,3,5,8,13,Je 18,Jl 1,Ag 12,O 6 1846
TxU 1846

JEFFERSONIAN republican. d D 11? 1844-45||
Followed by Jeffersonian
DLC D 21,30 1844;Ja 3-O 30 1845
MWA Ja 20,F 10,12-13,15,18-19,Mr 7-8,25,Ap 12,15,21,25,My 14,17 1845

JEFFERSONIAN republican. w D 13 1844-
DLC Ja 25 1845

New Orleans JOURNAL. w S 3 1860-
In German
NNHi S-N 5 1860

Le JOURNAL de tout le monde. sw Ja 15? 1848-
In French
LNM F 24 1848

Le JOURNAL de ville. w
In French
LNA Jl 22 1825-Jl 18 1826

LEDGER. w Ja 3 1880-
MWA Ja 10 1880

LEVY'S letter sheet price current. w
F 1 1834-Ap 20 1839 as New Orleans wholesale price current
MHi Jl 16,Ag 13 1836;N 4 1837
MWA F 1 1834;D 9,23-30 1837;Ja 13,F 10,Mr 3,Ap 7,D 15-22 1838[Ja-Ap 20,O 12-D 21 1839]

*LOUISIANA advertiser. sw,tw,d Ap 19 1820-
DLC Ap 25-27,29-30,My 1 1822;Jl 15 1824;Ja 14,My 10 1828;My 30,Je 16-17 1831;Je 22 1833; Mr 5 1836;O 29 1840;Je 23 1841
LNH Ap 20-My 13 1840;N 6 1842
LU S 28-D 1841
MWA Je 23,Jl 4,31 1823;Ag 18 1826;F 6 1827
N Jl 30 1827
NNHi D 8 1827;Ja 8,11 1828
WHi [1821-Je 11 1824]O 6 1826-S 1828

LOUISIANA weekly advertiser. w
CSmH Jl 17 1830
DLC Je 22 1833
LNA 1826;Jl 1828-My 1829;30-32;34-Mr 1835
LNH Ja 1 1825
NNHi D 13 1828
PHi Je 11 1825

LOUISIANA advertiser letter sheet price current. sw?
CSmH Ja 27 1836
MWA Je 26 1824;S 19 1832

*LOUISIANA courier. Le Courier de la louisiane. tw,d O 14 1807-N 24 1860||
Suspended from Ap 7-S 18 1859
In French and English
A 1858
CSmH Ag 20-21 1830;F 19 1853
Ct Mr 14-15 1835
DLC O 7-18 1824;Jl 11-O 24 1825;Jl 3-N 29 1827;30-38;Mr 30,Jl 11-O 19,D 2,6 1839;40-49; O 26,N 3 1852;Mr 8 1853-F 5,D 29,31 1859-N 24 1860
ICU [Ja-F,Ap-My 1848]
IU [N-D 1849]
LNA Ja-O 1821;Ap 1822-Jl 1823;24-27;Mr 1828-Ja 1829;30-33;Je 1836-My 1837;40-41;Jl 1842-Je 1859;Jl-N 1860
LNC O 3,5-6,9-10 1860
LNH Ap 2,My 5[O-D 1842;N 1849-F 1850;Ja-Ap,O 1851;Ap,Jl-D 1853]Je 7-10,Ag 11 1854; Ja 10-13[Je,Ag-D 1855;Mr-My 1856;Mr-Ap, Jl,O 1857;Je 1858]
LNM 1822-O 14 1834;O 1835-O 1836;37-42;Ap 7,10,12 1843
LSfD Ap 9 1845;F 2 1854;Jl 2 1856
MBAt F 22 1822
MHi Ap 16 1821;Ja 7,31,S 29 1824;Mr 24,My 9 1825;N 3,18 1826;D 16 1843
MWA F 11 1822(supp);F 2 1825;Mr 7 1837;Jl 22,N 23 1852;Je 12-14 1855;Je 5 1856
MsHi Mr 17 1857
N O 1 1833
NNHi D 19 1827;O 1 1833
NNT Ja 8 1821;Je 11 1823;Ja 18-D 13 1832; Ap 2 1839;Ap 14,27 1841[F-Jl, S-D 1852]Ja 23,Mr 23,Ap 5-7,My 18 1843;Ap 8 1847;My 31 1849;My 21 1852;F 17,Ag 27 1854;O 11 1855; Ag 17 1856;Mr 18 1857;Ap 7 1859
NcD D 8 1858
NhD Ja 10 1832
OOxM Ja 12,26,F 9,16,19,27,My 26 1829
PHi Mr 8-9 1827
TxU 1842

*LOUISIANA courier for the country. Le Courrier de la louisiane pour la compagne. w,tw O 14 1807-
Title varies slightly
In English and French
DLC 1821-N 1827;Mr 1829-31[36;39]
LSfD D 16,27 1853;My 23 1854
MWA Ag 31-S 1824;F 3,D 7 1827

LOUISIANA Floridian. w
LNM S 10 1845-N 23 1859

*LOUISIANA gazette. La Gazette de la louisiane. w,sw,tw,d Jl 24 1804-
Subtitle varies
1804-My 1817 in English only
w 1804-Ja 1805;sw Ja 15 1805-Ap 1810;tw S 6-N 1811,Ag 11 1812-Ja,F 18 1817-Ja 1818
DLC Ap 25-27,29-30,My 1 1822;N 1,3-5 1823; Mr 25-26,Ap 1-3,5,My 3-4,18-19,S 8-9 1824,My 25,D 1825
LNA Jl-D 1821;Jl 1822-Je 1824;25-N 1826
LNC D 18 1822
LNM My 27-D 20 1827
MHi O 10 1825;Ja 11,15 1826
MWA Ja-My 1822]N-D 1823
N My 24,Je 1 1824
WHi [Mr 13 1823-Je 10 1824]
—country ed *See* Louisiana state gazette for the country

LOUISIANA guardian. w My 9 1931-
LNH 1931-Ja 9 1932

Weekly LOUISIANA review. w N 28 1888-94||?
LNC Ag 17 1892
LNH Mr 27 1889;O 26,D 13 1892
LU 1888-O 25 1893
TxU 1888-N 19 1890

LOUISIANA signal. tw
LNA Ag 29-N 5 1860
LNC S 3 1860
MWA N 1 1860
OClWHi S 18,O 4-25,30-N 3 1860

LOUISIANA spectator. w
LNA 1850-Ap 1851;Ag-D 1853
LNM Mr 1850-F 14 1851

LOUISIANA staatszeitung. w Jl 9 1850-Mr 1 1866||
Merged with Wöchentliche deutsche zeitung
In German
LN Jl-D 1850;Jl 1852-64
LNA My-N 1855;O 1861-Je,Jl 10,O 23 1862-65

LOUISIANA standard. w 1884-90||
DLC Je 8 1889
LNH N 1 1884;Ap 6,My 11 1889
LSfD Ap 26 1890
TNY Ap 6 1890

LOUISIANA state gazette for the country. La gazette d'état de la louisiane. tw
In English and French
DLC [Ja-D 7 1826]
MWA Jl 26 1826
—city ed *See* Louisiana gazette

LOUISIANA state republican.
LNA Ap 1854-Je 1855

LOUISIANA statesman. tw 1845?-
DLC O 30 1852
LNA Je-D 1848

LOUISIANA weekly. w 1930?+
LNH Mr 22,My 17-31,Je 14,28 1930+

LOUISIANA whig. Le Republicain de la Louisiane. d Ap 19 1824-Mr 1835||
Follows Louisianian and the friend of the laws. 1824-Ag 6 1834 as New Orleans argus.
Merged with L'Abeille
In English and French
CSmH Ag 9 1830
DLC N 29-30 1824;F 6,My 25 1827;Ja 19-D 19 1828;Je 9,Jl 18,21,Ag 13 S 8,O 15,N 14,D 3 1829;S 29 1832
LNA Ag 19-30 1824;F-Ap 1825;26-28;My 1829-Ap 1830;Ja-Je 1833;Ap 1834-Ja 1835
LNC Ap 22 1831
LNH Je 4 1831
LNM My-D 1824;My 1826-27
MWA Ap 13 1825
N O 17 1833
WHi Jl 10-11,14,17,19,21,28,31 1832

Le LOUISIANAIS et l'ami des lois. *See* Louisianian and the friend of the laws

La LOUISIANE. sw S 12 1841-
In French
CtY S 12 1841
DLC S 16,O 14 1841
NN Mr 29,O 7 1841
NNT S 12-N 11 1841

Weekly LOUISIANIAN. sw,w D 18 1870-Je 17 1882||
1870-My 7 1871 as Louisianian; My 11 1871-Ap 21 1872 Semi-weekly Louisianian sw 1870-Ap 21 1872
Negro
DLC 1870-Ja 25 1873;Ag 15 1874;Mr 27 1875; N 30 1878-Je 17 1882
TxU My 14 1871;F 28 1874-F 5 1876[S 29 1877-Je 17 1882]

LOUISIANIAN and journal of commerce. d Ja 14 1839-
In English and French
DLC [Ja 14-Mr 2 1839]
MWA Ja 14 1839

LOUISIANIAN and the friend of the laws. Le Louisianais et l'ami des lois. tw,d N 1809-Ap 15 1824||
1809-S 19 1822 as Friend of the laws. L'ami des lois (Sub-title varies... et journal du soir;... et journal du commerce) Followed by New Orleans argus, later Louisiana whig
tw 1809-Ap 1815;Jl-N 1820
In English and French
LNA Jl 26-D 1821;My 28-Je 29,S 4-O 1822; 23-24
LNC My 1 1823
NcD F 1 1823

MASCOT. w F 19 1882-1900||?
LSfD S 2 1882;Mr 6 1886
MWA Mr 25 1882;Ja 12 1884;N 10-D 22 1894; Ja 5-19 1895

MERCANTILE advertiser. d 1820?-
DLC My 14-15,Jl 12,14-15,21-22 1824;Je 2-5, Jl 13,15,S 2,4,7,9,O 9,12,D 9-10 1829;Ja 8,11 1830
LNA F-D 1831;Ja-Jl 1834
MBAt S 11-13 1827
N O 17 1833
NNHi Ja 11-12 1828
NjR My 18-19,22-31,Je 2-6 1826
OOxM Je 3-4 1828

MERCANTILE advertiser for the country. tw
CSmH Ag 3 1830
DLC Mr 10-D 10 1825[Ja,Mr,N-D 1826]O 16 1829
MWA Ja 27 1831

MERCANTILE advertiser. m?
LNA D 1851-Ja 1852

MERCHANT. d Ja? 1838-
CSmH My 17 1838
Ct Mr 3 1838
MWA Ap 12 1838

MERCHANTS daily news. d Ja 21? 1834-
DLC Ja 23 1834
LNA F-D 1834

MERCHANT'S transcript. sw Ja 28 1839-
Title varies slightly
DLC Ja 28 1839;O 24 1840
MWA D 3 1838[1840-Mr 23 1842]
NhD Ja 27 1841

Evening MERCURY. d D? 1846-
LNH F 1 1847

Weekly MERCURY. w N 14 1846-
OClWHi N 14 1846
WHi N 14 1846;Ja 30,Mr 28,My 30,Je 13,Jl 18,Ag 15,S 11-18,O 2,30-N 13 1847

Weekly MIRROR. w
DLC Mr 12 1859
LNA S 1858-Jl 1859
LNC My 4 1861

El MISISIPI. sw 1834-
In Spanish
LNH Mr 14 1835

New Orleans MITRAILLEUSE. w 1870-
MWA Ag 23 1871;F 4 1872
NNHi Ag 23 1871

Le MONITEUR du Sud. Il Monitore del Sur. w,sw,tw Ag 5 1849-
w Ag-O 1849;sw N 1849-Ja 1850
Ag-O 1849 in French and Italian
LNM Ag 5 1849
NNT 1849-My 24 1850

Il MONITORE del Sur. *See* Le Moniteur du Sud

Le MOUSTIQUE. w S 14 1892-
In French
LNM S 14 1892
NNT O 26 1892

Le NATIONAL. d O 1855-58||?
In French
LNA O 1855-Je 1856
LNM O 24 1856
NNT Mr 27 1856

NATIONAL advocate. d 1861-
LNC [Je 25-D 1862]
LNH S 8,O 7,N 1,3 1862
LNM Je 30,Jl 12 1862
LSfD D 20 1862
MWA O 21,23 1862
NNHi [O 1862]
NcD D 4 1862
VRC Jl 13 1862
WHi Jl 12,Ag 26,D 26 1862

NATIONAL republican. d 1871-D 22 1872||
Merged with New Orleans republican
DLC Ja 2-D 22 1872
LNH D 11-15,17-22 1872
LNM N 1871-72

Weekly NATIONAL republican. w 1871-D 22 1872||
Title varies slightly
LNA Ja-N 1872
LNM D 1871-72
NNHi N 22 1871

NATIVE American. d Jl 1839-
DLC Ag 3 1839
MWA S 19,N 11 1839

Weekly NATIVE American. w Jl 12? 1839-
DLC F 9 1840
LNC F 29 1840
NN Ja 24 1846
P-M D 3 1845

NATIVE American repealer. d Je 13 1841-
DLC Je 13 1841

NEUE deutsche zeitung. sw 1907-18||?
Follows Wöchentliche deutsche zeitung
In German
LN 1907-Ap 1909
LNH 1908-S 1909;Jl 10 1910-14

LOUISIANA (*Continued*)

NEW ORLEANS—*Continued*

NEW delta. w 1890-92||
LNA Ja-Je 1891
LNH Ag 19 1890;O 2,D 10 1891;Ja 15,My-Ag 28 1892
LNM S 1890-My 10,O-D 1891

NEW South. w 1896-1904||?
DLC Ja 13 1900
LNH Mr 24,Je 2 1900

New Orleans daily NEWS. d 1901-11||
LHi O 9-D 16 1905;06;Ap-S 1907;Ja-S 1908; Ap-Je,O-D 1909;Ap-Je,O-D 1910;Ap-Je 1911

El OBSERVADOR ibero. w 1888-93||?
In Spanish
CLM Ap 14 1889

New Orleans OBSERVER. w F 14 1835-
MWA 1835-F 6 1836
OOxM F 14,28-Mr 14,Ap-My 9,30-Jl,Ag 22-S, O 17-N 7,21-D 12 1835
PHi O 24 1835-D 17 1836

L'OMNIBUS. tw D 17? 1840-
In French and Spanish
DLC D 22 1840;Ja 5 1841
LNH D 31 1840;Ja 25-26,F 10,17 1841

L'OPINION. w,d 1886-O 30? 1888||
w 1888-S 1888
In French
LNH Ja 9 1887;Ja 1 1888

L'ORLEANAIS. 1847-58. *See* Daily Orleanian

L'ORLEANAIS. d 1887-92||
In French
LNH D 21,28 1889;Ja-Ag,S 20,27,O 4,N 4,8,15, 22,29,D 13,20,27 1890;Ja 10,24,F,Jl 19,S 21,24, O 28 1891[Mr-Jl 1892]

Daily ORLEANIAN. L'Orleanais. d My 1847-Ap 18 1858||
In English and French
DLC [N 19 1847-Mr 18 1848]
LNA Ja-Je 1848;49-Je 1851;52-Ap 1858
LNH [Jl 1847-51]Ja 10,N 19 1852;Je 28,Jl 19, S 15,N 4 1857
MWA N 23 1852
NNT Ap 23 1849;Ja 1 1850;Je 5 1853
WHi S 12 1848

*ORLEANS gazette and commercial advertiser. tw,sw,d D 20 1804-
sw Je 1805-Ag 1812;tw 1804-Je 1805,Ag 10 1812-20?
DLC Ap 25-27,29-My 1 1822

La PATRIA. d 1846-
In French
CtY O 25,N 11 1847

Le PATRIOTE. d My 13? 1838-
In French
LNM My 27 1838

Le PATRIOTE. w Jl 2 1876-
In French
NNT Jl 2-Ag 13 1876

Weekly PELICAN. w 1886-89||
Negro
DLC My 4 1889
LNH Ap 21 1888;My 11-18,Je 8 1889
LNM D 1886-N 1889
MWA N 24 1888
TNY N 26 1887

PEOPLE. d O 2 1848-
In French and English
LNH O 3 1848

Daily PICAYUNE. *See* Times-picayune

Weekly PICAYUNE. *See* Weekly times-picayune

El PORVENIR del pueblo. *See* L'Avenir du peuple

New Orleans evening POST. d
InVi N 19 1841

La PRESSE des deux mondes. sw 1848-49||
In French
LNH Ja 10-17,24-31,F 11-14,21-Mr 14,21-28, Ap 4 1849

New Orleans PRICE current. *See* Commercial bulletin

PROGRESS. w 1888||?
TNY Je 9.23 1888

Le PROPAGATEUR Louisianais. w Ja 6-Jl 21? 1827||
Follows Le Reveil (New York)
In French
NNT Jl 21 1827

New Orleans PROSPECT. L'Avenir de la Nouvelle Orléans. w,sw Ag 19 1866-74||
In English and French
sw 1870-71?
LNH 1866-N 18 1867;D 8 1870-[71]73;Ja 4 1874
LNM My 26 1867
NNHi Ap 13 1873

La RÉFORME. sw Ag 23 1845-Ap 1846||
In French
LNH Mr 29 1846
NNT [S 25 1845-Je 17 1846]

La RENAISSANCE. d My-Jl 1862||?
In French
LNH My 20,26,Je 2-14,18-19,21,23-26,28,Jl 1-23 1862
LNM Je 25 1862
NNT [Je-Jl 1862]
WHi [My 19-Jl 19 1862]

La RENAISSANCE louisianaise. w My 5 1861-D 24 1871||?
In French
LNH 1864
LNM N 17 1861
LU Ap 23 1862(extra)
NNT My-S 8 1861;Jl 13 1862-Ap 12 1863;66-71
WHi [F 2-Ag 17 1862]

Le RENARD démocrate. sw My 15? 1834-
In French
LNC My 18,Je 12 1834
LNM Je 26 1834

REPUBLIC. w 1822-
NN Ag 30 1823

Daily REPUBLIC. d Mr 3 1848-
DLC Mr 4,6-11,14-18,20-21,24-25 27-Ap 1,3-8 1848

Le RÉPUBLICAIN. sw Jl 4-D 23 1845||
In French
LNH complete
NNT complete

Le REPUBLICAIN de la Louisiane. *See* Louisiana whig

New Orleans REPUBLICAN. sw D 10 1842-
DLC D 17 1842;N 4-8 1844
TxU Je 14 1844

REPUBLICAN. d D 16? 1842-
LU Ja 7 1843

New Orleans REPUBLICAN. d Ap 10 1867-78||
CtY 1867;Ap 1870-Ja 21 1877
DLC Ap 11-D 28 1867;S 28 1868;Ag 10 1871 [O-D 1872;F,Ap 1873]Jl 14 1874-Je 9 1877
LNA Ap 30-D 1867;69-76
LNH 1873-Ja 3,12,31,F 3,10 1877
LNM 1867-N 10 1878
LU [1869]71-76;Ja 1878
MBAt [1867-69]
MWA Je 14 1867;N 19 1875
N Ja 10 1869
NN Ap 10 1867
NNHi O 5,9 1872;Ja 3,My 1 1873;S 15-17,20, 22-23 1874;Ja 6-9 1875;Ap 21,28 1877
NjR [S 1876]
OClWHi Ap 3 1869
TNY Jl-D 1874;F 1875-76
TxU Jl 1871-Je 1872;Jl 4 1874-76
WHi Ja 11-Ag 1871;Ja 14 My,O 1872-Ap 12, O 1873-Mr 8 1874;Mr 5-D 7 1876

New Orleans weekly REPUBLICAN. w Jl 6 1867-78||
CtY Ja 24-N 10 1877
MWA D 14-28 1867;Ja 18-F 1,My 30 1868-Je 26 1869
TxU Je 10 1872

New Orleans REPUBLICAN. w 1890-91||?
LNH Ja 9 1891

REPUBLICAN courier. w 1899-1900||
Negro
DLC Ja 27 1900
LNH D 2 1899

La RÉPUBLIQUE. d Ja 4 1863-
In French
LNH Ja 4,F 1 1863

Le RÉVEIL. sw,tw Jl 4 1897-1901||?
sw 1897-98
In French
LNH Jl 4[S-N 1897]Ja 7-12 1899

Le RÉVEIL des peuples. w Ap 11 1852-
In French
NNT O 24 1852

ROYAL gazette.
Mardi gras number
NNHi F 17 1874

Wöchentliche RUNDSCHAU. w
In German
LNH Mr 11-18,Ap 1908-Ja 1909

La SEMAINE de la Nouvelle Orléans. w 1851-52||
In French
LNC Jl 18 1852
LNH Ap 11 1852

SOUTH. w Ag 13 1865-
MBAt Ag 27,S 24-O 15 1865
TxU Ag 13 1865

SOUTHERN democrat. w Jl 4 1852-
MWA Jl 4 1852

New Orleans SOUTHERN pathfinder. w Ja 27 1860-
MsHi Mr 17 1860

SOUTHERN patriot. w
A F 1851-F 1857

SOUTHERN pilot. w Ag 29? 1862-
LNC F 21 1863

SOUTHERN republican. w 1898-1907||?
DLC Ja 18,F 8 1900
LNH S 2 1899;Ap 14 1900

SOUTHERN standard. d Jl ? 1849-
VRC Je 3 1855
WHi Jl 10 1849

Daily SOUTHERN star. L'Etoile du sud. d S 2 1865-Ap 1866||?
In English and French
DLC D 2 1865
ICHi N 16 1865
LNA S 1865-Ap 1866
LNC O 15 1865;F 8,13 1866
LNM O-D 1865;F-Mr 1866
LU 1866
MBAt [S 1865-Ap 6 1866]

SOUTHERNER. d Ap 20-O 2 1847||
DLC Ap 22-O 2 1847
LNA Ap 1847

SOUTHERNER and people's friend. d D 16 1837-
CSmH Mr 14 1838
Ct D 17 1837;Ja 25 1838

STANDARD. d O 10 1836-
MWA O 10 1836

New Orleans daily STATES. d 1879+
Sunday ed as Times-picayune New Orleans states
pub 1911+
CoU 1902;04;S 1906-Je 1909
DLC Ap 1917-Ag 1933
LBL My 14 1928+
LHi 1880-Je 1881;83-Je 1890;91-Ap,S 1892-94; Ap 1895-Je 1898;99-1901;Ap-Je 1902;03-07; Mr-Ap,S 1908-F,N 1910-D 1911;Ja-Ag,N-D 1912;My,Jl 1913-Mr,My,Jl,S-N 1914;Ja,Mr-Ap,Jl,O 1915-N 1916;17;F 1918-N 1923;Ja-N 1924;F-Je,Ag-D 1925;F 1926-Ap,N 1929-F,Ap 1930-Ja,Mr-Je 1933
LNA 1881-84;Jl 1886-Je 1891;Jl 1894-Je 1903;Je 1911-Je 1920
LNH Je 9,11,17,19,21-25,29-Jl 2,5-6 1880;My 13 1882;O 21 1886[F-O 1889]1900+
LNP S-N 1904;Je 1911-N 1916;17-S 1919;N 1920-25
LU Je 1889-Je 1890[1917-18]
MWA Ap 20 1884
NcD F 9 1887;My 20 1888;D 1 1889;Jl-D 1890; S 17,N 19 1905;D 30 1906 F 3,17 1907

Le SUD. sw Ja 16?-Ap 1861||
Merged with La Renaissance louisianaise
In French
WHi F 10,Mr 7,Ap 15(extra), 21 1861

Le SUD. sw Jl 4 1873-
In French
LNM Ag 14 1873
NNT Ag 7 1873

Der SÜDLICHE pionier. sm 1893||
In German
LNH My 31,Jl 15 1893

SUN. d D 2 1839-
DLC D 3 1839
MHi Ap 19 1840

SUNDAY illustrated. w 1887-88||
LNH Ja 15 1888

TÄGLICHE . . . *See under* next important word; e.g. Tägliche deutsche zeitung. *See* Tägliche DEUTSCHE zeitung

Le TAENARION. Journal du progrès. tw O 4 1846-
In French
NNT O 4-N 24 1846

El TELEGRAFO. sw O 30? 1825-
In Spanish
LNH N 8 1825

New Orleans TELEGRAM. d 1891-1902||?
DLC D 13 1897
LNH N 29 1897;F 7-8 1900

New Orleans daily TELEGRAPH. d Ja 2 1845-
Also dated at Lafayette
MWA Ja 3 1845

Daily TIMES. d O 23 1839-
1839? as New Orleans times
DLC O 23 1839;Ja 23,30 1840
MWA My 14 1840

Weekly TIMES. w Je 22 1840-
DLC Je 22 1840

Daily TIMES. d Ap? 1857-
DLC My 23 1857
LNA Ap-S 1857
LU Ap 28-S 1857

New Orleans TIMES. 1863-81 *See* Times-democrat

TIMES DEMOCRAT. d 1863-My 11 1914||
1863-D 3 1881 as New Orleans times.
United with Daily picayune to form Times-picayune
A 1882-Je 1887;Ja-Je 1889;O-D 1890;S-D 1893; Jl-D 1894;98-1902;Jl 1907-Ag 1910
C F 5 1887-F 1889
CSmH N 21 1867
CU-B [D 1884-My 1885]
Ct F 3 1905
CtY 1864-Je 1868
DLC N 25 1863;Ja 17 1864-65;Ap 27 1866-Mr, Jl 1867-68;O 1872;Mr 8 1873;Jl 1874-Ja 1908
ICHi Ap 19 1865;F 16 1882
ICM Ja 1 1879;F 6 1880
ICU N 18 1865;F 2,Ag 9 1866;S 21 1881
InLHi F 21 1882
KHi S 1883-85
KWiU O-D 1874
LHi 1901-O 1904;Ja-Je,N 1905-Ap,S 1906-Ap, Jl-Ag 1907;Mr 1908-O 1910 11-Jl,N 1912;13-Ap 1914
LNA S 1863-O 1867;69-Je,O 1877-81;Jl 1882-S 1893;94-95;Jl 1897-Ap,Jl 1909-14
LNC Ag 28,S 21,24,26,30,O 11,13,N 13,D 14 1864 Mr 27-29 1865;S 4,N 6 1869;S 23 1877
LNH S 20,O 6-7 1864[Mr 1865-66]F 10,14-16, 18-22,Ap 20 1867;Je 17 1868;Mr 29,My 9 1869; 73-Je 1883;84-1914
LNM S 21 1863-Mr 19,Je 20 1868-O,D 1870-Je 12 1881
LNP 1882-Je,S 1902-Je 1903;N 1904-F 1914
LNaS Ap 1906-Mr 1907;S 6 1908-My 3 1910
LSfD My 31,Je 1-2 1885;Je 15 1886
LU S 20 1863-S 19,D 4 1867-S 1872;73-Mr 1876; 79-Ap 1914
MB F-Mr 1874
MBAt Mr 5 1864;Jl 22-27,30,Ag 5,8-O 11,13-N 4,7 1865-[67-69]
MWA F 1,Ap 17,My 28,S 18 1864;Mr 11 1865; Ja 28,F 4,Je 17 1866;D 24 1869;Je 22 1870;Jl 2 1873;Ag 31-S 1 1879;S 1 1882;O 14 1883;O? 1884 Ja 5,My 5 1885;S 24 1913
MiU [1903-04]
MoSW [Mr 21-S 19 1864;S 1866;67-68;Ja-Mr 1870]

LOUISIANA (*Continued*)

NEW ORLEANS—*Continued*

TIMES DEMOCRAT. d 1863-1914||—*Continued*
MsSM [1895-98]-[1902]-[04-07]-[10-11]-[14]
MsHi 1886-1910
MsU [1887-88]
N My 11,30,O 5 1866
NN Je 12 1864;Ap 19 1865
NNHi [Ap-Ag 1865]O 13 1870;F 22,D 5(supp) 1871;F 14 1872;My 9 1873[S]D 3 1874;Ja 5,7-8 1875;Ja 7,Mr 1 1876;Ap 21,23,26,My 14 1877
NbHi F 21-25 1883;F 17,Ag 9 1885;Mr 1886
NcD N 18 1863;My 31,O 4 1874[82-88]Je 15 1887;D 12 1889;My 22 1903[06-08]
NjP [O 1863-D 21 1864]
NjR Mr 22 1868
OClWHi My 21,28,O 13,22 1864[Ap-My]Je 11, 18,Ag 12-13,D 17 1865;F 16,Je 27 1882;F 16 1883;F 16-17 1885;D 7-10 1889
OOxM O 20 1883
TNY 1882-84
Tx N 2 1868;Ja 20,My 22,Jl 9,24,Ag 7,S 19,O 22,N 6 1870;F 27,Mr 5,Ap 13-14,D 5,18 1871;F 11 1872;My 31 1874
TxGR My 25 1882;F 10 1884;Ap 22 1885;D 12 1889;Je 21 1904-14
TxU S 21 1863-Mr 19,S 20-D 1864;Mr 18 1865-Mr 23 1867;Ag-O 1868;Mr 20 1869-D 18 1870; Ap-D 1871;Ja-Mr 1873;Ap 1874-Mr 1875;80-S 1881;82-Je,O 1885-Mr,Jl 1886-S 1897;Jl 1898-1901;O 1903-07
WHi O 1882-S 1887;90-Ap 5 1914

Weekly TIMES-DEMOCRAT. w N 14 1863-1914||
1863-81 as New Orleans weekly times. United with Weekly picayune to form Weekly times-picayune
A Ja-Je 1867;Jl 1879-81
DLC Je 4 1864;F 18,Jl 22-30,S 2,30,N 18-25,D 23 1865;My 26,Je 9-16,Jl 28,O 13,27,N 10-24 1866
ICN 1863-64
ICU F 8 1871
In S 1865-N 1867
LNH Ap 16,My 1864-Je 17 1865
LNP 1863-64;73-80
LSfD My 31,Je 1-2 1885;Je 15 1886
LU 1882-Ag 4 1883;85-86;88;91-92
MBAt Je 2 1866;Ag 31 1867
MWA Ja 25 1868
MsHi D 1871;86-1910
NcD Jl 31-Ag 7,O 23 1886;Je 11,25,Jl 30,Ag 13,S 17-O 22,N 26 1887
TJT N 6 1900
TU F 20 1882
TxGR Ag 17 1889
TxU 1886
VRC O 21-28 1871

TIMES-PICAYUNE. d 1836+
1836-My 11 1914 as Daily picayune
Sunday ed as Times picayune-New Orleans states
A Ag 1854-Ag 1856;O 15 1877-Je,D 1882-Ap, D 1883-Ap,Ag 1884-89;F 1896-1910
C F 4 1887-90
CL Ap 17-30 1927
CSmH S 2 1846;Ja 26-Jl 1849;Ag 26 1853;Mr-Je 1855;Ag-O 1857;N 14 1860
CU Mr 1912+
CU-B D 15 1849
CoHi Je 22 1862
Ct F 10-11 1902;F 1 1905
CtY Ja 25-Ag 15,S-O 28 1837;S 1849-F,Jl 1851-O 1852;Mr 1854-Je 1855;Mr 1856-O 1857; 66
DA 1915+
DLC Ag 1845-53;56-62;S 1 1867;Ap 6 1873;Je 9 1876;Ag 24 1879;87+
IC Ja 8-Je 1841;Ja 26-Je 1844;Jl-O 1855
ICHi S 24 1865
ICM Ag 4,11 1878;F 23 1884;F 22,My 24,N 11 1885
ICN D 1917-Mr 1919
ICU Ja 25-Ap 1839;Jl 28 1840-Ja 24 1845;My 24,26 1846;Mr 21,O 17 1848-Ja 25,D 7 1849; My 6 1853;O 3 1856;Je 19,Jl 9 1861;F 11 1892; F 14 1897;1935+
IHi F 12 1909
IU N 7 1909-Ja 1,28-31,Mr-Ap 24 1910
IaSc current 6 months only
InNcHi My 14 1864
LBL My 1926+
LHi 1901-03;My-N 1914;F-Je,O-D 1915;My,Jl-S,D 1916;F 1917;F 1918-O,D 1919-Je,Ag 1920-F,Ap 1921-F,My-Jl,O,D 1922-F,Ap-Ag,O 1923;O 1924;F-Ap,Je,Ag-D 1925;F 1926-O,D 1932-Je 1933
LNA D 1839-47;Jl 1848-My,Jl 1864-Je 1865;Ap 1866-67;69-Mr,Jl 1874-Je,O 1878-S 1887;Ja-Mr,Jl-D 1888;Ap-S 1889;90-95;Jl 1897-1910; Ja-Mr,My 16 1911-13,Ja-Ap 5 1914
LNC N 4 1846;O 14 1855;D 9 1860;My 3,N 8,D 28 1861[62-64]Ja 4,13-14,20,25-My 9,17 1865;Ja 19-S 9 1866;Ap 20 1887
extras:Mr 25 1862;Mr 10 1864
LNH [1838-N 1839]My 17 1840[Je-N 1841]Ja 22,Jl 6 1842;Jl 13,S 2,16 1843;Ja 17-19,Mr 20, Ap 20,27 1844;F 28,Mr 1,6,My 4,Je 8,Jl 19 1845;Mr 23 1846;Je 6 1848;52-60;Ag 1861-[63] Ja 12-13,19,21,23,25-26,30,Ap 28-29,My 1,11-12,22,Je 3 1866;My 6,Je 15,Jl 4,6,Ag 1,22 1869;Ja 9,11,16,Ap 9,O 22,N 10,16 1870;73-89; Jl 1890+
LNM Mr 28 1840;O 23 1861;Ag 19 1863;S 1 1874;S 1 1876
LNP Ap 25 1837-N 1845;46-F,Ap 1867-S 1881; 82-1905;My 1906+
LNaS Mr 7 1905-09;F 1911+
LSfD F 15 1849;Jl 20-21,26,S 8,O 20 1861;Mr 18 1862[Ja-S 1863]Mr 6 1864;S 1 1885;N 10-12 1918
LU Jl 28 1840-Je 1841;42-45;S 1846-Ag 1847; Ja-Je,S 1849-Ja 25 1850;Mr 1851-Je 1852;N 1856-Ja,Ag 1857-Ja 1858;N 1859-Ja 1860;Ag 1861-62;65-Je 1866;68-Mr 1876;Ja-Mr 1877;Mr 9-D 1879;F 1880-Je 1881;89-Ag,N 1898-Je,O 1900-Je 1901;O 16 1903-F 1916;17+
MB [Mr 21-Ap 20 1841;Mr 30-Jl 23 1847]Je 23 1866;Ja 18 1873;N 19 1875;S 20 1881;N 4 1884; F 10 1891;F 13-14 1893;F 5-6 1894;F 18 1896; F 21-22 1898
MBAt F 13,Ap 17 1861;Ap 19-20,23,27,29,My 6-7,11,13,Je 6,17,Jl 1862;Je 18 1863[Ap 1865-69]
MDeHi Je 12,20 1862
MH Ap 26,My 2-3,7,Ag 20 1862
MWA Ja 18 1838;D 27 1839;Mr 17,Ap 24,My 21,29 1842;S 1-22,O 1843-Mr 20,Ap 20-21,27-28,My 9,12,25,28,O 1844-S 23,O 5 1845[F 15-Je 21]S 6 1846;47-57;D 26 1858;Je 9 1859;S 28,30, N 22-D 1861;Ja 26,My 1,6-7,Je 6,11-12,24,Jl 15,Ag 7-8,O 18-22,26 1862;F 23,Jl 23,O 8 1863; Mr 6 1864;Ap 1 1865;66;Je 22 1870;Ap 16 1873; Ag 25,S 1 1876;O 12 1883;O 21 1885;Mr 9,Je 9,Jl 22 1886;Ja 25,Ap 7 1887;D 12 1889;F 10 1891;F 22,26 1900;O 9,26,N 5,12 1914
MiU [1861]
MnU 1890-91;1906-12
MsHi S 21 1850-S 1851;Je 1902-10;Ap 1928+
MsSM 1914-[17-18]-[30-32]F 17 1934
MsU 1887[88]1915+
NN 1845-62;F 14,18 1863;Ap 12 1889;D 9,17, 19-27 1890;Ja 13,15,Mr 14-15,17,19,22,29 1891; Ag 4,D 11,13-14 1892;N 24 1896;Jl 5,S 26,O 31,D 12 1897;Ja 7,9,S 12,D 4 1898;N 2 1899;F 20 1901;My 2,30 1902;Jl-S 9,12-14,23-30 1903 [Ja-F 1908]
extras:F 15 1895;F 23,24 1903
NNHi Ag 8 1860;N 18 1863;Ap 22 1877;Ap 29 1884;F 18 1890
extras:Ja 7,8,9 1863
NbHi F 27 1876;F 22 1883;F 17 1885;F 14-17, 23,28 1889;N 1-8 1896;Jl 26 1901-Ja 11,13-F 1,3 1902-Je 1903;Ag 30-31,S 6,8,12,15-16,29,O 2 1907
NcD O 29 1843;Ag 26 1846;S 6 1861;Ap 27 1862;My 2,N 21 1863;My 31,Je 28 1885;Ja 29, D 12,26 1886;Jl 10,31,S 18,25,O 16 1887;Je 17 1891;Ag 12 1909
NjP [1861-63]
NjR Mr 18 1868
OClWHi F 1,9,15,Ag 29,S 10,18-19,22,N 2 1839; F 20,My 15,Je 16 1840;My 7,S 21,25,28,O 13, 20,23-24,30-31,N 5 1841;S 10 1845;Ja 21,Ap 16,My 7,17,Je 30,Jl 17,25,O 6,10,23,N 4,1846; Je 19,25 1847;Je 14 1848;Mr 5 1852;Jl 30 1853; Mr 1 1856;D 9 1860;Ja 22,F 17,My 2,31,Jl 6,23,Ag 3,1861;62;Mr 21,Ap 21,Ag 8 1863;F 12,Ap 12,29,My 25,Jl 15,26,N 11 1864;My 20 1866;D 6 1867;Ja 5 1869;Ap 15 1871;F 5 1876; D 16 1881;Mr 18 1883;F 17 1885
OHi 1914-22
OOxM D 10-11 1880
P Jl 1890-My 1917
PBL [Jl-D 1844]-[47]-[Ja-S 1858]
PHi Je 5 1862
PP [1927]+
PWbW F 18 1896
TNY Ag-O 1858
TU F 13 1893
TxCA 1861-71
TxF O 1926+
TxGR F 8 1860;Je 20,S 9,D 4 1861;Ap 12,15 1862;Ap 23 1864;My 25 1882;S 1 1908;Ap 6 1914+
TxU N 1837-My,N 1838-Jl 1839;40-Ja 25,S-O 1849;Ja 26-O 1850;N 1851-F,Jl 1852-F,Jl 1855-O 1856;F-Ap,N 1857-Jl 1858;F 1859-Jl 1861; Jl-D 1862;68-Ag 1869;Ja-Mr 1872;Ap 1904-06;Jl 1907-O 1911;12-13;N-D 1915;F 1917;18-23;Ap 27-My 29 1927
VHi S 12 1915
VP Jl 1853-54
VRC Ap 27,30,My 2,4 1862;F 2,Ap 7 1879
VU Ap 14-15,20 1902
WHi 1862;Ja 18,Mr 7 1863;My 12 1914+
WaPS Ap 16 1919[27]

Weekly TIMES-PICAYUNE. w,sw Ja 25 1837-1924||?
1838-98? as Weekly picayune; 1899?-Ap 2 1914 Twice-a-week New Orleans picayune
CSmH F 19 1844-F 10 1845;Ag 31 1846;F 15 1847-F 7 1848
CtNw 1841-43
DLC Ag 9-16,S 27-O 4,18 1841[42-43]S 22 1860; F 23,Ag 10 1861;Mr 4 1876;My 7 1881
ICHi N 20-27,D 11,25 1843;Mr 24 1844
ICU Ap 12,My 3,Je 28,O 11 1852;Mr 7,Ap 18 1853
IU Mr 25,O 14 1844;Ap 14,28 1845;N 29 1847
IaDH Mr 1905-14
KHi F 22 1841-F 8 1847
LNH Ja 12(supp)1857;N 1860-Ja 5,19-26,F 16,Mr-D 21 1861;Ja 4-18,F-Ap 1862
LNM F 28 1842
LNP Mr 1839-D 1840;F 1841-F 1843;N 8 1894-O 1897
LU Mr 1841-Ja 1842;Je-D 4 1843;Jl 30 1870-S 1 1871
MB [Ap 11 1842-Jl 1843]
MBAt F 1 1862;O 21,N 4,D 30 1865;Mr 3,31 1866;Mr 2 1867
MSaE N 11 1844;O 20 1845
MWA [Ap 16 1838-Je 3 1839;Je-S]D 21 1840; F 15 1841-[42]F 13,Ap 24 1843;Ja 1,F 12,Jl 8,S 16 1844;F 23,Mr 23,Je 29,S 21,O 12 1846-Ja 1854;Ja 19,F 2,Ap 13(supp)-20,D 14 (supp)-21 1857;F 1,Mr 22(supp)-29,My 25,D 27 1858;Ja 31 1859;Ja 12-Mr 9 1861[74]D 25 1875;86-93;1909-O,D 10 1914-Jl,S 1915-Ag,D 1916-19
MiU-C [1846;48-49]
MnHi D 14-21 1840
N N 28 1842
NN Mr 29 1841
NNHi D 9 1839-F 15 1841;F 7 1842[Jl-O 1848; Ap 1867-Ag 1868]
NcD F 28 1842-F 6 1843;My 3,Jl 12-19,Ag 16 1852[53] Ja 11-16,F 20 1854;Ag 22 1885;S 15 1898
NhD Mr 23 1840
NjHi Ag 13 1838
OClWHi Jl 6,O 12 1840;My 3,N 15 1841;Je 1, Ag 31,N 9,D 21 1846;Ag 30-S 6 1847;F 21,S 4 1848;D 12 1889
PBL [F 1843-O 1844]
Tx S 6 1847;Ap 10 1848
TxGR Ap 5 1862;F 2,Mr 1-8 1884
TxU F 26 1838-F 5 1849;F 25 1850-Ja 1859
VRC S 26 1874
WHi Ap 1845-F 8 1847;My 29 1848;Ag-S 6 1852;Mr 26 1859;F 15 1862;O 4 1864;92-96;D 15-26 1903

Le TOCSIN. tw Mr 30? 1844-
In French
LNH Ap 25-My 28 1844

Le TRIBUN. tw D 19? 1831-
In French
LNH Ja 1,Jl 26 1832

Morning TRIBUNE. d D 16 1924+
Sunday ed as Item-tribune
pub 1924+
LBL My 20 1932+
LNH 1924+
LNM 1924-25
MWA D 23 1924

Weekly TRIBUNE. La tribune de la Nouvelle-Orleans. tw,d,w Jl 21 1864-Mr 5 1870||?
tw Jl-O 12 1864;d O 14 1864-Ap 1869
In French and English
LNA 1864-65;Ap-D 1867
LNH [Ag 1864-65]Mr 7,My 19,Je 2,17,Jl 19 1866;Ja 19,Ap 12 1867
LNM Ja-F 1869
LNP Ja-F 1869
MBAt [Ag 1865-68]
MWA Ap 22 1865
NNT [1865-67,70]
OClWHi My 4 1865
TxU Ag 17 1867

Daily TROPIC. d O 3 1842-
Title varies slightly
DLC O 4 1842
LNA Jl 1843-Ap 1847
LNM O 1843-Ag 1846
MWA O 6-8,11,13-15 1842;Jl 6 1844;F 25 1845
NcU Mr 12 1846
TxU 1842-S 1845

Weekly TROPIC. w N 26? 1842-
DLC Ja 28 1843;O 26 1844
IHi Ag 10 1844
LNH F 1 1845;Je 27,D 19 1846
MWA S 13 1845;N 14-28,D 12,26 1846;Ja 9,F 6,20,Mr 6 1847
NcD Jl 27 1844
OClWHi Jl 4 1846

Le TROPIQUE. w S 1 1872-
In French
LNM O 27 1872
NjR O 6 1872

TRUE American. d My 4? 1835-
Ct My 6 1835
DLC Mr 9 1836
LNH Ag 1835

TRUE American. w
DLC N 26 1840
LNA My-O 1836;Jl 1838-39
LNM Mr 11-Ap 1837;39

Daily TRUE delta. d -Mr 30 1866||?
CSmH Jl 6,N 6,30 1860
DLC O 4 1853;My 23,N 18 1857-My 16,O 17 1858;59;N 18 1860-My 17,D 23-24,27 1862;Ap 5 1863;Je 19 1864-Je 1865;Ja-Mr 1866
ICHi O 22,N 1,9 1865
IG Jl 6 1865
LNA N 1849-Mr 1866
LNC F 16-17 1858;N 17,20-21,23-D 11,14-15, 22,25-26,29 1860[61-63]F 5,20-21,Mr 19-20,24, 29,My 4,6,8,14,22,Je 11(extra)1864
LNH N 18 1849-N 16 1856;My 19 1857-N 16 1861;My 18 1862-63
LNM My 18-Ag 17 1859;N 18 1860-My 17 1861; Je 3,Jl 12 1862
LSfD My 30,Jl 7,Ag 21,S 21,25,N 13 1861;Je 28,Jl 29,Ag 2,23,30,S 3,13,27 1863;S 8 1864
LU My 19-O 23 1852;My 18-N 16 1862;My 19 1863-My 19,N 21 1865-Mr 1866
MBAt Ap 19,23-25,29,My 7-8,11,13,Je 6-8,10-11 1862;S 24 1864[Jl-D 1865]Ja 2-16,19-21,25-26,28-Mr 1866
MH My 2 1862
MWA Ja 30 1852;Ap 6 1861;Je 15-16,Jl 6-12 1862;Jl 15,S 2 1863
MiU [1860-61]
N My 9 1862
NNHi [Ag-D 1860]Ja 11[My,S-N]1862;Ja 28 1863;N 9 1864;Mr 29,My 3,Je 23-24,Jl 30 1865
NcD Je 1-3 1862
NjP [Ag 3 1861-My 25 1864]
OClWHi Mr 31,D 8,15 1861;My 12,15 1865
PHi My 25,28 1862
Tx S 2 1859;D 28 1860
TxU N 2 1850;S 7 1852;Jl 30 1859;My 19 1863-My 19,N 21 1865-Mr 1866
VRC F 22,Ap 27,My 1,3,6-7,9-11,14 1862
WHi Ja 30,Mr 11,18,Ap 3,27,My 20-21,28,30, Je 29,Ag 2,5,19,31,S 23 1862;Ap 2 1863

Evening TRUE delta. d
CtW Ap 26 1862
CtY My 22,Ag 26 1862
DLC Ag 3 1861;F 6,Mr 25 1862
ICU Ap 16 1859;D 24 1860;Ja 21,Mr 2 1861
LNC [1861-62]Ja 13,29-F 9,Ap 13,S 3 1863;Ja 23 1865
LNM Mr 19,My 19,23 1886
LSfD D 2 1858
MBAt Ja 13,My 3,6,Je 2,17 1862;Ja 10,20 1866
MH Ap 28,My 5,Ag 5,20 1862
MWA O 14,N 13 1861;My 22,29,S 6 1862;F 24 1864
NN Je 17 1862
NNHi Ag 20,31,N 6,D 26 1860;Ag 29,O 31 1861 [My]Je 14,16[Jl-D]1862;My 12 1863;Jl 5 1862 (extra)
OClWHi My 20,Je 7 1862;Jl 20 1865
VRC Ap 28 1862
WHi My 27,Je 5,Jl 30 1862

LOUISIANA (*Continued*)

NEW ORLEANS—*Continued*

New Orleans weekly TRUE delta. w 1851-
DLC Ja 7,21,Mr 10,Ap 14,28,My 26-Je 2 1860; Ag 3 1861;D 27 1862
LNC Ap 11,25-My 9,30,Je 20-Jl 18,Ag 1,22-O 3,17-24,N 21-28 1863;Ja 23-F 6,Mr 12-Ap 16, Jl 23,Ag,S 10-30,O 1-22,N 12 1864;Ja 7, 28,F 11-18,Ap 8,Jl 1,15 1865
LNH My 10 1862-Ap 1864
MBAt S 30,O 28,D 30 1865
MWA F 23 1852;D 24 1853-Ap 21,Ag 25 1855
MsHi O 2 1858;59-Ap 21 1860;Ja 12 1861;62
Tx S 26 1857
TxU Ja 17 1858[Ag-N 17 1861]
VRC O 23,30 1856
WHi Ja 22 1853;My 2 1857

TRUE democrat. w
LNA Ap 17-My 15 1856

TRUE republican. w
LNH F 16 1870

Daily TRUTH. d 1891-94||
LNH Mr 17 1894

TWICE-a-week picayune. *See* Weekly times-picayune

New Orleans UNION. d S 21 1835-
DLC S 26 1835
LNM S 21-D 31 1837

L'UNION. d Jl 1-O 31 1857||
In French
LNA complete

UNION. L'Union. sw,tw 1862-Jl 1869||
Negro
In English and French
LNH Ja 13-15,29,F 24-28,Ap 9-16,My 14-19, 30-Je 2,30,Ag 1,D 25 1863
MBAt F 11 1864
MWA Jl 14 1863
OClWHi Jl 9 1863;Jl 12,19 1864
WHi [1862-64]

UNIVERSE. w Ag 12 1896-
LNH Ag 12 1896

VIEUX Carré news. w,sm 1925-28||?
w 1925?
LNH N 7-D 12 1925

La VOCE coloniale. Colonial voice. w My 15 1915+
In Italian
pub 1930—
IU D 8 1917+
LNH O 11 1930+

Le VRAI républicain. tw Ag 15? 1837-
In French
LNM D 28 1837

New Orleans WHOLESALE price current. *See* Levy's letter sheet price current

WÖCHENTLICHE ... *See under* next important word; e.g. Wöchentliche deutsche zeitung

NEW ROADS

PARISH courier journal. w Ja 1 1922+
pub Ag 1922+

POINTE Coupee banner. w 1880+
LNH Je 9 1917
LU My 18,Je 1,22,Ag 10-17 1889

NEWLLANO

LLANO colonist. w 1921+
LBL Mr 9 1929+
M [S 6 1929-Ag 9 1930]

OAKDALE

Oakdale AMERICAN. w O 1921+
pub 1921—

Oakdale JOURNAL. w 1913+
pub 1913+

OPELAUSAS

Opelousas CLARION-NEWS. w O 11 1890+
1890-1922? as St. Landry clarion; 1923?-29? Opelousas clarion progress
1890-92? in English and French
LNH Ja 3 1892
LU 1890-S 1902;O 10 1903-S 1909

Opelousas COURIER. Le Courrier de Opelousas. w D 11 1852-1910||
1852-Ap 18 1863 in English and French
DLC D 13 1862;Ap 18 1863
ICHi Je 24 1876
LLS [D 1852;D 1861;Jl 25 1863-65]Je 15 1867-78;87-Ja 22 1910
LNH Ja 18 1868
LNM S 24 1864
LU 1852-D 1 1855;56-D 1 1860;62-My 27,Ag 12 1865-S 21,O 28 1889-My,S 9 1905-F 5 1910
MB Ap 22 1863
MBAt Ap 30 1863
MHi D 27 1862;Ap 25,30 1863
MWA F 15,Ag 30 1862;Ap 25,30 1863;Je 11 1864
NN D 13 1862;Ap 18,Mr 7 1863
NNHi Ap 18,22,24 1863
NcD S 27 1862;Ag 8 1863
OClWHi O 25 1862;Ap 30 1863
WHi Mr 21 1857

Le DÉMOCRATE de St. Landry. *See* St. Landry democrat

Hebdomadal ENQUIRER. L'enquirer Lebdomadaire. w 1841||
In English and French
DLC Jl 27,Ag 17 1841

Opelousas GAZETTE. Gazette des Opelousas. w My 12 1827-
In English and French
CtY Ag 16 1828
DLC O 20 1832;Jl 27 1833
LNH N 9 1839;Ja 16,30-F 6 1841
LU N 20 1841-S 14 1844;S 25 1847-S 6 1848
MWA S 8 1827;Ja 7 1829;Jl 14 1852
NhD Ag 31 1839
OOxM Je 14,S 27-O 4,D 3,17 1828-My 6,20,Je 10,Jl 1 1829

Opelousas JOURNAL. Le Journal. w Ja 4 1868-78||?
In English and French
LU 1868-69;Ag 6 1870;71-D 8 1877;Ja 5 1878

Opelausas PATROIT. Le Patriote de Opelausas w Mr 3 1855-63||?
Follows St. Landry whig
In English and French
LU 1855-Ag 31 1861
MBAt Ja 3,Mr 7,21-28 1863

Le PROGRÈS de St. Landry. *See* St. Landry progress

ST. LANDRY clarion. *See* Opelousas clarion-news

ST. LANDRY democrat. Le Démocrate de St. Landry. w Ja 19 1878-F 24 1894||
In English and French
LU complete

ST. LANDRY progress. Le Progrès de St. Landry. w Jl 27 1867-S 26 1868||
In English and French
LU Jl 27-O 5,N 2-23,D 14-28 1867;Ja 25, F 22-Mr,Ap 11,My 2-S 26 1868

ST. LANDRY republican. w Ag 15 1876-
LU Ag 15-N 2 1876

ST. LANDRY whig. Le Whig de St. Landry. w S 5 1844-55||?
Followed by Opelausas patriot. . .
In English and French
DLC S 12 1844
LU 1844-Ag 1845;Jl 18 1846

La SENTINELLE du Sud. *See* Southern sentinel

SOUTHERN sentinel. La Sentinelle du Sud. w Ja? 1864-
In English and French
LU O 28 1865-Jl 6 1867

Le WHIG de St. Landry. *See* St. Landry whig

PARADIS

Paradis ENTERPRISE. w 1914-21||?
LNH S 23 1914

PLAQUEMINE

L'AMBASSADEUR d'Iberville. *See* Iberville ambassador

CONDENSER. w N 19 1835-
In English and French
N Mr 19 1836

GAZETTE des planteurs. *See* Planter's gazette

IBERVILLE ambassador. L'Ambassadeur d'Iberville. 1837-
In English and French
DLC My 19 1838

IBERVILLE gazette. w Ap 3 1852-
DLC O 23 1852
MWA Ag 7 1852;Jl 5 1862

IBERVILLE pioneer. *See* Pioneer and news

Weekly IBERVILLE south. Le Sud d'Iberville. w 1857+
Suspended 1875?-79?
In English and French
LBL Mr 9 1929+
LNC N 25 1893
LNH N 6 1869;Ap 23,Je 11,N 5 1870
MsHi Ap 17 1869

Daily JOURNAL. d 1891-1903||?
LNH N 14 1894

Weekly MAGNOLIA. w 1860-
MWA Mr 30 1861

PIONEER and news. w S 12 1868-74||?
1868-73? as Iberville pioneer
MBAt S 19-O 3,N 7,28 1868

PLANTER'S gazette. Gazette des planteurs. w D 1840-45||?
In English and French
DLC Je 24 1841[Ap 12-O 25 1845]

Le SUD d'Iberville. *See* Weekly Iberville south

POINTE A LA HACHE

L'OBSERVATEUR de Plaquemines. *See* Observer

OBSERVER. L'Observateur de Plaquemines. w 1873-84||
In English and French
ICHi Jl 24 1875

POINTE COUPEE

Pointe Coupée DEMOCRAT. Le Démocrate de la Pointe Coupée. w Ja 23 1858-62||?
In English and French
LNH Mr 6 1858
LSfD Jl 6 1861;Mr 8 1862

Le DÉMOCRATE de la Pointe-Coupée. *See* Pointe Coupée democrat

Pointe Coupée ECHO. L'Echo du la Pointe Coupée. w 1861?-71||?
In English and French
LNH Mr 25 1871
LSfD [1869-70]
NNHi Ap 15 1863

PELICAN. w 1877-78||
MWA Ag 31 1878

Pointe Coupée REPUBLICAN. w Je 9? 1871-
LNH F 10 1872

PONCHATOULA

ENTERPRISE. w Mr 1921+
pub 1921+

PONT-BREAUX. *See* BREAUX'S BRIDGE

PORT ALLEN

Port Allen OBSERVER. w Ja 5 1856+
1856-1925? as Sugar planter
LU 1856-58;Ja 29-N 26,D 31 1859-Ja 4 1862;Ja 27 1866-Ja 22 1870;S 3 1881;Ja 21 1882

SUGAR planter. *See* Port Allen observer

PORT HUDSON

Morning COURIER. d 1863-
DLC Ja 21,My 16 1863
MHi Ap 17 1863
MWA My 16 1863(extra)
NN Ap 20-21,My 11 1863
NNHi [Ap-My 1863]

Port Hudson FREEMAN. tr Jl 14 1863-
MWA Jl 14,20 1863
NN Jl 14 1863
NNHi Jl 14-15 1863
OClWHi Jl 15,21 1863

Port Hudson NEWS. w,tw D 1862-
NNHi Ap 14 1863
NcD Ja 14 1863

RAYNE

Rayne TRIBUNE. w 1893+
pub O 12 1904-22;25+
MsHi N 3,17 1894

RAYVILLE

RICHLAND beacon news. w 1869+
1869-87 as Richland beacon
pub 1873+
N Ja 1 1876

RESERVE

Le MESCHACÉBÉ. *See under* Lucy

RICHMOND

MADISON democrat. w 1860-
MWA Ap 4 1861
MsHi Jl 18 1861

MADISON journal. w 1845-
DLC My 14 1847

ROSELAND

Roseland HERALD. w 1891+
LBL Mr 1929-Je 1933

RUSTON

Ruston LEADER. w 1894+
pub 1929+

Ruston daily LEADER. d 1905+
1905-31 as Daily leader
pub 1929+

ST. BERNARD

St. Bernard weekly EAGLE. w 1877-85||
LNH Mr 2 1878;Mr 16 1882

Weekly HERALD. w Ag 13 1868-
MBAt O 29-N 5 1868

ST. FRANCISVILLE

*ASYLUM. w 1820-Jl 30 1825||
1820-Mr 20 1823 as Asylum and Feliciana advertiser
DLC N 8 1821-25
MWA My 29 1824

CRISIS. w
LSfD My 10 1828

St. Francisville DEMOCRAT w F 3 1892+
1892-N 1928 as True democrat
pub 1892+
LBL Mr 1929+
LNH Je 16-Jl,S 15-N 17,D 1,15 1900-F 9,23-My 11,25-Je 15,29 1901
LU Ap 13-D 1912;F 1913-[19-20]+

DUNN leader. *See* Feliciana ledger

FELICIANA herald. w S 25? 1896-D 14? 1898||
LSfD N 20 1896-D 14 1898

FELICIANA ledger. w 1872-77||
Follows Feliciana ledger (Bayou Sara).
1872-Je 12 1875 as Dunn leader
LSfD Ap 19 1873-Ja 6 1877

LOUISIANA (*Continued*)

ST. FRANCISVILLE—*Continued*

FELICIANA republican. *See* St. Francisville republican

FELICIANA sentinel. w 1876-92||?
1876-79? as West Feliciana sentinel
LSfD Ja 13 1877-80[82]-Ag 3,D 1889;S 13-D 13 1890;91-D 3 1892

FLORIDA gazette. w Ja 1829-
DLC Je 27 1829

LOUISIANA chronicle. w Ja 20 1838-
DLC F 10 1838;Ag 21 1841;Ja 1 1842
LSfD Jl 1-8 1843;D 13 1851
MWA S 24 1842;O 11,N 8 1845
TxU O 11-18 1845;Jl 4 1846

LOUISIANA journal. w Ja 15 1824-
DLC F 5,Mr 4,My 27,Jl 22 1824;Mr 24 1825-D 9 1826;Je 21 1828
InI F 3,17 1825
LNC F 18 1836
LNH Ja 30 1841
LSfD [S ? 1824]Jl 28 1827;Ap 19 1828;F 8 1838

PHOENIX. w 1832-
DLC S 21 1833
LSfD S 7 1833;Ag 1,O 28 1835

St. Francisville REPUBLICAN. w S 26 1868-74||?
1868-71? as Feliciana republican
LSfD My 8,Ag 17,O 30,N 20,D 18 1869;Ag 27 1870-Mr 22 1873
MBAt O 3-24,N 28 1868

TRUE democrat. *See* St. Francisville democrat

WEST FELICIANA sentinel. *See* Feliciana sentinel

ST. JOSEPH

NORTH Louisiana journal. *See* Tensas gazette

TENSAS gazette. w 1852+
1852-77 as Tensas gazette; (title varies: Tensan parish gazette) 1878-91 North Louisiana journal
pub 1872+
DLC Ag 23,S 6,N 8 1861
LNH Ag 15 1890
MsHi Jl 27 1867
VRC Ja 23,Ap 10 1863

TENSAS herald. w
TxU Ja 22-N 1853

ST. MARTINVILLE

ATTAKAPAS gazette. Gazette des Attakapas. w Ja 1 1825-
In English and French
CSmH My 15 1830
Ct N 2 1833
DLC D 19 1840
LNH Ja 29-F 13 1841
LU Ap 26-Jl 12 1834
MWA Je 25 1825

ATTAKAPAS sentinel. La Sentinelle des Attakapas. w D 1873-78||?
Je 1874?-S 1875? pub in Breaux's Bridge
In English and French
ICHi Ap 1 1876
LU Ja 8,Je 4 1874:N 6 1875
NNT Je 4-11 1874

COURIER of the Teche. Le Courrier du Têche. w 1850-72||
In English and French
ICU Ap 19 1851;Ap 10 1859;Ja 3 1863
MWA Ja 3 1863;Je 10 1865
NNT F 12 1859;My 11 1861

CREOLE. Le Créole de St. Martinville. w O 16? 1840-
In French and English
DLC Je 19 1841
LU O 14 1848
MWA Ag 25 1849
TxU O 25 1845;My 9 1846

St. Martin DEMOCRAT. Le Démocrate de St. Martin. w 1858-65||
In English and French
MBAt Mr 28 1863
MWA Je 17 1865
NNT Ap 29 1865

ECHO. L'Echo. w Mr 30 1872-78||?
In English and French
Negro
NNHi Mr 15 1873

GAZETTE des Attakapas. *See* Attakapas gazette

Weekly MESSENGER. w F 28 1886+
pub 1886+
LNH Jl 2 1898
LSfD Ap 19 1931

La SENTINELLE des Attakapas. *See* Attakapas sentinel

SHREVEPORT

Shreveport BULLETIN. w 1870-
DLC O 18 1870

CADDO free press. w
WHi Ap 30 1840

CADDO gazette. w 1841-69||?
DLC F 7-21 1844;Mr 17,26 1845;O 24 1849;Ja 30,F 6 1850;Ap 23,My 28,S 10-17 1853;F 3 1855;My 3 1862;N 3 1865
MBAt Jl 14-21,S 1,O 13,D 1 1865;Je 15,29-Jl 6,Ag 3-10,24 1867;Ja 25 1868
Tx D 6 1851
TxU Je 30 1865

Shreveport INTELLIGENCER and Caddo beacon. w
WHi Ja 14 1841

Shreveport JOURNAL. w Ap 3 1848-
DLC Ap 3-My 1 1848

Shreveport JOURNAL. d Ja 7 1895+
1895-97? as Shreveport evening judge
MWA Je 27 1935

Shreveport evening JUDGE. *See* Shreveport journal 1895+

MESSENGER. w
LU Ap 27 1865

Shreveport NEWS. w 1858-70||?
DLC My 10,Jl 1 1864
TxU S 1 1863;Jl 25 1865;Mr 6 1866;Ag 17 1867

Shreveport semi-weekly NEWS. sw N? 1861-
DLC Jl 1 1865
LNH D 2 1865
MBAt Ag 26-S 2,9-19,26,O 10-14,N 7,21,D 19 1865;Ja 13-27,F 17 1866
MiU Mr 25 1862
NNHi Ap 7,O 9 1863

PROGRESS. w 1892-1900||?
NcD [My-O 7 1899]

Shreveport SENTINEL. w
TxU Je 18,Jl 17 1865

SOUTHWESTERN. w 1852-72||
DLC F 4 1857;Jl 20 1864
MBAt O 18,N 8,D 27 1865;Ja 31,F 14 1866
Tx Ag 28 1869
TxGR Mr 25,Ap 15-22,Jl 29,Ag 19,S 2-23,D 2 1863
TxU Ag 23 1854-Ag 12 1857;S 8 1858-Ag 10 1859;Ag 15-S 19 1860;61-Mr 1862[Ap 1863-My 1865]-[71-Mr 15 1872]

Daily SOUTHWESTERN. d 1868-72||
LNH Ap 16-O 14 1869
TxU O 15 1868-O 14 1869

Shreveport evening STANDARD. d 1878-83||?
DLC F 18 1879

Shreveport SUN. w O 6 1920+
Negro
pub 1921+

Shreveport TIMES. d 1872+
Title varies slightly
pub 1872+
DLC Jl 3 1872;Ag 1 1877;Jl 18 1878;My 29 1886;Jl 2,27 1887;Jl-D 1898
LNH My 12 1887;S 28 1902
M Jl 11 1928
NNHi N 15 1873
NcD Ap 1 1873;Ag 10 1897

SLIDELL

Slidell ADVOCATE. w 1902-10||?
DLC F 24 1906
LNH Mr 3 1906

Slidell AMERICAN. w 1911-17||?
LNH O 31 1912

STOCK LANDING

PROGRESS. w
In French and English
LNH [My 26 1888-89]

TALLULAH

MADISON journal. w 1887+
pub N 1912-18;20+
LU Ap 13,My 4,18,Je 29 1889

THIBODAUX

BANNER of the ironsides. w Ap 4 1863-
OClWHi Ap 4,My 5 1863

CONFEDERATE banner. w
In English and French
MWA O 25 1862
NcD O 25 1862

L'ETOILE de Lafourche. *See* Star of Lafourche

INTELLIGENCER and Lafourche and Terrebone advertiser. Le Nouvelliste et moniteur de Lafourche et Terrebonne. w 1833-39||
In English and French
DLC Ag 2 1833;Ja 24 1834

LAFOURCHE comet. w Ap 1889+
pub 1890+
LNH Ag 1 1929

LAFOURCHE union. *See* L'Union de Lafourche

Le NOUVELLISTE et moniteur de Lafourche et Terrebonne. *See* Intelligencer and Lafourche and Terrebone advertiser

PATRIOT of La Fourche-interior. Le Patriot de la Fourche-interne. w Jl 19 1841-44||
In English and French
DLC Jl 19 1841

Weekly Thibodaux SENTINEL. La Sentinelle de Thibodaux. w 1861-1912||?
In English and French
ICHi Ag 26 1873
LNH Ag 30 1890
MHi O 25 1862
MWA O 17 1862
NNHi Ap 26 1873
NNT D 26 1891

STAR of Lafourche. L'Etoile de Lafourche. w Ag 13 1887-
NNT S 3,24-N 5,D 3 1887

STARS and stripes. ir F 24 1863-
MWA F 24,Mr 11 1863

L'UNION de Lafourche, Lafourche union. w Je? 1855-61||?
In French and English
LSfD Jl 17 1856;Je 24 1858;Mr 7 1860

UNION guidon. w My 18 1864-
NNHi My 18 1864

TRINITY

Trinity HERALD. w 1886-89||
LU Je 6-13,27 1889

VERMILIONVILLE. *See* LAFAYETTE

VIDALIA

CONCORDIA eagle. w 1873-90||?
Negro
LU S 4,O 2 1875;Mr 3,Ap 7 1877;Mr 27 1879;Ap 8 1880

CONCORDIA intelligencer. w 1842-
DLC Ag 26,S 2 1848;Jl 7 1849;N 1,29 1861
LU Ag 22 1846;F 27 1847;D 29 1849;Ja 5 1850; Jl 31 1852;F 5-12 1853
MWA My 18-25[Ag 17-N]1844[45-46]-54;O 26 1855;N 16 1860
MsHi My 20[Ag 1843-Jl 11 1846;58-62;67-69]
OClWHi Ja 24 1846
P-M Ap 6 1844
T My 9 1846
TxU Mr 8 1845;S 7 1850

Vidalia HERALD. w 1869-74||?
LU F 25,Ag 19-26 1870

VILLE PLATTE

Weekly GAZETTE. w 1914+
LBL Mr 1929+

VIVIAN

CADDO citizen. w F 20 1930+
pub 1930+

WELSH

RICE Belt journal. w 1901+
LBL Mr 1929+

WEST BATON ROUGE. *See* PORT ALLEN

WINNFIELD

Winnfield COMRADE. *See* Winnfield news-American

Winnfield NEWS-AMERICAN. w 1890+
1890-1914? as Winnfield comrade; 1915?-22? Winnfield times
LBL Mr 15 1929+
LNH F 15 1918

Winnfield TIMES. *See* Winnfield news-American

WINN Parish democrat. w 1887-90||
LU Mr 1-15,O 25 1889;Ap 25 1890

WINN Parish enterprise. w Jl 1 1924+
pub 1924+

MAINE

ALFRED

Alfred ADVOCATE. w 1915-16||
MeU N 4 1915-S 28 1916

COLUMBIAN star. w Jl? 1824-25||
MHi S 9-23,O 28 1824;Mr 24 1825
MWA Ap 28,My 26 1825
MeSY Jl 15 1824-S 8 1825

AUBURN

Auburn CLIPPER. w 1873-75||
MeAu Je 2 1873-[74]-Ja 2 1875

Auburn daily GAZETTE. d 1888-91||
MeBB Ja 10 1891

GREENBACK-LABOR chronicle. w 1875-80||
NcD Ja 23 1880

AUGUSTA

ADVOCATE of freedom. *See under* Hallowell

AGE. w,tw,d D 22 1831-63||?
d,tw during sessions of legislature
DLC 1832-33;Ja 20,Mr 13 1834;36-[44]45;47-49; 56;F 14,Ag 29 1861
MSaE Ja-Ap 5,N 9 1836;S 11 1841;Ja 17,Jl 22, D 2 1852;F 7-9,25-28 1854
MWA Mr 17 1836;Ag 8 1838;Mr 26 1839;Ja 4, 9-14,18 1840;Mr 23 1843;S 20 1844;Jl 30 1846; Jl 30(extra)N 12 1847;Ag 20 1850;Ja 10,F 5, 10,Mr 6,25,Ap 6,13-15,24,Jl 22 1852;Ja 20-F 5, 10,15 1853;Ja 21,F 25,Mr 30 1854;Ja-Mr 20, Ap 3,S 13 1855;Ja 7-Mr,D 9 1858;Ja 6-Ap 5 1859;Ja-F 7,Mr-Ap 24 1861;Mr 5 1863
MeAlC 1847-50;52
MeAuC 1854-56
MeBB Ag 12-15 1834;Ja 4 1844;My 20 1847;Ag 11 1849;Mr 5 1853;Ja-F,Ap 1-22 1854;Ja 15 1856;Mr 29-31 1859;Ja 30 1862
MeBa Ag 18 1840;Mr 5 1847;S 23 1852
MeBt Ja 6-Ap 5 1853
MeHi D 23 1831-D 19 1832;F 19,Mr 10-12,Ag 12-15 1834[F 10-28,Mr 14-26]Ap 15 1835;Ja 15-F 26,My 27,Je 24,Jl 1,5,S 16 1842[43]F 1 1845;My 7 1847;N 2 1848;Ja 10,F 5,Ap 5 1853; Ja 7-Ap 22 1854;Ja 11,F 5,18 1862
MeSY 1839-Ap 8 1845
MeP Ja 7 1836-Ap 1 1837;Ja 8-Ap 18 1857;Ja 7-Mr 1858;Ja 6-Ap 5 1859;Ja 5-Mr 22 1860;Ja 4-Ap 25 1861;Ja-Mr 1862;Ja 8-Mr 27 1863
NNHi Mr 21,D 19 1832;F 11 1833;Mr 6 1835;F 10,Je 17-24,S 16 1842;Ja 23 1844;Ja 28 1848
NcD Ja 25,F 5 1853;Ja 23,F 20 1858;Ja 3 1861
NhD Ja 9 1841
NjR Mr 29 1849
P-M F 14,Ap 3 1852

APPEAL to the democracy.
MWA Ag 7 1838
WHi Ag 17 1840

Augusta COURIER. w Ag 19 1831-N 26 1832||
Me 1831-Ag 17 1832
NN Ja 12 1832

DREW'S rural intelligencer. *See* Maine rural (Gardiner)

HONEST truth. w Jl 29 1879-
campaign paper
MWA Jl 29 1879
MeBa Jl 29-Ag 12,26-S 2 1879;Jl 28-S 8 1880
MeHi S 2 1879

Daily JOURNAL. *See* Kennebec journal

KENNEBEC age. w
MeMC Ja 18-D 1853;Ja 1-22 1857

KENNEBEC journal. w,d,tw Ja 8 1825-1914||
Title varies: Daily journal; Maine daily journal; Tri-weekly journal
d,tw during sessions of legislature
pub complete
CSmH Ag 27 1830
DLC Mr 24 1827;Mr 14-28,Jl 11,Ag 8 1828;Mr 13[Je-D 1829]-Ja 8,22,D 24 1830;Ja 14 1831; Je-D 1832-Ja-Mr,Ag 1839-43;Mr 22-D 1849; 51-52;64;66 D 8 1869
KHi 1890-My 17 1893
MB Ja 8 1825-D 23 1826;Ja 3,Mr 5 1833;Ja-Mr 14 1834;Ja 8 1835-Ap 5 1836;Ja 18-Jl 12 1837
MBAt Ja 30,S 18-25 1829
MHi O 29 1825;F 3-10 1827;N 7 1840;Mr 27 1841
MSaE Ap 5 1876;Jl 15 1852;F 6,20-24,Mr 1 1854;S 16 1868
MWA Ja 8-15,Ap 23,My 14-21 1825;Ja 14 1826; N 17 1827;My 22,Jl 24 1829;D 24 1830;Ja 27,Ap 13 1832;F 13,20-Mr 3 1834;F 5-7,Ap 22,Mr 19,O 7 1835;Ja 17 1838;F 2,14-16,Mr 21,26,O 1,15-D 3,24 1839-Ap 17,My 1,Je 19-O 8,29,N 12 1841[42-43]-52;Ap 2,Je 2,Ag 4 1853;Ja-Mr 19 1855;O 10 1856;F 9,Mr 25-27 1857;Ja 15,25-F 1 1858;Ja 7-Ap 6 1859;F 13,S 14 1860;F 20,Ap 24 1861;Jl 25,Ag 29 1862;D 4 1863;Ja 7-Mr 26 1864;Ja-F 1865;My 24 1867;F 23 1870;Ap 26 1871-[74]-92
MeAuC 1854-78;80-1906
MeBB Ja 5 1855;Ja 8-Mr 24 1864;Ja-Mr 9 1868;Ja 7-Mr 13 1869
MeBa Ja 8 1825[28-30]Ap 14,S 26 1840;Ja 16,F 13,Jl 16-23,S 17 1841;Ap 29 1842;My 26,O 13 1843;Ja 12,Je 7,O 11,N 15 1844;Jl 3 1846;D 10 1847;Ap 28,O 5 1848;Mr 5,Ap 21,S 9 1852; Ja 21,F 11 Mr 23 1853;Ja 11,F 6,15 1854;Ja 5-17,22,31,F 7-9,14-Mr 7,12,16,19 1855[Ja-Ap 1856]Ja 8-Mr 16,20-Ap 17,Jl 31 1857; Ja 13-18,F 10,15-22,26-Mr 26,31 1858;Ja 7-Mr 9,14-Ap 6 1859;Ja-F 13,17-Mr 21 1860;Ja 4-7,11-Mr 13,18,Ap 24-25 1861;Mr 10 1862;Ja 9-F 2,6-20,25-Mr 27 1863;O 28-N 4 1864[Ap-D 1865]Ja 5,10-F 26 1866[Ja-Mr 1868;Ja-Mr 1869]Ap 8 1874;Ap 18-20,N 21 1888;Je 24 1891; My 4 1892;Ja 16 1895
MeBt Ja-Ap 2 1853
MeBtC D 30 1859-D 20 1861
MeHa Ja-Mr 13 1832;Ja-Mr 14 1834;Ja-Mr 21 1838
MeHi Ja-Mr 14,D 30 1831-Mr 5 1833;35-36 [38-39]-Ap 4,O 17 1840-D 19 1845;D 25 1846-D 17 1847;D 21 1848-D 12 1850;Ap 21 1854[64]-F 1865;Ja-F 1866[Ja-Mr 1867]69
MeMC Ja 9-Ap 10 1841;Ja 6-Ap 21 1854;F 16 1855-Ja 10 1856;Ja 23 1857-1913
MeP [N 1833-Je 1852]56-Ap 17 1857;Ja 8-Mr 1858; Ja 10-Ap 6 1859;Ja 6-Mr 21 1860;Ja-Ap 1861;Ja-Mr 1862;Ja 8-Mr 27 1863;Ja 7 1864-F 1865
MeU Ja-Mr 1868;Ja-Mr 1869
MeWC 1869-My 23 1878
MiU 1842
N S 23,D 9 1831[32-34]Jl 20,O 21,N 25 1835; Ja 6,Jl 6,D 7-14 1836;My 3,24 1837;Ap 18, Jl 18,N 21,D 19 1838[Ja-Ag 1839]Ag 29 1840
NN Ja 7 1830;Mr 15 1836;F 11 1856
NNHi Ja 20 1832-[Ja-Jl 1833]Ja-Mr,My 1835-[37;39]Ag 31 1866;Ap 16 1868 [Ja-Mr 1869] My 30 1873
NcD Ag 9,N 22 1844;O 23 1851;Ag 19-26 1852;S 12 1856[Ja-Mr 1864]F 17 1865
NjR Ag 11-18 1848
OClWHi Ja 6 1865

KENNEBEC journal. d Ja 1 1870+
Title varies: Daily Kennebec journal
pub 1870
DLC Jl 15 1874+
KHi 1890-My 17 1893
M N 13 1929;Ap 6 1933
MSaE S 20,O 11 1916
MWA Ja-Ap 1,N 21 1870;Ja-Mr 1871;Mr 18 1872;Ja 28 1874;O 9 1882;D 20 1887;Ja 8 1925
MeHi [Ja 1873-S 15 1875]Jl 11 1879[F 9 1881-D 1 1883]Ja 17 1916
MeP 1870-F 27 1871;Ja 4 1872-Mr 1 1873;Ja 7-Mr 6 1874;Ja 7-F 26 1875;79-Mr 24 1880; 81-Mr 17 1883;Ja 7 1885-Mr 19 1887
MeU Ja-Ap 1895
MeWC 1870-My 23 1878
NNHi [Ja-Mr 1870]N 6 1872;My 30 1873

MAINE daily journal. *See* Kennebec journal

MAINE patriot and state gazette. w O 31 1827-D 1831||
CSmH Jl 21 1830
Ct [1828-31]
DLC Mr 11 1829-30
MBAt S 10 1828
MWA N 7 1827;Ag 13 1828;O 21 1829
MeBB Ja 9,Ap 16 1828
MeHi O 29 1828-O 21,N 4 1829;Je 16 1830; Ja 14,F 16 1831
NN Ag 25 1830

MAINE standard. w 1867-80||
MWA Jl 16,O 29 1869;Ja 21,Je 3,N 18 1870; S 20 1872;Mr 31 1876;F 6-13,27-Mr 5 1880
MeBa Ja 17,31-F 7,Mr 13-20,Ap 10,Ag 14 1868
NNHi Ap 4 1873
WHi Ap 1876-N 12 1880

MAINE temperance gazette. *See under* Portland

NEW age. w 1867-1920||?
MWA Jl 31 1885
MeHi F 9 1900

Daily STANDARD. d D? 1879-80||
MWA Ja 30-F 4,7-9,11-13,18,21,25-28,Mr 6,9,15 1880

VOICE of the people. w My 18 1838-44||
DLC My 25 1838
MB My-S 3 1838
MWA Je 8 1838
MeBB O 24 1844
MeBa Jl 4,18,Ag 1,15-S 12,26-N 14 1844
NN Jl 20 1838
NNHi Ag 24 1838

WASHINGTONIAN. w Je 9 1841-
MWA Jl 14-28,Ag 25 1841;F 16 1842

BANGOR

BANGOREAN. w Ja-O 1836||
Merged with Mechanic and farmer
MeBa Mr 17 1836

Weekly BUDGET. w
MeBa Je 17 1880

CLARION. w My 3 1828-
N Ja 17 1829

Bangor weekly COMMERCIAL. w F 15 1838-1925||?
1838-79 as Democrat; 1880-81 Bangor weekly commercial and democrat
DLC S 20 1838;O 26-N 2 1852;Ja-Ap 22 1856
IU S 27 1838
KHi Je 18,Jl 30-Ag 6 1861
MB [1838-45]
MHi Je 9 1846;Je 26 1855
MSaE Jl 13 1852;Ag 24 1876
MWA Jl 21 1840;O 9 1860;Mr 5 1868
MWiC Ap 16 1868
MeB F 1848-Ja 1850
MeBa 1838-F 8 1842;F 1843-Ja 19 1847;F 1848-[51]Ja 6,20,F 24-Mr 2,16,30-Ap 6,27-My 11, 25,Je 8,N 1,16-23 1852[Mr-D 1853]Ja 10,Mr 28-Ap,Ag 1-15,O 24-31 1854;Mr 6,27-Ap 17, My 22 1855;Ja 8,22 1856-Ja 6,27,Mr 31 1857; Ja 26,Ap 20-My 4,25,Je 15,Jl 13,Ag 3,31 1858; O 4 1859;My 21,Ag 6 1861;Mr 31 1863;Jl 4, Ag 1 1867;Ja 13,Je 2 1870;Mr 28 1902
MeHi Ja 7 1851;Ag 13 1861;Ja 5 1900
MeP My 28 1839-Je 8 1841

Bangor daily COMMERCIAL. d Ja 1 1872+
DLC N 26 1897-98;1900-Ap 1901
KHi [Je 14-Ag 2 1888]
MWA Ja 1-2,6,8-9,12-16,19,22,26,F 5-6,9-10, 12-13,16-17,21-23,26 1880;Ap 9 1881;Jl 23 1883; Ag 24 1885;F 22(supp)1897
Me My 1902+
MeBa Mr 29 1873;Ap 1,24,D 2 1875;S 10,21, D 3 1878;D 26 1879;Ag 18,N 26 1881;Mr 15, Jl 22,Ag 28 1882;Mr 9, Ap 2 1883;85;Ja 1, Jl 1886-87;Mr 31,Jl 1888-Je 1890;F 16,Mr 14, My 17,22-24,27,Je 4-5,7-8,12,18,21-22,26,28,Jl 1 1895;Ja 4,Mr 9,28 1896;F 22,My 6,O 15 1897; Ap 1,11,My 2,Je 17-18,22,Jl 4 1898;Ja-S,O 10 1899;Jl-S,N 10,15 1900 Ja-S 1901;Ja-Mr,S 1913+
MeHi Ap 19 1881;Ja 1,5 1900
MeU O 1930+
NNHi Ap 29 1873
NcD Mr 26 1892
NcU Ag 26 1875

Daily COMMERCIAL advertiser. d Ag 18 1835-D 1836||
Ct Ag 19 1835
DLC Ag 19 1835
MWA My 25 1836

Bangor COMMERCIAL advertiser. w Ag 18 1835-My 31 1836||
MWA D 15 1835
MeBa complete
NN Mr 22 1836

COON dissector.
MWA Ap 17 1844

Bangor COURIER. w Jl 2 1833-1900||?
DLC Jl 9 1833;O 2 1838
KHi Ag 3-10 1888
MSaE Jl 20 1852
MWA Jl 14 1835;O 22 1850;O 30-N 6,20 1860
MeBa N 29 1836;S 26-N 7 1837;Jl 1838-Je 18 1839;D 1 1840;Mr 31,Ap 14,S 15, 1829;N 30 1830;Jl 26 1831;Jl 10 1832;N 5,D 17 1833;Ja 7 1834; F 21 1837
MeBB Ag 30 1827;Mr 4 1828;Jl 30 1833
MeBa F 9-16 1830;My 1,22,Jl 30,S 18 1838
MeHi Jl 13 1830
NN Ag 24 1830;Ja 20 1835
NNHi D 27 1827-Ja,O 14 1828-Mr 3,17-Je 2,Ag 25 1829-Ja 5,19,F 2 1830
WHi My 10 1827;D 19 1837

Bangor GAZETTE. w Ap 30 1842-
DLC Je 11 1842;O 26 1844
MB [1842-F 23]N 7 1847
MWA My 11 1844;S 12 1846
MeBa Jl 15-22,S 28 1843;Ja 24,Mr 4,Je 22,Jl 18 1844;O 25 1845;Ja 24,S 26 1846
MeHi Ap 24 1844
NNHi My 11 1844;Ja 17 1846

Bangor daily GAZETTE. d 1843-
MWA O 4 1843
MeBa S 28 1843;Ja 24,Mr 4 Jl 18 1844

Bangor INDEPENDENT. w 1916||?
MeBa Mr 25-My 12,Jl 16-S 9 1916

Bangor JEFFERSONIAN. w Mr 1 1849-S 20 1870||
1849-F 1851 as Jeffersonian
DLC [1864-S 18 1866]
MHi Ap 5 1864
MSaE Je 8 1852
MWA Ag 18 1863
MeBa 1849-Je 1867
MeBaHi 1849-Je 4 1867;D 29 1868-70
MeHi Ja 6 1851;D 30 1856
NNHi Ag 23-30,S 6 1853;Jl 5 1870

JEFFERSONIAN daily evening news. d Je 28-Ag 2 1862||
MeBa Je 28 1862

Bangor JOURNAL. w Je 1 1837-My 24? 1838||
MSaE Mr 29 1838
MeBB 1837-My 24 1838
MeBa N 9 1837

Bangor daily JOURNAL. d Ag 26 1854-Jl 31 1857||
Followed by Bangor daily union
MWA 1854-F 24,Ag 27 1855-F 1 1856;F 16-Jl 1857
MeBa Jl 31,N 14,D 1 1855;Ja 3,8,14,17,My 22, S 20,30,D 20 1856
MeBaHi Mr 6-Ag 23 1855

Bangor LIFE. w
MeBa Ap 27 1890

MECHANIC and farmer. w F 6 1835-F 21 1839||
MSaE Mr 23 1837
MWA D 18 1835
MeBa D 4 1835;F 23,Mr 9,Ap 27,My 11-Je 1,15-22,Jl 6-13,S 14,28,O 12,N 2,D 28 1837-39
NN N 20 1835;Mr 17 1836

MAINE (*Continued*)

BANGOR—*Continued*

Bangor daily MERCURY. d Ap 15 1844-56||?
Merged with Bangor daily journal
DLC [Ap-Jl 1844]Jl 8 1845;Mr 26-31,Ap 2-5 1855
MSaE Jl 28 1852
MeBa Ap 27,Je 30,O 15-D 2,15 1844-Ap 12,Je 21,O 8,D 5,24 1845;Ag 14,28,S 30 1846;Ja 28,F 9,Mr 5 1847;Ja 4,11,Je 17 1848;Je 6,Jl 25 1850;Ja 16,23,30,Jl 1 1851;Ap 23 1852;F 19,Mr 11,S 17 1853;Jl 24,28,Ag 1 1854;N 10,D 15 1855;Ja 10,12 1856
MeBaHi Ap-O 14 1844;Ap 14-O 12 1845;Ap 14 1846-O 14 1848

Weekly MERCURY. w 1844?-54||
MSaE Jl 20 1852
MeBa Ag 27 1850
MeHi Ja 7 1851

Bangor MESSENGER. w 1881-83||
MeHi Ag 23 1882

Bangor daily NEWS. d Je 18 1889+
pub Mr 1900+
DLC Mr 5 1900-01;My 1902+
MWA Jl 4(extra)1889
MeBa 1902-Ap,N 1913+
MeU [1898-Ap]Jl 1930+

Bangor semi-weekly NEWS. w,sw 1889?-1920||?
1889-96? as Bangor weekly news (w)
Me Jl 1900-20
MeBa Jl 16-D 3 1896[S 1897-Je 1903;Jl-D 1906] Mr 8 1912

NORTHERN border. w Ja 4 1873-77||
MWA Ja-Mr 15,Ap 5 1873
MeBa Mr 22,My 24 1873;F 20,Jl 3 1875

PENOBSCOT freeman. w Ag 7 1834-Ag 4 1835||
MBAt My 5 1835
MeBa complete
NNNi N 18 1834

PENOBSCOT gazette. w 1824-F 1827||
Followed by Eastern republican
MSaE My 24 1826
MeBa O 19 1825
NNHi Mr 15 1826

PENOBSCOT journal. w Ag 9 1831-33||
Follows Bangor register
MeBa 1831-Jl 1832
NN Ja 31 1832

PLAIN DEALER. w Jl 28 1840-
MWA Ag 4 1840
WHi Ag 4 1840

Bangor POST. w
Ct Jl 18 1837

Bangor RECORD. w
MeBa Jl 29 1880

***Bangor REGISTER.** w N 25 1815-Ag 2 1831||
Title varies: Bangor register and Penobscot advertiser; Bangor weekly register. Followed by Penobscot journal
Suspended from Ag 23-D 25 1817
CtY Mr 15 1831
DLC 1821-26;Ja 23 1828;29
MBAt F 22 1821
MHi N 28 1822;Ja 26 1826;O 24 1827
MSaE Ag 11 1825
MWA Mr 30-Ap 6 1826;Ja 2 1828;Ap 6 1830
MeBa 1821;S 9 1824;D 14 1826;Ja 31,Je 27,Ag 29-S 5,D 12 1827;D 16 1828;Ap 7 1829;Jl 6 1830
MeBaHi 1828
NN D 7 1830

Daily REPUBLICAN. d 1833-
DLC Ja 17 1834

REVEILLE. d
MeBa D 21 1864

Bangor daily evening TIMES. d Je 19 1858-68||
DLC F 19-O 1866;Ja 3-Jl 1867
MWA S 24 1863;Je 23 1864;Ja 12-24,28-F 1,3-27,Ap 28 1865
MeBa Je 30 1858;My 13 1859;F 1,Ap 11,Je 5,11 1860[Ap-D 1861]Ja 6,24,28,31,F 3,8,13,Mr 15, 29,Ap 5,8,Jl 19,Ag 7,14,20,29 1862[63-S 1864] Ap 7,10,15,19,My 16,20 1865;Ja 24,Mr 26 1868
MeHi Ag 27 1862-S 26 1865
NcD F 15,17 1865

Bangor daily UNION. d Ag? 1857-
Follows Bangor daily journal
DLC 1859-Mr 4 1861

VELOCIPEDE. d
MeBa Mr 30-Ap 1 1869

Bangor daily WHIG and courier. d Jl 1 1834-Je? 1900||
1833-Je 1834 as Bangor courier; Jl-D 2 1834 Bangor daily whig. Merged with Bangor daily news
A 1850;Jl 1867
DLC N 28 1840;O 10 1848-99
MB Jl 25 1833;N 10 1836;F 25,Ap 4,O 7,9-10 1837;Je 4,Jl 5 1838;S 16,N 23 1839;Ag 26,N 6 1840;S 4 1841;Ag 23 1842;Ag 2 1843[Ap 18-N 25 1844]Ja 11,O 23 1845;Je 1 1852
MBAt Ap 17 1865
MHi Ja 16 1857
MSaE Ap 11 1839;Ja 28 1852
MWA D 2 1834;N 24-25 1836;N 4 1840;Ap 5, O 3 1843[Je 8-D 1849]N 5,22 1856;Je 30 1858[Ag-D 1861]O 31 1862[Je 19-O 24 1863] F 15 1864-My 13,Jl 28 1865;O 1 1869;Je 5,O 18-19 1871;Mr 5,D 2 1885;Mr 5 1888;Jl 6 1891
Me Jl 1893-Je 1900
MeBa Jl 1836-Ap 12,Jl 1845-Mr 3 1900
MeHi Je 6 1835;Ja 4 1851[Ja 30 1860-Mr 2 1885]F 7 1900
MeP Jl 2 1839-Jl 1 1840
MeU [1844-99]
MiU-C O 1 1869
NN Mr 20 1835
NNHi Mr 28,Ag 18 1838;Ap 7,N 30-D 1 1840; Ap 5,Ag 29 1842;Ag 18 1843;Jl 8 1845;Jl 1848-Je 1849;F 11,Je 5-6 1850;Je 29 1870;N 6 1872; Je 2 1873;Mr 13 1874
NcD Ag 22 1863;F 17,My 18,Je 21 1864;Mr 30-Ap 12,15-20,22-30 1865
NjR D 22 1865
OClWHi D 18 1865
P-M F 12 1845
WHi S 12 1856;68-71
—w ed *See* Bangor courier

BAR HARBOR

Daily HERALD. d Jl 6-S 4 1886||
MWA complete
MeHi complete
NcD complete

MAINE coast cottager. *See under* Portland

MOUNT DESERT herald. *See* Maine coast cottager (Portland)

Bar Harbor RECORD. w Jl 14 1887-1917||
United with Bar Harbor times, to form Bar Harbor times and record, later Bar Harbor times
MeBh 1887-[1909-16]

Bar Harbor TIMES. w Jl 11 1914+
1917?-25? as Bar Harbor times and record
MeBh [1916-24]
MeHi Ja 3 1900

Bar Harbor TOURIST. sw 1880-
pub in Summer only
MWA Ag 12 1885;Ag 13 1887
MeBa Ag 4 1883
NN Jl 25 1883

YOUNG democrat. m Mr 2 1935-
MWA Mr 2 1935

BATH

AMERICAN sentinel. w 1854-93||?
1854-Ag 1855 pub at Damariscotta
DLC Jl 21-28 1859
MWA Je 6,S 27 1855;Ap 29 1858;Ja 8,29 1863; Ap 18 1867-O 1868;Ag 31 1871;Ap 21,My 5,Je 16 1887
MeBHi S-9 1869-71;Mr 1872-83;Ja 10 1884-Je 4,18 1885-86
MeBa O 19 1865
MeBt 1855-56;Mr 14 1872-My 1889
MeBtC 1869-82;86
OClWHi O 27 1859;D 15 1864
—d ed *See* Bath daily sentinel; Bath daily times

Bath ANVIL. w 1905-08||?
MeBt Ja 13 1906-Ja 13 1907
MeHi My 11,Jl 20 1907;My 2 1908

Bath COMMERCIAL. w Je 2 1869-78||?
Follows Seaside oracle
MWA O 25 1879
MeHi Je 2 1877

DOLLAR weekly inquirer. *See* Maine inquirer

EASTERN times. w 1846-60||?
United with Bath daily tribune to form Bath daily tribune and Eastern times
DLC N 4 1852;My-D 1856
MSaE Jl 29,D 2 1852
MWA My 22,Je 20 1856;My 25 1860
MeBt Mr 14 1850-Ap 24 1856

Bath ENTERPRISE. sw 1890-1902||
Merged with Bath independent
MeBt complete
MeBtC complete
MeBtT 1890-92;96;1901-02

Saturday GAZETTE. w S 28 1839-71||
1839-50 as Maine cultivator and Hallowell gazette (title varies slightly); 1851-68 Hallowell gazette (Hallowell)
MSaE S 28-O 4 1839[40-41]Jl 24 1852;Mr 10 1866
MWA S-N 22 1839;Ja 17-D 5 1840;41-Mr 5,Ap 30 1842;Je 8,Jl 27 1844;Je 28,D 13-20 1845;Ja Mr 7,28,Ag 22,S 5,N 7,D 12-26 1846;Ja 30-F 6,27-Mr 6 1847;F 16 1856;Ap 3 1858;Ap 6 1861;Ag(supp)1871
MeHi O 1839-[40;Ap 10-S 1841]Ja 4 1851 extras:Ap 23,24,25,My 3 1861
NN D 12 1840
NNHi O 3 1840;Ja 28 1843
PPL N 9 1850
WHi [O 1839-Ap 17 1841]

***GAZETTE and inquirer.** w D 8 1820-Mr 17 1836||
1820-33 as Maine gazette. Followed by Lincoln telegraph
CSmH Ag 27 1830
DLC Ja 19-F 2,23,My 25,Je 1,Jl 27,N 30 1821; My 31,Je 21-Ag 2,30,S 12-27,O 18 1822;O 31,N 20 1823 [24-25;My-D 1829]
MBAt Ag 8 1828
MH 1821-22[27]
MSaE Ag 1 1823
MWA 1821-23;Mr 12,N 5 1824;D 21 1827;O 3, N 28 1828;Je 25 1830
MeBB 1822-23
MeHi [1834-36]
MeBt N 1832-33
NcD Jl 21 1821

Bath INDEPENDENT. w 1879+
MWA My 22 1886;D 3(supp)1887;Mr 13 1897
MeBa F 2,16,Mr 2,23,My 25,Je 8 1895;My 27, Je 10-Jl 1, N 4(supp)1899;F 24 1900
MeBt D 18 1880-D 3 1881;D 16 1882-D 10 1887[94-1924;26-30;32-33]
MeBtC 1889;94-1919;21-29;31
MeBtT 1868-69;95-1919

KENNEBEC courier. w 1861-
1861-Ag 1863 pub in Hallowell
MWA D 3 1863
MeHa Ag 1862-Ag 6 1863
ODW S 4,18,O 23,N 20,D 4-11 1862;My 28,Je 19 1863

LINCOLN telegraph. w Mr 17 1836-S 1846||
Follows Gazette and inquirer. Followed by Northern tribune
DLC Je 11 1840;Ap 21 1843
MWA My 10 1838;Ag 13-27,S 24,N 5 1840; Ja 28 1841;Je 2 1842;My 30 1844
MeBHi 1841-42
MeHi O 21,N 4-11,25-D 1 1836;My 25 1837; Ja 25 1838;Ja 31,Jl 11,Ag 15,S 12 1839
NNHi My 21 1840
OClWHi Ja 15-22 1846

MAINE gazette. *See* Gazette and inquirer

MAINE inquirer. w O 14 1824-36||?
Title varies: Maine inquirer and advertiser; Maine inquirer and Lincoln county advertiser. United with Maine gazette to form Gazette and inquirer
Ct Ap 11 1826[28]
MBAt D 17 1824;Je 23 1829
MSaE Je 12 1827
MWA 1824-O 10 1826;Ja 1 1828
MeBB O 30-N 6 1827;Ja 15,Mr 4 1828
MeBt 1824-O 7 1828;N 9 1830-N 9 1832;N 8 1833
MeBtT 1824-O 10 1826
MeHi Jl 5 1833
MeU 1827-31
MnHi Je 8 1832
N O 18 1833
NNHi O 22 1824-[Mr-D 1826]-O 2 1827;My 18 1828;D 1 1829
PEL Ag 15 1834

MAINE inquirer. sw Je 10-S 13 1842||
MWA complete

MAINE inquirer. w Je 22 1842-
Je-S 7? 1842 as Dollar weekly inquirer
MWA Ag 24,S 14 1842-Je 12 1844

MAINE reporter. sw
MeB Jl 31 1832

Weekly MIRROR. w 1849-S 23? 1853||
MSaE Ag 28 1852
MWA D 14 1850;Ag 12 1853
MeBtT Ag 23 1851-S 23 1853
MeHi Ja 4 1851

Bath daily MIRROR. d 1853-O? 1859||
United with Northern tribune to form Bath daily tribune, later Bath daily tribune and eastern times
DLC [Ag 18-D 5 1858;Ap 12-O 1859]
MWA S 26,29,O 20,N 8,15,D 20 1854;Ja 11,17, 23,F 7,28,Mr 6,27,Ap 3,My 1,16,23,29 1855
MeBtT Ag 23 1851-S 23 1853
MeHi Ja 4 1851

Tri-weekly NORTHERN tribune. d,tw 1848-My 1855||
1848-S? 1853 as Daily Northern tribune. Followed by Bath daily tribune, later Bath daily tribune and eastern times
MWA Ja 15,Je 25,Jl 2,8,17,20-22,Ag 21,S 7 1847;Mr 15-25 1848
MeBa D 25 1846-Ja 4 1847;O 24 1851;D 8 1853
MeHi Ja 2-3 1851

NORTHERN tribune and weekly mirror. w 1847-56||
Follows Lincoln telegraph
1847-S? 1853 as Northern tribune. Merged with Eastern times
DLC N 5 1852
MSaE My 21 1852
MWA F 4,Mr 17,Jl 21-28 1848[49]F 15 1850; Ja 17,D 12 1851[52-53]Ja 6 1854;Ja 5,N 30 1855;Mr 14 1856
MeBa D 25 1846-Ja 4 1847;O 24 1851;D 8 1853

SEASIDE oracle. m,smw Ja 1869-My 26 1877||
Followed by Bath commercial m 1869; sm 1870-71
1869-S 1876 pub at Wiscasset
MHi F 24(extra)1872
MWA complete
MeHi O 1876-77
NNHi 1872-My 10,Je 28,S 6 1873;Ja 10-Jl 4,25-S,O 24,N 21 1874;75-My 1876;F 7(supp)-14,28,O 10-N,D 12-26 1874
NcD 1872-S 23 1876;O 10 1874-[75]-My 13 1876

Bath daily SENTINEL. d Ag 11 1856-61||
United with Bath daily morning times to form Daily sentinel and times, later Bath daily times
MWA Ag 14 1856
MeBHi Ag-N 8 1856;61
—w ed *See* American sentinel

Semi-weekly SENTINEL. sw 1860-
MeBB [Ap 17 1861-My 31 1862]

Daily SENTINEL and times. *See* Bath daily times

TELESCOPE. w Ja 26 1838-
MWA Ap 13 1838
MeBa Ag 10 1838

Bath daily TIMES. d 1860+
1860-62 as Bath daily morning times; 1862-70 Daily sentinel and times
pub 1864-76;78-94;96+
DLC F 17,19-21,Mr 6-7,9 1863
KHi Jl 31,Ag 6-7 1888
M Ag 14 1922
MSaE My 3,5 1864;F 19 1866
MWA My 27 1861;My 7 1863;F 20 1872;My 5 1877;Mr 7,20,27 1879;Jl 9,O 5,N 20 1885;My 9, 16,Je 1,4,28 1887
MeBHi D 1866-N 1867;Je 23-D 1868
MeBa O 28,N 11-12 1861
MeBt 1866-67;69+
MeBtC Je 6 1862-Je 4 1867;68-92;94+
MeHi Je 12 1865-Je 2 1866
NcD Mr 20 1879
—w ed *See* American sentinel

MAINE (*Continued*)

BATH—*Continued*

Bath daily TRIBUNE and eastern times. d Je 5 1855-58||
1855?-S 4 1857 as Bath daily tribune
MWA Jl 27,Ag 3,17,O 1-2 1855;Jl 21,Ag 5 1856;Ja 23,F 4 1858
MeBt S 1855-My 8 1856;Ag 1857-Ag 12 1858
OClWHi S 10 1856

BELFAST

Belfast weekly ADVERTISER. w 1871-74||
MWA Jl 1871
MeBe D 30 1873-D 29 1874

Belfast ADVOCATE. *See* American advocate

Belfast AGE. w Jl 1 1854-99||
1854-S 5 1889 as Progressive age
MWA Jl 29,O 27 1854; Jl 1(extra)1856;N 26 1857;Jl 1 1858;O 20 1859;N 7 1861;Je 12,Ag 28 1862;Mr 16,S 21 1865;N 21 1873;Ag 26 1875; F 6-13,Mr 6,Ap 17,My 15,29-Je 19 1879;S 2 1880
MeBa [1854-64]Ag 7,28-S 11,O 9 1868;Ja 22 1869;My 12 1871;Je 21 1872;Ag 19 1875;My 3 1877
MeBe 1861-F 9 1899
MeHi Mr-Ap 1857[Ap 14-Je 23 1892]
OClWHi Ag 12 1866
P-M My 24 1855

AMERICAN advocate. w N 3 1830-Ap 28 1836||
Title varies: Maine advocate; Maine workingman's advocate
MWA My 4-11,S 1 1831;Jl 2-23 1835
MeBB N 3 1830
MeBe 1830-O 24 1832;N 6-13,27-D 4 1833;Ja 8-23,F 27,Mr 13-Ap,Jl 30,Ag 14,28-S 11,O 9,D 4-11 1834;Mr 7,12,Je 11,Jl 30,N 19,D 3, 17-31 1835;Mr 24 1836
MeHi 1830-O 1834
MeSY Je 26 1832-34

Belfast GAZETTE. w Je 28 1826-Mr 12 1828||
Follows Hancock gazette and Penobscot patriot. Followed by Waldo democrat
DLC complete
MWA Ag 22 1827;Ja 9 1828

*HANCOCK gazette and Penobscot patriot. w Jl 6 1820-Je 21 1826||
Jl-D 7 1820 as Hancock gazette. Followed by Belfast gazette
DLC Jl 1822-26
MBAt Ap 12-My 23 1821
MSaE Jl 30 1823
MWA 1821-S,N 6,22,D 1822;Ja 29,F 19,Je 25, O 22,D 31 1823;D 15 1824;O 19 1825
MeBe 1821-Je 14 1826
MeBeR 1821-26
MiU-C Mr 27-Ap 5 1821

Belfast INTELLIGENCER. w N 3 1836-Ja 12 1839||
MeBe complete

MAINE advocate. *See* American advocate

MAINE farmer and political register. w Ap 8 1829-O 1830||
CSmH Jl 7 1830
MHi F 24-S 22 1830
MWA My 5 1830
MeBB Ag 12,26-S 2,O 21 1829-Mr 1830
MeBe 1829-S 22 1830
MeHi complete

MAINE free press. w Je 15 1854-57||
United with United States democrat (Rockland) to form Democrat and free press, later Rockland tribune (Rockland)
DLC Je-D 1856
MWA Ja 18,Jl 12,26 1855;Ag 8-15 1856
MeBa S 6 1855;Ap 10 1857
MeBe 1854-S 5 1857
NNHi N 16 1855

MAINE workingman's advocate. *See* American advocate

NEW planet. w Jl 16-O 29 1847||
United with Waldo signal to form Signal and planet
MeBe Jl-S 24,O 8-29 1847

PEOPLE'S advocate and independent democrat. w Mr 1844-45||
NNHi Ap 10 1844

Belfast City PRESS. w 1886-89||
MeBe Ag 24 1886-Ja 8 1889

PROGRESSIVE age. w *See* Belfast age

PROGRESSIVE age evening bulletin. d Ap 23?-Je 29 1861||
MeBe Ap 23-Je 21 1861

REPUBLICAN journal. w F 6 1829+
Follows Waldo democrat
pub 1829+
DLC D 2 1829;Ja 20 1830;Ag 14 1834;Je 21 1844;D 21 1860[Jl-O 1866]D 29 1870
MBAt F 25,Ap 29 1829
MHi D 29 1870
MSaE S 10 1841;Jl 23 1852
MWA Ap 15 1829;Ja 12 1844;Mr 24-31 1848[Ja-O 12 1849;My 23-O 3 1851]F 6,Mr 12,My 28 1852;Jl 7 1854;Mr 23 1855;N 14 1856;Mr 26 1858[60]61;Ja 10-D 5 1862[63]-Ja 8 1864;F 10, Mr 10,Mr 10,24,Ap 28,Jl 14,Ag 25-S 1,15 1870;F 2-9,Mr 2 1871;Ag 22 1872;D 11 1873;F 5,19,O 8 1874;My 13 1875;Je 22 1882;Ja 10 1889;Ja 1 1891
MeBa S 25 1843;Ap 27 1849;S 1 1854;Mr 23,N 16 1855;Mr 7,S 5 1856;S 7 1860;Mr 15 1861[79-93]
MeBe 1829+
MeHi Ag 25 1830;F 4 1842;Je 30-Jl 14,Ag 4-18,S 15,29 1843;Ag 16 1844;F 20 1846;Ja 22,My 6 1847;My 18 1849;Ag 30,S 13 1850;Ap 4-11 1851;Ap 8 1853;Ag 17 1855;D 4 1857;Jl 27 1866; Ap 14-Je 23 1892;Ja 4 1900

NNHi D 3 1835;O 27 1836;Mr 15-22 1844;D 25 1846;N 14 1851;F 27,S 11,30,O 9 1863;Jl 10, O 1,N 26 1868;My 25 1873;D 10 1903
NjR Ag 18 1848
WHi F 27-Mr 12,Ap 2 1840;F 4,18 1841

SIGNAL and planet. w O 15 1840-N 1853||
1840-45 as Waldo signal; 1845-O 27 1847 State signal
DLC D 31 1840;Je 3 1841
MHi Ja 13 1853
MSaE Jl 21 1852
MWA Ap 15-22 1841;O 10 1844;D 25 1845;My 18,Je 29 1848;Jl 28 1853
MeBa Jl 16 1846;N 4 1852
MeBe O 17 1840-O 1844;N 1845-S 2 1852
MeHi F 10 1842;Mr 25,S 7,O 5-12 1843;Mr 15 1845

STATE signal. *See* Signal and planet

TAX payer. w
MeBe D 31 1881;Ja 14,28,F 11,25,Mr 11 1882;F 13-20,Mr 27 1886

TAX reducer.
MeBe F 13 1886

VOICE of the people. w?
MeBe Ag 1867

WALDO county herald. w 1908-19||?
MeBa Jl 30 1908
MeBe Jl 16 1908-Je 20 1918

WALDO democrat. w Mr 17 1828-Ja 31 1829||
Follows Belfast gazette. Followed by Republican journal
DLC complete
MWA Je 25 1828
MeBe My 21 1828
MeBeR complete

WALDO patriot. w D 30 1837-D 1838||?
Merged with Kennebec journal (Augusta)
MeBe Ja 26 1838
MeHi 1837-O 3 1838

Waldo SIGNAL. *See* Signal and planet

BETHEL

Bethel COURIER. w D 17 1858-Jl 26 1861||
MWA Ja 21 1859
MeHi Je 29 1860

Bethel NEWS. *See* Oxford county citizen

OXFORD county citizen. w Je 5 1895+
1895-My 7 1908 as Bethel news
pub 1895+
MeHi Ja 3 1900

BIDDEFORD

Daily CHRONICLE. d Mr 6 1876-
MWA Mr 7 1876
MeSY Mr 6-Jl 15 1876

EASTERN herald. w Jl 12 1860-
MWA Jl 19 1860

EASTERN journal and mercantile advertiser. w 1849-54||
1849-Ap 1852 as Eastern journal. United with Union to form Union and Eastern journal, later Biddeford weekly journal
DLC Je 18 1853
MSaE Jl 24 1852
MWA S 18 1852;Ap 30,D 10-17 1853
MeHi My 22 1852-D 10 1853
NNHi My 22 1852-Ja 1854

EASTERN star. *See* Kennebunk star (Kennebunk)

Weekly GAZETTE. w Ja 5 1857-61||
MSaE F 3 1858
MeSY Ja 6-D 1 1858

Biddeford weekly JOURNAL. w Ja 31 1845-1930||
1845-Ja 21 1852 as Union; F 4 1852-54? Union and eastern journal; 1855?-84? Union and journal Mr 1848-55? pub at Saco
CLM Mr 13 1890
DLC My 26 1854;N 11 1864
MHi Ag 24 1917
MSaE Ap 26 1850;Jl 14 1852;F 16 1866;Ap 7,Jl 28 1876
MWA [Mr 28-D 17 1845]Mr 10-17,Je 16,D 1, 29 1847[48-49]F 15,Mr 29,Ap 12 1850;O 8 1851[Ja 12-S 7 1853]Mr 24,Ap 14 1854;Ja 25 1856;Ap 23-30 1858;O 7 1859;Ap 5 1861;N 28 1862;Mr 6 1863
MeAC 1849-57;61-67;91-95;1901-30
MeBi O 13 1871;1908
MeHi D 9,10(extra)1846[50-51]F 1852-Ag 3 1853;My 8 1855;S 8,N 14,28 1856;Ja 23-30,Mr 13,Je 26 1857 [58-62;66]69[71]Ja 3,O 17 1873; F 9 1900
MeSY Ja 31 1845-D 12 1873;D 7 1883-Ja 5 1884;1900
NNHi My 5 1852;F 3-10 1854;Mr 21 1873
OClWHi Je 3,O 28 1864

Biddeford daily JOURNAL. d 1884+
DLC Ja 3-Je 30 1898
MWA O 6 1887;N 7 1894

La JUSTICE de Biddeford. w 1896+
In French
MeHi Ja 4 1900

MAINE democrat. w Ja 6 1828-78||
1828-67 pub at Saco
CSmH S 1 1830
Ct [1831-37]
DLC Mr 18,Ap 15 1835;F 12 1839;Ag 8 1843;S 3,O 22 1844;N 18 1845;Ap-D 1859;Je 5 1860
KHi Je 18,Jl 2 1861
MSaE Je 25 1839;Je 1 1852
MWA Jl 21 1830;N 16 1831;Ja 8-22 1834; Mr 18,Ap 15,O 14 1835;F 3,N 27,D 21 1836; Ja 11,F 15 1837;F 7, Ap 18,D 4 1838;F 12,26,My 7,28,Je 11-18,Ag 20-27,N 12 1839; Ja 21,Ag 25 1840;N 9 1841;My 24 Ag 30 1842;Ja 10,Mr 14 1843-O 9 1860;Jl 23(extra) 1861;62-My 10,Jl 12 1864

MeAlC 1846-67
MeBB S 24 1844
MeBi 1857-67;Je 17 1875
MeHi N 22 1842
MeSY Ag 1829-39;41-[70-Je 1878]
MnHi F 20 1833
N O 16 1833
NN Ja 11 1832
NNHi My 14-21 1834
NcD D 2 1845;Jl 28,N 3,D 22 1846;Mr 30,My 11,Je 22-29, Jl 27-Ag 3 1847
NhM 1860-61
OClWHi Jl 12 1842;D 6 1864

MAINE sentinel. w Mr 1? 1832-86||?
MWA Ag 9 1882

MERCANTILE advertiser. w Ap 1849-My 1852||
United with Eastern journal to form Eastern journal and mercantile advertiser
MSaE My 1 1852

Biddeford RECORD. d 1895-1926||
MeBi 1904-21

Weekly RECORD. w 1895-1926||
MeAlC 1901-23
MeHi F 9 1900
MeSY Ag 27 1891-Mr 24 1916[17-26]

Daily STANDARD. d 1888-94||
MWA O 14,23 1889
MeSY Ag 28 1891-Ja 3 1894

Weekly STANDARD. w 1888-94||
MeAlC 1891-94
MeSY Ap 10 1889-Mr 4 1891

Daily TIMES. d 1871-97||?
MWA Ja 4 1868;Ap 22,Je 8 1874;F 6 1877
MeSY Ap 13 1872-78
NNHi Ap 15,Je 2 1873;O 1874-75

Biddeford weekly TIMES. w 1879-96||?
MWA My 20 1882;Je 28 1889

UNION. *See* Biddeford weekly journal

UNION and eastern journal. *See* Biddeford weekly journal

UNION and journal. *See* Biddeford weekly journal

BINGHAM

Bingham HERALD. w 1891?-1914||?
MeHi Ja 3 1900

BOOTHBAY HARBOR

Boothbay REGISTER. w 1876+
MWA Jl 21 1877
MeHi Ja 5 1900

BRIDGTON

Bridgton NEWS. w S 1870+
pub 1870+
MHi Je 7 1916
MSaE Ap 7,S 1,22 1876
MWA O 13 1876;D 13 1895;D 11 1896;D 11 1897;S 15 1899; D 8 1905;D 3 1915
MeHi Ja 5 1900

Bridgton RECORD. w 1915-16||
MeU N 3 1915-Jl 26 1916

Bridgton REPORTER. w 1859-63||
Follows Nashua oasis (Nashua, N.H.)
MWA Ja 20,F 17,My 25 1860;Ap 12 1861

BRISTOL

PEMAQUID messenger. w 1886-97||?
1886-88? pub in Pemaquid
KHi Jl 19-Ag 1888
MWA S 26 1895

BROOKS

WALDO county advocate. bw 1905?-06||
MeBe Jl 22 1905;Ja 20 1906

BRUNSWICK

Brunswick and Topsham ADVERTISER. w
MeHi My 13 1848

ADVOCATE of freedom. *See under* Hallowell

ANDROSCOGGIN free press. w Jl 29 1828-30||?
D 10 1828-Jl 22 1829 as Free press and patriot
DLC Ag 26 1828
MWA Ag 19,S 16 1828;Jl 29 1830
MeB S 16 1828;My 6 1830
MeHi 1828-S 23 1829

BRUNSWICKER. w
MeB My 5 1842-My 11 1843
MeBa Ja 4 1844
MeHi My 1843-N 7 1844

FORESTER and Brunswick and Topsham messenger. w Ja 25 1845-Ja 31 1846||
MeBB F 22 1845
MeBa Ag 23 1845
MeBHi [1845-46]
MeHi complete

FREE PRESS and patriot. *See* Androscoggin free press

Brunswick HERALD. w Ag 1881-85||
MWA Ja 17 1885
MeB N 15,29 1884
MeBB Ag 9,30 1882

Brunswick JOURNAL. w Jl 1820-32||
MWA My 18 1831;Ja 7 1832
MeB O 20 1830

MAINE (*Continued*)

BRUNSWICK—*Continued*

*MAINE intelligencer and Brunswick and Topsham advertiser. w S 23 1820-21||
1820-Mr? 1821 as Maine intelligencer
MWA Ja-Mr 16,Ap 20 1821

PEJEPSCOT journal. Mr 21 1846-
MWA Mr 28,Jl 11 1846
MeBHi [Jl 1846-Mr 13 1847]

Brunswick RECORD. w N 28 1902+
MeB 1902+
MeBB 1902+
MeBHi 1902-N 18 1904

REGULATOR. w My 14 1836-38||?
MeB Jl 2 1836
MeBB Jl 30 1836

Brunswick TELEGRAPH. w 1853-Ag 26 1903||
DLC Ag 30(extra)1861
MSaE Mr 20,My 1,22-29,Je 19-26,Jl 10,Ag 7,S 25 1868;O 29 1869;Ja 14,Ag 5,S 30 1870;Ja 20, Mr 3 1871;Mr 31,Ag 18,S 8,29 1876
MWA Ag 1855-Jl 1856;F 10,My 4 1860;Ag 30(extra)1861;Ag 8 1862;S 4 1863;D 28 1866; Mr 15,Ap 26,My 24-O 18 1867;68-Ja,My 23,O 3 1873;Ap 10 1874;Je 18 1875;Ja 21,F 18,Mr 24,Jl 7-14,Ag 11,25 1876;D 14 1898
MeB My 1 1853-Ag,N 18 1854-S 1881
MeBB O 16 1857-93;My 1894-1903
MeBHi Je 14 1895-Je 1897
MeHi [S 1856-O 3 1862]-[O 1881-Ja 1 1886]
N S 21-O 5,19,N 2 1877
NNHi S 9,23 1870;F 27 1874
NcD [1868-72]

BUCKFIELD

Buckfield REPORTER. m,sm
m -D 1878?
MeBa Je 1878-F 15 1879

BUCKSPORT

Bucksport CLIPPER. w 1885-96||?
KHi Je 28 1888
MeBa [1886-89]

Bucksport HERALD. w 1898-1901||?
MeHi Ja 5 1900

RIVERSIDE echo. *See* Enquirer (Portland)

BUCKTOWN. *See* BUCKSPORT

CALAIS

Calais ADVERTISER. w Ap 14 1841+
Follows Gazette and advertiser
pub 1841-51;Ja 15 1857-64;70-Mr 1 1882;1927+
DLC My 5-19 1841;Ja 31 1844
MSaE Jl 29 1852
MWA Jl 27,Ag 17 1842;Mr 29 1843;F 1 1870
MeHi F 7 1900
MeMC 1843-52;Ja 16 1872-1933

DOWN easter. w F 18 1837-D 27 1838||
MWA Jl 10 1837

EASTERN democrat. w My 1832-Ap 14 1841||
Follows Northern light (Eastport)
Suspended from My 1837-Je 15 1839
1832-N 21? 1835 pub in Eastport
Ct Ag 31 1832
MeMC My 25-D 1832;O 1833-Ja 22 1834;Ja 14-D 1836;Je 15 1839-Je 13,Ag 18 1840-Ap 6 1841

FRONTIER journal. w Ja 9 1838-53||?
Suspended from Je 15 1839-Ap 14? 1841 (for this period *See* Eastern democrat)
CSmH Je 28 1853
MSaE Mr 3-10 1840
MeHi Ja 1 1851
MeMC Ja 16 1838-[52]

GAZETTE and advertiser. w 1836-Ap 7? 1841||
Followed by Calais advertiser

ST. CROIX courier. w F 4 1834-
Ct Mr 25-Ap 1,N 13 1834

ST. CROIX herald. w 1858?-64||
1858-62 pub in St. Stephen
MWA Je 1 1864

Calais weekly TIMES. w 1868-1916||?
KHi Ag 9 1888
MeHi Ja 4 1900
MeMC Jl 27 1877-1914

CAMDEN

Camden ADVERTISER. *See* Commercial advertiser (Rockland)

Camden HERALD. w Ja 1869+
pub 1881;91+
MWA Ap 4 1874;Ja-D 15 1877[Ja 14-S 23 1881]
MeBa Ja 3 1874
MeCm O 20 1927+
MeHi Ja 5 1900

CANTON

DIXFIELD citizen. *See* Rumford Falls times (Rumford Falls)

RUMFORD FALLS echo. w 1892-93||?
United with Canton telephone and Dixfield citizen to form Rumford Falls times (Rumford Falls)

RUMFORD FALLS times. *See under* Rumford Falls

Canton TELEPHONE. sm,ir S 27 1878-79||
S-N 1878 as Telephone
MWA N 30-D 1878;Ja 15,Je 28 1879
MeBa 1878-N 1 1879

Canton TELEPHONE. w 1883-93||?
United with Rumford Falls echo and Dixfield citizen to form Rumford Falls times (Rumford Falls)

CAPE ELIZABETH. *See* SOUTH PORTLAND

CARIBOU

AROOSTOOK republican. w 1880+
CLM Ag 28 1889
M S 18 1930
MeHi Ja 4 1900

CASTINE

AMERICAN. *See* Eastern American

EASTERN American. w Ja 20 1827-29||
1827 as American
MHi Jl 27 1827
MWA Je-Jl,O 19,N 23,D 5-19 1827;Ja 2,N 26,D 17 1828
MeBe Ag 29 1829

Castine GAZETTE. w 1884-85||
MWA Jl 16 1885

Castine monthly NEWS. m
MB Mr 1872-S 1873

CHASE'S MILLS

THEM steers. w Mr 15 1882-
MWA My 10,Je 7,Ag 30(and supp)1882

CHERRYFIELD

NARRAGAUGUS times. w 1897-1910||?
MeHi Ja 5 1900
MeMC N 1899-1906

CHINA

ORB.
MeHi S 30 1836

CORINTH

MIRROR. N? 1831-
MeHi D 26 1831

CORNISH

OSSIPEE VALLEY weekly. w 1908-16||?
MWA D 11 1913;D 17-24 1914;D 16 1915

CUMBERLAND

Cumberland GLOBE. *See* Portland globe (Portland)

SIX TOWNS times. *See under* Freeport

DAMARISCOTTA

AMERICAN sentinel. *See under* Bath

Damariscotta HERALD. w 1876-1919||?
1876-96? as Herald and record (inside sheets sometimes as Village herald and Lincoln record)
MWA Ag 11-18 1881
MeHi Ja 11 1900

LINCOLN advertiser. w Je? 1858-60||
Follows Thomaston journal (Thomaston)
1858-S 1859 pub in Thomaston
MWA S 9 1858;Ag 15 1860
NNHi Je 24 1858

VILLAGE herald and Lincoln record. *See* Damariscotta herald

DEER ISLE

Deer Isle GAZETTE. w Mr 15? 1882-88||?
MWA Mr 15 1883
MeBa My 8 1884

DEERING

Deering NEWS and enterprise and Westbrook globe-star. *See under* Westbrook

Deering REGISTER. w Ja 29 1887-
MWA S 3 1887

DEXTER

EASTERN gazette. w 1853+
1853-54 as Gem; 1855?-62? Gem and literary gazette; 1863?-91 Dexter gazette
pub O 13 1924+
MSaE Ja 4,28,Mr 18,Ap 22-My 13,27 1854;S 19,O 17,N 7,28-D 12 1857;Je 30 1876
MWA Jl 1856;Jl 14 1860;F 28 1878(extra)
MeBa Ag 6,S 3-10,O 8,N 5-12,D 24 1853;Ja 7, Mr 25,Ap 22-My 13,27,Je 10-Jl 15,Ag 5,S,O 14-D 1854;Ja 13,27-Ap 7,21-My 1855;Je 22 1883;O 29 1889
MeDB 1856
MeDW 1874

EASTERN state. w N 9 1882-91||
United with Dexter gazette to form Eastern gazette
MWA N 9 1882
MeBB S 24,O 15 1891

Dexter GAZETTE. *See* Eastern gazette

GEM. *See* Eastern gazette

DOVER

MYRTLE.
MeHi My 17 1845-Je 17 1848

DOVER-FOXCROFT

PISCATAQUIS farmer. *See* Piscataquis observer

PISCATAQUIS herald. *See* Piscataquis observer

PISCATAQUIS observer. w Je 1 1838+
1838-42 as Piscataquis herald; 1842-47 Piscataquis farmer
pub 1838-[1901]+
DLC S 27 1844
MSaE Jl 1 1852;F 1 1866
MWA N 2 1843;Ag 19 1858;F 11 1864;D 2 1875
MeBa Ja 18,F 8 1844;S 22 1881;D 11 1919
MeDo My 1897+
MeDoC 1862-[90]+
MeHi Je 20 1844;Ja 2 1850
NN Jl 29 1926

EAST THOMASTON. *See* ROCKLAND

EAST WINTHROP

KENNEBEC banner. *See* Winthrop banner

WINTHROP banner. w O 2 1889-97||?
1895?-96? as Kennebec banner
MeHi O 23 1889-Mr 21 1890

EASTPORT

EASTERN democrat. *See under* Calais

NORTHERN light. w Ap 16 1828-Ap 1832||
Followed by Eastern democrat (Calais)
CSmH S 8 1830
Ct Ja 21 1829;Ja 26,Mr 2 1831;Ja 4,18,F 22 1832
IU Ap 14 1830-Ap 4 1832
MWA Ap 30 1828

*Eastport SENTINEL. w Ag 31 1818+
Title varies: Eastport sentinel and Passamaquoddy advertiser
pub 1914+
CLM F 5 1850
DLC Mr 27,Ap 24,My 15,29,Jl 10 1824;Mr 18-25 1826;Mr 27 1827;Mr 21,Je 24,Ag 6,S,O 28,N 4,25 1829-Ja 13 1830;D 19 1832;Mr 12 1850
MHi My 26,D 24 1825;F 18 1826
MSaE Mr 29 1848;Jl 6 1852;F 14 1866
MWA Je 2 1821;Jl 26 1823;D 1 1827;Jl 26,S 13 1828;Jl 29 1829;Ag 8 1838;Ag 18 1841;Ag 4,18 1858;O 3 1860;Ap 3 1861;Mr 6 1895
MeBB S 3 1834
MeBa Ag 11,S 1,15 1858
MeEa 1821-32;79-90;1900+
MeHi Ja 1 1851
MeMC 1821-Ag 1 1832;53-1933

ELLSWORTH

Ellsworth AMERICAN. w O 17 1851+
1851-54 as Ellsworth herald
pub 1872+
KHi Je 28-Ag 16 1888
MHi Ja 3 1868
MSaE Jl 16 1852;Mr 9 1855;F 16 1866;Ap 6, Jl 27 1876
MWA Je 6 1856;O 20 1870;Ag 1871;D 4 1873; Ja 1,15 1874;Ap 1 1875;Mr 15 1883;Mr 17-Ag 4,25 1892;Je 28-Jl 5 1894;O 17 1895;F 6 1901
MeBa Ap 9 1852;O 14-21 1853;Ja 20,Mr 3 1854; Ap 27,My 18 1855[59-62]F 17 1865;D 25 1879
MeE 1886-92
MeEC [1851-60]-[65-70]-[72-73]-[75-76]78-79; 84;1904+
MeHi D 8 1865-Ja 3 1900
NNHi My 8 1873[Mr-Ag 1893]Je 28-Jl 12 1894
OClWHi My 12 1865

BEE. w F 12 1840-
MWA My 14 1840

DEFIANCE bulletin and Lowell's plain dealer. ir F 22 1849-
Title varies slightly
MWA F 22,Je 6 1849
NcD Je 6 1849

EASTERN farmer. w Ap 1860-61||
MWA Ag 31 1861

EASTERN freeman. w Ap 22 1853-Jl 28 1854||
MeEC complete

HANCOCK journal. w Ja 2-S 18 1866||
DLC Ja 16 1866
MeBa Ja 2,F 13-Ap 10,My,Je 12-19,Jl 10-Ag,S 11-18 1866

Ellsworth HERALD. *See* Ellsworth American

INDEPENDENT courier. w N 29 1826-30||
CSmH Ag 11 1830
DLC Je 13 1827;Ja 20 1830
MHi Jl 25,Ag 8 1827
MWA Ja 10 1827;Ja 9,S 3,O 30 1828
N N 29 1826

Ellsworth daily NEWS. d S 26 1933+
pub 1933+

Ellsworth RADICAL. w 1835-37||
MeBa S 30 1836

MAINE (*Continued*)

FAIRFIELD

AROOSTOOK VALLEY sunrise. w Ag 5 1863-77||
1863-Ag 2 1867 as Loyal sunrise; Ag 9 1867-Mr 24 1871 Sunrise; Ap 5 1871-My 17 1876 Presque Isle sunrise
1863-Ag 8 1877 pub at Presque Isle
MSaE N 8 1865;Ja 19 1866;Jl 29 1870;Mr 22,Jl 19 1876
MWA My 25 1864;69-Je 17 1870;D 20 1871
MeHi 1863-[75-My 1876]-[77]
NN N 15 1871
OClWHi Ja 25 1865

Fairfield weekly CHRONICLE. w My 1 1872-78||?
MeWC 1872-77

Fairfield JOURNAL. w 1872-1925||?
MeHi F 6 1900

FALMOUTH

Falmouth GAZETTE. w Ja 1 1875-
MeBa Ja 1 1875
WHi Ja 1 1875(facsimile)

FARMINGTON

Farmington CHRONICLE. w 1840-F 25? 1919||
United with Franklin journal to form Franklin journal and Farmington chronicle
CL Jl 14 1853
MB S 13 1883-86
MSaE Jl 29 1852;Ja 24 1866;Ag 17 1876
MWA O 26 1854;My 24 1860;N 20 1873;S 4 1879
MeF [1847-56;62-87;93-1914]-17
MeFC 1844-1914
NNHi Ja 30 1873[Mr 1875-76;Ap-Ag 1877]

DOWN EAST screamer. w
MSaE Jl 10 1852

FRANKLIN journal and Farmington chronicle. sw 1882+
1882-F 25? 1919 as Franklin journal
pub 1887+
MWA Jl 21 1883;Je 20 1885
MeFC 1879-O 1886
MeHi Ja 2 1851;Ja 1 1900

FRANKLIN patriot. w 1858-63||
1858-60? published in Lewiston
MeFC Ja 29 1858-Ja 20 1860
MeHi Mr 8 1861
NNHi N 6 1863

Daily PATRIOT. d O 29-N 19 1863||
pub during Wright & Doyle trials
MeBa complete
MeP complete

FRANKLIN register and Sandy River farmer. w F 1840-44||
1840-Ja 1843 as Franklin register
MWA Ja 4 1844
MeBB My 15 1841-N 14 1844
NNHi Je 27 1840
WHi Jl 11 1840

SANDY RIVER farmer. bw Je 16 1842-Ja 16 1843||
United with Franklin register to form Franklin register and Sandy River farmer
MeBB complete

SANDY RIVER yeoman. w 1831-32||
MeF 1831-32

FORT FAIRFIELD

FAIRFIELD aurora. w N 13 1875-76||
MeHi 1875-My 27 1876

NORTHERN leader. w 1892-1900||?
Followed by Fort Fairfield review
MWA D 21 1894
MeHi Ja 4 1899

Fort Fairfield REVIEW. w My 16 1902+
Follows Northern leader
pub 1902+

FRANKFORT

INTELLIGENCER. w
MeBa S 1 1838

WALDO gazette. w Mr 7 1839-
MWA Mr-S 14 1839

FREEPORT

SENTINEL. sm 1889-90||?
MeBB Ag 5,S 6,O 4,N 1 1889;F 8,Je 28 1890

SIX TOWNS times. w 1892-Ag 25 1916||
Dated also in Yarmouth
MeFr 1893-94;96-97;1900-01;03-15
MeP 1894-1900
MeU Ja 8 1892-1904;06-N 1913;Jl 17-24 1914;16
NNHi F 13-27 1903

FRYEBURG

Fryeburg POST. w N 2 1915-16||?
MBAt N 9 1915-Je 6 1916
MeU Ja-S 27 1916

GARDINER

Gardiner ADVERTISER. *See* Kennebec transcript

COLD WATER fountain. *See* Maine journal (Portland)

DAVID'S sling. w F 1-O 1845||
MHi Mr 13-20 1846

DREW'S rural intelligencer. *See* Maine rural

EASTERN chronicle. w O 19 1824-O 10 1826||
United with Christian intelligencer (Portland) to form Christian intelligencer and Eastern chronicle (not in this list)
Ct My 2 1826
MSaE Ap 18 1823
MWA D 28 1824;My 3,Je 7 1825;O 10 1826

FOUNTAIN and journal. *See under* Portland

Gardiner HOME JOURNAL. *See* Kennebec leader (w)

Gardiner INDEPENDENT. w Mr 25 1899-1905||?
MeHi Ja 6 1900

Gardiner JOURNAL. w 1918-30||
MeG complete

KENNEBEC leader. w Ja 1 1854-1917||?
1854-58 as Northern home journal; 1858-92 Gardiner home journal; 1893-1916 Reporter-journal
DLC My 16 1861;Ap 20-27 1865
MWA S 13 1876;Ag 10,31,S 14-21,O 5 1881;Ja 2 1888
MeG 1856-92;94-1913
MeHi 1893-Ja 5 1900

KENNEBEC reporter. w F 1865-D 1892||
United with Gardiner home journal to form Reporter-journal, later Kennebec leader
MWA D 8 1888
MeG 1866-90
MeHi D 8 1883-Ja 2 1886

KENNEBEC transcript. sw F 9 1850-57||
F 9 1850 as Gardiner advertiser
MSaE Jl 24 1852
MeHi My 18,29,Jl 24 1850 [51]56
DLC My 29-Je 1 1850

Gardiner LEDGER and farmer's journal. w N 10? 1842-D? 1843||
Follows Gardiner spectator
MWA Mr 3-10,Je 9 1843

MAINE rural. w Ja 6 1855-60||
1855-Mr 27 1858 as Drew's rural intelligencer; Ap 3 1858-F 12 1859 Rural intelligencer
1855-O 10 1857 pub in Augusta; O 10-D 26 1857 in Gardiner and Augusta
MWA 1855-Ap 21 1860
MeHi Ja-D 22 1855
NNHi 1855
NcD 1855;Ja 17 1857

Weekly NETTLE. w Ap 21- 1852||
MWA Ap 21,Je 12 1852

NORTHERN home journal. *See* Kennebec leader

REPORTER-journal. *See* Kennebec leader

RURAL intelligencer. *See* Maine rural

Gardiner SPECTATOR. w D 1839-O? 1842||
Followed by Gardiner ledger and farmer's journal
DLC My 29 1840;F 19,Mr 12,26 1841;Je 4 1842
MWA Ap 23 1842

YANKEE blade. *See under* Boston (Mass.)

GUILFORD

Guilford REGISTER. w Mr 25 1909+
pub 1909+

HALLOWELL

ADVOCATE of freedom. w Mr 8 1838-Je 12 1841||
1838-Ap 18? 1839 pub in Brunswick; Ap 25 1839-Ap 11 1840 in Augusta
MB [Ap 25 1840-Ap 1841]
MeBB 1838-F 21,Ap 25 1839-Ap,Je 12 1841
MeHi 1838-[Mr 1839-41]
WHi O 29 1840

***AMERICAN advocate.** w,sw Ja 23 1810-Ja 23 1835||
Jl 23 1814-Ja 14 1815 as American advocate and Kennebec advertiser; Ja 13 1821-N 5 1825 American advocate and general advertiser. United with Free press to form Free press and advocate
w 1810-29
CSmH S 4 1830
Ct Je 10,Ag 5 1826
DLC 1821-26;S 8 1827;28[Je-D 1829]Ja 15 1831
MBAt Ja 6,F 3 1821
MSaE Ag 16 1823
MWA My 18,Je 8,22-29,Jl 13-20,Ag 17-S 21,O 5,19-26,N 30-D 1822;Je 19 1824;My 7,Je 4 1825;N 17 1827;Ja 18 1828;My 15,29,Ag 28 1830;My 11,Ag 17,S 21 1832;F 27 1833
MeBB Ja 3,24-F 3,Mr 3,S 29 1827
MeBa Jl 26 1823
MeHa 1821-35
MeHi 1821-Ja 5,22,Jl 13,O 4,23,D 25,31 1832
NNHi Jl 9 1825;26;S 22 1827[28]F 13 1830
REdH 1828

CHRONICLE. w
MSaE My 19 1837

EASTERN examiner. w D 15? 1874-75||?
MWA S 22 1875

FREE PRESS and advocate. w F 4 1835-
Formed by the union of Free press and American advocate
DLC F 25 1835
MeHa 1835-O 12 1836
NNHi Mr 4,Ap 1-8,29,My 20 1835

FREE SOIL republican. w Jl 12 1841-Je 7 1849||
1841-Ag 24 1848 as Liberty standard. Merged with Portland inquirer (Portland)
MB 1841-Ja 1844
MWA D 14 1842;O 12 1848
MdBJ D 14 1842
MeBB complete
MeBa My 2,16,Je 6,20,Jl 11,Ag 1,O 10,N 14,D 26 1844;O 26 1848
NNHi N 3,D 8 1841;Ap 24 1845
OClWHi Ja 20,F 3,Mr 9 1843

***Hallowell GAZETTE.** w F 23 1814-D 12 1827||
DLC D 17 1823;F 4,25,Mr 31,My 12-19,Je 2,16,Jl 7,Ag 11,N 24 1824;Je 27-S 5 1827
MBAt My 8 1822
MHi O 12 1825
MSaE Jl 30 1823
MWA Ja 24 1821;My 8,29-Je 5,Jl,Ag 14-S 18,O 2-9,23,N-D 18 1822;Je 11 1823-My,Je 14 1826;D 12 1827
MeHa complete

KENNEBEC courier. *See under* Bath

LIBERTY standard. *See* Free soil republican

MAINE cultivator and Hallowell gazette. *See* Hallowell gazette

MAINE free press. w Jl 29 1831-
MB 1831-Jl 20 1832
MWA F 28 1834
NNHi Ja 16 1835
NjPa 1831-Ja 1835

Hallowell NEWS. w N 30 1894-My 19 1899||
MeHa complete

Hallowell REGISTER. w 1878-1913||
MWA Jl 2 1892
MeHa [1878-1913]
MeHi F 10 1878
NcD S 6 1879

'SEVENTY-SIX'. 1843-
MeHi Ja 1844

HARPSWELL

OCEAN breeze. w
MeHi Jl 13 1895

HARRISON

TRI-TOWN bee.
MeHi Ag 22 1908

HARTLAND

Hartland HERALD. w
MeHar My 30-Je 13,Jl 25,Ag 8,N 28 1912

PIONEER.
MeHar Mr 21 1884

HINCKLEY

GOODWILL record. m 1891?-
MeHi [1906-08]

HOLLANDVILLE

Hollandville TIMES. m
MeSY O 1876-Mr 1878

HOULTON

AROOSTOOK democrat. w Mr 21-N 1860||
MWA Ag 1 1860

AROOSTOOK pioneer. *See* Houlton pioneer-times

AROOSTOOK times. *See* Houlton times

Houlton PIONEER-TIMES. w 1857+
1857-Ja 11 1933 as Aroostook pioneer
1857-67 pub at Presque Isle
MSaE Ap 25 1865
MWA Ap 7,Je 30 1863;Ag 18 1874
Me 1857+
MeBa Jl 28 1863
MeHo D 1869-70;D 1905+
MeHoC 1857+
OClWHi Je 6 1865

Houlton TIMES. w Ap 13 1860-Ja 11 1933||
1860-1917 as Aroostook times. United with Aroostook times to form Houlton pioneer-times
MSaE Ag 17 1876
MWA Ap 5 1861;Jl 22 1864;Je 30 1871
Me 1875
MeHo Ap 10 1863-1933

KENNEBUNK

EASTERN star. *See* Kennebunk star

Kennebunk ENTERPRISE. w 1904-24||?
NNHi Mr 12 1919

***Kennebunk GAZETTE and Maine palladium.** w Mr 20 1805-My 28 1842||
1805-S 1833 as Kennebunk gazette
CSmH My 1 1830
MSaE Jl 19 1823
MWA Jl 7 1821-Je 1 1822;N 22 1823;Je 5 1824-My 28,S 3 1825;Ag 26 1826;My 12 1827;F 9 1828;O 5,N 9 1833;F 1 1834;Ja 3,Jl 25 1835;F 13,My 14,N 26 1836;Ja 7,F 4 1837;Je 30 1838;Ap 4,O 24 1840;My 8,Ag 7,D 25 1841
MeHi Ag 3 1833;My 31 1834
MeK [1822;25-29;31-42]
MeSY Jl 1821-My 1823
MeU S 15 1832
NN My 4 1822
NNHi Je 7 1821;Mr 9,Je 29-Jl 6,20-27,N 30 1822;Je 14,S 20 1823[Je 1824-25]

MAINE (*Continued*)

KENNEBUNK—*Continued*

Kennebunk STAR. w S 4 1877+
1877-1919? Eastern star
1877 pub at Biddeford
pub 1877+
MWA Je 10,Ag 26 1887;Ap 26 1889;Ja 27 1928
MeHi My 7 1880;Ja 5 1900
MeK 1881-91;99+
NNHi Ap 23 1880;My 26 1893

Weekly VISITOR. w Je 24 1809-
MWA Ja-Je 1821
NNHi Mr 10 1821

KEZAR FALLS

OSSIPEE VALLEY weekly. w 1908-10‖?
MeHi [O 29-D 10 1908]

LEWISTON

Lewiston ADVERTISER. m Jl 1866-70‖?
MWA Jl 1867

COURRIER du Maine. sw S 4? 1906-
In French
MWA N 6 1906

DEMOCRATIC advocate. w My 1852-61‖
United with Lewiston republican to form Lewiston herald
MWA S 27 1855;Jl 11 1861
MeAuC 1856-61

FRANKLIN patriot. *See under* Farmington

Lewiston weekly GAZETTE. w F 8 1872-81‖
MSaE F 26,Je 10,24,Jl 1,S 23 1876
MWA Mr 31(supp)1877[80-81]
MeAuC 1872-76;78-79
NcD F 7-Mr 23 1880

Lewiston HERALD. w 1861-62‖
Formed by the union of Democratic advocate and Lewiston republican

Lewiston weekly JOURNAL. w My 21 1847-1925‖
1841-66? as Lewiston Falls journal
pub Ag 13 1847-My 8 1852;My 13 1854-Ap 1860;My 1861-Ap 1862;My 1864-O 11 1866
MHi O 2 1920
MSaE My 29 1852;Ja 25 1866
MWA [My 19-D 22 1849]50-My 3 1851;F 28 1857;My 25 1860;Je 3,O 14,28,N 18 1880;Je 29,N 23 1882;Ja 11,F 22 1883-Mr 21,Ag 29-N 14,28,D 12 1884-F 13 1885;My-Je 11,25,O 22,N 12-19 1886;Ja 3 1889
MeAuC 1854-[1910]-[12]
MeBa Ja 15-22 1880
MeHi [N 18 1859-Mr 19 1863]
MeL F 17-Mr 19 1857;My 20 1869-73;My 29 1875-76;78-81;83-85;87
NbHi [Ja 1901]
WHi Jl 16 1853;S 26 1889-Mr 19 1891

Lewiston evening JOURNAL. d Ap 20 1861+
Title varies: Lewiston daily evening journal; Evening journal; etc.
Saturday ed as Saturday journal; Lewiston Saturday journal; etc
pub 1861+
CPo My 31,S 22-23 1882
Ct D 7,18 1897;Je 7,D 6 1899;Je 6,D 8 1902
DLC Ap 25 1863;64;68;94+
IC Ap 30 1889
M O 5 1929;Ag 28 1930
MSaE Mr 12,My 17 1867
MWA S 5 1861;S 20 1862;F 24 1876;Je 11,S 11 1879;Je 25 1889-91;Je 28 1894;O 12 1895;Ag 1908-[Jl-D 1926]+
MeAu Ap 22 1873+
MeAuC Ap 20 1861+
MeBB 1882-S 1924;30+
MeHi [F 10 1863-O 1872]Je 28 1894;Ja 1 1900
MeL Ap 20 1861+
MeLB 1903+
NNHi My 29 1873;Je 6-11 1903;Je 25-29,Jl 5,14,Ag 10 1904
NcD S 23 1863;O 7 1882

Lewiston JOURNAL magazine. w
MeBa Ja 27 1901;12;18-24

LEWISTON FALLS advertiser. w
NNHi D 5 1844

LEWISTON FALLS journal. *See* Lewiston weekly journal

MAINE independent. w Ap 3 1880-
MWA Je 19 1880

MAINE statesman. w Ja 2 1897?-99‖
CtY Ja 15-D 24 1898
MeAu Ja-D 18 1897
MeHi N 18 1899
MiU [1897]-[99]

Le MESSAGER. w,sw,tw 1880+
w 1880-90?; sw 1891?-1905?
In French
pub 1880+
IU O 19 1917+
MeHi Ja 1 1900
NhMA Ag 1906-Ap 1912

Lewiston REPUBLICAN. w 1860‖
United with Democratic advocate to form Lewiston herald

La REPUBLIQUE. w F 17-Ap 14 1887‖?
In French
MeBB F 17-24,Ap 14 1887

Lewiston daily SUN. d F 20 1893+
pub 1893+
MeAu 1906+
MeL Jl 1905-06;23+

LIMERICK

OSSIPEE VALLEY herald. w 1907-16‖
MeU N 8 1907-S 24 1915;Ja-S 27 1916

OSSIPEE Valley news. w 1876-82‖
MWA S 30 1882

REPOSITORY. w
MSaE Je 5 1852

Morning STAR. w My 11 1826-N 1833‖
MWA Je 29 1826;Jl 9 1828;F 20 1829;Jl 14 1830;S 16 1831;F 28,Mr 14 1833

VILLAGE register.
MeSY Ap 29-Ag 5 1840

LIMINGTON

MAINE recorder. w Ap 20 1832-D 31 1835‖
DLC Mr 27 1835
MWA Je 8 1832;S 27 1833;F 27,Mr 20-27,My 1-15 1835
MeHi Ja-D 19 1834
MeSY My 11 1832-D 25 1835

LISBON FALLS

Lisbon ENTERPRISE. w 1891+
pub [1907+]
MWA D 3 1895
MeHi Ja 5 1900;My 13 1904

LIVERMORE FALLS

Livermore Falls ADVERTISER. w 1891+
MeHi Je 7,Jl 26 1900

LUBEC

Lubec HERALD. w 1886+
MeMC 1910-33

MACHIAS

EASTERN star and Washington advertiser. w D 3 1823-Jl 21 1825‖?
1823-N 1824 as Eastern star
DLC My 20,Je 3,Jl 22 1824;Jl 21 1825
MSaE D 3,11 1823
MeHi Ag 5 1824
MeMC 1823-Jl 14 1825
N 1823-N 1824

MACHIAS VALLEY news. *See* Machias Valley news-observer

MACHIAS VALLEY news-observer. w Ap 2 1930+
1930-Jl 6 1932 as Machias Valley news
pub 1930+
MeAdS 1930+
MeMC 1930+

OBSERVER. w N 30 1927-Jl 6 1932‖
United with Machias Valley news to form Machias Valley news-observer
MeAdS complete
MeMN complete

Machias REPUBLICAN. w 1856-Jl 1 1920‖
United with Machias union to form Union-republican
MWA Ap 9 1861;My 4 1865;Je 28 1866;Ja 12 1871
MeBa Ag 31 1858;S 18 1860
MeHi O 27 1900
NcD D 13 1890

UNION-REPUBLICAN. w My 24 1853+
1853-1920 as Union
MWA [N 1853-N 1855]Ag 28 1860;Jl 31 1866; Jl 31 1866;F 12 1867;O 19 1869
MeHi Ja 2 1900
MeMC 1853+
NcD N 1 1853;F 28-Mr 7,My 30 1854;Mr 13, Ap 17,My 15,Jl 3-17 1855
OClWHi D 13 1864
WHi Je 2-9 1874

MADISON

Madison BULLETIN. w Ap 30 1885+
pub 1886+
MeMa 1886+

MECHANIC FALLS

ANDROSCOGGIN herald. w 1867-76‖?
MSaE F 24 1876

Mechanic Falls LEDGER. w 1884-1910‖?
MeHi Jl 1892-[95-96]-Je 1907

MILBURN. *See* SKOWHEGAN

MONSON

Weekly SLATE. w Je 9 1885-88‖?
MeHi 1885-Je 2 1886

NEWCASTLE

LINCOLN democrat. w 1850-58‖
MSaE My 19 1852
MWA N 10 1852;S 10 1856;Jl 8 1857;Je 30,S 1 1858
MeBa Je 6 1855
MeHi Ja 1 1851
NcD S 1 1858

NEWPORT

Newport TIMES. w 1879-80‖?
MeBa Mr 20 1880

NORRIDGEWOCK

PEOPLE'S press. w 1841-
MWA Ag 1 1843;N 21,D 12 1844

SOMERSET journal. w My 15 1823-42‖
Followed by Workingman, later Workman and people's press
Suspended Je 1837
Ct F 7 1826
DLC Je 13,S 5 1827;S 3 1839
M [My 25 1824-My 17 1825]
MBAt Ag 22 1827;Ag 5 1828
MH My 18 1831-My 9 1832
MSaE Jl 14 1823;Je 8 1824
MWA O 18 1826;D 26 1827;Jl 25 1832;S 17 1839
MeMH Jl 29 1828
WHi O 29 1840

WORKINGMAN and people's press. w O 12 1842-45‖
Follows Somerset journal
MBAt D 14 1843

NORTH ANSON

SOMERSET spectator. w Jl 23 1852-Je? 1856‖
DLC O 23 1852
MWA N 6 1852

UNION advocate. w Jl 23 1856-1910‖?
MWA Ap 29 1857
MeHi Ja 4 1900
OClWHi D 28 1864

NORTH BERWICK

North Berwick TIMES. m D 1879-80‖
MWA Ja 1880

NORTHPORT

Northport BUDGET. w
MeBe My 29 1908

NORWAY

Norway ADVERTISER-DEMOCRAT. w Mr 19 1844+
1844?-1934 as Norway advertiser (Title varies: N 1850-Je 1851 Pine state news; N 12 1875-N 17 1876 Oxford register and advertiser; 1882?-1905? Oxford county advertiser)
Suspended from N 1860-Ja 5 1872
pub 1882+
DLC 1844-Mr 1845
KHi [My 9 1845-Ap 8 1858]
MSaE O 27 1853
MWA Mr 19,Ap 12 1844-Mr 1845;Ap 14 1848-O 25 1850;Ja 2-23[Ag 21 1851-Mr 25 1852]Mr 4 1858;72-N 5 1875;D 1876-N 22 1878
MeHi Ap 17 1846-Ap 7 1848;Jl 6 1849;Ja 2 1851;Ja 5 1900
MeN 1882+
NNHi Mr 19-26,My 16 1844-Ap 3 1846;S 25 1851
NcD [O 13 1848-Mr 22 1850]Ag 30 1878[83]N 12 1886;Ja 7 1887
WHi Jl 29 1852

JOURNAL of the times. w Ap 25-Je 27 1832‖
KHi complete

OXFORD county advertiser. *See* Norway advertiser-democrat

OXFORD observer. w Jl 8 1824-Je 12 1832‖
1824-D 7 1826 pub in Paris
CSmH My 11 1830
KHi complete
MBAt Ag 7 1828
MHi Ag 5 1824
MSaE Ag 5 1824;N 27 1823;Jl 27 1826;Ag 14 1828
MWA 1824-Ja 20,F 10,Mr 3,Ap 14,Jl 9,21 1825; Jl 6-20,Ag 24,S 21 1826;O 18 1827;Ja 17,Ag 14 1828
MeHi 1824-Je 1828;O 18 1831;Mr 13 1832
NN My 22 1829

OXFORD oracle. w Je-Ag 1833‖
Ct Jl 22 1833
MeHi Jl 22 1833

OXFORD register. w O 1 1869-76‖?
United with Norway advertiser to form Oxford register and advertiser, later Norway advertiser-democrat
1869-75 pub at Paris
KHi F 21 1873-Jl 7 1876
MWA Ag 1 1873;Ja-N 17 1876
NN Mr 1872-N 5 1876
NcD N 12-D 1875

PINE state news. *See* Norway advertiser-democrat

POLITICIAN. w Je 26 1832-Ap 1833‖
KHi N 20 1832
MWA D 11 1832

OLD ORCHARD

Old Orchard BEACH sea-side reporter. *See* Old Orchard sea shell

Old Orchard NEWS. w Je 9 1914+
pub 1914+

Old Orchard SEA SHELL. d 1880-97‖?
1880-81? as Old Orchard beach sea-side reporter
d during Jl-Ag
MWA Jl 23,29-O 9,24 1880;Ag 23 1881;My 13 1883(special ed)Jl 30 1896

Old Orchard TRANSCRIPT. w N 2 1923-25‖?
MWA N 2 1923

MAINE (*Continued*)

OLDTOWN

Oldtown ENTERPRISE. w Mr 3 1888+
MeO 1888+
NN Je 16 1932

Oldtown HERALD. w Ja 4 1888-
MWA F 4 1888

Oldtown INDEX. w 1848-50|
MeHi D 7 1850

ORONO

OUTPOST. w
MeBa N 30-D 7 1918

ORR'S ISLAND

NEW dory. w
MeHi Ag 14 1891

PARIS

JEFFERSONIAN. *See under* Portland
OXFORD democrat. *See under* South Paris
OXFORD observer. *See under* Norway
OXFORD register. *See under* Norway

PATTEN

Patten VOICE. *See under* Sherman Mills

PEMAQUID

Pemaquid MESSENGER. *See under* Bristol

PHILLIPS

MAINE woods. w S 14 1878-D 31 1918||?
1878-D 7 1900 as Phillips phonograph. Merged with Farmington chronicle (Farmington)
DLC Ag 31 1900-Ag 8 1902
MWA S 1878;Jl 2,30-Ag 6,9(extra)1881;S 8 1882[Jl 10 1885-86]-92
MeF S 14 1878-Jl 18 1918
MeFC 1878-D 31 1918
MeHi Ja 5 1899

Phillips PHONOGRAPH. *See* Maine woods

PITTSFIELD

Pittsfield ADVERTISER. w 1882+
pub 1882+
MWA D 12-19 1895
MeHar Jl 26 1917
NNHi My 15 1883;Je 2 1904

PORTLAND

Portland ADVERTISER. sw N 8 1823-52||?
Title varies slightly: Portland advertiser and gazette of Maine
CSmH S 7 1830
DLC [1824]F 12-Jl 5 1825;Ap 3,Ag 24 1827;F 12 1828[Je 1829-Ja 1830]My 9 1843
MB [O 29 1833-Ag 1834]
MBAt Ja 22 1828;Mr 31 1829
MH 1831-39;42-Je 1843
MHi S 23 1825;My 19 1826;O 29 1832;F 21,Mr 14,Jl 9 1833
MSaE O 27 1824;Ja 19,Ap 27 1825;Mr 19 1830; F 4-12 1831;Jl 2 1852
MWA N 22 1823[Ja 31-N 20 1824]Ap 11 1826-Jl 22 1828;Ag 11 1829;Mr 9,Ag 20,O 5 1830;F 1 1831;O 29 1833;Mr 28,Ap 10-15 1834;D 8-11 1835;Jl 29,Ag 23,D 27 1836;Ja 3 1837;Mr 20 1838;F 18 1840
MeBB [Ag 12 1828-Ja 13 1832]
MeBa Ja 17,Ap 18,S 2,16 1834;Mr 24,Je 9,16, Jl 7,14,28 1835[36]Ja 24,31,Ap 11,N 21 1837; S 14 1852
MeHi S 10 1825-Jl 22 1828
MeP 1824-O 18 1833
NN S 2 1825
NNHi S 11 1824[Mr 1827-28]

Portland ADVERTISER. w 1830-1903||?
Title varies slightly: Portland advertiser and gazette of Maine; Portland weekly advertiser and star; etc.
Ct F 9 1836[37]
CtHi Ja-O 7 1834
DLC O 5 1830;My 8 1832;Ag 11 1846
MBAt D 19 1837
MH 1835-[39;45-46]
MWA Ja 20 1829-30;Ja 18,F 8,My 31,N 29 1831;Ja 31 1832-[Ja 21-D 10 1833]Ap 29 1834; F 10,N 10 1835;F 9 1836;N 21 1837;Ap 10 1838;Ja 29,My 7,S 10,N 12,D 3 1839;Mr 17, Je 16-N 10 1840;My 21 1844;Ja 7 1851;O 5,N 2 1852;Mr 1,Ap 19 1853;D 2 1856;64;F 25-D 23 1865;S 4 1868-70;Mr 8-29 1884
MeBB F 1,Mr 1-8 1831
MeHi Ag 1830-F 14 1832;D 24 1839-47
MeP O 11 1831-O 1 1832;D 19 1837-Jl 1841;51-55;60-61;Ja-Je 1866;69
MeU N 1873-76
MeWHi Je 3 1833;Jl 6 1846
NN Ag 31 1830
NNHi [Ja,Je-D 1835;Ap 1836-O 1837;Ap-My 1838;Ap,Je,S-D 1840;F-Ap,O 1842]Je 8 1852; Ja 17 1873
NcD Ap 13,Je 22,O 12 1830;Ap 15 1833;Ja-F 18 1865;71-N 21 1873;77-82;86-88
NhD Jl 16,O 29 1832;Mr 11,O 29 1833;Ja 7 1834;N 10,24,D 8 1835-Ja 5,19-Je,Jl 12-26,Ag 9-30,S 13-20 1836
OClWHi My 27 1865

Portland daily ADVERTISER. d Ja 1 1831-D 4 1909||
Title varies: Portland daily evening advertiser; Portland evening advertiser; Evening advertiser; Advertiser; etc. United with Portland evening express to form Portland evening express and daily advertiser, later Portland evening express. Suspended Jl 1866-Je 1868
DLC Ja 1,10,13,19 1831;O 2 1832;Ja 5 1841;My 27 1845;Jl 11-S 26 1848;Je 27 1849-D 17 1851; Mr 27 1861-63 Je 14,Ag 22-23 1898
IaDH Mr 7 1905-09
M [1855-F 7 1863]
MBAt Ap 15,20 1865
MSaE O 21 1851;Ag 25 1852;Mr 23 1854;Je 5, 7 1855;Ag 17 1857;O 24 1865;F 24,Mr 14,Ap 1,17 1876;D 17 1881
MWA 1831 33-[Jl 11 1836-Mr 18]S 7 1837;Ja 24 1838;D 17,28 1839;Mr 30,Ap 18,Ag 25,S 12, O 14,24,N 5,27-28,D 5,14 1840;Ja 16,Mr 8,Ap 7(extra)18 1841;F 13,My 10 1844;50-54;F 13, Mr 21,26,Je 7,Jl 1855-[57-58]-S 1860;64;F 21-D 1865;Jl-D 1866;69-89;Ja 23,Jl 1890-D 4 1909
MeBa Jl 6 1866;Je 1 1876;S 6 1878;S 9,D 26 1879;Ja 2,23,N 5,9 1880;Ja 22 1884
MeHi My 20 1831-Jl 1859;Ja 1,6 1900
MeP 1831-55;Jl 1836-Je 1866;Jl 1868-D 4 1909
MeU Ja-Je 1857;Jl-D 1868
N Mr 9 1837;Ja-Je 1855;Ag 20-22,25 1873
NN Mr 9 1836
NNHi 1831;Ja 26,Mr 10,Ap 1860;Ap 17 1862; Mr 24,Ap 10,N 7 1863;D 6 1868;Ja-Ap,N 4,D 27-31 1870[73-76]Ap 24 1880;O 2,20,D 1,21 1888[Ja-Ap 1889]
NcD S 8 1834[Mr 1835-Je 1836]Jl 15 1858;Ja 3-F 20 1865;Jl 10 1870
OClWHi My 30 1865
WHi Jl 16 1850;Ap 22 1865

Portland tri-weekly ADVERTISER. tw 1841?-65||?
DLC Mr 22 1859;Ap 20 1863
MWA O 27 1854;D 1-6,13-25,29 1865
MeBa Jl 16 1855;Ja 14 1856;F 15,20-Mr 20,25 29,Jl 2-5,12,15-22,26,29,O 16,N 15,D 18-25,30 1856
NN S 3 1862

ADVERTISER. Sunday issue. sw,w N 4 1866-70||
1866-F 1867 as Portland advertiser; Mr 1867-Ap, S 20-N 22 1868 Sunday advertiser, My-S 13 1868 Portland Sunday advertiser sw 1866-Ja 6? 1867
MWA 1866-69[F 20-S 1870]
NNHi F 16,Mr 1 1868

AMERICAN. w 1841-
DLC D 16 1843
MeP Ja 14-Ap 1843

Portland daily AMERICAN. d Ag 6 1842-F 15 1845||
DLC Ag 1 1842;Ap 13,O 8 1844-45
MWA Jl 10,D 14 1843;My 9,14,17 1844
MeP 1843-F 6 1845

AMERICAN citizen. w N 4 1875-76||
MWA N 11 1875
MeP 1875-Mr 30 1876

AMERICAN patriot. w My 20 1825-28||
Follows Independent statesman and Maine republican
DLC 1825-N 15 1828
MWA 1825-My 12,Je 23,S 8 1826;Ja 12,Mr 23, Je 1,Ag 24,N 23 1827;Ja 26,Jl 26 1828
MeP My 27 1825-My 11 1827
MeSY My 11 1827-N 15 1828
MiU-C [1825-26]
NN D 8 1826

ARGUS. *See* Eastern argus

BATTLE ax. w 1849-
MeHi Je 2,16,Jl 14,Ag 4 1849

CAMPAIGN argus. w Ag 2-S 7 1855||
MWA complete

Portland CITY item. *See* Portland evening item

COLUMBIAN. w 1894-1900||?
PPCHi [1897-1900]

Daily COURIER. d O 13 1829-40||?
CSmH S 18 1830
DLC [1829-Ja 1830]Ja 14 1831
MB [1837]
MSaE Ja 1 1830
MWA S 7,18 1830
MeBB 1829-O 12 1832
MeHi [1831]My 30 1833;Je 11 1839
MeP D 9 1830-Ja 17 1832;38-Ja 7 1840
MeWHi My 24 1833
NN Mr 17 1836
NNHi 1829-O 12 1830;Mr 16,26,Je 23 1831

Portland COURIER. w Ja 5 1832-
Follows Family reader. Title varies: Portland courier and family reader; etc
MWA N 21 1834
MeBa O 8 1839
MeHi Ap 10 1835-Ja 7 1840
NN Ja 5 1832
NNHi O 24 1834-Mr 10 1837;Ja 29,Jl 9 1839
NhD Jl 22 1836

Daily evening COURIER. d Je 12 1860-65||
1860-62 as Evening courier. Followed by Portland evening star
MHi Ap 20 1861
MWA [Je-N 22 1860]N 25 1861-F 8 1862;S 14 1863;F 25 1864;Ja 7,18-19 1865
MeBa Ap 17 1861
MeHi My 15 1861
MeP Ap-S 1864
NNHi Ja 26 1861

Portland weekly COURIER. w Ag 12? 1863-
MWA Mr 18,N 4,D 16 1864-Ja 6 1865

DOLLAR weekly American. w S 5 1843-
MWA S 5 1843

DOWNING gazette. w Jl 4 1834-Mr 26 1836||
DLC Jl 4,18,D 27 1834
MB [Jl 11 1835-36]
MSaE 1834-Ja 17,F-Mr 14,28-Ap,My 9-Je 13, 27 1835
MWA complete
MeBa Jl 4,O 18 1834
MeHi [1834-35]
NNHi D 6 1834

*EASTERN argus. w,sw S 8 1803-1921||
sw Ja 9-Mr 20 1821;F 18-25,Je 10-17 1823
Ct N 21 1826[27-28;37]Ja 17 1838
DLC 1821-Ag 22 1826;Ag 31 1830;Ja 18 1831; Jl 23 1833;D 8 1840
MB Ja 9,Ap 3,My 15-22,Je 12 1821[Ja-O 1822]
MBAt S 3 1822;S 9 1828
MHi Ja 23 1821;Ja 7,N 11 1823
MSaE Je 3 1823;Mr 5 1830
MWA [1821;F 26-D 24 1822]-D 6 1825;Je 6-13, Ag 29 1826;Jl 3,Ag 14,S 18,D 11 1827;Ap 8-15,My 20,Ag 26-S 2,N 11 1828;F 3,24 1829;Ap 27,Ag 3,24-S 7,O 12 1830;Ap 19 1831;Mr 20, Jl 17 1832;S 17 1833;Ja 21 1834;S 1,D 29 1835; Mr 3,My 17 1836;Ap 3,S 18,O 16 1838;F 19, Je 4 1839;Ag 1 1843;N 9 1852
MeBB 1821-O 5 1824;Ag 1833-Ja 5 1836;38-40; 48-59
MeBt 1821-Ja 3 1824
MeHi Ap 24 1821;N 6 1822[Jl-D 1826]-F 3 1829
MeMH Jl 10 1844
MeP 1821-26;29-Jl 1833;35-47;51-55
MeU 1860-1917
MiU-C [1822]
N O 15 1833
NN Ja-Jl 1821;Mr 4(supp)1828;O 27-30 1829; Jl 6 1876
NNHi [1821;23-24;47-N 1848]S 5 1872;Mr 6-13, Ag 14 1873;Mr 9,Ag 10,O 19 1876;Jl 10 1879; Jl 1,S 16 1880;Mr 10,My 26,O 6 1881;Je 29, Ag 17 1882;Je 28,Jl 19 1883;O 2,16,20,N 20 1884;Je 4 1885
NcD [1821-24]
OClWHi Je 1 1865
P-M F 6,Mr 6 1855

EASTERN argus. sw,tw S 30 1824-87||?
1844-47 as Tri-weekly argus
sw 1824-32
CSmH Ag 13 1830
DLC S 30,N 1,25 1824;F 21,Jl 7 1825;F 10 1826-Mr 23 1827;Mr 29 1829-S 18 1832;35
KHi D 26 1828
MBAt O 31 1826;S 25 1829
MH 1839-O 14 1846
MHi O 14 1824;F 24,Mr 7(extra)O 28,D 30 1825;D 29 1826
MSaE My 4,S 10 1841;Ja? 1843;F 23 1852
MWA S 30 1824;25[26-27]-[Ja-N 23 1830]Ag 30,D 23 1831;Ja 3,13,20-24,F 17 1832;N 12 1834;Jl 25 1836[My 6 1839-S 21 1840]O 20,D 1 1843;Ap 18,My 2,Jl 11,N 12 1845;Mr 13-18 1850;Mr 5,S 13,O 29,N 5-8,D 15 1852;F 23 1853
MeBB 1824-39;My 8 1840-47
MeBa Ag 30,S 22,D 17 1852;F 4 1853;Je 23 1854
MeBt 1825-30
MeHi Ja 10 1825-[Jl-D 1826]Jl 14[Ag-D]1829-31;33-34
MeP 1824-35
NNHi Ja-N 5 1833[34]O 20 1835;Ag 6 1838; Ja 21,F 8,29 1839
NcD Je 30,S 19 1826;My 23,O 7 1828;F 17,Ag 14 1829

Daily EASTERN argus. d Ja 1 1835-Ja 24 1921||
My 10 1844-47 as Daily argus. Followed by Portland herald
DLC O 14 1836;Mr 29,Ap 10,My 29,Je 15 1839; Mr 11 1840;F 17,Mr 10,24,Ag 27 1841;Jl 26, Ag 4 1845;Ag 22 1846-48;F 3 1854-[61-73]Jl 1874-1921
MHi O 18 1883
MSaE S 24 1841;O 19 1850;N 30 1852;D 14 1881
MWA F 25,S 2,O 3,7 1835;Ag 5 1837[Je 17 1840-45]-46[Mr-My]Jl 16 1847;Ap 8 1854;60-Je 1870;Mr 25 1872;Ag 20-25,27-28 1873;Ag 14,17 1874;Ag 11,N 29 1875;Jl 8 1880;Ag 3,5, 8-9 1881;Je 12,Jl 16 1883;Ja 24,My 23 1884;Jl (supp)1885;Jl 6-7 1886;Ap 21,O 3 1887;Mr 2 1889;D 7 1895;Ja 4 1896;F 2,15 1898;S 15 1899; Ag 8 1900;Je 11 1902;10-Mr,My 1920-Ja 24 1921
MeBa Jl 16 1838;F 17,Ap 6,Ag 29 1868;Ja 28, Mr 17 1869
MeHi 1835-36;Ja 12-D 1837;Ja 1,Je 30 1851
MeP 1835-1921
MeU 1866-1909
N Ag 21-27 1873
NNHi Ja-[Je-D]1836;F 6,D 12,26 1837;Ag 6 1838;Ja 21,F 6,22,D 15,28 1839[Ja-F]Mr 6,My 14 1840[Ja-Ap 1841]Je 21 1842;N 23 1843;N 25 1845;S 25,D 15 1846;S 17 1851;Ja 11 1853; Ag 10 1860;Jl 24 1867;F 13,Jl 30,O 15,N 18 1868;Ap 1-2 1870;Ap 6 1871;Je 2,6 1873;Ag 27 1874;My 20,Je 10 1875;Ja 12,F 3,11,Je 8 1876; Ag 17 1880;F 28 1882
NcD Jl 31 1840;Ja 7 1860[79-80;87;1907]
NcU Ag 29 1873
OClWHi Ap 8 1840;My 31 1865
WHi Je 17 1896

EASTERN argus-revived. sw Jl 1 1839-Je 22 1841||?
DLC 1839-Je 22 1841
MWA Jl 1 1839;O 27 1840;Ja 5,26-F 2,Mr 9, Je 11 1841
MeHi [1840-41]

EASTERN argus-revived. w Jl 2 1839-41||?
MWA S 17,O 1,22 1839

EASTERN farmer and journal of news. sm Ja 6 1842-43||
MWA Ja 6-D 22 1842
MeHi 1842
MeP 1842-Ja 1843
NNHi 1842

MAINE (*Continued*)

PORTLAND—*Continued*

Portland **ECLECTIC** and northern home. w O 5 1850-Ap 7 1855||
1850-52 as Eclectic. Merged with Portland transcript
MB O 11 1851-S 23 1854
MSaE Ap 10 1852
MWA O 8 1853-[54]55
MeBa S 18 1852
MeHi 1850-S 1851;O 8 1853-S 2 1854
MeP 1851-55
MiU-C Ja 4 1851
NNHi 1850-S 17 1853
NcD 1850-S 17 1853;Ag 12-19,S 9-30,O 21-N 4 1854;Ja 13,Mr 10-Ap 1855
P-M Ap 29 1854

ENQUIRER. w 1866-73||
1866-72 as Riverside echo
1866-68 pub in Bucksport
MSaE N 30 1867
MWA S 18 1869;70[Je 17 1871-N 23 1872]F 15,Ap 27,My 17,31 1873
MeBB 1870
NNHi N 17 1866;Ap 20 1867;F 15 1873
RW N 7 1868

Portland **EXPRESS.** d,tw Mr 18- 1844||
Mr 18-My 2 1844 as Daily express
d Mr 18-My 4 1844
DLC Mr 18-S 2 1844
MWA My 17 1844

Portland evening **EXPRESS.** d O 12 1882+
Title varies: Evening express; Portland evening express and daily advertiser; etc.
Ag 31 1932 is 50th anniversary no
pub 1882+
Ct D 24 1934
DLC N 11 1897-Je 1899
IaDH 1910-14
M S 1 1933
MWA D 23 1920;Ag 31 1932
MeBa S 5 1888;Ja 24 1903
MeHi Ja 1 1900;S 14 1901;S 1-2 1920
MeP 1885+
MeU 1922-Jl 1924
MiU-C O 12 1912
NN Mr 18-S 2 1844
NNHi O 31 1888
NcD [1890;93-96;1900-01;04-07;09;11]
OHi 1933+

Portland weekly **EXPRESS.** w 1888-99||?
MeBa N 29 1888;Je 20,Jl 4-18,O 17,31-N 7,21 1889
MeU Ap 1888-Ap 1889;My 1890-99
NNHi Mr 5 1896

FAMILY reader. w O 19? 1829-33||
Followed by Portland courier and family reader, later Portland courier
MWA Mr 23 1830;O 23 1831;Ja 31 1832
MeP 1829-31
NN O 8 1833
NNHi [Je 1830-O 1832]

*Portland **GAZETTE.** w Ap 16 1798-D 28 1824||
Title varies: Portland gazette; Jenks' Portland gazette; Jenks' Portland gazette and Maine advertiser; Portland gazette and Maine advertiser; etc. United with Portland advertiser to form Gazette of Maine.
sw during sessions of the legislature
MB 1821-S 21 1824
MBAt F 26 1821;S 3 1822
MSaE My 14 1822
MWA Ja 15 1821-[23]24
MeBB [1821-Ag 24 1824]
MeHi [1821-N 12 1822]
MeWHi N 26,D 3 1822
NN 1821 (extras:Ja 2,9,16,Ap 10,17,24 1821)
NNHi [1824]
NcD F 17 1824
NhD Ja 1-15,18-22,F 12-Mr 8,15,22,26,Ap-Mr 15,Je-S 18,O 2,16,20,N 20,D 1821-Ja 1,4-14,22-29,Je 4,18 1822

Saturday evening **GAZETTE.** w 1878||
DLC O 19-26 1878

GAZETTE of Maine. w Ja 1 1825-N 11 1829||?
Formed by the union of Portland gazette and Portland advertiser. Followed by Portland advertiser and gazette of Maine, later Portland advertiser
Ct D 6 1825;N 14 1826;Ja 3 1827
CtY S 2-9,O 21 1828
DLC F 8 1825-26;Ja 1,N 11 1828
MB Jl 25 1826;My 6 1828
MBAt S 9 1828
MSaE Ap 19 1825
MWA 1825-27;Ja 13 1829
MeHi Jl 3,O 23 1827-Ap,Je 3-10,Ag 29 1828;N 11 1829
NNHi [Ap 1825-Ap 1826]
NcD Je 19,S 11,O 9-30 1827;Ja 15,Je 17,Jl 22 1829

Portland **GENIUS.** sm 1840-
1840?-Je 1841 as Simon pure Portland genius
Suspended from Je 12 1841-D 28 1852
MWA Je 12 1841;D 28 1852
MeHi Jl 4 1853
MeWHi My 31 1854;Mr 7 1855;Ja 1 1856
NNHi F-My 1841

Portland **GLOBE.** w 1877-D 25 1897||?
1877-O 1878 as Cumberland globe (Cumberland)
MWA Ap 16 1881;D 29 1883
MeP Je 1877-O,N 15 1879-D 1897
NNHi Je 5 1880
NcD Mr 3 1883

Portland **HERALD.** w 1884-D 15 1898||?
MWA F 22,Mr 20 1894
MeBB N 13,27-D 4,18 1886-Ja 8,29 1887
MeHi N 15 1884-D 15 1898
MeP N 15 1884-D 22 1888;89-91
MeU [Mr 17 1888-Je 7 1890]

Portland **HERALD.** d Ja 25-N 19 1921||
Follows Daily Eastern argus. United with Portland daily press to form Portland press-herald
MeP complete
NcD O 11 1921

INDEPENDENT statesman and Maine republican. w Jl 14 1821-My 6 1825||
1821-Je 24 1822 as Independent statesman. Followed by American patriot.
DLC Ja 10 1822-D 21 1824;Ja 28,F 11-25,Mr 11,25-Ap 1,15-My 1825
MBAt Ap 12 1822
MHi O 24 1822;Ap 8 1825
MSaE Ja 24 1822;My 6 1825
MWA 1821[22]Ap 19[Ag 1823-24]Mr 4,Ap 1 1825
MeHi [1821-Jl 19 1823]
MeP [1821-My,Jl 12 1822-25]
MeSY [O 12 1821-25]
MiU-C [1824]
NNHi D 6 1823
NcD O 10 1822;F 7,Ap 2,23-30,Je 11,25,Jl 9, Ag 20 1824
NjR Ap 23 1824;My 20 1825
PDoHi Ap 22 1825

Portland **INQUIRER.** w 1848-55||
Titles varies slightly. United with Fountain and journal to form Journal and inquirer, later Maine journal
1848?-49 dated also at Bangor
DLC Jl-Ag 21 1849
MSaE Jl 22 1852
MWA Je 12-D 11 1849;Ja 23(extra)[F 20-D 11]1851;Je 24 1852;Ag 31 1854
MeBa F 24 1853;Ag 31 1854
MeHi N 11 1845;Ja 2 1851;D 1854-S 20 1855
NNHi S 30 1848;Mr 4,F 19 1852

INTERNATIONAL journal. *See under* Boston, Mass.

Portland evening **ITEM.** d 1879-82||?
Title varies :City item; Portland city item; etc. Merged with Portland eveining express
DLC [Ap-My 1880]
MeHi [1880]
MeP O 6 1879-My 8 1880;81-S 8 1882

JACKSON mirror and Maine Tory; or, Office holder's advocate. w S 4 1834-
MWA S 4 1834

JEFFERSONIAN. w Mr 21 1827-Ja 1 1838||
Merged with Standard
1828-Ap 301833 pub in Paris
CSmH Ag 24 1830
Ct Je 20,S 26 1827;F 6,27,Mr 5,Ap 9-16,Je 4, Jl 30-Ag 6,N 5 1828;Ja 21,Ap 1,My 20 1829; Ap 13,Je 29,N 16-20 1830;Mr 1,15-22 1831
DLC My 4 1830-38
MBAt S 10 1828
MWA Jl 11 1827;Ja 30 1828;N 24 1829;Je 14 1831;S 23-30 1833;Ja 27 1834;F 1 1836
MeBB Mr 29,Ag 8,22 1827;Mr 5 1828
MeBa Ja 6 1834;N 30 1835
N O 14 1833

JOURNAL and inquirer. *See* Maine journal

JOURNAL of reform. w 1836-37||
MeP My 25 1836-My 17 1837

LEADER. w Jl 8 1871-72||
1871-Jl 1872? as Monitor
MWA Jl 22 1871[Ag-N 16 1872]

Saturday evening **MAIL.** as O 18 1879-
MWA O 25 1879
MeHi O 18 1879

MAINE coast cottager. w 1881-1920||?
1881-Je 26? 1891 as Mount Desert herald
1881-Ag 1894 pub in Bar Harbor
1881-S 1882 sw during summer
MSaE Ag 21 1891
MWA Jl 14 1881-My 15,Jl 1891-Ag 1894;95;Jl 11-S 1896;Ja 21 1899-D 20 1902;Ja 23-D 1904
MeBHi [1881-92]
MeHi Jl 14 1881-My 15 1891[Je 23 1895-Ag 14 1897]Ja,Jl 1900;N 1904-Jl 1905;My 26 1917
NcD Jl 14-My 8,Jl 1891-93;Ag 4 1894;95;Jl 11-S 1896;99-1902;04

MAINE expositor. w Mr 2 1852-56||?
Suspended N 1-8 1854
MSaE Ag 11 1852
MWA Mr 2,Ap 5,D 1 1852;D 28 1853;F 1-8,Ap 26,S 20,O 25,N 15 1854
MeBa D 1 1852;Jl 2 1856
MeHi 1852-S 19 1855
NNHi Ag 30 1854

MAINE journal. w Je 24 1844-61||?
1844-Jl 19 1850 as Cold water fountain (title varies: Cold water fountain and Gardiner news-letter; Cold water fountain and Washingtonian journal); Jl 26 1850-D 31 1853 Fountain and journal; Ja 7 1854-O? 1855 Maine temperance journal; N 1855-D 30 1856 Journal and inquirer; Ja 1 1857-Ap 29 1858 Maine temperance journal and inquirer; My? 1858-Ja 26 1861 Maine temperance journal
1844-D 10 1853 pub in Gardiner
DLC N 10 1855
MSaE Mr 4,Jl 22 1852
MWA Ag 29 1845;N 20 1846;S 28 1849;Ja 18,F 15-22,Ap 12,My 24,Je 7,28-Jl 5,26Ag 30,S 12 1850[My-D 1852;F 10-D 1]17,31 1853 [54] Ap 17-My 8 1856;F 11-18,Ag 26-S 2,16,30 1858;D 27 1859;Jl 16 1860;Ja 19-26 1861
MeBa [S 15 1853]-[54-My 21 1860]F 16-Mr 2, 23,Ap 13,27-My 4,18,Je 1861
MeG Jl 30 1847-S 1848;Jl 26 1850-55
MeHi [1850-53]
MeP Ja-D 3 1854
NNHi D 29 1855;S 4 1856;F 2 1861
NcD Je 7 1850

MAINE standard. w My 11 1861-
MWA Je 29,Jl 13 1861
MeBa My 18,Je 8-15,Jl 6,27 1861

MAINE state press. w 1862-1924||?
Title varies: Maine weekly state press; etc.
MSaE F 1 1866
MWA Je 18 1863-N 9 1865;Je 28,Jl 12,Ag 2-9, 23 1866-94;97-98;1900;02-[13]-20
MeBa Je 16 1887
MeHi Ja 1900
MeU 1876;78-80;82-91;Ja-F 1895;1912-13;15-My 16 1916;17-20
NNHi [Ja-F,Ap 1864-My 1865]-[Mr-Ag]-[N-D 1866]-[F-Je,Ag-O 1868;Ja-F,Ap-My,Jl-S 1869;70-72] Ag 10,O 5 1876
NcD Jl 11 1872;Ag 1 1878;Mr-D 5 1895;Ja 9 1896-97
WHi Jl-D 1894;96
—d ed *See* Portland press-herald

MAINE temperance gazette and Washingtonian herald. w Ag 23 1838-43||?
1838-O 1841 pub in Augusta
MB Ag 29 1839-Ag 20 1840
MWA Ag 23,S 13 1838;Ja 10,24,Mr 7,S 19 1839;Jl 14,Ag 11 1842
MeBa N 8 1838
MeHi [1838-S 24 1840;41]-N 1 1843
NNHi Ag 20 1840;Mr 10 1842

MAINE temperance journal. *See* Maine journal

MAINE temperance watchman. *See* Temperance watchman

MERCANTILE bulletin. w
MeP O-D 8 1873

MONITOR. *See* Leader

Portland **MONTHLY.** m Ja 1860-
MWA Je-Jl,S 1860;D 1861

MOUNT VERNON. sw
MHi F 11-14 1859

NARRAGANSETT sun. w N 17 1892-1917||?
MWA 1892-9?
MeHi Mr 17 1892-96;Ja 3,Mr-Ap 18 1900;06-13
MeP 1894-1900
MeU 1896-1901;03-09[Ja 11-D 19 1912;Ja 9-N 20 1913]Ja-S 1916
MiU-C O 10 1895
NNHi Mr 5-12,Ag 20,S 3,24,O 15 1903

NATIONAL democrat. w S 5 1850-51||?
MeHi Ja 2 1851

NEW ENGLAND regulator. w 1866-71||
1870 as New England regulator and advertiser
MWA [O 15 1870-S 16 1871]
NcD [O 1870-S 1871]

Daily **NEW ERA.** d
NNHi [Jl 26-S 3 1878]

NEW ERA-LEADER. w 1877-80||
1877-78? as New era
MWA F 5-12 1880
MeP N 15 1877-N 18 1880
NNHi Ja 18 1880

Daily evening **NEWS.** d 1850-51||?
MeHi Ja 1 1851

Portland **NEWS.** d 1880?-82||?
1880?-D 12 1881 as Morning news
MeP Ja 29 1881-Ja 5 1882
NNHi N 24 1880

Daily **NEWS.** d 1891-92||
MeU D 9 1891-92

Portland evening **NEWS.** d O 3 1927+
pub 1927+
M S 18 1928;Jl 15 1933
MeHi 1927+
MeP 1927+

NORTHERN pioneer. w Jl 1-O 21 1848||
United with Portland transcript to form Portland transcript and northern pioneer, later Portland transcript
MWA complete
MeHi complete

ORION. w
MeHi Mr 11-D 13 1837;Mr 3 1838
NNHi Jl 29 1837

PEOPLE'S advocate. w
Ct [1836]

POLITICAL nostrum. w
MeHi O 5,27 1840

PORTLANDER. tw D 12? 1836-
Follows Daily times
MWA D 15 1836-[Ja-Je 13 1837]
MeHi [1836-37]

Portland **PRESS-HERALD.** d Je 23 1862+
1862-N 19 1921 as Portland daily press
pub 1924+
A Jl 13 1874-75
DLC Ja 22 1864;F 8,16,21,Mr 6 1871;72-81;N 21 1921+
IHi Ap 17 1865
MBAt Ap 15,17 1865
MSaE O 9 1871;Ja 24,Mr 14 1876;Ap 29,S 28,D 16 1881
MWA Je 25 1862-67;Jl 1868-70;S 10 1872;Jl 28,D 29 1875;Je 25,27,Jl 1,18,20 1878;Jl 1,14, 16,18-26,29,Ag 28-29,S 3-4,6,D 16 1879;Jl 5-6 1886; Mr 4 1887;F 22 1889;S 22 1897
Me 1924+
MeBB 1876-Je 1879
MeBa Mr 19,Ap 1 1863;My 29 1869;D 24 1874; Ja 8 1875;S 12 1876;Je 20,D 19 1879;Je 24 1880;S 14,D 22 1886;Je 11 1887;Ja 20 1890
MeHi 1862-94;Ja 1 1900;My 25-27, S 14,O 1 1911
MeP 1866-Je 1870;73+
MeU Jl-D 1875;F 19-Mr 17,Jl 1923

MAINE (*Continued*)

PORTLAND—*Continued*

Portland PRESS-HERALD. d 1862+—*Cont.*
N Ag 23,25,28-29 1873
NN Jl 6 1876
NNHi [Ap-My,Jl 1863;My,S-O 1864]Ap 17 1865;Jl 10 1866;Jl 24 1867[Mr-Ap,Jl,N 1868-Ja,Mr,S 1869]Ja-Ap 4 [Je-Jl]1870[F,D 1871-72]Je 6 1873[Ja,My-Ag,O-D 1874;supps: Ap 14,My 5,22 1866
NcD [1862-64;67-68;70-1903]-[13-18]-[21-23]
NcU Ag 22,24 1873
OClWHi D 21 1864;Ap 19 1865
VHaH Ap 17 1865;S 28 1881
WHi Ja-Mr,Jl 1894-Ja 1897

Portland PRESS-HERALD. w *See* Maine state press

Sunday PRESS-HERALD. *See* Portland Sunday telegram

Portland PRICE-CURRENT and shipping list. w 1861-84||
Title varies
MWA My 4,25,Je 8-22,Jl 27-Ag 3,17,31,S 21,O 5 1867
MeHi S 23 1861-S 1862;Ap 1864-S 1868[77-Mr 1 1879]
MeP Je 1877-My 8 1880
NNHi Ja 6,S 1866-68

Evening RECORD. d 1884||?
NNHi Mr 1 1884

Portland REGISTER. w
NNHi Je 23,30 1883

Saturday evening REVIEW. w S 13-N 20 1897||
MWA O 4-9,25-30,N 8-13 1897
MeHi complete
MeU complete

RIVERSIDE echo. *See* Enquirer

SENTINEL. ir Ap 2 1853-
Campaign paper
MWA Ap 2 1853
MeBa Ap 2,S 9,O 10,29 1853

SIMON pure Portland genius. *See* Portland genius

SPIRIT of '28. ir
Campaign paper
MWA O 29 1828
MnHi O 22 1828

SPIRIT of '40. w
Campaign paper
MSaE Jl 20,Ag 19,S 9 1840
MeHi Ag 12 1840
N Ag 5 1840
NNHi O 28 1840

STANDARD. w N 22 1837-
DLC 1837-D 11 1838
MWA F 28,O 30 1838

Portland weekly STAR. w 1864?-Ag 28 1868||
United with Portland weekly advertiser to form Portland weekly advertiser and star, later Portland weekly advertiser
MWA Je 5 1868
MeP Ag 23 1867-68

Portland evening STAR. d Je? 1865-68||
Follows Evening courier
MWA Jl 6 1866
MeHi Jl 6-7 1866
MeP Ja-Je 1868
MeU [Je 12 1865-Je 20]Jl 23 1866-Je 27 1868
NNHi Jl 7(broadside)Ag 15 1866;Ja 27 1868

Portland STAR. (Sunday ed) w 1866-75||
MWA Ja 14,F 26 1871;Mr 15-29 1874
MeBa Ja 10 1875
NNHi N 10 1872;Ja 26 1873

STATE of Maine. d Jl 25 1853-My 1859||
Title varies slightly
DLC D 26 1853-Je 1854
MSaE [1855-58]-[59]
MWA Ag 23 1853;D 19 1854;My 24,Jl 3(extra) 1855
MeBB N 14 1854-O 26 1858
MeP 1853-Je 1857
P-M S 28 1853

STATE of Maine. tw 1853-59||
MSaE D 23 1854;S 11 1855;Ja 10,Je 5,17,O 21,N 1 1855;Mr 26 1859

STATE of Maine. w Jl 1853-My 1859||
Merged with Portland advertiser
MSaE 1855-[57]Ja 12-26 1858
MeBB N 14 1854-O 26 1858

Portland Sunday TELEGRAM. w 1887+
Title varies: Portland Sunday press and Sunday press-herald; Sunday press-herald; etc.
MWA N 8 1891;D 22 1895;D 17 1899;Je 3,Ag 5-12 1900;S 8 1901;Je 23 1912
MeHi Ja 7 1900;S 15 1901;04;08;Je 4,25 1922;S 8 1929;My 21-28 1933
MeP 1910+
MeU 1913

TEMPERANCE watchman. w 1852?-53||?
1852 as Maine temperance watchman
MSaE My 22 1852;Ag 30 1853;D 24 1864;Ja 14 1865
MeB N 20 1852
MeBa Ap 3,Jl 3,17-Ag 7,S 11-17,O 23-30,N 20,D 11-25 1852;Ja 22-F,Mr 12,26-Ap 16,My-Jl 16,30-Ag 20,S 3-10 1853
MeHi S 11 1852
MeP Ja 8-S 10 1853
MeWHi Je 5-12,Ag 14-21,S 25,O 23 1852;S 3 1853
NNHi [F-Mr,Je-Jl,S 1853]

Daily TIMES. d Ag 18-D 10 1836||
Followed by Portlander(tw)
MWA [Ag 19-D 1836]

TIMES. d S 16? 1837-
MWA O 18,D 13 1837

Portland Sunday TIMES. w Ag 8 1875-D 26 1909||
Followed by Portland Sunday press and Portland Sunday times, later Portland Sunday telegram
DLC O 10 1897
MWA D 19 1875;F 20 1898;D 17 1899;My 20 1900;S 8,D 15 1901;D 14 1902
MeHi Ja 7 1900
MeP complete
MeU Ag 1881-Je 1883;Ag 31 1890-Ag 6 1893;S 9 1894-Jl,D 13 1895-1909
NNHi O 29 1876;My 25,S 7 1879
NcD Ag 1907-Jl 1908

Portland TRANSCRIPT. w 1837-1910||?
O 28 1848-Ap 14 1849 as Portland transcript and the Northern pioneer
DLC Ap 14 1838-Mr 1897
MB Ap 14 1838-Ap 6 1839[N 18 1848-Ap 13 1850;Ap 11 1857-Mr 1897]
MHi Mr 3 1860
MSaE O 17 1841-[42]-Ja 21,F 4,18-25 1843;Je 12 1852;Ap 17 1858[60]-Mr 1861[64]-Mr 1865; Mr 24,Jl 5 1866;S 4 1875;Ap 22 1876;S 8 1886; S 4 1889
MWA Ap 12 1837-Mr,N 27-D 4 1875;O 13 1877; My 31 1879;Ag 13-27 1881;Ap 1883-Ap 6 1904;D 1907
MeBB Ap 14 1838-Ap 10 1841;Ap 16 1842-Ap 10 1847;Ap 22 1848-Mr 1899
MeG Ap 15 1853-Ap 8 1854;Ap 12 1856-Ap 4 1857;Ap 9 1859-Mr 1860;Ap 1861-Mr 1863;Ap 1865-Mr 24 1866
MeHi Ap 12 1837-[44-47]-[52]-[54;58]-[66]-[72]-[92]-Ja 1901;Je 4 1902
MeP Ap 12 1837-Ja 1901
MeSY Ap 18 1839-Mr 1889
MeWC Ap 14 1838-Ap 6 1839
MeWHi Jl 11 1846
MiU-C [1847;56-57;61;63;68]
MnHi Ap 12 1856-Ap 4 1857
N Mr 1 1845
NN Ap 12 1837-Ap 7 1838;Ap 18 1840-Ap 10 1841;Ap 22 1848-Ap 4 1857;Ap 10 1858-Mr 1865;Mr 31 1866-Mr 1868;Ap 1869-Mr 1870;Ap 1884-Mr 1885;Ap 1886-Mr 1887
NNHi Ap 12 1837-45;F 7,21-28,Ap 4,18 1847-Ap 7 1855;56-Mr 1877;Ap 1878-Mr 1892;Mr-Je 1898
NcD [1838-41;46;48-49;59-60;62;66]F 3 1872[74; 91-93;95]
NhM Ap 14 1839-Mr 1840
NjR [1837-38;44;52-53]
OClWHi 1859;Ap 7-14,S 9-29,N 10 1860;Mr 9, 23 1861;Ap 4 1863;N 25 1865;Ag 5 1871;My 15-29,My 31,Je 29-Jl 5,Ag 16,S 6,17,O 4-18,N 1,D 20-27 1873
TJT Ap 1868-Mr 1869;Ap 1871-Mr 1872;Ap 1881-Mr 1882;Ap 1883-Mr 1885;Ap 1886-Mr 1888;Ap 1890-Mr 1891;Ap 1896-Mr 1897
TxU Ag 11 1849-50
WHi Ap 14 1838-Mr 14 1847;Ap 29 1848-Mr 1899

TRANSCRIPT advertiser. w
NNHi Ap 18-My 16 1840

Portland TRIBUNE. *See* Umpire

TRIBUNE and bulletin. *See* Umpire

TRUE patriot. Ag 20 1853-
NNHi Ag 20 1853

TRUE republican. w Ag 7 1880-
MWA Ag 7-14 1880

TRUE Washingtonian and Martha Washington advocate. w Jl 12 1842-Jl 10 1844||
MWA Jl 19 1843-44
MeHi Jl 19 1842-44

UMPIRE. w My 8 1841-49||?
1841-Je 14 1845 as Portland tribune; Je 20-S 19 1845 Weekly tribune and bulletin; S 26 1845-47 Tribune and bulletin
DLC N 20 1841-Ap 13,My 11-Je 6 1842;Ap 18 1843-Je 14,D 26 1845;F 15,20,Mr 6-13,Ag 21-28,S 25 1846
MB O 20 1846-Ag 1847;My 19-Je 16,S 15 1848; Mr 23,Ag 17,31 1849
MWA Je 5,Jl 31 1841-Ap 12,Je 13 1843-Je 1 1844;Mr 8,S 26 1845-Mr 19 1847;F 4,My 19 1848
MeBB Ap 20 1842-Ap 12 1843;Ap 13 1844-Ap 5 1845
MeBHi [1844]
MeBa Ap 13 1844-Mr 22,Ap 12-Je 20,Jl-Ag 22, S 1845-F,Mr 13-27 1846
MeG My 29 1846-47
MeHi Ap 20 1842-[43-44]-Ap 5 1845;Mr 26-D 1847;Mr 30 1849
NN Ap 20 1842-Je 14 1845
NNHi Ap 1841-Ap 5 1845;Ap 28,My 12 1848
OHi Jl 10-N 1841
TJT My 1846-Mr 19 1847
WHi Ap 13 1844-Ap 5 1845

Daily evening UMPIRE. tw,d Jl 19 1842-
Jl 19-S 10 1842 as Morning bulletin; S 13? 1842-S 28 1847 Portland bulletin; O 2-D 1847 Umpire
tw 1842-S 1847
DLC Jl-Ag 1842
MSaE S 21 1843;Je 3 1847
MWA 1842-44;D 30 1845-47;Ap 10 1849
MeBa Ap 20,My 18 1843
MeHi Ag 3,O 6 1849
MeMH Jl 10 1850
NcD S 8 1845

UNION chronicle. w
MeP N 1880-My 1881

VOICE from the belfry. sw Ag 17 1880-
Campaign paper
MWA Ag 17,S 18 1880

WASHINGTONIAN journal. w Jl 13 1842-46||
United with Cold water fountain (Gardiner) to form Cold water fountain and Washingtonian journal, later Maine journal
DLC 1842-Jl 5 1843
MWA Je 18 1845;Jl 29 1846
MeBa D 27 1843

WATCH tower. w 1846?-55||?
MsHi N 20 1852

WORLD in a nutshell. ir O 29 1829-
MeHi O 29 1829

YANKEE advertiser. w Ja 1828-Je? 1829||
MWA Ja 9-Jl 9 1828

PRESQUE ISLE

AROOSTOOK herald. w 1884-88||
United with North star to form Star-herald
KHi Ag 2 1888

AROOSTOOK pioneer. *See* Houlton pioneer-times (Houlton)

AROOSTOOK Valley sunrise. *See under* Fairfield

LOYAL sunrise. *See* Aroostook Valley sunrise (Fairfield)

NORTH-STAR. *See* Star-herald

STAR-HERALD. w 1871+
1871-88 as North star
MeHi Ja 4 1900
NN O 30 1886

Presque Isle SUNRISE. *See* Aroostook Valley sunrise (Fairfield)

RANGELEY

RANGELEY lakes. w 1895-97||
MeF My 30 1895-S 16 1897

RICHMOND

Richmond BEE. w 1880+
MWA Jl 10 1885
MeHi Ja 12 1900

ROCKLAND

COMMERCIAL advertiser. w 1851-55||
1851-My? 1853 as Camden advertiser (Camden)
MSaE Ja 23 1853
MWA Ag 16(extra)1854
NNHi Mr 23,Je 22 1853

Rockland COURIER. w 1874-81||
United with Rockland gazette to form Courier-gazette
MWA O 15 1878

COURIER-GAZETTE. w,sw,tw Ja 22 1846+
1846-Ja 2? 1851 as Lime Rock gazette; Ja 7? 1851-81 Rockland gazette
DLC My 15 1851
M 1902+
MSaE My 28 1852
MWA Ap 22-29 1847;49-O 10,D 5 1850-Ja 23 1851;Mr 4,Je 10-17,S 16-23,N 11-18 1858;Ap 5, N 22 1860;Ja 24,Jl 25,Ag 8 1861;My 22,Ag 9,N 1 1862;Ap 25,My 16, Jl 11,O 17-24,N 21 1863;F 7 1868;O 6 1871;Je 14-21 1872;Jl 4 1876;My 17-24 1877;Jl 29 1880;Jl 28 1881;My 24 1887;F 13 1894;Ag 8 1899;My 3 1902;Ag 20 1904;F 21-Mr 4,My 2,9-20 1905;F 3 1906;My 4,11,18, 25,Je 1,8,15,22,29,Jl 6,13 1907;Je 4 1918
MeBa Ap 5 1877
MeHi My 27 1847;My 9 1850;Ja 2 1851
MeR 1923+
MiU-C [1905]
NNHi Mr 13 1851;Je 24,Ag 12 1865;Jl 12 1877[My-Jl 1907]
NcD O 17,N 21 1863
NjR Mr 22 1849

DEMOCRAT and free press. *See* Rockland tribune

Rockland ENTERPRISE. m 1873-
MWA N 1873

Rockland FREE PRESS. *See* Rockland tribune

Rockland GAZETTE. *See* Courier-gazette

KNOX and Lincoln patriot. w 1868-69||
NNHi S 4 1868;Ja 30 1869

KNOX messenger. w 1918-24||?
Follows Rockland opinion

LIME ROCK gazette. *See* Courier-gazette

MAINE independent. w O 29 1872-74||?
MWA D 24 1872

OLD union. w
OClWHi S 10 1863

Rockland OPINION. w Ja 1 1875-D 27 1917||
Followed by Knox messenger
MWA Mr 23 1877;Ja 4,Ag 22,S 26 1884;Ap 12 1889;Ap 19[Je 19-S 25]1896;D 19 1902
MeR 1875-[93-95]-[97]-1917
MeRC complete
NNHi Ag 31 1883-Ag 15 1884

Rockland daily STAR. d 1894-1905||?
MeHi F 7 1900
MeR 1894-96

Rockland TRIBUNE. w N 1 1855-Mr 17 1897||
1855-57 as United States democrat; 1858-68 Democrat and free press; 1869-90 Rockland free press. Merged with Courier-gazette
DLC Jl 10-D 1856
MSaE F 7 1866
MWA Mr 11 1863;Ag 16,S 13 1865;Ja 13 1869;N 1 1871;O 23 1872;Je 27 1877;O 2 1878;F 5 1879;Mr 21 1883;Ap 22,S 16 1885;Jl 31 1889;O 8,N 15 1892;My 13,Ag 5,19-S 2,O 7,21 1893;O 13,N 24 1894[Ja 12-D 14 1895]F 13-Mr 13 1897
MeBa 1863-65]
MeR 1857-97
MiU-C Mr 13 1897
NNHi N 18 1868;My 28 1873;N 22 1876
NcD N 22 1876
OClWHi D 28 1864
WHi O 17 1860

UNITED STATES democrat. *See* Rockland tribune

MAINE (*Continued*)

RUMFORD

Rumford CITIZEN. w 1906-My 7 1908||
United with Bethel news (Bethel) to form Oxford county citizen (Bethel)

RUMFORD FALLS

Rumford Falls TIMES. w 1887+
1887-93? as Dixfield citizen (Canton)
pub 1921+
MWA D 13 1888;Je 8 1893;D 18 1896;Mr 30 1898
MeR [1913+]

SACO

Saco COURIER. w
MeSY Ja-Je 1869

Saco INDEPENDENT. *See* York county independent

MAINE democrat. *See under* Biddeford

MAINE palladium. w 1826-30||
United with Kennebunk gazette (Kennebunk) to form Kennebunk gazette and Maine palladium (Kennebunk)
Ct [1826-27]
DLC Ag 16 1826;Je 1828-Mr 3 1830
MBAt Ag 6 1828
MWA My 23,N 28 1827;O 8,29,N 19 1828;Mr 10,Ap 28 1830
NNHi O 1 1828
NhD F 21,My 23,Je 27-Jl 4,18,Ag 1-8,22 1827;O 8 1828

MERCANTILE advertiser. w Ap 1849-Ap 24 1852||
United with Eastern journal (Biddeford) to form Eastern journal and mercantile advertiser (Biddeford)
MeSY O 25 1849-52

NATIONAL republican. w O 24 1832-F 5 1834||
Followed by Thomaston republican (Thomaston)
MeSY O 24 1832-F 5 1834
MeWHi Je 5 1833

Saco NEWS. w O 9 1914+
pub 1914+

UNION. *See* Biddeford weekly journal (Biddeford)

YORK county herald. w Mr 1838-Mr 4 1843||
DLC Je 5,D 18 1841
MWA F 20,Jl 10,Ag 21,O 9 1841;F 11-18,25 (extra)Mr 4(extra)1843
MeHi Je-Jl 1838
MeSY Ap 1838-Ja 21 1843
NNHi F 12 1842

YORK county independent. w My 18 1869-79||?
1869-70? as Saco independent
MSaE Ag 31 1869;Ap 4,Jl 25 1876
MWA 1870-71;Ap 7 1874
MeP O 20 1874-O 16 1877
MeSY 1869-Ap 1878

ST. STEPHEN

ST. CROIX herald. *See under* Calais

SANFORD

La JUSTICE de Sanford. w Ja 15 1925+
In French
pub 1925+

Sanford TRIBUNE-ADVOCATE. w 1895+
1895-Ap 5 1923 as Sanford tribune
MeAlC 1917-23;25+
MeHi Ja 5 1900

SEARSPORT

GABBLE. w
MeBe Ja 29 1895

Searsport GUEST. w 1882-83||?
MeBe Je 5 1883

Weekly NEWS. w 1893-94||?
MeBe Ja 30 1894

SHERMAN'S MILLS

VOICE. m,w D 25 1866-74||
1866-Jl 1868 as Patten voice
1866-O 1867 pub in Patten; N 1867-74 in Patten and Sherman's Mills
m 1866-70
MWA 1866-70
MeHi [F 1869-Jl 1870]

SKOWHEGAN

To 1835 as Milburn

CENTENNIAL.
DLC S 22 1875
NNHi S 22 1875

DEMOCRATIC clarion. *See* Independent reporter

INDEPENDENT reporter. w Jl 1841+
Follows Skowhegan sentinel. 1841-Je 11 1857 Democratic clarion; Je 18 1857-Mr 1868 Republican clarion; Ap 1868-1907 Somerset reporter
DLC Je 9 1852
MSaE Jl 10 1852
MeBa Ja 3 1901
MeHi Ja 1 1851;F 8 1900
NNHi O 30 1852

PEOPLE'S press. w 1845-52||
MSaE Jl 27 1852
MWA F 20 1850
MeHi Ja 1 1851

REPUBLICAN clarion. *See* Independent reporter

Skowhegan SENTINEL. w D 12 1831-Ap 1841||
Follows Democratic Somerset republican (Somerset). Title varies slightly. Followed by Democratic clarion, later Independent reporter
MWA My 6-13 1835;Ja 24,Ap 10 1838;F 24 1840
MeHi D 7 1836
MnHi Je 15 1836

SOMERSET reporter. *See* Independent-reporter

SOUTH BERWICK

INDEPENDENT. *See under* Salmon Falls, N.H.

SOUTH PARIS

OXFORD democrat. w Ag 20 1833-N 7 1933||
United with Norway advertiser to form Norway advertiser-democrat (Norway)
Ct S 3 1833
DLC Ap 1 1834;My 16 1862
KHi Jl 1856-Jl 11 1876
MBAt Ap 21 1865
MH 1862-65;Ja 5-19 1866
MSaE Je 11 1852
MWA [Ja 28-D 2 1834]Jl 14 1840;Ag 18 1854; Ag 5 1864;Ag 19 1873;Je 16 1874;Ja 19 1875-86
MeBa My 5,Ag 11 1854;Ap 13 1855;Je 15,S 14 1886
MeHi Ja 14 1879-Ja 6 1880;Ja 9 1883-Ja 1 1884;Ja 2 1900
MeNA [1853]-1933
MeSoC Mr 1848-1933
MnHi Je 24 1834
NNHi Ja 30 1844;Je 24 1845;Mr 11 1873
NcD Je 26,Jl 24,D 11 1883;85;O 11 1910
NjR Jl 15 1870
OClWHi Jl 11 1848;Mr 3 1865
WHi D 8 1865

SOUTH PORTLAND

CAPE ELIZABETH sentinel. w 1881-1912||?
MWA D 14 1900;D 20 1907
MeHi My 4 1900[D 27 1901-Mr 7 1904]

COAST watch. w 1895-1916||?
1895-1905 pub at Cape Elizabeth
MWA Ap 6 1900
MeHi S 27 1895-D 1 1897;98-1901;03-09
MeP S 27 1895-S 24 1915
MeU 1903-[08]10-[16]
MiU-C Ap 6 1900
NNHi F 13-27 1903

SPRINGVALE

Springvale ADVOCATE. w Ja 1 1876-Ap 5? 1923||
1876-78? as Springvale reporter; 1879?-81? York county advocate. United with Sanford tribune (Sanford) to form Sanford tribune-advocate (Sanford)
MSaE Ja 8 1876
MWA Ja 29,Mr 4-11,25-Ap 1,15-My 6 1876;D 10-24 1915
MeHi Ja 5 1900;O 4,N 29 1901
NNHi F 6,Mr 6,My 27 1903

Springvale REPORTER. *See* Springvale advocate

YORK county advocate. *See* Springvale advocate

SQUIRREL ISLAND

Squirrel Island SQUID. w,sw 1876-81||?
pub for 6 weeks each year in Jl and Ag
w 1876-79
MWA Jl 14 1877;Jl 12,Ag 9 1879;Jl 10 1880;Jl 30,Ag 6 1881

THOMASTON

Thomaston HERALD. w 1877-1908||?
MWA My 25,Je 22,Jl 6 1905
MeHi Ja 4 1900
NNHi Jl 6 1905;Ja 25-F 8 1906

INDEPENDENT journal. w N? 1831-
Follows Thomaston register
MWA Je 18 1834
NN Ja 11 1832

Thomaston JOURNAL. w Mr 9 1854-My? 1858||
Followed by Lincoln advertiser (Damariscotta)
MWA Je 1 1854;S 3 1857;Ja 28 1858
P-M N 30 1854

LINCOLN advertiser. *See under* Damariscotta

LINCOLN miscellany. w Ag 7 1850-Ag 1853||
MSaE Jl 28 1852
MeHi Ja 1 1851

LINCOLN republican. w Ap 9-Je 4 1856||?
MWA My 7,Je 4 1856

NEW-ENGLAND chronicle. w My 14 1835-Ja 30 1836||
Merged with Lincoln patriot (Waldoboro)
Ct [1835]
DLC S 10 1835
MWA complete

Thomaston RECORDER. w Ag 23 1837-46||?
1837-Jl 18? 1844 as Recorder
DLC O 18 1838;D 19 1839;N 19 1840
MeHi 1837-Ag 16 1838
NNHi Mr 22 1838;Jl 15 1841;Jl 25 1844;S 3 1846

Thomaston REGISTER. w My 17 1825-S 1831||
Followed by Independent journal
CSmH Ag 18 1830
DLC S 27 1825;Jl 18,Ag 15 1826;Ap 3,S 27-O 2 1827;Ja 8-15,Ag 28,N 5,19 1828;Jl 20 1831
MBAt F 25 1829
MSaE My 27 1829
MWA Je 14 1825;Ja 8,Mr 4,Jl 15 1828;Ap 7 1830
NN S 10 1828;Ja 7 1831
NNHi Ja 9,D 4 1827

Thomaston REPUBLICAN. w F 12 1834-
Follows National republican (Saco)
DLC F 12 1834
NNHi Je 6 1834

UNION

Union weekly PRESS. w 1888-1904||?
MeHi Ja 13 1900

WALDOBORO

LINCOLN county news. w 1873-1909||?
MWA Ag 17 1876;Ag 29 1878;S 2-9,D 16 1881; Jl 27 1883;Jl 3 1885
MeHi Ja 4 1900
NcD Ag 29 1878

LINCOLN patriot. w D 5 1834-42||
MWA My 7,D 31 1839;Mr 9 1841
MeBa F 26 1836;Mr 17 1837
MeHi D 1836-Ja 11 1842
NNHi 1834-N 1836;S 17 1839

WATERVILLE

EASTERN mail. *See* Waterville mail

Waterville INTELLIGENCER. w My 1 1823-N 6? 1828||
Followed by Watchman
MSaE Jl 4,18 1823
MWA Ag 4 1824
MeBe Je 6,Ag 22,S 26 1823-Ap 9,21-Je 16,Jl, Ag 11,S 22 1824
MeWC My 23 1823-N 6 1828
NNHi Ag 7 1828

KENNEBEC democrat. w 1887-89||
MeWC F 1887-Ja 23 1889

Waterville MAIL. w Jl 19 1847-1906||
1847-58? as Eastern mail
MSaE Jl 22 1852;F 16 1866
MWA F 14 1850;O 7 1858;My 27 1864;D 13 1867[Ja 10-S 11 1868]Jl 11,25 1879;Jl 30-Ag 13 1880;S 2 1887
MeBa S 16 1858;Je 23-30,Jl 14,Ag 11-S 1,29-N 17 1865;Mr 23 1866;Jl 5 1867;My 7 1875;Jl 7 1876;O 3 1884;N 20 1885
MeHi Ja 2 1851;F 7 1900
MeWC 1868-99
NNHi Mr 21 1873

Waterville evening MAIL. d 1896-1906||
MeWC 1902-06

MAINE democrat. w 1908?-10||?
MeBa F 4,25 1910

Waterville SENTINEL. w 1881-1911||?
MWA Mr 16 1883;Jl 2 1885

Waterville SENTINEL. d Mr 4 1904+
pub 1904+
M Ja 12 1929
MeBa Mr 4,6-9,11 1912
MeW My 13 1905+

Waterville UNION. w Ap 1-Je? 1847||
MeWHi Ap 1 1847

WATCHMAN. w D 18 1828-D 30 1829||
Follows Waterville intelligencer
MeWC [1824;26-29;32]

WATERVILLONIAN. w 1841-42||
Followed by Yankee blade (Boston, Mass.)
MeWHi My 29 1841-My 1842
NNHi Ap 25-My 9 1842

YANKEE blade. *See under* Boston, Mass.

WESTBROOK

Westbrook CHRONICLE. *See* Westbrook chronicle-gazette

Westbrook CHRONICLE-GAZETTE. w 1882-1907||
1882-1902 as Westbrook chronicle
MWA D 21 1906;D 20 1907
MeHi Mr 2 1900;N 8 1907
MeU 1901;Je 19-26 1902;Ja 23-30 1903
NNHi Mr 13,O 2,23 1903

DEERING news and enterprise and Westbrook globe-star. w 1891-1916||?
1891-My 7 1898 as Deering news; My 14 1898-1904 Deering news and enterprise
1891-1904? pub at Deering
M 1894-1913
MeHi N 5 1910
MeP 1891-1904;06-D 3 1915
MeU 1903-04;06-07;Je 15 1911;Ja 25,Je 27,Ag 15 1912;Jl 17,N 27 1913;14-S 28 1916
NNHi F 7,Ag 29 1903

MAINE (Continued)

WESTBROOK—Continued

Westbrook GAZETTE. w O 13 1901-02||
United with Westbrook chronicle to form Westbrook chronicle-gazette
MWA D 8-15 1900;D 20 1901
MeHi Ja 26[S 20 1901-N 21 1902]

Westbrook GLOBE-STAR. w 1893-D 27 1900||
1893-95? as Westbrook globe. United with Deering news and enterprise to form Deering news and enterprise and Westbrook globe-star
MeHi Ja 4 1900
MeP 1894-1900
MeU 1897

Westbrook STAR. w 1894-95||?
United with Westbrook globe to form Westbrook globe-star
MeU Je 7,21,S 13 1894

WILTON

Wilton RECORD. See Wilton sentinel

Wilton SENTINEL. w Ja 1881-1900||
1881-99 as Wilton record
M Jl 24 1881-O 20 1883
MeFC complete

WINTERPORT

Winterport ADVERTISER. sm 1893+
MeHi F 15 1900

WINTHROP

Winthrop BUDGET. w 1881-Je 28 1918||
MWA My 7 1887;S 7 1889;Ap 21-My 5 1893; Je 20 1913;Je 14-28 1918
MeBa Ag 27 1881

Winthrop BULLETIN. w S 20 1867-
MWA D 27 1867

CITIZEN. w Ja 10 1828-N 26 1830||
CSmH Ag 20 1830
DLC Jl 10,Ag 7,S 4,25-O 9 1829;Ja 8 1830
MBAt S 25 1829
MWA 1828-[30]
NcD Ja 10,F 7 1828;Je 19 1829
NjHi 1828-Ja 2 1829
NjPa Ja 9 1829-30

Winthrop GAZETTE and rural intelligencer. w D 14? 1866-
MWA Ap 20 1867

WISCASSET

CITIZEN. w
WHi My 14,Je 4-11,25-Jl 2,16 1830

ECLECTIC miscellany. w Ja 6-Mr 24 1875||
MWA Ja-Mr 10,24 1875
NcD Ja 6-13 1875

LIGHT HOUSE and genius of temperance. w
NNHi [Ja-Mr 1829]

LILLIPUTIAN. w 1881-Ap? 1891||
Followed by Sheepscott echo
MeBB O 6 1883
MeHi N 28 1885;My 15-22,S 11 1886;My 19,Jl 21,Ag 18,S 1,15 1888

LINCOLN county republican. w 1839-43||
1839-41? as Lincoln republican
MWA My 1 1841;Jl 27 1843

LINCOLN intelligencer. w N 1 1821-O 1835||
CSmH Ag 27 1830
Ct [1827]N 19 1830
DLC Mr 5 Ap 2-9,My 28-Je 1 1824;D 2 1825;O 6 1826
MBAt Jl 6 1827
MH O 29 1824-27
MHi Mr 9 1827
MSaE Ag 7 1823
MWA D 12 1822;O 30 1823-O 22 1824;Mr 25-Je 10,S 23,O 14,N 11 1825;Ap 7,21,My 5 1826;O 26 1827-O 3,D 5 1828;Mr 20,N 26 1829;F 19,S 24 1830;Ag 30,S 13 1833;My 2 1834;O 30 1835
MeB Ap 3 1828
MeBa My 13 1836
MeHi [1821-O 19 1827]
NNHi Jl 23,O 29 1830
NjPa O 23 1829-O 15 1830
WHi Ag 13 1824

LINCOLN republican. See Lincoln county republican

LINCOLN telegraph. w Ap 27 1820-O 18 1821||
MBAt F 15 1821
MWA My 3,Jl 19 1821
MeHi Ap 26-O 1821

SEASIDE oracle. See under Bath

SHEEPSCOTT echo. w My 9 1891-1918||?
Follows Lilliputian
MWA 1891-Ap 1893
MeHi F 10 1900
NNHi Ag 11 1900

YANKEE and laborer's journal. w My 17? 1831-
MWA Mr 22,N 1 1832

YARMOUTH

EASTERN gazette. w Jl 13? 1887-Je 15 1888||
MWA Je 15 1888

SIX towns times. See under Freeport

YORK

York COURANT. See Old York transcript

OLD YORK transcript. w 1890+
1890-1901 as York courant
MeHi Ja 5 1900

MARYLAND

ABERDEEN

Aberdeen ENTERPRISE. w Je? 1889?-1920||?
United with Harford democrat to form Harford democrat and Aberdeen enterprise (Bel Air)
MdBE Mr 26-Je 11,O 1908-11;Ja 18,F 22,Je 13, Ag 15,29 1912;N 27 1913;Jl 18 1919

ANNAPOLIS

ADVERTISER. w S 22 1870-N 5 1908||
1870-Ag 11 1898 as Anne Arundel advertiser. United with Maryland republican to form Advertiser-republican, later Maryland gazette
MdAC Ag 10 1905-08
MdHi 1870-S 9 1875;S 12 1878-S 2 1880;S 1883-Ag 18,S 1887-N 16,D 14 1899-Jl 20 1905

Evening ADVERTISER. d Mr 2-D 31 1918||
Mr-Jl 14 1918 as Annapolis advertiser
MdAC complete

ADVERTISER-REPUBLICAN. See Maryland gazette w,sw

ANNE ARUNDEL advertiser. See Advertiser

ANNE ARUNDEL examiner. w S 5 1895-1908||
Follows Argus
MdBE Ag 4 1905
MdHi 1895-D 17 1896;98-1900;Je 15 1905-Je 26 1908

ARGUS. w D 20? 1894-Ag 29? 1895||
Followed by Anne Arundel examiner

Evening CAPITAL. d My 12 1884+
F 10 1910-Ag 2 1922 as Evening capital and Maryland gazette
My 12 1934 is 50th anniversary number
pub My 14 1884+
MdBE D 29 1902;O 3 1903;Jl 7 1905;My 12,29, 31,Je 15,19,21-23 1934
MdHi Ap 11 1888

CARROLLTONIAN; or Spirit of seventy six. w,sw 1826-Ja 28? 1829||?
sw during sessions of legislature
DLC Ja 10-Mr 7 1827;Ja 2,26-F 9,20-Mr 23 1828;Ja 14-28 1829
MWA Ja 21-28 1829
MdHi Ag 22,S 5-12 1828

Annapolis CHRONICLE. d S 29 1903-05||
MdBE Ap 24 1905

CRUTCH. w Ja 9 1864-My 13 1865||?
DLC My 28,Je 11-25,Ag 6,S 17-24,O 15,N 19,D 3-24 1864;Ja,F 11-25,Ap 15,My 6 1865
MHi 1864-65
OClWHi 1864-My 13 1865

DEMOCRAT. w Ja 30 1890-
MdBE F 20 1890

Annapolis GAZETTE. See Maryland gazette (1854-1910)

HAVERSACK. w Je 22? 1864-65||?
MHi [D 14 1864-65]

MARYLAND day star. See Maryland democrat and Maryland day star

MARYLAND democrat and Annapolis day-star. sw,w Mr 16? 1867-
Mr-My? 1867 as Maryland day star
MdBe My 29,S 28,N 16 1867;F 1 1868

MARYLAND examiner. w N 7 1868-
MdBE Ja 16,F 20-27 1869

MARYLAND free press. w Je 3? 1848-52||?
MdBE S 16 1848;Jl 20,O 20-27 1849;My 4,Je 1 1850
NN Mr 31 1849

*MARYLAND gazette. w Ja 17 1745-D 12 1839||
Title varies: Maryland gazette and political intelligencer; Maryland gazette and state register
Suspended from - 1765; from D 25 1777-Ap 30 1779
DLC S 14,N 2 1826;Ja 11 1827-Mr 8 1832
MBAt Mr 1 1821;F 14,Ag 21 1828
MHi Je 7 1821;Mr 11,D 30 1824;F 15 1827
MWA Ap 2 1822
Md 1821-39
MdHi Ja 18-25,Ap 5,19,Je 7-14 1821;N 3 1825; Ja 15 1829 S 22 1836
WHi D 23 1824

*MARYLAND gazette. w,sw Je 17 1809+
1809-N 7 1908 as Maryland republican (subtitle varies: . . . and political and agricultural museum; . . . or political and agricultural museum); N 12 1908-S 19 1918 Advertiser-republican; S 26 1918-Jl 27 1922 Weekly advertiser
S 19 1927 is "1727-1927: two hundred with the Maryland gazette
sw during session of legislature
pub Ag 1922+
DLC 1821-[29]-F 23,Jl 27,Ag 14,N 27,D 14,28 1830-Ja 8,22,F 15,Ap 12,Ag 2,S 20 1831;Ja-N 17 1832;N 7 1840
MBAt F 23 1822
MHi My 15 1824
MWA [Jl 24-D 4 1821;Ja-Je 15 1822]Ja 4 1823;F 24,Ag 21,O 9,D 4-11 1824;F 1,Mr 1, 29,N 15 1825;F 4,My 6,16 1826;F 24-Mr 10,My 8,S 1,18,O 9,27-N 17 1827[28]Ja-F 6,20-23 1830;Ja 22 1831;F 11,21 1832;My 10,N 15 1862; Je 25 1914;F 3 1915;S 19 1927
Md 1835-40
MdAC N 12 1908-20
MdBE S 25 1821;Ja 7,11,21-F 8,18,Mr 1-4,15 1822-[23]N 9 1867;Mr 21,Ap 4 1868;Mr 1878 (extra);Mr 1880(extra);Ap 7 1900;S 28 1922; Jl-D 1928;30+
MdEdC Ap 26 1828;O 4 1856
MdHi 1821-33;35-36;38-39;O 1845-Ag 7 1847;Je 11 1870-My 1 1880;Je 11 1881-Je 3 1882;Je 9 1883-86extra for Ja 1874;Mr 1876 Mr 1878; Mr 1880;Mr 1882
MdHi-H Ap 26 1828
NNHi O 24 1837
WHi F 4 1826;Mr 10 1827[28]F 28 1829[Ja-F 20 1830]

MARYLAND gazette. w S 1842?-
MdEdC Ap 5 1862

MARYLAND gazette. w,sw S 28 1854-F 3 1910||
1854-74 as Annapolis gazette (title varies slightly: Annapolis gazette and general advertiser). Merged with Evening capital
MdBE Jl 9 1903
MdHi 1854-S 5 1861;S 10 1863-Ag 1864;S 1865-Ag 1867;68-73 My 19-N 24 1874;Ja 26 1887-N 15 1891;D 31 1892-D 6 1896
MdHi-H Ja 23 1902

MARYLAND republican. See Maryland gazette 1809+

MARYLAND state capitol gazette. See Maryland state gazette

MARYLAND state gazette. w Ag 30 1851-
1851-52 as Maryland state capitol gazette
MdBE N 8 1851;Ja 31,N 13 1852;Jl 22 1854

NEGRO appeal. w S 22? 1899-1900||?
Dated also in Baltimore
DLC F 16 1900

Evening REPUBLICAN. d Jl 1 1886-
MdHi Jl-D 1886

UNIVERSAL advertiser. m 1869-
NNHi Mr 1869

ARLINGTON

Arlington ADVANCE. w Ap 8 1893-
MdHi Jl 8 1893

BALTIMORE

AFRO-AMERICAN. w Ag 1892+
1901-16? as Afro-American ledger
Negro
pub 1892+
M Ja 18 1930
MdBE Ap 30-My 21,Je 25,Jl 9-15,Ag 13-S 3, 17-O 1,D 24,31 1932+
NbHi Je 1908-O 1 1910;Mr 25 1911-Jl 1916
TNF 1933[34]+
TNY D 12-19,N 2,16,30-D 21 1929;Ja-My,Ag 23,S 13,27-D 6 1930

*Baltimore AMERICAN. d,w My 14 1799+
Title varies: American and daily advertiser; American and mercantile daily advertiser; American and commercial daily advertiser; American and commercial advertiser; Baltimore American and commercial advertiser
Ag 20 1883 is 110th anniversary number
d 1799-Mr 31 1928
pub O 1920-S 1921;22+
A 1824;26;62-64;78;80-81;86-87;1900-01
C F 4 1887-90
CSmH Ag 26 1830;Ag 20 1873(supp)
Ct [D 1826-31;33-34]
CtNcC Ap 20-21 1865
CtW Mr 31 1864
CtY O 1862-63;Ag 20 1883;Ap 24 1897
DLC 1821-26;Ja-S 1829;Ja 2,11,19 1830;F 15, Ag 26,N 21,D 8,14 1831;Mr 12 1833;Ja-Je 1834;Jl 6 1840;41-44;Je 26 1845;Mr 7 1849-Ap 1853;56-57;61-Ag 1896;98-1902;O 1924-Je 1928
DeHi Ag 20 1873
GAtCo Je 17-18 1839;Jl 1-2 1840
IC Ja-Je 1873
ICHi C 3,30 1865
ICM Mr 1 1876;My 15 1878;Ap 7,My 7 1883;Ja 16 1888;Je 1 1890
ICN Mr 11-D 1863;Jl 2 1864-65
IU N 17 1856;N 7,21,D 13 1862;Mr 7.N 10,12 1863[Ap 23-N 3 1864]F 22,Mr 3,13,Ap 3,5-6, 22,25,27 1865
MB [Ja 29 1831-My 9 1834]Jl 17,22,27,Ag 8 1835;Ja 23,My 7 1836;Ja 23,Je 28 1837[Je 19 1838-40;Mr 16 1850-F 26 1852;57-61]F 1 1862; Ja 13 1863;S 26 1864[65-Jl 27 1866]Ag 31 1867;Jl 27 1868;S 27,O 5 1869;My 31 1870;My 9,O 4 1873[Ja-Jl 2 1877]Ap 13 1878
MBAt Ag 28,O 4,N 29 1827[28]Je 2,D 24 1829; Ap 1,My 9,14 1862;O 9 1863-76
MH Ja-F 4 1823;Ag 7 1824;F 1845-Je 1855;Jl 1856-60;Jl 1863-S 28 1865;Ja-Je 1866;67-Je 8 1872
MHi Ja 14 1822;Je 7,16,Ag 28,D 12 1823;Ja 22,24,Ag 26 1824;Ja 13.Mr 11,24,D 3 1825;Ja 6,F 10,25 1826;Je 15,Ag 10 1827;N 5 1832

MARYLAND (*Continued*)

BALTIMORE—*Continued*

*Baltimore AMERICAN. d,w 1799+—*Continued*
MWA 1821-[29]-[37]-40;F 9,Mr 8-9,Ap 30,My 14,Je 8,Jl 1841-42;Mr 30 1843;44-Je 1855;Jl 1856-57;F 11 1858;Je 27,Jl 4,9 1859;My 11,S 24,O 20 1860;61[Ja-Je 5]Ag 4,S 7,N-8 1862; Ja 24,27,Mr 23,Jl 1863-Jl 3,N 22 1869;Je 13 1870;Jl 1874-Je 1895;98;S 1908-16
Md My 2 1862-Je 29 1867
MdBB N 23 1841-Je 1846
MdBE Ja 3 1823-Je 1824;25;Ja 26,F 3 1826;Jl 7,S 12 1827;F 15,Jl 14,26 1828;30;F 9,24 1831; F 20,S 9 1834[35]-Je 29 1836;Ja 4,9,13,16,21, 29,Jl-D 1837;Ja 9-Je,Jl 30,Ag 6,16,23,28,-31, S 4,20,22,25,O 18,21,1838;Ja 30,F 2,Ap 22,24, Jl 26-27,S 6,10,O 3,8,18,N 9,D 6,23 1839;Ap 20,My 5,Je 25,N 23,D 29 1840;Jl 10,21,28,Ap 7,17,S 27,O 19,N 24,1841;Ja 26,D 31 1842;Ap 16 1846;Ja 6 1847[Ap 22 1851-O 17 1853 Je 7 1854-Mr 1862]Ap 1862-Je 29 1867;Jl 25 1868;Ja 20,Mr 29 1869[Ap 5-S 20 1870]Ja 30, O 14(supp)1871;Ja 17,24,Mr 19-20,N 4,9,18,D 14,27 1872[73]-1920;N 4-5 1924;Mr 1926+
MdBG D 16 1836;Ap 18 1838;O 4 1841;Ag 7,O 3 1843;Mr 16 1847
MdBJ Mr 10 1858-1865;Ja 15-D 10 1873;Jl 2-D 29 1874;75
MdBLe Jl-D 1877;Jl 1878-Je 1880;Ja-Je 1886; 1921-32
MdBP 1821-Je,O-D 1920;Jl-S 1921;Ap-Je 1922; 23-Je,Ag 1927-Ja,My-O 1928
MdBSa Je 5,Jl 21,Ag 29 1917;Mr 5 1933
MdBSt 1821-41
MdHi 1821-Ja 14,Ap 1928+
MdWJ Ap 16 1865
N D 31 1827;O 15 1833;Mr 22 1834
NNHi D 5,10,17 1867
NPV [O 9 1861-D 21 1865]
NbHi Ap 8 1873;Mr 30 1877
NcD My 23 1848;N 18 1854;S 21 1855;57-59; Ap 13,My 23 1865;F 20,Mr 13,Ag 21,28,S 18 1871;Ja 17,24,27,Jl 2 1898
NcU F 26,Jl 12,D 29 1847;My 22 1848;Ap 12 1850;Ja 29 1876-Ja 1878
NhD Mr 11,My 2 1842;Ja 4 1847;Ap 20 1865
OClWHi N 5 1842;Je 19,21-22 1860;My 21,Je 18,20,26,O 6 1862;Ap 17-22,My 2,5-6,9,11 1865;O 17 1866;F 1,4-5,7-8 1870;N 23 1893; Je 15 1909
OHi Ag 1832-My 1834;Jl 1840-Ap 21 1842; S 25 1862;S 26 1865;Jl 12-D 1875
P-M Ap 19 1841
PBro Jl 7,29-30 1846
PHsHi Ag 20 1873
PPCHi [1921]
PPM 1863-67
PSuHi Ap 24 1885
PYHi Ap 20 1865
TJT [Ag 23 1914-Ag 1915]Mr 4 1917;Jl 13, Ag 3,10,17,S 21 1919
VHi Ja 11 1886
VRC Jl 1 1862;N 4 1863;Jl 15 1864
VU Ag 21 1821;S 19,26,O 12 1871;Mr 8 1896;My 27,Je 3,8,11,13,19,23,Jl 1,12 1898

Baltimore AMERICAN; twice-a-week edition. w,sw Mr 9 1850-S 1 1918||
1850-83? as Baltimore weekly American; 1883?-Mr 1894 Baltimore American: weekly edition; Ap 3 1894-Mr 22? 1895 Baltimore American: semi-weekly edition
CtW Ag 1 1868
ICN Mr 28 1864-65
MB Mr 16 1850-My 28 1853
MWA Mr 29 1851;Ag 3 1867;Ag 21-N 13 1869
MdBE Ag 22 1863;Ap 29,My 20,Ag 12 1865; Ag 1 1868;My 24,31 1873;F 18 1882;O 22, N 5 1887
MdHi Ag 21 1858;My 2 1863;Ag 1 1868;Jl 1893-S 1896;97-1917
MdHi-H [1866]N 16 1867[68-71]O 19 1872[73-78]Ja 1879;O 2 1880;Ja 10 1885
MiG D 6 1879
MnHi Ag 23 1873
NcD [1873-79]S 11,D 25 1880[Jl-D 1882]Je 2-16,S 15,O 6 1883;Je 7 1884
NcU S 27 1851;My 29,Jl 10,24 1852
OClWHi O 13 1866

Baltimore weekly AMERICAN *See* Baltimore American: twice-a-week edition

AMERICAN citizen. w F 8 1879-
Negro
MWA Ap 19 1879

AMERICAN cotton plant. *See under* Washington, D.C.

AMERICAN democrat. d S 10 1855-
MdHi 1855-Je 10 1856
NcD Ag 25 1856

AMERICAN republican and Baltimore daily clipper *See* Baltimore clipper

AMERICAN star. *See* Star (1908-20)

AMERICAN times. d *See* Times and ledger

AMERICAN times. sw
MB Ja 18-21 1854

AMERICAN times. w
MB [S 6-D 13 1853]

AMERICAN whig. w,d Ap 29 1843-N 9 1844||
Campaign paper
D 31 1844 is additional no. giving election results
w 1843-S? 1844
DLC Je 24 1843
MdHi F 10,O 5,N 2-9,D 31 1844
MoSM Je 29 1844
PHi Ag 19-N 9 1844
WHi O 30 1844

AMERICAN whig. w D 12 1846-47||?
MdHi Mr 13 1847

Daily ARGUS d N 2 1840-F 14? 1842||
United with Baltimore republican to form Republican and dailiy argus, later Baltimore republican
DLC D 9 1840;S 14 1841
MdBE N 3 1840
MdHi D 22 1841

Weekly ARGUS, w Ag 4 1849-S 5 1863||?
Ja 12 1850-O 28 1854 as Baltimore weekly argus
MdHi Ag 11 1849-Ag 2 1851;O 28-N 4 1854; Ja-F 3,24-My 19,Je,S-N 10,D 13-20 1855;F 2, Mr 1-8,29,My 24,Ag 23,N 8,D 13-20 1856
PHi F 7 1863
—d ed *See* Baltimore republican

Daily ARGUS. (1853) *See* Baltimore republican

ARGUS. w O 9? 1886-1905||?
MdHi Jl 30 1887;Jl 11 1891

BALTIMORE county advocate. *See under* Towson

BALTIMORE county sentinel. *See* Baltimore sentinel

BALTIMOREAN. w Je 8 1872-98||
DLC N 27 1875;F 26-Mr 4 1876
ICM Ja 10,Mr 20 1880;Ap 23,O 22,D 17 1881; Mr 11 1882
MWA Ap 24 1875;Jl 7 1877;Ja 10 1885
MdBE Ap 25 1874;S 16,O 7 1876;S 10 1887;O 6 1888
MdHi Ag 29 1874;O 2 1875
NNHi Jl 12 1873;Jl 25 1874
N Mr 31 1877;Mr 2 1878;Mr 15 1879
NcD Ja 21-F 7,Ap 4,18,Je 6,20 1874;S 27 1879;Ja 3 1880;S 27 1884
PHsHi S 17 1881
PSuHi Jl 1 1876

BAYERISCHES wochenblatt. w 1880-1919||
Followed by Täglicher Baltimore correspondent
In German

Baltimore BEE. *See* Baltimore morning herald

BIENE von Baltimore. *See* Baltimore volksfreund und biene

BUENA vista. w Mr 18-Jl 15 1848||
Campaign paper
MdHi Mr 25,Ap 15,29-My 20,Je 17-Jl 1, 15 1848

BULL and Tuttle's monthly clipper and general advertiser. *See* Baltimore monthly clipper

Monthly BULLETIN. m 1849?-
MWA N-D 1852

Evening BULLETIN. d O 2 1865-79||?
Follows Baltimore clipper. 1865-Mr 17 1868 as Baltimore daily commercial; Mr 18 1868-69? Evening commercial; -N 10? 1870 Evening bulletin; N 11? 1870-Ag 1871 Morning bulletin; S 4 1871-72? Baltimore evening journal. Merged with Baltimore news
Suspended from 1873-S 1876
DLC 1865-O 1866;My 31,Je 6 1868
ICHi O 4,N 4 1865
ICN O-D 1865
MB O 20 1866[Mr-D 1867]F 5,9,29 1868
MWA F 23,Je 3 1878
MdBE D 9 1865;O 15 1866; Ap 13 1867; Ja 21-22 1869;Ag 18 1879
MdBLe 1865-Je 1867
MdHi Ag 30 1867;Ja 12 1872;O 2 1876-D 19 1879
MdHi-H D 8 1865;F 13 1866;Mr 24,N 19 1868
N O 7 1870

Baltimore BULLETIN. w O 7 1865-S 23 1876||
Follows Weekly clipper
1865-69? as Baltimore weekly commercial; Ag 14 1870-My 4 1872 Sunday bulletin
ICM Ag 3-17 1872;F 8 1873;Ap 4,Je 20,N 14 1874;Ap 17,My 1 1875;Mr 25,My 6,Je 10 1876
ICN 1865
MdBE Ag 28 1869
PSuHi Je 24 1876

Weekly BULLETIN. w O 11? 1884-86||
DLC My 29 1886
ICM F 6-20,Mr 6,20-27,Ap 17-24,My 8,Je 12, Jl 17 1886

CAMPAIGN democrat. w S 2 1876-
NNHi S 2 1876

CAMPAIGNER. w Ja 31? 1850-52||?
CtY O 16-23 1852
MdHi Je 17-Jl 24,Ag 14-21, S 4,25-O 16,30-N 6 1852

CANFIELD'S lottery argus. sm, Ap ? 1826-1826? as Canfield's lottery register
Ct Ag 4 1828
DLC F 19,Mr 5,N 5-19 1827
MHi N 5 1827
MWA F 19 1827;Ap 7,Ag 18,S 15-O 20,D 1 1828;Ja 19-Ap 6 1829
MdBE Je 23 1826
N Jl 27-S 17 1827

Baltimore CATHOLIC review. w N 29 1913+
Je 15 1934 is tercentennial number
pub 1913+
DCU 1913+
MdBE Mr 31 1921;30+
MdBL 1913-N 18 1916
MdBSt 1913+

*CHRONICLE (for the country). tw Ap 8? 1819-40||?
1819-Je? 1825 as Morning chronicle and Baltimore advertiser (for the country); Jl? 1825-Ja? 1829 Commercial chronicle and Baltimore advertiser (for the country); F? 1829-30 Commercial chronicle and daily Marylander (for the country); 1831-F 13 1833 Chronicle and daily Marylander (for the country)
DLC Mr 21 1828;29-D 20 1834
MWA O 23 1821;Jl 16 1823;F 23,Mr 6 1824; Jl 14,D 1 1830;F 28,Ap 18-20,29,Je 8-10,Jl 22,N 30-D 2 1831; Mr 16,21,Ap 2,9-14,23,27, My 7,14-18,Je 20 1832;Ja 3,D 5 1834;F 5 1835;O 19 1837
N O 10-11 1833
NcD N 28-30 1835

Morning CHRONICLE and daily advertiser. *See* Commercial chronicle and daily Marylander

CHRONICLE of the times. *See* Baltimore times (1830-32)

Daily evening CHRONOTYPE. d Ja 10? 1867-
MdHi F 18 1867

Baltimore CLIPPER. d S 7 1839-S 30 1865||
Ja-N 5 1844 as Baltimore clipper and general advertiser; N 6-9 1844 Baltimore clipper and American republican; N 11 1844-D 31 1846 American republican and Baltimore daily clipper. Followed by Baltimore daily commercial, later Evening bulletin
A Jl-D 1848;62
CSmH Mr 28 1860
CtNlC Ap 15 1865
DLC complete
ICHi S 21 1865
ICN Ag 1863-S 1865
IU My 31 1845;N 12 1862
MB Ag 19 1841;S 9 1846;Je 3 1847;Ja 15,My 4 1850[Je 26-D 12 1841]Mr 4,22,Ap 12,Je 30, Jl 2 1852;S 29,D 5 1854;F 10,Je 15 1855;Jl 1 1856;Ag 12,O 31 1857[Ja 23-My 29 1861; My 6-28]S 24-25 1862;Ja 17,Mr 24 1863;O 7 1864;F 8,Ap 18,My 25 1865
MBAt Ap 18-20 1865
MWA S 18 1839;Mr 10-S 9,N 7,D 18 1840;Mr 13,N 25,D 16 1841;Mr 9 1842;Ja 3,14 1843;D 12 1844;Ag 6 1845;Je 8 1846;My 31-Je 1 1848; Je 4 1850;Ja 19,Ap 26,My 30,Je 15,28,O 19,N 7,23,D 14,28 1861[Ja 13-N 4 1862]Ja 29,D 2 1863;Ag 31 1864[Ja-S 1865]
MdBE Mr 18,31,Ap 27-S 7 1840;Ja 15 1842;Je 7 1847;F 11 1848;Ja 19 1855;My 8,Jl 27,S 13,O 6,8,N 1 1858;Ap 2,9 1859;F 27,Mr 17,My 22, Je 10,16,S 16 1862;Je 13,S 26 1863;Ap 15 1865
MdHi 1839-Jl 26 1843;N 11 1844-Je 1848;49-Je 27,Jl 4,7-8,S 6 1851[55-65]
MnHi D 30 1845
N My 26 1865
NN My 26(extra)1861
NcU O 17 1855
NhD My 28 1841;F 1 1842
NhM S 22 1857
TxU Ja 17,Ap 5,Mr 20 1859
WHi My 11(extra)1846;S 29 1860;Jl 10,12,26-27,Ag 6-7,S 6-7 1861

Weekly CLIPPER. w Je 27 1840-S 30 1865||
1840-46? as Ocean; 1847? Baltimore weekly clipper. Followed by Baltimore weekly commercial, later Baltimore bulletin
DLC Jl 4 1840;F 19 1842;O 30 1852
ICN Ag 13-D 1864;Ja 14-S 1865
MB N 3,D 22 1849;50-S 16 1854;Ja-N 22 1856
MWA F 24 1855;Ap 28 1860
MdBE 1854;F 2,23,Mr 8-15,Ap 26-My 3,24-Je 21 1856;Ja 2 1858;Ap 9 1859;Ap 13 1861
MdHi N 18 1843;Je 22,Jl 20 1861
MdHi-H Ag 21 1847;Mr 4,Ag 26 1848;Ja 11,F 1 1851;Je 12 1852;Jl 14-21 1855;F 9 1856;O 16 1858;Ag 20 1859;Ja 21,Mr 31,O 6 1860;Ag 13, D 9 1864
PWbW O 7 1861
TxU Ap 23,Ag 27-S 3,17,29,O 8,N 5,19,D 10 1842[Ja 28 1843-Mr 16 1844]
WHi Ap 20 1861

Baltimore monthly CLIPPER. m Je 1843-
1843-44? as Bull and Tuttle's new monthly Baltimore clipper and general advertiser (for the country); 1845?-Ap? 1847 Bull and Tuttle's monthly clipper and general advertiser (for the country)
IU My 22 1845
MWA Je 1 1852;Je 1 1854
MdBE My 1 1847
MdHi D 22 1843;My 22,N 22 1844
P-M N 1 1853
PP F 1848
TxU Ag 1 1848;Ja 1 1852

COLUMBIAN. sw N 2? 1836-
MdHi N 23 1836

Baltimore daily COMMERCIAL. *See* Evening bulletin

Baltimore weekly COMMERCIAL *See* Baltimore bulletin. w

*COMMERCIAL chronicle and daily Marylander. d Ap 8 1819-40||?
1819-Ap 6 1822 as Morning chronicle and Baltimore advertiser; Ap 8 1822-Je 1825? Morning chronicle and daily advertiser; Jl 1825?-Ja? 1829 Commercial chronicle and Baltimore advertiser
CSmH Ag 7-9 1827;Je 6 1829
Ct [1826-28]
DLC F 10 1821;Jl 15-16,Ag 28 1824;Ap 26,Jl 2 1825;Ag 15,S 22 1826;S 13,30 1827;F 2,Jl 2,D 11 1828[29-31;Mr-D 1832]Ja 3,12,14-17, 21-23,Jl 3,Ag 1,D 7,9,27 1833
MB [Ap 11-S 6 1831]O 10 1832;Je 21-22,24 1833[Ap 21 1834-37]F 13-22,Ap 9,Je 27 1838; Ap 13-18,Jl 13,N 8 1839
MBAt My 15 1822;O 30-31 1828;My 25-26,Je 3,S 16,O 7 1829
MHi D 9 1823;O 27 1824;Ja 4,22 1825;My 13 1826;F 16,Jl 11 1827
MWA Jl 13 1828;S 18,D 23 1830;F 9 1831;S 27,O 7,10,N 20,D 15 1834;Mr 6 1835;N 24 1836;N 28 1837
MdBE Ag 28-29 1822;Ap 29 1826;Jl 20-21 1830;N 1 1832;F 26 1834;S 17 1836
MdHi 1821-23;Ja 12 1824;Ap 1-7,Ag 31 1830; F 17-19 1831;S 8 1834;Je-D 1839
OC My 10 1832
WHi Ja-O 6 1821;Ap 8 1822-Ap 5 1823;Je 11, 15-17,22 1830;Ag-D 1834

COMMERCIAL chronicle and daily Marylander (for the country) *See* Chronicle (for the country)

COMMERCIAL enterprise and Baltimore advertiser. sm Ap 15? 1850-
MdBE D 2 1850

MARYLAND (*Continued*)

BALTIMORE—*Continued*

COMMERCIAL index. w Mr 30 1885-87||?
MdHi Jl 6 1885

Baltimore COMMERCIAL journal and Lyford's price current. w Mr 3 1838-49||?
1838-F 22 1840 as Lyford's Baltimore price current; F 29-My 16 1840 Baltimore weekly commercial journal and Lyford's price-current
DLC Ap 27 1844;Ja 23 1847-D 8 1849
MWA O 3 1840;N 25 1843
MdHi Ap 14 1838-Je 2 1849
MiU [1846-47]

Baltimore COMMERCIAL transcript. *See* Baltimore post and commercial transcript

CONSTITUTION. d,sw O 18 1844-D 25 1845||
Follows Spectator (Washington, D.C.)
1844-N 24 1845 pub in Washington, D.C.: d during sessions of Congress
DLC complete
MB [O 29-D 1844]-Mr 8,My-Ag 5 1845
MWA O 18 1844
NcD [1845]
NcU [1845]
OClWHi Je 12,26,Jl 10 1845
WHi O 22-N 5 1844;Ja 25,Ap 26 1845

Täglicher Baltimore CORRESPONDENT. sw,d 1919+
Follows Bayerisches wochenblatt. 1919-N 27 1930 as Baltimore correspondent
In German
sw 1919-O 1935
pub 1928+
MdBE Mr 12 1933+

COTTON plant. *See* American cotton plant (Washington, D.C.)

Sunday COURIER. w Ag 12? 1866-
MdBE S 16,D 9 1866

DAY. d Ap 17 1882-Ja 5 1885||?
Follows Baltimore gazette
MWA N 14 1883;Jl 2 1884
MdBE 1882-Ja 5 1885
MdHi My 4 1882;My 8,D 1,22 1883;Jl 22,26, 28,30 1884
V [Ap 1882-Je 27 1884]

Baltimore DEMOCRATIC herald. d Je 30? 1838-
IaDH Jl 20-O 16 1838

DEMOCRATIC standard. w 1847||
Campaign paper
MdBe Jl 10 1847

DEMOCRATIC telegram. *See* Telegram

Der DEUTSCHE correspondent. w,sw,tw,d F 6? 1841-Ap 28 1918||
In German
w,sw,tw 1841-44
DLC Jl 1881-1902;Ap 1918
IU N 1917-18
MdBE My 6-Ag 1887;88-Ag,O 18 1903-05; N 1910-18
MdHi My 26 1846;Ja-Je 1858;Ja-Je 1863;Ja-Je 1866;70-82;Ja 1883-F 1918

Baltimore DISPATCH. w Jl? 1853?-60||?
-F 28 1857? as Weekly dipsatch; -My 28 1859? Baltimore weekly dispatch
MdHi O 7 1854;F 28 1857;My 28 1859;Jl 21 1860
OClWHi S 13 1856

DOLLAR weekly exchange. w Jl 2 1859-S 14 1861||
1859-Je 1860? as Weekly exchange
MWA My 18 1861
MdHi Je 1,22 1861
NBuG F 9,22 1861
NcU Ap 6-13,27 1861
—d ed *See* Daily exchange

EASTERN Baltimore mail. w
PWaHi My 25 1846

EMERALD and Baltimore literary gazette. w Mr 29? 1828-Ap 11 1829||
Merged with Baltimore minerva, later Baltimore minerva, wreath, and Saturday post
CtY Ag 9 1828-29
MHi F 7 1829
MdHi Ap 19 1828-29

EVERY Saturday. *See* Saturday review

Daily EXCHANGE. d F 22 1858-S 14 1861||
Followed by Maryland times, later Maryland news sheet
CtY Ag 22 1859-F 21 1861
DLC complete
MBAt [1858]-[60]-Jl 9,11-S 10 1861
MWA S 6 1861
Md 1858-F 21 1861
MdBE [Jl 1858-Ag 4 1859 Mr-D 1860;Ap-S 14 1861]
MdBP complete
MdHi 1859-61
MoS Jl-Ag 1861
NBHi Ap-S 1861
NNHi S 7,13-14 1861
NcU F 10 1860
NhM S 22 1858
NjP [Ag 22 1860-61]
V [Mr 29 1859-F 21 1861]
VRC [Je 25-Ag 26 1859]Je 17,25 1861

Weekly EXCHANGE. *See* Dollar weekly exchange

Daily EXCHANGE prices current. w Mr 19? 1859-My 3? 1861||
MdBE Ja 2 1860

Evening EXPRESS. d 1859?-
MWA F 28-Mr 1,4,6-7,11,14,17,21,24,27 1862

FAIR journal. d Ap 2-13 1866||
MdHi complete

FEDERAL gazette. tw *See* Gazette (for the country)

FEDERAL gazette and Baltimore daily advertiser. *See* Baltimore gazette and daily advertiser

FEDERAL intelligencer, and Baltimore daily gazette. *See* Baltimore gazette and daily advertiser

***FEDERAL republican and Baltimore telegraph.** d Ap 1816-N 26 1834||?
Formed by the union of Federal republican and commercial gazette and Baltimore telegraph and mercantile advertiser (not in this list)
DLC D 12-13,15-17,19-20,22-23,25,27,29 1823-N 26 1824
MBAt Ap 18,My 25,D 10,21 1822;My 3,5 1824
MWA S 15 1821;Jl 26,30,Ag 3,6,8,28,S 10 1822; O 29 1824 ?
MHi My 12,Ag 28 1821
MdHi F 9 1821;Ja 29,F 18 1823
WHi O 4 1821-Ap 3,N 1 1822

***FEDERAL republican and Baltimore telegraph (for the country).** sw Ap 6 1816-
DLC Jl 20 1824
MWA My 1 1821;O 11 1822;Je 24 1823;N 2 1824
WHi Ja-My 29 1821

FELL'S POINT news letter and mercantile advertiser. sw,w Ja 13? 1835-
Ja?-My 8? 1835 as News letter-Fell's Point
sw Ja?-Ag? 1835
Ct My 8 1835
DLC Jl 7,24 1835
MWA Ag 12-28,O 9-16,N 21 1835;Mr 12 1836

FLAG of our union. w Ja 3? 1846-54||*
MdHi S 18 1847;F 18-Mr 25 1854
IU S 20 1851

FREEMAN'S banner. w Je 25 1831-O 13? 1832||
Campaign paper
DLC 1831-O 13 1832
MHi Ag 25,O 6 1832
MWA Je 25,Jl 23-30,S 17,D 10-17 1831;Ja 21,Je 9 1832
MdHi Ja 28 1832
NcD O 13 1832
OClWHi Je 25,Jl 9,30-Ag 19,S 24 1831

GAZETTE (for the country). tw
-1823 as Federal gazette (subtitle varies)
DLC N 19 1830;N 26 1831;S 26-D 2 1833;Ja 10,12,24-25 1835;Jl 14-15,23,25-29,Ag 4-5,11 12,25-26 1836
MWA Mr 17 1821;Ja 16,29-31 1822;Ag 19,N 8 1823;O 9,23 1824;My 29 1827;Je 14-17 1828; Je 4,Ag 7,D 8 1829;Ag 18 1835;Ja 23,F 11 1836

Baltimore weekly GAZETTE. w Jl 28 1832-Ja 18 1834||
DLC Mr 30 1833
MdBE N 24 1832
MdHi 1832-Ja 1834
—d ed *See* Baltimore gazette and daily advertiser

Daily evening GAZETTE. d Ag 20 1840-
DLC Ag 27,S 29-30,O 2-3,4-5 1840

Baltimore GAZETTE. d O 6 1862-Ap 15 1882||
Follows Maryland news sheet. 1862-S 16 1865 as Baltimore daily gazette; Ja 1876-Ap 30 1881 Gazette. Followed by Day
Suspended from S 30-O 6 1863
CSmH N 21 1866
CtY Ap 7-S 28 1863;Ap 6 1864-Ap 5,O 6 1866-69
DLC 1862-Je 1870;Ap 17 1871;72-My 1875;Ja-Je,Jl 3,13,22,Ag 26 1876;S 7,O 17 1877-Je,N 4 1879
DeWI F 14 1863
ICM Ag 6 1874;Ag 24 1876;Je 25 1878
MB D 8,31 1862[My 31-D 5 1863;Ja 4-S 8 1864;Jl 18-D 8 1877]Ja 8,F 2,Ap 3 1878
MBAt O 13,D 1,16-18 1862;63-65
MWA O 17,24-25,N 12,15 1862;Mr 2-31 1863 [Ap 25-D 1864]Ja 3,18[F-My 9]D 28 1865;Mr 6 1866;S 20 1869;Ja 25,F 17,My 4,Je 17,Jl 19,Ag 20 1872;Ja 23,Mr 4,D 29 1873;Je 24,Jl 3,O 10 1874 F 24,My 26-27 1875;Ap 22,D 11 1876
MdBE Ja 22,Ap 2,15,My 12,25,Je 17,22,30,Jl 1,9,11,15-16,23,O 26,N 4,24,D 1,12 1863;Ja 6,11, Ap 5,Ag 13,D 29 1864;Ja 4,F 5,Jl 18 1865;Je 27 1871;74-82
MdBJ O 3 1863-O 1864;S 17 1867-Ag 29 1868
MdBL N 1862-63
MdBLe Jl-D 1877;Jl 1878-Je 1880
MdHi 1862-72;Jl 1873-Jl 1874;75-80
MdHi-H My 12 1863
NNHi [Ap-My,N-D 1863;Ap 1865]D 5 1867;Je 2 1873
NbHi N 2 1871;My 19 1875
NcD Ag 25 1863;O 25 1865;F 7,25,Mr 5,N 8, 11,14,20-21,D 10,12 1867;Je 6 1868;Je 10,N 5 1869;O 17,N 11 1870;My 16 1877;Ja 28 1879; Ag 2,8 1880;F 18,Ap 8 1882
NcU S 2 1865;Ap 21,O 6 1876
NjP Ap 7 1863-65
OClWHi Jl 22 1863;F 8 1864
OOxM N 5 1864
V [Ap 7 1863-Ap 15 1882]
VRC O 24 1862;S 11 1863;Ag 17,S 12,O 1,6 1864 F 11,Ap 29,My 26 1865

Baltimore weekly GAZETTE. w Ja 3 1868-Ap 11 1882||?
DLC Jl 5,19-27,Ag 9-D 1873;Ag 8-D 19 1874; Ja 6 1875
MdHi My 23 1868
NcD Ap 26 1873

***Baltimore GAZETTE and daily advertiser.** d O 28 1793-Mr 31 1838||
Follows Baltimore daily repository (not in this list). 1793-O 29 1794 as Baltimore daily intelligencer; O 30 1794-95 Federal intelligencer, and Baltimore daily gazette; 1796-Je 1825 Federal gazette and Baltimore daily advertiser. Merged with Baltimore evening patriot
CSmH D 8(extra)1829;S 7 1830
DLC Jl 3 1822;Ja 17,20,25 1823[F 6-D 3 1829] Ja 13,25,F 12,Mr 24,D 30 1830;F 11,Ap 3,8, 12,28 Je 15,D 5,7,15,23,25 1831;Mr 1,N 10 1832
MBAt F 8 1822;S 19,28 O 9 1827;F 12,Mr 27, My 9,O 31 1828;Ap 25,Jl 14,S 22 1829;Ag 30 1830
MHi S 28 1821;Ja 10,16 1822;N 19 1823;Ja 14, F 15 1824;Ja 12,Ap 12,26,My 24,26,S 7 1825; Ja 23,N 1 1826;Ja 8 Mr 5 Ap 26,My 8 1827
MWA Ja 20 1827;F 14,O 3 1828;S 29 1830;F 7,15 1831;Mr 17 1836;N 21,D 12-13,26 1837;Ja 16,27 1838
Md Ja 26 1829-37
MdBE O 4-6,8-9,11-16,18-23 1824;Ja 8 1827; Ja 6 1832
MdBG Mr 21 1823;Ap 17,Je 16 1824;N 2 1826; Mr 27,D 6 1828;My 18-19 1829;S 23 1833
MdBP 1821-29
N N 2 1833
WHi Je 2 1832
—Country ed *See* Gazette (for the country)
—w ed *See* Baltimore weekly gazette (1832-34)

Baltimore Saturday HERALD. w My 8 1824-27||?
My-Je 5 1824 as Saturday evening herald; Je 12 1824-My 20 1826 Saturday herald
Suspended from My 8-Je 5 1824
Ct F 10 1827
DLC D 16 1826
MWA Jl 17 1824;Ja 1,D 17,31 1825[26-Ap 7 1827]
MdHi 1824-My 20 1826
NcD Ap 8 1826

Sunday HERALD. w S 19 1875-
Follows Baltimore Saturday night
MHi S 19-O 3 1875

Baltimore morning HERALD. d D 23 1875-Ag 31 1904||
D 23-24 1875 as Baltimore bee; D 25 1875-Ja 12 1878 Bee; Ja 14 1878-F 9 1900 Morning herald. Merged with Baltimore evening herald (1904-06)
DLC 1894;98-S 1900
ICM Ja 3 1877;F 25 1904
MdBE D 12 1876;Ja 14 1878-1904
MdBLe D 24 1875-Ag 22,S 2 1876-Ja 12 1878; 82-1904
MdHi D 13 1880;Ap 1,My 13 1882;N 1889;F 9-11,14-16,Mr 6 1904
NcD Mr 1879[Ap 26-S 14 1882]

Evening HERALD. d N 19 1879-Ja 2 1882||?
MdBE N 24 1879-My 15,N 19 1880-My 18 1881
MdHi D 9 14 1880

Baltimore Sunday HERALD. w My 16 1880-Je 17 1906||
1880-F 4 1900 as Sunday herald
ICM F 28 1904
MdBE 1881;Jl 1883-1906
MdBLe O 1898-1902;Ap 1903-Mr 1906
MdHi D 17 1880
N My 13 1883

Weekly HERALD. w Ja 5 1882-Je 15 1906||?
Mr 11-Jl 22? 1904 as Baltimore weekly herald
MdBE Jl 1883-Je 1903;Mr 11 1904-05
MdBLe Jl 1894-1901;Ap 1902-Je 1903;Mr 11 1904-05

Baltimore evening HERALD. d Ag 25 1904-Je 16 1906||
MdBE complete
MdBLe complete

INDEPENDENT. tw O 31-N 4 1882||
Campaign paper
MdBE complete

INDEPENDENT. O 5 1887-
Campaign paper
MdHi O 5 1887

INDEPENDENT press. tw Ap 10? 1841-
DLC Ap 20 1841

Baltimore daily INTELLIGENCER. *See* Baltimore gazette and daily advertiser

ITALIAN journal. w,ir Ag 18 1933-D 22? 1934||
In English
MdBE N 17-24,D 15 1933;Ja-F 16,Mr 9,23-My 11,Je-S 7,27-N 17,D 22 1934

JACKSONIAN and Baltimore county advertiser. *See* Jacksonian and general advertiser (Hereford)

JEDNOŚĆ-POLONIA. w 1907+
Follows Polonia. 1907?-16? as Jedność
In Polish
pub Ja 18 1917+
MdBE 1926-31;Jl 28 1933+

JEFFERSON reformer and Baltimore daily advertiser. d Ja 14 1836-
DLC Ja 14 1836
MdHi Mr 11 1836

Baltimore evening JOURNAL. 1871-72. *See* Evening bulletin

Baltimore JOURNAL. d F 13 1882?-1913||?
Suspended Je 18-D 18 1912
In German
MdBE Ap 13 1887-Ag,O 18 1903-Ap 1905;N 1910-Je 17,D 19-23 1913
—Sunday ed *See* Das sonntags-journal

Baltimore JOURNAL of commerce. w Je 20 1850-1908||?
1850-74? as Baltimore price-current and weekly journal of commerce; 1875?-88 Baltimore journal of commerce and price current
DLC Jl 31 1875-81;83-Je 4 1892;Je 1898-1907
MHi F 6 1858
MWA My 18 1855
MdHi 1850-Je 17 1854;Ja 16 1875
NNHi 1859-My 1862;Je 20 1863-[Ja-Je 11 1864]
PPiHi Ja 8 1853
WHi Je 25 1853-Je 12 1858

MARYLAND (*Continued*)

BALTIMORE—*Continued*

Baltimore JOURNAL of commerce. w Mr 4 1916-22||?
MdBLe 1916-Mr 6 1920

LEADER. w Ap 18-O 10 1868||
DLC complete
MdHi complete
NcU Jl 25 1868

LEE'S commercial and literary gazette. w Jl 2 1825-
IU Ag 20 1825
MWA S 10 1825

Baltimore LIST. *See* Baltimore price list

LOG CABIN advocate. w Mr 21-D 15 1840||
DLC Mr 21,My 9,23-Je 6,D 15 1840
GDE D 15 1840
ICHi D 15 1840
IU My 9,Je 9 1840
MHi O 3 1840
MWA My 9,D 15 1840
MdBE My 23,D 15 1840
MdHi Ap-[N-D]1840
MdHi-H Ap 25,Je 20-27,Ag 22,S 5,19-O 10,31 1840
MeBa My 9 1840
N My 9 1840
NcD My 9,D 15 1840
OClWHi Ap 4,18,My 16,Ag 29-S 5,O 24-31,D 15 1840
PNoHi D 15 1840

LOTTERY intelligencer. m S 28 1825-
MdBE S 28 1825

Baltimore evening LOYALIST. d Ag 12?-O 31? 1864||?
DLC O 6 1864
MWA S 24 1864

LYFORD'S Baltimore price current. *See* Baltimore commercial journal and Lyford's price current

M'PHERSON'S advertiser and miscellaneous journal. ir 1834-
MWA N 10 1835

MARION & Co's monthly reporter. m
MWA Ja-F 1854
P-M F 1 1854

Baltimore MARKET journal. w 1871-90||?
NbHi Ap 4 18 1874
NcD D 9 1872;F 1,Mr 10,S 2,30,O 21 1873;Ag 18 1874
VU Ja 6 1872

MARYLAND graphic. *See* Baltimore sentinel

MARYLAND leader. w N 9 1929-Ag 1 1936||
pub complete
MdBE N 23 1929-Ag 1 1936
MdBJ Je 1933-36

MARYLAND news sheet. d S 19 1861-Ag 14 1862||
Follows Daily exchange. S 19-23 1861 as Maryland times. Followed by Baltimore daily gazette, later Baltimore gazette
CtY Mr 19-Ag 1862
DLC complete
DeWI [1862]
MBAt O 2 1861-62
MHi [N 25 1861-Mr]My 1,3,20 1862
MWA N 12-13,22,25-28,30 1861-Mr 3,5-My 24, Jl 19-31,Ag 6,13-14 1862
MdBE S 21,N 30,D 19 1861;F 4,8,12-13,Mr 5, 15,Ap 14,16,18-19,My 8,26,29,Je 25 1862
MdBL O 29 1861;Mr-Jl 23 1862
MdHi complete
N Jl 12 1862
NBHi complete
NN Jl 26 1862
NNHi N 6,D 5 1861;Ap 1,Ag 14 1862
NcD Mr 14,Ap 2,17,24,26,My 1,Je 17-18,Jl 4, 9,23,28,Ag 4 1862
NjP S 19-D 1861
OClWHi 1861-Mr 18 1862
PHi N 23 1861
V complete
VRC S 25-26,O 1,3-4,7,9,11-12,14-17,24,28-29, 31-N 1,4-5,8,20,26 1861;Ap 4 1862
WHi Ap 5 1862

MARYLAND times. *See* Maryland news sheet

MARYLANDER. sw,d D 5 1827-Ja 7 1829||
United with Commercial chronicle and Baltimore advertiser to form Commercial chronicle and daily Marylander
d O 2-N 12 1828
Ct F 23 1828
DLC 1827-Ja 3 1829
IC F 16 1828
MWA D 8-22 1827[Ja 26-D 24 1828]
MdHi 1827-D 3 1828
N S 20 1828
NNHi Jl 19 1828
OOxM Ap 26,Je 21,Ag 2,20,30,S 6 1828
WHi complete

MARYLANDER. w Ap 18 1925-O 24 1931||
MdBE Ag 22 1925-31

MARYLÄNDISCHE teutsche zeitung. w Mr 7 1821-29||?
In German
CtY 1821-Mr 13 1822
DK Ja 16 1822
MdBG My 2-9,Jl 11-17 1821;Je 5,Jl 24 1822

MERCHANT. d My 24-N 11? 1837||
DLC My-O 17 1837
MB [My-N 4 1837]
WHi Jl-N 10 1837
—country ed *See* Reformer (Washington, D.C.)

MERCHANTS' and manufacturers' journal. w 1888-93||?
MdHi O 12 1889

Baltimore MESSENGER. d D 22 1842-
DLC D 22 1842

Baltimore MINERVA, wreath, and Saturday post. w My 2 1829-31||?
Title varies: Baltimore minerva and emerald; Baltimore minerva and Saturday post
CSmH S 11 1830
CtY 1829-Ap 3,My 8-Jl 3 1830
DLC Ja 27,Mr 1830;S 24,N 19,D 10 1831
MWA N 13 1830
MdBE F 27,Ag 28 1830;Ja 1,22 1831
MdHi Ap 10 1830

MIRROR. w 1890?-95||
MdHi F 13,27-Mr 6 1895

NATIONAL guard. w? 1860?-
CSmH Jl 4 1861
MWA Jl 4 1861
NNHi Je 26-Jl 4 1861

NEGRO appeal. *See under* Annapolis

NEW advertiser. w Ag 1 1870-
DLC Ag 1 1870
ICHi O 17 1870

NEW ERA. d Ap 18-My 2 1864||
MBAt Ap 19 1864
MHi complete
MdBE complete
NNHi complete

Baltimore daily NEWS. d S 10? 1834-
DLC S 20 1834

Daily Baltimore NEWS. d S 27 1851-My 10 1852||?
MdBE 1851-Ja 1852

Baltimore Sunday NEWS. w O 4 1874-D 30 1894||
Title varies: Sunday news
pub F 7-14,Ap 1875
DLC Jl 9 1876
ICM F 27 1876;Mr 7 1886;My 29 1887
MWA Mr 24 1878;N 16 1884
MdBE Jl 3 1881;S 17 1882;N 29 1891;O 1893-S 23 1894
MdHi D 13,27 1874[Mr 28-O 17 1875]S 17 1876; S 9 1877;Je 25 1882;N 3 1887

Baltimore NEWS; the Baltimore post. d N 4 1872+
Title varies: Evening news; Baltimore evening news; Baltimore daily news; Baltimore news; Baltimore news and the Baltimore star; Baltimore news and the Baltimore post
pub 1872-My 3,N 5 1877-N 3 1883;My 1884-My 3,N 4 1886-N 2 1887;My 4 1888-My 4,N 1895-1903;My 1904-Mr,Jl 1919-F,My 1923+
CtY Jl 2-D 1877
DLC 1898;Ja-Ag 1900;Ap 1919+
MWA Je 23 1874;Je 30(extra)1882;S 4 1883;Je 9 1884;My 8 1889
MdBE Ja 24 1876;O 13 1880;S 20 1881;Ja 6-O 13 1885;F 1886-92;My 7 1894-N 4 1897;98; 1905-20;Ag 29,S 16,30 1925;S 1928+
MdBLe 1921+
MdBP My-Je 1902;Ja-Ap 1905;Ja-Mr 1915;O-D 1918;Ja-Mr,Jl-S 1921;Ja-S 1922;23-Mr 1926;Ja-F,Ap-D 1927;Mr,My-Je,Ag-D 1928
MdBSa My 16,24,Je 6 1933
MdHi Mr 18,S 10 1873;Jl 29,Ag 6,19,O 24,31 1874;Ja 29,Je 26 1875;Ja 10 1877;Ja 16-21 1878;S 20 1881;My 9 1884;My 10 1887;Jl 1897-98;Ap 1899-Mr,Jl-S 1900;01+
MdTJ O 14 1874
NcD My 14,Jl 5,9,23,30 1898
PPCHi [1921]
VU O 5 1905;S 24 1918;Mr 12 1935
WHi My 17 1893

NEWS LETTER-Fell's Point. *See* Fell's Point news letter and mercantile advertiser

NICHOLSON'S lottery gazette. sm Ja? 1835-
DLC My 29 1835

OBSERVER. w Ap 26 1924+
MdBE 1924+
MdBLe My 10 1924-28

OCEAN. *See* Weekly clipper

OLIVE branch. m 1851?-
MWA N 1 1855
P-M Jl 2 1855

Baltimore PATHFINDER. ir Mr 1849-56||?
TxU Mr 10 1849

*Baltimore evening PATRIOT. d D 28 1812-61||?
Title varies: Baltimore patriot; Baltimore patriot and evening advertiser; Baltimore patriot and mercantile advertiser; Baltimore patriot and commercial gazette
CSmH Jl 23 1827
Ct [1826-27]
CtY S 20 1837-Jl 7 1838
DLC 1821-S,O 3,D 29 1829[Ja 11-N 25 1830] Je 13,20,Ag 26,S 24,D 3,13,28,30 1831[Ja-N 9 1832]Ag 24,S 14 1833;Je 3 1834;Mr 12,My 9,N 7 1840;Ag 28 1841;Mr 7 1849-51;D 6(supp) 1853;Ja 12 1857;Mr 5-D 1861
ICU Je 25 1839
IU Ag 2 1838
KyU My 6 1840
MB [Ap 11-D 1831;33-D 21 1835]Ja 12 1836-Je 1837;Je 16,D 19 1838;D 26 1839;Ag 15 1840; Ja 19;Je 10,S 24,O 30 1841;Ja 7,10 1842;Jl 24, Ag 10 1844;Ap 15 1845[F 5-Ag 1846]F 25,My 28,Ag 12,D 14 1847;Ap 13 1848;F 5,S 13 1852; My 20 1853;My 14,Je 14 1855;My 12,Je 28 1856[Jl 7-D 1857]
MBAt 1821-[27]-[38]-[60]
MHi Ja 14 1822;Ja 13,F 3 1824;D 24 1825;F 16,Mr 14 1827;D 2 1835;O 20 1836
MWA Ja 24,F 7 1821;Jl 27(supp)S 28,N 5,19, D 2,30 1824;Mr 7 1825;O 24,N 12,14,D 6 1827 [Ja-Mr 20]Ap 28,Ag 5,N 6,D 10-11,18 1828; Ap 14-16,29,Jl 10,14 1829;Jl 26 1830;Ap 17 1832;Ap 1 1833;D 15-16,18,21-23,28-29 1835 [Ja-F 1936]D 9 1837;Mr 14 1838;F 9,N 21 1839;F 7,My 9,18,S 10 1840;Je 19-21 1841;Je 3 1844;Ap 21 1846;Ap 3 1848;O 19 1849;Mr 18, O 31 1850;F 26 1851;Ja 11-Je 29,Jl 7,12 1853; Ja 12,Jl 3,O 27,N 2-3 1857;D 17 1861
MdBE F 11,Mr 19,21 1834;Ja 4,6 1840;Ja 19,F 3,Ap 5,17,21,24,29,My 1,5,10,17-19,26,29,Je 1 1841;Ap 7 1845;Je 16 1848;S 21-22 1849;F 3, Mr 1,N 8,19 1858;Mr 1 1859;F 14 1860;Ja 21 1861
MdHi 1821-24;S 19-20 1825;S 22,O 1 1827;34-Je 1835;Ja-My 1829;40-47;Jl 13 1850 Ap 20 1858;Ap 8 1859;My 13 1861
MdHi-H D 17 1859
MoSM My 2 1844
NcU S 27 1847;Jl 3,5 1848;Je 29-30 1852;Ag 28 1860
OHi Jl 27 1832-Ja 19 1833;34-42
PBro Ag 29-30 1842
TxU Mr 22 1832-Je 20 1833;Mr 5-N 11 1835; 39-45
WHi F 5 1829-Ja,Ap 8-Jl 1830;Je 4 1836-F 23 1837;N 24 1846;O 17 1849

Baltimore weekly PATRIOT. w D 28 1850-61||?
Title varies: Weekly Baltimore patriot
MBAt D 30 1854;55-56;58
MWA Ja 25 1856
MdBE Mr 22 1853;O 18 1856;O 24 1857
MdHi O 14 1854;D 22 1855
MdHi-H Ap 6 1861
WHi O 16 1852

*Baltimore PATRIOT and commercial gazette (country ed). tw,d 1812-
Ag 17 1813-Ap 30 1817 as Baltimore patriot and evening advertiser (for the country); My 1 1817-Mr 1838 Baltimore patriot and mercantile advertiser (country edition)
DLC Ja 28,F 17,Mr 13,Ap 15,20-22,My 15-18, 27,Je 3,8,19,23-24,Jl 1,13,31 1824;Jl 6 1825;Ap 23 1827;N 5 1829;Ja-Mr 25 1830;Mr 2-3,Ap 18,28,31,Jl 14 1831;F 28-29,Jl 28,30 1832;F 17-18,28-29,O 15 1842;Je 17 1843
KyLo O 8-D 1831
MWA Mr 1 1821;F 6,Jl 22,O 4 1823;S 28 1824; Ap 8,18 1825;Jl 28 1826[27]Ja 2,23,F 13,27[Je 13-N 7]1828;Ag 12,O 8,16,N 13 1829;Ja 13-18, Jl 12,S 1 1830;F 5 1831;D 19 1835;F 4,Jl 26 1836;D 21 1837;My 23 1838-43;Ja 17 1846
NcD [Jl-O 1855;Je 1856-Ag 1858]
PDoHi Ja 24 1825

PEOPLE'S weekly. w Jl 1864?-68||
MdBE Jl 4 1868

Weekly PILOT. w My 9 1840-Mr 20 1841||
DLC Je 6,Ag 15 1840;Ja 30 1841
GAtCo Jl 13 1840
ICU My-Jl 18 1840
MWA Jl 25 1840-41
MdHi Jl 25 1840-41
MiU-C [1840]
NNHi My-N 7 1840
NcD Ag 15 1840
OClWHi Je 19 1840

PILOT and transcript. d Ap 2 1840-Ja 25 1841||
Ap-My 2? 1840 as Pilot
DLC Ap-My 2,5 1840-41
MWA Ap 14,My 8,Je 9-10,S 11,19,24-26,O 22-23,26,N 7,19,D 25 1840;Ja 1 1841
MdBG Ap 2 1840
MdHi N 12,14-16-18,23-28,30 1840;Ja 20 1841
NjHi Ja 1 1841

PILOT for the country. sw Ap? 1840-
MWA N 5 1840

POLITICIAN. w Ap 3? 1880-
MdHi O 9-16 1880

POLONIA. w D 31 1891-1906||?
Followed by Jedność, later Jedność-Polonia
In Polish

Baltimore Saturday evening POST. w My 23? 1829-Je 26? 1830||
Merged with Baltimore minerva, later Baltimore minerva, wreath, and Saturday post
Ct Ap 17 1830

Evening POST. d Je 8 1864-Ap 6 1868||
MWA Ag 29 1864;N 21,D 28 1867
MdHi Jl 9 1864

Baltimore POST. d N 20 1922-Mr 24 1934||
1922-Ja 19 1929 as Baltimore daily post. Merged with Baltimore news
MdBE complete
MdBN Mr 1923-Ap,Ag 1924-S 1927;28;Ap 1929-33
MdHi Jl 2-11,16-20,23-30,Ag 1-14,20-22 1929

Baltimore POST and commercial transcript. d Mr 10 1836-Ap 22 1840||
Mr-Jl 1 1836 as Baltimore daily transcript; Jl 5? 1836-38? Baltimore commercial transcript
DLC D 22 1837;F 8,12,15,19,22,28,Mr 4,10,Ap 7,10 1840
MWA Je 8 1836;Mr 3 1838
MdHi 1836-38

*Baltimore PRICE CURRENT. w F 14 1803-D 25 1830||
1805-Je 12 1813 as Baltimore weekly price current
CSmH Ag 7 1830
MdHi 1821-D 25 1830

Baltimore PRICE-CURRENT and weekly journal of commerce. *See* Baltimore journal of commerce (1850-1908)

Baltimore PRICE LIST. w Je 27? 1883-88||?
1883?-86? as Baltimore list
KHi O 7-N 14 1885

Baltimore PUBLIC ledger. d Mr 2-Je? 1854||
United with Evening times to form Times and ledger

RACE standard. w 1894?-98||?
Negro
MdBE Ja 2,16 1897

Monthly REPORTER and advertiser. m D 1853-
MWA Ja-F 1854;S-O 1855
MdHi Je 1855
P-M My-Je 1855

MARYLAND (*Continued*)

BALTIMORE—*Continued*

Baltimore REPUBLICAN. (country edition) tw 1827?-
Title varies: Republican and commercial advertiser; etc.
DLC Mr 26 1829;Ja 10 1833;My 7 1841
MWA Jl 7,Ag 4,O 23,27,D 27 1827;Mr 3,My 14,19,Je 18,Jl 9,18,Ag 13,18,N 10 1828;F 25,My 18,Jl 3,N 10-18 1829;Ja 29,Mr 22,Ap 28 1830;Ap 22,My 4,Jl 18,O 28,N 28 1831;S 14 1832;N 29,D 6,18 1833;Ja 17,My 9 1834

Baltimore REPUBLICAN. d My 21 1827-S 11 1863||
Ja 1-Ap 2 1853 as Daily argus. Title varies: Baltimore republican and commercial advertiser; Republican and daily argus; Daily republican and argus; Republican and argus
CSmH Ag 10 1830;S 1 1853
Ct [1837-38]
DLC Ja 27 1827;N 7 1827;My 28 1829-My 17 1841;My 28,30 1844-45-48;Mr 3 1849;My 5 1853-60;Mr 26(extra)D 19 1861;S 2,6,11,13,17,29,N 28(extra)D 11,13,15,20,22,31 1862;Ja 10,23,F 4,My 7-8 1863
IU F 17,Mr 2,My 20 1840;My 22,Jl 9,14,29-Ag 1,5 1862
MBAt Je 17 1829
MHi Jl 16 1827
MWA Ja 2,Jl 10 1830;S 20 1831;O 1,N 17 1832;N 6 1834;D 7 1835;N 25 1836;Mr 6 1837;Mr 14,Ap 2 1839;My 22,D 3 1840;Mr 4,12,26,Ap 21,24,29,My 21 1845;Mr 24-D 8 1847;Ja 28,Mr 6 1848;D 20 1852;S 12 1857;My 20 1858;N 11,30,D 2,4,14,17 1861;Ja 7(extra)22,F 24 (extra)Mr 12,20,Ap 1,10,15,19-My 24 1862
MdBE N 10 1828;My 17 1843;Mr 15 1844;Jl 2 1845;My 3 1847;My 20 1848;My 28 1849;My 4,D 14 1858;F 8,Mr 3,Ap 26 1860;Je 3,10,Jl 8-9,S 27,N 2,27,29,D 4 1861[62]Ja 9 1863
MdBG Ag 21 1833
MdBP 1862
MdHi My 21-Ag 20,O 29 1827;Mr 6,29,Ap 24,29,S 2 1828;My 21-N 19 1829;S 2 1830;Mr 11 1831-S 10 1836;Mr 11 1837-Ap 1838;Ja 6 1840;F 15 1842-Je 1843;44-51;53-S 7 1863
MdHi-H D 30 1842
MiU-C Mr 7 1836
N O 15 1833
NN Jl 13 1829
NNHi Mr 5 1832;D 13-14 1833;Jl 12 1862
NcD Jl 8 1858;Jl 16,Ag 11 1862
NhD O 22 1831;My 28 1842
OC N 7 1832[Je 28 1833-S 19 1834]
PHi O 20 1850
TxU Mr 22 1832-Je 21 1833[Ap 9-S 9 1863]
VRC My 22 1862;Ap 9 1863
—w ed *See* Weekly argus

Saturday REVIEW. w O 6 1877-1910||?
1877-95? as Every Saturday; 1896?-99? Every Saturday review
MdHi O 9-16 1880

Il RISORGIMENTO Italiano. w Ag 5 1922+
In Italian
pub 1922+
MdBE O 26 1934

ROBINSON'S stock and exchange gazette. w
MBAt S 19 1823;D 17 1824

Baltimore SATURDAY night. w Ja 9? 1869-S 12? 1875||?
Followed by Sunday herald
DLC Jl 29-Ag 5 1871;O 12 1873
MH [Mr 1871-S 19 1874]
MdBE My 22 1869
MdHi [O 9 1869-Ap 17 1875]

Baltimore SENTINEL. w N? 1896-My 7 1919||
1896?-1900? as Maryland graphic; 1901?-18 Baltimore county sentinel
MdBE 1912-13;Jl 1918-19

SESQUI-CENTENNIAL journal. ir O 1-16 1880||?
Only three numbers issued?
MWA O 1,11 1880
MdBE O 11 1880
MdHi O 1,11,16 1880
NNHi O 16 1880

Das SONNTAGS-JOURNAL. w 1885?-N 1913||?
1885?-Jl 27 1913 as Die Sonntags-post
Suspended from Je 22-Jl 20 1913
In German
MdBE [Jl 1898-Ag,O 18 1903-Ap 1905;N 1910-Je 15]Jl 27,Ag-N 16 1913
—d ed *See* Baltimore journal

Die SONNTAGS-POST. *See* Das Sonntags-journal

Baltimore SONNTAGS WECKER. *See* Baltimore Wecker

SOUTH. d Ap 22 1861-F 17 1862||
Suspended S 14-18 1861
CtY Ap 23 1861
DLC 1861-F 11 1862
MSaE S 13 1861
MWA Ap 23-S 13,N 2,27,D 13,16-17,19-20,31 1861-F 17 1862
MdBE Ap 23,My 29,Je 14,Jl 1 1861;Ja 16,F 11,17 1862
MdBG Ap 22 1861
MdHi complete
MiU-C My 28 1861
NN Ap 23 1861-F 15 1862
NNHi complete
NcD Ap-S 13 1861
OClWHi complete
OHi Jl 31 1861
PHi Je 4,Jl 20,22 1861
WHi My 29 1861-F 17 1862

SOUTHERN herald. w F 3 1863-
OClWHi F 10 1863

SOUTHERN metropolis. w F 27? 1869-
MWA Mr 20 1869
NcD Ag 7 1869

SOUTHERN society. w O 5 1867-Mr? 1868||
MdHi Mr 7 1868
NcD O 5,19 1867

Weekly SOUTHERN spy. w Je 29 1861-
DLC Jl 6 1861
OClWHi Jl 6 1861

SPIRIT of democracy. d,tw Ap 25-O 26? 1840||
d Ap-Jl 31 1840; one issue only in Ag 1840
ICHi S 18 1840
IaDH My 4-O 26 1840
MdHi Ap-O 26 1840

SPIRIT of '70. w Je 24? 1854-
MdHi Ag 19 1854

Saturday STANDARD. w Mr 11 1876-79||?
Merged with Telegram
MdHi My 13 1878

STAR. d Mr 1 1882-
MdHi Mr 1 1882

Evening STAR. d O 10? 1885-
MdBE N 7 1885

STAR. d Ag 17 1908-N 30 1920||
Ag-N 15 1908 as American star. United with Baltimore news to form Baltimore news and the Baltimore star, later Baltimore news; the Baltimore post
MdBE complete
MdHi 1908-Je 1920

STAR spangled banner. w S 1846?-51||?
MdHi My 10,Jl 5 1851

STATESMAN. w O 17 1868-My 7? 1870||
DLC 1868-Ap 17,My 1869-Ap 1870

SUN. d My 17 1837+
My 17 1887 is 50th anniversary number
pub 1837+
A Jl 1895-96;1901-02
CSmH S 5 1846;Mr 7 1857;Ja 19 1861
CtW Ag 9 1869
DEHI My 17 1837
DGU S 15 1837-N 1840
DLC My 17(reprint),N 17 1837-Je 1844;45-O 11,N 15 1853;54-72;N 3 1873;Jl 1874-Je 1895;Ja-F 1896;97-Ag 1901;02+
IC Ap 30-My 1 1889
ICM O 19,21 1871;D 11 1876;Ja 3 1880;My 2-3,Je 14,N 29 1881;D 4 1884;Je 18 1885;Jl 4,28 1894;O 30 1901;My 24,Je 8,D 31 1902[03;Ag-D 1904;S-N 1913]F 7,My 24[D]1914;Ja 2-3,F 14 1915
ICN My 18 1846-N 15 1851;Mr 8 1852-N 17 1867
IU O 23 1846;O 21 1847;Ap 3 1848;My 20,Je 7 1859;Jl 25,31 1861;62
IaDH Ja 4 1851
KHi Jl 20-31 1932
M F 6 1932
MB My 17,S 9,O 7,16,28 1837[F 13-28]Ap 7,Jl 3 1838[Ap 8-D 16 1839]Ja,Ap 10,Ag 10 1840;Ja 22,Je 28,D 9 1841;Je 28,N 15,17 1842;Ja 6 1843;Je 17 1847[Je 7-15 1848;Ja-O 21 1850]Mr 24,Ag 26 1851[Jl 9-N 29 1852;Ja 24-S 1853]Je 30,Jl 11,13-14 1854[Ja-N 20 1857;Mr 22-D 14 1858]Ap 3,Jl 23 1860[61;F 17-Jl 1862;63;65]D 24 1866[Je-D 1867]O 30 1872;Je 11,Jl 1 1874[Ag 21-S 1 1875]
MBAt Ap 17,20 1865
MH 1860-66;Mr 19 1874[98-1920]
MWA D 27 1837-38;Ap 11,My 18-Je 5,Jl 11 1839;Ap 4,N 5 1840;Ja-My 15,Je 1,Jl 1,S 6,29 1841;42;F 17,22,Je 20,Jl 17 1843;Mr 5,My 27-28,30,Je 4-6 1844[45]-Ag 19 1848;O 1850-51;Ja 31[Je 2-22 1852]53[54-Jl 10 1855]56[57]D 25 1858[Mr-D 1859]Je 19-25,O 23,D 31 1860;Ap 24(extra)My 6,Jl 18,Ag 16 1861-N 15 1862;Ja 5,8-9,17,My 18-19,Jl 14,O 1863-Ja 2 [My 30 1864-Je 9 1865]Mr 5 1869;Jl 27,Ag 16,O 17,22 1870;Ja 8 1872;Ja 18,21,O 13,N 24,D 30 1873;Ag 24 1874;Ja 25,Ap 1,12,My 26,28 1875;Ja 1,4,18,25,F 19(supp)26,Jl 8(supp)1876 [F 1877]My 10(supp)1879;S 11,O 13 1880;O 22 1884;Ap 27 1885;My 17 1887;N 3,6,18,28 1888;S 18,O 30,N 6 1889;Mr 10,19,My 2(supp) 9(supp),S 22 1890;F 7,Mr 14 1901;O 1917—
Md Ja-Je 1892
MdBE N 17 1837-My 16 1838;Mr 8,29,My 6 1839-N 15 1845;Mr 26,N 17 1846-My 16,Je 11,Jl 19,N 17 1849-My 19 1851;N 18 1852-My 17,N 19 1855-N 16 1859;My 18 1860+
MdBJ D 27 1837-Ap 27,N 18 1839-My 16 1840
MdBLe 1874-Je 1880;1915+
MdBP N 17,22-D 16 1837[38-My 15 1841;F 1847-49]61-1909;Ap 1910-Je,O-D 1916;Jl 1917-18
MdBSa My 17 1838;N 10 1918[Ja-Jl 25 1933]
MdFF 1847-Mr 5 1853;54-71
MdHi 1837-40;Mr 2,Ap 5,26 1841+
MdHi-H My 17 1837;Mr 26 1838;Ap 20 1863
MiU [1838-47]-[52-53]-[56]-[60-61]-[72;74]-[86-87] - [94-1900;03]-[06]-[08;13-15]-[17-20;28 -29]+
MnHi Je 7 1841
MoS Jl 1861
MsU [1887]
NHuHi F 14 1855
NN My 17 1837(facsimile)Ja 31 1859;Ap 4-21 1898
NPV [N 6 1921-F 17 1922]
NbHi Ap 1 1873;D 20 1874;F 6 1882;My 30 (supp)Je 1(supp)1891;Ag 30 1892
NcD [1841-43;46-48;50-53;N 3 1856;N 10 1859;O 15 1860;[61-62;68]Ja 13 1872[75-76;78;81-82;84-86;88-89]My 3,27 1890[91-96;98;1900]Ja 10 1905;Mr 29 1915;Ap 26 1916[18]F 1 1925
NcU Mr 1 1850;N 6,10 1852;Ja 13 1855;Je 5,S 5 1856;Ja 23 1861;O 8 1890;Ag 26 1893;My 14 1906;Ja 20 1907
NhD N 6 1846
OClWHi My 29 1844;My 24,Je 8,Jl 26 1848;Ja 18 1851;Je 23,S 11,25,28 1860;F 22,Mr 6,10,25,Ap 13-D 1861;Ja 9 1863;Ap 25-26 1870;O 15 1911
OHi Ja 25 1860;Mr 20 1861;1917+
P 1890-Je 1917
PDoHi S 18 1890;F 23 1892;My 8 1896
PLaF S 28 1930+
PLaHi [1847-48]
PP 1933+
PPCHi [1921]
PU [1837]-[43-44]-[67]-[83]-94[96]-[99]-[1901-08]
PUn My 3 1856
PYHi [1847-48]
TJT Mr 18,My 27 1917
TSS 1875;77-78;Jl 1879-83;85-86;Jl 1893-94;98-Ag,N-D 1899
Tx D 8 1847
TxF O 1926+(Sunday issues only)
TxU Mr 26,28,Ap 12,14,19-20,26,30,My 4,11,17 1838[Ap-S 4 1839]Ja 2 1852;Mr 1 1854
VLyR Ag 28 1838
VU F 9,11 1853;Ap 29 1885;Ja 23 1889;Mr 9 1895;S 25 1896;My 5,Ag 7,21,S 4,11,18,25;N 1904-09(Sunday issues)Ja 20,O 25-27 1933
WHi F 26,Ap 13-14 1841;D 23 1844[45-My 1847]-Je 20 1848;N 18 1851-Mr 6 1852;54-56;N 17 1857-My 16 1863;64-Ap 18 1865
WvU My 1932-Je 1936
—**Overseas edition.** w Ap 22 1918-Ap 21 1919||
pub 1918-F 10 1919
MWA S 16,N 4 1918
MdBE Ag 5 1918
MdBLe complete

Baltimore weekly SUN. w Ap 14 1838-F 6 1904||
DLC Mr 14 1840;47-Ja 1902
ICM Ja 3 1880
ICN Mr 29 1851-Mr 18 1854;Mr 20 1858-Mr 10 1860;Mr 12 1864-Mr 3 1866
MB Ja 30 1847;Jl 9-30 1853;O 28 1854;Ag 1,15 1868
MWA Ja 1 1848;Mr 31 1849;My 15-Je 5 1852;Ag 10 1867
MdBE Je 29-D 1839;F 22-Mr 7,My 16-Je 13 1840;My 15 1841[F 7-D 1846]47;Ja 1,15-22 1848;Mr 31 1849-51;Ja 17,F 14,Jl 17 1852;Ja 8,Ap 23 1853;Mr 25 1854-Ja 18 1902;Ja 24 1903-Ja 16 1904
MdBLe Mr 1849-Mr 2 1851;Mr 25 1854-Mr 13 1858;Mr 17 1860-F 4 1888;D 1887-Ja 18 1902
MdHi N 28 1843;Ag 23 1845;S 22 1849;Ap 2-16 1853;Jl 16 1859;O 13 1860;O 2 1874;D 14 1889
NBuG Ja 14,19,Je 1 1861
NNHi Ap 9 1842;D 17 1867;D 22 1877
NcD [1850-56]O 16 1858[59]My 26,Jl 28,S 29,N 17,D 15-22 1860;Ja 5,19,Mr 10,Ap 13,My 11 1861[62]Je 6 1868;D 25 1869;D 21 1872;My 13,Ag 12 1876[78]D 20 1879[88-1900]
NcU [1881-82]S 1-15 1883;Ag 7 1886;Ap 2,Je 4-18,Ag 20,S,N 26 1887;Ja-F 11,Mr-Ap 7 1888
NhD F 5 1842
TxU [Je 9 1849-F 1 1851;Ja 18 1854-Ap 14 1855]
VRC O 13 1860-[64-65]
VU [Mr 11 1854-Ap 27 1861]My 12-19,Je 1866;D 14 1867;O 24 1874;D 31 1892;D 9 1893;Ja 5 1895;D 31 1903
WHi D 28 1895-99
WvU N 1857-S 1861

Evening SUN. d Ap 18 1910+
pub 1910+
ICM Mr 10,12,16 1914
MdBE 1910+
MdBLe 1926-32
MdBP Ja,My,Ag,D 1928
MdBSa N 9 1932;Mr 7,16-18,My 25,Jl 19 1933
MdHi 1910-22;O 1924+
MiU [1910-11]-[13]-[17-20;28-29]+
TxU Je 5 1913

Sunday SUN. Magazine section. w Mr 25 1923+
MdFrN My 18 1928;F 7,21-Mr 20,Ap-Je 12,O-N 13,27-D 18 1932;Ja 8-Je 11,S 10-D 3,17,31 1933+

TELEGRAF. w F 20 1909+
In Bohemian
pub 1909+
IU D 8 1917+
MdBE 1935+

TELEGRAM. w O 19? 1862-1915||?
1862-77? as Sunday telegram; 1907?-My 23 1914 Democratic telegram Merged with Saturday standard?
CtNlC Ap 16 1865
ICM Jl 27 1878
MB N 30,D 21 1862;Ag 30,O 11-25 1863;Ja-F 14 1864;Jl 7 1872
MWA O 23 1864;Ag 30 1874
MdBE D 7 1862;Ag 5,My 24,Jl 5,19 1863;N 20,D 11 1864;F 12,Ap 2 1865;D 30 1866;Ag 22 1869;Ap 28 1877;My 21 1881;Jl-D 1901;Ja 3,N-D 1903;Jl 1907-Je 1909;Ja-Je 17 1911
MdBLe 1912-F 27 1915
MdHi Ap 24 1864;Mr 17 1867;F 16-23,Mr 17 1868;N 27 1870;O 12 1873[Mr 1879-Ap 22 1882]
NNHi Mr 23 1873;Ag 30 1874
OClWHi Ap 24 1870
OHi Ja 28 1866
VRC N 20 1864

Baltimore TIMES. w O 2 1830-S 22 1832||
1830-S 24? 1831 as Chronicle of the times
MB [Ap-S 1832]
MWA Ag 11 1832
MdBE O 29 1831-32

Daily TIMES. d Ap?-O? 1852||
MWA Je 7,Jl 16 1852
MdHi S 24 1852

TIMES. w 1878?-
ICM N 23 1878

TIMES. w 1883?-Ja 17? 1885||
MdHi O 20 1883

TIMES. w,d My 10 1885-86||?
w My-O 12 1885
MdBE O 14 1885-Ja 30 1886
MdHi D 13-20 1885

TIMES; Baltimore's daily picture paper. d O 30 1922-Ja 25 1923||
MdBE O 30-D 1922
MdHi 1922-Ja 22 1923

MARYLAND (*Continued*)

BALTIMORE—*Continued*

TIMES and ledger. d Ag 8 1853-Jl 4 1854||
1853-F? 1854 as American times; Mr?-Je? 1854 Evening times
MdBE S 23,30 1853
MdHi S 19 1853

Baltimore daily TRANSCRIPT. *See* Baltimore post and commercial transcript

Evening TRANSCRIPT. d O 26 1863-65||?
MdHi N 28 1863
N 28 1863-1:27

TRIBUNE of Maryland. w Je 20- 1933||
MdBE Je 20-27,Jl 11 1933

TRUE democrat. ir O 12-30 1875||
Campaign paper
MdHi O 12,14,16,20,30 1875

TRUE republican. w Ag 16- 1879||?
Campaign paper
MdHi Ag 23 1879

Die TURN-ZEITUNG. w O 21? 1851-61||?
In German
MB O 6 1857-F 5 1861
MH O 18 1859-Mr 20 1860

VIPERS sting and Paul Pry. w Ja 13? 1849-
MWA F 9 1850
MdHi Ag 11-18 1849

Baltimore Saturday VISITOR. w F 4 1832-Ap 10? 1847||
Title varies: Saturday morning visitor. Merged with National era (Washington, D.C., not in this list)
Ct Ap 6 1833
MWA Mr 2,O 26 1833;N 29 1834;Ja 28(extra) D 19 1846
MdBE Mr 10,Ap 28,My 12,D 15 1832;Mr 2 1833
MdCt F 1833-Ja 1834
MdHi Je 30,Jl 14,Ag 4,25[S 22 1832-Je 14 1834]D 19 1840[41-47]
NhD Je 12 1841
OClWHi Ap 4 1840

Baltimore VOLKSFREUND und Biene. w F 22 1873-My? 1900||
1873-82? as Biene von Baltimore
In German
MdBE 1873-F 8 1879

WAVERLY gazette. *See* Woodberry news

Täglicher Baltimore WECKER. d O? 1851-S 1877||?
1851?-Mr 8 1867 as Baltimore wecker
MWA My 3-4 1858;Ja 1 1866
MdBE Ja 5-Je 1856;58-Je 1859;60-61;Jl 1862-Je 1869;70-72
MdHi Jl-D 1854

Baltimore WECKER. w Ja 4? 1856-1911||?
Title varies: Baltimore Wecker wochen-ausgabe; Wochenblatt des Baltimore Wecker; Baltimore sonntags wecker?
MWA D 22 1865
MdBE Ja 15-F 19,Mr-Ap 23,My 1858-Je 1859; Ja-Je 1860;Ja-Je 1869;71

WESTERN continent. w Ja 3 1846-49||?
DLC Mr 14,28-Ap 4,18 1846;O 21 1848
MWA F 14,Mr 14,28,O 17 1846;My 1,N 20 1847
MdBE Ja,F 7,Mr-My 9,23-Jl 11,25-N 7,28,D 19 1846-Ja 2,Ag 14 1847;Ag 19 1848
MdHi Mr 14,28 1846;Jl 22 1848-F 10 1849
MdHi-H Mr 28,D 26 1846;Ap 24,O 16,30 1847
N Ja 6 1849
PP Ap 25 1846

Baltimore daily WHIG. d My 14 1838-42?||
My-S 8 1838 as Whig
MdHi [My 15-O 16 1838]
NN Ag 19,27 1842

WOCHENBLATT des Baltimore wecker. *See* Baltimore wecker w

WOODBERRY news. w 1872-87||?
1872-74? as Waverly gazette
MdBE S 16 1876
NcD F 15 1879

Baltimore WORLD. d O 25 1890-Ap 16 1910||
1890-Je 1900 as World. Merged with Sun
MdBE O 26 1891-1910
MdBLe O 26 1893-Ap 28 1898;N 1899-1909
MdHi 1890-O 19 1891;MMr 18-O 1893;Je-Jl 1903

WREATH and literary shamrock. w O 1830-N 1831||
O 16 1830?- as Wreath. Merged with Baltimore minerva, later Baltimore minerva, wreath, and Saturday post
DLC Ja 8,Jl 23,Ag 13 1831

BEL AIR

ÆGIS. w Jl 11? 1857+
1857-F 1862? as Southern ægis; Mr 1862-Mr 4 1864 Southern ægis and Harford county intelligencer; Mr 11? 1864-Ja 26 1923 Aegis and intelligencer My 29 1831 is 75th anniversary number
pub 1894+
MdBE Ag 1,15,O 3-10,N 14-D 5,26 1857[58-69]N 10 1871;N 1 1872;Ja 10 1873;N 20 1874;F 4-11,Ap 28 1876;Ja 19 1877-[82-88]-91;Ap 1,S 30,O 7 1892[93-95]-S 24 1897[98-1907]+
MdHi Mr 15 1862-70;72-86;89-93
MdHi-H 1887-88
PDoHi N 12 1897[My 20-D 1914]

*BOND of union and Harford county weekly advertiser. w Mr 2? 1820-
1820?-S 1824? as Bond of union and weekly advertiser
DeHi Ap 3 1828
MdBE O 4 1821;O 9 1823;S 23-30 1824;Je 14 1827
MdHi Jl 28 1825
MdHi-H O 16 1823;O 13 1825;My 4,Ag 1,D 18 1826;Ja 25,Mr 1,My 31,Je 21 1827;Ja 17,Ap 24,My 8 1828

HARFORD citizen. w Jl 31 1828-
1828-33? as Independent citizen
CSmH Ag 19 1830
DLC 1828-D 3 1829;Ja 14-28,D 2-9 1830;S 15 1831;N 8-15 1832
MDeHi Ag 15 1832
MdBE [Ag 28 1828-31]Ja 19,F 9-16,Mr 1,29 1832;O 24 1833;S 12 1835
MdHi-H Ag 6 1829;D 29 1831;Ja 19,F 23,Ag 29,S 27 1832;D 12 1833

HARFORD democrat. w Ja 11? 1856-
MdBE Mr 28,Jl 18 1856

HARFORD democrat and Aberdeen enterprise. w O 2 1868+
1868-1921? as Harford democrat
pub 1920+
MdBE O 2,N 6 1868[69-74]-77;N-D 1886; 88-D 12 1919;20;My 18,Je 22 1934+
MdHi S 16 1870;73-86;Je 22-29 1894;D 12,26 1919-Ja 7,28-F 11 1921
MdHi-H O 8 1869;87-88;S 17 1890;F 10 1893;O 23 1896;Ja 22-29 1897;My 11,D 28 1900;Mr 29,Ap 5,My 31 1901;Je 27-Jl 11,25-Ag 8,D 12,26 1902;D 1 1905;Mr 9,My 11,Jl 6,30 1906; Ap 12 1907;O 30 1908;Ap 23,My 21-Je 18,Ag 12,S 3-10,N 5 1909;Mr 10 1911;Ja 31,Mr 28,Jl 11,O 10 1913;19-20
NNHi Ap 19 1878
PHi O 31 1913

HARFORD dispatch. sw,w Je 22 1895-F 24 1897||
Merged with Harford democrat, later Harford democrat and Aberdeen enterprise
sw Je 22-O 19 1895
MdBE Je-O 16,30 1895-97

HARFORD gazette and general advertiser. w My 26? 1848-
MdBE Ag 25 1848;S 17 1852;Ap 28,My 26,Je 2 1854
MdHi-H Ag 23 1850;My 30,D 5 1851;F 25 1853;D 8-22 1854

HARFORD republican and general advertiser. w 1830?-
1830?-54? as Harford republican
MdBE My 28 1840;F 17,Mr 31,O 27 1842;Ja 5 1843;Mr 25 1847;Mr 14 1850;Ag 31-S 7 1855
MdHi Mr 17 1836
MdHi-H Mr 29,Jl 19 1838;F 28 1839;Ag 10 1848;Ja 5,26-F 9,Mr 2,23,Ap 13-20,Ag 10,O 5 1855

HARFORD union. w O 2 1865-S 11? 1868||
MdBE Mr 30,Ap 20,My 25,Jl(supp)O 5-12 1866;Ja 4,F 22,Mr 1,My 17,Jl 19,N 8 1867;Ja 3,Je 5,19 1868
MdHi-H D 29 1865;N 23 1866;Mr 29,Ag 16,S 6,O 4,N 8-15 1867;Ja 3-10,24,Mr 6,Ap 3,My 29,S 11 1868

INDEPENDENT citizen. *See* Harford citizen

MADISONIAN and Harford and Baltimore advertiser. *See* Madisonian and Harford county weekly advertiser (Havre de Grace)

NATIONAL American. w F 1856?-66||?
MdBE Mr 5 1858;Mr 9,Je 8 1860[61-63;65-66]
MdHi Je 21 1861
MdHi-H [S 5 1856-Mr 16 1866]

Bel Air RECORD. w S 2 1869-F 24 1870||?
MdBE S 23,N 11 1869
MdHi-H F 10,24 1870

SOUTHERN ægis. *See* Aegis

STATE. w Je-D 1894||?
United with Bel Air times to form Bel Air times; The State, later Bel Air times

Bel Air TIMES. w Jl 1881+
1895?-Ja 1899? as Bel Air times; The State
pub 1881+
MdBE Mr 31,Je 30,N 17 1882;Jl 20,Ag 24 1883;Ja 18-25,Jl 4,25,Ag 8 1884;Ja 2,Jl 3,24-Ag 6 1885;Jl 30,Ag 13,N-D 1886;89-91;Ag 5 1892;93;Je 1,N 9 1894;95-S 1897;Ja 22-D 3 1898;S 23,O 14 1899;Ag 25,S 29-O 6,N 17 D 29 1900;Ja 26,Je 1 1901;My 17,Je 28-Jl 5,25-Ag 8,S 12,O 17,N 14,D 5 1902;Mr 1903-[04-05]F 29,Je 15 D 21 1906;Ja 25,F 8,Je 7,N 15-22 1907;08-[18]F 7,Mr-Ap 4,18-25,My 9-16, Je 13-Ag 8,22-S 12,O 17-24 1919;20+
MdHi O 2 1885;Ja 22,F 12,Jl 23 1886;F 14 1890

BELAIR. *See* BEL AIR

BERLIN

EASTERN SHORE times. w 1925+
1925-Jl 1932? as Berlin times
Dated also in Ocean City
pub Ag 1932+
MdBE My 10 1934+

Berlin-Ocean City NEWS. w 1929-32||
Merged with Eastern Shore times

Berlin TIMES. *See* Eastern shore times

BOONSBORO

FLAG. w Ja 29 1842-
CSmH Ap 16 1842

Boonsboro GUARD. w Jl 10 1840-
MdHK Jl-S 25 1840

MAN about town. w My 5? 1843-
MdHW My 19 1843

Boonsboro ODD FELLOW. *See* Hagerstown Odd fellow (Hagerstown)

TIMES. w 1880+
1880-1913 as Boonsboro times
pub [1899-1913]+
MdBE 1933+

BOWIE

INDEPENDENT farmer. w F 1? 1878-79||?
1878? pub in College Station
DLC My 24 1878
MWA D 12 1879
MdHi Ap 19 1878
MiU-C D 12 1879

REGISTER. w Ap 21 1927+
pub 1927+
MdBE 1927+

BRUNSWICK

BLADE-TIMES. w 1915+
1915-16? as Brunswick blade
pub N 20 1929+
NcD D 15 1921;Ap 14 1927

CAMBRIDGE

AMERICAN eagle. *See* Cambridge intelligencer

Daily BANNER. d S 21 1897+
pub F 1910+
MdBE My 29 1934+

Cambridge CHRONICLE. w Ap 20? 1822-54||?
1827?-My 17 1828 as Cambridge chronicle and Maryland weekly advertiser; Ja-Jl 13 1839 Cambridge weekly chronicle and farmers register
DLC Ap 29,Ag 5,S 23,O 14,N 11 1826;O 27 1827-My 19 1832;Je 30,Jl 28,S 15 1832;My 25,Je 1,15,O 12 1833-Ap 25,D 5 1840
MWA Ag 30-S 6,20-27 1828;D 25 1830;Jl 23 1831
MdCaB [S 1846-S 16 1854]

Cambridge CHRONICLE. w Ja 1870-1906||?
1870-71? as Cambridge telegraph. Merged with Daily banner
MdBE Je 25-Jl 2,16-23,Ag 13-20 1886
MdCaH 1887-97
MdHi Jl 30 1891

DEMOCRAT and news. w N 1845+
1845-66? as Cambridge democrat; 1867?-68? Democrat and herald
pub [1870-1913]+
MWA O 20-27 1852
MdBE Je 6,20,Jl 11-Ag 8 1885;1927+
MdHi N 16 1853

DORCHESTER aurora. w Jl 13 1835-40||?
DLC 1835-Ap 1840

DORCHESTER county era. w Mr 23 1878-1906||?
1878-O 1882 as Cambridge era; N 1882-1900? Dorchester era
MdBE 1878-Mr 11 1882;Je 20-27,Jl 18-25,Ag 15 1885

DORCHESTER era. *See* Dorchester county era

DORCHESTER news. w N 1865-70||?
United with Democrat and herald to form Democrat and news

Cambridge ERA. *See* Dorchester county era

HERALD. w 1866?-68||?
United with Cambridge democrat to form Democrat and herald, later Democrat and news

Cambridge INTELLIGENCER. w My 2 1855-
1855-64? as American eagle
DLC Ja 28 1865
MWA Je 30 1866
MdCaB Jl 23[S 24 1856-Ag 12 1857]

Cambridge ITEM. m F 1894-Ja 1901||
MdCaV complete

Cambridge RECORD. tw 1905+
Merged with Daily banner
pub S 5 1905+
M D 25? 1908

Cambridge TELEGRAPH. *See* Cambridge chronicle (1870-1906)

CAPITOL HEIGHTS

Weekly REVIEW. w N 14 1924+
pub 1929+
MdBE S 21 1928;O 26 1934+

CATONSVILLE

ARGUS. sm,w Ag 27 1881+
sm 1881-85?
pub O 1891+
MdBE Ap 2 1892[1912]Ja-Ap 5 1913[Jl-N 1915]Jl 15 1916-S 8 1917;Mr-Ag 24 1918;Ag 1919-O 2 1920;Ap 8,My 13 1922-F 23 1924; My 9-Ag 22 1925;O 8-D 10 1927;S 8 1928-F 2,Je 1929-Mr 21,Ag 15-O 24 1931;Jl 21,N 17,D 1933-Mr 16,N 1934+
MdHi D 17 1881;S 30 1899

Catonsville HERALD and Baltimore countian. w F 17 1928+
pub Je 29 1928+
MdBE My 18,O 26 1934+

CENTREVILLE

MARYLAND citizen. w Ja 1860-79||?
MWA Ap 9 1863
MdCeR My 26 1864

MARYLAND (*Continued*)

CENTREVILLE—*Continued*

MARYLAND sentinel. w F 18? 1839?-
1839?-47? as Weekly sentinel and general advertiser
DLC Ap 1 1845
MdBE S 29 1846;D 19 1854
MdChK D 21 1847

Centreville OBSERVER. w Jl 26? 1864-O 29 1936||
Follows Centreville times (1822-64). United with Queen Anne's record to form Queen Anne's record-observer
MdBE N 2 1869;S 27 1870;Je 27 1871;Ja 21 1873;Jl 4 1876;Ag 2 1907;O 3-10,N 21-28 1914; N 20-27 1915;S 16,30,N 25 1916[17-23]-[25-26] O 1927-N 6 1930;Je 14 1934-O 1936
MdCeR 1913-36
MdHi My 21,Ag 13 1891

QUEEN ANNE'S record-observer. w F 23 1933+
1933-O 29 1936 as Queen Anne's record
MdBE 1933-Jl,Ag 30,S 20-O 25,N 29 1934;35+

Centreville RECORD. w N 26 1874-Ap 14? 1932||
MdBE N 26,D 17-24 1874[75-85]-Mr 4 1886; Ja-Ag 20 1887;Ja-N 1888;Ja-O 1889;Ja 18-S 6 1890;Ja-S 12 1891;Ja-O 8 1892;Ja-D 12 1893;94-1908;Ja 19 1910-D 23 1911;12-My 20 1922;23-Ap 14 1932
MdCeO 1898

Weekly SENTINEL and general advertiser. *See* Maryland sentinel

Centreville STATE rights. w My 2 1857-64||?
1857-Jl 17 1860 as States rights advocate
MdBE Ja 31 1863
MdCeK Ja 24,Mr 6 1860-S 10 1861

STATES rights advocate. *See* Centreville state rights

Centreville TIMES. w 1822?-Jl? 1864||
1822?-40? as Centreville times and Eastern Shore advertiser; 1845?-46? Times and advertiser 1851?-53? Centreville times and Eastern Shore public advertiser. Followed by Centreville observer
DLC O 21 1826;Je 12 1828-O 4 1834;Ag 31 1839;Mr 29 1845;F 3 1853
MWA F 3 1827;F 5,Jl 30 1831
MdBE S 19 1846
MdChK My 1851-O 1853
MdHi My 13 1863

Centreville TIMES. w Ag 20 1932-N 1 1934||
MdBE S 29 1934
MdCeO complete

CHESAPEAKE CITY

CHESAPEAKE record. w Mr 16? 1878-D 1879||?
MdBE Mr 30 1878

CHESTERTOWN

ENTERPRISE. w S 27 1893+
pub O 1893+
MdBE My 30 1934+

KENT bugle; a political, literary and agricultural journal. w D 12? 1834-40||?
MdBE D 26 1834;My 8-29,Jl 31-Ag,N 6,D 11-18 1835

KENT inquirer. w N 12 1830-34||?
Follows Telegraph?
MdBE N 13,D 3 1830;Ja 7,F 18,Ap 29,My 13-27,Je 17,Jl 8,29 1831;D 1 1832;F 2,Je 29,S 14-21,N 2-16 1833

KENT news. w My 2 1840+
pub My 1 1841-O 6 1848;F 24,My 1849-57;60-61;N 19 1864-D 15 1866;67-71;76-78;87-93;Mr 9 1895-D 22 1900;01+
DLC My 9,N 28 1840
MdBE Ja 21 1843;Ag 5 1882;1903-06;10-11;17-18;Je 9 1934+
MdHi Ja 7 14 1851

TELEGRAPH. w O 21? 1825-30||?
1825-O 20 1826 as Chestertown telegraph
Followed by Kent inquirer?
CSmH Jl 16 1830
DLC Ap 11-25,Jl 11,25-Ag 1,15-S 12,26-O 10, N 7-21,D 5 1828;Jl 10-17,S 11,25-O 2,N 27 1829;Ja 1-8 1830
MdBE O 30,D 18 1829
MdChK O 28 1825-N 20 1829
MdHi D 1 1826

TELESCOPE, and Eastern Shore advertiser. w D 13 1833-
DLC D 20 1833;F 14 1834

Chestertown TRANSCRIPT. w My 20 1862+
pub 1889-Mr 1900;Ap 1902-15;18-19;22+
MdBE 1862-O 11 1919;Ja 10 1920+
MdChB Je 1896-Mr 1900
MdHi Mr 12 1875-My 10 1878

CLEARSPRING

Clearspring SENTINEL. *See* Potomac sentinel (Williamsport)

COCKEYSVILLE

BALTIMORE county advocate. *See under* Towson

COLLEGE PARK

PRINCE Georges post. w N 20 1935+
MdBE 1935+

COLLEGE STATION

INDEPENDENT farmer. *See under* Bowie

CRISFIELD

Crisfield INDEX. w 1872-73||
MdBE O 26 1872-Ja 18,F 1,15-Je,Jl 12-19,Ag-S 6,20-O 4,18-25 1873

Crisfield LEADER. *See* Crisfield tribune

Crisfield POST. w S 6 1935+
pub 1935+
MdBE O 4-N 8,29 1935+

SOMERSET republican. *See* Crisfield tribune

Crisfield TIMES. w 1889+
pub Jl 25 1891-95;1906-12;17+
MdBE My 21 1932;My 25 1934+
MdHi Je 17 1911

Crisfield TRIBUNE. w Ap 20? 1872-1908||?
1872-1903? as Crisfield leader; 1904? Somerset republican
MdPsM O 24 1885

CUMBERLAND

Cumberland ALLEGANIAN. w D 1838?-1926||?
1838?-43? as Alleganian; Ag 1845?-Ag 1861? Democratic Alleganian; Mr 1877?-Ja 1879? Alleganian and times; 1880?-92? Alleghanian?
Suspended from Ag 1861-My 1864
DLC S 1858-Je 1861;N 1867
MWA S 4 1858
MdBE Mr 30 1861;S 23 1915
MdCT Ag 1845-Je,Ag 1849-51;My 1857-59;My 1867-Ja 1879;93-94;Jl 1899-1900;02;04-06;08; 10-23
MnHi Ag 25 1844
NhD Je 5 1841
OClWHi Jl 20 1844

Daily ALLEGANIAN and times. *See* Cumberland evening times

Weekly CIVILIAN. sw,w F 7 1828-99||?
1828-Ag 22 1851 title varies: Civilian; Cumberland civilian; Phoenix civilian; Ag 29 1851-Mr 10 1859? as Cumberland miners' journal; Mr 17 1859-75 Civilian and telegraph
sw -N 5 1847
DLC Ap 17 1828-N 1829;Ja 15,29,N 19 1830;Jl 16,Ag 6 1831;F 7 1832;O 17 1840;Jl 23 1842;N 1846-S 1853;Mr 17 1859-77;Jl 7 1878
ICHi N 2 1865
MWA N 3 1848;Ja 30 1852;S 30 1853;Ja 7-21,F-Ag 14 1864;O 18 1866;Ag 27 1876
MdBE N 5 1833;92-97
MdCN 1877-79;81;90;92-97;Ag 14-D 1899
MdCT 1886-89
MdHi Mr 28 1828;My 22 1845
MnHi Ap 7,My 12 1846;F 19,Mr 4 1847
NhD Mr 27 1841
OClWHi O 9 1841
OOxM F 27,Mr 13-20,Ap 24,My 8,22-29,Je 26-Jl 3,17 1829

CUMBERLAND miners' journal. *See* Weekly civilian

DEMOCRATIC Alleganian. *See* Cumberland Alleganian

INDEPENDENT. w F 15? 1880-1903||?
MdCT F 15 1880-Ja 1883;F 1891-96;N 17 1900-F 28 1903

MARYLAND advocate. w S 17 1823-38||*
Mr? 1828-Je 4 1833 as Maryland advocate and farmers' and mechanics' register. Merged with Cumberland Alleganian
DLC 1823-O 1830
MWA Jl 25-O 3,N-D 12,26 1825-Ja 16,F 13-27,Ap 17 1826;Je 21,Ag 9,S 6-20 1828;Ja 24 1829
MdCK D 21 1831-N 19 1833

MOUNTAIN CITY times. *See* Cumberland evening times

Cumberland daily NEWS. d Ap 2 1871+
pub Ap 3 1872-Ap 3,Je 7 1875-80;Mr 17 1881-85;90-Ag 12 1899;1900;04+
MWA S 21 1871
MdBE Jl 18 1881;Ag 13 1927;N 1928-Ja,Ap, Je 1929-30;S,D 1933;F-Je,O-N 1934;Ja-Ap,Jl-S 1935
MdC 1873-1900;27+

PHOENIX civilian. *See* Weekly civilian

Cumberland TELEGRAPH and Maryland mining register. w Ap 22? 1852-Mr 10 1859||
1851?-My 1855 as Cumberland telegraph. Unites with Cumberland civilian to form Civilian and telegraph, later Weekly civilian
DLC My 31 1855-57;Ap 22 1858-59
MWA Ja 10 1856

Cumberland evening TIMES. d Ap 3 1869+
1869-Ap 1872? as Mountain City times; My 1872-75? Daily times; 1876-79? Daily Alleganian and times; 1880?-91? Cumberland daily times; 1892?-1912? Evening times
pub 1869-My 1876;79-Ja 1883;O 1884-O 1889;O 1890-O 1891;Ap-Jl 1894;95-S 1896;Ap 1897-1900;02+
DLC 1898
ICM Ap 9 1887
MdBE Mr 12 1887;F-Jl,N 9 1934;Ja-Ag 1935; 36+
MdC 1927+
VU N 16 1889

UNCLE SAM. w D 5? 1896-
WHi Ap 24,Je 5 1897

Cumberland UNION. w S 20 1862-68||?
1862-63? as Cumberland union and Allegany county gazette
DLC 1862-63;S 16 1865-S 7 1866;S 24-O 15, 29-N 19,D 31 1867

UNIONIST. w Ja 2 1851-
MWA F 27 1851

DENTON

AMERICAN union. *See* Caroline independent

CAROLINE advocate. w My 6 1834-37||?
DLC My 6 1834

CAROLINE democrat. w 1875-85||
MdBE Mr 3,Je 16-Jl 21,Ag 4-11 1885

CAROLINE independent. w Jl 17? 1860-1932||?
1860-My 6 1926 as American union; My 13 1926-Je 9 1927 as Independent
DeU Je 5 1879
MdBE O 23 1860;Je 27 1861;Ag 25,S 1 1864;Ja 17-D 12 1867;69-70;Ja 19-N 23 1871;Ja 14-D 23 1875;77;F 19-Jl 8,D 16-30 1880;Mr 5,Je 25-Jl 2,16-Ag 20 1885;Je 23-D 15 1892;98;Ap-D 1899;Je 19 1902-N 3 1904;Ja 20-Ap 7,My 12-S 29,O 13-N 3 1910;Ja 11-Je 13 1912;Ja-D 6 1913;S 23 1915;N 21 1918-O 3 1930;31-Jl 1 1932

INDEPENDENT. *See* Caroline independent

Denton JOURNAL. w D 11? 1847+
MdBE N 23 1850;Ap 28 1866;Ja 4,18-F,Mr 14-Je 20,Jl 4,18-Ag 8,29-S 19,O-N 21,D 5-12 1868;Ja 9-F,Mr 13,Je 12-19,Jl 24-31 1869;F 28,Je 20-Jl 4,18-Ag 8 1885;Ap 20 1927;Je 16 1934+
MdHi Ag 1 1891

Denton PEARL. w S 23 1840-
1840-45? as Pearl
MdBE S 30 1840;Mr 28 1846

DUNDALK

COMMUNITY press and Baltimore countian. w N 27? 1925+
1925?-Jl 19 1929 as Community press; O 28 1932-Ap 12 1935 Community press and Sparrows Pointer F 3 1928?-O 21 1932 pub in Sparrows Point
Suspended Ap 19-D 5 1935
pub 1925+
MdBE F 1928-32;34;Mr 8-Ap 12,D 12-26 1935; 36+

EASTON

Easton DEMOCRAT. w My 20? 1885-96||
1885-N 10 1886 as Easton independent; N 17 1886-Je 15 1889 Democrat. United with Easton star to form Easton star-democrat
MdHi Ja 20 1886-S 12 1891

EASTERN-SHORE star. *See* Easton star-democrat

EASTERN-SHORE whig and people's advocate. w S 9? 1828-Mr? 1841||
Followed by Eastern-Shore star, later Easton star-democrat
CSmH S 7 1830
DLC N 11 1828;Ag 4 1829
MdBE Ja 31 1837
MdET Ja 20-27,Mr 3,17,My 12,26,Je 30 1829;Je 8(extra)1830
MdHi Jl 13 1830-Mr 2 1841

*Easton GAZETTE. w D 15 1817-N 1 1929||
1817-Jl 28 1821? as Easton gazette and Eastern Shore intelligencer
DLC Jl 28 1821;N 6 1824;26-N 15 1828;My 23, Je 27,S 5-12,26-O 3 1829;Jl 24,N 13 1830;Jl 30 1831;D 15 1832;N 7 1840
MWA O 27 1827;O 18 1851;Je 30 1866
MdBE D 30 1826;Jl 24,O 2 1886;Mr 1895-O 16 1897;Jl 23 1913;Ag 2,O 4 1916;Ap 4 1917;S 7 1922;N 6-13 1924;O 22 1925;Ja 13 1928
MdChK Ag 10 1850
MdEJ Jl 15 1837;Je 18 1842;My 27,Ag 19 1854; Ja 9 1857;O 13,D 15 1860;Je 14 1862;N 10 1866;D 11-25 1897;D 28 1907;N 25 1914
MdET 1885-1908
MdHi 1821-S 1830;F 12 1831-48;Ag 16 1858-67; 69-93
PP N 30 1850

Easton INDEPENDENT. *See* Easton democrat

Easton JOURNAL. 1863-74 *See* Easton ledger

Easton JOURNAL. w Ag 20 1931+
pub Ag 20 1931+
MdBE S 17 1931;Je 22,S 28,O 12-26,D 7-14,28 1933-Ja 11,F 15,Mr 8-22,Ap 5-19,My 1934+

Easton LEDGER. w Ag 4 1863-1918||?
1863-O 22 1874 as Easton journal
MdBE Je 11 1885
MdHi 1863-91
OOxM Ja 29 1874

PUBLIC monitor. w Jl 1? 1858-
MdHi Jl 8,Ag 12-19,S 16,N 11-25 1858

*REPUBLICAN star and general advertiser. w S 1799-1833||?
1799-Ag 1802 as Republican star or Eastern Shore political luminary; S 1802-S 13 1814 Republican star or Eastern Shore general advertiser; S 20 1814 Republican star S 27 1814-16 Republican star or general advertiser.
CSmH S 14 1830
DLC 1821-24;F 18,25-26;Ja 8-D 1828;S 1829;Ag 16 1831
MdHi 1821-N 17,30 1830
WHi 1821-Je 12 1832

Easton STAR-DEMOCRAT. w Ap 20 1841+
Follows Eastern-Shore whig. 1841-My 16 1843 Eastern-Shore star; My 23 1843-96 Easton star
Suspended 1863-S 5? 1865
DLC Ap 1 1845;Mr 8-D 20 1853;59;F-D 1860
IU Ja 3,F 27,S 3,17-24,O 15,N 5 1844
MdBE My 30,D 26 1925;D 24 1927;N 24,D 22 1928;My 5-12,D 22 1933;Ja 26-F 2,Mr 9-30,My 18 1934+
MdHi 1841-63;S 26 1865-93;Mr 25 1911
NcD Ap 27 1858

MARYLAND (*Continued*)

EASTON—*Continued*

TALBOT county record. w Je 21-28 1935||
MdBE complete

ELIZABETH-TOWN. *See* HAGERSTOWN

ELKTON

Elkton APPEAL. w Ap 9 1884-1906||?
MdEkW 1884-Ja 2 1902

CECIL county news. w S 1880+
pub 1900+
MdHi Ja 29 1919

CECIL county star. w Jl 29 1882+
1882-85? as North East star; 1886?-1927? Cecil star 1882-Ag 1929? pub in North East
pub [Ag 1917-26]+
MdBE Jl 29 1882;O 23,N 1886-Jl,N 1889-My 4,Ag 24 1895-S 1899;Mr 17-Jl 21 1900;O 27 1906-S 7 1907;Ja-My 2 1908;My 1910-Mr 6,S 18 1915-Je 23 1917;Je 21 1934+

CECIL democrat. w F 19? 1842+
Follows Cecil gazette. 1842?-My 1850 as Cecil democrat and farmers' journal
pub [Je 1848-94]+
DLC Jl 23 1842
MdBE Ja 18 1862;Ap 1 1871;D 29 1877;Ja 18 1879;Jl 15 1882;Ap 30 1887;F 16 1889;O 5 1929-30;Je 20 1931;F 6 1932-33;Je 23 1934+
MdHi Ap 12 1845
MdHi-H N 4 1865

CECIL gazette and farmers' and mechanics' advertiser. w Ag 23 1834-F 1842||?
Follows Cecil republican. . . Followed by Cecil democrat
MdBE 1834-F 14 1835;S 12 1840

CECIL republican and farmers' and mechanics' advertiser w My 12 1832?-34||?
Followed by Cecil gazette. . .
MdEkC O 10 1833

CECIL whig. w Ag 7 1841+
pub 1841+
DLC N 4 1843;Mr 17 1860
MWA S 1 1866
MdBE Jl 7,S 29 1849;S 13 1851;My 8 1852;O 29 1853;S 22 1855;Ag 22 1857;Mr 5 1859;F 4 25 1860;N 9 1861;O 11 1862;Ja 27,F 10 1866; N 16-D 14 1867;Jl 8 1876;My 24 1879;S 17,O 8-15 1881;N 6 1886;My 25 1912;O 10 1914;Jl 26 1919;Je 22 1934+
MdChK Ag 9 1851
MdEKP S 25-O 2,30,N 20,D 25 1841[42-43;45-58;60-62;64-65]Ap 10 1869
MdHi [Mr 12 1842-58;60-65]Ag 17 1872

Elkton COURIER. w S 3 1836-37||?
MdBE S 24 1836

JACKSON picket guard. w Jl 16 1856-
NNHi S 3 1856

Elkton PRESS. w Jl 5 1823-32||?
1823?-Mr 7? 1829 as Elkton press and Cecil county advertiser
DLC F 14,N 13 1824;S 1 1827;Jl 19-Ag 2, 16-30,S 13-27,O 25-N 8 1828;Jl 11,S 12,26-O 3 1829;Ja 2,S 18,N 16,D 25 1830;Jl 23,Ag 6 1831
MdBE Ag 30 1828
MdCtS [O 19 1828-My 8 1830]
MdHi 1823-Je 12 1824;My 6 1826;N 1828-Ap 1 1829;Jl 10 1830

ELLICOTT CITY

AMERICAN progress. *See* Progress

COMMON sense. w 1867-71||?
MdBE Jl 29 1868
MdHi Ap 27 1871

Ellicott City DEMOCRAT. w Mr 3 1888-1902||?
MdBE N 12 1892

HOWARD county progress. *See* Progress

HOWARD district press. w Ag 22 1840-47||?
1840-Je? 1842 as Howard free press
DLC Ag 22 1840
MdBE Jl 30 1842
MdHi My 15-Ag 6 1847

HOWARD free press. *See* Howard district press

HOWARD gazette. w Ja 6 1849?-
MdElS 1853

PROGRESS. w O 13 1871?-1920||?
1871?-89? as American progress; 1890?-96? Howard county progress; 1914? Suburbanite progress
MdHi O 10 1873

SHANGHAI. w S 29 1855-F 9 1856||
WHi complete

SUBURBANITE progress. *See* Progress

Ellicott City TIMES. w Ja 1? 1870+
pub 1921+
MdBE 1877-79;92-1902;06-07;12-32;My 17,Jl 26 1934+
MdElS 1889-91
MdHi Mr 20 1909
NNHi Ap 6 1878

ELLICOTT'S MILLS. *See* ELLICOTT CITY

EMMITSBURG

Emmitsburg CHRONICLE. w Je 14 1879+
Title varies: Weekly chronicle
pub 1924+
MdBE Je. 20 1902;Ag 6 1915;O 1934+
MdEmJ 1879-My 13,S 16 1910-Ap 4 1913;Ap 23 1915-Je 1918
PPCHi [1891;1906]

GAZETTE. w Ag 17 1839-
DLC Ag 17 1839

ESSEX

STAR. w Jl 3 1924+
pub 1924+
MdBE My 24 1934

FEDERALSBURG

Federalsburg COURIER. w F 7 1872-1932||
1872-Je 23 1883? as Maryland courier; Je-D 1889? Courier and farmer
MdBE F 7 1872;F 1875-Je 23 1883;Ap 1884-S 1885;Jl 29 1927;31-Je 10 1932
MdHi Ap 7 1883

MARYLAND courier. *See* Federalsburg courier

Federalsburg TIMES. w Jl 26 1929+
pub 1929+
MdBE Ap 7 1933-My 4 1934;Ap 1935+

FELL'S POINT

Papers published in Fell's Point are listed under Baltimore

FREDERICK

ANTI-JACKSONIAN. w Jl 4-N 4 1828||
Campaign paper
DLC Ag 12,S 14,28,N 4 1828
MdHi complete

BARTGIS'S . . . gazette. *See* Political intelligencer or republican gazette

Frederick CITIZEN. *See* New citizen

DEMOCRATIC union. *See* Maryland union

*EXAMINER. sw,w Ag 9 1813-1913||?
1813-Ap 7 1841 as Political examiner (title varies slightly);Ap 14 1841-44? Frederick examiner
DLC 1821-26;28;F 4,Jl 15-22,Ag 19,S 23,D 30 1829-Ja 13,27 1830;Ja 19 1831;N 11 1840;S 18 1844;62
IU Ag 12 1861;Je 22,Jl 6-13 1864;Jl 17 1867;D 25 1888
MWA Ap 28,Ag 4,O 6 1821;Je 18,Jl 9-Ag 20,S 3,O 8,29-N 19 1828
MdFF Mr 9 1831-F 1835;F 1849-53;55-56;58-59;67-68;70-78;80-90;96-1913
MdHi [1821-Je] D 1835-S 4 1844;Mr 17 1847; 53-54;Je 1857-80
MdHiH [1906]
OCHi N 9 1836
OClWHi D 1 1841;O 19 1842
OOxM S 10,O 29 1829
V F 1829-Ja 1830
WHi N 14 1860;Je 19 1861

*Frederick HERALD. w Je 19 1802-61||?
1802-Ja 21 1832 as Frederick-Town herald
CSmH S 11 1830
DLC Ja 31,My 8,29 1824;Jl 29 1826;S 5-12,O 3,N 7,28 1829;Ja 30,Ag 28 1830;Je 11 1831;N 3 1832;N 14 1840;N 16 1850;Ag 5 1854
MdFN O 16 1830-O 20 1832
MdHW Ag 31-O 26 1844
MdHi [Ja-My 1821]-My 17 1823;24[25-34]Jl 15 1843;N 18 1848;Jl 25 1857;58-S 3 1861
PCarlHi Ag 26 1826

MARYLAND herald. w 1870?-72||?
DLC Ag 3,S 28 1872

MARYLAND sentinel. w Jl 13 1830-
Follows Reservoir and public reflector
CSmH Ag 24 1830
DLC Je 11 1833
MWA N 16 1830;Mr 26 1833

MARYLAND union. w Ja 5 1854-86||?
1854-Ag 9? 1855 as Democratic union
DLC Jl 24,Ag 14 1856;Mr 24 1859;Ag 28 1862
IU D 14 1854;Mr 6,D 4 1856;Mr 29 1860
MdFF S 14 1865-Ag 25 1870
MdHi D 27 1855;Ag 1856-80;Mr 10-17,31-Ap 7 1881
NNHi Ap 11 1878
NcD F 16 1878
WHi Ag 16 1855-Ag 7 1856;Ag 6,N 12 1857;N 10 1859;N 14,D 19 1861;Ag 21 1862-F 2 1865; N 14 1867;N 11 1869;S 1870-Ag 19 1875

NEW citizen. w Ap 8 1821+
1821-Mr 1923 title varies: Republican citizen; Citizen; Frederick citizen; etc.
Ap-S 1821 pub in Westminster
Suspended 1864- 1865
pub 1841-42;67;71-74;79-80;83-91;93;Ja 12 1894-97;99-1902;05-08;10-15;23+
Ct [1827-35]
DLC F 22,My 24 1839;F 13-20 1880
MWA Ag 29 1823;F 19 1847
MdBE Je 8 1832;S 26 1884;Jl 13 1923;My 1934+
MdFF Jl-D 15 1826;27-N 14 1849;Ja-D 7 1850; 51-52;F 4-18,Mr 4,18-25 1853
MdHi [Ag 31 1821-O 17]N 7 1828;Je 26 1829; Ja 29,Ap 22 1836;Ap 28 1837-Ja 5 1838;N 15 1844;Mr 17 1848-Mr 15 1850;51-Ap 11 1856;Ag 23 1865-80
MdWJ F 6 1824
MnHi Ap 4 1834;My 3 1844
N O 18 1833
NN S 14 1832
WHi S 6 1861

NEWS. d O 15 1883+
Title varies: Daily news
O 14 1933 is 50th anniversary issue
pub 1883+
CL O 14 1933
DLC O 14 1933
MWA Mr 2 1922
MdBE Ap 21,25,28,My 2,5,9,23-31,Je,Jl 2-3,5-28,Ag 7 1923;O 14 1933;My 5 1934+

OLIVE branch. w My 18? 1843-
MdHi My 16 1844

PEOPLE. w Ag 4 1828-
Campaign paper
MdHi S 1,15-22 1828

POLITICAL examiner. *See* Examiner

*POLITICAL intelligencer or republican gazette. w My 22 1792-1826||?
1792-Ap 1794 as Bartgis's Maryland gazette and Frederick-Town weekly advertiser; My 1794-Ag 23 1797 Bartgis's federal gazette or the Frederick-town and county weekly advertiser; Ag 30 1797-99? Bartgis's federal gazette or the Frederick county weekly advertiser; 1800?-Ja? 1814 Bartgis's republican gazette; F? 1814-Jl? 1821 Bartgis's republican gazette and general advertiser; Ag 4 1821-S 27 1823 Republican gazette and general advertiser; O 4 1823-Mr 6 1824 Republican gazette
DLC Mr 24-Ap 7,21-Je 23,Ag 18-25 1821;F 1823-F 1825
MWA Je 14-N 8,22-D 6 1823;Ja 3,24-Mr 20,Ap 3,Jl 17 1824
MdHi 1821-Mr 20 1824;Ap 27,D 29 1825;Ja 12,F 9,Je 1,29,Ag 17,S 28 1826
WHi Mr 13 1824;25-O 19 1826

Frederick POST. d D 10 1910+
1910-12? as Evening post
pub 1910+
MdBE Jl 26 1923;My 9 1934;36+

Evening PRESS. d Ag 2 1910-
MdFF Ag-D 1 1910

REFORMER and people's advocate. w Jl 30-O 29? 1844||
Campaign paper
DLC Ag 13-O 1844

REPUBLICAN citizen. *See* New citizen

REPUBLICAN gazette. *See* Political intelligencer or republican gazette

RESERVOIR and public reflector. w Jl 28 1823-Jl 6? 1830||
Followed by Maryland sentinel
CSmH My 18 1830
CaOLU [1824-26]
DLC 1823-Jl 19 1824;Je 17-N 4 1828
MWA Ja 9 1827
MdHi Ag 1823-Jl 1829

*STAR of federalism. w Ap 27? 1815-
Ap 27?-N 23? 1816 pub in Uniontown
MdHi N 23 1822

TIMES. w My 10 1832-35||?
Title varies: Weekly times
MdBE Ag 6 1835
MdHi 1832-My 1,Je 26,N 6 1834
NFre 1833

Frederick TIMES. w Ja 4? 1876-89||?
MdHi Ag 15 1876

Frederick TIMES and democratic advocate. w 1835-39||
1835-My? 1838 as Times and democrat advocate
Ct Ap 20 1837
MdHi Ap 27 1837-Ja 3 1839

TRUE democrat. w S 29-N 17? 1853||
MdHi S-O 20,N 1-17 1853

VISITER and temperance advocate. w Ag 30 1838-41||?
1838-O 7? as Frederick visiter (S 3 1840-F 25 1841 Visiter)
MdHi S-O 4,18-N 8 1838;Ja 10,24,F 7-21,Mr, Ap 11,My-Je 6,20,Jl 4,Ag 15,29-S 19,O 3,24-N 7,21-D 5,19-26 1839;Ja-F 13,27-Mr 12,26 1840-O 7,N 25-D 9 1841

WE, the people, a paper for the campaign. w Je 7-N 1 1856||
Campaign paper
MdFF complete
MdHi complete

FREDERICK-TOWN. *See* FREDERICK

FROSTBURG

Frostburg GAZETTE and miners' record. w D 18 1858-61||?
MdBE D 18 1858

Frostburg MINING journal. w S 30 1871-1911||
MdBE 1871-F 25 1911

Frostburg TRUE union, gazette and miners' record. w Ja 6? 1862-
MdBE Mr 11 1862

FULLERTON

BALTIMORE county independent news. w Ag 22 1934-
MdBE Ag 22,S 5,19,O 3-10,24 1934

GLEN BURNIE

SOUTHERN Maryland times. w N 25 1927+
pub 1927+
MdBE 1927-29;34+
MdHi-H 1927+

MARYLAND (*Continued*)

GREENSBORO

ENTERPRISE. w Je 20 1918+
pub Je 10 1926+
MdBE D 21 1933;Ja 4,S 13,O 17,N 1934+

FREE PRESS. w F 20? 1880-1914||?
Title varies: Greensborough free press
MdBE F 20,Mr 13,Ap 3,24,Je 19-Jl 3,17-Ag 14 1885
MdHi My 28 1897;My 18 1900

GREENSBOROUGH. *See* GREENSBORO

HAGERSTOWN

To Ja 26 1814 as Elizabeth-Town

ASHLAND star. w My 10?- 1844||
Campaign paper
MoSM Ag 16 1844

BLACK Hawk. w Ag 17? 1839-
MdHS O 12 1839

CAMP record. Je 27 1861-
N Je 27 1861
WHi Je 27 1861

Weekly CASKET. w Ap 8? 1848-
MdBE S 15 1849
MdHF Ag 5 1848
MdHi Ap 14 1849-O 1850

COURIER and enquirer. w My 28? 1834-
IU Ag 22 1838
MWA D 23 1835
MdBE D 17 1834;Je 17,Jl 1 1835

FARMERS' register and Maryland herald. w Ja 23? 1827-
1827-Ja 29 1828? as Maryland herald and Hagers-Town times
DLC Ja 29,Je 17,Jl 29-Ag 12,26,S 23,O 28,N 11-18 1828;S 15-29,D 29 1829-Ja 12,Ag 10-17 1830
MWA F 19 1828
MdHW Ja 19 1830-Ja 17 1832

Hagers-town FREE PRESS. w Ag 3 1831-
S 7-O 5 1831 as Free press; O 12 1831-Ja 9 1833 Hagerstown free press
MdBE 1831-Jl 24 1833;Jl 9 1834
MdHEves S 28 1831-Je 1833
MdHW Mr 26-Jl 23 1834

Hagerstown GLOBE. d Mr 1 1879-S 20? 1930||
1879-F 24 1930 as Evening globe
DLC 1898
MdBE Ap 9,Je 18,Jl 2,Ag 20 1898;My 30,Je 6 1906;N 11 1918;S 9 1924;My 21-Ag 1930
MdHW Ap 22 1879-S 1884;Mr 1885-Ag 1928;29-S 20 1930

Weekly GLOBE. w My 1 1879-S 1930||?
ICM F 6 1913
MdHW 1879-My 26,Je 21 1921-Jl 1926
MdHi My 1-22 1897

Morning HERALD. d 1891+
1891?-D 28 1895 as Daily herald and torch light
MdBE Je 7 1912;My 16 1918;Jl 9 1919;S 9 1924;Ap 1934+
MdHW D 30 1895-Je 1896;Jl 7-D 1897;Jl 1898-Je 1901;02;04-Je 1912;13-S 1917;18-S 1920;21-Je,O 1922-Je,O 1924+
MdHZ 1897
MdHi My 29,Je 8 1897;F 12 1904
NcD Ap 28 1922

HERALD and torch light. sw,w Je 5 1839-Ap 25? 1907||?
1839-Ap 6 1847 as Herald of freedom; Ap 14 1847-Je? 28 1848 Weekly herald of freedom; Jl 5 1848-Jl 30 1851 Hagerstown herald of freedom; Ag 6 1851-62? Herald of freedom and Torch light
sw 1846?-Ap 6 1847
DLC Je 5 1839
MWA Mr 11 1840;Mr 9 1864-F 7,21,Mr 7-14,28 1866
MdBoT Ja 23 1903
MdHK Mr 13 1862-N 23 1864
MdHW Je 1839-Je 1859;65-67;Mr 1868-82;Ag 23 1883-Ap 25 1907
MdHZ Mr 30,Ap 15,N 16,30 1864
MdHi [O 1839-My 1841]Je 16 1846-Ap 6 1847; Jl 1855-O 15 1862;Ap 15-22,S 16-23,O 21,N 11,D 20 1863;S 1877-83
OClWHi Ag 25 1841

HERALD of freedom and torch light. *See* Herald and torch light

LABOR vindicator. w O 6 1877-
MdHi O 6-20,N 3 1877

MAIL. w Jl 4 1828-1920||?
1828-Mr 25 1892 as Hagerstown mail (Jl 2 1830-Ap 1 1831 Hagerstown mail and Washington county republican advertiser)
CSmH Jl 23 1830
DLC Je 24,S 2-23,N 18 1831;F 3,Ap 13,S 7(extra)1832
IU Mr 27 1840
MWA N 14 1828;Je 24 1859;D 22 1876;S 21 1877-Mr 5 1880;82-83
MdBE Jl 4 1890;Ag 27 1915
MdHW 1828-Je 21 1833;Je 26 1835-Mr 4 1845;Ag 1861-O 20 1893;F 22 1895-1905;O 15 1909-Je 1911
MdHi N 21 1828;Ja 9 1829;Jl 1830-Je 24 1831; Mr 16 1849-Mr 15 1850
MnHi Ag 16-23 1844;Jl 2 1852
NcD O 10 1828;S 2 1831;Ag 2,S 20,O 11 1833; Ja 7 1881
NhD My 28 1841
P-M Ja 1 1868
VU D 10 1869;Jl 8 1870

Daily MAIL. d S 1 1890+
MdBE Je 28 1919;Ap-Jl,S 1934-35
MdHW 1890-Jl 1903;Jl-D 1904;J 1905-Je 13 1919;F 7 1920-Je,O 1928+
NcD D 28 1917[18]F 26-28 1923

MARYLAND free press. w 1866-68||
NNHi My 1867-Ap 1868

*MARYLAND herald and Hagerstown weekly advertiser. w Mr 2 1797-1826||?
Follows Washington spy (not in this list). 1797-F 19 1801 as Maryland herald, and Elizabeth-Town advertiser; F 26 1801-F 15 1804 Maryland herald, and Elizabeth-town weekly advertiser. Merged with Torch light
DLC N 20 1821
MWA S 4-11,O 23 1827
MdHW Ja-Je,Jl 10-31,Ag 21-S 4,18 1821-My 11,25 1824;Ja 3-10 1826
MdHi Ap 23 1822;Ag 22,S 1823

MARYLAND herald and Hagers-Town times. 1827-28. *See* Farmers' register and Maryland herald

NEWS. sw,w Ap 30 1842-47||?
w 1845
DLC Je 15 1842
MdBE Ap 30-My 4 1842
MdHL Je 22,Jl 2 1842
MdHi My 11-14,S 10 1842;Jl 18,Ag 12,N 3 1846;Ja 9-13,23-30,F 3,Mr 27 1847
MnHi Mr 20,My 1 1845;Mr 21 1846;D 11-13 1847

Morning NEWS. d F 1 1873-D 29? 1895||
1873-94? as Daily news (Jl 4 1879-D 19 1887 Hagerstown daily news; Jl 16-N 28 1894 Evening news) Merged with Morning herald
DLC F 1 1873
MdHW Jl 4 1876;My 2-Jl 1895
MdHi Mr 1874-N 1875;76-N 16 1883;84-89;91 My 1894-95

Weekly NEWS. w Je 21 1873?-95||?
MdHi [N 27 1875-Mr 1 1878]Mr 10 1882-Je 24 1887

Hagerstown ODD FELLOW. w D 17 1841-Ag 16? 1883||
1841-S 6 1881 as Boonsboro Odd fellow (Boonsboro); S 15-29 1881 Odd Fellow. Merged with Herald and torch light
MdHW N 23 1865-S 13 1876;S 20 1877-Ag 16 1883

OUR country. w Jl 4-N 1 1828||
Campaign paper
DLC Jl 26,Ag 23-N 1 1828
MdHi complete
NBHi O 18 1828

*TORCH LIGHT. w,sw N 1814?-Jl 1851||
Title varies: Torch light and public advertiser; Hagerstown torch light and public advertiser; Hagerstown torch light. United with Herald of freedom to form Herald and torch light
sw 1846
DLC D 16 1823;F 17,Mr 23,Ap 13,Jl 20-27,Ag 17 1824;D 6 1827[28;Jl-D 1829]-Ja 14,23,Ag 19, D 23 1830;N 8 1832;N 18 1841;Ap 3 1843
IU Ag 9,S 13 1838
MWA F 6-13 1821;O 29 1822;F 16 1837
MdBE N 27 1828;29-S 15 1831;S 17 1835
MdHW Ja-O 1821[22-O 21 1830]O 2-23 1834;S 14 1843-Jl 4 1844;Jl 1846-Ap 1 1847
MdHi N 8 1825-O 23 1828;N 24 1831-O 12 1837; Ag 20-24,S 3,14-17,O 5,12 1846;O 14-28 1847
MnHi Mr 27 1845
OClWHi Je 25 1840
OOxM F 15,O 4 1827[My 1828-Jl 1829]
P Jl 3 1828
WHi Ag 10-17 1824

Hagerstown TWICE-A-WEEK. *See* Yeoman's guard

WASHINGTON county democrat. w Mr 28? 1838-
DLC Ap 8 1840
IU My 5 1841

*Die WESTLICHE correspondenz. w Je 1799-
In German
DLC D 30 1825

YEOMAN'S guard. sw,w 1870-78||
1870?-1876? as Hagerstown twice-a-week (sw)
MdHL O 17 1878

YOUNG hickory. w Jl 2-N? 1844||
Campaign paper
MnHi Jl 9,Ag 26,S 30 1844

HAMPSTEAD

ENTERPRISE. w D? 1880+
1880-Mr 1883 pub in Manchester
pub Ap 25,My 8,Je 19,N 13 1885;Ja 3 1886;My 28,S 3 1897;O 1919+
MdBE S 28 1934;Ap 1935+

HANCOCK

Weekly GAZETTE. w Jl 1854-
DLC S 1 1854

Hancock NEWS. w Jl 2 1914+
Suspended from D 14 1934-Ja 25 1935
pub Ja 25 1935+
MdBE N 9-30,D 14 1934;Ja 25,F 8-My 17,31-Ap 23,S-D 20 1935;36+

STAR. w F 23 1889-O 2? 1919||?
Title varies: Hancock star
MdBE F 23 1889;Ap 13 1899-Mr 1916;Ap 1917-O 2 1919

HAVRE DE GRACE

DEMOCRATIC ledger. w Ap 14 1894+
pub 1894+
MdBE S 12 1896;D 28 1907;08-10;12-Ag 10 1918 Je 16-23 1934;Ap 1935+
MdHi My 9 1896

ELECTRIC light. w 1882-88||
MdBE Ap 4 1888

HARFORD county times. *See* Harford times

HARFORD dispatch. w Je 9? 1860-
MdBE N 17 1860

HARFORD Madisonian. . . *See* Madisonian and Harford county weekly advertiser

HARFORD times. w Ap 2 185?-
Ap 8? 1858-Mr 17? 1860 as Harford county times
MdBE Ap 9-16,30,My 14 1857;Ap 1,My 1 1858; Ja 29-F 5,Mr 19,Ap 23,Jl 2,30,Ag 27,S 24-O 15,29,D 3 1859;Ja 21-F 18,Mr 17,My 19-26,Jl 7, Ag 11,O 27-D 1,22 1860;F 23,Mr 16 1861
MdHi-H S 17,D 24 1857;My 22 1858;O 22 1859;My 5,19,Je 2,O 13,D 13 1860

HARFORD visitor, Susquehanna weekly advertiser. w Jl 14 1858-
MdHi-H Ag 4,S 4 1858

HAVRE republican. *See* Havre de Grace republican

MADISONIAN and Harford county weekly advertiser. w,sw S 22? 1836-57||?
Title varies: Madisonian and Harford and Baltimore advertiser; Harford Madisonian and Bel Air and Havre de Grave messenger; Semi-weekly Harford Madisonian, and Havre de Grace messenger; Harford Madisonian and Havre de Grave advertiser; etc.
MdBE D 28 1837;O 18 1838;N 21 1839;Ja 3,Ap 18 1845;Je 25,S 9 1846;Ja 1,Mr 19-26,Ap 23-30,S 4,17,O 22,D 2 1847;Ap 13,Ag 25 1848;Mr 21 1850;Ap 10,Ag 14,O 16 1851;Mr 18,S 17,O 18 1852;F 3,Ap 14,My 4 1853;Ap 20,My 26,Je 2,Jl 13;Ag 24-31 1854;Mr 1,O 11 1855;Ap 17,S 11,25 1856;Ja 15 1857
MdHi-H Ap 28 1838;Ap 8 1841;My 28,O 1 1847;S 7 1848;F 8-15 1849;My 6,Jl 28 1853;D 14 1854;Ja 25 1855

Havre de Grace REPUBLICAN. w Ja? 1868+
1868-81? as Havre republican
MdBE Je 3,Ag 12,N 4 1869;Ja 21 1870;Mr 31, Ag 4,18,S 22-O 6,N 10 1871;My 10,24,S 27,O 11,N 8 1872;84-86;89-91[93-94]-S 25 1897[Ja 22 1898-F 11 1899]Je 14 1902;My 2 1903;Ja 2, 23-30 1904;Je 9 1906;D 28 1907-[18-Mr 1920] Ap 27 1935+
MdHi N 27,D 11 1885;87-88,O 26 1895;Ag 15 1896
MdHi-H O 1 1868
OOxM F 13 1874

SUSQUEHANNA advocate and Havre-de-Grace advertiser. w S 30? 1839-
1839-Jl 27 1840? as Susquehanna advocate and Harrison democrat
DLC Jl 27 1840;O 23 1841

HEREFORD

JACKSONIAN and general advertiser. w My 11? 1850-52||?
1850?-51 as Jacksonian and Baltimore county advertiser (Baltimore)
DLC O 16 1852
MdHi O 23 1852
MdTJ N 23 1850

HIGHLANDTOWN

Papers published in Highlandtown are listed under Baltimore

HURLOCK

UPPER Dorchester news. w F 2 1923+
pub 1923+
MdBE Je 15,S 21,N 1934-Je 1935;F 14 1936+

HYATTSVILLE

Hyattsville INDEPENDENT. w Mr 25 1898+
pub 1929+
MdBE My 25,Je 29 1934+
VHi Mr 17 1906

KEEDYSVILLE

ANTIETAM VALLEY record. *See under* Sharpsburg

ANTIETAM wavelet. *See* Antietam Valley record (Sharpsburg)

KENSINGTON

MONTGOMERY press. w N 16 1888+
pub Ag 16 1895+
MdBE [1930-34]+

LA PLATA

CRESCENT. 1893-Ja 14? 1898||
United with Port Tobacco times (Port Tobacco) to form Times-crescent

MARYLAND independent. w Jl 1? 1874+
1874-92? pub in Port Tobacco
pub [1874-99]+
MWA D 16 1892
MdBE N 18,D 9 1874;F 10,24,Mr 10,Ap 7,My 5 1875;F 20 1880;Ja 11 1884;F 26-Mr,D 3 1926; Ag 5 1927[30-31]D 22 1933-[34]

MARYLAND (*Continued*)

LA PLATA—*Continued*

TIMES-CRESCENT. w Ja 21 1898+
Formed by the union of Crescent and Port Tobacco times (Port Tobacco)
pub Ap 8 1898+
MdBE [1899-1900]-[08-12]-17;O 11 1918;Ap 25-My 2,O 3,N 21,D 5 1919;Jl 10 1925[26-28]-S 2 1932;Mr 17,Ap 7,21-Je 9,23-S 1,N 10 1933+

LAUREL

ADVERTISER. w Ag 28 1889-N 26 1890‖
MdBE 1889-Mr 5,19-Ap 16,30,N 26 1890

Laurel BEACON. w D 17 1858-
DLC D 24 1858

Laurel DEMOCRAT. w 1889-1931‖?
MdLL [1925-31]

LEADER. w S 17 1897+
pub 1897+
MdBE Ap 27-My 11,25,Je 22-O 5,19 1934+

LEONARD TOWN. *See* LEONARDTOWN

LEONARDTOWN

Leonard Town HERALD. w D 25 1839-
DLC D 25 1839

SAINT MARY'S beacon. w 1863+
1891-94 merged with Saint Mary's enterprise
MWA Jl 20 1876
MdBE Ap 27-My 4,18-25,Je 29-Jl,Ag 10 1934+
MdHi F 17 1898

SAINT MARY'S enterprise. w Mr 31 1882+
1891?-94? as St. Mary's enterprise and beacon
pub Mr 31 1882;F 7 1891;Ja 13 1894;1928+
MdBE My 26 1933+

LIBERTYTOWN

BANNER of Liberty. *See under* Woodsboro

LONACONING

ADVOCATE. w S 29? 1910-17‖
MdBE S 9,23 1915

GEORGES Creek press. w Je 28? 1898-1907‖?
MdBE Ag 20,S 5 1907

MANCHESTER

ENTERPRISE. *See under* Hampstead

Manchester GAZETTE. w O 14 1870-Mr 1872‖
NNHi O 21 1870

MECHANICSTOWN

Papers published in Mechanicstown are listed under Thurmont

MIDDLETOWN

CATOCTIN enterprise. w Jl 31 1841-47‖?
Title varies: Catoctin enterprise and Middletown valley gazette
DLC Jl 31,Ag 21 1841;S 17 1842
MdMV [1841-47]

CATOCTIN whig. *See* Valley register

VALLEY register. w Ag 2 1844+
1844-56? as Catoctin whig (F 1855 Catoctin whig and general advertiser)
pub 1844+
MdBE N 1922-F,Jl 13-S 21 1923;Jl 20 1934;35+

MOUNT AIRY

COMMUNITY reporter. w N 29 1929+
pub 1929+
MdBE 1929+

Mount Airy MESSENGER. m Mr 3 1916-N 1922‖
United with Sykesville herald to form Herald-messenger, later Sykesville herald (Sykesville)
MdBE Mr 3 1916
MdWJ 1916-Je 10 1922

MT. RAINIER

PRINCE Georgian. w S 15 1916?+
MdBE O 26,N 2 1934;Ap 26 1935

NEWTOWN. *See* POCOMOKE CITY

NORTH EAST

CECIL star. *See* Cecil county star (Elkton)

North-East RECORD. w D 21 1878-81‖
MdBE D 28 1878;Ja 4,F 8-15 1879;Jl 17,S 25 1880;D 17 1881

North East STAR. *See* Cecil county star (Elkton)

OAKLAND

DEMOCRAT. *See* Mountain democrat

GARRETT journal. w Je 5? 1897-1914‖?
MdBE Jl 4 1901[Ap 10 1902-Ag 13 1914]

MOUNTAIN democrat. w F 2? 1878+
1878-81? as Democrat
pub Ag 11 1898+
MdBE Je 13-27 1901[02-10]Jl 11,N 28 1912;Jl 3,Ag 7 1913[14]Ag 26 1915[17-22]F 8,22,Ap 19,My 3-10,24,Jl 12-19,Ag 1934+

REPUBLICAN. w Mr 3 1877+
pub 1877+
MdBE 1877-Mr 3,17-24 1888;Ap 20,N 2-9 1889; F 8,Ap 19,Jl 11 1890-99;Mr 29,My 10 1900;Ja 3,F 14 1901;Ap 24,Jl 3,24,Ag,S 11,N 20,D 4 1902;F 12,26-Mr 5,19,Ap 2-23,O 1,D 3,17 1903;F 4-11,Mr 24-Ap 14,28-My 5,19-Je 9,23 1904;Mr 9-16,My 4,Je 29,O 19,D 7 1905;Mr 8 1906+

OCEAN CITY

EASTERN SHORE times. *See under* Berlin

Berlin-Ocean City NEWS. *See under* Berlin

PERRYVILLE

Perryville RECORD. bw,w Ja 4 1893-1906‖?
MdBE Ja 4 1893;96-97
MdHi-H Je 16 1897

POCOMOKE CITY

To Ap 5 1878 as Newtown

EASTERN shoreman. w 1889-91‖
MdCrT complete

LEDGER-ENTERPRISE. w 1885-1920‖?
1885-96? as Peninsula ledger. United with Worcester democrat to form Worcester democrat and the ledger-enterprise
MdBE S 19-O 3 1891;Ag 20 1898;D 2 1899;Ja 20-Mr,Ap 14-Je 9,Jl 14-Ag,S 29-N 17,D 1 1900;Mr 16-Je 15,Jl-N 1901;Je 29 1907;Jl-D 1913;Jl-S 5,N 7,28 1914-15;Ja-Jl 19 1919

NEW TOWN record. *See* Record and gazette

NEWTOWN gazette. w O 1866-72‖?
United with Newtown record to form Record and gazette

NEWTOWN record and gazette. *See* Record and gazette

PENINSULAR ledger. *See* Ledger-enterprise

RECORD and gazette. w O 28? 1865-88‖?
1865?-O? 1871 as New Town record; O? 1871-N 7? 1874 Newtown record and gazette
MdBE Je 30 1866;N 1872-O 1873;O 1874-N 4 1876;O 27 1877-O 18 1879
MdPW O 3 1885

WORCESTER democrat and the ledger-enterprise. w 1898+
1898-1920? as Worcester democrat
pub 1922+
MdBE Ja 13 1906-08;My 18 1934+

WORCESTER enterprise. w 1894-96‖?
United with Peninsula ledger to form Ledger-enterprise

POINT LOOKOUT

HAMMOND gazette. w N 17 1862-63‖
DLC S 29,D 23 1863
MBAt N 17 1862;S 1-15,D 9-23 1863
MH [1863]
OClWHi D 9 1863
PCHi D 2 1863

PORT DEPOSIT

CALL. w 1886-89‖?
MdBE Ap 28 1887

CECIL whig and Port Deposit weekly courier. w Ag 8? 1835-36‖?
DLC My 7 1836
MdHi D 26 1835

CENTRAL courant and Port Deposit intelligencer. w Mr 29? 1833-N 1834‖?
MdBE Ap 18,25(supp)1834
MdHi-H Ja 3,24,Ap 11 1834

PORT TOBACCO

MARYLAND independent. *See under* La Plata

Port Tobacco TIMES, and Charles county advertiser. w Ap 18? 1844-Ja 14 1898‖
United with Crescent to form Times-crescent (La Plata)
DLC My 2 1844;S 21 1865
MdBE [Je 26 1845-Ap 17 1862;My 1868-98]
MdHi Ja 21 1847
NNHi Ap 5,19 1878
PP N 20 1850

PRESTON

Preston ECHO. w Jl 28? 1866-
MWA N 3 1866

PRINCE FREDERICK

CALVERT gazette. w Jl 25 1885+
pub 1885+
MdBE Jl-Ag 1,29-D 19 1885;86-O 22 1898;1900-01;Ja-S 19 1903;04;08+

CALVERT journal. w Jl 1867+
pub 1890+
MdBE S 23 1876-F 16 1878;F 1-15,Mr 29,Ap 12-19,My-Ag,S 13-20,O-D 13 1879;Ja 3-10,31-Mr 1880;Ap 1882-Ja 6,20,F 17-Mr,Ap 21-Jl 7,21-Ag 11,S 15-29,O 27 1883;84-N 3 1888;Ja 12-19,F-N 1889;90-94;D 30 1905-10;12-20;22;N 17 1934+

PRINCESS ANNE

EASTERN shore republican. w Ag 29 1928+
pub S 12 1928+
MdBE S 17 1935+

HERALD. *See* Somerset herald 1827-41

MARYLANDER. w Ja 2? 1866-Ag 2? 1898‖
1866?-81? as True Marylander. United with Somerset herald to form Marylander and herald
MdBE S 18 1877

MARYLANDER and herald. w Ag 9 1898+
Formed by the union of Marylander and Somerset herald
Je 16 1928 is 100th anniversary number
pub D 30 1913+
MdBE Ag 17 1915;Je 16 1928;30;32—

PEOPLE'S press. w O 4 1836-38‖?
DLC 1836-Ap 24 1838
MWA Ja 23-30 1838

SOMERSET herald. w Ap 3 1827-41‖?
1827-My 15 1838 as Village herald; My 22-Ag 28 1838 Herald
CSmH Jl 27 1830
DLC Ap 10 1827-My 8,22 1838-N 1840
MWA Je 3,17,31,O 23,N 6-13,D 18-25 1827;Je 17-24,29-Ag,S 16-23,O 14,N 11 1828;Je 8,29-Jl 6,20,Ag 24 1830;Ja 4,Je 7 1831;D 22 1835; Ja 26 1836;D 5 1837;Ag 13 1839;Mr 24 1840
MdHi Ag 17 1830;My 22 1838-Je 22 1841
MdPsM Ap 13 1841
Mi-U-C [1827-28;30]

SOMERSET herald. w Je 11? 1861-Ag 1898‖?
United with Marylander to form Marylander and herald
OOxM F 3 1874

SOMERSET iris and messenger of truth. w Je 13 1828-29‖?
DLC 1828-Ap 7 1829
MWA Ag 19 1828
MdPsM O 28 1828
NNHi Mr 31 1829

SOMERSET news. w Mr 25 1925+
pub 1925+
MdBE My 19 1934+

SOMERSET union. w Ap 15? 1856?-
MdBE Jl 3 1860

TRUE Marylander. *See* Marylander

VILLAGE herald. *See* Somerset herald 1827-41

QUEENSTOWN

Queenstown NEWS. w Ja 1 1882+
pub 1882+
MdBE Je 1934+

REISTERSTOWN

COMMUNITY news and Baltimore countian. w Ja 13? 1928+
1928-31 as Community news
pub 1928+
MdBE My 18,O 26 1934+

RIDGELY

CAROLINE sun. w Mr 15 1902+
pub Mr 20 1926+
MdBE S 1933;Ja 6,27-F 17,Mr 17,31-Ap 14,My-Jl,Ag 25,S 8-15,29,O 27 1934+

RISING SUN

HOME journal. *See* Midland journal

Rising Sun JOURNAL. *See* Midland journal

MIDLAND journal. w O 26 1878+
1878-Ap 17 1880 as Home journal; Ap 24 1880-Jl 1885 Rising Sun journal
pub N 1878-85;87;90+
MdBE S 16 1882[1907-13]-29;N 7-21 1930;32; My 25 1934+

ROCKVILLE

AMERICAN journal. w Jl 20? 1855?60‖?
MdBE Je 3 17 1859

Rockville JOURNAL and Montgomery county advocate. w Ja 7 1841?-55‖?
1841-44? as Maryland journal and museum of politics, agriculture and foreign literature; 1845?-52? Maryland journal
DLC Ag 6 1853;Ja 27 1855
MdBE F,Mr 27,Ap 10,24-My 8,22-Je 19,Jl 3,17,31,Ag 21,S 4-18,O 9 1844;F 25-Mr 12,Ap 2-9,30,My 28,Je 11-Jl 16,Ag 20-27,S 17,O 1-8, 22-29,N 19,D 3-10,31 1845-F 21,Je 13-Jl 18,Ag 29,S 12 1846

MARYLAND free press. w My 12 1830
CSmH Jl 14 1830
DLC Jl 19 1838

MARYLAND journal. w Ag 4 1825-35‖?
1828?-F 1834 as Maryland journal and true American
DLC 1825-26;O 10 1827;28;S 9,30 1829;30-F,Ap 9-D 1834
MWA Ag 11 1825;Ag 28 1833;Jl 20-27 1836
MdBE Jl 8 1835
MdHi D 2 1829

MARYLAND journal. 1841-52 *See* Rockville journal and Montgomery county advocate

MONTGOMERY advocate. w N 7? 1872-1927‖?
MdBE Ap 11 1878;S 13,N 8 1883;Ap 4 1890; Ap 23(supp)1897

MARYLAND (*Continued*)

ROCKVILLE—*Continued*

MONTGOMERY county sentinel. w Ag 11 1855+
pub Jl 29 1932+
DLC Mr 13 1833;Mr 15 1872
MdBE D 20 1872[78-93]-[1906-08]+
NcD Mr 17 1871

MONTGOMERY independent. w S 1927+
MdBE 1934+

NATIONAL union. w O 4 1861-
OCHi Ja 3 1862
OClWHi O 4 1861

TRUE American and farmers' register. w F 2 1820?-26||?
United with Maryland journal to form Maryland journal and true American, later Maryland journal (1825-35)
DLC Mr 13,24,Ap 7,My 28-Je 4,Ag 13 1824
MWA My 28 1824

ST. MICHAELS

St. Michaels COMET. w S 1? 1866+
1868-1925? as Comet and advertiser (My-Je? 1870 Weekly phenix) 1928?-29? New comet
MdBE D 1935+
MdHi D 22 1866;Ap 27 1867;Ja 4 1868;Jl 31 1869;My 14,Jl 16 1870;F 1,Jl 12 1879;Ag 23 1890;S 1 1891

COMET and advertiser. *See* St. Michaels comet

NEW comet. *See* St. Michaels comet

Weekly PHENIX. *See* St. Michaels comet

SALISBURY

Salisbury ADVERTISER and the Wicomico countian. w 1867+
1867?-75? as Salisbury advertiser; 1875?-1922? Salisbury advertiser and Eastern shoreman
pub Ja 23 1886;1928+
MdBE Ap 19 1934+
MdSW 1871-77
OOxM Ja 31 1874

ADVOCATE. *See* Wicomico countian

COURIER. *See* Wicomico countian

EASTERN shoreman. w Mr? 1868-75||?
United with Salisbury advertiser to form Salisbury advertiser and Eastern shoreman, later Salisbury advertiser and the Wicomico countian
Prospectus is dated F 1868
MdBE F 1868

MARYLAND tribune. *See* Wicomico countian

Salisbury SENTINEL. w O 1 1859-60||?
DLC N 5 1859;Ja 21,F 4 1860

Salisbury TIMES. d D 3 1923+
Title varies: Evening times
pub 1923+
MdBE Mr 13,Ap 16-Je 11 1934;D 27 1935+

WICOMICO countian. w Ap 19 1899-1922||
1899-Mr 1913 as Courier; My 3-Ag 8 1913 Advocate; Mr 1914-19? Maryland tribune. United with Salisbury advertiser to form Salisbury advertiser and the Wicomico countian

WICOMICO news. w My? 1886+
pub F 9 1899+
MdBE Ag 1908

SHARPSBURG

ANTIETAM VALLEY record. w S 3? 1887-1903||?
1887-90? as Antietam wavelet
1887-Ag? 1896 pub in Keedysville
MdBE My 26 1898;Jl 27 1899
MdHW 1887-S 5 1890;S 1895-D 5 1903

SILVER RUN

NEWS. w My? 1881-86||
MdHi My 15 1886

SILVER SPRING

MARYLAND news. w,sw Ag 25 1927+
Follows Takoma news (Takoma Park, D.C.)
sw D 1929-D 14 1934
pub 1927+
MdBE My 9,Je 8 1934+

SMITHSBURG

TRUMPET. w O 30 1852-
MdHW 1852-S 17 1853

SNOW HILL

BORDERER. w F 11 1834-
MdBE Ap 29-Je 24,Ag 19-S 9,23 1834;Ja 6-13,27-F 3,17-My 5,Je 23-Ag 4,18,S 1 1835

DEMOCRATIC messenger. w Ja 30 1869+
pub 1881-D 23 1882;85+
MdBE S 1 1928;Mr 30,S 14 1929;My 17 1930;Mr 7 1931;D 27 1932;F 27 1936+

Snow-Hill MESSENGER. w S? 1827-
Title varies: Snow-Hill messenger and Worcester county advertiser
DLC Ag-N 4 1828;O 25 1830-Mr 11 1834
MWA My 14 1832
MdBE S 13,N 8,D 14 1830;Ja 11,25-F 1 1831;Ja 21 1834
MdHi Je 25 1832

WORCESTER banner. w N 20? 1838-40||?
DLC N 10 1840
MdBE Jl 16-Ag 6,20,S 24-O 8,N 19,D 3 1839;Ja 21,Je 23 1840

WORCESTER county shield. w Ja 6? 1846-90||?
Title varies: Worcester county shield and farmer's manual; Worcester shield and spirit of the Whig press; etc.
MH Jl 27 1847
MWA D 20 1862
MdBE My 19,O 20 1846[47-58]Jl 27 1861;Ag 22 1863;Ag 11 1866;Je 29 1867;S 18 1880[81-88]
MdChK D 29 1846

WORCESTER shield. *See* Worcester county shield

WORCESTER sentinel, and farmers' and mechanics' shield. w O 16 1835-
MdBE O 23 1835;Mr 25,Jl 26 1836;Ap 18 1837

SPARROWS POINT

COMMUNITY press. *See* Community press and Baltimore countian (Dundalk)

Sparrow's Point TIMES. w F 21? 1890-95||?
MdBE My 30 1890

SYKESVILLE

Sykesville HERALD. w S 18 1913+
N 23 1922-Ja 15? 1931 as Herald-messenger
pub 1913+
MdBE Ag 5,S 16 1915;S 1925-Ag 1928;Ag 24 1933+

HERALD-MESSENGER. *See* Sykesville herald

TANEYTOWN

CARROLL record. w Jl 7? 1894+
pub Jl 1894+
MdBE 1910-33;My 11 1934+
MdHi F 19-26 1932

RECORDER. w 1832-My? 1833||
Follows Regulator and Taney Town herald. Followed by Carrolltonian, later American sentinel (Westminster)

REGULATOR and Taney Town herald. w My 12 1830-32||?
My?-Je 16? 1830 as Regulator. Followed by Recorder
CSmH Je 16 1830
DLC Ag 2,23 1831

THURMONT

To F 9 1894 as Mechanicstown

CATOCTIN clarion. w Mr 4? 1871+
pub Ap 1871+
MdBE S 28 1934+
MdHi Jl 26 1873
MdWJ Je 22 1872

MECHANICSTOWN family visitor. w Je? 1860-
MWA Ap 5 1861

TOWSON

AMERICAN. w S 18 1858-D 30 1864||
1858-Ag 13 1861? as Baltimore county American. United with Baltimore county advocate to form Baltimore county union, later Union news
MdBE N 13 1858;Ag 16 1861;Mr 21 1862;S 9-D 1864

AMERICAN register and Baltimore county weekly advertiser. w O 4? 1856-
MdBE Jl 18 1857

BALTIMORE county advocate. w F 24 1850-D 31 1864||
D 14 1850-My 12 1855 as Baltimore county advocate and general advertiser. United with American to form Baltimore county union, later Union news F 24-Ag 24 1850 pub in Baltimore; Ag 31 1850-My 6 1854 in Cockeysville
DLC F 18 1854-F 10 1855;F 13 1858-F 4 1860;64;S 4(extra)1858
IR F 8 1862-64
MdBE 1850-F 15 1851;F 21 1852-F 9,Je 1856-64
MdTJ Ap 8 1845;N 17 1855

BALTIMORE county American. *See* American

BALTIMORE county democrat. *See* Democrat and journal

BALTIMORE county free press. w Ap 10 1867-68||
MWA Mr 18 1868
MdBE My 15,Jl 24 1867

BALTIMORE county herald. w Mr 19 1870-S 1885||
Followed by Baltimore county democrat, later Democrat and journal
MdBE Ap 2,S 3 1870;Ja 13,F 17-O,N 9 1872-D 5 1873;Ja 10 1874

BALTIMORE county union. *See* Union news

DEMOCRAT and journal. w 1885-1914||?
Follows Baltimore county herald. 1885-1905? as Baltimore county democrat. Merged with Jeffersonian
MdBE S 29 1888-S,O 12-26 1889;O 1892-My 2 1896;O 1897-S 5,O 11 1902-S 19 1903;1912

JEFFERSONIAN. w D 30 1911+
pub 1911+
MdBE My 19 1933;Ja 19,F 23,Mr 30,My 25 1934+
MdHi-H O 9 1915

MARYLAND journal. w Ja 7 1865-1905||?
United with Baltimore county democrat to form Democrat and journal
DLC 1872-75;79-85;91-92;95-96;extra:My 4 1874
MdBE 1865-87;89-96;Ap 29 1897
MdHi Ap 5 1865;Mr 13 1869;Je 21 1879;Ja 5-12 1884 Ja 15 1887
OOxM Ja 31 1874

NEW ERA. w O 25 1913-N 19 1921||
Merged with Jeffersonian
MdBE complete

Towson NEWS. w Je 17 1905-Ag 28 1909||
United with Baltimore county union, to form Union news
MdBE complete

UNION news. w Ja 7 1865+
Formed by the union of Baltimore county advocate and American. 1865-Ag 1909 as Baltimore county union; S 4 1909-Je 8 1912 Baltimore county union, the Towson news
pub Ap 1930+
DLC Ja 7 1865
IR 1865-Ja 7 1866
MdBe 1865-68;D 18-25 1869[73-79]-1900;02-20;D 4 1931;Ag 12 1932;34+
MdHi [1868-81]My 29-30 1930
MdHi-H S 13 1919;S 13 1920;Ja 8,F 26,My 4,Jl 2 1921;Je 17 1922;O 9 1925
P-M Jl 21,N 10 1883;Mr 7 1885

UNION BRIDGE

CARROLL news. w My 20 1886-97||?
MdUnP My 20 1886-Ag 1897

PILOT. w N 3 1899+
pub O 2 1908+
MdBE S 21 1934+
MdHi Je 14 1929;F 19 1932

UNIONTOWN

STAR of federalism. *See under* Frederick

UPPER MARLBORO

Marlboro' BANNER and weekly advertiser. w Mr 23? 1833-
DLC Ag 10 1833

COMMUNITY spirit of southern Maryland. w 1930-36||
MdBE Ap 26 1935;Ag 16-30,S 21-O 5,18,N 1-15,D 6-27 1935;Ja 24,F 14 1936

ENQUIRER-GAZETTE. w F 6 1924+
Formed by the union of Prince George's enquirer and Marlboro gazette and Prince George's advertiser
pub 1924—
MdBE Ap 27-My 4,18,Je 1,29 1934+

Marlboro' GAZETTE and Prince George's advertiser. w Jl 7 1836-Ja 1924||?
Title varies: Marlboro gazette and Prince George's county advertiser; Marlboro's gazette and Prince George's advertiser. United with Prince George's enquirer to form Enquirer-gazette
DLC Jl 7 1836
MdBE Ap 22,My 6,20-Je 10,Jl 15,Ag 12 1841; Mr 30 1843;Ag 1851-Jl 5 1854;Mr 30 1864;Mr 8 1865 Ja 1 1868;Mr 24 1869;Mr 18 1885;Mr 9,Jl 6 1887;Je 6,Ag 1 1888
VHi Ap 12-19,Jl 5 1899

PLANTERS advocate. w S 3 1851-61||?
1851-Ag 31 1853 as Planters' advocate and Southern Maryland advertiser
MdBE S 1853-N 22 1854;Ag 1860-O 16 1861
MdUE 1851-F 15 1860

PRINCE GEORGE'S enquirer. w 1883?-Ja 1924||
Follows Prince Georgian. D 22 1883?-D 2 1898? as Prince Georges enquirer and Southern Maryland advertiser. United with Marlboro' gazette and Prince George's advertiser to form Enquirer-gazette
MdUE D 22 1893-1924

PRINCE GEORGIAN. w 1862-82||
Followed by Prince George's enquirer
DLC S 3 1865
MdBE Je 6 1862;Mr 24 1865;N 26 1869-Mr 18, Ap-My 11,Je 10-24? 1870

WALKERSVILLE

GLADE VALLEY times. w N 3-D 15? 1933||
MdBE N 24-D 15 1933

WESTMINSTER

AMERICAN sentinel. w Je 25? 1833-1928||?
Follows Recorder. 1833-54? as Westminster Carrolltonian (Je 1845-Mr? 1848 Carrolltonian)
MWA S 30 1839
MdBE Je 8 1906
MdHi D 12 1835;N 18 1836[37;39-41;43-45;47-50;52-63;65-71]Jl 8-15 1876;Ap 16 1887
MdWJ 1850;56-60;62;65-72;74-87;89-1928
PP N 14 1850

AMERICAN trumpet. *See* Carroll county democrat

CARROLL county democrat. w F 1838-My? 1862||
1838-Mr? 1846 as Democrat and Carroll county republican; N 16 1854-My 31 1855 American trumpet. Followed by Western Maryland democrat
MdHi Ag 9,S 20 1838;Ag 7 1845;Mr 1,My 31 1855;My 13 1858;N 10 1859
MdWA Mr 31 1842-61
MdWJ 1857
PP N 14 1850

MARYLAND (*Continued*)

WESTMINSTER—*Continued*

CARROLL county democrat. w F 10 1887-
DLC O 27 1887
MdHi Ap 14 1887
MdWJ 1887

CARROLLTONIAN. 1833-54 *See* American sentinel

CARROLLTONIAN. w F 19? 1887-93||?
MdHi Ja 12 1889
MdWJ 1888-91;93

DEMOCRAT and Carroll county republican. *See* Carroll county democrat 1838-62

DEMOCRATIC advocate. w N 22? 1865+
pub 1865+
MdBE Ap 6 1901;S 24 1915;My 25 1934+
MdHi My 29 1875;Jl 15,Ag 19 1876;Ag 31 1878;Ag 30 1879;Ja 2 1886;Ap 16 1887;Jl 11 1891
MdWJ 1865-72;76-89;91-1906;08-16;19-21;23-24;26;28
OClWHi Je 28 1866
OOxM Ja 31 1874

HEAD-LIGHT. w D 17? 1887-89||
MdHi My 4 1889

REPUBLICAN citizen. *See* New citizen (Frederick)

TIMES. w O 6 1911+
pub O 6 1911+
MdBE Mr 23,O 5 1934+
MdHi F 19 1932
MdWJ 1913-16

WESTERN Maryland democrat. w Je 1862?-Ap 15 1865||
Follows Carroll county democrat
MdHi N 12 1863;Mr 2 1865
MdWA complete

WILLIAMS PORT. *See* WILLIAMSPORT

WILLIAMSPORT

MODERN times. *See* Times and journal

POTOMAC sentinel. w Ap 14? 1849-51||?
1849-F 20? 1851 as Clearspring sentinel (Clearspring)
DLC O 27 1849
MdHF N 3,D 15,29 1849;Ja 5,19,My 18,Je 1,Jl 27,Ag 10,23-S 6,O 11,25-N 7,21,D 19 1850;Ja 30,F 20,Je 12,Ag 1 1851

REPUBLICAN banner. w Ja 2 1830-
DLC Ja 2-9 1830;O 13 1832
ICHi Ag 2 1830-35
IU Ag 4,25 1838
MdHW Ja 22,S 17 1842
MdHi 1830-37;Ag 29 1840;My 8 15 1841
MnHi [1845]

TIMES and journal. w,sw F 7 1846-
F 7-Je 17? 1846 as Modern times; Je 24-Ag 26? 1846 Modern times and home journal
MdHW Mr 21 1846-Ap 11 1856
MdHi Je 24,Ag 5,26 1846
MnHi F 14,Ap 11 1846;My 8 1847

WOODBERRY

Papers published in Woodberry are listed under Baltimore

WOODSBORO

BANNER of liberty. w F 1850-1910||?
1850-1901? pub in Libertytown
MdBE S 17 1896-S 1901
MdHi F 25 1910
NcD Je 13 1856

MASSACHUSETTS

ABINGTON

Abington ADVERTISER. w 1890+
pub 1906+

Abington HERALD. w Jl 11 1884-My? 1885||
United with Plymouth county journal to form Plymouth county journal and Abington herald, later Abington journal herald (Whitman)
MWA Jl 11 1884

Weekly NEWS. w
MHi [1878-79]

PLYMOUTH county journal and Abington herald. *See* Abington journal herald (Whitman)

Abington STANDARD and Plymouth county advertiser. w O 6 1854-
MWA Jl 6 1855

ACTON

Acton ENTERPRISE. w 1884+
MWA Ap 19 1895

MIDDLESEX recorder. ir
MCheHi Ag 29 1885
MHi Ap 18 1885

MIDDLESEX recorder. ir 1894-
MWA Ap 19 1895

Acton MONITOR. w N 9 1882-
MH D 21 1882

ADAMS

Adams FREEMAN. w 1875-1907||?
1875-84? as Saturday freeman
MH Ag 6 1903

ALLSTON

Papers published in Allston are listed under Boston

AMESBURY

Evening CHRONICLE. w Ap 11-Ag 29 1833||
Follows New England chronicle. Ap-My 1833 as Amesbury chronicle
MAm Ap 18-Ag 1833
MSaE Ap 25 1833
MWA complete;extra:N 1832
MnHi Ap 18 1833

Morning COURIER. w Mr 6 1835-Ag 2 1839||
Mr-Ap 10 1835 as Evening courier; N 23 1837-Je 21 1838 News and courier. Followed by Transcript, later Essex transcript
Also dated in Salisbury Mills, Mass., and Portsmouth, N.H.
Ct My 8 1835
DLC S 30 1836;Ag 4,O 6,D 7 1837;Jl 26,Ag 2 1839
MAm Mr 25 1836-F 17,Mr 10-O 1837
MSaE Mr 13 1835[36]Jl 28,Ag 18 1837[38-39]
MWA Mr 13,27,Ap 17 1835-N 3(extra)23 1837-Ag 2 1839
N D 11 1835
NcD [Ap 1835-F 1836]
NhHi [D 21 1837-My 10 1838]

Amesbury DAILY. *See* Amesbury daily news

ESSEX transcript. w Ag 9 1839-Mr 1849||
Follows Morning courier. 1839-40 as Transcript; 1840-42 Village transcript. Followed by Villager
DLC D 1847-48
MAm F 21 1840-N 11 1842
MHi D 7 1842
MSaE [1839-49]
MWA Ag 9,23,D 27 1839;Ap 17,Ag 14 1840;Je 25 1846;My 13,S 16,30,D 16 1847;Mr 2,Je 8 1848
NhD F 2,My 31 1844

LIBERTY'S advocate. ir S 19 1843-
Campaign paper
DLC O 21 1843
MSaE S 19,O 7 1843;O 23,30 1846
MWA O 7,N 9 1843

MERRIMAC journal. w Mr 2 1872-81||?
MAm Mr 2-9 1872
MSaE [1872-81]
MWA Ap 19-My 3 1879

MERRIMAC VALLEY echo. w
MAm Ja-My 1916;D 17 1917

MERRIMAC VALLEY times. w S 1916-
MAm S-D 1916

NEW ENGLAND chronicle. w Ja 28? 1831-Mr? 1833||
Followed by Amesbury chronicle, later Evening chronicle
Ct Jl 12 1832
MAm Ja 28 1832-Ja 17 1833
MSaE Ap 12 1832
MWA My 31,N 1 1832
MnHi Je 21,O 25 1832

Amesbury NEWS. w Ap 2 1881-1904||?
1881-83 as Weekly news
MAm 1881-Mr 23 1888
MSaE [1882-99]
MWA Ap 20,Ag 3 1883;O 22 1886;Je 16,Jl 7,28 1899

Amesbury daily NEWS. d My 5 1888+
pub My 6 1888+
Ct Mr 4 1920
M Ja 29 1891[1928-Jl 1933]
MAm 1889-1927
MSaE F,Ag 20 1891[95-98]1900-[20-23]
MWA F 4-6,8,11,13-14,16,26,Mr 8,16,26,Ap 11,My 27,31,Jl 3,5,S 27- 1895;Ja 11,22,Jl 31 1896;Ja 29,F 10,Mr 10,26,Jl 26,S 7,O 12,D 7,10,14-15,31 1898;Je 3 1911;Ap 1,D 12 1916

NEWS and courier. 1837-38 *See* Morning courier

TRANSCRIPT. *See* Essex transcript

VILLAGE transcript. *See* Essex transcript

VILLAGER. w Ap 12 1849-1904||?
Follows Essex transcript. Title varies: Amesbury and Salisbury villager
dated also in Salisbury
DLC O 10 1850;Ja 7,21,Mr 11 1858;D 6-13 1860
MAm 1849-91
MBAt Je 24 1852;N 13 1856;Mr 4,D 2 1858;Mr 3,My 5,Jl 28,S 29,N 3 1859;Ja 19,N 15 1860;Ja 3-10 1861;Ap 24,My 8,O 23 1862;D 29 1864;My 4 1865;Ap 5,O 25 1866;Ag 8,S 12-26 1867;Mr 5,N 5 1868;D 2,30 1869;F 24 1870;Ap 6,Je 15,S 7,28 1871;N 28 1872;Mr 13,My 1,N 13 1873;F 18,Mr 4 1875;F 6 1879
MSaE [1849-50]-[52-57]-[63-70]-[79-81;83-91;95-1901]
MWA Jl 19 1849;F 14,Ap 25,O 24 1850[Mr-O 9 1851]F 12[Ap 29-D 9 1852]Ap 21,Je 16 1853;Ag 24,S 7,21,O 12 1854;F 1,Ag 2,O 18,N 1,22 1855;Ja 10,Ag 14,O 30 1856[57]-[63-73]-[75]F 24,Mr 2,23,My 25,Je 1 1876;Ap 26,N 1,29 1877;Je 16,Jl 7,21-28,Ag 18 1887;Mr 15,Jl 12-19,O 25,N 15 1888;Ja 24,F 14,Mr 7,My 16 1895;F 27,My 28,Jl 2 1896;O 21 1897;S 1 1898;F 2,My 18,Ag 3-10 1899;Ap 19,My 24,Jl 26 1900
MiU-C My 6 1852;Jl 16 1863
NNHi Ja 10 1850;Mr 13 1873
NcD Ap 14 1864

AMHERST

Daily EXPRESS. d Ap 20 1862-
MAJ [Ap 23-Jl 16 1862]
MBAt Ap 21 1862

Amherst GAZETTE and family miscellany. w Ja 24 1840-
ICHi F 7-Ap 17 1840

HAMPSHIRE and Franklin express. *See* Amherst record

HAMPSHIRE express. *See* Amherst record

Amherst MAIL POUCH. w 1870||
MAJ Jl-D 1870

NEW ENGLAND inquirer. w D 1 1826-N 13 1828||
DLC My 11 1827;Ja 17,My 15,29,Je 19 1828
MAJ [N 22 1827-N 6 1828]
MBC N 29 1827-28
MDeHi D 29 1826;Mr 9,30 1827
MWA Ja 26,N 22-D 6,20 1827[Ja-O 23 1828]
NNHi [N 22 1827-28]
NjHi N 22 1827-28

Amherst RECORD. w S 13 1842+
1842-Je? 1866 as Hampshire and Franklin express; Jl? 1866-Ap 30 1868 Hampshire express
pub Mr 30 1904+
DLC S 27 1844;Ja 12 1846;Ja 14 1847;Je 22 1849
M Ap 1933+
MAJ Ap 11 1845-Ag 1848;50-61;My 1866-Mr 23 1904;Mr 1925+
MDeHi Ag 1 1867
MH Mr 21 1862;Jl 25,Ag 15 1883
MNF [S 13 1844-Jl 11 1856]
MWA D 13 1844[45]O 15 1846[47-48;50-53]Ja 6 1854;Ap 15,29 1859;Ag 9 1860;Jl 12 1861;Jl 10 1863;Ja 6 1864;Jl 11 1864;Ag 27 1868;N 9 1870[Ja-Jl 1871]S 3 1879;Ag 17 1881[91]-94;O 19 1910+
MiU-C [1847]Ag 12 1853
NNHi Ap 19,My 3 1850
NcD Je 11-18,Jl 2,16-30 1852;Ag 25 1854;Ja 25,Mr 8 1871
OClWHi S 7 1865
P-M N 14 1845;Ja 28 1853;Mr 13 1857

Amherst TRANSCRIPT. w S 18 1877-79||
MWA S 18-25 1877;My 6 1879

ANDOVER

Andover ADVERTISER. w F 19 1853-F 10 1866||
United with Lawrence American to form Lawrence American and Andover advertiser (Lawrence)
DLC 1853-F 10 1855;F 27 1858;Ag 20 1864;N 10-17,D 1-8,22 1860
MBeHi 1853-60
MH D 24 1864;F 25 1865
MHi S 3 1853;Ja 6,F 3,17,S 15 1855;F 23 1856;F 14 1857;S 8,O 6 1860]Ja 12,Je 8,O 26 1861;Ja 4,D 27 1862;F 7,Je 27,Ag 29,N 7 1863
MSaE [1853-57]-66
MWA Ja 6-13,27,My 12 1855;N 13 1858;Je 18 1859;Ap 4,Ag 15 1863

Andover REGISTER. w 1867-69||
Mi My 1 1867

Andover TOWNSMAN. w O 14 1887+
pub 1887+
M 1887+
MAn 1887+
MBAt D 20 1895
MH Mr 30,O 19 1888-S 1889
MHi 1887-My 20 1921
MSaE 1887-1931
MWA F 17 1888;Ja 18-25 1889
MWo O 19 1888-S 1889
OClWHi Ja 18 1889
See also North Andover

ARLINGTON

Arlington ADVOCATE. w D 30 1871+
MAr 1871+
MWA My 3 1879;Jl 30 1881;Mr 16 1883;Ap 27,My 4 1928
MWo Mr 11 1898

Arlington INDEPENDENT. w Je 30 1922-29||?
MWA Ag 17-31,S 21 1923

Arlington NEWS. w,d 1914+
w 1914-31?
pub Ap 1932+
MAr My 1932+

STANDARD and advertiser. w
MWbHi Je 13,O 29 1856;F 4-11,Ap 15,My 20, Je 17,Jl 22,N 11 1859;Mr 21 1863

ASHBY

Ashby evening GAZETTE. d D 22 1869-
MH D 22 1869

MASSACHUSETTS (*Continued*)

ASHLAND

Ashland ADVERTISER. w Ag 27 1869-1914‖?
MWA Jl 23,O 29 1870;Jl 1 1871

ASSONET

Assonet REPORTER and Freetown advertiser. w Ag 5 1870-71‖
MWA Je 17 1871

ATHOL

Athol CHRONICLE. w Ja 24 1866-S 1935‖
1866-1908? as Worcester west chronicle; 1909-29? Athol and Worcester west chronicle
Ja 24-N 19 1866 pub in Barre
M S 23 1932
MAt 1866-1920
MAtN 1930-34
MHi Je 20 1912
MWA Ja 24,F 28-Mr 7,S 26 1866;F 19,Ap 8, Jl 8 1868;O 12 1870;Je 3 1875;Je 29,Jl 13-20, Ag 3 1876-Je 3 1880;Mr 2 1882;O 16 1884;Ja 6 1916

FREEDOM'S sentinel. w D 18 1827-
MDeHi Ja 1 1828
MWA 1827[28]Ja 19,Je 29,Ag 24 1829

Athol daily NEWS and transcript. d N 1 1934+
1934-S 19 1935 as Athol daily news
pub 1934+
MAt 1934+

Athol TRANSCRIPT. w 1871-S 1935‖
United with Athol daily news to form Athol daily news and transcript
M [Mr 1931-F 8 1933]
MAtN complete
MWA Je 24 1873;O 24 1876;D 9 1879;N 4 1884; Je 15 1886-D 1889;Mr 11 1890;Jl 28 1891;92-Ja 1893;S 28 1909
NN Je 18-S 3,17-O 15 1872

WORCESTER west chronicle. *See* Athol chronicle

ATTLEBORO

Attleboro ADVOCATE. w Mr 27 1875-94‖?
CtY D 16 1882
MAtt Mr 27 1875;My 31 1884;F 20,Ag 21 1886
MWA Je 25 1881

Attleboro CHRONICLE. w 1871-77‖?
CtY [1872-83]
MAtt F 1873;S 12 1874;Jl 4,O 14 1876;F 1 1883

Attleboro SUN. d S 3 1889+
Title varies: Daily sun; Attleboro daily sun
pub 1902+
M [O 4 1919-Je 8 1933]
MAtt N 16 1893;F 23,Mr 12-13,19,Je 16,O 9, 11,16-20 1894;S 7 1897;Mr 17-18 1898;Ag 3,7,S 3,5 1901;02+
MH Ja 6 1915
See also North Attleboro

AYER

Ayer ADVERTISER. sm
MHi Ag 15 1906

CITIZEN. sw
MHi D 17 1895;Ja 10,F 4-18 1896

Ayer EXPRESS. w
MHi Jl 4-S 12 1890

JUNCTION journal. w O 30 1885-
MHi N 5 1885
MWA D 11 1885

Ayer NEWS and times. w Ag 28 1907-S 7 1925‖
1907-21? as Ayer news
MAy complete
MHi Je 1 1911;Ja 8 1915;F 11 1916
MLa D 30 1922-Ja 2 1924

PEPPERELL clarion-advertiser. *See under* East Pepperell

PUBLIC spirit. *See* Turner's public spirit

Ayer REPORTER. d
MHi Mr 14-15 1883

Ayer SENTINEL. w 1879-80‖?
MHi O 7 1880

TURNER'S public spirit. w My 13 1869+
My-Je 10 1869 as Public spirit; Je 17 1869-My 1871 Weekly public spirit; Je 1871-F 1 1872 Groton public spirit; F 8 1872-F 6 1875 Public spirit
1869-Ja 11? 1872 pub in Groton
pub 1869+
CtY Ja 1 1874
DLC O 20 1883-O 11 1884;O 16 1886-O 8 1887;N 30 1895
MAy 1869+
MBAt Jl 5 1872;Ja 1,N 19-26 1874;Ap 3,Jl 10 1875;N 9 1878;My 15,Ag 7,28,D 18 1880;Ja 15,O 8,N 19,D 17 1881
MCheHi N 24 1883
MH My 13-S,N 4,D 9 1869[70-71]-O 18 1884; F 1886-Ja 13 Jl 20,O 8 1887;F 8 1890;S 30 1893;Jl 7-14,D 8,22 1928;Ja 5,F 2,23,Ag 31 1929;D 2 1933
MWA My-Je 3,17-S 1869;Jl 28,Ag 11-O 13 1870;Je 1,Jl 13,S 21 1871-[72-76]-[78-79]-[81]-83;F-Ap 17,My 1886-O 8 1887
MiU-C My 13-Je 3 1869
NcD D 19 1872
OClWHi Ap 3,My 1 1880

BARNSTABLE

BARNSTABLE county express. w 1825-
MWA Je 2? 1826

Barnstable JOURNAL, and county advertiser. w S 17? 1828-
MSanHi D 6 1832
MWA S 24 1829;Ap 19,Ag 30 1832;O 2 1834

Barnstable PATRIOT. *See under* Hyannis

BARRE

Barre GAZETTE. w My 20 1834+
DLC D 27 1839;Mr 13 1840;O 25(extra)1852
ICHi F 19 1836
MBa [1834-59]+
MDeHi Je 7 1839
MWA Je 5,N 27 1835;F 12,Ap 8-15,My 6,Ag 5,S 30,O 7 1836;F 17,Ap 14,My 12,N 24,D 29 1837;Ja 19-F 2,16-23,Ap 6,20-27,N 2 1838;Ja 18,Je 7 1839;S-O 16 1840;Ap 9-30 1841;Jl 22 1842;F 24,N 17-D 1,15-22 1843;My 10,Je 14-21 1844;F 14 1845;Ja 30,F 13,27,Mr 27 1846;N 12 1847;Mr 9 1849;Ag 23 1850;O 3 1851;My 26 1854;D 14 1855;N 2,D 21-28 1860;Mr 8,22, Ap 5,19-26 My-Je 21 1861;My 23,Jl 18-25,Ag 22,S-D 12,26 1862-Jl 21,Ag 18-O 6 1927;My 1928+
NcD F 10 1882
OClWHi N 24 1865
P-M N 28 1845;Je 30 1854

Barre PATRIOT. w Jl 26 1844-
DLC Ag 2 1844;Jl 20 1849-Jl 9 1852
MB Jl 23,Ag 6 1847;F 16,Mr 9,30,Jl 27,Ag 3, 31 1849[50-Ag 22 1851]
MH My 16 1851
MWA [1845]Ja 23-30,F 27,Je 5,Jl 10,N 13,27-D 4 1846;Jl 21 1848-Jl 12 1850;Ja 10,F 21-Je,Jl 11,25-N,D 12-26 1851;52-Mr 18,Ap-Jl 8,22,Ag 19-26,S 9-16,O 21-28,N 11-D 1853;Ja 13-F 3,17-Mr 10,24,Ap 7-14,28-My 12,Je 2-9,23 1854
NcD Jl 26,Ag 9,23-30 1844
NjR Mr 16 1849
P-M Ja 31 1855

WORCESTER west chronicle. *See* Athol chronicle (Athol)

BELCHERTOWN

HAMPSHIRE sentinel and farmers' and manufacturers' journal. w N 22 1826-
CSmH S 8 1830
Ct [1827]S 2 1828
MBAt N 21 1827
MBelHi 1826-My 4 1831
MDeHi Ag 20 1828
MHi Mr 21 1827
MWA D 27 1826;S 19 1827;F 4 1829
MiU-C N 29 1826;Mr 31 1829
P-M Mr 7 1827

Belchertown SENTINEL. w Ap 1 1915+
pub 1915+
MBel 1916+
MHi Je 27,Jl 25 1923

BELMONT

Belmont CITIZEN. w Mr 29 1919+
pub 1919+
M 1919+
MBelm 1919+

Belmont COURIER. w Ja 2 1889-
MBelm Ja 2,16,F 13,27-Jl 10,31-Ag,S 11,25-N 6,20-D 25 1889

Belmont COURIER. w 1914-D 29 1917‖?
MBelm 1914-Je 3,17,D 30 1916-D 1 1917
MBelmHi 1914-17

Belmont PATRIOT. w Ja 5-D 28 1918‖
M complete
MBelm complete
MH complete

Belmont TRIBUNE. w 1902-16‖?
MBelm N 14 1902-12
MH D 5 1908;My 22-Je 26 1915

Belmont WHIG. w Mr 1 1890-97‖
MBelm Mr 8,22-My 3,17,Je 14,Jl-S 6,20,O 4-11, N 1,15 1890-Ap 4,18-My,Je 27-Jl 4,18-O 10, 24,N-D 5,19 1891-Jl 23,Ag 13-20,S-O 1,15-N,D 10 1892-S 1 22,O 6,N 17-D 1 1894;Ja-Je 15, 29-Ag 3,17 1895-Ja 18,F-Jl 18,Ag-D 1896;Ja 16-Jl 24,Ag 14-O 9,23,N 6,20 1897

BEVERLY

Saturday morning CITIZEN. w 1851-1923‖?
1851-1900? as Beverly citizen
DLC O 13,27,N 10-24 1858[59]Ap 14,N 3,D 8-15 1860;Je 7 1862;Ja 26,Jl 13,O 5 1861;Ja 10,D 25 1863;O 24 1864;Ja 7,28,F 18,Ap 1-8 1865;Ap 21-D 15 1866;Ja 5-12,F 2,Mr 16 1867; S 1886-F 24 1893
M Mr 5 1892
MBe [1868-71]-[73-79]-[81-83]-[85-88]89
MBeHi 1851-1910
MH Ja 25,Mr 1,Ap 5-12,26-My 3 1862
MHi Mr 5 1892
MSaE 1851-[53-54;58-66]-[84-88]-1918
MWA N 24,D 29 1860;Je 7,O 5,26 1861;Je 28 1862;O 10 1863;Ja 2,Jl 23-Ag 20,S 17,O 8,N 19, D 3 1864;F 25,Ap 29 1865;O 30 1875;Je 21,O 25 1879;Je 5 1880;Je 30 1883;Mr 13-20,My 29,N 27-D 11 1886
NcD Je 28 1862

ORACLE. w
MSaE Mr 12 1868
OClWHi Mr 12 1868

Beverly RECORD. w
MSaE Je 23-Jl 14 1881

Beverly TIMES. w 1882-1902‖?
pub Je 1887-O 1893
MSaE [1882-88;93;95;97]99-[1902]
MWA My 31,Je(supp)1893

Beverly evening TIMES. d O 5 1893+
pub 1893+
M Mr 1917+
MSaE [1893;99]-1931

BEVERLY FARMS

Beverly Farms ADVOCATE. w Ja 1 1887-88‖
MBAt [1887-88]
MH F 25 1888
MHi D 24 1887
MSaE [1887-88]

BLACKSTONE

Blackstone CHRONICLE. w F 26-S 2 1848‖
DLC F 26,Je 3,Jl 29 1848
MHi S 2 1848
NN complete

BOSTON

ADOPTED citizen. sw Jl 26? 1842-50‖?
United with American celt to form American celt and adopted citizen
MWA Ag 17 1842

*Boston semi-weekly ADVERTISER. w,sw Ag 2 1768-1876‖
1768-My 2 1775 as Essex gazette; My 12 1775-Ap 4 1776 New England chronicle, or Essex gazette; Ap 25-S 12 1776 New England chronicle; S 19 1776-My 29 1817 Independent chronicle (N 7 1776-D 17 1801 Independent chronicle and the universal advertiser) Je 4 1817-My 23 1840 Independent chronicle and Boston patriot
1768-My 2 1775 pub in Salem; My 12 1775-Ap 4 1776 in Cambridge
Prospectus dated Jl 5 1768
w 1768-Ag 16? 1793
CSmH Ag 14 1830
Ct O 11 1826;Mr 20 1833;Ap 16 1834[35-38]
CtY Ag 20 1828-Mr 21,Je 17,D 23 1829;Mr 6 1830
DLC [J-Ap,Ag-D 1821]Je 4,Jl 6 1822;F 1823-Ag 1824;Mr 12,S 24 1825;O 14-21 1826;F 24,My 26 1827-My 3,Ag 9 1828;Ja-My,O-D 1829;Ja 23-30,Ap 24,Je 30,Jl 21,Ag 4 1830;O 26 1831; F 1832-My 23,Je 27-Jl 4 1840;My 6 1846;Ap 16 1851-Je-Ag 26 1863;Je 19 1875
ICU S 28 1850;N 8,26 1851;Ja 3,14 1852
IU D 13 1834
KHi Ja 1 1832-Ag 16 1837
M 1821-Je 1828
MB [1821-My 23 1840;Je 1845-N 1844]Mr 30 1845-D 30 1848[Ja 20 1849-Ap 19 1865]Mr 31 1869
MBAt 1821-My,Jl 6,10 1822;O 29 1823;F 21 1824;25[26]My 9 1827;Je 16 1830;S 17,N 30,D 28-31 1831;My 21 1836-[39]
MC 1821-39;62-64
MDeHi O 12 1844
MH 1821-S 1823;My 31 1826-50;52-54;56-58;My 21 1859-D 3 1860;Ja 27 1866
MHi 1821-22[25-38]42-43;F 3 1844[46-48;50-51; 59-66]Je 16 1869
MMarHi 1824;Ja 16 1836
MNaHi Mr 24 1841;Ja 26 1867
MNb 1823-30
MSaE [1832]-[34]Je 13-30,Ag 15,18,S 12,29 1838;39[40]
MWA Ja 3-My 5,Je 9,16,27,Jl 18,Ag 11-18 1821;My 29,Jl 10,S 21,O 12-N 20,D 7-18 1822; 23-[26]Ja 31,F 3,O 17,N 10 1827[F 20-D 1828]-Ja 16 1830[31]-[My 27-D 1840]-Ag 23 1872;Ag 22 1873;Je 19 1875;S 7 1877
MWo O 27 1869
MiU-C [1821-27;29-34;36;51;61;63]
N Jl 25 1821-25;Ap 1 1826;27;Mr 1,Jl 23 1828; 29-35;39;O 27 1852
NN Je 26 1833
NNC 1827-28
NNHi Mr 6 1824;32-39
NcD Mr 27,Ag 11 1824;Ap 17,S 25,O 9,30 1833;Ja 18-29,Mr 22,My 17-24 Ag 23-30,O 25 1834;Jl 11,S 30,D 23-30 1835;F 20,Je 4,Jl 9,28 1836;My 4 1839;F 20,Mr 10,Ap 14 1841;Ja 23 1850;Ja 4,Je 1854;O 10 1855;Ja 19 1856;N 9 1861;Ap 4 1863;Je 15,18 1864;F 15,Mr 18,O 7 1865
NhD My 14 1823-Mr 19 26-O 25,N 16-D 1825; F 15-13,Mr-Ap 22,29-Ag 26,S 9,13,20,30 1826-N 5,12-27 1828[29]30[My 1840-41]-Ja 5,15 1842;Je 11,S 24-O 1,15-25,N-D 1851;D 25 1852;Ap 9 1859;N 10 1860;Mr 15,29,Je 5,Jl 20-24,S 11,O 19-23,30-N 9 1861
OClWHi Ag 13 1864;Mr 11,Ap 12 1865
P-M Ap 20 1831
PPL [Jl-O 1826]
Vt 1867
VtU 1846-69;Ag 3,24-27,O 22 1870;F 25,O 25,D 9-31 1871
WHi 182?-Ja 20 1827;28;32-39;41-Ja 1843;D 1,8,22-29 1876

*Boston ADVERTISER. sw,tw Jl 6 1803-D 31 1831‖
1803-Ja 21 1804 as New-England repertory (Newburyport); F 3 1804-Je 28 1811 Repertory; Jl 2 1811-My 23 1827 Repertory and general advertiser
1803-Ja 21 1804 pub in Newburyport
sw 1803-F 1813
Ct [1826-27]Mr 27 1828;O 20 1831
DLC Mr 28 1822-24;F 11,Mr 18,25-30,Ap 4-22,Jl 20,N 4,D 7 1826;27;Je 17 1828[29]-Je 1831
MB 1821-My 22 1827;28-29
MBAt Jl 24 1821;Ap 9,20 1822;O 7 1824;My 27 1828 Mr 18 1830
MH Ap 2? 1825;30-31
MHi Mr 30 1822;Je 12 1823;Ap 6 1824

MASSACHUSETTS (*Continued*)

BOSTON—*Continued*

*Boston ADVERTISER. sw,tw 1803-31‖—*Cont.*
MSaE Ja 9,13,23-25,F 6-15,Mr 8,28 1821
MWA [1821]-My 24[29-D 1827]-31
NNHi 1821-S 1824;25-31
NcD F 11 1830;Ja 6 1831
NhD S 25 1821;My 30-Je 1 1822;Ja 29-31,N 6-11,23,D 21 1824;Ja 11,Mr 15-22,26,31,Ap 12-16,21-23,28,My 3-5,13-17,Je 23,Jl 7,19,Ag 9-16 1823;Ja 12,My 4 1826;F 10,My 10 1827
OClWHi Jl 29,Ag 3 1826

*Boston weekly ADVERTISER. w O 25 1811-1901‖?
1811-Ja 16 1861 as Boston weekly messenger (Mr 1 1832-Je 6 1833 Boston weekly messenger and Massachusetts journal; Ja 23 1861-D 5 1867 Boston daily advertiser. Weekly issue; D 12 1867-F 4 1869 Thursday spectator and Boston weekly advertiser; F 11? 1869-D 28 1871 Boston weekly spectator
CSmH 1821-Mr 13 1834;Mr 17 1836
CtY S 1862-Ap 1 1869;70
DLC 1821-N 6 1828;Ap 22 1830-Ag 17 1842;Ag 16,O 4 1843;Ja 8-Je 18 1845;Ja 7-21 1846;Ja 16,30-Mr 6,20-Je 12,26,Jl 3,17,31,Ag 14 1861; Ag 15 1863;N 26 1868;Je 17-24 1875
ICHi O 11 1832;Mr 7,My 2 1833;Ap 17 1834; Mr 19 1835;S 13 1836;Ja 26 1837;Ja 4 1838;D 3 1845;Ap 1 1846;Jl 19 1850;Ja 15,Ag 27 1851;N 14 1872;Ja 11-18,Mr 1-8,22 1877
IHi [S 20 1832-Ag 6 1851]
IaDH Ja-My 1821
M [1821-Je 1 1826]
MAm Mr-N 14 1884
MB [1821-Je 1843;45-46;57-58]D 12 1867-D 3 1868
MBAt 1821-[23-25]-[31]-Je 1842
MC 1821-My 1822;Je 1824-Je 1 1826
MDeHi D 20 1832
MH 1821-Je 17 1840;F 24,Mr 3,17,Ap 14 1841;O 9 1850;D 12 1867-O 1868
MHi [1821-26]32-34[37]F 9 1842;Ap 19-Je 21 1843;S 3 1856;N 6 1861;Je 22 1864;F 23,Ap 20 1865;Jl 5,O 17-24,N 7 1866;D 5 1867;My 24 1876
MNaHi Mr 27 1839
MSaE 1821-[32]-[35]-[37]-60
MWA 1821-My[Je 25 1829-31]-My 14 1835; 36-59;Ja 25,F 29,Mr 7 1860;Jl 15 1863;Mr 2 1864;Ja 12,F 2,16,Mr 2-16,Je 29,O 19 1865; Ap 16,30,N 26 1868;S 1869-70;F 9-16,Mr 9,Ap 6,O 12,D 14 1871;O 12 1883;N 12 1886
MeB O 6-20,N 3,24,D 22 1825;Ja 5,19,F 2,23, Mr 2-9,30 1826
MeBB 1821-S 26 1837;Ap 17 1839-44;48-Je 12 1850;My 30 1860-D 10 1862;D 23-30 1863
NN O 11,D 6 1821;Mr 21,My 30,Jl 25,Ag 29-N 21,D 1822-Ja 9,23,F 6,20-Je 5,19-S 4 1823; Ja 29,Jl 15,Ag 5,N 4 1824
NNHi Ja 25 1827;F 1 1838;F 7 1849
NPV 1821-24
NbHi [F 1885-Ag 1886]
NcD My 31,Je 9,D 6 1821;Je-S 4,25 1823;S 8 1825;Je 8,Ag 24,O 12,26,N 9,D 1826[27-S 1828]Ja 1 1835;N 26 1868;N 12 1886
NhD 1821[22-23]-[27-28]-[31]-Mr 8,Je 13,S 5, N 7,D 5 1833[34-37]N 7-14 1838;Ag 7,28-S 4 1839[Mr-O 7 1840]Je 1,O 5 1842;S 20,O 4,D 27 1843-Ja 3,Mr 27,S 4,N 20 1844;Ap 9,Je 4,Ag 27,S 24 1845;Ja 21,Mr 25,Ap 29,Je 24,Jl 15, Ag 19,D 9 1846[Ag 1847-O 11 1848]Ag 4-18,S 1,29,O 27 1852;O 19 1853;F 15,Mr 1,Je 7,Ag 16-23,S 1854;N 14-21 1872
OClWHi Ag 10 1864
P-M N 30 1826
WHi 1821-My,S 18 1823;24-Ja 19 1826[N 20 1828-My]Je 10 1830-Ja 1831;Ja 2-9 1861;71[72-75]-N 2,D 14 1876;77-D 18 1879

*Boston daily ADVERTISER. d Mr 3 1813-F 14 1929‖
Ja 2 1832-Je 1846 as Boston daily advertiser and patriot. Followed by Daily record
C F 4 1887-F 1889;Jl-D 1890
CL Ag 8 1921-Ja 1922
CP D 2 1845
CSmH Je 23 1829;Jl 1 1857;Ja 25 1879
Ct Je 18(supp)1875
CtY Ap 10,Ag 2 1827;Jl 15 1830;F 28,Jl 1831-Ja 24,Je 25 1844;46-53;56-81;86-93
DGU 1889-90
DLC Ja 9-10,19,24,26,F 6,15,Mr-[S-O,D]1821-Je 1822;23;Mr 1826-Ag 1827;Je 1831-Je 1844; Ja-Je 1845;46-49;Jl 1850-52;54-F 1929
IC 1854;F 12 1862;Jl 1863-64;72-79;N 24-26,28-30,D 3,6-8,10,12-16 1881;Ja 10 1884
ICM Jl 7,O 20 1885
ICU Ja 23,F 24 1854;Je 18 1855;S 22,O 31-N 1,4 1856;Ja 7-8,My 5,O 29 1857;F 18,26,Mr 1,8,10,13,15-16,18,24-26,30,Ap 10,12,My 6 1858; F 17,Ap 7,O 15 1859;F 4,Je 15 1860;Ja 21 1861
IHi Ap 15,19-22,24,26 1865
KHi Je 29-Jl 8,S 7 1865;F 5 1878;Ag 13-21 1890;N 1891-Ja 9 1913
LU 1844-53;55-Je 1856;57-71;76-79;Je 1880-86
M 1829-1929
MB 1821-[95]-F 11 1929
MBAt 1821-1902
MBr 1857-1900
MC Jl 1867-1917
MDeHi Ap 20 1875;S 23 1881
MH Ja 9,N 19 1821;Je 16 1824;My 28,O 24 1825;F 6 1826;S 1827-28;30-31;Ja 30 1836;40-N 1843;44-F,My 14,30,Jl 1 1918
MHi 1821-1919
MNb 1876-Je 1894
MSaE Ja 1-19,Ap 19,Ag 10 1821[23-24]Ja 15, 19 1825[26-27]28;Ja 17,24,28,My 27,N 7.25 1829;Ja 14,22,26,28,F 6,9,25,Ap 13 1830[31]F 18 1832;Je 17 1833;Mr 21 1834[35-41]-[44-48]-97
MSob 1872-73
MTa 1859-61;Mr 1862-Ap 1863;Ja-N 1864;Ap-Jl,S 1865-Mr 1866;79-Je 1917;Jl-Ag 1918
MWA 1821[22-25]-[27-31]-[34-36]-[43-45]-[59]-1909;Ap 19 1928
MWa Ja 13 1863-Je 1865
MeBB [Ap 1861-68]-My 11 1871;74-Je 1879;80-Je 1881;82-88
MeBa [1861-66]Mr 4-5 1869
MeU O 31 1832
MeWC D 1861-66
MiU 1864-[81]
MiU-C [1821-25;27-29;32-35]
MnHi 1859-66
NBHi 1868;Je 1869-Jl 1874
NN Ap 8,Jl 24 1843;My 1,Je 26 1844;O 8,N 6,11,13-14,D 24 1845[46-47]My 5,13,28 1848;Jl 27 1849;Jl 22,Ag 13,O 3-4 1850[51-52]Jl 21,23 1858;Jl 15,N 18 1863;Jl 20 1864;My 3,Je 15 (supp)1865;N 30,D 2 1868
NNHi D 19-20 1821;Mr 1-2 1822;Ap 2-3,My 2-3,Ag 30,O 31 1823-O 1831;32;D 23-24 1833;Mr 7 1834;Je 15 1836;O 27 1848;F 5 1850;O 20 1864;Ap 20 1865;Jl 1866-69;N 11 1872;Ja 20, My 20 1873;extra S 26 1831
NbHi [My 10-Ag 13 1855;Ja-S 7 1856;57;Mr-D 1868;Ja-S 1871;Jl-N 1872]Jl 3,5,8-9 1873;76 [Mr-D 1877]Ap 1-7,9-14,16-30,Ag 13 1880;Ja-Mr 1881[Ja-S 7 1885]
NcD Ja 5,11 1822;Ja 20 1824[27-28]Ag 3 1837;Jl 20 1846;N 17 1847;Ap 21 1854;My 2,8 1855[56;60-67]Jl 15 1868;Je 17 1869;Jl 1,8 1872; D 10 1873;75-94;Jl 1897-98
NcU Ag 28 1875;Ja 31 1876-Ja 1878
NhD Jl 1846-S 1872
NjR [1868-70;72;74;78]
OCHi Jl 15,17 1863
OCl Je 16 1821
OClWHi Je 20 1825;S 18 1861;Jl 1862-63;Ag 15 1864;Ap 15-20 1865;67;O 22 1874;O 2 1876;O 21,N 6,9,16 1897
OHi Je 25-30 1877
P-M My 31 1831;N 2 1844;Ap 18 1855
PU Je 6 1821[32]Ag 10,D 9 1833;Mr 2-3 1835
TxU 1862-63;Jl 1878-96
V N 1862-63
VHaH Ja 27,29,F 1,3,13,20-21,23-24,26,28,Mr 3, 7,9,13,14(supp)30 1866
Vt 1857;75
VtU 1871
WHi Ja-F,S 1821-F,S 1822-F 1823[27-Ap 17 1835]40;Jl 1841-Je 1843;Ja-Je 1844;Ja-Je 1845[Ja 14-D 1846]-48;My-D 24 1849;Jl 26 1850-54;Jl 16 1857-Je 1859;Ja-Je 1860;61-81

Boston Sunday ADVERTISER. w 1904+
DLC O 1924-27
M 1904+
MBAt D 9-30 1917

Boston daily ADVOCATE. d Ja 3 1832-D 1838‖
CSmH O 5(extra)1832
DLC 1832;S 18-D 1833;O 3,25,N 1834-S 23 1835; F 3 1836;Mr-My 1838
MB [D 1831-38]
MBAt 1832-35;Mr 7 1836
MHi N-D 1832;Ap 26 1833;N 14 1835;Ja 7,S 5 1836
MTaHi Ja 9-Mr 29 1834
MWA [1832-34;O 1835-36]Ag 9 1837;Ja 10,Ag 21 1838
NjR Mr 28 1836
OClWHi D 10 1836
WHi 1832;My-S 17 1833;Ja-O 1834

Boston ADVOCATE. w Ja 1885-88‖?
Negro
MB Je 27-Ag 22,S-O 17 1885[86]-Ja 22 1887
MHi [1885-86]

Boston ADVOCATE (1905-09) *See* Jewish advocate

ADVOCATE and West Roxbury advertiser. w 1885-90‖?
1885-88? as West Roxbury advertiser
MH D 28 1885
MWA D 10 1887

AGE. d Ag 8 1836-
Ct Ag 8-9 1836
MWA Ag 8 1836

ALLSTON news. w O 1 1935+
pub 1935+

ALLSTON record. w Mr 1919-N 1928‖?
MB-B 1922-26

AMERICAN. w O 21 1837-Mr 17 1838‖?
DLC N 25 1837
MB O 21 1837;Mr 17 1838
MWA Mr 17 1838

Boston daily AMERICAN. d Ag? 1842-
CtY Mr 11 1843
MB F 13,24,Mr 1,8,Ap 12-13 1843
MHi S 17,N 26 1842;F 3 1843

Boston AMERICAN. d Ja 15 1845-
NhM Ja-F 1 1845

Boston AMERICAN. d Mr 21 1904+
1904-Ap 14 1905 as Hearst's Boston American and New York journal; Ap 15 1905-Mr 16 1907 Hearst's Boston American
pub 1904+
CL [1904]-[22]
M 1904+
MB 1904+
MHi Je 7 1930
MWA Mr 21 1904
VU O 4 1905

AMERICAN bee, and guardian of liberty. w Ja 6 1855-
Follows Boston weekly bee
MB [Ap 2 1855-Jl 8 1861]
MWA Ja 13,Je 30 1855;D 20 1856
—d ed *See* Boston daily bee

AMERICAN cabinet and Boston athenaeum. w Ja 7 1848-Jl 19 1851‖?
MB [My 27 1848-D 8 1849;Jl-D 1850;Ja 25-Jl 5 1851]
MHi F 24 1849
MSaE 1850
MWA O 21 1848;F 3,My 5-12 1849;50;Ja 18,Ap 26,Jl 19 1851
NjR Mr 24 1849

AMERICAN Canadian. w Je 3 1874-76‖
MB [Je 10 1874-D 18 1876]

AMERICAN celt and adopted citizen. w Ag 31 1850-
- 1850 as American celt
CaQMF 1851;53-56
MWA Ag-S 21,O 12-N 2,D 7,21 1850;Ja 17 1852
NNHi 1850-51
PPCHi [1850-52]
WHi Ja 18 1851

Daily AMERICAN eagle. d D 3 1844-
DLC 1844-D 2 1845
MB [1844-Ja 1 1847]
MHi F 10,26 1846
MWA 1844-Je 2,30,Ag 29,S 23,N 25,D 9 1845

Weekly AMERICAN eagle. w D 28 1844-
MB 1844-45
MWA F 22,Je 21-28,S 20,D 6 1845
P-M D 20 1845

AMERICAN justifier. w N 30 1867-D 1874‖
1867-68 pub in Salem; 1873-Ja 24? 1874 in Boston, Salem and Wakefield
MB [1873-74]
MH Ja 25-Jl 25 1868
MHi F 15-22 1868
MSaE [1867-68;73-74]
MWA 1867-F,Ap-Je,Jl 11-18 1868;N 1-22,D 20-27 1873;Ja 10,17(supp)31-My 16,30 1874

AMERICAN nation and Yankee sentinel. *See* Yankee nation and American sentinel

AMERICAN patriot. w F 20 1852-
DLC D 30 1854;Ja 13,27-F 10 1855
MB My 1854
MWA N 13 1852;Mr 11,Je 3,N 25 1854;Ja 27, Je 2-9 1855;Je 6 1857
P-M Je 2-9 1855

AMERICAN republican. w N 9 1844-
MB N-D 21 1844
MWA N 9-16 1844

AMERICAN sentinel. w D 29 1849-My 3 1851‖
United with Yankee nation to form American nation and Yankee sentinel, later Yankee nation and American
DLC complete
MB Ap 13 1850
MWA F 2-23,Mr 2,Je 22 1850;Ja 25 1851

Daily AMERICAN signal. d My 20 1847-
MB My 20-O 20 1847;Jl 27-29 1848
MWA O 4 1847;Je 9 1848
P-M Ag 12,O 11,27,N 1,3,11-14 1848

AMERICAN statesman. *See* Boston statesman

AMERICAN traveller. *See* Boston traveller

AMERICAN union. w N 4 1848-76‖?
DLC S 16 1854
MB Jl 5 1851;Ag 14,N 20,D 11 1852[Ap 9-D 1853]F 18,Mr 4-11,S 16 1854;Ap 7 1855;Jl 26 1856;Ag 8 1857;Jl 16 1859;O 27 1860;F 16,Jl 20 1861;Ja 25 1862;Ag 2,16 1862
MH Mr 30,Ap 13 1850;Ag 23 1862;Je 9 1866;Mr 9-23,Je 29,Jl 20,Ag 10,S 7 1867;Mr 7 1868
MHi Ap 12 1856;O 6 1866
MWA 1848-[52-Jl 1857]Mr 6,O 23 1858;F 12,Mr 12,My 21 1859;Mr 24,Ag 25 1860;Ap 6,Je 1,22, Jl 6-13 1861;Ja 4,N 8 1862;Mr 14,Ap 18,My 2-9 1863;S 2 1865;Ja 12,26 1867;Je 13,Jl 4 1868;Mr 6,27,Jl 24 1869;Je 11 1870;My 6 1871
MiU-C [1849-51;53;55-57]
N Mr 4 1854
NNHi Ap 25 1863;Ap 11 1868;Ja 16,F 6-20,Mr 13-20 1869;Mr 26,My 14,Je 4,Jl 2-9 1870;My 3 1873
NcD My 26,Je 2 1849;Ja 11,N 22 1851;Ja 21 1854;Je 28 1856;Mr 21 1857
NjR N 6 1858
OClWHi My 18-Jl 13,D 21 1861;Ja 4-18 1862; Mr 20 1869
P-M Jl 1,O 14 1854
PWcHi N 15,D 13 1856;Ja 3-10,F 14-21,Mr 28,Ap 25 1857
TJT Ja 31 1874
WHi S 8 1860

ANGEL GABRIEL. w Ag 12 1854‖
MB complete
NjR complete

ANGLO-SACSUN. *See under* New York City

ANGLO-SAXON, European and colonial gazette. w D 22 1855-O 31 1857‖
CaOTA Jl 5 1856
DLC complete
KHi D 29 1855-D 13 1856
MB complete
MBAt D 20 1856-57
MWA Ja 26-F 2,Mr 15,29,Ap 19-My 3,24-Je, N 22 1856;Jl 18-Ag,S 19-26,O 10-31 1857

ANTI-KNOW-NOTHING: and true American citizen. w
MHi O 28 1854

ANTI-MASONIC free press. *See* Free press and advocate

Bostoner ANZEIGER. w 1888-1917‖?
In German
MWA Ag 27 1914;S 7 1916

ATEITIS. w 1913-18‖
In Lithuanian
IU Ja-Ap 26 1918

Boston weekly ATHENAEUM. w 1846-56‖?
United with Yankee blade to form Yankee blade and Boston athenaeum, later Yankee blade
MWA Jl 10,Ag 28 1847;Ja 22,F 26 1848

Boston semi-weekly ATLAS. sw Jl 1832-Ap 11 1857‖
Title varies: Boston atlas; Atlas; Semi-weekly atlas. Merged with Boston traveller
DLC 1841-42;Mr 18 1845;Ag 15 1849;Ja 10 1852
CtHi Jl 15 1835-39
IU O 31 1846
MB 1838-Ag 1842;Je 1843-N 1844;Ap 1850-53; 55-57
MBAt Ja 19,F 9.13 1839

MASSACHUSETTS (*Continued*)

BOSTON—*Continued*

Boston semi-weekly ATLAS. sw 1832-57||
—*Continued*
MH [O 24 1838-N 23 1839]Ja 1 1840;41-Jl,N 12 1845;Je 12,Jl 27,N 2,23 1850-Ap 11 1857
MHi Mr 4 1837;O 12 1839-40;S 21 1842;O 9,N 2 1844;S 10 1845;F 14 1846;Mr 20 1850
MWA Mr 19,Ap 2,16-26,My 7-21,28-31,Jl 4 1834[35;37]-[Ja-My 20 1843]N 2,D 14 1844;F 1,My 24,Je 21 1845;46-[52]F 21 1857
MiU Je 1 1844
MiU-C N 29 1844;Je 21 1848
NNHi 1839-40
NcD Ag 16 1834;S 25 1839;S 21,N 2 1844;O 28 1848;F 6-9,13-16 1850
NhD F 3,15 1838;Je 8 1839-Ja 15,22-Ap 15,22-Ag 12,19-S 9,16-N 25,D 1840;Ja 4 1854
WHi Ja 25,Ap 4 1840;Mr 25 1857

Boston daily ATLAS. d Jl 2 1832-Jl 8 1861||
1832-Ap 11 1857 title varies: Boston daily atlas; Daily atlas. Atlas. Ap 13 1857-My 16? 1858 merged with Boston traveller. My 17 1858-My 16 1860 as Atlas and daily bee; My 17 1860-Je 24 1861 Daily atlas and bee
A 1843-50
Ct [1832;35]Ja 25 1837
CtHi Jl-O 17 1832;D 25 1837-39
CtY S 24-25 1833;Ap 27 1841;Je 25 1844;O 10 1848;O 5 1859
DLC N 8 1832;Ja 16 1833;Jl-S 11,O 1834-Ap 20 1835[38]O-D 1839;Je 8,O 26,D 4 1840;Mr 6 1841-Ap 11 1857;My 6 1861
IaGG F 25 1852;Ja 24 1853;F 2,S 18 1856
KHi Je 15-O 1858
KyU Ja 22 1833
M 1832-57;Jl 8 1861
MB [My 17 1858-61]
MBAt 1832-[61]
MBr 1837-57
MH Ja 28,S 3 1833;F 3 1835;F 11,15-16,18-19, My 2,Je 9-O 6 1836;Ja 23 1837;S 11 1840;F 12 1841;42-55;F 20,26,Ap 1-11 1857;My 17 1858-Jl 8 1861
MHi Jl 3,N 27,D 3 1832[33]Ja 25,F 1834-[44-52]-[55-60]
MTa Ag 18-4-Je 1845
MWA S 18,O 18(extra)24(extra)N 19-20 1832; F 4 1833-[34]-[36-38]-[42-44]-[46-51]-[53-Ap 11 1857]My 17 1858-[59]-[Ja-Jl 8 1861]
MdBJ S 20 1844
MiU-C [1833-45;48;50-55;57-61]
MnHi N 12 1840
N [1841-42]
NIC 1843-47
NN Jl 30 1833-F 17 1852
NNHi Ja-O 19 1835[39-42]Mr 7 1843;Je 12 1848
NSchU Mr 9 1842
NbHi Ap 8 1839
NcD Ag 4 1834;Ap 21 1835;N 25,D 19 1840;D 8,18-26,28 1841-Je 1842[45]D 5 1846[49]Ap 24 1850;N 1 1852;My 5 1856
NhD My 11 1838;S 28 1840[Ja-Je 1841]S 4 1848;D 12 1853;Ja 17,Ap 27,Jl 8 1861
OClWHi Jl 11 1845
P-M Mr 4 1834
PEHi Je 16 1856
WHi O 4,16 1839;S 11,O 2,N 13 1840;Mr 27, Ap 1,23 1841 59-Je 24,1861
—campaign ed *See* Campaign atlas and bee
—evening ed *See* Boston evening atlas

Boston evening ATLAS. d My 16? 1860-
MHi My 21,Je 1,O 17,N 5 1860
MWA Je 8,19,O 10,N 2,9-10 1860

Boston weekly ATLAS and bee. w Ag 27 1843-61||?
1843-Ap 3? 1857 as Boston weekly atlas; Atlas. Ap 13 1857-My 16? 1858 merged with Boston traveller
MH [Ja 15-Je 11 1846]
MHi F 12 1846[48-49]Ap 10 1851[56]N 17,D 24 1859[60-61]
MWA Ja 4,18,Mr 1,Jl 26,S 13 1849
NcD O 12 1843;My 8 1856
OHi D 28 1854;F 28 1856
P-M N 27 1845;Ap 12 1848

ATLAS and daily bee. *See* Boston daily atlas

La AURORA. N 22 1845-
In Spanish and English
NNHi N 22 1845

AZK. (The nation) tw,d 1906-O 18? 1921||
United with Bahag to form Azk-bahag, later Baikar
tw 1906-O 11 1919
In Armenian
IU N 1917-19

AZK-BAHAG. *See* Baikar

BAHAG. *See* Baikar

BAIKAR. sw,tw,d 1913+
1913-O 18 1921 as Bahag; O 19 1921-D 30 1922 Azk-Bahag
sw 1913-Mr 1920;tw Ap 1920-O 15 1921
In Armenian
IU D 4 1917-Ja 1924[My 8-Jl 23 1930;Ja 13-F 22 1934]
M Jl 19 1930
MH 1923;Ja 28,F 19,Mr 1924+
PP [1934]+

BALANCE. w S 20 1836-
MWA S 20 1836

BALLOON-POST. d Ap 11-17 1871||
MB complete
MBAt Ap 11-15,17 1871
MHi complete
MSaE Ap 11 1871

BAY STATE. [election extra] w Ag 24 1838-
1838 as Bay state democrat
Campaign paper, pub for twelve weeks each year previous to November elections
DLC Ag 31,S 7 1838
M N 5 1838
MB Ag-N 9 1838
MBAt S 28 1839
MHi Ag-N 9 1838
MWA Ag-N 9 1838;Ag 31,N 2-16 1839;Ag 29,S 12,O 3 1840;O 13 1842
NN Ag-N 9 1838;N 16 1839
NNHi Ag-O 26 1838
NcD Ag 31,O 26,N 9 1838

BAY STATE democracy. w Ag 31 1839-
MB N 2 1839
OClWHi Ag-S 7 1839;Ag 29 1840

BAY STATE democracy. w D 27 1870-
MB D 27 1870

BAY STATE democrat. 1838 *See* Bay state [election extra]

Weekly BAY STATE democrat. w Mr 1 1839-
1839-N 15 1844 as Bay state democrat
CtY Mr-D 20 1839
DLC Mr 8,Ag 31,S 7 1839
MAt Ag 31 1842
MB 1839;Ag 18 1843[Mr 22-D 1844]
MBAt Ja 12,N 1 1844
MHi Mr-D 20 1839[40-42]
MWA 1839-[42]F 9,N 22 1844;Ja 31-Mr 6,21 1845
NNHi 1839-Je,Jl 31,Ag 4,S 10 1840
NcD Je 28,Jl 19,Ag 16,30,S 13,27-N 1,15,D 13 1839
NhD Mr 27 1840;S 8 1843
OClWHi S 27,O 8 1839
P-M Jl 5 1844
RP S 22,O 27 1843
Vt 1842
WHi Mr-D 20 1839
—Election extra. *See* Bay state

BAY STATE democrat. d Ja 1 1840-N 12 1844||?
Merged with Boston daily times
DLC Ja 4,Jl 1840-42
MB [1840-Mr 1843;Ja-Ap 18 1845]
MBAt [1840]42-[44]
MH O 1842-Mr,O 2 1843-Mr 1844
MHi 1840-N 16 1844
MWA Ja 22,Jl 31,S 25,D 4 1840;S 6,16,O 9,N 1 1841;Ap 15,My 6,Jl 1,13,23,26,Ag 9,12,23,S 1, 3,17,D 3,16 1842;Mr 29,Ag 12 1843;Jl 25,O 29,N 4,12 1844
MWo F 4 1840
MiU-C [1840-41;44]
MnHi Ja 22 1840;Je 15 1841
NN Jl-D 1841
OClWHi Jl 14,17[S 15-O]D 4 1840;Ag 4,N 15, 19-20,22 1841;Ja 14-15,18,27,F 24-26,Mr 25 1842;Jl 5,N 4 1844
WHi Ag 25 1840

BAY STATE democrat. sw Je 3 1840-
MB Je 24 1840-F 28 1844

BAY STATE democrat. [election extra] *See* Bay state

BEACON. w F 16 1884-D 31 1904||
United with Boston budget to form Boston budget and beacon
CtY 1884-Ja 24 1885
DLC 1884-88
InRE D 14 1889
MB 1884-N 1 1890;91-Je 1895;Je 13,Jl 25 1896; 98-1904
MH Mr 14 1885-Ja 5,19 1895
MSaE Ap 29 1899
MWA F 16 1884;Ag 1 1885;D 6 1890;Jl 1897-Je 1898;F 25,Ap 22,My 6 1899

Boston BEACON and Dorchester news gatherer. w 1873-83||
MB [Mr 25 1876-Ap 5 1879]Ja 22 1881-Ja 14 1882
MWA S 13 1879;Mr 17 1883

Boston daily BEE. d Ap 25 1842-My 14 1858||
Title varies: Daily evening bee; etc. United with Boston daily atlas to form Atlas and daily bee, later Boston daily atlas
C N 6-10 1849
CL Mr 17 1849
CSmH My 16 1853
CtY D 20 1842
DLC Jl 7,Ag 26 1842;Ag 3-4,14-15,26 1843;Ap 1849-50;S 11,O 30 1852;Ap 8 1853
MB [1842-My 5 1854;Ap 1855-58]
MBAt [1855]-58
MH [Mr 20 1850-Ag 27 1851]D 1 1852;Ja 1, Ap 18-19 1855;My 22 1857
MHi Ag 1 1842;Ag 16 1843;My 5 1845[46]S 17 1847[48-57]F 10,Mr 10,Ap 22,27 1858
MMarHi Ag 18 1842
MSaE S 27 1848;52
MWA 1842-Ap 24,Ag 2,25,S 25,N 14,16,D 13 1843;Mr 22,Jl 2,8,29,Ag 17,N 12,D 28 1844;Ja 1,16,18,Ap 3,My 8,Jl 4,N 15,D 31 1845;F 18,Mr 3 1846[47]Ja 12,F 29,Mr 13,28,Ap 11,Jl 13,O 27 1848[49-52]Jl 16,26,D 15,23 1853[Je-D 1854]-Ja 13,F 18 1858
MiU-C O 30(extra)1852
N Je 16 1842
NSchU Ag 12 1842
NcD Ap 25,My 31,Jl 1,N 2 1842;Mr 10,29,Ap 12 1843
PWcHi My 1857
WHi Ja 15-Ag 6 1856;O 16,26,N 2-4,11 1857
—w ed *See* American bee; Boston weekly bee

Boston weekly BEE. w F 11 1843-54||?
Followed by American bee
DLC N 29 1845;Ag 8 1846;N-D 11 1847;Mr-Ap 22 1848
MHi S 7 1844;N 22 1845;F 7,My 16 1846;F 10, Mr 3,My 12 1849
MWA [1843-45]-Ap 3 1852
MiU-C [1849]
NcD My 25 1844;F 7 1845
NhM Je 28 1845

BLAZE of glory. . . *See* Experiment and office holders' journal

BOSTON. S 17 1880||
pub on the 200th anniversary of the founding of Boston
MB complete
MeBa complete

BOSTONIAN. w N 14 1846-
MB Ja 5 1847
MWA 1846-My 1847
MiU-C D 5 1846

BOSTONIAN; or Dixon's Saturday night express. w N 26 1836-
MWA D 24 1836

BOSTONIAN and mechanics journal. w Jl 13 1822-
Jl 13-O 5 1822 as Independent Bostonian
MB Jl 27-D 21 1822[Ja-Je 1823]
MDeHi Je 14,Jl 26 1823
MWA Jl 20-Ag 10,31 1822-Je 1823

BRITISH AMERICAN citizen. w O 29 1887-1912||?
CtY O 29 1887
MB [1887-Mr 3,O 20 1888-F 2 1889]
MWA O-N 5 1887;O 19-D 1889;Ja 11-25,Mr-N 1 1890
OCHi O 29 1887

BROADSIDE. sm Ap 10 1878-80||?
DLC O 30 1880
MBAt Je 5,S 10,O 16-30 1878
MSaE S 10(extra)1878
NNHi Ag 14 1878

Boston BUDGET and beacon. w Je 29 1879-1917||?
1879-Je 24 1883 as Boston Sunday budget; Jl 1 1883-My 25 1905 Boston budget
KHi [N 25 1894-N 1896]
M [My 25 1901-D 17 1904]
MB [1879-F 17 1889;90-92]95;Mr 10-17 1895; 1901-06
MH [Mr 14-D 1880]-My 22 1881
MHi S-N 1879;My 12,D 15 1900;My 25,Je 15 1901;Je 1,D 13 1902;Je 6,D 12 1903;Je 11,Jl 24-31 1904;Je 3 1905;Je 2 1906;Jl 27 1907;S 26 1908;S 25 1909
MWA Je 29,Ag 24 1879;Mr 28,Ap 9,My 7,21-28, Je 1882;Ap 29,My 13,D 9-16 1883;My 18,Jl 27,Ag 17-24,S 21-O 12,N 2-9 1884;Jl 12,Ag 9 1885

Daily evening BULLETIN. d O 22 1842-
MHi O 31 1842
MNb [1842-43]
MWA O 29,31,N 4,8,16,19 1842;F 2,Mr 29,Ap 3,Je 14,21 1843

Boston weekly BULLETIN. w Ap 1 1843-
MWA Ap 15,My 13 1843

Boston evening BULLETIN and United States republican. d N 26 1827-Ap? 1830||
1827-28 as Boston evening bulletin
CSmH S 9 1829
Ct [1828-29]
DLC [1828-Ap 1830]
MB N 30 1827[F 7-D 25 1828]
MBAt 1827-29
MH Ag 22,26,29,S 4,8-9,11 17-19,22,24,26,29,O 2,7-8,10-14 1829;Ja 26-27,F 1-2,5,16 1830
MHi [1827-30]
MWA N 26-27,30-D 1,5,17,19,31 1827[Ja-Ag 1828]F 12,Mr 31,Ap 15,17,30,S 23-24,N 19,D 18-19,23,26,28-30 1829;Mr 8,30 1830
N Ja 15,Mr 26 1828
NN Ja 9 1828
NNHi [1827-Ap 1828]Ja 12,My 16,Ag 21,D 1 1829
NjCHi 1827-29
OClWHi O 22 1829

Boston evening BULLETIN and United States republican. sw D 13 1827-Ap 29 1830||
1827-D 29 1828 as Boston evening bulletin. Merged with New England palladium
CtY M 23 1829
MB D 20 1827;Ja 8,F 11,Ap 4 1828;29-30
MBAt D 20 1827;D 31 1829
MHi Ja 22-Mr 26,Ap 8 1829
MSaE F 22 1830
MWA complete
MiU-C [1828-29]
MnHi Ap 30 1829
NEhD D 13 1827-Je 1,N 30 1829-Ja 18 1830
NNHi [1827-Ap 1828]
WHi O 4,18 1828;F 5 1829

BUNKER HILL aurora and Boston mirror. w Ja 12 1827-S 24 1870||
Title varies: Bunker Hill aurora and farmers and merchants journal; Bunker Hill aurora and Middlesex county advertiser; etc.
Ct Jl 12 1834;Je 18 1836;D 16 1837
CtY Jl 19 1862
DLC Mr 15 1828;S 5,O 3,31,N 28,D 26 1829;Ja 9 1830;F 15,N 14 1840;Ja 14 1860-61;64-65
M Ja 26 1839-My 21 1870
MB complete
MBAt F 9 1828;Ja 17 1829
MH [Ap 20-S 14 1833]Je 22 1850;Je 5 1852; Ap 25 1868;Je 19 1869
MHi Ja 5 1828;S 15 1832;My 4,Je 1,22-29,S 21 1833[34-36]My 3 1845;F 27 1858;D 5 1863
MMal 1848-51;55
MWA [Jl 12-N 15 1827;Ja-N 1 1828]Ap 25,My 30[Jl 25-O]1829;F 6,Ap 17,Ag 28,D 4 1830;F 11 1832;Jl 5 1834[36-37]Ap 28,O 27 1838;Ap 6-13 1839;Ja 30-N 1841;Ja-N 1843;Ja 13 1844[45]46[48]Ja 27,F 24,N 3 1849;Ja-My 18, Je 22 1850;52-54;F 24 1855;My 9 1857;F 27 1858;59[Ag 10-D 7 1861]Jl 19 1862;F 14,O 17 1863;Mr 12,Ag 6,D 3 1864;O 28,D 23 1865;Jl 7 1866;Ja 12,My 11,O 5,19-N 9,23 1867-70
N D 27 1828
NNHi Jl 12,Ag 9,N 8-15,D 6-13 1827;Ja 19, Mr 22 1828;My 4,Je 15,Jl 20,S 21,N 16,D 14, 28 1833;N 12 1836
NcD Jl 30,Ag 13-S 3 1853;Ja 8 1859;O 23 1869;Jl 23,S 10 1870
NjR [Ja 19-My 10 1828]

BUNKER HILL centennial. Je 17 1875||
ICHi complete
MBAt complete
MiU-C complete
NNHi complete
NjCHi complete
REdH complete

MASSACHUSETTS (*Continued*)

BOSTON—*Continued*

BUNKER HILL chronicle. w Ap 6 1917-
MWA Je 15 1917

BUNKER HILL times, and Charlestown advertiser. w O 19 1872-97‖?
1872-O 11 1873 as Charlestown times; O 18 1873-D 9 1876 as Bunker Hill times
DLC F 14 1880
M [N 20 1875-Je 16 1894]
MB 1872-D 13 1879
MHi 1874-79;Je 26 1886;N 11 1893;Mr 17 1894; Je 15 1895
MWA Je 17,19-26 1875;O 7 1876;N-D 5 1880;Ja 8,Ap 9,Je 11 1881;Jl 29,N 18,D 2 1882;84[85-87]88;Mr 8 1890

CALIFORNIA bulletin. w Mr 15 1849-
CSmH Ap 5,19 1849

CAMPAIGN atlas and bee. w My 26 1860-
Campaign issues of Daily atlas and bee, later Boston daily atlas
MHi Je 23 1860
MWA Jl 14,28,S 1,29,O 20 1860

CAMPAIGN courier. w Ag 31?-N 23? 1864‖
MB S 7,21,O 26-N 2 1864
MSaE S 28 1864

CAMPAIGN for the union. sw O 8-N 8 1864‖
DLC O-N 5 1864
MB O-N 5 1864
MBAt O 31-N 4 1864
MHi complete

CAMPAIGN post. w Jl 3-N 6 1852‖
CSmH Ag 31,S 21 1866
GDE Jl 10,Ag 7 1852
MHi complete
MWA Jl 24,O 23 1852

CAMPAIGN post. w Jl 5 1856-
DLC Ag 30 1856
IU My 11 1860
InSHi Jl 12 1856
MB Jl-N 1 1856;O 27 1860
MHi Ag 30-O 11 1856;My 11 1860
MWA Jl 26-Ag 2,23-30,S 27,O 25 1856;S 1 1860;S 30 1864;S 28,O 19,N 2 1866;Jl 10,31,S 4,O 23 1868
MsHi My 2,Je 30,Jl 7,S 15,O 19,27,N 3 1860
N Jl 5,Ag 2-9 1856
NhM S 27 1856
OClWHi Jl-N 1 1856;O 27 1860;S 9-16 1864

CAMPAIGN republican. d O 29-N 3 1855‖
MB N 3 1855
MHi O 31,N 3 1855
MWA N 3 1855
N complete
NcD N 3 1855
OClWHi N 3 1855

CAMPAIGN times. w Je 28 1856-
MWA Je 28-Jl 12 1856

CAMPAIGN union. sw,w Jl 13? 1860-
MB Jl 27 1860
MHi O 19 1860
MWA Jl 27,O 26 1860
NNHi Jl-N 7 1860

CAPE COD sand. w Ap 19 1913-16‖?
Dated also in Yarmouthport
MWA My 3 1913

CARBINE. S 9 1843‖
MWA complete
NhD complete

Boston CASTIGATOR. w Ag 7 1822-
Title varies slightly: Boston castigator and independent quizzical examiner
CtY Jl 18 1828
M Ag-D 11 1822
MB N 13 1822;My-Je 4,21-Jl 19,Ag 2-9,23 1827; My 16,Ag 8 1828
MBAt S 27 1827
MeU Je 27,Jl 18,Ag 1 1828
OClWHi S 18 1822

CENSOR and evening star. d Ja 21 1836-
MWA Ja 25 1836

CENTENNIAL campaign. w Ag 15? 1876-
MB S 9 1876
MHi Ag 22 1876

Daily CENTINEL and gazette. d S 12 1830-My 1 1840‖
1830-Ap 10? 1836 as Daily Columbian sentinel. Merged with Boston daily advertiser
CSmH F 21-22,Ap 12,My 17 1832;O 16,27 1837-D 22 1838
DLC D 27 1830;Jl 20,Ag 25,O 2 1832;35;Ag 8 1838
GAtCo S 9 1839
MAtt D 17 1836
MBAt My 2,N 15 1838
MH My 2,4-13,16-18,20-Je 13,15,17 1831;Je 2, S 2 1835
MHi complete
MSaE Ja-Je 1837;38-39
MWA F 12-14,Je 18,24,27,29-30,S 12,21-27,30-O 4 1831;Ja 12 1832;Ap 26 1833;Ja 21 1834;Ap 2,D 2 1835[Ja-Ag 2 1836;F 10-N 28 1837;38]F 14-15,Ap 19,Ag 13,20,27,O 16 1839;Ja 2,Mr 2-My 1840
MiU-C [1830-31;37]
NNHi Ja 4 1840
WHi O 15 1831

CHARLESTOWN advertiser. sw,w Ja 3 1852-D 2 1876‖
1851-Ap 7 1852 as Charlestown city advertiser; Ap 10 1852-63 City advertiser. United with Bunker Hill times to form Bunker Hill times and Charlestown advertiser
O 25 1851 is prospectus
sw 1851-63?
DLC 1861-64;70-73
M [O 9 1858-76]
MB O 25 1851;52-N 25 1876
MH N 6 1858;D 3 1864;Ap 18,My 9,O 3,31 1868;Ja 30,F 13,D 4 1869;Ap 16-23 1870
MHi Ja 18,F 29 1868;N 26 1870;S 23 1871; D 11-18 1875
MWA Je 9,D 1 1852;Ap 21 1858;S 7 1859;Ag 15 1863;Ap 16,Je 25,S 3,O 29,D 3 1864;D 16 1865;Ja 27,Jl 7,S 8,O 20-27 1866[67-S 5 1868]O 29 1870;My 6,Jl 8 1871;75[76]
N Je 18 1864
NNHi F 13 1869;My 3 1873
NcD My 24 1873
OClWHi Ap 22 1865

CHARLESTOWN chronicle. w Ap 8? 1841-
M Mr 12 1842

CHARLESTOWN chronicle. 1868-70 *See* Saturday chronicle

CHARLESTOWN enterprise. w Ja 7 1882-O 13 1923‖
1882-83? as New Enterprise; Je 17 1889 Charlestown enterprise
M [Ja 11 1879-F 20 1886]-1923
MB 1878-86;Ja 8,N 12 1887-90
MB-C 1900-19;21-23
MH Mr 1880-Jl 16 1881;My 20 1882;Ja 13 1883
MHi Ap 9 1881;S 16 1882-F 20 1886;Je 1888-[1910]
MWA My 6 1882;Jl 5 1879;N 4,18,D 16 1882; Jl 14 1883;F 16,My 30,N 1-15 1884;86-87[Je-D 1888]F 23,Ap 27-My 4,Je 17,O 12,D 21 1889;F 8,Ap 5,O 4 1890;F 14,My 16 1891;Je 25-Jl 2 1892;F 11-18 1893;S 1,29,D 9,29 1894;Ja 5, 26,S 7 1895;D 17 1898;Ja 14 1899;S 2 1902; S 12 1903;Ag 26 1905;Je 18,O 6 1906;S 14,D 21 1907;My 8 1909
MiU-C N 18 1882[89-92;94-95;1907]

CHARLESTOWN news. w 1923+
pub Mr 1930+
MB-C 1924+

CHARLESTOWN times. *See* Bunker Hill times

Charlestown TRIBUNE. w N 19? 1886-87‖
M [Ja 15-Ap 1887]
MWA F 19-26,Mr 19-26,Ap 23 1887

CHRISTIAN SCIENCE monitor. d N 25 1908+
pub 1908+
A 1915-F 1919;O 1922-24;S 1925-Mr 1928
ArAH 1930+
C Ap 1910+
CClP O 26 1922-26[Je-Jl 1927]My 1928+
CL 1908+
CLO 1932+
CLSU Ap 1917+
CLU [1915-16]-[19]22+
CMiC Ap 1917-Ap 1918
CP Ap 1916-S 1919
CSt [1908]-[12-14]+
CU 1908-N 25 1913;14-S,N 1920-[Mr-Je 1921]+
CaNSa Ap 6 1934+
CaNU 1931+
CaSU [S 1923-N 1934]
CoAT 1925-32
CoS Ag 1924-N 1933
Ct S 26[O]1918-Jl 8 1919;O 24 1923;O 10-29,N 25 1932+
CtY 1919+
DL Je,N 1917;S 1922;Jl 1925+
DLC Je 17-22 1912;Mr 1913+
FCg Mr 1932-N 18 1933
FDe 1933-F 27 1934
FTS Ja 2-Ap 25,My 19 1931+
FU N 5 1921;N 8-14,16-27 1927;F 2,My 21,Ag 11 1928; D 7 1929;Mr 24 1931+
FWpR S 1931-My,D 1933+
GAA N 21 1925
GDE [1925-26]29
GU Ag 1928+
IAC D 7 1932-Ja 26,N 2 1933-Ap 22,S 10 1934+
IB current 2 years only
ICN 1908-29
ICU 1913+
IEN [1910]-[12]-[17]-[20;23-24]-[29]-[31]+
IEN-C D 1915-Je 1916;31+
IElC Ja 31 1935+
IF current year only
IGr current six months
IMaW current 2 months
IU O 4 1908-S 1919;20;Je 12-Ag 9 1922;F 1923+
IWW Jl 1934+
IaDH 1908-N 1934
IaDa current 3 months
IaGG [1916-21]+
IaMu current year only
IaSc current 6 months
IaU 1926-Ap,Jl 1932+
InU 1922+
KHi [N 1911-O 1924]
KWi Mr 1932+
LU Ap-Jl,N 1926-Ag 1927
M 1908+
MB 1908+
MH 1908-Ja 7,O 1,3 1910;Ap 26 1911[D 1916-18]+
MHi S 30-D 1909;Ja 5-F 5 1910;Ja 25-Ap 1913; 15-20;22-23
MNS [S 1922+]
MNort 1935+
MWA 1908-Je,Ag-S,N 1920;Ja 1-10,12-28,My 1921+
MiAC [1923-25;28-34]
MiD Je 1924+
MiG 1911+
MiU 1908-[14]-[21-22]+
MnHi [1909-16]+
MnU [1909]Ap 30,N 23 1910;Ap 29 1911;Ap-Jl 1916;17-O,D 1923-N 1925;26-Jl,O 1933+
MoFuW O 1933+
MoHi D 1 1925
MoS Je,O-N 1917;Ap,Je,D 1 1925;Je 1927-Ap, Je-D 1928;Mr 1929-[F]-[Ap-My 1931]-[F]-[Ap]-[O-N 1932]+
MoSP 1908+
MsU [1915]-[17-18;23]-25[32]
N 1908-[10-12]+
NBuG Jl-S 1914;15-Je 1920;Je 1922+
NCH 1926;31+
NIC 1908+
NN 1908+
NNC D 1916;Ap 1917+
NNQ My 1927-[30]
NNUT Mr 1911-Mr 1912;Je 18 1919-Ap 1920; 30+
NNW Je 14 1934+
NcD N 6 1926;28+
NhD N 25,27-D 24 1908;Ja-F 1 1909
NjBa 1926+
NvR [1932]-[34]
OAkU 1916-20;Ja-O 1 1926;Ja-Ag 1927;S 1929+
OCl 1908-[13]-15;S 1916+
OClWHi Je 3 1913;Jl 1917-19;Ap 10-Ag 1920;Ja 11,F 2 1923;S 1924-F 1925;Mr 15 1927+
OHi Ja-Je,N 1909+
OkAl [1934]+
OkCtH [1934]+
OkDS 1933+
OkEdC [1931-33]+
OkL 1927+
OkSt [1927-33]+
OkStO [1922-24;27-30]-[32]+
OkU [1916-17]-[19-22]-[24-26]+
OkWeS [1929]+
OrU [1927-31]+
P My-Je 1917
PA [1929-Ag 1933]
PMeA N 3 1924-Jl 3,N 2 1925-Je,O 15 1926+
PP 1917+
PU [1917-19]
TU [1929+]
Tx Ja-Je 1911;Ja-N 1912;Ap 1919+
TxGR 1908+
TxGroH Ap 6 1931-F 7 1933
TxH N 25 1913-Mr 1920;22+
TxHuS Ap 30,O 15 1930-Ap 1931;32—
TxLT O 1925+
TxU [F 17-N 17 1910]Ag 7 1911-N 4 1912[Je 2-O 1913]15-21;S 15 1922-34
VF 1934+
VHaH O 23 1934-Je 3,Jl 9-Ag 1935
VN 1930+
VU Jl 31 1934
WHi 1908+
WLc Ap 1917+
Wa D 1928-Ja 1930
WaPS Ap 1914-[15-16]-[19]20[22-23]-[27]-33
WaU N 28 1928-N 26 1930;F 17,My 13 1931-D 13 1933;Ja 19 1934+
WaWW 1915-Je 1920;Mr 1922+
WvU Mr 1933-Ag 1934

Morning CHRONICLE. ir F 23,Mr 1,15 1828‖
MBAt complete

Evening CHRONICLE. d Ja 1 1840-
MWA Ja 8,21,F 3,6 1840

Morning CHRONICLE. d Mr 22 1844-S 19 1845‖
DLC [1844]
MB complete
MDeHi S 6 1844
MWA 1844[45]
NhD Je 4,6-7,12 1844
WHi My 25 1844

Boston daily CHRONICLE. d Ag 9 1852-Ap 11 1857‖
Merged with Boston traveller
MB F 18,D 21,24,31 1853[Ap 19-Je 27]Jl 17 1854;My 5,Jl 18 1855[56]
MH Ag 23 1854;57
MHi O 30,D 11 1852;Je-D 1854;O 22,N 3-4 1856
MWA Ag 9,S 1,O 2,8 1852;Ja 5 1854[55-56]-Ap 10 1857
OOxM F 8 1868
WHi Ja 27,29,Mr 9 1857

Boston weekly CHRONICLE. w 1853-56‖
Merged with Boston traveller
MWA F 13(extra)1856
P-M F 9 1854

Sunday CHRONICLE. w O 20 1867-
MWA N 10 1867

Saturday CHRONICLE. w O 3 1868-O 4 1873‖
1868-S 3 1870 as Charlestown chronicle
DLC O 1 1870
M Ja 2,S 18 1869;O 1 1870
MB complete
MBAt 1868-S 1871
MH O 3 1868;Je 19 1869
MWA O 3 1868[69-73]
WHi Je 19 1869

Boston CHRONICLE. w 1915+
Negro
M [1928-F 1933]

CHRONICLE and reformer. w
Ct Mr 10 1835

Daily CHRONOTYPE. d F 11 1846-Ja 1 1851‖
Suspended from D 1849-Ag 1850
Merged with Boston commonwealth
Prospectus issued Ja 20 1846
C N 6-9 1848
DLC Mr 3 1846;Mr 14 1847;My 1,24,29,Je 3-4 1847[48]My 12,15,Je 12,N 15 1849;S 30 1850-51
IU D 25 1849
MB [Mr 1849-51]
MBAt 1846-[50]
MDeHi D 24 1850
MH F 29 1848-[49]O 22 1850-51
MHi [1848-50]
MWA 1846-[48-O 18 1849;S-D 1850]
MiU-C [1847]
N D 2,13(extra)1850
NNHi [N-D 1846]-Ap 17[Jl 1847-49]
NcD Ag 4 1846;My 27,S 7 1848;D 2,5,16 1850
PPoU Ap 23-S 12 1846
WHi N 9,11,19,22,D 14 1850

Weekly CHRONOTYPE. w My 28 1846-D 28 1850‖?
Ct S 22 1849
CtY 1846-My 20 1847
DLC 1846-My 20 1847;D 21 1850
ICHi D 24 1846-S 15 1849
MAm 1846-My 20 1847
MB 1846-S 1849

MASSACHUSETTS (*Continued*)

BOSTON—*Continued*

Weekly CHRONOTYPE. w 1846-50||?—*Cont.*
MBAt S 23 1847
MDeHi Mr 4,Ap 15-29,My 20,Je-Jl 22 1847
MH Ap 29 1848;S 15-D 1 1849;Ja 12 1850
MHi My 28-Je 4 1846;O 21 1847;Jl 21 1849
MWA S 24,N 26 1846;F 4,Je 10,O 1847-50
MiU-C [1850]
NNHi D 2 1848;My 26 1849-Ja 12 1850

Daily CIRCULAR. d Jl 25 1842-
MWA Jl 28,Ag 25,S 2 1842
NNHi Ag 15 1842

CITIZEN. sm N 14 1874-
MB N 14 1874-Mr 6 1875

CITY advertiser. *See* Charlestown advertiser

CITY crier and country advertiser. m F 1846-
MB My-Je Ag 1846
MWA Ap,Ag-O 1846
MnHi F 1846

CITY eagle. w Ag 16-D 20 1823||
Ag-S 20 1823 as Tea pot. United with Independent microscope to form Young galaxy
MWA Ag 16,30,S 27 1823

CITY firefly and humorous repository. w O 19 1822-
M [O 19 1822-F 25 1823]

Evening CITY gazette. *See* Saturday evening gazette

CITY watchman's alarm. ir My 25 1842-
NN Ag 12 1842
NNHi My 25 1842
OClWHi O 1 1842

CLASSICAL advertiser. sm,q 1832-
MBAt N 15 1833;F 15 1834
MeU Ja 15 1833
NcU D 15 1832

CLAY banner. w
MHi S 4 1848

***COLUMBIAN centinel.** sw Mr 24 1784-Ap 29 1840||
My 24-O 13 1784 as Massachusetts centinel and the republican journal; O 16 1784-Je 12 1790 Massachusetts centinel; Je 16 1790-O 2 1799 Columbian centinel; O 5 1799-D 1817 Columbian centinel: Massachusetts federalist; Ja 3-18 1818 Columbian centinel; Ja 21 1818- Columbian centinel. American federalist. United with Independent chronicle and Boston patriot to form Boston semi-weekly advertiser
C-S [Ja 1821]24-26;29
CSmH Ja 10 1821-22;Ja 18-25,F 1-5,Jl 19 1823; Ja 3-7,14-28,My 15 1824;F 12,Je 18,S 18,O 19 1825;Jl 8,12,N 22,D 30 1826;Ag 18-22 1827;Ja-Mr 12,Je 28,Jl 12-30,N 26 1828;Ja-Je 24,Ag 12,19,S 4,19 O 3,10 1829;Ag 9 1834;Ja-F,Mr 12,30 1836
CU Jl 8 1826
CtHi 1821-28
DLC 1821-30;Je 11,21 1834
ICU [1821-My-D 1822]23;Ja 5,29,F 9,16,23-Mr 2,19,Ap 23,30,My 14,25 1825;26-27;supp Mr 28 1827
IU Ja 3-5 1821;Ja 3,10,Ap 3,14,My 15,26,Je 26,Jl 11,Ag 11-14,S 29,O 16,25,D 29 1824;Jl 6 1825
M 1821-40
MB 1821-32
MBAt 1821-39
MBr 1821-28;31;33
MCam 1825
MDeHi O 8 1823
MH 1821-32;Ap 9 1834-My 23 1840
MHi [1821-34]
MSaE 1821-[30]-[32]-[36]
MSte D 11 1824
MStoR N 5 1904
MTaHi 1821-N 20 1824
MWA 1821-[31]-[33]Ja 11-15,22,29,My 2,Ag 29,O 1,N 5,29,D 6,13 1834[Ja-Ap 4,Je 17,Jl-O 1835]F 24,S 7,21,O 1,N 2,30 1836[37-O 3 1838] 39-Ap 17 1840]
MiU-C [1821-24]-[27]-[29-39]
MnHi 1821-27
MnU 1821
MoSW 1821-25
N 1821-[31-34]
NBHi 1821-29
NBuHi 1821-39
NChM Jl 23 1823
NIC 1821-29
NN 1821-S 10 1831;Ag 7 1833;Ja 10 1838
NNC 1830
NNHi 1821-Ap 1840;extras:My 14,21 1825
NcD Ja 3,21,Mr 24,Jl 25,D 8 1821;F 9 1822;N 12 1823[24]Mr 2,Jl 6 1825;Ja 4,Ap 12,29 1826;Mr 14 1827;Ja 26,F 27,Je 28 1828;Mr 21,O 24 1829;Ja 13,16,F 24,Ap 14,Ag 18,25 1830;Jl 18 1832 Ag 18 1838
NhD 1821-[33]-[36]-[39]-Ja 15,22-F 1,8-22,29-Mr 14,21-My 13,20-23 1840
NjR [1823-25-26]
PHi 1821-22;28
RW N 5 1823
Vt 1821
WHi 1821-29;F 17 1830

Daily COLUMBIAN sentinel. 1830-36 *See* Daily centinel and gazette

COMMENTATOR and Sunday times. w D 12 1829-
1829-N 14 1831 as Commentator
Ct Mr 20 1830
DLC D 19 1829-Ja 2,16-23 1830
MBAt [1829-31]
MHi Je 12-19 1830;Ap 21 1833
MWA D 26 1829;Ja 9,Mr 28 1830;F 6,Mr 6 1831
P-M Ja 16 1831

Daily evening COMMERCIAL. d Ja 15-D 31 1866||
Follows Boston evening courier
DHU-M N 16 1866
DLC Mr 6-15,Ap 20,Je 16 1866
MBAt complete
MH complete
MHi complete
MWA Ja-D 22,31 1866

Boston COMMERCIAL. w 1884+
MB S-D 1886[87-N 14 1891]

Boston COMMERCIAL and domestic advertiser. *See* Domestic advertiser

COMMERCIAL and shipping list. sw S 2 1843-86||?
1843-Ag 30 1848 as Boston shipping list, prices current, commercial and underwriters' gazette; S 2 1848-D 30 1874 Boston shipping list
CSmH My 2 1849
DLC 1858
DGE My 13 1848
M S 1850-Ag 1851
MB 1843-D 23 1868
MBAt S 1847-49;54-55;69-70
MH-BA 1843-Ag 1885
MHi D 20 1845;N 8,19-22 1862;Ja 10,21-24 F 14-21 1863
MSaE 1843-[48]-[58]-[60-61]-[64-70]
MWA S 2 1843;44-Ja 4,8-15 1845;51-Ag 1855; 56-57;My 19,S-D 1858;Ap 9 1859;Ja 1 1862;Ja 2 1864;O 3 1869;Ap 5-9 1884
MoSW [1844-49]
NNHi S 1862-Ag 1863;F 15 1873
OC [S 1844-Ja 24 1846]

COMMERCIAL bulletin. w Ja 1 1859+
DLC [1862-65]Ag 1 1868;72-74;Jl 17 1880+
IC O 14 1871
IU Jl 8-Ag 12,26 1916-Ag 1924;F 1925+
M Je 16 1932
MB 1859-63;69-70;72-80;82-83;97+
MB-K 1859—
MBAt 1865-75
MBr 1865-1909
MH-BA 1923-Jl 9 1932
MHi 1859-1901
MWA [1859]-92;1911[14]Ja 4 1919;27;Ja 6 1934
MiU-C [1860-67;81;86;97]
NNHi Ap 2 1870;D 21 1872;Mr 15 1873
NcD Ag 17 1861;Je 6,N 21 1868;Jl 10,24,Ag 7 1869
Vt 1860
WHi Ap 28 1860;62-64;68-69;Ap 23 1870;74-Je 1877;O 12 1889;D 20 1890-D 3 1892

***Boston COMMERCIAL gazette.** w,sw S 7 1795-My 25 1840||
1795-Je 4 1798 as Boston price-current and marine intelligencer; Je 7 1798-O 3 1800 Russell's gazette, commercial and political; O 9 1800-D 1802 Boston gazette, commercial and political; Ja 3 1803-D 1815 Boston gazette. United with Independent chronicle and Boston patriot to form Boston semi-weekly advertiser
CSmH Ja 8,Ap 16,Je 4,21,O 15,N 8,22-26,D 3,13,20-31 1821;Ja 7,My 20 1822;Ja 20,Ap 28 1823
Ct [1826-31]Jl 11 1833[35-36]
CtHi 1821-24;26-28
CtY D 3 1829
DLC 1821[22-28]
MB [1821-27;35]
MBAt 1821-27;Ja 10 1828;S 13 1830;Ag 13 1838;D 12,26 1839
MH 1821-O 6 1825;F 6,Jl 17 1826-My 25 1840
MHi [1821-33]Je 19 1837
MMarHi F 3 1823
MSaE 1821-26;My 31-Je 14 1827[28]Ja 29,F 26,Je 4 1829[30]Ja 3,10,17,Je 29 1831;N 3-6 1834;Mr 5,Ap 6 1836
MWA 1821-[Ja-N 27 1828]Mr 1829;Ja 7-11,21,F 1,11,Ag 12 1830;Ja 24,F 3-7,Mr 14 1831;F 16 1832;F 7,14,My 16 1833;Ag 6 1835;Ag 8 1836;Ja 16,Ag 7 1837;Ag 2 1838
MeBa Ja 28 1830
MeBt 1821-25
MeU Mr 15,O 7 1833
MiU-C [1821;23;25;27-29]
N 1822;N 10,D 29 1825[26-F 1,O 29 1827-D 22 1828]My 4-7,18,25,Je 8,S 24-28,O 8,19-22,N 5,12-16,30-D 10 1829[Jl-D 1830]
NN Mr 10-13,24-Ap 10,17-21,My 12-19,Je 5,O 20,N 13 1823;Ja 8,Mr 1,11,Ag 2,S 13 1824;My 12,S 12 1825;F 23,Jl 17,O 16 1826;N 26 1827
NNHi 1822-23;Je 28 1827
NcD My 14 1821[Je-S 1822;O-N 1824;25-27]
NhD 1821-Ja 7,N 14,21-28,D 5-26 1822;23[24-27]Ja 3,28,F 4,Mr 6,13,Ap 28,Ag 18,N 3 1828;F 9,Ag 3-10,N 9,16-19,D 7 1829;Ja 7,Mr 4 1830
NjR Je 26 1829
OClWHi N 29,D 13,31 1832;Ja 7-Jl 18,D 16-25 1833;Ja 9,20,Mr 13,Ap 14,My 8,Je 16-N 6 1834
PPL My 8[Jl 13-O]1826
WHi Mr 5 1821;My 25-30,Jl 1,25-29,Ag 8,22, S 2 1822;Mr 13 1828

Daily COMMERCIAL gazette. d My 10 1828-Ap 10? 1836||
United with Daily Columbian centinel to form Daily centinel and gazette
CSmH Ag 5 1830
DLC [My-Jl 1828;Je 1829-Ja 1830]My 14 1831; N 6 1832;Ag 29 1833
MBAt S 26 1831;F 21,N 13-14 1833;My 15 1834;F 28,Mr 27,My 4 1835
MH O 31 1829;31-32;Jl 3 1833
MHi [1830-36]
MWA Je 26,N 11,D 12-16,18-19,22,31 1828[Ja-F 11]Ap 7,29,My 14,Jl 9,14,D 22,29 1829;Ja 12,Ap 13,S 21,28,O 13,30,N 9 1830;F 10,12,Je 22,Ag 24,D 17 1831;Jl 6,Ag 15 1832;Mr 26,Ap 24,S 13 1833;Ag 23 1834
N O 28 1830;O 14 1833
REdH O 29 1828
WHi O 26 1829;Ja-Ap 9 1834

COMMONER. w Ja 1 1880-
MB Jl 24 1880-My 5 1881

Daily COMMONWEALTH. (evening ed) Ja 1 1851-S 21 1854||
Ja-Ap 7 1851 as Commonwealth. Title varies: Daily evening commonwealth; (evening ed). Followed by Evening telegraph, later Boston evening telegraph
DLC 1851-My,Je 5,20,23,27,Jl 18,21,26[Ag-S] 1854
InNcHi S 2,9,16,30 1865
KHi 1851-S 20 1854
MB complete
MBAt 1851-[54]
MH complete
MHi [1851-53]
MWA [Ja-N 1851]N 1 1852[53-54]
MiU-C [1851-52]
NN Je 7 1854
NNHi [Ja-O 1851;Mr 1852-O 1853]Je 5 1854
NcD Ja 1-26,28 1851;F 1,14,18,Mr 14,22,28,Ap 1,4,10,My 10-20,O 14,N 6,D 24 1851[52-Ag 14 1853]Ja 14,Mr 1,Je 7 1854
Tx F 27 1854

Weekly COMMONWEALTH. w Ja 4 1851-S 23 1854||
Ja-Jl 12 1851 as Commonwealth and emancipator. Followed by Weekly telegraph, later Boston weekly telegraph
CtY complete
IA [1851]
M [1851-54]
MB Ja 4,18,Ap 19 1851;O 15 1853;Ap 29 1854
MBAt Ap 19 1851
MH 1851
MHi [1851-54]
MSaE [1852-54]
MWA complete
MiU-C [1852]
WHi F 15-22,Mr 29,Ap 12-19 1851

Daily COMMONWEALTH. (morning ed) d Ap 8 1851-54||
Title varies: Daily morning commonwealth; Commonwealth (morning ed)
MHi Jl 20-D 1851;Jl-Ag 1853[54]
MSaE [1851-54]
MWA [Ap-Jl 12 1851]-[53]F 25,Ap 26,My 4 1854

Boston COMMONWEALTH. w S 6 1862-My 30 1896||
1862-Ag 28 1880 as Commonwealth
A Ja 5 1867
DLC 1862-88
ICHi O 28 1865
ICN 1862-Ag 1863
M [1862-Ag 1874]
MB S 1863-84;Mr 1885-95
MBAt 1862-Ag 1884
MC 1862-Ag 1864
MH 1880-96
MHi [1862-94]
MSaE [1862-65]-[74]-[76]
MWA 1862-Je 13 1896
MWo Ap 3 1869
N Ja 7 1863
NBuG 1862-Jl 1868
NN 1862-Ap 15 1871
NcD N 1 1862;S 1864-Ag 1870;F 25,Mr 25 1871
TNY N 22 1862;Je 5-12 1863;Ag 24-31 1867
WHi 1862-Ag 1886;Jl 5 1890;Mr 19 1892;D 15 1894

Sunday COMMONWEALTH. (Sunday ed) w My 5 1878-Mr 30 1879||
My 5-19 1878 as Commonwealth
DLC complete

CONSTITUTION. w My 24 1856-
MWA My 24 1856

Il CORRIERE di Boston. w 1893-1906||?
In Italian
MH [Je 1896-Jl 16 1899]

Boston COURANT. w 1890-1902||?
Negro
DLC Ja 6 1900

Boston daily COURIER. (morning) Mr 1 1824-D 31 1864||
1824-Ap 5 1851 as Boston courier. Merged with Boston evening courier
Ct Mr 26 1827;Je 2 1828
DLC [1824]-Je 1827[28-29]30;My 21,S 7-8 1831 [O-D 1832;F-My]Jl 1833-[34]-[36-37]-O 1839; Ja 11,Je 19,Jl 31,O 15,D 4,9,28 1840;Ap 23,Ag-S 1841;42-47;Mr 12 1849-52 Ap 30,My 13,Jl 16, Ag 15 1853;Je 7 1854[S-D 1856]S 1858-64
IU Je 23,26 1845
LU Mr-Ag 1826
M Mr 27 1861-Jl 1863
MB [1824-32;Je 22 1833-Je 1856;57-Je 13 1866]
MBAt 1824-[26-28]Ja 21,27 1829[30-33]Mr 25 1834 Ap 22,My 8,N 11 1835[36]-[38-40]42;44 [45]-48-64
MDeHi My 24 1830;O 21 1833;Je 23 1834;Mr 8 1858
MH 1825;F 2 1826;Ja-O 19 1827;S 29 1828;Jl-D 1830 F 8,D 10,15 1831;Ja 6-O 6 1832;Ap 22,My 13 1834;37-Je 1838;39;Ja 14,F 11,Mr 10,My 14,Je 25 1842;Ja 4 1844;S-D 1845;My-D 1846; Je 18 1847;48;Ja 22,Je 19,Ag 30,O 15 1850;51-64
MHi [1824-61]Jl 21 1863
MMarHi Ja 21 1826;My 29 1860-S 14 1863
MSaE [1826-27]Ja 9-10,31,Mr 27 1829[30]-[33]-36[38;40]O 13,F 14 1843;Ag 12,O 4 1844[45]-[47]-[50]My 7 1851[53]-[56]Ja 7,Mr 11 1857 [58]-[61]-64
MWA Ap 17,Jl 24,O 9,N 25,D 25 1824[25-27]-[29-34]-[37-39]-[41]-[57]-64
MiU-C [1825-27;30;32-33;35-36;38;42;45-52;55-56;58-60;62-64]
MoSW [1846-49]
N [Ap 1861-62]-64
NN N 11 1857
NNHi 1824-O 1831;Mr 4,Jl 1 1833;36;O 14 1837-S 12 1839;Jl 20 1840 Ap 7 20,22,My 13,Ag 19 1841;Ag 11 1842;D 25 1843;Je 10 1847;Mr 30 1859 Mr 4 1861;O 5,N 21 1863

MASSACHUSETTS (*Continued*)

BOSTON—*Continued*

Boston daily **COURIER.** (morning) 1824-64‖ —*Continued*
NcD [1835]Ag 16 1838;Mr 28 1839;S 25 1840;Je 19 1843;S 20,22 1844;Je 9 1847;Mr 30 1848;My 8,O 17 1849;Mr 6,O 17 1850;My 5 1856;N 16-17,25 1858;Ja 19,Ap 27,D 3 1859;Jl 26 1860[61-Je 16 1862;63-64]
NhD N 18 1851;Jl 9 1853;Ja 11 1862;Ap 6 1863
OClWHi Ja 19-30 1864
P-M My 1 1830;Ja 24 1845;My 11 1854
PEHi Je 14 1856
PHi F 6 1827
PWcHi Ja 26 1859
Vt 1839;41
WHi Ja-My,Jl-Ag,N-D 1825;My 20 1826;Ag 7-D 1827;Ag 1829-Je,S 3 1831-34;Jl-D 1855; 57-58;Jl-D 1859;Jl 2 1860-Je 29 1861;Ja-Je 1862;63-Je 1864

Boston semi-weekly **COURIER.** sw Ja 2 1826-66‖
1826-51 as Boston courier
CSmH Ag 5 1830;D 9(supp)1859
CtY Mr 12 1829;Jl 18 1836-40;Jl 23 1842;Ag 20 1851
DLC [1826-43;45]Mr 5,My 18-Je 1 1846;F 11, Ag 27 1847;[Ja-Ap 1850]51;Mr 4,Je 24,Ag 16,S 23-30,D 30 1852-Ap 7 1853;S 27-N 1 1858;Ja-Ag 18 1859;S 11 1862
MB [Ja 16-Mr 2 1826]Ja 24,My 8-12,Je 5-12 1828;F 12,23,Mr 9[N 19 1829-Ap 2 1832;33-Ap 18 1836]S 7,N 30 1837[S 16 1838-Ag 8 1839] Mr 9 1840;Je 7[N 8 1841-S 5 1845]S 17 1846 [48]Ap 23,Jl 16 1849[Ap 15-O 17 1850;Ap 17-O 25 1851]S 26,O 20-24 1853;Ja 30 1854[Ja 25-N 1 1855]Je 30,O 30,N 13-17 1856[Ja 11-Mr 15 1858]Mr 10 1859;Ja 26,S 3 1860;Ap 14 1864
MBAt [1826]-28;30-40;44-49;51-54;56
MH 1828;Mr 8 1830;Ja 31,F 3,21,Je 20 1831;Ja 28 1833;S 12 1836;Ap 10 1837;Jl-N 22 1838;My 20 1839;Ja 9 1840;O 21,N 11,D 20 1841;Mr 24, Ap 18,Jl 18 1842;S 18 1843-48;Ja 25 1849;Jl 15,S 30 1850;Ja 20 1851;D 2 1852;Ap 10 1854;N 1 1855;My 3 1858;Ja 16 1860;N 9 1866
MHi [1832-48]D 2 1852;Ag 14 1856[60-65]
MSaE [1828-47]-54
MWA [1826]-60;S 28,N 2,D 7 1863
MeBa Ag 29 1839
MeBt Ap 6 1829-Mr 18 1830
MeU [1848-N 1849]Ja-Je 10 1858
MiU-C [1842-45;47;51-52]
NN Ja 2,Ag 20 1832;Je 8 1833;My 28,N 3,D 1,8,16 1836;Ag 29,31 1837;O 29 1841;D 5 1842; Ja 10 1843;Ja 20,F 3 1846
NSchU Ap 21 1842
NcD [1830;32-34]Jl 30,Ag 6 1838;Ja 7 1839[40-41]F 3 1842[45]S 10 1846;S 4 1848[49-50]
NhD 1826-[37-40]-[45-48]Je 18-Jl 9 1849;F 7, 14,21,N 25,D 2-3 1850;Ag 25,N 10-D 1,8,29 1851;Ja-Je,S 7,N 1,27 1852;53-54;N 24 1856;Mr 5 1857;Ja 11 1862
NhED 1835-37;40
NjR Ja 24 1831
OClWHi Mr 18 1833;Jl 24 1839;F 10 1842;N 7 1846
OHi Jl 20-D 1829;Ja 10-N 3 1831;Ja 30 1832-O 14 1833
TxGR O 19 1829
WHi [Ja 14 1828-D 15 1845]46;Je 1864-Je 1865

Boston **COURIER.** w Ja 16 1837-O 27 1871‖
1837-Ja 3 1867 as Boston weekly courier. Merged with Boston courier (Sunday morning ed), later Boston courier and hotel news
DLC Ja 16 1837;Ap 20,Je 22,D 28 1865;Ag 27 1869;Mr 27,My 3 1870;F 5 1871
MB O 1 1846;D 16 1847[Ja-My 10 1848;F 19-D 1852]My 21 1857;Jl 10 1858[67-68]
MBAt 1837[38]41-49;51-54
MGb 1845-46;Je 1848-My 1850
MHi My 15 1840;My 19-Je 9 1842;Ja 29 1846; Ja 11 1849;Jl 24 1856;N 3-24,D 8-15 1860;Ag 2 1862;N 10-17 1864;Ja 24-F 7,My 23,Je 13-20 1867;F 5 1869
MNaHi F 27,Ap 24 1839
MWA Je 30-Ag 11 1837;Ag 10,31,N 2-16 1838; 39-41;45;Ap 29 1847;Ap 19-26 1849;N 4 1852; Ap-My 14,28 1857;N 5 1859;Jl 7-14 1860;Ja 14,28 1864;Je 8 1865;Ja-O,D 20 1867;68-[Ja-O 1871]
MiU-C [1840;42;59]
NNHi F 6,Mr 23 1865
NcD O 18 1867;My 3,22 1868

Boston evening **COURIER.** d O 6 1858-Ja 13 1866‖
Followed by Daily evening commercial
ArHi S 19 1859
DLC Ja-My 2 1865
MB 1865-66
MBAt 1865-66
MH 1858;Ja 1 1859;Ja-Ap 14 1860;65-66
MHi 1858-Ap 14 1860
MWA 1858-Je,D 3,9 1859;Ja 5,7,24,Mr 1,19 1860;65;Ja 1,4-6,8-13 1866
MiU-C [1859-60;65]
NNHi F 24,Ap 4,18,22,My 16 1865
NcD Ja 14,F 13,17 1865

Boston **COURIER** and hotel news. w Ja 3 1867+
Ja 3 1867 as Boston weekly courier; Ja 10 1867-Ap 10 1915 Boston Sunday courier: or Boston courier. Sunday ed
DLC Ag 2,D 6 1875;Ja 9-F 6 1876
M Ap 17 1915+
MBAt 1868;71-75;82-99
MH 1867-[1928-29]30
MHi Mr 12 1910
MWA Ap 19(supp)1868;Jl 18,Ag 1,S 26 1869;F 6,Ap 3,O 23,D 4 1870;Ja 8,Ap 23,My 7,S 24,O 22-N 12,26,D 10-24 1871;F 2 1873;Jl 12 1874; Je 18,D 17 1876;O 22 1882;S 30 1888;Mr 16-23 1890;D 13 1891

Boston **COURIER** for the country. tw 1824-
DLC S 18 1824
IU O 22 1824
MBAt D 28 1824
MShr Jl 18 1833
MWA Jl 22,S 16 1824;Ap 30 1825;F 18,Mr 9 1830

CRADLE of liberty. w Mr 23 1839-40‖?
Made up of selections from the Liberator
MAtt Ap 20 1839
MB [Ap-D 1839]
MHi Mr 23 1839
NIC 1839-Jl 18 1840
NNHi N 2 1839
NcD Ap 6-20,My 11-18,Je 15-Jl 6,27,Ag 17,N 9 1839;Mr 7,21 1840
OCHi Mr 23,Je 8 1839
P-M Ap 18 1840

Boston **CRITIC.** w Ag 26 1859-
MB Ag 26 1859
MHi [Ag-S 1859]

DEGRAND'S Boston weekly report of public sales and arrivals. *See* Boston weekly report. . .

DEMOCRATIC standard. w O 4 1850-
MWA O 4-11,26,N 9-16,30 1850;Ja 11,25-F 1, Mr 15,My 24 1851

Boston **DESPATCH.** d O 17 1842?-
MWA O 21 1842

Boston evening **DESPATCH.** d O 6 1896-
M O 14 1896
MBAt O 6-14 1896
MWA O 6 1896

DIAL of the Old South clock. d D 5-15 1877;D 4-15 1879‖
Issued during the fairs held for the preservation of the Old South Meeting-house
MB complete
MHi complete
MSaE complete
MiU-C [1877]
NNHi 1877

DIELLI. (The sun) ir F 15 1909+
In Albanian
IU S 1917-Ja,Mr 1918+
MH [1909]Ja 7-Jl 1,O 28 1910-D 25 1931;Mr 11 1932-D 15 1933
NN 1909+

DIME illustrated. w
NNHi D 14 1867-F 22 1868

Boston **DISPATCH.** An independent journal of the times. w N 7 1852-
N-D 5 1852 as Boston weekly dispatch; D 12 1852-53? Boston weekly dispatch, Sunday morning news; 1854? Sunday dispatch; 1855 Saturday evening dispatch 1856 pub in 2 eds Saturday pm and Sunday am
MB Ag 21 1853;Ap 5 1856
MHi [1856-57]
MSaE Ap 5-12 1856
MWA D 12 1852;Jl 9 1854;Jl 21 1855;My 24 1856

DOLLAR weekly Bostonian. w Ap 9 1842-
MWA Ap 9-16,Jl 9 1842

Weekly **DOLLAR** times. w Ap 4? 1848-
MB Ja 18,D 6-13 1849
MWA My 24,D 6 1849
—d ed *See* Boston daily times

DOMESTIC advertiser. w F 8 1849-51‖?
F-Mr 5? 1849 as Boston commercial and domestic advertiser
MB F 22,Ap 9,S 24 1849;Mr 25[N-D]1850;F 17-D 6 1851
MWA Mr 12,Ap 9,My 7,Je 25,S 24,N 19 1849; Ap 8 1850;Mr 3 1851

DORCHESTER argus-news. w O 1 1927+
1927-Ag 1 1932 as Dorchester news pub 1927+
M [F 24 1928-My 1930]
MB-D [Mr-My 1936]

DORCHESTER beacon. w 1868+
pub 1924+
KHi D 31 1892-Ap 24 1897
M N 30 1889+
MB-D 1915+
MHi [1892-94]Je 13 1908

DORCHESTER news. *See* Dorchester argus-news

DORCHESTER news-gatherer. w 1873-74‖?
MB S 27 1873-D 26 1874

EAST BOSTON advocate. *See* East Boston argus-advocate

EAST BOSTON argus. 1878 -87‖
United with East Boston advocate to form East Boston argus-advocate

EAST BOSTON argus-advocate. w 1868+
1868-87 as East Boston advocate
M [Mr 29 1930-S 16 1932]
MB Ag 27 1870-D 12 1875;Ag 26 1876;F 10 1877-D 23 1882;F 1883-89;N 21 1891-Mr 16 1895
MB-E D 30 1932;Mr 1 1934
MHi O 17 1874[80]
MWA Ap 1 1871;Je 18 1881;Je 1 1889
WHi 1872-74

EAST BOSTON free press. w Ap 17 1886+
pub 1886+
M [1928-Mr 25 1933]
MB [1886-89]
MB-E F 11 1933;My 19 1934

EAST BOSTON ledger. w Jl 21 1849-
DLC Je 12 1852
MB O 1 1859
MBAt 1849-Je 1850
MWA Ap 5-12 1851;Ap 17 1852
NNHi N 13 1858-N 5 1859

L'**ECHO** de la semaine. w 1897-99‖?
In French
CLM Ja 1 1898;O 28 1899
CtY Ja 1 1898

EMANCIPATOR and republican. w,m 1833-D 26 1850‖
1833-41 as Emancipator (1834-My 1835 Emancipator and journal of public morals) 1843-Mr 21 1844 Emancipator and free American; Mr 27 1844-O 8 1845 Emancipator and weekly chronicle; O 15 1845-S 13 1848 Emancipator; S 20-N 8 1848 Emancipator and free soil press
1833-D 3 1841 pub in New York City;D 10 1841-42 in New York City and Boston
Suspended from D 14 1833-Je 10 1834;from Mr 26-Ag 1835
m Ag 1835-Ap 1836
Ct Je 30,O 6 1836[39-42]N 23 1843[44-47]Mr 22 1848
CtY Ap 23 1836-48
DHU-M My 18 1833-Je,S 1835-Je 1836;My 1843-Mr 21,My 27 1844-Ap 1845
DLC Ag 8 1839-D 2 1841;My 10,26,Ag 11-S 15, D 22 1842;Ja 11,25,Mr 7,O 2,N 6 1844;Ja 8,O 29 1845-46;Ja 27-Mr 10,31-Ap 7,My 1847-[48-50]
ICHi F 12 1838;Ap 25,My 9-30,Je 13,Jl 4,18,Ag 22,N 7,D 19-26 1839;F,Ap 16,My 29-Je 5,O 22-N 5,19 1840;Mr 4,18,Ap 15,My 6,27,Je 10,Jl 29,Ag 19,O 28 1841;42;D 21 1843;My 29,Je 12,Jl 24,S 18,N 20 1844-F,Mr 12-Ap 2,16-23, My,Je 11-Jl 2,16-23 1845;Ap 15,Jl 15,Ag S 9-16,30,O 14,N 11-D 2,16 1846[47]
IU F 15 1838
KHi [O 1835-F 14 1839]
MAtt Je 7 1848;S 5 1850
MB Ag 6 1834;Mr 10,Je 23,O 20 1835;My 1836-[47-50]
MBC 1834-Je 1835[Ag 17 1837-Ap 22 1841]
MDeHi F 10,Mr 10 1842-Je 22,Jl,Ag 10 1843-Je 19,Jl-O 23,N 1844-F 5,19,Ap 2,My 7,Jl 2,S 17,O 15,D 17-24 1845;Ja 7,F 11,25-Mr 18,Ap-D 16,30 1846-[Ja-N 17 1848]My 3,17-24,Je-Jl 19,Ag 2,S 6-O 11,25 1849;F,Mr 11-Ap 11,25-My,Je 13-O 3,31-N 14,28-D 1850
MH Ja 17-Je 13 1850
MHi My 16 1839;Mr 5,D 24 1840;Ap 15,S 30 1841;Mr 7 1844[45-49]
MSaE S 14 1843;Ag 7,S 4-11 1844;Je 24,Ap 29 1846;Ag 16 1848;Jl 5,O 18-25 1849;Ja 10 1850
MWA F 10 1842-Ag[O 10-D 19 1850]
MiU Ag 30,N 1,15 1838;Ap 30-My 21,Je 4 1845
MiU-C Mr 27 1844[48-50]
MnU 1834[35]
N 1834-Je 1835;F 1836;F 3 1837;38-F 20,N 12 1840;Mr 31 1842;Mr 30,D 28 1843;F 26-Mr 19, Ap,My 14,28,Je 11-25,S 17,O 15,N 26 1845-[Ja 14-Jl 1 1846]
NHC 1838-48
NIC My 13-D 1834
NN Je 25(extra)Ag 10 1833;Ag 1835-Ap 23 1840
NNHi N 30,D 14 1833-Je 17,Jl 15,Ag 5-6,N 4 1834;Ja 20 1835-42
NSchU Mr 10 1842;My 1843-Ap 23 1845
NSyU F 1 1834;Mr 8 1848
NcU My 22 1840
NhD F 15,My 29-Je 5 1844;D 30 1846
OO 1835-[38-49]
OOxM Mr-Je 1835[Jl 1836-37]F 8,Mr 15-Ap 1838
P F 28 1839;My 6 1841
PPL Mr 23,My 1833-Je,Ag 1835-40
PSF Mr 9 1837
RP F 19,D 3 1845;Jl 8,22 1846
RPB Ap 6(extra)1834;F 11,S 16,30 1841
TNY Je 17(extra)1839
VtBr Jl 26 1838;O 24 1839;F 6-20,My 20,Je 10 1840;O 7 1841[42-N 9 1843]
VtMiM Ag 1835-F,Ap 1836-Jl 9 1840
WMeno [1842-46]

ERITASSARD hayastan. w My 9 1903-31‖?
In Armenian
NN 1903-10

ETHNIKE. National. w
In Greek
CtY D 7 1907-N 28 1908

EXAMINER or British, colonial and foreign weekly gazette. Ag 6 1829?-
MWA Ag 13,S 3,D 10 1829

EXCELSIOR. w 1847-My 26 1849‖?
MH My 1 1847-My 26 1849
MWA F 17 1847

EXPERIMENT and office holders' journal. w,sw My 5 1834-
Ag 13 1834 as Herald of glory and adopted citizens journal; Ag 18 1834 Blaze of glory and tories oracle
InNh Ag 7 1835
MB My 1834-Je 1835
MHi My-Je 1834
MWA Je 7,21-26,Jl-Ag 18,S 18,19,23,O 4,N 4 1834
MiU-C Jl 25 1834
MnHi Jl 4 1834

EXPOSITOR and Boston philanthropist. w Ap 2 1821-
MB [1821-Mr 1822]
MHi Je 18 1821
MWA My 28,Jl 14-21,Ag 18,S 29,D 15 1821

EXPOSTULATOR. w Ag 7 1839-
Campaign paper
MDeHi Ag 28 1839
MWA Ag 7-23,S 11,O 1839
MeBa Ag 21 1839

Boston daily **EXPRESS.** d D 11? 1837-
MWA D 14 1837;Ja 8,13,S 1,O 25 1838

Evening **EXPRESS.** d O 19? 1841-
DLC O 20,22 1841

Saturday evening **EXPRESS.** w 1857-85‖?
Title varies: Express; Saturday express
MBAt 1865-73
MWA Ap 21,My 4 1861;Ap 18,Ag 15 1863;My 7 1864;Ag 25 1865;Mr 23 1872;Mr 11 1876;Mr 20 1880;Ap 15 1882;My 5 1883
OClWHi S 17 1864
OOxM F 8 1868

MASSACHUSETTS (*Continued*)

BOSTON—*Continued*

FACTS for the people. w Ag 17-N 6 1839||
MB complete
MSaE Ag 17,S 7-14 1839
MWA Ag 17-31,O 19 1839
NcD Ag 24 1839
WHi Ag 17 1839

FATAT Boston. ir,m 1914-22||?
In Arabic
IU [D 28 1917-My 8 1919]

Boston FINANCIAL news. d 1893-1925||
DLC S 1924-Je 8 1925
MH-BA N 18 1896-Je 1907;09-23

Boston FINANCIAL news. w 1930+
PP 1930-[33]

FINANCIAL record. w F-O 30 1874||
MHi complete

FIRESIDE journal. w Ja 6 1855-
MWA Ja 6 1855
WHi Ja-F 3 1855

FLY. N 30 1850||
MHi complete

FOREIGN Protestant telegraph and European intelligencer. w
MHi F 7 1846

FREE American. w F 7 1839-41||?
1839-F 1841 as Massachusetts abolitionist. United with Emancipator to form Emancipator and free American, later Emancipator and republican
Ct 1839-F 18 1841
CtY Je 10 1841
DLC Mr-D 2 1841
DLC Mr-D 2 1841
MB Mr 7,My 9,Ag 8,S 19,D 12 1839;Mr 5 1840
MHi F 28 1839-F 18 1841
MWA Mr-D 2 1841
MiG 1839-F 13 1840
NIC S 1839-F 1841
NN Mr 13 1840
NNHi D 5 1839;Ja 16-Ag 13 1840;My 6,N 18 1841
NSyU Jl 28(extra)1839
NhD O 15,D 17 1840
OCHi 1839-D 10 1840;S 18(extra)1841
P-M O 15 1840

FREE PRESS. w N 22 1851-
C N 22 1851

FREE PRESS and advocate. w Ag 1 1828-38||
1828 as Anti-masonic free press; 1829-Mr 1832 Free press; Ap 1832-Ag 9 1837 Free press and Boston weekly advocate
CSmH S 10 1830
Ct O 11 1837
CtY Ag 21 1829
DLC Ja 26 1831-Mr 19 1834
MB [Ag-D 1828]D 1829-Mr 15 1831;Ag 1833-Ag 17 1836
MBAt Ap 17-24 1833;Ja 29 1834;N 16,D 14 1836;Ap 30,My 24,Ag 9,S 13,O 11 1837;Ag 29,O 10-17 1838
MDeHi Mr 26 1830
MH O 2,23,N 6-13,D 30 1829;Ag 27,S 24-31 1830;Mr 16 1831;N 27 1833;My 6 1834[Ap 1837-D 19 1838]
MHi S 5,19,O 17 1828
MSaE Ja 7 1835
MTaHi Ja 20 1833-Ap 18 1837
MWA Ag 22,O 24,N 7,21 1828;Ap 3,Je 12,Jl 17,Ag 21-28,S 18,D 18 1829;Ja-N 19 1830;F 2,Mr 2,Ag 3,S 28 1831;Mr 6,28-Ap 11 1832;Ja 30 1833;Ja 15,F-Mr 26,O 22-29,N 12 1834-Mr 4,18-Ap 8,D 9 1835;Ja 20-27,Mr 2,23-30 1836 [37]38
MeU Ag 8 1828
MiU-C Ja 9 1829
N My 2,S 26,O 3-10,24,N 28,D 12 1832;F 13,Mr 6-13,Ag 7-14,28-S 1835;O 16,30,N 20,D 18 1833;Ja 22-29,Mr 5-12,Ap 2,23,My 14-21,Je 11,Jl 9-23,Ag 6,20,S 17 1834
NNHi [D 1828-29]
NcD Ap 2,Jl 16,O 29,N 12 1830
P-M O 17 1833
RPB S 13 1837-D 26 1838
WHi N 17 1830-Jl 1833
—sw ed *See* Boston post

FREE SOILER. tw O 12? 1850-
Campaign paper
MB O 14,N 2 1850
MWA O 26,29 1850
NcD O 26 1850

FREEDOM'S sentinel. w
DLC Je 1 1830(supp)

Boston GAZETTE. sw 1800-15 *See* Boston commercial gazette

***Saturday evening GAZETTE.** w Ag 24 1814-1906||?
1814-Ag 10 1816 as Evening gazette and general advertiser; Ag 17 1816-O 17 1818 Boston intelligencer and morning and evening advertiser; O 24 1818-N 10 1821 Boston intelligencer and evening gazette; N 17 1821-50 Evening gazette (Mr 16-Ap 17 1822 Evening city gazette; D 29 1838-39 Evening gazette, New England galaxy and Boston pearl; 1841-42 Boston evening gazette)
CSmH S 18 1830
Ct [1826-28]
CtHi [1828]-35
CtY 1821-O 12 1822;Ap-D 1825;Ja 15-D 2 1826;Ja 20 1827-30;F 10 1838
DLC 1821-O 8 1825;Mr 1827-28;F 21,Jl 11-18,S 26 1829;Ja 23,Ag 21,O 9-16,30-N 13,27-D 4 1830;31-O 1832;33;Ap 5,19,Je 21-28,Jl 19,S 20,N 13,15 1834;My 5 1838;Ag 20 1841;My 15,O 30 1852;D 22 1855;F 2,My 8 1856;Mr 10,Ap 7,Jl 28,O 27-N 17 1860;Ja 12,F 23,Ap 20,Je 1-15,Ag 3,17,31,S 21,O 5,D 9 1861;O 18 1862;Ja 3 1863;Ap 15 1865;O 20,N 3 1900;Mr 16-My 4 1901

KHi 1888-Ap 17 1897
MB 1821-49[Ap 10-S 18]D 4 1852;53-[Jl-D 1854]55[Ag 22 1857-62;64-O 21 1876]D 24 1881;My 6 1882;Ja 6,Jl 7,21,Ag 4-11 1883[F 16 1884-Ag 1889]Ap 1 1893
MBAt Ja-Ag 10,S 7-14,N 9,23,D 14 1822-39;N 8 1851-54;56-61;65-76
MBeHi 1834-41
MBr 1835-36
MH Jl 10-17 1824[26-27]31-[43]-[90]-[95-96]-[1901-03]-N 26 1904;F 11 1905-O 13 1906
MHi [1821-40;44-69;71-73;81-91]
MSaE [1821-22]-25;N 14 1829;Ja 15,F 5,Mr 19 1831;Ap 28 1832;S 28 1833;S 12 1835;Ja 9,F 27 1836;Ja 28 1837;F 26 1842;Mr 10 1849;Ap 24,O 30 1852;Ag 4,N 3 1855;Mr 5 1859;Ap 15 1865;Ja 14 1860;Ap 23 1881
MWA 1821-[44]Ap 5 1845[46-57]-[59-64]-[67-68]Jl 16,D 17 1870;D 19 1874;Mr 13,My 22 1875;Mr 18-25,Ap 8,Ag 26 1876;Mr 3 1877;F 11,O 28 1882;Ja 6,Ag 11 1883;My 10,Ag 9 1884;Jl 25,Ag 22 1885;S 1 1888;Je 1 1889;Ja 10 1891;D 16 1893;Mr 16,D 1895-F,Mr 6(supp) 1897;D 8 1900;D 28 1901
MeBa Ja 17 1824
MeU Mr 3 1827;Mr 2 1833
MiU-C [1821;33;38;40]Ja 6 1883
N O 29 1831 Mr 31-Ap 7,21,My 19 1832;F 1,Ag 2,N 8 1834[Jl 1837-40]
NN [1821-22]N 14 1846
NNHi [1821-26]-[28-30]N 23 1844;Mr 20 1858;Ap 15-29 1865;My 3 1873
NNS Ja(extra)1831
NcD [1821;23-30;32-36]My 27 1837-40;Ja 16,30,Jl 24-Ag 7,21-28 1841;Ap 9,My 28,N 5,S 3-17 1842;Ja 21,Mr 25,Ap 3,Jl 15,Ag 19,N 11 1843;Jl 15 1854;Ap 7 1860;Ap 22 1882
NcU [1874-75]
NhD 1821-[22]F 6 1887;Ja 13-20,F 10-24,Mr 10,Ap 7,21 1894
OCHi Ag 4 1821
OClWHi Je 29 1861
OOxM F 8 1868
PEHi Je 14 1856
Vt Ap 1829-D 11 1830
WHi 1829-30;S 20 1856-65

Evening GAZETTE. d Ja 1-Ag 17 1822||
DLC Ja-Mr,Ap 27,Je 29 1822
MWA Ja 1 1822

GAZETTE and chronicle. [South Boston and Dorchester] w 1846-
1846-Ap 1851 as South Boston gazette; My 1851-S 18 1852 South Boston gazette and Dorchester chronicle
MB [O 7 1848-Ja 5 1856]
MB-S O 9 1847-Ja 6 1855
MHi 1850-55
MWA My 15 1852;Je 23 1855

Daily GAZETTE and general auction advertiser. d O 24 1840-
DLC D 5 1840
MWA O 24 1840

GAZETTE française. w S 14 1850-Jl 19 1851||?
In French
MB S 21 1850-Jl 19 1851
MH Ja,F 8,My 17,31,Je 28-Jl 5 1851
MWA O 19-N 23 1850;Ja 4-18,F 1-22,Mr 1,My 31,Je 21-28,Jl 19 1851

GAZZETTA del Massachusetts. w 1896+
In Italian and English
IU D 8 1917-Ag 1924;Jl 20 1925-29
M 1928+

GLEANER. sw My 23? 1834-
MB My 31 1834
MnHi Je 6 1834

Boston daily GLOBE. d 1832-33||
Ct [1833]
CtHi O 30 1832-Je 16 1833
DLC D 17 1832
MWA Ja 9,My 12,S 25,O 9 1833

Boston daily GLOBE. (morning ed) d Mr 4 1872+
Sunday ed (O 14 1877+) as Boston Sunday globe S 27 1881 is Garfield memorial ed; S 14 1901 President McKinley's death
pub 1872+
CL S 27 1881
CSt-H [1914-19]
Ct My 18 1906;O 24 1908;Ja 30 1909
DLC 1872-77;S 21,27 1881;Ag 22 1885;N 9 1886;87-92;Mr 3 1893-94;98+
KHi [S 1881-Ag 1889]
M 1872+
MAtt S 20 1881
MB 1872-91[Jl-S 1893;Ap-Je 1894]Jl-D 1894;Ap 1895+
MB-D [Ag 1936]
MBAt 1872-76
MH 1872-Je 19 1873;O 23 1874;Ap 20,Je 17,Jl 3-5 1875;S 7 1876-98;F 5,Mr 31 1899;O 9 1908;Mr 16 1915;Ap 21,Ag 7 1916;N 27 1921
MHi [1872-76]S 27 1881;My 4 1886
MTaHi Mr 17 1874
MWA 1872-[Ja-Je 1899]S 19 1901;12+
MeBa Jl 16,S 1881;S 14 1901
MiG Ag 26,28 1895
MiU-C [1872-76;78;81;83-84;86-87;99]1900;02-05
MnU S 27 1881
NN S 1873-Mr 1878;My 2,Je 24 1881
NNHi S 27 1881
NcD [1872-74]Ap 19,O 2 1875;Jl 11,O 7 1878[O 1879-Ja 1880]S 27 1881;F 4 1884;My 16,O 23 1887;Ja 1 1891;Ag 7 1892;S 19 1895;Mr 9-10 1896[1918-Ap 1920]
NcU Ag 29 1880
NhD Ap 30 1874;Ap 20,Je 17-18,N 23 1875;My 11,Je 24 1876;Ap 2 1877;F 25,Ag 25 1878;Ja 1 1881
NjR D 28 1877
OC N 2,27,D 5 1872;Mr 4 1873
OCHi Je 17 1875;F 2 1898
OClWHi Ag 7,15 1873;S 20,27 1881;O 19 1889;N 2 1890;Je 30-Jl 1 1913
OHi Je 25-30 1877
OOxM Je 18 1875
P Ag 1890-1917

PWaHi S 27 1881
REdH F 19-Ag 26 1898
VU O 3 1912
WHi S 6,N 13 1872;My 20,S 16,24,O 7,16,N 11 1873;Ja 17,F 17,O 12 1874 F 27,Ap 2,Je 17,O 6,9,18 1875;F 5,Jl 6 1876;Ap 12 1877;S 15 1884;Mr 5,Ag 9 1885;My 2,D 21 1887;Ja 15,30,Ag 10 1888;N 28 1889;Je 24-28,Ag 11-12 1890

Boston weekly GLOBE. w 1872-Ap 26 1892||
CLM Jl 18 1873;Mr 11 1879
IaHi Ja 13 1881-Ja 8 1884
KHi Jl 15-N 11 1884
MHi F 11-18 1879
MNaHi Ja 31 1877
MWA Ja 1875;F 13 1878;S 8 1880;Ap 26 1892
NbHi Jl 26 1876;F 7,Mr 7 1877
NcD N 10 1885
OCl My 16-S 5 1877
WHi Mr 30 1874;Je 18,S 3 1875;S 19 1877

Boston evening GLOBE. d Mr 7 1878+
1878- as Boston daily globe (Evening ed)
pub 1878+
MB F 1914+
MWA D 24,N 22 1889;O 1 1890;Ap 28 1898[Ja-Je 1909]Ap 11 1917;Je 12 1923;My 11 1931;Ja 5-7 1933

GOWARD'S real estate register. w Mr 18 1854-
MWA Mr 25 1854;Ag 18,O 6,20 1855;Ja 12-19,Mr 1,My 3,31,Je 21-28,Ag 16,D 20 1856;Ja 17-31,O 17,N 1-14,28 1857-[58-59]-[62]
MiU-C My 18 1861
P-M Mr 17,Ap 14 1855

GRIDIRON, and original know nothing. w
MSaE O 14,N 11 1854

GUARDIAN. w 1902+
M [Ja 11 1930-O 1931]

HAIRENIK. tw,d 1900+
In Armenian
pub Ag 22 1908+
IU D 1917+
MH F 18 1916+
NN 1931+
—English ed *See* Hairenik weekly

HAIRENIK weekly. w Mr 1 1934+
pub 1934+
IU 1934+
WHi F 13 1912
—Armenian ed *See* Hairenik

HARRISON democrat. w Ap 1-N 5 1840||
MDeHi Jl 7 1840
MH complete
MWA Ag 4-11,S 8,O 6-13,27 1840
NNHi Jl 14 1840

HEARST'S Boston American. *See* Boston American. d 1904+

Boston morning HERALD. d My 24 1836-
1836-37 as Boston daily herald
DLC My 31-Je 13,20,Jl 18,Ag 4,N 25 1836;Je 26-D 18 1837
MWA [My 25-D 1836]F 16,27,Mr 7,Ap 28,Je 8,13 1837;Mr 13,O 27 1838;N 26 1839;D 19 1840
NNHi F 27 1837;S 20 1839

Boston HERALD. d Ag 31 1846+
Ag 28 1921 is Diamond jubilee number
pub 1846+
C F 4 1887-89
CP Ja 13 1869
CSmH O 14 1846;My 1(supp)1889
CSt S 30 1861;Ja 1894;S 1901-Ag 1902
Ct Je 17-18 1875;Ja 30 1909;N 4 1921
CtSp O 1894+
DLC Mr 5,D 1849;O 25 1852;My 1856-Je 1861;My 9 1862;Je 10 1870;N 11 1872;Ap 2 1875;76-Je 1879;Ja-Je 1882;N 19 1885;Ap 1889+
ICM Ap 16 1883;Je 20,Jl 22-23,28,Ag 19,S 11,29-30 1885
IU N 6-D 1909;Ja 27-31,Mr 1-5 1910
KHi F 10 1848;F 1883-85 Ag 11 1890[D 12 1894-Ja 3]O 21 1897;Je 26 1914
M 1881+
MAm My 21,Jl 16,23, Ag 6 1898
MB [My 1848-O 1861;62-Je 1869;79]89+
MBAt Jl 24 1851[52]-56[61]+
MBr 1900-15
MDa 1933+
MH Je 16 1849[Ap 13-D 11 1850]Jl 1851-Je 1852;53;Ap-D 1854;Jl 1855-59;Ag 5 1870;N 11 1872;[1877-[84]-Je,O 1886+
MHi [1848-65]My 21 1870[N 1872]D 1 1874;Ap 20,Je 17 1875;Je 22 1877;S 18 1880;Ja 3-8,10 1884;Jl 24 1885;F 3,26 1886;My 1 1889;O 18 1891-F 1910[14-18]-33
MNaHi F 21-23 1854;D 1,5 1862;O 15 1864;D 6 1899
MNb 1888-93
MNort 1935
MW Jl 1892+
MWA Ag 31 1846[47-70]Ap 19,Je 26,O 9-11 1871[72-76]Mr 12,Je 26,O 11,N 9 1877[78-85]-[87]-F My 1906-15;F 25 1919
MWiC Ag 14-15 1861
MWo Jl 8 1865-N 7 1866;My 27 1875;Ja 25 1891;O 7-8 1892
MeBa Jl 7,S 20,23 1881;My 1 1889;Ja 27,30 1893;D 31 1898
MiU-C [1852;55-57;60;62;65;72;82-87;90;92-96;98;1901]
MnHi Mr 17 1841
NNHi S 29 1865;My 1 1873
NcD Ja 13 1849;O 30 1852;Ja-Je 1855;Jl 24 1861;My 3 1863;Ap 17 1865 My 10 1869;N 11-12 1872;Je 6 1874;Ja-Je 1877;Jl 24 1884;O 30 1885;S 1892-Je,S-O 1907;N 1909-10;Ag 1911;Ag,N 1912-Ja,Jl 1914;15;17 F,Ap-Ag 1918;Mr 1920;My 1922
NcU Ag 26,30 1880
NhD D 11 1872;Je 17-18 1875;D 1 1877;N 6 1878;Je 25 1880;Mr 23 1882;Jl 12,Ag 10,16,N 5-9 1884;F 2 1898
NjR Ja 29,Ap 25 1861;O 5 1862
OCHi Je 17-18 1875;F 1 1898
OClWHi Ap 10 1865;Jl 6-7,9 1860;S 7 1878;Ag 3-4 1900;S 9 1901;N 16 1904

MASSACHUSETTS (*Continued*)

BOSTON—*Continued*

Boston HERALD. d Ag 31 1846+—*Continued*
OOxM F 5-7,10 1868
PArL N 9,11-15,18-19,22 1918;Mr 5 1921
RW Je 26 1885
TSS [Jl-S 1891]
TxU 1860
VU Mr 2,N 23 1902;O 17 1905
Vt 1862
VtU 1897+
WHi O 6,20 1856;Jl 6 1857;D 19 1862;Jl 18 1863;D 15 1884;F 2,Ag 9,S 13 1885;D 27 1886; Je 22 1887;Mr 14,16,Jl 5 1888;Ap 7,N 27-28, 30 1889;Je 24-25;28,Ag 12 1890;93-F 1 1904;Ja 27 1930
WaPS [1916-17]O 20 1921;D 31 1922[23-24]

Weekly HERALD. w Ja 1848-
Ja-Ag 6 1848 as Boston weekly herald; Ag 13-D 23 1848 Sunday morning herald
MWA My 26 1849
NNHi 1848-49

Boston Sunday HERALD. w My 26 1861+
Title varies: Sunday herald; Boston herald: Sunday ed; etc.
DLC My 31 1863
MAtt Ja 8 1905
MCheHi F-S 13 1863
MH [F-S 6 1863;N 10-D 1 1872]My 6 1877;81; Jl 1883-Ap,S 1884-85;Ap-S 1886;Ja-Mr,Jl-S 25 1887;Jl-D 1888;Jl-D 1889;S-O 25 1908;My-Je 1909;My-Je 1910
MHi D 21 1862[63]Ap 16,Jl 9 1865;N 10 1872; My 27 1877;F 6,Ap 14 1881;Ja 1 1882;D 30 1883;D 21 1884;Ap 14 1889;Ja 4 1891;Ap 30 1893
MW Ap 14 1878+
MWA My 26 1861;Jl 6,S 21 1862[63]My 8 1864; Ap 16,Jl 2 1865;Mr 11,D 30 1866;My 22,Je 26 1870; Ja 21,N 10,D 22 1872;Ja 25 1874;Ja 10,S 5-26,O 17-N,D 19 1875-[76-79]-[82-84]-[86-91]92;Jl 1894-1900;Mr 1901-F,My 1906-15; N 26 1922;N 20 1927
MWo Ag 2 1885
MiG Je 21 1863
MnHi Ap 19 1863
NGL O 6 1912;Jl 27 1913[14-16]Ja 6,14,Ap 15, Je 10,24,Ag 19,S 2-9,30,N 4 1917;Ja 20-27 1918
NNHi Ap 12,My 17 1863;D 24 1871
NhD Mr 1 1874;My 26 1876;F 20 1881;D 10 1882;Jl 13 1890
OClWHi F 8-Ap 12 1863;S 25 1881;Ja 19 1890
PBf Mr 22-Je 1883
TxGR S 8 1889
WHi My 31-Je 14,Jl 5-12,26,Ag 9-23 1863;S 4 1864;Mr 5 1893

HERALD and star. sw 1836-38||?
MB [Je-N 1837]
MWA Ap 3,My 8 1838
NNHi Mr 9 1838

HERALD of glory. . . *See* Experiment and office holders' journal

Boston HOME journal. w 1846-1903||?
1846-Ap 15 1876 as Suffolk county journal (Ja 4-11 1873 Suffolk journal)
MB O 5 1850;My 16,20,Jl 25-N 1851;Je 26 1858[Ag 20-D 1859;Ja 14-O 1860;Mr-My 11 1861;F-S 13 1862;F-Jl 18 1863;Ap 16-D 3 1864]S 30 1865;Ja 27,Mr 30[Je 30-D 1]1866 [Ja-Mr 9 1867;Ja 18-O 1868;Ja 9-Jl 3 1869;Ja 8-O 22 1870;Ja 28-Ap 1871]Ja 16,O 16 1875; Ja 1,N 18 1876;Ja 13,My 1877-Ag 1887;Jl 7-14,D 22 1888;89-Ag 1891;92-95
MH Ja 11 1868-96
MHi Ja 14 1871;S 15 1877;Ap 6 1878;F 12 1881; Ja 21 1882;Mr 10 1883;87-88;Mr 3 1900
MWA Ag 14-21,D 4 1869;My 27 1871;Jl 5 1873;F 28,S 19,N 14-21,D 5,19 1874-[75]Ja 1, Mr 4,Ap 8-15,29 1876;Je 7 1879[80]Jl 23,O 8-22 1881;Mr 24,S 8 1883;Je 21-28 1884;Ja 3-10 1885;S 6 1888;O 10 1903
MWo Ag 3 1895

HOWARD gazette and Boston evening herald. w O 1 1823-Je 12 1824||
Ap 10-24 1824 as Howard gazette and middling interest herald
DLC F 14-21,Mr 6-20,Ap-My 22,Je 2,12 1824
MWA complete
MiU-C [1823-24]
WHi complete

IDISHER fihrer. *See* Jewish leader

IMPARTIAL citizen. w 1850-51||
DLC O 5-12 1850;Mr 15,My 10-17,31,Je 28,Jl 19,S 6 1851
MH [Ja-S 1851]

INDEPENDENT Bostonian. *See* Bostonian and mechanics journal

INDEPENDENT chronicle. sw 1776-1840 *See* Boston semi-weekly advertiser

INDEPENDENT chronicle and Boston patriot. d *See* Boston patriot and daily mercantile advertiser

INDEPENDENT chronicle and Boston patriot. sw *See* Boston semi-weekly advertiser

INDEPENDENT chronicle and Boston daily evening reformer. d 1835-
MHi Jl 8 1835

INDEPENDENT chronicle and Boston weekly reformer. w Ja 3 1835-
MSaE My 9,23,Ag 8 1835;Ja 8,F 5,Mr 18 1836
MWA Jl 4-11,Ag 8,22,S 19,D 19-26 1835;Ag 12 1836
N Ag 26 1836
NNHi Ja 15 1836

INDEPENDENT inquirer and journal of the times. w
MWA D 5 1846

INDEPENDENT messenger and weekly Bostonian. Ja 1 1831-39||
1831-38? as Independent messenger
Ja-Ap 1 1831 pub in Milford; Ap 8 1831-36? in Mendon
DLC [1831-32]
MB Ja 12 1832-D 5 1833[Ja-D 13 1834]My 15 1835-N 9 1838;Ja 4,O 18 1839
MHi 1831-Ja 1 1836
MMenHi 1831-32;Ja 11 1834-Ja 3 1835
MWA F 16 1832;Ap 4,17,My 29 1835;O 27 1837;S 13,O 11,D 13 1839
NN 1833-38
NNHi Ja 17 1833;Ja 1 1836

INDEPENDENT microscope. w S 19-D 19 1823||
United with City eagle to form Young galaxy
M complete
MWA complete

INDEX of the City of Boston. m,w Ja 1850-
Ja-My 1850 as Index, for Boston and vicinity, and country advertiser(m)
MHi S 24-D 10 ~~1850;51~~
MWA Ja,Mr,My,O 3,22 1850

Boston INTELLIGENCER and evening gazette. *See* Saturday evening gazette

Bostoner INTELLIGENZ-BLATT. w 1859-72||
In German
MB S 22 1866-[71-My 23 1872]

INTERNATIONAL journal. w F 27 1852-
Dated also in New York City and Portland, Me.
CaOAT Mr 31 1852;F 26 1853
DLC Ja 28 1854
MB [Jl 28 1852-53]D 9 1854
MWA Ag 28 1852;My 19,Ag 4 1855

Boston INVESTIGATOR. w 1831-1904||?
CL Ja 20 1869
Ct F 19 1836
ICHi Ap 27 1838
IU D 7 1859
IaDH My 10 1865-My 1 1867;My 1868-Ap 24 1872;Ap 30 1873-89
KHi Ap 27 1859-Jl 1904
MB Mr 24 1837-63;My 10 1865-My 25 1866; 69-76
MBAt Jl 7,N 10 1841;Jl 27 1842;70-71
MDeHi Ap 15 1846
MHi F 11 1846;Je 20 1855;Jl 21-28 1858;66-Mr 1895
MnHi Ag 23 1848
N Je 7,O 25 1833;My 8 1844-My 3 1848
NN S 7 1842;My 26 1846;Ap 27-D 1850;60;Ja-Ap 17 1861;My 1 1867
NNHi Mr 14 1834[F-D 1835]-F 1836;F 9 1838; O 22 1851;Jl 6 1870;Mr 26 1873
NbHi Ja 13,F 24 1875;D 11 1878
NcD Ap 2,D 16 1831;N 23 1832;Ap 12 1833;Je 13,27-Je 19,Jl 16 1835-Ap,My 27-Je,Jl 22,Ag 26 1836;Mr 19 1839-[Mr 1840-Jl 1841]My 16 1843-My 1,15 1861;My 1862-My 4 1864;Ja 5 1865; My 25,Jl 20 1870-Ap 14 1880;Ap 20 1881-Ap 12,Ag 30 1882;Ap 8 1891-Mr 1892;Ag 15 1903
NcU S 28 1838
NhD D 16-23 1840;Ap 14 1841;D 10 1845
OClWHi D 4 1835;My 20 1836;N 26 1851-Ja 7 1852;My 11 1859-O 2 1861;F 12-Ap 9 1862
OOxM Jl 24-Ag 21 1850
P-M Ag 23,N 22 1854;S 28 1853
TxU My 1868-Mr 1869

ITALIAN news. w F 1921+
M [Jl 1928-33]
MWA Ja 21 1922

Boston ITEM. w 1885+
M [Jl 1929-F 1 1930]

JACKSON republican. sw Ag 9-D 31 1828||
United with Boston evening bulletin to form Boston evening bulletin and United States republican
DLC Ag 13-D 27 1828
MB complete
MBAt Ag 16-27 1828
MHi complete
MWA complete
WHi [1828]

JEWISH advocate. w My 5 1905+
1905-My 21 1909 as Boston advocate
pub 1905+
M [Ap 19 1928-33]
NN 1905+

JEWISH chronicle. w 1890-S 9 1893||
MH S 25 1891-Je 2 1893

JEWISH leader. d,w S 7 1923-26||
d Je 20? 1924-N 19? 1925(sw during summer months)
In Yiddish and English
MWA S 7,21 1923;Ap 18,Je 20 1924
NN Ag 11 1925-O 15 1926

Boston JOURNAL. (morning) d F 5 1833-O 6 1917||
1867?-1902 as Boston morning journal (O 1891-F 2 1892 Boston journal). Merged with Boston herald
A 1870-Je 1879;Ja-Je 1882;93;Ja-Ap 1901
Ct Je 17 1875;Ap 16 1885;Ap 4 1900;Ja 30 1909
CtY Ja 19 1865
DLC Ja 21,F 24,28[Ap-D]1851;Je 12,Ag 25,O 25 1852;Ag 26 1853;Mr 15,My 29,O 4,7,19,31, D 21-22,27 1854;Ja 9-10,25,Mr 23,30,Ap 26,28, My 15,19,Je 25,Ag 20-21,23,S 28,N 9,D 13,28 1855[56]Ja 14,Je 25,Jl 3,24,S 3,O 9,26 1857;S 1 1858;Ja 11-12,My 14,23,25,Je 21 1859-[64]-Je 1869[70]-80;Jl 1881-O 6 1917
IC My 1 1889
ICM Jl 13 1885
ICU O 12,D 1 1852;F 11 1853;Ja 19-20 1854
IU Ap 9 1855
IaDH Ja-Je 1870;72-74;Jl 1875-77
M Ja 24 1853-54;57-1917
MAtt Je 21 1861
MB 1833-S 1892;93-1917
MBAt Ag 29 1865-[1903]
MDeHi Ja 1 1873
MH N 5 1867;Ja-Je 1890;D 19 1903
MHi [1851-61]-71;Je 17,D 6 1872[73-86]Ap 24 1893
MMal O 10 1860-Ja 1912
MNaHi O 28 1865;S 20 1881;N 28 1882;Mr 7 1883
MSaE Ag 29 1856
MWA [1851-63]-Je 1865[66-68]Ap 20 1875;Jl 9-17 1895;Ja 23 1901;D 15 1902;Mr 11,S 20 1913;Mr 23 1914;Ap 2,O 6 1917
MeBa D 3 1859;Ja 11,Ap 28,My 9,17,24,Ag 9 1862;Ap 10,Jl 7,9-10,13,20 1863;Ap 3-5,7-8,11, 28,My 4,23,Je 29,O 27 1865;Mr 5 1869;Mr 4 1876;Mr 5 1889
MiU-C [1846;48;50-52;56-78;80-81;83-84;86-87; 89;98;1913]
MnHi F 23,Mr 4,8 1865;F 9 1872
NFre Jl 23 1864
NN Ag 2 1862;F 11 1916-17
NNHi F 2 1854;Ag 16,D 25 1861;Ap 15 1865; Ap 22 1867;S 6 1877
NcD [1851-70;72;75;85-86;Jl 1903-Jl 1906]
NhD Ap 8 1852;N 5 1856[Ap-O 1861;Ja-O 1862]My 25,Jl 6-18,S 10 1863;F 12 1864;Ap 20 1865;Jl 30 1866[My-Jl 1868]Je 2 1874;Je 18 1875[My-S 18 1877]Ap 29 1878;Ag 6-9 1880;Mr 5 1881;Ja 3 1888
NjR [1860-71]
OClWHi S 15,O 15 1862;Ja 2 1863;O 1864-My 1,Je 17,21,26,Jl 1 1865;F 28-Ap 1 1870;S 23 1878;My 29,Je 5 1880
OOxM F 6-10 1868
REdH D 20 1864
TxU Ja-Je 1862;63-64
WHi D 4,27 1856;Je 11 1857;Ja 16-23,25,Ap 27,O 26-27,N 20 1860;61-65;Mr 6,Ap 10,Je 14, Jl 14,Ag 17 1866;Je 11 1867;Ap 10-My 28 1868;Mr 12 1869;Ja 26 1870

Boston daily JOURNAL. (evening) d Ja 30 1833-1903||
1833 as Boston mercantile journal; 1834-Mr 29 1845 Evening mercantile journal; Ap 5 1845-My 1872 Boston daily journal; Je 1872- Boston evening journal
Ct Mr 26 1833[34-36]F 9 1837
CtY O 25 1861;O 20 1862-63;Ja 19 1865
DLC Ja 29,F 15 1834;Ap 3,D 7 1840;Jl,O 18 1841;Ap 18,My 9,17,Jl 10-11,19,24,S 4-5 1844; Ap-Jl 18 1845[Ja-Ap 1846]-[Je-N 1847]48; 50-Ap 14 1851;Ja 24,Je 16,Ag 21,S 14,24,D 3 1852[53-54]F 22,My 19,Jl 5,Ag 20-21 1855;F 5,Je 2,6,N 3,D 2 1856;F 20,Mr 30,Ap 13,My 16,20,23,Je 9,Jl 1857-Je 1859;Jl 12,19,Ag 18, 20,24,D 1(supp)5,18,21,31 1860-84
IC O 26 1871
ICM N 11 1887
IaGG Ag 29,S 18 1856
KHi F 5 1836;37-43;Ap-D 1845
M F 18 1847-Mr 1868
MB 1836-39;41-42
MBAt 1833[35]Ja 18 1838[40]-[42]-Ag 28 1865
MBeHi 1861-63[65]
MH F 5 1833-39;Ja 30 1843;Ag 14 1847;49[Mr 1850-O 11 1851]My 11,25,D 17,29 1852;O 13,D 1 1853;My 30,Jl 14,Ag 4 1854[F 19-D 1856]Jl 3-D 1857;O 18-22,D 3 1860[61]-66;Je 28 1871-89;Jl 1890-98;Je 22 1899-Jl 8,O 1 1903
MHi S 14,N 7 1835;My 14,Jl 8,Ag 22-23 1836;Jl 19 1838[41-45]F 10 1846[49-62]-[65-85]Ja 26 1893
MMarHi Ap 30 1841
MNb 1862-Je 1867;69-70
MSaE [1837]-[60]-[64-66]-[69-77]
MShr Ap 15-20 1865
MTa 1848-49;66
MWA [1833-37]Ja 11,19,Mr 1,Je 15,O 12,D 4 1838[Mr-D 1839;Mr 1840-41]Ap 29-30,My 16, 21,N 5,23,D 1 1842;Je 5,24,Jl 13,Ag 8,O 7,N 3, 17,D 1,23 1843[44]F 27,Mr 29[Ap 5 1845-46]Ja 1,13,Je 15,Jl 1847-[48-Je 14]Jl 1850-[51-53]-[55-56]-[64-65]-95;Jl 1897-98
MWa Jl 22 1861-Je 1865;81-Je 1895;Je 1896-98; Ja-S 1900;Ja-S 1901
MWiC S 18 1861
MWo Ja 4 1871;Ja 1 1873;Ja 1 1879;F 20 1895
MeBB Jl 1888-Je 1889
MnM 1860-65
N Je 13 1835;Ag 23 1836;My 17 1837;Ja 30,F 21-22,Mr 4,6,16,18[N 25 1839-41]
NCanHi Je 18-19 1857
NN O 4 1841;Ja 26,Mr 17 1842;Jl 31 1844
NNHi Ag 29 1840;D 17 1863;Ja 30 1866;My 31 1873;Mr 5 1881;My 17 1882
NbHi S 18 1878
NcD Ap 28,N 10 1836;N 9 1837[45;47-48;50;54; 58-69]Ap 20,Je 18 1875;My 29 1879
NhD My 1 1846;S 10 1851;N 24 1855-66;N 10 1873;F 28 1874;Ap 20,N 22 1875;Je 11 1877;Mr 5 1884
NhM Ap 5 1858-Ja 6 1859
NhU [1859]-61
NjR Je 19 1875
OCl [Ja 31-Mr 14 1850]Ag 17 1858
OClWHi N 7 1860;Ap 3 1861;Jl 1 1865;Ap 19, 25-26,Jl 25,Ag 27,29,31 1866;D 7 1878;Ap 17 1880
RPB Jl 1852-67
RW Ap 12 1861
TJT Ja 2,16,F 6,21,Mr 2,8,Ap 1,3-4,My 23 1865
Vt 1863-64;72
WHi Ja-Je 1835;Ja-Je 1837[Ja 6-S 8 1838]-49;Ap 12 1850;Jl 1856-Je 1857;Ja 13-14,18,28,F 3-4,27,My 2 1860;Jl 3 1862-65;Ap 27,My 9(supp)19(supp)1866;Jl 16,Ag 12 1870;S 16,N 13 1872;73

Boston weekly JOURNAL. w My 22 1833-1905||?
1833-My 11 1837 as Boston mercantile journal and spirit of the age; My 18 1837-Mr 29 1845 Boston mercantile journal
CL F 6 1839;Mr 26 1840
DLC Mr 27 1834-N 17 1836;Je 13 1861;Ap 30, Jl 9,23-30,O 1,15,29 1863;Ap,Jl 7-14 1864;D 28 1865;S 27(supp)1881
ICHi N 14 1872
ICN My-D 1861
ICU My 6 1852;D 15 1859
IHi Ja 24 1867

MASSACHUSETTS (*Continued*)

BOSTON—*Continued*

Boston weekly JOURNAL. w 1833-1905||? —*Continued*
IaDuC F 26 1863
KHi 1844;F-Mr 1845
M 1841-42
MBAt Je 27,Jl 11 1839
MHi [1841;45-56]Ja 24 1857;N 14 1872;Mr 19 1874
MMarHi My 24 1860
MNaHi F 5 1851
MSaE [1834-37]-[39]
MWA Mr 27 1834-F 1,Mr 22,My 3,24,Je 21 1838;S 5 1839;Jl 2,O 8,N 12,D 17 1840;Mr 18,Je 17 1841;Ja 13,Mr 24-31,O 20 1842;My 18-D 1843;Ap 11 1844;Ja 16,O 9 1845[46-47]Ag 24-S 7,21-28,N 2 1848;O 25,N 1-15,D 27 1849 [50-51]-[Ja-N 2 1854]Ja 11-O 25 1855;F 4 1858;Ja 12-19,O 25 1860;Ap 25 1861;Jl 7 1864; Ja 5 1865;F 6 1868;O 14 1869;F 14 1878
MeBa S 22 1881
MeBaHi S 24 1847-S 4 1851
MiU-C [1846;50-51;56;59;66;74;76]
NNHi Ja 17 1861
NhD [1841]-Ja 4,Mr 7 1844;N 14 1872
OClWHi S 1 1864;Ag 14 1873

Boston semi-weekly JOURNAL. sw Ja? 1835-87||?
1835-Mr 28 1845 as Boston mercantile journal; Ap 5 1845-Ap 20 1849 Boston journal
DLC My-D 1849;D 13 1850;Ja 21 1862;Jl 6 1864
IU Jl 4,15 1845
MB 1836-39;41-42
MBAt Ap 24 1835[41]-43
MHi F 10,N 24 1846;Ag 17 1849
MMarHi N 20 1845
MWA Ja 3,27,S 4,D 19 1835;F 16 1836;N 26 1837;Je 15,O 11,N 6,D 11 25 1838;F 22-26,Jl-Ag 2,S 27,O 18,25,N 1-12 1839;40;Mr 19,26 1841;Ap 15 1842;Mr 21 1843;O 15 1844;45[49]-[52]S 23 1856
MWo Ja 7,Mr 11 1869
MiU-C [1846-51;55;60]
MnHi My 15,22-25 1860
NNHi [D 1835-37]38;40
NcD My 6 1856
TKL Ag 29 1856

Boston Sunday JOURNAL. w Je 6 1880-S 11 1904||
MBAt O 1893-Je 1903
MHi Je 6 1880
MWA Mr 5 1899
MWo Ja 2-9 1898

KELEIVIS. (Traveler) w 1905+
In Lithuanian
IU D 12 1917-Ap 26 1922

KNAPSACK. d D 14-21? 1863|
MB D 14-18 1863
NNHi D 16-19,21 1863

KNOW-NOTHING and American crusader. w My 6 1854-
CLM S 16 1854
CaOTA Jl 29 1854
MWA My 6,8,13,Ag 26,S 16 1854;F 17,Je 16 1855
N O 7 1854;F 17 1855
NN N 25 1854
P-M Je 3 1854

KNOW-SOMETHING; or, Guard of liberty. ir Jl 1 1854-
MWA Jl 1,S 16 1854

KOMBI. (The nation) w 1906-
In Albanian
MH [N 22-D 1907]-Ja 1 1909
NN Je 9 1906-N 25 1908

KURYER Bostoński. *See* Kuryer codzienny

KURYER codzienny. d 1915+
1915?-Mr 17 1919 as Kuryer Bostoński
In Polish
IU D 4 1917-20;O 4 1921-O 1922
M Jl 1930
MSaE O 12 1915;Mr 31 1916

LATIMER journal and North star. tw,ir N 11-26 1842;Ja 12,My 10 1843||
DLC N 11,26 1842
MB 1842
MHi complete
MSaE N 14 1842
MWA 1842;My 10 1843
MiU-C N 26 1842
NNHi N 8 1842
NcD 1842
WHi N 14 1842

Sunday morning LEADER. w O 9 1864-
O 9-16 1864 as Boston leader
MB 1864-F 5 1865
MHi O 9-23 1864
MWA O 9-16 1864;F 5 1865
MiU-C O 9 1864

Boston daily LEDGER. d Ap 4 1842-
MB Ap 6,My 15 1842
MNaHi Je 28 1850
MWA Ap 7,9,11 1842

Boston daily LEDGER. (evening) d Ap 28 1856-Jl 25 1859||
1856? as Evening ledger
DLC Jl 28 1856
MB Ap-N 22 1856;My 9,Je 20,Jl 6,29,O 31 1857;Ag 30,S 21 1858;Mr 1,Ja 6 1859
MH 1859
MHi [1856]Mr 15,17-21,26,Je 17,Jl 25 1859
MWA My 29,Ag 20,S 19,N 4,22 1856;57-Je,O 12,D 11 1858;F 2 1859
N Ap 28 1856
NhM Ag 6 1857

LIBERAL. sw Ag 21 1839-
MB O 12 1839
MWA [Ag 24-N 23 1839]

LIBERATOR. w Ja 1 1831-D 29 1865||
CLM Jl 12 1861
CPo Jl 27 1860
CSmH [My 9 1835-D 15 1865]
CSt 1850-65
CtY complete
DHU-M 1832;Ja 26,N 2,D 28 1833-37;45-48;Jl, Ag 8,S 26,O 24,N 21-D 5 1862
DLC complete
FTS My 5 1865
IC N 10 1854
ICN 1833-[37]38;40-65
ICU [1835-36;38;40;42-52]-[56]-[63-65]
IU [1847-48]My 4,O 12,N 2,30,D 7,28 1849[Mr-D 1850]-[56]-65
IaDH Je 23 1844
KHa [1847;49-Ap 7 1854]
MAm 1857-65
MB complete
MBC Ag 16 1834;D 5 1835;Ag 19(extra)1837; 39-40;Ag 24 1860-65
MCam 1836
MDeHi Ja 1 1831;D 15 1832;Ja 19,Jl 13 1838
MH complete
MHi complete
MMal 1840-65
MMarHi Jl 18 1839-D 15 1865
MNS 1847-62
MNaHi Ag 16 1839
MWA complete
MWalp [1849-65]
MWbHi [1837-39;41-64]
MeBB 1850-65
MeBa [1849-65]
MeBe My 5-12,Je 2-9,23,Jl 28 1832
MeP 1833-38;40-65
MeU D 5 1833
MiD-B 1833-43;45-60;62-65
MiU [1849-50]
MoS 1852-65
N Ja 1 1831;O 1835-39;Ag 21,S 25 1840;O 8,29 1841;Mr 31 1843[45-Ap 24 1865]
NB [1840-51]-65
NBHi Ja 1 1831;37-65
NBP S 10 1847;My 12,Je 9,23,Ag 11-18 1848;Ag 9,30,N 15,22-29,D 20-27 1850[51-53]-[56-58]-[65]
NIC complete
NN complete
NSyU My 28 1841;Ja 2 1846;Je 11 1847;Mr 10 1848
NcD F 25,Mr 12 1842[47]S 22-29 1848[Mr-Ag 1856]Ja 9-16 1857[58-60]
NhD Ja 26 1844
NhFr Ag 27,D 3 1858;Ja 28,O 7,N 11 1859;Ja 27 1860;N 13 1863[65]
NjN [Jl 1836-49]
NjP [1831-33]
OCHi Mr 15 1839
OCl O 17 1862
OHi S 15 1832-D 6 1834;Ja 25 1839-F 24 1843; F 14 1845-55
OO [1831-65]
OOxM Mr 7,21,Ap 9-Je 1835
P Ag 4 1848-65
PDoHi 1831
PHi 1831[32-65]
PLewL My 18 1833;Ja 18 1834
PNoHi Ja 8 1847
PPL [Ja-Je 1831]-65
PSF Ag 15,N 12 1831;My 17,D 20 1834;F 28,O 10,N 7 1835[36]Ja 5,N 23 1838
PU [1831]32;34-36[49]-[51-56]-[58-61]
PWcHi S 28 1838;My 16 1842;Mr 31 1843;Ja 15 1847;Ja 7 1848;Ja 26 1849;O 15 1858;Ja 21 1859;Jl 11 1862;My 6,27 1864;My 19 1865
RPB Mr 1857-Ap 16 1858
TJT Ap 14,Jl 21,Ag 18,S 8,N 17,D 8 1865
TNY Je 5,26,My 22 1840;41;Mr 11 1853;D 14 1855[60]Ag 28 1863
Tx Je 6,20-27,Jl 18,Ag 18,N 14-D 5 1856;Ja 16 1857;F 26-Mr 5 1858;D 23 1859-60;Ja 18-Ap 12,My 3-17,My 31-Je,S 6 1861[62-64]Ja 6,20-Mr 3,24,Ap 14,My 26 1865
TxDM [1863]Ja 15-29,F 12,Ap 1-8,22 1864;Je 23,S 22,O 6,D 29 1865
TxHuS 1833[38]F 8-15 1839;D 10,31 1841[44-Ag 1845]N 15 1850[F 1851-N 19 1852;53-N 10 1854;F 1855-N 1856]D 11-25 1857[F 1858-O 1859]D 29 1865
TxU 1832-33;35-F 11 1837;42-52;55-N 11 1865
VtBr D 10 1831;32-36;Mr 1837-[45]Ja 29 1847; Je 30,Ag 18 1848
VtNu 1834-35
WHi 1831[32]-[34-35]-65

LIBERTY. bw 1881-92||
CLM [1891-92]

LIFE in Boston and New York. w S 1848-
Title varies: Life in Boston; Life in Boston and New England police gazette
MB F 10 1849;F 2 1856
MWA S 1 1849;Ap 6,27,Ag 10 1850;Ja 4,Je 28 1851;Ap 15 1855;N 22 1856;Ap 11 1857

LITERARY and Catholic sentinel. *See* Pilot

LOUNGER. w Ap 22 1826-
Ct Ag 12 1826
MBAt Ap 22 1826

Boston daily MAIL. d D 8 1840-56||?
1840-O 30 1841 as Daily mail
Je 19 1843 is Bunker Hill monument dedication ed
CSmH Ja 25 1847
Ct Mr 12 1841
DLC Ja 22,Ap 21 1841;Ja 24,Mr 29 1844;Je 19(extra)1845;Ag 26,O 14 1847;Mr 28,Jl 10,Ag 31,O 2,20 1848;Mr 11 1850
M Je 16 1843
MB [1840-53]
MBAt Je 19 1843[47;49-50]
MH D 4,14 1849[Mr-D 11 1850]Mr 11,Ap 14,22, Jl 4,O 3 1851
MHi [1841-43]Jl 30 1844[45-46]Ja 25,Ag 14 1849[51-54]
MNaHi Je 26 1845;Ag 17 1849;S 6 1850;Ja 13 1851
MWA D 10,22,30 1840[41-43]-Je 29,Jl 29-30,S 14,19,O 21,N 9,13,16 1844;Mr 5,Je 17,23,28,Jl 1845-[52;Jl 1853-55]F 4,Mr 8,21 1856
MiU-C [1840-44;46-50]
MnHi Mr 4,12,17 1841;N 6 1844;Ja 14 1847;Ag 9 1850
N Ja 11 1842;S 22-O 7 1843
NNHi Ap 21,Je 1 1841;Je 7 1842;S 20 1844
NSchU Ap 28 1842
NcD Ap 21 1841;Je 27 1844;Ja 1-3 1849;Mr 29 1850
NhD My 30,Je 29,D 2 1848;My 29,Je 30,Ag 29,N 10,D 5-6 1849;Ja 27 1851
NjR O 7 1841
OClWHi Ap 21,O 13 1841;Ja 7,18 1844;Ja 25 1851
P-M Ag 11 1842
WHi S 1 1841;Ja 24 1842;Ja-Je 1846

Boston weekly MAIL. w Mr 19 1842-
CSmH Ja 23 1847
DLC Jl 5 1851
MHi My 17 1843;F 7 1846
MWA Ap 16-23 1842;Je 17 1843;D 12 1846;Ja 20,My 19 1849;Mr 23,Je 1 1850;Jl 5 1851;N 6 1852;My 20 1854
MiU-C Ap 6 1844

Saturday MAIL. w Je 12 1897-
MB Je 26-N 13 1897

MANUFACTURERS gazette. w 1881-99||?
MiU-C Je 24 1882;Je 24 1886

MASSACHUSETTS abolition st. *See* Free American

MASSACHUSETTS cataract. *See under* Worcester

MASSACHUSETTS journal. tw,sw Ja 3 1826-31||?
tw 1826-Ag 1829
Ct [1826-28]
DLC Ja 3,S 2-5,O 5-14,19,24,N 16,D 14 1826;F 1,Mr 1,27-29,Ap 12,My 1-10 17,26-29,Je 9,28,Jl 7,17,Ag 23,28,S 25,29,O 4,18,N 13,20,D 11 1827; Ja 5,F 24-26,Mr 11,20,Ap 8 My 13-D 1828;Ag 6,S 3,N 12,30-D 2,24 1829;Ja 4,10-14,28,Jl 3 1830
KyLo O 21 1826
MB 1826-D 23 1828;Mr 7-10,Je 2,9,Jl 1-23,S 16 1829;F 20,Mr 11,Ag 28,S 4 1830[Mr 5-N 12 1831]
MBAt 1826-[29]
MHi [1826-30]
MSaE [1826-31]
MWA [1826-N 16 1829]Ja 11-14 1830
MiU-C N 11 1828;F 19 1829
NNHi Jl 3 1827;Mr 25 1828
NcD Je 16,S 29,O 2,N 20 1827;Mr 13,N 22,D 6 1828
NhD Ag 29,O 21 1826;Ja 7,27,F 3,Je 7,11,23,Jl 12,S 4,O 4,9-11,16,20,25,N 1-3,13-15,20-22,D 4-6,11-13 1827;Ja 1,12-17,My 1,6,31,Je 26,O 16, 21,D 9 1828
OOxM N 3 1827[Jl 29 1828-Ag 6 1829]
P-M Je 19 1828
PDoHi N 10 1827
PP [Ag-O 1826]

MASSACHUSETTS journal. d Ja 1 1829-
Ja-D 1829 as Massachusetts daily journal
DLC [1829]F 6 1830
MBAt [1829]
MHi Jl 24,O 17 1829
MSaE [1829]
MWA [Ja-O 1829]
NhD Ja 7,Je 11 1829

MASSACHUSETTS journal and tribune. w S 3 1828-F 23 1832||
Title varies: Massachusetts weekly journal; Massachusetts weekly journal and tribune. United with Boston weekly messenger to form Boston weekly messenger and Massachusetts journal, later Boston weekly advertiser
CSmH Ag 28 1830
CtY 1831-32
DLC S 3 1828;Jl 1,O 4-D 26 1829;Ja 15 1831
MBAt N 19 1828;29-32
MHi [1828-30]
MWA S 3-17,O 22,D 24 1828-[29]-Ja 9,F 20, Mr,My 15,Ag-S 4,O 2-9,23-D 4,18 1830;Mr 5, Ap 30,My 21,N 5,19,D 17 1831
NN Jl 17-24,Ag 7 1830
NcD Mr 11,Ap 8,22 1829;O 23 1830
NhD S,O 8-N 19,D 1828;Ja 14,N 28,D 12-26 1829;Ja 9,30,F-Je 12,Jl 3,24,Ag 14-N 6,20 1830-32

MASSACHUSETTS life boat. w 1845?-54||
MB F-S 19 1854
MH O 13 1852;Ja 11-F 1,28,Mr 14 1854
MSaE F 25 1852
MWA Je 23 1852;O 12 1853-S 19 1854
P-M My 23 1854

MASSACHUSETTS spy. *See under* Worcester

MASSACHUSETTS sun; or, Thomas's Boston journal.
MCheHi Je 17 1875
NBHi Je 17 1875

MASSACHUSETTS whig. w Ag 24 1843-N 7 1844||
Campaign paper
DLC Ag-S 7 1843
MB Ag 31-N 7 1843;Ag 8-N 1844
MHi O 5-12,26 1843
MMarHi O 10 1844
MSaE Ag 8,22,S 5-12,26,O 10-N 1844
MWA S 7,28-O 5,N 9 1843;Ag 8,22-S 5, 9(extra)12,26-N 1844
NNHi S 9(extra)1844
P-M O 17 1844

MATTAPAN ledger. [South Boston] w F 5 1859-
MWA F 5 1859

MATTAPAN register. *See* South Boston register

Evening MERCANTILE journal. *See* Boston daily journal

Boston MERCANTILE reporter. w Mr 20 1857-
MB Mr 20 1857
MWA Ag 8 1857

MASSACHUSETTS (*Continued*)

BOSTON—*Continued*

MERCHANTS, manufacturers and bankers' tri-weekly guide and register. tw O 11?1866-
MB N 1 1866
MWA D 22 1866

Boston MERKUR. w N 21 1846-
In German
MB N 21,D 1846-Ja 1 1848

Thursday MESSENGER. w Je 5 1845-
DLC O 1,D 24 1846;Ag 19,S 2 1847;Ap 6 1848
MB Je 12,Jl 31,Ag 21 1845;F 19,Ap 2 1846
MWA Je 19-26 1845;Mr 12,Ap 23 1846;O 26 1848;Ag 16 1849

Boston weekly MESSENGER. *See* Boston weekly advertiser

Boston MIRROR. w 1830?-F 1834||?
United with Bunker Hill aurora to form Bunker Hill aurora and Boston mirror
Ct Mr 30,Jl 27 1833
MeBe Je 30-Jl 28 1832

Weekly MIRROR. 1898-1908 *See* Weekly review

Boston weekly MIRROR and theatrical journal. w N 7 1840-
MHi N 7 1840
MWA N 7 1840

MONUMENT. d S 8-15 1840||
MHi complete
MSaE S 10-12,15 1840
MeBa S 8-9 1840
MnHi S 8,12,14-15 1840

MUTUAL advertiser. w Mr 21 1846-
MB Ap 4,25-My 2,16-23,Je 20-Jl 4,Ag 8 1846
MWA Ap 25-My 2,16-23,Je 27 1846

Boston NATION. w O 5 1839-
ICHi N 23 1839
NhD F 12 1842;F 17,Ag 24,O 19 1844;S 13,O 18 1845;My 15,S 18 1847;F 12 1848
RW D 25 1841

NATION. w Ja 23 1864-D 26 1872||
Followed by Weekly news and nation
CLS Jl 28 1866
M Ap 22 1865
MB 1865[67-72]
MWA 1864-67;F 1,Mr 14,28,Ap 25,My 16 1868-D 7 1872
MiU-C D 16 1865
NNHi S 14 1871
NcD Mr 28 1864;My 11 1867;Je 26,D 18 1869

NATIONAL. w S 14 1907-N 28 1908||
MH complete

NATIONAL anti-slavery bazaar gazette. Ja 14 1848||
MB complete

NATIONAL champion. sw D 6 1842-
MB D 6 1842
MWA D 20 1842

NATIONAL democrat. w O 12 1853-
MWA O 12,N 9 1853;Ja 19,F 2,23-Ap 6,27-My 4 1854

NATIONAL union. w F 4 1860-
United with Spirit of seventy-six to form National union and spirit of seventy-six
MHi F 4-25 1860

NATIONAL union and spirit of seventy-six. w My 7 1859-
1859-N 10 1860 as Spirit of seventy-six
MHi N 17 1860-Mr 16 1861
MWA N 12 1859;F 25,S 1,N 17-24,D 15 1860

NATIONAL whig and star. d 1842-
MWA N 3 1847

NATIVE American republican. w N 9 1844-
CtY N 16 1844
MWA N 30 1844

NETTLE. w S 5 1838-N 6 1844||
Campaign paper
DLC S-N 22 1838;Ag 11 1840
MB O 9 1839-Mr 21,Ap 14 1840
MBAt [1838-39;44]
MWA S-N 22 1838;S 4 1839;Mr 21,Ap 14 1840; Jl 10,Ag 26-S 4,25,O 16-23 1844
NNHi Ap 14 1840
NcD Ag 26 1844
NhD Jl 28 1840

NEW age. w N 6 1875-Je 9 1877||
M complete
MB N 6 1875;N 18 1876
MH complete
MHi complete

NEW crisis. w Jl 12-N 3 1848||
Campaign paper
MWA Jl 12,S 8,O 27-N 3 1848
NNHi Jl 12 1848

NEW ENGLAND chronicle. *See* Boston semi-weekly advertiser

NEW ENGLAND democrat. w Ja 4 1844-F 20 1845||
MB Ja-N 14 1844
MDeHi F 20 1845
MHi S 19 1844;F 20 1845
MMarHi Je 27 1844
MWA My 30-Je 6,27,S 12-19,O 10 1844;F 20 1845
NN Ja-N 7 1844;F 20 1845
NNHi complete
NjR F 20 1845
T Je 1844-45

NEW ENGLAND democrat. w S 26 1846-
MWA O 3-10 1846

Der NEW ENGLAND demokrat. w,ir O 24 1857-
In German
MB N 21,D 5,30 1857-Ja 2,30-F 3,6,10 1858

NEW ENGLAND meridian. w Ja 5 1861-
MWA Ja 12 1861

NEW ENGLAND meridian. ir N 16 1861-Ap 11 1863||
These nine issues constitute the entire publication: N 16,30,D 14 1861;Jl 5,12 1862; Mr 16,21,28,Ap 11 1863
MBAt complete
NjR Jl 12 1862

NEW ENGLAND news letter. sm Je 15? 1927+
M [Ag 30 1928-S 1931]Jl,O 1936

Daily NEW ENGLAND palladium. d Ag 31-D 31 1830||?
CSmH Ag 31 1830
CtY Ag 31,D 1-2 1830
ICHi Ag 31-D 1830
MWA Ag 31 1830

*NEW ENGLAND palladium and commercial advertiser. tw,sw,d Ja 1 1793-My 26 1840||
1793-1800 as Massachusetts mercury (Jl 2 1793-N? 1794; Jl 8-D? 1796 Mercury) Ja 2 1801-Mr 8 1803 Mercury and New-England palladium; Mr 11 1803-D 31 1814 New England palladium. United with Independent chronicle and Boston patriot to form Boston semi-weekly advertiser
tw Ja-Je 1793;sw Jl 1793-Ag 1830
CSmH 1821-S 8 1826
Ct [1826-29;31]
CtHi 1825;29-30
CtY 1821;O 22 1824-34
DLC 1821-[30-Ap 1831]O 1 1839
ICHi 1824-27;29-S 3 1830
MB Je 19,N 23,D 16 1832[F 1834-N 1835;Jl-D 1836;My 12 1837-N 1838;39-40]
MBAt 1821-31
MH 1821-My 3 1831
MHi [1821-34]
MMarHi Jl 1 1828
MWA 1821-Je 17,Jl 5-8,Ag 12 1831;Ja 10,24,F 17,24-28,Mr 6,20,Ap 20,Je 5,O 26 1832;Mr 19, O 11,25,N 19 1833[34-Ag 21 1835]Je 8,15,22,N 6,D 11 1838;Ap 21 1840
MWo Mr 13 1821;D 31 1822
MeP 1821-23
MeU My 22 1829;My 24,S 23 1831
MiU-C [1822-23;25;30]
MoSW [1821-23]
N 1821-Ja 1826;O 1827-28;Ap 3-7,My 5-8,19-22, O 2,13 1829[Mr 26 1830-Je 7 1831]O 18 1833
NNHi 1821-[26-28]-30;35
NcD [1821;23]Ag 24 1824;Jl 7,S 22 1826;Je 12,D 25 1827[28-30]Ja 14 1831
NhD D 11 1821;S 10 1822;Ap 4,25,My 2,Ag 8, S 21,D 5,19 1823;F 6,Mr 30,Je 25,Jl 9,N 5-9 1824;Ja 11,F 11,My 17,Je 21,S 13,30,N 25 1825 [26-N 5 1833]
OClWHi 1827-Ag 29 1828
OHi Mr 9-16,Je 22 1821;F 14,21,My 30,O 10 1823;Ja 27-O 1 1824;Ag 3,D 25 1827;Ja 20-Ap 10 1829
PPL Jl 28,Ag 8,29 1826
WHi Je 1 1821;S 12 1826;Ja-S 21 1828;29,My 18-Ag 24 1830

NEW ENGLAND spectator. w N 5 1834-Ap 25 1838||
MB N 5,19,D 3,31 1834;Ap 8,My 13,Je 3,24, S 23,O 28-N 4 1835;36
MBAt Ag 1836-My,D 13-20 1837;Ja,F 14,28-Mr 21 1838
MWA N 5,26 1834-Ja 14,Jl 22,Ag 5,O 21 1835; F 24,N 23 1836;F 22,Mr 8,My 3,Ag 16,D 6 1837;Ja 17,31,F 21,Mr 14-Ap 11,25 1838
NNHi Ap 18 1838
WHi [My-D 9 1835]F 10,Je 8 1836

NEW ENGLAND staaten zeitung. w 1875-D 14 1901||
In German
M O 21 1893-1901
MB Jl-D 1877;79-90
MH D 5-12,26 1891-1901
MWA Ag 20 1881-92
—Beilage zur New England staaten zeitung. *See* Rhode Island wochenblatt (Providence, R.I.)
—Spezial-nachrichten. Beilage der New England staaten zeitung.
MWA D 22 1883-Mr 1 1884

NEW ENGLAND Washingtonian. *See* New Englander

NEW ENGLANDER. w 1842-
1842-N 18 1843 as Boston Washingtonian; N 25 1843-N 3 1849? New England Washingtonian; N 10 1849-Mr 1 1850 Washingtonian
MB Ag 23,S 6,N 22 1845;Mr 28,S 12 1846; S 18 1847[Ja-Ag 12 1848]F 2 1850
MBeHi 1848
MH N 10 1849-50
MWA My 20,S 30-O 7,N 25,D 30 1843;N 28 1846
NhD Jl 26,Ag 23,S 20 1845
NjR F 26 1848;Ap 21 1849
P-M D 6 1845

NEW ENTERPRISE. *See* Charlestown enterprise

NEW GALAXY. w
MHi My 21,Jl 16 1831

NEW WORLD. w Ap 17 1852-D 31 1853||?
MBAt Ap 24 1852-Ap 9 1853
MH 1852-53
MWA Ap 17,O 2 1852

NEWFOUNDLAND weekly. w Jl 19 1924-
M Jl 16 1927
MB N 29 1924
MWA Jl 19 1924

Boston daily NEWS. d Mr 13 1834-
Mr-Ap 12? 1834 as Boston news
MB Jl 1 1834
MWA Mr 19,Ap 5,12,Je 6 1834
NN Mr-S 10 1834

Daily evening NEWS. d O 2 1837-
1837 as Morning news
CtT O 18 1837
DLC 1837-Mr 24 1838
MB F 20-21,24,S 4 1838;F 18 1839
MNaHi Mr 11 1839
MWA N 10 1837;F 2,7,Ap 6,14,Je 12,22,Ag 6,8, 29,S 13 1838

Boston weekly NEWS. w Jl 17 1841-
MBAt N 6 1841

Sunday morning NEWS. w 1849-53||
1849-50? as Sunday news. United with Boston weekly dispatch to form Boston weekly dispatch, Sunday morning news, later Boston dispatch
MWA D 16 1849;F 10-17,Mr 3,24,Ap 14-21,My 26 1850;F 1,Mr 7,28,Ap 25-My 2,O 31 1852
N F 6 1853

Sunday NEWS. w 1853-
MWA Ag 27 1854;Mr 15 1857

Boston daily NEWS. d 1869-F 1 1876||
1869? as Boston daily news and tribune
DLC F 16,21,Ap 27,Je 8,Ag 9 1870-76
MB O-D 1869;Mr 13 1872;S 17 1875
MBAt Ag 29 1871-[72]-76
MHi O 26 1869;N 29 1875
MWA S 14,O 4,7-8,N 8,D 24 1869;70-72;N 8 1873-F 22,Ag 20,S 3,D 2,13,20 1875
WHi O 7,30 1875

Boston NEWS. d Je 1 1891-Je 12 1893||
MB Je 1 1891[Je 16-N 1892;Ap 7-Je 12 1893]
MWA 1891;Mr 19-O 1892;93
WHi S 7 1891;Jl 1892-93

Boston morning NEWS. w Ap 4-Jl 23 1901||?
M Ap 5-Jl 28 1901
MWA Ap 4 1901

Boston evening NEWS. d Ap 21 1903-Ap 23 1904||
MB complete
MWA Ap 21 1903

Boston NEWS. d Je 15 1921-
MB Je 15 1921

Weekly NEWS and nation. w Ja 3 1873-74||?
Follows Nation (1864-72)
MWA 1873-N 21,D 12-19 1874

Boston daily NEWS and tribune. *See* Boston daily news

Boston NEWS BUREAU. d Jl 25 1887+
pub 1887+
Ct Je 24 1920[Jl-O 1926]
CtY [1902-23]+
IEN-C Jl 1928+
M [S 8 1928-Mr 18 1931]
MB Mr 29 1910+
MH Mr-Jl 20 1918;Ja 7 1919;D 17 1920;D 3 1923;N 22 1924;F 7 1925
MH-BA 1905+
MHi D 21 1903;O 5 1910[11-13]Ja 12 1914;Mr 19 1915[16]Je 3,17,N 19 1918
MWA Jl 25 1887(reproduction)Mr 15 1906;Ap 13 1935
NIC [1909-16]
NN [1899-1912;17]
NNC-B O 1931+
PP [1921]
PPN 1925-Je 1926;27-Je 1932

NEWS-GONG. [East Boston and Chelsea] w My 28 1846-
MB [My 28-Ag 13 1846]

Boston NEWS-LETTER. d Je 2? 1835-
MHi Jl 1 1835
MWA Je 11 1835

Evening NEWS-LETTER. w
MHi O 11,24 1857

Boston NEWS-LETTER and city record. w N 5 1825-
MBr 1825-26
NBHi 1826

NORFOLK county American. w Je 4 1842-47||
Follows Dedham patriot (Dedham)
Followed by Roxbury gazette and Norfolk county American
1842-Mr 1846 pub in Dedham
MDHi 1843-My 3,Ag 30 1844;Ja 9 1846-Ag 24 1847
MWA D 26 1845;Ja 16,Ap 18 1846;Ja 16,30 1847

NORFOLK county democrat. (Roxbury) w O 6 1849-
MB O 6 1849-S 21 1850;O 1851-Jl 18 1857

NORFOLK county gazette: and manufacturers advocate. w 1824-26||?
1824-25? as Norfolk gazette: and manufacturers advocate
CSmH Jl 20 1826
MWA Ap 28,My 19,S 15 1825
NNHi Jl 13 1826
WHi D 31 1824

NORFOLK county journal. w O 6 1849-
DLC 1849-Ja 21 1865
MDHi [My-N 1859]F 21 1863-[Jl 1866-Ja 4 1868]
MHi F 1858-Ja,N 12 1859-Ja 21 1865;66-67
MWA N 17 1849;Ap 27,O 1850-O 11 1851;Mr 2,Ag 31 1861;Mr 15,My 17,Jl 12-19 1862;Jl 18 1863;Mr 12,My 14,Ag 13,S 17,O 29 1864;Ja 14, Ap 8,Jl 8,29,Ag 19-26 1865;N 9 1867
OClWHi Ja 28 1865

NORFOLK gazette: and manufacturer's advocate. *See* Norfolk county gazette: and manufacturers advocate

NORFOLK republican. w My 5-O 27 1827||
MBAt complete

Boston NORTH. w Ja 1 1859-
MWA Ja-F 19 1859

MASSACHUSETTS (*Continued*)

BOSTON—*Continued*

Boston NOTION. w S 28 1839-Ap 1848||
Suspended from Je 1842-Ap 22 1843. For this period *See* Quarto Boston notion
Ct F 1840-Ja 15 1842;My-Je 3,Jl 1,22,Ag-S,O 21,N 11-D 1843
M Ag 22 1840
MB N 16,D 7-21 1839;40-Ap 23 1842; D 16-23 1843;F 28 1846
MH N 16 1839;F 29-Ag,O 17 1840;Ja 2 1841
MHi [1839-46]
MSaE D 14-21 1839;Je 13 1840;Jl 15 1841;Je 21 1845
MWA 1839-43;Ja 15(extra) F 3,Ap 20,My 4-11,Jl 27,O 5-12 1844;Ja 31,F 28,Ap 18,Jl 11,D 5 1846;Mr 25 1848
MWo F 15 1840
MiU-C [1840-42]
NHuHi Je 27 1840
NN My 8,Jl 5,D 4 1841
NNHi F 29 1840;Ap 24,My 22,O 9 1841-Ap 2 1842
NcD O 26 1839;My 9,23,Jl 18,Ag 15,S 5 1840; Ja 30,Mr 13,Jl 15,Ag 7,S 4 1841
NjR Jl 25 1840
OClWHi D 23 1840;Ap 24 1841;My 27 1843
P-M S 20 1845
PWaHi Jl 15 1841
TKL F 13 1841
WHi Je 10(extra)1841
—Quadruple Boston notion. ir
ICN Jl 15 1841
MWA Je 10,Jl 15 1841
MeBa Jl 15 1841
NIC Jl 15 1841
PWaHi Jl 15 1841
—Quarto Boston notion. w O 9 1841-Ap 15 1843||
Contains "all the matter that appears in the folio Notion of the same week—including editorials, the news articles and general intelligence."
Title varies: Quarto Boston notion or Roberts' weekly journal of American and foreign literature, fine arts, and general news; Quarto notion
IaDH complete
MB complete
MBAt 1841-O 1842
MH 1841-O 1 1842
MSaE 1841-42
MWA complete
MiU-C [1842-43]
NcD complete
PWcL My 28 1842
TJT N 19 1842

La NOTIZIA. d F 1 1916+
In Italian
pub 1916+
M S 5 1931;Ag 28 1932

OLD Bay state. w,ir O 18? 1851-N 6 1852||?
MH My-N 6 1852
MWA O 25 1851;Jl 31 1852
N Je 12-19,Jl 10,Ag 7 1852
NcD S 4 1852

OLD countryman. . . *See under* New York City

ONE hundred years ago. Je 17 1875||
MB complete

OREM'S weekly bulletin of mining and finance. w 1904?-
Date line gives Boston and Salt Lake City
MB [Mr-Ag 10 1912]

OUR country. w Ja 10 1852-
Campaign paper
MB Ja 10,S 4 1852
MSaE My 29 1852
MWA Ja,Ap 10,My 15 1852
NNHi Ja 10 1852
NhD Ja 10 31-F 14,Mr 13-27 1852

OUR country. w
Title varies: Our country, and the American traveller
CtY Mr 19-Je 2 1892
MWA Ap 16 1892

OUR reporter. w D 24 1851-
MB D 24 1851

P.P.F. DEGRAND'S Boston weekly report of public sales and arrivals. *See* Boston weekly report

PARKWAY transcript. [Roslindale] w F 1930+
MDT 1930+

PARTHENON. w F 25-Jl 22 1905||
In Greek and English
MH complete
MWA Mr 4 1905

PATHFINDER and business intelligencer. sw 1846-
MB Je 3,S 23,N 1,D 27 1847;F 24 1848[Ap 12-N 15 1849]Ja 3,10,21,F 7,14 1850
MSaE My 6,O 14 1850
RW F 25 1850

*Boston PATRIOT and mercantile advertiser. sw,d Mr 3 1809-D 31 1831||
1809-Mr 6 1816 as Boston patriot; Mr 9 1816-My 31 1817 Boston patriot and morning advertiser; Je 2-D 1 1817 Independent chronicle and Boston patriot; D 2 1817-Je 30 1819 Boston patriot and daily chronicle; Jl 1 1819-Ap 1824 Boston patriot and daily mercantile advertiser; Ja 1-15 1825? Patriot and daily mercantile advertiser. United with Boston daily advertiser to form Boston daily advertiser and patriot, later Boston daily advertiser
sw 1809-My 31 1817
CSmH My 28 1829
CtY [My-Ag 15 1829]
DLC 1821-[30]31
MB 1821-Je 1823;24-31
MBAt 1821-31
MH 1821-[24]-27;N 10 1828
MHi [1821-30]
MMarHi S 13 1822;D 8 1825
MSaE 1821-[25]Ja 4,16,Ap 3,My 30,Je 16 1827 [30-31]
MWA [1821-31]
MeBa F 7 1825
MeU F 15 1830
MiU-C [1821-23;27-28]
N Mr 14 1821[23;Mr-Ag]N 1825-Je 1826;Ja 28,Jl 21,24,O 16,20-21 1828;29-Je 1830
NNHi N 1828-O 1831
REdH Ja 20 1826
WHi 1821;22-25;Mr 2-3,18 1826;Ja 4-5,31,F 21,Mr 14,22,24,Ap 26,Jl-D 1827;Ja 10-11,14, Je 6,Jl 11 1829[30]Ja 3,F 15,S 28 1831

PAUL PRY and the times. w Je 21 1828-F? 1829||
Je-Jl? 1828 as Paul Pry
Followed by Universe
MWA O 25 1828;Ja 3 1829
NN O 11,D 6 1828

PELLET. d Ap 16-27 1872||
CSmH complete
DLC complete
ICJ complete
MB Ap 16-17,25 1872
MBM complete
MH complete
MHi Ap 17-27 1872
MWA complete
MiU complete
RPB complete

FENNY gazette. *See* Scholar's penny gazette

Daily PENNY post. d Ag 25? 1833-
MBAt S 5 1833
MWA Ag 27,S 16 1833
MeU S 14 1833

PEOPLE'S paper. w N 7 1855-
MB Ja 19,F 16 1856
MWA N 7 1855;Ja 5 1856
WHi 1855

PEOPLE'S voice. w My 12 1922-
M My-N 17 1922
MBAt My-Je 9 1922
MWA My 12 1922

PILOT. w Ja 3 1835+
1835 as Literary and Catholic sentinel; 1836-56 Boston pilot
CSmH S 19 1846;Mr 27(supp)1869
CaOTA Ap 24,Je 19,O 30 1858;Ja 29,F 26 1859; Ag 24,S 14,N 16 1861;Mr 8,Ag 30,S 20,N 15 1862;Mr 7 1863;O 15,N 26 1864;Je 24 1865;My 5,N 17 1866;F 4 1871;Ag 21 1875
Ct [1836]
DGU 1836-Ja 1 1837
DLC Ja 11 1845;Mr 28,My 12 1846;50;54-56;59-60;66-67
ICHi O 14 1865
IHi Ap 22 1865
LNC Je 1,29 1861
M Je 13 1931
MB Ap 3 1841;52-64;70;72-75;94+
MB-D O 1935+
MH 1835-36;Ag 24 1844;Je 1863-Je 11 1864; O 7 1871;76-Je 9 1877;My 17 1890;Mr 8 1930
MHi S 10-17,O 22 1836;N 16 1844;F 16 1846; My 8,22 1869;Mr 5 1881
MWA My 21 1836;Ja 27 1838-Ja 19 1839;Ja 2, Mr 13,27-D 11 1841;Jl 13 1844;O 2 1852;O 8 1853;Ap 8 1854;Ja 19 1856;O 3 1857;D 10 1859; Ja 21,Mr 24,Jl 21,N 17 1860;D 6 1862;Ag 20 1864;Ap 15,29 1865;Mr 7 1870;Mr 25 1871;N 15 1873;Ag 4 1875;F 5,S 30 1876;F 8 1879-93; 1905;Ja-Mr 4,Je,Ag-O 7,N 4,D 2 1911;13;Mr 8 1930;Ap 14,Je 9 1934
MWa Mr 1855-57
MdBL Ja 26 1839-40
MoSU [1849-61]
N O 6 1855
NN Mr 25 1844;Jl 4 1874[Jl 1900-10]
NNHi 1842;Je 27 1846;Je 26 1847;Mr 4,25,Je 10,Jl 8 1848;52;Jl 8 1854;My 31 1873
NhD O 31 1885
OCX S 30 1843-44
PPCHi 1841-48[51-56;58-64]-90[98-1900]02-04; 06-10]14-[17;19;31;33]
PPL Ag 28-S 4 1874
WHi N 5 1853

PINE and palm. w My 18 1861-
Also dated in New York
DLC My 25-Jl 13,Ag 3-17,31-D 1861
MB [My 18 1861-Je 19 1862]
MWA My-D 12 1861;Ja 23,Je 26 1862
MiU-C [1861]
NIC Jl 24 1862
PLewL Jl 25,O 24,D 21 1861

POLITICIAN. w Ag 11 1900-
M Ag 11-O 1900

Boston PORTFOLIO. w N 3 1855-D 27 1856||
1855-Jl? 1856 as Portfolio. Merged with Boston olive branch, later Olive branch and Atlantic weekly (not in this list)
DLC 1855-Ap 1856
MB complete
MWA F 23,My-Je 14,Jl 26,D 20 1856

Boston POST. w Mr 10 1827-97||?
1827 as Saturday evening statesman; 1828-Ja 20 1855 Boston statesman; Ja 27 1855-81? Boston statesman and weekly post
CMa My 1858-Jl 5 1861;67-69;71
CSmH My 30 1829
Ct [1827]N 26 1831;Jl 9 1858
CtY My 29-Je 19,Jl 10-17,N 27 1852;Ja 8-F,Mr 12-Ap 16,30-My 21 1853
DLC My 19,Je 2 1827;F 16,26,Jl 12 1828;My 15, Je 13,O 26-N 9,D 28 1829;38;40;F 13,27,Mr 13, 27,Ap 3,24,S 18 1841;Jl 13 1860;Ja 3-17,F 7-21,Ap 3,24-Je 5 1868
ICHi My 21 1858
ICN My-D 20 1861
IU N 19 1836;S 15 1838;F 25,Je 24 1843
M [Je 1829-Mr 15 1834]
MB Ja 24 1829-S 1831[Ja 12-Mr 23 1833]S 22 1838[Ap 20-D 14 1839]F 1 1840;F 6[S-N 12 1842]F 11[Je 1843-F 19 1853]Ja-Ap 15,N 4 1854[55-59;62-O 5 1877]
MBAt Mr 17 1827;28-34;O 3 1862
MH Je 6 1829;Ja 23-30 1830;F 26 1831;F 9 1833
MHi [1827-49]Ag 26 1854;F 18 1859;F 17 1865; Ag 14 1868
MSaE [1829;31;36;46]
MTaHi [1833-37]
MWA [Mr 10-O 20 1827]28-[31-N 16 1833;Mr 22-N 1834]Ja 10,24,F 7,Mr 14,O 17 1835[Ja 16-Ap 2 1836]Ap 15,Jl 8 1837[Mr 10-D 15 1838]-[42-Jl 1845]N 20 1847-[49]-Ja 4,N 7 1856;Ap 10,O 30 1857[58]-[64]65;Ja 12-F,Mr 9-16 1866;O 4 1867;Ap 19 1869
MWo F 10 1888
MeBt Je 1829-30
MeU D 27 1828
MnHi F 18 1832
N Ja 12 1828-My 1829;Jl 10 31 1830;O 19 1833
NN Mr 3 1855
NNHi 1829-Jl 9 1831;S 1840-Ap 1841
NcD Mr 10,Ap 28,S 1 1827;S 27 1828;Je 1829-Je 5 1830;Ja 22-29,F 26 1831;D 13 1834;Ja 31 1835;Ap 2 1836;Jl 25 1840;F 7 1852;F 11 1854;Ap 18 1856;Je 7,21 1851[Jl 1862-S 1863]
NhD Ja 16 1863
OClWHi Ag 22 1873
P Je 4 1831
P-M F 14 1835
WHi My 9 1840[D 1877-D 12 1879]D 24 1880; Ja 14,Mr 4,Ap 15,Je 24[N 9 1881-Mr 23 1885]
—d ed *See* Boston statesman; Boston post
—sw,tw ed *See* Boston statesman

Boston POST. sw N 23 1830-84||?
1830-My 1832 as Boston press; My 20 1832-37 Boston press and semi-weekly advocate] 1838 Boston press and advocate; 1839-81? Boston press and post
CSb F 1855-N 26 1857
CSmH S 7 1852;Je 27 1867
CtY N 15 1832
DLC 1830-Ja 3 1832;S 30 1834;F 18 1845-Ap 4 1848;S 24 1852
DeWI [1865]
GAtCc N 28 1839
MB 1830-[35;37-41;44-45;49]
MBAt Mr 1 1833;Mr 27,My 12 1835;Ja 26 1847
MH 1830-N 18 1831;Ap 1832-[36]Ja 6-Mr,Jl 21 1837;O 22,D 11 1838
MHi Mr 18 1831;Jl 3 1835;39;41-42;F 6 1846;N 21,D 8,15,25 1848-[49]Jl 16 1863
MNaHi F 18 1839
MWA N 23 1830[Ja 18-S 20 1831]F 17 1832 [Ja 17-My 20 1834;Ja 25-Ap 3]O 14,D 18 1835[Ja 5-Ap 12]S 23,N 29 1836[Ja-F 10]Je 16,Jl 7,28,Ag 25,D 12 1837[Mr 20-Ap 27]N 27 1838;Ja 10,Mr 31,O 23 1840;Ap 2,Je 11,18,Jl 13 1841;Jl 26 1842;F 2,23,S 3,17,O 29 1844;Ap 3 1845[Ap-Jl 1846]Mr 5 1847;Ja 4,O 27 1848; Ja 19,D 4,14-18 1849;Mr 22-Ap 2 1850;Ja 14,21 1851;Ag 23 1853[55-70]Je 5,Jl 6,13,Ag 10,S 25 1871;Ja 18 1872
N O 18 1833
NN Jl 15 1831
NNHi D 31 1830;O 26 1838;Ap 27 1841-42;N 1844-Ag 1846;47;49-50
NcU O 15 1860
NhD Je 4,S 17 1844;N 3 1843
OClWHi F 14-D 12 1840;Mr 23 1841-32;My 25 1847
WHi [F 18 1831-Ap 2 1833]
—w ed *See* Free press and Boston weekly advocate; Boston post

Boston POST. d N 9 1831+
Title varies: Boston morning post; Daily morning post; etc.
CSmH Je 7 1844-69;Ja 2 1871;Mr 19 1888;My 8 1890
CSt-H [1914-15]-[18-19]
Ct [1832-38]Ja 18 1876
CtY [1861-65]
DLC [1832-40]N 13 1843-My 14 1844;Ja 14 1845-Ap 2 1849;Ja 13 1852-69;71-Je 1873;Jl 1874-O 1917;18+
ICHi Ap 15,Jl 28,S 28 1865
ICM Je 9 1876;O 20 1865
IU Ja 29 1835;Ap 18 1840
KHi [Jl 9 1838-Ap 9 1839]
M [Mr 18 1834-N 1836]44+
MB 1831-My 8 1832;S 13 1833-Mr 14 1834;D 1835-My 1836;39[49-91]My 1895+
MBAt 1831-Je 1895
MDeHi N 12,15,22-23,29,D 1,5 1831;Ja 20 1832
MH Ja 15,18,25,F 2,5,11,16,23 1842;47-D 12 1848[Ja-N 1849]-52[Ja-Je 3 1854]Jl-D 1856[Jl 1857-Je 1858]-[59;Ap 13-D 25 1863;Ag 15 1864-Jl 1866;Je 26 1869-Je 3 1887]O 8-N 7 1888; 90-92[Ag 3-O 10 1893]
MHi [1831-92]
MMarHi S 27 1833-Ja 1866
MSaE [1833-41]-97
MWA 1831-[33-37]-[49-52]-[54-56]-[60]-[62-68]-Je 1896;Jl 1897-98
MWaN Ja 4,Jl-D 1881
MWo My 16 1878;Mr 16 1881
MeBB F 24 1872-73;Jl-D 1879
MeBa Jl 15 1863;Ja 27 1893
MeU Ag 13 1832
MiU-C [1833;36;63;65;80-81;83-86;88;90-92]
MnHi Je 4 1836
MoS Jl 17-D 1855
N O 14 1833
NN D 4 1838
NNHi My 16 1832-Mr 9 1833;Ap 5 1834;Je 12 1835-45;47;Je 18 1857;Ja 12 1861;Ag 3 1867; F 26(supp)1868;Ap 28,My 9,Jl 8,10 1868;My 31 1873
NSyU O 13 1860
NcD N 22-D 1831;Je 4,Ag 30 1832;D 23,29,31 1835;Jl 15,18,O 17,D 27 1845[46-49;53-55]My 6 1856;Ja 18,Ap 5,Ag 13 1858;Jl 23 1861[Mr-Je 1863]S 25 1865[66;68-69;86;1918-Ap 1920]
NcU Mr 21 1876-Je 17 1878;Ag 31 1880

MASSACHUSETTS (*Continued*)

BOSTON—*Continued*

Boston POST. d N 9 1831+—*Continued*
NhD My 7,10-11,22-29,Je 2,4-14,16-19,22-28 1841;F 19 1844;O 16,18-21,23,28-N 2,5-6,8-11,N 26-28,30,D 6,11 1861;Ja 13,28,F 19,Mr 6,13,17, Ap 8 1862;S 19 1864;Mr 11 1865;Je 25 1867;O 3,5 1868;My 18,Je 3 1874;My 11,N 4,7 1876; Je 25 1880
NhM O 18 1853-S 15 1859;Ja 27 1870
NjR Ja 7,9-10,12-19 1832;Ag 22 1839
OClWHi N 20 1837;Ja 1,31,F 5,22,Mr 16,18,23, 26,Ap 9-10,15,29,My 9,Je 19,Jl 25,29,S 3-4,O 10,14,16,N 5 1840;F 12,Ap 27,Jl 13,16,O 14 1841;F 12,S 24 1842;Ja 21-Je 6,O 17-D 1864; Ap 15,22 1865;S 17 1887
OHi 1912-22
OOxM F 6-10 1868
P-M Mr 21 1832;Ja 13 1840
PEHi Je 14 1856
TxHuS Jl 13 1858;O 20,N 10 1864
VU O 17 1905
Vt 1845;66-73
WHi S 21 1839;Ap 27 1861-Ap 14[Jl 25-D 23 1862]Ap 20-O 1863;Ja 16-17,23,My 3-S 1865; Ap 28 1868;Ag 4(extra)S 12(extra)1888;Je-O 24 1914

Boston PRESS. . . sw 1830-81? *See* Boston post sw

Boston daily PRESS. d Ag 19? 1867-
MWA Ag 26 1867

Boston PRICE-CURRENT and marine intelligencer. *See* Boston commercial gazette

PURITAN. w
MHi Ja 15,F 5 1841

PURITAN recorder. *See* Boston recorder

QUADRUPLE Boston notion. *See under* Boston notion

QUARTO Boston notion. *See under* Boston notion

Saturday RAMBLER. w My 2 1846-D 14 1850‖
Merged with New England farmer (not in this list)
DLC 1848
MB [1846-47;Ag 2,26 1848;My 12,Je 9-23 1849; Jl 13 1850
MH Je 16 1849-50
MWA 1846[47]-[49]Ja 12,26,F 16,Mr 2,16,Je 29,Jl 13,S 7 1850
MiU-C Ja 27,My 12 1849
N N 10 1849
NcD Ja 15 1848;Ja 27 1849
NhM 1848-Mr 9 1850
NjR Ap 28 1849
P-M D 5 1849

Boston evening RECORD. d S 3 1884-Ag 8 1921‖
Merged with Boston daily advertiser
CL Ag 1-3,6 1921
M [Ag 1891-1921]
MB [Mr 1885-95]-1920
MHi 1884-S 4 1894
MWA D 1 1884;Ja 14-15 1887;Ag 2 1888;Je 3 1895;Ag 13,15 1898;F 4(extra)1917
MWo D 10 1887
MeBB 1885-87
NhD N 5 1884
WHi Mr 12 1885

Boston Sunday RECORD. w 1886-87‖?
MHi [1886-87]

Daily RECORD. d F 15 1929+
Follows Boston daily advertiser. F 15-23 1929 as Daily record. Boston advertiser; F 25-28 1929 Daily record and Boston advertiser; Mr 1-Je 3 1929 Daily record and Boston daily advertiser
MB 1929+
PP D 31 1934-Ja 23 1935

*Boston RECORDER. w Ja 3 1816-My 17 1867‖
1816 as Recorder; 1825 Recorder and telegraph; 1826-Je 30 1830 Boston recorder and religious telegraph; My 17 1849-My 13 1858 Puritan recorder. Followed by Congregationalist (not in this list)
CSmH D 27 1827;S 1 1830
Ct 1823
CtY complete
DLC complete
ICHi Ja 27,F 24 1821;Je 22 1822
ICN O 19,N 2,16 1831;Ja 11 1832
IU F 23 1838;Ag 9,23,S 13-20 1839[40]F 19,Mr 5,D 17-24 1841
KHi 1833-35
KyLo D 28 1838-Ja 4,18 1839
LU 1821
M [1821-28]
MB complete
MBAt 1821-48;Jl 24 1862
MBC complete
MDeHi 1821-Ag 1823;N 13 1824;O 6 1826;F 2, My 18-25,Jl 13,O 5,N 2 1827
MH 1821-[32]-48[Jl 29 1859-61]-[63-64]
MHi [1821-48]
MSaE 1821-49;59-66
MWA 1821-66;Ja 17 1867
MWiC 1821-43
MWo N 2 1866
MeBt 1821-30
MeWC 1821-25
MiU 1833-34
MnU 1821-24
N Mr 24 1821;Mr 23 1822-23;Ap 22 1825-34;36
NAubT 1821-23
NN 1821-35;Ap 6,D 14 1838;39-66
NNHi Jl 1830-32;34-35;O 6,D 29 1837
NNUT 1821-22;24-31;37-67
NSchU Ap-D 1824
NcD 1821-46;Je 28,S 13 1849;N 28 1850;F 5 1852;Ja 12,Mr 9 1854;Je 10 1858;D 29 1859;Mr 29,Je 14 1860;N 27 1863
NhK 1823-25
NjP [1821-24]
P-M F 27 1845
PEr [1825-30]
PHi [1834;41;43-O 12 1844]My 20 1858
RPB 1821-24
TxU 1821-26
VtMiM 1821-31
WHi [1823-24]-26;35

RECORDER. [Allston] w 1918-28‖?
MB-B 1924-28

Boston REFORMER and anti-monopolist. d,tw N 3 1834-
1834-My? 1836 as Daily reformer; Je?-Ag 1836 Boston reformer
d 1834-Mr? 1836
Ct [1834-36]
DLC F 25,27 1835
MB [Ap 23-O 21 1836;Mr 23 1838-Ja 4 1839]
MBAt F 16 1835
MHi N 3 1834;F 18 1835;Je 25,Ag 18,27 1836
MWA N 3 1834;Jl 26,30 1836;Ag 4-13,23-25 1836

Boston REFORMER and anti-monopolist. w 1835-38‖
1835-37? as Boston weekly reformer; or, Herald of union and progress
Ct F 21 1835
DLC D 2-23 1836;Ja 20,Mr 17-N 1837
IU S 28 1838
MB D 2 1836;Ap 21,My 12,Je 9,23,Jl 7 1837
MWA O 28,N 11,25,D 23 1836-Ja 6,O 13 1837; Ap 20-27,My 11-25,Je 15,N 9 1838
NNHi D 9 1836;My 4 1838
P-M Ja 31 1835

REFORMER and campaign times. ir Je 15-O 31 1872‖?
Campaign paper
DLC O 31 1872
MH Je 15,Ag 17,31-S 7,21-O 12,31 1872
MWA Ag 3 1872

Boston RELIANCE. w Ja 4 1912-
MB F 1,Mr 22 1913
MWA My 3 1913

REPERTORY and general advertiser. *See* Boston advertiser

Boston weekly REPORT. w My 1 1819-My 10 1828‖?
Title varies: Boston weekly report of public sales and arrivals; P.P.F. Degrand's Boston weekly report of public sales and arrivals
CSmH Jl 21 1827
CtY Ja-My 22 1821;22-25
DLC My 28-D 1825
MBAt 1821-27
MHi Ap 28 1821;22-23;25-27
MSaE 1821-[28]
MWA 1821-My 10 1828
MWo 1821-22
MiU-C [1822]25
NNHi 1822-24;26-My 10 1828
extras: My 1,Je 5,12,19 1824
NcD F 12,N 5 1825
NhD N 5 1825
PHi 1825-27

Boston REPORTER. w Ja 7 1847-49‖?
MAtt Ja 18 1849
MB [F-D 16 1847]F 10,D 14 1848
MH [F 25-D 16 1847;F 10-N 2 1848]Ap 12,26, My 10 1849
MWA N 25 1847[48]-Mr 22 1849
NN F 10 1848
WHi Mr 22 1849

Saturday REPORTER. w S 3 1859-
MB O 15 1859-O 10 1860

REPUBLIC. w 1835?-
MB Ja 11-D 27 1839
MWA Jl 19 1839

Le REPUBLICAIN. w Ja 22 1881-D 24 1884‖
In French
M complete
MB 1881-Ja 26 1884
MH F 5,D 24 1881;My 1882-F 1,Je 28,N 25-29 1883

Boston weekly REPUBLICAN. w O 24 1845-N 10 1848‖
1845-Ag 1848 as Boston weekly whig. United with Emancipator and free soil press to form Emancipator and republican
MB Je 26 1846;Ja 30 1847;Ag 11 1848
MDeHi Mr 31 1848
MHi F 6 1846
MWA O 24 1845;Jl 14,Ag 4,S 8-15 1848

Boston daily REPUBLICAN. d N 3 1845-N 15 1849‖
1845-Ag 8 1848 as Boston daily whig
DLC Ag 8 1848
MB [1845-46]Ja 9,28,Ap 23,27 1847;F 21[S-D 8 1848;Ja-Je 1 1849]
MBAt 1847[Ja-Ag 1848]-49
MH Je 1846-D 16 1848[Mr 17-O 27 1849]
MHi F 11,Je 1846-S 1849
MSaE 1846[Je 1847-88]
MWA N 8(extra)1845;Je 1-2,Jl 3,16-17,S 24,O 27 1846;F 5,Je 18,28,Jl 5,12,O 2(extra)15-16,N 19,25,D 1 1847;Ja 7,My 18[Je-Ag 8 1848]-O 15 1849
NNHi Jl 28 1848-F 6 1849
NSyU Mr 9 1848
NcD O 25,28,31 1848

Semi-weekly REPUBLICAN. sw Jl? 1846-50‖?
1846-Ag 5 1848 as Semi-weekly whig
DLC Mr 13 1847
MB Ja-My 1850
MBAt N 15-D 1849
MH S 26 1846;Jl-[Ja-S 15 1849]
MHi N 1,11,18 1848;Je 9,27,D 15 1849
MWA S 26 1846;Mr 31 1847;Ag 12,S 16,27-O 14,25-D 23 1848[Ja 17-O 24 1849]F 27,Mr 27, Ap 6 1850
NIC 1850

Boston REPUBLICAN, and Saturday evening visiter. w S 7 1833-
1833-S 1834 as Boston republican
MWA S 28,D 1833-S 6,O 18-25 1834

REPUBLIKA. w N 1 1930-Je 23 1932‖?
MH 1930-My,Je 9,23 1932

La RÉPUBLIQUE. *See under* Fall River

RESTITUTION. bw Ap 22 1863-
MH Ap-Jl 1863

Weekly REVIEW. [Allston] w Ja 1898-1914‖?
1898-Ag 29 1908 as Weekly mirror
M 1899-Ap 28 1911

RIGHT way. w N 18 1865-Mr 2 1867‖
DLC complete
ICHi N 18 1865
M complete
MB complete
MSaE [1865-67]
MnHi D 16 1865;F 2 1866
NIC complete
NNHi 1865-[66-F 1867]
NhD complete
P-M S 8 1866

ROUGH and ready. w 1847-
MB D 21 1848;Mr 10 1849
MWA Je 10,Ag 5 1848

ROXBURY advertiser. w Mr 18 1848-
MB 1848-49
MWA 1848[49]Ja 4,Jl 13,N 9 1850;S 6 1851

ROXBURY advocate. w D 2 1882-87‖?
MB D 9 1882-N 1886
MH O 19 1883
MWA Ag 1 1885

ROXBURY gazette. w My 1 1861+
1861-F 1863 as Roxbury city gazette; F 1863-Ap 1866 Roxbury city gazette and South end advertiser; Ap 1866-My 1895 Roxbury gazette and South end advertiser
M O 31 1890
MB N 13 1862;Ap 27-My 4 1865[Ja-N 15 1866] Ap 23 1868;Ap 30 1874
MH 1861-[86]-My 1895
MHi S 29 1870;Jl 1 1893
MWA D 17,31 1863
NNHi N 3 1864

ROXBURY gazette and Norfolk county American. w 1847-50‖?
Follows Norfolk county American. Followed by Dedham gazette (Dedham)
MB Ag 14 1847[Je 17-N 4 1848;49-F 2 1850]
MWA [1848]
MiU-C Ap 1 1848

ROXBURY Sunday telegram. w S 10 1916-
MWA S-O 29 1916

ROXBURY Sunday times. w N 26 1916-
MWA N-D 24 1916

Bostoner RUNDSCHAU. w 1884-86‖?
In German
MB Ag 2 1884;Ap 25-My 2,S 12 1885

SANDARA. w 1913-28‖?
In Lithuanian
IU My 1918-D 28 1928

Boston SATIRIST. w 1842-
MB Ag 18 1843

SATURDAY. . . *See under* next important word: i.e. Saturday evening gazette is alphabeted under . . . gazette

SCHOLAR'S penny gazette. w
Title varies: Penny gazette
MHi Ag 26 1848;F 17 1849

Daily SENTINEL and gazette. *See* Daily centinel and gazette

SHAMROCK wreath. Mr 17 1868‖
MB complete

Boston SHIPPING list. *See* Commercial and shipping list

Daily SOCIALIST. d D 1-16 1903‖?
M D 1-16 1903
MB D 2-15 1903
MWA D 1 1903

SOUTH BOSTON bulletin. w Ja 4 1890-99‖
MB 1890-95
MB-S 1890-D 9 1899
MHi 1892-98;F 4-18 1899

SOUTH BOSTON gazette. w 1906+
pub 1921+
MHi My 28 1910;Ap 22,My 20 1911

SOUTH BOSTON gazette and Dorchester chronicle. *See* Gazette and chronicle

SOUTH BOSTON inquirer. w Je 3 1871+
MB [Jl 8-N 18 1871;Ja 13 1872-My 10 1873;S 9 1876-77;80-89]
MHi Jl 26 1893;O 6 1894;F 27,Ap 24 1897;S 15, N 3 1900[Ja-My 1901]Ap 26 1902[03-11]
MWA Mr 31 1923
NcD Ag 13 1881;Ja 3 1885

SOUTH BOSTON mercury.
MB S 1854-Ag 1856

SOUTH BOSTON news. w 1885-1914‖?
MB Ap 3,Je 19 1886

SOUTH BOSTON recorder and monthly advertiser. m S 1862-
MWA S 1862

SOUTH BOSTON register. w Ap 30 1859-62‖?
1859-Je? 1861 as Mattapan register
MH 1859-Je 1,S 14 1861-[Ja-My 24 1862]
MWA Je 25 1859

SOUTH END reporter. w Ap 30 1854-
MB My 7-S 10,N 19 1853-Ja 7 1854

Boston weekly SPECTATOR. *See* Boston weekly advertiser

Thursday SPECTATOR. *See* Boston weekly advertiser

SPIRIT of seventy-six. *See* National union and spirit of seventy six

Boston SPY. w Ja 1840-
MB Je 10 1840

MASSACHUSETTS (*Continued*)

BOSTON—*Continued*

Boston weekly STAMPEDE. w Jl 6 1844-
MWA Ag 3 1844

STANDARD. w S 29 1835-36||?
Ct My 28 1836
MWA S 29-O 6 1835;Ja 6-13,Ap 30,My 21 1836

Evening STANDARD. d
MSaE Mr 4 1848

STANDARD. w My 2 1878-
MWA Je 20,Jl 18,Ag 22 1878

Boston daily STANDARD. d Mr 28 1895-Jl 11 1896||
KHi [Mr-Je 15 1895]
M complete
MB complete
MWA Mr 28,My 25,Je 17,Ag 3 1895
MiU-C Mr 28 1895
PPCHi [1895-96]

Boston daily STAR. d O 29 1845-
DLC N 3 1845(photostat)
MB O 29 1845-F 21 1846[Je 7 1847-Ap 1848]
MHi [1845-46]
MWA N 29,D 2 1845[46-47]
P-M F 17 1847

Boston weekly STAR. w N 13 1845-47||?
1845-46? as Streeter's weekly Boston star
MWA F 14-21,Ag 8,S 13 1846;O 14 1847
NjCHi Jl 29 1847

Evening STAR. d O 18 1880-85||
MB 1880-Jl 15 1885
MWA O 18,27,N 17 1880;Mr 24,Ap 28,My 2,6-7, 24,26,S 20 1881;Mr 4,30,Ag 2-3,5,7 1882;Ap 14, N 3 1883
MeBa Jl 5-7,11-12,16,18-23,27-Ag 2,4,6,8,10-13, 15,23,27,29 1881

Sunday STAR. w My 25 1884-85||
MWA My 25 1884

STAR spangled banner. w 1846?-
DLC Je 15,30-Jl 14 1849
IU N 8 1853
MB Mr 23,S 14 1850;Ja 29-F 19 1853;My 13 1854
MWA O 7 1848;My 26-Ag 11 1849[50-54]D 22 1855
P-M D 2 1854
PCarlHi Jl 29 1854

STATE. w S 19 1885-
DLC S 19,O 31 1885
MB O 24,N 21 1885

STATE HOUSE news. w F 24-Jl 20 1925||
M complete

STATE topic. w Je 16 1849-
MWA Je 16 1849
NNHi Je 16 1849

Boston STATESMAN. sw,tw F 6 1821-My 30 1829||
F 6-Ag 3 1821 as American statesman; Ag 6 1821-Jl 21 1823 American statesman and evening advertiser; Jl 24 1823-N 17 1827 American statesman and city register sw 1821-Ag 9 1824
CSmH F 4,21,Mr 11,18,My 6,Jl 4,29,Ag 1,8,19 1822
Ct [1826-27]
DLC complete
ICU N 24 1827;Ja 8,F 5,18-23,Mr 1-6,20-25,My 3-5 1828
MB [F 1823-Ja 1824]F 17 1827-29
MBAt 1821-Ja 26,Ap 2 1824;Ja-S 3 1825;My 6, Ag 22,S 9 1826;Ja 2,Je 12,Ag 28,S 25 1827;Ap 25 1829
MH F 6 1821-Ja 1823;Mr 10 1827[Je 17-D 1828]29
MHi My 6 1822;Jl 21 1823;Ap 2(extra)1824 [1827-29]
MNaHi Je 28 1834;F 27 1837
MSaE D 22 1823;S 14,O 26 1824
MWA 1821-[25]-My 28 1829
MeBa My 27 1826-Mr 6 1827
MeBt Ja 7 1824-25
MiU-C [1821-27]
N Jl 11 1826
NNHi Je 19-21,Jl 1-4 1828
NcD Ap 3 1823
NjR [1826]
PDoHi F 3,My 24 1825;Jl 18,S 23 1826
PPoU [1826]
WHi F 6 1821;Ja 12,Jl 19,S 14-18,23-28,O 2-12,16,21-25,28 1824;Je 23 1825;Je 1,12-22,Jl 24, Ag 13 1828

Boston STATESMAN. d S 5 1825-My 30 1829||
1825-N 18? 1827 as Boston daily American statesman
DLC S 5-6,8,O 13,18,N 4,14,D 28 1825;Ja 10, 26,Mr 27,Je 6,Jl 4,Ag 7,15,D 23 1826;Ja 9 1827;Jl 12,S 5 1828-29
MAm S 7 1827-Mr 4 1828
MB Ja-Je 1826[Ja-Mr 10]Ag 7 1827;Ja-Je 13 1828;29
MBAt complete
MH Ag 10 1826;Je 9-10 1828
MHi [1824-29]
MWA 1825[26-28]29
MeBa Ap 25 1826
N N 24 1826
NNHi S 9 1826;Mr 14 1828-29
PPL [Je 20-O 1826]
PToHi O 23 1826
REdH N 20 1828

Boston STATESMAN. w 1827-81 *See* Boston post w

Saturday evening STATESMAN. *See* Boston post w

STRAHDNEEKS. w,sw,tw 1905-19||
In Lettish
NN 1909-16
WHi My 27 1908-D 11 1917;D 31 1918;F 13 1919

STRAHDNEEKU rihts. w 1920+
In Lettish
WHi Ap 17 1926-Je 18 1932

STRAIGHT republican. w S 19-O 31 1857||
DLC S 26,O 17 1857
MB S 26,O 3,17-31 1857
MWA complete
MiU-C [1857]
WHi S 26,O 17-31 1857

STREETER'S weekly Boston star. *See* Boston weekly star

STRICT-CONSTRUCTIONIST. d Je 22 1882-Mr 2 1883||
MB [1882-83]
MH [Je-N 24]D 9 1882-F 17,Mr 2 1883
MWA Ag 3,29 1882

SUFFOLK county journal. *See* Boston home journal

Boston daily SUN. d Je 1845-46||?
MHi F 11 1846
MWA S 8,O 29,N 28 1845;Ja 30,Ag 4 1846

Boston SUN. w Je? 1845-
MB Mr 28,My 14,Je 9 1846
MHi F 14 1846

Boston Saturday SUN. w O 23 1897-
MWA O 23 1897

Boston SUN. m Ap 13 1918-
MWA Ap 13,Ag 17 1918

SUNDAY. . . *See under* next important word

SVENSKA nyheter. (Swedish news) w D 15 1914-18||
In Swedish
IRA 1916-17
MnHi D 15-22 1914;D 1917-F 5 1918

Weekly SYMBOL and Odd Fellows magazine. w My 20 1846-Ap 7 1849||
Title varies: Weekly symbol and home magazine; etc. Merged with Yankee blade
DLC Jl 1847-49
MB S 26 1846;Jl 15 1848
MH My 20,Jl 11,S 19 1846-F 13 1847
MHi Jl 29 1848
MWA F 13,Ap 10-24,My 22,Je 5,O 16,30 1847;Ja 20,F 3,17,Mr 31-Ap 7 1849

SYMPAN Hellenic newspaper. *See under* Ipswich

TEA POT. *See* City eagle

Boston evening TELEGRAM. d Jl 24 1893-
M Jl 24-O 18 1893

Boston TELEGRAM. d Mr 16 1921-N 6 1926||
M complete
MB 1921-O 3 1926
MWA Mr 17 1921

Boston TELEGRAPH. w Ja 1-D 23 1824||
United with Boston recorder to form Boston recorder and telegraph, later Boston recorder
CtY complete
DLC complete
IaDH 1824
M Mr 18-D 1824
MB complete
MBAt complete
MBC complete
MH complete
MHi complete
MSaE complete
MiU complete
MiU-C [1824]
NcD complete
PEr [1824]
WHi complete

Boston TELEGRAPH. w Ja 12 1831-35||?
CtHi 1831-32
CtW N 28-D 5,19 1832-F 13 1833
CtY Jl 25 1832
MB [1832-F 4 1835]
MBC Mr 6,Jl 3 1833
MWA My 14-21 1831[32]Ja 2,F 27 1833
NNHi N 14 1832;Je 5 1833
NhD N 5-12,26 1831-Ja,F 25-Mr 14,28-Ap 4, 18-Jl 11,25-N 7,21 1832

Daily evening TELEGRAPH. d N 15 1841-42||?
DLC N 15 1841
MWA Ap 5 1842
MeBB 1841-My 3 1842

Sunday TELEGRAPH. w S 27 1846-
MWA S 27 1846

Boston evening TELEGRAPH. d S 27 1854-Ap 10 1857||
Follows Daily commonwealth. S 27-O 4 1854 as Evening telegraph. Merged with Boston traveller
DLC S 28 1854;F 26-27 1856
KHi 1854-Mr 1855
MB complete
MH complete
MHi [1854-57]
MNaHi Mr 16 1855
MWA complete
MiU-C [1854-56]
NcD S 28-D 24 1854;D 21 1855
P-M N 24 1854;Ja 8 1855
WHi S-O 1854

Boston weekly TELEGRAPH. w S 30 1854-Ap 10 1857||
Follows Weekly commonwealth. S 30-O 14 1854 as Weekly telegraph
MB [1855-57]
MHi Mr 9 1855
MSaE 1854-56
MWA complete
MiU-C S 30 1854
P-M O 7 1854
PEr [1824]

Der Boston TELEGRAPH. d Mr 16 1885-D 18 1901||
In German
M S 25 1893-1901
MWA Mr 19 1885

Boston TELEGRAPH. w S 30 1926-Ap 22 1928||
M S 30-N 6 1926
MB O 1926-28

THOMAS'S Massachusetts spy. *See* Massachusetts spy. . . (Worcester)

THORN. w
Campaign paper
MB S 11-O 2 1838
MBAt O 23 1844
MSarHi Je 30 1840
MWA O 9,30,N 20-27 1838;Ag 28 1844
NN N 27 1838
NcD Ag 28 1844

TIME and the hour. w 1895-1909||?
MHi [1897-1900]

TIMES. w Je 23 1827-Jl? 1828||
United with Paul Pry to form Paul Pry and the times
MB Mr 15 1828
MBAt D 1,15 1827;Mr 29 1828
MWA S 22,D 8,29 1827
MeU F 16,Jl 19(extra)1828

TIMES d My 4 1835-
MB My 4 1835
MWA My 12 1835

Boston daily TIMES. d F 13 1836-Ap 23 1857||
Title varies: Boston daily times; Boston times; Evening times; etc. Merged with Boston herald
C Ag 30-31,N 28 1850;Ap 28 1851;Ja 12 1852
CSmH Ja 9,29 1849;Ag 30 1853
Ct [Jl-Ag 1836;Ja-F,Je 1837]S 2 1839
CtY Mr 11 1843;D 7 1848
DLC F 23-Je 7,S 12 1836-N 29 1837;D 14 1839; Je 15,D 5 1844;45-49
M Jl 1 1837;Je 24 1840;Ag 3 1854
MB [F 16 1836-Jl]Ag 7 1841-[42-O 2 1843;Ja 29-Ag 2 1844]N 27,D 31 1845[Ja 19-My 22 1846;Ja 26-D 9 1847;Ap 20-N 13 1848;Ja 24-D 14 1849;50-52]53
MBAt 1836-57
MDeHi Ja 25 1836
MH My 23 1836-Jl 20 1839;Mr 23,25,30 1848;Je 22,D 7 1849;Mr 20-23,Ap 18-19,My 25[Jl 6 1850-Ag 23 1851]S 4 1852
MHi [1836]Mr 23,Ap 9 1839;D 1,3 1840[41-57]
MMarHi Jl 21 1847
MNaHi Mr 13 1839;Mr 18 1850
MSaE [1836-50]Ja 26,Ap 6 1852[55]
MWA [Mr 15 1836-47]-[Jl 1848-52]Mr 3,7,21, My 21 1853;Ja 5,My 21 1854[55]Ag 26,S 5,D 16 1856;Mr 17,Ap 23 1857
MWo Ja 9 1849
MiU-C [1836;49-52]
MnHi Jl 15 1840;F 26,Mr 10 1841;Ja 30 1849;S 1852[Ap 26-D 24 1853]Je 26 1854
NNHi Jl 18 1839;Ap 7,Ag 14,16 1841;D 20,25 1847;F 21,28,Ap 24 1848
NSchU My 5,31 1842
NcD N 12 1844;Je 5,19,Jl 2 1845[Ap 1847-Jl 1848]
NhD D 2 1848[My-D 1849]Mr 26 1851
OC Ja 4 1843
OClWHi F 6 1839;O 26 1840;Mr 31,Ap 7-8,Jl 3,D 22 1845[Ja-Ag 18 1845]Ag 23,O 30 1847 [Mr 24-O 4 1848]
P-M O 29 1840;Ag 11 1855
WHi My 2,5,19-20,22-24,27,Ag 4,N 29,D 5 1845; Ap 3-4 1857
—w ed *See* Weekly dollar times

Boston weekly TIMES. w Mr 14 1838-
MB Mr 14 1838
MHi Jl 17 1839
MWA Jl 17-24 1839

Boston TIMES. d 1869-73||
Title varies slightly
MB Jl 19 1870
MH Jl 1872-My 27 1873
MHi Ag 10,S 18,O 6,N 5,D 30 1869;Je 28,O 15,N 19 1872
MWA S 8,28,O 20,N 4,D 17,23 1869;Ja 29 1870;S 23,26 1871
NNHi Mr 23 1873
NcD N 19 1872

Boston TIMES. d
Title varies: Boston evening times
MB Jl 11 1900-D 25 1915

Weekly TOCSIN. w F 20 1846-
MWA Mr 27,D 12-19 1846;Ja 2 1847

TODAY. w
MiU-C Ap 3 1852

Boston evening TRANSCRIPT. d Jl 24 1830+
Title varies: Daily evening transcript; Boston transcript; Boston daily evening transcript; etc.
Jl 24 1930 is 100th anniversary ed
pub 1830+
A Je-O 1906;08-Je 1923
ArHi F 9-11 1863
C Mr 12 1910-12
CL 1913-Je 1914;Ap 3 1917;N 29 1930
CPa current 2 years
CRed S 1904+
CSmH Ag 30 1830;Je 8 1838;43;45;47;50;52;54-56;58-67;70-74
CSt [1897-1906]+
CU My 1917+
CoCC 1862-Je 1863;1908-Ap 1913
Ct 1860-Jl 1861;1909+
CtY Jl 24 1830[46-49;57-75]-[78-80]-[90]-[95] 96[98-Je 1926]+
DLC 1830-49;Jl 1850+
FWpR N 1930+
IC O 21(supp)1871;Ja 10-Je 1873
ICHi Jl 24,30 1830;F 9 1874
ICM Jl 27 1885;Ap 28,My 5 1888
ICN 1865;D 1917-Je,S 22 1919+
ICU Jl 24 1830-Je 1836;37-1910;Mr 1912-34

MASSACHUSETTS (*Continued*)

BOSTON—*Continued*

Boston evening TRANSCRIPT. d 1830+—*Cont.*
IEN S 25 1913-[Je-Jl 1914]-[Je,N 1915]-S 23 1916
IHi [1921-28]
IU 1833;N 14 1908-My 14,N 16 1920+
IaDH 1906-14
IaDa current 3 months
IaSc current 6 months
IaU 1926-Jl,S-O,D 1927-F,Ap-My,Jl 1929+
In 1913-21
InTI Ap 1911-Je 1925
M [Ag 29 1832-92]+
MB Jl 1830-Jl 1867[68-N 1874]75+
MBAt 1830+
MBC 1904-Je 1909
MBNHi 1831+
MBr 1849;98+
MCam Jl 26 1830-F,Ag 25 1831-F,Ag 25 1832-F 1833
MDa 1933+
MDeHi Jl 24 1830;D 21(supp)1870;F 9(facsimile)1874;Mr 4(supp)1889
MH 1830-[33]Jl-D 1835;Jl 1837-Je 1838;40;Jl 1841-Je[Jl 14-O 14]1851;53;Jl-D 1857;Jl 1858-S 1898;99+
MHi [1830-45]+
MMarHi Jl 24 1830
MNaHi Jl 3 1847
MNb 1861-67;92-98;1916+
MSaE [1830-35]-[39-41]+
MWA Jl 24,Ag 28,O 26,D 11,14 1830[31-Jl 9 1832]-Je 1,18,Jl 18,21,Ag 5,16,19,23-24,D 21, 27 1836[37-39]-[41]-Je 29,S 10-11,O 19,23,28-29,31,N 2,30 1844;45-52;Ja 26,F 21,24,Mr 31,Ap 13,18,My 4,14,Jl 1853-[Ja-Je 1855]-[56-60]-[65]-97;Jl 1898-1906;Mr 1907+
MWa Ap 2-S 1898;Jl 1899-S 29,O 1900-Je,Ag 1905-Je 1906
MWo Jl 24 1830
MeBB Ja-Je 1890
MiU [1834]-[37]-41[61;94-97]1903-13;17-[19]+
MiU-C [1830-36;40-44;46;48-54;56;60-65;71-72; 74;80;98-99;1906-07]
MnHi 1893-Je 1920
MnU N 1922+
MoWeW [1931-Ja 1933]
N [1855-65]Jl 1896-Mr 1903;08+
NBHi Ag 14 1839
NMi Ja-Je 1832
NN Jl 24,Ag 30 1830;49-52;Jl 1 1874(facsimile) F 1902-[11]+
NNHi 1830-F[Je-Ag]1832-Je 1835;36-43;Jl-D 1844;Jl 1847-Je 1853;Ja-Je 1856;57-Je 1859-66] D 27 1871;N 11 1872;Je 2-3 1873;Ap 14 1874; Mr 11,18 1899;Ap 5 1924
NNY-H Jl 16 1831-Ap 11 1834
NPV 1914-16
NbHi Jl 24 1830
NcD N 21 1832[33-35]Je 14 1842;Ap 5,N 14 1843;O 13 1854[56-57]Ag 17 1858[60-62]F 11,21, 26 1863;Ja 18-19,23,25-29,Ap 9,13,16 1864;My 25 1865;Ja 2,23,Ag 28,S 13 1866;Je 2 1884 1900-01]06-My 1908;Jl 26,N 16 1907;D 1923-S 1928;Ja-N 1930;Ap-My,Jl 18 1928;Jl 1931+
NhD Jl 16 1866;Je 17,28 1872;F 28,Mr 17,Ap 29 1874;N 29 1875;Jl 5 1876;S 13,N 26 1877;S 25,N 14,D 19 1878;Jl 24 1880;D 30 1882;N 5 1884;Mr 5 1885;1904-Je,Ag 1926+
NhLa 1923+
NhM 1907[08]-[18]+
NjHi [1912-15]
NjR [1830;33-35;38;41]F 22 1855
OC Jl 24 1830;Mr 22 1872-S 1882
OCHi Jl 24 1830(facsimile)Ag 14 1839
OCl 1909-[15-16]+
OClWHi Jl 24 1830;Ag 14 1839;F 18 1851;D 26 1864;Ap 15-29,My 2 1865;N 6 1868;My 4 1889;Ja 19 1898;Ag 2,9 1905;09+
OHi 1849-71;1914+
P Jl 21 1835
PLaL Je 18 1875
PP [1927]+
PPi N 1895-Ap 1928
RP Ja 4 1923
RPB Jl 24 1830
TxF O 1908+
TxGR Ap 4 1914+
TxU Ja-Je 1834;35-36;Je-N 1856;Ja-Je 1859; Ja-Je 1860;O 1861-S 1862;Ap-S 1863;Ja-D 9 1864
VU N 16 1901
VtU Ja 18 1917+
WHi O 12-D 17 1831;F 18 1832;Ap-S,D 18 1833;34-Ja 1835;Je 3,O 25 1836;Ap 27,N 25,27, D 11-12,15 1837;F 20,23-26 1841;Ja-Je 1842; Mr 22,S 25 1844;O 12 1847;Je 2-D 1848;Ja-Je 1850;Jl 1851-Je 1853;Ja-Je 17 1854;57-58;Jl-D 1859;Jl 1860-64[Je 24 1869-S 13 1877]D 17 1903+
WaPS [1910-21;26+]
WaU Mr 17 1926+

Saturday morning TRANSCRIPT. w 1831-39||?
Ct N 19 1831[35-37]
DLC S 10 1831-Ag 1833;Ag 26 1837
MB S 1833-Ag 1836
MH S 1836-Ag 25 1837
MHi S 17 1836
MWA D 5,19 1835;36-Ja 14,Jl 8,S 16-23 1837 [38-39]
WHi S 24 1836

Boston weekly TRANSCRIPT. w 1852-1921||?
CClP [S-D 1904]Je 1905-[07-08]-Ag 25 1909
CLM Ja 16 1883
DLC Ja-Ap 3 1861
ICU Ap 17-D 1856;O 1866-71;73-1903
MDa Jl 1860-Je 1865
MH 1854-63;Ap 6 1864;Ja-S 26 1866;Je 22 1869;94-95
MHi [1885]
MNaHi Ap 20,Je 22 1875
MTaHi Mr 17 1874
MWA F 22 1855;Ja 27 1857;D 19 1860;Ja 28 1868;My 15 1891;D 2 1898;S 15 1899;S 20 1901;Je 12 1903;My 13 1910
MWa F 23 1875-98
MWo Je 17 1884
MiU-C [1899;1903]
MnU D 20 1889-O 1890
NcD Mr 21 1876
OCHi Ja 27 1893
OClWHi Ag 26 1873;Ja 20 1883
OrHi Je 1919-N 1921
WHi 1902-Ja 4 1904

Boston TRANSCRIPT for California.
MHi O 22 1860

Boston TRAVELLER. sw Jl 5 1825-90||?
1825-Je 1855 as American traveller. Title varies: American semi-weekly traveller; Boston semi-weekly traveller
pub 1825-90
CSmH S 17 1830
CoD O 30 1829-[Mr 1830-F 25 1831]
CtY N 16 1827-Ap 19 1833
DLC 1825-Je 1831;S 9-D 1832[Ja-S 1833]Ja 28 1834;O 25 1836;F 3,Mr 3,Ap 18 1837[Ja-O 1843;Ja-Jl 1844]
M [1825-S 19 1837]
MB 1825-Ap 1846
MBAt 1825-[36]37;Je 5,Ag 28 1838;39-[46-48] Je 3 1857
MDeHi My 8,N 30 1827;O 30 1835
MH O 17 1826;N 16 1827;Ap 30 1830;Ap 26,O 21 1831-Je 25 1841[O 6-D 1843]-Ap 8 1845;D 3 1859
MHi O 7-11,24,D 30 1825[26-33]F 21,My 6 1834;S 11 1835;S 2 1836;F 3 1837;F 6-9 1838; My 14 1839[40-42]S 3,10 1844;F 10 1846;My 23 1854[60;64-86]
MWA 1825-[42]-F 21,Ap 15-Je,D 26 1845;Ap 7 1846;D 19 1848;D 21 1849;Je 11 1850;N 27 1855;Je 14,Jl 2 1861;O 12 1866;Ja 1 1875;Ap 30 1880;Ja 17 1882
MnHi Ja 3 1832
N Jl 18,S 26-D 26 1826;27-Je 1833;Mr 6 1837
NNHi [Ag-D 1825]-Ja[Mr 1827-30]Ja 15,F 26,Mr 19,26 1833;S 4 1841;My 19 1851;Mr 8 1873
NcD [1829;32-33;36-39]F 3 1863
NhD Jl 5,S 6 1825[26-O 1828;29-35]Ja 1,22-29, F 9,19,Mr 8,Ag 5 1836;Je 24-Jl 1 1851
P-M Mr 20 1831;Mr 7 1846
PPL [Ag-O 1826]
RPB Jl 1826-Je 1827

Boston TRAVELLER. w Ja 1 1825-99||?
1825-88? as American traveller (title varies slightly)
pub 1825-99
CSmH Mr 4,O 31 1834
Ct [1825-28;30-36]
DLC Je 9 1849;Ag 28,D 18 1851;Ja 15-Ap 1 1852;Ap 9,30,Jl 2,30 1864;Ap 15 1865;Ap 8 1882
IHi My 11,Je 15,Jl 27,O 26,N 2 1850;D 18-25 1851
MB 1839-44
MBAt Ja 13-F 17 1849;D 14 1850;Ap 24-Ag 14 1857
MHi F 7,Mr 14 1846;O 20 1849;O 12 1850;Ja 18 1851;F 6-13,My 8,29 1851;Ap 23 1859;S 22 1860;61;Je 21 1862;S 12-19,N 14,28 1863;64-86
MNaHi Mr 8 1839
MWA Jl 20 1839;F 29,Mr 21 1840;Mr 27 1841; Ja 14 1843;Mr 16 1844;Ap 17,O 23-30,D 18 1847[48-N 17 1849]Ja,F 23,Mr 9,30 1850;Je 29, Ag 10 1854;Ja 12-19,Mr 8,Jl 5,Ag 30,D 27 1856;Ap 24-My 1857;Ja 30,My 29 1858;Jl 30 1859;Ja 20,Mr 24,Je 2,N 17-24 1860;O-D 1861; Mr 29 1862;O 31 1863;Ap 8,My 13 1865;Je 23 1866;Ja 5,Mr 9,N 1867;Ja 8,29 1870;Ja 6 1872; Mr 21 1874;S 22 1877;Je 24 1882;Ap 18,O 31, D 19-26 1885;Ja 2,23 1886
MWo N 6 1835;S 20 1839;Je 13 1843;O 27 1860
MiU-C [1849]
NN S 14 1850;D 8 1876
NcD [Mr-S 1861]Ja 11,F 1,15-22 1862
NhD F 13,O 8,N 3,12,15,19,22,26,D 12,13,16 1851;Ja 13 23,27,F 6,Mr 24,25,1852;Ap 2,Je 16,22,Jl 2,11,14,21,S 7,19 1853;Ja 30,31,F 8, 13,Mr 9,10,Je 10,15,19,27,Jl 1,12,S 4 1854;Ap 5 1855;F 1,S 11 1856;Je 5,15,21-22,26,29,Jl 26, 30,Ag 1,4,8,11 1860
WHi Ag 24-31 1850;Ap 1851-Mr 23,D 14 1854; Ag 21 1857

Boston evening TRAVELLER. d Ap 1 1845+
1845-Ja 31 1885 as Daily evening traveller; F 2 1885-S 30 1889 Boston evening traveller
pub 1845+
CSmH D 1 1852
CtY Mr 29 1859;D 31 1864
DLC Ap 25 1845-[48]-O 1,30,N 16-17,D 15 1852;Ja-Mr,Ap 20,My 3,20 1853;F 3,14 1855; S 18 1856;Ag 24 1857;My 3,12,S 6,O 25 1859-N 23,D 10,15 1860[Mr 9 1861-62;Mr 24 1863-Ja 4 1873;O 1874-Ag 4 1884;Mr 1885-Ap 21 1888] My-D 1898
ICU Je 3,28,Jl 16,Ag 18-19,S 15-16 1852;My 17 1855;O 13,N 22 1856;F 12,Je 27,N 3-4 1857;F 8,D 30 1859;Mr 7,N 14,19,22,24,26,28,D 6 1860; D 18 1861
KHi Ja-Je 1886
M Jl 18 1845+
MAtt Ap 27 1861
MB 1845-Mr,O 1854-O 1864;65-Je 1891;95+
MBAt S-O 24 1846;Ag 30 1848;Ja 15 1849[50; 57]-76
MBC Ap-Je 1857;59-S 1860;F 1861-F,Ap-Je 1862;Ja-Je,O 1863-Je 1868;69-72
MH 1845-47[Je 16-D 1849]-55;57-My 1906;Jl-D 1910;Jl-D 1911
MHi [1845-50]-[54-86]Ag 31 1905;Jl 6 1925
MMarHi My 31 1865
MSaE 1845-66;S 14 1867;Je 5 1875;My 10 1876
MWA 1845-[47]-[Jl-D 1853]-F 20 1858;O 25 1859-[64]-S 1889
MWa Ja 11-D 1881
MWo N 20 1863
MiU-C [1849-67;90;94;98]
N My 24 1845;F 12 1846[55-78]
NN Ag 21,25,N 28,30,D 5 1846;Mr 25,Ap 26-27,29,Ag 24 1847;Ap 20 1850;Mr 10,Jl 1,7,16, S 17-18,20,24 1851;Mr 9,Ap 9,O 26,28,30 1852; Jl 5 1876
NSchU Ap 22 1842
NbHi S 18 1878
NcD Ap 18 1851[Ja-My 1856]Jl 27 1861[Mr 1862-F 1863]Mr 19,Ap 11-13 1864;F 21,25,Ap 3-22 1865;Je 4 1866;Jl-D 1903;Ap-My 1916;F-Ag 1918;Mr 1920;My 1922
NhD Ag 13,17,S 5,O 1 1849;Ja 18,S 3 1850
NjR Ag 1 1868
OClWHi Ap 20,24 1850;Ap 15 1865
WHi D 30 1848[Ja-Mr 1849;Ap 12 1851-Ja 24 1874]Ja 4 1879

Boston TRAVELLER. (morning) d O 27 1856-98||?
1856-S 15 1857 as Boston morning traveller; S 16 1857-D 18 1894 Boston daily traveller
A 1862-Je 1866;Jl-D 1867;Jl-D 1868;Jl-D 1869; 71-79;Ap 1892-Je 1894
CtY Mr 19-Je 1 1892
DLC Ap 14 1857-59;Jl 2,O 4 1890
ICU Ap 27,Je 8-9,11,13,15,29,Ag 4,19,D 5 1857; My 25 1858
IU Ag 30 1858
KHi [O 26 1895-Jl 1896]
MBAt [1857]
MHi N 3-4 1856;Ag 4,11 1857[58-60]
MWA Ja 1,3,Mr 2,Ap 6,9,Je 13,Ag 14,S 16,N 20-21,24 1857;Ja 12,F 23 1858-O 24 1859;O 1889-98
NCanHi Je 18,27 1857
NcD Ap 28,My 8 1857
NhD S 30 1859
OClWHi Jl 20 1859

TRIBUNE. w My 28-Ag 6 1830||?
CSmH Ag 6 1830
MB My 28 1830
MWA My-Je 25 1830
MeBa My 28 1830
P-M Ag 6 1830

Boston daily TRIBUNE. d S 18 1844-
MNaHi F 17 1845
MWA N 30 1844
NNHi S 18 1844

Boston daily TRIBUNE. d S 1869-
MWA O 2 1869

Boston daily TRIBUNE. d Ja 1-O 31 1907||
M Ja-O 25 1907
MB complete
MWA Ja-Je 1907
MiU-C Ja 14 1907

Boston TRIBUNE. ir My 13 1933-
Issued irregularly as follows: My 13,27, Je 10,S 30,O 14,21,28,N 4
MB My 13-O 28 1933
MWA S 30-N 4 1933

Boston TRIBUNE and New England spectator. w Ja 23 1847-
MWA My 8 1847

TRUE American organ and Spirit of '76. w
DLC N 25 1854

TRUE democrat. ir O 11? 1845-
Campaign paper
MB O 18 1845
MWA O 18-25 1845

Boston TRUE whig. w S 22 1838-
MWA N 10 1838

UNCLE TOM'S journal. D 25 1852-
DLC D 25 1852

UNITED STATES literary advertiser, and journal of politics. w Je 12-O 16 1830||
CtY Je 19-N 6 1830
NjCHi complete

UNIVERSAL Yankee nation. w Ja 9 1841-
My 14-O 1 1842 as Yankee nation (Universal Yankee nation on inside sheets)
MB Mr 20,S 27,O 23-30,N 20 1841;F 20 1847
MWA Ja-Je 15,Jl 10,Ag 7-14,Ag 28-O,D 4 1841; Ja 1,Mr 19,My 14,Je 11,Jl 9,O 1 1842;Je 24 1843
MiG Ja 9 1841
NNHi Mr 13 1841
NcD Ap 17-24 1841

UNIVERSE. w Mr 3 1829-
Follows Paul Pry and the times
MB Mr 14 1829
MWA Mr 27 1829

Boston VINDICATOR. w Ja 21 1847-
OC Ja-Jl 1847

Weekly VISITOR. (Charlestown) w My 26 1846-
MB [My 26-Ag 11 1846]

Daily evening VOICE. d D 2 1864-O 16 1867||
MB [Jl 7 1866-67]
MBAt complete
MWA D 10-12,17 1864[66]
WHi complete

Boston weekly VOICE. w
MB O 18 1866-O 17 1867
WHi Mr 1866-O 11 1867

Boston WASHINGTONIAN. *See* New Englander

WEST ROXBURY advertiser. *See* Advocate and West Roxbury advertiser

WEST ROXBURY gazette. w Ap 3 1858-
MWA My 8 1858

WEST ROXBURY news. w 1872-1925||?
MH My 21 1881
MWA Je 8 1889

Boston daily WHIG. d S 23 1834-
MB [S 24 1834-Ap 24 1835]
MWA Ja 19 1835

Boston daily WHIG. d 1846-48 *See* Boston daily republican

Boston semi-weekly WHIG. *See* Boston semi-weekly republican

Boston weekly WHIG. *See* Boston weekly republican

WHIG republican. d Je 23 1840-
DLC Je 23,Jl 14 1840
MWA Jl 1 1840

MASSACHUSETTS (*Continued*)

BOSTON—*Continued*

WORKINGMAN'S friend. w Je 6 1840-
MBAt Jl 11,Ag 1 1840

WORKING-MEN'S advocate. w Jl 31 1830-
MWA D 4 1830;My 28,Ag 20 1831

WORKMAN. ir F? 1840-
Campaign paper
MB Je 11,Jl 8 1840
MSaE O 1840
MWA Mr 13,22,Je 11,Jl 8,1840
NNHi Je 26,Jl 8 1840
NhD Ap 15 1840

Boston WORLD. d D 12 1881-82||?
MHi S 29 1882
MWA D 12 1881;Jl 22,31 1882

WORLD in a nutshell. d Ag 19 1833-
MB Ag 19 1833;Mr 24 1834
MWA S 3 1833

YANKEE blade. w Jl 30 1842-95||?
Follows Watervillion (Waterville, Me.) F 2-Ap 26 1856 as Yankee blade and Boston athenaeum
1842-Ag 5 1843 pub in Waterville, Me.; Ag 12 1843-Ag 12 1845 in Gardiner, Me.
DLC 1842-Ag 12 1845;Mr 21 1849
M N 15-D 1851;Ja 17 1852-Mr 16 1889
MB [1842-51]S 11-18 1852;Mr 19-My 21 1853
MWA [Ag 14-D 4 1847]Je 10,N 11 1848[Ap 1849-55]-Mr 1856;My 12-Je 16 1888;D 28 1889-91
MeBa Ja 17,Ap 17 1844
MeHi O 19 1846
MeWC 1842-Jl,Ag 22 1843-Mr 18,Ag 28 1847-Ag 17 1850
NN Mr 8 1851
NcD Je 1-8 1850;O 18 1851;Mr 26,Ag 27,N 20,D 31 1853-Mr 16 1889
NjR Ap 28 1849
RPB 1842-Ag 5 1843
VU My 11 1889

YANKEE nation. 1842 *See* Universal Yankee nation

YANKEE nation and American sentinel. w N 17 1849-
1849-My 3 1851 as Yankee nation; My 10-Je 14? 1851 American nation and Yankee sentinel
DLC My 10-Je 14,28,Jl 12-19,Ag 2 1851
MWA N 24 1849;F 1,Ag 9 1851
NcD Ag 9 1851

YOUNG America Fremont journal. w Jl 26 1856?-
Campaign paper
MSaE Ag 2 1856
MWA Ag 9 1856

YOUNG galaxy. w D 27 1823-
Formed by the union of City eagle and Independent microscope
M 1823-F 14 1824
MWA 1823-F 28 1824

YOUNG galaxy, or bundle of stars. w F 15 1823-
M F 15,D 27 1823-Ja 3 1824

YOUNG guard. w Jl 4 1848-
Campaign paper
DLC Jl 4,15-29-S 9,23-O 21 1848
MWA Jl 15-Ag 19,S 16-23,N 4 1848

YOUNG hickory. w Ag 31 1844?-
Campaign paper
MBAt N 2 1844
MSaE S 21,O 12,26-N 9 1844
MWA S 21-28,O 19 1844

Bostoner ZEITUNG. w S 1 1865-
In German
MB [S 1 1865-F 23 1866]

BRADFORD

Bradford MESSENGER. w 1891-95||?
MHa S 1 1894-Ja 19 1895

Bradford SUN. w Mr 4 1876-
DLC My 6-20 1876
MHa Mr-Jl 15 1876
MSaE Mr-My,Je 10-24 1876

BRAINTREE

Braintree BEE. w D 22 1894-N 29 1919||
Merged with Braintree observer
MBra complete
MWA Ap 27 1895

Braintree CITIZEN. w Ja 13 1921+
pub [S 1928]+
MBra 1922-D 19 1924

Braintree NEWS-ITEM. w O 1933+
pub Ag 1936+

Braintree OBSERVER. w Ja 7 1878+
Title varies: Braintree observer-bee; Braintree observer-reporter
pub 1878+
Ct Mr 31 1894
M Ap 17 1897+
MBra [1878—]
MBraT 1878-1922
MHi N 25,D 16-23 1932;Ja 6-20 1933
MQ 1892-1908
MWA Ap 20 1878;Jl 11 1891

Braintree REPORTER. w My 21 1892-My 27 1899||
Merged with Braintree observer
Ct Mr 31 1894
MBra complete

BRIDGEWATER

Bridgewater ADVERTISER. w 1903-13||?
MH D 20 1911

Bridgewater INDEPENDENT. w 1879+
pub 1881+
M [Ja 9 1931-Ap 7 1933]

WE, the people and Old colony press. w
MWA S 4 1835

BRIGHTON

GEM. m S 1 1860-
MB S 1860-Ap,Je-Jl 1861

ITEM. w 1883+
pub 1885+
MB O 29 1887;My 1894[Je 19 1897-Jl 27 1907]
MB-B O 1885-Ja 5 1895;Ag 29 1914-Ag 17 1918;Ag 23 1919-Ag 13 1921;Ag 16 1924+

Brighton MERCURY. w D 31 1851||
MB complete

Brighton MESSENGER. w Ja 28 1871-76||?
MB-B 1871-Ja 22 1876

Brighton REPORTER. m Ja 1860-
MB Ja-Je 1860

BROCKTON

Brockton ADVANCE. w 1876-81||
MBro 1876
MWA Mr 16 1881

Brockton EAGLE. w 1884-
MHi My 23 1884

Brockton ENTERPRISE. w Jl 1879-95||
pub complete

Brockton daily ENTERPRISE and times. d Ja 26 1880+
1880-Mr 24 1934 as Brockton daily enterprise
pub 1880+
M 1916-17[28+]
MBro 1881-91;93+
MHi [Je 11-S 8 1886]
MWh Ap 1936+

Brockton weekly GAZETTE. w 1850-My 12 1894||
1850-Ap 30 1874 as North Bridgewater gazette (North Bridgewater)
CLM Ag 29 1890
MBro My 16 1851-94
MH Je 18 1852
MWA Ag 19 1857;Ja 27,Ag 18 1863;F 2,N 23 1864;Ag 10 1871

Brockton TIMES. d 1894-Mr 24 1934||
United with Brockton daily enterprise to form Brockton daily enterprise and times
M 1899-1915[28-34]
MBro F 1895-1934
MBroT complete
MH D 4 1902
WHi My 31 1895-Ja 1896

BROOKFIELD

Brookfield UNION. w 1892+
pub 1924+
MNob 1924+

BROOKLINE

Brookline CHRONICLE. w My 9 1874+
pub 1877+
DLC My 1 1875
MBr 1874+
MH S 11,O 2,16 1909
MWA Ja 9,My 8 1875;Jl 8 1876;Ja 4,O 5 1878;F 1,Ap 26 1879;O 17 1885;N 26,D 10 1887;D 1 1888;My 8 1924
MnU My 19 1894-Ap 24 1897
NcD Ap 6 1878

Brookline CITIZEN. w Mr 14 1935+
pub 1935+
MBr 1935+

Brookline INDEPENDENT. w Jl 4-N 29 1873||
MBr complete
MHi complete

Brookline NEWS. w Ag 7 1886-
MBr 1886-Mr 24 1888

Brookline NEWS. w D 10 1930-
MBr 1931

Brookline PRESS. *See* Brookline townsman

Brookline RECORDER. w F 24 1933-
MBr F 24,Mr 17-24 1933

SUBURBAN. w My 6 1899-1901||
MBr 1899-Je 14 1901

Brookline TOWNSMAN. w N 14 1903-S 20 1919||
1903-F 22 1913 as Brookline press. Merged with Brookline chronicle
MBrC 1907-19
MH Jl 10 1909

Brookline TRANSCRIPT. w O 15 1870-My 31 1873||
DLC O 22 1870-73
M complete
MB complete
MBr complete
MWA O 7,N 4 1871
OC Mr 1 1873

Brookline TRIBUNE. w 1931?-
MBr Ja-F 3 1933

BRYANTVILLE

Bryantville NEWS. w 1903-16||?
Ag 1912 is "Historic Pembroke, 1712-1912"
Ct Mr 20 1907
M Ag 1912

BYFIELD

Byfield ADVOCATE. w Ja 1898-1901||?
MSaE N 3 1899;Ja 26-F 2 My 18 1900;My 24 1901
MWA O 28 1898
NcD Ja 26-F 2,My 18 1900

CABOTVILLE

Papers published in Cabotville are listed under Chicopee

CAMBRIDGE

Cambridge CHRONICLE-SUN. w My 7 1846+
1846-My 1935 as Cambridge chronicle
pub 1846+
CtY Ja 13,O 12 1848;Jl 19 D 27 1849
DLC 1846-Je 17 1854
M 1875+
MB 1846-54;56-68;Ja 9,My 29,Je 12-19,Jl 10 1869[O 22 1870-Ap 18 1874;My 15-S 18 1875; F 19-D 1876]Ja 13-D 1877[Mr 29 1884-N 1885; F 11 1888-My 7 1904]
MBAt Ag 14 1852;Ag 13 1853;Ag 12-26,S 16,N 11-18,D 2-9 1854;Ja 13 1855;Ja 30,Jl 24 1858; Ap 30 1859;65-73
MCam 1846+
MH 1846-[86-Jl 23]Ag 1887-1933
MHi 1846-54;N 15,D 27 1856;Ag 7,D 11-18 1858; My 25,Ag 10,O 26 1861;My 10 1862;S 17 1864; Mr 2 1867;S 4 1869[71]Ja 13 1872;Jl 3-10 1875; My 1896
MWA My 28-Je 4,Ag 6,O 22 1846-[54-55]57-58;Ap 1859-64;66-75;77;Ap 20 1878;79-80
MiU-C [1846-49;53]
NN 1848-51
NNHi F 21 1850;Ap 5,My 24 1873;Jl 21 1877
NcD Jl 13 1848;Ja 3 1850 Mr 12 1853;D 12 1863
OClWHi Jl 23 1864
P-M N 4 1854
Vt 1848
WHi Ap 26 1849

Cambridge DAILY. d Ag 18-S 5 1888||
MH [1888]
MHi S 4 1888

Cambridge DEMOCRAT. w Jl 1 1901-D 19 1903||
MH [1901-03]

FROZEN truth. ir 1886?-93||
MH N 19,D 1 1887;N 28 1890;D 9 1893

Cambridge GAZETTE. w 1885-S 10 1887||
MH My 14-S 1887

GRIDIRON. w O 31 1914-Ja 14 1916||
MH complete

Cambridge HERALD. w Ja 8-Mr 9 1848||
MH complete

Cambridge JEFFERSONIAN. bw 1882?-83||
MH Je 9-O 27 1883

Cambridge MAGNOLIA. w O 22 1840-
1840-N 4 1841 as Magnolia
MH 1840-Jl 21 1842

Cambridge MIRROR. w 1906-09||?
Negro
MH Ag 25 1906

MOUNT AUBURN memorial. w Je 15 1859-
MB 1859-Je 6 1860
MH 1859-Mr 27 1861

MYRTLE. w O 16? 1839-
MH F 28-Mr 6 1840

Cambridge NEWS. d D 29 1873-
MB D 29 1873-Ja 24 1874

Cambridge NEWS. w Ja 4 1879-1901||
M 1881-95
MH [F 22-O 4 1879]My 6 1882;F 24 1894;N 14 1896;N 20-27 1897;98-F 9 1901
NcD Ja 14 1882

NEWS-BOY. bw F 20 1852-
MH Mr 20-Ap 3 1852

NON-PARTISAN advocate. w N 19 1904-
MH N 26-D 10 1904

Cambridge OWL. w Ap 13 1848-
MH Ap-O 12 1848
MHi Ap 20-Ag 24 1848
MWA Je 8 1848

Cambridge PALLADIUM. w Ja 7 1843-
DLC Je 17 1843
MH Ja-S 30 1843
MWA Ja 28 1843

PLAIN DEALER. w O 26 1848-
MH O-N 4 1848

Cambridge PRESS. w Ap 14 1866-1904||
M [1866-95]
MCam 1887-89
MH 1866-Mr 4,My 6 1903;Mr 30 1904
MHi Ja 5,N 30 1867-72
MWA Jl 10 1869;Ap 8 1876;O 9 1880
OClWHi Mr 13 1869
WHi Ap 13 1904

Cambridge daily PRESS. d My? 1898-99||
MCam O 25 1898-Ap 24 1899
MH [Jl 1898-N 21 1899]

Cambridge RECORDER. w Ag 12 1911+
pub 1911+
M [Ja 24 1931-O 1933]
MH N 4 1911

MASSACHUSETTS (*Continued*)

CAMBRIDGE—*Continued*

Cambridge REVIEW. w
DLC Ap 19,Jl 12 1860

Cambridge SENTINEL. w O 31 1903+
pub 1903-04;07+
M [Ja 21 1928-My 20 1933]
MCam 1903-12
MH 1903[04-05]Ja 6,Ap 28 1906;Jl 26-Ag 2,16 1924;F 7,O 2-10,N 7 1925;Ja 2-9,F-My,Je 26, S 18,O 2 1926;F 19 1927;F 4-11,Mr 24,Ap 7, 21,Jl 21 1928;My 18-25,O 19 1929;Ap 5,Jl 5,S 13,O 25,D 13 1930;Ag 1,15,S 19 1931;Je 11-18, Jl 9,S 10,O 15-22,N 19-26 1932[33-34]

Cambridge STANDARD. d 1911-17||?
MH Mr 9 1914

Cambridge TIMES. w Jl 10 1897-1916||?
MH 1897-[1900]D 11 1903;Ag 16 1907;Je 2 1911;Mr 1 1912
MHi Ag 28 1908-Ja 1 1909

Cambridge TRIBUNE. w Mr 7 1878+
F 20 1892 is Lowell memorial number; Jl 3 1925 Sesqui-centennial number 150th anniversary of Washington's taking command of the Continental army; Jl 21 1928 50th anniversary number
pub 1878+
CtY Je 1890
M 1878-96;Jl 1 1925;Mr 1927+
MBAt F 20 1892;Jl 3-4 1925;Jl 21 1928
MCam Mr 12 1887-Mr 2 1889;Mr 15 1890+
MH 1878-O 8 1904;Ag 5 1905;Jl 17 1909;Ja 8 1910;F 4,Ap 22,O 21 1911;Ap 19 1913;Ja 24 1914;Ap 24,O 30 1915;Jl 28-Ag 4 1917;S 16 1922-Mr 24,D 29 1923-26;Ja 8,F 12,Mr 5 1927; Jl 21,N 24 1928;Mr 2,9,D 28 1929;Ap 19,Je 21,S 27,O 18-26 1930;Ag 26-S 8 1932;Ja 20 1933;Ja 5,My 4 1934
MHi S 15 1882-F 1886;O 15 1887-F 11 1888; F 23 1889;F 3 1923;Jl 21 1928;Mr 8 1930
MWA My 2,Je 20,Jl 4 1878;Ja 31 1879;Ja 27 1882;F 23,Je 29,Jl 6,Ag 17,O 12 1883;Ja 11-25,F 8-15,Mr 7 1884;F 12,N 6 1886;N 17 1888; Je 1890[Ap-28-Jl 1900]Jl 21 1928
MiG Jl 3 1925
NN O 22-29 1921
NNHi D 31 1880;Mr 3 1882
OCHi N 17 1888
TxGR Jl 3 1925
WHi Jl 3 1925

WIDE-AWAKE. bw F 12 1865-
MH F 12 1865

CANTON

Canton JOURNAL. w 1867+
pub Je 1909+
MCa 1882+
NcD Je 3 1881

MASSAPOAG journal. w Ag 18? 1854-
MH Ag 4-11 1855
MHi [1854-57]
MWA Ag 11 1855

Canton MIRROR. w Je 13 1924-27||?
MWA Je 13 1924

CHARLESTOWN

Papers published in Charleston are listed under Boston

CHELMSFORD

Chelmsford COURIER. *See under* Lowell

Chelmsford EAGLE. ir Ja 1 1876-83||?
MH D 12 1877;D 12 1883
MWA Ja 1 1876;D 12 1877;D 15 1883

CHELSEA

Chelsea ADVERTISER. w Mr 19 1853-
MWA Mr 19 1853

Chelsea BULLETIN. w Mr 4 1865-
MWA 1865[66]Ja 5 1867

CATHOLIC citizen. w 1888+
MCh 1888+

Chelsea GAZETTE. w Ap 3 1886+
O 15 1910 is Achievement number
pub [1886-96]+
M [My 31 1930-My 1932]
MB Ap 18-O 3 1908
MCh [1886-1905]08+
NcD Mr 25 1893;Ag 4 1894

MYSTIC press. w S? 1869-
M [O 22 1870-Ag 19 1871]
MB Jl 9,O 1,15 1870-71

NEWS-GONG. *See under* Boston

Chelsea PIONEER. *See* Telegraph-pioneer

Chelsea RECORD. w 1875-95||?
NNHi N 22 1890

Chelsea evening RECORD. d D 17 1890+
pub My 15 1908+
M Je 1908+
MCh [1909+]
MH My 5 1923
MWA D 17 1930

Chelsea TELEGRAPH. w F 16? 1850-51||
United with Chelsea pioneer to form Chelsea telegraph and pioneer, later Telegraph-pioneer
MWA N 9 1850

TELEGRAPH-PIONEER. w Ja 1846-1906||
1846-51 as Chelsea pioneer; 1852 Chelsea telegraph and pioneer
DLC S 15 1862
MB Jl 12 1850;Ap 14 1861;F 15 1862;My 6 1865; Mr 23-30 1867[Ja 18-S 19 1868;Ap-N 20 1869;Ap 30-D 24 1870]F 4 1871;Jl 26 1873;F 7 1874;78-80

MCh O 1854-1904;06
MH Ap 27,Je 15,Ag 3,S 7,N 30 1861;S 15 1862; F 28,S 5 1863
MHi F 19,S 10-17,O 8 1881;F 28-Mr 7 1891
MWA Mr 23,D 14,28 1849;Ja 11 1850;Ag 1 1851;Ja 24,Je 19,S 10,D 4 1852;N 13 1858;N 22 1862;Ag-D 24 1864;65-Ja 5 1867;O 4 1871 [Mr 19-S 3 1881]N 3 1883
NcD My 21 1887;Jl 28 1888;D 13 1900
NjR F 20-Mr 6 1858
OClWHi Mr 19-S 3 1881;Mr 4 1882

Chelsea UNION. w 1850-
DLC Ag 16 1851
MWA S 27 1851;F 21,S 29 1852

WINNISIMMET chronicle. ir,w N 17 1838-
v 1 no 1-4 dated N 17 1838,D 26 1840,Mr 17 1841,S 11 1847
w S 11-D 18 1847
MB N 17 1838-D 18 1847

WINNISIMMET pioneer. sw 1847-
MWA Mr 3 1848

CHICOPEE

CABOTVILLE chronicle and Chicopee Falls advertiser. w 1839-
MChi Ag 13,N 12 1842
MWA Je 13 1840
OClWHi Je 8 1844
P-M My 6 1843

CABOTVILLE weekly courier. w Ja 2 1847-
KHi Mr 27 1847

CABOTVILLE mirror. w S 4? 1846-
MChi Ap 10 1847;S 7,N 2-9 1849
MWA Jl 6,20 1849

Chicopee HERALD. w F 22 1927+
pub 1927-Je 1930;My 1931+
MWA 1936(special flood ed)

Chicopee JOURNAL. w Ja 4 1854-
MChi Ja-Je 3,O 25 1854;My 24,N 1 1856;Je 5, D 11 1858;Ag 6 1859;Je 21,D 27 1862
MH F 17,Ap 7 1855
MWA Ja 10,Mr 21,Ap 11,Je 20-Jl 4,18-25 1857; N 20 1858
WHi Ap 24 1858

Chicopee JOURNAL. w 1912-15||
MChi [1913-15]

NOWA ANGLIA. (New England) w 1915+
In Polish
pub 1915+
M Je 3 1932

Chicopee TELEGRAPH. w F 11 1846-
MChi 1846-D 18 1850;D 17 1851;My 25 1853
MWA Ap 28 1847;My 26 1852

WILLIMANSETT reporter. w O? 1847-
MChi N 1847

CLINTON

Clinton ADVANCE. w S 14 1880-
MWA D 14-21 1880

Clinton COURANT. w Jl 4 1846+
1846-50? as Lancaster courant (Lancaster) 1851-62 Saturday courant
Suspended 1863-S 1865?
pub 1865+
MB My 31 1884;Ja 3,Ap 4,S 19 1885[Ja-D 18 1886;87-Ap 20 1889]
MC Ag 14 1846-Jl 14 1849;50+
MLan 1868+
MWA Ja 30 1847;Ap 19 1851;Jl 8 1854;Mr 10 1855;Ja 3,Jl 11 1857;Ja 30,Mr 20 1858;D 3 1859[Ja 28-N 24 1860;Mr 8-D 13 1862;Ja 13 1866;N 9 1867;Jl 31 1869;Jl 16 1870;My 4-11 1872;Je 7 1873;Mr 21 1874-[Ja-O 1875]Mr 27(extra)1876[Mr 31-D 1877]-Je 2 1883;O 19 1889-93

Saturday COURANT. *See* Clinton courant

ENTERPRISE. w,sw My 14 1886-98||?
w 1886-95?
MCl 1886-Je 1895

Clinton daily ITEM. d Jl 17 1893+
pub 1893+
M [1928-Jl 1933]
MC 1893-1935
MCl 1893+

Clinton weekly RECORD. *See* Clinton times

Clinton TIMES. w 1877-86||
1877-82? as Clinton weekly record
MC S 1877-N 18 1882;S 1883-86
MH Mr 18 1885
MWA Jl 16 1881;My 2(supp)1883;My 7,21 1884; My 26 1886

COHASSET

SOUTH SHORE life. w O 7 1926+
pub [1926+]

CONCORD

Concord ENTERPRISE. w 1888+
MC 1888+

Concord FREEMAN. 1834-47. *See* Middlesex freeman

Concord FREEMAN. w Ap 19 1875-96||?
Ap 19 1875 is Centennial ed
MBAt Ap 19 1875;Ap 27 1876
MC 1875-[77-78]-[80-82]-[84-85]-87
MHi Ap 19 1875
MWo Mr 18 1880
MiU-C Ap 19 1875
NNHi Ap 24 1876
NbHi Ap 19 1875
NcD Ap 19 1875;Mr 30 1876

Concord GAZETTE and Middlesex yeoman. *See* Yeoman's gazette

Concord HERALD. w 1929+
pub 1929+
MC 1929+

Concord JOURNAL. w 1928+
pub 1928+
M Jl 14 1932
MChe My 15 1930+

MIDDLESEX freeman. w D 11 1834-52||?
1834-47 as Concord freeman. Merged with Lowell patriot (Lowell)
Ct O 31 1835;S 9 1837[38]
DLC Ap 19 1875
IHi Mr 31 1843
MC D 1834-Mr 1847;Mr 1851-Jl 1852
MHi [1835-36]Ja 17-F 7 1845
MWA [Mr 14-D 1835]-Ja 9,30,Je 11,Jl 30,Ag 13 1836[F 11-D 9 1837]Ja 6 1838;O 4,D 6 1839;Mr 5-12,My 28,Jl 30,O 22 1841;My 6,Jl 30 1842;Ja 27,Mr 24,N 24 1843;F 9 1844-Mr 21,Jl 11 1845;Ja 9-16,Mr 20,My 15 1846;Ja 22 1847;Ja 4 1850;Je 13 1851;Ap 19 1875;S 18 1885
MnHi Ap 30 1841
NNHi [1843]O 27,N 17 1848
NcD Je 17,D 30 1837
OClWHi My 6,Je 3 1837;Jl 10 1840;S 8 1843

***MIDDLESEX gazette.** w Ap 20 1816-
Ap 18 1818-Ap 23 1819 as Middlesex gazette and advertiser
DLC O 12 1822;Mr 1,22-Ap 26,Je 24-Ag 9,O 18 1823
MC [Ja-S 1 1821]Je 22 1822-Je 14 1823
MWA Je 24,N 22 1823

MIDDLESEX patriot. w 1899-1904||?
MC 1900-02

Concord MINUTE MAN. w 1915-17||?
MHi O 7-14 1916

MONITOR. w Ap 19 1862-
MH My 3 1862

OBSERVER. w
MHi Je 1-D 7 1864

REPUBLICAN. w Jl 24 1840-D 1841||
Follows Yeoman's gazette
DLC N 20 1840;S 3 1841
MHi [1840-41]
MWA complete
NcD S 25 1840

SUNBEAM. w S 27 1839-
OClWHi S 27,O 11 1839

YEOMAN'S gazette. w N 29 1823-Jl 13 1840||
1823-F 25 1826 as Concord gazette and Middlesex yeoman. Title varies: Yeoman's gazette, mechanic's journal and Middlesex advertiser; Yeoman's gazette and Middlesex whig. Followed by Republican
DLC O 14 1826;Mr 24,Ap 21,S 22-29 1827;Ja 26,My 3-17,N 1 1828;Je 20,Ag 8,S 12,26,O 31 1829;Ja 23,D 25 1830;D 22 1832;F 15,Ap 18 1840
MB N 29 1823;F 25 1826;N 21 1829-N 13 1830; Jl 13 1833;Ag 23,S 6 1834
MC N 1823-N 1833;N 1835-N 1839;Ja-Jl 1840
MCheHi Ag 13 1825
MH Jl 31-Ag 7 1830
MHi [1824-25]Ap 13,Jl 13,O 26 1833;Ag 16-23 1834;S 5,O 31 1835;My 7,Jl 30,Ag 27,O 1,15 1836;Ap 28-My 12,O 6 1838;Ja 19-26,Ap 6 1839;F 15,Ap 18,Je 20,Jl 18 1840
MWA 1823-N 19 1825;Ja 14,F 11,Mr 1826-N 17 1827;Ap 5,O 11 1828;F 7,My 2,Jl 25,Ag 15,S 26,O 3,17,D 5,19 1829;Ja 1,30,Jl 31,O 9 1830;Ja 29,F 5,19,Jl 2,N 19 1831;Ap 27,S 14,28 1833;F 22,Ap 5,My 17-24,Je 7,N 29 1834;Ja 17-24,Mr 7,Ap 25,Je 20,Ag 15,O 3 1835[Ja-O 1836;37-38]-40
MiU-C [1825]
MnHi F 23 1833
NNHi Ap 23 1825;26-28;D 31 1831-Mr 9,23,Ap 6,Je 22,S 28 1833;extra Mr 3 1832
NcD O 7,N 25 1826;Ag 25 1829;N 27 1830;Jl 11 1835;Jl 9 1836;Mr 17 1838;Jl 27,Ag 3-10 1839;Mr 7 1840
P-M O 12 1833

COTTAGE CITY. *See* OAK BLUFFS

DANVERS

COMMON weal. w N 11 1910-
MSaE [1910]-[12-13]20-23
NcD N 25 1910[11]

Danvers COURIER. w Mr 15 1845-
United with Essex county mercury (Salem) to form Essex county mercury, and Danvers courier (Salem)
MSaE [1845]-47[49]
MWA O 1845-My 23,Je 6-13,Jl 11-Ag,S 19,D 12 1846;Mr,My 15,O 2 1847;F 12,Je 23,S 16 1848
NNHi [Mr-N 1845]

Danvers EAGLE. w S 6 1844-
MSaE [1844-45]
MWA F 15 1845

ESSEX county citizen. w Ja 26 1878-
MSaE [1878]
NcD Mr 16,Ap 20,Je 29 1878

ESSEX county review. w Je 12 1880-81||
MSaE [1880-81]
MWA Jl 17 1880

Danvers FIRE-FLY. Mr 7 1844-
First paper pub in Danvers

Danvers GAZETTE. w Ja 3 1868-
MH Ap 18,Jl 18 1868
MSaE [1868]
MWA Ap 4 1868

MASSACHUSETTS (*Continued*)

DANVERS—*Continued*

Danvers HERALD. w O 1920+
Follows Danvers mirror
pub 1920—
MDa 1920+
MSaE 1922-30

METEOR.
MSaE D 22-24 1868;D 21-23 1869;D 11-13 1877

Danvers MIRROR. w 1870-1920||
Followed by Danvers herald
Ct Ja 12 1895;N 12 1898
DLC Ag 31 1889
MDa 1878-1918;20
MSaE [1870-75]-1919
MWA Ap 22 1871
NcD F 19 Ap 8 1876;Mr 3 1877[81;84;87-90;94-95];S 21 1901;Je 21 1902;Mr 31-Ap 7 1910;F 4 1911;N 16 1915

Danvers MONITOR. w 1865-75||?
DLC D 23 1865
MSaE [1865-68]-72
MWA F 20-O 2,16,30,D 11-25 1867;Ja 8-15 1868;Jl 2? 1869
NcD My 18,Je 15-22,N 30 1870;O 9 1872
OClWHi Ap 4 1866

Danvers evening PRESS. d Je 1899-
MSaE 1899-1900
NcD Jl 12 1899

TRI-TOWN weekly press. [Middleton-Danvers-Topsfield] w O 1910-16||
MSaE 1913-[16]
NcD F 5 Mr 15,Je 4,S 17 1914;N 18 1915

Danvers WHIG. w
MHi O 5-12,N 9 1844
MSaE O 5-19,N 2-9 1844

DEDHAM

Dedham CITIZEN. w O 12 1889-1901||?
MDHi O 12-N 2 1889;O 15 1892;D 2,16 1893;S-N 26 1895

Dedham COMET. w Mr 30? 1844-
MWA Jl 27,D 1844

COUNTY recorder. w 1934+
MWA N 1 1935

Dedham GAZETTE. w 1849-F 19 1870||
Follows Roxbury gazette and Norfolk county American (Roxbury). Followed by Norfolk county gazette, later Hyde Park gazette-times (Hyde Park)
DLC F 16 1850-55;Ja 14-28,F 11 1860;Ag 30 1862;Ja 13,Mr 19 1864;O 21 1865;O 6 1866;Mr 1867-S 5 1868
MB [Mr 11 1849-Mr 11 1850]Je 21 1851;O 16 1852-70
MBAt F 1854-[55]56;65-70
MDHi F 23-Mr,Ap 20,Je 1,29,Jl 27,Ag 24-31,S 21,O 19,N 2 1850;O 16 1852-F 19 1870
MH N 2,D 14,28 1850;Ap 26,Je 19-28,Jl 19 1851-70
MHi Jl 12 1862
MHyHi 1852-70
MWA F 16,Je 15,N 2,23 1850[51-52]-Ja 7,F 4,My 13,S 9 1854-[Ja-O 23 1869]Ja-F 19 1870
MiU-C [1854]
NcD N 2 1850;F 3,Ap 21 1855;My 17-24 1856;57-N 9 1867[68]Je 5 1869
WHi Ja 16 Mr 19 1864

HAVERSACK. d Ap 6 1880-
ICHi Ap 6 1880
MDHi Ap 6-8 1880
MiU-C Ap 6-7 1880

INDEPENDENT politician. *See* Norfolk advertiser

Dedham JOURNAL. w D 10 1880-81||
MDHi D 10 1880;F 25 1881
MWA D 17 1880-F 18 1881

NORFOLK advertiser. w Ja 7 1831-F 2 1839||
1831-Jl ? 1832 as Independent politician and workingmen's advocate; Jl 13 1832-Mr 26 1836 Norfolk advertiser and independent politician. Followed by Norfolk democrat
DLC Mr 23 1832;F 9 1833
ICN S 29 1831
MB O 13 1838-39
MDHi Ap 23 1831-39
MH Je 23,N 3 1831
MHi Ag 1 1835;S 24 1836
MWA 1832-34 Mr 1836-38

NORFOLK argus. w 1860-
MAtt Ag 25 1860

NORFOLK county American. *See under* Boston

NORFOLK county gazette. *See* Hyde Park gazette-times (Hyde Park)

NORFOLK county news. w N 4 1911-
MDHi N 4- 8 1911

NORFOLK county republican. w D 3 1829-N 26 1830||
DLC D 3 1829
MB D 10 1829-30
MDHi complete
MWA Ja 2?,Ap 23,My 21,Je 25 1830

NORFOLK county republican. w
MDHi S 22,D 22 1888;Ja 4-18 1890

NORFOLK county star. w Je 17 1921-O 7 1922||
M complete

NORFOLK county whig. w O 7 1848-
MDHi O 14 1848

NORFOLK democrat. w F 9 1839-S 15 1854||
Follows Norfolk advertiser. Merged with Dedham gazette
DLC F 22-D 12 1840;F 1843-Ja 1848;F 9 1849;51-52
MB 1839-Ja 1843;47-Ja 18 1850;53
MDHi complete

MH Jl 15 1853
MWA complete
NN S 17 1841;Ja 2 1852
NNHi Ap 22 1842
NcD complete
NhD Je 15 1839;N 21 1840
OClWHi O 26 1839;Ja 25,F 1-8,S 12,26,N 14 1840;N 26 1841;F 4,S 16,O 14,N 11,D 2 1842;Ja 20,Mr 17,Je 9,30 S 8,O 13-17 1843;Ja 26,Jl 12-N 8 1844;Ja 31,Mr 21-D 12 1845;Ja-Mr 13,Ag 7 1846-Ap 23,Je 18,N 5-12 1847;Ja 14,Je 16 1848
P-M N 28 1845
RP Jl 8-15,Ag 5-12,26-S 2 1842

NORFOLK Washingtonian. w Ap 30 1843-
MWA My 5-O 20 1843

PARKWAY transcript. w F 28 1930+
pub 1930—

Dedham PATRIOT. w D 31 1830-Je 1842||
Title varies: Dedham patriot, and farmer's, mechanic's and manufacturer's advocate Dedham patriot and Canton gazette; Dedham patriot and Roxbury democrat; Mr?-Je? 1841 Patriot and democrat. Followed by Norfolk county American, (Boston)
Ct F 25 1836
DLC Ja 11 1838-O 17 1839;Ja 1 1840
MDHi 1830-[F 1837-S 26 1839]F 3,O 17 1840;Mr 13,My 29,Je 12,Ag 7,28 1841
MH Je 24 1831
MHi N 12 1835;S 22 1836
MNaHi Mr 21,My 9 1839
MWA 1831-D 17 1835 Je 9,Jl 7,Ag 18,O 27-N 3 1836[37-Jl 1839]Jl 3 1840;Ag 7 1841;My 7 1842
NN D 31 1830;F 6 1841
NcD Jl 4 1833;Jl 31,S 11 1834

SPIRIT of old Norfolk. w
NN Je 2,Jl 28,Ag 11,S 8,22-O 6,N 3 1840

Dedham STANDARD. w S 16 1882-1917||?
S 21 1886 is special ed "250th anniversary of the town".
KHi S 21 1886
M S 21 1886
MDHi 1882-Mr 21 1896[F-N 1898;Jl 1899-1913]
MWA Jl 10 1886-Je 1889;F 6,Ap 6,O 19 1895;Jl 24-31,S 18,O 2 1897;Je 4,S 3 1898;Ag 11 1900;Ap 25 1903
NcD Ag 21 1886
OClWHi S 21 1886

Dedham TRANSCRIPT. w Ap 9 1870+
1870 as Dedham transcript and Norfolk county advertiser
S 21 1886 is special ed "250th anniversary of the incorporation of the town of Dedham"
pub 1908+
M S 21 1886;95+
MB Ap 28 1883;D 12-19 1885;Ja 16[O 30-D 25 1886;F-Ag 20 1887]
MD 1870+
MDHi 1870+
MNaHi My 13 1876;81-83
MRa 1876-84
MWA [Ap 16-D 1870]-[98]Ja 7,Mr 25,Jl 8,Ag 19,D 23 1899-[1900]Ag 3-10,31,O 19 1901 [02]-Ap 17 1909[My 20-D 1911]
NbHi S 21 1886
NcD Ap 16 1870;F 18,Jl 15,29-Ag 12,26,S 2,16-23,N 18,D 2 1871;Mr 2,30,N 23 1872;Mr 15,Je 6,S 6,N 8,22 1873;F 14 1874;N 13 1875;76-N 1882;Ap 1881-S 1892;93-[98;1902-03]-[05]Je 2,Jl 14,N 3 1906;Ag 24 1907;Ap-My,S 26 1908

VILLAGE register and Norfolk county advertiser. w Je 9 1820-N 1829||
1820-23 as Village register
DLC Ja 11 1822;O 12 1826;N 8 1827;My 1-8,D 11 1828;Jl 2,Ag 6-13 1829
MDHi 1821-O 1829
MWA Ja 12-Ap 6,20,My 4-18,Je 15-29,N 23,D 8 1821;F 21,Mr 7 1823;My 5,Ag 4 1825;S 11 1828

DEERFIELD

FRANKLIN freeman. w Jl 25 1831-Jl 6 1832||
DLC Jl 25 1831
MH complete
NNHi complete
P-M Ag 1 1831

DORCHESTER

Papers published in Dorchester are listed under Boston

DUXBURY

UNION. w Ja 5 1856-
dated also at Scituate
MB Ap 5-S 13 1856

EAST BOSTON

Papers published in East Boston are listed under Boston

EAST BRIDGEWATER

East Bridgewater JOURNAL. w 1926+
pub 1926+
MWhT 1926+

LOG CABIN patriot. ir Ag 7-N 17 1840||
Campaign paper
DLC complete
ICU [1840]
MWA Ag 21 1840
OClWHi Ag 7,21,S 4 1840

East Bridgewater NEWS. w 1864-
MWA N 11 1865

EAST CHELMSFORD. *See* LOWELL

EAST DOUGLAS

Douglas HERALD. *See* Uxbridge compendium (Uxbridge)

WORCESTER south compendium. *See* Uxbridge compendium (Uxbridge)

EAST FOXBORO

COUNTRY times. w Ap 12 1856?-
MWA [Ap 26-D 1856]

EAST PEPPERELL

Pepperell CLARION-ADVERTISER. w 1868+
MH O 30 1926
MHi My 6-13 1893;My 19-Je 2,S 1,O 13 1894;F 23 1895-N 5 1904;Ja 6 1905
MLa Je 30 1917+
MWA S 19 1931

Pepperell FREE PRESS. w N 1929+
pub F 1930+

Pepperell NEWS. w Ja 1? 1909-21||
MHi F 19 1909
MPep D 30 1909-Ja 7 1921

EAST WEYMOUTH

Papers published in East Weyouth are listed under Weymouth

EASTHAMPTON

Easthampton ENTERPRISE. w O 14 1875-Ag 26 1881||
1875-My 1876 as Leader. United with Easthampton news to form Easthampton news and enterprise, later Easthampton news
MEa Je 1876-81
MWA F 25 1881

ENTERPRISE. w O 20 1897-1917||
MEa 1897-O 12 1898
MH D 13 1899

LEADER. *See* Easthampton enterprise

MIRROR. w
MDeHi N 15 1872;F 19 1873

Easthampton NEWS. w Je 4 1879-1928||?
S? 1881-87? as Easthampton news and enterprise
MEa My 12 1880-S 21 1894;Jl 26 1917-D 27 1928
NcD Je 3 1876

EASTON

Easton BULLETIN. w 1888+
pub Ap 1930+

EDGARTOWN

VINEYARD gazette. w My 14 1846+
pub 1846+
CSmH Jl 16 1853
DLC D 17 1875;F 11,Mr 3-10 1876;Ja 12,Mr 23-30 1877
M My 22 1931
MEd 1930+
MEdH 1846+
MOb 1930+
MWA D 18 1846;O 27 1848;Ja 23 1852;Je 19 1857;N 20 1863;S 8 1865;F 25,Mr 3-17,Ap 7 1876[Je 18-Ag 20 1886]
MWo Jl 28 1892
NcD Ap 18,Jl 18-25 1901
OClWHi My 6 1866;My 11 1893-Je 14 1894

ESSEX

Essex ECHO. w 1887-1920||?
MMaC 1895-1905
MSaE [1887-89;95-98]-[1918]
MWA S 16-D 1916
NcD My 12 1899;Ag 24-31,S 28 1900;D 30 1910

Essex weekly ENTERPRISE. w Je 12 1875-
MSaE Je 12 1875
MWA Je 12 1875

EVERETT

Everett GAZETTE. w O 4 1913+
pub 1913+
M Ja 9 1931-N 10 1932
ME 1913+

Everett HERALD and republican. w O 31 1885+
1885-91 as Everett herald
pub 1885+
ME 1885+

Everett evening NEWS. d Jl 25 1928+
pub Ja 1 1930
M Ja 16 1931
ME 1928+

FAIRHAVEN

O COLONIAL. w D 3 1925+
In Portuguese
pub 1925+

Fairhaven STAR. w F 18 1879+
F-Je 28 1879 as Star
M F 15 1929;N 23 1933
MFh 1879+
MNb 1879-95;99+
MWA [1879-80]Ja 8 1881
NN N 19 1920

MASSACHUSETTS (*Continued*)

FALL RIVER

Fall River ALL SORTS and Tiverton advertiser. sw 1843-
MWA Mr 16,Ag 14,21 1844
RHi Jl 10 1844;Ap 15 1848;Ap 17[My 1849-Ag 16 1851]
RW Ap 4,My 30 1846;O 20,N 10,24,D 22 1855; Ja 5,12,12,19 1856

ARCHETYPE. w Ja 7 1841-
MWA Ja 28,F 18,Ap 22,Je 10 1841

Fall River ARGUS. w My 5 1842-
MFa 1842-Jl 13 1843
MWA [Mr-Je 15 1843]

BORDER CITY herald. *See* Fall River herald-news

L'ECHO du Canada. w 1873-75||
In French
MWA Mr 28 1874-N 6 1875

FLINT and steel. w O 14 1842-
MWA N 11 1842

Fall River daily GLOBE. d Ap 27 1885-1929||
DLC 1898
M Je 1899-Ap 30 1823[1928-Ap 10 1929]
MFa Ap-O 29 1885;89-F 2 1929
MFaH complete
RW Je 15 1887

Fall River HERALD-NEWS. d 1872+
1872-75? as Border City herald; 1876?-1926 Fall River daily herald
pub 1877+
Ct Ap 3 1900
MFa F 16-D 1877;Jl-D 1878;Jl 1879+
MWA Ap 24 1873

L'INDEPENDENT. w,d Mr 27 1885+
In French
Also dated in New Bedford
pub Mr 27 1885-92;F 1928+
MB Mr 27 1885-Ja 1 1886
MWA Mr 27 1885-N 19 1886
RWoI My 1928+

Fall River JOURNAL. w S 17 1859-
MWA Ag 12 1865;My 6 1866

MECHANIC. w Ap 27 1844-
MFa 1844-Ap 1 1845

Fall River MONITOR. w Ja 6 1826-1904||?
Title varies: Fall River weekly monitor
CSmH Ag 21 1830
DLC N 28 1829;S 29 1832;D 5-12 1840
MFa 1826-27;S 27 1828-D 18 1830;Jl 26 1836-Je 1857;D 29 1865-Jl 20 1866
MH Ja 13 1827;F 7 1829
MWA Mr 11 1826;Ag 18 1827;Je 14 1828;Jl 10 1830;O 29 1842;Ap 27,N 30 1844;Je 22 1850; Je 5 1852;Jl 8 1854;F 23,Mr 8-15,My 3 1856; Ap 6 1861;D 4 1869
MnHi Ja 26 1833
NcD S 9 1876;Jl 2 1892
OClWHi Ap 28-My 5 1866
P-M S 16 1854
RW [D 18 1841-Je 22 1861]

Fall River daily MONITOR. d O 9 1865-
MWA O 9 1865;My 12 1866

MORAL envoy. w Mr 17 1830-
CSmH Je 9 1830
MWA Ag 18 1830
WHi Mr 24-D 8 1830

Fall River weekly NEWS. w Ap 3 1845-1926||
MFa 1845-Mr 1906
MH Ja 28 1858;Ag 1867-O 1895
MNb 1845-95
MWA 1845-Mr 17 1853[Ap 1854-Mr 1855]F 8 1866;Jl 20 1871
NcD D 31 1846
NjR Mr 29 1849
OClWHi F 1 1866
RW [S 26 1861-D 9 1880]

Fall River daily NEWS. d Ja 2 1860-1926||
Title varies: Fall River daily news; Fall River evening news. United with Fall River daily herald to form Fall River herald-news
MFa complete
MFaH 1860-1925
MBAt Ap 15 1865
MH Je 15 1887;Ag 31 1908
MWA [O 10-N 22 1860]Jl 25 1862;Ag 14 1863; Je 23 1864;Ag 11 1865;My 21 1890
NcD S 20 1881
OClWHi F 2 1866
RW Je 1-2 1859;D 14 1875;Je 30,Ap 8 1876;O 14 1878;F 14 1879;S 18 1882;Je 15 1887;S 9 1889

NOVIDADES. w 1907+
In Portuguese
pub 1923+
IU D 1917+

L'OUVRIER canadien. w Mr 27-Jl 10 1875||
Merged with L'Echo du Canada
In French
MWA Jl 10 1875

Fall River PATRIOT and Tiverton freeman. w Ja 5 1837-
Ct [1837-38]
DLC Ja 10-Jl,D 25 1839
MH F 23 1837
MWA Ap 19 1838-D 24 1840
NcD F 20-27 1840

PEOPLE'S press. tw D 10 1859-
MFa Ja 1 1863-S 9 1865
MWA D 15 1859;D 25 1860;Jl 30,Ag 6 1863

PRESS. w O 23 1903-
MFa 1903-My 13 1904

Le PROTECTEUR canadien. w D 17? 1875-
In French
MWA F 19 1876

Fall River weekly RECORDER. w Jl 11 1832-
MFa 1832-Ja 15 1834
MWA D 5 1832;F 1(extra)1834

La RÉPUBLIQUE. w 1875-77||
1875-F 5? 1876 pub in Boston
In French
MWA •Ja 1[F-Jl 1876]

Daily SPARK. d
NNHi S 20-N 4 1848

Daily evening STAR. d Ap 3 1857-
MFa 1857-Mr 31 1858
MWA Ap 20 1857

Daily SUN. d My 11 1880-
MFa 1880-Mr 25 1882

Morning TRIBUNE. d Mr 13 1890-
MFa Mr-O 7 1890

Evening TRIBUNE. d Mr 31 1890-
MFa Mr-O 1 1890

FALMOUTH

Falmouth ENTERPRISE. w 1894+
pub 1912+
M Ja 5,Ap 26 1928
MF 1896-1906;09-12;Ap 19 1913-Mr 1915;16-18;22+

Falmouth LOCAL. w 1886-89||?
MWA Ag 9,S 6 1888

NAUTICAL intelligencer, and Barnstable county gazette. w N 21 1823-
1823-Ap? 1824 as Nautical intelligencer and Falmouth and Holms-Hole journal
DLC Ap 9-16,30,My 28,Je 25,Jl-Ag 6,O 15,D 3 1824
MWA N 28 1823;Ap 16,Ag 27 1824

FITCHBURG

Fitchburg GAZETTE. w 1830-
MWA [Jl 12 1831-Ap 16 1833]

La LIBERTÉ. w 1919+
Also dated in Leominster and Gardner
In French
pub Mr 1921+
M N 3 1932
MWA My 2 1924

Evening MAIL. d O 3? 1888-97||?
MWA O 6 1888

MT. ROLLSTONE star. sm F 10 1848-
MWA F 10 1848

Fitchburg NEWS. w Ja 20 1852-
MWA Mr 3 1852
N F 15 1853

Daily NEWS. d 1904-19||
MFiHi complete
MHi [1918]

NORTH star. *See* Pohjan tähti

PIONEER. *See* Raivaaja

POHJAN tähti. (North star) d,tw, ir 1901-26||
In Finnish
IU D 6 1917-My 14 1926

RAIVAAJA (Pioneer). w,d Ja 1905+
w 1905-My 1911
In Finnish
pub Ja 31 1905+
WHi N 27 1909-Ja 17 1928

Le REVEIL. d,w 1895-97||
1895-My 5? 1897 pub in Worcester
d Je-O 1896
In French
MWA N 28 1895-Mr,Ap 30-Je 4,13-23,S 22-O 10,29 1896-Ap 8,My-D 16 1897

Fitchburg REVEILLE. w,sw Mr 27 1852-F 22 1877||
sw 1852-61
MB [My 1852-Ag 23 1854;F 14 1855-D 4 1862]
MBAt My 13-20,Jl 15,Ag 19 1869
MFiHi complete
MFiS Mr 31 1858-77
MWA [Ap 1852-Mr 15 1853]F 24 1855;Ap 4,Jl 22 1857;F 23,My 25 1859[60]F 13 1861;S,N 20-D 11,25 1862;F 5,19 1863[65]-[73]-77
OClWHi My 24 1866

Fitchburg weekly SENTINEL. w D 20 1838-Mr 31 1922||
pub complete
DLC D 20-27 1838
MBAt My 15,Jl 24-31,S 25 1869;My 5 1876
MF [1841-82]
MFiHi complete
MHi [My 1894-1914]-S 20 1918
MWA Ap 3 1839;My 5-12 1841[42-Je 19 1846] Ap 9 1847;Ja 18,F 22,My 17,Je 7,Jl 19,D 6,27 1850[51-52]-1917
MWo My 1 1894
N Ja 16 1863
NcD Ja 27 1865;Mr 1,22 1878
NhD Ap 26 1844
OClWHi O 27 1865

Fitchburg daily SENTINEL. d My 1873+
Je 18 1892 is 20th anniversary ed
pub 1873+
M Je 1899+
MFi My 6 1873
MFiHi 1873+
MH Mr 13 1880
MWA Ja 4 1882;Je 18 1892
WHi 1873-My 4 1874

WACHUSETT independent. w Mr 7 1845-
MWA Mr 22 1845

FOXBORO

EAGLE and the flag. m Ja-O? 1863||
Followed by Norfolk county chronicle
MB Ja 1863

Foxboro JOURNAL. w
MFo My 11-Je 8 1922

NORFOLK county chronicle. w,bw N 14 1863-
Follows Eagle and flag
bw 1863-S 17 1864
MWA 1863-Je,S 17-O 1 1864
NcD Ap 16 1864

Foxboro REPORTER. w S 24 1884+
pub 1884+
MFo Ja 11 1896;99+
MWA D 1 1888;Ap 2 1927

FRAMINGHAM

Framingham GAZETTE. w 1871-1913||
DLC Ja 23 1885
MFr [1871-1905]-13
MNaHi D 16 1874

Framingham evening NEWS. d Jl 1 1897+
pub 1897+
M Jl 1921+
MFr [1913-16]-[18]-[24-33]+

Framingham TRIBUNE. w O 26 1883-1912||?
MWA Ja 18 1884

FRANKLIN

Franklin MERCURY. w 1834-
MH 1835

Franklin SENTINEL. w 1878+
pub 1898+
MB Ag 18-D 1883
MHi Ja 19 1906

GARDNER

Gardner JOURNAL. w 1887-1913||
MGa 1890-1913

La LIBERTÉ. *See under* Fitchburg

Gardner NEWS. w Jl 3 1869-D 31 1904||
Je 27 1885 is illustrated centennial ed
pub complete
MGa 1870-1904
MWA Je 27 1885
NNHi Ap 5 1873;Je 27 1885

Gardner NEWS. d D 2 1896+
pub 1896+
Ct D 12 1903;N 14 1905;O 27 1908;F 12 1909
M [1928-Jl 1933]
MGa 1896+

GAY-HEAD (MARTHA'S VINEYARD)

Gay-Head LIGHT. w Ap 11 1866-
MH Ap 11 1866

GEORGETOWN

Georgetown ADVOCATE. w S 23 1874-1902||
M 1888-F 7 1902
MPe 1874-S 8 1899
MSaE [1874-75]-[1902]
NcD Ja 6 1877;F 26,Ap 23,Ag 13 1881;F 24-Mr 10,Ap 14,D 15-22 1883;Ja 12-26,N 15-22,D 6 1884;Ap 25,Je 20,Jl 25,S 26 1885-88

Georgetown BLUNDERBUSS. ir Jl 4 1878-
MSaE Jl 4 1878
MWA Jl 4 1878

Georgetown ERA. w Ja 3?-Jl 18 1868||?
MH My 23-Jl 18 1868
MSaE [1868]
MWA My 23-Je,Jl 11-18 1868

Georgetown EVANGELIST. ir O 14 1867-
MSaE O 14,N 25 1867
MWA O 14 1867

Georgetown EVANGELIST. w F 1-My 9 1868||
MH complete
MSaE complete
MWA complete

MASSACHUSETTS observer. w 1839?-48||?
MH Je 9-Jl 28 1848
MSaE [1848]
MWA Je-Jl 21 1848

Georgetown weekly REPORTER. w Je? 1850-
DLC Ap 5 1851
MSaE [1850-51]

STAR. m
MSaE [1871]
MWA My,D 1871

WATCHTOWER. *See under* Newburyport

GLOUCESTER

Gloucester ADVERTISER. *See* Cape Ann advertiser

Gloucester AMERICAN. w
MSaE O 10 1857

CAPE ANN advertiser. m,sm,w Ja 1 1856-Jl 1901||
1856-57 as Gloucester advertiser
m 1856-O 1857;sm N 1857-N 1858
DLC 1870-77;Ag 1 1879;S 22 1882
KHi Jl 9 1897;Ag 26 1898;Ja 27-F 3 1899
M 1887-88
MGlHi complete
MGlT complete
MSaE [1857-73]-[1901]
MWA D 20 1861;My 23,Jl 11,Ag 1 1862;Mr 4 1864;O 15,D 17(supp)1869;My 9 1873;N 2(supp)1877;Jl 29 1881;O 29(supp)1886
NcD [1874-77]O 8-15 1880[82-86]-99
OClWHi S 8 1865
VU N 18 1870

MASSACHUSETTS (*Continued*)

GLOUCESTER—*Continued*

CAPE ANN breeze. d Ag 29 1884-1901||
MSaE Ag 29 1884;F 23,D 5,9 1885[86-88;90;98]-1901
NcD Ja 3 1888;Je 1 1889;Mr 19,My 15,N 22 1900

CAPE ANN bulletin. w 1877-87||
Follows Gloucester telegraph
DLC N 10,24-D 22 1880
MSaE 1877[78]-[86-87]
NcD S 14,28 1881[Ap 1882-My 1883]N 29 1884; Ap 18,My 2,16-23 1885

CAPE ANN herald. sw
MSaE N 9,30-D 1876

CAPE ANN light and Gloucester telegraph. w 1843?-72||?
DLC Mr 30 1850
MSaE [1843-44;47-48;52;54-55]O 22 1859;D 8 1860;S 24 1864;F 11,N 4 1865;Je 15 1867;Je 6,S 26 1866
MWA My 3,Je 14 1845;Ap 18 1847;Je 4 1859;N 23 1861;Ag 2 1862;Ja 17,Je 27,Ag 8 1863;S 2 1871
NjR Ag 13 1864
OClWHi My 12 1866
—sw ed *See* Gloucester telegraph

CAPE ANN news. d 1900-09||
MSaE 1901-09
NcD Ap 22 1903

Gloucester DEMOCRAT. sw Ag 19 1834-
Title varies slightly
Ct D 15 1835[36-38]
MSaE [1834-38]
MTaHi F 12,23 1836
MWA Ag 19 1834;Mr 14,Je 27-30,N 24-28 1837

JEFFERSONIAN republican. sw O 15-N 23 1838||
MSaE complete
MWA complete

Gloucester NEWS. d 1884-86||
MSaE complete

Gloucester NEWS and semi-weekly messenger. sw 1849-51||
United with Gloucester telegraph to form Telegraph and news, later Gloucester telegraph
DLC Ja 22,Mr 8-12,19,26-29,My 17-21,28,Je 18,25,Jl 2,9,Ag 27 1851
MMarHi Je 23-27 1849
MSaE [1849-51]
MWA Ag 10 1850[Ja-O 4 1851]

PERLEY'S trade gazette. m
MSaE [1869-70]Ja 1871;N 1874

PROCTOR'S able sheet. m Jl 1 1853-O 1? 1855||
Merged with Gloucester advertiser, later Cape Ann advertiser
MGlT 1853-O 1 1855

Gloucester TELEGRAPH. w,sw 1827-76||
Followed by Cape Ann bulletin
1843-47 as Telegraph; 1852-66 Telegraph and news
w 1827-33;35;38
CSmH Ag 28 1830
Ct Ap 21 1827
DLC Ja-Mr,Ap 14-21,Je 23,Jl 21,N 10,D 8,22 1827;Ap 26-My 10,24,Jl 5,O 25 1828;Mr 14,Ag 8,S 1829;Ja 2 1830;My 14 1841;Ja 15,F 5-12,Mr 5-15,26,Jl 12 1851;Ja 14 1852;D 2 1854[67-68]O 6,23,N 13 1869;Ja 1,N 30 1870[71]Ag 19,S 9-16, 30,O 21 1874;Ja 13,Je 30,Jl 7 1875;F 2,Mr 1,My 17 1876
MB Ag 4 1838
MBAt Ag 8 1828;62-63
MHi O 24 1835;Ag 5 1848
MSaE F 17-24,My 12 1827;Ag 2 1828[32-40]F 24 1841;Ja 21 1843;Mr 23-27 1844[45-48;50-53]-[56-65]-76
MWA Mr 24 1827;Ja 5 1828;N 6 1830;S 21 1833;Ag 6 1834;Ap 14 1835;N 18 1838;Ja 25 1843;Mr 6 1844;My 24 1845;My 9 1846;Mr 10, Ap 3 1847;N 24 1849;D 4-18 1850;F 19,Mr 29[My 21-Ag 1851]F 14,Mr 3,13,My 26,O 27 1852[54-N 10 1855;Mr 28 1857;D 11 1861; Je 21,Ag 23,S 6,17-20 1862;Ja 28,F 11,My 13 1863;Je 14 1865[Mr 31-S 15 1866]Jl 2 1870; N 18 1871-Ag 11 1875
NN Ap 2 1831
NjR F 29 1860
OClWHi My 12 1866
—w ed *See* Cape Ann light. . .

Gloucester daily TIMES. d Je 16 1888+
pub 1888+
M 1888+
MH Ap 11 1890;F 1-3 1926
MHi Mr 2 1920
MSaE 1888-1919
NcD 1888;D 16-26 1889;S 3 1890;N 30 1891;My 15,D 20 1898;Ja-Je 10 1899;Ja 1,Ag 12 1901; Ag 29 1902;F 24,26,28-29 1912
WaPS S 5-6,9,11 1919

GRAFTON

Evening BUDGET. d My 28 1851-
MWA My 28 1851

Grafton HERALD. w 1874-1901||?
MWA [1884-85]-Ag 1 1888

GREAT BARRINGTON

BERKSHIRE courier. w O 16 1834+
Title varies: Berkshire courier and Great Barrington gazette; Berkshire courier and Housatonic mirror
N 1 1934 is 100th anniversary ed
pub 1855+
CL N 1 1934
Ct My 6 1841;Ja 5 1860
CtY Ja 9 1845-Je 4 1846
ICHi N 9 1865
IaDH 1900-My 1904
M [S 24 1931-Mr 9 1933]
MGb 1846-48;52-89;91-1929
MHi Je 2-9,23,O 13 1836
MPi S 10,N 26 1835;O 6 1836;Ag 3,17-24 1838; F 15,My 24,Jl 5-12,Ag-S 6 1838;Ap 15 1841; Mr 10,Je 23 1842;My 18-Je 1 1843;Ap 11,Ag 1,29,N 14,D 5 1844;Ap 3,My 29 1845;My 6,Je 18,Jl 9,Ag 13,O 29,N 19,D 3 1846;Ja 28,F 11, 25,Mr 11,My 6,20-27,Jl 15,Ag 6,S 9,30,O 14,D 9,23 1847;Mr 2,16,Ap 27,Ag 10,S 28 1848;S 4 1851;F 17-Mr 3,17 1859;D 23 1868;N 25,D 9-23 1874;F 10,Ap 28 1875;77,Ag 16,S 11 1878; 79-1901;03-11
extras:My 16,17,18,22 1878
MWA O 13 1836;Mr 22 1838;Ja 10,Mr 21,My 16,Ag 1 1839;F 6-13,Ap 16 1840[41]Mr 16,My 18 1843;Ag 7 1845;Jl 2 1846;F 25 1847;O 5 1848;Ag 9 1849;Je 12 1851;F 26 1852;Ap 13 1854;Je 19 1856;My 21 1857;D 8 1859;Ap 18,S 19 1861;My 8,Ag 7 1862;F 19 1863;Ja 19 1865; Ag 9 1866;Je 6 1867;My 26,S 29 1869;["70-73]F 4-13,Mr 18-Ap 1 1874;Ap 2,Je 21,Ag 3 1876;F 21-28,Mr 14 1877;My 22,O 16,D 25 1878;N 5,26 1879;F 4 1880;S 13 1882;S 5 1883[84]87;Jl 1888-90;F 16 1899
extras: N 7 1863;My 16,17,18,Ag 16 1878
MWiC Mr 3 1864
NHlH [1834-55]
NNHi My 15 1863;My 7 1873;Ja 2 1884
NcD F 6 1840;Ap 8 1841;Ap 26 1871;My 19,Je 4,Jl 23,Ag 6-13,27,S 10,O 22,N 5,26,D 10-17 1873;F 11 1874;My 17,O 16,D 25 1878;N 3 1886; Je 19 1889;Ap 2 1890
P Ap 3 1845
P-M O 6 1853

BERKSHIRE news. w 1889-Ap 1895||
M Ap 1894-95
MWA D 30 1893;D 1 1894

BERKSHIRE press. w D 13? 1906-
MWA My 17-24 1907

BERKSHIRE rambler. w Ja 4-Ap 19 1858||
MWA complete

Great Barrington GAZETTE. w Mr 30 1895-96||
M 1895-O 10 1896
MWA Mr 30 1895

HOUSATONIC mirror. w Mr 31-O 21 1846||?
United with Berkshire courier to form Berkshire courier and Housatonic mirror, later Berkshire courier
MWA [Ap 21-O 21 1846]

INDEPENDENT press. w S 20 1845-Ag 6 1847||
MWA D 27 1845;Ja 17 1846;Jl 30 1847
P-M N 15 1845

GREENFIELD

AMERICAN republic. w 1849-
MDeHi Ja 21,Je 17 1850;D 15 1851;Jl 5 1852 S 19-26,N 21,D 5 1853;Ja 16,Mr 6,Je 19,Jl 31,N 20 1854
MH My 27 1850
MWA Ja 12 1852

Greenfield COURIER. w 1838-Jl 13 1841||
United with Gazette and mercury to form Gazette and courier
MDeHi Jl 3 1838;Ap 9 1839-Mr,O 2 1840;Ap-Jl 1841
MWA Jl 9 1839;F 18 1840
NNHi Ag 18 1840
NcD S 15 1840

DEMOCRAT. *See* Franklin democrat

FRANKLIN county beacon. ir Ag 7 1873-
Campaign paper
MWA Ag 7,26 1873

FRANKLIN county reformer. w 1882-88||?
MWA Jl 16 1886

FRANKLIN county times. w 1871-78||?
MWA S 13 1872;Jl 17,Ag 14 1874;Ja 8 1875

FRANKLIN democrat. w Ap 21 1840-
1840-Ja? 1842 as Democrat
DLC My 21,Jl 2,Ag 6 1844;S 28,O 5,N 2-9 1847;Je 24 1850;F 21 1853;Ag 14,S 11 1854; My 21,Jl 2 1855;Ap 7 1856;F 9,23,Mr 2-30,Ap 20,S 7,28 1857;Ja 4,Je 21,Ag 16 1858;O 3 1859;Ja 2 1860
IU Jl 14 1840
MB 1840-Ap 10 1849
MDeHi [1840-48]Je 12 1854[Ap 1858-Ag 1859]
MH Mr 7 1848;Ap 17 1854;Mr 5 1855
MWA Jl 2 1844;S 15 1846;Ap 29 1850;Jl 28, Ag 18 1851;F 23,Mr 15,O 4 1852;S 5 1853; F 9,23-Mr 9,30,Ap 20 1857
MiU-C Mr 2,30 1857
NcD S 17 1844;N 2 1847
NhD My 28,Je 11 1844
OClWHi S 21 1841
P My 9 1843;Ap 22 1845
P-M O 11 1852
WHi Mr 2,Ap 20 1857

FRANKLIN freeman. w Jl 1831?-
DLC Ja 14 1833
MDeHi [Jl 25 1831-34]
MH Jl 30-D 1832[Ja 28-N 5 1833]
OClWHi My 13 1834

*FRANKLIN herald and public advertiser. w Ja 7 1812-Je 19 1827||
Follows Traveller (not in this list) 1812-S 3 1822 as Franklin herald. United with Greenfield gazette and Franklin county advertiser to form Greenfield gazette and Franklin herald, later Gazette and courier
DLC Ja 2-9,23,Ap 3,Je 19,Jl 3 1821-Je 10 1823 F 10-S 14 1824;F 15 1825;F 21-Mr 14,28,Je 6,Jl 4,18,Ag 8,S 19 1826-Jl 10 1827
MDeHi F 27,Ap 24,Je 19 1821;Jl 23,O 8 1822 Ag 12,S 9,D 9 1823;Ja 13,Mr 16,Ap 20,My 4,D 7 1824;25;Ja 10,Ap 11,D 5 1826;Ja 16,My 22 1827
MWA [F 20-D 18 1821]Ja 15-D 24 1822[Ja 21-N 1823;24-Je 12 1827]
MiU-C [1822;24]
NN S 10 1822
NNHi Ja 23,F 20,Mr 27,Ap 17,24,N 5 1821;F 5,Mr 19,Je 18,Ag 27 1822;F 4 1823;Mr 2-9 1824;S 13 1825;Ag 1 1826
WHi Ag 6-13 1822

FRANKLIN mercury. w S 7 1833-Je 27 1837||
United with Greenfield gazette and Franklin herald to form Gazette and mercury, later Gazette and courier
DLC Je 7,Ag 23,S 1834-Ag 23 1836
MB 1833-Ag 23 1836
MBAt D 1 1835
MDeHi S 28 1833;Jl 5,D 16 1834[35]F 2,Ag 30 1836-Je 20 1837
MGrR Ja 19 1836-37
MHi N 1 1834;Ap 7,Jl 28,O 1835;S 20,O 11 1833
MWA [1834-My 5 1835]
NcD [1833-Mr 1836]
Tx Ag 16 1836

FRANKLIN post and Christian freeman. *See* Old Hampshire post (Northampton)

FRANKLIN sentinel. w F 16 1830-
MWA Mr-Jl 1830

FREE soil. ir O 3 1848-
Campaign paper
MDeHi Ag 1,N 20(extra)1848
MH O 3 1848
MWA O 17 1848

FREEDOM'S sentinel. w F 13 1830-
CSmH Jl 6 1830
DLC Mr 9,Je 8-15 1830
MDeHi F 23,Je 1,29 1830
MH F-Ap 20 1830

GAZETTE and courier. w Jl 1 1823-Je 1932||
1823-S 12 1826 as Greenfield gazette; S 19 1826-Je 19 1827 Greenfield gazette and Franklin county advertiser; Je 26 1827-Je 28? 1837 Greenfield gazette and Franklin herald; Jl 4 1837-Jl 13 1841 Gazette and mercury. United with Greenfield daily recorder to form Daily recorder-gazette
F 1 1932 is centennial ed
pub 1845-1932
CSmH Ag 31 1830
Ct N 20 1827[30-31]
CtHi F 16 1885-Jl 1888
CtY S 9-16 1828
DLC F 24-O 26 1824;Mr 14 1826;S 25,D 25 1827;Ja 1-8,29-Mr 11,Je 3-10 1828;Je 30,Jl 7-14 1829;Ja 19 1830;F 15,Mr 15,Ap 5,26,Jl 19 1831;O 9-23 1832;O 22 1839;D 14 1841;Ja 11,F 1 1842
IU Ag 14 1838
KHi 1885-My 9 1891
M 1889-1932
MB Jl 20 1841-D 21 1847;60-62
MDeHi [1823-59]-[62-63]-[70]-[82]-[89]-91
MGr complete
MH Jl 22-D 1823]-Je 10 1828;N 4 1829;30-32; 35[42-N 1848]Ja 9-23,Mr 12 1849
MHi Je 14,O 4,N 1-22,D 6-20 1886;Ja 10,Ag 22 1887;Ag 1888-Mr 10 1894[97-1903]F 26 1921;Ag 8 1924
MN 1879-84
MWA Jl 15 1823;Ap 13,S 14,O 5 1824[O 1825-Je 19 1827]-[29-30]Ja 4,28,F 22,Ag 9,S 20 1831[32-33]S 16 1834;Ap 10 1838;Ap 23[Je 25 1839-Je 16 1840]Ja 14 1845;F 2 1847;49-[77]-84;D 5 1887;Mr 5 1888;89[90-91]-Mr 1893;Ap 28,O 6,N 10 1894;Je 27 1896;S 10 1898
MWo Mr 19 1877
MiU-C My 30 1837[49-55;57-62;67;70;82]
NNHi Ja 4 1825;Ap 27 1827;Ag 25 1862;My 18-Je 22 1863;My 19 1873
NcD [1823-37;40-47;49;65-66 76;89;91]
OClWHi O 3 1864;Ag 18 1884
OHi My 31 1858-Ap 9 1877
P-M Ap 19 1831
WHi Ag 25 1862

Daily RECORDER-GAZETTE. w,d Ja 1 1900+
1900-19 as Greenfield recorder(w) 1920-Je 1932 Greenfield daily recorder
pub 1900+
M Jl 31 1901;D 18(supp)1912[28-Jl 1933]
MGr 1920+
MHi F 23 1921

WORKINGMAN'S advocate, and democratic journal. w My 17? 1836-
MDeHi N 15 1836
MWA O 4 1836

GROTON

BROWN railroad mercury. *See* Railroad mercury

CENTENNIAL record. F 22 1876||
M complete
MH complete
MiU-C complete

Groton CITIZEN. m,w Ja 1884-90||?
m Ja-Jl? 1884
MB Ja,My-Jl,S 11-18,O 9 1884
MH Ja-Jl[S 11-N 6 1884]

Groton GEM. m My-Je 1859||?
MH My-Je 1859

GIVE 'em Jessie! ir Ag 25 1856-
Campaign paper
DLC S 25 1856
MH Ag 25,S 25,N 1 1856
MWA Ag 25,S 20,N 1 1856
MiU-C Ag 25,S 20 1856

Groton HERALD. w D 5 1829-S 4 1830||
MH D 29 1829;Ja 9-S 1830
MHi complete
MWA complete
MiU-C [1830]

MASSACHUSETTS (*Continued*)

GROTON—*Continued*

LANDMARK. w O 18 1884+
DLC D 31 1898
MGro 1902-06;08;10+
MH O 25 1884-Ja 1886;O 15 1887-1932
MWA 1884-Ja 1886;O 15 1887+
NcD O 23 1897
WHi My 25 1895-Ja 1917

GROTON mercury. *See* Railroad mercury

MIDDLESEX worker. w Ap 13? 1867-
MH S 14 1867

Groton NEWS. w
MHi Je 19,S 11 1914;S 10 1915;S 6 1918

PUBLIC spirit. *See* Turner's public spirit (Ayer)

RAILROAD mercury. m,sm,w Je 1851-S 26 1861||
1851-Ag 1852 as Groton mercury; S 1852-53? Mercury and spirit of the times; 1856?-57 Brown railroad mercury
m 1851-53?
MB 1851-My,Jl,S 1852;Mr,My 1853;Je 21 1860-61
MH 1851-Ap 1857;S 15 1859-61
MHi S 15 1859-61
MSte My 31 1860
MWA Je-Jl,S 1851;Ja,My,Ag 1852;S 15 1859-N 1860[Ja 10-S 1861]
MiU-C Je-Jl 1851;S 15-O 2 1852;Jl 20 1855; Ja 15 1857

SPIRIT of the times. w Jl 26 1848-
Campaign paper
DLC Jl,S-N 8 1848
MH Jl 1848
MWA Jl-D 7 1848
MiU-C Jl,S-D 1848

HAMPDEN

Hampden INTELLIGENCER. w O 24 1831-
N N 7-14 1832

HARVARD

Harvard HILLSIDE. w S 18 1909+
MH O 23 1909;Mr 2 1918;Mr 6 1920

HARWICH

Harwich INDEPENDENT. w Ap 1 1872+
pub 1872+
M [Mr 1930-Ag 10 1932]
NN My 23-D 12 1872

HAVERHILL

BREAK o'day. w F 7 1859-
MHa F 7 1859

Haverhill BULLETIN. d Jl 1 1871-98||
1871-Ja 26 1881 as Haverhill daily bulletin; Ja 27 1881-Mr 24 1895 Daily evening bulletin
DLC [1871-Ag 1872]Jl 3,Ag 10 1877;Ja 13,Mr 22[Ag 5 1880-89;Ap-N 1890;Je-N 1891;93-94]
MHa 1871-Jl 18 1898
MSaE [1871-73;75;78]98
MWA Jl 28 1871;Ap 17 1872;Ja 2-4 1890
NNHi 1871
NcD My 24 1872;Jl 1 1879[81-88;91-94]

Haverhill weekly BULLETIN. w Ja 5? 1872-98||
MH F 2 1878
MHa 1873-Je 10 1898
MSaE [1872-89]-[98]
MWA Ag 17 1872
NNHi 1872-O 1892;93-Ag 1895;97-Jl 15 1898
NcD N 28 1885-[91-96]

Le CITOYEN. w O 5 1905+
French
pub 1920+
M [Jl 29-N 1932]
MHa 1905+
MLT 1905+

CLARION and social democrat. w O 7 1899-D 14 1901||
1899-S 14 1901 as Haverhill social democrat
IU O 7-21,N 4,18,D 2-23 1899[1900-S 7 1901]
M complete
MB [Mr 1900-S 7]-D 1901
MH S 28-N 9,D 7 1901
MHa complete
MSaE [1900-01]
WHi 1899-S 7 1901

Saturday evening CRITERION. *See* Haverhill record

ESSEX banner. w Jl 5 1834-N 16 1888||
1834-Ap 10 1840 as Essex banner and Haverhill advertiser
Ct [1836-37]
DLC Ja 11,25-F 1,Ag 2 1851;Ja 10-F 14 1854; Jl 28 1855;Je 14 1856;My 3-N 21,D 19 1857; Ja 2,16,Je 12,Jl 3-10,24-31,Ag 14,O 16-23,N 20,D 11 1858;Ja 14,F 4-11,Mr 4-11,Ap 1-22, My 13,Jl 1,S 2-16,N 25 1859;F 24,Mr 16,Ap 6-13,My 4,25-Je 15,Jl 13-20,Ag 10,O 5,26 1860; Ja 4,F 1,My 17,D 6 1861;Ja 10,F 14,Ag 15,N 7,D 5-26 1862;Ja 23-30,Je 19 1863;Ja 6-29,Mr 11,My 6,27-Je 3,Ag 19,O 28-D 1864;My 19 1865;Ap 12,My 17-24,Je 21-28,Jl 19 1867;Jl 31, O 1,16-30,N 13 1868;Jl 9-16,D 24 1869;Je 17, Ag 5-O 28,N 11,25,D 9-16 1870;Ja 6,27,F 10, Mr 17,31-My 5,Jl 21-Ag 4,25-S 1,22 1871;Mr 29,My 17,Ag 23-30 1872 Ja 1,22,D 17,24 1875; Ap 6 1877;Ap 4 1879-82
MHa complete
MHi Ag 1 1835
MSaE [1834-39]D 4 1841[42-45]Ap 4 1846[48-57]-81;83-[88]
MWA Jl 5,N 1 1834;Je 27 1835;O 7 1837;My 19 1838-S 6,N 22 1851;Jl 1 1859[60]Ag 21 1863; Jl 2 1869

ESSEX chronicle. w S 17 1830-Ja 20 1832||
1830-Ag 19 1831 as Essex chronicle and county republican
Ct [1830-31]Ja 6 1832
MHa complete
MSaE S 24 1830[31]
MWA N 12,26 1830 Ja 7-14 1831
NNHi O 15 1830

ESSEX county democrat. w N 9 1859-61||
DLC Ja 11-18,F 8,22,Mr 7,21,O 3-10,31-N 7, D 12,26 1860
MB F 22,Je 2,20-27,Jl 11,Ag 22-29,N 14,28-D 5 1860;Ja 2,16,My 1-8,29,S 4,18 1861
MHa 1859-Mr 6 1861
MSaE [1859-61]
MWA My 2,D 5,19 1860;Ag 7 1861

ESSEX gazette. *See* Haverhill gazette

*ESSEX patriot. w My 10 1817-Ja 25 1823||
United with Haverhill gazette to form Haverhill gazette and Essex patriot, later Haverhill gazette
DLC Mr 3,24-Ap 7,Jl 28,S 1,29 1821;N 23 1822
MBAt Ja-My 5 1821
MHa Ja-My 12 1821
MSaE [1821-22]
MWA Ja 13 1821-23
MeWC 1821-23
NNHi F 10 1821

Haverhill GAZETTE. w Ja 6 1821-Mr 22 1895||
F 1 1823-Mr 6 1824 Haverhill gazette and Essex patriot; Mr 13 1824-D 24 1825 Gazette and patriot; D 31 1825-F 3 1827 Haverhill gazette and patriot; F 10 1827-My 2 1840 Essex gazette (1837 Haverhill gazette; 1838 Haverhill Essex gazette)
CSmH S 4 1830
CtSp Ap 1 1826
CtY S 9-13,N 15,29-D 6 1828;N 20 1832
DLC 1821-[24]F 26-Mr 5 1825;Ap 29,My 27,Je 10-17,29,N 18-25 1826;F 10,Je 30,Ag 25,O 20,N 10 1827;Ja 5,My 3,17,Je 14,28-Jl 4,N 1 1828 [29]-Ja 9 1830;Ja 1-8 1831;Ja 19,D 1-7 1833;N 22-30,D 13,27 1834;Ja 17,My 9,30,Jl 25,O 3,17 1835;Ja 30 1836[37]N 30 1838;F 1 1839;S 5, 19-26,N 8 1840[41-43]Mr 16,Ap 20-27 1844[45] Ja 9-16,Ag 21 1847;F 22,Ap 19 1851;Ja 9,30,Je 26 1858[59]-69
MB Je 28-D 1834;Jl 11-N 1835[Mr 13-D 1 1836]S 8,D 8 1837;D 20 1839[Ja 17-D 19 1840] Ja 21-28,F 11[O 28 1843-Mr 8 1845]Je 22 1850;Mr 10 1855
MBAt Ag 9 1828;My 30,O 31 1829;Ja 16 1830; Ag 10 1833;F 13 1836
MH Je 23 1821;D 20 1823;Ja 17 1835
MHa complete
MHi S 24 1831;My 30-Je 6 1835
MSaE 1821-[26-27;29-43]-[46]-[50-52]-[70]-[77-95]
MWA 1821-[24-25]N 10 1827;Ja 26,Jl 12 1828; Ag 8 1829;Mr 20,S 18 1830;Ja 1,Jl 2,16,Ag 20 1831;O 26 1833;Jl 4 1834[35]36[Ja 12-Ag 3 1838;39-Ap,Je 1840-41]-[43]-[45]Ja 17,Jl 25, S 19 1846[47-51]-[65-69]
MeWC F 8-Mr 22 1823
NNHi 1821;D 13 1823;My 4 1833;Je 14,Ag 9, D 20 1834
NcD Jl 21 1821[Ap-D 1822]F 12,Mr 5,19-26 1881
NhD Jl 23 1825
NjR Jl 23 1825
NjR Ja 13 1821-23
OCHi N 24 1821
OClWHi My 11 1866
P-M D 2 1854

Haverhill semi-weekly GAZETTE. sw Ja 4 1870-D 4 1877||
DLC [1870-73]O 6,20 1874;O 22 1875-Je 26, Jl 20,Ag 3-21,31-S 14 1877
MWA [1870-71]-73[Mr 1874-75]
NcD F 18,Mr 1 1870

Haverhill morning GAZETTE. d D 15 1877-80||
1877-My 8 1878 as Haverhill daily gazette
MHa complete
MSaE [1878-79]
MWA D 15 1877

Haverhill evening GAZETTE. d 1879+
1879-81 as Evening telephone
pub D 1893+
DLC 1898
ICM Jl 2-3 1890
M Je 1899+
MH F 10-Je 1879
MLa 1879+
MSaE N 1 1879[1880-89]-1931
MWA Jl 2-3 1890;S 14 1901;Ja 30 1904;My 6 1916
NcD N 10 1883[91-96]

Haverhill HERALD. d N 17 1913-14||
MHa 1913-N 28 1914
MSaE N 29 1913

Haverhill IRIS. w O 22 1831-D 20 1833||
Followed by Iris (Methuen)
Ct [1831]
MB [1831-33]
MHa complete
MSaE [1831-33]
MWA Ja 28,Mr 17-24,Ap 7,21,My 5-12,26,Je 16-23,Jl 14,D 22 1832;My 17,Ag 30 1833

Le JOURNAL. w Mr 30 1928+
In French
M S 26 1930
MHa 1928+

KOSMOS-WORLD. American weekly Hellenic newspaper. w Mr 24 1928-
MHa Mr 24-My 5 1928

LIFE. m Ag 1885-
MH Ag 1 1886
MHa Ag-S 20 1885

MERRIMACK register. w
MSaE Jl 23 1837

NEWS-REGISTER. w F 4? 1836-
MHa Je 17-N 25 1836

Haverhill OUTLINE. w S 16 1882-85||
MHa 1882-O 3 1885
MSaE complete

Haverhill daily PRESS. d Ap 12 1902-
MHa Ap 12-Jl 9 1902
MSaE [1902]

Tri-weekly Haverhill PUBLISHER. tw,sw Ja 1 1859-78||
Title varies: Tri-weekly publisher; Semi-weekly publisher
DLC Ap 20,N 30,D 28 1861;Ja 28,F 18,Ap 25, Jl 11-Ag 8,S 2-5,23,D 23 1863;Mr 29-31,Ap 9,My 28,Je 30,Ag 6-9 1864;Je 8,N 13,D 7 1869;D 9 1871
MHa 1859-F 2 1878
MSaE 1859-[70-73]-[76-78]
MWA Ja 5,12,Mr 29 1860;Ap 20 1867;Ap 21-23 1868;Mr 20,Ap 10 1869

Haverhill Sunday RECORD. w S 7 1902+
pub 1902+
M Ap 23-Ag 13 1933
MHa 1902+
MSaE 1902-19
MWA F 15 1903;F 14 1932

Haverhill RECORD and theatrical review. w Je 9 1900-16||
1900-D 5 1907 as Saturday evening criterion; D 12 1907-O 15 1915 Haverhill record and criterion
ICU My 16,Je 27-S 12,26 1903
MHa 1900-S 15 1916
MHaR 1900-01
MSaE 1900-[16]

Haverhill SOCIAL democrat. *See* Clarion. . .

STAR. Ag 13 1836-
MHa Ag 13 1836

Evening SUN. d 1900-
MHa Jl 16-Ag 17 1900

Haverhill Sunday SUN. w Ag 19-O 21 1928||
MHa complete

SYMPAN Hellenic newspaper. *See under* Ipswich

Weekly TATTLER. w Ja 16 1915-
MHa Ja 16-Mr 27 1915
MWA Ja 23 1915

Haverhill TELEGRAM. w S 22 1916-17||?
MHa 1916-S 22 1917

Haverhill TELEPHONE. w -1881||
Merged with Haverhill gazette
MHa Je 24-S 28 1881

Evening TELEPHONE. *See* Haverhill evening gazette

TRUE midnight cry. w?
MSaE Ag 22 1844

HINGHAM

Hingham GAZETTE. w Ja 5 1827-Je 1838||
Followed by Hingham patriot
Ct [1836-37]
DLC 1827-36
M 1827-36
MBAt O 5,N 2 1832
MHi S 23-30,O 14 1836;O 6 1837
MHin complete
MHinHi complete
MWA 1827-[Ja-N 13 1827]
MiU-C [1831-32]
NcD 1827-N 14 1828;O 23,N 6,27-D 4 1829;Ja 1,29,O 15 1830;Ja 7,S 2 1831[32-33]My 2,23,D 26 1834;S 23-O 1,21,D 1 1836
NjR 1827-28[30]

GOSPEL witness and old colony reporter. w
MHinHi Ap 1838-O 18 1839

Hingham JOURNAL. w Ja 4 1850+
Follows Hingham patriot. 1850-Je 1880 as Hingham journal and South Shore advertiser
pub N 1900+
DLC Jl 19,Ag 9-16,30-S 20,O 18,N 1,15,D 13 1850
M 1888+
MBAt Ag 12 1881
MH Jl 1871-72
MHi N 30 1854
MHin 1850+
MHinHi 1850-93
MWA 1850-59;Ap 20 1860-F 4,Je 17 1870-Ja 20, Jl 1871-1905;S 15(supp)1916
MiU-C [1850-59;61-64;83]
NcD [1851-52]Ap 4 1861;Je 5 1863;F 12 1864; Ag 10 1877;Ag 12 1881
OClWHi F 9 1866
WHi F 24 1860

Hingham PATRIOT. w Jl 2 1838-D 29 1848||
Follows Hingham gazette. Followed by Hingham journal
DLC 1838-41
MBAt Jl 2 1838
MHin complete
MHinHi complete
MWA 1838-[Jl-D 1844]-S 5,O 17,D 12 1845-[S 25 1846-Je 18 1847]-48
NcD [1839-46]
NjR Ag 11 1838;Jl 1840-Je 3,26 1841
WHi [Jl 9 1847-D 1 1848]

SPUNKVILLE chronicle.
NNHi Jl 4(extra)1854

HOLBROOK

Holbrook TIMES. w 1889+
pub 1889+
MHo 1899-1903

MASSACHUSETTS (*Continued*)

HOLLISTON

Holliston ADVERTISER. w F 9 1856-
MWA Mr 15 1856

HOLYOKE

AMERICAN telegraph. w S 6? 1854-
Also dated in South Hadley Falls
MWA Mr 15 1855
NNHi Mr 22 1855

CONNECTICUT staats-zeitung. *See under* Hartford, Conn.

Holyoke Saturday DEMOCRAT. w 1907+
M Jl 14 1928;Ja 25 1930;Je 23 1934[Mr 1935+]

Holyoke FREEMAN. w 1849-
1849-52 as Hampden freeman
CSmH Ap 23 1853
IaDH [1853]
MWA S 28 1850;Ag 28 1852

HAMPDEN freeman. *See* Holyoke freeman

Holyoke INDEPENDENT. w Jl 27 1854-
P-M Jl 27,Ag 10 1854

La JUSTICE. w 1903+
In French
pub Ap 1909+
IU D 1917+
M N 3 1932

Holyoke MIRROR. w Ja 7 1854-
Title varies slightly
IaDH 1854-N 10 1855
MWA Ja 7 1854;N 8 1856;F 21-28 1857

NEU ENGLAND rundschau. w Ja 1 1883+
In German
pub 1883+
M N 4 1932

Holyoke evening TELEGRAM. d 1898-D 30 1926||
United with Holyoke transcript to form Holyoke transcript-telegram
M Ap 1912-26

Holyoke TRANSCRIPT. w 1863-1913||
pub complete
MBAt N 1 1877

Holyoke TRANSCRIPT-TELEGRAM. d 1882+
1882-1926 as Holyoke transcript
O 10 1932 is "Romance of a paper through 50 years" ed.
pub 1882+
M 1927+
MHol 1906+

HOPKINTON

Hopkinton BANNER. w 1880-1901||?
NcD Je 29 1881;Ag 14 1889

Hopkinton GAZETTE. w 1883-1901||?
NcD N 29 1883

Hopkinton NEWS. w 1876-82||?
NcD N 16 1877;Jl 12-19 1878

Hopkinton OBSERVER. w 1874-
NcD O 7 1874;F 3 1875

Hopkinton TIMES. w 1863-
NcD O 17,N 7 1863

HUDSON

Hudson ENTERPRISE. w S 29 1883-1910||?
United with Hudson news to form Hudson news-enterprise
MWA Ja 5-19,Mr 15-22,Ap 19,D 27 1884;S 5 1901

Hudson NEWS-ENTERPRISE. w My 1 1899+
1899-1901 as Hudson news
pub 1899+
M F 2 1933

Hudson PIONEER. w 1865-96||?
MHi Jl 9,30 1870;My 20 1871
MWA Je 29 1867
OClWHi Mr 31,Ap 7,My 12,Ag 4 1866

Hudson SUN. d 1902+
pub 1923+
M Ag 15,N 10 1928;Mr 22 1929

HULL

Hull BEACON. w 1895+
M Ap 17 1897+

Saturday CHAT. w Jl 3-S 4 1909||
M complete

Hull-Nantasket TIMES. w Je 30 1930+
pub 1930+
M S 1,N 3 1932

HYANNIS

ATLANTIC messenger. w 1858-
MWA Jl 7 1859
P-M O 7 1858

BARNSTABLE patriot: w Jl 1830+
Title varies: Barnstable patriot and commercial advertiser; Barnstable patriot and county advertiser
1830-85 pub in Barnstable
CSmH Mr 2 1852
DLC N 18 1840
M Ag 8 1854;86+
MB Mr 13 1833;S 27 1848;88-My 13 1890
MBar 1830-1900
MHi My 2 1842;N 26 1843;Ag 23 1915
P-M Ag 6 1845

CAPE COD colonial. d O 9 1936+
MWA 1936+

HYDE PARK

Hyde Park GAZETTE-TIMES. w F 26 1870—
Follows Dedham gazette (Dedham) 1870-D 31 1898 as Norfolk county gazette; Ja 7 1899-F 24 1912 Hyde Park gazette 1870-N 7 1874 pub in Dedham
DLC D 10 1870;71;Ap 13,My 25-Je 1 1872
M F 9 1928;Ja 7 1932;Jl 6 1933
MB 1870-73
MBAt 1870-71
MDHi 1870-F 18 1882[86-91]-[93-95]98
MH 1870-73;D 31 1887
MHi [O 15 1870-Je 1871]
MHy 1874+
MHyHi 1870-98;1912+
MNaHi F 12 1876
MQ 1872-77
MWA Ag 27 1870;Je 17,N 11 1871;O 26 1872 F 6 1875;F 12,26,Ap 17,Ag 12 1876
NNHi O 7 1876

INDEPENDENT. w Ag 23-N 20 1884||
Campaign paper
MWA complete

Hyde Park JOURNAL. w O 6 1849-F 26 1870||
1849-Ja 4 1868 as Norfolk county journal. United with Dedham gazette to form Norfolk county gazette, later Hyde Park gazette-times
MH 1849-Ja 4 1868
MHyHi 1868-70

Hyde Park MONITOR. w Mr 28 1874-
MWA Ap 11 1874

NORFOLK county gazette. *See* Hyde Park gazette-times

NORFOLK county journal. *See* Hyde Park journal

Hyde Park TIMES. w 1884-Mr 6 1912||
United with Hyde Park gazette to form Hyde Park gazette-times
MHy 1887-1901

IPSWICH

Ipswich ADVANCE. w
MSaE [1871-72]

Ipswich BULLETIN. w O 12 1866-
MH Ja 25-Jl 18 1868
MSaE O 12,26,N 23 1866;Ja 4,18,Je 7,21,Jl 5 1867;Ja 25-Jl 18 1868

Ipswich CHRONICLE. w Mr 16 1872+
pub 1891-1925;28+
DLC Mr 16-23,Ap 1872-Mr 8 1873
MH N 30 1872
MI 1875+
MSaE [1872]-[78-81]-[91-93;97-98]-1907;Je 12 1908;10-21;28-[31]
MWA N 21 1885
MWo Ag 16-23 1884
NcD Je 28 1879;Jl 4-12,N 15-29,D 13-27 1884; Ja 17,31,My 2 1885[Jl 1886-F]Mr 5,S 24 1887 [1913-S 1919]
OClWHi Je 13 1874
WHi F 1 1873

Ipswich CLARION. bw
MSaE My 11 1850

Ipswich INDEPENDENT. w 1886-1912||?
MH Ja 13 1898
MHaR S 1896-99
MI 1886-1901

Ipswich JOURNAL. w
MSaE O 20,N 3 1827[28]

Ipswich REGISTER. w Je 27 1837-
MH D 15 1837-Ja,F 16,Ap 6 1838;N 29 1839
MI Je 2 1837-My 25 1838

SYMPAN Hellenic newspaper. w Ja 7 1911-
Ja 4-28 pub in Haverhill; F 1911-Mr 23 1912 pub in Boston
In Greek?
MHa 1911-Je 8 1912

JAMAICA PLAIN

Papers published in Jamaica Plain are listed under Boston

LAKEVILLE

CAMP gazette. (Camp Joe Hooker) w S 3 1862-
MWA O 8 1862

LANCASTER

Lancaster COURANT. *See* Clinton courant (Clinton)

Lancaster GAZETTE. w Mr 4 1828-Ap 13 1830||
DLC Mr 25 1828
MB Ja 13-O 12 1829
MBAt Je 2 1829;Ja 5,Mr 30-Ap 6 1830
MH complete
MHi 1828-29
MWA 1828-Jl 7 1829;Ag 11,O 20,N 3,24 1829[Ja 26-Ap 13 1830]
MeU Mr 4 1828

RED rose. w My 17 1859-
DLC Je 21 1859
MWA My 17-Je 28 1859
MiU-C Je 21 1859

LAWRENCE

Lawrence daily AMERICAN. d 1865-Je 30 1914||
United with Lawrence sun to form Lawrence sun-American
DLC Ap 7 1876;Ap 7,N 24 1879;Jl-D 1898
M Je 1899-Je 15 1914
MLa O 1866-91;Jl 1892-Jl 1893;94-S 1901;02-13; Ap-Je 1914
MMet 1877-91
MSaE [1869-73]Mr 10 1875[77-87]88;Ag 6 1896; Ag 15 1899;S 30 1901[04]Ap 3 1905;Jl 25 1912
MWA Je 12 1869
MnU Jl 21-N 1904
NcD N 24 1883

Tri-weekly AMERICAN. tw
MSaE O 19 1865[66-67]

Lawrence AMERICAN and Andover advertiser. w 1855-1920||?
1855-66 as Lawrence American. Title varies slightly
DLC S 29-O 20,N 3-10,D 29 1860;Ap 22 1865
MHi D 17 1859;Jl 6 1861;Ap 15 1865;O 26 1866
MMet 1878;82-90
MSaE [1855-57]-[59]-[95]O 30 1899
MWA My 29-Je 5 1858[Ja 14-Mr,N 17-D 15 1860]O 5,N 9-23,D 1861;Ja 18,F 1,Mr 1,Jl-D 1862;Ap 11,Ag 8,D 5 1863;Ap 10-17 1868;My 26,S 1 1871;Ag 1 1890
NNHi Ap 22 1865;My 10 1878
NcD O 25 1867;D 2 1870;O 22 1875;Ja 14,F 11,Mr 31,D 1,22 1876[Ja-Mr 1877]Ja 9 1885; Ja 3 1887
OClWHi Ja 28 1865
WHi Jl 17 1865

AMERICAN herald. w Mr 1848-
MWA Mr 25 1848

ANZEIGER und post. w O 1 1882+
In German
pub 1882+
MSaE [1899]-1931

Lawrence COURIER. w O 10 1846-62||
1846-Ap 17 1847 as Merrimack courier
1846 pub in Merrimac
DLC Ja 27 1847;Ja 8(extra)1848;Ag 25 1849; Mr 30,Jl 27,S 28-O 12,26 1850-Ja 3,17-24,F 14, Jl 3 1852;Ap 5,My 24 1853;Mr 14 1854
MH 1846-D 14 1854
MLa Ap 24-Ag 24 1847;Ag 25 1850-Ap 17 1862
MSaE 1846-[52-62]
MWA O 10 1846;Ja 27,F 20,Je 19,Jl 24 1847; Ja 8(extra)My 13,S 16 1848-[Ja-N 17 1849]Ja 19-F 16[My-N]1850;Ap 19-26,My 10,Ag 16,O 25 1851;F 28,My 29 1852;Jl 30 1853;F 18 1858; My 17 1860
NN Ja 27 1847
NNHi S 11 1847;Ja 8 1848
NSyU F 10,Mr 17 1849
NcD Ag 23 1851
P-M Ja 27 1847

Lawrence COURIER. sw,tw
Jl 26 1853-F 10 1854 as Lawrence semi-weekly courier. United with Daily journal to form Journal and courier
sw 1852-55
DLC Ag 26 1853
MWA Ag 24,O 1 1852[Mr 11-Jl 26,S-D 20 1853; 54]Ag 14 1855;Je 26 1857

Le COURRIER. w 1898+
1898-Ap 8 1932 as Le Courrier de Lawrence
In French
IU D 1917-N 18,D 16 1921;F 3-10,Mr 24,Ag 11 1922+
M Je 1911+
MSaE 1915

Lawrence daily EAGLE. d Jl 20 1868+
pub 1868+
DLC 1898
M [1928-Jl 1933]
MLa 1877;Jl 1905-07;Ap 1908-Ag 1910;11;Ja-Je, O 1913+
MSaE Jl 21 1868[69-70;72-83;85-87]N 15 1888; F 12 1896;D 28 1898[99]Je 4 1903[05]F 11 1907
MWA Ap 2 1872

ESSEX county sentinel. w 1848-
DLC O 23,N 13,D 25 1850;Ja 8-15,29-F 5,19 1851

ESSEX weekly eagle. w 1867-97||*
pub 1867-68
DLC My 30 1874
MCheHi Ag 10 1872
MSaE [1867-78]Ag 4-18 1883;Ag 9 1884[86-87]D 8 1888

HAVERSACK. d Ap 29-My 1 1863||
DLC Ap 30 1863
MH complete
MSaE complete

HOME review. w F 18 1854-
MSaE [1854-55]
MWA F 18,Mr 18-25,Ap 8-15,My 20 1854

Lawrence INDEPENDENT. w S 9 1932-
M [1932-Ja 19 1934]
MWA S 23 1932

Lawrence JOURNAL. w 1871-91||?
MLa O 13 1877-82
MSaE [1874-88]
MWA Jl 19,Ag 2-9 1873
WHi My 2,O 10 1874;My 2 1876

JOURNAL and courier. d,tw 1861-
1861-S* 1862 as Daily journal
MHi Jl 15 1862
MSaE [1861-63]
MWA O 21 1862;Mr 21,My 5-12,20,Je 16,18, 25,Jl 18,28,30,Ag 18,20,29,S 15,29 1863

Lawrence Sunday LEADER. w O 19 1901+
M O 27 1929;Mr 1 1931
MSaE [1901]Jl 24 1904[05]-[07]-[17]
MWA D 30 1906

MERRIMAC mirror. w
MSaE S 13 1854

MERRIMACK courier. *See* Lawrence courier

MASSACHUSETTS (*Continued*)

LAWRENCE—*Continued*

Weekly MESSENGER and Massachusetts era. w 1844-
1844-47? as Weekly messenger
MSaE Mr 8-15 1849
MWA O 21 1847

Lawrence Sunday NEWS. w N 1 1925+
pub 1925+
M N 4 1928;O 26 1930;O 9 1932
MLa N 8 1925-33

PLOUGH-BOY. w
MSaE S 28 1864

Le PROGRèS. w 1888-1908||
In French
MSaE D 30 1898-[1908]
NcD My 4 1905

Lawrence REPORTER. m Mr 21 1857-
DLC Mr 21 1857
MWA Mr-My 1857

Lawrence REPUBLICAN. w 1857-
MWA N 10 1859

Lawrence SENTINEL. w 1848-1916||?
DLC O 9 1850;Ap 2,Je 4-11,25 1851;N 11 1852
MLa 1861-76;78-83
MSaE [1850-79]-[83]-[94]
MWA O 9,N 6 1850;Ap 9-23,My 28,Ag-S 24,O 8 1851;Ja 2 1858;My 26 1860;N 4 1871
NcD D 9,23-30 1881;My 11,29 1888
OClWHi My 5 1866

Sunday STAR. w Je 14 1896-
MSaE [1898-1900]
NcD O 25 1896

Sunday SUN. w 1855+
pub 1890+
M Jl 1918+

Lawrence SUN-AMERICAN. d 1893-My 1924||?
1893-Je 1914 as Lawrence sun
M Je 1899-My 1924
MLa Ja-S 1905;06-13;Ap 1914-Je 1917;18
MSaE My 28 1895;Mr 19,Je 18 1896;N 16 1904;N 15 1906;F 14 1908
MnU Ag 19 1904-Ja 9 1905

Sunday TELEGRAM. w 1884-97||?
pub 1884-97
MSaE S 4,30 1887;D 21 1890

Daily TELEGRAM. d 1895+
pub 1895+
M [1928-33]
MH F 22 1907
MLa Mr 4 1896-1924;Ja-Je 1926;My 1927+
MSaE Ap 17 1895;My 4 1897[99]-31
NcD Jl 19,21,29,S 1 1906

Evening TRIBUNE. d 1890+
Title varies: Lawrence daily tribune
F 9 1929 is "75th anniversary of the city of Lawrence"
pub Ap 12 1890+
M [1928-33]
MLa Ap 1890-94;1905-S 1910;Ap-D 1911;Je 1913+
MWA Jl 1915;Mr 21 1936

VANGUARD. w S 1848-
MSaE O 21 1848
MWA S 2 1848

Al-WAFA. sw
In Arabic
MSaE [1907]-[10]

LEE

BERKSHIRE chronicle. w 1868-
1868-70? as Central Berkshire chronicle
Suspended 1871-75?
MWA [F 18-D 1869]Ja 13,27,Ap 28,S 29 1870; D 29 1876

BERKSHIRE democrat. w O 20 1840-
MWA Ja 20 1841

BERKSHIRE gleaner. w 1857+
1857-1901? as Valley gleaner (title varies slightly)
Ct F 24 1876;S 12-19 1877;D 25 1878;Jl 22 1891
DLC D 20 1860
MH Ja 15 1863
MLee 1929+
MWA Ja 15(extra)S 3 1863;O 15 1890
NNHi Ja 15(extra)1863;Ja 2 1873
P-M Ap 3 1862

CENTRAL BERKSHIRE chronicle. *See* Berkshire chronicle

VALLEY gleaner. *See* Berkshire gleaner

LEICESTER

Leicester BANNER. w 1892+
pub [1892+]

LENOX

BERKSHIRE herald. w Ja 5 1832-
MWA Ja-Je 1832

BERKSHIRE journal. *See* Berkshire county eagle (Pittsfield)

BERKSHIRE star and county republican. *See* Berkshire county eagle (Pittsfield)

JOURNAL and argus. *See* Berkshire county eagle (Pittsfield)

MASSACHUSETTS eagle. *See* Berkshire county eagle (Pittsfield)

LEOMINSTER

Leominster daily ENTERPRISE. w,d Je 4 1873+
1873-N 1895 as Leominster enterprise (d)
pub 1873+
M 1894+
MH Jl 25 1922
MLeo Je 4 1873+
MWA Je 4 1873;Ap 17 1908;Jl 2 1915

La LIBERTÉ. *See under* Fitchburg

LEXINGTON

Lexington INDEPENDENT. w 1901-14||?
MWA Mr 29 1906

Lexington MINUTE-MAN. w D 29 1871+
1871-Ag 19 1927 as Lexington minute-man; My 1 1925-D 9 1932 Lexington times-minute-man; D 15 1932-Ja 19 1933 Lexington townsman and Lexington times-minute man
pub 1932+
MH F 17,Jl 6,S 7,28 1872;Ja 1874;Ap 24 1875
MLeHi Ap 20 1875;Ap 20 1888;Ap 20-27 1900; Jl 21 1906;Ja 6 1922;O 26 1923;Ap 10,24 1925
MWA Jl 20 1872;F 1 1873
OClWHi My 23,O 10 1874

Lexington TIMES. w S 1 1922-Ag 19 1927||
United with Lexington minute-man to form Lexington times-minute-man, later Lexington minute-man
MLeHi O 26 1923-S 5 1924;Ap 1925
MLeM 1927

Lexington TIMES-MINUTE-MAN. *See* Lexington minute-man

Lexington TOWNSMAN. w Jl 30 1931-D 8 1932||
United with Lexington times-minute man to form Townsman and times-minute man, later Lexington minute-man
MLeM complete

Lexington TOWNSMAN and Lexington times-minute man. *See* Lexington minute-man

LOWELL

To 1825? as East Chelmsford

Daily evening ADVERTISER. d Je 1835-
Title varies: Daily advertiser; Lowell daily advertiser
MWA Jl 4 1835;Ag 27 1852;Jl 8 1854;N 13 1856;My 26 1860

Lowell ADVERTISER. tw 1836-
DLC Ap 7 1846
MHi [1842]
ML 1838-D 23 1839
MWA F 22 1837;S 14 1838;My 22 1840;Jl 9 1841;Ja 20 1852

Lowell AMERICAN. w Je 2 1849-
MH Je 9 1849-53
MWA Jl 24 1852

Lowell tri-weekly AMERICAN. tw 1850?-
MWA F 2 1852

AMERICAN citizen. w 1854-94||
DLC Mr 9,Je 15 1866
MWA S 25 1857-Ja 1 1858;Je 15 1860;Ap 15 1864
—d ed *See* Lowell daily citizen

AMERICAN citizen. d S 10 1855-Ap 25 1856||
United with Daily morning news to form Lowell daily citizen and news, later Lowell daily citizen
MLHi complete
MWA N 16 1855

Sunday ARENA. w Je 21 1891-93||
ML 1891-Mr 5 1893

CENTRALVILLE news. *See* Lowell news

CHELMSFORD courier. w Je 25 1824-Je 10 1825||
Followed by Chelmsford phoenix
DLC 1824-Je 3 1825
MBAt Je 10 1825
MCheHi Ag 6 1824;Ap 29 1825
MH My 19 1825

CHELMSFORD phoenix. w Je 28 1825-F 24 1826||
Follows Chelmsford courier. Ag 4-S 23 1825 as Phoenix. Followed by Merrimack journal
DLC complete
MCheHi Je 28 1825
MH Jl 22 1825
MWA S 9-16,O 1825-26

Lowell daily CITIZEN. d 1850-F 1906||
1850-Ap 25 1856 as Daily morning news; Ap 28 1856-Ap 1 1876 Lowell daily citizen and news. United with Lowell daily courier to form Lowell courier-citizen
MB [Jl 1860-65]
MH Ja 8 1884
ML 1862-1906
MLHi Ap 28 1856
MWA S 2 1851;F 7,N 11 1852;Ap 23 1858;Ja 27,F 9[O 17-N 23 1860]Mr 9 1871;Je 27,N 28,D 19 1874;Ap 5-6 1876;My 9 1885
MiU-C [1866]
NcD F 24 1876
OClWHi D 1 1864
WHi Ap 28 1856-79
—w ed *See* American citizen

Le CLAIRON. w 1905+
In French
pub 1905+
M [1930-N 1932]
MLT 1905+

Lowell COMPEND. w 1832-
MWA Je 14 1833
MnHi Ag 9,O 4 1833

Lowell COURIER. tw 1835-45||
Followed by Lowell daily courier, later Lowell courier-citizen
DLC Ja 2,21,26-30[Je 1836-Ja]My 2,S 16 1837; D 20 1838;N 28 1840;Ja 8 1842
MB [Ja 12-My 24 1836]My 6-O 23 1837[Ja 12-My 24 1838]39;F 4,O 9 1840;N 11-18,D 18,28-30 1841;Mr 19,Ap 14,D 3 1842;Ja 21,F 4-9 1843
MBAt Ja 2 1836
MC 1842-45
ML 1837
MWA Mr 3,N 10 1835;Ja 2,S 8 1836;Ja 6 1838; D 10 1839;Je 25,Jl 21 1840;My 6 1841;Jl 9 1842;F 22-24,O 18,24,N 23 1844
OCHi S 7 1840
WHi Je 27 1835-38[Mr 14 1839-Je 14 1845]

Lowell COURIER-CITIZEN. d 1845+
Follows Lowell courier (tw). 1845-F 28 1906 as Lowell daily courier (1849-60? as Lowell daily journal and courier)
1906-18? pub both morning and evening ed. Evening ed followed by Lowell evening leader
pub 1912+
CLS Ap 19 1911
DLC O 19 1849;Mr 20-S 9 1850;Jl 30-D 1867;D 20 1871
M Je 1895+
MB Mr 19 1863;Ap 17-29,My 2,6,Je 3 1865;Jl 9,21 1866;N 4 1868;Mr 2 1876;N 8 1879
MBAt 1853;Ap 15,19 1865
MC 1845-1917
MCheHi Jl 5,8 1876;F 8 1892;Mr 29 1936+
MH Jl 26-29 1862
MLG 1920+
MTaHi N 29 1876
MWA F 21,My 4(extra)1846;N 9 1849;Ja 15,S 24 1852;Ag 31 1853;Mr 4 1854;O 30 1858;Mr 19 1860;O 12 1861;Ja 14 1862;F 23 1864;D 18 1865[F-Ag 1870;71]N 25 1874;Mr 2 1876;Je 29 1878;Ja 4 1879;O 9 1880;Mr 17 1881;O 2 1884;Ja 1 1915;Mr 21 1933[Mr 26-Ap 21 1934] Mr 14,26 1936
NSyU Ag 10,S 27,O 19,26,N 2,4,6,8-9,13 1848
NcD Mr 2 1876;O 25 1878;O 18,24,30 1882;Jl 3 1884
OClWHi Ja 9 1866
WHi Jl 8 1845-47;49-65;Jl-D 1883;Jl 1884-86

Sunday CRITIC. w S 18 1887-S 13 1891||
ML complete

DIXON'S daily review. d My 24 1835-
Ct Je 4 1835
MWA My 25 1835

L'ETOILE. d 1886+
In French
M Ag 17 1929;D 3 1930;Ja 10 1933

Lowell GAZETTE. w Ag 7 1847-
MB 1847-F 10 1849
MWA Ag 19 1848

Lowell GAZETTE and meteor of the western hemisphere. w F 19 1831-
MWA Mr 19 1831

GLOBE-MERRIMAC and Massachusetts general advertiser. w
MiU-C Jl 23 1825

HENOSIS. w N 3 1906-Je 15 1907||
MH complete

Daily morning HERALD. d Ag 20? 1843-44||?
1843-Ja 4 1844 as Morning herald
ML Ag 25-26 1843;Ja-Je 7 1844

Lowell weekly HERALD. w Ja 4? 1844-
MWA My 3 1844

Morning HERALD. d O? 1853-
MWA F 8 1854

Lowell HERALD. w D 9? 1854-
MWA Ap 15 1854

L'INDEPENDENCE. w Ap 4- 1890||
ML Ap-S 1890

Lowell weekly JOURNAL. w Mr 2 1827-1904||?
Follows Merrimack journal. Title varies: Lowell journal; Lowell journal and bulletin; Lowell journal and mercury; Lowell journal and Middlesex county republican; Lowell weekly journal and courier
DLC Je 15 1827;Ja 25,F 29 1828;My 6,20 1829; Ap 29,D 2,16-30 1842;Jl 21,Ag 4-18,S 1,O 6-13,27,D 22 1843;F 6,My 29,Je 5,19-D 11,25 1846;F-Mr 26,Ap 9,Je 11,Jl 2,25 1847
MB Jl 6 1831[32-D 18 1835]Mr 4 1836;O 4 1837;My 23 1838;S 29 1841;Je 16 1854;60-Je 1861
MBAt Je 8,Jl 20,D 7 1827;O 31 1828;Ja 13 1836;Mr 10 1841;50-59
MCheHi Je 2 1865;S 20-27 1867;D 1 1871;Mr 28 1875;My 2 1879;Mr 11 1887;F 14 1890;Mr 6 1891;F 19 1892;Je 23 1899
MH S 15-D 8 1830;O 19 1831;47-1904
MHi S 26 1828;Jl 18 1832
MSaE F 2 1844
MWA 1827-30;Ja 26,F 16-Mr 9 1831;Ag 20 1834;Ja 28-F 4,Mr 6,Je 19,Jl 17,Ag 14 1835; Ap 1,Jl 6-13,27 1836;Ja 11,F 22[Je 28-O 25]D 13 1837;Ja 31,Mr 7 1838;Ja 23,O 16 1839;Mr 4, 25,Ag 26,O 10 1840;Mr 6(extra)1841[S 23 1842-N 22 1844]Ap 28 1848;Je 14 1850;Ja 9 1852;Ag 21 1863;Ja 31 1868;Jl 30 1869;Ja 14 1870-93
MnHi N 6 1833;Ja 15 1834
NNHi Mr 21 1828;Ja 5 1831
NcD Ap 7 1876
NhD Je 25 1852;Ap 29,Jl 8 1853
OCHi S 12 1840
OClWHi Ja 6 1843;Ja 5 1866
WHi 1826-F 23 1831

Lowell daily JOURNAL. tw,d Jl 1 1831-
1831-32? as Lowell journal and tri-weekly advertiser. United with Lowell daily courier to form Lowell daily journal and courier, later Lowell courier-citizen
DLC N 12 1832
MWA Jl 1 1831;O 4-5 1833;O 25 1834
P-M Ag 23 1834

MASSACHUSETTS (*Continued*)

LOWELL—*Continued*

Le JOURNAL. w Ap 2 1916-
In French
ML Ap-Je 1916

Lowell daily JOURNAL and courier. *See* Lowell courier-citizen

Lowell evening LEADER. d Mr 1 1921+
Follows evening ed of Lowell courier-citizen
pub 1921+
M My 7 1921+
MCheHi Mr 28-Ap 24 1936
ML My 7 1921+
MWA Mr 24-25 1936

LIFE in Lowell. w Jl 26? 1843-
MWA Ag 23 1843

Lowell morning MAIL. d 1879-1908||?
Title varies: Morning mail; Lowell mail
DLC 1894
MH Je 1 1882
MWA N 6 1881;D 23 1885;F 5,Jl 20,N 1 1886
NbHi Ja 13 1884

Lowell MERCURY. w N 13 1829-D 26 1834||
1829-Ap 24 1830 as Lowell mercury and Massachusetts gazette
CSmH Jl 17 1830
Ct [1831-35]
DLC 1833
MBAt O 8 1831
ML 1834
MWA Ja 30,F 13,Ap 24,N 20 1830;Ja 15,Ap 23,Je 25,Jl 16,S 3,O 28 1831;My 25,N 9 1832;My 1(extra)Ja 5(extra)1833
MnHi My 16 1834
NNHi Ag 21 1830
OClWHi Ja 3 1834
WHi N 14 1829-N 6 1830

MERRIMACK journal. w Mr 3 1826-F 23 1827||
Follows Chelmsford phoenix. Followed by Lowell journal
DLC N 3 1826
MCheHi N 17 1826;F 2 1827
MWA complete

METANASTIS. sw 1905-07||?
In Greek
MWA Ap 5 1907

MIDDLESEX democrat. w 1871-73||
MH My 3 1873

MIDDLESEX mercury. w S 11 1839-
MWA S 11 1839
WHi S-D 4 1839

MIDDLESEX standard. w Jl 25 1844-Mr 13 1845||
United with Worcester county gazette to form Worcester and Middlesex gazette, later Worcester county gazette (Worcester)
MLHi 1844-F 13,27,Mr 13 1845
MWA [1844-F 1845]

MIDDLESEX telegraph and manufacturers and farmers advocate. w S 12 1831-
MBAt Jl 14 1832
MWA O 31 1831
NNHi F 11 1832

MIDDLESEX Washingtonian and Martha Washington advocate. w F ? 1843-
MWA O 27 1843;F 16,Mr 29 1844

Le NATIONAL. w 1883-95||
In French
ML Je 13 1890-O 4 1895

Lowell NEWS. w My 5 1916+
My-N 12 1916 as Centralville news; N 19 1916-27? Lowell Sunday news
ML 1916-My 16 1920

Daily morning NEWS. *See* Lowell daily citizen

NIAGARA. w Ap 18 1846-
MHi Jl 25,Ag 22 1846
MWA Ag 1 1846

Lowell OBSERVER. w Ap 7 1832-
DLC S 5 1834
MWA 1832-Ap 26 1833;Ja 3,24-31,Ap 25,Je 27,Jl 25,Ag 22 1834
NNHi Mr 22-Ap 26,Je 28,D 20 1833

Lowell PATRIOT. w N 7 1834-
Title varies: Lowell patriot and republican; Lowell patriot and advertiser; etc.
Ct [1835-37]
DLC Je 26 1836;Mr 15 1850
MCheHi Ag 15 1845
ML 1834-36
MWA 1834-F 19 1836;Ja 5,F 9-Ap 13,1837;S 20 1838;F 21,Ap 25 1839;S 3,24 1840;Ap 14 1841[Ja-Mr 1844]Ag 6-13 1847:O 27 1848;N 22,D 6 1850;My 7 1858;My 18 1860;N 20 1863
MeAu O 19 1837
NNHi Mr 18 1836

A PAZ. w 1912-15||?
In Portuguese
MWA My 28 1915
NN Ap 1913-15

La RÉVEIL. d S 14 1908-09||?
In French
ML S 14 1908-Ja 1 1909

Lowell SENTINEL. w F 9 1861-
MSaE Ap 20 1861
MWA Ap 13 1861

Evening STAR. d Mr 31 1890-Je 30 1896||
DLC Mr 31-Jl 1890;91-Je 1892
MB complete

Lowell SUN. w,d N 11 1878+
w 1878-91?
pub 1878+
DLC Ja-Je 1898
M [1928-33]
MCheHi Ag 18 1888-Jl 1889
ML 1894+
NcD Jl 24 1880

Lowell Sunday TELEGRAM. w Ap 2 1899+
1899- as Sunday telegram
pub 1899+
ML 1899+
MLG 1920+

TIMES. bw Ag 31 1833-34||
ML 1833-Ja 24 1834

TIMES. w Je 2? 1839-
MWA D 29 1839

Lowell weekly TIMES. w 1872-86||?
MH Ja 11 1884
MWA Ja 15 1875;Jl 9 1880
NcD Ap 7 1876

Lowell morning TIMES. d 1873-96||
CtY D 17 1879-80;82;Jl 1883-Je 29 1895
M S 1879-Je 1896
MCheHi Je 13 1890
MWA Ja 16 1875;Mr 14,Jl 4 1883;Ja 23 1884

Lowell Sunday TRIBUNE. w Ja 1 1910+
pub 1934+
M My 11 1930;F 22 1931

L UNION. w Mr 8 1879-80||
In French
ML My 17 1879-Mr 20 1880

La VÉRITÉ. tw Ag 15-N 19 1910||?
ML Ag-N 19 1910

Lowell daily VOX. d S 16 1851-69||?
MB S 16-O 20 1851

VOX populi. w My 29 1841-91||
C F 15 1851
CtY Jl 1,D 2 1864
DLC Je-O 23 1841;Jl 27 1849-N 11 1853;54-N 9 1855;My 24,N 8,28 1861;My 14 1881
MB D 25 1841;Mr 26,Ap 16 1842;Ja 20 1843;Je 17 1859
MSaE My 25 1841
MWA Ap 11 1845;Ja 9 1846;My 28,Jl 30 1852;My 5 1854;Ap 13 1860;F 6 1863;Ap 21 1865;Ja 5,N 23 1866;Ap 4 1883;My 20 1885
NcD Mr 20-27 1875;Mr 1 1876;F 7 1883
P-M D 26 1845
WHi Ja 17 1845-46;N 8 1861-O 1865;66-O 4 1867

LYNN

AWL. w
MSaE N 30,D 14 1844

BAY state. w O 14 1849-
DLC Ja 1 1852;57;61
MB O 25 1849;Ap 4 1850;Ap 14 1853;O 11 1855
MH Ja 8 1857
MSaE [1849-65]
MWA O 31,N 14,D 12,26 1850[Ap 10-O 16 1851]Je 10-17,Jl 1 1852[Ag 11-D 1853]Ja 5,My 18,Jl 13 1854;Je 28,D 6 1855;Ap 10 1856;D 3,12(extra)1857;Ja 1,Jl 29-S 1858[Mr 17-D 22 1859;Ja 12-O 18 1860]Ja 3,Ap 4,Jl 18 1861;Ag 13 1863
Mi D 10 1857
P-M Jl 29 1852

Lynn BEE. d 1880-91||
MSaE [1881-91]
MWA Je 9 1884

Lynn BULLETIN. sw,w
MSaE [1865]
Mi Mr 28,Ap 11,My 10,24 1865

Lynn CHRONICLE. w Ap 13? 1835-
MHi N 7 1835
MWA N 23 1835

Le COURRIER de Lynn. *See* Lynnois

Lynn DEMOCRAT. w
MSaE N 2 1838

ESSEX county republican. w 1899-1901||
M Je 2,30 1900
MSaE [1899-1900]Ja 5 1901

ESSEX county Washingtonian. w Mr 16 1842-
MWA [Mr-D 8 1842]S 19 1844
NcD Ag 11 1842

ESSEX county whig. *See* Lynn news

ESSEX democrat. w
Ct [1831-32]
MSaE Je 24,O 28 1831

ESSEX tribune. w S 14 1833-
MSaE S 14,N 9 1833
MWA O 5 1833

Lynn FORUM. w 1846-
MSaE Je 23 1846;Ja 16,Jl 31 1847;S 16,N 11 1848
MWA Ja 16 1847;F 19,My 13,Jl 22 1848

FREE democrat. w
MSaE N 11 1848

FREE soil pickaxe. ir Ag 19 1848-
Campaign paper
MH S 16 1848
MSaE Ag 19 1848

Lynn FREEMAN and Essex county whig. w 1838-
1838-39? as Lynn freeman
MBeHi 1840
MH Je 26,N 20 1841
MHi Ap 10 1841
MSaE N 10 1838[40-41]-Ja 8 1842;Ja 28 1843
MWA My 9 1840
NNHi D 1 1838

Lynn city ITEM. w 1876-My 31 1913||
M O 1881-1913
MSaE 1876-77;Jl 27 1878;D 27 1879[80;87;89]Ag 15 1890;My 15 1891;Ag 25,30 1893;94-1913
NcD Jl 1,S 30,D 9 1876;Ja 27,F 17-Mr 3,17 1877-Jl 27 1900;D 4 1903;N 3 1911

Daily evening ITEM. d D 8 1877+
pub 1877+
DLC 1898;Ja-Ag 1900
M F 1895+
MB My 10-18 1900
MLy 1877-D 8 1887;D 18 1889+
MSaE [1877-94]F 19 1895[93]-1931
MWA O 1 1888;N 27 1889;D 8 1927
MWo Ja 28 1892
NcD [1919]

JEWISH advocate. w,sw 1900+
MH Ap 12 1923;N 13 1931;Je 28,D 13 1932
MWA S 15,N 13 1931;Ja 19 1932

JOSSELYN'S Lynn daily. d Ja 8 1855-
MSaE [1855]
MWA Ja 8,20,26 1855

LITTLE giant. w 1869-72||
MSaE [1869]-[72]

LOCOMOTIVE. *See under* Salem

LYNNOIS. w 1895-Jl 26 1935||
1895-D 23 1914? as Le Courrier de Lynn
In French
IU F 20 1918-24;27-35
M Je 20 1911-35
MSaE 1915

Weekly MESSENGER. w Ap 14 1832-
MSaE [1832-33]
MWA Ap 14-21,D 8 1832
NNHi S 15 1832

Lynn MIRROR. w 1825-
Title varies: . . . and mechanics museum; . . . and Essex democrat; . . . and independent whig
CtY Mr 6 1830
MBAt [1830]Ag 20 1831
MDeHi My 8 1830
MHi Je 9,Jl 7 1827;F 2 1828;Jl 4 1829
MSaE [1825-26]Ap 28 1827[28-30]My 28 1831;N 9 1836[37]
MWA Ap ? 1826;O 25 1828;Mr 6,Ap 3 1830;Ap 16 1831;Mr 12 1836
NNHi Ja 28 1832;D 12 1835

Lynn NEWS. w Ja 5 1844-
1844-45 as Essex county whig
MHi Ap 16 1847;Mr 31 1848;Ap 26-My 2 1850
MSaE [1844-45]Je 26 1846;D 17 1847;Mr 31 1848;49-[52-57]-[60-61]
MWA Ap 17,31,D 5(extra)1844;My 3 1845;Ja 10 1846-47;S 1 1848;Ja 26-Mr 2 1849;N 28 1850[Ja 17-O 17 1851]Ja 20 1854;F 2-23,Ag 31 1855[F 23 1858-59]Je 13 1860 [F 13-Jl 3 1861]
Mi O 27,D 22 1857;F 16,Mr 2,S 21 1858;D 7 1859
N Mr 3 1857
WHi Je 29 1855

Lynn evening NEWS. d 1897-1918||
United with Lynn telegram to form Lynn telegram-news
MSaE D 29 1898-[1918]
NcD [1899-1901;11-12]

OLD tunnel. d
MSaE Ap 14-15 1868

ORGAN. bw Mr 20? 1854-
MSaE [1854]
MWA Ap 24 1854

Lynn PIONEER. d Mr 23 1921-
MWA Mr 23-25 1921

PIONEER and herald of freedom. w 1841-
1841-O 1846 as Lynn pioneer
MB [N 19 1846-Ap 22 1847]Mr 15 1848
MHi Ja 28 1847;D 13,28 1848
MSaE [1845-49]
MWA S 10 1845;My 27,Jl 23 1846;Mr 15 1848
NIC [1845-48]
OClWHi Jl 23-D 24 1845;Ja 1-21,Ap 15,29,Je 10,Jl 26 1846

Lynn daily PRESS. d S? 1889-95||?
MMarHi N 27 1889
MSaE Mr 21,My 19 1890;S 8 1891;S 21 1892 [93]

Lynn RECORD. w Ja 23 1830-
CSmH S 11 1830
DLC Ja 23 1830-Ja 12 1831
M F 27 1833-F 23 1842
MHi O 8,N 5 1835
MSaE 1830;Jl 6,Ag 3 1831;D 26 1832[33]F 12-19,Ap 2 1835[36;39]Mr 1841
MTaHi F 5,19,Mr 19 1834
MWA 1830-Ja 12 1831;Ag 1,22 1832;N 13 1833;F 5,D 10 1834;My 7,S-O 8,D 31 1835;Jl 20 1836;Mr 7,Je 20 1838[F 20-N 9 1839]Ag 19 1840[Je 30-N 10 1841]Ja 19-26,F 16 1842
MiU-C S 1 1841
MnHi D 29 1841
N [Ap 24 1830-Ja 5 1831]
NNHi Ap 11 1832;37-38;Ap 17 1839

Lynn RECORD. w Jl? 1872-81||
MSaE [1872-73;75-78]Jl 12 1879[80-81]
MWA Jl 20 1872
NcD My 25,Je 29,Jl 20-Ag 10 1872
WHi Ja 8,F 12 1876

MASSACHUSETTS (*Continued*)

LYNN—*Continued*

Lynn REPORTER. sw,w Mr 25 1854-89||?
1854-65 as Lynn weekly reporter sw 1870-78
DLC Mr 22 1856-Mr 14 1857;61-62;Ja 23,My 14-Je 4,Jl 11,30,O 1-8,29-D 3,17,31 1864-Ja 14 1865;Ap 14,28 1866;Jl 15 1868
MH Jl 20,S 21 1861;Ag 29 1863;Mr 5 1864
MSaE 1854-[79-88]
MWA Jl 29 1854;Mr 3,Ap 28,Ag 18 1855;Mr 1-22,N 29-D 6,20-27 1856;Ja 10,D 12-19 1857;Ja 9-F 6,20,Mr 6-13,Ap 3,17-Je 5 1858;Ap 30 1859;Mr 10,Jl 14,S 15 1860;Ja 12,My 11,N 2-9 1861;My 31,Jl 19 1862[63]Ja 2 1864[Ap 29-D 1865]F 7 1866;My 23-30,D 16 1868-Ja 2 1869
MWo Mr 25 1854-Mr 17 1855
Mi N 7,D 19 1857;F 2,N 2 1861;D 5 1863;My 13,27,Je 17-24,S 9,O 14 1865;Ag 22 1866;F 6, 23,Ap 27-My 1,Je 19,22 1867;Je 27,Jl 1,D 30 1868;Ja 2,6,9 1869;Jl-D 1870;Jl 1874-Je 1875; Jl-D 1878
N O 4 1856;Mr 27 1858
NcD [1866-77]S 21 1878
P-M Ap 15 1854

SIZZLER. w
MSaE [1848]

Lynn SPECTATOR. w D 4 1848-
MWA D 4 1848

STAR. w Jl 30 1836-
MWA Jl 30 1836

Lynn SUN. w D 20 1931-32||
M D 20 1931;Ja 24 1932
MWA D 20 1931

Lynn TATTLER. w
MSaE [1848]

Lynn TELEGRAM-NEWS. d 1912+
1912-18 as Lynn telegram
M [1928-Jl 1933]
MLy D 17 1912+
MSaE 1919-31

Lynn weekly TIMES. w 1895-1916||?
MSaE 1898-1914
NcD [1909-12]

Lynn TRANSCRIPT. w D 21 1867-96||?
DLC Ja 10,F 21 1874;D 18-25 1875;My 4,Jl 6 1888-My 10,Je 14,Jl 12,Ag 9-16,S 6,20-27,O 17-N 1 1889;My 30,Je 27-Jl 4,18-25,Ag 8,S 5,N 13,28,D 5-12 1890;Ja 23-F,Je 19,O 30 1891;F 5,Ap 8,Jl 5,Ag 12,S 2-9,O 21,N 4-18,D 9 1892;Ap 21 1893
MSaE D 21 1867[68-69]-[96]
MWA D 28 1867;N 26 1870;Je 29 1883
NcD S 25 1869[70-77;81-82;87;89-93]
OClWHi Ag 9 1873

Saturday UNION. w 1870-88||?
O-N 16 1883 as Lynn union
MH [O-D 8 1883]
MMarHi Mr 8 1884
MSaE D 23 1881-[82]Ap 6 1883;S 26 1885

VINDICATOR. w D 23 1876-79||?
MH D 23 1876
MSaE 1876[77-79]

VOICE of the people. w
MSaE N 4 1843

YOUNG hickory. w Jl 27 1844-
Campaign paper
MWA O 12-N 9 1844

MALDEN

Malden FREE PRESS. w Mr 20 1914-21||
Follows Malden mirror
MMal 1914-Mr 18 1921

HEADLIGHT. w O 19 1881-82||
MMal complete
MWA N 9 1881

Malden evening MAIL. w Ap 4 1887-1919||
MMal 1887-Je 28 1919

Malden MESSENGER. w Jl 16 1856-72||
MHi D 27 1865;My 2,16,S 5 1868
MMal 1856-N 27 1872
MWA Ag 24 1867;Ap 3,My 8,29 1869;Ja 14 1871
NNHi Jl 11 1868

Malden MIRROR. w My 27 1871-Mr 14 1914||
Followed by Malden free press
MMal complete
NcD S 24 1881;Ag 4 1888

Malden evening NEWS. d Mr 16 1892+
pub 1892+
M [1928-S 1933]
MMal Mr 23 1893+
NcD S 8 1888

Malden OUTLOOK. w S 17 1904-Mr 3 1905||
MHi complete
MMal complete
MWA complete

Malden city PRESS. w O 2 1880-95||
MMal 1880-Ag 24 1895
MWA D 10 1881;D 9 1882;O 1 1885

Malden PRESS. w Ja 10 1934+
pub 1934+
MMal 1934+

Malden TELEGRAM. d Mr 24 1921-22||
MMal 1921-F 11 1922

Malden TRIBUNE. w Mr 2 1872-75||
MMal 1872-Ag 13 1875
MWA F 7 1874

MANCHESTER

BEETLE and wedge. m 1875-78||?
MSaE [1875]-77
MWA F,Ap 1876

BREEZE. w 1904+
1904-31 as North shore breeze
MSaE 1904+

Manchester CRICKET. w My 19 1888+
pub 1888+
MSaE Jl 11 1895;Je 27 1896;Mr 13 1897;D 31 1898-1931
MWA Jl 13 1895
NcD Je 5 1909

NORTH SHORE breeze. *See* Breeze

MANSFIELD

Mansfield ENTERPRISE and Foxboro journal. w
MFo Ap 6-27 1922

Mansfield NEWS and Foxboro times. w Mr 1873+
pub 1873+
M Mr 8 1929;O 31 1930
MFo 1914-22

MARBLEHEAD

AMERICAN statesman. w 1881-83||
MSaE [1882-83]
WHi S 4 1882

CHRONICLE. w Ja 3-Jl 18 1868||
Ja-My 9 1868 as Marblehead chronicle
MH Mr-Jl 1868
MSaE [1868]
MWA Mr-My,Je 20-27,Jl 11-18 1868

Marblehead COD.
Issued Jl 4 each year
MSaE 1880;83-86;92;1903;07;09-14;16;19

CRITIC. m
MMarHi S 1871
MSaE Ag,O 1871

Marblehead ENTERPRISE. d O 9? 1890-
MMarHi O 27 1890;Ja 17 1891

ESSEX county statesman. w,sw Ja 6 1881-84||
Ja-D 22 1881 as Essex statesman w 1881-82?
MSaE complete
NcD Ap-Je,S-D 1881

Marblehead GAZETTE. w Ap 7 1832-34||?
MB D 21 1833-Ap 19 1834
MMarHi Jl 21-28,Ag 25-S 1 1832;My 18,Je 29, D 26 1833
MSaE [1832]33

Marblehead LEDGER. w Jl 6 1859-D 27 1862||
DLC Jl 13-20,Ag 17,31,S 14-21,O 5,24,N 9-30, D 14 1859-Ja 18,F 8,Ap 4,25,My 2-9,23-Ag 8,29-S 19 1860;Je 26 1861
MB Jl 13 1859-My 10 1862
MMarHi complete
MSaE [1859]-62
MWA Jl 13-20,Ag 31,S 14-21 1859[F 8-My 16] Je 1860-62

MARBLEHEADER. m N 20-D 20 1876||
MMarHi complete
MSaE complete

Marblehead MERCURY. *See* People's advocate and Marblehead mercury

Marblehead MESSENGER. w Ja 6 1872+
S 2 1929 is 300th anniversary ed
pub 1872+
DLC Mr 18 1876
M S 2 1929;D 15 1933
MHi S 4 1914;Jl 3-24 1931
MMar 1872+
MMarHi 1872-1909
MSaE [1872-74]-1931
MWA 1873;Mr 21 1874;Je 19-26,Jl 10,24-Ag 7,D 4 1875;Ag 17 1877[My 31-N 1878]My 23,Je 6 1879;Mr 12,D 3 1880;Ja 7-14,Mr 11-S 1881; Ag 25 1882[83-84]My 22,Je 5,Ag 14 1885;Ja 8,Je 4 1886;Ja-Mr 20 1914;Ag 16 1935
MiU-C [1883-86]
NcD 1876-77;S 30 1881;N 14 1884-Ja 9 1885; Jl 26 1918;Jl 25 1919

Marblehead MIRROR. w F 21-Jl 4 1863||?
MMarHi F 21-Je 20 1863
MSaE [1863]
MWA Mr 7,Ap 18,My 2-16,30-Je 8,27-Jl 4 1863

PEOPLE'S advocate and Marblehead mercury. w N 27 1847-
1847-D 9? 1848 as Marblehead mercury
MB 1847-[50-Jl 3 1858]
MMarHi 1848-N 24 1855
MSaE D 11,25 1847[48]S 15 1849[50-53]Je 10 1854;55-[58]
MWA Mr 11,25,O 21,D 30 1848[49]Ja 5,S 21 1850;Ja 18,F 15-22,Mr 8,My 10 1851;Je 5,S 4 1852;Je 11,Ag 13 1853;N 25 1854
P-M S 9 1854

Marblehead REGISTER. w Mr 13 1830-My 8 1833||?
MH 1830-Mr 5 1831
MMarHi 1830-33
MSaE [1830]-[33]

MARLBORO

Marlboro ENTERPRISE. d 1887+
pub 1887+
M [1928-33]
MWA Ag 26 1936

Marlboro JOURNAL. w 1861-75||?
United with Marlboro mirror to form Marlboro mirror-journal, later Marlboro republican
MWA Ag 1 1863
OClWHi D 19 1863;Ja 20,Mr 3,Ag 18 1866

Marlboro MIRROR. *See* Marlboro republican

Marlboro daily MIRROR-JOURNAL. d D 13 1886-
M D 13 1886-My 13 1889

Marlboro MIRROR-JOURNAL. w *See* Marlboro republican

Marlboro REPUBLICAN. w N 12 1859-96||?
1859-75? as Marlboro mirror; 1876?-90? Marlboro mirror-journal
MH 1859-Ap 13 1861
MWA Ap 7,O 27-N 10 1860;Ap 13 1861;D 30 1865;S 14 1867;F 24 1872
NcD S 20 1884

Marlborough STAR. w 1890-93||
PPCHi [1890-93]

Marlboro TIMES. w Ap 12 1877-1919||?
1877-Ag 13 1885 as Times
MB [1877-79;82-89]
MHi Ag 1879-Mr 24 1892
MWA S 8 1881;N 22 1883;Jl 23-Ag 13 1885;Ap 15,My 13-20,Je-Jl 22,Ag 5-19 1886
NcD O 25,N 8-D 1883;Ja 17,31-F 7,21,Mr 6,27-Ap 1884

MEDFORD

Medford CITIZEN. w D 5 1900-02||
Merged with Medford mercury
M N 22 1901-O 24 1902
MMe O 1901-02

Medford LEADER. w D 17 1903-D 24 1908||
M 1904-08
MMe complete

Medford MERCURY. w,d D 16 1880+
w 1880-1926?
pub 1902+
M Je 23 1905[29-O 1933]Ja-Jl 1934;Ja-Ag 16 1935;36+
MH F 22 1884;S 9 1898
MMe 1884-89;94-95;97-1901;03+
MWA My 11 1883;S 29 1911;Ja 15 1932

Medford MERCURY and messenger. w O 10 1913+
1913-26 as Medford messenger
MMe 1913+

Medford MESSENGER. *See* Medford mercury and messenger

Medford city NEWS. w?
MMe 1891;93

MEDWAY

Medway GAZETTE. w 1882-1902||
MMed 1885;87;89;91;93-96;98-1902

Medway MAGNET. w 1872-78||?
MWmB F 10 1872-78

MELROSE

Melrose FREE PRESS and Melrose home sector. w 1901+
1901-N 23 1933 as Melrose free press
pub 1901+
M 1908+
MMel 1901+
MWA N 23-30 1933

Melrose GAZETTE. w Ag 2 1856-
MWA N 22 1856

Melrose HOME sector. w 1920-N 23 1933||
United with Melrose free press to form Melrose free press and Melrose home sector
MWA N 23 1933

Melrose JOURNAL and reporter. w 1869-1907||?
1869-1905? as Melrose journal
MMel 1871-1903
MWA D 21 1900
OClWHi Ja 30 1886

Melrose LEADER. w Ja 18 1934+
MWA Ja 18 1934

Melrose evening NEWS. d 1906+
M [1928-Ag 4 1933]

Melrose RECORD. w 1875-76||
MMel complete

Melrose REPORTER. w 1887-1905||?
United with Melrose journal to form Melrose journal and reporter
MMel 1887-1903

Melrose weekly VISITOR. w 1878-80||
MMel complete

MENDON

Mendon AURORA and advertiser. w
MMenHi F 7 1854

INDEPENDENT messenger. *See under* Boston

MERRIMAC

Merrimac BUDGET. w Mr 21 1884-1910||?
MMer 1890;97-98;1900-02;07
MSaE [1884-95]D 30 1898-[1910]
NcD Jl 11,S 12-19,N 14 1884;Ja 30 1903

Merrimack COURIER. *See* Lawrence courier (Lawrence)

RIVER-SIDE press. w 1876-79||?
MSaE [1876]Ag 22 1878

METHUEN

Methuen ENTERPRISE. w 1879-83||?
MSaE [1880-83]

Methuen-Falls GAZETTE. w Ja 2 1835-
MSaE [1835]O 6 1837
MWA Je 5 1835
MnHi Mr 6 1835
NNHi S 1 1837

Methuen GAZETTE. m
MSaE N 16 1872[73]

IRIS. w D 27 1833-
Follows Haverhill iris (Haverhill)
MB [Ja 19-D 19 1834]
MHa 1833-D 6 1834
MSaE [1834]
MnHi Ja 23 1835
NNHi My 16,Je 13 1834
OClWHi Je 27 1834

MASSACHUSETTS (*Continued*)

METHUEN—*Continued*

Methuen TRANSCRIPT. w 1876+
pub 1876+
MMet 1876+
MSaE [1875-90;93-97]99-1921;24-31
NcD Ag 9 1884;Ja 13-27,Mr 2 1888;Mr 23,Ap 6 1900;Ag 18 1916

MIDDLEBORO

Middleboro GAZETTE. w O 7 1852+
1852-58? as Namasket gazette; 1859?-69 Middleboro gazette and Old colony advertiser
pub [1852-58]+
Ct 1855-58
DLC Mr 6 1857
ICM Jl 18 1855
MB Je 18 1859-O 1860
MMi 1852-Ag 1866[67-68]1905+
MWA Ja 28 1853;Ap 21 1854;D 12 1857;Mr 10, My 12 1860
N Je 23 1860
OClWHi Mr 11 1865;Mr 3,Ap 7,My 21 1866

NAMASKET gazette. *See* Middleboro gazette

Middleboro NEWS. sw,w 1881-1914||?
sw 1881-97
Ct D 17 1886

OLD COLONY democrat. w 1834-
MWA F 5 1835

MILFORD

BAY STATE chronicle. w Jl 4 1860-
MWA O 24,N 21 1860

INDEPENDENT messenger. *See under* Boston

Milford JOURNAL. w Je 18 1852-1902||
DLC 1852-Je 9 1854;Jl 20 1867
MMenHi complete
MMil complete
MMilJ complete
MWA Jl 2 1852;Je 10 1853;O 20-N 3,17 1860; F 1[Ag-D]1862;Ja 3,17,F 7,Mr 7 1863;Mr 26, My 21 1864;F 10 1866;Je 18 1870;Je 18 1874;O 27 1875;Je 2 1876;Je 9 1880;My 31(extra)1884
NcD Ja 15 1859;Ap 6 1861;S 23 1865;Ap 26 1876
WHi F 8,22,Mr 1-15 1862;Mr 12 1864;Mr 25 1865

Milford daily JOURNAL. d 1888-Jl 18 1918||
Merged with Milford daily news
MMenHi complete

Milford daily NEWS. d 1887+
pub 1927+
M [1928-Jl 1933]
MMil 1927-31

MILL RIVER

RISING sun. m N 15 1854-
MWA 1854-O 1855

MILLBURY

Millbury JOURNAL. w 1893+
pub 1893+
MWA Jl 20 1894

Millbury PATRIOT and Worcester county workingman's advocate. w Ja 5 1831-
1831-Jl? 1832 as Plebian and Millbury workingman's advocate
MWA [Ja-O 1831]Ja 25,Ag 29 1832
P-M O 17 1832

PLEBIAN and Millbury workingman's advocate. *See* Millbury patriot and Worcester county workingman's advocate

MILTON

Milton LEADER. w S 1 1899-Ap 24 1903||
MMilt complete

Milton NEWS. w 1882-Ja 15 1904||
MMilt Ap 1882-Ap 9 1887;Ap 1888-1904

Mattapan-Milton NEWS. w Ag 22 1923+
pub 1923+
MWA Ag 9 1924

Milton RECORD. w F 13 1904+
pub 1904+
MMilt 1904+
MMiltHi 1904—

MONSON

Monson REGISTER. w 1895-1925||
United with Palmer journal to form Palmer journal-register (Palmer)
MPR complete

NANTUCKET

Nantucket INQUIRER. w Ap 11 1840-
MWA Ap 11,Je 20,S 19,O 10 1840;O 23 1841; D 20 1843;N 28 1857

Nantucket daily INQUIRER. d 1844-
CtY O 11 1844
DLC S 23 1844;Ap 17-19,21-26,My 22,27,29,Jl 15 1845
N Ag 13 1845

INQUIRER and mirror. w,tw,sw Je 23 1821+
1821-65 as Nantucket inquirer
sw 1833-41;O 1860;tw 1852
pub 1821+
CSmH S 4 1830
Ct [1826-27]Ap 17 1830
CtY Mr 11,17 1843;F 9 1846
DLC F 9,23,Mr 15,29-Ap 5,19-26,My 17,31,Je 21,Ag 9,O 18 1824;Mr 7(extra)1825;Ap 1 1826; Ap 7,N 10 1827;Mr 21,My 9,30-Je 13,27-Jl 11, 25-D 19 1829;Ja 23,Ag 14-21,N 6,20-D 4 1830; Ja 1,Ap 16,30,N 26,D 17 1831;Mr 4,Jl 7,Ag 4,S 8 1832;Ag 27,N 23 1842;Jl 1 1843[Ap 1847-50]F-Mr 5,Jl 16,Ag 29 1851
M [Je 11 1932-S 1933]
MBAt N 4 1826;Jl 21,Ag 4-11 1827[33-35;37-39]D 19 1840;Ap 24 1841
MH D 31 1836;My 4 1867;Ag-N,D 8 1894
MHi Mr 18 1823;Ag 27 1834;Ag 5,O 10,D 9 1835;Ja 27,Jl 30,S 3,10 1836
MWA D 20 1821[22-23]N 29-D 6,20 1824;25-27; F 9,Mr 22,S 6 1828;S 12,26 1829;F 6,Mr 6,Ap 3,Ag 14 1830[31-32]-[36-37]-[39-41]Jl 26 1852; O 2,16-26,N 14-21 1860;Ap 15-O 14 1865;66-69;O 8 1870;Ja 14,D 2,16-23 1871;S 7 1872;D 5 1874[75-77]-91;Mr 10 1934
MWiC Jl 5 1861
MiU-C [1834-37;39]
MnHi F 20 1833
N Jl 26,S 20 1821-D 23 1823;D 13,27 1824;F 25 1825-Ja 23 1826;S 29,O 27 1827;My 2,S 5,O 2 1829;N 13 1830;Ja 15,F 9,Mr 26,Ag 13,N 19 1831;Je 15 1833;My 30 1835;Je 30,Jl 11 1838;O 19,N 9 1872
NEh [F 23-D 20 1828;F-My 1829]30[Ja 16-Jl 20 1833]F 11-19 1834
NN Ag 15 1838
NNHi [Ja-My 1823]N 29 1824-26;D 29 1827-[Ap-D 1828]29;D 4 1833
NjCHi D 20 1826-N 3 1827;Mr 9,23-30 1839
NjR F 16 1824
OCHi My 17 1843
OClWHi S 30 1823;O 21 1865;My 20 1893-Je 23 1894

ISLAND review. sw Ag 22 1874-78||
MH Ag 22 1874
MHi 1874-Ag 1878
NhD Ag 24 1878

ISLANDER. w Mr 1840-Mr 18 1843||
Followed by Weekly telegraph
DLC Ja 1 1842
MWA Mr 26 1842-43
MnHi D 11 1841

Nantucket JOURNAL. w 1826-
MWA S 28 1827;Ja 11 1828
N [Ja-Ag 1827;Ja-Ap 1828]

Nantucket JOURNAL. w 1878-99||?
NN Ag 18 1881

Nantucket weekly MIRROR. w 1845-65||
United with Nantucket inquirer to form Inquirer and mirror
DLC Mr 7 1846;N 23 1850;Je 7,Jl 12,26 1851; Ja 7,Ap 30,My 7,Jl 1853-Mr 11,Ag 19 1854
MWA Ag 14 1852;Mr 10 1860

Morning TELEGRAPH. d 1843-
DLC N 1 1843;Je 26,Jl 30-31,N 26 1844;F 13-15 17,Mr 6-8,10-Ap 2,7,10-11,15 1845
MWA Jl 22 1844

Weekly TELEGRAPH. w Mr 31-S 29 1843||
Follows Islander
MWA [Mr-S 8 1843]

WARDER. sw Ja 3 1846-
MWA Ja 10-14,21-24,Je 10 1846
P-M Ap 11 1846

NATICK

Natick BULLETIN. w N 27 1869+
Follows Natick observer
pub 1869+
M 1912+
MH My 28 1875;Jl 26 1878;Jl 15 1881;My 26 1882;Je 3 1898
MNaHi N 27 1869;72-1932
MNaM 1869+
MWA D 1869-O 1870[Ja 20-Jl 1872]

Natick CITIZEN. w D 22 1877+
MH [Ja 25 1878-O 20 1882]
MNaHi 1877-1916
MNaM D 29 1877-D 18 1895
MWA S 20 1878
NcD Ag 15 1889
NcU D 28 1887

Natick HERALD. w 1924+
M [S 18 1930-Ag 4 1932]

Natick MIRROR. w O 21 1848-
MH O 21 1848

Natick OBSERVER. w 1856-68||
Followed by Natick bulletin
MNaHi Ap 5,19-26,Je 21,Ag 14,O 2 1858;S 3 1859;62-68
MNaM 1856-Ag 10 1861
MWA Je 16 1860

Natick TIMES. w O 28 1865-69||
Merged with Natick bulletin
MNaHi Mr 10,N 4,18 1865
MNaM 1865-F 13 1869
MWA D 26 1868

Natick TRIBUNE. w F 1914+
Suspended from Ag 1-N 2 1934
pub 1914+
M [Je 8 1928-D 1 1933]

NEEDHAM

Needham CHRONICLE. w N 28 1874+
Early years as Needham chronicle and Wellesley advertiser
pub 1874+
MHi S 16 1911
MNaHi My 6 1876
MNd 1874-89
MNdT Je 1935+
MWA D 5 1874;My 10-24,Je 14 1884

Needham TIMES. w Mr 10 1932+
pub 1932+

NEW BEDFORD

New Bedford ADVERTISER. w Ja 3 1826-
MNb [Ja-S 19 1826]

A ALVORADA. *See* Diario de noticias

Evening BULLETIN. tw,d D? 1841-
1843-44 as Daily evening bulletin (d)
MH D 3 1847
MNb 1842-43
MWA F 22 1842;D 21,23 1843;Ag 20,30,O 22 1844;Ag 13 1847

CONSERVATIVE, and weekly democrat. w Jl 18 1868-
MWA O 31 1868

New Bedford COURIER. w Je 5 1827-34||
United with New Bedford gazette to form New Bedford gazette and courier
CSmH Ag 31 1830
Ct S 4 1827;F 26,Mr 26-Ap 2 1834
CtY My 24 1831
DLC O 30 1827;Jl 24 1833
MH D 16 1828
MNb 1832-33
MWA D 4 1833
P-M S 25 1833

DIARIO de noticias. w,d 1910+
1910-Ja 23 1919 as A Alvorada; Ja 25 1919-D 31 1926 Alvorada diaria
w 1910-Ja 23 1919
In Portuguese
pub 1911+

Weekly ECHO. w Ap 7 1849-
MWA Ap 28 1849

New Bedford daily GAZETTE d
MHi S 1 1836
MNb 1837
MNbHi Ja-S 1834
NNHi S-O 22,N 1,4-7,10-17 1834

New Bedford GAZETTE and courier. w N? 1830-
1830-34 as New Bedford gazette
Ct [1831-36]Ja 18 1838
DLC D 19 1831
MWA S 5 1831;F 13 1832;Jl 30 1834;O 19-26, N 30 1835;Ja 11 1836
N O 14 1833

Morning HALCYON. sw O 18 1843-
MNb O-N 6 1843

L'INDEPENDANT. *See under* Fall River

INDEPENDENT. F 24 1849-
MWA Mr 3 1849

O JORNAL do povo. w 1923-24||
In Portuguese
IU Je 28-S 19 1924

New Bedford evening JOURNAL. d 1890-S 8 1896||
M 1891-96
MNb 1890-Je 1896

*New Bedford MERCURY. w Ag 7 1807-95||?
CLM F 1 1828
CSmH Ag 13 1830
DLC Ja 17-F 21 1823;O 13 1826;N 9 1827;My 2,Je 27,Jl 4 1838;Je 19,S 18 1829;Ja 8,22 1830
MH Ag 6 1824[Je 25-N 19 1841]S 2 1842;N 27 1845;F 21,N 7 1851
MHi O 30 1835;Jl 29,Ag 19 1836;Je 19 1863
MNb [1821-22]-24
MWA Ja 17,31 1823;24-Ja 5,Ag 11,N 3 1826;D 7 1827;Ag 29 1828-F 1830;Jl 27 1832;Mr 18,S 23 1836;O 27,N 10 1837;My 11 1838[44-Mr 1847]Mr 15 1850;Ja 23 1852;Mr 6 1857
N Ag 3 1827
NNHi Jl 20 1821-Jl 9 1830;S 16 1869
OOxM Ap 17 1829
PPL [Jl 14,Ag 11,S 1,O 13 1826]

Daily MERCURY. d F 28 1831+
Ag 7 1907 is 100th anniversary ed
Ag 8 1932 is 125th anniversary ed
DLC Je 2 1853;Mr 10 1856
ICM Jl 7,13 1885
MA O 6 1897;Ap 26,My 3,7,10,Je 2 1899;Ag 7 1907
MBAt Ap 15,20 1865;Jl 6 1900
MHi Jl 25 1836
MNb 1831+
MNbHi 1859
MWA Jl 30 1836;O 16 1837;Je 8 1839;My 26 1840;Jl 7,S 9 1841;S 2 1842;Jl 22,27,Ag 3 1843;Jl 10 1844;Ap 10,O 8 1847;My 31,N 9-10,16 1852;D 29 1854;Mr 7 1857[O-N 1860]Jl 1862-Je 1863;My 25,D 20 1872;Jl 4 1876;Ag 7 1907;Ja 24 1927;Ag 8 1932
N O 16 1833;Mr 20 1837
NNHi D 30 1869;Je 2 1873
OClWHi S 22 1864
PPoU Jl-D 1837

Le MESSAGER. w My 1927+
In French
pub 1927+
M N 6 1932

NEW ENGLAND gazette. w 1823-
DLC Ap 8,O 28,D 16-23 1823;Ja 13 1824-Mr 29 1825
MWA [My 20-Ag 5]D 23 1823 Mr 23,My 18-25,Jl 13,27,Ag 17,S 7 1824

O POPULAR. w 1913-31||
In Portuguese
IU N 29 1917-Ap 1924
M O 16 1930;Jl 9 1931
MH O 25 1917-N 11 1920

RECORD of the times. w Ag 26 1829-
CSmH Ag 30 1830
DLC Ag-S 16,30,O 26 1829
MWA S 2,D 7 1829;Ag 9 1830

New Bedford weekly REGISTER. w 1831-
DLC Ja 12 1831
MBAt My 16 1832
MNb 1843
MWA F 8 1832;F 27 1839;Jl 8 1840;Jl 16,30 1844;Ap 22,D 23 1845;Mr 3,17-24 1846

MASSACHUSETTS (*Continued*)

NEW BEDFORD—*Continued*

Daily evening REGISTER. d F 7 1839-1839-S 8 1845 as Morning register
MBAt S 5,O 20 1840
MNb [My 10 1839-O 1840;F 10 1841-Mr 25 1845]
MWA 1839-F 7 1840;41-Mr 14 1846
OClWHi D 22 1840

New Bedford REPORTER and seaman's weekly visitor. w Jl 30? 1846-
Title varies: New Bedford reporter and the family weekly visitor; New Bedford reporter and whaleman's weekly visitor
MNb [1847]
MWA F 26 1846;Ja 21 1847

REPUBLICAN standard. w 1850-1912||?
MH S 26 1901
MWA Mr 30-Ap 6 1854;Je 4 1857;Je 1860-My 1861;O 5 1865;F 22 1866;O 14 1869
OClWHi Je 29 1865

New Bedford STANDARD-TIMES. d F 15 1850+
1850-Ag 6 1932 as New Bedford evening standard (title varies slightly)
pub 1850+
Ct Jl 10 1901
DLC 1898
M Je 1899+
MBAt Ap 15,20 1865
MNb 1851+
MNbHi 1859
MWA F 15 1850(facsimile)N 9,11 1852;F 15 1853-F 14,Jl 25,D 8 1854;My 30 1855;N 15 1858;O 17-N 22 1860;F 18,Jl 24 1862;Ap 30, My 11,19,21,23,30 1864;Ap 15,My 4,6(supp) 1865;Ja 9,Jl 5,D 20 1866;Mr 4 1868;Je 12 1869;My 27 1871;S 1,D 15 1874-Je 1895;98;Jl 1908-20;Ag 8 1932
MiU-C F 14 1898
NcD Mr 12,Ap 2,My 21,Ag 13 1878;Mr 25,My 6,S 2,D 2 1879;Ja 20,Ap 6 1880
WHi My 25 1860

Sunday STANDARD-TIMES. w 1907+
1907-Jl? 1932 as Sunday standard
DA 1922+
MWA Ag 7 1932

New Bedford daily SUN. d O 27 1923-Je 5 1924||
M complete

New Bedford TIMES. w 1858?-
MWA F 18 1860

New Bedford TIMES. d 1901-Ag 6 1932||
United with New Bedford evening standard to form New Bedford standard-times
M 1916-32
MNb [Ap 1903-08]-32
MWA Ag 6 1932

WHALEMEN'S shipping list. w Mr 17 1843-D 29 1914||
1843-D 25 1883? as Whalemen's shipping list and merchants' transcript
CtY Ja 15 1862-D 28 1858;Mr 15 1829-F 27 1866
DLC Mr 12 1844-47;Jl 18 1848-77;79-84;F 5-19 Mr 5-Ap 23 1889
MB Mr 12 1844-F 1865;F 18 1879-Jl 6 1880
MH My 1860-S 10 1861
MNbHi complete
MSaE Ap 30,Jl 27 1852
MWA complete
MiU-C [1849;52;54;57;66;71;84]
N Ap 5,19-26 1859
NNHi [Mr 13 1860-Mr 5 1861]

NEWBURYPORT

Newburyport ADVERTISER. sw My 10? 1831-Jl 21 1832||
1831 as Newburyport advertiser and Merrimac journal of the times
MNp 1831
MSaE [1831-32]
MWA [My 21 1831-32]
MnHi Je 14 1832

Newburyport ADVERTISER. sw O 7 1845-
DLC 1845-O 6 1846
MNp 1845-49
MSaE 1845[46-49]
MWA My 22,Je 9,Ag 25 1848;N 25 1847;N 10, 17 1848;Mr 6 1849

AMERICAN sentinel and Essex north record.
DLC D 2 1854

ADVOCATE. w Mr 20- 1874||
MSaE [1874]
MWA Mr 20-27,Ap 17-24 1874

BEACON of liberty. w S 23 1848-
Campaign paper
MHi S 13,O 4 1848
MSaE [1848]
MWA O 28 1848

CITY advertiser. m S 1851-
MWA S 1851

COMET. w
MNp [1858]

Newburyport COURIER. sw Jl 4? 1844-
MSaE [1844-46]
MWA Ag 30,N 5,D 17 1844;F 14,21,Mr 14,My 16,Jl 12(supp)Ag 22 1845;Mr 7 1846

Daily COURIER. d My 2-Ag 1 1846||
MWA complete
MiU-C Jl 3 1846
NcD My 11-Je 26,30-Jl 1-2,4-7,9,16,18,20 1846

ESSEX county constellation. w
Also dated in Salem
MSaE Jl 16 1846;F 11-18 1847

ESSEX courant. w Je 9 1825-Mr 16 1826||
Followed by Free press
MHi complete
MSaE [1825]
MWA S 8,D 15 1825;Ja 5 1826
NNHi N 17 1825

ESSEX north register and family monitor. sm, w F 15 1834-D 29 1837||?
1834-36 as Essex north register
sm 1834
DLC S 22 1837
MSaE [1834]-[37]
MWA Mr 29 1834;Ja 31,S 12,N 21 1835;36-37
RW Mr 24 1837

FOSTER'S "Go a-Ahead" express and monthly advertiser. m Ja 1 1846-
MWA Ja 1,F 5,Ap 2 1846

FREE PRESS. w Mr 22 1826-
Follows Essex courant
DLC My 25,S 21 1826
MHi Mr-D 9 1826;Je 8(extra)1826
MWA Ap 20,Ag 24-31,S 24,O 19-28,N 11 1826
NNHi S 7 1826

Newburyport GAZETTE. *See* Newburyport herald

Newburyport daily GERM. sw,tw,d My 3? 1879-87||?
Title varies with periodicity
MSaE [1880-86]Ja 14 1887
MWA Jl 5 1879;Ja 3,F 11 1880
NcD Jl 29,Ag 8 1882

***Newburyport HERALD.** sw,w O 31 1797-1902||
Formed by the union of Impartial herald and Political gazette (not in this list) 1797-Ap 11 1815 as Newburyport herald and country gazette (Mr 4 1803-N 1811 Newburyport gazette) Ap 18 1815-Ap 18 1817 Newburyport herald and commercial gazette; Ap 25 1817-Ja 28 1818 Newburyport herald, commercial and country gazette
sw 1797-1879
CSmH S 3 1830
Ct [1826]
DLC Ag 13 1822;My 28,My 30 1823;N 19 1824; S 13,D 2,23 1825;O 13,N 28 1826;Ja 1,22-29, Ap 22,29,My 6,13,Jl 4,S 5,N 4 1828;Mr 3,Je 19,26,Jl 6-14,24,S 4-8,15,O 20,N 3,17,25 1829; Ja 1,26,F 2,9-12,26-Mr 2,9-12,19,Ap 27-Ag 17, S 14 1830;My 3 1841;N 3 1846
MAm 1837-39;41
MB Jl 23,Ag 20,27,S 21 1824[29]D 9 1831[N 14-D 6 1834]F 23 1836;S 21 1837[Mr 13-Je 19 1838]Mr 8,N 22-26,D 17 1839;D 31 1841;D 2 1842[Ja 21-31 1845]My 28-Je 1,25 1847;Mr 21 1862;D 20 1872
MBAt O 20 1826;My 4,S 11 1827;Ag 1 1828; My 22 1829;My 29 1835
MH Ap 1825-F 23 1827
MHi Ag 30 1825
MNp 1821-32
MNpN 1858-88
MSaE 1821-[24-27;30-33]-[35-36]-[38;40-42;44-45]-[49-53;55-69]-[79-80]Ap 15 1882;Ag 8 1883;My 20,D 1 1886[87]Ag 10 1888[90-93;S 17 1897;Jl 22 1898[99]-[1902]
MWA [1821]-[24-25]-[27-33]Jl 28,Ag 21 1835; Ja 29,My 3,S 20 1836;O 27 1840;Ag 18 1846;F 5 1856;Jl 17,Ag 7,18-21,S 15,D 4 1857;Ja 5-8, 29,F 19,Mr 16,Jl 27 1858;Ag 19,S 12 1862;Ap 30,Je 16-19,27,Jl 3,D 22 1863;Jl 7,N 7 1865;N 28 1872
MeU N 4 1825
MnHi Je 22 1832;N 21 1834
MnU O 2 1829
N N 12 1839
NN Jl 10 1821;D 20 1822;N 20 1823;Jl 5 1825; My 17 1834
NNHi Jl 23,O 8 1822;N 7 1826
NcD Ap 5 1821;S 9,O 11 1825[26;70-76;79-80; 85;88-89]
NjR Je 21-24 1842

Newburyport morning HERALD. d Ag 1 1832-O 2 1915||
Title varies slightly. Merged with Newburyport daily news
CtY Ja 8 1864
DLC Mr 11 1837;Ag,O-N 1839;40;47-56;Jl 1857-Je 1858[Ja-O 1860]61[Ja-Je 1863;Je 1865-Ap 1866]Jl 20 1870;D 12(extra)1840
ICHi My 19-20 1859
ICU D 2,13,27-29 1848[Ja-N 1849]
M Je 1899-1915
MB D 25 1832;D 25 1833[34-N 1840;Ap 29-D 1841;Jl 13 1842-Ja 15 1845;Jl 26-O 14 1848;Ja 10-N 21 1850]F 4,D 3 1851;Jl 5,Ag 31,S 18 1852;D 10 1856;Ap 24-25,Ag 6 1856;Ja 14,Ap 28,My 14,28,Je 7 1858;Mr 3,7,11 1859;Jl 30,Ag 6,O 26 1860;Ja 10,Ap 4,8,25[Ag 29-N 2 1861;F 15-N 24 1862;F 28-Ag 1863;Jl 30-O 13 1864] Ag 25 1871;Ap 28 1873;Ag 7,S 1 1874[Ja 7-F 9 1878]Ja 2,Jl 8 1879
MBAt Je 11 1833
MH Jl 23 1856;Jl 7 1865;Ag 2,O 8 1879;Ja 16, 19-23 1880;S 14 1909
MHi N 2 1832;Jl 30 1835;Jl 1,O 7 1836;Ap 7, 27 1841;D 24 1852
MNp complete
MNpN 1856-1915
MSaE [1832]-[62]65-[90]-[1915]
MWA Ag 4,11,D 7 1832[33]Jl 12,Ag 1834-Jl,D 26 1835;Ja 12,F 22,Ap 22,Je 2 1836;37-[46]-48; Ja 30,Je 4,Jl-D 1849;F 13,Ap 30,Jl 1850-71;F 17,24,29,Mr 2,9,16,30,S 7 1872;S 1 1873;74-75; F 11,D 14 1876;Ap 7,O 8-9 1877;78-[89-91]-[93-98]D 17 1906
MiU-C [1834-35;37-39]-[41-53]-[55-69;71;75;78-88;91-92;96-97]
N Jl 7 1865
NNHi Jl 2 1847
NcD Mr 6 1841;My 31 1851;D 13 1864;D 22 1866;D 8 1868;Ja 1-2,My 18 1869;Ja 1,Ap 13, Je 30,D 8 1870;Je 28 1873;Ja 6,F 14,Mr 24,S 1,25 1874;Ja 9,Ap 13 1878[80-89;1907-13;15]
OClWHi My 3 1841;O 27 1863;F 9 1866
TxU O 26 1847-O 24 1848

Daily evening HERALD. d 1880-1904||?
MSaE S 14 1881;Ap 15 1882;Ag 8 1883[84-86; 88-90;92-93;95-99]D 12 1900
MiU-C [1880-84;88-89]
NcD Ag 15 1884;D 4,10 1886;O 15,D 14 1888; Ja 21,23,F 8 1889;Ag 20 1896

Newburyport ITEM. w 1890-1909||
MSaE Je 8 1895;99-1909
NcD Ap 22 1899;D 1 1900

Newburyport LEADER and summer colonist. d 1906-11||
Title varies
MSaE [1908]-[10-11]
NcD Je 10,Jl 20 1908

MERCANTILE advertiser. bm Jl 1852-
MSaE Ag 1871
MWA Jl 1852
MiU-C Jl 1852

MERRIMAC journal. w
MSaE N 9 1842

MERRIMAC VALLEY visitor. w 1872-87||
Title varies: Valley visitor
M [Ja 20 1877-D 21 1878]
MSaE [1872-87]
MWA O 23 1875
NcD F 20,Ag 21-28,O 23 1875;Mr 4,25 1876;Ja 6,F 24,Mr 31-Ap 7 1877;Je 1,15 1878;My 4 1881;Ag 28 1882;Ja 13,Ag 18 1883

NEW ENGLAND repertory. *See* Boston advertiser. sw,tw (Boston)

NEW ERA. w
MSaE Je 1 1860

Newburyport daily NEWS. d 1888+
Title varies: Newburyport daily news and Newburyport herald
pub 1888+
M O 1915+
MH Mr 30 1933
MNb 1889+
MSaE [1888-95]My 22 1896[97-99]-[1913]-31
MWA Jl 18 1916
NcD My 10 1893;Ag 30,N 16 1894;My 8 1897 [98-1904;08;10]Ag 23 1912[16]

NORTHERN chronicler. w My 19 1824-
DLC Jl 7 1824
MSaE [1824]
MWA Jl 14,S 16,O 7 1824;F 3,24,Mr 17,Ap 7 My 5,19 1825

PEOPLE'S advocate and commercial gazette. sw Jl 6? 1833-
Ct [1833]
DLC Ag 24 1833
MSaE Je 26 1833
N O 19 1833

PUTNAM record. m?
MSaE N 1856;Mr 1857

Newburyport STAR. w 1865-
MNp 1865
MSaE [1865]

TIMES. sw Ag 1831-
DLC N 5 1832
MSaE [1832]
MWA N 1 1832

Daily evening UNION. d Ag? 1849-D 31 1853||
Merged with Newburyport morning herald
DLC Jl 1850-Je 1851
MNp 1849-53
MSaE [1849]-53
MWA Ja 8,My 9[S-D 1850] Ja 14-15,17,22, F 4(extra)My 29,Jl 8,N 28 1851;Ja 21,F 4, Jl 6,16,Ag 12,S 17 1852[Ja-Ag 10]D 27-31 1853
WHi Ja-S 18 1851

Saturday evening UNION and Essex north record. w Ja 21 1854-
1854-F 13 1855 as Saturday evening union and weekly family visitor
MNp 1854-55
MSaE [1854-55]
MWA 1854-D 1 1855

VALLEY visitor. *See* Merrimac Valley visitor

VOICE from the jail. w D 11? 1842-
MSaE D 11-25 1842
MWA D 18 1842

WATCHTOWER. w Ja 5 1838-
1846-Ap 7 1848 pub also at Georgetown
MNp 1838-39
MSaE 1838-[40-41;43-48]
MWA Ja 12,F 16,Mr 2,23,Ag 17,31,O 26,N 16 1838;Ja 18,N 28 1839[Mr-O 1840;41]Ja 26, F 9-16,N 1 1844;My 16 1845;S 4,18,O 16, N 13,D 18 1846;F 18,Ap 6(extra)7,Je 2,Ag 25,D 29 1848;Mr 23,My 25 1849
MiU-C D 10 1841;F 16 1844
NNHi S 13 1839;Ag 28 1846

NEWTON

Newton CIRCUIT. w D 17 1892-D 1922||
MNe complete

Newton FREE PRESS. w Ja 21 1915-D 1918||
MNe complete

Newton GRAPHIC. w Je 13 1873+
1873-81 as Newton republican
M Ja 18 1929
MNe 1873-81;O 21 1882+
MNeC O 21 1882-O 2 1891
MWA N 2 1888
NNHi O 12 1881

Newton JOURNAL. w S 8 1866+
Je 3 1921 is 55th anniversary ed
DLC 1866-Ag 26 1876
M My 29-D 1931
MB S 8,O 27 1866;Ja 5,19-Ap 20 1867
MNe 1866-Ag 1928
MNeC Ag 26 1882-Ag 22 1890
MWA Ag 1 1868;D 4 1875;Mr 17 1883;Je 3 1921
NjR [1867-70]

MASSACHUSETTS (*Continued*)

NEWTON—*Continued*

Newton PROGRESS. w Ap 26 1923-D 1930||
MNe complete

Newton REPUBLICAN. *See* Newton graphic

Newton TIMES. w Mr 1 1911-F 3 1921||
M complete
MNe 1911-Ja 5 1921

NEWTON CENTER

TOWN crier. w S 8 1898+
pub 1898+
MWA N 7 1924
MNe 1898+

NORTH ADAMS

ADAMS news and transcript. *See* North Adams transcript

BERKSHIRE advocate. w 1832-Je 18 1834||
DLC N 6 1833-34
MWA F 13 1833
MWiC O 31 1832-34

BERKSHIRE American and Adams manufacturer. w D 14 1825-
1825-F 13 1828 as Berkshire American 1825-F 16 1827 pub in Pittsfield
CSmH Ap 3 1830
Ct Je 6 1827
DLC D 31 1825
MPi Ja 28,Je 8 1826
MWA Mr 23-Ap 6,27,Ag 31,O 12,26,N 9,23,D 14-21 1826;27-Je 18 1828
NN Jl 30 1828
P-M Ja 11 1827

GREYLOCK sentinel. w 1851-
MWA F 13 1852

North Adams TRANSCRIPT. w 1843-1918||
Title varies: Weekly transcript; Weekly transcript and Berkshire county intelligencer; Adams news and transcript
pub complete
DLC Ag 9 1860
IU My 1 1856
M F 11 1886-1918
MH Je 15 1865
MNo complete
MWA F 26 1852;Mr 3,Ap 7 1853;Jl 27 1865;Ag 24 1871
MDeHi Jl 1,15-29,Ag 12,25,S 2 1852
OHi Jl 11 1868
P-M N 13 1835

North Adams TRANSCRIPT. d 1895+
pub 1895+
Ct D 15 1921
M 1895+
MAd current 5 yrs only
MNo 1895+

NORTH ANDOVER

SPECTATOR. w Jl 17 1936+
MNor 1936+

NORTH ATTLEBORO

Attleborough weekly BULLETIN. w My 16? 1857-
MAtt F 13 1858
MWA My 23-30,Je 13,Jl 18,S 5,N 7 1857;Ja 9,Mr 13-Ap 17,My 8 1858

North Attleboro evening CHRONICLE. d 1870+
pub [1884-85]1908+
M [1928-Je 1932]Ja-Je 1934;36+
MAtt S 7 1897;D 15 1917

Attleborough evening CHRONICLE. w,sw,d 1872-1931||?
w 1872-89?
My 12 1886 is historical ed
MWA My 12 1886

Attleboro weekly NEWS. w 1860-
MAtt Jl 13 1861
OClWHi Ap 22 1865

NORTH BILLERICA

Billerica NEWS. w F 2 1928+
pub 1928+

NORTH BRIDGEWATER

OLD COLONY reporter. w
DLC N 10(extra)1849
MBro O 27 1848
PP Ap 1821-Mr 1822
PPL N 29 1850

North Bridgewater REPUBLICAN and Old Colony press. w
MHi N 29 1835;F 12-26 1836

NORTH BROOKFIELD

North Brookfield JOURNAL. bw,w F 1 1875-1919||
bw 1875-Ag 1877
MNob [1875-95]99;1901-19
MWA 1875-77

NORTH EASTON

Easton BULLETIN. w 1888+
pub My 1931+

Easton JOURNAL and Bristol county advertiser. w D 9 1871-98||?
MWA D 23 1871

NORTH WRENTHAM

NEW-ENGLAND telegraph. w 1831?-
DLC Jl 24,Ag 28,S 18 1833;Jl 30 1834
MB Je 4 1834
MBC Jl 3,Ag 14,S 4,18,O 2,D 11 1833
NNHi Jl 17 1833

NORTHAMPTON

Le CITOYEN. w Ap 11 1908-
In French
MNF Ap-O 3 1908

Northampton COURIER. d D 28 1829-O 26 1858||
My 18-N 9 1831 as Northampton courier and Hampshire sentinel. United with Hampshire gazette to form Hampshire and Northampton courier, later Hampshire gazette
Jl 13 1832 has an extra "Handbill on the cholera epidemic"
CSmH S 8 1830
CtY Ag 5 1835
DLC D 28 1829;O 27 1830;Ja 5-19 1831;N 25 1840
GAtCo Ja 8 1840
IU Jl 11 1843
MBAt Ag 15 1843
MEa N 23 1831-D 19 1832
MH D 28 1829-Ja 6 1830;Mr 15 1837
MHi O 29 1834;Ag 5,S 9-16,O 21-28 1835; F 10,Je 8,22,Ag 31 1836
MNF complete
MWA [F-Ag 1831]Ap 4 1832;F 26 1834[35]-[37]O 17-24 1848;Ja 20 1852;Ag 2 1853
MiU-C [1829-35;42;44]
MnHi [1835]
N Ag 22 1838;Mr 27 1839;F 1 1842;O 22 1844
NcD S 16 1835[36]Jl 12,Ag 2,O 25 1837;Ag 29 1848;F 13,Je 19,Ag 7 1849;My 14,Je 18, N 12 1850;S 9 1851;Je 15 1852;O 11 1853
NhD Mr 20 1839
P-M Jl 18,Ag 1 1832
TxU D 21 1836-D 12 1838

Northampton DEMOCRAT. w D 16 1840-
Ja 27-Ap 27 1841 as Northampton democrat and Hampshire county advertiser
LU Ja 20-D 1841
MNF [D 23 1840-Jl 1854]
N F 13,Je 18 1844
NhD O 6 1846
P-M D 16 1840

Northampton FREE PRESS. sw,w Ap 13 1860-D 26 1874||
1869-70 as Northampton semi-weekly free press. United with Northampton journal to form Journal and free press, later Hampshire county journal
sw 1860-70
DLC Ap 11 1862-Ap 7 1863;Ap 12 1864-Ap 7 1865
MNF [1860-74]
MWA Ap 12 1861-Ap 7,Jl 28 1865;Ag 23 1870; My 24 1873
NNHi Jl 3 1863
NcD Ap 10 1863-Ap 7 1865

Daily GAZETTE. d My 27-Jl 20 1846||
MNF complete

Daily GAZETTE and courier. d Ap 25-Jl 22 1861||
DLC My 21 1861
MNF complete
MWA My 13 1861

HAMPSHIRE county journal. w Jl 1875-Ag 3 1895||
1875 as Northampton journal; 1876 Journal and free press
CtY O 1887
M [Ap 8 1882-83]
MN 1879-87
MNF 1877-95
MWA Ap 29,Jl 15 1876;Je 26 1886

*HAMPSHIRE gazette. w S 6 1786-Jl 9 1918||
Jl 9 1815-Jl 26 1817 Hampshire gazette and Northampton advertiser; Ag 2 1817-D 30 1818 Hampshire gazette and public advertiser. Merged with Daily Hampshire gazette
S 6 1886 is centennial ed
CSmH S 1 1830
Ct D 6 1826
CtY Jl 30,Ag 20-27 1828;S 6 1886
DLC 1821-25;Ag 27 1828;Ag 31,N 30 1831;Ja 25,Ap 18,D 12 1832;Ja 23,F 6-13,Jl 31-Ag 7, 21-28,O 9,D 11 1833;Ja 20,Je 4,25,Jl 16,Ag 6, 20-27-S 3,17,O 1,22,N 5,D 10-24 1834;Jl 1-22, Ag 12-29 1835;Mr 30,Ap 20-27,Je 1,15,Jl 13 1836;Ja 1 1844;Mr 4 1856;Je 17 1862;Mr 10 1863
ICHi Je 17 1862
ICN O 5-19,N 23,D 7 1831;Ja 4 1832
M S 6 1886
MAJ Mr 21,D 5 1838;Mr 10 1841
MBAt Mr 27 1822;Ap 22 1829
MEa 1821-D 13 1826;Ja 27 1827-N 1829;33-O 1881;S 6 1886
MH Mr 31 1824
MHi Ap 16,O 8 1834;O 28,N 11,25-D 2 1835;F 3,Ap 6,Ag 31 1836;S 6 1886
MN 1880-87
MNF [1821-1917]
MS 1821-30
MWA 1821-F 18,S 1,22,O 6,N 10-17,D 8-15 1824 [25]-[28-29]30;F 23 1831;D 18 1833;F 10 1836; Ap 26 1837;N 7 1838[Je 24-D 1840]-Mr 19,Ap 2,Jl 9,O 29 1844;F 4,Ap 8-15[Je 17-D 1845]-47;S 25,D 11 1849;Mr 18 1851;Ja 20 1852;D 2,16-23 1856;Ja 6-13 1857[Ap 13 1858-N 20 1860]F 12,Mr 5,26,Ap 9-16,My 7,D 3,24 1861; Ja 14,F 1862;D 22 1863;Ap 19,My 24,S 20,O 25,D 6,20 1864;Jl 25,N 28,D 12 1865;F 20,Mr 13,Ap 17 1866;Ag 17,S 14 1869;Je 14,Ag 9 1870;Ja 3,24-31,F 28 1871;My 28,Jl 23,S 17,D 31 1872;Je 19 1877;Jl 25 1882;S 6 1886
MiU-C [1821-22;24-34;36-37;39-44;46;53-55;57; 59-61]
MDeHi [My 8 1822-S 8 1824]D 10 1828;Mr 17, My 12,D 22 1830;Ja 12,Mr 9 1831;Je 17,24,S 9,16 1840;F 24,Mr 3,31,Ag 10 1841;Mr 28 1843;Je 9 1857;Mr 1 1859;S 6-7 1886
N F 14,Ap 11,25,Jl 4 1838;N 30 1841;Ja 4,Jl 12,Ag 2 1842;Ap 29,Je 17 1845;Ap 14,28 1863;F 27 1866
NN Ap-My 23,S 19,N 7,D 5 1838;O 23 1839;N 30 1841;Ja 11 1842;Ap 27 1852;Jl 4 1876
NNHi My 19-Je 23 1863;S 6,20 1886
NcD Ja 23,Mr 6 1821[23]Ja 14 1824;D 28 1825 [26-Mr]Ag 16,O 4,N 1 1842;D 23 1873;My 26 1874;Jl 4 1876;Jl 17-24 1877
NhD Ag 3 1869
OClWHi Ag 26 1840;My 17 1842;F 28,My 2 1843;My 25 1852;N 4 1856;D 15 1857;Ja 9-19, F 23 1858;S 5 1865
P-M Mr 13 1835;N 18 1840
PEL O 8 1834
PPoU Ja 16-D 1822
WHi N 28 1821;D 18 1822;25-26;D 10 1828;O 21,N 4 1829;60-63;65;Ag 28 1866

Daily HAMPSHIRE gazette. d N 1 1890+
Jl 2 1910 is Easthampton's 125th anniversary ed; S 5 1936 is 150th anniversary ed
M Jl 2 1910[28-Jl 1933]
MBAt Ap 18 1865
MNF 1890+
MWA O 24 1894;O 1 1896 S 5 1936
NcD S 8,O 19 1903;Je 6,13 1904

HAMPSHIRE herald. w F 4 1845-
DLC F 24 1846;Ja 29,Mr 9 1848
MAJ N 4 1845
MDeHi Mr 17 1846;Ap 25 1848
MNF 1845-O 1847;F-Ag 15 1848;N 16 1888
MWA Ag 26 1845;F 1847-Ja 1848
NcD N 10-24 1846;Ap 20,Je 15-22 1847;Ja 11-18 1848
P-M D 9 1845

HAMPSHIRE daily herald. *See* Northampton daily herald

HAMPSHIRE republican. *See* Republican, and Hampshire and Franklin advertiser

Northampton daily HERALD. d S 1 1882-Ap 11 1921||
1884-S 30 1885 as Hampshire daily herald
MNF complete
NcD S 3,N 14 1903

HOLYOKE mountaineer. ir
MNF Ap 14,O 27 1846

Le JEAN BAPTISTE. w F 24 1875-
Dated also in Springfield
In French
CLM F 24 1875

Northampton daily JOURNAL. d Je 19-Jl 25 1877||
MNF complete

Northampton JOURNAL. *See* Hampshire county journal

NORTHAMPTONIAN. w O 22-N 18 1921||
MNF complete

OAK. bw Jl 1852-My 5 1853||?
MNF 1852-My 5 1853

OLD HAMPSHIRE post. w Ap 19 1825-Ap 22 1828||
1825-Ap 10 1827 as Franklin post and Christian freeman (Greenfield)
DLC complete
MB 1825-Ap 11 1826
MDeHi Ap 19 1825-Ap 11,My 9-23,Je 20 1826; Jl 3 1827
MNF complete
MWA 1825-Ap 10,My 1827-Ap 15 1828
MiU-C [1825-28]

REPUBLICAN and Hampshire and Franklin advertiser. w F 18 1835-40||?
1835-38? as Hampshire republican
Ct [1835-37]F 7 1838
DLC Ap 22 1835;Je 22,Ag 3,D 28 1836;N 7 1838
MBAt N 4 1840
MDeHi O 7 1835;N 7 1838;Mr 27,Jl 17,Ag 14 1839
MHi Mr 11,O 21 1835
MNF [1835-Je 1838]-N 10 1840
MWA Mr 25,Ap 8,22,Jl 22,N 4 1835;O 3 1838; Ap 10 1839;Je ? (extra)1840
MiU-C (1836-37;40]
NhD My 15 1839
OClWHi F 26 1840

Northampton weekly TIMES. w Je 6-N 23 1924||
MNF complete

NORTHBORO

Northboro TIMES. w 1860-
MWA Ja 4 1862

NORTHFIELD

Northfield HERALD. *See* Northfield press

Northfield PRESS. w Ap 10 1931+
1931-Je 1935 as Northfield herald
pub 1931+

NORWOOD

Norwood ADVERTISER. w 1883-1912||?
1886-94 as Advertiser and review
MNr O 15 1888-D 15 1894
MWA D 22 1894

Norwood MESSENGER. w,sw 1895+
w 1895-1929
pub 1896+
M Ap 11-15 1930
MNr F 13 1898+

MASSACHUSETTS (*Continued*)

OAK BLUFFS

Earlier names of city: Wesleyan Grove; Vineyard Grove; Cottage City

CAMP MEETING herald. d Ag 6 1862-
Issued during period of meeting only
MEdV Ag 11 1862;Ag 19 1864;Ag 27 1866;Ag 14-17 1867;Ag 17 1869
MWA Ag 7-8 1862;Ag 21-22,24 1866

CAMP MEETING herald and Oak Bluffs gazette. w Jl 14 1862-71||?
1862-69? as Camp meeting herald
MEdV Ag 11 1862;Ag 19 1864;71

COTTAGE CITY star. w,sw My 22 1879-My 14 1884||
sw 1880
MEdV [Jl 14 1883-84]
MWA Ag 11,18 1880;Je 1,22,S 3 1882;My 23,O 31 1883

MARTHA'S Vineyard herald. w 1879-O 25? 1888||
CtY N 24 1887-O 11 1888
DLC Je 2 1887-O 11 1888
ICHi Ja 5-O 4 1888
KHi N 1887-88
M N 3 1887-O 11 1888
MB N 1887-O 11 1888
MH N 1887-O 1888
MHi N 1887-O 11 1888
MWA N 1887-Jl 21 1888
MnU N 1887-O 1888
P N 10 1887-88

SEASIDE gazette. sw,d 1872-75||
sw in summer; d during camp meeting week
MEdV Jl 1873-[75]
MWA Jl 25 1873

OAKHAM

Oakham HERALD. w Ag 6 1890-Je 18 1902||
MWA complete

ORANGE

Orange ENTERPRISE. w 1885-98||
United with Orange journal to form Orange enterprise and journal

Orange ENTERPRISE and journal. w Mr 25 1871+
1871-83 as Journal of industry; 1883-98 Orange journal
pub 1871+

JOURNAL of industry. *See* Orange enterprise and journal

OXFORD

MID-WEEKLY. w O 28 1885-Jl 25 1900||?
MOx 1885-1900
MWA 1885-Jl 1900
NcD [Ag 1886-Jl 1890]F 11,Ap 22,Je 10,S 23-30 1891;Jl 25 1894;Ja 30,N 6 1895

PALMER

Palmer JOURNAL-REGISTER. w Ap 6 1850+
1850-1925 as Palmer journal
pub 1850+
NcD Mr 26 1925
MWA My 8 1852;Jl 5 1856;O 20-27,N 17 1860;Je 24 1865;Je 30 1866;F 13,27 1869;Je 18 1886;Mr 26 1925
MWal N 23 1933+
P-M My 13 1854

PEABODY

To My 1868? as South Danvers

Peabody ADVERTISER. w 1876-Je 1 1895||
1876-N 4 1893 as Peabody reporter. United with Peabody press to form Peabody union
DLC O 1885-Ja 9 1886;D 9 1893
MSaE [1876]-[80-84]-[95]
MWA 1886-95

Peabody ENTERPRISE. w My 10 1912+
pub 1912+
M Mr 1917+
MSaE Ag 12 1912;Ag 1-8,D 5 1919

Peabody PRESS. *See* Peabody union

Peabody REPORTER. *See* Peabody advertiser

SOUTH DANVERS wizard. *See* Peabody union

TIMES. w
MSaE [1879-80]

Peabody TIMES. w Mr 3 1924+
pub 1924+
MSaE 1924[25]-31

Peabody UNION. w,sw D 7 1859-D 28 1895||
1858-N 28 1860 as Wizard; D 5 1860-My 13 1868 South Danvers wizard; My 20 1868-Je 1895 Peabody press (Je-Ag 1890 Peabody semi-weekly press)
sw Ja 28 1888-Ag 30 1890
DLC D 12 1860-My 29,N 27 1861-[63-Ap 1866] Ja 23-30,F 13,My 15,Je 26,Jl 17,O 9 1867;O 7,28 1868;69-84;88;93
ICHi My 1 1861
MBe 1881;85-86
MSaE [1859]-[68]-[95]
MWA 1859-F 13,O 9,23,N 7 1867;Ja 29 1868;90;S 3-10 1892;Jl-D 1895
NcD D 14-21 1859[F-N 1860]F 7 1870;78;S 5 1883
OClWHi F 7 1870

WIZARD. *See* Peabody union

PEMBROKE

BELLOWS. w Ag 12 1868-
MH Ag 12 1868
MiU-C Ag 12 1868

PITTSFIELD

ARGUS. w My 24 1827-S 1 1831||
United with Berkshire journal (Lenox) to form Journal and argus, later Berkshire county eagle
CSmH Je 5 1828
CtY Mr 4 1830
DLC S 10-26,D 3,24 1829-Ja 21 1830
LU [1829-30]
MWA Mr 27 1828;Jl 16,30,Ag 6 1829;Je 17 1830;Ap 7 1831
OClWHi N 22 1827

BERKSHIRE American. *See* Berkshire American and Adams manufacturer (North Adams)

***BERKSHIRE county eagle.** w D 1 1789+
1789-1806 as Western star (Je 17-F 27 1794 Andrew's western star) 1807-N 23 1815 Berkshire reporter; N 30 1815-28 Berkshire star; 1828-29 Berkshire star and county republican; S 3 1829-S 1831 Berkshire journal; O 1831-Ag 20 1834 Journal and argus; Ag 27 1834-49 Massachusetts eagle
Ap 13 1926 is anniversary no
1789-1806;N 30 1815-28 pub is Stockbridge; 1828-44 in Lenox (1842-43 pub in Lenox and Pittsfield
pub 1839-49;N 1853
Ct Ag 23,S 13-20 1877;S 19 1878
CtHi My 1855-Jl 24 1857
DLC 1821;Ag 28 1828;S 3,17,O 1,29,N 19,D 24-31 1829;Ja 21 1830;Ap 6 1837;S 19 1839
ICHi 1825-26
ICM O 18 1888
MB Ag 24 1837-Ag 16 1838;Ja 1 1845
MBAt My 13 1824;S 17 1829
MDeHi S 21 1843
MH Mr 1823-Ja 1 1824
MHi Ag 18,O 20 1836;O 29-N 5 1835
MPi 1821-22;My 24 1827-Mr 6,Ag 27 1835-Ag 9 1838;Ja 2,N 12 1840;Ap 12 1842;Je 29 1843;Ap 19,N 14 1845;Ja 30,My 15,Je 5 1846;Ap 16 1847;Jl 12,Ag 25-S 1,22,N 17 1848;Ja 4 1850;D 3 1851;O 29 1852;55-62;Jl 16 1863;65+
MWA S 23,D 23 1824;My 26,Je 9 1825;D 4 1828;D 1 1831;Ag 28 1834-Ag 20 1835;O 6 1836;O 12 1837;My 24,Je 14 1838;S 5 1839;D 15 1842[44]Ag 9 1845;Je 12,N 20 1846;Ja 25,Mr 15,S 13 1850;Mr 4,Ap 22-29,D 23 1853;My 12 1854;Mr 2-23 1855;F 20 1857;F 4,Ap 22 1859;S 12-19 1861;Je 25,N 5 1863;Ja 6,F 4 1864;N 2 1865;Mr 8-15 1866;D 3 1868;O 17-24,D 19 1872;S 2 1875;F 24,My 18,N 9 1876;Ap 12-19,N 22 1877[79]Ag 5,O 21-N 4 1880[82-83]Ja-O 1884;My 14-D 1885[88-90;93]Mr 7,Jl 25,Ag 8 1894 [95]My 10,Je 21,N 8 1899;Ag 8 1900;Ja 2 1901;S 3,O 15-22 1902;Mr 11,N 4 1903
MiU-C [1824]
N N 7 1833
NN S 8 1825
NNHi O-D 1821;Ag 18 1836;F 3 1842
NcD O 12 1882;O 4 1883;Ja 26 1888;F 6 1890
OClWHi O 23 1823;My 13,27,Ag 25 1824
P-M S 30 1830;F 20 1834;Mr 15 1838;N 26 1839;Ja 1 1843;O 31 1845;D 8 1854
PEL D 28 1826
PWbW [1836-37]

BERKSHIRE county whig. w 1841-
CtY Ja 27,F 3,10,My 10 1842
DLC Jl 8 1841
MPi Mr 11 1841-F 1849
MWA Ag 14 1845
N Ag 18 1842
P-M Ap 24 1845

BERKSHIRE culturist. *See* Culturist and gazette

BERKSHIRE evening eagle. d My 9 1892+
pub Jl 1892+
M Je 1899+
MAd current year only
MH F 4 1926
MWA Ap 13 1926

BERKSHIRE journal. *See* Berkshire county eagle

BERKSHIRE Sunday record. w 1893-96||
MPi Je 18 1893-Mr 29 1896

BERKSHIRE resort topics. w 1903-06||?
pub only during season
MPi 1903-04

BERKSHIRE star. *See* Berkshire county eagle

Sunday morning CALL. w 1888-1902||?
LU D 1894-N 1895
MPi N 22 1891-N 5 1899;N 1900-N 2 1902
MWA [F-S 1890]N 20 1892;Mr 14,Ap 4,My 2 1897

Morning CALL. d F 17 1896-
MWA F 17,Ap 25 1896

CULTURIST and gazette. w 1848-
1848- as Berkshire culturist
LU 1855
MPi Jl 12 1848-49;56-D 15 1858
MWA Je 30 1852;S 13,O 18 1854
P-M D 20 1854

Pittsfield JOURNAL. d 1880+
Jl 1 1911 is 150th anniversary ed
M Jl 1 1911

Evening JOURNAL. *See* Daily news

JOURNAL and argus. *See* Berkshire county eagle

MASSACHUSETTS eagle. *See* Berkshire county eagle

NEW ENGLAND cataract. w Je 27 1844-
CoHi Je 24 1845
MWA [Jl 18-D 1844]-Jl 1845
P-M Ap 22,D 10 1845
PPiHi Ja 9 1845

Daily NEWS. d S 27 1880-1917||
1880-1915 as Evening journal
LU [1880]-86
MHi [1884-89]
MPi 1880-94;96-1917
MWA Ap 8 1895

Pittsfield Sunday POST. w 1927+
M Ja 22 1928

***Pittsfield SUN.** w S 16 1800-S 27 1906||
1800-D 30? 1805 as Sun (My 23 1803-S 8? 1804 Pittsfield sun) Ja 6 1806-07? Pittsfield sun; or, Republican monitor S 27 1900 is Centennial ed
Index: 1800-1905
Ct [1830-31;33-38]S 19 1877
DLC D 3 1821;N 4 1828;N 1 1832;Je 7,Ag 2 1838
LU [1830]77-83
M S 27 1900
MPi 1821-1906(and index)
MWiC N 1 1860;O 28 1874;N 6 1878
MWA 1821-[57-Ap 1865]-Je 1869;S 22 1870;F 23,My 18 1871;My 29 1872;Mr 26-Ap 2 1873 [74]F 9,Mr 8,Je 28 1876;Ap 11-25 1877;S 3,O 29 1879;Je 9,N 3 1880;Je 8(supp)N 9 1881;D 7 1882;Jl 23,S 24 1885;Je 17,S 2,O 28-N 4 1886;N 15,D 20 1888;Ja 31,My 23 1889;F 6-13,Mr 27 1890;Ap 30 1891;Ja 21,Ag 11-25 1892;Mr 9 1893;Ag 9 1894;N 7,D 5-12 1895;Ja 7 1897;O 12 1899-F 8,Mr 29 1900;Je 25 1903
MiU-C [1821-22;24]
N My 1,D 19 1822;Je 19,O 2 1823;Je 1 1826;Ag 20 1829-30;O 17 1833;Jl 18 1850
NN [1822]-24
NNHi Ag 20-27 1829
NcD Ja 24 1821;S 19,O 3,17 1822;F 22 1827 [28-31;35-36;39;54;58;67-69;76;79-80;90;99]
OClWHi Ag 6 1840;Mr 4,Jl 15 1841;Ja 22 1879
P-M O 3 1833;D 4 1834;S 24 1835;My 19 1836;Jl 13 1837;Je 27 1839
WHi Jl 31,Ag 14,S 19 1822;O 16,30 1823;Mr 17 1825

PLYMOUTH

Plymouth daily JOURNAL. d D 21 1916-
MWA D 21 1916

Plymouth JOURNAL and the Massachusetts advertiser. d Jl 29-Ag 31 1896||
MDeHi Ag 1 1896
MSaE Jl 31 1896
NNHi complete
NcD Jl 29 1896

OLD COLONY democrat. w F 16 1833-
MHi F 16,Mr 30,S 14,O 19-26 1833;O 2 1834
MWA 1833-F 8 1834
P-M S 28 1833

OLD COLONY memorial. w My 4 1822+
1822-My 5 1827 as Old Colony memorial, and Plymouth county advertiser; 1864?-68? Old Colony memorial and Plymouth Rock
pub 1822+
CtY 1822-[24]Jl 28 1827;Ja 20 1837
DLC 1822-[24]-26;Ap 21,Ag 25,S 29 1827;28;Mr 28,Jl 4,Ag 8,S 26,N 28,D 26 1829;My 22 1841
ICHi Jl 1822;Mr 8-29 1823
M 1822-Ap 1824[1928-33]
MB 1822-Ap 22 1824
MBAt 1822-O 1823;O 9 1824;D 31 1825;Je 10 1826-My 5 1827;O 10 1829
MDeHi O 19 1822
MH Je 29,Ag 10,S 28,O 12 1822;S 22 1832;O 8 1915
MHi My 8,Jl 3 1824;O 1 1836
MTaHi 1822-Ap 1824
MWA 1822-[29-32]S 27 1834;D 19 1835;Mr 21,Je 13,S 5 1840;O 7 1843;Mr 23,Ap 20,Je 22 1844;D 20? 1845;F 14,Jl 10 1852;Ap 21 1855;Ag 20 1859;Jl 7 1860;F 23 1866;Je 17(extra)1868?;My 16 1872;D 21 1876;Ap 11,Je 20 1878;Ja 28 1886;Ag 9 1888;Je 1 1895;My 5 1922
MeBa Jl 8 1826
MiU-C [1822-24;28-48]
NN O 10(extra)1866
NNHi My 4,O 12 1822-[Ja-Ap 1825;36]My-D 1827;Jl 15 1837;My 22-Je 5 1863;F 20 1873
NcD F 10 1827;Ja 24,Mr 7,D 19 1829;Mr 2,Ap 6 1876
NjR [1824-25]
OClWHi Ap 12 1862
P-M S 14 1833;Jl 12 1834
WHi My 3 1828

OLD COLONY sentinel. w 1864-Je 1872||
Merged with Old Colony memorial
MWA Jl 25 1868
OClWHi Ja 20 1866

PILGRIM; or, Plymouth county chronicle and domestic and foreign intelligencer. w My 17 1832-
M 1832-Jl 4 1833

PLYMOUTH ROCK. w Ja 25 1838-63||
Title varies: . . . and Old Colony reporter; . . . and county advertiser. United with Old Colony memorial to form Old Colony memorial and Plymouth Rock, later Old Colony memorial
Ct Ja 25 1838
DLC O 25 1838;S 19 1839;My 28 1840;Je 3,Jl-D 9 1852;Ja 20,F 3,24,Ag 11 1853
MH [Mr 30-D 18 1851]
MHi Mr 21,My 9,23,Je 27-Jl 4 1839;Mr 5 1846
MWA Ap 5 1838;Jl 8 1841;Ja 20 1848;F 15 1849;My 20,Je 10 1852;O 13 1853;N 1,15 1860;Je 27 1861
NNHi Ag 9 1860
OClWHi F 27 1840;Jl 4 1844
P-M Je 1,Jl 27 1854

MASSACHUSETTS (*Continued*)

PLYMOUTH—*Continued*

PLYMOUTH ROCK free press. w Jl 20 1872-1903||?
MH Jl-Ag 10,23-30 1872

TOWN crier. w 1916-17||
MWA My 8-15 1917

WE the people. w O 27 1832-
1832-N 29? 1834 as We, the people and Old Colony press
MHi 1832-[35]
MWA My 18 1833

WHITMAN times and Plymouth county courier.
Je 7,14 1912 issues are in celebration of the 200th anniversary of the old town of Abington, Mass.
MeBa Je 7,14 1912

PROVINCETOWN

Provincetown ADVOCATE. w 1869+
pub 1869-75;79+
MWA Ag 10 1933

Provincetown BANNER. w 1855-
MWA Ap 9 1857;Ja 3 1861

Provincetown BEACON. w Ag 2 1890-1918||?
CtW Ag 9 1890

QUINCY

Quincy ADVERTISER. w,sw N 13 1884-Ja 30 1914||
w 1884-95?
MQ complete

Quincy AURORA. w Ja 1843?-
MWA Mr 27,S 11 1845

Quincy ENTERPRISE. w 1920-23||?
MQ [Je 25 1920-Je 2 1922]

Quincy HERALD.
NSyU Ja 29(extra)1844

Quincy LAMP. w 1888-
MQ F 4-D 1 1888

Quincy LEADER. w 1903-05||
MQ My 9 1903-F 4 1905

Quincy daily LEDGER. d Ap 8 1890-D 31 1915||
United with Quincy patriot to form Quincy patriot-ledger
MQ complete
MWA Ap 27 1895

Quincy MERCHANTS bulletin. m,w 1910-15||?
m 1910-11
MQ D 15 1911-Ap 16,My 7 1915

Quincy MONITOR. m Ap 1886-98||?
MQ 1886-94;96-My 1898

Quincy evening NEWS. d S 20 1928+
pub 1928+
M [1928-F 4 1933]
MQ 1928+

Quincy PATRIOT-LEDGER. w,d Ja 1 1837+
1837-1915 as Quincy patriot
w 1837-90
pub 1837+
Ct Ja 14 1837
DLC 1837-Ja 16 1847;Mr 3 1849;54-55
M [1928-Jl 1933]
MBAt Ja-Mr 10 1838;Je 9 1930
MH Jl 4-11 1885;Ap 10-17 1886
MHi Jl 8 1873
MQ 1837+
MWA Mr 18 1837;F 23 1839;D 12 1840;F 13 1841;Ag 19 1843;Ja 27 1844;Ag 17 1850;Ja 24, Ag 28 1852;Je 11 1853
NFj Mr 7 1840
NN Je 18,Jl 2-16 1842;Jl 28 1849
NNHi O 4 1856;Ag 1 1863;F 15 1873
NcD Ap 8 1876
NhD N 10 1849
OClWHi F 11 1837;O 24 1840;My 5 1866

Quincy evening TELEGRAM. d 1909-F 12 1927||
Merged with Quincy patriot-ledger
MQ 1909-27

THIRD HILL searchlight. w 1914-15||
MQ D 10 1914-Jl 30 1915

Quincy TRANSCRIPT. w 1927-
MQ Jl 15-O 14 1927

Quincy daily WHIG and republican. d
NjVi [O 1860-S 30 1861]

RANDOLPH

Randolph ADVERTISER. *See* Transcript and advertiser

EAST NORFOLK register. *See* Randolph register and Holbrook news

Randolph HERALD. w 1930+
pub 1930+
MRa 1931+

NORFOLK county register. *See* Randolph register and Holbrook news

Randolph REGISTER and Holbrook news. w 1865-1910||
1865-66 as East Norfolk register; 1887-89 Norfolk county register (title varies slightly)
pub 1886-1900
MHo 1873-84
MRa 1866-1910
MWA Jl 21 1866;Jl 15 1871

Randolph SENTINEL news. w 1909+
pub 1909+

TRANSCRIPT and advertiser. w 1857-65||
1857-62 as Randolph advertiser
Suspended from O 1863-D 1864
MRa 1858-65
MWA N 8 1862;My 16 1863;Ja 28-F 4,18,Mr 25,Ag 5 1865

READING

Reading CHRONICLE. w My 28 1870+
1870-D 18 1880 as Weekly news and chronicle
pub 1897+
MR 1870+
MWA [F 12-D 1881]-85;O 12 1889-F 8 1890[Ag 1892-93]-[95]-[98;1900]-[Ja-S 1902;F-Ag 1903; 04-07]09-[13]-[Ja-S 1915]
NcD Ap 22 1899;N 3,D 1900[01]-Ja 11,25 1902; My 6 1910

FATHER Abraham. w My 10 1864-
MH My 10 1864

Weekly NEWS and chronicle. *See* Reading chronicle

REHOBETH

Rehobeth TOWNSMAN. w 1884-94||?
My 12 1886 is historical number
MWA My 12 1886

REVERE

Revere BUDGET. w 1910+
Je 7 1930 is 20th anniversary and tercentenary ed
pub 1910+
M [Ag 1930-O 1932]

Revere HOME TALK. w 1924+
MReC 1936+

Revere JOURNAL. w F 5 1881+
pub 1881+
MWA F 27 1932

ROCKLAND

Rockland INDEPENDENT. w 1884-Ap 27 1933||
Merged with Rockland standard
pub complete
M [Mr 16 1928-33]
MH S 1900-Ap 21 1911;Mr 13 1925
MWA N 26 1915
NN S 1898-Ag 18 1899;S 1900-S 5 1902;Jl 24 1903-Jl 1907

Rockland STANDARD. w 1854+
pub 1854+
M 1900+
MRo 1876+

ROCKPORT

Rockport GLEANER. m Ja 1872-87||
MSaE 1872-81;Ap 1882;83-85
MWA Jl 1873;Jl 1875;My-Je 1877

Rockport QUARRY. w Ja 3? 1868-
MH Je-Jl 18 1868
MSaE [1868]
MWA Je,Jl 11-18 1868

Rockport REVIEW. w D 10 1881-1918||
MSaE [1881-90]F 11 1893[94]Jl 8,O 21 1899 [1900]-[08-09]-[17-18]
MWA Ja 28-F 4,Mr 4 1882
NcD [1883-85;87;94;1901-02;07;10-11]

ROSLINDALE

Papers published in Roslindale are listed under Boston

ROWLEY

Rowley ADVOCATE. w My 1898-1901||?
MSaE O 8,28-N 4 1898
MWA Ja 6 1899

ROXBURY

Papers published in Roxbury are listed under Boston

SALEM

Salem ADVERTISER. sw 1832-
Ct [1837]
MBeHi O 20 1841-F 18,O 22-D 1842;F-Ap 1843
MMarHi N 25 1846;N 13 1847
MSaE [1832-35]-[36-39;41-44]
MWA Ag 2,9,19-26 1837[Mr-Jl 1838;39]Ag 9 1848
NNHi S 5-N 14 1840

Salem ADVOCATE. w 1848?-
1848?-58 as People's advocate
MB O 29 1853;O 6 1855;Je 12-19 1858[Je 9-D 1860]-Ja 19,Ap 27,My 11 1861
MWA Mr 24 1860

AMERICAN justifier. *See under* Boston

Daily ARGUS. d Je 8 1881-
MSaE [1881-84]
MWA Je 8,11-15,22 1881

Saturday evening BULLETIN. w F ? 1833-
MSaE [1833-34]
MWA Mr 22 1834

Salem daily CALL. d 1890-91||
MSaE [1890-91]

Salem daily CHRONICLE. d Mr 1 1848-
MHi Mr 1-2,15-16,18,22,27-28,30,Ap 1,5,7,15,17, 19,26,28,My 10-11,19 1848
MSaE [1848]
MWA Mr 1-4,18,Ap 5-7,20-22,My 2,6,18 1848

COMMERCIAL advertiser and Essex county journal. w Ap 4 1832-
Title varies slightly
Ct [1834-36]
MBAt 1832-Ap 3,N 13 1835;N 2-9 1836
MMarHi D 17 1834
MWA Jl 29 1835;Je 29 1836
N O 16 1833

CONSTITUTIONALIST. w
MHi Jl 12,O 25,D 27 1834-Ja 3 1835
MSaE [1834]Ja 3 1835

Salem COURIER. w S 17 1828-S 9 1829||
DLC S 2 1829
MBAt complete
MHi 1828;Ja 14,26,F,Ap 22-Jl 1,S 9 1829
MSaE [1828-29]
MWA complete
MiU-C S 2 1829

Le COURRIER de Salem. w 1901+
In French
pub 1912+
M Ag 1908+
MSaE Jl 13 1905;S 27-O 4 1906[07]-31

Salem DEMOCRAT. w
MHi Jl 31-O 2 1852;Mr 15 1854

Salem DISPATCH. w My 26 1861-
My-O 13 1861 as Sunday morning dispatch
MSaE [1861]Ja 1 1862
MWA My-Je 2,O 13,30,N 13-27 1861

DISPATCH-GAZETTE. d 1908-17||?
1908-13 as Dispatch (running title: Howard's dispatch)
MSaE [1910-17]

Salem ENTERPRISE. w 1867-Ja 29 1868||
MHi Jl 12-17,31,Ag 14,S 25 1867
MSaE [1867-68]D 1876
MWA Ja 29 1868

ESSEX county constellation. *See under* Newburyport

ESSEX county democrat. sw N 2 1838-
DLC N 7 1838
MHi N 2,17,24,D 8 1838
MSaE [1838]
MWA N 6-9 1838

ESSEX county freeman. sw,w Ag 1 1849-
sw 1849-F 1 1854
MSaE [1849]-54
MWA Ag 1-3,15-18,N 28,D 8,19 1849[Ja 30-Je 1]Ag 1850-F 14,Mr 3,O 27,N 6,14-17 1852;O 12 1853;F 1,Mr 24,Je 14 1854
NSyU N 14-17 1852

ESSEX county mercury. w Je 8 1831-1902||?
1840-43? as Salem mercury. Subtitle varies: . . . and Danvers courier; . . . Danvers, Beverly and Marblehead courier; . . . and weekly Salem gazette; etc. Merged with Salem register to form Salem register and Essex county mercury, later Salem register
CSmH Ja 16 1861
DLC 1857-61;64-Ag 21 1867;70;74-[76]N 28,D 19 1877-Ap 17,Je 26-Jl 3,O 2,23-D 1878
ICM Je 2 1886
MB S 5 1848;Ja 28 1852[Ja 16-D 24 1862]Ja 7 1863 Jl 27-Ag 3 1864;Ja 18 1865;O 3 1866; Ag 5 1868;F 24 1869;Jl 19-26 1871;My 5 1875
MBe F 16-D 1898
MBeHi 1840
MH Ja 11 1865;Mr 5(supp)1884
MHi [1831-39]Ap 10 1861;S 21 1864;O 24 1883
MMarHi O 16 1844;Ag 1 1860;Jl 7,N 10 1875; D 3 1879;Ag 11 1880
MSaE 1831-[38-39]S 16 1840;45-1902
MWA Jl 13 1831-My 1832;33-My,O 15 1834;My 6,Jl 22 N 18,D 2,30 1835;Ap 13,S 21 1836;Jl 5,O 18,N 8 1837;F 27 1839;F 5,19,Mr 4,Ap 8 1840;Mr 30,Je 15,Ag 3 1842;D 13 1843[Ap 30-Ag 13]D 10 1845[Ja 14-Ap]O 28 1846;O 6,D 22 1847;Ap 26,O 18 1848;O 24,D 19 1849;Ap 17,Je 19,O 23,D 18 1850;Mr 26,My 28,Ag 13, S 10 1851;Ja 21,F 4,25,Je 23 1852;Ap 13-27 1853;Ag 19 1857;Ja-F,Jl 6 1859;Ja 15,F 12,Ap 30-My 7,S 3 1862;Ja 6-13,Jl 20,Ag 3 1864;Jl 5,Ag 2 1865;Mr 10,N 10 1869;My 22,S 18,D 25 1872;Ap 30,N 26 1873;Ap 22,D 23 1874;N 3 1875;S 5,19,D 5 1877;S 25 1878;Ja 29,O 29 1879;S 21(supp)D 7 1881;Ja 25(supp)Je 28 1882;Ag 8 1883-O,D 14 1892-[93]Ja 17,Mr 14, Ap 11,Ag 1-8 1894
Mi Ag 12 1857;F 24 1858;S 7 1859
NN D 7 1831;D 26 1832
NhD Ag 7 1880;Ap 30,Jl 9 1851;Ja 14,D 22-29 1852;Mr 23,Ap 20,Je 29,Jl 20-27 1853
OClWHi F 14 1866

ESSEX county reformer. w S 2 1843-
MHi S 2-16 1843
MSaE [1843]
NAubHi S 16-N 25 1843

ESSEX county Washingtonian. *See under* Lynn

ESSEX register. *See* Salem register

ESSEX statesman. sw,w Je 17 1863-Je 27 1868||
MH O 10 1863;Je 20-27 1868
MSaE 1863-[67]
MWA Je 17,Jl 22,D 5,20 1863;Ja 13-16,Ag 17 1864;Ap 28 1866;Je 20-27 1868
OClWHi Jl 25 1866

EVANGELIST. w Ag 12 1843-F 17 1844||?
MHi S 2,30-O 14,28-N 18,D 2-16,30 1843;F 10 1844
MSaE [1843-44]
MWA D 9-30 1843
NAubHi 1843-F 17 1844

FREE world. w Ag 14-N 3 1848||
Campaign paper
MHi [1848]
MSaE [1848]
MWA Ag-S 1,15-O 13,27-N 1848

MASSACHUSETTS (*Continued*)

SALEM—*Continued*

*Salem daily GAZETTE. w,sw,tw,d Ja 5 1790-Ag 29 1908||
Follows Salem mercury (not in this list) w 1790-My 1796;sw 1796-O 14 1892(tw 1847-51?)
CSmH [1821-92;Mr 20 1893-O 1 1898]
Ct [1826]
CtY O 17 1892-96
DLC 1821-22;D 5,9-12,19-23 1823[24]Ja 3,Mr 17,21,My 2,30,Je 9 1826;Mr 2,Jl 6,Ag 28[O-D]1827;Ap 8,29,My 16-20,Je 3,17,S 23,O 21,31 1828;Ja 30[Je-D]1829-[Jl-O 1830]Ja 4 1831; Mr 30 1838;My 26,D 8 1840;D 12 1845;Ja 2 1846;F 12,20,My 7 1847;O 20,28,N 4,10-11,17, 24 1848;Ja 27,Mr 6,10,17,Je 15-16,O 19 1849; N 11 1851;Mr 9,Ag 6,O 29 1852;N 29 1853;S 29 1854;S 18 1855;Mr 2 1858;Mr 17 1868[Ja-Ap 1869]Mr 22 1870;Jl 23 1872;D 26,O 22,D 3 1878;Ja 4,11,Mr 4,11-14,Ap 1 1879;Ag 26 1881-97
ICN [1822-Ap 11 1823]
ICU [1830]32[33]
M O 17 1892-1908
MB 1821-39;41-66;Je 21,N 5,D 10,20 1867;68-73; My 4,21 1875-90;O-1891;Ja 1892;S 30,O 28,D 9 1893;F 27 1894
MBAt 1821-22;24-26;Je 19 1827-30;32-33;39-70; D 19(supp)1871;N 30(supp)1875;81-86
MBC 1822;24;26
MBeHi 1822;24-33[37]-[39-41;61-85;88-89]
MH 1821-O 6 1826;Mr 9 1827[S 23-D 1828]-S 15 1829[30]-O 1831;O 3-7,14,D 23 1834[35-37; 40-41]N 6 1860;N 12 1880;N 9 1883;F 18 1890
MHi 1821-[30-38;42-44]-Je 8 1855;Ap 4 1861; Je 6 1865
MMarHi Mr 5 1821;Mr 27 1822;Mr 19 1846;Jl 17 1855-S 14 1860;F 10 1875;76;Ja 4,My 9-15, Jl 24 1877;Ja 22 1878
MSaE 1821-[1908]
MWA 1821-[23-24]-29;Ja 8,Mr 12,19,Ap 13 1830;F 25,Mr 15,N 18 1831;Ap 3 1832;N 24 1835;Ja 26,Ap 19,29,My 27,Jl 26-29,D 5 1836; My 23 1837;Ja 9,Mr 6,O 30,D 7 1838;Mr 8, Ap 2,N 1,D 24 1839;Ap 21 1840[41]Ja 23,My 24 1844;Jl 15 1845;Mr 24 1846;S 11,O 16 1847; O 28 1848;S 29,O 6 1849;Mr 29,D 31 1850;Mr 21,Ap 1 1851;O 19 1852;Ap 19,Ag 19,S 9,O 11, N 29 1853;Mr 28,Je 9,13,Jl 11,Ag 29 1854[55-Mr 1859]F 10,Mr 9,Jl 27 1860;Ap 2,Jl 26,O 15 1861;Ja 7,Mr 11,Jl 4 1862;Ap 14 1863;Jl 7 1865;My 17,D 31(supp)1867;S 8,O 13(supp)N 24 1868;Ja 4,25,F 18,O 28 1870;Mr 17,S 19,O 6 1871;Jl 23-26,S 3,N 15 1872;O 2 1874;N 30 1875;Jl 3,Ag 1 1876;Je 5 1877;My 30 1879[Je-D 1880]-95;Ja 25,My 10 1898;My 29 1909;O 2 1910
Mi Je 24 1851;Mr 9 1860
MiU-C [1821-25;59;87;89;91]
MnU 1828
N 1821-22;Ja-D 16 1828;D 15 1837;O 25 1839; 47-50
NN Ja 8 1822
NNHi O 19 1821;Jl 20 1824;Jl 11 1843;Mr 10 1871;Ap 11,My 30 1873
NcD [1825]
OClWHi Je 29 1830;F 9 1866
PPL [Jl-O 1826]
WHi 1821;23-24;Ap 14 1826-N 23 1827;41-42

Salem GAZETTE. 1892-1911 *See* North Shore gazette

HARRISONIAN. w,ir F 22- 1840||
Campaign paper
MSaE F 22,Mr-Ap[Je,Ag,N]1840
MWA O 1840
OClWHi My 1840

HOWARD'S dispatch. *See* Dispatch-gazette

INDEPENDENT democrat. w
MSaE [1843]

Salem evening JOURNAL. d Jl 24? 1854-
Jl-Ag 14 1854 as Salem daily journal
MSaE F 22,Mr-Ap[Je,Ag,N]1840
MWA [Jl 27 1854-My 1855]

JOURNAL de Salem. w 1902-
In French
MSaE [1902]

LANDMARK. sw Ag 20 1834-
DLC S 13 1834
MB 1834-O 1836
MBAt S 12 1835
MH Jl 4 1835
MHi Jl 23,27 1836
MSaE [1834]-[36]
MWA Ag 20,S 27,O 18 1834-Ag 8,22,S 9,N 18 1835;Ja 2,20,F 27,Mr 19,30,Ap 23,Je 27,Jl 9, 23,Ag 10,24,S 21-24,O 5 1836
NNHi 1834-N 2 1836

LIGHTHOUSE. w My 11 1835-
MHi My-O 1835
MSaE 1835
MWA Je 8,27,Ag 22 1835

Salem LITERARY and commercial observer. *See* Saturday evening observer

LOCOMOTIVE: an independent journal. w Ja 26 1842-Ja-D 7? 1842 pub in Lynn
CtY Jl 6 1842
MHi D 17,31 1842;Ja 31,F 4,18,Mr 4,Ap 1-8, 22-29,My 27 1843
MSaE [1842-43]
MWA Jl 13,O 12,D 31 1842

Salem evening MAIL. d S 30 1915-16||?
MSaE [1915-16]
MWA S 30 1915

Salem MERCURY. 1840-43 *See* Essex county mercury. . .

Salem MERCURY. w Ag 6 1914-My 20 1917||
M 1915-17
MSaE [1916-17]
MWA Ag 6 1914

NATIONAL democrat. w
MSaE My 24 1851

NEW ENGLAND Washingtonian. w
MSaE [1842-44]

Daily evening NEWS. d
MHi [1868]
MSaE [1868]

Salem evening NEWS. d O 16 1880+
pub 1880+
M Ag 1908+
MDa 1911+
MSaE [1880]-[83]-[86]-[91]+
MWA My 28,Jl 19,22,27,Ag 3,10,20 1881;Mr 16 1883;Ag 25 1898;Je 30,Jl 6-7,9-10 1926

NORTH SHORE gazette. d 1892-1913||
1892-1911 as Salem gazette. United with Dispatch to form Dispatch-gazette
MSaE 1908-13

Saturday evening OBSERVER. w Ja 6 1823-1918||
Ja-D 27 1823 as Observer; Ja 2 1824-Ja 8 1825 Salem observer; Ja 15-D 24 1825 Salem literary and commercial observer; Ja 5 1828?-Ja 11 1896 Salem observer
Ct [1826-33;35-36]
CtY Mr 15 1823;My 17 1828;S 18 1867;S 12 1868;S 11 1869
DLC 1824-25;F 17,Mr 24 1827-30;O 20 1877-93
ICN D 17 1831
IU 1823-25;28-33[34]-D 19 1835;Ja-Jl 9,S 3,O, N 19,D 3-10 1836;Ja 21 1837-N 24,D 22 1838; Ja 26 1839-[43]-45;F 14,Mr 21,Ap-Je,Jl 11-O, N 14 1846-[50]-[53]55;My 31-Je 7,S 6,N 15 1856;Ap 25,My 9,Je 20,Jl 14,S 12,26,N 7 1857 [Ja-S 1858;59-62]-[75]-[78]-[82]-Ja 12,Mr 15, 29,Ag 23 1884;Ja 10-F 14,Jl 11,Ag 15,O 31-N 14,D 19 1885;Ja 16 1886-[88]-Ja 12,Mr 2,O 26, D 7 1889;Ja 11,28,Je 14,S 6 1890;91-Ja 7,F 4, Mr 4,18,Ap 1,My 13,Je 10-17,Jl 1,Ag 5,26 1893[F 1894-Ag 24 1895]-[99-1900]-Ja 12,Ap 5-12 1901;02;Ap 8,Je 24,S 16 1905;S 22 1906; Je 8 1907;Jl 18 1908;F 10 1912;N 7 1914;My 1,Je 5,O 16 1915;Jl 29 1916;S 22-N 10 1917;My 11,Je 29,Jl 13-N 9,23,D 7 1918
MB 1824;N 1868;Ag 9 1884;Mr 7 1885
MBAt Ap 12 1823;S 18 1824;Jl 18-25 1829;30;N 17 1832
MH My 24 1823;S 1 1849
MMarHi Mr 4 1854
MNaHi Je 29 1844
MSaE 1823-44;48-86;89-91;93-95;97-1904;06-15
MWA 1823[24]-[Ja-Je]Ag 1 1829[30]F 12,26, Mr 19,Ap 9-16,Je 25 1831;Jl 27 1833;Ag 30 1834;36-37;F 24,My 19,Ag 4 1838;Mr 2-9,Jl 6, S 21,D 14-21 1839;Mr 14,Jl 18,O 3-10,N 28 1840;My 15,Je 26,Ag 7,D 18 1841;Ja 15-22,F 26 1842;Jl 1,Ag 26 1843;N 30 1844[My 10-S 6 1845]Mr 28 1846;47-Ja 5,N 26 1853;O 7,D 2 1854;D 15 1855;Ap 19,Je 14,S 6 1856;Ja 31 1857;60-65;N 7 1868;Jl 22 1871;Mr 6 1875;Ap 5,My 28 1879;S 30 1882;F 17 1883;Jl 24,O 2 1886;Ap 28,Ag 4 1888;O 22 1892;Jl 31 1897;S 9 1899;Ap 13 1907;O 19 1918
Mi Ja 3 1857;My 1 1858;Ja 4 1862
MiG D 29 1877
MiU-C [1823-26]
N Jl 1827-28;Mr 4 1843
NNHi 1825;30;extras:Je 5,Ag 21,D 11 1830
NcD O 7 1837;Jl 13 1850
OClWHi Jl 21 1866;S 3,D 3 1892
PPL [Jl-S 1826]
WHi S 10 1859

PEOPLE'S advocate. *See* Salem advocate

Salem POST. m,w N 1872-82||
1872 as City post; 1873 Salem city post
MH Ag 31 1881
MMarHi O 24 1877
MSaE [1872]-82
MWA D 1872;F 12,My 28,Je 11,Jl 16 1873-[74-Ag 18]D 22 1875;My 23,Jl 11,30 1877;Ap 7-14, 28,S 15 1880;Je 18-19,S 14 1881;Ja 11 1882

Salem evening POST. d 1879-84||
1879-N 30 1881 as Salem post
MSaE [1883-84]
MWA N 5-7,10,12,21-23,26-30,D 2 1881

Salem PUBLIC. w 1887-88||
DLC Jl 2 1887
MSaE 1887[88]
MWA F 11 1888

*Salem REGISTER. sw My 12 1800-My 22 1893||
My-Jl 1800 as Impartial register; Jl 31 1800-D 31 1801 Salem impartial register; Ja 4 1802-Jl 16 1807 Salem register; Jl 23 1807-D 31 1840 Essex register
CLM Jl 2,Ag 6 1885
CSmH S 26 1821;Ja 15 1827;S 2 1830;Ap 19 1832;F 21 1833;F 26 1835;O 20 1836;37-58;Ap-N 10 1859;F-D 6 1860;61-D 14 1865[66-69]Ja 20 1870-[74]Ja 21,Ap 8-O 14 1875;S 29,N 20 1879[80]-[86]F 14-Jl 7 1887;Ag 2 1888;Mr 4, Jl 1-4,11,22,S 2,N 21 1889[90]My 11-14,Je 18, Ag 13,N 26 1891[92]Ja 12,30,F 2,My 1,22 1893
Ct [1827;29]
CtY O 1 1827;N 26 1857;Mr 10 1862;Je 24 1880
DLC 1821-41;61;S 1881-93
M [S 21 1826-Ag 26 1839;51-92]
MB 1822-70;D 11 1871;72-73;Ja-Je 1877
MBAt Ap 3,My 15 1822;24;N 5 1827;28-76
MBeHi 1821-40;75-[87;89-90;92-93]
MH [1835]39-73;S 22,29 1881
MHi Mr 27,Jl 4 1823;Ja 5,Ap 10,Jl 10 1826; My 14,F 5 1827;Mr 28-31,My 5,O 6 1831;O 1 1832;Mr 3,Jl 18,Ag 18,29,O 6 1836;O 26 1837
MMarHi 1821-Ap 12 1886
MWA [1821]-[23-24]-[53]-[61]-[Ja-Je 1864]65 [67-74]Jl 15 1878;Je 13,23 1881;S 1 1884;Mr 25 1886;D 10 1888;Ja 28-F 4,Ap 18,My 16-20,27 1889;Ja 22 1891
MeU Jl 22 1830
Mi D 15 1864;Jl 6 1865;F 18,Mr 4-14 1867;Ja 4 1869
MiG D 13 1877
MiU-C [1821-22;25-26]-[28]-[30-43;45-53;56-63; 65-66;72]
N My 12 1821;Ja 23-Mr 23,Ap 17,My 18,29,Je-Jl 13,Ag 14,21-D 1822;25-27;D 24 1838;Ag 6 1840
NNHi 1822[23-24]26;Ag 19 1830
NcD [1826-27]-[30-34]Ap 17-20 1837;Je 10,Ag 22,O 31 1839[42-50;53-54;57]
NjR Ja 27 1834
OHi 1845
PPL [Jl-O 1826]
REdH N 17-20 1828
WHi Ap 28 1825;F 29,Ap 23,N 26,D 27 1827; Ap 15-Je 24 1830

Salem evening REPORT. d Mr 2 1912-
Mr 2 1912 as Salem report; Mr 7-Je 11 1912 Salem daily morning report
MSaE [1912]
MWA Mr 2,7-9,23,Je 6-11,13 1912

SPECTATOR. d
MSaE O 6-8 1869

Evening TELEGRAM. d 1885-88||?
MSaE 1885-[88]

Daily TIMES. d 1887-88||
MSaE [1887-88]

TIMES and Essex county chronicle. w 1879-80||
MSaE [1879-80]

Salem Sunday TRIBUNE. w 1926+
M Ap 17 1932

UNION democrat. sw
MSaE [1852;58]

VILLAGE record. sm Ag 15 1910-
MSaE Ag 15,S 7 1910;Ap 1911;Ag 2-16 1919; Ap 11 1920
MWA Ag-S 7 1910;Ag 2(extra)1919

VOICE around the jail. Ap 30 1843-
MHi My 28 1843
MSaE Ap 30,My 14,28 1843
MWA Ap 30 1843

WHIG. w?
MSaE F 29,Jl 27 1840

WHIRLWIND and Essex county advertiser. m Jl 1869-
Title varies slightly
MSaE [1869]
MWA Jl 1869

Salem WITCH. w D 16 1865-66||
MSaE D 23 1865-[66]
MWA Ja 10,F 28 1866

SALISBURY MILLS

Papers published in Salisbury Mills are listed under Amesbury

SANDWICH

CAPE COD advocate and nautical intelligencer. w 1850?-
MWA Ag 28 1858;Mr 17 1860

CAPE COD gazette. w 1867-72||?
MWA Ag 10 1871

Sandwich MECHANIC. w
MSanHi O 3 1851

Sandwich OBSERVER. w
WHi S 26 1847-My 24 1851

SAUGUS

Saugus HERALD. w 1887+
pub 1932+
M Mr 25 1932;Jl 7 1933
MSaE D 16 1899[1916]-31
MSau 1912+
MWo Je 9 1894

Saugus evening NEWS. d 1876?-1912||?
MLyI 1877-78
MSaE S 16 1876;Je 4 1881

Saugus REPUBLICAN. w 1899-1905||?
MSaE F 23-N 24 1900

SCITUATE

Scituate HERALD. w 1890+
M N 9 1928
MSc 1936+
MScT 1929-35

Scituate LIGHT. w 1895+
M Ja 16,31 1931;Je 16 1933

UNION. *See under* Duxbury

SHARON

Sharon ADVOCATE. w 1881+
M Ja 13 1934
MSh 1901-07;10-18

SHEFFIELD

Sheffield SENTINEL. w Mr 30 1895-96||?
MWA Mr 30,Jl 20 1895

SHELBURNE FALLS

DEERFIELD VALLEY sun. w
MDeHi 1886

Shelburne Falls GAZETTE. w
-Ag 1886 as Northwestern Massachusetts gazette
MDeHi Ag 25,S 18 1886

NORTHWESTERN Massachusetts gazette. *See* Shelburne Falls gazette

Shelburne Falls STANDARD. w
MDeHi Mr 30,Ap 6,20,My 4-11,25-S 21 1877

MASSACHUSETTS (*Continued*)

SHELBURNE—*Continued*

Weekly VISITOR. w 1887-88||?
MDeHi D 14 1887

Shelburne Falls WORLD. w 1889-
MDeHi D 7 1889

SHREWSBURY

Shrewsbury weekly NEWS. w 1874-95||?
1874-S 29 1881 as Shrewsbury news
MShrHi O 1874-O 8 1876
MWA O 17 1879;S 29 1881;Je 15-Jl 20,Ag 3-17 1886

SOMERVILLE

Somerville ADVERTISER. w Ja 1 1878-80||
NhD Ja 19 1878

Somerville CHRONICLE. w Ap 4 1874-75||
NNHi Ag 8 1874-O 9 1875

Somerville CITIZEN. w Ag 17 1888-1901||?
MWA Ja 11,Je 14 1895;Ag 20 1897;Ja 21 1898

Somerville JOURNAL. w D 3 1870+
pub 1870+
M 1885+
MH O 5 1900
MHi My 8 1880[91-1900]
MSo 1870+
MWA Je 12 1875;Ag 29 1885;F 8 1890;Mr 5,Je 18-25 1892;N 24 1894;Ja 21 1898;D 2 1904;Ja 2 1925
MiU-C Je 25 1892
NNHi Ag 31 1872-N 11 1882;Mr 22-Ap 12,Ag 30-S 6 1884
NhD Ap 17,Je 12,Ag 14 1875;Jl 8 1876;Mr 30 1878

Somerville NEWS. w Ja 6 1893-
M 1893

Somerville PRESS. w Je ? 1933+
M Ja 11,25 1934;Mr 21,Je 6 1935;Ap 9,My 7 1936

SOUTH ABINGTON

South Abington TIMES. *See* Whitman times and Plymouth county courier (Whitman)

SOUTH BERLIN

Berlin NEWS. w 1888-Jl 19 1893||
MBer Jl 24 1889-90

SOUTH BOSTON

Papers published in South Boston are listed under Boston

SOUTH BRAINTREE

Papers published in South Braintree are listed under Braintree

SOUTH DANVERS. *See* PEABODY

SOUTH FRAMINGHAM

Papers published in South Framingham are listed under Framingham

SOUTH HADLEY FALLS

AMERICAN telegraph. *See under* Holyoke

SOUTH NATICK

Pupers published in South Natick are listed under Natick

SOUTH READING

South Reading GAZETTE and Boston and Maine railway advertiser. w My 1857-
MH [N 10 1860-Jl 13 1861]
MWA Jl 23 1859

SOUTHBRIDGE

Southbridge COURIER. w Je 8 1839-
DLC Je 8,27-S 5 1839
MWA Jl 4 1839

Southbridge HERALD. w 1882-1930||?
MSob 1902-09;13-29
MWA Mr 15 1883;Mr 28 1889

Southbridge JOURNAL. w 1861-1900||?
DLC Jl 24 1868
MSob 1861-1900
MWA O 3 1862[63-70]D 29 1871;F 9,Mr 1 1872;Je 6 1873;Ja 5 1874;Ja 1 1875;Ja 31,Mr 7 1878;Jl 8 1887;My 24 1894
NcD O 3 1862;D 8 1865;F 2,Mr 16,Ap 6,Je 1, N 9 1866;D 6 1867;Mr 27,Ap 17,Je 24 1868;My 6,20 1870
OClWHi D 20 1861;My 12 1865

MORALIST and general intelligencer. w Ja 1-D 1828||
Ja-My 1 1828 as Reformer and moralist. Followed by Southbridge register. . .
MWA complete
REdH N 20 1828
WHi D 4 1828

Southbridge NEWS. d Ag 1923+
pub 1923+
M Je 1 1933
MWA Ag 27,30 1923

Southbridge PRESS. w O 8 1853-
MSob [1853-58]
MWA N 12 1853;Ag 13 1856
NNHi 1853-D 9 1854
P-M S 2,D 16 1854;F 10,Mr 17 1855

Southbridge PRESS. w My 9 1891+
MSob 1904+

QUINNEBAUG item. w O 18 1860-
MWA O 18-25,N 22 1860

REFORMER and moralist. *See* Moralist and general intelligencer

Southbridge REGISTER and farmers, mechanics and manufacturers advocate. w F 1829-F 1832||
Follows Moralist and general intelligencer. F-My 19 1829 as Southbridge register
CSmH S 7 1830
CtY Je 1,22 1830
DLC F 24,Jl 7 1829
MWA [1829-31]

VILLAGE courier. w F 7 1832-Ja 30 1833||
MWA 1832-Ja 22 1833

WELLSWORTH life. m F 1916-D 1917||?
MSob 1916-17

SPENCER

Spencer BULLETIN. w O ? 1885-88||
United with Spencer sun to form Sun-bulletin, later Spencer sun
MWA S 1 1886

Le CANADIEN. w 1883-84||
In French
MWA Jl 9 1884

Spencer LEADER. w Ap 1891+
pub 1891+
MSp 1930+
MWA Ag 7 1897;S 8 1900;Ja 18,F 8 1902;My 20 1910

Spencer SUN. w 1872-1901||?
Mr 22-Je 21 1888 as Sun-bulletin
MH F 13 1874
MLei [1872]
MSpL 1872-91
MWA Ag 15,N 7 1873;Mr 6,My 15,O 16 1874; Jl 9 1875[76-81]-[83-90]Ag 27,D 17 1891;My 18,S 7,O 5 1893;N 25,D 23 1897;Mr 10 1898
NcD N 8 1878;Mr 21 1879

SPRINGFIELD

Weekly AMERICAN. w 1855-
MWA Ap 26 1856

Daily AMERICAN. d Mr? 1856-
MWA My 2 1856

Springfield daily ARGUS. d Ja? 1856-
MWA F 9 1856

Weekly COURIER. w Ja 2 1847-
KHi Mr 27 1847

Springfield DEMOCRAT. w Jl 29-N 11 1876||
MS complete

Springfield DEMOCRAT. d S 24 1883-85||
MS 1883-Mr 23 1885
MWA S 26 1883

L'ECO coloniale. *See* L'Eco della Nuova England

L'ECO della Nuova England. w Ap 19 1913+
1913-20 as L'Eco coloniale
In Italian
pub 1913+
IU D 8 1917-O 3 1919
M N 4 1932

FEDERAL spy. w 1853?-
DLC My 4 1862

FEDERALIST and journal. *See* Hampden journal and advertiser

FOREST PARK times. w 1924+
M My 29 1931;S 16 1932
MH Ag 15-22 1930

Springfield GAZETTE. w S 14 1831-Je 28 1848||
Merged with Springfield republican
CtY 1831-Mr 1837;D 6 1843;O 30(extra)1844
DLC S 21 1831-S 5 1832
ICN S-N 1831;32-33
MH Jl 11 1837
MHi S 11 1833-34;S 9 1835;38;41-45
MS 1831-41;46-48
MWA F 3,O 19 1836;Jl 19 1837;Je 3 1840[41] Jl 3,31 1844;45-46
MiU-C [1839;45]
N 1831-Mr 5 1845
NN F 1836-F 1837;Je 19 1839;Jl 3 1844
NNHi O 1831-34;37;40
NcD 1839
P-M N 21 1832;Ja 7 1846
TxU 1831-S 4 1833;36-37;O 2 1839-41
WHi O 3 1838;Je 11 1845

Springfield daily GAZETTE. d Ap 1 1846-Je 30 1848||
MS complete
MWA Ja 18 1847
N Mr 1,28,Ap 7-11,Je 19 1848

Springfield GRAPHIC. w Ap 5 1890-94||?
CtY 1890-D 2 1893

HAMPDEN intelligencer. w O 25 1831-Ja 9 1833||?
MDeHi My 30 1832
MS 1831-32
MWA N 14 1832
P-M [1832]-Ja 9 1833

*HAMPDEN journal and advertiser. w Ja 7 1806-D 31 1834||
1806-Jl 23 1812 as Hampshire federalist; Jl 30 1812-Ap 21 1819 Hampden federalist; Ap 28 1819-D 25 1822 Hampden federalist and public journal; Ja 1-Mr 5 1823 Federalist and journal; Mr 12 1823-D 31 1828 Hampden journal. United with Springfield republican to form Republican and journal, later Springfield republican
Ct N 1 1826
CtY 1895
DLC Je 20,O 24,D 12 1821;Je 25-Jl 9,23 1823; 25-27;30;Ja-S 1832;F 13 1833
ICN N 16 1825;O 4 1826;27-[31]
M Ja-D 12 1821
MBAt N 26 1828
MCHi Ja 21-D 1824
MDeHi Je 5 1822;Je 18,Jl 30,Ag 20-S 3 1823; Ap 15-22,O 21 1829;N 21 1832
MHi 1825;34
MS 1821-34
MWA 1821-23;Ag 3 1825;Ag 29 1827;O 1 1828; Mr 21,Ap 11,O 17 1832;O 2,23,D 25 1833
MiU-C [1833-34]
N Ja 31 1827
NN F 12 1823
NNHi 1821;My 21 1823;24;Je 14 1826-32
NcD 1822
P [1821]
P-M My 26 1830

*HAMPDEN patriot and liberal recorder. w D 31 1818-Ap 28 1824||
1818-Ja 24 1821 as Hampden patriot
DLC Je-O 1821;O 9-16 1822
MDeHi Ag 1,15,29-S 12,D 12 1821;F 13-Mr 13, My 22,S 4,25 1822
MS complete
MWA 1821-23
MiU-C Ap 4 1821
N Mr 10 1824
NNHi Ap 2 1823;Ja-Mr,Ap 28 1824
NcD 1822

HAMPDEN post. w F 24 1830-
1830-S 5 1838 as Hampden whig
CSmH Ag 25 1830
Ct [1830-31]Ap 18 1832;Jl 9 1834[35-37]
CtHi 1830-F 11 1835
DLC 1830;Ja-Ag 1832;34-F 11 1835;Mr 6,S 4 1839;F 1847-O 18 1848
ICN O 12,N 30 1831
MDeHi S 1 1830;Jl 10 1839;F 5 1840;Je 9 1841; F 17,Mr 3,13 1847;Jl 12 1848
MH Ag 17 1831
MS 1830-47;My 31 1848-Mr 14 1849;50-Je 2 1852;F 9 1853-Ag 2 1854
MWA F 25 1835;Jl 6 1836;Ja 9 1839;Je 19 1844;My 7 1845;Jl 14 1852
MnHi My 12 1830
N Ja 5,O 16 1833;S 24,D 24 1834
NNHi 1830-32;O 25 1848[49-50]F 12 1851
P-M Ag 29 1832;F 27 1839
TC N 8(extra)1834
WHi My 30 1838

HAMPDEN statesman. w
DLC Ag 15-22,S 12,O,N 14,28 D 26 1846
NhD F 14,My 23 1846
P-M D 6 1845;Ja 17 1846;Jl 25-Ag 1 1855

HAMPDEN Washingtonian. w Ja 6 1842-Ja 1 1848||
DLC S 22 1842
MS 1842
MWA Jl 28 1842;S 28 1843
P-M D 4,25 1845;Ja 22 1846

HAMPDEN whig. *See* Hampden post

HARRISONIAN. w
WHi My 22 1840

INDEPENDENT democrat. w My 26 1841-Ja 1 1845||
MBAt Ja 13 1844
MS complete
MWA Jl 3 1844

Le JEAN BAPTISTE. *See under* Northampton

MECHANICS reporter. w 1850-
MWA S 25,O 9 1851
NN D 25 1851

Evening NEWS. d Mr 30 1868-70||
MS [1868-Ja 10 1870]
MWA [Mr-N 2 1868]

Springfield daily NEWS. d 1880+
M [1928-Jl 1933]
MS 1905+

ORACLE. w Ag 25 1866-
N S 22 1866

Springfield POST. tw 1845-
MS F 12,Ap 11,16-30,Jl 1846-47;Ja 1,F 15-22, 26-Je,Jl 19,24-Ag 11 1848
P-M S 16,D 23 1845

Springfield daily POST. d Je 1 1848-
DLC Je 23-1848;Jl 10 1852
MS 1848-Jl 6 1854
MWA Ag 28 1851;Jl 9 1852

Springfield REPUBLICAN. w S 8 1824+
Ja 10 1835-37 as Republican and journal
pub 1824+
CClP S 18 1903-D 1 1929
CSf 1891
CSmH S 1 1830;My 25 1861
CSt Je-D 1896
Ct S 5,8 1824;Ag 2 1826;Ap 2 1828[30]Jl 7 1832;Je 18 1875;Je 13,Jl 7 1886;Mr 16 1902; 09+
CtY S 22 1824-25;S 10,D 10 1828;N 25 1837;59-Ja 17 1863;64-74;89-1900;15-16
DLC S 8 1824(facsimile)25-30;Ja-S 1832;35-42;61-Jl 7 1871
IA S 1860-66
ICHi Ja 14 1854-56
ICN S 8 1824-[31]-33;D 13 1834-[37]-41
ICU N 20 1903;My 20 1904;Ja 24,Mr 21,Je 13 1907;F 4,18-Ap 8,22-My 6,20-Jl 15,Ag 12-O 13,N 11 D 2,16-23 1909;Ja 6 1910;23-24;Ap 22 1926-Ja 1933

MASSACHUSETTS (*Continued*)

SPRINGFIELD—*Continued*

Springfield REPUBLICAN. w 1824+—*Cont.*
IEN O 19-N 2 1916
IaDuC O 14 1865
KHi O 9 1838;Ja 26 1861;My 24 1862;Ja 27 1868;O 31 1887-Mr 12 1895;N 12-26 1897
LNH Ap 10 1896
LU My 13 1837-My 12 1838
MAS 1908-F 1918
MB Jl 5 1826;My 7-14 1842;S 25,O 16 1852[Ja-Mr 26 1853]My 12,Ap 21,N 17 1855;My 24 1856;F 12,My 16 1857;D 4 1858;D 24 1859;Mr 10,31,Ap 21 1860;Ap 13,Je 22 1861;63-64;My 27 1865-Ja 24 1876;Ja-N 1888
MBAt My 2 1827;Ag 6 1828;S 23 1829;S 30-O 7 1843
MC 1873-1914
MChi Je 2 1830;63+
MDeHi S 8 1824(facsimile),Mr 18,Je 17 1829; N 24 1832;Mr 18-My 24 1861;Ag 4 1863;F 20 1864
MGr 1899-1925
MH My 1 1852;68[69]-Mr 15 1872;Jl 25 1873: Je 5 1874;O 29 1875-76;D 12-19 1884[Je 1889-My 20 1892]Je 24 1904;F 13 1908
MHol [1856-60]61[64-86]1902+
MHi [1825;33-34]Ag 29 1835;My 28 1836[55-56]My 1858-N 1862[63-65;1911-17]-Je 27 1929
MNF 1866-84;93
MNS 1922+
MNb 1876-1905
MS 1824-48;F 10 1855-Je 1867;68+
MSob 1872-73
MWA 1824-[28]-[30-Ag 1834]35-36;Ap 22,Jl-Ag 19,O 7 1837;F 24[My 19-D 22]1838;My 16 1840[41]F 5 1842;Ja 29,N 23 1844;My 20 1848;Ag 25 1849[Je-D 10 1851]Mr 3,Ap 28 1852;54-Mr 1855;56-65[F-S 15 1866]67;Mr 21 1868;Ja 1,23,F 4,Je 5,21 1869-70;Je 16,Jl 14,S 1,22 1871;Ag 31-S 7,O 5,19 1877;Jl 1889-91;S 8 1899;1903-Ag,N-D 12 1918;S 11 1924
MWiC Je 15 1861;76-1925
MWo Ja 24,Mr 4 1892
MeBa [Je 1864-66]
MiAC [1896]
MiU-C [1836]Mr 27 1844(facsimile)[53;59-61; 67;86-87;91]
MnHi S 6 1824;Ap 13 1833
MnU [1923-24]+
N Mr 24,N 8 1826;F 14,Jl 11-18,Ag 1 1827;F 26 1828;Jl 15,Ag 12 1829;Ap 14-21 1830;D 9 (extra)17 1831;S 13 1834-[35-45]O 9 1847;Mr 24 1849
NCH Jl 11,25 1835;Ja 23,My 28-Je 4,S 10,N 19 1836;Ja 21,F 18,28,O 21,N 18 1837
NCor My 1858-73
NIC Jl 10-Ag 7,S 18 1903-07
NN Ag 11 1830;S 8 1824(facsimile)Mr 27 1844(facsimile)Ag 13 1853;Jl 19 1854;S 15 1878(facsimile)Ap 14 1888(facsimile)
NNHi S-D 1824;N 1 1826
NbHi O 19 1861
NcD [1827-28]D 17 1831;D 18 1832[36;39]Mr 24 1855;O 8 1859;Ja 26 1861;My 3 1862;S 3 1864;Jl 8 1865;My 5 1866;Ja 12,Mr 23,Je 29 1867
NhD My-Je,Jl 13-20,Ag-S,O 12-26,N 9-D 1861;Ja 11-Mr 1,15,29-Ap 12,26-O 4 1862;F 17 1866;Ap 4,My 30-Je 6,Jl 4 1868;Mr 27 1885
OClWHi N 30 1861;Jl 5 1906
OHi Mr 13 1869;F 18 1870
OrHi 1924-Je 25 1925
REdH Ap 18 1827
RPB 1880-86
TxU Je 1905-08
VU Je 23 1885;Je 24 1887;S 27-O 4 1917
VtRC 1905-07
WHi O 6 1856;O 13-27,N 10-17 1860;61-71; Mr 7 1873;Mr 6,27-Ap 3 1874;My 5,N 10 1876; 80;D 21 1884;88-94;98;1900-04
WaPS [1909-10]-[13;15-16]-[19-20]-22;24-[27]-33

Springfield REPUBLICAN. d Mr 27 1844+
Title varies: Daily evening republican; Springfield daily republican; etc.
pub 1844+
C F 1887-89
CU Mr 27 1844
CaOLU 1859
CoHi Je 26 1934
CtHi 1855-66
CtNIC [1861]
CtW F 1871-Ap,S 1883-F 1930
CtY Ja 15,Je 27,Ag 29 1849;63-65;73;Mr 23 1877;My 16-23 1935
DLC Mr 27 1844(reprint)Mr 1850-D 19 1851;F 1852-Je 1853;58-62;67-73;Jl 1874+
IC Ja-Je 1873
ICN [1849-50]-[52]-[54]-58;Jl 1859-Je 1925
IEN N 9 1916-Je,S 1919-F,Je-Ag 1920;Ap,Je-Jl,S,D 1921-Mr,My-Je,Ag,D 1922-F,Ap-My, Jl,S 1923-F,Ag-S,D 1924-Ja,Mr 1925-33
IHi F 12-13 1909
IU N 16 1908-Ap 10,Je 9,12-14,O 18,N 6 1909-Ja 3,28-31,Mr 2-Ap 26 1910
InU 1916;18;21+
M Mr 1877+
MB 1890-Ag 1898;1900+
MBAt 1863-Je 1895
MDeHi Mr 27 1844(facsimile),Ja 28,Je 22 1848; D 23 1862;S 11 1863;Jl 5 1867;S 28 1881;My 20 1906
MGr 1899+
MH O 10,N 6 1844;Ap 21 1849:Ap 16,23 1850: Mr 11,15,Ap 21 1851;Jl-D 1857:Ag 28 1863: Ag 11 1869[Mr 1872-Jl 26 1873]My 20,Je 16 1874;D 8 1879:O 18 1884;My 26 1886;Ag 4 1887;D 20 1889[Ag 9-O 12 1893]Je 30,Jl 16 1894;D 27 1896;My 13,Je 23,25,27-28 1898; Ap 21,Je 27 1899;F 17,Mr 16,Ap 21,My 7,Jl 7,14 1901;My 16 1904;Ja 6,F 2 1908;F 15 1909; Ja 10,Mr 7,Ap 18,My 2,23,O 10,N 14,21,D 12, 19,26 1910;Mr 6,Ap 3,10,17 1911;Ja 6-Ap 21 1918;N 12 1926:Mr 25,S 15 1932
MHi F 19 1847;Ja-Je 1851;60-Jl 1861;Jl 8 1863; Ja-Je,O 1 1866[69-75]Ja 17 1878;F 12 1884 [1910-16]
MNF 1857+
MPi Jl-D 1886;99-Mr 1927
MS 1844+
MSob 1872-73
MWA N 28 1845;Mr 19-27,30-31 1846;O 4 1848; Mr-D 1850;Jl 23,N 9 1852;53-[60]Ja 4 1861;F 20,25,28,My 19,Jl 19,25 1862;Jl 9,Ag 22,N 3 1863;Je 13-14,16,Jl 7,Ag 3,S 8,D 3,16-20,23,27-29,31 1864;F 8,Ap 21,My 23-D 1865;Ja 3,F 21,Mr 7,D 20 1866;Ja 23,Je 14,Jl 29 1867-Jl 24,D 26,29 1868;Ja 1,23 1870-Ag 1911;F-D 1913;My 16 1935
MWf 1858-1927
MWo Mr 27 1844(facsimile)Ag 17 1877
MiU 1926+
MnHi Mr 27 1844
MnU [1860]-63
N 1861-72;1911+
NBHi 1865-75
NBuHi 1858-65
NN O 8 1847-Jl 1848;Ag 9 1859;Je 29,Jl 8-12, 14-15,20-28,S 26 1864;Jl 2,6-7 1866;S 1-2 1869
NNHi D 30 1861-62;F 11 1869;Je 1873;D 30 1875
NRU Jl 7-Ag 3 1886
NcD [1844;52-53;58;62;65;71-73;76;96-99;1903-04; 06]
NcU F 1876-Ja 1878
NhD Jl 27 1868;Ag 30,D 12,17 1878
NjFHi Mr 27 1844(reprint)
OClWHi My 25,S 21 1861;S 7 1870;F 23 1885;O 18 1913
P-M Ag 17 1831;Mr 7 1840;D 9,19 1845;Ag 12,N 23,D 20 1853
PEHi Je 13 1856
PP 1927+
TxU Ja-Mr 1868;Jl-D 1869;Jl 1888-Je 1891; 92-S 1895;F 11 1919-25
WHi D 28 1914-Ja 1 1920

Springfield REPUBLICAN. tw Ja 2 1860-S 7 1863||
CtY 1860;62-63
MS complete
NhD Je 29,Ag 8 1860
OClWHi D 31 1862

Springfield REPUBLICAN. sw S 9 1863-D 29 1871||
CtY 1863
IHi [F 24-D 1869]
MS complete

Springfield Sunday REPUBLICAN. *See* Sunday union and republican

REPUBLICAN and journal. *See* Springfield republican

Springfield SENTINEL. sw,w 1846-
sw 1846-47?
MWA Jl 30 1847;Ja 5,O 11 1848

Saturday evening TELEGRAM. w Mr 18 1871-73||
MNF 1871-My 10 1873
MWA Jl 29 1871
NNHi D 21 1872

Sunday morning TELEGRAM. w Ap 6 1873-N 5 1876||
MNF 1873
MS 1874-76
MWA F 6 1876

Springfield UNION. (morning) d Ja 4 1864+
1864-Je 30 1892 as Springfield daily union; Jl 1892-95 Springfield morning union
For Sunday ed F 7 1926+ *See* Sunday union and republican
My 25 1886 is Anniversary ed; My 28 1902, pt 2, is "Story of Springfield and her golden jubilee"
pub 1920+
Ct S 22-25 1921
CtY Je 13 1872-Je 1878
DLC [1868]
M My 25 1886;My 28 1902;N 1921+
MH S 21 1867;Je 13,17 1874;Ag 18,23,28,31,S 2,6,15-O 2,5-N 10 1880[S 29 1893-Ja 4 1895]Jl 23,O 6 1896;Ap 21 1900;D 16 1909
MS 1864+
MWA D 1864;Ap 10 1865;S 14 1870;N 11 1872; Ja 1,My 3,Jl 19,O 16 1873;Je 27 1874;F 10 1875;Mr 21 1884;My 26 1886;My 23,O 29,D 12 1887;Mr 8 1888;Ja 3 1889;Ag 30 1890;O 29 1891;Jl 1892-Je 1895;98;My 16-17 1935
MiU [1872]-[1915-17]

Springfield weekly UNION. w O 6 1864-1902||?
MS 1879-Ja 9 1902
MWA Mr 14,Ap 11,O 3 1873;S 3,24 1875;Je 23 1876;Mr 8,29,Je 28 1878;Ja 24 1879
OClWHi O 14 1864

Springfield evening UNION. d Ja 1 1892+
M Ag 2 1922;Mr 16 1932
MS 1892-Mr 1918
MWf 1928+
MiU [1892]-96

Sunday UNION and republican. w S 15 1878+
1878-F 7 1926 as Springfield Sunday republican (title varies)
pub O-D 1915;Ap-Je 1917;19+
Ct 1909-Ag 1925;26+
CtY Ja 5 1893
ICN 1878-Je 1925
IEN O 22 1916-33
MGr 1925+
MS 1878+
MWA F 23 1936
MiU [1888]-[91-92]
See also West Springfield

STOCKBRIDGE

BERKSHIRE star. *See* Berkshire county eagle (Pittsfield)

Weekly VISITOR. w Mr 18? 1841-
MWA Ag 19-26,S 16,O 7 1841
P-M My 11 1843

STONEHAM

AMATEUR. w Mr 21 1870-74||
Followed by Stoneham independent
pub 1870-Je 27 1874

Stoneham INDEPENDENT. w Ja 4 1875+
Follows Amateur
pub Ja 11 1875+
M 1912+
MHi S 28,O 19,N 2,D 21 1901;Ja 11,Ag 3 1902
MSt 1875+

Stoneham NEWS. w S 11 1880-94||?
MSt 1883-88
MStI S 18 1880-D 9 1882

Stoneham PRESS. w 1935+
MSt 1935+

REGULATOR, and Middlesex advertiser. w Ja? 1840-
MWA D 10 1840
MWo O 7 1840

Stoneham SENTINEL. w Je 18-S 3 1864;D 5 1868-77||?
Merged with Middlesex journal, later Woburn journal (Woburn)
MWA Je 18,S 3 1864
MWo complete

Stoneham SENTINEL. w D 5 1868-76||
MSt 1874-76
MWA D 12 1868

STOUGHTON

Stoughton CHRONICLE. w 1930+
pub Ag 27 1930+

Stoughton NEWS-SENTINEL. w F 19 1864+
1864-S 8? 1911 as Stoughton sentinel
pub 1864-65;71+
MStou D 26 1863-1933
MWA Jl 23 1864
OClWHi Jl 23,D 17 1864;Je 17,Ag 19-26 1865

Stoughton RECORD. w 1886-1912||?
M Ap 1897-1909

Stoughton SENTINEL. *See* Stoughton news-sentinel

SWAMPSCOTT

Swampscott ENTERPRISE. w Ja 6 1877-1912||?
MLyI 1877-78
MSaE Mr 1 1884

Swampscott STANDARD. w Ja 6 1886-87||?
MSaE [1886-87]
NcD Ja 20,My 12 1886

TAUNTON

ADVOCATE. w F 23 1827-O? 1830||
My 4,Je 8 1827;N 27 1828 as Commonwealth's advocate. Followed by Sun
CSmH Ag 27 1830
MTaHi 1827-Ja 1829
MWA My 4,Je 8 1827;N 27 1828;F 27[Ap 17-D]1829-Ja 8,29,Ap 23,Jl 2,23 1830
REdH D 12 1828

AMERICAN republican. *See* Bristol county republican

AMERICAN whig. *See* Bristol county republican

AURORA. w Jl 9 1833-
MWA Jl 9 1833

BEACON of liberty. w Je 8 1844-
MAtt D 20 1845
MWA Je 15 1844;N 29 1845

BRISTOL county democrat and independent gazette. *See* Household gazette

BRISTOL county free democrat. *See* Household gazette

BRISTOL county republican. w 1821-1910||
1821-58 as American whig; 1859-Ag 24 1860 American republican
DLC Je 4 1845
IHi D 31 1845
MAtt Ja 15 1845;O 5 1860;S 6 1861
MB Ja 24 1844;D 17 1846;Jl 29,O 14 1847;F 10,Je 15 1848;Ag 23 1849;My 1 1851;Ag 25 1852;D 22-29 1853;F 16 1854
MH O 26 1860;Mr 11 1864
MHi Jl 17 1851;D 11 1856;Jl 26 1861
MTa [1838-1910]
MTaHi D 18 1844-1901
MWA Ja 22 1852;Ap 29 1858;Mr 8,Jl 12,O 19-N 2,16 1860;Ag 9 1861
NNHi Ja 15 1850
RP Ap 17 1863

BRISTOL county telegraph. w 1858-
DLC Ag 7,N 6 1858
MWA Jl 14 1860

CABINET. w D? 1829-
CSmH Mr 27 1830

CLAY whig. w
MoSM Ag 28 1844

COLUMBIAN reporter and Old Colony journal. w Ap 4 1821-32||
1821 as Old colony reporter. Followed by Old colony whig and Columbian reporter, later Taunton whig
CSmH S 1 1830
DLC D 31 1823;Ap 14,My 5,Je 9,O 20,N 10 1824;N 1 1826;My 9,23,D 26 1827;Ja 2,Ap 23-30,My 14,Jl 2 1828;Ag 12,S 9,O 27 1829
MAtt N 22 1826
MH F 16,Mr 2,O 26,D 7-14 1831;Ja,F 29,Mr 21-Ap 25,My 9 1832
MTa O 12 1831
MTaHi My 1821-32

MASSACHUSETTS (*Continued*)

TAUNTON—*Continued*

COLUMBIAN reporter. . . w 1821-32‖—*Cont.*
MWA Ap 4,O 10,N 14,D 26 1821;Je 26-Ag 7, 28 1822;Je 11,N 26,D 3-10,31 1823[Ja-N 24 1824]Ag 2 1826;Je 6,20 1827;My 28,O 29,N 19, 27 1828;Ja-F 4,Mr 4,Ap 22,Ag 26 1829;Mr 3, S 22 1830;Ag 24 1831;My 2,Ag 29 1832
NcD Je 5 1827
NjR Je 22 1831;F 29 1832
PPL [1821-22]Ap 9 1823-Mr 24 1824
REdH N 19 1828

COMMONWEALTH'S advocate. *See* Advocate

Taunton DEMOCRAT. *See* Household gazette

DEW DROP. w 1843-Ag 24 1848‖?
United with Massachusetts cataract. . . to form Massachusetts cataract, Worcester county waterfall, temperance standard and dew drop (Worcester)
MAtt D 7 1847
MTa 1843-48
MTaHi Ap 14 1846-Ag 20 1848
MWA D 7 1845;Jl 28 1846

FREE PRESS. w N 14 1823-N 5 1824‖
MTa [1823-24]
MTaHi D 12 1823
MWA complete

Taunton tri-weekly GAZETTE. tw Mr? 1833-
MTaHi Mr 16-D 30 1833
MWA Je 18 1833

Taunton weekly GAZETTE. *See* Household gazette

HARRISON eagle. w My 16-N 7 1840‖
Campaign paper
DLC My 23 1840
MB complete
MHi O 3 1840
MTa [1840]
MTaHi complete
MWA Je 20,O 10 1840

Taunton evening HERALD. d 1893-1900‖
United with Taunton evening news to form Taunton herald-news
MWA S 15 1900

Taunton HERALD-NEWS. d 1889-1914‖?
1889-1902? as Taunton evening news
MH Mr 5 1903
MHi Je 4 1889
MTa 1902-04
MTaHi 1887-Je 1902
MWA Jl 10 1901

HOUSEHOLD gazette. w Ja 5? 1832-93‖?
1832-37 as Independent gazette; 1838-My? 1849 Bristol county democrat and Independent gazette (title varies slightly); Je? 1849-50? Bristol county free democrat; 1851?-61 Taunton democrat; 1862-73 Union gazette and democrat; 1874-78? Taunton weekly gazette
DLC Ja 17 1834;Jl 23 1863
MAtt S 29 1881
MB Ja 11-18 1850[F 25-D 23 1853]F 17 1860; O 31 1861;S 1 1864;Jl 27 1865
MH F 10 1881
MHi O 18 1833
MTa N 1838-[50-61]-93
MTaHi 1832-61;O 29 1874-76;78-82
MWA Je 22 1832;O 12 1838-[39]My 28 1841;N 4-11 1842;Ap 14 1843;Ja 12 1844;D 25 1846;My 11,N 23 1849;Mr 7 1851;O 22,N 12 1852;Mr 17 1854;O 26 1855;O 22 1858;Je 13 1861;Ja 22 1863;Ja 4 1866
P-M S 8 1854

INDEPENDENT gazette. *See* Household gazette

LIFE BOAT. w 1846?-
MWA Ja 21 1852

MASSACHUSETTS cataract. *See under* Worcester

Taunton evening NEWS. *See* Taunton herald-news

OLD COLONY reporter. *See* Columbian reporter and Old Colony journal

OLD COLONY republican. w S 1846-
MTa 1846-49
MWA F 20 1847

OLD COLONY whig and Columbian reporter. *See* Taunton whig

SUN. w N 26 1830-
Follows Advocate
DLC S 2,O 21 1831;Ag 3 1832;Ag 9 1833
MTa N 1 1833
MTaHi D 1830-N 18 1831;Je 19 1835;F 10,24 1837
MWA 1830-N 9 1832;D 6 1833;Jl 4 1834
P-M N 25 1831

TRUE democrat. w Ag 24 1848-
MB Ag,S 13-20,O 4,N 9,15 1848
MTaHi 1848-D 29 1849

UNION gazette and democrat. *See* Household gazette

Taunton WHIG. w Ja 2 1833-
Follows Columbian reporter and Old Colony journal. 1833-S 26 1838 as Old Colony whig and Columbian reporter
CSmH D 5 1839;Ap 6 1841;D 5 1844
DLC Ja-Ag 14 1833;Ag 8 1838;Ag 25 1841
MAtt S 30 1840;Ap 14 1841;F 2,Jl 13,Ag 3-10 1842
MTa 1839-58
MTaHi 1833-Ja,O 1838-D 11 1844
MWA S 18 1833;Mr 19 1834;Jl 15-Ag 5,19,S 9,30 1835;O,N 21-D 19 1838;Ja-My 15,Je 5,Jl 3-10,24 1839[Ap-D 1840]-Je 23 1841;Ag 7 1844
NN Ap 6 1841(extra photostat)
NNHi Jl 24 1833
RPB [1840]

TOPSFIELD

Topsfield TOWNSMAN. w Ja 12 1895-Ap 29 1899‖
DLC Ja 12-19 1895
MSaE 1895-[99]
MTHi complete
MWA Ja 16-23,F 6,20,Jl 31,S 11,O 30 1897

TOWNSEND

Townsend TIMES. w D 27 1922-28‖?
MTo 1923+
MWA D 27 1922

TURNERS FALLS

Turners Falls REPORTER. w 1872-1920‖?
MTu Jl 3 1872-D 29 1920

UXBRIDGE

BLACKSTONE VALLEY news. w F 10 1916-23‖
1916-S 13 1917 as Uxbridge booster; Ja 20-Je 25 1920 Blackstone Valley news and Whitinsville press
Suspended from Ag 20 1920-N 25 1921
MUx 1916-Jl 9,Ag 6,20 1920-D 6 1923

Uxbridge BOOSTER. *See* Blackstone Valley news

Uxbridge COMPENDIUM. w Mr 7 1868-Je 27 1913‖?
1868-Ja 18 1873 as Douglas herald Ja 25 1873-D 29 1882 Worcester south compendium
1868-S 1873 pub in East Douglas; O 1873-D 29 1882 in Worcester
MUx 1868-Je 27 1913
MWA D 11 1869;Ag 16 1873;Ap 29,My 13,Ag 5-12 1876

Uxbridge TIMES. w S 27 1929+
pub 1929+
MUx 1929+

Uxbridge and Whitinsville TRANSCRIPT. w Jl 22 1904-19‖?
1904-05? as Whitinsville transcript (Whitinsville)
DLC Ag 4 1905
MUx 1904-18
MWA D 9 1904;Ag 4 1905

VINEYARD GROVE. *See* OAK BLUFFS

VINEYARD HAVEN

Vineyard NEWS. w 1919-21‖
MEdV [1919-21]

WAKEFIELD

AMERICAN justifier. *See under* Boston

Wakefield BULLETIN. w 1881-86‖?
MB My 24,Je,O 11-18,N 1 1884

CITIZEN and banner. w S 7 1872-1911‖
1872-73? as Citizen
MB [N 1872-73]
MWA N 3 1883;Ja 9-My 22,Je 26,Jl 24-Ag 14 1903
MWak S 7 1872-73;86-Je 23 1911
NcD [1876-85]

Wakefield daily ITEM. d My 7 1894+
pub 1894-My 6 1895;Ap 1900+
M [1928-Jl 1933]
MWA My 7 1895;D 29 1923
MWak 1894-95;My 1901+

WALPOLE

Walpole ENTERPRISE. *See* Norfolk county tribune

NORFOLK county tribune. w 1878-82‖
1878-81? as Walpole enterprise
MH Ag 26 1882

Walpole TIMES. w 1915+
pub [1915-22]+
MWA S 27 1924
MWalp F 6 1926

WALTHAM

Waltham COURIER. w N 27 1925+
M Ja 29 1931;N 3 1932
MWa 1925-N 18 1927;32-N 1 1934

DEMOCRAT. w 1916-20‖?
MWa F 3-10,Mr 9,30-Ap 6,20,My 4,Je 1,15,D 14,17 1916

Waltham FREE PRESS. w N 25 1863-1901‖?
DLC My 28 1875
MH 1863-Ja 1 1869
MWA 1863-N 15 1864;D 1865-68;N 20 1874
MWat F-Ap 2,N 12 1875-77
MWo Ja 24 1868
MNHi 1863-68
OClWHi Jl 13 1866

Waltham daily FREE PRESS-TRIBUNE. d Mr 24 1888-Mr 3 1924‖
1888-97? as Waltham daily free press. United with Waltham evening news to form Waltham news-tribune
MWa 1888-F 1924
MWaN 1889-1900;02-04;06-24

MASSASOIT balance and Waltham advocate. w Ap 24 1852-
DLC Je 26,Jl 17 1852
MWA Jl 17 1852
P-M My 15 1852

Waltham MIRROR. sm Jl 6 1848-
MWA S 28 1848
MWa 1848-Jl 26 1849

Waltham NEWS-TRIBUNE. d 1893+
1893-Mr 3 1924 as Waltham evening news
pub 1893+
M Mr 1916+
MWa Jl 1893+

Waltham RECORD. w D 1 1876-90‖?
MWa 1876-N 1883;F 21,N 13 1885-Mr 1886;D 30 1887
NcD F 16 1883

RUMFORD journal. w My 18 1850-
MWA Je 8,Jl 27,Ag 31 1850

Waltham SENTINEL. w F 15 1856-77‖
MB O 1856-Ja 1857
MH 1856;Je 23 1865
MWA Ag 7,21 1857;Ja 28,Mr 11,Ap 22,Jl 15,Ag 5,19 1859-[63-64;66-67]76;F 2-16,Mr 9 1877
MWa 1856-Mr 1877
NNHi 1856-57
NcD Ja 11 1861;Ag 26 1864;D 1 1865
NhD 1856-57
OClWHi Mr 4 1864

Waltham STAR. w 1836-
MWa My 7-Jl 2 1836

Waltham TRIBUNE. d O 2 1882-97‖
United with Waltham daily free press to form Waltham daily free press-tribune
MWA Mr 17,Jl 21 1883
MWa 1882-Je 30 1897

WATCH. w 1909-22‖
MWa [1909-22]

WARE

Ware STANDARD. w 1855-95‖?
MWA Ap 3,24 1858[59-69]Ag 26 1871

WARE RIVER news. w O 1887+
pub 1888+
M [O 22 1930-33]N 3 1935

WAREHAM

Wareham COURIER. w 1898—
pub 1896+

Wareham NEWS. w 1862-99‖?
MWA Ag 19 1871

Wareham TRANSCRIPT and advertiser. w
DLC Jl 20 1855

WARREN

Warren HERALD. w Ja 1877-1907‖?
MWA N 13 1879;F 23 1882;Ag 2 1901

WATERTOWN

Watertown ENTERPRISE. *See* Watertown tribune enterprise

Watertown OBSERVER. w 1877-79‖
MWat O 1877-Ja 1879

Watertown PRESS. w 1870-75‖
MWat Ap 15 1870-Ja,Ap 9-N 5 1875

Watertown SUN. w O 6 1921+
pub 1921+
M [F 21 1929-F 18 1932]
MWat 1921+

Watertown TRIBUNE-ENTERPRISE. w N 5 1879—
1879-Mr 20 1903 as Watertown enterprise
Jl 31 1925 is Sesqui-centennial number
M N 1890+
MH O 16 1908-Jl 6,N 10 1923-S 19 1930;31+
MWat 1879+

WEBSTER

Webster EAGLE. *See* Worcester county news

Webster JOURNAL. w Jl 17 1858-
MWA S 11,O 23,N 20 1858

Webster TIMES. w Mr 17 1859-1930‖?
1859-Jl 13 1867 as Webster weekly times
pub 1859-1930
MWA [1859-70]Je 3,Jl 15,Ag 5 1871;Ag 17,N 30 1872;Je 7,Ag 9,S 20,O 25,D 27 1873;F 14, Ap 25,N 28 1874;Ja 30 1875;Ap 8,Ag 19 1876; D 14 1878;My 31,Jl 19 1879;F 14,N 6 1880;Ja 20 1882;Ja 18 1884;O 15 1886;F 25,My 27,S 21 1887;My 4,Ag 17 1888;Mr 15 1889;O 12 1894;Mr 3,S 8 1899
MWeb Mr 16 1861-F 17 1877;F 22 1879-1922; O-D 1923
NcD Ap 19 1880;Ja 20 1882
OClWHi Je 22 1861

Webster evening TIMES. d,sw O 1 1923+
pub 1923+
MWA O 1-3 1923;Ja 16 1934;O 12 1935

WORCESTER county news. w 1880-88‖?
1880-86 as Webster eagle
MWA Jl 2 1880;O 28 1881;D 29 1883;F 8,Mr 28 1884;Ag 28 1885;Ja 8 1886;S 24 1887

WELLESLEY

Wellesley COURANT. *See* Our town

OUR town. w,m 1883-1904‖
1883-97 as Wellesley courant. Followed by Townsman
w 1883-97
MWel complete

Wellesley TIMES. w S 6 1929-
MWA S-N 22 1929

MASSACHUSETTS (*Continued*)

WELLESLEY—*Continued*

TOWNSMAN. w Ap 6 1906+
Follows Our town
pub 1906+
MWA Ap 6 1906;D 8 1911;My 24,Je 7 1912;My 30 1913;S 13,N 22 1918;F 4-11 1921;Jl 14 1922;Ag 22 1924;Je 12 1925;Jl 16,30-Ag 13 1926;Mr 9 1928[Mr 15-N 15 1929]Ja 10,Jl 11,S 26-O 3 1930;Mr 27-Ap 10[Ag 28-D 25 1931]Ja 1,Ap 15,D 16 1932;Ag 11,S 8 1933;Ja 12,Mr 9 1934-Jl 12 1935
MWel Ap 13 1906+

WENHAM

Wenham-Hamilton TIMES. w 1882?-1919‖?
MSaE [1897-98]-1902

WESLEYAN GROVE. *See* OAK BLUFFS

WEST CONCORD

Papers published in West Concord are listed under Concord

WEST NEWBURY

West Newbury ERA. *See* West Newbury messenger

West Newbury MESSENGER. sm Ja 23 1883-95‖?
1883-84? as West Newbury era
MSaE 1883[84]-[86-89]-[91-95]
MWA 1883-Ap 1 1884
MiU-C [1888]
NhD Ap 3 1883

West Newbury RECORD. w,ir Mr 16-O 12 1852‖
Campaign paper
DLC Mr 16,Ap 7,28,My 19,Je 9,30 Jl 21,O 12 1852
MH Ap 7 1852
MSaE [1852]
MWA Mr-Jl 21,O 12 1852
MiU-C Mr 16,Ap 28,Je 9,Jl 21 1852
WHi Mr 16,Ap 28,My 19,Je 9,30,Jl 21,O 12 1852

WEST ROXBURY

Papers published in West Roxbury are listed under Boston

WEST SPRINGFIELD

West Springfield NEWS. w Jl 20 1928+
pub 1928+
M Mr 7 1930
MWs 1928+

WESTBORO

Westborough CHRONOTYPE. w 1867+
1867-70? as Saturday evening chronotype
pub 1867+
MWA Je 3 1871;Mr 29 1873;D 25 1875;O 8 1926
NcD Je 3 1871

Weekly MESSENGER. w
Title varies slightly
NNHi S 22 1849-50

Westboro TRANSCRIPT. w 1861-
MWA My 7 1864
OClWHi D 12 1863

Westborough TRIBUNE. w 1889-Je 1891‖
Merged with Westborough chronotype
MWA Mr 13 1891

WESTFIELD

Westfield ADVERTISER. w 1875-80‖?
MWA My 4,18-25 1877

Evening BULLETIN. d
P-M Ap 22,My 18 1861

DEMOCRATIC herald. w Mr 31 1835-
Follows Westfield journal?
MWA N 3 1835

HAMPDEN register. *See* Westfield register

Westfield JOURNAL. w S 10 1833-
Followed by Democratic herald?
MWA S 10,D 24 1833

Westfield JOURNAL. w,d 1885-1925‖?
1885-1922? as Valley echo(w) 1923? Journal and Valley echo
MHi Ja 19 1912;F 19 1915

Westfield NEWS-LETTER. *See* Western Hampden times and Westfield news-letter

Westfield REGISTER. w F 17 1824-
1824-Mr? 1829 as Hampden register
CSmH S 1 1830
Ct Je 13 1827;Ja 17 1828
CtHi Ap 25 1827-N 12 1828
DLC S 2,O 14-21,D 23 1829
ICN S 20-27 1831
MWA [Je 9 1824-25]Ja 11,25,F 8,22,Mr 1-8, 29,Ap 12,My 10,Jl 26,S 13,D 13 1826;Ja 31,S 24,O 8 1828;F 11,O 7-14,D 23 1829;F 3,17-24, Je 16 1830;N 15 1831
N D 24 1828
NN Je 2 1824
OClWHi Je 22,D 7 1825;My 10,Jl 20 1826;Mr 25 1829
P-M [1824-25]Ap 12 1831

Westfield SPECTATOR. w Ap 10? 1839-
IU O 2 1839

Westfield STANDARD. w 1845-
MWA S 17 1851;Jl 13 1853
P-M D 10 1845;F 4 1846

VALLEY echo. *See* Westfield journal (1885-1925)

WARONOCO palladium. w
P-M D 29 1841

WESTERN HAMPDEN times. w Mr 17 1869-73‖?
United with Westfield news-letter to form Western Hampden times and Westfield news-letter
N O 6 1869

WESTERN HAMPDEN times and Westfield news-letter. w F 18 1841-83‖?
1841-73? as Westfield news-letter
MWA S 4 1844;D 2 1845;Mr 25 1846;S 7,O 26 1853
N S 22 1843
NSchU Mr 11 1842
NcD Ja 31 1883
OClWHi Ag 6 1862
P-M Ja 20 1843;Je 19 1844;Mr 24,Ap 28 1852; F 19 1856[57-64;66-67]
WaPS [Ja 10-O 10 1873;Ap 28-N 24 1875]

WESTFIELD VALLEY herald. w Mr 11 1926+
pub 1926+
M Ja 16 1930;Ag 6 1931
MWf 1926+

WIDE AWAKE American. w
P-M O 21,N 11 1845

WESTWOOD

Westwood JOURNAL. w
MDHi Ap 2 1897-D 20 1901

WEYMOUTH

Weymouth GAZETTE and transcript. w My 2 1867+
Title varies: Weymouth weekly gazette; Weymouth weekly gazette and Braintree reporter; etc.
pub 1867+
DLC 1867-Ap 1868;Je 16 1876-Ap 17 1885;1928+
MH Ja 21 1881
MWA S 5,O 10,31 1867;Jl 10 1868;Ja 21 1881; O 24 1924;Jl 9 1926
MWe 1867+

Weymouth ITEM. w O 24 1923-31‖
M [1923-My 7 1931]

Weymouth TRANSCRIPT. w My 1 1903-Ap? 1905‖
United with Weymouth weekly gazette to form Weymouth gazette and transcript
M 1903-04

Weymouth TRUTH. w Ap 1932+
pub 1932+

WHITINSVILLE

Whitinsville COMPENDIUM. w D 10 1870-Ja 8 1873‖
United with Douglas herald (East Douglas) to form Worcester South compendium, later Uxbridge compendium (Uxbridge)
MUx 1870-O 14,D 16 1871-73

Whitinsville TIMES. w S 27 1929+
pub 1929+

Whitinsville TRANSCRIPT. *See* Uxbridge and Whitinsville transcript (Uxbridge)

WHITMAN

ABINGTON journal herald. w 1872+
1872-My 1885 as Plymouth county journal; Je 1885-1932? Plymouth county journal and Abington herald
Dated also at Abington
pub 1872+
MWhT Mr 22 1878-My 8 1885;1936+

PLYMOUTH county journal. *See* Abington journal herald

Whitman TIMES and Plymouth county courier. w 1873+
1873-N 1885 as South Abington times; D 1885-Ap 25 1886 South Abington times and Plymouth county courier
1873-Ap 25 1886 pub in South Abington
pub 1873+
MWh 1934+

WILLIAMSTOWN

AMERICAN advocate. w Ap 12 1827-
DLC Ap 26,My 24,Jl 19,S 20 1827;Ja 3,Ap 2,23,My 14 1828;Ja 14,Mr 4,Je 24-Ag 5,S 2, 23,N 25,D 2,23 1829-Ja 20 1830
MBAt Ap 26 1827;Ag 6 1828
MDeHi Ap 9 1828
MWA Ag 30,N 8 1827;F 20 1828;Ap 28 1830
MWiC 1827-Ja 5 1831
MiU-C N 17,D 1 1830
OClWHi My 3 1827

WILMINGTON

Wilmington NEWS. w Ja 1928+
pub 1928+
MWA S 18 1931

WINCHENDON

Winchendon COURIER. w N 22 1878+
pub [1878-1919]+
MWA Mr 21 1879
MWinc [1907-22]+

Winchendon weekly MIRROR. w N 27 1852-
MWA D 4 1852

NORTH STAR. w S 9 1852-
Campaign paper
MWA S 9-16,30-O 14 1852

WINCHESTER

Winchester NEWS. w D 8 1905-Jl 10 1908‖
Merged with Winchester star
DLC F 2 1906
M complete

Winchester PRESS. w O 26 1900-D 2 1904‖
M 1900-O 17 1902
MWin 1900-O 17 1902
MWo 1900-02

Winchester STAR. w Je 24 1880+
pub 1913+
M 1903+
MWA D 1 1905
MWin Jl 1880+
MWo F 8-Je 5,Jl 1903-Je 1904

Winchester TRANSCRIPT. w Je 10-S 2 1864‖
Merged with Middlesex journal, later Woburn journal (Woburn)
MWA Je 17,S 2 1864
MWo complete

WINTHROP

Winthrop REVIEW. w 1919+
M Je 24 1932;Ja 26 1934
MWA My 25 1928
MWint 1919+

Winthrop SUN. w 1892-1905‖
United with Winthrop visitor to form Sun and visitor, later Sun. . .
MWint complete

SUN; Winthrop's pioneer newspaper. w Je 1 1880+
1880-1905 as Winthrop visitor; 1906-18 Sun and visitor; 1919-36 Winthrop sun
Mr 28 1902 is semi-centennial ed
pub 1900+
DLC Mr 28 1902
M Mr 28 1902
MWA Mr 28 1936
MWint 1882+

Winthrop VISITOR. *See* Sun. . .

WOBURN

Woburn ADVERTISER. w S 3 1846-Mr 30 1848‖
MWin 1846-S 6 1847

Woburn ADVERTISER. w Ja 20 1871-90‖?
MWo 1871-88

Woburn weekly BUDGET. w S 18 1857-D 31 1863‖
MWA Ag 12 1859;O 19,N 2,D 21 1860;Ag 16 1861;Mr 6-13,Ap 3,My 1,29,Ag 21,O 23,D 18 1863
MWo complete

Woburn CITIZEN. w 1932?+
MWo Ag 17 1935-Mr 21 1936

CORNER STONE. m 1896-98‖?
MWo Ap 1896-98

Woburn GAZETTE and Middlesex advertiser. sm,w Mr 15 1844-
Mr-O 1844 as Woburn gazette
Suspended from Ap 26-My 31 1844?
sm Mr-Ap 1844
MWA Ap 26,O 4 1844;Ag 7,D 4 1845
MWo Mr-Ap,My 31 1844;Mr 20-S 11,25 1845-Jl 29 1846

GRATTAN echo. w 1881-Jl 1882‖
MWo Mr 1,Jl 30,Mr 12 1881-Je 24 1882

Woburn ITEM. w Je 21? 1879-
MWA Ag 2 1879

Woburn JOURNAL. w O 18 1851-Ag 29 1913‖
1851-Mr 25 1854 as Woburn journal; Ap 2 1854-65? Middlesex journal; 1866-S 13 1873 Middlesex county journal
CtY Ja 20-F 3 1888
DLC Ja-O 6,D 1855-66;F 14-21,Mr-My,Je 13-27,Jl 11-25,Ag 8-22,S 5-12,O 3 1867
M 1880-1913
MH Ap 6 1878;Ja 6 1882;F 6 1891
MHi N 1851-S 3 1852
MWA Jl 17,31,S 18 1852;O 14 1854;Ap 7 1855; Ja 5-12,Ag 9-D 1856;D 4 1858;Ja 28 1860; Ja 12 1861;Ag 30 1862;Jl 29 1865;O 24 1868;S 24 1870;N 17(supp)1877;Ap 27(supp)1878
MWin 1851-Mr 1854;O 18 1881-N 23 1906
MWo complete
MiU-C Ja 6 1855
NNHi O 18 1851
OClWHi Jl 22 1871

MIDDLESEX county journal. *See* Woburn journal

MIDDLESEX journal. *See* Woburn journal

NEW ENGLAND family. w N 28 1844-45‖?
MWo D 1844-Ja 17 1845

Woburn NEWS. w,d Jl 19 1890-D 31 1912‖
Merged with Woburn journal
w 1890-1907
M O 1904-12
MH Ja 17 1891
MWo 1890-[92]-1912
VHi Ja 28 1899

OUR paper. m S 1875-My 1878‖
MWo complete

Woburn City PRESS. w,d N 28 1888-1912‖
MWo 1888-Jl 1892

REGULATOR and Middlesex advertiser. *See* Sentinel and Middlesex advertiser

MASSACHUSETTS (*Continued*)

WOBURN—*Continued*

SENTINEL and Middlesex advertiser. w 1840-
1840? as Regulator and Middlesex advertiser
MWA F 18 1841
MWo O 7 1840;Jl 1 1841

Woburn TELEGRAM. w My 2 1914-
MWo My-S 25 1914

Woburn daily TIMES. d O 21 1901+
M [1928-Jl 1933]
MWo 1901+

Woburn TOWNSMAN. w F 12 1864-
MWA Ap 1-8,Jl 1,29 1864
MWo F-S 2 1864

UNION weekly. w My 31 1884-85||
MWo 1884-Ap 25 1885

WORCESTER

Saturday evening ADVERTISER. w D 6 1879-
MWA D 6-20 1879
NcD D 20 1879

*AEGIS and gazette. w D 2 1801-95||?
1801-O 31 1857 as National aegis (Ag 31 1831-Jl 24 1833 National aegis and general advertiser; Jl 31-D 25 1833 National aegis and Massachusetts yeoman) N 7 1857-D 30 1865 Aegis and transcript
Suspended from 1834-Ja 17 1838
CSmH Ap 28 1830
Ct [1825-27;30-33]
CtY Jl 4 1821;Je 25,Ag 13,S 17,D 3-10 1828;O 3 1832
DLC 1821-[24]-[27]-[31-33]38-[47-48]N 20 1850 [51]-56;O 10-17,N 7-14,28 1857;N 10 1860;O 29 1864
KHi D 15 1824-D 20 1826;30;Ja 24 1838-40
MB [1821-D 19 1828;Je 10-N 11 1829]30-Ag 24 1831;33;41-42;45;49-50
MBAt Ja 24,F 21,N 7 1821;Ap 3,Jl 17-Ag,O 2 1822;D 31 1823;D 15 1824-33;38-Ja 3,Ag 22,S 26,D 5 1849[50]-[59]N 10 1860;O 28 1865
MH Ap 4 1838;Ag 15 1844;Ja 22 1887
MHi F 7,D 5 1827;Ja 24 1828-Ja 2 1839
MHu Jl 24 1822
MSaE My 19,Je 26 1844
MWA 1821-33;Ja 24 1838-[59-61]Ja 4,Je 14,28, Jl 12,Ag 2,N 22,D 6-13,27 1862-[63]-65[F 1866-67]-[69]-[84]-93
MeBa N 1 1826;Je 27 1827
MiU-C [1821;24-25;33;40-41;49;57;80]
N Ja-N 1825;Ja-Jl 21 1830;O 30 1833;40
NN D 6 1826;Mr 11 1829
NNHi [My-D 1822]
NcD D 14 1825;Mr 8 1826;Ap 23 1828;N 1830-N 1832;Ja 29,Je 24,Jl 15 1840[Ap-Je 1843;50] My 28,O 15,D 24 1851;My 26,S 29 1852;F 1 1854;Ja 17,F,Mr 14-28,Ap 17 1855;Mr 12,Ag 20,S 10 1856;F 18,O 17,31,D 19 1857-N 1858;Ag 4 1860;Ap 13 1861;N 7-14,D 5-19 1863;Je 25 1864[65]Ag 27 1870[Ja-Jl 1874]-Mr 1875;My 12-Je,Jl 21-D 8 1877;Ap 19 1879;F 12,S 10,O 22-29 1881;My 3,O 18 1884
NhD [1821-Ag 1833]
NjR [1849]
OClWHi O 31 1821;O 24 1874;My 3 1884
P-M Mr 19 1845
WHi D 15 1824-D 25 1833;Ja 24 1838-43;45
—d ed *See* Worcester evening gazette

ALBANIA. *See under* New York City

Weekly AMERICAN times. w O 3 1857-
MWA O 24 1857

AMERIKOS lietuvis. w 1907+
In Lithuanian
pub 1907+
IU D 13 1917-N 22 1928;Ap 1929+

ARBETARENS vän. *See* Nya fäderneslandet

ARGUS. *See* Saturday observer

ARROW. m Ja 1854-
MWA Ja-Mr 1854

Daily BAY STATE. d S 1 1856-F 6 1858||
MWA 1856-[S,N-D 1857]F 1858

Weekly BAY STATE. w S 6 1856-
MWA S 6-13,O 4 1856;Ag 29 1857;Je 5-12,Ag 7,S 11,O 30-N 20,D 11 1858-[59;F 24-Jl 7 1860]
NcD F 24 1860

BAY STATE farmer and mechanic's ledger. w Ja 7 1846-
MWA Mr 25,My 13-Jl 1,22-Ag 19 1846
NcD Jl 22,Ag 12 1846

BAY STATE press. w S 25-O 2 1869||
MWA complete
NcD complete

Le BIEN public. tw Ja 21 1879-80||?
In French
MWA 1879-Ap 3 1880
NcD F 8 1879

BRITISH and American world. m Ja 1887-
Follows British-American
MWA F-Je,D 1887

BRITISH-AMERICAN. m F-D? 1886||
Followed by British and American world
MWA F-S 1886

Evening BUDGET. d Ja 1 1847-
MWA Ja 8 1847

Worcester Sunday BULLETIN. w N 2 1912-
1912-F 22 1913 as Worcester bulletin
MWA 1912-Mr 2 1913

CAMPAIGNER.
Campaign paper
MWA O 30 1858

CATARACT and waterfall. *See* Massachusetts cataract. . .

CATHOLIC messenger. w Ja 1887+
1887-F 1 1907 as Messenger (My 7 1898 as Messenger and Saturday observer; My 14 1898-N 25 1902; Ja 1-22 1904 Messenger and observer)
MWA 1887-94;S 19 1896;Mr 26 1898+
NcD D 1 1888;F 20 1892;My 28 1898-S 1899; Ag 31 1903
PPCHi [1887-94]

COMMERCIAL advertiser. w Jl 4 1865-
MWA Jl 4 1865
NcD Jl 4 1865

COMMERCIAL advertiser. w,m,sm S 1867-
m S-N 1867;sm D 1867
MWA 1867;Ap 11-25,My 9-16,30-Je 6,Jl 4,Ag 24-S 14,N 21 1868
NcD S 1867

COMMERCIAL advertiser. w Ag 15 1871-73||
MH Ja 4 1872
MWA Ag,O 17-24,N 7-14,D 5-14 1871;F 1,29, Mr 14-28,Ap 11,25,My 9,Je 6,Ag 1-8,N 7,D 19 1872;Ja 16,30-F 6,27,Jl 31-Ag 21,23(supp)1873
NcD Ag 7 1873

COMMERCIAL advertiser and railway times. m N 1877-
MWA N 1877-Ja,Ap,Ag-S,D 1878
NcD D 1877

Le COURRIER du nouveau monde. w,sw 1880-91||
1880-Ja 10 1891 as Courrier de Worcester
Suspended Ja 11-23 1891
sw Ja 9-16 1885
In French
MWA F 20 1880-O 24 1891
MiU-C Ja 3-10 1891
NcD My 19 1885

Weekly DEMOCRAT. w S 15 1900-
MWA S 15 1900
NcD S 15 1900

Weekly DESPATCH. w 1887-Ap 1 1894||
Merged with Sunday recorder
MWA N 5 1892

Worcester ENQUIRER. w Mr 9-Ap 20 1913||
MWA complete

L'ETENDARD national. w,sw N 3 1869-74||
w 1869-My 5 1870
In French
MWA 1869-O 18 1870
MiU-C D 30 1869;Ja 13 1870
—supplement *See* Le Foyer canadien

Le FOYER canadien. w Mr 18 1873-74||
supplement of L'Etendard national
In French
MWA Mr 18 1873;S 29 1874

Sunday FREE PRESS. w F 23 1879-
MWA F 23,Mr 16-23 1879

Worcester FREEMAN. w Ja 6 1838-
CSmH Ja 6 1838

Worcester evening GAZETTE. d Je 9 1845+
1845-65 as Worcester daily transcript (title varies: Daily transcript; Daily morning transcript; Worcester transcript; etc.)
pub 1915+
DLC Je 8-14 1848;Ja 26,Je 24 1852;S 14 1853;54 [55]Je 10 1857[58;60]My 3,14,17,22 1861[62-63] Mr 12,My 14,Jl 1,13-14,20,S 27 1864;Ja 2,Mr 16,22,Ap 10 Jl 5,S 15,O 18 1865;Ja 1,3,F 20-27,Mr 1-3,Jl-D 1866;O 31 1879
KHi Jl 1853-55;66-85
M Mr 1897+
MB S 10-D 1855
MBAt N 13 1861[62-63]
MH N 26 1879;Jl 20 1887;Ag 17,23,26,O 13 1889[F 27 1890-94]-[98-1902]-[Ja-Ap 13 1906]
MHi [1862-63]
MW 1870+
MWA 1845[46-47]-Je 26 1848;Ap 1851-[60-61]-Ap,Je-Ag 1927;Ja-Je 1928;29+
MWo O 21 1892
MiU-C [1848;52-55;63-65;70;74-76;81;83-84;98-99;1906-11]
NcD Ag 6,15,18,O 9,16,D 9 1845;Jl 20 1846; Mr 17 1847[F,Je 1848;Jl-S 1851;52]Mr 11,S 3, N 15,D 31 1853[Ja-O 1854]56;Ja 3-28,30-F 4, Jl 10 1857;Mr 3 1858;Jl 8,Ag 1,N 14 1859;Mr 14,Jl 13 1860[My-D 1861]Mr 24,Ap 6,10 1863; O 6,N 12 1864;Mr 2,Ap 15,Ag 12,O 18 1865;D 22 1870;Mr 10 1871;Ap 6-7,Jl 4 1876[Je-O 1878;Ja-O 1879]Jl 27,S 10,11(supp)1880[81-96] F 26 1898
NhD Ag 27 1856
OClWHi O 18 1865;O 21 1870;Ap 26 1876;O 22 1877;O 21 1878;O 23 1882;Ap 30 1884
P-M D 30 1845
WHi S 10 1853;Jl 25 1892;1900-01;Jl 1902-05
—w ed *See* Aegis and gazette; Worcester transcript

Worcester GLOBE. tw D 1889-
MWA Ja 16-F 13 1890

GOSPEL messenger and Providence and Worcester journal. *See under* Providence, R.I.

HASWELL'S Massachusetts spy. *See* Massachusetts spy

Worcester HERALD. w Jl 31 1932+
Title varies: Worcester Sunday herald; Sunday herald
MWA 1932+

Worcester HOME journal. *See* New England home journal

L'IDEE nouvelle. The New idea. w My 27 1869-
In English and French
MWA Je-Jl 24 1869

INDEPENDENT journal and temperance agitator. w 1853-
MH D 22-29 1854;F 15 1855
MWA Je 1-8,22-29,S 21,N 24 1854
MiU-C Je 22 1854

Worcester daily JOURNAL. d S 1 1847-O 22 1849||?
DLC Ap 25 1848[O 2-22]1849
MWA [1847-48]O 2-22 1849
MiU-C O 3 1849
NcD [Ja-F 1848]

Semi-weekly JOURNAL. sw D 2? 1847-
MWA Mr 17 1848

Worcester daily JOURNAL. d Ag 30 1854-My 26 1855||
1854-Ap 3 1855 as Daily evening journal. Merged with Worcester daily transcript, later Worcester evening gazette
MWA [1854]55
P-M Mr 8 1855

Worcester weekly JOURNAL. w Je 21 1871-
MWA Je-Ag 9,O 18 1871
NcD Je 21,Jl 19 1871

Worcester daily JOURNAL. d N 10? 1871-
MWA N 11-D 11 1871

Saturday evening JOURNAL. w D 13? 1879-
MWA Ap 3,My 8-29,Jl 3-10 1880

LIBERTY of the press. *See under* Boston

MASSACHUSETTS cataract, Worcester county waterfall, temperance standard and dew drop. w F 28 1842-53||?
1842-D 20 1843 as Worcester waterfall and Washingtonian mirror; D 27 1843-Mr 13 1844 Cataract and waterfall; or Massachusetts Washingtonian. Subtitle varies: Mr 20 1844-D 16 1847. . . and Worcester county waterfall; D 23 1847-Ag 24 1848. . . , Worcester county waterfall and temperance standard; etc.
Some years dated also in Boston and Taunton
IHi F 28 1844
KHi Ja 17,Mr 27 1844
MB D 27 1843-Mr 9 1847;S 14-21 1848;Je 21 1849;Ap 25 1850
MBAt Mr 20 1844-Mr 9 1847
MH D 25 1847-Ap 21 1853;O 20-D 15 1854
MHi [1847-48]
MSaE [1851]Jl 22 1852
MWA Mr 5,My 7,Jl 16-23,S 10 1842;Ja 28,Jl 29,S 9,N 4,D 27 1843-Mr 10 1853
MiU-C [1846-47]
NN Ja 21 1843
NcD My 7 1845;Jl 29 1847
P-M D 24 1845

*MASSACHUSETTS spy. tw,sw,w Jl 17 1770-My 27 1904||
Title varies: Massachusetts weekly spy; Thomas's Massachusetts spy; Haswell's Massachusetts spy; etc. Subtitle varies
1770-Ap 1775 pub in Boston
Suspended from Jl 17-Ag 2 1770;F 1-Mr 7 1771;Ap 6-My 3 1775;F 23,Mr 8-Ap 5,19, My 31-Je 14 1776
tw Jl-O? 1770;sw N 5 1770-F 1 1771
C-S 1823-26
CtY D 21 1823;Ag 27 1828;Ja-Je 1864
DLC 1821-Ag 25 1830;Ja 19-26,F 9-16,Mr 9, Jl 13,D 21 1831;32[33]-[35-36]-[49]-Mr 1859; Ag 8,S 19 1860;Ap 24,Jl 3 1861;F 12-19,N 12 1862;My 24-31 1865;Ja 5,26-Ap 13,N 30 1866; Jl 26,D 20 1867;Jl 3 1868;Ja 15-F,My 7 1869; F 25,My 6,Jl 18,Ag 26 1870;F 3,17,Ap 14,Jl 28 1871;Ja 5,Ag 2,16 1872;Ap 25,Ag 1 1873; Mr 20 1874;F 25-D 22 1876
ICHi Ja 9,30 1822;Ap 16,Ag 27 1823
KHi 1822;Ag 20 1823
M [1821-S 9 1881]
MB 1821-Jl 2 1851;My 12,Je 16,Jl 28 1852;Mr 8,My 31,Ag 16,30,S 27,O 25,D 6 1854;Je 6,20, Ag 8,O 3,N 28 1855;F 27,D 29 1856;Je 24-Jl 1,S 30 1863;Ja 25 1865;Jl 22 1870
MBAt 1821-32[61-63]
MH D 21 1836[50-52]
MHi 1821-30;N 20 1861;Ap 16,S 17,O 22 1862; Ja 21,My 6 1863
MSaE Ag 29 1821;Jl 30 1823;D 15 1830;Ja 5 1866;Je 17 1875
MWA 1821-1904
MeBa D 6 1824;Mr 9 1825
MiU-C [1822-24;26;28-29;31-32;41;43;55;61-66; 68-70;73;75;78;80;86]
MoHi Jl 15 1852
NN F 7,Mr 14,Ap 4-11 1821;My 8,22,Je 5,Jl 10 1822;D 20 1826;Jl 30 1828;O 24 1849;N 28 1855
NNHi 1821-30;Mr 31(extra)1824
NcD N 26 1823;Ap 26 1826;Mr 28 1827;F 1830-32;Ja 27,Je 15 1836;Jl 17 1839[Ap-Je 1843]My 7-21,Jl 2-9 1845;Ap 18 1849;Ap 3 1850;Ap 23, Ag 6 1851;My 12,Je 23,S 15,N 24 1852;Mr 30,Ap 13 1853;My 31 1854;D 16,30 1857;F 10,S 22,O 27 1858[S 1859-60]-64;My 3,24,O 25,N 8,22,D 27 1867[68-Jl 1872]Ja 24 1873;Ja 23 1874[76-79]Ap 23,O 1880[81-90;95-O 1899]
OClWHi O 2 1822;Ap 26,O 11 1826;Mr 11 1829; Ja 2,Mr 12 1862;Jl 22 1870;My 6 1879
P-M F 13 1839
PPAm 1821-30
PPAp 1821-30
REdH N 19 1828
WHi 1821-97
—d ed *See* Worcester daily spy

MASSACHUSETTS yeoman. w S 3 1823-Jl 26 1833||
Ag 27 1825-Ap 20 1833 as Massachusetts yeoman and Worcester Saturday journal and advertiser; Ap 27-Je 21 1833 Massachusetts yeoman and Worcester journal. United with National aegis to form National aegis and Massachusetts yeoman, later Aegis and gazette
CSmH S 11 1830
CoD N 14 1829
CtY 1823-Ag 1824
DLC 1823-F 5,Mr 5,26,Je 11,Jl 9 1831;Ag 11 1832
ICHi N 19-26 1831;F 25-Mr,Je 9,Jl,Ag 11,O 6,N 3,D 8-22 1832;Ja 5,Je 7 1833
KHi S 10 1823-D 18 1830

MASSACHUSETTS (*Continued*)

WORCESTER—*Continued*

MASSACHUSETTS yeoman. w 1823-33||—*Cont.*
MB 1823-F 20 1830;32-Mr 2 1833
MBAt 1823-Ag 20 1831;32-Ap 6 1833
MH 1823-Ag 1824;25-Ag 16 1828
MHi Ap 20 1825;Ja 27 1827;My 24,Je 21 1833
MNaHi Mr 15 1828
MWA 1823-My 17,31,Je 14-21,Jl 26 1833
MiU-C [1826-27;33]
NNHi D 31 1823[24]
NcD Jl 14 1827;N 13 1830-My 5 1832
WHi S 10 1823-S 9 1826;S 1827-33

MESSENGER. *See* Catholic messenger

MINUTE gun. w S 25? 1845-
KHi F 5-Jl 2 1846

NATIONAL aegis. *See* Aegis and gazette

NEW ENGLAND home journal. w D 21 1882-My 4 1889||
Ag 2 1884-My 7 1887 as Worcester home journal. Followed by Worcester county register
MH Ja 26-F 2,O 19 1883
MWA complete
MiU-C [1884]
NN D 28 1882
NcD 1882-D 20 1884;D 19 1885-N 1887;88-89

NEW IDEA. *See* L'Idee nouvelle

Worcester daily NEWS. d Mr 15 1885-86||
MWA Mr 17,My 14-15,N 10 1885[Mr-Ag 1886]
MiU-C Jl 16 1886
NcD Jl 16 1886

Worcester NEWS. w Je 18-O 22 1933||
MWA complete

NO LICENSE advocate. w N 5-D 10 1886||?
Campaign paper
MWA D 1886
NcD D 10 1886

NORD-ÖSTERN. w 1883-85||
In Swedish
IRA 1884-85
MWA D 5 1884

NORTH bend. w Jl 11-O 31 1840||?
Campaign paper
DLC S 5 1840
MWA Jl 18-25,O 31 1840
MiU-C O 31 1840
NNHi Jl 11 1840

NYA fäderneslandet. w 1889-99||?
1889-98 as Arbetarens vän
In Swedish
IRA 1891-92;96-99

Saturday OBSERVER. w Ja 30 1897-Ap 30 1898||
Ja-S 4 1897 as Argus. United with Messenger to form Messenger and Saturday observer, later Catholic messenger
MWA Ap 24,S 11 1897-98
NcD Ap 24,O 30-N 13,D 4,18 1897;Ja-F 12,26, Mr 12 1898

OLD guard. d Ja 19 1886-89||
OClWHi Ja 20 1886;Ja 18-21 1887;F 7-10 1888; F 5-7 1889

OLD Massachusetts. w S 25-N 13 1841||
Campaign paper
MWA complete

Worcester OMNIUM gatherum. *See* Worcester sentinel and reformer

L'OPINION publique. sw,d Ja 27 1893-Je 30 1931||
sw 1893-Ap 27 1898
In French
MWA F 1893-[95]N-D 22 1896;97-F 1905;Ja-Mr,My-N 1907;08-31
MiU-C [1901-04]

ORACLE of liberty. O 22 1844-
MWA O 22,N 8(extra)1844

Worcester PALLADIUM. w Ja 1 1834-F 12 1876||
F 20 1839-F 12 1840 as Worcester palladium and Worcester county republican. Merged with Massachusetts spy
CSmH F 21 1866
Ct N 30 1836
DLC [1834-39]40;Ja 27 1841;Ja 24 1844-76
MB 1834-D 20 1837[Ja 17-D 19 1838]-40[Ja 27 1841-42]Mr 8 1843-76
MBAt D 7 1842;Ap 19 1865
MHi Ag 27 1834;N 18 1835;My 11,Je 1,Ag 17,31 1836
MNaHi Ap 17 1839
MWA complete
MiU-C [1834;36;39;47;57]
NN N 26,D 10-24 1834;Ja 21-28,F 11-18,Mr 11, 25 1835;S 20 1837;Jl 18,Ag 29,N 28 1838
NcD Ja 28 1835[Ap-Je 1843;45]Ap 18 1849;O 12 1853;F 1 1854;Ja 3-17,F 7,Mr 28,N 21 1855;Mr 12,Ap 30,My 14-21,Je 4 1856;Ja 14,O 28 1857;Ap 28 1858;S 7,21,N 10,D 7-14 1859;F 15-22,Mr 7,Ap 11,Jl 4-11,S 12 1860-[69-71;74-75]
OClWHi Mr 28 1838;F 12-Ap 8,Jl 22,S 9-N 24 1840;Ja 3 1841
WHi 1834-42;Mr 8 1843-74

Worcester evening POST. d S 23 1891+
Jl 1 1922 is Worcester 200th anniversary celebration ed
pub F 1928+
MH My 29 1926
MW 1907+
MWA S 23 1891[97]-99;Jl 1900-09;My 1910+

Worcester daily PRESS. d Ap 1 1873-Ap 27 1878||
Merged with Worcester spy
Suspended from Jl 1-O 17 1877
DLC 1873-76
KHi 1873-Mr 1878
MWA 1873-Je,O 18 1877-78
NcD Ap 24,S 6 1873;Ap 27 1878

Worcester weekly PRESS. w 1873-Ap 1878||
Merged with Massachusetts spy
MWA Jl-O 13 1877

Worcester evening PRESS. d F 2 1874-77||?
DLC 1875
NcD Mr 2 1874;D 30 1876;Ja 6 1877

Sunday RECORDER. w S 17? 1893-95||?
MWA Mr 18-Jl 8 1894

Worcester RECORDER. w Mr 25 1898-S 9? 1899||
Merged with Messenger, later Catholic messenger
MWA Ap 1,22,Jl 1,15,Ag 12,S 24,D 17-24 1898; Mr 25-Jl,Ag 12 1899
NcD Ap 22,Je 10 1898;My 6,27,Jl 8,29-S 2 1899
PPCHi [1898-99]

Worcester REFORMER and true Washingtonian. w O 8 1844-Mr 12? 1845||
United with State sentinel to form State sentinel and Worcester reformer, later Worcester sentinel and reformer
MWA 1844;Ja 28-Mr 12 1845
MiU-C Ja 28 1845

Le RÉPUBLICAIN. sw Mr 19 1892-
In French
MWA Mr-D 24 1892

Worcester REPUBLICAN. w Mr 4 1829-F 13 1839||
1829-Ag 1833 as Worcester county republican. United with Worcester palladium to form Worcester palladium and Worcester county republican, later Worcester palladium
CSmH S 1 1830
Ct [1829-37]
DLC Mr 4 1829;30;Ag 28,O 9 1833;34-38
KHi [Ag 19 1829-My 12 1830;D 18 1833-Ag 15 1838]
MB 1829-F 1833;Mr 1835-36;Ja-Ag 8 1838
MBAt 1829[30-33]F 18,D 23 1835;Ja 13-20,Ap 13 1836;My 17 1837[38]
MH D 30 1829
MSaE Ag 26(extra)1835
MWA 1829-38;Ja 9,F 6 1839
MeU Ap 13 1831
MiU-C [1829-30;34-36]
NcD S 8 1830
OClWHi O 4 1837
P-M Jl 25 1832;Mr 14 1838
WHi 1829-33;O 29 1834;35-38

Worcester REPUBLICAN. w S 8 1860-
Campaign paper
DLC S 15 1860
MBAt S-N 3 1860
MWA S-N 3 1860
NcD S 8,N 3 1860

Le REVEIL. *See under* Fitchburg

Worcester SENTINEL and reformer. w 1844-Ap 18 1846||
1844-Mr 19? 1845 as State sentinel; Mr 28-Jl 4 1845 State sentinel and Worcester reformer; Jl 12-D 1845 Sentinel and reformer; Ja 3 1846 Worcester omnium gatherum. Merged with Bay state farmer and mechanics ledger
DLC Jl 26-Ag 2,O 25,N 1 1845
MWA [1844-45]Ja 3,Mr 28-Ap 4,18 1846
NcD Jl 4-12,N 8 1845

SKANDINAVIA. w 1886-Ap 23 1918||
1886? as Veckoblad. Merged with Svea
In Swedish
CtY S 26 1890
IRA 1887-1918
MH Mr 1917-18
MWA Mr 1888-92;1914-18
MWS 1886-97
MnHi S 9 1908-[S 1910-Mr 24 1911]Mr 27-Ap 17 1918

Worcester SOUTH compendium. *See* Uxbridge compendium (Uxbridge)

Worcester daily SPY. d Jl 24 1845-My 31 1904||
1845-S 30 1850 as Daily spy
CtY F 26 1857;Mr 20 1863;64-65
DLC Jl 31,Ag 27,S 24 1845;O 19,N 9 1846; Mr 1 1847;Je 28-29,Jl 27,O 31,N 7-8,10,27,29, D 9,19-20,30 1848;My 3 1849[50-53]F 15-D 11 1854;S 21,O 1,15,19,25,N 1,5,D 20 1855[56]-My 1897;My 1901-04
ICM Jl 15 1889
KHi 1859-Je 1886
MBAt [1861-63]Ap 15,19 1865
MCheHi My 25 1880;Jl 12 1884
MH Ag 29 1850;Je 6,8 1854;Je 2 1856;F 25,O 6 1862;Jl 18 1870;F 8 1872;O 11 1880;O 13 1895;Je 4 1901-04
MHi S 25 1862;Ag 11,18,25,28 1863
MLei 1862-76
MNaHi S 13 1873
MSob 1872-[1900]-02
MWA [Jl 24 1845-Ap 27 1847;Je 28 1848-D 13 1852]53-[55-56]-1904
MiU-C [1861-65;70;72-73;75-77;81;84;88]
NcD O 29,N 6,D 12,18 1845;Ap 18,Je 18,27,Jl 29,31,Ag 5,7,D 1,7-9,11-12,14,17-19,21-23 1846; Ja 8,Mr 6,8-10,22,24-30,Ap 1-4,6-7 1847[Je 1848-54]Jl 21,23 1857;Jl 15 1858[59-62]-[67-98] Jl 22 1899;F 11,Jl 22 1900;Mr 15,S 14,16-20 1901[02]Jl 1,14,O 27 1903
OClWHi Ja 9,F 9,27,Mr 9,Ap 22,My 27,Je 22, Ag 22,27,O 9,N 27,D 9 1861;62-D 18 1863; Jl 1864-Je 1868;Jl 31,D 8-9 1873
PEHi Je 9 1856
WHi 1845-Jl 22 1847;Jl 26 1848-Ag 1852;53-1903
—w ed *See* Massachusetts spy

Worcester Sunday SPY. w Jl 22 1888-My 29 1904||
MWA complete

SPY. (War committee of the Worcester club) ir O 1 1918-Ja 9 1919||
MH O 1,N 11 1918;Ja 9 1919
NcD O 1,N 11 1918
OClWHi O 1,N 11 9118;Ja 9 1919

Worcester STANDARD. w O 2 1912-
O 2-30? 1912 as Worcester standard and commercial bulletin
MWA 1912;Ja 5,18-25 1913

Daily STAR. d Ap 4 1879-
Ap-Jl 2 1879 as Worcester evening star; Jl 3-Ag 13 1879 Daily evening star
MWA Ap-Ag 15 1879
NcD Ag 15 1879

Worcester Sunday STAR. w F 13 1881-
MWA Ap 10 1881

STATE sentinel. *See* Worcester sentinel and reformer

Worcester STATESMAN. w Ja 23 1847-
MWA Ja 23 1847

Daily SUN. d O 18-N 1 1869||?
MWA O-N 1 1869

Worcester SUN. w Je 29 1895-97||?
Je-Ag 16 1895 as Worcester weekly sun
MWA Je-S 6 1895;Mr 7 1896
NcD N 9 1895

Worcester SUN. bw N 4 1933||?
MWA N 4 1933

SVEA. w 1897+
Title varies slightly
In Swedish
pub 1897+
IRA 1899-1925;27+
MWA D 31 1898;Jl-Ag 16 1899;1914-15;My 1918+
MnHi Ja 17 1900+

Worcester Sunday TELEGRAM. w N 30 1884+
pub 1884+
M N 30 1884+
MW 1884+
MWA 1884-O,D 1925-Mr,My-Je,S,N 1927-Ag 1928;29+
MWHi 1884+

Worcester TELEGRAM. d My 19 1886+
1886-D 31 1889 as Worcester daily telegram
pub 1886+
MH D 21 1906;Ja 1,Mr 11 1907
MW 1886+
MWA 1886-O,D 1925-Mr,My-Je,S,N 1927-Ag 1928;29+
NcD S 23,30,D 2 1894;Ja 20,F 23,Ap 1,7,12,14, Ag 25,S 29,D 22 1895;Ja 17,Mr 17,24,28,Je 23, 29-30,Jl 8,10,18,Ag 2,18 1896;Jl 31 1919

Worcester TELEGRAM. The Evening gazette. Sunday telegram. Retail ad-viser. bw 1920?+
My 8 1924-My 25 1929 as Worcester telegram-gazette. Retail ad-viser; Je 8 1929-Je 22 1935 Worcester telegram and the gazette. Retail ad-viser
MWA My 8 1924-F,My-Je 17,S 9 1926+

Worcester daily TELEGRAPH. d My 8? 1847-Mr 15 1849||?
1847-Ag 23 1848 as Worcester telegraph
DLC Je 8-10,12,14 1848
MWA [Je 19-S 6 1847;48]Ja 5,20,Mr 10,15 1849
NcD Ja 24,F 21,My 1-2,18-20,23,Je 8,10,12-14 1848;Ja 5 1849

THOMAS'S Massachusetts spy. *See* Massachusetts spy

Worcester daily TIMES. d Jl 23 1860-
MWA 1860-Ja 22,F 21,25 1861

Worcester weekly TIMES. w 1860-
MWA N 30 1861

Worchester daily TIMES. d S 1 1879-90||
MWA 1879-N 14 1889;F 19-D 1890
MiU-C My 28 1880
NcD S-N 25 1879;My 28 1880

Weekly TIMES. w 1889-90||
MWA F 1 1890

Worcester TRANSCRIPT. w D 20 1851-S 26 1857||
Ag 25-D 1855 as Worcester weekly transcript and Massachusetts guardian; 1856-F 28 1857 Worcester weekly transcript. United with National aegis to form Aegis and transcript, later Aegis and gazette
MB 1851-54
MWA 1851-55;N 29-D 6 1856;F 28,Jl 11-25,Ag 8,22-S 5,19-26 1857
NcD S 3,D 31 1853

Worcester daily TRANSCRIPT. *See* Worcester evening gazette

Le TRAVAILLEUR. w,sw,tw O 16 1874-D 31 1892||
My 31-N 25 1875;F 5 1889-F 17 1892 as Le travailleur, journal canadien-francais w 1874-My 22 1879;sw S 29 1879-F 17 1892
In French
CaQ Mr 6 1885-92
MWA 1874-Je 24[Jl 8-N]1875;Ag 30,S 13,D 6 1877[F-My 1878]My 22[S 29 1879-O 22 1880; My 13-D 1881]Mr 8 1882[S 7-N 13 1883]Ja 29 1884;S 18,O 6,D 1,18 1885;O 15(supp)1886;Mr 15,Jl 8-15,O 18 1887-O 15 1889[F-O 17 1890]Mr 13 1891;Ja 15,F 17,Ap 8 1892

Le TRAVAILLEUR et le progrès. w S 10 1931+
1931-Ag 4 1932 as Le travailleur
Dated also in Manchester, N.H.
MWA 1931+
NhMA 1933+

Daily TRIBUNE. d N 14 1849-Mr 22 1851||
Merged with Worcester daily transcript, later Worcester evening gazette
MWA N 15 1849-51

Worcester TRUE republican. w? N 1 1860-
MWA N 1 1860

TRUE whig. d Jl 12-N 14 1848||
MWA [1848]
NcD Ag 19,23,O 16,20,N 11,13-14 1848

MASSACHUSETTS (*Continued*)

WORCESTER—*Continued*

TZAIN Hai-eniatz. w S? 1899-
In Armenian
MB [Jl 1900-N 1901]Ja-Mr 28 1903

VECKOBLAD. *See* Skandinavia

Worcester WATERFALL and Washingtonian mirror. *See* Massachusetts cataract. . .

WORCESTER county advertiser. w F 3 1869-
MWA F 3,25,Mr 11,Jl 27 1869
NcD Ap 24 1869

WORCESTER county cataract and Massachusetts Washingtonian. w Mr 22-D 20 1843||
United with Worcester waterfall and Washingtonian mirror to form Cataract and waterfall, later Massachusetts cataract. .
MB complete
MWA complete

WORCESTER county democrat. w Jl 14 1860-
MWA Ag 18 1860

WORCESTER county gazette. w Ja 1 1845-F 24 1847||
Ja 1-Mr 12 1845 as Worcester county gazette; Mr 19 1845 Worcester and Middlesex gazette; Mr 26-Jl 30 1845 Worcester county gazette and Middlesex standard
DLC 1845-46
MHi My 14,28 1845
MLoHi Mr 19-Jl 16 1845
MWA [Mr 26 1845-D 16 1846]F 3,17-24 1847

WORCESTER county weekly record. w
MiU-C Je 27 1908

WORCESTER county register. w My 11-Je 29 1889||
Follows New England home journal
MWA complete

WORCESTER county republican. *See* Worcester republican

WRENTHAM

Wrentham RECORDER and county register. w O 11 1872?-78||?
MWA Ja 3-10 1873

YARMOUTH PORT

CAPE COD item. w 1879-91||?
DLC S 8 1882
IU N 6 1888

CAPE COD item. d Ag 11- 1890||?
MWA Ag 27,S 3,19,25-26,O 3-20 1890

CAPE COD sand. *See under* Boston

Yarmouth REGISTER and Barnstable county weekly advertiser. w D 1836+
pub 1912+
DLC Ag 29 1839;O 30 1845
MH Jl 10 1845
MHi Ap 18 1850;Ja 21,F 25,Mr 4-25 1853;My 10 1861
MSanHi My 22 1863
MWA O 19 1837;S 5 1839;My 21 1840;D 28 1843;My 9 1850;Jl 22 1852;Ap 22 1864;Ja 14, Ap 8 1871
MY 1836+
MYa 1836+
P-M D 11 1845
PPL N 28 1850

MICHIGAN

ADRIAN

CONSTITUTIONALIST. *See* Michigan whig

Adrian daily EXPOSITOR. tw,d 1851-O? 1868||
Early years as Adrian evening expositor. Merged with Adrian daily times to form Adrian daily times and expositor, later Adrian daily times
tw 1851-55?
DLC D 28 1853
MiAd Je 1858-Ap 1862
—w ed *See* Michigan expositor

Adrian weekly JOURNAL. w 1867-79||?
MWA Je 2 1876

LENAWEE republican and Adrian gazette. *See* Adrian weekly times

MICHIGAN expositor. w O 15 1840-O? 1868||
United with Adrian weekly times to form Adrian times and expositor, later Adrian times
1840-Ag? 1843 pub in Jonesville
DLC F 27,Ap 24,Je 5,Ag-S 4,N 13-D 4,18-25 1849;Ja 2-F 4,25,Ap 15-22,My 13-Je,Jl 22,Ag 12-19,S 16,O 21-28,D 16-23 1851;Ja 6,20-F 10,Mr 2,Ap 6,27,Jl 6,Ag 3,17-24,S 21,O 19-26,N 9 1852;F 22,My 24 1853
MWA N 23 1852;F 17 1866
MiAd D 1849-58
N Ap 5 (extra)1842
OClWHi My 17 1843
—d ed *See* Adrian daily expositor

MICHIGAN messenger. w,sw 1886-98||?
w 1886-90?
MiAd 1890-97

MICHIGAN whig. w O 11 1837-42||?
1837-39? as Constitutionalist
MiD-B N 18 1837;S 30 1840
MiG N 13 1839
N Ag 21 1839;S 14 1842
OClWHi F 24 1841

Adrian weekly PRESS. w 1873-1908||
MWA Ag 25 1876;Ag 22 1879
MiAd My 1873-Ap 1904
N Je 13 1884

Evening RECORD. d 1881-87||?
NN Ag 23 1881

Adrian tri-weekly TELEGRAM. tw 1886?-1902||?
MiAd 1902

Adrian daily TELEGRAM. d D 2 1892+
1892-98? as Adrian evening telegram
pub 1892+
MiAd 1892-98;1900+
MiU 1926+
—**Michigan news index.**
MWA Ja-Ap 23 1925

Adrian weekly TIMES. w,sw tw O 15 1834-D 31 1913||
O-D 11? 1834 as Lenawee republican and Adrian gazette; D 18? 1834-Ag? 1865 Adrian watchtower; S? 1865-O? 1868 Adrian weekly times; N? 1868-1903? Adrian times and expositor. Merged with Adrian daily telegram
w 1834-1900?;sw Ja?-O 1901
DLC Ja 28,Jl 8 1835;Je 19 1845
IU Ap 20 1843
MWA D 21 1852;My 30 1879
Mi 1901-11
MiAd O 1852-N 1854;S 15 1857-O 1861
MiU Ag 8(extra)S 3 1840
NN F 27 1840
NcD Ja 18 1902

Adrian daily TIMES. d Je 1853-Ap 14 1914||?
1853-Ag? 1865 as Adrian daily watchtower; S? 1865-O? 1868 Adrian daily times; N? 1868-1903? Adrian daily times and expositor. Merged with Adrian daily telegram
MWA Ap 20 1876
MiAd 1853-Je 1863;Jl 1867-Ap 14 1914
NcD Mr 25 1899

Adrian WATCH-TOWER. *See* Adrian times

ALBION

Albion weekly HERALD. w 1861?-
MWA F 10 1866

Albion MIRROR. w O 11 1855-1910||?
MWA N 4 1869;My 22 1879
MiU [1855-56]

Albion RECORDER. w 1868-1918||?
MWA Ap 22 1876

Albion REPUBLICAN. w 1879-86||?
MiU My 2,Jl 25,Ag 29-S 5,O 3 1884

ALGONAC

Algonac COURIER. w 1894+
OClWHi Mr 10-17,Je 9-16,Jl 14,O 27 1911

ALLEGAN

ALLEGAN county democrat. w 1867-79||
MWA Ap 19 1876;Mr 26 1879
MiD-B Mr 15 1876;Je 5 1878

Allegan GAZETTE. w 1882+
pub 1882+
MiD-B [1922-23]-[25-26]-[28]

Allegan JOURNAL. w 1856-97||?
1882?-88? as Journal and tribune
MiAgG 1857-97

Allegan NEWS. w 1899+
pub 1899+
MiD-B [1922;24-25]-27

Allegan RECORD. w Ja 20 1843?-69||?
Ja?-Je? 1843 as Allegan and Barry record
MWA D 20 1852
MiD-B Jl 7 1843

Allegan TRIBUNE. w 1880-81||?
United with Allegan journal to form Journal and tribune, later Allegan journal

ALMA

Alma RECORD journal. w 1878+
1878-My 1929 as Alma record
pub 1878+
MiAC [1888-93]96-[98;1900]-[02-06;08-11]-[13-24]-[26]-[32]+
OClWHi Mr 7 1929

ALMONT

Almont HERALD. w F 15 1875+
pub 1875+
MWA Ap 27 1876

Almont LEADER. w 1853?-
MiAlH Je 27,Ag 15 1854;Je 20 1855;Ap 15 1865

Almont PALLADIUM.
MiAlH D 20 1853

ALPENA

ALPENA county pioneer. *See* Alpena pioneer

Alpena ARGUS-PIONEER. w Je 29 1871-1918||?
1871-1908? as Alpena weekly argus
Suspended from Jl 12-Ag 27 1872
MiAlp [1871]-[1917]

Alpena daily ECHO and Alpena farmer. d 1890-1916||?
1890-1915? as Alpena evening echo
MiAlp [1912-15]

Alpena NEWS. d 1899+
pub 1920+
MiAlp 1899-[1920-34]+
—w ed *See* Alpena pioneer

Alpena PIONEER. w Ap 30 1863-1908||?
1863-Ap 1866 as Thunder Bay monitor; My 1866-83? Alpena county pioneer. United with Alpena weekly argus to form Alpena argus-pioneer
MWA F 17 1866;Ap 14 1876
MiAlp Mr 9-23 1900
—d ed *See* Alpena news

THUNDER BAY monitor. *See* Alpena pioneer

ANN ARBOR

Ann Arbor daily ARGUS. d N 16 1898-Je 24 1907||
United with Ann Arbor news to form Ann Arbor news-argus
MiU complete

Ann Arbor weekly ARGUS and Ypsilanti sentinel and commercial. w Ja 28 1846-D 27 1907||?
1846-O 10 1879 as Michigan argus; O 17 1879-O 7 1898 Ann Arbor argus; O 14 1898-F 16 1906 Ann Arbor argus-democrat; F 23-D 7 1906 Ann Arbor weekly argus
MWA N 24 1852;Mr 12 1858;Ap 21,My 19 1876;My 23 1879
MiD-B Je 15 1853;F 2 1854;Mr 17 1876
MiU [1846-54]-[81-83]-[86-88]-[92]-[98]-[1906] 07

B'HOY'S eagle. sm? O 1848-D 29 1849||?
MiU My 8,Je,O 11,D 29 1849

Morning CHRONICLE. d Mr 14-Ag? 1839||
Follows Daily Michigan argus
MiU Mr 14 1839
—w ed *See* Michigan argus

COON hunter. w? Je 15- 1844||?
MiU Jl 6 1844

Ann Arbor daily COURIER. d O 16 1894-S 28 1895||
MiU complete

COURIER-REGISTER. w Je 13 1861-My 23 1906||
1861-Je 11 1863 as Peninsular courier; Je 21 1863 Peninsular courier and Ann Arbor visitant; Je 28 1863-Ap 7 1876 Peninsular courier and family visitant; Ap 14 1876-D 20 1899 Ann Arbor courier
Suspended 1895
MWA F 11 1864;F 8 1866;Ja 25 1878
MiU [1861-63;66]-[68;70]-[78]-[83]-[92]-1906
PLaL Ap 14 1876

Ann Arbor DEMOCRAT. w S 13 1878-O 7 1898||
United with Ann Arbor argus to form Ann Arbor argus-democrat, later Ann Arbor weekly argus and Ypsilanti sentinel and commercial
MWA My 8 1879
MiU complete

DEMOCRATIC herald. w Ag 28 1839-D 28 1842||
Follows Michigan argus
DLC D 30 1840-Je 6 1841
MiU [1839-42]

Der DEUTSCHE hausfreund. *See* Der Hausfreund und post

EMIGRANT. *See* Michigan emigrant

Der HAUSFREUND und post w Ja 1889-93||?
1889-92? as Der Deutsche hausfreund. Followed by Neue Washtenaw post, later Washtenaw post-tribune
In German
MiU [1890-92]

Ann Arbor JOURNAL. w Ag 11 1847-68||?
1847-Jl 25 1855 as Washtenaw whig; Ag 22-S 26 1855 Ann Arbor journal and Washtenaw whig
DLC F 9 1853-Mr 15 1854;Je 4 1868
MiU [1847]-[55]-[63]

Ann Arbor LOCAL news. w Jl 21 1857-Ag 21 1860||?
1857-Ja 4 1859 as Local news and advertiser
MiU [1857-60]

MICHIGAN argus. w F 5 1835-Jl 25 1839||
Followed by Democratic herald
Ct Ap 30 1835
DLC Ja 19 1837-38
MWA Ja 14 1836;Mr 1 1838
MiD-B Mr 19 1835
MiU complete
—d ed *See* Daily Michigan argus; Morning chronicle

Daily MICHIGAN argus. d Ja 14-Mr 12 1839||
Followed by Morning chronicle
MiU Ja 15,19,25,F 7,9,22,Mr 6 1839

MICHIGAN argus. 1843-45 *See* True democrat

MICHIGAN argus. 1846-79 *See* Ann Arbor weekly argus and Ypsilanti sentinel and commercial

MICHIGAN (*Continued*)

ANN ARBOR—*Continued*

MICHIGAN emigrant. w N 18 1829-N 13 1834||
1829-N 17 1830 as Western emigrant; N 24 1830-F 13 1833? Emigrant. Followed by Michigan whig, later Michigan whig and Washtenaw democrat
Suspended from N 18-D 2 1829
CSmH Ag 25 1830;S 28 1831
DLC F 17-D 15 1830;D 26 1832
MWA O 5 1831
MiD-B N 3 1832;D 26 1833
MiU 1829[30-34]
P-M Jl 21 1855

MICHIGAN state journal. w S 10 1835-50||?
Follows Michigan whig and Washtenaw democrat. 1835-My 10 1838? as State journal
DLC O 27 1840;F 5 1845
Mi My 12 1836-Ap 1837;40-N 19 1845
MiD-B Mr 2,Ag 10,N 16 1837;Je 6 1839;Mr 22 1843
MiU 1835[36]-[38]-[40]-[44-45]46

MICHIGAN state news. w 1857?-
CaOTA My 19 1866
MiU Ag 28 1860-[61-62]-Je 23 1863

MICHIGAN times. w? S 2 1837?-
MiU S 23 1837

MICHIGAN times. w My 2-O 27 1840||
DLC Je 16 1840
MiU My 9,Je 16-23,Jl 7,21,Ag 11-18,S 15-22,O 13,27 1840
NBuG Ag 25,S 8 1840

MICHIGAN whig and Washtenaw democrat. w D 4 1834-S 3 1835||?
Follows Michigan emigrant. 1834-Ap 2 1835 as Michigan whig. Followed by Michigan state journal
MiD-B F 26 1835
MiU [1834-35]

MILL boy of the slashes. w? 1844||?
MiU O 21 1844

NEUE Washtenaw post. *See* Washtenaw post-tribune

Ann Arbor daily NEWS. d N 28 1890+
1890-Ag 2 1898 as Washtenaw evening times; Ag 3 1898-Ap 12 1900 Evening times; Ap 13 1900-Ap 3 1902 Washtenaw times; Ap 6 1902-Ag 31 1903 Washtenaw daily times; S 1 1903-My 2 1908 Ann Arbor daily times; My 3-Je 6 1908 Ann Arbor news, times and argus; Je 8-13 1908 Ann Arbor times; Je 14 1908-Mr 31 1909 Ann Arbor daily times; Ap 1 1909-O 24 1919 Daily times news; O 25 1919-D 31 1927 Ann Arbor times news
MWA N 1 1906
MiU 1890+

Ann Arbor NEWS-ARGUS. d D 18 1905-My 2 1908||
1905-Je 24 1907 as Ann Arbor news. United with Ann Arbor daily times to form Ann Arbor news, times and argus, later Ann Arbor daily news
MiU complete

OBSERVER. S 30 1905||?
MiU S 30 1905

OLD hero. w Ap 24-O 1840||?
DLC My 1 1840
MiD-B O 9? 1840
MiU Jl 17,Ag 14 1840

PENINSULAR courier. *See* Courier-register

Ann Arbor RECORD. w S 21 1900-Ap 10 1903||
1900-Mr 7 1902 as Washtenaw republican
MiU complete

Ann Arbor REGISTER. w S 7? 1872-D 21 1899||
United with Ann Arbor courier to form Courier-register
Suspended from Ag 29 1873-D 22 1875
MWA My 17 1876;N 12 1891
MiU 1875-81;83-99
PLaL Jl 12-19,Ag 23 1876;My 30 1877;My 15, Jl 17 1878;Je 11,Ag 6 1879
WHi 1890-93

SIGNAL of liberty. w Ap 26 1841-F 5 1848||
Followed by Michigan liberty press (Battle Creek)
DLC N 20 1843
MdBJ D 29 1841-43;46;Ap 1847-48
MiBy 1845
MiD-B Ja 30 1843;My 20 1844
MiU Je 6,S 5 1846
NhD N 20 1843;Ja 29 1844

STATE journal. *See* Michigan state journal

Ann Arbor daily TIMES. d D 6 1877-
MiU D 6 1877;Mr 8 1878

Evening TIMES. *See* Ann Arbor daily news

Ann Arbor TRIBUNE. *See* Washtenaw post-tribune

TRUE democrat. w F 1 1843-Mr 8 1849||?
1843-D 16 1845 as Michigan argus; D 19 1845-Ja 1846 True democrat; F 5 1846-My? 1847 True democrat and Michigan argus
DLC 1844-Ja 16 1846
MiD-B Jl 5,O 25 1843;My 18 1847
MiU [1843-49]

WASHTENAW county tribune. *See* Washtenaw post-tribune

WASHTENAW post. w 1879-92||?
United with Der Deutsche hausfreund to form Der Hausfreund und post
In German
MWA Ja 14 1881

WASHTENAW post. 1905-27 *See* Washtenaw post-tribune

WASHTENAW post-tribune. w,sw,tw 1894+
Follows Der Hansfreund und post. 1894-1904? as Neue Washtenaw post; 1905?-S 9 1927 Washtenaw post; S 16 1927-Ja 1928 Washtenaw county tribune; Ja 24? 1928-Jl 20 1931 Washtenaw tribune; Jl 22 1931-F 6 1935 Ann Arbor tribune
sw S 16 1927-Jl 20 1931;tw Jl 22 1931-F 1934
1894-1917? in German
MiD-B O 22 1925-[28-Jl 1931]-[33]-F 6 1934;F 8 1935+

WASHTENAW republican. *See* Ann Arbor record

WASHTENAW daily times. *See* Ann Arbor daily news

WASHTENAW tribune. *See* Washtenaw post-tribune

WASHTENAW whig. *See* Ann Arbor journal

WESTERN emigrant. *See* Michigan emigrant

WOLVEREEN. sm Ap 25? 1836-
MiU O 24 1836

ARMADA

Armada TIMES. w 1889+
pub O 1921+

ATHENS

Athens TIMES. w,d 1883+
My 27 1931 is centennial ed
MiD-B [1922-23]My 27 1931

ATLANTA

MONTMORENCY county herald-tribune. *See* Montmorency county tribune

MONTMORENCY herald. *See* Montmorency county tribune

AUGUSTA

Augusta BEACON. w Mr 14 1902+
pub 1902+

BAD AXE

HURON county republican. w 1899-1901||?
United with Huron tribune to form Tribune-republican, later Huron county tribune

HURON county tribune. w 1875+
1875-1901? as Huron tribune; 1902?-06? Tribune-republican
pub 1907+
MiD-B F 2 1912[Mr 1922-23]-[26]

HURON tribune. *See* Huron county tribune

TRIBUNE-REPUBLICAN. *See* Huron county tribune

BALDWIN

LAKE county star. w My 1 1873+
pub 1903+
MiD-B Mr 16-23 1876;Mr 1922-[25]

BANCROFT

Bancroft BULLETIN. w 1879?-
MWA Ja 1 1880

Bancroft COMMERCIAL. w 1890+
MiD-B [Mr 1922-Je 7 1928]

BANGOR

ADVANCE. w 1873+
pub 1873+

BARAGA

BARAGA county herald. *See* Democrat

BARAGA county journal. *See* Baraga journal

DEMOCRAT. w 1892-94||
1892 as Baraga county herald
MiLaS [1892]

Baraga JOURNAL. w,ir 1910-22||
1910-11? as Baraga county journal
w 1910-16
MiLaS [1915-22]

BARRYTON

Barryton PRESS. w 1896-1927||?
MiD-B [Ap 20 1922-25]

BATTLE CREEK

Sunday morning CALL. w Ag 3 1884-91||?
MiBcS 1884-Je 20 1886
—mail ed *See* Weekly call

Weekly CALL. w S 5 1885-87||?
MiBcS S-N 7 1885
—city ed *See* Sunday morning call

CONSTITUTIONAL union. w F 19? 1868-
MWA F 26 1868

Battle Creek ENQUIRER-NEWS. d 1900+
1900-S 1 1918 as Battle Creek enquirer; S 3 1918-29? Battle Creek enquirer and evening news
MiBcS [Jl 1917-S 1 1918]-Ap 1919
—Annual New Years supp
MiBcS 1915-10;18-19;21-22;25;28+

Battle Creek JOURNAL. w 1850-1914||?
Title varies: Weekly journal
ICHi N 8 1871
MWA Ap 19 1876
MiBcS Mr 1852-[54]-[56-57]-Jl 24 1863;Ap 20 1865
OClWHi O 5 1865

Battle Creek daily JOURNAL. *See* Battle Creek moon-journal

MICHIGAN liberty press. w Ap 13 1848-49||
Follows Signal of liberty (Ann Arbor)
MdBJ Ap-Ag 1848

MICHIGAN tribune. w Ag 8 1846-48||?
Follows Western citizen
MiBcS [1846-Mr 18 1848]

MICHIGAN tribune. 1870-82 *See* Battle Creek republican

Battle Creek daily MOON. d Mr 25 1879-Je 6 1915||
1879-83? as Nightly moon. United with Battle Creek daily journal to form Battle Creek moon-journal
MiBcS Mr-My 4 1879;Ag 9-10,14 1909

Battle Creek MOON-JOURNAL. d 1872+
1872-Je 6 1916 as Battle Creek daily journal (1907-S 23 1911 Battle Creek journal)
MiBcS 1872-My 7 1873[Ap 1906-17]-[20-31]+
MiD-B [1919-22]
—w ed *See* Battle Creek journal

Battle Creek NEWS. d 1911-Ag 1918||?
United with Battle Creek enquirer to form Battle Creek enquirer and evening news, later Battle Creek enquirer-news

Battle Creek REPUBLICAN. w 1870-D 29 1882||?
1870-Je 17 1882 as Michigan tribune; Je 24-O 21 1882 Battle Creek tribune
MWA Ap 20 1876
MiBcS [O 20 1871-72]-74;S 1877-[79]-82

Battle Creek TRIBUNE. *See* Battle Creek republican

WESTERN citizen. w? Jl 1845-Ag 1846||
Followed by Michigan tribune
MiBcS Mr 7 1846

BAY CITY

Daily morning CALL. d Ap 13 1881-84||?
MiBy Ap-[O 1881-Ap]O 13 1882-Ap 12 1883

Weekly CHRONICLE. w F 17 1871-78||?
United with Bay City tribune to form Bay City chronicle and tribune, later Bay City tribune

Bay City CHRONICLE and tribune. *See* Bay City tribune

Le COURIER. w Ja 12 1884-87||?
In French
MiBy 1884

Bay City DEMOCRAT. w 1890+
MiD-B [1922]-[25]

Bay City EXPRESS. w Ap 28-Jl 18 1857||
Followed by Bay City press, later Bay City press and times
MiBy complete

Bay City JOURNAL. w O 1 1864-O 30 1873||
Merged with Bay City chronicle
MiBy O 14 1864-Ag 15 1868

Bay City daily JOURNAL. d 1871-O 1873||
Merged with Bay City chronicle
MiBy N 18 1871-F 24 1873

Tri-weekly JOURNAL. tw
MiBy Mr 20-O 28 1871

Bay City OBSERVER. w Ja 5 1876-79||?
MWA My 1 1879
MiBy 1876-Mr 1 1879

Le PATRIOTE. w S 6 1883-95||?
In French
MiBy 1883-84

Bay City evening PRESS. d N 1 1879-My 30 1891||
United with Bay City times to form Bay city times-press, later Bay City daily times
MiBy complete

Bay City PRESS and times. w S 14 1859-O 31 1864||
1859-Ag? 1860 as Bay City press
MiBy 1859-Ag,D 13 1860-[S-O 1863]-64

Bay City daily TIMES. d 1884+
Je 1891-Ap 30 1904 as Bay City times-press; Ag 1 1916-D 30 1927 Bay City times-tribune (other variations slight)
Mi Jl 1909+
MiBy 1889+

Bay City TRIBUNE. d Ap 5 1873-Jl 31 1916||
1879-80 as Bay City chronicle and tribune. United with Bay City times to form Bay City times-tribune, later Bay City daily times
ICM N 9 1879
MWA Ap 20,Ag 23 1876
MiBy Ap-[N 1873-Mr 1879]-1916

BEAR LAKE

Bear Lake BEACON. w S 1 1888+
pub S 1918+

BELDING

Belding BANNER-NEWS. w My 1889+
1889-My 1918 as Belding banner
pub 1889+
MiD-B [1922-24]-Je 7 1928
MiG 1916+

Belding NEWS. w 1896-My 1918||
United with Belding banner to form Belding banner-news

MICHIGAN (*Continued*)

BELLAIRE

Bellaire RECORD. w Jl 9 1931+
pub 1931+

BELLEVILLE

Belleville MIRADOR. w Ap 1 1881-84||?
MWA My 6 1881

BELLEVUE

Bellevue weekly GAZETTE. w 1871+
MWA Ap 20 1876

BENTON HARBOR

BANNER-REGISTER. w 1888-O 6 1922||
1888-93? as Berrien county banner. Followed by Benton Harbor herald
MiD-B [F 10-O 1922]

BERRIEN county banner. *See* Banner-register

Benton Harbor HERALD. w O 12 1922-N 11 1926||?
Follows Banner-register
MiD-B 1922[23-24]-N 11 1926

MICHIGAN democrat. *See under* Grand Rapids

Benton Harbor NEWS-PALLADIUM. d 1895+
1895-1903 as Benton Harbor evening news
pub 1895+

Benton Harbor PALLADIUM. w,sw O 9 1868-1903||
Jl 1 1881-83? Times and palladium (title varies slightly) United with Benton Harbor evening news to form Benton Harbor news-palladium
w 1868-95?
DLC F 23 1872-Mr 10 1882
MiBhN complete

Benton Harbor TIMES. w 1875-Je 1881||?
United with Benton Harbor palladium to form Times and palladium, later Benton Harbor palladium

TIMES and palladium. *See* Benton Harbor palladium

BERRIEN SPRINGS

BERRIEN county journal. *See under* Eau Claire

Berrien Springs ERA. *See* Journal-era

JOURNAL-ERA. w D 1875+
1875-S 1931 as Berrien Springs era
1934+ also dated in Eau Claire
pub 1875+
MWA Ap 19 1876
MiD-B [1922-26]-My 1928

BESSEMER

Bessemer FREE press. w 1901-09||
United with Bessemer herald to form Bessemer herald-free press, later Bessemer herald

Bessemer HERALD. w Ja 1 1886+
1886-94 as Pick and axe; 1910-19 Bessemer herald-free press
pub 1895-1914 20+
MiD-B [1922-23]-[25-27]-Je 8 1928

PICK and axe *See* Bessemer herald

BIG RAPIDS

Big Rapids CURRENT. w F 6 1879-91||?
Mi 1879-85

Big Rapids HERALD. *See* Mecosta county herald

Big Rapids MAGNET. w 1870-76||?
United with Big Rapids pioneer to form Pioneer-magnet, later Big Rapids pioneer
MWA Ap 20 1876

MECOSTA county herald. w 1876-1914||?
1876-1906? as Big Rapids herald (1878?-79? National greenback herald) United with Big Rapids pioneer to form Pioneer-herald, later Big Rapids pioneer
MiU 1894-1901
MoCaT S 20 1878

MECOSTA county pioneer. *See* Big Rapids pioneer

NATIONAL greenback herald. *See* Mecosta county herald

Big Rapids PIONEER. w 1862-1914||?
1862-73? as Mecosta county pioneer; 1877?-81? Pioneer-magnet
MWA F 17 1866

Big Rapids PIONEER. d 1881+
1881-1914? as Big Rapids pioneer; 1915-16? Pioneer-herald

BIRMINGHAM

Birmingham ECCENTRIC. w My 1878+
pub 1878+
NcD D 1 1905

BLANCHARD

Blanchard BANNER. *See* Tri-county banner

TRI-COUNTY banner. w O 1 1921+
1921-26? as Blanchard banner
pub 1921+

BLISSFIELD

Blissfield ADVANCE. w Ap 9 1874+
pub 1874+
MWA Ja 30 1879
MiD-B [1925-[28]

BOYNE CITY

Boyne CITIZEN. w,tw,sw 1880+
sw 1907-14?;tw 1915-24?;sw 1925-27?
pub 1881+
MiD-B [1922-24]-[26]

BRIGHTMOOR

Papers published in Brightmoor are listed under Detroit

BRIGHTON

Brighton ARGUS. w 1880+
Early issues as Brighton weekly argus and gazette
KHi O 19 1881
MWA Ja 25 1881

Brighton CITIZEN. w 1871-90||?
MWA Ag 25 1880

LIVINGSTON courier. *See under* Howell

BRONSON (BRANCH COUNTY)

Bronson HERALD. w Ja 3? 1867-71||?
MWA F 21 1867

BRONSON (KALAMAZOO COUNTY). *See* KALAMAZOO

BROOKLYN

Brooklyn EXPONENT. w S 1? 1881+
MWA N 17 1881
OClWHi Jl 30-Ag 6 1903

BROWN CITY

Brown City BANNER. w 1892+
1892-94 as Brown City bee
pub 1892+

Brown City BEE. *See* Brown City banner

BUCHANAN

BERRIEN county record. w,sw 1867+
1885?-1903? as Buchanan record
sw 1902?-09?;18?-25?
MWA F 3,Mr 17,Ap 14 1870;F 16,Ag 24-31,O 26 1871;F 29,Mr 21-28,S 5,26-O 3,24 1872;Ja 23,N 20 1873;F 19,Mr 5,19,Ap 2-9,My 7,Je 11 1874;Ap 20 1876;Ap 26 1888

MICHIGAN independent. w 1879-96||?
1879-80? as Buchanan reporter; 1881?-95? Michigan independent and reporter
MWA Ja 15 1885

Buchanan RECORD. *See* Berrien county record

Buchanan REPORTER. *See* Michigan independent

Buchanan weekly UNION. w 1863?-69||?
MBAt Ap 3 1865
OClWHi Jl 10 1865

BURR OAK

ST. JOSEPH county democrat. *See under* Three Rivers

BURTON HEIGHTS

Papers published in Burton Heights are listed under Grand Rapids

BYRON CENTER

Papers published in Byron Center are listed under Grand Rapids

CADILLAC

ARBETAREN. w 1900-04||
In Swedish
IRA Ap 26 1894

CALEDONIA

Caledonia FREE press. w D 1925-O 3 1930||
Merged with South Kent county news and Grand Rapids suburbanite (Grand Rapids)
MiG D 10 1926-30

CALUMET

COPPER country news. *See* Calumet news

HRVATSKA. w 1905+
1905-14? as Hrvatska sloboda
Dated also in Chicago
In Croatian
IU D 14 1917-Ag 15 1924
PPiHi N 12 1931+

MINATORE italiano. *See under* Laurium

Daily MINING gazette. *See under* Houghton

Calumet NEWS. w 1881+
1889?-97? as Calumet and Red Jacket news; 1898? Calumet, Red Jacket and Laurium news; 1899?-1908? Copper country weekly news
MiHoM F 22 1889-F 1892

Calumet NEWS. d 1892+
1892-O 22 1907 as Copper country evening news
MiC S 19 1898+
MiHoM 1893-[1927-28]+

SENTINELLA. w 1896-1906||?
In Italian
WHi F 6 1906

SLOVENSKE novice. w 1916-21||?
In Slovenian
IU D 14 1917-Je 1920

VALVOJA. sw,tw N 1915+
Title varies: Walvoja
sw 1915-23?
In Finnish
pub 1920+

WALVOJA. *See* Valvoja

CAMDEN

Camden ADVANCE. w Ag 1898+
pub 1898+

CARLETON

Carleton MESSENGER. w 1905+
pub 1905+

CARO

Caro ADVERTISER and citizen. *See* Tuscola county advertiser

Caro CITIZEN. w 1878-82||?
United with Tuscola advertiser to form Caro advertiser and citizen, later Tuscola county advertiser

Caro DEMOCRAT. *See* Tuscola county courier

TUSCOLA advertiser. *See* Tuscola county advertiser

TUSCOLA county advertiser. w Ag 21 1868+
1868-82? as Tuscola advertiser; 1883?-Ap 10 1884 Caro advertiser and citizen
pub 1868-72;Ag 1884-S 1887;S 1888-Ag 1891; My 1892+

TUSCOLA county courier. w 1878-O 15 1918||?
1878-95? Caro democrat; 1896? Tuscola county courier and democrat
MiCarA 1888-95;98-99;1901-02;04-09;11-O 15 1918

CARSON CITY

Carson City GAZETTE. w Ja 1881+
pub 1881+

CASNOVIA

Casnovia HERALD. *See* Kent City-Casnovia herald (Sparta)

CASS CITY

Cass City CHRONICLE. w 1899+
1899-1903? as Tri-city chronicle
pub 1904+
Mid-B [1922-24]-[26]27

TRI-CITY chronicle. *See* Cass City chronicle

CASSOPOLIS

NATIONAL democrat. w 1850-1925||
Merged with Cassopolis vigilant
MiD-B [1922]23
NNHi Mr 21 1873

Cassopolis VIGILANT. w My 16 1872+
pub 1872-O 1874;Ja 27 1876+
MWA Ap 20 1876

CEDAR

GLADWIN county record. *See under* Gladwin

GLADWIN county register. *See* Gladwin county record (Gladwin)

CEDAR SPRINGS

Cedar Springs CLIPPER. w D 1869+
1869-70 as Wolverine clipper
pub 1869+
MWA Ap 19 1876
MiG D 1905+

Cedar Springs LIBERAL. w 1890-1927||?
MiG S 8 1926-Je 2 1927

WOLVERINE clipper. *See* Cedar Springs clipper

CENTREVILLE

CRUSADER. w 1870-85||?
MWA Ja 9 1879

MICHIGAN liberator. *See under* Jackson

MICHIGAN (*Continued*)

CENTREVILLE—*Continued*

Centreville OBSERVER. w O 11 1890+
pub 1890+

PENINSULAR. w? Jl 2 1836-
Suspended from D 1836-Ap 1837
CtY Ap 25 1837

ST. JOSEPH county advertiser. *See under* Constantine

ST. JOSEPH county republican. w Ap 16 1869-90||?
1891 pub as part of St. Joe county news (Mendon)
MiD-B 1869-72;75-76;79-80

WESTERN chronicle. *See under* Three Rivers

CERESCO

Ceresco PIONEER. w 1873?-
OClWHi Ap 1 1875

CHARLEVOIX

Charlevoix COURIER. w 1883+
1883-98? as Charlevoix democrat
pub 1906+

Charlevoix DEMOCRAT. *See* Charlevoix courier

Charlevoix SENTINEL. w Ap 16 1869+
pub 1869+
MiD-B [1922-24]-[26-Je 7 1928]

CHARLOTTE

Charlotte ARGUS. w 1855-70||?
OClWHi O 3 1865

Weekly CALLER. w 1878-84||?
NcD F 16 1884

DEMOCRATIC leader. *See* Charlotte leader

EATON county republican. *See* Republican-tribune

Charlotte LEADER. w F 3 1871-1928||?
1871-73? as Democratic leader
MWA Ap 21 1876
OClWHi F 3,D 29 1871;D 4 1884;Mr 9,Jl 6 1900;N 30 1905

REPUBLICAN-TRIBUNE. w 1854+
1854-61? as Eaton county republican; 1862?-92? Charlotte republican; 1893?-98? Eaton county republican; 1899?-1928? Charlotte republican
MWA Ap 21 1876
Mi 1861
MiCh 1855-70;72;78-88

Charlotte TRIBUNE. w 1887-1928||?
United with Charlotte republican to form Republican-tribune
OClWHi Je 13 1900

CHEBOYGAN

Cheboygan DEMOCRAT. *See* Cheboygan observer

Cheboygan FREE press. w Ja 6 1876-Ap 4 1878||?
Follows Cheboygan independent
MWA Ap 20 1876
MiD-B [1876-Ap 4 1878]

Cheboygan INDEPENDENT. w D 4 1872-N 19 1875||?
Follows Cheboygan times. Followed by Cheboygan free press
MiD-B [1872-N 19 1875]

MANITOBA chronicle. w Ja 28-Je 3 1871||
Followed by Cheboygan times

NORTHERN tribune. *See* Cheboygan daily tribune

Cheboygan OBSERVER. w F 26 1880+
1880-1927? as Cheboygan democrat
pub 1900+
MiD-B 1880-[83]-[98]

Cheboygan TIMES. w Ja 18-N 18 1872||?
Follows Manitoba chronicle. Followed by Cheboygan independent
MiD-B [Ja-N 18 1872]

Cheboygan daily TRIBUNE. w,sw,d Jl 17 1875+
1875-Jl 2 1885 as Northern tribune; Jl 9 1885-1912 Cheboygan tribune
w 1875-1910?;sw 1911?
pub 1875+
MWA Ap 15 1876
MiD-B 1875-[77-80]-[83]-[85]-[87]-[89]-[97]
MiG N 25 1876;Ag 30 1894

CHELSEA

Chelsea HERALD. w 1871-1905||?
United with Chelsea standard to form Standard-herald, later Chelsea standard
MWA O 3 1878
MiU [1885;89-92]

Chelsea STANDARD. w 1889+
1906?-07? as Standard-herald
MiD-B [1922-23]-Je 7 1928
MiU [1890-92;97]

CLAM LAKE

Clam Lake weekly NEWS. w 1872-77||?
MWA Ap 28 1876

CLARE

Clare SENTINEL. w 1892+
MiD-B [1922-24]

CLIO

Clio MESSENGER. w 1907+
MiD-B [1922-24]25
MiF Ag 18 1932-[33]+

COLDWATER

BRANCH county gazette. w 1857-68||
1857-60 as Branch county republican
MWA D 25 1867

BRANCH county news. w Je 18? 1837-39||?
1837-38? as Coldwater observer
MWA D 30 1837

BRANCH county republican. *See* Branch county gazette

Coldwater OBSERVER. *See* Branch county news

Coldwater daily REPORTER. d 1895+
MiU [1926]+

Coldwater semi-weekly REPUBLICAN. sw 1875?-
MWA Ap 21 1876

Coldwater SENTINEL. w Ap 16 1841-Je 1854||?
DLC S 24 1841
MiCl 1841-49
MiU [1848]-[54]

COMSTOCK PARK

Papers published in Comstock Park are listed under Grand Rapids

CONCORD

HOME enterprise. *See* Concord news

Concord INDEPENDENT. *See* Concord news

Concord NEWS. w N 1871+
1878-87 Home enterprise; 1888-1918 Concord independent
pub 1895+
MWA Ap 21 1876

CONKLIN

Conklin ENTERPRISE. w Ja 1 1933+
pub 1933+

CONSTANTINE

ADVERTISER. *See* St. Joseph county advertiser

ADVERTISER record. w Je 1897+
1897-Je 15? 1900 as Record
pub 1897-1913;16+
MiD-B [F 8 1922-Jl 1928]

Constantine MERCURY. *See* St. Joseph county advertiser

RECORD. *See* Advertiser record

Constantine REPUBLICAN. w Jl 6 1836-Ag 1 1838||?
Ct [1837-38]
DLC N 8 1837
MiD-B Jl 13 1836-Ag 1 1838

ST. JOSEPH county advertiser. w F 12? 1845-Je 1900||
1851-60? as St. Joseph county advertiser; 1861?-70? Weekly mercury and St. Joseph county advertiser; 1871?-74? Constantine mercury; 1875?-76? St. Joseph county advertiser; 1877?-79? St. Joseph county advertiser and Constantine mercury; 1880? Advertiser; 1881?-82? Advertiser and mercury. United with Record to form Advertiser record
1845-My 1851 pub in Centreville
MiConA 1880;82-84;86;88-1900
MiD-B Ja 10 1861-70
OClWHi O 22 1845

COPPER HARBOR

LAKE SUPERIOR news and mining journal. *See* Mining journal (Marquette)

CORAL

Coral NEWS. w Ja 27 1897+
pub 1897+

CORUNNA

Corunna JOURNAL. w 1880-1913||?
1880-84? as Shiawassee county journal
MiCo 1897-1913

SHIAWASSEE American. *See* Shiawassee county American

SHIAWASSEE county American. w 1855-84||?
1855-80? as Shiawassee American
MWA F 22 1866

SHIAWASSEE county journal. *See* Corunna journal

SHIAWASSEE democrat. w 1839-56||
1839-40? as Shiawassee express and Clinton advocate; 1841-42 Shiawassee argus and Clinton advocate; 1843-Jl? 1848 Owasso argus and Shiawassee democrat
1839-49? pub in Owosso
MWA Je 1 1843;D 18 1852
MiG S 2 1854
NN N 27 1841;F 26,Mr 12,Ap 16-23,My 21 1842-Je 1 1843;Mr 7 1844

COVERT

Weekly REVIEW. w 1901||?
MiSoT Jl 5-N 8 1901

CRESTON

Papers published in Creston are listed under Grand Rapids

CROSWELL

Croswell DEMOCRAT. *See* Croswell journal

Croswell JEFFERSONIAN. *See* Sanilac Jeffersonian

Croswell JOURNAL. w 1880-1902||?
1880-1900? as Croswell democrat
MWA F 25 1881

SANILAC Jeffersonian. w O 7 1858+
1915-Ag 1 1935 as Croswell Jeffersonian
1858-N 16? 1894 pub in Lexington
pub O 1879+
CaOTA Ag 1 1863
MWA F 3 1866;Ap 22 1876
MiD-B 1858-[64-68]-[70]-[78]-[88-89]-[92-94]-[96-98]
NbHi My 27,Jl 15 1876
OClWHi Jl 22 1865

DAVISON

Davison INDEX. w Jl 1889+
pub 1889+
MiF Ag 19 1932-[33]+

DEARBORN

FORDSON independent. *See* Dearborn independent

Dearborn INDEPENDENT. sw,tw,w 1921+
Not to be confused with Dearborn independent (Ford 1899-1927,not in this list)
1921-D 1925 as Springwells independent; D 25 1925-N 13 1928 Fordson independent
sw F 1928-Je 1929;tw Jl 1929-Ap 1930
pub 1924+
MiD-B [1929-30;34-35]

SPRINGWELLS independent. *See* Dearborn independent

DECATUR

Decatur REPUBLICAN. w Je 5 1867+
1867-82? as Van Buren county republican
pub 1895+
MWA Mr 30 1876

VAN BUREN county republican. *See* Decatur republican

DEERFIELD

Deerfield RAY. bw 1875?-
MWA D 11-25 1875

Deerfield RECORD. w 1878-84||?
MWA Ap 9 1881

DETROIT

Detroiter ABEND-POST. d S 5 1868+
In German
MWA Ag 23 1876
MiD-B 1916-[18;23-28]-[30]+

ADVANCE and labor leaf. w N 1 1884-89||?
1884-F 12 1887 as Labor leaf
MiD-B S 10 1887-O 6 1888
WHi D 15 1888;F 23-My 11 1889

Detroit weekly ADVERTISER. w N 20 1829-Jl 1862||
1829-N 17 1830 as Northwestern journal; N 24 1830-F 1833 Detroit journal and Michigan advertiser; Mr 1833-Ja 14 1835 Detroit journal; Ja 21 1835-S? 1839 Detroit journal and courier
CSmH S 1 1830
Ct [1830-31]
DLC N 20,D 2-16,30 1829-Ja 6,N 24 1830;Ja 5 1831;O 10 1832;33;38;N 2 1852
MBAt Ap 7-14 1830
MWA N 20 1829;Ja 12,F 16,Mr 9,Je 1 1831;Ag 8 1837;F 5 1840
Mi 1829-N 14 1832
MiD 1829-30;N 27 1833-N 1835; S 1839-S 1 1841;42-Ag 1845
MiD-B 1829-N 17 1830[31-40]42[43-45;49;59-60]
MiG Ap 20,O 12 1831;Ja 11,F 1-8 1832;Ap 21 1841-42;Ja 10 1843-D 9 1845
MiU Mr 29 1838;59-Jl 1 1862
MiU-C S 8 1841;Mr 24 1846
OClWHi Mr 31 1830;Jl 18-O 1832;N 3 1840;O 30 1860-Ja 1 1861
OHi Ap 20 1835
PWCl Ap 20,Jl 13,27 1842
WHi Ja 28 1834
—sw,tw ed *See* Detroit journal and courier

Detroit daily ADVERTISER. d Je 11 1836-Jl 7 1862||
United with Detroit daily tribune to form Detroit advertiser and tribune, later Detroit tribune
DLC O 22,24(extra)1840;Mr 7 1842-F,Ap 9,21 1845;Mr 2 1846-Ag 1847;Ja 29 1850-Ag 4 1853; F 12-Jl 1862
MWA Jl 9 1844;Ja 23 1847;D 24 1852;O 16-N 3,10-21 1860
MdBJ D 13 1842
Mi Ag 14-D 1857;D 29 1858-62
MiD 1836-42;44[45]-47:49-62
MiD-B [1836-39]-[41-47]-[49-52;54-55;57-62]

MICHIGAN (*Continued*)

DETROIT—*Continued*

Detroit daily ADVERTISER. d 1836-62||—*Cont.*
MiEIS [Ja,Mr-Je,S-D 1861]
MiG [Ja-N 1845;Ja-My 3 1847]Jl 27 1849;Je 16-27,30-Jl 4,7-22,24-Ag 1 1851;O 1-2,D 4 1857;My 4 1858;Ja 25 1859
MiMu Ap 13-D 24 1860;Mr-D 1861
MiU [1836-38]-[45;61-62]
NN Ap 4[S 1840-Mr 1842]
NNHi D 19 1860
NcD S 7 1848
OClWHi Jl 11,20-21,Ag 31,S 10-11,N 21,28-29,D 6-15,28 1860;Ja-Mr 4 1861
PAtM Jl 13 1854
PPiHi Ja 10 1859
WHi N 1 1836;Ja 22 1839;Mr 10 1840-Ap 1842

Detroit ADVERTISER and tribune. [Evening ed] d 1849?-O 1877||?
1849?-Jl 1862 as Evening tribune?
DLC Ag 10,25 1869
MWA F 27 1854;Ja 23 1855

Detroit ADVERTISER and tribune. [morning ed] *See* Detroit tribune

Detroit weekly ADVERTISER and tribune. *See* Detroit weekly tribune

Detroit ADVOCATE. w Ja-Je 8 1901||?
MiD-B Mr 23-30,Ap 20-Je 8 1901

ALLGEMEINE zeitung von Michigan. *See* Michigan tribune

Detroit AMERICAN. w 1905-18||?
MiD-B [1907;09-11]

AMERICAN vineyard. w S 1843-My 19 1848||?
Title varies: Vineyard
MiD-B [1844;46-47]
MiU-C [1846-48]
NNHi D 24 1847
—d ed *See* Daily vine?

ANTI-ROMAN advocate. w N 20 1869-Ag 1870||
1869-F 1870 as L'Impartial
In English and French
MWA N 20 1869

Detroit weekly ARGUS. w D? 1863-
MiD-B Ja 25 1864

BRIGHTMOOR journal. w 1923+
pub 1923+

CITY life. w F 21 1897||?
MiD-B F 21 1897

COLONIAL review. bw O 8 1927-Mr 10 1928||?
MiD-B O 22 1927-Mr 10 1928

Detroit COMMERCIAL. w 1883-86||?
MiD-B S 1884-85

COMMERCIAL advertiser. *See* Detroit journal w 1861-1915

Detroit daily COMMERCIAL bulletin. d My 28 1848-Ap 16 1852||
DLC Je 27 1848

Daily CONSTITUTIONAL. sw,w,d My 25 1842-45||
1842-Jl? 1844 as Constitutional democrat
sw My-S 1842;w O 1 1842-Jl? 1844
DLC F 24,Ap 13,Je 1,Jl 8,Ag 7,20,30 1844
MdBJ Ag 6 1842
MiD-B [Je 1842-Je 1844]
MiU My 11 1844
WHi Ja 1 1843

CONSTITUTIONAL democrat. *See* Daily constitutional

Detroit CONTENDER. w 1920-My 7 1921||?
Negro
MiD-B N 13 1920;My 7 1921

Detroit COURIER. w D 23 1830-Ja 14 1835||
United with Detroit journal and Michigan advertiser to form Detroit journal and courier, later Detroit weekly advertiser
DLC 1830-D 22 1831;O 11 1832
ICN N 17 1831
MBAt Je 2-9 1831
MWA D 23 1830;Ja 6,Mr 24-31,Ap 21-My,Je 23,Jl-S 15,29-O 6,20 1831;D 6 1832;Mr 20 1833;F 5 1834
Mi 1830-D 15 1831;Ja 12 1832-Ja 1 1834
MiD-B [1831]-[33-34]35
MiU D 19 1832-D 11 1833
WHi S 6 1832

Detroit COURIER. w My 1870+
1870-71 as Wyandotte enterprise; 1872?-87? Wayne county courier
1870-75 pub in Wyandotte
MWA F 27 1880
MiD-B Mr 17 1876

Detroit daily DEMOCRAT. d Ap 3 1853-F 4 1855||
United with Detroit inquirer to form Detroit democrat and inquirer
MiD Ja 11-N 10 1854

Detroit DEMOCRAT and inquirer. d Ja 18 1854-N 19 1855||
1854-F 4 1855 as Detroit daily inquirer.
Merged with Detroit daily advertiser
MWA Mr 16 1854
Mi N 20 1854
MiD-B [Ja 28-Ag 5 1854]

DEMOCRATIC free press. *See* Detroit free press . . .

DEMOKRAT und volksblatt. *See* Michigan volksblatt. w

DESTEPTAREA. w 1914?-
In Roumanian
NN N 27-D 18 1921

DZIENNIK polski. [Polish daily news] d Mr 4 1904+
In Polish
pub 1904+
MWA N 1 1906
PP Mr 20 1897[1922]+
PPiHi N 24 1931+

ECHO. w O 15 1878-92||?
MWA N 20 1879
MiD-B O 15 1878;Mr 24 1880
N F 6 1879
TJT N 30 1887
—d ed *See* Detroit news

Detroit evening EXPRESS. d Je 2-N 29 1845||
Merged with Detroit daily advertiser
MiU Je 9 1845

Detroit FREE press. d S 28 1835+
1835-Mr 1 1842 as Detroit daily free press; Mr 2 1842-Ja 4 1846 Democratic free press
Suspended from Ja 4-Je 5 1837,Ja 3-11 1842
My 10 1931 is centennial ed
pub 1874+
ArHi Ag 30 1888
CL My 5,12 1931
CLM My 14 1884;F 27 1886
CP Jl 23,25 1885
CU-B S 20,22-24,26 1881
Ct O 8 1835;Je 23 1837;My 10 1931
CtY 1864-65
DLC Je-O 14 1837;Mr 25 1840;N 12 1842;Jl 8 1844;Je 9 Ag 25 1846-47;F 5 1854-56;D 24 1859;60-61;63-N 2 1866;67-72;Jl 10 1874-Je 1883;Je 19 1884+
ICHi Mr 12 1838;Jl 3 1840;O 16,23,N 9,16,21 1858;S 21 1860;Ap 15,Jl 18 1864;O 9 1871
IaDH Ap 12 1905-14
KHi Ja 7 (supp)1873;N 24 1877
M F 23-27,My 10 1931
MBAt Ap 15-18 1865;My 10 1931
MH Je 25 1885;Ap 27 1905;O 23-28,30-N 4,6-11,13-14 1911;My 10 1931
MWA N 27,29 1852;Ja 8-Je,D 20 1853;Ja 13,Jl 18,Ag 5,7,O 25,N 1,D 25 1860;N 3 1862;My 5 1871;Je 16 1875;Mr 13,D 10 1877;Je 30 1885;Ja 29 1888;My 3 1891;O 30 1899;My 1 1913
Mi Ag 19 1839-Mr 11 1841;43-Je 19 1844;F 25 1845;Mr 11,S 17,21 1856;Ja 28,Je 15,Jl 22,Ag 20,S 4,9-12 O 22,N 28 1858;59+
MiD 1835[36]-[45]-[52]-[56]-[70]-[1911]+
MiD-B [1835-58]-[61]-[63-69]-[71]-[83]-[87]-1915;19[20]-[29]-[32]+
MiG Je 13,S 24 1840;Ja 11 1842;F 6,S 19 1843;Ap 6,My 28,N 15-16,18-20-21 1844;Ja 10,16,Mr 7,19,O 30,N 16,D 21 1861;Mr 11 D 12 1862;Mr 20,Ap 8,11,22 1863 [F-D 1864]Mr 1,3,S 16 1865 Mr 29 1866;O 12 1871;Ap 30 1889;Jl 31 1908;11+
MiEIS N 1885-[1924;26]28;30+
MiLS 1904-Mr 1907
MiCw Ja-Ag 1878
MiU [1836 38;40-41;49-50;54;63-64;85]+
MnU [1918-21]
NIC 1893-1905
NNHi Mr 13 1863;Mr 25,Je 1-2,Jl 30 1873
NcD O 9 1840;Ja 11 1863;Ap 1 1892
NcU Ag 13 1875[77]My 10 1931
OClWHi D 20-21 1864;Ag 19 1881;Ja 3 1888;S 14 1913
OHi 1923-Jl 1931
T My 10 1931
TJT F 7 1855;Ja 25 1898
WHi My 1902-My,Jl 1904-09;15+

Semi-weekly FREE press. sw Je 19 1835-
1835? as Democratic free press
Suspended from Ja 4-F 28 1837;Ja 3-11 1842
DLC Mr-Je 2 1837
MiG Je 9 1835

Daily FREE press (for the country). sw
DLC 1838-39;Ja 15/16 1845;S 28 1846-49

Detroit FREE press. tw -1884||?
MiEIS [Ja-O 1880]

Detroit FREE press and live stock journal. w,sw My 5 1831-1905||?
1831-N 28 1832 as Democratic free press and Michigan intelligencer; D 5 1832-Ja 10 1848? Democratic free press; Ja 17 1848-95? Detroit free press; 1896?-1904? Twice-a-week Detroit free press
w 1831-95?
C 1887-90
Ct [1834-37]
CtY My 1864-D 11 1865
DLC 1832-D 7 1842;F 25,Ag 18 1845;Ja 5-19,F 16-Mr 9,23-30,My 11,Je 22-29,Jl 20,Ag 3,17-S 7,21,O 5-19,N-D 14,28 1846-Ja 11,F 1-8,Mr 1,29-My 17,31-Je 14,Jl 12-19,O 25,N 15,D 13,27 1847;Ja 7,F 7 1848;O 29 1860
ICHi My 5 1831
ICM D 11 1880-D 29 1883[84-My 1885]-[Mr-Je 1887]Ap 24,N 20 1890;Ja 12,Jl 20,Ag 10,S 28,O 19,N 23,D 28 1893[94]Jl 4 1895[Jl 1897-1903]
ICN My 5 1831
IHi [F-D 22 1877]
MWA My 5 1831;Mr 2 1836;Ja 17 1837;Ja 5 1842;Mr 7 1877;S 13 1879;N 19 1881;Ap 22,My 20,Jl 1-8,Ag 5 1882;N 27 1886;F 28-Mr 7,21,Ap 11,25-My 15,Je 6-13,Jl 4-11,Ag 1,29,S 19 1889-Ja 16,30-F 6,20 1890;F 13 1900
Mi 1831-Ap 23 1834
MiD 1831-N 22 1832;Mr 29 1843-Je 17 1844
MiD-B [1831-36 38-41;43-48]
MiEIS N 24-D 1880
MiG My 5,D 29 1831-Ja 5,Mr 15,Je 7 1832;D 24 1834;F 4 1835;Ap 17,My 29,Jl 10,N 13-20 1839;My 20 S 9 1840;Ap 21,My-Jl,Ag 11-18,S,N 3,24 1841-N 11 1844;Ag 18 1856
MiPoHi My 5 1831;D 17 1855
MiU My 5 1831 My 23 1844;Ap 22 1845
NBuG N 8-29 D 13-27 1837;Ja 10,O 17,D 19 1838-Ja 9,31-F 20,Mr 13-Ap 1839;My 6,20-27,Je 17-Jl 8,Ag 5,S 4,D 23 1840
NN N 18 1840-My 12 1841

NbHi O 30 1875;S 20 1879;O 3 1889
NcD My 30 1895
NcU F 28 1885
OClWHi My 5 1831;D 18 1884

Detroit FREE union. sm,w Jl 18 1863-Ja 11 1864||
Merged with Detroit advertiser and tribune, later Detroit tribune
sm Jl-O 8 1863
MH Ag 31-S 15 1863
MiD-B [1863]-Ja 7 1864

* **Detroit GAZETTE.** w Jl 25 1817-Ap 22 1830||
DLC Ag 21 1827;Ag 14 1828;Ja-F 18,Mr 4,Ap 1 1830
IU complete(photostat)
MBAt Ja 24 1823
MHi F 22 1822
MWA 1821-30(photostat)
Mi 1821-22
MiD-B 1821-[28-30]
MiG complete(photostat)
MiU-C 1821-30(photostat)
MnHi complete(photostat)
NBu Jl 24 1828-Jl 2 1829
NNHi D 28 1821-Jl 12 1822
TxU 1821-Ap 8 1830
WHi 1821-Jl 3 1828

Detroit daily GAZETTE. d D 19 1842-45||?
Mi Mr 28 1843
MiD 1842-Je 13 1843
MiU [1842-43]

GAZETTE van Detroit. w 1914+
In Flemish
IU Ja 11 1918-F,Jl 10 1925—
MiD-B [1922-24]-26

Detroit GRAPHIC. w Jl 12 1879-F 1881||
Jl-O 4 1879 as Public spirit
MiD-B [N 8 1879-N 1880]

HAMTRAMCK news. w 1902-28||?
MiD-B [1922]-[25]

Sunday HERALD. w 1880-81||?
MWA My 29 1881

HEROLD. w Je 13 1855-My 31 1918||
1855-Mr 1876 as Michigan journal; Ap 1876-89? Michigan journal und herold; 1890? Herold; 1891?-93? Journal und herold
In German
WHi [1902]-18

HIGHLAND PARK times. w 1911-N 1923||
United with Highland Parker to form Highland Parker and Highland Park times

HIGHLAND PARKER and Highland Park times. sw,w 1919+
1919-N 1923 as Highland Parker
sw 1923?
MiD-B [1924-30]+

L'IMPARTIAL. *See* Anti-Roman advocate

INDEPENDENT. *See* Michigan independent

Detroit INFORMER. w 1897-1916||?
Negro
DLC Ja 13 1900

Detroit daily INQUIRER. *See* Detroit democrat and inquirer

Detroit JEWISH chronicle. w 1916+
PP [1917]+

Detroit JEWISH daily. *See* Jewish daily press and der weg

JEWISH daily press and der weg. d F 21 1919-N 5 1920||?
1919-Ag 21? 1920 as Der Weg; Ag 22-N 5 1920 title varies: Jewish way; Detroit Jewish dialy
In Yiddish
NN 1919-N 5 1920

JEWISH way. *See* Jewish daily press and der weg

Detroit JOURNAL. w 1833-35 *See* Detroit weekly advertiser

Detroit JOURNAL. w,sw 1861-1915||?
1861-66 as Commercial advertiser; 1867-93? Detroit commercial advertiser and Michigan home journal
w 1861-95?
MWA F 13 1864;D 19 1874
MiD-B [1864;74;76;81-82;86]My 24 1894
MiU [1871-73;75]
NbHi N 1 1878
OHi F 14,Mr 28,N 14 1879
VU D 8 1870

Detroit JOURNAL. d S 1 1883-Jl 21 1922||
1883-F 1888 as Detroit evening journal.
Merged with Detroit news
CP Jl 23,28 1885
DLC 1893-1922
IC My 1 1889
ICM My 14 1884
Mi 1901-Je 1918;19-22
MiD My 1884-[1919]-[21]-Je 1922
MiD-B [1884-89]-[91-92]-1901[08]-15[18-22]
MiDN Ja-Mr,S 1884-Ag 1886;87-1922
MiG Mr 4 1897;S 1 1898
MiU 1899-1902[15]
NbHi F 11 1904

Detroit JOURNAL and courier. sw,tw Mr 1 1833-
1833-Ag 1835 as Detroit journal and advertiser (sw)
MiD F 28 1834-Jl 1835
MiD-B [1833-35]
—w ed *See* Detroit weekly advertiser

JOURNAL und herold. *See* Herold

LABOR leaf. *See* Advance and labor leaf

LAKE SUPERIOR journal. *See* Mining journal (Marquette)

LAKE SUPERIOR news and journal. *See* Mining journal (Marquette)

MICHIGAN (*Continued*)

DETROIT—*Continued*

Detroit daily LEDGER. d S 4-8 1923||
MiD-B complete

LINCOLN PARK news. w 1918-33||?
MiD-B [1924-26]-[31-32]33

Detroitské LISTY. *See under* Chicago

MAGYAR banyászlap. w 1913+
1917?-O 20 1921 pub in New York City; O 27 1921-Ag 30 1928 in Himlerville, Ky.; S 6 1928-O 29 1931 in Columbus, Ohio; N 5 1931-F 2 1933 in Cleveland, Ohio
In Hungarian
IU D 1917+

MAGYAR hirlap. *See* Magyar napilap

MAGYAR napilap. w,sw,d N 1917?-S 9 1933|| 1917-Je 6 1933 as Magyar hirlap. Merged with Detroiti ujság
w 1917-D 5 1919; sw D 9 1919-Jl 6 1933
In Hungarian
IU N 9 1917-33
PPiHi [N 23 1923-D 8 1931]

MICHIGAN free democrat. w S 22 1852-
DLC N 3 1852
MiG Ja 12 1853
P-M F 13 1855

MICHIGAN herald. w My 10 1825-Ap 30 1829||
DLC 1826;Ja-Ag 14,D 18 1828-29
MWA S 13 1826;Ja 29 1829
MiD-B 1825-[27-29]
WHi S 20 1825;Je 26,Jl 3-10,Ag 28,O 2 1828

MICHIGAN independent. w Mr 11 1922+
1922-Mr 24 1935 as Independent; Mr 31-S 1935 Northwestern news
Negro
pub 1922+

MICHIGAN journal and herold. d Je 13 1855-1905||?
1855-Mr 1876? as Tägliches Michigan journal
In German
NNHi Ap 22,1870;Je 3,Jl 24 1873

MICHIGAN journal und herold. w *See* Herold

MICHIGAN staats zeitung. *See* Michigan tribune

MICHIGAN sun. *See under* Jackson

MICHIGAN tribune. sw,w S 21 1844-54||
1844-45 as Allgemeine zeitung von Michigan; 1846-50 Michigan staats zeitung
In German
MiD-B O 5 1844

MICHIGAN volksblatt. w 1853-1911||?
1853-69? as Demokrat und volksblatt
In German
MWA O 11 1871

MICHIGAN volksblatt. d N 1860-1915||
MWA Ag 28 1876
MiD-B 1870-74;76-1911

Der MICHIGAN volksfreund. w 1848?-
MWA N 20 1852

Detroit week-end MIRROR. w 1932-
MWA Ag 6 1932

Detroit NEWS. d Ag 23 1873+
1873-Ag 22 1905 as Evening news
F 1 1915-16? Sunday ed as Detroit news-tribune
pub 1873-[89]-[93]-[1907]+
DLC 1873-[95-98]Ag 23 1905+
ICM Jl 15 1882;D 4 1891
ICU Mr 1934+
MWA Ap 24 1876;F 17 1880;Je 28 1882;My 9 1888
Mi 1873+
MiD 1873-[84]-[1911-12]+
MiD-B [1873;75-79]-[81-88]-[91-92]-[94-95]-1901[04]-15[19]-[25]-[27-28]+
MiG 1930+
MiMn current year only
MiU 1897+
MnU My 1930+
N Ag 14,16-17 1875
NN Ag 23 1873
NNHi Ag 12 1878
NcD My-Je 1910;Ja 1911
NcU Ag 11 1875
OHi 1933-Je 10 1934
—w ed *See* Echo

Detroit NEWS. [morning ed] *See* Detroit tribune

Detroit NEWS-TRIBUNE. [morning ed] *See* Detroit tribune

Detroit NEWS-TRIBUNE. [evening ed] *See* Detroit news

Detroit NEWS-TRIBUNE. [Sunday ed] *See* Detroit news

NORTHWESTERN journal. *See* Detroit weekly advertiser

NORTHWESTERN news. *See* Michigan independent

OLD hero. w? 1840||?
Mi S 18 1840

OLIVE branch. w O 6 1848-
DLC D 11 1848

PENINSULAR freeman. w 1848-49||?
Merged with Detroit tribune
MdBJ O 11-D 1849

Detroit PLAINDEALER. w My 16 1883-95||?
KHi S 20 1889-My 19 1893

POLISH daily news. *See* Dziennik polski

Detroit weekly POST. w Ag 4 1837-
DLC S 30 1844
MiD-B 1837-Ag 8 1838
NNHi Ja 9,23,Mr 20,Ap 3 1839

Detroit morning POST. d 1838-
NNHi Ja 28,Mr 13,19,24,29 1839

Detroit daily POST. d Mr 27 1866-O 13 1877||
Title varies: Daily post; Detroit post. United with Detroit advertiser and tribune, to form Detroit post and tribune, later Detroit tribune
MWA Mr 26,My 2 1876
Mi complete
MiD complete
MiD-B [1869;72-77]
NcU Ag 14 1875
OHi Ja 10 1870

Weekly POST. w 1866-77||?
CaOTA O 2 1869
NNHi Ap 5,My 2 1873

Detroit POST. 1884-85 *See* Detroit tribune

Evening POST and craftsman. d Jl 3 1837-40||
1837-38 as Detroit morning post;Ja-My 1839 Morning post and craftsman
Suspended from S-N? 1839
MiD-B [1837-39]

Detroit weekly POST and craftsman of Michigan. w 1837-40||?
MWA Mr 27 1839

Detroit POST and tribune. tw 1849?-Jl 24 1884||?
1849?-Jl 1862? as Detroit tribune; Ag 1862?- O 1877? Detroit advertiser and tribune
DLC [Ag-D 1861]-Jl 1 1862;Ja 12,N 1 1864
MWA O 17 1867
MiD-B Mr 3 1874
MiElS [Mr 1867-O 1868]
MiG Ja 20,F 8,N 4 1876

Detroit POST and tribune. d *See* Detroit tribune

Detroit weekly PRICE current. w D 2 1875-N 1882||
MWA Ap 20 1876

PUBLIC spirit. *See* Detroit graphic

REDFORD record. w 1900+
pub 1925+

REKORD codzienny. d N 28 1913+
In Polish
Ct F 17 1920
IU D 8 1917-Ap 15 1918

DER REPUBLIKANER. w Jl 10?-D? 1852||
In German
MWA D 18 1852

RIVER ROUGE herald. Jl 27 1914+
pub [1914+]

Detroit SATURDAY night. w Mr 2 1907+
MdBJ Ap 4,O 10 1914;My 1,15,Jl 31 1915
Mi 1907+
MiD F 1908+
MiD-B [1907-17]-[20]-[22]-[25]-[28]+
MiG 1914+
MiU Ja 10 1914;28+
WHi Je 15 1935

SHRAPNEL. w Jl-N? 1864||
MiD-B S 17 1864

Detroit evening SPECTATOR and literary gazette. sw O 20 1836-My 20 1838||?
MWA D 3 1836
MiD-B Ap 26 1837(photostat)
MnHi Je 14 1837
NFre 1836

SPIRIT of '76 and Theller's daily republican advocate. d Ag 17 1839-40||?
Mi 1839-Ap 1,O 15 1840
MiD-B F 15 1840

SPY in Michigan. w Je 12 1837-40||?
Suspended from N 13 1838 to early in 1839
Mi N 14 1838
MiU S 26 1838

Detroit evening TELEGRAPH. d O 15 1877-N 15 1878||
MiD complete
—morning ed *See* Detroit tribune

Detroit daily TIMES. d My 14-N 1842||
DLC Je 7 1842
MdBJ My 28,31,Je 4,7-9 1842
MiD-B My-Ag 12 1842

Detroit daily TIMES. d Mr? 1853-56||
MiD-B Ap 21 1853

Detroit TIMES. d D 4 1883-F 26 1885||
MiD 1883-N 1884

Detroit TIMES. d O 1 1900+
1900-02 as Today; 1903? Detroit evening times
M N 17 1929;S 20 1931
MBAt N 17 1929
Mi Ag 15 1901-Je 2 1902
MiD 1900-[16]17[21]-[23]-[30]+
T S 21 1931
WHi N 17 1929

TODAY. *See* Detroit times 1900+

LA TRIBUNA italiana d'America. w My 1909+
In Italian
IU D 1917+

TRIBUNA romana. w 1924+
In Roumanian
PP O 29-N 26 1933

Detroit TRIBUNE. d N 19 1849-Ja 31 1915||
1849-Jl 7 1862 as Detroit daily tribune; Jl 8 1862-O 13 1877 Detroit advertiser and tribune; O 14 1877-Jl 31 1884 Detroit post and tribune; Ag 1 1884-O 31 1885 Detroit post; N 1 1885-Mr 22 1886 Detroit daily tribune; Mr 23 1886-My 23 1887 Detroit morning tribune; Ag 24 1905-Jl 6 1912 Detroit news [morning ed] Jl 7 1915-S 30 1913 Detroit news-tribune
CP Jl 23 1885
CtY Ja 24-D 1863;O 13 1871
DLC Ja 31 1850-Jl 21 1852;D 25 1861;Jl 8 1862-65;Jl 1874-Je,S 1894-98;1900-Ag 23 1905
ICHi S 30,O 6,20,26-27 1865
ICM O 4 1885
MB [Ja 22-O 1856]
MBAt Ap 15-19 1865
MWA D 11 1852;Jl 23 1862;Ag 23,S 16 1863; My 6 1871;My 2,Ag 4 1876;My 30(supp) 1880; Je 12 1881;My 9 1888;S 8 1889;Ja 30 1915
Mi 1859-1915
MiD 1849-My 18 1850;57-58;60-61;Jl 1862-Jl 3 1863;64-74;Jl 1875-[81]-Ag 1905;N 1913-15
MiD-B [1849;52-55;57;59]-[61-62]-[64-72;74-76]-[84-85]-[92]-[94]-[97]-99
MiElS S 1858-60;Jl 1861-[N 1862-N 1863;Ja-F,Jl-D 1871;Ag-N 1872;Jl-D 1873;Jl-D 1874]-O 1885
MiG Mr 21,O 2 1857;Jl 26 1858;Ap 15 1863;Ap 15,17,N 30 1865;O 11,13 1871;Mr 4 1889
MiPoHi Ja 30 1850;Mr 21(extra) 1857
MiU Jl 5 1859;S 27 1881;Jl 17 1882[98]-[1905]
MnHi Ap 16,My 17 1865
NNHi Jl 16 1863
NcU Ag 12,16 1875
P-M Mr 6,18,1854
WHi Je 28 1862

Detroit weekly TRIBUNE. w 1849-99||?
1849-Jl 15 1862 as Detroit weekly tribune; Jl 22 1862-O 11 1877? Detroit weekly advertiser and tribune; O 18 1877-Jl 31 1884 Detroit post and tribune; Ag 7 1884-O 29 1885 Detroit weekly post; N 5 1885-My 21 1891 Detroit weekly tribune; My 28 1891-Je 28 1892 Detroit tribune
DLC N 6 1855;D 11 1860-Ja 8,29,F 26,Mr 19,My 21,Je 11-18,Jl 9 1861
MWA My 16-N 7 1865;66-92
Mi D 27 1859-D 4 1860
MiElS [Mr,Je-O 1872]
MiU [1852-59]-[63]
OClWHi F 11 1875;F 14 1882
WHi Mr 12 1861-F 1865;96-99

Evening TRIBUNE. *See* Detroit advertiser and tribune. [evening ed]

Detroit TRIBUNE. tw *See* Detroit post and tribune tw

TRUMPET. w? 1841||?
MiU S 25 1841
PWCl S 11 1841

Detroiti UJSÁG. w 1922+
In Hungarian
IU N 17 1933+
PPiHi [Ja 30 1923-D 12 1931]

Detroit daily UNION. d Jl 4 1865-Jl 27 1876||
Merged with Evening news, later Detroit news
MiD [1868-69]-73
MiD-B O 12 1869;S 21 1872
MiG My 5 1871
MiPoHi Mr 7 1866
WHi S 20 1869

Daily VINE. d Jl 1846-
MiD-B Jl 11 1846
—w ed *See* American vineyard

VINEYARD. *See* American vineyard

LA VOCE del popolo. w S 1910+
In Italian and English
pub 1910+
IU D 14 1917+
MiG Ap 20 1911+

WAYNE county courier. *See* Detroit courier 1870+

Detroit WEEKLY. w Mr 21-Ap 11 1913||?
MiD-B Mr 28,Ap 11 1913

DER WEG. *See* Jewish daily press and der weg

DEWITT

CLINTON express. *See* St. Johns democrat (St. Johns)

DEXTER

Dexter LEADER. w Ja 1 1869+
pub 1870+
MWA My 2 1879
MiD-B 1924-25
MiU [1890-92]

Dexter NEWS. w D 24 1891-93||?
Merged with Dexter leader
MiU [1891-92]

DOWAGIAC

CASS county republican. w 1856-1907||?
1881-88? as Weekly republican. United with Dowagiac herald to form Herald-republican, later Cass county weekly
MWA Ap 20 1876
MiDoN 1869-[79-84]-[86]-[88-90]-1907

CASS county weekly. w 1892-1913||?
1892-1907? as Dowagiac herald;1908?-Ap 1912? Herald-republican;My?-D 1912? Moon's weekly
MiDoN 1909-Jl 1910;11-Ap,My 23-D 1912;Ja 23-N 6 1913

Dowagiac HERALD. *See* Cass county weekly

Dowagiac MONITOR. tw 1875||?
MiDoN [Ag-N 1875]

MOON'S weekly. *See* Cass county weekly

Dowagiac daily NEWS. d F 6 1897+
pub 1897-Je 1902;04;06+
MiU 1926+
—w ed *See* Dowagiac times

MICHIGAN (*Continued*)

DOWAGIAC—*Continued*

Weekly **REPUBLICAN.** *See* Cass county republican

Dowagiac **TIMES.** w 1880-1906||?
MiDoN 1887-1906
—d ed *See* Dowagiac daily news

DUNDEE

Dundee **ENTERPRISE.** w O 10 1871-76||?
MiD-B Mr 18 1876

Dundee **LEDGER.** w Jl 15? 1881-82||?
MWA Ag 19 1881

Dundee **REPORTER.** w 1876+
pub F 19 1826+
MWA My 3 1879
MiD-B [1922-Je 5 1925]

DURAND

Durand **EXPRESS.** w 1887+
pub 1900+

EAST JORDAN

CHARLEVOIX county herald. w 1896+
MiD-B [1922-23]-[25]-Je 8 1928

EAST LANSING

East Lansing **PRESS.** w 1919+
MiElS [O 19 1928-31]

EAST SAGINAW

Papers published in East Saginaw are listed under Saginaw

EAST TAWAS

IOSCO county gazette. w N 1 1868+
1868-80? pub in Tawas City
MWA Ap 20 1876
MiD-B Mr 16 1876[1922-25]
MiOs 1881+

IOSCO county news. w Ap 1 1922-D 26 1924||
MiLiH complete

EATON RAPIDS

Eaton Rapids **JOURNAL.** w 1864+
pub 1864+

Eaton Rapids **REVIEW.** w 1895-1926||
Merged with Eaton Rapids journal
MiD-B [1922-23]-26
MiErJ 1900-26

EAU CLAIRE

BERRIEN county journal. w 1874-S 1931||
United with Berrien Springs era to form Journal-era (Berrien Springs)
1874-82? pub in Berrien Springs
MWA Ap 22 1876

JOURNAL-ERA. *See under* Berrien Springs

EDMORE

Edmore **TIMES.** w 1902+
pub 1925+

EDWARDSBURG

ARGUS. w O 23 1875+
MiD-B Mr 18 1876

ELK RAPIDS

Elk Rapids **PROGRESS.** w My 1872+
1872-81? as Traverse Bay progress
MWA Ap 14 1876
MiD-B [1922-23;25-28]

TRAVERSE BAY progress. *See* Elk Rapids progress

ELSIE

Elsie **SUN.** w 1885+
pub 1908+

EMPIRE

Empire **LEADER.** *See* Northport leader (Northport)

LEELANAU leader. *See* Northport leader (Northport)

ESCANABA

DELTA. w Ap 30 1886-89||?
Merged with Gladstone delta (Gladstone)
MiE 1886-Ja 19 1889

IRON port. w,sw,d D 9 1869-1912||
1869-O 9 1877 as Escanaba tribune;N 28-D 23 1899 Evening iron port
sw My 5 1891-Mr 11 1892;d N 28-D 23 1899;sw D 1899-1904?
MWA Ap 15 1876
MiE 1869-D 2 1876;F 10-N 17 1877;S 21 1878-Ja 18,Je 27,O 4,N 22,D 6 1902-04;06;08-Jl 1910

Escanaba **JOURNAL.** w 1892-1923||?
MiD-B [1922-23]

MEDBORGAREN. w,m 1892-S 24 1920||?
w 1892-Jl 1920?
In Swedish
IRA 1895-1920
IU D 21 1917-[Ja-S 24 1920]
MnHi Ja 25 1918-S 24 1920

Escanaba daily **MIRROR.** d 1885-Je 28 1924||
MiE Ja-Ag 1906;Mr 15 1910-11;N 1912-My,Jl 1913-Je 1916;17-22

Escanaba daily **PRESS.** d 1909+
1909-24 as Escanaba morning press
MiE Jl 1910;Je 7 1912-Je 1914;15+
MiMn current year only

Escanaba **TRIBUNE.** *See* Iron port

EVART

Evart **REVIEW.** w O 10 1872+
pub 1872+
MWA Ap 14 1876
MiD-B [1922-24]25

EWEN

CLOVERLAND press. w 1912+
pub D 1912-23;My 1934+

FARMINGTON

Farmington **ENTERPRISE** and Garden City review. w 1888+
1888-1923? as Farmington enterprise
Also dated in Garden City
pub 1888+
MiD-B [1922-26;28]

FARWELL

Farwell **REGISTER.** w 1872-95||?
MWA Ap 13 1876

FENNVILLE

Fennville **HERALD.** w Jl 1892+
pub 1892-1903;08+

FENTON

Fenton **COURIER.** w,sw 1882+
1882-1907 as Genesee county courier
w 1882-S 1934
pub 1882+
MiF Ag 18 1932-[33]+

Fenton **GAZETTE.** w 1865-82||?
MWA Ap 25 1876

GENESEE county courier. *See* Fenton courier

FLAT ROCK

HURON VALLEY sentinel. w D 10 1920+
pub 1920+

FLINT

BEACON. w 1928?-31||?
Title varies: Murray Hill beacon
MiF [My 10 1929-31]

Flint **FLASHES.** *See* Flint weekly review

FLINT RIVER gazette. w Ja 26 1839-41||?
MiD-B S 28-O 5 1839

GENESEE county democrat. w My 4? 1843-
MiU N 16 1843

GENESEE weekly democrat. w O 29 1845-1905||?
1845-S 1853 as Flint republican
DLC Ja 19-26 1860
MWA F 21 1867;My 24,Je 14 1879
MiD-B [1876]-1904
OClWHi D 23 1882

GENESEE democrat and daily city news. d Mr 21 1859-
MiF [Mr-S 15 1859]

GENESSEE republican. w Ap 17 1845-
MiD-B O 2 1846

GENESEE whig. *See* Wolverine citizen

Flint daily **GLOBE.** d S 10 1900?-S 8 1902||
Title varies: Flint evening globe. United with Flint evening journal to form Journal and globe, later Flint daily journal
MiFJ S 10 1900-02

Flint **GLOBE** and news. w Ag 1866-1912||?
1866-D 21 1899 as Flint weekly globe;
D 28 1899-1906? Flint globe
MiFJ D 21 1899-Je 1902;04
MiU [1894]-99
—d ed *See* Flint daily globe; Flint daily journal

Flint **INDEPENDENCE.** *See* Flint news-advertiser

Flint **JOURNAL.** w,sw 1875-1902||?
pub My 30 1899-1900
MWA Je 11 1879
OClWHi Jl 1 1882

Flint daily **JOURNAL.** d Mr 3 1883+
1883-S 8 1902 as Flint evening journal;
S 9-D 1902? Journal and globe
pub 1898+
Mi 1921+
MiF 1912-[15]-[25]-[27]+
MiG 1927+

Flint **LABOR** news. *See* Flint weekly review

MURRAY HILL beacon. *See* Beacon

Daily **NEWS.** d Ag 18 1884-1905||?
Title varies: Flint daily news
MiD-B 1884-[1905]
MiF Je 8 1905

Flint **NEWS-ADVERTISER.** w,sw 1931+
1931-Ap 28 1933 title varies: Flint independent; Flint independent advertiser
Suspended from Ap 28-D 22 1933
w 1931-Ap 1933
pub 1931+
MiF [1932-33]+

NORTHERN advocate. w Ap 18 1840-42||?
DLC Jl 11 1840
MiD-B D 25 1841
NN O 2 1841

Flint **REPUBLICAN.** *See* Genesee weekly democrat

Flint weekly **REVIEW.** w 1910+
1910-11 as Flint flashes; 1912-16? Flint labor news
MiF [1927-34]+

Flint **SATURDAY** night. w 1919-31||?
Suspended from N 5 1921-My? 1928
MiF 1920-21; My 1928-My 16 1931
MiFN 1931
MiG Jl 24 1920-N 5 1921

WOLVERINE citizen. w F 23 1850-1911||?
1850-55 as Genesee whig; 1856 Wolverine citizen and Genesee whig
MWA Jl 16 1853;Ja 27 1866;S 5 1874;Ap 15 1876
MiF 1850[51]-73[75]-[77]
N N 7 1874
NNHi 1850-Mr 16 1867;Mr 27 1869-F 5 1887;F 9 1889-Ja 1893
OClWHi S 2 1865

WOLVERINE daily citizen. d Ag 25 1859-
NNHi 1859-N 17 1860

FLUSHING

Flushing **OBSERVER.** w Je 15 1882+
pub 1882+
MiF Mr 16 1935+

FORDSON

Papers published in Fordson are listed under Dearborn

FORT GRATIOT

Weekly **ENTERPRISE.** w 1878?-
MWA My 28 1881

FOWLERVILLE

Fowlerville **REVIEW.** w Je 19 1874+
MWA Ap 21 1876
MiD-B [1922]-[24]-[26]-[28]

FRANKENMUTH

Frankenmuth **NEWS.** w Jl 1 1906+
pub 1906+

FRANKFORT

BENZIE county patriot. w 1895+
MiD-B [1922-23]-[25-27]
MnHi [O 18 1934-Mr 14 1935]

FRASER

Warren-Fraser **HERALD.** *See under* Warren

FREMONT

Fremont **NEWS-INDICATOR.** *See* Fremont times-indicator

Fremont **NEWSLETTER.** *See* Fremont times-indicator

Fremont **TIMES-INDICATOR.** w 1884+
1884-87? as Fremont newsletter; 1888-1900? Fremont news; 1901-11? Fremont news-indicator
MiD-B F 5 1884[1922]-[24-25]-[27]

GALESBURG

Galesburg **ARGUS.** w,sw 1898—
Also dated at Richland
sw 1901-18?
pub 1921+
MiD-B [1922-23]-[25-28]

GARDEN CITY

FARMINGTON enterprise and Garden City review. *See under* Farmington

Garden City **REVIEW.** w -1926||?
United with Farmington enterprise to form Farmington enterprise and Garden City review (Farmington)

GLADSTONE

Gladstone **DELTA.** w 1887-Ja 22 1918||
United with Delta county reporter to form Delta county reporter and the Gladstone delta, later Delta reporter
MiE Je 14 1887-Ap 19 1890;My 11 1901-Mr 17 1917

MICHIGAN (*Continued*)

GLADSTONE—*Continued*

DELTA county reporter. *See* Delta reporter

DELTA reporter. w,sw 1902+
1902-Ja 22? 1918 as Delta county reporter; Ja 29 1918-O 21 1920 Delta county reporter and the Gladstone delta
sw 1913?-23?
MiG Ap 25 1935

GLADWIN

GLADWIN county record. w 1877+
1877 as Gladwin county register
1877-80? pub in Cedar
pub 1877+
InRE Je 7 1889
MiD-B [1922-23]-[26]

GOBLES

To 1921? as Gobleville

Gobles NEWS. w 1889+
pub Ag 18 1905+

GOBLEVILLE. *See* GOBLES

GRAND HAVEN

Grand Haven weekly CLARION. w Ap 1855-N 1862||
MiGh Je 9 1859;Mr 5(extra) Ag 6,20 1861
N Jl 7 1859
OClWHi My 26 1859

GRAND RIVER times. w Jl 2 1851-
MWA D 15 1852
MiD-B O 6 1852
MiGh 1851-O 1857

Grand Haven HERALD. w Ag 28 1869-91||?
MWA Ag 28,O 2 1869;Ap 22 1876

Grand Haven NEWS-JOURNAL. w 1858-84||?
1858-76? as Grand Haven news;1877?-81? News and journal
MiGh 1858-67;Ag 20 1868;N 26 1869
OClWHi S 20 1865

Grand Haven PRESS. w 1899-1902||?
MiGh Je 15 1899

Grand Haven daily TRIBUNE. d 1885+
Title varies: Evening tribune
pub 1886+
MiG Jl 3 1894
MiGh D 24 1898;Mr 25 1903;Ag 30 1913;Je 6,N 11 1918;N 12 1919;O 13 1922;Jl 30,N 11,D 31 1924;D 31 1925

Grand Haven UNION. w 1862-72||?
MWA Ja 9 1866
MiGh Jl 16-28 1863;F 9 1864;Ag 6 1867;Je 2,Ag 4 1868;Ja 3 1871;My 21 1872
OClWHi Jl 4 1865

GRAND LEDGE

Grand Ledge INDEPENDENT. w 1870+
pub 1870+
MWA Ap 21 1876

GRAND RAPIDS

AMERIKAANSCHE stoom post. w 1859-66||?
In Dutch
MiG S 28,O 26 1860-Jl 15,D 2 1863;Jl-Ag 9,S 1865-S 5 1866

BREZEE'S herald. *See* Semi-weekly herald

BURTON HEIGHTS leader. w My 1 1913-Je 4 1914||
United with Madison Square sun to form South end weekly sun
MiG complete

BURTON HEIGHTS record. w Je 23 1921+
MiG 1927+

BYRON CENTER progress. w O 3 1926-O 3 1930||
Merged with South Kent county news
MiG D 17 1926-30

Grand Rapids CHRONICLE. w 1884+
1884-O 1897 as Workman
MiG S 17 1887;F 4-11 1897;1905+
NN Je 1899-Je 7 1900
WHi Ag 12 1897

COMSTOCK PARK news. w 1925+
MiG Ap 8 1926+

CRESTON news. w 1906+
MiG D 19 1908+

Grand Rapids DEMOCRAT. d *See* Grand Rapids news

Grand Rapids weekly DEMOCRAT. *See* Middle West

Grand Rapids weekly EAGLE. w D 25 1844-O 1894||?
1844-My 26 1851 as Grand River eagle
Suspended Mr 9-Je 8 1849
DLC Mr 12 1845
MiG My 7 1845;Jl 8-15 1846;My 26 1847-Ap 5,21-My 12,Je 23-N,D 9 1848-Ap 4,22-S 2,16, 30-O 21 1851;Jl 10 1852;F 29-Mr 8 1853;Ja 7,S 2 1854;Ag 20 1857;Mr 12 1863;F 25 1864-Mr 16,30-Ap 20,My,Je 8-Jl 6,20-Ag 17,S-O 5,N 2-23,D 1865-Ap,My 9-23,Je-S 5,19-N 14 1867; Ja 9-16,30,F 13,27-Je 1868;Ag 11 1870;Je 22 1876;N 3,17,D 1 1887;F 28 1889;D 4 1890
MnHi Ap 20 1865

Grand Rapids daily EAGLE. d My 26 1856-94||
Suspended from Ja 7-F 22 1864
CLM F 22,Ap 27 1888
DLC Ja-Ag 1866;Jl 24-D 1867;Ja 28,Ap 20-21 1871;F 19 1879
MWA S 14-O 20 1868;F 15 1871;Ap 20 1876
MiD-B D 4 1857;Ag 29 1861;D 12 1863;Mr 15 1876;O 5 1886; F 12,Jl 30 1894
MiG [1856]-Ag 3 1860;Je 13,N 8 1861[F-D 1863]Ja 6 1864-F 19,Je 30,Ag 27,N 6 1894
TKL My 6 1888

EAST END advocate. w N 13 1920-O 11 1930||
MiG complete

EAST END star. w D 12 1917-
MiG D 19 1917

ECHO. w 1904+
In Polish
MiG 1905+

Grand Rapids ENQUIRER. w Ap 18 1837-My 1863||
1837-My 11? 1841 as Grand River times (title varies slightly). Followed by Grand Rapids weekly democrat, later Middle West
CtY Jl 3-10 1837
DLC F 28,O 2 1840;Ap 12 1843;Ag 5(extra) 1848
MWA N 15 1839;N 10 1852;Ap 25 1877
MiD-B Jl 15 1837
MiG Ap 18 1837;S 11 1840;Je 22 1841-F,Ap 18 1845-O 8 1856;Ap 22,My 13 1857-Ap 1858;Ag 22-S 12,O 3,17-N 21,D 5,6(extra)12 1860-Jl 2 1862
WHi Ap 18 1837;Ja 2 1850

Grand Rapids daily ENQUIRER and herald. d,ir N 19 1855-Je 1863||
1855-My 1 1857 as Grand Rapids daily enquirer. Followed by Grand Rapids daily democrat, later Grand Rapid news
ir 1860-63
Suspended from Ap 9-25 1856
MiG 1855-Ap,My 29 1860-My 5 1861

FREE coinage independent. w 1893-My 13 1897||
United with Middle West and weekly democrat to form Middle West, weekly democrat and free coinage independent, later Middle West
MiG S 1895-97

GERMANIA. w,d 1882-1916||
d 1882-96
In German
MiG O 3 1895-Mr 29 1916
—Sunday ed *See* Sonntagsbote

Saturday GLOBE. w Jl 1883-84||?
MiG Jl 28-Ag 4 1883

GRAND RIVER eagle. *See* Grand Rapids weekly eagle

GRAND RIVER times. *See* Grand Rapids enquirer

GRANDVILLE AVENUE record. *See* Record

Grand Rapids HERALD. d Mr 26 1855-My 1857||
United with Grand Rapids daily enquirer to form Grand Rapids daily enquirer and herald
MiG [1855-Je] Ag 18 1856

Grand Rapids HERALD. d S 23 1884+
1884-Ap 16 1886 as Grand Rapids morning telegram; Ap 17 1886-Ja 2 1892 Telegram-herald
DLC 1898+
Mi 1893+
MiG 1884-S 4 1885:Ap 17 1886-94;O 6 1895+
MiGh Jl 5 1898;N 11,28 1918
MiU 1926+

Semi-weekly HERALD. w,sw 1884-1903||?
1884-Ap 1886 as Brezee's herald; Ap 1886-Ja 7 1892 Weekly telegram herald; Ja 14 1892-O 1894 Weekly herald; N 1894-Ag 1895 Herald; S 1895-Je 16 1896 Grand Rapids semi-weekly herald
w 1884-Ag 1895
MiG [1890-1902]

HOBBIES. *See* Town news

KURYER z Grand Rapids. w Jl 27 1906-Je 1 1907||
In Polish
MiG complete

Grand Rapids daily LEADER. *See* Evening press and leader

Grand Rapids weekly LEADER. w F 20 1879-92||?
MWA D 4 1879
MiG 1879-F 6 1884;F 24 1886-F 5 1890

Grand Rapids LIFE. w O 13 1888-
MiG O 13 1888

MADISON SQUARE advertiser. w,sw N 27 1913-O 6 1933||
w 1913-24
MiG N 21 1924-33

MADISON SQUARE sun. w N 27 1913-Je 4 1914||
United with Burton Heights leader to form South End weekly sun
MiG complete

Evening MAIL. d Je- 1876||
MiG S 20 1876

MICHIGAN democrat. w Jl 11 1930-N 26 1935||
Also dated in Benton Harbor
MiG complete

MICHIGAN journalen. w 1897-
Follows Michigan posten?
In Swedish
IRA 1898

MICHIGAN news-digest. w F 10-Ag 11 1917||
MiG complete

MICHIGAN posten. w 1896-
Followed by Michigan journalen?
In Swedish
IRA My 1 1897

MICHIGAN republican. w? 1920?-
MiG Ag 28 1920

MICHIGAN staats zeitung. w N 25 1874-86||?
1874-79? as Michigan staats zeitung; 1880-81? Sonntagsblatt (Michigan staats zeitung)
MiD-B Mr 30 1876

MICHIGAN state news. w 1920-25||
Negro
MiG F 9 1922-Ja 3 1925

MIDDLE West. w Je 1863-1907||?
Follows Grand Rapids enquirer. 1863-Ap 8 1897 as Grand Rapids weekly democrat; Ap 15-My 13? 1898 Middle West and weekly democrat; My 20-D? 1898 Middle West, weekly democrat and free coinage independent
MiG [Ag 1868-Jl 15 1874]-[Jl 26 1876-D 19 1883]Jl 1885-Ja 1892;O 1893-Jl 7 1898
—d ed *See* Grand Rapids news

Grand Rapids daily NATIONAL. d Ap 1878||
MiG Ap 2 1878

Grand Rapids NEWS. d Je 1863-D 19 1922||
Follows Grand Rapids daily enquirer and herald. 1863-Ja 26 1902 as Grand Rapids democrat (title varies slightly) Ja 28 1902-F 13 1903 Evening post democrat; F 14 1903-My 1 1906 Grand Rapids post; My 2 1906-Ap 13 1911 Daily news
DLC D 28 1867;Ap 16 1868
MWA Ap 21 1876
Mi Jl 28 1909-22
MiD-B N 7 1894;Mr 27 1895[Je 1902]
MiG Je 18 1863[S 4 1865-My 1]Jl 1,O 20 1867; S 6 1868-[70-Mr 3 1885]-Je 1886;Ja-Mr,Ap 19,My 15,Jl 1887-Mr,Ap 7,19,Jl 1888-99;S 1900-22
MiGh N 11 1918
MiU [1886]89-1902
N O 2 1875
OClWHi N 9,11 1876
WHi 1917-19
—w ed *See* Middle West

Daily evening NEWS. d D 3 1874-75||
MiG Ja 30 1875

NEWS item. d 1876-77||
MiG Ap 5 1877

NORTHWESTERN weekly. w 1914+
My-Je 5 1914 as North-westerner
pub 1926+
MiD-B [1922-28]
MiG My 15 1914+

NORTH-WESTERNER. *See* Northwestern weekly

OBSERVER. w O 5 1907-My 31 1926||
MiG 1908-26

Grand Rapids PLAIN DEALER. w O 1907-Ap 8 1910||
MiG Ja 29 1909-10

Saturday evening POST. sw,w O 4 1873-86||
Title varies: Grand Rapids post; Saturday post
sw 1873?
MiG 1877;F 1879-D 9 1882;Ja 13,F 10,N 10 1883;Ja 19 1884
MnHi S 30 1876-F 15 1879

Grand Rapids POST 1903-06 *See* Grand Rapids news 1863-1922

Grand Rapids weekly PRESS. sw,w S? 1858-
1858? as Semi-weekly press (sw)
ICHi O 22 1858
MiG My 11 1859

Grand Rapids PRESS. d S 1890+
1890-O 3 1913 as Grand Rapids evening press
Mi Jl 1909+
MiD-B F 11 1893[1901-02;05-18]
MiG S 10 1890;My 5 1894;O 1895-1900;My 1901+
MiGh Jl 4 1898;Ap 3 1917;N 11 1918

Evening PRESS and leader. d F 14 1879-D 31 1892||
1879-My 30 1880 as Grand Rapids daily leader; My 31 1880-D 25 1892 Evening leader. Merged with Grand Rapids evening press, later Grand Rapids press
MiG F 15 1879-F 14 1882;F 15 1883-92

Grand Rapids RADICAL. w F 16-S 1884||
Merged with Grand Rapids democrat, later Middle West
MiG Mr 8 1884

RECORD. w Mr 1910-Ja 17 1919||
Mr 1910-Ap 23 1915 as Grandville Avenue record
MiG Ap 1911-19

Saturday REVIEW. w 1879-83||
Followed by Michigan tradesman (not in this list)
MiG F 21 1880

SEYMOUR SQUARE news. bw 1928-Ap 29 1932||
MiG [Je 26 1930-32]

SIXTH WARD news. *See* West Side news 1909-19

SONNTAGSBLATT (Michigan staats zeitung). *See* Michigan staats zeitung

SONNTAGSBOTE. w 1887-1916||
In German
MiG Jl 1898-Mr 1916
—d ed *See* Germania

SOUTH END leader. w Mr 2 1922-Mr 29 1923||
MiG complete

MICHIGAN (*Continued*)

GRAND RAPIDS—*Continued*

SOUTH END news. w Ag 30 1923-Ja 10 1930||
MiG Ag-N 22 1923;Ag 10 1928-30

SOUTH END weekly sun. w Je 1914-N 22 1918||
Formed by union of Madison Square sun and Burton Heights leader
MiG complete

SOUTH KENT county news and Grant Rapids suburbanite. w O 10 1930+
MiG 1930+

SOUTHWEST community alliance. w 1923+
pub 1928+
MiG [1926]28+

De STANDAARD. *See* Standard-bulletin

STANDARD-BULLETIN. w,sw Ja 20 1875+
1875-1919? as De Standaard
sw 1877?-1919?
1875-1919? in Dutch; 1920?+ in Dutch and English
MiD-B Mr 15 1876
MiG N 27 1894;Jl 28 1908;S 5,26 1916-S 7 1917; Mr 15 1918+

Een STEM des volks. w 1892-1903||?
In Dutch
MiG O 27 1899

Morning TELEGRAM. *See* Grand Rapids herald 1884+

Weekly TELEGRAM herald. *See* Semi-weekly herald

Daily TIMES. d Ap 17 1870-Jl 21 1886||
Title varies slightly. Merged with Grand Rapids democrat, later Grand Rapids news
MWA Jl 7-14 1870;Ag 26 1876
MiD-B Mr 15 1876
MiG 1870-[72-73]-85

Grand Rapids weekly TIMES. w Ap 1870-86||
MiD-B Mr 17 1876
MiG 1883-Jl 2 1886

TIMES. w 1895-D 30 1921||
Merged with Grand Rapids chronicle
MiG Ja 13 1906-21

TOWN news. w Ja 10 1889-F 15 1890||
Ja 10-N 14 1889 as Hobbies
MiG complete

Weekly VISITOR. w F 1913-
MiG Mr 29 1913

VRIJHEID'S banier. w N 1 1868-1904||?
Title varies: Vrijheids banner
In Dutch
MiD-B Mr 16 1876
MiG O 16 1897

Grand Rapids WEST SIDE news. w 1886-93||
MiG Ag 16 1888

WEST SIDE news. w Ap 28 1909-Ja 10 1919||
1909-Ap 13 1917 as Sixth Ward news. Merged with Northwestern weekly
MiG complete

WOLVERINE cyclone. w 1884-89||
MiG Ap 4 1885;D 22 1888

WORKMAN. *See* Grand Rapids chronicle

YOUNG hickory. w? 1844||
MiG S 20 1844

GRANDVILLE

Grandville NEWS. *See* Grandville star

Grandville STAR. w 1907+
1907-11 as Grandville news
pub 1921+
MiG [My 15 1908-Je 16 1911]Ja 25 1912+

GRANT

Grant HERALD and independent. w 1910+
1910-17 as Grant herald
pub 1925+

Grant INDEPENDENT. w 1898-1917||
United with Grant herald to form Grant herald and independent

GRASS LAKE

Grass Lake NEWS. w 1879+
MWA S 3 1880

GRAYLING

CRAWFORD avalanche. w 1878+
pub 1878+
MiD-B [1905;22]-[25]-[28]

GREENVILLE

Greenville CALL. d 1879-1923||?
1879-82? as Daily news. United with Greenville independent to form Independent daily news, later Greenville daily news
MWA S 28 1879

Greenville INDEPENDENT. *See* Greenville daily news. 1854+

MONTCALM reflector. *See* Greenville daily news. 1854+

Greenville daily NEWS. w,d S 19 1854+
1854-F 24 1857? as Montcalm reflector; Mr 1857?-1923? Greenville independent; 1924?-25? Independent daily news
w 1854-1923?
MWA Ap 20 1876

MiGr [1854-F]My 18 1857;D 20 1859;Mr 10,O 10-16 1860;Mr 11 1863;Ja 5,26,F 16,Mr 2-9,Ap 7,My 16,O 25 1864;Mr 28,My 16,Je 6,Ag 16 1865
OClWHi Jl 24 1866

Daily NEWS. 1879-82 *See* Greenville call

HALFWAY

Halfway NEWS. w 1921-28||?
1921-22? as Roseville news; 1923-24? Halfway-Roseville news
1926 pub in Mount Clemens
MiD-B [1926]-[28]

HAMTRAMCK

Papers published in Hamtramck are listed under Detroit

HANCOCK

AMERIKAN suometar. w,tw Je 8 1899+
w 1899-1912?
In Finnish
pub 1889+
IU 1918+

Evening COPPER journal. w,tw,d 1884+
1884-1900? as Copper journal
w 1884-97?;tw 1898?-1900?
MiHoM D 13 1892[93;1901]-[16]-[32]34+

TYÖMIES. *See under* Superior, Wis.

HANOVER

HANOVER-HORTON local. w Je 13 1891+
Also dated in Horton
pub 1891+

HARBOR SPRINGS

EMMET county graphic. w 1875+
1875-1925 as Harbor Springs republican
MiD-B [1922-23]-[26-28]

Harbor Springs. REPUBLICAN. *See* Emmet county graphic

HARRISVILLE

ALCONA county review. w Ap 27 1877+
pub 1877+

HART

Hart JOURNAL. w 1869+
1869-82? as Oceana county journal
pub 1875+

OCEANA county journal. *See* Hart journal

HARTFORD

Hartford DAY spring. w S 1 1871+
pub [1871-73]+

HASTINGS

Hastings BANNER. w,sw My 1 1856+
1856-80? as Republican banner
sw 1877?-80?
pub 1856-[80-90]+
MBAt Ap 12 1865
MiD-B S 16 1874;My-N 1879[98-99 1910-15]17 [18]-[21-25]-[28-32]
NNHi Je 10 1863

BARRY county democrat. *See* Hastings herald

BARRY county pioneer. w Mr 1851-N 1 1856||
Title varies: Barry pioneer. Followed by Independent
Suspended at various intervals in 1851
MiD-B [1851-54;56]
MiG Ag 16 1854

BARRY county review. w 1853-Je 1854||
Merged with Barry county pioneer
MiD-B Ap 5 1854

BARRY pioneer. *See* Barry county pioneer

DEMOCRAT. *See* Journal-herald

Hastings HERALD. w 1880-1910||
1880-96? as Barry county democrat. United with Hastings journal to form Journal-herald
MiD-B Jl 13 1899

Hastings HOME journal. *See* Journal-herald

INDEPENDENT. w 1867-68||
Follows Barry county pioneer. Followed by Democrat, later Journal-herald

JOURNAL-HERALD. w 1868-1921||?
Follows Independent. 1868 as Democrat; 1869-84? Hastings home journal; 1885-1910 Hastings journal
MiD-B S 17 1874;D 11 1902

REPUBLICAN banner. *See* Hastings banner

HEMLOCK

Hemlock TRIBUNE. *See* Saginaw county tribune (Saginaw)

HERSEY

OSCEOLA county outline. w 1870-1909||?
1870-82? as Osceola outline
MWA Ap 21 1876
OClWHi Mr 28 1872

OSCEOLA outline. *See* Osceola county outline

HESPERIA

Hesperia UNION. w 1895+
pub 1910+

HIGHLAND PARK

Papers published in Highland Park are listed under Detroit

HILLSDALE

Weekly BUSINESS. w 1870-86||?
IU S 9 1871

Hillsdale COURIER. w? Ja 15-O 1 1845||
OClWHi Ap 22 1845

DAILY. *See* Hillsdale daily news

Hillsdale DEMOCRAT. w 1852-1908||?
MWA Ap 15 1881
NN N 23 1866

Hillsdale GAZETTE. w Ap 13 1839-O 1852||
1839-My 1843 as Hillsdale county gazette (Jonesville)
OClWHi Ap 13 1839;Ja 16 1845
P-M Ap 7 1843

Hillsdale LEADER. w,sw 1882-1919||?
sw 1911?-15?
MiG Ja 15 1909
MiH S 26 1884-1902;08-09

Hillsdale daily NEWS. w,d Je 30 1846+
1846-Ja 1851 as Whig standard; F 1851-1908 Hillsdale standard; 1909 Hillsdale daily standard-herald; 1910-14 Hillsdale daily
w 1846-1908
pub 1849+
IU Ag 6 1872
MWA D 14 1852;Ap 18 1876
MiH 1846+
N S 21,O 5 1875;D 19 1876

Hillsdale STANDARD. *See* Hillsdale daily news

WHIG standard. *See* Hillsdale daily news

HOLLAND

Holland CITY news. w 1871+
MiG Ag 28-S 4 1897

De GRONDWET. w My 1860+
In Dutch
pub 1872+
MWA D 2 1863;Ja 10 1866
Mid-B [1922-23]-[27-28]
MiG Ag 24-31 1897;Ja 30 1906+

De HOLLANDER. w 1850-
In Dutch
MWA D 2 1863
MiG Ag 20 1856

OTTAWA county times. w 1892-1907||?
MiG Ag 27 1897

Holland daily SENTINEL. d 1895+
1927-28 as Holland evening sentinel
Ag 25-26 1897 are semi-centennial eds
pub 1912+
MiD-B [1922-28]
MiG Ag 25-26 1897
WHi S 1 1926

STEM uit het westen. Ag 23 1867-
In Dutch
MiG Ag 23 1867

HOLLY

Holly REGISTER. w 1865-82||?
CSmH Jl 18 1867

HOMER

Homer INDEX. w 1871+
MWA Ap 19 1876

HORTON

Hanover-Horton LOCAL. *See under* Hanover

HOUGHTON

Daily MINING gazette. d S 14 1899+
Also dated in Calumet
pub 1899+
M S 17 1932
Mi 1921+
MiC O 2 1899-Ag 1931
MiHo O 1913+
MiHoM 1899+
MiU 1926+
—w ed *See* Portage Lake mining gazette

PORTAGE LAKE mining gazette. w Jl 1858+
pub 1885+
DLC Ag 8 1878-80
MB My 17 1862-Ja 17,F 21,D 12 1863;Ja 16-S 3 1864
MNaHi S 24 1864;Ja 21 1865
MiD-B [1863-64;75-76]
MiHoM 1862-Jl 24 1867;Mr 1869-Jl 17 1872;Jl 11 1873-Je,Ag 1879-Ja 8 1885;86-Ja 1,Jl 1889-Jl 8 1891;Ja 1,Jl-O 1897
—d ed *See* Daily mining gazette

HOWARD CITY

Howard City RECORD. w My 20 1872+
pub 1872+
MWA Ap 20 1876

MICHIGAN (*Continued*)

HOWELL

LIVINGSTON county press. *See* Livingston county republican-press

LIVINGSTON county republican. *See* Livingston republican

LIVINGSTON courier. w Ja 10 1843-Ap 1857||
Followed by Livingston democrat, later Livingston republican-press
Ja-N 1843 pub in Brighton
ICHi D 4 1855
MiHw Ja 10,F-O 4,N 22,D 1843-Mr 1846

LIVINGSTON democrat. *See* Livingston republican-press

LIVINGSTON herald. w 1886-1908||?
MiHwC 1886-91

LIVINGSTON reporter. tw,w,sw 1906-20||?
1906-16? as Livingston tidings
tw 1907-15?;w 1916?
MiHwC 1906-12;19-20

LIVINGSTON republican. w My 1855-1928||
1890?-95? as Livingston county republican. United with Livingston county press to form Press-republican, later Livingston county republican-press
MWA Ap 19 1876
MiHw 1906-28
NNHi Je 16 1863;Ja 8 1873

LIVINGSTON republican-press. w Ag 5 1857+
Follows Livingston courier. 1857-1927? as Livingston democrat; 1928 Livingston county press; 1929? Press-republican
pub 1880+
MWA Ap 19 1876
MiHwC 1896+

LIVINGSTON tidings. *See* Livingston reporter

PRESS-REPUBLICAN. *See* Livingston republican-press

HUBBARDSTON

ADVERTISER. w 1870-91||?
MWA Ap 20-27 1876;Ap 8 1880

HUDSON

Hudson GAZETTE. w 1858-1919||
United with Hudson post to form Hudson post-gazette
MWA Ag 22 1879
MiHu complete

Hudson weekly HERALD. w 1863?
MBAt Ap 19 1865

Hudson NEWS. w My 23 1933-
MiHu [My 23 1933-Mr 29 1934]

Hudson POST-GAZETTE. w,sw 1869+
1869-1919 as Hudson post
w 1869-1904?
MWA Ap 20 1876
MiHu 1895+
N O 7 1875

Hudson REPUBLICAN. *See* Hudson vibrator

Hudson SENTINEL. w
P-M Jl 6 1855

Hudson VIBRATOR. w 1894?-98||?
1894?-N 4; 1896 as Hudson republican
MiHu Mr 27 1895-N 4,D 16-23 1896

HUDSONVILLE

Hudsonville HOME news. w Je 1927-Mr 2 1933||
Merged with Grandville star (Grandville)
MiG Ag 1927-33

IMLAY CITY

Imlay City TIMES. w 1888+
MiI 1888;90-93;97;1915-16

IONIA

Ionia GAZETTE. w Ja 2 1849-67||
MiG Ag 25 1854

IONIA county news. w N 1921+
pub 1921+

IONIA county sentinel. *See* Ionia sentinel-standard w

Ionia JOURNAL. w F 1843-46||?
DLC Ag 30 1843;S 11 1844

Ionia SENTINEL-STANDARD. w 1866-1920||?
1866-69? as Ionia county sentinel; 1870?-1918? Ionia sentinel
MWA Ap 8 1880

Ionia SENTINEL-STANDARD. d 1879+
1879-1918? as Ionia daily sentinel

Ionia STANDARD. w 1868-1918||?
United with Ionia sentinel to form Ionia sentinel-standard

Ionia daily STANDARD. d 1887-1918||?
United with Ionia daily sentinel to form Ionia sentinel-standard

IRON MOUNTAIN

IRON range. *See* Range tribune

MENOMINEE range. *See* Range tribune

MICHIGAN veckoblad. w 1903-13||?
In Swedish
IRA 1904-10
MnHi F 22 1908-Je 18 1910

MONITOR. w 1900-08||?
In Swedish
IRA 1903-08

Iron Mountain PRESS. w 1896-1920||?
MiIm 1896-1917

RANGE tribune. w 1879-1920||?
1879-90? as Menominee range; 1891?-Mr 1893? Iron range
1879-82? pub in Quinnesec
MWA S 1 1880
MiIm 1885-99

Daily TRIBUNE. d 1896-99||?
MiIm 1897-Jl 3 1899

IRON RIVER

IRON county reporter. *See* Iron River reporter

Iron River REPORTER. w,d,sw 1885+
1885-1901? as Iron county reporter; 1902?-21? Iron River-Stambaugh reporter; w 1885-1921?;d 1922?-23?
Pub 1922+

IRONWOOD

FRIHET. w -Ag 18 1904||
Merged with Svenska Amerikanska tribunen (Superior, Wis.)
In Swedish
IRA 1904

GOGEBIC mining record. *See* Ironwood news record

INTER-STATE news-record. *See* Ironwood news record

Ironwood NEWS record. w 1885-1921||?
1885-90? as Gogebic mining record; 1891? Inter-state news-record
MiHoM Ja-Ap 1899;Ja 1,Ap 30-D 1900;05-20
MiIr 1912-21

Ironwood TIMES. w 1888+
MiIr 1912-21

ISHPEMING

AGITATOR. *See* Iron ore

IRON agitator. *See* Iron ore

IRON home. w 1874-79||?
MWA Ap 22 1876

IRON ore. w 1878+
1878-82? as Agitator; 1883-86? Iron agitator
MiD-B [1922-23]-[25]-[27-28]
MiHoM Jl 19 1891-My 20 1892;O 1896-Ag 16 1918;Mr 9 1919+
WHi O 4 1930

PENINSULAR record. *See* Ishpeming record

Ishpeming RECORD. w 1884-1931||?
1884-1905? as Peninsular record
WHi Ag 24 1895

SUPERIOR posten. w 1888-1918||?
In Swedish
IRA 1888-1916

ITHACA

GRATIOT county herald. w 1869+
1869-87? as St. Louis herald (St. Louis)
pub [1890+]
MWA Ap 14 1876
MiD-B [1922-23]-[28]

GRATIOT county journal. w,sw 1866-1914||?
sw 1905?-11?
MWA Ap 28 1876
MiG Je 14-21 1889

JACKSON

To 1833 as Jacksonburg

AMERICAN citizen. *See* Jackson citizen

Jackson CITIZEN. w,sw 1849-1909||?
Follows Michigan state gazette. Early years as American citizen
sw 1896?-1905?
DLC Je 23 1852
MWA My 21 1851;S 1 1859;Jl 29 1879
OClWHi Jl 5 1865

Jackson CITIZEN patriot. d 1865+
1865-1904? as Jackson daily citizen; 1905?-17? Jackson citizen press
Jl 7 1929 is diamond jubilee ed
DLC Jl 27 1867-68;Ja 23-D 1874
M Jl 7 1929
MWA Ja 24 1866;Ap 20 1876
Mi 1921+
WHi Jl 7 1929

Weekly CLARION. w
MiU-C [1868]

MICHIGAN democrat. w Mr 8 1838-45||
Followed by Jackson weekly patriot
DLC Jl 11 1844
Mi Mr 8,Ag 25 1838;N 7 1839;Ap 25 1844
MiU Ag 15 1839;Ja 18 1844

MICHIGAN liberator. w 1880?-81||?
1880? pub in Centerville
MiTh 1880-81

MICHIGAN state gazette. w Ag 13 1840-49||?
Follows Jackson sentinel. Followed by American citizen, later Jackson citizen
DLC S 24 1840
Mi 1840-Ag 5 1841

MICHIGAN sun. w Ja 14 1879-
Ja-S 1879 pub in Detroit
MWA My 10 1879

Jackson weekly PATRIOT. w 1845-1917||?
Follows Michigan democrat. United with Jackson citizen press to form Jackson citizen patriot
MWA N 24 1852;My 7 1879

Daily PATRIOT. d Ag 1870-1917||?
United with Jackson citizen press to form Jackson citizen patriot
MWA My 2 1876
NbHi Mr 10-12 1911

Jackson evening PRESS. d 1884-1904||?
United with Jackson daily citizen to form Jackson citizen press, later Jackson citizen patriot

Jackson SENTINEL. w My 20 1837-40||
1837-Mr 1838 as Jacksonburg sentinel. Followed by Michigan state gazette
Mi My 20,Je 3,S 30,O 28 1837;Ja 6,Mr 10,Ap 21,My 26 1838;My 29,Je 12,S 25 1839

Saturday evening STAR. w 1878+
pub 1926+

Jackson TRIBUNE. d,sw 1925+
sw O 13 1925-My 24 1926
pub 1925+

JACKSONBURG. *See* JACKSON

JONESVILLE

HILLSDALE county gazette. *See* Hillsdale gazette (Hillsdale)

Jonesville INDEPENDENT. w F 23 1850+
1850-Jl 1 1855 as Jonesville telegraph
pub 1850+
IU My 11,Jl 20 1871
MWA D 22 1852;Ap 22 1876
MiD-B [1922-23]-[26-28]
MiJ 1869+
OClWHi S 14 1852;Ja 14 1875

MICHIGAN expositor. *See* Adrian times (Adrian)

Jonesville TELEGRAPH. *See* Jonesville independent

KALAMAZOO

To Mr 30 1836 as Bronson

Kalamazoo ADVOCATE. w 1905-26||?
MiK 1918-Je 1922

Kalamazoo CITIZEN. w
MiK O 9 1931-Ja 22 1932

GATEWAY.
MiK N 1926-O 1930

Kalamazoo GAZETTE. w,sw D 10 1833-1905||?
1833-Ja 17 1835 as Michigan statesman and St Joseph chronicle; Ja 24 1835-D 15? 1836 Michigan statesman; D 22? 1836-Mr 1900 Kalamazoo gazette; Mr 23 1900-04? Semi-weekly gazette news 1833-Jl 30 1835 pub in White Pigeon
Suspended for a time between O 15 1836 and Ja 28 1837
Ct [1834-35]Mr 4 1837
DLC Ja 24-D 1835[39-40]Ag 6 1852;S 23 1853
ICHi O 22,D 24 1858
MWA S 8,O 29 1838;Ap 21 1876
MiD-B O 16 1835
MiG Ja 27,N 17,D 8 1838
MiK Je 28 1834-Jl,O 1835-O 15 1836;Ja 23 1837-O 13 1843;My 15 1846-N 7 1862;S 23 1870-Mr 1878;Ap 1880-93;95-97
MiU 1900-01
NSchU My 12 1834

Kalamazoo GAZETTE. d Mr 26 1872+
1872?-D 1901 as Daily gazette (title varies slightly) Ja 1902-D 1903 Kalamazoo gazette-news; Je 19-N 25 1916 Gazette-telegraph
MWA S 15 1882
Mi 1921+
MiG Jl 4 1876;1932+
MiK Mr-N 10 1872;Mr 28-D 1876;Jl 1877-S,N 1899-O,D 1910;16+

Kalamazoo HERALD. w 1913-21||?
United with Kalamazoo Saturday night to form Kalamazoo Saturday night and herald
MiK 1918-Mr 1920

HOLLANDSCH weekblad. *See* De Hollandsche Amerikaan

De HOLLANDSCHE Amerikaan. w,sw,tw S 1 1889+
1889-92? as Hollandsch weekblad
w 1890-92?;tw 1895?-Je 2 1920
In Dutch
pub 1898-[1900-02]+
IU D 1917+
MiG 1905+

Kalamazoo INDUSTRIAL news. w Ag 1920-
MiK 1920-Jl 7 1921

MICHIGAN statesman. *See* Kalamazoo gazette

MICHIGAN telegraph. *See* Kalamazoo telegraph

Kalamazoo NEWS. sw 1894-Mr 1900||
Merged with Kalamazoo gazette to form Semi-weekly gazette-news, later Kalamazoo gazette
MiU [1895]-1900

Kalamazoo evenings NEWS. d 1894?-Mr 1900||
United with Daily gazette to form Gazette-news, later Kalamazoo gazette
MiK Ap 1898-Mr 1900

Kalamazoo NEWS. w F 26 1932-
MiK F-Je 1932

PEOPLE. w 1915-22||?
MiK Mr 1918-Je 8 1922

Kalamazoo PRESS. w 1908-11||?
MiK N 20 1908-My 1911

MICHIGAN (*Continued*)

KALAMAZOO—*Continued*

Kalamazoo evening PRESS. d F 8 1909-My 13? 1911||
United with Kalamazoo evening telegraph to form Kalamazoo telegraph-press
MiU [F 13 1909-My 15 1910]

Kalamazoo SATURDAY night and herald. w D 6 1919-30||?
1919-Ap 10 1920 as Kalamazoo Saturday night
MiK D 1919-Je 1921

Kalamazoo TELEGRAPH. w,sw S 10 1844-My 1916||?
1844-65 as Michigan telegraph (Je 1847-Ja 1850 Kalamazoo telegraph)
Suspended from Ja-Ap? 1850
w 1844-Je 1897
DLC 1851
MWA D 10 1851;F 7 1866
MiG Jl 13 1876
MiK [O 24 1845-56]S 16 1857-Ap 1859[60-O 5 1866]-67;70-75;78-Je 1914
MiU 1893-98;1910;13
NN Jl 12 1876
OClWHi Jl 5 1865
P-M D 5 1845

Kalamazoo TELEGRAPH-PRESS. d Ap 6 1868-My 1916||
1868-Ap 27 1901 as Kalamazoo daily telegraph; Ap 29 1901-My 13 1911 Kalamazoo evening telegraph. United with Kalamazoo gazette to form Gazette-telegraph, later Kalamazoo gazette
CLM Ja 5 1899
MWA S 1 1874;Ap 17 1876;My 4 1881
MiK 1868-Ap 11,O 20 1870-Mr,O 1871-Je 1887; 88-90;Jl 1891-Je 1892;93-1916
MiU [1898]-[1901]-[11-13;15]
NN Ja-S 1875

WESTERN banner. w Ap 1839-44||?
CtY Jl 30 1839
DLC My 28 1839

KENT CITY

Kent City-Casnovia HERALD. *See under* Sparta

Kent City JOURNAL. w 1916-20||?
United with Casnovia herald to form Herald-journal, later Kent City-Casnovia herald (Sparta)
MiG F 14 1919

KINGSTON

Kingston ENTERPRISE. w F 5 1915+
pub 1915+

LAINGSBURG

Laingsburg PRESS. w O 22 1921+
pub F 4 1926+

LAKE CITY

ERA and republican. *See* Missaukee republican

Lake City JOURNAL. *See* Missaukee republican

MISSAUKEE independent. *See* Plain dealer

MISSAUKEE republican. w 1877+
1877-83? as Lake City journal; 1884?-86? New era; 1887?-88? Era and republican
pub 1883+

NEW era. *See* Missaukee republican

PLAIN DEALER. w 1887+
1887-92? as Missaukee independent
MiD-B [1925-26]-[28]

LAKE LEELANAU

To 1921? as Provemont

Provemont COURIER. *See* Suttons Bay courier (Suttons Bay)

LAKE LINDEN

NATIVE copper times. w 1884+
1884-F 21 1893 as Torch Lake times
MiC My 24 1887-N 6 1928
MiD-B [1922-26]-[28]
MiHoM 1889+

TORCH LAKE times. *See* Native copper times

LAKE ODESSA

Lake Odessa WAVE-TIMES. w,sw 1888+
1888-1909? as Lake Odessa wave
sw 1888-94?
pub [1900-04]+
MiD-B [1922]-[28]

LAKEVIEW

Lakeview CITIZEN. w Ja 21 1876-78||?
MiD-B Mr 17 1876

L'ANSE

BARAGA county herald. m,w 1928-Mr 1933||
1928? as L'Anse vox republica (m)
MiLaS [1928-33]

LAKE SUPERIOR sentinel. *See* L'Anse sentinel

L'Anse SENTINEL. w 1880+
1880-87? as Lake Superior sentinel
pub [1880-My 1896]+
MiD-B [1922-24]-[26-28]
MiHoM Ja 1,S 21 1890-Ag 1904

L'Anse VOX republica. *See* Baraga county herald

LANSING

Lansing CAPITAL news. d My 26 1921-Jl 1933||
Mi complete
MiEIS My 1922-23
MiLS Jl 1921-32

FREE PRESS. *See* Michigan state journal

Lansing JOURNAL. w Jl 18 1872-1907||?
MWA Ap 27 1876;My 8 1879
Mi 1872-Jl 5 1889
MiD-B 1872-[82]
MiLS 1879-85
MiU [1894]-[99]

Lansing JOURNAL. d 1887-Ja 22 1911||
United with Daily state republican to form Lansing journal-republican, later State republican
Mi 1887-1910
MiLS 1902-11

MICHIGAN state digest. w My 21 1926+
pub 1926+
MiU [1926]+

MICHIGAN state journal. w Ja 11 1848-62||?
Ja-D 18? 1848 as Free press. Followed by Lansing state democrat (1866-72)
MiU Je 11 1849

Lansing daily NEWS. d Jl 3 1882-D 31 1883||
Mi complete

Lansing PRESS. d N 11 1912-Ap 8 1916||
1912-My 29 1915 as Lansing evening press
Mi N 29 1912-16
MiLS 1912-Je 1915

Lansing REPUBLICAN. w *See* Lansing state republican

Lansing daily REPUBLICAN. d Jl 30?-Ag 12 1872||?
Mi Jl 30-Ag 12 1872

Lansing tri-weekly REPUBLICAN. sw,tw Ja 12 1875-Ja 1886||
1875-79 as Lansing semi-weekly republican (sw)
MWA Ja 28,F 11,25,Mr 10,Ap 25,My 2, Je 30 1876;My 27 1879
Mi complete
MiEIS [1875-78]-[80]-[82-85]
PLaL Ap 12,16,23-My 3 1878

SOUTH LANSING news. w S 1929+
pub 1929+

Lansing STATE democrat. w Je 6 1866-72||?
Follows Michigan state journal

Lansing STATE democrat. w S 5 1889-95||?
MiD-B 1889-[93-94]

STATE journal. d Ja 1 1886+
1886-Ja 22 1911 as Daily state republican; Ja 23-F 11 1911 Lansing journal-republican
pub 1887+
Mi 1886+
MiEIS 1886-1923;25;27;29-[33]+
MiG Ja 6 1897;My 9 1905;23+
MiLS 1902+
MiU 1895-F 13 1911
WHi 1917-19;Ja 1 1930

Daily STATE republican. *See* State journal

Lansing STATE republican. w,sw Ap 28 1855-Ja 5? 1906||
Ja 3 1875-85? as Lansing republican
sw Ap 7-D 30 1861; S 1898-1901
pub complete
DLC Ja-O 1866
MWA Ja 31 1866;My 3 1876
Mi Ap 28 1857-Ap 17,My 15,Je 5,Jl 10,Jl 31, Ag 28 1861;Ja 29-F 12,26-Ap 23 1862;63-Ap 12 1865;F 20 1867;Ap 1869-74
MiEIS [N 1857-Ja 1 1875]
MiMu O 27 1880-O 19 1881
MiU F 5 1875
NNHi N 17 1857;Mr 13 1873;Ap 24 1874
—d ed *See* State journal
—tw ed *See* Lansing tri-weekly republican

LAPEER

Lapeer CLARION. w 1856-1925||?
United with Lapeer county press to form Lapeer county press and Lapeer clarion, later Lapeer county press
OHi F 13 1879

Lapeer DEMOCRAT. *See* Lapeer county press

LAPEER county democrat. *See* Lapeer county press

LAPEER county press. w 1873+
1873-84? Lapeer democrat; 1885?-94? Lapeer county democrat; 1895?-96? Lapeer county press and democrat; Mr? 1925-Lapeer county press and Lapeer clarion
pub 1880+
MWA Ap 24 1876

PLAIN DEALER and Lapeer county democrat. w 1839-45||
DLC Ap 17 1840

Lapeer REPUBLICAN. w? 1858?-
OClWHi Jl 28 1865

Lapeer SENTINEL. w N 1839-40||?
CtY Jl 14 1840
DLC My 5,Ag 4 1840
OClWHi Mr 10-S 17 1840

WHIG. w Mr 15? 1842-
MiAlH Mr 22 1842

LAURIUM

CALUMET. Red Jacket and Laurium NEWS. *See* Calumet news (Calumet)

MINATORE italiano. d,tw Ja 1 1897+
1897-1912? pub in Calumet
d 1897-1919?
pub 1897+

LAWRENCE

Lawrence ADVERTISER. w F 10 1875-80||?
MiD-B Mr 15 1876

Lawrence TIMES. w 1897+
pub 1934+
MiD-B 1926-[28]

LAWTON

Lawton LEADER. w 1886+
MiD-B [1925]-[28]

LESLIE

Leslie HERALD. w 1869-76||?
MWA Ap 22 1876
MiD-B Mr 18 1876

LEVERING

Levering LOCAL. w 1915-25||?
MiD-B [1922-23]

LEXINGTON

SANILAC county leader. w 1854-60||
1856-58? as Sanilac county leader and Huron county republican
MiD-B Ag 27 1856

SANILAC Jeffersonian. *See under* Croswell

LINCOLN

ALCONA county herald. w Ja 1 1908+
1908-Mr 3 1910 as Lincoln herald
pub 1908+

LINCOLN PARK

Papers published in Lincoln Park are listed under Detroit

LINDEN

Linden LEADER. w 1896+
MiF S 9 1932+

LITCHFIELD

Litchfield GAZETTE. w O 2 1871+
pub S 1901+
MWA My 29 1880

LOWELL

Lowell JOURNAL. w,sw Jl 1865-Jl 7 1932||
Merged with Lowell ledger
w 1865-1915?
MWA Ap 19 1876
MiD-B Mr 22 1876
MiG S 15 1916-32
MiLo N 1870-Mr,Jl 1873-Je,O 1881-Je 1896
MiU-C [1872-74;77;81]

Lowell LEDGER. w Je 1893+
pub 1893+
MiG N 30 1905+

LUDINGTON

Ludington weekly APPEAL. w Je 27 1873-1900||?
United with Ludington record to form Ludington record-appeal
MiD-B Mr 17 1876
MiLu 1890;92;96-1900

Ludington DEMOCRAT. w,sw 1881-98||?
w 1881-93?
MiU [1894]-[96]

MASON county record. *See* Ludington record-appeal

Ludington daily NEWS. d 1901+
1901-06? as Ludington sun
pub Je 20 1933+

Ludington RECORD-APPEAL. w S 17 1867-1913||?
1867-80? as Mason county record; 1881-1900? Ludington record
MWA Ap 19 1876
MiD-B Mr 15 1876;Ag 13 1885
MiLu 1867-74;1902-06
MiLuN 1897-1906

Ludington SUN. *See* Ludington daily news

LYONS

Lyons HERALD. w 1882+
pub Ap 28 1899-1904;06+

MANCELONA

Mancelona HERALD. w 1879—
pub 1879+

MICHIGAN (*Continued*)

MANCHESTER

Manchester ENTERPRISE. w O 10 1867+
pub 1867+
MWA My 8 1879
MiD-B Mr 16 1876

MANISTEE

Manistee ADVOCATE. w 1871-O 1914||?
MiMa Ja 9 1875-D 7 1878

Manistee daily ADVOCATE. d 1895-O 1914||
United with Manistee daily news to form Manistee news-advocate
MiMa Je 1905-Je 1911;12-14

Manistee GAZETTE. *See* Times 1864-1914

Manistee INDEPENDENT. w 1879-81||?
MWA Ag 27 1880

Manistee NEWS-ADVOCATE. d 1894+
1894-O 1914 as Manistee daily news
MiD-B [1922-28]
MiG Ap 2,My 14,21,Jl 2,9,31-Ag 3 1918
MiMa Ap 1894-1902;Je 1905+
—w ed *See* Times 1864-1914

NORDENS medborgare. w 1889-90||?
In Swedish
IRA 1890

SENTINEL. *See* Times 1864-1914

Manistee STANDARD. w 1871-S 5 1874||
Merged with Manistee times (1864-1914) to form Times and standard, later Times
MiMa Mr 25 1871-74

STANDARD. *See* Times 1864-1914

TIMES. w,sw Mr 1864-1914||?
1864-66 as Manistee gazette; 1867-Ag 1874 Manistee times; S 1874-82? Times and standard; 1883-85? Standard; 1886? Sentinel; 1887-1903? Times-sentinel
w 1864-1903?
MWA Ap 22 1876
MiD-B Mr 18 1876
MiMa N 17 1864-66;72-76
—d ed *See* Manistee news-advocate

TIMES. w My 1873-86||?
Not to be confused with Times 1864-1914
MiD-B S 29 1881
MiMa F 15 1883-84

MANISTIQUE

Manistique HÄROLD. w 1894-1909||?
In Swedish
IRA 1894-1909

Manistique semi-weekly PIONEER. w,sw,tw Ap 29 1880-96||
1880-84 as Schoolcraft county pioneer; 1885-86 Semi-weekly pioneer; 1887-92? Manistique tri-weekly pioneer. United with Manistique tribune to form Manistique pioneer-tribune
w 1880-84; tw 1887-92
MWA N 12 1881
MiMan 1884-92
MiManP complete

Manistique PIONEER-TRIBUNE. w 1893+
1893-96 as Manistique tribune
pub 1897+
MiD-B [1922-23]-[25]-[28]
MiMan 1897-My,Jl 1924-25

SCHOOLCRAFT county pioneer *See* Manistique semi-weekly pioneer

Manistique TRIBUNE. *See* Manistique pioneer-tribune

MAPLE RAPIDS

Maple Rapids PRESS. w My 1930+
pub 1930+

MARINE CITY

Marine City INDEPENDENT. w Mr 1919+
pub 1919+

MARQUETTE

Marquette CHRONICLE. d 1907-19||?
Some years as Marquette daily chronicle. Merged with Daily mining journal
MiMa Ja-Mr,Jl-D 1913;Ja-Je 1919

LAKE SUPERIOR journal. *See* Mining journal

MINING journal. w,m Jl 11 1846-1917||?
1846-Ap 1850 as Lake Superior news and mining journal; My 1850-67 Lake Superior journal Jl-O? 1846 pub in Copper Harbor; Je 1847-55? in Sault Ste. Marie in summer and Detroit in winter
Suspended from O 1846-Je 1847?
m in winter 1846-57?
DLC Je 8,Jl 6 1849;My 14,28-Je 4,Jl 9-30, Ag 13-O 1,15,29-N 5,D 1 1851;Ja-My 1,22-Je 5,16-30,Jl 21-N 10 1852;My 28,Je 11,25, Jl 16,O 1,29-N 12 1853;Ja 2,Mr 1,My 17-N 7 1854;My 24,Je 7-14,Ag 11,25,S 15-O 20,D 1 1855;My 17,31-Je 7,Jl 26 1856;N 21 1861
InLHi Ag 25 1855
MH [1846-N 11 1848]
MWA Jl 3 1847;S 11 1850;Ag 13,D 1 1851; Ap 1,My 1,22-N 10 1852;My 28-S 3,24-N 12 1853;Ja 2,Mr 1,My 17-O 21 1854;My 31, Je 21-Jl,Ag 18-O 1855;My 17-N 8 1856; Ja 3,Mr 7,Ap 5,18,My 16,Je 6-20,Jl-Ag,S 19-O 17,D 5 1857;F 6 1858;Je 26 1863
MiD-B [1875]80-81
MiHoM 1884-86
MiMar D 1 1855;68[69]-[71-74]-[76]-[97-98]-1917
NN Jl 1 1864
NNHi Je 5 1863
OClWHi Jl-S 19 1846
OOxM Jl 17 1850
WHi 1846-N 8 1849;My 1850-N 4 1854;96-N 12 1904

Daily MINING journal. d Je 2 1884+
MiG Jl 16 1897
MiHoM 1884-[86]+
MiMar 1896+
MiMn current year only
MiU 1889[1929]+
WHi 1917+

MARSHALL

CALHOUN county patriot. *See* Democratic expounder

Evening CHRONICLE. d Ag 1879+
1879-1910 as Daily chronicle
MiMars 1879-[81-1920]25+

DEMOCRATIC expounder. w O 2 1836-1909||
1836-40 as Calhoun county patriot; 1841-F 1875 Democratic expounder and Calhoun county patriot. Merged with Evening chronicle
Ct [1837-38]
DLC Mr 29,Ap 18,Ag 29 1844;O 16-N,D 11, 25 1846;Ja 15 1847-49;51-53;My 17 1855
MWA Ja 17 1840;Ag 21 1879
MiD-B Mr 16-N 1838
MiG S 27 1839
MiMars 1840-N 17 1842;F 14 1851-52;55-71
MiU N 27 1840
N Je 25 1840
NN D 27 1839-Ja 3,17-24,F 14,28 1840;Ja 15 1841

NEWS-STATESMAN. d 1899-1919||?
1899-1912? as Marshall news

Marshall STATESMAN. sw,w S 12 1839-1913||?
1839-O 5 1843 as Western statesman (title varies slightly). Merged with Marshall chronicle
sw Ap 19-Ag 12 1887
MWA F 14 1866
Mi Jl 30 1856-Ag 17 1859;F 29 1860-N 1864
MiG O 3 1839
MiU-C [1839-41]-[44-48]-[50]-[57]-[59-60]-[65-66]-[68]-[72]-[92]-[94-96]-[98-1900]-[04-05;07-09;11]
NSchU Ja 29 1842
OClWHi Jl 5 1865
WHi Mr 12 1851

Evening STATESMAN. d Ja 15- 1887||?
MiU-C [1887]

Evening STATESMAN. d 1911-13||?
United with Marshall news to form News-statesman
MiU-C [1911-13]

Marshall TIMES. w D 16 1836-Ag 1837||?
MWA S 22 1837
MiD-B Ag 11 1837

WESTERN statesman. *See* Marshall statesman

MASON

INGHAM county democrat. w 1875-1915||
Merged with Ingham county news
MiMasN complete

INGHAM county news. w Je 30? 1859+
pub [1859-70]+
MWA D 29 1859;Je 14 1860;Ap 20 1876
OClWHi Jl 19 1865

MEARS

Mears NEWZ. w 1914+
NcD Ag 23 1929;Ja 24,F 7 1930;N 4-11,D 2, 23-30 1932;Ja 20-27,F 17 1933;extra N 5 1932

MECOSTA

Mecosta NEWS. w 1913-25||?
MiD-B [1922-25]

MEMPHIS

Memphis BEE. w 1893+
MiD-B [1922-23]-[28]

MENDON

Mendon GLOBE. w 1875-1912||?
United with Mendon leader to form Globe leader

GLOBE leader. w 1894+
1894-1912? as Mendon leader
MiMen O 12 1916+

Mendon LEADER. *See* Globe leader

ST. JOE county news. w 1886-91||?
1891? part of paper as St. Joseph county republican (Centreville)

MENOMINEE

Menominee DEMOCRAT. w? 1885-1901||?
MiD-B F 27 1892
MiMe N 1885-My 1896

HERALD-LEADER. w,sw 1864+
1864-1904 as Menominee herald (w)
MWA F 17 1866;Ap 20 1876
MiMe 1887-1900
OClWHi Jl 22 1865
WHi Ap 14 1866-N 2 1867

Menominee HERALD LEADER. d,tw 1894+
1894-1904 as Menominee herald;1905-Mr 1910 Daily herald leader
tw 1900-01?
MiHoM S 1896-S 11 1897
MiMe Mr 1894-Ja,My 1899-Ap 1901;Mr 1905-Mr,My 1910+

Menominee daily LEADER. tw,d 1893-1904||
1893-1901? as Evening leader. United with Menominee herald to form Menominee herald leader
tw 1893-1901?
MiMe F 22-My 14 1904

MERRILL

Merrill MONITOR. w My 1902+
pub 1921+

MIDDLETON

Middleton NEWS. w Je 1935+
pub 1935+

MIDDLEVILLE

BARRY county republican. *See* Middleville sun and Caledonia news

Middleville REPUBLICAN. *See* Middleville sun and Caledonia news

Middleville SUN and Caledonia news. w 1870+
1870-79? as Barry county republican;1880?-93? Middleville republican;1894?-1922? Middleville sun
MWA Ap 20 1876

MIDLAND

Midland INDEPENDENT. w 1866?-80||?
MWA Ap 15 1876

Midland REPUBLICAN. w Ja 1 1881+
F 22 1934 is oil and industry ed
pub 1881+
MiG F 22 1934

Midland SUN. w 1881-1927||
Merged with Midland republican
MiMdR complete

MILAN

Milan LEADER. w 1881+
pub 1881+
MiU [1890-92]

Milan morning SUN. d 1881||?
MWA Je 4 1881

MILFORD

Milford TIMES. w F 18 1871+
pub [1871-80]+
MiD-B [1922]-[28]

MONROE

Monroe ADVOCATE. *See* Monroe commercial

Monroe COMMERCIAL. w Ja 1 1841-My? 1904||
Follows Monroe times. 1841-48 as Monroe advocate. United with Monroe record to form Record commercial
DLC D 26 1844;My 15 1845
MWA F 25 1864;F 22 1866;Je 20 1879
MiD-B [1859;76;86]
MiMD Ag 1856-[66]-N 21 1867
MiMN Je 30 1853-N 13 1862;N 23 1865-O 24,D 1872-75;77-85
MiU 1867-87

Monroe DEMOCRAT. *See* Monroe evening news

Monroe GAZETTE. w S 2 1837-Ag 31 1841||
MWA S 16 1837
MiD-B [1839-40]
MiMD complete

Monroe GAZETTE. w My 21 1845-
MiD-B My 20 1846

Monroe INDEX. w Mr 16? 1881-83||?
MWA Je 22 1881

Monroe JOURNAL and Michigan inquirer. w Jl 31- 1834||
MiD-B Ag 7 1834

MICHIGAN sentinel. w Je 3 1825-Jl 16 1836||
Some issues as Monroe sentinel. Followed by Monroe times
DLC Je 10 1825-Ja,F 21,Mr-My 23,Je 13-Jl 4,18,O 24,N,D 19 1829;30;Ja-Jl 19 1834
InRE D 5 1835;Jl 10 1836
MWA Ja 6 1827;Jl 18 1829
MiD-B [1825;28-29;31;35]
N Jl 7 1827
OClWHi Ja 24-My 16,S 12 1835

Monroe MONITOR. w My 28 1862-80||?
MWA Ap 19 1876;Ja 14 1880
MiMD 1862-My 16 1866

Monroe NATIONAL press. w 1856-62||
MWA Ap 3 1861
MiD-B Je 29 1859

Monroe evening NEWS. w,d Mr 17 1880+
1880-Mr 12? 1915 as Monroe democrat(w) Mr 19? 1915-Je 20? 1918 Monroe news courier
pub Mr 13 1884-F 16 1893;F 22 1894-F 13 1896;F 18 1897-F 2 1906;F 1908-Je 19,O 16 1916+
MWA S 2 1880
MiAdT S 1927+
MiG S 9 1904;My 6,Je 10 1910
MiMD 1880-Mr 13 1914;30-32

MICHIGAN (*Continued*)

MONROE—*Continued*

RECORD COMMERCIAL. w 1900-20||?
1900-My 19 1904 as Monroe record. Merged with Monroe evening news?
MiG S 8 1904;Je 9 1910
MiMN My 31 1900-Ap 1917

Monroe **SENTINEL.** *See* Michigan sentinel

Monroe **TIMES.** w Jl 28 1836-N? 1840||
Follows Michigan sentinel. Followed by Monroe advocate, later Monroe commercial
CtY Ja 13 1837
DLC Jl-N 1836;Ja 5 1837
MiD-B 1836-Jl 20 1837;Ap 26 1838

MONTAGUE

Montague **LUMBERMAN.** *See* Montague observer

Montague **OBSERVER.** w 1872+
1872-88? as Montague lumberman
MWA Ap 22 1876

Montague **SYNDICATE.** w 1871-73||?
NNHi Ja 4 1872

MORLEY

Morley **JOURNAL.** w 1905-20||?
MiHcR 1905-09

MOUNT CLEMENS

HALFWAY news. *See under* Halfway

Mount Clemens daily **LEADER.** d 1889+
MiAC [1933-34]
MiU 1926+

MACOMB county herald. w My 30 1849-
MWA D 22 1852
MiD-B Ap 23 1851

MACOMB gazette. w 1839-
MWA D 15 1852
MiD-B Ag 19 1852

MACOMB statesman. w S 22 1837-
MiD-B [N 10 1837-Ag 8 1840]

Mount Clemens **MONITOR.** w 1864+
pub 1880+
MiD-B [1926]27

Mount Clemens **PATRIOT.** w Ag 24 1839-
CSmH Ja 27 1842
MWA S 5 1840
MiD-B [S 11 1841-Jl 15 1847]

MT. MORRIS

Mt. Morris **TIMES.** w Ag 30 1928+
pub 1928+
MiF Ag 25 1932-[33]+

MT. PLEASANT

ISABELLA county enterprise. w 1865-1925||?
MWA Ap 19 1876

ISABELLA county times-news. w,d 1895+
1895-1930? as Mt. Pleasant times
d 1928?-30?
MiD-B [1922-24]-26

MORGAN'S watchtower. w 1873?-76||?
MWA Ap 11 1876

Mt. Pleasant **TIMES.** *See* Isabella county times-news

MUIR

GRAND RIVER herald. w 1871-78||?
MWA Ap 20 1877

MUNISING

CLOVERLAND farmer. *See* Wright's illustrated weekly

Munising **NEWS.** w 1896+
MiMn Je 1923+

WRIGHT'S illustrated weekly. The Cloverland farmer. w 1915-28||?
1915-23? Cloverland farmer;1924?-25? Wright's weekly
MiD-B 1924-25

MUSKEGON

Muskegon **CHRONICLE.** w Ja 30 1869-1906||
MWA Ap 21 1876
MiMu 1869-97

Muskegon **CHRONICLE.** d My 1879+
F 19? 1909-Mr 26 1913 as Muskegon news chronicle
MiG 1912-S 1913;14-S 1918;30+
MiMu Ag 26 1880+
NbHi O 16 1890

Muskegon **ENTERPRISE.** w Ja 1869-Ja 24 1873||
MiMu Ja 28 1870-73

FÄDERNESLANDET. w 1890-1901||?
1890-1900? as Frihets-baneret
In Swedish
IRA 1901

FRIHETS-BANERET. *See* Fäderneslandet

Muskegon **JOURNAL.** w D 18 1877-81||?
Merged with Muskegon chronicle
MiMu 1877-Jl 26 1881

Muskegon **LAKESIDE** register. w F 25 1874-77||
1874-Je 30 1875 as Muskegon lakeside weekly
MWA Ap 19 1876
MiMu 1874-Je 1875;My 1876-Ap 14 1877

Muskegon **LAKESIDE** weekly. *See* Muskegon lakeside register

Muskegon morning **NEWS.** d Ag 2? 1882-F 18 1909||
United with Muskegon chronicle to form Muskegon news chronicle, later Muskegon chronicle
MiMu Ag 4 1882-Je 1885;Mr 15 1889-Ap 8,Jl 29 1890-1909

Muskegon **NEWS** chronicle. *See* Muskegon chronicle

Muskegon **NEWS-REPORTER.** w,sw 1864-1904||?
1864-65 as Muskegon news; 1866-79? Muskegon news and reporter
sw 1875-83?
MWA My 23 1866
MiMu F 1870-87;My 1889-90;Jl 30 1891-93;97-S 1899
NN S 9(supp) 1865

Muskegon **OBSERVER.** w 1918+
pub 1924+
MiD-B 1927

Muskegon **REPORTER.** w Ap 1857-O 1865||?
United with Muskegon news to form Muskegon news-reporter
MiMu Ap 28 1859-S 1864

Muskegon weekly **TIMES.** w 1864?-
OClWHi S 9 1865

Muskegon daily **TIMES.** d Je 7? 1911-Mr 31 1916||
MiMu Je 9 1911-16

MUSKEGON HEIGHTS

RECORD. w D 2 1921+
pub 1921+

NASHVILLE

Nashville **NEWS.** w O 3 1873+
MWA Ja 8 1881
MiD-B [1876;1922-24]25

NEGAUNEE

Negaunee **IRON** herald. w N 1873+
pub 1873+
MiHoM O 9 1896-O 1 1897

LAKE SUPERIOR mining and manufacturing news. w My 15 1867-Ag 15 1868||
MiMar 1867-68

MARQUETTE weekly plain dealer. w O 1867-70||?
MiMar S 10-O 8,22-N 5 1868;Je 11,25-Jl 2 1870
OClWHi N 20 1869

Negaunee **MINING** review. w Jl 28 1870-72||?
MiMar Jl-Ag 1870

NEW BUFFALO

New Buffalo **INDEPENDENT.** w 1860?-
WHi O 26 1860

NEWAYGO

Newaygo **REPUBLICAN.** w 1856+
MWA Ap 19 1876
MiG O 12 1881
OClWHi Jl 12 1865

NEWBERRY

Newberry **ENTERPRISE.** w F 8-N 19 1894||
MiNeN complete

Newberry **INDEPENDENT.** *See* Luce county democrat

LUCE county democrat. w My 2 1889-Ap 25 1892||
1889-Ja 24 1891 as Newberry independent
Suspended between Ja 24 and My 2 1891
MiNeN complete

Newberry **NEWS.** w Je 10 1886+
pub 1886+

NILES

BERRIEN county freeman. w 1856-F 1866||
United with Niles inquirer to form Niles weekly times, later Niles republican
MWA Ja 20 1866

Niles **COURIER.** *See* Niles express

Niles **DEMOCRAT.** w O 25 1839-89||?
1839-67 as Niles republican
DLC D 3 1839;N 19 1840[Ap 1841-47]
ICHi O 20 1877
MWA D 25 1852
Mi Ap 1842-Je,N 10 1849-Mr 1862
MiN 1839-Ap 1889

Niles **ENQUIRER.** *See* Niles inquirer

Niles **EXPRESS.** w Ja 1 1845-50||?
1845-47? as Niles courier
DLC N 1-8,D 13-20 1849;Ja 17 1850

Niles **GAZETTE** and advertiser. w S 5 1835-Ja 1838||
Followed by Niles intelligencer
Ct [1836-37]
MiN S 12 1835-F 1837
WHi 1835-S 1836

Niles **INQUIRER.** w Ja 1855-F 1866||
Title varies: Niles enquirer. United with Berrien county freeman to form Niles weekly times, later Niles republican
CSmH Ja 4 1860
MWA D 27 1855;Ja 8,Ap 3,Jl 24,O 2 1856;Ja 22,F 26,Je 11,Jl 2 1857 Mr 25,O 7,N 11,D 2,23 1858;F 3,Mr 3,N 10 1859;Ja 25,Mr 21 1860;N 12 1862

Niles **INTELLIGENCER.** w F 21 1838-Mr 10 1841||
Follows Niles gazette and advertiser. Merged with Niles republican, later Niles democrat
ICHi Jl 10 1839
MiN complete
WHi F 28 1838-41

LOCO foco. w 1840||?
NBuG Ag 21 1840

Niles **MIRROR.** w 1876-1901||?
MiN Mr 22 1876-My 3 1899

Niles **REPUBLICAN.** 1839-67 *See* Niles democrat

Niles **REPUBLICAN.** w Mr 1 1866-1915||?
Formed by the union of Niles inquirer and Berrien county freeman. 1866-Mr 1868 as Niles weekly times
MWA F 19 1874;Jl 29 1875;Ap 20 1876;Ja 13 1881
MiD-B Ja 3 1867
MiN 1866-81;83-84;87;Ap 26 1888-92;Ap 1893-Ap 14 1895;Mr 1901-Ja 1905
OClWHi Je 21 1866

Niles daily **REPUBLICAN.** d Ag 26 1880-
MWA Ag 26 1880

Niles daily **STAR.** d 1885+
O 21? 1919-Je 1924 as Star-sun
MiN Mr 22 1905+

Niles daily **SUN.** d 1893-O 20 1919||
United with Niles daily star to form Star-sun, later Niles daily star
MiN My 4 1909-Ap 19 1911;Je 1914-Je 20 1916

Niles weekly **TIMES.** *See* Niles republican 1866-1915

WESTERN union. w 1852?
MWA Mr 24 1853

NORRIS

Norris **SUBURBAN.** w F 7? 1876-78||?
MWA Ap 21 1876

NORTH BRANCH

North Branch **GAZETTE.** w 1879+
pub 1879+

North Branch **OBSERVER.** w 1875-79||?
MWA Ap 19 1876

NORTHPORT

Northport **LEADER.** w 1893+
1893-98? as Leelanau leader;1899? Empire leader
1893-99? pub in Empire
pub [1914+]

NORTHVILLE

Northville **RECORD.** sm,w 1869+
1869-70? as Wayne county record
sm 1869-79?
pub 1869+
MWA Ap 22 1876;Jl 1 1881

WAYNE county record. *See* Northville record

NORWAY

Norway **CURRENT.** w F 7 1885+
pub 1885+
MiHoM 1890-Ag 6 1920

Norway **IRON** chronicle. w F? 1880-84||?
MWA Ag 28 1880

OLIVET

Olivet **NEWS.** w 1886-87||?
MiOC 1886-87

Olivet **OBITER.** w My 9 1885-86||?
MiD-B [1885-86]

Olivet **OPTIC.** w Ap 13 1889+
pub 1889+
MiD-B [1922-23]-[27-28]
MiOC 1889-1911

ONAWAY

Onaway **OUTLOOK.** w 1898+
pub 1898+

ONTONAGON

Ontonagon **HERALD.** w 1881+
pub S 1896+
MiHoM O 28 1890-[96]-[1918]+

LAKE SUPERIOR miner. *See* Ontonagon miner

Ontonagon **MINER.** w Ag 1855-98||?
1855-65? as Lake Superior miner
InLHi Ag 18 1855
MWA Ap 15 1876
MiU F 18 1865
N S 14 1861
WHi Ja 5,O 1855-Ag 16,D 1856-N 13 1858;S 10 1859;Ag 31 1867-S 10 1870

MICHIGAN (*Continued*)

OSCODA

Oscoda PRESS and Huron shore resorter. w 1879+
1879-1932? as Oscoda press
MiOs [1911+]

OTSEGO

ALLEGAN county record. w 1863-71||?
1863-68? as Otsego herald
MiOtU [1863-71]

Otsego HERALD. *See* Allegan county record

Otsego UNION. w 1875?+
1875?-87? as Otsego weekly union
pub [1875-90]93+

OTSEGO LAKE

OTSEGO county herald. w 1875-78||?
MWA Ap 14 1876;My 31 1878

OVID

CLINTON and Shiawassee union. w 1859-86||?
United with Ovid register to form Ovid register-union
MWA S 16 1881

Ovid REGISTER-UNION. w 1866+
1866-86? as Ovid register
MWA F 21 1867;Ap 21 1876;Ag 29 1879

OWOSSO

Owosso AMERICAN. *See* Press-American

Owosso ARGUS. 1843-49 *See* Shiawassee democrat (Corunna)

Owosso ARGUS-PRESS. d 1892+
1892-S 1919 as Owosso evening argus; O?-D? 1919 Argus and press-American
pub [1892+]

NEW ERA. w Mr 1874-76||?
Mr? 1874 as New era and grange index; Ap? 1874-75? New era and northern granger
MiU S 17 1874

Weekly PRESS. w S 1862-1906||?
MWA Ap 26 1876;My 21 1879
MiOw O 1862-N 1865;O 1866-67;O 1868-Ag 1878;O 1879-O 1886;O 1887-90;O 1892-1901;O 1903-06

PRESS-AMERICAN. d 1894-1919||?
1894-99? as Owosso American. United with Owosso evening argus to form Owosso argus-press
MiOw D 24 1900-04;Ap 1905-15

SHIAWASSEE argus and Clinton advocate. *See* Shiawassee democrat (Corunna)

SHIAWASSEE county reporter. *See* Shiawassee reporter

SHIAWASSEE express and Clinton advocate. *See* Shiwassee democrat (Corunna)

SHIAWASSEE reporter. w 1887-1900||?
1887-97? as Shiawassee county reporter
IU Je 8 1888

SHIAWASSEE republican. w 1879?-
MWA Ja 7 1880

Owosso TIMES. w 1878-1925||?
MiD-B [1922-23]-[25]

VALLEY CITY stereoscope. w 1874-77||?
MWA Ap 25 1876

OXFORD

Oxford LEADER. w 1881+
pub 1881+

PARCHMENT

Parchment NEWS. w 1928?+
pub 1928+

PARMA

Parma NEWS. w Je 13 1868+
pub 1868+
MWA Je 13 1868

PAW PAW

COURIER-NORTHERN. w Ja 1 1873+
1873-76? as Courier; 1877-1919? Free press and courier
pub 1873+
MiD-B [1922-24]-[28]

Paw Paw FREE PRESS. w? 1843-76||?
United with Courier to form Free press and courier, later Courier-northerner
MWA D 25 1852
MiPaC [1800-69]

FREE PRESS and courier. *See* Courier-northerner

TRUE northerner. w 1855?-1919||?
United with Free press and courier to form Courier-northerner
MWA Ap 5 1861;Ap 21 1876
MiPaC [1890-1919]

PENTWATER

EAST SHORE news. *See* Pentwater news

Pentwater NEWS. w 1871+
1871-72? as East Shore news
MWA Ap 20 1876

OCEANA times. w 1861-70||?
OClWHi Ag 25 1865;S 17 1869

PETOSKEY

Petoskey evening NEWS. d 1883+
1883-1901? as Resorter; 1902?-13; Evening news and resorter; 1915?-24? Petoskey news; 1925?-27? News and resorter
1883-1901? pub only during summer season
pub Je 1917+
MiP 1922-25

RESORTER. *See* Petoskey evening news

PIGEON

Pigeon PROGRESS. w S 5 1897+
pub 1897+

PINCKNEY

Pinckney DISPATCH. w Ja 1 1883+
pub 1883+

PINCONNING

Pinconning JOURNAL. w 1885+
1885-Mr 1925 as Pinconning press
pub 1905+

Pinconning PRESS. *See* Pinconning journal

PIONEER

TELEPHONE-NEWS. *See under* Reading

PITTSFORD

Pittsford REPORTER. w 1903+
MiD-B [1922]-[27]

PLYMOUTH

Plymouth MAIL. w S 16 1887+
pub 1887+

PONTIAC

Pontiac BILL poster. *See* Oakland county post

Pontiac COMMERCIAL. w 1876-79||?
MiPoHi Je 20 1876-Ap 23 1878

Pontiac COURIER. w Ja 28 1835-N 23 1842||
1835-Ja 1836 as Oakland whig; 1840? Jeffersonian
MiD-B F 8 1839
MiPoHi My 2,Je 20-O 24,N 14,28,D 19-26 1836;My 18-25,Je 8-22,Jl 6-Ag 24,S 7 1838

Pontiac GAZETTE. w F 7 1844-1910||?
1844-My 24 1851 as Oakland gazette
MWA D 18 1852;F 16 1866;Ap 21 1876
MiD-B [1844-46]-[48;50-51]-60;62;64-72;74-75;77-[1900-04]
MiPoHi F 12 1848-F 2 1850;71-79;83-94
MiU-C [1844-45]
—d ed *See* Pontiac daily press

Pontiac daily GAZETTE. d 1895-96||?
MiPoHi 1895-Mr 21 1896

Pontiac JACKSONIAN. w Mr 24 1838-73||?
MWA D 3 1863
MiPo Mr 24 1840-Mr 1844
MiPoHi [Jl 1838-Jl 1839]My 1842-[43]-Mr 1844

JEFFERSONIAN. *See* Pontiac courier

OAKLAND chronicle. w My 31 1830-Ap 22 1831||
Suspended from My 31-Je 11 1830
MiD-B O 1 1830
MiPoHi complete

OAKLAND county post. m,w Ja 1 1868-1915||?
1868-89? as Pontiac bill poster; 1898?-1904? Pontiac post
m 1868-Jl? 1869
MWA Ap 26 1876;My 28 1879
MiD-B [My 1878-F 22 1882]
MiPo 1874-90
MiPoHi 1874-89;S 1 1893

OAKLAND gazette. *See* Pontiac gazette

OAKLAND patriot. w D 1834-Mr 1836||
MiD-B O 21 1835

OAKLAND whig. *See* Pontiac courier

Pontiac POST. *See* Oakland county post

Pontiac daily PRESS. d 1900+
1906?-18? as Press-gazette
MiPo F 1924+
MiRo 1930+
MiU 1926+
—w ed *See* Pontiac gazette

PORT AUSTIN

HURON county news. w 1863-86||?
MWA Ap 20 1876

PORT HURON

Port Huron COMMERCIAL. w 1849-87||?
United with Port Huron tribune to form Commercial-tribune, later Port Huron tribune
MWA D 18 1852;My 22 1861

Sunday COMMERCIAL. w 1873-89||?
MWA Ap 16 1876;Ag 24 1879

COMMERCIAL-TRIBUNE. *See* Port Huron tribune

Port Huron FREE PRESS. w Mr 1 1919+
pub 1919+

Weekly HERALD. w -1869||?
NN F 3 1862(photostat)

Port Huron daily HERALD. d Ag 1? 1900-Ap 3 1910||
United with Port Huron daily times to form Port Huron times-herald
MiPh Ag 1900-10

LAKE HURON observer. *See* St. Clair observer (St. Clair)

NORTHERN miscellany. w 1841||
DLC N 18 1841

Port Huron OBSERVER. *See* St. Clair observer (St. Clair)

Port Huron TIMES. w,sw Je 25 1869-D 24 1909||
w 1869-97?
MWA Je 25 1869
Mi Mr 1871-72;74-75;Ja 30-D 1906;Ag 1907-F, O 13 1908-09
OClWHi S 11 1879

Port Huron TIMES-HERALD. d Mr 23 1872+
1872-Ap 3 1910 as Port Huron daily times
pub current 3 years only
DLC 1898
ICM O 28 1882
MWA Mr 23 1872;Ap 19 1876
Mi 1875;Jl-D 1882;87-Je 1892;Jl 1896-Ap 15 1909
MiD-B Mr 15 1876;S 19 1891
MiPh 1872-Je 1880;81-Je 1886;88-90;Jl-S 1891; 92-Ja 2 1903;04-11;Ap 1912-S 1913;14-23;25+
OClWHi F 11,Mr 4 1875;D 20 1878

Port Huron TRIBUNE. w 1881-94||?
1881-84? as Sunday tribune; 1887?-90? Commercial-tribune
ICM 1884(no day)

PORTLAND

Portland OBSERVER. w 1867+
MWA Ap 25 1876
MiPor O 1867-1903;10-14;19-24

Portland REVIEW. w Je 3 1885+
pub 1885+

POTTERVILLE

Potterville NEWS. w Mr 28 1929+
pub 1929+

PROVEMONT. *See* LAKE LEELANAU

QUINCY

BRANCH county democrat. w 1868-81||?
1868-Ag 25 1880 as Quincy times
MWA Ag 25-S 1 1880

Quincy HERALD. w 1878+
MiQ 1891+

Quincy TIMES. *See* Branch county democrat

QUINNESEC

MENOMINEE range. *See* Range tribune (Iron Mountain)

RAVENNA

Ravenna TIMES. w 1888+
pub 1926+

READING

Reading HUSTLER. w N 11 1891+
pub 1891+

Reading NEWS. w?
MiRH My 25,Jl 20 1878

Weekly PRESS. w 1872-77||?
MiRH Mr 20,Jl 24 1875;Jl 29,Ap 22,D 16, 1876;Ja 6,Mr 17,Je 23 1877

Reading REVIEW. w 1869?-70||?
MiRH O 15,N 5 1869;Ap 27 1870

ROUGH notes. w O 12 1872-74||?
MiRH [1872-74]

TELEPHONE-NEWS. w Ap 1879-1908||?
1879-Jl 1893 as Reading telephone
F 1896-97 pub in Pioneer
MiRH Je 5,O 14 1880;S 1882-84;86-99

RED JACKET

CALUMET and Red Jacket news. *See* Calumet news (Calumet)

REDFORD

Papers published in Redford are listed under Detroit

REED CITY

Reed City CLARION. w My 9 1873-1915||?
1873-76? as Reed City weekly clarion. United with Osceola county herald to form Osceola county herald-clarion, later Osceola county herald
MWA Ap 20 1876
MiD-B Mr 23 1876;Ag 14 1885;O 26 1894

OSCEOLA county democrat. *See* Osceola county herald

OSCEOLA county herald. w 1886+
1886-1909? as Osceola county democrat; 1916-17? Osceola county herald-clarion

MICHIGAN (*Continued*)

REESE

Reese REVIEW. w 1900+
pub S 1920+
MiFrN S 1930+

REMUS

Remus COURIER. w N 20 1930+
pub 1930+

RICHLAND

GALESBURG argus. *See under* Galesburg

RIVER ROUGE

Papers published in River Rouge are listed under Detroit

RIVERDALE

Riverdale PROMOTER. w 1911+
pub 1920+

ROCHESTER

Rochester CLARION. w Ag 19 1898+
pub 1898+
MiD-B [1922-23]-[25-29]

ROCKFORD

Rockford REGISTER. w F 6 1871+
pub 1871+
MiD-B [1876;1922-28]
MiG 1906+

ROCKLAND

Rockland REPORTER. w S 1 1898+
pub 1898+
MiD-B [1922-25]-[27-28]

ROMEO

Romeo ARGUS. w My 14 1857-
MiD-B 1857-My 6 1858

Romeo OBSERVER. w My 1866+
MWA Ap 19 1876
MiD-B Mr 15 1876

ROMULUS

Romulus ROMAN. w 1892+
pub Ap 1914+
MiD-B [1925]-[31]+

ROSEVILLE

Roseville NEWS. *See* Halfway news (Halfway)

Roseville RECORD. w 1925-31||?
MiD-B 1927[28]

ROYAL OAK

Daily TRIBUNE. w,d 1904+
1904-O 8 1925 as Royal Oak tribune (w)
pub O 1912+
MiD-B [1922]-[25;28-31]33+
MiRo [1912-16]+

SAGINAW

Saginaw COURIER-HERALD. w,sw Je 16 1859-1912||?
1859-79? as East Saginaw courier; 1880?-89 Saginaw courier
w 1859-97?
MiS [1859-D 6 1866;76-90]

Saginaw COURIER-HERALD. d Mr 5 1868-Jl 30 1918||
1868-S 18 1889 as Saginaw daily courier. United with Saginaw daily news to form Saginaw news courier, later Saginaw daily news
CtY O 14 1871
MWA Ap 20 1876
Mi S 19 1889-1918
MiD-B 1868-[1902-03]-[07]
MiS 1876-1918
N D 10 1882
NNHi S 11 1869
NbHi S 19 1877
PLaL Je 20 1878;Je 20 1879

Saginaw weekly ENTERPRISE. w S 8 1853-Ap 1874||
DLC Ag 19 1858; undated extra
MiS [1853-73]
OClWHi Je 22 1865

Saginaw semi-weekly ENTERPRISE. sw Ja 1 1858-
MiS Ja 1-5,12-19,26-29 1858

Saginaw ENTERPRISE. tw
MiS My 24-S 1 1859

Saginaw daily ENTERPRISE. d S 1866-73||
MiS D 20 1866;O 4 1867;F 13,Ap 27,My 1,O 2,10 1868;F 26,O 1 1869;O 9-14 1871

Saginaw GLOBE. d 1890-97||?
MiS Ja-Je 1891

Saginaw daily HERALD. d 1874-S 7 1889||
United with Saginaw daily courier to form Saginaw courier-herald
Mi 1880-89

Evening JOURNAL. d 1886-90||?
MiD-B Ap 1 1887

Saginaw JOURNAL. w 1901-Ja 1925||?
In German
IU D 1917-Ja 16 1925

Daily NEWS. d 1875-80||?
MWA Ag 28 1875
N Ag 20 1875

Saginaw daily NEWS. d My 2 1881+
1881-Mr 16 1910 as Saginaw evening news; Ag 1 1918-Ag 31 1927 Saginaw news courier
DLC 1898
Mi Ag 1918+
MiD-B Ag 29 1888
MiG Je 1? 1934
MiS 1890—

Saginaw REPUBLICAN. w 1858-79||?
MWA Ap 20 1876

SAGINAW county tribune. w 1929+
1929-33 as Hemlock tribune (Hemlock)
pub Mr 1935+

SAGINAWIAN. w My 1 1869-1917||?
MWA Ap 15 1876;Jl 5 1879
MiD-B Mr 18 1876

SPIRIT of the times. w 1849-60||?
MWA D 16-23 1852
MiD-B S 16 1852
MiS [F 17 1853-My 1859]
NjR Je 9 1853

Saginaw evening STAR. d Mr 15 1923-Ag 11 1924||
MiS complete

VALLEY news. w,sw 1874-1916||?
1876?-78? as Semi-weekly valley news (sw)
MWA Ap 18 1876

Saginaw ZEITUNG. w S 1 1868-97||?
In German
MiD-B Mr 16-Ap 6 1876

ST. CLAIR

St. Clair BANNER. *See* St. Clair democratic banner

St. Clair DEMOCRATIC banner. w Mr 27 1842?-56||
1842-Je 1843 as St. Clair banner. Merged with St. Clair republican
OClWHi D 4 1843

LAKE HURON observer and St. Clair county advertiser. *See* St. Clair observer

St. Clair OBSERVER. w F 11 1837-56||
1937-Jl 14 1845 as Lake Huron observer and St. Clair county advertiser; Jl 21 1845-Ag 1849 Port Huron observer
1937-Ag 1849 pub in Port Huron
Suspended from Ja 1-Ap 1842
CSmH D 11 1848
DLC My 9 1842
MiD-B S 27 1845;Ag 18 1849

St. Clair REPUBLICAN. w My 1856-1925||?
MWA F 20,Je 5 1857;Ap 26 1876;Ja 15 1879
MiD-B [1857;76;1922]-[24-25]

ST. CLAIR county press. w 1900+
pub D 20 1912+
MiD-B [1922]-[24-28;33]

ST. CLAIR SHORES

St. Clair SHORE NEWS. w 1925-28||?
MiD-B [F 15 1926-28]

ST. IGNACE

St. Ignace ENTERPRISE. w 1894-F 1932||?
United with Republican-news to form Republican-news and St. Ignace enterprise

St. Ignace NEWS. w 1883-99||?
United with St. Ignace republican to form Republican-news, later Republican-news and St. Ignace enterprise

REPUBLICAN-NEWS and St. Ignace enterprise. w 1878+
1878-99? as St. Ignace republican; 1900?-F 1932 Republican-news
pub Mr 10 1910+

ST. JAMES

NORTHERN islander. w D 12 1850-Je 19 1856||
MiD-B [1850-Ag 1851;Mr-N 11 1852]Ap-My 1853[F-N 1 1854;My 31-D 6 1855]Ja 24-Je 1856(photostat)
WHi [1850-56]photostat

NORTHERN islander. d Ja 24?-Je 20 1856||
MiD-B Je 20 1856(photostat)

ST. JOHNS

CLINTON county republican-news. w 1856+
1856-Ap 24 1924 as Clinton republican
pub 1864-70;82+
DLC F 25 1870
MWA D 22 1865
MiD-B [1922-24]-[28]

CLINTON democrat. w 1873-1908||?
1873-1903? as Clinton independent
MWA Ap 27 1876

CLINTON independent. *See* Clinton democrat

CLINTON republican. *See* Clinton county republican-news

St. Johns DEMOCRAT. w 1850-58||
1850-56 as Clinton express (DeWitt) 1857 North Side democrat
MiG Ag 12 1854
NBuG Je 3-10,24 1856

St. Johns NEWS. w 1889-Ap 1924||
United with Clinton republican to form Clinton county republican-news
MiD-B [1922-23]
MiSjR complete

NORTH SIDE democrat. *See* St. Johns democrat

St. Johns UNION democrat. w 1856?-
MWA D 5 1863

ST. JOSEPH

St. Joseph ADVERTISER. w S 5? 1867-
MWA S 12 1867

Saturday HERALD. w 1866-1916||?
1866-88? as St. Joseph herald (1875?-85? Traveller herald)
MiSa [1868-S 20 1872] My 11 1874-S 16 1916

Daily evening HERALD. d 1881-82||?
MiSa Mr 8 1881-Jl 22 1882

St. Joseph evening HERALD. d 1901-15||?
United with St. Joseph press to form St. Joseph herald-press
MiSa D 14 1901-D 11 1915

St. Joseph HERALD-PRESS. d 1891+
1891-1915? as St. Joseph press
MiSa S 9 1916;34+

LAKE SHORE daily news. d 1876-81||?
MiSa S 1880-Ja 1881

St. Joseph PRESS. *See* St. Joseph herald-press

St. Joseph TIMES.
TxU D 7 1867

Saint Joseph TRAVELLER. w 1859-74||?
United with St. Joseph herald to form Traveller herald, later Saturday herald
MWA N 20 1869;Ja 7,F 18 1871;My 4,Ag 10,24,S 14,N 2,D 21 1872;Ja 4 1873
MiSa Mr 18 1859-Mr 10 1866

ST. LOUIS

St. Louis HERALD. *See* Gratiot county herald (Ithaca)

St. Louis INDEPENDENT. w F 6 1890-1915||?
MiD-B 1890[92-96]-[98-99]-[1901-03;05-06]

St. Louis LEADER. w Ag 12 1879+
1890?-1909? Republican leader
MiD-B 1879-[81]-[83-84]-[86]

St. Louis evening PRESS. d My 1 1894-96||?
MiD-B 1894[95]96

St. Louis REPUBLICAN. w,sw 1882-89||?
United with St. Louis leader to form Republican-leader, later St. Louis leader
sw 1882-87?
MiD-B [1886;88-89]

REPUBLICAN-LEADER. *See* St. Louis leader

SALINE

Saline OBSERVER. w N 18 1880+
pub 1885+
MWA D 2 1880
MiD-B [1922-23]-[25]-[28]
MiU [1890-92]

Saline STANDARD. w D 1877-79||?
MWA O 17 1878

SANDUSKY

SANILAC county republican. *See* Sandusky republican tribune

Sandusky REPUBLICAN tribune. w 1885+
1885-My 1926 as Sanilac county republican
MiD-B [1926-28]

Sandusky TRIBUNE. w 1905-My 14 1926||
United with Sanilac county republican to form Sandusky republican tribune
MiD-B [1926]

SARANAC

Saranac ADVERTISER. w Ap 1893+
pub 1893+
MiD-B [1922-28]

Saranac REPORTER. w Jl 14 1875-76||?
MiD-B Mr 15 1876

SAUGATUCK

COMMERCIAL record. w 1868+
1868-1901? as Lake shore commercial
pub 1880+

LAKE SHORE commercial. *See* Commercial record

SAULT SAINTE MARIE

CHIPPEWA county news. *See* News and upper Michigan farm journal

Evening JOURNAL. d 1902-
NbHi O 25 1902

LAKE SUPERIOR journal. *See* Mining journal (Marquette)

LAKE SUPERIOR news and mining journal. *See* Mining journal (Marquette)

MICHIGAN (*Continued*)

SAULT SAINTE MARIE—*Continued*

Evening NEWS. d 1901+
Ag 2-3 1905 are semi-centennial celebration eds
Mi D 16 1910-Ap 1,Ag 2 1915+
MiG Ag 2-3 1905
MiU 1926+

NEWS and upper Michigan farm journal. w 1878+
1878-87? as Chippewa county news; 1888?-1910? News
OClWHi Jl 23 1887

SCHOOLCRAFT

BRADY news. *See* Dispatch and news

DISPATCH and news. w 1869-83||?
1869-72? as Schoolcraft dispatch (1870? Brady news?)
NbHi My 18 1878
WHi Jl 24 1869

SCOTTVILLE

ENTERPRISE. *See* Mason county enterprise

MASON county enterprise. w,sw 1885-1929||?
1885-1918? as Enterprise
sw 1919?-Ag 1925
MiD-B [1922-24]25

SEBEWAING

Sebewaing BLADE. w 1890+
pub 1900+

SHELBY

OCEANA herald. w 1888+
MiD-B [1922-28]

SOUTH HAVEN

South Haven MESSENGER. w 1881?-D 1902||?
United with Weekly tribune to form Tribune-messenger
MiSoT 1882-Ja 18 1895

South Haven daily TRIBUNE. d My 1899+
pub 1899+

TRIBUNE-MESSENGER. w,sw 1897-1917||?
1897-D 26 1902 as Weekly tribune
sw 1898?
pub 1900-06;08-09;11-Je 1912

SOUTH LYON

South Lyon EXCELSIOR. *See* South Lyon herald 1881+

South Lyon HERALD. w S 25? 1879-
MWA Ag 2 1879

South Lyon HERALD. w 1881+
1881-89? as South Lyon excelsior; 1890?-1902? Oakland excelsior
MWA Ap 12 1881
MiD-B S 13 1881

OAKLAND excelsior. *See* South Lyon herald 1881+

SPARTA

Kent City-Casnovia HERALD. w 1878-1930||?
1878-1920? as Casnovia herald; 1921?-26? Herald-journal
1878-1926? pub in Casnovia

Sparta LEADER. w 1895-99||?
United with Sparta sentinel to form Sparta sentinel-leader

Sparta SENTINEL-LEADER. w 1876+
1876-99? as Sparta sentinel
MiG D 1905+
MiSp 1919+

SPRINGPORT

Springport SIGNAL. w 1876+
pub 1910+

STAMBAUGH

Iron River-Stambaugh REPORTER. *See* Iron River reporter (Iron River)

STANDISH

ARENAC county independent. w Je 1 1883+
1883-94? as Arenac independent
pub 1883+

ARENAC independent. *See* Arenac county independent

STANTON

CLIPPER-HERALD. w 1879+
1879-1912? as Stanton clipper

MONTCALM county journal. w 1875-79||?
MWA Ap 28 1876

MONTCALM herald. w S 11 1867-1912||?
United with Stanton clipper to form Clipper-herald
IU Ja 4 1879

STEPHENSON

MENOMINEE county journal. w Ag 24 1893+
pub 1893+

STURGIS

Sturgis JOURNAL. w,sw,d 1859+
1876? Sturgis journal and times; 1877-79? Sturgis journal-times; 1880? Sturgis journal-leader
w 1859-1910?; sw 1911-16?
pub 1860+
MWA Ap 20 1876
MiD-B Jl 1861-64;69-70;Mr 16 1876;83-84
MiSt 1889+

MICHIGAN democrat. *See* Sturgis times-democrat

Sturgis TIMES. w 1874-75||?
United with Sturgis journal to form Sturgis journal and times, later Sturgis journal
MiU [1874-75]

Sturgis TIMES-DEMOCRAT. w,tw,d 1880-S 15 1917||
1880-1904? as Michigan democrat; 1905?-09? Michigan democrat and times. Merged with Sturgis journal
w 1880-1909?; tw 1910-12?
MiD-B My 1887-88;O 18 1915
MiU-C Ag 25 1886

SUNFIELD

Sunfield SENTINEL. w 1889+
1889-95? as Sunfield sun
pub Mr 12 1896+

Sunfield SUN. *See* Sunfield sentinel

SUTTONS BAY

Suttons Bay COURIER. w O 20 1915+
1915-Mr 1921 as Provemont courier (Provemont)
pub 1915+
MiD-B [1922-24]

TAWAS CITY

Tawas HERALD. w Ja 1 1884+
pub 1884+
MiD-B [1922-23]
MiOs 1884+

IOSCO county gazette. *See under* East Tawas

TECUMSEH

Tecumseh CHIEF. w?
MiAd My 19 1859-My 1860

Tecumseh DEMOCRAT. *See* Village record

HAYDEN'S Tecumseh globe. m? 1925-
MiD-B Mr 1 1926

Tecumseh HERALD. w My 25 1850+
pub 1850+
MWA Mr 24 1864;Ap 24 1879
MiD-B Mr 16 1876
MiT 1850-52;54-58[62-65]74-75;77-94;1903-16

Tecumseh NEWS. w 1884-1914||?
MiT 1884-96
MiU [1892]

RAISIN VALLEY record. w S 20 1866-76||?
MiD-B Mr 16 1876

VILLAGE record. w 1834-47||?
1834-Ap? 1837 as Tecumseh democrat
DLC My 14 1839
MiD-B Ag 16(extra)1836?
NOHi F 18 1837

TEKONSHA

Tekonsha PATRIOT. w 1922+
pub Mr 20 1931+

THOMPSONVILLE

Thompsonville NEWS. w 1893+
pub 1903+

THREE OAKS

ACORN. w 1891-1928||?
NN D 18 1905

THREE RIVERS

Daily COMMERCIAL. d 1907+
MiTh 1911;17-18;23

Three Rivers HERALD. w,sw 1869-1905||?
1869-Jl 1875 as St. Joseph county democrat
1869-72? pub at Burr Oak
sw Ag 23-D 1890?
MiD-B [1888]-90

Three Rivers NEWS reporter. w Ja 1 1861-92||?
1861-79? as Three Rivers reporter
MWA Mr 20 1880
MiD-B [1861]62;68-70;73-74[76;83]-88
MiTh 1862-66;70;73;75-77;80-81

Three Rivers REPORTER. *See* Three Rivers news reporter

ST. JOSEPH county democrat. *See* Three Rivers herald

Three Rivers TRIBUNE. w Ag 15 1878-1905||?
MiD-B 1878-86
MiTh 1879-81

WESTERN chronicle. w S 29 1849-1849-54? pub in Centreville
DLC O 21 1852
MiTh 1850-63

TRAVERSE CITY

Traverse City EAGLE. d 1893-1910||?
United with Evening record to form Record-eagle
—w,sw ed *See* Traverse Bay eagle

GRAND TRAVERSE herald and Traverse Bay eagle. w,sw 1858-1915||?
1858-1909? as Grand Traverse herald
w 1858-1906?
MWA Ap 20 1876
—d ed *See* Record-eagle

RECORD-EAGLE. d 1897+
1897-1909? as Evening record
OClWHi N 18 1905
—w,sw ed *See* Grand Traverse herald and Traverse Bay eagle

TRAVERSE BAY eagle. w,sw 1864-1909||?
United with Grand Traverse herald to form Grand Traverse herald and Traverse Bay eagle
w 1864-1905?

TRENTON

CENTENNIAL. w Ap 13 1876-
MWA Ap 13 1876

Trenton TIMES. w 1887+
pub 1912+

UBLY

Ubly COURIER. w 1894+
pub 1902+

UNION CITY

Union City REGISTER-WEEKLY. w 1869+
1869-1901? as Union City register
MWA Ap 22 1876

ROBINSON'S weekly. w 1896-1901||?
United with Union City register to form Union City register-weekly

UTICA

Utica SENTINEL. w Ag 11 1876+
pub 1876-79;81-95;Jl 1928+
MWA F 7 1880
MiUtF Ag 18 1876-1928

VASSAR

Vassar PIONEER-TIMES. *See* Tuscola county pioneer-times

Vassar TIMES. w 1881-1912||?
United with Tuscola county pioneer to form Vassar pioneer-times, later Tuscola county pioneer-times

TUSCOLA county pioneer-times. w N 24 1857+
1857-1912? as Tuscola county pioneer; 1913?-29 Vassar pioneer-times
pub [1857+]
MWA Ap 19 1876
NNHi Ag 19 1863;Ag 16(supp)1865;Ap 16 1873

VERMONTVILLE

Vermontville ECHO. w 1875+
1875-84? as Hawk
MiD-B [1922-23]-[26-27]

Vermontville ENTERPRISE. w 1874-80||?
MWA Ap 20 1876

HAWK. *See* Vermontville echo

VICKSBURG

Vicksburg COMMERCIAL. w,sw 1879+
w 1879-1901?
pub 1879-1919;23+

Vicksburg MONITOR. w,sw 1875-85||?
1875-76? as Vicksburg semi-weekly monitor (sw)
MWA Ap 26 1876

WALDRON

Waldron RECORDER. w 1892+
MiD-B [1922;24]

WARREN

Warren-Fraser HERALD. w 1892-1931||?
1892-Ap 10? 1924 as Warren watchman
MiD-B [1922-28]

Warren WATCHMAN. *See* Warren-Fraser Herald

WATERVLIET

Watervliet RECORD. w 1881+
pub Mr 1890+

MICHIGAN (*Continued*)

WAYNE

Wayne DISPATCH. w 1914+
1914-28 as Wayne weekly
pub 1918+

WAYNE county tidings. w 1876-80||?
MWA Ag 15 1879

Wayne WEEKLY. *See* Wayne dispatch

WEIDMAN

Weidman MESSENGER. w 1912+
pub Ap 1928+

WENONA

Wenona HERALD. w Mr 9 1869-77||?
MWA Ap 15 1876
MiD-B Mr 9-16 1869

WEST BRANCH

OGEMAW county herald. w 1878+
pub 1878+

WHITE CLOUD

White Cloud EAGLE. w 1897+
pub Jl 25 1910+

WHITE PIDGEON

GAZETTE. w Ag 1837-38||?
Followed by White Pigeon republican and St. Joseph county advertiser

MICHIGAN statesman. *See* Kalamazoo gazette (Kalamazoo)

White Pigeon NEWS. w 1912+
pub Ag 15 1927+

White Pigeon REPUBLICAN. w Jl 4 1865-66||?
MiD-B [Ag 1865-66]

White Pigeon REPUBLICAN and St. Joseph county advertiser. w F 6 1839-40||?
Follows Gazette. Followed by St. Joseph county republican
DLC F 6,20 1839

ST. JOSEPH county republican. w My 5 1841-42||?
Follows White Pigeon republican and St. Joseph county advertiser
DLC My 5-12 1841

WHITEHALL

Whitehall FORUM. w O 28 1869+
pub Jl 1876+
CtY N 19 1897

WILLIAMSTON

Williamston ENTERPRISE. w Je 6 1873+
MiD-B [1876;1922-23]-[25-28]

WOODLAND

Woodland NEWS. w 1889+
IU Je 21 1917-31

WYANDOTTE

DOWN RIVER daily record. d 1928-My 1935||
United with Gateway chronicle to form Wyandotte daily news

Wyandotte ENTERPRISE. *See* Detroit courier (Detroit)

GATEWAY chronicle. w 1926-My 1935||
United with Down River daily record to form Wyandotte daily news

Wyandotte HERALD. w Je 2 1879+
pub Jl 1886—
MiD-B [1922]-[25-26]27
MiW 1915+

Wyandotte daily NEWS. d My 23 1935+
Formed by union of Down River daily record and Gateway chronicle
pub 1935+

WAYNE county courier. *See* Detroit courier (Detroit) 1870+

YALE

Yale EXPOSITOR. w 1882+
1882-94 as Weekly expositor
pub 1882+
MiD-B [1922]23

YPSILANTI

Ypsilanti COMMERCIAL. w Mr 1 1864-1900||
United with Ypsilanti sentinel to form Ypsilanti sentinel-commercial
MWA Ap 22 1876;Je 21 1879
MiD-B Mr 18 1876
MiG Jl 13-20 1872
MiU [1878;83;87;89]-[91]
MiY 1864-F 1879;Mr 1880-N 1895;Jl 24 1896-Ag 1898

Ypsilanti daily PRESS. d Mr 10 1904+
1913?-Mr 10 1928 as Daily Ypsilantian press
pub 1904+
MiG Je 25-Jl 3,6-7 1923
MiYM 1904+

Ypsilanti RECORD. w O 28 1915-My 28 1925||
MiYM complete

Ypsilanti REPUBLICAN. w Jl 11 1838-39||?
DLC Jl 11 1838

Ypsilanti SENTINEL-COMMERCIAL. w D 20 1843-1906||
1843-1900 as Ypsilanti sentinel. United with Ann Arbor weekly argus to form Ann Arbor weekly argus and Ypsilanti sentinel and commercial (Ann Arbor)
CtY Ja 10 1844
MWA Ag 20 1879
MiD-B F 28,Je 17(extra)1844;Jl 29 1846; Jl 3?(extra)1847;Mr 15 1876
MiG Jl 14 1847;F 12 1851
MiU [1844;90-92]1900[01]-03
OClWHi Ag 20 1862

WASHTENAW times. *See* Ann Arbor daily news (Ann Arbor)

YPSILANTIAN. w 1880-1912||?
United with Ypsilanti daily press to form Daily Ypsilantian press, later Ypsilanti daily press
MiU [1886;90-92;95]-99

Daily YPSILANTIAN press. *See* Ypsilanti daily press

ZEELAND

Zeeland EXPOSITOR. *See* Zeeland record

Zeeland RECORD. w O 1 1893+
1893-97 as Zeeland expositor
pub 1915+

MINNESOTA

ADA

Ada ALERT. *See* Norman county index

NORMAN county herald. w Ap 28 1888+
MnHi 1888+

NORMAN county index. w Ap 1880+
1880-82? Ada alert
pub 1882+
MnHi F 7 1890+

PUHLER'S Red River Valley journal. w Mr 20 1885-86||
MnHi Ap 10 1885-Ja 15 1886

ADAMS

Adams REVIEW. w 1897+
pub 1899-[1905-09]-[21-25]+

ADRIAN

Adrian GUARDIAN. w 1883-1905||
MnHi S 26 1890;91-O 18 1905

NOBLES county democrat. *See* Nobles county review

NOBLES county review. w 1891+
1891-1924? as Nobles county democrat
MnHi [1895;97]-Je 5 1903

AITKIN

Aitkin AGE. *See* Aitkin independent age

Aitkin INDEPENDENT. w 1901-Jl 27 1912||
United with Aitkin age to form Aitkin independent age
MnAiI complete
MnHi [1903]-12

Aitkin INDEPENDENT age. w Ap 1883+
1883-Jl 27 1912 as Aitkin age
pub 1883+
MnHi [1883;90]+

Aitkin REPUBLICAN. w Jl 27 1894+
pub 1894+
MnHi [1894]+

AKELEY

Akeley HERALD. *See* Akeley herald-tribune

Akeley HERALD-TRIBUNE. w Je 28 1899+
1899-1904? as Akeley independent; 1905-Mr 1909 Akeley herald
pub My 1928+
MnHi O 9 1913+

Akeley INDEPENDENT. *See* Akeley herald-tribune

Akeley TRIBUNE. w 1904-Mr 1909||
United with Akeley herald to form Akeley herald-tribune

ALBANY

Albany ENTERPRISE. w Mr 3 1910+
pub 1911+
MnHi Ag 25 1910+

ALBERT LEA

Albert Lea ENTERPRISE. w 1872-1905||
United with Freeborn county times to form Times-enterprise
MnHi My 8 1879;My 23 1889;O 16 1890-1905

FREEBORN county eagle. w S 11 1858-My 19 1860||
MnHi [S 25-D 18 1858;Ja 15 1859-My 12 1860]

FREEBORN county standard. sw,w My 26 1860-Ap 30 1931||
sw My 1915-Mr 1921
MWA N 16 1871
MnAlT complete
MnHi 1868-Ja 7 1875,F 20 1879-Ap 30 1931

FREEBORN county times-enterprise. *See* Times-enterprise

Albert Lea POSTEN. w 1882-Mr 17 1885||
Merged with Nordvesten (St. Paul)
In Norwegian
IaDeL Mr 16 1883-85
MnHi [1883]-85

SOUTHERN Minnesota star. w Jl 9 1867-
MnHi Jl 9 1867

TIMES-ENTERPRISE. w 1895-S 25 1923||
1895-D 22 1905 as Freeborn county times; D 27 1905-Je 6 1906 Freeborn county times enterprise
MnHi 1895[96-97]-Ap 4 1923

Evening TRIBUNE. d O 15 1897+
1897-My 1915 as Albert Lea evening tribune
pub 1897-[1901]+
MnHi N 28 1899+

ALDEN

Alden ADVANCE. w Ap 1890+
pub [1890+]
MnHi D 14 1897-[1900]Ja 25 1923+

Alden EAGLE. w S 5 1879-Je 4 1880||
MnHi complete

ALEXANDRIA

CENTRAL citizen. *See* Alexandria citizen

Alexandria CITIZEN. w 1894-Ap 1 1920||
1894-D 2 1897 as Central citizen. United with Alexandria post-news to form Douglas county news, later Alexandria citizen news
MnHi Ap 8 1897-1920

Alexandria CITIZEN-NEWS. w Ag 1 1878+
1878-Ap 19 1894 as Douglas county news; Ap 26 1894-Ap 1 1920 Alexandria post-news; Ag 25 1932-Ap 13 1933 Douglas county news
pub Ap 25 1894-[1932]+
MnA Ap 8 1920+
MnHi 1878+

DOUGLAS county news. *See* Alexandria citizen-news

DOUGLAS county sentinel. w 1892-93||?
MnHi [Ap 20-D 21 1893]

Alexandria POST. w S 23 1868-Mr 30 1894||
United with Douglas county news to form Alexandria post-news, later Alexandria citizen-news
MnAC 1874-94
MnHi 1868-[70]-[77-78]-[84]-94
MWA Jl 22 1881

Alexandria POST-NEWS. *See* Alexandria citizen-news

PARK region echo. w 1891+
1891-Ag 27 1908 as Brandon echo (Brandon)
pub 1923+
MnHi 1898+

Alexandria REPUBLICAN. w F 24 1894-Je 2 1897||
MnHi D 22 1894-97

Alexandria TRADE-NEWS. m 1922?-D 17 1932||
1933+ as monthly supp of Park region echo
MnHi Mr 26 1927-32

AMBOY

Amboy HERALD. w 1890+
MnHiS 19-O 17 1890;N 25 1891-Ap 12 1895

ANNANDALE

Annandale ADVOCATE. w Ag 5 1897+
My 25 1899-1903 as Annandale advocate-post; Ja-N 1904 Annandale advocate and Annandale post
pub 1899+
MnHi 1897+

Annandale POST. w 1890-My 19 1899||
United with Annandale advocate to form Annandale advocate-post, later Annandale advocate
MnAnA complete
MnHi Ap 18 1891-99

ANOKA

ANOKA county press. *See* Anoka herald

ANOKA county republican. *See* Anoka herald

ANOKA county union. w S 5 1865+
S 3 1868-Jl 8 1869 as Anoka weekly union
pub 1865—
MnHi D 13 1866+

MINNESOTA (*Continued*)

ANOKA—*Continued*

Anoka city DEMOCRAT. w Mr 3 1870-
MnHi Mr 3 1870

Anoka FREE PRESS. w Ag 15 1901-N 10 1910||
Merged with Anoka herald
MnHi complete

Anoka HEADLIGHT. w F 26 1885-
MnHi F 26-Ag 14 1885

Anoka HERALD. w 1866+
1866-Jl 5 1873 as Anoka county press; Jl 12 1873-76 Anoka county republican; 1877-78 Anoka sun and republican
pub [1884]+
MWA S 3 1887
MnHi [Ja 26 1869-74]O 18,N 2 1878;N 30 1889+

Anoka REPUBLICAN. w 1860-63||?
Followed by Anoka star
N O 12,D 14 1861

Anoka SENTINEL. w Ap 7-Je 30 1865||
MnHi complete

Anoka STAR. w O 3 1863-64||
Follows Anoka republican
MnHi 1863-S 3 1864

Anoka SUN and republican. *See* Anoka herald

Anoka weekly UNION. *See* Anoka county union

APPLETON

Appleton INDEPENDENT. w 1922-24||
MnHi Mr 9 1923-24

Appleton PRESS. w Ap 3 1880+
pub 1880+
MnHi Ap 22 1897+

SWIFT county republican. w 1912-25||?
MnHi 1924-O 23 1925

SWIFT county standard. *See under* Benson

Appleton TRIBUNE. w S 12 1896-1906||
MnHi 1896-[1901]-Mr 28 1906

ARGYLE

MARSHALL county banner. w D 23 1882+
pub 1882+
MnHi [Ap 15 1897-Mr 10 1898] Ag 12 1915+

ARLINGTON

Arlington ENTERPRISE. w 1884+
My 14 1891-Mr 28 1895 as Sibley county enterprise
MnHi Mr 2 1887 [88;91]+

SIBLEY county enterprise. *See* Arlington enterprise

ASHAWA

NORTHLAND farmer. w D 10 1903-08||
MnHi D 31 1903-[07-08]

ASHBY

Ashby AVALANCHE. w Ag 31 1883-86||?
MnHi 1883-85

GRANT county farmer. *See* Elbow Lake tribune (Elbow Lake)

Ashby POST. w N 14 1903-22||
MnHi 1903-[04-05]-[08]-My 12 1922

Ashby TRIBUNE. w 1897-My 18 1899||
United with Barrett lake breeze (Barrett) to form Elbow Lake tribune (Elbow Lake)

ASKOV

Askov AMERICAN. w S 17 1914+
pub 1914+
MnHi Ap 9,N 5 1925+

ATWATER

Atwater PRESS. *See* Republican-press

REPUBLICAN. w My 30 1895-F 16 1900||.
United with Atwater press to form Republican press
MnAtR 1895-96;99

REPUBLICAN-PRESS. w Ja 9 1880+
1880-84? as Western Minnesota press; 1885?-F 16
1900 Atwater press
1880-Ap 15 1881 pub in Willmar
pub 1896;99;1907+
MnHi [1880-Ap 1881]Mr 1887-[88-89]+

WESTERN Minnesota press. *See* Republican-press

AURORA

Aurora NEWS. w Je 20 1907+
pub 1909+
MnHi Ja 31 1919+

AUSTIN

Austin DEMOCRAT. *See* Austin weekly herald

Austin weekly HERALD. w O 1886-1923||
1886-N 23 1897 as Austin democrat
pub complete
MnAu 1886-N 23 1897
MnHi [F 1891-98]-1920

Austin daily HERALD. d N 9 1891+
Suspended Ja 26 1895-Ja 25 1896
pub 1891+
MnHi 1891 [92]-Ja 26 1895;Ap 20 1923+

MINNESOTA courier. w 1860-
MnHi [Mr 26 1862-Ja 6 1864]
MnAu [1860-64]

MOWER and Fillmore county republican. *See* Preston republican (Preston)

MOWER county mirror. w S 30 1858-
MnHi N 4 1858-O 13 1859

MOWER county news. w 1868+
1868-My 1919 as Mower county transcript; Je 1919-O 7 1920 Mower county transcript-republican
MWA O 28 1869;D 8 1870;Mr 26(supp)O 15 (supp)1874
MnAu [1868]-[1914]Je 1919+
MnHi Jl 15 1869-[77-78]-[1919]+

MOWER county republican. w -S 17 1875||
United with Fillmore county republican to form Mower and Fillmore county republican, later Preston republican (Preston)

MOWER county republican. w 1908-15||
United with Mower county transcript to form Mower county transcript-republican, later Mower county news

MOWER county register. *See* Austin register

MOWER county transcript. *See* Mower county news

MOWER county transcript-republican. *See* Mower county news

NATIONAL republican. *See* Preston republican (Preston)

Austin REGISTER. w Jl 2 1863-1908||
S 30 1869-Je 22 1871 as Mower county register
MWA Ap 30,S 3 1868;Mr 11 1875;Ja 2 1879
MnAu 1863-96
MnHi [1864]67-My 29 1908

AVOCA

MURRAY county independent. w 1892-1904||?
MnHi Ap 14 1893-Ja 24 1902

BACKUS

Backus NEWS. w Ag 30 1903-S 22 1904||
O 15 1903-Ag 25 1904 as Backus news and Pillager post. United with Pine River sentinel to form Pine River sentinel and the Backus weekly news (Pine River)
MnHi complete

Backus TIMES. w Mr 3 1906-
MnHi Mr 3-S 29 1906

BADGER

HERALD-RUSTLER. w 1896+
1896-99? as Badger herald
MnHi My 1 1909+

BAGLEY

CLEARWATER crystal. w 1903-My 2 1913||
MnHi O 7 1909-13

FARMERS independent. w 1918+
pub 1918+
MnHi D 22-1921+

BALATON

BYSTANDER. w Mr 23 1900-
MnHi Ap 6,My 4,18-S 1 1900

Balaton JOURNAL. w 1887-90||
MnHi S 20-N 1 1890

Balaton PRESS-TRIBUNE. w 1903+
1903-Mr 1910 as Balaton press
pub 1910+

BARNESVILLE

Barnesville HEADLIGHT. w 1890-Jl 1919||
United with Clay county leader and Moorhead independent to form Country press (Moorhead)
MnHi Jl 18 1913-O 4 1917

Barnesville RECORD. w Ja 28 1897-S 11 1903||
United with Review to form Barnesville record-review
MnHi Ap 8 1897-[1900]-[02]

Barnesville RECORD-REVIEW. w 1885+
1885-S 11 1903 as Review
MnHi S 19 1890+

REVIEW. *See* Barnesville record-review

BARNUM

Barnum ADVOCATE. w O 6 1893-94||
MnHi 1893-94

GAZETTE. w O 1 1896-F 5 1903||
United with Moose Lake star to form Star-gazette (Moose Lake)
MnHi complete

Barnum HERALD. w 1909+
MnHi Ja 5 1923+

BARRETT

Barrett LAKE breeze. *See* Elbow Lake tribune (Elbow Lake)

BATTLE LAKE

Battle Lake REVIEW. w My 1884+
pub 1884+
MnHi F 21 1889-[1903]-[06]My 24-S 27 1917

BAUDETTE

RAINY RIVER region. *See* Baudette region

Baudette REGION. w 1904+
1903-12? as Rainy River region
MnHi Ap 1925+

BAYPORT

Bayport HERALD. w 1923+
pub 1923+
MnStG 1923+

BEAR RIVER

Bear River JOURNAL. w 1906-19||
MnHi My 25 1911-Ja 30 1919

BEARDSLEY

Beardsley NEWS. w 1897-1907||
MnHi Ap 6 1900-S 26 1907

Beardsley NEWS. w Ap 10 1908+
pub 1908-[10]-[14]-[23-24]+
MnHi 1908+

BEAVER CREEK

Beaver Creek BANNER. w 1901-09||
MnHi [O 2 1908-N 5 1909]

Beaver Creek BOOSTER. w Je 22 1922-23||
MnHi 1922-Je 14 1923

BEAVER FALLS

Beaver Falls GAZETTE. w Ap 5 1870-
Ap-My 1870 as Beaver Falls weekly gazette
MnHi Ap 26-N 18 1870

RENVILLE times. *See* Olivia times (Olivia)

Beaver Falls TIMES. *See* Olivia times (Olivia)

BECKER

Becker HERALD. w Jl 1 1913+
pub 1913+

BELGRADE

ENTERPRISE. w 1890-91||?
MnHi F 26-Je 18 1891

Belgrade TRIBUNE. w Je 1 1899+
pub 1915+

BELLE PLAINE

Belle Plaine ENQUIRER. w D 2 1857-O 5 1861||
DLC Ja 6-D 17 1859
MnHi [Mr 18 1858-61]

Belle Plaine HERALD. w Ja 5 1882+
pub 1882+
MnHi 1894+

SCOTT county journal. w N 7 1861-
MnHi N 28 1861-Ag 28 1862

BELLINGHAM

Bellingham TIMES. w 1889+
pub [1916-20]+
MnHi N 14 1895-S 7 1916;Ap 1927+

BEMIDJI

BELTRAMI county news. w 1898-1908||?
MnHi F 11 1904-[06]-Mr 7 1907

BELTRAMI eagle. w 1896-97||?
MnHi Ap 1897-O 29 1897

Bemidji HERALD. w Ag 19 1915-16||
MnHi 1915-My 25 1916

Bemidji INDEPENDENT. w Ag 1 1924-
MnHi Ag 1-N 28 1924

Bemidji weekly PIONEER. w Mr 19 1896-1926||
pub 1898-1926
MnHi [Ap 30 1896-Ap 22 1897] 1900-17

Bemidji daily PIONEER. d Ap 20 1903+
pub 1903+
KHi [F 7-My 8 1923]
MnB 1920+
MnHi Jl 12 1904+

Bemidji SENTINEL. w N 27 1901+
pub 1901 [02-11]+
IU D 14 1928-Ja 3 1930
MnB 1922-32
MnHi O 7 1903-Ja 18 1906;Je 28 1918+

BENSON

STANDARD. *See* Swift county standard

SWIFT county advocate. w S 7 1877-78||
MnHi [1877-78]

SWIFT county monitor. w 1886+
pub 1888-1919;22+
MnHi O 24 1890+

MINNESOTA (*Continued*)

BENSON—*Continued*

SWIFT county news. w 1892+
1892-Ag 3 1900 as Murdock review (Murdock) Ag 10 1900-Ag 26 1900 Swift county review
pub 1903—
MnHi Mr 12 1897+

SWIFT county press. w 1882-85||
MnHi F 28 1883-Jl 3 1885

SWIFT county review. *See* Swift county news

SWIFT county standard. w Ag 8 1890-94||
1890-O 9 1891 as Standard
Dated also at Kerkhoven, Appleton, and Willmar
MnHi 1890-[92]-[94]

Benson TIMES. w 1876-1912||
MnHi [Mr 3 1877-N 22 1878]S 26 1882-Ag 13 1912

BIG FALLS

Big Fork COMPASS. w Ja 7 1903+
pub 1903+

BIG LAKE

Big Lake HERALD. w Mr 25 1898-1909||?
1898-99 as Big Lake mirror
MnHi N 25 1898;Mr 31-S 29 1899

Big Lake MIRROR. 1898-99 *See* Big Lake herald

Big Lake MIRROR. w 1921-25||
MnHi Ja 19 1922-S 3 1925

Big Lake WAVE. w Je 24 1910-14||
MnHi 1910-Jl 31 1914

BIGELOW

MINNESOTA signal. w F 27 1896-1907||?
Jl 2-D 31 1897 as Bigelow's Minnesota signal
MnHi Je 19 1896;Ap 9 1897-[1901]

BIGFORK

Big Fork SETTLER. w O 8 1903-14||
MnHi 1903-[07-08]-S 17 1914

Bigfork TIMES. w F 12 1925-33||
MnHi 1925-Ag 9 1933

BIRD ISLAND

Bird Island BLIZZARD. w Ap 21 1881-
MnHi N 17-D 1,22 1881

Bird Island POST. *See* Bird Island union

RENVILLE county union. *See* Bird Island union

Bird Island UNION. w Ag 22 1879+
1879-80 as Bird Island post; 1881-N 20 1903 Renville county union
MnHi O 3-10,N 7,21-D 12 1879;Ja 16-F 6,20, My 14,28,Je 11 1880[S 8 1881-Ap 3 1891]+

BIWABIK

MESABA range. w Jl 14 1892-D 21 1897||
Suspended S 3 1896-Je 1897
MnHi complete

Biwabik TIMES. w Ja 25 1907+
pub 1907+
MnHi N 3 1922+

BLACKDUCK

Blackduck AMERICAN. w D 2 1901+
pub 1901+
MnB 1922-32
MnHi O 16 1907+

BLOOMING PRAIRIE

Blooming Prairie TIMES. w My 18 1893+
pub 1893+
MnHi S 15 1898-[99]Je 21 1917+

BLUE EARTH

BEE. w 1864-85||?
1864-71? as Minnesota southwest; 1872?-74? Blue Earth City mail
MnHi [1868-S 2 1871]75-O 1 1881

FARIBAULT county journal. w O 4 1880-D 19 1881||
MnHi N 8 1880-81

FARIBAULT county register. w Ja 1888+
pub 1899+
MnHi Mr 6 1891-Ap 23 1908

Blue Earth City MAIL. *See* Bee

MINNESOTA southwest. *See* Bee

Blue Earth City NEWS. w Ap 20 1861-
MnHi N 1861-[62]

Blue Earth POST. w My 29 1869+
Title varies slightly
MnBl 1869+
MnHi Je 5 1869-[70]My 31 1873-S 1 1882;Je 30 1887-[88]-[89]+

SOUTH-WEST Minnesotian. w 1861-
MnHi Ag 2-S 13 1862

BOCK

Bock NEWS. w My 5 1915-20|
MnHi 1915-Je 10 1920

BOVEY

Bovey PRESS. w D 8 1932+
pub 1932+

BOWLUS

Bowlus ADVANCE. w Ap 5 1917-My 1 1925|
Follows Bowlus independent. Followed by Bowlus hustler
MnHi complete

Bowlus HUSTLER. My 8 1925-
Follows Bowlus advance
MnHi My 8-Jl 10 1925

Bowlus INDEPENDENT. w N 3 1916-Mr 30 1917||
Followed by Bowlus advance
MnHi N 10 1916-17

BOYD

Boyd BULLETIN. w Je 4 1897+
pub 1897+

BRAHAM

Braham JOURNAL. w Jl 28 1899+
pub 1899+
MnHi 1906—

BRAINERD

Brainerd ARENA. w Mr 1 1899-1910||
MnHi 1899-[1909]-Jl 8 1910

Brainerd DISPATCH. w D 21 1881-1932||?
pub 1883-1932
MnHi S 19 1890-My 5 1932

Brainerd daily DISPATCH. d Je 3 1901+
pub 1901+
MnHi O 3 1924+

Weekly JOURNAL. w 1882-D 1 1898||
MnHi Ja 22,My 28 1891-98

Brainerd JOURNAL-PRESS. w D 9 1910—
pub 1915+
MnHi 1910—

Daily NEWS. d Je 6 1887-88||
MnHi 1887-Je 30 1888

Weekly NEWS. w N 23 1887-88||
MnHi D 7 1887-Je 21 1888

Brainerd TRIBUNE. w F 10 1872+
pub 1872+
MnHi 1872-77;81-My 6 1882[Mr 5 1887-90]+

BRANDON

Brandon ECHO. *See* Park region echo (Alexandria)

BRECKENRIDGE

GAZETTE-TELEGRAM. w 1884+
1884-S 1 1920 as Wilkin county gazette
pub 1886+
MnHi 1906-Ja 19 1912;20+

RECORD. w O 13 1894-1904||
1894-Ja 2 1903 as Rothsay record (Rothsay)
MnHi 1894-Ja 2 1904

REPUBLICAN. w O 1 1890-
MnHi [1890]

Breckenridge TELEGRAM. w 1891-S 1 1920||
United with Wilkin county gazette to form Gazette-telegram
MnBrG complete
MnHi 1906-20

WILKIN county gazette. *See* Gazette-telegram

BREWSTER

Brewster BEACON. *See* Brewster tribune

Brewster TRIBUNE. w Jl 1896+
1896-97? as Brewster beacon
pub 1932+

BRICELYN

Bricelyn SENTINEL. w Ag 29 1899+
pub 1899-[1909-12]+
MnHi Ap 14 1911+

BRONSON

Bronson BUDGET. w O 1904+
pub [1920]+
MnHi [Ag 31 1905-07]-F 27 1913

BROOTEN

Brooten CO-OPERATOR. m
MnHi Ap,Ag-O,D 1922

Brooten REVIEW. w Mr 7 1908+
pub 1910+
MnHi My 15 1930+

BROWERVILLE

Browerville BLADE. w 1906+
pub [1931]+

Browerville WAVE. w Ag? 1902-03||
MnHi My 1-Ag 7 1903

BROWNS VALLEY

FOOTPRINTS. *See* Traverse county traveler (Wheaton)

INTER-LAKE tribune. w S 23 1885+
F 19 1891-Ap 23 1892 as Inter-lake tribune and Traverse county times
MnHi [O 28 1885-98]1900-03;05+

Brown's Valley REPORTER. w My 20 1880-89||
United with Wheaton gazette to form Wheaton gazette-reporter, later Wheaton gazette (Wheaton)
MnHi 1880-Je 27 1889

VALLEY news. w Ap 16 1926+
pub 1926+
MnHi 1926+

BROWNSVILLE

Brownsville NEWS. w 1885-1920||
MnHi 1904;06-O 21 1920

SOUTHERN Minnesota herald. w Ag 1855-
N My 17 1856

BROWNTON

Brownton BULLETIN. w S 8 1892+
pub 1892+
MnHi 1892-1904;06-13;15+
MnLaS [1892-93]

BUFFALO

Buffalo JOURNAL. *See* Wright county journal-press

Buffalo Lake NEWS. w 1894+
pub 1895+
MnHi Ap 9 1897;98-1901;06-08

Buffalo STANDARD. w S 8 1897-Ap 25 1900||
Merged with Buffalo journal, later Wright county journal-press
MnHi 1899-1900

WRIGHT county journal-press. w 1887+
1887-N 27 1930 as Buffalo journal
MnHi [Mr 14-D 1888]-1903;05+

WRIGHT county press. w 1919-N 1930||
United with Buffalo journal to form Wright county journal-press

BUHL

Buhl-Kinney TRIBUNE and the Cook journal. w
MnHi Mr 2-My 4 1922

BUTTERFIELD

Butterfield ADVOCATE. w 1896+
pub [1896]+
MnHi 1906+

BYRON

Byron BULLETIN. w
MnHi [1913-14]

CALEDONIA

ARGUS. w 1879+
My 14 1909-D 26 1919 as Caledonia argus
MnHi [N 24-D 1888]1906-Ja 23 1920

HOUSTON county journal. *See* Caledonia journal

Caledonia JOURNAL. w 1865+
1865-84? as Houston county journal
pub 1865+
MnC 1868;71-72;79
MnHi Mr 14 1906+

Caledonia TRIBUNE. w D 7 1897-98||
MnHi 1897-[98]

CALLAWAY

Callaway TOMAHAWK. w O 1926?-27||?
Follows Tomahawk (White Earth)
MnHi Ja 13,F 3,Mr 24-31,Je 2 1927

CAMBRIDGE

Cambridge INDEPENDENT. w O 5 1898-Jl 1907||
United with Isanti county press to form Independent-press
MnHi [1898-99]

INDEPENDENT-PRESS. w 1874-Ja 22 1920||
1874-Jl 18 1907 as Isanti county press
MnHi S 15 1887;N 10 1897;S 21,O 26,D 28 1893 [1906]-20

ISANTI and Chisago county news. w D 18 1919-Ja 15 1931||
MnHi complete

ISANTI county press. *See* Independent-press

NORDSTJERNAN. *See* North star

NORTH star. w Ja 1 1905+
1905-Je 1 1913 as Nordstjernan (in Swedish)
pub [1913]+
IRA F 12 1907-10
MnHi My 24 1917+

MINNESOTA (*Continued*)

CANBY

Canby NEWS and press. w 1878+
1878-Jl 1932 as Canby news; Ag 5-D 9 1932 Canby news-press
pub 1885+
MnHi 1906+

Canby PRESS. w 1917-Jl 28 1932||
United with Canby news to form Canby news and press
MnHi Ja 25 1928-32

CANNON FALLS

Cannon Falls BEACON. w Ag 4 1876+
pub 1876+
MnHi 1906+

GOODHUE county news. *See* Red Wing free press (Red Wing)

CARLTON

CARLTON county vidette. w D 1887+
pub 1909+
MnHi 1906+

CARMAN

Carman COURIER. w Je 22 1882-83||
MnHi [N 16 1882-Je 7 1883]

CARVER

CARVER county democrat. w My 10 1859-
MnHi My 17-Ag 3 1859

Carver weekly FREE PRESS. w 1874-My 13 1897||
MnHi 1884-97

VALLEY transcript. *See* Weekly Valley herald (Chaska)

CASS

CASS county pioneer. *See under* Walker

CASS LAKE

Cass Lake INDEPENDENT. w Mr 17 1899-
MnHi Mr 17-Je 9 1899

Cass Lake TIMES. w Ap 26 1899+
pub 1899+
MnHi 1899-[1906]+

Cass Lake VOICE. w D 16 1899-1910||
MnHi 1899-[1902]-[07]-[09-10]

CENTER CITY

CHISAGO county news. w 1908-Ap 5 1917||
MnHi F 1916-17

Center City PRESS. w N 5 1903-Ap 27 1905||
Follows Nya pressen (Lindstrom)
MnHi complete

CHASKA

Chaska REVIEW. w 1898-1907||
MnHi N 25 1904-Ap 26 1907

Weekly VALLEY herald. w O 6 1861+
1861-S? 1862 as Valley transcript (Carver)
pub 1875+
MnHi F-Jl 23,S-N 6 1862;64-[74]-Ja 17 1875;S 18 1890+
N O 16 1861

CHATFIELD

Chatfield DEMOCRAT. *See* Chatfield news

Chatfield NEWS. w,sw N 26 1856+
1857-My 15 1902 as Chatfield democrat; My 22 1902-31 Chatfield news-democrat
sw N 27 1894-95
pub [1878-1905]18+
DLC Ja 28-Jl 7 1860
MWA F 5 1857
MnHi 1857+
MnU Ap 27 1878
N S 14,28 1861

Chatfield NEWS. w 1894-My 15 1902||
United with Chatfield democrat to form Chatfield news-democrat, later Chatfield news
MnHi My 20 1897-1902

Chatfield NEWS-DEMOCRAT. *See* Chatfield news 1856+

Chatfield REPUBLICAN. w O 25 1856-O 15 1861||
Followed by Fillmore county republican, later Preston republican (Preston)
MnHi 1856-[58-O 15 1861]
N My 15,Jl 24 1860;O 8 1861

CHISAGO CITY

Chisago City TRIBUNE. *See* Taylor's Falls times (Taylor's Falls)

CHISHOLM

Chisholm HERALD. w 1901-Ja 28 1910||
United with Tribune to form Tribune-herald
MnHi N 18 1904-[07]10

MESABA miner. w My 31 1909+
MnCh Jl 6 1917+

TRIBUNE-HERALD. w 1904+
1904-Ja 1910 as Tribune
pub 1910+
MnCh 1915+
MnHi F 1910+

CHOKIO

Chokio TIMES. *See* Morris times (Morris)

CLARA CITY

CHIPPEWA county herald. *See* Clara City herald

Clara City HERALD. w O 4 1895+
1895-Ag 7 1903 as Chippewa county herald
pub 1895+
MnHi N 22 1895-[96-97]+

CLAREMONT

COSMOPOLITAN. w N 25 1880-81||
MnHi 1880-Je 9 1881

Claremont NEWS. w 1909+
pub 1909+
MnHi Mr 24 1922+

CLARISSA

Clarissa INDEPENDENT. w Jl 27 1900+
1900-Mr 11 1910 as Todd county independent
pub 1900+

TODD county independent. *See* Clarissa independent

CLARKFIELD

Clarkfield ADVOCATE. w 1893+
1893-Mr 1 1906 as Reform advocate
pub [1893-95]+
MnHi Ap 22 1897+

REFORM advocate. *See* Clarkfield advocate

CLEAR LAKE

SHERBURNE county times. *See* Clear Lake times

Clear Lake TIMES. w 1892+
1892-Ap 10 1919 as Sherburne county times
MnHi Ap 29 1897+

CLEARBROOK

Clearbrook JOURNAL. *See* Clearbrook leader

Clearbrook LEADER. w My 22 1902+
1902-Je 1910 as Olberg journal (Olberg) Jl 1910-D 1917 Clearbrook journal
pub [1910]+
MnHi 1902-17

CLEARWATER

Clearwater HERALD. w My 22 1903-O 30 1930||
MnHi complete

Clearwater NEWS. w Ag 19 1892-Ag 28 1896||
MnHi 1892[93-95]-96

CLEVELAND

LE SUEUR county herald. w 1858-
N O 19 1861

CLIMAX

Climax CHRONICLE. w Je 12 1897-98||
MnHi [Je 12 1897-D 2 1898]

CLINTON

Clinton ADVOCATE. w S 1895+
pub 1895+
MnHi Ap 15 1897+

CLOQUET

INDUSTRIAL vidette. w Ag 18 1887-89||?
United with Pine knot to form Pine knot vidette, later Pine knot
MnHi Ag 18 1887

PINE knot. w Jl 12 1884+
1889?-D 13 1890 as Pine knot vidette
pub [1918]+
MnCl [1918]+
MnHi S 13 1890-[94;96-99]+

PINE knot vidette. *See* Pine knot

COKATO

COMMONER. *See* Cokato enterprise

Cokato ENTERPRISE. w 1883+
1883-91 as Cokato observer; 1892-Mr 27 1896 Commoner
pub [1889-96]+
MnHi Ja 17 1889-My 7 1891;N 9 1892+

Cokato OBSERVER. *See* Cokato enterprise

COLD SPRING

Cold Spring RECORD. w N 1899+
pub [1899-1909]+

COLERAINE

ITASCA iron news. w O 5 1904+
pub [1904+]
MnHi Ag 12 1915+

COMFREY

Comfrey TIMES. w Mr 9 1900+
pub 1900+
MnHi 1900+

COOK

Cook HERALD. w Mr 2 1922-My 22 1930||
Follows Cook journal. United with Cook newsboy to form News-herald
MnCoN complete
MnHi [1922-30]

Cook JOURNAL. w 1906-F 16 1922||
Followed by Cook herald
MnHi F 28 1919-[20-21]22

Cook NEWSBOY. w 1915-29||
United with Cook herald to form News-herald
MnCoN complete

NEWS-HERALD. w My 22 1930+
Formed by union of Cook herald and Cook newsboy
pub 1930+
MnHi [1930]+

COSMOS

Cosmos NEWS. w Jl 31 1925-D 4 1925||
Absorbed by Hector mirror (Hector)
MnHi complete

COTTONWOOD

Cottonwood CURRENT. w 1890+
pub 1890+
MnHi Ap 24 1897+

CROOKSTON

Crookston BROAD-AXE. d D 21 1881-
MnHi 1881-F 14 1882

Daily CHRONICLE. d 1890-
MnHi Jl 25-D 31 1890

Crookston daily JOURNAL. d 1901-My 29 1909||
Merged with Crookston daily times
MnHi F 1903-09

NORTHERN tier. w O 25 1879-80||
MnHi 1879-Jl 17 1880

Daily NORTHERN tier. d Je 18 1883-
MnHi Je 18,29 1883

Weekly NORTHERN tier. w Jl 14 1883-
MnHi Jl 14 1883

PEOPLE'S press. *See* Polk county leader

POLK county journal. w My 1 1877-My 27 1909||
Merged with Crookston weekly times
MnHi N 25 1880;Ap 23 1891-1909

POLK county leader. w My 19 1898+
1898-My 1920 as People's press
My-Jl 14 1898 pub in Fosston
MnHi 1898-N 1906;Ap 20 1911+

RED RIVER tidende. w O 17 1895-D 19 1899||
Merged with Nordvesten (St. Paul)
In Norwegian
IaDeL 1895-D 19 1897
WHi complete

Crookston weekly TIMES. w O 24 1885-Mr 31 1923||
MnHi 1885-87[89]-[1923]

Crookston daily TIMES. d N 25 1891+
Suspended Ja 30 1911-Ap 2 1923
pub 1891+
MnCr [1926+]
MnHi 1891+

TRIBUNE. w 1890-99||
MnEgR 1895-99
MnHi My 20 1891-94

Crookston daily TRIBUNE. d 1891-99||
MnEgR 1895-99
MnHi F 27 1892-Ap 16 1892

VESTERHEIMEN. w 1892-1918||?
1892-99? pub in Hatton or Mayville, N.D.
In Norwegian
IaDeL S 9,D 23 1896[Je-S 22 1897]D 28 1898; Ja 10 1899[N 29 1900-F 1902]Ap 29 1914
MnHi Je-Ag 1917

CROSBY

Crosby COURIER. w 1910+
pub 1924+
MnHi My 17 1918+

Crosby CRUCIBLE. w Mr 22 1913-My 10 1918||
Merged with Crosby courier
MnCroC complete
MnHi complete

Crosby RANGER. w Mr 6 1931+
1931-O 25 1932 pub also at Ironton as Ranger
pub 1931+
MnHi 1931+

MINNESOTA (*Continued*)

CURRIE

Currie INDEPENDENT. w Je 3 1908+
pub 1908+

MURRAY county pioneer. *See* Slayton gazette and Murray county pioneer (Slayton)

Currie PIONEER. 1878-80. *See* Slayton gazette and Murray county pioneer (Slayton)

Currie PIONEER. w Ag 14 1890-1905||
MnHi [1893]-Jl 14 1905

SOUTHWEST Minnesotian. w Jl 6 1880-Je 1881||
United with Currie pioneer to form Southwest Minnesotian, later Slayton gazette and Murray county pioneer (Slayton)

SOUTHWEST Minnesotian, 1881-87. *See* Slayton gazette and Murray county pioneer (Slayton)

CUYUNA

CUYUNA Range miner. *See under* Ironton

CYRUS

Cyrus LEADER. w N 4 1904+
pub 1904+

DASSEL

Dassel ANCHOR. *See* Meeker county news (Litchfield)

Dassel DISPATCH. w D 20 1918+
pub [1918+]
MnHi Ja 30 1919+

DAWSON

LAC QUI PARLE county vidette. w Ja 5 1899-1903||
MnHi 1899-My 14 1903

Dawson SENTINEL. w 1885+
1885-Mr 4 1898 as Sentinel
MnHi My 7 1886+

WESTERN guard. *See under* Madison

DEER CREEK

Deer Creek MIRROR. w N 1905+
pub 1905+

DEER RIVER

ITASCA news. *See* Deer River news

Deer River NEWS. w O 16 1896+
1896-My 1 1924 as Itasca news
Suspended S 25 1897-Ap 23 1898
pub 1898+
MnHi Ap 10 1897+

Deer River TIMES. w 1911-13||?
MnHi Mr 23 1911-Jl 5 1913

DEERWOOD

Deerwood ENTERPRISE. w 1910+
MnHi F 24 1922+

Deerwood TIMES. w Ag 29 1913-
MnHi 1913-[17]

DELANO

BIG WOODS citizen. w Mr 29-S 20 1872||
Followed by Wright county eagle, later the Delano eagle
MnHi complete

BUFFALO gazette. w 1888-1901||
MnHi Ap 17 1891-S 20 1901

Delano EAGLE. w S 27 1872+
Follows Big woods citizen. 1872-S 15 1881 as Wright county eagle
pub [1872+]
MnHi 1872+

WRIGHT county eagle. *See* Delano eagle

DELAVAN

Delavan BEE. w Je 8 1872-74||
MnHi 1872-1874

Delavan HERALD. w 1886-1903||
MnHi Ap 1897-Je 1898;F 20-O 9 1903

DELHI

Delhi BUILDER. w Ja 14 1925-Mr 10 1926||
MnHi complete

DETROIT

DETROIT free press. w 1890-95||
MnHi Mr 1894-Je 7 1895

DETROIT LAKES

Detroit HERALD. *See* Detroit Lakes tribune

Detroit NEWS-tribune. *See* Detroit Lakes tribune

Detroit RECORD. w Ag 31 1871+
Title varies slightly
pub 1872+
MnHi My 18 1872-[73]-Je 16 1875;91+

Detroit STANDARD. w D 30 1903-Je 30 1905||
MnHi complete

Detroit Lakes TRIBUNE. w 1908+
1908-Mr 27 1924 as Detroit herald; Ap 3 1924-N 1 1928 Detroit news tribune
pub [1920+]
MnHi Mr 5 1924+

DEXTER

DEXTERITE. w F 1896-1906||
MnHi Ap 16 1897-N 1 1906

DODGE CENTER

DODGE county record. *See* Dodge Center record

DODGE county star. w 1890+
pub 1903+
MnHi Ap 15 1897+

Dodge Center INDEX. w 1880-Ap 3 1885||
Followed by Dodge county record, later Dodge Center record
MnHi O 7 1882-85

Dodge Center PRESS. w 1874-80||
MWA N 8,D 6 1878;Ja 10 1879
MnHi 1876-[79]-F 27 1880

Dodge Center RECORD. w Ap 10 1885+
1885-1906? as Dodge county record
MnHi 1885-S 13 1888;S 19 1890+

DOVER

Dover INDEPENDENT. w Ja 6 1905+
pub 1905+

DULUTH

Duluth ADVERTISER. *See* Duluth free press

BEDE'S budget. w,m 1893?-1931||?
1893?-Ag 3 1930 as Duluth times; Ag 15-N 1930 Times
w 1893-S 1930
MnHi 1927-Ap 1931

Buffalo Bill's press. *See* Duluth press

Morning CALL. d D 1870-My 28 1871||
MnHi Ja 4,Mr 6-My 28 1871

Daily COMMERCIAL record. d D 1894+
MnHi 1895-[99 N 18 1907-09]+

Duluth COMMONWEALTH. d 1890-Ap 14 1896||
MnD Ag 1 1893-Ap 1 1896
MnHi O 20 1892-Ap 13 1896

Le COURRIER de Duluth. sw Jl 9 1890-
In French
MnHi Jl 16-D 4 1890

Duluth DEMOCRAT. w Ap 2 1871-
MnHi [Ap 2-O 1 1871]

Duluth daily DEMOCRAT. d Jl 25 1888-
MnHi [Jl 25-O 30 1888]

Duluth FREE PRESS. w Mr 12 1904+
1904-22 as West and advertiser: 1923-S 5 1930 Duluth advertiser
pub 1904+
MnD Ag 28 1931+
MnHi O 11 1928+

Duluth daily HERALD. d Jl 3 1871-S 6 1875||
Title varies: Duluth morning herald
MnHi Jl 22 1871
OClWHi D 1 1871
WHi Jl 3 1873

Duluth weekly HERALD. w Ag 30 1873-Ag 1875||
United with Duluth Minnesotian to form Duluth Minnesotian-herald
MnHi Ag 30 1873;Je 12-Ag 7 1875
OClWHi Ag 30 1873

Duluth HERALD. w Je 1-Ag 3 1878||
Follows Duluth Minnesotian-herald. United with Duluth weekly tribune to form Duluth tribune and herald; later Duluth weekly tribune
MnHi complete

Duluth HERALD. d Ap 9 1883+
1888-My 31 1910 as Duluth evening herald
pub 1883+
DLC D 28 1897-98;Jl 2 1900-Je 29 1901
MWA Jl 18 1931;Ap 10 1933
MnD Jl 1892+
MnHi [1887]+
WHi Mr 6-D 1896;1917-21

Duluth weekly HERALD. w My 15 1889+
MnHi 1889-1917

Duluth evening HERALD and journal and Saturday evening journal. w Ap 2 1887-88||
1887 as Saturday evening journal
MnHi [Ap 2 1887-Ag 25 1888]

INDUSTRIALISTI. d Mr 19 1917+
In Finnish
pub 1917+
MnHi Je 3 1919-Jl 19 1920;F 2-Ag 11 1926;S 25 1934+
NN D 1917+

Saturday evening JOURNAL. *See* Duluth evening herald and journal and Saturday evening journal

LABOR leader. *See* Truth

LAKE SUPERIOR news. *See* Duluth news-tribune

LAKE SUPERIOR review and weekly tribune. w My 4 1870-92||
1870-O 17 1890 as Duluth weekly tribune (Ag 16-O 25 1878 Duluth tribune and herald)
InRE Ag 10-24,S 7 1877
MnHi My-Jl 6 1870;S 14 1871-N 3 1882;Ag 24 1883-O 21 1892

Duluth MINNESOTIAN-HERALD. w Ap 24 1869-My 18 1878||
1869-S 4 1875 as Duluth Minnesotian. Followed by Duluth herald
KHi S 9 1876
MWA Ag 5 1876
MnD 1869-S 1 1877
MnHi complete
NBuG Jl 16 1870
WHi D 23 1871;Ap 26 1873

Duluth daily NEWS. *See* Duluth news-tribune

Weekly NEWS-TRIBUNE. w Jl 4 1878-1921||?
1878-87? as Lake Superior news; 1888?-92? Duluth weekly news
MB 1878-Ag 7 1879
MnHi 1898-1918
NjR Mr 27 1886
WHi Jl 11 1878

Duluth NEWS-TRIBUNE. d 1886+
1886-O 5 1892 as Duluth daily news
pub 1892+
MWA Jl 19 1891
MnD Jl 1887-F 10 1889;92+
MnHi [1887]+
OClWHi S 5 1888
WHi 1890-99
WS N 31 1888-Ja 1889;Mr 25-Ap 15 1893

NORDVESTERNS handelstidning. w 1902-06||
Merged with Duluth posten
In Swedish
IRA [1902-06]

NORDVESTERNS nyheter. w 1906||
Merged with Nordvesterns handelstidning
In Swedish
IRA Ap 26,My 11 1906

PAIVALEHTI. d Ja 1900+
In Finnish
pub 1900+
IU Mr 1918-My 19,Jl 9 1925-Ag 18 1926

PARAGRAPHER. w Ja 29 1887-89||?
MnHi Ap 9,[Je 1887-O 1888]

PEOPLE'S press. *See* Duluth press

PLAIN dealer. w F 11 1933+
pub 1933+

Duluth POSTEN. w My 1888-D 31 1920||
United with Svenska Amerikanska tribunen to form Svenska Amerikanska tribunen-Duluth posten, later Svenska Amerikanska posten (Minneapolis)
In Swedish
pub 1906-18
IRA 1891;98-1918
MnHi 1906-20

Duluth PRESS. w N 27 1891-
Ap 23-My 28 1892 as Union workman: the people's press; O 22 1892-S 23 1893 People's press; My 9-Je 6? 1896 Buffalo Bill's press
MnHi Ja 30 1892-Je 20 1896
WS Mr-D 1893

PUBLICITY. w N 8 1930+
MnHi 1930+

Weekly RECORD. w 1904-13||
F 11-Ag 6 1910 as Saturday record
MnHi Ja 28,F 11 1909-[10]-Je 28 1913

Duluth REPUBLICAN. *See* Sun

SCANDIA. *See under* Chicago, Ill.

Daily SHORT LINE. d 1890-O 1892||
Merged with Duluth commonwealth
Dated also at Superior, Wis.
MnHi D 31 1891-S 8 1892

SIIRTOLAINEN. sw,w 1893+
In Finnish
pub 1893+
MnHi Ja 2 1917-Je 17 1925

Duluth SKANDINAV. w F 1887+
In Norwegian
pub 1917+
IU 1918-
IaDeL Je 16 1916[Mr 11-D 1917]Ja 25-Mr 15 1918;26+
MnHi [1917-18]+
PP [1922-27]+
WHi Ja 10,Je 27,O 3 1930;My 4,O 19 1934

Duluth daily STAR. d Je 21 1907-Je 3 1909||
MnD complete

SUN. w 1899-1903||
S 7 1899-Ja 1 1903 as Sun and Metcalfe's x-ray; Ja 8-Je 18 1903 Duluth republican
MnHi Ap 29 1897-O 1 1903

Duluth TIMES. d Jl 1-D 13 1890||
Merged with Duluth herald
MnHi complete

Duluth TIMES. w *See* Bede's budget

Duluth TRIBUNAL. w 1894-1907||
MnHi Jl 31 1897-[99]-[1901-1902]

Duluth weekly TRIBUNE. 1870-90 *See* Lake Superior review and weekly tribune

Duluth daily TRIBUNE. d 1881-O 5 1892||
United with Duluth daily news to form Duluth news-tribune
MWA F 12 1888;Jl 19 1891
MnD Ja-O 1892
MnHi N 12 1882-[83]D 5 1884-[86-88]-92

Duluth TRIBUNE and herald. *See* Lake Superior review and weekly tribune

TRUTH. w Je 22 1917-Ap 13 1923||
Je 22-O 5 1917 as Labor leader
MnHi complete
WHi O 15 1920-23

UNION workman. *See* Duluth press

VOIX du lac *See under* Minneapolis

MINNESOTA (*Continued*)

DULUTH—*Continued*

Duluth-Superior VOLKSFREUND. w 1888-1901||
1888-Mr 17 1898 as Duluth volksfreund
ICJ Jl 1894-98
MnHi [Ap-D 1897]-[1901]
WHi Ja-O 5 1899

Duluth WEEKLY. w Mr 19 1881-
MnHi Mr 19-Jl 2 1881

WEST-END advertiser. *See* Duluth free-press

DUMONT

Dumont JOURNAL. w Jl 5 1902-04||
MnHi 1902-Ap 16 1904

DUNDEE

Dundee weekly ADVOCATE. w 1897-1904||
MnHi [Ag 20 1903-Ap 7 1904]

Weekly NEWS. w
InRE S 22 1877

DUNNELL

Dunnell PROGRESS. w O 5 1934-F 22 1935||
MnHi complete

EAGLE BEND

TODD county news. w 1892+
pub [1892-31]+

EAGLE LAKE

Eagle Lake NEWS. w Jl 24 1899-1904||?
MnHi D 1899-Ja 1900

EAST GRAND FORKS

East Grand Forks COURIER. w 1883-F 12 1904||
MnHi S 26 1890-1904

Weekly RECORD. w F 24 1900+
1900-Ap 25 1901 as Saturday valley view; My 2-23 1901 Valley view and East Grand Forks tribune; My 30 1901-F 14 1913 Valley view
pub 1905+
MnHi 1900+

VALLEY view. *See* Weekly record

EASTON

Easton LEADER. w N 11 1904-09||
MnHi 1904-S 11 1909

ECHO

Echo ENTERPRISE. w Ja 4 1894+
pub [1905]+
MnHi 1894-Ap 13 1906

EDEN VALLEY

COUNTY line. w 1897-Ap 27 1900||
MnHi Ja 7 1898-1900

Eden Valley JOURNAL. w 1892+
pub 1892+
MnHi S 26 1912-[17]+

EDGERTON

Edgerton ENTERPRISE. w 1883+
pub 1913+
MnHi F 26-N 12 1887;Ap 18 1891-[92-Jl 8 1893]F 5 1897-[1902]-[05]-[08]-[11]-S 12 1913
MnLaS [1884-85]

ELBOW LAKE

GRANT county herald. w 1878+
1878-85? as Herman herald (Herman)
MnHi O 31 1889+

Elbow Lake TRIBUNE. w 1887-1903||
1887-96 as Grant county farmer (Ashby); 1897-My 18 1899 Barrett Lake breeze (Barrett)
MnHi S 25 1890-[91]-My 14 1903

ELGIN

Elgin FREE PRESS. w N 6 1896-1900||
MnHi 1896-Mr 23 1900
MnLaS 1896-[1900]

Elgin JOURNAL. w Mr 1882-
MnElM 1882-F 1883

MINNESOTA union. w Jl 4 1879-
MnElM Jl 4, Jl 19 1879

Elgin MONITOR. w D 2 1904+
pub [1905]+
MnHi 1904+

ELK RIVER

Elk River daily NEWS. d 1872-78||?
MnHi O 25-N 1 1875

Elk River weekly NEWS. w Ja 1872-81||
United with Sherburne county star to form Sherburne county star-news
MnHi Jl 1875-[76-77:80-81]

SHERBURNE county star-news. w S 24 1875+
1875-81 as Sherburne county star
pub [1888+]
MnHi 1875[76]S 21-N 16 1877[78]Mr 4,D 30 1880;N 17 1881;F 9 1888[89]+

SHERBURNE county tax-payer. w O 29 1875-
MnHi O 29 1875

SHERBURNE county weekly. w O 8 1869-71||?
MnHi Mr 19 1870

ELLENDALE

EAGLE. w Mr 30 1901+
pub 1901+

ELLIS

CASS county pioneer. *See under* Walker

ELLSWORTH

Ellsworth NEWS. w 1885+
MnHi Ap 17 1891-[1916-18]+

ELMORE

Elmore EYE. w Ja 15 1892+
Ja 15-S 21 1892 as Elmore weekly eye;S 28 1892-Mr 31 1899 Eye
pub [1922]+
MnHi 1892-Jl 18 1918

ELY

Ely IRON home. w 1888-Ap 6 1892||
MnHi O 14 1890-92

Ely MINER. w Jl 24 1895+
MnHi 1895+
MnEyC 1895+

Ely TIMES. w D 12 1890-1903||?
MnHi 1890-My 11 1900

ELYSIAN

Elysian ENTERPRISE. w 1893+
pub 1910+
MnHi Ap 23-N 5 1897

EMMONS

Emmons LEADER. w N 7 1901+
pub 1901-04;25+

ERSKINE

Erskine ECHO. w 1899+
pub 1899+
MnHi D 14 1906+

ESTERDY

CASS county pioneer. *See under* Walker

EVANSVILLE

Evansville ENTERPRISE. w 1890+
MnHi My 24 1895-Ap 7 1899

EVELETH

Eveleth CLARION. w Je 16 1921+
pub 1921+
MnHi 1921+

Eveleth MINING news. *See* Eveleth news

Eveleth NEWS. w 1901+
1901-Ja 2 1907 Eveleth mining news
sw 1901-Je 17 1909
pub 1902-[15]+
MnHi Mr 28 1903+

EXCELSIOR

Excelsior COTTAGER. w Je 1876-O 8 1897||
1876-Mr 3 1877 as Lake Minnetonka tourist; Mr 10 1877-S 9 1879 Tourist and sportsman; S 16 1879-S 1880? Tourist; O 1880?-My 4 1894 as Northwestern tourist; My 11 1894-Ag 23 1895 Minnetonka news
MnHi Je 1876[77-80;Je 30 1888-89]-97

INVESTOR. w My 2 1888-
MnHi My 2-9,Je 13,27-Jl 11 1888

LAKE Minnetonka tourist. *See* Excelsior cottager

MINNETONKA mirror. w D 1885-My 25 1889||
MnHi Ag 7 1886-[87]-89

MINNETONKA news. *See* Excelsior cottager

MINNETONKA record. w Ag 1 1901+
pub 1901+
MnHi D 20 1901+

NORTHWESTERN tourist. *See* Excelsior cottager

TOURIST. *See* Excelsior cottager

Excelsior WEEKLY. w Ap 25 1883-My 1885||
MnHi complete

EYOTA

Eyota ADVERTISER. m Ap 1 1869-78||?
MnHi Ap 1 1869-[76-77]-Jl 1878

FAIRFAX

Fairfax CRESCENT. w 1890-My 19 1899||
Merged with Fairfax standard
MnHi Ja 14 1898-99

Fairfax STANDARD. w Jl 14 1898+
pub 1898+
MnHi 1898+

FAIRMONT

Fairmont CHAIN. w O 15 1873-Jl 22 1874||?
MnHi [N 5 1873-Jl 22 1874]

MARTIN county atlas. w Ap 11 1868-D 25 1869||
Followed by Wells atlas (Wells)
MnHi complete

MARTIN county democrat. *See* Martin county independent

MARTIN county independent. w,sw,d O 8 1892-O 26 1929||
1892-96? as Martin county democrat
w 1892-Ag 3 1905;sw;tw 1917
MnHi 1902-O 1895;Ap 22 1897-1929

MARTIN county review. w Ag 27 1870-72||
MnHi [1870-Ag 23 1872]

MARTIN county sentinel. *See* Fairmont daily sentinel

Fairmont NEWS. w 1885-Jl 28 1905||
Merged with Martin county independent
MnHi O 1887-1905

Fairmont daily SENTINEL. w,sw,d Jl 4 1874+
1874-1918 as Martin county sentinel
w 1874-1913; sw 1913-18
pub 1874+
MnFC 1874
MnHi 1875-[82]

FARIBAULT

CENTRAL republican. *See* Faribault republican

Faribault DEMOCRAT. w Ag 2 1870-1920||
1870-Ag 29 1871 as Faribault leader
MWA Ag 21 1874;Ag 3 1877;O 11,N 15 1878;F 6 1880
MnHi [1870-Jl 11 1873]Jl 10 1885-1920

Faribault HERALD. w N 26 1856-Je 16 1858||
Followed by Central republican, later Faribault republican
CaOTA Jl 9 1857
MnHi Ap 2,My 28,Ag 13,D 17-24,1857;F 10, Mr 3-Je 16 1858
P-M Je 11 1857

JEFFERSONIAN. w 1897?-1900||?
Followed by Madison Lake new era (Madison Lake)

Faribault JOURNAL. w O 26 1897+
MnHi 1897+
MnFaC 1917-S 1919;22-23;25;30-31

Faribault LEADER. *See* Faribault democrat

Faribault daily NEWS. d D 1 1914+
MnFa 1914+
MnFaC My 1918-[23]-28;31
MnHi F 21 1920+

NORTHERN statesman and western farmer. w N 12 1861-
MnFaC My 1862-63
MnHi [N 12 1861-Mr 18 1862]

Faribault PILOT. w Ag 9 1888-Ja 26 1928||
Merged with Faribault daily news
MnFaC 1923
MnHi D 20 1888-1928

REFERENDUM. w 1899-1917||?
MnHi Je 24 1911-16
WHi D 6 1902;Je 6 1903;Mr 18,Je 18,O 29 1904;My 20 1905

Faribault REPUBLICAN. w Je 23 1858-1920||
Follows Faribault herald. 1858-My 18 1870 as Central republican
CtY O 15 1873
ICM My 25 1881
MBAt Ap 19 1865
MWA Ap 8 1863;My 25 1864;Ja 31 1866;Ap 22 1868;Jl 24 1872;Mr 17 1875;S 11,N 13-20 1878; Ja 8,F 5,19-26 1879;F 25 1880
MnFaC 1860-61;64-81;Ja-Ap 1918
MnHi 1858-[1917]O 9 1919-F 19 1920
N Jl 7 1861

FARMINGTON

DAKOTA county breeze. w Ap 13 1898-Ja 11 1899||
Follows Lakeville and Rosemount arbitrator (Lakeville). Merged with Dakota county tribune
MnHi complete

DAKOTA county tribune. w Mr 6 1884+
Early years also dated at Lakeville
pub 1923+
MnHi 1886-F 28 1908;Ap 7 1911+

Farmington JOURNAL. w Mr 21 1883-Ap 17 1884||
MnHi Je 13 1883-84

Farmington PRESS. w Ag 4 1870-Je 6 1883||
MnHi complete

Farmington REPORTER. w F 27 1883-
MnHi F 27-Je 5 1883

Farmington TELEGRAPH. w Je 4 1868-Ag 26 1869||
MnHi complete

MINNESOTA (*Continued*)

FERGUS FALLS

Fergus Falls ADVOCATE. w,sw Ap 15 1871-76||
w 1871-74?
MnHi [Ap 22 1871-N 12 1876]

Fergus Falls ADVOCATE and Otter Tail county representative. 1878-81 *See* Fergus Falls independent

ALLIANCE advocate. w 1892-96||
Dated also at Henning
MnHi Ja 2-O 1 1896

Daily FARMER. d O 7 1888-
MnHi O 8-D 18 1888

Fergus Falls FORUM. w Ja 18 1894-96||?
1894-95? as Pelican Rapids sentinel (Pelican Rapids)
MnHi [1894] Ap 30-Ag 27 1896

Weekly Fergus Falls FREE PRESS. w,sw O 23 1900-29||?
sw O 23 1906-Je 28 1907
MnFf [1900]-06
MnHi Ap 18 1902-O 27 1927

Fergus GLOBE. w 1888-1910||
MnHi Jl 10 1890;Ag 27 1891-1910

Fergus Falls INDEPENDENT. w,sw Ap 12 1878-My 1883||
1878-Je 24 1881 as Fergus Falls advocate and Otter Tail county representative. Merged with Fergus Falls daily telegram
w 1878-S 1881
MnHi complete
NdHi Mr 3 1881

Fergus Falls weekly JOURNAL. w Jl 24 1873+
pub 1873+
MnFf 1910-30
MnHi 1873-80;84-87;89-1917
WHi 1873-Ja 10 1879

Fergus Falls daily JOURNAL. d 1883+
pub 1883 —
MnHi [188?]+

RED RIVER tidende. *See under* Crookston

RODHUGGEREN. w 1893-98||
United with Den Fjerde Juli og Dakota to form Fram (Fargo, N.D.)
In Norwegian
IaDeL N 2- 1893-97[Ja 11-My 10 1898]
MnHi 1893-96

SENTINEL. *See under* Minneapolis

Fergus Falls daily TELEGRAM. d S 1882-84||
MnHi [O 1-82-O 1884]

Fergus Falls weekly TELEGRAM. w N 2 1882-84||
MnHi Jl 6 1883-N 27 1884

Fergus Falls TRIBUNE. w S 19 1895+
1895-Ag 26 1920 as Wheelock's weekly
pub 1895-[1920-21]+
MnHi 1895—
MnFf 1895-[1920-21]-[32]+

Fergus Falls UGEBLAD. w 1881+
In Norwegian
IU S 1917-S 25 1918
IaDeL O 22 1907-[08]-[11]-[14-S 11 1918]
MnHi 1886—

WHEELOCK'S weekly. *See* Fergus Falls tribune

FERTILE

ARBEIDSMANDEN. w My 11 1900-01||
In Norwegian
MnHi 1900-Mr 29 1901

Fertile JOURNAL. w 1886+
pub [1896+]
MnHi O 2 1890-O 18 1894

FINLAYSON

Finlayson REGISTER. w Mr 14 1919-Je 10 1921||
MnHi complete

FISHER

Fisher BULLETIN. w My 15 1880-1905||
Ap 16-Mr 14 1881 as Fisher's Landing bulletin
MnHi 1880-84;95]-1905

FOLEY

Foley INDEPENDENT. w 1899+
pub 1900+
MnHi Ap 1?-Je 14 1901;Mr 11 1909+

FOREST LAKE

Forest Lake TIMES. w 1906+
pub 1928+

FOSSTON

Fosston JOURNAL. w 1919-Ap 30 1924||
MnHi S 19 1923-24

PEOPLE'S press. *See* Polk county leader (Crookston)

THIRTEEN towns. w 1884+
pub [1893]+
MnHi F 1894+

FRANKLIN

Franklin NEWS. w 1891-
MnHi S 19 1891

Franklin TRIBUNE. w 1898+
pub [1901]+
MnHi Ja 8 1920+

FRAZEE

Frazee FREE PRESS. *See* Frazee press

Frazee NEWS. w N 1896-N 25 1904||
1896-Mr 1898 as Frazee news; Ap 1898-O 20 1899 Park region news. Merged with Detroit standard (Detroit Lakes)
MnHi O 21 1898-1904

PARK region news. *See* Frazee news

Frazee PRESS. w 1904+
1904-Mr 27 1914 as Frazee free press
MnHi Jl 14 1905+

FROST

Frost RECORD. w 1900-18||?
MnHi My 30 1902-Mr 27 1903

FULDA

Fulda FREE PRESS. w 1881+
1881-Ap 24 1896 as Murray county republican; My 1 1896-Mr 29 1912 Fulda republican
pub 1913+
MnHi Ag 1889+

FREE PRESS. w Mr 1897-F 7 1907||
MnHi Mr 31 1898-1907

MURRAY county republican. *See* Fulda free press

Fulda REPUBLICAN. *See* Fulda free press

GARDEN CITY

HERALD and journal. w O 23 1867-Ag 5 1870||
1867-My 13? 1870 as Garden City herald
MWA Je 10-24,Jl 15-22,Ag 5 1870
MnHi complete

GARY

Gary GRAPHIC. w F 3 1900+
pub [1909+]
MnHi 1900-Ja 22 1904

GAYLORD

Gaylord HUB. w Mr 13 1886+
pub 1886+
MnHi Ap 18 1891-F 7 1908

GIBBON

Gibbon GAZETTE. w Ap 1894+
pub [1894]+

GILBERT

Gilbert HERALD. w 1908+
WHi Je 23 1922-O 30 1925

GLENCOE

Glencoe ENTERPRISE. w 1873+
1873-Je 30 1880 as McLeod county enterprise
pub [1900]+
MnHi O 1873+

MCLEOD county enterprise. *See* Glencoe enterprise

MCLEOD county register. *See* Glencoe register

MCLEOD county republic. w Ja 3 1919+
MnHi 1919+

Glencoe REGISTER. w Ag 8 1857-F 1 1907||
Ja-Ap 1863 as Glencoe register and soldier's budget; Ja 9-Ap 2 1863 Glencoe weekly register; Ap 9-Jl 2 1868 McLeod county register
MnHi [1857-Ap 17 1863]Ja 9-Jl 2 1868;F 25 1869-1907
N S 21 1861

GLENVILLE

Glenville PROGRESS. w 1897+
pub 1903+

GLENWOOD

Glenwood EAGLE. w N 4 1871-S 26 1874||
MnHi complete

Glenwood GOPHER-PRESS. w 1900-D 4 1913||
1900-Ja 12 1905 as Glenwood gopher
MnHi Jl 9 1903-13

Glenwood HERALD. w 1887+
MnHi S 12 1890+

Glenwood MESSENGER. w 1882-S 25 1885||
MnHi My 11 1883-85

POPE county press. *See* Glenwood press-bulletin

POPE county tribune. w 1920+
pub 1920+
MnHi N 10 1921+

Glenwood PRESS-BULLETIN. w 1874-87||
1874-84? as Pope county press
MnHi O 6 1882-F 20 1885

GLYNDON

RED RIVER gazette. w Je 27 1872-74||?
MnHi 1872-Jl 17 1873

RED RIVER valley news. w O 30 1878-1929||
MnHi F 27 1879-[87-88]-Je 1 1923;D 11 1924-D 5 1929

GONVICK

Gonvick BANNER. w Jl 3 1910+
pub 1910+

GOOD THUNDER

Good Thunder HERALD. w S 1 1891+
pub [1914]+
MnHi 1901+

GOODHUE

Goodhue ENTERPRISE. *See* Goodhue county tribune

GOODHUE county tribune. w S 28 1896+
1896-My 20 1926 as Goodhue enterprise
pub 1896+
MnHi Ja 21 1898+

GOODRIDGE

Goodridge BANNER. w 1906-23||
1906-My 23 1918 as Eleven towns; My 30-Je 6 1918 Goodridge banner and the eleven towns
MnHi Ag 12 1915-Mr 2 1923

ELEVEN towns. *See* Goodrich banner

GRACEVILLE

Graceville DEMOCRAT. w My 3 1888-Jl 25 1889||
Merged with Graceville transcript.
MnHi complete

Graceville ENTERPRISE. w N 1892+
Ap 6 1894 as Graceville enterprise and transcript Ap 13-S 28 1894 Graceville transcript-enterprise
pub [1892-1924]+
MnHi Ap 6 1894-[1930]+

PHENIX. w 1894-1914||?
MnHi Ap 15 1897-1912

Graceville TRANSCRIPT. w O 6 1883-Mr 31 1894||
Ag 10-24 1889 Transcript-democrat. Merged with Graceville enterprise
MnHi complete

GRANADA

Granada TIMES. w Ag 10 1906-10||?
MnHi 1906-08

GRAND MARAIS

COOK county herald. *See* Cook county news-herald

COOK county news-herald. w My 30 1891+
1891-92? as Grand Marais pioneer; 1892?-1911 Cook county herald
pub 1890+
MnHi [Je-O 16 1891]Je 24 1893-[94-96]-1907; My 1915+

Grand Marais PIONEER. *See* Cook county news-herald

GRAND MEADOW

NEWS. w 1878-80||
MnHi My 14-Ag 27 1880

Grand Meadow RECORD. w 1883+
MnHi S 27 1890-[91]-[95;1901-Mr 1904;Ag 1905-O 18 1906]

GRAND RAPIDS

Grand Rapids HERALD-REVIEW. w 1893+
pub 1894+
MnHi [1898]-[1911]16+
MnG 1894+

ITASCA county independent. w N 1 1902+
pub 1902+
MnG 1902+
MnHi 1902+

Grand Rapids MAGNET. w Je 11 1891-1906||
Follows La Prairie magnet (La Prairie)
Merged with Itasca county independent
MnG [1895-96;99]
MnHi 1891-N 17 1897;Je 1903-O 24 1906

GRANITE FALLS

Granite Falls JOURNAL. w 1875-N 17 1922||
Merged with Granite Falls news
MnGrN 1902-07;14-17
MnHi Ap 20 1876-My 9 1878;My 22 1890-1922

Granite Falls NEWS. w S 28 1923+
pub 1924+
MnHi 1923-Jl 10 1931

NORGE. w Ag 18 1899-1901||
In Norwegian
IaDeL 1899-S 24 1901

Granite Falls TRIBUNE. w Ag 7 1883+
pub 1883+
MnHi Ag 14 1883+

MINNESOTA (*Continued*)

GRASSTON

Grasston ADVANCE. w 1911-Je 27 1924||
MnHi Je 7 1917-24

GREEN ISLE

Green Isle RECORD. w Jl 21 1905+
pub [1908]+

GREENBUSH

Greenbush TRIBUNE. w O 15 1908+
pub 1908+

GREY EAGLE

GAZETTE. w 1901+
pub 1901+

GROVE CITY

Grove City TIMES. w 1892-Ap 7 1922||
MnHi Ap 16 1897-1922

GRYGLA

EAGLE. w 1903+
pub 1903+
MnHi D 1915+

GULLY

SUNBEAM. *See under* Sunbeam

HACKENSACK

CASS county independent. w 1920+
1920-Ap 9 1926 as Hackensack independent
MnHi S 16 1921-[22]+
Hackensack INDEPENDENT. *See* Cass county independent

HALLOCK

KITTSON county enterprise. w 1882+
pub [1882+]
MnHi Ap 30 1897-[1901]29+
Hallock weekly NEWS. *See* People's press
PEOPLE'S press. w 1889-D 28 1928||
1889-O 23 1920 as Hallock weekly news. Merged with Kittson county enterprise
MnHi [F-D 1890]Ap 18 1891-[1921]-28

HALSTAD

Halstad JOURNAL. *See* Western Norman county journal-review
WESTERN Norman county journal-review. w 1907+
1907-O 9? 1931 as Halstad journal
pub [1926]-[31]+
MnHi O 16 1931+

HAMLINE

Papers published in Hamline are listed under St. Paul

HANCOCK

Hancock RECORD. w F 24 1899+
pub 1899+
MnHi 1899+

HANSKA

Hanska HERALD. w Je 1900+
pub D 30 1904+

HARDWICK

Hardwick NEWS. w 1888-1906||
MnHi 1901-Jl 6 1906

HARMONY

Harmony NEWS. w D 15 1897+
MnHi 1898+

HARTLAND

Hartland VIDETTE. w -My 23 1895||
Supp to New Richland north star, later New Richland star
MnHi Ag 15 1889;Ag 14 1890-95

HASTINGS

Hastings BANNER. w 1866-86||
1866-Mr 1870 as Dakota county; Ap 1870-S 12 1884 Hastings union
MnHi O 23 1867-Je 25 1886
Hastings CONSERVER. w Ap 18 1861-N 13 1866||
Ap 18 1861-Je 30 1863 as Minnesota conserver. United with Hastings independent to form Hastings gazette
MWA S 26 1865
MnHi 1861-62;Ag 30 1864;Ap 11 1865-66
N N 21 1861
DAKOTA county union. *See* Hastings banner
DAKOTA weekly journal. w My 24 1856-
MWA S 20 1856
MnHi Je 21 1856;S 12 1857
Hastings DEMOCRAT. w D 3 1859-Ap 27 1861||
MnHi [1859-61]
Hastings DEMOCRAT. w 1887-S 19 1919||
Followed by Dakota county globe, later West St Paul booster and Dakota globe (South St. Paul)
MnHi Ap 9 1891-1919
Hastings GAZETTE. w Jl 27 1857+
1857-N 8 1866 as Hastings independent
pub 1857+
MWA Ap 25 1861;D 3 1863;Ja 4 1866
MnHi N 12 1857;N 4 1858;Ja 27 1859-62;Ja 28 1864+
N O 24 1861
NbHi Jl 3 1875
Daily GAZETTE. d 1883-S 1 1917||
MnHi Mr 22 1888-1917
Hastings HERALD. w Je 1 1924+
pub [1926]+
MnHi Ag 28 1930+
Hastings INDEPENDENT. *See* Hastings gazette
Daily LEDGER. d 1858-
MWA N 23,D 30 1858
Hastings weekly LEDGER. w Mr 12 1859-
MWA Jl 16 1859
MnHi [Mr 26-O 8 1859]
MINNESOTA conserver. *See* Hastings conserver
Hastings NEW ERA. w 1875-83||
MnHi S 26 1882-My 8 1883
Hastings NEWS. w O 21 1920-Ag 19 1921||
MnHi complete
Hastings UNION. *See* Hastings banner

HAWLEY

CLAY county herald. *See* Hawley herald
Hawley HERALD. w 1882+
1882-F 17 1927 Clay county herald
MnHi Jl 24 1903-12 [22]+
Hawley-Hitterdal STANDARD. w 1921-Je 1 1933||
1921-30? as Hitterdal standard (Hitterdal)
MnHi S 15 1921-My 6 1926;F 12 1931-33

HAYFIELD

DODGE county herald. *See* Hayfield herald
DODGE county transcript. *See* Hayfield herald
Hayfield GUARD. w Ap 27 1905-Jl 27 1917||
United with Dodge county transcript to form Hayfield herald
MnHi complete
Hayfield HERALD. w Ag 21 1895+
1895-Ag 3 1899 as Dodge county herald; Ag 10 1899-Jl 26 1917 Dodge county transcript
MnHi 1895+

HECTOR

Hector MIRROR. w Ag 1 1889+
pub 1900+
MnHi Ap 22 1891+
RENVILLE county union. *See* Bird Island union (Bird Island)
Hector UNION. w 1881-90||?
An edition of Bird Island union (Bird Island)
MnHi Jl 10 1884;Ja 4 1886;Ja 14 1887

HENDERSON

Henderson weekly DEMOCRAT. w Ap 3 1856-
MnHi [1856-58]-Mr 4 1861
N F 11 1860
NbHi My 5 1860
Henderson INDEPENDENT. w 1873+
1873-Mr 3 1922 as Sibley county independent
pub [1892+]
MnHi O 1890+
SIBLEY county independent. *See* Henderson independent
Henderson TIMES. w Ja 6 1872-75||
MnHi 1872-[75]

HENDRICKS

Hendricks PIONEER. w Ap 12 1900+
pub [1900+]

HENDRUM

Hendrum NEWS. w N 25 1898-99||
MnHi [1898-99]
RED RIVER review. w 1899-1931||
United with Halstad journal to form Western Norman county journal-review (Halstad)

HENNING

Henning ADVOCATE. w Mr 12 1891+
Mr 12 1891-D 26 1895 as Alliance advocate.
pub 1891+
CtY S 17 1891
MnHi 1891-[1896]+
ALLIANCE advocate. *See* Henning advocate

HERMAN

Herman ENTERPRISE. w My 12 1887-1905||
MnHi My 19 1887-Je 1 1905
GRANT county review. *See* Herman review
Herman HERALD. *See* Grant county herald (Elbow Lake)
Herman REVIEW. w O 11 1900+
1900-O 25 1917? as Grant county review
pub 1920+
MnHi Jl 11 1901-O 25 1917;Je 16 1931+

HERON LAKE

GUARDIAN. w O 1 1880-82||
MnHi [1880-1882]
JACKSON county times. w 1895-1913||
MnHi Ap 10 1897-Jl 19 1913
Heron Lake NEWS. w 1886+
pub 1914+
MnHi [Je. 22-D 1889]+

HEWITT

Hewitt BANNER. w 1904+
1904 as Hewitt enterprise
pub [1904-18]+
Hewitt ENTERPRISE. *See* Hewitt banner

HIBBING

MESABA ore and the Hibbing news. *See* Hibbing daily news and the Mesaba ore
Hibbing NEWS. *See* Hibbing daily news and the Mesaba ore
Hibbing daily NEWS and the Mesaba ore. w,d 1893-D 2 1927||
1893-O 1901 as Hibbing news; N 1901-Ja 1920 Mesaba ore and the Hibbing news w 1893-Ja 1920
MnHb [1920-27]
MnHbT complete
MnHi complete
ST. LOUIS county independent. w F 1 1922+
pub 1922+
MnHi Ag 25 1922+
Hibbing SENTINEL. w F 8 1894-1901||
MnHi 1894-O 6 1900
Hibbing daily TRIBUNE. w,sw,d 1899+
Title varies slightly
w 1899-My 5 1908;sw My 1908-O 15 1909
pub 1899+
MnHb 1916+
MnHi N 7 1907+

HILL CITY

Hill City NEWS. w My 5 1910+
pub 1910+
MnHi 1910+

HILLS

Hills CRESCENT. w 1893+
pub 1896+
MnHi [Ja 10 1895-96]+

HINCKLEY

Hinckley ENTERPRISE. *See* Hinckley news
Hinckley HERALD. w 1909-17||
Merged with Hinckley news
MnHi D 14 1910-17
Hinckley NEWS. w Jl 1891+
1891-Je 1893 as Pine-wood dart: Jl 1893-Mr 1921 Hinckley enterprise
pub [1891+]
MnHi Ag 27 1891+
PINE-WOOD dart. *See* Hinckley news

HITTERDAL

Hitterdal STANDARD. *See* Hawley-Hitterdal standard (Hawley)

HOFFMAN

TRIBUNE. w Ag 1 1922+
pub 1922+

HOKAH

Hokah BLADE. w S 16 1875-80||?
Merged with Hokah chief
MnHi [Mr 11 1876-O 6 1877]
Hokah CHIEF. w Jl 15 1857+
Ja 18 1894-Ap 21 1927 as Houston county chief
pub 1899+
MnHi Mr 27,Ap 23,Je 5-12,Jl 10 1858-F 5 1859;F 7 1860-N 18 1862;S 28 1882+
N O 15 1861
WHi Jl 15 1857
HOUSTON county chief. *See* Hokah chief
Hokah SUN. w Ja 14 1886-99||
Merged with Hokah chief
MnHi 1886-99

HOLDINGFORD

Holdingford ADVERTISER. *See* Holdingford herald

MINNESOTA (*Continued*)

HOLDINGFORD—*Continued*

Holdingford HERALD. w N 12 1908+
1908-Je 1 1925 as Holdingford advertiser
pub [1908-25]+
MnHi D 9 1909+

HOLLAND

Holland INDEPENDENT. w Je 22 1922-F 26 1932||
MnHi complete

HOLT

Holt weekly NEWS. w Ag 4 1911+
1911-Mr 20 1914 as Northern light
pub 1911-[13-14]-[19-20]+
MnHi 1911+

NORTHERN light. *See* Holt weekly news

HOPKINS

HENNEPIN county enterprise. *See under* Robbinsdale

HENNEPIN county review. w 1904+
1904-Ap 23 1925 pub in Minneapolis
pub [1925]+
MnHi 1923—
MnHo 1934+

HOUSTON

Houston SIGNAL. w Ag 17 1882+
1882-Ap 27 1905 as Houston valley signal
pub 1882-[95-96]+
MnHi F 27 1890+

Houston VALLEY signal. *See* Houston signal

HOWARD LAKE

Howard Lake HERALD. w Je 14 1877+
1877-N 1881 as People's advocate
pub [1880+]
MnHi 1877-My 7 1885;F 21 1889+

PEOPLE'S advocate. *See* Howard Lake herald

HUGO

Hugo INDEPENDENT. w O 1 1919-O 1 1932||
pub complete

HUTCHINSON

Hutchinson INDEPENDENT. w,sw 1893-1906||
N 21 1901-Jl 24 1902 as Independent-times
sw Ag 4-N 13 1897
MnHi Ap 15 1897-1906
MnHuC 1895-1900

Hutchinson LEADER. w Jl 17 1880+
pub 1880+
MnHi Ap 23-Ag 27 1886;Jl 29-O 28 1887;Ap 13-Je 22 1888;1901+
MnHu 1915+

Hutchinson PRESS. w 1910-Mr 27 1934||
Merged with Hutchinson leader
pub [1922-34]
MnHi Ap 16 1925-34

INTERNATIONAL FALLS

To Mr 8 1904 as Koochiching

BORDER budget. w 1899-Je 10 1909||
Merged with International Falls press
MnHi My 7 1903-1909

Daily JOURNAL. d 1907+
MnHi Jl 28 1923+

KOOCHICHING press. *See* International Falls press

International Falls PRESS. w D 21 1904+
Follows Laurel press. (Laurel)
1904-Mr 15 1905 as Koochiching press
MnHi 1905+

RAINY Lake herald. w Je 28 1894-1901||
Je 28 1894-O 21 1897 as Rainy Lake journal and Koochiching advertiser
MnHi 1894-Ja 3 1901

RAINY Lake journal. *See* Rainy Lake herald

Falls evening TRIBUNE. d O 16 1922-Jl 7 1923||
MnHi complete

IONA

Iona JOURNAL. w 1898+
pub 1899+
MnHi Jl 20 1905-12

IRONTON

CUYUNA range miner. w 1911-20||
Merged with Deerwood times (Deerwood) 1911-16? pub in Cuyuna
MnHi Ap 12 1912-S 1915;Jl 20 1917-Jl 7 1920

Ironton NEWS. *See* Ranger

RANGER. w 1913-O 25 1932||
1913-Mr 1930 as Ironton news
pub 1912+
MnHi Ja 31 1924-[32]
See also Crosby ranger (Crosby)

ISANTI

Isanti INDEPENDENT. *See* Isanti news

Isanti NEWS. w Ja 24 1901-F 28 1924||
D 21 1922-Ja 11 1923 Isanti independent
pub [1901-24]
MnHi complete

ISLE

Isle ADVANCE. w 1917-O 18 1928||
Merged with Onamia herald (Onamia) to form Mille Lacs messenger
MnHi Je 7 1923-28

MILLE LACS messenger. w O 25 1928+
Formed by the union of The Isle advance and Onamia herald (Onamia)
pub 1928+
MnHi 1928+

IVANHOE

Ivanhoe TIMES. w Jl 20 1901+
pub 1901-[27+]

JACKSON

JACKSON county pilot. w 1889+
pub 1912+
MnHi [Ap 16-D 1891]-S 6 1894;Ja-N 7 1895;Ag 29 1929+

Jackson REPUBLIC. w Mr 5 1870-Ap 6 1934||
Merged with Jackson county pilot
pub complete
MnHi 1870-O 7 1887;F 14 1890-1934
MnJHi 1873-95

JANESVILLE

Janesville ARGUS. w 1873+
pub 1873+
MnHi S 29 1890+

WASECA county democrat. w,sw O 7 1897-1904||
sw Ap 17-Ag 14 1900
MnHi 1897-F 10 1904

JASPER

Jasper JOURNAL. w Jl 27 1888+
pub 1888+
MnHi Mr 7 1890;Ap 17 1891-[93]-[96]-[1902-04]

JEFFERS

Jeffers MIRROR. *See* Jeffers review

Jeffers REVIEW. w Mr 8 1900+
Follows Madison Lake mirror (Madison Lake) 1900-Ja 3 1901 as Jeffers mirror
pub [1900]+
MnHi 1900+

JORDAN

Jordan ADVOCATE. w Ag 29 1878-84||
1878-Ag 18 1882 Scott county advocate
MnHi S 5 1878-S 12 1884

Jordan INDEPENDENT. w 1884+
pub 1884+
MnHi Ap 20 1887;O 19 1893+

MINNESOTA volksfreund. w S 1 1892-1907||?
In German
MnHi 1892-Ag 17 1899

PEOPLES weekly. w Jl 11 1919-Ap 4 1929||
Merged with Jordan independent
MnHi complete

SCOTT county advocate. *See* Jordan advocate

KARLSTAD

Karlstad ADVOCATE. w 1901+
1901-Jl 12 1905 as Karlstad news
pub 1911+
MnHi [1905]+

Karlstad NEWS. *See* Karlstad advocate

KASOTA

Kasota TIMES. w Mr 27 1896-98||
MnHi My 15 1896-My 27 1898

KASSON

Kasson CALL. w D 12 1928-Ja 16 1929||
MnHi complete

DODGE county republican. w Je 29 1867+
MWA Je 20,Ag 1,N 7 1868;S 12,N 14 1878;Je 25 1879
MnHi Ag 10 1867-75;My 14 1885-1913;16+
MnK 1867-99

KEEWATIN

Keewatin CHRONICLE. w 1917-Mr 11 1927||
MnHi S 16 1921-27

KELLOGG

Kellogg ENTERPRISE. w D 1903-18||
MnHi D 8 1904-Jl 11 1918

WABASHA county enterprise. w D 23 1926-Mr 31 1927||
Merged with Wabasha county herald-standard (Wabasha)
MnHi complete

KENNEDY

Kennedy STAR. w 1900+
pub [1918+]
MnHi F 1931+

KENYON

Kenyon LEADER. w 1885+
pub 1885+
MnHi O 1890-S 1907;N 1924+

MINNESOTA signal. w Je 1 1900-05||
MnHi 1900-05

Kenyon NEWS. w Ap 11 1906+
pub [1906+]
MnHi 1906-[13]-[27]

KERKHOVEN

Kerkhoven BANNER. w 1897+
pub [1897]+
MnHi 1898+

SWIFT county standard. *See under* Benson

KIESTER

Kiester COURIER. w 1900+
pub [1907+]

KINBRAE

Kinbrae HERALD. w 1894-1900||
MnHi S 16 1897-Mr 1 1900

KOOCHICHING. *See* INTERNATIONAL FALLS

LA CRESCENT

CO-OPERATOR. w 1886-Jl 1 1892||
MnHi Mr 24,My 25,D 7,21 1888;Ja 3 1889;Ap 10,D 18 1891;92

Weekly PATROL. w Ap 24 1888-89||
MnHi [1888-89]

PLAIN DEALER. w D 3 1860-
MnHi [Ap 16 1861-N 11 1862]
N O 15 1861

LAC QUI PARLE

LAC QUI PARLE county press. w D 20 1872-78||
MnHi 1873-[77-78]

Lac qui Parle PRESS. *See* Independent press (Madison)

LAFAYETTE

Lafayette LEDGER. w My 14 1904+
pub [1904+]

LAKE BENTON

Lake Benton NEWS. w 1880+
pub 1887+
MnHi Mr 23 1892+

LAKE CITY

Lake City GRAPHIC. *See* Lake City graphic-republican

Lake City GRAPHIC-REPUBLICAN. w Ag 5 1865+
1865-Je 15 1881 as Lake City leader;Je 22 1881-S 6 1882 Review; S 12 1882-Ag 30 1887 Lake City graphic; S 6 1887-Ag 30 1910 Graphic-sentinel
MnHi [1865-67]-Mr 1 1905;S 1910+

GRAPHIC-SENTINEL. *See* Lake City graphic-republican

Weekly JOURNAL. w O 29 1859-
1859-D 8 1860 pub in Wabasha
MnHi [1859-Ag 31 1861]

Lake City LEADER. *See* Lake City graphic-republican

Lake City REPUBLICAN. w Mr 8 1888-S 3 1910||
United with Graphic sentinel to form Lake City graphic-republican
CtY Je 23,S 29,O 27 1888;F 10 1894
MnHi [1888-89]-1910

REVIEW. *See* Lake City graphic-republican

SENTINEL. w O 12 1870-Je 15 1881||
1870-D 23 1874 as Wabasha county sentinel; D 30 1874-N 26 1879 Wabasha county sentinel. United with Lake City leader to form Review, later Lake City graphic-republican
MnHi complete
WHi F 3 1871-D 15 1880

Weekly Lake City TIMES. w S 28 1861-
MnHi D 7,D 21 1861;Mr 1-22,Ap 19,My 17,Jl 26-S 6,20,D 27 1862
N O 12 1864

WABASHA county leader. w 1919+
MnHi Ja 30 1925+

WABASHA county sentinel. *See* Sentinel

MINNESOTA (*Continued*)

LAKE CRYSTAL

Lake Crystal MIRROR. w 1888-93‖
MnHi S 19 1890-Ag 25 1893

Lake Crystal TRIBUNE. w 1882+
1882-D 1 1921 as Lake Crystal union
MnHi [1889]-1917;Mr 10 1921+
MnMaHi 1884-1919

Lake Crystal UNION. *See* Lake Crystal tribune

LAKE HARRIET

Papers published in Lake Harriet are listed under Minneapolis

LAKE PARK

BECKER county journal. *See* Lake Park journal

Lake Park JOURNAL. w Ja 1 1897+
1897-S 1 1927 as Becker county journal
pub 1928+
MnHi N 9 1922+

LAKE WILSON

Lake Wilson PILOT. w Ag 23 1901+
MnHi [1903]

LAKEFIELD

Lakefield HERALD. w N 15 1895-My 18 1904‖
MnHi complete
MnLaS complete

MINNESOTA citizen. *See* Lakefield standard

Lakefield STANDARD. w N 30 1883+
1883-Ap 2 1886 as Minnesota citizen
pub 1883-1908;10+
MnHi [1891]-[94-97]+

LAKEVILLE

Lakeville and Rosemount ARBITRATOR. w D 3 1892-Ap 6 1898‖
1892-F 22 1893 as Lakeville arbitrator. Followed by Dakota county breeze (Farmington)
MnHi 1892-O 2 1895-Ja 5-Ap 6 1898

DAKOTA county tribune. *See under* Farmington

LAMBERTON

Lamberton LEADER. w 1889-My 19 1893‖
MnHi Mr 28 1890-1893

Lamberton LEADER. w 1893-1924‖
1893-Ap 5 1923 as Lamberton star
MnHi My 15 1896-[97]-[1924]

Lamberton NEWS. w N 26 1919+
1919-N 7 1929 as Northern light
pub 1919-23;25+
MnHi 1922+

NORTHERN light. *See* Lamberton news

Lamberton STAR. *See* Lamberton leader

LANESBORO

Lanesboro CLARION. w S 10 1868-73‖
1868-N 14 1871 as Lanesboro herald
MnHi 1868-Ap 22 1873

HARDING'S herald and Lanesboro journal. w
InRE Jl 10,S 4-11,O 2-9 1880

Lanesboro HERALD. *See* Lanesboro clarion

Lanesboro JOURNAL. w 1874-1907‖
MnHi N 27 1875-My 1876;O 1890-Je 1907

Lanesboro LEADER. w O 15 1898+
My 20 1915-My 11 1933 as Levang's weekly
pub 1898-[1902-15]+
MnHi 1898+

LEVANG'S weekly. *See* Lanesboro leader

LAPORTE

Laporte NEWS. w S 11 1908-27‖
MnHi 1908-O 28 1927

LA PRAIRIE

La Prairie-Itasca COUNTY news. w 1891-94‖
1891-S 9 1893 as La Prairie news
MnHi S 1892-F 3 1894

La Prairie MAGNET. w 1890-My 28 1891‖
Followed by Grand Rapids magnet (Grand Rapids)
MnHi Mr 19-My 28 1891

La Prairie NEWS. *See* La Prairie-Itasca county news

LAUREL

Laurel PRESS. w Mr 27 1903-D 16 1904‖
Followed by Koochiching press, later International Falls press (International Falls)
MnHi complete

LAX LAKE

LAKE county advocate. w 1904-09‖?
MnHi F 23 1907-[09]

LE CENTER

To 1931 as Le Sueur Center

LE SUEUR Center leader. *See* Le Center leader

LE SUEUR county democrat. w Ag 9 1900-Je 27 1907‖
United with Le Sueur county leader to form Leader-democrat, later Le Center leader
MnHi complete
MnLcL complete

LE SUEUR county leader. *See* Le Center leader

Le Center LEADER. w 1896+
1896-Je 27 1907 as Le Sueur county leader; Jl 1907-Je 5 1924 Leader-democrat; Jl 12 1924-Ja 1931 Le Sueur Center leader
pub 1907+
MnHi D 23 1897+

LEADER-DEMOCRAT. *See* Le Center leader

LEECH LAKE

CASS county cruiser. w S 21 1892-Ag 2 1893‖
MnHi complete

LE ROY

Le Roy INDEPENDENT. w 1875+
pub [1917]+
MnHi Mr 21 1890-[96]

LESTER PRAIRIE

Lester Prairie JOURNAL. *See* Lester Prairie news

Lester Prairie NEWS. w My 25 1895+
1895-Je 7 1901 as Lester Prairie journal
pub 1895+
MnHi [1897]+

LE SUEUR

Le Sueur COURIER. w 1866-Ag 27 1873‖
MnHi D 11 1867-73

Le Sueur ECHO. w 1876-D 25 1877‖
MnHi My-D 1877

Le Sueur HERALD. *See* Le Sueur news-herald

Le Sueur NEWS. w 1880-My 1 1924‖
United with Le Sueur herald to form Le Sueur news-herald
MnHi Mr 19 1887[89-91]92[97]-1924

Le Sueur NEWS-HERALD. w Ja 24 1917+
1917-My 7 1924 as Le Sueur herald
pub 1917+
MnHi 1917+

Le Sueur SENTINEL. w 1873-D 9 1911‖
Followed by Waterville sentinel
MnHi My 17 1877-1911

LE SUEUR CENTER. *See* LE CENTER

LEWISTON

Lewiston JOURNAL. w D 28 1929+
pub 1929+

LINDSTROM

CHISAGO county courier. w O 28 1899-
Follows Inter State park press (Taylors Falls)
MnHi 1899-Ap 22 1905

CHISAGO county news. w Ap 19 1888-1905‖
1888-Je 14 1894 pub in Taylors Falls
MnHi 1888-S 21 1905

CHISAGE county press. w 1898+
pub My 11 1905+

MEDBORGAREN. w 1898-1905‖
In Swedish
IRA 1905

NYA pressen. w Ap 4-O 17 1903‖
In Swedish
Followed by Center City press (Centér City)
MnHi complete

LISMORE

Lismore FREE PRESS. w 1913-29‖?
MnHi S 16 1921-N 5 1926

LITCHFIELD

Litchfield INDEPENDENT. w My 30 1876+
pub [1876]+
MnHi 1890+
MnLi [1904]+

Litchfield LEDGER. *See* Litchfield news-ledger

MEEKER county news. w 1868-My 26 1874‖
United with Litchfield ledger to form Litchfield news-ledger
MnHi 1871-74

MEEKER county news. w 1894+
1894-1917 as Dassel anchor (Dassel)
pub [1918]+
MnHi Jl 16 1903-O 18 1917;Mr 18 1926+

Litchfield NEWS-LEDGER. Ap 30 1872-Mr 18 1920‖
1872-Je 4 1874 as Litchfield ledger. Merged with Litchfield independent
DLC My 16,S 19 1878
MnHi complete
MnLi [1904]-20

Litchfield REPUBLICAN. w Ja 24 1871-
MnHi Ja 24-S 6 1871

Litchfield REVIEW. w Jl 1884+
1884-Ag 14 1925 as Litchfield Saturday review
pub 1890+
MnHi D 21 1889[90]+
MnLi [1904]+

ROTHUGGAREN. w O 1880-Mr 1886‖
In Swedish and English
IRA [1880-81]
MnHi S 1885

LITTLE FALLS

Little Falls HERALD. w 1889+
MnHi 1896+
MnLf 1927+

MORRISON county democrat. w 1887-1909‖
MnHi N 1891-Jl 29 1909

NORTHERN herald. w
DLC S 2 1857
MnHi Ja 14,21,Ag 19,O 28 1857

Little Falls TRANSCRIPT. w,sw 1877-Ja 1 1901‖
w 1877-Ja 28 1898
MnHi N 1-17 1877;Jl 11 1878-Ag 13 1880;My 1891-1901

Daily TRANSCRIPT. d Ag 16 1880+
pub 1892+
MnHi [1880-81]1901+
MnLf [1919]+

LITTLEFORK

Littlefork GUARDIAN. w 1903-09‖?
United with Littlefork times to form Littlefork times and guardian

Littlefork TIMES and guardian. w 1905+
1905-09? as Littlefork times
MnHi N 17 1921+

LONG PRAIRIE

Long Prairie DEMOCRAT. w Ag 15 1902-08‖
MnHi 1902-[08]

Long Prairie LEADER. sw,w 1883+
sw F 19 1907-N 12 1909
pub 1902+
MnHi My 1891+

TODD county argus. w 1876-N 29 1917‖
Merged with Long Prairie leader
MnHi Ja 19 1883-1917

TODD county tribune. w Je 6 1918-22‖
MnHi 1918-[22]

LONSDALE

Lonsdale TIMES. w 1917-20‖
Merged with New Prague times (New Prague)
MnNpT complete

LUCAN

Lucan LEADER. w N 5 1920-23‖
MnHi 1920-[23]

LUVERNE

Luverne JOURNAL. *See* Rock county leader

ROCK county herald. w My 23 1873+
pub 1873+
MnHi F 1877-[78-81]+
MnLu 1900+

ROCK county leader. w Ag 1898-1919‖?
1898-1918? as Luverne journal
MnHi Je 29 1899;1901-[03-04]

ROCK county news. w 1888-1900‖
MnHi O 1890[91]-1900

ROCK county star. w 1918+
MnHi S 23 1920+

LYLE

Lyle TRIBUNE. w 1891+
pub [1896]+
MnAu [1896-97]
MnHi Ap 1897-[1903]

MABEL

Mabel ENTERPRISE. *See* Mabel sentinel

Mabel RECORD. w 1906+
MnHi Ag 22 1930+

Mabel SENTINEL. w 1884-1905‖
1884-Jl 11 1895 as Mabel enterprise; Jl 18 1895-Ap 30 1903 Mabel tribune
MnHi Ja 16 1890-[1905]

Mabel TRIBUNE. *See* Mabel sentinel

McGRATH

McGrath TRIBUNE. w Ag 5 1924-26‖
MnHi 1924-My 5 1926

McGREGOR

McGregor PILOT review. w S 25 1925-Mr 15 1934‖
Followed by Kanabec county progressive (Mora)
MnHi complete

MINNESOTA (*Continued*)

McINTOSH

NEWS. *See* Nordstjernen

NORDSTJERNEN. w My 14 1891-93||
Follows McIntosh tribune (1888-91). My 18 1891-Ag 9 1893 as News
In Norwegian and English
MnHi [1891]-93

McIntosh TIMES. w O 8 1888+
pub 1888+
MnHi [1891]+

McIntosh TRIBUNE. w 1888-My 6 1891||
Followed by News, later Nordstjernen
MnHi Ap 22-My 6 1891

McIntosh TRIBUNE. w Jl 12 1893-1904||
MnHi complete

MADELIA

Madelia HERALD. w O 30 1874-
MnHi [1874]

Madelia MESSENGER. w 1893-Ag 28 1903||
United with Madelia times to form Madelia times-messenger
MnHi Ap 16 1897-1903

Madelia RECORD. w 1889-F 27 1891||
MnHi S 19 1890-91

Madelia TIMES-MESSENGER. w 1871+
1871-Ag 28 1903 as Madelia times
MnHi Ja 29 1886+

MADISON

INDEPENDENT-PRESS. w Ap 7 1882+
1882-Ap 23 1886 as Lac qui Parle press (Lac qui Parle); Ap 30 1886-Mr 30 1894 Lac qui Parle county press
MnHi 1882+
MnMd 1884+

LAC QUI PARLE county independent. w 1879-Mr 30 1894||
United with Lac qui Parle county press to form Independent-press
MnHi [Je 20-D 1890]-94

LAC QUI PARLE county press. *See* Independent-press

MINNESOTA tidende. w 1894-99||
1894-Ag 5 1897 as Madison tidende
In Norwegian
IaDeL [1895]-[Ja 13-Ag 1899]
WHi Jl 8-D 1898

Madison TIDENDE. *See* Minnesota tidende

WESTERN guard. w 1890+
1890-O 28 1891 pub in Dawson
MnHi 1891+
MnMd 1890+

MADISON LAKE

Madison Lake MIRROR. w 1896-F 15 1900||
Followed by Jeffers mirror, later Jeffers review (Jeffers)
MnHi Ap 15 1897-1900

Madison Lake NEW ERA. w D 7 1900-03||
Follows Jeffersonian (Faribault)
MnHi 1900-S 4 1903

Madison Lake TIMES. w D 3 1904+
pub 1904+

MAGNOLIA

Magnolia ADVANCE. w 1893-1920||
MnHi 1898-[1920]

MAHNOMEN

Mahnomen PIONEER. w My 12 1905+
1905-Ap 10 1910 as Mahnomen plaintalk
pub [1905-10]+
MnHi [1914]—

Mahnomen PLAINTALK. *See* Mahnomen pioneer

MANKATO

Mankato FREE PRESS. sw,w 1857-1924||?
1857-63? as Mankato independent (title varies: Semi-weekly Mankato independent)
sw 1860?-Mr 7 1861
DLC [Ag-D 1861;Ja-Je 1863;Je 1882]
MnHi [Ag 9 1860-Jl 11 1863]O 31 1879-80[87-88;90]-1918
MnMa [1857]-[62]
N O 24 1861
WHi Je 6 1857

Mankato FREE PRESS. d Ap 4 1887+
pub 1887+
MnHi N 23 1887[88]+
MnMa 1901-[10]+

Mankato INDEPENDENT. *See* Mankato free press

Mankato LEDGER. w 1879+
MnHi Ap 13 1891-[92]+

Mankato NEWS. w 1916+
pub [1926]+
MnHi 1925-Mr 11 1926

Mankato POST. w 1886-1917||?
In German
MnHi D 25 1891-[92]
MnMa 1901-02

Mankato RECORD. sw,w Jl 5 1859-O 25 1879||
Title varies: Semi-weekly record: Mankato weekly record
sw Jl 1860-63
MWA My 2,Jl 25,Ag 29,N 21 1863;Ag 20,D 10 1864;Ap 1 1865
MnHi Ag 2-9,S 5-12,27-O 4,25 1859-Je 1860[Mr 29 1861-S 3 1864;My 27-D 16 1865]Jl 12 1867-79
MnMa 1859-68
N S 6,O 15 1861
WHi S 5-12 1874;Mr 20-27,Je 5,Jl 10 1875

Mankato REGISTER. w 1885-F 5 1891||
Merged with Mankato free press
MnHi S 26 1889-91

REVIEW. w 1869-1919||?
Title varies slightly
MnHi 1871[72-74]-O 13 1887;S 16 1890-1917
MnMa [1872]-[80-98]-1905

Daily REVIEW. d S 12 1892-N 8 1919||
Merged with Mankato free press
MnHi complete
MnMa 1892-[99-1902]-[11]-[14]-19

Mankato TELEGRAM. w O 5 1922-Mr 28 1924||
Merged with Mankato news
MnHi N 9 1922-24

Mankato weekly UNION. w Jl 17 1863-O 24 1879||
DLC Jl 24 1863-Mr 10 1865
MWA F 2 1866
MnHi 1863-65;67-79
MnMa [1863-68]-[79]

UNION news. w S 27 1918-Mr 16 1923||
Merged with Mankato telegram
MnHi complete

MANTORVILLE

Mantorville EXPRESS. w Jl 16 1857+
S 3 1880-O 22 1886 as Mantorville and Kasson express
MWA F 16-23 1866;Ag 12 1870;Ja 9 1874;Mr 19-26 1875
MnHi 1857+
N O 18 1861

MAPLETON

BLUE EARTH county enterprise. w 1884+
1884-Je 3 1898 as Mapleton enterprise
MnHi S 19 1890+

Mapleton ENTERPRISE. *See* Blue Earth county enterprise

MARIETTA

INTERSTATE messenger. *See* Marietta messenger

Marietta MESSENGER. w Ag 17 1900-07||
1900-N 24 1905 as Interstate messenger
MnHi 1900-My 10 1907

MARINE FALLS

Marine Mills MASCOT. w My 12 1904-08||?
MnHi [1904]

MARSHALL

FARMERS reporter. w 1889-F 24 1921||
1889-O 17 1918 as Lyon county reporter. Merged with Marshall messenger, later Marshall news-messenger
MnHi [1890-91]-1921
MnMdHi 1891-1909
MnMrM complete

LYON county news. w 1879-85||
Merged with Marshall messenger, later News-messenger
MnMdHi My 1879-My 1884
MnMrM complete

LYON county reporter. *See* Farmers reporter

Marshall MESSENGER. *See* News-messenger

NEWS-MESSENGER. w,sw,d Ag 23 1873+
1873-S 24 1875 as Prairie schooner; O 1 1875-Ag 1932 Marshall messenger (title varies slightly)
w 1873-1931; sw Ja-Ag 1932
MnHi [1873-76]-[80]-84;D 1886+
MnMdHi S 1873+

PRAIRIE schooner. *See* News-messenger

MAYNARD

Maynard HERALD. w
1899-1900 as Maynard news
MnHi [1899-1901]

Maynard NEWS. 1899-1900. *See* Maynard herald

Maynard NEWS. w Ap 9 1909+
pub [1925]+
MnHi [1909-10]

MAZEPPA

Mazeppa INDEPENDENT. w 1895-D 24 1897||
Followed by Zumbro Falls independent and Mazeppa independent, later Zumbro Falls independent (Zumbro Falls)
MnHi Ap 16-D 1897

Mazeppa JOURNAL. w 1903+

Mazeppa TRIBUNE. w O 27 1877-Je 26 1908||
Merged with Mazeppa journal
MnHi [F 1887-88]S 11 1889-1908

MELROSE

Der ANZEIGER. w 1895-1901||
In German
MnHi 1898-1901

Melrose BEACON. w 1890+
MnHi Ja 31 1902+

MENAHGA

Menahga JOURNAL. *See* Menahga messenger

Menahga MESSENGER. w 1906+
1906-25 as Menahga journal (1915-Jl 21 1916 Wadena county advertiser)
MnHi N 19 1909-[25]

WADENA county advertiser. *See* Menahga messenger

MENTOR

Mentor HERALD. w Ap 8 1903-D 5 1906||
Merged with Erskine echo (Erskine)
MnHi complete

MERRITT

MESABA Range news. w Mr 12 1892-94||
MWA Mr 12 1892

MIDDLE RIVER

Middle River PIONEER. w 1903-23||
MnHi Jl 1909-[13]-[23]

Middle River RECORD. w 1906+
1906-24 as Oslo tribune (Oslo)
MnHi S 16 1909-10;Mr 20 1924-31

MILACA

MILLE LACS county times. w Ag 19 1892+
pub 1892+
MnHi Mr 11 1893+

Milaca TRIBUNE. w Jl 24 1919-28||
MnHi 1919-Ja 12 1928

MILAN

Milan STANDARD. w 1900+
pub 1900+
MnHi My 1903+

MILROY

Milroy ECHO. w 1905+
pub 1929+
MnHi N 4 1915+

MINNEAPOLIS

ADVERTISER. w Je 6 1862-
MWA Je 13 1862

AFRO-AMERICAN advance. w My 27 1899-1905||?
Follows Twin City American
MnHi 1899-N 17 1900

AFRO-INDEPENDENT. *See under* St. Paul

AMERICA-HEROLD. w D 4 1924+
Follows Minneapolis freie presse-herold Minneapolis ed of America-herold pub in Winona
In German
MnHi 1924+

Weekly ARGUS. *See* East Minneapolis argus

BUDSTIKKEN. w S 2 1873-D 26 1894||
Merged with Minneapolis tidende
In Norwegian
IaDeL 1873-Ag 10 1886;F 22-Ag,D 12 1888-94
MnHi Je 9 1874-94
WHi Ap 1880-85

BUSINESS weekly. w 1918+
1918?-Jl 1925 as South side weekly; Ag 1925-S 1926 South town sentinel
pub [1925]+

CELTIC world. w D 3 1881-82||?
MnHi 1881-D 9 1882

CHAT. *See* Courier-journal

Minneapolis CHRONICLE. w Je 9 1866-
MnHi Je 16-S 29 1866

Minneapolis daily CHRONICLE. d S 20? 1866-
MnHi S 21 1866-Ap 30 1867
MnM 1866-My 1867

Minneapolis CHRONICLE. 1883-1928. *See* Spectator

CITIZEN. w 1873-77||
MnHi Ja 13 1876-D 8 1877

Minneapolis COMMERCIAL. m Mr 1870-
MWA Mr 1870
MnHi Mr-O 1870

CONWELL S star of the north. *See* Minneapolis weekly star

COURIER-JOURNAL. w Je 22 1894-Je 8 1895||
1894-Mr 30 1895 as Chat
MnHi complete

Saturday CYNIC and weekly star. w 1895-1902||?
1895-N 6? 1900 as Saturday cynic
MnHi N 17,D 1-22 1900

DANSKE amerikaner. w 1894-Ag 20 1896||
In Danish
WHi O 17 1895-96

Minneapolis DEMOCRAT. w
Early years as Minnesota democrat
DLC [Jl 19 1856-My 30 1857]

MINNESOTA (*Continued*)

MINNEAPOLIS—*Continued*

Weekly DEMOCRAT. w O 15 1869-Ja 9 1873||
1869-Mr 28 1872 as St. Anthony Falls democrat. Merged with Dollar weekly times
MnHi complete
MnM 1869-Mr 1872

Minneapolis DEMOCRAT. w Ap 1 1898-1901||
MnHi 1898-Jl 26 1901

DOLLAR weekly times. w Ja 17-D 20 1873||
MnHi Ja 17-Je 13 1873

Minneapolis DOWNTOWN shopping news. w
MnU [1929-34]

EAST Minneapolis argus. w Ja 2 1892+
Ja-Ag 18 1892 as Weekly argus; Ag 15 1892-1922 North east argus; 1923?-Ag 27 1926 East side argus
pub [1892+]
MnHi N 17 1922+

EAST SIDE argus. *See* East Minneapolis argus

L'ECHO de l'ouest. w 1884-Ja 4 1929||
In French
IU 1914-28
IaHi O 31 1889-Ag 28 1890
MnHi Ja 14 1885-1929
MnM 1898-1928

FÄDRELANDET og Emigranten. w Ja 14 1864-94||
1864-Ag 24 1868 as Fädrelandet. Merged with Minneapolis tidende
1864-85 pub in La Crosse, Wis
In Norwegian
IaDeL Mr 1 1865;F 1,22,Ag 7-S 4,27-O 4 1866; S 1868-[69]-93
MnHi [Mr 16 1887-Mr 21 1888]
MnSL 1864-79

FALLS evening news. (St. Anthony) d,tw S 28 1857-My 18 1861||
d S-D 7 1857
DLC 1857-58
MWA O 31 1857
MnHi 1857-[59]-61

FELT raabet. w My 13 1887-89||
In Norwegian
MnHi 1887-F 22 1889

FINANCE and commerce of the Twin Cities. d Ja 16 1888+
pub 1888+
MnHi 1912-14;16-27

FOLKEBLADET. m,w Ag 1877-1915||
m 1877-O 1880
1916+ pub as a Lutheran church paper
In Norwegian
IaDeL N 1879-80;82-1915
MnHi Ap 14 1897-1915
MnSL [1899]

FOLKETS RÖST. (Voice of the people). w,sm 1904-25||
1904-O 26 1918 as Gaa paa
1904-06 pub in Girard, Kan.
w 1904-Je 7 1924
In Norwegian
IU D 21 1918-Ag 29 1925
MnHi Jl 1917-O 31 1925
WHi Ja 16,Ap 2 1904;Jl 17,N 13 1909-O,D 21 1918-O 31 1925

FREE FLAG. w D 6 1876-77||
Suspended from Ag 9-N 5 1877
MnHi 1876-N 5 1877

FREE PRESS. w,sw D 11 1897-98||
sw F 12-My 20 1898
MnHi 1897-Ag 12 1898

FREIDENKER. *See under* New Ulm

Minneapolis FREIE PRESSE-HEROLD. w 1869-N 28 1924||
1869-Ja 2 1891 as Minneapolis freie-presse. Merged with America-herold (Winona) Ap 30 1920-N 30 1923 dated also at Winona
In German
MnHi N 12 1870-[89-90]-1924

GAA PAA. *See* Folkets röst

Minneapolis GAZETTE. w F 2 1858-
MnHi Mr 16-O 15 1858

GAZETTE. w Ja 26-Ag 8 1891||
Ja-Mr 14 1891 as New Boston gazette.
MnHi complete

GOPHER mirror. *See* Minnesota mirror

HARRIET news. w Je 21 1919-21||
MnHi S 12 1919-D 9 1921

HEM och härd. w F 2 1897-F 8 1898||
In Swedish. Supp to Svenska Amerikanska posten
MnHi complete

HENNEPIN county herald. w My 30 1912-21||
1912-O 24 1918 as Wayzata reporter
1912-My 15 1919 pub at Wayzata
MnHi 1912-[20]

HENNEPIN county mirror. *See* Minnesota mirror

HENNEPIN county review. *See under* Hopkins

Minneapolis HEROLD. w 1884-91||
United with Minneapolis freie-presse to form Minneapolis freie-presse-herold
In German
MnHi N 15 1890-[91]

ILLUSTRERET familie journal. w 1881-90||?
1881-O 25 1888 as Illustreret ugeblad; den literäre afdeling
In Danish
MnHi Mr 29,My 31 1888-Je 6 1889;D 18 1890

ILLUSTRERET ugeblad. . .
—**Literäre afdeling.** *See* Illustreret familie journal
—**Nyheds afdeling.** *See* Det Danske ugeblad (Tyler)

INDEPENDENT. ir O 15 1924-
MnHi O 15 1924;F 4,Mr 9,31 1925

IRISH standard. w N 7 1885-1920||
1885-Ap 10 1886 as Northwestern standard
IU 1918-My 1920
MnHi 1885-[1920]
PPiHi [1886-90;1905;13;15;20]

Minneapolis JOURNAL. d N 26 1878+
Title varies: Evening journal; Minneapolis evening journal
pub 1878+
CtY F 24-Mr 2,Jl 1-7 1933
DLC 1895-1902;06+
ICM Je 1 1882
ICN D 1917-N 1919;Mr-Ap 1920
ICU 1935+
IaDH Mr 8 1901-14
IaSc current 6 months
KHi S 28 1895;F 25,Mr 1-2 1923
MWA My 25 1893
MiU [1906-07]26+
MnHi [My 2-Jl 1883]Ag 1[S-D 1885]+
MnM N 26 1878+
MnU Je 1934+
NcD Ag-S,N-D 1906;F-Mr,My,Jl 1907-My 1908;F 24-Mr 3 1933
NdVS Mr 2 1895-Mr 1896
OClWHi Jl 26 1914
WHi Jl 1891-96;S 1900-Ja 13 1908;17-19

LAKE district advocate. w 1917+
Mr 6 1925-O 29 1926 as Lake district life
MnHi F 10 1922;Mr 16 1923-30

LAKE HARRIET weekly leader. w 1925-
MnHi D 15 1927-Je 21 1928

LAKE HARRIET news. w Mr 31 1932-33||
MnHi 1932-My 25 1933

LAKE HARRIET record. w Mr 3-Je 23 1922||
MnHi complete

LYNNHURST herald. w 1917+
MnHi Je 1923-32

Minneapolis evening MAIL. d 1874-75||
MnHi [1875]
MnM Je 13 1874-D 11 1875
WHi D 5 1874

Daily MARKET record. d 1884+
pub 1884
DLC 1914+
MnU 1892-1901;08-09
MnU-A 1920-33
NdHi 1919-Je 20 1920

Minneapolis MESSENGER. *See* Minnesota messenger

MINNESOTA. w 1871-73||
In Norwegian
IaDeL O 25 1871-Ap 17 1872;My-Ag 7,S 4,20 1872;Ja-Ap 4 1873

MINNESOTA beacon. bw Ja 1860-
Ag 1-15,S 15 1860 pub at Wasioja
Jl 15 1860 never published
MnHi Je 15-Jl 1,Ag 1-15,S 15 1860

MINNESOTA democrat. *See* Minneapolis democrat (1856-57)

MINNESOTA independent. w Ja 2 1868-
MnHi Ja 23 1869;Mr 6-My 8 1869

MINNESOTA leader. ir F 16 1918+
1918-Mr 27 1920 pub in St. Paul; Ap 10 1920-N 15 1924 in Olivia
IU 1919-N 15 1924;My 4 1926
MnHi 1918-[25-26]Mr 8,N 1 1927;Je 10 1930
MnU [1918;24;26]N 1 1927
MnU-A 1921-O 15 1924
WHi Ja 17 1920-N 15 1924;My 4,Je 5 1926;Ap-O 5 1935

MINNESOTA messenger. w My 7 1921-F 9 1924||
1921-Ap 1 1922 as Minneapolis messenger
MnHi complete

MINNESOTA mirror. sw,w O 31 1873-84||
Title varies: Sunday mirror; Gopher mirror; Mirror; Hennepin county mirror; Minneapolis mirror
sw Ag 29-S 19 1874;78
MWA Ja 11 1874
MnHi F-D 1874;Ag 7 1878-[79-80]-O 10 1884

MINNESOTA republican. w O 5 1854-
Suspended Mr 20-Je 26 1856
MWA N 27 1856
MnHi 1854-D 24 1858

MINNESOTA searchlight. w S 3 1915-F 16 1917||
MnHi complete

MINNESOTA daily star. *See* Minneapolis star (1920+)

MINNESOTA state news. w 1855-
MWA O 20-27,N 10 1860
MnHi Ap 7 1860-[61]-62;My 9-Jl 4 1863
N O 12 1861

MINNESOTA stats tidning. *See under* St. Paul

Daily MINNESOTA tribune. *See* Minneapolis tribune

MINNESOTSKY pokrok. *See under* St. Paul

Minnetonka NEWS. *See* Excelsior cottager (Excelsior)

MIRROR. -1873-84 *See* Minnesota mirror

Weekly MIRROR. w 1894+
MnHi Ap 27 1912+

Sunday MIRROR. *See* Minnesota mirror

NEW BOSTON gazette. *See* Gazette

NEW TIMES. w S 16 1910-Ja 1919||
MnHi N 25 1910-19

Daily evening NEWS. d 1871-73||
MnHi My 29 1872-My 30 1873

Daily NEWS. d 1903-Je 27 1923||
Merged with Minneapolis tribune
MnHi Mr 30 1922-23

NORDISK volkeblad. w Mr 12 1868-Jl 7 1875||
Merged with Skandinaven (Chicago, Ill.)
Mr-My 14? 1868 pub in Rochester
In Norwegian
IaDeL [My 1868-Mr 5 1873;Ap 16 1874-75]
MnHi [1868-69]-75
MnSL [1868]

NORMANNA. w O 6 1888-94||
IaDeL 1888-90
MnHi [1888]

NORTH. w Je 12 1889-Ja 24 1894||
IRA [1889-94]
MnHi complete
WHi complete

NORTH EAST argus. *See* East Minneapolis argus

NORTH MINNEAPOLIS news. *See* Spectator

NORTHERN headlight. w 1921+
pub 1921+

Minneapolis NORTHSIDER. w Ag 12 1920+
1920-N 22 1928 as Northsider
MnHi 1920-[28]-S 21 1929

NORTH-WESTERN democrat. w Jl 13 1853-
1853-Ag 12 1854 printed in St. Anthony
DLC F 22-Ag 2,19 1854-Je 28 1856
MWA F 1 1854
MnHi Jl 13 1853[Ag 12 1854-O 17 1857]

NORTHWESTERN standard. *See* Irish standard

NORTHWESTERN tourist. *See* Excelsior cottager (Excelsior)

NORTHWESTERN-vine. w 1901-03||?
Negro
MnHi [O 1902-03]

NOWINY Minnesockie. *See under* St. Paul

NY TID w,m 1894-Je 1909||?
1894-Jl 19 1904 as Nye Normanden; Jl 26 1904-O 29 1907 Politiken
1894 pub in Moorhead
w 1894-1907
In Norwegian
IaDeL Ag 25 1896;Ja 13,O 1897-[Jl 26 1904-Ja 8 1907]
MnHi O 29 1895-S 14 1897;N 1907-Je 1909
WHi N 1895-Ag 1897;99-1909

NYA världen. w 1889-91||
In Swedish
IRA [1889-91]

NYE Normanden. *See* Ny tid

Minneapolis OBSERVER. w Ag 16 1890-
Negro
MnHi Ag 16-S 27 1890

ODALMANNEN. *See* Western American

L'OEIL. w D 17 1892-
Dated also at St. Paul.
In French
MnHi D 17 1892-S 6 1893

PENNY press. *See* Evening press

PLAIN dealer. w 1859-
MnHi F 4-O 27 1860

POLITIKEN. *See* Ny tid

POSTEN. *See* Chicago posten (Chicago)

Evening PRESS. d O 1 1893-Jl 3 1897||
1893-D 21 1896 as Penny press; D 22? 1896-Mr 1 1897 Evening penny press
MnHi complete
MnM 1893-[96-97]
WHi 1893-96
—**Sunday ed.** *See* Sunday review

PROGRESS-REGISTER. w 1884+
1884-Ap 21 1923 as Progress
pub [1919]+
MWA My 13 1905
MnHi Je 29,Ag 10,S 1889-[93]+
MnM 1894-1911;13-14
MnU Je 2 1917;O 5 1918[19;N 20 1920-21]N 1924+
NIC Ap 1898-Je 20 1908
TJT S 8 1900
WHi Ap 29 1889-Mr 1904;My 13 1905

REGISTER. w 1887-Ap 21 1923||
Merged with Progress to form Progress-register
MnHi 1889-1923

Sunday REVIEW. w N 25 1894-Ap 7 1895||
Sunday ed. of Penny press, later Evening press
MnHi complete

ST. ANTHONY express. w My 31 1851-
DLC O 27 1855;Ap 14-O 6 1860
MWA D 23 1852;Ja 14,F 25 1853
MnHi 1851-[54;60-61]
MnS 1851-Ja 28 1853

ST. ANTHONY FALLS democrat. *See* Weekly democrat

SATURDAY night. *See under* St. Paul

SENTINEL. w 1891-F 18 1899||
1891-98 pub at Fergus Falls
MnHi N 10 1898-99
WHi N 10 1898-99

SKANDINAVEN. w
A Sunday ed of Skandinaven (Chicago)
In Norwegian
MnHi 1908[09]-[11-12]-[14]-[17]

SOUTH Minneapolis press. w Ap 3 1901-Jl 28 1903||
MnHi complete

SOUTH Minneapolis telegram. *See* Minneapolis telegram

SOUTH SIDE weekly. *See* Business weekly

MINNESOTA (*Continued*)

MINNEAPOLIS—*Continued*

SOUTH TOWN sentinel. *See* Business weekly

SOUTHEAST review. w
MnHi D 3-17 1921

Saturday evening SPECTATOR. w 1880-Jl 6 1895||
MWA My 14 1887
MnHi My 2 1885;Ja 21 1888-95
MnM Je 1881-Je 1883;90-[95]

SPECTATOR. w Ag 8 1883+
1883-1928 as Minneapolis chronicle; Mr 1-Ag 10 1929 North Minneapolis news
MnHi D 14 1889-[91;96]+
MnM 1888-90

Minneapolis weekly STAR. w F 8 1868-
F 8-My 30 1868 as Conwell's star of the north
MnHi F-Je 6,Ag 1-15 1868

Minneapolis STAR. d S 22-N 6 1900||
United with Saturday cynic to form Saturday cynic and weekly star
MnHi complete

Minneapolis STAR. w N 29 1906-Ja 26 1911||
MnHi complete

Minneapolis STAR. d Ag 19 1920+
1920-Je 30 1924 as Minnesota daily star
pub 1920-24
ICU D 1920-Ap 1926
M Ag 5-10 1929
MnHi 1920+
MnM 1920+
MnU Mr-D 1934

Evening STAR and news. *See* Minneapolis tribune

Daily STAR-NEWS. *See* Minneapolis tribune

STATE atlas. w 1859-67||?
Merged with Minneapolis tribune
MnHi Ja 14 1860-[61-62]-Ag 1864;Ja-My 8 1867
N Jl 31,O 16-23 1861;F 5 1862
NjR D 21 1864

SVENSKA amerikanska posten. w 1883+
1883-1903? as Wisconsin svenska tribunen; 1904?-20 Svenska amerikanska tribunen; 1921-Jl 21 1922 Svenska amerikanska tribunen-Duluth posten
1883-1919? pub at Superior, Wis.
In Swedish
IRA [1889-91]-1924;30-33
IU D 1917+
MnHi [1891-93]+
WaPS [1915]-[18]-[24]-33

SVENSKA folkets tidning. w O 5 1881-Ag 25 1927||
Merged with Svenska amerikanska posten
In Swedish
IRA 1881-1918
KHi F 7 1923
MnHi complete
NdHi Ja 24 1906-13

Minneapolis TELEGRAM. w S 13 1890-1910||
1890-N 30 1900 as South Minneapolis telegram
MnHi 1890-[1902]-[04]-Je 17 1910

Minneapolis TIDENDE. w 1880-Mr 21 1935||
1880-87 as Grand Forks tidende (Grand Forks, N.D.); 1887-88 Tidende. Merged with Decorah posten (Decorah, Iowa)
In Norwegian
IU 1917-35
IaDeL 1885;87-88;94-1935
IaDeP 1888-1935
MnHi 1895-1935
WHi O 18 1895-1935
WaPS [1915-16]-[22-23]-[25-26]-33

Minneapolis daglig TIDENDE. d Ja 24 1887-Ap 29 1932||
In Norwegian
IaDeL complete
MnHi [1908]-16
MnSL [1897]
MnU 1921-24
WHi My 18 1908

Minneapolis evening TIMES. d 1872-D 20 1873||
MnHi [1873]

Minneapolis daily TIMES. d O 1 1889-S 24 1905||
1889-N 30 1901 as Minneapolis times
CtY Ja 1 1890
DLC 1898;Ja 4 1902
KHi My 21 1899(supp);F 21 1902
MWA Ja 1 1890
MnHi complete
MnM 1890-1905
NN S 12-18 1901
WHi Mr 2 1895-96

TOWN talk. w Ag 11-N 3 1894||
MnHi complete

Minneapolis TRIBUNE. d My 25 1867+
1867-Ap 30 1876 as Minneapolis daily tribune; My 2-O 28 1876 merged with St. Paul daily pioneer press as Pioneer press and tribune; N 19 1882-Mr 21 1884 Daily Minnesota tribune; Mr 22 1884-Je 3 1886 Minneapolis daily tribune; D 13 1909-F 1 1930 Minneapolis morning tribune
pub [1897-1900]—
A N 1887;Ja-S 1888;89-Je 1892
CLM N 27 1890
CoU 1900-01;03;S 1906-My 1910
DLC Ag 9-N 24 1867;Ag 13-20 1869;O 17 1883+
IC My 1 1889
ICHi Ja-F,S 1881;82-My 1883;Ja-F 1885;O 1886-S 1887
ICM Mr 25 1882
KHi Je 6 1884;D 9 1917-My 15 1923]
MWA D 11 1869;Ag 16 1876;Ja 4 1879;O 8 1882;Ja 1 1885;Ja 1 1886;Ja 1 1887;Ja 1 1888; Ja 1 1889;Ja 3 1893
MnHi 1867+
MnM 1870+
MnU 1867;Je-D 1869;Je 1934+
NjHi My 7-9 1871
OClWHi Je 6,11 1892
OHi Ja-N 1933
PPL Ag 24 1883
VU F 14 1909
WHi N 7 1867;Je 3 1883-Ag 20 1884

Minneapolis weekly TRIBUNE. w 1867-76||
CoBoC Ja 1,Ap 19-26,Je 19 1874
MWA N 18 1869
MnHi Ja 27,F 17,Mr 17 1870
N O 1867-Ja 1868
WHi S 24,O 1 1874

Minneapolis TRIBUNE. (evening ed) Jl 1887+
1887-Ja 31 1888 as Daily star-news; F-Ap 6 1888 Evening star and news; Ap 7? 1888-Ag 24 1889 Evening star; Ag 26 1889-Ap 5 1890 Minneapolis tribune-star; Ap 7 1890-1923? Minneapolis evening tribune
MnHi O 18 1887[88]-1907;Je 28-O 4 1923
MnM Ap 1894-[98]-Mr 1900

Minneapolis TRIBUNE-STAR. *See* Minneapolis tribune

TRUTH. *See under* St. Paul

TWIN City American. w My 4-18 1899||
Followed by Afro-American advance
MnHi complete

TWIN CITY guardian. *See under* St. Paul

TWIN CITY herald. w
MnHi Ap 2 1932+

TWIN City reporter. ir 1913-29||?
KHi My 10 1918
MnHi Ja 8 1915-N 25 1927

TWIN CITY star. w Je 2 1910-Ja 25 1919||
Suspended N 27 1915-Ja 1 1916
MnHi complete

UGEBLADET. *See* Det Danske ugeblad (Tyler)

VÅRT hem. *See under* St. Paul

Les VEILLÉES Canadiennes. m D 1889-
In French
MnHi D 1889;Ja 1890

VESTERN-Amerikanen. *See* Western American

VOIX du lac. w Mr 9 1892-93||?
Dated also at Duluth and West Superior
In French
MnHi 1892-S 6 1893

La VOIX du peuple. 1900-Je 1904||
United with Canadien (St. Paul) and Le courier de l'Ouest (Chicago) to form Courier franco-americain (Chicago)
In French

WEST end life. w My 27 1891-
MnHi My 27-Je 24 1891

WESTERN American. sm,w 1904-15||?
1904-Ag 15 1912 as Odalmannen; S 1 1912-My 7 1914 Vestern-Amerikanen
sm 1904-S 1912
1904-My 7 1914 in Swedish
MnHi 1912-Je 18 1914

MINNEOTA

Minneota MASCOT. w 1891+
pub 1891+
MnHi Ap 30 1897+

MONTEVIDEO

Montevideo ADVANCE. w 1896-1916||?
MnHi 1898-[99-1900]

Montevideo AMERICAN. d,tw,sw,w S 1911+
d 1911-Je 30 1924;tw Jl 1924-O 29 1925;sw N 1925-Mr 30 1926
pub 1924+
MnHi [1917]+

CHIPPEWA county commercial. *See* Commercial

COMMERCIAL. w Je 12 1883-S 21 1917||
1886-N 11 1887 as Chippewa county commercial
MnHi complete

Weekly ITEMIZER. w 1881-83||
MnHi S 28 1882-Ap 26 1883

Montevideo LEADER. *See* Montevideo news

Montevideo NEWS. w 1877+
1877-S 27 1911 as Montevideo leader
pub [1890-1917]-23;25+
MnHi Ja 19 1883+

MONTGOMERY

ČECHO-Amerikan. w Ap 29 1887-
In Czechoslovakian
MnHi Ap 29 1887

Montgomery MESSENGER. w 1888+
Ag 28 1903-My 6 1904 as Messenger
pub [1888]93+
MnHi My 1891-N 1895;1902+

Montgomery STAR. w Jl 17 1886-Ap 29 1887||
Follows Montgomery sun
MnHi complete

Montgomery SUN. w My 13-Jl 15 1886||
Followed by Montgomery star
MnHi complete

MONTICELLO

COURIER. w Ap 25 1863-
MnHi My 2-Jl 25 1863

Monticello NEWS. *See* Monticello times (1912+)

NORTH western-weekly union. w N 30 1861-
Follows Wright county republican
MnHi [1861-63]

NORTHERN statesman. w Ag 27 1863-71||
MnHi [Ap 9-D 1864;66-71]

Monticello TIMES. w My 21 1857-Ap 6 1859||
MnHi [1857-59]

Monticello TIMES. w Je 3 1871-My 30 1918||
1871-My 31 1906 as Wright county times
MnHi 1871-S 13 1882;F 28-S 19 1889;Ap 24,Je 19,O 2,N 13 1890-1918

Monticello TIMES. w O 9 1912+
1912-O 16 1919 as Monticello news
MnHi 1912+

WRIGHT county republican. w Je 30 1859-N 23 1861||
Followed by North western-weekly union
MnHi [1859-61]
N O 12 1861

WRIGHT county times. *See* Monticello times (1871-1918)

MOORHEAD

Moorhead ADVOCATE. *See* Moorhead weekly news

Daily ARGONAUT. d D 4? 1881-Mr 4 1882||
Followed by Moorhead daily news
MnHi D 23 1881-[82]

Moorhead ARGONAUT. w *See* Moorhead weekly news

Daily ARGUS. *See under* Fargo, N.D.

Moorhead CITIZEN. w 1902-17||
MnHi Ap 21 1909-Ja 31 1917

CLAY county advocate. *See* Moorhead weekly news

CLAY county leader. w 1890-Jl 18 1919||
United with Moorhead independent and Barnesville headlight (Barnesville) to form Country press
MnHi O 12 1917-19

COUNTRY press. w 1890+
1890-Jl 18 1919 as Moorhead independent
pub 1928+
MnHi Ap 17 1896-Jl 11 1913

Moorhead DISTRICT herald. w Je 27 1923+
MnHi [1923]

Moorhead ENTERPRISE. d C 3?-D 30 1882||
MnHi O 6 1882

FOLKETS ven. *See under* Fargo, N.D.

Moorhead INDEPENDENT. *See* Country press

Moorhead daily NEWS. d Mr 6 1882+
Follows Daily argonaut
pub [1883]+
MnHi [1882-F 23 1883;Mr 1885-87]-Ap 1906+

Moorhead weekly NEWS. w Jl 6 1872-1930||
1872-Mr 1877 as Red River star; Ap 1877-My 1878 Moorhead advocate; Je 1878-80 Clay county advocate; 1881 Moorhead argonaut
pub 1883-1930
MnHi 1872-Mr 3 1881;92;[93]-Ap 11 1895;Ap 21 1909-Ja 31,S 6 1917-Mr 29 1923
NdHi Ag 3 1872;Je,Jl 5,Ag 9,O 11 1873;Ap 5 1879

NYE normanden. *See* Ny tid (Minneapolis)

RED RIVER star. *See* Moorhead weekly news

MOOSE LAKE

STAR-GAZETTE. w 1896+
1896-Ja 3 1907 as Moose Lake star
MnHi Ap 29 1897+

MORA

KANABEC county forum. w 1920-23||
MnHi Mr 31 1921-O 18 1923

KANABEC county progressive. w My 3 1934+
Follows McGregor pilot review (McGregor)
MnHi 1934+

KANABEC county times. w O 6 1884+
Follows Mora times
pub [1884+]
MnHi 1884-[97-98]+

Mora NEWS. Ag 4 1883-
MnHi Ag 4,25 1883

Mora TIMES. w O 8 1882-84||?
Followed by Kanabec county times
MnHi Ap 16 1883

MORGAN

Morgan MESSENGER. w 1890+
pub [1890-91;97-98]1902+
MnHi My 2 1891-Ap 27 1899;O 23 1902+

MORRIS

Morris JOURNAL. w Ag 12 1882-Ja 6 1883||
MnHi [1882]
MnMoHi complete

REPUBLICAN times. *See* Morris times

Morris SUN. w 1883+
1883-Ja 31 1895 as Sun
MnHi S 13 1884[89-90]+
MnMoC [1886]
MnMoHi 1883

Morris TIMES. w F 17 1898-1906||
F 17-S 7 1898 as Chokio times (Chokio); S 14 1898-Je 6 1900 Republican times
MnHi 1898-[1906]

MINNESOTA (*Continued*)

MORRIS—*Continued*

Morris TRIBUNE. w Je 1876+
pub [1883+]
MnHi [Mr 9 1887-88;91]+
MnMoC [1881-91]
MnMoHi 1876+

MORRISTOWN

NEW ERA. *See* Morristown press

Morristown PRESS. w Jl 5 1892+
1892-Ag 3 1893 as New era; Ag 10-N 2 1893 Morristown press and new era
pub 1900+
MnFaC 1928;34
MnHi F 16 1893-1904

Morristown PRESS and new era. *See* Morristown press

MORTON

Morton ENTERPRISE. w 1886+
pub [1887+]
MnHi [Ap 17 1891-92]Je 4 1897+

MOTLEY

CASS county pioneer. *See under* Walker

Motley CITIZEN. w Ag 9 1901-02||
MnHi 1901-Ag 29 1902

Motley MERCURY. w 1901+
MnHi Mr 3 1911+

MORRISON county democrat. w 1887-91||
1887-O 1891 as Motley register
MnHi Ap 28 1888-[91]

Motley REGISTER. *See* Morrison county democrat

MOUND

MINNETONKA pilot. w Je 22 1922+
pub 1930+
MnHi [1922]+

MOUNTAIN IRON

Mountain Iron REPORTER. w My 23 1918-Ja 5 1922||
MnHi D 30 1920-[21]
MnMt complete

MOUNTAIN LAKE

Mountain Lake OBSERVER. w Ag 13 1925+
pub 1925+
MnHi 1925+

Mountain Lake VIEW. w 1896-1931||
Merged with Mountain Lake observer
pub [1896-1931]

MURDOCK

Murdock LEADER. w 1900+
pub 1924+
MnHi 1916+

Murdock REVIEW. *See* Swift county news (Benson)

Murdock VOICE. w Ag 30 1900-15||
MnHi [S 13 1900-01]-15

NASHWAUK

EASTERN Itascan. w 1909+
1909-26 as Nashwauk herald
pub 1913+
MnHi O 16 1915-F 12 1916

Nashwauk HERALD. *See* Eastern Itascan

NERSTRAND

Nerstrand HERALD. w 1911-27||
MnHi Mr 12 1915-Ag 19 1927

NEW BRIGHTON

New Brighton JOURNAL. d Je 6 1894-
MnHi [1894]

TWIN CITY live stock reporter. *See under* St. Paul

NEW LONDON

New London TIMES. w 1886+
MnHi Ap 23 1903+

NEW PRAGUE

New Prague TIMES. w S 6 1889+
pub [1889+]
MnHi 1889-Je 1892;Mr 30 1893;My 14-21 1896; Ap 15 1897-98;Je 21 1917+

NEW RICHLAND

NORTH star. *See* New Richland star

New Richland REVIEW. w S 24 1884-85||
MnHi 1884-[85]

New Richland STAR. w 1885+
1885-Ap 5 1906 as North star
MnHi [Mr 1887-88;90]+

NEW ULM

BROWN county journal w 1898+
MnHi O 18 1902-30

DAKOTA freie presse. *See under* Bismark, N.D.

Der FORTSCHRITT. w Mr 26 1891-D 25 1915||
Merged with New Ulm post
In German
MnHi complete

FREIDENKER. w,sw Ap 1 1872+
1872-Mr 1874 as Milwaukee freidenker 1872-My 7 1916 pub in Milwaukee, Wis; My 14 1916-S 8 1918 in Minneapolis
IU O 19 1884
TxU Jl 14 1878-80;Jl-D 18 1881;O 1882-84
WHi 1872-1909;14+
WM 1879-84;88;90-1916
WaSp 1907-08

New Ulm HERALD. w Ja 31 1873-78||
Follows New Ulm plaindealer
MnHi 1873-[78]
MnU My 3 1878

New Ulm NEWS. w 1892-1910||?
MnHi My 13 1893[97]-98

New Ulm PIONIER. *See* New Ulm post

New Ulm PLAINDEALER. w O 29 1870-D 6 1872||
Followed by New Ulm herald
MnHi complete

New Ulm POST. w Ja 1 1858-My 12 1933||
1858-Ag 16 1862 as New Ulm pionier
In German
MWA F 23 1866
MnHi 1860-F 16 1861;F 1864-1933
MnNuH 1858-62
MoKR 1858-62

New Ulm REVIEW. w 1878+
pub 1878+
MnHi Ag 24 1887;Je 18 1890-Ag 9 1893;Je 5,Jl 10 1895;Ap 14 1897-F 1 1899;N 19 1913-[18]+

New Ulm VOLKSBLATT. w 1892-1921||
N 7 1919-O 28 1921 dated also at Winona
In German
MnHi S 11 1902-O 28 1921

NEW YORK MILLS

New York Mills HERALD. w 1916+
pub 1917+

New York Mills JOURNAL. w 1901-06||
MnHi Ag 6 1902-[06]

MINNESOTAN uutiset. sw S 24 1932+
In Finnish
pub 1932+

UUSI kotimaa. *See under* Superior, Wis.

NEWPORT

COMMUNITY life. sm O 17 1929-31||
MnHi 1929-[31]

NICOLLET

Nicollet LEADER. w My 16 1896+
pub [1896]+

NININGER

EMIGRANT aid journal. w
WHi Mr 10 1858

NORTH BRANCH

North Branch REVIEW. w 1889+
pub [1889+]

NORTH MANKATO

North Mankato REVIEW. w S 8 1921+
pub 1921+
MnHi 1921-My 31 1923

NORTH ST. PAUL

North St. Paul COURIER. w Ap 14 1920+
pub 1920+
MnHi 1920+

SENTINEL. w Ag 27 1887-1919||
MnHi D 17 1887[88]Ap 17 1891-Ap 26 1919

NORTHFIELD

DUNDAS news. *See* Northfield news

Northfield ENTERPRISE. w D 20 1866-Je 30 1870||
1866-S 18 1868 Northfield recorder
MnHi S 13 1867-70

Northfield INDEPENDENT. w D 15 1887+
pub [1890-93]1904;06;08+
MnFaC 1915-16
MnHi D 15 1887[88]+

Northfield NEWS. w N 4 1876+
1876-N 1 1879 as Dundas news
pub [1884]+
MnFaC 1914;17-18;20-21;34
MnHi Mr 5-26 1887;S 15 1888+
MnN 1891+
MnNC 1908+
MnNS 1908+
WHi Ja 1 1926

NORWEGIAN American. *See* United American

Northfield RECORDER. *See* Northfield enterprise

RICE county journal. w 1872-84||
Merged with Northfield news
MWA Ja 2 1879
MnN 1872-82

Northfield STANDARD. w Ja 6 1870-75||
MnHi complete

Northfield TELEGRAPH. w Mr 13 1861-Mr 19 1862||
MWA Ap 3 1861
MnHi complete
N O 10 1861

UNITED American w S 4 1908-23||
1908-Mr 29 1918 as Norwegian American
In Norwegian and English
IU N 1912-Mr 5 1920
MnHi 1908-Jl 13 1923

NORTHOME

Northome NEWS. w 1901-05||
1901-Je 26 1903 as Bridgie news (Phena Postoffice)
MnHi D 5 1902-[05]

Northome RECORD. w 1902+
Title varies slightly
KHi Mr 9,23 1923
MnHi Ag 13 1915+

NORWOOD

Norwood TIMES. w My 15 1889+
pub 1890+
KHi F 9 1923
MnHi Ag 7 1890;91-94[97]+

OAK PARK

Oak Park LEADER. w Mr 30-O 29 1926||
Mr-Ap 20 as Oak Park what. Merged with Foley independent (Foley)
MnHi complete

Oak Park WHAT. *See* Oak Park leader

ODIN

Odin weekly RECORD. w 1921-26||
MnHi 1924-Ag 13 1926

OGEMA

Ogema NEWS. w Ap 29 1920-22||
MnHi 1920-22

OGILVIE

Ogilvie SENTINEL. w 1904+
pub [1904-22]
KHi Mr 9 1923
MnHi Ag 13 1915+

OKABENA

Okabena PRESS. w 1920+
MnHi O 1925+

OKLEE

Oklee HERALD. w My 14 1914+
pub 1914+
MnHi [1914]+

OLBERG

Olberg JOURNAL. *See* Clearbrook journal (Clearbrook)

OLIVIA

MINNESOTA leader. *See under* Minneapolis

PEOPLE'S voice. m N 1919-
MnHi [1919-20]

Olivia PRESS. w 1895-Jl 17 1901||
Merged with Olivia times
MnHi Ap 14 1897-[1901]

RENVILLE county journal. w 1899+
1899-Jl 12 1918 as Sacred Heart journal 1899-Ag 29 1919 pub in Sacred Heart
pub [1921]+
KHi Ap 19,My 3 1923
MnHi F 21 1913+

RENVILLE county republic. w My 26 1926-27||
MnHi [1926-27]

RENVILLE times. *See* Olivia times

Olivia TIMES. w 1872+
1872-90? as Beaver Falls times (Beaver Falls); 1891-My 31 1900 Renville times
pub [1902]+
MnHi F 15 1877+

ONAMIA

Onamia HERALD. w Ja 3 1924-O 18 1928||
United with Isle advance to form Mille Lacs messenger (Isle)
MnHi 1924-[28]

MILLE LACS lake breeze. *See* Onamia teamwork

MINNESOTA (*Continued*)

ONAMIA—*Continued*

Onamia TEAMWORK. w 1908+
1908-Je 23 1921 as Mille Lacs lake breeze
MnHi Ag 1920-30

Onamia TRIBUNE. w D 12 1928-
MnHi Ja-Ag 8 1929

ORMSBY

Ormsby REVIEW. w My 16 1924-25||
MnHi 1924-Ja 30 1925

ORTONVILLE

BIG STONE county herald. *See* Herald-star

BIG STONE county journal. *See* Ortonville journal

Ortonville HEADLIGHT. w 1884-98||?
Also dated at Big Stone, S.D.
MnHi [Mr 1887-88]

HERALD-STAR. w 1879-1912||
1879-87 as Big Stone county herald
MnHi O 12 1882-1912

Ortonville INDEPENDENT. w My 13 1920+
pub 1920+
MnHi 1920+

Ortonville JOURNAL. w Je 24 1892-S 29 1927||
1892-1912 as Big Stone county journal; S 23 1926-Ja 6 1927 Journal-star. United with Ortonville star to form Ortonville journal-star
MnHi complete

Ortonville JOURNAL-STAR. w 1919-30||
1919-S 29 1927 as Ortonville star (S 23 1926-Ja 6 1927 Journal-star)
MnHi D 22 1921-Ap 17 1930

Ortonville NORTH STAR. w Je 1878-D 14 1887||
United with Big Stone county herald to form Ortonville herald-star
MnHi S 25 1882-F 20 1883;Ag 24 1886-87

PEOPLE'S vindicator. w S 18 1884-
MnHi O 23 1884

Ortonville STAR. *See* Ortonville journal-star

OSAGE

BECKER county blade. w Mr 13 1890-91||
MnHi [1890-91]

OSAKIS

LAKE review. *See* Osakis review

Osakis OBSERVER. w Je 30 1881-
MnHi O 27-N 10 1881

Osakis REVIEW. w 1890+
1890-Ag 22 1901? as Lake review
pub 1896+
MnHi Ap 10 1891-[92]+

OSLO

Oslo TRIBUNE. *See* Middle River record (Middle River)

OSSEO

HENNEPIN county herald. *See under* Wayzata

HENNEPIN county review. *See under* Hopkins

Osseo PRESS. w N 29 1923+
MnHi 1923+

OTTER TAIL CITY

Otter Tail City RECORD. w S 2 1871-72||
MnHi S 30 1871-My 11 1872

OWATONNA

Owatonna CHRONICLE. w 1896-Mr 9 1906||
United with Owatonna journal to form Owatonna journal-chronicle
MnHi Jl 19 1901-06

Owatonna JOURNAL-CHRONICLE. w 1863+
1863-Mr 9 1906 as Owatonna journal
DLC Ja-N 1872
MWA Ja 2 1868;F 29 1872;O 18 1889
MnHi Ja 9-Ap 1868;D 8 1870-O 14 1875;77+
WHi S 10 1874;Ap 1,My 20,Jl 1 1875;Ja-Je 8 1917;N 11 1918

PEOPLE'S press. w 1874-S 23 1921||
pub complete
MWA N 25 1876;D 6 1878;F 28,Ag 15 1879
MnHi Ag 17 1888-1921

Daily PEOPLE'S press. d 1915+
pub 1915+
MnHi S 27 1921+

Owatonna PLAINDEALER. w Ap 30 1863-Jl 19 1866||?
MWA Ja 4 1866
MnHi O 1 1863-[65]-Jl 19 1866

Owatonna REGISTER. w Je 26 1867-
MnHi O 23 1867-F 19 1868

REPRESENTATIVE. w D 11 1860-
MnHi Ja 9-Mr 13 1861

Owatonna REVIEW. w 1875-79||
MnHi Ag 17 1877-Ap 11 1879

STEELE county citizen. w 1907-16||
1907-Ja 28 1916 as Owatonna tribune
MnHi Ag 13 1915-[16]

STEELE county democrat. w F 19 1889-90||
MnHi Mr 7 1889-[90]

STEELE county news-letter. w
WHi O 16 1860

Owatonna TRIBUNE. *See* Steele county citizen

Owatonna UNION express. w D 10 1861-
N D 31 1861

Owatonna WATCHMAN and register. w Jl 22 1856-
CaOTA Jl 22 1856

PALISADE

Palisade AMERICAN. w Ag 30 1924-Mr 31 1933||
MnHi complete

PARK RAPIDS

Park Rapids ENTERPRISE. w Jl 25 1882+
Jl 13 1883-My 7 1908 as Hubbard county enterprise; My 14 1908-Jl 3 1919 Enterprise
pub 1882+
MnHi 1882[83-84]+

HUBBARD county clipper. *See* Hubbard county journal

HUBBARD county enterprise. *See* Park Rapids enterprise

HUBBARD county journal. w Je 11 1896+
1896-Ap 23 1914 as Hubbard county clipper
pub [1896+]
MnHi [1897-98;03]-[16]

PARKERS PRAIRIE

INDEPENDENT. w 1902+
pub 1902-[06-07]+
MnHi Jl 1 1920[22]+

PAYNESVILLE

Paynesville LEADER. w Ap 23 1908-F 24 1910||
Merged with Paynesville press to form Paynesville leader-press, later Paynesville press
MnHi My 28 1908-[10]

Paynesville LEADER-PRESS. *See* Paynesville press

Paynesville PRESS. w 1887+
1887-F 24 1910 as Paynesville press (title varies) Mr 3 1910-Ap 25 1912 Paynesville leader-press
MnHi O 2 1890+

PELAN

Pelan ADVOCATE. w N 19 1902-Jl 13 1905||
1902-My 21 1903 as Pelan post
Followed by Karlstad advocate (Karlstad)
MnHi F 12 1903-1905

Pelan POST. *See* Pelan advocate

PELICAN RAPIDS

Pelican Rapids BLADE. w D 4 1891-92||
MnHi 1891-Ag 17 1892

PARK region pioneer. w Je 1 1882-95||
1882-D 18 1885 as Pelican Rapids times
Suspended from My 28 1891-S 29 1894
MnHi S 28 1882-[95]

Pelican Rapids PRESS. w 1897+
pub 1897-[1907+]
MnHi 1935+

Pelican Rapids SENTINEL. *See* Fergus Falls forum (Fergus Falls)

Pelican Rapids TIMES. *See* Park region pioneer

PERHAM

Perham BULLETIN. *See* Perham enterprise-bulletin

Perham ENTERPRISE. w 1899-Je 19 1913||
United with Perham bulletin to form Perham enterprise-bulletin
MnHi D 12 1907-13

Perham ENTERPRISE-BULLETIN. w 1882+
1882-Je 12 1913 as Perham bulletin
MnHi Je 14 1888;O 9 1890+

Perham JOURNAL. w 1881-83||
MnHi O 26 1882-Ja 4 1883

Perham NEWS. w Jl 30 1875-76||
MnHi F 5 1875-Je 16 1876

PHENA POSTOFFICE

BRIDGIE news. *See* Northome news (Northome)

PIERZ

Pierz JOURNAL. w 1909+
pub 1909+
MnHi O 23 1924+

PILLAGER

Pillager HERALD. w 1908+
MnHi Mr 11 1921+

Pillager LEADER. w 1903-07||
MnHi My 1905-[07]

Pillager POST. w Ag 17 1900-O 9 1903||
United with Backus news to form Backus news and Pillager post, later Backus news (Backus)
MnHi O 12 1900-03

PINE CITY

PINE county news. w My 3 1873-77||
Suspended D 19 1875-Mr 21 1876
MnHi My 3 1873,F 21,My 2,Jl 11,Ag 1,S 26-D 19 1874,Mr 28 1876-Jl 10 1877

PINE county pioneer. w D 12 1885+
pub [1885+]
MnHi F 22 1889[91]+

PINE county record. w D 26 1878-85||
Suspended from Ja 19-S 20 1884
MnHi F 12 1879-[80]-F 16,S 20 1884-Mr 21 1885

PINE county record. w S 22 1898-Ja 5 1899||
Merged with Pine poker
MnHi complete

PINE poker. w S 23 1897+
pub 1915+
MnHi 1897-1905

PINE ISLAND

Pine Island JOURNAL. w 1882-My 8 1891||
Merged with Red Wing journal, later Red Wing times (Red Wing)
MnHi [1882]-[85;90-91]

Pine Island RECORD. w Jl 8 1891+
pub 1891+
MnHi D 25 1891+

PINE RIVER

PINE tree blaze. *See* Pine River sentinel-blaze

Pine River SENTINEL and the Backus weekly news. w 1904-Jl 18 1913||
United with Pine tree blaze to form Pine River sentinel-blaze
MnHi [1904]-05

Pine River SENTINEL-BLAZE. w Je 21 1901+
1901-Jl 18 1913 as Pine tree blaze
MnHi 1901+

PIPESTONE

FARMERS' leader. *See* Pipestone leader

Pipestone LEADER. w 1889+
1889-D 31 1914 as Farmers' leader
pub 1889+
MnHi Ap 15 1897+

PIPESTONE county star. w,sw Je 19 1879+
w 1879-1907
pub 1879+
MnHi Je 19 1879,O 17 1890+
MnPHi 1879+

Pipestone REVIEW. m Mr 1887-
MnHi Mr 1887

Daily STAR. d Ap 4? 1892-My 29 1899||
MnHi [1892-99]

WEEK'S review. w Jl 4 1902-05||
MnHi [1902]-[05]

PLAINVIEW

Plainview ENTERPRISE. w 1864-
MnPlN Ap 22 1864

Plainview NEWS. w 1877+
Ap 1 1899-N 20 1903 as Plainview news-gleaner
MnHi O 18 1879+

PLUMMER

Plummer PIONEER. w 1904-30||?
MnHi D 14 1907-[13]

PLYMOUTH

WAYNE county review. *See under* Wayne

PRESTON

Preston COURIER. w 1893-F 8 1900||
MnHi Ap 22 1897-1900

Preston DEMOCRAT. *See* Preston times

FILLMORE county republican. *See* Preston republican

MOWER and Fillmore counties republican. *See* Preston republican

NATIONAL republican. *See* Preston republican

Preston REPUBLICAN. w N 2 1861+
Follows Chatfield republican (Chatfield). 1861-65 as Republican; 1866-70? Preston republican; 1871?-S 17 1875 Fillmore county republican; S 23 1875-O 16 1879 Mower and Fillmore counties republican; O 23 1879-D 28 1900? National republican
S 23 1875-O 16 1879 pub in Austin
pub 1881+
MnHi 1861-[63-64]-Je 1865;Ja 5-19,Ap 20,Jl 20,D 28 1866-Ap 1887;F 21-28 1889;Jl 24 1890;Mr 19-Jl 2 1891;Ja 13-27 1899;1900;D 1903+
NbHi D 23 1875

Preston REPUBLICAN. 1875-84 *See* Preston times

MINNESOTA (*Continued*)

PRESTON—*Continued*

Preston TIMES. w O 28 1875+
1875-F 21 1884 as Preston republican; Mr 6 1884-Je 24 1886 Preston democrat
pub 1890+
MnHi [1875-Je 1886;Ag 22 1889-91]+

PRINCETON

Princeton APPEAL. w Ja 1875-Ap 27 1877||
MnHi Jl 1 1874;Ja 13-20,My 13 1875-77

Princeton NEWS. w F 1903-Jl 20 1917||
Merged with Princeton union
MnHi complete

Princeton UNION. w D 1876+
pub 1876+
MnHi Je 1877-[81-82]Mr 17-24 1887[90]+

PROCTOR

Proctor JOURNAL. w Je 23 1906+
pub 1906+
MnHi N 29 1929+

RAYMOND

Raymond NEWS. w N 23 1900+
pub [1900+]
MnHi S 20 1929+

READ'S LANDING

Read's Landing PRESS. w 1876-Mr 29 1878||
MnHi My 11 1877-78

WABASHA county herald. *See under* Wabasha

RED LAKE

Red Lake NEWS. m,sm 1912-20||?
Chippewa Indian
MnHi Jl 1917-Mr 20 1920

RED LAKE FALLS

Red Lake COURIER. w 1898-Jl 4 1907||
1898-O 29 1903 as Red Lake county courier. Merged with Red Lake Falls gazette
MnHi N 7 1901-07

Red Lake Falls ERA. *See* Red Lake Falls weekly messenger

Red Lake Falls GAZETTE. w 1883+
pub [1916]+
MnHi Ag 26 1887[91-92;97]+

Red Lake Falls weekly MESSENGER. w Je 29 1882-85||
1882-F 21 1883 as Red Lake Falls era
MnHi [1882]-[85]

Red Lake Falls NEWS. *See* Thief River Falls news (Thief River Falls)

RED LAKE county courier. *See* Red Lake courier

RED WING

ADVANCE. w O 1873-N 19 1884||
1873-Ag 1 1877 as Grange advance. United with Republican to form Advance-republican, later Red Wing republican
1873-75? dated also at St. Paul
ICM My 21 1885
MnHi My 20 1874-84
MnRe [1873]-84

ADVANCE-REPUBLICAN. *See* Red Wing republican

ADVANCE SUN. *See* Red Wing republican

Red Wing ARGUS. w 1864-My 11 1900||
Merged with Goodhue county news, later Red Wing free press
MnHi 1868-1900
MnRe [1869]-[97]

Red Wing daily EAGLE. d 1911+
pub 1911+
MnHi Mr 31 1923+
MnRe 1924+

Red Wing FREE PRESS. w 1899-1913||
1899-S 18 1909 as Goodhue county news
1899-Mr 15 1900 pub at Cannon Falls
MnHi F 15 1900;01-13

GOODHUE county news. *See* Red Wing free press

GOODHUE county republican. *See* Red Wing republican

GOODHUE volunteer. w Ag 1 1857-
1857-Ap 24 1861 as Red Wing sentinel
MnHi [D 25 1858-Ap 24 1861]F 19 1862-[63]-Ag 31 1864

GRANGE advance. *See* Advance

Daily INDEPENDENT. d N 30 1891-92||
MnHi 1891-Mr 10 1892

Red Wing JOURNAL. *See* Red Wing times

MINNESOTA gazette. w
WHi F 27 1857

MINNESOTA posten. w 1857-58||
Merged with Det gamla och det nya hemlandet (Chicago, Ill.)
In Swedish
IRA 1857-58

NORDSTJERNEN. w 1895-98||
In Norwegian
IaDeL Ag 23 1895-S 24 1897;F 11 1898
MnHi Ja 4 1895-N 18 1898

NORTH star. w D 10 1871-
MWA My 21-O 22,N 12-D 3 1872

ORGANIZED farmer. w Je 12 1919-My 6 1932||
MnHi complete

Red Wing REPUBLICAN. w,sw S 4 1857+
Ag 12 1859-Jl 29 1880 as Goodhue county republican; Ag 7 1880-N 22 1884 Republican; N 26 1884-O 14 1885 Advance-republican; O 21 1885-Ja 2 1895 Advance sun
sw Jl 22 1893-Ap 11 1894
IRA N 17 1897;Ap 19 1899;Ja 24 1900
MWA Je 26 1863;Ja 26 1866
MnHi 1857-O 22 1858[F 1860-61]-[S-D 1864]67-[70]-[72]+
MnRe 1884-Jl 1885
N O 18 1861

Red Wing daily REPUBLICAN. d O 12 1885+
MnHi [F 6-S 30 1886]Ag 4,N 23,25,28 1887;Mr 15 1888+
MnRe 1885-O 10 1896;O 12 1903-O 12 1906;24+

Red Wing SENTINEL. *See* Goodhue volunteer

SUN. w Ja 17 1884-O 14 1885||
United with Advance-republican to form Advance sun, later Red Wing republican
ICM My 15 1884
MnHi complete

SVENSKA Minnesota bladet. w Ja 16 1869-
In Swedish
MnHi Ja 16-Jl 24 1869

Red Wing TIMES. w 1883-D 17 1897||
1883-My 8 1897 as Red Wing journal. Merged with Red Wing argus
MnHi My 14 1890-1897

REDWOOD FALLS

Redwood GAZETTE. w S 17 1869+
1869-Ap 25 1873 as Redwood Falls mail
pub [1875+]
MnHi 1869-[73-74]-Ja 19 1882;Ja 23 1890+

Redwood Falls MAIL. *See* Redwood gazette

REDWOOD county sun. w 1886+
1886-Je 21 1910 as Redwood reveille; Je 28 1910-O 26 1928 Redwood Falls sun
pub 1925+
MnHi Ja 14 1887[88]Mr 16,Ag 10,31,S 14 1889-D 12 1896;Jl 26 1899+

Redwood REVEILLE. *See* Redwood county sun

Redwood Falls SUN. *See* Redwood county sun

REMER

Remer RECORD. w 1911+
MnHi Je 1923+

RENVILLE

Renville weekly NEWS. w N 4 1887-89||
MnHi D 2,23 1887;My 16,S 26 1888;Je 14,O 4 1889

Renville RECORD. w 1896-1904||
1896-N 1 1899 as People's watchman (Sacred Heart)
MnHi Ap 14 1897-S 21 1904

RENVILLE county independent. w Mr 30 1916-17||
MnHi Jl 20 1916-[17]

STAR farmer. w 1888+
pub [1890+]
MnHi F 17 1893+

REVERE

Revere RECORD. w 1901-Ag 5 1915||
MnHi N 26 1903-15

RICE

BENTON county review. w O 9 1908-11||
MnHi O 23 1908-[11]

ROBBINSDALE

HENNEPIN county enterprise. w 1912+
1912-D 13 1928 pub in Hopkins
MnHi My 26 1927+

NORTHERN headlight. sw 1921+
MnHi F 15 1922+

Robbinsdale park PROGRESS. w D 1903-05||
MnHi My 26 1904-[05]

Robbinsdale TELLIT. w Jl 3 1908-D 31 1920||
MnHi complete

ROCHESTER

Rochester daily BULLETIN. *See* Rochester post-bulletin

CENTRAL record. *See* Record and union

Rochester DEMOCRAT. *See* Democrat (Winona) 1857-60

FEDERAL union. w 1866-D 26 1873?||
United with Minnesota record to form Record and union
MnHi 1868-73

Rochester FREE PRESS. w F 3 1858-
MnHi Mr 17 1858-Ag 20 1859

Rochester HEROLD. w 1880-Je 8 1894||
In German
MnHi S 26 1890-[94]

Rochester daily LEADER. *See* Rochester daily post and record

MINNESOTA record. *See* Record and union

NORDISK folkeblad. *See under* Minneapolis

OLMSTED county democrat. w 1886-1916||
MnHi O 23 1890-95[97]-[1916]

POST and record. w N 5 1859-S 29 1916||
1859-65? as Rochester City post; 1866?-Ja 27 1899 Rochester post
MnHi N 12 1859-Ag 2 1862;Ap 18 1863-S 3 1864 [66-67]-1916
MnRP [1899]-[1906]-16
N O 12 1861

Rochester daily POST and record. d F 1 1892-Mr 28 1925||
1892-S 2 1893 as Rochester daily leader; S 3? 1893-Ja 28 1899 Rochester daily post; Ja 29? 1899-S 29 1917 Daily post and record. Merged with Rochester daily bulletin to form Rochester post-bulletin
MnHi complete
MnRP 1899-1925

Rochester POST-BULLETIN. d 1891+
1891-Mr 28 1925 as Rochester daily bulletin
pub 1891+
MnHi [1923-25]+

RECORD and union. w F 4 1871-Ja 27 1899||
1871 as Central record; 1872-Mr 7 1874 Minnesota record. United with Rochester post to form Post and record
MnHi 1871-76;80-[99]
MnRP [1871]-[74]-[76-77]-[98]

Daily RECORD and union. d 1893-94||
MnRP 1893-[94]

Rochester REPUBLICAN. w 1863-
MWA Je 1 1864;F 15 1866
MnHi [Mr-Ag 24 1864]Mr 22,Ap 26,Jl 5,N 29 1866
MnRP [1862]-64
N O 9 1861

Die WACHT. w 1893-94||
In German
MnHi My 10 1893-Ap 25 1894

ROOSEVELT

Roosevelt REPORTER. w 1914-Mr 3 1932||
United with Roseau county leader to form Roseau county leader and Roosevelt reporter, later Northern Minnesota leader and Roosevelt reporter (Roseau)
MnHi Mr 23 1921-[30]-32

ROSEAU

NORTHERN Minnesota leader and Roosevelt reporter. w Ja 20 1932+
Ja-Mr 2 1932 as Roseau county leader; Mr 9-D 1 1932 Roseau county leader and Roosevelt reporter
MnHi 1932+

Roseau PLAINDEALER. *See* Warroad plaindealer (Warroad)

Roseau REGION. *See* Roseau times-region

ROSEAU county leader. *See* Northern Minnesota leader and Roosevelt reporter

ROSEAU county times. w Jl 26 1895-Je 29 1917||
United with Roseau region to form Roseau times-region
pub complete
MnHi 1895-Jl 10 1896;F 19 1897-1917

Roseau TIMES-REGION. w 1892+
1892-Je 1917 as Roseau region
pub 1917+
MnHi D 6 1895[96-98]1917+

ROSEMOUNT

Rosemount RECORD. w S 2 1921-
MnHi 1921-Ja 27 1922

ROTHSAY

Rothsay ENTERPRISE. w Ap 4 1903+
MnHi 1903+

Rothsay RECORD. *See* Record (Breckenridge)

ROUND LAKE

Round Lake GRAPHIC. w 1898+
pub 1898-[1902-13]+
MnHi [1930]+

ROYALTON

Royalton BANNER. w Ja 21 1886+
pub [1912+]
MnHi [1887]-Ja 2 1889;F 11 1891+

Royalton RECORD. w 1884-85||
MnHi [Jl 17-D 2 1885]

RUSH CITY

CHISAGO county post. *See* Rush City post

Rush City POST. w Ja 6 1875+
1875-D 29 1876 as Chisago county post
pub 1896+
MnHi 1875-[89]+

RUSHFORD

SOUTHERN Minnesotian. w 1867-
MnHi Ja 4-Ap 16 1868

Rushford STAR-REPUBLICAN. w Ap 1873-S 6 1923||
1873-S 6 1923 as Rushford star. Merged with Tri-county record
MnHi F 15 1877-[84;89]-[93]98-1923

MINNESOTA (*Continued*)

RUSHFORD—*Continued*

TRI-COUNTY record. w N 4 1915+
pub [1915+]
MnHi 1915+

RUSHMORE

Rushmore MAGNET. w S 16 1897-98||
MnHi F 18-Ap 22 1898

RUSSELL

Russell ANCHOR. w 1907+
pub 1909+

RUTHTON

Ruthton TRIBUNE. w 1914+
MnHi Je 25 1925+

SACRED HEART

Sacred Heart JOURNAL. *See* Renville county journal (Olivia)

Sacred Heart NEWS. w My 1 1920+
pub 1930+
MnHi 1920+

PEOPLE'S watchman. *See* Renville record (Renville)

RENVILLE county journal. *See under* Olivia

ST. ANTHONY

In 1872 annexed to Minneapolis. Papers published in St. Anthony are listed under Minneapolis

ST. BONIFACIUS

St. Bonifacius STAR. w S 19 1913-20||
MnHi 1913-O 29 1920

ST. CHARLES

Saint Charles HERALD. w D 20 1867-74||
MnHi 1867-[73]-Mr 14 1874

INTER-COUNTY press. w 1877+
1877-Ag 28 1919 as St. Charles union; S 4 1919-F 3 1922 Union free press
MnHi N 24 1887;O 3 1890+

Saint Charles TIMES. w Jl 19 1873-Jl 26 1901||
MWA Ag 2 1873
MnHi Ja 24 1874-82;Ap 17 1891-1901

St. Charles UNION. *See* Inter-county press

UNION free press. *See* Inter-county press

ST. CLOUD

Der ANZEIGER. w 1895-1907||
In German
MnHi 1902-07

St. Cloud DEMOCRAT. *See* St. Cloud journal press

St. Cloud JOURNAL PRESS. w D 10 1857-1918||
1857-Jl 22 1858 as St. Cloud visitor; Ag 5 1858-S 1866 St. Cloud democrat; S 13 1866-My 18 1876 St. Cloud journal
CLM Ag 8 1889;Ap 17 1890
DLC O 1858-Ag 1859
MWA My 20 1858;My 24 1860
MnHi 1857-66;Je 27 1867-1918
MnScT Ag 1858-1918
N O 3 1861;F 4,Mr 3,Ag 25 1864
NNHi Jl 23 1863
OClWHi Je 24,D 20 1858;Je 2 1859;Je 25,D 18-25 1862;F 12,Mr 5-12 1863

Daily JOURNAL-PRESS. d S 3 1892-Ag 31 1929||
United with St. Cloud daily times to form St. Cloud daily times and the daily journal-press
CLM Ap 26,28 1893
MnHi complete
MnScT complete

MINNESOTA advertiser. w Ja 15 1857-
DLC Jl 9 1857
MnHi F 26-Ap 16 1857

MINNESOTA union. *See* St. Cloud times

Der NORDSTERN. w 1874-Ag 27 1931||
In German
IU D 6 1917-S 26 1929
MnHi F 17 1876-Ja 3 1878;N 21 1889-1931
MnScT D 1 1894-1931

St. Cloud PRESS. w F 22 1872-My 18 1876||
United with St. Cloud journal to form St. Cloud journal-press
MnHi complete
WHi My 27-Je 3 1875

St. Cloud SENTINEL. w Mr 31 1932+
Follows Sauk Rapids sentinel (Sauk Rapids)
pub 1932+
MnHi 1932+

STEARNS county leader. w 1900-20||?
1900-My 2 1919 as Richmond standard
1900-Ag 29 1919 pub in Torah
MnHi Mr 5 1909-Je 3 1921

St. Cloud TIMES. w Je 13 1861-1920||?
1861-62? as Minnesota union; 1863?-Mr 31 1864 St. Cloud union
MnHi Je 13-21,Ag 16 1861;My 1 1863;F 25-Mr, Ap 9-N 5 1864;S 15 1866-1918
MnScT 1872-1918
N O 11 1861

St. Cloud daily TIMES and the daily journal-press. d S 27 1887+
1887-Ag 31 1929 as St. Cloud daily times
pub 1887—
CLM Ap 17 1890;My 2 1893
MWA Mr 27 1929
MnHi 1887+

TRIBUNE. w 1880-88||
MnHi [Jl 30 1887-88]

St. Cloud UNION. *See* St. Cloud times

St. Cloud VISITOR. *See* St. Cloud journal-press

ST. HILAIRE

St. Hilaire SPECTATOR. w 1882+
MnHi O 15 1890+

ST. JAMES

St. James GAZETTE. w 1896-Mr 9 1906||
United with St. James journal to form Journal-gazette
MnHi Je 4 1897-1906

St. James HERALD. w Mr 7-Jl 25 1874||
MnHi complete

St. James INDEPENDENT. *See* Watonwan county leader

JOURNAL-GAZETTE. w 1878-S 13 1917||
1878-Mr 9 1906 as St. James journal. Merged with St. James plaindealer, later Watonwan county plaindealer
MnHi 1891-1917

St. James PLAINDEALER. *See* Watonwan county plaindealer

WATONWAN county leader. w 1914-Ap 4 1929||
1914-N 7 1928 as St. James independent. United with St. James plaindealer to form Watonwan county plaindealer
MnHi 1924-Ja 1929

WATONWAN county plaindealer. w S 3 1891+
1891-Ap 4 1929 as St. James plaindealer
pub 1909+
MnHi 1891-Ja,Ap 11 1929+

ST. LOUIS PARK

St. Louis Park HERALD. w My 6 1915-
MnHi My 6-O 14 1915

ST. PAUL

St. Paul ADVERTISER. *See* St. Paul financial, real estate, and railroad advertiser

AFRO-INDEPENDENT. w Je 9 1888-
Dated also at Minneapolis
Negro
MnHi S 22 1888

ANTI-MONOPOLIST. w Jl 16 1874-78||
MnHi 1874-[77]-D 12 1878
NbHi O 31 1878

APPEAL. w Je 6 1885-N 24 1923||
1885-D 29 1888 as Western appeal. United with Northwestern bulletin to form Northwestern bulletin-appeal
Negro
MnHi Je 13-Jl 18 1885[87-92]Ap 17 1897-1923

Der BEOBACHTER am Mississippi. w S 12 1889-90||
In German
MnHi Ja 3,30 1890

BREEZE. w,m 1887-99||
1887-95 as Lake breeze
1887-Je 10 1897 pub in White Bear Lake
w 1887-Ap 27 1899
MnHi Ag 29 1891-[92-94]-Jl 1899
MnLaS [1891-92]

BROAD axe. w S 17 1891-Je 11 1903||
MnHi complete

Morning CALL. d S 1 1894-Je 1 1895||
Merged with St. Paul globe
MnHi complete
WHi D 1894-F 1895
See also Noon-day call

CALL of the north. w Ja 27 1923-
MnHi 1923-F 15 1924

Le CANADIEN. w Ag 16 1877-Je 19 1903||
United with Le Courrier de l'ouest (Chicago), Le Courrier de l'Illinois (Chicago) and La Voix du peuple (Minneapolis) to form Le Courrier-Canadien, later Courier franco-americain (Chicago)
In French
IHi [Ja 18 1901-Ag 12 1904]
MnHi [1887-88]-1903
WHi Ag 27 1896-1903

COURIER. ir 1923+
MnHi O 15 1923+

DAKOTA tawaxitku kin; or Dakota friend.
ICHi My 1852

DAY. d S 21-D 29 1884||?
MnHi S 24-D 29 1884

St. Paul daily DEMOCRAT. My 1 1854-O 31 1855||
United with Daily Minnesota pioneer to form Daily pioneer and democrat, later St. Paul daily pioneer
MWA Je 8 1854
MnHi [1854-O 24 1855]
MnS complete
N [My-O 1854]

St. Paul DEMOCRAT. w Ag 3 1895-D 19 1901||
MnHi Mr 4 1897-1901

St. Paul DISPATCH. d F 29 1868+
Title varies: St. Paul daily dispatch
pub 1868+
DLC Ap 1869-74;98+
ICHi [Ja-N 1885]
KHi Ag 31 1891-Mr 1906;F 20,Mr 2 1923
MWA F 1 1877;Jl 15 1891-Ag 19 1905
MnHi 1868-[85]+
MnS Mr 1868-71;N 1873-76;89-Ag 1892;93-F,My 1908-09;My 1910-Ag 1910;Ag 1912;Jl 1918+
N S 22 1870
NdHi Mr 1868-[Ag 1880-Je 1881]-Mr 5 1885
OCl [1874]93;98[1903;08;10]
WHi F 29-Je 24 1868;Ap 12 1878-My 1882;89-96

St. Paul tri-weekly DISPATCH. tw
DLC Ja 10,24 1871
NNHi D 17 1872;F 7,Je 5 1873

St. Paul weekly DISPATCH. *See* Farmer's dispatch

EAST St. Paul examiner. *See* Examiner

EAST side daily. ir
MnHi S 1 1931-F 26 1932

EAST side journal. w 1922-
MnHi Jl 17 1924-O 17 1930

EAST SIDE leader. w Jl 6 1900-Ag 3 1917||
1900-S 22 1916 as East side star
MnHi 1915-17

EAST SIDE star. *See* East side leader

EAST SIDE tribune. w Ag 28-O 30 1931||
United with Progress to form Progress and East side tribune
MnHi complete

St. Paul ECHO. w N 7 1925-
MnHi 1925-Je 25 1927

St. Paul ENTERPRISE. w Ag 5 1910-D 16 1919||
Followed by the New era enterprise (denominational, not in this list)
MnHi complete

EXAMINER. w O 9 1919-Ja 5 1923||
1919-N 24 1921 as East St. Paul examiner
MnHi complete

FARMER labor advocate. ir F 9 1923-F 1 1927||
MnHi complete

FARMER labor leader. *See* Minnesota leader

FARMER'S dispatch. w,sw 1868-Ag 26 1926||
1868-O 1 1903 as St. Paul weekly dispatch (title varies); O 8 1903-Ag 31 1905 Farmers' weekly dispatch and St. Paul weekly dispatch; S 7 1905-Ja 30 1913 Farmers' weekly dispatch; F-N 11 1913 Farmers' twice a week dispatch
sw F 4 1913-Ja 30 1925
DLC N 11 1870;S 29 1871
IU 1917-26
MnHi Jl 14 1871-73;Ap-Jl 1874;Ap 22 1875-80;F 21 1889-1926
OClWHi Je 10 1921

St. Paul FINANCIAL, real estate, and railroad advertiser. w N? 1854-Je 19 1858||
Title varies: St. Paul financial and real estate advertiser; St. Paul advertiser; etc. Merged with St. Paul pioneer-press
DLC [Ja-Ap 1857]
IU O 31 1857
MSaE Ag 29 1857
MWA Je 13,Ag 8 1857
MnHi F 16-23 1855;F 1856-58
MnS Ja 26 1856-58
N S 19 1857
WHi Mr 7,My 30,N 14 1857;Mr 13 1858

FOLKEBLADET. *See* Skaffaren

FOLKETS röst. sm Jl 10 1858-N 20 1858||
In Norwegian
MnHi complete
MnSL complete

St. Paul daily FREE PRESS. d O 4? 1856-
MnHi [O 11-Ap 5 1856]

FREMTIDEN. w,ir 1919-21||
In Norwegian
MnHi Mr 31-N 10 1921

FRIA ordet. w Mr 14-O 24 1896||
In Swedish
MnHi complete

St. Paul GERMANIA. w S 20-N 29 1890||
In German
MnHi complete

St. Paul GLOBE. d Ja 15 1878-Ap 30 1905||
1878-F 9 1884 as Daily globe
DLC O 26 1878-1902
IC My 1 1889
ICHi S-N 1881;Ja-Je 26 1885
MWA Je 16,O 11,28 1887
MnHi complete
MnS 1878-Mr 1883;Jl 1885-88;90;F 1891-S 1899; 1900-05
OCl [1886]87;91[96;1901-05]
WHi Ap 12 1878-My 1882;Mr 4 1885;88-96

St. Paul semi-weekly GLOBE and farmers' family journal. w,sw Ja 17 1878-Je 28 1900||
1878-S 7 1899 St. Paul weekly globe (title varies)
MnHi 1878-83,94-1900

GRANGE advance. *See* Advance (Red Wing)

GREAT West. w O 18 1889-Ja 12 1894||
MnHi complete

GREATER St. Paul bulletin. w Mr 6 1924-Jl 5 1929||
1924-Jl 2 1925 as Hill herald
MnHi complete

HEIMDAL. *See* St. Paul tidende

St. Paul HERALD. w 1881+
pub 1901+
MnHi F 16 1889+

HILL herald. *See* Greater St. Paul bulletin

MINNESOTA (*Continued*)

ST. PAUL—*Continued*

St. Paul **INDEPENDENT.** w Ap 19 1924-
MnHi Ap 19-My 3 1924

INTERURBAN. Ja 3 1896-99||
MnHi 1896-99

INTER-URBAN graphic. *See* Midway news

IRISH times. w S 27 1872-
MnHi D 13 1872

Saint Paul **JOURNAL.** w Ja 1 1862-
MnHi Ja 1-O 31 1862
N Ja 9 1862

St. Paul evening **JOURNAL.** d N 24? 1872-Jl 17 1874||
MnHi N 26 1872-74

St. Paul **JOURNAL of commerce.** w 1886-93||?
MnHi Mr 17,Ap 7 1887

MIDWAY advertiser. w 1906-Jl 27 1933||
MnHi Mr 30 1907-33

MIDWAY circle. w N 9 1923-F 1 1924||
MnHi complete

MIDWAY news. w My 19 1888+
My 19-Jl 21 1888 as Inter-urban graphic
pub [1924]+
KHi Ap 2 1892
MWA Jl 25 1891
MnHi 1888+

MINNEHAHA. w 1867-
In German
MnHi [1868]
—d ed *See* Täglisches Minnesota volksblatt

MINNEHAHA. w,sw 1877-1933||?
w 1877-
MnHi My 26 1889-1901
—d ed *See* Tägliche volkszeitung

MINNESOTA. w 1849-
MH O 23 1851-Ja 20 1853

MINNESOTA chronicle and register. w My 31 1849-F 10 1851||
My-Ag 9 1849 as Minnesota chronicle. Merged with Minnesota democrat
DLC [Ag 1849-F 17 1851]
MWA Je 10 1850;Ja 13,27 1851
MnHi complete
MnS S 1849-51

MINNESOTA democrat. w D 10 1850-O 31 1855||
United with Minnesota pioneer to form Pioneer and democrat, later St. Paul pioneer
DLC S 21 1853-55
MWA Ja 14 1851;Je 8,O 19,D 7 1853;Ja 3-10, My 17-24,Ag 16-23,S 6,20-27,D 6-20 1854;Ja 17-Mr 7,21-My 23,Je-Ag 15,29-O 1855
MnHi complete
MnS D 17 1850-55
N 1851-My 1854
OClWHi D 24 1850;Ja 7 1851

MINNESOTA evening democrat. d O 7? 1863-
MnHi O 9 1863

MINNESOTA deutsche zeitung. w 1856-
In German
MnHi [Ag 1857-My 22 1858]

MINNESOTA free press. *See* St. Peter free press

MINNESOTA journal of commerce. w 1871-73||
MnHi [Jl 24 1872-Ap 3 1873]

MINNESOTA leader. 1918-20 *See under* Minneapolis

MINNESOTA leader. w Ja 15 1930+
1930-34 as Farmer labor leader
MnHi 1930+

MINNESOTA national demokrat. w 1857-
In German
MnHi [Mr 6 1858-O 8 1859]

MINNESOTA pioneer. *See* St. Paul pioneer

MINNESOTA posten. w 1890-94||
Merged with Folkets nyheter (Rockford, Ill.)
In Swedish
MnHi Jl 30,O 29 1890;F 4 1891;Ap 26 1893

MINNESOTA register. w Ap 7-Ag 18 1849||
Merged with Minnesota chronicle to form Minnesota chronicle and register. The issue of Ap 7 was reprinted Ap 28 and wrongly dated Ap 27,v 1 no 1
MnHi Ap 7,Jl 28,Ag 5-18 1849
OClWHi Ap 7 1849
OHi Jl 28-Ag 4 1849
WHi Ap 7 1849

MINNESOTA staats-anzeiger. w Ap 18 1889-90||
In German
MnHi 1889-Je 13 1890

MINNESOTA staats-zeitung. w,tw Jl 24 1858-Ag 30 1877||
United with Minnesota volksblatt to form Volkszeitung
w 1858-Ag 1867
In German
MnHi [1858-60]-[62-66]67[69-70]-[73-75]-77
N O 26 1861

MINNESOTA stats tidning. w 1877+
1877-82 pub in Minneapolis
For Mr 14 1882-O 23 1895 See Skaffaren
In Swedish
IRA 1878-82;95+
IU D 19 1917+
MnHi 1877+
MnM 1878-81
MnU O 1925+
NbHi Mr-D 10 1913;Ja 7,21-Ap 22,My 27 1914-Ja 3,17,F 14-21,Mr-My 16,Je 13-27,Jl 11-S 19, O 10-24,N 7,21-28,D 26 1917
NdHi 1906-12
WHi O 12 1898+
WaPS S 22 1915-Ag 1918

MINNESOTA tidning. *See* Svenska monitoren

MINNESOTA weekly times. w My 23 1854-
United with St. Paul weekly Minnesotian to form Weekly Minnesotian and times, later St. Paul weekly Minnesotian
MSaE Je 21 1856
MnHi 1854-My 23 1857,Ja 9 1858
MnS 1854-My 23 1857

Tägliches **MINNESOTA volksblatt.** d 1861-77||
United with Minnesota staats-zeitung to form Tägliche volkszeitung
In German
MnHi O 7 1866-68
—Sunday ed *See* Minnehaha

MINNESOTA volksblatt. w 1861-Ag 30 1877||
United with Minnesota staats-zeitung to form Die wöchentliche volkszeitung
In German
MnHi [My 14 1864-65]-O 6 1866

St. Paul weekly **MINNESOTIAN.** w S 17 1851-61||
D 17 1859-Mr 1860? as Weekly Minnesotian and times
DLC Ap 28 1855
MWA D 17 1853
MnHi 1851-59;Mr 10 1860;Ja 11 1861
MnS My 1 1852;Je 1853-My 6 1854
N Je 1853-My 1854
P-M F 18 1854
WHi [My 1855-My 8 1858]

Daily **MINNESOTIAN.** d My 11 1854-Ja 25 1861||
D 14 1859-Je 17 1860 as Minnesotian and times
CtY Je 7 1859
InLHi S 17 1855
MWA F 19 1860
MnHi 1854-[59]-Ja 10 1861
MnS 1854-Mr 15 1859
N Je 17 1859

MINNESOTSKÉ noviny. w 1904-14||
In Polish
MnHi D 30 1909-My 28 1914

MINNESOTSKE pokrok. w F 19 1908-20||?
Dated also in Minneapolis, and Omaha, Neb.
In Polish
MnHi [1917]-My 20 1920
NbHi 1908-Jl 1909

Sunday **MIRROR.** *See under* Minneapolis

NEGRO world. w Jl 2 1892-
MnHi Jl 23,30,Ag 20,S 3 1892;Mr 10-Je 9 1900

Monday morning **NEWS.** w Je 30 1873-
MnHi Je 30 1873

St. Paul daily **NEWS.** Je 23 1879-Ja 2 1880||
MnHi complete

Saturday evening **NEWS.** w 1883-1901||
MnHi [1889]-D 14 1901

St. Paul daily **NEWS.** d D 13 1887-Ap 6 1894||
Followed by St. Paul news-record
MnHi 1887-[88]-94
MnS 1890-94
WHi Mr 1889-94

St. Paul daily **NEWS.** d Mr 1 1900+
pub [1907]+
MnHi 1900+
MnS Ja-Je,O 1906-10;Jl 1921+

St. Paul and Minnesota **NEWS-LETTER.** w
MnHi D 1 1860

St. Paul **NEWS-RECORD.** d O 1-D 31 1894||
Follows St. Paul daily news
MnHi complete

NOON-day call. d My 4? 1875-
MnHi My 28 1875
See also Morning call

NORDVESTEN. w Je 1 1881-Je 27 1907||
Merged with Minneapolis tidende
In Norwegian
IaDeL 1882-[1901-03]-07
MnHi F 5,Ap-My 21 1885;Ap 13 1893;96-1907
WHi 1893-98;Ja 11 1900-06

NORTH CENTRAL progress. *See* Progress and East side tribune

NORTHWESTERN bulletin-appeal. w Ja 21 1922-Ag 15 1925||
1922-Ja 5 1924 as Northwestern bulletin
Negro
MnHi Mr 11 1922-25

NOWINY Minnesockie. w 1916+
1916-S 26 1919 pub in Minneapolis
In Polish
pub 1925+
IU S 1917-Ap 9 1926
MnHi Je 21 1917+

OBZOR. w 1891-93||?
In Bohemian
MnHi Ap 19 1893

L'OEIL. *See under* Minneapolis

St. Paul **PIONEER.** w Ap 28 1849-Ap 9 1875||
1849-N 1 1855 as Minnesota pioneer; N 8 1855-N 10 1865 Weekly pioneer and democrat (title varies). United with St. Paul weekly press to form Weekly pioneer-press
DLC O 25 1849;Ja 16 1850;Ja 16,Mr 20,My 8-15,Ag 7 1851;O 14 1852;Ja 3 1856;S 1857-59
MWA Ap 28 1849;D 12 1850;Mr 20 1851;Ja 3-17,31,F 14-S 18,O-N 13,27 1856;Ja 15-Je 4,18-Jl,Ag 13-S 3,O 1,22-29 1857;Ja-Jl 11,25-D 1862;F 13,Ag 1863-F 17 1865;F 16-23 1866;Ag 6 1869;My 5,N 3 1871
MnHi 1849-Ag 1859;62-75
MnM S 1857-Ag 1858
MnS Ap 24 1851-Ap 15 1852;N 1855-59;Jl 1860-66
N S 20,O 3,D 1861-My 1862
NNHi Jl 17 1863;Ap 4,Je 6 1873
NjHi My 5 1871
OClWHi Ap 12 1861
P-M Ja 25,My 10 1855
PWCl D 9 1852
WHi D 27 1849[Jl 25-D 1850]-[52-F 17 1853]D 24 1857;Ja 21-My 6 1858;66;N 1872-75

St. Paul daily **PIONEER.** d My 1 1854-Ap 10 1875||
1854-O 30 1855 as Daily Minnesota pioneer; N 1 1855-Jl 13 1860 Daily pioneer and democrat; Jl 14 1860-S 24 1862 Pioneer and democrat; S 25 1862-O 27 1867 St. Paul pioneer. United with St. Paul daily press to form St. Paul pioneer press
DLC Ja 18 1856-Ja 22 1860;Ja 17-S 25,D 31 1862-Ja 24 1863;F 24-D 1867;Ag 17 1869;Jl 12 1874-75
IU My 11,17 1863
InRE D 10,13 1870
MBAt Ap 15,O 29 1865
MHi Mr 28-D 1871
MWA Mr 24,Je 25,Jl 19 1856;Mr 15 1861;D 22 1865;My 5 1871
MnHi complete
MnS complete
MnU 1867;Ag-D 1868;Ja-My 1870;71-72
N F 14 1864;Jl 17 1867;O 9 1868
NN Ja 22 1858
NbHi Mr 22 1868
NdHi Mr 5 1868-[Ja]-[Jl 1870-Je]-D 1872
WHi Ap 5 1859

PIONEER and democrat. *See* St. Paul pioneer

Weekly **PIONEER-PRESS.** w Ja 1861-My 3 1906||
1861-Ap 8 1875 as St. Paul weekly press; Ap 16 1875-Ap 27 1876 Pioneer press; My 4-O 26 1876 Pioneer press and tribune; N 2 1876-D 25 1879 Pioneer press
ICHi S 25 1862
KHi 1878-F 13 1879
MBAt Ap 13 1865
MWA Ja 8(supp)11-25,F 8-22 1866;Ja 17,31,F 14-Mr 7 1867;Ja 13-27,F 10-Mr 3 1870;Ja 12-19,F 2-9 1871;N 5 1874
MnHi [Ja 10 1861-81]84-1906
MnS 1877-78
MoS Ap 1899-Ag,O 1903-06
NbHi Mr 22 1868
OClWHi Ag 3 1865
WHi Jl 20 1871-75

St. Paul **PIONEER-PRESS.** d Ap 11 1875+
Formed by the union of St. Paul daily pioneer and St. Paul daily press. 1875-Ap 30 1876 as St. Paul daily pioneer press; My 2-O 28 1876 Pioneer press and tribune; O 29 1876-D 26 1879 Pioneer-press; D 27 1879-D 21 1909 Daily pioneer-press
pub 1875+
CaM 1884-92
CoU 1899-1902;S 1906-My 1910
CtY Jl 8 1893
DLC 1875-Ap 1890;91-1901;Ap-D 1902;S 1906+
IC My 1 1889
ICHi Mr 8 1879-S 1887
ICM My 8 1880;Ag 13,17-18 1881;Mr 24-25,S 6 1882;F 27 1884
IaDH Je 15 1881-84;Ap-S 1885;Jl 1894-Ap 1914
KHi Je 30 1913-F 9,25 1923
MB Jl 12-D 1888
MWA Jl 9,Ag 16,O 10,N 16 1876;Ja 30-31,F 27, Jl 20 1877;Je 18,N 22,D 7 1878;Ja 2,11,F 28,Ap 23,27-28 1879;F 21,Mr 7,9 1880;Jl 14-19 1891;Je 25 1893;S 24 1895
MnHi 1875+
MnS Ap-Je,O 1885-87;89-1912;Jl 1918—
MnU N 9 1899;Ja-F,My-Ag,N 1921-26
MoS Ap 1899-Ag,O 1903-S 1907;Ja-Je,Ag,O 1908-Je,Ag-D 1909;Ja 1912
NbHi Ag 9-10 1883;S 5 1889;N 8 1890;Jl 21 1901-Ja,F 2 1904
NcD S 1906-My 1908
NcU Mr 9 1884
NdHi F 24 1879-[Ag 1880-87]-[Ap-D 1888]-[Ja-Mr 1890]-[Jl-S 1893]-[O-D 1896]-[O 1901-Je 1902]-Je 1905
NdV Ap 1896-1902
OClWHi Jl 12 1881;Jl 18 1885;Je 8 1892;Ag 16, S 1-5 1896
P Jl 1890-1917
PP O 2 1928;34+
PPL S 4 1883
WHi 1887+

Evening **PIONEER-PRESS.** d Ag 17 1908-09||
MnHi 1908-My 31 1909

St. Paul **POST.** d O 22 1890-
MnHiO 22-D 13 1890

Evening **POST.** d Ap 28-My 19 1894||
MnHi complete
WHi complete

St. Paul daily **PRESS.** d Ja 1 1861-Ap 10 1875||
Mr 24 1864-D 31 1865 as St. Paul press. United with St. Paul daily pioneer to form St. Paul pioneer-press
CU-B Ja 1 1871
DLC [My 12-O 12]19-D 1861;Ap 5 1863-Ap 19 1865;Ja 20-Jl 1 1866;Jl 1874-75
IU S 1 1861
MBAt Ap 16,18 1865
MWA Mr 25-26,Je 18 1862;Ag 4 1865;F 14,28, Ap 2 1868;Ag 31,S 10,D 14 1869;Mr 4 1870
MnHi complete
MnS 1861-74
MnU 1867-69;71-72
N O 19,N 1 1861
NcD My 12 1863
NdHi Mr 7 1868-Je 1869
OClWHi My 2 1861;Ag 4 1865
WHi Ap 16 1865

St. Paul weekly **PRESS.** *See* Weekly pioneer-press

MINNESOTA (*Continued*)

ST. PAUL—*Continued*

PROGRESS and East side tribune. w Mr 2 1911+
1911-Je 24 1927 as North central progress; Jl 2 1927-Mr 10 1932 Progress
pub 1932+
MnHi 1911+

St. Paul REGISTER. w Je 17 1867-
MnHi Ag 12 1867

St. Paul REVIEW. w S 17 1892+
F 10 1894-F 22 1896 as St. Paul Saturday review
MnHi 1892+

ST. ANTHONY hill graphic. w N 9 1888-91||
MnHi D 14 1888;F 8-15,Ap 5 1889-N 6 1891

SATURDAY night. w D 16 1916-18||
Dated also at Minneapolis
KHi Ja 12 1918
MnHi 1916-Ja 12 1918

SKAFFAREN. w 1878-O 23 1895||
1877-Mr 7 1882 as Folkebladet; Mr 14 1882-O 23 1895 Skaffaren och
In Swedish
IRA complete
MnHi Je 12 1889-95

STATE. w 1890-92||?
MnHi F 21 1891-F 25 1892

SVENSKA Minnesota bladet. w -1869||
Followed by Minnesota tidning, later Svenska monitoren

SVENSKA monitoren. w 1870-72||
Follows Svenska Minnesota bladet. 1870 as Minnesota tidning
IRA 1870-72

SVENSKA nybyggaren. 1872-76||
In Swedish
IRA [1872-76]

St. Paul TIDENDE. w 1891-My 6 1927||
1891-1902 as Heimdal. Merged with Ugebladet (Minneapolis)
In Norwegian
IaDeL [1892-94;97;1900-01]Ja 10-F 21 1902
MnHi Ap 16 1893;S 18 1903-27

St. Paul daily TIMES. d My 5 1854-
MWA Ja 22 1857
MnHi 1854-N 8 1856[Jl 1858-D 10 1859]Je 21-D 1860
MnS 1854-My 14 1857
N My-N 1854;Ja 30 1856;My 15 1866
WHi My 15 1854-My 14 1856

TRUTH. w D 24 1892-
Dated also at Minneapolis
MnHi 1892-Mr 25 1893

TRUTH. ir My 30 1896-
MnHi 1896-Je 1899

TWIN CITY guardian. w N 16 1895-1923||?
Dated also at Minneapolis
ICJ N 12 1898-[1902]
MnHi 1895-Ja 17 1920
WHi [Ja 21-D 1899;Jl 28 1900-Ap 1901]03-Mr 22 1919

TWIN CITY live stock reporter. d,sw 1890-94||
1890-S 1893 pub in New Brighton
MnHi Ap 13 1891-S 23,O 21 1893-Je 29 1894

St. Paul daily UNION. d 1862-F 28 1863||
Merged with St. Paul daily press
DLC Ja 21-F 28 1863

VÄRT hem. w Ag 1890-96||?
1890-Ja 23 1891 pub in Spring Lake; Ja 30 1891-Ja 13 1893 in Minneapolis and Spring Lake; Ja 20 1893-Ja 18 1895 in Minneapolis
In Swedish
MnHi [S 15 1890-S 11 1891]F 1892-96

VOICE of the people. w Ap 21 1888-
MnHi My 12-Je 23 1888

St. Paul VOLKSFREUND. w S 22 1894-95||
In German
MnHi 1894-My 25 1895

Tägliche VOLKSZEITUNG. d S 9 1877+
Formed by the union of Minnesota staats-zeitung and Minnesota volksblatt
In German
pub 1877+
MnHi S 9 1877;Ja 4-S 28 1878;My 22 1889+
—Sunday ed *See* Minnehaha

Wochentliche VOLKSZEITUNG. w 1877-1921||?
In German
KHi [O 31 1888-F 6 1889]
—Sunday ed *See* Minnehaha

WEST St. Paul times. w Ja 1 1887+
pub 1887+
MnHi Mr 5 1887+

WESTERN appeal. *See* Appeal

WORLD. w 1895-
MnHi Ap 25 1896-[97]

ST. PAUL PARK

St. Paul Park REVIEW. w My 20 1915-
MnHi My 20-N 11 1915

ST. PETER

St. Peter ADVERTISER. *See* St. Peter commercial advertiser

Saint Peter's CATECHIST. w Ag 28 1874-
MnHi Ag 28-O 30 1874

St. Peter COMMERCIAL advertiser. w 1865-76||?
1865-74? as St. Peter advertiser
MWA N 17,D 1 1870;Jl 27 1871

St. Peter COURIER. w Ja 4 1855-58||
Title varies slightly
DLC O 30 1857
InLHi O 18 1855
MnHi [Ap 26 1855-Ja 1 1858]
WHi Ag 13 1856[Ja-Ap 1 1857]

St. Peter FREE PRESS. w My 27 1857-
1857-N 17 1858 as Minnesota free press
Suspended from N 17 1858-Ap 20 1859
MnHi 1857-N 17 1858

St. Peter FREE PRESS. w 1894-D 30 1925||
Merged with St. Peter herald
MnHi Ag 1896-1925
MnSpH complete

St. Peter HERALD. sw 1884+
pub 1884+
MnHi O 3 1890+

Saint Peter JOURNAL. w 1883-1903||
MnHi [1888]Ap 10 1897-Je 30 1903

MINNESOTA free press. *See* St. Peter free press (1857-)

MINNESOTA statesman. w Je 11 1858-
MnHi [O 8 1858-D 23 1859]
N My 27 1859;O 4 1861

St. Peter TRIBUNE. w F 15 1860-Ja 21 1920||
Merged with St. Peter herald
DLC S 12-26,O 10 1860
MnHi complete
MnSp complete
N Ja 8 1862

ST. VINCENT

St. Vincent NEW ERA. w 1884-1929||?
MnHi Mr 17-N 7 1890

SANBORN

Sanborn SENTINEL. w 1890+
pub [1896+]
MnHi N 1915+

SANDSTONE

PINE county courier. w D 27 1894+
pub 1903+
MnHi 1894+

Sandstone TRIBUNE. w D 22 1910-14||
MnHi 1910-O 30 1914

SAUK CENTRE

Sauk Centre AVALANCHE. w 1887-D 29 1904||
1887-1900 as Avalanche; 1901-02 Twentieth century avalanche. Merged with Sauk Centre herald
MnHi Jl 26,Ag 30 1888;Ag 28 1890-1904
MnSk [1890]-1904

Sauk Centre HERALD. w 1867+
Title varies slightly
pub 1867+
MnHi 1868-[72]-Ja 19 1905;My 20 1915+
WHi S 12 1874;Ap 24 1875

Sauk Centre NEWS. w N 15 1923-D 2 1926||
Merged with Sauk Centre herald
MnHi N 29 1923-26
WaPS [1924-26]

TWENTIETH century avalanche. *See* Sauk Centre avalanche

SAUK RAPIDS

Sauk Rapids FREE PRESS. w 1885-N 7 1903||
Merged with Sauk Rapids sentinel to form Sentinel free press, later Sauk Rapids sentinel
MnHi My 15 1886;Ja 24,My 9,S 12 1890-1903

Sauk Rapids FRONTIERMAN. w Ap 26 1855-
DLC Jl 26,Ag 8-16,O 4 1855
InLHi Ag 9 1855
MnHi [1855]-O 30 1856;Ap 16,Ag 20,S 24 1857; F 18-Je 24 1858

Sauk Rapids SENTINEL. w Mr 28 1868-Mr 24 1932||
N 13 1903-N 2 1910 as Sentinel free press
Suspended F 16 1872-Mr 25 1873
MnHi 1868-F 16 1872;Mr 25 1873-[74-75]-[77]-1913;Je 17 1917-32
MnScS 1887-89;93-95;1903-32

SENTINEL-free press. *See* Sauk Rapids sentinel

SEAFORTH

Seaforth ITEM. w 1901-Jl 30 1920||
MnHi N 1915-20

SHAKOPEE

Shakopee ARGUS-TRIBUNE. w N 30 1861+
N 30 1861 as Scott county argus; D 1861-S 11 1884 Shakopee argus; S 18 1884-1919 Scott county argus; 1920-Mr 26 1926 Shakopee argus
pub 1861+
ICHi S 19,O 3 1865
MWA F 21 1867
MnHi 1861[62-64]-S 1865;F 14 1867+
MnU Ap 25 1878

Shakopee COURIER. w 1877-My 4 1893||
Merged with Shakopee argus, later Shakopee argus-tribune
MnHi Ag 10 1882-93

Shakopee INDEPENDENT. *See* Weekly valley herald

MINNESOTA post. w 1884-85||
In German
MnHi Mr 20 1890-95

REPUBLICAN advocate. w O 17 1856-
MWA F 28,My 2,S 5,O 10 1857

SCOTT county argus. *See* Shakopee argus-tribune

SCOTT county democrat. w F 12 1859-
MnHi Ap 9 1859-Ag 24 1861

Shakopee SPECTATOR. w Ag 3 1867-
MnHi 1867-Ap 2 1868

Shakopee SPY. w D 17 1863-
MnHi 1868-70

Shakopee TRIBUNE. w 1896-Mr 25 1926||
United with Shakopee argus to form Shakopee argus-tribune
MnHi Ap 16 1897-O 19 1917;S 19 1920-26

Weekly VALLEY herald. w N 3 1855-
1855-S 17 1856 Shakopee independent
CSmH N 24 1855
IHi [1855-N 18 1857]
MSaE D 17 1856
MWA Je 18 1856
MnHi N 10 1855-O 28 1857

SHERBURN

Sherburn ADVANCE-STANDARD. w 1887+
1887-Ag 16 1906 as Sherburn advance
pub 1925+
MnHi S 27 1890-O 21 1898;Mr 21 1906+

MARTIN county standard. w 1897-Ag 9 1906||
United with Sherburn advance to form Sherburn advance-standard

SILVER LAKE

Silver Lake LEADER. w D 1901+
pub [1901-12]+
MnHi Ja 17 1903;Ag 27,D 17 1904;Ja 21,Ap 29,D 2-9,23 1905;Mr 10 1906;Ja 5,19,Mr 2,Jl 13-27,S 6 1907[08-12]-[16]-[18]-[21]-[25-26]+

SLAYTON

Slayton GAZETTE. w 1883-N 23 1893||
United with Murray county pioneer to form Slayton gazette and Murray county pioneer
MnHi Ag 18 1887[88;90]-93

Slayton GAZETTE and Murray county pioneer. w Ja 24 1878-Jl 4 1918||
1878-My 27 1880 as Currie pioneer; Je 1880-Je 1881 Murray county pioneer; Jl 1881-D 28 1887 Southwest Minnesotian; Ja 5 1888-N 23 1893 Murray county pioneer. Merged with Murray county herald
1878-Ag 7 1890 pub in Currie
MnHi [1878]-1918

MURRAY county herald. w 1893+
MnHi O 6 1897-1915;Ag 12 1920+

MURRAY county pioneer. *See* Slayton gazette and Murray county pioneer

SLEEPY EYE

BROWN county pioneer. *See* Brown county republican

BROWN county republican. w Jl 15 1881-
Jl-Ag 5 1881 as Brown county pioneer
MnHi Jl 22 1881-S 5 1883

Sleepy Eye DISPATCH. w Jl 3 1890-Je 19 1908||
United with Sleepy Eye herald to form Sleepy Eye herald-dispatch
MnHi complete

FARMERS criterion. w N 6 1875-
MnHi N 27 1875

Sleepy Eye HERALD-DISPATCH. w 1880+
1880-Je 19 1908 as Sleepy Eye herald
pub 1924+
MnHi Mr 25 1882+
MnSl [1923+]

Sleepy Eye PROGRESSIVE. w Jl 12 1916+
pub [1918+]
MnHi 1916-Ja 2 1930
MnSl [1923+]

Sleepy Eye WIDE-AWAKE. w F 25 1879-
MnHi Jl 29 1879

SOLWAY

Solway PRESS. w Jl 28 1899-1901||
MnHi 1899-Ap 19 1901

SOUTH ST. PAUL

DAKOTA county globe. *See* West St. Paul booster and Dakota county globe

South St. Paul daily REPORTER. d Ja 17 1891+
DA [D 1914-15]+
IU Jl 1919-N 1924;Ja 19,Ap 1925+
MnHi 1891+
MnU-A 1920-1933

WEST ST. PAUL booster and Dakota county globe. w S 26 1919+
Follows Hastings democrat (Hastings). 1919-S 25 1925 as Dakota county globe
pub 1919+
MnHi 1919+

MINNESOTA (*Continued*)

SPICER

GREEN LAKE breeze. w 1904+
pub [1904+]
MnHi Jl 9 1914+

SPOONER

NORTHERN news. w 1907-Mr 27 1925||
Merged with Baudette region (Baudette)
MnHi O 16 1908-25

SPRING GROVE

Spring Grove HERALD. w 1891+
pub [1895+]
MnHi S 7 1893+

SPRING LAKE

Vårt hem. *See under* St. Paul

SPRING VALLEY

Spring Valley MERCURY-VIDETTE. w 1880-O 3 1929||
1880-O 27 1904 as Spring Valley mercury. Merged with Spring Valley tribune
MnHi F 1887-1929

Spring Valley SUN. w S 2 1892-1913||
MnHi 1892-Ag 31 1913

Spring Valley TRIBUNE. w Mr 1 1928+
pub 1928+
MnHi O 3 1929+

Spring Valley VIDETTE. w 1869-O 27 1904||
1869-S 12 1877 as Western progress. United with Spring Valley mercury to form Spring Valley mercury-vidette
MnHi Ag 10 1870-S 12,22 1877-Mr 12 1880;F 25-Mr 4,Ap 1,Jl 15-O 14,D 2 1887[88-91]O 5, N 16 1894-Ja 11 1901

WESTERN progress. *See* Spring Valley vidette

SPRINGFIELD

Springfield ADLER. w D 27 1889-91||
In German
MnHi 1889-Ja 2 1891

Springfield ADVANCE-PRESS. w 1887+
1887-Ag 15 1918 as Springfield advance
MnHi Ap 20 1894-18;Ja 11 1922+

STAPLES

PRESTO change. *See* Staples world

Staples WORLD. w 1890+
1890-F 20 1892 as Presto change
pub 1893-[1925+]
MnHi Ap 18 1891+

STARBUCK

Starbuck TIMES. w 1898+
MnHi Ag 6 1915+

STEPHEN

MARSHALL county leader. *See* Stephen messenger and Marshall county leader

Stephen MESSENGER. w Ap 1910-S 1915||
United with Marshall county leader to form Stephen messenger and Marshall county leader
MnSteM [1910-15]

Stephen MESSENGER and Marshall county leader. w 1883+
1883-S 1915 as Marshall county leader
pub [1887-1905;15]
MnHi Ja 17-S 22 1888;Ap 24 1891-O 2 1903

STEWART

MESSENGER. *See* Stewart tribune

Stewart TRIBUNE. w N 4 1892+
N 4 1892-95 as Messenger
pub 1896+
MnHi N 4-25 1892;Ag 11,S 15 1899;N 30 1900+
MnLaS 1892-95

STEWARTVILLE

Stewartville STAR. w 1891+
pub 1891-[1907-12]+
MnHi My 19 1893-Mr 2 1894;D 21 1906-Ja 15 1915

Stewartville TIMES. w 1897-1906||
MnHi 1898-1906

STILLWATER

Daily CALL. d Ag 11-D 31 1890||
MnHi complete

Stillwater DEMOCRAT. w D 17 1858-
MnHi Ja 8 1859-F 2 1861

Stillwater DEMOCRAT. w Ja 2 1887-91||
MWA S 17 1887
MnHi F 27 1887;90-Jl 2 1891

Stillwater GAZETTE. w Ag 6 1870+
pub 1870+
MnHi 1870-74;98+

Stillwater daily GAZETTE. d 1884+
DLC 1898
MnHi Mr 14 1888+
MnSt 1900+

Stillwater daily JOURNAL. d Mr 15 1915-
MnHi Mr 15-My 17 1915

Stillwater LUMBERMAN. w Ap 25 1875-83||?
MnHi 1875-[78]-Ja 17 1879

Stillwater MESSENGER. *See* Stillwater post-messenger

Stillwater NEWS. w F 14 1900+
1900-Ap 24 1931 as Trade news
pub 1900+
MnHi Mr 14 1930+

Stillwater POST-MESSENGER. w S 15 1856+
1856-F 22 1928 as Stillwater messenger
MWA N 3 1863;Ja 16 1866
MnHi Je 8 1858-[64-66]+
MnSt 1905-27
N Ja 7 1861

Stillwater REPUBLICAN. w Mr 18 1868-D 9 1870||

ST. CROIX post. w 1877-F 2 1911||
MnHi F 1878-1911

SAINT CROIX union. w O 23 1854-N 13 1857||
DLC Mr 7 1856-57
MnHi 1854-N 3 1855;Ja 26,F 7,Je 20-27 1856

Stillwater daily SUN. d S 12 1881-Je 4 1884||
MnHi complete

Daily TIMES. d O 4 1897-98||
MnHi O 4 1897-Ag 10 1898

TRADE news. *See* Stillwater news

WASHINGTON county journal. w Mr 3 1893-O 11 1918||
MnHi 1893-F 21 1896;Ap 16 1897-1918
MnStG complete

WASHINGTON county post. w Mr 11 1920-F 24 1928||
United with Stillwater messenger to form Stillwater post-messenger
MnHi complete
MnSt 1924

STORDEN

Storden TIMES. w Ap 25 1915+
pub 1915+

STRANDQUIST

Strandquist PRESS. w 1922+
pub 1932+

STRATHCONA

Strathcona STAR. w D 9 1920-22||
MnHi 1920-N 23 1922

SUNBEAM

SUNBEAM. w Ap 20 1901-Ja 17 1919||
Merged with Thief River Falls tribune (Thief River) 1901-Jl 7 1905 pub in Gully
MnHi complete

TAYLORS FALLS

CHISAGO county news. *See under* Lindstrom

INTER STATE park press. w F 27 1897-O 21 1899||
Followed by Chisago county courier (Lindstrom)
MnHi complete

Taylors Falls JOURNAL. w Jl 22 1873+
Follows Taylors Falls reporter
pub [1924+]
MnHi 1873-[74]-Ag 1 1912;24+

Taylors Falls REPORTER. w F 23 1860-Jl 11 1873||
Followed by Taylors Falls journal
MWA F 10 1866
MnHi 1860-[61]-Jl 31 1862;S 10-N 19 1864;Mr 31 1865-[66]-S 29 1870;Ap 6 1872-Jl 11 1873

Taylor's Falls TIMES. w 1912-16||
1912-My? 1915 as Chisago City tribune (Chisago City)
MnHi Je 30 1915-My 17 1916

THIEF RIVER FALLS

Thief River Falls FORUM. w Ap 6 1932+
pub 1932+
MnHi Ja 12 1933+
MnTr [1932]+

Thief River Falls NEWS. w 1884-My 23 1912||
1884-Ag 3 1893 as Red Lake Falls news (Red Lake)
United with Thief River press to form Thief River Falls news-press
MnHi O 16 1890-[93]-1912

Thief River Falls NEWS-PRESS. w My 30 1912-D 20 1917||
Formed by union of Thief River Falls news and Thief River press. Merged with Thief River Falls times
MnHi complete

Thief River PRESS. w 1889-My 24 1912||
United with Thief River Falls news to form Thief River Falls news-press
MnHi F 1909-12

Thief River Falls TIMES. w 1910+
pub 1916-1917;19+
MnHi D 27 1917+

Thief River Falls TRIBUNE. sw Ja 3 1919-Ag 31 1927||
Merged with Thief River Falls times
MnHi complete

TINTAH

Weekly CALL. w 1902-07||
MnHi Je 25 1903-Ap 5 1907

TORAH

RICHMOND standard. *See* Stearns county leader (St. Cloud)

STEARNS county leader. *See under* St. Cloud

TOWER

AMERIKANSKI slovenec. w 1892-98||
In Slovenic
PPCHi 1892;97-98

Tower weekly NEWS. w Je 1 1900+
pub 1900+

VERMILION iron journal. w 1885-1900||?
MnHi Mr 29 1888;N 20,D 4-11 1890;Ap 1891-D 2 1897

TRACY

Tracy HEADLIGHT. *See* Tracy headlight-herald

Tracy HEADLIGHT-HERALD. w 1885+
1885-Ja 11 1901 as Tracy republican; Ja 18 1901-10? Republican-trumpet; 1911?-My 1 1920 Tracy headlight
pub 1920+
MnHi Ap 28 1893;Mr 13 1896;D 10 1897-[1902]-F 14 1908
MnU Ag 19 1932

Tracy HERALD. w S 4 1894-My 1 1920||
United with Tracy headlight to form Tracy headlight-herald
MnTraH complete

Tracy REPUBLICAN. *See* Tracy headlight-herald

REPUBLICAN-TRUMPET. *See* Tracy headlight-herald

Tracy TRUMPET. w 1880-Ja 8 1901||
United with Tracy republican to form Republican-trumpet, later Tracy headlight-herald
MnHi Mr 10 1893-Je 1894;D 10 1897-1901

TRIUMPH

Triumph-Monterey JOURNAL. *See* Triumph-Monterey progress

Triumph-Monterey PROGRESS. w 1899+
1899-F 8 1923 as Triumph progress; F 15 1923-F 21 1924 Triumph-Monterey journal
pub 1900+
MnHi Je 19 1903+

Triumph PROGRESS. Triumph-Monterey progress

TRUMAN

Truman TRIBUNE. w Ja 5 1900+
pub 1900+
MnHi 1900-[07-08]+

TURTLE RIVER

Turtle River PINE tree. w Jl 26 1899-1904||?
MnHi Jl 26 1899-N 1 1900

TWIN VALLEY

Twin Valley TIMES. w 1896+
pub 1909+
MnHi Ap 14 1897+

TWO HARBORS

Two Harbors CHRONICLE. w 1890+
1890-O 29 1909 as Two Harbors iron news; N 4 1909-Jl 29 1920 Journal-news; Ag 5 1920-Jl 31 1930 Lake county chronicle
pub 1918+
MnHi Ap 21 1893+
NNRa 1926+

Two Harbors IRON news. *See* Two Harbors chronicle

Two Harbors IRON port. w 1887-91||
MnHi Ap 7-14,O 6,27 1888[Ap 19 1890-N 5 1891]

IRON port-advocate. w 1908-11||
1908-D 1 1909 as Two Harbors iron port
MnHi S 29 1909-[11]

IRON trade journal. w N 4 1897-O 28 1909||
United with Two Harbors iron news to form Journal-news, later Two Harbors chronicle
MnHi complete

JOURNAL-NEWS. *See* Two Harbors chronicle

LAKE county chronicle. *See* Two Harbors chronicle

MINNESOTA (*Continued*)

TYLER

Det DANSKE ugeblad. w Ap 1 1881+
1881-Mr 27 1890 as Illustreret ugeblad; nyheds afdelingen; Ap 3 1890-Mr 7 1929 Ugebladet 1881-Ap 1887 pub in Chicago; My 1887-S 1931 in Minneapolis
In Danish
pub 1932—
IaDH 1893-1914
IaDeL Ag 13-20,S 3 1891;96-[1903-05]-[08-13; 16-19]
MnHi My 31 1888-1931;Jl 14 1932+
WHi O 15 1895-S 24 1931;Jl 14 1932+

Tyler HERALD. w 1907+
pub 1907+
MnHi My 28 1908+

Tyler JOURNAL. w 1882+
1882-Ja 22 1892 as Lincoln county journal
pub [1882-93]+
MnHi N 14,D 5,26 1890;Ap 17 1891+

LINCOLN county journal. *See* Tyler journal

ULEN

Ulen UNION. w O 23 1896+
pub 1896-[97-98]+
MnHi Ja 28-Jl 22 1898;Je 16 1916+

UPSALA

Upsala NEWS-TRIBUNE. w N 15 1915+
pub 1915+

VERGAS

Vergas GRAPHIC. w Je 11 1926+
pub [1926-27]+
MnHi 1926+

VERNDALE

Verndale JOURNAL. *See* Wadena pioneer-journal (Wadena)

Verndale SUN. w 1895+
pub 1918+
MnHi Ap 2 1897-[1901-02]-[05]+

WADENA county tribune. w Mr 10 1877-
1877-N 16 1878 as Wadena tribune (Wadena)
MnHi [1877-78]-Je 21 1879

VIRGINIA

Virginia ENTERPRISE. w Jl? 1893-N 5 1915||
pub complete
MnHi [1894-95]-Jl 1896;Ja-My 1897;98-1915

Virginia daily ENTERPRISE. d 1914+
pub 1915-17;19+
MnHi N 11 1914+

Virginia daily PRESS. d F 1 1912-Je 30 1923||
1912-My 7 1923 as Daily Virginian. Merged with Virginia daily enterprise
KHi [Mr-Ap 1923]
MnHi complete

QUEEN city sun. w F 1 1922+
pub 1922+
MnHi 1922+

RANGE labor news. w 1919-D 30 1921||
Merged with Eveleth clarion (Eveleth)
MnHi O 21-D 30 1921

VIRGINIAN. w,sw My 2 1895-1922||?
sw My 5 1908-Ag 6 1909
MnHi [1895]-1916

Daily VIRGINIAN. *See* Virginia daily press

WABASHA

Wabasha DEMOCRAT. *See* Wabasha standard

Weekly JOURNAL. *See under* Lake City

MINNESOTA patriot. w D 24? 1858-
MnHi Ja 8-D 1 1859

Wabasha STANDARD. w 1888-Ap 11 1929||
1888-S 28 1898 as Wabasha democrat; O 7 1898-D 29 1899 Standard and Wabasha democrat; Ja 6 1900-N 2 1922 Standard. United with Wabasha county herald to form Wabasha county herald-standard
MnHi O 1899-1929

WABASHA county herald-standard. w 1857+
1857-D 8 1860 pub in Read's Landing
sw Ja 30 1861-O 8 1862
MWA Mr 15-22;D 27 1866
MnHi Ja 29 1859-[61-65]-S 3 1868;Ja 27 1870-S 1875;D 13 1876-O 3 1877;S 11 1878-82;Ja 27 1890;Ap 15 1891+
MnW [1865-69]+
N D 21 1861

WABASSO

Wabasso STANDARD. w 1900+
pub 1900-[06-23]+
MnHi S 1923+

WACONIA

CARVER county news. *See under* Watertown

Waconia PATRIOT. w 1897+
pub 1900+
MnHi [1903]+

Der WIEDERHALL. w Ja 1-Mr 19 1889||
In German
MnHi complete

WADENA

Wadena NEWS. w Je 26 1919-S 30 1926||
1919-F 9 1922 as Progressive news. Merged with Wadena pioneer journal
MnHi complete

Wadena PIONEER-JOURNAL. w 1879+
1879-N 2 1893 as Verndale journal (Verndale); N 9 1893-Jl 30 1897 Wadena county journal
pub [1897-1925]+
MnHi S 29 1882+

PROGRESSIVE news. *See* Wadena news

Wadena TRIBUNE. 1877-78 *See* Wadena county tribune (Verndale)

Wadena TRIBUNE. w 1888-1905||?
MnHi [1899]-[1901]-[04]

WADENA county journal. *See* Wadena pioneer-journal

WADENA county pioneer. w 1878-Jl 1897||
United with Wadena county journal to form Wadena pioneer journal
MnHi F 13 1890-[91-92]
MnWadP [1878-97]

WAHKON

Wahkon BOOSTER. w Ap 12 1923-Je 18 1926||
MnHi complete

Wahkon ENTERPRISE. w N 28 1907-Ja 19 1923||
MnHi complete

WALKER

CASS county pioneer. w Ja 16 1894+
1894-My 2 1896 place of pub varies: Ellis; Esterdy; Motley; Cass
pub 1894+
MnHi 1894-[1901]-[05]-[18]+

Walker PILOT. w 1897+
MnHi Mr 13 1903+

WALNUT GROVE

RURAL center. *See* Walnut Grove tribune

Walnut Grove TRIBUNE. w Ag 13 1891+
1891-O 19 1900 as Rural center
pub [1891-1906]+
MnHi 1891-N 1 1900;O 31-D 5 1901;Mr 1906+

WANAMINGO

Wanamingo PROGRESS. w Ap 9 1909+
MnHi 1909+

WANDA

Wanda PIONEER press. w Ap 24 1902-03||
MnHi 1902-03

WANKE

Wanke HERALD. w 1901-
MnHi Je 19-S 25 1902

WARREN

Warren REGISTER. w 1887-D 27 1928||
Merged with Warren sheaf
MnHi S 17 1890-[92]-1928
MnWa complete

Warren SHEAF. w D 1 1880+
pub [1901-02]+
MnHi 1880-Mr 16 1882;S 18 1890-F 18 1904; Mr 2 1905+

WARROAD

Warroad PIONEER. w S 9 1897+
1897-Ap 27 1899 as Roseau plaindealer (Roseau); My 1899-Ag 31 1911 Warroad plaindealer
MnHi 1897-Ap,Je 1899-N 1912

Warroad PLAINDEALER. *See* Warroad pioneer

WASECA

CAMPAIGN. w Ag 22-N 7 1872||
MnHi complete

Waseca HERALD. w O 4 1877+
1877-Ap 6 1906 as Waseca county herald
pub 1886+
MnHi Ja 25 1878-Ag 1 1879;S 29 1882+

Waseca JOURNAL. w Je 4 1895+
Ja 9 1902-N 23 1921 as Waseca journal-radical
pub [1895+]
MnHi 1895+

Waseca JOURNAL-RADICAL. *See* Waseca journal

Waseca LEADER. w 1875-78||
MWA S 15 1877
MnHi D 30 1876-Ap 6 1878

MINNESOTA democrat. w D 23 1887-
MnHi Ja 14 1888

MINNESOTA radical. *See* Waseca radical

Waseca NEWS. *See* Waseca radical

Waseca RADICAL. w 1863-Ja 1 1902||
1863-D 30 1874 as Waseca news; Ja 7 1875-Mr 21 1883 Minnesota radical. United with Waseca journal to form Waseca journal-radical, later Waseca journal
pub [1883-1902]
MWA Ja 8 1879
MnHi O 10 1867-1902

RECORD. w O 4 1873-
MnHi N 22 1873-F 21 1874

WASECA county herald. *See* Waseca herald

WASIOJA

Wasioja GAZETTE. w 1858-
MWA Jl 1 1859

MINNESOTA beacon. *See under* Minneapolis

RURAL Minnesotian. w N 14 1860-
MnHi F 28,Ag 29 1861

WATERTOWN

CARVER county news. w My 6 1887+
1887-Ag 27 1897 pub in Waconia
pub 1897+
MnHi 1887-[91]-O 29 1903

WATERVILLE

Waterville ADVANCE. w S 10 1884+
MnHi 1884-1885,S 24 1890-Ap 1 1908

Waterville GAZETTE. w Ag 5 1892-S 30 1904||
Merged with Waterville advance
MnHi S 30 1892-1904

Waterville SENTINEL. w D 15 1911-Mr 28 1919||
Follows Le Sueur sentinel (Le Sueur)
Merged with Waterville advance
MnHi complete

WATSON

Watson VOICE. w 1926+
pub 1926+
MnHi 1928+

WAUBUN

Waubun FORUM. w 1907-28||
MnHi O 7 1921-Ja 27 1928

WAVERLY

Waverly STAR. w 1904?-08||?
United with Waverly tribune to form Waverly star and tribune

Waverly STAR and tribune. w 1890+
1890-1908? as Waverly tribune
pub 1916+
MnHi 1898-Mr 26 1908

Waverly TRIBUNE. *See* Waverly star and tribune

WAYZATA

MINNETONKA herald. w My 23 1930+
pub 1930+
MnHi 1930+

MINNETONKA pilot. w 1923?-My 15 1930||
MnHi Ja 16-My 15 1930

Wayzata REPORTER. *See* Hennepin county herald (Minneapolis)

WELCOME

Welcome MESSENGER. w F 12 1890-
MnLaS [1890]

Welcome TIMES. w 1896+
MnHi 1898-S 27 1907

WELLS

Wells ADVOCATE. *See* Wells forum-advocate

Wells ATLAS. w Ja 20 1870-75||
Follows Martin county atlas (Fairmont)
1870-D 16 1874 as Wells atlas; D 23 1874-Ap 14 1875? Faribault county leader
MnHi 1870-My 12 1875

FAIRBAULT county leader. *See* Wells atlas

Wells FORUM. w 1894-O 11 1906||
United with Wells advocate to form Wells forum-advocate
MnHi 1898-1906

Wells FORUM-ADVOCATE. w 1870-Ja 1 1925||
1870-O 11 1906 as Wells advocate. Merged with Wells mirror
MnHi Ja 13-Ap 21 1881;My 22 1885-1925

Wells GAZETTE. w O 7 1875-
MnHi O 7 1875

Wells MIRROR. w S 3 1913+
pub 1913+
MnHi [1913-14]+

WENDELL

Wendell TRIBUNE. w 1914-S 14 1923||
Merged with Grant county herald (Elbow Lake)
MnHi Ag 24 1917-23

MINNESOTA (*Continued*)

WEST CONCORD

CONCORD people. w Ap 21 1892-93||
MnHi N 10 1892-Ag 26 1893

West Concord ENTERPRISE. w 1892+
pub [1901]-[21-23]+
MnHi Ap 29 1897+

WEST DULUTH

Papers published in West Duluth are listed under Duluth

WEST SUPERIOR

VOIX du lac. *See under* Minneapolis

WESTBROOK

Westbrook SENTINEL. w Je 11 1901+
pub 1901+

WESTPORT

Westport WORLD. w N 5 1920-Ap 12 1923||
MnHi complete

WHEATON

FOOT PRINTS. *See* Traverse county traveler

Wheaton GAZETTE. w Mr 6 1885+
1889?-Ap 24 1925 as Wheaton gazette-reporter
pub 1919+
MnHi 1885-S 23 1887;Ap 10 1891+

TRAVERSE county star. w Ag 31 1922-Ja 25 1924||
MnHi N 16 1922-24
MnWhG complete

TRAVERSE county traveler. w Mr 28 1890-N 8 1918||
1890-Mr 31 1916 as Foot prints (title varies slightly). Merged with Wheaton gazette-reporter, later Wheaton gazette
1890-S 7 1894 pub in Browns Valley
MnHi Ag 1 1890;Mr 27 1891-1918

WHITE BEAR LAKE

BREEZE. *See under* St. Paul

LAKE breeze. *See* Breeze (St. Paul)

White Bear LIFE. *See* White Bear press

White Bear PRESS. w Ap 17 1896+
1896-Ap 2 1914 as White Bear life
pub [1914]23+
MnHi 1896+

WHITE EARTH

PROGRESS. w O 8 1887-Jl 13 1889||
MnHi O 29 1887-89

TOMAHAWK. w Ap 9 1903-O 21 1926||?
Followed by Callaway tomahawk (Callaway)
MnHi Ap 1903-S 8 1904,N 18 1915-My 27 1926

WILLIAMS

Williams NORTHERN light. w F 3 1916+
pub 1916+

WILLMAR

ALLIANCE standard. w 1891-92||
MnHi F 2,Ap-D 1892

Willmar weekly ARGUS. w 1885-1900||?
MnHi [1887]-Ja 5 1893;F 4 1897-Ag 17 1899

Willmar GAZETTE. w Ja 28 1871-
1871-75? as Willmar republican; 1876?-Ap 24 1930 Republican gazette
MnHi 1871-Ag 1873;S 25 1890+

Willmar JOURNAL. w Jl 16 1904+
MnHi 1904+

Willmar REPUBLICAN. *See* Willmar gazette

REPUBLICAN-GAZETTE. *See* Willmar gazette

Willmar TRIBUNE. w,sw F 19 1895+
sw D 3 1902-D 2 1903
MnHi F 19 1895+
MnWi 1898+

Willmar daily TRIBUNE. d Ja 3 1928+
MnHi 1928+
MnWi 1928+

SWIFT county standard. *See under* Benson

WESTERN Minnesota press. *See* Republican-press (Atwater)

WILMONT

Wilmont INITIATOR. *See* Wilmont tribune

Wilmont TRIBUNE. w D 1900+
1900-09 as Wilmont initiator
pub 1906+

WILTON

Wilton weekly NEWS. w 1864-
MWA F 21 1867
MnHi Ja 3-O 3 1867

WASECA citizen. w D 26 1860-
MnHi [1860-Mr 27 1861]

WASECA home views. w Mr 14 1860-
MnHi [Je 13 1860-S 26 1861]

WINDOM

COTTONWOOD county citizen. sw,w 1883+
sw Mr 11 1908-Ja 6 1909
pub [1883+]
MnHi Ap 18 1891+

Windom REPORTER. w S 7 1871+
pub 1883-84;1908+
MnHi 1871-S 14 1872;S 11 1884+

WINGER

Winger ENTERPRISE. w 1915+
pub 1922+
MnHi S 28 1922+

WINNEBAGO

Winnebago ADVERTISER. w F 29 1872-
MnHi F 29-Je 6 1872

Winnebago City ENTERPRISE. w 1893+
MnHi My 30 1901-Ag 18 1904

FREE homestead. w 1863-70||
1863-Ap 1864 as Whig of '76
MnHi Mr 28 1866;Ja 23-Ap 10 1867;68-Je 8 1870

Winnebago NEWS. w 1881-84||?
United with Winnebago press and times to form Winnebago City press-news

Winnebago City PRESS. w Je 23 1870-80||?
United with Winnebago times to form Winnebago press and times, later Winnebago City press-news
MnHi Jl 1870-D 14 1871[77-78]

Winnebago PRESS and times. *See* Winnebago City press-news

Winnebago City PRESS-NEWS. w 1872-Ja 18 1930||
1872-80? as Winnebago times; 1881-84? Winnebago press and times
MnHi Ap 25 1891-1930

Winnebago TIMES. *See* Winnebago City press-news

WHIG of '76. *See* Free homestead

WINONA

Winona ADLER. w O 9 1873-88||?
In German
MnHi 1873-S 29 1875

AMERICA-HEROLD-LINCOLN freie presse. w Ja 21 1881+
1881-N 25 1924 as Der Westlicher herold
Prints ed. for Minneapolis; Chicago; La Crosse, Wausau, and Manitowoc, Wis.
In German
pub 1881+
IU D 21 1920-Ag 2 1932
MnHi 1881+
WHi Mr 24 1887-S 3 1907;O 29 1918-27

Winona ARGUS. w O 3? 1854-57||?
Followed by Winona times
DLC [N 22 1854-N 26 1856]
MnHi Ap 25 1855;F 26-S 3 1857

Winona BANNER. w Jl 14 1866-
In German
MnHi Jl 14-S 8 1866

DAKOTA rundschau. *See* Dakota freie presse (Bismarck, N.D.)

DEMOCRAT. w Ag 5 1857-
1857-O 21 1858 as Rochester democrat (Rochester)
DLC D 30 1857[59-N 3 1860]
MnHi Mr 18-O 21,N 20 1858-N 17 1860

Winona DEMOCRAT. w S 17 1864-
MnHi S 24 1864-S 9 1865
MnWn 1865-67
MnWnR 1864-68

Winona daily DEMOCRAT. d Ja 8 1868-
MnHi Ja 8-N 14 1868
MnWn 1868
MnWnR 1868

Evening DEMOCRAT. d O 8 1900-
MnHi O 8-N 10 1900

DEMOCRATIC press. w S 9 1865-
MnHi O 21,D 16 1865

ELGIN herold. *See* Illinois wochenblatt. (Elgin, Ill)

Winona weekly EXPRESS. w Ag 14 1855-
MnHi Ag 14-O 16 1855

HEIMATBOTE. *See under* Chicago, Ill.

Winona HERALD. w My 7 1869-F 18 1901||
United with Winona weekly republican to form Winona weekly republican-herald
DLC Jl 7 1876
MnHi 1869-F 1884;Ap 1889-Ap 11 1890;O 31 1891-O 13 1893
MnWn 1869-98
MnWnR 1869-[75-76]-[81-82]-[90]-[96]-1900
MnU Ap 26 1878

Winona daily HERALD. d 1886-F 17 1901||
United with Winona daily republican to form Winona republican-herald
MnHi Mr 21 1888-1901
MnWn 1888-97
MnWnR 1888-[95-96]-1900

ILLINOIS wochenblatt. *See under* Elgin, Ill.

Winona INDEPENDENT. d 1902-My 29 1919||
Merged with Winona republican-herald
MnHi O 1902-19
MnWnR 1907-[12]-19

Winona LEADER. w,d My 9 1890-Ap 15 1922||
Title varies slightly
w 1890-O 6 1921
MnHi 1890-[95]-1922

Der MISSISSIPPI bote. w N 5 1870-71||
In German
MnHi 1870-Mr 17 1871

Winona weekly NEWS. w O 24 1893-1905||
MnHi 1893-O 16 1894;N 9 1897-N 8 1898
MnWn 1893-96
MnWnR 1894-[96-97]1900-05

Winona daily NEWS. d S 14 1916-
WHi S 14-O 6 1916

Winona weekly REPUBLICAN-herald w N 20 1855-Ag 1907||
1855-F 18 1901 as Winona weekly republican
MWA Je 8 1859;O 17-31,N 14 1860;S 17 1862;Je 13 1866
MnHi 1855[56-58]-[60]-62;D 7 1864;67-78;80
MnWn complete
MnWnR 1855-74;76-86;88-91;94-95;97-99
N O 2 1861
WHi S 9 1856;S 16 1874;Ap 28,My 12 1875;94-1907

Winona REPUBLICAN-HERALD. d 1859+
1859-F 18 1901 as Winona daily republican
pub 1860+
DLC [F 23 1865-O 15 1866;Ap 6 1867-69;Ja 30-Ap 16 1872]
MWA My 30 1866;Jl 25,Ag 7,O 5,N 12 1868
MnHi O 2 1861-[62]-[96]+
MnWn 1859+
WHi F 25 1870

Die RUNDSCHAU. w 1879?-
In German
MnHi D 2 1924-D 17 1929

Der SEEBOTE. *See under* Milwaukee, Wis.

TIMES. w Ja 30 1858-
Follows Winona argus
MnHi F 6-Jl 17 1858

Winona daily TRIBUNE. d
MnWnR 1881-82

VOLKSBLATT des westens. w N 23 1898-
In German
MnHi 1898-[1916]-[19-Jl 23 1920]

Der WESTENS. w
In German
IU N 4 1921-N 28 1924
MnHi D 10 1920-N 28 1924

Der WESTLICHER herold. *See* America-herold-Lincoln freie presse

WIARUS. w,sw 1886-1919||?
In Polish
w 1886-N 20 1917
MnHi Ag 12-D 16 1919

WINONA. w My 21 1887-D 31 1920||
In German
MnHi complete

WINSTED

Winsted JOURNAL. w O 12 1922+
pub 1922+

WINTHROP

Winthrop NEWS. w D 17 1887+
pub 1887+
MnHi D 24 1887+

WOODLAKE

Woodlake LEDGER. *See* Woodlake news

Woodlake NEWS. w 1898+
1898-N 2 1900 as Woodlake ledger
pub 1913+
MnHi D 17 1897-[1904]-O 1915;O 26 1916-S 6 1923

WOODSTOCK

Woodstock EAGLE. w Ag 12 1891-92||
MnHi 1891-Mr 11 1892

Woodstock NEWS. w 1898+
MnHi F 12 1909-Jl 28 1916

WORTHINGTON

ADVANCE-HERALD. w 1872-Mr 25 1910||
1872-Jl 3 1908 as Worthington advance. Merged with Worthington globe
MnHi Mr 1874-1910
MnWoG S 1874-[92]1900-01;06-08

CLAIM shanty vindicator. w O 7 1874-
OClWHi O 14,N 11 1874

Worthington GLOBE. sw Mr 1886+
pub 1886-[92]95-97;1902+
MnHi S 25 1890-My 18 1899;Mr 31 1910+

Worthington HERALD. w S 1894-Jl 1908||
United with Worthington advance to form Advance-herald
MnHi Ap 12 1895-1908
MnWoG [1894-97]1904-05

NOBLES county times. w 1911+
pub [1917]+
MnHi Ag 1923+
MnU Ap 16 1926+

MINNESOTA (*Continued*)

WORTHINGTON—*Continued*

Worthington PROGRESSIVE. w Mr 9 1911-My 27 1915||
1911-Ja 30 1913 as Worthington republican
MnHi complete

Worthington REPUBLICAN. *See* Worthington progressive

WYKOFF

Wykoff ADVERTISER. *See* Wykoff enterprise

Wykoff ENTERPRISE. w 1893+
1893-98? as Wykoff advertiser; 1899-1909 Wykoff enterprise; Ja-Jl 8 1910 Messenger enterprise
MnHi Ap 16-N 1897;1910+

Wykoff MESSENGER. w 1903-D 31 1909||
United with Wykoff enterprise to form Messenger-enterprise, later Wykoff enterprise
MnHi F 15-D 1909

MESSENGER-ENTERPRISE. *See* Wykoff enterprise

YOUNG AMERICA

Young America EAGLE. w Ag 12 1904+
pub 1904+
MnHi Ag 12-S 2 1904;Ag 5 1909+

ZUMBRO FALLS

ENTERPRISE. w O 1 1908+
pub 1908+

Zumbro Falls INDEPENDENT. w Ja 7 1898-Ag 8 1902||
1898 as Zumbro Falls independent and Mazeppa independent
MnHi Ja 14 1898-1902

ZUMBROTA

Zumbrota INDEPENDENT. w 1875-1906||
MnHi Ap 24,N 20 1890-My 10 1906

Zumbrota NEWS. w 1885+
MnHi Jl 25 1890+

MISSISSIPPI

ABERDEEN

Weekly CONSERVATIVE. w 1842-
MsHi Je 9 1855

Aberdeen EXAMINER. w 1866+
DLC Jl 10 1879;O 26 1882-Ja 8 1885
MsAbC 1879+
MsHi 1881;83-89;91;93-1910;13-15
NcD Ag 22 1872

Daily Aberdeen EXAMINER. tw,d 1866-85||?
Title varies: Tri-weekly examiner
GAtCo Ja 17 1867
MsHi Ap 8 1881;83-85

Weekly INDEPENDENT. w Ja 8 1848-53||
Merged with Weekly conservative
DLC Ja 8 1848-D 7 1850;Ja 11,F 15-Mr 8,Ap 19-My 10,24 1851;Ja 29-Je 16,Jl 16 1853
MWA Mr 10 1849-Ja 12,26-F 2,16-23,Mr 2-16 1850
MsHi D 21 1850-D 10 1853
PPL N 30 1850

MISSISSIPPI advertiser. w Mr 5 1842-
Followed by Monroe democrat
DLC D 14 1844-F 22,Mr 8,My 10 1845
MsHi 1842-Ap 14 1847
NSchU Ap 30 1842

MONROE democrat. w Ap 19 1848-
Follows Mississippi advertiser
DLC 1848-Mr 13 1850
MsHi My 3 1850-D 22 1852

NORTH Mississippi advocate. w Jl 14 1838-
WHi Jl 21 1838

SUNNY South. w Ja 10 1856-
DLC 1856-D 22 1859
MWA 1855-O 1 1857
MsLE Ag 12 1858
TM F 5 1863
WHi [Ja 24-D 11 1856]

Aberdeen daily SUNNY South. d 1865-
GAtCo D 3 1866;Ja 4 1867

TRUE republican. w Ja 19 1874-76||
MsAbE O 29 1875

Aberdeen WEEKLY. w 1875+
MsHi 1902-10

Aberdeen WHIG and North Mississippi advocate. w My 7 1839-
MsHi My 7 1839

ACKERMAN

CHOCTAW plaindealer. w 1887+
MsHi Ja 6-O 24 1902

ASHLAND

BENTON county argus. w 1872-82||?
MsAsC 1879-Ja 1880

Ashland CHRONICLE. *See* Ashland register

Ashland REGISTER. w 1879-1907||
1879-90? as Ashland chronicle
MsAsC complete

SOUTHERN advocate. w 1905+
pub [Je 1906-O 12 1912]+
MsAsC 1907+

BATESVILLE

PANOLIAN. w F 1 1881+
pub 1881+
MsBaC 1882—
MsHi Je 1902-N 1910

BAY ST. LOUIS

GULF coast progress. w 1895-1919||
Merged with Sea coast echo
MsBayC complete

SEA coast echo. w 1892+
MsBayC 1892+
MsHi S 1902-N 1910

BAY SPRINGS

JASPER county news. w 1896+
1896-N 15 1917 as Bay Springs news
MsLE 1908-25

JASPER county review. w
MsHi O 1902-N 1904

Bay Springs NEWS. *See* Jasper county news

BELEN

Quitman QUILL. w 1890-
MsHi My 30 1902-D 18 1903

BELZONI

Belzoni BANNER. w 1910+
MsBC Je 1918+

BENTON

NORTH Mississippian. w Jl 14 1830-
NcD S 22 1830

YAZOO banner. w Ja 20? 1838-
MsHi Ja 27 1838-Je 1 1844

BILOXI

Daily HERALD. *See under* Gulfport

SEA shore sentinel. w 1850-
MWA Ja 14 1854

BLUE MOUNTAIN

NEW standard. w 1901-05||?
MsHi My 1902-04

BOONEVILLE

Booneville BANNER. w 1897+
MsBoC 1898+

Booneville INDEPENDENT. w N 1923—
pub 1923+

BRANDON

Brandon DISSEMINATOR. w D 28? 1844-50||?
MsHi F 8 1845-My 6 1846

FREE state. w 1898-1904||?
Negro
WHi Ja 20 1900

MISSISSIPPI intelligencer. w
DLC Ag 12 1841
MsHi 1839-40

Brandon NEWS. w 1892+
pub D 1924+
MsBraC 1932+
MsHi 1902-10

Brandon REPUBLIC and Eastern advocate. w Ap? 1837-
MsHi Je 24 1837-S 12 1838

Brandon REPUBLICAN. w 1850-90||?
CSmH Ap 30 1863
MWA D 16 1852;Mr 23 1865
MsLE Mr 2,23 1865
MsU Ap 23 1874-Je 29 1876
NcD Mr 2,23 1865;My 30 1872
PHi S 24 1863
PPL Ja 18 1851

BROOKHAVEN

Brookhaven ADVERTISER. w 1859-
MsHi O 26 1861

Brookhaven LEADER. sw 1883+
MsHi 1902-10

LINCOLN county times. w 1889+
pub 1889+
MsBrC F 17-D 21 1893
MsHi Je 1902-N 1910

MISSISSIPPI weekly citizen. w
-1869? as Southern journal
InRE F 27 1875
MWiC N 20 1869
MsBrC 1869-77

SOUTH Mississippian. w 1905-09||
Merged with Brookhaven leader
MsBrC Ja-D 20 1906

SOUTHERN journal. *See* Mississippi weekly citizen

CALHOUN CITY

DIXIE herald. w 1903-19||?
United with Calhoun monitor to form Calhoun City monitor-herald
1903-09? pub in Pittsboro
MsHi Ap 5 1906-D 17 1908

Calhoun MONITOR-HERALD. w 1900+
1900-19? as Calhoun monitor (Pittsboro)
MsHi Je 22 1905-N 16 1910

CANTON

AMERICAN citizen. w,tw,d 1850-88||?
DLC F 1851-Ja 20 1855;64-65
MBAt O 22 1865
MsCaC 1851-81
MsLE O 26,D 26 1864

COMMONWEALTH. w 1855-
DLC My 9 1862
MsCaC 1852-60
NcD Jl 27 1857

Canton HERALD and Mississippi intelligencer. w 1836-39||
Followed by Madison county Whig advocate
MWA My 30 1838
MsHi Ap 21 1837-Ja 2 1839

INDEPENDENT democrat. w S 17 1842-44||
Follows Madison county whig advocate
Followed by Mississippi Creole (1844-51)
DLC S 17 1842;My 11,Jl 6 20,Ag 14-21,S 7-O 9,30-N 13,23 1844
MsCaC complete
MsHi O 1 1842-N 13 1844

MADISON county herald. w Je 1906+
Follows Canton times
pub 1906+
MsCaC 1906+

MADISON county whig advocate. w Ja 12 1839-42||
Follows Canton Herald and Mississippi intelligencer. Followed by Independent democrat
MsCaC complete
MsHi Ja 19-26 1839
GAtCo S 7 1839

MADISON democrat. w Ja 11-D 23 1882||
MsCaC complete

MADISONIAN. w 1848-55||?
Merged with American citizen
MsCaC 1848-55

Canton MAIL. w 1865-79||
MsCaC 1871-79

MISSISSIPPI creole. w My 29 1841-51||?
Follows Independent democrat
DLC S 25,N 20 1841
GDE N 24 1849
MsCaC 1844-51
MsHi 1841-Je 4 1842

PICKET. w 1883-1907||
MsCaC complete
MsHi My 1902-N 1907

Daily PICKET. d 1886-93||
MsCaC complete

Canton PROGRESS. w 1891-93||
Followed by Canton times
MsCaC complete

Canton TIMES. w 1893-1906||
Follows Canton progress. Followed by Madison county herald
MsCaC complete
MsHi My 30 1902-F 26 1904

CARROLLTON

Carrollton CONSERVATIVE. w 1865+
1865-79? as Mississippi conservative; 1880? Carrollton courier conservative
MsHi 1902-10

Carrollton COURIER conservative. *See* Carrollton conservative

Carrollton HORNET. w Jl 11 1843-
MsHi 1843

MISSISSIPPI conservative. *See* Carrollton conservative

MISSISSIPPI democrat. w 1847-
MWA D 22 1848

SOUTHERN pioneer. w D 5 1840-42||?
MsHi 1840-N 5 1842

WESTERN statesman. w Je 20 1844-Jl 8 1845||
Followed by Greenwood reporter (Greenwood)
MsHi complete

WHIG creed. w S 6 1845-
MsHi N 29-D 6 1845

MISSISSIPPI (*Continued*)

CARTHAGE

CARTHAGINIAN. w 1872+
Ja 14-Je 1909 as Carthage-Mississippian
pub 1909+
MsCarC 1881+
MsHi 1902-06

MISSISSIPPIAN. w Jl 1908-Ja 7 1909||
United with Carthaginian to form Carthage-Mississippian, later Carthaginian
MsCarC complete

CENTREVILLE

Centreville JEFFERSONIAN. w 1890+
MsWoC F-D 1895

CHARLESTON

DEMOCRATIC herald. *See* Mississippi sun

MISSISSIPPI sun. w 1892+
1892-Mr 1908 as Democratic herald; Ap 1908-Ap 7 1920 Tallahatchie herald; Ap 14 1920 Tallahatchie herald and Mississippi sun
pub 1919+
MsCC 1919+
MsHi My 1902-N 9 1910

TALLAHATCHIAN. w 1862-68||?
MWA F 16 1867

TALLAHATCHIAN. w 1903-D 25 1907||
MsHi O 5 1904-07

TALLAHATCHIE herald. *See* Mississippi sun

CLARKSDALE

Clarksdale BANNER. w 1884-1910||
MsHi O 1902-O 1907;F 1908-N 1910

Clarksdale CHALLENGE. w 1896-1919||?
MsHi Je 1905-Mr 1906

Clarksdale daily REGISTER. d 1908+
MsClR 1908+

CLEVELAND

BOLIVAR commercial. w,sw Mr 30 1917+
w 1917-30?
pub 1917-19;21+

Cleveland ENTERPRISE. w 1899+
pub 1899+
MsHi 1902-10

CLINTON

CONSTITUTIONAL flag. w
Ct Ap 6 1832

Clinton GAZETTE. w 1833-40||?
MsHi [1833-D 9 1837]

MISSISSIPPIAN. w N 8 1832-
MsHi My 31 1833
N S 27 1833

SOUTHERN marksman. w S 1838-
DLC D 4 1838
MsHi D 1838-Ja 1839

COFFEEVILLE

Coffeeville COURIER. w 1891+
MsHi [My 24 1902-D 10 1903]

SOUTHERN appeal. w 1851-
MWA Ja 14 1854

COLLINS

Collins COMMERCIAL. w 1902+
MsHi F-D 1905

COVINGTON county news. w My 20 1931+
pub 1931+

COLUMBIA

COLUMBIAN-progress. w 1901+
1901-35 as Columbian
MsCoC 1901+

MARION county progress. w 1908-35||
United with Columbian to form Columbian-progress
MsCoC 1911-27;29-35
MsHi Jl 1909-N 1910

PEARL RIVER news. *See* Columbia times

Columbia TIMES. w 1883-1908||?
1883-1903 as Pearl River news
Merged with Marion county progress
MsHi Ag 29 1902-O 16 1903
MsPu 1884-98;D 1901-02

COLUMBUS

Columbus COMMERCIAL. w 1895-Mr 5 1922||
United with Columbus dispatch to form Commercial-dispatch
MsHi 1902-10

COMMERCIAL dispatch. w,tw 1880+
1879-Mr 5 1922 as Columbus dispatch (w,tw)
pub 1900+
MsColC 1929+
MsHi S 18 1902-10
NcD My 9 1886;My 29 1887;O 2 1929

Columbus DEMOCRAT. w 1830-58||
Followed by Mississippi democrat
DLC 1837;39-[41;43-44;53]-[55-56]
ICHi N 13 1852
MWA Je 19 1852;O 28 1854
MsHi Ag 1836-41;S 1848-F 6 1853
NcU My 2 1840;O 12 1844

Columbus DEMOCRAT. w 1869-78||?
LNC D 23 1871
NcD Jl 6 1872

Tri-weekly Columbus DEMOCRAT. tw 1885-86||
NcD Ap 30 1886

DEMOCRATIC Whig. w S 22 1842-43||
DLC S 22 1842
MsHi N 17 1842-N 2 1843

Columbus DISPATCH. *See* Commercial dispatch

Columbus INDEX-DEMOCRAT. w 1865-95||?
1865-68 as Mississippi index; 1869-94 Columbus index
NcD D 17 1865;Ap 16 1867;F 14 1868;Ag 1,3 1872
OClWHi Ja 28 1873

MISSISSIPPI democrat. w 1858-
Follows Columbus democrat
NcD Jl 24 1858
TxU F 5 1859

MISSISSIPPI index. *See* Columbus index-democrat

Daily MISSISSIPPIAN. d
DLC D 10 1863(extra)
TM N 22 1863(extra)

PATRON of husbandry. w 1873-82||
TxU Jl 12 1879;Mr 18,My 6 1882

PLUG-UGLY. Ag 27 1857-
NcD Ag 27 1857

Columbus PRESS. w 1869-76||
KHi N 1873-Ap 15 1876
NcD Ag 24 1872;Jl 12 1873

PRIMITIVE republican. w 1842-52||
MsHi Ja 9 1851-N 25 1852

Columbus daily REPUBLICAN. d 1864-
NcD Mr 15 1865

SOUTHERN argus. w 1833-
DLC [1835;41]
MsHi S 28 1841-S 6 1842
NcU D 6 1834;Je 27,Jl 11,O 5 1835;My 19 1840

SOUTHERN republic.
GAtCo S 18 1861

SOUTHERN sentinel. tw,sw 1866-69||
NcD F 13 1866;My 11 1869

SOUTHERN standard. w 1851-
DLC O 16 1852
MsHi 1851-53

STATE advocate. w 1832-
N S 24 1833

CORINTH

Corinth CHANTICLEER.
MnHi Jl 31 1863
OClWHi S 18 1863

Daily CORINTHIAN. d 1895+
MsHi N 1902-Jl 1903

Weekly CORINTHIAN. w 1894+
MsCorC 1906;18+

Corinth HERALD. w 1879-1907||
MsCorC 1906

MISSOURI army argus. ir O 26 1861-My 1862||?
Confederate Army paper
O 28 1861 pub near Neosho, Mo.; N 16 1861 Pineville, Mo.; N 22 1861 Greenfield, Mo.; N 30-D 15 1861 Osceola, Mo.; D 25 1861-F 13 1862 Springfield, Mo.; Mr 2 1862 Cove Creek, Ark.
DLC O 28 1861-Mr 2,My 7-25 1862 extras:N 23,D 3 1861;Ja 5 1862
MnHi N 30 1861
MoSHi N 30 1861

Corinth WAR eagle. w Jl 31 1862-
MWA Jl 31 1862

CRYSTAL SPRINGS

SOUTHERN argus and crisis. sw Ag 1 1868
MBAt Ag 1 1868

DE KALB

KEMPER county messenger. w 1932+
MsDC S 1934+

KEMPER democrat. w 1857-
NcD Ap 8 1858

De Kalb SENTINEL. w 1926-My 1933||
Merged with Kemper county messenger (Scooba)

SOUTHERN star. w 1898-
MsHi O 24 1900

DREW

Drew LEADER. w O 1918+
pub 1918+
MsRR 1918+

DURANT

Durant NEWS. w 1882+
MsHi My 1902-08

EASTPORT

NORTH Mississippi union. w
TxU My 1 1852

ELLISVILLE

JONES county item. w 1922-23||
United with Ellisville progress to form Progress-item

JONES county news. w 1888-1924||
1888-1905 as New South; 1906-09 New South-news
MsEC 1892-1924
MsHi S 6 1902-Mr 12 1904

NEW SOUTH. *See* Jones county news

NEW SOUTH news. *See* Jones county news

Ellisville NEWS. w 1892-1904||
United with New South to form New South-news, later Jones county news
MsEC complete

PROGRESS-item. w 1921+
1921-23 as Ellisville progress
MsEC Mr 23-30,Ap 13,My 25 1922;24+

ENTERPRISE

CLARK county times. w 1887-1907||
MsHi D 5 1902-Je 16 1904;F 1905-S 1907

Enterprise COURIER. w 1870-85||?
MWA F 28 1880

Weekly NEWS. w 1859-
MWA Ja 26 1860

STAR. *See* Star of Pascagoula (Pascagoula)

EUPORA

PROGRESS. *See* Progress warder

PROGRESS warder. w 1889-1919||?
1889-1907? as Progress. Followed by Webster progress
MsHi 1902-03;F 1905-N 1910

WEBSTER progress. w 1923+
Follows Progress warder
pub 1923+
MsHi My 23 1902-Ja 9 1903;05-N 1910

FAYETTE

Fayette ADVERTISER and Jefferson county advocate. w
DLC F 14 1839

BOND payer. w
DLC S 24 1841

Fayette CHRONICLE. w 1866+
MsFC 1890+
MsHi My 1902-1907

JEFFERSON whig. S 26 1840-
Follows Rodney telegraph (Rodney)
MsHi 1840-My 4 1841

SOUTHERN watch-tower. w Ja 1843-
MWA Ja 4,11 1854
NcD 1843-Ja 1846

FOREST

NEWS. w 1911-15||
United with Register to form News-register

NEWS-REGISTER. w 1867+
1867-1915 as Scott county register
pub 1924+
MsHi Jl 2 1902-Ja 14 1903;Mr 1905-06

SCOTT county register. *See* News-register

FORT ADAMS

Fort Adams ITEM. w S 2 1854-
Follows Fort Adams times
LSfD F 9 1856
MsHi 1854-N 10 1855

Fort Adams TIMES. w,m 1853-54
Followed by Fort Adams item
MsHi My 21-N 12 1853

FRANKLIN

Franklin ADVOCATE. w
MsHi O 1902-07

FRIAR'S POINT

Friar's Point COAHOMIAN. w
MsHi 1865-66

Friars Point COAHOMIAN. w 1886-1931||?
1886-94? as New Coahomian
MsHi My 1902-N 1910

FULTON

Fulton HERALD. w 1892-1904||?
MsHi O 10 1902-Ag 20 1903

GAINSVILLE

Gainsville ADVOCATE.
MsHi 1845-46
P-M N 1 1845

MISSISSIPPI (*Continued*)

GALENA

NORTHWESTERN gazette and Galena advertiser.
DLC S 20 1834

GALLATIN

Gallatin INTELLIGENCER. w Ja 18 1834-
DLC Ja 25,Mr 1 1834

RADICAL democrat. w Jl 1844-
MsHi Jl 20-Ag 17 1844

SOUTHERN star. w N 11 1837-
MsHi D 16 1837-S 8 1841

GARDEN CITY

SOUTHERN progress. w 1889-91||?
MsMaF 1889-91

GLOSTER

Gloster RECORD. w F 1888+
1888-1904 as Valley record
pub 1888+
MsHi O 16 1903-Ja 15 1904

VALLEY record. *See* Gloster record

GRAND GULF

Grand Gulf ADVERTISER. w,sw,tw F 17 1834-Ct Mr 17 1835
DLC F 24 1834[39]
MsHi 1835-39

GREENVILLE

Weekly DEMOCRAT-TIMES. w 1888+
1888-1917 as Weekly democrat
pub 1924+

Daily DEMOCRAT-TIMES. d S 6 1896+
1896-1917 as Daily democrat
pub 1924+
MsHi O 1902-N 1910
MsSM [O 6-D 27 1916]

Weekly TIMES. w 1868-1917||
United with Weekly democrat to form Weekly democrat-times
MsGD 1868-69
MsHi F 1905-N 1910

Greenville TIMES. d 1907-17||
United with Daily democrat to form Daily democrat times

GREENWOOD

Greenwood weekly COMMONWEALTH. w 1896+
pub 1905+
MsHi Je 13 1902-O 10 1903;05-10

Greenwood daily COMMONWEALTH. d 1916+
pub 1916+

Greenwood ENTERPRISE. w 1896-1918||?
MsHi My 23 1902-My 24 1903

Greenwood REPORTER and commercial reporter. w F 18-Jl 8 1845||
Follows Western statesman (Carrollton)
MsHi F 18-Je 3 1845

GRENADA

BOWIE knife. sw Mr 29-Ap? 1839||
Followed by Southern reporter
DLC Ap 2 1839

Grenada GAZETTE. w 1885-90||
MsGrC 1889-Ja 3 1890

GRENADIAN. w D 7 1838-
MsHi 1838-39

HARRY of the West. w F 1844-Mr 14 1846||
MsHi Mr 16 1844-46

Grenada HERALD. w S 1 1842-
MsHi S 8 1842-D 15 1843

MISSISSIPPI sentinel. *See* Grenada sentinel

NEW SOUTH. w 1878-81||
MsGrC N 4 1880-D 17 1881

Weekly REGISTER. w Ja 6 1842-Mr 8? 1843||
Followed by Panola weekly register (Panola)
DLC Ja 13 1842
MsHi 1842-F 4 1843

Grenada REPUBLICAN. w 1849?-
MWA Ja 14 1854

Grenada SENTINEL. w 1854+
1854-70? as Mississippi sentinel
pub 1854+
MsGrC 1870+
MsHi S 1902-N 1910

SOUTHERN reporter. w My 18 1839-
Follows Bowie knife
MsHi 1839-My 22 1841
NhD My 22 1841

Daily STAR. d My 1 1935+
MsGrC 1935+

GULFPORT

GULF Coast guide. *See* Mississippi guide

Daily HERALD. w,d O 4 1884+
1884-1903 pub in Biloxi
w 1884-Ag 1898
pub 1888+
MsGuC 1913+

MsHi My 1902-N 1910
TxGR Ap 17 1933
WHi Je 1893

MISSISSIPPI guide. w S 17 1925+
1925-Je 15 1928 as Gulf Coast guide
pub 1925+

Gulfport RECORD. w 1900-09||
MsHi 1905-09

RECORD-TRIBUNE. d 1907-08||?
MsHi 1907-O 1908

HANDSBORO

Handsboro DEMOCRAT. *See* Pascagoula chronicle-star (Pascagoula)

HATTIESBURG

Hattiesburg AMERICAN. d O 2 1917+
Follows Hattiesburg news
pub 1917+
MsHC 1927+
MsSM [O-D 1931]+

Saturday evening EYE. w 1903?-
MsHi 1905

Hattiesburg NEWS. d O 16 1907-O 1 1917||
Followed by Hattiesburg American
MsHA complete
MsHC [1912-17]

Hattiesburg daily PROGRESS. d 1890-1909||?
MsHi My 24 1902-03

HAZLEHURST

COPIAH county news. w 1860-
MsHi Ag 15 1860-Ag 21 1861

Hazlehurst COURIER. w 1895+
MsHaC 1895+
MsHi Jl 1902-N 1910

HERNANDO

DE SOTO times. w 1848-1901||
United with Promoter to form Times-promoter

Hernando FREE press. w Je 6 1839-Jl? 1840||
MsHi Je 6-O 19 1839

NORTH Mississippian. w F 1 1840-
MsHi F-Mr 7 1840

PEOPLE'S press. *See* Hernando press

Hernando PHOENIX. w
MsHi 1845

Hernando PRESS and times. w 1846-79||?
1846?-68? as People's press; 1869-70? Hernando press
MsU F 15 1866-F 6 1868;F 11 1869-Ja 23 1873

PROMOTER. *See* Times-promoter

TIMES-promoter. w 1897+
1897-1901 as Promoter
MsHi 1902-09

HILLSBORO

Hillsboro ARGUS. w N 16 1842-
DLC N 16,30,D 30 1842

HOLLY SPRINGS

Holly Springs BANNER. *See* Southern banner

Holly Springs CONSERVATIVE. 1869-70. *See* South

CONSERVATIVE and Holly Springs banner.
1839-41 *See* Southern banner

EMPIRE democrat. w
DLC Mr 3-23,Ap 13-27 1855

Holly Springs GAZETTE. w Jl 28 1841-
MsHi 1841-Ag 14 1846
TxU N 15 1858

GUARD. w Ja 12 1842-
DLC Ja 3-10,F 7,Mr 14 1843;Ap 24 1844
MsHi 1842-Ag 5 1846
P-M Mr 5 1845

INDEPENDENT South. *See* South

MARSHALL county republican and Free trade advocate. w Ag 4 1838-
DLC Ag 4 1838
MsHi 1838-39

MARSHALL democrat. w S 1 1855-
DLC S 1-O 13,27,D 8-15 1855

MARSHALL Jeffersonian. w O 1851-
ICHi 1852 O 28

MISSISSIPPI palladium. w Ap 25 1851-Jl 1 1852||
DLC complete
MWA complete
NcD complete
TxU complete

MISSISSIPPI times. w 1853-
MWA Ja 18,F 1,Ap 20 1854

Holly Springs REPORTER. *See* Holly Springs south-reporter

SOUTH. w 1869-1919||
1869-70? as Holly Springs conservative; 1871?-73? Independent South. United with Holly Springs reporter to form Holly Springs south-reporter
MsHi 1902-10
MsHoC 1889-19

Holly Springs SOUTH-REPORTER. w 1865+
1865-1919 as Holly Springs reporter
pub Ja 13 1898+
MsHi 1902-10
MsHoC 1887-1919

SOUTHERN banner. w Ja 18 1839-
Title varies: Holly Springs banner; Southern banner and conservative; Conservative and Holly Springs banner
DLC Ja 25 1839;Mr 21 1840;Jl 23 1841
MsHi 1839-N 12 1841

SOUTHERN herald. w 1855-
NcD Jl 27 1860
Tx Je 21 1861

HOLMESVILLE

SOUTHRON. w 1852-
MWA Ja 12 1854

HOUSTON

CHICKASAW county times. w 1910-13||
United with Houston post to form Times-post
MsHouC 1912-13

Houston PETREL. w 1857-
MWA Mr 2 1860
VRC O 3 1861

Houston POST. *See* Times-post

SOUTHERN argus. w Je 19 1850-
Follows Southern patriot
DLC Je 19 1850-Jl 26 1854

SOUTHERN herald. w 1860-
MLei D 14 1860

SOUTHERN patriot. w -Je 9 1850||
Followed by Southern argus
DLC F 14 1849-Je 9 1850

TIMES-POST. w 1904+
1904-13 as Houston post
MsHouC 1907+

INDIANOLA

Indianola ENTERPRISE. w 1896+
MsHi 1902-03

SUNFLOWER tocsin. w 1886+
pub 1922+
IU Je 21 1917-D 22 1921

IUKA

BADGER bulletin.
Pub by Wisconsin soldiers occupying Iuka
WHi Je 14 1862

Iuka REPORTER. *See* Iuka vidette

Iuka TELEGRAPH. w F 6 1838-
CSmH F 13 1838

Iuka VIDETTE. w 1881+
1881-89? as Iuka reporter
MsHi O 16 1902-Mr 3 1904
MsIC S 30 1925+

JACKSON

Tri-weekly CLARION. d,tw,sw 1863-72||?
1863?-My 5 1866 as Daily Mississippi clarion; My 15-Ag 2 1866 Daily clarion and standard; Ag 1866-67? Daily clarion
d 1863?-67?; tw 1868-70?
DLC N 25,D 6 1865;Ap 3 1866-Je 1 1867
MBAt F 12 1868
MsHi Je 12 1869

Weekly CLARION-LEDGER. w 1837-1912||?
1837-64 as Eastern clarion; 1865-Ja 11 1888 Weekly clarion
1837-62 pub in Paulding
DLC [1854-My 12 1855]58-O 1860;N 10-D 3 1865;O 25 1866;Je-O 1867;Jl 23 1873-93;1900-01
LNC Je 12 1878;Ap 20 1887
MWA My 4 1859
MiU-C [1868]
MsHi [1858-62]-83;My 1902-10
MsLE Je 14 1851;Ja 28 1854;Ag 23 1856;My 31-Je 7 1861
MsSM Ja 19-D 21 1911
MsU Ag 8 1872-N 21 1877
NcD O 28 1869;Je 26 1873
NcU Je 7,Jl 19 1845

Daily CLARION-LEDGER. d 1888+
1888 as Clarion
DLC 1928+
MsU 1888-89[98-99]-[1901-04]-[06]-10
OClWHi Ap 16(supp)1908
PU [1890]

COMET. w 1877-81||?
MsU Ja 11 1879-D 25 1880
OClWHi Ap 10,My 29 1880

EASTERN clarion. *See* Clarion-ledger

ENQUIRER. tw,w Ja 7 1840-
tw during sessions of the Legislature
MsHi Ja 1840

FLAG of the union. w N 22 1850-
Follows Southron
DLC N 22 1850-D 30 1855
MWA Ja 31,O 31 1851
MsHi Ja 16 1856

Jackson HEADLIGHT. w 1899-1900||
DLC Ja 27 1900

INDEPENDENT journal. Ag 24-O 12 1839||
DLC S 6 1839
MsHi complete

MISSISSIPPI (*Continued*)

JACKSON—*Continued*

ISSUE. w 1908-18||?
MsSM Ja 30 1909-F 17 1911;Ap 16 1914-Ap 22 1915
NN Ap 4,18-My 9,23 1908
OkHi [1908;10]11
WHi Ap 11-18 1908

Daily MISSISSIPPI clarion. *See* Tri-weekly clarion

MISSISSIPPI free lance. w 1923-27||
MsJC O 17 1923-27

Weekly MISSISSIPPI pilot. w 1868-76||
DLC Je 24 1876
MsHi 1869-70;D 26 1874-N 1875
MsU Jl 20 1872-Je 21 1873;75-Je 24 1876

Daily MISSISSIPPI pilot. d,sw
sw N 13-D 26 1871
DLC Ja 4-D 31 1871
MsHi F 6-12 1874
MsU D 30 1874-Ag 1 1875

Daily MISSISSIPPI standard. d 1865-
DLC Mr 23-My 9 1866
MWA Ap 1 1866
MsHi Mr 28 1866

MISSISSIPPI state journal. w 1868-
NcD Ap 21 1868

Weekly MISSISSIPPIAN. w 1832-65||?
1851-59? as Mississippian and state gazette pub daily during sessions of the legislature
Ct [1835-36]
DLC Ja 10 1834-38[41;43]-[50]-[54-56]
ICHi Jl 1 1865
MWA F 21 1834[Ja-Jl 22 1846]-[47;Ja 28-Mr 24 1848]Ja[F 14-My 9 1851]Mr 5 1852;Ja 18-20 1854;O 21 1855;Ap 25 1860;Ap 15,Jl 8 1863
MsHi 1835-44;Jl 22 1853;57[59-63]
NcD Je 20,Jl 11 1855;S 1-8 1858
NcU Ja 7 1846
OClWHi Jl 8 1863
OOxM Jl 8 1863
TKL Ja 30 1835
TxU Mr 12-D 20 1850;Ja 17 1851-52

Semi-weekly MISSISSIPPIAN. sw,d Jl 4 1854-
d during session of legislature
D 2 1856-Ap 18 1859 as Mississippian
DLC 1854-56,58-60
MWA N 17 1854;Jl 8 1856
OClWHi F 5 1861

Daily MISSISSIPPIAN. d 1862-Je 4 1867||
United with Vicksburg daily herald (Vicksburg) to form Herald and Mississippian, later Vicksburg herald
Ag? 1863- 1864 pub in Selma, Alabama
CtY D 14 1862
DLC Jl 11,15 1862[Ap 3-Jl 7 1863;Jl 13-N 23 1865]
ICHi My 13 1863;F 3,(extra)Jl 1 1865
ICN Je 21 1864
LNC O 8 1862
LNH Ag 13 1862
MBAt Ap 18-19 1863;Mr 12,16-17,19,Ap 19 1864;Ap 14 1867
MWA Je 20-21,Jl 5,N 15,D 3-4,6-8,10,13-14,17-21,24-25,27-28 1862;Ag 20 1863
MnHi N 15 1864
MsHi Mr 6 1862-Ap 2,My 12 1863-N 11 1865
NN N 18 1864
NNHi O 28 1863
NcD N 20 1864
OCHi D 2,10 1863;Ja 7,My 22 1864
PHi N 3,27 1863
V O 20 1862;Je 3,5,9,14-16,22,Jl 2-3,6-8,10 1864
VRC Ja 28 1863
WHi D 20 1862

Jackson daily NEWS. d 1860-
MsHi 1860;O 22 1865
DLC My 5,O 22,25,N 19 D 3 1865
NcD Mr 7 1865

Jackson weekly NEWS. w
DLC O 30,N 6 1865
MsHi O 22 1865

Jackson daily NEWS. d 1892+
Title varies: Jackson evening news
pub 1907+
LNH D 10 1904
MsHi My 1902-Ja 8 1911
MsLE O 1925-Mr 1927
MsSM [1908-15]+
MsU 1911[12]-20;22+
Tx Ap 26-30,My 2-9 1934

OLD soldier. w Ag 4-N 1840||
MsHi Ag-O 13 1840

PEARL River gazette. w 1823-Ag 1824||
Followed by Southern luminary
DLC F 7,Ap 27,My 25,Je 1-8,22,Jl 6 1824

Daily SOUTHERN crisis. d D 30 1862-Mr 30 1863||
DLC Ja-Mr 23 1863
MsHi Ja-Mr 30 1863

SOUTHERN luminary. w Ag 17 1824-
Follows Pearl River gazette
sw during sessions of the legislature
DLC 1824-N 15 1825
MWA N 2 1824

SOUTHERN mercury. w 1854-
MsHi D 13 1854

SOUTHERN reformer. d,w S 26 1843-My 15 1846||
d during legislature
DLC D 26 1843;Ja 22 1844-D 27 1845;F 2,Mr 23 1846
MWA O 11 1845
MsHi 1843-Mr 23 1846
NcD [Ap-D 1848]
NcU Je 21 1845;Mr 23 1846
TxU O 25 1845

SOUTHERN republican. sw My 28? 1876-
MWA Je 10 1876

SOUTHERN star. w 1850-
MsHi N 23 1852

SOUTHERN sun. w Mr 17 1838-
GAtCo Ja 23 1840
DLC Mr 24 1838
MsHi 1838-40

SOUTHERN whig. w Ag 16 1837-
DLC Ag 16 1837

SOUTHERNER. w Ja? 1840-
MsHi D 31 1840-F 18 1848

SOUTHRON. w,tw D 24 1840-N 15 1850||
Followed by Flag of the union
DLC D 31 1840;Jl 20 1841;S 7 1844;Mr 9 1849-50
MWA Ja-F 1,15-22,Mr 8-Ap 19,My 3-10,24,Je 14-Jl 5,26-S 6,O-N 1850
MsHi My 15 1844
NcU D 15 1845
TKL Ap 13 1849

STATE journal. w Ja 4 1826-
DLC Ja 4,28,My 3-S 27,O 11,25-N 8,22-D 6, 20 1826

STATE rights banner. w Je 6 1833-
DLC Ja 24 1834
MsHi Je 13 1833
NcU D 29 1836

STATE telegraph. w Ag 17 1842-
DLC O 5 1842
MsHi Ag 17-O 12 1842

STATESMAN. Jl 15-N 1843||
Campaign paper
MsHi Jl 22-N 4 1843

Jackson daily TIMES. d My 13 1875-My 27 1878||
Follows Vicksburg daily times (Vicksburg) 1875-Mr 17 1876 as Daily times
DLC complete
MsHi O-D 1877
MsU Jl 16 1875-Je 1876

Jackson weekly TIMES. w
DLC Je 15-Jl 26 1878

TRUE issue. w,sw Jl 7 1840-
DLC Jl 14,Ag 4 1840;Ja 22,F 19 1841

KOSCIUSKO

ATTALA register. w Ap 23 1843-Jl 6 1844||
Followed by Central journal
MsHi Ap-O 7 1843

CENTRAL journal. w Jl 6 1844-
Follows Attala register
MsHi Ag 6 1844-S 20 1845

CENTRAL register. w Je 2 1838-
1838-Ag? 1839 as Spirit of Kosciusko
MsHi 1838-Ag 31,S 21 1839-S 12 1840

CENTRAL star. *See* Star-herald

Kosciusko CHRONICLE. w Ja 3 1846-72||?
DLC F 14 1846
MsHi 1846

Kosciusko COURIER. w 1910-15||?
MsKoC 1912-14

Kosciusko HERALD. w 1900-19||?
United with Star-ledger to form Star-herald
MsKoC 1901-18

JEFFERSONIAN. w Ja 1844-Jl 12 1845||
MsHi F 17 1844-45

Weekly NEWS. w Je 21 1862-
MBAt D 20 1862

SOUTHERN sun. w 1850-
DLC O 13 1852[Mr 18 1854-D 1 1855]

SPIRIT of Kosciusko. *See* Central register

STAR-HERALD. w 1866+
1866-80? as Central star; 1881?-94? Kosciusko star; 1895?-1919? Star-ledger
MsHi 1902-10
MsKoC 1911+

LAMAR

INDUSTRIAL tattler. w Jl 7 1884-Ja 1 1885||
MsAsC 1884

LAUREL

Laurel ARGUS. w 1911-14||
Merged with Laurel chronicle
MsEC S 21,O 5,N 30,D 8 1911

Morning CALL. d Mr 3 1926-Ja 1930||
1926-D 30 1928 as Jones county call.
United with Laurel daily leader to form Laurel leader-call
MsLE 1926-Mr 16 1927
Tx O 13 1928

Laurel CHRONICLE. w 1897-1915||?
MsEC 1898-99;1904-09;11
MsHi N 1902-S 1903;04-N 1910

JONES county call. *See* Morning call

JONES county times. w 1914-18||
MsEC 1916-18

Laurel LEADER-CALL. d Ag 1911+
1911-F 2 1930 as Laurel daily leader
MsLE 1923+

Laurel LEDGER. w My 5 1902-10||?
MsLE N 15 1902-04

LEAKESVILLE

GREENE county herald. w S 1 1898+
MsHi O 31 1902-N 1910
MsLeC 1898+

LELAND

Leland ENTERPRISE. w 1900+
pub Jl 1902+

LEXINGTON

Lexington ADVERTISER. w 1841+
pub 1927+
MWA Ja 17 1854;Mr 17 1876
MsHi N 1892-N 1910
TxU Ap 3 1855

DEMOCRATIC advocate. w 1853-
MWA Ja 17 1854
MsHi My 5 1859

HOLMES county times. w Ap 13 1906-
MsHi Ap 13-N 23 1906

Lexington STANDARD. *See* Lexington union

Lexington UNION. w Je 12 1838-
Je-N 10 1838 as Lexington standard
MsHi 1838-D 23 1843
NhD My 22 1841

WHIG republican. w O 21 1840-
MsHi O-D 24 1840

LIBERTY

Liberty ADVOCATE. w 1835-76||?
DLC Jl 1,29,Ag 19 1841
LU Jl 1844-45
MsHi Ja 24 1837-Ag 1 1846

AMITE democrat. w 1860-
MWA Ap 3 1861

PINEY Woods planter and Amite union literary reflector. w F 10 1838-
DLC Jl 21 1838
MsHi 1838-F 23 1840

Liberty PRESS. w 1828-
MWA D 12 1828

SOUTHERN herald. w 1866+
MsHi Je 16,D 1 1866;N 1902-Ja,Ap 1905-S 1910
MsLiC 1889+

LOUISVILLE

Louisville MESSENGER. w Je 25 1842-
MsHi Jl 9 1842-N 11 1843

TIME'S tablet and Mississippi gazette. w My 1 1841-
MWA My 15-29,Je 19 1841
NcD My 22 1841
—*See also* same title under Natchez and Washington

WINSTON county journal. w S 22 1892+
pub 1892+
MsHi My 23 1902-Ja 2 1903

LUCEDALE

GEORGE county times. w 1904+
1904-My 1910? as Plaindealer
MsLuC Je 1910+

PLAINDEALER. *See* George county times

MABEN

Maben PRESS. w Ag 12 1904+
pub 1910+
MsStC D 7 1828-Ag 19 1932

McCOMB

McComb ENTERPRISE. w 1889+
pub 1889+
MsHi Ag 1902-Ag 1909
MsMagC 1901-11;23-32

McComb JOURNAL. w,sw 1902+
w 1902-25
pub 1902+
MsMagC 1923+

MACON

Macon BEACON. w Ag 1849+
1849-61 as Union beacon
pub [1849-93]+
MsHi F 1908-N 1910
MsMacC 1860+
NcD N 20 1875[Mr 1881-Ag 1927]

DEMOCRAT-SUN-TRIBUNE. w 1889-1904||?
1889-90? as Noxubee democrat; 1891?-96? Farmers democrat
NcD O 12 1889

FARMERS democrat. *See* Democrat sun-tribune

Macon HERALD. w Jl 10 1841-
MsHi Jl 17 1840-N 16 1842

INDEPENDENT. w Mr 15? 1843-
MBAt S 26-O 3 1844
MWA Ja 25 1844

Macon INTELLIGENCER. w My 9 1838-40||
MsHi My 16 1838-N 7 1840

MISSISSIPPI sun. *See* Macon sun

NOXUBEE democrat. *See* Democrat sun-tribune

Macon SUN. w 1875-96||?
1875-92? as Mississippi sun. United with Farmers democrat to form Democrat-sun-tribune
NcD Ap 21,Je 21 1876[84]Ag 14 1885[88]Ja 2, F 20,Ap 24,O 23,N 6 1891;Ja 8,22 1892

UNION beacon. *See* Macon beacon

MISSISSIPPI (*Continued*)

MAGEE

Magee COURIER. w 1926+
pub 1927+

MAGNOLIA

Magnolia GAZETTE. w 1872+
LU My 11 1918
MsHi Je 1902-N 1910
MsMagC 1882-1909;12-15;17-22;25-28;31+

Magnolia HERALD. w 1875-78||?
LU Ja 5-19,F 2-9,23-Ap 6 1877

MANCHESTER

Manchester GAZETTE. w
DLC Ag 4 1838

Manchester HERALD and Yazoo advertiser. w
DLC Mr 1,15 1834

MARION

LAUDERDALE republican. w 1852-
A Ja 3 1854
MWA Ja 10 1854

MARKS

QUITMAN county democrat. w 1905+
1905-25 as Quitman county leader
MsMarC Mr 22 1928-Mr 20 1930

QUITMAN county leader. *See* Quitman county democrat

MARSHALL

TIMES. w
Ct D 16 1856

MAYERSVILLE

ISSAQUENA democrat. w Ja-D 1931||
MsMC Ja 2-D 4 1931

Mayersville SPECTATOR. w 1877+
MsHi S 27 1902-Je 16 1903
MsMC 1915+

MEADVILLE

FRANKLIN advocate. w 1891+
pub N 1909+
MsHi 1902-07

FRANKLIN county banner. w O 1909-Ja 1910||
MsMaC complete

MENDENHALL

SIMPSON county news. w 1872+
1872-1903 as Westville news (Westville)
pub 1925+
MsHi My 1902-Jl 1908
MsMeC 1872+

WESTVILLE news. *See* Simpson county news

MERIDIAN

Meridian CHRONICLE. w,sw 1867-68||?
DLC [1868]

Daily CLARION. d Jl 1? 1863-
DLC Je 16 1865
LNC Ag 16 1864
MWA Ag 30 1863;F 24 1865
MsHi Jl 6 1864
OClWHi Je 19 1864
PHi N 25 1863
TM Ag 26 1864
TxU Ag 14 1864
V Je 4,6,9-10,13-15,17,22-23,25,Jl 2,6-8 1864

Daily MISSISSIPPIAN. d
MsHi 1865

Meridian NEWS. w 1932+
MsMerC 1932+

Meridian PRESS. w Ja 14 1902-
MsHi [O 1902-Ag 1903]

Meridian STAR. d 1897+
Title varies: Evening star; etc
pub Jl-S 1905;Ja-Mr 1908;Ap-Je,O-N 1909;13-S 1914;15-16;Ap 1917-Mr,Jl 1925-Mr,Jl 1927+
DLC 1930+
MsHi My-D 1902
MsMerC 1897-1911;O 1928+
MsU 1927+

MONTICELLO

Monticello GAZETTE. w Ap 5 1823-
DLC F 2,Mr 2-30,Ap 26,My 18-25,Je 22-29,Jl 13 1833
MWA Mr 22-O 4 1823
NcD Je 21-28,Jl 12-19,S 13-20 1823

LAWRENCE county press. w 1888+
MsHi My 1902-N 1910
MsMoC 1888+

PEARL River advocate and Eastern advertiser. w
DLC My 7,Je 11-18,Jl 23,Ag 13,S 24,O 30-N 27 1830

PEARL River banner. w Jl 1837-
MsHi 1837-39

PLANTER'S museum. w S 26? 1828-
MWA Ap 11 1829

SOUTHERN journal. w 1841-
DLC My 11 1850-Jl 1 1854
ICHi Je 13 1846

MOSS POINT

Moss Point ADVERTISER. w S 1909+
pub 1909+
MsMpC 1909+
MsPaC 1909+

NATCHEZ

ARIEL. w Jl 20 1825-
Ct Je 8,Ag 17 1827;S 13 1828
DLC [F 9-Jl 6 1827]Jl 26 1828;F 28-Ag 1829; 30-Ap 2 1831
extras:O 6 1828;My 8,S 29,D 28 1830
LU Jl 27 1827-Jl 1828
MWA F 6-Jl 14 1826;Ag 1827-Jl 19 1828
MsHi Ap 14,My 26 1826;My 4,Je 2,Jl 13 1827; Jl 26,N 15,D 8 1828;Ja 3-10 1829
MsNF 1825-Ja 1826
MsNH 1825-Ja 1826
MsNK 1825-Ja 1826
OClWHi Jl 4 1829

Natchez evening BULLETIN. d 1898-1906||?
MsLE Jl 24 1899-Ap 1900

Natchez weekly COURIER. w 1830-71||?
Follows Southern galaxy.
1830-32 as Natchez;1833-34 Natchez courier and Adams, Jefferson and Franklin advertiser;1834-39? Weekly courier and journal
CSmH D 20 1833
CtY Mr 13 1854
DLC Ja 1-9,My 8(extra)N 20,D 25 1831;O 26 1832;Ap 10 1850-51;F 12-19,Ap 9-16,My 21, Je 25,S 3,O 8-22,N 19-26 1862;Ja 21-Jl 1 1863;O 22-29 1866;Ag 17 1867
ICHi Ap 2,Jl 2,16 1862
KyLo D 31 1847-My 1854
LU D 27 1848-My 1 1850
MWA Ag 19,O 14 1831;F 17,D 7 1832;Ja 4 1833; D 26 1834-Ja 23 1835;Ap 19 1839;D 26 1849-54;Jl 3 1861;N 12 1862
MsHi 1830-33[36;46-47]
NN Mr 15 1833
NcD D 4-18 1850;F 12 1862
OClWHi O 21 1831;Ja 22,My 27,S 10 1840
TxU D 18 1835;Ap 11 1849;52-55;F 18 1867

Natchez daily COURIER. d 1836-44||?
Ct N 3 1835
DLC Jl 2-D 1841;O 3 1844
MsHi 1837-38
OClWHi S 8 1840
TxU [O 9-N 17 1844]

Natchez COURIER. sw,tw 1836-71||?
Title varies with periodicity: Tri-weekly courier; Semi-weekly courier (other slight changes)
tw 1836-45?;Je 1865?-67?
Ct [1836-37]
DLC Ag 20 1850-51;N 20,D 15-29 1863;Ja-S 23 1865
LU Ap 30 1847-Ap 1850
MBAt Ag 15-S 23 1865
MWA My 6/7 1840;Ap 13,My 29 1849;O 23 1863;F 16,Mr 8,29,My 17,31,Je 7,14,28,Jl 5,22, Ag 23-S 2,O 25,N 11-15,D 13 1864;Jl 22,27 1865
NcD D 4-18 1850;F 12 1862;Jl 22,27 1865
OClWHi My 19 1846
TxU Mr 10 1846[Jl 16-D 24 1847;Ap 25-D 1848]-O 11 1850
WHi F 26 1850-D 23 1851

Natchez daily COURIER. d 1852-71||?
Title varies slightly: Daily morning courier; Courier. United with Natchez daily democrat to form Natchez daily democrat and courier, later Natchez democrat
DLC [Ja-S 1856;Ja-Mr,O 1860]My 22-23,Je 1[D]1861;Ap 25,S 11,O 31,N 19 1862;Ja 23,Ap 4,7-10,15-16,21-24 1863[O-D 1865,Ag 1866]
ICHi O 7 1862
LNH F 14 1863;O 13 1865
MB [Ja 12-Mr 27 1861]
MBAt Ap 4 1863;S 26-28,30,O 3-5,7,11,13-14, 17-21,24-28,31-N 9 1865
MWA My 20,Ag 10 1853;N 6 1855;Mr 16 1858; Ap 10,13[N 20-D]1861;Ja 3,Je 14,28[S 19 1862-Jl 10 1863]
MsLE D 15 1855
NcD Ja 22,29 1856;Ja 19,F 25,28,O 3-4,9-11,18-20,23-25 1860;D 3,5-7,13-18,27 1861;Ap 24 1863
OClWHi Ap 13-14,17-18,20-24,27,My 1,Jl 8,31,O 5 1861;Mr 26,My 14,Jl 11 1863;Ap 11 1865
TxGR Jl 26,S 18 1862

Natchez DEMOCRAT. tw,d 1865+
1872?-Jl 7 1875 Natchez daily democrat and courier
pub 1865—
DLC [O 7-D 1865]Jl 14 1874-Mr 11 1930
LSfD Ag 27 1878
MsHi 1865-75;O 7 1876;F 8 1884;My-1902-N 1910
MsNCC 1931+
MsSM 1865+
NcD Je 17 1879

Natchez weekly DEMOCRAT. w 1865+
MsHi 1866-68;70;Jl 19 1876
NcD Je 18 1879

Natchez daily FREE trader. d F 1858-
Follows Mississippi free trader (sw)
MWA Mr 22 1861
MsU 1858-Jl 1859
TxU F 2 1858-Jl 1859

Natchez GAZETTE. 1825-32. *See* Mississippi gazette

Evening GAZETTE. d D 1861-
MWA Ja 9,28,F 5 1862

MISSISSIPPI free trader. w Ag 4 1835-61||?
1839?-55? as Mississippi free trader and Natchez gazette
CSmH S 17 1839
DLC Jl 30 1839-40;My 10,N 1 1843;Ag 28,O 16 1844;My 28-Je,D 10 1845[46-N 14 1849]N 17 1852;Ja 24 1859
LSfD O 2 1857
MWA D 26 1839;Mr 12,D 3 1840;Ja 7,F 25,S 16 30 1846-Ag,O 1853-Mr 1854
MsHi 1835-58;Ap 1860-My 1861
NhD F 10 1841
OClWHi S 5 1844;Ap 22 1846

MISSISSIPPI free trader and Natchez gazette. tw,sw 1838-Ja 1858||
Followed by Natchez daily free trader
tw 1838-48
DLC Ja 9,30,Mr 20-Ap 23,My 6,13-24,29-Je 7, 12-14,21-Jl 1,8,15,19-22,S 20 1845;Mr 11 1847; S 12,N 30,D 12-14,19-29 1848;Ja 6-10,17-F 10,17-Mr 7,14,21-31,Ap 7-14,25-28,My 16,30, Je 13,S 22 1849
MWA My 15-17,Je 3 1845;Ja 30 1855
MsLE O 12 1847
MsU Jl 30 1839-41;52-57
Tx Ja 30-F,Mr 25-Ap 3,5-My 4,8-29,Je-O 9, 14-D 25 1847
TxU Ja 6 1857-Ja 22 1858

*MISSISSIPPI gazette. w,sw Ap 13 1813-Ag 31 1833||
1813-N 10 1815 as Washington republican; N 17 1815-17 Washington republican and Natchez intelligencer 1818-My 14 1825 Mississippi state gazette; My 18 1825-F 7 1827 Natchez gazette; F 14-N 22 1827 Mississippi statesman and Natchez gazette; N 29 1827-F 20 1830 Statesman and gazette; F 27 1830-33 Natchez gazette. Followed by Time's tablet and Mississippi gazette
sw S 9 1818-Jl 1819;23
CSmH Ag 4 1830
Ct F 7-14,Mr 15,Ap 12,My 24,Je 14,Jl 19,Ag 9,23-S 13,O 4 1827;My 1-8,22,Ag 7-14,O 2,23-N 6,D 4 1828;F 7 1829;Je 5,Jl 28,Ag 11,S 1,O 6,20,N 3-10 1830;F 6-9 1831
CtY Jl 17,Ag 7 1828
DLC 1821-D 16 1826;F 14 1827;Mr 7 1829-33
KyLo Ap-N 1826;My 31-D 1831
MWA [F-Ag 1821]F 2 1822[23-24]-My 18,Jl 13, 23-Ag 3,24,N 12 1825;F 25,Je 3,O 21,D 2 1826[F 1827-29]Ja 5,F 2,Mr 20-27,Ap 17-Jl, S-O 20,N-D 1830;Mr 9,Je 8-15,Jl,N 2-9,30-D 1831;F 8,29,Mr 22,Ap 27,S 12,O 17-24 1832;Ja 12,F 23,Mr 9,Ap 27,Je 8-22,Ag 3-17, 31,S 7 1833
MsHi 1821-29;Ag 1833
NcD 1821;23-My 1825;F 7,22-Mr 22 1827;Ja-F 7,21-Mr 7,21-28,Ap 11-18 1829;Ap 27 1833
OCHi [Ap 17-D 8 1830]
WHi Je 23,Jl 14-28 1832

MISSISSIPPI journal and Natchez advertiser. w 1832-
CSmH D 27 1833

*MISSISSIPPI republican and literary register. w Ap 8 1812-24||?
1812-23 as Mississippi republican?
DLC F 9 1821-Ja 28,D 1 1824
MWA Ja 16,Mr 13-20,Jl 24 1823;Je 2,Jl 7,21, S 1,15,N 17,D 1,22 1824
MsHi 1821-23
NcD Ja 16,Mr 20 1823;D 1 1824

MISSISSIPPI state gazette. *See* Mississippi gazette

MISSISSIPPI statesman. w D 23 1826-F 7 1827||
United with Natchez gazette to form Mississippi statesman and Natchez gazette, later Mississippi gazette
Ct [1827]
MWA D 23 1826;F 7 1827

MISSISSIPPIAN and Natchez advertiser. w Ap 12? 1822-24||?
DLC Ag 17 1822-O 22 1824
MBAt F 8 1823
MWA Mr 20,Jl 10 1824
NcD F 7 1824

NATCHEZ. *See* Natchez weekly courier

NEW south. w 1869-76||?
MWA Mr 9 1872-Ag 16 1873

Natchez NEWSPAPER and public advertiser. w
DLC Ap 25-D 6 1826

SOUTHERN clarion. w Ap 29 1831-
Ct My 13-20,Je 10,Jl 8,Ag 5-12,26-S 2,O 21-N 18 1831

SOUTHERN galaxy. w My 22 1828-30||
Followed by Natchez weekly courier
CSmH My 6 1830
Ct [1828-29]
DLC Ag 27,N 12,D 3-24 1829;Ja 7 1830
MWA My 22,Je 5-12,D 18 1828;Mr 18 1830
MsHi Ja 22 1829-My 13 1830
OClWHi Ap 2,Jl 23 1829

TIME'S tablet and Mississippi gazette. sw S 18-28 1833||
Follows Mississippi gazette
DLC S 18 1833
MWA S 28 1833
MsHi S 18 1833
See also same title under Louisville and Washington

Natchez UNION courier. w Ag 15 1863-
ICHi Ag 15 1863

WASHINGTON republican. *See* Mississippi gazette

NEW ALBANY

New Albany GAZETTE. w 1887+
pub 1917+
MsHi Jl 1904-Ag 1907
MsNaC 1936+
MsNaS 1898-1912

MISSISSIPPI (*Continued*)

NEW ALBANY—*Continued*

New Albany TIMES. w 1931+
MsNaC 1936+

UNION county times. 1907-17||?
Follows New Albany vidette
MsNaS 1911-17

New Albany VIDETTE. w 1904-07||
Followed by Union county times
MsNaS Ja 10-S 26 1907

NEW AUGUSTA

PERRY county herald. w 1926+
Follows Perry county telegram
MsNagC 1926+

PERRY county telegram. w 1906-26||
Followed by Perry county herald
MsNagC [1910-26]
MsRD complete

NEWTON

Newton RECORD. w D 5 1901+
pub 1901+
MsLE 1901-F 12 1925
MsHi 1902-03;My 1905-Mr 1907;08-10

OCEAN SPRINGS

JACKSON county times. w 1916+
Follows Ocean Springs news
MsPaC 1916+

Ocean Springs NEWS. w 1897-1916||
1897-1904? as Progress. Followed by Jackson county times
MsPaC 1909-16

PROGRESS. *See* Ocean Springs news

OKOLONA

CHICKASAW messenger. *See* Okolona messenger

CHICKASAW sun. *See* Okolona sun

Okolona MESSENGER. w 1872+
1872-94? as Chickasaw messenger; 1895?-99? People's messenger
pub [1881-85]1911+
MsHi Je 1902-Ag 1910
MsOC 1906+

PEOPLE'S messenger. *See* Okolona messenger

PRAIRIE news. w 1851-75||?
CSmH Jl 7 1855
MsHi F 1858-S 1859
NN F 11 1854

Okolona SUN. w 1892-1912||?
1902-05 as Chickasaw sun
MsHi 1902-Mr 1910

OSYKA

Daily DISPATCH. d
LNC N 3-14,D 14 1864

OXFORD

CONSTITUTION. w Mr 22 1851-
Follows Organizer
MsHi 1851

DEMOCRATIC flag. w Mr 10 1852-
MWA N 17 1852
MsHi 1852

Oxford EAGLE. w 1876+
MsHi Je 1902-Ag 1904

Oxford FALCON. w 1865-87||
OClWHi My 28 1885

LAFAYETTE county press. w 1906-14||?
MsHi O 1908-N 1910

Oxford OBSERVER. w Ag 12 1843-44||
Followed by Organizer
MsHi Ag 19 1843-Je 22 1844

ORGANIZER. w N 1844-51||
Follows Oxford observer. Followed by Constitution
MsHi 1849-50

PANOLA

Panola LYNX. w Ja 11 1845-
MsHi 1845-Ag 1 1846

Panola weekly REGISTER. w Mr 15 1843-D 28 1844||?
Follows Weekly register (Grenada)
MsHi 1843-44

Panola STAR. *See under* Sardis

PASCAGOULA

Pascagoula CHRONICLE. w 1897-1914||
United with Pascagoula democrat-star to form Pascagoula chronicle-star
MsPaC 1900-11

Pascagoula CHRONICLE-STAR. w 1845+
1845-78? as Handsboro democrat (Handsboro) 1878?-1914 Pascagoula democrat-star
pub 1911+
MsHi My 1902-O 1910
MsPaC 1874+
MsPaS 1928+

Pascagoula DEMOCRAT-STAR. *See* Pascagoula chronicle-star

STAR of Pascagoula. w 1866-78||
1866-72? as Star of Enterprise (Enterprise). United with Handsboro democrat (Handsboro) to form Pascagoula democrat-star, later Pascagoula chronicle-star
MsPaC 1874-78

PAULDING

Weekly AURORA. w 1843-
NcU Jl 10 1844

Weekly CLARION. *See* Clarion ledger (Jackson)

EASTERN clarion. *See* Clarion ledger (Jackson)

JASPER county review. w 1890-1904||?
MsHi O 1902-N 1904

TRUE democrat. w Ap 28 1845-
MsHi My 1845-Ag 18 1847

PHILADELPHIA

NESHOBA democrat. w Ag 6 1881+
MsHi My 29 1902-Ja 8 1903
MsOM [1906-10]
MsPhC 1900+

PICAYUNE

Picayune ITEM. w Je 1 1904+
MsP 1904+

PITTSBORO

CALHOUN monitor. *See* Calhoun City monitor-herald (Calhoun City)

DIXIE herald. *See under* Calhoun City

PITTSBURG

Pittsburgh BULLETIN. w Mr 27? 1835-
MsHi N 19-26 1835

PITTSBURG. w F 26 1835
MH F 26 1835

PONTOTOC

ADVANCE. w 1900-19||
Follows People's banner
MsPoC 1900-17

AMERICAN sovereign. w 1850-
MWA Ap 23 1853

CHICKASAW union. w Jl 1 1836-38||
DLC Jl 1 1836
MsHi 1836-Mr 8 1838
PSuHi S 14 1836

Pontotoc DEMOCRAT. *See* People's banner

EXAMINER. w
MsPoC O 30 1857-59

Weekly FOLIO. w 1876-77||?
VRC O 7-20 1876

MISSISSIPPI intelligencer and general advertiser for the new counties. w 1836-
GAtCo Ag 14 1838

Pontotoc OBSERVER. *See* People's banner

PEOPLE'S banner. w 1877-99||
1877-85 as Pontotoc observer; 1886-My 7 1887 True democrat; My 12 1887-Mr 1892 Pontotoc democrat. Followed by Advance
GU F 5 1887
MsPoC 1884-99

Pontotoc PROGRESS. w F 1929+
pub 1929+
MsPoC 1929+
Tx O 6 1932;S 28,N 16 1933[F 1934-Ap 1935]

Pontotoc SENTINEL. w 1893-1929||
MsHi Je 12 1902-O 1910
MsPoC 1894-1902;04-Jl 1929

SOUTHERN tribune. w S 14 1842-
Follows Spirit of the times
DLC S 21 1842
MsHi 1842-Ag 5 1846
TxU O 22-29,D 13 1845

SPIRIT of the times. w My 9 1841-S 3? 1842||
Followed by Southern tribune
MsHi 1841-S 3 1842
TxU Ja 8 1842

TRUE democrat. *See* People's banner

POPLARVILLE

Poplarville FREE-PRESS. w 1890+
MsHi Mr 1902-N 1910

PORT GIBSON

AMERICAN times. w S 2 1824-
MdHi D 30 1824

*Port-Gibson CORRESPONDENT. w N 1818-
Je 1824-32 as Port Gibson correspondent and Mississippi general advertiser. United with Port Gibson herald to form Port Gibson herald and correspondent
DLC 1821-[Je-N 1829]N 27 1830;S 29 1832;O 6 1840
CSmH Je 5 1830
MWA Ja 22,Ap 8,My 6,27,N 18,D 2-9 1824;F 15 1827;Ag 30,N 1 1828;Mr 14 1829
MsHi 1821-25;Je 1 1833;35-46
MsPgC 1830-S 1832
NcD D 3 1836
OClWHi D 20 1834
WHi Ag 30 1828

Port Gibson HERALD and correspondent. w 1842-
1842-Ag? 1851 as Port Gibson herald
MWA Ja 13 1854
MsHi 1843-Ag 22 1851
MsPgC S 1842-Ag 1851

MISSISSIPPI watchman. w Jl 3 1832-
MWA Jl 3 1832

Weekly RECORD. w F 4-N 16 1887||
Merged with Southern reveille, later Port Gibson reveille
MsHi complete
MsPgC complete

Port Gibson REVEILLE. tw,w 1850+
1850?-90? as Southern reveille (title varies)
Suspended My 1861?-Ja 1876
Ag 29 1926 is Semi-centennial ed
DLC Ag 16 1860
LSfD Ag 29 1926
MWA Ja 11 1854
MsHi 1852-54
MsPgC S 1856-Je 1859;F 1876-Mr 1891
N 1887-96;Je 1902-N 1910
NcU S 19 1890
OClWHi N 20,D 1 1860;Mr 15-Ap 12 1861

Daily SOUTHERN reveille. d
MsPgC S 1858-Je 1859

SOUTHERN reveille. *See* Port Gibson reveille

Weekly STANDARD. w N 9 1865-75||
MsHi 1865-Je 3 1866;Ag 24 1867
MsPgC D 1865-Ag 1875

PRENTISS

Prentiss HEADLIGHT. w 1906+
MsPrC 1910+

QUITMAN

CHICKASAHAY advertiser. w 1856-
MWA Ja 19 1861

CLARKE county tribune. w 1909+
MsQC 1920+

Quitman INTELLIGENCER. w 1853-
MWA Ja 5 1854

RALEIGH

SMITH county reformer. w 1892+
MsHi Ag 21 1902-Ja 7 1904

RAYMOND

Raymond COMET. w Jl 17 1840-
MsHi Jl-D 11 1840

Raymond FENCIBLE. w Ag 22 1849-
MsHi Ag 22-S 12 1849

HINDS county gazette. w 1844+
1883-1906? as Raymond gazette
MWA Ja 18 1854;Je 29 1870
MsHi 1845-89;1902-10;20+
MsRaC 1920+

SOUTHWESTERN farmer. w 1842-45||
Follows Raymond times
MsHi Mr 28 1845

Raymond TIMES. w 1835-F 7 1842||
Followed by Southwestern farmer
DLC N 13 1840
MsHi Ap 21 1837-42

RICHTON

Richton DISPATCH. w 1906+
1906-12? as Perry county review
MsNagC 1926+

PERRY county review. *See* Richton dispatch

RIENZI

Rienzi CLIPPER. w -F 14 1857||?
MWA F 14 1857

RIPLEY

Ripley ADVERTISER. w Ag 1843-94||?
DLC [1855-56;58;60]
MWA Mr 20 1861
MsHi S 9 1843-Jl 11 1846
MsRipC 1880-81;84-87;90-91;93-94

SOUTHERN sentinel. w My 1 1878+
MsHi 1905-10

Ripley STANDARD. w 1897-99||?
MsRipC 1897-99

Ripley TRANSCRIPT. w Je 26 1837-
MsHi O 5 1837-Ja 25 1838

RODNEY

Rodney PHOENIX and Jefferson gazette. w
TxU O 1852-N 21 1853

SOUTHERN telegram. *See* Rodney telegraph

Rodney STANDARD. w N 14 1837-
MsHi 1837-Ap 14 1838

Rodney TELEGRAPH. w 1833-S 12? 1840||
1833-D 15 1838 as Southern telegraph. Followed by Jefferson whig (Fayette)
MsHi Ag 1 1837-S 12 1840

MISSISSIPPI (*Continued*)

ROLLING FORK

DEER Creek pilot. w Ja 1 1876+
pub 1876+
MsHi O 24 1902-Ap 24 1903

ROSEDALE

BOLIVAR county democrat. w 1888+
MsHi 1902-04

RULEVILLE

Ruleville RECORD. w O 1918+
pub 1918+

SALEM

Salem FREE press. w Jl 13 1839-
DLC Jl 13 1839

SARDIS

PANOLA star. w 1855-86||?
1855-79? pub in Panola
DLC Ja 7 1857
MBAt Ja 23 1862
MsHi Ag 1902-N 1910
MsSaC 1861-86

SOUTHERN reporter. w 1855+
1855-79? as Panola star (Panola)
pub 1888+
MsSaC 1885+

SCOOBA

KEMPER county messenger. w Ag 1932+
pub 1932+

KEMPER herald. w 1876-O 1933||
MsHi O 1902-Jl 1908

SCRANTON. *See* PASCAGOULA

SENATOBIA

Senatobia DEMOCRAT. *See* Tate county democrat

NORTH MISSISSIPPI democrat. *See* Tate county democrat

TATE county democrat. w 1891+
1891-96? as North Mississippi democrat; 1897?-1925? Senatobia democrat
MsHi My 1902-07

SHIP ISLAND

SOLDIER'S news-letter.
MBAt My 10 1862
MWA My 2 1862

SHUBUTA

MISSISSIPPI messenger. w 1879-1925||?
MsQC 1905-20

Weekly SOUTHERN republic. w
V Je 4 1864

STARKVILLE

EAST Mississippi star. *See* Weekly star

EAST Mississippi times. w 1866-Ag 20 1926||
Merged with Starkville news
MsSM Jl 7 1922-26
MsStC 1903-10;13-19;21-26

Starkville NEWS. w 1901+
pub 1901+
MsHi 1902-10
MsSM [Ja 11 1907-14]Ap 22 1921+
MsStC 1908-10;12+

Weekly STAR. w Je 1933+
1933-My 11 1934 as East Mississippi star
pub 1933+
MsSM [1933]+
MsStC Jl 20 1934-Je 13 1935

SUMMIT

CONSERVATIVE times. *See* Summit times and intelligencer

Summit SENTINEL. w 1873+
pub 1928+
MsHi 1902-07
MsMagC 1882-96;1900-01;06-07;14-15;19-20;23-24
NcD D 12 1889;Ja 29 1891;Je 9,23 1892

Summit TIMES and intelligencer. w 1867-83||?
1867-79? as Summit times; 1880 Conservative times; 1881-82? Summit times and sentinel
MsLE Ja 25-My 2 1872;Mr 31 1876-My 23 1880

SUMNER

Sumner SENTINEL. w 1908+
pub 1916+

TUNICA

DELTA democrat. *See* Times-democrat

Tunica weekly INDEPENDENT. w 1888-97||?
DLC My 28 1892

Tunica TIMES. w 1908-18||
United with Delta democrat to form Times-democrat
MsTuC 1910-18

TIMES-DEMOCRAT. w 1895+
1895-1918? as Delta democrat
pub 1923+
MsHi Jl 7 1902-Je 19 1909
MsTuC 1907-17;26+

TUPELO

Tupelo JOURNAL. w,sw 1872+
1872-78 as Lee county journal; Ap 1924-Je 1926 Journal-review
w 1872-1924?
pub [1872+]
MsHi 1902-10
MsTC 1873+

JOURNAL-review. *See* Tupelo journal

Tupelo weekly LEDGER. w 1887-92||?
MsTC 1890-92

LEE county journal. *See* Tupelo journal

Tupelo REVIEW. w 1911-Ap 1924||
United with Tupelo journal to form Tupelo journal-review, later Tupelo journal
MsTC 1910-11

Tupelo STANDARD. w 1872-75||?
MsTC O 1872-Ag 1873

Tupelo TIMES. w My 1894-97||
MsTC complete

Tupelo TRIBUNE. w 1909-11||?
MsTC 1910-My 1911

TYLERTOWN

Tylertown TIMES. w 1907+
pub 1926+

UTICA

Utica HERALD. w 1897-1904||
MsHi Mr 1903-O 1904

VICKSBURG

ADVOCATE and register. *See* Vicksburg register

Vicksburg AMERICAN. d 1901-10||
MsHi My 1902-My 1904[N 20 1905-F 1910]

CAMPAIGN sentinel. w Je 7 1848-
Campaign paper
MsHi S 6-O 11 1848

Daily CITIZEN. d -Jl 4 1863||
Title varies: Vicksburg daily citizen Jl 2 1863 re-issued on Jl 4 1863 by Union Army, with additions. Many facsimiles of this number; originals reported by C, CSmH,DLC,MWA,MdBJ,MnHi,NN,OC,Tx
ArHi Jl 2 1863
C Jl 2 1863
CL Jl 2 1863
CLM Je 30,Jl 2 1863
CSmH Jl 2,4 1863
CoHi Je 25,Jl 2 1863
CU Je 25,Jl 2 1863
Ct Jl 2 1863
CtY Je-D 1861;Jl 2 1863
CoHi Jl 2 1863
DLC Je 9,O 7 1860;Je 18,20,30,Jl 2 1863
GAA Jl 2 1863
ICHi Je 16,27,Jl 2 1863
ICU Jl 2 1863
IHi Jl 2 1863
KyFM Jl 2 1863
LNC Je 18,Jl 2 1863
LSfD Jl 2-4 1863
MBAt Jl 2 1863
MCheHi Jl 2 1863
MHi Jl 2 1863
MWA Jl 4 1863
MdBJ Jl 2 1863
MeBa Jl 2 1863
MiU-C Je 18,Jl 2 1863
MnHi Jl 2 1863
N Je 25,Je 27,Jl 2 1863
NN Jl 2 1863
NbHi Jl 2 1863
NcD Je 29,Jl 2 1863
NjHi Jl 2 1863
NjR Jl 2 1863
NjWdHi Jl 2 1863
OC Jl 2 1863
OCHi Jl 2 1863
OCl Jl 2 1863
OClWHi Je 27,Jl 2 1863
OHi Je 30,Jl 2 1863
P Jl 2 1863
PArdL Jl 2 1863
PEHi Jl 2 1863
PHi Jl 2,4 1863
PHs Jl 4 1863
PLatL Ja 10 1864
PNoHi Jl 2 1863
PPFfHi Jl 2 1863
PPeS Jl 2 1863
PPiHi Jl 2 1863
PScrGr Jl 3-4 1863
PScrHi Jl 3 1863
PUn Jl 2 1863
PW Jl 3 1863
T Jl 2 1863
TKL Jl 2 1863
TU Jl 2 1863
Tx Jl 2 1863
TxGR Je 27,Jl 2 1863
TxU Jl 2 1863
WHi Je 18,Jl 2 1863

Vicksburg daily COMMERCIAL. d 1877-82||
United with Vicksburg daily herald to form Vicksburg commercial-herald, later Vicksburg herald
DLC Mr 21 1877-D 28 1882

CONSTITUTIONALIST. sw F 22 1844-
MsHi 1844-F 19 1845

Vicksburg HERALD. d 1863+
1863-Je 4 1867 as Vicksburg daily herald; Je 5-Ag 25 1867 Herald and Mississippian; Ag 26 1867-83 Vicksburg daily herald; 1883-97 Commercial-herald
pub 1865+
CtHT F 1 1865
DLC F 16 1865-O 26 1866;Ja-O 20 1867;98+
InNcHi Je 1,6 1864
MBAt Ap 13,Jl 6,8,S 17-O 6,8-10,12-13,15,18-20,22-N 4,22,25,D 2-3 1865;Ja 3,19,21,25,F 8 1866
MHi Je 1,D 7-9 1864;Ja 7 1865
MWA Mr 12 1865;D 25 1867
MnHi Ag 9-10,N 17 1864;65-Ap 1910
MsV 1869-Je 1870;O 8 1911-Jl 21 1918
MsVJ 1899-1913
OClWHi Je 30-Jl 2,6 1864;Ja 7,17,Mr 1865; Ap 20 1866

Vicksburg weekly HERALD. w 1864+
pub 1864+
DLC S 9 1865-S 1 1866
MWA Ap 28 1876
MsHi O 9 1865;1878-Ap 1910
VRC Mr 3 1878

Vicksburg JOURNAL. d My? 1865-Je 16 1866||
MBAt [Jl 31-N 23 1865]
MsHi O 19-D 27 1865
MsV complete

LIGHT. m 1891-1922||?
DLC Ja 18 1900

MISSISSIPPI advocate. w 1828-S 12 1831||
United with Vicksburg register to form Advocate and register, later Vicksburg register
MsHi S 12 1831

MISSISSIPPIAN. w Ja 9-N 8 1832||
DLC S 12 1832
MsHi complete

Vicksburg MONITOR. w S 18 1829-
DLC S 18 1829

Vicksburg evening POST. d My 3 1883+
Ap 23 1934 is 50th anniversary ed
pub 1883+
LSfD Ap 23 1934
MsHi Ap 23 1934
MsV 1926-32

Vicksburg REGISTER. w S 16? 1829-39||?
S 30 1831-32? as Advocate and register
CSmH Jl 15 1830
DLC O 18,N 21 1832
MHi O 29 1835
MWA D 17 1835
MsHi 1831-32;34-38

Vicksburg REGISTER. tw,d 1836-
tw 1836
DLC My 4 1838
ICHi Ja 28 1837
MWA Ja 2 1838
MsHi Ja 23-Je 12 1838

REPUBLICAN. w Mr 1825-
Title varies
DLC My 4 1825
MsHi Mr 8-23 1826

Vicksburg REPUBLICAN. sw,d My 1867-
sw My-S 1867
MBAt [Jl-N 22 1867]
MWA Je 12,25-28,Jl 9-18,26-Ag 2,9-13,20-S 24 1867

Vicksburg weekly REPUBLICAN. w O 7 1867-
1867-Mr 2 1868 as Vicksburg republican
DLC Ja 21-D 1868
MBAt O 14-28,D 1867-Ja 1868
MWA D 31 1867;Ja 14,Mr 23(supp)31 1868

Vicksburg weekly SENTINEL. w D 1836-
1836-S 22 1846 as Sentinel and expositor; S 29 1846-47? Weekly sentinel
DLC [1839-41;44-46]Je 22 1853-55
LNC Ap 14 1847
MsHi 1837-38;Jl 1839-46;48-51
NcD [Je-Jl,O, D 1847]Mr 1,15 1848
OClWHi Jl 9 1844

Vicksburg SENTINEL. d,tw 1838-60||?
d 1838-51?
DLC Ap 22 1844;O 28 1852
MWA Je 19 1854
MsHi [1838-51]

SENTINEL and expositor for the country. w D 27 1836-46||
DLC Je 14,Jl 5 1842;F 21,Mr 14 1843
MWA Jl 16 1839
MsHi 1836-38;45-S 22 1846

SOUTHERN newspaper. w S 6 1827-
1827-F 1829? as Southern newspaper and Mississippi impartial politician
DLC S 12 1827;F 6 1829
MWA S 20 1827;Mr 20 1829

Vicksburg weekly SUN. w
DLC D 6 1858-D 24 1860

Vicksburg evening TELEGRAPH. d 1867-
CSmH N 29 1867

Vicksburg daily TIMES. d 1863-Ap 26 1875||
Followed by Daily times (Jackson) later Jackson daily times
CSmH Jl 12 1868
DLC 1873-75
MsHi Ag 29 1866-70
MsU Ap 11 1873-75
MsV Je 19-O 18 1866;Jl 1870-Je 1872

MISSISSIPPI (*Continued*)

VICKSBURG—*Continued*

Vicksburg TIMES. w 1866-75||
MsHi N 10 1868-Ap 12 1870

Daily Vicksburg WHIG. d Ap 8 1839-My 2 1863||
Title varies: Vicksburg daily whig
CoHi Mr 21 1863
DLC N 25 1860;Ag 10 1861;Ap 1 1862
LNC Ap 3 1847;Ja 18,F 4 1861;Je 17 1862
MBAt Ap 16 1863
MWA O 3 1845
MsHi 1839-46;N 1854-Ap 1855;56;58-60
MsLE Jl 14 1859
OClWHi My 7 1846;Ag 9 1862;My 14 1863
VRC Ap 8 1863
WHi O 27 1840-Ap 28 1842;My 27 1862

Vicksburg WHIG. w,tw 1839-My 2 1863||
Title varies slightly
CSmH Ag 23 1853
DLC F 6 1839;D 1844-48
MBAt Ap 22 1863
MWA Mr 6 1861
MsHi 1842-50;52-53;My-D 1855;58-My 8 1861
NcD Ap 15 1863
WHi Je 15-N 1 1841

WALTHALL

Walthall WARDEN. w 1881-1907||
MsHi S 8 1902-Ag 21 1903

WASHINGTON

TIME'S tablet and Mississippi gazette. sw S 2 1836-
MWA S 2 1836
See also same title under Louisville and Natchez

WATER VALLEY

NORTH Mississippi herald. w 1888+
MsHi My 1902-N 1908
MsWaC 1935+

Water Valley PROGRESS. w 1882-1907||
MsHi 1902-Ag 1906

WAYNESBORO

Waynesboro BEACON. *See* Waynesboro news-beacon

Waynesboro NEWS-BEACON. w 1898-1918||
1898-1903? as Waynesboro beacon
Followed by Wayne county news
MsHi N 8 1902-Je 27 1903
MsWayC 1906-18

WAYNE county news. w N 28 1918+
Follows Waynesboro news-beacon
MsWayC 1918+

WESSON

Wesson ENTERPRISE. w 1899+
MsHi 1905-10

WEST POINT

West Point CITIZEN. w 1871-74||?
NcD Je 20 1873

CLAY county leader. *See* West Point times-leader

DIXIE press. w 1892-1907||
MsHi My 22 1902-Jl 1907

West Point LEADER. *See* West Point times-leader

TIMES-HERALD. d 1904-28||
United with West Point leader to form West Point times-leader

West Point TIMES-LEADER. w,sw,d 1880+
1880-91? as Clay county leader; 1892?-1928 West Point leader
pub 1928+
MsHi My 29 1902-10
MsWeC 1880+

WESTVILLE

Westville NEWS. *See* Simpson county news (Mendenhall)

WIGGINS

Wiggins ENTERPRISE. *See* Stone county enterprise

STONE county enterprise. w 1911-
1911-16 as Wiggins enterprise
pub 1927+
MsWgC 1916+

WINONA

Winona DEMOCRAT. w 1899-1903||
MsHi 1902-03

Winona TIMES. w 1883+
pub 1910+
MsWiC 1883+

WOODVILLE

Woodville COURIER. w N 1888-96||?
MsWoC Je 11 1890-91

MISSISSIPPI democrat. *See* Woodville republican

Woodville REPUBLICAN. w D 11 1823+
1823-30 as Woodville republican; 1831 Mississippi democrat; 1832 Southern planter; 1833-Ja 27 1844 Woodville republican; F 3 1844-Ja 30 1847 Republican
pub 1878+
DLC Ap 6 1824;Jl 10 1841;D 28 1844;N 21 1858
InI My 18-25 1824
LSfD O 18,D 20-27 1853;D 10 1863;Ag 27 1864;F 27 1904
LU Ja 26,My 14 1918
MWA O 28 1828;N 30 1844;Ag 8 1846;Mr 9 1889
MsHi O 6 1832;1850-53;S 30 1865;N 1902-N 1910
MsU D 18 1823-D 19 1848
MsWoC 1881-89;92-1908;10+
TxGR N 14,28 1863
TxU 1866-Ag 1869

SOUTHERN planter. *See* Woodville republican

WILKINSON gazette. w Ap 10 1858-
LSfD S 18 1858
MWA N 6,20 1858;Ag 27 1859;D 15 1860

WILKINSON journal. w 1861?-
FTS Ja 26 1866

WILKINSON whig. w Ja 26 1848-
LSfD Jl 28 1848
MWA Mr 9,O 20 1848;N 23,D 7 1849;My 31,Jl 19 1850;My 30,Je 20 1851;O 9,1852;N 6,D 4-11 1852;Jl 16,Ag 6,O 1,N 19-D 3 1853;Ja 28,Jl 1,29,S 23,N 4,D 9 1854;Ja 6,My 26,Je 9-16,30 1855;Ag 1 1857
TxU Ja 28 1854-Ja 17 1857

YAZOO CITY

Weekly AMERICAN banner. w My 18 1855-
LNC D 14 1860
MsHi 1855-D 26 1856

Yazoo BANNER. w
MsHi 1838-41

Yazoo DEMOCRAT. sw,w Ag 10 1844-
CtY Jl 20 1850
DLC Mr 31 1849-Ag 3 1850
MWA Ag 8 1848;My 25 1853
MsHi 1844-47;Ag 1850-O 11 1854
MsU S 1858-Ag 1860

Yazoo City HERALD. sw,w 1872+
pub 1905+
MsHi 1902-10
MsYC [1872-74]+

MISSISSIPPI democrat. w Ja 1 1868-
MBAt Mr 12,Ap 23-30,My 14-21,Je 11,Jl 30,Ag 20,S 17 1868

Yazoo SENTINEL. w,sw 1874+
MsHi 1902-10
MsYC 1875+

SOUTHERN banner. w
WHi Jl 3 1863

STATE'S rights and democratic union. w Jl 23 1839-
MsHi Ag 13-N 27 1839

Yazoo city WHIG. w Jl 12 1839-My 25 1855||
MWA S 7 1849;Je 3 1853
MsHi 1839-F 1847;53-My 18 1855

Semi-weekly WHIG. sw Ja? 1849-
MWA Ag 7 1849

Yazoo daily YANKEE. d
OHi Jl 20 1863
WHi Jl 20 1863

YAZOO county news. w 1901-31||?
MsYC [1915-31]

MISSOURI

ADRIAN

Adrian JOURNAL. w N 1889+
MoHi Ag 14 1903+

ADVANCE

Advance GUARD. w Jl 1902-08||?
MoHi Ap 20 1906-N 6 1908

Advance NEW era. w Mr 1911-19||?
MoCaT 1917-19
MoHi My 1916-O 1918

ALBANY

Albany ADVOCATE. w 1890-97||?
MoHi N 14 1890

Albany CAPITAL. w O 1890+
MoHi Ag 1901+

Albany LEDGER. w My 1868+
pub 1883+
MWA O 5 1876
MoHi O 23 1903-Ap 1904;My 1909+

ALEXANDRIA

Alexandria DELTA. w,tw 1856-63||
w 1856?
MoHi Ap 17 1861

NORTH Missourian. w 1854-
MoHi F 20 1855

ALTAMONT

Altamont TIMES. w 1900+
pub 1908+

ALTON

OREGON county democrat. w Ap 1898-My 1909||
United with South Missourian to form South Missourian-democrat
MoHi Jl 1901-D 22 1905

OREGON county South Missourian. *See* South Missourian-democrat

SOUTH Missourian-democrat. w 1871+
1871-Ag 3 1905 as Oregon county south Missourian; Ag 10 1905-My 6 1909 South Missourian
MoCaT 1906+
MoHi D 1898-Je 7 1900;01-06;Jl 1907-N 1925;F 1926+

AMORET

Amoret CHIEF. w Je 20 1890-92||?
KHi O 1890-92

Amoret LEADER. w 1913-23||?
KHi O 7 1915

AMSTERDAM

BORDER chief. w 1890-93||?
KHi Ja-Je 1893

ENTERPRISE-LEADER. w 1902-24||?
1902-23? as Amsterdam enterprise
MoHi Jl 9 1903-N 21 1918

Amsterdam TEMPEST. w 1900-02||?
OkHi [1900-02]

ANDERSON

Anderson ARGUS. *See* McDonald county republican

MCDONALD county republican. w 1900-08||?
1900-05? as Anderson argus
MoHi 1901-D 8 1905;D 1906-S 6 1907

Anderson NEWS-REVIEW. w My 1900+
1900-My 8 1914 as Anderson news
pub 1914+
MoHi My 15 1914-O 1920

Anderson REVIEW. w D 1912-My 1 1914||
United with Anderson news to form Anderson news-review
MoHi 1914

APPLETON CITY

Appleton City JOURNAL. w Jl 15 1881+
pub 1881+
MoHi 1903-1905;13+

Appleton City TRIBUNE. w 1900-09||?
MoHi Jl 14 1903-O 1909

ARMSTRONG

Armstrong HERALD. w 1888+
MoHi Jl 20 1894;1903+
MoSHi O 14 1915

ARROW ROCK

Arrow Rock STATESMAN. w N 1893-1919||?
MoHi N 25 1898-Ag 1900;01-Ap 1919

ASH GROVE

Ash Grove ADVANCE. w 1897-1904||?
MoHi 1903;F-Je 1904

Ash Grove COMMONWEALTH. w My 1881+
Title varies: Commonwealth
MoHi Jl-D 1904;Mr 30 1905;Jl 16 1908;14+

ASHLAND

Ashland BUGLE. m,w 1875+
1875-Ap 1877 as Bugle (m) (Columbia)
pub 1908+
MoHi Je 27 1895;1903-07;10+

ATLANTA

Atlanta EXPRESS. w 1908+
pub 1924+
MoHi O 10 1913-Mr 1933

Atlanta NEWS. w Ap 1896-1907||?
MoHi 1903-07

AUD

Aud VISITOR. w Je 1895-O? 1896||
Followed by Osage county republican (Linn)

MISSOURI (*Continued*)

AURORA

Aurora ADVERTISER. w 1889+
1889-Ag 6 1903 as Advertiser-herald; Ag 11 1903-04? Christian herald; 1905-06? Aurora advertiser and southwest miner
MoHi 1903 Mr 20 1908+
MoMon 1931+

Aurora daily ARGUS. d 1891-1911||?
MoHi Jl 1903-Je 1904;Mr 13 1908

CHRISTIAN herald. *See* Aurora advertiser

SOUTHWEST miner. w 1901-04||?
United with Christian herald to form Aurora advertiser and southwest miner, later Aurora advertiser

Aurora weekly TIMES. w 1886-90||?
MoHi O 24 1890

Aurora daily WORLD. d 1914-16||?
MoHi Jl 6 1914

AURORA SPRINGS

Aurora Springs DEMOCRAT. w Mr 30 1888-89||?
MoHi 1888-Ag 1889

AUXVASSE

Auxvasse REVIEW. w F 1 1888+
pub 1888+
MoHi O 30 1890;Jl 25 1901+
MoSHi F 16 1911;Je 12,Jl 31-Ag 7,21,S 4 1913

AVA

DOUGLAS county advocate and the Ozark breeze. w 1905-09||?
1905-08? as Ozark breeze
MoHi F 25 1909

DOUGLAS county capital. w Mr 1930+
pub 1931—

DOUGLAS county democrat. *See* Douglas county journal

DOUGLAS county herald. w Mr 3 1887+
pub 1887+
MoHi 1899[1900]+

DOUGLAS county journal. w Ja 1916-20||?
1916-18? as Douglas county democrat
MoHi F 20 1919-S 9 1920

DOUGLAS county record. w Ap 1910-16||?
1910-O 1915 as Enterprise
MoHi O 1913-S 14 1916

ENTERPRISE. *See* Douglas county record

OZARK breeze. *See* Douglas county advocate and the Ozark breeze

AVONDALE

SENTINEL. w My 1926-30||?
MoHi Jl 23 1926-Ap 11 1930

BAKERSFIELD

Bakersfield NEWS. w Ap 15 1905-12||?
MoHi 1905-06;09-10

Bakersfield NEWS. w Ap 1928+
pub 1928+

BELL CITY

Bell City NEWS. w
MoCaT 1919

BELLE

Belle BANNER. w D 1924+
pub 1925+
MoHi S 12 1929+

REPUBLICAN star. w O 1902-Ag 14 1903||
United with Belle times to form Star-times, later Belle times
MoHi 1903

Belle REVIEW. w Mr 1904-08||?
MoHi Ap 5 1906-07;Ja 3 1908

STAR-TIMES. *See* Belle times

Belle TIMES. w F 1896-1916||?
Ag 21-D 18 1903? as Star-times
MoHi Ag 21-D 1903;Mr 22 1906-09

BELLEVIEW

OZARK banner. w 1905-08||?
1905? as People's banner
MoHi Ap 29 1905

PEOPLE'S banner. *See* Ozark banner

BELLFLOWER

Bellflower NEWS. w D 1903+
1903-Jl 1906 as Bellflower telegram
pub 1903-[21-24]+
MoHi 1904-Je 1918

Bellflower TELEGRAM. *See* Bellflower news

BELTON

CASS county leader. w 1880-95||?
MoSHi Jl 31 1886

Belton HERALD. *See* Star-herald

Belton STAR. w 1916-Ap 1923||?
United with Belton herald to form Star-herald

STAR-HERALD. w N 1891+
1891-My 10 1923 as Belton herald
KHi Mr 3 1921;D 27 1923
MoHi Ag 16 1901-06;13-28

BENTON

Benton RECORD. w 1879-1908||
Followed by Scott county democrat
MoHi O 31 1890;N 25 1898-99;1903-08

SCOTT county democrat. w 1908+
Follows Benton record
MoCaT 1909+
MoHi 1909+

SCOTT county kicker. w 1902-17||?
MoCaT 1917

BERNIE

Bernie NEWS. *See* Star news

Bernie NEWSBOY. w Ja 4 1923+
pub 1923+
MoHi F 22 1923-27

Bernie STAR. w 1906-15||?
United with Bernie news to form Star news
MoHi Ag 2-23,S 20,O-N,D 20 1912;Ja 3-10, 24 1913

STAR news. w O 17 1913-19||?
1913-15? as Bernie news
MoCaT 1917-19
MoHi 1913-Jl 1915;16;My 1917-Ag 1919

BETHANY

Bethany CLIPPER. w O 7 1905-Ja 30 1929||
United with Bethany republican to form Republican-clipper
MoHi complete

Bethany DEMOCRAT. w F 1877-1920||?
MoHi Jl 24 1901-O 1920

HARRISON county herald. w Ag 4 1859-75||
1859-D 1865? as Bethany star; Ja 4? 1866-71? North Missouri tribune; 1872?-74 Bethany tribune
MWA Ja 25 1866

HARRISON county times and Gilman City guide. w 1931+
Ja-S 1931 as Harrison county times
pub 1931+
MoHi 1931+

NORTH Missouri tribune. *See* Harrison county herald

Bethany OWL. w 1901-03||?
MoHi Jl 8-D 1903

REPUBLICAN-CLIPPER. w Ap 1873+
1873-Ja 1929 as Bethany republican
KHi Je 1 1927
MoHi Jl 1901+

Bethany STAR. *See* Harrison county herald

Bethany TRIBUNE. *See* Harrison county herald

BEVIER

Bevier APPEAL. *See* Macon county journal and Bevier press-appeal

MACON county journal and Bevier press-appeal. w S 1889+
1889-1923? as Bevier appeal; 1924?-32? Bevier press-appeal
MWA Ap 8 1932
MoHi O 31 1890;Jl 26 1901-S 1921

Bevier PRESS-APPEAL. *See* Macon county journal and Bevier press-appeal

BIGELOW

Bigelow ENTERPRISE. w S 15 1902-Jl 15 1904||
MoHi Ja-Jl 1904

BILLINGS

Billings weekly TIMES. w 1883+
pub Je 1927+
MoHi O 23 1890;D 1898-N 1899;Je 1900-20; 25+
MoSHi D 4 1919

BIRCH TREE

Birch Tree RECORD. w 1893-1907||?
MoHi D 1898-Je 1905

SHANNON county herald. w O 1907+
pub 1908+
MoCaT 1917-19
MoHi 1914-18;Je 1919-22

BISMARCK

Bismarck BANNER. w 1904||?
WHi Ag 20,S 3 1904

Bismarck GAZETTE. w Ja 1901+
pub 1913+
MoHi My 1906-16; My 1932+
MoCaT 1917-19

BLACKBURN

Blackburn RECORD. w 1889-1914||?
MoHi Jl 26 1901-12;Ja-S 1914
MoSHi S 26 1913

BLACKWATER

Blackwater NEWS. w 1898-1923||?
MoHi Jl 26 1901-My 1917

BLAIRSTOWN

Blairstown BANNER. w 1891-92||?
MoHi N 19 1891

BLAND

Bland COURIER. w My 6 1904+
pub 1904+
MoHi 1904-24

BLOOMFIELD

STODDARD tribune. w Ag 1913+
pub 1913+
MoCaT 1917-19
MoHi 1919-Je 1922;23+

Bloomfield VINDICATOR. w O 1 1877+
pub 1877+
MoCaT 1907+
MoHi My 1902+

BLOOMINGTON

Bloomington GAZETTE. *See* Bloomington weekly journal

Bloomington weekly JOURNAL. w My 28 1850-54||
1850-Je 1852? as Bloomington gazette
MoSHi Jl 2 1853
NcD Jl 9 1853

BLUE SPRINGS

Blue Springs HERALD. w Mr 23 1923+
MoHi 1923+

SNI-A-BAR voice. w Ap 1901-D 21 1923||
Merged with Blue Springs herald
MoHi 1903-23

BOGARD

Bogard DISPATCH. w 1900+
MWA Je 27 1924

BOLCKOW

Bolckow HERALD. w Jl 1 1906+
pub 1906+

BOLIVAR

Bolivar FREE press. w My 15 1868+
pub 1891+
MoHi Je 24 1869;O 23 1890;N 14 1901+

Bolivar HERALD. w 1871+
pub 1889+
MoHi O 30 1890;D 1 1898—
MoSHi Ap 1,D 9 1886;My 26-Je 2,23 1887;Jl 3 1890

POLK county news. w Je 24- 1914||?
MoHi Je-Jl 1 1924

Bolivar weekly SENTINEL. w Ag 25 1865-
MoHi [1865-66]

BONNE TERRE

DEMOCRAT-REGISTER. *See* Bonne Terre register

NEWS-REGISTER. w 1912-S 11 1919||
1912-D 5 1918 as Bonne Terre weekly news. United with Star to form Star-news-register
MoCaT 1917-19
MoHi D 12 1918-19

Bonne Terre REGISTER. w 1890-D 1918||
1890-Ja 18 1905 as Democrat-register. United with Bonne Terre weekly news to form News-register
MoCaT 1917-18
MoHi N 25 1898-1918

STAR news-register. w 1896+
1896-S 12 1919 as Star; S 17-N 28 1919 Bonne Terre star and news-register
pub 1923+
MoCaT 1917-19
MoHi N 1898-D 1899;1912-22

BOONVILLE

ADVANCE. w Ap 1902-Ap 7 1904||?
Merged with Central Missouri republican
MoHi 1903

Boonville weekly ADVERTISER. w,sw Mr 13 1840+
1840-D 12 1850 as Boonville observer; D 19 1850-Je 8? 1862 Boonville weekly observer; Je 15 1862-S? 1873 Central Missouri advertiser; O? 1873-O 15 1875 Boonville Missouri advertiser; O 22 1876-S 1921 Boonville weekly advertiser; O 4 1921-S 1922 Twice-a-week advertiser
sw O 4 1921-S 1922
pub 1927+
IUr Jl 5 1872
MoBoH D 1878-Ja,Mr 1884-F 1888;Jl 1895-96;1904-06;11-24
MoHi Mr 13 1844-Jl,D 1846-Ja 12 1848;Mr 21 1850-My 1851;Mr 1854-56[My-D 1868]-My 1 1869;My 23 1873+
MoSHi F 3 1855;Ap 22,S 2 1865
NbHi F 11,19,Je 9 1876;F 2,O 12,N 9 1877;F 8,My 17,D 6-13 1878;Ag 29 1879
—tw ed *See* Tri-weekly observer

MISSOURI (*Continued*)

BOONVILLE—*Continued*

ADVERTISER. d O 25 1875-79||?
MoHi 1875-O 24 1877

Boonville BULLETIN. w
-S 9 1847 as Boonville commercial bulletin
MoSHi Ap 11 1846-Ap 1848

Boonville evening CALL. d 1908-
MoHi 1909-Mr 1910

CENTRAL Missouri advertiser. *See* Boonville weekly advertiser

CENTRAL Missouri republican. w Jl 1 1884-1927||?
Merged with Boonville daily news
MoBoH Jl 29 1884-87;91-92;96;1904-19
MoHi O 30 1890;Jl 1901-Je 1926

CENTRAL Missourian. *See* Boonville daily news

CENTRAL Missourier. w 1868-1907||?
In German
MoBoH N 1883-96
MoHi O 22 1874-1907

Boonville COMMERCIAL bulletin. *See* Boonville bulletin

COON hunter. w Ap 26-N? 1844||
MWA Ap-My 3,24,Je 7-14 1844
MoSM Je 14,S 6 1844

COOPER county democrat. *See* Missouri democrat

Boonville weekly DEMOCRAT. w
ILeM N 29 1859-D 5 1860
MoSHi My 5-12,D 22 1848;Ja 12,26-F 1849;Mr 8 1850

Boonville weekly EAGLE. w O 7? 1865-Jl 12 1878||
Followed by Sedalia weekly eagle (Sedalia) later Sedalia weekly eagle-times
MWA O 21 1865;F 3 1866;O 20 1871
MoHi My 1868-78

Daily EAGLE. d
MoHi S 29-O 1 1869

FIFTH Iowa register.
MoSHi F 3 1862

Boonville GAZETTE. d Ap 8 1909-10||?
Ap-Je 17 1909 as Missouri democrat
MoHi Ap-Jl 7 1909
—w ed *See* Missouri democrat

Boonville HERALD. w Ag 1 1833-
DLC O 3 1833
ICHi N 29 1833
MoHi Ag 8 1834
MoSHi Mr 28 1834

Friday morning INDEPENDENT. w Jl 8-1898||?
Jl 8-15 1898 as Independent
MoHi Jl 8-22,Ag-S 9,23-D 2,16-30 1898

Boonville MISSOURI advertiser. *See* Boonville weekly advertiser

MISSOURI democrat. w 1890?-1909||?
1890?-Je 30 1893 Cooper county democrat; Jl 7 1893-N 2 1894 Missouri democrat; N 9 1894-O 16 1896 Boonville Missouri democrat
MoHi 1890-Jl 1898;Je 23-Jl 7,Ag 4-11,25-N 24 1899;My 23 1902;Jl 10 1903;Ap 7 1909

MISSOURI democrat. d *See* Boonville gazette

MISSOURI register. w Jl 18? 1839-54||?
MWA Ag 8 1839;Jl 19 1845
MoHi My 1840-Je 1841;Ag 1843-F,Jl,N 1845

Boonville MONITOR. w F 13 1864-
MoHi F-Ag 6 1864

Boonville daily NEWS. d S 1919+
1919 as Boonville daily republican; 1920-Ag 4 1928 Central Missourian
pub 1919+
MoHi D 1926+

Boonville OBSERVER. w *See* Boonville weekly advertiser

Tri-weekly OBSERVER. tw D 31 1850-
MWA 1850-Mr 8 1851

Boonville daily REPUBLICAN. *See* Boonville daily news

REPUBLICAN-SUN. w,d Ap 1929-Ja 31 1934||
1929-My 1933 as Republican(w) Merged with Boonville daily news
MoBoM complete

Semi-weekly STAR. sw N 1886-94||?
MoBoH S 1888-My 1894
MoHi My 18 1890-Je 3 1893

Boonville SUCCESS. w 1902-
MoHi My 3 1902

Boonville tri-weekly TOPIC. w,tw Ag 1877-90||?
1877-Jl 17 1888 as Topic(w)
MoBoH 1886-87
MoHi S 19 1884-89

WESTERN emigrant. w Ap 19 1838-
MWA O 31 1839
MoHi 1839-Mr 1840
MoSHi Mr 26 1840

BOSWORTH

Bosworth ADVERTISER. w 1888-90||?
MoHi N 1 1890

Bosworth SENTINEL. w 1891+
KHi Mr 22,N 29 1923

BOURBON

Bourbon STANDARD. w 1906+
pub 1919+
MoCaT 1917-19

BOWLING GREEN

DEMOCRATIC banner. *See under* Louisiana

Bowling Green JEFFERSONIAN. w Jl 9 1924-27||?
MoHi 1924-N 1927

MISSOURI journal. w My 1844-48||
MoHi S 14 1844

PIKE county express. *See* Bowling Green times

PIKE county post. w 1871-1918||?
1876-85? as Post-observer
MoHi O 30 1890;D 17 1913;14-O 1918

RADICAL. *See* Democratic banner (Louisiana)

SALT RIVER journal. *See* Democratic banner (Louisiana)

Bowling Green TIMES. w Ag 1875+
1875-79? as Pike county express
1875-76? pub in Curryville
MoHi 1903-07;14+

BRANSON

Branson ECHO. w N 17 1905-09||?
MoHi 1905-N 5 1909

Branson SENTINEL. w O 1901-15||?
MoHi N 14 1913-O 9 1914

TANEY county democrat. w F 10 1910-11||?
MoHi F-N 17 1910

WHITE RIVER leader. w My 9 1913+
MoHi 1913-Je 1919;25+

BRASHEAR

Brashear NEWS. w 1885+
pub 1926+
MoHi 1903-Je 1906;My 1912-Jl 1926;32+

BRAYMER

Braymer BEE. w Je 1887+
MoH F 10 1921+
MoHi D 1898-N 1916

Braymer COMET. w 1891-1914||?
MoHi Ja-Je 1898;N 1908-13

BRECKENRIDGE

Breckenridge BULLETIN. w 1875+
pub 1875-93;95+
MoH 1921-Jl 8 1927;Mr 28-My 1930
MoHi D 31 1897;Ja 21-F 4,18-25,Mr 11-My 6, 20,Je 3,17-24 1898;Jl 26 1901+

BRONOUGH

Bronough JOURNAL. w Jl 14 1904+
pub 1904+

BROOKFIELD

Daily ARGUS. w,d 1884+
1884-O 1914 as Brookfield argus(w)
MoBr [Ap-D 1919]-[23-25]+
MoHi S 19 1903;04+
MoM F 10 1930+

Brookfield BUDGET. *See* Linn County budget-gazette

Brookfield GAZETTE. w Ap 1867-Ap? 1927||
United with Linn county budget to form Linn county budget-gazette
MoHi 1867-70;Mr 25 1871-75;77-1926
MoSHi Ja 4 1919

LINN county budget-gazette. w,sw,d,tw 1895+
1895-1904? as Brookfield budget; 1905-Ja 24 1927 Linn county budget
w 1895-1909,22-25;sw 1910-20?;d 1921?
pub 1895+
MoHi F 1895-My 22 1897;F-D 1898;1901-My 1904;Mr 1905+

BROWNING

Browning LEADER-RECORD. w 1893+
1893-96? as Browning leader
MoHi Mr 1905+

Browning RECORD. w 1886-96||?
United with Browning leader to form Browning leader-record

BROWNINGTON

Brownington NEWS. w 1889-90||?
MoHi O 23 1890

BROWNSVILLE. *See* SWEET SPRINGS

BRUNSWICK

Weekly BRUNSWICKER. w O 14 1847+
1857?-65? as Central City Brunswicker
DLC Je 12,S 25-O 9,23,N 27,D 11-25 1869
MWA F 3 1866
MoHi D 23 1881;Jl 11 1896;Ag 1901-03;My 23 1930+
MoSHi 1847-S 19 1853[59-72]85-1917
WHi Ja-S 9,O 28 1854-Mr 1857

CENTRAL CITY. w -1856||?
United with Weekly Brunswicker to form Central City Brunswicker, later Weekly Brunswicker

Brunswick NEWS. w 1875-93||?
MoSHi O 30 1875-F 4 1893

BUCKLIN

Bucklin HERALD. w S 26 1886+
MoHi 1899+

BUCKNER

Buckner RECORD. w 1907+
pub 1907+

Buckner TRIBUNE. w 1897-1906||?
MoHi Mr 7 1903;N 18 1904
NN Je 20 1903

BUFFALO

Buffalo COURIER.
MoBoH Ag 25 1901

DALLAS county republican. w 1926+
pub S 1928+

Buffalo RECORD. w Je 1894-1921||?
MoHi Ja-O 1902;Ap 2 1908;09-10;14-Mr 1921

Buffalo REFLEX. w 1869+
pub 1869-[73-1901]+
MoHi S 11 1869;F 8 1878-F,Mr 19 1880;Ja-Ag 1902;03+

Buffalo REGISTER. w 1879-84||?
MoHi Ap 17 1879-Mr 18 1880

BUNCETON

Bunceton weekly EAGLE. w 1888+
pub 1894+
MoHi Jl 26 1907+

Bunceton ENTERPRISE. w 1887||?
MoHi Jl 1 1887

Bunceton TRIBUNE. sw,w Jl 1895-Je 20 1911||
w 1895-1902?
MoHi D 15 1899;Ag 9 1901-11

BURLINGTON JUNCTION

Burlington Junction LEDGER. w 1890-98||?
MoHi O 23 1890

Burlington Junction POST. w Ag 1879+
pub 1934+
MoHi N 1 1890;Jl 27 1901+

BUTLER

BATES county democrat. w D 16 1869+
pub 1869+
MoHi S 1903-F 1904;My 16 1907;08-09;11+

BATES county record. w Jl 9 1866-1918||?
MoHi Jl 1868-Je 22 1872;Je 28 1873-Je 1886;88-Ap 1918

BATES county times. *See* Butler weekly times

Butler daily DEMOCRAT. d 1889+
pub 1889+

Butler FREE press. *See* Republican press

LOCAL news. *See* Republican press

REPUBLICAN press. w 1888+
1888-89? as Local news; 1890?-95? Weekly union; 1896-Ag 2 1901 Butler free press
MoHi Ag 1901+
NbHi Ag 13 1891
NcD Je 7 1895;My 29,Ag 14 1896;D 23 1898

Butler weekly TIMES. w N 1878+
1878-81? as Bates county times
MoHi O 29,N 12 1890;Jl 25 1901+

Weekly UNION. *See* Republican press

CABOOL

Cabool ENTERPRISE. w Mr 23 1906+
Ja 18 1917-28 as Cabool enterprise-press
pub 1913+
MoHi Ap 20 1906-Ag 1908;14-Ap 1921
MoSHi Ja 18 1897

Cabool PRESS. w 1913-16||?
United with Cabool enterprise to form Cabool enterprise-press, later Cabool enterprise

CAINSVILLE

BOOSTER. w D 11 1914-15||?
MoHi 1914-O 8 1915

Cainsville INDEPENDENT. w S 25 1913-14||?
MoHi 1913-Jl 23 1914

Cainsville NEWS. w My 1 1886+
MoHi O 30 1890;Jl 25 1901+

CALHOUN

Calhoun CLARION. w Mr 25 1902-O 1 1918||
MoHi complete
NN Jl 4 1903

Calhoun STAR. w O 1919+
pub 1934+

CALIFORNIA

CENTRAL Missouri push. w Ag 5 1899-1902||?
MoHi 1899-Jl 12 1902
WHi O 12 1901

California DEMOCRAT. w O 1858+
1858-69 as California news; 1870-71 Moniteau county democrat
pub 1858+
MoHi F 1873-79;81-86;88-1902;Je 25 1903+

MISSOURI (*Continued*)

CALIFORNIA—*Continued*

California DISPATCH. w Jl 16 1896-1907||?
MoBoH Mr 1897
MoHi 1896-1900;03-F 12,Jl 22 1904;S 22(extra) 1897
NN My 15-22 1903

GREENBACK derrick. w Mr 25 1882-83||?
MoHi 1882-F 2 1883

LOYAL Journal. *See* Moniteau journal

LOYAL Missourian. *See* Moniteau journal

MONITEAU county democrat. *See* California democrat

MONITEAU county herald. w My 23 1889+
pub [1889]+
MoHi 1889-93;Mr 1894+

MONITEAU journal. w Je 14 1866-
1866-Ag 1867 as Loyal Missourian; S 1867-N 1869 Loyal journal
MoHi 1866-D 9 1875;Je 8 1881
MoSHi O 5 1871

MONITEAU monitor. w Mr 3 1880-82||?
MoHi Mr 24 1880-Mr 15 1882

California NEWS. *See* California democrat

NEWSPAPER. w My 8 1884-96||?
MoHi 1884-85;Ap 8 1886-Jl 9 1896

CALLAO

Callao JOURNAL. w 1907+
pub 1907+

CAMDEN POINT

PLATTE county news. w D 7 1917-18||?
MoHi 1917-N 1 1918

CAMDENTON

REVEILLE. sw,w Je 23 1879+
1879-Ap 17 1931 pub in Linn Creek
sw 1902-04?
pub Je 10 1885+
IaHi N 20 1902-O 3 1903
MoHi S 1881-Mr 1883;My 22 1890;92-94;96+
MoSHi F 11 25-Mr 3,Ap 14-28,Je 9 1916

CAMERON

HAMMER. *See under* Turney

Cameron MISSOURI sun. *See* Cameron sun and the weekly observer

NEWS-OBSERVER. d 1905+
1905-S 15 1920 as Cameron daily news
pub 1905+
MoHi O 1913+

OBSERVER. d 1892-S 15 1920||
United with Cameron daily news to form News-observer
MoCamN complete
MoHi Ag 8 1901-20

Cameron PROGRESS. w S 1923+
pub 1923+

REPUBLICAN. w 1898-
MoHi Mr 16 1900

Cameron SUN and the weekly observer. w 1887+
1887-S 19 1902 as Cameron sun; S 26 1902-Ap 16 1914 Cameron Missouri sun
pub 1887+
MoH Ja 27 1921+
MoHi Jl 10 1896;Ag 1902+

VINDICATOR. w Je 8 1876-92||?
MoHi 1876-Je 5 1879
MoSHi O 24 1884

Daily VINDICATOR. d Je 10 1881-92||?
MoHi 1881-S 21 1888

CAMPBELL

CITIZEN. w Je 15 1900+
1900-Ap 1901 as Dunklin county citizen
pub Je 22 1900+
MoCaT 1917-19
MoHi O 1903-N 1904;08+

DUNKLIN county citizen. *See* Citizen

CANTON

CANTONIAN. w F 10 1916-19||?
MoC [Mr 30 1916-Je 5 1919]
MoCC 1916-18

LEWIS county journal. *See under* Monticello

MISSISSIPPI sawyer. *See* Canton news

MISSOURI plebeian. *See* Northeast reporter

Canton NEWS. w 1880-N 15 1928||
1920-Jl 1922 as Mississippi sawyer. United with Canton press to form Canton press-news
MoC Ap 7 1882;91-1928
MoCC 1880-91;1908;10;26-28
MoHi O 24 1890;Jl 25 1901-N 1908;F 13 1913-S 3 1919

NORTHEAST reporter. w Je 9 1848-61||
1848-Ap 1849 as Missouri plebeian
MoHi Je 16 1848-My 20 1850;Je 24 1852-O 2 1856
MoSHi Je 30 1853

Canton PRESS-NEWS. w Jl 4 1862+
1862-N 16 1928 as Canton press
MoC [Ag 1880-1922]+
MoCC 1928+
MoHi Jl 16 1862+

Canton RECORD. w O 17 1929+
MoC 1929+
MoCC 1929+
MoMontL 1929+

CAPE GIRARDEAU

Cape Girardeau weekly ARGUS. w 1863-70||?
MoCaT Ap 21 1870
MoHi Jl 19 1866

CAMP FREMONT register. ir? S 25 1861-
WHi S 25 1861

CAPE county herald. w 1898-1913||?
MoHi [Mr-N 1911]My 24 1912

CAPE daily tribune. d 1914-18||?
Followed by Morning sun
MoHi Mr 13 1914-O 16 1918
MoSHi F 20 1916
—w ed *See* Weekly tribune

Cape Girardeau DEMOCRAT. w 1876-1909||?
MoCaT 1891-1900;07-09

DEMOCRAT. d 1889-1909||?
MoCaT 1893-1900;02-09

Cape Girardeau EAGLE. w 1847-
1847-51? as Western eagle
MWA D 16 1853
MoSHi Ap 11 1851
WHi My 11 1849-Mr 21 1851

Daily EAGLE. d 1861-
MoHi Je 25 1861
OClWHi Ap 30 1862

Cape Girardeau eagle, union series. w pub by Union Army
WHi My 10-24,Je 28-Ag 2 1862

Cape Girardeau HERALD.
MoCaT 1919-Ja 1924

MARBLE CITY news. *See* Cape Girardeau news (1865-88)

MISSOURI democracy. w 1868-70||?
MoCaT F 9 1870

Cape Girardeau NEWS. w 1865-88||?
1865-74? as Marble city news
MoCaT Ap 13 1870
MoHi Mr 9 1881

Cape Girardeau NEWS. w 1909-10||?
MoHi 1909-Jl 1910

Cape Girardeau NEWS. w O 10 1929+
MoCaT O 1929+

Cape Girardeau PROGRESS. sw,w Ja 1902-09||?
sw S 1902-03
MoCaT 1907-09
MoHi Ap 1902-09

Weekly REPUBLICAN. w 1901-18||
MoCaT 1908-18
MoHi F-D 4 1908;09-18
MoSHi F 1908-Ja 1913
—d ed *See* Southeast Missourian

Daily REPUBLICAN. *See* Southeast Missourian

SOUTHEAST democrat. w 1857-
MoCaT N 25 1857
MoHi My 5 1858

SOUTHEAST Missourian. d 1901+
1901-F 1918 as Daily republican
pub 1905+
MoCaT Ag 20 1903;18+
MoHi D 1903-S 9 1904;My 18 1905;My 28 1912;18-20,23+
—w ed *See* Weekly republican

SOUTHEAST radical. w 1865?-
MWA Mr 9 1866

SOUTHERN advocate and state journal. *See* Jackson courier (Jackson)

SOUTHERN standard.
MoSHi S 5 1849

Morning SUN. d Ag 16 1919-Ag 12 1922||
Follows Cape daily tribune
MoCaT complete
MoHi Ag 27 1919-Je 1922

Weekly TRIBUNE. w 1902-19||?
MoCaT 1914-19
MoHi O 25 1918-Je 20 1919
—d ed *See* Cape daily tribune

WESTERN eagle. *See* Cape Girardeau eagle

CARDWELL

Cardwell OUTLOOK. w 1913-23||?
MoCaT Jl 26 1918-19

CARL JUNCTION

GRAPHIC. d
MoHi Ja-Ap 1907

JASPER county world. w 1900-07||?
MoHi O 26 1906-07

PLAINDEALER. *See* Carl Junction times

Carl Junction STANDARD. w 1890+
Suspended from 1907-10; and from My 22-Ag 2 1918
MoHi D 16 1898-1906;Ja 20 1911+

Carl Junction TIMES. w 1900-17||?
1900-Ap 1915? as Plaindealer
MoHi 1908-Ap 16,My 20 1915-F 1 1917

CARONDELET

Papers published in Carondelet are listed under St. Louis

CARROLLTON

CARROLL county journal. *See* Carrollton journal

Carrollton DEMOCRAT. w 1875+
O 13 1933 is centenary ed
pub 1875-91[93]+
MWA O 13 1933
MoHi D 23 1898+
MoSHi O 31 1919

Carrollton DEMOCRAT. d 1882+
pub 1882-91[93]+
MoHi Ap 30 1896;O 6 1927+

Carrollton JOURNAL. w,sw O 6? 1865-89||?
1865? as Carroll county journal; 1866?-76? Carroll journal
w 1865-87?
MWA O 13 1865
MoHi N 16 1877-N 14 1879

Carroll RECORD. *See* Republican-record

REPUBLICAN. w 1891-N 1894||
United with Carroll record to form Republican record

REPUBLICAN RECORD. w Ja 1868+
1868-Ag 10 1878 as Wakenda record (Wakenda) Ag 17 1878-N 1894 Carroll record
pub 1904+
MoCarrD N 1904-24
MoHi N 6 1869;O 31 1890;1904+

CARTERVILLE

Carterville FREE press. w 1890-91||?
MoHi N 1 1890

CARTHAGE

Carthage BANNER. w D 1866-92||?
MoCar 1866-75;77-78;80;82-91;S-D 1892
MoHi [Je 18 1868-My 17 1877]

Carthage daily BANNER. d 1878?-92||?
MoHi F 5,Jl 18 1879

Carthage DEMOCRAT. d 1884+
MoHi Ja 12 1909;Je 28,Ag 20 1910-Ja 12 1917
—w,sw ed *See* Jasper county democrat

JASPER county democrat. w,sw Ag 30 1884+
w 1884-1904?
MoHi 1884-Ag 21 1885;D 8 1898+
—d ed *See* Carthage democrat

JASPER county news. w O 1 1901-04||?
MoHi 1901-Ja 5 1904

Carthage PATRIOT. w 1876-8?||?
MoCar Je 27 1876-77

Carthage daily PATRIOT. d 1878-87||
MoCar 1878;Je 1879-81;Jl 7-O 28 1882
MoHi F 29 1879

PEOPLE'S press. *See* Carthage press

Carthage PRESS. w 1872+
1872-Jl 14 1881 as People's press
pub 1872+
MWA Ag 17 1876
MoHi Jl 25 1901-20

Carthage evening PRESS. d 1883+
pub 1897+
MoCar 1898+
MoHi Jl 23-25 1914;21+

Carthage REPUBLICAN. w O 1878?-79||?
MoHi [S-O 1879]

REPUBLICAN. w Je 19- 1884||?
MoHi Je-D 18 1884

SOUTHWEST news. w D 1859-
MoCar Mr 29 1861

CARUTHERSVILLE

DEMOCRAT-ARGUS. w,sw 1868+
1868-91? as Gayoso democrat; 1892?-1901? Caruthersville democrat; 1902-N 1921 Twice-a-week democrat
1868-91? pub in Gayoso
w 1868-1900?
pub 1894-1911; 13+
MoCaT 1917-19;22+
MoCaru 1927+
MoHi D 1898-F 1900;O 1903-My 1904;O 1908+

PEMISCOT argus. w Jl 1 1898-N 30 1921||
United with Twice-a-week democrat to form Democrat-argus
1898-1907 pub in Hayti
MoCaT 1907-21
MoCaruD complete
MoHi Ja 13 1905-07;S 24 1908-21

PEMISCOT press. w,sw 1895-1908||?
w 1895-Ag 1906
MoHi 1902-D 12 1906;S 25-D 1908

REPUBLICAN. w 1910+
pub 1925+
MoCaT 1917-19
MoCaru 1926+
MoHi 1925+

SOUTHEAST scimitar. w My 23-D 26 1901||?
MoHi 1901

CASSVILLE

Cassville DEMOCRAT. w 1872+
pub 1876+
MoHi 1903-04;06-09;11+

Cassville REPUBLICAN. w 1872+
1872-78 as Valley press
pub 1893+
MoHi O 18 1878;O 30 1890;Jl 9 1896;D 29 1898+
MoMon 1931+

VALLEY press. *See* Cassville republican

MISSOURI (*Continued*)

CEDAR CITY

CHRONICLE-REPORTER. w 1894-1914||?
1894-My? 1903 as Cedar City chronicle
MoHi N 1899-My 21,Jl 1903-06

Cedar City REPORTER. w 1899-My 1903||?
United with Cedar City chronicle to form Chronicle-reporter

CENTER

Center HERALD. w 1904+
pub 1910-23
MoHi 1919+

Center INTELLIGENCER. w 1898-1902||?
1898-1901? as Rolls county intelligencer
MoHi Ap 11 1902

ROLLS county intelligencer. *See* Center intelligencer

CENTERVIEW

Centerview RECORD. w 1898-1906||?
MoHi Ja 26-F 9,23-Mr 23 1906

CENTERVILLE

Centerville REFORMER. w 1891-1911||?
MoHi Mr 1904-07

REYNOLDS county courier. w 1924+
MoHi N 18 1926+

REYNOLDS county outlook. w 1877-1925||?
MoCaT 1907-13

CENTRALIA

Centralia COURIER. w My 21 1891+
pub 1891+
MoHi Ap 9 1908;Ja 29 1915+

Centralia FIRESIDE guard. w O 1868+
pub [1868-70]+
MoHi Mr 27 1903+

CHAFFEE

Chaffee SIGNAL. w S 2 1910+
MoCaT 1917-19

CHAMOIS

OSAGE county enterprise. w 1888-1918||?
Suspended 1911
MoHi O 23-30 1890;Jl 9 1896

CHARLESTON

Charleston COURIER. w 1901-Ap 15 1915||
United with Weekly enterprise to form Enterprise-courier
MoHi 1903-[11]-15

Charleston DEMOCRAT. w Ag 15 1929+
pub 1929+
MoHi F 17 1933+

Daily ENTERPRISE. d 1891-1903||?
MoHi D 20 1898-Ap 24 1899

ENTERPRISE-COURIER. w Ag 1875+
1875-Ap 16 1915 as Weekly enterprise
pub [1875-1928]+
MoCaT 1907+
MoHi My 16 1902+

INDEPENDENT. 1862-
KHi Mr 10 1862

Daily INDEX. d 1919-23||?
KHi Ja 31 1923

Charleston REPUBLICAN. w O 6 1906-Ap 19 1917||
MoCat 1917
MoHi 1906-Ag 13 1914;Mr 15-22, Ap 1917

TIMES. w Je 24 1921-S 7 1928||
Merged with Enterprise-courier
MoChE complete
MoHi 1925-28

CHILHOWEE

Chilhowee BLADE. w 1915-21||?
MoHi Ja 22 1915-D 16 1921

Chilhowee NEWS. w 1896+
MoHi N 18 1898-99;1901-O 1 1914

CHILLICOTHE

CONSTITUTION-TRIBUNE. w 1860+
1860-F 1928 as Chillicothe constitution
MWA Ap 12 1866
MoHi Ja 12 1865;99+
MoSHi Ap 6 1865

CONSTITUTION-TRIBUNE. d 1887+
1887-F 1928 as Chillicothe constitution
MoHi Mr 1928+

Weekly Chillicothe CRISIS. w 1877-1903||?
MoHi S 17 1903

Chillicothe daily DEMOCRAT. d 1892-1905||?
1892-99? as Chillicothe mail and star
MoHi My 22,S 8 1903-O 9 1905

Chillicothe DEMOCRAT. w 1893-1905||?
1893-99? as Chillicothe mail and star
MoHi D 1898-N 1899

FIRST Kansas. O 16 1861-
KHi O 16 1861

Chillicothe JOURNAL. w 1870-72||?
MoHi Ap 28 1870
TKL S 22,O 20-27,N 10 1870;Ja 19,Mr 30-Ap 1871

Chillicothe MAIL and star. *See* Chillicothe democrat

MISSOURI world. w 1888-1908||?
MoHi Jl 24 1901-08
NbHi Ag 26 1896
NcD Ag 23 1893;Mr 4,Ag 12 1896
NcU Jl 17 1895
WHi Ap 8 1908

NEWS-CHRONICLE. w,sw 1928+
1928? as Chillicothe news; 1929-31? Chillicothe news and Chula chronicle w 1928?
MoHi O 12 1928+

Chillicothe SPECTATOR. *See* Chillicothe tribune

Chillicothe TRIBUNE. w 1866-F 1928||
1866-67? as Chillicothe spectator. United with Chillicothe constitution to form Constitution-tribune
MoHi Mr 8 1866-Mr 7 1867;F 9 1893;1919

Chillicothe daily TRIBUNE. d 1881-F 29 1928||
United with Chillicothe constitution to form Constitution-tribune
MoHi S 15 1910-Mr 1 1917;N 1924-28

CHULA

Chula CHRONICLE. w 1923-28||?
United with Chillicothe news (Chillicothe) to form Chillicothe news and Chula chronicle, later News-chronicle (Chillicothe)

NEWS of Chula. w Ap 1899-1923||?
MoHi Mr 30 1906-D 22 1910;Ja 12 1911

CLARENCE

Clarence COURIER. w 1881-Mr 14 1928||
United with Shelby county independent to form Independent-courier
MoCll 1916-28
MoHi O 22 1890;Jl 31 1901-28

FARMER'S favorite. *See* Clarence republican

INDEPENDENT-COURIER. sw,w My 5 1925+
1925-Mr 16 1928 as Shelby county independent (sw)
pub 1925+
MoHi 1925+

Clarence REPUBLICAN. w 1889-1912||?
My 19 1899-1911? as Farmer's favorite
MoHi D 1898-N 1899[1901]

SHELBY county independent. *See* Independent-courier

CLARK

Clark CHRONICLE. w D 1902+
MoHi 1904-N 1924

CLARKSBURG

Clarksburg CRESCENT. w 1888-99||?
MoHi O 9 1890

Clarksburg MESSENGER. w 1885-86||?
MoHi Ja 29 1886

CLARKSDALE

Clarksdale JOURNAL. w S 1902-O 11 1928||
United with Stewartsville record (Stewartsville) to form DeKalb county record-journal (Maysville)
MoHi F 19 1904-08;14-25

CLARKSVILLE

Clarksville BANNER. w 1898-1907||
1898-D 22 1899 as Calumet banner. United with Clarksville sentinel to form Clarksville banner-sentinel, later Clarksville sentinel
MoHi D 22 1899;S 18 1903

Clarksville BANNER-SENTINEL. *See* Clarksville sentinel

CALUMET banner. *See* Clarksville banner

Clarksville PIKER. w D 1903-17||?
Merged with Clarksville banner-sentinel, later Clarksville sentinel
MoHi My 24 1906-N 1 1917

Clarksville SENTINEL. w Jl 1866+
1908-28 as Clarksville banner-sentinel
pub 1867-68; 88+
MoHi Je 10 1869; D 10 1913;14-27
MoLo 1867-69

CLARKTON

Clarkton GAZETTE. w 1913-17||?
MoCaT 1917

CLAYTON

Clayton ARGUS. w 1877-1920||?
MoCaT 1917-19
MoHi N 25 1899-1920
MoSHi D 18 1891

PEOPLE'S advocate. *See* St. Louis county advocate

ST. LOUIS county advocate. w 1896-1903||
1896-98? as People's advocate. United with St. Louis county watchman to form Watchman-advocate
MoHi Jl 10 1903

ST. LOUIS county leader. w F 16 1923+
pub 1923+
MoHi 1923+

ST. LOUIS county sentinel. *See* Sentinel-democrat

ST. LOUIS county wächter. w 1878-1910||?
In German
MoHi 1903

ST. LOUIS county watchman. *See* Watchman-advocate

SENTINEL-DEMOCRAT. w 1919-25||?
1919-23? as St. Louis county sentinel
MoHi 1921-24

WATCHMAN-ADVOCATE. w,sw S 1881+
1881-S 1903 as St. Louis county watchman
sw My 1923-27
pub 1881+
MoCaT 1907+
MoHi O 24 1890;Jl 26 1901-05;Ap 1908+
MoSHi O 14 1910-D 7 1917
MoWe 1933+

CLEARMONT

Clearmont LEDGER. *See* Clearmont news

Clearmont NEWS. w Ja 11 1911+
1911-12 as Clearmont ledger
pub 1913+

CLIMAX SPRINGS

CLIMAX advocate. w 1889-
MoHi O 29-N 19 1890

CLINTON

Clinton ADVOCATE. w Ja 1866-91||?
1866-69? as Weekly Clinton advocate
MoHi Je 3 1869;Ja-Mr 1875;Mr-Ap 1881;83; 85-87;89-Mr 1891

Daily ADVOCATE. d 1883-89||?
MoHi S 1883-Ja 1884;85-[87-88]-S 21 1889

Daily DEMOCRAT. d 1886+
Title varies slightly
pub 1890+
MoHi N 19 1891;O 1893-1903;F-D 1905;Ag 3 1908;Mr-D 1911;My 9 1914

Clinton EYE. w N 14 1885+
pub 1885+
MoHi O 25 1890;Je 27 1914;19+

HENRY county democrat. w 1868+
pub 1885+
MoHi Je 24 1869;Jl 1875-Jl 1883; My 30,Jl 4,O 24,Jl 18 1889;O 30 1890;O-D 1893; F-D 1894;98+
MoSHi N 25 1920-Je 2 1921

HENRY county republican. w 1865-1917||?
For O 1 1914-Mr 18 1915 *See* Progressive Missourian
MoHi Ap 1891-95;Ag 15-O 1896;F 1898-S 1902; 03-07; Jl 30 1908;09-17
—d ed *See* Republican

Clinton JOURNAL. w Ap 26 1858-61||
KHi Jl 4 1861

PROGRESSIVE Missourian. w O 1 1914-Mr 18 1915||
Replaces Henry county republican
MoHi complete

REPUBLICAN. d O 11 1904-17||?
1908? as Evening republican
MoHi 1904-Mr 13 1906;Ag 3 1908;S 1910-Je 1911; Mr 27-Ap 1916
—w ed *See* Henry county republican

Daily TRIBUNE. d 1913-16||?
MoHi Je 27 1914

CLYDE

Clyde TIMES. w 1893-1914||?
MoHi 1904-14

COFFEY

Early years as Coffeyburg

Coffeyburg ENTERPRISE. w 1904-12||?
MoHi Mr 23 1905

Coffeyburg SUN. w My 25 1899-1901||?
MoHi 1899-N 1901

COFFEYBURG. *See* COFFEY

COLE CAMP

Cole Camp COURIER. w Ag 1894+
MoHi Jl 25 1901+

COLUMBIA

BOONE county journal. *See* Columbia Missouri herald

BOONE county sentinel. w 1877-87||?
MoHi My 19 1877

BUGLE. *See* Ashland bugle (Ashland)

DOLLAR Missouri journal. *See* State argus

Columbia GLOBE. w Ap 22 1847-48||
MoSHi D 1,10 1847-Mr 24 1848

MISSOURI (*Continued*)

COLUMBIA—*Continued*

Daily HERALD. d 1906-09||?
MoHi Ag 26 1908;My 31 1909

***Columbia HERALD-STATESMAN.** w Ap 23 1819+
Ap-O 1819 as Missouri intelligencer and Boon's Lick advertiser; N 1819-D 5 1835 Missouri intelligencer; D 12 1835-42 Columbia patriot; 1843-O 17 1851? Missouri statesman; O 24 1851-60? Weekly Missouri statesman; 1861?-Ap 1905? Columbia Missouri statesman; My 1905?-S 4 1913 Columbia statesman
1819-Je 22 1826 pub in Franklin; Je 29 1826-Ap 9 1830 in Fayette
CtY Ja 30 1846
DLC Ja 1821-D 21 1826;Ag 9 1827[Je-D 1829]Ja 8,D 4 1830;O 6 1832;Mr 6 1841;Ja 20 1843;My 1844[Ap-D 1849]Ja-D 19 1851;O 29 1852;D 30 1859;Mr 16 1860;Ag 30 1861;Ag 30 1867;O 27 1871;My 23 1879;Jl 9 1880
ICHi Mr 1831
MWA Jl 1 1823;Mr 6,27,My 8,22,Je 12,Jl 10,Ag 21-S 11 1824;Ja 13 1826;D 16 1853;Mr 15 1861
Mo My 1845-F 1849
MoMaD 1840-1912
MoHi 1821-35;D 8 1838;Mr 1841+
MoSHi Ag 1822-Ap 3 1824;Je 16 1826;Ja 27 1843
N O 28 1842

Columbia MISSOURI herald. w F 5 1869-S 1913||
1869-70 as Boone county journal. United with Columbia statesman to form Columbia herald-statesman
DLC Jl 7 1870;Jl 31 1879
MoHi 1869-Ja 11,My 30-N 7 1872;Ja 16-My 15,S 18 1873;Ap 5,Ag 23 1877;Ap 11 1878-Ag 1913
MoSHi D 17 1897;D 16 1898;D 15 1899;Ja 6 1905;D 23 1907

MISSOURI intelligencer. . . *See* Columbia herald-statesman

Weekly MISSOURI sentinel. *See* State argus

Weekly MISSOURI state journal. *See* State argus

MISSOURI statesman. *See* Columbia herald-statesman

Columbia PATRIOT. *See* Columbia herald-statesman

PROFESSIONAL world. w N 1 1901-20||
Also dated at Jefferson City
Negro
MoHi 1901-08;Ap 23 1909

SENTINEL. w N 15 1907-08||?
MoHi 1907-My 8 1908

STATE argus. w F 25 1852-60||
1852-D 15 1853 as Weekly Missouri sentinel; D 22? 1853-D 13 1855 Dollar Missouri journal; Ja 17-O 2? 1856 Weekly Missouri state journal; O 16 1856-Ap? 1857 Union democrat
Suspended from D 13 1855-Ja 17 1856; from O 2? 1858-Ap 7 1859
DLC Mr 1852-D 8 1853;Ja-D 13 1855;O 16-D 1856;Ap 16 1857
KHi Mr 1852-D 8 1853(photostat)Ja 17-O 2 1856(photostat)1855(photostat)
MoHi Mr-D 1852;Ja 27-D 8 1853(photostat)Je-Jl 6,27-Ag 3 1854;55;Ja 17-O 2 1856(photostat)
MoSHi S 17 1857

Columbia STATESMAN. *See* Columbia herald-statesman

Columbia daily TIMES. d Je 8 1911-19||
MoHi 1911-[Ja-D 1917]-Ja 12 1919

Columbia daily TRIBUNE. d S 13 1901+
1901-Ja 25 1904 as Daily tribune
pub 1915+
MoHi 1901-06;08+
MoSHi Ap8,Je 1,22 1915

UNION democrat. *See* State argus

CONCEPTION JUNCTION

Conception COURIER. w 1908—
MoCon 1917-19;21-30

CONCORDIA

CONCORDIAN. w S 1 1892+
MoHi D 1898-1900;14-Ap 1919

CONWAY

Conway weekly RECORD. w 1891+
MoHi F 15 1915-18;20+

CORDER

Corder JOURNAL. w Ja 22 1909+
pub 1909;21+
MoHi 1914+

MISSOURI thalbote. *See under* Higginsville

COWGILL

CALDWELL county democrat. w 1897-98||?
MoHi Ja 13-27,F 24,Mr 10-17,31-My 5,19-Je 23 1898

Cowgill CHIEF. w Ap 1887+
pub 1887+
MoH [1921-O 20 1922]+
MoHi O 23 1890;Ap 21 1899-Ap 19 1907;17+

Cowgill NEWS. w Mr 15 1921-26||?
MoHi S 9 1921-F 1926

CRAIG

Craig LEADER. *See* Holt county democrat and the Craig leader (Mound City)

Craig TRIBUNE. w Jl 28 1933+
Follows Fairfax tribune (Fairfax)
pub 1933+

CRANE

Crane CHRONICLE. w Ja 1905+
pub 1905-13;27+
MoHi Ap 26 1906+
MoSHi Ja 14,Jl 29 1915

CREIGHTON

Creighton BANNER. w 1927+
pub 1927+

Creighton LEDGER. w 1889-90||?
MoHi O 25 1890

Creighton NEWS. *See* Cass county news (Pleasant Hill)

CROCKER

Crocker IMPETUS. *See* Crocker news

Crocker NEWS. w Ag 4 1905+
Follows Iberia impetus (Iberia) Ag-S 22 1905 as Crocker impetus
MoHi 1905-Ag 16,S 13-27,O 11-18 1907

CRYSTAL CITY

Crystal City PRESS. w My 15 1916+
pub 1916+
MoCaT Ag 1918-19
MoHi 1919+

CUBA

Cuba REVIEW. w O 1894+
1894-O 1903 as Cuba telephone
pub 1894+
MoCaT 1917-19
MoHi 1899-N 1918

Cuba TELEPHONE. *See* Cuba review

CURRYVILLE

PIKE county express. *See* Bowling Green times (Bowling Green)

DANVILLE

Danville STAR. w
MoSHi Je 27 1867

DARLINGTON

Darlington RECORD. w Ja 29 1891-1907||?
MoHi F 1891-1907

DEARBORN

Dearborn DEMOCRAT. w N 1890+
pub 1898+
MoHi Jl 1898-1900;Jl 26 1901-04;06-Je 1922

DEEPWATER

Deepwater WORLD. w Ja 1 1890+
pub 1900+
MoHi Jl 8 1896;Jl 24 1901-O 1902;03;14-Jl 1918

DeKALB

DeKalb TRIBUNE. w O 1897-1925||?
MoHi 1903-N 1922;Mr-Ag 1923

DESLOGE

Desloge SUN. w 1908-Je 23 1925||
Merged with Lead belt news (Flat River)
MoCaT 1917-19
MoHi 1925

DE SOTO

De Soto FACTS. *See* Jefferson county republican

INDEPENDENT De Soto press. w
WHi S 1 1869

JEFFERSON county herald.
Reverse side called U.S. American volunteer
MoSHi My 21 1861

JEFFERSON county republican. w 1888+
1888-1903 as DeSoto facts; 1903-Ag 31 1906 Weekly republican
pub 1895-96;99;1903-04;08-15;17+
MoCaT 1917-19
MoHi S 27 1901+

De Soto PRESS. w 1891+
pub 1891-1906;13+
MoCaT 1917-18
MoHi 1902-O 1908;14-17

Weekly REPUBLICAN. *See* Jefferson county republican

DeSoto TIMES. w My 28 1915-18||?
MoCaT 1917-Ap 5 1918
MoHi 1915-17

U. S. American volunteer. *See* Jefferson county herald

DeWITT

CARROLL farmer's herald. *See* DeWitt herald

DeWitt HERALD. w 1888+
1888-1920? as Carroll farmer's herald
pub 1888+
MoHi Jl 26 1901+

DEXTER

Dexter ENTERPRISE. *See* Dexter messenger

Dexter MESSENGER. w 1875—
1875-78? as Dexter enterprise; 1879?-93? Enterprise-messenger
MoCaT 1917-19
MoHi O 23 1890

Dexter STATESMAN. w Mr 20 1910+
pub 1910+
MoCaT 1917-19
MoHi 1910+

STODDARD county democrat. w 1891-1903||?
MoHi N 24 1898-99

DIXON

Dixon ECHO. w Je 1891-1905||?
MoHi 1903-05

Dixon PILOT. w F 23 1911+
pub 1911+
MoHi 1914+

DONIPHAN

CURRENT River news. w 1877-N 23 1883||
United with Prospect to form Doniphan news-prospect
MoDP complete

HUSTLER. w 1898-1904||?
MoHi My 22 1903

Doniphan PROSPECT-NEWS. w 1874+
1874-N 23 1883 as Prospect
pub 1874+
MoCaT 1907+
MoHi Ja 23 1891;N 24 1898+

Doniphan REPUBLICAN. w D 1905+
pub 1905+
MoCaT 1917-19
MoHi D 9 1915+

RIPLEY county democrat. w N 1898-1920||?
MoCaT 1917-18
MoHi N 17 1905-S 1918

DREXEL

Drexel STAR. w Ap 1892+
pub 1892+
MoHi N 25 1898-Ag 24 1900;Jl 26 1901-O 1904;14+

EAST PRAIRIE

East Prairie EAGLE. w Ap 20 1905+
1905-D 7 1906 as Prairie eagle
pub Ap 20 1905;S 14 1934+
MoCaT 1917-19
MoHi Je 1905+

PRAIRIE eagle. *See* East Prairie eagle

EDGERTON

Edgerton JOURNAL. w Ap 1895+
pub F 1908+
MoHi 1898-1900;S-D 1903;Jl 12 1912;14+

EDINA

DEMOCRAT. *See* Knox county democrat

KNOX county democrat. w 1870-1925||
Ap 25 1905-Jl 9 1915 as Democrat. United with Edina sentinel to form Edina sentinel and Knox county democrat
MoES complete
MoHi 1874-Mr 18 1886;D 7 1893-1925

KNOX county independent. *See* Knox county republican

KNOX county register. w 1898+
MoHi Jl 25 1901-05

KNOX county republican. w 1883-97||?
1883-94? as Knox county independent
MoHi O 30 1890

Edina NATIONAL. w N 6 1879-80||?
MoHi 1879-My 12 1880

PELL mell greenbacker. w 1881||?
Also dated in Kirksville
MoHi Mr 31-Ap 7,Je 16 1881

Edina SENTINEL and Knox county democrat. w Ap 1868+
1868-1925 as Edina sentinel
pub 1868+
MoHi F 26 1874-83;O 16 1890;Jl 1905+

EL DORADO SPRINGS

El Dorado MASCOT. w 1890-95|
MoHi O 23 1890

El Dorado Springs NEWS. w O 1897-1920||?
MoHi Mr 30 1905-20

El Dorado SUN. w 1895+
O 1896 is historical ed
MoHi O 1896

UNCLE SAM. w Jl 30 1881-91||?
MoHi O 24 1890

MISSOURI (*Continued*)

ELDON

Eldon ADVERTISER. w Je 1894+
pub [1894-1902]+
MoHi 1903+
MoSHi Jl 3 1913

Eldon EAGLE. w S 11 1903-
MoHi S 11-D 1903

ELLINGTON

Ellington PRESS. w Ja 4 1906+
MoCaT 1913+
MoHi 1906-09;11+

ELMO

Elmo REGISTER. w 1890+
pub 1899+
MoHi Jl 10 1896

ELSBERRY

Elsberry DEMOCRAT. w Mr 26 1900+
pub 1908+
MoHi Ag 28 1903-Mr 1904;14+

ELVINS

LEAD BELT post. w 1917-19||?
MoCaT 1918-19

ST. FRANCOIS county record. w 1912-17||?
MoCaT 1917
MoHi [F-N 1916]Mr 2-23,Ap 6,My 4 1917

EMINENCE

CURRENT wave. w Je 1874+
pub 1885+
MoCaT 1907+
MoHi Je 13 1901+

ENGLEWOOD

Englewood SUBURBAN items. *See* Suburban items (Independence)

ESSEX

Essex LEADER. w My 15 1908-21||?
MoCaT 1917-19
MoHi My 15 1908-20
MoSHi Ja 6 1921

EVERTON

DADE county journal. w 1892+
1892-Ap 30 1904 as Everton eagle
pub 1892+
MoHi 1899;Jl 1901-F 1903;Ja-My 1904;14-Mr 1916

Everton EAGLE. *See* Dade county journal

EXCELSIOR SPRINGS

Excelsior Springs daily CALL. d 1883-Ag 9 1925||?
United with Excelsior Springs daily news to form Excelsior Springs daily news-call
MoHi Ag 14 1903-O 1918

Excelsior Springs weekly CALL. w O 19 1911-25||?
MoHi 1911-O 1916

Excelsior Springs JOURNAL. w,d 1886-1916||?
w 1886-Ag 22 1907?
MoHi O 25 1890;Ag 18 1905-06;Jl 1907-09;Mr 1913-S 1915;Ja 18-Ap 27 1916

MISSOURI state journal. w Ja 30- 1926||?
MoHi Ja-S 18 1926

Morning NEWS. d Mr 7 1926-
Follows Northwest Missourian
MoHi Mr 9-Je 1926

Excelsior Springs daily NEWS-CALL. d D 1923-Ja 3 1926||
1923-Ag 9 1925 as Excelsior Springs daily news. Followed by Northwest Missourian
MoHi Jl 17 1925-26

NORTHWEST Missourian. w Ja 7-Mr 4 1926||
Follows Excelsior Springs daily news-call. Followed by Morning news
MoHi complete

Excelsior Springs daily STANDARD. w,sw,d 1887+
1887-1918? as Excelsior Springs standard
w 1887-1914?;sw1915?-18?
pub 1894-97;1910+
MoHi 1903;07-09;13-Ja 17 1920;F 22 1927+

FAIRFAX

Fairfax FORUM. w D 10 1892+
MoHi Ag 1901+

Fairfax TRIBUNE. Jl 18 1930-Jl 21 1933||
Followed by Craig tribune (Craig)
MoCrT complete

FAIRMOUNT

BLUE VALLEY inter-city news. *See* Inter-city news

INTER-CITY news. w Mr 1912+
1912-28 as Mount Washington news; Ja-O 4 1929 Inter-city news; O 11 1929-30? Blue Valley inter-city news
MoHi S 24 1926+

MOUNT WASHINGTON news. *See* Inter-city news

FAIRPLAY

ADVOCATE. w 1893+
MoHi 1919+

FARBER

Farber FORUM. w 1891-1915||?
MoHi Jl 10 1896

FARMINGTON

Farmington NEWS. w 1883+
MoCaT 1917-19
MoHi Ja 3 1919+
MoSHi S 22 1916-Ja 12 1917

Farmington PRESS. w O 25 1928+
pub 1928+

ST. FRANCOIS county democrat. w 1886-91||?
MoHi O 25 1890

ST. FRANCOIS county republican. w 1910-12||?
MoHi My 10 1912

ST. FRANCOIS herald. w 1892-1900||?
United with Farmington times to form Farmington times and herald, later Farmington times

Farmington TIMES. w Ja 1874-F 1926||
1901-03? Farmington times and herald. Merged with Farmington news
MoCaT 1906-26
MoHi N 6 1890;D 1898-1926
MoSHi S 15 1916-S 1917

FAYETTE

Fayette ADVERTISER. w S 1 1840+
1840-Ag 1848 as Glasgow news;S 1848-60 Howard county banner; 1861-1916? Howard county advertiser
1840-52 pub in Glasgow
Suspended from Je? 1864-66
DLC O 28 1852
MoFaC My 19 1859;1911-15;Ja-Ag 1931;32-Ag 1933
MoHi Ag 8 1861;Je 17 1864;Ag 16 1866;Jl 1 1869;Jl 26 1876;S 23 1887;Je 7 1888;Ja 25 1894;Jl 27 1901+
MoSHi Je 12 1845-Je 1847;Ag 29 1907;Ja 2 1913

Fayette BANNER. w 1880-92||?
United with Howard county democrat to form Democrat-banner, later Democrat-leader
MoHi Mr 11 1891

BOON'S LICK democrat. *See* Missouri democrat

BOON'S LICK times. *See* Glasgow weekly times (Glasgow)

DEMOCRAT-BANNER. w *See* Democrat-leader

Daily DEMOCRAT-BANNER. d 1894-96||?
MoHi Je 26 1896

DEMOCRAT-LEADER. w,sw 1879+
1879-88? as Missouri independent; 1889?-92? Howard county democrat; 1893?-94? Democrat-banner; 1895?-97? Semi-weekly democrat-banner (sw)
MoFaC Ja-Ag 1931;32-S 8 1933
MoHi F 8 1888;O 31 1890;D 23 1892;Ag 24 1897;S 15,D 8 1898-99;Jl 1901+
MoSHi Ap 21 1904;D 12 1907;08-Ap 8 1909

HOWARD county advertiser. *See* Fayette advertiser

HOWARD county banner. *See* Fayette advertiser

HOWARD county democrat. *See* Democrat-leader

HOWARD county leader. w 1894-97||?
United with Democrat-banner to form Democrat-leader
MoHi S 5 1895;My 28 1896

MISSOURI democrat. w D 17 1834-Ag 1850||
1834?-Ja 20 1844? as Boon's Lick democrat
Ct D 17 1834
DLC Ap 2,Jl-D 17 1845
IU Je 30 1838
KHi [Ap-D 1845](photostat)
MWA Jl 23 1845
MoHi My 9 1837[Ap-D 1845](photostat)S 16 1846
MoSHi F 25 1846-Ja 1849

MISSOURI independent. *See* Democrat-leader

MISSOURI intelligencer. *See* Columbia herald-statesman (Columbia)

MISSOURIAN. See Glasgow weekly times (Glasgow)

WESTERN monitor. *See* Glasgow weekly times (Glasgow)

FERGUSON

Ferguson TOWN talk. w My 4 1923+
pub 1923+

FESTUS

CRYSTAL mirror. w 1885-87||?
MoCaT Ja 28,F 11,Ap 1 1886;My 12-19 1887

Festus NEWS. w My 1 1903+
MoCaT 1917-19

TRI-CITY independent. w S 1908+
pub 1909+
MoCaT 1917-19
MoHi F 1913-Ag 1916

FILLMORE

Fillmore GEM. w F 1931+
pub 1931+

FLAT RIVER

LEAD BELT news. w 1898+
pub 1912+
MoCaT 1917-19
MoHi D 1915-Ja 21 1916;Ap 26 1918+

FLORIDA

MONROE county democrat. w Ag 16 1882-84||?
MoHi Ag 16 1882

FLORISANT

Florisant NEWS. w 1911-13||?
MoHi Ag 11 1911;Ap 17-24 1912
MoSHi Ja 15-N 15 1913

FOREST CITY

Forest City NEWS. w Je 1907-Jl 1918||
suspended O-N 1907
MoHi N 5 1909;14-18

FORNFELT

Fornfelt TRIBUNE. w 1915-17||?
MoCaT 1917

FORSYTH

TANEY county republican. w N 1895+
pub 1895+
MoHi My 9 1901-08;N 1911+

FOSTER

Foster NEWS. w 1889-
KHi O 21-N 11 1892

FRANKFORD

Frankford CHRONICLE. w 1878+
pub 1878+
MoHi F 6 1914

FRANKLIN

MISSOURI intelligencer. *See* Columbia herald-statesman (Columbia)

FREDERICKTOWN

ADVANCE guard. Ag 28 1861-
pub by 17th Regiment Illinois Volunteers
MWA Ag 28 1861

BEE. w 1868-74||?
MoHi S 11 1869

CONSERVATIVE. *See* Weekly Perryville union (Perryville)

DEMOCRAT-NEWS. w 1893+
1893-1900? as Madison county democrat
pub 1893+
MoCaT 1919+
MoHi Jl 27 1901+
MoSHi Je 9 1910

MADISON county democrat. *See* Democrat-news

MADISON county press. w 1895+
MoHi 1934+

Fredericktown NEWS. w 1895-1900||?
United with Madison county democrat to form Democrat-news
MoHi F 15 1896
MoSHi O 16 1897

Fredericktown PLAINDEALER. w 1874-90||?
MoHi O 25 1890

TRIBUNE. w 1898-1918||?
MoCaT 1907-18
MoHi Jl 26 1901-O 1918

FULTON

BANNER of liberty. *See* Missouri telegraph

CALLAWAY county journal. w 1891-O 1915||
1891-1912? as Fulton journal. Followed by Fulton weekly times
MoBoH My 1896
MoHi Jl 25 1901-02;04-15

CALLAWAY gazette. *See* Fulton gazette

CALLAWAY watchman. *See* Missouri telegraph

Fulton GAZETTE. w Je 1 1877-D 30 1926||
1877-My 1890 as Callaway gazette. United with Fulton daily sun to form Fulton daily sun-gazette
MoFuB complete
MoHi Je 8 1877;D 6 1878;D 19 1879;O 23 1890;N 25 1898-1926
MoSHi [Jl 22 1910-N 7 1913]

Fulton JOURNAL. *See* Callaway county journal

MISSOURI (*Continued*)

FULTON—*Continued*

MISSOURI telegraph. sw,w Mr 30 1839+
1839-41 as Banner of liberty; 1842-43 Callaway watchman; 1844-45 Western star; 1845-50 Fulton telegraph
sw 1896-1905?
pub 1878+
DLC Mr 30 1839;Ap 21 1865
MWA N 15 1845
MoFuW S 1932+
MoHi N 2 1839;Ja 11 1840;Ag 1848-Jl 1851;Ap 16-My 14,Je 25 1852;S 8,O 13 1854;Ag 29 1856; Je 19 1857;Mr 23,Ap 13,O 26-N 2,23 1860;Ja 4-11,Mr-Ap 19,My 31,S 6-13,O 4-11,N 15,D 6 1861;Mr 7-14,Ap 4-11,25-My 9,23-Jl 4,18,Ag 8,O 17,31 1862;Ja 16,My 29 1863[Ja-S,D 1864]My 12,N 10 1865;F 14,Jl 10,D 4 1868;69-77;F 7,Mr 7,My 2,16 1879;Ja 2,My 14,N 26 1880;F 11 1881;N 29 1898-99;Ja 26,F 6,27,Mr 16,Jl 3,O 9-16,26-30,N 6,16,27 1900;Ag 1903-08;10+
MoSHi My 17 1861;S 3 1886
WHi Ap 7 1865
—d ed *See* Fulton daily sun-gazette

Fulton REFORMER. w My 28 1840-
DLC Je 18 1840

Fulton SUN. w,sw 1887-1909||?
sw 1904-05
MoHi Ag 1901-09

Fulton daily SUN-GAZETTE. d Ap 1888+
1888-1925 as Fulton daily sun
pub 1888+
MoFuW S 1931+
MoHi S 18 1903;My 13,N 29,D 6 1904;Je 6,23, 30,Ag 1,8,N 21,30,D 5,27 1905;Ja 5,26 1906;Je 5 1908;F 6 1913+
—w ed 1927— *See* Missouri telegraph

Fulton TELEGRAPH. *See* Missouri telegraph

Fulton weekly TIMES. w 1915-
Follows Callaway county journal
MoHi Mr-My 18,Je 1,15-29 1916

TWENTIETH century. w Ja 1901-03||?
MoHi 1902-Jl 1903

WESTERN star. *See* Missouri telegraph

GAINESVILLE

OZARK county news. w 1882-1906||
Merged with Ozark county times
MoGaT [1896-1906]
MoHi N 19 1903-S 1904

OZARK county times. w O 1901+
pub N 1907+
MoHi 1903;06+

GALENA

JAMES RIVER republican. w My 1911-14||?
MoHi Ja-N 19 1914

RECORDER-ADVERTISER. w 1907-08||?
MoHi Ap 30,Je 4-18,Jl 16-Ag,N 3 1908

STONE county news. w Ap 9 1903-04||?
MoHi Ap-O 3 1903

STONE county news. w 1914-My 9 1917||
United with Stone county oracle to form Stone county news-oracle
MoHi 1915-17

STONE county news-oracle. w 1884+
1884-My 9 1917 as Stone county oracle
pub 1904+
MoHi Mr 1903-F 1912;13+

STONE county oracle. *See* Stone county news-oracle

GALLATIN

Gallatin DEMOCRAT. w Jl 1869+
DLC N 8,D 6 1923;Ja 3 1924
MoHi O 23 1890;N 25 1897;N 24 1898+
MoSHi Jl 31 1886

Gallatin NORTH Missourian. w Ag 28 1864+
MoH Jl 28 1921+
MoHi S 15 1864-Ag 20 1866;Ag 19 1892-1900;Ag 1901+

GALT

Galt HERALD. w 1887-1906||?
United with Galt sun to form Sun and herald
MoHi F 9 1905

SUN and herald. w 1900-21||?
1900-06? as Galt sun

GARDEN CITY

Garden City VIEWS. w 1889+
KHi Ap 26 1923

GAYOSO

Gayoso DEMOCRAT. *See* Democrat-argus (Caruthersville)

GERALD

Gerald JOURNAL. w O 1 1915+
pub 1915+
MoCaT 1917-19

GILMAN CITY

Gilman City GUIDE. w 1898-S 1931||
United with Harrison county times (Bethany) to form Harrison county times and Gilman City guide (Bethany)
MoBeT [1898-1931]
MoHi Jl 26 1901-N 1921

Gilman City TRIBUNE. w Ag 3 1933+
pub 1933+

GLASGOW

CENTRAL Missourian. *See* Glasgow Missourian

Weekly GLOBE. w 1897-1907||?
MoG Ja 7,N 19 1903-[05]-My 10 1907

Glasgow GRAPHIC. w 1909-10||
Merged with Glasgow Missourian
MoG D 16 1909-Ag 25 1910

HOWARD county banner. *See* Fayette advertiser (Fayette)

HOWARD county echo. w 1898-Je 2 1904||
Merged with Glasgow Missourian
MoG Ag 30-N 15,D 26 1900[01]-04

HOWARD union. *See* Glasgow weekly times

Glasgow JOURNAL. w 1867-89||?
1880-81 as Glasgow weekly journal.
Merged with Glasgow Missourian
MoG D 23 1880[81]Ag 24-S 7,O 5-12 1882;F 1,Mr 1-15, Ap 19,My 3 1883;My 22-Je 5,N 27-D 4,25 1884-Ja 8,22,F 5-12,Ap 9 1885;Je 17,O 21-28,D 16-23 1886[87-88]Mr 7,Jl 11-18, Ag 2,S 12-19 1889

Glasgow MISSOURIAN. w 1879+
1879-S 10 1891? as Central Missourian
Mog Ag 21,O 23 1879;F 12-19 1880;Mr 17,N 1 1881;Ap 27-My 4,25-Je 1,15,29-Jl 6,20 1882 [83-84] My 27 1886[87-90]D 17 1891;Ja 7,21-28,Mr 10-24 1892[S 1900-01]-[06-07]-[12-13]-[24-32]+
MoHi O 30 1890;Jl 1901+

Glasgow NEWS. *See* Fayette advertiser (Fayette)

Glasgow weekly TIMES. w S 1 1827-70||?
1827-36 as Western monitor; 1837-Mr 14? 1840 Missourian; Mr 21 1840-S 29 1848 Boon's Lick times; O 1848-61 Glasgow times; Je 15 1865-Ja 1866 Howard union
1827-S 29 1848 pub in Fayette
Suspended from 1861-Je 15 1865
Ct [S 8 1827-29]Mr 7 1837
DLC F 21-Mr,Ap 11,25,Jl 4-11,Ag 8,29-O 10, 24-N 14,28-D 19 1829;Ja 9-D 15 1830;Mr 21 O 3 1840
KHi [F 21 1829-D 15 1830](photostat)
MoG [Mr 28 1840-S 1848]-F 1858
MoHi [F 21 1829-D 15 1830](photostat)Mr 28 1840-F 1858(photostat O 1848-F 1858)Je 15-D 7 1865;Ag 24-S 7 1866;O 1 1869
MoSHi S 22 1827;Je 14 1828;Mr 15 1836
N S 27 1833

GLENWOOD

Glenwood CRITERION. w Je 8 1870-92||?
DLC F 18 1876
IaHi Mr 24-N 15 1876
MoHi 1870-Ap 1874;Je 17-24,Jl 8-Ag 19,S 2 1875;D 14 1876-My 1884;O 31 1890

NATIONAL issue. w S 13-O 8 1879||
Printed on two pages of Glenwood criterion
MoHi complete

Glenwood PHONOGRAPH. w 1894-1909||?
1894-96? as Weekly phonograph
IaHi F 15 1895-Ja 17 1896
MoHi My 4 1900;My 1902-09

GOLDEN CITY

Golden City FREE PRESS. *See* Golden City register

Golden City HERALD. w S 9 1881+
pub 1881+

Golden City REGISTER. w 1892-1912||?
1892-1905 as Golden City free press
MoHi D 1,22 1898-99;Jl 1901-S 1911

GORIN

Gorin ARGUS. w 1890+
pub 1917+

MISSOURI state news. w F 26 1903-12||?
MoHi Mr 5 1903-12

GOWER

Gower ENTERPRISE. w 1905+
pub [1906-21]+

Gower EPITOMIST. w 1898-1904||?
MoHi Jl 25 1901-04

GRAHAM

Graham POST. w 1891-09||?
MoHi Ja-F 11,F 25-Ap 22 1909

GRANBY

Granby MINER. 1873-77 *See* Miner and mechanic (Neosho)

Granby MINER-MISSOURIAN. w Ja 1892-1920||?
1892-F 1914 as Granby miner; Mr 1914-Ap 7 1916 Granby Missourian
MoHi 1892-N 1903;F 21 1913-20

Granby MISSOURIAN. *See* Granby miner-Missourian

Granby NEWS-HERALD. w 1920+
1920-25? as Granby news
KHi D 17 1925

GRANDIN

Grandin HERALD. w -1909||?
MoVC 1899-1909

GRANDVIEW

JACKSON county times. w 1890+
1890-My 1931 as Grandview times
pub 1890+

Grandview TIMES. *See* Jackson county times

GRANT CITY

ENTERPRISE. *See* Grant City star

Grant City STAR. w Ap 1867-Mr 22 1922||
1867-Ap 1869 as Enterprise
MoGrT [1870-1913]
MoHi F 15,29-Ap 4,25,My 16,Ag 8,29-S 5,O 10,31,N 28 1872;O 14 1886;1903-22
NbHi Mr 30 1876

TIMES-TRIBUNE. w 1872+
1872-1928 as Worth county times
pub 1872+
MoGr 1931+
MoHi Jl 25-S,D 1901-O 1925;Ap 21 1927+

WORTH county times. *See* Times-tribune

WORTH county tribune. w Mr 12 1913-D 26 1928||
1913-D 9 1914 as Worth tribune. United with Worth county times to form Times-tribune
1913-N 18 1914 pub in Worth
MoGrT complete
MoHi Ap 30 1913-28

WORTH tribune. *See* Worth county tribune

GREEN CASTLE

Green Castle JOURNAL. w S 9 1904-Je 8 1933||
Merged with Weekly graphic (Kirksville)
MoHi S 16 1904-33

GREEN CITY

Green City JOURNAL. w 1890-91||?
MoHi O 24 1890

Green City PRESS. w 1899+
MoHi Jl 26 1901+

GREEN RIDGE

PETTIS county enterprise. w 1882-92||?
MoHi Je 16 1892

GREENFIELD

DADE county advocate. w D 1874+
MoHi O 23 1890;Ja 1 1891;99[1900]+

MISSOURI army argus. *See under* Corinth, Miss

Greenfield VEDETTE. w Ag 20 1866+
1866-69 as Greenfield vidette
pub [1866-85]+
MoHi O 23 1890;1903;14+

Greenfield VIDETTE. *See* Greenfeld vedette

GREENVILLE

Greenville REPORTER. w 1869-71||?
MoCaT My 27,Jl 1 1869; Mr 23,Ap 27,Jl 13 1870

Greenville SUN. w My 1893+
MoCaT 1907+
MoHi F 1913+

WAYNE county journal. *See* Wayne county journal-banner (Piedmont)

HALE

Hale HUSTLER. w 1894-1905||
United with Hale leader to form Hale hustler leader, later Hale leader
MoHi Jl 1901-Ja 1,Mr 11 1904

Hale HUSTLER-LEADER. *See* Hale leader

Hale LEADER. w 1899+
1899-1905 as Hale leader; 1905-D 7 1923 Hale hustler-leader
MoHi Jl 3 1903+

HALLSVILLE

Hallsville EAGLE. w My 24-D 1903||?
MoHi My-D 1903

Hallsville NEWS. w 1907-09||?
MoHi Ja 15 1909

HAMILTON

Hamilton ADVOCATE-HAMILTONIAN. w Jl 6 1878+
1878-F 25 1919 as Hamilton Hamiltonian
pub 1890+
MoH 1878-Je 13 1912;[Jl 22 1920-Jl 14 1921]+
MoHi Jl 1887-Je,Ag 1901+

MISSOURI (*Continued*)

HAMILTON—*Continued*

Hamilton FARMER'S advocate. w 1890-F 27 1919||
United with Hamiltonian to form Hamilton advocate-Hamiltonian
MoHi [Ja 12-Je 15 1898]Ag 1901-19

Hamilton HAMILTONIAN. *See* Hamilton advocate-Hamiltonian

HEAD light. 1885-
S 1889 is special ed
MoHi S 1889

Hamilton NEWS graphic. w Ag 9 1877-99||?
MoHi 1877-Jl 1882;Jl 31 1884-Mr 10,N 24 1898-Ap 13 1899

HANNIBAL

Hannibal weekly CHRONICLE. w 1862?-
MWA Ja 18 1866

Hannibal CLIPPER-HERALD. w Ja 1871-80||?
1871-79? as Hannibal clipper
MoHi F 21 1874-76

Hannibal CLIPPER-HERALD. d 1874-80||?
1874-79? as Hannibal clipper
MoHi S 28 1874-75;77

Hannibal COMMERCIAL advertiser. w N 1837-39||
MoHi Ja 4,Je 22,S 18-25 1838;F 27 1839

Hannibal COURIER. w 1832-90||?
1832-62? as Missouri courier; 1863-71? North Missouri courier
1832-S? 1848;55-62 pub in Palmyra
MWA Jl 27 1865;S 7 1871
MoHi Jl 7 1838;My 16 1844;F 5 1846[O 12 1848-Je 8 1854]Je 24 1869
MoSHi My 5 1853;O 18 1860;N 9 1865
OClWHi S 7 1871
WHi Ja 18,My 24 1849-Ja 5 1855

Hannibal COURIER-POST and journal. d 1863+
1863-71? as Daily North Missouri courier; 1872-91? Hannibal courier; 1892?-Mr 2 1918 Hannibal courier-post
DLC Je 14 1865
MWA Jl 26 1871
MoHa 1931+
MoHi D 1903+
OClWHi Ag 1 1865

Hannibal DEMOCRAT. w O 2 1856-63||?
1856-59 as Hannibal national democrat
MoHi 1856-Mr 12 1857

Hannibal GAZETTE. w N 12 1847-My 3 1848||
Merged with Missouri courier, later Hannibal courier
MiU-C Ja 27 1848

Hannibal HERALD. w 1876-79||?
United with Hannibal clipper to form Hannibal clipper-herald

Hannibal JOURNAL. 1843-50 w *See* Western union

Hannibal JOURNAL. d Mr 14 1853-
MoHi Mr 15-S 21 1853
—w ed *See* Western union

Hannibal weekly JOURNAL. w 1871?-1915||?
MoHi 1901;03;05
MoSHi 1915(anniversary ed)

Morning JOURNAL. d 1877-Mr 2 1918||
United with Hannibal courier-post to form Hannibal courier-post and journal
DLC D 10 1880
IU S 1,8 1917-F 27 1918
KHi Ap 13 1916
MWA D 10 1880
MoHi N 7 1890;Ja 19 1894[F 15-My 5 1896]F 1900-Ap,Je-Ag,O 1901-Ja,Ap,Je,Ag, O-N 1902;Ja-Mr,Je-Ag,N 1903;Jl 1905-18

Hannibal MESSENGER. w D 16 1851-65||?
1851-Ap 17 1856. as Whig messenger. Merged with North Missouri courier, later Hannibal courier
MoHi S 15 1852-S 1 1859

Hannibal daily MESSENGER. tw,d Jl 15 1852-65||
1852-N 1858 as Tri-weekly messenger(tw)
Merged with Daily North Missouri courier, later Hannibal courier-post and journal
DLC N 6 1859
MoHi 1852-O 13,N 8 1853-N 13,D 7 1858-D 6 1859

MISSOURI courier. *See* Hannibal courier

MISSOURI state register. *See* Hannibal register

NORTH Missouri courier. *See* Hannibal courier

Hannibal NATIONAL democrat. *See* Hannibal democrat

PACIFIC monitor. *See* Western union

Evening POST. d 1886-91||?
United with Hannibal courier to form Hannibal courier-post, later Hannibal courier-post and journal
MoHi O 27 1890

Hannibal REGISTER. w 1919+
1919-26 as Missouri state register
Negro
pub 1919+

Weekly TRUE American. w Ja 18 1855-56||
MoHi 1855-S 11 1856

Hannibal daily TRUE American. d My 19-1856||
MoHi My-Je 21 1856

WESTERN union. w Mr 9 1840-53||
1840 as Pacific monitor; Ja-D 1841 Journal and price current; Ja-D 1842? Hannibal journal and native American; 1843?-Ag? 1850 Hannibal journal. Merged with Hannibal messenger
MoHi [S 1848-Ag 1850]-[S 1851-S 15 1853]
MoSHi S 20,O 21-28,N 11,D 16 1852;Mr 31,Je 30 1853
—d ed *See* Hannibal journal. 1853

WHIG messenger. *See* Hannibal messenger

HARDIN

Hardin NEWS. w F 1888+
Early years as News of Hardin
pub 1888+
MoHi Jl 25 1901-Je 1921;24+

HARRIS

Harris HERALD. w 1913+
pub 1931+

HARRISON

BOON county advocate. w 1868-
MoHi Ag 18 1870

HARRISONVILLE

CASS county democrat. w Mr 24 1881+
MoHi Je 20 1889;My 8 1890;Ag 20 1891;D 8 1898-Ag 1905;08+
MoP 1932+

CASS county leader. w Mr 1898-1925||?
MoHi Ap 1906-25

CASS county news. w S 19 1878-1917||?
1878-1901? as Cass news
MoHi O 1878-Ag 1893;S 1894-Jl 1917

CASS news. *See* Cass county news

Harrisonville DEMOCRAT. w 1865-72||?
MoHi N 18-D 2 1865;My 22,O 2 1867;Ja 15,N 11-18 1868;S 15 1869

MISSOURIAN. w Je 19 1931+
pub 1931+
MoHi Jl 30 1931+

RETORT. w 1901-03||?
MoHi Ja 9-Jl 1903

HARTSBURG

Hartsburg TRUTH. w My 1899+
MoHi 1903+

HARTVILLE

Hartville DEMOCRAT. w 1889-S 19 1929||
1889-97? as Hartville press. Merged with Wright county republican
MoHi N 26 1898-S 1899;Jl 1901-[Ja-My 1904] 06-08;10-19;Ap 1920-25;27-29

Hartville PRESS. *See* Hartville democrat

WRIGHT county progress. w D 1893-1912||?
MoHi N 25 1898-1910

WRIGHT county republican. w Ja 1892+
pub 1916+
MoHi F 1911-Ag 7 1930;Mr 12-S 10 1931

HAWK POINT

Hawk Point TRANSCRIPT. w 1912-17||?
MoHi Ja 22 1914

HAYTI

CRITIC. *See under* Piggott, Ark.

Hayti HERALD. w O 29 1908+
pub 1908+
MoCaT 1917-19
MoHi 1909-N 20 1931;32+

PEMISCOT argus. *See under* Caruthersville

HERCULANEUM

Herculaneum INDEPENDENT. w 1916-18||?
MoCaT 1917-18

Herculaneum TIMES. w Mr 15 1920+
pub 1920+

HERMANN

ADVERTISER-COURIER. w 1873+
1873-76? as Hermann advertiser
pub 1873+
MoCaT 1907+
MoHi N 19 1890;D 28 1904;O 18 1905;14+
MoSHi O 15 1919

Das CALUMET. w N 25 1869-
In German
MoHi N 25 1869

GASCONADE county courier. w 1874-76||?
United with Hermann advertiser to form Advertiser-courier

Hermann LEDGER. w 1888-96||?
MoSHi D 21 1888

Hermanner VOLKSBLATT. w 1856-Ap 18 1928||
In German
MWA Ja 6 1866;Ag 23 1876
MoCaT 1917-Ag 2 1918
MoHeA complete
MoHi N 14 1890;D 1904-28
NN My 18 1861

HERMITAGE

Hermitage ENTERPRISE. w 1870-73||?
MoHi Mr 5,Ap 30 1870

Hermitage GAZETTE. w O 16 1895-1902||
United with Index to form Index-gazette, later Index
MoHerI complete

HICKORY county republican. w Ja 1898-1905||?
MoHi My 28-D 1903

INDEX. w Jl 1885+
1895-1903 as Index-gazette
pub 1885+
MoHi My 28 1903+

HIGBEE

Weekly NEWS. w F 5 1887+
pub Je 1890+
MoHi My 1926+

HIGGINSVILLE

ADVANCE. w S 1879+
MoHi Ag 14 1903+

Higginsville DEMOCRAT. *See* Higginsville leader

Higginsville JEFFERSONIAN. w,sw 1894+
w 1894-1916?
pub 1894+
MoHi Ag 10 1901-Je 1902;Jl 1903+
MoSHi S 25 1914

LAFAYETTE leader. *See* Higginsville leader

Higginsville LEADER. w,sw My 1888-1909||?
1888-91? as Higginsville democrat; 1892?-99? Higginsville leader; 1900-01? Lafayette leader
sw 1895?-96?
MoHi O 24 1890;D 17 1898-Jl 1901;Je 1905-06; 09

MISSOURI thalbote. w Ap 1871-1918||
1871-79 pub in Lexington; 1880-92 in Concordia
In German
MWA Ag 26(supp) 1876
MoHi 1903

HILLSBORO

JEFFERSON county leader. *See* Jefferson democrat

JEFFERSON county record. w Ja 1905+
1905-10? as New era
MoCaT 1917-19
MoHi Mr 1911+
MoSHi Mr 22 1917

JEFFERSON democrat. w Ja 6 1866+
1866-69? as Jefferson county leader
MoCaT 1907+
MoHi My 27 1870;71-88;90-1917;N 1924+

NEW era. *See* Jefferson county record

HOLDEN

Holden ENTERPRISE. w Mr 1867+
pub 1884-88;90+
MoHi Jl-S 1901;03-04;26+

Holden INDEPENDENT. w 1890||?
MoHi O 30 1890

Holden PROGRESS. w O 1 1904+
pub 1904+
MoHi 1907+

HOLLISTER

Hollister NEWS. w My 1911-20||?
MoHi D 1911-18

HOLT

Holt RUSTLER. w S 1889+
KHi Je 1 1923
MoHi Ap 3 1903

HOPKINS

Hopkins JOURNAL. w Mr 1875+
pub 1875+
MoHi 1903-28

HOUSTON

Houston DEMOCRAT. *See* Houston republican

Houston HERALD. w 1878+
pub 1878+
MoHi O 22 1890;D 1898-99;1901+

Houston REPUBLICAN. w My 15 1899+
1899-O 22 1903 as Texas county democrat; O 29 1903-06? Houston democrat
MoHi Jl 9-D 18 1903;My 1909-Jl 1925;F 1926+

TEXAS county democrat. *See* Houston republican

TEXAS county pioneer. w Mr 28? 1868-75||?
1868-69? as Texas county record
MWA Ap 25 1868

TEXAS county record. *See* Texas county pioneer

TEXAS county sentinel. w 1890-92||?
MoHi O 23 1890

TEXAS county star. w D 1893-1914||?
MoHi O 15 1903-Jl 1911

MISSOURI (*Continued*)

HUMANSVILLE

Humansville STAR-LEADER. w Je 1877+
MoHi 1913+

HUME

BATES county globe. w 1894-95||?
MoHi F 2 1895

BORDER messenger. w Mr 1889+
1889-S 10 1925 as Border telephone
pub 1896+
MoHi O 2 1890;Jl 27 1901+

BORDER telephone. *See* Border messenger

Hume NEWS. w 1883-
MoHi Ag 7,O 19 1883;Mr 28 1884

Hume STAR. w 1883-88||?
MoHi Mr ,My 8 1885;Mr 18 1887;F 3 1888

HUMPHREYS

Humphreys BLADE. w 1890-91||?
MoHi O 30 1890

HUNNEWELL

Hunnewell BEE. *See* Hunnewell graphic

Hunnewell ENTERPRISE. *See* Hunnewell graphic

Hunnewell GRAPHIC. w D 23 1886+
1886-87? as Hunnewell enterprise; 1888?-92? Hunnewell bee
MoHi O 24 1890;S 1903-20

HUNTER

SOUTHEAST Missourian. w 1913-28||?
MoCaT 1917-19
MoHuM 1913-23
MoVC 1920-21

HUNTSVILLE

Huntsville HERALD. w Ja 20 1869-Mr 12 1931||
1869-Ja 1 1871 as North Missouri herald. United with Randolph county times to form Randolph county times-herald
MoHi 1869-75;77;79-92]-1931

INDEPENDENT Missourian. w N 16 1854-56||
Merged with Randolph citizen
MoHi N 16,30 1854-My 3 1855

NORTH Missouri herald. *See* Huntsville herald

RANDOLPH citizen. w N 30 1854-75||?
Suspended for some time during Civil War
MoHi My 1855-My 23 1861;Ag 17 1866;Ja 15 1874
WHi S 27 1867

RANDOLPH county times-herald. w Ag 11 1911+
1911-16? as Huntsville times; 1917?-Mr 12 1931 Randolph county times
MoHi Mr ,Ap 3 1914;15-O 1916;31+

RANDOLPH democrat. w Jl 1897-99||?
MoHi N 25 1898-99

Huntsville TIMES. *See* Randolph county times-herald

HURDLAND

KNOX county news. w 1926+
pub 1926+

Weekly NEWS. w 1890||?
MoHi O 29 1890

IBERIA

Iberia IMPETUS. w 1885-Jl 28 1905||
Followed by Crocker impetus, later Crocker news (Crocker)
MoHi Je 23-Jl 1905

Iberia SENTINEL. w 1905+
MoHi 1914[15]19-20

ILLMO

Illmo JIMPLICUTE. w D 24 1914+
pub 1914+
MoCaT 1917-19
MoHi 1914+

INDEPENDENCE

BORDER star. w 1847-
KHi Ag 11-13 1862(facsimile)

Independence CHRONICLE. *See* Independence messenger

Independence EXAMINER. d My 16 1905+
pub 1905+
MoHi 1905+
MoI 1905-My 21 1918
MoSHi D 29 1915
—w ed *See* Jackson examiner

JACKSON county democrat. *See* Jackson democrat

JACKSON county judge. w Ja 1901-07||?
MoHi 1903

JACKSON democrat. w Je 1907-Jl 23 1914||
Follows Richmond democrat (Richmond) 1907-Mr 1912 as Jackson county democrat. United with Independence tribune to form Independence tribune with which is combined the Jackson democrat
MoI 1915-34
MoIN 1916-34
MoK [1907-Mr 1912]

JACKSON examiner. w F 10 1898-F 3 1928||
pub complete
MoHi Jl 1901-28
MoI F 19 1898-F 15 1918
MoK 1907-28
—d ed *See* Independence examiner

Independence JOURNAL. *See* Key City commercial (Weston)

LETTER. *See* Daily record

Independence MESSENGER. w Ap 3 1840-70||?
1840-My 1841 as Independence chronicle; Je 1841-Je 1843 Western Missourian; Jl 1843-49 Western expositor; 1850 Missouri commonwealth; 1851-61? Occidental messenger
Suspended from 1861-Je 1865
DLC Ap 3 1840
KHi S 3 1859
MWA Ja 22 1841;D 10 1853
MoHi Je 19 1869

MISSOURI commonwealth. *See* Independence chronicle

Independence NEWS. d 1901+
pub 1901+

OCCIDENTAL messenger. *See* Independence messenger

Independence PROGRESS. w 1881-99||?
MoHi N 1 1890

Daily RECORD. d 1898-
1898-Ja 9 1904 as Letter
MoHi Jl 12 1901-Je 1905

Independence SENTINEL. w 1866+
MoHi Ag 5 1876;Ja 2 1886;99-1902;F 7-21 1903
MoKHi 1916-20

Evening and morning STAR. m
Reprint of Evening and morning star, Je 1832-Jl 1833
MoHi 1911-Je,O-N 1914
MoSHi Je 1911-Je 1913

SUBURBAN items. w 1920+
1920-27 as Englewood suburban items (Englewood)
pub 1928-29

Independence TRIBUNE with which is combined the Jackson democrat. w 1933?+
1933?-Jl 1934 as Independence tribune

WESTERN dispatch. w Ja 6 1854-
KHi Ja 13 1854

WESTERN expositor. *See* Independence messenger

WESTERN Missourian. *See* Independence messenger

INDIAN SPRINGS

Indian Springs ECHO. w D 1881-82||?
KHi Mr 10 1882

IRONTON

ARCADIA VALLEY enterprise. w S 1904+
MoCaT 1917-19
MoHi My 1906-My 1916;25+

Tri-weekly BLAND register. tw Jl 9 1861-
WHi Jl 9 1861

IRON county eagle. w Ap 1897-1903||?
MoHi Jl 25 1901-03

IRON county register. w 1867+
MoCaT 1907+
MoHi D 24 1874;Je 26 1890;Jl 25 1901+
WHi Mr 23 1893-Je 20 1901

LIBERAL. w 1870-71||?
MoSHi Jl 23 1870

OZARK record. w My 24 1927+
pub 1927+

SOUTHEAST Missouri enterprise. w My 1866-75||?
MoHi My 14 1868-Mr 1870;S-N 1871;My-S 1873

JACKSON

CAPE county post. w Mr 11 1886+
1886-Je 1918 as Deutscher volksfreund (in German)
pub 1886+
MoCaT 1917-19;25+
MoHi My 17 1912

CAPE Girardeau patriot.
MoCaT Jl 23(extra)1838

Jackson COURIER. w N 25 1820-61||
1820-F 1831? as Independent patriot; Mr 1831-N 1835? Jackson eagle; D 1 1835-37? Southern advocate and state journal; Ja?-F 24 1838 Southern Missouri advocate; Mr 3? 1838-44? Southern advocate; 1845-N 1849? Jackson review; D 1849-My 1850? Southern advocate; Je 1850?-52 Southern democrat.
D 1835-37? pub in Cape Girardeau
CLS Je 20 1850
DLC 1821-N 16 1822;F 8 1823-D 13 1826;Ja 20-D 1838
ICU Ag 26,S 9 1843
KHi [1821-D 15 1826](photostat) Ja 23-D 1838(photostat)
MWA Je 28 1823;Je 19,Jl 3,Ag 25 1824;S 14 1850
MoCaT Ja 7,17,Mr 19,My 7 1827;Je 29,Jl 28 1838;My 31,O 25-N 1,15-22,D 1851-Ja 24 1852
MoHi 1821-N 16 1822;F 8 1823-O 8 1825;Mr-D 15 1826(photostat) Mr 24,D 22 1832;My 15 1836;Ja 20-D 1838(photostat)Jl 11,25,Ag 29 1840;Ap 5,Je 24,Jl 12 1845;Je 6,O 24 1846;D 2 1848;Ag 3-10 1850;My 10 1851;F 4 1854
MoSHi Ja 25 1822;S 27 1823;Ap 26 1851;Ja 24 1852;O 4 1854

DEUTSCHER volksfreund. *See* Cape county post

Jackson EAGLE. *See* Jackson courier

Jackson EXAMINER. w 1898-1927||?
MoHi O 30(supp)1903

Jackson HERALD. w N 1897-1910||?
MoHi Jl 25 1901-D 4 1910

INDEPENDENT patriot. *See* Jackson courier

Jackson ITEMS. w 1910-16||?
MoHi Je 13 1912

JEFFERSONIAN. w 1852-
MoHi Ja 8,Ap 9,Jl 16 1853
MoSHi Je 11 1853

Jackson MERCURY and Cape Girardeau farmer. w D 13 1828-
DLC D 13 1828;O 3 1829
MoCaT D 11 1830
MoHi D 31 1831

MISSOURI cash-book. w Ag 6 1871+
pub 1871+
MoCaT 1907-25
MoHi Ap 24 1884;O 30 1890;D 10 1908+

Jackson REVIEW. *See* Jackson courier

SOUTHERN advocate. *See* Jackson courier

SOUTHERN democrat. *See* Jackson courier

SOUTHERN Missouri advocate. *See* Jackson courier

JAMESON

Jameson GEM. w S 25 1913+
pub 1913+
MoHi 1913+

JAMESPORT

Jamesport GAZETTE. sw,w Ja 1 1876+
Ja-Mr 1876 as Trenton gazette?; Ap? 1876-Jl? 1913 Jamesport semi-weekly gazette (1892? Gazette-herald)
sw 1876-Jl? 1913
Ja-Mr 1876 pub in Trenton
MoHi D 11 1900;03-Ag 1915;Jl 1922+
MoSHi 1904-Ag 7 1913

Jamesport HERALD. w N 1885-91||?
United with Jamesport gazette to form Gazette-herald, later Jamesport gazette
MoHi D 1889-D 4 1891

JASPER

JASPER county news. w S 12 1896+
1896-1925? as Jasper news
pub 1896+
MoHi Jl 26 1901+

Jasper NEWS. *See* Jasper county news

JEFFERSON CITY

Daily CAPITAL news. d 1910+
Sunday issues as Jefferson City post-tribune and daily capital news
MoHi 1919-[Ja-Mr 1930]+
MoJ 1910+

Jefferson City COURIER. w 1896-98||?
1896-D 10 1897 as Republican courier
MoHi Je 19 1896-Mr 4 1898

COLE county democrat. w Je 6 1884-F 1910||
United with Jefferson City weekly tribune to form Jefferson City weekly democrat-tribune
MoHi 1884-My 1893;My 16 1895;My 14-21 1896; S 15 1898;Ap 1900-Jl 1907;Ja 8 1910
MoJ 1901-10

COLE county daily democrat. d 1902-F 1910||
United with Jefferson City daily tribune to form Daily democrat-tribune, later Jefferson City post-tribune
MoHi Jl 31 1903

COLE county rustler. w 1896-1926||?
1907-18 Russellville weekly rustler (Russellville)
MoHi 1919-26
MoLozF 1907-22
MoSHi Je 27 1913

Jefferson City weekly DEMOCRAT-TRIBUNE. w O 4 1865-1917||?
1865-85 as People's tribune; 1885-Ja 4 1899 Jefferson City tribune; Ja 11 1899-1904 Missouri state tribune; 1905-F 1? 1910 Jefferson City weekly tribune. Followed by Mosby's Missouri message
MoHi 1865-98;Ja 11-F 1,Je 22,D 21 1899[Mr-O 1909]
—d ed *See* Jefferson City post-tribune

Daily DEMOCRAT-TRIBUNE. *See* Jefferson City post-tribune

Daily ECLIPSE. d D 1878-82||?
MoHi N 3 1879;80-Ja 6 1881

Jefferson EXAMINER. w S 14 1852-62||
Follows Metropolitan. Followed by Weekly Missouri state times, later Missouri state times
DLC My 24-31,Je 21-28 1853;55-57
MoHi 1852-S 6 1853;55-57(photostat)Ap 24 1858-O 1 1859;Ap 14,28,S 15-O 20,N 10 1860;S 13-27,C 11,N 1-22,D 6-13 1862

Daily Jefferson EXAMINER. d 1852-62||?
Followed by Daily Missouri state times
MoHi Ja 12,19-20,23,F 1,7,13-14,16 1855;Ja 6, 18,F 4-5,10-11,Mr 3,10-11,N 30-D 1,3,13-14,22 1859

MISSOURI (*Continued*)

JEFFERSON CITY—*Continued*

Der FORTSCHRITT. w 1866-75||?
Followed by Missouri volksfreund
In German
MoHi Je 9 1869

Weekly HERALD. w Jl 30 1913-15||?
Negro
MoHi 1913-Ag 1914

Jefferson weekly INQUIRER. w Mr 31 1838-1838?-O 21? 1854 as Jefferson inquirer
DLC Ap 17 1845-49;51-53;55-57
MWA Ap 11,Ag 1,O 17 1844;Jl 31-Ag 7,S 18,N 13,D 31 1845[Ja 14-Jl 1846]Jl 3-10,O 23,N 6, 27-D 18 1847[Ja-Mr 1848]O 21,D 23 1854
MoHi S 10 1840-49;F 23 1850-O 14 1854;55 (photostat)56-S 1859;Je 10 1860-Ja 1861
MoSHi Je 15 1850;Je 28 1851;Je 30(supp)1853

Tri-weekly INQUIRER. tw N 3 1846-
DLC N 9-14,19-D 1,5-15,19,29 1846;Ja 2-7 1847

Daily INQUIRER. d D 19 1850-
Title varies: Daily Jefferson inquirer
Issued only during political campaigns and sessions of legislature
KHi 1850-Mr 2 1851
MoHi Ja 9,19-20,23,26-27,31,F 3,13,16-17 1855; My 27-Ag 28 1856;Ja-Je 17 1857;Ja-Mr 14 1859;Ja 1-28 1861

JEFFERSONIAN republican. w O 1825-44||
1825-Mr? 1831 as Jeffersonian
1825 pub in St. Charles
CLM My 1 1830
DLC Ja 1 1830[Ap 30-D 17 1831]33-[37]-40
KHi [Ap 30 1831-40]photostat
MoCaT D 18 1830;Ja 12 1833
MoHi S 9 1826;Ap 1830-31;33-Ag 10 1844(1831-40 photostat)
MoSHi D 25 1826;Ag 7-14,28 1830;Mr 9 1831; Ap 10,29 1833;Ag 21 1844

METROPOLITAN. w O 6 1846-S 7 1852||
Follows Missouri herald. Followed by Jefferson examiner
DLC O 5 1847
MWA F 1 1848
MoHi 1846-S 1848;O 1849-S 1850
MoSHi Ap 18 1848;Ja 27,Ag 31 1852

MISSOURI herald. w -S 1846||?
Followed by Metropolitan
MoSHi My 10,Je 7,Jl 8 1845

MISSOURI state journal. w Ja 17 1920-24||?
MoHi 1920-Ap 5 1924
MoSHi Mr 20,Ap 3,17 1920

MISSOURI state times. w 1863-72||?
Follows Jefferson examiner. 1863-70? as Weekly Missouri state times
ICHi S 22,N 12,24 1871
MBAt Ap 15-22 1865
MoHi 1865-Jl 1868;69;Je 3 1870

Daily MISSOURI state times. d 1863?-72||?
Follows Daily Jefferson examiner
DLC Ja 24 1867;Mr 7 1871
MoHi Ja 26 1864
WHi F 20 1865

MISSOURI state tribune. w *See* Jefferson City weekly democrat-tribune

MISSOURI state tribune. d *See* Jefferson City post-tribune

MISSOURI volksfreund. w 1876-1927||
Follows Der Fortschritt
In German
MoHi O 29 1890;1913-Mr 1917

MISSOURI watchman. w Mr 29 1838-
DLC Ap 26 1838

MOSBY'S Missouri message. w Ja 11 1918-Jl 26 1922||
Follows Jefferson City weekly democrat-tribune
MoHi 1918-19
MoSHi Ap 1 1921

Weekly NEWS. w O 12 1888-89||?
MoHi 1888-Ja 11,25 1889

PEOPLE'S tribune. *See* Jefferson City weekly democrat-tribune

Daily POST. d Jl 15 1908-F 2 1927||
United with Jefferson City tribune to form Jefferson City tribune-post, later Jefferson City post-tribune
MoHi F 3 1913-S 1917;D 6 1924-27

Jefferson City POST-TRIBUNE. d D 6 1871+
1871-98 as Daily tribune; 1899-1904 Missouri state tribune; 1905-Ap 1 1909 Jefferson City tribune; Ap 2 1909-F 7 1910 Jefferson City daily tribune; F 8 1910-N 1924 Daily democrat-tribune; D 1924-F 2 1927 Jefferson City tribune; F 3-My 4 1927 Jefferson City tribune-post Sunday issues as Jefferson City post-tribune and daily capital news
MoHi D 11 1871-Mr 1872;Ja-Mr 1873;74-My 1881; Jl 1882-87;Jl 1888+
MoJ 1901+
MoK Jl-D 1925
MoSHi Ag 12 1914
WHi 1917-19
—w ed *See* Jefferson City weekly democrat-tribune

Jefferson City daily PRESS. d 1899-1901||?
MoHi Je 7 1899
MoJ 1901

PROFESSIONAL world. *See* under Columbia

REPUBLICAN courier. *See* Jefferson City courier

SPY. w Je 1844-
MoSM Jl 13 1844

STATE journal. w *See* State times

Daily STATE journal. d S 9 1873-86||?
MoHi 1873-Mr,S 9 1874-Je 1879;Ja,Mr 1880-Je 1881;Ja-Je 1882;83-Je 1884

STATE republican. w 1871-96||?
Merged with Jefferson City courier
MoHi 1890-Mr 1896

STATE sentinel. w O 26 1844-
DLC N 2 1844
MoHi D 14 1844
MoSM D 14 1844

STATE times. w D 27 1872-88||?
1872-Ag 6 1886 as State journal
MoHi 1872-74; Ja 21-F 4,18-25,D 24 1875-O 5 1888
—d ed *See* Daily state journal

Daily TRIBUNE. *See* Jefferson City post-tribune

Jefferson City weekly TRIBUNE. *See* Jefferson City weekly democrat-tribune

Jefferson City TRIBUNE-POST. *See* Jefferson City post-tribune

WESTERN messenger. w 1901-17||?
Negro
MoHi Ja 9 1914-N 1917

WESTERN monitor.
MoCaT Ap 27(extra)1829

JERICO SPRINGS

Jerico Springs OPTIC. w Ja 1 1889+
pub 1889+
MoHi N 7 1890;Jl 26 1901+

JONESBURG

Jonesburg JOURNAL. w N 1879-Ap 25 1927||?
MoHi Ag 8 1901-N 1922

Jonesburg MESSAGE. w Ag 2 1928+
pub 1928+
MoHi 1928+

JOPLIN

Joplin ADVANCE. w My 10 1895-
KHi My 10 1895

FREE PRESS. w 1912-
MoHi Ja 17-[Je-O 3]1914

Joplin daily GLOBE. d Jl 1896+
pub 1896+
KHi S 1921+
MoHi Jl 27 1901+
MoJo 1904+
NcD Ja 31 1904

Joplin daily HERALD. d Mr 4 1877-Mr 3 1900||
United with Joplin daily news to form Joplin daily news-herald
CLM Ag 17 1890
MoJo N 1877-87

Joplin daily NEWS-HERALD. d 1872+
1872-Mr 3 1900 as Joplin daily news
pub 1872+
KHi [O 24 1919-O 27 1920]
MoHi My 16 1899-O 1 1900;01+
MoJo 1904+
NcU Ag 2 1878

Joplin evening TIMES. d N 1900-12||?
MoHi N 8 1906-S 1910

Joplin morning TRIBUNE. d 1911-Ap 11 1913||
MoHi F 9-Ap 1913

KAHOKA

CLARK county courier. w N 1 1895+
pub 1395+
MoHi Ja 3 1896-97;99+

CLARK county gazette. *See* Kahoka gazette-herald

Kahoka DEMOCRAT. d O 8 1879-80||?
MoHi [O 1879]Ag 7 1880

FREE press. sw 1910+
KHi Jl 24 1928

Kahoka GAZETTE-HERALD. w Ja 1 1872+
1872-88 as Clark county gazette
MoHi Jl 26 1901+

REVIEW. w 1888-1905||?
MoHi D 7 1898-1905

KANSAS CITY

Kansas City AMERICAN. w Ap 12 1928+
Negro
MoHi Je 21 1928-Ja 12 1933

BLUE VALLEY press. w 1902+
1902-28 as Sheffield press
pub D 25 1906+

BORDER star. w 1855-68||?
1855? as Frontier news; 1856? Border times; 1857? Star of an empire
KHi O 6 1855;Ja 17-24,Mr 21,S 5 1857;Ja 28 1859

BORDER times. *See* Border star

Kansas City weekly BULLETIN. w 1868-72||?
MoK [1872]

Kansas City CALL. w My 1919+
Negro
pub 1923+

CATHOLIC register. w 1899+
pub 1900+
MoCon 1924+
MoHi 1903+

Daily COMMERCIAL advertiser. d 1865?-
OHi Jl 26,O 3 1865

COMMERCIAL indicator. *See* live stock indicator

El COSMOPOLITA. w Ag 30 1914-19||?
In Spanish
IU D 8 1917-N 15 1919
KHi N 27 1915
MoHi My 1915-18
MoSHi My 15 1915
NN S 25 1915

Kansas City daily DEMOCRAT. d Je 10 1926+
pub 1926+
MoHi 1926+
MoK 1926+
—w ed *See* Missouri democrat

Daily DROVERS' telegram. d 1881+
1881-85 as Daily live stock record and price current
pub F 28 1884+
DA My 1908-[09]-[11-14]-[16]-[19-20]-[28]+
IU [1908]-O 1914;Ja-Je 1916;S-O 1917:Ja-O 1918;Jl 4 1919-O 1924;Ap 1925+
MoHi Ag 1,14 1905
MoU Ag 1902-07;Jl 1908-Ag 1915
NcD Ap 23 1896

Kansas City ENQUIRER. w Ap 19 1860-
DLC Ap 19 1860
MWA My 24 1860

Kansas City ENTERPRISE. *See* Kansas City journal

EXCHANGE journal. w Ap 24 1890-
KHi My 8-29 1890

EYE. w 1889-93||?
KHi Jl 10-S 18 1890

FRONTIER news. *See* Border star

GATE CITY press. w 1880-89||?
KHi S 8 1888

Kansas City GLOBE. w F 10 1889-Jl 29 1909||
1895?-Mr 1900 as Sunday world
KHi 1889-Ap 19 1891
MoK 1889-Ap 1891;Ap-Jl 1900
—d ed *See* Daily news and Kansas City world

INDEPENDENT. w 1899+
Mr-Je 20 1908 as Newsbook
pub 1899+
KHi Ag 9 1924+
MoHi Jl 1901-11;13+

ITALIAN press. La Stampa-italiana. w 1914+
1914?-Je? 1931 as La Stampa
1914?-My 18 1918 pub in Omaha, Neb.
In Italian and English
IU O 27 1917-Je 1918;Mr 8 1919-[Ja-Je]D 25 1931+
NbHi Je 21-28,Jl 19,D 1918-21

Kansas City JEWISH chronicle. w 1920+
pub 1920+

Kansas City JOURNAL. w S 23 1854-1927||?
1854-O 3 1857 as Kansas City enterprise; O 10 1857-My 1863? Western journal of commerce; My 1863?-My 1878 Weekly journal of commerce; Je 1878-90? Weekly journal; 1891-99? Journal and agriculturist; 1900-19? Weekly journal; 1920-25? Journal and Missouri and Kansas farmer
pub [D 1855-O 1857]
CSmH O 28 1854
KHi O 28 1854;Mr 7,S 12 1857;Jl 16 1859;60-Ag 6 1861;72-[79-98]
MWA O 14 1854
NbHI My 12,26 1898; Ap 15,My 3,24,Je 7,Ag 30 1900
P-M O 28 1854
VU Ag 9-S 12,O 4,25-N 1,15-22 1917;Ap 11-18, S 5-12,O 24,N-D 12 1918;Ja 9,F 6 1919
WaPS [1901;18;26-27]
—d ed *See* Kansas City journal-post

Weekly JOURNAL of commerce. *See* Kansas City journal

Daily JOURNAL of commerce. *See* Kansas City journal-post

Kansas City JOURNAL-POST. d Je 15 1858+
1858-Mr 7 1861 as Daily Kansas City western journal of commerce; Mr 15-16 1861 Daily journal of commerce; Mr 17-Ag 21 1861 Daily western journal of commerce; Mr 18 1862-My 1863 Daily Kansas City western journal of commerce; My 1863-My 27 1878 Daily Kansas City journal of commerce; My 28 1878-F 8 1897 Kansas City daily journal; F 9 1897-O 3 1928 Kansas City journal
Suspended from Mr 7-My 15,Ag 21 1861-Mr 18 1862
pub 1858+
DLC Jl 11 1876;Mr 1890+
ICM D 15 1884;S 24 1885
ICN D 16 1917-My 21 1920
IHi Ap 18 1865
IU Je 10 1920-My 1925
KBB O 1883;Ap-My 1884;89[94]Je-D 1905 [08;13-14;16;18]+
KHi Ap 18,20 1865[77-78]Jl 1879+
MWA Ap 14 1876;Ja 1 1889
MoHi My 11 1879;S-N 1884;Ja-Mr 1885;O 28 1890;Je-Jl 15,S-O 1893;Mr 10,20 1894;Ag 16 1896-[98-99]-1900;Ag 1901+
MoJ 1901+
MoK Ja 16-N 7 1877;78+
MoSHi Ag 28-29,D 12 1886
NbHi D 16 1897;Ja 15,F 2-3 1898;N 4 1900; Je 7 1903;Jl 1 1906
OClWHi D 21 1879;Ja 9 1880
OOxM O 12,15,26 1882
OkHi [1893]-[1902]-[07]
TJT N 29 1894;Mr 19 1903;D 11 1904
VHi F 17 1899
WHi F 7 1865;Ja 6 1876;Ja 1 1887
—w ed *See* Kansas City journal

MISSOURI (*Continued*)

KANSAS CITY—*Continued*

KANSAS Citian. w 1911+
pub F 1913+

KANSAS daily pioneer. d 1879-80||?
MoHi Jl 25 1879

LIBERATOR. w F 1901-10||?
Negro
MoHi 1903

LIVE STOCK indicator. w Ap 4 1878-1903||?
1878-D 29 1881 as Commercial indicator; Ja-Je 8 1882 Live stock indicator and farmer's gazette
DLC S 11 1902
KHi 1884
MoHi Ag 1901-Jl 1903
MoK 1878-92
NbHi Ag 8 1878

Daily LIVE STOCK record and price current. *See* Daily drovers' telegram

Kansas City evening MAIL. d 1875-Ja 1882 ||
1875-79? as Daily Kansas City mail
KHi Ag 24 1877
MoK N 22 1875-Mr 21 1876;S 19 1877-O 24 1881

Kansas City MAIL. d 1892-1902||?
KHi Mr 23 1892-O 4 1902
MoHi Mr 10 1894;99-O 1902
MoK Jl 11 1892-O 11 1902
OkHi [1893]-[95]

Kansas City MAIL. w My 14 1895-1901||?
MoHi 1895-1900
MoK 1895-My 5 1896
NbHi D 27 1898

El MERCURIO. w 1883-84||?
In Spanish
MoHi Ag 1 1884

Il MESSAGGIERO. bw Ap 12 1928+
In Italian
MoP 1929+

MIRROR of progress. w Jl 12 1879-82||?
KHi O 1879-Ap 23 1881

MISSOURI democrat. w O 16 1925+
pub 1929+
MoHi 1925+
—d ed *See* Kansas City daily democrat

MISSOURI post. *See* Post und tribune

MISSOURI staats-zeitung. w 1894-1917||?
In German
MoHi 1899-1907;09-17

NEUE KANSAS staats-zeitung. w 1894-F 8 1918||?
In German. Not to be confused with Missouri staats-zeitung
KHi 1917-F 8 1918
MoHi D 4 1908;14-F 8 1918

Kansas City evening NEWS. d 1885-90||?
1885-86? as Kansas City daily news
KHi My 12 1888-O 8 1890
MoK Mr 1887-O 1890
MoSHi D 13 1886

Daily NEWS and Kansas City world. d Ja 11 1894-Ap 11 1908||
1894-Mr 25 1908 as Kansas City world
CLM Ag 1897
DLC F-Je 1897
IaHi O 1901-02
KHi Jl 11,S 11 1895-Je 1907
MoHi O 30 1895;S 1901-Je 1907
MoK complete
OkHi [1894]-[97]
WHi Ja 12 1896
—Sunday ed *See* Kansas City globe

NEWSBOOK. *See* Independent

Kansas City NEWS-PRESS. w 1914+
1914-18? as South city press; 1919?-23 South Kansas City press
pub 1919+

Kansas City OBSERVER. w 1896-1901||?
Negro
DLC Ja 27 1900

L'OSSERVATORE. w 1908-
Merged with La Voce dell'emigrante
In Italian
MoHi O 11 1912;14-Ag 1915

PENNY press. d F 15- 1890||?
KHi F-Je 19 1890

Kansas City PIONEER. w 1873-81||?
KHi O 23 1878;Jl 18 1881
MoHi 1880

Kansas City POST. d Mr 14 1906-Ag 31 1928||
United with Kansas City journal to form Kansas City journal-post
KHi My 16 1906-O 1927
MoHi Ap 6 1906-28
MoK complete
MoKJ complete
NbHi F 25-Mr 2,4-6,8-9,Ap 10 1912-S 25,O 24 1916-Jl 10 1918
WaPS [1926-27]

POST und tribune. w 1858-96||?
Early years as Missouri post; 1881?-85? Westliche volkszeitung
In German
MWA Ag 20-S 17,O 1-15,29,N 19-26 1859; Ja 14 1860

Tägliche POST und tribune. d 1858?-96||?
1858?-71? as Tägliche post (other variations slight)
In German
MWA Ag 25, 27 1876

Kansas City PRESSE. d,sw,w 1884+
Since 1924 has section called St. Joseph volksblatt
d 1884-My 1918;w My 1918-24?
In German
pub 1884+
KHi Jl 18 1918+
MoHi N 18 1890;Ja-Mr 1914;O 1915-21
MoK 1898-Je 1917;F 1918-27

Kansas City PRICE current. w 1873-82||?
KHi Je 25 1880-O 1881

REFORM. d,w 1890?-1909||?
1890?-99 pub in St. Louis
d 1890?-99
In German
MoHi S 4-D 9 1899;Mr 17 1900-07;Ja-Je 1909
WHi N 30 1895

Daily REPORTER. d 1873-74||?
KHi F 3 1874

RISING son. w 1896-1918||?
Negro
DLC Ja 27 1900
MoHi Ja 16 1903-07

SHEFFIELD press. *See* Blue Valley press

SOLDIER'S letter. sm,w Ag 20 1864-
Also dated in Fort Riley, Kansas
sm 1864-Ja? 1865
CSmH [S 17 1864-Ja 17 1865]
KHi 1864-O 14 1865
MnHi 1864-Ja 9 1865

SOUTH city press. *See* Kansas City news-press

SOUTH Kansas City press. *See* Kansas City news-press

La STAMPA-ITALIANA. *See* Italian press

Kansas City STAR. d S 18 1880+
Ag 7 1921 is Missouri centennial ed
pub 1880+
DLC D 22 1891-D 16 1897;Ag 1898-Ja,Mr 1910+
FTS Ja 1,F 23,25,Ap 13,15,Je 7,9,D 25,27 1931; Ja 3,5,F 9,11,Mr 3,5,31,My 1,Jl 8,10 1932;Ja 22,24,Mr 13,15,S 4,6,O 5,7,N 17 1933
IC My 1 1889
ICU S 19 1881-S 17 1883;S 18 1884-S 17 1885;S 18 1886-Mr 13 1890;S 18 1891-Mr 18 1892;Mr 20 1893-S 17 1895;Mr 18 1896-Jl 1926
IU Ja-Mr,My 1909+
IaHi Mr 1890-Jl 1894;1901-S 1903;Je 4-30 1928
KBB My 1929+
KHK 1903-My 1933
KHi Ag 19 1886+
KK 1905+
MWA S 18 1880;Ag 7 1921;Ag 9 1925;S 18 1930
MiU [1921-25]+
MnU [1918-21]
MoCaT 1933+
MoFuW S 11 1931-Je,S 8 1932-Je 2,S 10 1933+
MoHi S-O 1893;N 26 1898-Mr,My 1899+
MoJ 1901+
MoK 1880+
MoMaryT 1933+
MoSHi My 4,15,25,Je 1 1917
MoSp 1917+
MoSpD 1934+
NNRo Ap 1917-Ja 1919
NbHi N 5,11 1884;Ag 2,N 21 1899;N 4-11 1900; Jl 30 1901-F,Ap 1907-Ag 1908;Ja-F,Jl-Ag 1909;Mr 1910-F 1914;My 12-Je,S-D 1917;Ja 23-28,F 1918-F 1921
OCHi Ja 19 1898
OHi 1917+
OkHi [1897]-[1906;08]
TJT Jl 25-26 1900;S 10,13 1905;N 1, 4 1908
Tx Ag 1916+
TxGR current year only
WHi N 14 1913-N 1923
WaPS Ap 9 1928;Mr 1929;D 29 1931
—morning ed *See* Kansas City times

Weekly Kansas City STAR. w 1890+
KHi S 16 1891+
MWA [1904]-F 3 1915
MoF 1932+
TJT F 2 1898;Ap 23-My,Je 11,25-Ag 20,D 17-24 1913;F-Mr 11,25,S 23-O,N 11 1914-Ja 13,F-Ap 19,28-My 5 1915;Ap 26-Jl 12,Ag 9 1916-Mr 21,Ap 11-My,O 24-N 1917;Ja-Mr,Ap 17,My 22-S 11,25-D 1918;Mr 2 1920
TxU 1914-O 23 1918
VU [1902]
WaPS [1918-21]

STAR of an empire. *See* Border star

Kansas City Sunday SUN. w Mr 2 1889-98||?
1889? as Kansas City sun
KHi Mr-My 4 1889
MoBoH Jl 1898
NbHi N 8 1891
OkHi [1893]-[95]

Kansas City SUN. w 1908-24||?
Negro
KHi D 7 1912
MoHi Ja 10 1914-Je 1924

SVENSKA harolden. w 1879-85||?
In Swedish
KHi 1882-Ap 22 1885

SVENSKA pressen. *See* Kansas City tribunen

SVENSKA sydvestern. *See* Kansas City tribunen

SVENSKA tidningen och Skandia. w 1891-98||
1891-Ag 16 1895 as Skandia (Sioux City, Ia.)
In Swedish
IRA 1893-98
MnHi Ag 11 1892-Ag 9 1895

SVENSKA weckobladet. w 1883-91||?
In Swedish
MoHi N 21 1890

SYDVESTERN. *See* Kansas City tribunen

TÄGLICHE. . . *See* next important word: e.g., Tägliche post is alphabeted as Post

Kansas City TIMES. d S 8 1868+
pub 1868+
C 1898
CU Ja 3 1880
DLC 1893-Ap 1896;98-Ap 1899
IC Ap 30 1889
ICU Ja 22-F 1898;S-O 1900;Ag-S,O 20,27,N 3 1901-Jl 1926
KBB My 1929+
KHK S 1918-Ap 1933
KHi Jl 1874+
KK 1905+
MWA D 31 1886;F 4-D 1915
MoCaT 1933+
MoFuW S 11 1931-Je,S 8 1932-Je 2,S 10 1933+
MoHi Je-Jl 15,S-O 1893;Mr-Ap 15 1894;Je 16-Ag 15,O 1896-Ag 15,S 16 1897-F,Mr 16 1898-S,D 1899-1900;Jl 1902+
MoJ 1901+
MoK Ag 20 1871-73;Je 21 1874;75+
MoMaryT 1933+
MoSHi D 5 1885;My 23,N 20,30 1886;My 17,Je 1 1917
MoSp 1924+
MoSpD 1934+
NbHi S 22,24,O 27 1881;D 8 1902;Ja-F,My 1903-Ap,S 1908;Jl-S,D 31 1909;Ap 1910-13; Ja-Mr,My 1918-S,N 1919-F 14 1921
NcD D 14 1883
OClWHi Ja 11 1880;D 12 1881
OHi 1933+
OkHi [1902-03]
TJT N 4 1908
Tx Ag 1916-20; Mr-Ap,Jl 1921-24;Jl 1925-Jl,S 1928+
TxGR current year only
WHi S 21 1888;N 14 1913-Je 1915
WaPS [1916]Mr 12 1918;Mr 1929;N 14,23 1932
—evening ed 1901+ *See* Kansas City star

Kansas City weekly TIMES. w sw 1869-1901||?
sw 1894?-Ap 1901
IaHi Mr 1877-Mr 1878;N 1882-Ap 1884;1900-O 1901
MoSHi Ap 6 1882
N D 1 1871
NbHi O 6,D 8 1881;Mr 30 1882
TJT N 9 1900

Kansas City evening TIMES. d O 9 1890-D 12 1891||
MoK complete

Kansas City TRIBUNE. w 1869-71||?
United with Post to form Post und tribune
In German

Kansas City TRIBUNEN. w 1892-1914||
1892-96 as Svenska sydvestern; 1897-1900 Sydvestern; Ja-My 1901 Svenska pressen
In Swedish
IRA [1895-99]1901-14
MnHi [Je 24 1904-Jl 16 1914]
MoHi 1903-O 1914

Kansas City TRUTH. w 1903-05||?
MoK 1904-Ja 5 1905

La VOCE dell'emigrante. w Ja 1909-
In Italian and English
MoHi Ag 11 1915-O 1917

WESTERN journal of commerce. w *See* Kansas City journal

Daily WESTERN journal of commerce. *See* Kansas City journal-post

WESTERN metropolitan. w 1858-
DLC Ag 18 1859;Mr 8 1860

WESTLICHE volkszeitung. *See* Post und tribune

WESTPORT border times. w 1856-
N Ap 5-12 1856

WESTPORT examiner. *See* Westport sentinel examiner

WESTPORT sentinel. d 1892-My 1894||?
United with Westport examiner to form Westport sentinel examiner

WESTPORT sentinel examiner. w 1893?-99||?
1893?-Je 9 1894 as Westport examiner
MoK Ag 19 1893-Ag 8 1899

Kansas City WORLD. *See* Daily news and Kansas City world

Sunday WORLD. *See* Kansas City globe

KEARNEY

Kearney CLIPPER. w 1894-1918||?
MoHi O 3 1904;13-O 1917
MoSHi Ag-D 1894

KENNETT

Kennett CLIPPER. *See* Dunklin democrat

DUNKLIN county herald. *See* Dunklin county republican

DUNKLIN county mail. w 1900-05||?
MoHi Ja 12,26,Mr 2,16-Ap 1905

DUNKLIN county news. w 1916-My 22 1931||
Merged with Dunklin democrat
MoCaT 1917-19
MoHi Mr 16 1917-31
MoKeD complete

DUNKLIN county republican. w F 1 1907-Ap 22 1910||
1907-F 11 1910 as Dunklin county herald
MoHi complete

DUNKLIN democrat. w,sw Ap 19 1888+
1888-93? as Kennett clipper
w 1888-1923?
pub 1888+
MoCaT 1906+
MoHi O 23 1890;1901+
MoKe 1932+

MISSOURI (*Continued*)

KENNETT—*Continued*

SOUTHEAST Missouri republican. w 1910‖?
MoHi Ap 29-D 1910

Kennett TIMES. w 1900-06‖?
MoHi Jl 21 1905-06

KEYTESVILLE

CHARITON county news. *See* Chariton county union

CHARITON county union. w Ag 1866?-72‖
1866-69? as Chariton county news. Followed by Keytesville herald, later Chariton courier
MWA Ag 31-S,O 12,26,N 30 1867[Ja 11-N 13 1868]
MiU-C S 18 1868

CHARITON courier. w 1872+
Follows Chariton county union. 1872-My 1878 as Keytesville herald
MoHi Mr 1872-My 15,Je 1878-1900;Jl 1901+

CHARITON recorder. w 1905-F 1 1918‖
Merged with Chariton courier
MoHi N 22 1907-18

Keytesville HERALD. *See* Chariton courier

KIDDER

Kidder DISPATCH. w 1886-1900‖?
1886-99? as Kidder optic
MoHi O 23 1890

Kidder INDEPENDENT. w 1903-13‖?
MoHi Mr 11 1910-11

Kidder OPTIC. *See* Kidder dispatch

Kidder STAR. w 1921-25‖?
MoH [D 29 1921-D 18 1924]

KING CITY

King City CHRONICLE. w Mr 1880+
pub 1893+
MoHi Jl 26 1901+

King City DEMOCRAT. w 1892-1918‖
MoHi N 25 1898-Je 1899;1903;05-S 1918
MoKinN 1905;10-18

TRI-COUNTY news. w Je 11 1920+
Follows Union Star herald (Union Star)
pub 1920+
MoHi 1920+

KINGSTON

CALDWELL banner of liberty. w 1864-66‖
Follows Caldwell county beacon
MoH [My 20 1864-Je 23 1865]

CALDWELL county beacon. w O 1860-64‖
Followed by Caldwell banner of liberty

CALDWELL county news. w S 1921+
MoH [My 18 1922-S 1928]+

CALDWELL county sentinel. w 1867-87‖?
MoHi My 4,Je 8,22-Jl 6,O 12-N 9 1883;Ap 1886-Ag 1887

Kingston HAMPTON'S mercury. *See* Kingston mercury

Kingston MERCURY. w 1895-1921‖?
1895-1917? as Kingston Hampton's mercury
MoHi N 1902-O 1903;Ag 12,N 1904-Ap 1921

Kingston TIMES. w 1885-1901‖?
MoHi F 11 1886-89;O 24,D 5 1890;91-99;F-S 1901

KIRKSVILLE

ADAIR county farmer. w 1890-94‖?
IaHi S 1891-Mr 1894

Kirksville DEMOCRAT. *See* Kirksville daily news

Kirksville daily EXPRESS and news. d N 1901+
1901-22 as Kirksville daily express
pub 1908+
MoHi Ag 6 1912;N 10 1917+

Weekly GRAPHIC. w 1880+
pub [1882+]
MoHi 1903+

Kirksville JOURNAL. w,d D? 1865-N 26 1926‖
Follows Kirksville patriot. 1925? as Journal-news. Merged with Kirksville daily express and news
w 1865-F 1926
MoHi O 23 1890;Ag 1901-25;Mr-N 1926

Kirksville daily NEWS. w,d 1870-D 31 1922‖
1870-1914 as Kirksville democrat. United with Kirksville daily express to form Kirksville daily express and news
w 1870-1919
KHi Ag 3 1913
MoHi O 23 1890;Jl 26 1901-F 6 1916

NORTH MISSOURI register. w S 1870-79‖?
S-D 1 1870 as North Missouri tribune
MoHi D 1870-N 1871;Mr 9 1876

NORTH MISSOURI tribune. *See* North Missouri register

Kirksville PATRIOT. w Ag 23 1864-N 23 1865‖
Followed by Kirksville journal
MWA Ag 17 1865

PELL MELL greenbacker. *See under* Edina

KIRKWOOD

Kirkwood COURIER. w 1902-19‖?
1902-S 17 1904 as Weekly courier
MoCaT 1917-19
MoHi 1903-12;15-18
MoKirM S 23 1911-S 21 1912

Weekly MAIL. w Ja 31 1877-78‖?
MoHi 1877-F 20 1878
MoSHi F 14-21 1877

Kirkwood MESSENGER. w Je 22 1923+
1923-Je 4 1925? as St. Louis county messenger
pub 1923-Je 4 1925;N 8 1928+

Kirkwood MONITOR. w O 1 1915+
pub 1915+
MoCaT 1918-19
MoHi 1919+

ST. LOUIS countian. w 1902+
MoHi 1919+

ST. LOUIS county messenger. *See* Kirkwood messenger

ST. LOUIS county news. w 1907-14‖?
1907-Ap 1912 as Kirkwood tablet
MoSHi Je 27 1908-S 20 1912;Ag 15,S 25 1914

Kirkwood TABLET. *See* St. Louis county news

KNOB NOSTER

Knob Noster GAZETTE. w Je 25 1870-
MoHi Je 25 1870

Knob Noster GEM. w 1870+
pub 1919+
MoHi Ja 8 1914+

Knob Noster NEWS. w 1869-70‖?
MoHi S 18,O 9 1869

KNOX CITY

Knox City BEE. *See* Knox City enterprise

Knox City ENTERPRISE. w 1893-1917‖?
1893-1913? as Knox City bee
MoHi 1904-05

Knox City NEWS. w 1927+
pub 1927+

KOSHKONONG

OREGON county leader. *See* Oregon county times-leader

OREGON county times-leader. w 1902+
1902-15? as Oregon county leader
MoCaT 1917-19
MoHi Jl 10 1903-S 1904;Jl 16 1908;12-14;F-O 21 1915;Ja-O 18 1918;19+

Koshkonong TIMES. w 1914-15‖?
United with Oregon county leader to form Oregon county times-leader

LA BELLE

La Belle STAR. w Ap 14 1883+
pub 1883+
MoHi Ag 16 1901+

LACLEDE

Laclede BLADE. w My 10 1890+
pub 1890+
MoHi O 25 1890[Jl 1902-03]+
MoSHi Je 23 1916

LADDONIA

Laddonia ENTERPRISE. w 1882-84‖?
MoHi Mr 5 1884

Laddonia HERALD. w Mr 1884+
MoHi O 30 1890;N 24 1898-1907;13+

LA GRANGE

La Grange DEMOCRAT. w Jl 4 1872-Jl 1 1891‖
United with Lewis county herald to form Herald democrat
MoHi 1872-Je 1882;Je 19 1884-D 16 1886;F 17 1888-91

HERALD DEMOCRAT. w Ag 1889-95‖?
1889-Je? 1891 as Lewis county herald

La Grange INDICATOR. w Mr 31 1893+
pub [1893+]
MoHi N 24 1898+

LEWIS county herald. *See* Herald democrat

La Grange NATIONAL American. w Ag 29 1857-72‖
Suspended from Je 1861-Ja 1864?
MWA F 8 1866
MoHi 1857-O 20 1860;Ja 5,F 2,Mr 9,Ap 20-27, My 25 1861;Ja 30-Mr 5,Ag 11,25-S 22,O 13 1864;Mr 2,30-Ap 20 1865[F-D 1868;Ja-N 1870]Ja 20 1871

LAMAR

BANNER of truth. w N 30 1869-
MoHi N 30 1869

Lamar DEMOCRAT. w,sw 1871+
w 1871-1929?
MoHi 1899+
NNHi D 12 1872

Daily DEMOCRAT. d 1901+
KHi Ja 20 1923
MoHi Ja 16,Jl 1,25 1914

FLAG of the Free. w 1867-
InNcHi Mr 15 1867

INDUSTRIAL leader. *See* Lamar leader

INDUSTRIAL union. *See* Lamar leader

Lamar LEADER. w 1890+
1890-96 as Industrial union; 1896-1902 Industrial leader
pub 1902+
MoHi Jl-N 1901;O 1902-Jl 1913;Ja-Jl 1914

Daily LEADER. d 1896-1910‖
pub complete

Lamar REPUBLICAN. w 1868+
1868-99? as Southwest republican; 1900-Je 10 1920 Republican-sentinel
N 1905 is semi-centennial ed
MoHi Ag 8 1901-S 18 1902;N 1905;N 28 1907+

SOUTH-WEST Missourian. w 1868-74‖?
MoHi Je 10 1869
NNHi D 12 1872

SOUTHWEST republican. *See* Lamar republican

LAMONTE

Lamonte RECORD. w 1880+
pub 1909+
MoHi Ag 9 1901-28

LANCASTER

Lancaster EXCELSIOR. w Mr 15 1866+
pub 1914+
IaHi My 23 1891-Je 1892
MoHi 1866-S 23 1871;My 1902+

SCHUYLER county avalanche. *See* Schuyler county republican

SCHUYLER county republican. w O 18 1899+
Early issues as Schuyler county avalanche
MoHi Ap 1902-16;O 1922+

LA PLATA

La Plata HOME press. w My 13 1875+
My 13-Je 17 1875 as Moberly signal (Moberly)
pub 1875+
MoHi F 20 1913+

La Plata REPUBLICAN. w 1892-1925‖?
MoHi D 23 1904;13-25

LAREDO

Laredo TRIBUNE. w 1900-24‖?
MoHi 1905

LA RUSSELL

SPRING RIVER news. *See* Miller news-herald

LATHROP

Lathrop HERALD. w 1896-N 3 1906‖
United with Lathrop monitor to form Lathrop monitor-herald
MoHi Je 1901-06

Lathrop MONITOR-HERALD. w 1869-1913‖?
1869-N 3 1906 as Lathrop monitor
MoHi Je 4 1886;1903-Jl 1913
MoSHi Ag 13 1886

Lathrop OPTIMIST. w 1909+
MoHi F 1913-Ag 1915;19+

LAWSON

COURIER. *See* Lawson review

Lawson LEADER. *See* Lawson review

RAY county review. *See* Lawson review

Lawson REVIEW. w 1888+
1888-93? as Lawson courier; 1894?-98? Lawson leader; 1899?-My 4 1916 Ray county review
MoHi Ag 20 1908;My 27 1909+

LEBANON

LACLEDE county republican. w 1889+
MoHi N 14 1890;Ag 9 1901-10;Ag 11 1911+

LACLEDE county sentinel. w 1873-1907‖?
MoHi D 1898-1907

Lebanon RUSTIC. w 1873+
MoHi S 20 1894;Jl 1903+

LEE'S SUMMIT

Lee's Summit DEMOCRAT. sw 1932+
MoHi Mr 1933+
MoL 1932+

Lee's Summit JOURNAL. w 1883+
pub 1894+
MoHi N 25 1898+
MoL 1932+

LEWISTOWN

Lewistown NEWS. w Mr 1 1928+
pub 1928+

Lewistown RECORD. w Ap 1914-Ap 1931‖
MoMontL complete

MISSOURI (*Continued*)

LEXINGTON

AMERICAN citizen. w 1855-
MoLe S 4 1855-Ja 21 1857

Lexington APPEAL. w
MoSHi Ap 7-14 1847;F 15,My 9-23,Jl 4 1848

Weekly CAUCASIAN. w Ap 4 1840-Ag 14 1875||
1840-46? as Lexington express; 1847?-61? Lexington weekly express; 1862?-65? Central union; 1866? Lexington express. Merged with Lexington intelligencer
MWA O 2?,D 12 1840;Ja 16,F 6,Mr 6,20-Ap 3 1841;N 30 1853
MoHi [O 14-D 1865;My-S 22 1866]Je 19-S 1867;Ja 1?,My 2 1868;Ja 22 1870-D 9 1871;N 1 1873;74-75
MoLe Jl 20 1844-Je 2 1846;Ag 10 1852-Ja 21 1855;Ag 27 1859-S 5 1860;Ap 25 1866-Mr 1869;70-75
NcU Je 22 1872

CENTRAL union. *See* Weekly Caucasian

Lexington EXPRESS. *See* Weekly Caucasian

FIRST Kansas.
KHi Ja 18 1862

HARRY of the west. w My 3-N? 1844||
MWA My 3,17-Je 21,Jl 19-Ag 9,23-30,S 27,O 18 1844
MoSM [My-O 18 1844]

Lexington HERALD. w 1889-94||?
1889-93? as Saturday herald
MoHi F 21 1894

Lexington INTELLIGENCER. w Ap 1871+
pub 1871+
CLM D 14 1889
MoHi [1872-85]87-[93]+
MoLe Ja 20 1872-73;S 1875-80;F 26 1881-Mr 11 1882;F 24 1883-F 1884;Ja 21 1885-1905
MoSHi D 18 1897

Daily INTELLIGENCER. d 1898+
MoHi Ap 10 1909

LAFAYETTE county post. w 1883-89||?
1883-87? as Post
MoHi D 22 1887

LAFAYETTE county sentinel. w 1873-80||?
MoHi Ag 25 1876-Ag 24 1879

LEXINGTONIAN. w Ag 1909-15||?
MoHi 1910-My 1915

MISSOURI thalbote. *See under* Higginsville

MISSOURI VALLEY register. *See* Lexington register

Lexington NEWS. w,d 1889+
w 1889-1932
MoHi N 18?4[Ja-My 1895]99-1907;18-F 17 1933

POST. *See* Lafayette county post

Lexington REGISTER. w 1866-90||?
1866-68? as Missouri Valley register
MoHi [1866-Mr 5 1868]Jl 1 1869[Ja-S 1875;77-N 1878]88-Ap 1890
MoLe 1866-Ap 1886

Lexington weekly UNION. w
DLC Ag 22 1863
MoHi S 5 1863;Mr 5 1864

LIBERAL

ENTERPRISE. w 1892-1913||?
MoHi Jl 26 1901-Jl 1913

Liberal INDEPENDENT. w 1891-1905||?
MoHi S 16 1904-05

LIBERAL. w 1879-86||?
CtY Je 3 1886
MoSHi Je 6 1883;Ja 8 1885

Liberal NEWS. w F 25 1910+
pub 1910+
MoHi 1910-

LIBERTY

Liberty ADVANCE. w 1875+
pub 1895+
MoHi O 31 1890;N 22 1901+
MoLiW 1905-14
MoSHi [Ja-S 1885]Jl 2,Ag 13,S 24,N 12 1886; Ja 28,Ap 15 1910;F 4 1916;N 14 1919

Liberty CHRONICLE. w Ap 27 1933+
MoHi 1933+

CLAY county democrat. w 1894-1904||?
MoHi Jl 25 1901-03

CLAY county flag. w
MoSHi Mr 23 1861

CLAY county progress. w 1888-94||?
MoHi O 22 1890

DEMOCRATIC platform. w 1853-54||
KHi Mr 23-O 5 1854

FAR west. w 1836||?
MoSHi Ag 18 1836

Liberty TRIBUNE. w Ap 4 1846+
pub 1895+
MWA N 18 1853
MoHi 1846-Ap 8 1853(photostat)Je 9 1854;Ja 8 1886;My 1 1896;1903+
MoLiW 1846-86;1908-13
MoLiW 1848-86
MoSHi 1846-Je 18,Jl 23 1852-[60-64]-[86;92-93; 95;97;99;1903;09-10;15;19]

Liberty weekly UNION. w My 10 1867-
MoSHi 1867-My 6 1869

UPPER MISSOURI enquirer. w Ja 11 1834-40||
DLC Ja 11,25 1834
MoSHi Ja 25 1834

WESTERN journal. w Je 1 1838-44||?
1838-41 as Western star
DLC Je 15 1838;Ap 9 1841
MoSHi F 5,My 28 1841;Jl 22 1842

WESTERN pioneer. w My 24 1844-
DLC Je 21 1844
MoSHi N 1 1844

WESTERN star. *See* Western journal

LILBOURN

Lilbourn BANNER. w 1927+
MoHi O 27 1927+

Lilbourn HERALD. w 1912-26||?
MoCaT 1917-19
MoHi 1914-O 1918;25-26

LINCOLN

Lincoln REPUBLICAN. w 1893-1906||?
MoHi Ag 19 1903-06

LINN

OSAGE county news. *See* Unterrified democrat

OSAGE county republican. w N 20 1896+
Follows Aud visitor (Aud)
pub 1896-99;1902-08;11;13+
MoHi 1902-My 1921;25-26

UNTERRIFIED democrat. w Jl 1866+
1866-74 as Osage county news
pub My 1911+
MoHi Ap 19 1906+

LINN CREEK

CAMDEN county news. w D 18 1902-04||?
MoHi 1902-03

CAMDEN county rustic. w 1902-
MoHi D 31 1902-03

CAMDEN county sentinel. *See* Osage Valley sentinel

OSAGE VALLEY sentinel. w 1889-92||?
1889-90? as Camden county sentinel
MoHi Jl 16 1891-92

REVEILLE. *See under* Camdenton

LINNEUS

Linneus BULLETIN. w My 1871+
pub 1871+
MoHi 1899-1900;02+
MoSHi D 14 1898;Jl 1913-Ag 8 1917

LINN county news. w,sw 1881+
w 1881-1914?
pub 1882+
MoHi Jl 25 1901+

Linneus MISSOURIAN. w My? 1865-71||?
MWA D 27 1865
MoHi Je 12 1869

LOCKWOOD

Lockwood LUMINARY. w Ag 1882+
MoHi Jl 26 1901-19;25+

Lockwood MISSOURIAN. w 1901-15||?
MoHi D 29 1904-06;N 1911-Je 1915

LOUISIANA

AMERICAN union. *See* Lousiana journal

DEMOCRATIC banner. w O 16 1833-52||
1833-41 as Salt River journal; 1841-Ja 22? 1845 Radical
1833-Mr 1846 pub in Bowling Green
DLC D 4 1833;O 22 1842
ICHi Ag 23-30 1834;F 20 1841
IHi My 28 1849
MoHi F 26 1835;N 29-D 13,27 1837;F 27,S 1 1838;Ja 5,26 1839;S 18 1841;Ag 10 1844;Mr 15 1845

Louisiana DEMOCRATIC herald. w 1857-
MWA O 15,N 5 1857
MoHi My 21 1857;O 6 1859
MoSHi Ag 4 1859

Louisiana HERALD. w 1896-Ag 1 1903||
MoHi [N 26 1898-99]-1903

Louisiana JOURNAL. w Je 22 1854-Mr 20 1902||
1854-Je 1859 as American union. United with Louisiana Missouri press to form Louisiana press-journal
MoHi Ja 30 1862;Je 19 1869
NcD N 8 1873

Louisiana MISSOURI press. *See* Louisiana press-journal

NORTH-EAST Missourian. d
MoSHi Jl 1,8 1853

PIKE county news. w 1890-Ag 30 1917||
Merged with Twice-a-week times
MoHi Ag 1901-17
WHi Ja 9-Je 1892

Louisiana PRESS-JOURNAL. w 1872+
1872-Ap 16 1885 as Riverside press; Ap 23 1885-Mr 20 1902 Louisiana Missouri press
MoHi My 25 1899+
MoLo 1872+

Louisiana weekly RECORD. w 1849-
MoHi S 29 1851

RIVERSIDE press. *See* Louisiana press-journal

Twice-a-week TIMES. w,sw 1898-O 28 1927||
1898-Mr 9 1906 as Louisiana times (w)
Merged with Louisiana press-journal
MoHi Jl 26 1901-06;F 10 1914-27

TRUE flag. w 1864-Ja 1867||
DLC Jl 22-Ag 5,S 9-O 14,29-N 5 1865

LOWRY CITY

Lowry City INDEPENDENT. w 1888+
pub 1908-Ja 1918]+
MoHi Jl 26 1901-08;10+

LUCERNE

Lucerne STANDARD. w 1888-1917||?
MoHi O 24 1890

LUDLOW

Ludlow HERALD. w 1903-05||?
MoHi Ja 6,Ap 14 1905

LURAY

Luray NEWS. w 1890-
CLM Mr 1890

LUTESVILLE

Lutesville BANNER. w 1891-1922||?
MoCaT 1917-19
MoHi Jl 1903-04[Ag 1916-17]

Lutesville HERALD. w 1872-75||?
1872-74? as Missouri herald
NNHi O 17 1872

MISSOURI herald. *See* Lutesville herald

McFALL

McFall MIRROR. w 1890-1907||?
MoHi O 31 1890;1903

MACK'S CREEK

CENTRAL Missouri leader. w O 8 1902+
pub 1902+

MACON

Macon ARGUS. w 1864-70||?
MWA Ja 31 1866
MoHi Je 19 1867-F 1870

CAMP news (Camp Gilbert) w? S 14 1861-
DLC S 14 1861

Macon daily CHRONICLE-HERALD. d Jl 11 1910+
1910-Ja 13 1916 as Macon daily chronicle
MoHi 1910+

Macon CITIZEN. w 1893-Ag 30 1901||
Merged with Macon republican
MoHi D 1898-1901

Macon DEMOCRAT. w 1883-Ag 23 1901||
United with Macon times to form Macon times-democrat
MoHi N 25 1898-1901

Macon GAZETTE. w Ja 15 1862-
MoHi Ja-Ag 6 1862;Ja 14 1863-My 4 1865

Macon daily HERALD. d N 15 1913-Ja 13 1916||
United with Macon daily chronicle to form Macon daily chronicle-herald
MoHi complete

Weekly Macon JOURNAL. w N 7 1867-75||?
MoHi 1867-O 1868

MISSOURI granger. w Mr 3 1874-76||?
MoHi 1874-Je 1876

NORTH MISSOURI register. w 1870-82||?
MoHi Je 27,O 1879-S 23 1881

OUR whole union; or, the Missouri register. (Union army paper) *See note under* Sunday register and leader

Sunday REGISTER and leader.
My 31 1914 has reprint of Our whole union; or, the Missouri register, for Je 15 1861
MWA My 31 1914

Macon REPUBLICAN. w 1860-Ap 19 1929||
Merged with Macon daily chronicle-herald
MoHi Ap 1871-F 20,Ap 1890-Ag 1891;Ja-Je 1892;93-98;F 1899-1929

Macon TIMES-DEMOCRAT. w 1865-Ja 27 1916||
1865-Ag 1901 as Macon times
MoHi 1889-96;Ag 1901-16

Daily TIMES-DEMOCRAT. d Ja 17- 1916||?
MoHi Ja-N 28 1916

MADISON

ADVANCE. *See* Madison weekly times

Madison weekly TIMES. w 1887+
Follows Watchman. 1887-Jl 1893? as Advance
pub My 9,Ag 11 1889;Jl 21 1892;1903+
MoHi Jl 25 1901+

WATCHMAN. w 1885-86||
Followed by Advance, later Madison weekly times
MoMdT Je 17 1886

MISSOURI (*Continued*)

MAITLAND

Maitland HERALD. w 1887+
pub 1921+
MoHi O 30 1890;Ag 1901-17

MALDEN

DUNKLIN county news. *See* Dunklin news

DUNKLIN news. w 1886-1912‖?
1886-96? as Dunklin county news
MoHi O 24 1890;Jl 1901-12

Malden MERIT. w 1904+
MoCaT 1917-19

MALTA BEND

Malta Bend COMMUNITY weekly. *See* Saline county republican

Malta Bend NEWS. w Ap 9 1909-10‖?
MoHi Ap-O,D 1909-10

Malta Bend QUI VIVE. w 1887-1908‖?
MoHi O 17 1890;Jl 26 1901-08

SALINE county republican. w 1926-D 28 1933‖
1926-N 1931 as Malta Bend community weekly. Followed by Saline county record (Marshall)
D 14-28 1933 pub at Marshall
MoHi Ap 1930-33

MANSFIELD

Mansfield MAIL. w 1894-1908‖?
O 28-D 1899? as Mansfield republican
MoHi D 1898-O 1899;Ja 22-D 17 1904;O 14,28 1905;F 24-D 1906

Mansfield MIRROR. w 1909+
MoHi D 26 1912+

Mansfield PRESS. w O 9 1908-12‖?
MoHi 1908-09

Mansfield REPUBLICAN. *See* Mansfield mail

MAPLEWOOD

Maplewood CHAMPION. See Maplewood news-champion

Maplewood HERALD. w
MoSHi F-Mr 15 1912

Maplewood JOURNAL.
MoSHi S 9 1911

Maplewood NEWS. w -Ja 1914‖?
United with Maplewood champion to form Maplewood news-champion
MoSHi [1912]Ja 10-17,Mr 21 1913

Maplewood NEWS-champion. w D 12 1912+
1912-Ja 2 1914 as Maplewood champion
MoCaT 1917-19
MoHi 1912+
MoSHi 1912[13-14]-[17]

MARBLE HILL

Marble Hill BANNER-PRESS. w 1881+
1881-My 10 1923 as Marble Hill press
MoCaT 1906+
MoHi Jl 1901+
MoSHi D 31 1903;Ag 26 1915

BOLLINGER county standard. *See* Missouri standard

MISSOURI standard. w 1868-74‖?
1868-73? as Bollinger county standard
MoCaT Ag 29,N 7 1868
MoHi Mr 24 1870

Marble Hill PRESS. *See* Marble Hill banner-press

MARCELINE

Marceline HERALD. w 1913-My 29 1929‖
United with Marceline journal-mirror to form Marceline news
MoHi My 30-Je 6 1913;14-S 15 1916;Mr 1917-29

Marceline JOURNAL-MIRROR. w 1888-My 29 1929‖
1888-1912? as Marceline journal. United with Marceline herald to form Marceline news
MoHi O 23 1890;F 24 1898-Je 1900

Marceline MIRROR. w 1888-1912‖?
United with Marceline journal to form Marceline journal-mirror
MoHi O 31 1890

Marceline NEWS. w Je 7 1929+
Formed by the union of Marceline herald and Marceline journal-mirror
MoHi 1929+
MoM 1930+

MARIONVILLE

BUZZ SAW. *See* Marionville free press

Marionville COMMERCIAL. *See* Marionville free press

Marionville FREE PRESS. w 1883+
1883-85? as Marionville commercial; 1886?-89? Buzz saw; 1890-93? Marionville republican
pub 1883+
MoHi O 24 1890;Jl 8 1903-S 1904;13+

Marionville REPUBLICAN. *See* Marionville free press

MARSHALL

Marshall BANNER. w 1868-
MoHi Je 4 1869

Marshall CAPITAL. w 1888-92‖?
KHi Ja 4 1889

Marshall DEMOCRAT. w
MoSHi Ja 15 1858-F 20 1861

Weekly DEMOCRAT-NEWS. w 1873-O 22 1931‖
1873-88? as Saline county democrat. Merged with Saline county citizen
MoHi D 24 1898-1931

Daily DEMOCRAT-NEWS. d Je 28 1879+
1879-88? as Daily news
pub 1879+
CLM Je 7 1888
MoHi My 22 1903;D 8 1908;Ap 8 1909;Ja 19 1932+
MoMaM 1928+

Daily NEWS. *See* Daily democrat-news

Marshall REPUBLICAN. w 1892-1914‖?
1892-My 1899 as Saline republican
MoHi D 23 1898-1914

SALINE citizen. w *See* Saline county citizen

SALINE county citizen. sw,w S 6 1894+
1894-1930? as Saline citizen
sw 1896-1900?
pub 1894+
MoHi 1901-18;My 15 1931+

SALINE county democrat. *See* Weekly democrat-news

SALINE county index. w 1874-1905‖?
MoHi Mr 1900-05
MoSHi Jl 7 1904

SALINE county progress. w Je 1865-Jl 1917‖
MoHi Je 25 1869;1902-17
MoMaD complete

SALINE county record. w Ja 4 1934+
Follows Saline county republican (Malta Bend)
MoHi 1934+

SALINE county republican. *See under* Malta Bend

SALINE republican. *See* Marshall republican

MARSHFIELD

Marshfield ADVERTISER. w 1869-
MoHi Ag 26 1869

Marshfield CHRONICLE. w 1877-1926‖?
MoHi Jl 30 1908-09;11-S 1920

Marshfield DEMOCRAT. w D 25 1869-79‖?
MoHi D 25 1869;Ja 15 1870

Marshfield HERALD. w 1930?+
pub 1930+
MoMar 1933+

Marshfield MAIL. w 1892+
pub D 1892+
MoHi Ag 1901+
MoMar 1923+

MISSOURI yeoman. w 1866-70‖?
MoHi Je 5 1869

REPUBLICAN standard. w 1884-92‖?
1884-91? as Webster standard
MoHi O 17 1890

WEBSTER standard. *See* Republican standard

MARTHASVILLE

Marthasville RECORD. w 1898+
pub 1898+
MoHi Jl-D 18 1903;27+

MARTINSBURG

AUDRAIN county oracle. *See* Martinsburg monitor

Martinsburg ENTERPRISE. w 1901-04‖?
MoHi 1903-Ja 7 1904

Martinsburg MONITOR. w 1900?+
1900?-F 1908 as Martinsburg sunbeam; F 1908-N 10 1919? Audrain country oracle
pub 1920+

Martinsburg SUNBEAM. *See* Martinsburg monitor

MARYVILLE

Weekly DEMOCRAT-FORUM. w N 13 1869+
1869-Je 2 1910 as Nodaway democrat; Je 16 1910-24 as Democrat-forum; 1925-My 15 1929 as Weekly democrat-forum and Maryville tribune
pub 1869+
MoHi D 9 1880;N 24 1898+
OClWHi Jl 13 1876
—d ed *See* Maryville daily forum

Daily DEMOCRAT-FORUM. *See* Maryville daily forum

Maryville daily FORUM. d Je 4 1910+
1910-Ap 1925? as Daily democrat-forum; My 1925-My 21 1929 Democrat-forum and Maryville tribune
pub 1910+
MoHi Ag 1915+
MoMaryT 1930+
—w ed *See* Weekly democrat-forum

NODAWAY county republican. *See* Maryville republican

NODAWAY democrat. *See* Weekly democrat-forum

NODAWAY forum. w 1900-Je 1910‖?
United with Nodaway democrat to form Weekly democrat-forum
MoHi S 1903-Je,O 21-D 1909
MoMaryF 1903-10

Maryville REPUBLICAN. w Ag 2 1870-Je 9 1910‖
1874-79? as Nodaway county republican. Merged with Democrat-forum, later Weekly democrat-forum
MoHi 1870-Jl 12,N 29, D 13-20 1894;99-1910
MoSHi Ja 30 1908
NNHi D 19 1872

Maryville REPUBLICAN. d 1906-10‖?
MoHi O 19 1908-Ag 3 1909

Maryville TRIBUNE. w 1887-My 1925‖?
United with Democrat-forum to form Weekly democrat-forum and Maryville tribune, later Weekly democrat-forum
MoMary Ap 1896-Ag 18 1899;F 27-D 1902
MoMaryF complete

Daily TRIBUNE. d 1900-My 2 1925‖
United with Daily democrat-forum to form Democrat-forum and Maryville tribune, later Maryville daily forum
MoHi Ja 24,F 7 1905;13-25

MAYSVILLE

DE KALB county democrat. w 1896-1914‖?
MoHi D 8 1898-99;Ag 1901-O 1903

DE KALB county herald. w 1866+
MoHi Ag 18 1904;Ap 23 1925+

DE KALB county record-journal. w O 18 1928+
Formed by the union of Stewartsville record (Stewartsville) and Clarksdale journal (Clarksdale)
MoHi 1928+

DE KALB county republican. *See* De Kalb county sun

DE KALB county sun. w 1877-1924‖?
1877-83? as De Kalb county republican; 1884?-D 5 1912 Republican pilot; D 12 1912-13? Maysville pilot
MoHi N 24 1898-Ag 1899;Ag 1901-20

Maysville PILOT. *See* De Kalb county sun

Maysville REGISTER. w 1867-80‖?
1867-70 as Weekly western register
MoHi My 28 1868-S 8 1875
NbHi F 16 1876

REPUBLICAN pilot. *See* De Kalb county sun

STEWARTSVILLE record. *See under* Stewartsville

Weekly WESTERN register. *See* Maysville register

MEADVILLE

Meadville MESSENGER. w 1881+
pub 1915+
MoHi N 24 1898-Jl 1900;Ap-D 1905;Mr 6 1919+

MEMPHIS

Daily CHRONICLE. d 1899-1904‖?
MoHi F 5,O 27 1902

Memphis CONSERVATIVE. w 1866-81‖?
MoHi F 26 1869-Jl 16 1874;N 23 1876-Jl 1 1880

Memphis DEMOCRAT. w 1873+
1873-79? as Scotland county democrat
pub 1900+
MoHi Jl 1901+

FARMERS' union. *See* Herald-democrat

GREENBACK tribune. w Ag 21 1880-
MoHi Ag 21-S,O 9-23 1880

HERALD-DEMOCRAT. w 1891-96‖?
1891-Ja 24 1895 as Farmers' union; Ja 31 1895-Ja 1896? Herald
MoHi 1891-Ja 1896

NATIONAL. w 1882-88‖?
MoHi N 16 1882-N 22 1888

NATIONAL democrat. w 1859-65‖
Followed by Memphis reveille

PEOPLE'S messenger. w 1891-98‖?
IaHi Mr 26 1896-Je 17 1897
MoHi Mr 19 1896-F 1898

REGISTER. w D 20 1888-90‖?
MoHi 1888-Ja 1890

Memphis REVEILLE. w S 9 1865+
Follows National democrat
pub 1865+
MoHi O 26 1871;Ag 13 1874;O 23 1890;D 1898-Ag 10 1916;Mr 1917+

SCOTLAND county democrat. *See* Memphis democrat

SCOTLAND county news. w S 10 1873-79‖?
MoHi 1873-O 9 1879

Semi-weekly STAR. sw 1901-03‖?
MoHi N 6 1901-F 1903

MENDON

Mendon CITIZEN. w 1889-1904‖?
MoHi 1902-03

Mendon CONSTITUTION. w 1904+
pub Je 1925+
MoHi Ja 10 1914+

MERCER

Mercer SEARCHLIGHT. *See* Princeton post (Princeton)

MISSOURI (*Continued*)

MERWIN

Merwin CLIPPER. w 1904-11||?
MoHi S 15 1904

META

Meta HEADLIGHT. *See* Meta herald

Meta HERALD. w O 27 1902+
1902-17 as Meta headlight
pub 1902+
MoHi Mr 1923+

METZ

Metz TIMES. w Ja 2 1902+
pub 1902+

MEXICO

AUDRAIN county banner. w 1858-61||
MoHi Ap 1861

AUDRAIN county press. *See* Mexico press

INTELLIGENCER. w 1855+
pub [1880—]
MoHi 1902+
MoSHi 1903-Ag 3 1916;F 1 1917

Daily INTELLIGENCER. d 1880+
pub [1880+]
MoHi Jl 27 1903-Je,D 19 1908;09+

Mexico weekly LEDGER. w 1865+
1865-67? as North Missouri messenger; 1868-76? Missouri messenger
pub 1876+
DLC My 2 1867
MoHi O 23 1890;D 29 1892;99+
MoSHi S 29 1927

Mexico evening LEDGER. d 1886+
pub 1886+
MoHi Ag 1901+
MoSHi Ap 21,Jl 3 1913

MISSOURI citizen. w
MoSHi Je 5 1863

Mexico MISSOURI message. w 1899-1919||?
MoHi Ja 15 1903-N 7 1918

MISSOURI messenger. *See* Mexico weekly ledger

NORTH Missouri messenger. *See* Mexico weekly ledger

Mexico PRESS. w 1879-83||?
1879-82? as Audrain county press
MoHi Ja 1 1880

MIAMI

CABLE. *See* Miami weekly news

Miami DEMOCRAT-NEWS. w Mr 3 1921-22||?
Not to be confused with Miami weekly news
MoHi 1921-Ap 13 1922

Miami INDEX. *See* Miami weekly news

Miami weekly NEWS. w My 7 1870-D 28 1922||
1870-73? as Cable; 1874?-80? Miami index
MoHi My 7 1870;O 25 1890;99-1922

MIDDLETOWN

CHIPS. w 1882+
MoHi Ag 21 1903-09

MILAN

Milan weekly ACORN. w 1872-73||?
NNHi N 15 1872

Milan RADICAL. w 1864?-
OClWHi S 28 1865

Milan REPUBLICAN. w F 19 1875+
pub 1875+
MoHi Mr 1875-F 1888;Jl 25 1901+

Milan STANDARD. w 1872+
1872-88? as Sullivan standard
MoHi O 24 1890;1903-04;Ag 27 1908;13+

SULLIVAN standard. *See* Milan standard

MILLER

Miller NEWS-HERALD. w Ja 1916-D 10 1925||
1916-19 as Spring River news (La Russell)
MoHi Mr 15 1917-25

MIRABILE

HAMPTON'S Mirabile mercury. w 1895-98||?
MoHi F 4,18 Mr 4,18-Ap 8,22-My 6,Je 3,17-24 1898

MISSOURI CITY

Missouri City HERALD. w Je 25 1869-
MoHi Je 25 1869
MoSHi 1869-Jl 2 1870

MOBERLY

Moberly weekly DEMOCRAT. w 1871-1915||?
1871-89? as Moberly headlight
MoHi O 16 1908

Moberly evening DEMOCRAT. d 1873-Mr 1925||
1873-89? as Moberly headlight. United with Moberly daily monitor-index to form Moberly daily Monitor-index and democrat
MoHi O 28 1890;N 25 1903-06;O 15,N 1908-25
MoMoM complete

Moberly DEMOCRAT leader. w Ap 1926-32||?
1926-Ja 29 1932 as Moberly home press
MoHi 1926-Je 17 1932

Moberly HEADLIGHT. 1871-89 *See* Moberly democrat

Moberly HEADLIGHT. w 1891-1902||?
McHi Ag 1901-02

Moberly HOME press. *See* Moberly democrat leader

Moberly daily INDEX. *See* Moberly daily monitor-index and democrat

Moberly MESSAGE. w Ap 1930+
MoHi My 1930+

Moberly MONITOR, sw,w 1871-My 19 1932||
w 1908-10
MoHi O 23 1890;1903-10;16-32

Moberly daily MONITOR. d 1873-Je 1919||
United with Moberly daily index to form Moberly daily monitor-index, later Moberly daily monitor-index and democrat
MoHi O 12,16 1908
MoMoM complete
MoSHi Jl 3 1899

Moberly daily MONITOR-INDEX and democrat. d 1916+
1916-Je 1919 as Moberly daily index; Jl 1919-Mr 1925 Moberly daily monitor-index
pub 1916+
MoHi D 31 1918+

Saturday SENTINEL. w 1890-91||?
MoHi O 25 1890

Moberly SIGNAL. *See* La Plata home press (La Plata)

Moberly TRIBUNE. w 1904-06||?
MoHi D 22 1904-05

MOKANE

Mokane HERALD. *See* Mokane Missourian

Mokane MISSOURIAN. w 1894+
1894 as Mokane herald; 1895-98 Mokane times-herald; 1899-1900? Mokane herald; 1901?-Je 1 1909 Herald-post
pub 1899+
MoHi Jl 23 1901-08;10-20;Jl 1922-25;Ap 1926-27;30+

Mokane TIMES-HERALD. *See* Mokane Missourian

MONETT

Monett EAGLE. w 1888-1906||?
MoHi O 31 1890;Ag 1903-Je 1904

Monett daily RECORD. w 1902-15||?
1902-13? as Monet daily star
MoHi Ap 10 1906-My 8 1911;14-Ag 20 1915
MoSHi Ja 14 1915

Monett daily STAR. *See* Monett daily record

Monett TIMES. w S 7 1899+
pub 1899+
MoHi Je 25 1903-Je 2 1904;My 29 1908,13+

Monett TIMES. d 1908+
pub 1908+
MoMon 1927+

MONROE CITY

Monroe City APPEAL. *See* Monroe county appeal (Paris)

Monroe City DEMOCRAT. w 1888-1923||?
MoHi D 1893-1919

Monroe City NEWS. w,sw 1875+
1910-Ja 10 1930 as Semi-weekly news (sw)
MoHi O 30 1890;1903;14+

MONTGOMERY CITY

MONTGOMERY county republican. w 1892-1900||?
MoHi N 25 1898-S 21 1900

MONTGOMERY standard. w 1869+
MoHi 1880-1901;Mr 1902+
MoSHi Jl 31 1908
NNHi D 26 1872

MONTGOMERY tribune. w 1892-1910||?
MoHi 1901-10

MONTICELLO

LEWIS county journal. w 1878+
D 27 1907-Je 1908 as Observer
pub at Canton, dated at Monticello O 10 1929+
pub 1881+
MoC N 16 1833+
MoHi O 1889+

OBSERVER. *See* Lewis county journal

MONTROSE

Montrose RECORDER. w 1899-1918||?
MoHi Jl 26 1901-Ag 1918

Montrose SIGNAL. w 1891-93||?
MoHi N 12 1891

Montrose TIDINGS. w D 26 1918+
pub 1919+
MoHi 1918-Ja 1928;Ja 17 1929+

MOREHOUSE

Morehouse HUSTLER. w Mr 8 1907-19||?
MoCaT 1917-19
MoHi Mr 15 1907-10

MORLEY

SCOTT county banner. w 1895-1921||?
MoCaT 1917-19
MoHi 1914-Ag 1921

SCOTT county citizen. w 1903-09||?
1903-Mr 1908 pub in Oran
MoHi O 18 1907-09

MORRISVILLE

Morrisville JOURNAL. w 1910-18||?
MoHi Ja 12 1912-13

Polk county advocate. w S 19 1923-Je 26 1924||

MOUND CITY

HOLT county democrat and the Craig leader. w N 1886+
1886-1932 as Craig leader (Craig)
Suspended from Jl 12-N 15 1907
MoHi N 14 1890;O 9 1903-[06]21—

HOLT county independent. w Je 4 1927-Ag 30 1929||
United with Mound City news-Jeffersonian to form Mound City news-independent
MoHi S 22 1927-29

JEFFERSONIAN. w 1891-Ja 29 1914||
United with Mound City news, to form Mound City news-Jeffersonian, later Mound City news-independent
MoHi N 24 1898-Mr 1900;Jl 1903-14

Mound City JOURNAL. w 1915-D 24 1925||
MoHi complete

Mound City NEWS-INDEPENDENT. w 1879+
1879-Ja 1914 as Mound City news; F 1914-Ag 1929 Mound City news-Jeffersonian
pub 1884+
MoHi Jl 1901+

MOUNDVILLE

Moundville TIMES. w 1890-93||?
MoHi O 30 1890

MOUNT VERNON

Mount Vernon ERA. d N 13 1905-07||?
MoHi 1905-[Ja-Mr 1907]

FOUNTAIN and journal. w 1867-1916||?
MoHi O 9 1890;1903;Je 19 1914

LAWRENCE chieftain. w Mr 1 1876+
pub 1876+
MoHi Jl 2 1914;19+

LAWRENCE county record. w 1898+
MoHi Jl 25 1901-Je 1902;My 1903-Jl 1904;05-Ag 1913;Jl 2 1914

PROGRESSIVE era. w Jl 3 1914-
MoHi Jl 3 1914

MOUNTAIN GROVE

Mountain Grove ENTERPRISE. w 1903-
MoHi N 26-D 1903

Mountain Grove JOURNAL. w 1897+
Follows Mountain prospect
pub 1899+
MoHi D 1898-O 1900;Jl 1901—

MOUNTAIN prospect. w Mr 31 1882-94||?
Followed by Mountain Grove journal
MoHi O 10,31 1890
MoMgJ 1883-Je 1894

MOUNTAIN VIEW

POSTMAN. w 1901-05||?
MoHi Jl 1903-[Ja-S 16 1904]

Mountain View STANDARD. w D 4 1908+
pub 1909+

NEOSHO

Neosho daily DEMOCRAT. d Ja 25 1905+
pub 1905+
MoHi F 6-Jl 22 1913;Jl 17 1914

Neosho FREE press. w 1902-
MoHi O 9 1903-04

INVESTIGATOR. w N 24 1869-70||?
MoHi N 24 1869;Mr 31 1870

Neosho JOURNAL. w 1871?-81||?
MWA Je 8 1871
WHi D 26 1872

MINER and mechanic. w 1873+
1873-77 as Granby miner (Granby)
pub 1890+
MoHi Jl 1903+

MISSOURI army argus. *See under* Corinth, Miss.

NEWTON county tribune. w 1866-
MoHi Je 9 1869

Neosho TIMES. w N 1869+
pub 1869+
MoBoH Mr 1897
MoHi N 6 1890;N 24 1898-99;Ag 1901+

NEVADA

Nevada DIRECTOR. w 1892-99||?
MoHi Jl 20-N 2 1894[Ap 15 1897-F 3 1898]
WHi Ap 22 1897

MISSOURI (*Continued*)

NEVADA—*Continued*

Nevada daily DIRECTOR. d Ja 22 1894-
MoHi S 22-N 6 1894

Nevada HERALD. w 1888+
pub 1888+

INDUSTRIAL review. w 1890||?
MoHi O 31 1890

Nevada daily MAIL and post. d 1895+
1895-1917? as Nevada daily mail
KHi D 29 1924

Nevada NOTICER. w 1886-94||?
MoHi N 6 1890

Weekly POST. w 1868-O 1917||
United with Southwest mail to form Southwest mail and post
MoHi Jl 1901-17

SOUTHWEST mail and post. w 1879+
1879-O 1917 as Southwest mail
MoHi Jl 1901-15;20+

NEW BLOOMFIELD

New Bloomfield NEWS. w 1901+
MoHi Je 1903-Je 1905;Jl 1912-20;24+

NEW CAMBRIA

New Cambria LEADER. w 1913+
MoHi Mr 25 1927+

New Cambria PRESS. w 1888-91||?
MoHi O 25 1890

NEW FLORENCE

MONTGOMERY county leader. w 1887+
pub 1887+
MoHi O 31 1890;D 1898-1902;06+

OPTIC. w 1877-90||?
MoHi O 24 1890

NEW FRANKLIN

New Franklin NEWS. w 1893+
MoHi N 25 1898-Mr 1900;Jl 1903-Jl 1904;13+

NEW HAMPTON

New Hampton HERALD. w 1896-1920||?
MoHi Jl 25 1901-Je 1920

NEW HAVEN

New Haven LEADER. w 1895+
MoCaT 1917-19
MoHi Jl 1903-Ja 1904;13+

New Haven NOTES. w 1885-98||?
MoHi Ja 18,F 8,Ag 9,N 29,D 27 1889;Ag 10 1894

NEW LONDON

RALLS county record. w Je 29 1865+
pub [1865+]
MoHi Jl 26 1901-07;Ja-F,Mr 13 1908;09+

RALLS county times. w 1898-1916||?
MoHi Ap 20 1906-Je 2 1916

NEW MADRID

HEADLIGHT. *See* Southeast Missourian (Portageville)

JOURNAL of the times. w
MoSHi Je 24-Jl 1 1853

Weekly RECORD. w 1867+
pub 1898+
MoCaT 1907+
MoHi N 15 1890;N 1901-10;13+
MoPoM 1880+
MoSHi F 22-Mr 7,28 1908[09]Ap 27 1912

SOUTHEAST Missourian. *See under* Portageville

NEWBURG

PHELPS county record. w Ja 30 1914-1922||?
MoHi 1914-O 1921;Ja-N 1922

NEWTONIA

NEWTON county news. w 1890-1906||?
MoHi O 30 1890;1903-06

NOEL

NOEL-OZARK press. w My 24 1929+
pub 1929+

NORBORNE

Norborne DEMOCRAT-LEADER. w Ja 1 1902+
1902-Jl 1923 as Norborne democrat
MoHi Ag 10 1923+

JEFFERSONIAN. w 1888-1900||?
United with Norborne leader to form Leader-Jeffersonian
MoHi D 1898-1900

Norborne LEADER. w 1884-Jl 31 1923||
1901-04? as Leader-Jeffersonian. United with Norborne democrat to form Norborne democrat-leader
MoHi O 24-31 1890;Jl 1903-Ag 1904;Ja 5-12,S 21-N 30,D 21-28 1905;Ja 11 1906-22

NORTH KANSAS CITY

CLAY county news. *See* North Kansas City news

INDUSTRIAL press. w S 1930+
MoP D 1933+

North Kansas City NEWS. w Je 15 1920+
1920-Je 1923 as Clay county news
pub 1920+
MoHi Ap 17 1930+

NOVINGER

Novinger FREE press. *See* Novinger herald

Novinger HERALD. w 1904+
1904?-12? as Novinger record; 1913?-14? Novinger free press
MoHi Ap 1906-Ja 21 1910;F 28 1913-Ag 1916

Novinger RECORD. *See* Novinger herald

OAK GROVE

Oak Grove BANNER. w Ag 1889+
pub 1889+
MoHi Jl 27 1901+

OAKRIDGE

INDICATOR. w S 6 1906-11||?
MoHi 1906-10

ODESSA

ADAIR'S Odessa democrat. w S 1883+
1883-1910? as Odessa democrat
pub 1905+
MoHi O 3 1890;N 1901+

Odessa DEMOCRAT. *See* Adair's Odessa democrat

MISSOURI ledger. w 1892+
MoHi 1914+

Odessa ORACLE. w Jl 1901-03||?
MoHi F 27 1902-Mr 19 1903

ORAN

SCOTT county citizen. *See under* Morley

OREGON

HOLT county sentinel. w Je 30 1865+
MoHi S 10 1869;O 31 1890;O 7 1898;Jl 1901+
MoSHi 1865-Je 1869

ORONOGO

Oronogo INDEX. w 1896-1908||?
MoHi Jl 26 1901-06

ORRICK

Orrick TIMES. w Ap 15 1891+
pub 1928+
MoHi Jl 9 1896

OSBORN

Osborn ENTERPRISE. w 1894+
MoHi 1916+

Osborn INVESTIGATOR. w 1873-91||?
IU S 8 1888
MoHi N 1 1890

OSCEOLA

Osceola DEMOCRAT. 1859-60 *See* Osage Valley star

Osceola DEMOCRAT. 1871-76 *See* St. Clair county democrat

Osceola HERALD. w 1866-74||?
MoHi Je 17 1869

Osceola INDEPENDENT. w
MoSHi Ja 18 1851;O 30,D 25 1852[Ja-Ag 1853]

MISSOURI army argus. *See under* Corinth, Miss.

OSAGE VALLEY star. w 1859-61||
1859-Jl 1860? as Osceola democrat
MoHi Je,Jl 12,N 8 1860-F 1861

ST. CLAIR county democrat. w Jl 1 1870+
1870-76? as Osceola democrat; 1877?-78? Sentinel-democrat; 1879-92? Osceola sun
MoHi 1906+

ST. CLAIR county republican. w S 5 1888+
MoHi Jl 9 1908;14+

Osceola SENTINEL. w 1875-76||?
United with Osceola democrat to form Sentinel-democrat, later St. Clair county democrat

SENTINEL-DEMOCRAT. *See* St. Clair county democrat

Osceola SUN. *See* St. Clair county democrat

OTTERVILLE

Otterville MAIL. w 1892-1924||?
MoHi D 9 1898-1902

OWENSVILLE

Owensville ARGUS. w My 8 1903-05||
United with Republican banner to form Gasconade county republican
MoHi 1903-04
MoOR complete

GASCONADE county republican. w 1905+
Formed by union of Republican banner and Owensville argus
pub 1905+
MoCaT 1917-19
MoHi 1910+

REPUBLICAN banner. w 1897-1905||
United with Owensville argus to form Gasconade republican
MoHi 1903-05
MoOR complete

OZARK

CHRISTIAN county republican. w My 1888+
MoHi N 24 1898-1911;13+

Ozark DEMOCRAT. w 1900-28||?
MoHi Jl 17 1908

Ozark DEMOCRAT. *See* Ozark news-leader

Weekly MAIL. w 1890-91||?
MoHi O 24 1890

Ozark NEWS. w 1884?-93||?
WHi O 15 1885

Ozark NEWS-LEADER. w My 1900+
1900-S 6 1929 as Ozark democrat
pub 1900+

Ozark TRIBUNE. w Je 22 1905-08||?
MoHi 1905-08

PACIFIC

Pacific CITY herald. w 1880-91||?
MoHi F 21 1889;Ja 2,30,Ap 3,S 11-18,N 6,D 11, 25 1890-Ja 1 1891

MERAMEC VALLEY transcript. w S 11 1891+
1891-1924? as Transcript; 1925?-Ja 16 1931 Pacific transcript; Ja 23? 1931-N 1 1932 Plowman-transcript; N 8 1932-O 6 1933 Pacific transcript
MoCaT 1917-19
MoHi Jl 26 1901+

Pacific PLOWMAN. w -Ja 16 1931||
United with Pacific transcript to form Plowman-transcript, later Meramec Valley transcript

PLOWMAN-TRANSCRIPT. *See* Meramec Valley transcript

Pacific TRANSCRIPT. *See* Meramec Valley transcript

PALMYRA

Palmyra COURIER. *See* Missouri courier

MARION county herald. w Ja 1882-1925||?
MoHi O 30 1890;N 24 1898-Je 1921;O 1922-24

MARION county standard. w Ag 9 1933+
MoHi 1933+

MISSOURI courier. *See* Hannibal courier (Hannibal)

MISSOURI whig. *See* Palmyra spectator

SOUTHERN sentinel. w Ap 16 1856-58||
United with Palmyra weekly whig, later Palmyra spectator
MoHi Ap 23 1856-S 15 1858

Palmyra SPECTATOR. w Ag 3 1839+
1839-N 27 1841 as Missouri whig and general advertiser; D 14 1841-53? Missouri whig; 1854-Ap 3 1863 Palmyra weekly whig
pub 1839+
DLC O 31 1840
MWA Ap 11 1873
MnHi Ap 2 1846
MoHi 1839-45(photostat)[1852-53]Je 1856-S 2 1858;90;F 28 1896;99;1901+
MoSHi O 15 1846;Je 17 1852;Ag 12 1908-O 1916

Palmyra weekly WHIG. *See* Palmyra spectator

PARIS

Paris MERCURY. w 1837+
1837-72 as Paris sentinel
MWA Mr 30 1866
MoHi Ag 8 1846;N 23 1853;Ja 3 1862;My 22,Jl 3 1863;Ja 29 1864;Mr 10,N 22 1865;My 11 1866;My 12,Ag 4,D 1,22 1868;Ap 6,My 18,Je 15 1869;Ja 25 1870;N 21 1871;Ag 12 1873;Ja 14 1887;O 31 1890;Je 1901+

MONROE county appeal. w O 6 1865+
1865-72 as Monroe City appeal (Monroe City)
pub 1874+
MoHi 1903;Jl 1906+

Paris SENTINEL. *See* Paris mercury

PARKVILLE

Parkville INDEPENDENT. *See* Platte county gazette

PLATTE county gazette. w Mr 1885+
1885-Jl 6 1899 as Parkville independent
pub 1885+
MoHi D 16 1897-1900;S 1901+
MoP 1924+

Weekly SOUTHERN democrat. w Je 9 1855-
KHi Je 30 1855

MISSOURI (*Continued*)

PARMA

NEW MADRID county courier. w My 28 1908-21||?
1908-13? as Parma victor. Followed by Parma press
MoCaT 1917-19
MoHi Jl 1908-Je 1909

Parma PRESS. w 1921-27||?
Follows New Madrid county courier

Parma VICTOR. *See* New Madrid county courier

PARNELL

NODAWAY county times. w 1891-93||
Followed by Ravenwood gazette (Ravenwood)
MoRG complete

Parnell SENTINEL. w 1894-1922||?
MoHi D 1898-O 1909;10-22

PATTERSON

MISSOURI weekly. w
MoCaT Ap 15-S 3 1868

PATTONSBURG

Pattonsburg CALL. w S 6 1881+
MoHi 1902+

STAR-PRESS. w 1895-99||?
1895? as Star
MoHi N 25 1898-99

PERRY

Perry ENTERPRISE. w Ja 26 1899+
pub 1899+
MoHi O 30 1890;My 10 1906+

PERRYVILLE

Perryville CHRONICLE. w 1885-
KHi Ja 10,F 7 1889

NEW era. w My 22 1913-22||?
1913-18? as New republican era
MoCaT 1917-19
MoHi Je 19 1913-My 4 1922

NEW republican era. *See* New era

PERRY county republican. w S 1889+
MoCaT 1917-19
MoHi Jl 25 1901+

PERRY county sun. w 1880+
MoCaT 1906+
MoHi O 31 1890; D22 1904;F 23 1933+

Weekly Perryville UNION. w Je 1862-82|
1862? as Conservative (Fredericktown)
Merged with Perry county sun
MoHi Jl 2 1869

PIEDMONT

Piedmont weekly BANNER. w Je 1 1892-N 1919||
United with Wayne county journal to form Wayne county journal-banner
MoCaT 1917-19
MoHi S 17 1903;14-19
MoPiJ 1893-1919

JOURNAL-BANNER. *See* Wayne county journal-banner

WAYNE county journal-banner. w 1876+
1876-N 1919 as Wayne county journal; D 1919-Ja 1925 Wayne county journal-banner; F 1925 Journal-banner 1876-1919 pub in Greenville
pub 1876+
MoCaT 1917-19
MoHi O 16-23 1890;My 1902-Ag 1904;05-07;09+

PIERCE CITY

Pierce City DEMOCRAT. w 1884-1904||?
MoHi 1903

Pierce City EMPIRE. w 1875-1902||?
MoHi D 1898-1900

Pierce City daily EMPIRE. d 1881-1905||?
MoSHi Ag 1 1900

Pierce City JOURNAL. w O 12 1901-Ja 10 1919||
1901-16? as Southwest journal. United with Pierce City leader to form Leader-journal
KHi 1901
MoHi Je 1906-19

LEADER-JOURNAL. w 1905+
1905-Ja 10 1919 as Pierce City leader
pub 1905+
MoHi F 1913-Ap 1926;F 10 1927+

SOUTHWEST journal. *See* Pierce City journal

PILOT GROVE

COOPER county leader. w 1882-92||?
MoHi Mr 27 D 1890;N 27 1891;Ja 8-15,29,F 19,Mr 4,Ap 1,15,My 13,27 1892

Pilot Grove ENTERPRISE. w 1899-1907||?
MoHi Jl 25 1901-My, N 1905-Ja 1907

Pilot Grove HERALD. w 1882-1900||?
MoHi 1892-N 17 1893

Pilot Grove RECORD. w 1881+
MoHi D 24 1909-Ag 1916;S 25 1931+

PINEVILLE

Pineville DEMOCRAT. w 1875+
1875-N 1893 as Pineville news
MoHi 1899+
MoPinH Mr 1883-N 1893
MoSHi Je 27 1903

Pineville HERALD. w N 1894+
Suspended from 1898-S 1901
pub 1894+
MoHi 1903+

INDEPENDENT. w 1890-91||?
MoHi O 25 1890

MISSOURI army argus. *See under* Corinth, Miss.

Pineville NEWS. *See* Pineville democrat

REPUBLICAN. w Jl 15 1904-05||?
MoHi 1904-F 17 1905

PLATTE CITY

Platte City ATLAS. w Ap 4 1857-Ja 1864||
Suspended from 1861-S 5 1863
MoHi S 5,O 3-10,31,D 19 1863;Ja 30 1864

LANDMARK. w S 28 1865+
1865-78 as Platte county landmark
1865-Je 1871 pub in Weston
pub 1871-73;90+
MoHi [1866]F 8,Jl 15,Ag 30,S 13,O 18 1867;Mr 1898-1915;Ja-Jl 1917;Jl 1921-Ag 1925

PLATTE argus. *See* Platte county conservator

PLATTE county argus. *See under* Weston

PLATTE county conservator. w 1842-64|
-N? 1842 as Platte eagle; D 1842-F 1844 Platte eagle and Weston gazette; Mr 1844-Je 14? 1862 Platte argus (1856? as Weston weekly Platte argus)
Suspended several months in 1862
D 1842-F 1844;56? pub in Weston
DLC S 26 1845;S 24 1847;O 31-N 14,D 1856
IHi F 26 1847
MoHi Ja 10,F 21,Mr 7,21,Ap 4 1863
MoSHi [1848-F 16 1849]Jl 19-D 6 1862

PLATTE county landmark. *See* Landmark

PLATTE county reveille. w Jl 6 1866-Je 1871||
Merged with Landmark
MoHi Jl 12 1867
MoPlL 1866-69

PLATTE county sentinel. w 1862-Jl 1864||
1862-F 1864 pub in Weston
MoHi Mr 24,Ap 7,Je 23 1864
MoSHi My 14 1863

PLATTE eagle. *See* Platte county conservator

Weekly TENTH legion. w D 1860?-61||
MWA Mr 30 1861

PLATTSBURG

CLINTON county democrat. w 1866+
1866-83? as Clinton county register; 1884?-94? Register-lever; D 2 1898-1906 Democrat-lever
pub 1907+
MoHi D 1898-1900;N 23 1906+
MoSHi D 6 1878;Jl 14-S 15 1899;F 16 1900

CLINTON county register. *See* Clinton county democrat

CLINTONITE. w 1897-98||?
MoSHi Jl 15 1897

DEMOCRAT-LEVER. *See* Clinton county democrat

Plattsburg LEADER. w 1895+
MoHi Jl 26 1901+

Plattsburg LEVER. w 1873-83||?
United with Clinton county register to form Register-lever, later Clinton county democrat

REGISTER-LEVER. *See* Clinton county democrat

PLEASANT HILL

CASS county news. w 1901+
1901-O 1927 as Creighton news (Creighton)
pub O 27 1927+
MoHi N 18 1927+

CASS county republican. w 1920-25||?
MoHi O 1920-25

Pleasant Hill GAZETTE. *See* Pleasant Hill times

Pleasant Hill weekly LEADER. w 1869-73||
Followed by Las Animas leader (Las Animas, Col.)
CoHi O 18 1872-Mr 21 1873
MoHi Je 11 1869
MoSHi My 14 1869-O 11 1872

Pleasant Hill LOCAL. *See* Pleasant Hill register

Pleasant Hill POST. *See* Pleasant Hill times

Pleasant Hill REGISTER. w 1872-1924||?
1872-86? as Western dispatch; 1887?-S 1915 Pleasant Hill local
MoHi Je 7 1889;O 24 1890;F 27 1891;Ap 19 1892;Jl 6,N 30 1894;Ag 1901-O 5 1917

Pleasant Hill REVIEW. *See* Pleasant Hill times

Pleasant Hill TIMES. w 1890+
1890-99? as Pleasant Hill gazette; 1900? Pleasant Hill review; 1901? Pleasant Hill post
pub 1890-91;1901+
MoHi O 30 1890;1904+

Pleasant Hill UNION. w 1866-
MoHi S 17 1869

WESTERN dispatch. *See* Pleasant Hill register

POLO

Polo HERALD. w Ap 29-Jl 15 1915||
United with Polo news to form Polo news-herald

Polo NEWS-HERALD. w 1902+
1902-Jl 15 1915 as Polo news
pub 1919+
MoH [Ja 27 1921+]

Polo POST. *See* Vindicator

VINDICATOR. w 1887-1901||
1887-1900? as Polo post
MoHi O 30 1890

POPLAR BLUFF

AMERICAN republic. d 1916+
1916-Jl 29 1923 as American; Jl 30 1923-Mr 10 1928 Interstate American
pub 1923+
MoHi S 7 1917+
—w ed *See* Poplar Bluff republican

BLACK RIVER news. *See* Weekly citizen-democrat

BLUFF citizen. *See* Weekly citizen-democrat

BUTLER county democrat. d 1904-S 1908||?
United with Poplar Bluff citizen to form Daily citizen-democrat
MoHi [Ja 1904]06-07

BUTLER county democrat. w 1904-O 1 1908||?
United with Poplar Bluff citizen to form Weekly citizen-democrat
MoHi Ja 14-28 1904;S-D 1906

Weekly CITIZEN-DEMOCRAT. w 1869-1927||?
1869-73? as Black River news; 1874-75? Bluff citizen; 1876-O 1 1908 Poplar Bluff citizen
MoCaT 1907-My 24 1917
MoHi S 10 1869

Daily CITIZEN-DEMOCRAT. d 1893-1915||?
1893-Jl 1905? as Evening citizen; Ag 1905?-S 1908? Poplar Bluff citizen
MoHi Ag-S 1905;My-S 1906;Je-Jl 1907;Ap 16 1913-15

INTERSTATE American. *See* American republic

Evening JOURNAL. d 1902-03||?
MoHi Ag-D 1903

Poplar Bluff RENOVATOR. w 1886-87||?
MB [Ap 17-D 18 1886]

Poplar Bluff REPUBLICAN. w 1891+
pub 1891+
MoCaT 1917-19
MoHi D 30 1915+
—d ed 1916+ *See* American republic

Poplar Bluff REPUBLICAN. d 1902-D 1915||
MoHi Mr 12 1913-15

PORTAGEVILLE

SOUTHEAST Missourian. w D 1894+
1894- as Headlight
1894-1908 pub in New Madrid
pub 1896+
MoCaT 1917-19
MoHi Jl 25 1901+

POTOSI

Potosi EAGLE. w 1889-90||?
MoHi O 30 1890

INDEPENDENT-JOURNAL. w Ja 1 1873+
1873-1928 as Weekly independent; 1929-Ja 18 1934 Weekly independent and Potosi journal
MoCaT 1907+
MoHi Jl 1901+

Potosi JOURNAL. w 1894-D 26 1928||
United with Weekly independent to form Weekly independent and Potosi journal, later Independent-journal
MoCaT 1917-19
MoHi Jl 22 1903;D 1915-28

MINER'S prospect. w S 1846-49||?
MoSHi S 20 1849

WASHINGTON county journal. w 1867-75||?
MWA Jl 8 1869

POWERSVILLE

Powersville HELPER. w 1900-26||?
1900-16? as Powersville record
MoHi Mr 20 1908;Mr 12 1909;Ap 16 1915

Powersville RECORD. *See* Powersville helper

PRINCETON

PEOPLE'S press. *See* Princeton press

Princeton POST. w 1896+
1896-97 as Ravanna searchlight; 1897-1900 Mercer searchlight
1896-97 pub in Ravanna; 1897-1900 in Mercer
Suspended from 1900-Ja 1901
pub 1901+
MoHi Jl 12 1903+

Princeton PRESS. w 1881-1907||?
1881-Ag 20 1902 as People's press
MoHi N 1901-07

Princeton TELEGRAPH. w 1873+
pub 1873+
MoHi O 29 1899; Ag 1901-24;26+

MISSOURI (*Continued*)

PUXICO

Puxico HERALD. w 1895-1930||?
1895-1924? as Puxico index
MoCaT 1917-19

Puxico INDEX. *See* Puxico herald

QUEEN CITY

Queen City LEADER-TRANSCRIPT. *See* Queen City monitor-leader

Queen City MONITOR. w 1924||?
United with Queen City leader to form Queen City monitor-leader

Queen City MONITOR-LEADER. w 1896+
1896-1924? as Queen City leader (Ap 6 1917-19? Queen City leader-transcript)
MoHi Jl 26 1901-19

Queen City TRANSCRIPT. w 1888-Mr 1917||
United with Queen City leader to form Queen City leader-transcript, later Queen City monitor-leader
MoHi Jl 26 1901-17

RAVANNA

Ravanna SEARCHLIGHT. *See* Princeton post (Princeton)

RAVENWOOD

Ravenwood GAZETTE. w N 3 1893+
Follows Nodaway county times (Parnell)
pub 1893+
MoHi Ag 1901+

RAYTOWN

Raytown NEWS. w 1925+
pub D 30 1926+

REA

ANDREW county times. w 1889-92||?
MoHi O 25 1890

REEDS SPRING

STONE county democrat. w 1910-
MoHi Ag 25-N 17 1910

REPUBLIC

GREEN county republic. w 1888-93||?
1888-90? as Republic
MoHi O 23 1890

Republic MONITOR. w 1894+
pub 1894+
MoHi N 21 1907+

REPUBLIC. *See* Green county republic

RHINELAND

Rhineland RECORD. w 1902+
pub 1902+

RICH HILL

BATES county critic. *See* Critic

BATES county republican. w 1881+
MoHi 1920+

CRITIC. w 1898-
1898-1900? as Bates county critic
WHi Mr 2,16,Ap 6,My 11 1899;Ap 13 1900;F 15 1901

MINING review. w O 29 1880+
MoHi N 24 1898+

Daily REVIEW. d 1886+
—w ed *See* Mining review

Rich Hill TRIBUNE. w 1890-1911||?
MoHi Ja 25 1900;Ag 1901-10

WESTERN enterprise. w S 16 1881-1919||?
MoHi My 23,Jl 1902-S 1904;05-19

RICHARDS

Richards CHRONICLE. w 1890-92||?
MoHi O 16 1890

Richards PROGRESS. w Ap 1901-Ap 30 1933||
MoMeT complete

RICHFIELD

Richfield ENTERPRISE. w
MoSHi N 25 1854-S 7 1855

Richfield MONITOR. w
MoSHi D 8 1855-Je 23 1856

RICHLAND

Richland CYCLONE. w 1885-1909||?
MoHi Ja-S 10 1903

Richland MIRROR. w 1908+
pub 1932+
MoHi 1913+

Richland SENTINEL. w D 1872-80||?
MoHi Ja 10-24 1873

RICHMOND

Richmond CONSERVATOR. w Mr 17 1852+
1852-Ja 1853? as Richmond herald; F? 1853-58? Richmond weekly mirror; 1859?-Ap 23 1863 North-west conservator; Ap 30 1863-64? Conservator; 1865?-Mr 3 1866 North-west conservator; Mr 10-D 1866 Conservator
Suspended from S 13 1861-Jl 10 1862;Jl 7 1864-My 13 1865
MWA N 18 1865
MoHi Mr-O 1 1852[F 18-S 2 1853]54-Ap 21 1855[S 11 1857-O 16 1858]Ap 1861-66;86-97; 1900+
MoSHi O 15,N 26-D 3 1852

Richmond DEMOCRAT. w 1873-1906||?
Followed by Jackson county democrat, later Jackson democrat (Independence)
MoHi My 22 1879-88
NN F 2 1882

Richmond HERALD. *See* Richmond conservator

Richmond weekly MIRROR. *See* Richmond conservator

Richmond MISSOURIAN. w S 1898+
pub 1898+
MoHi Jl 25 1901+
MoSHi D 21 1905-Je 1907

Richmond NEWS. tw S 1914+
pub 1914+
MoHi Jl 8-S 1915;19+

NORTH-WEST conservator. *See* Richmond conservator

RAY county republican. w 1890-1908||?
N 1906-Ap 1907? as Richmond republican
MoHi N 8-15,29 1906-F 28,Mr 14-25,My 16,Je 7,20-27,Jl 11-O 17,30-D 12 1907

Richmond REPUBLICAN. w 1866-72||?
MoHi Je 23,D 1 1869

Richmond REPUBLICAN. 1905-07 *See* Ray county republican

RIDGEWAY

Ridgeway JOURNAL. w Ap 3 1891+
pub 1891+
MoHi 1891-My,O 1894;99+

ROCHEPORT

BOONE county democrat. w
MoHi O 16 1876

Rocheport COMMERCIAL. w 1878-1900||
MoBoH 1887-1894

Rocheport DEMOCRAT. w
MoBoH 1886-1906;14

Rocheport PROGRESS. w 1906-17||?
MoHi N 13 1908

ROCK PORT

ATCHISON county journal. w S 19 1863-Ap 1927||
Merged with Atchison county mail
MoHi Ag 30 1879-Ag 1892;93-1927
NN Jl 12 1923
NbHi Mr 29,My 24,Jl 5 1894;F 19 1897

ATCHISON county mail. w Ag 29 1878+
1878-Jl 8 1880 as Democratic mail
pub 1878+
MoHi O 18 1883-90;D 1898-N 1899[Mr-D 1900]+
VU Mr 3 1912

ATCHISON democrat. w 1876-81||?
MoHi Ag 14 1879-Jl 14 1881

Rock Port DEMOCRAT. w N 12 1884-89||?
1884-Jl 1888 as Missouri agitator
MoHi D 24 1884-Je 1889

DEMOCRATIC mail. *See* Atchison county mail

MISSOURI agitator. *See* Rock Port democrat

SUN. w 1876-82||?
MoHi Jl 21 1881-82

ROCKVILLE

Rockville BOOSTER. w 1908-16||?
MoHi Ja 14,28-F 4,25-Mr 24,Ap 7 1916

Rockeville LEADER. w O 1923+
pub 1923+

ROLLA

CAMP SWEENY spy.
IHi Jl 4 1861
MoSHi Jl 4 1861

Rolla EXPRESS. w 1859-75||?
1859-69 as Rural express
MWA Ja 20 1866
OClWHi Jl 31 1865
WHi Ja-Mr 3,Ap 28 1866

Rolla HERALD. w S 1866+
1866-69 as Herald of liberty; 1869-99? Rolla weekly herald; 1900-10? Rolla herald-democrat
pub 1869+
MoHi D 1898+

NEW era. w 1875+
MoHi 1903;14+

RURAL express. *See* Rolla express

Rolla TIMES. w 1907-29||?
MoHi Mr 10 1910-26

ROSENDALE

Rosendale SIGNAL. w 1892+
pub Ap 1931+

RUSSELLVILLE

Russellville weekly RUSTLER. *See* Cole county rustler (Jefferson City)

ST. CHARLES

St. Charles ADVERTISER. *See* St. Charles cosmos-monitor

St. Charles BANNER. w 1889-97||?
United with St. Charles news to form St. Charles banner-news

Evening BANNER. d 1890-97||?
United with St. Charles news to form St. Charles daily banner-news

St Charles BANNER-NEWS. w 1864+
1864-65 as News; 1866-97? St. Charles news
1864-65 pub in Wentzville
pub [1889;1900-02]+
MoHi Jl 25 1901-02;Jl 9 1903;Ap 23,My 1908-09;11+
OOxM Jl 26 1879-81

St. Charles daily BANNER-NEWS. d 1889+
1889-97 as St. Charles news
pub [1889;1900-02]+
MoBoH 1897
MoHi 1903-My 1905;Ap 23,My 1908-09;N 1910-Ja 11 1911
MoSHi O 26-31 1912
MoSc 1934+

St. Charles CHRONOTYPE. *See* St. Charles cosmos-monitor

CLARION. *See* St. Charles cosmos-monitor

St. Charles COSMOS-MONITOR. w 1835+
1835-39 as Clarion;1840-44 Free press; 1845-Ap 1846? St. Charles advertiser;My 6? 1846-O 21? 1847? Missouri patriot; O 28 1847?-48 Western star; 1849-53 St. Charles chronotype; 1854-65? St. Charles reveille; 1866?-F 5 1902 St. Charles cosmos (1867-68 Cosmos-sentinel)
pub 1908+
IHi Ja 1 1846;Jl 15 1847
MWA Jl 1 1863;Mr 22-29 1876
MoHi Je 17,D 9 1869;N 25 1874; D 22 1897; F 8 1899-1907;S 1909-18;20+
MoSHi My 1846-O 21 1847;Jl 2 1853;Je 3 1854;Ap 20 1860;Mr 6 1873
NcD Jl 24-31 1852

St. Charles daily COSMOS-MONITOR. d 1894+
1894- F 5 1902 as St. Charles daily monitor
pub 1908+
MoHi O 10-D 1894;F-Je 1895;Ja-Ag 1896

St. Charles DEMOKRAT. w Ja 1 1852-D 28 1916||
In German
MWA O 19 1865
MoHi O 30 1890;F 4 1909
MoSHi complete

FREE press. *See* St. Charles cosmos-monitor

JEFFERSONIAN. *See* Jeffersonian republican (Jefferson City)

MISSOURI advocate. w D 24 1824-F 19 1825||
United with St. Louis enquirer to form Missouri advocate and St. Louis enquirer (St. Louis) later St. Louis enquirer
MoSM complete

MISSOURI gazette. w N 1823-24||
MWA Je 10 1824
MoSHi My 6 1824

MISSOURI patriot. *See* St. Charles cosmos-monitor

***MISSOURIAN.** w Je 24 1820-22||?
DLC 1821-O 24 1822
KHi 1821-O 24 1822(photostat)
MWA Je 27 1821
MoHi 1821-O 24 1822

St. Charles MONITOR. w 1894-Ja 1902||?
United with St. Charles cosmos to form St. Charles cosmos-monitor
MoHi O 5 1894

St. Charles daily MONITOR. *See* St. Charles daily cosmos-monitor

St. Charles NEWS. *See* St. Charles banner-news

St. Charles REVEILLE. *See* St. Charles cosmos-monitor

St. Charles SENTINEL. w 1866||?
United with St. Charles cosmos to form Cosmos-sentinel, later St. Charles cosmos-monitor

WESTERN star. *See* St. Charles cosmos-monitor

ST. CLAIRE

St. Clair CHRONICLE. w S 1924+
pub 1924+
MoHi Mr 17 1927+

St. Clair TIMES. w 1916-18||?
MoCaT 1917-Ap 1918

STE. GENEVIEVE

CORRESPONDENT. w Ap 1821-
1821-Mr? 1822 as Correspondent and Ste. Genevieve record
MBAt D 25 1821;Mr 19 1822
MoSHi My 28 1822

MISSOURI (*Continued*)

STE. GENEVIEVE—*Continued*

DEMOCRAT. w Ja 7 1916-19||?
MoHi Ja 7-My 19 1916

FAIR play. w 1872+
pub 1872+
MoCaT 1917-19
MoHi Je 17 1875;Je 15 1876;Mr 23 1901;Ag 30 1902+
MoSHi Ap 23 1874;Je 17,O 15 1875;Je 15 1876;Je 10,24 1916

Ste. Genevieve HERALD. w My 6 1882+
In English and German
MoCaT 1907+
MoHi Ja 10 1903-Ja 14,S 1905-06;09+

MISSOURI citizen. w
MoSHi N 25 1859

NEWS and advertiser. w 1868-72||?
In English and German
MoHi Mr 11 1869

Ste. Genevieve PIONEER.
MoSHi F 16,My 4 1850

Ste. Genevieve PLAINDEALER. w 1851-
MoHi [1853]F 22-Mr 22 1861
MoSHi O 23,D 11,25 1852;My 7,Jl 9,23,Ag 6 1853;F 2,Mr 30,Je 29,Jl 13,27,S 7 1860

RAILROAD extra.
MoSHi F 24 1872

Ste. Genevieve REPRESENTATIVE. w Mr 3? 1866-
MoHi Ap 21 1866
WHi Ap 7 1866

ST. JAMES

St. James JOURNAL. w Ag 28 1896+
Ag-O 22 1896 as Vindicator
pub 1896+
MoHi Jl 26 1901-Mr 1923

St. James LEADER. w Ap 28 1928+
pub 1928+

ST. James REPUBLICAN. w 1912-16||?
MoHi Ja-Mr 9 1916

VINDICATOR. *See* St. James journal

ST. JOSEPH

ADVENTURE. w My 5 1848-
MoSj 1848-Ap 21 1854

St. Joseph Saturday ARGUS. w Ja 14- 1893||?
KHi Ja 28 1893

St. Joseph BALLOT. d 1890||?
MoHi N 8 1890

CATHOLIC tribune. w Ja 1 1878+
pub 1932+
MoCon 1913;18+
MoHi O 25 1890;Jl 27 1901+

St. Joseph COMMERCIAL cycle. w 1848?-
1848?-53? as Weekly commercial cycle
DLC 1855-D 5 1856
MWA D 6 1853
MoSHi Je 24 1853

EYE. w 1905-17||?
MoHi D 4,19 1908; Ja 9,D 24 1909-N 1916

St. Joseph FREE-DEMOCRAT. w 1859-
1859-My 1860? as St Joseph weekly free democrat
KHi O 29 1859-My 12,S 8-D 15 1860
MWA O 13-27,N 17 1860

St. Joseph GAZETTE. d 1845+
Ag 1900-Mr 1902 as St. Joseph gazette-herald
CLM Je 24 1891
MoHi Je 1868-Je 1870;83-Je 1884;85-Mr,Jl-D 1886;N 1887-Je 1889;O 27 1890;S 1893;98+
MoSHi N 14 1885;D 14 1902;D 20 1903
MoSj Jl 1868-Je 1870;72-Je,D 1874-94;96+
NbHi N 1 1891

St. Joseph GAZETTE. w Ap 25 1845-1903||?
Ag 1 1900-Mr 1902 Gazette-herald
DLC [1845 Ap-D 1846]S 7 1876
IaHi 1883-84
KHi 1845-D 4 1846;S 13 1877-N 15 1902
MWA N 30-D 7 1853
MoHi 1845-D 4 1846(photostat)85-86;My 1888-Je 1889;Ap-D 1890;Ja-Mr 1892;O 1900-N 1901
MoSj 1845-D 4 1854

St. Joseph morning HERALD. d F 12 1862-Jl 1900||
D 12 1865-Jl 24 1866? as Morning herald and daily tribune. United with St. Joseph gazette to form St. Joseph gazette-herald, later St. Joseph gazette
CtY Ja 2 1888
DLC D 12 1865-O 1866;67-N 11 1868;98-Je 1900
KHi Mr 14-Ap 1 1877;Ja-Je 1882; Ja 2 1888
MB Mr 18-F 17 1872
MoHi S 1865-F 1875;76-S 1885;86-1900
MoSHi Ja 1 1875
MoSj 1862-72;Jl 1883-1900
NbHi S 30 1876-N 1877;S 1878-80; Ag 23-D 1881;Jl 1882-Je 1883;85;88-Je 1889;Jl 1891-[93:Ja-Je 1900]
OClWHi Je 14 1862
WHi S 19,23 1863;Jl 21,Ag 1 1864

St. Joseph weekly HERALD. w Mr 10 1862-Jl 1900||
Title varies: Weekly herald. United with St. Joseph gazette to form Gazette-herald, later St. Joseph gazette
KHi Ap 1877-1900
MH 1862-O 1864
MWA O 30 1862;Ja 11 1866
MoHi F-D 1869;83-88;90-93
NbHi D 13 1894

St. Joseph weekly JOURNAL. w 1847-
DLC Ja 6 1860
MWA N 15 1861

Daily JOURNAL. d
MB [Ap 24-Jl 21 1862]
N F 5, Mr 4 1862

St. Joseph LEADER. w 1884-89||?
MoHi Ag 7 1886

MISSOURI vindicator.
MoSHi My 23 1868

Weekly New era. w Mr 24 1862-
KHi Ap 14 1862

St. Joseph NEWS. w 1879-85||?
1879-Ag 1883? as Western news
MoHi [Ag 12 1881-N 11 1882;Ja-Ag 1883]Jl 29 1884;Ja-Ap 21 1885

St. Joseph NEWS-PRESS. d My 3 1879+
1879-Jl 17 1885 as Evening news; Jl 20 1885-Ag 1903 St. Joseph daily news; S 1-20 1903 St. Joseph news; S 21-D? 1903 St. Joseph news and press
KHi Ap 25 1915-O 17 1921
M Ja 1 1892
MWA Ja 1 1888
MoHi O 25 1890; Ag 1 1891;Ag 27 1903+
MoSj 1879-Je 1880;F 1881-86;My 1888+
NbHi D 3 1901;Ja 23,F 3,6,Ap 4 1902;Ap 9, Jl 3 1903;N 29 1907
WHi 1917-Ja 1 1920

Evening PRESS. d Ag 26 1902-S 1903||
United with St. Joseph press to form St. Joseph news-press
MoHi 1902-Jl 1903
MoSj complete

St. Joseph STANDARD. w 1871-
KHi S 29 1873
MoHi 1871-Ag 1873

STAR. w 1887-93||?
MoHi O 24 1890

St. Joseph STAR. d N 1905-09||?
MoSj 1905-Mr 1909

St. Joseph STOCKYARDS daily journal. d S 3 1897+
pub 1899+
DA Je 23 1908-[12]-[14-15]-F 1917;22[23-25]+
IU F-Mr 1918;Jl 1919-N 1924;Ap 1925+
MoHi S 25,O 3-4 1905;F 16,21 1906
MoSj 1903-Ag 1917

St. Joseph daily TIMES. d S 13 1897-98||?
MoHi 1897-Mr 16 1898

Saint Joseph daily TRIBUNE. d O? 1862-
WHi Ap 19,Je 10,24,Jl 19,27,Ag 24 1864

St. Joseph weekly TRIBUNE. w O? 1863
WHi Mr 10 1864

Daily evening TRIBUNE. d 1870-
MoHi O 24 1870

St. Joseph UNION. d 1864?-
Title varies slightly
MoSj [Ap 23-D 1 1869;F 1870]
N S 23,N 7,D 14 1865
WHi S 27 1866;My 22 1867

St. Joseph weekly UNION. w 1865-72||?
MoHi Ja 6 1870
MoSj F 23 1871

St. Joseph VOLKSBLATT. d 1858?-1911||?
1858?-79? as Das Westliche volksblatt
MWA Ag 26 1876

St. Joseph VOLKSBLATT. w 1858-1924||
1858-79? as Das Westliche volksblatt. Since 1924 printed as part of Kansas City presse (Kansas City)
In German
KHi O 19-D 21 1924
MWA F 10 1866
MoHi F 3 1906

WATHENA gazette. w 1887-
KHi Ap 11-Ag 8 1891

Weekly WEST. w My 1858-
MoSj My 1859-Ap 1860

Daily WEST. d
MsHi 1860

WESTERN news. *See* St. Joseph news

Das WESTLICHE volksblatt. *See* St. Joseph volksblatt

ST. LOUIS

ABEND. . . *See* next import word: e.g., Abend post is alphabeted as Post

AGE.
MoSHi F 20 1847

St. Louis AMERICAN. d 1845?-
MoS S 8 1845-Ap 23 1847
MoSHi Mr 17 1845
NhD Jl 19 1845

Weekly AMERICAN. w 1845?-
MoS Ja 9 1846-Ap 22 1847
OHi O 2 1846

St. Louis AMERICAN. d My 23 1924-
MoS My-Je 1924

St. Louis AMERICAN. w 1928+
Negro
MoS 1928+

AMERICAN Celt. w 1888-93||?
MoHi F 7 1891

AMERICAN eagle. 1894-1907||?
Negro
MoHi D 17 1905

AMERICAN tribune. d O 1874-
DLC O 16 1874

AMERICAN tribune. w Mr 8- 1883||?
IHi Mr 8 1883

AMERIKA. d O 1872-N 9 1924||
In German
IU Jl 1917-Jl 8,O 2-N 1924
MoHi Jl 1914-20
MoS 1903-Je 1914;21-24
MoSC 1872-Ap 1921
MoSHi My 20,Je 24 1906;Je 4 1916;Ap 16 1922
—w, sw ed *See* Amerika und herold des glaubens

AMERIKA und herold des glaubens. w, sw 1872-N 9 1924||
1872-1920 as Amerika
w 1872-1902
In German
KHi Ag 1 1888
MoCon 1921-23
MoSC O 23 1872-[O 23 1921-Je 1924]
—d ed *See* Amerika
—Beilage. w
KHi Ag 1888-Mr 20 1889

Abend-ANZEIGER. d O 31 1835-1912||?
1835-Ja 7 1898 as Anzeiger des westens
In German
IHi D 11 1847;My 13 1848
MWA [O 17-N 21 1860]Ap 13 1862
MoS 1835-O 20 1838;O 20 1841-O 10 1843; O 19 1844-O 22 1848;O 21 1849-O 20 1862; Jl 21 1863-Je 7,O 1898;S 1901-07;Ap-Je 1908; 09-Ap 1912
MoSHi D 8 1848;Jl 13 1850-51;Ap 21,D 22-23 1857;Ja 16,18,20 1863
PP F 7 1851
WHi O 25 1860

ANZEIGER des westens. w
In German
IU N 12,D 8-10,15,20,24-29 1842;Ja 5,10,21, F 9,21,Ag 17,O 26 1843

ANZEIGER des westens: abend blatt. *See* Abend-anzeiger

ANZEIGER des westens: Sonntagsblatt. w 1835-Je 1898||?
1835-60? as Westliche blätter. Merged with Westliche post
In German
MWA O 21 1860;Ap 13 1862
MoS Jl 24 1864-Je 5 1898
MoSHi D 2 1860

ANZEIGER des westens: wochenblatt. w 1835-Je 1898||?
In German
IHi [D 28 1839-Ja, Jl 23 1863-Jl 15 1869]
MoS O 19 1844-O 17 1846;68-Je 5 1898
MoSHi O 16 1847-F 17 1849
PPL F 8 1851

ARBEITER-ZEITUNG. w Ag 27 1898-1931||
Follows Abend post und tageblatt
In German
ICJ 1903-N 4 1916;N 1917-Ap 10 1931
IU My 4,Jl 20 1901;03-Ag 1905
MWA Ag 1 1914
MoHi Ap 18 1908
MoS 1903;12-15;17+
MoSHo complete
NNC [1903-31]
PU 1909-14
WHi 1898-N 4 1916

Daily ARGUS. d
WHi F 24-25 1841

St. Louis ARGUS. w 1912+
Negro
MoHi 1915-18;F 1919+
MoS Ag 1932+
TNY O 11-18,N 1929-My,Ag 15,S 26,O 1930-S 11,O 23-N 13,27,D 11 1931; Ja-F 19,Mr 18, Ap 15-22,My 20,Je 24,Jl 15,Ag 5,O 14,N 11-D 1932;N 1933-Mr 1934

BARNBURNER. 1849-50||?
Followed by Morning signal

St. Louis BEACON. w Mr 2 1829-32||
Follows St. Louis enquirer. Mr 2-9 1829 as Beacon
Ct [1829-31]
DLC Ap 13 1829-D 6 1832
KHi [Ap 13 1829-D 6 1831](photostat)
MWA Mr 1-8,Jl 26 1832
MoHi Ap 13-N 14 1829;30-32(photostat)
MoS 1829-31
MoSM Jl 21 1831

St. Louis BEACON (for the country) w Ag 29 1829-
CSmH Ag 29 1829
DLC Ag 29,S 12,O 3 1829

BREEZE. w 1884||?
CtY My 3 1884

St. Louis daily BULLETIN. d Jl 18 1859-Jl 11 1861||
O 18 1859-Ap 18 1860 as Evening bulletin
MWA Jl 19 1859
MoS Ap 19-O 13 1860
MoSM O 18 1859-Ap 18 1860
MoSj 1859-Mr 1860

Weekly BULLETIN. w 1860?-
DLC Jl 17 1860

Daily BULLETIN. d Jl 12-Ag? 1861||
Not to be confused with St. Louis daily bulletin. Follows Daily Missouri state journal
DLC Jl 12-13,Ag 7 1861
MoS Jl-Ag 1861
MoSHi Ag 8 1861

Morning CALL. d Je 1884-
MoHi Je 5 1884
MoS Je-Jl 1884

MISSOURI (*Continued*)

ST. LOUIS—*Continued*

CARONDELET new era. w?
MoSHi F 1859-Ja,O 27 1860

CARONDELET news. w 1900+
pub 1900+
MoHi Ja 31 1903+
MoS 1919;23+

CARONDELET progress. *See* South St. Louis progress

CATHOLIC news letter. w N 22 1845-Ap 1 1848||
MoSHi My 2 1846
MoSU [1845-N 14 1846]-48
OCX complete

CAVALIER. w
MoSHi Ja 20 1867

CENSOR. w 1896+
1896-99 as Dyer's news letter
MoHi Jl 25 1901+
WHi Ap 21 1904

Die CENTRAL post.
In German
MoSHi O 22 1870

CHRONICLE. w
NcU Ag 31 1878

St. Louis CHRONICLE. d Jl 31 1880-Je 5 1905||
1880-90? as Evening chronicle; United with St. Louis star to form St. Louis star-chronicle, later St. Louis star-times
MoHi S 10 1887;D 2 1889;O 28 1890;F 11 1892;F 18,Mr 7,16,Jl 4,22,O 3,D 6 1893;Ja 31, My 12 1894;Je 9 1896;S 20 1898;Jl 29,Ag 5 1899;Jl 24-Ag 1901
MoS 1880-S 1892;Ja-Mr,Jl 1893-1905
MoSHi Je 30 1882;Ap 30 1889;My 27 1896;Ap 20,O 10 1898;S 1901-05

CIMETER. w, sm Ja 3 1884-87||?
w 1884-85?
IHi [1884-F 5 1885]

St. Louis COMMERCIAL advertiser. w N 7? 1826-
Ct My 23 1827

Daily COMMERCIAL bulletin. tw, d My 18 1835-
1835-Ap 19 1836 as St. Louis commercial bulletin and Missouri literary register; Ag 22 1836-Je 17? 1838 Daily commercial bulletin and Missouri literary register tw 1835-Ap 19 1836
MWA O 4 1841
MoHi N 24 1840; Mr 24 1841
MoSHi Je 3 1835;N 10 1841
MoSM [1840]
WHi 1835-38

St. Louis COMMERCIAL bulletin and Missouri literary register—for the country. w 1835?-
MWA N 4 1840

St. Louis COURIER. w Mr 12 1892-95||?
KHi Mr 19 1892
MB 1892-95
MoS 1892-94

St. Louis CRITIC. w 1876-1900||?
DLC O 31 1888
KHi S 16 1888
MWA Jl 19,Ag 9 1884
MoHi N 1 1890
MoSHi O 12 1889

St. Louis DEMOCRAT. d Ja 3 1842-My 19 1875||
1842-F 1843? as Native American bulletin; Mr 2 1843-F 1844? Old school democrat and St. Louis herald; F 1844-51? St. Louis democrat; 1852-72 Daily Missouri democrat. United with St. Louis daily globe to form St. Louis globe-democrat
CL Ap 10 1865
CSmH F 3 1868
DLC Ja-S 29 1842[Mr-D 1843]F 20-S 2 1844;O 13,17,29,31 1852;55;Mr 24 1857;Mr 28 1861-65; F 19 1866[67-72]Jl 1874-75
IC Ja 11-Je 21 1873
ICHi N 27 1861; D 27 1862;Ag 10,28 1865
ICU Jl 23 1862;F 17-18,21,21,Mr 2-4,7 1865
IHi [N 1861-My,Ag-N 1862;64-Jl 1866]
IU Mr 9,18,S 14 1861;O 10,12 1871
KHi [Mr-D 1843](photostat)F 20-S 2 1844 (photostat)N 14 1857;F 10 1864[S 15 1866-Ja 3 1875]
MBAt Ja 27,Jl 17,S 9 1862;63-75
MWA F 14,Je 5,Ag 27 1857;Mr 19,31, Ap 5, Jl 22 1859;My 12 1860-Je 30 1864;F 8,My 12, Ag 29-S 2,D 7,27 1865;Ja 3,Ap 26,Jl 6, Ag 13,N 19,29,D 25 1866;S 17 1867; F 10,16, Mr 13,My 11 1868;My 2,N 18 1870; Ap 9 1872; Ja 1,S 1 1874;Ja 1, My 14 1875
Mo S 1866-Jl 1874
MoHi Ja-S 29 1842(photostat)[Mr-D 1843] (photostat)F 20-S 2 1844(photostat)Ja-D 1 1855(photostat)[58-73]
MoS My 1855-Je 1857;58-59;Ja 14-Mr 1861; 62-75
MoSG 1854-75
MoSHi N 15 1842;Mr 23 1855;O 15 1859-75
MoSM Jl 1857-58;61-[63]-Je 1864;Ja-Je 1865; 67-[71-75]
N F 7 1859;N 6 1861;F 14,Je 25 1862;Ja 1 1875
NN Ag 25 1863;S 26,29,D 18 1865
NNHi S 1 1862
NSyU N 9 1873
NbHi Ja 1 1874
NcU O 5 1870
OClWHi Ap 1870-Ja 14,Mr 15-22 1871
OHi Mr 10 1863;N 20 1866
PPM 1863-Je 1865
TU S 17 1867
WHi [Ag 25 1862-F]Mr 7-Je 2-Jl 28,O 12 1864;Ja 31,F 11,,21,My 30,Ag 21,D 21 1865; My 25,Je 4,Ag 24,S 22,O 1,D 21, 1866,Mr 23, O 11 1867;Ja 9,F 11,Mr 16,31,O 8,N 20, 24-25 1868;Ja 1,My 13,21,Jl 13,22,29,Ag 2 1869
—w ed *See* Old school democrat and St. Louis weekly herald; Missouri democrat

Weekly DEMOCRATIC free press. w 1864-
MoHi Jl 2 1864

Tägliche DEUTSCHE tribüne. d Jl 15? 1844-
In German
IU F 17 1848
MoSHi Jl 15 1844-Mr 1852

Die DEUTSCHE tribüne. w Jl 25 1844-
In German
MoSHi S 20 1848-F 1849
OCoC Jl-S 12, O 3-17,31 1844-Mr 20 1845

St. Louis DISPATCH. d 1864-D 1878||
United with St. Louis evening post to form St. Louis post-dispatch
CSmH S 16 1867;Ja 4,Ap 2,Je 17 1868
DLC D 12 1865-N 1 1866;Je 3 1874
IHi My 2 1865
MWA Je 13 1866; O 20 1869
MoHi F 24,Ap 3,10,17,My 2,26,29,31 1865;My 17 1866;Ag 20 1870;F 7,Mr 27,D 21 1876; Ja 2,13 1877;Ja 2,21,31 1878
MoSHi N 28 1864-D 14 1866;Ap 6-D 1869
MoSM N 21 1864-Je 1866;Jl 1867-70;73
MoSPo 1874-78
MoSW N 1864-66
N F 18,23 1876
NNHi Je 17 1869;Mr 1,Ap 4,Je 25 1873
NhD Mr 3 1870
Tx S 21 1869

St. Louis weekly DISPATCH. w
MWA Je 9 1866

Tri-weekly DISPATCH. tw
MWA Je 13 1866

DYER'S news letter. *See* Censor

*St. Louis ENQUIRER. sw,w My 1815-F 1829||?
1815-My 10 1817 as Western journal; My 17 1817-Ag 1818? Western emigrant; S 1818-F 21 1825? St. Louis enquirer; F 28 1825?-D 7 1826 Missouri advocate and St. Louis enquirer. Followed by St. Louis beacon sw S 1819-Ag 1820
Ct [1827]
DLC 1821[22-24]Ja 10-31,My 7 1825;S 7 1826
KHi 1821-D 18 1824(photostat)
MBAt Ag 23 1823
MoHi 1821-S 2 1822;23-24(photostat)
MoSHi Ja 13 1821-D 16 1822;Ja 25 1823-D 18 1824;Ja 10-Jl 15,D 10 1825-Ap 8 1826; F 15 1827(photostat)
MoSM F 28 1825-26
N Ag 20 1825
NN Ag 23 1823;My 27 1826

St. Louis ENQUIRER (Country edition). w S 1819?-
DLC N 12 1821

EQUALITY. w Ap 3 1905-
MoSHi Ap 3 1905

St. Louis ÉS VIDÉKE. w 1913+
D 27 1918 is jubilee number
In Hungarian
IU 1918+
MoS D 27 1918
PPiHi [Ap 27 1923-Ag 14 1931]

EXPRESS. d Mr 20 1860-
MoSM [Mr-O 1860]

FARMERS' and mechanics' advocate. w O 31 1833-
Ct N 7 1833; Mr 13 1834
DLC 1834-Ap 18 1835
ICHi D 19 1833
MH N 1833-O 23 1834
MoHi 1834-Ap 18 1835

Weekly FOUNTAIN. w
MoSHi My 12 1849

FRANKLIN AVENUE weekly bulletin. w 1875-
MoHi O 23 1875

St. Louis FREE press. w Ap 13 1832-
Ap-S 20? 1832 as Missouri free press; S 27? 1832-My 23 1833 Free press
Ct Mr 28 1833
DLC Ja-O 24 1833
ICHi My 24,S 27 1832
KHi Ja-O 24 1833(photostat)
MWA N 5 1832
MnHi S 20 1832
MoCaT S 26 1833
MoHi Ja-O 24 1833(photostat)
N O 3 1833
TxU 1832-Ap 6 1833

FREIE blaetter. w Mr 18 1851-
In German
MoS 1851-Mr 5 1853

Evening GAZETTE. d Jl 3 1838-
Title varies: Daily evening gazette
DLC O 28 1840;D 11 1845
MHi Je 18 1846
MWA S 3 1838;Ag 12 1841
MoSM Jl 1839-44
P-M Mr 4 1845

St. Louis weekly GAZETTE. w 1840-
ICHi Mr 22 1845
IHi D 13-20 1845
P-M D 6 1845

St. Louis daily GLOBE. d Jl 18 1872-My 19 1875||
United with St. Louis democrat to form St. Louis globe-democrat
C F 18-D 1874
DLC complete
IHi S 14 1874
InRE Ja 10 1875
Mo Ja-F,My-D 1873
MoHi [1873-75]
MoS Ag 1872-Je 1874
MoSG 1874-75
MoSHi complete
MoSM complete

St. Louis weekly GLOBE. w 1872-My 1875||?
United with Missouri democrat to form Weekly globe-democrat
MoHi My 30-Je 13,Jl 11,Ag 1,29 1873
NbHi Ja 4,17 1873
TJT D 11 1874

St. Louis GLOBE-DEMOCRAT. d My 20 1875+
Formed by the union of St. Louis daily globe and St. Louis democrat
pub 1875+
A O 1877-78;Jl 1879-Je 1881;My-D 1900;02
C F 3 1887-F 23 1889
CLM Ag 8 1897
CtW My 24 1893
DLC 1875-84;Ap 4 1885-87;Jl 1888-My,Jl 1901+
I 1914-21
ICHi Jl 24 1885
ICM Ap 24,Je 5 1882[Mr 1883]Mr 2 1884
ICU [1892-94]-[98]-[1900]-28
IEa 1901-18
IHi [Jl 1899-1934]
IU Mr 5,My 5-22 1908;09-F 13,Ap 4 1925-Jl, S 1927+
IaDH 1889-1914
InLHi Mr 15 1879
InMovHi S 13-17,19 1901
MWA 1875-Je 1879;Je 24 1880;O 19-21,N 5 1881; Ap 20 1883;Ag 8 1892
MiU 1889;1903-[08]26-Ap 20 1934
MiU-C Je 23 1876[92]
MnU Jl 15 1918-[19]-Ja 1920;S-N 1921
Mo Ap 29 1891+
MoCaT 1913-20
MoFuW S 19 1932-Je 1,S 8 1933+
MoHi [1875-76]-[78-87]+
MoJ 1901+
MoS 1875+
MoSHi Je 5-26,O 1876-Ap 1894;1900-O 1918; Ja,O 1919
MoSM Je 1875+
MoSW 1885-89;94-1901
MoWeW S 1932+
N F 17,23 1876
NbHi My 3 1877;S 1,8-10 1880;Je 15-16 1890; S 18 1892;F 27,Ag 10,28,S 7,O 9,12 1894; Ap 21,Jl 10,19,Ag 11,25,S 13,N 1-8 1896; My 15,N 4-11 1900;Jl 21 1901-F,My-Ag 1909; Mr 1910-16
NcU Ag 24-25,27-30 1878
OClWHi F 1 1878
OHi 1912-Jl 1931
OOxM Ap 15-16,Jl 24-25 1879;D 9-10,15 1881; S 27,O 11, 27 1882
P Jl 1890-Ag 1917
PP Je 1 1927;34+
TKL Ag 18 1891
Tx Je 1904+
TxGR Ja 25 1878;S 11 1900;current year
WHi N 11-13,16 1880;O 19-20 1881;Je 13-16 1890;Jl 22 1896;1904+
WaPS D 12,15 1915;Ap 23 1924;Ap 17 1925

Twice-a-week GLOBE-DEMOCRAT. w,sw My 28 1875-1926||?
Formed by the union of St. Louis weekly globe and Missouri democrat. 1875-Ja 20 1921 as Weekly globe-democrat (w)
C 1915-23
IaHi N 1881-N 1882
KHi My 6 1886
MBAt 1875-76
MWA 1875-92;Ap 11-18,My 30 1899
MoHi [1880]Mr 10 1881;F 14 1884;F 18 1886-F 17 1887;92-94;96-Mr 1898;Ja-My,Jl-Ag 1,N 18 1902
MsSM 1909
OClWHi Jl 21 1881;O 3 1899;S 20 1901
TJT O 24 1889;Ja 29 1898;Jl 24,N 9-16 1900; Ja 18-Ap 19,26,My 3-10,30,S 24-O 18,N 6, 20,26-D 1901;Ja 9-31,Ap-My 9,Ag 19 1902-Mr 17,Ap 10,17,Jl 19 1903
TU-J O 25 1888

GOLDEN era. w? 1851?-
Also dated in Alton, Ill.
IGK F 11-18 1854

GUARDIAN. w D 30 1865-
MoSHi 1865;Ag 17 1867;Ja 2,13,Ag 18, N 17 1886
MoSU 1865-[Ja-N 14 1868]

Evening HERALD. d 1834-34||?
MoSM [Je 5-N 9 1835]

Sunday HERALD. w 1850-
DLC Mr 30,Ap 20-27,Je 15 1856
MoHi O 26,D 7,21 1856;Ja 25,F 8,Ap 5 1857

St. Louis daily morning HERALD. d D 20 1852-
DLC Ag 14(extra)1861
MoHi D 31 1856
MoS 1852-Ag 13 1854;Je 1855-56
MoSHi 1852-Jl 2 1853;Mr 9 1854;Ja 20 1856; S 1857-Je 1859;Ja-Je 1860

St. Louis HERALD. w 1876?-78||?
NbHi S 16 1876

St. Louis HIRLAP. w
In Hungarian
MoSHi Ag 15 1913

HLAS. w,sw O 1 1873+
w 1873-S 1905
In Bohemian
pub 1873+
ILiS 1928+
IU D 1917-N 1919
MoS 1917
MoSHi 1901-Ap 1929

MISSOURI (*Continued*)

ST. LOUIS—*Continued*

ILLUSTRATED graphic news. w 1885?-
MoS Mr-D 1886

INDEPENDENT live stock reporter. d 1904-
MoHi D 29 1905

Daily St. Louis INTELLIGENCER. d Ja 1 1850-O 12 1857||
1850 as St. Louis intelligencer; Ja 2-Je 21 1851 St. Louis daily intelligencer. United with St. Louis daily evening news to form St. Louis daily evening news and intelligencer, later St. Louis daily evening news
DLC 1850-51;D 16 1852
IU Jl 26 1854;Mr 20 1856
MWA N 24 1852;Je 7,D 23 1853
MoHi Ap 11 1856
MoSHi Ja-S 2 1853
MoSM 1850-55;Jl 1856-57
N N 21 1853

Daily St. Louis INTELLIGENCER. d Evening ed
MoSM O 14 1850-51

Weekly St. Louis INTELLIGENCER. w 1850?-O 13 1857||
United with St. Louis weekly news to form Weekly St. Louis news and intelligencer, later Weekly St. Louis evening news
ICHi F 29 1856;Ja 16 1857
MWA S 23 1852
MoHi F 27[Je 29 1852-Je 28 1853]Jl 18 1854; 56-57

Tri-weekly St. Louis INTELLIGENCER. tw
MoHi Je 3 1854

St. Louis JEFFERSONIAN. w Ag 8 1884-
WHi S 26 1884

JEWISH record. w 1915+
In English and Yiddish
MWA F 22 1918
PP 1928+

St. Louis daily JOURNAL. d 1857?-N 15 1878||
Title varies slightly. United with St. Louis daily times to form St. Louis times-journal, later St. Louis times
DLC N 9 1874;75-78
KHi O 29 1876-O 2 1877;Mr 18,Ap 18 1878

St. Louis weekly JOURNAL. w 1857-78||?
United with St. Louis times to form St. Louis times-journal, later St. Louis times
MWA Ag 17 1876
NbHi O 3,24 1872;D 16 1875;Je 1 1876

St. Louis evening JOURNAL. d 1895-97||?
MoS Je 1896-Je 1897

LEADER. w Mr 10 1855-
CtY Mr-S 1855
DGU 1855
DLC N 22,D 13-27 1856
MWA My 16-Je 13,Ag 1,S 12-19 1857
MoHi Ja 4,O 16 1857;Ap 6 1858
MoS Mr-S 1855
MoSM 1855-Mr 1 1856
MoSU [O-D 1856]
MoSW D 1856-F 6 1858
NNHi Je 30-Jl 14 1855

St. Louis LEADER. d Jl 1856?-
Jl?-O 11 1856 as St. Louis daily leader
MoS Ap-S 1857
MoSHi Jl 7,14 1855;Ja 19 1856;My 27 1857
MoSM O 13 1856-F 3 1858
MoSU [Jl-D 1856]
MoSW O 13 1857-My 11 1858

La LEGA italiana. w O 9 1914-21||?
In Italian
IU Ja 25 1918-20
MoHi 1914-20

LIBERIA advocate.
IU Mr 25,O 26 1846
MsHi D 1847-Ja 1849
NN Je 29? 1847

St. Louiské LISTY. w 1902+
In Bohemian
IU D 1917-F 6 1932

St. Louis daily LIVE STOCK reporter. *See under* National Stockyards, Illinois

LOG CABIN hero. w My 7- 1840||?
DLC My 7 1840
MoSM My 7 1840

LOUISIANA gazette. *See* Missouri gazette

St. Louis LUMINARY. w N 22 1854-D 15 1855|
MWA N 22 1854
USlC complete

MILL boy. w 1844-Ja 21 1845||
DLC F 10 1844
In complete
MWA F 10 1844-45
MoHi My 4,O 26 1844
MoSHi Ja 28,Mr 1844-45
MoSM F 10-D 1844;Ja 21 1845
OHi Je 29 1844
TxU Ag 10 1844

Daily evening MIRROR. d
MoSHi Je 19 1855

MISSISSIPPI blätter. w 1857-Mr 7 1932||
In German
IU S 1917-32
KHi N 10 1918
MBAt Ap 16 1865
MoHi My 1914-20
MoS 1903-07;09-Ap 1914;21-Jl 1929
MoSHi My 5 1901;Mr 11 1906;Ja 1 1918;Jl 22 1923-S 18 1927
NN Mr 14,O 3 1909
Tx F 15,My 31-S 6,27-O 11,N 1 1874
—d ed *See* Die Westliche post

MISSOURI advocate and St. Louis enquirer. *See* St. Louis enquirer

MISSOURI argus. w Ap 24 1835-41||?
Followed by Missouri reporter
Ct [1835-36]
DLC My 22 1835-N 25 1839
KHi My 22 1835-O 1840
MoHi My 22 1835-My,N 18-D 23 1837;Ja 6 1838-N 22 1839(photostat)
MoSM My 26-Je 2,N 25,D 9 1837;Ja 20 1838; Ag 19,D 2 1841

MISSOURI argus. sw 1835-41||?
MoHi Je 6-N 11 1837(photostat)
MoSM Je 9-O 18,25-N 15,29-D 9,13-30 1837; Ja 8-13,23-29 1838
WHi My 16-20,O 14,28 1840

MISSOURI argus. d 1838-41||?
Followed by Missouri reporter
DLC Jl 4-S 14 1839;F 3-D 1840
IHi [Jl 4-Ag 9 1839](facsimile)
MWA F 26,Je 6(extra)29 1840
MoHi Jl 4-S 14 1839;Mr 5- D 1840(photostat)
MoSHi Jl 4,Ag 1 1839;F 27 1840-Jl 16 1841
MoSM Jl 31 1838-Ja 1839[41]
WHi D 16-17 1840

MISSOURI democrat. w 1852-My 20 1875||
1852?-My 12 1868 as Weekly Missouri democrat. United with St. Louis weekly globe to form Weekly globe-democrat
DLC My 5,Jl 28,D 15-22 1854;Jl 15,Ag 26,S 23-30,O 14-28 1856; Ja 20,F 17 1857;My 19, Je 16 1863;Ag 9,S 27-O 18-25,N 15,29-D 20 1864;Ja 10 1865-Je 23 1868;Ja 5-12,26,F 16-23,Ap 20-S 1869
ICHi Ja 30 1855;Jl 3,31 1866
KHi F 24,My 5 1863
MWA D 9 1856;My 30-Ag 1,29,S 26,O 17-24, N 7,21 1865-N 6 1866;My 14 1867-75
MeBa [F-D 1861]-Ja 21 1862
MoSG 1854-75
MoHi [1857]-N 1859;61-62; Jl 14 1863;Ap 25, D 12 1865;Ap 28 1868
MoSHi D 11 1860;F 26 1861;Mr 20 1866
NN Ag 27 1858
NNHi D 24 1863;S 16 1868;Mr 4 1873
NbHi O 11,25 1864-Mr,Ap 18 1865;D 9 1869; D 12 1873
PPot S 11 1866
TKL Mr 22 1872
TxU O 30 1852
WHi Ap 2 1861;Mr 6,My 15 1866;S 10, N 17 1867;Ja 5,My 11,Ag 10,S 14 1869

Tri-weekly MISSOURI democrat. tw
IHi N 25,D 2,6,11-13,20 1861;Ja 29-31,Mr 14, 17,24,31 1862
KHi Ja 7 1861-Ap 17 1865
MWA My 17 1865-Ap 17 1867
MoHi N 18 1861;D 31 1862-Je,S 1864-67;F 28 1868-Je 1870;71-72
PPL [1862]
WHi Ag 14-D 1861;F 26 1862-F 22 1864

Daily MISSOURI democrat. *See* St. Louis democrat

MISSOURI free press. *See* St. Louis free press

*MISSOURI gazette and public advertiser. w Jl 12 1808-Mr 6 1822|
1808-N 23 1809 as Missouri gazette; N 30 1809-Jl 11 1812 Louisiana gazette; Jl 18 1812-F 19 1814 Missouri gazette; F 26 1814-Jl 8 1815 Missouri gazette and Illinois advertiser; Jl 15 1815-My 1 1818 Missouri gazette; My 8-Jl 3 1818 Missouri gazette and Illinois advertiser. Followed by Missouri republican
DLC 1821-22
KHi [1821-22](photostat)
MHi F 7 1821;O 15 1823;S 6 1824
MoHi 1821-22
MoSM F 7,Mr 14 1821

MISSOURI herald and St. Louis public advertiser. w N 8 1826-
Ct [1826-27]
MoHi [N 22 1826-Mr 14 1827]
MoSHi F 21,Jl 25 1827

MISSOURI Saturday news. w 1840-
MoHi O 17 1840

MISSOURI observer. w O 31? 1826-
1826-27 as Missouri observer and St. Louis advertiser
Ct [S 12 1827-28]
MWA N 21 1827;Ja 30 1828

MISSOURI reporter. d 1841-Ag 15 1846||
Follows Missouri argus. United with Daily morning Missourian to form St. Louis daily union
DLC F 3 1845-46
MoHi Mr 28 1842;Ag 23,S 8,12,15,26, N 25, D 2 1843;Ja 15,26,F 10,N 28 1844;F 8 1845-Ag 15 1846(photostat)
MoSHi 1842-S 1843;Mr 13 1844;Je 28,Jl 1845-Ag 14 1846
MoSM [Jl 27-Ag 1846]
NSchU Jl 1,Ag 9 1842
Whi [N 14 1843-46]
—campaign ed 1844 *See* Slasher

MISSOURI reporter. w 1841-Ag 1846||?
Follows Missouri argus. United with Weekly Missourian to form St. Louis weekly union
DLC Ja 4-25 1845
MoSHi Ja 2 1845
—country ed *See* Reporter (for the country)

MISSOURI republican. w Mr 20 1822-D 4 1919||
Follows Missouri gazette and public advertiser. Merged with St. Louis globe-democrat
A 1878-Je 1881;82-83
ArHi Je 27 1897
C Ja 9,Mr 13 1852;F 5 1854
CtD S 10 1877
DLC 1822-28[Je-D 1829]Ja 4 1831;Mr 19 1852-Je 1855
IC Ap 20 1852-Ap 19 1853
ICHi N 26 1823;O 15 1871
ICU D 1-8 1865
IHi Ap 14 1865
IU Jl 1 1859
KHi [1822-28](photostat)Ap 7 1871[Ap 13 1874-Je 23 1895]
MBAt Je 30 1829
MWA Mr 29,Ap 26,My 17-24,Je 14,Jl 26 1824; F 22 1827;D 11 1832;extra 1838;Je 20,N 28 1840;My 21,Jl 4 1849;Ja 15 1850;F 27,D 10-31 1852;Ja 28-F 11,My 6-Jl 1,Ag 26-S 2,23 1853;F 28,Mr 14,21,My 23 1854;Ja 16,O 26-N 2 1855;F 22,Ag 22,O 10,1856;S 10 1858; Jl 10 1863
MoCaT N 29-D 6,27 1867
MoHi 1822-28(photostat)Ap 14,S 22-29,O 13-20 1838;Mr 2,S 28 1839;Ag 28 1849;O 30,N 9, 20-D 11,25 1855-[Je-N 1856]Ja-Ap 1860;F 11 1862;S 1 1863
MoSHi Mr 27 1822-Ap 2 1833;D 22 1843-Ja 1 1847; Jl 10 1884-O 16 1890
MoSM [1827]-[29-30]Mr 22 1831
MoSW Ja-O 1850;51-52;56;65-66
N Ap 26-My 17,O 25 1824-F 12 1827; Ap 8-15 1828; Je 14 1859
NNHi Je 1-8 1849
NbHi My 6 1886;My 3 1887
NcD F 25 1875
OClWHi Ap 13,My 4,18 1830;F-My,Jl-N 1878; Je 27 1880
TxU F 26,Mr 7,Jl 13-27,Ag 3,17 1890;Ap 9, O 9 1892
WHi [Ja 31-Jl 1832]
—d ed *See* St. Louis republic

Tri-weekly MISSOURI republican. tw 1823-
CLS Mr 22 1852
ICHi O 28 1858
ICU N 14-23,28-D 14,28 1864-Ja 2,6-F 24,Mr 2-22,27,31-Ap 7,12-My 1,8 1865
IHi [D 20 1862-O 15 1866]
IU [1859-60;62]Ja 5-9,12-14,19-21,26-F 2,6,11-13 1863
KHi [N 3 1856-S 15 1863]
MWA D 19,24-31 1835;Ja 5-23,30,F 4,9 1836; F 18 1847;Ja 14 1852; Mr 10 1863
MoHi F 8 1844;N 2 1857[Jl 1859-60]-[62]-Je 1865;66-Je,S 11,30,N 15 1867;Ja-Je 1868
MoSHi F 16,Mr 22 1827;Mr 25 1828-Mr 22 1855;F 5 1861-Ap 2 1863
PP 1862

MISSOURI republican. sw Ap 9 1833-S 1836||?
CSmH F 3 1834
MoSHi 1833-Ap 28 1835
NN Jl 5 1833

Daily MISSOURI republican. *See* St Louis republic

MISSOURI republican. d Evening ed
MoS Jl-S 1861
MoSHi Ap 20,My 5 1862;My 25,Jl 27,O 26 1863;My 5,16 1864;F 17 1865
MoSM Jl 18-D 1861
N N 6 1861

MISSOURI state atlas. w S 7 1871-72||?
DLC 1871-My 9 1872

Daily MISSOURI state journal. d Mr 11-Jl 11 1861||
Suppressed and followed by Daily bulletin
MoHi Jl 6 1861
MoS Ap-Jl 1861
MoSHi My 18,21,24,30,Je 15,Jl 6,11 1861
MoSM complete
NSyU My 1,15,22,Jl 11 1861

MISSOURI state journal. w Mr 2 1868-
CSmH Ap 6 1868

MISSOURI state republican. w,tw,d 1901-09||?
tw O 22-31 1903; d N 2 1903-Ja 2 1904
IU [My 11 1906-Ap 1907]
MoHi Ja-Jl 10,N 1903-06
MoSHi Ja 31 1902-My 23 1907
WHi Ap 13 1906-Ap 1907

Weekly MISSOURIAN. w Ag 9 1843-Ag? 1846||
1843? as Missourian. United with Missouri reporter to form St. Louis weekly union
DLC N 8 1843;Ap 5-23,My 28 1845
MoSHi D 14 1843-F 1845

Daily morning MISSOURIAN. d 1844-Ag 15 1846||?
Title varies: Daily Missourian. United with Missouri reporter to form St. Louis daily union
DLC My 1,3,7,9-10,12-15,17,19 1845[Ja-Jl 1846]
MoSHi O 7 1845-Jl 28 1846
MoSM O 21-23 1844

St. Louis daily NATIONAL live stock reporter. *See* St. Louis daily live stock reporter (National Stockyards, Ill.)

NATIVE American bulletin. *See* St. Louis democrat

Die NEUE welt. d 1868-71||?
In German
MoS N 16 1868-N 13 1869
MoSHi N 15 1868;O 7 1870
Tx S 23 1869

Die NEUE zeit. d
In German
MoSHi D 2,9,11 1863;Mr 31 1864

St. Louis NEW era. w Mr 30 1840-
DLC Mr 30 1840;Mr 26 1841
MoSHi S 25 1841;Ap 28 1842;My 25 1848
MoSW 1846

St. Louis daily NEW era. d 1840-
DLC Jl 28,D 12,23 1845[Mr 5-D 29 1849]
MWA Jl 13 1842;Jl 27 1843
MoSHi Mr 17 1847
MoSM Ap-S 1840;Mr 30 1841-Mr 1842;43;Ja-Mr 1845;46-Je 1848;49;F-D 1850
MoSU [Ap 1845-Mr 1846]

St. Louis NEW era. [For the country] tw?
DLC Mr 5/6 1845

NEW St. Louis star. *See* St Louis star-times

MISSOURI (*Continued*)

ST. LOUIS—*Continued*

Weekly St. Louis evening **NEWS.** w 1850-67||?
1850-O 13 1857? as St. Louis weekly news; O 20 1857-Je 1859 Weekly St. Louis news and intelligencer
KHi O 27 1857
MoHi Jl 20 1854-Ag 2 1855;O 20 1857-F 8 1858;Jl 10 1862

St. Louis daily evening **NEWS.** d Ap 17 1852-67||
O 13 1857-Je 24 1859 as St. Louis daily evening news and intelligencer. Merged with St. Louis dispatch
DLC S 30 1853;Ag 11,D 14 1865-O 5 1866
MWA D 22 1853; Je 3 1859
MoHi Jl 6 1852[56-63;65]
MoS Jl-D 1859
MoSHi Mr 8 1855;Je 14,Ag 13,D 4 1856;F 14, O 9 1861;F 20 1862;Ag 1,28,S 22,26,N 9 1863
MoSM 1852-63
N S 27 1859
Tx S 27 1860

Tri-weekly evening **NEWS.** tw
MWA Ag 5 1865

St. Louis daily **NEWS.** d 1881-82||?
DLC N 23 1881
MWA N 23 1881
MoHi D 6,12,18-19,23 1881;Ja 6 1882
MoS 1881-82

St. Louis **NEWS.** w 1898-1908||?
MoHi N 22 1908

St. Louis daily **NEWS.** d 1904?-
MoHi D 18 1905
MoSHi 1906-07

St. Louis **OBSERVER.** w N 21? 1833-
ICHi F 11 1836
IHi [S 1835-Jl 21 1836]
MWA D 26 1833;N 5(extra)1835

OLD school democrat and St. Louis weekly herald. w D 2 1842-
DLC Ja-F 1843
MWA Ja 13 1843
—d ed *See* St. Louis democrat

Daily **ORGAN** and reveille. d 1839-
1839-50? as Daily people's organ
DLC N 29, D23-24 1845
ICHi Ap 2 1845
MoCaT O 28 1851
MoS Ja 31 1842-F 20 1845;Ja-Je 9 1846
MoSHi Ja 31 1844;Je 29 1847
MoSM [Ja-O 1844]
NSchU Ag 25 1842

PALADIN. w Ja 12-Ap 6 1918||
WHi complete

St. Louis **PALLADIUM.** w 1884-1908||?
1884-My 1903 as Palladium
Negro
MoHi Ja 10 1903-O 1907;Ag 15 1908

Die **PAROLE.** w 1884-91||?
In German
MoHi N 15 1890

Le **PATRIOTE** et le phare des lacs. w 1878-87||?
1878? as Le Patriote
In French
IaHi My 28 1885-86
MoS 1878;86-87

Daily **PENNANT.** d 1839-
DLC D6 1839;N 3 1840
MoSHi Ap-O 19 1840

Weekly **PENNANT.** w O 26 1839-
DLC D 7 1839

PEOPLE'S weekly organ. w
IU Ap 21 1849

Daily **PEOPLE'S** organ. *See* Daily organ and reveille

PEOPLES voice.
MoSHi O 25 1914

PICKET guard. d Ag 18 1842-
DLC Ag 19 1842

Weekly St. Louis evening **PILOT.** w 1854-
1854?-Jl 26 1856 as Weekly St. Louis pilot
DLC 1855-N 15 1856

St. Louis morning **POST.** 1846?-
OClWHi F 8 1847

Saturday evening **POST.** w
MoSHi Jl 17 1847

St. Louis evening **POST.** d Ja 10-D 11 1878||
United with St. Louis dispatch to form St. Louis post and dispatch, later St. Louis post-dispatch
DLC My 23,Jl 13 1878
MWA My 28,Jl 13 1878
MoHi complete
MoS complete
MoSHi Ja 10,Je 29 1878
MoSM complete

Abend **POST** und tageblatt. d 1888-Jl? 1898||
1888-Jl? 1897 as St. Louis tageblatt. Followed by Arbeiter-zeitung
In German
MoHi O 28 1890
MoS Ap 1888-Je 1897
NN [1888-96]
WHi Je 1891;Mr 13-15,22,24-25 1893;F 25, 27-28,Mr 2-3 1895;Je 20,O 11 1897

St. Louis **POST-DISPATCH.** d D 12 1878+
Formed by union of St. Louis evening post and St. Louis dispatch. 1878-F 15 1879 as St. Louis post and dispatch
D 9 1928 is 50th anniversary ed
pub 1878+
ArHi Ap 24 1898
CL D 9 1928
CU Je 1934+
CtW My 23 1893
CtY Ap 7 1889
DLC Mr 13 1879;Je 2 1881;O 10 1883;S 1893-94;S 1918+
ICM D 9 1879;Ja 26,F 22,Mr 3 1884;Jl 10 1904
ICU D 9 1928;35+
InRE Ja 30 1884
InU O 1931+
MWA Mr 13 1879;Je 2 1881;S 18 1882;D 14 1913
MoCaT 1933+
MoFuW S 19 1932-Je 1,S 8 1933+
MoHi 1878-F 15,Mr 19 1879[F-S 1885]S 4, N 19,D 11 1886;D 2 1889;Ja 12,N 7 1890; N 13 1892;O 21-D 1 1893;Ag 1901+
MoMaryT 1934+
MoS 1878-Je 1881;82-84;S 1886+
MoSHi Jl 1884-S 1885;Ap-S,O 28,D 27 1886; Ag 10 1888;F 22,Mr 14 1891;Mr 5,D 10 1893; My 28 1896;F 16 1897;Ja 30,F 6,21,Ap 21, My 17,Jl 4,14 1898;1900-Ap,Jl 1918-O 1919
NBuG D 9 1928
NN D 9 1928
NNC D 9 1928
NbHi O 3 1892;N 1-8 1896;Ja 31 1904
NhD D 9 1928
OHi 1933+
OOxM D 16 1880;D 14 1881;O 27 1882
OkU [1932]

St. Louis **POST-DISPATCH.** w 1878-88||?
IaHi Je 24 1880-Jl 14 1881;S-O 1887

St. Louis daily **PRESS.** d 1864-
ICHi O 1,N 12 1864
MoSHi Ap 16 1865
MoSW D 1864-Ag 1866

St. Louis **PRICE-CURRENT.** w 1850?-
1850?-52? as St. Louis price current and merchants' commercial record
MWA Mr 31 1864
MoSHi Mr 9 1850-D 11 1852;55-Ja 1 1856
WHi My 19 1856-Ap 1857

St. Louis **PRICE CURRENT** and trade journal. w 1874?-
DLC N 22 1877
MWA N 22 1877

PRZEWODNIK polski. w 1899+
In Polish
IU D 20 1917+
MoSHi 1903-10;13-28

St. Louis **REFERENDUM**
MoSHi Ap 23 1902

REFORM. *See under* Kansas City

St. Louis **REGISTER.** w My 12? 1821-
MoSM D 8 1821
N S 22-29 1821;Mr 16,Ap 6 1822

REPORTER (for the country). tw
DLC Mr 1845-Mr 25 1846
MoSM Jl 28-Ag 21 1846
—d,w ed *See* Missouri reporter

St. Louis **REPUBLIC.** d S 20 1836-D 4 1919||
1836-N 3 1873? as Daily Missouri republican; N 4 1873-D 15 1876? Saint Louis republican; D 16 1876-My 30 1888 Missouri republican. Merged with St. Louis globe-democrat
Jl 12 1908 is centennial ed
A 1884-88;Jl 1889-Je 1894
ArHi O 15 1864
C Ja 11 1877-My 1887;My 31 1888-F 27 1889;Jl-D 1890
CLM Mr 18 1890;S 17 1902;D 13 1903
CSmH S 16,O 11,27 1867;F 3,Je 26,Ag 8 1868
CSt-H [1914-15]
CtW My 19,24 1893
CtY 1859-65; S 10 1877;D 23 1891
DLC Ag 17 1839;O 30 1840;Mr-D 1841;D 5 1845;My 27 1846;Mr 1849-54;S 23,D 23-24 1856;Mr 18,Ag 22 1857;Ja 8 1858-60;S 3 1861; Mr 5,Ap 15,O 23 1862;F 8-14 1865;F 14,S 25 1866;Ja 18,F 26,Mr 6,8,11-12 1867[Ja-Mr 1868] F 13,15,17 1869;F 18 1871;73-Mr 1899;1900-19
I 1914-N 1919
IAl Je 1847-48
IC Ja 13-Je 1873;My 1 1889;Jl 12 1908
ICHi O 16,N 6,21 1865
ICM My 29 1876;Ja 31,Je 21,24 1882[Ap-My 1883]F 23,My 15 1884
ICN F-D 1873
ICU [Ag-D 1863]D 19 1864;F 17,19-21,24,Mr 3-4,7,Ap 9-10 1865
IEa 1901-19
IHi [Mr 14 1850-N 16 1865]Jl 12 1908;S 14 1914
ILeM Jl 12 1908
IU Ja 7,Ag 9 1859;Mr 15 1861;Ja 24,29-30, F 5,22,Mr 30,Ap 17-18,23,25,My 12,N 12 1862;Mr 27,My 11,Jl 22,O 10 1863;Mr 23-24 1865;Ja 12,Mr 23 1867;Mr 10 1868;My 14 1869[S-D 1871;F 1872-S 1873;My-D 1874; Ja-Ag 1875;76-N 1877;80-82;84-N 1887]F 21,Mr 20,30,Ap 3-8,12,My 14,17-18 1888;My 1909-N 1919
IaDH Ap 10 1852
IaHi Mr 1898-Mr,Ag 1902-Ag 1903
InMovHi S 15 1901
InRE D 16 1872
KHi Mr-D 1841
LNH Ag 29 1864;Jl 31 1865
MB Ap 20 1850;Ag 23 1852;D 31 1856[Jl-D 4 1864]Ja 16-17,22-23 1865;D 15 1883
MBAt 1862-Je 1864;Ap 15,17,19 1865
MNaHi My 3 1860
MWA My 6 1841;My 10 1848;Mr 6,Jl 10-23, O 6-13,O 21,N 11-D 9 1849;Ja 1,6-13,F 6, 10,N 4,17-24,D 22 1850;D 7 1852;My 14,O 6, D 23 1853;N 9 1854;My 28 1856;Je 26[Jl 7-Ag 25]1857;Je 6,16,Jl 20,Ag 17-18,21,24,29-S 1,6-11,29,N 11 1858;Mr 27,Ap 16(supp)19,Jl 10,13,S 10(supp)25 1859;Ja 10 1861;Ja 28 1862-63;S 14,16 1867;S 14 1868;Mr 13,15,O 22 1869; Ja 9 1873;F 11-Mr 29 1874;Ap 2,O 15 1876; S 10 1877;F 5-D 1879;Mr 15 1882;S 29 1883; Mr 2 1884; O 5 1885
MiU [1880]81
Mo S 1866-Jl 1874;Jl 1879-Mr,Jl 1880-S 1889; Ap 1892-1919
MoCaT D 3 1843;Jl 27 1882;My 2 1889;1913-19
MoHi Mr-D 1841;Mr 1849-50(photostat)[56-65]-Jl,N 17,22 1872;N 1874-Ag,O 1888-N 1891;Ap 16-17,24,Je 26,Jl 10,17,Ag 21,D 16 1892;Ap 15-My 15,Jl 8,S,N 1893;Mr 20,Ap 1-15,Je-Jl 15,Ag 16-D 15 1894;Ja 16 1895-O, N 16-D 16 1897;Ja 16 1898-1919
MoJ 1901-19
MoK Ap 15-N 1904;Jl 12 1908
MoS 1851-53;Ap-D 1854;Mr 1855-59;S 1860-Je 1869;70-84;Jl 1885-1919
MoSHi complete
MoSM [1847-48]-[50-51]53-Je 1862;63-Je 1869; My 26 1870-1919
MoSU 1859-S 1916
MoSW 1847;49-55;57-Je 1869;My 1870-1914
MsHi [1857-58]Ag 24 1863[66]
N N 6 1861;Jl 17,N 29 1862;F 11,My 1 1863; Ag 24 1864;S 10 1866;Jl 19 1867;F 10,17 1876
NBuG Ag 8-S 12 1856
NN S 28,30,N 16 1865
NSchU Ap 5,My 10 1842
NSyU My 1,Ag 13,20-21 1862;Jl 29 1873
NbHi Ap 5,Je 24 1892;Ap 4-5,Je 16,30 1893; F 16,Mr 9,Ag 16,S 2,12,14,N 15,19 1894; N 1-8 1896;My 26 1899;N 4-11 1900;Je 1 1903; My 13 1904;Ag 26 1906;Jl 12 1908
NcD Ag 25 1861
NcU Ja 26 1876-Mr,Jl 1877-Ja,S 1 1878
NhD Mr 10,13 1861
OClWHi My 26 1861;Ap 12 1862;Mr 16 1864; My 21 1868
OHi F 23 1863;Ja-O 1919
OOxM N 4 1876;D 15 1881;O 11 1882
PEHi My 28 1856
PPGr Ap 13 1865
PWaHi Jl 12 1908
TJT O 15 1900
Tx D 29 1870
TxU [N 21 1899-Mr 21 1900]
WHi My 28 1860;65
—w ed *See* Missouri republican

St. Louis **REPUBLIC.** sw My 1888-1919||?
Jl 12 1908 is centennial ed
MoHi F-D 1892;My-D 1893;F 1894-Mr 1895
MoSHi O 23 1890-Je 28 1894;Jl 1909-Ja 13 1910;12-14
MsSM 1906-[13]
WHi 1892-O 1893;Jl 12 1908

St. Louis **REPUBLICAN.** *See* St. Louis republic

REPUDIATOR. w F 20? 1868-
DLC Mr 5-12,26 1868
MWA Mr 12 1868

St. Louis **REVEILLE.** d My 14 1844-50||?
United with Daily people's organ to form Daily organ and reveille
CLS Ag 18 1850
CSmH S 9 1846
DLC N 19,22,D 1,13,25 1844;Ag 7,N 28-29,D 4, 20-21,24 1845;Ja 7,15 1846
ICN 1844-My 12,Je-O 6 1850
MHi S 27 1847
MoSHi Ag 16,S 26,O 4,20,D 18 1847;Ja 24,F 22 1848
MoSU 1844-N 13 1845
WHi S 28 1845

Weekly **REVEILLE.** w Jl 15 1844-50||?
ICN 1844-S 1850
MWA N 2,D 14 1846-Ja 4,Ap 5,19,My 24, Je 7,21,Jl 5-12,Ag 2,15,30-S 20,O 4,D 13 1847
MoS 1844-46
MoSHi 1844-O 7 1850
MoSM 1844[45]-Jl 5 1847
MoSU 1844-Jl 7 1845
NNHi O 22-N 5,D 17 1848[49]-Ap 19 1850
OHi Ja 5 1849

REVUE de l'ouest. Ja 7 1854-65||?
In French
CaQMF 1862-S 1865

REVUE icarienne.
LNM O 15 1858

ROLLING ball.
MoSHi Je 16 1850

ST. LOUIS county watchman. *See* Watchman-advocate (Clayton)

St. Louis **SATURDAY** night. w Mr 6 1920-
MoHi 1920-S 1921
MoS 1920

SAYINGS. *See* St. Louis star-times

Morning **SIGNAL.** d 1851-53||?
Follows Barnburner. Merged with Missouri democrat
MoSM Ja-Jl 8 1852

SLASHER. w Ap 4-N? 1844||
IU Ap 4 1844
MWA Ag 24 1844
MoSM Ap 27 1844
OHi Je 25 1844
—d ed *See* Missouri reporter

SOUTH ST. LOUIS progress. w 1891-1902||?
1891-Ap 29 1899 as Carondelet progress
MoHi N 26 1898-99

SQUATTER. w 1848||
MoHi O 14 1848
—d ed *See* St. Louis daily union

St. Louis evening **STAR.** d 1878-79||?
DLC F 19 1879

MISSOURI (*Continued*)

ST. LOUIS—*Continued*

St. Louis STAR-times. w,d My 4 1884+
1884-N 13 1887 as St. Louis Sunday sayings; N 20 1887-Ap 15 1888 Sayings; Ap 19 1888-Mr 28 1895 Evening star-sayings; Mr 29-D 1895 St. Louis star-sayings; 1896-Je 23 1932 St. Louis star (Je 6 1905-O 24 1908 St. Louis star and chronicle; O 1913-O 9 1914 New St. Louis star) Je 24-Jl 23 1932 St. Louis star St. Louis times; Jl 25 1932-D 2 1933 St. Louis star and times
w 1884-Ap 15 1888
IU My 16,20,27,29[Je-S 1]N 19 1909;My 16 1914-Je 1918
MWA O 23 1887
MoHi S 22 1890;N 20 1891;F 17 1892;O 29 1899;O 14 1903-F 1904;Jl-S 1905;14+
MoS 1884-O 28 1888;Ja 29 1889-Ag,O 1902-Mr,My 1904+
MoSHi Je 14 1896;F 16 1897;Mr 6,17,Jl 14,31 1898;F 27, My 8 1900;Ap 2 1901;O 25 1902; Ap 29 1903;Je 13 1903;Mr 13 1904;F 17 1906; O 9 1913;O 15 1917;O 3 1919
TJT D 4 1904

STEAMER City of Memphis reporter. d 1858-
CL My 1 1858

St. Louis TAGEBLATT. *See* Abend post und tageblatt

St. Louis TAGES-CHRONIK. d 1852-
In German
MoS 1858-59

TÄGLICHE. . . *See* next important word: e.g., Tägliche volkszeitung is alphabeted as **Volkszeitung**

Le TELEGRAPHE. sw Ap 11 1840-
In French
DLC Ap 25 1840
NN Ap 15 1840
WHi Ap 11,29 1840

St. Louis TIMES. w Jl 7 1829-
CSmH Ag 28 1830
Ct [1830-31]
DLC Jl 7-21,Ag 31 1829
ICHi F 4-My 19,Je 2-16,30-Jl 14,Ag 11,S 15,O 6-15,27 1832-Ja 19,F-My 11,25,Je 8-Jl 13,Ag 3,30 5,19,D 7,21 1833-Ja 4 1834
MWA Ap 10 1830;F 12,D 10 1831;My 5 1832; F 23-Mr 2,30 1833
MoSM Jl 10-D 1830;Ja-Mr 1832
N S 28 1833
WHi F-My 12 1832

Daily St. Louis TIMES. d Ap 1850-
MoSM My 27-D 1850
TxU My 1850-Ap 1851

St. Louis TIMES. d Jl 21 1866-81||?
1866-N 15 1878 as St. Louis daily times; N 16 1878-O 22 1879 St. Louis times-journal
CSmH O 27 D 20 1867;Ja 4,Ap 29 1868
DLC [Ja-Mr 1868]F 17,S 14 1869;O 15 1871; N 3 1872 O 12 1873;F 19,Je 7,27,D 5 1874; N 28 1875;Jl 1877-D 26 1879
ICM F 15 1880
IU F 15 1881
KHi Ag 25 1869;Mr 22 1870;Jl 23 1872
MWA N 26 1870;S 30 1875
MoHi S-D 1870;Ap 14 1872;76-S 1877;Ja-Mr,Jl-D 1878
MoS 1866-Ja 10 1881
MoSHi Mr 28 1874
MoSM 1866[67-68]-[70]-[72]-[75]-Je 1880
OClWHi F 3 1876
OOxM S 5 1874;N 4 1876

St. Louis TIMES. w 1866-81||?
N 16? 1878-O 22 1879 as St. Louis times-journal
C Ja 9 1873-Ja 1874
ICHi O 15(supp)1871
MoSM Jl 1877-Je 1880
NcD 1879
TJT Mr 25 1875

St. Louis TIMES. d 1895-Je 23 1932||
United with St. Louis star to form St. Louis star-times
MoHi My 1907-Je 1916;Je 23 1932
MoS Ap 15 1907-32
MoSHi Ap 15 1907-17

St. Louis daily TRIBUNE. d 1869-71||?
MoHi Ag 21 1870
MoSM O 25 1869-Je 1870

St. Louis TRIBUNE. d 1880-97||?
In German
MoS S 1880-97
MoSHi Ap 2,14 1881

TWICE-A-WEEK. . . *See* next important word: e.g., Twice-a-week globe-democrat is alphabeted as **Globe-democrat**

St. Louis daily UNION. d Ag 17 1846-67||?
Formed by the union of Daily morning Missourian and Missouri reporter. Title varies: St. Louis daily morning union. Merged with St. Louis dispatch
DLC 1846-Ap 6 1849
IHi My 18 1849
IU S 14 1858;S 5,O 23,N 29 1862;F 20,Mr 20, O 14 1863
MWA D 12 1846;N 22 1852
MoS Je 10 1862-Je 19 1863
MoSHi Ag 27 1846;Ap 21 1847;Jl 28 1848; S 12 1851 Je 30 1863-N 12 1864]
MoSM 1846[47-48]-51;Je 9 1862-Je 8 1863
MoSW Je 1853-N 1864
WHi [1846 Ja 6-Ap 1847;Ja 1-10,My 31-Ag 12,S 23-24 1848;My 21 1850
—**Campaign ed.** 1848 *See* Squatter

St. Louis weekly UNION. w Ag 25? 1846-
Formed by union of Missouri reporter and Weekly Missourian
MoSHi Jl 28 1848
MoSM Ag 25 1846-47

St. Louis daily evening UNION. d
MWA My 9 1848;F 11 1851;Ap 24 1852

St. Louis tri-weekly UNION. tw
MoHi Ap 7-10,Je 22 1847

VOLKSSTIMME des westens. d S 3 1877-80||?
Prospectus S 1 1877
In German
MoS S 1 1877-Je 19 1880
NN S 21,O 4-5,D 14 1877;F 20,S 9 1878
WHi S 1 1877-78

Tägliche VOLKSZEITUNG. d 1865-69||?
In German
WHi Mr 21-Jl 13 1866

St. Louis WASHINGTONIAN. w Ap 23? 1842-
MWA Jl 16 1842

WESTERN atlas, and Saturday evening gazette. w Ja 10 1839-
DLC Mr 21 1840
MWA D 12 1840-[41]-Ja 5,19-26 1842
MoSHi Ja 11 1840
MoSM Ja 16 1841- Je 1842

WESTERN banner.
MoSeR 1858-59

WESTERN emigrant. *See* St. Louis enquirer

WESTERN home press. w Ja 7 1860-
DLC Ja 7-14,Mr 3-17,31 1860

WESTERN journal. *See* St. Louis enquirer

WESTLICHE blätter. *See* Anzeiger des westens: Sonntagsblatt

De WESTLICHE post. d S 27 1857+
In German
pub 1857+
IU D 2 1906;S 1917+
MoHi S 26-27,29,D 18-20,22 1905;Ja 17 1906; Jl 1914-20
MoS 1857-59;D 1898+
MoSHi O 26 1861;S 29 1881;Ja 30 1899;F 26, Ap 24 1900;D 13 1915;Ja 1 1918
NN O 7 1904
NNHi Mr 5,My 2,O 9 1873
OkU [1933]34
Tx My 24 1874[75]
—**Sunday ed.** *See* Mississippi blätter

Die WESTLICHE post. d
Country ed
In German
MoS S 13-D 1909;My-Ag,D 1910-12;Jl-D 1915

Die WESTLICHE post. sw
In German
MoS 1899-1901

WOMAN'S national daily. *See* Woman's national weekly

WOMAN'S national weekly. d,w N 1 1906-My 1916||?
1906-Mr 16 1911 as Woman's national daily (d)
C Ag 1915-My 6 1916
Ct Je 26 1915
DLC 1906-15
MnHi [1911-16]
MoHi D 1908-My 1916
MoSHi Je 6,8 1908
NN My 23 1908;Mr 25,N 30,D 15 1909;Ja 26 1910
NbHi D 31 1909[10-Mr 15 1911]
OO [1906;08-16]
Tx S 14,19,O 20,N 18-19,29,D 16,29 1910;Ja 6, 13-14,17-18 1911
VU N 5,9,20 1907;My 1,Jl 14,24,Ag 14,O 15, N 11,D 4 1909;Ja 29,My 16 1910;Je 29 1912

St. Louis WORLD. d 1902-18||?
MoHi 1903-O,N 8,D 3,5,9,15 1904
MoS Je 1902-S 1906
MoSHi Mr 3 1918

ST. MARYS

St. Marys weekly REVIEW. w 1907+
MoCaT 1917-18

SALEM

DEMOCRAT-BULLETIN. w 1899-O 28 1931||
1899-1904? as Democratic bulletin. Merged with Salem post
MoHi 1902-11;Ap 1930-31
MoSalP 1928-O 1929

DEMOCRATIC bulletin. *See* Democrat-bulletin

DENT county post. *See* Salem post

Salem MONITOR. w 1868-1920||?
MoCaT 1907-20
MoHi My 4 1872;Mr 8,Ap 12 1873-76;81-99; 1901-20

Salem NEWS. w 1909+
MoCaT Je 1918-19
MoHi Ag 12 1909-Jl 13 1911;Je 1918-Ja 1919; 20+

Salem POST. w 1912+
1912-19? as Dent county post; 1920?-27 Post
pub 1913+
MoCaT 1917-19;21-26
MoHi O 1912-21;N 1931+

Salem REPUBLICAN. w 1880-
MoHi O 27 1880

REPUBLICAN. w,sw 1895-1918||?
1895-My 1906 as Republican-headlight (sw)
MoCaT 1917-My 1918
MoHi 1905-06;Ja 11 1907-My 1918

SOUTHERN Missouri argus. w 1860-
MoHi Je 30 1860

SALISBURY

Salisbury BULLETIN. *See* Salisbury press-spectator

CHARITON county democrat. *See* Salisbury democrat

Salisbury DEMOCRAT. w 1883-D 21 1917||
1883-90? as Chariton county democrat. Merged with Salisbury press-spectator
MoHi O 24 1890;Ja 9 1903-17

Salisbury PRESS-SPECTATOR. w F 26 1869+
1869 as Salisbury bulletin; 1870-Jl 8 1881 Salisbury press
pub 1869;D 1877+
MoHi Jl 26 1901+

Salisbury SPECTATOR. w N 1880-Jl 1881||
United with Salisbury press to form Salisbury press-spectator

SARCOXIE

Sarcoxie LEADER. w 1893-1908||?
1893-F 6 1903 as Sarcoxie tribune
MoH D 1898-F 1908

Sarcoxie RECORD. w 1901+
MoH O 30 1903-05;14+

Sarcoxie TRIBUNE. *See* Sarcoxie leader

Sarcoxie VINDICATOR. w 1881-91||?
MoHi O 23 1890

SAVANNAH

ANDREW county democrat. w Ag 1876-S 1925||
1876-1908? as Savannah democrat. United with Savannah reporter to form Savannah reporter and Andrew county democrat
MoHi O 24 1890;N 25 1898-1925
MoSaR 1880-1925

ANDREW COUNTY new era. w 1864-72||?
1864-70? as New era
MoHi My 19 1870

ANDREW COUNTY republican. w 1871-76||?
MoSaR 1872-74

Weekly COURIER. w Ja 1 1868-69||?
NbHi Ja 1 1868

Savannah DEMOCRAT. *See* Andrew county democrat

MISSOURI plaindealer. w 1861-
MoHi Ap 2 1864

NEW era. *See* Andrew county new era

NORTHWEST democrat. w 1854-57||?
MoSaR 1854-57

Savannah REPORTER and Andrew county democrat. w Ap 28 1876+
1876-S 1925 as Savannah reporter
pub 1876+
MoHi O 24 1890;Jl 26 1901+
MoSa 1912+

Savannah SENTINEL. w N 1 1851-53||
DLC Ja 10 1852
MoHi N 1,15-22,D 6,20 1851;Ja 3,17-24,D 11 1852[53]
MoSaR complete

Savannah TRIBUNE. w 1870-
MoHi My 28 1870

SCHELL CITY

Schell City NEWS. w S 4 1880+
pub 1890+
MoHi O 30 1890;N 17 1904

SEDALIA

Sedalia ADVERTISER. w Ag 20 1864-
MoSe 1864

Sedalia ADVERTISER. w? N 15 1877-
MoHi N 15 1877

ADVOCATE. w Ja 24 1891-
MoHi Ja-Mr 7 1891

Daily BAZOO. d 1869-95||?
MoHi O 12 1869[Mr-Je 1873]-[Jl-D 1874]-75;Ag 20 1876;77-Je 1887;Ja-[N-D]1888-93; F 17,21,Mr 17 1895
MoSHi Mr 21-Ag 1870
MoSe S 20 1870-Je 1872;Ja-Je 1873
OOxM O 11 1882

Sedalia BAZOO. w Je 1 1869-1904||?
Title varies: Sedalia weekly bazoo
MoBoH Jl 1895-My 1896
MoHi Je 15 1869;Je 1877-87;89-93;F 12 1901; Jl 19 1904
MoSe My 30,Jl 18-25,Ag 15-29,S 12,26 1871; 72-Mr 18 1873;74-O 9 1895

BLUE ribbon. w Ag 15 1877-
MoSe Ag 15,O 6 1877

Weekly BULLETIN. w 1885-
MoHi O 31-N 7,21-28,D 19 1885

Saturday evening CALL. w 1879-81||
MoHi Ja 24 1880;Mr 7 1881

Sedalia daily CAPITAL. d My 7 1895+
pub 1922-Ap 1924;25-My,S 1931+
DLC Jl-D 1898
MoHi My 1895-97;F 1898;Ja-Mr,My-S,N-D 1899;Ag 15 1900;F 1901+
MoSe My 1895-Ap 1905

Sedalia weekly CONSERVATOR. w My 8 1903-09||
Negro
MoHi 1903-[06-S 1908]

MISSOURI (*Continued*)

SEDALIA—*Continued*

Sedalia DEMOCRAT. d 1868+
1907-Mr 1912 as Sedalia democrat-sentinel
pub 1892+
DLC S 4 1879
ICM My 18 1884
MoHi D 1871-My,Jl 1872-Je,O 3 1875;76;Jl 1877-Je,Ag 29 1882;83-85;Jl 1886-Je 1887; Ja 29,Ap-Je 1888;D 1891-Ag,S 26,N 30 1893;94; F 7,My 14,D 5-6 1895;96-F,Ap 1898-Mr 1901; Jl 24,N 6,9-10 1904;Ja 27 1905;19+
MoSe D 19 1871-82;84-Je 1885;D 1893-O 1894; 96;My 1899-Jl 1901;Ja-Je 1902;08-O 1918;19+

Sedalia weekly DEMOCRAT. w 1868+
1868? as Democratic press; 1869-Ja 18 1882 Sedalia democrat
pub 1892+
InRE Mr 16 1873
MoHi F-D 17 1868;Mr 18 1869-Ja,Je 20 1878; 82;F 24-My,Je 9,O 6,17 1883;N 3 1893
MoSe 1870-71;76-84;86

DEMOCRATIC press. See Sedalia weekly democrat

Sedalia daily EAGLE-TIMES. d 1878-82||?
1878-81? as Sedalia daily eagle
MoHi N 14 1880;F 13,20,Mr 6,13,20,Ap 10,17, Jl 3 1881
MoSe 1879;F 22 1882

Sedalia weekly EAGLE-TIMES. w Ag 2 1878-82||?
Follows Boonville weekly eagle. 1878-81? as Sedalia weekly eagle
MoHi 1878-Jl,N 14 1879;F 27,Mr 9 1881

EARTH. w 1885-87||?
MoHi D 19 1885;Mr 27-Ap 10,24,My 1-15,Je 26,D 18 1886

Sedalia FREE press. d 1877-
MoSe [Mr 23-Ag 17 1877]

Sedalia FREE press. w 1877-79||?
MoSe Ag 25 1877

Saturday FREE press. w Mr 2 1895-
MoHi Mr 2,30-Ap 6 1895

Sedalia morning GAZETTE. d 1888-Ag 1895||
Merged with Sedalia daily capital
MoBoH 1892
MoHi D 1888-Mr,Je 14,Jl 1894-95
MoSe 1888-Je 1890;91-Mr 1892;93-95

INDEPENDENT press. w Mr 31 1866-
MoHi Mr 31,Ap 12,Jl 19,D 20 1866;Ja 10, Mr 28-Ap 4,My 30,S 19,O 4(extra) 1867
PWcHi O 11 1866

Sedalia JOURNAL. w 1877-1917||?
In German
MoHi D 1898-1906;09-My 10 1917

MISSOURI new age. w Ag 3 1882-83||?
MoSe Ag 10 1882-O 6 1883

Evening NEWS. d 1880-85||?
MoHi F 18,Mr 30,Ap 7,17,23,27,My 11,24-25, 27,Jl 15,Ag 30 1880
MoSe Mr 9 1885

ONWARD republican. d 1888-
MoHi My 14 1888

PENNY earth. Ja 7 1900-
MoHi Ja 7 1900

Sedalia evening REPUBLICAN. d 1870-
1870? as Daily republican
MoHi O 14 1870;My 9,Ag 25-O 7,N 18 1884
MoSe Ag 25 1884-Mr 1885

Sunday REPUBLICAN. w 1876-
MoSe S 3 1876

ROSA PEARLE'S paper. w 1893-1910||?
MoHi 1902-09
MoSHi Ap 6 1907
MoSe S 16-23 1899;N 9 1907;Jl 18,S 19-26, O 10-24 1908;Mr 26 1910

Sedalia SENTINEL sw,w 1886-D 1906||
1886-92? as Central Missouri sentinel; 1893-95? Enterprise-sentinel. Merged with Sedalia democrat sw 1900-01?
MoHi N 20 1886-Ja 1889;N 1 1890;Ja 14-24, Mr 14 1891[93]Je 16,S 29 1894;My 11,O 12 1895
MoSeD S 1898-Jl 1 1906

Sedalia evening SENTINEL. d 1895-D 1906||
Ja-Je 5 1896 as Evening star-sentinel. United with Sedalia democrat (d) to form Sedalia democrat-sentinel, later Sedalia democrat
MoHi Ja-Ag 1896;97-1906
MoSe S 1901-O 19,N 1902-06
MoSeD 1898-Ap 1 1899;S 1900-02

SOCIAL messenger. w 1912-18||?
MoSe Ja 18-25,Ap 26,My 31 1913;My 16,S 19, O 24,N 7,D 12 1914;D 11,25 1915-Ja 1,N 18 1916;Mr 3 1917

Sedalia morning STAR. d -D 31 1895||
Merged with Sedalia evening sentinel to form Evening star-sentinel, later Sedalia evening sentinel
MoHi N-D 1895

Evening STAR-SENTINEL. *See* Sedalia evening sentinel

Sedalia weekly TIMES. w Mr 31 1865-81||?
United with Sedalia eagle to form Sedalia eagle-times
MoHi Mr 31 1865;F 9 1866-S 1872;73-80
WHi N 24 1865

Sedalia daily TIMES. d 1872-81||?
United with Sedalia daily eagle to form Sedalia daily eagle-times
MoHi N 1872-My 3 1873;N 7 1881

Sedalia TIMES. w 1894-1905||?
Negro
MoHi Ag 31 1901-D 19 1903;Ja 21,F 4 1905

TRUTH. w F 21- 1889||?
MoHi F 21 1889

SELIGMAN

Seligman SUNBEAM. w N 5 1881-97||?
MoHi N 1 1890

SENATH

DUNKLIN county republican. w Ap 1 1910+
1910-O 1921 as Senath leader
MoCaT 1917-19

Senath LEADER. *See* Dunklin county republican

SENECA

Seneca DISPATCH. *See* Seneca news-dispatch

Seneca HUSTLER. w 1903-08||?
Merged with Seneca dispatch, later Seneca news-dispatch
MoHi D 22 1904

Seneca NEWS-DISPATCH. w 1881+
1881-1908? as Seneca dispatch; 1909?-11? Dispatch hustler; 1912? Seneca dispatch
pub 1897+

SEYMOUR

Seymour CITIZEN. w Ja 18 1907+
MoHi Ag 1923+

Seymour ENTERPRISE. w 1886-95||?
MoHi O 10 1890

SENTINEL. w Ja 22- 1904||?
MoHi Ja-Ag 1904

SHELBINA

Shelbina DEMOCRAT. w 1869+
pub 1870+
MoHi O 29 1890;Jl 24 1901+

Shelbina TORCHLIGHT. w 1882-1922||?
MoHi N 7 1890;Ag 9 1901-22

SHELBYVILLE

SHELBY county herald. w 1870+
pub 1870+
MoHi O 22 1890;1904-05;25+

SHELDON

Sheldon ENTERPRISE. w 1881+
pub 1895+
MoHi Ag 1901+

Sheldon NEWS. w 1889-92||?
MoHi O 30 1890

SHERIDAN

Sheridan ADVANCE. w 1888+
F 14-Ap 11 1902 as Sheridan advance-news
MoHi O 30 1890;1902-22

Sheridan NEWS. w 1901-Ja 1902||?
United with Sheridan advance-news to form Sheridan advance-news, later Sheridan advance

SIKESTON

Sikeston ENTERPRISE. w 1884-1909||?
MoHi My 1906-09

Sikeston HERALD. w 1900+
pub F 1916+
MoCaT 1917-19
MoHi F 21 1919+

Sikeston STANDARD. w,sw 1911+
w 1911-17?
MoCaT 1917-19
MoHi 1914+

SILEX

Silex INDEX. w 1893+
MoHi Jl 25 1901+

SKIDMORE

NEW era. *See* Skidmore news

Skidmore NEWS. w 1895+
1895-F 9 1905 as Skidmore standard; F 16 1905-15 New era
MoHi Ag 12 1898-1904;F 16 1905-Mr 1927

Skidmore STANDARD. *See* Skidmore news

SLATER

Slater MISSOURI index. w 1880-99||?
MoHi D 1898-D 14 1899
MoSHi D 15 1898

Slater NEWS. w 1907+
MoHi 1913+
MoSl O 1930-O 7 1933

Slater RUSTLER. w F 25 1885+
pub 1885+
MoHi 1903+
MoSl O 1930-O 7 1933

SMITHTON

Smithton REVIEW. w 1872-
MoHi Mr 19 1872

Smithton SUNBEAM. w 1896-1907||?
MoHi Ja-O 18 1907

Smithton TIMES. w 1908+
KHi Ja 5 1928

SMITHVILLE

DEMOCRAT-HERALD. w 1889+
1889-1908 as Smithville democrat
pub 1915+
MoHi 1914+

Smithville HERALD. w 1889-1908||
United with Smithville democrat to form Democrat-herald
MoHi Jl 1901-08

Smithville STAR. w 1901-08||?
MoHi Ag 13 1903-07

SOUTHWEST CITY

REPUBLIC. w Ag 1902+
pub 1902+
MoHi S 1903-04;Ja-Ap 1906;19+

SPARTA

CHRISTIAN county leader. w 1900-07||?
MoHi Ag-D 1903

SPICKARD

GRUNDY county gazette. w 1887+
Ap 25 1907-Jl 7 1910 as Spickard herald and Grundy county gazette
MoHi Jl 31 1901+

SPICKARD herald and Grundy county gazette. *See* Grundy county gazette

SPRINGFIELD

Springfield ADVERTISER. w My 14 1844-
MWA Ap 2 1861
MoHi 1844-Je 22 1847(photostat)
MoSHi Jl 11 1848-F 10 1849
MoSp [1844-47]

Springfield ADVERTISER. w 1871-76||?
United with Missouri patriot to form Patriot-advertiser, later Springfield patriot

AMERICAN negro. w 1890-
MoHi O 15 1890

COMMERCIAL events. w F 12 1928+
Follows Springfield express
pub 1928+
—d ed *See* Daily events

Springfield DEMOCRAT. d 1890-94||?
United with Springfield daily leader to form Springfield leader-democrat, later Springfield leader and press
MoHi O 26 1890
WHi Ag 20 1894+

Daily EVENTS. d Jl 1928+
pub 1928+
— w ed *See* Commercial events

Springfield EXPRESS. w Ap 1 1881-F 5? 1928||
Followed by Commercial events
MoHi 1881-Mr 9 1894;Jl 10 1908

Springfield daily HERALD. d 1883-91||?
KHi S 1-2 1888
MoSHi My 31 1885

HERALD. w 1906-11||?
MoHi Jl 17 1908

Weekly Springfield JOURNAL. w My 21 1862-65||?
MWA Mr 31 1863;O 2 1865

Springfield LABORER. d 1916-26||?
IU D 8 1916-Jl 16 1917
MoHi [D 12 1916-Je 15 1917]

Springfield LEADER and press. d 1882+
1882-94? as Springfield daily leader; 1895?-1901? Springfield leader-democrat; 1902? Springfield leader and democrat; 1903?-My 14 1933 Springfield leader
Sunday issues as Springfield news and leader
KHi [Ag 29 1888-Ja 1889]N 26 1924;Jl 7,11 1927
MoHi My 8 1870;O 23 1890;D 1892;My 1902+
MoSHi D 2 1886;Mr 3 1912;F 25 1918
MoSp [1911+]
MoSpD 1934+
OkMT My 15 1933+
WHi 1917-19

MILITARY news.
MoSHi Je 29 1861

MISSOURI army argus. *See under* Corinth, Miss.

MISSOURI weekly patriot. *See* Springfield patriot

MISSOURIAN. *See* Springfield patriot

Springfield daily NEWS. d 1892+
1892-Ja 2 1927 as Springfield republican
KHi Ag 18 1926;Ap 13 1927
MoHi Je 5 1892;Jl 14 1903-My 1904;Jl 16,O-N 1908;Je 11,Jl 4,10,22,S 19 1909;Ap 6,Ag 1910+
MoSp 1910+
MoSpD 1934+
OkMT 1928+

MISSOURI (*Continued*)

SPRINGFIELD—*Continued*

Springfield PATRIOT. w Mr 1 1862-83||?
1862-63 Missourian; 1864-76 Missouri weekly patriot; 1877-81? Patriot-advertiser
MWA O 19 1865;Ja 18 1866
MoHi Jl 1 1869

Semi-weekly PATRIOT. d,tw,sw S 11 1866-
S-D 1? 1866 as Missouri daily patriot; D 13 1866-Jl 1867 Tri-weekly patriot
MoHi 1866-S 13 1867

Springfield PRESS. d Mr 4 1929-My 14 1933||
United with Springfield leader to form Springfield leader and press
MoHi complete
MoSp complete

Springfield daily REPUBLICAN. d 1884-89||?
KHi S 15-D 16 1888

Springfield REPUBLICAN. 1892-1927 *See* Springfield daily news

SOUTHWEST union press. w
WHi D 2 1866

Springfield WHIG. w S 11 1848-
C 1848-S 15 1849

STANBERRY

GENTRY COUNTY headlight. *See* Stanberry headlight

Standberry HEADLIGHT. w 1894+
1894-Ap 5 1910 as Gentry county headlight; Ap 12 1910-Ag 1913 Stanberry owl-headlight
pub F 1922+
MoHi N 22 1898-1900;02-Mr 18,Ap 12 1910-Ag 1913;F 4 1926+

Stanberry HERALD. w 1887-D 3 1925||
Merged with Stanberry owl-headlight, later Stanberry headlight
MoHi Ja 3 1914-25

Stanberry OWL. w 1900-Ap 5 1910||
United with Gentry county headlight to form Stanberry owl-headlight, later Stanberry headlight
MoHi Ag 26 1902-10

Stanberry OWL-HEADLIGHT. *See* Stanberry headlight

STEELE

ENTERPRISE. w 1921+
pub [1921-My 1931]+

STEELVILLE

CRAWFORD county democrat. *See* Steelville ledger

CRAWFORD mirror. w Ap 7 1872+
MWA My 24,Je 21 1872
MoCaT 1919
MoHi 1908-[Ja-F 1928]Ap 1929+

CRAWFORD sentinel. w
MoHi N 1890

Steelville LEDGER. w 1887+
1887-O 7 1905 as Crawford county democrat
pub 1896+
MoCaT 1917+
MoHi O 30,N 20 1890;1902+

STEWARTSVILLE

Stewartsville INDEPENDENT. w 1877-91||?
MoHi O 25 1890

Stewartsville RECORD. w 1892-O 11 1928||
Jl 5-O 11 1928 pub in Maysville. United with Clarksdale journal (Clarksdale) to form DeKalb county record-journal (Maysville)
MoHi Mr 10 1905-28

STOCKTON

CEDAR county republican. w D 10 1886+
pub 1896+
MoHi Ja 22 1914+

Stockton JOURNAL. w Ja 1869+
MoHi Ja 5 1870;O 16 1890;1903-Ja 7,21 1904; My 29 1913;14+

SOUTH-WEST tribune. *See* Stockton tribune

Stockton TRIBUNE. w 1866-74||?
1866-70? as South-west tribune
MoHi Je 25 1869

STOTTS CITY

Stotts City SUNBEAM. w 1899-1907||?
MoHi Jl 23 1901-07

STOUTLAND

CAMDEN county herald. w 1909-10||?
MoHi 1910

STOUTSVILLE

Stoutsville BANNER. w 1890-1914||?
MoHi O 30 1890;N 24 1898-99;1903-Ag 1913

STOVER

Stover NEWS. *See* Tri-county republican

TRI-COUNTY republican. w Ap 1911+
1911-Mr 1922 as Stover news
pub 1919+

STURGEON

Sturgeon LEADER. *See* Omar D. Gray's Sturgeon leader

OMAR D. GRAY'S Sturgeon leader. w 1866+
1866-Ag 13 1888 as Sturgeon leader
pub 1904+
MoHi O 25 1890;Ag 1901+

SUGAR CREEK

JACKSON COUNTY herald. w 1924+
pub My 22 1925+

SULLIVAN

Sullivan NEWS. w Je 9 1910+
pub 1910-17;19-24;26+
MoCaT 1917-N 21 1918
MoHi 1910+

Sullivan SENTINEL. w 1896-Je 26 1914||
Merged with Sullivan news
MoHi Jl 26 1901-14

TRI-COUNTY democrat. w O 13 1916+
pub 1916+

SUMMERVILLE

OZARK MOUNTAIN news. Jl 3 1930+
pub 1930+

SWEET SPRINGS

To 1887 as Brownsville

BROWNSVILLE herald. *See* Sweet Springs herald

Sweet Springs HERALD. w 1874+
1874-87? as Brownsville herald
MoHi Ag 20 1874-S 12 1884;My 27 1904+

TANEY CITY

TANEY county times. w 1887-90||?
MoHi O 23 1890

TARKIO

ATCHISON county world. w 1898-1903||?
MoHi Ja-Jl 1903

Tarkio AVALANCHE. w 1884+
MoHi Ag 15 1885-90;99-1902;08+

INDEPENDENT. w 1890-1908||?
MoHi 1902-08

TEBBETTS

Tebbetts POST. w 1899-1900||
United with Mokane herald (Mokane) to form Herald-post, later Mokane Missourian

THAYER

Thayer NEWS. w 1900+
1900-17 as Ozark news
MoCaT 1917-19
MoHi 1919+

OREGON county tribune. *See* Thayer republican-tribune

OZARK news. *See* Thayer news

REPUBLICAN. w 1900-N 1904||?
United with Oregon county tribune to form Thayer republican-tribune

Thayer REPUBLICAN-TRIBUNE. w 1888-1905||?
1888-99? as Thayer tribune; 1900?-N 18 1904 Oregon county tribune
MoHi O 18-25 1890;99-F 17 1905

Thayer TRIBUNE. *See* Thayer republican-tribune

TINA

HERALD. w 1884-1911||
Merged with Tina interior journal
MoHi O 31 1890

Tina INTERIOR journal. w 1912+
MWA Je 19 1924

TIPTON

Tipton weekly ADVANCE. w Ag 18 1871-72||?
MoHi 1871-S 1872

Tipton GAZETTE. w 1895-Je 1897||?
United with Tipton times to form Tipton times-gazette, later Tipton times
MoHi My 16 1895;Mr 19,My 14,Jl 30-Ag 6, S 3,17-25,O 8,N 26 1896

Tipton MISSOURI mail. w 1898-1907||?
MoHi Jl 26 1901-07

Tipton TIMES. w 1875+
Jl 1897-1906? as Tipton times-gazette
pub 1875+
MoHi [Mr-D 1877]Ja 10 1878-1900;Jl 1906+

TRENTON

Trenton GAZETTE. *See* Jamesport gazette (Jamesport)

GRAND RIVER news. *See* Trenton republican-times

GRAND RIVER republican. *See* Trenton republican-times

Trenton weekly LEADER. w
MoSHi Je 10 1915

Trenton NEWS. w 1907-11||?
Merged with Weekly republican-tribune, later Trenton republican-times
MoHi N 1907-11

Trenton REPUBLICAN-TIMES. w 1861+
1861-65 as Grand River news; 1866-72? Grand River republican; 1873?-Mr 12 1903 Trenton republican (1885? as Republican-star) Mr 19 1903-Mr 17 1927 Weekly republican-tribune
pub S 1869+
MoHi S 1869+
MoSHi [N 23 1920-Je 2 1921]
WHi D 22 1866

Trenton REPUBLICAN-TIMES. d 1881+
1881-Mr 1903? as Daily evening republican; Mr 1903?-Mr 1927 Daily republican-tribune
pub 1881+
MoHi 1884-1902;04-13

Trenton STAR. w 1879-84||?
United with Trenton republican to form Republican-star, later Trenton republican-times

Trenton weekly TIMES. w 1872-F 22 1927||
United with Weekly republican-tribune to form Trenton republican-times
MoHi O 30 1890;Ag 1901-12;19-27

Trenton morning TRIBUNE. d 1889-Mr 1903||
United with Daily evening republican to form Daily republican-tribune, later Trenton republican-times
MoHi Ja 23 1891-97

Trenton weekly TRIBUNE. w 1889-Mr 1903||?
United with Grand River republican to form Weekly republican-tribune, later Trenton republican-times
MoHi D 31 1890-99;1901-02

WESTERN pioneer. w
MoLe Je 28 1851-Je 19 1852
MoSHi O 11-25,N 22-29 1851;Ja 24-31 1852

TROY

Troy DISPATCH. w -Je 4 1873||
United with Lincoln county herald to form Troy herald

Troy FREE press. w Jl 1878+
pub 1881+
MoHi O 24 1890;D 21 1900;Ag 1901+

Troy GAZETTE. w
WHi S 21 1865

Troy HERALD. w D 1865-O 30 1878||
1865-Je 4 1873 as Lincoln county herald
MoHi Ag 24,D 28 1866-Je 4,18 1873-78

LINCOLN county herald. *See* Troy herald

LINCOLN county news. w 1887-90||?
MoHi O 23 1890

TURNEY

HAMMER. w 1896-
Also dated at Cameron
MoHi Ag 14 1896

Turney TIMES. w 1901-03||?
MoHi D 12 1902;03

TUSCUMBIA

HELMET. w 1874-78||?
MoHi Ap 1876-Mr 1877

MILLER county autogram. w Mr 15 1883+
pub 1883+
MoHi Ag 27,S 10 1885-Jl 1894;1906+

MILLER county vidette. w 1872-79||?
MoHi [Ja 15 1875-1876;Mr-D 1878]

MILLER county vindicator. w 1879-88||?
MoHi [S 9 1881-Ap 1884;Mr 1885-Mr]Ap 15 1887

OSAGE VALLEY banner. w Ja 9 1879-82||?
MoHi [Ja 16 1879-N 10 1881]

OSAGE VALLEY sentinel. w 1870-72||?
MoHi Ja 20 1871-N 1872

UNION

Union APPEAL. w 1865-71||?
MoHi Je 10 1869;Ja 20 1870

FRANKLIN county progress. w 1865?-
MWA Mr 16 1866

FRANKLIN county record. w S 3 1874-90||?
KHi O 25 1888
MoHi 1874-[80]-84;F 1885-Je,N 1889-N 1890

FRANKLIN county tribune. *See* Republican tribune

REPUBLICAN headlight. w Mr 4 1904-F 28 1919||
United with Franklin county tribune to form Republican tribune
MoCaT 1917-19
MoHi Mr-Ag 19 1904;14-19

MISSOURI (*Continued*)

UNION—*Continued*

REPUBLICAN tribune. w Je 17 1887+
1887-D 5 1890 as Tribune; D 12 1890-D 11 1896 Tribune-republican; D 18 1896-F 28 1919 Franklin county tribune
My 7 1915 is fiftieth anniversary ed
MoCaT 1907+
MoHi 1887+
MoS My 7 1915
MoSHi My 7 1915;Mr 1919-F 1922

TRIBUNE. w *See* Republican tribune

UNION STAR

Union star COMET. w 1883-99||?
1883-86? as Toothpick
MoHi O 24 1890

Union Star COMET. w 1920+
pub D 18 1928+

Union Star HERALD. w 1898-My 1920||
Followed by Tri-county news (King City)
MoHi Jl 1901-20
MoKiT 1915-20

Union Star HERALD. w Jl 1923-N 30 1928||?
1923-Mr 5 1925 as New Union Star herald
MoHi 1923-N 1928

NEW Union Star herald. *See* Union Star herald 1923-28

TOOTHPICK. *See* Union Star comet 1883-99

UNIONVILLE

Unionville DEMOCRAT. *See* Putnam democrat

Unionville INVESTIGATOR. w 1886-88||?
IaHi F 1886-Je 1888

NEW century. *See* Putnam democrat

Evening NEWS. d D 1 1897-
MoHi D 1-21 1897

Unionville daily PANTAGRAPH. d D 22 1897-98||?
MoHi 1897-Ja 6 1898

Unionville PANTAGRAPH. w,sw 1897-D 29 1904||
sw 1898-1900
IaHi 1898-1900
MoHi 1898-1904
MoSHi 1904

Unionville PROGRESS. *See* Putnam democrat

PUTNAM county journal. w 1889-1926||?
1889-98? as Putnam county leader; 1899?-1903? Putnam journal; 1904? Putnam journal-news
IaHi My 1891-93;97-O 1903
MoHi Ag 22 1901-26

PUTNAM county leader. *See* Putnam county journal

PUTNAM democrat. w 1876-97||?
1876-85? as New century; 1886?- Je 1891 Unionville democrat; Jl 1891-Ja 1892? Unionville progress
IaHi Ag 1876-Ja,Mr 1892-F 1897
MoHi O 30 1890

PUTNAM journal. *See* Putnam county journal

Unionville REPUBLICAN. w S 11 1865+
pub 1870+
IaHi N 1879-Ap 1885;Ap 1888-1900
MoHi O 1892-96;1903+
MoSHi Jl 1 1903;My 7 1919
NNHi S 26 1867-O 6 1870

Evening TRIBUNE. d 1897||?
MoHi N 22-30 1897

URICH

Urich CHRONICLE. w 1886-92||?
MoHi O 24 1890

Urich HERALD. w My 11 1893+
pub 1893+

VALLEY PARK

Valley Park SUN. w 1906-16||?
MoSHi Ja 21 1911

VAN BUREN

CARTER county journal. w 1912-14||?
MoHi Ja 9-D 4 1914

CURRENT local. w 1884+
Follows Van Buren times
pub 1884+
MoCaT 1907+
MoHi N 24 1898-99;Jl 1901+

Van Buren ECHO. w D 22 1904-05||?
MoHi D 22 1904-05

Van Buren TIMES. w 1879-84||
Followed by Current local
MoVC complete

VANDALIA

Vandalia LEADER. w 1875+
pub 1893+
MoHi 1915+

Vandalia MAIL. w Ag 1893+
1893-1903? as Mail and Express
pub 1893+
MoHi Ag 28 1902;O 8-D 1903;05+

VERONA

Verona ADVOCATE. w 1892-1923||?
MoHi Mr 9 1917-D 20 1918

VERSAILLES

Weekly ARGUS. w Ja 19 1871-72||?
MoHi Ja 26 1871-Je 13 1872

Weekly GAZETTE. *See* Messenger gazette

Versailles JOURNAL. w 1882-
MoHi Je 1,15,Jl 20 1882-Ja 1883

Versailles LEADER. w Ja 6 1887+
1887-90? as Morgan county leader
KHi S 13-N 22 1888
MoHi 1887-94;97+

MESSENGER gazette. w F 4 1871-87||?
1871-86? as Weekly gazette
MoHi 1871-Jl 1879;80-Jl,O 13-N 3 1881;Ap 1882-Mr 17 1887

MORGAN county banner. w 1866-
MoHi Mr 16 1867-68;Mr 27-O 16 1869[70]

MORGAN county democrat. *See* Morgan county republican

MORGAN county leader. *See* Versailles leader

MORGAN county republican. w 1900-14||?
1900-Ag 17 1906 as Morgan county democrat
MoHi Jl 10 1903-12;Ja-Ag 1914

MORGAN messenger. w O 9 1884-86||?
United with Weekly gazette to form Messenger gazette
MoHi 1884-O 21 1886

Versailles STATESMAN. w S 1887+
pub 1887+
MoHi 1902+

Versailles VINDICATOR. w Jl 12 1866-70||?
MoHi Jl 12,S 27 1866-Ja,F 12,26-Mr,Ap 9-My 7,Je 11 1869

VIENNA

HOME adviser. w N 12 1903+
pub 1904+
MoHi My 17 1906+

MARIES county gazette. w 1874+
MoHi O 30 1890;Ag 1902-N 1905;Mr 1906-Ja 1907;Ja 9-Jl 10,31,Ag 14,28,S 11-18,D 18 1914

WAKENDA

Wakenda ALERT. w Je 29 1888-
KHi Jl 20-27 1888

Wakenda RECORD. *See* Republican-record (Carrollton)

WALKER

Walker HERALD. w Ja 1882+
pub 1882+

WALNUT GROVE

Walnut Grove TRIBUNE. w 1903+
MoHi 1904-18

WARRENSBURG

Warrensburg DEMOCRAT. w S 23 1871-O 13? 1876||
1871-D 18 1874 as Johnson weekly democrat. United with Warrensburg journal to form Journal-democrat
MoHi 1871-Mr 1872;Ap 25 1874-Ap 14 1876

JOHNSON county democrat. w 1913-18||?
MoSHi S 12,26-N 14,28 D 12-26 1917;Ja 9, F 13 1918

JOHNSON county star. *See* Warrensburg star-journal

JOHNSON weekly democrat. *See* Warrensburg democrat

JOURNAL-DEMOCRAT. w 1866-1912||?
1866-O 13 1876 as Warrensburg journal
United with Johnson county star to form Warrensburg star-journal
MoHi Ap 18 1866;My 8 1867-Jl 4 1868;Je 13 1874-D 12 1879;Jl 8 1881-D 29 1882;O 31 1890;Ja-N 1892;94-1907

MISSOURI tribune. w 1864-
MWA O 14 1865
MoHi Jl 1 1865
NN O 14 (supp)1865

Warrensburg STANDARD-HERALD. w,sw Je 17 1865+
1865-92? as Warrensburg standard
sw 1892-96?
pub 1865-99;1901;03+
MoHi Ap 26,My 10 1867-Ja 27,Ap 21 1870; Je 7 1877;Ja 3 1879;S 25 1903+
MoSHi Je-N,D 28 1917

Warrensburg STAR-JOURNAL. w,sw 1882+
1882-1912? as Johnson county star w 1882-1916?
pub 1911+
MoHi Ag 8 1891-Ag 6 1892;My 5 1916+
MoSHi N 13,D 7 1917

WESTERN Missourian. w
MoSHi Ag 21 1858

WARRENTON

Warrenton BANNER. w 1865+
Follows Nonpareil. 1865-82? as Missouri banner;. 1889?-90? Economist-banner
MoHi N 7 1890;Ag 29 1902-F,S 1910+

CHRONICLE. w 1869-75||?
MoHi D 9 1869

ECONOMIST-BANNER. *See* Warrenton banner

Warrenton HERALD. w S 13 1898-1905||?
MoHi 1898-N 15 1905

MISSOURI banner. *See* Warrenton banner

NONPAREIL. w 1857-64||
Followed by Warrenton banner

Die UNION. w Ag 31 1876-
In German
MoHi Ag 31 1876

Warrent VOLKSFREUND. w 1880-1918||?
In German
MoHi F 1902-Ap 1918

WARREN county economist. w 1887-88||?
United with Warrenton banner to form Economist-banner, later Warrenton banner

WARSAW

BENTON county enterprise. w 1881+
1881-97? as Missouri enterprise
MoHi Jl 26 1901+
MoSHi Jl 11 1913

Daily BUGLE call. d S 20 1899-
KHi S 20-23 1899

Warsaw DEMOCRATIC review. w
MoSHi S 30,D 9 1852;Ap 14,My 12,Je 30 1853

MISSOURI enterprise. *See* Benton county enterprise

OSAGE banner. w Ag 6 1840-
DLC Ag 13 1840

OSAGE yeoman. w 1843-
DLC N 28 1844

Warsaw TIMES. w N 1865+
pub [1891]+
MoHi O 1905+

Saturday morning VISITOR. w
MoSHi Je 10 1848-Mr 3,Ap 28,My 12-26 1849

WASHINGTON

Washington CITIZEN. w Ag 25 1905+
pub 1905+
MoCaT 1917-19
MoHi 1905+
MoW Ja 27 1933+

Die DEUTSCHE welt. w 1889-90||?
In German
MoHi Ap 26 1889

FRANKLIN county observer. *See* Washington Missourian

Washington MISSOURIAN. w 1861+
1861-1926 as Franklin county observer
pub Ag 1926+
MoCaT 1917-19
MoHi Je 18 1869;Ja 1 1904;O 13-27 1905;13-26
MoW Ja 27 1933+

Washington REPUBLICAN. w 1888-90||?
MoHi O 24 1890

WASHINGTONER post. w 1869-1910||?
In German
MoHi O 24 1890

WAVERLY

Waverly EXPRESS. w 1870-72||?
MoHi My 7 1870

Waverly TIMES. w 1887-1900||?
MoHi O 16,N 6 1890

WAYNESVILLE

PULASKI county democrat. w 1882+
MoHi 1902-14;D 1915-S 1917

WEBB CITY

Webb City daily REGISTER. d 1891-1917||?
MoHi S 18,N 2 1903-S 1910;14-Ja 1917

Webb City daily REPUBLICAN. d 1890-91||?
MoHi O 25 1890

Webb City daily SENTINEL. d 1890+
pub 1913+
MoHi Ag 8 1901-Ap 1906

Webb City daily TIMES. d 1890-94||?
MoHi N 19 1891

WEBSTER GROVES

Webster NEWS. w 1910-Ja 1914||
United with Webster Groves times to form Webster news-times
MoHi My 17 1912-13

Webster NEWS-TIMES. w 1908+
1908-Ja 14 1914 as Webster Groves times
pub Ja 14 1914+
MoCaT 1917-19
MoHi Ja 9 1914+
MoWe Jl 26 1929-[30-31]+
MoWeW S 1930+

Webster Groves TIMES. *See* Webster news-times

YE olde towne crier. w O 27 1932+
MoWe Mr 9 1933+
MoWeW N 1932+

MISSOURI (*Continued*)

WELLINGTON

Wellington NEWS. w 1904-22||?
MoHi Ag 1916-S 1920

WELLSTON

Wellston JOURNAL. w 1928+
pub 1928+

Wellston LOCAL. w 1914-29||
Merged with Wellston journal
MoSHi S 6 1917

ST. LOUIS county herald. m 1903-30||?
MoHi 1903-24

WELLSVILLE

Wellsville OPTIC-NEWS. w 1886+
1886-90? as Wellsville news
MoHi My 22 1896;Jl 18,N 14 1902;Jl 17 1903-Jl 1904;14-S 1921

Wellsville RECORD. w 1879-1906||?
MoHi Ag 1901-03

WENTZVILLE

NEWS. *See* St. Charles banner-news (St. Charles)

Wentzville UNION. w 1891+
MoHi 1914+

WEST PLAINS

HOWELL county gazette. w 1881+
MoHi N 25 1898+

HOWELL county news. w Jl 1 1895-D 26 1907||
Merged with West Plains weekly journal
MoHi N 25 1898-1907
MoSHi complete

Wet Plains weekly JOURNAL. w 1870+
pub 1896+
MoHi D 1898+

West Plains weekly QUILL. w S 5 1885+
pub 1885+
MoHi Je 14 1907-Ag 1908;19+

West Plains daily QUILL. d Ja 9 1903+
pub 1903+

WESTBORO

Westboro ENTERPRISE. w O 1901-22||?
MoHi My 1906-07;My 1914-21

WESTON

BORDER times. w F 13 1864-71||
MoHi 1864-Ag 9 1867;F 28 1868-F 18 1870
WHi F 13,27,Mr 12,26,Je 10-17,Jl 22-29, Ag 12,N 4 1864;F 10,Mr 3,17 1865; Mr 15 1867
—d ed *See* Weston daily times

Weston CHRONICLE. w Jl 1872+
1872-82 as Weston commercial
pub Ap 23 1886+
MoHi 1898-1900;O 1929+

Weston COMMERCIAL. See Weston chronicle

Weston JOURNAL. *See* Key City commercial

KEY CITY commercial. w S 12 1844-58||
1844 as Independence journal (Independence) Ja 4 1845-O 1849 Weston journal; N 1849-56 Weston reporter
DLC S 12 1844
MoSHi S-O 1844;Ja-Ap 19 1845

LANDMARK. *See under* Platte City

Weston weekly PLATTE argus. *See* Platte county conservator (Platte City)

PLATTE county argus. w 1884-S 26 1929||
Merged with Weston chronicle 1884-1925 pub in Platte City
KHi S 28 1922
MoHi 1898-1929
MoP 1924-29

PLATTE county sentinel. *See under* Platte City

PLATTE county world. w 1896-1901||?
1896-Ag 9 1900 as Weston world
MoHi F 28 1898-1901

PLATTE eagle and Weston gazette. *See* Platte county conservator (Platte City)

Weston REPORTER. *See* Key City commercial

Weston TIMES. w N 27 1863-
WHi N 27 1863

Weston daily TIMES. d 1867-
MoHi S 18 1867
—w ed *See* Border times

Weston WORLD. *See* Platte county world

WESTPHALIA

OSAGE county volksblatt. w 1896-1917||?
In English and German
MoHi Ag 13-D 1903;05-11;13-Jl 1917

WESTPORT

Papers published in Westport are listed under Kansas City

WHEATLAND

HICKORY county mirror. w Ja 7 1870-75||?
MoHi Ja 14 1870

WILLIAMSVILLE

TRANSCRIPT. w 1888-92||?
MoHi O 23 1890

WILLOW SPRINGS

Willow Springs ADVOCATE. w 1925-Ag? 1931||
United with Willow Springs republican to form Willow Springs news

Willow Springs INDEX. w 1884-1910||?
MoHi 1903

Willow Springs NEWS. w 1890+
1890-Ag 13 1931 as Willow Springs republican
MoHi S 29 1904-Jl 1908 F 1913+

Willow Springs REPUBLICAN. *See* Willow Springs news

WINDSOR

Windsor REVIEW. w 1875+
MoHi D 29 1898-S 1899;Ja-O 1909;Ja-Mr,Je, Ag-O,D 1914-N 1916;Jl 1917+
MoSHi Mr 1896-Ja 1901

WINONA

OZARK news. *See* Shannon county democrat

SHANNON county democrat. w 1895+
1895-96 as Ozark news
pub 1895+
MoCaT 1917-19
MoHi Ag-D 1903;11+

WINSTON

Winston NEWS. w F 24 1910-
MoHi F-Jl 14 1910

Winston SENTINEL. w 1901-28||?
KHi [F 21-Ap 17 1924]
MoHi Ap 8 1901-F 1928

WORLAND

Worland WATCHMAN. w Ap 15- 1892||?
KHi Ag 15-Ag 26 1892

WORTH

Worth TRIBUNE. *See* Worth county tribune (Grant City)

WRIGHT CITY

Wright City NEWS. w 1905-17||?
MoHi Ja 15 1909;My 12 1911

WYACONDA

CLARK county news. *See* Wyaconda news-herald

LEADER. *See* Reporter-leader

Wyaconda NEWS-HERALD w 1888-1924||?
1888-1922? as Clark county news
MoHi 1904-24

REPORTER-LEADER. w 1926-31||
1926-30? as Leader
MoWyH complete

MONTANA

ABSAROKEE

Absarokee ENTERPRISE. *See* Stillwater enterprise

STILLWATER enterprise. w 1912-Ap 27 1934||
1912-Je 21 1928 as Absarokee enterprise
MtHi N 1922-34

ALZADA

Alzada FAIRPLAY. w Jl 1 1910-My 3 1934||
MtHi O 19 1923-34

ANACONDA

Anaconda RECORDER. w,d Jl 21 1894-O 5 1899||
w 1894-S 1896
MtHi complete

Anaconda weekly REVIEW. w My 1884-Jl 12 1894||
Followed by Railway review, later Mining and railway review (Butte)
MtHi 1886-94

Anaconda STANDARD. d 1889-S 11 1928||
Butte ed united with Butte miner (Butte) to form Montana standard (Butte)
Suspended Je 21-Jl 4 1927
CU-B F 23 1893
CoU S 1906-My 1910
DLC 1898-1902;Jl 1924-28
MtBu Ap 1898-1928
MtHi Ap 7 1891-1928
MtU-J 1903-S 1910
NbHi [O 1899-Ap 2 1902]
WHi S 5 1899;O 30 1912-28

ANTELOPE

Antelope INDEPENDENT. w 1913-N 7 1924||
Merged with Producers news (Plentywood)
MtHi 1923-24

ASHLAND

Ashland PIONEER press. w 1916-N 9 1928||
MtHi D 30 1921-[28]

AUGUSTA

Augusta NEWS. w S 19 1917+
Suspended Ap 29 1926-Je 20 1929
pub 1917+
MtHi 1917[26-29]+

Augusta TIMES. w N 20 1914-Je 21 1918||
United with Gilman optimist (Gilman) to form Gilman times-optimist
MtHi complete

BAINVILLE

Bainville DEMOCRAT. w O 13 1933+
MtHi 1933+

VALLEY tribune. w 1907-N 3 1932||
MtHi Jl 20 1911-32

BAKER

FALLON county times. w 1915+
1915-18 as Fallonite
MtHi F 1916+

FALLONITE. *See* Fallon county times

Baker JOURNAL. w
MtHi Ap 4 1934+

Baker SENTINEL. w 1909-D 27 1928||
MtHi 1912-N 1917;O 1923-28

BALLANTINE

PROJECT pioneer. w Mr 1912-Ap 30 1915||
Followed by Park City Pioneer (Park City)
MtHi Ap 12 1912-15

BASIN

Basin PROGRESS and mining review. w 1898-Ja 30 1909||
1898-F 27 1904 as Basin progress
MtHi 1899-1909

Basin TIMES. w F 10 1894-Ap 25 1896||
Followed by Butte times (Butte)
MtHi complete

BELFRY

CARBON county news. w S 3 1908-Ja 26 1911||
MtHi complete

BELGRADE

GALLATIN county journal. *See* Belgrade journal

GALLATIN farmer and stockman. *See* Belgrade journal

Belgrade JOURNAL. w S 20 1902+
S 20 1902-O 5 1904 as Gallatin farmer and stockman; O 12 1904-My 11 1933 as Gallatin county journal
MtHi 1902+
WHi O 24 1912

BELT

Belt MOUNTAIN miner. w Ag 26 1891-Ja 27 1894||
MtHi complete

Belt VALLEY times. w Je 21 1894+
pub 1894+
MtHi 1905-08;D 29 1910-Jl 1918;22+
WHi O 31 1912

BENZIEN

Benzien NEWS. w F 17 1917-Mr 9 1918||
Followed by Sand Spring news (Sand Spring.)
MtHi complete

MONTANA (*Continued*)

BIG ARM

Big Arm GRAPHIC. w Ja 3 1912-S 15 1915||
MtHi complete

BIG FORK

Big Fork ARCADIAN. w Ag 7 1915-Je 30 1916||
Follows Flathead county news
MtHi complete

FLATHEAD county news. w Ag 14 1908-Jl 30 1915||
Followed by Big Fork Arcadian
MtHi complete

BIG SANDY

BEAR Paw mountaineer. *See* Mountaineer

MOUNTAINEER. w Mr 1 1911+
1911-Ag 11 1918 as Bear Paw mountaineer
pub 1911-[18-20]+
MtHi Je 22 1911+

Big Sandy SENTINEL. w 1913-S 22 1916||
MtHi S 24 1915-16

BIG TIMBER

Big Timber EXPRESS. w O 2 1895-Mr 2 1901||
Follows Columbus express (Columbus)
MtHi complete

Big Timber PIONEER. w N 20 1890+
MtHi Ag 18 1891-1917;Je 1923+

SWEET Grass news. w Ap 1924+
pub 1924+

SWEET Grass tribune. w 1910-D 3 1913||
MtHi [Je 16 1911-13]

YELLOWSTONE leader. w S 30 1899-Ap 10 1906||
Merged with Big Timber pioneer
MtHi complete

BILLINGS

Billings GAZETTE. d 1901+
pub 1901+
MtB 1902+
MtHi 1901+

Billings GAZETTE. w See Midland empire news

Billings daily HERALD. d 1882-83||?
MtB [Ap 2-N 19 1883]

Billings HERALD. w Je 12 1882-My 2 1885||
United with Billings post and Billings rustler to form Billings gazette, later Midland empire news
MtHi My 12 1883-85

Billings evening JOURNAL. d D 12 1906-Ap 30 1918||
D 12 1906-Jl 31 1908 as Billings daily journal; Je 17-D 31 1915 as Billings evening journal-tribune
MtB My-D 1903;D 1906-Ap, My 11 1907-Ja 2,Ap 30 1908
MtHi complete

MIDLAND empire news. w My 11 1885+
1885-1930 as Billings gazette
pub 1885+
MtB 1902+
MtHi My 1888

MIDLAND review. w S 1 1927+
Ap 1934-N 2 1934 as Montana state journal
MtHi My 11 1934+

MONTANA state journal. *See* Midland review

Billings NEWS. sw S 8 1900-F 28 1902||
MtHi complete

Billings POST. w Ja 26 1882-Ap 30 1885||
United with Billings herald and Billings rustler to form the Billings gazette, later Midland empire news
MtB [Mr 25 1882-85]
MtHi F 7 1882-85

Billings RUSTLER. w 1884-85||
United with Billings herald and Billings post to form Billings gazette, later Midland empire news

Billings SENTINEL. w Mr 19-Jl 9 1914||
Follows Laurel sentinel (Laurel). Merged with Billings daily tribune
MtHi complete

Billings STAR. m
WHi My 18 1919-O 16 1920

Billings TIMES. w Ap 11 1891+
pub 1913+
MtB Ap 16 1896-Ap 8 1897
MtHi 1891+
WHi O 10,24-31 1912

Daily TIMES. d Jl 21 1902-Ap 30 1903||
MtHi complete

Billings daily TRIBUNE. d Jl 21 1914-Je 16 1915||
Merged with Billings evening journal
MtHi complete

YELLOWSTONE valley recorder. w D 5 1894-Ag 26 1896||
Follows Stillwater bulletin (Columbus)
MtHi complete

BOULDER

Boulder AGE-SENTINEL. w Mr 21 1888-Je 3 1909||
1888-1904 as Boulder age
CU-B Mr 27-Ap 10,Jl 3-10 1889;F 12-26,Ag 6,20 1890;Ag 3-17 1892
MtHi complete

JEFFERSON county sentinel. w 1885-D 29 1904||
United with Boulder age to form Boulder age-sentinel
CU-B Ja 9,Mr 8-15,29,Jl 5-12,Ag 30-S 13 1889;Ja 16-30 1890
MtHi 1886-1904

Boulder MONITOR. w S 14 1907+
MtHi 1907+

BOX ELDER

Box Elder VALLEY press. w 1901-28||
MtHi Ja 19 1902-28

BOZEMAN

Bozeman AVANT courier. *See* Bozeman courier

Bozeman CHRONICLE. w Mr 1883+
pub 1883+
CU-B Mr 6,Jl 3-17,O 16 1889;Ja 1-8,O 8-29 1890
MtBo 1883+
MtHi My 30 1883+

Bozeman CHRONICLE. d 1912+
pub 1912+
MtBo 1912+
MtBoS O 1933+
MtHi 1912+

Bozeman COURIER. w D 15 1871+
1871-1904 as Bozeman avant courier (title varies slightly); Jl 1905-Mr 1912 Republican-courier
Suspended S 25-N 13 1874
pub 1871+
CU-B Ja 18,F 22-N 20,D 1874-S 8,D 8-22 1876;F 8 1877-Ja 3 1878[Ja 25-Mr 1 1883;S 1886-D 22 1887]Mr 21-Ap 11 1889
MtBo 1871-Je 1906
MtHi Ja 25 1872+
NNHi F 14 1873

GALLATIN county republican. w S 4 1900-Jl 4 1905||
United with Bozeman avant courier to form Bozeman courier
MtHi complete

GALLATIN county welfare. w My 6-S 23 1887||
MtHi complete

GALLATIN news. w 1881-Ag 23 1882||
MtHi My 20 1882

MONTANA pick and plow. w Ja 13 1870-
CU-B Mr 10,Jl 29 1870

MONTANA register. w Ap 1888-Ag 23 1890||
MtHi O 28 1888-90

NEW issue. w 1890-96||?
MtHi Ja 13 1893-N 22 1895

REPUBLICAN-courier. *See* Bozeman courier

Bozeman TIMES. w N 13 1874-Ag 27 1878||
Merged with Bozeman avant courier, later Bozeman courier
CU-B Mr 9,30-Ap 6,My 11,Je 1876
MtHi 1874-S 14 1875;76-78

BRIDGER

Bridger ADVOCATE. *See* Clark Fork herald

CLARK Fork herald. w 1906-D 19 1907||
1906-Mr 28 1907 as Bridger advocate
MtHi Ja 24-D 19 1907

FREE press. w Je 27 1902-04||
MtHi 1902-S 2 1904

Bridger TIMES. w 1909+
MtHi Je 16 1911-18;20+

Bridger TRIBUNE. w O 6 1904-Ja 19 1905||
MtHi complete

BROADUS

POWDER River county examiner. w 1918+
MtHi Jl 11 1919+

BROWNING

GLACIER county chief. w 1931+
MtHi Je 15,N 1934+

Browning REVIEW. w 1915-F 27 1925||
MtHi Je 23 1922-25

BUTTE

Butte BULLETIN. d,w 1918-Ja 11 1924||
1918-O 28 1921 as Butte daily bulletin
d 1918-O 1921
ICU D 28 1920-24
MtHi Ja 16 1919-24
NN D 8 1920-Je 1,24,Jl 1,15-S 23,O 7 1921-Mr 3,Jl 28,Ag 4,11,25,S 1-15,29,O 13-N 23,D 8,15 1922-Mr 23,30,Ap 13-Jl 6,20-N 1923;Ja 4,11 1924

Butte BYSTANDER. w 1891-97||?
MtHi Ag 27 1892-D 18 1897

EXAMINER. w 1895-N 7 1896||
MtHi My 18 1895-96

Butte INDEPENDENT. w Ag 1 1900-
MtHi Ag 1-O 25 1900

Daily INTER-MOUNTAIN. *See* Butte daily post

INTER-MOUNTAIN. sw *See* Butte semi-weekly post

INTER-MOUNTAINS freeman. w Mr 21 1881-D 24 1882||
Formed by the union of Ogden freeman (Ogden Utah) Frontier index, Atlantis (Glendale), Jeffersonian, Workingmen's union and Inter-mountains
MtHi My 1 1881-82

JOURNAL. w F 10 1900-Je 20 1903||
MtHi [1900-03]
MtU-J F 9 1901-F 7 1903

Butte MINER. w,sw Je 1 1876- 1917||?
sw 1885?-90?
CU-B Ja 6-Jl 7 1886
MWA N 8 1881
MtBu 1888-1916
MtHi Ag 12 1876-95
WHi 1896-1902

Butte MINER. d *See* Montana standard

MINING and railway review. w Jl 19 1894-Jl 1928||
Follows Anaconda weekly review (Anaconda) Jl 19-D 6 1894 as Railway review. United with Weekly review to form Tribune-review
MtHi complete

Butte MINING journal. w,sw 1886-92||?
MtHi Ag 27 1887-Mr 27 1892

MONTANA American. w 1915-27||
MtHi [1916-27]

MONTANA free press. d S 17 1928-My 19 1929||
MtHi complete

MONTANA journal. w 1897 -Ap 4 1903||
Merged with Montana staats-zeitung (Helena)
In German
MtHi S 21 1901-03

MONTANA socialist. w 1912-D 1 1917||
MtHi Mr 9 1913-17

MONTANA standard. d Ag 5 1879+
1879-S 11 1928 as Butte miner
CU-B F 14-Ag 1 1882;D 31 1885;Ja-Jl 1886
DLC 1928+
MWA N 8 1881
MtBu 1888+
MtHi My 1893+
MtU-J O 1903-S 1910
WHi N 3-4,7 1912;S 12 1928+
WaPS F 1917-Ap 1919

MONTANA state journal. w Ja 17 1900-O 10 1903||
In German
MtHi complete

NEW age. w My 30 1902-F 7 1903||
Negro
MtHi complete

Butte evening NEWS. d Mr 1 1904-F 3 1911||
MtBu 1904-Ja 1911
MtHi complete
MtU-J 1904-S 1910

PEOPLE. w
MtHi Ag 6 1901-Mr 31 1902

POPULIST tribune. *See* Tribune-review

Butte daily POST. d Mr 1881+
1881-1912 as Daily inter-mountain
CU-B 1887[88]-F 1890;Mr 3-D 1891
DLC 1898;Ja-Je 1900
MnU Ja-Mr,S-O 1920
MtBu 1894+
MtHi Ap 20 1881+
MtU My 1903-S 1910
WHi N 6 1912

Butte semi-weekly POST. sw 1885-1920||?
1885-1912 as Inter-mountain
CU-B My 25,Je 5,Jl 13-20 1887[88]F 3-6,10, Ap 7,14-17,My 26,Je 23,Ag 18 1889[91]

QUINN'S review. w Ag 1897-Ja 15 1898||
MtH complete
MtHi S 1897-98

RAILWAY review. *See* Mining and railway review

REVEILLE. w 1898 -O 22 1909||
Suspended Mr 31-Ag 28 1902
MtHi S 1900-09
MtU-J Ag 28 1902-05

Butte TIMES. w My 9 1896-Jl 12 1902||
Follows Basin times (Basin)
MtHi complete

Daily TOWN talk. d Je 8 1885-86||?
MtHi 1885-My 29 1886

Weekly TRIBUNE. *See* Tribune-review

TRIBUNE-REVIEW. w 1893-D 25 1920||
1893-N 17 1894 as Populist tribune; N 24 1894-Jl 30 1898 Weekly tribune
MtHi Ja 20 1894-1920
WHi Je 22,S 21,O 19-N 2 1912

CAMAS

SANDERS county signal. w Ja 25 1906-O 9 1924||
1906-15 pub in Plains
MtHi complete
WHi N 1 1912

CASCADE

Cascade COURIER. w Ja 21 1910+
MtHi 1910+

Cascade ECHO. w N 14 1912-Mr 16 1916||
MtHi complete

MONTANA (*Continued*)

CASTLE

Castle NEWS. w Mr 15-S 13 1888||
MtHi complete

Castle REPORTER. w 1890-93||?
MtHi S 9 1892-Mr 1893

WHOLE truth. w 1896-S 24 1898||
MtHi 1897-98

CHESTER

Chester DEMOCRAT. *See* Chester reporter

Chester REPORTER. w 1912+
1912-21 as Chester democrat
MtHi N 19 1915+

Chester SIGNAL. w F 23 1905-Jl 23 1915||
MtHi complete

CHINOOK

Chinook NEWS. w Je 7 1930-Jl 1934||
1930-Ag 7 1931 as Hogeland herald (Hogeland); Ag 13 1931-S 7 1933 Big Flat news (Turner) Followed by Fort Peck press (Fort Peck)
MtFp complete
MtHi complete

Chinook OPINION. w My 8 1890+
pub [1890-1904]+
MtHi 1890+
WHi O 31 1912

CHOTEAU

Choteau ACANTHA. w Mr 24 1904+
Follows Dupuyer acantha (Dupuyer)
pub 1904+
MtHi 1904—

Choteau CALUMET. w D 18 1885-Je 29 1889|
MtHi complete

MONTANIAN and chronicle. w 1890-1905||?
1890-Je 14 1901 as Montanian
MtHi S 18 1891-Ag 1 1902

Choteau MONTANAN. w Jl 4 1913-1924||
MtHi complete

TETON chronicle. w S 10 1897-Je 14 1901||
United with Montanian to form Montanian and chronicle
MtHi complete

TETON times. w Ap 16 1892-94||?
MtHi 1892-Ap 10 1894

CIRCLE

Circle BANNER. w 1914+
MtHi Mr 5 1920+

McCONE county pioneer. w 1912-D 27 1920||
MtHi F 21 1919-20

McCONE county sentinel. w Ag 13 1931+
pub 1931+
MtHi My 31,D 13-27 1934

CLANCEY

Clancey MINER. w Ja 5 1895-Jl 15 1899||
1895-96? as Lump City miner (Lump City)
MtHi complete

CLYDE PARK

Clyde Park HERALD. w Mr 12 1910-S 19 1924||
MtHi 1910-18;20-24

COFFEE CREEK

Coffee Creek HERALD. w 1914-Ja 12 1924||
MtHi Je 1915-24

COLUMBIA FALLS

COLUMBIAN. w Ap 23 1891-F 26 1925||
Followed by Whitefish independent (Whitefish)
MtHi Ag 27 1891-1925

COLUMBUS

Columbus EXPRESS. w Je 13-S 25 1895||
Followed by Big Timber express (Big Timber)
MtHi complete

Columbus NEWS. w Ag 8 1901+
1901-09 as Tri-county news
MtHi 1901+
WHi O 31 1912

STILLWATER bulletin. w 1892-N 10 1894||
Followed by Yellowstone Valley recorder (Billings)
MtHi Ja 27-N 10 1894

STILLWATER county democrat. w Mr 15 1913-D 23 1916||
MtHi complete

TRI-COUNTY news. *See* Columbus news

CONCORD

Concord TRIBUNE. w S 13 1911-Mr 7 1913||
MtHi S 20 1911-13||

CONRAD

Conrad INDEPENDENT-OBSERVER. w 1907+
1907-22 as Conrad independent
MtHi 1911+

Conrad OBSERVER. w Ap 27 1905-D 29 1921||
United with Conrad independent to form Conrad independent-observer
MtHi complete

PONDERA county news. w Jl 28 1929+
pub 1929+
MtHi 1929+

CORVALLIS

NEW idea. w Ap 30 1887-89||?
MtHi Je 11 1887-Mr 30 1889

CULBERTSON

Culbertson REPUBLICAN. w Ag 9 1907-Jl 11 1913||
United with Searchlight to form Searchlight and republican
MtHi N 15 1907-13

SEARCHLIGHT and republican. 1902+
1902-Jl 11 1913 as Searchlight
Suspended from Mr 6 1925-Mr 22 1929
MtHi 1907+

CUT BANK

Cut Bank PIONEER press. w 1909+
MtHi D 16 1910-16;N 1923+

Cut Bank TRIBUNE. w Ja 17 1912-My 13 1915||
MtHi O 1912-15

DARBY

Darby SENTINEL. w Mr 1894-D 18 1896||
MtHi 1895-96

DAYTON

Dayton LEADER. w Mr 10 1911-D 20 1917||
MtHi complete

DEER LODGE

Evening BULLETIN. sw F 1 1926+
MtDes 1926+

Weekly INDEPENDENT. *See* Helena independent (Helena)

NEW northwest. w Jl 9 1869-Ap 30 1897||
Merged with Silver state, later Silver state post
CU-B 1869-O 3,D 19 1879;80-82[F-Mr 1883;Je 1886;87-Je 1888;Ja-N 1889
DLC 1871-72
MtDe 1869-Je 26 1885
MtHi [1870-73]-97
NNHi D 7 1873

POWELL county post. w Ap 30 1909-Mr 5 1925||
United with Silver state to form Silver state post
MtG My 3 1912
MtDes complete
MtHi 1917-18;20-25

SILVER state post. w My 21 1889+
1889-Mr 5 1925 as Silver state
pub 1889+
MtHi 1893-98;1900+

De MERSVILLE

INTER-LAKE. *See* Daily inter-lake (Kalispell)

DENTON

Denton RECORDER. w 1913+
MtHi S 1923+

DEVON

Devon REGISTER. w Ap 12 1915-D 28 1917||
MtHi [Ag 23 1915-17]

Devon TRIBUNE. w 1911-F 13 1915||
MtHi Mr 28 1913-15

DEWEY

TOBACCO Plains journal. w Ag 21 1903-Mr 1904||
Followed by Tobacco Plains journal (Eureka), later Eureka journal
MtHi complete

DILLON

Dillon EXAMINER. w S 16 1891+
pub 1891+
MtD 1903+
MtHi My 24 1893+

Dillon TRIBUNE. w F 19 1881+
pub 1881+
MtD 1903+
MtHi 1881+

DRUMMOND

GRANITE county news. *See* Drummond news

Drummond NEWS. w 1912-Mr 4 1925|
1912-Ap 6 1916 as Granite county news
MtHi Ag 29 1912-25

DUNKIRK

Dunkirk PRESS. w S 20 1911-S 26 1914||
MtHi N 1911-14

DUPUYER

Dupuyer ACANTHA. w S 15 1894-Mr 17 1904||
Followed by Choteau acantha (Choteau)
MtHi complete

DUTTON

Dutton SENTINEL. w 1915+
MtHi Je 23 1922+

EAST HELENA

East Helena RECORD. w N 19 1897-Je 7 1902||
Followed by Powell county record (Elliston)
MtHi complete

REPUBLICAN. w N 1 1899-N 2 1909||
MtHi complete

EDWARDS

GARFIELD county journal w 1915-F 19 1927||
MtHi O 1923-27

Edwards JOURNAL. w 1919-25||
Merged with Jordan tribune (Jordan)
MtJT [1919-25]

EKALAKA

Ekalaka EAGLE. w Ja 1 1909+
MtHi Ap 1909+

ELLISTON

POWELL county record. w Jl 18 1902-Ja 13 1905||
Follows East Helena record (East Helena)
MtHi complete

ETHRIDGE

Ethridge WORLD. w S 13 1913-O 28 1916||
MtHi N 1913-16

EUREKA

Eureka JOURNAL. w Ap 1904-D 29 1927||
Follows Tobacco Plains journal (Dewey) 1904-11 as Tobacco Plains journal. Merged with Western news (Libby)
MtHi complete
WaPS N 30 1922[23]

TOBACCO Plains journal. *See* Eureka journal

FAIRFIELD

Fairfield TIMES. w 1916+
MtHi 1923+

FAIRVIEW

Fairview NEWS. w Ag 1 1918+
pub 1924+
MtHi Jl 15 1920+

Fairview TIMES. w 1910-Jl 1 1920||
MtHi 1915-O 4 1917;20

FALLON

Fallon HERALD. w Je 1 1916-19||
MtHi complete

FORSYTH

Forsyth DEMOCRAT. *See* Forsyth independent

Forsyth INDEPENDENT. w 1913+
1913-My? 1923 as Forsyth democrat
MtHi Jl 15 1915-17;19-20;Jl 1923+

Forsyth JOURNAL. w Ag 1907-O 13 1909||
United with Forsyth times to form Forsyth times-journal
MtHi D 18 1907-09

ROSEBUD county news. w Mr 28 1902-My 15 1906||
Follows Miles City weekly news (Miles City) Merged with Forsyth times, later Forsyth times-journal
MtHi Ap 10 1902-06

ROSEBUD county record. w 1915-D 1926||
1915-Ag 1923 as Rosebud record (Rosebud)
MtHi Je 16 1922-26

Forsyth TIMES-JOURNAL. w S 29 1894+
1894-O 13 1909 Forsyth times
MtF 1921+
MtHi O 1894+
WHi O 31 1912

FORT BENTON

CHOTEAU county independent. w Ap 1 1910-Jl 31 1925||
MtHi complete

Fort Benton RECORD. w F 1 1875-F 1885||
F-Je 1875 as Benton weekly record
MtHi 1875-My 10 1884
NN Ja 1 1883

MONTANA (*Continued*)

FORT BENTON—*Continued*

RIVER press. w O 27 1880+
pub 1880+
CU-B Ja 2 1884[87-S 1888]
MWA D 17 1884
MtHi 1880-82;85-97;Jl 1898+

FORT PECK

Fort Peck PRESS. w Ag 2 1934+
Follows Chinook news (Chinook)
pub 1934+
MtHi 1934+

FOX LAKE

Fox Lake PROMOTER. *See* Richland county leader (Lambert)

FROID

Froid TRIBUNE. w 1910+
MtHi Je 30 1911-My 1916;F 1923+

GALATA

Galata JOURNAL. w 1910-D 30 1920||
MtHi Je 15 1911-20

GARDINER

WONDERLAND. w My 17 1902-05||?
DLC Ap 30 1903
MtHi 1902-D 7 1905

GEBO

CARBON county sentinel. w 1896-Ap 25 1902||
MtHi 1898-1902

GERALDINE

Geraldine REVIEW. w Ag 15 1913+
MtHi 1913+

GEYSER

Geyser TIMES. w Mr 23 1911-O 13 1916||
MtHi Je 15 1911-16

GILMAN

Gilman OPTIMIST. *See* Gilman times-optimist

Gilman TIMES-OPTIMIST. w 1913-D 30 1921||?
1913-Je 21 1918 as Gilman optimist
MtHi D 20 1918-21

GLASGOW

Glasgow COURIER. w 1911+
pub Ag 1913+
MtHi Ag 1913+

Glasgow DEMOCRAT. 1909-10. *See* Montana citizen

Glasgow DEMOCRAT. 1913-25. *See* Glasgow times

MONTANA citizen. w My 19 1899-Je 24 1911||
1899-F 6 1909 as North Montana review; F 13 1909-Jl 2 1910 Glasgow democrat
MtHi Complete

NORTH Montana review. *See* Montana citizen

Glasgow RECORD. w Mr 21 1895-O 29 1896||
MtHi Complete

Glasgow TIMES. w Je 1913+
1913-25 as Glasgow democrat
pub 1913+
MtHi 1914-26

GLENDALE

ATLANTIS. w 1879-Mr 23 1881||
United with other papers to form Inter-mountains freeman (Butte)
CU-B D 28 1879
MtHi [S 1880-81]

GLENDIVE

DAWSON county review. w F 17 1898+
pub 1898+
MtHi 1898-1917;20+

Glendive INDEPENDENT. w Je 14 1884-N 7 1916||
MWA Je 20 1896
MtHi S 10 1887-1916

INDEPENDENT voice of western Montana. w Mr 1935+
MtHi Jl 1935+

Daily NEWS. d
MtHi Ag 3-S 16 1892

Glendive TIMES. w Ag 11 1881-Ap 30 1887||
MtHi Ja 19 1882-87

VALLEY county gazette. w 1893-99||?
MtHi Ja 20 1894-D 23 1899

VALLEY county independent. w 1911-Ag 1 1913||
MtHi 1912-13

VALLEY county news. w Ap 22 1904-Ag 10 1923||
MtHi complete
WHi N 1 1912

YELLOWSTONE monitor. w Mr 2 1905-S 27 1928||
Merged with Dawson county review
MtGD complete
MtHi complete

GLENTANA

Glentana REPORTER. w D 18 1913-S 13 1918||
Merged with Opheim observer (Opheim)
MtHi complete

GRANTSDALE

BITTER Root bugle. w 1888-93||?
CU-B O 2,16 1889

VALLEY advertiser. w My 19 1894-Jl 6 1895||
MtHi O 1894-95

GRASS RANGE

Grass Range REVIEW. w 1912+
MtHi Ap 19 1917+

GREAT FALLS

Great Falls CALL. w 1920 -N 25 1922||
MtHi O 1921-22

CENTRAL Montana farm news. *See* Treasure-belt news

INDLANDSPOSTEN. w D 10 1915-Ap 11 1917||
In Norwegian
IaDeL complete

Great Falls TRIBUNE. d My 14 1885+
Follows Sun River sun (Sun River)
pub 1885+
CU-B Ja 31,Mr 27 1892
MtBoS O 1933+
MtGf Je 1904+
MtHi 1885-S 1916;O 1917+
WHi Ja-S 1913;17-19
WaPS [1919]Jl 2,9 1923

GUILFORD

Guilford TRIBUNE. w 1912?-Ap 30 1925||
MtHi Je 29 1922-25

HAMILTON

BITTER Root times. w 1890-N 24 1899||
Merged with Ravalli republican
MtHi F 23 1894-99

RAVALLI county democrat. w Ja 3 1900-Ap 25 1902||
Merged with Ravalli republican
MtHi complete

RAVALLI republican. w S 22 1894+
1894-D 7 1898 pub in Stevensville
pub 1894+
MtHi 1894+

WESTERN news. w 1889+
1889-Ag 9 1893 pub in Stevensville
pub 1889+
MtHi My 1893+
MtU-J O 12 1921-O 6 1922

HARDIN

Hardin HERALD. w Jl 1919-Ja 14 1924||
United with Hardin tribune to form Hardin tribune-herald
MtHi Je 9 1922-24

SEARCHLIGHT. w Ja 25 1925-D 29 1926||
MtHi complete

Hardin TRIBUNE-HERALD. w Ja 1 1908+
1908-Ja 14 1924 as Hardin tribune
pub 1908+
MtHa 1925+
MtHi F 7 1908+

HARLEM

MILK River valley news. *See* Harlem news

Harlem NEWS. w Mr 23 1904+
1904-Je 11 1908 as Milk River valley news
MtHi 1904+

HARLOWTON

MEAGHER county democrat. *See* Harlowton press

MUSSELSHELL news. *See* Harlowton press

Harlowton NEWS. *See* Harlowton press

Harlowton PRESS. w Jl 12 1906-Ap 12 1923||
1906-Ja 18 1909 as Musselshell news; Ja 25 1909-Ja 23 1914 Harlowton news; Ja 30 1914-N 26 1915 Meagher county democrat
MtHi complete

Harlowton TIMES. w Jl 1917+
pub 1917+
MtHi 1923+

HAVRE

Havre ADVERTISER. w Je 20 1893-F 28 1895||
MtHi Je 27 1893-95

Havre EAGLE. w Mr 27 1897-F 1 1902||
1897-Jl 20 1901 as Milk River eagle
MtHi My 21 1897-1902

Havre HERALD. w Jl 6 1904-S 30 1908||
MtHi complete

HILL county democrat. *See* Hill county Sunday journal

HILL county journal. *See* Hill county Sunday journal

HILL county Sunday journal. w My 25 1912+
1912-28 as Hill county democrat; 1929-33 Hill county journal. 1934 + as Sunday ed of Havre daily news
MtHi 1912+

Havre INDEPENDENT. w O 29 1931+
pub 1931+

MILK River eagle. *See* Havre eagle

Havre daily NEWS. w,d Jl 16 1909+
1909-D 7 1914 as Havre promoter; D 14 1925-N 24 1928 Havre promoter-news
w 1909-14
MtHav Je 1920+
MtHi 1909-14;16-O 1918;Je 1923+
—Sunday ed. *See* Hill county Sunday news

Havre PLAINDEALER. w F 8 1902-My 14 1921||
MnU [1903-21]
MtHav 1903-F 1920
MtHi complete

Havre PRESS. sw N? 1902-O 17 1903||
MtHi Ja 21-O 17 1903

Havre PROMOTER. *See* Havre daily news

HEDGESVILLE

Hedges HERALD. w 1909-18||?
MtHi Ja 6 1914-D 28 1917

HELENA

Morning CAPITAL. d Mr 2-D 31 1880||
MtHi complete

Helena CLOCK. w O 23 1894-Je 1 1895||
MtHi complete

COLORED citizen w S 3 1894-
MtH 1894
MtHi S 3-D 15 1894

Daily GAZETTE. *See* Daily Rocky Mountain gazette

Helena HERALD. w N 15 1866-D 27 1902||
Follows Montana radiator
CU-B Ag 13 1868-Ja 21,Mr 20-Je 12,D 11-25 1869;Ja-My 21 1874;O 1875-76;Ja 2 1879[Jl 15-D 1886]
CoHi Ja 1 1881
MWA Ja 14 1869;Ja 2,Je 12 1879
MtHi 1870-1902
OClWHi S 29 1881

Helena evening HERALD. d Ag 2 1867-D 27 1902||
Title varies: Helena daily herald; Helena herald
C D 11 1868
CU-B F 10,O 22 1869;F 17,Mr 1871-My 19,Je 30 1874-76;O 1879-[80]87-91
DLC 1870-76;89-Je 1898
MWA Ja 14 1880
MtHi complete
NNHi Ap 30 1873

Helena INDEPENDENT. w,sw O 12 1867-1914||
1867-Mr 7 1874 as Weekly independent (Deer Lodge)
w 1867-Ag 15 1899
pub complete
CU-B [1867-Je 5 1869;Mr 25 1871-80;O 8 1885-O 20 1887] Ja 12,26,F 9,Je 21 1888;N 12-19 1891;N 10 1892;F 2,My 18,O 26,D 21 1893;Ag 9 1894[Ja 24-N 14 1895]Ap 16,Ag 6,O 8 1896[Mr 18 1897-98;Ap 13 1899-Ja 1901]
MtHi S 30,O 17,27 1871;F 24,Mr 30,Ap 6-13,Jl 13 1872;F 1873-93
NNHi Ja 18 1873
WHi S 27 1896;N 1, 5 1912

Helena INDEPENDENT. d Mr 1874+
pub 1874+
CU-B Ap 25 1874-Ap 1875;D 1879-80;S 25-27,29 1885-[86] D 22,28 1887-Jl 1888;Jl 7 1889
DLC 1898+
MtH 1897+
MtHi Jl 1874+

Helena JOURNAL. d S 7 1888-N 9 1892||
1888-Mr 16 1889 as Helena daily record
DLC Ap 30 1889
MWA N 9 1889;Ja 1 1890;Ja 29 1891
MtHi complete

Helena JOURNAL. w 1888-92||
1888-Mr 1889 as Helena record
MtHi 1891-92

MONTANA freie presse. w Ag 5 1886-88||?
In German
MtHi 1886-Ag 4 1888

MONTANA lookout. w Jl 25 1908-Je 3 1911||
MtHi complete

Daily MONTANA news. d Je 12 1875-F 1876||
MtHi S 1875-76

MONTANA news. w S 17 1902-09||
1902-03? as Judith Basin news
1902-Je 29 1904 pub in Lewiston
MtHi 1902-Mr 4 1909
WHi O 26,N 9,23-30 1904;F 8,Mr 15-22,Ap 5-19,My 3 1905[D 23 1909-11]

MONTANA (*Continued*)

HELENA—*Continued*

MONTANA post. w Ag 27 1864-Je 11 1869||
1864-Ap 18 1868 pub in Virginia City
CSmH Mr 11 1865
CU-B N 11-D 16,30 1865;Ja 13,F 3-10,24,Mr 10,24-Ap 14,28,My 12 1866-Je 12,Jl,Ag 14,N 13,27-D 11,25 1868-69
CoD S 9 1865
DLC 1868-69
MtBuL complete
MtDe 1866-S 4,O 23 1868-69
MtHi complete
NNHi S 10 1864-Ap 2 1869
OHi Ap 8 1865
OrHi F 18 1865

Daily MONTANA post. d Ap 20 1868-
C D 12 1868
CU-B [Ap 20-S 30 1868]
MBAt My 11,25,Jl 21 1868

MONTANA progressive. w Ja 9 1913-16||?
MtHi 1913-15
WHi O 30 1912

MONTANA radiator. w D 17 1865-O 13 1866||
First paper pub in Helena. Followed by Helena herald
MtHi [Ja 20-O 13 1866]

MONTANA record-herald. d Ag 20 1900+
1900-Ap 1916 as Montana daily record
DLC 1903+
MnHi [1918]-Ja 18 1930
MnU My-Jl 1918
MoHi S 22 1901
MtH 1900—
TxGR Jl 28 1906
WHi N 1-2,6 1912

MONTANA record-herald. w *See* Helena record-herald

MONTANA staats-zeitung. tw,sw,w 1885-S 27 1917||
In German
MtHi O 1889-1917
WHi S 27,O 11-18,N 1 1912

Helena NEWS. w,d S 28 1893-Ap 25 1896||
1893-Ja 17 1895 as Helena evening telegram
d O 5-D 19 1894
MtH 1893-D 19 1894
MtHi complete

PRESS. sw S 13 1902-O 8 1904||
MtH 1902-S 1903
MtHi complete

Helena RECORD. 1888-89. *See* Helena journal

Helena RECORD-HERALD. w D 5 1901+
1901-16 as Montana record; 1917-23 Montana record-herald
MtHi 1901-02
OrHi 1902-Ag 1 1916

REPORTER. sm
Negro
DLC F 1 1900

Tri-weekly REPUBLICAN. *See* Tri-weekly post (Virginia City)

ROCKY Mountain gazette. w Ag 11 1866-Ja 9 1874||
CU-B My 23[D 1868-F 3 1869;My 30 1870-Ag 5,S-N 1872;Ja 7,Ap-D 1873]
MtHi [Ag 18 1866-73]
NNHi Mr 19 1873

Daily ROCKY Mountain gazette. d Mr 30 1868-74||?
1868-70? as Daily gazette
CU-B [My 29 1870-D 16 1872;F 4 1873-Ja 9 1874]
DLC Ap 3-4,14-19,24,26,28-29,My 2-3,9-10,13-14,19-20,24,26-29,Je 1-2,11,19-21,26-28,30,Jl 3-4,9 1868;O 29 1870
MtHi Ja 15-O 24 1870
NNHi My 1 1873

Helena evening TELEGRAM. *See* Helena news

TREASURE state. w My 9 1908-D 30 1911||
MtHi My 16 1908-11

WESTERN progressive. w Ja 11 1932+
MtHi 1932+

HINGHAM

Hingham AMERICAN. w Ap 21 1911+
1911-D 5 1918 as Hingham review
pub 1911+
MtHi Je 16 1911-Ag 21 1919

Hingham HERALD. w Je? 1913-14||
MtHi My 2-Jl 11 1914

Hingham REVIEW. *See* Hingham American

HINSDALE

MONTANA homestead. w My 11 1904-Ja 13 1912||
MtHi complete

Hinsdale TRIBUNE. w Je 5 1912+
MtHi 1912-S 22 1921;O 12 1923+

HOBSON

JUDITH Basin star. w O 15 1908+
pub 1908+
MtHi 1908+
WHi O 31 1912

HOGELAND

Hogeland HERALD. *See* Chinook news (Chinook)

HUNTLEY

Huntley JOURNAL. w Ap 20 1912-20||
United with Pompeys Pillar rock (Pompeys Pillar) to form Yellowstone (Worden)
MtHi My 1912-13

HYSHAM

Hysham ECHO. *See* Midland empire farmer

MIDLAND empire farmer. w 1911+
1911-N 16 1933 as Hysham echo
MtHi My 15 1919+

INGOMAR

Ingomar INDEPENDENT. w O 23 1913-F 19 1927||
1913-N 28 1918 as Ingomar index
MtHi Ja 16 1914-N 28 1918;O 1923-27

Ingomar INDEX. *See* Ingomar independent

INVERNESS

Inverness NEWS. w S 1 1917-Ag 31 1918||
MtHi S 8 1917-18

ISMAY

ISMAY. w My 20 1908-10||?
MtHi 1908-O 5 1910

Ismay JOURNAL. w Mr 25 1910-Ja 27 1933||
MtHi O 21 1910-33

JOLIET

CARBON county journal. *See under* Red Lodge

Joliet JOURNAL. w Je 25 1904-09||
MtHi 1904-F 19 1909

JOPLIN

Joplin INDEPENDENT. *See* Joplin times

LIBERTY county farmer. w F 8 1924+
pub 1924+
MtHi Mr 1924+

Joplin TIMES. w 1910-Jl 25 1918||
1910-Je 1911? as Joplin independent
MtHi Jl 1911-18

JORDAN

Jordan GAZETTE. w 1913 -N 30 1922||
Merged with Jordan times
MtHi O 1914-22

Jordan TIMES. w Jl 4 1919 -S 16 1932||
Merged with Jordan tribune
MtHi O 14 1921-32
MtJT [1919-32]

Jordan TRIBUNE. w N 1927+
pub 1927+
MtHi 1927+

JUDITH GAP

Judith Gap JOURNAL. w N 20 1908-O 3 1924||
MtHi D 11 1908-24
WHi D 13 1912

KALISPELL

Kalispell BEE. sw,tw,d,w Je 15 1900-Jl 28 1921||?
sw Je-N 7 1900,S 1901-17;tw N 9 1900-F 1901;d Mr-Ag 1901
MtHi 1900-17
MtK 1900-[D 1919-Jl 1921]

CALL. w Mr 12-O 15 1896||
MtHi complete

FLATHEAD herald-journal. *See* Kalispell journal

FLATHEAD monitor. w Je 3 1920+
pub 1924+
MtHi D 1920-21;Je 1923+

Kalispell GRAPHIC. w 1891-N 6 1895||
Merged with Inter-lake
MtHi My 25 1892-95

Daily INTER-LAKE. w,sw,d Ag 10 1889+
1889-Ap 6? 1908 as Inter-lake (w)
1889-91 pub in De Mersville
pub 1890+
MtHi 1893-N 1917;Mr 15 1921+

Kalispell JOURNAL. w 1892-D 5 1918||
1892-My 30 1907 as Flathead herald-journal
MtHi My 1893-1918

Kalispell TIMES. w Je 18 1910+
pub 1910+
MtHi 1910+

KENDALL

Kendall CHRONICLE. w Mr 25 1902-N 3 1903||
MtHi complete

Kendall MINER. w D 8 1905-F 24 1911||
MtHi complete

KEVIN

Kevin COURIER. *See* Kevin review

Kevin REVIEW. w My 5 1922-Je 6 1929||
My-O 5 1922 as Kevin courier
MtHi complete

KREMLIN

Kremlin CHANCELLOR. w 1913-Ja 25 1929||
MtHi N 24 1922-29

LAMBERT

Lambert PROMOTER. *See* Richland county leader

RICHLAND county leader. w Je 16 1913+
1913-17 as Fox Lake promoter (Fox Lake); 1918-20 Lambert promoter
pub 1913+
MtHi Je 30 1922+

LAREDO

Laredo TRIBUNE. w 1917 -D 30 1926||
MtHi N 11 1922-26

LAUREL

Laurel OUTLOOK. w Jl 14 1909+
MtHi 1909-S 8 1918;Ja 16 1920+
WaPS [1922-25]+

Laurel SENTINEL. w S 22 1906-Mr 12 1914||
Followed by Billings sentinel (Billings)
MtHi complete

LAVINA

Lavina INDEPENDENT. w 1910-S 28 1923||
MtHi O 28 1921-23

LEWISTOWN

Lewistown DEMOCRAT. w 1890-N 18 1904||
1890-Jl 7 1895 as Montana democrat; Jl 14 1895-Ag 16 1900 Lewiston democrat; Ag 23-O 25 1900 Fergus county democrat
MtHi Mr 1893-1904

Lewistown DEMOCRAT-NEWS. d 1905+
1905-Je 1915 as Lewistown daily news
pub 1905+
MtHi F 9 1921+
MtLe Je 1914-16

FERGUS county argus. w Ag 9 1883+
1883-Ag 5 1886 as Mineral argus (Maiden)
pub 1883+
MtHi D 20 1883+

FERGUS county democrat. w 1900. *See* Lewistown democrat

FERGUS county democrat. w 1904-19. *See* Judith Basin farmer

JUDITH Basin farmer. w Ag 16 1904+
1904-Jl 17 1919 as Fergus county democrat
pub 1904+
MtHi Ag 23 1904-30

JUDITH Basin news. *See* Montana news (Helena)

MONTANA democrat. *See* Lewistown democrat

MONTANA news. *See under* Helena

Lewistown daily NEWS. *See* Lewistown democrat-news

LIBBY

Libby HERALD. *See* Lincoln county herald

KOOTENAI times. *See* Libby times

LINCOLN county herald. w Ag 17 1911-Jl 3 1914||
Follows Troy herald (Troy) 1911-Ag 1913 as Libby herald
MtHi complete

Weekly MONTANIAN. w 1894-Ap 18 1903||
MtHi Je 1897-1903

Libby NEWS. w Mr 1898-My 30 1901||
MtHi Ja 26 1899-1901

SILVER standard. w Jl 13-N 9 1895||
MtHi complete

Libby TIMES. w D 1913-D 26 1919||
1913-O 7 1916 as Kootenai times
MtHi My 1914-O 7 1916;Ja 19 1917-19

WESTERN news. w Jl 17 1902+
pub 1902+
MtHi 1902+

LIMA

Lima LEDGER. w 1912+
MtHi 1923+

LIVINGSTON

Livingston ENTERPRISE. d Je 4 1883+
MtHi 1914+
MtL 1883-N 8 1884;Mr 20 1911+

Livingston ENTERPRISE. w Je 4 1883-Mr 14 1914||
CU-B Mr 9,Jl 13,S 7-14 1889;Ja 25,F 22 1890
MtHi Ag 10 1883-1914
MtL N 25 1884-My 25 1912

Livingston HERALD. w Ap 23 1891-My 9 1898||
MtHi My 24 1893-[98]

MONTANA (*Continued*)

LIVINGSTON—*Continued*

PARK county news. w N 2 1917+
pub 1917+
MtHi Je 24 1921+
MtL 1917+

PARK county republican. w D 23 1894-My 31 1902||
Merged with Livingston enterprise
MtHi complete

Livingston POST. w Ap 18 1889-1915||
MtHi complete
MtL 1889-Mr 3 1904

Livingston daily POST. d 1908-15||
MtL F 10 1909-O 16 1913;My 6-O 28 1915
WHi N 1 1912

LODGE GRASS

BIG Horn county news. w 1926+
MtHa [1926+]
MtHi My 18-S 28 1934

LOMA

Loma LEDGER. w 1913-16||
MtHi Ja 22 1915-Ap 27 1916

LUMP CITY

Lump City MINER. *See* Clancey miner (Clancey)

MAIDEN

MINERAL argus. *See* Fergus county argus (Lewistown)

MALTA

Malta ENTERPRISE. w 1899-Ap 15 1926||
Merged with Phillips county news
MtHi 1909-26

PHILLIPS county news. w My 1 1924+
MtHi 1924+

MANHATTAN

Manhattan COMMUNITY searchlight. w 1928+
WaPS [1930]

Manhattan RECORD. *See* Rocky Mountain American

ROCKY Mountain American. w D 6 1906+
1906-19? as Manhattan record
MtHi 1906-18;Je 22 1922+

MARYSVILLE

Marysville GAZETTE. w 1893-94||?
MtHi Ja 18-O 18 1894

Marysville MESSENGER. w Ja 19 1895-96||?
MtHi 1895-Mr 14 1896

MOUNTAINEER. w 1892-1907||
MtHi My 1893-F 14 1907

MEDICINE LAKE

Medicine Lake WAVE. w 1909+
MtHi F 6 1911+

MELSTONE

Melstone GRAPHIC. w O 6 1911-D 27 1912||
MtHi complete

Melstone MESSENGER. w 1912+
MtHi 1922+

MILES CITY

Miles City AMERICAN. w 1911-26||
MtHi 1915-26

Daily COURIER. d S 28 1888-N 10 1894||
MtHi [1888-94]

Miles City INDEPENDENT. *See* Miles City weekly star

Miles City weekly NEWS. w Ap 16 1898-F 28 1901||
Followed by Rosebud county news (Forsyth)
MtHi 1898-Ap 1900

Miles City daily PRESS. d F 19 1882-Je 6 1884||
MtHi Jl 1882-S 19 1883

Miles City daily RECORD. d Ag 14-O 30 1884||
MtHi [S 13-O 1884]

Miles City weekly STAR. w Ag 27 1903+
1903-22 as Miles City independent
pub 1903+
MtHi 1903-22
WHi N 1-8 1912

Miles City daily STAR. d My 23 1911+
My 24 1934 is Golden jubilee ed
pub 1911+
MWA My 24 1934
MtHi My 27 1911-Ag 1916;F 13 1921+
MtMi Jl 1930+
WHi N 6-8 1912

STOCKGROWERS journal. w,sw 1884-Ag 1917||
Merged with Miles City American
sw Ap 29 1908-10
MtHi 1893-1910; 13-16

YELLOWSTONE journal. w Jl 24 1879+
pub 1888 [90-1920]+
CU-B Je 26-Ag 14,28 1886-F,Mr 12-Je 26 1887;N 3 1888;Ag 23-S 15 1890;Ja-Mr 7,21-Ag 22,S 12-O,N 14-D 19 1891
MnHi Jl 24 1879
MtHi Ag 28 1879-95;1927-[32]+
MtMi 1879-Je 1900

Daily YELLOWSTONE journal. d O 19 1882-Ja 15 1918||
MtHi 1894-1918
MtMi 1882-F,S 1883-Mr,S 1895-Mr 1901
WHi N 2 1912

MISSOULA

Evening DEMOCRAT. *See* Missoula daily democrat-messenger

Missoula daily DEMOCRAT-MESSENGER. d 1895-D 3 1903||
1895-Je 2 1897 as Evening democrat
MtHi 1896-1903

Missoula GAZETTE. w,d Ap 29 1888-Ag 16 1892||
d 1891
MtHi complete

Missoula HERALD. w,d F 2 1906-Ja 31 1911||
w F-Mr 1906
MtHi complete

Evening ITEM. d Jl 4-S 1 1888||
MtHK complete

Missoula JOURNAL. w,d,sw D 12 1903-06||?
1903-Jl 30 1904 as Missoula times
w 1903-Ja 21 1904;d Ja 22-Jl 30 1904
MtHi 1903-06

Missoula MESSENGER. d S 19 1896-Je 2 1897||
United with Evening democrat to form Missoula daily democrat-messenger
MtHi complete

MISSOULA county times. w N 15 1882-Mr 7 1888||
CU-B Ja,F 15-22,Mr 7 1888
MtHi O 3 1883-88

MISSOULA county times. w N 19 1931+
MtHi 1931+

Weekly MISSOULIAN. w F 28 1873-1910||
Follows Missoula pioneer
pub 1891-1910
CU-B [1873]-Ap 1874;S 13-O 4 1876;Ja-N 18 1887;My 16 1888-[90]91
MtHi complete
NNHi My 16 1873

Daily MISSOULIAN. d 1888+
1888-95 as Morning Missoulian (title varies)
pub My 1905+
CU-B Ja 29,Jl 4-5,7,9,17,D 24,27 1889
MWA O 6 1908
MtHi 1889+
MtM O 31 1901+
WHi Ag 29 1906;O 31 1912

MONTANA populist. *See* Montana silverite

MONTANA silverite. w 1890-Ja 1 1897||
1890-Mr 23 1894 as Montana populist
MtHi My 1893-97

Missoula NEW northwest. *See* Missoula daily northwest

Missoula daily NORTHWEST. w,d 1915-My 18 1929||
1915-27 as Missoula new northwest
w 1915-19;21-27
MtHi D 5 1919-20;22-29
WHi D 15 1916-Mr 5 1920

Missoula PIONEER. w 1871-F 21? 1873||
Followed by Weekly Missoulian
CU-B N 2-23,D 9,23 1871-Mr 2,30,Ap 6,20-My 11,Je 1,15 1872-F 8 1873

Evening REPUBLICAN. d Je 12 1895-Ag 28 1896||
Merged with Evening democrat, later Missoula daily democrat-messenger
MtHi complete

Missoula SENTINEL. d Mr 1911+
pub 1911+
MtHi 1911-Ag 1918;S 1922-Mr 1930

Missoula TIMES. *See* Missoula journal

WESTERN democrat. w,d Je 1892-Mr 4 1895||
F 25 1895 as Daily democrat. Merged with Montana silverite
MtHK complete
MtHi 1894-95

MOCCASIN

INDEPENDENT. w 1920-My 8 1924||
United with Judith Basin county press (Stanford)
MtHi N 8 1923-24

MONARCH

MONARCH. w 1890-Jl 7 1891||
MtHi Jl 7 1891

MONDAK

YELLOWSTONE news. w 1905-Ap 24 1920||
MtHi Mr 10 1906-20

MONTAGUE

Montague HERALD. w N 15 1917-Jl 2 1919||
MtHi complete

MOORE

Moore INDEPENDENT. w 1915-Ja 1931||
MtHi D 8 1921-31

INLAND empire. w S 14 1905-Mr 18 1915||
MtHi complete
WHi O 31 1912

NASHUA

Nashua INDEPENDENT. w 1912-Mr 23 1933||
MtHi Ag 29 1914-33

Nashua MESSENGER. w Ag 1934+
MtHi O 1935+

NEIHART

Neihart HERALD. w 1890-Ja 5 1901||
MtHi My 29 1891-1901

Neihart MINER. w D 25 1891-Ja 1899||
MtHi 1894-98

OPHEIM

Opheim OBSERVER. w 1916-N 13 1931||
MtHi 1919-31

PARK CITY

Park City HERALD. w S 12 1912-O 23 1913||
MtHi complete

Park City PIONEER. w My 1915-S 4 1925||
Follows Project pioneer (Ballantyne)
MtHi complete
WaPS [1921-22]-25

PAXTON

Paxton PILOT. w 1913-N 1 1917||
MtHi Mr 23 1916-1917

PHILIPSBURG

CITIZENS call. w Mr 1 1893-S 6 1905||
MtHi Ja 10 1894-1905

Philipsburg MAIL. w Ja 28 1887+
pub 1887+
MtHi Ap 28 1887+
WHi O 25 1912

Philipsburg PRESS. w D 18 1913-Je 17 1914||
MtHi complete

PINIELE

Piniele LEADER. w F 6 1914-Je 23 1926||
MWA My 14 1914
MtHi O 10 1921-26

PLAINS

PLAINSMAN. w N 9 1895-O 31 1896||
MtHi complete

PLAINSMAN. w Mr 16 1900-N 22 1929||
MtHi 1900-N 22 1917;S 8 1922-29

SANDERS county democrat. w O 22 1909-D 1910||?
MtHi D 3 1909-10

SANDERS county signal. *See under* Camas

PLENTYWOOD

Plentywood HERALD. w 1908+
pub 1908+
MtHi 1909+

PRODUCERS news. w 1918+
MnHi [1919-20]
MtHi N 24 1922+

SHERIDAN county farmer. w O 12 1923-N 7 1924||
MtHi O 19 1923-24

SHERIDAN county news. w 1909-Ag 29 1919||
MtHi My 23 1913-1919

PLEVNA

Plevna HERALD. w 1914-Ag 7 1931||
MtHi Ja 13 1922-1931

POLSON

FLATHEAD courier. w 1910+
MtHi Ja 6 1911+

LAKE county herald. w Jl 23 1923-F 21 1924||
MtHi complete

LAKE county vista. w S 1929+
MtHi 1929+

LAKE shore sentinel. w S 9 1909-Ag 11 1911||
Merged with Flathead courier
MtHi complete

POMPEYS PILLAR

Pompeys Pillar ROCK. w 1917-20||
United with Huntley journal (Huntley) to form Yellowstone (Worden)

MONTANA (*Continued*)

PONY

Pony DISPATCH and express. w Ja 7 1908-O 31 1913||
1908-11 as Pony express
MtHi 1908-11;Mr 22 1912-13

Pony EXPRESS. *See* Pony dispatch and express

MADISON county monitor. *See under* Twin Bridges

Pony SENTINEL. w Ap 1 1899-Ap 27 1906||
MtHi complete

POPLAR

ROOSEVELT county independent. w 1912-D 5 1924||
Ag-D 1924 pub in Wolf Point
MtHi N 17 1922-24

Poplar STANDARD. w My 12 1910+
pub 1916+
MtHi 1910-Jl 1918;O 1923+

QUIGLEY

ROCK Creek record. w My 16 1896-My 1 1897||
MtHi complete

TIMES. w My 22-O 30 1896||
MtHi My 29-O 30 1896

RADERSBURG

BROADWATER county taxpayer. w Je 29-O 31 1908
MtHi complete

RED LODGE

CARBON county chronicle. w Je 25 1901-N 1 1904||
MtHi complete

CARBON county chronicle. 1924. *See* Carbon county news

CARBON county democrat. w N 29 1899-My 29 1901||
MtHi complete

CARBON county gazette. w Mr 2 1905-F 16 1906||
MtHi complete

CARBON county journal. w Je 26 1909-N 11 1918||
1909-11 pub in Joliet. United with Red Lodge picket to form Picket-journal
MtHi complete
MtRP complete

CARBON county news. w Mr 17 1924+
Mr-O 1924 as Carbon county chronicle
pub 1924—
MtHi Mr 28 1924+
WaPS [1-25]-Mr 1927
—d ed. *See* Red Lodge daily news

CARBON county republican. w Mr 3 1906-O 11 1907||
Merged with Red Lodge picket, later Picket-journal
MtHi complete

NEW idea. w O 5 1893-O 17 1895||
MtHi complete

Red Lodge daily NEWS. d,tw,sw O 13 1931-D 30 1932||
d 1931-Je 10 1932;tw Je 11-27 1932
MtRC complete
—w ed *See* Carbon county news

PICKET-JOURNAL. w S 1 1889+
1889-N 11 1918 as Red Lodge picket;
pub 1912—
MtHi D 28 1889+
WHi O 3 1912

REDSTONE

Redstone REVIEW. w 1911+
MtHi Je 22 1923+

REED POINT

Reed Point REVIEW. w 1915-D 30 1921||
MtHi Ap 23 1920-21

RICHEY

Richey PILOT. w 1913+
pub 1916+
MtHi N 24 1921+

RINGLING

Ringling INDEPENDENT. w 1919-Mr 7 1925||
MtHi N 1922-25

RONAN

Ronan PIONEER. w 1910+
MtHi F 1911+

ROSEBUD

Rosebud COURIER. w Mr 20 1913-Jl 9 1915||
MtHi complete

Rosebud RECORD. *See* Rosebud county record (Forsyth)

ROUNDUP

Roundup RECORD-TRIBUNE. w Ap 3 1908+
1908-29 as Roundup record
pub 1908+
MtHi 1908+

Roundup TRIBUNE. w Je 1910-D 31 1929||
United with Roundup record to form Roundup record-tribune
MtHi Je 15 1911-29
MtRoR complete

RUDYARD

Rudyard DISPATCH. w F 6? 1914-Ag 16 1918||
MtHi D 25 1914-18

RYEGATE

Montana CLARION. w Ag 24? 1910+
1910-My 2 1934 as Ryegate reporter
MtHi Je 15 1911+

Ryegate REPORTER. *See* Montana clarion

SACO

Saco INDEPENDENT. w 1909+
MtHi Jl 12 1912-15;N 10 1922+

ST. IGNATIUS

St. Ignatius POST. w 1912-Ja 14 1927||
MtHi N 10 1922-27

SAND SPRINGS

Sand Springs NEWS. w Mr 16? 1918-19||
Follows Benzien news (Benzien). Merged with Jordan tribune (Jordan)
MtJT [1918-19]

Sand Springs STAR. w Ap 25 1919-D 18 1920||
MtHi 1920

SAVAGE

YELLOWSTONE valley star. w 1910-D 30 1920||
MtHi 1912-20

SCOBEY

Scobey CITIZEN. w 1916-Jl 1 1920||
MtHi O 12 1917-20

DANIELS county free press w. O 11 1935+
MtHi 1935+

DANIELS county leader. w F 9? 1922+
MtHi N 23 1922+

Scobey SENTINEL. w Je 22 1912-Je 24 1927||
Merged with Daniels county leader
MtHi D 28 1912-27

SHELBY

Shelby INDEPENDENT. w Ag 29 1901-N 17 1904||
MtHi complete

Shelby NEWS. w Je 21 1900-Ja 3 1901||
MtHi complete

Shelby NEWS. w Ap 22 1910-Je 25 1915||
Merged with Shelby promoter
MtHi complete

Shelby PROMOTER. w My 15 1912+
pub 1916+
MtHi N 15 1918+

TRIBUNE of Shelby. w 1910+
MtHi 1927+

SHERIDAN

Sheridan weekly CHINOOK. w 1896-D 16 1903||
MtHi Ap 21 1899-1903

Sheridan ENTERPRISE. w Ja 8 1904-Ag 13 1909||
MtHi complete

Sheridan FORUM. *See* Madison county forum

MADISON county forum. w F 2 1911+
1911-F 16 1923 as Sheridan forum
MtHi F 23 1911+

MESSENGER. w 1879-Mr 19 1881||
MtHi Ja 10 1880-81

Sheridan PAPER. w N 26 1896-Ap 14 1899||
MtHi Ja 8 1897-99

SIDNEY

DAWSON county chief. *See* Richland county chief

Sidney HERALD. w Mr 13 1908+
MtHi Jl 24 1908+

RICHLAND county chief. w 1913-Ap 24 1928||
1913-14 as Dawson county chief. Merged with Sidney herald
MtHi Ja 16 1920-28

SQUARE BUTTE

Square Butte TRIBUNE. w 1915-S 29 1922||
MtHi O 13 1916-22

STANFORD

JUDITH Basin county press. w F 19 1909+
1909-N 1920 as Stanford world
pub 1931+
MtHi F 26 1909+

Stanford WORLD. *See* Judith Basin county press

STEVENSVILLE

NORTHWEST tribune. w 1887—
CU-B S 20 1889;Ja 10-24,Ag 15-22,O 24-31 1890
MtHi 1888;My 27 1893+
WHi O 4 1912

RAVALLI republican. *See under* Hamilton

Stevensville REGISTER. w S 27 1902-S 13 1918||
MtHi complete

WESTERN news. *See under* Hamilton

SUMATRA

Sumatra SUN. w 1921-S 3 1925||
MtHi N 23 1922-25

SUN RIVER

RISING sun. w Ag 13 1885-D 23 1896||
CU-B Mr 20,Je 26-Jl 3,S 4-11,D 11,25 1889;Ja 8,29-F 5,O 22-29 1890
MtHi complete

Sun River SUN. w F 14 1884-Ap 30 1885||
Followed by Great Falls tribune (Great Falls)
MtHi complete

SUPERIOR

MINERAL county press. w 1913-D 19 1918||
MtHi Jl 9 1914-18

MINERAL independent. w My 7 1915+
MtHi Je 1915+

SWEET GRASS

Sweet Grass EXAMINER. w Mr 4-D 30 1932||
MtHi complete

Sweetgrass SUNBURST sun. w 1910-Jl 15 1926||
MtHi N 15 1923-26

TWIN City advocate. w Ja 27 1927-D 8 1932||
MtHi N 10 1927-32

TERRY

Terry TRIBUNE. w O 20 1905+
pub 1905+
MtHi O 11 1907+

THOMPSON FALLS

INDEPENDENT enterprise. w 1916-18||
United with Sanders county ledger to form Sanders county independent-ledger

Weekly MONTANIAN. w O 13 1894-D 26 1896||
MtHi complete

SANDERS county independent-ledger. w F 24 1905+
1905-Ja 17 1918 as Sanders county ledger
pub 1906+
MtHi 1905-S 8 1921;Ap 23 1929+

SANDERS county ledger. *See* Sanders county independent-ledger.

THREE FORKS

Three Forks HERALD. w S 24 1908+
pub 1908+
MtHi 1908+

Three Forks NEWS. w D 1910+
MtHi Je 15 1911-D 7 1916

TOSTON

CROW Creek journal. w Je 19-D 19 1907||
MtHi complete

TOWNSEND

BROADWATER opinion. w Ag 22 1910-Je 29 1914||
MtHi S 11 1910-14

Townsend FORUM. w Ap 26 1900-Jl 25 1901||
Merged with Townsend star
MtHi My 30 1900-01

Townsend INTER-MOUNTAIN. w Ag 20-D 31 1914||
MtHi complete

MEAGHER county news. *See under* White Sulphur Springs

Townsend MESSENGER. w D 11 1890-Ja 10 1901||
Merged with Townsend star
CU-B Ja 8,22-29,F 12-Mr 4,18-25,Ap 8-My 6,20,Ag 12-S,O 14-28,N 18 1892
MtHi 1891-1901

Townsend STAR. w Ap 24 1897+
pub 1897+
MtHi 1897+

Townsend TRANCHANT. w D 1884-Ja 23 1890||
MtHi 1886-90

MONTANA (*Continued*)

TROY

Troy ECHO. w O 2 1914-My 27 1927||
MtHi 1914-Ja 1925;26-27

Troy HERALD. w My 20 1910-Jl 28 1911||
Followed by Libby herald, later Lincoln county herald (Libby)

Troy RANGER. w Je 21 1934+
MtHi 1934+

Troy TRIBUNE. w 1922-Je 9 1933||
Merged with Western news (Libby)
MtHi D 19 1924-33

TURNER

BIG FLAT news. *See* Chinook news (Chinook)

TWIN BRIDGES

Twin Bridges INDEPENDENT. w S 24 1915-S 19 1924||
MtHi complete

MADISON county monitor. w Ap 1 1892-O 27 1922||
1892-Je 1 1893 pub in Pony
MtHi complete

VALIER

VALERIAN. w O 1 1909+
MtHi 1909-Jl 18 1918;F 8 1924-Ap 9 1926;N 14 1935+
WHi O 25 1912

VIRGINIA CITY

CAPITAL times. tw S 1869-70||
CU-B [Mr 14-Je 13 1870]

MADISONIAN. w N 16 1873+
F 26 1915-Mr 12 1920 as Madisonian times
pub 1873+
CU-B Ag 24,S 14 1876;My 17 1877-Ja 1878[N-D 1879]80;Ja-O 7 1887
MtHi D 20 1873+

MADISONIAN times. *See* Madisonian

MONTANA capital times. w N 19? 1869-70||
CU-B Ap 9,23,Je 11 1870

MONTANA democrat. w,tw N 1865-Ag 1869||
w 1865-F 2 1869
CU-B [S 21 1867-Je 26 1869]
DLC Ap 12 1866;Mr 7,D 19 1867 [68-69]
MtHi Mr 29,Ag 30,S 6 1866;F 22 1868;F 2,11, 13 1869
NNHi Jl 14 1868

MONTANA post. *See under* Helena

MONTANA republican. w Jl 9 1869-
CU-B Ag 20-S 17 1869

MONTANIAN. w Jl 21 1870-Mr 9 1876||
Merged with Madisonian
CU-B [1870-72]-[74]-76
DLC Jl 1874-O 14 1875
MtHi Ap 13 1871-76
NNHi Mr 6 1873

Virginia City tri-weekly POST. tw Je 28 1866-68||?
Je-S 27 1866 as Tri-weekly republican (Helena)
CU-B Ag 18 1866-Mr 28 1868
MtHi Jl 26,Ag 28,S 25 1866
NNHi O 3 1867

TIMES. w Je 9 1899-F 19 1915||
United with Madisonian to form Madisonian times, later Madisonian
MtHi complete
MtVM complete

Virginia City TIMES. w 1921-Ap 23 1923||
MtHi Ja 31 1922-23

WALKERVILLE

Walkerville TELEGRAPH. w 1891-Ap 21 1893||
MtHi O 2 1891-93

WESTBY

Westby NEWS. w 1913-22||
MtHi N 16 1914-22

WHITE SULPHUR SPRINGS

MEAGHER county news. w O 31? 1889-My 1 1897||
1889-Ag 23 1890 pub in Townsend
CU-B Jl 15-Ag 6 1892
MtHi Ap 18 1890-97

MEAGHER county news. w Jl 20 1900+
1900-Jl 1934 as Meagher county republican
MtHi 1900+

MEAGHER county republican. *See* Meagher county news

WHITEFISH

Whitefish INDEPENDENT. w Mr 20 1925+
Follows Columbian (Columbia Falls)
pub 1926+
MtHi 1925-Je 1930

Whitefish PILOT. w Ja 23 1904+
MtHi 1904+
MtU-J O 1919-Ag 1921
WaPS Ag 11 1925;F 15 1929;Mr 3 1931;Ja 5 1932

WHITEHALL

JEFFERSON county zepher. w N 29 1894-O 25 1901||
MtHi complete

JEFFERSON Valley news. w 1911+
pub 1915+
MtHi N 9 1911-14;18+

MONTANA sunlight. w F 14 1902-Jl 7 1911||
MtHi complete

WIBAUX

BEAVER Valley gazette. w 1910-O 19 1918||
United with Wibaux pioneer to form Wibaux pioneer-gazette
MtHi Ja 30-O 19 1918

Wibaux PIONEER-GAZETTE. w Ja 7 1907+
1907-O 19 1918 as Wibaux pioneer
MtHi 1907-Ag 1920;23+

WICKES

Wickes PIONEER. w Ag 10 1895-Ap 25 1896||
MtHi complete

WILSALL

SHIELDS valley record. w 1913-D 26 1924||
Merged with Park county news (Livingston)
MtHi F 15 1917-24

WINIFRED

Winifred TIMES. w 1913+
MtHi Je 22 1923+

WINNETT

Winnett TIMES. w 1915+
MtHi Ap 1921+

WINSTON

Winston PROSPECTOR. w My 13 1897-Jl 1899||
MtHi My 27 1897-99

WISDOM

BIG HOLE Basin news. w 1912-Ap 30 1925||
MtHi N 16 1922-25

BIG HOLE breezes. w 1898-N 21 1913||
Merged with Big Hole Basin news
MtHi S 15 1899-1913||
WHi N 1 1912

WOLF POINT

Wolf Point HERALD. w 1913+
MtHi O 12 1917+

Wolf Point PROMOTER. w Ap 1919-Jl 13 1922||
MtHi S 21 1919-22

ROOSEVELT county independent. *See under* Poplar

ROOSEVELT county news. w My 17 1935+
MtHi S 19 1935+

WORDEN

YELLOWSTONE. w 1921+
Follows Pompeys Pillar rock (Pompeys Pillar) and Huntley journal (Huntley)
pub 1926+
MtHi O 13 1922+

ZORTMAN

LITTLE Rockies miner. w Jl 4 1907-D 4 1909||
MtHi complete

NEBRASKA

ADAMS

Adams weekly GLOBE. w Ja 1890+
Title varies slightly
pub O 1907+
NbHi Jl 22 1892;O 18-25,D 13-20 1895;Ja 31,Mr 6,Ap 17,My 8-22,Je 5,19-26,Jl 17-O 23,N 6,20-D 18 1896;97-Jl 1,15-Ag 19,S-O 7,28-N 18,D 1898-F 10,24,Mr 31-My 12,26-Jl 14,28,Ag 18-S 1,15-O 13,27-N 3,17-D 8,29 1899-1900;Ja 25,Ap 26,My 3,17-Je,Jl 19-S 20,O 1901-Ja 17,31-Mr 21,Ap-My 2,16-23,Je 13-Ag 15,S 5-19,O 10 1902;O 1907-35

AINSWORTH

BROWN county democrat. w Ja 1906+
pub 1909+
NbHi Ag 20 1909+

Ainsworth HERALD. w Ag 1889-1903||?
1889-My 31 1900 as Home rule
NbHi Jl 28 1892;Ag 31 1893;Ja 18,Jl 19-26 1894;N 7,D 12 1895;F 20-Mr,Ap 23-My 21,Je 4-11,Ag 6,N 12 1896;Ja 6,F 11,N 4-18,D 9 1897;Ja 13-N 3 1898;F 15,My 1900-Ja,F 14-Mr 1901

HOME rule. *See* Ainsworth herald

Ainsworth JOURNAL. w Jl 8 1884-My 7 1891||
United with Ainsworth star to form Ainsworth star-journal
NbHi Jl 8,10-17,31,Ag 14-28,S 11 1884-Je 18,Jl 9-S 17 1885;Ja-F 4,Mr 25,Ap 22-My 6,27-Ag,S 9-D 16,30 1886

KEYA PAHA press. *See under* Springview

Ainsworth STAR-JOURNAL. w Ag 10 1886+
1886-My 7 1891 as Ainsworth star
MWA Ag 1 1894;Jl 17 1895
NbHi Ag 31-S 14,O-D 22 1886;Ja-Ap 6,27-S 8,22-N 17,D 1-22 1887;88-Je 4,Jl-N 19,D 1891-Ja 3,17-31,F 14-Ap 4,25,My 16-S 19,O-N,D 12-26 1894;Ja 16,30-Ag,S 19-25,O 9 1895-98;Ja 12-Je,Jl 13,27-Ag 17,S 14 1899-F 6 1914;O 1915+

WESTERN news. w Ja 1882-91||
1882-My 1883 as Long Pine news (Long Pine). Merged with Ainsworth star-journal
NbHi Mr 30 1882;Ja 25,My 2 1884;S 27 1888

ALBION

Albion ARGUS. w Jl 30 1876+
1876-93? as Boone county argus
pub 1876+
NbHi S 16 1892;Ag 2,O 18,N 1,15,29-D 20 1895;Ja 31,F 14-21,Mr 27,Ap 24,My 15,Je 12-26,Jl 17-Ag 21,S 4-11,25-O 23,N 13,D 1896;Ja 8-29,F 19-Ag 13,27,S 10 1897-F 11,25-Ag 5,19-S,O 14 1898+

BOONE county argus. *See* Albion argus

BOONE county blade. w D 2 1896-Mr 30 1898||
Merged with Albion argus
NbHi [1896-98]

BOONE county news. *See* Albion news

CALLIOPE. w Ja 1891-D 6 1895||
United with Boone county republican to form Boone county outlook, later Cedar Rapids outlook (Cedar Rapids)
NbHi D 2 1892;S 20,O 18-N 1,15-29 1895

Albion daily CRITIC. d 1896-
NbHi Ja 28-F 2,4-9,11-16,18,20-23,25-Mr 1,3-4 1896

Albion weekly NEWS. w,sw O 1879+
1882?-86? as Boone county news; 1887?-91? Albion semi-weekly news (sw)
pub 1879+
NbHi Ap 13,My 27 1887;My 20 1892;Ag 9 1895+

ALEXANDRIA

ALEXANDRIAN. *See* Alexandria news

Alexandria ARGUS. w My 1894+
pub 1894+
NbHi N 1,15-D 13,27 1895[96-97]Ja 7,21-F 4, 18-Mr,Ap 8,22-S 23,O-D 1898;Jl 1899+

Alexandria HERALD. w 1883-93||?
1883-91? as Thayer county herald
NbHi Jl 15 1892

Alexandria NEWS. w O 1878-88||?
1878-Mr 29 1879 as Alexandrian
NbHi Ap-Je,Jl 26 1879-Jl 17 1880;Ag 3 1882

THAYER county herald. *See* Alexandria herald

ALGERNON

Algernon CHAMPION. *See* People's advocate (Ansley)

ALLEN

Allen NEWS. w Ag 12 1890+
NbHi Je 16 1892;D 12-19 1895;Ja 2,16,F 20-27, Mr 12-Ap,My 14-21,Je 4-18,Jl 16-23,Ag 13 1896;Mr 18,Ap 30,D 9 1897;O 27,N 10 1898; N 7,21-D 12 1901;Ja 23 1902

ALLIANCE

GUIDE. w 1887-Ja 13 1898||
1887-D 21 1894 as Hemingford guide (Hemingford)
NbHi N 4 1892;N 10 1893-D 21 1894;95-98

NEBRASKA (*Continued*)

ALLIANCE—*Continued*

Alliance **HERALD.** w F 1895-Je 30 1922||
 1895-1901? as Hemingford herald (Hemingford) United with Alliance semi-weekly times to form Alliance times and herald, later alliance times-herald
 NbHi Jl 26 1895-Ja 8,22,Je 11-18 1897;Mr 18-Ag 1898;F 21,Jl 11-18,Ag 8-29,S 12,26,O 17-D 12,26 1902-Ja 16,30-Ap 10,My 1-15,29,Je 26,Jl 10,31-Ag 14,28-D 11,25 1903;04-N 2 1905; Mr 19 1908-22

Alliance **NEWS.** w F 1914+
 S 1917-S 1922 Antioch news (Antioch)
 NbHi Je 25 1914;18+

PIONEER grip. w 1885-S 22 1905||
 1885-90? as 'Gene Heath's grip (Nonpariel) Merged with Alliance times-herald
 NbHi Je 10 1892;O 13 1893-Ja 19,F 2,16-23,Mr 9-16,30-Jl 20,Ag 1894-1905

Alliance **TIMES-HERALD.** w,sw Je 1887+
 1887-Ag 1890 as Alliance times; Ag 22 1890-Je 1922 Alliance semi-weekly times (sw) Jl 1922-28? alliance times and herald
 pub Ag 22 1890+
 NbHi Ag 22,O 17 1890;Ja 9 1891;Jl 22 1892;F 14 1896-[98]+

ALMA

Alma **BEACON.** *See* news-reporter

HARLAN county journal. w Jl 1897+
 NbA [1902-04]-07;09-32
 NbHi Ag 27-D 24 1897;Ja 7,21-Ap,My 13,27,S 9-23,O 21,N 4-11,25,D 30 1898;Ja 27-F 3,17, Ap-My 12,26,Je 9-O 13,27-N 3,17-D 1,22 1899-Mr 9,25-S 14,O 19-N 1906;Ja 18-25,F 15-Mr 15,Ap,My 17-Je 7,21,Jl 12,26,Ag 9 1907-14;F 20,Mr 12 1920-21;24+

HARLAN county news. w 1875-91||?
 United with Alma beacon to form News-reporter
 1875-81 pub in Republican City

HARLAN county standard. *See* Alma herald

Alma **HERALD.** w Ap 11 1879-83||?
 1879?-80? as Harlan county standard
 NbHi O 12 1882

NEWS-REPORTER. w 1888-99||?
 1888-91? as Alma beacon
 NbHi Jl 21,D 15 1892;N 7 1895;Ja 9-Mr 20,Ap-My 22,Je 5-11,24-Jl 16,30-S 3,17-O 1,15,29-N 19,D 3-10 1896;Ja 14,28-Ap 15,29,My 20,Je 3, Jl 2,16-Ag 13,27,S 10,30,O 21 1897-F,Mr 10-Je 2 1899

Alma **RECORD.** w D 1892-Je 26 1925||
 1908?-13? as Shaffer's Alma record (other variations slight) Merged with Harlan county journal
 NbHi O 25-N 1,15-22,D 1895-Ja 3,F 7,28-Mr 6, 20,Ap 3-10,24-Jl 3,17-Ag 14,28-O 16,N 1896-Ja 15 1897;Je 21,Jl 12-19,S 27-O,N 15-D 1901;Ja 17-24,F 14-Je Jl 11-N 21 D 5-19 1902;03-F 19,Mr 4-11 1904;Je 7 1907;08-My 4,18-Je 1,15-22,Jl 6,20-Ag 3,24-S 7,21,O 1923-Ja 9,23-F 20,Mr-Je 1925

SHAFFER'S Alma record. *See* Alma record

Alma **STANDARD.** *See* Alma herald

ALVO

Alvo **ADVANCE.** w 1891-My 26 1921||
 NbHi N 30,D 28 1895-[96-98]Ja 7,F 4-11,Ap 1-8,My 13,27-Je 17 1899;D 14 1901-Ja,F 14-Mr 7,21-Ap 4,18-My 2 1903;Mr 21 1908-21

AMELIA

Amelia **JOURNAL.** w Ja 17 1887-My 2 1895||
 Merged with Atkinson plain dealer (Atkinson)
 NbHi O 27 1892

AMHERST

ALERT. w My 5-D 1897||
 NbHi My 26-Je,Jl 9-16,30-Ag 20,S 1-3,10,22,29, O 6-D 1897

ANOKA

Anoka **HERALD.** w Mr 6 1903-09||?
 NbHi Mr-My 8,29 1903-Ap 2,16-N 12 1908;Ja-F 26 1909

ANSELMO

Anselmo **ENTERPRISE.** w My 11 1906+
 NbHi Mr 20-Ag 14,28-N,D 11 1908-F,Mr 19-Ap 9 1915;Ja 4,18-F 1,15,Mr 1918+

ANSLEY

ARGOSY. w 1884-Jl 1914||
 1884-86 as Western echo (Westerville) 1887-S 26 1902 Ansley chronicle; O 3 1902-S 26 1907 Chronicle-citizen; O 3 1907-Je 1910 Argosy and chronicle-citizen
 NbBb [1894-1902;07-09]
 NbHi Je 10 1892;O 15,N 1,15-22,D 6 1895[96-97]-Mr,Ap 14-21,My-Je,Jl 14 1899-[1904-05]-O 3,17-24,N 28,D 26 1907-Jl 2 1914

Ansley **CHRONICLE.** *See* Argosy

CITIZEN. w My 17 1901-S 26 1902||
 United with Ansley chronicle to form Chronicle-citizen, later argosy
 NbBb [1901-02]
 NbHi My 24-S 19,O,N 8-29,D 13,27 1901-Jl 11,25-Ag 15 S 5 1902

Ansley **HERALD.** w S 1890+
 1890-S 7 1911 as Custer county beacon, S 14 1911-My 7 1914 Custer county herald 1890-My 7 1914 pub in Broken Bow
 NbBb [1888-89;96-97;1900;08-10]
 NbHi Mr 24,D 1 1892;Ag 15 1895-N 18 1897 [98;Ap-Ag 1900;Ap-O 1901]-F 6,Ag 1902-My 7 1913;Jl 16 1915+

PEOPLE'S advocate. w 1886-98||?
 1886 as Algernon champion (Algernon) 1887-D 6? 1895 Mason City advocate (Mason City)
 NbBb [1897-1900]
 NbHi Je 3 1892;D 13-20 1895;Ja 24-31,F 14,Ap 10,My 1-15,29-Je 5,26-Jl 10,31 1896-Ja,F 12-26, Ap 26,My 28-Je 11,25-Jl 2,23,S 10,O 10,24,D 3 1897;Ja 28,F 11,Je-Jl 22,O 28-N 11,25 1898
 NcD Ja 20 1888

ANTELOPEVILLE

NEBRASKA observer. w Ap- 1885||?
 NbHi Jl 24 1885

ANTIOCH

Antioch **NEWS.** *See* Alliance news (Alliance)

ARAGO

SOUTHERN Nebraskian. w Ja 1866-71||?
 Follows Falls City broad axe (Falls City) 1866-Je 1867? pub in Falls City
 NbHi Mr 5 1867;N 13 1868

ARAPAHOE

Arapahoe **PIONEER.** w Jl 3 1879-1911||?
 NbArH 1879-Je 1882
 NbArP Jl 7 1882-Ag 22 1884
 NbHi S 12 1879;Jl 22 1892;S 27,O-D 6,20 1895-98;My 12,Je 2,16-S 1,29-D 15,29 1899;F-Ap, My 11-N,D 14 1900-05;08-Ag 24 1911

PUBLIC mirror. w 1882+
 pub 1908+
 NbHi S 1895-Ja 20,F-Mr 3,24-My 5,19-Jl,Ag 11-S 15,29,O 13-20,N 10 1898-Ap 20,My 4,13, Je-Ag 10,31,S 14-28,O 12 1899-[1903]-F,Mr 11 1904;10-N 1919;20+

ARCADIA

ARCADIAN. w 1927+
 Follows Arcadia champion and Arcadia tribune
 pub 1929;31;35+

Arcadia **CHAMPION** and Arcadia tribune. w 1886-O 7 1926||
 1886-My 1895? as Arcadia courier; Je 1895-Jl 15 1926 Arcadia champion. Followed by Arcadian
 NbHi My 20 1892;Je 21,S 20,O 25,N-D 13 1895; Ja 24,F 21,My 29-Je,Jl 17-S 4,18 1896-[98] 1901-Jl 20,Ag,S 14-28 1906;07-S 4 1913;My 28-Je 18,Jl 2,16-D 17 1914;F 4 1915;Ja 4,D 28 1917-Mr 14 1924;S-D 3,17-24 1925;Ja-F 11,25-Je 10,24-O 1926

Arcadia **COURIER.** *See* Arcadia champion and Arcadia tribune

Arcadia **TRIBUNE.** w 1925-Jl 15 1926||
 United with Arcadia champion to form Arcadia champion and Arcadia tribune

ARLINGTON

Arlington **HERALD.** *See* Arlington review-herald

Arlington weekly **NEWS.** w 1891-97||?
 NbHi O 26-N 2,30-D 14 1895;F 1,22,Je 6,Ag 1-8,22-29,S 26,O 10-17,N 7-14,28 1896-F 6,20-Mr 13,27,Ap 10,24-Jl 17 1897

PEOPLES defender. *See* Arlington review-herald

Arlington **REVIEW.** w F 24 1899-1904||
 United with Arlington herald to form Arlington review-herald

Arlington **REVIEW-HERALD.** w N 17 1882+
 1882-91? as Peoples defender; 1892?-1900? Arlington times; 1901?-04 Arlington herald
 NbHi S 13 1889;Je 24 1892;N 1,15,29-D 20 1895; 96-My 1898;Ja 27-F 3,Mr 24-31,Ap 14-My 12, 26-Je 9,30-Jl 21,Ag 11,S-N 3,17-24,D 29 1899 [1900]My 11-Je 22,Jl 20,Ag 3-17,31-O 4,19-N 9,23,D 21-28 1901;Ja 11-25,F 8,22-Mr 1,22 Ap-My 3,17-24,Je 21,Jl-Ag 2,S 5-19 1902;Mr 19-My,Je 11-O 22,N 5,19 1908+

Arlington **TIMES.** *See* Arlington review-herald

ARNOLD

Arnold **NEWS.** w 1886-94||
 1886-Ja 1889 as Callaway standard (Callaway)
 NbHi Jl 1 1892

Arnold **SENTINEL.** w Jl 20 1911+
 NbHi Ja 15-22,S 17,O 15,D 24 1914;Ja 7,F 11-25 1915;My 22 1919+

ARTHUR

Arthur **ENTERPRISE.** w My 1912+
 KHi S 7 1928
 NbHi F-Mr 12,26-Ap 16,30-My,Je 18-S 3,17-D 10,24 1920-Mr 3,17-31,Ap 14-28,My 26,Je 2,Ag 25,S-N 1,15 1922+

ASHLAND

Ashland **GAZETTE.** w 1878—
 1878-79? as Saunders county reporter; 1880? Saunders county pioneer
 pub 1900+
 NbHi D 2-9 1892[F-D 1893]-My,Jl 13-20,S 7 1894;N 1 1895;Ja 24,F 7,Ap 3,My 22,Je 26,Jl 17-Ag 14,28,S 11,25-O 23,N 1896-S 1917;F 6,N 21 1918+
 supps:N 15,29,D 6,13 1895

Ashland **JOURNAL.** w Ja 14 1897-1907||?
 1897-N 3 1905 as Saunders county journal
 NbHi Mr 11-25,Ap 8-29,My 27-Jl 22,S 2,D 30 1897-F 3,24,My 12-Jl 7,28-Ag 11,O 13-N 10, 24-D 1 1898;My 16,30-Jl 4,18-Ag 1,S-N 14,D 12,26 1901-N 24 1905;F 2,16,Mr 2-16,30-Jl 20, Ag-S 1906;F 8,Mr 1-15 1907

Ashland **NEWS.** w Ja 1894-S 25 1896||
 NbHi N 1894-F,Mr 15-My,Je 14-Ag 23,S 27-N 8,22-29,D 13 1895;Ja 10-31,F 14,Mr 13-S 1896

SAUNDERS county journal. *See* Ashland journal

SAUNDERS county pioneer. *See* Ashland gazette

SAUNDERS county reporter. *See* Ashland gazette

SUMMER breeze. d Je 22 1896-
 NbHi Je-Jl 18 1896

ASHTON

Ashton **HERALD.** w 1915-N 2 1934||
 NbHi F 13-O,N 13 1925-[Ag-S 1932]-34

ATKINSON

Atkinson **GRAPHIC.** w Ag 10 1882+
 Je 17 1897-Jl 1900 Atkinson plain dealer and graphic; Ag 1900-N 1901 Atkinson plain dealer
 pub F 1895-Ja 1910;F 1911+
 NbHi S 28 1882;F 15,N 29 1883;Ag 18,N 24-D 1 1892;N 30,D 14 1893-My 1898;Ja 26 1899-[1902]08-Je 1914;18+

HOLT county republican. w Ag 19 1899-Jl 1900||
 Merged with Atkinson graphic
 NbHi Ag-S 23,O-N,D 29 1899-F 16,Mr-Ap 13, 27-Je 1,22-Jl 6 1900

Atkinson **PLAIN DEALER.** w Ag 1893-Je 16 1897||
 United with Atkinson graphic to form Atkinson plain dealer and graphic, later Atkinson graphic
 NbHi Ja 1-8,Jl 11,O 16-23,N 6,27-D 11 1895;S, O 21,N 4-18,D 1896-97

Atkinson **PLAIN DEALER** 1897-1901 *See* Atkinson graphic

AUBURN

GRANGER. w Ja 23 1874-D 28 1915||
 Follows Brownville democrat (Brownville) 1874-Ja 8 1892 as Nemaha county granger (title varies slightly) Merged with Nemaha county republican
 1874-N 14 1884 pub in Brownville
 NbHi Jl 14-21,Ag 25,O 27 1876;Ja 26 1877;78;Ja 24,Je 27,Ag 15,D 12 1879;80-[84]-Ja 1,Je 25,Jl 16-D 1886;N 11 1887;88;O 4 1889;90-[97]-1900; Mr 8,Ap 19-Ag 2,16-S 6,20 O 1901-15

NEBRASKA advertiser. *See under* Nemaha

NEMAHA county herald. w F 1888+
 1888-98? pub in South Auburn
 pub 1888+
 NbHi Ja 11,Je 21,Ag 23 1889;Mr 7,Jl 11,Ag 8 1890;Ja 29,D 2,16 1892;Mr 17 1893;Ja 29,O 25, N 1,15-29,D 13-27 1895;Ja 24,F 21,Mr 20-27, Ap 17-24,My 8,Je 19-S 11,25 1896-Ap 22,My, Je 10,24-Jl 1,15-22,O 28-N 4,18-25 1898;N 9 1900;Jl 1901+

NEMAHA county journal and Nebraska advertiser. w O 21 1882-
 NbHi N 18 1882-Ap 19 1883

NEMAHA county republican. w 1879-N 1929||
 1879-Je 1882 as Sheridan post (Sheridan) Jl 1882-1903? Auburn post. Merged with Nemaha county herald
 NbHi Ag 9,S 6,O 11-18,N 8-15,D 6 1883;Ja 31-F,Mr 27,Ap 10,24,My 29-Je 19,O 23-30,D 4,18 1884;Ja 8-15,29-Mr 5,Ap 2,23,My 7,21 1885;Ja 12,F 3,Mr,Ap 14,My 12,Je 2-9,23 1887;Ap 4, My 2-9,23-Je 6,20-Jl 11 1889; O 8 1891;Jl 7,D 1 1892;Mr 22-29,Ap 19-Je 21,Jl-Ag 9,23-S 13, 27-D 20 1894;95-Ja 6,20-Jl 14,Ag 4-18,S 1-8, 29-N 10 1899;1900-My 16,S 26,O 3,17-24,N 1913-14;17-29

Auburn evening **POST.** d Ap 2- 1887||?
 NbHi Ap 8,12-13,15,19-21,23,Je 1-3,7,9-10 1887

Auburn **POST.** w *See* Nemaha county republican

AURORA

HAMILTON county democrat. w S 17 1895-
 NbHi S 17-24,O 8-15,N 5,19,D 1895-Ja 14,28-F,Mr 10,24-Je 2,16-23,Jl 14,Ag 11 1896

HAMILTON county register. w,sw D 6 1890-Mr 22 1923||
 United with Aurora republican to form Hamilton county republican-register
 sw Mr 17 1922-Mr 30 1923
 NbHi D 6 1890;Ja 10-Mr 7,21,Ap-O,N 14-D 19 1891;N 26,D 31 1892;94-F 6,20-Ap 3,17-My 1,22,Jl 3-24,Ag 28,O 16-23,D 1897-99;F 3,Mr-Je 16,30,Jl 14-28 1900;01-My 17,31-Ag 9,23-S 13,27-O 4,18-N 22 1902;Jl 11-S 5,19 1903-29

NEBRASKA (*Continued*)

AURORA—*Continued*

HAMILTON county republican-register. w Je 1873+
1873-Mr 22 1929 as Aurora republican
pub 1890+
NbHi Ap 25 1877;Mr 11 1886;Ja 10,24-31,F 22,Mr 15,My 3,S 13,O 18,N 1,15,D 6 1889;My 21,Jl 4,O 1,N 26,D 17 1891;Je 30,Jl 21 1892;N 17 1893;Jl 6,Ag 3,N 2,16-23 1894;O 1895-Je 17 1898;Ja 27,Mr 24-Ap 14,28-My 12,26-Jl 14, Ag 18-25,S 8,O 6,20,N 3,25 1899+

Aurora NEWS. w Jl 1873-Je 22 1887||
1873-Ag 14? 1885 as Hamilton county news. Merged with Aurora republican, later Hamilton county republican-register 1873-76? pub in Orville City; 1877?-F 1879 in Hamilton
NbHi Ap 13 1877-F 22,Mr 8 1879-S 1881;F 17 1882-[Je 1884-Je 1887]

Aurora NEWS. w Ag 8 1885+
1885-Ap 12? 1929 as Aurora sun
Suspended from N 19 1926-My 3 1928
NbHi Ag-O 17 1885;My 29-Je 12,Jl 10,S 18,O 2-9,23,N 6-13,D 18 1886[87-88]Ja,Mr 9,My-Je 15,Ag 10,24,S 28,O 19,N 2 1889;Mr 29,Jl 26-Ag 2 1890[91]92;Ag 10 1895-Ja 9,23,F 6-20,Mr 13, 27,Ap 10-S 4,N 6,D 4 1897;98[99]1900[02]08-N 19 1926;My-Je,Jl 12-S 6,20-N 22,D 6,20 1928-Ja,Ap 19-26,My 10 1929+

Aurora REPUBLICAN. *See* Hamilton county republican-register

Aurora SUN. *See* Aurora news 1885+

Aurora TELEGRAPH. w D 27 1877-F 1879||
Merged with Hamilton county news, later Aurora news (1873-87)
NbHi 1878-F 13 1879

AXTELL

Axtell ADVERTISER. *See* Axtell times

Axtell REPUBLICAN. w O 10 1889-Ja 30 1896||
NbHi complete

Axtell TIMES. w My 1 1896+
1896-1901? as Axtell advertiser
NbHi My 22,Je 5,19,Jl 17-31,Ag 21-28,S 11-O 16,N-D 18 1896;Ja 22,F-Mr 12,26,Ap 9-Ag 13, 27,S 17-N 5,19-D 10,24 1897-Ja 23,F-Mr 3,24-My 6,19-Je 2,23-Ag 18,S 1,15,29,O 13,N 17-D 8,29 1899-Mr 7,21-Je 6,Jl 4 1902;F 26-My 14,28-Jl 1909

BANCROFT

Bancroft BLADE. w Ag 1889+
1889-92 as Bancroft independent
NbHi Ja 19 1894;Ja 24,N,D 13-20 1895;F 14,Ap 24,My 8,22-29,Ag 28,S 18-26,N 6,27 1896[97-1902]-S,O 11,N 1903;04+

Bancroft ENTERPRISE. w F 1895-My 8 1896||
Merged with Bancroft blade
NbHi Je 14,Ag 2,O 11,25-N 8,29-D 1895;Ja 24,F 28,Mr 27,Ap 10-My 8 1896

Bancroft INDEPENDENT. *See* Bancroft blade

BARNESTON

Barneston STAR. w 1888-1907||?
NbHi N 8-22,D 5 1895;My 15-22,S 11-25,O 9, N 13,D 11-18 1896[Ja-N 12 1897]S 30-O 14, N,D 9 1898-[1900]Ja 4,18-F 15,Mr 15,Ap-Jl, Ag 9 1901-02;Ja 9-F 20,Mr,My 22-29 1903; Ag 11-S 8,22-O,N 17-D 1,15 1905;Ja 12-19,F 23,Mr 9,30-Jl,Ag 31-O 5,19 1906-Ja 4,18-F 8 1907

BARTLETT

WHEELER county advance. *See* Wheeler county republican

WHEELER county independent. w Ja 1891+
NbHi F 11 1897-S 8,O 20-27,N 17,D 1 1898 [99-1900]Ja 24,Ap 25-Jl,Ag 15 1901-My 22,Je 26,Jl 10-Ag 7,21-S,O 16 1902-Ap 14,28-My 5 1904;My 11 1905;Mr 14 1907;Jl 23,Ag-O,N 12 1908-My 6,20-Je 17,Jl 8,22 1909;Jl 7,21,Ag 11 1910-Ja,F 16,Ap 6-13,Je 15-Jl 13,27-Ag 10, 31,S 14-O 12,N 1911+

WHEELER county news. w Jl 20 1895-F 3 1897||
Merged with Wheeler county independent
NbHi Jl 22-N 11,25,D 9 1896;Ja-F 3 1897

WHEELER county republican. w Je 3 1886-92||?
1886? as Wheeler county advance
NbHi Je 10 1886;O 6,27 1887;F 9,Je 10,Jl 26-Ag 2 1888

BARTLEY

Bartley INTER-OCEAN. w O 1886+
NbHi Ag 20 1892;O 25 1895;Je 5,Jl 24-Ag 14, S 25,D 25 1896[Mr 1899-1900]Ja 25,My 10,24 1901;F 2,Ap 11,26-My 3,Je 14 1902;09[10]-12; 14-Jl 8 1915;16+

BASSETT

Bassett EAGLE. *See* Newport eagle (Newport)

Bassett HERALD. *See* Republican statesman

REPUBLICAN statesman. w 1884-93||?
1884-89? as Bassett herald; 1890?-91? Republican herald
NbHi Ap 27,Jl 20 1888;Je 16,D 8 1892

ROCK county leader. w D 3 1897+
pub 1902+
NbHi 1897-98;Ag 17 1900-[01-02]-[15]-Ag 17, 31-S 7,28,O 19,N 2-16,D 1916-Ja 11,25-F 8, 22-Je 15,29,Jl 12 1917+

ROCK county republican. w 1889||?
United with Bassett herald to form Republican herald, later Republican statesman

BATTLE CREEK

Battle Creek BLADE. w Ap 2 1885-88||?
NbHi Ap 2,My 1-8,Ag 14 1885

Battle Creek ENTERPRISE. w Ap 1887+
NbHi Ap 19,Jl 5,Ag 23,S 20 1888;D 9 1892;Ja 31-F 14 1896;Mr 5-12,26-Ap 9,23,My 7,28-Je 11,25,Jl 23-30,Ag 13,27-S 10 1897;N 25 1899; Ap 30,My 14,Jl 9,Ag 20,S 3,17-24,O 15-N,D 24 1908;09-[30]-[33-35]+

Battle Creek REPUBLICAN. w 1894-1905||?
NbHi O 25 1895-[96-97]-Je 19,Jl-O 1903

BAYARD

CHIMNEY ROCK transcript. *See* Bayard transcript

FARMER'S exchange. w S 1 1917-O 1923||
1917-18? as Merrill county news
NbHi Mr 6,My 29-Jl 3,17 1919-Ag 2,16-S 1923

MERRILL county news. *See* Farmer's exchange

Bayard TRANSCRIPT. w D 1888+
1888-Je 12 1891 as Chimney Rock transcript
1888-Je 1889 pub in Chimney Rock
NbHi My 27 1892;O 18-D 6,27 1895[Ap 24 1896-97]-Ja 14,28,F 25-Mr 4,18-25,Ap 8-My 5,19,Je 2-23 1898;Mr 24-Ap,Je 23,Jl 7-21,Ag 4,S 1-22,O 6,27-N 3,24-D 1,29 1899[1900;Ap 1901-O 1902]O 24 1908+

BAZILE MILLS

KNOX county times. w 1880-89||
Suspended from 1884-Mr 1885
NbHi Jl 8 1881;Ap 20 1887

BEATRICE

BLUE VALLEY record. w Jl 8 1868-69||
Followed by Beatrice clarion
NbHi O 7 1868

Beatrice CLARION. w 1869-Mr 1870||
Follows Blue Valley record. Followed by Beatrice express

Beatrice COURIER. w Ja 5 1875-N 1881||
Followed by Gage county independent, later Beatrice republican
NbHi Jl 13 1875;My 23,Jl 11 1876

Morning CRITIC. d Mr 1 1899-
NbHi [Mr 14-O 8 1899]

Daily DEMOCRAT. d 1886-92||?
NbHi O 30 1888;Ag 1 1890;Mr 11-12,14-19,21-26,28-Je 1892
—w ed *See* Gage county democrat

Beatrice EXPRESS. w,sw Ap 1870-Mr 7 1912||
Follows Beatrice clarion. Title varies slightly
sw O 1901-Ag 10 1906; Ja 19 1909-O 6 1911
ICM Jl 12 1877
MWA Ag 20 1874;Jl 13 1876
NbHi Ap 15-O,N 11-D 23 1871;72-Ap 5 1877; Ja 28 1878;Ja 26 1880;Jl 24 1883;S 1891-1912

GAGE county democrat. w 1879-1909||?
NbHi Je 11 1880;Ap 24,Je 9,S 1 1882;Ja 26,Jl 6,S 14-21,N 9-16,D 7 1883;Ja 21 1884;Ja 15 1886;Ag 4 1887;Je 13 1889;Ag 5-12,S 16,O 14 1892-1909
—d ed *See* Daily democrat

GAGE county herald. w D 1884-1905||?
NbHi Ja 18-F 1,15-22,Mr 15,Ap,My 10-17,31, Je 14,28-Jl 19,Ag,S 13-O 4,18,N 1,15,29-D 6, 20 1901-Ja 3,24,F 21-28,Mr 28,Ap 11,25-My 2, Je 6,Ag 15-22,S 12-19,O 3-10,N 7,D 5,19 1902;Ja 9,F 13 1903;Ap 14,28 1905

Die NEBRASKA post. w Mr 1892-97||?
1892-Mr 25 1897 as Beatrice post
In German
NbHi S 1895-My 13 1897

Weekly NEWS. w S 1898-1900||?
NbHi Ja 4,10,25,Mr 15,Ap,My 17-Je 7,21,Jl 26,Ag 16-23,S 13,27-N 1,15-29 1900

Beatrice NEWS. w Je 24 1926+
pub 1926+
NbHi 1926+

Beatrice POST. *See* Die Nebraska post

Beatrice REPUBLICAN. w D 10 1881-92||?
Follows Beatrice courier, 1881-83? as Gage county independent
NbHi 1886-F 6,Je 25 1892

Beatrice daily SUN. d Jl 8 1902+
KHi F 27 1925;Jl 15 1926
NbHi [Jl-S 26 1902]Mr 18 1908-Ag 20 1918; 20+

Beatrice evening TIMES. d Jl 1 1892-O 1902||
1892-F 6 1898 as Beatrice daily times
NbHi [1892]-Ja 27 1894[S 1895-1902]

Beatrice weekly TIMES. w 1892-F 4 1909||
Merged with Beatrice express
KHi Mr 9 1899;Ja 25 1900;N 12 1908
NbHi D 3 1892;N 1-15,D 27 1895;Ja 24-31,F 21-28,Mr 27,Ap 9,My-D 1896;F 11,Mr 25-Ap 1,My 27,Je 24,Jl 8,S 23,D 2 1897;Ja 20-27, Je 30,S 22 1898;F 8-22,Mr-Ap 5,19-Ag,S 20-27,O 11-D 6,20 1900-[02]-09

TRIBUNE. w O 1892-98||?
NbHi Ag 9-16,30 1895-96;Ja 29,F 19,Mr 5,19, Ap 30,Je 25,Jl 9,23-Ag 6,20,S 3,O 8 1897;Ag 26-S,O 14-21 1898

BEAVER CITY

BEAVER VALLEY tribune. w 1886-Ja 10 1902||
United with Beaver City times to form Times-tribune
NbHi Je 17-24 1892;O 25-N 1,15-D 20 1895; Ja 17-24,Ap 17-My 1,15-Je 5,19-26,Jl 17-Ag 21,S 11-O 21,N 1896-1902

FOR revenue only. w 1894-N 1 1895||
United with beaver City times to form Times-revenue, later Times-tribune

TIMES-TRIBUNE. w N 1875+
1875-78 as Western leader; 1879-Ja 10 1902 Beaver City times (N 8 1895-My 22 1896 Times-revenue)
NbHi Mr 17 1881;Ag 11 1887;My 24 1888;Jl 21 1892;Ja 11 1894;Ag 23,S 20-27,O 18-N 1,15 1895-[96]-F 11, 25,Mr 11-My,Jl 29,S 30,O 28-D 9 1898;Ja 6,20-F 10,Mr 24-My 12,25-Ag 11, 25-O 13,27-N 3,17-D 8,29 1899-F 16,Mr 2,16-Je 1,15-Ag 17,S 14,28,O 19-N 2,16-D 1900;Ap 26-S 20,O-N 15,29 1901-Ap,My 11-Jl,Ag 10, 31,S 21-O 5,19-26 1906;07+

WESTERN leader. *See* Times-tribune

BEAVER CROSSING

Beaver Crossing BUGLE. w Ap 24 1887-Jl 1889||
NbHi complete

ECHO. w Ja 10 1913-
NbHi Ja 17,31,F 14,Ap 11-18,My 2,Je 6-20,Jl 4-18,S 19-26,D 22 1913

INDEPENDENT examiner. w Mr 11 1905-06||?
NbHi 1905-N 1906

NEW ERA review. *See* Beaver Crossing times

PRIDE of Beaver Crossing. *See* Beaver Crossing times

Weekly REVIEW. *See* Beaver Crossing times

Beaver Crossing TIMES. w My 5 1892+
1892-Mr 25 1904 as Weekly review; Ap 22-D 16 1904 New era review; 1905-Jl 5 1906 Pride of Beaver Crossing
Suspended from Mr 25-Ap 22, from D 16 1904-Ja 1905
NbHi 1892-My 21,Je 4,18-Ag 20,S-O 1896;Ja-F,Mr 12-Ap 16,My 14-Je 14,18-Jl 9,D 24 1897-F 4,25-Ap 8,My,N 18,D 1 1899;Mr 30-Ap 6 1900;01-04;Mr 31-Ap 21,My 5-12,Je 9,23 1905-Je 1909;O 12 1911+

BEEMER

Beemer TIMES. w Mr 11 1886+
pub 1886+
NbHi Mr 18,Ap 1886-S 11 1891;D 9 1892;Mr-N 4 1898;Jl 28 1899;1900[01-S 19 1902]06-O 14 1908;09-My,Jl 4,18-Ag 1918;20+

BELDEN

Belden PROGRESS. w 1902+
NbHi D 28 1911-Ja 8,21-29,F 12-Mr 5,19-Ap 2,16 1914;Ja 4,Mr 9-My 11,25-Ag 24,S 14-D 1922;Ja 11-F 1,15-22,Mr 15-My,Je 14-S,O 11 1923+

BELGRADE

Belgrade HERALD. w S 1900+
pub 1900+
NbHi Mr 13 1908-Ap 16,Je 25 1909-Je 17,Jl,Ag 12,26-O 7,21,N 1910-My 23,O 24,N 14-28,D 12 1913-Ja 9,30,Ap 17,Jl 24 1914;Je 18 1915

BELLEVUE

Bellevue BROADCASTER. w D 1930-
NbHi Ag 11,S 1-22,O-N 17,D 1932-F 2,23,Mr 31-Ap,My 12 1933

Bellevue GAZETTE. w N 1856-O 1858||
NbHi Ja 15-22,Je 18 1857;Ja 21 1858

Bellevue GAZETTE. w Ap 1904-10||?
NbHi Mr 1906-Ap 15 1910

NEBRASKA palladium. w Jl 15 1854-
Jl-O 21 1854 pub in St. Mary, Iowa
CSmH N 15 1854
KHi 1854-55
NbHi Jl 15,Ag 30,S 13,O 11-N 15,29 1854-Ja 10,24-F 7,21-Mr 7,21-Ap 11 1855;Mr 19 1856 (extra)

BELLWOOD

Bellwood GAZETTE. w Ja 10 1886+
pub Je 1917+
NbHi N 1-8,22 1895-[96-97]Ja 14,28-Mr 11,25-My 1898[99-1900]Ja 4,25,Ap 26,Jl 19,Ag 2,30-S 13,27-O 4,18-N 1,15,D 6,20-27 1901;F 7-21, Mr-Ap 11,My 2,30-Je 6,20-Ag 1,15-22,S 5-12 1902;N 1935+

BELVIDERE

BRUNING banner-Belvidere news. *See under* Bruning

Belvidere INDEPENDENT. w Je 2 1899-1908||?
NbHi Je-Jl 21 1899;Ag 21-D 4,18-25 1908

Belvidere NEWS. w 1890-1900||?
NbHi Ja 27 1892;S 18-O 9,N 13-20,D 4,18 1896-Mr 5,26-Ag 13,27-O 15,29-N 5,26-D 10 1897;Ja 14-F,Ap 8 1898;Jl 21,N 10,D 1 1899; O 26,D 7 1900

NEBRASKA (*Continued*)

BENEDICT

Benedict HERALD. w Mr 16 1900-Je 27 1902||
United with Benedict news to form Benedict news herald
NbHi Jl 13,D 14 1900;Ap 26-My 3,17,31-Je,Jl 19,Ag 2-23,S-N 15,29,D 13 1901;Ja 3-17,31-F, Mr 21-My 23,Je 13-27 1902

Benedict NEWS HERALD. w F 1897-1910||?
1897-Je 1902 as Benedict news
NbHi Jl 1-Ag 15,29-S 19,O 3,17 1902-S 16,O 7-14,28-N 4,18-D 9 1903;08-Je 15 1910

BENKELMAN

Benkelman CHRONICLE. w 1894-My 1906||
United with Benkelman news to form News-chronicle
NbHi S 1,O 1897-F 4,18-Ag 5,S 1898-Ja 6, 20-F,Mr 10-My 5,19-S,O 13 1899-[1904]-06

NEWS-CHRONICLE. w 1893-Ap 28 1922||
1893-My 11 1906 as Benkelman news. United with Benkelman post to form Benkelman post and news-chronicle
NbHi Mr 24,My 19,Jl 14,28,Ag 11,25-S 1,15,O 27-N 3 1899;O 5-12,26,N 23-30,S 28-D 1900; Ja 25,Ap 19-My,Je 14-21,Jl 19,Ag 2-16,30-S 6,20-O,N 22-29 1901;Ja 17,F,Mr 14-Ap 18,My 9,23,Je 20-Jl 4,18,Ag 8-S 12,O 10 1902;My 18 1906-22

Benkelman POST and news-chronicle. w Ja 1 1916+
1916-Ap 28 1922 as Benkelman post
NbHi 1920—

BENNET

ENTERPRISE. w Ja 1908-10||?
NbHi O 22,D 24 1908;F 1909-O 21 1910

Bennet SUN. w Ja 1911+
pub 1924+
NbHi D 15 1911-S 21,N 16 1922;23+

Bennet UNION. w 1888-1908||?
NbHi N 2 1892;F 28 1895-F 1,15-22,Mr-Je 1900

BENNINGTON

Bennington HERALD. w 1904+
NbHi 1908-Ja 12,Mr 9-D 14 1917;18-Jl 22 1927

BENSON

Benson TIMES. w N 1903+
pub 1903+
NbHi 1907- 34-35]+

BERLIN. *See* OTOE

BERTRAND

Bertrand HERALD. w 1888+
1888-91? as Phelps county herald; 1892?-N 23 1928 Independent herald
NbHi D 3 1892;Ap 13-Jl,S 1901-My 7,Jl 1926+

INDEPENDENT herald. *See* Bertrand herald

Bertrand LEADER. w S 19 1896-98||?
NbHi S 19-26,D 12-19 1896;Ja 9,23,F 6-13,27-Mr 13,27-My 8,22,Je-Ag 7,S 4-11,O 9-16,30,N 20,D 1897-Ja 8,29,F 10,24-Mr 1898

PHELPS county herald. *See* Bertrand herald

Bertrand TIMES. w D 1894-96||?
NbHi O 18,N 1 1895;Ja 3,F 21-Mr 13,27,Ap 10-17,My 1 1896

BETHANY

LANCASTER press. w F 19 1898-
NbHi Mr-Ap 9,23,My 7-14,Je-Jl 9,30 1898

BIG SPRINGS

DEUEL county herald. w Je 30 1930+
1930-Ap 4 1935 as Big Spring news
pub Je 27 1931+
NbHi Mr 12-Je,Jl 16,Ag 13-N 12,D 10 1931+

Big Springs JOURNAL. w 1911-12||?
NbCR Ap 1911-O 1912

Big Springs NEWS. *See* Deuel county herald

BLADEN

Bladen ENTERPRISE. w D 1893+
NbHi O 24 1895-[96]-[98-1900]Ja 3,24,O 18,N 1 1901;S 19 1902;Ap 26-Ag 23,S 6-20,O 1907-Ja 13,F 17-Mr 24,Ap 7,21,My 12-19,Je 23-Jl 21,D 1-8,22 1911-Ja,Mr,My 2,S 17 1920+

BLAIR

Blair COURIER. w Jl 6 1889-Ag 15 1907||
United with Blair democrat to form Democrat and courier, later Pilot-tribune
NbHi Jl 1889-[99]-Ag 21 1906

Blair DEMOCRAT. *See* Pilot-tribune

ENTERPRISE. w N 21 1896+
1896-Ag 19 3 as Kennard enterprise (Kennard)
pub 1914+
NbBl 1929+
NbHi [1897-Mr 3 1899;O 1902-Ja 1903]Ag 23 1908+

Weekly LEADER. w O 12 1895-97||?
NbHi N 2,16-D 21 1895[96]-Ja 21 1897

Blair PILOT. w My 1872-F 7 1929||
1872-Ag 1874 as Tekamah pilot? United with Blair tribune to form Pilot-tribune
1872-Ag 1874 pub in Tekamah
NbHi Jl 27,Ag 31-N 9,23 1876;Ja 4-11,25,F 22-Mr 1,O-N 8 1877;Ja 3,Ap 25,My 16-23,Je 6 1878;Ap 3 1879;Ja 22,Je 17-24,Jl 29-Ag 5, S 9,23,O 7-14,N 4-11 1880;Mr 3,My 12 1881; Jl 20,Ag 3-10,31-S 7,28 1882;Ja 3,S,N 27 1884;Ja 22,Ap 9 1885;S 16 1886;F 17,O 6,27 1887;My 10-24,Je 28 1888;D 19 1889;Ag 21-S 4,18,N 27 1890-[91-93]-[1902]-29

PILOT-TRIBUNE. w Jl 1870+
1870-Ag 1880 as Blair times; Ag 1880-F 26 1905 Blair republican; Mr 4 1905-N 8 1917 Blair democrat (Ag? 1907-12? Democrat and courier) N 15 1917-F 7 1929 Blair tribune
pub O 191 +
NbHi Mr 3 1873;My 6 1875;Ja 6,Ap 6 1876;F 15,Ag 30,O 11 1877;My 16,Je 6 1878;Je 12 1879;Jl 20,S 28,O 19 1882;Jl 31 1884;Ap 21 1887;Je 13 1889;Je 30 1892;O 17-N 7,21,D 12 1895-[97-94]Ja 5,19-F,Ap 20,My 11,25-Je 1, 15,Jl 6,20-27,Ag 31 1899;N 9 1900;N 1902-N 8 1917;F 14 1929+
NjR Mr 19 1874

Blair REPUBLICAN. *See* Pilot-tribune

Weekly TELEGRAM. w D 13 1894-95||*
NbHi 1894-F 7,21-Mr 7,Jl 11-18,Ag 22,S 26-O 3,24 1895

Blair TIMES. *See* Pilot-tribune

Blair TRIBUNE. *See* Pilot-tribune

WASHINGTON pulse. w Mr 17- 1898||?
NbHi Mr 31,My 26,O 6-20 1898

BLOOMFIELD

Bloomfield GERMANIA. w S 1896-1914||?
In German
NbHi Ap 9-Jl 23,Ag 1908-My 1914

Bloomfield JOURNAL. w My 1892-O 20 1921||
NbHi Jl 30 1896-1902;Ap 17-S 4,18 1908-N 4, 25 1910;My-D 1 1911;Je 11 1914-21
supps:Jl 23 1896;My 12 1898;My 17 1901

Bloomfield MONITOR. w D 1890+
NbHi Je 24 1892;O 16-N,D 11 1895-[96-97]98; Mr 22-My 10,31,Je 14-21,Jl-O 1,N 24 1899 [1900-01]+

BLOOMINGTON

Bloomington ADVOCATE. w S 1 1881+
1881-96 as Republican Valley echo; 1897-My 31 1901 Bloomington echo; O 13 1922-Ja 22 1931 Bloomington advocate-tribune
pub 1881—
NbHi 1897-[1900]Ja 4,My 10,24 1901+

BANNER-GUARD. *See* Riverton review (Riverton)

Bloomington ECHO. *See* Bloomington advocate

FRANKLIN county guard. *See* Riverton review (Riverton)

FRANKLIN county tribune. w F 1916-O 5 1922||
United with Bloomington advocate to form Bloomington advocate-tribune, later Bloomington advocate
NbHi D 27 1917-22

Bloomington GUARD. *See* Riverton review (Riverton)

PRICKLY pear. w Je 9 1899-My 31 1901||
United with Bloomington echo to form Bloomington advocate
NbHi Je 9 1899;1900-01

REPUBLICAN VALLEY echo. *See* Bloomington advocate

BLUE HILL

Blue Hill LEADER. w D 1887+
pub 1900+
NbHi Je 25 1892;S-O,N 16-23,D 1895[96-97] Ja 21-F 4,O 28-N 4,18-25 1898;Ap 19-My 10, 31,Je 21-28,Jl 12-26,S 13-27 1901;Jl 17,O 9,N 13,D 11,25 1908-Ja 8,22-29,My 28 1909+

BLUE SPRINGS

Blue Springs BEE. w Ja 1926+
NbHi Ap 28-S,O 13 1927-Ap 11,25-My 2,16-Je 20,Jl 4,25-S 12,O 3,17-31,N 14 1929—

Blue Springs REPORTER. *See* Wymore reporter (Wymore)

Weekly SENTINEL. w Ja 1886-1919||?
NbHi Mr 10 1892-My 4 1893;S 1895-S 5 1918

BODARC

Bodarc RECORD. w O 21 1886-87||?
NbHi N 11,D 31 1886;Ja 14-21,F 11,25,Mr 11-18,Ap 22 1887

BOONE

Boone ENTERPRISE. w Ja 1905+
NbHi Mr 26-Ap 2,30-O 15,29 1908-10;D 14 1911-Je 20 1912

BRADSHAW

Bradshaw MONITOR. w Ag 20 1896+
1896-Ap 29 1909 as Bradshaw republican
NbHi Ag 27 1896+

Bradshaw REPUBLICAN. *See* Bradshaw monitor

BRADY

Brady VINDICATOR. w Je 1 1908+
pub 1908+
NbHi Ag 13 1909+

BRAINARD

Brainard CLIPPER. w Jl 16 1897+
NbHi Jl-Ag 13,27-S 3,17,O 15,29-N 5,19,D 31 1897-Ap 8,My 6,20,N 4 1898;Mr 31 1899;Mr 9,23 1900;Ap 27-Je 8,Jl 20,Ag 10-24,S 7-21, O 5,26-N,D 28 1901-F,Mr 15,29,Ap 12,My 17, Jl 10,24-31,S 11-18,O 9 1902;O 30,D 11 1924+

BREWSTER

BLAINE county news. *See* Brewster news

Brewster NEWS. w Jl 26 1884+
1890? as Blaine county news
pub 1888+
NbHi S 19 1884;Je 17 1892;Ag 1895+

BRIDGEPORT

Bridgeport BLADE. *See* Bridgeport news-blade-herald

Bridgeport HERALD. w F 1911-Je 6 1929||
1911-12? as Herald (Northport). United with Bridgeport news-blade to form Bridgeport news-blade-herald
NbHi Ap 1925-Mr 15,N 15 1928-29

Bridgeport NEWS-BLADE-HERALD. w Jl 1900—
1900-Jl 17 1908 as Bridgeport blade; Jl 24 1908-My 30 1929 Bridgeport news-blade
NbHi 1901+

PLATTE VALLEY news. w S 26 1902-Jl 17 1908||
United with Bridgeport blade to form Bridgeport news-blade, later Bridgeport news-blade-herald
NbHi O-D 19 1902;Ja 2-16,Mr 6,My 22,Je 19, Jl 17,31,Ag 28 1903

BRISTOW

Bristow ENTERPRISE. w Je 1901-F 18 1932||
United with Lynch herald to form Lynch herald-enterprise (Lynch)
Suspended from S 26 1918-F 6 1919
NbHi Ap 24-My 8,Ag 21-D 1908;Ja 8-Ap,My 14,28,Je 25-Jl 9,30,Ag 20-N,D 17,31 1909[10]-32

BROADWATER

Broadwater NEWS. w Mr 1911+
NbHi F 19 1920+

BROCK

Brock BULLETIN. w Ag 1895—
1895-97 as Brock champion
pub 1928+
NbHi N 1-8,22,D 6,20 1895[96-97]My 20-27, Jl 15,Ag 5 1898;O 20-N 10,24-D 8,22 1899-1902;Ag 19 1909-25;S 23-N,D 16 1926-Ja 13, 27,Mr 10,24 1927+

Brock CHAMPION. *See* Brock bulletin

BROKEN BOW

CUSTER county beacon. *See* Ansley herald (Ansley)

CUSTER county chief. w,sw Ap 16 1892+
w 1892-1929
pub 1892+
NbHi Ja 13 1893;Ag 16-23,S,O 11-18,N 1-8, 22,D 6,20 1895+
NbM 1917+

CUSTER county herald. *See* Ansley herald (Ansley)

CUSTER county republican. w Je 29 1882-Ja 20 1921||
Merged with Custer county chief
NbBb 1882-93;95-99;1904-05;09]
NbHi O 24-31,N 21 1895-[96-97]-1920
—d ed *See* Daily evening republican

CUSTER leader. w Je 13 1881-Ja? 1894||
NbHi Ag 11 1887;Je 9 1892

Daily evening REPUBLICAN. d 1888-Jl 1911||
Title varies slightly
NbBb [1898]
NbHi My 9-11,14,17-18,20-21,23-24,Je 3,6-7,9-11,13,15,Jl 26 1898
—w ed *See* Custer county republican

BROWNVILLE

Brownville BIOGRAPH. O 17 1902-03||?
NbHi N 14 1902;Mr 27 1903

Brownville DEMOCRAT. w Jl 11 1868-73||
Followed by Nemaha county granger, later Granger (Auburn)
NbHi S 27 1872;Ag 15 1873

Brownville daily DEMOCRAT. d Jl 19 1870-
NbHi Jl 21-24,26-Ag 4,6-8,10-14,16-21,23-28,30-31,S 2-4,6-11,13-14,16,20-21,23-25,27-O 2,4-5, 8-9,11-12,14,16,18 1870

Brownville LETTER. w My 1904-06||?
NbHi O 14 1904;Ag 18,O 13 1905;Ja 16 1906

NEBRASKA advertiser. d S 5 1870-71||?
NbHi S-D 1870

NEBRASKA (*Continued*)

BROWNVILLE—*Continued*

NEBRASKA advertiser. w *See under* Nemaha

NEMAHA county granger. *See* Granger (Auburn)

Brownville NEWS. w F 1889-91||?
NbHi O 4 1889;Mr 15,Ag 28,S 5,O 10-24,D 5 1890

Brownville REPUBLICAN. w Ap 27 1882-83||?
Merged with Nemaha county granger, later Granger (Auburn)
NbHi 1882-83

Brownville TELEGRAPH bulletin. d D 1 1860-
Suspended from Ja 1-11,15-20 1861
NbHi D 1,4-10,12-19,21-23,25,27-30 1860;Ja 1, 11-13,15,20,22-24,26-27,29-F 3,5,10,12-15,17,19, 21,26-27 1861

BRULE

Brule CITIZEN. w Je 1928+
pub 1928+

BRUNING

Bruning BANNER-Belvidere news. w Ap 1918+
Follows Bruning booster. 1918-32? as Bruning banner
Also dated in Belvidere
pub 1918+
NbBr 1918+
NbHi O 9 1930+

Bruning BOOSTER. w Mr 1913-17||
Followed by Bruning banner, later Bruning banner-Belvidere news
NbBrB My 1913-D 22 1917
NbHi My 29 1914-16

Bruning COURIER. w Je 30 1899-1920||?
NbHi Je-Jl 7,21-N 3,17 1899-[1905]-Ap 5,19 1907

BRUNSWICK

Brunswick INDEPENDENT. w Ap 1908-F 9 1928||
NbHi Ag 19 1909-25;Ja 8-S 10 1926;Ja-Je 17 1927

BURCHARD

Burchard NEWS. w F 1884-88||?
1884-Je? 1885 as Plaindealer
NbHi Je 13-Ag,S 12-N 15,29 1884-F 7,Jl-S,N 1885;Ja 2,23-D 4 1886;O 8-22 1887

PAWNEE county times. *See* Burchard times

PLAINDEALER. *See* Burchard news

Burchard TIMES. w 1889+
F 1894-Jl 24 1896 as Pawnee county times
NbHi O 25,N 1895-[96-98]-F 1899;O 18-D 6,20 1901-02;F 13-Mr 13 1903;Ag 20 1909-Je 3,17, Jl 1-8,Ag 19,S 30,O 14-21,N-D 1910;Ag 18 1911-S 13 1912

BURNETT

Burnett BLADE. w Ag 14 1884-Je 1890||
NbHi Ag-D 18 1884;Ja-Mr,Ap 9,My 15 1885-Ja 1887;Je 15 1888

BURR

urr STAR. w Mr 20- 1897||
NbHi Mr-Jl 9,23-30 1897

BURTON

urton INDEPENDENT. w 1906-17||?
NbHi D 1911-Mr 14,28-O,N 14 1912;My 28-N 19,D 1914-My 13,Je-S 16,O 1915-[16]-Jl,Ag 9-16 1917

BURWELL

EYE. w Ja 1890-98||?
1890-94 as Loup Valley alliance
NbHi Jl 7 1892[95]-Ja 16,F 20-Mr 19,Ap-Je, Jl 9-Ag,O 1896-My 12 1898

GARFIELD enterprise. *See* Burwell mascot

Burwell LEVER. *See* Burwell mascot

LOUP VALLEY alliance. *See* Eye

Burwell MASCOT. w 1888-1903||?
1888-89? as Burwell lever; 1890-94? Garfield enterprise; 1895?-96? Burwell progress. Merged with Burwell tribune?
NbHi Je 23 1892;Ag 15-S 5,26,O 31,N 14-D 19 1895;Ja 23-F 6,20,Mr 19,Ap 9,23-My,Je 18, Jl 16-Ag 13,S-O 15,N 12-D 17 1896;97[98]-1902;Ja 15-O 8 1903

Burwell PROGRESS. *See* Burwell mascot

Burwell TRIBUNE. w O 27 1898+
pub 1908+
NbHi F 2,Mr 23,Ap 20-My 11,Je-Jl 6,20-O 12,26-N,D 21-28 1899;Ja 18,F 8-Mr,Ap 19-26, My 10-Je 7,21,Jl-Ag 2,23-30,S 13,O 4,18 1900-My-Je 20,Jl 11-Ag 15,29-D 5,26 1901;Ja 9,F 20,Mr-Ap 17,My 8-22,Je 12-Ag 14 1902;O 1908-Je 1918

BUSHNELL

Bushnell RECORD. w F 8 1917+
pub 1917+
NbHi Jl 24-O 2,16-D 11,25 1919-Mr,Ap 13,My 18-25,Je 8-29,Jl 13-27,Ag 10,24 1932+

BUTTE

BOYD county register. w S 17 1896-1909||?
1896-Ap 29 1898 pub in Spencer
NbHi 1896-Jl 22 1898;Je 9 1899;Je 1908-09

Butte GAZETTE. w 1892-F 9 1933||
United with Spencer advocate to form Spencer advocate and Butte gazette (Spencer)
NbHi D 3 1892;Ag-D 1895;Ja 31-My 15,29-O, N 20,D 4-18 1896;Ja-F 5,19-Mr,Ap 9,23-Jl 9, 30-O,N 19,D 3-17,31 1897-Ja,F 11-Jl 15,29, Ag 12-19,S 23,O-N 18,D 9 1898-Ja 19,F-Je 1,29-Jl 6,Ag 17,31-S 4,21,N 2,30-D 7 1900 [Ap 1901-02]-My 1,15-N,D 11-25 1903;04-Ag 21,S 18-25,O 16,30-N 1924[25-26]Ja 6,20,Mr 3,24 1927-33

BYRON

Weekly Byron BLADE. w N 1904-Ja 10 1913||
Title varies slightly
NbHi 1908-13

Byron HERALD. w N 20 1896-1906||?
NbHi D 25 1896-F 12,26-N 19,D 1897-Mr 11, 25,Ap 8-My,Je 10,Jl-S 2,16-30,O 21-N 4,18-25,D 9-30 1898

CADAMS

Cadams PROGRESS. w Je 1-D 14 1916||
Merged with Nelson gazette (Nelson)
NbHi Je-O 12,26-D 14 1916

CAIRO

Cairo RECORD. w Ap 1903+
NbHi Ap 26 1907-Ag 20 1909;F 1920+

CALLAWAY

COURIER-TRIBUNE. w Ag 1887-Ap 9 1914||
1887-Mr 2 1905 as Callaway courier
NbBb [1897-1902;06-09]
NbHi Je 24 1892;F 16-Ap 20,My 4-18,Je 1-8, 22-Jl 20,Ag 17 1894;O 25-N 1,22,D 6-20 1895; Ja 31,Mr 6,Ap 24,My 15,Je 12,Jl 24,Ag-O 9, N 13-D 18 1896;Ja-F 5,26,Mr 12-Ap 2,16-Jl, Ag 13-20,S,O 8-22,N 1897-F,Mr 9,23-30,Ap 14-O 20,N-D 8,29 1905;Mr 9-Ap 20,My-S,O 12 1906-Ja 22,F 5-12,Mr 12,26-Ap 9 1914

LOUP VALLEY queen. w Je 20 1902+
NbBb [1906-09]
NbHi Mr 19 1908-O 1917

Callaway STANDARD. *See* Arnold news (Arnold)

Weekly TRIBUNE. w Je 2 1892-F 1905||
United with Callaway courier to form Courier-tribune
NbBb [1897-1902]
NbHi D 3 1892;F 20-Je 18,Jl 2,23-Ag 6,20-27,S 10-17,D 10 1896;Mr 20-27,Ap 17,My 8, 29,Je 12,20,Jl 10 1897;Ja 29,Ap 2 1898;Mr-My 20,Je 10-17,Jl 22-Ag 19,S 2-16,O 7-21,N 11-25,D 9,23 1899[1900-01]-05

CAMBRIDGE

Cambridge CLARION. w,sw Jl 1885+
1885-Ja 1899 as Cambridge kaleidoscope
sw 1909-Je 1916
NbHi My 20 1887;Je 3 1892;O 25 1895-[98]-[1904-05]O 23-30 1908;Ag 20 1909+

Cambridge KALEIDOSCOPE. *See* Cambridge clarion

CAMPBELL

Campbell CITIZEN. w Ja 1901+
pub My 1928+
NbHi Mr 13-20,Ap-Je,Jl 16-D 10,24 1908-09; D 28 1911-Ap 16,30,My 21,Je 4 1914

Campbell PRESS. w O 1885-1903||?
NbHi Mr 18 1892;O 25,N 29 1895;Ap 17-24, My 15-Je 19,Jl 17,31-Ag 7,21,S-O 16,N 6,20 1896-My 21,Je-Jl 9,23,Ag 6-13,S 17-O 22,N-D 17,31 1897;Ja 14-F 11,25-Mr 4,18-25,Ap 8-My,D 9 1898-Ag 7 1903

CARLETON

Carleton ENTERPRISE. w N 21 1919+
pub 1919+
NbHi 1919+

Carleton LEADER. w 1893-1918||?
NbCaB 1906-13
NbHi Ag 24,S 21,N 1906-N 19 1909;Ja-S 1, 15-22,D 8 1910;Ja-Je 1,22,Ag 3,N 23,D 7 1911;Ja 4,Je 20,S 26,D 12 1912;Je 19,Jl 3,O 10,N 20-27 1913

Carleton VISITOR. *See* Southern Nebraskan (Fairbury)

CARROLL

Carroll INDEX. w Ap 3 1901-My 30 1928||
NbHi N 29,D 20 1901;Ja-N 1902;03-Ja 21,Ap 15 1910-11;25-28

CEDAR BLUFFS

Cedar Bluffs OPINION. *See* Cedar Bluffs standard

Cedar Bluffs STANDARD. w 1891+
1891-94? as Cedar Bluffs opinion
pub O 1917+
NbHi O 25-N 15,29 1895-[96-97]-[99]+

CEDAR RAPIDS

BOONE county outlook. *See* Cedar Rapids outlook

Cedar Rapids LEADER. w Jl 17 1933+
pub 1933+
NbHi My 30,Je 13-D 1935

Cedar Rapids OUTLOOK. w N 1885+
1885-D 6 1895 as Cedar Rapids republican; D 13 1895-Ap 8 1898 Boone county outlook
pub 1885+
NbHi Je 10,N 25 1892;O 18-25,N 15,29,D 13 1895-Ja 3,24,F 7,28,Mr 13-Ap 3,17-My 22,Je 1896-[97]-1909;Ja 13,27,My 5-12,Je 16,Jl 14-21,Ag 11-S 1 1910;Mr 28 1912;Je 4,18 1914+

Cedar Rapids REPUBLICAN. *See* Cedar Rapids outlook

CENTER

OUTLOOK. w N 29 1901-
NbHi D 1901;Ja 3,17-F 14,Ap-My 2,23,Je 20-Jl 18,Ag 8-D 1902

Center REGISTER. w 1903-06||?
Merged with Crofton journal (Crofton)
NbHi Jl-Ag 18,S 1905-Je 22,Jl-Ag 10,S 7 1906

CENTRAL CITY

To Mr 1875 as Lone Tree

Central City COURIER. w Ap 9 1874-D 27 1894||
1874-Mr 1875 as Lone Tree courier
NbHi Jl 27 1876;Mr 31 1892-94

Central City DEMOCRAT. *See* Central City record

MERRICK county item. w Ja 14 1880-
NbHi 1880

Central City NONPAREIL. w Ja 1882+
Title varies slightly
NbHi Je 30 1892;O 3,24-31,N 14,D 5-19 1895 [96]-Mr,Ap 12-19,My 10-24,Je-S 20,O 4-18,N, D 13 1900-[01-02]+

Central City RECORD. w Je 1893-1909||?
1893-Ja 12 1905 as Central City democrat. United with Central City republican to form Republican and record, later Central City republican
NbHi Ag 15-S,O 10 1895-N 1909

Central City REPUBLICAN. w Jl 1893+
1910?-14? as Republican and record
NbCc 1929-33
NbHi F 29,Mr 14-21,Ap-My 16,30-Je 20,Jl 25, Ag 8 1896;Ja 2,My 1 1897;Ja 15,Ap 30,My 14,N 5,D 31 1898-Ja 7,Ap 1,22-29,My 13,D 2-9 1899;My 12 1900;Je 15-22,Jl 20,Ag-S 14,28-O 19,N 2,D 14 1901;N 15 1902-Ja 3,17-F 14,28-Je 20,Jl 4-11,25,Ag 15-D 1903;Ja 16,30,F 13, Mr 12-My 14,28-D 3,24 1904-17;19-F 1924;25+

CERESCO

Ceresco COURIER. w Ja 1892-Je 18 1925||
NbHi Jl 23,D 3 1892;O 6 1894;N 2-9,D 21 1895[96]-[98]Mr 21 1908-S 23 1910;Ja-O 24 1912;13-25

Ceresco NEWS. w D 4 1924+
Follows Kennard news (Kennard)
pub 1924+
NbHi Jl 9 1925+

CHADRON

Chadron ADVOCATE. w N 17 1887-Ja 1892||
1887-Ag 2 1889 as Northwestern temperance advocate. Merged with Dawes county journal, later Chadron journal
NbHi D 22 1887[88-89]-Ja 1,15-22 1892

CHADRONIAN. *See* Chadron times

Chadron CHRONICLE. w 1909+
pub S 1918+
NbHi S 11-25,O 9,30-N 6,27-D 4,18 1919;20+

Chadron CITIZEN. w Ag 27 1885-95||?
1885-90? as Chadron democrat
NbCrN 1885-D 15 1887
NbHi Ag 27,S 24 1885;F 18,Ag 5,O 28,N 11 1886;Jl 25,Ag 11,S 1,22,O 6,N 14,D 1 1887;88 [89]Ja 9-23,F 13,My 22,Je 12,Jl 3,31,D 4,25 1890-Ja 1,15,Mr 19,Ag 10,N 12 1891[F 1892-D 6 1894]Je 7-14 1895

Chadron DEMOCRAT. *See* Chadron citizen

DAWES county journal. *See* Chadron journal

Chadron JOURNAL. w N 1884+
1884-F 12 1897 as Dawes county journal; F 19-D 31 1897 Journal
pub 1885+
NbHi N 6 1885;Mr 4 1887;S 25 1891;Ap 15-My 13,27-Je,Jl 15,29-Ag 5,S 9,30 1892-Ja 18,O 11, 25,N 29-D 20 1895;96-1906;Ja 11-18,F 8-Mr 1, Ap 1907-O,N 20,D 1908+

NEWS. w My 27 1898-1900||?
NbHi My-Je 3,Jl 29 1898;Jl 14,D 15 1899-Ja 19,F 2,16-Mr 3 1900

NORTHWESTERN temperance advocate. *See* Chadron advocate

Chadron RECORDER. w S 3 1892-97||?
1892-Ap 23 1896 as Chadron signal; Ap 30 1896-Mr 18 1897 Signal-recorder
NbHi O 1 1892;F 4,Mr 4-11,Ap 1,29,My 13-20, Jl 22-29,Ag 12-19,S 7,28,O 26,N 2,23,25,D 9 1893[94-96]Mr 18-Ap 8,29-My 6,20,Je 3-10,Jl 8,Ag 6,20-27 1897

NEBRASKA (*Continued*)

CHADRON—*Continued*

Chadron RECORDER. w Jl 22 1893-Ap 23 1896||
United with Chadron signal to form Signal-recorder, later Chadron recorder
NbHi Jl,Ag 12-19,S 7,28,O 26,N 2,23 1893;F 1,15,Mr-Ap,My 31,Je 21,Jl 5-12,27-Ag 10,O 19,N 9-D 20 1894[95]-F,Mr 13-Ap 23 1896

Chadron SIGNAL. *See* Chadron recorder 1892-97

Chadron TIMES. w 1898-1905||?
1898-1902 as Chadronian
NbHi Ag 13-S 10,24 1902-Jl 1905

CHAMBERS

Chambers BUGLE. *See* Chambers sun

Weekly JOURNAL. w N 20 1886-87||?
NbHi N 20 1886;F 19,Ap 20,Je 18-25 1887

PICKINGS. w Ap 19 1887-89||?
NbHi D 2 1887;F 10,Ap 20,My 4,Je 1-8,22-29 1888

Chambers SUN. w D 1891+
1891-Ag 30 1917 as Chambers bugle
NbHi Jl 14 1892;O 31-D 1895;F 6,20-27,Mr 12-19,Je 25,Jl 16,30-Ag 6,20,S 3-17,O 1-8,N 5,19-D 17,31 1896[97]-Ja 20,F-My 5,19-Je 2 1898[F 1899-1901]-Ja 9,27 1902;Mr 19-Jl 2,16-30 1908; 09+

CHAMPION

CHASE county champion. w My 1886-92||?
NbHi Je 13 1889;Jl 21-28 1892

CHAPPEL

Chappel REGISTER. w Ap 1887+
pub 1887+
NbHi Je 16 1892;O 31-D 1895;Ja 23,F 20,My 14-Je,Jl 16 1896-F 14,Mr,Ap 25-Je,Jl 18-Ag 15,29-S 12,26-N 14,28-D 5,19 1901-Ja 2,16,F 20-27,Mr 20-27,Ap 10 1902-Ap,My 12-Je 2,16-Jl,Ag 11,25-O 6,27-D 1,29 1904-Ag 3,24-O 5, 19 1905-Mr 1,15-D 6,20 1906-[25]+

CHESTER

Chester HERALD. w Jl 1885+
Suspended from 1895-Ag 21 1896
pub 1885[86-94]96-Je 1906;07-12[15-16]-19;22; 32+
NbHi Ag 30-S 6,O 4,25,D 13 1889-[90-92]Ag 28 1896-[1900-02]F 13-O 2,16 1903-10;Ja 26-Mr,Je 8 1911;N 29,D 13 1923+

CHIMNEY ROCK

Chimney Rock TRANSCRIPT. *See* Bayard transcript (Bayard)

CLARKS

Clarks ENTERPRISE. w Jl 1891+
1891-97 as Clarks leader
pub Jl 21 1933+
NbHi N 25 1892;O 9-23,N 20-D 4 1896;Ja-F 12,26-Mr 5,26-My 7,21-Je 11,25-Ag,S 9-O 21, N-D 3,17 31 1897-F 11,25-Ap 15,29-My 1898 [99]-Mr 9,23,Ap 20,My-Je 22,Jl-Ag 10,24 1900-Ja 15 1903;Jl 4 1904;Je 1914-S 6 1918; 19+

Clarks LEADER. *See* Clarks enterprise

CLARKSON

COLFAX county press. w 1904+
1904-My 30 1916 as Clarkson herald; Je 6?- 1916? Colfax county press and Clarkson herald
1923?-24? also dated in Schuyler
NbHi S,D 1909-13;F 10 1914;15-My 16,30,Je 8-Jl 20,Ag 1916-25;30+

DOMACI noviny. w,sw D 1904-Mr 25 1924||
sw D 9 1910-F 24 1911
In Bohemian
NbHi Ag 27 1909-24

Clarkson HERALD. *See* Colfax county press

POKROK. w F 1903-09||?
In Bohemian
NbHi S 29 1904-Je 17 1909

CLATONIA

Clatonia OBSERVER. w Je 13 1907-Ap 2 1909||
NbHi Je 13,Jl 4,18-25,Ag 8-S 5,26-N,D 13 1907-Ja 1,15-Ap 1909

CLAY CENTER

CLAY county patriot. *See* Clay county republican

CLAY county republican. w My 1892-Ag 1921||
1892-O 28 1920 as Clay county patriot
NbHi O 11-25,N 22 1895-[96-97]-[1902-05]-21

Clay Center SUN. w Ag 22 1884+
pub My 1912+
NbClP [1884-My 1912]
NbHi My 20 1887;D 16 1892;Jl-N 1,15 1895-[99-1900]-Ja 3,17,31-O,N 20-D 12,26 1902-Ap 3,24-S 11,O 2,16-23,N 1903-O 7 1910;D 27 1917-Ap 11,25-Jl 11 1918;F 1920+

CLEARWATER

Clearwater HEADLIGHT. w S 30 1886-87||?
Followed by Clearwater message?
NbHi 1886-Je 2,16 1887

Clearwater MESSAGE. w Jl 8 1887-96||?
Follows clearwater headlight?
NbHi 1887-S 1888;My 9 1890;My 30,Je 17 1892; Mr 15,O 11,25,N 8-22,D 1895;Ja 17-24,F 21-Mr 13,27-Ap 10,My 8-Je,Jl 17-Ag 14,28-S 11,O 2-16 1896

Clearwater RECORD. w Ap 23 1897+
NbHi 1897-Jl,Ag 12,29 1904;Jl 7 1905;My 25,S 23,28,N 30 1906;Mr 3,8,My 17 1907;Ag 28,S,O 9 1908-[32]+

CODY

Cody COW BOY. w D 6 1900-Je 10 1927||
Merged with Valentine democrat, later Cherry Valley news (Valentine)
NbHi 1900-Ag 16,30-O 11,25,N 15 1912;Ja 17 F-Ap 4,18,My 1916-27

COLERIDGE

Coleridge BLADE. w 1891+
pub [1891-1920]+
NbHi Je 16 1892;Ap 30-My 21,Je 4,Jl 23-Ag 6,D 17 1896-[97-99]-[Ja-S 1902]Jl 20-D 21 1906[07]-Je 18,Jl 2-9,Ag 6,27,O 22 1909-S 19,O 10-31,N 21-D 5,19-26 1918;Je 30 1927-Ja 19,F 1933;Ja 17,Ag 25,S 1935+

COLLEGE VIEW

College View ADVOCATE. w Mr 23-D 1917||
United with College View gazette to form College View gazette-advocate
NbHi complete

College View GAZETTE-ADVOCATE. w N 10 1910-29||?
1910-17 as College View gazette
NbHi N 10 1910;Ja 12,26-F 16,Mr 9-23,My 4, 25,D 8,29 1911;Ja 12,Mr 29,Ap 26-My 3,17,Je 7-14,28,Jl 16-Ag,S 10-O 1,29-D 12,26 1912-21;Ja 26,F 9-Mr 16,30-Ap 6,20,My-Je 22 Jl 6,20,Ag 3,S 7,21-O 12,N 2-9,30,D 14 1922;F-Mr 22,My 17-31,Je 14,28,Jl 12,Ag 2,O 4,25 N 1,29 1923;Ja 8-15,My 8,Je 25,Jl 2,16-30 1924; Ag-S 17 1925

COLUMBUS

Columbus DEMOCRAT. *See* Columbus telegram

Columbus JOURNAL. w My 16 1870-1917||?
Follows Platte Valley journal
N N 16 1870
NbCoC 1872-76;79-1909;13-15
NbHi Ja 12 1876;Ap 16,30,My 14 1890-Mr 15 1893;1905-Ag 1906;16-Jl 12 1917

NEBRASKA biene. w 1894-1918||?
In German
NbHi 1897-1900;O 18 1901-Je 1918

NEW PLATTE county argus. *See* Platte county argus

Columbus NEWS. w Ap 1933+
NbHi N 17 1933+

PLATTE county argus. w Ag 1886-1905||
1886-Ap 1892 as Platte Center argus (Platte Center) S 15-N 10 1899 New Platte county argus. Merged with Columbus journal
NbCoC 1896
NbHi Jl 1 1892;N 29-D 10 1895[96-N 1898]Je 9-N 10 1899;S 1901-05

PLATTE county sentinel. w 1889-Ap 1892||
United with Platte Center argus (Platte Center) to form Platte county argus (Columbus)

PLATTE county times. *See* Columbus times

PLATTE VALLEY journal. w 1864-69||?
Followed by Columbus journal

Columbus SENTINEL. w
NbHi Ja 12 1876

Columbus TELEGRAM. w,d 1880+
1880-Mr 1889 as Columbus democrat
w 1880-Mr 1922
NbCoC 1881-82;84-88;95+
NbHi My 22 1892;Ag 15 1895+

Columbus TIMES. w Ap 18 1896-1903||?
1896-Ap 1 1899 as Platte county times
NbHi My 30,Je 20-Jl 4,18-25,Ag 8,22,S 12,26-O 17,31-N 7,21-28 1896[97]-Ja 15,F 19-26,Mr 19, Ap 2-16,My 14-28 1898;Ja 28,Mr 25-My 20,Je 3,17-Jl 8,Ag 19,S 2-16,O 7,21-N 11,25-D 9,23 1899-[1900-01]Ja 11-25,Mr 1,15-My 3,Jl 5,19-26,Ag 23,S 13 1902

Columbus TRIBUNE. w O 3 1906-My 17 1911||
Merged with Columbus journal
NbHi O 10 1906-Ja 23,Ap-My 22,Je-N 13,27 1907-F 1,15-22,Mr-My 17 1911

COMSTOCK

Comstock NEWS. w Ag 1907+
NbHi Ag 27 1909-Ja 21,F 11-18,Mr 25,Ap 15, 29-My 6,Je 10-17,Jl 1910-17;20+

CONCORD

TRI-COUNTY times. *See* Emerson advocate (Emerson)

COOK

Cook weekly COURIER. w 1892+
pub [1892-1909]+
NbHi N 23,D 14 1895;Ja 18,F 1-8,Ap 18,My 9,30,Je 6,20,Ag 1,S 12,O 17,N 7,D 26 1896-Ja 2,16,30-F 6,27,Mr 13-Ap 3,24,My 8-Ag,S 11, O 23,N 6-20,D 4,18 1897;Ja 1,F 12-O,N 12 1898-N 16 1906;Mr 22 1907+

CORTLAND

Cortland HERALD. w D 13 1887-1900||?
NbHi F 8,N 16,D 7 1888;N 24 1892;O 24-31,N 21-28,D 19-26 1895;Ja 23 F 6,20,Mr 19,Ap 23-My,Je 18,Jl 9,23-Ag 20,S 10-N 12,26 1896-Jl, N 30,D 14 1899-F 1,22-N 19,D 2,16-30 1900

Cortland NEWS. w 1897-Ap 24 1925||
1897-Ap 6 1916 as Cortland sun (title varies slightly)
NbHi Jl 23,S 10,24-O 1,15-22 1897;Ja 21-F 4, 18-Ap 7,21,My-Je 2 1898,F 2,Mr 23-My 4,Je-Jl 13,27-Ag 17,31,S 21-28,O 12,N 16-30 1899; 1900-[04]-Ja,F 16,Mr 16-Ap 11,25,Je 15-Jl 13,27,Ag 10-17,31 1911-S 1918;Mr 7-14,28-Ap 4,25-My 16,30-Je 6,Jl 4,S 12-26,O 10 1919-20;S 16 1921-25

Cortland NEWS. w Ap 6 1933+
NbHi 1933+

Cortland PILGRIM. w 1927-Ap 26 1934||
NbHi F 24 1927-34

Cortland SUN. *See* Cortland news 1897-1925

COZAD

Cozad LOCAL. w,sw Jl 16 1897+
Title varies slightly
w 1897-F 15 1924
NbHi Jl-Ag 20,S-N 5,D 3,24 1897-[98]Ja 27-F, Je 23,N 17 1899-F 9,23-Mr 2,30,Ap 27,Jl 6-13 1900;Ap 12-19,My 3,17-Jl Ag 30-S 6,20-D 20 1901;Ja 17,My 9,S 26 1902-Ja,F 13-20,Mr 6,20-Ap 10,My 1903-Jl 5,19,Ag 23-30,S 13-N 22,D 13 1907+

MERIDIAN star. w Ja 1896-F 12 1897||
NbHi My 28-Je 4,19,Jl 17-S 11,O 9,N 6,20-27 1896;Ja 8-15,29-F 1897

Cozad MESSENGER. *See* Cozad tribune

Cozad REPORTER. *See* Cozad tribune

Cozad REPUBLIC. w Ap 10 1908-10||?
NbHi Ag 28-N,D 18 1908-F 1910

Cozad TRIBUNE. w 1886-Jl 13? 1908||
1886-90? as Cozad messenger; 1891? Cozad reporter. Merged with Cozad republic
NbHi Jl 15 1892;O 25-D 1895;Ja 24,My 15-Je 5,19,Jl 17-Ag,S 25-O 16,N-D 18 1896[97-99]-Ja 12,F 2-16,Mr 1900-[06]-Ja 11,25,Mr 15-N 1907

CRAB ORCHARD

Crab Orchard HERALD. w 1889+
pub Mr 1906+
NbHi Ag 26 1892;N 9 1894-97;Ja 14-Je 10,Jl 8,Ag 5,19-S 2,16-O 14,28 1898-1901;Ja 31,F 21-Mr 21,Ap-Je,Jl 18-25,Ag 8,29-S 19,O 10, 24-N,D 12 1902-Mr 6,My 1903-Ja 12,F 9-16, Mr-D 7,21 1906+

CRAIG

Craig ADVERTISER. w Jl 1904-06||?
United with Burt county news to form Advertiser and Burt county news, later Craig news
NbHi Ja-F 1,15,Mr 1,Ap 5-19,My 3,Jl 5,Ag 10,31,S 21 1906

ADVERTISER and Burt county news. *See* Craig news

BURT county news. *See* Craig news

Craig NEWS. w Ag 1887+
1887-1906? as Burt county news; 1907?-08? Advertiser and Burt county news
pub My 11 1909+
NbHi Ja 2-9,23-30,D 17 1892-N 1893[95]Ja 10, 24-Je,Jl 10 1896-Ja,F 12-26,Mr 19-26,Ap 9,23, My 7-Je 18,Jl 2-23,Ag 6-13,S 17-O 15 1897; 98-Mr 3,17-Je 2,16-O,N 17 1899-Mr 2,16-Ag,S 14-21,O-D 21 1900;Ag 12-N 11,25 1909-14;18-S 1927;28+

CRAWFORD

ALLIANCE boomerang. *See* Crawford gazette

Crawford BULLETIN. w Ja 1897-Ag 5 1904||
Merged with Crawford tribune
NbCrT complete
NbHi Ag 28 1897;My 13,Je 17-24,Jl 8-22,Ag 19,O 28,N 25 1899-Ja 6,27-Mr,Ap 14-Je 9,Jl 7-14,O 5 1900;Ja 4-11,F 8-22,Mr-O 4,25,N 8 1901-04

Crawford CLIPPER. *See* Crawford tribune

Crawford COURIER. *See* Northwest Nebraska news

Crawford GAZETTE. w Ag 1890-1902||?
1890-92? as Alliance boomerang
NbCrN O 10 1890;96-98;Ag 23 1901-Ag 15 1902
NbHi Je 1,22 1892;O 13,27,N 10 1893-F 2,Ap 13,My 4,Je 1,22,Jl 6 1894;S 6-13;N 1 1893;Ag 15-22 1902

NORTHWEST Nebraska news. w Ja 1906+
1906-N 21 1929 as Crawford courier
pub [1907]-15[23;25-26]-S,N 28 1929+
NbHi My 30-O 16 1914;N 28 1929+

Crawford TRIBUNE. w 1888+
1888-91? as Crawford clipper
pub Mr 1910+
NbHi Je 24-Jl 8,22,D 9 1892;Jl 17-Ag 21,S-O 16,N 6,20,D 11 1896-Ja 14,28-F 11,Mr-My,Jl 8,22-29 1898[99]+

CREIGHTON

Creighton COURIER. *See* Creighton liberal

KNOX county news. *See* Creighton news

NEBRASKA (*Continued*)

CREIGHTON—*Continued*

Creighton LIBERAL. w Je 13 1889-1917‖?
1889-1905 as Creighton courier; 1906-S 11 1912 Nebraska liberal
NbHi Je 13 1889;S 1895-N 3,17-24,D 29 1898; Ja 12-F,Mr 9-Je 15,29,Ag 8-15,S 21 1899;Ja 4 1900;Ap 3,24-My 1,15,Je 12-19,Jl 3-17,Ag-S 18,O-D 1902;Mr-Je 19,Jl 10-O 2,16-23,N 6,27,D 18 1903-Ja 8,29,F 19-Mr 4,18-Ap 15,My 20-27, Jl 8,29,Ag 12-19,S 9,N 19 1904;Ja 27-F 3,17, Mr 10-17,31,Ap 14-My,D 22 1905-Ag 9 1917

NEBRASKA liberal. *See* Creighton liberal

Creighton NEWS. w My 1879+
1879-91? as Knox county news; 1892?-My 1904 People's news
1879-84 pub in Niobrara
pub 1904+
NbHi My 29,Je 19-Jl 2,D 24-31 1879;Ja 15-29, F 19-Mr 4 1880;Mr 19 1885;S-D 5,19 1901-Ja 9,23,F 6,20,Mr 6,20,Ap 17,O 2-9,22,N-D 19 1902;Ja 2,F 13-Mr 6,20-27,Ap 17-My 15,29-S 11,25-D 18 1903;Ja-My,Je 10-Jl,Ag 12,26-S 2,16-23,O 28,N 18 1904-[05-06]-09;12+

PEOPLE'S news. *See* Creighton news

Creighton PIONEER. *See* Niobrara pioneer (Niobrara)

Creighton TRANSCRIPT. w D 17 1885-87‖?
NbHi Ap 7 1887

CRESTON

Creston STATESMAN. w 1897-Je 1 1932‖
Merged with Leigh world (Leigh)
NbHi Ag 15-S 12,26 1902-32
NbLeiW 1926-32

CRETE

Crete CHRONICLE. w My- 1891‖?
NbHi My 29-Jl,Ag 21,S 4-18 1891

Crete DEMOCRAT. w O 8 1874-Ap 12 1922‖
1874-Ap 11 1889 as Opposition
1874-Mr 8 1877 pub in DeWitt; Mr 15? 1877-Ap 11 1889 in Wilber
NbHi O-N 12,D 10-24 1874;75;Ja 13,27-Je 1, 22-Ag 3,17-D 14 1876;Ja-F 8,22,Mr-Ap 12,26-D 20 1877;78-Ja 1,Ap 2,23-Ag 13,S 10-D 1, 15,30,N 19,D 24 1890-[93]-[95]-1922

Crete DEMOCRAT. 1878 *See* Saline county democrat

Crete GLOBE. w 1873-90‖?
1873-77? as Saline county news; 1878?-83 Saline county union
NbHi Je 28,Jl 19 1877;My-Je 20,Jl-S,O 10,24-N 21,D 5-19 1878;F 7-14,Mr 21 1879-[82-83]-F 14,Mr 6-13,Ap 3-17,My 8-Jl 3,17-Ag 21 1884;85-Ap 11,25,O 10 1889;Mr 29-Ap 12,26-My,Je 14-Ag 22,S 5-19,O 1890

Crete daily GLOBE. d Ag 11 1884-
NbHi [Ag-D 1884]

Crete HERALD. w D 21 1893-Je 25 1902‖
United with Crete vidette to form Crete vidette-herald, later Crete vidette
MWA Je 1 1894
NbCreN [1897;99]
NbHi 1893-Ja 18,F-Ap,Je 12,Ag 2-9,23 1895-1902

Crete NEWS. w Mr 14 1908+
pub 1908+
NbCre [1921+]
NbHi 1908-Je 10,Jl 1,S 23 1920+

Cretesky POKROK. w F 8 1905-09‖?
In Bohemian
NbHi 1905-Je 1909

SALINE county democrat. w Ja 1878-79‖?
1878? as Crete democrat
NbCreN O 2 1878

SALINE county express. *See under* Friend

SALINE county news. *See* Crete globe

SALINE county standard. w N 27 1879-83‖?
Follows Wilber record (Wilber)
NbHi N 27-D 11 1879[80]-[83]

SALINE county union. *See* Crete globe

Crete SENTINEL. w D 1875?-My 1876‖
NbHi F 26,Mr 25-Ap 15 1876

STATE vidette. *See* Crete vidette

Crete VIDETTE. w My 10 1883-Je 14 1928‖
1883-S? 1891 as State vidette; My 1 1902-My 30 1918 Crete vidette-herald
NbCreN 1883-88[92-1901;03;05]
NbHi 1883-[89]Ja 9-F 20,Mr-D 11 1890;Jl 23-30,Ag 13-S 3,17-24,D 1891[92-N 8 1894]Ja 17, 31,F 28-Ap,Jl 25 1895-97;Ja 20-27 1898;Mr 16, O 5 1899;1900-01;F 6-13,Mr 6-20,Ap 3-17,Mr 20,My 1902-F 9,23,N 30,D 1911-[13]-Mr 8,22-Je 1928

CROFTON

Crofton JOURNAL. w D 1905+
NbHi O 25-D 13,27 1906;Ja 10-17,31-Je 13,Jl 11-Ag 22,S 19,O 17 1907-Ja 21 1926;Ap 1933+

CROOKSTON

HERALD-MESSENGER. w Ag 15 1913-1922‖?
1913-My 21 1920 as Crookston herald
NbHi S 26 1913-F 6,27-O 15,N 5 1920;Ja 14,Mr 4,Ap 1-8,22,My-Jl 1 1921

CULBERTSON

Culbertson BANNER. w Ag 18 1905-My 27 1921‖
Merged with Palisade times (Palisade)
NbHi [1908]-[20]Ja 7,21,F 11-My 1921

Culbertson ERA. w O 1893-1915‖?
NbHi O 11,N 13 1895-[1896-1900]Ap 25-Je 13 1901;04

HITCHCOCK county herald. w -Ja 26 1904‖
NbHi F 13 1903-04

HITCHCOCK county republican. w Ja? 1885-92‖?
1885-89? as Hitchcock county reveille
NbHi Ja-Jl,Ag 10,24-D 21 1888;Jl 11-O 1890; My 20 1892

HITCHCOCK county reveille. *See* Hitchcock county republican

PROGRESS. w Je 24 1920+
1928-30 as Culbertson progress
pub Jl 30 1920+
NbHi Jl 1920+

Culbertson SENTINEL. *See* People's sentinel (Trenton)

Culbertson SUN. w O 1880-92‖?
NbHi F 16-Mr 8,Je 23-Ag 11,25,S 8-D 1 1883;Mr 22-Ap 5,My-Ag 9,30 1884

CUMMINSVILLE

WHEELER county gazette. S 6 1883-88‖?
NbHi S 13-O 18,N 15,29,D 13-20 1883;Ja 10-F 7,21-Mr 13,My 1-8,Je 26,Jl 31-Ag 7,S 4-18,O 2,16-30,N 13 1884;Ja 1-15,F 5,26-Mr 19,My 21, O 1,N 19 1885;F 18,My 13,Jl 29,S 16,O 21,N 11-18,D 9,30 1886;Ja 13-20,Jl 28 1887;Mr 29-Ap 5 1888

CURTIS

Curtis COURIER. w 1885-1916‖?
NbHi Je 24 1892;D 6 1895[96]-[99-1901]-03;05-[14-16]

Curtis ENTERPRISE. w O 1891+
NbHi Jl 15-22,N 18 1892;Je 8 1894;F 21-28,Mr 20,My 29-Je 5,26,Jl 24,Ag 7,S 11,N 27 1896-Ja 1,22-Ap 2,16-Je 4,18-25,N 5,26,D 24 1897-[1905-06]-09;Ja 14-21,Mr 4,S 30,O 21-28 1910; My 12 1911-[23]+

Curtis REPORTER. w Ja 1 1914-17‖?
NbHi Ja 8 1914-My 17,Ag 30-S 6 1917

DAKOTA CITY

DAKOTA county herald. w 1895+
pub 1900+
NbHi D 2 1899;Ja 20 1900;F 6-20,Mr 12,Ap 9,23-30,Ag 27 1904;07+

Dakota City HERALD. w Jl 15 1857-60‖?
DLC [Ap 28-Ag 25 1858;Ja 7-Ap 21 1860]
NbHi Ag 13,27-O 8,N-D 3,24 1859;Ja 7,21,F 4,18,Mr 10,Ap 7-My 4 1860

Dakota City MAIL. w Jl 29 1870-Mr 1 1878‖
Merged with North Nebraska eagle, later Eagle (South Sioux City)
NbHi O 25 1872;Mr 17 1876;Ja 26-F 2 1877

NORTH NEBRASKA argus. *See* Argus (South Sioux City)

NORTH NEBRASKA eagle. *See* Eagle (South Sioux City)

DALTON

Dalton DELEGATE. w Ag 1914+
pub 1914+
NbHi My 16-23,Je-O,D 12,26 1919[20]+

DANBURY

Danbury NEWS and Lebanon advertiser. w My 1894-S 7 1922‖
1894-S 1918? as Danbury news. United with Marion enterprise (Marion) to form South Side sentinel
NbHi S 27-N 8,22-29,D 13 1895;Ja 24-31,F 14-21,Ap 24,My 8,Je 5,19,Jl 31-O 16 1896;Je 21 1900-Je,Jl 11 1901;Ap 1902-[07]-[10-11]12; D 1913-22

SOUTH SIDE sentinel. w Jl 30 1909-N 1 1934‖
1909-Mr 3 1910 as Marion citizen; Mr 10 1910-S 7 1922 Marion enterprise
1909-Ag 20 1925 pub in Marion
NbHi 1909-S 7 1922;Ag 27 1925-34

DANNEBROG

Dannebrog NEWS. w 1898+
pub [1903-04]+
NbHi O 22 1908+

DAVENPORT

CHRONICLE. w 1898-99‖?
NbHi Je 11-Jl 16,30,Ag 12-O 14,28 1898-F 3,17-24,Mr 10-My 5,26-Je 2 1899

PEOPLE'S journal. w 1890+
KHi Ap 10 1896
NbHi Jl 22 1892[97]S 28 1900-Mr,Ap 12-26,My 10,31,Je 28,Jl 12-26,S 13 1901;Ag 1902-[06-S 3 1907]Ag 20 1909-20;23+

DAVEY

Davey MIRROR. w 1891-1921‖
NbHi D 2 1892;O 19 1894;D 21,25 1895-F 8,Mr 7,21,Ap,My 9,30-Je 6,20-Jl 18,Ag 1,15-O,N 14, 28 1896-Ja 23,F 6,20-O,N 13 1897-Ja 22,F,Mr 26-Ap 9,23,My 21,Je-Jl 2,23,Ag 6,S 3,24,O-N 5,19,D 10 1898-Ja 7,21-28,F 11,Ap 15-29,My 13-27,Je 24,Jl 15-29 1899;1908-21

DAVID CITY

BUTLER county press. w,sw S 25 1873+
sw Ja-Ap 10 1901
pub 1910+
NbHi Jl 22 1892;S 20 1895-Mr 18,Ap-Jl,Ag 12 1898-F,Mr 10,Ap-Je 16 1899;1901-Ja 13,27-Ag, O 5-12,26 1904-06;Ap 17 1907+

BUTLER county republican. w F 5 1897-Je 17 1898‖
NbHi F 5-19,Mr-D 10,24 1897-Je 3,17 1898

HOME record. w D 19 1901-03‖?
NbHi Ja 2,F 27-Je 19,Jl 1902-Ap 23 1903

David City NEWS. w 1891-1901‖?
NbHi S 5,O 1895-[99]-Ap 18,My 2-23 1901

PEOPLE'S banner. w 1890+
pub 1913+
NbHi Ja 2,O 23,N 20,D 18-25 1895;Ja 15,F 20,Mr 5-12,Ap 2-16,30-My 7,21-28 1896;Ja 1, 29-Ag 6,27,D 3,17-24 1897;Ja 14-Ag 12,26-S 16,30 1898-1922;25+

David City REPUBLICAN. w F 6 1877-84‖?
NbHi N 20 1877

David City TRIBUNE. w 1884-93‖?
NbHi Jl 16 1885-Ja 7 1886;Ja 13 1887-Ja 5 1888;N 24 1892

DAWSON

Dawson HERALD. w My 19 1921+
NbHi 1921+

Dawson NEWS BOY. w Je 1888-Ap 30 1909‖
NbHi Ag 9 1889;S 16 1892;N 8-D 20 1895;Ja 24,F 7,Mr 6,Ap 17,My 1,Je 5,19-26,Jl 24,Ag-S 4,25,N 7 1896-1909

Dawson REPORTER. w 1913-My 1920‖?
NbHi Jl 10-17,31-Ag 21,S-O 9,30,N 13 1914-Mr,My 1919-F 13,27-Ap 16 1920

DAYKIN

Daykin HERALD. w Ap 7 1900-03‖?
NbHi My 26-Je 16,30-Jl 14,S 1900-Mr 23,Ap 6-13,27-My 4,18-Jl 6,20-Ag 10,24-S,O 12,26,N 9-16,D 28 1901-Mr 1 1902

Daykin HERALD. w O 1927+
pub 1927+
NbHi Ag 24 1928+

DECATUR

Decatur HERALD. w 1902+
NbHi Ag 21-28,S 11-18,O 1902-Ap,My 9,Je 6,20-27,Jl 18-O 3,N 21-D 5,19 1918;Ja 9-23,F 13,27-Ap 17,My-Je,Jl 17,31,S 4,O 30-N 13,D 25 1919-Jl,S 13-20,O 25 1923+

Decatur NEWS. w 1892-96‖?
NbHi Je 21 1895-Ja 3,17-Ap 17,My 8,22-Je,Jl 10-Ag 1896

VINDICATOR. w Ap 3 1877-Ap 30 1878‖
NbHi Ap-O 2,N 13-D 1877;Ja 8-Ap 2,16-30 1878

DESHLER

Deshler CHRONICLE. *See* Deshler rustler

Deshler CITIZEN. w 1892-97‖?
NbHi N 1,15 1895-Ja 3,24-Mr 14,Ap 17-24,My 8-Je 5,19-Jl,Ag 14-N 6,D 1896-F 5,19,Mr 5,19 1897

Deshler RUSTLER. w 1899+
1899-Je? 1906 as Deshler chronicle
NbHi Je 23-D 1899;Ja 12 1900-F,Jl 1905-F 2,23,Mr-My,Je 15,N 30 1906-Jl 11,25-Ag 1 1918;19+

DE SOTO

NEBRASKA enquirer. w Jl 21? 1860-
NbBlP Ap 19 1860
NbHi Ag 18-S 15,O 6 1859;Ag 16 1860;Ja 17-24,F 28,Jl 16-Ag 13,S 3,24 1861

De Soto PILOT. w Ap? 1857- S? 1858‖
DLC [My 30 1857-My 4 1858]
NbHi Jl 11-18,S 12-19,N 17 1857

DEWEESE

Deweese BOOSTER. w 1915-18‖?
NbHi Ap 16 1915-[18]

DE WITT

De Witt ADVERTISER. sm My 30 1874-77‖
NbHi My 30,Jl-Ag 1,S 1-15 1874

DEMOCRATIC guide. *See under* Wilber

De Witt EAGLE. w Ag 29 1894-1921‖?
1894-D 11 1903 as Saline county independent; D 18 1903-O 1 1904 De Witt record
NbHi Ag 29,S 12,26-O 2,10,31-N 14,D 26 1894; Ap 3,Jl 24-Ag 7,21,O 9,23-30,N 13 1895-Ja,F 19-Je,Jl 10-21,Ag 1896-F,Mr 14-Ag 15 1902;Ja 15-F 5,19-Ap 2,16-D 11 1903;04-S 19 1907;Ap 30-Jl 2,23,S 10,D 17 1908;Ag 19-D 9 1909

NEBRASKA (*Continued*)

DE WITT—*Continued*

FREE PRESS. w 1877-80||?
1877-My 3 1879 as De Witt free press
NbHi F 4,Ap 18-Je 19,Jl 4-18,O 17-31,N 14, 28-D 12,28 1878;F 15,Mr 22-Ap 19,My-S 6,20-27,O 11-D 6 1879;Ap 16 1880

De Witt NEWS. w Ag 22 1902-My 8 1903||
United with De Witt times to form De Witt times-news
NbHi complete

OPPOSITION. *See* Crete democrat (Crete)

De Witt RECORD. *See* De Witt eagle

De Witt REPUBLICAN. w Ja 8-S 26 1904||
United with De Witt record to form De Witt eagle
NbHi Ja 8-22,F-Mr 11,25-Ag 12,26-S 1904

De Witt RIP-SAW. w Jl 18-N 8 1888||?
NbHi Jl 18,Ag 15,S-N 8 1888

SALINE county independent. *See* De Witt eagle

De Witt TIMES-NEWS. w Ag 18 1881+
1881-My 7 1903 as De Witt times
NbHi S 8-15,O 6,20,N 3,17 1881-[82-86]-91;Je 16 1892[93-94]-Ap,Ag 1895-[1900-01]-07;O 22 1908+

DILLER

JEFFERSON county record. *See* Diller record

Diller RECORD. w 1887+
1887-D 5 1901 as Jefferson county record
pub 1887+
NbHi O 26 1888;Ja 18 1889;Je 24 1892;N 8-D 20 1895;Ja 17,My 15,Je,Jl 24,Ag 7-14,28-S,O 16-23,N 6,20 1896-[97]Ja 7,21-Ap,My 13-27 1898 [99]+

DIXON

Dixon JOURNAL. w 1908+
NbHi Ag 20-O 22,N-D 3,17 1909-Mr 11 1910; Ja 29-Mr 4,18-Ap 15,29-O 1920;Ja-Ap,My 12-19,Je 2,16 Jl 14,28,Ag 25,S 8-22 1921;25+

DODGE

Dodge ADVERTISER. *See* Dodge criterion

Dodge CRITERION. w 1888+
1888-94? as Dodge advertiser
NbHi N 2-D 1 1892;O 11,25 1895-[96-97]Ja 7,28-Mr 4,18-Ap 22,My 13 1898;Ap 7,Je 2,S 22,O 6,N 24,D 15 1899;Ja 5,F 2-9 1900;My 31-Je 14,28,Jl 12-19,Ag 2-16,S 1901+

DONIPHAN

Doniphan ENTERPRISE. w 1914-21||?
NbHi Jl 28-Ag,S 10 1914-Ag 5 1921

Doniphan HERALD. w Ag 10 1923+
NbHi 1923-[30]+

Doniphan INDEX. w Jl 11 1896-97||?
NbHi Jl 25,Ag 15-O,N 14-28,D 12,26 1896-Ja, Mr 13-20,Ap,My 15-Ag 14,S 11-O 2,16-23 1897

DORCHESTER

Dorchester LEADER. w 1933+
NbHi Je 22,Jl 13 1934+

SALINE county express. *See under* Friend

Dorchester STAR. w Ag 25 1881+
NbHi S 8-15,O 13-N 3,17-D 1,15 1881[82]My 3-10,24-Ag 23,S,N 8,D 6,20 1883-[84]-[88]-Ap 4,Ag 15,D 12,26 1889[90]-[93]-My 3,24-Je 14 1894;Ja 17,31,F 28-Ap,Jl 25 1895-[96,97]-Je,Jl 28,Ag 11 1898[99-1905]Mr 8,22,My 3-17,31,Je 14,Jl 27,Ag 17,31 1906;Ja 31-Mr 7,21-28,Ap 18-My 9,23-Je,Jl 11,25-Ag 15 1907;08+

DOUGLAS

Early years as Hendricks

Douglas ENTERPRISE. w 1889+
1889-90? as New era
pub [1895-1905]+
NbHi O 25-N 15,29,D 13-27 1895;Ap 11-18,My 23-Je 6,20-27,Jl 18-Ag 22,S-N 7,21-D 19 1896; Ja-F 6,20-O 9,23-N 13,D 4 1897;Ja 8-15,F 10, Ap 23,My ",Je 11,S 24,O 15,29-N 12,D 17 1898;S 1909-Ja,F 10,Mr 3 1921;Mr 9,23,Ap 13,My 4,Je-Ag,S 14-28,O 12 1922-S 1934

NEW ERA. *See* Douglas enterprise

DU BOIS

Du Bois ITEM. *See* Du Bois times

NEWS-RECORD. *See* Our homes and the news-record

OUR homes and the News-record. w Je 1900-08||?
1900-06 as News-record
NbHi Je 8 1900-My,Jl 1907-Ja 1908

Du Bois PRESS. w 1904+
NbHi 1912+

Du Bois TIMES. w 1886-Je 1 1900||
1891?-Ag 1- 1896 as Du Bois item
KHi Ag 23 1895-Ag 1896
NbHi My 27,Je 17 1892;F 17-24 1893;S 1895-Ap 6 1900

DUNBAR

Dunbar REVIEW. w 1899+
NbHi O 11,N 22,D 1900;Ja 24,Ap 18-Je,Jl 18-S,O 10 1901-Ja 16,F,Mr 20-My 22,Je 12-19, Jl,Ag 14,S 4-18 1902;Ag 19 1909-Je,Ag 1912-My 8 1913;S 23 1915-My 1917;F 1,15,Mr 8,My 3,31,Je 7 1935

DUNNING

BLAINE county booster. w 1909+
NbHi Je 25,Ag 1914+

EAGLE

Eagle BEACON. w My 3 1889-1933||?
NbHi Je 24,Ag 18-N 17 1899[Ap 1900-01]-Mr, Ap 18-Jl 4 1902;Je-Jl 10,24 1908-Mr 10,Ap-Je 14 1911;14-[17]-Ja 17,O 10 1929-My 4 1933

EAGLET. w S 19 1890-1900||?
NbHi S 19-N 7,21-D 19 1890;Ja-F 6,27 1891-[92]-[94]Ja 11,Mr 14,28-Ap,Jl 18,Ag 1,S-N 7,28 1896-[97-98]F 25,Mr 25,My 20,Je 3-10, 24-Jl 8,29 1899

EDDYVILLE

Eddyville ENTERPRISE. w 1906-20||?
NbHi D 14 1911-Ja,F 12,26-Mr 4 1920

EDGAR

CLAY county call. *See* Edgar post

Edgar INDEX. w S 1898-Je 20 1900||?
NbHi O 14,N 11,25,D 16,30 1898-Ja 6,27-F 3, 17,Mr 31-Ap 7 1899

Edgar POST. w,sw 1884-Ap 22 1921||
1884-Ap 1885 as Clay county call
w 1884-Je 9 1905
NbHi O 25 1895-[1907]-Ap 19 1921

Edgar SUN. w Je 1900+
pub 1922+
NbHi My 2,16-30,Je 20-27,Jl 11-S 12 1902;Ag 20 1909-[13-14]+

EDISON

Edison ECHO. w Ja 2 1925+
NbHi 1925+

Edison NEWS. w F 1906-Ag 1916||
1906-09? as Republican Valley news
Suspended from Mr 12-Ap? 1909
NbHi Mr 20-O 16,30 1908-Ja 15,F 5-12,26-Mr 12;D 21 1911;My-Je,Ag 1-15,S 5,19,N 14,D 5,19 1912[13]Ja 15,29,F 12,Ap 2,23,Je 11 1914-Jl 22 1915

Edison RECORD. w S 4 1915-17||?
NbHi 1915-Ja 19 1917

REPUBLICAN VALLEY news. *See* Edison news

ELGIN

Elgin REGISTER. *See* Neligh register (Neligh)

Elgin REVIEW. w Ja 1 1897+
pub F 1908+
NbHi Ja 1-8 1897;N 25 1898;Ja 20,Je 2,16,Ag 4,18 1899;F 16,Ap 27,Je 8,Ag 17,N 9 1900; Mr 22,Ap 5,Jl 26 1901;Mr 14,Ap-Ag 22,S 26 1902;F 6,Mr 13,Ap 17,My 8-15,29,Je 12-19,Jl 3,17,31,Ag 7-14,28,S 11 1903+

ELK CREEK

Elk Creek HERALD. w 1894-1910||?
NbHi O 24-N 21,D 12 1895-[96]-98;Mr 23,Jl 1899-Jl 19,S 1906-Mr,Ap 14-Ag 18 1910

ELKHORN

Elkhorn EXCHANGE. w 1891+
NbHi N 25 1892;Ja 18 1907;Jl-D 11 1914;15-Mr 8,22-Jl 19 1918;Ap 17 1931

ELM CREEK

Elm Creek BEACON. w 1898+
pub 1914+
NbHi Je 10 1898-1904;Ja 20-My 1905;18+

Elm Creek PILOT. *See* Buffalo county pilot (Kearney)

ELMWOOD

Elmwood ECHO. w N 1886-Jl 10 1896||
United with Elmwood leader to form Elmwood leader-echo
NbHi N 18,D 2 1892[96]

Elmwood LEADER-ECHO. w S 1891+
1891-Jl 3 1896 as Elmwood leader
NbHi D 23 1892;O 25-N 1,15,29,D 13,27 1895; Ja 3,Mr 20-27,My 15,29 1896[97]-Ja,F 18-Ap 8,29-My 13,27,Je 17,Jl 22,S 2-9,30 1898;Jl-Ag 11,S 1,15,N 3-10,D 15,29 1899[1900-01]+

ELSIE

Elsie LEADER. w O 4 1894-1902||?
NbHi O 10,24 1895-[96-97]-Ag 8 1902

ELSMERE

NEBRASKA news. w Je 1908-Mr 8 1917||
NbHi O 1912-17

ELWOOD

Elwood BULLETIN. w Ag 5 1896+
Title varies slightly
NbHi Ag 13-O 8,22-29,N 12-19,D 10 1896;Ja 8,F 18,Jl 8 1897;Je 28 1900-Mr 21,My 23-30, Je 13-20,Jl 18,Ag 1,15-29,S 19,O 24-N 14,D 5 1901;Ja 2,30-My 1,15-22,Je 12-Jl 3,Ag 1, 14-S,O 9,23 1902;Ag 27-N 19,D 3-17,31 1908-Je 1917;18+

GOSPER county citizen. *See* Elwood republican

GOSPER county enterprise. w Je 15 1899-1901||?
NbHi Je 15,29-O 12,26 1899-Mr 1901

Elwood REPUBLICAN. w 1884-97||?
1884-93? as Gosper county citizen; S 9-O 12 1897 Western Nebraska eye
NbHi O 12,26-D 14-21 1895;F 15,My 8-15,29, Je 19-25,Jl 17-24,Ag 7-21,S 4,10,30-O 21,N 12 1896;Ag 26-S 2,N 4,18,D 2-9,23-30 1897

WESTERN Nebraska eye. *See* Elwood republican

EMERSON

Emerson ADVOCATE. w 1894-1903||?
1894-97? as Emerson times; 1898? Tri-county times
1898? also dated in Concord, Hubbard and Thurston
NbHi Je 5 1896;F 19,Ap 23,O 15-22,N 5,19 1897;O 13,27-N 17 1898;Ap 19,My 10,O 11-N, D 27 1901

Emerson CRESCENT. w N 1 1903-05||?
NbHi Je 9 1904-My 4,18-S 7 1905

Emerson ENTERPRISE. *See* Tri-county press

Emerson TIMES. *See* Emerson advocate

TRI-COUNTY press. w Ap 1891+
1891-1925? as Emerson enterprise
pub S 1930+
NbHi Ag 5,D 1 1892;S 11-O 16,N 6,20-D 18 1896[97]Ja 14-F 11,25-Mr,Ap 15-My 20 1898 [99-1900]Ap 26,My 10-Je,Jl 12-Ag 16,30-D 14,28 1901[02-S 1903]Mr 16-Ag,O 5-12,26-N, D 21 1906-Je 4,18-25,Jl 30 1914;Mr 29-Ag 5, 19-26,My 17-Je 7,Jl 5,19-S 13,27 1934+

TRI-COUNTY times. *See* Emerson advocate

ENDICOTT

Endicott CALL. w My 1882-Jl 1885||?
NbHi D 2-9,23 1882;N 16-23,D 28,1883;My 18 1884

ERICSON

Ericson JOURNAL. w 1912+
NbHi My 27,Je 10,24-Ag 19,S 9 1914+

EUSTIS

Eustis NEWS. w 1904+
pub 1911+
NbHi Je 10,24 1904-[05-07]+

Weekly RECORD. w Ja 1891-1901||?
NbHi D 17 1892;O 24 1895[96-97]Ja 13-My 5, 19 1898-Je 6 1901

EWING

Ewing ADVOCATE. w D 13 1891+
1891-Ap 1927 as People's advocate
pub 1901+
NbHi N 25 1892;F 26 1897;N 4 1898;Je 16 1899;F 2,16-Mr,Ap 20-My,O 26-N 2 1900;My-Jl,Ag 23-O 4,18,N-D 20 1901;Ja 17-31,Mr 21, Ag 22,S 19 1902;S 28,N 23 1906;Mr 1,29,My 10 1907;Ag 28 1908-Ap 1911;21+

Ewing DEMOCRAT. w Je 6 1888-95||?
NbHi Je-Jl 18,Ag-S 19,O 3 1888;O 23,N 6 1889;Ap 22-29 1891;Ap 27,Jl 20 1892

Ewing ITEM. w 1884-90||?
NbHi Ja 10,Mr 13,Ap 10,My 8,S,O 16-23,N 13 1884;Ja 15,Ap 2 1885;Ag 12,N 11 1886;Jl 28 1887;Mr 29,My 24,Je 7-14,28-Jl 5,19-26,Ag 16, S 27 1888;Mr 28,My 23,O 10,24 1889

PEOPLE'S advocate. *See* Ewing advocate

EXETER

Exeter ENTERPRISE. w S 29 1877-Je 4 1909||
Merged with Nebraska signal (Geneva)
NbHi S 29-D 1 1877;78[79-Ag 4 1882]N 1-22 1884;O 10,24 1885-Ja 8,22-29 1887;88[89-92]F 11,Mr 4,My 27,Je 17,Jl 1-22,Ag 5 1893[Ap 1894-96]97[Ap 1898-99]-[1901]Ja 10-31 1902; Ja 12-19 1905[06-08]

Exeter EYE. *See* Fillmore county news

FILLMORE county news. w F 6 1892+
F-Ag 1892 as Exeter eye; S 1892-98 Fillmore county democrat
pub 1892+
NbHi S 7-14,28 1895-My 1898[99]+

FAIRBURY

Fairbury DEMOCRAT. *See* Fairbury sun

Fairbury ENTERPRISE. w 1888-Ag 1902||
Merged with Fairbury gazette
NbHi Ag 17 1895-1902

Fairbury GAZETTE. w,sw S 3 1870-S 15 1911||
United with Fairbury news to form Fairbury news and gazette
sw Je 14 1907-Ag 1909
NbHi N 15 1873;Je 20,Jl 11 1874;D 6 1879;Ja 24-Mr 6,27,Ap 13,My 1,Je 5 1880;F 4,Jl 29,S 16 1882 My 12-26,Ag 25-S 1,29-N 10 1883;S 12 1885;F 27,D 4 1886;S 8,Ag 11 1887;Ap 6, Je 8 1889;My 28 1892;Ag 17 1895-1911

NEBRASKA *(Continued)*

FAIRBURY—*Continued*

JEFFERSON county journal. *See* Fairbury journal

JEFFERSON county news. *See* Fairbury news and gazette

Fairbury JOURNAL. w Ap 9 1892+
1892-My 24 1902 as Jefferson county journal
pub Ap 1893+
NbHi My 21,Je 25 1892;O 26-N 2,16,30 1895-[97-98]+

Fairbury LIBERATOR. *See* Fairbury sun

NEBRASKA telegraph. w Jl 1879-80||?
NbHi N 14,D 19 1879;Ja 2,30,F 3,6,20,Mr 12, Ap 16 1880

Fairbury NEWS and gazette. w D 1897+
1897-1902? as Jefferson county news; 1903?-S 15 1911 Fairbury news
pub 1897+
NbHi Mr-My 20,Je 10-Ag 5,19-S,O 14-28,N 11-18,D 9-16 1898;My 19,Je 30 1899;Mr 20 1908-16,My 15 1919+

SOUTHERN advance. *See* Southern Nebraskan

SOUTHERN NEBRASKAN. w S 6 1879-Ap 1885||?
1879-80? as Carleton visitor (Carleton) 1880-81? Southern Nebraska advance (Steele City) 1882? Southern advance
NbHi My 18,D 5 1882;F 3-9,23,Mr 9,30-Je 8, Jl 27,Ag 24,S 7-21,O 26-N 9,30 1883;F 6-13, 27,Mr 13-20,Ap 10 1885

Fairbury SUN. w Mr 1889-Mr 1892||
1889-90 as Fairbury democrat; 1891 Fairbury liberator
NbHi Jl 20 1889

FAIRFIELD

Fairfield AUXILIARY. w O 1911+
pub O 10 1911+
NbHi Jl 15,29-D 9,23 1914-[21]-Ja 12,26,F 15-22,My 4,Je 1,S 7,21,O 5 1922;F 10-Je 18, Jl 1925+

Fairfield HERALD. w Je 7 1877-1907||?
1877-91? as Fairfield news; 1892?-My 1902 Fairfield news-herald
NbHi O 15,29 1885;O 11,25-N,D 13 1895-[96-97]-Je 9 1898[99-1902;F 1903-04;F 1905-O 11 1906]Mr 28-Jl 11,Ag-D 1907

Fairfield HERALD. w 1881-91||?
United with Fairfield news to form Fairfield news-herald, later Fairfield herald

Fairfield INDEPENDENT. w 1902-17||?
NbFaA N 7 1902-O 4 1907;O 9 1908-O 1 1909
NbHi 1908-[10]-Ag 9,S 7-14,O 5,19-D 14,28 1916-F 8 1917

Fairfield MESSENGER. w 1892-1902||?
1892-F 1900 as Fairfield tribune
NbHi O-D 13 1895;Ja 10,24,F 14-21,Mr 6 1896; Ag 28,S 16-30,O 21-N 11,25 1898-F 3 1899[F-D 1900]Ja 4,18-F 1,15-22,Mr-D 6 1901

Fairfield NEWS. *See* Fairfield herald 1877-1907

Fairfield TRIBUNE. *See* Fairfield messenger

TRUE light. w Ag 1898-F 1900||
United with Fairfield tribune to form Fairfield messenger
NbHi Ja 20,F-Mr 24,Ap 14-Ag 4,18 1899;Ja 19,F 2 1900

FAIRMONT

Fairmont BULLETIN. *See* Fillmore chronicle

FILLMORE county bulletin. *See* Fillmore chronicle

FILLMORE chronicle. w My 1 1872+
1872-74? as Fillmore county bulletin 1875?-Je 1885 Fairmont bulletin
pub 1872+
NbHi Jl 21,N 24 1892;O 31-D 5,19 1895-[96]-[1901]-14;16+

NEBRASKA signal. w O 27 1881-Ap 9 1896||
United with Republican journal (Geneva) to form Nebraska signal (Geneva)
NbHi N 19,D 24 1891-94;Ja 10-Mr 21,Ap-Ag 1,15-22,O 24 1895-F 13,Mr-Ap 9 1896

Fairmont TRIBUNE. w Ja 15 1897-99||?
NbHi [1897-98]Ja 13,27-F 3,Mr 24-Jl 14,28 1899

FALLS CITY

Falls City BROAD AXE. w N 1857-65||
Followed by Southern Nebraskian (Arago)
NbHi N 20 1860;Ja 1-15,F-Mr 12,Ag 13-27,S 10,O 1,15,29,N 19 1861;Mr 11 1862
OHi Jl 26 1865

GLOBE-JOURNAL. *See* Falls City journal

Falls City JOURNAL. w,d 1868+
1868-S? 1875 as Nemaha Valley journal, O? 1875-81 Globe-journal
w 1868-N 1908
pub 1920+
NbHi Mr 1879-[85-86]-[88]-F 6,8,10-12,15-17, 19,22-27,Mr 1-20,22,30-31,Ap 2-3,5,My 25 1909;D 11 1911+

LITTLE globe. w 1873-S? 1875||
United with Nemaha Valley journal to form Globe-journal, later Falls City journal

NEBRASKA staats-zeitung. *See under* Nebraska City

NEMAHA VALLEY journal. *See* Falls City journal

Falls City NEWS. w,d 1875-1934||?
1875-O 1879 as Falls City press. Merged with Falls City journal
w 1875-Je 1919
pub 1878+
NbHi Ja 22 1880;Ap 1 1886;Mr 9 1888;Ag 16 1895-[1921]-[23]-[33-Ap 11 1934]

POPULIST. *See* Falls City times

Falls City PRESS. *See* Falls City news

SOUTHERN Nebraskian. *See under* Arago

Falls City TIMES. w,sw 1892-99||?
1892-Je 8 1898 as Populist
w 1892-Jl? 1898
NbHi O 22-N 12,26,D 10-31 1895;Ja 14,F 18-25,Mr 10-24,Ap 14-Je 9,23,Jl 7,Ag 4 1896;O 19 1897-Ap,My 11-Je 8,17,Jl 1-8,S 14,O 22-N 12 1898

Falls City TIMES. w Ag 2 1928-N 22 1929||
Merged with Falls City news
NbHi complete

Falls City TRIBUNE. w Ja 8 1904-11||?
NbHi 1904-Je 2,16-Jl 14 1911

FARNAM

Farnam ECHO. w D 5 1903+
NbHi D 12 1903-F 4,18-Je 3,17-24 1905;My 7, 28 1914+

FILLEY

Filley REPUBLICAN. w Jl 1894-1901||?
NbHi O 10,24-D 1895;Ja 23,F 20,Mr 19,Ap 16, 30-My 7,21,Je 18-25,Jl 30-Ag,S 10-O 8 1896; Mr 11-My 20,Je-Jl 8,22-29,Ag 12,S 9-N 18,D 2,16 1897-Mr 3,17,31,Ap 14-My 12,26,Ag 19-S, O 28-N 4 1898;Ja 13-F,Mr 10-24,Ap 13-My 11,25,D 9 1899;Ap 13-My 11,25 1900

Filley SPOTLIGHT. w Ap 1916-D 3 1926||
NbHi Ag 16-S 13,27-O 4,18 1918-26

FIRTH

Firth GRAPHIC. w 1893-1910||?
NbHi O 26,N 16,30-D 21 1895;Ja 11,Mr 28-My 9,30-Je,Jl 18-Ag 1,29,O 17-24,N 7,21-D 12 1896;Ja 16,30,F 13-Jl 17,31,S 4,18-O,D 18 1897-Ja 1,15-F 12,26-Mr 5,Ap 2-23,My 7-21, Je 11-Jl 9,30-Ag 13,27,S 17-O 8,N 19-D 1898; Ja 21,F 4,Mr 18,Ap 29,Je 3,17-24 1899;Mr 21 1908-Ap 1,15-S,N 4-18 1910

FLORENCE

Papers published in Florence are listed under Omaha

FORDYCE

Fordyce PRESS. w Ja 7 1914-Mr 17 1915||
Merged with Hartington herald (Hartington)
NbHi Ja 28-My,Je 10 1914-15

FORT CALHOUN

Fort Calhoun CHRONICLE. w My 20 1915+
pub 1915+
NbHi S 19-O 17,N-D 5,19 1918-[19]+

FRANKLIN

FRANKLIN county news. sw,w F 9 1910-My 17 1929||
Merged with Franklin county sentinel
w N 30 1916-Mr 14 1929
NbHi F 12,Mr 23 1910-F 14,28-My 1929

FRANKLIN county sentinel. w 1889+
1889-94? as Independent press; 1895?-S 19 1912 Sentinel; S 26-O 21 1920 Franklin sentinel
NbHi O 25-N 1,29-D 20 1895[96-97]-S 1899; Je 29 1900[My 1901-03]-[19]+

FRANKLIN county times. w F 12-My 23 1929||
Merged with Franklin county sentinel
NbHi F 12,26,Mr 5,26 1929

Franklin FREE PRESS. w Ap 4 1900-My 26 1906||
Merged with Franklin county sentinel
NbHi Jl 1900-06

INDEPENDENT press. *See* Franklin county sentinel

SENTINEL. *See* Franklin county sentinel

FREEPORT

Freeport GAZETTE. *See* Early day (Harrisburg)

FREMONT

DODGE county leader. *See* Tri-weekly leader

Fremont HERALD. w,sw,tw Ag 1871-O 27 1928||
Jl 28 1903-F 1904 as Fremont tri-weekly herald-leader (other variations with frequency)
sw N 12 1892-Jl 24 1903;S-O 1927;tw Jl 28 1903-09?
MB [My 8-D 1 1872]Ja 8-15 1873[Ap 26-D 1874]-Ap 19 1876
NbFrP 1906-27
NbHi F 9,Mr 1,O 3,N 1 1876;My 2,O 10 1877; F 14,Ap 4,Ag 8,S 12 1878;F 27-Mr 3 1879;Ap 15 1880-N 3 1881[82]Mr 8-29,Ap 12-19,My-S 13,27-D 1883;Ja 17-24,F-Mr 6,Ap-My 15,Je 1884-85;Jl-S 16 1886;Ja 20-Mr 10,Ap 6,21-Je, O 1887-Mr,Je 14,26 1890-1900;Jl 1901-Ap 11 1905;12-27

Fremont HERALD. d 1871-1910||?
Jl 1903?-F 1904? as Herald-leader
MB Jl 31,S 17 1872;Ja 16 1873;Ag 23 1875;Ap 25 1876
NbHi [1877-78]Mr 3 1879;My 25,Je 1,9,Jl 29 1880;N 1881-Ja 17 1882;Ja-F,Je 12-22,Jl 2-3,5-7 1883[85;87]Ja 1 1888[90]S 1891-[95-Je 1897]Jl 1900-[01-02]Ja,My 1904[05-06]-Jl 1910

Tri-weekly LEADER. w,tw Mr 1891-Jl 25 1903||
1891-92? as Dodge county leader; 1893?-Ja 9 1903 Leader. United with Fremont semi-weekly herald to form Fremont tri-weekly herald-leader, later Fremont herald
w 1891-Ja 9 1903
NbHi N 1-8,D 13 1895-Ja 3,17,F 21-Je,Jl 10, 24,Ag 7,S-N 6,20 1896-Ja 15,29,F 12-26,Mr 12 1897-1903

PLATTE RIVER zeitung. w 1883-1917||?
In German
NbHi Ag 16 1895-Ja 11 1917

Fremont tri-weekly TRIBUNE. w,sw,tw Jl 24 1868-Ag 4 1917||
Title varies with frequency
w 1868-90?;sw 1891?-Ap 19 1892
pub complete
MWA F 20 1897
NbHi Ap 23,S 23,D 23-30 1869;Ap 14 1870;Je 15,Ag 10 1871;My 2 1873;Jl 13 1876;Ja 25,S 27 1877;S 12 1878;Je 10,Ag 19-26,S 23,O 14 1880;Mr 24 1881;S 1 1882;Ag 29 1891-1917

Fremont daily TRIBUNE. d My 12 1883+
pub 1883+
NbHi My 28,S 3 1884;Ag 31 1891-[98-1900]-[02-04]-Ja 27 1910;Jl 27,Ag 5 1918-O 10 1923; Ja 8 1924+

FRIEND

To 1883? as Friendville

Friendville ADVOCATE. w F 1877-Ja? 1878||
Followed by Friendville telegraph, later Friend telegraph
NbHi My 4-18,Jl 13,O 5,19,N 2,16 1877

Friend FREE press. w Jl 9 1885-90||?
1885-F 11 1886 as Saline record; F 18 1886-S 15 1887 Saline county gazette; S 22 1887-Ap? 1889 Weekly free press
NbHi Jl 16-30,Ag 13,27-D 1885;Ja 14-21,F 11-Je 10,24,Jl-S 2,16 1886-S 1,22 1887-[88]-Ja 18,F 1,15-22,Mr 8-Ap 5 1889;Ap 11,25,My 23-Jl 18,Ag 1-22,S 12-O 1890

SALINE county democrat. *See under* Wilber

SALINE county express. w 1892-D 1893||
United with Saline county standard to form Standard-express, later Weekly standard
D 1892-Je 1893 pub in Crete; Jl-Ag 1893 in Dorchester
NbHi D 17 1892[Ja 20-My 12,S 29-D 1893]

SALINE county gazette. *See* Friend free press

SALINE county standard. *See* Weekly standard

SALINE record. *See* Friend free press

Friend SENTINEL. w D 23 1897+
pub 1897+
NbHi Ja 6,Mr 3,Ap 21,My 12,26-Je 9,23-30, Jl 14-21,S-O 20,N 24 1898-F,Mr 9-Ap 6,20,My 4 1899;My,Je 14-28,Jl 12-19,Ag-S 1900;Ja 3, 17-Mr 7,21-Ap,S-D 1901;Jl 9,Ag 21,S-D 1902; My-Jl 23,Ag 1903;My-D 1904;S 1905-F 15, Mr 1-22,Ap 5-12,26-My 24,Jl 19-Ag 16 1906; F-Mr 7,21-Je 13,27-Ag 1 1907;Ag 20-S 3,17-O 1908;D 28 1911;Mr 14-28,Jl-N 21,D 26 1912+

Weekly STANDARD. w 1890-1900||
1890-My? 1892 as Saline county standard; D 1893-Je 8 1894 Standard-express
NbHi F 19-Ap,My 9-Je 6,20-O,D 5-12 1890; Ap 8,Je 3-17,D 2,16,30 1892;Ap 1,14,My 5-19,Je 2-9,23-Jl 14,28-S,O 13-20,N 3-17,D 8,29 1893-[94-95]-Mr 16 1900

Friend TELEGRAPH. w F 7 1878+
Follows Friendville advocate. 1878-Je 29 1883 as Friendville telegraph
pub 1887+
NbHi [1878-85]-[87-90;92-95]-[97]-N 1905;06+

FRIENDVILLE. *See* FRIEND

FULLERTON

NANCE county journal. w 1878+
Ja 1 1897 as Fullerton news-journal; Ja 8 1897-S 13 1928 Fullerton news and Nance county journal
pub 1878+
NbHi My 20 1887;D 15 1892[Mr 1895-96]+

Fullerton NEWS. w 1893-96||
United with Nance county journal to form Fullerton news-journal, later Nance county journal
NbFuN complete
NbHi Ag 16-O 4,18 1895-96

Fullerton NEWS-JOURNAL. *See* Nance county journal

Fullerton POST. w Je 8 1888-Jl 19 1928||
NbFuN complete
NbHi D 15 1892;Mr-Jl 5,19 1895-[1904]Ja 20-F 17,Mr 10-24 1905;Mr 28 1907-28

NEBRASKA (*Continued*)

FUNK

Funk ENTERPRISE. w S 30 1898-1903||?
NbHi S-N 11,25-D 16,30 1898-F 3,17-Mr 3 1899

GANDY

LOGAN county independent. *See* Logan county pioneer

LOGAN county pioneer. w 1886+
1889? as Pioneer-republican; 1890?-91? Pioneer; 1892?-94? Logan county independent
ICM O 9 1891
NbHi O 25 1895-[96]-[Ja-Jl 1898;F 1899-1900; Ap 1901-S 1902;Mr-D 1908]-[10]-[24]-Ap 6, 27,My 18-Je 1,15-Jl 6,20-27,Ag 10 1934+

PIONEER-REPUBLICAN. *See* Logan county pioneer

GARLAND

Garland HERALD. w 1920?+
NbHi 1920-21;24-Ap 1934

GARRISON

Garrison ARGUS. w My 1902-08||?
NbHi Je 22 1905-Ap 4,18-My,S 5,19-N 7 1907; Ja 1908

GENEVA

FILLMORE county republican. *See* Nebraska signal

FILLMORE county review. *See* Nebraska signal

Geneva GAZETTE. w 1894?-1911||?
NbHi N 15 1895;Ja 3,Mr 6-13,27-Ap 3,17-My 8,22-29,Je 12-19,Jl 3,24 1896-[97-99]-Ja 12, Ap 27,Ag 10 1900;Ap 26-My 3,17,31-Je 21,Jl-Ag 2,S 20,O 4-11,N 15 1901-Ja 3,17,31,Ag 8-O 24,N 14 1902-Ap 20 1911

Geneva JOURNAL. w 1890-93||?
United with Fillmore county republican to form Republican-journal, later Nebraska signal

NEBRASKA signal. w 1875+
1875-82? as Fillmore county review; 1883?-85? Geneva review; 1886?-93 Fillmore county republican; 1894-Ap 21 1896 Republican-journal
pub 1894+
NbHi Je 8 1892;95-1922;25+

REPUBLICAN-JOURNAL. *See* Nebraska signal

Geneva REVIEW. *See* Nebraska signal

GENOA

Genoa ENTERPRISE. *See* Genoa leader-times

INDIAN news. m? 1897-My 1933||
Suspended Je 1920-S 1930
NbHi Ap-My 1903;Mr,S 1906;Ja-Je,S-N 1907; Ja-Je,S 1908-Ap,Je,N 1909-Je,O-D 1910;F-Ap,O 1911-Je,S 1912-My,S-D 1913;F-Je,S 1914-Je,S 1915-Je,O 1916-Je,O 1917;Ja-Je,S,N 1918;Ja-Je,O 1919-Je 1920;S 1930-F,Ap-My, S-O,D 1931;F,Ap-My,S,N 1932-Ap 1933

Genoa LEADER-TIMES. w 1879+
1879-Je 25 1926 as Genoa leader (1884?-86? Genoa enterprise)
NbHi O 25,N 15,D 6,20 1895-[96-97]Ja 14-F 11,25-My 1898[99-1900]Ap 26-Je,Jl 19 1901-[Ja-S 1902]S 11,O 13,D 18 1908+

NANCE county populist. w 1890-97||?
NbHi O 18,N 8-29,D 13-20 1895;Ja 12-17,F 7, 21-28,Mr 13-My 22,Je 5-19,Jl 17-S 4,18,D 11, 25 1896;Ja 29,F 19,Ap 2,23-30,My 14-Je 25 1897

Genoa TIMES. w Ja 17 1902-Je 25 1926||
United with Genoa leader to form Genoa leader-times
NbHi 1902-[06]-26

GERING

Gering COURIER. w Ap 27 1887+
pub 1887+
NbHi 1887-98;Ja 27-F 3,17,Mr 3-10,24,Ap 14, Ag 18-S 1,22-D 1899;Ja 12-19,F 2,16,Mr 9,23-My,Je 8,29,Jl 13,27-S 21,O,N 9-23,D 14 1900; Ja 18,F 1-8,Mr 15-22,Ap 5,My 3-10,Je-S 6, 20-27,O 11-N 1,15-29,D 20 1901-[04-05]-Je 1906;07+

Gering MIDWEST. w 1918-Jl 1 1927||
NbHi Ja 30-N 7,21 1919-26;Ja 14-Ap 22,My-Jl 1 1927

NEBRASKA homestead. *See* Mitchell index (Mitchell)

TWIN CITY times. w Ja 25 1912-N 19 1914||
1912-O 9 1913 as Wasp
Ja-O 1912 pub in McGrew
NbHi F 12 1912-Je 12,Jl-Ag 7,21-O 9,23 1913-14

WASP. *See* Twin City times

GERMANTOWN

Germantown GLEANER. w 1894-97||?
NbHi N 30,D 14-21 1895;Ja 11,F 28,Mr 14-21, Ap 4-11,25,Ag 8,S-O,N 28-D 5,19-26 1896;Ja 9-16,F-Je,Ag 1 1897

GIBBON

BUFFALO county beacon. w 1882-96||?
NbGi [1882-96]
NbHi Je 24,N 18 1892;O 11,25-N 1,15-22,D 6-20 1895;Ja 17,F 28,Ap 10-Je 5,26-Jl 3,24,Ag 7-21,S 4-11,25-N 13 1896

Gibbon REPORTER. w Je 1890+
pub 1890+
NbHi Je 23,D 8 1892;Mr 12,Ap 23,Je 4,Jl 23 1896;Mr 11,My 20,Je 10 1897;Je 2,16,Jl 7,N 10,24 1898;F 8-22,Mr-Ag 23,S-D 1900;02-12, 14-F,Mr 12,Ap 1,15-My,Je 10-Ag 5 1920;Je 1921+

GILTNER

Giltner GAZETTE. w 1901+
NbHi Ja-O 17,31,N 21,D 1918+

GLENVIL

To 1915? as Glenville

Glenville BEE. w Mr 1899-1905||?
NbHi N 10 1899-Ag,O 19-N 9,30,D 14-21 1900;Ja 4-11 1901

Glenville GLOBE. w 1915-17||?
NbHi F 12-26,Mr 19-S,O 8 1915-17

GLENVILLE. *See* GLENVIL

GOEHNER

Goehner NEWS w S 22 1899-
NbHi S-O 20,N-D 8 1899;F 16,Mr 9-23,Ap 20 1900

GORDON

Gordon JOURNAL. w,sw N 1891+
sw Ja 2-Ap 4 1919
pub 1905+
NbHi O 28 1892[96-97]-My 6,20-27 1898[Mr 1899-1900;Ap-N 1901;F-N 1902]-Ja,F 10,Mr 3,24-Ap 14,28 1905;Jl 27 1906;Mr 22 1907-N 4 1910;Mr 17,D 15-22 1911;12-Ja,F 10,Mr 2-9,23-Ap 13,My 4,18-O 12,26-N 14,28 1916+

GOTHENBURG

Gothenburg INDEPENDENT. w 1885-Ja 1925||
Merged with Gothenburg times
NbHi Je 15-22 1892;O 26 1895-Ja 12,Ap 20-27, My 11-Je 22,Jl 13-27,Ag 24-31,S 14 1901-N 1904;Ja 5 1905;09-25

Gothenburg SUN. w Ap 1900-04||
Merged with Gothenburg independent
NbHi Ap 19-26,My 10-Je 7,21-Jl,Ag 30,S 13, 27-O,N 15-D 20 1901;Ja 17-31,My 16 1902-04

Gothenburg TIMES. w Ag 7 1896-S 10 1897||
NbHi 1896-F 5,19-S 10 1897

Gothenburg TIMES. w Jl 17 1908+
pub 1908+
NbHi 1908+

GRAFTON

Grafton SUN. w F 25 1898-1909||?
Merged with Nebraska signal (Geneva)
NbHi Mr 18-Ap 1,15-My 1898;Ja 20-Ap 21, My 5-19,Je 9 1899-[1900-01]-Ja 11,F 1,My 16-23,Je 13-Ag 8,S 12-19,O 10 1902

GRAND ISLAND

Grand Island ANZEIGER. w S 1889-92||?
United with Der herold to form Grand Island anzeiger und herald, later Grand Island herald
NbHi Je 10,24 1892

Grand Island ANZEIGER und herold. *See* Grand Island herald

CENTRAL NEBRASKA republican. w 1894-99||
NbHi S 14,O 26 1895-Ap,My 1897-99
—d ed *See* Grand Island daily press

Grand Island DEMOCRAT. w Jl 3 1884-1908||?
1884-N 1901 as Democrat
NbHi Mr 3 1891;Je 10-17,D 2 1892;Ag 1895-Ja 24,Mr 6,20-Ap 3 17-24,My 15-Je 19,Jl 17-Ag 7,21-N 20,D 1896-98;F 3 1899;Ja 11-25,My 10,24 1901-[04]-N 13 1908

FREE PRESS. w 1894-1915||?
NbHi Ag 1895-[97]-Ag 1898;N 8 1901;Ag 22-S 5,19,O-D 12 1902;08-13;Ja 22-F,Mr 11-Ap 9 1915

Morning FREE PRESS. d Ag 2 1914-15||?
NbHi [1914-F 1915]

Grand Island HERALD. w O 29 1880+
1880-92? as Der herold; 1893?-Mr 8 1901 Grand Island anzeiger und herold; Mr 15 1901-Jl 4 1918 Nebraska staats-anzeiger und herold
1880-Jl 4 1918 in German
pub 1880+
NbHi My 26,Je 16 1892;Ag 16-S,O 11 1895-S, N 2-9,23 1906-[32-33]+

Grand Island INDEPENDENT. w,sw 1869-1918||
1869-82? as Platte Valley independent
w 1869-N 26 1892
pub complete
NbHi Mr 18-25 1876;F 10 1877;F 2,Je 22,Jl 20, Ag 3-17,31-O,N 9,23-D 14,28 1878[79]Ja 17-31 1880;Ap 9 1881;Ag 26 1882;85-89;Mr 8-Ap 19 1890;91-[95-99]Ja 13 1906

Grand Island daily INDEPENDENT. d Ja 1 1884+
pub 1884+
NbHi 1887;Ja-Je 1888;90-Je,N 1891-[93-95]-[98]-1918;F 13,19,My 13,Jl 29 1919;20[21]+

NEBRASKA staats-anzeiger und herold. *See* Grand Island herald

NEW WEST. w My 21-O 29 1890||
NbHi My 21,Je-Jl 2,16-23,Ag,S 10-O 1,29 1890

PLATTE VALLEY independent. *See* Grand Island independent

Grand Island daily PRESS. d Jl 19 1897-1903||?
1897-N 24 1900 as Grand Island daily republican
NbHi [1897-1900]-[02]
—w ed *See* Central Nebraska republican

Grand Island daily REPUBLICAN. *See* Grand Island daily press

GRANT

PERKINS county herald. w 1893-94||?
United with Perkins county sentinel to form Perkins county herald-sentinel, later Perkins county sentinel

PERKINS county herald-sentinel. *See* Perkins county sentinel

PERKINS county news. *See* Tribune-sentinel

PERKINS county sentinel. w Je 1888-Ja 1911||
1895?-My 27 1897 as Perkins county herald-sentinel. United with Perkins county tribune to form Tribune-sentinel
NbHi O 25-N 1,15 1895-[96]-My 5,19-Je 3,Ag 25-S 1,15-D 1,29 1898[99-O 9 1902]

PERKINS county tribune. *See* Tribune-sentinel

TRIBUNE-SENTINEL. w D 10 1897+
1897-My 1909 as Perkins county news; Je 1909-Ja 1911 Perkins county tribune
NbHi D 17 1897;98-My,S-O 19,D 7,21-28 1900; Ap 26,My 17-Jl 19,Ag 2-9,23,S 6-13,27-O 4,25, N 15 1901;08-17;D 1918+

GREELEY

Greeley CITIZEN. w,sw 1892+
sw Jl 1 1918-Mr 29 1923
NbHi O 18,D 6,20 1895-Ja 3,24,F 21-Mr,Ap 10-24,My 22-29,Jl 17,31,Ag 7 1896;Ap 29-My 13,Je 4,Jl 30,Ag 20,O 1,22 1897;N 4-11,25 1898; Jl 20,Ag 1900-Ja,F 14-28,Mr 14-28,My 30 1918+

Greeley INDEPENDENT. w 1890-93||?
United with Greeley leader to form Leader-independent

LEADER-independent. w 1886-D 18 1924||
1886-93? as Greeley leader. Merged with Greeley citizen
NbHi Jl 1 1892;O 26-N 1,15-D 19 1895[96]-[99]-My 1906;Ja 23-D 1908;Ja 14-O 7,21 1909; 10-D 11 1924

GREENWOOD

Greenwood GAZETTE. w 1889-Ap 1934||
Merged with Lancaster county weekly (Lincoln)
NbHi Jl 22,D 2 1892;D 14-21 1895[96-Ag 5 1899]D 14 1901-My 2 1903;Mr 21 1908-N 13 1919;20-34

Greenwood NEWS. w Ap 27 1900-03||?
Jl 6 1900-My? 1901 News-record
NbHi Jl-Ag 3,17-D 7,21 1900;01-Je 5 1903

Greenwood RECORD. w S 1897-Je 29 1900||
United with Greenwood news to form News-record, later Greenwood news
NbHi O 29 1897-1900

GRESHAM

Gresham GAZETTE. w 1887+
1887-93 as Gresham review
NbHi My 15,29,Jl 27,S 14 1896;Ap-My 7,21-Je 4,18,Jl 9,O 29 1897;Ja 7,N 25 1898;Ap 21 1899; Mr 14,My 22 1902;Mr 20-27,Ap 10-D 11,25 1908-27;Ja 13,F 24,Mr 1928+

Gresham REVIEW. *See* Gresham gazette

GRETNA

Gretna BREEZE. w Je 16 1899+
pub 1899+
NbHi 1899-Ja,F 13-Mr,D 1931+

Gretna NEWS. w S 1896-Je 18 1897||
United with Gretna reporter to form Gretna news-reporter
NbHi Mr 25-My,Je 18 1897

Gretna NEWS-REPORTER. w Jl 1888-Je 1900||
1888-89? as Sarpy county democrat; 1890? Sarpy county reporter; 1891?-Je 1897 Gretna reporter. Merged with Gretna tribune
NbHi S 3 1891;Ag 4,S 8 1892;Ja 26 1893;N 15-22,D 1895-My 1898;Ja 27-F 17,Ap 21-My 19,Je-Jl 14,28-S 8,22-O 6,20-N 1899;Ja 19-F 16,Mr-Ap 6,27-My 4,18-Je 1,15 1900

Gretna REPORTER. *See* Gretna news-reporter

SARPY county democrat. *See* Gretna news-reporter

SARPY county reporter. *See* Gretna news-reporter

Gretna TRIBUNE. w Jl 13 1900-Mr 1901||?
Merged with Gretna breeze
NbHi Mr 29,Jl 13-27,Ag 10-24,S 14,28 1900;Mr 1901

NEBRASKA (*Continued*)

GROSS

Gross ARGO. w My 22 1901-02||?
NbHi Je 5-12,Jl 24,Ag 14,O 23 1901

GUIDE ROCK

Guide Rock SIGNAL. w Ja 1883+
pub 1904-05;24+
NbHi Ja 9-Mr 6,20 1886-Ja 1 1887[88-89;92]D 26 1896-[98]Ja 1899;1908-Ag 21 1919;20+

GURLEY

CHEYENNE county citizen. w 1921-25||?
NbHi F 13-Ap 10,My 22-Je 19,Jl 3-10,24,S 18, O 2-16 1925

GAZETTEER. w 1930+
pub Je 1934+

HAIGLER

Haigler NEWS. w S 1907+
KHi O 3 1913
NbHi Ag 20 1909-Je,Jl 8,O 22,D 20 1910;Ag 23 1918+

HALLAM

Hallam PROGRESS. w O 25 1905-
NbHi O 25 1905;N 1,15-D 1907;Ja 10-Mr,Ap 10-Jl 2,16-30,Ag 14-S 1908

HAMILTON

HAMILTON county news. *See* Aurora news (Aurora)

HAMPTON

Hampton HERALD. w F 21 1884-87||?
NbHi 1884;Ja 21,F 26-Ag,S 10-O,N 12-D 1885

Hampton TIMES. w S 19 1891-97||?
NbHi O 3-10,N 21,D 5 1891;Ap 19,N 1,D 13,27 1895;Ja 24,F 21,My 15-Je 12,26,Jl 10-31,Ag 14-21,S 11,25-O 2,N 13-20,D 1896-Ja,F 19-Je 11,25-Jl 10,23-Ag 13 1897

HARDY

Hardy HERALD. w S 11 1880+
pub 1880+
NbHi D 2 1892;Ja 24,F 14,Ap 24-My 22,Je 5,19-26,Jl 24-O 23,N 1896-F 19,Mr 5-12,26-My 21,Je-Ag 13,S 10-O 8,22-N 19,D 3,24 1897-Ja 7,21-Ap 22,My,S 30,O 14-D 2,16 1898+

HARRISBURG

BANNER county news. w Ja 1893+
NbHi N 16 1894-Jl 1906;07-Je,Jl 8,22-29,Ag 19-S 2,O-N 4,25-D 23 1920;21+

BANNER county republican. w Jl 1895-96||?
NbHi N 22-29,D 13-20 1895;Ja 17-F 7,Ap 24,My 29-Je,Jl 17,31-Ag 21,S 11-O 2,16,N 6-13 1896

EARLY day. w Mr 22 1888-92||
1888-F? 1889 as Freeport gazette (Freeport) Mr?-S 1889 Harrisburg gazette
NbHi Jl 15-22 1892

Harrisburg GAZETTE. *See* Early day

HARRISON

INDEPENDENT. w S 1 1892-93||?
NbHi S 1,22-O 1892;Mr 16-Jl 6,20-27 1893

NORTHWESTERN press. w Mr 7 1896-Jl 1899||
United with Sioux county journal to form Harrison press journal
NbHi Ap 25-My 2,16-Je 13,27,Jl 18,Ag 8,S 5-12,26-D 1896;Ja 16,30,N 13,D 4 1897;Ja 22,My 14 1898;My 27,Je 10 1899

Harrison PRESS-JOURNAL. w Ag 1888-1904||?
1888-Jl 1899 as Sioux county journal
NbHaS 1888-Ag 1894
NbHi Jl 7 1892;Ag 22,S 1895-98;Ja 26-F 2,Mr 23-My 11,Je-Jl 20,Ag,S 14,28-O 12,26-N 2,16-23,D 14-28 1899;Ja 11-Je,Jl 12-N 1,15-D 6,20-27 1900;Ja 24-F 14,Mr 14,Ap 4,25-My 2,16-23, Je 1901-Je 16 1904

SIOUX county journal. *See* Harrison press-journal

Harrison SUN. w My 1900+
pub 1900+
NbHi Ag 24-D 14 1900;Ja 25,Ap 26,My 17-Je 21,Ag 2,16-30,S 13-O 4,18-N 8,22-D 1901;Ja 17-24,F 7,21-Mr 7,Ap 11-25,My 23,Je 13-20,Jl-Ag 1,15,S 12 1902;My 1908-N 5,19-26 1909;Ja 28,Mr 20-27,Ap 10-24 1910;Jl 30 1915+

HARTINGTON

CEDAR county leader. w 1892-Jl 1898||
1892-94? as Hartington leader. Merged with Hartington herald
NbHi Ag 9-S,O 11-18 1895

CEDAR county news. w Ja 6 1898+
pub 1898+
NbHar 1914+
NbHi F 24-Mr 3,17,31-Je,Jl 14-S 8,22-O,N 10, 24-D 8,22 1898-Ap 20,My 4,18,Je,Jl 13-D 7,21 1899-1901;F 13 1902+
NbO O 1913

CEDAR county wächter. w 1898-Ag 22 1918||
In German
NbHi 1908-18

Hartington HERALD. w 1883+
NbHar 1883+
NbHi O 4 1888;Je 11-18,Jl 16 1892;Mr 31 1894;My 25 1895-Ja 20,F-Je,Ag-S 18,O 13,27-N 3,24-D 1 1899;1900-Je 23 1905;N 13 1908+

Hartington LEADER. *See* Cedar county leader

HARVARD

Harvard COURIER. w Ja 10 1885+
pub 1885-95;99+
NbHav 1885-95;99+
NbHi Je 4,Ag 13 1892;O 26 1895-1901;Ja 11, 25-Mr 8,22-Jl,Ag 9-O 18,N-D 6,20 1902-Ja,F 14-Mr 7,21-Ap 4,18-25,Je 20-27,Jl 11-Ag 22,S 5-19,O 17-D 19 1903;Ja 2-23,F 6,Mr 12,Ap 2, 23,My 14-N 12,26-D 17,31 1904+

HASTINGS

ADAMS county democrat. w *See* Morning spotlight

ADAMS county gazette. *See* Sunday gazette-journal

Hastings CENTRAL Nebraskan. *See* Hastings weekly Nebraskan

Sunday GAZETTE-JOURNAL. w Ja 10 1872-90||?
1872-80? as Adams county gazette; 1881?-89? Gazette-journal
1872-Je 1878 pub in Juniata
NbHM 1872-83
NbHi Jl 3,17-S 4,18-O 2 1878

Daily GAZETTE-JOURNAL. d 1883-89||?
Suspended Ja-Je 1889
ICM F 20 1884
NbHi Mr 1,My 20,25 1887

Hastings INDEPENDENT. w 1886-Ja 1891||?
United with Hastings tribune to form Hastings independent tribune, later Hastings tribune

Hastings INDEPENDENT tribune. *See* Hastings tribune

Hastings JOURNAL. w My 1873-80||?
United with Adams county gazette to form gazette-journal, later Sunday gazette-journal
NbHi D 16 1875;D 7 1876

Hastings JOURNAL. w 1894-1906||?
1894-1902? as Public journal
NbHi N 22,D 13-20 1895;Ja 10,24,F 14,28,Mr 13,27-Ap 24,My 15-Je,Jl 10-Ag 21,S-O 2,16 1896-Ja,F 12-19,Mr-Ap 2,16-Ag 6,27 1897-[1900]My 17,Je 14-21,Ag 2,30,S 20-O 11,25-D 6,20 1901;Ja-F 7,21,My 7,21,My 2-9,Je 27-Jl 11,Ag 1-15,S 19,O 17 1902

NEBRASKA volksfreund. w Ag 1892-99||?
In German
NbHi N 22 1895-Ag 1896;Ja 6,20,F 17-Mr 3 1899

Hastings weekly NEBRASKAN. w F 1878-95||?
Follows Kenesaw times (Kenesaw) 1878-79? as Hastings Central Nebraskan
NbHi Mr 23,Jl 20 1878;S 1891-92;F 23-My 18,Je-Ag 3,S-N 23,D 14-28 1893;Ja 11-F 22,Mr 1894-F,Mr 14-28 1895

Hastings daily NEBRASKAN. d 1888-O 8 1894||?
Merged with Hastings daily republican
NbHi Ag 28 1891-[92-93]-O 7 1894

Hastings daily NEWS. d Ap 1897+
NbHM 1897+
NbHi [My-Ag 1897]

Hastings weekly NEWS. *See* Williams' Hastings news

PUBLIC journal. *See* Hastings journal

Hastings evening RECORD. d S 20 1897-1900||?
NbHi [1897-Ag 22 1898;99-N 1900]

Hastings REPUBLICAN. sw,w 1889-1917||?
Title varies slightly
w 1889-1903?
NbHi S 26,O 17,N 7-21,D 5 1896;Ja 9,F 20-Jl 17,31-Ag 21,S 4,25,O 23-30,N 13-20,D 11 1897-Ja 15,29-Ag 23 1898;F 4-11,Ag 12,26-S 9,23-O 14,28-N 4,18-D 2,16 1899-F 16,Mr 9-30,Ap 13 1900;Ap 19,My 17-Je 7,21-Jl 5,19-Ag 2,S 27-D 20 1901;Ja 17-24,F 7 1902

Hastings daily REPUBLICAN. d 1891-S 1915||
Merged with Hastings daily tribune
NbHi My 27 1892;O 2,26,28 1895-[96-97]Ja 24-27,31-Ap,My 2-3,11,20,23 1898[99-1900;My 1902-05]-S 4 1915

Morning SPOTLIGHT. w,d Jl 10 1880+
1880-My 1935 as Adams county democrat (w)
pub 1880+
NbHM 1895-1914
NbHi Je 24-Jl 1 1892;Ag 9-23,S 1895+

Hastings TRIBUNE. w 1886-1917||?
F 1891-N 29 1895 as Hastings independent tribune
NbHM 1892-1914
NbHi S 2,D 16 1892-Ja 20,F 10-17 1893;Ag 1895-Jl,Ag 10 1917

Hastings daily TRIBUNE. d O 2 1905+
pub 1905+
NbHi S 28,D 12 1911;My 27 1914+

WILLIAMS' Hastings news. w 1897-1906||?
Title varies: Hastings news; Hastings weekly news
NbHi Ag 6,20-27,S 10-N 19,D 10 1897-F 9,24-N 23,D 7-14 1900;F 1,22,Mr 8,22-Ap 5,19-My, Je 21-28,Jl 12-19,Ag 2,16,S-O 18,N 1,29 1901-Ja 10,31-F 7,28-Je 13,27-Jl 4,18-Ag 15,O 3-17, 31-N 1902
—d ed *See* Hastings daily news

HAVELOCK

Papers published in Havelock are listed under Lincoln

HAY SPRINGS

Hay Springs ALERT. w Ag 1885-87||?
NbHsN [1885-86]

Hay Springs ENTERPRISE. w 1885-1915||?
1885-88? as Northwest news; 1889?-92? Hay Springs review; 1893?-F 16 1894 Sheridan county democrat; F 23 1894-1902? Hay Springs leader. Merged with Hay Springs news
NbHi F 24,O 28 1893-Mr 9,30-Ap 6 1894;Ja 4,D 20-27 1895;Ja 17,F 7,21,Mr 13-20,Ap 10-17,My 1-15,Je 19-24,Jl 31-Ag 7,28,O 16,D 18 1896;Ap 16,My-Jl 2,Ag 27 1897;My 13-20,Je 3,17-24,Jl 8,22-29,N 1898;Ap 19,My 3-17,Je 7-21,Jl-Ag 2,S 6,20-27,N 15,29,D 13-20 1901; Ja 24 1902;S 30-O,N 11-25,D 30 1904;05;Ag 21-O 2,16-N,D 11 1908;My 18 1915
NbHsN [1889;91-92;96-1900;02-07;09-11]

Hay Springs LEADER. *See* Hay Springs enterprise

Hay Springs NEWS. w S 1910+
NbHi Jl 1915+

NORTHWEST news. *See* Hay Springs enterprise

Hay Springs REVIEW. *See* Hay Springs enterprise

SHERIDAN county democrat. *See* Hay Springs enterprise

HAYES CENTER

HAYES county herald. *See* Hayes county republican

HAYES county republican. w Ap 5 1885-F 1903||
1885-87? as Hayes Center news; 1888?-Ap 1889 Hayes county herald. United with Hayes county times to form Hayes county times-republican, later Times-republican
NbHi Ap 9-23,My 21 1885-Ap 15 1886;Ag 1888-Ag,S 17,O 1891-Je,Jl 27 1893-1902

HAYES county times. *See* Times-republican

Hayes Center NEWS. *See* Hayes county republican

TIMES-REPUBLICAN. w N 1886+
1886-F 1903 as Hayes county times; Mr 1903-My 1907 Hayes county times-republican
NbHi Jl 20,N 23 1892;O 2-9,23 1895-Ja 1,22-F 12,Ap 15-My 20,Je 17-24,Jl 15-22,Ag 5-19,S 2-23,O 7-14,N 1896-S,O 13-N 17 1898;Ap 25,Je 6,Jl 4,S 12-O 3,N 14 1901;Ja 30,Ag-S 4,18-O 16,30 1902;Mr 1903+

HEARTWELL

PRAIRIE home. *See* Minden news (Minden)

HEBRON

Hebron CHAMPION. w Je 1895-Ja 28 1916||
1895-F 15 1901 as People's champion. United with Hebron register to form Register-champion, later Hebron register
NbHi Ja 10,F 28,Mr 13-27,Ap 17,Je 19,Jl 24-31 1896;F 26-Ap 9,23-Ag,S 17-N 5,19,D 24 1897;Mr 4,18-Ap 15,29-My 6,Jl 1,29-S 16,30,O 14 1898-1916

Hebron JOURNAL. w F 9 1871+
NbHi Ap 23 1874;Ap 22 1875-77;Ag 1 1878; My 22-S 18,O 23 1879-N 13 1885;86-1923;26+

PEOPLE'S champion. *See* Hebron champion

Hebron REGISTER. w,sw 1883+
F 4 1916-Ag 21 1930 as Register-champion (title varies slightly)
sw O 7 1919-Ja 16 1920
NbHi Jl 22,Ag 5 1892;Jl 7,N 10 1893-Ja 19,F-Mr 9,Ap 13-Ag 17,31-S 21,O 5-N 9 1894;Ag 16 1895+

Hebron REPUBLICAN. w N 1890-1900||?
1890-94? as Thayer county mail
NbHi N 15-29,D 20-27 1895;Ja 24,F 14,My 15, 29-Je 12,26,Jl 17-Ag 21,S,O 9 1896-Ja,F 19,Mr 5-12,26-Ap 16,My 7,21-28,Je 18-Jl 2,16,30-Ag 13,S,O 22,N 5-19,D 1897-F 4,18-My 1898;Ja 27,F 3,Mr 31-Ap 7,21-My 19,Je 9,23-Jl 21,Ag, S 8,22-29,O 13-D 1,15 1899;Ja 5-12,F 2-16,Mr 9-Je 1,22-Ag 17,S-D 1900

THAYER county mail. *See* Hebron republican

THAYER county sentinel. w Ja 1876-80||?
NbHi Ja 1,Mr 27,My 23-30,N 20 1879;F 12,Je 10 1880

HEMINGFORD

Hemingford GAZETTE. *See* Guide (Alliance)

Hemingford GUIDE. *See* Guide (Alliance)

Hemingford HERALD. *See* Alliance herald (Alliance)

JOURNAL. w 1907-O 14 1915||
Title varies slightly. Merged with Alliance times, later Alliance times-herald (Alliance)
NbHi O 22,N 5,19-D 10,24 1908-Mr 11,25-Ap 1,15-29,My 13-O 7 1909;Ja 13 1910;Ag 24 1911-Ag 5,19-O 14 1915

Hemingford LEDGER. w O 1915+
NbHi D 18 1919;F 5-19,Ap 22-29,My 13 1920-Ag 3 1933

NEBRASKA (*Continued*)

HENDRICKS. *See* DOUGLAS

HERMAN

Herman CYCLONE. w 1906-07||?
NbHi Ap 26 1906-Ap 7 1907

Herman NEWS. w S 1892-95||?
NbHi D 29 1892;Mr 15-22,My 24-Je 14,28,Ag-O 11,25-N 1,15 1894-Ja 1895

Herman RECORD. w 1908+
NbHi 1920-23;26+

Herman REVIEW. w Jl 23 1896-98||?
NbHi S 17 1896-Ja 8,22-Ag 13,27-O 7,23-N 20, D 4-11,25 1897;Ja 1898

HERSHEY

Hershey REVIEW. w My 7 1896-97||?
NbHi My 7,Jl 30,Ag 13-20,S 3,17-O 22,N-D 3,17,31 1896-Ap 1897

Hershey TIMES. w Je 1 1911+
pub 1911+
NbHi My 28-Je 4,18 1914-18;Ja 9,23-Je 12,26, Jl 10-Ag 14,O 16,N 6,27 1919;20-Jl 14,28,Ag 8,S 29,O-N 3,17-D 8,22 1921+

HICKMAN

Hickman ENTERPRISE. w 1886+
pub 1891+
NbHi D 3-10 1892;O 26-N 23,D 7,21 1895-Je 10,Jl 8-22,O 21-28,N 25,D 30 1898;F 10,24,Mr 24-My 19,Je-Ag 18,S 1,22,O-D 1,15 1899-Ja 5,19-F 16,Mr 9-30,Ap 13,My 4,18-Je 1,22-29,Jl 13-Ag 24,S 14-D 1900;Ja 25,Ap 26-My 3,17 1901-Mr,My 16 1913+

HILDRETH

Hildreth TELESCOPE. w 1887+
NbHi D 3 1892;N 23,D 1895-Ja 1,F 1-8,29-Mr 7,21,Ap 11,25,My 9-23,Je 27-Jl 11,Ag 29,S 18,O 2-9,23-D 11,25 1896+

HOLBROOK

Holbrook HERALD. w Ag 1893-1905||?
NbHi O 25-N 8,15,29,D 20-27 1895;Ja 10,F 21,Mr-Ap 3,10-My 1,15,22-Je 19,Jl 17,31-S 11, 25,O 9-16,N 6-20,D 11-18 1896;97-Ap 22,My 6-13,27,Jl 15-Ag 26-S 2,O 7-14,28,N 25-D 9,30 1898;Ja 20-27,F 10-Mr 3 1899

Holbrook OBSERVER. w My 1905+
NbHi Ap 30 1908-F 18,Mr-Ag 12,S 30 1915; 18+

HOLDREGE

Holdredge CITIZEN. w,tw 1884+
1884-86? as Republican; Mr 12 1897-Je 10 1898 as Holdrege citizen-forum
w 1884-Jl 21 1932
pub 1896+
NbHi My 31,Je 28 1892[96]-1901;Mr 7-14,Ap 11-18,My 2-9,23,Je 27,Jl 11-25,Ag 8-15,S 1902-[03]+
NbHo 1908+

POLITICAL forum. w Mr 1892-F 1897||
United with Holdredge citizen to form Holdrege citizen-forum, later Holdrege citizen
NbHi Je 29,D 7 1892;Ag 1895-97

Holdrege PROGRESS. w,sw 1887+
Title varies slightly
w 1895-Ja 1933
pub 1907+
NbHi O 11 1895-97;N 25,D 30 1898-F 12,D 30 1904+
NbHo 1908+

REPUBLICAN. *See* Holdrege citizen

HOLMESVILLE

HUMMER. w Ap 1901-
NbHi Ap 7,17-My 14,Je 4-11 25-Jl 2,10,11,23, Ag 8-D 2,30 1902;Ja 10 1903

HOLSTEIN

Holstein REPORTER. w Jl 1924-N 20 1925||
NbHi F 13-N 1925

HOMER

Homer FREE PRESS. w S 1899-1910||?
NbHi Ag 17 1905-Ap 1910

Homer PATRIOT. w Je 1895-97||?
NbHi Ag 7-14,28 1896-Ja,F 12,26-Mr 12 1897

Homer STAR. w Je 1910+
pub 1910+
NbHi 1918+

HOOPER

Hooper SENTINEL. w Ap 1885+
pub [1885-89]+
NbHi Ap 1,D 8 1892;O 24 1895-Ja 7 1904;Ag 20 1908+

HOSKINS

Hoskins HEADLIGHT. w Je 1905-Ag 28 1924||
Suspended from My 21-Jl 1923
NbHi Ag 27 1905-S 16,O 1909;D 21 1911-Ag 21 1924

HOWELL

Howell JOURNAL. w O 2 1888+
pub 1888+
NbHi N 18 1892;O 25,N 8,D 20 1895;F 21-28, Mr 13-27,Ap 10,24-My 1,Je 26,Jl 24-Ag 21,S 18-O 23,N 6,27 1896-[97-O 1898;Mr 1899-O 1902]08-[11]+

HUBBARD

TRI-COUNTY times. *See* Emerson advocate (Emerson)

HUBBELL

Hubbell STANDARD. w S 29 1899+
Suspended from F-D 1918
NbHi S-O 6,20-N 17 1899;F 9,23,Mr-Je,Jl 27,S 15,29 1900;Ag 9-N,D 13 1902-F 18,Mr-Jl 15,29,S 1910-Ap 1,15,My 6,27,Je 10-Jl 8,22-O 7,21 1921-22

Hubbell TIMES. w 1892-99||?
NbHi D 3 1892;O 11,N 8 1895;Je 19-26,S 25,D 18 1896;Mr 5,Ap 15,My 7,S 3,O 15,29,D 17 1897;Ja 14,28-Je,Jl 8-15,29-S 2,23 1898-My 5,Jl 14-Ag 11,25-S 8 1899

HUMBOLDT

Humboldt ENTERPRISE. w Ap 1883-1905||?
1883-86? as Nebraska enterprise
NbHi 1888-Ap,My 11-Je 1,15-22,Jl 6,20-27 1889;My 20,Je 10,Jl 29 1892;O 25 1895-Je 16 1905

Humboldt LEADER. *See* Humboldt news

NEBRASKA enterprise. *See* Humboldt enterprise

Humboldt NEWS. w My 21 1897-Je 8 1923||
1897-Ap 30 1920 as Humboldt leader (Ag 13 1897-S 8 1899 united with Humboldt standard to form Standard-leader)
NbHi My 21,Je 11,25,Jl 2,16-Ag 6 1897;O 6-13, 27-N 3,17-D 1,22 1899-F,Mr 9,30,Ap 13,27-My 4,18-Je 1 15-Ag 3,17,S 14-21,O 5-D 1900;Ap 26,My 10-31,Je 14-27,Jl 19-Ag 2,16,30,S 13,27-O 4,18-25,N 8-15,D 13-20 1901;Ja 17-24,Mr 7, 21-Ap 25 My 9-23,Je 13-20,Jl 4-11,Ag 15,S 5-12 1902;Mr 20 1908-Ja 5,26 1923

Humboldt STANDARD. w Jl 1882+
Ag 13 1897-S 8 1899 as Standard-leader (title varies)
NbHi Jl 3,27,Ag 10-17 1888;Je 10 1892;O 20 1893-Ag 19,S 9 1898[99-1900]Ap 12-19,My 17-24,Je,Jl 19-Ag 2,16,S-O 4,25-N 22,D 13-27 1901;Ja 17,F 14,28-Mr 7,21,Ap 18-25,My 16-23,Je 13,Jl 11,Ag 1-8 1902;Mr 1908-[34-35]+

HUMPHREY

Humphrey DEMOCRAT. w F 1887+
1887-S 1895 as Democrat
pub 1889+
NbHi Je 17 1892;F 17 1893;S 27-O 18,N-D 13, 27 1895;Ja 31,My 1,Je 5-12,Jl 17-24,Ag 7-21,S 4-11,O 2-16,N 1896-F 5,19-Mr,Ap 23-30,My 28-Je 4 18,Jl 2-9,Ag-S 3,O 29 1897;Ja 28-F 4,My 13-27,Je 17,Jl 1-15,29 1898;Ja 29-F 19,Mr 1904+

Humphrey HERALD. w O 4 1895-96||?
NbHi O 18,N 1-15,D 6,20 1895;S 11 1896

HYANNIS

GRANT county tribune. w 1888+
NbHi Je 14 1892;Ag 1895-Mr 19,Ap 8-15 29-Je 5,Jl 29-Ag 5,S 9-O 14,N,D 9 1897-Jl 7 1898;O 5 1902-04;Ag 30-S 20,O-D 6,20 1906-Ja,F 18-My 6,20-S 9,30-O 14,D 2,23 1909-Ja 6,27-F 3, 24,Mr 24-31,Ap 14-21 1910;Ag 24-31 1911

IMPERIAL

CHASE county enterprise. w 1890-Mr 2 1899||
Merged with Chase county tribune
NbHi O 10,24-D 5,26 1895;F 6,My 14-21,Je 4, Ag 6-13,S 10,24,O 8,N 24 1896;F 11,Ap 15-22, My 6-13,Je 17-24,Jl 8,29,Ag 26,S 30,O 14,D 30 1897;Ag 18 1898-99

CHASE county tribune. w Jl 30 1897-1907|
Merged with Imperial republican
NbHi Jl 30-S 10,O 1,29,N 12,26 1897-F,O 28-D 2,23 1898;Mr 24-31,Ap 28-My 12,26-Je 2,23-Ag 11,S 1,22-29,O 27-N 3,17,D 1,29 1899;Ja 5,19,F 16,Mr 8-23,Ap 6-13,27-My 4,Je 1,15-S,O 19,N 9-16,30-D 1900;Ja 25,Ap 26-My 3,17 1901-[02]-07
NbIR 1897-98

PEOPLE'S voice. w 1892-96||?
NbHi D 1 1892;O 24,N 7-14,D 5,26 1895;Ja 9, 20-27,Mr 12-Ap 16,My-Je 11,Jl 2,23-Ag 6 1896

Imperial REPUBLICAN. w 1887+
pub 1920+
NbHi Ag 11-25,S 29,N 3,D 29 1899;Ap 1908-Je 23,Ag 18,O 6-20,N 24 1911;Mr 29,My 3,24,Je 7,Jl 19,S 6,20-27,D 6 1912;O 17 1913;Je 5-19,Jl 17-31,Ag 14-21 1914;Mr 5-19,Ap 30 1915;My 23 1919-22;25+

INDIANOLA

Indianola weekly COURIER. *See* Weekly courier (McCook)

Indianola INDEPENDENT. 1893 94 *See* Indianola reporter

Indianola INDEPENDENT. w S 14 1900-N 14 1902||
Merged with Indianola reporter
NbHi S 14-O 12,N 23-D 7,28 1900;Ja 25,My 17-Je 7,21,Jl 12,Ag 9-16,30,S 13,27-O 11,N 8 1901-Ja 17,31-F 7,21-Mr 21,Ap-My 2,16-23,Je 13-Ag 1,15,29-S 5,19,N 7-14 1902

RED WILLOW county republican. w Ag 1900-Ag 2 1901||
Merged with Indianola reporter
NbHi O 12,26-N 2,D 28 1900-Ja 4,25,Ap 19-26, My 17-24,Je 7-21,Jl 19,Ag 2 1901

Indianola REPORTER. w Mr 1893+
1893-94? as Indianola independent
Suspended from Ag 1898-Jl 1901
pub 1904+
NbHi Ap 24,My 15-Je 5,19-26,Jl 17,Ag 7-14 1896;Ap 29,My 13,27-Je 10,24-Jl 22 1898;Ag 16,S 6,20 1901-Ja 3,S 19-D 19 1902;Ja-F 6,20-Ag 14,28,S 11-25,O 9-23,N 6,20-27,D 18 1903; Ja 8-Ap,My 13-Je,Jl 8-Ag 1904;08+

INMAN

Inman INDEX. w S 6 1884-88||?
NbHi S 6-20 1884;My 8,D 18 1885;F 18-25,My 20 1887

Inman NEWS. w O 1892-1907||?
NbHi Ag 6-13 1895;Ja 14,Mr 3,17-24,Ap 14,Je 2-9,Jl 7,S 8,D 8 1896-[1901-02]-Je 13,27-Ag 1, 15-22 N 2-16 1905;Jl 10-O 16,30 1906;Ja 8,22-F 5,26-Mr 5,19-Ap 2,16-Je 1907

JACKSON

Jackson CRITERION. w 1886-1904||?
NbHi Jl 23 1896;Ja 14-21,F 11-25,Mr 11,Ap 8-Ag 19,S-O 7,21-28,N 11-18,D 1897-F 10,24-Mr 17,Ap,My 12-Je 2,16-Jl 14,28-Ag 4 1898;F, Ap 6-20,My-Ag 24,S-O 12,26,N 9-16,30 1899;Ja 4-18,F 1-15,Mr 1-22,Ap 5-12,26-My 24,Je 14-28,Ag 2-23,S 13-20,D 13 1900;Ap 25,My 16,O 10,24,N 7,21 1901;Ja 23 1902

JANSEN

Jansen NEWS. w Ap 11 1915-Ap 30 1925||
Merged with Fairbury journal (Fairbury)
NbHi 1925

JENKINS MILLS

LITTLE blue. *See under* Washington, Kansas

JOHNSON

Johnson CITIZEN. w F 1898-99||?
NbHi My 13-Je 17,Jl,S 9 1898-F 10,24 1899

Johnson NEWS. w 1892+
NbHi O 25-D 6,20-27 1895;F 21-28,Mr 20,Ap-My 22,Je 12,26,Jl 24-31,Ag 21,S 11-25,O-D 4 1896;97-Mr 3,Je 9 1899;My 3,17-Je 21,Jl 12-Ag 9,30-S 6,27-N,D 13-20 1901;Ja 10-F 21,Mr 14-21,Ap,My 9-16,Je 20,Ag 8 1902-[08]-F,Ap-Je 7,21-Ag 2,16 1909+

JUNIATA

ADAMS county gazette. *See* Sunday gazette-journal (Hastings)

Juniata HERALD. w N 26 1876-1917||?
NbHi N 26-D 26 1877;78-F 12,Mr-My 21,Je 20-O 17 1879;Ja 9,23-Ap 2,16-O 7,21-D 9 1880;81-Jl 6,Ag 17-S 7,21-N 2,D 14 1882-[83]-N 20 1884;Ag 1885-N 1917

KEARNEY

BUFFALO county pilot. w 1896-1900||?
1896-Mr 1898 as Elm Creek pilot (Elm Creek)
NbHi [Je 12 1896-My 1898;99-F,Je-N 1 1900]

BUFFALO county sun. *See* Sun

CENTRAL Nebraska press. *See* Kearney hub

CENTRAL star of empire. w? 1897-1906||?
KHi Jl 1901
NN F 1900
NbK N-D 1906

Kearney DEMOCRAT. *See* Sunday tribune

Kearney HERALD. w 1865-
NbHi Je 13,Jl 3,Ag 29,O 6 1866
NcD O 30 1866

Kearney HUB. sw,w F 1873-1923||?
1873-88? as Central Nebraska press
sw 1891?-1917?
NbHi Ap 24 1873;Ap 16 1874;S 14 1876;Ja 11, Ap 19,My 3,S 6,27,O 18-N 1 1877;Ag 8 1895-1906
NbK 1896-1906;18-21
NbLeD Ag 10 1876

Kearney daily HUB. d O 1888+
pub 1888+
KHi D 3 1925;N 16 1927
NbHi My 2 1891;Je 18 1892[O 1895-97]-[1905-06]+
NbK 1889-1933

NEBRASKA standard. w D 1891-93||?
United with New era to form New era-standard, later Kearney weekly times
NbHi Jl 1,D 2 1892

NEW ERA. *See* Kearney weekly times

PLATTE VALLEY Sunday tribune. *See* Sunday tribune

SUN. w 1894-1900||?
1894-O 23 1897 as Buffalo county sun
NbHi Jl 27 1895-F 8 1900

NEBRASKA (*Continued*)

KEARNEY—*Continued*

Kearney TIMES. w O 12 1872-77||?
NbHi Jl 20 1876;Ap 19,Je 21,Jl 19,Ag 9 1877

Kearney weekly TIMES. w 1880-F 1 1913||
1880-93? as New era; 1894?-Je 10? 1909 New era-standard
NbHi Ag 9 1895-[1900-01]-Ja 23 1913
NbK Je 9 1909

Kearney morning TIMES. d Je 15 1909-O 1917||
Merged with Kearney daily hub
NbHi [1909-17]

Sunday TRIBUNE. d,w 1892+
1892-Jl 1926 as Kearney democrat; Ag 1926-1932 Kearney tribune (N 1932-34? Kearney daily tribune); 1934?-Ag 17 1935 Platte Valley Sunday tribune
d N 1932-34?
NbHi Ag 13,S 1896-F 4,18-Ag,S 9-30,O 21-28,D 9,23 1897;Ja-My,Je 16,Jl 7-14,28-S 1,15,29-N, D 8-29 1898;Ja 12-F,Mr 23-My 4,18,Je 15,29-Jl 6,Ag 17,O 5,19,N 2,23,D 14,28 1899;Ja-F 1, 15,Mr 1,15,29-Ap 5,My 3-10,Ag 16-23,O 4,N 8,29-D 6,20 1900-Ja 3,Jl 25-Ag 8,22,S 5,N 21 1901[02]-32;Jl 1935+

WART nya hem. w 1877||
In Swedish
IRA complete

KENESAW

Kenesaw CITIZEN. *See* Kenesaw sunbeam

Kenesaw KALEIDOSCOPE. *See* Kenesaw sunbeam

Kenesaw PROGRESS. w Mr 1917+
NbHi My 23-Ag 1,29-S 5,O-D 12,26 1918-F 4,Mr-Ap 15 1920;O 20 1921-Mr 1,15-Ap,My 10-Je,Jl 12-Ag 9,23,S 20-27,O 18,N 1923+

Kenesaw SUNBEAM. w 1890-Mr 6 1919||
1890-1908? as Kenesaw citizen; 1909?-13? Kenesaw kaleidoscope. Merged with Kenesaw progress
NbHi N 24 1892;O 25,N 8-22,D 1895[96-97]Ja 7,28-My 6,27 1898[99-1902]Mr 16,Ap 27 1906; Jl 12 1907;S 16-N 11,25 1910-F 10,24,Mr 10,24, Jl 21;Jl 9-23 1914;F 1915-19

Kenesaw TIMES. w Je 6 1876-Ja 1878||
Followed by Central Nebraskan, later Hastings weekly Nebraskan (Hastings)

KENNARD

Kennard ENTERPRISE. *See* Enterprise (Blair)

Kennard NEWS. w 1916-O? 1924||
Followed by Ceresco news (Ceresco)
NbCeN Je 14 1916-O 1924

KILGORE

CHERRY county messenger. w 1918-My 21 1920||
United with Crookston herald to form Herald-messenger (Crookston)

KIMBALL

WESTERN Nebraska observer. w 1885+
pub [1885-88]+
NbHi My 19 1892;N 21-28,D 19-26 1895;Ja 23,F 6,20,Ap 30-Je,Jl 23-O 15,N,D 10 1896-Ja,F 11-Jl,Ag 12,26-S 2-9,23-O,N 11 1897-1914;17+

LAKESIDE

Lakeside SUN. w O 10 1918-20||
NbHi 1918-Ja 8 1920

LA PORTE

WAYNE county review. *See* Wayne herald (Wayne)

LAUREL

Laurel ADVOCATE. w Mr 1893+
pub 1893+
NbHi O 12,26-N 2,16,D 7-21 1895;F 8-15,My 30-Je 6,20,Jl 25-Ag 8,22-O 17,N 7,21-D 1896; Ja 9-16,30-F 6,20-Mr 6,20-My 1,15-Je,Jl 10, 24-31,Ag 14,S 11-O 2,16-30,N 13-20,D 4 1897; Ja 8-Mr 19,Ap-Je 11,25-Jl 2,16-Ag 13,27-S 3, 17-24,O 15,N-D 10 1898;Ja 14-28,F 18-N 4,18-D 16,30 1899-Ja 6,20-F 17,Mr-Ap 14,My-Je 2, 15-29,Jl 27-Ag 17,S 1900+

LAWRENCE

Lawrence ENTERPRISE. w Ja-N 1 1928||
NbHi My 31-N 1928

Lawrence LOCOMOTIVE. w 1887+
pub Ap 1896-Mr 1898;Ap 1900-Mr 1902;04+
NbHi Ag 4 1892;My 11,25,Je 8,22,Jl 6-27,Ag 31-O 5,19-N 2,16,30-D 7 1901;Ja 16,25,F 8-15 1902

LEBANON

Lebanon ADVERTISER. w F 1 1912-S 1918||
United with Danbury news to form Danbury news and Lebanon advertiser (Danbury)
NbHi Mr 1912-F,Mr 13-Je 19 1913;Ja 11-18, Jl 1914-Ap,Je 6-13 1918

LEIGH

Leigh WORLD. w 1885+
pub 1926+
NbHi D 2 1892;N 15,29,D 27 1895;Ja 3-10,Mr 13-Ap,Je 12,Jl 3,24,Ag 7-14,O 9 1896;Ag 6-13,S 17 1897-1903;My 1908+

LEWELLEN

DEUEL county news. *See* Garden county news (Oshkosh)

GARDEN county news. *See under* Oshkosh

Lewellen GAZETTE. w 1911-17||
NbHi Je 10,Jl-Ag 12,S 2-9,23,O 14,N 4,25-D 2 1911;Ja 6,F 24 1912;S 1914-17

Lewellen OPTIMIST. w Mr 22 1917-22||?
NbHi Mr-My 10,Je 14-21,Jl-O 11,N 15,D 27 1917-Ja 10,31-F 7,Mr-Jl,Ag 8,D 5 1918;Je 1919-Ja,F 12 1920-My 19,Je-N 10,24,D 1921

WEST NEBRASKA beacon. *See under* Oshkosh

LEWISTON

Lewiston POST. w Ap 4 1913-Je 10 1921||
United with Steinauer star to form Steinauer star-post (Steinauer)
NbHi 1913-[18]-21

LEXINGTON

To 1889? as Plum Creek

Lexington CLIPPER. sw,tw,w 1888+
1895?-Mr 1922 as Clipper-citizen
sw O 4 1910-F 12 1912;tw F 3 1930-N 18 1931
NbHi Je 23 1892;O 18,N 29,D 13-20 1895;Ja,F 21-Mr,Ap 17,My 8,Jl 24 1896;Ap 2,23-30,My 21,Je-Jl 2,23,S 1,10 1897[98;F-D 1899]-Ja 12,F 9-16,Mr 1900+
NbLeD My 30 1902

DAWSON county enterprise. w 1895-97||?
NbHi O 11,N 1 1895;My 1,22-Je 5,19,Jl 24-N 6,27 1896-Ja 22 1897

DAWSON county herald. w 1884-94||?
NbHi Je 10 1892
NbLeD S 8 1886-Ja 13 1887;Jl 26-Ag 9 1888; My 9,Ap 18 1889;S 25 1890;Je 8 1894

DAWSON county pioneer. w N 29 1873+
pub Jl 20,Ag 10 1876;O 13,N 13 1879;F 5,My 13,Ag 5 1880;Je 9 1881;O 21,D 2-9 1882;Ja 20 1883;My 17,O 4 1884;Ja 17,Mr 14 1885;O 2 1886;O 22,N 19 1887;F 25,Mr 24,Ap 14,My 5,Je 16,Ag 4 1888;Ap 20,My 11 1889;Ap 4 1891;Ja 5,Je 9 1894;N 30 1895;Ja 4 1896;Ap 8 1899;Ag 25,D 8,25 1900;My 24 1902;Ag 11,S 1 1922
NbHi Je 2 1894;Ag 1895-[97-1900]-[03]-18;F 1920+

Lexington GAZETTE. w 1884-93||?
NbHi Je 10 1892
NbLeD O 3 1890;Ap 24,O 9,N 27 1891;Mr 10 1893

Lexington NEWS. w S 1897-99||?
NbHi O 29 1897-Ag 1899

LIBERTY

GAGE county farm journal. *See* Liberty journal

Liberty JOURNAL. w 1882+
1925?-My 7 1931 as Gage county farm journal
NbHi My 20 1892;D 13-20 1895[96-O 1901]Mr 28,O 24-N 14,28-D 1902;Ag 28 1908-Ag 4 1916; F 19-Je 11,25,Jl 9-O 22,N 5,19 1925;26-[28-29]Ap-Je 19,O 16 1930-S 3,17-24,O 8-N 5,19-26 1931;32[33-34]

LINCOLN

Lincoln evening CALL. d Je 19 1879-Jl 16 1898||
1879-Je 1888 as Daily state democrat (other variations slight) United with Lincoln evening news to form Evening news-call, later Lincoln daily news
NbHi Je-O 24 1879;F 18 1882;Jl 15,S 4 1884;Ja 17,21,28[O 1885-O 1888;Ap 1889-90]Ja 22,29,31, Mr 1891-[97-98]
OClWHi Mr 12 1888

Lincoln weekly CALL. w O 17 1879-97||?
1879-87? as Weekly state democrat (1883?-85? Nebraska free trader)
NbHi O 24 1879-F 17 1882;S 16 1887;Ag 5,N 18,D 3 1892;S 25 1896

CAPITAL CITY courier. *See* Courier

CAPITAL CITY times. w S 23 1932-
M [D 16 1932-F 24 1933]
NbHi S-O 14,N 11-18,D 2 1932

COUNTY merchant. w My 1899-S 18 1909||
1899-O 12 1901 as Weekly produce reporter and prices current
NbHi Jl 1-S 9,O 21,N 1899-Ja 4 1904;Ap 15 1907-09

COURIER. w D 1885-Mr 28 1903||
1885-Je 3 1893 Capital City courier; Je 10?-25 1893 Sunday morning courier; Jl 1893-Mr 10 1894 Saturday morning courier
NbHi D 25 1890;S 19-26 1891;92-My 15 1897;Ja 5 1901;F,Mr 8-S 13,27 1902-Mr 7,21-28 1903

EAST LINCOLN news. *See* University Place news

FARMER'S alliance. *See* Independent

FARMERS alliance leader. *See* Nebraska state leader

Lincoln FREIE presse. w Ag 8 1884-1929||
United with Westlicher herold (Winona, Minn.) to form Amerika-herold-Lincoln freie presse (Winona, Minn.)
In German
IU Ja 20 1915-Ap 30 1929
MnHi 1884-Jl 23 1929
NbHi S 1891-92;Je-Jl,Ag 1893-Ap 16,Je,Jl 9-30 1896;97-N 1924

Lincoln daily GLOBE. d Ap 1876-81||?
NbHi Jl 6,S 26 1876;Ja 2-3,6,17,F 15,Jl 19,Ag 13 1877;Ja 15 1878;Ja 20,28,F 11,Je 11,S 30 1879;Jl 26 1880;Ja 19,21-22 1881

Lincoln GLOBE. w,d 1889-90||?
Early issues as Sunday morning globe (w)
NbHi S 30-[N]D 1889

HAVELOCK post. w Ja 1913-Ap 30 1925||
United with Havelock times to form Havelock times-post, later Lancaster county weekly
NbHi F 1918-25

HAVELOCK times. *See* Lancaster county weekly

HAVELOCK evening watchman. d My 28 1902-
NbHi My 28,Je 3,21,28,Jl 1,7-8,11,14-17 1902

Lincoln weekly HERALD. w 1890+
MWA Ap 28 1894
NbHi Mr 8 1890-Ag,S 8,22-N 2 1894;Je 28,O 1895-My,Ag 21,S 4,18,O 2-9,23-N 4,20 1896;Ja 8,Ap 23-30,S 3 1897;Ag 19 1898;Je 9,D 22 1899; N 1904+

INDEPENDENT. w Je 19 1889-Ap 25 1907||
Je-D 7 1889 as Alliance; D 14 1889-Mr 1892 Farmer's alliance; Ap-Je 1892 Farmer's alliance and Nebraska independent; Jl 1892 Mr 8 1894 Alliance-independent; Mr 15 1894-Ja 9 1896 Wealth makers; Ja 16 1896-O 1902 Nebraska independent. Followed by Independent farmer and western swine breeder, later Nebraska ruralist (not in this list)
NNC [Jl 14 1898-Je 1906]
NbHi 1889-[Je-N 1892]-1907

Lincoln INDEPENDENT. w My 1893-Ja 3 1896||
1893-S 18 1895 as Weekly independent. United with Wealth makers to form Nebraska independent, later Independent
NbHi Ag 22 1895-96

Sunday JOURNAL and star. *See* Nebraska state journal; Lincoln daily star

LANCASTER county citizen. w D 30 1915-My 19? 1926||
NbHi 1915-25

LANCASTER county weekly. sw,w Jl 1891+
1891-Ap 1925 as Havelock times; My 1925-Mr 7 1933 Havelock times-post
sw Jl 9-S 26 1929
NbHi 1911+

LIBERTY. w Mr 1892-93||?
NbHi Jl 2,23,S 24,O 8,D 3 1892;Ja 7,F 25-Mr 11,25 1893

LIVING issue and new republic. *See* New patriot

NATION'S anchor. w Mr 1894-1901||?
1894-1900? as Our nation's anchor
NbHi My 19,Jl 21-Ag 4,D 8 1894[95]Ja 4,25,F 8,Mr 9,28,Ap 18,Je 20,25,Jl 4-11,Ag 29,N 21,D 5 1896;Ja 9-16,F-Mr 13,Ap-O,N 27 1897;F 26,Mr 19-26 1898;Mr 9 1901

NEBRASKA beacon. w 1898+
NbHi My 18 1933-34

NEBRASKA blizzard. w O 22 1898-My 1904||
United with Shelby sun to form Nebraska blizzard and Shelby sun, later Shelby sun (Shelby)
NbHi complete

NEBRASKA commonwealth. *See* State journal

NEBRASKA free trader. *See* Lincoln weekly call

NEBRASKA independent. w D 1890-Mr 1892||
United with Farmer's alliance to form Farmer's alliance and Nebraska independent, later Independent
NbHi S 4-O,N 13-20,D 1891-92

NEBRASKA independent. 1896-1902 *See* Independent

NEBRASKA independent patron. *See* Nebraska patron

NEBRASKA leader. w Je 14 1919-N 19 1921||
MnHi [1919-21]
NbHi complete

NEBRASKA news. *See* University Place news

NEBRASKA patron. w Jl 1874-
S-O 1876 as Nebraska independent patron
NbHi Jl 1 1874;Mr 31,Ap 1,S-O 1876

NEBRASKA staats-anzeiger. w My 1880-Mr 7 1901||
United with Grand Island anzeiger und herold to form Nebraska staats-anzeiger und herold, later Grand Island herald (Grand Island)
In German
NbHi N 3 1883;Ag 20 1885;S 1891-1901

NEBRASKA staats-demokrat. *See* Nebraska state republican

NEBRASKA state capital. w Ag 1889-1912||?
KHi S 29 1900-Ap 13 1901
NbHi Jl 2,Ag 6 1892;S 28,O 19-26,N 9 1895-S 9,O 28-N 4 1899;D 1900-Ja 12,26-F 9,Mr-Ap 13,Jl 27 1901;Ap 25,My 9,Je 6,27,Jl 4,18-25,Ag 15-29,S 12-19 1902;Jl 31 1908-Ja 5,19-S 6 1912

NEBRASKA state democrat. *See* Nebraska state republican

NEBRASKA (*Continued*)

LINCOLN—*Continued*

NEBRASKA state journal. d Jl 20 1870+
1870-Jl 5 1878 as Daily state journal; 1894?-95? State journal (other variations slight) Sunday issues as Sunday state journal; Sunday journal and star
pub 1870—
DLC Ap 30 1890+
IaDH Mr 10 1901-14
KHi Ag 15 1879-D 16 1904;S 11 1925
Nb Ap 1889-97;Ap 1898-Mr,Jl 1899-Je 1927;34+
NbHi Je 9 1871;Je 1872;Ja 16,O 5 1873;F 11, 28,Mr 18,21,Ap 9,My 1,17,23,Je 4,26,Jl 28,S 3, O 16 1874;Ja 17,F 3-4,12,21,23 1875;Ja 9,My 17,Jl 4,8,Ag 13,S 26-O 1,3,24,N 25,D 5,16,30 1876;Ja 1,17-19,21,23,25,F 6-7,11,13,16,18,My 20,O 11,N 16,20,27 1877;Ap 18,Jl 5,7,26 1878 [79]Ja 22,27,29,F 1,4,6,8,10,Je 1,8,O 15,N 9 1880[81]S 22,24,O 11,15,19,22,26 1882;Ja 3,My 18,D 11 1883;My 15,17,21 Je 12,Jl 29,O 28-29, 31-N,D 12 1884[85-89]-[92]+
WHi 1917-19
—Evening ed *See* Evening state journal

NEBRASKA state journal. w *See* State journal

NEBRASKA state leader. w F 25 1893-
F-Jl 14 1893 as Farmers alliance leader
Suspended from Jl 14-O 14 1893
NbHi 1893-F 24 1894

NEBRASKA state register. w 1873?-74||?
Follows Nebraska statesman?
NcD My 22 1874

NEBRASKA state republican. w Ag 1888-1921||?
1888-89? as Nebraska staats-demokrat (in German) 1890?-Ap 1921 Nebraska state democrat
NbHi S 1891-Ja 7,28-Mr 4,25,My 6,27-Je 3,17-Ag 5,19,S 30 1899;Mr 14 1908-Ap 1921

NEBRASKA statesman. w Ap 4 1866-73||?
1866-N 1867? pub in Nebraska City
NbHi Ap 4,21-Je,Jl 14-O 13 1866;Jl 2,21,Ag 4,25-S 22,O 6,20,N 3,24-D 1,15-22 1868;Ja 5 26,Mr 9,20-Ap 3,24,My 8 1869-F 19 1870;My 16 1873
—d ed *See* Daily Nebraska statesman (Nebraska City); Lincoln daily statesman

NEW economy. w D 10 1892-95||?
NbHi D 24 1892;F-Ap 15,29-My 13,Je 3,17,Jl,D 30 1893-Ja 13,F 24,Ap 14 1894

NEW patriot. w Mr 28 1885-1908||?
1885-F 1902 as New republic (Mr 24-N 10 1887 as Living issue and new republic)
MWA My 23 1889
NbHi Ap 4-18,My 16-Je,Jl 18-Ag,S 12-19,O 17,D 12,26 1886-Mr,Ap 17-24,My 8-29,Je 12, Jl 10,S 11,O 9,23 1886;F 5-19,Mr 1887-[91-92]-[1902]F 1,Ap 5 1903
NcD Mr 13 1890
WHi D 8 1887-Ap 4 1889

NEW republic. *See* New patriot

STATE democrat. *See* Call

Lincoln daily NEWS. d 1881-S? 1917||?
Jl 17? 1898-99? as Evening news-call (title varies slightly) United with Evening state journal to form Evening state journal and Lincoln daily news, later Nebraska state journal
NbHi S 26,Ap 19 1887;S 24 1888;Je 11-N 1890; Mr 1891-[92]-[1900]-[02]-D 8 1909;Mr 12 1912-S 1917

Lincoln weekly NEWS. w S 1885-97||?
NbHi Mr-Je,Jl 9-S,O 8-D 3,24-31 1891;Mr 24-My 5 1892;Je 18 1896;My 13,Je 3,16,Ag 5,27,S 10-O 8 1897

OUR nation's anchor. *See* Nation's anchor

Weekly POST. w S 1896-98||?
NbHi Mr 4-11,Ap 15-22,My 6-20,Je 10-17,Jl 1,15,29,S 9,23,O 28 1897;F 17,Je 30-Jl 1898

Weekly PRODUCE reporter and prices current. *See* County merchant

Weekly REVIEW. w Ja 5 1933-
Negro
NbHi Ja 5-12,26-Mr 2 1933

SPOTLIGHT. w Ag 18 1933-
NbHi Ag 18-S 1,22,O 6-13,N 17,D 15 1933;Ap 13,Je 25,Ag 10 S 21,D 21 1934

Lincoln daily STAR. d O 2 1902+
Sunday issues as Sunday state journal and star; Sunday journal and star
pub 1902+
NbHi 1902+

STATE journal. w,sw S 7 1867-Ap 1907||
1867-70? as Nebraska commonwealth; 1871?-91 Nebraska state journal
Merged with Independent farmer and western stock breeder, later Nebraska ruralist (not in this list)
sw 1892?-1902?
DLC N 7 1879
NbHi S 7,N 2,23 1867-F 8,22-Mr 14,My-Je 20, Jl-S 5 1868;Je 9 1871;Mr 12,My-Je 18 1875; Je 16,Jl 7,21,Ag 4-11,S 1,15-N 10 1876;Ja 1, 18-25,F 23 1877;F 15-22,Mr 8-15,Je 7-14,28-Jl 5,19 1878-Mr 7,28 1879;Ja 23 1880;F 23 1883;F 27 1885;Ja 14-21,F 6,Mr 13-27 1887; My 31,O 27 1889;My 7 1891;D 9 1892;Ja 20 1893

Evening STATE journal. d 1916?+
1916?-D 7 1917 as Evening state journal and Lincoln daily news
NbHi O 1917+

Daily STATE journal [morning ed] *See* Nebraska state journal

Sunday STATE journal and star. *See* Nebraska state journal; Lincoln daily star

Lincoln daily STATESMAN. d Ja? 1872-73||?
OClWHi S 15 1872
—d ed *See* Nebraska statesman

Lincoln SVENSKA tribun. *See* Vesterns svenska tribun (Omaha)

UNIVERSITY Place gazette. w 1894-98||?
NbHi My 24 1894;O 18-N 22,D 1895;Ja 10,F 14-28,Mr 14-My 16,Je,Jl 17-24,Ag 28,O 3-24, N 21 1896-Ja 16,30-F 6,20-26,Mr 12-Ap 2,16-My 21,Je 4,18-Jl 9,23-30,Ag 13,S 10,24,O-N 19,D 3 1897;Ja 14-21,F 11-Ap 22,My-S 3 1898

UNIVERSITY PLACE news. w Mr 1905+
1905-Ap 1913 as Nebraska news; O 14-28 1926 East Lincoln news; N 1926-O 1928 East Lincoln news and University Place news
pub 1929+
NbHi N 13,20-D 7 1905[06-10]-31

UNIVERSITY Place times. w S 1890-99||?
NbHi My 9,Je 20-Jl 11,25,Ag 8,O 17-24,N 7, 28,D 19 1896-Ja 16,F 20,Ap 3,17-24,My 15-Jl 10,31-Ag 14,28,S 11,25-O 23,N 20,D 4 1897; Ja 1,15,29-Ap 16,My 21-Je 11,Jl 2-16,S 10,O 1,15-N,D 17-31 1898;Ja 14-21,F,Mr 13 1899

WEALTH makers. *See* Independent

WELT-POST. w Ap 13 1916+
Dated also in Omaha
In German
pub D 1917+
NbHi Ap 13,27-My 4,18 1916+

LINDSAY

Lindsay POST. w 1897+
NbHi My 1-22,Je-Ag 21,S 4,18-N 6,20 1908-Ap 7 1911;Ja 14 1915;F 24 1916

LISCO

Lisco TRIBUNE. w Jl 5 1912-Mr 5 1926||
NbHi 1912-[16]-My 18,Je 8,22-Jl,S 7,21-D 7, 21 1922-My 17,31-Je 7,21-O 11,25-N 1,22-29 1923;Ja 10,31,F 28-Mr 20,Ap 3,17-My 22,Je-O 9,23 1924-25

LITCHFIELD

Litchfield MONITOR. w D 1 1887+
pub 1887+
NbHi Je 6 1890;Je 6 1892;D 12 1895-[96-97]-Mr 18,Ap-My 1898;S 25,O 30,N 13 1908-F 10,24-S 15 1911;D 12 1913;Jl-Ag 17,S 4-18,O 1914+

LODGE POLE

Lodge Pole EXPRESS. w F 1886+
1886-89? as Lodge Pole magnet
pub 1893+
NbHi Je 9-16 1892;N 21,D 5-12 1895[96-97]-My 5 1898;Ap-My 6,20 1899+

Lodge Pole MAGNET. *See* Lodge Pole express

LONE TREE. *See* CENTRAL CITY

LONG PINE

BROWN county bugle. w 1885-89||?
1885 as Long Pine sentinel
NbHi F 17-Mr 3,Ag 11 1887;My 17,Jl 5-19 1888

Long Pine JOURNAL. w 1881+
1895-Ag 1899 as Republican journal
NbHi My 5,Ag 18,S 8-N,D 22 1883-Ja 12,Mr 23,Ap 5 1884 O 24-D 5,19 1895-[96-97]-My 1898[99-1900]+

Long Pine NEWS. *See* Western news (Ainsworth)

REPUBLICAN journal. *See* Long Pine journal

Long Pine SENTINEL. *See* Brown county bugle

LOOMIS

Loomis SENTINEL. w N 18 1910+
pub 1910+
NbHi S 19 1913+

LOUISVILLE

Louisville weekly COURIER. w 1882+
1882-89? as Louisville observer; 1890?-94? Louisville courier-journal
NbHi Jl 29 1892;S 6-13,O-N 14 1902;Ag 29,S 12-D 19 1908;09+

Louisville OBSERVER. *See* Louisville weekly courier

LOUP CITY

Loup City LEADER. w 1919+
1919-Mr 7 1935 as People's standard
pub Ap 1922-My 14 1935
NbHi 1925+
NbLo 1930-My 1935

Loup City NORTHWESTERN. w 1881-S 20 1917||
United with Sherman county times-independent to form Sherman county times
NbHi My 27,Je 17 1892;S 20 1895-Ag 19,S-D 2,23 1898;99-1917

PEOPLE'S standard. *See* Loup City leader

SHERMAN county times. w 1877+
1891?-Ag 1915 as Sherman county times-independent
pub 1880+
MB [Ja 24 1879-Mr 14 1880]
NbHi S 25 1891;Je 24 1892;O 25-N 1,15 1895-[96-98;My 1900-02]08-N 1925;Jl 9-16 1926;Ap 8 1927+
NbLo 1930+

STANDARD gauge. w 1905?-Ag 10 1911||
NbHi Mr 13 1908-11

LOWELL

Lowell REGISTER. w Ja 1872-78||?
NbHi D 31 1875
NbMi Ag 18 1876-N 9 1877

LYMAN

Lyman LEDGER. w My 5 1927+
pub 1927-[31-33]+
NbHi 1927+

LYNCH

Lynch HERALD-ENTERPRISE. w Je 30 1897+
1897-1918 as Lynch journal; 1919-Ja 1932 Lynch herald
NbHi 1897-[1900-02]Mr 1908-Jl 1918;Ap 1919-Jl,Ag 10-S 14,28-N 23 1933,34+

Lynch JOURNAL. *See* Lynch herald-enterprise

LYONS

LOGAN VALLEY mirror. *See* Lyons mirror

LOGAN VALLEY sun. *See* Lyons mirror-sun

Lyons MIRROR. w D 1881-D 21 1917||
1881-85? as Logan Valley mirror. United with Lyons sun to form Lyons mirror-sun
NbHi My 1 1884;S 25,O 30,N 27,D 11 1890-1916

Lyons MIRROR-SUN. w 1888+
1888-Jl 21 1897 as Logan Valley sun; Jl 28 1897-D 21 1917 Lyons sun
pub N 1896+
NbHi D 2 1892;N-D 19 1895[Ap 1896-97]-F 9, 23,Mr 9,23-Je 1 1898[Mr 1899-1902]-Je 17 1915;18+

Lyons SUN. *See* Lyons mirror-sun

McCOOK

Weekly COURIER. w Ja 1 1880-1901||?
1880-Je 1895 as Indianola weekly courier (Indianola)
Merged with McCook republican
NbHi Ag 22 1895-D 19 1901

McCook DEMOCRAT. *See* McCook republican

McCook daily GAZETTE. d 1924+
KHi S 20 1927
NbHi 1925-[27-29]+
— sw ed *See* Red Willow county gazette

RED WILLOW county gazette. sw 1911-25||?
NbHi D 27 1917-24;Ja 22-26,F 9 1925
—d ed *See* McCook daily gazette

McCook REPUBLICAN. w Je 13 1885+
1885-O 1889 as McCook democrat; N 1889-My 29 1896 McCook times-democrat
NbHi O 26-N 1,15,29-D 13,27 1895-[96]-[99-1901]+

McCook TIMES-DEMOCRAT. *See* McCook republican

McCook TRIBUNE. w,tw Je 8 1882+
w 1882-Jl 10 1924
pub 1882—
NbHi D 9 1892;S 6-27,O 18-D 13 1895;96-My, Jl 1911-24;26+

McCOOL JUNCTION

BLUE VALLEY journal. w Je 18 1897+
pub 1897+
NbHi Je 25,S 1897+

McCool Junction RECORD. w 1887-96||?
NbHi My 26 1892
NbMcB My 1887-S 1896

McGREW

WASP. *See* Twin City times (Gering)

MADISON

Madison CHRONICLE. w,sw D 13 1878-Ap 1 1921||
1878-83? as Madison county chronicle. Merged with Madison star-mail
sw D 1918-13?
NbHi Ap 29,D 18 1879;Ap 1,My 20,S 2,D 23 1880;S 3,17-24 1884;Ag 18 1886;Ag 24 1887; My 9,Jl 5,Ag 1 1888;Ja 20 1892-93;F 8 1894; 95-1921
NbMa 1916-21
NbMaS 1901-21

Madison INDEPENDENT reporter. *See* Newman Grove reporter (Newman Grove)

MADISON county chronicle. *See* Madison chronicle

MADISON county reporter. *See* Newman Grove reporter (Newman Grove)

MADISON county review. *See* Madison review

NEBRASKA (*Continued*)

MADISON—*Continued*

Madison MAIL. w Ja 17 1902-F 20 1903||
United with Madison star to form Madison star-mail
NbHi Ja 24-My 6,30-Je 6,27 1902-03
NbMaS [1902]

Madison NEWS. w Ja 27 1927-Jl 1933||
Merged with Madison star-mail
NbHi 1927-Ja 12,F 16-23,Mr 9,Ap-Jl 1933
NbMa 1927-Je 1933
NbMaS 1927-Je 1933

Madison REVIEW. w Ja 23 1874-O 1878||
1874? as Madison county review (title varies slightly)
NbHi F 20 1874;D 17 1875;F 15,My 12 1876
NbMaB 1874-76

Madison STAR-MAIL. w,sw N 17 1893+
1893-F 1903 as Madison star; My 19 1927-Mr 29 1928 Star-mail and Elkhorn Valley mirror
sw F-My 12 1927
pub 1893+
NbHi Je 19-26,Jl 31-Ag 21,S-O 9,N 1896-Ja, F 12,26-Ag 6,27 1897;Ja 14,28,My 13-Je 10, 24-Jl,Ag 12,O 21 1898-F 17,Mr-Je 23,Ag 31 1899;F 9,23,Mr 16,Ap 13,My 11,Je 22,Jl 7,21-Ag,S 15,O 13,27,D 8 1900-Ja 5,26,Ap 26-S,O 11,N 1,D 1901[02]N 13 1903;Ap 1905+
NbMa 1916-33

MADRID

Madrid HERALD. w Ja 1920+
pub 1920+
NbHi F 21 1935+

Madrid NEWS. w 1887-97||?
NbHi D 2 1892;D 27 1895-Ja 17,F 28,Mr 13-20, Ap 10,My 8-15,29,Je 12,Jl 24 1896;F 26 1897

MALCOLM

Malcolm MESSENGER. w 1891-Ap 1934||
Merged with Lancaster county weekly (Lincoln)
NbHi Ja 11,F 15,Mr 14,Ap,My 9-16,Ag 1,29-O,N 28 1896-Ja 8,22-29,F 12-Mr 5,26-Ap 2, My 21,Je-Jl 9,Ag,S 17,O-N 19,D 3,17,31 1898; Mr 21 1908-Ap 18 1934

MARION

Marion CITIZEN. *See* South Side sentinel (Danbury)

Marion ENTERPRISE. *See* South Side sentinel (Danbury)

SOUTH SIDE sentinel. *See under* Danbury

MARQUETTE

Marquette INDEPENDENT. w Ja 2 1884-F 5 1885||
NbHi complete

MARTEL

Sprague-Martel LEADER. w 1911?-Ap 1934||
1890-Jl 1932 as Martel leader. Merged with Lancaster county weekly (Lincoln)
NbHi My 28 1914-34

MASON CITY

Mason City ADVOCATE. *See* People's advocate (Ansley)

Mason City STAR. w Je 19 1903-Ap 7 1910||
Merged with Mason City transcript (1909+)
NbHi Je 19-26,Jl 10-24,Ag 7-14,28,S 11-N 13,D 4-18 1903;Ja 1-15,F 5-19,Mr-S 9,23,O 21-28,N 18 1904[08-09]-F 18,Mr 4-11,31 1910

Mason City TRANSCRIPT. w 1886-1902||
NbBb [1897-1902]
NbHi Ag 4 1892;O 10,24 1895-[96-97]-Mr 17, Ap,My 26 1898[99;F 1900-S 18 1902]

Mason City TRANSCRIPT. w Ap 27 1909+
NbHi Ap 14-My,Je 9-Jl 22 1910;S 21 1911-S 17,O 8,29-N 4,D 31 1914+

MAYWOOD

Maywood EAGLE-REPORTER. w N 1891+
1891-Ja 16 1902 as Maywood eagle
NbHi My 25,Jl 20 1892;O 24-D 1895[Ap 23 1896-97]-Mr 17,31-Ap 21,My 5-12,25 1898[99-1900]Ja 28,Ap 25-My 2,16-Je,Jl 18,Ag 1-22,S-O 3,17,31-N,D 12-26 1901;Ja 9-23,F 6-20,Mr 6,27-My 1,22,Je 12-26,Jl 10-24,Ag 7,28-S 11 1902;18+

Maywood REPORTER. w 1901-02||?
United with Maywood eagle to form Maywood eagle-reporter

MEADOW GROVE

Meadow Grove NEWS. w 1906+
pub 1917+
NbHi My 16 1919+

Meadow Grove TRIBUNE. w 1890-Je 1898||
United with Norfolk times to form Norfolk times-tribune (Norfolk)
NbHi N 15 1895;Mr 19-26,Ap 9,23-Je 11,25,Jl 9,30-Ag 6,20,D 31 1897;Ja 14-21,F-My 6,20 1898

MERNA

Merna MESSENGER. w F 17 1905+
1905-Ap 13 1917 as Merna postal card
pub 1905+
NbBb [1906-09]
NbHi F 24 1905;Ag 21 1908+

Merna POSTAL CARD. *See* Merna messenger

Merna REPORTER. w N 1891-Jl 1894||
NbBb [1894]
NbHi D 8 1892

MERRIMAN

Merriman MAVERICK. w Mr 11 1910-Ja 11 1929||
NbHi Mr 25 1910-28

MILFORD

Milford MONITOR. *See* Milford review

Milford NEBRASKAN. *See* Milford review

Milford OZONE. *See* Milford review

Milford REVIEW. w,sw F 1882+
1882-F 14? 1884 as Seward county democrat; F 22 1884-F 13 1885 Milford ozone; F 20 1885-Ap 30 1909 Milford Nebraskan (title varies slightly) My 7 1909-10? Milford monitor
sw O 20-D 1886
pub O 1910+
NbHi F 22-Ap 18,My 1884-[1900-S 1902]Ap 1903-[05;Ap-D 1906]Ap 12 1907-D 10 1909;O 19 1911+

SEWARD county democrat. *See* Milford review

MILLARD

Millard COURIER. w N 1893+
1893-94? as Douglas county courier
NbHi O 29 1897;Jl 1914-Ja 4,18-F 15,Mr 1-8, 22-Jl 19 1918

DOUGLAS county courier. *See* Millard courier

MILLER

Miller FORUM. w O 8 1908-11||?
NbHi 1908-Je,Jl 13-Ag 3 1911

Miller GAZETTE. w D 30 1897-1900||?
NbHi 1897-S 28 1900

MILLIGAN

Milligan JOURNAL. w 1897-1901||?
NbHi S 4,O 16 1897-Jl 5 1901

Milligan REVIEW. w F 18 1933+
NbHi Mr 10 1933+

Milligan TIMES. w Mr 9 1901-N 9 1920||
NbHi 1901-[06]-Mr,My 21,Je 14-N 15,D 1907-O,N 9 1920

MINATARE

Minatare FREE PRESS. w F 18 1908+
F-Mr 12? 1908 as Minatare sentinel; Mr 19 1908?-1912 Minatare free press and sentinel
pub 1923+
NbHi Mr 19-S 17,O 1-8 1908;Ja 21-Mr 12,Ap 16 1909-Ja,F 11-18,Mr 11,Ap 22,My 13-Ag,S 9-O,N 11 1910+

Minatare SENTINEL. *See* Minatare free press

MINDEN

Minden COURIER. w O 9 1890+
1890-Je 22 1892? as Workman
pub 1890+
NbHi Je 22 1892;O 17-31,N 21,D 5-12 1895 [96]+
NbMi 1890+

Minden GAZETTE. *See* Minden new gazette

KEARNEY county bee. *See* Minden new gazette

KEARNEY county gazette. *See* Minden new gazette

KEARNEY county news. *See* Minden news

Minden NEW gazette. w 1878-F 26 1904||
1878-S 15 1882 as Kearney county bee; S 22 1882-91 Kearney county gazette; 1892-1902 Minden gazette. United with Kearney county news to form Kearney county news and Minden new gazette, later Minden news
NbHi Je 30-Jl 7 1892;O 10,24-31,N 14-D 1895; Ja 23,F 6,20,Ap 30-My,Je 18-Jl 2,16 1896-1902
NbMi N 22,D 5 1878-S 15 1882;84-Ag 13,N 20 1903-04

Minden NEWS. m,w 1894-S 21 1922||
1894-O 25 1901 as Prairie home; N 1 1901-F 1904 Kearney county news; Mr 1904-Ap 6 1906 Kearney county news and Minden new gazette; Ap 13-Ag 10 1906 News-gazette
1894-S? 1901 pub in Heartwell
m 1897-98
NbHi Ja 1897;Mr-Jl 1898;S 27 1899-S 20,D 13-20 1901;Ja 3,17-F 7,21-28,Mr 14 1902-22
NbMi Mr 1900-13

NEWS-GAZETTE. *See* Minden news

PRAIRIE home. *See* Minden news

WORKMAN. *See* Minden courier

MITCHELL

Mitchell INDEX. w 1893+
1893-Ap 26 1901 as Nebraska homestead (Gering)
pub 1901+
NbHi Mr 20,Jl 17,My 8,Jl 24,N 20,D 25 1896; Ja 15-Ag 20,S 1897-[99]Ja 5,19,F 2-16,Mr 9, 23-Ap 20,My 18-Je 1,15-Ag 17,S 7-21,O 5-19,N 2-16,30 1900-Ja 4,25,Ap 26-Jl 5,19 1901+

STAR. *See* Scottsbluff star (Scottsbluff)

MONOWI

Monowi NEWS. w Mr 1904-10||?
NbHi Mr 27 1908-Mr 11 1910

MONROE

LOOKING GLASS. w 1889-N 22 1917||
NbHi Je 23,D 22 1892;O 1895-[96]-[1900-02]-13

Monroe NEWS. w My 28 1894+
1894-1919 as Monroe republican
NbHi O 11,25-N 22,D 6-20 1895[96-97]-Mr 18, Ap 1-22,My 6-13,27 1898[99]-[1925]+

Monroe REPUBLICAN. *See* Monroe news

MORRILL

Morrill MAIL. w Je 1 1907+
pub 1907+
NbHi Ap 17 1908-[11]+

MULLEN

Mullen ENQUIRER. w Jl 1888-96||?
NbHi D 2 1892;Ag 23-O 1,25,N 15,D 13 1895; Ja 17-24,F 7,28,Mr 27 1896

HOOKER county tribune. w 1895+
NbHi S 5-12,26,N 7-14,28-D 1902;D 28 1917+

MURRAY

Murray BANNER. w Ap 1891-93||?
NbHi Jl 2-9 1891;N 17 1892
NbMuG [Ag 11 1892-Mr 1893]

Murray BANNER. w Mr 30 1895-96||?
Mr-S 1895 as Murray mirror
NbHi My 18,Ag 3,17-31,N 9,D 14 1895;F 8-15 1896
NbMuG Mr-[S 14 1895-F 22 1896]

Murray MIRROR. *See* Murray banner

NAPER

BOYD county democrat. *See* Naper independent

Naper INDEPENDENT. w Mr 1916-17||?
Mr-Je 1916 as Naper press; Jl-Ag 3 1916 Boyd county democrat
NbHi Ap 13-D 1916;Ja 11-F 1 1917

Naper NEWS. w F 9 1900-05||?
NbHi F 9-23,Mr 16-My,Ag 24-O 9,N 23-D 21 1900;Ap 19 1901-Ap 1,15-29,My 13-Je 17,Ag 12,26 1904

Naper PRESS. *See* Naper independent

NAPONEE

Naponee HERALD. w 1911-17||?
NbHi My 29-S 11,25,O 16-23,N 27 1914-Ap,My 14-Jl,Ag 12-S 9,23,O 21-N 18,D 30 1915-F 10, 24-Mr 9,Ap-My 18,Je 1,Ag 31-D 14 1916;17

NEBRASKA CITY

Nebraska City daily CHRONICLE. d Ag 1868-75||?
Ag-O 1868 as Daily plebian (other variations slight)
DLC Jl 19 1870-F 22 1872
NbHi O 18 1873

CONSERVATIVE. w Jl 14 1898-My 29 1902||
Followed by Nebraska City weekly
ICU My 23-30,Je 13-Jl 4,18,Ag-O 17,31-N 21,D 12 1901-F 6,20-My 1902
IaDH Je 12 1900-02
KHi complete
NbHi Jl 14-Ag 11,25 1898-F 9,23,Mr-Ap 6, 20-My,Je 8,22-O 12,26,N 16,30,D 21 1899;D 27 1900-Ja 3,17,F 7,Mr 21-Ap 4,18,My 9,Je 6,Jl 4-11,Ag 8,S 12,N 14,D 12,26 1901;Ja 2, My 22 1902

Nebraska City FERRET. w,sw Mr 1896-98||?
1896-97? as Otoe chief
w Mr-Je 1896
NbHi Mr 12-26,Ap 9-23,My-Je 11,25-Jl 1896

Nebraska City HERALD. *See* Nebraska press

NEBRASKA news. *See* Nebraska City news

NEBRASKA daily news-press. d 1858+
1858-N 19 1925 as Nebraska daily press (N 30 1907-F 12 1910 Nebraska press and Nebraska City daily tribune) other variations slight
pub 1858+
CtY My 15 1887
DLC 1868-69:F 11-Jl 16 1870;Ja 25 1873-76
NbHi S 9 1875;Jl 5,O 24,D 30 1876;My 15 1887; Ap 23 1889;Ap 8,Je 1,8,Jl 21,N 29 1892;S 24, 26 1893-F 3,O 16,27,29 1895-[99-1906]-[11]+

NEBRASKA (*Continued*)

NEBRASKA CITY—*Continued*

NEBRASKA press. w,sw 1858-1910||?
1858?-F 1862 as Nebraska City herald?; Mr? 1862-65? People's press (other variations slight)
sw 1894?-1904?
DLC S 18 1861-F 27,My-D 4 1862;64-Je 8 1865;Ja 28,F 15-22,Mr 8,29,Ap 26 1873
KHi D 25 1907-F 11 1910
NbHi N 17 1859;N 30 1872;Mr 20 1873;Ja 8,Jl 3,D 11 1875;F 19,D 30 1876;Ap 28 1888

NEBRASKA staats-zeitung. w 1877-Ja 1912||
Merged with Omaha tribüne, later Freie presse und wochentliche tribüne (Omaha)
Also dated in Falls City
In German
NbHi Je 14-21,Jl 1907-12

Daily NEBRASKA statesman. d S 10? 1866-
NbHi S 17-22,28,O 3,6,8 1866

NEBRASKA statesman. w *See under* Lincoln

NEBRASKA volksblatt. *See under* Westpoint

Nebraska City NEWS. w,sw N 14 1854-N 6 1925||
1854-My 8 1858 as Nebraska news
sw 1894?-Ag 23 1918
pub 1854-55 61-1925
DLC [1856-61]
MWA Ja 12 1856
NbHi [1857]-[59-S 14 1861]Ja-Je 7,21-N 1 1862;O 18 1873;Ja 27 1877;D 18 1880;Ap 26 1889;N 9 1894-1909;14-[16]-25
TU F 7 1857

Nebraska City NEWS. d,tw 1863-Je 10 1870||?
Merged with Nebraska City daily times
d 1863-65?
N Je 17-29 1865
NbHi D 3-24 1864[65;67-68]Ja 6 1869

Nebraska City NEWS. d 1879-N 6 1925||
Title varies slightly. United with Nebraska daily press to form Nebraska daily news-press
NbHi D 7 1892;O 26,28,N 1,16,22,27,29,D 5,7, 10,14,19,26 1895[96-My 1898;F 1899-S 1902] My 11 1914-Jl 25,31,Ag 2,7,10,14,17 1916;O 27 1917
NbNeN complete

OTOE chief. *See* Nebraska City ferret

PEOPLE'S press. *See* Nebraska press

Daily PLEBIAN. *See* Nebraska daily chronicle

Nebraska City daily TIMES. d Ap 25 1870-71||?

Daily TRIBUNE. d My 27 1901-N 25 1907||
United with Nebraska City daily press to form Nebraska daily press and Nebraska City daily tribune, later Nebraska daily news-press
NbHi [My-D 1901]-07
—w ed *See* Nebraska City weekly

Nebraska City WEEKLY. w My 30 1902-N 25 1907||
Follows Conservative
IU My-S 19 1902
IaDH 1902-Mr 17 1905
KHi complete
MnU My-S 13 1902;Ja 20 1903-Mr 17 1905
NbHi Je-S 19 1902
WHi Jl 15 1902
—d ed *See* Daily tribune

NEHAWKA

Nehawka ENTERPRISE. w Mr 1922+
NbHi Jl 1931—

NEWS-LEDGER. w Je 1910-20||?
1910-N 1 1917 as Nehawka news; N 8 1917-18 Nehawka news and Union ledger
NbHi O 13,27 1911-17;Ja 10-Ag 22,S 5,26-N 1918;Ja-Ag 21 1919

Nehawka REGISTER. w Ag 12 1892-1910||?
NbHi Ag 26 1892;O 25 1895-Je 17,Jl-S 9,23,O 14,D 2 1898;Ja 1,F 17,Mr 3 1899;O 11 1901 [02]-Ap 1,Jl 15 1904[06-07]-Ag 1909

NELIGH

Neligh ADVOCATE. w 1881-1901||?
Ja-Jl 1881 as Antelope county eagle
NbHi Ja 1,26,F 16,Mr 9,Ap-Jl 13,Ag 1881-Ag 1,29,S 12-19,O 3,17 1885;86-N 1894;96-N 1901

ANTELOPE county eagle. *See* Neligh advocate

ANTELOPE tribune. w O 3 1879-Mr 9 1898||
1879-My 4? 1887 as Neligh republican
MWA My 14 1880
NbHi 1879-F 17,Mr 10-N 3 1882;F 9 1883-My 4,21,Je 1,Ag 2- 1887;Ja 11,F 22,Ap 11,My 9, Jl 25,Ag 22,S 19-26,N 7,28 1888;Mr 27,Ap 10, My 22,S 18,D 4 1889;F 26,Mr 26,N 5,S 24 1890;91-98

Neligh INDEPENDENT. w Ja 1-Ap 18? 1878||
NbHi Ja-Mr,Ap 11-18 1878

Neligh JOURNAL. w My 1874-N 7 1877||
NbHi O 8,12 1875;Ja 11-25,Mr 14,Ap 18,My 23,Jl 26,Ag 16,S 6-20,O 25,N 15-29,D 13 1876; Ap 4,18,My 2,16-23,Je 27,Ag 15,S 12,O 3-17, 31-N 1877

Neligh LEADER. w Je 1885+
pub 1885+
NbHi 1885+

Neligh NEWS. sw w 1914+
1914-S? 1916 as Neligh semi-weekly news (sw)
NbHi S 20 1923+

PUBLIC opinion. *See* Neligh yeoman

Neligh REGISTER. w 1903-D 1924||
1903-Ap 1905 as Elgin register (Elgin)
Merged with Neligh news
NbHi F 16-23,Mr 16,30-Ap 6,Je-N 5,16,30,D 21 1905;Ja 11,F 1-8,22,Mr 1-15,Ap 12,26-My 10,24,Je 28,Jl 12-19,Ag 1906-24

Neligh REPUBLICAN. *See* Antelope tribune

Neligh YEOMAN. w F 18 1890-Ap 13 1905||
1890-O? 1893 as Public opinion; N? 1893-S 1902 Yeoman
NbHi Mr 13 1891;N 25 1892;Ja 27-F 3,Mr 31, O 13,D 1 1893;Ag 17-24,S 7-21,O 19,N 2 1894;Ja 18,F 22,Mr 29,My 3,Je 7,21-Jl 5,O 11,25 1895 F 21-Mr 6,My 8 1896-1905

NELSON

ALLIANCE herald. *See* Nuckolls county herald

Nelson GAZETTE. w My 3 1884+
pub 1884+
NbHi O 24 1895-[96]-My 26 1898[F 1899-1900] Ja 3,24,Ap 25-My 2,16-30,Ag 22 1901;F 6,27 Mr 13,27,Ap 10,24,My 22-29,Je 7-12,Jl 10,Ag 14-S 18 1902;Ag 20 1908+
NbN 1926+

NUCKOLLS county herald. w My 10 1877+
1891?-Ap 20 1894 as Alliance herald
pub 1921+
NbHi D 2 1892;93-1921;24-25;27+
NbN 1926+

NUCKOLLS county republican. *See* Nuckolls county sun

NUCKOLLS county sun. w Ag 1899-1906||?
1899-F 1900 as Nuckolls county republican
NbHi Mr 1,29,Ap 12-19,My,Jl 5,19 1900

NEMAHA

NEBRASKA advertiser. w Jl 7 1856-1908||?
1856-Ag 1882 pub in Brownville; S 1882-87? in Auburn
DLC Je 7,D 1856-Ag 12 1858[62-Mr 1864;72]
KHi S 12 1867
MWA F 25,Jl 29 1858;D 17 1868
NbHi 1856-Ap 10 1862[64-65;Mr-D 1866]-N 9 1882;Je 24 1892;My 5 1894;Je 7,O 18-D 20 1895[96-97]-My,O 21-28,N 11-D 2 1898[99-1900]Ja 4,Ap 26-My 3,17-31,Je 14 1901-[02]-F 7,21-Ag 21,O 23,N 6,D 18-25 1908
—d ed *See* Nebraska advertiser (Brownville)

NEBRASKA herald. w N 24 1859-
NbHi N-D 22 1859;Ja 12-26,F 9-Mr 1,15-My 24,Je 21-Ag 16,30-O 4,25-N 22 1860;Ja 3,19-26,F 9-Mr 9 1861

NEWARK

Newark HERALD. w N 14 1880-Ap 1882||
Merged with Kearney county bee, later Minden new gazette (Minden)
NbMi Je 9 1881-Mr 1882

NEWCASTLE

Newcastle TIMES. w Mr 1890+
pub Ag 1925—
NbHi O 29-N,D 10-31 1895;Ja 21,F 11-Mr 17, Ap 7,My 1896-Ap 14,28-Je 9,23 1898;Ja,F 8-15 1900;O,N 13-D 18 1902;Ja 8-29,F 12-My 7, Jl 23-D 1903

NEWMAN GROVE

Newman Grove ADVERTISER. *See* Weekly herald

Newman Grove weekly GAZETTE. w D 13 1894-D 17 1896||
United with Newman Grove advertiser to form Weekly herald
NbHi O 24-31,N 14-D 19 1895;Ja 16,F 20,D 17 1896

Weekly HERALD. w 1887-1907||?
1887-92? as New era; 1893?-D 18 1896 Newman Grove advertiser
NbHi O 25-D 1895;Ja 24-31,F 14,Ap 24,My 15, 29-Je,Jl 17-Ag 21,S-O 16,30-N 20,D 1896;Ja 14,F 4-18,Je 24-Jl 22,Ag 5-12,26-S 9,23,O 14, 28,N 18,D 16-30 1897;Ja 27-F,Ap 7-21,Je 16,Jl 28,S 15-O 6,20-27,N 24-D 1,15 1898-Ja 12,F 9,Mr 2 1899;F 8-Mr,Ap 12-Je 21 1900

MADISON county reporter. *See* Newman Grove reporter

NEW ERA. *See* Weekly herald

Newman Grove REPORTER. w Mr 1886+
1886-Ap 6 1911 as Madison county reporter
1886-My 1899? pub in Madison
pub Je 1899+
NbHi Je 7,Jl 12 1888[92]-My 1899;Ap 11 1907; Ap 1908+

NEWPORT

Newport EAGLE. w 1895-1903||?
1895-F 1902 as Bassett eagle (Bassett)
NbHi Ag 22 1895-Ag 28 1903

Newport REPUBLICAN. w 1883-1917||?
NbHi Jl 31,Ag 21-28,S 11,25-O 9,23,N 6,D 18 1896-F,Mr 12-Ap,My 14-Ag 20,S 1897-F 4,18-My,Je 10-Jl 1,15-Ag 19,S 2,16-D 9,23 1898-F, Mr 11-My 13,27-O 7,D 16 1910-Ja 28,Mr-Ap 10,24-Je 5 1913

NIOBRARA

KNOX county news. *See* Creighton news (Creighton)

Niobrara PIONEER. w S 4 1874-1904||?
1852-87? as Creighton pioneer (Creighton)
NbBf 1874-79;S 9 1881-82;85;87;96;1902-03
NbHi S 22-D 24 1874[Ja-N 11 1875;JeD 1876]-S,O 18-25 1878;Ja-Jl,Ag 23,O 17,N 7,D 9,23 1879-Ja 6,S 28-D 1880;Ja 14-28,F 18,Mr 4-11,Ap 22,My 6,Je 3-17,N 11 1881;Ap 28,Je 23,Jl 21 1882;Ap 8,S 16-N 11,D 2-16 1892;Ja 27-F 3,Je 3,Jl 14,S 1 1893;Mr 23 1894;S 13 1895-S,N 1900-[01]-03;Ja 15-Ap 15,29-My 6, 27-Je 3,Jl 1-15 1904

Niobrara TRIBUNE. w 1890+
NbHi Mr 22-29,Ap 12 1895+

NONPARIEL

GENE HEATH'S grip. *See* Pioneer grip (Alliance)

NORFOLK

ELKHORN VALLEY mirror. w My 13 1926-My 12 1927||
United with Madison star-mail to form Star-mail and Elkhorn Valley mirror, later Madison star-mail (Madison)
NbHi complete

ELKHORN VALLEY news. *See* Norfolk weekly news-journal

Norfolk INDEPENDENT. *See* Norfolk times-tribune

Norfolk JOURNAL. w,sw N 30 1877-N 16 1900||
United with Norfolk weekly news to form Norfolk weekly news-journal
w 1877-97?
NbHi N-D 14 1877;F 15-22,My 3,Jl 26-Ag 9, 30,S 13,O 11-18,N 8 1878;Ja 3-10,F 21,My 7, 21,Ap 25,My 9,Je 20,Jl 11 1879[80-81]-Ap 19, My-S 20,N 29,D 13 1888-F 14,Mr 14-21,My 2, O 24 1889;My 10,S 1,O 6 1892;Ja 3,O 18-D 20 1895;96[97-98]-1900

MADISON county times. *See* Norfolk times-tribune

Norfolk daily NEWS. d 1887+
pub Jl 1888+
NbHi Ap 19 1888;D 10 1892[O 1895-99]-S,N 1909-[12]-Je 1919;20+
NbNo 1915+

Norfolk weekly NEWS-JOURNAL. w S 1881-O 19 1917||
1881-88? as Elkhorn Valley news; 1889?-N 16 1900 Norfolk weekly news
NbHi My 25 1882;S 4-11,25 1884;S 15 1887; Ap 26,Je 21 1888;F 13 1896-O 12 1917
NbNo Je 1895-97

Norfolk PRESS. w 1900+
Title varies slightly
pub 1907+
NbHi S 23 1904;Ag 24 1906;Mr 8,Je 21 1907; 08+
NbNo 1922+

Norfolk TIMES. w S 16 1880-N 1881||
NbHi S 16-30,O 14,28,N 11-D 23 1880;Ja-Mr 24,My 25-Jl 6,20-S 7 1881

Norfolk TIMES-TRIBUNE. w,sw F 28 1896-1909||?
1896 as Norfolk independent; Ja-O 2 1897 Madison county times; O 9 1897-Je 1898 Norfolk times
sw 1898?
NbHi F-Mr 13,27-Ap 3,My 1-22,Je 5,Jl 31 1896;Ja 8,F 1897-[99]-1903;Ja 3 F 26,Ap 1904-[06-07]08;Ja 15 1909

NORTH BEND

North Bend ARGUS. w Ap 10 1890-O 1897||
United with North Bend republican to form North Bend eagle
NbHi 1890-Ap 2,Ag 21-S 4 1891;N 25,D 2 1892[S 1895-O 1897]
NbNbE complete

North Bend EAGLE. w N 4 1897+
Formed by the union of North Bend argus and North Bend republican
pub 1897+
NbHi 1897+

North Bend REPUBLICAN. w 1892-O 1897||
United with North Bend argus to form North Bend eagle
NbHi [S 1895-97]
NbNbE [1892-97]

NORTH LOUP

North Loup LOYALIST. w 1887+
NbHi Je 2 1892;1903-[10-11]-[13]+

NORTH PLATTE

ENTERPRISE. *See* North Platte republican

FARMER-LABOR herald. *See* North Platte herald

North Platte HERALD. w D 28 1923-
1923-Mr 6 1925 as Farmer-labor herald
NbHi O 1924-Mr 6 1925

INDEPENDENT democrat. w 1889-1905||?
1889-My 1904 as Independent era
NbHi Je 17 1892;F 20-Ap,My 21-Je 25,D 31 1896;Ja 21-28,F 25-My 20,Je 10,24-Jl 15,O 7, D 30 1887-F 3,My 12-19,Je 2,23-30,Jl 14-Ag 3,N-D 1 1898;D 20 1900;Ap 18,My 9-Jl,S 26-O 17,N 1901-Ja 2,16-30,Mr 20,Ag 21-28,S 11 1902-Jl 13 1905

INDEPENDENT era. *See* Independent democrat

NEBRASKA (*Continued*)

NORTH PLATTE—*Continued*

LINCOLN county journal. w My 18 1904-My 3 1907‖
Merged with North Platte telegraph
NbHi Jl 28,Ag 11-S 15,O-D 8 1905;Ap 26-My 1907

LINCOLN county tribune. w,sw 1885+
1892?-1922 as North Platte tribune (title varies slightly)
sw 1899?-1932
NbHi O 25-N 1,12 1895-[Ja-My 1898;Jl 1899-1902]My 29 1908+

North Platte daily RECORD. d N 1895-96‖?
NbHi D 12,16 1895;Ja 13,22-25,27,F 5,8,11,17, Ap 15-16,22-23,27,29,My 1,5,7-8,14-15,21-22,27, 29-30,Je 2,5-29,Jl 15,17-18,23-Ag 26 1896

North Platte REPUBLICAN. w 1868-81‖?
1868-73? as Enterprise
NbHi Ap 12 1873;Ja 1 1876;Ja 20,F 3 1877

North Platte TELEGRAPH. w,sw 1880-1927‖
Title varies slightly
sw 1899?-1908?
pub complete
NbHi Je 25 1892;O 26-N 16,30-D 7,21 1895-97[Mr-D 1900]My 10-28 1907;My 1908-Ja,F 21-Ag 8 1918

North Platte daily TELEGRAPH. d 1896+
Title varies slightly
Suspended from 1905?-08?
pub 1896+
NbHi [Ap 1896-O 13 1902]

North Platte TRIBUNE. *See* Lincoln county tribune

NORTHPORT

HERALD. *See* Bridgeport herald (Bridgeport)

OAK

Oak LEAF. w Ap 14 1914-20‖?
NbHi Ap 23-My 14,28-Je 4 1914;F-N 3,17-24, D 1915-F,Mr 11-Ap,My 13-Je 10 1920

Oak NEWS. w Je 18 1897-1911‖?
NbHi S 17,O 1-22,N-D 1897;Jl 7-14,28-S 8,22-O 6,27 1899-Jl 13,27,Ag 10,31-S 7,N 16,30 1906;F 1,Mr 29-My 24,Ag-D 6,20 1907-Ag 11 1911

Weekly TRIBUNE. w Jl 11 1911-13‖?
NbHi Jl-N 14,28 1911-My 21,Je 4,25-Jl 16,30-Ag 3,17 1912-S 2 1913

OAKDALE

ELKHORN pen and plow. *See* Oakdale guard

Oakdale GUARD. w Ap 7 1877-92‖?
1877-F 20 1891 as Oakdale pen and plow (Ap 17 1879-O 11 1883 Elkhorn pen and plow) F 27- 1891? Oakdale journal
NbHi My 26,S-O 13,27 1877-Ja 11,25-F 8,22-Mr 22,Ap-Je,Jl 12-O 1883;Ja 28 1887-Ap 17 1891

Oakdale JOURNAL. w S 16 1873-Ja 21 1887‖
Merged with Oakdale pen and plow, later Oakdale guard
NbHi S 23 1873;Je 4-11,S 3,O 15-22 1874;Ja 26,Ag 3,31,S 28,O 5 1875;O 25,N 1883-87

Oakdale JOURNAL. 1891 *See* Oakdale guard

Oakdale PEN and plow. *See* Oakdale guard

Oakdale SENTINEL. w Je 25 1887+
pub 1904+
NbHi N 5 1887;Mr 24,Jl 7-14,S 1,29,N 3 1888; Ag 23 1890;Jl 11,S 7 1891;Jl 30 1892;O 12,26 1895-O,N 28 1929;Ja,Mr 13,Ap-My 15,29 1930+
NbOaC 1887-1904

OAKLAND

Oakland INDEPENDENT and republican. w N 1880+
1880-Jl 19 1907 as Oakland independent
pub 1907+
MnHi [Mr 20 1908-N 19 1915]
NbHi N 30 1881;O 11-25,N,D 20 1895[96-98]+

Oakland REPUBLICAN. w 1894-Jl 26 1907‖
United with Oakland independent to form Oakland independent and republican
NbHi O 24,N-D 1895;Ja 23,F,Ap 1896-Ap 12 1907

OCONTO

Oconto REGISTER. w My 1 1905-Je 3 1920‖
NbHi 1908-[14]-Ap 1,15-22,My-Je 1920

ODELL

Odell ORACLE. w D 11 1919+
pub 1919+
NbHi 1919+

Weekly WAVE. w Ap 1892-Jl 1919‖
NbHi O 25-N 1,22-D 13 1895;Ja 24,F 7,21,Mr-My 22,Je,Jl 24,Ag 21,S 11 1896-[99-1902]-12; F 14-28 1913;Je 1914-19

OGALLALA

KEITH county news. w S 18 1885+
1890? as Keith county news and Ogallala reflector; F- 1905? Keith county news and republican argus
pub [1885+]
NbHi 1885-Jl 15,29 1892;Ag 16 1895[96]-S 3 1897;Ja 7 1898[1900]-[02]Ja 9-30,F 20,Mr 27, Jl 17-24,Ag 7-14,S 4,O 23 1903;Ja 8,F 12,My 20 1904-[13-14]+

Ogallala REFLECTOR. w 1884-90‖?
United with Keith county news to form Keith county news and Ogallala reflector, later Keith county news

REPUBLICAN argus. w Ja 15 1898-Ja 27 1905‖
United with Keith county news to form Keith county news and republican argus, later Keith county news
NbHi [1898]Ja 14-21,F,Mr 23-30,Ap 13,My,Je 15,Jl 6,Ag 3-10,24,N 9,D 7,21 1899[1900]-05

Ogallala TRIBUNE. w Jl 1916-D 12 1918‖
Merged with Keith county news
NbHi Jl 28 1916-S 12,26-D 1918

OHIOWA

Ohiowa ADVERTISER. w 1922-Ja 17 1930‖
Merged with Nebraska signal (Geneva)
NbHi F 12 1925-30

OHIOWAN. *See* Ohiowa spotlight

Ohiowa OPINION. w Mr 14 1930-Ja 19 1934‖?
NbHi 1931-Ja 19 1934

Ohiowa SPOTLIGHT. w 1885-S 7 1917‖
1885-1912 as Ohiowan (title varies slightly)
NbHi O 24-N 14,28 1895-[96-97]Ja 13-F 10, 24-My 19,D 15 1898[99-1900]Ap 18-25,My 9-16,Je 13-20,Jl 18-25,Ag 15,29 1901-Mr 14 1907; 08-12;My 28 1914-17

OMAHA

AFRO-AMERICAN sentinel. w O 1893-99‖?
Negro
NbHi F 22,Ap 25,Je 1896-S 1898;Ja 28-F 4,25, Mr 25 1899

AMERICAN homestead. w 1883-1908‖?
NbHi D 2 1893;O 26-N 2,D 7-14 1895;Ja 18,F 8,29-Mr 14,Ap 4-11,25-My 9,30,Je 20-Jl 11, 25-Ag 1,15,S 5-12,O 10,N 7,D 5-12,26 1896;Ja 2,23,Ap 17-24,Je 19-Jl 3,Ag 14 1897;Jl 2-16, Ag 6 1898;My 10-17,31-Jl 4,19-S 1902

AMERICAN nonconformist. *See* Central farmer

Omaha ARROW. w Jl 28 1854-
DLC Jl-Ag 4,S 8 1854
MWA Ag 4,O 20 1854
NbHi Jl-Ag 4,S 1-15,29-O 20,N 3-10,D 29 1854
NbO Jl-S 7,22-N 10 1854

Omaha BEE. w S 6 1871-99‖?
Title varies slightly
ICM D 17 1890;Ja 14 1891
MWA N 30 1887;D 2 1896
NbHi N 24,D 8-22 1875;My 10,24-S 1876;Ja-Mr,N 1877-Ja 3 1883;Ja 2,Ap 30,O 8,22 1884;F 4,18-Mr 11,N 4,18-25 1885;Ja 13-20,F 24,D 8 1886;Mr 2,O 7-14 1887;Mr 25 1891;My 25,Je 8 1892;Ja 16,O 23,N 6,27-D 4 1895[96]F 17,Mr 3,17,S 1,D 1 1897;My 11,Ag 24-31,S 21,N 9-30 1898[99-Jl 4 1900]
NbO 1873-81
WHi 1896-99

Omaha BEE-NEWS. [morning ed]. d Je 19 1871+
1871-F 14 1927 as Omaha bee (title varies slightly) F 15-O 2 1927 Omaha morning bee Omaha daily news
pub 1871+
A 1888-Je 1894;Mr 1896-1902
CaOTA Ap 26-27 1875
CoU Ja 1 1881;Ja 7 1899-1901;05;S 1906-My 7 1910
DLC Jl 14 1886+
IEN O 1902-D 6 1906
IU O 12 1915-16
IaDH Je 1890-1914
MB O 15 1889-90
MiU [1893]1926-30
Nb Ap 1889-Je,O 1893-Mr,O 1894-Je,O 1895-Je, O 1896-Je 1927
NbHi D 31 1872;Ap 15 1873;S 3 1874[Je 19 1875-Ap 1877]Ja 18,Ap 9,14,22,S 2,O 1,3 1879 [80]-[82]-[1927-29]+
NbO F 1878+
NcD 1903-My 1908
PP Ja 1 1929;34+
WHi Jl 3 1892;My-Je 1900;15+

Omaha evening BEE-news. d 1871+
1871-F 14 1927 as Omaha evening bee (other variations slight)
NbHi My-Ag 22,25 1898;Je 16 1922;Ap 2 1925;My 28 1926;F 14-O 2 1927
OClWHi F 8-9 1900

Omaha BEOBACHTER. w 1869-74‖?
United with Omaha post to form Omaha post und beobachter, later Omaha post
In German

CENTRAL farmer. w 1897?-Jl 1903‖
1879-98 American nonconformist; 1899-1900 Nonconformist; Ja-Mr 21 1901 Central farmer and nonconformist. Merged with Farmers' advocate (Topeka, Kansas)
NbHi Mr 24,My 12-26,Je 30,Jl 14-28,Ag 11,S 1-8,O 27,1898;N 9-D 21 1899;Ja-F 1,15,Mr 1-8,22-Ag 9,23-D 20 1900;01-Ja 8,22-Jl 1903

Omaha COMMERCIAL exchange. *See* Omaha journal of commerce

COMMERCIAL exhibit. w S 1893-96‖?
NbHi Ag 15-D 19 1895;Ja 1896

Den DANSKE pioneer. w 1872+
In Danish
pub 1872+
CtY Ag 25 1921
IU D 1917+
IaDeL F 9 1894;My 21 1896;Ja 17-D 19 1901
MnHi Ap 16 1918+
NbHi Ag 22 1895+
WHi O 17 1895-Ag 20 1896;O 1898+
WaPS S 23 1915-O 10 1918

DĚLNICKÉ listy. *See* Květy Americké (1894-1919)

Omaha evening DISPATCH. d Je 30 1883-Ap 17 1885‖
Je-Jl 23? 1883 as Omaha daily union
NbO Je 30,Jl 1-2,30,D 31 1883-85

Omaha DISPATCH. 1887-89 *See* Evening republican and evening dispatch

DROVERS' journal. [South Omaha]. d 1887-99‖?
United with Omaha daily stockman to form Drovers' journal-stockman, later Omaha daily journal-stockman

DROVERS' journal-stockman. *See* Omaha daily journal-stockman

ENTERPRISE. w Ja 1893-1914‖?
Negro
DLC Ja 12 1900
NbHi Ag 10-24,S 21,O 19,N 16,30 1895-Ap 18, My,Je 20-Jl,Ag 8,22,S 5,19-O,N 14-D 5,19 1896-Ja 9,23-F 6,20-Ap 3,17-My 1,15-29,Je 19-26,Jl 3 1897;Ag 21-S 18,O 2-16,D 1908-Je,Jl 9-30,Ag 20-O 8,29 1909-Ap 22,My 13-Je 17,Jl 15,Ag 1910-Ja 6,20-F 1911

EXAMINER. w S 1900-Jl 1924‖
NbHi S 1901-Je 21 1924
NbO complete

Omaha EXCELSIOR. w Ja 1884-D 1921‖
NbHi Ap 2 1887;S 1891-1915;18-[21]
NbO complete

FLORENCE courier. w
P-M Jl 9 1857

FLORENCE fontanelle and Minne Lusa review. w Jl 9 1916-Mr 2 1933‖
1916-28 as Florence fontanelle
NbHi Ag 1919-[29]-32;Ja 13-F 3 1933

FLORENCE gazette. w Je 5 1903-1908‖?
1903-Jl 17 1908 as Florence items
NbHi Je 5,26,Jl 24-31,S 4-18,O 30 1903-Ja 15 1904;Je,Jl 13 1906-Jl 5,19-Ag 16,30-S 13,27, O 11-N 8,22,D 20 1907-Jl 10,24-S,O 9-23,N,D 18-25 1908

FLORENCE items. *See* Florence gazette

FLORENCE tribune. w Je 4 1909-16‖?
NbHi 1909-N 10,D 8 1916

FOLKETS nya tidning. w 1873-78‖
1873-N 23 1876 as Kansas monitoren (Topeka, Kansas) N 30 1876-D? 1876 Folkets tidning. Merged with Svenska tribunen (Chicago)
In Swedish
IRA 1877-78

FOLKETS tidning. *See* Folkets nya tidning

FREIE PRESSE und wöchentliche tribüne. w 1883-Ag 25 1926‖
1883-91? as Nebraska tribüne; 1892?-1919 Omaha tribüne (1908-My 13 1909 Nebraska tribüne und westliche presse; other variations slight) 1920-Ja 3 1923 Council Bluffs freie presse und wöchentliche tribüne
For 1895?-98? *See* Nebraska vorwärts
1920-26 also dated in Council Bluffs, Iowa
In German
IU Jl 27 1917-26
NbHi O 25 1894;My 1908-21;24-26
—d ed *See* Tägliche Omaha tribüne

GLOBE-CITIZEN. [South Omaha] 1905-13‖?
1905-Ag 6 1909 as South Omaha citizen
NbHi Mr 27 1908-Ag,D 17,31 1909-Mr 11 1910

Omaha GUIDE. w 1927+
Negro
NbHi Jl 16-23,Ag 6,S 1932+

GWIAZDA zachodu. w 1904+
Title varies: Gwiazda z zachodu
1904-15? pub in South Omaha
IU D 14 1917-Ap 15 1921
NbHi Ja 11-F,Mr 22,Ap 26-My 3,S 12-19,27-O 11,25-D 20 1918;19-Ja 2,16,30,F 13,Mr-Ap 2, 16,30-My 21,Je 4-18,Jl-D 17,31 1920[21]Mr-Ap 21,My-Je 2,16 1922+

Omaha weekly HERALD. w O 2 1865-89‖
United with Omaha weekly world to form Omaha world-herald
CtY Jl 14 1869
NbHi My 6,Ag 12,S 16 1868;F 24,Mr 17,Ap 4,Je 9,N 17,D 22 1869;My 17,S 6 1871;Je 12 1872;Ag 11 1876;N 16 1877;F 14-21,Mr 21,Je 6, O 17 1879;Ja 9,My 21,Je 25,Ag 13-O 1 1880;Ja 28,D 23 1881;Je 11 1882;Mr 30 1883;Ja 11,Je 27 1884;Jl 21,S 1 1887;Ja 12-19,Ag 12,O 17,N 28 1888
NbO O 9 1865-O 13 1869;70-87

Omaha daily HERALD. d O 7 1865-Jl 14 1889‖
Title varies slightly. United with Omaha daily world to form Omaha daily world-herald, later Omaha morning world-herald
CtY Jl 20,23 1869
DLC Mr 24 1866;My 26 1867;O 29 1878-89
MWA Ja 16,Ag 11 1872
NbHi Jl 23,Ag 18,O 7,13-16,18,23,N 7-8,D 4 1868;Ag 28,My 14,16,Je 25 1869;My 17,N 18, 20,22 1870;Mr 4 1871;My 1,Je 12,O 17,30,N 3,5,11,D 13,29 1872[Mr 1873-76]Ja 23,F 20-21, My 5,Ag 23,O 12,N 7,27 1877;Ja 9,Mr 29,My 31,Jl 26,S 4-5,12,26,O 2,N 1,16,19 1878;My 22,Je 3,6,Jl 20,S 3,O 2-3,17,20,25,N 2,21,29,D 11,13 1879[80]-[Jl 1884]-[Je 1886-87]-[89]
NbO complete
OClWHi S 23 1881

Omaha INDEPENDENT. w 1877-
NbHi S 17 1877;Ja 3 1878

INVESTIGATOR. w F 8 1906-10‖?
NbHi 1906-Mr 7 1907;Mr 26-My 14,Je 11-18 1908

Omaha ISSUE. w Ag 1907-N 5 1909‖
NbHi Ag 13,S-O 1909

JEWISH bulletin. w F 1916-23‖?
NbHi Ap 1919-Ap 1 1921

NEBRASKA (*Continued*)

OMAHA—*Continued*

JEWISH press. w D 16 1920+
NbHi 1920+

Omaha JOURNAL. w,sw F 7 1930+
sw 1933?
pub 1930—

Omaha JOURNAL of commerce. w S 1876-79||
1876-S 1878 as Omaha commercial exchange; S? 1878-Mr 17 1879 Omaha commercial exchange and journal of commerce
NbHi My 24,Jl 26,O 28-N 18,D 29 1878;Ja 20,F 3,Mr 3-17,31,Je 16 1879

Omaha daily JOURNAL-STOCKMAN. d Je 12 1886+
1886-99? as Omaha daily stockman; 1900?-23? Drovers' journal-stockman
1886-1900? pub in South Omaha
pub 1886+
DA [O 1918-22]+
IU D 18 1920-N 1 1924;Ap 1925+

KVĚTY Americké. w 1894-Je 4 1919||
1894-Jl 12 1898 as Dělnické listy; Jl 18 1898-1900? Osvěta; 1901?-Ag 1916 Osvěta-Americká
In Bohemian
KHi Je 17 1914-Ag 1916
MnHi Je 1914-Ag 1916
NbHi Ag 12 1895-Jl,S 1896-N 1899;Mr 29 1900;S 9 1903-19

Květy Americké. w N 1 1900-Jl 30 1903||
In Bohemian
NbHi complete

Omaha MERCURY. w 1879-1906||?
1879-88? as Nebraska watchman
KHi My 1883-Mr 2 1906
NbHi F 11,S 16 1882;My 10-17 1889;Ag 29 1889;Jl 10,N 20 1891-S 15,N 24 1893;94-99;Jl-N 16,D 21 1900;01-[04]-My 5,19,Je 16-D 8,22 1905;Ja 12,F 23,Mr 2-9,Ap 13,Jl 6 1906
NbO 1901-Jl 1906

MIDWEST labor news. *See* Mid-West news

MID-WEST news. w Mr 1915-24||
1915-Jl 1 1916 as Omaha unionist; Jl 8 1916-19? Unionist; 1920-F 8 1924 Midwest labor news
IU Je 24 1915-17[F 21 1921-S 22 1922]Je 29-Ag 3 1923;Je 15-O 21,N 28,D 1924
NbHi N 20,D 10 1920-O,N 28-D 1924

Omaha MONITOR. w Jl 3 1915-Ja 11 1929||
Negro
NbHi Jl-S 4 18 1915-29

NARODNI pokrok. w Ag 12 1921+
In Bohemian
pub Ag 12 1931+
NbHi 1921+

NEBRASKA banner. *See* Nebraska vorwärts

NEBRASKA democrat. [South Omaha]. d,w 1901-21||?
1901-Jl 15 1915 as Nebraska daily democrat (d)
NbHi [My 1902-03]-Ap 11,My 4 1906-[07]-[12]-Ag 14,S,O 9 1915-Ja 13,27,F 17,Mr 24-N 3,17 1917-20;Ja 15-F 19,Mr 12-Ap 9,23 1921

Omaha tri-weekly NEBRASKA republican. tw -1870||?
DLC Ja 13 1862-Je 22[Jl 1863-Ja 1864]
NbHi My 7,28,Je 13,25,Jl 11-23,Ag 13-29,S 12-17,24,O 6-8,N 17,24,D 1 1869;Ja 26 1870

NEBRASKA republican. w,d *See* Republican

NEBRASKA tax reform. w O 7 1893-95||?
NbHi O-N 11 25 1893-F 10,24 1894-My 4 1895

NEBRASKA trade journal. *See* Omaha trade exhibit

NEBRASKA tribüne. w *See* Freie presse und wöchentliche tribüne

NEBRASKA tribüne. d *See* Omaha post-tribüne

NEBRASKA vorwärts. w 1887?-98||?
Follows Omaha post? 1887?-90? as Westlicher courier; 1891?-93? Nebraska banner
In German
NbHi S 27 1894;My 23(extra)1895;Mr 19 1896-Mr 18,My 20-Je 3,17-24,Jl-S 9 1897
—d ed *See* Omaha post-tribüne

NEBRASKA watchman. *See* Omaha mercury

Omaha NEBRASKAN. *See* New Nebraskan

Omaha NEBRASKIAN. w 1855-Je 15 1865||
1855-My 27 1857 as Nebraskian
DLC 1856-O 12 1861
ICHi D 8 1858
NbHi Ja 8,13 1858;59
NbO Jl 10 1863-N 16 1864;65
NcD N 7 1855
PEHi Je 24 1857
PWCl D 29 1860

Daily Omaha NEBRASKIAN. d D 8? 1859-
DLC D 13 1859-Ja 12,S 19-N 15 1860
IaCb Ag 7,10,14 1861

NEW era. w S 1920-Ag 6 1926||
Negro
KHi Ag 21 1925
NbHi Jl 21 1922-My,Je 11,Jl-Ag 1926

NEW Nebraskan. w 1905-S 16 1920||
1905-Ag 14 1919 as Omaha Nebraskan
NbHi Ja 1,D 1914-S 9 1920

Omaha evening NEWS. d My 29 1878-Je 15 1880||
1879 as Evening news
DLC D 16 1879
NbHi Mr 11,My 24,Je 17 1879;Ap 24,My 15,20 1880
NbO complete

Omaha daily NEWS. d O 9 1899-F 13 1927||
United with Omaha bee to form Omaha bee-news
NbHi 1899-1906;Mr 1907-Jl 6,8-9,12,23 1918-[23]-27
NbO complete
NbOB complete

Omaha daily NEWS-REPUBLIC. d Mr? 1894-96||?
NbHi [Ag-D 13 1895;F 6-Mr 11 1896]

NONCONFORMIST. *See* Central farmer

NOVA doba. w,sw O 1911-18||?
w 1911-14?
In Bohemian
NbHi [My-D 6 1918]

OSVĚTA. *See* Květy Americké 1894-1919

POKROK západu. w Ag 1 1871-D 15 1920||
In Bohemian
IU Je 11-18,Jl 16 1919-My 19 1920
KHi 1915
NbHi S 15 1871;My 11 1875-My 2 1877;My 8 1878-80;N 10 1881-Ap 1883;Jl 27 1892-1905;Ja 10-17,My 30 1906-20

Omaha POST. w 1872-87||?
1875?-77? as Omaha post und beobachter; 1884?-85? Post und telegraph. Followed by Westlicher courier, later Nebraska vorwärts?
In German
MWA Ag 26 1876

Omaha POST. d 1897-99||?
In German
—evening ed *See* Omaha post-tribüne

Omaha POSTEN. w 1886+
1886-Ja 1892 as Svenska tribun; F- 1892? Svenska journalen-tribunen; 1892?-1908? Svenska journalen
In Swedish
pub 1886+
IRA S 9 1914+
MnHi Ap 1897-O 7 1904
NbHi F 1892-[96]+

Omaha POST-TRIBÜNE. d 1881?-99||?
1881?-91? as Nebraska tribüne; 1892?-93 Tägliche Omaha tribüne
Suspended from 1893-98?
In German
NbHi [Mr-D 1892]
NbOT [1881-93]
—w ed *See* Nebraska vörwarts; Freie presse. . .
—morning ed *See* Omaha post

PROGRESS. w 1889-1904||?
Negro
DLC Ja 26 1900
NbHi Mr 22,N 29 1890;Mr 7 1891

Omaha weekly REPUBLICAN. w My 12 1858-91||?
1858-Mr? 1864 as Nebraska republican
DLC [1861;64-65]
MWA O 20 1858
NbHi N 9,23 1859-Mr 21,Ap-My 23,Je 20-S,O 10-24,N 7 1860;My 6,Jl 8,Ag 12,S 16 1868;D 6,27 1873;My 9,Je 20,O 17,31,N 28-D 5,21 1874 [75-77]-S 1881,O 20,N 3,D 1,15-22 1882;Ja 12,F 2,16,Mr 2,D 7 1883;My 23,D 18 1884;Ap 28-My 5,Jl 19 1889
NbO Ap 8 1864-O 19,N-D 21 1883

Omaha REPUBLICAN. d 1858-Je 30 1890||
1858-64 as Daily Nebraska republican
CtY Jl 23 1869
DLC Ja 22 1864;O 10 1865-O 1866;F 4-N 8 1873;Jl 12 1874-90
ICHi Ja 14,F 4 1868
ICM O 10 1881
MWA F 24,S 24 1869;S 26 1875;Ag 8 1876;O 31 1888
NbHi S 18,26,O 9,14-15,22,N 6-7,D 3,18,23 1868;Ja 10,Ap 15,My 30,Ag 25,O 13 1869;Mr 7,20,My 8,14,Je 17,20-22,24-25,Jl 2,O 14,D 20 1873;S 3,D 9-13 15-18,23-24 1874;S 7 1875[Ap-D 1876]Ja 3,9,12,14,18-19,27,F 14,20-21,Ap 20,O 12,19,D 19 1877;Ap 2,My 18,Je 20,Jl 7,25,S 21,N 4,28,D 14,17 1878;F 27,My 20,Jl 2,Ag 30,S 5,7,O 2,D 1 1879;Ja 21-22,F 14,20,Mr 13,Ap 10-11,13-1880-[81]-88[Ap 1889-90]
NbO My 17 1861;Ja 1 1875;D 2-31 1876;F 1878-Je,S 1886-90
—tw ed *See* Omaha tri-weekly Nebraska republican

Evening REPUBLICAN and evening dispatch. w D? 1887-D 30 1889||
1887-N 23 1889 as Omaha dispatch; N 25-29 1889 Evening republican and Omaha dispatch
NbHi O 27 1888-[Ja-N 1889]

ROZHLEDY. w 1914-19||?
In Bohemian
IU 1918-O 23 1919

SOCIALIST herald. m,w Ja 1907-S 30 1908||
m Ja-S 1907
NbHi complete

SOUTH OMAHA citizen. *See* Globe-citizen

SOUTH OMAHA daily sun. d N 27 1895-My 15? 1901||
Merged with South Omaha daily times
NbHi N 30,D 3-4,7 1895[Ap 4 1896-Je 2 1898;99-1900]Ja 2,18,22,28-30,Ap 20,22-27,29-30,My 9-11,14-15 1901

SOUTH OMAHA sun. w,tw,sw 1921+
w 1921-23?;tw 1924-F 12 1932
NbHi F 13 1925-[Je-S 22 1926]-[32-Jl 12 1933] F 27,Ap 5,10-12,17,24-26,My 1934-Ja 4 1935

SOUTH OMAHA daily times. d 1900-02||
Merged with Nebraska daily democrat, later Nebraska democrat
NbHi D 22,24,26-29 1900[My-D 1901]-D 30 1902

SOUTH OMAHA wasp. w Ag 1897-99||
NbHi Ja 29,F 12-19,Mr 5-12,Ap 9-My,Je 11-S 3,17-24,O 8-29,N 12 1898-Mr 6,Ap 10-My 8,25-Je 16,30 1899

La STAMPA. *See* Italian press (Kansas City, Mo)

Omaha daily STOCKMAN. [South Omaha] *See* Omaha daily journal-stockman

SVENSKA journalen. w Ja 3 1889-Ja 28 1892||
United with Omaha Svenska tribun to form Svenska journalen-tribunen, later Omaha posten
In Swedish
IRA 1890
NbHi O 24-31,N 19-26 1891;Ja 7,21-28 1892

SVENSKA journalen-tribunen. *See* Omaha posten

SVENSKA posten. w Ja 1881-95||?
In Swedish
NbHi D 9,23 1893-Ja 20,F 17-Mr 3,31,Ap 21,My 15,Ag 7-14,28-S 4 1894

SVENSKA pressen. w 1903-06||
Merged with Minneapolis veckoblad (Minneapolis, Minn.)
In Swedish
IRA complete

SVENSKA tribun. *See* Omaha posten

SVENSKA veckobladet. w
In Swedish
IRA 1890-91

TÄGLICHE. . . *See under* next important word: e.g., Tägliche Omaha tribüne is alphabeted as Tribüne

Daily TELEGRAM. d F? -Ag 7 1861||
Dated also in Council Bluffs, Ia.
IaCb F 22-Ag 5 1861
NbO Mr 2-Ap 10,Je 10-Jl 27 1861

Omaha TELEGRAPH. w 1880-83||?
United with Omaha post to form Post und telegraph, later Omaha post
In German

Omaha TIMES. w 1857-
DLC [1858-Mr 1859]
NbHi Je 10-Jl,Ag 26,S 23-O 21,N 25 1857;Mr 9 1858
NbO Je 11 1857-Mr 24 1859

Omaha evening TIMES. d N 1868-69||?
NbHi D 10-11,14,16,21,29-31 1868;Ja 2,15,20,F 5,Mr 1,12 1869

Omaha evening TIMES. d
NbHi O 15-27,N 1884-Ja 10 1885

Omaha TRADE exhibit. w,m S 1890-Ag 1927||
1890-F 15 1896 as Nebraska trade journal
w 1890-Ap 1927
NN Je 20,Jl 4,Ag 15-22 1908;O 30,N 13-D 4 1909;F 5-12,Ag 6 1910
NbHi N 24 1893-Ja 12,26,F 9-My 4,18-Je 8 1894;S 21,N 2,23,D 7 1895;Ja 11,F 15 1896-Ja 9,23-30,F 13-27,Mr 13,Ap-N 13 1897;My 20 1899;1908-Je,Jl 29,Ag 19 1922-27

TRAIN ligue. w N 25- 1871||?
MWA N-D 9 1871
MiU-C N 25 1871

Tägliche Omaha TRIBÜNE. 1892-93 *See* Omaha post-tribüne

Tägliche Omaha TRIBÜNE. d,tw Mr 14 1912+
tw Ag 31 1926-Ja 15 1928
In German
pub [1912+]
IU S 1926-Ap 22 1928
NbHi Mr 14 1912;My 22 1915+
—w ed *See* Freie presse. . .

Omaha TRIBUNE. d Jl 20 1870-Je 1871||
Merged with Omaha republican
NbHi Ja 19,Mr 6 1871

Omaha weekly TRIBUNE. w Jl 20 1870-Je 10 1871||
Merged with Omaha republican
NbO Ag 1870-71

Daily TRIBUNE. [South Omaha] d 1890-My 21 1902||
Merged with South Omaha daily times
NbHi Ja 2,4-8[My 1896-98]-[1900]-My 21 1901

TRUE populist. w F 1 1900-02||?
ICJ F-N 1 1900
NbHi F-Mr 22,Ap-N 1,29-D 6 1900

Omaha daily UNION. d 1873?-74||?
NbO Ja 15-O 22 1874

Omaha daily UNION. 1883 *See* Omaha evening dispatch

UNIONIST. *See* Mid-West news

VÄKTAREN w Ag 20- 1868||
In Swedish
IRA O 1-8 1868
NbHi Ag 20 1868

VESTERNS svenska tribun. w Ag 2 1899-1904||?
1899-1902 as Lincoln svenska tribun (Lincoln)
IRA Ja 22 1902
NbHi Ap 10 1901-Ja,Ap 2,My 14-28,Jl 23-30,Ap 27 1902-Mr 16 1904

VIKINGEN. w 1894-1905||
Dated also in Moline, Ill.
In Swedish
IRA 1894-1905
MnHi F 8 1899-D 20 1900

WELT-POST. *See under* Lincoln

WESTLICHER courier. *See* Nebraska vorwärts

WESTRA posten. w 1879-83||
In Swedish
IRA 1880-83

NEBRASKA (*Continued*)

OMAHA—*Continued*

Omaha WORLD-HERALD. d Ag 24 1885+
1885-Je 12 1889 as Omaha daily world (other variations slight)
pub 1885+
CtW Ag 10 1891
DLC 1889+
ICU Je 1935+
IaSc current 6 months
KHi Ag 11-D 7 1896
MWA S 7 1885
Nb Mr 1891-Mr,Jl 1899-S 1904;05
NbHi Ja 18,Je 12,18,S 9,12-13,15,O 12 1887;Ja 1,18 1888;My 6,Je 10,12,O 5 1889[90-91]-[93]-[1903]+
NbO 1885+
NdHi D 29 1909-10
OClWHi Je 12 1891

Omaha WORLD-HERALD. w,sw F 1887-1910‖?
1887-89 as Omaha weekly world
w 1887-98?
IaHi F 1895-F 1896
NbHi Mr 13,Ap 17,My 15-Jl 17,O 9 1889;F 19 1890;Ap 8 1891;Mr 16,N 16 1892;My 24 1893 [Mr 1895-97]Ja 14-21,F 1-4,18-25,Mr 1-8,22-25, Ap 26,N 25 1898

O'NEILL

ALLIANCE tribune. w 1883-94‖?
1883-My 1890 as O'Neill tribune
NbHi Je 9,Jl 7,28-Ag 11,25,O 13,N 3,D 8-15 1887;Ja 12-19,F,Mr 8,29-Ap 5,26-Ag 23,S 6,O 4,N 15-22 1888;F 7,28-Mr 21,Ap 4,18-My,Ag 1,15-22,S 19-N 14,D 12 1889;Ja 9,Mr 20,Ap 3,D 19 1890;Ag 7-14 1891;O 21 1892

BEACON light. *See* Holt county independent 1892+

FRONTIER. w Jl 29 1880+
pub Jl 22 1886+
NbHi S 30 1880;Ja 13,Ap 21,My 12-19,Je 2,Ag 18-25,S 22,O 6,D 1,29 1881-Ja 5,26-F,Mr 9-My 4,18,Je-N,D 14 1882-[83]-F,S,O 30 1884;Ap 2 1885;Ag 4 1887;Mr 15,N 22,D 19 1888;Ja 3,Mr 14,Je 13,D 6 1889;S 14 1890;Je 30,S 15,29,N 24 1892;S 1895-[1900-01]

HOLT county banner. w Mr 14 1882-84‖
Merged with Frontier
NbHi Ap 25,Je 13 1882;Ja 23,Jl 31,S 11,26,O 23,N 13,D 25 1883;Ja 22 1884
NbOnF 1883-F 26 1884

HOLT county independent. w My 1892-Ja 1895‖?
United with Beacon light to form Beacon light and Holt county independent, later Holt county independent
NbHi D 2-9 1892

HOLT county independent. w 1892+
1892-Ja 1895? as Beacon light; F? 1895-Ja 11 1897 Beacon light and Holt county independent
pub Jl 5,27 1895;Ja 15 1904+
NbHi F 1,15,O 18-N 1,D 1895[Ja-Ag 1896;F-S 1897]-Jl 1903;05+

HOLT county record. w Je 2 1879-82‖
1880 as Holt record
NbHi Je 16 1879;Ap 12,Je 28 1880;Je 18,Jl 23 1881

HOLT record. *See* Holt county record

O'Neill SUN. w My 8 1890-97‖?
NbHi Jl 28 1892;Ag 15 1895-97
NbOnH 1890-Ap 25 1895

O'Neill TRIBUNE. *See* Alliance tribune

ORCHARD

Orchard NEWS. w N 1902+
pub 1902+
NbHi Ag 20,S 10 1903;My 17,31-Ag 14,D 1 1904;Mr 16-23,Ap 13,My 11 1905;Ja 18,Ag 9,S 27 1906;Mr 8,29,My 10-17,Ag 16 1907;08-[12-14]+

ORD

Ord JOURNAL. w,sw 1887?-D 27 1928‖
My 1898-Ap 7 1899 as Ord semi-weekly journal (sw) Merged with Ord quiz
NbHi Je 17 1892;Ja 3,S 27,O 4,18 1895-[96-98]-1928
NbOrQ Ja-Ap 19 1917;20;S 11 1924-S 3 1925;S 9 1926-28

Ord OBSERVER. w D 18 1930-Mr 10 1932‖
NbHi D 18 1930;31-32
NbOrQ complete

Ord QUIZ. w Ap 6 1882+
pub 1882[83]-86;89-90;92-93;Ja 12,Mr 9,D 14 1894-[99]-1901;Ja,F 15,D 31 1903-[17]-[22]Ap 5 1923;24;Ap 11 1925;26+
NbHi F 27,Ap 3,N 21 1885;Je 10,O 7 1892;S 1895-[1905]+

VALLEY county journal. w 1879-87‖?
NbHi Je 24,Jl 29,Ag 12,S 2-9,O 7 1881;F 8,S 5,19 1884;Mr 10 1886

VALLEY county times. w My 14 1897-1902‖?
NbHi [1897]-[1900-01]

ORLEANS

Orleans CHRONICLE. w 1889+
1889-98? as Southwest Nebraska courier; 1899?-Jl? 1906 Orleans courier; My 21 1914-S 14 1916 Shields' Orleans isser
pub 1919+
NbHi Je 10 1897;Ja 20-27,F 17-Ap 7 1898[My 1901-Je 1903]-Jl 20 1906;S 27-D 6 1907;Mr 27 1908+

Orleans COURIER. *See* Orleans chronicle

Orleans PROGRESS. w 1894-98‖?
NbHi O 25-N 8,22-D 13,27 1895;F 7-14,Ap 24, My 15,Je 5,Jl 24-Ag 21,S 11-O 23,N 1896-Ja, F 26-Ap 2,16-Je 4,18-25,Jl 9-30,Ag 13,S 3,17, O,N 12-19,D 17-24 1897;Ja 14-Jl 1 1898

SHIELDS' Orleans isser. *See* Orleans chronicle

SOUTHWEST Nebraska courier. *See* Orleans chronicle

ORVILLE CITY

HAMILTON county news. *See* Aurora news (Aurora)

Osceola HOMESTEADER. *See* Osceola record

POLK county democrat. w 1888+
NbHi O 24,N 14 1895-[96-97]F 3,My 12,26-Je, Jl 14,Ag 11,O 27-D 1 1898;Ap 18-25,My 9-16, 30-Jl,Ag 29-S 5,26-D 19 1901;02-17;F 14 1918-F 4,Ap 1,Je 24,Jl 8 1926+

POLK county independent. *See* Polk county republican

POLK county republican. w Ap 1 1892-My 15 1902‖
1892-D 13 1900 as Polk county independent. Merged with Osceola record
NbHi Ja 12 1893;Ap 4,Ag 22 1895;Ja 22,F 20-27,Mr 26,Ap 2,16,My 14,28,Je 16,Jl 2,16,Ag 13, D 24 1896;My 12,O 27-D 1 1898;Ap 6 1899; Ap-S 13,27-N 22,D 1900;Ap 25,My 16-Je,Jl 25, Ag 8-22,S 12-N,D 12-26 1901;Ja 16-23,F 20-27, Mr 13,27-My 1 1902

Osceola RECORD. w 1873+
1873-Ja? 1876 as Osceola homesteader
NbHi [1880]-Ja 20,F 10,Mr 3,17-24,Ap 21,My 12-19 1881;Ja 26,Mr 23,Ap 6,20,Je 1-8 1882;N 8 1894;Ja 10-17,Ap 4,N 21-D 12,26 1895[96]-[98]-[1900-02]Ap 20-My 18,Je-Jl 20,Ag 17,S 14,28 1905;Ap 11,25-My 9,Jl 4-11 1907;Mr 19-O 18,29 1908-My 11,25-Ag 10 1911;16-17;Je 5-12,26,O 2,30-D 11,25 1919+

OSHKOSH

GARDEN county news. w Ja 3 1909+
1909-Ja 22 1910 as Deuel county news
1909-S 12 1913 pub in Lewellen
pub 1913+
NbHi Jl 3-10,24-O 2,D 25 1909-Ja 1,29 1910+

Oshkosh HERALD. w My 1905-F 20 1919‖
NbHi Ag 28-S 11,25,N 6-20,N 27-D 18 1908;09 [10-11]-[17]-F 6,20 1919

WEST NEBRASKA beacon. w F 1 1929+
1929-N 1931 pub in Lewellen
pub 1929+
NbHi 1929+

OSMOND

Osmond REPUBLICAN. w N 1891+
pub 1904+
NbHi D 8 1892;O 10,24,N 28-D 12,26 1895[96-N 4 1897]Ja 6,20,Mr 31-Ap,My 12 1898;F 2, Mr 30,Ap 27,My 18,Jl 13-Ag 10,S 14,O 26,D 28 1899-Ja 4,18-25,F 15,Mr 29,Ap 26,Je 14,S 20,D 13-27 1900;Ap 25-My 2,16,Je 13,27,O 24, N 7,D 12 1901;F 13,Mr 27-Ap 10,My 15,Je 19,Jl 10,24,Ag 7 1902;S 26-O,N 14,28-D 5,19 1907-[08-09]+

OTOE

To S 1918 as Berlin

Otoe weekly TIMES. w N 1915-21‖?
1915-S 3 1918 as Berlin weekly times
NbHi Ja 15 1918-S 1921

OVERTON

ALFALFA herald. *See* Overton herald

Overton HERALD. w Je 23 1900+
1900-Jl 29 1904 as Alfalfa herald
pub [1900+]
NbHi [My 1902-O 1904]-[16-17]+

OXFORD

Oxford STANDARD. w 1887+
Suspended from S 1920-Mr 10 1921
pub Ag 1920+
NbHi Je 23 1892;Ap 30-My 7,21,Je 11,Jl 16-23,Ag,S 10,24-O 22,N 5,D 24 1896-Ja 21,F-Mr 5,Ap 30,My 21,Jl 9,Ag 27 1897;Mr 11,O 6,20-27,N 24-D 8,22-29 1898;Jl 20 1899;Ag 8-S 5,N 14-28 1902;Ag 27-O 22,N,D 10 1908-Mr,Ap 14-S 1910;Jl 2 1914;18-Ag 1920;Mr 10 1921+

PAGE

Page REPORTER. w N 7 1902+
pub 1902+
NbHi Ja 2 1903;Ja 8 1904;Mr 31,D 15 1905;F 2 1906;Jl 2 1914

PALISADE

FRENCHMAN VALLEY times. w S 1888-N 26 1896‖
NbHi O 24-N,D 12 1895-Ja 9,23,F 13,27,Mr 12,Ap 2,16-30,My 14-Je 11,Jl 16,30-Ag 20,S 3-17,O 1-22,N 5-26 1896

Palisade PRESS. w S 4 1897-1901‖?
NbHi S-N 13,27,D 11 1897;Ja 8,22 1898;Ag 11-D 8 1900;F 9,23,Mr 9-16,30,Ap 13-27,My 11-18,S 26,N 7-14 1901

Palisade TIMES. w F 26 1909+
NbHi F 26,My 1909-21;24+

PALMER

Palmer JOURNAL. w Je 29 1911+
pub [1918-19]+
NbHi Je 1914-Ja 1,F 5-19,Mr-Ag 19,S-D 23 1920;21+

PALMYRA

Palmyra ITEMS. w 1887+
pub 1925+
NbHi Ag 23 1895-1902;F 1903-F 5,19-Ap 8 1904;Mr 20,Je 20,Jl 3,Ag 21 1908-My 16 1913

PANAMA

Panama RECORD. w O 29 1913-15‖?
NbHi 1913-Mr 4,18,My-D 16 1915

PAPILLION

SARPY county herald. w F 18 1898-1901‖?
NbHi Ap 14,My 12,26,Je 16-30,Jl 21-Ag 11,O 27-N 1898;N 16-30,D 14-21 1899;Ja 18-My,Je 21-Ag 23,S-O 18,N 1 1900

SARPY county republican. w Ap 1906-11‖?
NbHi 1908-F 17 1910;Ag 24 1911

Papillion TIMES. w 1874+
NbHi D 10 1874;Ag 26 1875;Ap 28 1881;Ag 8 1884;Je 24,Jl 15 1892;O 10,24-31,N 21-D 1895; Ja 23,Ap 23-My 14,Jl 16-Ag 6,S 3-10,24 1896-F 18,Mr-Ag 12,26-N 18,D 2,16 1897-[98]Ja 26-F 2,Mr 23,Ap 27-My 11,Je 1,15,29,Jl 13-Ag 10,24 1899-F 2,My 25 1922+

PAWNEE CITY

Pawnee CHIEF. w 1900+
pub 1903+
NbHi Ap 18-25,My 9-Ag 1,15,29-S 12,26-O 17, N-D 12 1901;Ja 16-23,F 6,My 1902+

ENTERPRISE. *See* Pawnee press

Pawnee City INDEPENDENT. w 1894-F 1896‖
NbHi Je 1 1894;Ja 18,Ag 23,S 27 1895-F 14 1896

Pawnee PRESS. w,sw 1877-1908‖
1877-O 17 1883 as Enterprise. One page as Steinauer press
sw Mr 1896-N 1903
NbHi My 15-Ag 21,O 23-30 1878;Ja 8,Mr 12-Ap 23,My 7-14,Je 11,25-Ag 20,S 3,17 1879-Ag 11,S 22,O 13-N 22 1880;Ja-Mr 16,30,Ap 13-Jl, Ag 10-O 5,19-D 21 1881;Ja 4,18-25,F 15-22, Mr 8,22-My,Je 14-D 20 1882;83-F 15 1888;N 23 1892;N-D 1894;Ja 16-F 6,20 1895-[97-98]-Jl 24 1908

Evening daily PRESS. d 1895?-96‖?
NbHi Ag 15 1895-[Ja-F 1896]

Pawnee REPUBLICAN. w 1868+
pub 1882+
IaDH D 28 1876
NbHi N 6,20,D 1884;Ja 8-Ap 2,16-Je 4,N 6,20 1885;Ap 14 1887;My 26 1892;Ag 15-D 19 1895; 96-My 1906;Ja 16-23,F 13,Mr 12-S,O 8,22 1908+

Daily REPUBLICAN. d Je 11- 1894‖?
NbHi Je 11,15-16,20,22,26-27,29,Jl 7,19-21,23, 25-28,31-N 3,5-10 1894

PAXTON

Paxton TIMES. w O 1 1920+
pub Jl 1923+
NbHi Je 20,Jl 11 1924+

PENDER

LOGAN VALLEY times. *See* Pender times

NEW ERA. w Ja 16 1901-03‖?
NbPR Ja 16 1901-Mr 25 1903

Pender REPUBLIC. w O 30 1889+
1889-92 as Thurston county republican; 1892-F 18 1898 Thurston republic
pub 1889+
NbHi Ag 16-23,S 13-O 11,25-N 1,15,D 20 1895; My 1,29-Je 5,19-26,Jl 17-24,Ag 28-S 18,O 2, N 13 1896-[97]-F 11,25-Mr 11,25-My,D 2-23 1898;99+

THURSTON county republican. *See* Pender republic

Pender TIMES. w 1886+
1886-Ja 20? 1899 as Logan Valley times
pub [1886-89]+
NbHi Ja 27-F 3,Mr 24-31,Ap 14-28,My 12,26-Ag 18,S 1,15,N 17 1899;Ja,Mr 2-9,Ap 20-My, Je 22-Jl,Ag 17,S-O 19,N 2,16,30-D 1900;Ja 25,Ap 19-My 3,17 1901+

PERU

Peru ENTERPRISE 1897-98 *See* Peru pointer

Peru ENTERPRISE. w O 4 1934+
NbHi O-N 1934;Ja 24,F 21,Mr 7,Ap-Jl 18,Ag-O 17,31 1935+

Peru POINTER. w Ag 1897+
1897-98 as Peru enterprise
pub 1897+
NbHi Jl 30-Ag 13,27-S 10,24-O 1,22-D 3,17 1897-Ja 7,21,F 4-11,25,Mr 11,25-Ap 1,15,My 6-13,27,Jl 8 1898;Ja 27,F 10-17,Mr 24-Ap 14, My 5-12,26-Je,Jl 21-S,O 13-N 17,D 1899-[1902]+

Peru TIMES. w N 1893-97‖?
NbHi D 7 1894;N 16-22,D 20 1895;My 15,Je 5,Ag 7 1896

NEBRASKA (*Continued*)

PETERSBURG

Petersburg INDEX. w 1887+
1887-93? as Petersburg press
NbHi S 8,O 20,D 1-8 1892;O 24 1895;F 20-My 21,Je 18,Jl 23-30,D 10,24 1896;Ja 7-14,28-F 11,25-Jl 8,29,Ag 26,S 23,O 14 1897-F 16 1899;N 1 1900;Ap 4 1901;Ja 16,30-F 6,Mr 13-My 8,Je 19-Jl 17,Ag 7,S 4-18 1902;Ja 7,Mr 17 1904;D 21 1905;F 22 1906;Je 6 1907;S 1911-Jl 1918;F 21-S 5,26 1919-[24]-[27-33]-Ja 12,26-Mr 20,Ag, O 1934—

Petersburg PRESS. *See* Petersburg index

PIERCE

PIERCE county call. w O 6 1877+
pub [1877;84-87]+
NbHi Je 4,18 1878;Ap 28 1880;Ag 5 1881;F 23 1883;S 5-12,O 3-10,24-N 14,D 5-12,26 1884[85]-F,My 7 1886;N 17-24 1887;Ja 25,Ap 19,Ag 23, S 20,O 4,N 1,22 1889;F 7 1890;S 2,23,D 2 1892;Ja 13 1893;O 11,25-N 1,15-29,D 13-27 1895[F-D 1896]97;Ja 28-My 1898;Ja 27,F 17, Mr 24-S 8,O 6 1899[1900]Ap 19 1901-17;20-28;30+

PIERCE county leader. w Jl 1889+
pub [1889-1913]+
NbHi Jl 22 1890;S 9 1892;Ag 16 1895-[96]-[1901-02]F 27,Je 26 1903;Je 13 1907;S-O 1908; My 6-20,O 14 1909-Ap,My 9-N 7 1918;Ap 9-16,My 28-N 19,D 1925+

PILGER

Pilger HERALD. *See* Stanton county news

STANTON county news. w 1901+
1901-30 as Pilger herald
pub Jl 15 1925+
NbHi S 20,N 1901-F 6 1903

PLAINVIEW

Plainview GAZETTE. *See* Plainview republican

Plainview NEWS. w S 1892+
NbHi S 6-13,27-O 18,N-D 6,20 1895-[96;98-99]-F,Mr 23-Ap 13,27-Je 15,29,N 2 1900;Mr 16,F 18 1905;Ap 30,O 22-29 1908;Ag 26 1909-17;19+

Plainview REPUBLICAN. w 1884-Mr 13 1919||
1884-99 as Plainview gazette
NbHi S 29 1887;Ja 31 1889;My 15,Je 12 1890 [91-94]-N 1899[1900-O 1902]Ap 24 1903;F 18 1905;O 22-29 1908;My 20-Jl 8 1909;My 28-Ag 6,20 1914-Ap 1,15-My 13,27-Jl 8,22-S 23 1915; D 27 1917;Ja 10-17,31-Mr 8,21-N,D 19 1918-Ja 16,30-Mr 1919

PLATTE CENTER

Platte Center ARGUS. *See* Platte county argus (Columbus)

Platte Center SIGNAL. w 1893-Jl 26 1923||
NbHi O 25-D 1895;Ap 17-My 1,15,Je 26,Jl 24-Ag 21,S 4-11,25,O 16-23,N 1896-Ja,F 12-Jl 2, 16,30,Ag 13,27,S 10-O 1,15,N 19-26,D 10,24 1897-Ja 14,F 4,18-25,Mr 18-25,Ap 15-22,My 20-Jl 1,15-Ag 12 1898;1908-21;Ja 13-Ag 18,S, N 3-10,D 1,15 1922;Ja 11-Jl 1923

PLATTSMOUTH

CASS county democrat. sw,w Mr 17 1898-1902||?
1898-1900 as Plattsmouth post (sw)
NbHi D 21 1900;Je 7-21,Jl 19-Ag 2,16-O 4,18-N 15,29,D 20 1901;Ja-F,Mr 21-My 2,16-23,Je 27-Jl 18,Ag 1-15,S 5-12 1902

CASS county sentinel. w F 1858-O 28 1865||
NbHi Mr 17 1859

CASS county tribune. w Je 1895-97||?
NbHi O 11 1895;O 9-23,N 6-20 1896;Ja 15-22,F 19-26,Mr 12-19,Ap 9 1897
—d ed *See* Plattsmouth daily tribune

Plattsmouth weekly HERALD. w Ap 10 1864-94||
1864-Jl 1882 as Nebraska herald. United with Semi-weekly news to form Plattsmouth news-herald
NbHi Ap 19-Je,Jl 12 1865-F 1872;F 27,Ap 10, My 8,Jl 24-31,Ag 14,28 1873;Jl 6 1876;Mr 8 1877;S 1891-Ap 13 1893
NbO Ap 1870-Mr 1882

Plattsmouth HERALD. d 1887-92||?
NbHi S 1891-92

Plattsmouth daily JOURNAL. d N 5 1881+
Suspended from 1900?-04?
NbHi D 31 1884;Ja 3 1885;92[93]Jl 2,Ag 19,21, 27,30-S 1,4,O 1,3,5,D 4,8 1897;Ja 3,7,17,31,F 3,5,8,10,12,Mr 30,My 11-13,23-26,28,Je 3-4,6-7, 10,14-18 1898

Plattsmouth JOURNAL. w,sw 1881+
w 1881-1906?
pub 1902+
NbHi 1894-My 1896;Ap 16 1897;Je 24-Jl 23,Ag 6,O 19,26,N 5-26 1898;Ap 8-12 1899;Ap 19, 26,My 10,17,31-Ag 2,S 20,O 4-18,N 8-22,D 1901-Ja 3,17-24 1902;09+

NEBRASKA herald. *See* Plattsmouth weekly herald

Evening NEWS. d 1891-D 7 1908||
NbHi D 14 1892;Ag 16 1895-[98]-[1901-08]

Plattsmouth NEWS-HERALD. sw,w 1892-N 15 1912||
1892-94 as Semi-weekly news; 1895-Ja 11 1909 Semi-weekly news-herald. Merged with Plattsmouth journal
sw 1892-1910
NbHi D 14 1892[96-97;My 1899-1900]D 17-21, 28 1908;09[10]-Ja 20,F-My 19,Ag 4-11,S 29,O 1911-Ap 12,26-Jl 6,19-N 1,15 1912

Daily POST. d Mr 12 1898-1900||?
NbHi Mr 12,19,22,Ap 1-2,4,9,13,18-21,25-30,My 4,6-7,9-10,12-14,17,19,21,23,26-27 1898[99-1900]

Plattsmouth POST. sw *See* Cass county democrat

Plattsmouth daily TRIBUNE. d 1895-96||?
NbHi S 4,O 1,3,5,N 12-15,21,25-26,28,D 4,8,13 18-20,27 1895[F 5-S 18 1896]
—w ed *See* Cass county tribune

Plattsmouth TRIBUNE. w 1898-1904||
NbHi Ja 27,Mr 24-31,Ap 14-My 5,26-Je 16,Jl 7-14,28-Ag 4,S 15-O 13,N 3,24-D 8,29 1899;Ja 12,26-F 2,Mr-Ap 13,27-My 4,18-Je 2,Jl,Ag 10, S 7-14,28-O 19,N-D 14,28 1900;Ja 25,Ap 26-My 3,17-Ag 16,30,S 20-O 4,18,N-D 13,27 1901; Ja-F 7,21-28,Mr 21-My 16,Je 13,27,Jl 11-18,Ag 8-O 24,N 14-D 19 1902;03-Ja 8 1904

PLEASANT DALE

Pleasant Dale QUIZ. w Jl 11 1890-1902||?
NbHi 1891-[94-95]Ja 11,25,F 8-My,Je 13-20,Jl 4-18,Ag-S 5,26,O 31,N 14,D 5,19 1896-[98]Ja 14,F 18,My 27,Ag-N,D 9-30 1899;F 17,Mr 10, 24,Ag 21 1900

PLEASANT HILL

Pleasant Hill NEWS. w Ag 1873-Jl 22 1876||
NbHi Ja 15,F 12,Mr 4-18,Ap 1-22,My 6-20,Je 3-17,Jl 1,15-22 1876

PLUM CREEK. *See* LEXINGTON

PLYMOUTH

Plymouth ENTERPRISE. *See* Plymouth news

Plymouth NEWS. w Je 8 1893+
1893-95 as Plymouth enterprise
pub [1893-1919]+
NbHi Je 15 1893;O 25-D 6,20 1895[F 28-D 1896]-Jl 10,31,Ag 14,28,S 11-D 4,18 1897-My 7,28,O 8,D 31 1898-[1902]+

POLK

Polk PROGRESS. w Mr 17 1907+
pub [1907-15]+
NbHi Ag 19,S 30-D 23 1909;Ja-F,Mr 17,31,Ap 14-My 19,Je 2-16,Jl-D 8,22-29 1910

PONCA

DIXON county advocate. w Ag 1915-29|
NbHi D 27 1917-Ja 9,23-F 20,Mr-Je 12,26,Jl 31,S-N 13,27 1919-28

DIXON county leader. w Jl 12 1894-Mr 13 1913||
United with Northern Nebraska journal to form Nebraska journal-leader
NbHi N 26-D 11 1895;F 19-Ap 22,My 6-13,Je 4,Jl 1,22-Ag 5 1896;Ap 24-Jl 3,17-S 11,25-O 23,N-D 1901;Ja 15-F 5 1902;Ap 30 1908-11

Ponca GAZETTE. *See* Ponca grit

Ponca GRIT. w Ag 1890-1901||?
1890-Ap 12 1900 as Ponca gazette
NbHi Jl 21-28 1892;Ag 15 1895-Mr 19,Ap 2,23-30,My 14 1896-My 12,26,D 8 1898-Mr,Ap 12,26, My 10-17,31 Je 14-Jl 12,Ag 2,16-30 1900

NEBRASKA journal-leader. w,sw Ja 16 1873+
1873-Mr 13 1913 as Northern Nebraska journal
pub 1885+
NbHi O 24-31,N 14 1895[96]-Ag 6,S-O 1 1908; F 11-Ag 5,12-O 14,28 1909-F,Mr 13-Ap 3,24-My 15,Je 1913+
NbWnH 1880-D 17 1891

NORTHERN Nebraska journal. *See* Nebraska journal-leader

POTTER

Potter REVIEW. w Mr 1912+
pub 1912+
NbHi Je 1914-S,N 12 1926-D 13 1929;30—

PRIMROSE

Primrose PRESS. w 1911+
pub 1911+

Primrose RECORD. w Mr 1904-10||?
NbHi My-O 9 23 1908-Ap,My 14-S 10,O 29-N 5 1909

RAGAN

Ragan JOURNAL. w 1906+
pub Ag 1927+

Ragan weekly NEWS. w Jl 1893-1903||?
NbHi S 27,O 13,N 1,15-29,D 13 1895-[96-99]-Mr,Ap 14 1899-[1900-01]Ja 24-31,F 14-28,Mr 14-Ap 18,My 2,16-23,Je 6-20,Jl-Ag 1,S 5-19 1902

RANDOLPH

Randolph ENTERPRISE. w 1907-N 1914||
United with Randolph times to form Randolph times-enterprise

Randolph RECORD. w 1893-Ap 23 1897||
United with Randolph reporter to form Randolph reporter and record, later Randolph reporter

Randolph REPORTER. w sw Ap 1893-1909||?
Ap 30 1897-Ap 1898 as Randolph reporter and record
sw Ja 22-N 18 1904
NbHi O 11,25-N 8,28-D 1895;Ja 23,F 6-13,Ap 20-My,Je 11 1896-Ja 21,F-Ap 15,30-O 22,N 1897-N 1898;Ja 28-F 3,Mr 24,Ap-Jl 22,Ag 5-11,S 1,15-D 16,30 1899-1900;Ja 26,Ap 26-D 20 1901[02-N 1903;04]-05;Ja 12,26-Mr 23 1906;D 10 1908-My 6 1909

Randolph TIMES-ENTERPRISE. sw,w Jl 1888+
1888-N 1914 as Randolph times
sw Je 23-Ag 31 1896
pub 1915+
NbHi O 11,25-D 1895;Ja 24-F 14,Je,Jl 17-O 22, N 1896-[97]-Ap 22,My 1898[99-1901;My 1902-03]Ja 1,F 12,26-Mr 4,Ap 1-8,22,My 6 1904;N 25 1909+
NbR 1925+

RAVENNA

Ravenna NEWS. w 1886+
pub 1886+
NbHi Je 23 1892;N-D 6,20 1895-[96-97]-My 1898[Mr 1899-S 19 1902]Mr 20,Ap 3-17,My 15 1908-21;24+
NbRa F 1921+

RAYMOND

Raymond REVIEW. w 1891-Ap 1934||
Merged with Lancaster county weekly (Lincoln)
NbHi Jl 21 1892;N 2-9,D 14-21 1895[96-98]D 21 1901-Ja 4,18-D 1902;Mr 21 1908-Ap 12 1917,18-Mr 7,21-Ap 1934

RED CLOUD

Weekly ADVERTISER. *See* Commercial advertiser

Red Cloud CHIEF. w Jl 3 1873-N 22 1923||
Merged with Webster county argus
NbHi Jl 3 1873;Je 10-17 1892;O 19 1894;O 25-N 1,15-D 20 1895[96]-My,Je 10 1898[99-S 19 1902]Mr 9-16,30 1906-My,Je 28,Jl 19-Ag,S 20, O 1907-23
NbRcC 1873-76;Ag 9,S 20-D 20 1877;78-Jl 8,S 16 1880-S 10 1886;88-Je 13,Ag 22-D 10 1890; 91-98 F 10 1899-1901;Mr 7 1902-O 14 1904;05-23

Evening CHIEF. d S 1887-88||?
NbHi N 11 1887
NbRcC D 1887-Ja 1888

COMMERCIAL advertiser. tw 1902+
Friday issue as Weekly advertiser
pub [1902+]
NbHi My 1908-[17-20]-[23]+

GOLDEN belt. w 1892-96||?
NbHi F 22,Ag 16-S 13,O 25,N 22-D 1895;Ap 10-17,My 15,29-Je 5,19-26,Jl 17-31,Ag 15,S 5,19,O 3,9 1896
NbRcC My 5-D 22 1893;Jl 6-D 21 1894;Ja-N 1895 Ja 10-O 24 1896

Red Cloud NATION. sw,w F 1891-Mr 12 1908||
1891-97 as Nation
sw N 24 1903-Ja 8 1904
NbHi Jl 13 1892;O 24 1895;Ja 25,F 20,Mr 19,Ap 9,23-30 My 14-21,Je 4-11,Jl 9,23 1896;Je 10-17,Jl 1,15-29,Ag 12,26-S 9,N 4 1897;Ja 13,My 12-Je 2,16-30,Jl 14-21,O 27-N 1898;My-Jl,Ag 29-S 12,26-O 17,N 5,19-D 1901;Ja 16-23,F 13, My 3-Je,Jl 10-Ag 7,21 1902-F,Mr 12-Jl,Ag 14,27 1903-F,Mr 10-S 1,15 1904-08

WEBSTER county argus. sw,w Ag 1878-Ag 21 1930||
Merged with Commercial advertiser
sw D 2 1912-Ja 30 1913
NbHi Mr 10 1881;F 9-23 1893;O 2,31 1895-[99]Ja 12-F 16,Mr 1900-30
NbRcC Ag 18 1881-84;Je 1885-D 1 1887;88-1930

REPUBLICAN CITY

HARLAN county democrat. w 1884-My 30 1902||
Followed by Harlan county ranger, later Republican City ranger
Suspended from My 2-30 1902
NbHi Jl 13,Ag 24,S 7,21,O 26,N 2,16-D 21 1895;Ja 4,18,F 8,29,Mr 14,28 1896-97;Ja 22-Mr 5,19-Ap 23,My 7-14,28,D 30 1898[99]-1902

HARLAN county news. *See under* Alma

HARLAN county ranger. *See* Republican City ranger

Republican City RANGER. w Je 3 1902+
Follows Harlan county democrat. 1902-O 12 1922 as Harlan county ranger
pub 1923+
NbHi Je 20-27,Jl 11-Ag,S 12 1902+

RISING CITY

Rising City INDEPENDENT. w S 17 1880+
NbHi Jl 21 1892;Je 14 1894;O 11-D 19 1895 [96-98]-Jl 3 1930

NEBRASKA (*Continued*)

RIVERTON

FRANKLIN county guard. *See* Riverton review

Riverton REVIEW. w Ag 1872+
1872-93? as Franklin county guard (1876?-80? Bloomington guard; 1881? Banner-guard) 1872-89? pub in Bloomington
pub [1905-15]+
NbB!A [Ag 22 1872-75]
NbHi N 1,15-29,D 27 1895;96-Ja 6 1899;S 1901-[04]-Ag 1906;07-Ag 1908;My 11 1909;Ag 24,S 14 1911-My 4,O 26,N 9,23 1922+

ROSALIE

Rosalie RIP-SAW. w 1909+
pub 1909+
NbHi O 13-20,N 1911-[13-15]Ja 7,28,F 4,25-Ap 7,21,My 5 1916[Ap 24 1918-19]-23;Ja 25-Mr 7,21-O 17 1924;Ja 30-My 1,15-Jl,Ag 14-S 4,18-O 2,16-D 18 1925;26+

ROSELAND

ADAMS county gazette. w Jl 1891-1906||?
1891-1905? as Roseland gazette
NbHi Ap 23 1897;Mr 4 1898;Jl 19,Ag-O 4,18-25, N 8-D 20 1901;Ja-F 7,21-Mr 14,28-Ap 4,My 10,23,Je 13-Ag 8,S 5-19 1902;Ja 2-9 1903

Roseland GAZETTE. *See* Adams county gazette

RULO

NEBRASKA register. w 1864-My 1871||?
NbHi Jl 5 1866

Rulo REGISTER. w N 18 1903-04||?
NbHi D 1903-Jl 20 1904

Rulo REGISTER. w 1907-17||?
NbHi Ag 11 1909-Jl 1916

Rulo REPORTER. w Ja 1896-D 14 1900||
NbHi Jl 24,S 25,O 9,N 27-D 4 1896;Ja 8,14,29, F 19-Je 4,18-Ag 6,S,O 8,22,N-D 1897;Ja 21-Ap 22,My 6,27 1898;F 3-17,Mr,Ap 14-My 12,Je-S 1,22-O 13,27-N 3,17-D 1,22 1899-Ja 19,F 2-16, Mr 9,30,Ap 13-My 11,25-Je 1,15-Ag 3,17-O 19, N 2-23,D 7 1900

Rulo WESTERN guide. w Je 18 1858-
DLC Je 18-S 10 1858

RUSHVILLE

Rushville DEMOCRAT. *See* Sheridan county star

Rushville RECORDER. *See* Sheridan county star

SHERIDAN county star. w My 6 1895+
1895-Jl 10 1896 as Rushville democrat; Jl 17 1896-Mr 9 1933 Rushville recorder
NbHi O 23-D 20 1895;F 7-14,Ap 17-24,My 8-Je 12,26,Jl 10-Ag 21,S 4,25-O 2,16-23,N 20-D 18 1896[97-99]-1901;F 21 1902-My 18,Jl 12 1933;34+

Rushville STANDARD. w,sw Ag 1885-Ap 6 1933||
sw 1892
NbHi Ag 16-30,S 13 1895-Mr 1933

RUSKIN

Ruskin LEADER. w 1900-S 22 1911||
NbHi Ja 30,F 13,27-Mr 6,26-Ap 10,My 1-22,Je 5-19,Jl 30,Ag 14,D 25 1903-Ja 22,F 5,26-Mr 4,18-D 1904;08-Ja 21,F 11-Mr,Ap 8-Ag 12,S 16-30,O 14-21,N-D 9,30 1910-Ja 13,27-My 5,26-Je 9,23-Jl 14,28-S 8 1911

Ruskin NEWS. w Ap 1912+
NbHi My-Ag 20,S 1914-F 17 1916;F 12 1925+

ST. EDWARD

St. Edward ADVANCE. w Je 1900+
1900-N 8 1929 as Boone county advance
pub 1930+
NbHi 1908-15;18+

BOONE county advance. *See* St. Edward advance

St. Edward SUN. w Je 1891-1916||?
NbHi O 25-D 1895[F 1896-97]-F 4,25-Mr 11 1898;Jl 7,28,Ag 11,S,O 20 1899-Je 1904;05-16

ST. HELENA

CEDAR county bulletin. *See* Cedar county nonpariel

CEDAR county nonpariel. w Ap 4 1877-84||?
1877-78 as Cedar county bulletin
NbHar 1877-Mr 27 1878

ST. PAUL

St. Paul DEMOCRAT. *See* St. Paul press

St. Paul FREE PRESS. *See* St. Paul press

HOWARD county advocate. w Je 20 1873-Ap 20 1881||
United with St. Paul democrat to form St. Paul free press, later St. Paul press
NbHi Jl 20 1876

HOWARD county herald. w Je 1891+
1891-D 12 1918 as St. Paul republican; D 19 1918-Jl 6 1922 Republican; Jl 13 1922-Ag 16 1923 Howard county herald and the republican
NbHi Je 17 1892;N 10 1893+

PHONOGRAPH. sw,w Ag 29 1878+
F 1902-10 Phonograph-press
sw My 10-S 30 1898
NbHi S 26 1878;S 1880-Ja 12 1893;S 20 1895-S 1898;99-Ja,F 28 1902+

St. Paul PRESS. w Mr 16 1881-Ja 1902||
Mr-Ap 20 1881 as St. Paul democrat; Ap 27 1881-88? St. Paul free press; Mr 19 1897-Mr 8 1901 Press. United with St. Paul phonograph to form Phonograph-press, later Phonograph
NbHi My 18 1888-Ja 6,Je 8 1892;S 20,N 1895-[96]-[98-99]-1902

St. Paul REPUBLICAN. *See* Howard county herald

SALEM

Salem INDEX. w 1883-Mr 11 1910||?
NbHi Jl 29 1892;O 11,25-N 1,15-22,D 1895[96-97]Ja 7,21-F 11,25,Mr 11-18,My 6-13,27 1898 [F-D 1899]Ja 5,19-F,Mr 9,Ap,My 11-Je 1,15-29 1900;Je 26 1903;Ag 19-26,S 10-N 12 1909;F 11-25,Mr 11 1910

Salem STANDARD. w S 1910-F 18 1916||
United with Verdon visitor to form Verdon visitor and Salem standard (Verdon)
NbHi O 1911-16

SANTEE AGENCY

IAPI oaye. m
MB [Ag 1879-O 1880]

SARGENT

COMMONER. *See* New era

Sargent LEADER. w Je 1899+
NbBb [1899-1902;07-09]
NbHi My 25-Je 15,29-Ag 3,17-S 21,O 5,19-26,N 16-D 14,28 1900;Ja 25-F 1,15-Mr 1,15,29-S 4, 18-O 16,30,N 13-D 18 1901;02-Jl 10 1903;Mr 11,My 27,Jl 1,15,Ag 26,O 21 1904;D 14 1911+

NEW ERA. w N 5 1898-1902||?
1898-Ap 23 1899 as Commoner
NbBb [1899-1901]
NbHi Ap 30-Ag 19,S 1899-F 1,15-My 24,Je-O 11 1902

SCHUYLER

COLFAX county call. w Jl 27 1933+
NbHi 1933+

COLFAX county press. *See under* Clarkson

FREE LANCE. w 1903-08||?
NbHi My 8 1903-My 1904

Schuyler HERALD. w Ja 1880-98||?
Ja-S 1881 as Schuyler news. Merged with Quill
NbHi N 18 1882;Ag 8-O 3,31 1895-Je 24 1898

Schuyler MESSENGER. w N 26 1909-S 9 1920||
Merged with Schuyler sun
NbHi 1909-Ja 16,30,F 20,Mr 6-13,27 1914-Je,Jl 8-S 1920

Schuyler NEWS. *See* Schuyler herald

QUILL. w Jl 1886-Ja 17 1908||
Title varies slightly
NbHi Ap 9 1890;Je 8 1892;O 9,23-D 4 1895[Mr 12 1896-98]Ja 27-F 3,Mr 24-O 13,27-N 3,17-D 1,29 1899-F 16,Mr 9,23-Ap 6,20-Ag 24,S-D 14,28 1900;Ja 25,Ap 12,26-My 3,17 1901-08

Schuyler REGISTER. *See* Schuyler sun

Schuyler SUN. sw,w S 30 1871+
1871-76? as Schuyler register
sw My-Je 1902
pub 1916+
NbHi S 22 1881;Jl 19 1883-87;Ja 12,26,Mr 1-15, Ap 19-26,My 17 1888-Ja 10 1889;Ja 2-9,30-F 6,27,Mr 13,27-Ap 17,My,Je 12 1890;O 13 1892; Ag 15,29-O,N 14 1895-[1901-S 19 1902;05-07]-Ja 17,F 21,Mr 6,27-O,N 13-D 1908;O 13 1911-Je 13,27-Ag 1918;Ja 30-Mr 6,20 1919+

SCOTIA

Scotia REGISTER. w 1895+
pub F 1925+
NbHi O 24 1895-[96-97]-Mr 3,17-My,O 27-N 1 1898[99-S 18 1902]Ag 27 1908-S,O 13-27,N 10-24 1910;12-Jl 11 1918;19-Je,Jl 8-Ag,S 16, 30,O 21,N 18,D 2,23 1926;27+

SCOTTSBLUFF

Scottsbluff HERALD. *See* Scottsbluff daily star-herald

Scottsbluff PIONEER. *See* Scottsbluff tribune

Scottsbluff REPUBLICAN. w,sw My 4 1900+
1900-Ap 1916 as Scotts Bluff county republican (w)
pub 1912+
NbHi Jl 13,S-O 19,N-D 14,28 1900[01;F 1902-03]-Ja 8,22,F 5,Mr 4,Ap 1,15,My 13,Je 17,Jl 1 1904;08-F 6,Mr 13-27,Ap 10 1914+

SCOTTS BLUFF county republican. w *See* Scottsbluff republican

Scottsbluff STAR. w 1906-S 1912||
1906-Ja 1911 as Star. United with Scottsbluff herald to form Scottsbluff daily star-herald
1906-07 pub in Mitchell
NbHi O 23 1908-11;Ja 12-S 1912

Scottsbluff daily STAR-HERALD. w,sw,d My 17 1901+
1901-S 1912 as Scottsbluff herald
w 1901-Jl 10 1917;sw Jl 14 1917?-Je 1924
pub 1914+
NbHi My 17-24 1901;Mr 28 1902;O 1912+

Scottsbluff TRIBUNE. w Jl 31 1930+
1930-32 as Scottsbluff pioneer
pub D 1932+
NbHi S 18 1930+
NbSS D 1932+

SCRIBNER

Scribner NEWS. w Ap 11 1884-O 4 1912||
United with Scribner rustler to form Scribner rustler and Scribner news, later Scribner rustler
NbHi Ag 28 1886;Jl 2 1887;Ag 18,S 1,N 10, D 1,15 1888;Mr-My 18,Je-D 1889;F 1,15,Mr 1890;My 27 1892;O 25 1895-[96-99]-N 12 1909; 11-12

Scribner RUSTLER. w N 1894+
O 10 1912-N 1927 as Scribner rustler and Scribner news
NbHi O 25-N 1895;F 7,21,My 1,22,Je 28,Jl 16-Ag,S 24,O 1-22,N 19-D 10,31 1896-My 1898 [99]+

SENECA

THOMAS county clipper. w Jl 1910-S 20 1928||
United with Thomas county herald to form Thomas county herald-clipper (Thedford)
NbHi Ja 29-F 5,Mr 4,18 1920-Ap 7,My 5,Ag 18-S 8,N 3,D 22 1927;Ja 5,Mr 29,My 24-Je 7,21-28,Jl 19-S 1928

SEWARD

BLUE VALLEY blade. w F 1877+
1877-78 as Seward county advocate
pub 1879+
NbHi Ag 17-O 5,19-26,N 9-23 1887;Ag 14 1889; N 23 1892;Ag 21 1895-[1901-02]+

DEUTSCHES journal. *See* Seward journal

Seward INDEPENDENT. w Je 1 1893+
Je 17 1897-1930 as Seward independent-democrat
pub Mr 11 1897+
NbHi Je 30 1894;Ja 3-10,Mr 9,O 18-25,N 15,D 1895;Mr 13-20,My 15-22,Je 5,19-26,Jl 17-O 10, N-D 1896[F 1897-98;F 1899-1901]+

Seward JOURNAL. w 1899-D 3 1931||
1899-1912 as Nebraska deutsche farmer-zeitung; 1913-Je 1918 Deutsches journal
1899-Je 1918 in German
NbHi Ja 24-31,F 14,Mr 13-20,Ap-Jl,Ag 14 1908-F 16,Mr 1-8,Je 7-14 1912;D 1913-31

NEBRASKA atlas. w Mr 24 1870-74||?
1870-72? as Nebraska atlas and peoples' journal
NbHi O 18 1872

NEBRASKA atlas. w N 19 1879-80||?
NbHi D 3 1879

NEBRASKA deutsche farmer-zeitung. *See* Seward journal

NEBRASKA weekly reporter. *See* Seward weekly reporter

Seward weekly REPORTER. w,sw O 1870-1900||?
1870-81? as Nebraska weekly reporter; S 6-N 8 1892 Seward semi-weekly reporter (sw)
NbHi Ja 20-F 10,24 1874-78;Ap 10 1879;Ap 28 1881;83-84;87-89;91-1900

SEWARD county advocate. *See* Blue Valley blade

SEWARD county democrat. w S 1 1891-Je 17 1897||
United with Seward independent to form Seward independent-democrat, later Seward independent
NbHi Je 9 1892;Ag 22 1895-O 1896;Mr 25-Je 1897

SEWARD county tribune. w Ja 5 1915-Ja 22 1920||
NbHi S 30 1915-Ja 1,22 1920

SHELBY

NEBRASKA blizzard and Shelby sun. *See* Shelby sun

Shelby SUN. w 1889+
Je 9-Jl 21 1904 as Nebraska blizzard and Shelby sun; Jl 28-O 6 1904 Nebraska blizzard-sun
NbHi Je 23 1892;Ag 29,O 10,24-31,N 14-D 19 1895;Ja 2,16-Mr,Ap 9-O 8,22 1896-My 12,26, N-D 1 1898;F 2-9,Mr 23-My 4,18,Je-Jl 6,20-O 5,19-N 2,23-30 1899;F 8-15,Mr 1-8,29,Ap 12-O 1900;Ap 18-Ag,S 12,26-O 24,N-D 19 1901; Ja-Mr 6,20-Je 5,19-Ag 21,S-O 9,23-D 18 1902; 03-Je 23,Jl 14-S 8,29-O 6 1904;Jl 20 1905+

SHELTON

Shelton ADVISER. *See* Shelton star

Shelton CLARION. *See* Shelton clipper

Shelton CLIPPER. w 1879+
1879-S 1880 as Shelton clarion
pub Jl 17 1880+
NbHi My 27,Je 24 1892;O 25-D 1895;Ja 24-31, F 14,Ap 24,My 15,29-Je 5,19,Jl 24-Ag 14,28-O 16,N 6,20,D 11 1896+

Shelton STAR. w Mr 3 1899-1900||?
Mr-D 18? 1899 as Shelton adviser
NbHi 1899-Ja 5,19-Mr 2,16,30,Ap 13-27,My 11-Je 1,14-28 1900

NEBRASKA (*Continued*)

SHERIDAN

Sheridan **POST.** *See* Nemaha county republican (Auburn)

SHICKLEY

HERALD-SENTINEL. w 1886-1925||
1886-F 10 1922 as Shickley herald
NbHi O 25-D 20 1895[96-O 17 1902]Mr 26,Ap 30-My,Je 12-Ag 14,28 1908-09;Ja 14-28,F 25, Mr 11-18,Ap 8,29,My 13-Je 3,24,Jl 15-22 1910; Je 16,30-Jl 7,21-28,S 1,15-22 1911;N 27-D 19 1913;Ja 2,My 29 1914-17;F 1918-19;My 6-21, Je,Jl 9-30,Ag 13-S 17,O-N 19,D 1920-Ja 8 1925

SHUBERT

Shubert **CITIZEN.** w Mr 1893+
NbHi Mr 12 1897;F 14-21,My 23,Je 27,Jl 11 1902;Mr 20 1908-[10]Ag 25-S,O 13-N 3,17 1911;Mr 20,My 29-Je 12,Jl 24,S 18,O 9,30-N 13 1914;Ja 15-29,F 12,Mr 19-My,S 17,D 17 1915;Mr 3,17,Je 2,16,Ag 11,S 29,D 1,15-29 1916;F 2,16-Mr 2,23-30,S 28 1917[F-D 1920]-S 3,17,N 25 1925;Je 10,S 9,N 4 1926

SIDNEY

CHEYENNE county record. w Ag 2 1934+
pub 1934+
NbHi Ag 9,30,S 13,27-N,D 13-20 1934;Ja 10-O 17,31-N,D 12-19 1935

Sidney **ENTERPRISE.** *See* Sidney news

Sidney **NEWS.** w 1917-Ja 1930||
1917-27? as Sidney enterprise. United with Sidney telegraph to form Sidney telegraph-news
NbHi O 14 1926-30

PEOPLE'S poniard. w 1891-99||?
NbHi S 2 1892;Ag 16-D 13,27 1895-F 7,21,Mr 13-Ap 3,My 8-29,Je 18-Ag 22,S-O 17,N 1896-Ja 7,21 1899

Sidney **PLAINDEALER.** w O 10 1878-F 1881||
United with Sidney telegraph to form Sidney plaindealer-telegraph, later Sidney telegraph-news
NbHi O 10 1878

Sidney **PLAINDEALER-telegraph.** *See* Sidney telegraph-news

Sidney **TELEGRAPH-NEWS.** w,sw 1873+
1873-Ja 1930? as Sidney telegraph (Mr 1881-84? Sidney plaindealer-telegraph) F 1930?+ Friday issues as Sidney telegraph w 1873-S 17 1926
pub 1879+
NbHi Jl 15 1876;Ja 6 1877;N 12 1892;Ag 10,24 1895-F 11,25-Je,Jl 15-22,Ag 5,S 1899-N 9 1907; Mr 1908+

SILVER CREEK

Silver Creek **SAND.** w O 3 1903+
NbHi Ja 10,Mr 20-Ag,O 2-9,23 1908+
NbSc 1903+

Silver Creek **TIMES.** w N 6 1891-1902||?
NbHi 1891-96;Jl 16 1897-1900;Ap 19-26,My 10-Jl 12,26-Ag 2,16-30,S 20-N 8,22-D 13 1901;Ja 3,17-Mr 7,21-Ap 18,My 2-9,23,Jl 4,Ag 1-8,29-S 12,O 10-17 1902

SMITHFIELD

Smithfield **ENTERPRISE.** w Ap 3 1908-13||?
Suspended from O 19 1911-Ja 30 1913
NbHi My 8-29,Je 12-19,Jl 24-31,O 23 1908-Mr 9,23-30,Ap 20,My-S 21,O 1911-Jl 17 1913

PRACTICAL farm news. w Ap 10 1896-Ap 23 1897||
NbHi Ap-My 15,29-Je 12,26,Jl 10,31-Ag 7,O 16, N 1896-Ja,F 19-Ap 1897

SNYDER

Snyder **BANNER.** w Mr 1906+
pub Ap 1906+
NbHi 1908-Ja 21,F-Ap 22,My 6-13,27-O 21 1910;14-S,N 20-27 1925;N 10-17,D 8-22 1927;F 16,Mr 29-Ag 23,S,O 11-N 1,15-D 6,20 1928-Ja 3,F 7,Mr-Ag 8,22-S 19,O-N 21,D 1929-[31]Ja 14-21,F 11-18,Mr 3-10,24-Ap 7,21-28,My 26,Je 30 1932

SOUTH AUBURN

Papers published in South Auburn are listed under Auburn

SOUTH OMAHA

Papers published in South Omaha are listed under Omaha

SOUTH SIOUX CITY

ARGUS. w 1880-S 19 1902||
1880-N 13 1891 as North Nebraska argus (Dakota City). Merged with Dakota county record
NbHi N 20,D 1891-Mr,Ap 14-S 22,O-N 10,D 1,22 1893;Ja 5 1894;O 11,25-N,D 20 1895[96-97]Ja 7,21-My,Je 17-Jl 1,Ag 5,O 21-28,D 2 1898[99-1901]-F 14,28,Mr 14-My 23,Je 13-Jl 18,Ag 1,15,S 1902

DAKOTA county democrat. *See* South Sioux City press

DAKOTA county record. w 1895-1919||
NbHi O 12,26-N 2,16-D 1895;Ja 25,F 8-22,Ap 4,My 2,30-Je 6,20-27,Jl 25-O 3,17,N 1896-Ag 14,S 11-O 9,23-30,N 13-20,D 1897-Ap,My 28 1898;Ja 28,Mr 25-My 13,27-Jl,Ag 12,26-S 23,O 14-N 4,18-D 9 1899;1900[Ap-D 1901]F 15,Mr 22,Ap 5-19,My 3-10,Ag 2-9,30,S 13-20 1902;N 14 1908-16;F 2,16-23,Mr 9,Ap 13,27,Ag 17 1917-Ja,F 14-Mr 7,21-28 1919

EAGLE. w My 24 1876+
1876-Jl 5 1928 as North Nebraska eagle 1876-S 12 1923 pub in Dakota City
pub 1876+
NbHi O 31 1877;S 12 1879;Jl 17,S 11,O 9,23-N 20,D 4-18 1890;F-Ap,N 11-19,D 24 1891-[92]-[1900-02]+

South Sioux City **MAIL.** w Ap 1920+
NbHi Je 11-Jl 2,16 1926-27;F 3,Mr-Ap 20,My 4,18 1928+

South Sioux City **NEWS.** w 1887||?
United with South Sioux City sun to form Sun and news, later South Sioux City press

NORTH NEBRASKA eagle. *See* Eagle

South Sioux City **PRESS.** w 1887-98||?
1887-90? as South Sioux City sun (1888?-89? Sun and news) 1891?-96? Dakota county democrat. Merged with Dakota county record?
NbHi Jl 15-22,D 9 1892;O 11,25-N 1,15-D 1895; Ja 24,F 14,My 1,15,29-Je,Jl 10-Ag 21,S-O 23,N 1896-Ja,F 12-Jl 23 1897

South Sioux City **SUN.** *See* South Sioux City press

SPALDING

Spalding **DEMOCRAT.** w F 1913-17||?
NbHi My 29,Je 12-N,D 11 1914-My 11 1917

Spalding **ENTERPRISE.** w Ja 12 1901+
pub 1925+
NbHi Ja 12,Mr 9 Ap 20-Ag 10,24-31,S 14,O 12-N 9,30 1901-Ja 10,31,F 14-Ap 4,Je 23 1903;Je 3 1904;Je 9 1905;08-Je 18 1909;Ag 21-28,S 11 1919-Ja 8,22-Mr 18,Ap,My 13-Jl,Ag 12-26,S 23-30,O 21 1920+

SPENCER

Spencer **ADVOCATE and Butte gazette.** w 1892+
1892-1902? as Boyd county advocate (1896?-98? Boyd county advocate and democrat) 1903?-F 9 1933 Spencer advocate
NbHi Ja 3-10,F 21,My 8,Je 19 1896;N 3 1898; Je 22 1899;1908-21;24+

BOYD county advocate. *See* Spencer advocate and Butte gazette

BOYD county register. *See under* Butte

BUTTE county democrat. w 1894-95||?
United with Boyd county advocate to form Boyd county advocate and democrat, later Spencer advocate and Butte gazette

SPRAGUE

Sprague-Martel **LEADER.** *See under* Martel

SPRINGFIELD

Springfield **MONITOR.** w D 1882+
pub 1882+
NbHi D 8 1892;Ja 2-9,30,F 27-Mr 5,19,Ap 2,23, My-Je 4,Jl 2-9,23 1896+

SPRINGVIEW

ALLIANCE herald. *See* Springview herald

Springview **HERALD.** w 1891+
1891-94? as Alliance herald
For S 30 1897-Mr 13 1902 *See* Keya Paha call and Springfield herald
pub 1902+
NbHi D 18 1895;Ap 15,29,My 27,Je 24,Jl 22-S 16,O 14 1896-Ja,F 14,Mr,Ap 14,My 5-19,Je 2, 23,Jl 7-14,Ag 4-11,S 1897;Mr 20-Ap 17,My 8, 22,Je 12,Jl 3-17,31-Ag 14,28-S 18 1902;07-F,Mr 10-24,Ap 21-28,My 19-Ag 11,S 1 1910;Ag 24-S 1911;12-Ja 11,25-D 6,27 1917-Ja 17,31-My 16, 30-O,N 14-28 1918;Ja 2-23,F-My 1919;Jl 7-21,Ag-D 1921

KEYA PAHA call and Springview herald. w F 5 1897-Mr 13 1902||
F-S 1897 as Keya Paha call
NbHi Mr 26,Ap 29,My 20,Je 4,25-Jl 2,16,30-Ag 6,20-S 3,N 5 1897;My 13-Je 17,Jl 1-15 1898;Jl 18,Ag 1,15,29,S 12-O,N 14,28,D 18 1901;Ja 16, F 6-13,27-Mr 1902

KEYA PAHA press. w Ja 1885-89||?
Ja-My 1885 pub in Ainsworth
NbHi F 18,Mr-Ap 22,My 13-Je 3,24-Jl 15,29, Ag 19-S 2 1887

STAMFORD

Stamford **POST.** w Je 28 1907-11||?
NbHi Ag 23-O 4,18 1907-Ja 6 1911

Stamford **STAR.** w O 1914+
pub Mr 1919+
NbHi 1925+

STANTON

Stanton **DEMOCRAT.** w 1883-Je 25 1897||
Merged with Stanton register
NbHi S 13 1895-Ja 22,Mr 12-19,Ap 9,23,My 7-21,Je 11-25 1897
NbStR 1885-97

Stanton **INDEX.** w O 5 1877-79||?
NbHi O 12 1877;Mr 8,My 10,Jl 19 1878

Stanton **weekly PICKET.** w 1893-1922||?
NbHi N 3 1893;O 25-N 1,D 13 1895[96-1900; Ap 1901-02]-Ja,F 10,24-Mr 2,16 1905-Ja 11 1906

Stanton **REGISTER.** w,sw O 1879+
Ap 23-Ag 23 1901 as Semi-weekly Stanton register (sw)
pub [1879-80]90+
NbHi Mr 17,Ap 7,Je 23,Jl 14 1880;S 4-11,25 1884;My 3,17,S 27 1888;Jl 10 1890;Jl 28 1892;D 5-26 1895;F 13 1896-My,O 28,N 18-D 2 1898 [99-1902]-12;Jl 16 1915+

STAPLEHURST

Staplehurst **SENTINEL.** w S 29 1921-23||?
NbHi D 22 1921-22;Ja 11-Jl 21,S 20-O 1923

STAPLETON

ENTERPRISE. w Je 25 1912+
pub Jl 1912-[15-17]+
NbHi Jl 25-N 7,21-D 12 1912;13+

STEELE CITY

Steele City **NEWS.** w Ja 18 1929+
NbHi 1929+

Steele City **PRESS.** w 1904-O 18 1928||
Suspended from Jl 6-N 2 1923; from Mr 7-My 1 1924
NbHi Mr 28,O 24 1908-Ap 12,My-Ag 23,S 6-13,O 18 1928

SOUTHERN Nebraska advance. *See* Southern Nebraskan (Fairbury)

Steele City **STANDARD.** w 1892-Ap 1900||
NbHi N 26 1892;O 12,26 1895-Ja 11,F 1896-1900

STEINAUER

Steinauer **PRESS.** *See* Pawnee press (Pawnee City)

Steinauer **STAR-POST.** w O 1893-Je 28 1925||
1893-Ja 27 1921 as Steinauer star
Suspended from Ja 27-Je 17 1921
NbHi N 1,22,D 6 1895[96]-98[F-D 1 1899;F 9-D 1900]Ja 25,Ap 26-Je 7,21-28,Jl 19 1901-Ja 6,20-27,Je 17 1921-My 1925

STELLA

NEBRASKA free press. *See* Stella press

Stella **PRESS.** w 1882+
1882-87? as Stella tribune; 1888? Nebraska free press
NbHi Ag 12 1892;O 25,N 15,29-D 1895;F 7,Ap 17-24,Je 19-26,Jl 17-Ag 21,S-O 16,N 6,27-D 4,24 1896-Ja,F 12,My 21 1897;Mr 18,Ap 15,My 6,Ag 5,S 2,30-O 7,21-N 4,18-D 2 1898;Ja 6-13, O 20 1899;O 12-N 9,D 1900[01-N 1902]Mr 13 1903;Ap 10-17,My 1908+

Stella **TRIBUNE.** *See* Stella press

STERLING

Sterling **EAGLE.** *See* Sterling record

Sterling **RECORD.** w 1893-1906||?
1893-Jl 1899? as Sterling eagle; Ag 1899-Ap 13 1900 Sterling record and eagle
NbHi S 19,O 24 1895-[96]-F,Mr 9,23-Jl 13,Ag 11 1899-My 11,Je 8 1900-[03]Ja 28,Mr 3-10, My 26-Je 2,23,Jl 21 1904-Ag,O 5-12,N 1905-Mr 15 1906

Sterling **SUN.** w,sw Ag 1886+
sw 1892-1910
pub Jl 1911+
NbAdG 1888-1910
NbHi Je 10 1892;Ap 23,Ag 20 O 22 1895-[96]-[1903-05]-Je 13,27-N 7 1912;Mr 27 1913+

STOCKVILLE

FABER. w My 1884-1928||
1884-94? Frontier county faber; 1895-N 1904 Faber; D 1904-Ap 1913 Republican-faber. Merged with Curtis enterprise (Curtis)
NbHi My 20 1887;Jl 29,S 23 1892;Je 27,Ag 15 1895-Ag 1906;Ag 20 1908-28

FRONTIER county faber. *See* Faber

FRONTIER county republican. *See* Republican

REPUBLICAN. w Jl 1892-N 1904||
1892-Jl 2 1903 as Frontier county republican. United with Faber to form Republican-faber, later Faber
NbHi N 25 1892;O 24-D 19 1895[96-97]-Ja 13, F 17-My 1898[99-1900]Ap 13,My 2,16-Je,Jl 18,Ag 1,29-N 7,21,D 19 1901;F 20,Mr 13-Ap 3,17-24,My 8-15,Je 12-Jl 24,Ag 1902-04

REPUBLICAN-FABER. *See* Faber

STRANG

Strang **REPORTER.** w 1889-1912||?
NbHi S 9 1892;Ap 26,My 10-17,31-Jl 5,19-Ag 2,30-O 11,N 8-22,D 1901-Ja 3,17-F 7,My-Ag 15,29-S 1902;Ag 19-N 1909;D 28 1911-Mr 1912

NEBRASKA (*Continued*)

STRATTON

Stratton HERALD. w Ap 1885-94||?
NbHi O 15 1885;Ag 12 1887;F 26,Jl 1 1892

Stratton NEWS. w D 15 1910+
pub [1910+]
NbHi Ag 31 1911-[18]-26;Ja 13,Ag 4,S 22 1927;30;32+

Stratton SIGNAL. w Mr 12 1895-1913||
NbHi N 29 1895;Mr 6-20,D 25 1896[97]Ja,F 11,25,Ap 22,My-Jl,Ag 12-S 9,O-N 11,25-D 23 1898;Ja-F 10 1899

STROMSBURG

FOLKETS vän. w 1885-S 20 1887||
Merged with Svenska Amerikanska posten (Minneapolis, Minn)
In Swedish
IRA 1885-87

HEADLIGHT. w My 14 1885+
NbHi Je 23 1892;S,O 10 1895+

Stromsburg NEWS. w 1880-N 21 1918||
1880-90? as Stromsburg republican
NbHi N 11 1892;Ap 14 1893;O 11,25-N 1,15-22,D 6-20 1895;Ja 31-F 7,Mr 20,Ap 24,My 8, Je 12-26,Jl 17,31 1896-Ap,Je 13-20,Jl 11-18,Ag 8,22 1907-18

Stromsburg REPUBLICAN. *See* Stromsburg news

STUART

Stuart ADVOCATE. w F 1906+
pub 1908+
NbHi Ag 27-S 3,17-24,O 8 1908-N 14 1918;19+

Stuart LEDGER. w Ag 1883-1903||?
NbHi D 15 1887;Ja 19-26,Ag 30 1888[95]96;Je 28 1897-My 12,26,Je 9-23,Jl 7,21,Ag-N 17,D 2, 10 1898[Mr 24 1899-N 15 1901]O 24-31,N 14 1902-F 6,20-Mr 6 1903

SUMNER

Sumner NEWS. w My 1907+
NbHi Je 11-O 22,N,D 10 1914+

SUPERIOR

Superior EXPRESS. w Ja 11 1900+
F 15-Mr 29 1900 as Express and the Superior sun
pub 1915+
NbHi F 15,Mr 8 1900-F 1902;Mr 12 1908+

Superior daily EXPRESS. d 1908-17||?
pub 1915-My 1917
NbHi N 26 1913

Superior weekly JOURNAL. w 1882+
pub [1882-1915]+
KHi 1897-N 13 1913
NbHi Mr 9,Jl 27 1892;Ja 2,23-F 20,Mr 13-20, Ap 17,My 15,29,Jl 10-17,31-Ag,S 11 1895+

Superior daily JOURNAL. d 1888-1916||?
NbHi F 6 1893[O 1895-Je 2 1898;99-O 13 1902]

Superior SUN. w 1880-F 8 1900||
United with Superior express to form Express and the Superior sun, later Superior express
NbHi N 2,16,30-D 21 1895;Ja 18-25,F 15,My 16,Je 6-13,27,Jl 11-O 3,17,N 14-D 19 1896;Ja 2-16,F 20-My,Je 17-Jl 8,D 16 1897;98-1900

SURPRISE

Surprise CITIZEN. w 1895-1908||?
1895-1900? as Surprise herald
NbHi Mr 27 1896-Je 10 1898;Jl 14,O 27 1899-Ja 12,F-My 4,25-Je,Jl 27,Ag 10,31,S 21-O 1900;D 18 1902

Surprise ENTERPRISE. w My 1914-21||?
NbHi N 27-D 4 1919;20-S 8 1921

Surprise HERALD. *See* Surprise citizen

SUTHERLAND

Sutherland COURIER. w 1895+
1895-F 14 1918 as Sutherland free lance
pub 1899+
NbHi My 27 1897-Je 23,D 1898-Je 19,Jl-D 21 1899;1900-Ja 19 1905;Ag 27 1908+

Sutherland FREE LANCE. *See* Sutherland courier

SUTTON

ADVERTISER. *See* Sutton news

CLAY county globe. w Je 14 1875-80||?
Merged with Sutton register
NbHi Ja 19 1877;N 19 1880

Sutton NEWS. w 1887+
1887-93? as Advertiser; 1894? News; 1895?-Mr 6 1903 Advertiser-news
NbHi S 1895-[1905]Ja 5,Je 22,Jl 13-20,S 7,D 14 1906-F 15,Mr 15,29-Ap 12,My 3,17 1907+

Sutton REGISTER. w F 12 1880+
NbHi Mr 24 1881;O 12-N 2,16 1895;My-Ag 7, 28-S 1902;Ag 20 1908-N 22 1917;F 12 1925+

SWANTON

Swanton ECHO. w Mr 1 1895-96||?
NbHi Mr-Ap,Jl 26-O 18,N-D 13,27 1895-My 15,29,Je 12 1896

Swanton ITEMS. w N 21 1896-My 1897||
NbHi 1896-Ja 9,23,F-Ap 2,16-My 1897

Swanton NEWS. w Je 19- 1890||?
NbHi Je-Jl 10,31,Ag 14,S 4,18-25,O 23-30 1890

Swanton NEWS. w 1896?-1911||?
NbHi 1903-Ja 12,26-Mr 9,23-30,Ap 20-Je 15, 29-Ag,S 14-21 1907;O 24 1908-F 4 1911

Swanton RECORD. w 1892-1902||?
NbHi Mr 4,18-Ap 1,15,My 6-20,Je 3-10,24-Jl 15,29-D 16,30 1893-94;Ja 19-Ap 1895;98-N 1902

SYRACUSE

Syracuse DEMOCRAT. w Jl 1 1896-Ap 1917||
United with Syracuse journal to form Syracuse journal-democrat
NbHi Jl 1896-1902;Ap 1903-17

Syracuse HERALD. w 1885-98||?
NbHi O 4-11,N 8 1888;Ja 7,28,Mr 25,My 13,27-Jl 1,29,O 28-D 2 1897;Ja 9,F 17,My 5, Ag 19,S 30,O 14,N 4,D 9-30 1898

Syracuse JOURNAL-DEMOCRAT. w,sw Ja 1878+
1878-Ap 1917 as Syracuse journal
sw S 6-D 18 1896
NbHi S 7,21,N,D 14,28 1888;F 1,15 1889;Ja-N 1892;S 1895-N 17,D 1-8,18 1896;S 10-O 8 1897[98]Jl-Ag 11,S 8-15,O-D 15 1899[1900-S 12 1902]Ag 23 1907;Mr 27,My 8-22,Je 1908+

TABLE ROCK

Table Rock ARGUS. w My 25 1882+
pub 1891+
NbHi My 5,Jl 21-28,Ag 25-S 22,O,N 10-17 1883; Jl 18,S 26-O 3,N 1884-My 22 1885;Je 24 1892;O 25,N 15,29-D 6,20 1895[96]-Ja 8,22-29,F 12 1897+

Table Rock HERALD. w Ap 27 1893-94||?
NbHi Ap-Ag 10,24-D 22 1893;Ja-N 23 1894

TALMAGE

Talmage TRIBUNE. w F 1883+
pub Je 10 1898;1906;12;20+
NbHi [F-N 1899;1900-O 10 1902]Mr 27-S 4,18 1908-My 2,Je 27-Jl 4,18,Ag 1919-My 8,D 18 1924;25+

TAMORA

Tamora LYRE. *See* Shield's Tamora lyre

Tamora weekly REGISTER. *See* Shield's Tamora lyre

SHIELD'S Tamora lyre. w 1893-Ag 28 1913||
1893-Mr 26 1909 as Tamora weekly register; My 1909-F 16 1911 Tamora lyre
NbHi N 1-8 1895;Ja 24,My 15,Je 25,N 27 1896; My 6-13 1898;S 15-O 13,N 17,D 22 1899-[1900-N 1902]Ja 9-Mr,Ap 10-D 1903[08]-F 5,26,Mr 12-26,My 1909-F 20,Mr 13-Ag 1913

TAYLOR

Taylor CLARION. w Ag 1883+
1883-Ap 1896 as Loup county clarion; My 1896-Ja 12 1899 Clarion
NbHi S 18 1884;Ap 19,Je 14,Ag 9 1888;Je 23 1892;Ag 22 1895+

LOUP county clarion. *See* Taylor clarion

LOUP county news. w O 25 1901-15||?
NbHi D 20 1901-D 13 1902;O 9 1908-O 7 1910

TECUMSEH

Tecumseh CHIEFTAIN. w 1868+
1868-S 1869 as Tecumseh gazette; O 1869?-70? Nebraska gazette
pub 1884+
NbHi S 5 1891+

Tecumseh GAZETTE. *See* Tecumseh chieftain

JOHNSON county journal. w Mr 1879-S 1929||
D 2 1909-Ja 1916 as Johnson county journal-tribunal. Merged with Tecumseh chieftain
NbHi Ja 24,Je 27,Jl 11 1889;D 1-8 1892;Jl 12 1894;D 5 1895;F 27-Mr 12,Ap 23,Je 25-Jl 2, 30,Ag 13,27,S 24-O 1,D 24 1896-98;Ja 12-19,F 23-Mr 2,Je 29,N 2,16 1899-D 3 1903;Mr 26 1908-14;17-29
NbTeC 1880

JOHNSON county tribunal. w N 19 1898-N 1909||
United with Johnson county journal to form Johnson county journal-tribunal, later Johnson county journal
NbHi [1899-1901]-09

NEBRASKA gazette. *See* Tecumseh chieftain

TEKAMAH

BURT county herald. w 1882+
NbHi Je 24 1892[95-99]-N 1906;07+

BURT county plaindealer. w Ap 19 1934+
NbHi Ap-Jl 12,26 1934+

BURTONIAN. w S 1873-D 27 1901||
Title varies slightly. Merged with Tekamah journal
NbHi Je 25-Jl 9,23-D 1874;Ja 7-14,28-Ap 8,22-S 2 1875;F 24,S 30 1876-Ag 22,S 19-26,O 10-17,N 14 1878-My 6,27,Je 10-Ag,S 16 1880-Ap, S 8,O 20,N 17,D 8-15 1881[Ja-Jl 20 1882]S 20 1883-S 11 1884;S 24-D 23 1885;86-S 1888;O 1892-1901

Tekamah JOURNAL. w D 7 1899-1918||?
NbHi F 1900-My 9,23-Ag 15 1918

Tekamah PILOT. *See* Blair pilot (Blair)

THEDFORD

Thedford BANNER. w 1889-D 3 1897||
1889-Jl 12 1894 as Thedford tribune
NbHi D 8 1892;Ja 18,F 1-8,Je 28-Jl 5,26,Ag 30,O 24-31 1894;N 14 1895-[96-97]

THOMAS county herald-clipper. Je 1888+
1888-S 20 1928 as Thomas county herald
NbHi N 17 1911-13;20+

Thedford TRIBUNE. *See* Thedford banner

THURSTON

Thurston MAIL. w O 10 1912-15||?
NbHi 1912-Jl 1 1915

TRI-COUNTY times. *See* Emerson advocate (Emerson)

TILDEN

Tilden CITIZEN. w Ja 21 1893+
NbHi Ja 21,F,Jl 22,Ag 5,N 4-11 1893;O 11 1895;My 23,Ag 15,29,O 10 1896-[98]Ja,O 14 1899-Ja 6,27,F 17-Mr,Je 9,O 27-N 3 1900;Mr 30,Ap 27,My 25,S 21 1901 [02]-Ja 17,31,F 14, 28-Mr 7,21,Jl 25,S 12 1903;F 20,Mr 19-26,Ap 29,Je 11,O 8,N 12 1904;Mr 18-25,Ap 15,O 21 1905;Ja 26,F 23,Ag 17 1906;My 17 1907; Je-O 3,17 1919-20;23-S 23 1926;Ja 20 1927+

TOBIAS

Tobias EXPRESS. w O 18 1895-1922||?
1895-Jl 12 1901 as Saline county gazette (D 6 1895-O 16 1896 Saline county gazette-tribune)
NbHi O 18,N 1895-Je 5,19-Jl 3,17 1896-Jl,Ag 12-S 2,16-O 14,28-N 11,25-D 2,16,29 1904[05-S 13 1907]08-Ja 21,F-Mr 4,25-My,Je 17-Jl,Ag 12,S 9,O 14,N-D 2 1921;Ap 23,My-Je 9,Jl 7-21,Ag 5-19,S 1,22-O 6,27 1922

Tobias weekly INDEX. w Mr 1 1889-O 24 1890||
NbHi Mr-Ap 19,My-Je,Jl 12-19,Ag 9,S 13-O 4,N 8-D 6,27 1889-Ja 10,31-Ap 11,25-My,Je 13-Jl 11,25-O 1890

Tobias NEWS. w Ap 22 1923-F 11 1927||?
NbHi D 27 1923-F 11 1927

SALINE county gazette. *See* Tobias express

Tobias TIMES. w Ap 15 1927+
NbHi Je 1927+

Tobias TRIBUNE. w Jl 24 1884-N 29 1895||
United with Saline county gazette to form Saline county gazette-tribune, later Tobias express
NbHi Jl-Ag 7,21-O 24,N 7,21 1884-[85-N 25 1887;88-93]-My 18,Je 1-15 1894;Ja 18-F 1,Mr-Ap 5,19-26,Jl 19-N 1895

TRENTON

Trenton DEMOCRAT. *See* Trenton register

Trenton LEADER. *See* Republican-leader

PEOPLES sentinel. w S 1891-96||?
1891-92? as Sentinel; 1893?-D 27 1895 Culbertson sentinel
1891-95 pub in Culbertson
NbHi Jl 22 1892;N 15-D 1895[F 21-Ag 7 1896]

Trenton REGISTER. w D 11 1885+
O 29-N 16 1888 as Trenton democrat
pub D 18 1885+
NbHi D 2 1892;Ag 16-23,S 1895+

Trenton REPUBLICAN. w F 12 1904-05||?
United with Trenton leader to form Republican-leader
NbHi 1904-Mr 10 1905

REPUBLICAN-LEADER. w,sw My 1897+
1897-1905? as Trenton leader
sw 1916-19
NbHi My 13-Je 17,Jl 1-15,29,O 21,N 11-18,D 2 1898;Ap 7 1899;Ap 27 1900;Ap 19,My 17-Je 7,21-Jl,Ag 23-30,S 13,27-O 11,N 8,D 1901-Ja 3,17-31,My 2-9,23-Je 6,20-Ag 1,15-S,N 14 1902;08-Ag 1916;N 20 1917;20+

TRYON

Tryon GRAPHIC. w Ja 1 1887+
1887-95? as McPherson county news
pub 1922+
NbHi Jl 27,S 1,28-O 19,N 2,16,D 7-21 1900[01; Ag-D 1902]F-Jl 9,30-O 8 1903;My 28-Jl,Ag 13 1914-[18]-O,N 13-20 1919[F 1920-N 10 1921]Mr 16,Jl 20-N 23,D 1922+

MCPHERSON county news. *See* Tryon graphic

UEHLING

Uehling MESSENGER. w Ja 7 1926+
NbHi 1926+

Uehling POST. *See* Uehling press (1919-25)

Uehling PRESS. w Ja 30 1906-17||?
NbHi Mr 20-My 22,Je,Jl 10 1908-Ja 12,26-Ag 1917

Uehling PRESS. w 1919-D 11 1925||
1919-N 2 1923 as Uehling post
NbHi Ja 2-16,29-N 13,27-D 1925
WaPS [1924-25]

Uehling TIMES. w Mr 1906-10||?
NbHi Mr 27 1908-Ja 7,F 11-Ap 1,15-22,My 6-13 1910

NEBRASKA (*Continued*)

ULYSSES

Ulysses DISPATCH. w My 6 1880+
NbHi My 27 1880;N 30 1892;O 9,D 4-11 1895 [96]Mr 3-10,21,My 5-19,Je 9,30-Jl 7,Ag 25,O 6-20,D 5 1897;My 18-Jl 20,Ag,S 14-20,O 12, 26-N 9,23 1898-Mr 1,29-Ap 5,26-Ag,S 13-N 8,22 1899-[1904]Ag 19 1908+

SATURDAY NIGHT review. w Mr 1911-Ag 18 1917||
Merged with Ulysses dispatch
NbHi Mr 30 1914-17

UNADILLA

OTOE union. w N 7 1896-D 1928||
NbHi D 5 1896;Ja 16-S 1897;Ja 25-Mr 7,21,Ap-My 2,Je 20-Jl 18,Ag 1,15 1902-[07]-[11]-28

UNION

Union LEDGER. w 1888-O 1917||?
United with Nehawka news to form Nehawka news and Union ledger, later News-ledger (Nehawka)
NbHi N 26 1892;O 25,N 8-15,29-D 20 1895;Ja 31,My 16,29-Je,Jl 24-31,Ag 21,S 18-O 9,N 7,20-D 4,25 1896;Ja,F 19,Mr-My,Je 11-25,Jl 23,S 10-24,O 8,N 5,26-D 12 1897;Mr-My 13,27, Ag 5,D 23 1898-[99-S 19 1902]08-09

UNIVERSITY PLACE

Papers published in University Place are listed under Lincoln

UPLAND

Upland EAGLE. w O 1899+
Suspended from Ag 25 1932-Ap 27 1933
pub Ap 27 1933+
NbHi My 10 1901;Ag 15,29-S 19,N 21,D 19 1902;Ap 30-Je 18,Ag 1908-[10]Ja 6,20,F 10,Mr 3-24,Ap 7,21-28,My 12-26 1911;Je 18-N 5,19 1914-Ag 1932

UTICA

Utica SUN. w S 1887+
NbHi N 26 1892;O 26-N 16,30-D 14,28 1895[96-97]Ja 1,15-Je 23,Jl-O 1,29 1898;F,Mr 25-Je 17,Jl,Ag 11-N 4,18-D 2,30 1899[1900-O 16 1902] Mr 1908-J 3,15 1919;S 15 1921-23;Ja 29,F 19-Je,Jl 16 1925;Ja 28-F,Mr 11-18,Ap 1-8,22,My-Je,Jl 15 1926;N 15-D 6 1928;N 1929-Ap 1931; Jl 11-O 17 31 1935+

VALENTINE

CHERRY county gazette. *See* Cherry county news

CHERRY county independent. *See* Cherry county news

CHERRY county news. w S 18 1885+
1885-89? as Democratic blade; 1890?-92? Cherry county gazette; 1893?-Ap 2 1896 Cherry county independent; Ap 9 1896-F 6 1930 Valentine democrat (S 22 1898-1900 Western news-democrat)
pub My 26 1892+
NbHi Ag 1 1887;D 8,22 1892;O 17,N 14,28-D 5,19 1895;Mr 5-12,Ap 1896-98;1901+
NbVD 1885-S 7 1888

Valentine DEMOCRAT. *See* Cherry county news

DEMOCRATIC blade. *See* Cherry county news

MINNEKAHDUSA republican. w 1884-85||?
United with Valentine reporter to form Republican reporter

Valentine REPORTER. *See* Republican reporter

REPUBLICAN. w D 3 1887+
pub Ap 13 1888+
NbHi Ap 13 1888+

REPUBLICAN reporter. w My 3 1883-86||?
1883-85? as Valentine reporter
NbHi My 3 1883
NbVD 1883-Ap 3 1884

SEARCHLIGHT. w Ja 1909-N 8 1918||
NbHi S 19 1913-18

WESTERN news. w Ag 12 1896-S 15 1898||
United with Valentine democrat to form Western news-democrat, later Cherry county news
NbHi Ap 23 My 14-21,Je 4,Ag 13 1897;S 1-15 1898

WESTERN news-democrat. *See* Cherry county news

VALLEY

Valley ENTERPRISE. w Ap 1887+
pub 1887+
NbHi D 2 1892;O 25-D 1895;Ja 31,Ap 17-24, My 15,29,Je 19-26,Jl 17-Ag,S 11-O 2,N 27 1896;Ja 22,F 5,19-My 7,21,Je 4,Ag 13,S 10 1897;F 4 1898;Je-Jl,Ag 10 1906-[10-S 1911]18-Ag 1920;Je 17 1921-[26]Ja 20,Mr 10-17,My 19, S 12,N 10,24,D 1927-Ja 18,29-F 5,19-Jl 2,D 31 1931-Je 1932

VALPARAISO

Valparaiso AVALANCHE. *See* Valparaiso visitor

Valparaiso VISITOR. w 1879+
1879-90 as Valparaiso avalanche
pub 1929+
NbHi My 26 1892;O 24,N 21,D 5 1895[96]-[99]-[1901-S 18 1902]O 28 1908+

VERDIGRE

Verdigre CITIZEN. *See* Verdigre eagle

Verdigre EAGLE. w 1899+
1899-F 5 1931 as Verdigre citizen
pub [N 10 1910-F 5 1931]+
NbHi 1908-[23]-25;28+

KNOX county recorder. w 1889-97||?
NbHi D 1 1892;Ap 17-24,My 15,29-Je 19,Jl 17-Ag 21,S 18-O 23,N-D 18 1896

VERDON

Verdon DELPHIC. w Mr 18 1920-My 5 1921||
NbHi complete

Verdon VEDETTE. w 1883-1919||?
NbHi N 13 1885-87;N 16 1888-[1900-N 1901]Ja 17,S 19 1902;My 29 1914-Mr 10,24-Jl 14,28 1916

Verdon VISITOR and Salem standard. w Ja 1922-28||?
1922-S 3 1925 as Verdon visitor
NbHi F 19-Mr 19,Ap,My 21-Je 18,Jl 9-Ag 6, 20 1925-Mr,Ap 12-My 3,17-Je 21,Jl-Ag 1928

WACO

Waco STAR. w Mr 17 1916-18||?
NbHi Ap 21-Jl 7,S 8 1916-18

WAHOO

Wahoo DEMOCRAT. w S 1884+
NbHi Ap 20 1893;My 21-28,Je 18-25,Jl 23-Ag 13,S 10-N 5,19 1896-Ja 21,F 4-18,Mr-Jl 22,Ag 5-12,S 1897-Jl 3,Ag 7,S 11 1902;08+

Wahoo INDEPENDENT. *See* Wahoo wasp

Wahoo NEW ERA. *See* Saunders county new era

SAUNDERS county new era. w,sw Ag 7 1890-1906||?
1890-Ja 20 1899 as Wahoo new era (title varies slightly)
sw Ag 3-O 22 1897
NbHi 1890-Jl 22,Ag-S,O 14 1898-My 17 1906

Wahoo WASP. w S 1875+
1875-86? as Wahoo independent
pub 1875-85;94-97;99+
NbHi Ag 19 1880;Je 16 1892;O 24-31,N 14-28,D 12,26 1895;F 6,Ap 30,My 14-28,Je 18-25,Jl 30, Ag 13-20,S 10,24-O 1,15-N 5,19 1895-F 4,18-Mr 11,25,Ap 15-Ag 12,26,S 9 1897-1916;O-N 1,15 1917+

WAKEFIELD

Wakefield JOURNAL. w D 19 1895-1900||?
NbHi Ja 23,F 6,Ap 16-30,My 14,Je 18-25,Jl 23-S,O 8-22,N-D 17 1896;Ja 14,28,F 11-18,Mr-Jl 8,22-Ag 12,26-S 9,O-D 9,23 1897-Ap 14,28-My 1898;Jl 13-Ag 17,31,S 14-O,N 16,30,D 28 1899-Ja 4,18-F 1 1900

Wakefield REPUBLICAN. w 1882+
pub 1906+
NbHi D 15 1892;O 24-D 19 1895[96-97]-My 1898;F 2,Mr 23-My 11,Je-S 14,O 12-19,N D 22 1899[1900]Ap 25-My 16 1901;Mr 11,Ag 8-S 19. O 3,17-24 1902[03-06]08-Ag 1922;23+

WALLACE

Wallace HERALD. w Ja 24 1888-96||?
NbHi Ja 29-F 19,Mr,My 13-Je 3,17-O 21,N 1892;Ja 6-20,F 3-17,My-Jl 21 1893;O 18-N 8, 22,D 6-20 1895

Wallace STAR. w Jl 24 1891-94||?
NbHi Jl 24-31,D 18 1891-Ja 22,F 12,Mr 11,25-Ap 1,My 13,Jl 22-O,N 18-D 23 1892;Ja-Ap, My 12,Jl 14 1893

WALTHILL

Walthill CITIZEN. w N 19 1915+
pub 1923+
NbHi 1918-Ja 20,F 3,24-Mr 3,Ap-My 5,19,Je 9-16,30-Jl 14,28-Ag 18,S-O,N 10 1933+

Walthill TIMES. w N 16 1906+
NbHi N 16-23,D 1906-Je 3,17-Jl 15,S 16-23, O 7-14,28,N 11,25 1910-Mr,Ap 20-My 4,25,Je 15,Jl 6,27-Ag 10,31-D 7 1917;F 8-22,Mr-My 3,17 1918-19 Ap 9,Je 4 1920;F 11-D 23 1921; 22-N 11 1926[Mr-D 1927]-Je 2,Ag 25 1932-Je 15,Ag-O 5,N 9-D 21 1933;Ja-Jl 12,Ag 30-D 6,27 1934-F 14,Mr 21 1935+

Wallace TUG. w F 24 1896-98||?
NbHi Ap 24,29,Je 5,Jl 31-Ag,S 11-O 23,N-D 18 1896;Ja 8-15,29-F 5,19-Je 18,Jl-Ag 6,S-O 8,22-N 19,D 1897-Ap 22 1898

Wallace WINNER. w 1908+
S 27 1917 is Hoosier holiday ed
pub 1926+
EHi S 27 1917
NbHi Je 4,18-Jl 9,23-Ag 13,27,S 10,O 8 1914;F 25 1915

WATERLOO

DOUGLAS county gazette. w Mr 8 1895+
1895-Ja 5 1934 as Waterloo weekly gazette
pub [1895-96;1917-23]34+
NbHi 1895-Ja,F 11,25,Mr 11,25,Ap 8,22,My 6, 20-27,Je 17,S 9,N 11,25,D 9-16,30 1898;F 17, Mr 3-10,Ap 14-21,My 13 1899-O,N 16,30-D 14 1900[01-02]-My,Je 12,26,Jl 10 1903-05;Ja 11-Mr 8,22-29,Ap 12-Ag 16,S 1906-[07-08]-[10]-Ja 5 1934

Waterloo weekly GAZETTE. *See* Douglas county gazette

WAUNETA

Wauneta BREEZE. w Ja 1887+
pub 1887+
NbHi My 19 1887;N 24 1892;O 24-D 12 1895; Ja 2-9,F 6,Mr 5,19,Ap 16-23,My 7-14,Je 4,25, Jl 23-30,Ag 13,27-O 8,22-N 12,D 3-24 1896; 97-Mr 2 1899;Ag 14 1902+

WAUSA

ENTERPRISE-HERALD. w 1890-1902||?
1890-94? as Wausa enterprise
NbHi Je 17-24 1892;N 1,15-D 20 1895[96-97]Ja 14,28,F 11,25-My 1898[F 1899-D 6 1901]Ja 17-24,Mr 21-Ap 4,My 2-9 1902

Wausa GAZETTE. w D 1 1898+
NbHi D 22-29 1898;Ja 13 F 2-9,Mr 2,16,Ap 13-My,Je 8,22-N 16,30,D 21 1899-N 1,22 1900+
NbWa 1898-My 1911;12-13 F 18 1915+

WAVERLY

Waverly WATCHMAN. w D 1891-Ap 1934||
NbHi D 3 1892;O 5,26,N 9,30-D 7,21 1895[96-98]Ja 7,21,F 25,Mr 8,25-Ap 1,My 13-20,Je 10-24 1899;D 14 1901-Jl 5,19-S 13,27 1902-Ja 1903;Mr 21 1908-Ap 18 1934

WAYNE

Wayne DEMOCRAT. *See* Nebraska democrat

Wayne GAZETTE. w *See* Nebraska democrat

Wayne semi-weekly GAZETTE. sw 1884-
NbWC [1884-88]

Wayne HERALD. w Ag 1875+
1875-79? as Wayne county review; 1880?-81? Wayne review; 1882?-Ag 8 1884 Logan Valley herald; Ag 15 1884-85 Wayne herald-tribune
1875-82 pub in La Porte
pub My-Je,Jl 11,25-Ag 15 1884;S 3 1885;D 20 1886 Ja 27 1887;My 10 1888[89-Ag 7 1890]F-Je,Jl 9-23,Ag-D 24 1891[95]Ja 9-30,F 13 1896-[97]Jl 14 1898-Ja 11,25-Ap 12,My-Je,Ag 23 1900+
MWA O 2 1879
NbHi Je 30-Jl 7 1892;Ag 29-D 5,26 1895;Ja 16-Mr,Ap 16 1896-O 10 1918;Ja 30 1919+
NbWC Ja-Jl 12,26-N 6,20 1884-Mr 19,Ap-My 7,21-Jl 9,23-O 8,22-N 1885;88-89;Ja 16-Je,Jl 10-31,Ag 14-S 4,18,O 2,16-23,N 6-13,27 1890-[91-93]-Ja 2 1896;97-Ap,My 19-26,Je 16-Ag 4,18-25,S 15-N,D 8 1898+

LOGAN VALLEY herald. *See* Wayne herald

NEBRASKA democrat. w,sw 1884+
1884-90? as Wayne gazette; 1891?-93? Wayne county democrat; 1894-N 1 1898 Wayne democrat
sw Je 1897-N 1898
NbHi My 27 1892;S 27,N 15,D 6,27 1895-Ja 1,24-31,F 14,Ap 17-24,My 20-Je 5,19-26,Jl 17, Ag 7-21,S 11-18,O 9,23,N 6,20,D 1896-Mr 12, Ap 9-23 1897;Jl 20 1900;Ja 4,Ap 26,My 10-Je 21,Jl 12-19,Ag 1901-[Ja-S 19 1902]Ag 20-S 3, 17-O 1,15 1908-11;My 15 1919-Mr 1932;N 15 1934;Jl 1935+
NbWC D 18 1885;Ja-Je,D 17 1886;Jl-Ag 16 1887;Ja-F 8,22,Mr-Jl 5,Ag-S 13,27 1889-Ja 4 1890;Ja 13 1893;96-97;F 18-Mr 18,29-Jl 1,8-Ag 13,30-N 1 1898;99+

Wayne REPUBLICAN. w F 17 1894-O 13 1904||
Merged with Wayne herald
NbHi Ag 17-D 21 1895;96-Mr 12,26-Ap 16,30-Jl 2,16-O,N 12-26,D 24 1902-Ja 8,22-Je 3,17-24,Jl 8-15 1904
NbWC D 8,29 1897-Ap,My 11-Je 1,15-Ag 3, 17,31,S 14,28-D 1898;F 8-15,Mr 8-15,My 31-Jl 5,19-S 6,N 22-29,D 13-20 1899

Wayne REVIEW. *See* Wayne herald

Wayne TRIBUNE. w -Ag 1884||?
United with Logan Valley herald to form Wayne herald-tribune, later Wayne herald

WAYNE county democrat. *See* Nebraska democrat

WAYNE county review. *See* Wayne herald

WEEPING WATER

NEBRASKA register. w S 25 1875-76||?
NbHi S-O 2,16,N 6-13,27 1875-Ja 15 1876

Weeping Water REPUBLICAN. w 1882—
NbHi My 5-12,Je 1,16-30,Jl 14-N 3,17 1892-Ja,F 9-23,Mr-Je 8,22-Jl 5,20-Ag,S 14-28,O 12-19,N 2,16-D 14,28 1893;Ja 18-F 22,Mr-Ap 5,19-Je 14,Jl 5 1894;S 1895+

SILVER blade. w S 18 1896-97||?
NbHi O 30,N 20 1896;Ja 1-22,F 26-Mr 19 1897

WEST UNION

West Union GAZETTE. w 1884-Ag 28 1896||
NbHi My 20,Je 10 1892;O 18 1895-[96]

WESTERN

Western REPORTER. w N 7 1889-
NbHi N 7,21-28 1889;Ja 16-Mr 6 1890

Western WAVE. w Mr 26 1885+
NbHi [1885]-88;Ag 15-29,S 26-O 10 1889[Ap-D 1890]Ap 14,N 17 1892[Mr 1893-95]+

WESTERVILLE

WESTERN echo. *See* Argosy (Ansley)

NEBRASKA (*Continued*)

WESTPOINT

West Point ADVOCATE. w N 1 1870-
NbHi N 1 1870

CUMING county advertiser. w Ap 24 1889-N 1900||
Merged with West Point republican
NbHi complete

CUMING county democrat. w Ag 10 1876+
1876-98? as West Point progress (title varies slightly)
pub 1900+
NbHi Ag 10,N 23 1876;Ja 4,F 8,22,Mr 22-29,O 11,N 22-D 6 1877;Ja 3-10,24-31,F 21-28,Mr 14,Ap-S 5,19-26,O 10 1878-[83]-N 1886;O 25, N 8,D 1895[96-97]Je 13-Jl 18,Ag 1,S 5-12 1902;Ja 25 1907;Ag 20 1909+

CUMING county vindicator. w O 4 1875-
NbHi O 4 1875

NEBRASKA volksblatt. w F 16 1868-1916||
1868-79? pub in Nebraska City?
In German
NbHi S 24 1879;D 9 1892;Ja 24 1896-Ap 19 1901;15-16

West Point NEWS. w O 15 1872-74||?
NbHi O 15,D 24 1872;Je 24,O 14,D 16 1873;Ja 27-F 10 1874

PROGRESS. *See* Cuming county democrat

West Point REPUBLICAN. w 1870+
pub N 1870+
NbHi Ja 27,My 12,Jl 21 1871;Je 17,D 11 1873; Ja 22,Mr 5,19,Ap 23-30,My 21,Je 4,S 3-17 1874;Mr 11,Ap 29,Jl 8,S 16,N 4 1875;Mr 2, 23,My 18,Jl 6,20,Ag 31,O 26,D 14 1876;F 22-Mr 1,Je 28-D 20 1877;Ja-S,O 10 1878[79]My 13-20,S 2-9,23,D 16 1880;Ja 13-F 3,Mr 31,Jl 14,Ag 11 1881;Ja 12-19,Mr 9,30,Ap 27,Je 29, O 26 1882;F 21,My 1 1884;My 14 1885;O 28 1886;My 17,D 13 1888;O 30 1891;Ja 22,O 7,D 2 1892;Ag 9-O 11,25-D 1895;My 15-22,Je 5,26, Jl 17-Ag 21,S 1896-Je,Jl 20 1900-Ja 3,17-My 16,30-Je 20,Jl 1902+

WHITMAN

Whitman SUN. w Ap 17 1897-1901||?
NbHi Ap-My 8,Jl 23-31,Ag 14,28-S 4,O 8,N 13-20,D 1897-My,S 16 1898-Mr 3,24-S 1,15-N 3,24-D 2,15 1899-Ag 1901

WILBER

BLUE VALLEY blade. w Ja 24 1884-86||?
NbHi F 7,28,Mr 20,Ap 3,My 29,Je 12,Jl 31,Ag 21,S-D 4,25 1884-Ja 1,22,F 12,Ap 9,My 14-21, Je-S 17,O 1-15,29-N 12,D 3-17 1885;Ja 7,21-F 11 1886

DEMOCRATIC guide. w 1888-90||?
1888-Ap 11 1889 pub in DeWitt. Merged with Saline county democrat?
NbHi 1888-F 13 1890

FREE PRESS. w D 12 1879-80||?
NbHi D 12-19 1879[80]

LISTY. *See* Přítel lidu

OPPOSITION. *See* Crete democrat (Crete)

PŘÍTEL lidu. w S 1891-1904||
1891-94? as Listy
In Bohemian
NbHi Ag 15-D 5,19 1895[96-98]Mr 9-N 2,16-D 14,28 1899[1900-02]-Mr 9 1904

Wilber RECORD. w 1878-79||?
Followed by Saline county standard (Crete)

Wilber REPUBLICAN. w F 3 1887+
pub 1887+
KHi Mr 4 1927
NbHi [1887-88]-Ap 18,My 30,Ag 15,O 10,24,D 5 1889;Ap 10-O 1890;92[Ja-N 1893]F 2-9,Ap 27,My 25,N 9 1894[Jl 1895-96]-[1907]+

SALINE county democrat. w N 3 1888+
1888-F 1890 pub in Friend
NbHi 1888-Ja 5,19-Ap 6,20-My,Je 13-Jl 11,25-Ag 8,S 19,O 10,24-31,N 14-D 12,26 1889-[90-91]-Ja 14,28,F 11-Mr 17,31,Ap 14-21,D 1 1892;Ap 2-9,23-Jl 23,Ag 13 1895-1931;Mr 17-Je 16,30-Jl 7,21 1932-Mr 9 1933;Je 27,Jl 11 1935+

Wilber UNION. w Ap 1 1886-Ja 27 1887||
NbHi Ap-Je 10,Jl 1-8,29-Ag 5,19-S 2,23-O 7,D 9-23 1886;Ja 1887

WILCOX

Wilcox BANNER. w Jl 1904-Je 1908||
Merged with Wilcox herald
NbHi Ja 4,25-F 1,15-Mr 15,29-Ap,My 10-24, Je,S 13 1907

Wilcox HERALD. w Mr 1895+
Suspended from Ap 15 1927-D 21? 1928
pub Ap 1895-1908;Ja 23-30,Mr 27-Ap 3,O 10-17,N 20 1919;Ja 20 1920-Ag 22 1921;F 1923-Ap 15 1927;D 21 1928+
NbHi N 8,D 6-13 1895[96-97;F 1898-99]My-Jl 13 1900;D 8 1905;Ja 19-N 23,D 1906-Je 5,Jl 1908;S 15,O 13 1911-Ja 2,16-F 20,Mr 6,20-Ap 2,Jl 2 1914;21-Ap 15 1927;My 16-Ag 22,S 1929+

Wilcox POST. w 1890-94||?
NbWiH 1893-94

WILSONVILLE

Wilsonville REVIEW. w Mr 1887+
KHi S 7 1928
NbHi O 25-N 15,D 6,20 1895;F 21-Je 5,19,Jl-D 11,25 1896-[97]-1906;Ja 11-My 17,31-Je 7,21, Jl 5,26-S,O 11,N 1907-F 2,16-23,Mr-Je 1,Ag 10,31-O 12,26 1923+

WINNEBAGO

Winnebago CHIEFTAIN. w N 1907-N 10 1932||
Merged with Walthill citizen (Walthill)
NbHi Ag 20 1909-S 1914;My 22-Ag,O 30 1919; Jl 7-14,28 1921-N 1926;Ag 1929-Ag 12 1932

WINSIDE

Winside TRIBUNE. w 1889+
1889-93? as Winside watchman
NbHi Je 1 1892;O 24 1895-[96-97]-F 17,Mr 3-10,24-31,My 1898[99-1900]Ap 25-Je,Jl 18-Ag 15,29 1901-[Ja-S 11 1902]Ja 9,Mr 26 1908+
NbWC [1897-98]F 2-16,Mr 9,Ap 6,27,My 25-Je 1,22-S 7,28,O 26,N 30 1899

Winside WATCHMAN. *See* Winside tribune

WISNER

Wisner CHRONICLE. *See* News chronicle

Wisner FREE PRESS. w Mr 11 1898-1916||?
NbHi Mr 18-My 6,20-27,O 28-N 18,D 1898-[1900]-F 9,23,Mr-Je 8,22-S 14,O,N 10 1906; 09;Je 5,19-Ag 14,28 1914-S 22 1916

NEWS chronicle. w 1886+
1886-Ja 3 1924 as Wisner chronicle
NbHi Mr 26,O 8,D 3 1892;O 12,26-D 1895[F-D 1896]-[98]-[Ja-N 9 1901]Mr 22,Ap 5-19,My 17,Jl 19,O 1902-[Ja-N 14 1903]F 6-20,Mr 5, Ap 2,My 21-Je 4 1904[05]-Mr 10,Ap 7 1906; Ap 20-My,Je 8,22-29,Ag 17,N 2-9 1907;Ja 2, My 8 1909;My 22-Jl 24,Ag 7-14,28-S,O 16 1924+

WOLBACH

Wolbach ADVERTISER. *See* Wolbach messenger

Wolbach MESSENGER. w 1902+
1902-04? as Wolbach wave; 1905?-06? Wolbach advertiser
NbHi N 19,D 10 1908;F 18,Je 17,Jl 29 1909+
NbPaJ 1926-32

Wolbach WAVE. *See* Wolbach messenger

WOOD LAKE

Wood Lake STEAMER. *See* Stockman

STOCKMAN. w Jl 1 1911+
1911-Ap 3 1914 as Wood Lake steamer
NbHi Ag 1911-D 3 1915;Ja 28 1916+

WOOD RIVER

Wood River GAZETTE. w S 9 1881-N 17 1894||
NbHi Je 23 1892

Wood River INTERESTS. *See* Wood River sunbeam. 1894+

Wood River SUNBEAM. w N 7 1894+
1894-Jl 11 1919 as Wood River interests
NbHi N 1-8,22 1895[96-97]Ja 14-28,F 11-18, Mr 4-11,25-My,O 21 1898[99-1900;Ap 26 1901-02]-04;F-Mr 3,17-Ag 4,25-O 20,N-D 22 1905; 06-[10-11]-[13]-23;26-[30]+

Wood River SUNBEAM. w N 1902-O 1913||
Merged with Wood River interests, later Wood River sunbeam
NbHi Mr 2,16-23,Ag 10-N 9 1906;F 13 1908-13

WOOD RIVER CENTER

HUNTSMAN'S echo. w Ap? 1860-Ag 1 1861||?
NbHi Je 14,Jl 26-Ag 2,S 6-13,27,O 28 1860;F 7,21,Ap 25-My 2,Ag 1 1861

WYMORE

Weekly ARBOR state. w 1880+
1874?-89? as Wymore democrat
Suspended from 1890?-93?
pub 1914+
NbHi Je 14,Jl 5-12,O 4,D 20 1895;Ja 13 1896-Ja 8,25,29-Je 18,Jl 1897-Je,Jl 10 1903;04-Ja 7 1910;Jl 1911-[14-15]-F,Ap 14,28,My 26 1916; 25+

Wymore DEMOCRAT. *See* Weekly arbor state

Wymore REPORTER. w 1878-1903||?
1878-81? as Blue Springs reporter (Blue Springs)
NbHi Ap 26 1893;O 23,N 6-20,D 4-18 1895[96-97]-Ap 20,My 4,18-25 1898[F 1899-1901]F 21 1902

Weekly WYMOREAN. w 1882+
NbHi Ag 25 1895-[99-S 1902]Ja 10-24,Je 27,Jl 11-18,Ag-S 5,19,O 3,17,31,D 26 1903[04]05;Ja 11-My 10,24 1906;07-F 15,Mr 8-Ap 12,Ag 1934-[35]+
NbWyA 1889-1906;08+

WYNOT

Wynot TRIBUNE. w D 1907-33||
Merged with Cedar county news (Hartington)
NbHarC complete
NbHi Ag 20 1909-Ja,F 17,Mr-Ap 7,21-Je 16, 30-Ag,S 15-O,N 10-D 15,29 1910;18-Ja 1,15 1920;Je 10 1926-33

WYOMING

Wyoming TELESCOPE. w O 1856-
NbHi Je 11,Ag 13,S 3-10 1857;Mr 5-19,Ap 9, My 7,Jl 30,S 3 1859

YORK

York DEMOCRAT. w 1883-N 6 1924||
NbHi D 8 1892;O 24 1895-[96]-F 3,24,Mr 17-Je,Jl 16-23,Ag 1898;F 2,Mr 30-My 18,Je-Ag 17,S 21 1899[1901-02]-[05-08]-[13-S 22 1915] Ja 19,Mr 22,Ap 12-19,Je,Jl 19,Ag 2,16,30,N 1,D 20 1916;My 16 1919-O 23,N 6 1924

NEW teller. w Ag 19 1897+
1897-N 1911 as Teller (O 1899-Ja 17 1901 Teller-democrat)
NbHi S 9-23,O 14,28-N 11,25 1897-Ap,My 11-18,Je-D 21 1899;1900-F 5,19-26,Mr 20-Ap 3, 24,My 8-15,Je 19,Jl 3,17 1901-Ja 8,22,F 1902-[20]Ja 19-26,F 9,Mr,Ap 20,My-Je 1,15,29,Jl 27,Ag 10,24-S 7,N 9,23,D 1921-Ja 4,25-F 8,Mr 8,22,Ap 1922+

York daily NEWS-TIMES. d D 1908+
1909-O 1913 as York daily news
NbHi [1911-13]Je 5 1924+

York REPUBLICAN. w Ap 1876+
pub 1876+
NbHi My 22 1878;N 18-25,D 23 1891-Ja 1,15-F 5,19 1896+

TELLER. *See* New teller

York TIMES. w,sw Ag 13 1880-Jl 20 1912||
Merged with York republican
w 1880-N 28 1908
NbHi Ag 17 1887;N 24 1892[96-97]-My 5,19-26 1898;Ja 2,Mr 1899-1912

York daily TIMES. d 1888-O 1913||
United with York daily news to form York daily news-times
NbHi [O 14 1895-99]-[Ja-S 19 1902]

YUTAN

Yutan BREEZE. w Ja 1895-1908||?
NbHi Ap 18-25,My 9,30,Je 27,S 12,O 3-10,N 14,28 1896-Ja 22,F 5-12,26,Ap 9-23,My 14-21, Jl 30,Ag 20-O 1,22,N 5-19,D 3-17,31 1898;Ja 21,F 18-25,Ag 22-29,Je 17-24,Jl 15-Ag 5,26, D 14-28 1899;D 14 1901-Mr 7,21-My 23 1903

CONSUMERS commercial cyclone. w D 1901-10||?
NbHi Mr 25 1905-Mr 5 1910

NEWS advocate. w F 1915-18||?
1915-F 15 1917 as Yutan news
NbHi F 22,Mr 1917-S 12,26 1918

SMITH press. w 1931+
NbHi My 19-Je 20,Jl 1935+

NEVADA

AURORA

ESMERALDA herald. *See under* Hawthorne

ESMERALDA star. w,sw My 10 1862-Mr 1864||
1862-S 23 1863 as Star
w 1862-Je 24 1863
CU-B N 18 1863
OClWHi My 17 1862

ESMERALDA union. w Mr 21 1864-O 3 1868||
Suspended from Jl-N 23 1867
CU-B N 23 1867-68
Nv F 1867-68

STAR. *See* Esmeralda star

Aurora TIMES. w,d Ap 1863-Ap 1865||
w 1863-My 9 1864
CU-B Je 11,O 7 1864

AUSTIN

Daily morning DEMOCRAT. d Ag 8 1882-Jl 8 1883||
C [Ag 13 1882-83]
CU-B Ag 9 1882-83

PEOPLES advocate. w,sw My 19 1890-D 31 1892||
w 1890-Ja 1891
CU-B D 10 1890-92
Nv complete

REESE River reveille and Nevada progressive. w,sw,tw,d My 16 1863+
w My-Je 6 1863,My 29-S 11 1869,Mr 21 1890-91;sw Je 10-N 25 1863,93-99;tw N 27 1863-My 21 1864
pub 1863+
C N 22 1864-Jl 1865;My 22 1866-[68]N 1888-Je 1889

NEVADA (*Continued*)

AUSTIN—*Continued*

REESE River reveille and Nevada progressive. 1863+—*Continued*
CU-B [My-S 1863]-O 20,N 21 1867-73;F 1878-80;D 3 1885-Ap,Je,S 18-30, D 1886-91;93-99
KHi N 11 1922
MWA Jl 18 1863
NNHi Ap 3 1873
Nv 1867-78;83-1923
NvAC 1865+
NvU Je 1907+
OClWHi S 13 1869

BATTLE MOUNTAIN

CENTRAL Nevadan. *See* Battle Mountain herald and Central Nevadan

Battle Mountain HERALD and Central Nevadan. w 1885-1912||?
1885-1907 as Central Nevadan
CU-B Mr 17 1887;Jl 4,25,D 12 1889;Ja 9-23,F 6 1890;O 15 1891
Nv 1885-88;90-1908;10
NvU D 19 1908-My 18 1911

LANDER free press. w Jl 8 1881-83||?
Nv 1881-82

MEASURE for measure. w D 26 1873-O 1875||
CU-B Ag 28 1875
Nv Mr-O 1875

Battle Mountain MESSENGER. w,sw My 19 1877-D 26 1884||
sw Jl 23-S 17 1881;Ap 26-D 1884
CU-B D 15 1877-[78]-80;Jl 23 1881-[82;83]-84
Nv Je 1881-84

Battle Mountain SCOUT. w 1912+
Nv 1919-24;26-27
NvU 1913+

BEATTY

Beatty BULLFROG miner. *See* Rhyolite herald (Rhyolite)

BELMONT

Belmont COURIER. w F 11 1874-Mr 2 1901||
CU-B O 1876-Ag 17 1878;My 8 1880;F 25 1882;Jl 1889-Ja 1890
ICHi Je 9 1876
MnHi Jl 14 1876
Nv 1875-76;O 1882-1901

MOUNTAIN champion. w Je 3 1868-69||
CU-B 1868-Ap 10 1869

SILVER Bend reporter. w,sw Mr 30 1867-Jl 29 1868||
w 1867-Je 6 1868
CU-B [Mr 30-Je]D 14 1867-68
DLC complete

BLAIR

Blair PRESS. w O 1906-10||?
NvU Ja 17-Je 17 1910

BUTLER

TONOPAH bonanza. *See under* Tonopah
TONOPAH miner. *See under* Tonopah

CALIENTE

Caliente EXPRESS. *See* Caliente lode express

Caliente HERALD. w Ja 12 1928+
pub 1928+
NvU Mr 31 1932+

Caliente LODE-EXPRESS. w 1904-08||?
1905-06 as Caliente express
CLM [1905]
NvU S 7 1907-D 12 1908

Caliente NEWS. w 1920-26||
Merged with Lincoln county record (Pioche), later Pioche record
NvCH 1922-26

PROSPECTOR. w Mr 20 1909-D 28 1912||
Nv complete
NvU complete

Caliente weekly RECORD. w
Nv Ap 1925

CANDELARIA

CHLORIDE belt. Ja 7 1891-D 24 1892||
Nv complete

TRUE fissure. w Je 5 1880-D 4 1886||
CU-B Je 12 1880-[81]-Jl 1882;F 10 1883
Nv complete

CARLIN

COMMONWEALTH. *See under* Deeth

WESTERN home builder. w Je 6 1914-16||?
Nv Ag 1914
NvU 1914-N 23 1916

CARRARA

Carrara OBELISK. w 1913-16||?
NvU F 7 1914-S 9 1916

CARSON CITY

Carson City APPEAL. *See* Carson City appeal-news

Carson City APPEAL-NEWS. d My 16 1865+
1865-D 25? 1870 as Daily appeal; D 29 1870-S 8? 1872 Daily state register; S 9 1872-Mr 9 1873 New daily appeal; Mr 11 1873-76 Carson daily appeal; 1877-1906 Morning appeal
C O 10 1868
CU-B 1865-70;F 22 1871-Ap,Je-D 1880;Ja 9,11 1881;Jl 12,D 29 1882;Je 7-26 1883;F 5,My 1 1884;Ja 26-N 8 1885;86-91
DLC D 29 1870-Mr 5,D 1871-Mr 6 1872
ICHi Ag 15,27 1865
MWA Ja 16 1867;O 29 1868
Nv 1865+
OClWHi O 2 1881

Carson FREE lance. w 1885-86||?
Nv 1885-86

Daily evening HERALD. d Jl-S 1875||?
Nv Ag-S 1875

Daily INDEPENDENT. d Jl 27 1863-O 11 1864||
CU-B Je 17 1864

Daily INDEX. *See* Nevada index-union

NEVADA index-union. d D 25 1880-88||?
1880-81 as Carson index; 1882-85 Daily index; 1886-Jl 1887 Carson daily index
Nv 1880-87

NEVADA patriot. Jl 11 1876-
CU-B Jl 11 1876

NEVADA tribune. sw,d Jl 16 1873-Jl 15 1896||
sw 1873-Ja 24? 1874
CU-B [S 19 1873-My 15,Jl 27 1875;S 1879-80]Je 11 1881;Mr 9,Ap 9 1883
ICHi O 5 1876
Nv Mr 1875-96
NvRW Ap 22-Jl 1896

NEVADA union. w Ag 4 1886-Jl 2 1887||
United with Daily index to form Nevada index-union
Nv complete

NEVADIAN times. w Jl 1927+
pub 1927+

NEW daily appeal. *See* Carson City appeal-news

Carson City NEWS. d 1891-My 1 1930||
Title varies: Carson morning news; Carson daily news, etc. United with Carson City appeal to form Carson City appeal-news
CU-B Jl 20 1927-30
Nv 1894-97;1900-30

Carson City POST. d Ag 27 1864-Mr 22 1865||?
Title varies: Daily evening post; Daily morning post
CU-B D 28 1864
Nv Ap 18 1865

SILVER age. w,d D 1860-N 2 1862||
Followed by Virginia daily union (Virginia City)
w 1860-Ag 1861
CU-B O 2 1862

Daily STATE register. *See* Carson City appeal-news

TERRITORIAL enterprise. *See under* Virginia City

Carson daily TIMES. d Mr 18 1880-81||
CU-B Ap 21,My 19,22[Je 28 1880-F 15 1881]
Nv Jl-D 1880

Carson WEEKLY. w 1891-N 7 1918||
Nv 1891-98;1900-08;12-18
NvU Ja 20 1907-18

CHAFEY

Chafey NEWS. w S 24 1908-09||?
NvU O 10 1908-Ja 23 1909

CHERRY CREEK

Cherry Creek INDEPENDENT. w D 6 1877-Mr 1878||
CU-B Ja 18,F 24 1878

WHITE pine news. *See under* Ely

COLUMBUS

BORAX miner. w Ag 1873-77||
Nv F 1875-My 19 1877

COMO

Como SENTINEL. *See* Lyon county sentinel (Dayton)

DAYTON

ESMERALDA news. *See under* Hawthorne

LYON county sentinel. w Ap 16 1864-66||
Ap-Jl 9 1864 as Sentinel
Ap 16-Jl 9 1864 pub in Como
CU-B 1864-O 6,20 1865-Ap 7,Je 30 1866

LYON county times. *See* Yerington times (Yerington)

Dayton SENTINEL. *See* Lyon county sentinel

DEETH

COMMONWEALTH. w 1909-O 28 1914||?
1909-Ap 16 1911 pub in Carlin
Nv 1912-Ap 29 1914
NvU N 14 1910-Ap 16,My 3 1911-O 28 1914

DELAMAR

Delamar LODE. w 1892-1906||?
Nv 1895-1905

ELKO

Elko ARGONAUT. d Ja 3 1898-F 4 1899||
Nv complete

Elko weekly CHRONICLE. sw,w Je 5-D 4 1870||
Je-S 1870 as Elko chronicle; S-N 1870 Elko semi-weekly chronicle
CU-B Je-N 20 1870
Nv complete

Elko ENTERPRISE. w D 1 1916-17||?
NvU 1916-F 9 1917

FREE press. w 1881-1916||
pub complete
CU-B [F 16-Ap]N 30 1883;Mr 14-28,My 9 1884;Mr 16,Ap 27,Ag 31,D 28 1889[Ja-My,Ag 20-N 1892]O 7 1893;F 3 [Mr-Je]Jl 14-21 1894
Nv 1883-90;92;1900-16
NvU 1883-1916

Elko daily FREE press. tw,d 1904+
tw 1920-31?
pub 1904+
NvEl O 1934+
NvU 1904-Je 1932

Elko INDEPENDENT. sw,w,tw Je 19 1869+
Title varies: Weekly Elko independent; Elko weekly independent, etc.
sw 1869;w 1870-D 22 1933
pub 1870+
CU-B [Je 19 1869-Jl 1882]Mr 3-17,Je 30, O 13 1889
MWA Je 19-Jl,Ag 7-11,28-S 4,11,18,25,29 1869
Nv 1869-71;77-1914;16-Je 1918;Mr 1930+
NvU My 1912+

Daily INDEPENDENT. d 1874-1919||?
CU-B Ja 4 1877[78-Ag 2 1882]Mr 1,O 11, D 26-28 1889
DLC Jl 1885-F 19 1887
Nv 1915

NEVADA silver tidings. w 1896-99||?
Nv 1897-Jl 1899

Elko weekly POST. w S 11 1875-Ap 1881||
CU-B Ja 15-22,Ap 22 1876-Je 1880
Nv 1876-S 1877

ELY

Ely weekly MINING expositor. w 1906-12||
Nv 1907-12
NvU Je 1907-12

Ely daily MINING expositor. d 1907-14||?
Nv My 1910-D 20 1914
NvU F 12 1908-13

MINING record. *See* Ely record

Ely RECORD. w Mr 1905+
1905-06 as Mining record; 1907-08 Ely mining record
pub Jl 16 1906+
Nv 1905-23;26-27
NvU O 12 1907+

Ely daily TIMES. d Ap 20 1920+
pub 1920+
CU-B S 19 1925
NvU F 12 1928+

WHITE Pine news. d,w D 26 1868-Je 24 1923||
1868-Ja 1870 pub at Treasure City; F 1870-80 at Hamilton; 1881-84 at Cherry Creek
d Ap 1869-My 23 1872
CU-B 1868-My 1869;Mr 20-My 23 1872;O 16 1875-Ap 14 1877;Je 15 1878;My-D 16 1880;81-Jl 1882;Jl 1889-Ja 4 1890
ICHi Jl 22 1876
Nv 1870-76;81-87;90-1923
WHi Je 15 1869

EUREKA

ESMERALDA news. *See under* Hawthorne

Eureka evening LEADER. d Je 25 1878-85||?
1878-8? as Eureka daily leader
CU-B Je 25 1878-D 1880;Ja 6,Ap 9 1881
MnHi Ap 22 1879
Nv 1878-79;84-My 16 1885

Eureka daily REPUBLICAN. d Ja 4 1877-Je 24 1878||
CU-B Ja 4,10 1877-78
NbHi My 18 1878
Nv 1877-My 15 1878

Eureka daily SENTINEL. w,d Jl 16 1870-87||?
w 1870-My 20 1871
CPo [1881-82]
CU-B N 12,26 1870-Ap 29,My 3 1871-[73]My 14 1874-75[76-78]-F 1 1881;Ja-Jl 1882;F 12,Mr 19 1884
ICHi Ag 24 1876
MnHi Ap 11 1875;Ag 11 1878[79]
NcD O 17 1877
Nv Ag 1875-S 30 1887

Eureka SENTINEL. w Ag 30 1879+
1879-1903 as Eureka weekly sentinel
CPo Mr 11-S 9,O 7-14,N 25 1882
CU-B Ag 30-S 6,27 1879;N 14,D 1885-N 5, D 3-17,31 1887;Ja 21-Je 1888;Ja 12 1889-Ja 2 1892
Nv 1889-1924;26-Je 1927

Eureka tri-weekly STANDARD. tw 1885-86||?
Nv 1886

FALLON

BALLOT box. w Ap 15 1911-13||?
NvU 1911-Je 28 1913

NEVADA (*Continued*)

FALLON—*Continued*

CHURCHILL county eagle. *See* Fallon eagle

CHURCHILL county standard. *See* Fallon standard

Fallon EAGLE. w O 11 1906+
1906-S 17 1927 as Churchill county eagle
pub 1906+
Nv 1908;10;12;14-23;28-29
NvU My 23 1907+

Fallon STANDARD. w D 1902+
1902-Jl 6 1921 as Churchill county standard
pub Ap 1914-24;26+
Nv 1903-05;07-20;23-30
NvU 1908+

GARDNERSVILLE

Gardnersville RECORD. w Ag 1898-Mr 1904||
United with Courier (Genoa) to form Record-courier
Nv complete

RECORD-COURIER. w Jl 23 1880+
1880-98 as Genoa weekly courier (Genoa); 1899-Mr 1904 Courier (Genoa)
CU-B O 3-17 1890
Nv 1880-98;1900-30
NvFE Ag 1884-O 4 1895
NvU N 1914+

GENOA

CARSON Valley news. sw,w F 20 1875-80||
sw F 16-Ag 14 1877
CU-B [O-D 1875]-[Ja-S 1877]-Je,D 6,27 1878-Ja 10,Je 13,Ag 8-D 5 1879;Ja 2,23-30,Mr 12,My 28,Jl 9 1880
Nv 1875-F 1876

Genoa weekly COURIER. *See* Record-courier (Gardnersville)

DOUGLAS county banner. w O 7-D 23 1865||
CU-B N 18 1865
Nv complete

FREE lance. *See under* Hot Springs, Cal.

Genoa JOURNAL. w Je 2 1880-Ja 1 1881||
CU-B O 13-D 22 1880

TERRITORIAL enterprise. *See under* Virginia City

GILBERT

Gilbert RECORD. w F-My 1925||?
Nv F-My 1925

GOLCONDA

Golconda NEWS. w My 4-D 28 1899||?
Nv My-D 1899

GOLD CREEK

Gold Creek NEWS. D 24 1896-D 10 1897||?
Nv 1896-97

GOLD HILL

Gold Hill daily morning MESSAGE. d My 23-Je 29 1864||
CU-B Je 16 1864

Gold Hill daily NEWS. d O 12 1863-Ap 8 1882||
C Ap 17 1865;N 6 1866;D 29 1868
CSmH Ag 9 1864
CU-B complete
DLC Ap 20-22,My 6-10,24-29,31,Je 2-10,13-29,Jl 6-10,13-14,18,20,24,31,Ag 22,S 1,9,12,21,23,25,D 14 1865;Ap 21-D 1874
ICHi O 5 1876
MWA Ja 26 1866
NNHi My 2 1873
Nv Ap 15 1865;O 1867-Je 1871;F 1875-82
NvU Ap 13 1866-Mr 10 1877

GOLDFIELD

Goldfield CHRONICLE. d 1906-F 27 1909||
NvU Je 5 1907-09

Goldfield daily NEWS. d F 23 1909-Mr 18 1911||
Nv 1909-Je 1910
NvU complete

Goldfield NEWS and tribune. w 1904+
1904-11 as Goldfield news
MWA F 26 1926
Nv Jl 1905-10;Ag 1925;Je-D 1930
NvU My 31 1927+

Goldfield REVIEW. w 1905-F 13 1909||
Nv 1905-08
NvU O 1907-09

Goldfield daily TRIBUNE. d 1905-29||
Merged with Goldfield news and tribune
Nv S 1906-22;Ag 1929
NvU Ja 15 1909-My 1927

GOOD SPRINGS

Good Springs GAZETTE. w My 19 1916-My 21 1921||
Nv Ap-D 1919
NvU Jl 1916-My 14 1921

GRANTSVILLE

Grantsville BONANZA. w 1880-84||?
Nv 1883;Mr-N 1 1884

Grantsville SUN. w O 18 1877-Je 1879||
CU-B Ja 4,O 19,N 30,D 1878;Ja 11-Ap 16 1879

GREENFIELD

MASON Valley tiding. w Mr 1893-N 29 1894||
Nv complete

HAMILTON

Daily INLAND empire. d Mr 27 1869-N 9? 1870||
Follows Daily safeguard (Virginia City)
Suspended from Ap 10-O 4 1870
C Ap 1 1869
CU-B Mr 27-D 1869;F-Ap 10;O 4-N 9 1870
MWA Mr 27 1869
Nv Ap-S 1869
WHi Je 16,S 21 1869

WHITE pine news. *See under* Ely

HAWTHORNE

ESMERALDA herald. w O 13 1877-84||?
1877-Jl 1882 pub in Aurora
CU-B N 1877-Jl 1882
Nv Ag 1883-Ap 19 1884

ESMERALDA news. w 1886-89||?
Early years pub in Dayton, and in Eureka
Nv 1887;89

Hawthorne LUCKY-BOY post. w My 12-O 2 1909||?
NvU My 12-O 2 1909

Hawthorne NEWS. w Ag 29 1928+
pub 1928+

WALKER Lake bulletin. w 1883-My 11 1924||
CU-B [Jl-D 1888]
Nv 1883-85;89-1904;12-24
NvU Mr 21 1911-Ja 25 1919

IONE

NYE county news. w Je 15 1864-My 1867||
CU-B Je 25-Jl 9 1864;S 15 1866

JUMBO

Jumbo MINER. w Ap 4-Jl 15 1908||?
NvU My 16-Jl 15 1908

KIMBERLY

Kimberly NEWS. w F 17-D 17 1910||?
NvU F 17-D 17 1910

LAS VEGAS

Las Vegas AGE. d,tw 1905+
Nv 1909-20;23+
NvU S 21 1907+

CLARK county review. *See* Las Vegas evening review-journal

Las Vegas REVIEW. *See* Las Vegas evening review-journal

Las Vegas evening REVIEW-JOURNAL. w,tw,d Ja 1 1909+
1909-22 as Clark county review; 1922-28 Las Vegas review; Ja-Jl 18 1929 Las Vegas evening review
w 1909-22;tw 1922-28
pub 1909+
Nv 1912-16;20+
NvU 1909-Ja 25 1919;Je 1927+

LOVELOCK

ARGUS. w Ja 5 1901-04||?
Nv 1901-D 23 1904

NORTHERN Nevada weekly mine review. w D 2 1914-15||?
NvU Mr 11-D 29 1915

Lovelock REVIEW-MINER. w 1906+
1906-11 as Lovelock review
pub 1906+
Nv 1913-19
NvU Ja 28 1910-Ja 13 1911;12+

Lovelock TRIBUNE. w 1897-D 28 1911||
United with Lovelock review and Seven troughs miner (Mazuma) to form Lovelock review-miner
Nv 1898-F 1911
NvU 1908-11

LUCKY BOY

Lucky boy MINING record. w Jl 8 1908-09||?
NvU Je 10-S 10 1909

McGILL

COPPER ore. w F 2 1909-14||?
NvU 1909-Je 11 1914

MANHATTAN

Manhattan NEWS. w Ap 7 1906-07||?
Nv Ap-D 1906

Manhattan POST. w 1909-My 30 1914||
Nv 1912-14
NvU 1910-14

Manhattan TIMES. w Jl 13 1907-08||?
Nv Jl-D 7 1907

MAZUMA

SEVEN troughs miner. w 1907-12||
United with Lovelock tribune and Lovelock review to form Lovelock review-miner (Lovelock)
Nv 1908
NvLR complete
NvU N 1908-D 1 1910

METROPOLIS

Metropolis CHRONICLE. w S 15 1911-D 15 1913||
NvU complete

MINA

WESTERN Nevada miner and Mineral county news. w 1907-30||?
1907-29 as Western Nevada miner
Nv F 1914-O 1926
NvU 1909-N 9 1918

MOUNTAIN CITY

Mountain City TIMES. w Ja 21- 1898||
Nv Ja 21-My 13 1898

NATIONAL

National MINER. w Jl 22 1910-13||?
NvU D 9 1910-S 26 1913

PARADISE

Paradise REPORTER. w My 10 1879-N 1880||
CU-B My 17-Ag 30 1879;Ap 10-Ag 28,O 9 1880

PIOCHE

ELY record. *See* Pioche record

Pioche JOURNAL. d D 15 1874-My 3 1876||
CU-B [Ap 1875-Ap 1876]

LINCOLN county record. *See* Pioche record

LOCAL messenger. w 1898-99||?
Nv Je 1898-My 23 1899

Pioche RECORD. sw,tw,d,w S 17 1870+
1870-S 15 1872 as Ely record; S 17 1872-99 Pioche record; 1900-28 Lincoln county record
sw N 13 1870-Ap 11? 1872;tw Ap 14-S 15 1872;d S 17 1872-73?
Cu-B D 7,17 1871;S 15,17,22,25-N 9,30,D 18 1872-Ja, F 1-14,16-Mr 1873;F 5 1881;F 11,Mr 25,Ap-Jl 1882[Mr 9-Ap 20 1889]
ICHi S 23 1876
Nv 1875-1928
NvCH 1928+
NvPC 1870+
NvU My 18 1907+

Daily Pioche REVIEW. d S 23-N 9 1872||
Merged with Pioche record
CU-B complete

RAMSEY

Ramsey RECORDER. w 1905-08||?
Nv 1907-N 8 1908
NvU 1906-O 25 1908

RAWHIDE

Rawhide PRESS-TIMES. d,sw,w F 1 1908-11||?
d F-My 1908,09-10;sw Je 1-D 1908?
NvU Mr 10 1908-Ja 13 1911

Rawhide RUSTLER. w 1907-09||?
Nv 1907-08
NvU F 22 1908-My 17 1909

RENO

BOLLETINO del Nevada. w Je 12 1915+
Italian
pub 1915+
NvU 1915+

Reno CRESCENT. d,w Jl 4 1868-Je 16 1875||
Followed by Daily Nevada democrat
d O 22-N 12 1870;Mr 31 1874-75
C O 10 1868
CU-B Jl 11 1868-[69-71]-S 14 1872;O 23 1873
N F 20 1869
Nv F 12-Je 16 1875
NvRW Jl 1868-My 10 1874

Reno DEMOCRAT. w D 17 1883-84||?
Nv 1883-Ag 21 1884

Reno evening GAZETTE. d Mr 28 1876+
C Jl 8 1904+
CSt Je 7 1895
CU-B Ap 26 1877-Ap 1883;Mr 7,Je 20-Jl 18,S 1877;88-91
KHi Je 1917;Je 21 1919
MWA N 12-15,22-23 1935
Nv Mr 1880+
NvR [1929-33]+
NvRW 1876+
NvU My 1900+

GAZETTE and stockman. w,sw Ap 14 1877-1905||?
1877-87? as Reno gazette
w 1877-1901
CU-B Ap 14 1877-78;Mr 6 1879-80
DLC My 1900-02

Reno LEDGER. w N 6 1899-1904||?
Nv 1900-02
NvRW 1899-O 31 1903

NEVADA (*Continued*)

RENO—*Continued*

Daily NEVADA democrat. d Je 30 1875-Jl 1878||
Follows Reno crescent. Followed by Reno daily record
Nv Je-Jl 1875

NEVADA home builder. w 1916-21||?
NvU O 13 1917-Ja 1 1919

NEVADA mines and farms. w 1909-13||
w ed of Nevada state journal
NvU O 23 1911-Ag 19 1913

NEVADA mining news. w My 2 1907-09||?
NvU D 5 1907-F 25 1909

NEVADA mining press. w 1918-31||?
Nv S 192.-23;Jl 1926-27

NEVADA news letter. w 1913-27||?
KHi Ja 3-10 1916;Je 21 1919

NEVADA rock-roller. w Je 27-S 19 1914||?
NvU Je 27-S 19 1914

NEVADA state journal. w,sw N 23 1870-1902||?
sw F 29 1873-Mr 24 1874
C D 10 1870-Je 21 1873
CU-B 1874-Mr 25,Ap 11 1874-D 1880;Ja-Je 1886
DLC 1872-D 13 1873
ICHi Ag 12 1876
Nv 1870-S 3 1871
NvRW 1870-Mr 25 1874
NvU 1870-72

NEVADA state journal. d Mr 31 1874+
CU-B N 18 1876-78;F 1879-80;My 4,N 11 1882;Ja 18 1883;86-87
CoU 1903;S 1906-My 1910
DLC Jl 1893-1902
ICHi S 27 1876
KHi Jl 28 1912;Ap 18 1920;F 11,My 5 1922
Nv F 1875—
NvR Jl 29 1929+
NvRW Mr 26 1874+
NvU 1874+
WaPS My 21-27 1917;Ap 7 1919;Mr 30 1929
—w ed. 1909-13. *See* Nevada mines and farms

Reno NEVADA weekly. w Jl 25 1907-Mr 11 1911||?
1907-Ap 5 1910 as Reno reveille
NvU F 21 1908-Ap 5,30 1910-Mr 11 1911

Reno PLAINDEALER. w,sw Mr 28 1881-O 31 1884||?
sw during two months preceeding elections
Nv Mr-D 1881;Jl-S 1882;My 1883-S 1884
NvRW Mr 28 1881-O 31 1884

Reno PLAINDEALER. w 1895-99||?
NvRW D 14 1895-O 23 1899

Reno daily RECORD. d Ag 5 1878-N 1878
Follows Nevada daily democrat
Nv Ag-N 15 1878

Reno REVEILLE. *See* Reno Nevada weekly

Reno TIMES. ?
NvRW Ja 13-S 13 1882

WESTERN miner. w My 10 1915-27||?
Nv Mr-My 14 1927
NvU My 31 1915-Je 16 1919
WHi N 15 1927

RHYOLITE

Rhyolite daily BULLETIN. d S 23 1907-09||?
NvU 1907-My 31 1909

BULLFROG miner. *See* Rhyolite herald

Rhyolite HERALD. w Mr 30 1906-Je 22 1912||
1906-S 12 1908 as Beatty bullfrog miner; S 19 1908-S 25 1909 Bullfrog miner
CLM F 8 1907
Nv S 28 1907-S 17 1909
NvU Je 1907-S 25,O 11 1907-12

ROCHESTER

Rochester MINER. w Ja 22 1913-17||?
NvU 1913-Ja - 1917

ROUND MOUNTAIN

Round Mountain NUGGET. w 1906-10||?
NvU Ja 4 1906-Ap 2 1910

RUBY CITY

OWYHEE avalanche. w S 1865-
Nv S 1865-66

RUBY HILL

Ruby Hill MINING news. w Ap 24 1880-84||?
CU-B Ap 24,O 30,D 11 1880-Ja 22,Ag 29 1881-Jl 1882
Nv 1883-N 3 1884

SEARCHLIGHT

Searchlight BULLETIN. w 1902-13||?
Nv 1905-10
NvU O 11 1907-Ja 3 1913

SHERMANTOWN

WHITE pine telegram. d Je 2- 1869||
CU-B [Je 2-Ag 18 1869]

SILVER CITY

LYON county times. *See* Yerington times (Yerington)

MINING reporter. *See* Silver City reporter

Silver City REPORTER. d,w,tw Mr 10-D 5 1876||?
Mr-Ag? 1876 as Mining reporter
d Mr-My 9? 1876;w Je-Ag? 1876
CU-B Ap 22-My,Je 25-Ag 6,O 6-8,N 2-5,12-D 5 1876
Nv Mr-My 1876

SPARKS

Sparks DISPATCH. sw Ja 21 1905-06||?
Nv Ja 21-D 27 1905

Sparks daily FORUM. d,tw Ja 30 1906-10||?
CU-B F 15 1910
Nv Ja-Mr 1910

Sparks TRIBUNE. tw 1909+
Nv S 1910-29;Ap,Je-Jl,S-D 1930

SUTRO

Sutro INDEPENDENT. w Jl 1 1875-N 29 1880||
C-S Ap 21 1879-N 22 1880
CU-B O 16-N 20 1875;Mr 18-O 21,D 1876;Jl-D 7,28 1878;Ja 4,Mr 1,Ap 21-N 22 1880
ICHi Je 24 1876
Nv S 25 1875-78

TAYLOR

WHITE Pine news. *See under* Ely

TONOPAH

Tonopah BONANZA. w Ja 4 1902-09||?
1902-Mr 4 1905 pub in Butler
Nv 1901-D 25 1909

Tonopah daily BONANZA. d 1906-29||
United with Tonopah daily times to form Tonopah times-bonanza
Nv 1912-O 1918
NvU F 1907-Ag 3 1915

Tonopah MINER. w 1901-N 5 1921||
Early numbers pub in Butler
NN Je 25 1910-13
Nv Jl 1902;03-21
NvU Je 1907-21

Tonopah NEVADAN. d O 8 1912-Je 5 1913||
NvU complete

Tonopah daily SUN. d Jl 1905-10||?
Nv 1905-Ap 1910
NvU S 20 1907-Jl 16 1910

Tonopah TIMES-BONANZA. d 1915+
1915-N 15 1929 as Tonopah daily times pub 1915+
NvU N 10 1927+

TREASURE CITY

WHITE pine news. *See under* Ely

TUSCORORA

MINING review. sw,d My-D 30 1877||
United with Weekly Tuscorora times to form Tuscorora times-review
CU-B O 24,31-D 1877

Tuscorora TIMES-REVIEW. d,w Mr 24 1877-1905||?
1877 as Weekly Tuscorora times
w 1877
CU-B Mr 24,Ap 21,My 5,19-Je,23 1877;Ja 10 1878-Jl 1882
MWA Je 18 1878
Nv S 1880-O 1895;97-1903

TYBO

Tybo SUN. w My 19 1877-N 1879||
CU-B S 15 1877-[78]-Ag 9,S 6 1879

UNIONTOWN. *See* WINNEMUCCA

VIRGINIA CITY

Monday BUDGET. w D 24 1917-18||?
Nv 1917-O 28 1918

Monday BUDGET. w Ag 29 1927-
C 1927-[F 18-Ag 12]-O 14,D 9,23 1929

Virginia evening BULLETIN. d Jl 7 1863-My 1864||
CU-B Ap 29 1864

CAMPAIGN notes. w? 1900-01||?
Nv N 1900-Ja 1901

Virginia CHRONICLE. d,tw Ap 8 1872-My 3 1927||
1872-D 28 1905 as Virginia evening chronicle
C Ap 17 1874-Ap 2 1875;S 30 1876-Ap 6,O 12 1878-Ap 4 1879;Je 1880-O 7 1882
CPo [1881-82]
CU-B Ap 8,11,13-D 1872;F 1873-78;Mr 1879-80 87-91
CoU 1901;06-My 1910
DLC Ap 8-O 7 1875
MWA My 4 1876
Nv F 1875-1927
NvU Je 1907-27

Daily CONSTITUTION. d O 26 1864-Ja 1865||
CU-B D 23 1864

FOOTLIGHT. d 1881-87||?
Nv My 24 1883-84;O-D 31 1886

Daily INDEPENDENT. d Je-D 1874||?
CSmH O 31 1874 (supp)
CU-B Jl 15-D 1874
NNHi O 31 1874 (supp)

OLD Piute. d Ap 16 1864-Ja 8 1875||
CSmH My 17,Ag 25,27 1864
CU-B Je 18 1864

Evening REPORT. d F 4 1887-1904||?
CU-B N 18 1887
Nv 1887-N 1888;93-1903

Daily SAFEGUARD. d O 5 1868-Mr 4? 1869||
Follows Trespass. Followed by Daily inland empire (Hamilton)
C O 26 1868
CU-B O 10,12,14-23,26 1868-F 1 1869

Daily TERRITORIAL enterprise. w,d D 18 1858-My 30 1916||
1858-O 1859 pub in Genoa; N 1859-O 1860 in Carson City.
Merged with Virginia chronicle
w 1858-1860
C O 30 1868
CPo Mr 7,Ap 6,O 26,N 21 1882
CU-B Je 9 1860-[67]Ja 10 1868-[72]-[78]Je 1879-80;Jl 11,23,S 6 1890
DLC Jl 1874-Jl 18 1882;89-92
ICHi Ag 5 1876
MWA Ap 6 1865;S 6 1879
MnHi [1879]
NNHi My 6 1873
NcD F 4-Je 25 1879
Nv My 1875-92;94-1916
NvU Ap 1866-1912

Daily TRESPASS. d F 6 1867-O 3 1868||
Follows Union. Followed by Daily safeguard
CU-B F 16 1867-68

Virginia daily UNION. d N 4 1862-F 5 1867||
Follows Silver age (Carson City). Followed by Trespass
C Mr 19,Ap 18 1865
CU-B Ja 1,3,5 1864-67
NvU O 21 1864-O 21 1865

WADSWORTH

Wadsworth DISPATCH. sw 1891-1903||?
NvRW S 21 1892-D 29 1903

WARD CITY

MINER. sw,tw O 1876-Ap 1877||
sw 1876;tw 1877
CU-B N 24,D 7-11 1876;Ja 15-18,29-Mr 9,21-29 1877

Ward REFLEX. sw,w Ap 19 1877-82||?
sw Ag 9-S 30 1877
CU-B 1877-Jl 1882

WASHOE

EASTERN slope. w D 9 1865-Je 27 1868||
CU-B 1865-Mr, Jl 1866-68
Nv Ap 1866-N 1867
NvRW complete

Daily evening Washoe HERALD. d Jl 1-Ag 8 1864||
CU-B Jl 2 1864

OLD Pah-Utah. w O 18 1862-Ap 16 1864||
1862-D 5 1863 as Washoe times
CU-B Jl 11,D 26 1863

STAR. *See* Washoe weekly times

Washoe TIMES. w 1862-63. *See* Old Pah-Utah

Washoe weekly TIMES. w Ap 16 1864-N 20 1865||
1864-Ja 21 1865 as Star
CU-B N 19 1864[65]
Nv S-O 1865
NvRW Ja 28-N 11 1865

WELLS

NEVADA state herald. w 1897+
Nv 1897-Je 1927
NvU N 14 1916+

WINNEMUCCA

Winnemucca ARGENT. w Jl 23-N 21 1868||
CU-B complete
Nv complete

HUMBOLDT register. w My 2 1863-D 1 1876||
F 13-Ap 17 1869 as Humboldt register and workingman's advocate
1863-N 29 1869 published in Unionville
C O 10 1868
CU-B 1863-My,N 27 1869-Ag 6 20 1870-76
DLC D 23 1863 (supp)
MH My 3 1873
Nv Ja-N 3 1876
NvWC 1863-Ap 23 1864

HUMBOLDT star and silver state. d 1906+
1906-Jl 14 1925 as Humboldt star
pub 1906+
Nv 1912+
NvU Je 7 1907+

NEVADA news. w Ja 6 1900-01||?
1900 as News
Nv S 13 1900-Mr 4 1901
NvU Ja-S 3 1900

NEWS. *See* Nevada news

NEVADA (*Continued*)

WINNEMUCCA—*Continued*

PEOPLES advocate. d 1898-99||?
Nv Ja-Ap 1899

SILVER state. d,sw,tw 1869-Jl 14 1925||
1904-06 as Daily silver state; 1907-10 Silver state news. United with Humboldt star to form Humboldt star and silver state
1870-S 3 1873 pub in Unionville
d 1870-1908;sw 1908-10
CU-B Mr 22 1870;Ag 5 1871-S 3,10 1874-Jl 28 1882;Je 29 1885;86-91
DLC My 26 1877
Nv F 1875-1902;04-10;Jl 1911-25
NvU Je 1907-25
NvWH 1876-1925

SILVER state news. *See* Silver state

WONDER

Wonder MINING news. w 1906- N 13 1912||
Nv 1908-12
NvU D 28 1907-12

YERINGTON

LYON county monitor. w 1900-02||?
Nv 1900-Mr 7 1902

LYON county times. *See* Yerington times

MASON valley news and times. w 1910+
1910-Ja 22 1932 as Mason valley news
NvU Ag 1928+

Yerington RUSTLER. F 28 1895-1900||?
Nv 1895-99

Yerington TIMES. d,tw,sw,w Jl 5 1874-Ja 22 1932||
1875-1907 as Lyon county times. United with Mason Valley news to form Mason Valley news and times
1875-88 pub in Silver City; 1889-99 in Dayton
tw 1874-Mr 2,Je 9 1876-Ja 8 1877;d Mr 4-Je 7 1876;sw Ja 13 1877-D 18 1880
CU-B Jl 9 1874-Mr 2,4-Je 7,9 1876-Ja 8,13 1877-D 6 1879;Ja 17,Mr 6,17,Ap 17-D 1880;Je 25 1881;Jl 1,22 1882;S 22-29,O 13 1883;F 9,Mr 15-D 1884;Jl 1888-91
Nv 1880-1909;11-23;26-27
NvU Jl 1912-Ja 1919;25-32

WASP. w S 3 1912-13||?
NvU 1912-F 27 1913

NEW HAMPSHIRE

ALSTEAD

To 1868? as Paper Mill Village

AMERICAN citizen and militia advocate. w
MWA Jl 25-Ag 1 1845
NhD My 2,Ag 22,N 14,D 26 1845-Ja 2,My 22 1846
NhHi F 28 1845

COLD RIVER journal. w Ap 9 1883-Mr 18 1905||
NhHi Ap 9 1891-Ap 21 1897
NhK [1884-87]

INDEX. *See* World's index

WORLD'S index. w Ja 20 1847-
Mr 17 1847 as Index
MWA Mr 17,N 24-D 1,29 1847;Ap 19-26,My 10 1848

AMHERST

FARMER'S cabinet. *See* Milford cabinet (Milford)

HAMPSHIRE express. w
MiU-C My 2 1867

Amherst HERALD. w Ja 1 -N 26 1825||
Merged with New Hampshire statesman (Concord)
DLC Ja 15,Ap 23,My 7,21,Je 11,25,S 17-24,O 22 1825
MBAt Ja 1,F 19,N 12 1825
MWA Ja 8-15,Mr 12,Ap 2-9,23-My 7,21,Je 11-Jl 9,30-Ag 13,S,O 8-N 5 1825
NhA complete
NhHi [1925]

*HILLSBORO telegraph. w Ja 1 1820-Jl 13 1822||
DLC Jl 21,Ag 4 1821;Ja 5,Mr 23 1822
MWA F 10-17,Mr 24-Ap 14,28-My 5,19,Je 2,16,30-Ag 18,S 8-22,O 20,D 15-22 1821;Ja 5-12,F 2,Mr 9,23,Ap,My 11-18,Je 1,Jl 6 1822
MiU-C Jl 2 1821
NhD Ja 6,Mr 10,Je 23,Ag 25,S 15-29,O 27,N 10,D 8 1821
NhHi 1820[21]22

ANTRIM

REPORTER. w 1882+
pub [1882-N 1892]+
Nh 1902+
NhHi 1891-1901

ASHLAND

Ashland ADVANCE. w 1881-86||?
NhHi Ap 21 1883-N 1885[Ja-N 1886]

Ashland CITIZEN. w 1881+
1881-1901 as Ashland item
Nh 1901-25
NhHi 1891-1901

Ashland HERALD. w
Nh 1903-06

Ashland ITEM. *See* Ashland citizen

BATH

CONTEST. w 1894-99||?
NhHi 1895-[97-Ap 1899]

BEDFORD

Bedford MESSENGER. m 1883-
MWA D 31 1884
NhD 1884-Mr,Je-D 1885
NhHi 1883

BENNINGTON

Bennington weekly NEWS. w
NhHi [Jl 19-D 1900]-11

BERLIN

Berlin INDEPENDENT. sw,w Ap 11 1888-1908||?
Nh 1900-08
NhHi 1888-89;Ap 15 1891-99

Berlin REPORTER. w O 8 1897+
pub 1911+
Nh 1899+
NhHi 1897-98

BETHLEHEM

WHITE MOUNTAIN echo. w 1878-1928||?
1878-79? as White Mountain echo and tourists' register (title varies)
pub during summer only
MSaE Ag 18 1883;Ag 23 1884;S 3 1887
MWo Ag 11 1883
MiU-C Ag 27 1887
NN Jl 13-S 14 1878;Je 28-S 13 1879
NhD 1889-94;98
NhHi 1878-96[Jl 13 1918-S 1919;21]

BRADFORD

LAKE and Mountain pathfinder. *See* Bradford pathfinder and visitor

Bradford PATHFINDER and visitor. w D 15 1898-1916||?
1898-N 9 1899 as Lake and mountain pathfinder
Nh 1900-16
NhHi 1898-Ja 17 1901

BRISTOL

Bristol ENTERPRISE. w Je 28 1878+
Title varies: Weekly enterprise; Bristol weekly enterprise
pub 1878+
MWA Je 29,Jl 27 1878;Ag 21,D 4,25 1924;Ja 8,22,F 5 1925
Nh 1900+
NhBr 1878+
NhD 1925
NhHi 1878-[1908]-[11]My 23 1912-[21-22]+

Bristol weekly NEWS. w 1869-72||?
NhHi Je 5,O 16 1869

CANAAN

Canaan REPORTER. w Je 1867+
pub [1905]23+
MWA S 7 1917
Nh 1900+
NhCa Ja 1,F 5,Mr 12-My,Je 4 1869;N 17 1876
NhD F 10 1871
NhHi [O 22 1869-76;F 16 1877-F 1886;87;Mr 16 1888-91]-99

CANDIA

Candia BANNER. w 1877-81||?
NhD Jl 30 1881
NhHi [Ja-My 1880]

CENTER OSSIPEE

CARROLL county independent and pioneer. w O 21 1881+
1881-Jl 11 1924 as Carroll county pioneer
1881-1900? pub in Wolfeborough Junction; 1901-Jl 11 1924 in Sanbornville
pub 1924+
Nh 1901-Ag 2 1918;S 9 1921+
NhCe [1925-28]+
NhHi 1891+
NhO [1925]+
NhWo My 1925+

CHARLESTOWN

Charlestown COMET.
NhHi D 13 1881

OLD No. 4. m D 1882-Ag 1886||?
NhD F-Mr,Je,S,D 1883-Ja,My-O,D 1884;Ja, Ag 1886
NhHi 1882[83]-[86]

SULLIVAN mercury. w D 18 1829-
CSmH Ag 27 1830
DLC D 25 1829;Ja 1,29,Mr 12-19,My 28,Je 25 1830;Je 3 1831
MWA O 15 1830;S 23 1831
NhHi [1830-32]
OClWHi F 26,Jl 30,N 19-26 1830

CHESTER

METEOR.
NhHi Ap 23 1868

CHICHESTER

Chichester REGISTER.
NhHi D 17 1883

CLAREMONT

Claremont ADVOCATE. w 1848+
1848-My 1849 as Northern intelligencer; Je 1849-N 25 1882 Northern advocate
pub 1881+
DLC My 16 1894
MH Je 24-D 23 1879
MSaE F 13 1866
MWA Ja 29,Je 18-25 1850;F 18 1851;My 8 1860;Mr 8 1864;Ap 6 1875
NNHi My 4 1852;Mr 4 1873
Nh 1901+
NhC Je 12 1855+
NhD Ap 2 1867;S 19 1890;N 22 1893-[94-Ap 1898]
NhHi S 26 1848[54;56]Mr 13-D 18 1860[61]-[77]-[79-84]-[87-88]-[1901-My 1902]
OClWHi Ap 24 1866

Daily ADVOCATE. d
NhHi F 21,23 1891

ARGUS. *See* Argus-champion (Newport)

COMPENDIUM. w,sm My 1870-Ja 1875||
Followed by Narrative (not in this list)
Suspended Ap-D 1871
NNHi Ap 17 1873
NhC 1874

Daily EAGLE. d O 5 1914+
NhC 1914+

GRANITE state journal. w 1869-84||?
MWA Ag 15 1874
NhD Ap 22-My 6,S 23 1871[72-75]My 20,Je 3, 24,Ag 19 1876
NhHi Ap 26 1873

IMPARTIALIST. w 1832-35||
DLC S 13 1833
MBAt N 22 1834[35]
NhC complete
NhHi O 20 1832-Ag 2 1834

INDEPENDENT advocate. w
NNHi Ap 24 1833

NATIONAL eagle. w N 1 1834+
DLC D 11 1840;O 15 1841;Ap 21 1843;Ja 22 1847[63-65]
MBAt Ja 26 1838
MH [1879-88]
MSaE 1834-[57]
MWA Mr 25 1836;D 1 1837;F 23 1838-Mr 15 1839;Ja 10,25,O 16 1840;O 15 1841;F 11,O 7 1842;Ja 27,F 10 1843;Ag 7 1856;Ap 19 1860;Ja 29,D 16 1876;Ag 3 1907
NNHi [O 1863-S 1864]-Ja 18 1868;Mr 8 1873
Nh 1901+
NhC 1834+
NhD [O 1835-36]Ja 31,O 14 1845;O 14 1852;O 6 1866;D 31 1870
NhHi [1835-36]-[38;Mr-S 1850]Ap 20 1854-O 6 1856[My-D 1874]-S 11 1875;77-[79-80]-1900
OCHi Ap 13 1838;Ja 17 1840
OClWHi F 2 1838;O 30 1840;Ap 21 1866
P-M Ap 4 1845;S 21 1854
WHi O 30 1835-[1836-Je 1837]Ja 21 1871-S 11 1875

Claremont NEWS. tw Mr 18-Jl 3 1913||
NhC [Mr-Jl 1913]
NhHi complete

NORTHERN advocate. *See* Claremont advocate

NORTHERN intelligencer. *See* Claremont advocate

Claremont SPECTATOR. w Ag 29 1823-S 3 1824||
Followed by New Hampshire spectator (Newport)
MBAt Ap 30 1824
MSaE S 12 1823
NhC complete
NjR S 19,N 7,D 19 1823

COLEBROOK

Colebrook weekly NEWS. w 1876-O 4 1889||
United with Northern sentinel to form News and sentinel, later Colebrook sentinel
NhHi D 15 1876

NEWS and sentinel. *See* Colebrook sentinel

NORTHERN sentinel. *See* Colebrook sentinel

NEW HAMPSHIRE (*Continued*)

COLEBROOK—*Continued*

Colebrook SENTINEL. w N 18 1870+
1870-O 4 1889 as Northern sentinel; O 11 1889-Ag 28 1913 News and sentinel
pub 1871-90;1905-21;27+
MHi Ja 3,F 24 1871
NN Ja 9 1918
Nh 1900—
NhCo 1931+
NhHi 1870-75;D 15 1876-Jl 1880;O 11 1889[95]-99

CONCORD

ABOLITIONIST. *See* Herald of freedom

Concord ADVERTISER. sw Mr 8? 1831-
United with Penacook chameleon to form Penocook chameleon and Concord advertiser
MWA Ap 12 1831
NhHi Mr 11-Ap 15 1831

ADVOCATE of democracy. w Ja 9-Mr 11 1843||
Campaign paper
MWA Ja 2,F 20 1843
MnHi F 13 1843
NhHi F 13 1843
NhM complete

AMERICAN patriot. *See* New Hampshire patriot

Concord daily BLADE. *See* Saturday blade

Saturday BLADE. d,w S 1 1880-N 1883||?
S-D 7 1880 as Concord daily blade. Merged with Concord tribune
Suspended from D 7-18 1880
d S-D 7 1880
MWA S 2[N 11-D 7]1880;Ja 1,22,F 5-12,26-Mr 12,Ap 2 1881
NhHi 1880-D 16 1882

CHAMELEON. *See* Penacook chameleon and Concord advertiser

COURIER and inquirer. *See* New Hampshire courier

CRUSADER and New Hampshire state temperance journal. w 1852-
Title varies: Crusader and reformer and family circle. Merged with New Hampshire phoenix
d during legislative session
MWA Ap 2 1853
NhHi Ap 10 1852-S 22 1853

Daily DEMOCRAT and freeman. *See* Daily independent democrat

DEMOCRATIC standard. w Je 14 1856-Ag 3 1861||
DLC Je 28 1856;Ap 25 1857-S 17 1859;Ja 7-My 5 1860
MB O 4-11,D 21-28 1850;Ja 18-Jl 1851[59-61]
MWA 1856-[Ja-Jl 20 1861]
MiU-C [1856;58-61]
NhHi complete
NhM Jl 19 1856-N 7 1857

Concord ENTERPRISE. w F 22 1892-
Nh 1900-08
NhHi F 22 1892

EXPOSITOR. bw N? 1834-
InI Ag 3 1835
MWA Mr 30 1835
NhHi F-D 7 1835

Daily FREEMAN. d
United with Daily independent democrat to form Daily democrat and freeman, later Daily independent democrat
DLC Je 9,Jl 1 1846

GRANITE column. w Jl 21 1842-
WHi Jl 21 1842

GRANITE freeman. w Je 20 1844-Ap 23 1847||
United with Independent democrat to form Independent democrat and freeman later Independent democrat
DLC Je 20 1844
MHi Ag 22 1844;Ja 16,O 9 1845
MWA 1844[45-O 1846;Ja 15-Ap 9 1847]
MiU-C [1844-47]
NNHi Ap 3 1845
NhD Je 20,Jl 18 1844;O 16-23,N 6 1845;Ja 22 1847
NhHi complete

GRANITE state courier.
NhHi [S 1924-My 1926]

HERALD of freedom. w,sm Ja 24 1835-O 23 1846||
Ja-F 1835 as Abolitionist
Suspended from Je 14-Jl 5 1844;D 6 1844-Mr 14 1845
w 1835-45
Ct D 9 1837
CtHi Mr 14 1845-O 2 1846
DLC Mr 1835-46
IP S 1 1838
MB S 21 1839;Ja 18,F 29-D 1840;41-45
MBAt Ja 3 1835
MHi Je 14 1844;My 9,Jl 11,Ag 22-29,S 12 1845;Ja 9,F 27,Je 5,19,O 23 1846
MSaE D 12 1835;Je 27 1845
MiU-C [1835-37;41;43-45]
MnHi Ap 8 1842
NNHi [1835-36]F 1837-Ag 1838;39-[41]43;45
NSyU Jl 8 1837
NhD [1835-38]Ag 28 1840[41-46]
NhHi F 7,Mr 1835-[41-42]-[45-46]
NhM [My 14 1836-37]
TNY S 28 1839;S 24 1841;Jl 4-18,Ag 8 1845

HILL'S New Hampshire patriot. w Ag 12 1840-My 27 1847||
Merged with New Hampshire patriot
CtHi N 11 1840-Jl 21 1842
DLC Ja 5 1843-D 31 1846;Mr 4 1847
MWA 1840-[Ja 14-My 13 1847]
MiU-C [1841-47]
NcD [Ag 1840-45]
NhD Ag 26 1840;F 21 1842;My 26-Je 13,Jl 14,N 3,D 3 1842-Ja 5,19-Mr,Ap 13-20 My 11-Ag 3,17-31,S 14-28,O 12,26-N 2,16-23,D 7-28 1843;Ja 11,25-F 1,15,Ap 18,My 30,S 12-O 17 1844
NhHi complete
NhLa O 1840-My 20 1847

HILL'S daily patriot. d Je 3 1841-
Merged with Daily patriot
d during sessions of legislature
DLC Je 7-8 1842
MWA Je 3,12 1841
NhHi [1841-Je 17 1842]

Daily INDEPENDENT democrat. d
1847-49 as Daily democrat and freeman
d except Mondays, during legislative sessions
DLC Je 17 1857;[Je 12-Jl 5 1861]S 6 1866
MWA Je 7-Jl 13 1855;Je 4-27 1857;Je 25 1858;Je 2-29 1859;Je 7-Jl 5 1860;Je 6-Jl 5 1861
MiU-C [1856;57;59-61]
NhD Je 6-Jl 5 1861
NhHi Je 8,Jl 5 1847;55-61

INDEPENDENT democrat. w My 1 1845-S 29 1871||
My 1847-F 1849 as Independent democrat and freeman. United with Republican statesman to form Independent statesman
My 1-? 1845 pub in Manchester
DHU-M Ja 27,F 17,Mr 2-9,23,Ap 20-27,S 24 1848
DLC F 24 1848;Je 21 1849;D 22-29 1859;Ja 5 1860[Je-N 1861]N 6-20 1862[64-65]-70
IHi Ap 20 1865
MBAt Ap 20 1865
MHi Mr 12 1846;Mr 16,Je 1,D 7 1848;Ja 4 1849;Ja 7 1869
MSaE Ag 5 1847
MWA 1845-Ap 1846;My 1847-My 2[23-D 12] 1850;51-71
MiU-C [1857;59;69]
NNC Mr 16,My 25,Je 1,15 1848;Mr 13,Jl 31 1851;Je 2 1852
NNHi 1845-Ap 1847;My 1848-Ap 1850;Mr 29 1855
NhCon 1847-65
NhD S 18 1845;Mr 16 1848-Mr 22 1849;D 5 1861;F 27 1862[1868]
NhHi complete
NjR My 1848-Ap 1849
OClWHi Je-Jl 5 1860;Je-Jl 5 1861;Mr 11 1863
OrHi F 22 1866
P-M Je 29 1854

INDEPENDENT statesman. w O 6 1871-1924||?
Formed by the union of Independent democrat and Republican statesman
CtW S 27 1883
DLC 1871-S 1874;Ja-Je,1 Jl 6 1882
MWA 1871-S 24 1891;O 1892-S 1917
MiU-C 1871-[77]-80[82]-[84]-86;91-[93-94]
NNHi O 6-13,N 9-16 1871;Ja 18-Mr 7 1872
NbHi Ja 22 1874;O 10,31 1901
NcD 1875
Nh O 1900-S 1916;Ja 8 1923-F 1924
NhD Jl 19,D 27 1883-S 1900;Je 29 1905-My 1907;O 21 1909-S 1923
NhHi 1871-[1919-20]-S 24 1923
OClWHi S 2 1880
—d ed *See* Concord daily monitor and New Hampshire patriot

LEGISLATIVE reporter. d Je 7 1849-
Issued daily during legislative sessions
DLC Jl 9 1863;Je 25 1864;Je 13-15,27-28 1865
MWA Je-Jl 7 1849;Je 5-Jl 9 1862;Je 4-Jl 11 1863;Je-Jl 15 1864;Je 8-Jl 3 1865;Je 7-Jl 9 1866
MiU-C Je 8 1849[62-65]
NhCon [1849]
NhHi Je 7-Jl 7 1849;62-66
WHi Je 5-Jl 10 1862

Morning LIGHT. w
NhHi N 23 1854
P-M D 11 1854

LOCAL news. d F 3 1879-
DLC [F 3-Mr 3 1879]
MWA [F-D 1879]Ja 2-7,12,16,27-30,F 20,23,26,28-Mr 1,13-15 1880

LOCOMOTIVE. w My 20-? 1842||
NhD My 31,Je 3 1842
NhHi My-Jl 12 1842

Weekly MESSENGER. w
NhHi [1910]

MONITOR. sm,w 1830-
sm 1830-Ap 20 1836
DLC [My 7 1834-Ap 20 1836]
MWA My 1834-35;Ja 27-My 4,O 14 1836
MiU-C Je 15 1834
NjR My 7 1834

Concord daily MONITOR and New Hampshire patriot. d My 23 1864+
1864-Mr 14? 1884 as Concord daily monitor; Mr 15? 1884-Mr 1923? Concord evening monitor
pub 1871+
DLC Ja 14,Ap 15 1865;Je 13 1867;My 5 1870;Je 15 1871;Jl 9 1874-Je 1875;76-1902
MWA My 25,Jl 20,N 3,23 1864-My 20 1865;Mr 14,Je 6 1866;Mr 7 1868;Mr 24,My 28,Je 8,11 1869;Je 21,30 1870;Jl 6,D 27 1876;D 27(supp) 1877;F 28,Jl 12 1881;Je-S 15 1883;Jl 25 1884;My 23(supp)1885;Je 21 1894;My 30 1896;My 24 1915
MiU-C [1864;69;83]
NNHi My 1 1873;O 1 1875
Nh My 23 1864-[84-85]-[95]-[1901-06]-[13]-[21-24]-[29-31]+
NhCon 1871+
NhD Jl 7 1864;Jl 1924+
NhH 1864-1926
NhLiT Je-Jl 3 1875
NhM D 1881-Ja 4 1883
NjR D 27(supp)1877

Concord MONITOR. w O 14 1865-Ja 5 1867||
Merged with Independent democrat
MWA 1865[66]Ja 5 1867
NhHi complete

Concord morning MONITOR. d Mr 15-N 15 1885||
MWA Jl 24,Ag 11 1885

NEW HAMPSHIRE courier. w D 14 1832-
Title varies: Courier and inquirer; New Hampshire courier and Concord gazette; etc.
DLC Ap 29 1835[36]F 8 1839;Mr 13 1840;Ja-D 1 1842
MBAt D 14 1832;Ja 11,F 15-22 1833;Je 13-27 1834;F 6,Mr 27,My 15,Ag 28,S 25 1835;F 19 1836;F 16,Mr 23-30,Ag 17 1838
MWA D 1832[S 27-D 1833]Ja 10 1834-My 1836;S 23-N 23,D 15 1837[F-N 16 1838]Je 7,Jl 26,N 1,D 13 1839;Je 5,26,O 16 1840;Ja 15,F 12,Ap 2,16,S 3,D 10 1841[42-N 3 1843]Jl 5 [O 1844-D 19 1845;F 1846-Mr 1847]
MeU 1832-Ja 4 1833
MiU-C [1834;38]
MnHi Je 16 1840;Ja 8,My 7 1841;Mr 17 1843
N 1832-Je 3 1836;Ap 1 1846
NNHi [1832-Je 1836]My 27 1840;Ap 2 1841;N 22 1844;N 25 1846
NcD Mr 30, My 4 1838
NhD Jl 5 1839;F 7 1840;Ja 3, Ap 23 1841;My 31 1844
NhHi 1832-Je 3 1836;S 26 1837-Mr 1847
NhM Je 1834-Je 3 1836
VtNU 1833-34

NEW HAMPSHIRE journal. w S 11 1826-My 16 1831||
United with New Hampshire statesman to form New Hampshire statesman and state journal, later New Hampshire statesman
Ct [1826-27]
DLC complete
ICHi D 17 1827[28-29]Mr 15 1830
MB F 3-10 1872
MBAt 1826-F 7 1831
MHi Je 23 1827
MSaE O 30 1826;Ap 21-S 1,D 20,N 3 1828;Ja 12 1829;N 1 1830;My 9 1831
MWA complete
MeU Je 16 1828;Ap 25-My 2 1831
MiU-C [1826-31]
MnHi Ja 4 1830
N F 12 1827;S 15 1828
NcD O 29 1827;Ag 25,S,O 6 1828;Mr 28 1831
NhD complete
NhHi complete

*NEW HAMPSHIRE observer. w Ja 4 1819-38||
1819-Mr 25 1822 as Concord observer; Ap 1 1822-Je 24 1826 New Hampshire repository; Jl 1 1826-Jl 5 1827 Repository and observer; Jl 12-O 3 1827 New Hampshire repository and observer. Ap 15-Ag 5 1830 United with Christian mirror to form Christian mirror and New Hampshire observer (Portland, Me) (not in this list) Jl 12 1827-My 11 1831 pub in Portsmouth
CSmH F 24 1830
DLC Jl 14-28 1821;Jl 22-D 9 1822;Je 14,N 8-23, D 6-13 1824;O 24 1827-34
ICN Ja 7 1832
MBAt [1821]My 27 1822;Ap 14,28,S 29,N 3 1823;My 10 1824;O 31 1825;S 29,D 23 1826;Ag 30 1827;O 20 1830;My 21 1831;D 1 1832;Jl 20 1833
MSaE S 22 1823;Mr 3 1832
MWA 1821-Mr,Ap 15 1822-[23-24]25;Ja 23,Ap-[Jl-D 1826]-Je,Jl 12 1827-Ap 12[Ag 11-D 1830]-[36-37]38
MiU-C [1821-22;27-35]
MnHi My 27 1829;F 23 1832
N My 6-20,Je 17,Jl 1,Ag 5,N 4,D 16 1822;Ja 13,Mr 31,Ap 21-28,Jl 7,21,D 8 1823;Ja 12,F 2,Mr 22-29,My 3,Jl 5,S 27,N 15 1824;F 28,S 19 1825;Je 1,Ag 9 1827;30
NNHi F 12 1821;Ap 1822-Jl 6,S 27 1827;Ja 2,F 6,Mr 5 1828
NcD [1823;25-Ja 6 1830]
NhD [1821-N 2 1838]
NhHi 1821-38
NhM My 21 1831-Ap 10 1835
NjR N 22 1824;Ja 2 1826
OClWHi Ag 23 1879

*NEW HAMPSHIRE patriot. w O 18 1808-1921||?
1808-Ap 4 1809 as American patriot; Ap 18 1809-Ja 26 1819 New Hampshire patriot; F 2 1819-68 New Hampshire patriot and state gazette (1863-O 16 1867 New Hampshire patriot and gazette); O 10 1878-Mr 1901 New Hampshire people and patriot (title varies: People and patriot; People and New Hampshire patriot
CSmH S 6 1830
Ct [1827-29]
CtHi [Mr 1839-Je 16 1842]
CtY Ja 9 1826-N 19 1832;Mr 21 1834-40;My 19 1841-44;S 1845-S 21 1848;Jl 12-27 1849;Je 20-D 1850;Mr 22 1851-62;Ja 18,F 1 1871
DLC 1821-[29]-[43-44]-69[73]N 1877-O 2,17 1878-[80]-[82]-Ap 10 1890
GAtCo Je 3 1839
ICHi Ag 12,D 9 1822[23-F 4 1828]
IU D 1 1834
MAm Jl-D 1917
MB Jl 30 1821;S 18 1826;Mr 12-19,O 1 1827;Je 23 1828;Mr 12 1856;Ja 22,O 22 1862;Jl 1 1863;Mr 16 1870;Jl 15 1874
MBAt 1821-28;Mr 16,Jl 13 1829;Mr 8,Ag 30,N 1 1830;O 10 1831;F 13,Je 11 1832;Je 3,O 14,D 2 1833;Ap 28,My 5-12,D 8 1834;Ap 20,Je 29 1835;F 29,Ap 25 1836;N 20 1837;Ja 1,F 12 1838;O-D 1840;S 9 1841;42-43;Ja 7 1847;53;Ja 2-16,My 7 1856;Ap 1865
MH 1821

NEW HAMPSHIRE (*Continued*)

CONCORD—*Continued*

*NEW HAMPSHIRE patriot. w 1808-1921||?
—*Continued*
MHi 1822-25;27;29;O 4-11,N 1-8 1830;34;37-38;O 22 1862;My 5 1869
MSaE D 31 1821-23;25[28]O 24 1831;Ap 7,My 12,Jl 2,23-30,Ag 13-20,S 3,O 15,N 12,D 17 1832;Ag 3,O 5 1835
MWA 1821-[68-69]-71[F-Ag 14 1872]Ja 8,My 28 1873;Ag 26,S 9 1874-O 2,10 1878-90;Ag 31 1899;Ag 19 1903
MeBa [1829-Je 1832]Mr 5 1838
MeU Je 16,O 6,D 15 1828;Ag 9,S 6 1830;S 19 1831;Jl 30,D 1,5,8,24 1832;Ja 14-30,F 4, 9,Mr 4-11,27,My 8,Jl 1 1833;F 13(extra)1851
MiU-C [1821]-[23]-[29-65;67;81-82]
MnHi D 30 1822[F-N 17 1823;F 13 1826-N 1829]O 11 1830;Jl 20 1835;Jl 18 1836;Je 24 1839;Mr 30,O 19-31 1840;Ap 2,30 1841;Je 16,N 10[D 22 1842-44;46;49]-Ap 1853;Jl 2 1856[58-60;62]
N 1821-24;N 7 1825;S 24 1827
NBHi Ap 2 1821
NBuG Je 22,Ag 3,O 24 1840
NN S 5 1855;F 4 1857
NNHi 1821-[26;Jl-D 1827]-[35-37]Jl 16,N 12 1838;Ja 14,S 2,N 11 1839;Ag 12 1840-1847;S 1856-O 14 1857;59;S 12-26 1860;61[62]Ja 5 1869;My 1,O 9 1873;Ag 19,O 2 1875;Ap 18 1889
NcD [1821-25;29;33-34;36-49]-[60-68]
NcU Jl 29 1857
NhCon [1821-S 23 1863]
NhD 1821-32;F 18,Ap 22,Jl 29-O 14,28 1833-Ap,My 14-Jl 16,30-Ag 12,26-D 1841[42-78]-Ap 7 1892
NhHi 1821-[94]-[98]
NhK Ag 20 1827-Je 1843
NhLa My 26 1828-32;41-Jl 1842;My 1847-My 17 1849
NhM [1821-28]-[32]-[63]-Ag 17 1870
NjR [1825-26;29;35;42;44-45;47;49]
OClWHi D 31 1821;My 19,Je 30 1823;Ap 19, 26 1824;Ja 12,19,O 19,26,N 2 1829;O 29,N 6 1832;Ap 13,D 14 1835;Je 22 1840;Ap 14 1842; Jl 22 1847;Ja 11 1849
P-M My 11 1835
RPB Mr 4 1843
TxU 1827-Ag 18 1828
VtNU 1825-26
WHi [O 1882-Mr 3 1887]Je 4 1900

NEW HAMPSHIRE patriot. . . sw *See* Semi-weekly patriot

NEW HAMPSHIRE people and patriot. d *See* Concord evening patriot

NEW HAMPSHIRE people and patriot. w *See* New Hampshire patriot

NEW HAMPSHIRE phoenix. w Ja 28 1854-
Merged with Weekly chronicle, later Rockingham chronicle (Portsmouth)
MWA My 27,Ag 12,S 9,N 11,25 1854;Ja 27,F 24,Ap 28,My 12,N 3 1855
NN Ap 8 1854
NhHi 1854[55]-Mr 8 1856

NEW HAMPSHIRE repository and observer. *See* New Hampshire observer

NEW HAMPSHIRE statesman. w Ja 6 1823-D 25 1868||
O 22 1825-My 14 1831 as New Hampshire statesman and Concord register; My 21 1831-Jl 16 1847 New Hampshire statesman and state journal. Followed by Republican statesman
CSmH F 24 1823
Ct [1831]Jl 14 1832;Mr 29 1834
CtY F-D 1856;Je 28 1862;Mr 16 1866
DLC [1823-24]-68
IU Je 20 1845
MB [O 16 1824-My 20 1826]S 1,22,N 3 1827 [28]
MBAt [1823-25]Ja 7,27 1826[27-28]Ja 3,Mr 14, Ap 18,My 2,30 1829;Mr 6,27-Ap 3,24-My 1,Je 12 1830;My 21,N 19 1831[32-33]Ap 26,My 24 1834;Ja 24-31,F 14,Mr 21 1835;N 4 1837;F 10, N 10-17 1838
MSaE [1826-30]Ja 1,22-29,F 12-Mr 5,19-Ag,S 10-O 1 1831
MWA Ja 13 1823-24;Je 6,O 22 1825-36[Ap-D 1837]-[40]-[42]-[Ja-O 1844;Ja 24-N 1845]46-68
MeU Je 11 1831;Mr 22 1834[35-41]S 30-O 7 1842[43]Je 21 1844;Ja 3 1845
MiU-C [1823-26;28-44;46-47;49-58]-[60-64]
MnHi My 2,Jl 18 1840
N Jl 28,N 17 1827;My 30,Je 25 1830;Ja 21 1832;O 19 1833;Ag 30 1851-52;Jl 16 1853
NN F 10 1823
NNHi Mr 24,Je 1823;My 29 1824;Jl 16 1825-Jl 18 1829;My 21 1831-My 11,Ag 17 1833[36]Mr 9 1849;Ja 31,Je 6,Ag 2 1851;D 17 1859-Ja 1861;D 13 1862;63-65;Ja-F,Mr 3-17,Je 21 1867
NSchU Mr 25-Ap 1,My-Je 10 1842
NcD [1823-25]-29[37]52-68
NhD [1823-S 1848]
NhHi complete
NhM Ja 19-Je 21 1824;O 22 1825-[28-32]
OClWHi Ap 26,My 31,Je 21-28,Ag 2 1824; Ja 10 1825;D 16 1826;D 7 1833;S 17 1836;63-64
WHi My 13 1826;Jl 23 1847-Jl 13 1849;S 6 1851

NEW HAMPSHIRE statesman. d Je 2 1852-Jl 5 1861||
1852-58 as Daily statesman
d during legislative sessions
MWA Je 19 1851;Je 9-10,14,Jl 11 1854;Je 8, 22,Jl 4 1855;Je 12-14,25,27,Jl 3,10 1856;Je 9,24-26 1857;Je 3-26 1858;Je 2,4-15,17-27 1859; Je 6-7,11,13-15,19-20,28,Jl 2,5 1860;Je 6,10,13-14,18-19,Jl 2,5 1861
MiU-C [1856-57]
NcD Je 2,10 1859;Je 6,13 1860;Je 13,15,27 1861
NhD Ja 28 1842;Je 9-Jl 10 1846;Je 3-Jl 3 1847;Mr 21 1857;Ja 1 1859
NhHi Jl 4 1846;48;51-52;54-61
P-M Jl 12 1855
WHi Je 2-18 1852;Je 8-Jl 15 1854;Je 7-Jl 14 1855;Je 5-Jl 12 1856;Je 4-27 1857;Je 5,16 1858;Je 2-28 1859;Je 6-Jl 5 1860;Je 5-Jl 5 1861

NORTHERN indicator. w Ja 1- 1853||
NhHi J 1-15 1853

Concord OBSERVER. *See* New Hampshire observer

OLIVE branch. w Ja 5 1832-
DLC Mr 1 1832
MWA Ja 19-Je 14 1832
MiU-C F 16 1832
NjR Ja 5 1832

Semi-weekly PATRIOT. sw N 20 1832-Mr 19 1834||
1832-33? as New Hampshire patriot and state gazette
DLC Ag 14 1833;F 5 1834
MWA [N 20 1833-34]
NhHi 1832-Mr 19 1834
NjR Ja 30 1833

Concord PATRIOT. w Ja 13 1835-
MBAt Mr 10 1835
NNHi F 3 1835
NhHi Ja 13-Mr 17 1835

Concord evening PATRIOT. d 1839-F 28 1923||
1839-Ap 26? 1885 as Daily patriot; Ap 27 1885-My 1889 Daily people and patriot; Je 1 1889-Mr 1901 People and patriot (Ag 7 1893-F 19 1898 New Hampshire people and patriot) F 1 1901-O 26 1919 Daily patriot. United with Concord daily monitor to form Concord daily monitor and New Hampshire patriot
pub only during legislative sessions and political campaigns through 1861
CtY Je-Jl 13 1850;Je-Jl 5 1851
DLC Jl 1 1843;Je 3-5 1847;Je 8 1848-Ja 5 1849; Je 6-Jl 13,N 7 1850-Ja 4 1851;Je 3 1852-Ja 10, Je 2-Jl 2 1853;Je 8 1854-Jl 14 1855;Je 5-Jl 12 1856;Je 4-27 1857;Je 3-26 1858[Je 1859;Je-Jl 1860]Je 6-Jl 3 1861;Jl 1869-Ja 1 1870;Jl 10 1874-O 1877[80]F 17,24 1881;Jl 8 1889-1902
MB Je 9 1842;N 7 1850-Ja 2 1851
MBAt Je 4-27 1857;Jl 3-26 1858
MHi N 20 1868
MWA N 5,17,D 2 1842;Je 26 1843;Je 6-19,N 21-D 10,13-18,21-28 1844;Je 4-Jl 9 1846;Je 3-Jl 5 1847;Je 9,12-16,19-24,N 25 1848-Ja 5 1849;Je 6-Jl 13,N 7 1850-Ja 4,Je 5-Jl 5 1851; Je 3-19,Ag 12 1852;Je 2-Jl 2 1853;Je 8-Jl 15, N 20,24-27,29 1854;Je 7-Jl 14 1855;Je 5-Jl 3 1856;Je 5-10,12-27 1857;Je 3-26 1858;Je 2-28 1859;Je 7-Jl 5 1860;Je 6-Jl 4 1861;Je 3 1868-69;Je 16,Jl 1870-72;My 31 1873-Jl 6,Ag 1,8,11, 17-18,27-28,31,S 14,17 1874;Je 14 1875;Jl 20 1876;Ap 7 1877;Ag 11,17,23,31,S 4 1883;D 15 1908
MiU-C [1846-47;50-53;58-61;69]
MnHi Je 8,15,17,19,24 1841;D 20 1842
NN Je 5,17,19,22-Jl 1 1849;Je 5-Jl 3 1851;Jl-D 1871
NNHi N 7 1850-Ja 4 1851;Ag 19 1852;Je 12 1855-Jl 12 1856; Ap 18 1889
Nh Je 6 1844-[46]-61;68[69]-[73-75]-81;85-[92]-[96-1902]-[05-07]-[12]-[15-23]
NhCon 1847;50;52
NhD N 11-12,14-19,D 2,6,24-25,29 1842;F 1,Je 4 1844-Je 13,15-20,22-27,29-Jl 4,7-10 1845;Je 8-10,12-14,16-17,19-24 1848;Je 21-23,27 1855;D 17 1868;Jl 19,26,Ag 20,S 16 1887
NhHi 1841[Je 1842-Je 1843]44-[77-79]80;[Je-D 15 1883]Ap 27-D 1 1885;86-92
NhLiT Je 2-Jl 6 1875
NjR [Je 10-Jl 15 1854]
OClWHi Ja 4-5 1849

PENACOOK chameleon and Concord advertiser. sm,w
Title varies: Chameleon; Penacook chameleon
NhHi [My 10 1834-Ja 1 1835]

PEOPLE. w Je 11 1868-O 3 1878||
United with New Hampshire patriot to form People and New Hampshire patriot, later New Hampshire patriot
DLC Je 11 1868;Jl 1869-Je 1870;Je 29-S 7,N 1871;F,Je 27-D 1872-Je 13,S 12 1878
MSaE Ap 29-Ag,S 9 1869-Ja 1871
MWA complete
MiU-C [1871-72;76-77]
NNHi O 9 1873;Ag 19 1875
NcD [Je-D 1868]-[72-75]
NhD 1869-78
NhHi complete

Daily PEOPLE. d Je 1 1870-78||
United with Daily patriot to form Daily people and patriot, later Concord evening patriot
MWA Je 7-Jl 18 1871;Je 6-Jl 9 1872;Je 5-Jl 3 1873;Je 3-Jl 10 1874;Je 2-Jl 3 1875;Je 8-Jl 21 1876;Je 7-Jl 21 1877;Je 6-Ag 20 1878
MiU-C [1873-74;77]
NhD Jl 11-12,14 1871;Je 11,14,20,26,Jl 3 1872
NhHi 1870-74

Daily PEOPLE and patriot. *See* Concord evening patriot

PEOPLE and patriot. w *See* New Hampshire patriot

Twice-a-week PEOPLE and patriot. sw
NhHi 1892[Ja 3-Ag 4 1893]

PEOPLES advocate. w Ag 12 1841-44||
DLC Ag 19-26 1841
MdBJ Jl 1-8,22,Ag 11-26,O 7-14,N 4,25,D 2, 24-31 1842
NhHi [Je 17 1842-Ja 23 1844]

PLAIN dealer. w
NhHi S 6 1845

Concord REGISTER. w My 29 1824-O 15 1825||
United with New Hampshire statesman to form New Hampshire statesman and Concord register, later New Hampshire statesman
DLC complete
MBAt Ag 7 1824;Ja 1,Je 18 1825
MSaE Ag 7 1824
MWA complete
N complete
NNHi My 29 1824;Jl 16-O 1825
NcD complete
NhD Je 11 1825
NhHi complete
NhM Jl 31-O 15 1824
TxU complete

REPOSITORY and observer. *See* New Hampshire observer

REPUBLICAN statesman. w Ja 1 1869-S 29 1871||
Follows New Hampshire statesman. United with Independent democrat to form Independent statesman
DLC complete
MHi Ja 1,Ap 23 1869
MWA complete
MiU-C 1869[70]71
NNHi Jl 9-30 1869;Je 10-N 11,D 23-30 1870; Jl 14-21,Ag 4-11 1871
NcD [1869-71]
NhD Ja-Ag,O 14-D 10,24-31 1869
NhHi complete

ROLLIN's mercantile advertiser. m
NhHi [F 1850-O 1852]

ROUGH and ready. w D 12 1846-
campaign paper
DLC F 20,Mr 6-13 1847
MWA 1846-Mr 13,D 18 1847-Mr 11 1848
MnHi D 12,26 1846;Ja 2-Mr 13 1847;Ja 15,F 12,Mr 4 1854
NcD F 5 1848
NhHi [1846-Mr 18 1848]

SPIRIT of inquiry. w Je 18 1833-Je 10 1834||
Merged with New Hampshire courier
MBAt complete
MWA complete
NhHi [1833-34]
NjR S 17 1833

SPIRIT of the republican press. w Ja 7 1829-
MWA Ja 21,F 11 1829
MnHi Mr 11-18,Ap 1 1829
NhHi Ja-Ap 1 1829

STATE capital reporter. sw Ja 1 1852-S 5 1854||
DLC Ja 18 1853-S 5 1854
MWA complete
MiU-C [1852;54-55]
NNHi 1852
NhD Ag 24 1852;Je 20 1854
NhHi complete
NhM complete

STATE capital reporter. w Jl 16 1853-D 26 1856||
Merged with Independent democrat
DLC S 8 1854-56
MWA Ap 29,Je 10[Ag 12 1854-F 1,Je 27-D 5 1856]
NhHi [Ag 27-D 1853]-56
NhM 1853-F,N 23 1855

Daily STATESMAN. *See* New Hampshire statesman d

Concord evening TELEGRAM. d 1925-27||?
Nh [Ag 13-D 1925]-Je 20 1927

TELEGRAPH bulletin. d Ap 24-Jl 6 1861||
NhHi [1861]

TIMES mirror.
NhHi O 20 1828

TOUGH and steady. w F 2-Mr 16 1847||
Campaign paper
DLC F 2,16,Mr 2-9 1847
MWA complete
MnHi F 16 1847
NhHi complete

TRANSCRIPT. w,bw Ja 20 1835-
Suspended from Mr 14-My 1 1835
w Ja-Mr 14 1835
MWA F 14,28-Mr 14,Je 15-29 1835
NhHi [Ja-My 19 1835]
NjR Ja 27 1835

Concord TRIBUNE. w S 4-N 27 1852||
campaign paper
MWA O 15-23 1852
NhHi S 18 1852

Concord TRIBUNE. w 1880-1918||?
MWA O 14 1899
Nh 1901-18
NhHi 1884-90;92-99

TRUE whig. w O 24 1846-Ap 10 1847||?
DLC D 26 1846
NhHi [Ja 9-Ap 10 1847]

Concord daily UNION. d
CtY Jl 7 1867

VOICE of the masses. w
NhHi D 18 1851

VOICE of the stockholders. w
NhHi D 23-30 1854;Ja 27-Mr 3 1855

WHITE MOUNTAIN torrent. w Ap 14 1843-Jl 20 1846||
MSaE Ja 2,30 1846
MiU-C Je 6 1845
NhD N 10,24,D 29 1843-Ja 5,Mr 29,My 17-Je 14,O 4-11,25-N 15,29-D 6,20 1844;Ja 17,F 14-28,Mr 14,28,Ap 18,25-Je 20 1845
NhHi [Ap 28 1843-Ap 10 1846]
NhM 1843-Mr 29,Ap 19,Je 7 1844

WILMOT proviso. w D 25 1847-Mr 25 1848||
campaign paper
MWA Ja 1,F 26-Mr 11 1848
NhHi 1848

CONTOOCOOK

Contoocook evening ADVERTISER.
NhHi Ja 21 1875

HOPKINTON times. w S 15 1880-D 31 1884||?
S-O 6 1880 pub at Hopkinton
DLC Je 4 1884
NhD 1883-84
NhHi 1880-84

NEW HAMPSHIRE (*Continued*)

CONTOOCOOK—*Continued*

Contoocook INDEPENDENT. w 1892-Ja 18 1902||
NhHi complete

Contoocook INQUIRER. w Ja 21 1875-
Nh 1902-My 13 1908

DERRY

Derry ENTERPRISE. w,d O 20 1905+
1932-33 West Rockingham times and Derry enterprise
w 1905-33
pub 1905+
Nh 1905-18

Derry NEWS. w D 3 1880+
pub 1880—
Nh 1900-19
NhD Ag 29 1902
NhDe [1910+]
NhHi F 20 1891-99

Derry TIMES. w 1898-1908||?
Nh 1898-1908

WEST ROCKINGHAM times and Derry enterprise. *See* Derry enterprise

DOVER

CAMPAIGN press. w
MWA Ja 28 1876

DEMOCRATIC press. *See* State press

Dover ENQUIRER. w F 25 1828-F 16 1900||
F-Ag 5 1828 as Strafford inquirer; D 2 1828-29 Times and Dover enquirer
DLC Jl 8,Ag 19 1828[29-30]O 3 1832;Ag 27 1833;D 6-20 1842;N 11-25 1845[50-51]-[54]-58 [61]
MB S 2 1834;Ja 12,My 17 1836[50-F 15 1855] My 10 1859
MBAt D 2-16,30 1828-Ja 13,F 3-17 1829;My 3 1831;S 3 1833
MHi O 8 1868;S 29 1881
MSaE Mr 22 1831;My 21 1857
MWA 1828-Je 19,S 18,O 1832-71;O 30 1873;My 11,D 14 1876;N 1 1877;Ja 3,24,Mr 14-21,Ap 25,Je 20,Jl 4-11,25,Ag 8-15,29-S 12,26-O 3 1878;N 24 1893
MiU-C [1830-31;59]
MnHi N 6 1832;Ag 20,N 19 1833[34-37]F 13, My 1-15,Jl 31 1838;Jl 30,Ag 20,S 10-17,D 10, 24 1839;F 25 1840
NNHi Mr 6,23 1873;Jl 28-Ag 18,S 8-15,O 15-22 1899;Ja 5 1900
NcD [1834-36;38;40-41;44-48;50-65;67]
NhD D 29 1828;Ja 13,F 10,24,Mr 3-10,Ap 14, S 1,O 27,D 29 1829;30-[33]-Ja 4 1834;F-My,O 11-17,N 8 1842;Ja 24 1843;Ag 12 1858;N 17 1859;D 19 1861;Ja 23,My 8,Je 26,D 25 1862; Je 25,O 8,D 24 1863;O 11 1866;68-69;Je 20 1872;S 11 1873;Ja 29,Jl 30,O 22,N 26,D 17 1874;O 21,D 9 1875;S 7,N 2 1876;Ja 18,Je 15, Ag 2,O 11 1877;Ja 3-10 1878;Ap 10-17,O 30 1879
NhHi 1828-50[Je 19-D 1891]1900
WHi 1828-Je[Jl 26 1831-35]Je 28 1836;S 12 1837-Je 9[Ag 25 1846-50]-My 10 1866

FOSTER'S daily democrat. d Je 20 1872+
MWA My 3 1882;D 17 1891
Nh 1895-[97-98]-[1900]-[04-06]-[14]-[20-21]-[25]
NhHi S 20 1881;D 12 1886;Jl 13 1887

FOSTER'S weekly democrat and enquirer. w 1872+
Follows Public forum (Manchester)
1872-F 13 1900 as Foster's democrat (title varies slightly)
NNHi F 22 1873
Nh 1901+
NhHi 1891-99

Dover GAZETTE. w D 14 1825-77||?
1825?-Mr 3 1860 as Dover gazette and Strafford advertiser. Merged with Middlesex democrat (Lowell, Mass)
Ct [1828-29;31]
DLC [1827]D 9 1828-D 13 1831[32-56]58-Ja 5 1861[63;65]
MBAt Je 28 1826;My 1,29 1827;Je 12,N 1 1836
MSaE Je 25 1839;N 17 1840;Mr 4 1843
MWA My 10,S 5 1826;Je 5,Jl 3,D 11 1827;Ap 8,22,Je 3,O 14-21,D 16,30 1828;Mr 9,24,Ap 7, 28-My 5,26-Je 2,Jl 21,Ag 18,N 3,D 29 1829;F 9,Mr 30,Je 29-Jl 13,Ag 10,S 7,O 12 1830;My 17,Je 7-14,Jl 26,S 13,O 11-25 1831;F 14,O 16 1832;Je 18 1833;D 22 1835;Mr 15 1836;Ja 14 1840;My 14,Ag 13,O 29 1842;D 9-16 1843;D 28 1844;Mr 1 1845;Mr 18 1848;Ja 20,F 10 1849; My 29 1852;My 28 1853;Ja 23,S 25 1858;Ja 1 1859;Mr 31 1860;F 5 1864;O 15 1869
MeU D 30 1840
MiU-C N 3 1829
MnHi Je 22 1830;D 13 1831;Ja 3,17,F 7,Jl 10, Ag 21,D 4 1832;Jl 16,Ag 20,S 17 1833;F 25, Ap 22,My 27,Ag 5 1834;Je 21 1836;O 16 1838; Ja 22 1839;F 25,Mr 3 1840;Ap 27 1841[42-44] 46;Ag 19,S 30 1848
NNHi N 27 1838-39;N 9 1850-O 1854
NhD D 28 1830;O 2,D 18 1833;Ja 15 1839;S 7 1841;Mr 2 1844;Ap 1,Ag 26 1854;S 29,O 20 1855;O 11,25 1856;My 16,Je 20,Ag 8 1857;Ja 7,Jl 13 1860;O 5 1861;Ja 17 1862;O 14 1864;Mr 12,O 29 1869
NhHi 1825-71
NhWo [N 1831-Ja 27 1835]
OClWHi Mr 18,Je 3 1828;Ap 27 1866

Weekly INVESTIGATOR. w
NhHi D 23 1879

LOCAL record. m D 1869-71||?
MWA D 1869
NhD Je 1 1870
NhHi S 1871

NEW HAMPSHIRE chronicle. w Je 5 1830-Mr 17 1832||
Merged with New Hampshire observer (Concord)
CSmH Je 5 1830
MeBa complete
NhHi [Ag 1830-Je 18 1831]

NEW HAMPSHIRE globe. w My 18 1833-S 27 1834||
MWA Je 15 1833;Ap 19,My 24 1834
MeBa complete
NhHi [Jl 27 1833-S 6 1834]

NEW HAMPSHIRE palladium and Dover advertiser. w S 7 1830-Ag 28 1832||
CSmH S 14 1830
MeU S 7-14,N 16 1830;Ja 11,Ap 5,S 6 1831;Ap 10 1832
NhHi Mr 6 1832

NEW HAMPSHIRE republican and county advertiser. w Ja 8 1823-O 30 1829||
Follows Strafford register. 1823-N 14 1826 as New Hampshire republican
DLC Jl 15,O 28-N 11 1823;O 19,N 16-30 1824; N 15-29 1825;Jl 10,24-31,S 25,O 2 1829
MBAt Ja 22-F 19 1823;My 1 1827
MSaE S 3 1823
MWA 1823-24;F 1,My 17 1825;F 28-N,D 26 1826;Mr 6-13,S 25,O 16 1827;Mr 18,My 27,O 28,D 23 1828
NcD Jl 25-S 5 1826
NhD 1823-Jl 16,30-O 1,N 21 1826;Mr 4,O 14 1828
NhHi complete
NhWo [N 23 1824-N 28 1826]

Dover evening NEWS. d 1911-13||?
Nh [1912-13]

Dover REPORTER and Cochecho advertiser.
NhHi Mr 2 1844

Dover daily REPUBLICAN. d 1880-1900||?
Nh [1891-F 16 1900]
NhHi [1884-N 5 1896]

Dover SENTINEL. w My 1 1860-61||
DLC My 1 1860
MWA Ap 19 1861
NhHi Ap 5 1861

SPIRIT of inquiry. w 1833-
NcD D 24 1833

SPIRIT of '76. w Mr 8 1843-
RPB Mr 8 1843

Evening STAR. d 1889-95||?
NhHi N 8 1895

STATE press. w My 22 1874-83||?
1874-My 12? 1876 as Democratic press
MWA 1874-My 12 1876;Ja 5 1877
NhHi My 8 1874-[76;Mr 15-O 1878]-[Ja-N 2 1883]

STRAFFORD inquirer. *See* Dover enquirer

*STRAFFORD register. w S 5 1795-D 17 1822||
Follows Phoenix (not in this list). S-N 11? 1795 as Sun; N 18? 1795-Je 1812 Sun. Dover gazette and county advertiser; Jl 1812-Jl? 1818 Dover sun. Followed by New Hampshire republican
Suspended D 25 1810-Ja 1811
DLC Jl 23-30,Ag 13,27-S 3,O 15,D 3-10 1822
MBAt S 17 1822
MWA Ja 9-23,Jl 17-24 1821;My 14-Je 18,Jl 2-9,23-O 1,15,29 N 12,26-D 3,17 1822
NcD D 17 1822
NhD Ap 17,Jl 31,Ag 28 1821;Ja 15,S 24 1822
NhHi 1821-22

SUN. *See* Strafford register

Dover TELEGRAPH. w,d S 25 1846-My? 1848||
w 1846-Ap 1848
MWA 1846-S 23,O 21 1847
NhHi Ja 21 1847

Weekly TIMES. w 1886-96||?
NhHi F 26-Jl 16 1891[93]-[95]96

TIMES and Dover enquirer. *See* Dover enquirer

Dover TRIBUNE. w 1910+
Nh 1910-[32]

DUNBARTON

ANALECTA. *See* Valley times (Pittsfield)

SNOWFLAKE. *See* Valley times (Pittsfield)

DUNSTABLE

Papers published in Dunstable are listed under Nashua

DURHAM

Durham NEWS. w Je 2 1932-Jl 8 1933||
NhDuP complete
NhU Jl 1932-33

EAST JAFFREY

JAFFREY recorder and Monadnock breeze. *See under* Jaffrey

EASTPORT

EASTERN democrat. w 1832-33||
MnHi F 15 1833

ENFIELD

Enfield ADVOCATE. w Ap 27 1894+
Nh 1902-18
NhEN 1894-[1911-16;20-26]+
NhHi 1894-99

EPSOM

Epsom NEWS letter. w Ja 4 1896-1901||?
Nh 1900-01
NhHi 1896-99

EXETER

AMERICAN ballot and Rockingham county intelligencer. w N 21 1854-O 1865||
1854-Jl 15? 1858 as American ballot
1854-55? pub in Portsmouth
DLC My 3 1860
MWA N 21,D 19 1854;F 20,Ap 3,Jl 10 1855;Jl 8,22,Ag 19-26,O 21-28,N 11 1856;Ag 13 1857; Ja 27-F 3,Mr 3,My 12,Jl 14 1859;Mr 8 1860; Ag 13 1863;Ap 13,27 1865
MiU-C N 11 1856;F 3 1853
MnHi Ja 15,Jl 3,S 18 1862;Ap 30,Ag 6-13,S 10 1863;D 29 1864
NNHi N 27 1855;D 4 1862
NcD S 17 1863
NhHi [1854-Je 1865]

Exeter GAZETTE. w,sw 1876-1900||?
w 1876-99?
NhHi O 7 1876-S 7 1900

Evening GAZETTE. d D 2 1878-1900||?
Title varies: Daily gazette; Exeter daily gazette
Suspended from D 1899-F 25 1900
MWA D 2,13,16,26,31 1878;F 19,Mr 6,14,19,22, Ap 11-29,My 1-16,19-22 1879
MiU-C [1879]
NNHi O 24-25,29-30,D 22 1879
Nh [O 12 1896-1900]
NhHi [1878-Ja 1880]

GRANITE state democrat. w F 1 1840-Mr 9 1843||
DLC N 6 1840
MB F 17 1842-F 9 1843
MWA Mr 21,Ap 11,S 5,O 30 1840;Ja 1,Mr 12 (extra)D 16 1841;F 3,Ap-My,Je 9-23,Jl-Ag 4, 18,S 1,15-22,O 6,D 15 1842;Mr 9 1843
MnHi F 26,O 1 1841;Je 16 1842
NhHi 1840[41-43]

GREENBACK lever. *See under* Manchester

NEW HAMPSHIRE gazette. *See under* Portsmouth

Exeter NEWS-LETTER. w My 10 1831+
My 17 1831-Ap 30 1833 as Exeter news-letter and Rockingham probate advertiser; My 7 1833-Ap 21 1840 Exeter news-letter and Rockingham county advertiser; Ap 28 1840-Ja 7 1867 Exeter news-letter and Rockingham advertiser
CtY Jl 5,28 1858;Mr 7,Ap 4 1859
DLC [1831-39;41-44]46-[48]-[50]-[52]-[56-58]-[61-63]-[66-69;71;73-74]
MAm 1831-Jl 24 1832
MB My 15,Je 26,Jl 10,31 1832;N 12 1833;Ja 7, F 4 1834;Ag 11-D 15 1835;S 18 1838-39]Mr 24,Ap 21 1840;Ap 22,My 20 1844;Ap 29 1850; Ja 6 1860;F 18 1861
MBAt Ag 16 1831;Ag 28,D 25 1832;Ja 8,S 17, O 1 1833;Ap 15 1834;O 20 1835[36]Je 27,N 28-D 5 1837[38-39]F 4,My 12,D 22 1840;S 28 1841
MH My 1837-40[45-46]-55
MSaE N 17 1835;Ag 30 1836;Ap 25 1843
MWA 1831-My 21,Jl 2-16,Ag 13,O 1866-O,N 18,D 23 1867[68]69;F 11,Mr 4,Ag 19,D 9-16 1870;Mr 24-D 1871;F 2,23,Mr 8,22-Ap 5,My 10-24,Je 7-21,Ag 30 1872;73-87;My 11,Je 8-15 1888;Ag 15 1890;92-95;Ap 7 1899;Ag 17 1917
MiU-C [1831-39;45;48-51;56-57;59-62;65-66;68-69;73-74;78]
MnHi Je 12,S 18,D 4,25 1832;F 19 1833;My 19 1835;My 18 1846;N 19 1866;Ja 7 1867;S 4 1868;N 19 1920
NN [Mr-S 1872]
NNHi Je 26 1843;D 15 1851;Ap 9 1855-Mr 1865;My 9 1873;S 13 1901
NcD [1831-95]
Nh 1900+
NhD My 5,19-26,Je 9,23,Ag 11,25,S 8,22,O 27, N 10,24,D 22 1835;Ja 5,19,F 9-Mr 15,29-My 3,17,Je 15-21,Jl 26,Ag 9-23,S 3-N 15,D 6 1836
NhE 1831+
NhHi 1831-[70-71]-1917;19;32;O 1-8 1891
NjR D 20 1836;S 4 1848
OCHi Ja 2 1838;Je 15 1841
OClWHi My 24 1842
VtBr Mr 26 1839

NORTHERN republican. w
MBAt Ap 30,My 21,Ag 6 1821
MSaE Mr 6 1821
MWA Jl 9-16,30 1821
NhHi F 13-Ag 6 1821

Weekly PROTEST. w 1880-89||?
NhHi [Je 3 1881-Ap 20 1883]Jl 23 1886

ROCKINGHAM county record. w 1898+
MnHi O 27,N 17 1927
Nh 1901-05
NhER F 24 1933+
NhHi S 22-29 1900

ROCKINGHAM gazette. w S 21 1824-O 16 1827||
United with Portsmouth journal of literature and politics to form Portsmouth journal and Rockingham gazette, later Portsmouth journal of literature and politics (Portsmouth)
DLC S 28,O 19 1824;Je 28 1825;Je 27 1826;F 13 1827
MB N 16-1824-[Ja-N 1 1825;Ja 17-Je 5 1826]
MBAt S 21 1824[25]
MSaE F 22,Ap 26,Jl 12-19 1825
MWA S 28-N 9,D 21 1824;F 8,Mr 1,Ap 12,26-My 3,17,Je 14,28-Jl,Ag 9,23,S 27,O 18 1825; Ja 24,F 21,Mr 7,Ag 8,29,O 17,N 21,D 12 1826; Ja 2,Ap 17 1827
MnHi S 12 1826
NN F 8 1825
NNHi complete
NhD 1824-N,D 13 1824-My 2,16-Ag,S 12 1826-Je,Jl 17-O 1827
NhHi complete

NEW HAMPSHIRE (*Continued*)

EXETER—*Continued*

ROCKINGHAM newspaper. w
NhHi F 2,Mr 9 1878

WEST ROCKINGHAM republican. w
NhHi Ag 18 1876

FARMINGTON

Farmington ADVERTISER. w Ap 21 1866-79||?
NhHi Je 16 1866;Ja 5,My 11 1877

HERRINGS advertiser. w
DLC Ap 1852

Farmington NEWS. w Mr 14 1879+
MWA Ja 6 1888
Nh 1901-19
NhF 1879+
NhHi [1879-80]-99

SANDY RIVER yeoman. w O 20 1831-
NhF 1831-O 17 1832

FITZWILLIAM

JAFFREY recorder and Monadnock breeze. *See under* Jaffrey

FRANCESTOWN

Francestown AGE. w
NhHi F 7 1891-S 21 1895

Francestown weekly HERALD. w Ap 10 1902-19||?
NhHi 1902-11

FRANKLIN

Franklin CORRESPONDENT. m Ap 15 1879-
MWA Ap,S,N-D 1879

JOURNAL-TRANSCRIPT. w F 23 1872+
1872-Je 1898 as Merrimac journal
pub 1872+
MWA D 15 1876;Jl 16 1903;S 6 1917
MiU-C My 25(supp)1911
Nh 1900+
NhHi 1872[75-76]-99

MERRIMAC journal. *See* Journal-transcript

Franklin TRANSCRIPT. w Jl 1 1882-Jl 1 1898||
United with Merrimac journal to form Journal-transcript
NhFrJ complete
NhHi 1882[83]-90;96-Je 1898

Franklin UNION. w Je 19 1869-70||?
NhHi [Je 26-Ag 21 1869]

GILFORD

DEMOCRATIC spy. w O 21 1829-Je 1830||
1829-Mr? 1830 pub in Sanbornton
NhHi [N 1829-Mr 9 1830]

REFORMER. F 14-Jl 1832||
MBAt F 14 1832
MnHi F 14 1832

STRAFFORD republican. w My 17-Je 7 1831||
MWA My 24 1831
NhHi My 17,31 1831

GILMANTON

MESSENGER. w
NhD N 15 1883
NhHi O 15 1883

GORHAM

Gorham MOUNTAINEER. w Ap 6 1877-1916||
MSaE Ja 11 1878
MWA N 7 1887;Ja 8-22 1892
Nh 1912-13
NhG complete
NhHi My 1891-1911

GREAT FALLS. *See* SOMERSWORTH

GREENLAND

NEW HAMPSHIRE gazette. *See under* Portsmouth

GROVETON

Groveton ADVERTISER. w 1909-21||?
Nh 1910-[20]-Ap 1 1921

Groveton ENTERPRISE. w 1892-95||?
NhHi F 14-Jl 11 1895

HAMPTON

Hampton UNION and Rockingham county gazette. w Ja 1 1898+
1898-Ap 18 1929 as Hampton union
pub 1930+
Nh 1901+

HANCOCK

Hancock JOURNAL. w
Nh 1902-08

HANOVER

AMULET. w My 4 1840-
My-N 10 1840 as Experiment
Suspended from Je 22-Jl 22 1841
NhD My-N 17 1840;Je 15-S 24 1841

Hanover CHRONICLE. w Mr 18 1828-
NhHi Mr 18 1828

DARTMOUTH advertiser. w Mr 1 1853-
NhD 1853-Je 1 1854;Je 1857

***DARTMOUTH herald.** w Je 21 1820-
NhD Ja-Mr 14,28,Ap 11-My 23,Je 6-20,Jl 4, 18-25 1821
NhHi [Ja-Jl 11 1821]

EXPERIMENT. *See* Amulet

FAMILY visitor. w F 14 1844-
NhD F 21-28,Mr 20,Ap 10,My 15-22 1844

Hanover GAZETTE. w My 23 1885+
DLC Je 20 1929-33
MWA Je 28 1906
NBuG N 7 1918
NNHi Je 19 1886
Nh 1900-Jl 11 1918;Ap 28 1921+
NhD 1885+
NhH 1914+
NhHi [Je 13 1885-S 22 1888;91]-99;1929-30;32

INDEPENDENT chronicle. w
WHi O 22,N 5 1835

VALLEY star. w S 13 1850-
NhD O 4 1850

HAVERHILL

Haverhill COURIER. w 1890-97||?
NhHi [D 19 1890-91]-Ap 16 1897

DEMOCRATIC republican. w Jl 23 1828-63||
1828-38 as Democratic and republican general advertiser
CSmH D 22 1830
Ct [1828-29]
DLC D 11 1831;Ja,Mr 14-28,Ag 29 1832;My 29, Je 12,N 27-D 4 1833;Ja 8 1834;Ja 13,Jl 13-20 1836[37]-[41]-[43]Ap 8,29,My 20-27,Je 10,Jl 8 1846;F 3,My 26,O 6,27-N 4,D 29 1847;O 3-10 1849;Mr 20,Ag 14 1850;My 7,Ag 27,S 24 1851;F 18,Mr 24,My 26,D 1-15 1852;F 9,My 25,Je 8-15,S 14-21,O 19 1853;D 6 1854[55-56] Ap 1,S 16 1857;Ap 28,D 8-15 1858;Mr 23,Ap 6 1859;Je 27,Ag 22,S 12-19,O 17,D 5 1860;Je 26,Ag 7,28 1861
MBAt S 28 1831
MWA Ag 13,N 19 1828;Ap 1 1829;S 8,O 20-27, N 24 1830;Mr 23,N 9,D 7,28 1831;F 29,Ap 11-18 1832;Ag 1 1838;F 20,Mr 13,Ag 28 1839; Ag 12,S 9-23,O 14 1840;S 8 1847;D 1 1852;Mr 21 1860;Ap 10 1861
MnHi F 27 1833;Mr 26 1834;O 2 1839
N O 16 1833
NN D 15 1830
NNHi My 5-12 1830;Ap 3,My 15-22,S 4,O 2,N 9 1839
NSchU Ag 10 1842
NhD [Ap 20 1828-62]
NhHi [1828-30]-[32-O 16 1833;Mr 11 1835-N 16 1836;Mr 14-N 14 1838;39]-[41-N 15 1843;S 1849-Ag 14 1850;Ap 20 1853-Ap 1858;F-D 17 1862]
OClWHi O 13 1830
VtNU 1834-36

GRAFTON and Coos intelligencer. *See* New Hampshire intelligencer

GRAFTON county register. w Ja 1886-89||?
NhD O 1-15,20,N 12-D 1886;Jl 15 1887
NhHi 1887-89

GRAFTON county signal. w O 23 1882-87||
1882-Je 3 1884 as Signal; Je 10 1884-My 20? 1885 Grafton county signal and democratic republican
MWA D 11 1882
NhD [1882-N 26 1887]
NhHa O 23 1882
NhHi [N 20 1883-D 16 1885]

Haverhill HERALD. w My 17 1879-80||
NhD D 20 1879

***NEW HAMPSHIRE intelligencer.** w N 30 1820-27||
1820-21 as Grafton and Coos intelligencer
CSmH F 21 1821
Ct [1826-27]
DLC S 11 1822;O 20-28,N 24 1824;N 9 1825;O 25 1826,F 17,Mr 3 1827
MBAt Ja 31,O 17,N 14 1821;Ap 17 1822
MSaE My 15 1822;N 26 1823
MWA Ja 16 1822;N 2 1825;Ja 11,Ag 16 1826
NN Ja 31,F 7-14,28 1821;D 31 1823
NhD Mr 31 1824;N 15 1826
NhHi [1821-My 19 1827]

NEW HAMPSHIRE post and Grafton and Coos advertiser. w Jl 6 1827-33||
DLC Ag 14-24,S 14-28 1827;Mr 28-Ap 11,Je 6, 20,O 17(extra)1828;Je 24,Jl 8-15,Ag 5,S 30,N 11,25 1829;Ja 6-20,F 24-Mr 10 1830;Ja 12,N 30,D 28 1831;O 31-N 7 1832
MBAt Ag 6,S 10 1828;D 8 1830;Ag 24 1831;O 24 1832;F 27 1833
MSaE F 1 1828;Ap 29 1829;Ap 28-My 5 1830; Jl 6 1831
MWA 1827-Ap,O 21 1829;Ja 2-16,F 6 1833
NNHi Mr 4 1829;N 3,D 8 1830;F 9,My 11,D 21 1831;Ja 25,F 1,Ag 15,S 5,O 1832
NhD 1827-My 1 1833
NhHi [S 28 1827-29;Ag 11 1830-Mr 20 1833]

Haverhill RECORD. w Jl 3 1897-Mr 28 1908||
NhHi complete

SIGNAL. *See* Grafton county signal

TRUE democrat and granite state whig. *See* Granite state free press (Lebanon)

WHIG and aegis. w Je 4 1839-42||
Follows White Mountain aegis (Lancaster)
DLC 1839;N 26-D 1841
MHi Ap 10 1841
MSaE N 1839;Mr 7,Ag 1,S 12 1840;Ja 30,Ap 10,My 29,Je 26,N 12,D 24 1841
MWA Jl 9 1839
MiG Ap 18 1840
NhD Je 18-25,Jl-Ag 6,O 8,N 5-D 3,17,24 1839-F 4,29-My 9,23-Je 20,Jl 4-Ag 22,S 5 1840-Ja 9,23-Ap 10,24-Je 12,26-Jl 10,24-Ag 28,S 11-D 1841;F 4-18,Mr 4-11 1842
NhHi 1839-My 1 1841

HENNIKER

Henniker weekly COURIER. w 1886+
NhHi [Ap 15 1886-Jl 24 1889]Jl 1895-1911

HILLSBORO

To 1908? as Hillsboro Bridge

Hillsboro ENTERPRISE. w 1893-99||?
NhHi [Ag 7 1895-96]-[98-99]

Hillsboro MESSENGER. w 1868+
Nh 1902+
NhHi 1891-1901
NhHil Je 25 1927+

HILLSBORO BRIDGE. *See* HILLSBORO

HINSDALE

PLAIN truth. m? 1892||?
NhHi O 1892

VALLEY record. w 1885-96||?
NhHi 1891-Ag 28 1896
NhHin [1889]

ZION'S hill press. w D 4 1900-
NhHi [1900-My 1901]

HOLLIS

Hollis TIMES. w O 14 1886-1921||
Title varies: Hollis times and brookline reporter
MHi Jl 11-18,Ag 15-22 1890;F 13,Mr 6,Ap 17, Je 15-26 1891;Ja 1,15,29,D 30 1892
Nh 1902-[21]
NhHi 1886-1901

HOPKINTON

Hopkinton TIMES. *See under* Contoocook

JAFFREY

MONADNOCK breeze. *See* Jaffrey recorder and Monadnock breeze

Jaffrey RECORDER and Monadnock breeze. w Je 8 1898+
1898-Mr 1932 as Monadnock breeze
Also dated in Fitzwilliam, Ridge and Troy
pub 1923+
Ct My 11 1907
Nh 1901+
NhFi 1923+

JEFFERSON

JEFFERSONIAN. w 1891-96||?
pub only during Jl-O
NhHi [Jl 13 1895-Jl 1896]

Jefferson TIMES. w 1893-1918||?
Nh 1907-13

KEENE

AMERICAN news. w Ja 4 1851-
MWA Ja 4-11,F 15,Mr 15-29 1851;Ap 16,Ag 13,O 8,N 12 1852;Ap 29,D 16 1853
NhHi [Jl 4 1851-My 19 1854]
NhK Ja 6 1854;Ja 9-Mr 9 1855

Keene BLIZZARD.
NhHi Ag 1890

CHESHIRE county republican and farmer's museum. *See* Cheshire republican

CHESHIRE republican. w,sw S 14 1827-1914||?
1827-S 26 1834 as Farmer's museum (revival of Farmer's museum, Walpole); O 2 1834-35? Cheshire county republican and farmer's museum; 1836-42? Cheshire republican and farmer's museum; 1843?-52 Cheshire republican and farmer; 1853-N 1910 Cheshire republican; D 2 1910-Ja 9 1914 Cheshire republican and Keene free press
1827-N 7? 1828 pub in Walpole
w 1827-1913?
CSmH Jl 9 1830
Ct [1828-38]
DLC O 12,N 2-9,23-D 7,28 1832;Ja 11-18,F 15,Mr 1-15,29-Ap 12 1833;O 30 1834;N 28 1838;Ag 25,S 8,29,D 22-29 1841[42;44-45]Jl 14 1852;F 8 1854-S 24 1856;Mr 10 1866;Jl 20 1872
MBAt Mr 6 1862
MWA S 28-N 2 1827;Ja 4,18-25,F 8,22-Mr 21,Ap 11-18,My 2,30,Jl 4-11,Ag 8,S 5-12,O 3-17 1828;F 20,Ap 24-My 1,15-22,Je 12,26,Jl 10-31,Ag 14,S 11,25,O 9,D 4 1829;Ja 22,Mr 5,26-Ap 2,30,My 14,Je 4,Jl 16,30,O 1 1830;Mr 11,Je 17,Jl 1,22-29,O 28,N 25-D 2,23 1831;Ja 6-13,27-F 3,17-Ap 6,20-My 4,S 21-O 1832;O 2,N 20-27,D 11 1834;Ja 22-29,Mr 5,Ap 2-16 1835;F 7,21 1838;S 14 1842;My 8,O 23 1845; Jl 16 1846;N 25-D 2,16 1847;O 1-8 1851;52; My 10,S 27 1854;Jl 25 1855;F 6,Mr 5,Ag 1856-1911;Ja 2-9,13-My 22 1914

NEW HAMPSHIRE (*Continued*)

KEENE—*Continued*

CHESHIRE republican. w,sw 1827-1914||? —*Continued*
MiU-C D 2 1832[59;61;63;65]-[69-71]-[75-1904]Ja 23 1914
N Je 13 1828;O 18 1833
NNHi Ja 30 1829;91-96
Nh 1912-13
NhD Ja 16 1829-N 6 1836;Jl 13 1842;N 29 1849;O 1 1851;F 11 1857
NhHi [1828-43]-1911
NhK [1827-28]45-[80-Ap 11 1913]
NhW 1827-S 4 1829
OClWHi O 14 1865
RP Je 22,Ag 3,24,S 7,21-28,O 19,N 16 1842

FARMERS museum. *See* Cheshire republican

Keene FREE PRESS. w Ap 9-N? 1910||
United with Cheshire republican to form Cheshire republican and Keene free press, later Cheshire republican
NhK Je 11,O 22 1910

FREE soil palladium. w Ag 15 1848-
MBAt Ag 22,S 19-26 1848

GRANITE state journal. w 1869-1909||?
NhHi Je 14,28 1873
NhK [D 11 1869-My 1871]

NEW ENGLAND observer. w 1878-89||?
NhHi O 23 1889
NhK [Je 1883-89]

*NEW HAMPSHIRE sentinel.** w Mr 23 1799+
pub 1905+
DLC 1821-26,29;Ja 8,22,D 3-10 1830;D 2-10 1831;D 23-30 1840[42-My 1843]S 24 1845[50] N 7 1861[62]Ja 1,29,Ap 2-10 1863
M Ap 17 1929[Ap 22 1931-Jl 1933]
MBAt [1824]Ja 7-21,F 4,25 1825;Ag 24 1827; Ag 8 1828;Ap 20 1865
MSaE Ja-Mr 17,S 8 1821;Ag 1,15 1823
MWA 1821-Je 8,S 20 1832-[33]-Je 10 1853; Jl 14 1854;F 15,Je 13,S 26 1856;Ap 1859-60; My 23,Jl 18,D 26 1861;Ja 2 1862;S 14,O 12 1865;Ja 11 1866;S 10,N 12-26,D 10-31 1868;S 4,N 20 1873;Mr 2 1876;My 13 1891;D 7 1898
MiU-C [1821-22;37-40;51;53]
NcD [1840-41;43;49;52-53]
Nh 1900-24
NhD 1821-58
NhHi [1821-22]-[25]-[37]-[52]-[59]-[63-65]66; 68-[70-78]80;82-90;Je 17 1891-Mr 15 1899
NhK 1821+
NjR [1832;52-66;68-69;83-84]
OClWHi S 21 1837;F 15 1838;Ag 19-26,N 11 1840;Ja 27,F 24 1841;Mr 22 1843;N 7 1844;My 3 1866
PAtM Ja 17 1833
RP My 25,Je 29-Jl 13,Ag 10 1842

Keene daily NEWS. d Ap 15-Je 12 1905||
NhK Ap 15,Je 12 1905

OBSERVER. w 1890-93||?
NhHi [O 4 1890-91]-My 20 1893

PHILANTHROPIST. w N 18 1845-
MWA Je 18 1847;Ap 28,Je 16,Jl 7,S 15-22,O 27 1848
NhHi N 17 1848
NhK N 18 1845;Ja 1 1846

PRESS and printer. w
MHi D 3,17,31 1887-Ja 7,21-28 1888

Keene evening SENTINEL. d O 20 1890+
Mr 23 1899 is New Hampshire sentinel-centennial number
pub 1905+
MWA Mr 23 1899
Nh S 10 1896-[99-1900]-[02-04]-[06-07]-[11]-[21-22]+
NhK 1890+

SPIRIT of the times. w Ja 4 1849-
DLC N 15 1849
MWA Ap 5,My 17,Jl 12,Ag 30,S 27-O 4,18, D 13,27 1849;F 21,Mr 7-14,My 30,Jl 18-25, Ag 29,S 19,O 3,N 7,21-D 12 1850
NhHi Ja 3 1850

Keene daily TRIBUNE. d Je 15 1889-S 8 1890||
NhHi [1889-90]
NhK [1889-90]

KINGSTON

Kingston ADVERTISER. w
NhHi N 1882;D 1893

LACONIA

To 1862? as Meredith Bridge

Laconia ADVOCATE. w,sw Ja 1887-93||?
1886-O 18 1887 as Labor advocate
sw Mr 1887-88?
MWA 1887-88;Je 19 1890
NhHi 1887-91;Mr 24 1892
NhLa Ap 24-D 1888;Mr 27-D 12 1889;F-D 1890;Ja 30-Ap 14 1892;93

Daily ADVOCATE. d O 8 1888-
NhHi O-N 1 1888

BELKNAP gazette. w Ag 4 1841-
Title varies: Belknap gazette and Carroll county advertiser; Belknap county gazette
DLC Ag 4 1841;51-Ag 28 1852
MWA S 7 1841;F 8 1842;D 16 1848;Jl 24 1852; Je 20 1863
MiU-C S 20 1842
NNHi N 6 1852
NhHi [S 1842-S 1 1849;Ap-S 1854;Mr 28 1863-Ap 23 1864]
NhLa Ag 1843-Jl 23 1844
P-M Mr 18 1845

BELKNAP tocsin. w My 19 1881-83||?
NhHi Ap 19,N 25 1883
NhLa My 19 1881-82

Laconia evening CITIZEN. d Ja 4 1926+
M D 16 1932
Nh [1927-28]-[31-32]+
NhLa 1926+

CITIZENS' press. w N 7 1834-
MWA N 7 1834;Ja 23-F 6,Mr 6,Ap 3-10 1835

CITIZEN'S times. N 7 1834-
NhHi 1834-My 22 1835

Laconia DEMOCRAT. w Ja 4 1849-Jl 8 1933||
1849-63? as New Hampshire democrat
Merged with Laconia evening citizen
pub 1888-1933
DLC 1849[Jl 1856-Jl 1857]
MWA F 13 1851;Jl 15 1852;F 12,Ap 2 1858;N 18,D 23 1859;Mr 23 1860;S 5 1863 My 6 1864; O 14 1869;Jl 1 1875;Ap 23(supp)1880
NNHi Ap 10 1851;N 4 1852
Nh 1900-22;25-33
NhHi [O 7 1852-58]-[1864-65;Mr 1867-O 14 1869;Ja 19 1871-F 15 1872;Mr 26 1874-S 20 1877;Je 22 1883-My 15 1885]My 1891-99
NhLa 1849;51;54;58;1862-81;Ja-Je 1882;83-1933

LABOR advocate. *See* Laconia advocate

NEW HAMPSHIRE democrat. *See* Laconia democrat

Laconia NEWS and critic. w Mr 5 1889+
pub 1889+
Nh 1900+
NhHi Je 17 1891-99
NhLa 1889+

PRESENT age. w Ja 4 1877-
NhHi Ja 11 1877

Laconia PRESS. d 1895-98||?
Nh [1896-Je 1898]

WINNIPISAUKEE gazette. w 1843?-
DLC Ap 20 1861
MWA O 9 1858;Mr 10,Ap 7-14,My 19 O 13-20, N 3 1860;Ja 5,F 23,Mr 2 1861;Ap 5 1862
NNHi Ap 4 1855
NcD F 20 1858;D 29 1860;[61]
NhD S 25 1858
NhHi [Ap 7 1855-N 1 1862]

LAKE VILLAGE. *See* LAKEPORT

LAKEPORT

To 1890? as Lake Village

BELKNAP republican. w Ja 3 1868-98||?
1868-87 as Lake Village times
NhHi [My 1868-Ja 13 1872;Ap 1874-76;Ap 12-O 12 1878;My 17 1884-My 23 1885]Je 19 1891-98
NhLa 1868-85
NhM [1868]-[88]

LAKE VILLAGE times. *See* Belknap republican

LANCASTER

COOS county democrat (1838-60) *See under* North Stratford

COOS county democrat. w S 15 1886+
Nh 1901+
NhHi [1886-N 1888]-1901
NhL [1886-1900]

COOS republican. w D 11 1855-84||?
DLC Mr 18 1856;My 17 1859;My 1,15,O 2-9,30-N 6 1860;Ap 23,My 14,Je 18,Jl 9,S 3,17-24,O 8-22 1861;F 25,N 4,25 1862;Ja 27,Mr 3-10,Jl 21,O 13,D 15 1863;Ja 12-19,D 27 1864;Ag 8 1865;Ag 14-21 1866;Je 2 1868;Je 22 1869
MB O 16 1866-Ag 18 1874
MWA Ag 19,S 2 1856;S 28 1858;N 29,D 13 1859;Mr 13,Ap 3,My 22,Jl 17,O 9,30,N 6,27 1860;Ja 8,22-29,F 19-Mr 12 1861;Ag 1863;Ja 23,S 11 1866
NNHi D 11 1855
NhD [D 11 1855-O 4 1870]
NhHi 1855-[71-Ag 21 1878;Mr 31 1880-82]

Lancaster GAZETTE. w Ja 3 1872-1916||?
1872-78 as Independent gazette
Suspended from S 25 1885-Ja 19 1886
MWA Ja 17 1872;Ap 16 1879;Mr 23 1881;Jl 25, Ag 22,O 3,17,N 14,D 5,19-26 1884
Nh 1900-16
NhHi 1872-73[My 19 1875-Je 19 1878;Ag 17 1883-N 19 1890]91-99
NhL 1874-78;80-85

INDEPENDENT gazette. *See* Lancaster gazette

REVEILLE. D 20 1889-
NhHi 1889-Ja 10 1890

WHITE MOUNTAIN aegis. w My 22 1838-39||
Followed by Whig and aegis (Haverhill)
DLC My 22 1838
MWA Ja 15 1839
NhHi 1838-My 14 1839

LEBANON

GRANITE state free press. w O 5 1844+
1844-My 1848 as True democrat and granite state whig; Je 9 1848-Jl 8 1859 Granite state whig
1844-47? pub in Haverhill
DLC S 21 1849;O 5 1855;My 27,Jl 11-18,N 7 1862;Jl 2,16,30-Ag,S 10-24,O 8-29,N 12,26-D 10,31 1864;Ja 7-14,F 4-18,Ap 1-8,My 13,Je 3-10 1865[66-70;73-75]Mr 9,30 1877;Je 4 1879; S 29,O 13,N 10-17 1882;My 13 1887;My 14 1897;Ja 3 1908;Jl 7 1911;Ja 7 1927;Ap 25 1930
IU Jl 18 1845
NNHi D 31 1847;Je 22 1849;Ag 10 1855
MSaE N 15 1844;N 13 1846;Ja 15,29,Mr 12-19, Ap 2-23,Ag 13,D 3 1847[48-49]Ap 26-My 10, 24-S 20,O 4-11,N 15 1850;Ja 31,Je 27-Jl 11 1851;Ag 29,D 19 1863

MWA My 30,O 10-17,31,N 14,D 12 1845[46] My 7 1847;F 23 1851;S 14 1855;Jl 13 1860;D 27 1861;Jl(supp)D 20-27 1872;F 21 1873;F 12 1886
NNHi D 31 1847;Je 22 1849;Ag 10 1855
Nh 1900-[19]+
NhD N 15 1844;45;Ja-S,O 10 1846[1848-Ja 1931]
NhHi [1845-Mr,Je 16-Ag 11 1848;49-57;61-75]-[80] - [1907]-[11-12]-[19-20]-[23-28] - Mr 20 1931
NhLe 1859+

GRANITE state whig. *See* Granite state free press

METEOR.
NhHi F 14 1850

NEW HAMPSHIRE weekly news. w
NhHi My 6,Je 1 1876

TRUE democrat and granite state whig. *See* Granite state free press

LISBON

Lisbon HERALD. w 1882-1901||?
1882-Mr 18 1897 as Northern herald
NhHi Je 17 1891-Ap 25 1901

Lisbon INDEX. w 1882-89||?
NhHi [My 17 1884-My 23 1885]

Lisbon NEWS-LETTER and Grafton county news. w Ap 19- 1902||
NhHi [Ap-Ag 2 1902]

NORTHERN herald. *See* Lisbon herald

Lisbon TRANSCRIPT. w 1920-30||?
Nh [1921-22]-My 1930

LITTLETON

AMMONOOSUC reporter. w Jl 4 1852-D 23 1854||
Followed by White Mountain banner
NhHi [Ag 27 1853-My 13 1854]
NhLiT S 11 1852-54

AMMONOOSUC VALLEY argus. *See* Littleton argus

Littleton ARGUS. w D 25 1875-My 3 1878||?
Je 15-D 22 1877 as Ammonoosuc valley argus
NhHi D 15 1876;F 22 1878
NhLiT Je 15 1877-78

Littleton COURIER. w D 4 1889+
Nh 1903-18
NhHi 1889-1902
NhLi 1912-13;16+
NhLiT 1889-N 17,D 1897-1913

Littleton GAZETTE. w N 10 1865-S 20 1867||
MWA Mr 16 1866
NhLiT complete

Littleton JOURNAL. w Ja 21 1881-S 8 1889||
United with White Mountain republic journal to form Republic-journal, later White Mountain republic journal
NhHi [My 16 1884-My 22 1885]
NhLi 1881-84
NhLiT 1881-Ja 4 1884;85-89

PEOPLE'S journal. w Je 6 1855-D 24 1864||
Merged with Granite state free press (Lebanon)
MWA O 24 1856;S 28 1860;O 24 1862
NhD O 31 1863;F 13 1864
NhHi [Ja 23 1856-Jl 17 1857;D 16 1859-N 1864]
NhLiT complete
OClWHi N 5 1864

REPUBLIC-JOURNAL. *See* White Mountain republic-journal

WHITE MOUNTAIN banner. w Ja 20 1855-Je 4 1859||
Follows Ammonoosuc reporter. Merged with New Hampshire patriot (Concord)
MWA Jl 12,Ag 2 1858
NhLiT Ja-Ag 4,S 29 1855-59

WHITE MOUNTAIN republic-journal. w O 4 1867-Ag 4 1914||
1867-S 7 1889 as White Mountain republic; S 14 1889-S 11 1891 Republic-journal
DLC Jl 29,Ag 26 1892
MWA Jl 31 1868;S 10 1869;D 6 1884
Nh 1900-13
NhD Je 5,19,Jl 24,S 25,O 30 1891;My 6,20,Je-Ag 26,S 9,23-D 9,23 1892-Ja 6,F 3-17,Mr,Ap 15 1893
NhHi [Je 12 1868-Ap 1870;Je 30 1883-S 7 1889]S 11 1891-99
NhLiT 1867-S 24,O 8 1869-S 25 1893;94-1914

LONDONDERRY

Londonderry TIMES. w 1864?-
MWA Ja 1 1867
NhHi [1867-F 1878]

MANCHESTER

Semi-weekly ADVERTISER. sw N 28? 1842-
MWA D 6 1842

Manchester ADVERTISER. w 1889-1908||
1898?-99? as Manchester herald and advertiser
Nh 1902-08
NhHi [1895]-[98-99]-1901
NhM 1897-1908

Manchester ADVOCATE. w
Nh N 1 1912-Jl 13 1915

Manchester ALLODIUM. w Ja 14-Ap 8 1843||
Followed by Manchester transcript
NhM complete

NEW HAMPSHIRE (*Continued*)

MANCHESTER—*Continued*

Semi-weekly AMERICAN. sw S 1 1845-Ap 9 1846||
MWA S 8 1845-46
MnHi complete
NhHi complete
NhM complete

Manchester daily AMERICAN. d O 23 1852-D 31 1863||
United with Manchester daily mirror to form Daily mirror and American
MSaE Ja 24 1857
MWA Ap 18,My 19,21 1859;Mr 3[O 17-N 21 1860]Mr 13,Ag 26 1863
NhD My 15 1858;N 14,D 22 1860
NhHi O 25-N 3 1852[S 18 1854-Ap 22 1863]
NhM [1856-63]
WHi S 28 1854;Ja-Je 1855;Ja-Jl 12 1856;58-Je 1863

Manchester AMERICAN and messenger. w S 6 1844-F 14 1857||
1844-Je 11 1852 as Manchester American; Je 19-Jl 24 1852 American and messenger. United with Manchester democrat to form Manchester democrat and American
CtY S 11 1852
DLC S 6 1844;51;F 13 1852
MWA Ap 1(extra)D 5(extra)1845;Ag 14 1846; Mr 7 1847;Jl 14 1848;Ja 25 1850;Jl 3,31,O 16, N 6 1852;Jl 23 1853;Mr 18,Je 17,Jl 29 1854; Je 9,Jl 28,S 22 1855
NNHi Je 13,Jl 11,O 3,24,D 5(extra)19 1845;F 6,20-27 1846;My 6,O 14 1854-O 1855
NhHi [S 8 1848-52]53
NhM complete

L'AMI du foyer. w F 5 1901-05||?
In French
NhM 1901-Ja 1902

AMOSKEAG bulletin. sm,m D 2 1912-F 1922||
NhHi complete
NhM 1912-21

AMOSKEAG memorial. *See* Manchester memorial

AMOSKEAG representative. *See* Manchester representative

ANZEIGER und post. w 1890-1907||?
1890-94? as New Hampshire post; 1895?-S 26 1896 Deutsche post
In German
NhHi 1895-99

L'AVENIR canadien. *See* L'Avenir national

L'AVENIR national. w,sw,d S 11 1888+
1888-91? as L'Avenir Canadien
Nh [1899-1908]-[12-16]-[20-22]-[27]-[31-33]+
NhHi [1891;95]-98
NhM 1888-O 1890;Jl-S 1910;13-16;Jl 1918+
WHi O 23 1916

Manchester weekly BUDGET. w Je 16 1883-1907||
1883-97 as Manchester budget
MSaE Ja 26 1889
MWA N 9 1889
Nh 1901-05
NhD Je 16-Jl 7,S 8-22,O-N 3 1883
NhHi S 29 1883;Ag 2 1884;97-99
NhM 1883[84;92-93;97]-[1901]-03;05-07

Le BULLETIN. w 1896-99||?
In French
NhHi [S-D 1896]-98;Ja 26-Ap 2 1899

Manchester illustrated BULLETIN. ir
Followed by Pickering's weekly bulletin
NhM Fall,winter,1873

BUSINESS advertiser. m,sm F 27 1869-70||
F 27-Ap 24 1869 as Manchester business index
NhHi F 27 1869
NhM F-Ap 24,Jl 24 1869-My 7 1870

Manchester BUSINESS index. *See* Business advertiser

BUSINESS monitor. m D 1866-
NhHi D 1866;S,N 1867
NhM 1866-67

Le CANADO-AMERICAIN. m O 13 1900+
In French
Nh 1900-[21]+
NhMA 1900+

CITY messenger and true republican. w F 4 1859-60||
Title varies: Manchester republican; True republican
MWA Ap 7 1859
NhHi S 29 1859
NhM Mr 3 1859

CONSTELLATION. *See* Nashua gazette (Nashua)

Manchester COURIER. bw S-N 1874||
NhM complete

Daily DEMOCRAT. d
NNHi Je 12 1850
NhHi Je 12,Jl 5 1850

Manchester DEMOCRAT and American. w Ap 26 1842-D 24 1863||
1842-F 1857 as Manchester democrat. Merged with Dollar weekly mirror, later Mirror and farmer
CSmH Ap 2 1845;N 11 1846;D 8 1847
DLC 1859[My-Ag 1861;Ap 1862-My 1863]
MB Ag 1848-Jl 1849;Ag 1851-Jl 22 1852
MHi F 7 1844;My 28 1845
MWA Ag 2,D 7 1842;Ja 25-F 1,Mr 22-29,Ap 26,My 24 1843;Mr 27 1844;Mr 5,Ap 2(extra) 16 1845;Ap 8,O 7 1846;Je 13(extra)23,O 26 1848;Ja 11,Ag 30,S 13 1849;Ap 18,N 14-21 1850;F 13(extra)Jl 22 1852;Ja 3 1854;Ag 11 1859;Mr 8 1860
MnHi Ap 26,My 10,Ag 23,D 7 1842
NN S 22 1847
NhD Ja 11-25,Mr 15-My,Je 14 1849-Ja 2,Ap 1851-Ap 21,My 12,26-Je 23,Jl-Ag 25,S-N 24, D 8 1853-Ja 19,F-Mr,Ap 13,26-My 17,Jl 12-19,Ag 9,30-N 15,29-D 13,27 1854
NhHi S 13 1842-[43;F 21 1844-50;My-N 8 1854;F 20-O 1 1856]
NhM [Ag 1842-43]47[48]-[50]-[52]-[56-57]58
NjR Mr 29,S 27 1849
WHi F 22 1843;Je 5 1850;S 20 1860-63

DEUTSCHE post. *See* Anzeiger und post

Saturday night DISPATCH. w Ja 24 1874-F 23 1878
S 1877-Ja 5 1878 as Manchester dispatch
NhHi 1874-Mr 1877
NhM complete

DOLLAR weekly mirror. *See* Mirror and farmer

L'ECHO des canadiens. w,sw Jl 2 1880-84||?
In French
NhM 1880-83

ENTERPRISE. O 6 1882-
NhM O 6 1882

ERGATIS. sw Mr 10 1910+
pub 1910+
NhD [Ap 1933+]

GLEANER. w N 5 1842-My 23 1846||
DLC N 5 1842
MWA F 17,Je 1 1844;F 22,Ag 30 1845
MnHi Je 15,N 23,D 14 1844;S 13,O 4 1845
NN Jl 6 1844
NhHi N 18 1843-D 6 1845
NhM complete

GRANITE farmer and visitor. w F 26 1850-Je 6 1857||
1850-53 as Granite farmer. Followed by Granite state farmer
DLC [1854-57]
MH [1854-Je 6 1857]
MSaE O 16 1855
MWA [1854]-[56-Je 6 1857]
NcD Je 25 1851
NhHi 1850-[53]-[57]
NhM [1850-57]

GRANITE state. w S 21-N 9 1878||
NhM complete

GRANITE state farmer. w Jl 18 1857-D 4? 1858||
Follows Granite farmer and visitor. Followed by New Hampshire journal of agriculture
MH [1857-O 15 1858]
MWA [1857-Ap 24 1858]
NhHi [1857-58]
NhM 1857-F 20 1858

Daily GRAPHIC. d N 15 1895-
NhHi 1895-Ja 4 1896

GRAPHIC. w N 2 1895-98||?
NhHi N 9 1895

Manchester GRAPHIC. sw Ja 8 1896-99||?
NhHi 1896-S 1899

GREENBACK lever. w Je 22-S 14 1878||
Je 22 1878 pub in Exeter
NhM Je 22,Jl 20,Ag 10-S 1878

GREENBACK press. ir Ja 29 1880-
NhM Ja-My 15,Je 2 1880

Manchester GUARDIAN. w Jl 14 1883-84||?
NhM 1883-My 17 1884

Manchester HERALD and advertiser. *See* Manchester advertiser

INDEPENDENT democrat. *See under* Concord

Daily ITEM. d D 12 1877-Ja 9 1878||
NhM complete

LITTLE live daily. d S 1-16 1896||?

ITEMIZER. w My 10 1878-
NhHi My 12 1883
NhM 1878-Jl 10 1880

Manchester LEADER and evening union. d O 9 1912+
1912-Ag 1914 as Manchester leader
pub 1912+
Nh 1912[13-14]-[16]-Je 1918
NhD 1912-Ap 1913
NhM 1912+

LITTLE live daily. d S 1-16 1896||?
NhM S 1-16 1869

Manchester MAGAZINE. w D 21 1839-40||
NhM 1839-Mr 14 1840

MASSABESIC. w Je 1-S 28 1878||
NhHi Je 1-8 1878
NhM complete

Manchester MEMORIAL. w Ja 1 1840-Ag 30 1844||
1840-41 as Amoskeag memorial. Followed by Manchester American, later Manchester American and messenger
CSmH Ap 15 1840;Ja 6 1841
DLC Ap 14 1843;Mr 29 1844
MWA My 6,Je 17-Jl 1 1840;Jl 14,D 8,22 1841; Ja 26,Ap 20,My 27 1842;My 19 1843;Je 7 1844
NN Jl 29 1840
NNHi S 22 1841
NSchU N 17 1841
NhD Je 7 1844
NhHi [Ja-N 18 1840;Mr 1841-42]-44
NhM 1840-[42-44]
PWCl D 22 1841

Manchester MERCANTILE advertiser. w Jl 3 1845-
MWA Jl 17,31-Ag 7 1845

MERRIMACK VALLEY sun. d S 1928-30||
NhM [O 18 1928-O 8 1929]

Saturday MESSENGER. w N 29 1845-Je 11? 1852||
United with Manchester American to form Manchester American and messenger
MWA Jl 18,O 24 1846;Ja 23 1847;S 2 1848;N 24 1849-O 18 1851;Ja 10,24,F 21,Mr 6,Ap 17, Je 5 1852
NhD F 9 1850
NhHi [O 1847-Ag 9 1851]
NhM 1845-48;N 1849-[50]-O 1851

Daily MIRROR and American. d O 28 1850-D 1924||
1850-D 26 1863 as Manchester daily mirror
DLC My 8 1862;Ja 16-O 1864
MHi Ag 13,15 1857;S 14 1859;O 30 1862
MSaE S 7,O 9 1858;S 15 1859;Je 19 1865
MWA Ja 1,N 19 1851;Ap 30 1852;Je 28,Jl 30 1853;F 11 1854;My 9 1859;Mr 29[O 17-N 23 1860]Ja 19(extra)Jl 25 1862;My 2,Je 5, Jl 26-27,Ag 8,17,23 1865; Jl 13,N 21 1867;Mr 10(extra)1869;Jl-D 1871;Je 4 1874;S 11 1879;S 4 1883;Je 17,24 1886;O 8 1888;Je 19 1890;O 30,N 3 1891
NNHi O 29 1850-S 27 1851;D 24 1862
Nh complete
NhD Mr-1858-S 24 1859;Ap 11 1860
NhHi [F 28 1851-Ag 2 1859;O 6 1863-N 7 1864;65]-[72]-Ja 24 1873-Mr 3 1881]
NhM [1850]-F 20 1852[Ag 1856-66]-[71]-[77-95]-[1917-20]-24
NhMA Ja-Je 1864

MIRROR and farmer. w F 22 1851-1917||
1851-61? as Dollar weekly mirror; 1862?-Jl 1 1865 Dollar weekly mirror and New Hampshire journal of agriculture
DA [1895-97]-[99]-[1902-03]
MB Ja 18 1862-72;Mr 23 1878
MSaE 1858[59]Jl 22 1871
MWA [Mr-N 24 1860]Ja 31,F 21,Mr 7,Ag 15 1863;Je 18 1864;68-70;72;Je 14 1873;S 4 1875;N 11,25,D 9,23 1876;Ja 18,Jl 12 1883-My 15 1890;Ag 8 1912-Ja 16 1913;Jl 23 1914
NN [1901;04-05;08]
Nh 1900-18
NhD F 12 1859;Ja 21 1860;Mr 24,Jl 14,28-Ag 11,D 1-21 1861[62-75]Ja 20 1877
NhHi [1852;My 28 1853-Ap 1854;56]-99
NhM [1851]-52[54-57]-[59]-[61]-[63-64]-[72-73]-1911;13;15-17
TJT O 18 1900

Le NATIONAL. d Ja 3 1893-94||?
In French
NhM 1893

NEW HAMPSHIRE. w Ja 21-Mr 4 1882||
NhD Ja 21,F 14-Mr 4 1882
NhHi complete

NEW HAMPSHIRE weekly advertiser. w
MB Je 14-D 6 1866
NhHi Je 14-21 1866

NEW HAMPSHIRE farmer and weekly union. w Ja 24 1851-1921||
1851-N 11 1879 as Union democrat (My 28-D 29 1861 Weekly union) N 18 1879-Je 10 1880 Union democrat and New Hampshire agriculturist; Je 17 1880-O 30 1901 Weekly union
DLC Jl 14,D 22 1857-[58-O 1 1861;Je-D 1867]
MHi F 14,28,Mr 21,Ap 23,My 7-14,Je 18,Jl 16, S 10 1851;F 4,Mr 17 1852;Je 1,S 14 1853;My 3,31 1854;F 12 1861;N 23 1868
MWA F 9,Mr 23 1853;My 8 1860;62-71;My 7 1876;89-91
MiU-C [1867-70]
NN Mr 9 1853;Jl 11 1876
Nh 1891-1918
NhHi [1851]-[72-80]
NhK D 30 1862[63-O 10 1865;66-Mr 1868]My 18,Je 1,15,D 7,1869-F 22,Mr 1-22,Ap 5,My 24-Jl 12,Ag 16,30 1870;Ja 3,17 1873
NhM 1851-[56]-[63]-[69]-[87]-[96]-[1902]-11, 14-16

NEW HAMPSHIRE Sunday globe. w F 7 1875-
MHi [F-D 17 1875]
NhHi [Ap 2-D 17 1876]
NhM [1875]D 31 1876

NEW HAMPSHIRE journal of agriculture. w D 11 1858-Ja 12 1863||
Follows Granite state farmer. Merged with Dollar weekly mirror, later Mirror and farmer
DLC Ja 15 1859;Je 2,Jl 7,S 1,O 20 1860;Je 15, Jl 17 1861
MHi D 8 1860-N 1862
MB S 15 1859-Ja 12 1863
MWA Ja 29[Je-D 1859;F-Mr 1860]-O,D 15 1862
NcD Je 15 1861;Je 11-18 1862
NhD 1858-Ag 2 1861;S 7-O 1,15-N 1862
NhHi 1858[59]-[61]62
NhM [1859]-[61]

NEW HAMPSHIRE post (German) *See* Anzeiger und post

Daily NEWS. d Ja 1 1869-
MWA F 4 1869
NhHi Ja 5-F 8 1869
NhM Ja 1-My 6 1869

Manchester NEWS. d O 27 1900-Ag 18 1904||?
Nh [1901-Ag 18 1904]
NhM 1900-Ag 18 1904

NORTHERN advocate. w N 28? 1847-
MWA Mr 14 1848

OLD hero. w Je 13 1848-
campaign paper
MWA Je 20 1848

Manchester PALLADIUM. w Mr 4 1846-F 18 1847||
NhHi Je 11-O 1846
NhM complete

Manchester PHONOGRAPH. w O 5 1878-
NhHi O 26 1878
NhM O 1878

NEW HAMPSHIRE (*Continued*)

MANCHESTER—*Continued*

PICKERING'S weekly bulletin. w O 2-D 25 1878||
Follows Manchester illustrated bulletin
NhM complete

PIONEER. w S 20 1879-
NhHi S 20 1879
NhM 1879-F 7 1880

Daily PRESS. d Mr 5 1888-92||?
NhHi Ja 15 1891
NhM 1888-Ag 31 1892

PUBLIC forum. w S 30 1871-Ja 1872||
Followed by Foster's democrat, later Foster's weekly democrat and enquirer (Dover)
MWA N 25 1871

PUTNEY'S weekly advertiser. w Je 3 1845-
NhHi Je 3,17 1845

Semi-weekly RECORD. sw,w D 1 1883-84||
Title varies: Weekly record
NhHi Ja 26 1884
NhM 1883-Ap 26 1884

Manchester REPRESENTATIVE. w O 18 1839-D 2 1842||
1839-Ja 15 1841 as Amoskeag representative. Merged with Manchester democrat, later Manchester democrat and American
MHi Jl 9,O 22,N 5,19-D 1841
MWA O 18 1839;Ap 10-My 1,O 9,N 27-D 4 1840;Ja 22,Ap 23,My 7-14,S 3,24,O 1,15 1841-D 2 1842
MnHi Ag 7 1840
NNHi 1839-O 9 1840
NcD S 25 1840
NhD Ja 22 1841
NhHi [1840-42]
NhM [1840]-O 15 1841
WHi Jl 31 1840;N 19 1841

Manchester REPUBLICAN. w 1859. *See* City messenger and true republican

REPUBLICAN. D 5 1868-
NhHi D 5 1868

REPUBLICAN volunteer. w Ag 12-O 28 1880||
Campaign paper
MWA Ag 25-S 9 1880
NhHi [1880]
NhM complete

Le REVEIL. d S 1 1908-Je 1910||?
In French
NhM 1908[09]-Je 1910

Manchester SPY. w Ag 1850-52||
NhM [1850]-N 1851

STARS and stripes. w S 23 1854-
MWA S 23 1854;Ap 28,My 19-26,Je 16,Jl 6,S 1, 15-22,N 17 1855;Ap 11 1857
NNHi Ap 7 1855
NhHi [1854-O 4 1856]

Saturday SUN. w N 23 1889-
NhHi N 23-30,D 14 1889

Sunday SUN. w S 29 1889-90||?
NhHi [1889]

Saturday TELEGRAM. w O 26 1889-95||?
NhHi 1891-Ag 3 1895
NhM 1889-[93]94

Manchester TELESCOPE. w S 9 1848-Ap 27 1850||?
MWA Ja 19 1850
NhHi Mr 26 1849;Ja 19 1850
NhM 1848[49]-Ap 27 1850

Manchester weekly TIMES. Ja 26 1878-Mr 3 1883||
NhHi Ja 26,D 14 1878
NhM complete

TIMES. w 1893-95||
NhHi Ja-My 8 1895

TRADERS' advertiser. w O 25 1865-
MWA Mr 28 1866
NhHi N 15 1865-Ja 3 1866

Manchester TRANSCRIPT. w Ap 21 1843-
Follows Manchester allodium
DLC Ap 21 1843
NhHi Ap-Ag 4 1843

Le TRAVAILLEUR et le progrès. *See under* Worcester, Mass

TRUE republican. *See* City messenger and true republican

Daily UNION. d O 15 1852-
MWA N 3 1852
NhHi 1852

Manchester daily UNION. d Jl?-N 8 1856||
MHi O 21 1856
MWA O 20,N 8 1856

Manchester UNION. d Mr 31 1863+
Title varies: Manchester daily union; Daily union; Daily union and American; etc.
pub [1864-1902]+
Ct Mr 31 1913
CtY N 15 1880
DLC [Ag-S 1863;65-Jl 1866]My 29 1878;98+
M [My 1931-My 1932]
MB Ag 1864-80
MHi N 23 1863
MWA [1863-F 19 1868]F 9,13,16,20,23,Mr 16,Je 15 1869;My 27,Je 4 1870;Ja 24,My 11,16 1871; Ap 12 1872;Ap 1(supp)1873;D 1,13 1876;O 24 1877[N 20-D 10 1879;Ap 28-Jl 22 1880]Mr 5(supp)1889;Jl 1908-21
Nh [1891;93]-[97-98]-[1900]-[18]-[22-25]+
NhD [Ap 1863-S 1865;66-68;Ap;S 1870-My 9 1871]Ja 25 1875;1904-Ja,Mr 1930+
NhHi [F 15 1855-N 7 1856]63-80;Je-N 5 1887; Je-Ag 17 1889
NhLa D 1903+
NhM 1863+

NhU 1908-13;32+
OClWHi D 27 1864;N 18 1878;Jl 30,Ag 30 1880
PAtM Ag 29 1866
PU [1902]
TxGR F 22 1932

Sunday UNION. w F 13 1910-
NhM F 13-N 27 1910

Weekly UNION. *See* New Hampshire farmer and weekly union

UNION democrat. *See* New Hampshire farmer and weekly union

La VOIX du people. w,ir F 25 1869-
In French
MB F 25,Mr 18,Ap-Jl 15 1869
MWA F 25 1869

MEREDITH

Meredith EAGLE. w 1880-86||?
?-Jl 23 1880 as Meredith eagle and blue ribbon advocate
NhHi Jl 1880-[Ja-O 1886]

Meredith NEWS. w Jl 1880+
pub [1880-1922]+
MWA Jl 17,Ag 28-O 1912;Je-Ag 20 1913;Ap 29-My 1914;Ja 24 1923
Nh 1900-My 1901
NhHi [1884-My 1885]95-99

Meredith REVIEW. sw D 25 1880-81||?
NhHi Ja 8-Je 11 1881

MEREDITH BRIDGE. *See* LACONIA

MERIDEN

Meriden ENTERPRISE. w 1908-15||?
Nh 1908-15

MILFORD

Milford ADVANCE. w Ja 4 1887-Jl 5 1891||
NhHi 1887
NhMi complete

*Milford CABINET. w N 11 1802+
1802-Je 28 1900 as Farmer's cabinet
1802-Jl 5 1900 pub in Amherst
pub Jl 1894+
DLC 1821[22-29]-[31-32]-[37]-[40;43-44;47-49; 52-57;60-67;69-73;77-81;84]
ICHi F 16 1828
ICN O 8,N 19-D 3 1831;Ja 14 1832
MBAt My 5 1827;Jl 18 1829;Ag 6 1831;Ja 13 1837
MHi D 11 1830
MSaE S 3 1908
MWA 1821-[43]-55;F 14 1856-99;1901-S 1910;S 6 1917
MiU-C [1821-42;44-47;73-83;85-86;89-90;93;97-98]
N My 11,D 28 1822;Ja 10,My 15-D 18 1824;O 1827-S 6,O 4,D 27 1828;My 5 1832;S 19,D 19 1834;My 1 1835
NNHi O 15 1825;Mr 25,Ag 5 1826;My 26,Je 30,D 22 1837;Jl 25 1844;Jl 1 1852;D 8 1853;Mr 2 1854;N 1 1855;Ja 11 1860
NcD [1821-42;44-61;64-78]-82;N 13 1902-Je 23 1910
Nh 1901-[19-21]+
NhA 1821+
NhD 1821-Ag 20 1841;Ag 19 1842-Jl 15 1869
NhHi 1821-1900
NhM Ap 27 1865
NhMi Jl 1891+
OHi N 18 1826
PPL N 28 1850
WHi D 1 1827;Ja 3,17 1834;Je 19 1835;Mr 25, Ap 8,My 6,Jl 15-22 1836;Jl 27 1838;D 5 1841;D 14 1865

Milford ENTERPRISE. w D 30 1873-D 28 1886||
MSaE D 15 1874;Ja 26,D 14-21 1875;Je 13 1876;D 18 1877;F 19,Mr 26,O 15-29,N 12,26,D 24 1878;Ja 28,F 18,Ap 8,29,My 13-27 1879;My 25-Je 8,Jl 13,S 14,O 1880;Ap 12-19,My 24 1881;O 24 1882;Ag 14,O 9 1883;S 23-30 1884; Je 23 1885
MiU-C Ag 31 1886
NhHi Ag 11 1874-[76]-[86]
NhMi complete

Weekly MIRROR. w S 17 1847-Ag 11 1848||
Followed by Souhegan standard
NhMi complete

*NEW HAMPSHIRE sentinel. w Mr 23 1799-
NhMi 1832-33

Milford daily POINTER. d Jl 16 1894-1909||?
Nh [1894-1908]-Jl 15 1909
NhMi 1894-[97-Ja 27 1909]

Milford REPUBLICAN. w Ja 7 1857-61||
MWA Ja 28 1857;My 2 1860;Mr 27 1861
MiU-C [1858-61]
NhHi [Ja 21-S 1857]
NhM Mr 3 1858

SOUHEGAN standard. w Ag 18 1848-N 10 1848||
Follows Weekly mirror
NhMi complete

MOULTONBORO FALLS

REFORMER. w 1833-34||
MnHi [1834]

MT. WASHINGTON

AMONG the clouds. d Jl 20 1877-1917||
1877-84 as Burt's Among the clouds
Suspended from Je 18 1908-Jl 5 1910
published during summer season only
M [1877-1917]
MB 1877-90[92-1904]Jl 1 1907;Je 18 1908

MH Jl 8-S 15 1886;Jl 14-S 19 1899
MSaE S 11 1890;Ag 6,26 1901
MeAu S 6 1904
N Jl 20-S 11 1877;Ag 20 1880;Jl 1 1907
NN Jl 9,Ag 20 1879;Ag 9 1886;Ag 5 1899; 1900-07;10-12
NNHi [1911]S 11 1912
NhD [1877-1904]
NhG 1877;80-98;1901-07;10-12
NhHi [1877-1917]
NhM Ag 21 1879-S 10 1913
OClWHi Ag 21 1877;Ag 22-23 1882

BURT'S Among the clouds. *See* Among the clouds

NASHUA

CAMPAIGN points. w
campaign paper
NhHi N 1 1888

Nashua CHIMES. w
NhHi N 3 1885

CONSTELLATION and Nashua advertiser. *See* Nashua gazette

CONSTELLATION and Nashua gazette. *See* Nashua gazette

EMERALD. d My 2 1887-
NhHi My 2-6 1887

Nashua GAZETTE. w D 16 1826-95||?
1826 as Constellation and Nashua advertiser; Ja-Ag 11 1827 Constellation and Nashua gazette; Ag 18 1828-78? Nashua gazette and Hillsborough county advertiser
CSmH Ag 27 1830
DLC [1829-66;73-78]
MBAt Jl 21 1827
MHi Ap 10 1862;D 3 1868
MSaE Je 15 1832;Je 21,N 1 1833;Ja 31,My 16, Je 6,Ag 1,S 26,O 24,N 29,D 19 1834[35-37]Ap 7,Ag 4,25, N 3-10 1837;F 22,Mr 16 1838;Je 7, S 20,N 8 1839;S 13 1840;Mr 14 1850;58;59;60-Ja 22 1863
MWA Ag 2,30 1828;Jl 24 1829;Je 15 1832;Ja 11-F 1,Mr 29,Ag 2,O 11 1833;F 7,Ag 22,S 26, D 12 1834;Ja 23,F 6,Mr 13,My 15,Je 19,Jl 17, Ag 28 1835;My 27 1836;My 5,D 8 1837;F 16, N 16 1838[F 1839-40]F 5,Ap 9,N 12 1841;My 13,Ag 25,N 3 1842;Mr 21 1844;Jl 3,S 11 1845; Ja 13 1848;D 11 1851;Ja 8,Ag 12 1852;My 11, Jl 20-27 1854[Mr 1855-S 4 1856]F 12,Mr 26,Jl 23-30 1857;Jl 7 1859;Je 14 1860;Mr 21 1861; Mr 12 1863;Ap 20 1865;D 27 1866;F 13 1868;Je 29 1871;D 21 1876;Ap 25 1878
MiU-C Ag 22 1834
MnHi Ja 15,Mr 2,26,Ap 9-23,My 14-21,Jl 30 1841
NNHi Je 17 1836;Jl 7 1870
NhD F 28 1839;Jl 1841-Mr 23 1843;Ap-My 2 1844;F 27,My 16 1845-Ja 4 1849;Jl 22 1852
NhHi [Mr 1827-28]-[31-32]-[38]-[42-F 5 1846; Mr 1848-Je 1850]-52;54-59;93-Ja 23 1896
NhNa 1826-D 12 1889
NjR Mr 24 1859
OClWHi Je 6,20-27 1850;Ag 24 1865
P-M Mr 23 1854

Nashua daily GAZETTE. d S 5 1872-N 9 1895||
MWA Mr 28 1876;Je 19,Ag 23,25 1877;O 15 1889
NNHi My 7 1873;D 30 1880
Nh Ja-N 9 1895
NhHi 1872-89
NhNa [1872]-[89-90]-[95]

GRANITE state beacon light. w D 3 1853-Mr 18 1854||
MWA 1853-F 18,Mr 11 1854
NNHi D 3 1853
NhHi complete

GRANITE state register. w My 8 1857-
NhHi 1857-Ap 8 1859
NjR Ja 1 1858

HARRISON eagle. w My 7 1840-
NhHi My 28,O 8 1840

L'IMPARTIAL. tw F 1 1898+
In French
pub 1898+
Nh [1912-15]-[18-25]-[29]+
NhHi F-S 1898

KING'S effort. S 10 1867-
NhHi S 10 1867

NEW HAMPSHIRE republican. d My 25 1892-F 11 1893||
Nh D 1892-93
NhHa complete
NhHi complete

NEW HAMPSHIRE spectator. w Ja 1? 1832-
MnHi Ja 14 1832

NEW HAMPSHIRE telegraph. *See* Nashua weekly telegraph

Nashua NEWS. d 1904||?
Nh S 12-D 2 1904

Nashua OASIS. w Ja 4 1843-O 6 1858||
1843-51 as Oasis (Jl 1851-S 21 1853 Nashua and Nashville oasis). Followed by Bridgeton reporter (Bridgeton, Maine)
DLC Mr 6 1844;F 18-Mr 25 1846;O 31-D 26 1849;[Ja-O 1851]My 12,N 24 1852;O 11 1854
MSaE Ja 18 1843
MWA D 27 1843;Ja 31 1844;Ja 29,Je 4 1845; 47-48;Ag 15 1849-[55]-F 6,Mr 6,Ag-S 1856;Ag 5 1857
MiU-C [1848;51-52;54]
NhHi complete
NhNa 1843-[51-55]
NjR O 21 1846;D 29 1847
P-M Ja 3 1855

Nashua daily PRESS. d N 11 1895-Jl 19 1905||
Merged with Nashua daily telegraph
Nh 1895-[96-1905]
NhHa [1895-96]-1905

NEW HAMPSHIRE (*Continued*)

NASHUA—*Continued*

SQUARE deal. w 1914-15‖
DLC S 1914-S 16 1915
NhHi Ap 1914-S 16 1915

Nashua weekly **TELEGRAPH.** w O 20 1832-S 25 1918‖
1832-S 13 1873 as New Hampshire telegraph
DLC D 23 1843;My 23,Ag 29,S 5 1846[49-51;60;62-66]
MBAt O 20 1832
MSaE Ap 29 1843;Ap 8,Jl 22-29 1876
MWA O 20 1832;Mr 9,Ap 27 1833;Mr 22,D 9 1834;Ja 27,Ag 11-18,S 8 1835;O 24,D 19 1837;Ja 2,Je 12 1838;Ja 21,Mr 4,Je 17,Jl 15,S 3 1843;Ja 11,S 20 1845;Je 20,Ap 15,D 9 1848[49]Mr 30,Je 1,Jl 6,Ag 31,O 12,N 2 1850;Jl 12,S 6 1851;Ja 24,Mr 27,Jl 24,S 4,O 16,N 27 1852;Mr 26,Ap 2,N 5,D 17 1853[54-Ag 1856;Jl 18-D 1857]Ja 2,Ap 10 1858[F 1859-60]Je 15 1861;Ja 18,F 8,Mr 1-8,Ap 5,Je 14,N 15 1862[F 14-D 12 1863;Ap 9-D 1864]-Ap 22 1865;F 17 1866;N 30 1867;O 23 1869[F 11-D 2 1871;F 10 1872-N 22 1873]O 24 1874;O 1875-S 1879;S 18(supp)N 10 1883;Mr 3 1894;O 1898-S 1899
MiU-C [1849;54;57;60]
MnHi F 10 1835;Ja 19,F 2,My 18,Jl 27 1841
NNHi S 9 1854;Je 14 1862;My 30 1863;Ap 22 1865
NcD [1849;55-57;59-60;71-73]
NhD Ja 12 1841;D 9 1843
NhHi 1832-[34-35;Mr 1836-48]-[51]-[59]-[61]-[64]-81[Ap 1882-85]-[1908-Ag 1909]-18
NhM Ag 6 1859
NhNa 1832-63
OClWHi My 1 1912
P-M N 25 1854

Nashua daily **TELEGRAPH.** d Mr 1 1869+
pub 1928+
DLC Mr 31 1869
MWA Mr 7-9,Ap 21(extra)1870;Jl 28 1871;O 28 1873;Je 30,S 7 1877;Ag 29 1883;My 30,O 15 1889;Ap 6 1891-Jl 1893;Ja 1 1896;N 20 1916;S 6-8 1917
Nh F 13-28 1893;95-Jl 10 1918
NhHi 1869-1920
NhNa 1899+

NELSON

Nelson **CLARION.** ir Mr 1870-
DLC Mr 1870;My 1871
NhHi Mr,My 1870

NEW IPSWICH

NEW ENGLAND star. m
NhHi My 1875

NEWS-GATHERER. w D 1 1835-
MBAt Ja 7 1836
NhHi My 26 1836

New Ipswich **REGISTER.** w F 26 1833-
MWA My 28 1833

NEW LONDON

HIGHLANDER. w 1928?-Je 30 1931‖
NhHi Ag 8 1928-31

NEWCASTLE

Newcastle **OBSERVER.** Fort Constitution. S 3? 1863-
DLC O 3 1863

NEWMARKET

Newmarket **ADVERTISER.** w
MSaE N 22 1844

Newmarket **ADVERTISER.** w S 4 1873-1932‖?
1873-75? as Weekly advertiser; 1876?-79? Rockingham county advertiser
MWA D 24 1874
Nh 1900-[19]-Mr 17 1932
NhHi F 21 1891-99

ROCKINGHAM argus. w Mr 1843-44‖?
NhHi Jl 28 1843

ROCKINGHAM county advertiser. *See* Newmarket advertiser

NEWPORT

Tuesday **ARGUS.** w O 16 1923-25‖?
NhHi [O 23 1923-O 20 1925]
—Thursday ed *See* Argus-champion

ARGUS and spectator. *See* Argus-champion

ARGUS-CHAMPION. w S 1833+
1833-S? 1834 as Argus; O 14 1834-Jl 18 1835 New Hampshire argus; Jl 25 1835-1926 New Hampshire argus and spectator (Je 17 1842-49? Argus and spectator)
1823-O? 1834 pub in Claremont
pub 1930+
DLC N 25 1833;F 15 1834;Ag 5-19,N 11 1837;F 24-Mr 3 1838;F 16-23,Ap 13,27-My 4,Je 1,Ag 10-24,S 14-21,O 26 1839;Ja 11,25,Ap 18 1840;Mr 28 1845;47-49;My 25 1860; D 24 1869;Ja 3 1890;Ja 19 1894;Ja 29 1897;Je 17,Jl 8-Ag 19 1898;F 2,Je 15 1900;Ja 4,18-25,My 3,1901;Ja 9 1903
MB Jl 28,S 9,O 4,D 16,29 1842-Ja 1843
MBAt N 23 1839
MSaE N 13 1841
MWA D 27 1834;Ja 17,31,F 21-Mr 7,My 30,O 24-31 1835;Jl 23,Ag 27,O 8 1836[F 18 1837-S 19 1840;41]Jl 22 1842;S 22,D 8 1843;Mr 8,My 31 1844;Ja 10 1845;F 6,Je 19,Jl 31 1846;Ja 15,D 24 1847;Ag 24 1849;Je 18 1852[Ap 14-D 1854]Jl 20 1855;F 22,Jl 25,Ag 8-22 1856;Ja 30,F 20,Mr 13,Ap 9,Jl 23 1858;Ja 14,Jl 15,29,Ag 19,S 9 1859[60]-[62]-Ja 6,27-F 3,Ag 11 1865;F 21,S 4,25 1868;F 26,Mr 19,Ap 16-23 1869
MnHi S 21 1839
NcD Ag 6,O 1,29,D 3,17 1869
Nh 1900-O 1 1920;F 25 1921+
NhD Je 20 1840;Mr 9 1849;Ap 12 1867;N 14 1873;S 18,O 28 1874;Je 10,Ag 26,S 23 1881;F 10-24,Ap 7-14 1882;Ja 12,F 9, Mr 9,30,Je 1, Jl 27-Ag 3,31,O 12,N 16 1883;F 1,O 17 1884; Mr 27,Ap 17,Jl 31 1885;Je 18-25,S 17 1886; Mr 25-Ap 1,15,My 20 1887;Mr 9,Ap 27 1888; Ja 4,O 11-18, N 15,29 1889;Ja 3-24,F 7,21, Mr 28,Je 6-13,Ag 1,15 1890[91-98]Ja 6,Ag 18,D 29 1899[1900]-My 3,Ag 30,D 30 1901-Ja 3 1902;Ja 9,My 29-Je 5,Jl 24,O 16 1903
NhHi [O 11 1834-36]-[40]-[48-51]-[55]-[59]-[66]-[73]75[76]-[78]-[1904]-[12]-[24-25]
NhNe 1902+
NhNeB [1878+]
RP Jl 15 1842
—Tuesday ed *See* Tuesday argus

FARMER'S advocate and political adventurer. w Ap 7 1831-32‖
MWA My 12 1831
NhHi Ap 14 1831

NEW HAMPSHIRE argus and spectator. *See* Argus-champion

NEW HAMPSHIRE spectator. w Ja 12 1825-Jc 1835‖?
Follows Claremont spectator (Claremont)
United with New Hampshire argus to form New Hampshire argus and spectator, later Argus-champion
CSmH Jl 10 1830
Ct [1827-33]
DLC O 9 1827;Ap 14 1829-Ap 6 1830;Ja 1,15, 26 1831;Ja 26,F 2-9,Mr 2-9,Ap 6-13,My 4-11, Je 8-22,Jl 27,Ag 17,S 21-28 1833
MBAt Ja 12-26,F 9,23 1825
MWA F 23 1825;Ag 15 1826;My 1,O 9,N 20 1827;Ag 4,O 20 1829;O 30 1830[31;Ap 14 1832-33]
N Ag 10-17 1825;Ap,Jl 18-N 1826;My 1827-28;O 19 1833
NNHi O 23 1827
NhHi 1825-[29]-[32]-[34-Je 13 1835]
NhW Ja 22 1828-Mr 3 1829
WHi Ap 4 1835

REPUBLICAN champion. w Ja 6 1881-1926‖
United with New Hampshire argus and spectator to form Argus-champion
DLC Ja 18 1894,S 2,D 25 1897;Ja 27,Mr 3, 24,Ap 7 1898;Ap 5,19-26,My 24,Jl 12 1900;Ja 18-25, Ap 25-My 2, Je 27 1901
Nh 1900-25
NhD O 11-18 1883;Ja 3,Mr 27,N 20 1884;Ja 1,Ag 6 1885;F 25 1886;Mr 24-31,S 29-O 6 1887;F 9,Mr 22-29,Je 21 1888;My 8,Jl 24-Ag 7,N 27 1890[91]Mr 24,Ap 7,Je 9,S 8,N 24 1892;Mr 23 1893;Ja 18-25,Mr 29,Ag 23,N 29 1894-[95-96]S 1897-S 1,N 17 1898;Jl 20,S 21, O 26 1899[1900-01] Je 19-26,N 13 1902;03;F 4,18-25,Ap 14,28 1905;D 6,27 1906
NhHi 1881-[86-87]-1924
NhNe 1902-26

SULLIVAN republican. w Ja 1859-61‖
MWA Ap 6 1860
NhHi [F 26 1859-S 1861]

WHIP and spur. w Ja 1 1839-
campaign paper
MWA Ja 1,F 5,19-26,Mr 12-19 1839;S 11,O 23-30 1852;S 13-27,O 11-N 1 1856
NjR Ja 8 1839;N 11 1844

NORTH CONWAY

IDLER. *See* Reporter

REPORTER. w Je 22 1880+
1880-My 1887? as Idler; Je 1887?-1916 White Mountain reporter
pub Jl 1907+
MWA S 27 1900
MiU-C S 27 1900
NNHi Je-S 7 1880
Nh 1900-[20]+
NhConw [1902-10]-[12-15]-[18]-[20]-[22-23]-[25]-[27]-[32]+
NhHi Mr 14 1895-99

WHITE MOUNTAIN record. w N 28 1879-81‖?
NhHi 1879-Ja 14 1881

WHITE MOUNTAIN reporter. *See* Reporter

NORTH STRATFORD

COOS county democrat and Northern press. w S 11 1838-62‖?
1838-59 as Coos county democrat (Lancaster)
MB Ag 9,S 13,27,O 4 1842;Ja 4-18,F 1-8 1843
MWA Jl 30 1839;D 28 1841;Ja 4 1842;Jl 17 1844;My 19,Je 2,S 1-8 1846;Ja 19,F 9-16 1847; O 25-N 1 1848;Mr 14,My 2 1849;D 4 1850;Ag 11,N 3 1852;D 6 1854;F 13,Jl 16,Ag 27 1856;Mr 24 1858;Mr 21 1860;Mr 27 1861
NNHi O 4 1854
NhD S 18 1838-Ag 6,20,S 3-O 8,22 1839-Je 16, 30 1840-Ag 17,31 1841-Ap,My 10-Je 14,28,Jl 5,19-Ag,O 4 1842;Ag 30-S 20,O-D 6,20 1848-Ja 10,31-F 7,21,28-Mr 14,Ap 18-My 9,23,Je 6-13,27,Jl 25-Ag 8,22-29,S 12-26,O-N,D 12,26 1849;Ap 3,Jl-Ag 21 1850;Ag 20 1855
NhHi [O 1838-Ag 1839;43-46]-[Je 1853-N 1854;55-57;Ja-Jl 1861]
NhL 1847-60

NORTH WOODSTOCK

North Woodstock **TIMES.** w Ag 4 1899-
NhHi 1899-Ag 3 1900

NORTHAMPTON

Northampton **DEMOCRAT** and Hampshire county advertiser. 1840?-
IU F 24 1841

OSSIPEE

CARROLL county register. w Je 2 1859-
NhHi [O 14 1861-S 1864]

PAPER MILL VILLAGE. *See* ALSTEAD

PENACOOK

Penacook **NEWS LETTER.** sw,w Mr 1874-1924‖?
1874-1901? as Rays of light
sw 1874-1901?
Nh 1902-24
NhHi [Mr 10 1876-79]-[87]-1901

RAYS of light. *See* Penacook news letter

PETERBOROUGH

CONTOOCOOK transcript. *See* Peterborough transcript

HILLSBORO' county republican and state clarion. w Ja 1 1830-
Ja? 1830 as Hillsborough republican
CSmH Jl 2 1830
DLC Ja 8 1830
NhHi Ja 15 1830

HILLSBOROUGH republican. *See* Hillsboro' county republican and state clarion

Peterborough **MESSENGER.** w O 13? 1847-
MWA Ja 21-28,Mr 3 1848
NhHi F 11 1848
NhP Mr 18 1848

Peterborough **TRANSCRIPT.** w Je 2 1849+
1849-53? as Contoocook transcript
pub 1923+
ICHi Ag 13 1864
CSmH O 15 1908
MWA My 26 1860;S 27 1862;Ag 24 1871;Ag 18 1910
NNHi F 20 1873
Nh 1900+
NhHi Ag 14-S 4 1850[My 24-D 1854;F-S 3 1856]91-99
NhP 1849-My 11 1853;My 24 1854+
T Ag 1934

PITTSFIELD

ANALECTA. *See* Valley times

SNOWFLAKE. *See* Valley times

Pittsfield **STAR.** w 1873-82‖
1873-74? as Weekly star
NhHi Jl 12 1873;F 21 1874;Ja 12 1875
NhPi [1873]

SUNCOOK VALLEY times. *See* Pittsfield times

Pittsfield **TIMES.** w O 15 1868-75‖?
1868-Ap 22? 1871 as Suncook Valley times
MWA 1868-O 7 1869;F 17-Mr 10,Je 9-O 1870
NhHi 1868-O 1870;Ap 29 1871-Je 8 1872
NhPi [O 29 1868-O 7 1869]

VALLEY times. m,sm,w D 1877+
1877-83 as Snowflake; 1884-95? Analecta
1877-84? pub in Dunbarton
m 1877-79;sm 1880-82
pub [1901+]
MWA F-M 1878;Je 1(supp)1880;84-Je 1886;S 16 1890
Nh 1900+
NhHi [1879-Je 1882]-90
NhM 1877-[86]87
NhPi 1883;85+

PLYMOUTH

GRAFTON county democrat. w Ja 5 1878-86‖?
MWA Ag 13 1881
NhHi [Ap 1878-My 1885]

GRAFTON county journal. w 1874-86‖?
Followed by Plymouth record
MWA D 25 1875;Ja 22-F,Mr 11-25,Ap 15-22 1876
NhHi [S 11 1875-79]-86
NhM Je 24 1876-[77-78]-[81]-N 6 1886

GRAFTON journal. w Ja 1 1825-
DLC Ja 15-29,Mr 26,My 14 1825
MBAt 1825-Mr 25 1826
MWA [Ja 8-D 24 1825]
NhHi 1825-Mr 18 1826

Daily Plymouth **JOURNAL.** d
NhHi Jl 14 1876

NEW HAMPSHIRE advertiser.
NhHi F,Ap 1893

Plymouth **RECORD.** w Ja 1 1887+
Follows Grafton county journal
pub 1914+
MWA My 25 1935
Nh 1900-S 21 1918;26+
NhD Ag 15 1900;Jl 19 1913
NhHi 1887-99
NhM 1887[88-89]-1907

REPUBLICAN star. w 1880-86‖?
NhHi 1881-[86]

WHITE MOUNTAIN bugle. w Ja 1 1848-
MBAt Ja 15 1848
NhHi Ja 8 1848

NEW HAMPSHIRE (*Continued*)

PORTSMOUTH

ADVERTISER. m N 1879-
MWA N 1879
NhHi D 1879

AMERICAN ballot. *See under* Exeter

Portsmouth morning **CHRONICLE.** bw Je? 1822-
MSaE Jl 18,Ag,S 12,O 10,D 5 1823
MWA S 12,N 7 1823
NhHi Jl 1-D 19 1823

Portsmouth daily **CHRONICLE.** d Ag 2 1852-Je 13 1921||
1825-67? as Portsmouth morning chronicle
CLM F 9 1874
MSaE S 5 1855
MWA Ag 2-7,O 29 1852;Ap 20,Jl 2-7,D 10 1853[F 18-4-N 1855]F 18,Mr 14,Ap 2,18,O 18 1856;My 6,29,Jl 15,O 2 1857;Ja 1,Mr 3,My 19, Je 28,O 23,N 12 1858;Ap 11 1859;Ap 26,My 6, O 24,N 21 1861;Ag 30,N 4 1862;F 14,18,Mr 6, Ap 3,O 23 1863;Ap 17,S 25 1865;F 20,Ap 11 1866;Mr 12 1868;69-Je 1877;D 2 1879;Ag 2 1902;My 28 1903
Nh My 1893-Jl 1918
NhD Ja 11-14 1881
NhHi [O 29 1852-53]-[55]-[58-N 1 1860]61-[65-O 1881]
NhM F 13 1871
NhPo Ag 2 1852;Jl 31 1856
NhPoH complete
OClWHi My 9 1865
—w ed *See* New Hampshire gazette
—Evening ed *See* Portsmouth herald and times

Weekly **CHRONICLE.** *See* Rockingham chronicle

CHRONICLE and phenix. *See* Rockingham chronicle

COMMERCIAL advertiser. w Jl 8 1825-29||
DLC Ag-D 22 1825;Je 25-Jl 2 1829
MBAt S 16-23 1825;Ja 31,Ag 7 1828;Mr 5 1829
MSaE S-O 7,21-D 22 1825;27-[29]
MWA Jl-Ag 1825;Ja 5,My 25,Ag 24 1826;N 1-8 1827;My 22,Jl 31 1828;F 12 1829
NhD F 16 1826;D 18 1828
NhHi [Jl 22 1825-S 6 1827]28-S 17 1829

Evening **COURIER.** w O 24 1832-
MAm N 21 1832
MWA 1832-Ja 3 1833
NhHi 1832-Ja 9 1833

FOWLE'S New-Hampshire gazette and general advertiser. *See* New Hampshire gazette

FRANK W. MILLER'S Portsmouth N.H. weekly. w My 12 1877-81||?
NhHi 1877-Ap 23 1881

FREEMAN'S friend.
CSmH O 14 1840
MWA O 14 1840

FREEMAN'S journal; or, New-Hampshire gazette. *See* New Hampshire gazette

Daily evening **GAZETTE.** d Jl 20 1849-My 22 1856||
1849 as New Hampshire gazette and city advertiser
MWA F 1,Ap 19,26 1856
NNHi 1856
NhHi [N 30 1849-Ja 23 1850]Ja 21-My 1856
—w ed *See* New Hampshire gazette

Portsmouth **HERALD** and times. d S 23 1884+
1884-My 1925 as Portsmouth herald
pub 1884+
Nh Je 1897-[98]-[1905]-Je 1918;25+
—w ed *See* New Hampshire gazette
—morning ed *See* Portsmouth daily chronicle

HOME budget. w? Jl 3 1878-
NhHi Jl 17 1878

HORNET. w Mr 4 1837-
MWA Ap 13,Je 1 1837
NhHi Mr-Ag 24 1837

Daily Portsmouth **JOURNAL.** d Je 4-10 1834||?
MWA Je 4-6,9-10 1834
NcD Je 9-10 1834
NhHi Je 9-10 1834

*Portsmouth **JOURNAL** of literature and politics. w,sw Je 4 1793-My 16 1903||
1793-99 as Oracle of the day; 1800-O 10 1801 United States oracle of the day; O 17 1801-O 15 1803 United States oracle and Portsmouth advertiser; O 29 1803-Je 30 1821 Portsmouth oracle; O 20 1827-Je 1 1833 Portsmouth journal and Rockingham gazette. Merged with New Hampshire gazette
sw 1793-95
CSmH Ag 4 1827
CtY 1823-Je 1825;26-28;37;Ja 11 1840;41-S 14 1844;49-53
DLC Jl 1821-33;35-52;54-66;68-[73]-[80]
GU Jl 12 1873
ICN [Jl 20 1822-Ap 12 1823]
IU Ja 16 1836;S 10 1848
IaDH F 8 1840
MB [Ap 10-My 1824;Je-Ag 3 1833]D 23-30 1837;Je 1 1842;Ja 21 1843;D 30 1862;Ag 25 1878
MBAt Ja 27,Mr 3,Je 16,Jl 7,Ag 18,S 8,O 13, D 8 1821;22-[42]-Ja 14 1843[49]-[52-53]
MH Jl 17 1821-Je 1825[38-39;41-43]
MHi 1821-Je 1 1833
MSaE N 24 1824
MWA Ag 18-D 8 1821;22-[30]-1903
MnHi N 25 1826;O 10 1829;Ja 14 1832;D 17 1842;F 4 1843
N 1822-24;Ja 7,Mr 18,My 6,Je 10,Jl 1826-D 19 1829
NN Je 1821;32-33
NNHi [1822]25;Jl 8 1826;Mr 24 1827;Mr 8 1828;30;Ap 9 1831;32[33-34]-36;Je 1838-[45-54]-[58]-Ap 9 1870;Je 17 1871;Ag 24 1872-Mr 1873;extra:Jl 2 1834
NcD Mr 15 1823;D 4 1824;My 10 1828;Ja 14 1832[35-42;47;51;60-64;73;76]
NhD 1821-[42]-[44-50]-[81]-My 16 1903
NhHi 1821-1903
NjR D 31 1831
TxU 1836-55;64
WHi Jl 7 1821-Je 28 1890

Portsmouth **JOURNAL** of literature and politics. tw
MWA D 9,13-15,D 23 1834-Ja 3 1835
MiU-C [1822-33]36-[38-40]-[44-45]-[50-56]-[61-63;66-83;88-92]-[94]-[97]-1901
NcD D 13 1834
NhHi D 9 1834-Ja 1 1835

MERCANTILE transcript. w
WHi N 19 1846-D 16 1847

Portsmouth **MERCURY.** w S 28 1843-S 17 1845||
Followed by Republican union
DLC [1845-46]
MWA [1844-45]46
MiU-C [1844-45]
NNHi S 12 1844
NhHi O 12 1843-46

*NEW **HAMPSHIRE** gazette. w O 7 1756+
Mr 11 1763-Ja 9 1776 as New-Hampshire gazette and historical chronicle; My 25 1776-Je 9 1778 Freeman's journal; or, New-Hampshire gazette; Je 16 1778-S 1 1781 New-Hampshire gazette; or, State journal and general advertiser; S 7 1781-Ap 9 1793 New Hampshire gazette and general advertiser (D 24 1784-Je 2 1787 Fowle's New-Hampshire gazette and general advertiser); Ja 12 1847-Mr 17 1853 New Hampshire gazette and republican union
25 1776
N 1775 pub in Greenland; Je 16 1778-S 1 1781 in Exeter
pub 1859+
Ct [1827-37]
DLC 1821-31[33]-Je 1849;53-57[60;69]-75
ICHi O 12 1872;S 1 1881
MBAt 1821-S 14 1861;O 12 1872
MSaE Ap 30 1822;S 2 1823;Je 21 1836
MWA [1821]-[30-Je 1831]Jl 22,O 21 1834[35]-[41-43]-[Ja-S 2 1845]Ja 20,Ap 7,My 26,Je 9, 30,Jl 28 1846;47-[Ja-S 1850]Ag 26 1851;Ja 27, Je 8 1852;O 28,D 2 1854;O 11 1856;Je 13 1857; My 5 1860;S 14 1861;S 2 1865;Ja 1,29,Ap 2,Je 11 1870;Ja 21,Ap 8,Jl 1(supp)15, O 28 1871; Mr 16,O 12 1872;Ap 11-My 2,23-Je 6,27 1889; S 18-O 2 1890
MeU Ag 17,S 28,N 9 1830;Ja 10,S 11,N 20 1832;Mr 5,Jl 2,23,Ag 6 1833
MiU-C [1821-30;35-49;56;65;70;96]
MnHi D 20 1825;Ja 18 1831;Ja 24 1832;Jl 28 1835[36-37]Mr 5 1839;Je 23,Jl 7 1840
N Ja 30,F 27-Mr 13,Ap 10,My 29,Je 12,S 4 1821;Ja 22,F 5-12,26,Mr 19-Ap 9,23-30, My 21, S 24,O 1,N 19 1822-Mr 10,My 13,N 11 1823-24
NNHi 1821-Ap 13,Je 1,N 9 1824;F 8,Mr 29,N 29 1825;My 29,Je 12,Jl 10,Ag 7,S 25 1827;F 12,Mr 10,Ap 8 1828;Ja 15 1870;Mr 10 1873
NcD [1822;49;56]
Nh 1900-18
NhD [1821-24]-[29]-[32-Ag 1836]
NhHi 1821-[32-33]-[36-37]-[51]-[58;69-70]-72 [Ag 1876-77]78;My 1891-99
NjR [1832-33]
OCl Ja 24 1895
—d ed *See* Portsmouth daily chronicle

NEW HAMPSHIRE gazette and city advertiser. d *See* Daily evening gazette

NEW HAMPSHIRE observer. *See under* Concord

NEW HAMPSHIRE repository and observer. *See* New Hampshire observer (Concord)

NEWS and courier. *See* Morning courier (Amesbury)

NOVATOR. w N 7 1822-24||
1822-Ja? 1823 as Paraclete and tickler; F-Ap? 1823 Novator and independent expositor
DLC Jl 15 1824
MBAt Ja 16,F 13-20,Mr 20-27 1823;Ap 29 1824
MSaE Ag 7 1823
MWA Jl 10 1823
NNHi N 7 1822
NhHi [1822-Ja,Mr 13-Jl 8 1823]

OLIVE leaf. w 1841-45||?
1841-N 2 1843 as Portsmouth Washingtonian (O 13 1842-Jl 27 1843 Washington and banner) N 9 1843-N 27 1844 Washingtonian and philanthropist
MWA F 10,O 13 1842-O,D 21 1843;Ap 25,O 2 1844
NhHi [O 14 1841-N 1844]-Ja 1 1845

Portsmouth **ORACLE.** *See* Portsmouth journal of literature and politics. w,sw

PARACLETE and tickler. *See* Novator

PENNY post. *See* Evening post

Evening **POST.** d S 23 1884-91||?
1884-My? 1890 as Penny post
MWA 1884
NhHi [S 29 1887-My 29 1890]

REPUBLICAN daily news. d O 1-N 12 1892||
MWA complete
NhHi complete

REPUBLICAN union. w S 24 1846-Ja 7 1847||
Follows Portsmouth mercury. United with New Hampshire gazette to form New Hampshire gazette and republican union, later New Hampshire gazette
MWA complete
MiU-C S 24 1846
NhHi complete

ROCKINGHAM chronicle. d 1853-
MWA Ap 7 1860

ROCKINGHAM chronicle. w Ja 1 1853-S 21 1861||
1853-55? as Weekly chronicle; 1856? Chronicle and phenix; 1857-59? Rockingham weekly chronicle. Merged with New Hampshire gazette
MWA F 23,Mr 22 1856
NhHi 1853 [My-D 1856] N-D 5 1857
—d ed *See* Portsmouth daily chronicle

ROCKINGHAM messenger. w S 1847-55||
MSaE Je 8 1848
MWA [Je 9 1852-Ja 5 1853]My 17,Jl 5 1854
MiU-C [1852]
NhHi [F 11 1852-S 6 1855]

SIGNS of the times. *See* Times

STATE herald; the manufacturers' and mechanics' advocate. w Ja 6 1831-My 1833||
Ja-Mr 1831 as State herald: the factory people's advocate. Merged with Portsmouth journal of literature and politics
MBAt Ja 19 1832
MWA Mr 1831-N 1 1832
MeU O 25-N 1 1832
MnHi D 8 1831;Mr 1 1832
NcD Je 23-30,Jl 14,Ag 18-O 6 1831
NhHi [1831-32]

STATES and union. w Ja 2 1863-1919||?
MSaE Ap 30 1869
MWA Ag 21 1863;N 4 1864;Ja 27,F 10,Je 29, Ag 10-17,S 21 1865;My 1 1868
NNHi Mr 28 1873
Nh 1900-18
NhD D 23 1870;Mr 17 1871
NhHi 1863[65-66]-[68-69]Jl 16 1891-99
—d ed *See* Daily evening times

TIMES. w Jl 4 1827-N 25 1828||
1827-Ja 1 1828 as Signs of the times. United with Dover enquirer to form Times and Dover enquirer, later Dover enquirer (Dover)
DLC S 25,N 13 1827;Ja 8,22,F 12,26-Mr 4,18, Ap 1,15,29,Je 3,Jl 1,N 25 1828
MBAt 1827-N 18 1828
MWA [Jl-N 20 1827]Ja 1[8-O 7]1828
MeBa complete
MiU-C [1827-28]
NNHi complete
NhD 1827
NhHi complete

Daily evening **TIMES.** d Mr 16 1868-My 1925||
United with Portsmouth herald to form Portsmouth herald and times
DLC Jl-D 1898
MWA Mr 17 1868;O 30 1871;Jl 5 1888;D 23 1890;My 9 1891
NNHi My 1 1873
Nh F 1895;Mr 6 1898-[99]-Je 5 1925
NhD Jl 9 1889
NhHi [Mr-My 13 1868;70-N 1872;My 1879-S 1880;F 18-Ap 4 1893]
NhPo 1868-86
—w ed *See* States and union

UNITED STATES oracle. *See* Portsmouth journal of literature and politics. w,sw

Evening **VISITANT** and public advertiser. w Ja 3 1823-
MWA Ja 17,My 9 1823
NhHi Ja-Je 1823

Portsmouth **WASHINGTONIAN.** *See* Olive leaf

RIDGE

MONADNOCK breeze. *See* Jaffrey recorder and Monadnock breeze (Jaffrey)

RINDGE

Rindge evening **JOURNAL.** D 1861||?
NhHi D 1861

ROCHESTER

ANTI-MONOPOLIST. *See* Strafford county record

Rochester **COURIER.** w Ja 22 1864+
Title varies slightly
pub 1885+
MHi N 6 1868;Ag 24 1917
MWA Mr 4,Ap 1 1864;S 22 1865;O 12 1866;Ap 12 1867;Mr 27 1868
NNHi F 17,Mr 31-Ap 14,28-My 5,19,Je 2, 30,S 15,29 N 17-24 1865;Ja 31 1873
Nh 1900+
NhHi [F 17 1865-Ap 3 1868;My-D 1891]-99
NhR 1864+

Rochester **LEADER.** w 1885-1900||?
MWA Je 20 1888
NhHi 1895-Ja 1900

RECORD. *See* Strafford county record

Rochester **REVIEW** and Carroll county advertiser. w S 16 1858-Ag 30 1860||
Followed by New Hampshire review (Somersworth)
MWA Mr 22 1860
NhHi S 16 1858
NhR complete

STRAFFORD county record. w O 19 1878-D 18 1917||
1878-My 1890 as Anti-monopolist;Je 3 1890-Ag 25 1908 Record
Nh 1900-17
NhHi 1895-99
NhR complete

NEW HAMPSHIRE (*Continued*)

SALMON FALLS

INDEPENDENT. w 1894-1922||?
Also dated at South Berwick, Me.
MeSb F 26,D 29 1903;Ja 7-14,F 18-D 1904;Ja 19-My 4,18-N 9,23-D 1905-[07]-Mr 4,Je 10 1909-10;Ja 2-My 21,O 15-D 1911
Nh 1900-[22]
NhHi 1895-99
OCHi Ag 13-20 1896

SANBORNTON

DEMOCRATIC spy. *See under* Gilford

Strafford GAZETTE. w O 23 1824-26||
1823-F 12 1825 as Weekly visitor
DLC N 13 1824
NhHi Ja[F 19-O 15 1825]

Weekly VISITOR. *See* Strafford gazette

SANBORNVILLE

CARROLL county pioneer. *See* Carroll county independent and pioneer (Center Ossipee)

SANDWICH

Sandwich NEWS. w 1922?+
NhCe [Je 21 1922-25]+

Sandwich REPORTER. w N 1881+
pub 1881+
Nh Je 1898-[1920-21;23]-[28]-[32]+
NhCe [O 21 1915-18]+
NhHi Je 1883-My 1898
NhSHi Je 1885-86

SEABROOK

CHRONICLE. w -1933||
Merged with Exeter news-letter (Exeter)
Nh S 27 1929-[33]

SOMERSWORTH

To 1892 as Great Falls

CHANDELIER. d D 17 1850-
MWA D 17 1850

Somersworth FREE PRESS. w My 5 1876+
1876-F 17 1893 as Great Falls free press (F 4 1881-D 19 1884 Free press and journal)
pub 1876+
MWA D 15 1876;F 27,S 14,D 7-14,28 1880-90; Ag 1891;Jl 14 1893;N 16 1916
MiU-C [1882-86]
Nh 1900-[20]-[27]+
NhD 1894-99
NhHi 1876[77-79]-Ag 1909;32
P-M Ag 14 1885
WHi D 1 1876;S 21,O 12 1877;D 28 1880[84-85]

FREE PRESS and journal. *See* Somersworth free press

GREAT FALLS advertiser. w F 23 1856-
DLC D 5 1857;Mr 24 1860
MWA [1856-57]-[60]-Jl 20 1861
NhHi 1856-60
WHi Mr 22 1856;Je 11,Jl 23 1859;D 1 1860;Mr 16,Ap 27 1861

GREAT FALLS semi-weekly advertiser. sw My 4 1867-
MWA My-Ag 10 1867

GREAT FALLS democrat. w My 29 1852-
MWA My-Je 5,Jl 10,Ag 21 1852
WHi Je 5 1852

GREAT FALLS free press. *See* Somersworth free press

GREAT FALLS journal. 1832-36 *See* Village journal

GREAT FALLS journal. w N 11 1847-55||
1847-S 1850 as Thursday sketcher; O 1850-51 Great Falls sketcher and journal
MWA N 18,D 16 1847;Ja 13,O 26 1848-[Ja-Jl 1850]O 9-30,N 27,D 11-18 1851[Mr 1852-55]
MiU-C [1848-49]
NhHi 1847-[50-51]-55
WHi [1848-49;51-53]Ag 18,N 3 1855

GREAT FALLS journal. w Ja 5 1867-Ja 28 1881||
United with Great Falls free press to form Free press and journal, later Somersworth free press
MWA Ja 11 1868;Mr 18 1871;N 29 1873;D 15 1876;Ap 13 1877;Ap 12 1878;N 19 1880-81
NhD 1867-D 23 1871
NhHi complete
NhSF 1867-69;71-81

GREAT FALLS weekly news. w Ap 7 1866-
MWA Ap 21,My 19 1866
NhHi Ap 21,My 19 1866

GREAT FALLS reporter and Somersworth and Berwick register. w F 27 1831-
NhHi Mr 5 1831

GREAT FALLS sketcher and journal. *See* Great Falls journal

GREAT FALLS transcript. w 1845-
1854-47 as Strafford transcript and Great Falls advertiser; 1848-49 Great Falls transcript and Strafford and York advertiser
MWA Ap 18,My 16 1846;Ja 23,S 4,N 6 1847[Je-Ag 12 1848;Mr 10-O 20 1849;50]F 1 1851
WHi N 6 1847[O 26 1848-My]Je 22 1850

NEW HAMPSHIRE review. w S 1860-
Follows Rochester review and Carroll county advertiser (Rochester)
MWA S 21,N 2 1860

NORTHERN light. w N 14 1840-
MWA O 9,D 11 1841;Mr 11,Ap 29,Ag 5,O 21 1843
NhD N 7 1840;Ja 23 1841
NhHi Jl 10 1841-Jl 1842
VtU 1842-44

STRAFFORD transcript and Great Falls advertiser. *See* Great Falls transcript

THURSDAY sketcher. *See* Great Falls journal 1847-55

VILLAGE journal. w 1832-36||?
1832-Ap 30 1836 as Great Falls journal
DLC F 23 1833-D 5 1835
MWA Je 1 1833[Ja 11-Ap 12]N 15,D 6 1834; Ja 9-Ap,My 14-Jl 1836
MeU Ap 25,My 12,Je 16-23,S 15-22,D 1 1832; Mr 2,16,My 11,Je 22 1833;N 29-D 6 1834
NhHi N 3 1832;S 6 1834
WHi F 1-8 1834;N 27,D 11-18 1851[Ap 22 1852-N 3 1855]

SOUTH WOLFBOROUGH

CARROLL county republican. w Mr 3 1841-
MWA Jl 7 1841
MnHi Mr 31 1841

SUNAPEE

LAKE SUNAPEE echo. w 1890-96||?
NhHi [Je-D 1891]-96

SUNCOOK

Suncook weekly JOURNAL. w 1874-1900||?
1874-D 17 1898? as Suncook journal
MWA Ja 7 1882
NhHi O 28 1876-My 18 1878[79]-[82]-[91]-[94]-[99-1900]

Suncook PRESS. w 1894-1931||?
Nh D 14 1895-Ap 1931

THE WEIRS

CALVERT'S Weirs times and tourists' gazette. w,sw Je 29 1883-98||
1883-90? as The Weirs times and tourists' gazette
pub only during summer season
sw 1883-87?
MWA Ag 15 1883;Jl 4 1885;Je 26-S 4 1886;Jl 16-S 21 1887;Jl-Ag 1888;Jl 17-S 7 1889;Ag 13-S 17 1890;Ag 17 1895;Jl-S 12 1896;Je 26-S 11 1897;Jl 23-S 3 1898
MiU-C [1896-97]
NhHi 1883-98
NhM Je 26 1886-[91]-93

LAKESIDE daily news. d Jl 22 1880-
pub only during summer season
NhHi Jl-Ag 19 1880

The Weirs TIMES and tourists' gazette. *See* Calvert's Weirs times and tourists' gazette

TILTON

Tilton ADVOCATE. w 1889-90||?
NhHi Ja 2-9 1889

TROY

HOME companion. m
NhHi 1897-My 1901

WALPOLE

CHESHIRE gazette. w
MSaE Ja 13 1826

CHESHIRE gazette. w Ap 8 1825-Je 2 1826||
MWA Ap 8 1825
NhHi Ap 8 1825;F 10 1826
NhW complete

FARMER'S museum. *See* Cheshire republican (Keene)

Walpole GAZETTE. w 1891?-98||?
NhHi Ap 30 1891-Ap 21 1897

WARNER

INDEPENDENT and times. *See* Kearsarge independent

KEARSARGE independent. w Ap 4 1884+
1885-Je 3 1887 Independent and times; Je 10 1887-1926 Kearsarge independent and times
Nh 1903-[20-21]+
NhHi 1885-90;Mr 27 1891-99

WARREN

Warren NEWS. w 1883+
Title varies: Warren weekly news
Nh 1900-[20]-[22]
NhHi [1895]-99

WARREN SUMMIT

NORTH country times. w
NhHi Ja-Jl 1895

WASHINGTON

Washington and Marlow TIMES. w Ap 25 1901-17||?
NhHi [1901]-My 21 1903;04-11

WEARE

Weare SENTINEL. w 1868+
NhHi Ag 14 1902-10

WELLS RIVER

JOURNAL.
Also dated in Woodsville
NhD Je 29 1885

WEST STEWARTSTOWN

ENTERPRISE. w F 20 1907-09||?
1907-Ap 15 1908 as New enterprise
NhHi 1907-Mr 10 1909

FRONTIER gazette. w My 28 1892-1917||?
NhHi 1892-[1903]

NEW enterprise. *See* Enterprise

WHITEFIELD

Whitefield TIMES. w Ja 1 1897+
1897-Ja 1904 as White Mountain times
Nh 1900-16
NhD 1897-99
NhHi 1897-99;1901-03
NhWh 1898-1903

WHITE MOUNTAIN news. w 1890-99||?
NhHi F 25 1891-99

WHITE MOUNTAIN times. *See* Whitefield times

WILTON

Wilton JOURNAL. w 1873?+
NhHi N 12 1891

WINCHESTER

NORTHERN advocate. *See* Claremont advocate (Claremont)

Winchester STAR. w O 18 1895-1918||?
MWA Jl 31-Ag 7 1900
Nh 1900-18
NhHi 1895-99

WINNIPESAUKEE

Winnipesaukee TIMES. w Je 7 1924-
pub only during summer
NhHi [1924;My 30 1925-Ag 1926]

WOLFEBORO

CARROLL county democrat. w Ap 23 1868-71||?
NhHi Je 25 1868

CARROLL county pioneer. w Ja 24 1856-
NhHi [F 28 1856-Jl 1858]

CARROLL county pioneer (1881-1924) *See* Carroll county independent and pioneer (Center Ossipee)

GRANITE state news. w N 1 1860+
pub 1891-93;99
MBAt S 13 1869
MSaE O 11 1869
MWA Ag 20 1862;Mr 11 1863;Ja 31 1866;Jl 15 1868;Ap 10 1931
Nh 1904-[19-21]22;25+
NhHi N 28-D 12 1866[Ap 28 1873-Ja 5 1880; 91]-[99]1901-03
NhWo 1903+

WOODSVILLE

Woodsville ENTERPRISE. w 1883-89||?
NhHi My 30-Je 13 1884

JOURNAL. *See under* Wells River

Woodsville NEWS. w 1883+
MWA Je 2 1893
Nh 1901-[20-21]+
NhD Ag 29 1902[03]04
NhHi 1891-1900;32

Woodsville TIMES. w Ag 12 1921+
pub 1921+

NEW JERSEY

ABSECON

ATLANTIC democrat and Cape May county register. w
MWA Jl 11 1863

ALLENDALE

Allendale ARGUS. w 1924+
pub 1924+

ALLENTOWN

Allentown INDUSTRY. w 1880-
NjHi Ag 19-S 16 1880

Allentown MESSENGER. w O 22 1903+
pub 1903+
NjFHi O 22 1903;Ja 24 1935+

Allentown TRANSCRIPT. w Mr 26 1875-
NjR Jl 16 1875;Ja 28 1876

Allentown TIMES. w My 5 1881-
NjFHi My 5 1881

ARLINGTON

OBSERVER. w 1889+
NjHi [1917-19]

ASBURY PARK

ARTESIAN. w,ir 1884-87||
NjFHi D 8 1886;Ja 21 1887

Asbury Park JOURNAL. w Ja 8 1876-1911||
MWA F 25 1876
NIC N 15 1901-Je 19 1908
NjAs 1876-Jl 1881;82-Je,O 1897-1905
NjFHi [1877-82] 1901-02[11]
NjR 1910[11]

Asbury Park daily JOURNAL. d Je 4 1883-1911||
Title varies slightly. Usually issued Je-Ag only
NjAs Je-Ag 1884;Je 15-Ag 1885;86-93;Jl-Ag 1894;95;Je-Ag 1896;Je-S 1897;O 1899-My,O-D 1900;06-11
NjFHi Je 4 1883[Mr-S 1911]
NjR 1908;10[11]

MONMOUTH republican. w Je 9 1883-O 1884||
Merged with Asbury Park journal
NjFHi Je 9 1883;Mr 15 1884

PEOPLE'S advocate. w 1912-13||
NjFHi [1912-13]

Asbury Park evening PRESS. d 1879+
Title varies
IaHi 1906
NjAs 1887-88;Je-Ag 1889;Je-Ag 1890;Je-Ag 1891;F-Ag 1895;Ap 1896-Ag,O 1897-Je,O 1898-Ag,O 1899-Ap,Je-S 1901;Ja-Mr,Jl 1902-My,Jl 1903-My,Jl-Ag,O,D, 1906-Mr,My-Ag 1907;Ja-Ap,S-D 1908;Jl 11-N 1909;10+
NjHi N 23 1911;17+
NjR [1935+]

Asbury Park morning PRESS. d 1886-1918||?
Usually issued Je-Ag only
NjAs [1904-05;08-14]

Asbury Park Sunday PRESS. Shore press. w Jl 10 1879+
1879-1920? as Shore press
Jl 7 1929 is 50th anniversary ed
IaHi 1906
NjAs 1888-91;Ja-Ap,Je-D 1896;98-My,O 1899-Je 1900;Ja-My 1901;03
NjFHi [1879;81-84;1904-05;29;32-F 1934]+
NjR Jl 7 1929

PROGRESSIVE citizen. w Mr 30 1929+
NjFHi Mr 15 1935+

SHORE press. *See* Asbury Park Sunday press

Asbury Park TIMES. d 1912-14||
NjFHi My 14 1914

ATLANTIC CITY

ATLANTIC county review. *See* Atlantic City gazette-review

ATLANTIC review. *See* Atlantic City gazette-review

Atlantic City Sunday GAZETTE. w 1879-My 16 1925||
Merged with Atlantic City press

Atlantic City GAZETTE-REVIEW. w 1872-My 1925||
1872-81 as Atlantic county review; 1882?-1914 Atlantic review. Merged with Atlantic City press
ICHi Jl 3,S-O 9,23-N 13,27-D 4,18 1875;Ja-Ap 1,15-My 13,27-Je,S 9-16,O-N,D 9 1876;77
MWA Ja 1,15-F 5,19,Mr-My 13 1876;Ap 7 1888
NNHi [Ja-Je]S 9 1876;Ja 27-F 17,Mr 3 1877
NjHi 1915-18
RP O 4 1913

NEWS. w 1920+
PP [1935]+

Atlantic City PRESS. d Mr 4 1895+
Mr 3 1929 is 75th anniversary number
NjR Mr 3 1929
PP 1928+

Atlantic City evening UNION. d S 3 1888+

ATLANTIC HIGHLANDS

Atlantic HIGHLANDER. *See* Atlantic Highlands journal

INDEPENDENT. *See* Atlantic Highlands journal

Atlantic Highlands JOURNAL. w 1885+
1885-94 as Independent; 1895-1914 Monmouth press; 1915-18 Atlantic highlander
pub 1923+
NjAt Ap 24 1930+
NjFHi [1895;1911-16]-S 1920;Mr 1935+

JOURNAL. w 1892-Ja 3 1919||
United with Atlantic highlander to form Atlantic Highlands journal
NjFHi [1894-95;1911-15;18-19]

MONMOUTH press. *See* Atlantic Highlands journal

AUDUBON

CITIZEN and Oaklyn record. w 1923+
pub Ja 15 1924+

BALLENTINE

YOUNG Hickory. (A Jersey flag staff) w
DLC Ag 21,N 27 1844

BAYONNE

Bayonne HERALD. w 1869-1923||?
1902?-20? as Bayonne herald and Greenville register
NjBa 1904-06;09-11;13-15
NjHi D 14,28 1901;Ja 18,25 1902

Bayonne evening NEWS. d 1911-30||
NjBa 1923-S 6 1930

PUBLIC opinion. d 1922-30||
NjBa 1922-27

Bayonne TIMES. d 1870+
NjBa D 1914+

BELLEVILLE

Belleville NEWS. w 1915+
pub 1925+

Belleville PRESS. w 1889-98||?
1889-90? as Belleville sun
NjHi 1890-94

Belleville SUN. *See* Belleville press

Belleville TIMES. w 1909-O 11 1935||
Merged with Belleville news
NjBeN complete

BELMAR

Early years as Ocean Beach

BEACH patrol. w Ja 15 1887-88||?
NjFHi [1887-S 1888]

COAST advertiser. w 1892+
NjFHi Mr 8 1935+

CRAB. w Jl 23 1881-84||?
NjFHi Jl 23,N 5 1881

BELVIDERE

APOLLO. w Ja 11 1825+
1825-30 as Belvidere Apollo (S? 1829-F? 1830 Belvidere Apollo and Warren patriot) 1849-69 Belvidere intelligencer
Ct Ja 8 1828
IU My 17 1831
MWA Mr 1 1825;D 11 1827;Jl 28 1829
N O 8 1833
NjHi Ag 1 1826;F 26,O 21 1828;My 26,Ap 28,N 3 1829;Ja 12,F 9,Je 22,Jl 12,27 1830[59-67]
NjR Je 13 1843;D 15 1846;N 7 1848;Je 29 1860;O 31,N 28 1862;Mr 6 1863
OClWHi Ag 10 1866
PEL [S 1848-F 1849]

Belvidere INTELLIGENCER. *See* Apollo

WARREN journal. w 1832+
pub 1926+
NNHi My 9 1873
NjHi N 1848-50[67]
NjR N 30 1841;S 13 1842

BERGENFIELD

INTERBORO review. w 1911+
1911-21 as Saturday review
NNHi Mr 15 1919
NjR Ap 22 1927

Saturday REVIEW. *See* Interboro review

BERLIN

ATCO breeze. *See* Breeze and Saturday evening news

BREEZE and Saturday evening news. w S 30 1921+
1921-Jl 7 1922 as Atco breeze; Jl 14 1922-Ag 17 1923 Breeze
pub 1921+

BERNARDSVILLE

Bernardsville NEWS. w 1892+
Some years as Bernardsville news-recorder
pub 1916-[20]+
NjR [1907-08]

BEVERLY

Beverly BANNER. w 1877+
NjR O 16 1880
PP O 12 1928+

Beverly LEADER. w 1926+
PP [1930]+

Beverly NEWS. w Ja 1 1849-
NjR Ja 1 1849

BLACKWOOD

Blackwood OBSERVER. w 1927+
pub My 1934+
NjBerB My 1934+

BLAIRSTOWN

Blairstown PRESS. w 1877+
pub 1877+
NjHi Ag 14 1878
NjR Ag 8 1883

BLOOMFIELD

Bloomfield CITIZEN. *See* Bloomfield-Glen Ridge independent press

Saturday GAZETTE of Bloomfield. w S 7 1872-N 15 1875||
1872-Ja 26 1873 as Bloomfield gazette. Merged with Arlington journal (Arlington)
Suspended from Ja 26-F 22 1873
NjBl 1872-Ja 1873;74-75
NjBlI complete
NjHi complete

Bloomfield INDEPENDENT. w F 7-D 26 1891||
NjBlI Ap 11-Ag 22 1891
NjHi complete

Bloomfield-Glen Ridge INDEPENDENT-PRESS. w My 6 1882+
1882-1915 as Bloomfield citizen; 1916-Independent press and Bloomfield citizen
My 6 1932 is 50th anniversary number
pub Ap 28 1883-[N 1890-1915]+
MWa Ja 20 1928
NjBl [1884-87;89-93]1916+
NjFHi My 6 1932
NjHi 1883-88;91-1906;10+
NjR My 6 1932

INDEPENDENT PRESS. w My 9 1913-15||
United with Bloomfield citizen to form Independent press and Bloomfield citizen, later Bloomfield-Glen Ridge independent press
NjBl complete
NjHi complete

Bloomfield MAIL. w Jl 1933-N 1934||
NjBlI [1933-34]

Bloomfield RECORD. w 1873-99||?
NjBl Ja 23 1873;Je 11 1875 Jl 2,16,Ag 12-S 2,N 4 1892;Ja 27,F 10,Mr 24,Ap 14,D 29 1893;Mr 30,My 11-25,Je 15 1894;S 11 1896
NjHi 1873-82;93;95-97

Weekly REPUBLICAN. w S 16 1880-
NjHi S 16,D 16,30 1880

BOONTON

LITTLE paper called Boonton. 1894-97||?
NIC [1894-97]

NEW JERSEY freeman. w 1844-
MWA S 4 1847
NjHi Je 1844-Mr 1850
PP O 8 1846

Boonton TIMES. w 1896-1927||?
United with Boonton bulletin to form Boonton times-bulletin

Boonton TIMES-BULLETIN. w,sw 1870+
1870-1927? as Boonton bulletin (title varies)
w 1870-
NjHi F 10 1871;Ja 15 1874;Je 30 1881;Ja 17 1884

BORDENTOWN

PALLADIUM. *See* Bordentown register

Bordentown REGISTER. w 1845+
1845-50 as Palladium
MWA Ag 31 1866
NjCHi [O 1876-77]
NjHi [1867]77-1919
PHi O 27 1876-My 23 1879

BOUND BROOK

CHRONICLE. w Ag 8 1868+
1868-77? as Family casket
1868-Ja 23 1878 pub in White House Station
pub 1894+
NjBb 1892+
NjR My 10 1884[1904-07]

NEW JERSEY (*Continued*)

BOUND BROOK—*Continued*

Bound Brook DEMOCRAT. *See* State centre-record

SOMERSET argus. w 1869-70||
NjHi N 1869-Ap 1870

STATE centre-record. w 1890+
1890-97 as Bound Brook democrat; 1897-1902? State centre
pub Mr 9 1899+

UNION. w Jl 30 1856-
NjR Ag 13 1856

BRANCHVILLE

SUSSEX record. w
NjHi [1867]

BRICKSBURG

Bricksburg INTELLIGENCER. w O 4 1866-
MBAt N 1 1866

BRIDGETON

Bridgeton AURORA. w Ap? 1862-
NjWdHi F 11 1863

Bridgeton CHRONICLE. w D 23 1837-1906||?
Follows West Jersey observer
DLC [1839]Ja 6 1849
NjBrC N 13 1852-88
NjBrHi 1837-65;77-78
NjHi [1862-67]
RW Ap 11 1868
WHi 1837-50

CUMBERLAND county patriot. *See* New Jersey patriot

Bridgeton DAILY. d 1874-
NjWdHi F 23 1875

DOLLAR news. w 1876+
NjBrC 1915-31
NjVi [1881-83]
—d ed *See* Bridgeton evening news

NEW JERSEY patriot. w S 30 1865-D 25 1914||
1865-Mr 1868 as Cumberland county patriot
NjBrC Je 1871-N 1872;89-1914
NjHi Jl 8 1869

Bridgeton evening NEWS. d F 1 1879+
NjHi Ag 24 1889;Ag 16 1919
NjWdHi Ja 8 1904
PP [1928]+
—w ed *See* Dollar weekly news

Bridgeton OBSERVER and Cumberland, Cape May and Salem advertiser. w O 5 1822-Je 17 1826||
United with Washington whig to form Washington whig and Bridgeton observer and Cumberland, Cape May and Salem advertiser, later West Jersey observer
DLC Je 14,28,Jl 12,Ag 2,10,23-S 20,O 4,25-N 9 1923;Je 12,26,Jl 17,31-Ag 7 1824;Ja 1 1825
NjBrHi O 19 1822-D 18 1824;Ja-F 18 1826;O 16 1830
NjHi Jl 31 1824;N 19-26 1825;26
WHi O 1823-26

Bridgeton PIONEER. w 1847-
1847-Ja 3 1884 as West Jersey pioneer
NjBrC N 20 1852-O 11 1917
NjHi Ap 6 1863;Ap 18 1873;Ja 8-22 1885
WHi Ja 8,O 22 1851-53

Daily PIONEER. d 1886-1930||?
NjHi Jl 26 1892;O 13 1908
NjR Jl 26 1892

Bridgeton VIDETTE. m,w Ap 1872-
m Ap-S 1872
MWA S,O 5 1872

WASHINGTON whig. w Jl 24 1815-Je 13 1826||
United with Bridgeton observer. . . to form Washington whig and Bridgeton observer, later West Jersey observer
DLC 1821-26
MWA My 1-8,Jl 24-31 1824;Mr 29 1828
NjBrHi 1821-26
NjR D 20 1823
PWcHi Mr 3 1823

WASHINGTON whig. w Jl 15 1826-D 1837||
Publisher claims that this is the original Washington whig, established 1815. Merged with West Jersey observer
CSmH Ag 28 1830
DLC 1826;S 1 1827;28-29
NjBrHi 1826;Ag 25 1827-37
NjHi Mr 22 1828;Mr 28,My 2-23,O 10 1829; Mr 20,Ag 14,O 30 1830;Ap 7,My 19,Je 1 1832

WASHINGTON whig and Bridgeton observer. *See* West Jersey observer

WEST Jersey observer. w Je 24 1826-D 16? 1837||
1826-D 1 1827 as Washington whig and Bridgeton observer. . . Followed by Bridgeton chronicle
CSmH Je 19 1830
DLC 1826-27;F 2,Ap 5 1828;Mr 14 1829-30;32-33;36
MWA Jl 11,O 3,31,N 14-21 1829;Ja 9,D 4,25 1830
NjBrHi 1826-O 16 1830;32-O 21 1837
NjHi 1826-F 2,My 31,N 29 1828;Mr 7,21-Ap 4,S 12-19 1829;Ja 2 1830

WEST Jersey pioneer. *See* Bridgeton pioneer

BURLINGTON

Burlington semi-weekly ADVERTISER. sw 1876-
MWA Mr 7 1877

Daily ENTERPRISE. d 1884+
NjR [1902-03]
—w ed. *See* New Jersey enterprise

Burlington FREE press. w
NjR Ag 27 1847

Burlington GAZETTE. w D 16 1835-73||?
Title varies slightly
Ct [1836]
DLC S 10 1841
NjHi S 1852-Jl 1855

NEW JERSEY enterprise. w 1868-1931||?
MWA [Je 25 1869-Ag 12 1870]
—d ed. *See* Daily enterprise

Burlington PRESS. w O 1928+
pub 1928+

Saturday evening VISITOR. w Ja 1-D 1825||
NjR complete
WHi complete

CALDWELL

Caldwell NEWS. w 1891-96||?
NjHi 1893-96

Caldwell PROGRESS-Verona news. w Ja 6 1911+
1911-34 as Caldwell progress
pub 1911+
NN Mr 24 1923
NjR S 1923+
NjVe 1930+

CAMDEN

AMERICAN banner. *See under* Philadelphia, Pa

AMERICAN eagle. *See* Camden semi-weekly phoenix. . .

AMERICAN star. *See* West Jersey press

Camden ARGUS. m,w O 1896+
1896- 1901 as New Jersey sand burr; 1902-O 26 1907 East Side press; N 2 1907-Camden argus and East Side press
m O- 1906
pub 1926+
NjCHi N 26 1931

ATLANTIC Coast guide. w D 1887-1903||
1887-Ja 1888 as Atlantic Coast pilot
NjFHi My 21 1896

ATLANTIC Coast pilot. *See* Atlantic Coast guide

CAMDEN county courier. w My 1878-1906||?
1878-O? 1879 as Haddonfield courier (Haddonfield)
NjCHi F 1883-N 21 1885;87-89
—d ed *See* Camden evening courier

CAMDEN county journal. w Mr 3 1883-1918||?
In German
NN 1883-Ja 19 1889

Camden CITIZEN. *See* Camden independent

Camden evening COURIER. d Je 2 1882+
Title varies slightly
special ed 1909 "Greater Camden"
special ed Je 1917 "Story of Camden"
Nj 1930+
NjCHi [Ap-D 1883]Ag 3 1885;F 13 1928
NjHi Jl 21 1887;O 2 1890[S-O 1907]
NjWdHi S 22 1885;My 8 1887;F 13 1928;S 19(supp)1930
PP N 26 1927+
PPR O 1927;F 1928-31
—w ed *See* Camden county courier

Sunday COURIER-POST. w 1929-30||
PPR Mr 24 1929-Ag 17 1930

Camden evening DAILY. d Ja 4-Mr 6 1858||
Ja 4-5 as Camden daily
NjCHi complete
NjWdHi [1858]

Camden DEMOCRAT. w 1832-Je 6 1908||
1832-N 1846 as Franklin advertiser. Merged with Spirit of '76
DLC Ja 23 1847
NNHi Ap 22 1855;Mr 15 1873
Nj Je 1860-My 1865
NjCHi Ag 27 1859-60;N 23 1861-F 8 1862;63-99;1901-S 6 1902;03-08
NjHi [1865]
NjR S 19 1844;D 20 1862
NjWdHi D 22 1855
OClWHi S 6 1862

DEMOCRAT. w Ap 15 1840-Je? 1841||
Follows Village herald and Gloucester advertiser (Woodbury) Ap 15-Ag 1840 as West Jersey democrat

EAST Side press. *See* Camden argus

FRANKLIN advertiser. *See* Camden democrat

GAZETA niedzielna przyjaciel ludu. *See* Nowiny

GLOUCESTER farmer. *See* Village herald and Gloucester advertiser (Woodbury)

HICKORY club. w
DLC My 17 1844(extra)

Camden INDEPENDENT. w 1893-99||
1893-F 1 1896 as Camden citizen

Camden daily JOURNAL. w,d Ap 1857-Ap 1865||
1857-64? as Camden weekly journal. Merged with West Jersey press Ap-S 1857 printed in Philadelphia
w 1857-64
FGS Ag 22 1864
NjCHi Je 25 1864
NjHi [1862]O 3 1863
WHi F 1860-Mr 22 1862;O 10-17 1863

Camden MAIL. . . *See* West Jersey press

NEW JERSEY coast pilot. w Mr 4 1882-88||
Followed by Atlantic coast pilot, later Atlantic Coast guide
NjHi Mr 4,18,Ap 8-15 1882;Ja 13-20,F 10,Mr 10,Je 23 1888
PP Mr 10 1883

NEW JERSEY sand-burr. *See* Camden argus

NEW JERSEY statesman. w -N 1 1828||
DLC My 31,Je 7,21,1828
NjR My 31 1828

NEW republic. w N 30 1867-78||
DLC Mr 11 1876
NjCHi D 14 1867-[69]-Ap 13 1878
WHi F 15 1873

NOWINY. (News) w 1885+
1895-O 1934 as Gazeta niedzielna przyjaciel ludu (People's friend)
In Polish
pub 1885+

Camden semi-weekly PHOENIX and West Jersey democratic journal. w,sw S 29 1842-1860?||
S 29-D 24 1842 as American eagle; D 31 1842-N 16 1844 American eagle and West Jersey advertiser; N 23 1844-Ja? 1850 Camden phoenix and farmers' and mechanics' advertiser
w 1842-Ja? 1850
DLC F 12,22 1850
NjHi N 13 1847
PHi S 29 1842-Ja 11 1845

Morning POST. d O 2 1875+
1875-Je 10 1899 as Camden daily post; Je 12 1899-D 31 1925 Camden post-telegram
Nj Je 12 1899+
NjCHi Ja 14 1876[O-D 9 1876]-Mr 1877;78-87; 90-97;Je 12 1899-1922;Ap-D 1923
NjWdHi Mr 1,3,Ap 2 1934
PHi 1879-81;83
PP N 28 1927+

Camden POST-TELEGRAM. *See* Morning post

Camden Sunday REVIEW. w Ap 15 1889-Ag 1892||
Followed by Daily review
NjHi My 17-24 1891

Daily REVIEW. d S 6 1892-D 31 1902||?
Follows Camden Sunday review
NjCHi 1894-1902

Camden SPY. m Ja 1872-
NjCHi Ja-D 1872

Camden daily TELEGRAM. d F 24 1886-Je 10 1899||
F-S 1886 as Camden evening telegram. United with Camden daily post to form Camden post-telegram, later Morning post
Nj F 27-Je 10 1899
NjCHi 1887-Ag 1890;92-99

Camden TIMES. w F 17 1894+
1894-1908? as Stockton times
1894-99? pub in Stockton

Camden TRIBUNE. m 1871?-
NjCHi Ja-D 1874

Evening VISITOR. w Ja 1 1874-N 1876||
PHi Jl 2-N 16 1874;Ja-Je 1875

WEST Jersey bugle. *See* West Jersey press

WEST Jersey democrat. *See* Democrat

WEST Jersey mail. *See* West Jersey press

WEST Jersey press. w Ap 17 1821+
1821-D 22 1824 as American star; D 29 1824-Ja 5 1831 American star and rural record; Ja 12 1831-32 American star and New Jersey advertiser; 1832-35 Camden mail and New Jersey advertiser; 1836-Ag 27 1845 Camden mail and general advertiser; S 3 1845-F 24 1847 West Jersey mail; Mr 3 1847-59 West Jerseyman; Ja 4-Ap 18 1860 West Jersey bugle
DLC D 1 1824;M 15 1826;Ag 12,N 18 1829;Ja 5 1831;Ja 30 1833
MWA Ag 14 1821;Ap 16 1834
N N 8 1854
NjCHi O 31 1827;O 8 1828;Ap 1834-Ja 4 1860;61-89;92-1913
NjHi Je 19,N 21,D 25 1821;Jl 23 1822;Mr 23, My 4,Ag 10,1825;Ja 7,Jl 16,S 10,O 15,29 1828;S 16 1829;Jl 1830;Ap 18 1832;My 1915-20;22+
NjWdHi Ap 1834-Ap 8 1840;Ja 29 1868
NjWdN Jl 29 1863
OHi Mr 8 1865
PHi O 26 1842-N 1844

WEST Jerseyman. *See* West Jersey press

CAPE MAY

OCEAN wave. *See* Star and wave

STAR and wave. w 1854+
1854-75? as Ocean wave; 1876?-1907 Cape May wave
pub 1854+
MWA Ap 9 1863
NjHi [1865-67]
NjR S 7 1889
PHi Je 5 1856-My 28 1863

STAR of the cape. w 1868-1907||
United with Cape May wave to form Star and wave
NNHi Ja 22 1892

Cape May WAVE. *See* Star and wave

CARTERET

Carteret NEWS. w Je 17 1908+
1908-N 10 1922 as Roosevelt news
pub 1908+

ROOSEVELT news. *See* Carteret news

NEW JERSEY (*Continued*)

CHANCEVILLE. *See* NEW MONMOUTH

CLAYTON

PRESS. w Ag 1925+
pub 1925+

CLEMENTON

Clementon NEWS. w
PP D 11 1930-N 21 1931

CLIFFSIDE PARK

PALISADIAN. w 1906+
pub S 1906–

CLIFTON

Clifton LEADER. w O 14 1926+
pub 1926+

NEW American. Italian-American weekly. w S 1933+
NjClL 1933+

Clifton TIMES. w 1901+
pub Mr 23 1933+

CLINTON

CONSTITUTIONAL democrat. *See* Clinton democrat

Clinton DEMOCRAT. w Ap 11 1868+
Ap 11-D 8 1868 as Constitutional democrat
pub 1868+
NjHi Jl 29 1870;Ap 28 1887;Jl 4 1901
NjR Ja 21 1932+

NEW JERSEY leader. w 1859-F 1865||
1859-61 as Clinton times
MWA My 23 1863
NjR Je 3 1865

Clinton TIMES. *See* New Jersey leader

CLOSTER

BERGEN review. w Ag 16 1922+
pub 1922+

COLLINGSWOOD

Weekly RETROSPECT. w 1902+
pub 1906+

CRANBURY

Cranbury PRESS. w Jl 17 1885+
pub 1885+

CRANFORD

Cranford CHRONICLE. w 1893-1921||
United with Cranford citizen to form Cranford citizen and chronicle
NjCrC complete

Cranford CITIZEN and chronicle. w 1898+
1898-1921 as Cranford citizen
pub 1898+
NjR [1917-20]

DECKERTOWN

SUSSEX county home journal. w My 19 1867-
NjHi My 19 1867

WANTAGE recorder. w 1894-1900||?
NjHi Je 26-Jl,Ag 14 1896

DOVER

Dover ADVANCE. sw Ap 11 1903+
1904?-26? as Dover advance and iron era
pub 1903+
NjD 1903-06
NjHi 1907

Dover DAILY. d My 9-D 3 1904||
NjD My 9-Ag 14,31-D 3 1904
NjHi complete

Dover INDEX. w 1875-1933||
Merged with Dover advance
NjD Je 1897-98;Jl 1899-Ja 1907
NjDA complete
NjHi [1881-83;87-88]O 17 1890;92-[1908]Mr 3-10,Je 2,30 1921
NjR [1885]-1933

IRON era. w 1870-My 11 1914||
United with Dover advance to form Dover advance and iron era, later Dover advance
NjD D 30 1871-F,O-D 1883;95-Ja 1907
NjHi [1870-71;80]D 1881-[1906]07
NjR S 27 1879

Dover daily JOURNAL. d 1895-96||
NjHi Ag 1895-My 1896

Dover evening MAIL. w 1924-
NjHi Je 9-Ag 11 1924

MORRIS county journal. w O 17 1890-1900||
NjD Je 1897-Ja 1900
NjHi 1890-F 1900
PPCHi [1891-92;94-95]

EAST ORANGE

East Orange CITIZEN. w 1921+
Title varies slightly
Nj S 1925+
NjEo Ag 28 1925-F 18 1932

East Orange COURIER. w
NjEo S 26-O 17,D 5,19 1896

East Orange GAZETTE. w O 1873-Je 1908||
Nj 1873-Ap 1897;My 1898-1908
NjEo complete
NjHi O 1 1881;S 19 1901

MORRIS and Essex record. w 1886-N 7 1889||
1886-My 2 1889 as Record; My 9-Je 27 1889 Morris and Essex news and the Record
Nj [1889]
NjEo 1889
NjO complete

RECORD. 1886-My 2 1889 *See* Morris and Essex record

East Orange RECORD. w 1899+
pub 1899+
Nj 1912+
NjEo 1912+

East Orange TIMES. w F 3 1922-Ja 30 1925||
Merged with East Orange courier
Nj complete
NjEo complete

EATONTOWN

Eatontown ADVERTISER. w 1877-1925||?
1878-79 as Monmouth county Jerseyman
NjFHi Ja-F 1877;O 10-17,31-N 7 1878;F 20,Mr 27-Ap 17,My 22 1879;Mr 9 1882
NjHi 1883-84

MONMOUTH county Jerseyman. *See* Eatontown advertiser

EDGEWATER

BERGEN citizen. w Ja 1925+
pub 1925+

EGG HARBOR CITY

ATLANTIC democrat. w 1863-89||?
NjHi Je 1 1867

NEWS. w Mr 7 1907+
pub 1907+

ELIZABETH

Evening BULLETIN. d
NjNb [1867]

CENTRAL New Jersey herald. w 1861-94||?
1861-70? as Union county herald; 1871-72? Elizabeth herald
KHi Mr 12-14 1892
MWA O 15 1864
NjHi 1867
NjR D 24 1864

CONSTITUTIONALIST. w Mr 9 1864-
MWA Jl 16 1864

ESSEX standard. w
NjHi F 26 1846(extra)
WHi Mr 2 1847

FREIE presse. sw,w 1871-1905||?
sw 1871-84?
In German
MWA Ag 26 1876

***Elizabeth-town GAZETTE.** w S 8 1818-21||
United with New Jersey journal to form New Jersey journal and Elizabeth-town gazette, later New Jersey journal
NjR [1821]

HERALD. w Mr? 1864-
NjR D 24 1864

Elizabeth HERALD. 1871-72. *See* Central New Jersey herald

ISSUE. w 1911-19||?
WHi F 23 1915

Elizabeth daily JOURNAL. d Jl 20 1871+
F 16 1929 is Sesqui-centennial ed
InU F 16 1929
MWA F 16 1929
MnU F 16 1929
NNHi My 1 1873;F 16 1929
NjE 1910+
NjHi 1913-My 1918;31
NjN F 16 1929
NjR F 16 1929
OClWHi F 16 1929
TxGR F 16 1929
—w ed *See* New Jersey journal

Sunday LEADER. w 1883-90||
NjHi [1886-88]

Elizabeth daily MONITOR. d 1868-80||?
NjHi Ag 1868-O 1869;Jl-D 1873

***NEW JERSEY journal.** w O 14 1783-Ap 1900||
1783-My 3 1786 as Political intelligencer and New Jersey advertiser; My 10 1786-Je 6 1792 New Jersey journal and political intelligencer; Je 13 1792-1820 New Jersey journal; 1821-25 New Jersey journal and Elizabeth-town gazette
1783-Ap 5 1785 pub in New Brunswick
CSmH S 7 1830
CtY O 22 1822
DLC O 30 1832;Ap 9 1833
MWA My 1,Jl 17 1821;O 18 1825;Jl 19 1864; Mr 2 1869;Ag 12 1879
NN Jl 2,16-Ag 6 1822;Ja 7,21,F 11-Mr 4,S 23,O 7-14 1823;25
NNHi N 21 1826
NjFHi Jl 12 1836
NjHi 1821-28;35-37;43-53;55-57[65-67]
NjR [1821]-[23]32-[35;46;49]
PDoHi Ap 26 1825;Je 12 1827
WHi Ap 10-17,O 2 1821;Ap 1 1823;F 17,My 25, Je 22,S 28 1824;Je 28,N 29 1825;F 14,Jl 18,Ag 22 1826;Ja 9,Ap 10 1827;Ap 10 1828;O 27 1829 Ap 27 1830
—d ed *See* Elizabeth daily journal

POLITICAL intelligencer. *See* New Jersey journal

Elizabeth evening TIMES. d
NjHi O 26-29 1914

TRUE Jersey blue. sw 1865||
Campaign publication for Marcus Ward for governor
NjHi O 21,N 4,10 1865

UNION county herald. *See* Central New Jersey herald

Elizabeth UNIONIST. w
NjHi [1862]

ELMER

Elmer GAZETTE. *See* Elmer times

Elmer TIMES. w Ag 8 1885+
1885-Je 30 1886 as Elmer gazette
pub 1885+

ELWOOD

ATLANTIC democrat and Cape May County register. w
NjHi [1862-67]

ENGLEWOOD

Englewood NEWS. w 1928+
pub D 1928+

Englewood PRESS. w 1888+
Je 1 1934 is 60th anniversary number
pub 1890+
MWA O 4 1890
NjR Je 1 1934

Englewood STANDARD. w 1879-84||
NjEnP complete

Englewood TIMES. w 1874-1906||?
NjEnP 1874-78
NjHi O 18 1879

FLEMINGTON

DEMOCRAT-ADVERTISER. w Je 11 1881-1925||
1881-82 as Hunterdon advertiser
NjHi Je 11,S 24-O 1 1881;S 16 1882;83-90;92-97
NjR [1902]10-[25]

HOME visitor. w 1883-99||
MWA Je 6 1894
NjHi Jl 1893-O 1895
NjR Je 6 1894

HUNTERDON advertiser. *See* Democrat-advertiser

HUNTERDON county democrat. w 1838+
MWA Je 8 1864
MdBJ O 5 1844;Jl 30 1845
NbHi Ag 27 1862
NjFlC 1853+
NjHi 1848-58;71-94;1915-23
NjR [1871;75;77;79;83;92;94]
PSuHi [1927]

HUNTERDON gazette and farmer's weekly advertiser. w Mr 24 1825-Jl 10 1867||
Title varies slightly. Merged with Hunterdon county democrat
Suspended from My 1832-Jl 18 1838
CSmH S 1 1830
DLC Jl 18 1838;Ap 19,N 24 1841;My 11 1842
MWA S 3 1828;Ja 29 1834;Mr 23 1836;D 5 1838
NbHi O 18 1837;S 2 1840;Ja 11,Jl 19 1843;My 15 1844
NjHi Ap 14 1825-Je 9 1830
NjR My 17 1826;N 10 1841;S 7 1842;Ap 8-15 1863;Mr 7 1866
PHi Mr 19 1828-Mr 16 1831

HUNTERDON republican. w O 15 1856+
pub 1926+
MWA Mr 15 1861
NbHi Ap 6 1866;N 29 1867
NjFlC 1856+
NjHi [1862-67;81-88]93-95
NjR [1864;66-68;70;72;74-76;78;80;82-83;Ap 9 1884;85;88;93]

FREEHOLD

FREEHOLDER and Irvington tribune. w F 1 1928-31||
Title varies slightly
NjR [1928-Ja 23 1931]

MONMOUTH democrat. w Ap 12 1834+
Sub-title varies
Ap 12-Jl 5 1834 pub in Princeton
Ap 12 1934 is 100th anniversary issue
Ct Ja 15 1835
DLC Ap 2 1874;Jl 6 1916;Ap 12 1934
MWA S 9 1858;F 22 1866;N 20 1884
NNHi Ap 20 1865;My 3 1873;Je 27,N 7 1878
Nj 1854-1903
NjFHi [1834-35;37-40;42-49]51+
NjHi [1865-67]73-96
NjR Jl 11,S 26 1844;Mr 29 1894;1910+
OClWHi Ag 1 1866
P-M S 20 1834
PWCl Je 2,30-Jl 7,28 1842

NEW JERSEY (*Continued*)

FREEHOLD—*Continued*

MONMOUTH weekly herald. w N 1 1854-Mr 1860||
United with Monmouth inquirer to form Monmouth herald and inquirer, later Monmouth inquirer
NjFHi [1854-60]

MONMOUTH herald and inquirer. *See* Monmouth inquirer

MONMOUTH inquirer. w Jl 7 1829 Ja 1933||
1829-33 as Monmouth enquirer; 1838-41 Monmouth inquirer and general advertiser; Ap 1860-65 Monmouth herald and inquirer. Merged with Freehold transcript
CSmH Jl 3 1830
DLC Ag 18,S 15 1829;O 25 1832;Ag 29 1833
IU Ag 22-N 14,D 5 1861
MWA My 5 1831;Je 27 1878;N 13 1884
N Ag 18 1842
NN Je 20-Jl 11 1878
NNHi Ag 13 1863;Je 20,Jl 18-25 1878
NcD N 13 1884
NjFHi [1829-69]72-[1921-22]-[25-26]-32
NjHi Ap 12 1828;Jl 7 1829;D 12 1839[65-67]78-1931
NjR [1835;42;45;1925-26]

MONMOUTH daily inquirer. d Ja 6 1858-
NjFHi Ja 7,9,13,My 8,Je 13 1858

MONMOUTH journal. w D 26 1826-
Ct F 27 1827
NjFHi Mr 27,Ap 3,My 1-8 1827;Ap 8-15,My 6 1828

***MONMOUTH star.** w N 2 1819-
NjHi Je 11-18,O 8 1821

PEOPLE'S advocate. w S 23 1850-
NjFHi [1850]

ROUGH and ready. w Jl 15 1848-
Campaign paper
NjFHi [1848]

SPIRIT of democracy. w Ag 18 1860-
Campaign paper
NjH Ag 18,S-O 1860

Freehold TRANSCRIPT. w S 7 1888+
pub 1888+
NjFHi 1888+
NjHi Je 5 1895;O 23 1925
NjR [1903;31;34-35]

FRENCHTOWN

DELAWARE Valley news. w 1879+
1879-Ag 1932 as Frenchtown star
pub 1879+

HUNTERDON independent. w 1871+
NbHi Ja 29,Je 17,Jl 22-29,N 25 1876;My 12,26, Je 23-30,Ag 11,25-S 8,O 6-13,27,N 10-17,D 1-15 1877;Ja 5,F 21 1878
NjR N 11 1871;Ja 19-Je 22 1917

Frenchtown PRESS. w Ap 2 1868-79||?
MWA Jl 16 1868;Ap 26 1876
NbHi Jl 16 1868;F 18 1869

Frenchtown STAR. *See* Delaware Valley news

GARFIELD

Garfield NEWS. w 1917+
pub 1917+

SZABAD-SATTO. (Free press) w 1908+
In Hungarian
pub 1928+

GLASSBORO

Glassboro ENTERPRISE. w 1880+
pub 1930+
IU Mr 20 1886
NjWdHi F 12 1904

GLEN RIDGE

Glen Ridge PAPER. w Ap 19 1935+
pub 1935+

GLEN ROCK

Glen Rock RECORD. w 1924+
pub 1924+

GLOUCESTER CITY

CITIZEN. w Ag 12 1915-16||?
NjCHi Ag 12-D 23 1915

Gloucester City NEWS. w S 1927+
pub Jl 1928+

Gloucester City RECORD. w Ja 20 1929+
pub 1929+

HACKENSACK

BANNER of truth. w
NBHi D 1867-Ja 1 1868

BERGEN county democrat. w 1861-
Title varies: Bergen county democrat and New Jersey state register
NjHi [1865-67]Mr 5-11 1869;Mr 26 1886;Mr 11,My 27 1887;Mr 11 1904

BERGEN county herald. w 1870-1902||?
United with Evening record to form Evening record and Bergen county herald, later Evening record

BERGEN index. w,sw 1875-1907||
NjHi Mr 1876-95

NEW JERSEY republican and Bergen county watchman. *See* Hackensack republican

Hackensack REPUBLICAN. w 1870+
1870-78 as New Jersey republican and Bergen county watchman
pub 1870+
MWA S 25 1879
NjHi 1890;98[1901-08]
NjR [1871-89]

Evening RECORD. d 1895+
1902?-13 as Evening record and Bergen county herald
pub My 1906+

Hackensack STAR and Bergen farmer. w
DLC Je 30,D 22 1824
NNHi S 1 1824

HACKETTSTOWN

Hackettstown GAZETTE. w 1857+
1857-67? as Warren gazette
pub 1857+
NjHi [1862;65-67]

Hackettstown HERALD. w 1872-81||?
NjHi 1875-80

WARREN gazette. *See* Hackettstown gazette

WARREN republican. w 1883-1920||
NjR [1894-1920]

HADDONFIELD

Haddonfield COURIER. *See* Camden county courier (Camden)

HAMMONTON

Hammonton FARMER. m 1857-
MWA S,D 1859

Hammonton ITEM. w 1872-77||?
NNHi D 14 1872

Hammonton NEWS. w 1863+
1863-1924? as South Jersey republican
NjHi [1867]
NjR [1935]

SOUTH JERSEY republican. *See* Hammonton news

HASBROUCK HEIGHTS

Hasbrouck Heights OBSERVER. w 1924+
pub 1926+

HIGHLAND PARK

Highland Park PRESS. w D 1 1920+
pub 1920+
NjR [1921-31;35]

MIDDLESEX review-press. w Ja 1 1930+
NjHp 1930+

TRI-BORO review. w Jl 1924+
NjHp 1924+

HIGHTSTOWN

Hightstown GAZETTE. w Je 1849+
1849-63 as Village record
pub 1849+
NjFHi 1849-Je 1850;Jl 1852-54
NjHi D 28 1860[61-67]

VILLAGE record. *See* Hightstown gazette

HILLSDALE

Hillsdale HERALD. w 1926+
pub 1935+

HOBOKEN

Hoboken ADVERTISER. w F 2 1878-Je 2 1883||
United with Hudson county democrat to form Hudson county democrat advertiser
NjH [F 12 1881-83]
NjT complete

CITY gazette and Hudson county weekly chronicle. w 1854-
Follows Hoboken gazette
NjH My 29 1858-Je 1859

Sunday DISPATCH-INQUIRER. 1896-Jl 9 1916||
1896-1901 as Inquirer; 1902-D 17 1904 Inquirer and republican; D 24 1904-Mr 25 1911 Inquirer; Ap 1 1911-Ag 28 1915 New inquirer; S 5 1915-Ap 23 1916 Sunday inquirer
NjH 1902-04;06-16

FREE lance. w 1930+
NjFHi Ag 23 1930

Hoboken FREIE PRESSE. w S 8 1902-
In German
NjH [S 8-O 29 1902]

Hoboken GAZETTE. w S 10 1853-54||
Followed by City gazette and Hudson county weekly chronicle
NjH S 10 1853-Ag 26 1854

HUDSON county daily democrat. d
NNHi My 11 1870
NjHi [My 1869-Ap 1872]

HUDSON county democrat-advertiser. w 1854-Ap 27 1889||
1854-83 as Hudson county democrat
NjH [O 13 1855-Ap 24 1869;Ap 12 1873-81;Je 9 1883-89]
NjHi [1865]
NjJ O 11 1856-S 1857;O 1860-Mr 1867;Je 9 1883-89

HUDSON county journal. w 1874-95||?
In German
NjR D 2 1876

HUDSON county socialist. w
NN Ap 1914-Ap 10 1915

HUDSON county volksblatt. w 1868-71||?
In German
NjJ My 14 1870-Ja 10 1871

HUDSON observer. *See* Jersey observer

INQUIRER. *See* Sunday dispatch-inquirer

JERSEY observer. d F 6 1892+
1892-Ja 11 1911 as Observer; Ja 12 1911-Ja 30 1924 Hudson observer N 12 1927 is Holland Tunnel historical number
NNHi O 24 1931
NjH 1892+
NjJ 1892-93;Jl 1904+
NjU 1924+

NEW inquirer. *See* Sunday dispatch-inquirer

Evening NEWS. d 1870-98||
NjH D 11 1886-My 7 1898

OBSERVER. *See* Jersey observer

REPUBLICAN. w Ja 15 1897-D 28 1901||
United with Inquirer to form Inquirer and republican, later Sunday dispatch-inquirer
NjH complete

Hoboken STANDARD. w Je 13 1857-76||?
1857-O 8 1859 as Hoboken City standard; O 15 1859-S 28 1861 Hoboken standard and gazette; O 5 1861-S 27 1862 Hoboken standard weekly
NjH Je 27 1857-Jl 2 1864
NjHi [1862-67]

HOPEWELL

Hopewell HERALD. w 1874+
pub 1874+

JAMESBURG

ADVANCE. bw,w Mr 1 1888+
bw 1888-Je 1889
Nj 1888-F 28 1901
NjHi 1889-1901
NjR [1891;1900-21]+

Jamesburg RECORD. w 1882-1904||
NjR F 15 1890[99-1904]

JERSEY CITY

Jersey City ADVERTISER and Hudson republican. sw,w D 2 1837-D 1 1846||
1837- as Jersey City advertiser; - Jersey City advertiser and Bergen republican sw 1837-D 14 1838
IaDH N 6,27 1839
NjJ complete
NjR N 23 1841

Jersey City daily ADVOCATE and Hudson county observer. d Ap 16 1863-Ag 30 1864||?
Ap 16-My 6 1863 as People's advocate and Hudson county observer
NjJ 1863-Ag 30 1864

AMERICAN standard. d Ag 8 1859-Ag 8 1875||
Follows Daily telegraph
MB D 21 1860;Ja 22-25 1861
MWA Je 4 1875
NjHi [1861-67]
NjJ complete
NjR N 30 1859

Jersey City ARGUS. w Ap 10 1875-Mr 23 1891||
1875-F 2 1884 as Argus
NjHi Je 1 1887;N 5 1890
NjJ complete

BERGEN county courier. w
NjJ F 1-N 14 1832

BERGEN county gazette and Jersey City advertiser. w
NjJ S 18 1829-My 1831

Jersey City CHRONICLE. sw F 14 1863-Ag 24 1864||
N My 1863-64
NjJ complete

Semi-monthly COURANT. *See* New Jersey monthly courant

Jersey City COURIER. w 1855-64||?
1855?-My 14 1857 as Hudson county courier
NjJ Ja 10 1856-Ag 30 1864

Daily COURIER and advertiser. d Ag 29 1845-Jl 28 1862||
1845-My 16 1848 as Evening sentinel; Mr 17 1848-Jl 4 1856 Daily sentinel and advertiser; Jl 5 1856-O 28 1857 Jersey City daily sentinel
MWA Mr 11 1854
NjHi O 1848-54;My 16 1855-Ap 6 1857
NjJ complete
NjR [1852-53]

GAZETTE. w,d
Jl 18-D 20 1870 pub each Saturday as Evening gazette
NjJ My 4 1870-My 13 1871

Evening GAZETTE. d *See note under* Gazette

Jersey City GAZETTE and Bergen county advertiser. w
MWA Jl 25 1835
NjHi O 10 1835
NjJ My 1835-Ap 15 1837

Jersey City HERALD. w 1870-1920||?
MWA S 30 1876
NjJ Je 4 1870-Ap 29 1871;Je 21 1873-My 4 1889

NEW JERSEY (*Continued*)

JERSEY CITY—*Continued*

HUDSON county courier. *See* Jersey City courier

HUDSON county ledger. *See* New Jersey ledger

HUDSON Jewish news. sw 1922+
In Yiddish and English
pub 1926-28

JERSEY journal. d My 2 1867+
1867-O 1909 as Evening journal
My 2 1917 is Golden jubilee number
DLC 1894;-8
MWA Ja 5,Je 13 1876;Je 29 1883;My 2 1917
NcU Ap 11 1878;Jl 9 1879
NjBa 1867-Ag,N 1910+
NjHi [1865-67]
NjJ 1867-1909
NjR N 9 1877

JERSEY review. w 1920+
NjBa Ap-Ag,O 1924-Je 1929
NjJ Ag 23 1928+
NjHi Mr 12-D 24 1930;My-D 1931
NjFHi Jl 23 1921

JERSEY Sunday press. w S 30 1928+
NjJ 1928+

JEWISH standard. w D 18 1931+
pub 1931+

Evening JOURNAL. *See* Jersey journal

NEW JERSEY monthly courant. sm,m -1851 as Semi-monthly courant
DLC Je 16 1849
MWA Je 8 1848;Mr 24,Jl 25,Ag 23,O 20 1849;Ja 21,Ag 3 1850;Jl 17 1851;Mr 1852
N Ag 1 1860
NjR O 21 1850

NEW JERSEY morning journal. d
NjHi Jl 23 1887;Ap 19,Ag 30-31 1888

NEW JERSEY ledger. w 1878-87||
1878-83 as Hudson county ledger
NjR S 8 1883

NEW JERSEY press. w My 20 1824-
N Jl 8 1824

NEW JERSEY weekly times. w 1866-
MWA N 3 1868

Sunday morning NEWS. w 1882-D 27 1891||
1882-S 1883 as Sunday tatler and Jersey City express
NjJ D 28 1884-91

Jersey City NEWS. d F 25 1889-1906||
NjHi Ap 17 1891;Ja 22,F 1,Ap 7 1892;D 4 1893
NjJ F 25 1889-D 22 1906

PEOPLE'S advocate and Hudson county observer. *See* Jersey City daily advocate and Hudson county observer

Daily SENTINEL. *See* Daily courier and advertiser

SQUARE. w
NjJ D 4 1915-F 19 1916

SVOBODA (Liberty). w,tw,d 1893+
w 1893-1914?;tw 1915-20
In Ukrainian
pub 1893+
CSt-H [1916]35+
DLC 1912;15-15
IU 1915+
MWA Jl 25-27 1936
PPiHi D 24 1931-Mr 1932

Sunday TATLER and Jersey City express. *See* Sunday morning news

Daily TELEGRAPH. sw,d Je 5 1847-Je 25 1859||
1847-F 10 1850 as Jersey City telegraph (sw) Followed by American standard
DLC F 4-O 21 1854;Mr 16 1855-N 8 1856
MWA My 16 1851
NSyU D 3 1852
NjJ complete
NjR Je 7 1848

Jersey City TIMES. d S 14 1864-N 8 1873||
1864-S 16 1868 as Jersey City daily times; S 17-N 4 1868 Daily times; N 5 1868-Mr 31 1870 Daily evening times
DLC 1868
MWA S 14 1864
NbHi Jl 19 1865
NjJ complete
NjR Jl 19 1865

Jersey City TIMES. w
NjHi Ag 1864-65

Jersey City UNION. tw 1852?-
MWA N 3 1853

UNITED STATES telegraph. w
NSchU Mr 3 1842
PWCl N 17 1841;Mr 24,Ap 7,22-29,My 25 1842

KEANSBURG

Keansburg BEACON. w 1913+
NjFHi Mr 8 1935—

Keansburg NEWS. w 1925+
pub 1925+
NjFHi Mr 1935+

KEY-EAST

Key-East KEYNOTE. w 1883-85||
1883 as Seaside keynote
PLanA Je 4 1883-Ja 17 1885

SEASIDE keynote. *See* Key-East keynote

KEYPORT

Keyport ENTERPRISE. w 1879+
pub 1922+
NjFHi N 5 1881;O 14 1882;[1911-15]Mr 1935+

NEW JERSEY standard. w 1852-
MWA N 29 1855
NjFHi S 12 1855;Ja 24-31,My 1 1856;Ja 14,Mr 4 1858

Keyport PRESS. sm S 24 1863-
NjFHi S 24,O 15,N 4,D 16 1863

Keyport WEEKLY. w 1868+
pub [1870+]
NjFHi My 5 1875;77-79;81+

KINGSTON

RECORD. w My 1932+
NjR [1935]

LAKEWOOD

Lakewood CITIZEN. w 1900+
pub 1900+

LAMBERTVILLE

Lambertville BEACON. w 1845+
Title varies: People's beacon; Beacon
pub [1845]80+
MWA Je 19 1885
NjHi N 25-D 23 1853[65-67]
PNoHi D 15 1854[Ja-My 1855]

DELAWARE Valley diarist. w 1849-
NjHi [Ja 4-Ap 5 1851]

PEOPLE'S beacon. *See* Lambertville beacon

Lambertville RECORD. w 1872+
MWA Jl 8 1885
NjHi 1879-97
PNhF O 21 1885;S 22 1886

LEONIA

NORTH Jersey life. w 1922+
pub 1934+
NjHi 1920+

LINDEN

AZ UJSAG (The news). w
In Hungarian
PPiHi Ag 27,D 3 1929

Linden NEWS. w N 1927+
pub 1932+
NjL Mr 1929+

Linden OBSERVER. w 1919+
NjL Mr 1929+

LITTLE FALLS

Little Falls HERALD. w 1923+
pub F 1925+

LODI

Lodi BULLETIN and news letter. w S 1925+
pub S 17 1925+

Lodi INDEPENDENT. w 1921+
pub 1921+

Lodi MESSENGER. w S 4 1929+
pub 1929+

LONG BRANCH

MONMOUTH American. w O 17 1917+
NjFHi Mr 8 1935+

Long Branch NEWS. w,tw,d 1866-1910||
United with Long Branch press to form Long Branch press and Long Branch news
d,tw during Jl-Ag
NjFHi [1866-73]O 19,N 9 1878;N 5,12 1881;Jl 6 1882;Ap 21 1883
NjHi [1867]F 12 1881;Je 20-Jl 4,11,16 1885;Ag 5 1886
NjR Ag 11 1879

Long Branch PRESS and Long Branch news. w 1898-1918||
1898-1910 as Long Branch press
NjFHi [1911-15]

Long Branch RECORD. w 1883-1912||
NjFHi [1887]1900-04[11-12]

Long Branch daily RECORD. d 1902+
NjFHi [Ap-Je 1911]Ja 17,Mr 16 1912;D 19 1932+

LORNS RIVER

OCEAN county sun. w N 12 1926+
pub 1926+

LYNDHURST

COMMERCIAL leader. w Je 1921+
pub 1921+

SOUTH Bergen eagle. w 1913+
pub 1913+

MADISON

Madison EAGLE. w 1880+
pub 1880+
NjHi Mr 18 1892;O 29 1897

OUR bulletin. sm S 1890-
KHi [O 1890-Mr 1892]

MANASQUAN

COAST star. w 1880+
NjFHi Je 6 1902;Ap 15,29 1910;N 23,D 14 1928[30-Ja 5 1934]Mr 1935+

SEASIDE. tw,w Je 14 1877-89||?
Followed by Seaside gazette, later Spring Lake gazette (Spring Lake)
NjFHi Je 14-Jl 3 1877;N 9 1878;N 4 1881

Manasquan RECORD. w 1929+
NjFHi O 10-24 1930;Mr 17,Je 9,N 3-10,24 1933;F 1935+

MAPLE SHADE

Maple Shade PROGRESS. w N 1916+
pub [1916-29]+

MAPLEWOOD

HOME news. *See* Maplewood news

Maplewood NEWS. w Ja 1 1915+
1915-My 14 1925 as Home news
NjMa 1915+

Maplewood RECORD. w O 6 1922+
NjMa 1922+

MATAWAN

Early years as Middletown Point

ATLANTIC and Monmouth county advertiser. w Ap 24 1855-
NjFHi O 30,D 11 1855;F 20,Ap 15,Je 17,O 14 1856

DEMOCRATIC banner, and Monmouth County advertiser. w 1845-Mr 1852||
Followed by New Jersey standard, later Red Bank standard (Red Bank)
MWA F 19 1852
NjFHi [O 1848-52]

Matawan JOURNAL. m,sm,w Jl 1869+
m Jl 1869-My 1870;sm Je 1870-Jl 8 1871
NjFHi 1869-93;95-Jl 1906;07+

NEW JERSEY standard. *See* Red Bank standard (Red Bank)

OLIVE branch. w 1845-
NjFHi [O 1847-Je 1848]

UNION. w S 18 1845-
NjFHi [N 1845-Jl 1847]

MAY'S LANDING

ATLANTIC county record. w 1877+
1877-1908? as May's Landing record
NjHi Ja 3-24,F 21 1885

ATLANTIC journal.
NjHi [1852]

MERCHANTVILLE

COMMUNITY news. w 1923+
pub 1928—

MIDDLETOWN

NEW JERSEY standard and independent family journal. w
NNHi Ja 15 1852-Ap 1 1854

MIDDLETOWN POINT. *See* MATAWAN

MIDLAND PARK

Midland Park POST. w Mr 1924+
pub 1924+

MILFORD

Milford LEADER. w 1880+
MWA Ap 14 1880
NbHi 1890-Ja 23 1908

MILLBURN

Millburn-Short Hills ITEM. w 1888+
pub 1929+

MILLSTONE

Millstone MIRROR. w Ap 18 1861-
NjHi [1862]
NjN Ap 18 1861

MILLTOWN

Milltown REVIEW. w 1926+
NjR O 14 1927

MILLVILLE

Millville REPORTER. *See* Millville daily republican

Millville daily REPUBLICAN. d 1864+
1864-1901? as Millville reporter
pub 1922+
NjHi [1867]

NEW JERSEY (*Continued*)

MONTCLAIR

Montclair-Glen Ridge BULLETIN. w O 13 1922+
pub 1928+

Montclair HERALD. m 1873-74||
NjHi Je 1873-Je 1874

Montclair REGISTER. w 1888-89||?
NjHi My 10,Je 6,21 1888

Montclair TIMES. w 1877+
NjHi F 10,24 1883;O 8 1887;S 8 1888;Jl 22 1916
NjMo 1894+
NjMoT F 17 1877+

MOORESTOWN

CHRONICLE. w 1879+
NjR [1934]+

Moorestown NEWS. w 1926+
pub Je 1926+

MORRISTOWN

Morristown BANNER. w,d Je 6 1838+
1838-44? as Democratic banner (title varies) 1845?-1915? True democratic banner; 1916?-32? True republican banner
DLC Je 13 1838
MWA O 31 1878;Jl 12-26,Ag 16,S 13 1883
N Ap 9 1856
NjHi O 1848-[54-55;63;65;82-89;92-93;1901]F 21,28,Mr 28,My 30 1918;My 29,Je 5 1919;Ag 7 1930
NjR [1845;64-65;69-72;79]
OClWHi Ag 3 1865

Evening EXPRESS. d 1890-1907||?
NjHi Ap 13 1901

JERSEYMAN. w,d O 4 1826-O 9 1931||
w 1826-1918?
DLC 1832-D 17 1834;Mr 25 1835-38;Jl 10,S 4 1839;Je 16 1841
MWA Ag 22 1829;Jl 24 1839
N O 30 1833
NjHi [1827-29]-[31-32]-[35-69]-1918;O 4,S 30 1926
NjM 1926-31
NjR Jl 1867-[Jl-D 1869;74]
OOxM F 4 1829
P-M D 10 1845

MORRIS county chronicle. w N 2 1877-1914||
United with Daily times to form Daily times and the Morris county chronicle
NjHi [1882;87-89;94;97]98[1902]
NjR S 12 1885

MORRIS county whig. w 1834-
Follows Palladium of liberty
MWA Jl 30 1834
NNHi S 9 1835
NjHi [1834-36]

MORRIS herald and workingman's advocate. w
NjHi D 24-31 1834

MORRIS republican. w 1872-76||?
NjR Je 18 1875

*PALLADIUM of liberty. w Mr 31 1808-1834||
Followed by Morris county whig
CSmH S 8 1830
DLC Ag 5 1824;Jl 1-8,Ag 5,S 23-30,O 28,N 18-25,D 30 1829-Ja 13 1830;F 5 1834
MWA My 19 1825;D 6 1827;O 3 1832
N N 21,D 5 1822
NNHi O 10 1822;N 25,S 16,O 7-14,D 2-9 1829; Ja 13,27,F 17-Mr 10,Ap 28 1830;Ap 6 1831;Ap 4 1832
NjHi 1821-Ja 1833[34]

RECORD. m Ja 1880-84||
OClWHi 1880-81;83-84

Morristown daily RECORD. d Je 25 1900+
pub 1900+
NjM 1932+

Daily TIMES and the Morris county chronicle. d O 4 1915-F 29 1916||
NjM complete

Morristown TOPICS. w 1920-30||
NjM complete
NjHi [1920-29]

TRUE democratic banner. *See* Morristown banner

WHIG standard.
Campaign sheet
MWA S 26 1838

MOUNT HOLLY

BURLINGTON county herald. *See* Mount Holly herald

BURLINGTON mirror. *See* New Jersey mirror

FAMILY casket and Burlington county herald. *See* Mount Holly herald

Mount Holly HERALD. w 1826+
1826-32 as New Jersey chronicle; 1832-46 Burlington county herald; 1847-49 Family casket and Burlington county herald
pub 1865+
CSmH Je 22,Ag 20 1830
DLC Mr 5 1829
MWA S 10 1830;S 4 1931
NNHi F 10 1832
NjCHi Jl 26-Ag 2 1924
NjHi D 17 1840;N 2-9,23-D 1848[65-67]
NjWdHi Ja 20,My 12 1933
PHi Ja 31 1828-Jl 21 1829
PP S 20 1873

NEW JERSEY chronicle. *See* Mount Holly herald

*NEW JERSEY mirror and Burlington county advertiser. w S 16 1818+
1818-S 8 1819 as Burlington mirror
D 20 1893 is 75th anniversary number
pub 1821+
CtY D 20 1893
MWA N 20,D 4 1822;O 10 1872;O 16 1873;O 15 1874;O 12 1876
NjHi 1821-O 1827
NjR 1821-[Je-D 1826]
P-M F 15 1855
PP S 2 1852

Mount Holly NEWS. w 1879+
pub 1879+
NjHi Je 30,Jl 14-21 1885
PP N 24 1885

MULLICA HILL

Mullica Hill MESSENGER. w F 2-Ag 31 1899||
NjWdHi [1899]

NEW BRUNSWICK

*New Brunswick FREDONIAN. w,sw Ap 17 1811-1900||
1811-Ap 11 1854 as Fredonian. Title varies slightly. Followed by New Brunswick press
sw F 7 1882-D 30 1884
CSmH S 8 1830
DLC Ag 23,S 6,20,O 3-25,N 8-D 12,27 1821-Ja 6,27,Ag 11 1830;F 9 1831;O 31 1832;D 24 1834;D 2 1840
MWA Ja 16 1823;Mr 25,Je 2-9,Ag 4,N 17 1824;Ja 3 1827;F 20,Mr 26 1828;Jl 1-8,29-Ag 12,S 16,30 1829;D 30 1830
NNHi My 21 1863
NjHi O 3,D 11 1822;O 18 1837;48-[59-67]D 23 1875;Jl 9 1886
NjR 1821-[27;38]-[44;47]-[51;53]-85
PDoHi D 27 1825
WHi Ag 15 1855

New Brunswick daily FREDONIAN. d Ja 15 1855-Ag 31 1900||
1855-Ja 14 1856 as New Brunswicker; Ja 15 1856-Mr 21 1859 Daily New Brunswicker. Followed by Daily press, later New Brunswick daily press
Ct [1826-27]
NjCHi Ja 7 1897
NjFHi My 27 1880
NjHi My 27,31,Je 18 1867;Je 25 1886;F 18 1887
NjNb Jl-D 1889
NjR 1855-[65-66]-1900;S 8(extra)1855

Daily HOME news. d 1879+
pub 1906+
NjR [1879-84]+

Weekly HOME news. w 1880-1921||?
NjR [1882;87;93-94]

MAGYAR hirnok (Hungarian herald). w O 1909+
In Hungarian
pub 1924+
PPiHi [N 22 1923-Je 11 1931]

New Brunswicki MAGYAR ujsag (New Brunswick Hungarian news). w 1916-28||?
In Hungarian
PPiHi [D 13 1923-Jl 1926]

MIDDLESEX county gazette. w Ja 4 1922-
NjR Ja 4 1922

MIDDLESEX Jeffersonian. w Je-D 1899||
NjR complete

MIDDLESEX mail. w 1889-95||?
NjR Ja 10,S 11 1892

MIDDLESEX republican. w N 4 1905-
NjR N 4 1905

MIDDLESEX true democrat. sw 1858-
NjR O 5,12,22,N 1 1858

NEW BRUNSWICKER. *See* New Brunswick daily Fredonian

NEW JERSEY pilot. bm 1928-
NjR My 15 1928

NEW JERSEY union. w Je 2 1847-Mr 1851||
Followed by New Brunswick daily news
DLC Je 2-9,24,Jl 8-Ag 19,S 2,16-23,O 7-22,N 4-18,D 8(extra)9,23 1847;Ja 20-27,F 10,24,Mr 2-9,Ap-My 18,Je,Jl 13,27-Ag 3,17-31,S 14,28-O 12,26-N 9,23-D 7 1848
NjR Ag 10 1848;D 13 1849

New Brunswick daily NEWS. d 1851-61||?
Follows New Jersey union. Merged with New Brunswick daily times
NjR [1852-53;55-58;60]

New Brunswick OBSERVER. w 1919-21||
NjR [1919-20]

POLITICAL intelligencer. *See* New Jersey journal (Elizabeth)

Sunday morning POST. Ap 6-Ag 31 1884||
NjR complete

New Brunswick daily PRESS. d S 1 1900-F 1909||
Follows New Brunswick daily Fredonian. 1900-Ag 8 1902 as Daily press
NjNb 1903-Je 10 1908
NjR 1900-[07]

New Brunswick PRESS. w 1900-09||
Follows New Brunswick Fredonian

New Brunswick SPOKESMAN. w S 25 1925+
NjR 1925+

New Brunswick evening STAR.
My 24-Je 25 1884||
NjR complete

*New Brunswick TIMES. w Je 1 1815-Ap 1 1902||
Follows Guardian, or New Brunswick advertiser (Not in this list). 1815-O 1 1818 as Times and New Brunswick general advertiser; O 8 1818- 1826 Times and New Brunswick advertiser; 1826-Ja 7 1858 Times; Ja 14 1858-D 6 1860 Times and New Jersey union
CSmH S 8 1830
Ct [1826]Ap 28 1830
DLC O 13 1824
MWA Ag 29 1822;N 25 1840
N O 16 1833
NNHi O 17-24 1832;Jl 29 1840
NUHi Jl 4 1827
NjFHi Mr 15 1843
NjHi Ja 25,My 17 1821;Ap 11 1822[65-67]
NjNb 1855-58;68-70;1903-06
NjR [1821-29;32-33;35;38-40;43;51;54;58-68]
PDoHi D 27 1825

New Brunswick daily TIMES. d O 8 1869-Ja 4 1917||
NNHi Ap 28 1871;My 1 1873
NjNb 1859-62;D 28 1871-83;Jl 1884-Je 1885; 86-90;92-Ag 1916
NjR [1870;72-73]-[1917]

Sunday TIMES. w F 18 1917+
Follows New Brunswick times
pub 1917+
NjNb 1917+
NjR Je 7 1917[18]+

New Brunswick WASP. Ag 2 1855||
NjR complete

WATKINS weekly. w Ag 3 1895-
NjR [1895-96]

NEW EGYPT

New Egypt PRESS. w 1899+
My 9 1929 is 30th anniversary ed
NjR My 9 1929

NEW MONMOUTH

Early years as Chanceville

DIRECTORY: devoted exclusively to Monmouth county intelligence. sm,w Je 15 1858-
1858 as Monmouth county directory
NjFHi S 15 1858;My 1,S 15,O 11,N 1,D 15 1859

MONMOUTH County directory. *See* Directory

Semi-monthly SHANGHAI.
NjFHi [1858]

SHANGHAI: something tall.
NjFHi [1855-56]

SPIRIT of the age. sm Ja 1 1873-75||?
NjFHi [1873-Ja 27 1875]

NEWARK

Newark weekly ADVERTISER. w O 5 1832-
MWA O 5 1832

Newark daily ADVERTISER. *See* Newark star-eagle

ANTI-Jacksonian. w Ag 18-N 3 1828||
NNHi Ag 18 1828
NjHi complete

Newark Sunday CALL. w My 19 1872+
1872-81 as Newark call
Mr 29 1936 is Newark centennial number
pub 1873+
ICM Mr 26 1882
MWA Ap 12 1931;Mr 29 1936
Nj 1916+
NjHi O 1913-30;32+
NjN Je 1872+
NjR 1935+

CARTOON. w 1873-74||
NjHi Ag 29 1874

CENTINEL of freedom. *See* Sentinel of freedom

Newark CHRONICLE. w 1830-
NjHi Ap 29,O 21 1830;S 23 1831

Newark daily COURIER. d 1866-77||
1866-Ap 7 1876 as Newark evening courier
DLC Ap 3 1872;75-76
MWA S 6 1871
NNHi Ja 3 1874
NjHi Je 1866-Je 1875;My-Ag 1877
NjN Jl 11,Ag 15,23,30,S 23,N 14,23 1870;Ja 1871-N 1877

Newark DEMOCRAT. Ag 18 1860-
NjHi Ag 18 1860

Newark daily EAGLE. d Je 10 1847-O 31 1857||
1847-Je 13 1853 as Newark morning eagle. Followed by Newark journal
DLC 1847-O 17 1850
NhD My 18 1852
NjHi Je 14 1852-57
NjN complete

Newark EAGLE and the Newark star. d O 22 1906-Ja 29 1916||
1906-F 2? 1908 as Morning star and Newark advertiser; F 3 1908-F 21? 1909 Star and Newark advertiser; F 22-Mr 11? 1909 Newark star; Mr 12-19? Star and Newark advertiser; Mr 20 1909-Ag 1? 1915 Newark star. United with Newark evening star to form Newark star-eagle
MWA N 6 1852;Ag 2,N 18 1853
NjHi 1907-15
NjN complete

Newark ECHO. w 1872-73||?
NjN Ja 4 1873

NEW JERSEY (*Continued*)

NEWARK—*Continued*

ESSEX county press. w 1872-80||?
During 1878 campaign pub d as Newark daily press
MWA F 2- 1877
NjHi 1876-78

FACTS for the people. w
NjN S 26 1839

Newark GAZETTE. w
Title varies: Newark gazette and mercantile advertiser; Newark gazette and farmer's journal
DLC N 7 1832;F 24 1841
MiU-C D 7 1842
NhD N 9-13 1843

Newark INQUIRER. bw 1833-
NjN Jl 3 1834-35

Newark INTELLIGENCER. w 1825-30||
CSmH My 22 1830
DLC Ag 25 1828;F 12,26,Je 25,Jl 16 1829
NjHi [1827-30]
NjN Ag 9 1828;Je 12 1830
NjR [1828]

INVISIBLE spy. w 1830-
NjHi Mr 3,24 1830

ITALIAN tribune. w Jl 29 1931+
NjR 1934+

JERSEY review. w Ja 1 1926+
pub 1926+

JERSEYAN and Newark evening advertiser. w
NNHi Jl 16,30 1823

JEWISH chronicle. w 1921+
pub 1921+
M Jl 8-15 1932

Newark JOURNAL. d N 2 1857-Ja 29 1895||
Follows Newark daily eagle. Title varies slightly: Newark evening journal; Newark daily journal
DLC S 15 1859-D 14,16-21,23-24 1861
MBAt D 21 1863;Ap 15-18,25 1865
MWA Mr 22 1860;N 2 1881
NNHi S 1858-N 1860;O 1 1886;Ap 6 1874
Nj My 1865-95
NjHi 1857-8-;My 8 1890;Je 24(extra)1891;92-Je,O 2 1894
NjN 1857-94
NjR [1879-82]

Newark weekly JOURNAL. w N 24 1857-O 30 1866||
Follows New Jersey weekly eagle
NjHi My 13 1862
NjN complete

Newark LEDGER. d,w,sw O 1916+
1916-19? as Newark morning ledger
NjHi F-Mr 1932
NjN 1916-Je 1919;F 1928+

Newark daily MERCURY. d 1848-D 31 1863||
DLC Ag 1861-63
MWA S 3 1861;Ap 10,S 5 1862;Je 9,22 1863
NN Ap 29 1857[O 10 1860-Mr 1861]
NNHi S 26 1850
NjHi Ja 13-D 1849;S 1850-63
NjJ 1852-53;56-61
NjN 1849;Ap 1850-Je 1854;55-63

Newark MONITOR. w Ja 6 1830-Jl 27 1834||
CSmH S 7 1830
NNHi D 30(extra)1830;Ag 2,N 8-22 1831;Ja-F 7,Jl 3,24-31,Ag 14,28-S 4,O 9-N 13,D 4 1832
NjHi complete
NjN Ja 10,N 27 1832
NjR Mr 24 1831

MORGENSTERN. (Jewish morning star) sw O 1921+
In Yiddish and English
pub 1922-28

NEW JERSEY American.
NjHi [1859]
NjR D 10 1859

NEW JERSEY deutsche zeitung. w 1872-
In German
NjHi 1880-98
NjN Ja 16 1886

*NEW JERSEY weekly eagle. w,sw Mr 3 1820-N 17 1857||
Mr-O 27 1820 as New Jersey eagle, and Newark, Orange and Bloomfield early intelligencer; N 3 1820-Je 8 1847? New Jersey eagle. Followed by Newark weekly journal
CP Ag 2 1842
Ct [1833-36]Mr 6 1838
DLC Jl 31,Ag 13 O 1-8,29 1824;Ag 31 1827;Ag 2 1833;My 23 1834;D 6 1836:S 15 1837;D 11 1838;40-Ag 10 1841;S 22 1846-My 21 1847
MWA F 8,Ap 26,My 31,Je 14,Jl 26,Ag 9,23-S 13,27-O 11,25,N 15,D 6 1822;Ap 18 1823;Ja 7 1824;Ap 20 1827;Mr 20 1829;Je 24 1831
N Ja 21 1825;Ja 26-F 9 1827;O 18 1833
NNHi Ja 31,Jl 5,18,S 19,D 19-26 1823;F 6,Mr 19,S 10-17,N 19 1824;Ap 27,My 20 1825;Ja 27,N 24 1826;Ja 26,D 14 1827;Ja 18 1828;Ja 22,F 19,Ap 16-23,My 7 1830;Ja 27,Ap 13,Jl 6, Ag 3-10,24 1832
NjHi 1821-Ja 2- 1843;My 23 1845-Je 8 1847
NjN 1821-[23-28]F 26 1839;57
NjR Ag 21(extra)1838

NEW JERSEY freie zeitung. d Ap 26 1858+
Follows Newark zeitung
Ag 26 1908 is golden jubilee number
In German
MWA Ag 23 1876
NN Ap 26 1908;Ja 20-F 3 1933

NEW JERSEY freie zeitung. w 1882-1912||?
NjHi 1890-1912

NEW JERSEY herald. w
OClWHi O 9,22 1873

NEW JERSEY weekly post. w 1843-
MWA Ag 13 1844

NEWARK es videke (Newark and vicinity). w 1928-32||?
In Hungarian
PPiHi F 29,Ap 18 1928

NEWARKI hirlap (Newark journal). w
In Hungarian
PPiHi [Ag 28 1930-Jl 16 1931]

Morning NEWS. d S 16 1841-
DLC S 16 1841
NjHi S 27-O 1 1841

Newark evening NEWS. d S 1 1883+
pub 1883+
CSt [1929]
DLC 1898+
MWA O 6 1888;S 1 1933
NNHi [Jl-Ag 1903]
Nj 1897+
NjEo 1903+
NjHi Ap 1900-30;32+
NjN 1890+
NjR F 19 1895[1902-04]+
PP [1931]+
TxGR Ja 5 1929

Newark Sunday NEWS. w 1901-05||
Nj F 1901-F 1905

Daily PATRIOT. d S 11-N 9 1865||
N O 11 1865
NjHi complete
NjN [1865]

PEOPLE'S paper. d My 2 1871-
NjN My-N 1871

Newark morning POST. w 1841-
NN Ag 9 1844
NjHi Ja 11,Jl 1,30,Ag 21 1844;O 3 1867
NjN My 21 1844

Saturday POST and merchant's journal. w 1868-
NjHi Jl 4 1868

Newark PRESS. w N 21 1868-70||?
NjHi D 12 1868

Newark daily PRESS. d Jl 12 1873-Mr 1 1886||
United with Newark morning register to form Newark press-register
NjHi N 6 1878;O 15-D 13 1884;85-86

Morning PRESS. d Ap 7-D 6 1890||
Follows Newark press-register. Merged with Evening press
NjHi Jl 21,23 1890
NjN complete

Evening PRESS. d D 1 1890-Ap 25 1891||
Follows Newark press-register
NjN complete

Newark PRESS-REGISTER. d Mr 9 1886-Ap 4 1890||
Followed by Morning press; Evening press
MWA O 17 1889
NjHi 1886;Ag 31,S 3-4,6-7 1888;My 31,S 9 1889
NjN O 1889-90

Newark REGISTER. w
NjHi [1859]

Newark morning REGISTER. d My - 1869-Ap 30 1886||
United with Newark daily press to form Newark press-register
MWA Ag 24-25,N 8 1876
NNHi D 24-25 1875
NjHi 1869-74;76-Mr 1886
NjN O 10 1877

Newark REPUBLICAN. w D? 1829-
CSmH Jl 8 1830

La RIVISTA. The Review. w 1905-21||
In Italian and English
IU D 8 1917-Ag 23 1921

ROSEVILLE weekly. w 1898-1914||
NjHi S 8,22-29,O 13,N 3 1899

*SENTINEL of freedom. w O 5 1796-1909||?
Title varies: Centinel of freedom; Sentinel of freedom and New Jersey advertiser; Sentinel of freedom and Newark weekly advertiser
CSmH Jl 13 1830
CtY S 16,N 25,D 9 1828;F 23 1830
DLC Ja 9-Jl 3,17-24,Ag 7,21-28 1821;O 31 1832
GAtCo Ja 1 1881
MWA 1821-Mr 18,Ap 1,Je 1823-S 16 1828;Ap 9 1839;S 2,N 11 1845;Ja 6,F 10-17 1846;Je 1 1847;Ag 26 1856[Ja 20-N 24 1857;My-D 21 1858;Mr 8 1859-63]-[65]Ja 19-26,Mr 1869-[70] F 13,Jl 23,S 24 1872
MiD-B [1839-49]
NN S 3 1821;S 8 1822
NNHi Ja 23,My 20,S 23,D 23 1823;Ja 27 1824; Ap 12 1825;Ja 16,F 13,My 22,O 9,30,D 18 1827;F 16,Mr 2-9 1830;Jl 10 1832;Ap 14 1840; My 22 1849-Jl 9 1850;Mr 4 1873
NjHi 1821-95
NjN S 1823-S,N 1825-Mr,S 1836-49;Jl 1850-95
NjR [1821-23;25-30;32-35]
OClWHi Ag 27 1878
P-M S 4 1832
PCA Je 17 1873
PDoHi Je 26 1827

Sunday STANDARD. w 1887-96||
NjHi [1889]90-92;1895-96
NjN D 1889-Ap 1896

Newark STAR. Morning edition. *See* Newark eagle and the Newark star

STAR and Newark advertiser. Evening ed. *See* Newark star-eagle

STAR and Newark advertiser. Morning ed. *See* Newark eagle and the Newark star

Newark STAR-EAGLE. d Mr 1 1832+
1832-O 14? 1904 as Newark daily advertiser; O 15 1904-Ap 27 1907 Newark advertiser; Ap 29 1907-F 2? 1908 Evening star and Newark advertiser; F 3 1908-Ap 1? 1909 Star and Newark advertiser. Evening ed.; Ap 2-31? 1909 Newark star and Newark advertiser. Evening ed.; My 1-N 26? 1909 Newark star and Newark advertiser; N 27 1909-Ja 29 1916 Newark evening star and Newark advertiser
CoD Ap 15 1865
CtY Mr-Je 7 1832;My 9 1843;S 20 1852
DLC Mr 28-Ag 1832;33-Je 1855;56-58;Ja-Je 1860;61-66;F-Ap,Jl 11-D 1867;Ag 7 1868;Ja 18,Ap 30,My 6,10,12,15 1869;70+
IU O 31,N 24 1849;My 1 1850;F 20 1851;F 24 1852;F 8 1853
MBAt Ap 18,20,27 1865
MWA Mr 4 1830[Je 21 1832-33]Ap 4,O 22 1834;Mr 5 1835;F 25,Mr 7,19,Jl 25-28 1836;Mr 23 1837;O 6 1838;Mr 6,My 6-7,S 21,D 7-30 1839[Ja-My 25 1840]Jl 16 1841;Ja 3,Je 28 1842;Ja 3-Jl 8 1843;Ag 14 1845;Ja-F,Ap,My 9,Je 1846-Ag,S 28,N 1-29 1847;Ja-S,N 1-29 1848;Ja-Ap,Je-N 1849;50-[O 3-D 1853]-[Ja-My]S 1858;Ja 21,Ap 29-Ag,N 22 1859;Ja 21 1860;Je 3 1861;Jl 23 1863-[65]F 10-27,My 17-18,29-Jl,D 1866;Ja-F,S 29-30 1868;Ja 4-F 23, N-D 1869;My 26 1870;Mr 12 1875;My 21 1878; My 4,26 1881;Ag 4,D 1 1885;Ja 21,My 31,N 7 1888;O 16 1889
MiU-C Ja 17 1846
NN Ja 3 1843;Ja 16 1845;Ap 17 1850;Ja 23 1854;Jl 19 1856;Mr 10 1864;My 18 1866
NNHi [F 10 1837-Mr 6 1839]F 19 1846;O 30 1848;Jl 11 1850;D 11 1855;My 7 1863;O 2,7 1874
NhD Ag 20 1849;Ag 6 1852
Nj 1832+
NjHi 1832-1906;F 1916-Je 1918;23+
NjJ 1840-51
NjN 1832+
NjP [1838-39]-75
NjR [1836;40;48;62-64;69;85;89;93-94]
OClWHi Jl 6 1850;My 15,D 6,10,23 1864;Ja 7-28,Mr 20-My 19,Je 21-29 1865
P F 7 1834;Ag 23 1854
PEL D 24 1845-F 16 1852
PP Jl 28 1847;My 25 1848
WHi Je 16 1847;Ag 11 1849:Jl 11 1850;62;Ja 14 1867

TARIFF advocate. d Jl 23 1844-
DLC Ag 3 1844
NNHi Ag 15 1844
NjHi Jl 23-N 12 1844

Newark TIMES. d 1891-94||
NjHi [1891-94]
NjN F 6 1894

Newark ZEITUNG. d F 9 1853-53||
Followed by New Jersey freie zeitung

NEWFIELD

Weekly ITEM. w O 14 1873-1931||?
NjVi [Ag 24 1877-Ag 24 1883]
NjWdHi N 1 1878;Je 25 1880

NEWTON

NEW JERSEY herald. w 1829+
Title varies: New Jersey herald and Sussex county democrat; New Jersey herald and Sussex county democratic republican
pub 1844+
DLC 1840-Jl 12,26,O 18 1841;D 5-19 1857;Ja-F 13,27-Mr 6,20,Ap 17-24,My 8-Je 5,19,Jl 3, 31,Ag 14-28,S 11,O 2,16,30-N 13 1858
NNHi F 19 1839;Mr 13 1873
Nj Ag 1855-Ag 21 1858
NjHi [1865-67]75-81;F 28,Mr 21-28,N 28 1883; D 17 1891;Je 7 1917

SUSSEX democrat. w 1858
NjHi Ja 5-12 1860

*SUSSEX register. w Jl 6 1813+
CSmH Jl 12 1830;Ap 14 1834
DLC D 21 1824;Jl 15,Ag 19 1839;Ag 14 1847
MWA Ja 15 1827;Jl 29 1833
NN S 4 1842;S 4 1843
NNHi Je 25 1821;Ap 7,Jl 28,Ag 25,N 13 1822; Jl 24 1826;S 10-O 1,D 17 1827;Mr 24 1828;N 16 1829;Ap 26,D 27 1830;O 15,N 5 1832;Je 12 1863;My 15 1873
NjHi [1821-F 9 1835]My 5 1849[65-67]Je 1 1887;97-S 1900
NjR [1873;1918-19]
PMilD F 5 1822
PMilHi Je 23 1845

NORTH PLAINFIELD

SOMERSET advocate. w Ja 16 1931+
pub 1931+

NUTLEY

Nutley NEWS. w 1927+
pub 1927+

Nutley SUN. w 1894+
pub 1905+
NjNu D 9,23 1916;N 10,D 15 1917;Ja 26 1918; Ja 4 1919;Jl 23 1927;Ap 22,Ag 1 1930

OCEAN BEACH. *See* BELMAR

OCEAN CITY

Ocean City PRESS. w 1929+
NjWdHi Mr 12 1931

NEW JERSEY (*Continued*)

OCEAN GROVE

PHILADELPHIAN and Ocean Grove record. *See* Ocean Grove record

Ocean Grove RECORD. w Je 5 1875-1908||?
1877-79 as Philadelphian and Ocean Grove record. Merged with Ocean Grove times
NjAs Je 1875;77;80;83
NjFHi Ap 9 1881;N 4 1882;O 20 1883
NjHi 1885-87;90-91
NjR 1875-79

Daily SPRAY. d during summer months
NjAs Je-Ag 1882-86;Je 20-S 2 1887;Je-Ag 1891-92;Jl-Ag 1896-1900

Ocean Grove TIMES. w 1893+
pub D 28 1895+
NjFHi Mr 15 1935+

ORANGE

Orange ADVERTISER. w 1898-1924||
NjO 1899-1900;04-05;07-24

Orange ADVOCATE. w 1909-10||
NjHi [Ag 6 1909-Ap 15 1910]

Daily CHRONICLE. w,d 1869-1913||
1869-1908 as Orange chronicle
w 1869-1908
ICM S 23-30,O 14 1893
Nj 1903-13
NjEo 1903-13
NjHi [1889-1908]
NjO complete

COURIER. *See* North Jersey courier

Orange JOURNAL. w Jl 1 1854-1907||
CoD Ap 8,20-22 1865
MWA D 26 1863;Mr 9 1872;Ap 1 1876;Ja 30 1886
NjHi [1875-1908]
NjN My-Je 1907
NjO 1854-58;85-1907
OClWHi Je 11 1864

Orange evening MAIL. d 1888-91
NjO 1889-91

NORTH Jersey courier. w,d F 6 1925+
1925-O 20 1926 as Courier; N 8 1926-S 30 1930 Daily courier
w 1925-O 29 1926
Nj 1925+
NjEo 1925+
NjO 1925+

PALISADES PARK

INFORMATION. w 1930+
pub Ap 1930+

PASSAIC

Passaic Sunday EAGLE. w 1927+
pub 1927+

HERALD-NEWS. d Ag 6 1872+
1872-1932? as Passaic City herald
NjHi [1875]Mr 25 1886;Ja 30,F 27,O 16 1890;Je 6 1898;Jl 18,20-21 1903;Je 1 1922

ITEM. w Jl 9 1870-1908||?
Nj 1870-79

JEWISH record. w 1927+
1927-28? as Passaic county Jewish record (Paterson)
pub 1928+

Passaic City RECORD. w My 21 1890-N 30 1907||
Nj complete
NjHi [Je 11 1890-Ap 16]O 2,16 1891

SZABAD sajto (Free press). w 1907-31||?
In Hungarian
PPiHi D 15 1923

Passaic WOCHENBLATT. w 1888+
In German
pub 1901+

PATERSON

Morning CALL. d 1885+
DLC N 27 1897-Je 30 1899
NjPa O 1885-89;92+

Paterson Sunday CALL. w 1885-89||
NjPa O 1885-Ja 27 1889

Paterson weekly CALL. w 1885-89||
NjPa O 1885-Ja 17 1889

Paterson CHRONICLE and Essex and Bergen advertiser. w 1822-
CSmH Ag 24 1825
MWA Je 4 1823
NjHi O 8 1823

Paterson Sunday CHRONICLE. w 1894-1927||?
NjPa 1899;1902-08

Paterson COURIER. w 1833-
Ct My 6 1835
MWA Ja 28,O 7 1835
N O 15 1833
NjR Mr 25 1834

Paterson GUARDIAN. d 1836-S 25 1915||
Title varies: Passaic guardian and Paterson advertiser] Daily Patersonian; Paterson guardian and Passaic and Bergen advertiser; Paterson daily guardian and Falls City register United with Paterson daily press to form Paterson press-guardian
NNHi F 1 1845;Jl 4 1848
NjHi [1865-67]
NjPa 1856-[58-63]67-[72]-[1900-01]-15
NjR Mr 5 1839

Paterson GUARDIAN. w 1836-1900?
1836-64? as Passaic guardian and Paterson advertiser; 1865?-67? Patersonian
Ct [1836]
MWA S 13 1864
NjPa N 17 1857-59;62;68-71;Jl 1874-Je 1875; 83-84
NjR Mr 5 1839

Paterson HOME journal. *See* Paterson journal

INDEPENDENT democrat and Paterson intelligencer. w -F 1857||
Follows Paterson intelligencer
NjHi Ag 1856-F 18 1857

Paterson INTELLIGENCER. w 1829-Ag 1856||
Followed by Independent democrat and Paterson intelligencer
CSmH S 15 1830
DLC Jl 8-29,S 16,30,D 2 1829;D 8-15 1830;Ja 12-19 1831
NNHi Jl 15 1829;Ja 11 1832;D 27 1837;Mr 7,21-Ap 4,18,My 9,Jl 11-18,Ag,S 26-O 3,24,N 21-D 12,26 1838;Mr 6 1839
NjHi Ap 22 1829;O 14 1835;O 1848-56
NjPa Mr 1833-F 1836

Paterson JOURNAL. w 1880-83||?
1880-81 as Paterson home journal
WHi Mr 26,My 7 1881

NEW JERSEY flying post. w S 25 1893-
NjPa S-N 30 1893

Paterson evening NEWS. d 1890+
pub 1890+
NjPa Ja 14 1902+

Het OOSTEN. w 1904+
In Dutch
IU D 7 1917-Ja 2 1920
MiG Ap 1906-F 13 1920

PASSAIC guardian and Paterson advertiser. *See* Paterson guardian

PATERSONIAN. *See* Paterson guardian

Paterson PEOPLE. w 1894-1902||?
WHi O 15 1898

Paterson weekly PRESS. w 1863-1902||?
NjPa S 1863-66;68-71;75-77;80;89-91;95;98

Paterson PRESS GUARDIAN. d S 19 1863-Je 1920||
1863-Je 14 1907 as Paterson press; Je 15 1907-S 25 1915 as Paterson daily press
S 19 1913 is 50th anniversary number
DLC Jl 25 1867-74;98;Ja-Je 1900
ICM F 12 1885
MBAt Ap 15,26 1865
MWA My 5 1868;S 19 1913
Nj 1899-Je 1915
NjHi [1871-74]-[77-1913]
NjPa complete

Paterson daily REGISTER. d
NjHi [1865]

De TELEGRAAF. w 1880-D 28 1921||
In Dutch
IU D 1917-21

Paterson morning TIMES. d 1922-N 1923||?
NjPa N 1922-N 1923

PAULSBORO

HERALD and report. *See* News-herald

HERALD-SUN. *See* News-herald

Paulsboro NEWS. w 1924-28||
United with Herald-sun to form News-herald
NjWdN 1927-28

NEWS-HERALD. w 1910+
1910-18? as Paulsboro report; 1919?-20 Herald and report; 1921-27 Herald-sun
pub 1924+
NjWdHi My 21 1925
NjWdN 1924-34

Paulsboro REPORT. *See* News-herald

Paulsboro SUN. w 1905-20||
United with Herald and report to form Herald-sun, later News-herald

PENNS GROVE

Penns Grove RECORD. w N 23 1878+
pub 1878+
NjPg O 12 1929+
NjWdHi Ja 22-29 1931

PERTH AMBOY

Perth Amboy CHRONICLE. d 1890-1913||
NjR Je 21 1904
NjPe 1891-Jl 29 1896;Ag 1898-[1907-12]-Mr 5 1913

Perth Amboy GAZETTE. w 1874-79||
NjR F 21 1878
NjPe Ag 3 1876-Ag 29 1878;Ja 10-Ag 29 1879

Weekly GUARDIAN. w 1873-75||
NjPe Jl 4 1873[74]-Jl 22 1875

HIRADO (Herald). w 1920+
In Hungarian
pub 1920+
PPiHi [N 13 1923-Jl 16 1931]

JERSEY mosquito. *See* Mosquito

Perth Amboy JOURNAL. w Ja 1 1858-
NjPe Ja 1,N 13 1858-S 7 1861

MIDDLESEX county democrat. w Jl 28 1859-1907||?
Suspended from F 23 1860-My 16 1868
N O 30 1869;Ap 2,Ag 20 1870
NjHi N 22 1879;Mr 12 1887
NjPe 1859-[99]
NjR [1874-76]
PP Je 30 1883

MOSQUITO. w 1910-31||?
1910-23? as Jersey mosquito
NjPe [Ag 1922-25]-Mr 15 1926
NjR [1917-18;20-26]

NEW JERSEY era. w 1867-68||
NjHi [1867]
NjPe S 1-O 20,N 3 1866-Ag 24,S 7,S 21-D 21 1867;Ja 1868
NjR Ag 3 1867

Perth Amboy evening NEWS. 1903+
NjPe 1906+
NjR Je 16,22 1904[32;34]

Perth Amboy RECORD. w 1923-29||
NjPe [O 1923-25]-[1928-29]

Perth Amboy TIMES. O 2 1858-Jl 6 1859||
NjPe complete

PHILLIPSBURG

Phillipsburg DEMOCRAT. *See* Warren democrat

WARREN advocate. w Ja 24 1825-
PE F 2,16-23 1825

WARREN county democrat. *See* Warren democrat

WARREN democrat. w 1868-74||?
1868-69 as Phillipsburg democrat; 1870?-72? Warren county democrat
MWA Ag 19 1869

PISCATAWAYTOWN

RARITAN independent. w 1910?-
NjR O 28 1921

PITMAN

LEADER. w My 1924+
pub 1924+

Pitman Grove REVIEW. bw 1903+
pub 1903-16;19+
NjWdHi F 4,Mr 6-11 1931;D 21 1932;Mr 29 1933

SOUTH Jersey progressive. w 1913-
NjVi [1913]

PLAINFIELD

CENTRAL New Jersey times. w 1868-99||?
MWA Ap 8 1875-Mr 27 1879
NjHi My 21 1885;Ag 12 1886;N 19 1890

Plainfield COURIER. d 1891-N 3 1894||
United with Plainfield evening news to form Plainfield courier-news
NjPl 1893[94]

Plainfield COURIER-NEWS. d Je 2 1884+
1884-N 3 1894 as Plainfield evening news
pub 1884+
NjPl 1893-[1900-03]-[07]-[09]-[11]-[13]+
NjR Je 2 1934

Plainfield GAZETTE. w 1848-F 1864||
NjHi 1850-51

Plainfield evening NEWS. *See* Plainfield courier-news

Plainfield daily PRESS. 1887-O 7 1916||
Merged with Plainfield courier-news
NjPl Jl 23 1888;93-1916

Plainfield UNION. w 1837-68||
NjHi [1862-67]
NjPl [1837-41;43-45;47;50-52;67]
NjR N 29 1864
OClWHi Jl 25 1866

PLEASANTVILLE

Pleasantville PRESS and Ventnor news. w 1893+
1893-Ag 1929 as Pleasantville press
pub 1898+

POINT PLEASANT

BEACON. w 1883-1915||
Followed by Ocean county leader and beacon
NNHi F 5 1909

OCEAN county leader and beacon. w 1916+
Follows Beacon

PRINCETON

Monthly ADVERTISER. m F 1871-Ja 1872||
NjT My 1871-72

Princeton COURIER and literary register. w 1831-35||
NNHi Jl 28,O 6 1832
NjHi Ja 28,Mr 17,Ap 14 1832
NjP Ja 9 1832

Princeton HERALD. N 1 1923+
pub 1923+
NjP 1923+

JERSEY blue. w S 17-N 5 1844||
NjP complete

MERCER county mirror. w Ap 3 1855-56||
Merged with Princeton standard, later Princeton packet
NjP [1855-56]

NEW JERSEY patriot. w Ag 10 1826-
DLC S 27,O 12,26-N 30,D 14(extra)15-28 1826; Ja 4-11,25-Ap 5,19-My 5,24,30,Je 14-28,Jl 1-19,Ag 2-O 12 1827
MWA N 16 1826
NjP [1826-27]photostat of DLC's copies

NEW JERSEY (*Continued*)

PRINCETON—*Continued*

Princeton PACKET. w S 7 1832+
S-D 1832 as American system and farmer's and mechanic's advocate; Ja 1833-Ag 18 1854 Princeton whig (subtitle varies) Ag 25 1854-D 28 1860 Princeton press; Ja 4 1861-Ap 1 1870 Princeton standard; Ap 7 1870-D 28 1872 Princetonian; Ja 4 1873-F 5 1916 Princeton press
DLC N 8 1832;D 18 1840;Mr 26,Ag-S 10,O 1, 15-D 1841;Ap 22-Jl 8,22-Ag 12,26-N 11 1842
ICM Mr 28 1885
MWA 1835-37;Ag 14 1840;Ap 4 1845;N 29 1850;F 28,Mr 28 1851;S 16-23,O 14 1853;O 20-N 17,D 8 1854[55]Ja 9,F 27,Mr 27-Ap 3, 17-My 8 1857;Jl 10 1863;Jl 2 1869
NN S 23 1842
NNHi O 18 1861
NjHi Ap 28 1837;My 17 1839;Ap 16,28 1841; 55-58;68-7-;73-1908
NjP O 9 1835;36-37[39-44]-97;1909+
NjR O 2,13 1835;N 10 1837;Ag 27 1841;Je 7 1844;F 9 1849[58-59;65;70-84;86;1910
OClWHi Jl 20 1866

Princeton PRESS. *See* Princeton packet

PRINCETONIAN. 1870-72. *See* Princeton packet

Princeton STANDARD. w Ag 24 1859-D 1860||
United with Princeton press to form Princeton standard, later Princeton packet

Princeton STANDARD. 1861-70. *See* Princeton packet

Princeton WHIG. *See* Princeton packet

RAHWAY

Rahway ADVOCATE. *See* New Jersey advocate

BRIDGETON museum. . . *See* New Jersey advocate

DEMOCRATIC republican. *See* Union democrat

Rahway HERALD and New Jersey general advertiser. sw
NjHi Ap 15 1837

Rahway MUSEUM. *See* New Jersey advocate

NATIONAL democrat. *See* Union democrat

NEW JERSEY advocate. w Jl 13 1822-1911||?
Jl 13-Ag 3 1822 as Bridgeton museum and New Jersey advocate. Ag 10 1822-27? Rahway museum and New Jersey advocate: 1827 New Jersey advocate and Middlesex and Essex advertiser; 1828-S 5 1850 New Jersey advocate; S 12 1850-63 Advocate and register; 1864 Advocate and times; 1864-81 Weekly advocate and times; 1882-87 Rahway advocate
CtY Mr 11 1823
DLC O 27 1829;Je 4 1833
KHi Jl 21 1864
MWA S 12,26,D 12 1845;Mr 20-27 1846;Ag 21 1852
NNHi O 9 1852
Nj S 27 1831-S 22 1834
NjHi S 1848-Ag 1853[65-67]My 21-28 1881[83-94]
NjR N 30 1830;S 1 1843;Mr 1 1844;D 26 1845
OClWHi Jl 19 1866
OHi Ja 20 1854

Daily RAHWEGIAN. d S 1878-
NjR N 13 1878

Rahway RECORD. sw 1822+
O 7 1932 is 110th anniversary number
pub 1822+
KHi [My 11 1915-Ag 8 1919]
NjR O 7 1932

REGISTER and times. w
NjHi [1862]

TOWN news. w Ap 14 1888-
NjHi Ap 14,Jl 7,O 6-13,N 5,D 28 1888

UNION democrat w 1840-94||
1840 as Democratic republican; -1862 Union democrat and Rahway republican; 1862-90 National democrat
NjHi [1862;85-91]-94

RAMSEY

Ramsey JOURNAL. w 1892+
pub 1899+

RARITAN TOWNSHIP

RARITAN weekly times. w D 5 1929+
NjR 1934+

RED BANK

ECHO. w 1904+
Negro
NjFHi [1911]

NEW JERSEY standard. *See* Standard

Red Bank REGISTER. w Je 1878+
pub 1878+
NjFHi 1878+

Red Bank STANDARD. w Ap 1 1852+
Follows Democratic banner and Monmouth county advertiser (Matawan) 1852-1903;O 21 1904-10? as New Jersey standard 1852-58 pub in Matawan and Keyport
NjFHi Ap 8,My 20,D 8,22 1852[Ap 1853-Ap 1854;59-60;62-64;69;78-81;88]1901-04;Je 1906-My 1910[12-13;21]28+
NjHi [1867]

RIDGEFIELD PARK

Ridgefield Park BULLETIN. w 1900+
pub 1900+
NjRp Ap 2 1926+

RIDGEWOOD

Ridgewood HERALD. w N 1 1898+
pub N 1904+

Ridgewood NEWS. w 1890+
pub 1895-98;1904-05;11-13;15-19;21+

RIVERTON

NEW ERA. w 1892+
pub 1892+

ROCKAWAY

Rockaway RECORD. w 1888+
NjHi N 23 1899-Je 28 1900;My 2-Je 6 1901

ROSELLE

NORTH Jersey enterprise. w 1898-1901||?
MWA Ag 10 1899

SPECTATOR. w Ap 16 1916+
pub 1916+

ROSENHAYN

Rosenhayn ADVOCATE. w 1890-95||
NjVi [1894-95]

ROSEVILLE

Papers published in Roseville are listed under Newark

RUTHERFORD

BERGEN advertiser. w 1907-17||?
NjR Ja 3 1913

BERGEN county herald. w 1872-97||
NjHi N 1896-N 1897

SALEM

AMERICAN statesman and literary journal. w My 22 1830-
CSmH Jl 10 1830
MWA Ag 7,N 13 1830
N O 12 1833
NjR My 26 1832

FREEMAN'S banner. w
DLC D 16 1835
PEL O 17 1834

HARRISONIAN democrat. w
Nj Ap 18-O 31 1840

Salem MESSENGER. *See* Salem standard and Jerseyman

NATIONAL standard. *See* Salem standard and Jerseyman

SOUTH Jerseyman. w 1881-1904||
United with National standard to form Salem standard and Jerseyman
NjSS complete

*__Salem STANDARD and Jerseyman.__ w S 19 1819+
1819-22? as Salem messenger; 1823?-39? Salem messenger and public advertiser; 1840-1904 National standard
pub 1851+
DLC Jl 28,N 17 1824
MWA Ap 15 1829;Ap 11 1866
NNHi Je 15 1870;Ap 9 1873
NjCHi Ja 28-F 11,25 1932
NjHi Ap 24 1822;D 29 1824;Ag 17,D 7 1825[Ap 12 1827-N 10 1830]Ap 11,25 1832;73-[1904-18]
NjPg O 12 1929+
NjWdHi Ap 9 1823;O 10 1824;My 24 1826;My 23 1827;Mr 11 1829;Ja 17 1849;S 4 1895;Mr 13 1912[Ja-My 1931 My-Je 1932]

Salem SUNBEAM. w 1844+
pub 1860+
DLC D 7 1844
MWA O 8 1858 Ja 9 1863;My 7 1869;Ag 5 1931
NNHi Je 10 1870;Mr 21 1873
NjHi [1861-67]
NjR Je 17 1853
NjWdHi Je 14,N 1 1861;O 14 1931;Jl-[S]1933

SEA ISLE CITY

CAPE MAY county times. w 1886+
pub 1915+
NjV 1887-98

Sea Isle City GAZETTE. w 1888-
In German and English
NjVi 1888-89

Sea Isle REVIEW. w 1886-87||
NjVi [1886]

SEABRIGHT

Seabright NEWS-SENTINEL. w 1925+

Seabright SENTINEL. w 1879-1918||
NjFHi O 1897-N 10 1905;S 21 1918

SEASIDE HEIGHTS

OCEAN county review. w 1912+
PP O 4 1918;D 12 1924[27]+

SERGEANTSVILLE

MILITARY review. w
NjFHi F 1,Je 1 1859

SHORT-HILLS

Short-Hills ITEM. m,w,bw 1888-1915||
1888-89 as News item
m 1888-89
NjHi 1888-89;Ja 10,24,F 7 1891;Ap 11 1901;O 15 1903

NEWS item. *See* Short Hills item

SOMERVILLE

POLITICAL intelligencer. *See* Somerset messenger-gazette

SOMERSET county news. w D 1 1859-63||
United with Somerset whig to form Somerset unionist, later Unionist-gazette
NjHi O 1862
NjR [1860;62]

SOMERSET democrat w 1888-1931||?
NjHi Ag 30,O 4 1889

SOMERSET gazette. sw,w D 21 1848-Ap 1 1882||
Title varies slightly. United with Somerset unionist to form Unionist-gazette
sw 1877-Ja 17 1878
NjHi [1867]76-82
NjR [1878-80]

*__SOMERSET messenger-gazette.__ w,sw 1820+
1820-S 1823? as Political intelligencer; O 1823-1930 Somerset messenger (Title varies)
pub 1931+
DLC S 28,30 O 28,N 17 1829 O 19 1841;1931+
MWA F 3 1876
NNHi D 16 1823-Mr 1831
NjHi Ap 24 1828;My 21 1829;Ap 11 1832;Ag 28 1833;Je 4 1834;D 29 1835;Mr 5 1844;O 11 1848-(59-67) S 1870-76;Mr 1 1877
NjR [1824;31;34-37;52;70-71]97-1910[15]-30;Je 1934+
OClWHi My 4 1865

SOMERSET whig. w 1834-
MWA O 6 1835

UNION. w Jl 30 1856-
NjR Ag 13,S 3 1856

UNIONIST-gazette. w Ag 12 1834-D 30 1930||
1834-F 26 1863 as Somerset whig; Mr 5 1863-Mr 26 1882 Somerset unionist. United with Somerset messenger to form Somerset messenger-gazette
DLC Je 27 1929-30
MBAt Ap 20 1865
MWA F 15 1866
N Ag 16-30 1842
NNHi D 31 1851
NjHi O 1848-S 1854[58;62]Mr 1870-Ja 1871;My 1882-[91]
NjR [1834-35;40-41;49;51;54;59;62;64-66;80;82; 84;93;96]-1930
NjSoM 1834-59;64-1930

SOUTH AMBOY

ARGUS. w 1873-79||
NjR [1875]-[79]

South Amboy CITIZEN. w. 1881+
pub 1899+
NjR [1882;87;1908;13;19;22;24-29]

SOUTH ORANGE

South Orange BULLETIN. m,sm,w 1869-1906||
NNHi D 1870;Ja 1 1873
NjHi [D 15 1872-O 18 1877]
NjO 1871-74;76-92;94-96;98-1906

South Orange RECORD. w 1919+
NjMa Ja 2 1920-S 29 1922

SOUTH RIVER

South River SPOKESMAN. w 1919+
pub 1919+

SPRING LAKE

Spring Lake GAZETTE. w 1881+
Follows Seaside (Manasquan)
1881-1913? as Seaside gazette
NjFHi Mr 7,S 12 1891;Ja 15 1897 O 12 1906;Mr 7 1935+
TxGR Ap 20 1889;Ap 4 1891

SPRINGFIELD

Springfield SUN. w S 27 1929+
pub 1929+

STOCKTON

CAMDEN times. *See under* Camden

STONE HARBOR

AVALON coast reporter. *See* Seven mile beach reporter

SEVEN mile beach reporter. w 1910+
1910-16 as Avalon coast reporter
pub 1918+

NEW JERSEY (*Continued*)

SUSSEX

Sussex INDEPENDENT. w 1870+
pub 1870+
NjHi Ap 1917-1926

WANTAGE recorder. w 1894+
pub 1894+
NjHi 1909-Jl 1910;14-17

SWEDESBORO

Swedesboro NEWS. w 1890+
pub 1927+
NjWdN 1927+

Swedesboro TIMES. w 1870-87||?
NNHi N 14 1872

TEANECK

TIMES-REVIEW. w 1913+
pub 1932+
NjRp 1926+

TOMS RIVER

FREE press. w My 21 1863-
MWA Jl 2 1863

NEW JERSEY courier. w 1850+
1850-66 as Ocean emblem
pub 1866+
DLC Ag-O 7,21 1868-Ap 7,Je 9-Jl 21,Ag 11-18 1869
MWA F 20 1856;O 4 1866;O 21 1868-F 3 1869
NNHi O 22 1856-O 24 1860;Ja 23 1873
NjFHi Ag 28-N 1850;58[64-65]66-72,74,79-88
NjHi N 1865
NjR [1861-62;65;78;83-84;86]

OCEAN emblem. *See* New Jersey courier

OCEAN signal. w 1851-S 1 1852||
MWA S 1 1852

TRENTON

Trenton Sunday ADVERTISER. *See* Trenton Sunday times-advertiser

ARGUS. w Ja 1 1835-
pub Ap 16,My 14-21,Je 11,Jl 2,Ag 20 1835
DLC F 13 1835
PP F 25 1836

Evening ARGUS. d N 16 1872-D 1873||
United with Daily sentinel to form State sentinel and argus, later State sentinel
Nj 1872-Ag 15 1873
NjHi 1872-73

CLAY banner. w Mr 6?-S 4? 1844||
NjHi Jl 11 1844
NjR Ap 10,S 4 1844

CRISIS. w
DLC S 26 1832

DETECTIVE. Je 1 1871-
NjHi [Je-N 2 1871]
NjR Jl 9 1874

EGYESITES (Consolidation).
In Hungarian
PPiHi Mr 1931

Daily EMPORIUM. d Ag 5 1867-92||
NjHi Ag 24 1865

EMPORIUM and true American. w Je 2 1821-N 13 1849||
1821-Jl 4 1829 as Emporium. United with Trenton daily news to form True American
CSmH Jl 10 1830
Ct [1826-28;30-31;33-37]F 23 1838
DLC Jl 10-17,Ag 7,21,N 13 1824;Ag 25 1827;Ja 5,D 6 1828;Je 27,Jl 4,18-25,Ag 8,O 3,N 21-28 1829;Ja 2-16,F 6,Mr 6 1830;31-Mr 12 1841; Mr-Je 23,Jl 21,Ag 18,N 24,D 8 1843;Mr 1844-S 10 1847
MWA O 4 1823;Jl 17 1824;D 9 1826;D 1 1827;S 6 1828
N O 12 1833
NN D 9 1826
NNHi S 13-20,O 25 1823;Ap 30,S 3 1825;O 20-27,N 4,D 1,8(extra)1827[Mr 3,22 1828;N 28-D 5 1829;Ja 9,30,F 13-Mr 13,Ap 24,My 8 1830;Ja 28 1832;Ap 7 1837
Nj 1821-F 24 1843
NjFHi 1831[33;35]37;Mr 1843-My 1845]
NjHi 1821-My 1827;Je 1830-33;Ap 1837-40
NjP 1824-25
NjR [1825;27-28;33;40;43]
NjT 1821-My 1823
PEL D 9 1826
PP Mr 9 1833[Jl 12 1839-Ap 15 1842]
WHi D 15 1821

EMPORIUM and true American. d
DLC [Ja-F 1840]

*Trenton **FEDERALIST.** w Jl 9 1798-Je 29 1829||
1798-Je 30 1800 as Federalist; New-Jersey gazette; Jl 8 1800-My 4 1802 Federalist and New Jersey state gazette. Followed by New Jersey state gazette, later Trenton state gazette
CtY Jl 28,Ag 18,S 1,15,D 8-15 1828
DLC 1823-24;S 19 1825
MWA Jl 2 1821;Jl 22 1822;D 13 1824;Ap 17 1826
N N 29 1824
NNHi Mr 26,Ap 16,S 3 1821;Mr 31,Ap 28,Ag 25 1823;My 24,Je 28,S 13,D 20 1824;Ja 10,24,F 14,28,My 16,O 24 1825;Ja 16,My 15,Je 12,S 18 N 20(extra)1826;Ja 22-29,Ap 30,My 21,D 17 1827;My 12,Ag 25 1828
Nj 1821-29
NjHi 1821-24
NjR [1821-22;24;26-29]
NjT [1821-25]
OHi O 6,D 1 1823;My 3 1824
PDoHi Je 25 1827;Ap 20,My 11 1829

FUGGETLENSEG (Independence). w 1913+
In Hungarian
pub 1913+
PPiHi D 20 1919[Mr 6 1924-D 9 1931]

Trenton weekly JOURNAL. w 1845-
Follows Sheet anchor of democracy
NNHi O 3 1845

MERCER standard. w N 11 1854-F 22 1856||
Nj complete
NjR Jl 18 1857

Trenton daily MONITOR. d Ja 27 1864-D 1865||
Merged with Trenton state gazette
MBAt Ap 15,17,19 1865
Nj 1864-Ap 1 1865
NjHi [1865]

Trenton weekly MONITOR. w 1864-65||
Merged with Trenton state gazette
NbHi O 26 1865
NjHi Ag 24 1865

NATIONAL union. w N 26 1830-
1830-31 as Union. Followed by New Jersey democrat
DLC Ja 8 1831;O 13 1832
MWA D 14 1830;My 21 1831
NjFHi Jl 28 1832-Jl 27 1833
NjHi Jl 2,16,S 10,O 8 1831;Ja 14,28,My 12,Jl 7,O 20 1832

NEW JERSEY democrat. w
Follows National union
NjFHi Ap 19 1834

NEW JERSEY staats journal. w 1867+
In German
NNHi D 28 1872

NEW JERSEY state gazette. *See* Trenton state gazette

NEW JERSEY weekly visitor. w
NjFHi Je-O 1846
NjWdHi Mr 15 1848

NEW JERSEY volunteer. w Jl 27 1865-
MWA S 21,N 16 1865
NbHi O 5,26 1865
NcD N 16 1865
NjFHi N 16 1865
NjHi Jl 27-O,N 16 1865

Trenton daily NEWS. d Mr 2 1846-N 10 1849||
United with Emporium and true American to form True American
DLC My 21 1846
Nj Mr 29-S 21 1847;N 10 1849
NjR Ja 4,Mr 30,Je 9 1848;Ag 20 1849
NjT 1846-Mr 1847

PATRIOT. d
NjHi O 20 1862
NjR N 19 1861

PEOPLE'S visitor and trade index.
PHi 1878

Weekly PLAINDEALER. w N 27 1846-
MdBJ N 27 1846

Sunday PRESS and Anglo-American. w 1886-90||?
NjHi My 19,S 1 1888

PRZYJACIEL wolnosci (Friends of freedom). w 1919+
In Polish
pub 1919+

PUBLIC opinion. d Ja 1 1874-My 1 1875||
Nj complete
NjHi complete

Weekly PUBLIC opinion. w 1874-78||
Nj 1875-N 7 1878
NjHi 1875-Ja 10 1878
NjR Ag 15 1874

REPUBLICAN. d -Jl 1857||
United with State gazette to form Daily state gazette and republican, later Trenton state gazette
NjR Je 5-6 1857
NjT Ja-Jl 1857

Daily SENTINEL. d -1873||
United with Evening argus to form State sentinel and argus, later State sentinel

SHEET anchor of democracy. tw Ap 25 1843-Jl 12 1845||
Followed by Trenton weekly journal
DLC My 24 1844
MWA My 29,Je 29 1844
Nj Ap-O 20 1843
NjR Ag 18,S 1-8,22-29,O 27,N 2 1843
NjT complete
PP Je 7 1844

STATE capital. w Ag 22 1872-
MWA D 12 1872

Trenton STATE gazette. w Jl 4 1829-1913||
Follows Trenton federalist. 1829-39 as New Jersey state gazette
A Jl 1874-79
CSmH Jl 10 1830
DLC Jl 11-25,S 5,19,N 21,D 5-12,26 1829;30;Ja 15 1831;S 29 1832;Jl 1841-D 16 1842;N 6 1843; F 22-D 1850
MWA My 29 1846;F 19 1880
N Mr 10 1832;Mr 22 1834
NN Ap 6,Je 2 1852
NNHi F 20,Mr 13,Ap 24,My 8 1830;Ag 11,S 8,N 3 1832[Ag 1838-39]-Ja 10 1840;O 28-N 11 1842;Mr 13 1868
NbHi Ja 25,My 24,Ag 19 1877;Ja 6 1881
Nj 1829-39
NjFHi Mr 13,O 6 1830;F 8 1839
NjHi [1830-37]48-58;69-1913
NjR [1845;69-70;79]Ja 25 1883
NjT 1840-89
NjTT Jl 1857-63;84-93;1906-10
PDoHi N 1829;Mr 5 1831
PP [My 26 1871-N 1872]O 23 1873;S 3,O 1 1874;Je 17 1875;Ag 14 1879;S 13-27 1888

STATE gazette. tw Ja 14 1840-D 30 1846||
Followed by Daily state gazette, later Trenton state gazette
Nj complete
NjR [1841-42]

Trenton STATE gazette. d Ja 12 1847+
Ja 12- 1847 as Daily state gazette; F? 1847-Jl 16 1857 State gazette; Jl 17 1857-My 11 1863 Daily state gazette and republican; My 12 1863-Ja 17 1918 Daily state gazette; Ja 18 1918-Ja 29 1927 State gazette
pub 1847+
DLC F 20 1850-Jl 25,Ag 1853-61;63-82;84;98;Jl 1913+
MBAt Ap 18-19 1865
MWA 1850;52;Je 9 1865;Mr 21 1879;Ja 3,Mr 21 1919
NNHi My 20 1873
Nj 1847+
NjHi 1849[61]F 9-20,23 1863
NjR [1908-18;24-29]+
NjTT 1839-Jl 1857;90+
NjWdHi 1847-50
OClWHi Ag 31 1861;S 26,O 3,N 25 1862
PP D 15 1928+

STATE republican news. w Ja 16? 1915-
NjHi N 13 1915-Jl 8 1916

STATE sentinel. w 1866-73||?
1866-70 as Union sentinel; 1871-73? Title varies: State sentinel and argus; State sentinel and capital; etc.
NjFHi S 9 1869
NjHi [1867]Ap 10,My 16 1873

Trenton evening TIMES. d O 12 1882+
1882-Ag 9 1895 as Trenton times
pub 1882+
MWA D 26 1901
Nj 1882+
NjHi 1891[1914]-Jl 13 1918
NjR F 6 1911[31;35]
NjTT 1882+

Trenton TIMES. w Ja 1883-94||?
NjHi 1891

Trenton Sunday TIMES-ADVERTISER. w Ja 7 1883+
1883-1912 as Trenton Sunday advertiser
pub 1883+
MWA Ja 20 1883;Ja 12 1919
Nj 1883-1908
NjR O 27 1929
NjTT 1883+
NjWdHi O 27 1929
VHi Ap 16 1916

TOWN talk. w Ja 31 1891-D 22 1894||
1891 as Trenton town topics
Nj complete

Daily TRENTONIAN. d 1848-51||
NjR My 6 1850

***TRUE American.** w Mr 10 1801-Je 27 1829||
United with Trenton federalist to form New Jersey state gazette, later Trenton state gazette
DLC 1821-28;Mr 21,Je 27 1829
IU Mr 31 1821
MBAt My 25 1822;Ag 6,S 6 1828
MWA [Ap 27-D 14 1822]F 1,22 1823;Mr 20,Ap 24,Je 26,Jl 31,O 9 1824;N 3 1827;Ja 30,Mr 29,Je 20,Ag 2-9,O 4,N 8-15 1828
N My 25 1822
NNHi Je 8,N 23 1822;My 10,Je 28,Jl 12,Ag 2,O 25 1823;Je 19,S 18 1824;Ag 5 1826;Ja 13, 27,Ap 28,N 17,D 8-15 1827
Nj 1821-28
NjHi My 25 1822
NjP [1821-28]
NjR [1822;24-28]
PDoHi Jl 30 1825;D 20 1826;My 5-19 1827;Mr, My 14-21,Je 7,11 1829
PWcT O 12 1822;Mr 29 1823;Mr 16 1826
T S 8,N 3,14,D 1,15 1821

TRUE American. tw Ag 28-O 8 1838||?
Nj Ag-O 8 1838

Trenton evening TRUE American. d N 13 1849-Ag 8 1913||
Formed by the union of Trenton daily news and Emporium and true American. 1849-N 15 1908 as Daily true American; N 16 1908-O 12 1912 Trenton true American
DLC 1854-56;Mr 31 1858-60;O 23 1878-1902
MWA N 2,30 1852[My 23-S 1853;Ja-F]Ag 2,4, O 30 1854;55-[57-My 1858]Ag 19 1859;My 17 1876
Nj 1849-Je 1913
NjCHi Mr 19 1878
NjR [1852;57;78;94]
NjT 1850-62;Jl 1863-Je 1877;78-Je 1886;87-Je 1892;Ja-Je 1893;94-1912
NjWdHi O 19 1893
PP Mr 14,Ap 16,My 3 1856

TRUE American. w N 13 1849-Ag 1913||
Formed by the union of Emporium and true American, and Trenton daily news
DLC 1849-N 1853
MWA N 1 1850;Ja 17,F 14,Mr 7-14 1851[My 27-D 16 1853;54]-[Ja 25-Jl 11 1856]Jl 22 1864
NjHi Jl 1855-Je 1869
NjR [1850;55;57]
NjT 1850-Mr 1853;Jl 1855-Je 1886;Ap 1887-Mr 1888;90-Mr 1900
OClWHi Ag 11 1865

UNION. *See* National union

UNION sentinel. *See* State sentinel

TUCKERTON

Tuckerton BEACON. w 1889+
pub 1889+

NEW JERSEY (*Continued*)

UNION

Union REGISTER. w Ap 30 1925+
1925-O 30 1928 as Register
pub 1925—

UNION BEACH

Union Beach RECORD. w Ap 1925+
pub 1925+

UNION CITY

HUDSON dispatch. d 1872+
NjJ F 1930+
NjU 1924+

HUDSON news. w 1904+
pub 1904—

VENTNOR

Ventnor NEWS. w 1907-Ag 1929||
United with Pleasantville press to form Pleasantville press and Ventnor news

VERONA

Verona NEWS. w Mr 1929-Ja 9 1935||
United with Caldwell progress (Caldwell) to form Caldwell progress-Verona news (Caldwell)
NjCaP [1929-35]
NjVe complete

VINELAND

Vineland ADVERTISER. sm,w D 13 1867-Jl 25 1879||
1868-Ja 2 1869 as Vineland democrat; N 18 1872-My 1874 Vineland advertiser and Cumberland county news
Suspended 1869-N 11 1872
MWA D 28 1867-Ja 25 1868[Mr 1875-S 2 1876]
NjHi Ap-D 1875
NjVi [1867-79]

Daily ADVERTISER. d Je 1-S 25 1875||
MWA [1875]
NjHi Je 1 1875
NjVi [1875]

Vineland CITIZEN. w Jl 27-N 7 1910||
NjVi [1910]

Vineland DEMOCRAT. *See* Vineland advertiser

Vineland daily ENTERPRISE. d Mr 19-Je 30 1888||
Follows News-times
NjVi [1888]

Vineland ENTERPRISE. w Jl 22-O 14 1911||
NjVi [1911]

EVERY Saturday. w Je 20 1891-S 1 1900||
United with Vineland republican to form Vineland republican and Every Saturday
NjVi [1891-1900;]

Morning HERALD. d My 9-My 29 1898||
NjVi [1898]

Vineland INDEPENDENT. w,m Mr 2 1867-1931||?
Ag 1 1880-F 1 1890 as Weekly independent
MWA Ap 22 1876
NNHi My 20 1870
NNS Ap 10 1919
NjBrHi F 28 1872-F 1875
NjVi 1867-1908
WHi O 2 1903;Ap 1,Jl 1 1904;O 18,N 8 1907;Jl 6 1916-O 17 1918;Mr 13 1919-Je 1931

Daily INDEPENDENT. d O 14 1876-Ja 17 1877||
NjVi [1876-77]

INGLESIDE. w 1881-Jl 8 1882||
NjVi [1881-82]

Weekly ITEM. w O 1874-Jl 20 1877||
MWA D 9 1875
NjVi [1875-77]

Evening JOURNAL. d Je 7 1875+
1875-D 13 1890 as Daily journal
NjVi [1875]90+

Weekly JOURNAL. w Je 14 1879-Mr 11 1882||
1879-D 3 1880 as Peoples advocate
NjVi [1879-82]

Evening LEDGER. d Jl 9 1888-Ja 22 1889||
Jl 9-N 24 1888 as Morning ledger
NjVi [1888-89]

Morning NEWS. d O 29 1881-F 10 1882||
United with Daily times to form News-times
NjVi [1881-82]

Vineland weekly NEWS. d,w F 4 1889-N 27 1908||
1889-Je 1890 as Vineland daily news (d)
NjVi [1889-1908]

Vineland evening NEWS. d S 11 1905-Mr 17 1906||
NjVi [1905-06]

NEWS-TIMES. d N 17 1877-N 28 1887||
1877-F 10 1882 as Daily times. Followed by Vineland daily enterprise
NjVi [1877-87]

PEOPLES advocate. *See* Weekly journal

POST. w S 18 1925+
NjVi 1925+

Vineland REPUBLICAN and every Saturday. d,sw,w 1891-Je 18 1904||
1891-1903 as Vineland republican
d 1891-S 1 1900;sw S 8 1900-Mr 1901
NjVi 1892-[94-95;1900-04]

Millville and Vineland daily REPUBLICAN. d F 7 1907—
NjVi [1907]+

ROSTRUM. bw N 17 1883-Mr 19 1887||
NjVi complete

Vineland RURAL. m
MWA My 1863;F(supp)N(supp)1867;F 1868
NN Jl,S 1866(supp);Ja,D 1877
NNHi Ap 2 1870
NjR Ag 1864
PWCl N 1864

SOUTH Jersey leader. w Mr 13-Jl 24 1878||
NjVi [1878]

SOUTH Jersey sun. w My 4 1906-Ja 3 1907||
My- 1906 as Vineland sun
NjVi [1906-07]

SOUTH Jersey telephone. w O 25 1895-1903||?
NjVi [1895-96;1903]

Morning STAR. My 1894-D 28 1895||
NjVi [1894-95]

Vineland SUN. *See* South Jersey sun

Morning TELEPHONE. d Ap 23-My 3 1887||?
NjVi [1887]

Daily TIMES. 1877-82. *See* News-times

Vineland TIMES. w,sw,d 1887+
Suspended 1902-O 1925
w 1887-Mr 30 1926;sw Ap 1926-D 9 1927
pub 1925+
NjVi [1887-1902]25+

VALLEY ventura. w Ja 30 1903-D 7 1907||
NjVi complete

Vineland WEEKLY. w S 9 1865-Ag 1 1880||
Merged with Vineland independent
CtY F 24 1872
KHi My 29 1875
NNHi My 21 1870;Mr 8 1873
NjVi 1865-[76]-[78-80]

WALLINGTON

Wallington REVIEW. w 1921+
pub 1921+

WASHINGTON

Washington STAR. w 1868+
NjR Jl 14 1876[1929-30]+

Washington SUN. d
PMcT Ja 2-7 1879

WARREN tidings. w 1877-1915||?
NjR My 21-28 1913

WATERTOWN

JEFFERSONIAN. w
InRE O 4 1841

WEST ORANGE

Weekly REVIEW of West Orange. w 1931+
pub 1931+
NjO 1931+

WESTFIELD

Westfield LEADER. w S 1890+
pub 1911+

Westfield STANDARD. w 1884+
1884-1913? as Union county standard
NjHi Ja 27 1894;F 25,My 14 1909;Mr-Ap 1 1910
NjR [1916]

UNION county standard. *See* Westfield standard

WESTVILLE

Westville NEWS. w Ap 29 1926-31||?
NjWdHi O 1 1931

WESTWOOD

Westwood CHRONICLE. w 1895+
pub 1935+

Westwood NEWS. w O 1922+
pub 1922+

WHITEHOUSE STATION

FAMILY casket. *See* Chronicle (Bound Brook)

Whitehouse REVIEW. w Ap 1 1897+
pub 1897+

WILDWOOD

FIVE Mile Beach journal. *See* Wildwood tribune-journal

Wildwood JOURNAL. *See* Wildwood tribune-journal

Wildwood LEADER. w 1920+
pub 1921+
NjW Jl 1 1926+

Wildwood SUN-TRIBUNE. w 1900-24||?
1900-18? as Wildwood journal. United with Five Mile beach journal to form Wildwood journal, later Wildwood tribune-journal
NjWT 1901-02;23-24

Wildwood TRIBUNE-JOURNAL. w 1890+
1890-1924 as Five Mile Beach journal; 1924-25 Wildwood journal
pub 1890-1923;25+
NjW Jl 22 1898-My 1923

WILLIAMSTOWN

PLAIN dealer. w O 1926+
pub 1926+

WOODBRIDGE

Woodbridge GAZETTE. w 1866-
NjHi [1867]
NjR [1866-67]
OClWHi Jl 23 1866

INDEPENDENT hour. w Ap 13 1876-98||?
NjR N 6 1879;F 14 1895

Woodbridge LEADER. 1891+
1891-1910? as Weekly register, devoted to the interests of Woodbury, Carteret, Sewaren and vicinity
NjR My 5,14 1904

Woodbridge NEWS; an independent family newspaper. w 1899-1909||?
NjR Mr 20 1903

Weekly REGISTER. *See* Woodbridge leader

WOODBURY

CONSTITUTION and farmers' and mechanics advertiser. w Ag 19 1834+
Title varies slightly
pub 1834-[1915-27]-[29]+
CtY N 20 1849
DLC D 1 1840
MWA S 23 1834
NjCHi N 9-30 1904;Je 27 1903
NjHi [1865-67]
NjR S 13 1922
NjWdHi 1834-[1915]16;24[25-34]
NjWdN N 24,O 8 1857;O 2 1860;My 3 1865
PP Jl 9 1839

GLOUCESTER county democrat. *See* Evening news and Gloucester county democrat

GLOUCESTER farmer. *See* Village herald and Gloucester advertiser

HERALD and Gloucester farmer. *See* Village herald and Gloucester advertiser

LIBERAL press. w 1877-97||?
NjWdHi N 19 1897

Evening NEWS and Gloucester county democrat. w,d O 1878+
1878-1932 as Gloucester county democrat
pub 1878+
NjCHi [1905-23]
NjHi 1904-O 17 1907
NjWdHi [1894-95;1903-31;33]Je 16 1934

Woodbury daily TIMES. d F 2 1897+
NjCHi N 21 1908
NjHi S 30-O 21 1907
NjWdHi F 2 1897[99;1903;10-12 16-17;19-21;23-25;27-28;31-33]

VILLAGE herald and Gloucester advertiser. w Ja 1 1817- 1840||
1817-F 13 1820 as Gloucester farmer; D 20 1820-S 8 1824 Herald and Gloucester farmer; S 15 1824-F 20 1833 Village herald and weekly advertiser. Followed by West Jersey democrat, later Democrat (Camden) 1819-D 13 1820 pub in Camden
DLC D 19 1832
MWA S 23 1829;S 29 1830
NjCHi 1821-Mr 26 1823;S 15 1824-Ag 26 1829
NjHi S 17 1823;Jl 7 1824;N 22 1826;S 22 1830
NjP 1826-S 21 1836
NjWdHi Ap 17 1822;Ag 4 1824;My,O 1826;Je 16 1830-Mr 2 1831;N 5 1834;F 4 1835;Ja 9 1838
NjWdN Je 16 1824
NjWdS S 1829-F 20 1833
PP F 27 1833-Ag 16 1837

WOOD-RIDGE

Wood-Ridge INDEPENDENT. w 1926+
pub 1926+

WOODSTOWN

Woodstown MONITOR. w 1884-91||?
United with Woodstown register to form Woodstown monitor-register

Woodstown MONITOR-REGISTER. w 1869+
1869-91? as Woodstown register
NjElT Mr 1921-Je 1923
NjHi Ag 16,30,S 13,27,O 18 1907
NjWdHi Jl 1 1926

Woodstown REGISTER. *See* Woodstown monitor-register

WYCKOFF

Wyckoff NEWS. w 1926+
pub 1926+
NjHi [F 1929-My 1930]

NEW MEXICO

ALAMOGORDO

ADVERTISER. w 1927+
1927-28 as Southwestern advertiser
pub 1927+

CLOUDCROFTER. w 1913-Jl 1922||
Merged with News
NmHi 1917
NmU [1917-My 1920]

NEWS. w 1898+
1898-1920 as Otero county news
pub 1898+
KHi Jl 1 1905
NmHi 1917-20

OTERO county news. *See* News

SOUTHWESTERN advertiser. *See* Advertiser

ALBUQUERQUE

La BANDERA americana. w 1903+
In Spanish
pub 1903+
IU 1917-Ag 15 1924;Jl 10-N 1925;26
NmHi 1917-21;26-28
NmU [1917-25;29+]
WHi Jl 30 1920

Evening CITIZEN. *See* Evening journal

Albuquerque DEMOCRAT. w 1881-93||?
CU-B Ag 3-10,31-S 7 1890

Albuquerque morning DEMOCRAT. *See* Albuquerque journal 1880+

DEMOCRAT and journal. *See* Albuquerque journal 1880+

HEALTH city sun. w 1929+
pub 1929+
NNHi Ag 28 1931
NmA O 1929-Mr 1933

Evening HERALD. *See* Evening journal

Sunday HERALD and New Mexico ruralist. w 1918-22||
1918-21 as New Mexico ruralist
NmU [My 1918-F 1920]

El INDEPENDIENTE. w 1894+
1894-1932 pub at Las Vegas
In Spanish
pub 1932+
IU [D 1917-O 10 1918]
NmU [Mr-Jl 1935]

Albuquerque JOURNAL. w 1879-86||?
KHi My 1881-Jl 12 1886

Albuquerque JOURNAL. d 1880+
1880-89 as Albuquerque morning democrat; 1889-90? Democrat and journal; 1891-98? Albuquerque morning democrat; 1899?-S 1903 Albuquerque journal-democrat; O 1903-25 Albuquerque morning journal
pub 1882+
CLM Ap 18 1889
CSmH Mr 13 1884
CU-B Ap 7-11,O 19,D 3,15 1884;Je 8-10,14, 18,Ag 27,S 2,O 22 1887;Ja 30 1890
Ct Ag 17,25-S 1 1903
DLC 1900-Je 1901;Ja-Je 1904;06+
KHi Ag 5 1915[N 1920]F 5 1929
NmA [O 1907+]
NmAC 1912+
NmHi O 1882-83;88-90;N 1912-Mr,Jl 1915-O,D 1918-Mr,My 1919-Jl,O 1921-Mr,Jl 1922-23;F 1924-Ag,N 1929;Ap 1931+
NmLS F 1909+
NmU 1907-17;21+
OClWHi Ja 1 1898;D 8-9 1899

Albuquerque morning JOURNAL. d 1881-86||
CLM My 2,O 8 1886
CU-B My 5 1881;Ja 14,21,28,Jl 22,26 1883; Ja 1[Ap 8-Ag 14 1884]Ja 27,29 1885
CoU S 1906-Je 1908;Jl 1909-My 1910
DLC S 4 1885
MWA Ag 1 1883;Je 15 1884
NjR My 4,10 1881
NmHi Mr-D 1882;Ap-Jl 1883;Ap-Jl 1884

Evening JOURNAL. d 1886-1933||
1886-Ag? 1909 as Evening citizen; S?-D? 1909 Tribune-citizen; 1911?-Jl 1926 Evening herald
pub complete
CLM O 6 1890
CU-B Je 14-15,Ag 29,O 14,N 13,15 1889;Ja 7-9 1890
CU Ja-Je 1907;Jl 1908-Je 1909
DLC 1898-Ag 1909
KHi Je 7 1887-Jl 16 1906
NmA Jl 1926-32
NmAC 1912-33
NmU 1927-33

Albuquerque morning JOURNAL. 1903-25
See Albuquerque journal 1880+

Albuquerque JOURNAL-DEMOCRAT. *See* Albuquerque journal. 1880+

KILLGLOOM gazette. w Ja-Ag 1914||
NmAH complete

MAGEE'S independent. *See* Albuquerque tribune

NEW MEXICO democrat and independent. w 1912-20||?
1912-15? as New Mexico state democrat
NmHi 1916-20
NmU [F 1916-Jl 1918]

NEW MEXICO press. *See* Albuquerque weekly press

NEW MEXICO ruralist. *See* Sunday herald and New Mexico ruralist

NEW MEXICO state republican. w 1911-22||
NmU [Jl 1919-20]

NEW MEXICO state tribune. *See* Albuquerque tribune

NUEVO mundo. w 1897-1901||?
In Spanish
CoU F-N 1899

Albuquerque OPINION. w Jl 17- 1886||?
KHi 1886

PEOPLE'S news. w N 1935+
In English and Spanish
pub 1935+
NmU 1935+

Albuquerque weekly PRESS. w Ja 20 1863-67||?
1863-Jl 12 1864 as Rio Abaja weekly press; Jl 19 1864-Ja 9 1867 as New Mexico press
CSmH F 7 1865;Ap 10 1866;O 19 1867
MWA D 27 1864-Ja 9,F 9-Mr 9 1867
NmHi 1863-O 4 1864

REPUBLICAN review. *See* Albuquerque review

Semi-weekly REVIEW. sw 1867-69||?
DLC Ap 21 1868-D 11 1869
NcD D 25 1868;Ap 16,My 7,Jl 4 1869

Albuquerque REVIEW. w Mr 16 1870-82||
1870-73 as Republican review
CSmH S 13 1879;Ap 24 1880
CU-B Ap 24 1880
DLC 1870-Je 21 1873
NcD [1870-F 4 1871]
—Spanish ed *See* La Revista

Albuquerque evening REVIEW. d 1882||?
OOxM O 17 1882

La REVISTA. w 1870-82||?
1870-73? as La Revista republicana
NcD My 14-28 1870
—English ed *See* Albuquerque review

RIO Abaja weekly press. *See* Albuquerque weekly press

SOUTHWEST review. w 1921-30||
NmU 1925-27

Albuquerque TRIBUNE. w,d 1922+
1922 as Magee's independent (w) 1923-F 1933 New Mexico state tribune
pub 1933+
DLC S 1930+
NmA 1933+
NmAC 1922+
NmHi [1922]
NmU [1922-F 1933]+

TRIBUNE-CITIZEN. *See* Evening journal

ARTESIA

Artesia ADVOCATE. w 1903+
KHi [S 26 1919-23]-F 22 1924;Ja 7-21 1926

AZTEC

INDEPENDENT review. w 1914+
1914-32 as Independent
pub 1932+
NmAzC 1924+
NmU 1917-Ag 1918;23 [27-28] Ag 1934+

SAN JUAN county index. w 1889-1913||?
CoU 1899-Ap 1910

SAN JUAN review. w 1920-32||
United with Independent to form Independent review
NmAzC 1924-32
NmAzI complete
NmU [Ap-My 1922;D 1929-Ap 1932]

BELEN

HISPANO-americano. w 1911+
1925+ as section of News
NmU [1921-Ja 1925]

NEWS. w 1912+
NmU 1917-Ja 1918
—Spanish ed *See* Hispano-americano

BERNALILLO

El ESPEIO del Valle de Taos. w 1878-79||
In English and Spanish
CSmH Mr 8 1879

Bernalillo NEWS. w 1881-82||?
CU-B S 23-O 21,N 11-D 2,16-23 1881

Bernalillo TIMES. w 1929+
In English and Spanish
pub 1932+

BLAND

Bland weekly HERALD. w 1895-1902||?
CoU N 1899-Ja 1902

CARLSBAD

Carlsbad ARGUS. w 1889-1927||
United with Current to form Current-argus
KHi Jl 23 1920;O 5 1923

CURRENT-ARGUS. w,d 1892+
1892-1927 as Current (w)
pub 1928+
NmU [Jl-S 1928;S 1929+]

EDDY county news. w 1929+
1929-32 as Lovington tribune (Lovington)
pub 1932+
NmU Jl 1934+

Carlsbad SUN. d 1933+
pub 1933+

CARRIZOZO

LINCOLN county news. w 1900+
1900-25 as Carrizozo news
KHi My 7 1920
NmHi 1918-21
NmU [1917-25]Ag 1926-31

Carrizozo NEWS. *See* Lincoln county news

OUTLOOK. w 1907+
NmHi 1918-21;26-28

CERRILLOS

Cerrillos BEACON. w 1890-92||
CU-B Ja 19 1891

Cerrillos COMET. w F 24 1882-
MWA F 24 1882

CHLORIDE

BLACK range. w 1882-99||?
CU-B Ja 24,F 7,21-28,O 1890
NmHsS 1882-89

CIMARRON

CITIZEN. *See* News and citizen

NEWS and citizen. w 1908-17||
1908-10 as Citizen

NEWS and press. w 1870-1910||
1870-74 as News. United with Citizen to form News and citizen
CSmH D 6 1877;S 6 1878 (extra)
DLC Ja 17,F 7,My 30-Je,Jl 11,25-Ag 8,22-S,O 10,25 1874
ICM D 23 1880
NmHi 1875-82

CLAYTON

CITIZEN. w 1904-27||
Merged with Clayton news
NmCN complete

LANCE. *See* Clayton news

Clayton NEWS. w 1908+
1908-09? as Lance
pub 1910+
NmCC 1925+
NmHi 1918-20
NmU Ap 1922-Ap 1923;D 1929+

UNION county leader. w 1929+
NmCC 1929+
NmU S 1934+
TxU F-S 4 1930;S 24 1931-33

UNION del pueblo. w 1913-22||
In Spanish and English
NmU [S 1920-Mr 1921]

CLOVIS

CURRY county times. w 1932+
pub 1932+
NmU Ag 1934+

Clovis JOURNAL. w 1909-29||
United with News to form Evening news-journal
NmHi 1918-Jl 1921
NmU [1920-21]

Evening NEWS-JOURNAL. w,d 1907+
1907-29 as News (w)
pub 1929+
NmU D 1929-32;Je 1934

COBRA SPRINGS

CHRONICLE. *See under* Las Vegas

COLUMBUS

Columbus COURIER. w 1911-21||
NmU [1917-Mr]Ag-D 1920

Columbus COURIER. d 1919-21||
NmDC 1919
NmU My-Jl 1920

CUERVO

CLIPPER. w 1908-23||
NmHi 1917-18

NEW MEXICO (*Continued*)

DEMING

Deming GRAPHIC. w 1902+
NmDC 1903+
NmHi S-D 1917;Mr 1918-Je 1920;26-28
NmU 1917+

Deming HEADLIGHT. w 1882+
CU-B F 1886-87
KHi Ja 28 1893
NmDC 1901+
NmHi 1882-86;1918-S 1920
NmU 1920+

Deming HERALD. w 1900-05||
NmDC 1901-03

Deming TRIBUNE and Lake Valley herald. w 1883-85||?
1883-84 as Deming tribune
CSmH Mr 13 1884;O 1885; legislative bulletins Mr 1,24 1884
CU-B F 5 1885

DES MOINES

SWASTIKA. w 1907-25||
NmHi 1913-21

EAST LAS VEGAS

Papers published in East Las Vegas are listed under Las Vegas

EDDY

Eddy ARGUS. *See* Pecos Valley argus

PECOS Valley argus. w 1889-99||
1889-96 as Eddy argus
NcD N 7 1891

ELIDA

ENTERPRISE. *See* Roosevelt county record

ROOSEVELT county record. w 1916-34||
1916-24 as Enterprise; 1925-27 Enterprise-record
NmHi 1917-24

ELIZABETHTOWN

NATIONAL press and telegraph. *See* Railway press and telegraph

RAILWAY press and telegraph. w O 1869-74||?
1869-70 as National press and telegraph
CSmH D 18 1869
MDeHi D 7 1872
NNHi O 5 1872;Ja 10,Jl 11 1874

THUNDERBOLT. w F 20 1871-
NNHi F-Mr 12 1871

ESPANOLA

El PALITO. w 1925-27||
Follows El Nuevo estado (Tierra Amarilla)
In Spanish
IU My 8 1925-Jl 1926

La VOZ del Rio Grande. w 1909+
In Spanish
IU [Ag 6 1926+]
NmHi 1926-28

ESTANCIA

Estancia HERALD. w 1910-13||?
In English and Spanish
United with Estancia news to form Estancia news-herald

Estancia NEWS-HERALD. w 1904+
1904-13 as Estancia news
1906-07 in English and Spanish
NmHi 1911-2?
NmU [1918-19;30+]

FARLEY

Farley EXAMINER. w 1932+
pub 1932+
NmFP 1932+
NmU Ag-S 1934

FARMINGTON

Farmington ENTERPRISE. w 1905-19||
NmHi 1905-06;08-09;12-14;19

HUSTLER. w 1901-05||
United with Times to form Times-hustler

REPUBLICAN. *See* Sentinel

SAN JUAN times. *See* Times-hustler

SENTINEL. w 1926+
1926-My 1935 as Republican
NmAzC 1927+
NmU [1930-34]

TIMES-HUSTLER. w 1890+
1890-91 as San Juan times; 1891-1905 Times
CoHi 1910-18
CoU 1899-Je 1900
KHi [Je 14-O 1894]
NmAzC 1924+
NmHi 1917-18;20-27
NmU 1918-19[30]+

FOLSOM

METROPOLITAN. w 1888-95||
Title varies: Springs metropolitan
CU-B Ja 30 1892

SPRINGS republican. *See* Metropolitan

FORT BAYARD

Fort Bayard NEWS. w 1917-O 24 1919||
IU Mr 1918-O 1919
OHi Ap-Ag 8 1919
WHi Ap-O 1919

FORT SUMNER

Fort Sumner LEADER. w 1909+
NmU D 1929+

Fort Sumner REVIEW. w 1908+
NmHi 1918-20
NmU 1919-Jl 1923

GALLUP

CARBON City news. w 1888-1925|
NmGC 1901-25

Gallup CHIEFTAIN. w 1928-33||
NmGC complete

Gallup GLEANER. sw 1888-1905||
CU-B Mr 11,18,27 1889;Ag 6,13 1892
NmGC 1901-05

Gallup HERALD. w,d 1915-31||
United with Independent to form Independent and herald
w 1915-30
KHi N 20 1920
NmGC complete
NmU S 1920-22;F 1930-Ap 1931

INDEPENDENT and herald. w,d 1909+
1909-31 as Independent (w)
pub 1931+
NmU [1929+]

MCKINLEY county republican. w 1888-1915||
NmGC 1901-15

GLENRIO

Glenrio TRIBUNE-progress. w 1910+
1910-33 as Glenrio tribune
MWA Ag 18 1922
NmHi 1926-28
NmU [1918-32]
WaPS [1925]

GOLDEN

Golden RETORT. w 1881-84||
CSmH Jl 28 1882;Ag 17 1883

GRANT

Grant REVIEW. w 1928+
pub 1928+
NmU Ap-Ag 1934

HAGERMAN

Hagerman MESSENGER. w 1901+
KHi O 3-10 1919
NmArA 1901+
NmU [Jl 1926;Ag-S 1934]

HATCH

Hatch REPORTER. w 1926+
1926-29 as Rio Grande reporter
pub 1930+
NmU [1930+]

RIO GRANDE reporter. *See* Hatch reporter

HILLSBORO

Hillsboro NEWS. w 1931+
pub 1931+

SIERRA county advocate. *See under* Hot Springs

SIERRA county record. w 1925-33||
NmHC 1925-30

HOBBS

Hobbs NEWS. sw 1929+
pub 1929+

Hobbs REPORTER. w 1929+
pub 1929+

HOPE

PENASCO Valley news. w 1909+
1909-29 as Penasco Valley press
pub [1909-29]+

PENASCO Valley press. *See* Penasco Valley news

HOT SPRINGS

Hot Springs HERALD. w 1930+
pub 1930+
NmU Ag 1934+

SIERRA county advocate. w 1884+
1884-1925 pub in Hillsboro
pub 1884+
NmHC 1925+
NmHi 1884;1917

KENNA

Kenna RECORD. w 1907-24|
United with Enterprise (Elida) to form Enterprise-record, later Roosevelt county record (Elida)

KINGSTON

Kingston CLIPPER. w F 1- 1884||?
CSmH Mr 8 1884

SHAFT. *See under* Rincon

LAKE VALLEY

Lake Valley HERALD and Deming tribune. w 1881-84||?
United with Deming tribune to form Deming tribune and Lake Valley herald (Deming)
PPL D 20 1883

LAS CRUCES

BORDERER. w 1871-77||
CU-B Ja 24,F 21-28,My 8 1872-Ag 16,S 27,D 27 1873;Ja 10 1874
NmU [Mr 1871-72]

Las Cruces CITIZEN. w 1902+
Early years in English and Spanish
pub 1902+
KHi D 4 1920
NmHi 1917-22;26-28
NmLS [1917+]
NmU D 1929+

El FRONTERIZO. w 1874-77||
In Spanish
CSmH F 11 1875

NEWMAN'S thirty-four. *See* Thirty-four

Las Cruces daily NEWS. w,d 1881+
1881-1914 as Rio Grande republican; 1914-22? Rio Grande republic; 1923?-34? Rio Grande farmer; 1935? Las Cruces daily news and Rio Grande farmer
w 1881-34
pub 1934+
CU-B 1887;Mr 16-23,Ap 6,Je 29-Jl 6,S 7,N 16 1889;Ap 16,30-S 6, O 4-11,25,D 27 1890
CoU F 1899-F 1901
NmHi 1888-89;1917-19;26-28
NmLS 1923-24;34+
NmU [Ag-O 1934]

RIO GRANDE farmer. *See* Las Cruces daily news and Rio Grande farmer

RIO GRANDE republic. *See* Las Cruces daily news and Rio Grande farmer

RIO GRANDE republican. *See* Las Cruces daily news and Rio Grande farmer

THIRTY-FOUR. w 1878-83||
Title varies: Newman's thirty-four
CSmH N 19(supp)26 1879;S 24 1880(extra) Ja 20 1881(extra)

El TIEMPO. w 1882-1913||
In Spanish
KHi D 31 1885

LAS LUNAS

VALENCIA vindicator. w S 15 1883-
CU-B S 15 1883

LAS VEGAS

Las Vegas ADVERTISER. w 1870?-78||
In English and Spanish
CSmH Jl 12 1873

CHIHUAHUA enterprise. m D 15 1882-
1882-83 pub in Chihuahua, Mexico
CU-B D 1882-Ap, Je,Ag-N 1883;Ja 1884

CHRONICLE. w 1880-86||
Jl 31-S 22 1886 pub at Hommel's ranch, Cobra Springs
In English and Spanish
CU-B [Ja 24 1885-N 1 1886]

Las Vegas EUREKA. m,w N 1879-80||
m 1879-Ja? 1880
CU-B Ja 1880
KHi N 1879

FISK'S great southwest. m 1884-
CLM F 1886

FREE press. d 1891-92||?
CU-B Ja 5 1892

La GACETA. w 1873-79||
In Spanish
NmHi 1873
—English ed *See* Las Vegas gazette

Las Vegas GAZETTE. w 1872-87|
Title varies: Sunday gazette
CSmH Jl 5 1879
CU-B O 25 1885
KHi Ap 25-S 1883
NcD Ap 12 1873
—Spanish ed *See* La Gaceta

NEW MEXICO (*Continued*)

LAS VEGAS—*Continued*

Las Vegas daily GAZETTE. d 1880-87||
CU-B Ja 24 1883;D 6-7,14 1884
NmHi 1881-83
OOxM O 19 1882

HADLEY'S pointers—mines, money and commerce. w S 7 1882-
MWA S 7-14 1882

El INDEPENDIENTE. *See under* Albuquerque

Morning LAS VEGAN. sw,w 1932+
sw 1932-S 1935
pub 1932+
NmU S 1934+

Daily OPTIC. d 1879+
pub D 1879;1908+
CSmH Mr 5 1884
CU-B D 5 1884
KHi My 17 1881;S 18 1888-Jl 14 1906;N 7 1927
NmHi 1881-82;88-91;1912-20;N-D 1921
NmLv 1925+
NmU D 1929+
OClWHi S 20,27,O 13,17 1881;Ja 1 1892
OOxM O 18 1882

OPTIC and livestock grower. w 1879-1922||
1879-84? as Las Vegas weekly optic
pub Ag-N 1879
CU-B Mr 20 1884
KHi [Mr-Je 14 1883]-Ag 21 1884
NbHi Mr 1898-1908;F 18 1911-19

POINTERS. w
KHi [S 21-N 16 1882]Mr 20 1883

POLITICAL comet. 1882||?
CSmH N 4 1882

LA VOZ del pueblo. w 1889-1925||
Some years dated at East Las Vegas
In Spanish
CU-B O 18 1890
IU D 8 1917-Je 16 1923; F-Mr 22,Je-O 1924
NmHi 1917-20
NmU [1917-24]

LINCOLN

Lincoln INDEPENDENT. w 1880-95||
CU-B D 6-13,27 1889-Ja 3,Mr 7,Jl 25,Ag 15-22 1890

LORDSBURG

Lordsburg ADVANCE. w 1883-87||
NmHi 1883

Lordsburg LIBERAL. w 1887+
1887-1919 as Western liberal
CU-B [Mr 8 1889-O 1890;92-94]
NmHi 1919-20;26-28
NmU 1930+

WESTERN liberal. *See* Lordsburg liberal

LOVINGTON

Lovington LEADER. w 1910+
NmU N 1934+

Lovington TRIBUNE. *See* Eddy county news (Carlsbad)

MAGDALENA

Magdalena NEWS. w 1910+
NmHi Ap 1917-21
NmU D 1929+

MANZANO

GRINGO and greaser. sm Ag 15? 1883-84||?
CSmH Ja 15-F 1 1884
MWA F 15 1884
NBHi F 15 1884

MESILLA

Mesilla INDEPENDENT. w 1877-79||
Early issues as Mesilla Valley independent
CU-B Mr 16 1878
TxE N 1878-Jl 12 1879

MESILLA Valley independent. *See* Mesilla independent

Mesilla MINER. w Je 9 1860-
CSmH Je 9 1860

Mesilla weekly TIMES. w O 18 1860?-
CSmH O 25-N 1 1860;Jl 15 1867
NNHi Ja 15 1862

MILLS

DEVELOPER. *See* Harding county developer (Roy)

MORA

La CRÓNICA de Mora. w
In Spanish
CU-B Jl 18-25,Ag 29-S 12,N 23-30 1889

El DEMOCRATA de Mora. w 1888-89||
In Spanish
CU-B Mr 1889

MORA county patriot. *See* Mora county star

MORA county star. w 1921+
1921-30 as Mora county patriot
pub 1931+

MOSQUERO

DEVELOPER. *See* Harding county developer (Roy)

HARDING county developer. *See under* Roy

MOUNTAINAIR

INDEPENDENT. w 1916+
In English and Spanish
NmU Ag 1934+

PORTALES

Portales DAILY. w,d 1913+
1913-Ag 1935 as Portales Valley news (w)
pub 1916+
NmPC 1916+
NmU [1917-22;28-Ag 1934]

Portales HERALD and times. w 1902-16||
1902-13 as Herald. Followed by Portales journal
CoU My 1902-F 1903
NmPD complete

Portales JOURNAL. w 1917-20||
Follows Portales herald and times
NmPD complete

PORTALES Valley news. *See* Portales daily

ROOSEVELT county herald. w 1926-30||
Merged with Portales Valley news, later Portales daily
NmU [Ag 1928-Ja 1930]

Portales TIMES. w 1903-13||
United with Herald to form Portales herald and times

QUEMADO

CATRON county news. w Mr 1935+
pub 1935+

CATRON county stockman. w 1922-24||
NmMN complete

QUESTA

Questa GAZETTE. w 1910-15||
NmHi N 1912-Ja 1914

RATON

Raton COMET. w 1881-86||
NmHi 1881

Raton GAZETTE. d 1931||?
United with Raton daily range to form Range and gazette, later Raton daily range

Raton INDEPENDENT. d 1883-98||
CU-B F 28-Mr 2,5,9,Je 13-15,25,28,Jl 6,13 1889
NmHi 1883

NEW MEXICO news and press. w 1870-92||
ICM Mr 11-18 1882

Raton daily RANGE. w,sw,tw,d 1881+
1881-1925 as Raton range; 1926-29 Raton daily range; 1930-31 Range and gazette
w 1881-1907,26-28;sw 1908-25;tw 1931?
pub 1932+
CoU 1900
KHi Ag 22 1924
NmHi 1881;1917-20
NmRC 1912+
NmU Je-Jl 1921;O 1928+

Raton REPORTER. w,sw 1890-1930||?
w 1890-1914?
CU-B O 18,25,N 1 1893
CoU 189[illegible]-1910
KHi N 1 1921
NmHi 1917-21
NmRC 1914-30
NmU 1917-19;O 1920-Mr 1930

RINCON

SHAFT. w 1886-94||?
1886-93? pub in Kingston
CU-B O 25 1890;Ag 6-13 1892;O 7 1893;My 30, Je 13 1894

ROSWELL

Roswell DISPATCH. sw,d 1925+
1925-28 as Southwestern dispatch (sw)
NmU D 1929-Mr 1930

Roswell evening NEWS. d 1911-25||
KHi Ap 17-Jl 22 1920

PECOS Valley register. *See* Register and tribune

Roswell daily RECORD. d 1903+
pub 1903+
KHi O 31 1919-Mr 11 1932
NmHi 1916-17;19-25;O 1926-My 1928;S-D 1929
NmRoC 1903+
NmU D 1921-Ag 1932;Ag 1934+

Roswell weekly RECORD. w,sw 1891-1913||?
w 1891-1912?
CoU Mr 1899-1904

REGISTER and tribune. w 1888-1911||
1888-90 as Pecos Valley register; 1890-1907 Register
CU-B O 18 1890;Ja 2,16-23,F 27-Mr 5,Ap 2, 16,30 1892
CoU 1899-My 1910

SOUTHWESTERN dispatch. *See* Roswell dispatch

Roswell STAR. w 1915-20||
NmHi 1917-19

ROY

HARDING county developer. w 1914+
1914-20,32-34 as Developer
1914-20 pub in Mills; 1921-34 pub in Mosquero
pub 1934+
NmHi 1922-23;26-27
NmU N 1929-Mr 1930;32

OBSERVER and reporter. *See* Roy record

Roy RECORD. w 1903+
1903-05 as Observer and reporter; 1905-27 Spanish American
1905-27 in English and Spanish
pub 1916+
NmHi 1917-21
NmU [1917-25]N 1929+

SPANISH-American. *See* Roy record

SAN LORENZO

RED RIVER chronicle. w 1880-83||
In English and Spanish
NmHi 1882-83

SAN MARCIAL

San Marcial BEE. w 1892-1906||
KHi [My 27-D 9 1893]

San Marcial REPORTER. w 1886-93||
KHi Je 1889-Mr 1 1893

SANTA FE

Santa Fe AMERICAN. *See* New Mexico examiner

El BOLETIN popular. w 1885-1910||
In Spanish
CU-B Jl 4,18-25,Ag 22-29,S 12-19 1889;Ag 28 1890;Ja 7 1892
KHi O 13 1892-1904

CAPITAL. w 1900-05||
NmHi Je 1900-Ap 1903

El CLARIN mejicano. w 1873-
In Spanish
CSmH Ag 10 1873

Santa Fe weekly DEMOCRAT. w 1879-81||
CSmH N 5 1880;Ja 6 1881
CU-B N 5 1880;Ja 6 1881
ICM O 6-13 1881
MWA D 23 1880

Santa Fe daily DEMOCRAT. d 1880-92||
In English and Spanish
MnU O 7 1880

EAGLE. w 1900-15||
NmHi Ag 1913-15

Weekly ERA southwestern. w 1879-83||
CSmH Jl 15,Ag 5 1880

Santa Fe weekly EXPRESS. w Je 1 1887-
CSmH Ag 13 1887

Santa Fe GAZETTE. w Ap 12 1851-S 1869||?
Title varies: Santa Fe weekly gazette
CSmH [Mr 8 1856-N 1859]My 8 1860;O 3 1863;Ap 16 1864;F 3 1866;O 5-12 1867
CU-B Je 1868-S 1869
DLC N 1852-58[Jl 1860-O 1861;62]F 21 1863-65;D 28 1867;Ja 11 1868-S 1869
ICHi My 28 1864
MWA My 17 1851;Ja 24,O 23 1852;D 24 1853; Jl 29 1854;Ap 20-27,Jl 6,S 14-21 1861;Je 8-15,Jl 27 1867
N O 25 1856
NmHi 1864-66
PDoHi [D 24 1853-F 16 1856]

Sante Fe HERALD. w,d 1887-90||
w 1887-88
NmHi Jl-D 1888

Santa Fe weekly LEADER. w My 9 1885-87||
CSmH My 30 1885;My 22 1886
KHi [1885-86]

Daily MOUNTAIN sentinel. *See* Rocky Mountain sentinel

NEW MEXICO (*Continued*)

SANTA FE—*Continued*

Santa Fe NEW MEXICAN. w,d 1848+
1848-N? 1849 as New Mexican review; N 24 1849-Je 5? 1883 Santa Fe New Mexican (title varies slightly) Je 6-11? 1883 Santa Fe New Mexican and review; Je 12 1883-Jl 7 1885 Santa Fe New Mexican review w 1849-N? 1849
CLM Jl 11 1891
CSmH Ag 26 (extra) S 28 1875;Ag 14,21,O 22 1877;F 24 1880;S 21,27 1881;F 14 1882;Je 6 1883-Je 1884;Ja 25(supp) 1886;O 21 1901
CU-B Je 15 1869;Je 24 1883[S-D 1884]
CoHi F 20 1901-F 18 1905;F 15 1908-Ap 19 1909;F 1 1911-Ag 13 1913;Jl 1917+
DLC [Ap 23-D 3 1870]71-S 21 1872;Jl 17 1874-77;Mr 1880-Ag 2 1883;Ag 21 1888+
GU Ja 11 1919
ICM D 11,18 1881
IU N 24 1849;Ag 6 1909;19-My 18 1926
KHi Jl 17,Ag 19 1881-Jl 19 1883;Jl 1888-D 2 1901;Ag 3 1926
N S 15 1882
NbHi Jl 22 1901-Ap 14 1906
NmHi 1868-77;80-87;91-1932
NmU O 1920+
OOxM O 19-21 1882
TJT D 15 1898
TxU Ja 3-My 27 1883
WHi N 2? 1849;S 15,29 1865;Ap 20 1866;F 28 1914+
—Spanish ed *See* El Nuevo mexicano

Weekly NEW MEXICAN. w 1863-83||
1863-O 27 1868 as New Mexican
CSmH Ag 22 1863;Ja 9,31,F 27 1864;D 29 1866;F 24 1874;Je 16 (extra),Ag 31 1875[78] Ap 5 1879-Mr 28 1881;Ja 2,My 29 1882;My 28 1883 (extra)
CU-B Ag 28 1877
DLC O 15 1872;73-My 12 1874;78-79
NmHi My 1864-83

NEW MEXICAN review. 1848-49 *See* Santa Fe New Mexican

Santa Fe NEW MEXICAN review. d 1862-Je 5? 1883||
Merged with Santa Fe New Mexican to form Santa Fe New Mexican review, later Santa Fe New Mexican
NmHi 1883

NEW MEXICAN review. w 1862-1918||?
1862-Mr? 1884 as Weekly New Mexican review (title varies slightly); Ap? 1884-85 New Mexican review and live stock journal
CLM Ja 7 1909
CSmH Jl 1?,Ag 9 1883;D 24 1885
CU-B S 4,18-O 2,16-30,N 13-20,D 4-11 1884; Ja 15,F 12,Ag 27 1885
NmHi 1884-85
WHi Je 28 1906-F 1914
—d ed 1883-1918 *See* Santa Fe New Mexican

Santa Fe NEW MEXICAN review. 1883-85 *See* Santa Fe New Mexican

NEW MEXICO examiner. w 1933+
1933-34 as Santa Fe American
pub 1933+

NEW MEXICO state record. w O 1914+
NmHi 1914;16 18-21;23-24;27-28

NEW-MEXICO union. w 1872-75||
In English and Spanish
CSmH Jl 3,D 30 1873
DLC Ja 2,F 27-Mr 20,Ap 10-17,My 8-Je 5 1873

NEW MEXICO war news. w Jl 1917-18||
NmU complete

El NUEVO Mexicano. w 1862+
In Spanish
CSmH Ap 2? 1863;D 7 1878;S 24 1881
CoAT [1930-32]
IU D 1917-Ag 8 1918
NmHi 1890-91;93;95-1901;06-22;24
NmU My 1922+
OOxM O 7 1882
—English ed *See* Santa Fe New Mexican

Santa Fe weekly POST. w O 2 1869-73||
CU-B O 2 1869;Mr 12 1870
DLC O 2-9,N-D 1869;Je 25 1870-Je 1872
MWA Ap 30 1870

Santa Fe daily POST. d 1871-73||
DLC F 6-8,10-11,13-14,16-18,20,22-23,27-Mr 3 1872

Santa Fe REPUBLICAN. w 1847-
CSmH [N 20 1847-N 1848]Ag 8 1849 (extra)
DLC Ap 28 1849

Santa Fé REPUBLICAN. w Je 14 1862-
CSmH Je 21 1862
DLC Jl 5-12 1862

ROCKY Mountain sentinel. w 1878-80||?
1878-79? as Daily mountain sentinel
CSmH Ja 30,F 27-Mr 13,Ap 3,17,My 29,Je 19,Jl 10,Ag 14,O 30,N 20,D 11,25 1879

El VERDAD. w N 1842-Ja 1845||
In Spanish
CSmH S 12 1844
NmHi S 12 1844

SANTA ROSA

La VOZ pública. w 1906-22||
In Spanish and English
NmHi Je 1917-19

SILVER CITY

Silver City ENTERPRISE. w 1882+
pub 1896+
CSmH Je 5 1893
CU-B N 15-29 1889;Ja 17 1890
MWA Ja 3 1890
NmHi 1917-21;26-28
NmU 1917+

GRANT county democrat. w 1897-98||
NmU complete

GRANT county herald. *See* Southwest sentinel

Silver City INDEPENDENT. *See* Daily press and independent

Silver City MINING life. w 1873-75||
TxU My 31 1873-My 1874

Daily PRESS and independent. w,d 1896+
1896-Je 1935 as Silver City independent (w)
pub 1896+
KHi N 2 1920;Mr 18 1924
NmHi 1917
NmU 1917-Ag 1918;D 1929-Je 1935

Daily SOUTHWEST. d 1880||?
CSmH Je 9 1880

SOUTHWEST sentinel. w 1875-96||
1875-83 as Grant county herald
CU-B Ja-Je 1886
NmU [1875-85]
Tx My 1 1888

SOUTHWEST sentinel. d 1887-88||?
CU-B 1887-Ja 1888

TRIBUNE. w Ag 21 1873-74||?
CSmH Ag 21-30 1873

WATCH-DOG. w 1882-
WHi S 11-25,O 16 1883

SOCORRO

BULLION. w 1883-88||
CSmH Mr 1 1884
CU-B Ap 24 1886

CHIEFTAIN. w 1882+
CU-B O 3-10,24-31 1890;My 19 1893;D 8 1923;Ja-My 10 1924
NmHi 1917

El DEFENSOR del pueblo. w 1904+
In Spanish
NmU [Ap-My 1927;30;Ja-Ap 1931;Mr 1935+]

Socorro SUN. w 1880-85||
MWA My 7,Jl 16 1881
NN Extras:Ag 14,15,16 1881

SPRINGER

Springer BANNER. w Je 27 1889-94||
CU-B Je 27,Jl 11-18,O 17,D 12-18 1889;Ja 23-F 6,O 1890;Ag 11-18 1892
NmHi 1890
—Spanish ed *See* El Estandiarte de Springer

COLFAX county stockman. w 1882-1929||
CU-B Mr 23, Je 15,29,O 12 1889
NmHi 1927-28

El ESTANDIARTE de Springer. w 1889-94||?
In Spanish
CU-B D 31 1891;F 4 1892
—English ed *See* Springer banner

Springer TIMES. *See* Springer tribune

Springer TRIBUNE. w 1912+
1912-29 as Springer times
pub 1929+
NmHi 1917-19;26-28
NmU [1933+]

TAIBAN

VALLEY news. w 1907-23||
NmHi 1918

TAOS

CRESSET. w 1894-1902||
United with Revista de Taos to form Revista de Taos and cresset, later Revista popular
NmHi complete

HERALD. *See* Taos Valley herald

El HERALDO. w Jl 1 1884-89||
CU-B 1884-Mr 20,D 1885-F 6,My 13-S 9 1886[87]-Ja 14,28,F 25,Mr 10,Ap 9 1888;Mr 9-16,Ap 6 1889
—English ed *See* Taos Valley herald

REVISTA popular. 1900+
1900-01,07-25 as La Revista de Taos; 1902-06 Revista de Taos and Cresset
In Spanish
IU D 1917-18;F 1919-Ag 20 1920
WHi N 29 1918

TAOS county republican. w 1904-19||
NmHi complete

TAOS Valley herald. w Jl 1 1884-90||
1884-89 as Herald
In English and Spanish
CU-B 1884-[Ja-F 6 1886]
NmHi 1884
—Spanish ed *See* El Heraldo

TAOS Valley news. w 1910+
1917-19? as Taos Valley news and El crepusculo (in English and Spanish)
KHi D 21 1915
NmHi 1910-26;28

TEXICO

Texico TRUMPET. w 1904-13||
WyToT 1908-11

TIERRA AMARILLA

El NUEVO estado. w 1901-25||
1901-07 as El Republicano. Followed by El Palito (Española)
In Spanish and English
IU [D 24 1917-24;F 9-Mr 2 1925]
NmHi 1912-19

El REPUBLICANO. *See* El Nuevo estado

TUCUMCARI

Tucumcari AMERICAN. w 1915+
pub 1915+
KHi S 9,N 25 1920
NmHi 1917
NmTC 1915+

Tucumcari NEWS. w O 1901+
1919-21 as News-times
NmHi 1917-19
NmTC 1910+

Tucumcari SUN. w 1908-21||
NmHi 1917
NmU [1917-Jl 1918]

Tucumcari TIMES. w 1903-19||
Merged with News to form News-times, later Tucumcari news

TULAROSA

Tularosa BEACON. w 1931+
pub 1931+

VAUGHN

Vaughn NEWS. w 1917+
1920-21 as News-times
pub 1917+

WAGON MOUND

ARROW-pioneer. w 1885-88||
1885-86 as Arrow
NmHi 1885
—Spanish ed *See* La Flecha

El COMBATE. w 1900-20||
For 1911-13 *See* Sentinel
—English ed *See* Sentinel

La FLECHA. w 1885-88||
In Spanish
NmHi 1885
—English ed *See* Arrow-pioneer

MORA county news. w 1925+
In English and Spanish
NmU [D 1929-Ja 1932]

MORA county sentinel. *See* Sentinel

PANTOGRAPH. w 1909-21||
NmHi 1917

SENTINEL. w 1909?-21||
1909?-10 as Mora county sentinel; 1911-13 Sentinel and El Combate (in English and Spanish) 1914-15 Mora county sentinel
NmHi 1917

Wagon Mound TRIBUNE. w 1932+
pub 1932+

WATROUS

MORA county pioneer. *See* Pioneer journal

PIONEER journal. w 1881-86||
1881-85 as Mora county pioneer
NmHi 1881

Watrous PLAINDEALER. w 1887-88||
NmHi 1887

WHITE OAKS

White oaks weekly EAGLE. w 1885?-1902||?
CoU 1899-S 1900

LINCOLN county leader. w 1882-84||
NmHi 1882

NEW MEXICO interpreter. w 1885-91||
CU-B Mr 8-Ap 12,D 6 1889;Ja 3,F 14-28,Jl 4,Ag 15-S 12,O 1890
NmHi 1891

WILLARD

Willard RECORD. w 1908-1932||
NmHi 1917-20

NEW YORK

ADAMS

JEFFERSON county journal. w 1844+
NNHi Ap 11 1872-Mr 16 1886

ADDISON

Addison ADVERTISER. w 1858+
pub 1878+
MWA S 8 1869
NNHi My 9 1860;F 20 1861;F 26 1873
OClWHi My 16 1866

AKRON

Akron NEWS. w 1882+
pub [1891-92;97]O 1925+

ALBANY

***Albany daily ADVERTISER.** d S 25 1815-Ap 14 1845||
CSmH S 1 1830
Ct Ag 21 1834
DLC Ap 15,22(extra)Je 4(extra),S 10,20,30,O 18,N 23 1824;My 18 1825;F 29,My 3,D 9 1828; Je 15,20,Jl 9,11,27-28,30-Ag 1,6-7,11,S 11,29-30, O 6 1829;Ja 6,23,28,D 22 1830;Ja 5,14,Je 15 1831;O 9 1832;33;Jl 7 1834;D 2 1840
MBAt Ja 30 1824;F 26-27 1829;D 12 1831
MWA Ag 22 1823[24-N 4 1825]Ap 3 1826;Mr 11,Jl 7 1828;My 30,Je 16 1829;N 9 1830[F-Mr] D 31 1831;Ja 1,3,Je 20,Jl 14,O 10,N 18 1835; Jl 1-3 1837;S 21,N 1,D 4-5 1838;Ap 6,Je 6 1842;Ap 7 1845
MHi Ap 10 1823;F 16 1827
MiU-C [1824-25]
N S 27 1822-S 29 1823;Ap 25-S 29,N 3-4,10,12, 24-25,D 15 1824;Mr 11,Ap 27,Jl 16,Ag 12,S 30,O 30,N 3-4,D 2 1825;Ap 3,N 17,D 5 1826; F 12,17,20,24,My 27,Jl 7,O 12,N 2,5 1827;Ja 5,18,Ag 26 1828;F 27,O 16 1830;S 14 1831;Ja 11 1832;N 5 1833;Je 27 1834;Ja 31,F 13,20-21, 25[S 26-D 1835]Je 2,Ap 1836;Ap 14 1845
NN D 20 1822;Ap 30,My 11 1823;S 27(extra) 1824;Ja 18(extra)1825;D 2 1834;N 8-9,11 1825; Ja 4,F 21,Mr 22,Ap 19,25,Je 27,Jl 10,S 29[O-N]1826[27-32]Je 21 1833[Mr-O 1837]Ap 16 1841
NNHi [O-N 1822;Ja,Je-N 1823]Jl 25 1827;Ap 6 1829;Ap 1,11,19 1831;S 25 1841;F 17,Mr 28(extra)1842;Jl 26,Ag 4,17,N 21,D 25 1843;Ja 5,F 29 1844
NSchU N 8 1824-31;Je 12,24 1835;Ag 14 1827;N 3 1828;Ap 19,22,28,Mr 30 1842
NjR N 28 1822
OClWHi S 15 1835;O 22 1838
P-M D 2 1841

AGE. w Ja 22? 1828-
MWA F 26 1828
N Ja 19-Ap 19 1828
NNHi F 9 1828

ALBANIAN. sm Ja 30 1828-
N F 3,Mr 3,Jl 14 1830

ALBANIAN. d 1844||
N [My 30-S 3 1844]

ALBANIAN. m D 1851-
N F-Jl 1852;Ja 1853

ALBANIAN. sm S 1857-
N Mr 13-Je 18 1858

Daily AMERICAN citizen. d Je 1842-
DLC Jl 6-D 1842
MWA F 18,Mr 9 1843
N F 18-O 1843;F 8,Ap 8,Je 12 1844;Je 17 1846
NN D 1 1843
NNS Ja-Jl 29 1843
NSchU Jl 18-20,22,25-28,Ag 1-3,15-16,18-19,23-24,27,30-S 1,3,6 1842
WHi Ap 18 1845

ANTIDOTE. w My 19 1827-
Ct Ag 25 1827
N My 19-26 1827
NNHi My 7 1828

ANTI-RENTER. w Ag 16 1845-
N S 13,O 4 1845;Ja 17,31,F 14-28,Ap 4-11,Je 6,20,O 24 1846

Albany ARGUS. w 1813-94||?
Title varies: Argus; Weekly argus; etc. 1841-42? as Argus and rough hewer; F 18 1856-My 15 1865 Atlas and argus
A N 1879;My-Je,S 1880-Je 1882
CSmH 1841-42;44-55
ICHi 1841
IG 1853
IU O 22 1836;S 2 1842;52
MB 1841-F 5 1842
MBAt Ap?(extra),S 5 1828;Je 3 1836
MWA Jl 5,19 1834;41-42[F 23-D 1856]Ja 3,17-31,Je 27[Ag-D 1857]Mr 13 1858-O 1859;F 11-D 15 1860[Je 11 1868-Jl 1 1869]
MWiC Ja 9 1841-42
MiU 1838-39;O 27 1840;Ap 23 1844
MiU-C [1821-25;28-29;33;35-36;38]41
MsHi 1837-45
N 1841-55
NBu Ja 1 1858;Ja 8-15 1859;Je 30 1860
NBuHi Ja 9 1841-54
NCanHi Ja 27 1844;Je 23 1855
NHerHi 1843-45;48-51
NHi S 27 1833;O 28 1837
NI 1821
NN D 29 1832;33-D 2,15 1838-39;Ja 9-S,O 9-N,D 11-31 1841;46;S 3(extra)-N 1842;49
NNHi Jl 26 1834;Ap 16,My 28,D 10 1836;Ag 4 1838[My,Ag-D 1840]-42;44-52
NPuD 1846-D 18 1847
NSchU Ja 8,Mr 12 1842
NSyU Mr 12 1839
NUHi 1833-34;37-40
NWat 1840-41
NjR [1845-46;53-59]
OClWHi O 9 1840;D 28 1887
P-M O 9 1832
PEL F 26,Mr 18 1828
PWCl Ja 26 1841
Vt • Ja 9 1841-D 3 1842;45-N 1846;Ja 23 1847-49
WHi 1841
WM 1836;D 27 1845-S 16 1846

***Albany ARGUS.** sw Ja 26 1813-1907||?
F 18 1856-My 15 1865 as Atlas and argus
CtHi [N 30 1827-N 1838]
CtY 1828-My 19 1829;Je 7 1833;S 3 1881
DLC 1821-Ja 15,D 14 1830-Mr 13 1832;Je 13 1834;O 17-20 1848;Jl 19,Ag 2,O 18-N 22,D 6 1856;Ja 17,Ap 25,My 9 1857
MB [Je 1840-Je 3 1842]
MHi [1821-25;27]O 5 1835
MWA 1821-23;Ja-[Jl-D 1824;F 25-Ap 16]N 8 1825;26-Ap 27,My 7,Ag 13,N 30[D]1830[32]-[34]-F 26,Mr 29 1836-[38]-Mr 5,S 14,21,28-O 5 1841;Ag 9 1842;45;Ja 5,Ap 17 1855;F 27 1857;Mr 12 1868;Je 8 1876
N 1821-Ap 1843
NBu Jl 17,S 14,21 1832-[34-35]-Ja 8,15-Jl 1,8-15 1836;Ja 18 1859
NBuHi 1833-D 22 1843
NCH My 1,S 4-7,14,O 23-26,N 2-9,30 1821
NCanHi Je 11 1840
NN 1821-D 14 1825;O 17-N 3 1826;27-S 1833; Ja-N 10 1835;Ja 16 1838-D 12 1845;O 6,11-N 6 1846;Ap 30-D 21 1847;Ja 7 1848-D 1 1854;Jl 2 1877
NNHi 1821-[44]-53[56-60]Ap 16 1865
NPyC D 9 1831-32
NR Jl 31 1829-Jl 20,N 9 1830;N 2,D 15 1832-33;Mr 1834-37;Ap 27-N 27 1838;39-Ja 3 1840; Ag 17-D 1843
NSchU S 1841-D 12 1842
NcD 1830-O 1832;33-39
NhD Je 12,22,Jl 31,O 12-16 1832;Jl 18 1834
NjHi Ag 11(extra)1834
NjR [1824;49]Ja 18 1859
PEL F 20,Mr 18(extra)1828
WHi Mr 9,Jl 23 1824[Mr 21 1834-35;Ja 13-D 1837]-[40-43]-45

Daily Albany ARGUS. d Ap 17 1826-1920||
Title varies: Albany argus; Albany argus and daily city gazette; etc. F 18 1856-My 15 1865 as Atlas and argus. Merged with Daily press and knickerbocker
Ja 26 1913 is centenary ed
CLM Jl 18 1886
CSmH Jl 2 1830
CSt Ap 20,24,27,N 14 1838;D 14 1831;Ja 3,Ap 25 1843;S 27 1881
Ct [1826-28]Ap 4 1834
CtHi N 9 1838-Je 1840;S 24 1841-N 2 1842
CtW Ag 25,S 21 1893
CtY Ja 25 1827;Mr 7,Ap(extra)1828;Ja 17 1829-34;36-Je 1846;Ag 21 1848;D 12 1897
DLC Mr 11 1826;D 14(extra)18(extra)19(extra) 1827;Ja 1(extra),S 2(extra)1828;Ja 23 1829-30;Ja 5 1831;32-N 16 1841;Jl 8 1845-48;Mr 21 1853-60;F 6 1862;My 21 1864;S 18 1875;98
DeHi O 25 1828
KHi Ap 16 1865
MBAt N 21 1828;F 11,My 8 1830;F 25,D 14 1831;Ap 8,19,26 1865
MH Ap 11 1848-Ja 10 1850
MWA N 4 1825;My 17,Je 21,Ag 10,25,30 1826 [27;Ap-D 1828]Mr 27,My 7(extra)Jl 17,Ag 29 1829;F 10,Mr 4,My 5,24,N 26,D 9(extra)1830; Ja 19,Mr 18,My 5,10,Je 6,13,Jl 4,O 10,N 14,26 1831;Ja 25,F 10,Mr 3,Ap 10,S 15,21 1832;D 18 1833;Ja 18-20,My 19 1834[Ja-Mr 1836]Mr 25, 1843;Mr 25,My 20,Je 14 1844;Ag 31,N 8 1852 [Jl-D 1853]My 21 1856;Jl 24,N 17 1862;S 26 1863;S 24 1867;S 12 1868;N 30 1871;Ja 22 1878; N 25 1879;O 9 1883;Ja 6,Jl 20-21 1886;S 10 1891;Ja 26 1913
MiU-C Je 23 1826
MnHi Ja 22 1862
N complete
NAubHi D 22 1829-S 20 1831
NBu 1848[49;F-D 1850]-Ap 21,Ag 8-D 5,7 1851-[52]-[56]-[59]-[67]-[69-71]-73[Ap 1874-79]-F 17,19,21-My 22,24,S 30 1880-82;F 1883-Je 1884;86-Ap 1888
NBuG N 5,8,29,D 6,13,17,20,24,27 1839-[40]Ja 5 1851[Jl-Ag]N 28-D 5,7-12,14-19,21-25,29-31 1857
NHuHi D 16 1828
NIC N 1826-73;Jl 1879;85-87
NN F 16,25,Ap 27[S-N]1826;Ap 28(extra)[My 1828-33]Mr-Ap,Je-Jl,S-D 1834;Ap-Ag,S 24 1835-F 18,Mr 5-My,Jl-D 13 1836;37-40;Mr 27, Ap 8,Je 22-23,Jl 16,19,21,N 13,15 1841;Mr 28 (extra),N 28 1842;Mr 30,Ap 2,S 12,D 28 1846; S 6 1848;F 19 1849;F 25,Ap 11,19 1851;Mr 8 1853;Mr 17,Ap 1 1854;Ja 29,F 21,My 14,Je 20,S 19,N 28 1855[F 1856]-F 4,Mr 1,23,Ap 20 1858;Ag 12-13,O 22 1859;Ja-Je 1861;Mr 30,N 30 1863;Je 20,S 23 1864;F 13,18,Ap 15,Je 12 1865;Jl 26 1866;My 3,24-Je 8 1867;Jl 6,21,D 5 1868;Ja 1,My 4 1870;72-86
NNHi Ap 12 1830[Ja-Je 1834]Ap 17 1835[Ja-My 1836]Ag 3 1840[Ja-Je 1843]Ag 23 1848[Ja-Ap 1850]F 4,13,26 1851[Ja-Mr 1858;N 1859;Jl-O 1867]My 1 1873
NSchU 1827-[36]Jl 1837-Je 1841;Ap 15,My 3, Ag 1 1842;43-48
NSyU F 17,Mr 3 1857;My 12,Je 13,Ag 12,O 18(supp)1859;Ag 18,31,D 15 1860;Ja 21,24,F 1, Ap 23,27,My 7,13,28-29,Jl 27,S 4,O 4,29,N 19-20 1861;F 5,22,Mr 4 1862
NT [1835-76]
NcD [Mr 1831;D 1836]
NhD Ja 24 1839
NjR Ag 15 1826;Ag 20 1827;Mr 13 1858;N 11 1859
OHi F 24 1860;Ja 7-My 20 1861;F 22-My 22 1862
P-M Ja 30 1834;Je 13 1837
Vt 1838
WHi Jl 23,S 4,30 1839;Mr 3,S 3 1840;F 3 1864-65

Albany ARGUS. [Sunday ed] S 5 1877-1916||?
MWA Mr 3 1878
N 1877-80
NN [1877-86]

Albany evening ATLAS. d D 10 1840-F 16 1856||
Ap 16 1841-Mr 25 1843 as Albany morning atlas. United with Daily Albany atlas to form Atlas and argus, later Daily Albany argus
CtY 1840-S 1841;Ag 8 1842-F 14 1844;S 19-22,N 4-6 1845;F 6-12 1846
DLC Mr 12 1845;Ag 26 1846-50;D 2 1853;Mr 29 1854-55
MWA Ja 15 1845;Je 1846;F 16 1850;Jl 31,Ag 24,D 7 1852;Jl 13 1855
MWiC My 6 1865
MiU-C Je 25 1844
N complete
NN Mr 1,14,16,Ap 24-25,D 21 1849;N 15 1850
NNHi D 11 1840-Ap 14,19-S 9 1841;My 26,Ag 5,S 19-20,22,N 4-6 1845;F 6-8, 10-12,Mr 3 1846; Mr 9,29,Ap 1,4-5,9 1850[Ja-Ap 1851]
NjR Mr 28 1854
P-M Ja 6 1846

Albany weekly ATLAS. w Je 15 1842-F 15 1856||
1842-F 15 1843 as New York democrat; F 22-D 13 1843 Albany atlas. United with Albany argus to form Atlas and argus, later Albany argus
IA [1854]
MWA S 18,D 11 1852[53]-F 16 1856
N O 19 1842;S 20 1843-F 14 1844
NN Ag 3-24,S 7-21,O-N 16,30,D 14-21 1842;Ja-My 17,31-Je 7,22,Jl-N 1,15-D 20 1843;Ja 3-10,24,F 7-14 1844;Ja 25-S 6 1845
NNHi Je 24 1848;My 17 1851;O 22,N 26 1853
NSchU Ag 3 1842
PSF D 9 1848

Albany ATLAS. sw Mr 1 1844-F 15 1856||
United with Albany argus to form Atlas and argus, later Albany argus
CSmH F 27 1849-F 21 1851;F 24 1852-F 25 1853
CtY Mr 1 1844-F 23 1849
DLC S 29 1846-48;50-Je 3 1851
MWA 1844-F 1845;Je 27,O 17-20 1828
N F 28 1845-F 24 1846;F 24 1848-F 23 1849;F 26 1850-F 15 1856
NNHi F 28 1845-F 1847;F 25 1848-F 1849;Ag 13,23,S 10,N 1 1850;Ap 15,Ag 15,O 28,31,N 7, 25-28,D 9 1851;F 6,24,Mr 22-26,Ap 2,23,My 7, 18,O 12,D 7 1852;Je 24,Ag 5,D 20 1853;F 17, Ap 21-25,My 9-16 1854[F-D 1855]Ja 1,11,F 1 1856
WHi Ag 8 1848

ATLAS and argus. *See* Albany argus

BEACON and watchman. w Ja 4 1834-
CSmH Mr 8-15 1834
NNHi Ja 18,F 1 1834

Albany BEE. d Je 17 1840-
DLC Jl 11 1840
N Ag 20 1840

CANTEEN. d F 22 1864-
NNHi F-Mr 5 1864

CARSON league. w Je 12 1851-
Suspended from F 6-Mr 25 1854
1851-F 6 1854 pub in Syracuse; Mr 25-Ag 5 1854? in New York City
MWA Jl 1 1852;My 6 1854
N 1851-Ag 5 1854;F 23 1856-D 18 1858

CASTIGATOR. w
NNHi Jl 17 1847

Albany CHRISTIAN register. *See* Albany telegraph and Christian register

Morning CHRONICLE. d Ag 13? 1822-
MWA Ag 23 1822
NNHi N 14 1822

Daily CHRONICLE. d Ag 22-N 7 1826||
N complete
NN Ag 22 1826

Albany CHRONICLE. sw Ja 18? 1828-
MWA Mr 22,Jl 26 1828
NNHi D 2 1828

Albany morning CHRONICLE. d Ja 19 1828-
DLC Mr 27,S 1,O 25 1828
MWA [Ja 29-N 11 1828]
N Je 6 1828
NSchU Ap 26,Jl 14 1828

Albany CITIZEN. d N 26 1928-Ap 6 1929||
MWA complete
N complete

CITY advertiser. d Jl 14 1834-
Followed by Saturday politician and Albany city advertiser
Ct Jl 17,N 28,D 19 1834
DLC Jl 21 1834
InNh Ag 5-9,12-16 1834

COMET. w Ag 4 1827-
N Ag 4 1827

Albany CONSTITUTION atlas. sw
PPL Ja 2-Jl 13,20-D 28 1848

Evening COURIER. d S 19 1860-F 28 1861||
United with Albany morning times to form Albany times and courier, later Times-union
N complete

Albany DEMOCRAT. w
IaDH S 9,O 28 1846

DEMOCRATIC republican. sw D 5 1822-
MWA D 12,19 1822;Ja 2 1823
N F 27,Mr 27 1823
NN Jl 14-17,S 22 1823
NNHi Ap 24,My 22,Jl 14,24,31-Ag 4,S 1 1823

NEW YORK (*Continued*)

ALBANY—*Continued*

Albany DUTCHMAN. w Jl 1849-
Jl-Ag 1849? as Sunday Dutchman
CtY Ap 5 1851
N My 3,O 11 1851
NNHi S 8 1849

Albany daily EAGLE. d S 1 1851-
CtY S 2 1851

EXAMINER. w 1841||
NNHi F 3,17,27,Mr 6,13,20 1841

Albany EXPRESS. d S 13 1847-D 1898||
Merged with Daily press and knickerbocker
Suspended from Mr 22 1856-My 4 1857
Jl 20 1886 is Bicentennial number
CLM Jl 20 1886
CtY 1847-Mr 22 1856;O 14 1874-O 12 1877
ICM Ag 21 1885
KHi O 24-25 1881;My 17-Ag 5 1885;Mr 3 1891
MWA Ag 28 1852;Ap 27 1859;My 24 1871;S 7 1876
N Jl 22,S 13 1848-F 22 1849;My 1,Ag 22,D 4 1850;F 1,17 1851;N 21 1853-Mr 1856;My 4 1857-60;My 6 1861-98
NBu Ap 9 1881-S 13,O 1882-Ja 1,Mr 13,15-18, 21-Ap 16,18-21,23-My 4,6-11,13-18,20-Je 27,30 1884-Je 1885;Jl-N 17,19-D 11,13-30 1885
NN Mr 17 1849;O 27 1874;Mr 8 1881
NNHi N 21 1853-My 19,N 20 1855-Mr 1856;O 3,21 1861[F,Ap-My,Jl,S 1862-Ja,My-Jl,S 1863-Ja,Mr-Ap 1865]
NjR My 2 1865
OClWHi Ap 26 1865
WHi F 15 1860

Albany weekly EXPRESS. w 1851?-
1851?-My 25 1854 as Weekly express
N D 1853-N 17 1855

FAMILY newspaper. *See* Southwick's family newspaper

FARMERS', mechanics' and workingmen's advocate. w N 3 1829?-
CSmH S 11 1830
NNHi [Ap 1830-Mr 1831]

Albany FREEHOLDER. w Ap 9 1845-
MWA [O 1845-N 18 1846]Ja 6-13,27-F 3,17,S 8 1847-Je 11 1851
NNHi F 25 1846
RPB S 24 1845

Daily FREEMAN'S advocate and farmers', mechanics' and workingmen's champion. d,sw
MWA Je 7 1831
NNHi My 10,Je 21,28 1831

***Albany GAZETTE.** sw,w Mr 27 1817-45||
Mr 27- 1817 as Albany gazette for the country. Continues volume numbering of Albany gazette (1874-) when that paper became a daily
sw 1817-38?
CoD Ap 7 1829
Ct F 10 1826;O 29 1830[31]Mr 26 1833
CtY S 12 1828;Ja 9 1829;Mr 28 1837-Mr 23 1838
DLC Ap 2,9,23,My 21-Je 8,29,Jl 27 1824;S 28,O 9 1832;Ag 6 1839
IC 1832[33-35]-[39]-41
ICU S 25 1827
MBAt F 27 1829
MHi Je 21 1823
MWA F 16 1821;Ja 1,F 22 1822;F 28,My 13, Ag 5 1823;My 11,Ag 20,27,O 12,N 26 1824;Ja 7,Ap 26-29,Je 14 1825;Mr 10 1826;Ap 6,Jl 10,N 2,23 1827,Jl 11,O 17 1828;S 8 1829;F 19 1830;Mr 18 1836;Ap 30 1839
N 1821-Mr 22 1822;Je 18-22,Ag 31-O 5,22-26, N 5-12 1824;Ja 11,O 1825-Ja 22 1829;S 10 1830;Ja 14,F 25,Ap 15,Je 28-Jl 1,12,N 4 1831; Ap 1832-Ap 8 1833;S 11-18,O 4-11,D 11-18 1838[39]S 8,22,O 6,N 17 1840;Ja 5-12,Je 4,O 29 1841
NN [1821]Ja 11 1822[23-26]
NNHi F 12,19-22 1822;Mr 19 1824;F 29 1828;Jl 29 1831;Mr 22 1842
NSchU Ag 12 1823-N 5 1824;Mr 18,Jl 15 1842
NUHi Jl 1830-Mr 1831;40-41

***Albany GAZETTE and daily advertiser.** w,sw, d My 28 1784-1822||?
1784-Mr 22? 1817 as Albany gazette
sw My 25 1789-Mr 1817;d Mr 25 1817
MBAt Ap 8 1822
MHi 1821-22
N 1821-S 26 1822
NN Ja 29,Ap 23,Jl 20 1822
NNHi My 6,Jl 30 1822

GRIP, a weekly truth teller. w Ag 14 1880-
N Ag 14,28,S 11,25 1880

HOUR and the man. d Ag? 1858-
Campaign paper
N S 27 1858

INDEPENDENT whig. Jl 4 1823||?
Jl 4 1823 is a prospectus, the first number was to be issued Ag 2
NN Jl 4 1823(photostat)

Albany INQUIRER. w 1881-85||
N O 1 1884
NNHi Ja 14 1885

JEFFERSONIAN. w F 17 1838-F 9 1839||
CoHi Mr 24-Ap 14 1838
CtY complete
DLC complete
ICN complete
MWA complete
MiG complete
MiU complete
N complete
NBuG complete
NIC complete
NN complete
NNHi complete
NjP complete
NjR complete
PHi complete
RW Je 1838
WHi complete

Albany JOURNAL. sw 1830-99||?
MWA Ja 4 1831[32]-Ja 24,Mr 18 1834-35;Mr 5 1861
MiG N 29 1839
WHi Ag 21 1838-39;Jl 7 1857

Albany evening JOURNAL. d Mr 22 1830-F 6 1925||
Merged with Albany evening news
CLM Jl 23 1885
CSmH Ag 25 1830
CtW S 20 1893
CtY Ag 11 1830-S 27 1832;Ap 27,O 12,D 11 1833;Ap 2,Je 20 1834;40-75
DLC Je 20-21 1831;O 16 1832;F 19 1839-My 5 1840;42-Je 1846;Mr 20 1849-O 27 1852;F 18 1853;Mr 4 1861-N 3 1866;67-68;71;Jl 6 1874-1902;S 1924-25
ICM Ag 4,10 1885
ICN [1865]
IHi Ap 15,17,20-21 1865
IU Jl 8 1846;O 9 1850
KHi [F 15-S 9 1865]Mr 22 1890
MBAt Ap 18,25-26 1865
MH 1895-S 7 1898
MHi Ap 1 1836;My 7,13 1864;Jl 5 1865
MWA S 22 1830-Mr 21 1832;S 22 1835-S 22 1836;Mr 23 1837-Je 1896;97-Je 1899;Jl 1900-Je 1903;04-Je 1905;06-16;F 6 1925
MiSa O 20 1837-My 5 1840
N complete
NBu Ag 6-N 21,23 1847;Mr 11-Ap 3,5-O 27,29 1848-72;Ag 1873-Je 1884
NBuHi S 15 1830-Je 1866
NCort F 21,Mr 15 1835
NHerHi F 18-Ag 16 1839
NHf 1863
NIC 1862;66-73;85-87
NN Ja 3-8,12-17,24-25 1850
NNHi Mr 22 1830[Ja-My 1834;Ja-My,Jl 1836] My 1838-S 13 1839;Ja-O 1840[Ja-O 1841;Ja, Jl 1843-Jl 1844]Mr 5 1845;My 24-D 1852;My-D 1854[Ja,Mr 1858]N 9 1860;Jl 20 1861[F-Mr, Jl-N 1862]My 21,23,Jl 7,18,D 23 1833[Ja,Ap-Jl,S-O,D 1864;F-My 1865]F 1,Ap 3 1873;extra N 9 1838
NSchU S 22,24,29[O 1834-F]Mr 2,10,12-14,Je 17,S 5,N 14 1835;Mr 30,Ap 4 1842
NSyU F 22 1849;F 21,Mr 29 1850;F 24,Mr 21 1857;Ag 14 1861;Je 21,S 13,27 1862;F 18,O 14 1864
NT Ja-Je 1876
NcD 1842-[44;60-63]Jl 11 1865;Ja-Je 1895;Ja-Je 1896;Jl-D 1898
NhD Ja 30 1843
NjR Ap 17 1849;Ja 13 1855;Ja 23 1858;O 20 1886
OCHi Mr 22 1830(facsimile)Mr 22 1890
OClWHi Ag 2 1831;Ap 8 1841;Ap 12 1852;Mr 17,24 1857;Ja 15,F 22-23,My 3,7,Je 4,13,S 25,O 15 1861;F 4,My 27,Je 17,Ag 22 1862;Ap 10 1865;Mr 1870-Mr 15 1871;Ag 31 1874;Ja 6 1912
P-M O 27 1837;O 1 1841
PAtHi Ap 20 1865
PAtM Ap 20 1865
WHi My 6,9 1844;S 29 1856;Ag 14 1862;Jl 6, 18,20,22,26-27 1867

Albany weekly JOURNAL. w N 19 1831-99||?
Follows Albany telegraph and Christian register. 1831-S 13 1834 as Journal and telegraph
CtY D 1832-N 23 1833
MNaHi S 30 1843;Ja 9 1847
MWA O 24 1840;D 15 1855;My 30 1857;N 12 1864
N 1831-D 22 1832;F 23,Mr 2,Je 1833-My,Jl 21,Ag 30,S 13 1834
NN Ja(extra)1832
NNHi [1831-32]F-Mr[My-N]1833-S 13 1834
NSchU Jl 27 1833
WHi [Jl 15 1854-Mr 12 1864]

Albany daily KNICKERBOCKER. *See* Daily press and knickerbocker

LIFE in Albany. w N 11 1859-
N Ja 21 1860

LOG cabin. *See under* New York City

Albany MERCURY. For the country. w Ja? 1835-
MWA Ag 15,S 26 1835

Albany MERCURY, and independent examiner. sw Ag? 1834-
MWA Ap 22 1835

Albany daily MESSENGER. d
CtY My 21 1849

Albany MICROSCOPE. w Mr 10 1821-
Title varies: Microscope and herald of fancy; Microscope and independent examiner
CSmH S 11 1830
Ct Jl 16 1831
GMM [Je 22 1822-Mr 22 1823;Ap 17 1824-O 29 1825;26]Je 9 1827
IaDH F 15,Ag 15 1840
MHi Mr 9,Ap 13 1839
MWA Je 1 1833;My 17 1834-F 1836;N 4,D 30 1843
N Mr 24 1821-27;F 28 1829-F 20 1836;Mr 11 1837-F 25 1843
NBHi Mr 11 1826
NFre N 5 1842;Ja 14,F 18,Ap 1,Mr 4 1843
NN Mr 20,Ap-My,Je 12 1824-Je 18,Jl 2,Ag 20,S-O 1,15,N 12-D 3,17 1825-My 13,Jl 22,Ag 5,S 2,O 7,21,D 2 1826;Ja-Mr 3,Jl 28,Ag 11-27, S 17,O 13,23,N 3,17,D 29 1827
NNHi 1821-Mr 6 1824;Ag 1829-Jl 1830[My 1834-Ja,Mr-My 1835]Jl 16 1836;My 27,S 9 1837-[Ap-O 1838]N 16 1839;Ag 21,S 25,O 23,N 13 1831-[Ja]F 5,Mr 5,Ap 2,Jl 2,D 10 1842;Mr 18,Ap 22 1843;Ja 27,My 18 1844;N 22 1845
NSchU Mr 26,Jl 16,Ag 20 1842
OClWHi My 11,D 14 1833;F 1,Mr 22-Ap 5,Je-N 1834;Ja 10-Je 6,O 17,N 21,D 26 1835-Ja 2, My 7,28-Je 1 1836;F 11 1837

Albany MINERVA. sm Ja 1-Mr 25 1828||
N complete

Albany MIRROR and public spirit. w 1879-80||
Title varies slightly
N O 18 1879-My 6 1880

NATIONAL democrat. sw O 8 1823-25||?
Followed by Albany patriot
Suspended from Mr 15-Ap 20 1824
DLC F 14,Ap 27-My,Ag 6-10,20,31-S 7 1824;Je 28,Jl 1 1825
MWA Ja 4,28 1825
N 1823-Mr 15,Ap 20-O,D 21 1824;F 5 1825
NNHi O 8,11,25 1823;Ja 7,Ap 23,Ag 27,S 17,O 29 1824
NSchU O 8,N 26 1823-Jl 26 1825

NATIONAL observer. sw,w Jl 25 1826-D 12 1828||
sw 1826-Ja 12 1827
DLC 1826;Ag 24 1827
MHi Ja 11 1828
MWA Ag 8,25-29,S 5-19,O 24 1826;Ja 12,F 23, Ap 13 1827;F 15 1828
N S 19,N 10 1826;F 9,Mr 23,Ap 6-13,Je 8,Jl 27-D 7 1827;F 8,Mr 4,7,Ap 12,Je 20,Ag 22-D 12 1828
NSchU Ag 17 1827;Mr 14,Ap 4,18,Jl 18,Ag 22, N 14,D 5-12 1828
OClWHi Ag 17 1827-28

NATIONAL observer and anti-masonic pioneer. sw Mr 4 1829-
1829? as National observer
CoD Jl 22 1829
DLC Mr 4(supp),Jl 15-22,Ag 11,D 2,30 1829;D 4 1830;Ja 1-15 1831
MHi My 1 1829
MnHi Ag 21 1829
NNHi F-[Jl-D 1829]Ja 6 1830
NSchU [Mr-N 1829]S 11-18 1830
OClWHi Mr-S 1829;Ja-Jl 21 1830

NEW ALBANY gazette. w
NLi My 13 1841

NEW YORK democrat. *See* Albany weekly atlas

***NEW YORK statesman.** sw My 16 1820-Ja 1 1822||
Follows Albany register (not in this list). United with New York evening journal to form New York statesman and evening advertiser, later New York statesman (New York City)
CtY Ja 19,N 13 1821
DLC Ja-N 1821
MBAt Ja 5 1821
MWA [1821]
N Ja 19,S 11,18-21,D 28 1821
NI Ja-Jl 1821
NN F 27,Ap 3,17,N 13 1821;Ja 1 1822

Albany daily NEWS. d Ap 5-Jl 12 1834||
MWA complete

Albany evening NEWS. d 1922+
M F 16 1933
PScrHi My 26 1931

NORTH star and freemen's advocate. w Ja 20 1842-
Negro
MWA F 10 1842
N F-Ap 14,D 8 1842;Ja 2 1843
NSchU My 17 1842

NORTHERN star. w Ag 5 1837-
DLC S 2 1837

Albany PATRIOT. sw Ag 12 1825-26||?
Follows National democrat
CtY S 20 1825
MWA Ag 23,O 21,N 15-29,D 6-9,16-27 1825[Ja 10-My 23 1826]
N F 3,Ap 21 1826

Albany weekly PATRIOT. w O 15 1841-48||?
1841-42 as Tocsin of liberty
DLC D 29 1847;My 31 1848
DLC D 24 1841;D 29 1847;My 31 1848
MB [D 31 1841-42]-O 1844
MWA D 17 1841
MdBJ Je 28,Jl 27,Ag 10-S,O 12 1842-Mr 23,Ap 13-Je 8,22-Jl,Ag 22-O 10,24-D 1843; 47-Je 14 1848
MiBy 1845
N N 18 1846;Ap 5 1848
NCanHi Ja 26,Mr 2,Ap 6,20,My 11,Ag 22,S 19 1843;My 8,Je 12 1844
NIC 1847-48
NNHi N 24(extra)1841;N 10 1842;N 13 1844-N 4 1846
NSchU D 3(extra)1841;Ja 7,12,26-F 2,Mr 16 1842
NSyU O 28 1846
NhD Je 12 1844
OClWHi Je 12,Jl 24,N 13 1844,Ja 29,Ap 9-30 1845
WHi O 1842-O 1844
WMeno 1843-O 1844

Albany daily PATRIOT. d Ja 3 1843-
DLC F 3 1843
MdBJ Ja 3 1843

Albany PATRIOT and daily commercial intelligencer. d
MWA N 4 1825

PLAINDEALER. d S 10 1840-
NNHi S-D 9 1840

Saturday POLITICIAN and Albany city advertiser. Ja 17 1835-
Follows City advertiser
DLC F 14 1835

Albany evening POST. d O 23 1865-94||?
N O 24 1865;N 8 1866;Ag 5 1885
NNHi Ap 14 1873

Sunday PRESS. w 1870+
CLM Ap 11 1886
CtY O 19,N 16 1873
MWA Ap 14 1872
N Jl 30 1871;F 23,Mr 2 1873;Jl 21 1878;D 28 1884;Ag 9 1885;S 21 1892;Je 17 1900
NNHi Jl 3 1870;Mr 9 1873

Daily PRESS. d F 26-Ag 11 1877||
United with Albany daily knickerbocker to form Daily press and knickerbocker
DLC complete

NEW YORK (*Continued*)

ALBANY—*Continued*

Daily PRESS and knickerbocker. d S 4 1843+
1843-Ag 11 1877 as Albany daily knickerbocker; Ag 13 1877-Mr 15 1879 Daily press and Albany knickerbocker; Ja 9 1899-My 20 1910 Press-knickerbocker-express
CL N 24 1928
CLM Jl 19,23 1886
CoU 1903;05;S 1906-Je 1910
CtY N 25 1847;Mr 24,Je 14,Jl 6,8,18 1848;My 22 1849;F 26,29 1916
DLC N 15 1850;77-91;Mr 20 1919+
M Mr 21 1933
MWA F 6 1844;Ag 19 1848;O 24,31 1850;F 4 1858
MnHi Ja 21 1862
N D 30 1845;Mr 1,My 14,O 12 1846;Ag 16,D 4-5 1850;My 19,Je 30,Ag 6,S 6,D 24 1852;Ap 20,Jl 25 1853;My 20,Je 4 1856;Jl 8 1858;O 17-18 1861;S 20,22,24 1862;Jl 15 1863;Ap 27,29, My 3-4,17-20,Jl 11,13,27,29,N 16,22 1864;Ja 23,Ap 10,15,17-22,26-29,Je 10,D 4 1865;66;Ja 24 1868;O 5 1870;F 22,24-25 1873;O 13 1874;F 20 1879;S 26,O 9 1883;Jl 19 1886;Jl 2,Ag 31 1888; Mr 11,14 1889;Jl-D 1905;Jl-D 1906;Jl-D 1907; Jl-D 1908;Jl 1909-Je 1910;Ja-S,N 1911-Je 1912;13+
NGL [Mr 1925-My 1927]N 24-28 1928
NN Mr 9 1848;Ap 14,16 1852;Ap 1,Je 2-Jl 10,13-Ag 8,10-S 13,15-N 1854;Ja 1,5-Je 1858
NNHi Ag 19 1847;O 18 1862;My 25,S 16 1864; Ap 20 1865;Ap 1 1873
NSyU Ap 20,24 1861
OClWHi Mr 31,Ap 7 1852;Ja 5 1912
WaPS Ap 7-8,10 1919[23-25]

RECORD. w Je 14-N 15 1879||
NNHi complete

*Albany REGISTER. w,sw O 1788-
Suspended from My 12 1820-Mr? 1821
w 1788-Ag 10 1822
DLC Ap 3 1822
MWA S 5,O 17-N 7,D 19 1821;Ja 23,Mr 6-13, 27,Je 22-Jl 6,27,Ag 10,16-30,S 13-20,27-O 4, 15-22,N 1,8,18,D 2 1822
NI Ap-D 1821
NNHi N 25 1822

Albany REGISTER. w Mr 1850-
NIC 1850-Mr 1854

REPUBLICAN statesman. w 1851-
NSyU Ap 20,Ag 31-S 14,O 12,N 2,16 1861;Ap 2,29 1862

REPUBLICAN statesman. d
MWA Je 17 1862
MWiC F 15 1862
N Je 17 1862

ROUGH and ready. w S 25 1848-
Campaign paper
N S 25 1848

ROUGH hewer, devoted to the support of the democratic principles of Jefferson. w F 20-D 24 1840||
United with Albany argus to form Argus and rough hewer, later Albany argus
Suspended from O 30-D 24 1840
Ja 18 1840 is Specimen number
CSmH complete
CtY Je 26 1840
DLC complete
ICU [1840]
IU Je 25,Jl 9,Ag 20 1840
MB complete
MH complete
MWA complete
MiU Jl 30 1840
N complete
NIC complete
NN complete
Tx complete
TxU complete
WHi complete

SIGNS of the times. w O 13 1827-N 8 1828||
Ct [1827-28]
CtY complete
MHi complete
MWA F 16-Ag 16 1828
N complete
NNHi 1827-O 11 1828
T complete

SOUTHWICK'S family newspaper. w Ja 6 1838-N 30 1839||
1838-Ja 12 1839 as Family newspaper
MWA Ja 27 1838-Ja 12 1839
N complete
NN Je 23 1838

STANDARD. w My 22 1827-
N My-Ag 21 1827

Albany evening STANDARD. d D 18 1858-
N 1858-Ap 28,O 2 1860-Ap 27,Jl 16 1861-Ja,F 3-S,D 29 1862
NSyU S 15 1860;Ja 31,My 18,25,Je 1,Jl 20,Ag 3,31,S 7,14,O 12,N 2,16 1861

Albany daily STATE register. d Mr 23 1850-
DLC S 19-D 1850
MWA Ag 31 1852
N F 14 1852;F-Ag,O 1853-55
NBa 1850-Mr 22 1856
NBu O 15 1855
NN Mr 25-27,29,Ap 1-3,5-30,My 2-3,6,9-Je 1 1850;My 4 1854
NNHi 1850-Mr 1851;O 12 1854;F 23 1855;Ap 19,26 1856
NUHi 1850-51

Albany STATE register. sw 1850-
NN Mr 25,Je 4-Ag 9,16-S 6,13,27,O 8-26 1850; Ja 21-F 4,11-Mr 4,11 1851

Albany STATE register. w 1850-
MWA Ag 25 1852
N Mr 12-Ap 9,D 3,17,31 1851;F 4,18-Mr 3,17, N 2 1852;S 18 1855
NjR D 4 1855
VtBr Mr 26-My 7,21-28,Jl 11-S 3,17-N 19,D 1851-Ja 21,F-Mr 10 1852

STATESMAN. d Mr? 1847-
N Je 21 1847

Albany STATESMAN. w Mr 18 1856-
N N 11 1856
NjR O 12 1858

Albany daily STATESMAN. d 1856-
MWA S 21 1858
N Jl 16 1856;Ja 20,Je 8,10,N 17 1857
NN Mr 26 1857
NNHi Mr 24 1856-S 23 1857[Ja-Mr 1858]
NSyU F 19 1857

Daily SUN. d 1838-
MWA O 21 1839

Albany SWITCH. w 1842-
IU Jl 29 1854
N F 24 1844[D 20 1845-D 5 1846]
NEh Je 15 1844
NNHi S 5,19-26,O 31-N,D 12,26 1846;F 13,27, Ap 24-My 8,Jl 10,N 13 1847;F 12-19,Mr 4,Jl 10,N 13 1848
WHi My 3 1851

Albany TELEGRAPH and Christian register. w My 19 1827-
1827-N 6 1830 as Albany Christian register. Followed by Journal and telegraph, later Albany weekly journal
N Ja 8-O 15 1831
NNHi My 17 1828-S 1831

Albany weekly TIMES. w Jl 16 1872-1908||?
N 1872-83;88-N 19 1891
NNHi Ag 28 1873

TIMES-UNION. d Ap 21 1856+
1856-F 1861 as Albany morning times; Mr 1861-S 23 1866 Albany times and courier; S 25 1866-N 16 1891 Evening times
DLC S 12 1892-93;97-Ap 26 1929
KHi Je 6 1877
MWA Ja 1 1857;Ap 27,O 12 1859;Mr 17 1860; D 1 1871;Ja 21 1873
N 1856-O 20 1860;Mr 1861-F,Je 20 1863-64;Mr 1865+
NN Ap 24 1861;Ap 7 1862;Je 9,D 10 1863; Je 5 1865
NNHi S 20,22 1862;Mr 16 1864;My 2 1873
NSyU Mr 17 1857;Ag 16 1861

TOCSIN of liberty. *See* Albany weekly patriot

Albany daily TRANSCRIPT. d O 12 1835-
Ct N 10,D 9,11 1835;Ja 30,F 2,Mr 9,14,17-19, 22-23 1836
N Mr 5 1836
NNHi D 10 1835

Albany TRANSCRIPT. w
Ct N 10 1835

Albany evening TRANSCRIPT. d Ja 31 1853-
Title varies slightly
MWA O 30 1857
N 1853-55;S 16-19 1856;Ja 31,F 4 1857;Je 18,Jl 3 1858
NjVi F 26 1858-Ja 22 1859
WHi 1853-Ja 30 1855

Albany weekly TRANSCRIPT. w 1857-
NjVi Ag 1 1857-Jl 31 1858

Albany UNION. w Ja 9 1858-
NjR Ap 24 1858

Albany evening UNION. d My 20 1882-N 16 1891||
United with Evening times to form Times-union
N complete

UNIONIST. d S 19 1840-
DLC S 19 1840

Albany WHIG. w Ag 2 1834-
Merged with Albany gazette
N N 29 1834;Ja 3 1825

ALBION

Albion ADVERTISER. w N 8 1929+
pub 1929+

ALBION. w
NBi S 4 1858-N 26 1859

Albion HERALD. w N 10 1859-
N Mr 3 1860

ORLEANS advocate. *See* Orleans telegraph

ORLEANS American. w S 5 1832+
Follows Orleans telegraph
DLC F 12 1834
GU My 23 1872
MWA D 2 1852;Je 27 1878
N D 26 1832;Ja 2,23,F 6-13,Mr 6,My 8 1833;O 17,D 5 1861;N 24 1864;O 12 1871
NNHi Ja 23 1873
NjHi S 12,O 3,24,N 7 1832

ORLEANS anti-masonic telegraph. *See* Orleans telegraph

ORLEANS democrat. w 1849-
DLC O 30 1852

ORLEANS republican. w O 1829+
CSmH S 8 1830
MWA N 3 1852;My 16 1866
N O 16 1833;O 21 1835;Ag 18 1852;D 15 1857; Mr 5 1862;My 19 1880;N 1913+
NCanHi Mr 20 1844
NMeT 1870-Ja 1 1871
OClWHi My 17,Je 14-28 1848

ORLEANS telegraph. w 1826-31||
1826-F 20 1828 as Orleans advocate; F 27 1828-F 4 1829 Orleans advocate and anti-masonic telegraph; F 11-Je 3 1829 Orleans anti-masonic telegraph. Followed by Orleans American
CSmH S 8 1830
DLC Ag 5 1829
MWA Ag 22 1827-Ag 6 1828;Ja 14 1829-Je 1830
N Je 1 1831

ALDEN

Alden ADVERTISER. w 1914+
pub 1927+

ALEXANDER

FARMERS' and mechanics' journal. w N 4 1837-Je 13 1840||
Followed by Batavia times and farmers' and mechanics' journal (Batavia)
DLC S 28,O 12 1839;My 30 1840
MBAt My 19 1838
WHi complete

ALEXANDRIA BAY

THOUSAND ISLANDS sun. w Ap 1901+
pub 1923+

ALFRED CENTER

Alfred SUN. w 1885+
NAlU 1885;87-1924;26+
RW Jl 21 1887

ALLEGANY

Allegany CITIZEN. w 1896+
pub 1896+

ALTAMONT

Altamont ENTERPRISE. w 1884+
pub 1884+

AMENIA

HARLEM VALLEY times. w Ap 7 1852+
1852-1911 as Amenia times
pub 1926+
MWA Jl 12 1864;F 25 1868;N 5 1877;Jl 30 1883
N My 4 1874
NAmeB 1926-33
NN F 4 1857
NNHi Ja 28 1873;D 8-15 1879
NP [1852-1911]+

Amenia TIMES. *See* Harlem Valley times

AMITYVILLE

LONG ISLAND enterprise. w 1900-10||
NRiHi Ap 7 1900-Mr 19 1910

LONG ISLAND sun. w Ap 8 1911+
pub [1916+]

Amityville RECORD. w My 4 1904+
pub 1904+

AMSTERDAM

Amsterdam daily DEMOCRAT. *See* Amsterdam evening recorder and daily democrat

INTELLIGENCER and Mohawk advertiser. w 1835-53||
Title varies: Amsterdam intelligencer; etc.
DLC F 11,N 18 1840
NFj Ja 14 1846;Jl 8 1851
NNHi My 14 1845
NSchU D 22-29 1841
NhD N 18 1851
WHi Mr 10 1835

MOHAWK gazette. w N 28 1832-
NNHi D 19-26 1832
WHi D 4 1833

MOHAWK herald. w D 26 1821-23||
Followed by Johnstown herald (Johnstown)
NFj 1822-D 10 1823

Amsterdam evening RECORDER and daily democrat. d Ag 20 1879+
1879-Ag 19 1902 as Amsterdam daily democrat
pub 1879+
ICM Ag 6,S 15-16 1885
N Ag 20 1913-Jl 1922

ANDES

Andes RECORDER. w 1867+
pub 1892+
IU F 5 1897

ANDOVER

Andover NEWS. w 1887+
pub 1904+
NAn 1922+

ANGELICA

Angelica ADVOCATE. w 1900+
pub Jl 1908-Je 1919;Ag 1920+

ALLEGANY county advocate. w Ja 1842-
N S 23 1852

ALLEGANY republican. w 1820-
DLC O 3 1833
NjHi [1821-25]

ALLEGANY republican. w 1843-
1843-55 as Whig and advocate
DLC S 27 1855
MWA Jl 27,Ag 24 1854;Jl 10 1856
N Ap 20 1854
NNHi D 6 1855

Angelica REPORTER. w 1834-
MWA Ja 6 1836
N N 4 1835

Angelica REPUBLICAN. w 1827-
OClWHi My 14 1828

WHIG and advocate. *See* Allegany republican

ANGOLA

Angola RECORD. w 1879+
pub 1884-1934

NEW YORK (*Continued*)

ANTWERP

Antwerp GAZETTE. w 1873-Ap 1925||
MWA Jl 27 1876;S 18 1889
NAnt 1876-88

ARCADE

Arcade ENTERPRISE. w Mr 31 1859-
NAr Mr 31,Ap 29,Je 10,Jl 21,S 30,D 30 1859; Ja 13,Mr 5,9-16,Ap 6-13,27-My 11 1860;Ja 24, Ap 21 1865;Jl 11 1866
Arcade HERALD. w 1891+
pub 1891+

ASSEMBLY POINT

LAKE GEORGE mirror. w 1890-
1890-1900 pub Je-D only
N Je 1891-1900;02-15

ASTORIA

Papers published in Astoria are listed under Long Island City

ATLANTA

Atlanta NEWS. *See* Cohocton index (Cohocton)

ATTICA

Attica ATLAS. w Ja 1 1851-70||
N S 4 1852;S 9 1870
Attica BALANCE. w 1835-37||?
Ct N 3 1835
Attica DEMOCRAT. w 1838-46||
N Ag 6 1845
Attica REPUBLICAN. w 1832-34||
N O 16 1833
NNHi Ja 7 1834

AUBURN

ADVERTISER-JOURNAL. d 1844-My 1931||
1844-1913 title varies: Auburn daily advertiser; Auburn daily advertiser and union; etc. United with Auburn citizen to form Citizen-advertiser
DLC 1866;My 21 1875
KHi N 15 1888
MBAt Ap 5 1865
MWA N 6 1852;O 22 1860;O 11 1876
N Je 8 1843;Ag 2 1876
NAub Ap 1903-31
NAubHi My 25 1848-Ag 23 1849;78-1931
NN F 26 1849;Jl 18,Ag 28,30,S 1 1851
NNHi Ap 1873
NSyU S 28-29,N 3-4 1848;F 2 1849;Je 1 1861
OClWHi My 18 1846;My 2,8,11,16 1861;Jl 8 1862;F 8 1865
Auburn AMERICAN. *See* Auburn union
Auburn ARGUS. w Ja 1891-D 31 1897||
United with Auburn democrat to form Auburn democrat-argus
MiU O 23 1891
NAubC 1891-95;97
Evening AUBURNIAN. d 1877-84||
United with Auburn news and bulletin to form Auburn news-bulletin-Auburnian, later Citizen-advertiser
MWA N 26 1880
NAubC N 8 1870-My 1879;D 9 1880-My 7 1881
NAubHi 1878-80;83-Je 1884
Weekly AUBURNIAN. w 1883-94||
NAubC 1885-88;Jl 1892-94
Auburn BANNER. w 1832-
NAubHi 1833-My 21 1834
PToF Ja 3 1838-O 2 1839
Auburn BANNER and Genesee, Oneida and Black-River conference record. w Ja 5 1837-
Title varies
KyLo D 12-19 1838
NAubHi 1838
NNHi 1837-38
PToF 1838-O 2 1839
Auburn weekly BULLETIN. w 1882-1911||
NAubC 1895-1911
Auburn daily BULLETIN. *See* Citizen-advertiser
CAYUGA county independent. *See* Cayuga county news
CAYUGA county news. w F 8 1874-1921||?
1874-1910 as Cayuga county independent
NAubC 1896
NAubHi F 28 1879-S 24 1891;N 12 1908-20
CAYUGA new era. w Je 22 1847-57||
Formed by the union of Cayuga tocsin and Cayuga patriot
DLC O 17 1855
MWA Ag 17,S 7-14 1853
NNHi N 17 1847;N 21 1849;N 20 1850
*CAYUGA patriot. w O 19 1814-Je 1847||
United with Cayuga tocsin to form Cayuga new era
CSmH S 8 1830
Ct [1827-28;30-37]
DLC My 13,N 4 1829;D 17 1834;D 23 1835;S 4 1839
MiU [1836]-[38]
N N 1,D 27 1826-28;D 19 1832;F 13,O 23 1833;D 17 1834;D 20 1837;My 10,Jl 5 1843
NAub Jl 1825-S 1826;Ap 1829-Mr 1834;Mr 1835-Mr 1847
NAubHi [1821-O 16 1832]
NCor Je 11 1828
NN O 18 1826
NNHi Je 17,O 28 1829;Ja 1,F 26 1834;N 17 1841;D 4,18 1844
NSchU O 26 1842
WHi Ap 17 1839
*CAYUGA republican. w Mr 24 1819-My 15 1833||
Follows Auburn gazette (not in this list). United with Free press to form Auburn journal and advertiser, later Auburn journal
CSmH My 6 1829;S 8 1830
DLC O 19,26 1824;Je 24-Ag 4,S 2-23,O 21,D 23-30 1829;Ja 6-20 1830
ICHi N 23 1825
MWA Ap 13,My 18-25 1825;My 17 1826;My 13 1829;My 25 1831
N Ag 27 1823;D 1 1824;N 30 1825;Mr 28 1827
NAubHi Mr 10,24 1824-F,Mr 12 1828-My 15 1833
NNHi O 6-13,27-N 10 1824;N 16-23 1831;N 21 1832
P-M O 10 1832
TxU Ap 1831-My 15 1833
WHi Ag 20 1823;O 20 1824;Ja-Mr 1825;S 3 1828;My 27 1829
CAYUGA tocsin. w Ap 5 1839-Je 1847||
United with Cayuga patriot to form Cayuga new era
MWA My 11 1842
N Mr 4 1840
NAubC Ap 8 1840-Mr 24 1841
NNHi N 16-23 1842;N 6 1844
NSchU Jl 27-S 7 1842
OClWHi Jl 16 1846
Daily CAYUGA tocsin. d 1845-
OClWHi Mr 19,Je 18,24,Jl 6 1846
CITIZEN-ADVERTISER. d F 16 1870+
1870-S 1905 as Auburn daily bulletin (Je 2 1879-84? Auburn news and bulletin; 1884-85 Auburn news-bulletin-Auburnian; 1885-1904? Auburn bulletin) O 1905-My 1931 Auburn citizen
pub 1870+
N Mr 1913+
NAub F 17 1870-78;Ap 1903+
NAubHi 1870-Je 1881;Je 1931+
NNHi 1870-Jl 3 1871;Ap 2 1873
NjR Je 8 1876
COON killer. w Jl 26 1844-
Campaign paper
MWA S 6 1844
Auburn DEMOCRAT-ARGUS. w,sw S 17 1868-1929||?
1868-74 as Auburn democrat; 1875-97 Auburn weekly news and democrat w 1868-1909?
NAubC S 17 1868-S 2 1869;75-97;1900-13
Morning DISPATCH. d 1882-88||
1882-89 as Evening dispatch
ICM Je 18,21 1888
KHi O 19 1888
NcD S 23 1884
PNbF Ag 3 1888
EXAMINER. w F 18 1826-
N F 18 1826
FREE PRESS. w Je 2 1824-My 1833||
United with Cayuga republican to form Auburn journal and advertiser, later Auburn journal
CSmH Jl 28 1830
DLC Ag 22 1827;S 16,O 28 1829;Ja 20-27 1830; Ja 12 1831
MWA My 4,S 21,N 9-16 1825
N D 15 1824-N 1826
NAubHi 1825-Mr 1,My 31 1826-My 21 1828
NNHi O 13 1824
NjH Je 4,S 10 1828;Mr 4,My 27 1829
P-M D 8 1832
Auburn INDEPENDENT. w 1856-
PAtM Ap 16 1857;S 17 1859
Auburn JOURNAL. w,sw My 22 1833-1913||?
1833-46 as Auburn journal and advertiser w 1833-94?
MWA Ag 23 1876;Mr 21 1894
N O 16 1833 Ap 19 1854
NAubHi 1833-My 21 1834
NCor My 31 1837-Ap 10 1850
NNHi N 22 1848;F 5 1873
NSchU Ap 13 1842
NSyU Je 8-15 1870
OClWHi Ap 16 1862
P-M S 25 1833;Jl 16 1854
TxU 1833-My 10 1837
Auburn MISCELLANY. w My 28 1835-
N O 1-8 1835
NATIONAL reformer. *See under* Rochester
Auburn daily NEWS. w F 9 1833-Ag 31 1838||
NAubHi complete
Auburn morning NEWS. d Jl 6 1868-My 31 1879||
United with Auburn daily bulletin to form Auburn news and bulletin, later Citizen-advertiser
CtY Ap 19 1869
DLC My 20-21 1875
NAubC complete
NAubHi complete
NNHi My 15 1873
Auburn weekly NEWS. w Ag 12 1872-D 31 1874||
United with Auburn democrat to form Auburn weekly news and democrat, later Auburn democrat-argus
NAubC complete
Auburn NEWS and bulletin. *See* Citizen-advertiser
Auburn weekly NEWS and democrat. *See* Auburn democrat-argus
Auburn daily UNION. d F 1 1855-Mr 7 1861||
1855-Je 1859 as Auburn American
MWA O 18 1850
NAubC 1855-Ja 21,Je 6 1860-61
NAubHi Jl 1860-61
Auburn weekly UNION. w F 7 1855-
1855-Je 22 1859 as Auburn weekly American
NAubC 1855-My 30 1860

AU SABLE FORKS

ADIRONDACK record-Elizabethtown post. w Mr 6 1908+
1908-N 19 1920 as Adirondack record
pub 1908+
N Je 12 1914-N 10 1916
NHi 1934+

AVOCA

Avoca HERALD. w Mr 20 1931+
pub Ag 24 1933+

AVON

AVON SPRINGS herald. *See* Avon herald
Avon HERALD. w 1876+
1876-87? as Livingston county herald. Some issues as Avon Springs herald
pub O 1882+
NN Ja 18 1912;Ja 17 1918
INDEPENDENT news. w O 23 1907+
1907-30 as Avon news
pub 1907-20;28+
NGe F 20,Mr 20,Ap 10-24,My 22-29,Je 19,Jl 10,31,Ag 14-S,O 30-N 13 1918;Ja 1,15,29,F 28, Mr 14-Je 1919
LIVINGSTON county herald. *See* Avon herald
Avon NEWS. *See* Independent news

BABYLON

Babylon BUDGET. w 1876-88||?
N Jl 24 1880-N 1881
NBHi My 1877-Ja 1883
NRc N 16 1878
Babylon EAGLE. w F 6 1929+
pub 1929+
Babylon LEADER. w Jl 8 1910+
pub 1910+
SOUTH SIDE signal. w 1869-
N My-Ag,N 2 1895;S 1917-19
NBHi 1884-1920
NNHi Mr 15 1873;S 29 1911
NRc My 11 1872;F 22,Mr 1873;Ap 24 1875;Ja 1,15,N 25 1876;Ja 27,Mr 24,Je 16,D 8 1877; Mr 15,Je 28 1879
NRiHi Jl 15 1876
NSm Je 10 1871;Jl 22 1876;Ag 30 1884;Jl 11-18 1891;O 21 1893;Ag 21 1909

BAINBRIDGE

Bainbridge REPUBLICAN. w 1871+
pub 1875+
KHi O 24 1874;Je 1 1922
N F 19 1886

BAINBURG

Bainburg EAGLE. w Ap 29 1845-
Follows National archives (Ithaca)
NIC Ap 29-D 4,18 1845

BALDWIN

Baldwin CITIZEN. w Ja 1925+
1932-33 as Nassau citizen
pub 1925+
NNQ S 28 1934+
NASSAU citizen. *See* Baldwin citizen

BALDWINSVILLE

Baldwinsville GAZETTE and farmers' journal. w O 1846+
1846-79? as Onondago gazette
pub 1846-N 20 1857;Ap 20 1865;Mr 1866-F 1869;N 25 1874;86+
MWA N 5 1852
NN D 1 1847
NNHi Jl 16 1863;F 19,Ap 2,My 14,Je 4,25 1873;Jl 22,S 2-9,O 21 1874[75-78]
ONONDAGO gazette. *See* Baldwinsville gazette and farmers' journal

BALLSTON SPA

Ballston ATLAS. w
N My 25,N 26 1858;Je 13 1862
NNHi Je 13 1862
Ballston DEMOCRAT. w 1845-53||?
MWA N 26 1852
N O 1847-S 21 1849
NHi S 12 1845(extra)
Ballston DEMOCRATIC whig journal. w Ap 20 1847-49||
Follows Ballston Spa gazette. Followed by Ballston Spa journal, later Ballston journal
NN N 9 1852
NSyU O 24 1848;Mr 13-20 1849
Ballston Spa GAZETTE. w N 1821-47||
Follows Saratoga farmer. Followed by Ballston democratic whig journal
CSmH Jl 13 1830
CoD O 4,18-N 8 1825;O 11,D 23 1828;29-Ja 5,O 5 1830;Ja 25-S 1831[F 1832-F 4 1834]
DLC My 18-25,Je 22,Jl 27,S 21,O 12,N 2,16,D 6 1824;S 4 1827;D 16 1828;Mr 24,S 15-23,O 27 1829;S 30 1832
MBAt Ap 3 1822
MWA S 14,N 9 1824;N 20 1827;O 21 1828;Ap 4 1843
N Ag 19 1823;Ag 2,16,N 14 1825;O 16 1827;N 1 1831
NHi My 10 1831
NN N 20 1827
NNHi F 20,O 22-N 5,19-D 10,24 1822;Ag 26-S 16,D 9-16 1824;F 24,S 21,O 26-N 2 1824; N 22 1825;O 24-N 6,21-28,D 12 1826;Je 26,O 30-N 6,20 1827;O 28,N 25 1828;N 17 1829; S 21-N 16 1830;Jl 15,S 16 1834;S 8,O 1 1840; Je 15,S 28 1841;F 23 1847
NSchU Ap 26-My 3 1842
P-M S 25 1832

NEW YORK (*Continued*)

BALLSTON SPA—*Continued*

Ballston JOURNAL. w 1849-1913||?
Follows Ballston democratic whig journal. Title varies: Ballston Spa journal
IU Jl 14 1857
N Ap 15 1856-65;Ja 13 1866-My 24 1913
NHi D 14 1872[80]
NNHi Ja(extra)1863;Mr 29 1873

Ballston Spa daily JOURNAL. d Je 2 1871+
pub 1930+
N Je 2,S 11 1871;S 1894-1929

NEW YORK palladium. w Ag 30 1830-
CoD Ja-My 3 1831
NNHi S 14-N 16 1830

Ballston Spa REPUBLICAN. w Jl 23 1833-
CoD Jl 30-D 10 1833
NHi [1836-37]
NNHi Jl 15,22 1834

SARATOGA and Schenectady standard. w Ja 18 1831-33||
Ja-O? 1831 as Schenectady and Saratoga standard (Schenectady)
N Ag 22,S 5,19,O 3 1831
NSchU Jl 25,Ag 8-15 1831;My 29 1832

SARATOGA county exchange. w F 5 1839-
DLC F 19 1839

SARATOGA farmer. w O 1820-O? 1821||
Followed by Ballston Spa gazette
DLC Ag 1 1821
NNHi Ja 17-24,F 7 1821

BARKER

Barker REGISTER. w D 10 1904+
pub 1904+

BATAVIA

BATAVIAN. w F 1868-97||
1868-Je 1895 as Progressive Batavian
MWA S 22 1871
NBat 1868-Ja 1897

GENESEE county herald. w 1854-
1854-56 pub in Le Roy
NBat 1857-Je 1861

GENESEE democrat. w 1857-
MWA Ap 11,Jl 4,D 5 1863
NBat 1857-59
NSyU Je 1,S 7,N 16 1861

Daily HERALD. d 1858-
OClWHi S 8 1859

MORGAN investigator. w Mr 29 1827-
MWA Jl 12,S 20 1827
N Mr 29 1827

Batavia daily NEWS. d 1878+
pub 1879+
MWA Ja 1 1879
N Ap 1913+
NBat My 1879-Ag 1881;Je 25 1891+

PEOPLE'S press. w 1825-
Merged with Spirit of the times, later Batavia times
Ct Ag 18 1827;My 10 1828
MWA N 10 1827
N D 9 1826;Ja 13 1827
NN O 21 1826

PROGRESSIVE Batavian. *See* Batavian

***REPUBLICAN advocate.** w N 9 1811-82||?
Title varies slightly
CSmH S 10 1830
ICM Ag 2 1877
MBAt Ja 5 1821;O 11 1842;Ja 3,S 26 1843
MWA My 14,Jl 30,O 8-15,N 5,D 3,24 1824;F 4,Jl 15 1825;My 8 1829;O 21 1831
N Jl 16,N 5 1824;F 11,Jl 29,O 28 1825;S 29,N 3-10 1826;Mr 23-30,Ap 13,My 25,Jl 20,Ag 31-N 23 1827;F 18,Mr 11,Ap 1,Jl 1,15,29-Ag 5,S 16 1834;Ag 31 1852;Ap 4 1854
NBat Ap 1822-76
NN S 29(extra)1826;Jl 3 1829;My 26 1870
NNHi O 3-10 1823;Mr 20 1873
NR F-D 7 1827
NjHi N 16 1827;Mr 27,S 11 1829;My 21 1830
OClWHi My 4,Jl 6-13 1841;Jl 22 1851;S 26 1854;Je 26 1855;Ap 1 1856;My 19 1857
REdH D 5,N 14 1828

SPIRIT of the times. *See* Batavia times

***Batavia TIMES.** w F 3 1819+
1819-1901? as Spirit of the times
pub 1819+
Ct Mr 10 1835;Mr 2 1837
DLC 1821-25
MWA N 30 1852;Ja-Ag,N 14 1854;Ja 9-Jl 21 1855;Ja-N 1 1856
N F 28 1823;O 15 1833;O 20 1835;Ap 4 1854;Je 15 1861-63;68;70-75;Mr 1913-20
NBat S 1830-N 1833;Jl 1840-N 1856;64-69
NNHi N 13 1829;Ap 26 1873
OClWHi Ap 30 1840;Je 2 1866
WHi O 11,N 15 1853;Mr 21,Jl 18 1854

Batavia TIMES and farmers' and mechanics' journal. w Je 1840-43||
Follows Farmers' and mechanics' journal (Alexander). Merged with Spirit of the times, later Batavia times
IU S 6 1843

BATH (STEUBEN COUNTY)

CONSTITUTIONALIST. w Ag 23 1837-44||
DLC Ag 28 1839
MWA Ag 29 1838
N S 21 1842
NCorL 1837-Ag 11 1841;S 7 1842
WHi Jl 22 1840

FARMERS' advocate and Steuben advertiser. *See* Steuben farmer's advocate

Bath HERALD. w
N N 15 1823;N 27 1824;My 13,Je 24,Jl 1-8 1826;Mr 10 1827

Bath PLAINDEALER. w 1883-1930||?
NIC Ap 27 1889-Ap 10 1898

STEUBEN American. w 1855-My 1857||
NCorL 1856-My 6 1857

***STEUBEN and Alleghany patriot.** w N 26 1816-22||?
1816-18? as Steuben patriot. Followed by Farmers' advocate, later Steuben farmers' advocate
MBAt Mr 14 1821

STEUBEN courier. w S 20 1843+
pub 1843+
DLC S 27 1843
KHi S 19 1924
N D 29 1858;Ja 19 1859
NBa 1874-80;1906;17
NNHi Jl 29 1863;Mr 12 1873
PAtM Je 28 1876

STEUBEN democrat. w Je 14 1848-52||
NCorL [Je 21 1848-Je 1849]

STEUBEN farmer's advocate. w 1823+
Follows Steuben and Alleghany patriot. 1823-57 as Farmers' advocate and Steuben advertiser
Ct [1837]
DLC Ag 31 1831;D 17 1834
MWA F 12-19 1840
N Mr 31 1825;Je 24,Jl 8 1830;Ap 20 1831;O 14 1835;D 23 1840;Ja 22 1845;Ja 23-30 1856; F 21,Ap 25 1873;O 17 1888;O 30 1889
NCanHi Ja 31 1879
NCor 1830-32;35-D 8 1847;D 13 1848-Mr 1854; Ap 1855+
NCorL My 12 1858-My 4 1859;Ja 7,D 29 1876-Ja 4,D 27 1878;Ja 5,D 28 1881
NHaK 1861+
NIC My 1860-Ap 1864
NN Ja 31 1879
NNHi F 11 1830;My 23 1855;Ap 26 1873
WHi O 31(extra)1839

STEUBEN messenger. w Ap 17 1828-34||
CSmH S 9 1830
DLC Ag 12 1830
N O 16 1833
P-M O 10 1832

STEUBEN patriot. *See* Steuben and Alleghany patriot

STEUBEN whig. w Ag 4- 1828||
Campaign paper
DLC Ag 4-11,25,S 16 1828

BATH-ON-THE-HUDSON (RENSSELAER COUNTY)

RENSSELAER county republican. *See under* East Albany

RENSSELAER eagle. *See under* Rensselaer

Evening STAR. *See* Rensselaer eagle (Rensselaer)

BAY SHORE

Bay Shore JOURNAL. w Ap 1874+
1874-86 as Suffolk county journal (Northport)
pub Mr 1926+
NRc Mr 11 1876
NRiHi Je 11 1931+
NSm S 15,D 15 1888;S 17 1892;Ag 14 1897;Ag 6 1898;Ap 1 1911

Bay Shore PRESS. *See* Bay Shore sentinel

Bay Shore SENTINEL. w Ag 20 1925+
Title varies: Bay Shore press; South shore sentinel
pub 1925+

SOUTH SHORE sentinel. *See* Bay Shore sentinel

SUFFOLK county journal. *See* Bay Shore journal

SUFFOLK every week. w O 18 1931+
1931-32? as Suffolk every Sunday
pub 1931+

BEACON

Beacon LIGHT and Fishkill standard. w Ag 2 1842+
pub 1842-[1920-22]
NPV N 25 1932

BELFAST

Belfast BLAZE. w 1899+
NBe 1916+

BELLMORE

Bellmore ADVOCATE. w Ja 12 1934+
pub 1934+

BELMONT

Belmont DISPATCH. w 1889+
pub 1904+
N F 28 1913+

BINGHAMTON

BROOME county courier. w Ag 4 1831-Jl 20 1837||
Title varies slightly. Followed by Binghamton courier and Broome county democrat
CtY D 29 1831
DLC F 6 1824
N O 31 1833
NBi complete

BROOME county republican. *See* Broome republican

BROOME republican. w Je 21 1822-1910||?
Title varies: Broome county republican; Republican and standard; Republican and times
CSmH Ag 26 1830
CtY D 29 1831
DLC Ag 15 1828
KHi Je 22 1842;D 1856;F 11 1857
N Mr 15,My 1832-Ap 25,My 9,O 17 1833;Mr 29 1843;S 29 1852;Ap 19 1854
NBi [Jl 25 1839-Ja 14 1841;Ag 1848-Jl 25 1849]
NIC S 20 1822
NNHi Ap 12 1865;Ja 27 1869;Ap 2 1873
P-M Mr 6 1834
PEL Ap 21 1831;Jl 19-26 1832
WHi O 24 1833;Ap 18 1866

Binghamton COURIER and Broome county democrat. w Ap 4 1839-46||?
Follows Broome county courier. Followed by Binghamton democrat
N S 3 1840;Jl 11 1844
NBi Ap-S 25 1839

Binghamton DEMOCRAT. w D 15 1846-1903||
Follows Binghamton courier and Broome county democrat
DLC 1846-D 5 1848
MWA Ap 29 1852;D 7 1854
N S 23 1852;Ap 13 1854
NBi 1846-O 1 1903
NIC 1846-48
NNHi Ja 23 1873
WHi D 12 1848-D 4 1849

Binghamton daily DEMOCRAT. d 1868-94||?
NBi 1869-81
NNHi Ap 30 1873

DEMOCRATIC leader. w S 10 1869-Je 29 1905||
NBi [S 1887-88;92;94]
—d ed *See* Daily leader

Binghamton weekly HERALD. w 1889-1900||
MWA My 1 1890
NBi S 11 1890-O 3 1900

Evening HERALD. d F 28 1889-Mr 30 1912||
United with Binghamton daily republican to form Republican herald, later Binghamton sun
NBi complete

IRIS. sm,w Jl 1839-53||
sm 1839-Je 1841
NBi Mr 28 1851-Mr 19 1852
PAtM O 10 1846

Daily IRIS. *See* Binghamton sun

Daily LEADER. d Ap 26 1878-Je 29 1905||
NBi [N 1878-O 1879]
—w ed *See* Democratic leader

Binghamton PRESS. d 1904+
N Mr 1913+
NBi 1907-Je 3 1920

Binghamton daily REPUBLICAN. *See* Binghamton sun

REPUBLICAN and standard. *See* Broome republican

REPUBLICAN and times. *See* Broome republican

Binghamton STANDARD. w,sw N 1853-74||
Merged with Broome republican
w 1853?-69
DLC Ag 10 1859-S 21,O 12-D 14,28 1864-D 12 1866
KHi D 26 1860
MBAt Ap 19 1865
MWA Ag 17 1864
NBi O 19 1853-O 11 1854;Jl 1870-[Jl 1872-Je 1873]-Je 1874
NNHi My 24 1873

Binghamton SUN. d 1848+
1848?-My 2 1849 as Daily iris; My 4? 1849-Mr 1912 Binghamton daily republican (title varies: Binghamton daily republican and morning sun; etc.); 1912-S 30 1919 Republican-herald; O 1 1919-23 Morning sun; 1924-26 Sun
pub 1918+
DLC Ag 29 1866
MBAt Ap 15,17 1865
MWA My 14 1849;Ja 12 1871;Ag 30 1876
NBi F 32-My 2 1849[Ag 21 1851-F 1852;Ag 18 1855-F 1856;Jl-S 1901]19-[O-D 1920]+
NNHi Je 5,15 1863;My 2 1873
OClWHi My 23 1866

Binghamton daily TIMES. d 1871-78||
United with Binghamton daily republican to form Binghamton daily republican and morning sun, later Binghamton sun
MWA Je 4 1873;S 9 1876
N Je 1874-77
NBi D 4 1872-Je 19 1878
NNHi [D 1872-Mr,My-Ag]-D 1873

Binghamton TIMES. w 1871-78||
United with Binghamton republican to form Binghamton republican and times, later Broome republican
NBi Ap 6 1871-Ja 17 1878

BLACK ROCK

Papers published in Black Rock are listed under Buffalo

BLOOMINGBURG

SULLIVAN county whig. *See* Sullivan county republican (Monticello)

SULLIVAN whig. w 1821-
MBAt Mr 13 1822

NEW YORK (*Continued*)

BLOOMVILLE

Bloomville MIRROR. *See* Stamford mirror-recorder (Stamford)

BOLIVAR

Bolivar BREEZE. w 1891+
pub 1891+
NBo 1933-34

BOONVILLE

BLACK RIVER herald. *See* Boonville herald

Boonville HERALD. w Mr 1852+
1852-O 19? 1855 as Boonville ledger; O 26 1855-71? Black River herald
pub 1852—
ICM Ja 29,Mr 5 1885
N Ap 20,N 30 1855;F 18 1864;My 21,D 24 1868;Je 3,O 14 1869;Ja 20,Mr 24 1870;S 18 1873;N 16 1882
NUHi 1852+

Boonville LEDGER. *See* Boonville herald

BREWSTER

Brewster GAZETTE. *See* Brewster standard

PUTNAM county standard. *See* Brewster standard

Brewster STANDARD. w 1869+
1869-70? as Brewster gazette; 1871?-82? Putnam county standard
pub 1869+
N Ag 17 1917-19

BRIDGEHAMPTON

Bridgehampton NEWS. w 1895+
N Ag 24 1917-D 19 1919
NSo 1911+

BROCKPORT

Brockport DEMOCRAT. w 1870-1925||?
United with Brockport republic to form Republic-democrat

Brockport FREE PRESS. w O 6 1830-
MWA Ja 11 1832
N 1830-S 25 1833
NUHi My 18,Ag 3 1831

MONROE chronicle and Brockport advertiser. w O 2 1833-
DLC F 14 1834
MWA F 7 1834
N O 16 1833
NCH N 1-8,29 1833;Ja 3 1834
P-M F 14 1834

MONROE republican. w Jl 11 1832-
NSyU Jl 25 1832

Brockport RECORDER and Clarkson advertiser. w 1828-30||
CSmH Je 30 1830
DLC Jl 14 1830
MWA O 8 1828

REPUBLIC-DEMOCRAT. w O 15 1856+
1856-1925? as Brockport republic
pub [1856-Je 25 1925]
CaOTA Je 7 1866
MWA My 31 1866

Brockport WATCHMAN. w 1844-
N Jl 3 1845

BRONXVILLE

Bronxville PRESS. sw 1925+
pub 1925+
NBro 1933+

Bronxville REVIEW. w 1901+
NBro 1922+

BROOKFIELD

Brookfield COURIER. w 1875+
pub 1875+
NLeC 1876+
NN Ag 26 1886

BROOKLYN

Brooklyn evening ADVERTISER. d 1834-
Title varies: Brooklyn morning advertiser; Brooklyn daily advertiser. Followed by American citizen and Brooklyn evening advertiser, later Native American citizen
C S 5-6,11 1834
Ct [1834-35]
MWA Ag 3 1835
NBHi Ap-O 16 1835

Brooklyn daily ADVERTISER. d Ja 19 1844-
MWA Ja 20 1844;Ja 17 1846;O 26,28-29,N 5 1852
NBHi S 10 1844-53

Brooklyn daily ADVERTISER. d O 18? 1864-
NBHi O 22 1864;N 1871;Je-Jl 1872

Brooklyn ADVOCATE. w S 2 1833-
Follows Long Island patriot
1833-35? as Brooklyn advocate and Nassau gazette
MWA Ja 2 1834;Mr 15 1836
N O 17 1833
NBHi 1833-Ap 1835
NN N 14 1833
NNHi N 8 1837-Ja 3,F 21-Je 27 1838;extra N 6,D 6 1837

Daily ADVOCATE. *See* Long Island daily advocate

AMERICAN citizen and Brooklyn evening advertiser. *See* Native American citizen

Brooklyn ANZEIGER. w 1874-81||?
In German
NBHi Ap 10 1875

Brooklyn daily ARGUS. d S 15 1873-77||
United with Brooklyn daily union to form Brooklyn union argus, later Standard-union
DLC S 14 1876
MB [1873-F 15 1877]
MWA S 19,26 1873;N 2 1875;O 23 1876
NB 1873-Je 1876
NBHi 1873-F 17 1877
OClWHi Ag 23 1876

BROADWAY news. w S 1925+
pub 1934+

BROOKLYNITE. 1926-28||
NBHi 1926-28

BROWNSVILLE and East New York American. w O 20 1911-18||
Title varies: Brownsville and East New York Jewish progress; Brooklyn Brownsville and East New York Jewish progress; Brooklyn Jewish progress
Suspended from N 10 1912-N 7 1913
In Yiddish
IU O 20-N 3 1911;S 15 1912-17
NN S 15 1912-Jl 26 1918

CHAT. w S 14 1900+
NNQ My 1927-[30]+

CHRONICLE. d F 5 1893-
NBHi F 5-My 12 1893

Brooklyn CITIZEN. d O 4 1886+
DLC Ja 1898-Je 1899
MWA O 4 1887;My 30 1890;Je 24 1891
NB 1887+
NBHi 1886-Mr,Jl 1919+

CITY national intelligencer. w S 25 1871-
1871 as City of Brooklyn; Ja 1872 City of Brooklyn and national intelligencer
NBHi 1871-F 10 1872

Brooklyn CITY news. d N 28 1859-
MWA My 13 1863
NBHi 1859-N 10 1863
NSyU F 25 1860;My 24 1861;Ap 1 1863

CITY of Brooklyn. *See* City national intelligencer

CONSTITUTION. O 24 1863-
NBHi O 24 1863

CRITERION. F 14 1878-
NBHi F 14-N 14 1878

DEMOCRAT. d N 5,7 1832||
NBHi complete

DEMOCRATIC advocate. w Ag 24 1844-
NNHi S 14 1844

DRUM beat. d F 22-Mr 5 1864||
CSmH complete
IaGG F 22,24,26-27,29,Mr 2-3 1864
KHi complete
MBAt complete
NBHi F 22-Mr 11 1864
NNHi complete
NjHi complete
NjP complete

Brooklyn daily EAGLE. d O 26 1841+
1841-50 as Brooklyn eagle and King's county democrat
F 28 1885 is Beecher memorial ed; O 26 1911 70th anniversary ed; O 26 1916 75th anniversary ed
pub 1841+
A 1893-Je 1894;98;1900-02
CLM Je 26 1887
CSt-H [1914-15;18-19]
CtY 1903-09
DLC O 26,29(facsimile)1841;F 12 1845;F 22-D 1848;F 20 1863;Je 23 1871;S 20 1881;Ja-Je 1888;89;Jl 1890-94;Jl-S 1895;Ja-N 1896;97-Mr 1899;1900-Ag,N 1905+
IC 1913
ICM Mr 30 1884;S 14,22,O 13 1885
ICN O 26 1841;D 3 1863-Je 1864;65;72-73;75-78
ICU Ag 24 1873
IU Jl 1908-Ap 14,Ag 14 1918-Ja 6,26,Mr 4,11 1919-Mr 1920
IaHi S 1901-Ja,Ap,Jl 1902-03
InU Mr-Je 1922
KHi O 26 1911;Je 13 1927
M O 26 1911
MWA [O-N 1852]Ja 2,N 5 1855;Ja 31 1863;Je 9,S 25 1866;O 19 1867;Jl 14,20 1869;Je 16 1871;Ag 14,29 1874;Mr 27 1877;Jl 17 1878;Mr 13,My 24,Jl 2 1883;Ag 31 1884;F 28 1885;Mr 13,My 8 1887;O 1 1890;My 28 1893;98;Ja-Mr,Jl-D 1913;O 26 1916;O 26 1926
MiG O 26 1911
MiU 1898-1904
MiU-C My 24 1863;Mr 18 1887
MoS Ja-N 1913
N My 24-25 1883;1911+
NB Jl 1863-67;Jl 1868+
NBHi 1841-48;56+
NBP 1892+
NEh F 21 1843;Mr 15 1847;O 20 1849
NHuHi O 26 1841;Ja 6,My 31 1919
NN Ap 5,9-10 1844;O 4 1862;63-[66-67]+
NNHi O 26(facsimile)1841;S 9 1861;Ap 10,12 1865;F 22 1880
NNU-H 1900-08
NOHi 1928
NPV [D 1862-Ap 25]Je 28 1865
NRiHi O 26 1841
NSyU S 3 1860;My 16,Je 14,Ag 16 1861
NcD [D 1894;Ap 1895]1900-01;Ap 1902-My 1908
NjHi 1913
NjO O 26 1841
NjP 1913
OCl 1902[03]-[15]
OClWHi Mr 13,Je 14,24 1865;Ag 4 1866;O 15 1882;Ap 6 1884;Mr 18 1887
P 1913-Jl 1917
WHi Ap 19 1896;Ag 31 1900-Ag 26 1914;Ap 2 1928

EAST New York journal. w S 2 1858-
NBHi [S 9 1858-Mr 24 1859]

EAST New York weekly sentinel. w O 27 1866-
NBHi O 27,D 8 1866

Brooklyn ERA. w
NNHi D 12 1861-Je 1862

EXPONENT. m 1885-91||
1885? as Pro bono publico
NBHi 1886-91

FINSKA Amerikanaren. w 1896+
In Swedish
pub 1906+
IRA 1901-18
IU Ja-Jl 18 1918;Mr 13 1919+
MnHi 1928+

FLATBUSH observer. w N 9 1909+
pub 1909+
NBHi [1917]

FRAMÅT. *See* Österns härold

Brooklyn daily FREEMAN. d 1849-
IaU-L [Jl 1-D 28 1850]
MWA F 2 1850
NNHi Mr 23,Ap 20,23-26,My 4 1850

Brooklyn GAZETTE. w 1874-78||?
NBHi S 15 1873;S 26 1874

GREATER Brooklyn. w Ap 5-N 22 1895||
NB complete
NBHi complete

GREATER Ridgewood news. *See* Long Island daily advocate

GREENPOINT globe. w 1877-98||?
MWA My 24 1879
NBHi 1877-98

GREENPOINT home news. w Mr 1914+
pub 1934+

GREENPOINT weekly star. w Mr 27 1875+
pub 1875+
MWA O 18 1919
NGr 1875+

IGAZSAG (Truth). w
In Hungarian
PPiHi F 27 1927

Daily INDEPENDENT press. (Williamsburg) d Jl 16 1850-55||
NBHi complete
NNHi [D 28 1852-Ag 13 1853]

ITALIA nostra. w S 4 1915-Mr 4 1916||
In Italian
NN complete

Brooklyn JEWISH voice. w Jl 5 1929+
In Yiddish
NN 1929+

Brooklyn morning JOURNAL. d 1851-
MWA Ag 10,O 26,N 1 1852;O 8 1855
NBHi F-Ag 1852

KINGS county advertiser and village guardian. sm My 6 1857-
NBHi My 6-20,Je 17-Jl 15 1857

KINGS county gazette. w Ap 1872-O 1885||
1872-F 1880 as Kings county rural gazette; Mr 1880-S 1882 Kings county and Brighton gazette; O 1882-S 1885 Kings county and Brooklyn gazette
N F 11 1888
NB complete
NBHi S 7 1872;76-85
NNHi Mr 29 1873;O 14 1882
NjR S 6 1873

KINGS county journal. w S 27 1861-
Title varies: Kings county weekly journal
NBHi 1861-62;My 9 1863

KINGS county journal. w 1884-97||?
N Ja 25 1888

KINGS county leader. *See* Leader (1906-09)

KINGS county patriot. (Williamsburg) w 1848-
NjFHi S 5 1848

KINGS county rural gazette. *See* Kings county gazette

KNICKERBOCKER news. *See* Long Island daily advocate

LEADER. w,sw 1906-09||?
My?-N 27 1906 as Kings county leader w 1906-07?
NN My 8 1906-Ja 1,15,29 1907-Ap 14,28 1908

Daily LEDGER. d O 1877-
NBHi O-D 1877

LONG ISLAND daily advocate. w,d 1911+
Title varies: Knickerbocker news; Greater Ridgewood news; Advocate and Greater Ridgewood news; Daily advocate
pub 1925+

LONG ISLAND family circle. *See* Schroeder's family circle

LONG ISLAND life. 1915+
NBHi [1915-33]

LONG ISLAND life illustrated.
NBHi S 1869;Ap 1870;Je 1871

NEW YORK (*Continued*)

BROOKLYN—*Continued*

LONG ISLAND patriot. w Mr 7 1821-Ag 1833||
Followed by Brooklyn advocate
CtY My 1-8,22,Je 19,Jl 17,Ag 21 1822
DLC Ap 25 1821;F 18,Ap 7,21,My 13-27,Je 17,N 18 1824;Mr 3 1825
MWA Je 6,Jl 18,O 17-24,N 14-21,D 5,19-26 1821[22]Ja 1,Ap 23 1823;F 3 1825;Ag 31,N 23 1826;N 22 1827;Je 25 1829
MiU-C Jl 18 1821
N Je 17-N 1824;O 20 1825
NBHi 1821-30;33
NN Je 13,Ag 1,O 17 1821;O 9 1822
NNHi Mr-Jl 4 1821;Ap 28-Jl 15,29-S 16,30-O 20,N 4-21,D 2-16,30 1824-O 7,21 1825-Mr 2, 16-23,Je 1-8,22,Jl-Ag 17,31-S 14 1824;S 6,N 1,D 27 1832;Mr 14 1833
NSm Je 26 1822;Je 3 1823
NhD S 7 1826
NjHi Ja 27 1825;Ag 11 1831;F 16,Mr 1,22,Ap 12 1832

***LONG ISLAND star.** w Je 8 1809-52||?
Merged with Brooklyn evening star
CSmH S 8 1830
CtY N 20 1828
DLC N 27 1823;Ja 29,F 19,Mr 25,Ap 8,22,My 12,20,Je 17-24,Jl 22,S 23,N 18 1824;D 20 1827; Jl 30,S 3,17,O 1,29,N 26,D 24 1829-Ja 14,28,D 21 1830;N 28 1839
DeHi N 20 1834
MWA Ja 3,D 6 1821;F 14 1822;Ag 12 1824;Ja 20 1825;Mr 12,My 14 1829;N 21 1832;Ag 28 1840[F 18 1841-Mr 3 1842]D 28 1843;F 17 1847
N [D 14 1826-Mr 6 1828]O 16 1833
NBHi 1821-41
NEh Ag 31 1826;Ja 3 1828
NHuHi N 9 1835
NN O 5 1826;F 20 1833;My 16,Jl 9 1839;S 28 1840
NNHi [Ja-F,Ap]-[Je-O]1821-Ja 3,F 7,Mr 7, Ap,My 9,Jl 11,N 14 1822;Ja 16,F 27,Ap[My 1823-Ap]My 12-Je 22[Ag 1824-Ja,Mr-Ap,Jl 1825-[Mr-Ap]-[S-D]1826-S 1828[F,Ap]-[S-N] 1829-F 4,25-Mr 4 1830
NNQ F 8 1827-50
NSchU Jl 14 1842
NSm S 15 1852
OClWHi Jl 16 1829

LONG ISLAND star for the country. w O 5 1837-
N O 23 1840
NEh Ja 12 1838;Ja 17 1840
NNHi D 22 1837-Je 1,Jl 20 1838-My 3 1839

LONG ISLAND daily times. d O 20 1840-
NBHi O 21 1840

Daily LONG ISLANDER. d N 4 1845-
NBHi N-D 1845

NATIVE American citizen. d,tw S? 1835-
Follows Brooklyn evening advertiser. S?-N 1 1835 as American citizen and Brooklyn evening advertiser
d 1835-36?
CSmH Mr 17 1836
CtY Mr 1 1837
MWA Mr 14 1836;F 1 1838
N My 12 1836
NBHi Jl 6 1836;S 26 1837
NNHi O 20 1835-Mr 1836;extra D 11 1835

NEW YORKIN uutiset. w,sw,tw 1907+
w 1907-11?;sw 1912?-22?
In Finnish
pub 1912+
NN Ap 12-29,Jl 8 1919;20-Je 1925;26+

Brooklyn daily NEWS. d 1840-N 1843||
Title varies slightly: Brooklyn daily news and Long Island-times; etc.
MWA [Ag 9 1842-Mr 9]My 12-13 1843
NBHi Mr 2 1840-43
NN Mr 31,Je 30 1841;Ja 10 1842;Mr 7,O 23 1843
NNHi My 6-D 16 1841

NORDISKE blade. w 1878-1902||
1900-02 pub in New York City
In Norwegian
IaDeL [1901-F 13 1902]
WHi N 16 1895-Ag 8 1896;99-Ag 8 1902

NORDISKE tidende. w 1891+
In Norwegian
IU D 1917+
IaDeL [F 15 1917-Jl 11 1918;Jl 17-S 4 1919]N 7 1921
MnHi My 14 1914-17;28+
PP [1928]+
WHi F 23 1922;O 8 1925;F 18 1926;Ja 9,O 9 1930

NORDLYSET. w O 1 1891+
1916?-D 1 1932 pub in New York City
In Danish
pub 1891+
IU D 12 1917-N 1921
IaDeL O 1896-S 16 1897[Je 9 1898-Ja 5 1899]S 21 1900-F 13 1902
MnHi Ap 25 1918+
NN O 1908+
WHi 1896-Je 1897

NORGESPOSTEN. w My 8 1924-F 1933||
In Norwegian
IaDeL 1924-Ja 1933
NN complete
WHi S 11 1924;Jl 30 1927;O 1 1929;O 14 1930;Ja 20 1931

ÖSTERNS härold. w 1892-
1892-Ap 1896 as Framåt
In Swedish
CtY Jl 1 1897
IRA 1892-1913
MnHi My 1896-S 17 1898

Brooklyn daily POST. d
NBHi S 30 1874
NN Mr 28 1874

Brooklyn-Brownsville POST. w 1909-24||?
In Yiddish
IU D 1917-19

Brooklyn PRESS. w
NN Je 18-S 17 1867

PRO bono publico. *See* Exponent

Brooklyn daily PROGRAMME. d O 1 1863-75||?
MWA Mr 21 1870
NN [Ap 4 1867-Ja 8 1870]

PUTNAMITE. w 1902-
NBHi 1902-04

QUEEN'S busybody. *See* Queens county American

QUEENS county American.
-Jl 9 1919 as Queen's busybody
NN My 28,Je 11 1919-Ap 6 1920

Brooklyn RECORD and reform. w 1871-1921||?
1871-1918? as Weekly record
NN [S 19 1903-Ja 20 1911]

Brooklyn REVIEW. w Mr 1873-95||?
1873-74? as Brooklyn Sunday review
NB 1873-74
NBHi Mr-D 1873

RIDGEWOOD times. w Ag 1 1908+
pub 1908+
NNQ 1913-18;24-26

SCHROEDER'S family circle. w Mr 6-Ag 14 1852||
Mr-Ag 7 1852 as Long Island family circle
NBHi Ap 3,Je 12,26 1852
NNHi Mr-Ap 10,My-Je,Jl 31,Ag 14 1852

SOUTH Brooklyn flag. w Ag 3 1872-
NBHi Ag-D 14 1872

Brooklyn STANDARD. w O 29 1859-Ap 25 1887||
1859-Ja 21 1860 as Standard. United with Brooklyn union to form Standard-union
MWA Ag 4 1860;Je 24 1865
N 1859-O 20 1860;O 1864-O 1866
NB 1859-O 1866
NBHi 1859-66
NNHi 1859-O 19 1861;O 25 1862-O 13 1866

Brooklyn daily STANDARD. d Je 3 1861-
Je-D 3 1861 as Daily standard
MWA Je 28 1861
NNHi Je 3-D 14 1861

Brooklyn STANDARD. d Ap 1 1885-87||
United with Brooklyn union to form Standard-union
MWA Je 25,28-29 1886
NBHi Ap-S 8 1885

STANDARD-UNION. d S 14 1863-Mr 9 1932||
1863-F 18 1877 as Brooklyn daily union; F 19 1877-Mr 25 1883 Brooklyn union argus; Mr 26 1883-Ap 25 1887 Brooklyn union. United with Brooklyn daily times to form Brooklyn times-union
CtY 1872-78
DLC F 12,Mr 25,Ap 3,My 13 1868;Ap 11 1872
IC My 1 1889
MWA Ja 9,Ag 20 1864;S 18 1865;Jl 10,15 1869; Je 29-Jl 9,12 1870;Jl 24 1871;Mr 5 1883;My 19 1890
N S 1864-69;O 11 1918-24
NB 1863-Ag 1875;76-1932
NBHi complete
NN [1863-69;71-74]
NNHi S 28 1867-Mr 1869;Ap 8 1873
NPV Ap 15-N 4 1865
Nc 1863-Mr 13 1869
OClWHi F 13 1878;Ag 9 1879
OHi Ap 11 1866

Brooklyn evening STAR. d Ap 1827-
CtDe My 1 1851
CtY Ap-Je 1827
MWA Mr 31 1842;S 1 1845;O 25,30,N 4 1852; Je 29,O 9 1855;Je 29 1860;Je 25 1862;Je 27 1863
NBHi Ap-Je 1827;42-63
NN D 6 1842;Mr 24,Ap 19,O 6 1843;D 28 1844; My 7 1845;N 8 1862;My 30-Je 13 1863
NNHi My 15 1857;Ag 20,D 17 1861
NNQ 1842-50
NcD My 25 1859
WHi O 12 1844

Brooklyn Sunday SUN. w N 30 1873-76||
LNC Jl 8-23,Ag 20,D 17-24 1876
NB 1873-N 19 1876
NBHi 1873-Jl 12 1874;N 28 1875-N 19 1876
NN My 17 1874

SYRIAN eagle. tw,d 1914+
1914-Ap 23 1920 as Eagle (New York City)
In Arabic
IU S 5 1917+
NN Ja-Je 1916

Brooklyn TIMES-UNION. d F 28 1848+
1848-Ja 5 1855 as Williamsburg times; Ja 6? 1855-Mr 10 1932 Brooklyn daily times (title varies slightly)
pub 1848+
CLM My 24 1883
DLC Mr 1900-02
MWA S 15 1852;S 11 1876;Ap 20 1894;My 30 1914
N Ap 22 1872
NB Ja-Je 1872;81-Je,O 1894-99;Jl 1900-Mr 1903;08-Ja 1916;17+
NBHi Ja 15 1849;Je 5 1851;1866-73;76-78;81+
NHuHi F 28 1846(facsimile)
NN O 21 1865;S 25,O 1 1866;Jl 16,24,Ag 7, 14,S 6-7 1867
NNHi My 1 1873
NNMC My 24 1883
OClWHi D 26 1863

Brooklyn daily UNION. *See* Standard-union

Brooklyn UNION-ARGUS. *See* Standard-union

UNIONIST. w Ag 8 1833-
DLC D 19 1833;Ap 10 1834

New Yorkin UUTISET sw,tw 1907+
sw 1907-Ja 8 1918
In Finnish
IU D 7 1917+
NN Ap 12-29,Jl 8 1919;20+

VIENYBE. w,sw,tw 1866+
1866-1917 as Vienybe lietuvniku
1866-1907 pub in Plymouth, Pa.
w 1866-Ja 26 1921;sw F 4 1921-Ag 28 1923
IU 1918-D 23 1924
NN 1897+

Brooklyn daily WHIG. d 1864-
MBAt Ap 15 1865

WILLIAMSBURG democrat. w Je 3 1840-
NbHi Je 5 1841
NjR My 21,Jl 30,Ag 13 1845

WILLIAMSBURG gazette. w,sw,d My 1835-53||?
My 1838-Ap 1848 as Williamsburg gazette and Long Island advertiser
w 1836-Ap 1848;sw 1835;My 1848-D 1849
Ct Ja 22 1838
NB My 25,28,Jl 23,O 12,30,N 10,13,D 16 1835;Ag 19-26,S 23,O 7,D 16 1837;F 1838-52
NBHi Ap 28 1835-38;My 1841-53
NSm My 29,Ag 7 1839

WILLIAMSBURG times. *See* Brooklyn times-union

BRUSHTON

FACTS and fallacies. w 1899+
pub My 11 1899+

BUFFALO

AGE of progress. w 1854-58||
NN Ja 13 1855
NNHi Jl 12 1856

AMERICAN celt. *See under* New York City

BLACK ROCK beacon. w Ja 10 1823-S? 1824||
DLC Mr 18,My 13 1824
NBu Mr 20 1823-Ag 12 1824

BLACK ROCK gazette. w D 20 1824-28||
DLC Mr 1-15,Ap 5,19 1825;O 27 1827
MWA Je 15 1826;Mr 31 1827
N S 13,N 1 1825

Weekly BUFFALONIAN. w D 25 1837-Ja 19 1839||
United with Weekly mercury to form Weekly mercury and Buffalonian
NBu Jl 7,N 17 1838;Ja 19 1839

Daily BUFFALONIAN. d 1838-39||
United with Daily mercury to form Daily mercury and Buffalonian
NBu [Ap 23 1838-Je 24 1839]
OClWHi N 16,D 4 1838

Buffalo BULLETIN. w Je 11 1830-My 1835||
United with Buffalo republican to form Buffalo republican and bulletin, later Buffalo weekly republican
Ct [1834-35]
MWA S 28 1833
N O 12,26 1833
OClWHi Ja-My 1831;Jl 14-D 15 1832
P-M Jl 14 1832

Buffalo COMMERCIAL. d Ja 1 1835-D 15 1924||
1835-F 1890 as Buffalo commercial advertiser (title varies: Commercial advertiser and journal; etc.). Followed by Evening post, later Buffalo post
CLM Mr 12 1874
CtY Ja 30,F 23,Mr 7,9,13 1838
DLC Ja 1(facsimile)1835;51-53;Je 3-4,6 1862; Ja 20-N 7 1863;Ja 16 1864-65;67-Je 1885;Jl 2 1894-1900
IC Ja 11-Je 1873
ICHi N 12,18 1864;Ja 26,28,F 1,8,10,15,25,Mr 11,24,27,Ap 18,22,25,29,My 1-2,Je 5,8,16,19-22, 28-30 1865;Ap 17,O 30 1866
ICM Ja 30 1833
MBAt Ap 17-18,20 1865
MH Ja 17-28 1857
MWA O 8 1840;S 3 1842;S 14 1844;Ag 9,11 1848;Ag 27 1852[53]-Ja 13 1854;Jl-D 1863;Jl 1864-Je 1865;Ap 7 1866;67-Je 1868;69;Jl 1870-Je 1871;D 5 1873;Ag 23-28 1876;Ag 14-16 1883;Jl 10 1884
MiU [1874]-[82-83]
N Ja 1 1835;Mr 10 1837;Ja 10,Jl 22 1846;Ap-D 1847;F 22,S 16 1858[Ap-N 1861]S 8 1862; Ap 17-18,27 1865;Ap 17 1869;Mr 12 1874
NBu Jl-D 1835;Mr 1842-My 14 1843;Mr 26 1844-Mr 11 1845;Mr 11 1846-My,S 13 1849-Je, Ag 2 1852-My,Jl 1853-1924
NBuG Mr 3-28,30,O 5,8-15 1845;N 19 1847;Je 21,S 8 1848;Jl 14 1849;Ja 2-21,23,Jl 17,19,D 11,13-31 1850;Mr 7,Ap 30,My 22,O 23 1857;F 25,N 12 1858;Ja 20 1859;F 16,Mr 24 1860[61-65]
NBuHi complete
NFre 1835;Ap 21 1836;Ja 5 1866
NKenHi N 11 1918
NN O 18 1864;D 16 1875;Jl 5 1876;S 20-21 1881
NNHi D 26 1863;My 1,16 1873
NOsC Jl-D 1851
NSyU My 18 1861
NcU Ag 30 1876
OClWHi Ap 21,Ag 22,D 31 1846;Ap 15 1865; Mr 1870-N 2 1872;D 30 1873;S 22 1881
OHi D 6,13-15,27 1860
P N 29 1841
PWCl D 22 1840
TKL Ag 21 1860
WHi O 11 1844-46;My 6 1850[Ap 18 1851-Ap 24 1852]N 24 1854;S 7-8 1901
—w ed *See* Buffalo patriot and journal

Buffalo COMMERCIAL advertiser. *See* Buffalo commercial

NEW YORK (*Continued*)

BUFFALO—*Continued*

Il CORRIERE italiano. w 1898+
In Italian
pub 1898-1933
NBuG My 1919-22;Ja 13-Je 14,Jl 5,Ag 7,S-O 18 1923;Ap 3-24,Je-Jl,Ag 14-N 1924;F 1925-26; Ja 13-30,F-Jl 7,21 1927-30;Ja 8-Je 11,25-N 9,D 10,24 1931-D 20 1934;Mr 21-Ap 18,My 1935+

Buffalo weekly COURIER. w 1849-1917||?
MWA F 12 1851;N 10 1852
NNHi Jl 4-N 14 1860;Ja 15 1873
OClWHi My 23 1866

Evening COURIER and republic. *See* Evening republic

COURIER-EXPRESS. d 1842+
1842-Ja 1843 as Daily mercantile courier and democrat economist; F 1843-Je 13 1926 title varies: Buffalo daily courier and economist; Daily courier and pilot; Buffalo courier-record; Buffalo courier-express
pub [184?-1926]+
CoU 1903-04
CtY Ag 23 1888
DLC Ap 15,My 18 1864;D 22 1866;Ja-Je 1893; 94-Mr,Jl 1896-1900
IaDH N 4 1857
KHi My 22 1896
MBAt Ap 15,17,19,27 1865
MWA N 2,29 1852;Mr 14,Ap 2,My 12 1855;Je 24,29-30,Jl 6-7 1875;Ag 22,24-30 1876;F 8 1880;Ap 7 1882;Ag 17-18 1883;Ja 9 1884;Ap 3 1887;S 7 1901
N Mr 23 1861;Ag 23-31 1876
NBu N 1842-Ja 21,F 25-Ag 25,S 1843-Mr 12 1844;Mr 12-Ag 1845;Ja 5-My 9,S 16 1846-48; Mr 21 1849-Je 1872;73+
NBuG Mr 21 1848;Jl-N 12 1856;Jl,D 1857;Ag 6 1858;Ag-S 1860[Ja-S 5 1861]Ja-Ap 1862; 63;Ap 15-D 28 1865;Mr 31,Ag 28 1866;68-96;S 12,14-15 1901;Ap 1926+
NBuHi O 3 1842+
NKenHi My 2-3 1898
NNHi My 1 1873
NNiU 1873-75
NSchU Ag 6 1842
NcD Jl 6 1875
NcU Ag 27 1876
NjR S 4 1878
OClWHi My 24 1866;D 1 1869;My 8 1895;Ag 21-28 1897
PWCl O 14 1864
WHi My 7 1850;Ap 26 1860;Ag 21 1901

DEMOCRACY. d My 10 1854-Ag 10 1855||
Merged with Express
NBu complete
NFre Je 17 1854
NSyU S 11 1854
PU complete

DEMOKRAT w D 2 1837-Jl 1918||
1837-52 as Der Weltbuerger; 1853?-91? as Weltbuerger und demokrat
In German
NBu 1837-N 24 1852
NBuG D 1890-1918
PU Jl 29 1854

Buffalo DEMOKRAT. d 1851-Jl 17 1918||
Title varies: Täglicher Buffalo demokrat
In German
MWA Ag 28 1855
NBu Jl 1856-Je 1897;98-1918
NBuG N 1886-N 1888;My 1889-1918
NBuHi Ap 19 1853-1918
NSyU S 11 1851

Buffalo daily DISPATCH and evening post. d 1877-79||
1877? as Buffalo daily dispatch
NBu Jl 1877-My 18 1878

DZIENNIK dla wszystkich. Polish everybody's daily. d 1907+
In Polish and English
pub 1907+
IU D 4 1919-O 29 1934

Weekly ECONOMIST. w
MnHi [1845-46]
NSchU Je 15 1842

Buffalo EMPORIUM and general advertiser. w,sw S 4 1824-
1824-Mr? 1827 as Buffalo emporium(w)
Ct Mr 25,My 20 1826
DLC Jl 9 1825;Ag 23 1827
MWA Ja 15-22,F 5,Mr 26 1825;N 1,17,26 1827
N N 13 1824;F 26,S 17,N 19 1825;Jl 29 1826; Mr 29 1827
NBu 1824-D 6 1827
NBuG D 1826-S 1827
NNHi O 9,D 4 1824

Buffalo ENQUIRER. *See* Daily star

ERIE county independent. *See under* Hamburg

ERIE county republican. w 1930?-Ap 28 1932||
NBu Mr 8 1930-32

Buffalo weekly EXPRESS. w 1846-1901||
DLC 1881-N 1 1883
ICHi O 12 1871
ICN Ja 12 1864-65
NBuG Ja 2 1854;Ja 9 1855;Je 24 1856
OClWHi Ja 15 1856-Je 8 1858
WHi My 20 1852
WaPS [1897]S 21-27 1881[1901]

EXPRESS. d Ja 15 1846-Je 13 1926||
Title varies: Morning express; Buffalo morning express; Buffalo express; etc.
United with Buffalo courier to form Courier-express
S 20 1881 is Garfield memorial ed; S 4-14 1888 is Souvenir ed(in 1 issue)
Sunday ed as Sunday morning express; Buffalo illustrated express; etc
CL S 20 1881
DLC 1850;F 11 1863-65;O 16 1866;Jl-D 1867;My 25,27,Jl-D 1876;79-80;Jl-D 1881;Jl-D 1882;85-90;Jl 1891-Je 1893;98-Ap 1901;02;S 1924-My 3 1926
ICHi S 15,O 1,N 24,D 24 1864;Ja 28,F 4,11,Mr 4,25,Ap 18,21,Je 19,30 1865;Je 1-5,27,Jl 9,Ag 1 1866
ICN [1864-65]
IHi Ap 17 1865
KHi S 4-14 1888;Je 2,Jl 20 1895
MBAt Ap 15,17 1865
MNaHi S 26 1864
MWA Ja 15 1846;Jl 15 1848-Jl 14 1849;Ja 15 1850-Jl 15 1851;Ja 16-Jl 15,N 2 1852;Jl 16-D 13 1853;Jl-D 1854;Mr 10 1855;Ja-Je 1856;57-59;Jl 1860-61;Ja-Je 1863;S 21 1864;Ap 17 1865;Jl-D 1866;Jl-D 1867;Ja-Je 1868;Jl 4 1871;Jl-D 1872[Ja-Je]-D 1875;My 3 1876;Jl-D 1877;S 20 1881;Jl-D 1884;Jl 1885-Je 1886;Mr 3 1889;Mr 16 1890;My 23,Jl-D 1891;Jl 1892-Je 1893;Ag 27,S 7 1901
MiU [1873]-[75;85;87]
MiU-C O 25 1859[84;86]
MnHi Ap 17 1865
N S 8 1860;Ag 31 1876;Mr 1913-Jl 1922
NBu 1846-Je 1847;48-1926
NBuC [1847-1926]
NBuG 1846-59;Jl 2 1860-Je 1864;65-Je 1867;Jl 1868-Je 1872;S 20,26-27 1881;86-Mr 1926
NBuHi Je 15 1846-1926
NCanHi S 20 1881
NFre Jl 17 1921
NIJ S 14,21 1901
NKenHi Ap 17 1865;S 20,27 1881;S 29 1884;Jl 23 1885;S 14-15,22,O 6 1901;Ap 16 1912;N 11 1918;Mr 5 1921;Ag 3 1923
NNHi N 20 1863;S 7 1864;My 2 1873
NcU Ja 27 1863;Ag 19 1875;Ag 25,28-30 1876
OCHi Ja 15(facsimile)1846;Mr 8 1887;Ja 15 1896
OClWHi N 15 1862;F 9 1863;Ap 17,21 1865-Ag 3 1875;S 20 1881;D 23 1894;Ap 14 1895;Mr-D 1900;Ja 13,Jl 28,S 14-15 1901;Ja 19 1902;Mr 27 1904
OHi Mr 19 1870
VU My 22 1883;Ag 27,O 20 1884
VtMS [1901-03;05-06]
WHi Ja 15 1846;D 25 1849;S 4-14 1888;Ap 14 1895;Ja 15 1896;Ag 28,S 8,14-16,20,22,25,29 1901;15-20

FORT PORTER reporter. w
NBuG F 14-My,Je 13-S 5 1919

Buffalo FREIE PRESSE. d 1872-N 14 1914||
In German
MWA Ag 29 1876
NBu 1886-Je 1897;98-1914
NBuHi complete

Buffalo GAZETTE. w 1841-44||
MiU N 1 1844

Buffalo daily HERALD. d
NBuG Ag 6-13 1869

Buffalo HERALD. m,w Mr 1905-
m 1905-Mr 1906
WHi 1905-Ag 18,D 22 1906-Je 11 1908

Buffaloi HIRADO (Buffalo herald). w 1920+
In Hungarian
PPiHi [Ja 21 1922-Jl 17 1931]

ILLUSTRATED Buffalo express. *See note under* Express

INTERNATIONAL gazette. w D 25 1885+
pub Je 10 1899+
NBuHi Ja 9 1886-D 10 1892;98-1915

Buffalo JEWISH review. w Ja 1912+
pub 1925+
NBuG S 14 1928+

***Buffalo JOURNAL.** w Jl 4 1815-35||
1815-20 as Niagara journal. Title varies: Buffalo journal and general advertiser; etc. Merged with Buffalo whig
DLC O 26,N 9 1824;D 27 1825;Ag 11,S 1,29, O 20-27 1829;Ja 5,27,Ag 25 1830
MBAt Mr 26 1822
MWA N 27 1821;Jl 20,S 18,O 12 1824;F 22,N 1 1825;Ja 9,D 18 1827;My 18 1831
N Jl 2 1822;My 6 1823;N 9 1824;Ja 25,Jl 12, Ag 2,S 6 1823
NBu D 29 1829-Mr 1833
NSchU Jl 14 1829
NhD Jl 7 1829
OClWHi S 23 1834
WHi Jl 14,S 1,15-22,O 20-N 3 1829

Daily Buffalo JOURNAL. d My? 1836-
United with Daily commercial advertiser to form Commercial advertiser and journal, later Buffalo commercial
MWA N 19 1836
NBu Ag-N 1836

Buffalo morning JOURNAL. d
NBu O 28-N 2 1897

Daily MERCANTILE courier and democrat economist. *See* Courier-express

Daily MERCANTILE review. *See* Buffalo review

Daily MERCURY and Buffalonian. d N 21 1838-
1838-Ja 19 1839 as Daily mercury
NBu [N 1838-Mr 21 1839]
OClWHi D 4 1838

Weekly MERCURY and Buffalonian. w D 1 1838-40||
1838-Ja 19 1839 as Weekly mercury
NBu 1838-Ja 26 1839
WHi F 2 1839

Daily NATIONAL pilot. d F 12 1845-Je 27 1846||
United with Buffalo courier to form Daily courier and pilot, later Courier-express
NBu complete
NN My 10 1845

NEW age. w 1912-25||?
ICJ F 16-Je 8 1918

Buffalo Sunday NEWS. w D 7 1873-1915||?
1873-95? as Buffalo Sunday morning news
MWA Ag 27 1876
N Ag 27 1876
NBuG Je 28 1874

Buffalo evening NEWS. d O 11 1880+
O 11 1930 is fiftieth anniversary ed
pub 1880+
CoU 1901-03;S 1907-My 1910
DLC Mr 1926+
KHi Ja 26 1893
MWA Je 27 1889;O 11 1930
N Mr 1913+
NBu O 11 1880-Ap 9 1881;89+
NBuG [Je-O 1906;Ap-D 1908;My-D 1909]O 1913-[17]-[20-26]+
NBuHi 1888+
NKenHi My 2 1898;S 14 1901;Mr 4-5 1921;F 3 1932
OClWHi Ag 21-28 1897;Jl 15 1908
PPiHi S 6 1901
VU O 3 1905
WHi S 13 1901

NIAGARA journal. *See* Buffalo journal

NIAGARA patriot. *See* Buffalo patriot and journal

OLD SCHOOL Jeffersonian. w 1842-43||
WHi Ja 21 1843

***Buffalo PATRIOT and journal.** w O 3 1811-
1811-Ap 14 1818 as Buffalo gazette; Ap 21 1818-My 1 1821 Niagara patriot. Title varies: Buffalo patriot and western advertiser; Buffalo patriot and commercial advertiser
CSmH Je 22 1830
Ct Mr 11,Je 14 1837
DLC Mr 8 1825-26;D 30 1828
ICHi Mr 26 1851;O 20 1852
IHi Je 16,30 1852
MWA Mr 25 1828;Je 23 1829;Je 7 1831;Ja 17 1832;N 26 1833
N My 21 1822;Ap 10,My 1,29,N 13,D 11 1832; Ja 15,F 26,Ap 16,My 7,21,S 3,O 22,N 19 1833
NBu Mr 6-20,My 1 1821
NBuG O 27 1846;Mr 1848-Jl 1854;55-72
NFre 1835
NNHi My 23-D 1860
OClWHi N 5 1822;Jl 18 1826;Ja 23,Je 26,S 11 1827;Ap 15,O 21,N 4 1828;Ja 13-20,Mr 24, Ap 7,O 27,D 8 1829;D 7 1831;N 30,D 18 1844
PWCl [1841]
WHi Ap 22-29 1846
—d ed *See* Buffalo commercial

POLAK w Ameryce. *See* Buffalo telegram

POLISH everybody's daily. *See* Dziennik dla wszystkich

Buffalo evening POST. d 1852-77||
Follows Daily Queen City. United with Buffalo daily dispatch to form Buffalo daily dispatch and evening post
MWA O 30 1852;N 1859-60;Jl 29 1861-Ja 27 1863[64-Ja 25 1865]Ag 22,23 1876
NBu O 11 1852-Je 25,Jl 29 1863-Ja 22,28-Je 19,Jl 7 1864-Je,Ag 1866-Je 28 1877
NBuG My 9,15,Je-O 10 1856;D 2-24 1857;F-My 1 1861
NBuHi 1857-Ja 27 1871
OClWHi F 1853-S 22,N 2-26 1854;55-Je,S 19 1857-Mr 26,Je 22 1858-F,Jl 12 1859-60;Ja 29 1861-63;Ja 28 1864-Ja 27 1865;Ag 1866-Ja 24 1867

Buffalo POST. d D 16 1924-F 6 1926||
Follows Buffalo commercial. 1924-D 6 1925 as Evening post
NBu complete
NBuG Je 1-4,6-21,23-24,26-29 1925

PROGRESS. *See* Buffalo republic

Daily QUEEN city. d Ja 28 1850-52||
Followed by Buffalo evening post
DLC F 20 1850
OClWHi Ja-Ag 19 1850;Ap 14 1851-My 10 1852

Buffalo weekly REPUBLIC. w 1847-
MWA N 23 1852
N Ag 8 1854;O 7 1856;S 15 1857
NBu Ja 17 1854-56;F 1857-Ag 1859
NBuG Ja 4 1868;Ja 11-My 17,31-Je 21,Jl-Ag 30 1869
OClWHi Je 1847-N 11 1848
WHi Ag 10 1852

Buffalo daily REPUBLIC. d Ja 26 1847-My 22 1861||
Title varies: Republic; Daily republic; Buffalo republic and times; etc. United with Evening courier to form Evening courier and republic, later Evening republic
MWA D 2 1852
N Ap 12,Ag 28 1856;N 8 1858
NBu F 20 1847-Je,Ag 1852-61
NBuG 1852;Je 1853-F,Ag 1854-Je 1855;Mr 26, Jl-Ag 1856;Ja-Je 1858;59
NBuHi 1852-59
OClWHi Ap 17 1858;Ag 18 1860
PWCl D 10 1849
WHi My 13 1853

Evening REPUBLIC. d 1860-84||?
1860-My 22 1861 as Evening courier; My 23 1861-75? as Evening courier and republic
ICHi Je 2 1866
MWA N 3 1862;O 6 1864
NBu My 23 1861-Je 1863
NBuG [My 23-S 5 1861]N 9 1864
NKenHi Ja 4,D 30 1862;Je 12,19 1865
OClWHi My 23 1866
WHi D 2 1861

Buffalo REPUBLIC. w N 1899-D 28 1911||
1899-Ja 1903 as South Buffalo progress; F 1903-Ag 1908 Progress
WHi Jl 18 1906-11

NEW YORK (*Continued*)

BUFFALO—*Continued*

Buffalo weekly **REPUBLICAN.** w Ja 25 1828-41||
1828-My 1835 as Buffalo republican; Je 1835-36? Buffalo republican and bulletin
CSmH S 4 1830
Ct [1828-38]
DLC Je 28 1828;Je 27,Jl 18-25,Ag 8,29,S 5,26, O 24,N 14-28 1829;Ja 2,23 1830
MWA Jl 31 1835;Mr 11 1836;Jl 25 1839
N N 2 1833;F 22,D 20 1834
NBu Mr 14 1826-F 13 1830
NNHi S 29 1832-Mr 1836;F 14 1839-41;extra D 1 1832
NhD Jl 4 1829
REdH N 15,D 6 1828
WHi O 15 1840

Buffalo daily **REPUBLICAN.** d F 5 1839-
MWA My 20 1840
N Mr 29 1841
NBu 1839-Ja 21 1842
PWCl Mr 1 1841

Buffalo daily **REPUBLICAN.** d Ja 26 1847-57||
DLC Jl 9 1849
NBuHi 1848-Ja 7 1852
NNHi O 24 1857

REPUBLICAN press. w
OClWHi N 6 1821

Buffalo **REVIEW.** d 1882-1903||
1882-Mr 1898 as Daily mercantile review
DLC Ja-Je 1898
NBu 1898-Je 11 1903
NBuHi 1898-Je 10 1903
OClWHi [Mr 22-Je 2 1899]
WHi S 16 1901

ROUGH notes. d Mr 1852-54||
Merged with Democracy
MWA N 6 1852
NBu My 19-Je,S 1-21,24-N 25,27-D 13,18-25,28 1852-Ja 1,4-Jl 2,4,6-27,29-O 4,6-N 24,26-D 1, 3-26,28-31 1853;Ja 2,4-F 7,9-My 9 1854

Buffalo **SENTINEL.** w F 27 1840-
CaOTA Ag 18 1855;Jl 16 1859;N 16 1861
DLC Mr 3-12 1840
NBuG Jl 4-D 26 1857;F 25,Mr 3,Jl 21,S 21,D 15 1860;F-Mr,Ap 13-20,My 13,Je,Jl 13-Ag 24 1861

Buffalo **SOCIALIST.** w Je 6 1912-My 30 1914||?
NNRa [1912]-[14]

SOUTH BUFFALO news. w F 1921+
pub 1921+

SOUTH BUFFALO progress. *See* Buffalo republic

Buffalo **SPECTATOR.** w
Ct Mr 16 1837
NOHi F 20 1836
WHi F 27 1836

Buffalo daily **STAR.** d 1834-
Merged with Buffalo daily republican
Ct Ja 15 1835
NBu N 10 1834-D 6 1838

Daily **STAR.** d Ap 9 1891-Je 19 1926||
1891-1924 as Buffalo enquirer. Merged with Courier-express
DLC Jl-D 1895;Jl-D 1896;99-1900
NBu complete
NBuC Ag 1891-1926
NBuG 1891-94
NBuHi 1892-1912
OClWHi S 16 1901

Buffalo **TELEGRAM.** d,w 1886-1933||?
1886-1919? as Polak w Ameryce
d 1886-1927?
In Polish
CSt-H [1919]
NBuG S 25,O 3 1925;Jl 1926-Mr 1927;Ja 10, Je-D 1928

TELEGRAPH. d 1880-81||
NBu O 30,N 2-13,16-24,26 1880-Ja 11,13-25, 27-Je 30 1881

Buffalo daily **TIMES.** d Ag 31-D 16 1857||
Merged with Buffalo daily republic
NBu complete

Buffalo **TIMES.** d 1879+
Title varies: Daily times; Daily morning times; Buffalo evening times; Buffalo daily times; etc.
CoU 1902;04;S 1906-09
IC My 1 1889
N Mr 1913-N 15 1922
NBu Mr 31-My 28 1881;D 13 1883-S 1884;97+
NBuG [Jl 1930+]
NBuHi D 13 1883-Je 1917
WHi S 7,13 1901

Buffalo daily **TRANSCRIPT.** d
NBu [D 31 1881-83]

Sunday **TRUTH.** w Ja 1 1888-D 25 1892||
MWA My 18 1890
NBu complete

Buffalo **VOLKSFREUND.** d 1868+
In German
pub 1868+
NBu 1891+
NBuG 1915-O 1918;19-S 1931;Ja-My,O 1932+
NBuHi 1896+

WELTBUERGER und demokrat. *See* Demokrat (1837-1918)

WESTERN advertiser. w D 10? 1827-Mr 25 1828||
United with Buffalo patriot to form Buffalo patriot and Western advertiser, later Buffalo patriot and journal
MWA F 8,Mr 12 1828

WESTERN star. d
Ct Jl 22 1834
NBu Jl 21,S 4-22,24-O 2,7-8,10,13,16-18 1834

Buffalo **WHIG.** w Je 18 1834-39||?
DLC Jl 2 1834

WORKING MEN'S bulletin. w Je 5 1830-
CSmH S 4 1830

WORKINGMEN'S organ. w D 24 1847-
NNHi F 26 1848

YOUNG Hickory.
NNHi O 28 1852

CALEDONIA

Caledonia **ADVERTISER.** *See* Tri-county weekly

Caledonia **ERA.** w My 8 1901-19||?
United with Caledonia advertiser to form Caledonia advertiser-era, later Tri-county weekly
NCalA 1901-15

TRI-COUNTY weekly. w My 7 1878+
1878-1919? as Caledonia advertiser; 1920-32? Caledonia advertiser-era
ICM Jl 1-8 1926
MWA O 15 1936
NGe Ja 31,F 21,Mr 14,28-Ap 5,26-My 3,17,O 18,N 1,29,D 13,27 1917;Ja 10,My 2,Ag 8,22,O 31,N 14 1918;Ja 16,30,Ap 10,24 1919

CAMBRIDGE

CAMBRIDGE VALLEY news. w My 1861-
MWA Jl 2 1863
NFeH Je 18 1863

***WASHINGTON** county post. w My 24 1804+
1804-34 as Northern post; Ja 7 1835-My 10 1837 County post and North star
1804-48 pub in Salem
pub N 9 1825;Jl 13 1831;Ja 11 1843;Ja 3,31 1844;49-51;54+
CSmH Ag 25 1830
ICN F 19 1823-[28-29]
MWA S 1-8,O 6-13,27 1824;Jl 30 1828;Ja 16,F 13,27,D 31 1840
N Ja 18,Ap 5-12,My 10,Ag 2 1821[Ap 18-D 5 1822]Ag 25,S 29,N 10 1824;O 12,N 9 1825;Ag 9 1826;Je 25 1828;Ja 27,Mr 31,Ap 28,My 12, Jl 28,Ag 4,18,S 29,O 13,N 3,24,D 1,15 1830;Ja 12,F 2,Ap 1831-45[48-49]54-81
NFeH Ja 28 1824;Mr 2 1831;F 18,My 13,N 11 1835;Ja 16,D 31 1840;S 30 1841;Ja 11 1843;Ja 3 1844;Ja 8 1845;Ja 6 1846;Je 6 1848;S 23 1881
NHfS 1882-88
NHi Ja 8 1845
NN Ag 1 1822
NNHi N 19 1823;O 12 1825;S 13 1826;33
NSalC Jl 11 1822;D 25 1835;N 20 1842
NT My 21 1828;30-33
NjHi [1823-28]

CAMDEN

Camden **ADVANCE-JOURNAL.** w Jl 1873+
1873-85 as Camden advance
pub 1873+

CAMILLUS

Camillus **ENTERPRISE.** w 1888+
pub 1888+
NCam 1923+

CANAJOHARIE

Canajoharie **COURIER.** w Ag 9 1878+
pub 1878+

Canajoharie **INVESTIGATOR.** w 1833-36||?
NCanjB Je 2,Jl 5 1834

MOHAWK VALLEY gazette. w 1848-49||
ICHi Mr 8,Ap 5 1849

MONTGOMERY county union. w 1849-53||
NCanjJ D 2 1852

Canajoharie **RADII.** w Ja 20 1837+
1837-40 as Radii; 1841-F 8 1849 Montgomery phoenix and Fort Plain advertiser (Fort Plain). Title varies: Canajoharie radii and deaf-mutes' journal; Canajoharie radii and tax-payers' journal
DLC Ag 11 1837;F 23,Ag 31 1841
MWA Ja 27-Mr 17,Je 23,Jl 7-21 1837;Jl 9 1863
N O 6 1840;F 24 1848-F 12 1852
NCanj 1858-59;71-77;79-91
NCanjB Mr 4 1844;59-1919
NN Jl 10 1862
NNHi My 14 1863;Mr 24,Jl 21 1864;Mr 1,Ap 19,Je 21 1866;Mr 6 1873
NSchU F 22 1842

Canajoharie **SENTINEL.** w Ap 23 1825-
CoD O 15 1825
CtY D 16 1828;Jl 7 1827

Canajoharie **TELEGRAPH.** w 1825-
CtY Je 5 1830
NCanjB D 7 1832
NN O 13 1827;Mr 28 1828

CANANDAIGUA

Canandaigua **CHRONICLE.** w N 24 1827-
N N 24 1827

CLAY club. w Ap 20-N 1844||
Campaign paper
NCanHi My 11,O 26 1844

FREEMAN and messenger. w
NFre Je 17 1843

GENESEE messenger. *See* Ontario messenger

ONTARIO county chronicle. w 1900-07||
N Ja 4 1905
NCanHi 1902-Mr 1904

ONTARIO county journal. w 1873-Ap 1930||
United with Ontario county times to form Ontario county times-journal
N [Mr 15 1878-Ja 11 1880]Ap 25,Je 27 1884;Ja 16,D 23 1885;My 27 1887;O 25 1889;Je 5 1891; Ap 22,Ag 5 1892;Je 9 1893;Ja 5,My 4,Je 29 1894;O 20 1905;F 9-16,Mr 30,My 11 1906;S 25 1908;Ja 13 1911;Ap 12 1912

ONTARIO county times-journal. w Ja 15 1852+
1852-Ap 24 1930 as Ontario county times
pub 1852+
CtY D 23 1863
N D 4 1877[My 1878-O 1879]My 9,N 28 1883; My 12 1885;Ja 6,N 24 1886;Mr 30 1887;Ja 14, Ap 22 1891;F 10,My 18,Ag 3,31 1892;Ja 11,D 20 1893[94-1903]-13[15]
NCan 1875-1928
NCanHi 1852-Ap 24 1930
VU F 20,Jl 16 1884;Mr 25 1885

ONTARIO freeman. w 1823-
DLC F 25,Mr 31,Ap 14-21,My 19,O 6-13 1824
N O 28 1823,Ap 14,N 1,10 1824

ONTARIO freeman. w Mr 18 1828-N 30 1836||
1828-Ag 29 1832 as Ontario phoenix. United with Ontario repository to form Ontario repository and freeman, later Ontario repository and messenger
CSmH Ag 4 1830
MWA Ap 15 1823;Jl 21,O 13 1824;Ja 5 1825;Ja 14 1835
N Mr 2,Je 8,N 16 1831;Ap 17,Je 12,Jl 31 1833; Ja 22,F 5,Jl 30,Ag 20-S 3 1834;Je 29 1836
NCanHi D 16 1829;Jl 7,Ag 29 1832-Ag 1834[F-Jl 1]O 14 1835-36
P-M O 10 1832

***ONTARIO** messenger. w N 25 1806-Ja 1862||
1806-N 27 1810 as Genesee messenger. United with Ontario repository to form Ontario repository and messenger
DLC Jl 17 1833;N 3 1852
MWA Ja 9,F 27,Ag 27 1828;F 22 1843;S 22 1852;My 30 1855
N Ja 7 1823;N 23 1825;N 8 1826;O 30 1833;D 17 1834;N 22 1837;Jl 3 1839;Jl 19 1843;Ja 1-22,F 5-12,Mr 5 1845;Ja 7,Je 17 1846;Mr 31, Je 16 1847;N 8 1854;Je 25,Jl 15 1856;Je 12 1861
NCanHi My 21 1822;O 19 1825;Ap 5 1826;F 4 1834;Ag 7 1839;Ag 19 1841;F 9 1892;My 9, Ag 30 1843;D 3 1845;Ja 5,13,Ap 7,My 12 1847; Mr 29 1848;N 21-28 1844;O 21 1851;Ag 8 1855; Je 24 1857
NCorL S 18 1850
NNHi Jl 30 1822;N 1 1826

ONTARIO phoenix. *See* Ontario freeman

***ONTARIO** repository and messenger. w My 3 1803-1904||?
1803-Ap 18 1809 as Western repository; Jl 23 1811-My 25 1813 Ontario repository and Western advertiser; D 14 1836-39 Ontario repository and freeman
CSmH Mr 17 1830
CtY Ag 13,S 10-17 1828;Ja 26 1831
DLC Ap 8 1823;Ja 7,F 25,Mr 10,Ap 21,Je 2,O 13 1824;F 23 1825;Ag 27 1827;My 31 1828; Je 17,Jl 1-8,24-Ag 5,S 9,O 28,D 30 1829;Ja 13,Ag 11-18,D 8 1830;O 3 1832;S 16 1840
ICHi Ja 22 1822;O 7-14 1823;Je 21 1837
ICN O 5 1831
MBAt S 3 1828
MWA Ja 2 1828;Je 19 1833;Je 6 1838;Je 17 1840;Ap 28 1841;D 25 1844
N Jl 12 1826;Mr 14,Ag 27 1827;Ap 1828-Ap 13 1830;O 16 1833;O 21 1835;Ja 8,Je 26,S 4 1839;D 16 1840;Ja 8,22,Mr 19,Ap 2-9 1845;Je 30,Jl 23 1846;F 6-15,25,Mr 13-18 1847;Jl 26 1848;O 24 1849;Ja 3 1861;Ja 27 1864;N 15 1865; S 5 1866;O 30 1867;F 16-23 1870;Ag 21 1872; Je 23 1875[78-79]Ja 17,Jl 6,N 30 1882;D 20 1883;Ag 4 1892;Ap 19,Jl 16-23,Ag 2,27 1895; Ap 1 1897[S-D 1904]
NBa 1880
NBuG N 2 1840
NCan Mr 26 1826;D 14 1836-Je 14 1837
NCanHi Ap 1824-Mr 1828;Mr 30 1831-Mr 21 1832;Mr 27 1833-N 7 1839;My 27,Je 10-17,Jl 22,S 16 1840;Ap 7 1841;Ja 26-F 2,My 3 1842;Ja 11,25,Ap 12,Ag 30,N 1 1843;Ja 3,17-24,F-Mr 20 1844;Jl 30,O 8 1845;Je 23,Jl 18-21,Ag 13-22,D 1 1846;F 6,Mr 4,My 11,20, Je 29,Jl 29,Ag 12,24,O 5,D 10 1847;Ja 14-25, Mr 1-3,10 1848
NCorL O 13 1824;O 14-21 1829;F 4 1834;Mr 4 1835;N 7 1849
NNHi Ap 9 1873
OClWHi Ap 18 1825;N 17 1863

ONTARIO republican. w F 20 1821-
NCanHi My 1,Ag 7 1821
NNHi O 1 1822

Daily **TIMES.** d S 3 1878-
N S 3-6 1878

WESTERN repository. *See* Ontario repository and messenger

CANASTOTA

Canastota **BEE-JOURNAL.** w 1865+
1865-87? as Canastota herald; 1888?-F 1921 Canastota bee
N N 19-26,D 23 1868
NCana N 1875-87;Je 1889+

COURANT. d,tw,w 1902-23||
1902-10? as Evening courant
d 1902-04?;tw 1905?-14?
NCana Jl 29 1902-10;My 1914-23

Canastota **HERALD.** *See* Canastota bee-journal

Canastota **JOURNAL.** w 1884-F 1921||
United with Canastota bee to form Canastota bee-journal
CLM Jl 25 1885

NEW YORK (*Continued*)

CANDOR

Candor COURIER. w 1899+
pub 1899+
NCandC F 22 1900

Candor FREE PRESS. w O 9 1867-Ap 8 1873||
NCandC O 9 1867

Candor GLEANER. w Ag 11 1892-93||?
NCandC S 15 1892

Candor REVIEW. w 1874-75||
NIC N 25 1875

Candor weekly STANDARD. w Ja 14? 1885-86||
NCandC Ja 14 1886

CANISTEO

Canisteo TIMES. w Ja 7 1875+
pub 1875+

CANTON

Weekly COMMERCIAL advertiser. w 1873+
pub My 1874+

Canton DEMOCRAT. w Jl 11 1833-
N O 31 1833

LIVELY times. w F 25 1875-
N My 20 1875

NORTHERN telegraph. w Jl 4 1832-
DLC O 31 1832
N Ap 18 1833

REPUBLICAN and advertiser. w 1827-
CSmH Jl 15 1830
MWA My 28 1829
N N 5 1829

ST. LAWRENCE plaindealer. w 1856+
pub Jl 17 1873+
MWA Jl 19 1866
NSyU Je 9 1870
OClWHi N 8 1899

CAPE VINCENT

Cape Vincent EAGLE. w 1872+
Follows Frontier patriot
pub [1872+]
MWA Jl 6 1876
NCpHi [1874-94]+

FRONTIER patriot.
Followed by Cape Vincent eagle
NCpHi [1862]

Cape Vincent GAZETTE. w 1858-
NCpHi [1858-61]

CARMEL

PUTNAM county courier. w 1842+
DLC F 23 1856
MWA My 19 1866
N N 8 1878
NCar [1849-1934]
NNHi Ap 12 1873

PUTNAM free press. w Je 12 1858-
CSmH Ap 7 1860

CARTHAGE

BLACK RIVER budget. w D 8 1858-
N Mr 24,Ap 14,28 1859

CARTHAGENIAN. w D 19 1839-43||
DLC Ja 2 1840

Carthage DEMOCRAT. w Ap 30 1881-
N Ap 30 1881

Carthage REPUBLICAN-TRIBUNE. w My 1860+
1860-1922? as Carthage republican (title varies; Carthage republican and The northern New Yorker
pub 1860;65-1909:11+
MWA Mr 21 1865;Jl 25,S 5 1876
N F 23 1869;My 9 1876

Carthage TRIBUNE. w 1887-1922||?
United with Carthage republican to form Carthage republican-tribune

CASTILE

CASTILIAN. w 1874+
NN Je 29 1906

CASTLETON

CASTLETONIAN. w O 25 1913-Ja 22 1916||
N complete

CATSKILL

AMERICAN eagle. w 1854-55||
N N 24 1855

Catskill DEMOCRAT. w 1843-49||
Merged with Catskill recorder
NNHi Mr 4 1844;Jl 1,22 1846

EXAMINER. w 1831+
1831-48 as Catskill messenger; 1849-57 Greene county whig
DLC D 17 1840
N N 8 1832-34;D 2 1843;F 17 1844;My 3 1845; Je 19 1847
NCatHi 1831-1927
NN D 3 1842
NNHi N 14 1857;F 15 1873
WHi [Ja 15 1876-Ap 13 1878]

GREENE county republican. w N 15 1826-29||
Merged with Catskill recorder
DLC F 21 1827
MBAt My 2 1827
MWA F 14 1827
N Ag 1 1827
NEh N 5 1828
NNHi Ja 10,Ap 4 1827

GREENE county whig. *See* Examiner

Catskill MESSENGER. *See* Examiner

Catskill MOUNTAIN star. w O 7 1922+
pub 1922+

*Catskill RECORDER. w My 14 1804+
Follows Western constellation (not in this list). Title varies: Catskill recorder and Greene county republican; Recorder and democratic herald
pub 1927+
CSmH S 9 1830
Ct [1829-33]
CtY S 5,19,D 12 1828
DLC Mr 5,Ap 9,Jl 30,Ag 13 1824;Jl 3 1834;Mr 17 1836
N O 17 1833;D 18 1834;F 16 1836;My 24,N 15 1838;Ap 4 1844;Mr 23 1854;Jl 26 1867;Ag 1911+
NCatHi 1821-Ap 16 1829[40-60]62;71-1927
NN My 9 1839;O 5 1848
NNHi Ja 26 1843;Je 11-18 1846;Ag 13 1869;My 23 1873

CATTARAUGUS

Cattaraugus TIMES. w 1885+
pub 1908+

CAZENOVIA

Cazenovia ABOLITIONIST. w F 25 1840-42||
MdBJ Jl 19-Ag 2,S 20 1842
NSyU Mr 11 1840

Cazenovia DEMOCRAT. w S 9 1836-F 20 1837||
Ct N 18 1836
NCaz complete

Cazenovia GAZETTE. w O 28 1851-My 5 1852||
NCaz complete
NN Ap 7 1852

MADISON and Onondaga abolitionist. w S 20 1841-43||
DLC Ja 4 1842
NSchU Mr 8 1842

MADISON county abolitionist. w S 21 1841-
MWA D 7 1841
NN O 19,D 7 1841
OClWHi N 23 1841

MADISON county eagle. *See* Madison county whig

MADISON county news. *See* Madison county whig

MADISON county whig. w F 1840-Ja 1857||
1841-My 21 1845 as Madison county eagle; My 28 1845-Ag 11 1852 Madison county news
N Ja 5-11,F 15,Mr 22 1842;Ja 4,18,Jl 12,O 25,N 15 1843;Ag 7,28,D 25 1844;Ap 30,S 24,D 10 1845;Ja 2 1849;Mr 20,Ap 17,My 13,29 1850; Mr 26 1851;F 4,18,Mr 3,My 19-26,S 15,O 6,20 1852;Ja 4,19-26,D 21 1853;Ja 18,Ap 19-26,Je 14,Jl 5,19,N 22-29 1854[F-My,O-N 1855;My-D 1856]
NCaz My 17 1843-Ag 11 1852
NN Mr 4,31,Ap 21-28,My 12,O 30 1841;F 22, S 21-28 1842;Jl 5,19,Ag 30 1843;O 2 1844;O 28 1846;My 5,Je 9,Jl 14,Ag 18 1847;Mr 22,S 20 1848;Ja 2,Mr 7-21,My 2,Je 27 1849;Mr 13,My 1,O 2 1850;Mr 5-12 1851;N 10-17,D 1,15 1852; D 21 1853;Ja 18 1854;Ap 18,N 6(extra),D 19 1855;F 27,Mr 12,Jl 9 1856
NOHi Ap 12 1843;O 7 1846
NSyU N 22 1843;N 12-19 1845;N 18 1846;Ja 5 1848

MADISON observer. *See under* Morrisville

MADISON republic. w Ja 1- 1850||
NCaz Ja-Ap 9 1850

*PILOT. w Ag 10 1808-Ag 7 1823||
NCaz 1821-23

Cazenovia REPUBLICAN. w My 1 1854+
pub My 1854+
MWA S 14,O 26 1876;Je 21 1917
N N 22 1917-19;Jl 26 1923+
NCaz Jl 30 1862-Mr 1900;Ja 10 1901-09;11-17; 19+
NN 1854-S,O 13,N 3,24 1858-Ag 7 1898;Ja 2,Mr 27,Ap 24,My 15,29,Je 19-Jl 3,17-S 4,18-O 9,D 4 1902;Ja 1-8,22,F 5,Ap 16,30,Je 4-18,Jl-Ag 20,S-O 1903;Ja 21-F 4,Je 16 1904;Ja 6 1905
NNHi Je 23 1858;Mr 13 1873
NOHi Jl 17 1902;25
WHi Ag 5 1868

REPUBLICAN monitor. w S 1823-Mr 4 1841||
CSmH Jl 20 1830
MWA Ag 17 1825;N 28 1837
N O 5 1825;N 11-18,D 9,30 1828;Mr,10,24,D 30 1829;Mr 24 1830;O 15 1833
NAubW 1829;33-34
NCaz My 10 1826-Ag 1832
NN Mr 30 1825-Ag 1832;Je 4,18,Jl 2,S 10,D 24 1833-Ja 14,F 4-18,Mr 11,25,Je 17,Ag 5-12, 26 1834-F 23 1841
NNHi O 18 1836
NOHi S 24 1823;Ap 5 1831
NjHi N 21-28 1827;O 14,D 2 1828;Mr 10,24 1829;F 9 1830

Cazenovia STANDARD. w 1878-79||
NCaz N 12 1878-Jl 23 1879

UNION herald. w,sm My 1835-Ap 21 1842||
MWA Ag 24 1839
N My 16,D 5 1837[Ap 1838-39]S-N 1840;My 1841-42
NN Je 8,Jl 27-O 5,19 1839-Mr 7,21-Je 4,15,Jl 9-30,D 17,31 1840;F 4-11,25,Ap 1-15 1841
NNHi Mr 16 1838-Ja 12 1839;My 1841-42
OClWHi Ag 24 1838

CENTER MORICHES

Center Moriches RECORD. w 1900+
NRiHi Je 14 1931+

CENTRAL SQUARE

Central Square NEWS. w 1877+
pub 1910+

CHAMPLAIN

CLINTON county herald. w Mr 1877-79||
1877-78? as County herald
NChM N 30 1877;Ja 3,17-F 7,Mr 28-Ap 4,Je 20,Ag 1 1879

Champlain COUNSELOR. w Mr 9 1883-S 1909||
Follows Champlain interview and Rouses Point star
NChM complete

COUNTY herald. *See* Clinton county herald

Champlain INDEPENDENT. w 1883-
NChM N 14,D 12,20 1884

Champlain INTERVIEW and Rouses Point star. w Ja 7 1881-82||
Followed by Champlain counselor
NChM F 4,18,My 6,Jl 15,O 7-14,D 16,30 1881;F 17,Mr 10-17,Je 9,Jl 21,Ag 4,S 1 1882

Champlain JOURNAL. w N 3 1865-79||
N N 3,17 1865;Je 1,N 9 1866;O 14 1871
NChM [1866]-[79]

LAKE CHAMPLAIN beacon. w Jl 12 1850-52||
NChM Jl 12,26-Ag 4 1850;My 17 1851

CHAPPAQUA

NEW CASTLE tribune. w Ap 21 1927+
pub 1927+

CHARLOTTESVILLE

Charlottesville PHOENIX. w
N 1881-Mr 29 1882

CHATEAUGAY

Chateaugay JOURNAL. w 1863-72||
NChaF Jl 13 1872

CHATHAM

Name varies: Chatham Four Corners; Chatham Village

COLUMBIA democrat. w 1847-
NN My 24 1848

Chatham COURIER. w 1861+
MWA O 27 1864;Jl 20 1907
N S 20 1923+

CHAUTAUQUA

To 1879 as Fair Point

Chautauqua ASSEMBLY herald. *See* Chautauquan

CHAUTAUQUA LAKE journal. Jl 1873-
NChau Jl 1873

CHAUTAUQUAN. d,m Je 15 1876+
1876-1905 as Chautauqua assembly herald
1876-77 pub d during season; m during winter
pub 1880-1933
MB [Je 1879-Ag 1880]
MdBJ 1892-97
NChau 1876+
NWe Ja 1886;Jl 3 1905
NcU Jl 14 1916
PScrHi [1877-80;95-96;98]
PWayW Jl 1878-Ag 22 1881

CHAUTAUQUAN weekly. w 1880+
pub 1880-1933
NChau 1906-16;19-32
PMeA 1918-31

IRVING democrat. w
NFre Je 30 1847

CHERRY CREEK

Cherry Creek NEWS. w 1885+
pub 1885+

CHERRY VALLEY

*Cherry Valley GAZETTE. w O 1818-F 5 1933||
Mr 26-Ap 2 1857 as Gazette and examiner; Ap 9-D 24 1857 Otsego gazette and examiner. Merged with Cobleskill times (Cobleskill)
CSmH S 7 1830
DLC Ap 12 1825;Mr 21 1826;Ag 28,S 25 1827;F 25,Mr 25,Ag 5 1834;Ja 16 1836[37]Ap 22 1846-Ag 15 1849;F 1855-S 1865;N 1866-Je 1867
MWA Ja-S 25 1821;S 30 1823;My 31,Jl 12 1825;Je 16 1829
N O 15 1833

NEW YORK (*Continued*)

CHERRY VALLEY—*Continued*

*Cheng Valley GAZETTE. 1818-1933||—*Cont.*
NChe S 28 1824-25;Mr 3 1829;Ja 18 1831;Jl 5 1836;N 6 1839;Je 25 1845;N 5 1856;Ap 1 1858;O 15 1857;Ag 14 1861;Je 4 1862;Mr 25, Ag 26,S 2 1863;Ja 13 1881;1927-33
NN Jl 2 1822;S 30 1823;Mr 9,Ap 27 1824
NNHi Ag 19 1846;My 22 1850;Ja 4 1873

Cherry Valley NEWS. w O 13 1932+
pub 1932+

OTSEGO gazette and examiner. *See* Cherry Valley gazette

WATCH TOWER. *See under* Cooperstown

CHEWANGO

NEW BERLIN herald. w
NFre 1832

CHITTENANGO

Chittenango HERALD. w Mr 1 1831-
InLoHi O 15 1833
MWA My 6 1840
N O 15 1833
NChiM Mr 1 1831

MADISON county times. w 1869+
pub 1933+
NChiH 1884-1930

MADISON democrat. w
NOHi 1846-98

Chittenango PHENIX.
NN N 27 1850

CINCINNATUS

Cincinnatus REVIEW. w N 1930-Ag 1931||
NCinS complete

Cincinnatus TIMES. w 1898-S 10 1925||
NCinB complete
NCinS Ag 4 1898;S 19 1901;F 15 1912;Ag 28 1919;Je 12 1924;S 10 1925

CLAYTON

Clayton INDEPENDENT. w 1872-84||?
ICM N 23 1881;Ap 12,N 29 1882
MWA Jl 20 1876

ON the St. Lawrence. w 1883+
pub 1883+
NPhN Ap 25 1879+

CLEVELAND

LAKESIDE press. w 1873+
NNHi F 24-Ap 1911;N 15 1912

CLIFTON

NEW ERA. w Ap 17 1884-
ICM Ap 24,My 8 1884

Clifton Springs PRESS. w Ap 26 1877+
pub O 13 1886+
Ct O 13 1881
ICM [Jl 1878-O 1881]Mr 1 1883;S 1 1892
N Jl 13 1882

CLINTON

Clinton ADVERTISER. w 1899-1911||
NCli D 16 1899-Mr 4 1911

Clinton COURIER. w S 1857+
Follows Oneida chief
pub S 1861+
IU D 29 1859;Jl 19 1860;Ja 10 1861
N D 29 1859
NCH 1857-Ag,O 1863-S 3 1868;S 1870-Ag 1872

ONEIDA chief. w 1851-57||
Follows Clinton signal. Followed by Clinton courier
DLC S 14 1855
IU Mr 23 1854;Ag 17 1855
MWA Mr 17 1853
N Je 23 1853;Ag 17,N 2 1855;Ag 8 1856
NCH 1851-57
NCli 1852

Clinton SIGNAL. w Jl 1 1846-51||
Followed by Oneida chief
N F 25 1847;Ag 9,D 27 1849;Ag 30,O 11 1850
NCH Ja 12-Je 1847;Je 21 1849-Mr 14 1851

CLYDE

Clyde COMMERCIAL. w F 1861-
KHi Jl 19 1862

Clyde HERALD. w Ja 1 1888+
pub 1888+

Clyde TIMES. w O 1 1840-My 3 1929||
United with Lyons republican to form Lyons republican and the Clyde times (Lyons)
KHi Je 25 1850;F 4 1860;Ag 24 1861
MWA F 20 1864
NLyR complete
NN N 18 1851;My 9 1857;Jl 6(extra)1861;Ag 22 1863

COBLESKILL

Cobleskill HERALD. *See* Cobleskill times

Cobleskill INDEX. w 1865+
pub 1901+
N My 1869-82
NCob 1921+

SCHOHARIE county republican. w 1852-
N Ap 28 1853

SCHOHARIE county sentinel. w Ja 21 1852-
MWA Ag 19 1852

Cobleskill TIMES. w 1877+
1877-85 as Cobleskill herald
N Ag 8-O 24,D 19-26 1879;Ag 20-27 1880;Ja 4,F 29,Mr 11 1884;Ag 27 1885
NCob Ag 1916-Jl 1919;21+

COEYMANS

Coeymans GAZETTE. w 1863-73||
N F 1 1873

COHOCTON

COHOCTON VALLEY times-index. w 1873+
1873-O 1 1902 as Cohocton Valley times
pub O 8 1902+

Cohocton INDEX. w Je 1 1892-O 1 1902||
1892-Je 5 1893 as Atlanta news (Atlanta). United with Cohocton Valley times to form Cohocton Valley times-index
NCohT complete

COHOES

Cohoes ADVERTISER. w F 9 1847-
N 1847-F 9 1848

Cohoes AMERICAN. w 1920+
Follows Cohoes republican
N 1920-Jl 1922

Cohoes CATARACT. w Ja 1 1849-80||?
Suspended from Ja-Je 1865
N 1849-52;Je 1853-79
NN Ag 2 1873

Cohoes DISPATCH. d 1884-1919||?
Title varies: Evening dispatch
N F 1894-Je 1898;99;1901;04-07

Cohoes daily NEWS. d S 22 1873-99||?
N 1873-S 22 1876;77-Mr 1894;95-S 22 1899

Cohoes REPUBLICAN. d Jl 15 1892-D 1919||
Followed by Cohoes American
N 1892-1906;Ap 1913-19

COLD SPRING

Cold Spring RECORDER. w Mr 1 1866+
MWA F 15 1867;Mr 7 1868

CONSTABLEVILLE

NORTHERN blade. w 1854-Ap 1857||
Title varies: Dollar weekly northern blade; etc.
N 1854

COOPERSTOWN

To Ap 3 1807 as Otsego

*FREEMAN'S journal. w O 22 1808+
1808-My 27 1809 as Impartial observer; Je 3 1809-17 Cooperstown federalist; 1817-S 27 1819 Freeman's journal and Otsego county advertiser
pub 1808+
CClP O 10 1831
CSmH Je 28 1830
Ct Jl 21 1828;N 20 1831;D 29 1834[35-38]
DLC D 11 1837
ICHi My 12 1823;D 11 1826;Je 14 1830;D 24 1852;F 13 1868
MWA Je 5 1826;Jl 29 1839;D 27 1845
MiU-C S 18 1837
N S 27 1824;O 31 1825;Ap 3,My 17,31 1830;O 21 1833;D 21 1835;D 11 1837;Je 2 1845;O 29 1852;Ap 7 1854
NCoo 1821-42;44;46+
NN N 26 1832;S 30 1839
NNHi Jl 28,Ag 25 1823;Ap 19-26,Je 28,O 25, N 8 1824;Ap 24 1873
NOn Je 9 1845
OClWHi Ag 4 1823
WHi 1821-32;O 21 1833;D 1 1834;Jl 13 1835;37-Jl 1851

GLIMMERGLASS. d Jl 1909+
pub 1909+

OTSEGO democrat. w 1846-O 1855||
United with Otsego republican to form Republican and democrat, later Otsego republican
N N 28 1849

OTSEGO examiner. w S 28 1854-57||
DLC Ja 12 1855
MWA F 2,N 16 1855

OTSEGO farmer. w D 5 1885+
pub 1885+

*OTSEGO herald. w Ap 3 1795-1821||
1795-S 12 1805 as Otsego herald; or, Western advertiser
NCoo Ja 1-29 1821

OTSEGO republican. w Je 1 1829-1910||?
1829-31 as Tocsin; N 1855-77? Republican and democrat
CL S 14 1861;Jl 12 1862
CSmH S 6 1830
CtY S 21 1861
DLC Ag 10 1829;Je 8 1840;Ap 12 1841
ICHi Ja 25,F 8-15 1868
ICM Je 15 1881
MWA D 20 1830;Jl 10 1852;My 9 1874
MeBa Jl 27 1861
N F 13,Ap 2,My 28 1832;O 21 1833;O 13 1834; O 30 1852
NChe Ja 3,Ag 30,S 27,O 25,D 6 1847;O 16 1848;Ag 20 1849;S 21 1881
NCoo Ag 1840-My 9 1842
NNHi O 1 1849;Ja 14,Ap 29 1850;Jl 19 1851; Mr-O 1852;Ja,Mr-Je,O,D 1853;Ja 21,Mr 4,18-25,Ap 8 1854;Mr 15 1873

OTSEGO spy. w
MeU D 9 1826

REPUBLICAN and democrat. *See* Otsego republican

TOCSIN. *See* Otsego republican

*WATCH TOWER. w Ap 6 1814-31||
1813-14 pub in Cherry Valley
CSmH My 3 1830
CtY O 11 1830
DLC D 20 1824
NCoo Ja 28 1828-S 19 1831
NNHi O 5 1829
PEL Ap 12 1830

COPENHAGEN

Copenhagen INDEPENDENT. *See* Copenhagen news

LEWIS county independent. *See* Copenhagen news

Copenhagen NEWS. w My 20 1880-Jl 17 1902||
1880-My 11 1881 as Copenhagen independent; My 18 1881-83? Lewis county independent
N 1880-My 11 1881[98-99]-1902

Copenhagen NEWS. w S 11 1888-97||?
1888-91? as Copenhagen visitor
N S 18 1888

Copenhagen VISITOR. *See* Copenhagen news

CORFU

Corfu ENTERPRISE. w 1898+
pub 1898+

CORNING

Corning and Blossburg ADVOCATE. w Jl 31 1840-43||
Merged with Steuben courier (Bath)
NCor Ag 21 1840-Jl 27 1842

Corning weekly DEMOCRAT. w Ap 15 1857-1900||?
N F 22 1882
NCor Ap 18 1860-Ap 7 1864;Jl 1866-Je 1868;Jl 1876-Je 1878;Jl 1882-N 24 1887
NCorL Ap 22 1857-Ap 10 1862;Jl 1878-N 1884; D 1885-96

Corning daily DEMOCRAT. *See* Corning evening leader

Corning JOURNAL. w My 12 1847-1905||
N S 23 1875;N 8 1883
NCor Jl 21 1847-92;94;98-99;1903-Je 28 1905
NNHi Mr 14 1873
NjVi F 9 1848-My 8 1849
WHi D 7 1855

Corning daily JOURNAL. d S 7 1891-Ja 21 1920||
Merged with Corning evening leader
NCor S 9 1891-1917;Jl-D 1918;Ag 1919-20

Corning evening LEADER. d My 26 1884+
1884-S 18 1902 as Corning daily democrat
pub S 19 1902+
NCor D 1884-N 1885;Je 1886-My 1887
NCorL 1884-N 1885;Je 1886-My,D 1896-S 18 1902

CORNWALL

Cornwall LOCAL. w Ap 15 1871+
pub 1871+

Cornwall REFLECTOR. w 1877-86||?
MnHi [1880-Ap 1883]
NNHi My 7 1881;O 25 1884

CORTLAND

Cortland ADVOCATE. w O 7 1831-
N D 9 1831;F 15,O 17,D 12 1833;D 18 1834;O 21,N 12 1835
NCort S 29 1836
NOHi Je 1 1834

Cortland CHRONICLE. w Ap 18 1828-
CSmH O 30(extra)1828
N N 14 1828
NCortHi Ag 22 1828

CORTLAND county democrat. *See* Cortland democrat 1864+

CORTLAND county standard. *See* Cortland standard

CORTLAND county whig. w My 25 1840-55||
Follows Republican and eagle. Followed by Cortland county republican, later Homer republican. . . (Homer)
DLC Jl 21 1840
MWA S 6 1842
N Ag 22 1844;S 30 1852;Ap 6 1854
NCort My 11 1841;My 30 1844-My 13 1852
NCortHi Ag 3 1853
NHom [Ag 24 1840-Ag 23 1855]
NSyU S 28,O 26,N 9 1848;F 15,Mr 1-15 1849

Cortland DEMOCRAT. w My 12 1840-
MWA My 12 1841
MiU Ag 4 1841
N N 24 1841;S 11 1844;O 14 1852;Ap 6 1854
NCort 1840-My 4 1842;My 8 1844-D 20 1849
NHom Je 30,Jl 14,O 13 1840;F 23,Mr 9-16 1841

Cortland DEMOCRAT. w 1864+
1864-78 as Cortland county democrat
pub 1868-70;75+
NCort O 1926-[30]32+
NCortHi Ja 13 1871
NIC [1869-O 1885]

NEW YORK (*Continued*)

CORTLAND—*Continued*

Cortland evening DEMOCRAT. d My 1875-
NCort Je 12 1875
NIC Je 1. 1875

GAZETTE and banner. w O 3 1861-69||?
ICHi F 1 1868
NCort F 20 1869
NCortHi D 26 1861;D 18 1862;N 30 1867

Cortland JOURNAL. w My 27 1869-Ap 1872||
United with Cortland county standard to form Cortland standard and journal, later Cortland standard
NCort D 2 1869

Cortland NEWS. w 1880-85||?
NCortHi D 29 1880;Ja 14 1881;N 10-17 1882

REPUBLICAN and eagle. w 1832-My 18 1840||
1832-Mr? 1836 as Cortland republican. Followed by Cortland county whig
CtY S 22 1833
N Ap 10,O 15 1833;S 22 1835;Ja 16 1838
NCort My 17 1836-40
NCortHi Ap 26 1836
NHom Ap 23 1833;Ja 28 1834[Ja-Ag 1835]Mr 1,Ag 9 1836[Ja-Jl 1837]Ag 21 1838;F 26 1839; F 25 1840

REPUBLICAN banner. w S 1 1858-
CtY [1861]
NCort 1858-S 18 1861
NSyU Ag 1861

Cortland STANDARD. w,sw My 1867-1919||?
1867-72? as Cortland county standard; 1873-78? Cortland standard and journal
w 1867-92
pub complete
MWA N 1 1876;N 15 1888;D 1895
NCort 1892-98
NCortHi [Mr 14 1877-F 8 1926]
NHom 1894-1901
NIC [My 1876-O 1885]S 20 1910
NMac 1868-72

Cortland STANDARD. d Mr 8 1892+
NCort 1892—

COXSACKIE

GREENE county advertiser. w 1831-36||
Followed by Standard
DLC N 8 1832
N O 17 1833

Coxsackie NEWS. w 1867-1906||?
United with Coxsackie union to form Coxsackie union-news
NNHi Ja 11 1873

Coxsackie REVIEW. w Mr 15 1934+
NCox 1934+

STANDARD. w 1836-38||?
Follows Greene county advertiser
NNHi Ag 16 1838

Coxsackie weekly UNION. w Ap 23 1851-
N Ag 20,S 24 O 15,N 5,D 24-31 1851;Mr 3 1852
NNewHi [1854]

Coxsackie UNION-NEWS. w 1899+
1899-1921? as Coxsackie union
NCox 1915+

CROTON-ON-HUDSON

CROTON journal. *See* Croton-on-Hudson news

Croton-on-Hudson NEWS. w Je 1894+
1894-D 1910 as Croton journal; D 1910-Jl 4 1930 Croton-Harmon news
pub [1894-1906]-09;20+

CROWN POINT

Crown Point BUDGET. *See* Essex county times

ESSEX county times. w D 26 1877-84||?
1877-80? as Crown Point budget
NHi O 3 1883

CUBA

DEMOCRATIC-TIMES. *See* Cuba free-press

Cuba FREE-PRESS. w 1881-1908||?
1881-96 as Cuba post; 1897?-1902? Democratic-times. United with Cuba patriot to form Cuba patriot and free press
NOl 1896

Cuba PATRIOT and free press. w 1862+
1862-74? as True patriot; 1875?-1908? Cuba patriot
pub 1886-1904;11+
MWA S 22 1871
NjHi F 21 1879

Cuba POST. *See* Cuba free-press

TRUE patriot. *See* Cuba patriot and free press

DANSVILLE

Dansville ADVERTISER. w Ag 2 1860-1912;Ja 13 1925-D 10 1931||
United with Dansville express to form Genesee county express and advertiser
ICM Je 29,N 30 1882
MWA S 6 1860 Mr 16 1882;O 22 1885
N Ap 22 1875
ND 1860-1912
NDG 1925-31
NN Ap 10 1862

Dansville BREEZE. w,d N 27 1883+
w 1883-1908
pub 1883+

Dansville CHRONICLE. w 1830-
N O 16 1833

Dansville weekly CHRONICLE. w Jl 21 1847-51||
N S 29 1847
NMmE O 6 1848
NNHi D 22 1847

Dansville COURIER. w O 1848-
N Jl 3 1849

Dansville EXPRESS. *See* Genesee county express and advertiser

GENESEE county express and advertiser. w My 23 1850+
1850-Ag 2 1865 as Dansville weekly herald; Ag 9 1865-D 10 1931 Dansville express
pub My 31 1877+
MWA S 21 1871
N O 21 1857
ND 1850-My 14 1851;My 19 1852;My 10,D 14 1853;My 17 1854;My 7 1856;My 25,N 30 1859; Ja 11 1860;Je 9,Ag 31,S 14,28,O 12-N 16 1864; Ja 4,10,31,Ag 2 1865
NGe Ja 18,F 1-8,Mr 1,22,Je 7-14,28 1917;Je 12,Jl 24 1919

Dansville daily HERALD. d Ja 20 1860-
ND Ja-Mr 21 1860;My 11-15,17-21 1861

Dansville weekly HERALD. *See* Genesee county express and advertiser

LIVINGSTON democrat. w Jl 7 1860-
N Jl-D 29 1860

LIVINGSTON sentinel. w O 27 1857-60||
NDG 1857-59
NMmE Ag 23 1859

Dansville REPUBLICAN. w 1842-
N Ag 22 1844

Dansville daily SENTINEL. d Ja- 1860||
N Mr 28 1860

VALLEY CITY register. w 1859-60||
NNHi S 10 1859

VILLAGE chronicle. w Ap 20 1830-
CSmH Ag 3 1830

DELHI

DELAWARE express. w Ja 30 1839+
DLC Ja 30 1839
MWA N 2 1876
N N 27 1839;Mr 18 1840;S 1,N 17 1841;D 28 1842;1913+
NDe Ap 1918+
NNHi Ja 20 1841;Ja 27 1843

*DELAWARE gazette. w N 18 1819-N 3 1915||
Ct D 20 1837
MWA Ja 29 1840;D 2 1863
N Je 30,O 13 1824;N 24 1826;N 7 1827;My 20 1829;O 16 1833;Mr 29 1837;Ja 16 1839;Je 17 1840;N 10-17 1841;D 21 1842;Ap 17 1844;Ja 25 1854
NDe complete
NNHi Ap 21 1873
WHi Ja 16 1856

DELAWARE republican. w S 1 1830-
CSmH S 8 1830

DELAWARE republican. w My 1860+
pub 1860+
NDe Ap 1918+
NNHi Mr 8 1873
OClWHi Jl 21 1866

DEPOSIT

Deposit COURIER. w 1846+
pub 1932+
MWA Jl 13 1866

DE RUYTER

BANNER of the times. w My 14 1851-55||
MWA Ag 27,D 3 1851;Mr 17 1852;F 23 1853

De Ruyter GLEANER. w S 18 1878+
pub 1878+

De Ruyter HERALD. w 1835-
NOHi Jl 8 1835

De Ruyter weekly NEWS. w 1862-
MWA D 2 1863

DOBBS FERRY

Dobbs Ferry REGISTER. w 1899+
NN D 28 1906-[1912]-14

DOLGEVILLE

Dolgeville FREE PRESS. m,w My 1889-1904||?
1889-1900? as Dolgeville herald
m 1889-Ag 5 1891
MWA Je,N 1889;Jl 1890
MnHi My 1889
NHerHi 1892-Ag 1899;1901-Jl 1902

Dolgeville HERALD. *See* Dolgeville free press

Dolgeville REPUBLICAN. w S 1897+
NHerHi 1902-04

DRYDEN

COMMUNICATOR. *See* Tompkins county rural news

Dryden weekly HERALD. w 1871-1919||
NCortS 1876-1918
NIC 1879-1919

Dryden NEWS. w 1856-70||?
NCortHi S 17 1857
NDr Mr 6,Ap 3-10,24,Ag 21-28 1862;Ag 20 1863; Ja 28,My 5 1864;My 3,Je 21-28,Ag 16,N 1 1866;D 24 1868

TOMPKINS county rural news. w Jl 1933?+
1933-Jl 1934 as Communicator
NDr 1933+

DUNDEE

Dundee EXPOSITOR. w
NNHi Jl 2 1869

Dundee OBSERVER. w Je 20 1878+
pub 1878+

Dundee RECORD. w Ja 25 1844-
KHi Ag 6 1856
N Ja 30 1850
NNHi O 20 1852

DUNKIRK

ADVERTISER and union. w Jl 4 1851-1913||?
1851-68 as Fredonia advertiser (Fredonia)
NBuG F 3 1860
NFre 1851-Ag 12 1864;Ap 19 1867;Jl 17 1868

Dunkirk BEACON. w Ag 1834-45||
1834-35? as Chautauqua whig
Ct [1837]
NDu [S 1835-Je 1841]
NFre Ap 5 1836;S 19 1844;Ag 14 1845
NJ 1835-45

CHAUTAUQUA journal. *See* Dunkirk journal

CHAUTAUQUA whig. *See* Dunkirk beacon

Dunkirk weekly JOURNAL. w My 1850-85||?
1850? as Chautauqua journal
ICHi S 23 1864
MWA D 31 1852
NDu N 1863-Mr 1866;S 1869-S 1870;My 1874-My 1883
NJ 1851-54
NWe Ag 3 1860

Dunkirk evening OBSERVER. d 1882+
NDu 1882+

Dunkirk PRESS and western argus. w 1859-
Follows Western argus (Westfield)
NWe Je 10 1859

Dunkirk UNION. w 1867-68||
United with Fredonia advertiser (Fredonia) to form Advertiser and union (Dunkirk)
NFre Ja 23 1867

EARLVILLE

Earlville STANDARD. w D 1 1887+
pub 1887+
NOHi Ap 19 1926

EAST ALBANY

RENSSELAER county republican. w 1880-
Also dated at Bath-on-the-Hudson
ICM O 15 1881

EAST AURORA

East Aurora ADVERTISER. w 1872+
pub [1872+]

EAST HAMPTON

East Hampton STAR. w D 1 1885+
pub D 1885+
NEh Jl 1927+

EAST NORWICH

East Norwich ENTERPRISE. w S 11 1880-1925||?
NBHi 1880-F 1925

EAST ROCHESTER

East Rochester HERALD. w 1909+
1909-25? as East Rochester realities
pub My 1926+

East Rochester REALITIES. *See* East Rochester herald

EAST SYRACUSE

ONONDAGA gazette. w 1891-95||?
N Ag 25 1893

EDMESTON

Edmeston LOCAL. w 1882+
1882-85 Wharton Valley echo
pub 1882+

WHARTON VALLEY echo. *See* Edmeston local

ELIZABETHTOWN

ESSEX county reporter. w Ja 4- 1849||
Follows Westport patriot and Essex county advertiser (Westport)
NHi Ja-Ag 16 1849
NNHi Ja-My 17,Je 7,21-Jl 5,19-26,Ag 9-23 1849

ESSEX county times. *See* Westport patriot and Essex county advertiser (Westport)

Elizabethtown POST. w 1851-N 19 1920||
United with Adirondack record to form Adirondack record-Elizabethtown post (Au Sable Forks)
MWA N 12 1852
N D 22 1864;Ag 12 1869;Jl 30 1908-18
NEIB 1894-96;1900-09
NHi 1860-70;79-93;97-99
NN F 5 1920

NEW YORK (*Continued*)

ELLENVILLE

BANNER of liberty. w 1852-87||?
DLC Je 2 1877

Ellenville JOURNAL. w 1849+
DLC F 20 1852
NNHi Mr 15 1873
NcD O 22 1864

Ellenville PRESS. w S 1870+
1870-72 as South Ulster press
pub 1893+
DLC My 17 1872;F 14 1873;Mr 5 1875;My 19 1882
NNHi F 28 1873

SOUTH ULSTER press. *See* Ellenville press

ELLICOTTVILLE

CATTARAUGUS freeman. w Ag 25 1840-
1840-54? as Cattaraugus whig
MWA N 23 1854;Ja 25 1855;Ap 24,Ag 28 1856; Ap 9 1857
N F 10 1841;Ap 15 1844;Mr 6 1847
NNHi My 28 1863

CATTARAUGUS republican. w My 17 1833-
1833-39? as Ellicottville republican
MWA Ja 4 1855
N O 18 1833
PW S 1840
PWCl Je 6,Ag 1 1842
WHi Je 9 1841

CATTARAUGUS union. w 1853-
DLC O 26 1855
MWA Ja 26,O 12 1855
NNHi F 27 1873

CATTARAUGUS whig. *See* Cattaraugus freeman

POST. w 1884+
pub N 1919+
NBuG F 1935+

Ellicottville REPUBLICAN. *See* Cattaraugus republican

ELMHURST

To 1828 as Newtown

NEWTOWN register. w,sw Jl 17 1873+
1873-98? pub in Newtown
w 1873-1900?
NBHi 1877-1920
NNQ 1873-1905;09+

ELMIRA

Elmira weekly ADVERTISER. w 1853-1914||?
Title varies: Elmira weekly advertiser and Chemung county republican
MWA N 3 1876
DLC F 28 1879
NCor 1870-72;74
NEmS [1858;60-61]
NNHi Ap 2,Ag 13,N 12 1864;Mr 1873

Elmira ADVERTISER. d N 3 1853+
pub N 1881;89-Ja 1890
DLC Ap 27,My 2 1881
ICM My 31 1878
MWA Je 3 1873;Ag 26 1876;Ag 23 1879;F 9 1884
MnHi Jl 6 1865
NEm 1864+
NEmS N 1881-Ja 1890
NNHi Jl 2 1860;Ap 16 1873
PAtM N 18 1857
PWeA [1854]

CHEMUNG county journal. w 1875-78||
PScrHi [1875]-[78]

CHEMUNG county republican. w
Merged with Elmira weekly advertiser
NEmS [1858]

CHEMUNG democrat. w 1847-51||
NNHi F 1,Ap 12,S 6 1849;Ag 8 1850

Elmira weekly FREE PRESS. w 1873-81||
United with Elmira gazette to form Elmire gazette and free press, later Elmira star-gazette
NEmS 1881

Elmira GAZETTE. *See* Elmira star-gazette

*INVESTIGATOR. w D 1819-22||?
Followed by Tioga register
MWA S 1 1821

Evening NEWS. d 1894-1906||?
NEmS Ag 1898-99
PPCHi [1894]

Elmira daily PRESS. d My 30 1859-
MnHi D 29 1863
N Je 6 1862
NEmS 1860-61

Elmira daily REPUBLICAN. d 1851-
MWA N 10 1852
NEmS Mr 1852;S 1857

Elmira REPUBLICAN and general advertiser. w 1829-57||
Follows Elmira whig. Title varies: Elmira republican; Elmira republican and canal advertiser
CSmH S 7 1830
DLC N 23 1833;F 8 1834
MWA O 15(extra)1844
N O 26 1833
NN D 24 1836;F 4 1837
P-M O 28 1831
PWbW F 27 1841

Saturday evening REVIEW. w Mr 13 1869-71||
NCor O 30 1869-Mr 4 1871

SOUTHERN TIER leader. w F 28 1874-
NCor 1874

Elmira evening STAR. d 1888-1906||?
United with Elmira gazette and free press to form Elmira star-gazette

Elmira STAR-GAZETTE. w 1829-1914||?
Follows Tioga register. 1829-81 as Elmira gazette; 1881-1913? Elmira gazette and free press
pub 1841;43;89;1901
MBAt Ap 20 1865
MWA Jl 28 1832;D 3 1863;O 19 1871
N Ap 16 1831;O 12 1833;Ap 6 1877
NCanHi Ja 20 1842

Elmira STAR-GAZETTE. d 1861+
1861-81 as Elmira daily gazette; 1881-1908? Elmira gazette and free press
pub 1875;78;82-83;85;current files only
DLC 1898
MWA O 20 1871
N Mr 1913+
NEm 1891+
NNHi My 2 1873
PAtM N 22 1876
PToHi Ja 5 1843;S 3 1856;S 6 1881

Elmira TELEGRAM. w My 5 1879+
Title varies: Elmira Sunday telegram; Sunday morning telegram
pub 1879+
KHi Je 6 1886;My 30 1891;My 28 1893
MWA Jl 6 1890;My 24 1891
PBlosM Ap 29 1889
PPCHi [1894]
PScrHi My 28 1893;D 2 1917
TxH Ja 27 1884
VU Ja 1 1884

TIOGA register. w 1824-28||
Follows Investigator. Followed by Elmira gazette, later Elmira star-gazette
N Ap 9 1825

Elmira WHIG. w S? 1828-29||
Followed by Elmira republican and general advertiser
DLC Jl 30 1829

ELMSFORD

Elmsford EAGLE. w N 11 1911+
pub 1935+
NNHi 1911-N 4 1916

ELYRIA

Elyria REPUBLICAN. w
Ct [1835-37]

ENDICOTT

Endicott BULLETIN. sw Ag 20 1914+
pub 1914+
NEnT 1917+

Il NUOVO Americano. New American. w 1920-29||
In Italian
NEnC [1920-29]

Endicott TIMES. w 1851+
1851-Ja 1919 as Union news (1906?-Ja 1918 Union-Endicott news); F 1919-29 Union news-dispatch
1851-1929? pub in Union
pub Ap 1915+
DLC Mr 4 1870
N S 12 1917-19

UNION news. *See* Endicott times

ESSEX

ESSEX county republican. *See* Essex republican

Essex REPUBLICAN. w Je 28 1823-33||
1823-31? as Essex county republican
CSmH Ag 14 1830
MWA Ag 30 1823
NHi Ja 6,N 17 1827;O 4 1828;Jl 30 1831;Mr 24,S 29,N 2 1832;O 13 1833

FABIUS

AMERICAN patriot. w 1835-
NN Ap 29,My 13,27,Je 3,17-24,Jl 15-Ag 19, S 2-16,30,O 21-D 9 1835;Ja 6-27,F 10-Mr 2 1836

FAIR HAVEN

Fair Haven REGISTER. w 1874+
pub 1914+

FAIR POINT. *See* CHAUTAUQUA

FAIRPORT

Fairport HERALD. w F 6 1872-Ap 30 1925||
United with Monroe county mail to form Herald-mail
N F 19 1886
NFpH complete

HERALD-MAIL. w My 1 1925+
Formed by the union of Fairport herald and Monroe county mail
pub 1925+

MONROE county mail. w Ja 3 1881-Ap 30 1925||
United with Fairport herald to form Herald-mail
NFpH complete

FAR ROCKAWAY

ROCKAWAY news. sw 1899+
pub 1899+
NNQ 1910-[19-20;24]-[29]+

FARMINGDALE

Farmingdale POST. w N 19 1920+
pub 1920+

FAYETTEVILLE

Fayetteville BULLETIN. *See* Eagle bulletin

EAGLE bulletin. w 1895+
1895-Jl 1933 as Fayetteville bulletin
pub 1904+
NF [1900-Jl 1933]+

Fayetteville LUMINARY. w 1837-
MWA O 3 1839
NSyU S 26 1839

Fayetteville weekly RECORDER. w 1866-98||
NF [1866-98]
NN F 18 1875

FILLMORE

NORTHERN ALLEGANY county observer. w My 11 1888+
pub 1888+

FISHKILL

Fishkill JOURNAL. w Ag 5 1854-82||?
MWA Ag 11 1864
NNHi Ag 5 1854;Je 23 1855;Jl 17 1862;Mr 21 1873
WHi Ag 10 1865-Jl 3 1879

FISHKILL LANDING

Fishkill STANDARD. w Ag 2 1842-1913||?
DLC Ag 2 1842
MWA O 25 1860;Ag 31,N 9,D 14 1867;Ja 11,F 8,29,Ap 4,My 2,Je 6 1868
N My 13 1847;Ap 22 1876
NNHi Je 11 1868;Mr 8 1873;Mr 28 1874
OClWHi Ag 2 1866
WHi Jl 6 1867

FLATBUSH

Papers published in Flatbush are listed under Brooklyn

FLORAL PARK

GATEWAY. w 1926+
pub 1926+

ISLAND review. m 1892-1900||?
NBHi Ag 13 1898

NASSAU event. 1904-17||?
NBHi 1904-17

FLUSHING

Flushing JOURNAL. *See* North shore daily journal

LONG ISLAND times. w Mr 1 1855-1902||?
MWA Mr 10 1864;Ag 29,O 10-17 1867
NBHi 1855-N 8 1860;64-82
NEh Mr 19 1863;O 5 1865;My 24,Je 21,Ag 9 1866
NN My 12-19 1859
NNHi Ap 17 1873
NNQ F 21 1861-63;F 21 1867-75
NSm D 15 1864;N 22 1883

NORTH SHORE daily journal. w,d Mr 19 1842+
1842-F 1879 as Flushing journal; Mr 1879-Ja 17 1931 Flushing evening journal
A specimen number was issued O 9 1841
w 1842-F 1879
pub Ap 1927+
MWA Ag 23 1845;O 14(supp)1846;Mr 4(supp) 1847
N [1843-47;50-64]
NBHi 1845-47;51-93
NEh Mr 19 1842;Ap 15 1848;N 25 1865
NN My 7 1842
NNQ 1910-[20]+
NSm My 16 1863;F 28 1880

NORTH SHORE news. sw 1921+
pub [1921+]

PUBLIC voice. w 1853-54||
NBHi complete

Flushing daily TIMES. d S 4 1865-1925||?
NBHi S 4 1865
NNQ Mr 3 1859-Ja 16 1860;73-83;1903-18

FONDA

Fonda HERALD. w 1836-
N D 8 1837

Fonda HERALD and Montgomery county advertiser. w 1841-
Follows Johnstown herald (Johnstown)
CtY D 7 1841
N O 11 1841
NSchU Ja 4,Mr 8 1842

MOHAWK VALLEY democrat. w 1859+
Follows Fonda sentinel
pub 1897+
MBAt Ap 18 1865
N Mr 1913+
NNHi F 22 1873

NEW YORK (*Continued*)

FONDA—*Continued*

MONTGOMERY democrat. w
NNHi 1868-54

Fonda SENTINEL. w O 13 1843-59||
Followed by Mohawk Valley democrat
CtY Mr 5 1847;Je 24 1851
DLC O 2 1842;Mr 28 1845;Ja 1 1850
N N 17 1843
NAmsB Mr 22 1844

FOREST HILLS

Forest Hills-Kew Gardens POST. w 1922+
pub O 1923+

FORESTVILLE

Forestville FREE PRESS. w 1891+
pub 1891+
CtY Jl 4-Ag 18 1933

PEOPLE'S gazette. *See under* Fredonia

WESTERN intelligencer. w Ag 29 1833-
N O 17 1833

FORT COVINGTON

FRANKLIN gazette. *See under* Malone

FRANKLIN republican. w Ap 24? 1828-33||
CSmH My 5 1830
MWA F 13 1828
NNHi D 16 1829;F 9 1831

Fort Covington SUN. w My 13 1885+
Follows Athelstan sun (Athelstan, Quebec)
pub 1885+
CaQHC 1885-N 1887

FORT EDWARD

Fort Edward ADVERTISER. w N 26 1879-1922||?
1879-O 5 1881 as Sandy Hill commercial advertiser (Hudson Falls); O 12 1881-88 Washington county advertiser
NFe 1879-88 1905-22
NHfP 1881-83;1905-22
NHi 1882-88

Fort Edward COURIER. w N 2 1853-My 1 1854||
Followed by Morning star (Mechanicville)
NHi complete

Fort Edward GAZETTE. w N 10 1866-85||
N [1866-69]Ja 26,D 6 1872
NFeH Ap 3 1868
NHi Ja 12 1872

Fort Edward LEDGER. w 1855-
1855-57 as Public ledger
MWA Ap 10,O 4 1863;F 12 1864
N [1856-64]

LOCAL observer. w Ag 10 1865-
N Ag 10 1865

PUBLIC ledger. *See* Fort Edward ledger

WASHINGTON county advertiser. *See* Fort Edward advertiser

WASHINGTON county clipper. w O 31 1885-87||
NHfS 1885-87
NHi 1885-Jl 21 1887

FORT PLAIN

Fort Plain FREE PRESS and Mohawk Valley register. w Ap 8 1884+
1884-N 1921 as Fort Plain free press
pub 1884+

Fort Plain JOURNAL. w 1836-41||
DLC Jl 10 1838
NFplM Ap 29 1837-S 18 1839;My 20 1840

Fort Plain JOURNAL. w Je 27 1847-
NUHi D 26 1847

MOHAWK VALLEY register. w F 3 1841-N 1921||?
1841-F 185- as Montgomery phoenix. United with Fort Plain free press to form Fort Plain free press and Mohawk Valley register
NNHi Ap 4 1873;Ag 6 1874
NUHi My 1856-61

MONTGOMERY phoenix. *See* Mohawk Valley register

MONTGOMERY phoenix and Fort Plain advertiser. *See* Canajoharie radii (Canajoharie)

Fort Plain STANDARD. w Mr 1877+
pub 1895+
N Ap 12 1917-19
NNHu [1933]+

FRANKFORT

Frankfort CITIZEN. w 1885-1919||?
N O 27 1917-19

HERKIMER county democrat. *See* Herkimer democrat (Herkimer)

Frankfort REGISTER. w Ja 1 1881-1904||
1881-S 8 1883 as Newport advertiser; S 15 1883-Ja 15 1886 Newport register
1881-Ja 15 1886 pub in Newport
NHerHi S 26 1885-Ja 15 1886;92-1904

FRANKLIN VILLAGE. *See* FABIUS

FRANKLINVILLE

Franklinville ARGUS. *See* Chronicle-journal

CHRONICLE-JOURNAL. w 1875+
1875-88? as Franklinville argus; 1889?-1911? Chronicle
pub 1929+

FREDONIA

Fredonia ADVERTISER. *See* Advertiser and union (Dunkirk)

Fredonia CENSOR. w 1821+
1821-24 as New York censor
pub My 9 1838+
CSmH My 19 1830
Ct Ja 16 1828
DLC Ja 2 1833
ICHi D 14 1864
KHi Ja 15 1840
MWA O 19 1847;My 18 1852;Ja 6,Mr 23 1864; F 7 1866;Ag 3 1881
MiU-C F 21 1838
N O 2 1833;F 8 1871
NBuG Ag 12 1840;Jl 8 1891
NFre N 13-20,D 4,18-25 1821;Ja 23-F 13,Mr 6,20-27,Ap 10-17 1822;Ap 9 1823-Je 1824;25+
NJ [1821-22]My 25 1825-Ag 5 1829;S 1830-60
NWe Jl 6 1825;Mr 23 1864;Je 18 1873;F 1 1899
NNHi Ag 12(extra)1840;Ap 9 1873
OClWHi Je 18 1873
PW F 6 1828;My 8 1832
WHi Je 15,29,Jl 13 1825

CHAUTAUQUA advertiser. w S 14 1824-25||?
United with Chautauqua gazette to form Fredonia gazette and Chautauqua advertiser
MWA O 1824;Ja 26-F 2 1825
N Mr 30 1825

CHAUTAUQUA gazette. *See* Fredonia gazette and Chautauqua advertiser

FRONTIER express. w Je 1846-48||
NFre 1848

***Fredonia GAZETTE and Chautauqua advertiser.** w Ja 7 1817-27||
1817-25? as Chautauqua gazette. Merged with Chautauque phoenix (Westfield)
N My 8-15 1822
NFre Mr 13 1821;My 8,O 16 1822;S 2 1826; Mr 1 1828
NJ Jl 24 1821;Je 26 1822[27]
NWe Jl 31 1822

NEW YORK censor. *See* Fredonia censor

PEOPLE'S gazette. w 1824-26||
United with Chautauqua gazette to form Fredonia gazette
1824-26? pub in Forestville

WESTERN democrat and literary enquirer. w 1834-36||
MWA Mr 8 1836
NFre D 23 1834-S 6 1836
NJ complete

FREEPORT

Freeport weekly BULLETIN. w 1858-
OClWHi Ja 8 1866

NASSAU county review. *See* Nassau daily review

NASSAU daily news. w,d Ag 29 1928+
1928-My 14 1934 as Nassau news(w)

NASSAU post. w 1914-18||
NRcN Ag 8 1914-Jl 19 1918

NASSAU daily review. w,d N 8 1895+
1895-99 as Queens county review; 1899-Mr 7 1921 Nassau county review
w 1895-Mr 7 1921
pub Mr 7 1921+
NBHi My 26 1921-28
NFr 1930+
NHe Je 25 1929+
NRc N 12-D 1920
NRcN 1895-N 1906

QUEENS county review. *See* Nassau daily review

SOUTH SHORE news. w F 13 1931+
1931-O 13 1933 pub in Merrick
pub 1931+

SOUTH SIDE messenger. w 1908-13||
NRcN 1908-O 24 1913

FRIENDSHIP

Friendship REGISTER. w 1869+
pub D 24 1870;D 9 1871;72;74;79-81;86 88-95; 98;1900-02;07-10;16+

FULTON

Fulton CHRONICLE. w N 1837-40||
NBi D 13 1837-N 21 1838

OSWEGO county gazette. w 1853-58||
United with Fulton patriot to form Fulton patriot and gazette, later Fulton patriot

Fulton PATRIOT. w 1856+
1858-91? as Fulton patriot and gazette
MWA Mr 31,Ag 25 1876
NFu 1899;1916+

Fulton TIMES. w 1868-1917||
NFu 1881-1917

FULTONVILLE

MONTGOMERY county republican. w O 24 1839-N 26 1916||
1839-Ap 15 1851 as Montgomery whig; Ap 22 1851-S 12 1856 Montgomery county whig
DLC Mr 10 1840
N O 19 1844
NFoM 1839-43;Ap 25 1845;S 19 1848;50-71;Ag 18 1874;S 21 1875;88-1904;06-16
NSaE D 13 1845
NSchU F 4,25,Mr 12,Ap 9 1842

MONTGOMERY county whig. *See* Montgomery county republican

MONTGOMERY whig. *See* Montgomery county republican

GARDEN CITY

Garden City NEWS. w S 23 1923+
pub 1923+
NHe [O 16 1924-Mr 16 1929]Ap 1933+

GENESEO

LIVINGSTON county leader and democrat. w Ag 12 1885+
1885-Ja 24 1930 as Livingston democrat
pub 1885+
MiU-C Je 14 1836
N My 21 1925-S 21 1928
NGe 1907-Je 14,Ag-N 17,D 1,29 1916-Je 1924; 25;27-Ja 1928
NMmE Je 28 1836

LIVINGSTON courier. w Ap 13 1831-
NMmE My 4-11,Ag 31,D 2 1831

LIVINGSTON democrat. *See* Livingston county leader and democrat

LIVINGSTON journal. w 1821-34||?
CSmH S 8 1830
DLC O 24(extra)1829
MWA S 8,O 13 1824;O 30,D 4 1827;Ap 1 1828
N O 16 1833

LIVINGSTON register. w Je 28 1824-
CSmH Ag 18 1830
CtY Mr 1 1845
DLC N 9 1835
N Ja 16,Ap 17-My 1,Je 5,26,O 16,D 25 1833; F 5-12,Mr 12,Je 18,Jl 9,Ag 13,O 27,N 24 1834
NGe Ja 27 1837-N 19 1839
NjHi N 18 1829;Ag 29,O 10-17,N 14 1832
WHi Ja 12 1825

LIVINGSTON republican. w S 19 1837+
pub 1885—
MBAt N 15 1842
MWA D 2 1852;Ag 16 1866
MiG Je 27 1889
N O 28 1852
NGe 1838-39;50-57;Ap 22 1858 My 16 1861;My 12-19 1864;S 23 1880;Je 11 1883;Je 1 1885; Ap 7,S 29 1887;S 5 1889;1905-06;08-19;21-23; 27-Je 1,Ag-S 18,O 16-N 20,D 1929+
NSchU Ag 16 1842

GENEVA

Geneva ADVERTISER-GAZETTE. w 1880-Ag 31 1917||
1880-Mr 4 1902 as Geneva advertiser
NGen S 10 1908-S 2 1915
NGenH Mr 11 1902-17

Geneva AMERICAN. w S 20? 1831-
MWA F 1 1832

Geneva CHRONICLE. w N? 1827-
1827-Ap? 1829 as Ontario chronicle; My?-S 16 1829 Chronicle of Geneva
DLC Jl 22,Ag 5,S 16,N 25,D 30 1829-Ja 6 1830
MBAt S 3 1828
MWA Ja 28 1829
NjHi Ap 29,Ag 19,S 2,N 25,D 9 1829

Geneva COURIER. w Ja 5 1831-1902||
Merged with Geneva daily times
DLC Ag 3 1864
MWA Je 9 1852;Ja 31 1866;S 17 1879
N S 20 1842
NCanHi Je 12 1842;N 14 1843
NGen Ja 12 1831-33
NGenH O 25 1854-62;F 23 1876-83
NN D 5(supp)1845
NNHi My 7 1873;Ap 24 1878
NjR Ag 24 1841
OClWHi Je 16 1840
RPB Ap 30 1834

***Geneva GAZETTE.** w Je 21 1809-Mr 7 1902||
Follows Expositor (not in this list). Title varies: Geneva gazette and general advertiser; Geneva gazette and mercantile advertiser. United with Geneva advertiser to form Geneva advertiser-gazette
CSmH Ag 19 1829
DLC Mr 9 1836;O 22,N 5 1852;S 8 1871
MWA My 31 1826;Mr 27 1833;Mr 15 1872;Ap 14 1876
MiU Ja 6 1836
N D 15 1824;O 26 1825;Ap 5 1826;N 1(supp) 1830;Mr 23 1831;O 16 1833
NCanHi Ap 2 1824
NCorL 1821-Ag 21 1839;45-1902
NGen D 25 1833-36
NGenH Je 13 1827-My 1834;Ag 29 1838-Ag 21 1839;Je 1847-49;My 1866-1902
NN O 19,D 21 1825;Ja 14 1829
NNHi My 16 1873
NjHi [1823-28]
NjR My 4 1849
OClWHi O 1 1845;Ag 30 1872
P-M O 17 1832
PErW Ag 30 1826
WHi N 20 1846

NEW YORK (*Continued*)

GENEVA—*Continued*

Geneva daily GAZETTE. d
NNHi D 18 1846;Ja 13,15-16,19,25 1847

Geneva INDEPENDENT. w 1853-
MWA F 2 1854

INDEPENDENT American. w Jl 14 1830-
CSmH Jl 28 1830

Geneva LEDGER. w 1857-
NCanHi Jl 2 1859

MISCELLANEOUS register. w Je 20 1822-D 13 1823||
NGenH complete

ONTARIO chronicle. *See* Geneva chronicle

ONTARIO whig. w
WHi O 14 1832

*Geneva PALLADIUM. w Ja 10 1816-28||
MWA Ja 21 1824;Ja 19 1825
NFre 1821
NGen 1821-22
NjHi Mr 28,Je,Jl 18,Ag 1,N 14 1821;Ap 24-My 1,Je 19,O 16 1822

Geneva daily TIMES. d My 28 1895+
My 31 1935 is 40th anniversary ed
pub 1895+
N Mr 11 1913+
NGen Ap 1 1915;Je 30,O 1,D 31 1922;Ap 1923+
NGenH 1920+
NN O 29 1834
NRU S 21 1929
TxGR My 31 1935

GILBERTSVILLE

OTSEGO journal. w My 1876+
pub O 4 1876+

GILBOA

Gilboa MONITOR. w Je 13 1878-1918||?
N D 19 1878[85-90]O 14 1909

GLEN COVE

CITY record. *See* Glen Cove record

COUNTY gazette. w My 1857-1900||
1857-91 as Glen Cove gazette
DLC My 10 1862
NBHi complete
NNHi F 1 1873

Glen Cove ECHO. w Je 23 1875+
NGc Je 13 1914+
NNHi Ag 26 1876

Glen Cove GAZETTE. *See* County gazette

PLAINDEALER. *See under* Roslyn

Glen Cove RECORD. w O 1917+
1917-O 1926 as City record
NGc 1929+
pub 1917+

Glen Cove SENTINEL. w My 6-Ag 12 1854||
MB complete

GLENS FALLS

Glens Falls CLARION. w Je 1841-50||
Follows Glens Falls gazette. Followed by Glens Falls free press
DLC My 23 1844
MWA My 26 1841
N S 1841-50
NGf [1844;46-47]Je 7 1849
PPL N 26 1850

Glens Falls FREE PRESS. w 1851-
Follows Glens Falls clarion
N N 5 1853;F 24-Ag 25 1855;F 1856-58
NGf My 7 1851;Mr 10 1852;My 1,Ag 7 1858; Ja 22,F 26,Ap 30 1859;F 25 1864

Glens Falls GAZETTE. w D 1 1839-My? 1841||
Follows Warren county messenger. Followed by Glens Falls clarion
DLC Ap 28 1840
NGf My 14,N 25,D 23 1840;Mr 31 1841

HICKORY leaf. w Ag 8 1844-
NGf Ag 15 1844

Glens Falls INDEPENDENT. w D 2 1868-
NGf D 2 1868

Glens Falls MESSENGER. w 1855-1916||?
Merged with Glens Falls times
KHi O 24 1873
MWA Je 7 1878
N Je 4 1857[My 1858-60]-72;Jl 1873-Jl 1880[82; 91-92]Ja 13 1893
NGf [1864-78;82;86-90]
NGfP 1858-62
NHi S 11 1868;D 25 1874
NNHi Ja 31 1868;Mr 12,Je 18 1869;Ja 31 1873

Sunday NEWS. w 1893-95||
N [Mr 1894-95]

Daily NEWS. d 1901-04||
NGfP My-D 1904

Glens Falls OBSERVER. w Ja 1 1827-
MWA Ja 28 1828
N My 28 1827-N 19 1828
NGf Mr 19,Jl 9 1827;Mr 24 1828

POST-STAR. d 1904+
1904-Je 1909 as Morning post
pub 1905-14;21+
N [1908-09]+
NGf D 16 1905;D 15 1906

Glens Falls PRESS and union.
NGf Je 4(extra)1864

Evening RECORD. d O 21 1891-Mr 3 1892||
N complete

Glens Falls REPUBLICAN. w S 27 1843-1905||
N O 4 1843-S 1846;S 1848-S 1850[51]S 1855-Je 1889[91-92]Jl 1893-N 1905
NGf [Ap 1844-47;50-55]-D 21 1858[59-60;64; 67;75-76]83[84]86[87;92-93]
NGfP 1896-97;1900-01
NHfH S 30 1846-F 15 1848
NHi F 23 1864
NN O 11 1864
NNHi Ja 7 1872
WHi N 20 1883-Ap 1884

Glens Falls SPECTATOR. w My 19 1837-
N 1837-Ap 1841
NGf F 16 1838;N 2 1839;N 19 1840

Morning STAR. d Ap 2 1883-Je 1909||
United with Morning post to form Post-star
N 1883-Je 1888[90-Mr 1892]93-Je 1909

Weekly STAR. w 1883-1909||
NGf Jl 14 1889;D 20 1895;F 12 1897

Glens Falls TIMES. d Je 21 1879+
pub 1899;1901-13;21
N Je 28 1879-87;Jl 1890-1922
NGf [1879-Ja 1896]

Glens Falls weekly TIMES. w 1881-92||?
MWA Je 15 1883;O 31 1884

WARREN county messenger. w 1829-N 1839||
Followed by Glens Falls gazette
CSmH Jl 8 1830
MWA F 9 1836
N Jl 18 1824-Ap 24 1835
NGf Jl 1 1830;Ap 2 1831;S 7 1832;33;Ag 22 1834;D 21 1836
NHi S 21 1832
NNHi Ap 9 1829

WARREN county times. w O 29 1869-71||
NGf 1869-Mr 25 1871

WARREN county whig. w 1854-55||
N F 24-Ap 21 1855
NGf Ag 5 1854;Ja 6-20,My 5 1855

WARREN recorder. w 1824-
NGf My 6 1825;S 13 1826

GLOVERSVILLE

DEMOCRAT. w Je 6 1868-70||
DLC [1868-My 1870]

FULTON county republican. w 1869-1927||?
1869-1911? pub in Johnstown
NGlL D 30 1875
NNHi F 27 1873

Morning HERALD. d 1897+
Follows Gloversville standard
pub 1904+
N Mr 1913+
NGl Mr 1897+

Gloversville INTELLIGENCER. w Ja 15 1867-89||
1877-81 as Gloversville intelligencer and republican
NGlL 1867-74;77-89

LEADER-REPUBLICAN. d Ag 30 1887+
1887-F 14 1912 as Daily leader
pub 1888+
NGl 1891+

Gloversville STANDARD. w D 1856-96||
Followed by Morning herald
N Jl 23 1857
NGl 1891-96

GORHAM

Gorham NEW AGE. *See* Gorham new age and Rushville chronicle (Penn Yan)

GOSHEN

Goshen CLARION. w S? 1843-49||
1843 as Democratic standard
DLC O 14 1847

Goshen DEMOCRAT. w Ja 4 1834+
Follows Orange county patriot. Title varies: Democrat; Goshen democrat and whig
pub [1837-1933]+
DLC Jl 3 1846
MBAt Ap 20 1865
MWA N 30 1849
N [1834-55]
NNHi My 3,Je 28,S 13,O 11 1834;Ja 30,S 24 1836;Jl 10,24 1840;O 1,D 3 1841;Jl 15 1842;O 20,D 15 1843;Ja 3,Je 28,S 13 1844;Mr 7,My 16,N 21,D 5,19 1845[46]Jl 9 1847;Ja-O,D 1848-[50]-[S-O 1857]-[Mr-N 1859;60-61]62;My 21, Jl 23 1863;Jl 14 1864[Ja-F,Ap-Je,N 1865;Mr-Jl,O 1866-F,Ap-Je,Ag-O,D 1867]Ja 9,30,F 27, Ap 2,Je 10,Jl 16,D 17 1868;Ja 7,F 11-25,My 20, S 2,16 1869;Ja 6,27-F 10,My 5,Ag 18,O 27,N 17-24,D 29 1870;F 2,8,Mr 7 1871;N 28 1872;Mr 13,N 13-20,D 25 1873;Ap 23-30 1874;Jl 27,O 26,N 9 1876;Ja 18-25,O 4 1877;Ap 11 1907

DEMOCRATIC recorder. w F 10 1834-
CSmH My 26 1854

DEMOCRATIC standard. *See* Goshen clarion

*INDEPENDENT republican. w,sw 1813+
sw 1904-20
pub [1850+]
Ct [1835]
DLC Je 22-Jl 6,20 1829;O 25 1844
MWA F 13 1852;Ag 23 1876;D 1 1880[1914-F 24 1920]-29;N 23 1909[Jl 13 1911-My 7 1912]
N O 28 1833;S 3 1852;D 28 1855;Mr 1913+
NNHi Ag 19 1822;Ja 9,Mr 12 1832
NcD D 3 1868
NjHi Ja 19 1824[1901]-[04]
NjR Jl 26 1901;F 11-14 1902
P-M Ap 29 1832

NEWS. w 1888-1902||?
NNHi O 27 1888

*ORANGE county patriot. w F 7 1809-33||
Follows Orange patrol (not in this list). Followed by Goshen democrat
Mr 26 1811-Ap 1812 pub in Newburgh
CSmH N 27 1820;Jl 5 1830
DLC Mr 16,Jl 20,O 5 1829
MWA Ja 22 1821;D 30 1822;S 8 1823
N N 6 1826
NHi Ag 19 1822
NNGe My 1828-31
NNHi N 23,D 7 1829;Ag 9 1830;Mr 5,19-26,Ap 30-My 7,Je 4,18,Jl 16,S 3,O 22 1831;S,N 10, 24 1832
NjHi [1821-32]

TRUE whig. w Ag 5 1842-45||
United with Goshen democrat to form Goshen democrat and whig, later Goshen democrat
NjHi 1842-N 1844

GOUVERNEUR

FREE PRESS. w 1882-Ap 1929||
United with Northern tribune to form Tribune-press

Gouverneur HERALD. w 1873-78||
N O 31 1878

NORTHERN tribune. *See* Tribune-press

TRIBUNE-PRESS. w S 1 1887+
1887-Ap 29 1929 as Northern tribune
pub 1887+

GOWANDA

Gowanda ENTERPRISE. w 1914+
pub Ap 14 1914+
NGo Je 1933+

Gowanda NEWS. w 1905+
pub 1908-12;14[15]-[19]+
NGo S 28 1933+
NWe Mr 10 1921

GRANVILLE

Granville NEWS. w S 22 1865-
N N 24 1865;Je 5 1868
NFeH O 5,N 2 1866;Jl 9 1867

Granville REGISTER. w My 1859-64||
NFeH Jl 21 1860

Granville REPORTER. w 1869-72||
N O 12 1872

Granville SENTINEL. w S 1875+
pub 1875-91;1919+

Granville daily SENTINEL. d 1879-80||
N Ja-My 1880

Granville TELEGRAPH. w My 1847-
1847-50? as Washington telegraph
DLC Jl 5 1851
NFeH Ap 9 1853
WHi F 21 1852

WASHINGTON telegraph. *See* Granville telegraph

GREAT NECK

LEDGER. w Ap 1 1927+
pub 1927+

Great Neck NEWS. w 1925+
pub 1925+

NORTH HEMPSTEAD times. w Ja 15 1898-1906||?
NBHi Ag 13 1898

GREENBUSH. *See* RENSSELAER

GREENE

CHENANGO American. w S 20 1855+
pub 1929+
KHi N 6 1873
MWA S 7 1876
NGr 1857+
NNHi D 30 1858;F 6 1873
NSyU Jl 18,O 10 1861;Ja 20-27,N 10 1881

CHENANGO democrat. w S 10 1833-
N O 15 1833
NSyU Mr 11,S 16,30,O 28,N 11 1834

CHENANGO news. w 1851-
KHi O 13 1854
NSyU S 16 1853

CHENANGO patriot. w N 17 1829-
CSmH Ag 18 1830

Weekly NEWS. w Ja 1 1881-83||?
NNHi 1881

GREENPOINT

Papers published in Greenpoint are listed under Brooklyn

GREENPORT

BULLETIN. Mr 1854-
NBHi Mr 1854

REPUBLICAN watchman. *See* Watchman of the Sunrise trail (Mattituck)

SHELTER ISLAND news. w
NShi My 10-Je 28 1923

NEW YORK (*Continued*)

GREENPORT—*Continued*

SUFFOLK times. w Ag 1857+
NBHi 1858-66
NNHi N 21 1867;Ja 7 1869;Ja 4 1873
NRiHi S 1862-Ag 11 1864
NShi S 4 1897;Ag 3,S 28,O 19 1901;D 23 1927

Greenport WATCHMAN. *See* Watchman of the Sunrise trail (Mattituck)

GREENWICH

To 1845? as Union-Village

ANTI-MASONIC champion. w Mr 4 1829-
CSmH Jl 28 1830
CoD [O 1-D 1829]
NNHi [O-D 1829]

BANNER. w Ja 4 1831-
N [My 31 1831-Jl 15 1834]

Greenwich JOURNAL. w O 13 1842+
1842-50 as Washington county journal; 1851-53? Union Village journal; 1854?-67? Washington county people's journal; 1868?-95? People's journal; 1895?-Ap 1 1896 Washington journal
pub 1842-67;76+
MWA 1842-D 14 1843;F 25 1869
N F 26 1846[F 1852-Ap 1853]S 20 1855;Jl 30,S 17,O 1-8,D 11 1868;F 8,Mr 11,Ap 28,Jl 15 1869
NFeH D 10 1857;N 17 1859;My 28-Je 4,Jl 9,S 10 1863;Ag 22 1873;S 16 1875;D 14 1876
NNHi Ja 8 1846;My 31,Jl 12,26,Ag 23,S 6 1849; Ja 2 1851

PEOPLE'S journal. *See* Greenwich journal

UNION VILLAGE courant. w My 11 1830-
CSmH Ag 31 1830

UNION VILLAGE democrat. w 1839-
DLC N 10 1840

UNION VILLAGE journal. *See* Greenwich journal

WASHINGTON county journal. *See* Greenwich journal

WASHINGTON journal. *See* Greenwich journal

WASHINGTON sentinel and Union Village free press. w Ap 4 1837-
ICN My 2,11,23-30,Je 20,S 5-12,20-27,O 11 1837

HAMBURG

ERIE county independent. w 1875+
Also dated at Buffalo
NBu N 9 1894-N 1 1895

HAMILTON (CATTARAUGUS COUNTY). *See* OLEAN

HAMILTON (MADISON COUNTY)

CIVILIAN. w Je 27 1830-N 1831||
CSmH Jl 27 1830
NCaz complete
NN N 5 1831 (extra)

Hamilton COURIER. w Mr 19 1834-38||
Title varies: Hamilton courier and Madison county advertiser
DLC Mr 26 1834
NHC 1834-Mr 11 1835

DEMOCRATIC reflector. *See* Hamilton republican

DEMOCRATIC republican. *See* Hamilton republican

DEMOCRATIC union. *See under* Oneida

Hamilton EAGLE w 1839-
NH Mr 20 1839-My 6 1840
WHi N 13 1839

LANDMARK. w 1850||
Campaign paper
NOHi Ag 1 1850

LIBERTY press. w
NHC Ag 1844;Je 14,Ag 2,N 22 1845;N 12 1846;Ap 29,My 27 1847

MADISON county journal. w S 19 1849-N 28 1855||
United with Democratic reflector to form Democratic republican, later Hamilton republican
N Ap 17,My 8 1850;Ja 15,F 19-Mr 5,S 3 1851; Mr 18,Je 10,D 21-28 1852;Ja 27 1853;F 11-17,Mr 25-Ap 1,Jl 1,15,N 1,29 1854;Ja 24,F 7, 28,Ap 11,N 7-14,28 1855
NCaz 1849-O 2 1851
NN Jl 17,D 18 1851;Ja 8,F 5 1852

Hamilton PALLADIUM. w 1838-42||
MWA Mr 18,My 13 1842
NHC Jl 19 1839-Jl 10 1840
NOHi Ap 16 1841

POLK-ER and Young Hickory advocate.
Campaign paper
NN S 19 1844

Hamilton RECORDER. w Jl 2 1822-F 14 1827||
United with Madison observer (Morrisville) to form Observer and recorder, later Madison observer (Morrisville)
DLC F 14 1827
NH 1822-Je 23 1824
NHC Ja 5,N 23 1825
NOHi Ja 12 1823

Hamilton REPUBLICAN. w 1843+
1843-N 1855 as Democratic reflector; D 1855-87 Democratic republican
pub F 12 1863-89 F 19 1891-94;Ja 21 1895-96; F 11 1897-98
MBAt Ap 20 1865

MWA Mr 26 1845;Ap 6 1854;S 7,N 2 1876
N F 11 1847;My 10 1849;Ag 20,S 3,24,O 1,15,N 5-19,D 31 1856;Ja 15 1857;My 25 1876
NCaz Ag 30-O 25 1849
NH N 18 1852-N 2 1854
NHC Ja 3 1843;F 10,Mr 23 1848;Ja 4 1849;Ag 26 1852;Ap 23 1857;O 7 1858;F 12 1863;80;Ja 20 1881-89;F 19 1891-94;Ja 21 1895-96;F 11 1897-98;N 1899+
NN O 25 1849
NOHi Jl 26 1888
NOrHi My 24 1934+

HAMMOND

Hammond ADVERTISER. w 1886+
pub 1886+

HAMMONDSPORT

Hammondsport HERALD. *See* Keuka grape belt and herald

KEUKA grape belt. w Ag 1 1929-N 19 1931||
United with Hammondsport herald to form Keuka grape belt and herald
NHa complete

KEUKA grape belt and herald. w Ap 28 1874+
1874-N 19 1931 as Hammondsport herald
pub My 1876+
NBaS 1874+
NHa 1920-Ag 1 1929;N 26 1931+

HAMPTON BAYS

Hampton Bays NEWS. w Je 11 1930+
pub 1930+

HANCOCK

Hancock HERALD. w Ap 1873+
pub 1873+

HARLEM

Papers published in Harlem are listed under New York City

HARRISON

CITIZEN-OBSERVER. w 1898+
pub 1898+
NHarC 1899+
NYW [1914-28]+

HASTINGS

Hastings NEWS. w 1897+
NHaS [1921+]
NN Ja 5-Ap 5,19-Jl 19,Ag 2-D 27 1912

HAVANA. *See* MONTOUR FALLS

HAVERSTRAW

NORTH RIVER times. w Ag 22 1834-
N 1834-Ag 11 1837
NNHi 1834-Ag 14 1835

ROCKLAND advertiser. w My 9 1833-
MWA Jl 11 1833
N O 31 1833

ROCKLAND county messenger. w My 1846+
pub [1846-Ja 1927]+
NNHi D 26 1872;Ja 2 1873;Ja 13 1881

ROCKLAND county times. w O 1889+
pub 1893-1933

HEMPSTEAD

Hempstead INQUIRER. w My 16 1830-N 12 1920||
My-O 14 1830 as Long Island telegraph and general advertiser; O 21-28 1830 Long Island telegraph and friend of education; N 1830-My 4 1833 Inquirer; My 11 1833-Ja 1835 Hempstead inquirer and Long Island advertiser. Merged with Nassau county review, later Nassau daily review (Freeport)
CSmH My 30 1830
CtY My 16 1830;F 2 1882
MWA Je 24 1848;Mr 31 1849;D 5 1863;F 21(supp)1868
N [Jl 18 1833-Ap 22 1837]F 21(supp)1868;83-89
NBHi My 13 1831;Je 16 1849;51-1920
NEh Je 14,D 6 1832;Ja 27 1836;F 13,Mr 12 1841;My 2,Je 20 1846;Jl 13 1877
NHe My 20-Jl 1 1830
NNHi 1830-My 1850;51-52;O 1855-My 3,O 1856-Mr 1857;D 19 1863;64;O 1868-69;Mr 25-Je 3,N 11-18,D 9-16 1870;Ag 11-S 8,22-29 1871;My 10 1872;Ja 17 1873;D 18 1874;extras: Jl 26 1832;D 6 1834;D 11 1835
NHeN 1870-1919
NSm Ap 27,Jl 20,N 2 1850;My 10-17 1851;S 18 1852;Ja 8,F 19,Jl 2 1853;Ja 28,Ap 29,Ag 19,S 23,N 4,18 1854;Je 14,Jl 12 1856;Ja 14 1860

JOURNAL. w Ag-D 7 1917||
NHe complete

LONG ISLAND telegraph. *See* Hempstead inquirer

QUEENS county sentinel. *See* Hempstead sentinel

SCHOOL master. bw Jl 5 1830-
NBHi 1830-Mr 15 1831
NEh Jl 5 1830
NHe 1830-Mr 15 1831
NUHi Jl 5,Ag 2,16,30,S 13,27,O 11 1830

Hempstead SENTINEL. w Je 1858+
1858-Je 1899 as Queens county sentinel
pub 1858-Je 1865;Je 1872—
MWA N 27 1862;D 3 1863;D 14 1865;F 1,S 13-O 4 1866;My 16,Ag 8,S 26,O 17 1867
NBHi 1859-86
NHe My 12 1887-S 9 1893;O 29 1914+
NNHi My 26,Ag 4 1881;D 1 1864;F 27 1873

HERKIMER

***Herkimer AMERICAN.** w Ja 4 1810-32||
1810-Ag? 1814 as American
CSmH S 8 1830
N N 10 1825;D 30 1828;F 3,Mr 31,Je 2-16 1829; Jl 14 1830
NHerHi My 18 1831-N 7 1832
NN Ja 17 1828
NNHi O 14 1824

Herkimer CITIZEN. w 1863-1922||
NHerHi 1868-70;72-1907;11-22

Herkimer DEMOCRAT. w,sw 1842-1908||?
1842-43 as Herkimer county democrat (Frankfort); My 1869-72 Herkimer democrat and Little Falls gazette. United with Herkimer county news to form Herkimer county news and democrat, later Herkimer county news (Little Falls)
N S 28 1843;Je 9,Ag 4-11,D 1 1869
NHerHi 1865-66;68-72;75-1906
NNHi Ap 16 1873;D 17-24 1879
OClWHi Je 6 1866

Herkimer HERALD. w O 1 1828-
NHerHi 1828-S 22 1829
NUHi N 26 1828

HERKIMER county journal. *See* Journal and courier (Little Falls)

Herkimer JOURNAL. *See* Journal and courier (Little Falls)

REPUBLICAN farmers' free press. w Je 9 1830-34||
CSmH Ag 11 1830
N Je 16,Ag 14,N 24 1830;Ja 19,F 9-16,Mr 23,Je 1(extra),Ag 3-17,31,N 23 1831
NN Je 9 1830

Evening TELEGRAM. d N 1 1898+
pub Ja-O 24 1906;O 26-D 1907;Ja-Je,O 1909-10;Jl 1912-Je 1914;15;19-20;23+
NHerHi 1898-1918;20-31
NIl Mr 29 1934+

TELEGRAM-RECORD. w D 20 1888+
1888-Ag 1900 as Wide awake Herkimer county record
NHerHi 1891-1904;21-31

WIDE AWAKE Herkimer county record. *See* Telegram-record

HICKSVILLE

CENTRE ISLAND news. w O 31 1917+
1917-N 3 1933 as Hicksville courier
pub D 7 1921-F 7 1924;N 10 1933+

Hicksville COURIER. *See* Centre Island news

HIGHLAND

Highland POST. w 1887+
pub 1910-12;19+

SOUTHERN Ulster. w 1889-1903||?
DLC Ap 9,O 1 1897
NN O 17 1898

HIGHLAND FALLS

NEWS of the Highlands. w Mr 5 1891+
pub 1891+

HILLSDALE

Hillsdale HARBINGER. w 1887+
pub 1887+
NHIH 1887+

HILTON

Hilton RECORD. w Ap 1 1897+
pub Mr 3 1910+

HINSDALE

PEOPLE'S gazette. w O 1 1840-42||
DLC O 1 1840

HOBART

Hobart FREE PRESS. w Ja 11 1855-
MWA F 22 1856
N Ag 2-16,S 6 1855

HOLLEY

Holley BULLETIN. sm N 1868-69||
Followed by Holley standard
NHoS complete

Holley STANDARD. w 1870+
Follows Holley bulletin
pub D 27 1878+
N F 24,Je 2 1877

HOMER

CORTLAND county republican. *See* Homer republican and Cortland county journal

CORTLAND county whig. *See under* Cortland

NEW YORK (*Continued*)

HOMER—*Continued*

CORTLAND observer. w S 28 1825-36||
Follows Cortland repository
CSmH Jl 2 1830
NCort 1825-S 14 1832
NCortHi O 31 1828
NHom F 8 1828-Ag 6 1830
NN F 22 1828(photostat)
P-M My 6 1831

*CORTLAND repository. w D 8 1813-24||
Followed by Cortland observer
N O 9 1821;Mr 31 1824
NCortHi N 20 1821

Homer POST. w 1931+
NCort [1931+]

Homer REPUBLICAN and Cortland county journal. w 1855-1919||
Follows Cortland county whig (Cortland) 1855-78? as Cortland county republican; 1879?-1918? Homer republican
MWA Je 5 1879
NCortHi S 18-O 2,16,30 1879;S 22 1881
NHom [O 30 1856-Je 14 1860]1876-1919
NNHi Ja 12 1860;My 15 1873
NSyU My 30 1861

*WESTERN courier. w O 1820-
MWA Jl 17 1821

HONEOYE FALLS

Honeoye Falls STANDARD. w 1838-
MWA My 16-Je 13,27 1839

Honeoye Falls TIMES. w Mr 2 1882+
pub 1882+
NCanHi F 13 1919

HOOSICK FALLS

Hoosick Falls INDEPENDENT. w O 29 1865-
DLC N 4-11,D 2-23 1865;Ja 6-27,F 10-17,Mr 10-31 1866

Hoosick Falls PRESS. w S 15 1920-Mr 29 1933||
United with Rensselaer county standard to form Hoosick Falls standard press
NHsS complete

RENSSELAER county standard. *See* Hoosick Falls standard press

Hoosick Falls STANDARD press. w S 10 1873+
1873-Mr 31 1933 as Rensselaer county standard
pub 1873+
ICM Jl 9 1881

HORNELL

CANISTEO VALLEY times. *See* Hornell times

DEMOCRATIC vidette. w O 4 1865-
OClWHi My 31 1866

Evening PRESS. d Mr 9 1889-93||
NHor 1889-Je 1893

STEUBEN signal. w Ap 4 1883-Ap 4 1888||
N 1883-Ja 23 1884
NHorT complete

Hornell TIMES. w Ja 17 1867-1905||?
1867-76 as Canisteo Valley times
pub 1867-N 7 1877
MWA S 20 1871
NHor 1877-D 12 1878;83;88-89

Hornellsville morning TIMES. d N 5 1877-Mr 14 1908||
1877-86 as Hornellsville daily times. United with Hornell evening tribune to form Evening tribune-times
pub 1879-1908
NHor F 25 1878-87;Ap 29 1889-Je 1906

Hornellsville weekly TRIBUNE. w N 26 1851-1911||
pub D 1851-D 22 1911

Evening TRIBUNE-TIMES. d S 2 1873+
1878-Mr 14 1908 as Hornell evening tribune
pub 1873+
N Mr 18 1913+
NHor 1880-88;92-97;99-Je 1902;Jl 1903-23

HORSEHEADS

CHEMUNG VALLEY reporter. w Ap 24 1887+
pub 1894+

HUDSON

COLUMBIA and Greene county envoy. w Ag 10 1830-
CSmH S 21 1830

*COLUMBIA republican. w S 12 1820-Je 30 1923||
Merged with Hudson daily star
CSmH Ag 31 1830
CtY Ja 26 1830;Ap 19 1831
DLC N 16 1824;F 24,Jl 7-14,Ag 4,S 22-29,O 6,27 1829;O 2 1832;Je 11 1833;D 8 1840
KHi D 27 1888-F 13 1890
MBAt Jl 4 1865
MWA Ap 1 1823;S 6 1824;Ap 12 1825;Jl 7 1829; Ja 5,Ap 6,My 11,Ag 31,S 14,O 5,19-N 9,D 21-28 1830;Je 7 1831;Ja 3,Jl 31 1832;Ap 18-25 1843
N O 22 1833;Jl 25 1865;Ag 13 1885;Ap 21-28, Jl 27-Ag 11 1887;Ag 2,D 6 1888;Ja 24,My 9-16,O 17 1889;Ja 16,Mr 13,O 2 1890;Ja 22,Ap 16-23,My 7-21 1891
NBHi Mr 12 1833
NHudS S 1824-Ag 1826;Ag 1834-Jl 1835;Jl 26 1836-Jl 1837;Jl 31 1838-Jl 20 1841;Ag 23 1842-Ag 13 1844;Ag 18 1846-Jl 13 1852;53-69;74-1923
NNHi Ja 15 1822;Je 3,S 2,D 23 1823;F 10,O 5 1824;Ja 5,F 22,Mr 5,N 15,D 13-20 1825;My 9 1826;Mr 27,Ap 10-24,My 8-22,Je 12-19,Jl 3-10,Ag 14-S,O 9,30-N 20,D 4-11 1827
NcD Mr 16 1830
NjR Ap 19 1836
OHi F 19 1861

COLUMBIA Washingtonian. *See* Hudson weekly star

COLUMBIAN. w
NNHi Ja 16-23,F 27 1827

DEMOCRATIC freeman. w 1848?-
N F 12 1854

Hudson FLAIL. w S 10 1840-
Campaign paper
N S 10-17,O 22-29 1840

Hudson GAZETTE. w 1824-1930||?
Ap 9 1885 is centennial ed
CSmH Jl 13 1830
Ct S 2 1828[30-38]
DLC Mr 8 1836;O 8 1844;Ap 9 1885
KHi Ap 9 1895
MBAt S 19 1843
MWA D 2 1828;S 15 1829;Ap 9 1885
N S 1825-Ag 1826;S 1829-Ag 24 1830;Ap 29 1831;D 17 1833;D 12-19 1837;Je 18,O 8,D 31 1844;Ja 28,Mr 25,Jl 29,Ag 5 1845;Mr 17 1870; 85-86
NNHi Ap 12 1825;Ap 4,My 23 1826;My-Je 19, Jl 17,31-S 11,25-O 2,30 N 13,27,D 11,25 1827; Ja 1 1828;N 6 1832;Ja 28,Ap 8 1845;N 28 1872
P-M Je 10 1831

MESSENGER of peace. sm Mr 13 1824-F 26 1825||
N complete
NNHi complete

Hudson MIRROR and Columbia county farmer. w My 18 1839-
NNHi My 18 1839-Ap 18 1840

*NORTHERN whig. w Ja 3 1809-
Follows Balance (not in this list)
DLC N 16 1824
MWA My 10 1825
N Ja 14-N 11 1823;S 21 1824
NN My 15 1821
NNHi Ap 1,My 6,N,D 9,23 1823;Ja 13-F 10,Mr 2,30,My 25,Jl 13-20,Ag,S 14-O 19,N 9 1824-Ja 4,F 8-15,Mr 1-15,29-My,Je 21,Jl 5-12,O 4,18, N 1-8,22-D 1825;F 7,Mr 7,Ap 25-My 2,30-Je 13,Jl 11-Ag 1,15-22,S,O 10,D 12 1826
NhD Ap 27 1824

Hudson evening REGISTER. d 1846?-
N N 3 1849

Hudson evening REGISTER. d 1866+
pub 1866+

Hudson REPUBLICAN. *See* Hudson daily star

Hudson weekly STAR. w F 1842-Ja 6 1876||
1843-Ap 1851 as Columbia Washingtonian
pub Ap 22 1852-Ag 13 1874;75-76
MWA Ag 21 1851
N Ja 16,Mr 27,My 22,Jl 31,Ag 7 1845;Je 14,Ag 2,D 6 1849;Ja 2,Mr 21-28,Ap 4,18 1850;F 6,Mr 6-13,Ap 3 1851;F 2 1860
NN O 12 1854;N 15 1855
OClWHi Jl 26 1866

Hudson daily STAR. d D 28 1847+
My 1 1876-Je 30 1923 as Hudson republican
pub Ag 1848-49;Jl 1850-Ap,S 18 1852-Je 1853; 54-66;Jl 3 1867-72;Jl 1873-Ap 1876;Jl 1923+
MWA F 27 1873
N 1913-Jl 1922;My 1923+
NHi Ap 15 1865
OClWHi Jl 24 1866;Ap 30 1875

THRASHER. w S 4 1840-
Campaign paper
MWA S 25 1840
N S 18 1840

HUDSON FALLS

To 1910 as Sandy Hill

Hudson Falls HERALD. w Ag 3 1824+
1824? as Political herald; 1825?-Mr 10 1910 Sandy Hill herald
pub 1929+
DLC N 16 1824;Ap 21 1831;D 17 1833;D 16 1834
MWA F 17 1829;F 21 1867;Je 14 1888
N My 12,N 3 1829;D 23 1830;Ja 10 1833;D 16 1834;D 12 1837;O 15 1839;Je 29 1852;My 23 1854-My,Je 26 1855;O 1858-59;Je 25 1861;Je 1864-S 12 1865[66-68]70-1911
NFe 1879-80
NFeH 1827-[30;32;35;37;41;59-60;67;71;97]
NGf Ap 19 1825;Mr 24 1857-D 8 1863
NHf 1833;35;49;52;63-85;87-1911;14-19;21+
NHfH D 23 1834[F 1841-Mr 3 1863]
NHi [1837;39-40]
NN Je 24 1845;D 17 1850
NNHi Ja 9 1873
NhD Ap 21 1835;Ag 30 1836;O 20 1846
WHi F 23 1847;Je 14 1888

POLITICAL herald. *See* Hudson Falls herald

SANDY HILL commercial advertiser. *See* Fort Edward advertiser (Fort Edward)

SANDY HILL herald. *See* Hudson Falls herald

SANDY HILL sun. w D 1825?-D 16 1828||
N S 11 1827
NNHi S 21 1826

SANDY HILL times. w 1819?-
DLC F 13,Mr 12 1824

WASHINGTON county observer. Ja 8 1886-
NFeH Ja 8,F 5 1886
NGf 1886-88

HUNTER

Hunter PHOENIX. *See* Hunter review

Hunter REPUBLICAN. *See* Hunter review

Hunter REVIEW. w 1884+
1884-89? as Hunter phoenix; 1890?-1901? Hunter republican
pub [1906+]

HUNTINGTON

*AMERICAN eagle. w O 18 1817-My 9 1826||
Title varies: American eagle and Suffolk county general advertiser
1817-Jl 1821 pub in Sag Harbor
MWA Ag 29 1824
N N 10 1825;F 2 1826
NBHi My 30 1822-D 4 1823
NSm My 2,O 24,N 7-21,D 1822-Mr 6 1823;F 12,N 11 1824

LONG ISLANDER. w Je 5 1838+
pub 1838+
MWA F 2 1866
NBHi F 18 1853;60-1918
NEh Jl 28 1848;Ap 23 1858
NHuHi 1839+
NNHi Ap 30-N 19 1847;Mr 10-D 1848;Mr 21 1873
NRc O 4 1850;O 3 1851
NRiHi Je 1931+
NSm O 2,23,N 13 1846;Mr 13 1863;F 9,My 4, Je 22 1866;S 27 1867;S 17 1892;N 25 1893;Mr 30 1900

PORTICO. w Mr 30 1826-Mr 1827||
NBHi Mr 30,Je 29 1826;Ja 25-F,Mr 29 1827
NEh Ap 20,N 16 1826
NHuHi complete

SUFFOLK bulletin. w F 19 1847+
1847-68 as Suffolk democrat
Je 10 1903 is 250th anniversary of Huntington ed
pub 1924+
CSmH Mr 19 1847
DLC O 20 1848
N S 1917-19
NBHi 1859-65
NEh F 26,Mr 26,Ap 23,Je 4,25-Jl 9,23,Ag 13,S 17,N 26-D 3 1847;F 18,Jl 28,O 20 1848;D 20 1850
NHuHi Ap 14 1854;Je 10 1903
NNHi Mr 11 1859-Jl 21 1865
NRc My 14 1847;N 2 1849;F 25,S 2 1853;O 27 1854;Jl 30,S 10,O 8 1858;Ap 26,Ag 30 1861; Ja 30,F 13,27,S 5 1863;My 17 1872
NSm O 29 1847;Ag 22 1851;O 24,N 14 1856; Ap 29 1859;Je 27,S 12 1862;Ja 8,30,F 13,27,My 1 1863
NSyU My 3,S 13 1861
P-M My 26 1854

SUFFOLK democrat. *See* Suffolk bulletin

Huntington TIMES. w O 12 1928+
pub 1928+

ILION

BOOSTER. w D 7? 1922-Jl 5 1923||
Follows Ilion citizen. Followed by Community review, later Ilion sentinel
NIl D 21 1922-23
NIlS complete

Ilion CITIZEN. w,d 1862-N 25? 1922||
Followed by Booster
w 1862-1919?
DLC S 26 1884
N Mr 23 1877;S 27 1917-19
NIl 1879-82;F 1920-N 25 1922
NIlS complete
NNHi Mr 13 1873

COMMUNITY review. *See* Ilion sentinel

Ilion INDEPENDENT. *See* Central independent (Utica)

Ilion NEWS. w 1889-1918||
N Ag 23 1917-Jl 11 1918
NHerHi 1892-1904
NIl D 1893-1918

Ilion SENTINEL. w S 12 1923+
Follows Booster. 1923-Jl 6 1933 as Community review
pub 1923+
NIl 1923+

WATCHWORD. w 1870-75||
N Ag 19 1875
NbHi Mr 26 1874

IRVINGTON

Irvington GAZETTE. w 1907+
N S 1917-19
NIr O 16 1907+

ISLIP

Islip BAY SHORE messenger. w 1924+
pub 1924+

Islip PRESS. w My 28 1912+
pub 1912+

ITHACA

AMERICAN citizen and Old Ithaca chronicle. w 1855-63||
Follows Ithaca chronicle. 1855-57 as American citizen. Followed by Ithaca citizen and democrat
NIC complete

AMERICAN journal. *See* Ithaca journal

NEW YORK (*Continued*)

ITHACA—*Continued*

Ithaca CHRONICLE. w Mr 3 1830-55||
Followed by American citizen, later American citizen and Old Ithaca chronicle
CSmH S 8 1830
DLC Je 19 1844
NCor S 12 1838
NI 1830-F 3 1847
NIC 1835-37;39-45;48-55
NN My 23 1832;My 17 1841
NNHi Ag 7 1830
NSchU Mr 23 1842
OClWHi S 24 1834

Ithaca daily CHRONICLE. d 1846-50||
NIC complete

Ithaca CHRONICLE and democrat. w 1820-1912||
1820-O 19 1906 as Ithaca democrat
MWA 1874-Je,Jl 31,N 1884-My 9,Je 20 1889
N 1886-1903;O 26 1906-11
NIC 1867-1912
NNHi Ja 16 1873
NcD Jl 5 1877;S 2 1886
OClWHi N 20 1884

Ithaca CITIZEN and democrat. w F 25 1863-Jl 4 1867||
Follows American citizen. . .
MWA Je 4 1864
NI 1863-F 14 1865

Ithaca daily DEMOCRAT. d Je 2 1884-
MWA Je 2-27,O 16 1884
NIC Je-N 5 1884
NcD Je 2,O 16 1884

Ithaca DEMOCRAT. w *See* Ithaca chronicle and democrat

Ithaca morning HERALD. d O 5 1894-Ja 4 1895||
NIC [1894-95]

Ithaca INDEPENDENT. w Je 22 1907-N 7 1908||
NIC complete

ITHACAN. w N 28 1868-Jl 31 1869||
NIC complete

Weekly ITHACAN. w 1871-1921||?
NIC D 10 1875;Mr-Ap,N-D 13 1878;Ag 8-29 1884;My 8-O 23 1885

JEFFERSONIAN and Tompkins times. w My 13 1835-
Ct Je 15 1835
DLC My 27 1835
NI 1836-37

***Ithaca JOURNAL.** w Ag 20 1817-
1817-Jl 9 1823 as American journal. Title varies slightly
pub 1892-1914;Jl 1915-Je 1916;Ja-Je 1917
Ct N 14 1827;D 10 1828[30-38]
DLC Jl 16 1823-Je 1824;O 28 1829
MWA Ja 12,Mr 2,Jl 13,27 1825;My 15(extra) 1833
MiU-C O 11 1837
N S 28 1825;O 16 1833;O 21 1835;Jl 27 1842; My 21 1845;Mr 29 1854;74;80;82;86;88;90-93;95
NCortHi Ag 22 1821
NI 1831-33
NIC 1821-72;S 27 1873-Ap 17 1874
NN O 25 1826
NNHi Jl 21,S 1,O 13-20,N 3-10 1824;Mr 11 1873
NSyU S 27 1848
NcD Je 6 1832;Ja 6,20 1858-62
NjHi [1821-Jl 9]Ag 13,S 3 1823;Ja 7,My 12 1824;Ap 16 1828
OClWHi F 3 1858
P-M O 17 1832
PAtM Mr 1 1826
PEL Jl 7 1833

Ithaca daily JOURNAL. d Je 27 1870+
D 1919-33 as Ithaca journal-news
Ag 28 1915 is Centennial ed
pub Ja-Mr 1900;Ap-Je 1905;Ja-Je 1934
MWA Ag 28 1915
N 1916+
NIC Je 27-N 14 1870;Jl 1872-N 1919;34+
NNHi My 2 1873
TxH Ag 8 1885

Ithaca daily LEADER. d 1869-73||
NIC F-Mr 3,My 12-Je 6,9-25 1870
NIJ O 16 1871-Ja 2 1873

NATIONAL archives. w F 6-Mr 13 1845||
Follows Tompkins democrat. Followed by Bainburg eagle (Bainburg)
NIC complete

Ithaca daily NEWS. d Ap 6 1895-N 30 1919||
United with Ithaca journal to form Ithaca journal-news, later Ithaca daily journal
N Ag 10 1895-Ag 1919
NIC complete
NIJ S-N 1919

Ithaca weekly NEWS. w Ag 29 1895-1908||?
N 1895-My 12 1898;N 15 1899-Ag 15 1900

Ithaca OBSERVER. w Ja 5-F 2 1934||
NIC complete

Ithaca REPUBLICAN. w Je 16 1830-
Follows Republican chronicle?
CSmH Ag 25 1830
NNHi Jl 14 1830;Mr 30-Ap 6 1831

REPUBLICAN chronicle. w Je 1820-28||?
Followed by Ithaca republican?
DLC Jl 23-30,N 5-12 1828
NI 1820-23

TOMPKINS American. w O 16 1833-34||
N O 16 1833

TOMPKINS county democrat. w S 1856-F 1863||
NIC S 18 1857-S 6 1861
NNHi D 19 1856
NSyU My 24 1861

TOMPKINS democrat. w Ap 11 1843-44||?
Followed by National archives
NIC 1843-D 12 1844

TOMPKINS volunteer. w N 16 1841-Ap 4 1843||
NIC complete

JACKSON HEIGHTS

Jackson Heights HERALD. w 1921+
pub 1921+

JAMAICA

DEMOCRATIC pilot. w S 3 1852-
NBHi O 29 1852

INDEPENDENT. ir Ja 16? 1865-
NBHi Ja 30-Mr 13 1865

LONG ISLAND democrat. w My 1 1835-S 25 1912||
KHi Je 19 1895
MB F 13,Ap-My 22,Je 19,Jl 24-Ag 21 1877;D 26 1882[83-90]
MWA O 21 1845;Mr 4,Ap 21 1862;D 8 1863;Ap 4 1865;Ap 30,Ag 13,S 24 1867
N [1837-41;45-62;65-66]
NBHi 1835-73;75-80;82-83;D 2 1884;85
NEh Je 15 1847;Je 20 1848;Ja 28 1851
NNHi My 19 1846;Jl 8,D 2-9 1856;Jl 14,28,S 22,O 20 1857;Ap 13 1858;F 14,My 1 29,Je 12-19,Jl 3,O 23,D 18 1860;Ja 22,F 12 1861;N 20 1866;Ja 22,My 28,S 10 1867;Mr 31,Ap 7,Je 16,S 8,N 17,D 8-15 1868;Ja 26,N 16(extra) 1869[71]D 26 1873[74-My 1875;Ja-O 1876]77-[Je 1878-79]-[81-My 1882]-[Ap 1883]-[N 1887-88]-[90]Ja 27 1891-95;S 1,15 1896;Ap 24,My 8,22-Je 5 1906;O,N 12,D 1907[S 1908-S 1909]-11
NNQ complete
NSm Mr 31 1863;Je 28 1892

Daily LONG ISLAND democrat. d F 24 1911-S 1912||
NNHi [1911]-12

LONG ISLAND farmer. w Ja 4 1821-D 31 1920||
1826-61 as Long Island farmer and Queens county advertiser. Merged with Long Island daily press
CSmH S 9 1830
MWA Jl 19 1821;Jl 14 1827;Mr 31,Ap 21 1831; O 21 1845;D 30 1862;O 11 1864;Jl 16,Ag 8 1867
N O 2 1826;O 16 1833;Jl 5 1842;O 3 1843
NBHi 1821-23;26;31-33;35-36;40-47;50-72
NEh S 25,O 2 1828;D 31 1829;Ap 12,My 10 1842; Je 13 1843;Mr 5 1844;Jl 22 1845;Ja 25,Mr 14 1848;Ap 23 1850;D 30 1862;F 12 1867;O 9-16 1873;My 30 1878;Ag 16 1883;Je 19 1890
NN [F-My,O 1840-41]-[44;F,Je 1845-47]
NNHi F 21 1822;O 2 1823;Jl 1828-Je 11 1829;Ag 16 1832;F 7,Mr 14 1833;D 15 1846;Ap 24,My 29 1849;Jl 15 1862;Ja 23 1873
NNJaL F-D 1892;96
NNQ O 1856-67
NSm Mr 26 1861;O 14 1862;Mr 8 1864;O 9 1879

LONG ISLAND daily press. d 1898+
1898-D 31 1920 as Long Island farmer; Ja 3 1921-Jl 11 1926 Long Island daily press and daily Long Island farmer
pub 1901-02;Jl 1903-09;Jl-D 1910;Jl-S 1911;Ja-Mr,Jl-S 1912;Ja-Mr,Jl-S 1913;Ja-Mr,Jl 1914-Mr,Jl-D 1915;Ap-Je 1916;Jl-D 1917;Ja-Je 1919;Jl 1920+
NNQ 1912-[25]-[27]+

QUEENS county news. *See* Queens evening news

QUEENS evening news. w,d Jl 24 1915+
1915-F 1928 as Queens county news(w)
pub Mr 1915+
NNQ 1927-[28]-[30]+

Jamaica STANDARD. w Ag 20 1868-1911||?
NBHi F 13,Ap 24 1869

STAR. w
NNHi F 3,Ag 11,S 29 1825

JAMESTOWN

CHAUTAUQUA county daily democrat. d 1872-79||
MWA S 15 1877
NJ Ag 1872-Mr 1879

CHAUTAUQUA democrat. w F 16 1853-91||
Follows Northern citizen
MBAt Ap 19 1865
MWA F 29 1860;S 22 1869;Ap 19 1882
NJ complete
NWe Mr 9 1853;Ja 27 1858

CHAUTAUQUA republican. w F 27 1828-33||
CSmH S 15 1830
Ct [Mr 19-S 1828]N 17-D 8 1830
DLC O 15 1828
MWA My 7 1828
NJ complete

FOLKETS röst. *See* Vårt nya hem

Jamestown HERALD. w Ag 1852-53||
NJ complete

Jamestown JOURNAL. w,sw,tw Je 21 1826+
w 1826-92;sw 1893-1904
CSmH S 8 1830
MWA Ja 16 1828;S 9 1829;Ag 6 1852;Jl 10 1857
N Ag 22 1827;O 16 1833;S 23 1881
NJ 1826-1906;08-16
NWe Ap 9 1880;Je 27 1902
OClWHi Jl 22 1866
PW F 7 1827;O 14 1841

Jamestown evening JOURNAL. d 1870+
1870-80 as Jamestown daily journal
pub 1924+
CLM S 19 1891
DLC 1898
MWA Je 3 1882;Ja 8,23,Ap 28,My 15,D 30 1885;F 22,26,Mr 9 1886;N 3 1887;F 24,Mr 28, My 4 1888;Je 12 1926
N Jl-D 1888;Jl-D 1889;Jl-D 1896;Jl-D 1897
NJ 1870-1924
NNHi My 1 1873
OClWHi Ja 5 1884

LIBERTY press. w
NJ 1845-46

LIBERTY star. *See* Northern citizen

***MONTGOMERY republican.** w Ag 1806-
CSmH S 1 1830

Morning NEWS. d 1885-96||?
CLM Jl 30 1894
MWA S 25,29,D 7,21,28 1886;Ja 4,11,18,F 8,22, N 22,29,D 13,20 1887;Ja 24,F 7,28 1888
NJ 1887-94

Jamestown weekly NEWS. w 1888-96||?
NJ 1888-94

NORTHERN citizen. w 1847-53||
1847-49 as Liberty star. Followed by Chautauqua democrat
MWA O 20 1852
NJ 1848-53

ÖSTERNS väktare. *See* Vårt land

Jamestown POST. d S 2 1901+
pub 1901+
CtY 1934+
MWA S 2 1910
N Jl 1913+
NWe S 2 1910

SKANDIA. w 1903+
In Swedish
pub 1903+
CtY [1933]
IRA 1909+
MnHi Ap 25 1918+

Jamestown STANDARD. w 1879-86||?
United with Sun to form Sun and standard
NJS 1879

SUN and standard. w 1884-97||?
1884-86? as Sun
WHi Je 17 1888

VÅRT land. w 1888-1922||?
1888-90 as Österns väktare
In Swedish
IRA 1889-90
MnHi D 15 1892-[N 1907-S 3 1920]

VÅRT nya hem. w 1875-91||
1875-My 1 1884 as Folkets röst. Merged with Vårt land
In Swedish
IRA Ja 14,F 5-11,25-Ap 14,My 5,19-Je 16,Jl 21,S 1-8,22,N 24 1876;Ja 1877;Ap 19 1883

JEFFERSON. *See* WATKINS GLEN

JEFFERSONVILLE

Jefferson COURIER. w 1872-1918||?
1872-79? as Jeffersonian
N Ja 16,My-O 1,D 17-31 1884;Ja 6-20,Ag 25-D 1886

JEFFERSONIAN. *See* Jefferson courier

LOCAL record. *See* Sullivan county record

SULLIVAN county record. w My 1868+
1868-80 as Local record
pub [1868-F 1891]+

JOHNSON CITY

Johnson City-Endicott RECORD. w 1896-1921||
NEnT 1915-21

JOHNSTOWN

Johnstown AMERICAN. *See* Johnstown independent

FULTON county democrat. w 1838-1925||?
CtY My 12 1841;N 23 1843;Je 6 1844;Je 24 1845;S 14-21 1847;Mr 21,N 30,D 19-26 1848;F 6,Mr 20,Ap 3,17-My 9 1849;Jl 8,Ag 12 1851
DLC Ap 1 1845
MWA O 12 1852
NJo 1849-54
NNHi Mr 4 1873
NSchU F 25 1842

FULTON county republican. w 1839-
DLC Mr 5 1845
MiU My 8 1844
N O 25 1852;Ap 23 1855
NN Ja 19 1841
NSchU Ja 12,My 4 1842
WHi Ap 24 1839

FULTON county republican. 1869-1911? *See under* Gloversville

Johnstown HERALD. w 1826-37||
Follows Mohawk herald (Amsterdam) Followed by Fonda herald (Fonda)
DLC N 11 1828;D 24 1833
MWA Ap 21 1829
N Ja 20,N 3 1829;Ap 14,D 18 1832;D 15 1835
NN D 15 1835
NNHi Je 17 1828;O 27 1829
P-M Ag 5 1834

NEW YORK (*Continued*)

JOHNSTOWN—*Continued*

Johnstown INDEPENDENT. w Ja 1856-90||?
1856-Mr 1858 as Johnstown American
MWA Je 3 1864;Je 15 1866

***MONTGOMERY republican.** w Ag 1806-N 1836||
Suspended 1834-O? 1836
N O 5 1825;O 29 1833

KATONAH

Katonah RECORD. w My 13 1913+
pub 1913+

KEESEVILLE

Keeseville ARGUS. w Ag 1832-38||?
N My 22 1833
NNHi O 16,30,N 27 1833;Ap 15 1835;Jl 27 1836; Je 21 1837
WHi Mr 22(extra)1837

AUSABLE RIVER gazette. w N 8 1849-
NChM D 20 1849

Keeseville DEMOCRAT. w
Campaign paper
NHi O 28 1858

ESSEX county news. w 1906+
pub 1906+

ESSEX county republican. w S 1839+
pub D 10 1840;68+
IaDH N 19 1853
MWA F 15 1851;Jl 31 1852;My 6 1875
N Ap 24 1858;Ag 13 1896;Ag 28 1908-S 21 1917
NChM Mr 24 1855;Ap 24 1879
NHi 1840-[46;55]63-[67]79-[91]-93;96;98-1901; 04-05;34+
NSchU Jl 13 1842
NhD Jl 3 1852
NjR Jl 4 1872

Keeseville HERALD. w 1825-41||
Title varies slightly
DLC S 17,N 19 1840
MWA Mr 18 1828[Jl 25 1831-F 21]-Ag 1832
N N 4 1828;Ap 26 1831;D 25 1832;O 22,D 17 1833;Ja 7,D 16 1835
NHi 1831-[39]
NNHi D 28 1830;Ap 1831-Ap,S 1832-My 7,S 1833-F 1834;Ja-O,D 1835-[36-37]-40
NhD N 18 1828
NjR F 16 1830

Keeseville INTELLIGENCER. w O 22-D 31 1834||?
Merged with Keeseville herald
N D 17 1834

JOHNSONIAN. w
Campaign paper
NHi O 24 1840

NORTHERN gazette. w 1851-
MWA N 25 1852
WHi Ag 4 1853

NORTHERN standard. w 1854-D 27 1860||
NKeE Ap 22 1858-60

OLD SETTLER. m D 1847-
1849 pub in Saratoga Springs
MWA F 1854
NChM Ja 1848
NEh Mr 1857
NElP 1847-Mr 1848;Mr-N 1850;F-Mr,My-Jl,O-D 1851
NjR [1850;53]

TRUE democrat. w My 1848-
NHi Ag 30 1848

KENMORE

Kenmore INDEPENDENT-RECORD. w 1913+
1913-F 9 1933 as Kenmore independent
pub 1933+
NKen S 19-26,O 10,N 7,21-D 12 1928;Ap 25-My 2,16-Je 6,20,Jl 3,11-18,Ag 8-15,S 5-12,O 17 1929;N 13-D 1930;Ja 29-F 19,Mr 5,Ap-My 7, Je 11-18,Jl-D 1931;Ja 21-Je,Jl 14 1932-Ja 12, 26-S 7,O 12-N 23,D 1933-Ja 18,F 15,Mr 8-15, Ap-Ag 2,16-D 13,27 1934-Mr,Ap 11-My 2,16-Je 13,27,Jl 11-25,Ag 8 1935+

Kenmore RECORD. w 1916-F 9 1933||
United with Kenmore independent to form Kenmore independent-record
NKen S 20,O 4-18,N 1,15-D 20 1928;Ja 3-10,24-31,Mr-S 19,O 3-24,D 12 1929-F 13,Mr 13-Ap 10,24-My 8,22-O 16,30,N 13-D 1930;Ja 29-My 14,Je 11-O 1,15 1931-F 11,25-Ap 21,My-Je,Jl 14,28-O 20,N 1932-Ja 19,F 2-9 1933
NKenHi O 24,N 14,D 12 1918

Kenmore TRIBUNE. w 1932+
NKen 1933+

KINDERHOOK

Kinderhook ADVERTISER. w 1866-74||?
1866-71? as Columbia county advertiser
N S 20 1873

COLUMBIA county advertiser. *See* Kinderhook advertiser

COLUMBIA sentinel. *See* Kinderhook sentinel

ROUGH notes. *See under* Valatie

Kinderhook SENTINEL. w Ja 1832-54||?
1832-35 as Columbia sentinel. Followed by Rough notes (Valatie)
Ct Ag 16 1832;My 30,O 3,24 1833;Ja 1,Jl 17,S 4 1834;Ja 8,Je 4,Ag 13,27 1835;Ja 28,Je 23 1836
MWA F 8 1838;My 30,Jl 25 1850
N My 13 1847;Je 12 1851
NNHi D 5,19 1844
NSchU D 30 1841

KINGSTON

Kingston ARGUS. w My 22 1833-1908||?
1833-Ap 10 1861 as Kingston argus; 1861-62? Kingston argus and Ulster republican
CSmH D 28 1842
CtW [S 17 1834-N 18 1836]
DLC Ag 14 1833;My 13 1840-My 4 1842;Je 26 1844;S 27 1848;O 18 1871
MWA Je 12 1861;Je 7 1865
N O 16 1833;My 1835-Ap 1850;Je 11 1851-Ap 10,My 22 1861-My 13 1863;My 18 1864-My 21 1884
NBHi [1852-59]
NKiJ 1833-My 13 1835;My 13 1840-Je 23 1852; Ap 26 1854-O 1869;Mr 1872-My 13 1874;Je 1878-84
NN Mr 11,O 14,D 23 1863;O 4 1865;N 6 1872
NNHi N 26 1845;O 7 1863;S 8-15 1869;Ja 29 1873;Jl 23 1879
OClWHi Je 20 1866
P-M D 6 1854

Kingston evening ARGUS. d O 20? 1871-
DLC O 30 1871

Sunday ARGUS. w 1906-15||?
United with Kingston leader to form Kingston leader and argus, later Kingston leader

CAMP WARD journal. d Ag 20? 1855-
DLC Ag 23 1855
MWA Ag 23 1855

Kingston daily CHRONICLE. d 1859-
MWA Ag 1,O 6 1859

COURIER. w 1847-83||
1847-69 as Rondout courier
DLC D 28 1860;Ap 26 1879
MWA O 8 1852[My 26-D 22 1854]56-67;Ja 23 1877
MiU-C [1858-60]
N Ap 1868-O 1 1869;N 17 1877-Ap 1881
NN N 13(supp)1868
NNHi Jl 10,S 11 1863;Ag 13 1879;F 18 1873;Ag 21 1880;S 3-10,24 1881;My 13 1882
NcD Je 9 1865

Morning COURIER. d O 4? 1877-83||
MWA O 21,24 1877;My 15 1878;Ag 2 1882
N O 19 1877-F 3 1883

***CRAFTSMAN.** w Mr 29 1820-
DLC O 8 1823
MWA S 12,O 10,D 19 1821;Ja 29 1823
NN Ja 6-Mr 21 1821
NNHi N 24 1824

Kingston DEMOCRATIC journal. *See* Kingston freeman and journal

Kingston FREEMAN. w Jl 26 1845-80||?
1845-68 as Rondout freeman. United with Kingston journal to form Kingston freeman and journal
CSmH O 4 1845
DLC My 9 1846
MWA O 19 1859
NNHi Je 27 1873;Mr 8,22 1878

Kingston daily FREEMAN. d O 18 1871+
1871-Mr 30 1872 as Rondout daily freeman
pub 1871+
DLC O 25 1871;Ja 24 1879
MWA S 20 1881;S 6 1901
N 1871-O 17 1884
NNHi My 1 1873
NSchU O 1872+

Kingston FREEMAN and journal. w N 25 1840-Jl 29 1932||
Formed by the union of Ulster sentinel and Political reformer. 1840-Jl 1868 as Kingston democratic journal; Ag 1868-80? Kingston journal; 1881?-83? Kingston journal and weekly freeman
pub Ap 24 1872-Ap 17 1874
DLC My 27 1846;Ja 9-Ap 3,24-My 15,29-Je 12,26-Jl 24,S 4,O 23-N 13,D 1850;Ja 14 1852;S 6 1876
MWA Mr 19 1845;Ap 7 1847;Jl 7 1852;Ap 29 1868;S 19 1901;O 2 1908
N N 16 1842;My 29 1844;N 9 1845-S 4 1878
NKiJ My 1856-N 17 1858;N 21 1860-N 13 1867
NN Je 5 1850
NNHi Ja 10 1844;S 9 1863;S 15 1869;F 5,Mr 5,N 26 1873;S 1,O 6 1881;Je 7 1883
NSchU complete
NjHi My 3 1854

HARRISON advocate. w Je 18- 1836||
Campaign paper
CSm Je 18 1836
OHi Je 18-Jl 9,23-Ag,S 10 1836

Kingston JOURNAL. *See* Kingston freeman and journal

Kingston LEADER. w 1881-1924||?
1915?-19? as Leader and argus

Kingston daily LEADER. d 1882+
DLC Ag 7,O 16,N 13 1882;Jl 13 1886
N F 19 1883-My 6 1889

Kingston daily NEWS. d Je 1? 1878-
DLC Je 29 1878

PEOPLE'S advocate. w S 13 1824-
DLC Ja 19 1825;Mr 29,N 1 1826
NNHi O 13 1824

PEOPLE'S press. *See* Kingston press

PLEBEIAN and Ulster county advertiser. *See* Ulster plebeian

POLITICAL reformer. w My 31 1837-N 18 1840||
Follows Ulster county whig. United with Ulster sentinel to form Kingston democratic journal, later Kingston freeman and journal
N complete

Kingston PRESS. w My 28 1853-76||?
1853-59 as People's press
DLC Mr 25 1859
N 1853-My 15 1857
NN Jl 18 1856
NNHi F 1858-S 1859;Jl 24,S 25 1862
OClWHi My 21 1863

RONDOUT courier. *See* Courier (1847-83)

RONDOUT freeman. *See* Kingston freeman

ULSTER and Delaware gazette. *See* Ulster gazette

ULSTER county gazette. *See* Ulster gazette

ULSTER county whig. w S 17 1834-
Followed by Political reformer
CSmH Mr 18 1835
CtW [S 17 1834-N 16 1836]
DLC S 17 1834
MWA N 2 1836
NNHi S-O 15,N 19-26,D 10 1834[35-36]Ja 4,F 18 1837

ULSTER democrat. w 1846-
Follows Middletown courier (Middletown)
DLC S 10 1850
NNHi Ja 30 1862;S 16 1869

***ULSTER gazette.** w My 5 1798-1822||
Title varies: Ulster county gazette; Ulster and Delaware gazette
MWA Jl 4 1870

ULSTER daily gazette. d 1870-71||
DLC Mr 9 1871

ULSTER Huguenot. w Jl 20 1843-
DLC Ap 27 1844
MWA My 4,Jl 13 1844
N Mr 9 1844

ULSTER palladium. w My 3 1828-
Title varies: Ulster palladium and anti-masonic journal; Ulster palladium and manufacturers journal
1828 pub in Saugerties
CSmH Mr 4 1829;S 8 1830
DLC S 27(extra)1832
MWA My 3 1828;Ag 1,O 31 1832
N N 30 1831
NN [Mr 18-D 1829]Ja 12 1831
NNHi My 3 1828[Mr 1830-N 1833]
NjHi Mr 11 1829
P-M S 1832

***ULSTER plebeian.** w Je 29 1803-
1803-Jl 25 1815 as Plebeian; My 31 1826-27? Plebeian and Ulster county advertiser
CSmH Je 30 1830
Ct [1827]
DLC Je 1 1825;O 18 1826;Ja 13 1830;Ja 26 1831
MWA O 20 1824;Ja 12,F 2,Mr 9 1825;N 26 1828;O 21 1829;Ja 12? 1831
N O 6 1824;S 19 1827;F 3 1830
NN My 17,31,N 8 1826
NNHi O 31 1821;Ag 27,S 10,24-O 1,N 5 1823;Ap 21,Jl 28,O 13 1824;Ag 25(extra)1832
NjHi [1821-26]

ULSTER republican. w Ag 15? 1827-My 15 1861||?
United with Kingston argus to form Kingston argus and Ulster republican, later Kingston argus
DLC Je 25 1828
MWA D 26 1827;F 20 1828

ULSTER sentinel. w Je 14 1826-N 18 1840||
United with Political reformer to form Kingston democratic journal, later Kingston freeman and journal
CSmH Je 4 1828;S 1 1830
Ct [1830-31]
DLC Je 14,O 25 1826;O 23 1833;Je 18 1834;Mr 9 1836
MWA N 3 1830
MeU Ap 30 1828
N N 29 1826;O 8 1828;O 16 1833
NNHi O 29,D 2 1829;Jl 6 1831;F 1,D 19 1832;N 1 1839

ULSTER star. w 1832-
N O 17 1833

ULSTER true American. w
Ct N 13 1827

Kingston weekly UNION. w D 8 1898-
DLC Mr 3 1899;Ja 26 1900
MWA O 13 1899

LAKE GEORGE

GUARDIAN. w 1820-
NGf N 23 1821
NHi Ja 17 1823

Lake George MIRROR. w 1890+
NHi 1931+
NLg Je 20 1914+

LAKE PLACID

ADIRONDACK. *See* Lake Placid news

Lake Placid NEWS. w 1895+
1895-1905? as Adirondack
pub 1914-[19-20]-[24-25]+
NHi S 24 1897;S 23 1898;My 18-25,Je 14,N 23 1900;S 7 1906;35+

LAKE RONKONKOMA

Lake Ronkonkoma MIRROR. w 1926+
pub 1926+

LANCASTER

Lancaster ENTERPRISE-TIMES. w 1895+
1895-98 as Lancaster enterprise
pub 1895+

NEW YORK (*Continued*)

LANCASTER—*Continued*

Lancaster STAR. w 1878-80||
NBuG [My 31 1878-Mr 4 1880]
NLaE complete

Lancaster TIMES. w Jl 8 1880-98||
United with Lancaster enterprise to form Lancaster enterprise-times
NBuG complete
NLaE complete

UNION and republican sentinel. w
WHi Je 23 1846

LANSINGBURGH

Papers published in Lansingburgh are listed under Troy

LARCHMONT

Larchmont TIMES. w 1901+
pub D 1910+
NLar O 1926+

LE ROY

Le Roy GAZETTE-NEWS. w Ja 7 1826+
1826-29? as Genesee gazette; 1830?-1911? Le Roy gazette
CSmH S 9 1830
DLC Ja 7 1830
IG D 8 1847
MBAt Ja 12 1832
MWA Ja 21 1826
N O 11 1827;Ja 22 1845;S 4 1878;Ag 16 1917-19
NN Je 18 1829;F 9 1859
NNHi Mr 5 1873
NSchU S 21 1842
OClWHi Mr 11,Ap 1 1840
WHi Ja 11 1827-Ja 3 1828;D 12 1840(extra)

GENESEE county herald. *See under* Batavia

GENESEE gazette. *See* Le Roy gazette-news

Le Roy NEWS. w 1899-1911||?
United with Le Roy gazette to form Le Roy gazette-news

LETICIA

LIBERTY press. w
NhD N 28 1843

LEWISTON

NIAGARA democrat. *See under* Lockport

Lewiston SENTINEL. *See* Niagara sentinel. . . (Lockport)

Lewiston TELEGRAPH. w 1837-
NGe Ap 11,25,Jl 4,Ag 1 1838;Ap 19 1839

LIBERTY

Liberty GAZETTE. w S 17 1892+
pub 1892+

Liberty REGISTER. w 1869+
pub 1910+

Liberty STAR. w
NJ 1847-48

LIMA

Lima RECORDER. w O 1 1869+
pub S 1929+
NLivG 1929+

LINDENHURST

Lindenhurst STAR. w S 21 1927+
pub 1927+

LISLE

Lisle GLEANER. w 1871-1928||
NLi F 2,My 2 1874;My 5 1875;My 7 1884;Ap-My 7 1885;Mr 16 1887;Ja 27,F 5 1890;F 9,Ap 20-27 1899;F 22,Mr 22,Ap-My,Je 21-28,Jl 19,Ag 30,D 1900[01-04]-06;My 2,O 3 1907;F 3,Ag 18,S 1,N 1910;11-Je 5,D 25 1913-Ap 1916 [17]-Jl 1 1926;My 17,S 14 1927-28
NLiT 1921-25

LITTLE FALLS

ASTORAGAN enterprise and Mohawk Valley record. w
DLC Jl 17 1847

Saturday BUDGET. w F 11 1893-
NHerHi F 18-Ap 29 1893

Evening HERALD. d 1889-90||?
NHerHi S-D 1890

HERKIMER county news. w 1868+
Title varies slightly
NHerHi 1872-77;92-1904;18-31

HERKIMER freeman. Je 28 1844-50||
Followed by Mohawk times (Mohawk)
Ct Ag 5 1845;Jl 27 1847;Jl 4 1848
MnU 1844-Je 20 1845

Little Falls INQUIRER. w Ag 22 1832-
MWA Je 27 1833
N [F 21-N 26 1833]

JOURNAL and courier. w D 27 1837+
Title varies: 1837-Ja 1 1864 Herkimer journal; Herkimer county journal
1837-49 pub in Herkimer
Ct F 28,Mr 13 1844;S 1 1846
CtY Jl 28 1853;Ja 28 1864;O 10,N 5 1867;D 1 1870;Jl 30 1872;Ag 14 1877
N Ap 5,26,Je 6-20,Jl 18 1838;Ap 24 1839;Ja 1,N 4,25 1840;Ap 10 1844
NHerHi 1868-1904
NLit My 8 1856-58;60-Ja 17 1861;62-1924
NN D 25 1839;F 16 1842
NNHi My 28 1872;Mr 11 1873
NSchU Mr 9 1842

MOHAWK courier. w S 1821-Ja 1 1864||
1821-31 as People's friend. Title varies: People's friend and Little Falls gazette; Mohawk courier and Little Falls gazette. United with Herkimer journal to form Journal and courier
Ct D 31 1857
CtY D 14 1848
DLC 1829-Jl 1 1830;Ap 14-21 1831
MWA N 15 1826;Ja 17 1827;Je 25 1829;Ja 2 1834;Jl 18 1839;Jl 13 1843;N 4 1852
N Mr 16 1825;Jl 24 1828;O 22 1829;Jl 19,D 20 1832;Je 14 1833;Ja 9-F 6,Mr 13-20 1834
NHerHi Jl 12 1832-Ag 14 1834;Ja 28 1836-Je 1839;Jl 1840-47
NLit Ja 1824;29-Je 21 1832;F 18 1836-Jl 1 1858
NLitJ 1836-38
NN Ap 24,Je 19 1834;D 17 1835
NNHi 1843-49;extras:Ja 7,D 2 1845;Ja 6,O 22 1845;D 9 1847;Ja 4,F 16,Je? 1848;Ja 2 1849
NUHi D 31 1829
NhD S 17 1846

MOHAWK mirror and independent chronicle. w 1841-44||
NN D 9 1842
NUHi N 18 1842

PEOPLE'S friend. *See* Mohawk courier

Evening TIMES. d My 10 1886+
pub 1891+
N 1925+
NHerHi 1886-1904

TRIBUNE and spirit of ninety-eight. w Jl 4 1840-
MiU Jl 18 1840
N S 12 1840

LITTLE NECK. *See* GREAT NECK

LITTLE VALLEY

CATTARAUGUS union. *See under* Salamanca

LIVONIA

Livonia GAZETTE. w O 1 1875+
O 2 1925 is 50th anniversary number
pub 1875+
NLiv 1875+
NNC O 2 1925

LOCKPORT

Lockport daily ADVERTISER and democrat. d F 1854-
NLoC Mr 1859-F 1861;62-63
NSyU Ap 20,My 18,25,Je 1,10,Jl 20,Ag 10,17,S 20 1861;N 7 1862
WHi Ag 18 1858

Lockport BALANCE. w 1831-38||
Title varies slightly: Balance and gazette; etc. Merged with Niagara democrat. . .
Ct [1835-38]
N Ap 3 1832;Jl 22 1835-F 28 1838
NBuHi 1832-D 30 1834

Lockport weekly BEE. w Je 18 1864-
MWA Jl 9 1864

Lockport CHRONICLE. w Ap 9 1859-
NBuG Je 14 1862
WHi Ag 9 1862

Lockport daily COURIER. d 1851-59||
United with Lockport daily journal to form Lockport daily journal and courier, Lockport daily journal
MWA N 26 1852
NBuHi Je 2 1851-O 1854
NLoC Ap 1858-F 1859
—w ed *See* Niagara courier

FREEMAN'S advocate. w
WHi Ja 11 1839

Lockport GAZETTE. w 1829?-1834||
United with Lockport balance to form Balance and gazette, later Lockport balance
NNHi N 14 1829

Lockport INTELLIGENCER. *See* Niagara county intelligencer

Lockport JOURNAL. w Ap 10 1828-
Follows Niagara sentinel and Lockport observatory
MWA Ap 17 1828

Lockport JOURNAL. w 1851-54. *See* Niagara county journal

Lockport daily JOURNAL. d 1851-1914||?
1860-71 as Lockport journal and courier. United with Lockport union-sun to form Lockport union-sun and journal
MBAt Ap 15,18 1865
MWA N 26 1852;Je 1 1870
NBuG Jl 29 1863
NLoC F 1858-Ag 1890
NN My 8,12 1863
WHi O 19 1860;Ap 3,10,15,22-23 1865;Jl 13 1895
—w ed *See* Niagara county journal

NIAGARA cataract. w 1846-51||
NBuHi [Ap 1 1846-Jl 23 1851]
WHi N 18 1846

NIAGARA county intelligencer. w Mr 2 1859-
Title varies: Lockport intelligencer; etc.
MWA S 7 1859;F 4 1863
WHi Ap 27 1864

NIAGARA county journal. w,sw 1851-1910||?
1851-54? as Lockport journal; 1855?-1900? Niagara journal
w 1851-89?
DLC S 19 1855
MWA D 1 1852
N S 22 1852
NBuHi Jl 30 1851-Ap 5 1856
VU My 28 1884;My 26 1886

NIAGARA courier. w My 1 1823-
CSmH Ag 26 1830
DLC My 7 1834;Ap 21 1841
MWA D 1 1852
N Je 26-Jl 3,Ag 21-S 4,O 9,23 1828;N 15-22,D 6 1831;F 21,Je 26,O 20,D 18 1832;Ja 23,Mr 20,Ap 17,Ag 7,S 4-11,N 6 1833[Ja-S 1834]Ap 5 1854
NBuHi My 22 1828-Ag 18 1841;45-D 3 1851
NNHi Jl 15 1840
P-M O 16 1832
—d ed *See* Lockport daily courier

NIAGARA democrat and Niagara sun. w,sw 1821-1911||?
1835-Mr 2 1838 as Niagara democrat and Lockport balance; Mr 9 1838-95? Niagara democrat
1821 pub in Lewiston
w 1821-89?
Ct Mr 18 1836
DLC O 28 1852
MWA D 21 1854;O 17 1863;Ja 7 1865;F 9 1867
N O 27 1837;Ap 3 1839;O 7 1852
NBuHi S 19 1835-S 4 1844;O 15 1845-Mr 1854
NNHi Ap 11 1838;Ap 3 1839;Ap 5 1873
OClWHi Je 18,Jl 2 1845
VU Ja 2 1883;My 29 1886
WHi S 16 1846;My 4,Je 8 1854-Je 14 1855
—d ed *See* Lockport union-sun and journal

NIAGARA journal. *See* Niagara county journal

NIAGARA sentinel and Lockport observatory. w 1822-Ap 3 1828||
1822? as Lewiston sentinel (Lewiston) 1823?-Ag 10? 1827 as Niagara sentinel. Followed by Lockport journal
MWA D 7 1827
N D 30 1825;Ja 6,20,F 17 1826
NNHi F 17 1826

Lockport OBSERVATORY. w 1823-27||?
United with Niagara sentinel to form Niagara sentinel and Lockport observatory
DLC Ap 28 1825
N Mr 23 1826

Daily SUN. d 1891-94||?
United with Daily union to form Lockport union-sun, later Lockport union-sun and journal

Lockport UNION-SUN and journal. d 1860+
1860-94? as Daily union; 1895?-1914? Lockport union-sun
O 8 1921 is centennial ed
pub Mr 29 1890+
MWA O 8 1921
NLo 1924+
NLoC 1867-70
VU My 22,Je 19 1883;Ap 9,26 1884
—w ed *See* Niagara democrat

LONG BEACH

Long Beach LIFE. w 1917+
NN My 22 1922

LONG ISLAND chronicle. w D 10 1926+
pub 1926+

LONG ISLAND CITY

ASTORIA gazette and Newtown sentinel. w Ag 5 1852-53||
NEh S 23,N 25,D 30 1852;F 3-10,Mr 3,31,My 26,Je 16 1853
NNHi 1852-Jl 7 1853

ASTORIA herald and Newtown gazette. Je 6 1863-
NBHi Ag 29 1863

ASTORIA times. w Ap 1931+
pub 1934+

MAGYAR szo (Hungarian voice) w
In Hungarian
PPiHi Ap 2 1931

Long Island weekly STAR. w O 20 1865-1921||
Title varies slightly
NBHi N 3 1865;80-1921
NNHi Mr 20 1868

Daily STAR. d Mr 26 1876+
NN N 3 1917[18]
NNQ Jl 1909-[19-20]+

LOWVILLE

BLACK RIVER gazette. w O 19 1825-
MWA Ap 1 1829
P-M O 10 1832
PDoHi Je 19 1827

Lowville HERALD. w S 22 1846-1916||
1846-Ag 1910 as Lewis county democrat
1846-49 pub in Turin
N 1846-50,O 31 1866-Ap 16 1884 91-96;F 1898-1909;S 1910-14
NN Ja 2,F 6,27-D 15 1849
OClWHi Je 20 1866

NEW YORK (*Continued*)

LOWVILLE—*Continued*

JOURNAL and republican. w F 22 1838+
 1838-59 as Northern journal
 pub D 1883+
 DLC Mr 1 1838;S 20 1871
 MWA Ap 23 1862;O 16 1872
 N My 30,O 10 1839;Ja 9,Ag 20 1840;O 14 1841;D 29 1842;S 21 1843;Ag 1,D 12 1844;Ja 16 1845;Ja 29,F 19,Mr 12,Ap 9,Je 26,S 17-24 1846;47-58;Jl 6,S 28,O 5,19-26,N 16,D 28 1859; 60-[90-96]Ja 27 1898;Ap 20,Je 8,Jl 27 1899;Je 7 1900;Ag 7 1902;Ap 24 1913+
 NSchU My 5 1842
 WHi S 16 1841;Je 17 1847

LEWIS county banner. w S 3 1856-
 MWA S 10 1856;D 30 1857
 N O 15 1856;Ja 7,N 11,25 1857;Ap 14-21 1859; Mr 28 1860;Ja 16 1861-N 2 1864

LEWIS county democrat. *See* Lowville herald

LEWIS county republican. w My 18 1830-D 1859||
 United with Northern journal to form Journal and republican
 NN N 7,D 5 1848;Ja 2,30,F 13-D 25 1849

LEWIS democrat. w Mr 25 1834-
 N O 21 1834

NORTHERN journal. *See* Journal and republican

Lowville TIMES. w 1876-1908||?
 Title varies slightly
 MWA O 30 1884
 N Jl 1876-[92-94]
 NNHi N 13 1884

LYNBROOK

NASSAU daily star. d 1927+
 NRcN 1930+

ROCKAWAY times. w 1911-16||
 NRc Ja-D 14 1916

LYONS

Lyons ADVERTISER. w My 31 1822-
 N N 2(extra)1825;N 28 1827

Lyons ARGUS. w 1830-
 1830-36 as Western argus
 MWA O 13 1830;F 17,Mr 9 1836
 N D 6 1831;O 9-16 1833;N 4 1835;O 4 1837;Jl 31 1844
 NN Ag 15,N 21 1832;Ja 28 1835
 NNHi O 1830-S 1834;S 30 1835-S 1836

Lyons COUNTRYMAN and anti-masonic recorder. w Ja 26 1830-32||
 Follows Palmyra freeman (Palmyra)
 CSmH S 14 1830
 MWA Mr 2 1830;My 24 1831
 P-M O 17 1832

FLAIL. w
 NNHi Jl 19-N 1 1844

GRIN and bear it. w 1882-84||
 KHi S 27 1884

Lyons REPUBLICAN and the Clyde times. w Ag 3 1821+
 1821-My 3 1929 as Lyons republican (title varies)
 pub 1821+
 KHi Mr 11 1927
 MWA My 24 1866;Je 30 1881;Ja 25 1883;Ag 3 1921;Jl 30 1926
 N 1910+
 NN S 22 1881
 NNHi My 15,Je 26 1863;F 20 1873

WAYNE county review. w Je 3 1892-Je 1 1907||
 Merged with Lyons republican
 NLyR complete

WAYNE democratic press. w Ag 1 1821+
 pub Ap 1872+

WESTERN argus. *See* Lyons argus

MACEDON

Macedon JOURNAL. w O 12 1923+
 pub 1928+

MCGRAWVILLE

CENTRAL reformer. w 1856-
 NSyU My 19 1858

McGrawville EXPRESS. w
 WHi My 25 1848

MACHIAS

Machias SENTINEL. w Ap 9 1931+
 pub 1931+

MADRID

Madrid weekly NEWS. w Ja 7 1875-77||?
 N My 27 1875

MALONE

Malone FARMER. w 1881+
 pub 1900+

FRANKLIN gazette. w 1837-1910||?
 1837-47 pub in Fort Covington
 N Mr 21 1857
 NChaF N 19 1845
 NNHi [1849-S 1854]Mr 7 1873

*FRANKLIN telegraph. w Ag 31 1820-30||
 CSmH Ag 26 1830
 MWA Ag 13 1829
 N N 21 1822;Mr 27,Je 26 1823
 NMa 1821-Je 25 1829
 NN Ag 29,S 5 1822;Ap 10 1823;N 29 1827
 NNHi [Mr-D 1826]F 8,Ap 26,O 4 1827;O 15 1829

FRONTIER palladium. *See* Malone palladium

JEFFERSONIAN. w Ja 18 1853-D 5 1854||
 DLC Ag 30 1853
 MWA Ap 25-My 2,D 5 1854
 NNHi Ja 25 1853-Je,Ag 29 1854

NORTHERN spectator. w 1830-35||
 NNHi Ja 5,26,Mr 9 1831

Malone PALLADIUM. w Mr 1835-1909||
 Title varies: Palladium; Frontier palladium
 MWA N 11 1852;Mr 29 1860;Jl 14 1864
 N My 5 1842;O 30 1845
 NMa complete
 NNHi N 1 1836;Ja 18(extra)1851;S 17 1863; F 27 1872

Malone evening TELEGRAM. d N 1905+
 pub 1905-07;13+

MAMARONECK

Daily TIMES and the Mamaroneck paragraph. d O 1 1925+
 pub 1925+
 NPV 1925+

MANHASSET

Manhasset MAIL. w Jl 22 1927+
 pub 1927+

MANILA

Manila AMERICAN. 1900-05||?
 NIC [Jl 4 1902-S 14 1905]

MANLIUS

Manlius EAGLE. w 1889+
 NN My 17 1906

ONONDAGA county republican. w 1821-24||
 NN Ja 9 1822

Manlius REPOSITORY. w 1831-
 N Ja 8,O 29 1833;D 16 1834
 NN Mr 8 1831

MARATHON

Marathon INDEPENDENT. w 1870+
 pub 1870-76;84-1912;14+
 N My 5 1874
 NCortHi Ja 8 1908

Marathon LEADER. w 1864-
 MWA F 19 1867

MARCELLUS

Marcellus OBSERVER. w 1879+
 pub 1879+
 NMar 1913+

MARGARETVILLE

CATSKILL MOUNTAIN news. w 1894+
 N F 4-11 1916

MARION

Marion ENTERPRISE. w S 24 1880+
 pub 1880+

MARLBORO

Marlboro RECORD. w 1885+
 NNHi [Ag,N-D 1892]Mr 8,16 1895

MARTINSBURG

AMERICAN union. w
 NN Jl 4 1861

LEWIS county republican. w 1829-59||
 United with Northern journal to form Journal and republican (Lowville)
 WHi [My 27 1834-O 18 1836]

LEWIS county sentinel. w O 12 1824-
 N N 16 1824

MASSENA

Massena OBSERVER. w D 1 1891+
 pub 1891+
 NMaS 1891+

MATTITUCK

WATCHMAN of the Sunrise trail. w S 16 1826+
 1826-1921? as Republican watchman; 1922-25? Greenport watchman
 1826-S 1844 pub in Sag Harbor; O 1844-1924? in Greenport
 pub Jl 14 1927+
 Ct My 16 1835
 MWA F 13 1864;O 14 1876
 N O 12-19 1833;Ja 16 1869
 NBHi 1864-1917
 P-M Ag 29 1863

MAYVILLE

Mayville SENTINEL. w D 1 1834+
 pub 1933+
 CtY [1933]
 DLC F 4 1841;D 28 1843
 MWA Ap 10 1861
 NJ 1834-53
 NWe O 1 1840;N 28 1844-48;52-N 1898;Ap 14, My,Jl 28,Ag 18,S 1,15,N 24 1899;Mr 9,D 14 1900
 P-M Jl 16-23 1840

MECHANICVILLE

Morning STAR. w Ag 29 1854-55||
 Follows Fort Edward courier (Fort Edward)
 N 1854-S 17 1855
 NHi S 5 1854

Mechanicville STAR. w Mr 11 1871-72||
 N 1871-Mr 2 1872

MEDINA

Medina REGISTER. w 1876+
 VU Je 7,28 1883

Medina TRIBUNE. w 1852+
 pub 1860-65;71+
 MWA S 28 1865
 VU My 31 1883;F 7 1889

Medina WHIG. w Jl 1 1852-
 MWA D 2 1852

MERIDIAN

Meridian SUN. w 1854-
 WHi F 16 1855

MERRICK

SOUTH SHORE news. *See under* Freeport

MEXICO

Mexico INDEPENDENT. w Mr 21 1861+
 pub 1921+
 DLC Ja-Je 19 1873
 MWA O 3,D 19 1861;Mr 20 1862;D 24 1863;Mr 8 1866;Ag 9 1871
 NNHi Mr 28 1873;Jl 3 1879
 WHi Ap 25,Je 13 1861-[62-Ag 1866]Je 8 1870

MIDDLEBURGH

Middleburgh GAZETTE. w O 11 1871+
 N 1871-84;87-90

MIDDLEPORT

Middleport HERALD. *See* Niagara herald

NIAGARA herald. w,sw S 13 1885+
 1885-1921? as Middleport herald
 sw 1908?-20?
 N F 18 1886

MIDDLETOWN

Middletown daily ARGUS. *See* Middletown daily herald

BANNER of liberty. *See under* New York City

Middletown COURIER. w Ap 23 1841-46||
 Followed by Ulster democrat (Kingston)
 MWA 1841-Ap 13 1843
 NNHi [Ap-S 1841]-S,N 24 1842;Ap 20 1843-Ap 10 1845

Middletown daily HERALD. d 1876-1926||
 1876-1918 as Middletown daily argus. United with Middletown times-press to form Middletown times-herald
 NMi complete
 NNHi S 20-21,23 1882;S 19-21 1883;My 4 1895

LIBERAL sentinel. w Ap 23 1881-
 KHi Ap 30-O 1 1881

Middletown MERCURY. w,sw O 1 1859-1917||?
 w 1859-83?
 N 1859-67
 NNHi Jl 13 1860[F-O 1868]Jl 23,Ag 6,S 10 1869;Ap 18,Je 13 1873
 —d ed *See* Middletown daily herald

ORANGE county news. w Jl 1846-49||
 NNHi S 18 1846;Ag 17 1848

ORANGE county press. *See* Orange county times-press

ORANGE county times. sw 1891-1906||
 United with Orange county press to form Orange county times-press
 NMi complete

ORANGE county times-press. w,sw N 26 1851-1928||
 1851-N 15 1865 title varies: Whig press; Whig press and Orange county local record; N 22 1865-1906 Orange county press
 NMi complete
 NNGe 1851-Mr 1868
 NNHi 1851-N 16 1853;Je 30-Jl 14,S 1 1858;Jl 4,N 7 1860;Jl 24-Ag 14,28-S 11,O 9-16,N 20-D 11 1861;Ja 15-22,F 12-26,Ap 2,16-30,Je 11,Jl 30,D 10 1862;F 4 1863;Jl 13,Ag 3 1864;My 17 1865;O 1(extra)1869;Je 12 1874;Ja 3,S 20 1878-Jl 11 1879;D 28 1883;My 30,Ag 22 1890

Middletown daily PRESS. *See* Middletown times-herald

NEW YORK (*Continued*)

MIDDLETOWN—*Continued*

Middletown daily TIMES. d 1891-F 1 1906||
United with Middletown daily press to form Middletown times-press, later Middletown times-herald
NMi complete

Middletown TIMES-HERALD. d 1870+
1870-Je 1873 as Middletown evening press; Jl 1873-F 1 1906 Middletown daily press; F 2 1906-26 Middletown times-press
N Mr 1913-O 1922
NMi 1871+
NNHi O 25 1870(extra);S 18 1883

Middletown TIMES-PRESS. *See* Middletown times-herald

WHIG press. *See* Orange county times-press

MILLBROOK

Millbrook MIRROR and round table. w 1906+
NMil [1923+]

MILLERTON

NEWS. w Ag 31 1932+
CtS 1932+

Millerton TELEGRAM. w N 1 1876+
NGL Ap 10-N 13 1930

MILTON

NATIONAL pioneer. w O 20 1829-
CSmH S 8 1830
DLC Jl 7 1830

MINEOLA

NASSAU county gazette. *See* Nassau weekly

NASSAU weekly. w 1898+
1898-1923? as Nassau county gazette
N Ap 18 1913-14

MOHAWK

Mohawk EAGLE. *See* Herkimer county farmer

HERKIMER county farmer. w 1872-1905||?
1872-90? as Mohawk independent; 1891?-99? Mohawk eagle
NHerHi 1892-99

Mohawk INDEPENDENT. *See* Herkimer county farmer

MOHAWK VALLEY register. w Ja 1855-
NHi Je 6 1855

Mohawk TIMES. w 1850-53||
Follows Herkimer freeman (Little Falls)
Ct Ap 22,My 13 1853

MOIRA

Weekly JOURNAL. w 1868-80||?
MWA Mr 25 1873

MONROE

Monroe GAZETTE. w Mr 1 1908+
pub 1908+

Monroe REPUBLICAN. w
WHi Ja 1 1822

Monroe TIMES. w 1880-1904||*
NNHi D 18 1891

MONTGOMERY

ORANGE farmer. w 1820-
DLC O 16,30,N 27 1824

Montgomery REPORTER. w 1888-99||?
United with Standard to form Standard and reporter

Montgomery REPUBLICAN. w 1864-Ap 16 1869||
United with Standard to form Republican and standard, later Standard and reporter
NNHi [S 1868-69]

REPUBLICAN and standard. *See* Standard and reporter

STANDARD and reporter. w Jl 1860+
1860-99? as Standard (Ap 16 1869-Ap 22 1871 Republican and standard; Ap 29 1871-80 Republican and standard and Wallkill Valley times)
A prospectus was issued Je 1860
pub 1890+
MWA D 30 1865
NMoQ 1890+
NNHi Je(prospectus)Jl 31,S 1860-Ja 19,F 2,Ap 20,Ag 31 1861-[66-67]-[69-Jl 1884]Ja 8 1914

WALLKILL VALLEY times. w 1868-Ap 1871||
Merged with Republican and standard, later Standard and reporter
NNHi Ap 1868-69;Je 24,Ag 5,19,S 2,16,30,D 2 1870

MONTICELLO

REPUBLICAN watchman. w 1826+
pub 1826+
Ct Je 28 1831
DLC O 5 1847
MWA My 26 1829
N O 17 1833
NNHi Mr 29 1831;O 15 1840;Ap 15 1873
NNS My 7 1862
NSyU Ag 7 1861

SULLIVAN county republican. w 1844+
1844-56? as Sullivan county whig; 1857?-62? Sullivan county democratic republican
1844-62? pub in Bloomingburg?
DLC Je 15 1849
N Ag 14 1846;D 31 1847;Mr 18 1853;Mr 24 1865;Mr 7 1913+
NNGe My 15 1845-N 15 1850
NNHi O 21 1824;S 22-29,O 20,D 1-8,22 1854;Ja 5,Jl 6 1855;Ap 4,My 9 1856;Je 12 1863

UNION democrat. w 1854-56||
United with Sullivan county whig to form Sullivan county democratic republican, later Sullivan county republican
NNHi My 2 1856

MONTOUR FALLS

To 1895 as Havana

CHEMUNG democrat. w 1838-42||
Followed by Democratic citizen (Watkins Glen)
NCor O 30 1839
OrHi N 1838-Ja 8 1840

CHEMUNG whig. w
NNHi Mr 15,Ap 12 1843

Montour Falls FREE PRESS. w 1889-1923||
1889-95? as Havana free press
NMn complete

HAVANA enterprise. w 1869-77||
NMn F 28 1877

HAVANA free press. *See* Montour Falls free press

HAVANA journal. w S 1 1849-93||
CtY O 19 1867;Je 13 1868
MWA Ja 20 1872
N Ap 29 1854;N 13 1858
NIC complete
NMn complete
NNHi Mr 2 1850;My 23 1851;Ag 20 1853;Je 3 1854;F 22 1873

HAVANA observer. w Je 10 1829-
DLC Je 10-19,Jl 8 1829

HAVANA republican. w Jl 3 1833-
N O 16 1833
NMn 1837-42
NNHi N 3 1841;Ja 31,F 21 1851
OrHi Ja 9 1839-Ja 15 1840

MORAVIA

CAYUGA county courier. *See* Republican-register

Moravia CITIZEN. *See* Moravia republican

MORAVIA VALLEY register. *See* Republican-register

Moravia REPUBLICAN. w 1876-Ja 1906||
1876-82? as Moravia citizen. United with Moravia Valley register to form Republican-register

REPUBLICAN-REGISTER. w 1863+
1863-69? as Cayuga county courier; 1870-Ja 1906 Moravia Valley register
NMor 1871+

MORRIS FLATS. *See* MORRISVILLE

MORRISANIA

In 1873 incorporated as part of New York City. For papers published in Morrisania *See under* New York City

MORRISVILLE

MADISON county advertiser. w My 1817-22||
1817-19 pub in Peterboro
NHC Ja 24 1821

MADISON observer. w Ja 1821-
F 27 1828-34 as Observer and recorder
1821-22 pub in Cazenovia
CSmH S 7 1830
Ct [1831;33-38]
DLC Ap 26 1831;D 26 1832;F 13,D 18 1833;D 17 1834
MWA Jl 25,N 28,D 19 1861;Ap 15 1868
N Jl 14 1829;My 3 1831;F 13,O 16 1833;F 13 1834;D 30 1835;Je 6-13,D 19 1837[41-47;49-56] Ja 22 1857;D 8,29 1859;Ja,S 27,O 11-25,N 15 1860;Ap 4-11 1861
NCan Jl 21 1840-44
NCana Jl 21 1840-44
NCaz Ag 13 1823-Ag 1834
NHC Ap 23 1823;Mr 19 1828;Mr 10 1829;Mr 30,Ag 31,O 26,N 9 1830;O 18 1831
NNHi N 16 1825;My 18 1830;D 2-16 1845;N 16,30,D 7 1847;D 5 1848;Ja 2,D 4 1849;Ja 15,D 10 1850;Je 7 1856;N 12-19 1857
NOHi N 21 1827;Jl 17 1849
NSyU My 6 1846;N 20 1849
PWCl Ag 11 1841;Ag 17 1842

OBSERVER and recorder. *See* Madison observer

MOSCOW

LIVINGSTON gazette. w
NNHi D 27 1821;My 9 1822

LIVINGSTON register. w
NNHi Jl 1 1824

MOTT HAVEN

Papers published in Mott Haven are listed under New York City

MT. KISCO

NORTH WESTCHESTER times. w My 25 1878+
pub 1910+
NMkF [1910+]

Mt Kisco RECORDER. w Ap 24 1874+
NMk 1874+

MOUNT MORRIS

Mount Morris ENTERPRISE. w Mr 2 1875+
pub 1875-84;1924+
NGe Ap-Ag 7,28-O 16,30-D 18 1918;F 5,26-Mr 12,Ap-Je 18,Jl 2-23 1919
NMn Ap 1913+

LIVINGSTON county whig. w N 30 1843-Ja 25 1848||
United with Mount Morris spectator to form Livingston union, later Mount Morris union
NGe complete

LIVINGSTON union. *See* Mount Morris union

PICKET line post and Mt. Morris union. w Je 16 1899+
1899-Je 1918 as Picket line post
pub 1899+
NMm S 16 1910+

Mount Morris SPECTATOR. *See* Mount Morris union

Mount Morris UNION. w Ja 24 1834-Je 1918||
1834-F 2 1848 as Mount Morris spectator; F 9 1848-F 1862 Livingston union; Mr 1862-79? Union and constitution. United with Picket line post to form Picket line post and Mount Morris union
N O 28 1869
NGe 1848-49
NMm Mr 26,O 29 1846;S 15 1903-Je 27 1918
NMmP [1834-61]
NN D 6 1838
NNHi N 5 1867;F 6 1873

Mount Morris daily WHIG. d Je 22-Ag 15 1846||
NGe complete

MOUNT PLEASANT

WESTCHESTER herald. *See under* Ossining

MOUNT VERNON

Daily ARGUS. d Ap 1 1892+
DLC 1898
N Ap 1913+
NNHi 1903-15;Ja-Je 1917;Jl 1918-F 1919

CHRONICLE. *See* Mount Vernon record

La CRONACA illustrata. w D 1915+
In Italian
pub 1915+

Daily EAGLE. d,w 1900-10||?
d 1900-06?
NNHi Ag 14 1903

Mount Vernon RECORD. w 1869-1910||?
1869-98? as Chronicle; 1899?-1901? Chronicle-record
N Mr 16 1877
NNHi F 1 1873;S-D 1898;1901

Mount Vernon RECORD. w 1884-98||?
United with Chronicle to form Chronicle-record, later Mount Vernon record
NNHi 1893

STANDARD. w Ja 18 1873-
MWA F 8 1873

WESTCHESTER county democrat. w 1870-72||
MWA D 14 1872

WESTCHESTER times and East Chester news. w
NNHi D 23-30 1882

NAPLES

Naples weekly EXPENSES. w Je 13 1860-
NNaR Je 13 1860

FAMILY visitor. w F 17 1862-
NNaR Ap 14 1862

NEOPOLITAN. w My 22 1840-
NNaR My 27 1840-Ja 13 1842

NEOPOLITAN. w 1880-84||
United with Naples record to form Neopolitan record, later Naples record
NNaR complete

NEOPOLITAN record. *See* Naples record

Naples NEWS. w 1897+
NNaR 1897+

Naples RECORD. w,d F 1 1870+
1884-87 as Neopolitan record
d Ap 26-My 21 1875
pub 1870+
MWA Jl 3 1875

NARROWSBURG

DELAWARE VALLEY news. w Je 1 1929+
1929-31 as Narrowsburg news
pub 1929+

Narrowsburg NEWS. *See* Delaware Valley news

NEW BERLIN

New Berlin GAZETTE. w 1849+
pub [1908-16]+
MWA S 2 1876

NEW YORK (*Continued*)

NEW BERLIN—*Continued*

New Berlin **HERALD.** w 1833-
MWA Mr 16 1836
N O 16 1833
NNbG Jl 17 1833

NEW BRIGHTON

Papers published in New Brighton are listed under Staten Island

NEW DORP

RICHMOND county independent. w 1907-
NN Ag 31-N 9 1907

NEW HYDE PARK

PUBLICITY. w Ap 3 1930+
pub 1930+

NEW JERUSALEM

New Jerusalem **MESSENGER.** w
NhD Jl 25,Ag 1 1866

NEW PALTZ

INDEPENDENT and times. w 1868+
1868-1919? as New Paltz independent
pub 1868+
DLC Je 21 1877;Ja 18 1889
N Je 29 1883
NNHi S 16 1869;F 13,Mr 20 1873;N 3-10 1882; Ja 5,My 4,N 23,D 7,21 1883;F 15,Je 20,Jl 4-18 1884

New Paltz **TIMES.** w Jl 1860-1919||?
United with New Paltz independent to form Independent and times
DLC S 28 1876
MWA Ap 5,19-26 1861;Jl 3 1863;F 15 1867
NN Jl 4 1878
NNHi D 31 1868;S 2,16 1869

NEW ROCHELLE

New Rochelle **PARAGRAPH.** w 1891-Je 4 1920||
NNr 1897-1920

New Rochelle **PIONEER.** w Mr 24 1860-O 2 1920||
MWA Je 23 1860;Ap 12 1862;N 5 1864;Ap 22 1865;Mr 11,25-Ap 1 1871;F 1 1873
NN Je 4,25 1864
NNr 1897-1920
NNrS [Ap 14 1860-Mr 17]My 26 1900-O 1903

New Rochelle **PRESS.** w My 1875-My 24 1919||
MWA Je 1 1878
NNr 1897-1919
NNrS [My 20 1876-Ap 16 1898]Je 27 1903-S 14 1907

New Rochelle **STANDARD.** d 1908-Je 30 1923||
United with New Rochelle star to form Standard-star
NNr 1909-23

STANDARD-STAR. d Jl 1 1923+
Formed by the union of New Rochelle standard and New Rochelle star
NNr 1923+

New Rochelle **STAR.** d 1911-Je 30 1923||
United with New Rochelle standard to form Standard-star
NNr complete

WESTCHESTER news. *See under* Yonkers

NEW YORK CITY

ABEND blatt für die arbeiter zeitung. d 1895-Ap 12 1902||
In Yiddish
NN Jl 1 1897-1902

New Yorker **ABEND post (New York Jewish abend-post).** d F 3 1899-D 5 1901||?
In Yiddish
NN [1899-1901]
—w ed *See* Idischer journal

Die **ABEND zeitung (Evening times).** d Mr 18-My 12 1906||
In Yiddish
NN complete

ABENDBLATT der New Yorker staats-zeitung. *See* New Yorker staats-zeitung. Abendblatt

ADOPTED citizen. d Ap? 1834-
NNHi Ap 4 1834

New York **ADVANCE.** *See* Bronx record and times

*New York **ADVERTISER.** sw Mr 26 1817-O 31 1836||
Followed by New York advertiser and express, later New York semi-weekly express
CSmH S 14 1830
Ct [Ja-Je 1821]Je 2 1826;My 26,Ag 23 1829[30-36]
CtHi 1821
CtY Ja 23 1822;Mr 8,D 3 1823;Ag 11 1824;Ap 26 1831;D 7 1832;Ja 1,Mr 19-22 1833
DLC 1821-Mr 13 1824;Ag 17-S,O 5,19 1825-Ja 17,24-Ap 14,25-My 5,12,Ag 11 1826
ICU 1821-[25]28-[30]-O 29 1836
MWA Ja-Ag 1821;O 5 1822;My 11,Jl 31 1823;D 22,29 1824;Ja 1,Je 11,Jl 23,N 19,D 16,23 1825; Mr 31,Ap 28 1826-S 26,N 21 1828;Ja 13,D 22 1829-Ja 5,12,26-29,Mr 26,Jl 9 1830;Ja 4 1831; Mr 7,Je 21 1834;Je 3 1835;Jl 27 1836
MiU-C [1826-28]
N 1821-[28]-[30]S 16,D 9,20 1831;Ja 4,F 13 1832;Ja 7 1834;Ag 6 1836
NNHi Jl 21,28 1829
NcD Je 13 1828;Je 25 1830
NjHi N 1821-Ap 1823
OCU Ja 14-F,Mr 17,24-Ap 7,My 19-22,Jl 31,Ag 7,S 11-15 1824
OClWHi Je 29 1822-Ag 25 1824;My 4-S 18 1834;S 17,24 1836

*New York daily **ADVERTISER.** d Ap 9 1817-O 31 1836||
Follows New-York courier (not in this list). Merged with New York express, later New York morning express
Ct Je 19 1821;Ag 30 1834
CtY Ap 5 1823;Ap 19 1824
DLC Ap 25,My 22-31,Jl-D 1821;D 11-13 1822; Ja 8-13,F-Je,Ag 7 1823;F 18,Jl-D 1824;29-36
LU 1823-32
MBAt Ja 6 1821;My 19,N 26 1828;Mr 3,5 1829
MHi Ap 4 1821;Ja 3,F 28 1822
MWA S 14,29,N 19 1821;S 24,O 26 1822;S-D 1823;Jl 26,Ag 31 1824[Ja-Mr,Ag-D 1825]F 18, D 30 1826;N 27,D 8-9,25 1828;Ja 29,D 17 1829; F 23 1830;Je 8,O 3(extra)D 7 1831;Ja 24 1832;Ja 29,F 21,D 9 1835
MiU-C [1822;25;27]
NBHi Ja 12 1821;N 8 1828
NN Ag 30 1821;O 19 1826[N 19 1830-32]D 7 1833;Mr 3 1834
NNHi 1821-27
NNMT N 1833-S 1834;35
P-M Ap 7 1831;Ap 4 1834
WHi D 19 1826;N 6 1827

New York **ADVERTISER. (For the country)** w Ja 1 1834-
MWA Ja 1,My 24 1834
NNHi Ja 8 1834
WHi Ja 8 1834

New York **ADVERTISER.** d Je 7? 1841-42||?
MWA Jl 3,Ag 6,10 1841
NSchU Mr 7 1842

Morning **ADVERTISER.** d Je 8 1891-Ap 1 1897||
Follows Daily continent. United with New York journal to form New York journal and advertiser, later New York American
A [1893-94]
DLC 1891-96
MWA complete
NBHi 1891-92
NN complete
OHi Ja 16 1892-93

New York **ADVERTISER and express.** *See* New York semi-weekly express

ADVERTISER and uptown journal. 1851?-
NNHi O 4 1851

Weekly **ADVOCATE.** 1837. *See* Colored American

New York **ADVOCATE.** d Ap 11 1891-93||?
NNHi Ap 11 1891-Mr 18 1893
—w ed *See* Westchester times. . .

New York **ADVOCATE and journal.** d Ag 17 1831-Ap 20 1833||
1831-Je 9 1832 as New York American advocate. United with New-York mercantile advertiser to form Mercantile advertiser and New York advocate, later Mercantile advertiser
Ct [1831]
CtT Ja 5 1836
DLC S 23 1831;F 17-20,N 8 1832
MBAt N 14 1831;Ja 11 1833
MWA 1831-Je 7,Jl 18 1832-33
NNHi complete

New York **ADVOCATE and journal.** sw Ag 23 1831-F 16 1836||?
1831-Je 12 1832 as New-York American advocate for the country; Je? 1832-Ap 20 1833 New York advocate and journal for the country
Ct [1833-36]
CtHi N 1831-O 16 1832
CtY Ag 13 1832[My 1833-34]Ja 13,S 29 1835; N 17 1837
DLC Ap 20 1832
MB [Je 29 1832-Ja 4 1833]
MWA D 16 1831;Ja 30,Mr 20,Je 12 1832
N F 21,Mr 2,S 7 1832
NNHi Ag 23-S 6 1831;O 12,N 12,27,D 25 1832-Ja 5,11,22,29-F 15,22 1833
NjHi F 7-10,Ap 10,My 8-15 1832;Ja 5,F 12 1836
OOxM [N 1831-Mr 1832]
P-M S 7 1832
PBL [My-D 1834]-My 8 1835
—d ed *See* Mercantile advertiser

AGE. w Je? 1830-31||?
CSmH S 18 1830
DLC Ja 8-15 1831
NNHi Je 25 1831

AGE. d My? 1836-
NNHi Je 3 1836

AGE. d My 12 1838-
NNHi My 12-25 1838

AGE. w My 4 1861-
MWA My 4 1861(specimen no.)

New York **AGE.** w 1880+
1880-N 8? 1884 as New York globe; N 22-D 6 1884 Freeman; D 13 1884-O 8 1887 New York freeman
Negro
CtY My 2 1885
DLC N 18 1882;83-N 19 1892;Ja 4 1900
MB [Ap 1887-Ap 7]Je 9-16,S 1 1888[F-S 7 1889;Ag 16 1890-F 1892]
N Mr 7 1885
NN 1906-09;11+
NNHi F 13 1892
TNY [F 1931-S 2 1933]

AGE of reason. w,sm 1847?-49||?
w 1847?-48?
NNHi My 14 1848;Ja-D 1 1849

ALBANIA. F 28 1918-
1920? pub in Worcester, Mass.
In Albanian
NN F-Ap 25,My 23-Jl 25,Ag 8 1918;Ja 23 1919-Jl 8 1920;N 21 1931

ALBION. w Je 22 1822-76||
Title varies slightly
A 1830-41
CSto 1835-37
CaNS Je 17 1826-Je 9 1827;Jl 31 1830-Je 4 1831;34-37;41;50;56
CaNU 1822-46
CaNW F 1834-35:60
CaNs O 30 1830-Ag 20 1831;Je 9-D 1832;Ja 11 1834-35;37
CaOKU 1822-55
CaOLU 1839-44;46[50-60]-[64-70]
CaOT Je 1826-57;59-61;63-64;67
CaQMF 1836-40
CaQMM 1822-Je 14 1823;Je 19 1824-47;49-59;61-75
CaQMS 1840;46-47
CtHT [Je 1826-28]-[30]
CtHi 1822-N 1827;Je 1830-35;39;41-44
CtW Je 18 1825-Je 10 1826;Je 16 1827-Je 7 1828;36-37;40
CtY Je 29 1822-66
DGU Je 17 1826-Je 4 1831;36-38;Je-D 1839
DLC Ag 17 1822-66
GAtCo My 2 1840
GMM 1852
GU Jl 3 1858
IHi Ap 22 1865
KyLo 1835-Je 18 1836[Ja-N 1856;Jl 24 1858-My 21 1859]
LNH Ag 16 1827;Ag 15,S 5-12,O 3-10,D 19 1829[30]-F 5,19-26,Mr 12-Ap 16 1831[33]Ja 11 1834;36-56
LSfD Je 4 1842;Ag 27 1853;Mr 18 1869;Je 10 1876
LU 1846
MB O 14 1826-S 1828;Je 9 1832-55;58[59]-61 [Ja 11-Ag 2 1862]Ap 22-29,Je 1865-75;Ja 29-D 23 1876
MBr 1833-44
MH O 19 1822-26;28-31;34;36-46;48;Ag 24 1850; 54-60;My 10 1862-N 7 1863
MHi 1822-Je 12 1824;Ag 11,28,S 29,D 1 1838;Ag 3-10 1839
MWA 1822-69
Md Je 16 1827-Je 4 1831;41-48;Ap 1853-Mr 11 1854
MdBE 1835-Ja 7 1837
MdBJ Je 19 1824-Je 17 1826;44-47;49-74
MdHi O 20 1849-Ag 1850
MeB 1841[42]
MeWC 1846
MiD Je 1825-My 1827
MiU 1838-42
MnHi 1844
MoS 1874
MsNF Mr 14 1840-S 1841
N [1822-My 1823;32-54;56-74]
NB 1847
NBHi 1822-31;33-34;36-40;47-50;52-55;57
NBuG N 1836-F 10 1838
NHfH 1838
NMi Ja-D 20 1840
NN 1822-S 1855;56-63;71-[74-75]
extras:Ap 18 1829;N 23 1831;Mr 9 1840
NNHi Ap 5,Je 14 1823-Je 2 1827;Je 14 1828-Je 6 1829[S 1831-32]-48[51]-[53]-Ja 2 1858;My 18-Ag 24 1861;Je 6-13,S 5-12 1863
NT 1839-50
NcD [1829-32;34-36]-[53]62-65;67
NcU Jl 24 1824-Je 1833;39-44
NjP 1825-46;63
OCo 1851-56
OO [1846]
OY Ja-F 11 1836
PAg N 1830-41
PHi O 1823-N 17 1838
PPL [1822]34-35;43;My 8,Jl 24 1847;Ag 12,26 1848
PPM O 21 1837-46;60
PPi [1830]-50
PWCl Ag 9,30,O 4,D 20 1828;Mr 14 1829[30] Ja 1,22,Ap 16,N 19 1831;Ag 18,O 13 1832[36-38]
RPB 1831-54
ScHi Je 19 1824-59
T 1851
THi Je 1824-Je 1826;Je 1831-Je 1832
TU [1844-47]
Tx Je 14-N 22,D 1828-Je 6 1829;Je 1832-D 24 1853
TxHuS S 18 1847
TxU 1833;O 13 1849-S 17 1853
VHi 1829;34;40-41
VP 1823-25;27;29-35;37-39
VRC Ja 20,D 1 1838;F 16-23,Jl 27 1839;S 12 1840
VtBr Je 19,Jl 19 1847

ALLGEMEINE zeitung. w O 10 1835-
In German
MB [O 12-D 20 1839;Ja 18-Jl 11 1840]
NNHi 1835-O 1 1836

New Yorker **ALLGEMEINE zeitung.** 1877-78 *See* New Yorker herold. Morgenblatt

Daily **AMERICA.** d My 10 1893-Ja 11 1894||
Merged with Daily mercury
NjR complete

La **AMERICA.** w N 11 1910-D 26 1924||?
In Ladino and Yiddish
NN 1910-24

*New-York **AMERICAN.** sw,d Mr 3 1819-F 15 1845||
1819-S 8 1821 as American. Merged with Morning courier and New York enquirer
Suspended from Mr 1-8 1820
sw 1819-Mr 1 1820
CSmH S 6 1830
CtHi My 30 1826-Ap 3 1829
CtY 1821-O 1827;N 12 1828-O 1829;Ja-Je 11, Jl 24 1830-31;Je 13,Ag 10 1832;My 1833-S 11 1839[40]-Je 1841
DLC 1821-[29-Ja 1830]31-Ap 1832;D 19 1837; N 13 1840;My 24,Ag 12 1843

NEW YORK (*Continued*)

NEW YORK CITY—*Continued*

*New York **AMERICAN.** sw,d 1819-45‖—*Cont.*
KHi Jl 20 1827-Jl 1835
LU 1824-30
MBAt D 8 29 1823;Mr 12,My 18 1824[27-28]Mr 3,Ap 20 1829
MHi [1821]
MWA Ja 2-3,6,Mr 5,7 1821;Je 9 1823;O 5-6 1824;Ja 21,F 4,7,Mr 10 1825;Ja 18 1826;Ap 16,My 1 1827-F 4[25-Jl 18 1829]F 18,Mr 30, Jl 13,30(suppl)Ag 28-30 1830[31]Ap 27,My 23,Je 2,11 1832-34;Ja 19 1835;S 5,O 14 1836;F 10(extra)28,Je 29(extra)O 26 1837;Ap 20 1840;Je 1,O 27 1841;Ap 13,My 19,Jl 5,Ag 8 1842;My 24 1843;Je 6,Ag 30,S 7 1844
MiU 1821-[23]-[25]26;28[32]36-[38]-[40]-43
MiU-C [1821]
MnS S 13 1831-32;Jl 1833-Ag 15 1837
N Mr 18 1824-Mr 8,11,23,29 1825;Ja 7,10 1826; N 9 1827;F 6,Mr 21,28,Ap 1,Jl 14 1828;Ap 5,N 30 1830;F 19,N 8 1831;32;Ag 10,O 16 1833;34-35;Ja-Je 1840;Ap 22 1842
NAubHi S 8,15-23 1821
NHuHi Ja 3 1825;Mr 9 1831
NN Ag 6,F 29 1824;N 29 1827;F 19,Mr 1,Ag 18-19 1831;Je 14,Mr 26 1834;Ap 20-27 1837;N 25,D 3,7-11,14-15,19,24 1840-Je 1841;My 2,O 19,27 1843
NNC My 1828-Ap 1834[42]44
NNHi 1821-Ap 1843
NNMC O 27-28 1824;N 4 1830
NNMT N 5 1834-41;43-44
NNS 1821-34;36-F 14 1845
NNUnC Je 4 1839;Ap 7-8 1841
NRiHi 1834
NSchU N 20 1830;Je 10,29,Jl 8,23,26-28,Ag 8-9,18,29,S 8,D 14 1831;Ap 18-19 1832
NSyU D 6 1833
NT 1821-Ja 14 1845
NUHi 1833
NcD [Jl-O 1823;Ja-F 1826;F-Ap 1827;29-Ja 1830;S-D 1831;My 1833-Mr 1834]
NjR [1834;40;43]
OClWHi Mr 25 1825;Ap 6 1832;Mr 21 1835;Jl 22 1836;F 16 1838;S 15 1841;Mr 21 1844
P-M Ag 31 1832
PAtM My 31 1834
RPB Ag 13,S 21 1830;Ap 10,Je 12 1834
WHi 1823-27;Ja-Je 1829;F 9-D 1831

*New York **AMERICAN** (for the country). sw Mr 11 1820-F 17 1845‖
1820? as American. Merged with Semi-weekly courier and New York enquirer
CSt D 21 1843;Ap 8,My 9 1844
CtY 1821;Ag 7-11,28-S 1 1824;S 7 1827[Ap-N 1831]Je 19 1832;D 12 1840
DLC Jl 24 1822-25;Ag 4 1826-Ap 13 1827;O 9 1829-45
GDE [1824-25]-[27]
IC My 3 1823-Ap 1825;My 1831-Ap 1834
ICHi S 7 1830
IU Ap 15 183_
MB [1824-F 19 1825]
MBAt Je 18 1823-29;Ap 27 1830
MH [Je 26 1840-My 16 1842]
MHi Ja 9,Ap 18,Je 5,O 9 1822;Ja 10,Jl 24,O 10,17,N 11 1823;Ja 8,Ap 20,Je 26,D 10 1824;Mr 16,My 17 1825;Ja 4,31,F 22 1826[27-28]Ap 11 1833;Ag 26 1840;Jl 10 1843
MWA 1821-[35]-45
MdBJ My 2-5,12-Je 16,27-30,Jl 14-25,Ag 1-4, 18-N 17 1842
MeBC Jl 20 1827-28
MeU Je 25 1830;Ja 10 1832
MiU-C [1821-24;27-29;34;37;41]
N Ja 5 1821-Ap 3 1822;O 2 1824-[32-39]Ja 7-Je 12,Jl 14 1840
NBHi Jl 19,29-Ag 2,16,26-S 9 1825
NBi Ja 16 1829-Jl 9 1830;My 1834-My 19 1835
NCH S 15 1821-My 25 1822;23-O 2 1824;O 20 1829-Mr 22 1831;Ap 17,Je 10 1837
NCanHi D 2-9 1834;Ja-F 13,24-Mr 27 1835
NN F 4 1824;D 30 1828;Jl 1829-Ag 1831[32]-Ja, Mr 1834-[Mr-Ap 1837]-O 1843
NRU O 2,26,N 2,D 4,11 1827;F 1,8,My 9,16,O 14,21 1828;My 22,29,Je 9,16 1829;Mr 9,16,Ap 30,My 7,S 7,14 1830;Jl 8,15,O 14,21,N 8 1831
NSchU Ag 30 1842
NcD [1821-23;25;27;29-31;34-35;37;41]
NjHi 1822-40
OCU O 19-23 1827[28-29]Ag 27 1830-Ja 7,Mr 8,Ag 5 1831-[32-33]-Jl,D 5-9 1834[35]
OHi Jl 29 1829;Jl 1841-Ap 23 1842
PAtM My 30(extra)1834
PDoHi Ja 29 1825
WHi Ja-D 24 1823;N 6,20,27,D 21 1827;Ap 26, My 27 1831-D 25 1832[Ja 15 1833-My 5]O 1835-Ap 1837

New York **AMERICAN.** tw 1832?-35‖?
DLC F 19-23,Mr 18-21,Ap 4,11-13,20,25,My 11,18,Jl 15,27,Ag 1,6,10-13,24,29-30,S 3,7,12-21, 26,O 1-12,19,21,29-31,N 14,21,26,D 4 1833;Ja 18 1834-Mr 1835
NcU D 4 1832;N 27 1834;F 3,28,Mr 17,My 9-11, Jl 9,25,O 15 1835
PEL F 17 1833-N 18 1834

New York **AMERICAN.** d 1882+
1882-N 6 1895 as Morning journal (My 27 1888-My 5 1895 New York morning journal) N 7 1895-Jl 18 1896 Journal; Jl 19 1896-Ap 1 1897 New York journal; Ap 2 1897-N 10 1901 New York journal and advertiser; N 11 1901-Mr 9 1902 New York journal and American; Mr 10 1902-Mr 1 1903 New York American and journal
Mr 13 1888 s Snowsheet-blizzard extra
CL Ap 1904-Mr,Jl 1907-16
CSt-H [1914]-1_
CU Jl 8,26 1914-19
CtY F 4 1897;S 4 1901
DLC O 19 1884-1902;My 1905-Ja 1908
KHi D 14 1884[Jl 14-O 13 1896]
M Ja 23 1929;Ja 4 1932
MB [Je-O 1884]Je 17 1886
MWA N 16 1882;Ag 6-7 1885;Mr 13 1888;Ja 12 1894;F 15 1897;N 6 1901
MiU N-D 1896;Je-S 1901
MiU-C Je 16 1892
N Ag 5 1885;Mr 13 1888;Ap 1913-O 1922
NN N 16 1882-My 15 1883;O-D 1895;Ap 1896+
NNCom Mr 1916+
NNMC Mr 13 1888
NcD My 1905-My 1908[19;25]
NcU Ap 12 1898
NjCHi S 23,O 11-13,15-18,24,D 2,5,23,27,29,31 1897;Ja 15,25,27,29,F 11-28,Mr 6-My 6,Je 3-Jl 21 1898
NjR Mr 1897-Ja 1898
PCHi F 20 1898
PLaF [1924]+
PPL Ap 10 1884
PPeS N 6 1932
PWbW S 12 1909
REdH S 15 1901
VU F 3,O 5-9,21 1905;S 28,O 1,4-5 1909
WaPS Je 10 1919[23]Je 1,Jl 6 1924
—evening ed *See* New York evening journal

New York **AMERICAN** advocate. 1831-32 *See* New York advocate and journal

AMERICAN advocate. w S 1 1841-
DLC S 1-7 1841
NhD O 7 1841

AMERICAN advocate for equal rights for men. d N 1844-45‖?
Merged with Daily plebeian?
OHi D 17,21 1844

AMERICAN artisan. w 1847-Mr 1854‖
1847 as Weekly artisan. United with Banner of the union to form Banner of industry
MWA S 30-N 11 1848;S 18 1852;Ja 8 1853-Mr 4 1854
NEh F 16 1850
NNHi Ja 29,Ap 16,S 17 1853
NcD Jl 5 1851
WHi D 30 1848

Daily **AMERICAN** artisan. d Je? 1847-
DLC Jl 31 1847

AMERICAN Celt w 1849-
1849-53? pub in Buffalo
MWA D 24 1853
P Jl 14 1855
PPCHi [1853]-[55-57]

AMERICAN citizen. d Je 30? 1835-
DLC Jl 1 1835;Ja 5,9 1841
NNHi Jl 25,Ag 3 1835

AMERICAN ensign. d O 7-N 20 1844‖?
DLC O 14 1844
MWA N 20 1844
NNHi O 31,N 20 1844

AMERICAN life. w O 8 1886-
NN O 8 1886

AMERICAN mail. w Je 5-Ag 21 1847‖
IU Jl 10 1847
MB Je,Jl 31 1847
MH complete
MWA Jl 10 1847
NNHi complete

Weekly **AMERICAN** patriot. w Ag 25 1841-46‖?
Merged with Gazette and times. For the country
CtY Ag 25 1841
MWA Ag 25 1841

AMERICAN patriot. d 1843-D 30 1845‖?
Merged with Gazette and times
MWA O 28,D 30 1845

AMERICAN ploughboy. *See* Ploughboy

New York **AMERICAN** republican. d 1843-1845‖?
1843 as American republican; Ja-Ap 23 1844 New York citizen and American republican
IU My 29 1844
MWA Mr 19 1844;Ap 24-O 14 1844
NNHi 1844

Weekly **AMERICAN** republican. w S 7 1844-45‖?
N Je 14 1845

AMERICAN statesman. w F 3-D 4 1847‖?
NNHi F-D 4 1847

AMERICAN whig. *See* Constitution

AMERICA'S own. w Ap 14 1849-
Je 16 1849-S 4 1852 as America's own and fireman's journal
MWA My 13,D 9 1854;Mr 31,My 12,Je 23 1855
NNHi 1849-Je,Ag 21,S 11 1852-Jl 14 1855

AMERIKAI magyar népszava. w,sw,d O 22 1899+
w 1899-1901?;sw 1902?-04?
In Hungarian
pub F 14 1900+
PPiHi F 13 1915-Ja 1 1916;N 24 1931+

AMERIKAI magyarsag. w 1909?-24‖?
In Hungarian
PPiHi S 13 1922-Je 28 1923

AMERIKANISCHE schweizer-zeitung. w 1868+
In German
DLC Jl 21 1900-N 29 1902

AMERIKANSKIE izvestiia. w 1917?-
In Russian
CSt-H [1920]-24
DLC Mr 26 1924

AMERIKANSKII pravoslavnyĭ viestnik. w 1896+
In Russian
DLC 1897-1902;08-10;12-16;22-24[26]+
NN [1899]-[1906]-[10]-[17]18

AMÉRIQUE. w S 17 1933+
In French
MWA D 10 1933;Ap 14 1935
PP S 16,N 25 1934+

L'**AMÉRIQUE** française. w D 1902?-
In French
NN F 8-Jl 5 1903

New York **AMSTERDAM** news. w D 7 1909+
1909-Ag 6 1919 as Amsterdam news
Negro
pub 1922+

ANGLO-AFRICAN. w 1859-
1859-62? as Weekly Anglo-African
Suspended S 23-30 1865
DLC Ap 27,Ag 10 1861-Ap 1862
MWA N 24,D 15 1860-Mr 23,Ap-My 11,Ag 10 1861;Ag 12-D 23 1865

ANGLO-SACSUN. w,m D 5 1846-F 1 1850‖?
Suspended from Ap 17-My 16 1847
1846-Ap 17 1847 pub in Boston
w 1846-49
Phonetic newspaper
CtY F 26,Je 17 1848
DLC D 5 1846;Je 19,S 18-25 1847;My 20,Je 17, Ag 5 1848
ICN Ja 14 1847-S 16 1848
MB D 5 1846;Ja 14,23,F 6,Ap 3 1847
MH D 5 1846;47-48
MWA D 5 1846[47]Mr 18,My 6,27-O 1848;Ap 1849;Ja-F 1850
N F 20 1847
NN D 5 1846;Ja 14-D 25 1847;Ja 8-My 14 1848
NbHi My 22,Je 12-Jl 3,17-N,D 11 1847-Ja,F 12-Mr 4,18,Ap 1,My-Jl 22,Ag 5,S 16 1848
VtBr Ja 14 1847
WHi Je 19 1847

ANGLO-SAXON. *See* Anglo-sacsun

L'**ARALDO** italiano. d 1889-1921‖?
In Italian
IU D 7 1917-[18]-D 16 1919
NN 1895-96;98;F-Je,Ag-N 1900;Ja-Ap,Jl-D 1901;Jl 1902-Ap,Jl 1904-Je 1919

ARBEITER. w Mr 27 1858-
In German
WHi Mr-My 8 1858

New Yorker **ARBEITER-ZEITUNG.** w S 3 1864-
In German
WHi 1864-65

ARBEITER-ZEITUNG. 1873-74 *See* Neue arbeiter-zeitung

ARBEITER ZEITUNG (Workman's paper). w 1890?-1902‖
In Yiddish
NN 1890-1902

New York **ARENA.** d Mr 14 1842-43‖?
Merged with Daily plebeian
MWA Ap 8 1842
NNHi Ap 12 1842
NSchU Jl 6 1842

New York **ARGUS.** w D 7 1861-
CSmH Ap 5 1862
MWA D 7 1861
N 1861-Ja 15,Ap 9-16,30,My 21,Je 4-11,Jl 16, Ag 27-S 3,17-24 1863
NN 1861-O 8 1863
NNHi 1861-N,D 18 1862;Ja-Je 11,25-Jl 9,23-30, Ag 13-S 17,O 1-8 1863
OClWHi Ap 12 1862

ARGUS. d O 20 1887-
NN O 20 1887

ARISTOCRATIC monitor. w Ag 28 1847-
Ag 28-N 13 1847 as Monitor
MWA N 20-D 1847
MdHi 1847-S 1848

Weekly **ARTISAN.** *See* American artisan

ASSYRIAN American. *See* Persian American courier

ATBALSS. w F 15 1918-
In Lettish
WHi F-Jl 13,N 18,D 9 1918

ATLANTIS. w,sw,tw,d Mr 3 1894+
w 1894-1900;sw 1901?-03;tw 1904?-Ja 2 1905
In Greek
pub 1894+
CP Ja 12 1905
KHi Ap 29 1919
MB N 12 1900-F 1902;Mr 1903-04[06-Mr 1922]
NN 1894-F 1898;Mr 1899-F 23 1900;03+
VU N 12 1907
WHi Mr 2 1895

ATLAS. w S 20 1828-N 2 1833‖
1828-S 11 1830 as Atlas; or literary, historical and commercial reporter. United with Constellation to form New York atlas and constellation, later Constellation
CSmH D 19 1829
CaNS [1828-S 1829]
CaQMS [S 18 1830-S 10 1831]F 16-O 1833
CtY 1828-O 26 1833
DLC S 1829-Ag 1831
GAtCo S 19,O 10-24,D 5 1829;F 13-Mr,Ap 10, Je 12-Jl 24,Ag 7,28,O 9,23,N 6,D 18 1830-[Ja-Jl]N 19 1831
MB S 17 1831-S 8 1832
MWA 1828-Ag 1831
MiAC [1828-32]
N 1828-S 10 1831
NN 1828-D 1833
NNC 1828-[32-33]
NNHi 1828-S 17 1831;Ap 14,My 26,Jl 21,S 15 1832-S 7 1833
NT F-N 1829
NcD [Je 1829-Ap 1831]
NjHi Je 19 1830
RPB [S 1829-32]
WOc 1828-29

New York **ATLAS.** w Ag 12 1838-81‖?
1838-O 11 1840 as Sunday morning atlas; O 18 1840-Je 19 1853 Atlas
CSmH Ap 19 1840
DLC Mr 31,My 5 1844;Je 25,S 3,O 1,15-22 1848; N 11 1849;N 30 1851;Ap 25 1852;My 20 1860-My 12 1861;Je 13 1863
GAtCo F 24 1839
In F 1859-Jl 1860
KHi Ap 29 1862

NEW YORK (*Continued*)

NEW YORK CITY—*Continued*

New York ATLAS. 1838-81||?—*Continued*
MH Je 9 1844-Je 1 1845;S 29 1850-D 23 1855
MMarHi 1838-Ag 4 1839
MWA 1838-My,S 26,O 10 1841;Je 5 1842-S 6 1857;My 23 1858-62;Jl 1864-D 7 1872
MiU-C Ap 29 1862
N Ap 14,28-My 5,Jl 21,Ag 4,21 1839;Je 21,Ag 23 1840
NEh O 16 1842
NN 1838-Ag 4 1839;Mr 4,8 1840;My 29 1853-My 21 1854;58-Ag 4 1859;My 5 1861
NNHi Mr 8,22,Ap 12,26,My 10-24,Je 7,21-Jl 5,19-O 11 1840;F 23 1845;O 11 1846;Mr 3,24 1850;Ap 11 1852;D 4 1853;F 5,Ap 30,Ag 6,20,O 8 1854;Ja 2 1862
NSyU D 24 1864
NcD Mr 17 1844;O 3 1847
TJT My 1 1878
WHi Ag 9 1840-My 1841;Jl 30 1843

New York ATLAS and constellation. *See* Constellation

AUCTION bulletin and general advertiser. d Ag 24? 1840-
DLC Ag 25 1840

New York AURORA. d F 1 1842-My 1844||?
Mr 18-Ag 1843? as New York aurora and union. Merged with Daily plebeian
DLC Mr 11,Ap 22,S 25,D 22 1843
MB My 31,My 27,Je 13,20 1842[Ja-F 11 1843]
MWA [Ag 17-O 1843]Ja 17,F 9,12,14,17,Mr 21, Ap 3,My 3 1844
NNHi Mr 18,23,Jl 17,Ag 2-3,11,S 5,26,O 7 1843
NSchU Jl 6,Ag 1,S 1 1842
NjPa N 24 1842-N 23 1843

AUSTRO-HUNGARIAN gazette. *See* Oesterreichisch-ungarische zeitung

BADGER'S weekly messenger. *See* New York weekly messenger and young men's advocate

BAGATELLE. w? 1839?-
DLC Je 16 1842

BALLOT box. d O 3-N 1840||?
Campaign paper
DLC O 28 1840
MB O-N 4 1840
MWA O 24,31 1840
NN O 31 1840

BANNER of industry. w 1847-
1847-Mr 1854 as Banner of the union
MWA Ap 1-8,22-29,My 13-20 1854

BANNER of liberty. w 1848-72||?
1848-64? pub in Middletown
GAtCo Je 20,Ag 1,S 19 1860;D 7 1870
IU O 7 1849
InSHi Je 10 1857
MWA F 1 1853;N 26 1856;Ag 24,S 14,O 5-19,N 2-23 1859;S 14 1870
MnHi My 24 1864
N F 1854-56
NMi 1859-S 3 1861
NSyU Jl 16,S 3 1861
NcD S 21,O 24 1859
OrHi N 30 1859;Je 6 1860
P-M Je 15 1855
THi 1857-S 1861
Tx Ag 16 1869
TxU Jl 1867-Ag 1868
WHi Jl 1 1857;Ja 22 1872

BANNER of the union. *See* Banner of industry

BARNBURNER. w Jl 1-N 18 1848||?
Campaign paper
N Jl 1 1848

Al-BAYAN. w,sw,tw 1910-19||?
sw 1915?;tw 1916?-18?
In Arabic
NN S 10 1912-15

New York daily BEE. d Mr 5 1834-36||?
Suspended in 1835?
NNHi Mr 5 1834

Der BEOBACHTER am Hudson. *See* Revue

BERMUDA-AMERICAN. w 1915-25||?
Also dated in Hamilton, Bermuda
NN D 25 1915-N 22,D 13 1916;Ja 17,F 28,Mr 7,28,Ap 11,My 2,16,Jl 25,Ag 23,S 5 1917;Mr 27,Je 22 1918

BLACK republican and office-holder's journal.
MWA Ag 1865
NNHi Ag-S 1865

BOLLETTINO della sera. d 1898-1932||?
In Italian
NN Ja 2 1901;11-18;Ap 5 1919-S 29 1922
NNPro [1915-29]

La BOS del pueblo. *See* La Epoca de New York

BOYS in blue. w Ag 14-N 1880||?
Campaign paper
MWA Ag 21 1880
NN Ag 14 1880

BRITISH chronicle. w
CaOT Jl 30 1842-Jl 22 1843

BRITISH North American. w
CaNs [1850-53]-55

BROMLEY morning news. d F 29 1908-
CtY [1908]
MWA F 29 1908
NcD F 29 1908
NjR F 29 1908

BRONX borough record. *See* Bronx record and times

BRONX home news. *See* Home news

BRONX record and times. w 1891?+
1891?-98? as New York advance (1894?-95? New York advance and Westchester gazette); 1899?-1900? New York advance and Bronx borough record; 1901?-09? Bronx borough record; 1910?-14? Bronx borough record and times
NNHi O 26-N 2,D 7-21 1901;Ja 11-18,My 10, Jl 19,D 20 1902;Ap 12,N 1,D 20 1903;Ja 10,D 20 1904;Je 14,S 17,N 19,D 10 1905;Mr 4,Ap 12,My 10,24,Ag 1,D 5 1906;Mr 31 1907;Mr 15, Ap 12,My 10,24,Ag 1,D 5 1908;O 12 1918;S 15 1923;S 27 1924
—CHRISTMAS number. an
NN 1906
NNHi 1901-05

BRONX sentinel. (Westchester) w 1901+
1901-02? as Westchester sentinel
NNHi O 26-N 2 1901

BRONX star. w F 1 1908-
NNHi 1908-15;D 21 1918[19]Mr 6,20,Ap 3-10,D 11-18 1920;Ja 1,Mr 12,Jl 2,Ag 13-20,O 15 1921;Ja 30 1923;My 17,31,Je 21 1924

BROTHER Jonathan. w Jl 13 1839-
CSmH 1842-D 23 1843
CoHi S 15 1848
CtHi My-S 1843
DLC D 14 1839;Ap 10,D 11 1841;Jl 4 1845;Jl 4 1846;Jl 4 1848;Mr 4,Jl 4 1849;My 29 1852;Jl 4 1853;Jl 4 1854;Mr 29,My 17-24,Je 24,Ag 23,S 6,27,O 25-N 1,15,29,D 13-20 1856;Ja 31-F 14, Mr 14,28,My 16-23,Je 13 1857;Ag 4-11 1860
ICHi N 23 1839;Jl 4 1845;Je 12 1852;Jl 4 1856; D 10 1859;D 21 1861
IHi Ja 14 1854
IU F 24,Ap 27,My 4 1844;N 15 1847
IaU Ja 1 1845
KHi F 8 1840
MB N 23-D 7 1839[Ja-D 12 1840]My 28 1842;Jl 4 1845;Ja 1 1846;Jl 4 1848;Jl 4 1850;N 22 1851; Jl 4 1854;S 13 1856;Jl 4 1858;Jl 4 1859
MH [Ag 10-N 23 1839]Je 19,Jl 3 1841;D 30 1843-Je 22 1844
MHi D 21 1839;Ja 1 1843;Ja 1 1846;Mr 4,Jl 4 1849
MNaHi Jl 4 1848
MWA [Ag 31-D 1839]-41;Ja 8,Ap 2,My 21 1842;Ja 1 1843;Ja 1,27 1844;Ja 1,Jl 4 1845;Ja 1,Jl 1846;Jl 4,D 25 1847-Ja 1,Jl 4,D 25 1848-Ja 1,Mr 4,D 25 1849-Ja 1,Jl 4,D 25 1850-Ja 1,Je 12,D 25 1852-Ja 1,22[My 28-D 24 1853;My 13 1854-55]F 23 1856-[57-58]D 25 1859-Ja 1,S 15,D 25 1860-Ja 1 1861
MiG O 10 1840;Jl 4 1848
MnHi Je 20 1840;Ap 17 1841
N Jl 4 1844;Jl 4 1846;Jl 4 1847;Mr 4 1849;Jl 4 1850;Jl 4 1851;Ja 1,Jl 4 1853;Ja 12 1856
NEh Ja 1 1846
NHuHi D 26 1840
NIC 1842;My-D 23 1843
NN N 23 1839;Ap 10,D 25 1841;Mr 26 1842;Ja 1 1844;Jl 4 1845;Jl 4 1848;Mr 4 1849
NNHi N 23 1839;S 12,O 10 1840;D 25 1841-Ap 1843;Ja 1,Jl 4 1845;Jl 4 1850;N 22 1851-[52]55-60[62]
NSalC Jl 4 1845
NcD [1840-41;46;49;53;55;57-61]
NcU F 7,My 2 1840
NhD Ap 24 1841;42
NjHi Mr 6 1841
OCHi Ag 10 1839;Mr 4 1849
PAtM Jl 4 1845
PDoHi D 25 1856;Ja 1 1857;Ap 16 1859
PPot Ja,Jl 1848;Ja 1849
PWCl [1842]
PWbW Jl 1845-53
PWcHi Je 12 1841;Jl 1847
RW [1843-Ja 1854]
T Jl 4 1848
TKL Je 25 1859
TU Je 16 1855
WHi Ap 4 1840;42-43;Ja 1,Jl 4 1845;Jl 4 1846; Jl 4 1848
—d ed *See* Evening tattler
—GREAT pictorial battle sheet, Christmas and New Year ed.
DLC 1845-46;48-50;52
ICHi D 1851
IG 1847-48;49-50
MiU 1842
N 1846-47;49-50;57-58
NHuHi 1852
NN 1847;55;60
NNHi 1848-49;56-57
NNMC 1853-54
NSalC 1845
NjO 1845-59
PDoHi 1856
V 1848-49

BRYAN democrat. w O 16 1898-Je 28 1900||
Suspended from O 23 1898-Ap 16,N 9 1899-Ap 5 1900
Campaign paper
DLC complete
NN 1898-[1900]

BUCCANEER. w Mr 13- 1842||
MWA My 8 1842
NSchU Ag 13 1842

New-York BULLETIN. w 1840?-D 25 1850||?
DLC Ap 2 1844
IU Ja 9 1844;Je 10 1845
MWA Ap 2 1844;D 25 1850
NNHi Mr 27 1850
WHi Ag 8 1843;Ja 9 1844

New York Sunday morning BULLETIN. w Mr 19 1843-
NNHi Mr 19 1843

New York monthly BULLETIN. m Mr 15 1846-
1846? as Monthly bulletin and New York general advertiser
MWA Mr 15,My 15 1846;Je 15 1847

Daily BULLETIN. 1865-74? *See* Daily commercial bulletin and auction record

New York BULLETIN. d Je 19 1924-
MWA Je 19 1924
NN Je-Jl 31 1924

BUNKER HILL. w Jl 27 1844-
MWA Ag 24,N 30 1844
PDoHi D 21 1844

BUSINESS reporter and merchants' and mechanics' advertiser. d F 12 1835-
MWA F 12 1835

CALIFORNIA herald. w? D 26 1848-
Title varies slightly
CU-B Ja 3 1852;Ja 5 1853
NN D 26 1848;Ja 8 1849;Ag 1850-N 1854;59; Ja-Je 1861;62
RPB D 26 1848
WHi Ja 16(extra)1849
—d ed *See* New York herald. 1835-1924

CALIFORNIAN. w,ir S 8 1855-
CSmH D 7 1855
CU-B S 8,20,D 7,22 1855;Ja 5 1856
MWA S 8 1855

Evening CALL. d O 25 1890-91||?
NN O 25 1890

New York CALL. d 1908-23 *See* New York leader

CAMPAIGN. w S 7-N 2 1844||
DLC complete
N O 5 1844

CAMPAIGN democrat. w 1856||?
IHi My 22 1856
MWA Ag 11,S 1 1856
PNoHi Ag 11 1856

CAMPAIGN express. w?
MiG N 2 1848

CAMPAIGN of freedom. w Ag 26-N 1848||?
Campaign paper
DLC Ag 26,S 2 1848
MWA Ag 26 1848
WHi S 16 1848

CAMPAIGN times. w 1852||?
NN Je 26-O 16 1852

CANFIELD'S American argus, commercial and exchange telegraph. w Je 1 1829-My 3 1830||?
DLC Je 1 1829
MWA Mr 8-22,Ap 12-My 3 1830
NNHi Je 1 1829

CARPATHO-RUSSIA. w,sw 1914-24||?
1914-Mr 16 1920 as Sfên otechestva
sw F 5 1919-N 1920?
In Russian
DLC N 13,27,D 11-25 1918
IU N 13 1918-N 2 1920

CARSON league. *See under* Albany

CASTIGATOR and New York anti-abolitionist. sw Ag 1835-
NNHi Ag ? 1835

New York CATHOLIC register. w 1839-D 1840||
United with Freeman's journal to form New York freeman's journal and Catholic register
MoSU Jl 16-D 24 1840

New York weekly CAUCASIAN. *See* New York weekly day book

CENSOR. d Ap 1838-
NNHi Ap 10-14 1838

CENTURY. w D 25 1858-61||?
Title varies slightly
DLC Mr 24 1860-Je 15 1861
ICHi 1858-Mr 17 1860
MB 1858-D 17 1859
MH 1858[59]-F 1860
MWA Ja 1,29,N 19 1859
N 1858-Mr 10 1860
NN 1858-Mr 17 1860
NNHi 1859;Mr 24 1860-Mr 4 1861
OHi Mr 24-S 13 1860
PPL 1858-Mr 17 1860
PToHi 1859[60]

CHAMPION of American labor. w Ap 3-Ag 14 1847||?
NNHi Ap-Ag 14 1847

CHINESE American. w F 3- 1883||?
In Chinese
DLC F 3 1883
N F 3-10 1883
NN F 3 1883
NNHi F 3 1883
WHi Mr 31 1883

CHINESE nationalist. d 1916?+
Suspended F 1-Mr 11 1931
In Chinese
NN Ja 21 1927+
NNHi My 9 1930
WaU D 7 1927+

CHINESE daily news. d
In Chinese
CtY F 1932-My 1933
M Je 8 1932
WHi F 21-22,Mr 7,13,16-28,30,Ap 27 1932

CHINESE reform news. sw,w 1904+?
sw 1904?-D 28 1918
In Chinese
IU Ag 22 1917-28
NN Mr 10 1904-My 10 1913

CHINESE republic news. w,d 1912?+
F 1-Mr 8 1932 as Chinese republic daily (d)
In Chinese
IU S 1917-My 2,N 29 1931+

CHINESE vanguard. w 1934?-Ag 17 1935||?
In Chinese
DLC Ja-Ag 17 1935

Morning CHRONICLE. d Mr 1 1827-
MWA Ap 12 1827
NNMC Mr 1 1827

NEW YORK (*Continued*)

NEW YORK CITY—*Continued*

Evening CHRONICLE. My-Jl 1837 *See* Evening herald

Morning CHRONICLE and New York penny-a line advertiser. d S 7 1842-Ja 30? 1843||?
1842-Ja 4 1843 as Morning chronicle
CtY N 22 1842
DLC S 15 1842;Ja 5 1843
MWA Ja 30 1843
NSchU S 19 1842

Morning CHRONICLE and Tippecanoe advertiser. d F 11 1840-41||?
1840? as Morning chronicle
DLC F 12 1840
MiU F 27 1840
NN F 11-Ap 28 1840
NNHi Mr 27 1840

CHRONICLE of the times. w Ap 5 1828-My 2 1829||?
DLC Jl 28 1828-My 2 1829
GMM [Jl 12 1828-Ja 10 1829]
MWA Ap 5-12,26-My 3,Je 7-14 1828
NNHi Ap 12 1828-My 2 1829
NjR O 4 1828

New-York CITIZEN. d N 27 1832-
DLC D 7 1832

New-York CITIZEN. w Ap? 1839-
DLC Jl 27 1839

Weekly CITIZEN. w Mr 9 1844-
MWA Mr 30,Ap 13-20 1844
NNHi My 25 1844

CITIZEN. w Ja 7 1854-
ICN Ja 14 1854-55
MB Ja-Jl 1 1854;Mr 1-8 1856
MsHi Ja-D 23 1854
N Ja-Jl 1 1854
NB 1854-55
NIC 1854
NN 1854-O 17 1857
NNHi 1854-56
NNIHi 1854-55
NcD [Ja-Jl 1854]Ag 11 1855
NjHi Ja 21 1854;56
OCl O 24-D 12 1857
P-M Mr 11,Ag 5 1854;Ap 28 1855
THi 1854
WHi Ja 14 1854-55

New York CITIZEN and American republican. *See* New York American republican

New York CITIZEN and round table. w Ag 13 1864-73||?
1864-F 25 1865 as Citizen; Mr 4 1865-Je? 1869 New York citizen
CtY Jl 10 1869-Ag 5 1871
DLC 1865-[68]Je 12 1869;Ag 12 1871-Ap 1872
MB [Jl 10 1869-Ja 18 1873]
MBAt F 25 1865
N D 10-17 1870;F 11,25,Mr 25 1871
NBHi Jl-D 1869
NCH Ag 14-N 1869;F 26-My 21 1870
NNHi 1864-Je 1865;N 12 1870-Mr 23 1872
WHi Je 17 1865;F 24-Mr 3 1866

CITIZEN of the world. w Mr 22? 1834-
MWA Mr 29 1835

Il CITTADINO. w 1910?-19||?
In Italian
IU [S 20 1917-Ag 28 1919]

Evening CITY gazette. w Mr? 1828-
Ct [1828]
DLC D 6 1828
MWA Jl 12 1828;Ap 4 1829
NNHi N 1 1828

New York CLARION. w S 8-D 15 1849||?
NNHi S-D 15 1849

CLAY tribune. w My 4-N 2 1844||
Campaign paper
DLC complete
MWA Je 1,Ag 24,O 5 1844
MiG My 4 1844
MoSM Jl 20 1844
N Jl 20 1844
NN complete
NNHi Je 1,Ag,S 14-21,O 1844
NcD Ag 17,31 1844

COLORED American. w Ja 7 1837-42||?
Ja-F 1837 as Weekly advocate
Also dated in Philadelphia, Pa.
Ct Je 29 1839;Ag 29,O 24 1840;Mr 13 1841
CtY Ja 19 1839
DLC Mr-Ap 1,15-22 1837;S 29-D 1838[39]My 30,Ag 15 1840
MB [Mr 1837-F 1841]
N Mr 18 1837
NIC Mr 1837-N 23 1839
NN N 17 1833
NNHi F 18,Mr 1837-38
NSchU D - 1841

COLUMBIAN. 1809-17 *See* New York evening journal and patron of industry

*COLUMBIAN, for the country. sw D 16 1809-Je 1821||?
Ap 1817-18 as New-York Columbian
MBAt Ja - 1821
MWA Mr 6 1821
NBHi 1821
NNHi Ja 9 1821

COMBINED New York morning newspapers. d S 19-26 1923||
Joint issues of morning newspapers during printers' strike. Holdings are listed under individual newspapers except where joint issues are the only holdings
CLM S 19 1923
CSmH S 19,22,24,26 1923
PHsHi S 23 1923

*New York COMMERCIAL. w,sw,d F 21 1815-D 31 1925||
1815-S 10 1816 as General shipping and commercial list; S 13 1816-S 9 1820 New-York shipping and commercial list; S 12 1820-23 Turner's New-York shipping and commercial list; 1824-25 Shipping and commercial list; 1826-Ja 10 1893 Shipping and commercial list and New York price current (S 1840-Mr 1849;Je 1868-74? Shipping and commercial list) Ja 11-F 28 1898 Commercial America and shipping and commercial list and New York price current; Mr 1 1898-O? 1902 New York commercial and shipping and commercial list and New York price current; N 1902-Je 1904 New York commercial and price current. United with New York journal of commerce and commercial bulletin to form Journal of commerce and commercial
sw 1815-94? (w Jl 21-Ag 11 1832) w 1895?-Ja 10? 1898
A Je 1907-08
CSmH My 1831-35;O 1839-43;50-56;Je 1857-My 1858
CaQMF 1864-65
CtY 1823-24;28-57;59-60;S 17 1870;Ja 18,Ap 26,My 6 1871
DA Jl 1913-26
DLC 1821-Je 1894;97-1926
IU Mr 1923-Je 1926
M Ja 22 1917
MB 1838-52;54-57;Je 1865-Ja 1869;O 13-N 17 1883[S-N 5 1884]
MH-BA Ag 21 1917-26
MHi [1855-75]
MWA 1824;Ja 8 1825;26-[67]F-Ap 22,N 14,D 1868-Mr 20 1869;Ja 4 1898
MiU [1824]-[30]33-34;46-48;51;54;58[59]61;63-64[75;82]-88[1901-02]05-12
MiU-C [1830-32;34;44]45[47-48]
MnU 1844;46-49[Ag 8 1907-Ap 6 1908]
NB N 5 1836-37
NBuG Mr 26 1864-Mr,Jl 1867-Ap 1872
NN 1821-Je 1894;Mr 9 1895;D 23 1909-26
NNHi 1821;24-88
NSchU Ja 23 1833
NcD 1828-29[31]-33;37;40;42-44[48]-[53]55-56;73;Jl 24 1915
NcU 1824-26
OC Ag 1844-45
OrU [1922-26]
PHi F 9 1825-38;40-50
PPL Ja 25 1851
RPB Mr 23 1838-57
TxU F 16-O 12 1908;Ja-Ap 17 1909
V Je 26 1830-D 23 1837;39-44;76
—evening ed *See* New York price current

*Weekly COMMERCIAL advertiser. sw,w O 4 1797-1879||?
Follows Herald; a gazette for the country (not in this list). 1797-1875? as New York spectator (-Mr 1867 New York spectator and semi-weekly commercial advertiser) 1876? Spectator and commercial advertiser
sw 1820-Mr 1867
CSmH S 7 1830
CaOTA S 28 1827
CoD Ja 17 1823-26;28;31-43
Ct D 24 1822-N 23 1824[25-27]Ag 23 1831
CtDe N 25,D 4 1833
CtHi 1823-34;Mr 31 1841-42
CtW 1845
CtY 1821-65
DLC 1821-[26]-[28-30;33;40;43]Ap 1848-49
ICHi N 1823-24;S 26 1833;Ap 12,Je 3,Jl 1,11,S 9,20,27,O 11,N 4,11 1834[Ja-N 1844:45-O 1848]-Ja 4,22 1849
KHi Mr 4 1861
MB 1821-Je 1 1824;D 13 1838[Ja 7-D 28 1839;Ja 6-D 13 1840]
MBAt Ja 9 1821;Ja 15,Ap 2 1822;O 10 1828-O 1831
MHi 1821-Ag 7 1837;S 11 1841
MWA My 9 1821-23;My 21 1824-My 24 1825;26-My 23 1828;O 1833-35;D 11 1837-[57-59]-F 20 1860
MWiC 1821-55
MeB Ag 12,19,My 10-O 1825
Mi S 28 1821;Je 27-D 1823;O 30 1829-30
MiU-C [1822-23;27-29;40]
MnHi Je 9 1826-Je 5 1827
N 1821-22;Mr 11 1823-Ag 27,O 5,N 5 1824[Ja-Je]Ag 23,S 2,9,16,O 7-10,D 9,16,30 1825;F 23,Mr 16,Ap 3-6,My 14-25[Je 1827-O 1828]D 1829-Jl 11 1832
NBHi Ja-F 22 1822;Jl 15 1828;30-32;34-43;45-47
NBu O 14 1823-24;26-My 11 1827
NBuG My 11 1848
NCH 1821-[31-38]43-44[O 11 1845-47;49-56]N 1858-[59]
NCIM Mr 30 1840-41
NFre Mr 9 1821
NHuHi O 10(extra)1828
NN 1821-25;27-32;Ap 18,Je 17-20,Jl 22,S 2,30-D 4,12 1833[34-35]Ap 4,25,S 15,26 1836;Ja 27,Jl 24,30 1837[38]S 9 1840;Je 9,19 1841;O 5 1848;Ap 4 1864;67-69
NNHi 1821-65
NNS S 14,25 1822-My 6,11,Jl 14,Ag 21 1825
NPalC [Ja 21 1839-F 8 1845;64;S 16 1866-Ap 13 1876]
NSchU O 8 1824-O 4 1831;Mr 2,30,My 11 1842
NSm Ap 14 1836
NcD [1826;50]
NhD Ja 15-Mr 2,19,30-Ap 3,10-13,My 2,18,Je 12,Jl 3,14 1821[22-N 1825;26-N 1827;F-Je 1828]F 3 1829;Mr 6,Ap 23,D 14 1830 Ja 25,Ap 1,Ag 26,O 28 1831[F 13 1832-N 1833]Ja 13-20,27-30,F 6-20,Mr 6-14,20-24,31-Ap 3,23,Je 3,10,Jl 24,D 4 1834;Ja 14,19,1835;Ja 25,D 15 1836;Ja 13,My 20 1837;Ag 19,20,S 5 1839;Ap 20,27,My 18-21,Je 1,Jl 13,30 1840;Jl 6 1844;Ag 24-28,O 16,N 22 1849
NjHi 1821-Je 18 1828
NjR 1833-36
P-M [1832-36;38-39]
PAtM N 6 1829
PHi Mr 1826-27
PNoHi D 3,31 1824
PToHi N 6 1829
PWbW [1832-35]Mr 6 1841
RPB 1821-22;S 7 1830;Ap 4,Ag 22,O 31 1833;F 24 1834;Ap 27 1837;F 5 1838;My 7,21-25,Je 11,29 1842
TxU My 16 1823-My 18 1824;My 24 1825-My 16 1826;My 27-D 16 1828;22-Je 1833;N 20 1834-N 1835
Vt 1821-22
VtBr D 23 1823-Mr 1,Ap 29-Je 17,Ag 18,N 25 1825[26]27;Ap 3-7 1829
VtMiM [Ag 26 1843-Ap 25 1850]
VtU 1840-43
WHi [N 18 1823-Mr 7]My 12 1826-Ag 22 1828;Ag 11 1829-Ap 1863

COMMERCIAL advertiser. d *See* Globe and commercial advertiser

Daily COMMERCIAL bulletin and auction record. d 1865-Je 10 1893||
1865-69? as Daily bulletin; 1869?-74? New York daily bulletin; 1875?-79? New York daily bulletin and auction record. United with New York journal of commerce to form New York journal of commerce and commercial bulletin, later Journal of commerce and commercial
DLC Jl 12 1867-F 27 1868;Mr 28 1870;81;Jl-D 1882;Jl-D 1883;N 1888-93
GU D 11 1872
KHi Je 2 1884
MWA Je 17,S 5 1867;Ja 2 1868;My 19 1870;Ag 25,S 8 1871;My 15 1872;N 12 1873;79-[Jl 1884-Je 1885]-Ag 1888;F 18,Mr 11-Jl,D 28 1889-92;My-Je 1893
NBHi 1882-85
NN Mr 14-27,30-My 12,14-Jl 21 1885[My-Je,N 1885]-Ap 1887
NNHi F 1889-Mr 17 1890
NhD Je 9,11 1879;My 26 1880;Je 29,Jl 6 1881
PHi My 23 1876-Je 1878;Ja-Je 1879

New York COMMERCIAL gazette. w N 29? 1840-
MiU Je 8 1841
NSchU Mr 22-Ap 12 1842

COMMERCIAL register and spirit of '76. d *See* Spirit of '76

New York COMMERCIAL times. w S 18 1858-
MWA D 25 1858;Ja 8-22,F 12-Ap 16,30-My,Je 18-Ag 10 1859
WHi Ja 5-15,F 12-26,Ap 16,My 14 1859

COMMONWEALTH weekly. w Ap 30? 1910-
NN My 28,D 17 1910;F 25,Mr 4,18-Ap 1,15,My 20,27-Je 3 1911;12-O D 1914-Ap 7,21,Je 2 1915;Mr 22,My 16,Ag 26 1916;17-Ap 14,D 29 1920-21;F 21-28,Mr 14,28,My 30,Je 30,Jl 18,Ag 1,15,29-S 6 1923

CONSTELLATION. w N 21 1829-Ag 2 1834||?
N 9- 1833? as New York atlas and constellation; My 17-Jl 5 1834 Constellation, with which the Merchant's intelligencer is incorporated
CSmH S 11 1830
CoHi Ja 8 1831
Ct Ja 2,N 29 1831[32]
CtY [1830]Ag 20 1831-Je 23 1832;N 9 1833
DLC N 28 1829;Ja 16-23 1830;My 14 1831[Ap-Jl 1832]-S 7 1833
MB N 20 1830-Ap 7 1832
MH N 20 1830-Ja 1832
N 1831-32;N 9 1833
NN N 21 1829-33
NNHi N 21 1829-[32-33]My 17-Ag 2 1834
P-M D 3 1831
WHi Ap 27 1833

CONSTELLATION. Illuminated quadruple sheet. Jl 4 1859||
Ct complete
CtDe complete
CtNcH complete
DLC complete
IP complete
MWA complete
MiU complete
N complete
NFre complete
NIC complete
NN complete
NNHi complete
NNMC complete
PPFfHi complete
RW complete
WHi complete

CONSTITUTION. d My 18?-O 31 1834||?
My-Ag? as American whig
DLC My 21,S 20,O 7-18,21-23,27,29-31 1834
MWA My 21 1834

Daily CONTINENT. d F 1-Je 7 1891||
Follows New York star. Followed by Morning advertiser
DLC complete
MWA F 1-2 1891
NBHi complete
NN complete

CONTINENTAL. w 1847?-49||?
NNHi Je 2,23,Jl 21 1849

El CONTINENTAL. w 1861?-
In Spanish
MH Ag 4-D 22 1862;Ja-F 21 1863

New York COPPERHEAD. w My 16 1863-
CLM Je 13 1863
CtY Je 27 1863
DLC My 23 1863
KHi Je 13 1863
MBAt Je 27 1863
MWA My 23 1863
NN My 16,30-Je 20,Jl 11-25 1863

CORAM'S champion. sw Jl 4 1826-
DLC Jl 4,Ag 26,O 7 1826
MWA Jl 4-26,Ag 2,9-12,19,26,S 6,20-O 11 1826

NEW YORK (*Continued*)

NEW YORK CITY—*Continued*

CORRIERE d'America. d D 27 1922+
In Italian
pub 1922+
ICU D 27 1922-O 27 1926
IU D 16 1925+
NNPro 1923+
PP 1934+

CORRIERE della sera. d -1933‖?
In Italian
NNPro 1932-33

CORRIERE Siciliano. w Mr 7 1931+
In Italian
pub 1931+

Il CORRIERE tirolese. sw 1915-My 4 1918‖
In Italian
1915-Mr 1917 pub in Mt. Carmel, Pa.
NN F 7 1917-18

CORSAIR. d Ap? 1840-
DLC My 26 1840

New York COURIER. w Mr 20 1825-26‖?
"First Sunday newspaper printed in N.Y."
CtY [1826]
MWA Mr 20 1825(photostat)
N Mr 20 1825
NN Mr 20 1825(photostat)
NNHi Mr 20 1825(photostat)
WHi Ap 3 1825

Sunday COURIER. w F 5 1848-80‖?
1855?-76? as New York courier
Ct F 8 1857
DLC F 18-25 1866;Jl 14 1867
InI My 19 1866-69
MWA D 31 1848;Ap 25 1852;S 30 1855;F 20 1859;F 12 1860;Jl 16 1876;Je 20 1880
NNHi Jl 29 1849;Ap 11 1852;F 6-13,Mr 6-20,Ap 10-My 15,29 1859
OClWHi Ja-Ap 13 1861
P-M Je 26 1858

New York Saturday COURIER. w Ja 13 1855-
MWA [Mr 17-O 20 1855]Ja 19,F 23,Je 14-21,S 6 1856

Morning COURIER and New York enquirer. d My 3 1827-Je 29 1861‖
1827-My 23 1829 as Morning courier. United with World to form World, morning courier and New York inquirer, later World
CSmH Je 15 1829
Ct [1827;29]Jl 5 1831
CtSp Mr 1 1838;S 12,O 1 1840[41;43-44]
DLC Ja 12 1828;29-30;Ja 8(supp)Mr 4,8,11 1831;32-33;S 22 1834-36;Ag 17 1837;Jl 4 1838-Je 18,D 7 1840;41-45;Mr 23,Jl 7 1847-Je 21 1848;Mr 8 1849-Ja 1 1853;Ja-Je 1854;Jl-D 1855;Ag 1856-61
GAtCo S 23 1838
IP [1831]
MB O 1 1830;Ap 18-D 1831;Ja 11 1833[F 19-My 13 1836]D 12,19,22 1837;Ja 3-Je 7 1853
MBAt Jl 6 1829;Ja 5 1831;Ja 1 1851
MWA D 5,29 1827;Ja 3,5,8-9,11,15,S 24,O 15-20,N 13,D 19 1828;My 26,S 16 1829;Mr 8,Ap 23,S 6,N 26 1830;Ja 17,Mr 18-19,Jl 25,O 12,N 9 1831;Ag 6,D 10 1832;Ja 1,Jl 1833-My,Je 23,Jl 7-8 1834;Mr 12,My 27 1835;Ap 10,My 6-7,27 1836;Ja 28,O 3 1837;Jl 15 1840;Ap 6 1844;Mr 30,N 16 1847;Ja 1 1851;Ja 1,Jl 2,26 1852;Ja 1,F 5 1853;Ja 31 1856;F 22 1860;Je 29 1861
supps:F 20 1830;Ja 8,F 5 1831;Ja 4 1853;F 3 1857
MiU O 14 1841
N My 8(supp)1830;Ag 26(extra)1832;O 31 1833;Mr 25 1834[Je 1835-47]
NBHi D 9(extra)1829;S 27 1831;33;36-53
NBu 1830-Ag 21 1832
NN S 1-6,10-18,28-D 12,14 1827-S 8,O 1828-My 23 1829[30]-61
NNHi My-Ag 1827;N 1828-29;D 1 1830;Ag 6 1835;Ap 1837-S 13 1839;My 1843-Mr 1846;F 7 1851;58-Je 1859;Jl 1860-61
NNMC My 24 1831
NNMT 1833;36-45;47-49;56-Je,Ag 1860-61
NNS My 1829-Je 1846
NNUnC D 21 1835
NSchU Ap 30 1827;Ap 19 1828;37-Mr 15 1838
NT [1834-N 24 1836]
NcD [1832-34;57-59]
NhD [1830-53]
NjHi Ap 14,My 8,Je 11,N 25-26 1828;36-Mr 1837
NjR [1834;36-37;43]
OCHi Jl 8 1831
P-M O 21 1831;Ag 29 1832
PBL Ap 1839-O 11 1844
PEL Ja 16 1832-Ap 19 1833
PMilA O 11 1830
PP My 5 1831[38-39]My 5,S 21 1840;My 12,Jl 14,Ag 10,13-14 1841
PPM Ja 12-Mr 17 1838
RW F 24 1837;Ja 1 1838
VtMoC My 22 1828-D 17 1830
WHi My 18 1827

Semi-weekly COURIER and New York enquirer. sw 1827-Je 1861‖
1827?-My 23? 1829 as Morning courier; My 26 1829-F 8 1842 Morning courier and New York enquirer, for the country
CtY Ja 1-8,15-25 1833;S 15,N 13,24,D 1-11,22 1835-Je 9 1836[Ja-S 1837;Ja,Mr-N 1838;39-40]
DLC Je 2 1829;Je 10 1834;Ag 14-28,O 5,12,19,N 9 1844
IP My 29-D 1829
MBAt Mr 2 1830;O 26 1832
MHi N 28 1827-Mr 1830
MWA My 22,N 30 1827;F 5,16,D 9 1828;My 29 1829-D 10 1830;My 18 1832;F 18,Je 10 1834;N 14 1837-F 16,N 2 1838;My 17 1843;F 19 1845-My 1,15,26-Je 5 1847;Ap 28,D 1 1849;D 13 1851;Mr 20 1852;S 6 1854;Mr 31 1860
MeBt Je 1829-30
MiU-C O 21 1827
N Je 2,O 18 1839[My 7-O 4 1845]O 7 1848-Ag 7 1852
NN [1827;Je-D 1829;F-O 1830;Mr 1831-32]33;Ja 9 1835;O 4-22,29 1839-42;Ap 1843-Mr 1844;51-56
NNHi Mr 2,17,Ag 3 1829;My 3,13,Je 14,Jl 8,Ag 5,S 16,N 15,D 13,23 1831;S 8 1837;F 12,26-Mr 26 1853
NcD D 11 1829;Ag 2 1831; D 11 1832
NcU Ag 12,S 2,N 11 1854;Ja 5 1855
OCHi D 10-17 1845;N 17-20,D 25 1847;Ja 1-5,Mr 11 1848-Je 1861
OClWHi Je 21-24,Ag 5,16 1831;Ag 1838-F 1 1839;Mr 14 1844;My 13 1861
P Je 6 1829-S 10 1830
VRC O 9 1852
WHi 1830-Mr 1831

Weekly COURIER and New-York enquirer. w Ja 28 1832-
DLC F 23 1833
IHi D 22 1832;Ag 24 1833
MWA Ja 28,Ap 21,My 19,Ag 18,S 1,22-O 20,N 10 1832;Je 22 1833;F 21 1835;O 28 1837;Mr 16,My 4 1839
N Ja 28 1832;Mr-N 1836;Ag 12 1837;Ap 14 1838
NN 1833-34;N 18 1837-Mr 1839;Ap 10 1841-Mr 25 1843
NhD D 1832-Je,D 1834-Je 1835
OClWHi N 7 1835;My 14-S 1836;Ag 31 1844
OHi Ag 9 1833-35
PAtM Je 1 1833
PBro D 12 1846
PW Jl 7 1832

COURRIER des États-Unis. w,sw,tw,d Mr 1 1828+
sw N 18 1829-N 9 1839;tw N 12 1839-Je 10 1851;d Je 1 1851-Je 3 1932
In French
pub 1828+
C 1889+
CLM Jl 12,26 1837
CSmH N 21 1829
CSt 1898-99;1934+
CSt-H [1887-91]
CU [1915;17]
CaM 1885-87
CaQME 1928+
CaQMF 1842-72
CaQMSm 1838-59
CoAT My 1933+
Ct Ag 17 1833
CtHT [Ag 1846-Ap 1847]
CtW [1919;21]-[24]
CtY [1828]30-31[44-46]
DGU 1828-Ja 12 1831
DLC 1828-F 1833;S 19 1835-Ap 19 1837;Je 22,N 9 1839-N 1851;52-N 1863;64-71;98+
GMM Mr 1851-Je 1 1852
IAC My 14 1933-D 2 1934
IC Ja-Je 1873
ICHi 1828-F 26 1842;Jl 6,10-11,15-16 1861;62-67;69-70;75-80
ICU Ja 28 1835-F 1841;42-F 1848;Mr 1849-[52]53[Je 13-D 1854]-Je 1855
IEN [1838]-[40]D 20 1856-Jl 25 1857
IHi S 20 1834
KHi Ja 7 1879[Ag 1888-F 1918]Mr 13,21 1925
LNA O-N 18 1852
LNH 1828;Mr 4 1841-F 1843;N 19 1844-N 1846;Mr 1848-F 25 1850;62-68;71-72;74;76-Je 18,Jl 27-D 3 1882;1924+
LNM Mr 1843-F 1848
M D 8,11 1929
MB [1846-F 1848;S 1850-F 1851]
MHi Jl 1828-Jl 25 1829;Ap 18 1835;N 5 1863;F 18-19 1864;Jl 26 1867;Ag 31,S 2-17 1869[S 1871]Je 5 1875
MNS [O 1927-Je 1932]
MWA 1828-86;1925+
MdBE 1886-1903
MdBP 1828-86
MeBa S 28,O 21 1916;D 22 1917;F 3 1918
MeWC Mr-Jl 5 1834
MiU 1828-[30;41-43]-[47;63]-[65]O 6 1917
MnU N 1851-N 1852
MoKS 1933+
MoS Mr 1839-F 1840;Mr 1841-Jl 20 1855;57;Je 30-D 1866
MoSU Mr 30 1841-Ag 8 1843
MoScR 1864-67
N 1828-F 1829;Jl 24-S 18 1830;45:63[Ja-Ap 1864]
NAlU 1933+
NCH O 30 1928-Ja 23 1929
NN 1828-29;Mr 1838-F,My 29 1839-48;Mr 1849-52;64+
NNCC 1828-F 1838
NNHi 1828-Ja 4,Mr 1832-F 1833;Jl 12 1837-Mr 1838;D 1841-42;Mr 10 1846-F 1847;S 1848-F,S 1849-52;F 1853-Je 1858;N 1860-Je 1861;Jl 1862-[Jl-N 1866]-67
NSW O 15 1933+
NcD 1828-[30-31]-[33;40;44;47-52]54;Jl 1855-Ja 17 1856
NjR [1923]-[34-35]+
OC Mr 1848-Ap 1852;N 1874-Je 1882
OO [1875-78;1913;15-18]-[21-22;25]
OkU [1933]+
P-M My 1830
PHi 1828-36
PP D 29 1860-Ja 5,26-F 2 1861;Jl 26 1896;D 25 1915;O 14 1916[28]+
PPL D 29 1860;Ja 5,26,F 2 1861
PPM Mr 1828-[33;39]-F 1848
THi 1828-F 1829;S 1830-O 1831
TU Je 17 1934;Mr 10-17 1935
Tx D 8,22 1860
TxGR My 2 1926;N 17 1929;My 1933+
TxU Mr 1840-F 1841;Mr 1842-F 1844;Mr 1845-F 1846;S 1848-F,S 1849-F 24 1851;Jl-D 1933
VHi D 30 1915
VRC Ag 17 1867;Mr 27 1869
VU [1848-49]-55;Mr 1-9,11-Je 3 1932
WHi Mr 1831-F 1832[43]44;My 1845-My 1846;Mr-D 1847;S 1867-O 1871

—Edition speciale pour l'Europe. ir
LNH 1862-69

—Editions des steamers.
CSmH Ag 25(supp)S 1 1860

COURRIER des États-Unis. Éd. hebdomadaire. w Je 21 1851-Je 11 1932‖?
In French
LNH Je-D 2 1885;1929-Je 11 1932
MB Je 29 1851-73;76
MWA 1852-Ap 1 1854;Je 26 1858;Jl 30 1859;Je 30 1860;F 8,Ag 16-23,O 4,25,N 15 1862;Ja 10,31-Mr 21 1863;My 1865-66;F-My 25,Ag 3 1867;D 26 1868;Ag 28(supp)1869;F 12 1870;My 16,Je 20-Ag 1874;F 9(supp)1878;86-95;Ja 1924
N [F 13-S 11 1853]
NBuG D 30 1915;O 7 1916
WHi 1851-Je 1855

CRISIS. tw Mr 20? 1834-
DLC Mr 27 1834

La CRÓNICA. *See* El Cronista

El CRONISTA. tw,sw 1848-77‖?
1848-My 1867 as La Crónica
tw 1848-Ja 1853
In Spanish
CU-B O 27 1850
DLC Ja 27 1849-Jl 20 1850;N 1851-54;Mr 1856-D 12 1859;D 16 1860-64;Ja 11 1866-67
MB S 5-12 1849;Ap 1850-Jl 1854[57-D 15 1858]Ag 10 1861
MWA N 20 1862;F 11,Mr 28,Ap 15 1863
NcD My 30 1849

CULTURA obrera. w
In Spanish
NNC D 7-14 1912;Je 11 1913-O 13 1917

Al-DALIL. *See* Guide

DAWN. d Ap 21- 1885‖?
NN Ap 21 1885

DAY. d O 26 1886-
MWA O 28 1886
NN O 26 1886

DAY. (Der Tog) d N 5 1914+
Mr 1 1919-F 3 1922 as Day and the Warheit
In Yiddish and English
pub 1914+
IU 1918-My 9 1927
MWA N 9 1915
NN 1914+
PPDa 1914-34
PPiHi Ja 18 1932+
WHi Ja 22-23,Mr 21 1916+

DAY. 1922-26 *See* Den

Evening DAY-BOOK. d Ja 3 1848-S 24 1861‖
Title varies slightly
DLC Mr 9 1860;S 24 1861
MWA Je 21 1851[52]-Ja 20 1853;My 8,Je 1,N 15 1855;Jl 11,15 1856;My 21 1857;Ap 29,Mr 4,31-Je 1,Ag 17,S 14 1861
NN Ja 19-D 24 1852;Ja-N 1856;57;Ap 1858-O 1860;Ja-Ag 1861
NNHi D 4-20,22,26-30 1848;Ja 5-6,10-13,16-17,22-26,29-30,F 2,9,13,27-Mr 1,3,5,7 1849
NSyU S 15,24,O 10,D 20 1860;My 17,31,Jl 27,Ag 17 1861
NhD Mr 15,17,20-22,Ap 23,My 5,9,17,Je 9 1851
NjP Jl-S 1861
OCHi Ag 20 1861

—campaign ed *See* New York unionist

New York weekly DAY BOOK. w 1848?-79‖?
1848?-S 1861 as Weekly day book; O 5 1861-O 3 1863 New York weekly Caucasian; O 10 1863-My 1868 New York weekly day book. Caucasian
CaOTA Je 23-30,O 6 1855
CtY Ja-Jl 1 1848
DLC Ap 12 1856-Ap 3,D 4 1858;Ja 8,Mr 12 1859;F 9,Ap 6,O 1861;S 20 1862;Ja 24,O 24-N 14,D 1863;Ja 9-F,Mr 26,Ap 9-16,30,My 21-28,Je 25 1864-Ap,My 27 1865;Ja 26 1867;F 4 1871;N 30 1872
GU D 8 1866;Ja 22,F 2 1867
IHi [Jl 30 1864-O 19 1867]
IU D 5-12 1863;S 23,N 11 1865;Ja 20 1866
IaDH O 18 1850
IaHi Ja 20 1877-F 1878
In 1865
KHi Je 1856-N 13 1858;Jl 12 1862
LNC Ag 29 1863
LNH O 29 1859;Mr 7 1863;O 22 1864;Ap 15 1865
LSfD Ap 11 1863
MWA Ag 28 1852[Mr 26-D 1853]N 18-25,D 16 1854-Ja 6,My 12 1855-N 1856;Ja-Ap,My 16,Jl 18,Ag 1-8,N 7 1857[58;F 18-My]Jl 1860-Ap,O 12 1861-S 5,O 1863-S 20 1865;O 1866-S,D 18 1869;Mr 23 1872;Ja 3-18,Je 7 1873
MiU-C N 22 1856
MnHi S 27 1862
MsHi N 10-24 1860;Ja 5 1861
N O 18 1856;F 28,Mr 14,Jl 25,Ag 1-8 1863;Ja 2-9,23,F 20,Mr 12-19,Ap 2,My 7-14 1864;Je 1 1867;Jl 4 1868;N 13 1869;70-71;F 1 1873
NN Ag 14 1858;O 1861-S 1867
NNHi F 7 1857;N 15 1862
NNMC Ag 9 1862
NSyU Je 28,Jl 12 1862;S 17-24,N 26,D 17 1864
NbHi F 7 1863;Jl 24 1869;N 19 1870;N 16,D 7 1872;Ja 25,My 17-24,Ag 30 1873;Ja 3 1874;Ja 13,F 10 1877;Mr 2,D 25 1878;Ja 8-15,F 12-19 1879
NcD Jl 4 1863;Je 15 1867[Je 1868-F 1873]Je 2 1877
NcU F 11,25,Mr 31,Ag 25-S 1 1860;D 1 1866
NjP 1861-70
NjR N 11 1871;Ag 2 1878
OHi Ap 4 1857
P O 1861-S 1862
PBf Jl 27,N 23 1861
PNoHi Ag 17 1861
PMe O 20 1866
PPL Ja 26 1856
PPiHi My 7,21-Je 11,Jl 23-S 10 1859;S 8 1860;Je 8,Ag 10 1861[Ja 25-Ag 1862;64]-[67]-Ja 1,22,Ag 1870-Ja 14;28-Mr 4,18,Ap 8-Jl 1871
PWCl F 1,Jl 5,19,Ag 2 1862[63-65]Mr 3,24-Ap 7,21-28 1866

NEW YORK (*Continued*)

NEW YORK CITY—*Continued*

New York weekly DAY BOOK.—*Continued*
V O 1861-63
VRC Ag 8 1863
VU N 24 1866-67;Ja 25,Mr 21-Ap 4,9,23,Je,20-Jl 18,Ag-N 14,28 1868-S 11,O 30-N 20,D 1869-Ja 6,20-F 3,Mr 10-Ap 21,My 12 1877
WHi Je 9,N 10 1852;Je 27 1855[My 12 1860-D 10 1864]O 1865-D 4 1869;N 30 1872-Ag 9 1873[My 1873-O 14 1876]

DAY'S New York bank note list, counterfeit detector and price current. w,sm O 1826?-59||?
Title varies: New York bank note list and counterfeit detector
CSmH Ag 16 1830
MiU My 2 1837
NNHi Ap 20 1836
P Jl 4 1828;Je 15 1830
RW Ap 10 1840

DEMOCRAT. d,sw Mr 9-N 26 1836||?
Suspended from S 5-10 1836
d Mr 9-S 5 1836
Ct Ap 13-14 1836
NN Mr-My 21,S 5-O 8,15-N 26 1836
NNHi O 19 1836

New York DEMOCRAT. d Ja 7? 1841-
DLC Ja 8 1841

New York DEMOCRAT. d Ag 15 1868-71||?
Title varies slightly
MWA Ag 19 1868;My 19 1869
N My 1 1871
NN Ag 17-19,21,28,S 2,5,12,15-16,19,O 9,13 1868;Ja 3-11,13-My 13 1871
WHi 1868-Ag 14 1869

DEMOCRAT thunder. w Ag 26- 1868||?
Campaign paper
NNHi Ag 26-S 2 1868

El DEMOCRATA. d My? 1870-
In Spanish
CtY S 9-D 20 1870

DEMOCRATIC advance. w 1882-86||?
KHi Jl 8 1882
NN 1882

DEMOCRATIC chronicle. d Mr 8-Ap 28 1834||?
DLC Mr 14 1834
MWA Ap 16-17,24-28 1834
N Mr 24 1834
NNHi Ap 5-12 1834

DEMOCRATIC press. d S 7-N 14 1840||
DLC S 9 1840
MWA S 19-N 14 1840
MnHi O 26 1840
NN S 29,O 3,7,12,14,16 1840
NjR O 10 1840

Weekly DEMOCRATIC press. w S 19-N 14 1840||
NN O 17 1840

New York DEMOCRATIC republican. w Ag 14 1830-31||?
CSmH Ag 28 1830
Ct [1830-Je 1 1831]
MWA Ag 28 1830
NNHi Ja 1 1831

DEMOCRATIC republican new era. d O 3 1836-42||?
1836-Ap 18 1839 as New era
Ct N 25 1836
CtY Mr 25 1839
DLC My 25,O 30,D 13 1839;N 2,D 5 1840;41-Ag 1 1842
IU F 27 1840
IaDH O 24 1840
MWA Jl 31 S 6 1837;My 26,N 27 1838;Jl 27,D 17 1839;My 21 1840;Ap 10,Je 29 1841;My 28(extra)Je 18 1842
N Jl 1 1837;Mr 7 1840
NN D 9 1836[Ja-Ap,O-N 1837;Je-Ag,N 1838]O 28 1839
NNHi O 3,D 8 1836;Ja-Je 1840
NSchU Je 21 1842
NjR N 18 1839

Weekly DEMOCRATIC republican new era and American courier. w F 18 1837-42||?
1837-Ap 13 1839 as New era and American courier
DLC Mr 11 1837
IU Je 12 1841
NN Mr 9-S 21,O 25-N 2 1839;Ja 25,F 29,Ap 18-25,Je 6-13,S 19 1840
RPB My 28 1842

Wöchentlicher New Yorker DEMOKRAT. w 1845-76 *See* New Yorker zeitung

New Yorker DEMOKRAT. d 1857-76 *See* New Yorker herold. Morgenblatt

DEMOKRATISCHER volks-freund. w? My 8 1841-
In German and English
DLC My 8 1841

DEN (Day). d D 30 1922-26||?
In Carpatho-Russian
IU D 30 1922;Ja 13 1923-F 5 1926

New Yorský DENNÍK. d S 3 1913+
In Czechoslovakian
pub 1913+
M Ap 5 1930
NN D 31 1930+

Ha-DEROR. w S 1-D 22 1911||
In Hebrew
DLC complete
NN complete
NNJ complete
PPD [1911]

DEUTSCHE schnellpost für Europäische zustände, öffentliches und sociales leben Deutschlands. sw Ja 4 1843-
In German
MWA Mr 22 1849
NNHi 1843-Jl 26 1845
extra:Ap 12 1845
OCHi [S 16 1843-45]
extras:D 25 1845;D 19 1849

Wochenblatt der DEUTSCHEN schnellpost. w F 7? 1845-
OCHi Ap 10,N 27,D 11 1845-47;Ja 13,Mr 1848-49

DEUTSCHES journal. d 1890-Ap 21 1918||
1890-Ag 14 1912 as Morgen-journal; Ag 15-O 16 1912 Deutsches morgen-journal
In German
CtY F 20 1896
DLC 1895-97
IU My 1913-18
KHi My 28 1839
NN Ja 1 1900;Ja 1 1901;F 1911-Ja,F 21 1916-Ja,N 18 1917-18
PScrHi Je 20 1909

DEUTSCHES morgen-journal. *See* Deutsches journal

DIAL. d 1884-85||?
NN Mr 17 1884-Mr 25 1885

DIARY. . . *See* Mercantile advertiser

DICKSON'S uptown weekly. w 1883-1900||?
NNHi Ap 7-14,S 22 1888;Ja 5,Je 15 1889[92-93]-[96]-98

Morning DISPATCH. d Ap 13 1839-F 1840||
United with Evening tattler to form Dispatch and tattler, later Evening tattler
CtY Ap-O 12 1839
MWA My 27 1839;Ja 1 1840
NN Ap-S 20 1839
NcD Ja 22 1840

Weekly DISPATCH. w Ap 20 1839-F 15 1840||
Merged with Brother Jonathan
CoG complete
DLC Jl 13 1839-F 8 1840
MWA Je 22,Jl 20 1839
WHi complete

New York DISPATCH. w D 7 1845-99||?
1845-My 1854 as Sunday dispatch (1852? Penny weekly dispatch)
DLC 1845-N 15 1857;N 19 1859-O 9 1887;My 16,Jl 4 1897
KHi My 17 1896-Ap 1899
MB Je 13-Ag 1869
MWA S 26 1847;F 10,24 1850;F 7,Mr 20,Ag 21 1852;Jl 2,O 15 1854;Ap 29,Jl 1,Ag 12,S 16 1855;Mr 9,S 14 1856;F 15,My 31,O 10 1857;F 14,My 23 1858;Ap 27,D 1 1861;O 23 1864; Ap 16 1865;Mr 15 1868;Je 25 1871
N F 6 1848;Jl 24,O 23,D 11,25 1864;Ja 8 1865;S 2 1883
NBuG Mr 22-My 17,Jl 12,O 17-24,N 21 1857;Mr 8 1860
NN 1864-70
NNHi Ap 11,Je-N 13 1852
NcD Mr 25,S 30-O 7 1855;My 25 1856;F 24 1884;F 14 1897
NhD F 14 1858
OClWHi Mr 25 1866
TxGR F 24 1878
VU My 22 1852
WHi F 15 1857

Daily DISPATCH. d N? 1849-
OClWHi D 21 1849

DISPATCH and tattler. *See* Evening tattler

Ha-DOAR. d N 1 1921-O 19 1923||
In Hebrew
DLC complete

DOLLAR express. *See* New-York weekly express

DOLLAR weekly. w N 27 1841-44||?
MWA Ap 16,D 10 1842
N D 10 1842
NN Jl 23 1842
NhD D 10 1842
NjPa 1841-N 19 1842
OC Ja 22 1842

DOLLAR weekly herald. w S 4 1849-
NN S 10,24-D 17,31 1849
—d ed *See* New York herald 1834-1924

DOLLAR weekly sun. *See* Weekly sun

DOLLAR weekly true sun. w 1847||?
NNHi Ag 28 1847
—d ed *See* True sun

DOW JONES letters. *See* Wall Street journal [Evening ed]

EAGLE. d S? 1834-
DLC O 13 1834
N O 17 1834
NNHi S 30 1834

EAGLE. bw Ja 5- 1848||?
MWA Ja 19,F 16 1848

EAGLE. 1914-20 *See* Syrian eagle (Brooklyn)

EAST BRONX herald. sw,w Mr 21 1935+
Follows Pelham Bay herald
NNHu [1935]+

EAST SIDE news. w My 3 1930+
pub 1930+

New York ECHO and spirit of the age. w S 14 1833-
MWA S 14-21 1833

L'ECO d'Italia. w,sw,d 1849-94||?
w 1849-65? sw 1866?-81?
In Italian
DLC Ja-[C-D]1857-Ja 9 1858[59]D 3 1863;Ja-Mr 3,Je 11 1864[65]-S 1866;F 9 1867-[F-My] N,D 22 1869-D 14 1870[71]Ja 20 1872-D 5 1874;F-My 12,Je 20-30 1875;76-D 11 1878[79;81]
KHi [Jl 18 1888-F 20 1889]
ME F 8 1851-F 1852
MEAt Ap 22 1865
MWA Je 18,Jl 9,O 1853-O 28 1854

L'ECO d'Italia. w 1883+
1883-97? as Rivista italo-americana; 1898?-1905? L'Eco d'Italia; rivista italo-americana
In Italian
IU D 13 1917-Ja 1924
MWA D 31 1892;O 11 1917

Uj ELŐRE. *See under* Cleveland, Ohio

ELY'S hawk and buzzard. . . *See* Spy, and New York and Brooklyn Saturday courier and enquirer

EMANCIPATOR. *See* Emancipator and republican, Boston, Mass

Az EMBER. w
In Hungarian
PPiHi [S 20 1926-Jl 18 1931]

EMERALD. . . *See* Globe and emerald. . .

EMIGRANT. w Ja 9 1833-S 23 1835||
United with Old countryman to form Emigrant and old countryman, later Old countryman
CSto 1833;35
CtW [1833-Jl 1834]
CtY F 20 1833
DLC Ja 16-23,Ap 3-17,My-S 4,18-O 16,N 1833;S 10 1834-35
MWA Jl 23 1834
MdBG Ap 16,Je 4,O 15 1834

EMIGRANT. sw *See* Al-Mohajer

EMIGRANT and Old countryman. *See* Old countryman

EMPIRE state. w -Jl 25 1840||?
DLC F 13,Mr 12,Ap 23,Jl 4 1840
DeHi O 3 1839;Ja 2 1840
MWA Ja 9-Jl 25 1840
NNHi My 7 1840
NcD Ja 23,F 20,Ap 23,My 21,Jl 25 1840

Saturday EMPORIUM. w Je 29 1844-47||?
CtW 1844-Je 21 1845
MWA Ag 17 1844;My 17,Jl 5,Ag 23 1845
NN Ag 31 1844
NNHi S 13 1845
P-M O 30 1847
WHi F 6 1847

EMPROS. w 1918+
1918-Je 30 1923 as Voice of the worker
In Greek
NN [1918+]
NNHa 1935+

New York ENQUIRER. d Jl 6 1826-My 23 1829||
United with Morning courier to form Morning courier and New York enquirer
DLC 1826-[29]
MWA Jl 20,S 15 1826;F 17,Mr 14,Je 11,14,16,N 1 1827[Jl-D 1828]-My 1 1829
MeB complete
N 1826;Ja 30,My 30,Jl 11 N 17 1827;Ag-O 27 1828
NN Ja 5-Je 28 1827;Ja-Jl 4 1828
NNHi 1826-Ja 5 1827[Ja 16-F]Mr 1,Jl 7-[N]D 1828
NNS complete
NcD N 13,D 10 1828;F 9 14,19,26-28,Ap 13,16 1829
NjHi Ap 7,S 20 1828
PDoHi Ja 4 1828

New York evening ENQUIRER. w 1926+
NN S 19 1926-27

New York ENQUIRER for the country. sw 1826-My 23 1829||
United with Morning courier to form Morning courier and New York enquirer, for the country, later Semi-weekly courier and New York enquirer
Ct [1827-28]
CtHT [1828]
CtHi Jl 11 1826-28
DLC Mr 13 1829
IP complete
MWA Ag 8,O 13,D 12 1826;My 18,25-29,Je 8-12 1827;My 9,23,Je 3,Jl 4-8,D 10 1828;Ja 9, Ap 28-My 1829
MeBt Jl 11 1826-My 20 1829
MiU-C Jl 11 1828
N Ag 22 1826;Ja 5 1827
NN [Ja-Jl]S 21,N 30 1827;F 15,Ap 8,My 9,13 [O-N]1828;Ja 27,Mr 31-Ap 7,28,My 8 1829
NNHi O 31 1826[28-Ap 1829]
NSchU Ag 18 1826;F 23,My 29,Jl 27,Ag 14,21-24,S 11,25,N 23 1827;Ja 18 F 12-15,22,29,Mr 4, 11,Ap 11,My 9,27,Jl 15,22 1828-Ag 25 1829 [F 1830-My 1831]
NcD Ag 31 1827-[28]
NhD Jl 14,25,S 22-26,N 21,D 15-19 1826;Ja 26, Ap 13,My 21,Je 26,O 16,N 9 1827;Ja 22,Mr 7, 14-18,My 6,13,20,27,Jl 18,N 18,28,D 1828[29-N 1830]F 25,Mr 15-Ap 8,My 3,27 1831-F 3,28,Mr 9,Ap 6,17-My 4,15-22,Je 1,26,Jl 3,10-N,D 10,18 1832;Ja 1,7,20,F 1,12,22,26,Mr 1-19,26,Ap 2,My 17 1833;Ap 27-Je 4,11,15-18 1841
OOxM Ja 9 1827
P Jl 1828-29

La EPOCA de New York. w,sw 1915?-20||?
-D 3 1915 as El Progresso; D 10 1915-N 1918 La Bos del pueblo
w -D 3 1915
In Ladino
NN O 10 1915-Ja 13 1920

New York daily ERA. d 1856-
MnHi Je 3 1864
OClWHi Ap 20 1865

New York ERA. w,sw 1860-82||?
MWA Ag 29 1876
N Jl 12,Ag 16 1862
NNHi Je-D 1862
OClWHi O 8 1872

NEW YORK (*Continued*)

NEW YORK CITY—*Continued*

ERITASSARD hayastan. sw,tw,w 1904-32||?
1904-23? pub in Chicago
sw 1904?-Ag 28 1920;tw S 1 1920-23?
In Armenian
IU D 12 1917-21;Ja 14-Ap,Ag 7 1922-O 13 1923

ETHIOPIAN world. w,ir 1917+
1917-33 as Negro world; Ja 6-Ap 14 1934 World peace echo
Suspended from Ap 14-My 26 1934
w 1917-Ap 14 1934
Negro
MnHi Mr 14 1925-O 17 1933;Ja-Ap 14,My 26 1934+
MnU F 17 1923-[24-26]-[29-30]-[33]
PP D 20 1930-[32]Ja-Ap 14 1934

ETHNIKOS kerux. *See* National herald

EUROPEAN. w Mr 12? 1835-S 24 1836||?
MWA Ap 16-23,S 24 1836

EUROPEAN. w N 15 1856-57||?
CaOTA N 15 1856
DLC N 15 1856;Ja 10,F 21,Mr 21 1857
NN 1856-My 2 1857

EUROPEAN news. w Jl 10 1847-
MWA S 11 1847

EVENING paper. *See* Abend blatt für die arbeiter zeitung

EVERY afternoon. d Mr 17 1868-
KHi Ap 11 1868
MWA Mr 17 1868
NjHi Mr 17-Ap 11 1868

EXAMINER. d Ag 17? 1837-
Ct [1837]
DLC Ag 19 1837

EXPOSITOR and banking circular. w D 10? 1848-
MWA Ja 15 1849

EXPRESS; or, New-York weekly journal. w Jl 28? 1824-
DLC S 22 1824

New York morning EXPRESS. d Je 20 1836-64||?
Je-O 31 1836 as New York express; N 1 1836-Ap 16? 1843 New York daily express
CtSp Ap 12 1841;Ag 1 1843;My 31 1845
CtY Ag 25,N 1838-O 1840;Ap 3,Je 9,Ag 26,N 15 1843[Ja-O 10 1844]N 11,13 1845;Ap 30 1846; Jl 1 1847;Je 15 1848;My 10 1851;Je 29 1860; S 2 1864
DLC N 1836-39;41-42;Ap 18 1843-44;Mr-D 1845; F 1846-Mr 1847;Mr 23 1848;F 1849-52;F-Ap, Jl 1853-O 1854;F-N 1855;F 1856-57;F,Ap,N 1858;Ja-N 1859;F-My 1860;Ja-Ap 1861
IU N 9 1844
MB [N 24 1836-S 21 1837]
MWA Jl 14 1836;N 1836-[Ja-Ag 8 1840]Je 2, Ag 9 1841;Ag 5,16 1843;Ap 16,Je 25[N 6 1844-45]-[Jl 1846-48]-Mr 10,Je 27 1849[Ap 28-O 2 1851]N 11 1852;My 4 1855;Ag 15 1856;N-D 1858;F 10 1859
MiU-C [1836-38]
MoS Jl 6-D 1855
NBHi Mr 31 1842
NCor N 20 1839-62
NN 1836-50
NNHi N 10 1837-43;F 23 1858
NcU D 16 1844
NhD My 7 1845;Je 22,29,Jl 10,S 5 1850;Je 13, 24,26-27,Jl 8 1851;O 25-26,N 16 1852
OClWHi Ap 12 1844;N 14 1845
PPM [1838]40-41

New York semi-weekly EXPRESS. sw N 3 1836-79||?
Follows New York advertiser (for the country). 1836-N 16 1839 as New York advertiser and express
Ct [1836-F 1839]
CtY 1836-Je 24 1837
DLC D 8 1846-Mr 15 1850
GAtCo Ap 29,Ag 1,12 1840
ICU 1836-Jl 21 1843
IU Ag 2 1844
KHi Ag 1 1864
MB N 1836[38]Ag 18,N 17,24 1843
MWA D 10 1836;N 18 1837;Ap 7,My 23,Je 30,O 24,D 12,29 1838;O 21 1840;D 31 1842;Ag 26,O 7 1862[My 22 1863-O 1864;Ja 17-Ag 18 1865;Mr 13-D 18 1866]Je 4,Jl 2,12 1867
NCor [Ap 14-D 1838]-41
NN Jl 17 1839;Mr 9 1849-Ap 4 1851
NSchU Jl 6 1842
NcD Ag 31 1842
NcU My 20,O 7,D 19-23 1856
NhD S 11 1839;Ag 10 1849;Ag 27 1850;F 27 1852
NjR O 17 1838
P-M N 4 1837
WHi S 17 1847

New York evening EXPRESS. d 1839?-D 1881||
United with New York evening mail to form Mail and express, later Evening mail
CLM S 20 1881
CSmH D 14,17,21 1861
Ct Ag 29-30 1855
CtDe Ag 18 1846
CtSp Je 2 1845;D 30 1846
CtY Ja 23-25,28-F 14 1840;F 21,My 10 1841; Ag 17 1853;My 8,O 13,20,31,N 2,7,10-11,14,21, D 2,5-6,12,15-16 1854;Mr 26,Ap 2-3,5-7 1855; Jl 15 1860;S 12 1864
DLC N 4 1840;Mr 6-D 1841;Ap 18,Jl 9,13,16,23 1846;F 15-17,25,27,Mr 3 1847;Mr 17,Ap 10, 18,20 1857;Jl 1861;62-F 1863;Je 1864-O 1865; Ja 1866;Ag 13 1867;My 30 1868;My 30-31 1871;Ja 17 1874;Ap 11,14,22,25,My 1,4,15,17, Je 1-2,Jl 11 1876;N 2 1877
ICHi Ag 6,N 25 1864;Ja 25-Je 5 1865
ICN [Ap-S 2 1856]O 1863-[64]
ICU O 10 1839;Jl 26 1843-50;Jl 2,5,S 19,21,28-29 1881
IU Jl 16 1844
MB Ja 15,F 27,Je 3-4,10-12 1861
MBAt F 4 1843
MHi Mr 20,S 11 1841;Jl 10 1843;Je 19,N 9 1844[46]O 25-26 1847;Ap 8 1851
MWA [1840;Mr 19 1841-45;Mr-Ag 1846;Ja 11-My 1,D 1847]O 9 1848;Ag 15,S 1 1849;Mr 29, Ap 6,My 8,Je 7,O 24(supp),D 30 1850;Ag 6, 27,O 4 1851;F 5,Ap 22 1852;F 17,Ap 8,Je 7, 29 1854;F 6,D 20 1855;S 12 1856;Ja 15,Mr 4 1857;F 15 1858;My 27,O 26 1859;My 18,N 22 1860[Ap 18-N 20 1861;My 9-N 12 1862;F 10-My 2 1863;Je 7-Jl 20 1864];F 14,Ap 13,15,26, N 30 1865;Ap 3 1868;F 14 1870;O 2 1871;Ag 20,D 26 1873;Ja 8,D 23-24 1874;F 4,Ap 22 1875;Je 13 1876;Ja 9,Mr 9 1877;D 10 1879;O 23 1880
MiU-C S 15 1841
MnHi Mr 20,Je 3 1863;Ap 15 1865
N Ja 4 1851;Mr 26 1863
NBuG [F 28-Ag 1861]Mr 17,19,28,Ap 7 1862; Ap 7-8 1864
NCor [1854]Jl 27-S 7 1858;O 12-19 1860;Mr 4 1861-62
NHuHi Jl 7 1849
NN 1858-60
NNHi Mr 2 1843;N 24 1845;Mr 8 1850;My 16 1851;Ap 24 1854;Je 16 1859;O 9(supp)1860;Jl 1,10 1863;My 3,7 1867;Ag 16 1879;S 20 1881
NNMC Jl 24 1861
NNMT 1847-48
NNUnC Ap 10 1841
NSyU S 8,22,24,O 8-9(supp)12(supp)1860;O 9, 30,N 2 1861
NcD Ag 17-19,S 30 1840;N 25 1874
NhD Ag 8 1844;O 20 1845[Ja-S 7 1848]My 3 1851;Je 1,Jl 7 1852
Nj D 1864-66
NjR F 22 1861
OClWHi Je 22,Ag 22 1844;Ag 12 1845;D 26-27 1850;Ja 7,30 1851;Ja 7 1861;Ja 17,Ag 5 1862; Jl 17 1863;F 5 1864;F 25 1865;Je 21 1866
OHi Ag 10 1861;My 13 1866
PBf Jl 7 1881
PEHi F 4 1868
PPM Mr 16 1838-41
PWCl Je 29,Jl 12 1842
RPB Ap 27,Jl 6 1850;F 24 1851
V Ja-F 6 1864
VtMS 1843-44
WHi S 14,O 24 1848

New-York weekly EXPRESS. w My 5 1843-81||?
Title varies: Dollar express. United with weekly mail to form Weekly mail and express, later Saturday evening mail
DLC My 5,Je 9,N 10,D 8-15 1843;Ja 5,Mr 29,Ap 12,26-My 3,17 1844;N 27 1846
IHi N 30,D 14 1860
MB [N 28 1840-Je 18 1842]D 20 1859
MWA Mr 1,22 1844;Jl 4 1845;Mr 5 1847;Ja 23,F 20-27 1857;O 28 1864
N [1840-42;45-49]Je 15,29,D 14-21 1860;61;F 14 1862-Ja 6 1871
NN Ag-N 7 1856
NNHi N 1 1844;S 12 1856
NSchU Mr 12,Ap 9 1842
NcD Ja 26,Jl 5,S 13 1844
NcU Ag 8 1856
NhD My 1,Je 12-19 1841;My 10 1844;N 10 1853;O 5-12 1854;Ap 19,My 10-31,Je 14,Jl 5-10,Ag 2,23-30,O 4 1855;My 8,22 1856;Mr 6, Je 5,Jl 10,31-Ag 14,S 18,O 16-N,D 11 1857-Ja 15,24-Mr 5,26,Je 11-18,Jl 23-30,S 3,O 29 1858;Ja 7,18,F 1,18,Je 10-Ag,S 9-N 4,18,D 2-9 1859;Ja 13,27,F 10-24,Ap 6,Jl 13 1860
NjHi Jl 4 1845
OHi Mr 1 1844
P-M S 28 1854
TJT Mr 12 1875
TxGR Ag 31 1860
WHi N 1845-Ja 1847

New York FAMILY courier. w
MWA D 20 1856
NN 1852-57
TU Ap 19-26,My 17-24 1851
WHi Ja 22 1853

FAMILY herald. w Ag 5 1857-
NN 1858-Je 1861;Ja-N 1862
NNHi Ag 1857-Jl 1859;Jl 31 1861-Jl 1862
NcU Ap 24-My 8,22 1861

Al-FATAT. sw,w 1916-19||?
sw 1916-Mr 26 1918
In Arabic
IU D 12 1917-N 15 1918;My 24-Jl 12 1919

FATHER Columbia's paper. sm S 15 1883-84||?
campaign paper
M N 14 1883
MMarHi N 15 1883
MWA N 15-D 1 1883
NNHi S 15 1883
OCHi S 15 1883
PPot Ja 14 1884

FEMALE advocate. w Mr 8 1832-
Ct Je 29 1832
MWA Ap 5,O 19,N 2,16,30,D 14,28 1832;Ja 12-S 7,O 19,N 2,16,30,D 14 1833
N Ag 10 1832-Ag 7 1833
NNHi Ag 24 1832;Ja 26,F 23 1833

FIHRER. d Ap 1-Ag 19 1915||
In Yiddish
NN [1915]

FINANCIAL America. *See* Wall Street news

New York FINANCIAL examiner. w My 11 1916-
NN My-Ag,N 1916-Jl 14 1917;F 16-Ap 6 1918

FLAG of our union. w 1846?-
NjR D 30 1848
WHi Jl 31,S 25,N 6-13,27-D 4 1852;F 19 1853

FLAG of the free and people's own. w 1847-Ja 13 1849||?
1847-Ja 6 1849 as Flag of the free
DLC Ap 1848-Ja 13 1849

Le FRANCO-AMÉRICAIN. *See under* New Orleans, La.

FRANKLIN daily advertiser. d Ap? 1832-
MWA Jl 21 1832

FREE PRESS. w 1833-O 10 1835||?
Title varies slightly
DLC My-N 1833
NNHi Je-O 10 1835
NjHi Ja 24 1835

New York evening FREE PRESS. d Ag 31 1870-
DLC 1870-Ap 15 1871

FREE STATE advocate. w My 24 1856-
campaign paper
DLC Je 16 1856
MWA Jl 28-Ag 11,25-S 15,29-O 13 1856

FREEDOM'S journal. w Mr 16 1827-
DLC Ap,My 16-23,Je-N 21,D 20 1828-Ja 2, 24-Mr 28 1829
MB [1828-29]
MMarHi Mr 30 1827
N Ag 31 1827
NIC 1827-Mr 1828
NN Mr 30 1827(facsimile)
NNHi Mr 30-D 21 1827;Ja 18-Mr 21,D 12 1828;Ja 2,F 14 1829
NjHi Ap 20, My 11 1827
WHi [1827-28]

New York FREEMAN. *See* New York age

New York FREEMAN'S appeal. w Ag 31 1861-
ICN Ag 31 1861
NSyU Ag 31 1861

New York FREEMAN'S journal and Catholic register. w Jl 4 1840-1918||?
1840? as Freeman's journal
Suspended from Ag 24 1861-Ap 19 1862
ArHi Mr 12 1886
CSmH Jl 18 1846
CaQMS [Ja 16 1841-O 3 1846]
DGU 1840-F 14 1891
DLC Ag 3-10,24 1844;S 20 1862;Ap 18 1863-O 20 1866;N 23 1872-F 1886;Ja-My 1918
ICN Jl 1860-Je 22 1861;Ap 19 1862-Ap 9 1864; Ap 15 1865-Mr 23 1867
KAS Mr 25 1871-Mr 15 1873
LNC Jl 16-23,Ag 6-20,S 10-N 5,19 1859-Ja, Ap 26,N 17 1860;Jl 26-Ag 9,23,S-O 5,18,N 1-22,D 1862-Ja 17,31,F 14-Mr 23,Ap 4-11,25-My 16,Je 6-13,27,Jl 11,S 19-26,O 10-24,N 7-14,28 1863-Ja 2,16-F 6,Mr 5,Ap,My 28-Je, Jl 16-30,Ag 13 1864
MiU Ja 25 1845
MoSU [1841-Je 1843]57-61;72-79;81-82
MsHi 1840-41;68
N 1862-63;Ap 29 1871
NN Ap 19 1862-Ap 11 1863
NNU 1895-1905
NNiU 1849-51;67;70-71;73-76;78
NSchU Ja 22-F 19,Mr 19,Ap 9-16,30,Je 11, Jl 2-9 1842
NSyU My 17,Ag 9 1862;F 28 1863;O 29,N 19-D 3,24 1864
NcU Ja 1,N 26 1870;Jl 15 1871;My 29 1883
OCX S 23 1843-F 1849
WHi 1858-59;63;65-67;71

FRENCH-AMERICAN advertiser. w 1859?-
In English and French
DLC My 1-8 1861
MWA Ap 27,Jl 13 1861

FREIE arbeiter stimme. w 1898+
Also dated in Philadelphia
In Yiddish
NNRa [1928]+

Morning FREIHEIT (Morgen freiheit). d Ap 2 1922+
1922-Je 16 1929 as Freiheit
In Yiddish
pub 1922+
NN 1922+
NNRa 1927-[30]
PP [1931]+

FUSION flashlight. w O 4 1917-
Campaign paper
MWA O 18 1917
NNHi N 1 1917

FUSION record. w 1903||?
NNS O 15-29 1903

GAELIC American. w 1903+
pub 1903+
CU [1912]+
CU-B S 18 1915
CtY [1917-21;23]
ICU 1922[23-24]
IU D 8 1917+
KHi O 6 1928
MH [1923]
MWA My 3 1913
OO [1903;19]
PPeS Je 21 1919

Saturday evening GAZETTE. w My 5 1827-
N My-Je 9,Ag 4 1827

New York evening GAZETTE. d D 22 1866-
DLC 1866-N 1867
MWA Ag 31 1867
NN 1866-Je 29,S 26 1867

***New York GAZETTE and general advertiser.** d D 29 1788-Ap 30 1840||
Follows Independent journal (not in this list) 1788-95? as New-York daily gazette (title varies slightly); Ja 6 1820-Ap 1822 Lang, Turner & Co's New-York gazette and general advertiser. Merged with Journal of commerce and commercial
Suspended from Ag 31-S 5 1806
Ct Jl 31 1825;Mr 20 1829
CtY Je 19 1831;34
DLC 1821[23-24;27-28;31-33;39]
MB N 15 1836
MBAt Ap 10 1822;F 21(supp)1831
MHi Ja 21 1824;Ja 5 1825
MWA Ja 8,Mr 8,My 1,7,24,N 20,28 1821;F 20,Mr 13,Ap 24,29-30,My 22,O 26,D 28 1822; Mr 11-12,My 26,D 31 1823;S 22 1826;My 27, Jl 10 1828;Mr 14,Je 27-29 1829;Mr 6,S 21,D 8 1830;Ap 13 1831;N 26,D 8 1834;My 8,Jl 22,S 7,O 1 1835;Mr 22 1836;Ja 16,Ag 21,O 23 1837;My 4,Ag 1,S 12 1839;Ja-Mr 1840

NEW YORK (*Continued*)

NEW YORK CITY—*Continued*

*New York GAZETTE and general advertiser. 1788-18-0||—*Continued*
N Ag-O 27 1828;O 16 1833;34-35
NN Ag 18 1824;N 10 1825;Je 27 1829;Ap 14 1836;N 27 1838
NNHi 1821-35;N 10-D 1837;38-S 12 1839
NNMT N 1833-Jl 1839
NhD My 22 1830
NjHi [1821-35]-My 1836;Jl 1837-40
NjR Ap 7 1825
P O 31 1830
PDoHi My 13 1826
PPM 1827

GAZETTE and times. d Mr 3 1845-O 25 1847||
1845-F 17 1846 as Evening gazette
DLC Mr 11,Ag 13 1847
MWA Je 4-5 1845;Mr 1846-Ja 1847
NNHi complete
NNS 1845-Je 1846

GAZETTE and times. For the country. sw Ja 12-Je 30 1846||?
MWA Ja 12,19 1846

GAZETTE extraordinary. w Ap 30-D 26 1842||?
MWA My 7-21,Je 18,Jl 9-23 1842
MiU-C D 16 1842
N S 10 1842
NNHi D 23 1842
RP My 28,Je 25,Jl 16-Ag,S 24-O 1 1842

GAZETTE franco-américaine. w 1919-21||?
In French
NN N 8 1919-N 1921

GAZETTE of the United States. *See* United States gazette (Philadelphia)

New York GENERAL advertiser and daily commercial register. d Ap 1835-
P-M Ap 24 1835

GENERAL shipping and commercial list. *See* New York commercial

GENIUS of liberty. 1827||?
MWA S 18(extra)1827

GERMAN-AMERICAN. w Ja 1 1864-
ICHi Mr 11 1864
MWA Ja 1 1864

GERMANIA. w
PPG 1875[76]

GERRIT SMITH banner. d O 16-N 1 1858||
Campaign paper
M [1858]
NIC O 16-22,26-N 1858
NSyU O 30 1858
OO O 16-23,26-N 1858
WHi O 16-23,26-N 1858

New-Yorker GESCHAEFTS-BERICHT. *See* New-Yorker handels-zeitung

Il GIORNALE italiano. d 1908?-21||?
In Italian
IU D 8 1917-S 27 1919

GLAS naroda. d 1892?+
In Slovenian
IU D 5 1917+
NN 1911-28

New York GLEANER. w 1858?-
MWA F 27 1861

New York GLOBE. d O 29-N 29 1832||
DLC N 29 1832

New York weekly GLOBE. w 1845?-48||?
DLC S 16-D 1848
MWA Jl 29-Ag 5,N 4 1848
NN Ja 9-Jl 3 1847
NNHi Mr 7 1846

New York daily GLOBE. d Ag 25 1845-Ap 1851||
1845-46 as Daily globe
CtY Mr 22(extra)1850
DLC [1845-My 1846]-48
IU Jl 23 1846
MWA D 25 1845
N S 11-12 1850
NB S 1845-47
NN Ja-Jl,S 1847-[Ja-Ap]S 12-13 1848;F 16,Mr 26,Ap 16,24 Mr 14 1849
NNHi O 27 1845;F 14,18 1846

GLOBE. d 1868-71||?
DLC N 7 1870;My 10,17,Jl 11,O 13 1871
MWA Mr 24 1870;Ag 28 1871
NcU My 2 1868

New York GLOBE. 1880-84 *See* New York age

*GLOBE and commercial advertiser. d O 2 1797-Je 2 1923||
Follows Minerva (not in this list). 1797-Ja 30 1904 as Commercial advertiser (title varies slightly). Merged with Sun
D 9 1918 is 125th anniversary number
CSmH My 22 1830
CSt-H [1914]
CaQMM O 8 1836
CoD [Ja-My 4 1829;Ja-Je 1831;Ja 20-Je 1832]
Ct [Jl 7-D 1834]Je 19-D 1835
CtHi Mr 8 1839-F 1840
CtSp Je 5 1840
CtT Ja 3 1834
CtY S 20 1832;My 7 1835;Jl 23 1846;D 17 1898
DLC 1821;Ap 8,21,25 1823;Jl 27,31,Ag 2,11,24,S 17,21-22,28,N 1,D 2,16-17,20,23 1824;Mr 9 1825;O 17 1826;Mr 29,Ag 27 1827;My 13,15,D 29 1828-Mr 5,Jl 1,3,8,25,27-29,31,Ag 8,S 1-2,4-5,14,16,28,O 5,N 2,18,28,30,D 23-24,30 1829;Ja 9,15-16,26,28,My 6 1830;O 28 1831;Ap 2,S 24 1832;Je 7,10 13 1839;S 24 1840;F 20 1841;Mr 6-7,13-14,Ap 17,24 1843;O 16,N 25 1844;Je 26 1847;D 20 1848;Jl 17-19 1849;Ja 17,S 30,O-D 1850;59;Mr 1861-63;67-84;Ap 1885-86;Ap 27 (supp)1889;90-91;Jl 1892-Je 1894;My 20 1895-Je,S-D 1902;My 1904-23
ICHi Je 25 1824;D 28 1861;Ap 18 1865
ICM Ap 29,Je 16-17,O 3 1888
ICU Jl 5-6 1831
IHi Ap 24,27 1865
IU Ag 5 1834;Ap 15 1842;My 7,Ag 26 1844
IaGG Je 23,30 1911;D 16-19 1912
KHi [1821-95]S 2 1915
MB [O 1827-My 1876]
MBAt Ja 25,F 2 1821;Mr 8 1823[24]O 5,12,N 7 1827;Ja 25,29,N 11 1828;S 24,D 8(extra)28 1830;Ap 18 1865
MHi [1821-27]Ap 27,29 1889
MWA F 8 1821;Jl 16 1822;Mr 4 1823;S 23-24 1824;Ja 25,31,Mr 2,My 18,Jl 30,N 2-3,5 1825 [Ag 21-D 1828;My 5-D 1829]30;Ja 7,F 9,21, 25,Mr 17-18,Jl-D 1831;Mr 8,Ap 18,25,27[Jl 10 1832-33]Ag 2 1834[F 19-D 19 1835]Ja 21, Mr 24,Je 7 1836;O 26 1837;Je 16,Jl 11,16 1838;Ja-Je 1839;Ag 6 1840[4]Ag 8,10,17 1842; O 17,D 29 1843;F 5,Mr 16,Ap 29(extra)30,My 18 D 4 1844;Ja 8 1845;Jl 23 1846;Ag 6,19,26,S 4,O 1 1847;D 17 1850;F 28 1851;Ja 12 1853;O 13 1855;Ap 1858-61;F 15,Ap 14,Ag 22 1862 My 14,Ag 26,S 12 1863;Jl 21 1864;Ap 13,27,N 22 1865-N 1877;Ja 13-Jl 18 1879;F 19 1880;F 21,23 1881;Ap 3 1884;N 21 1885;Ja 4 1895;S-D 1898;Ap 1899-Mr 1906;D 9(supp)1918
MiU-C [1839;59]D 9(supp)1918
N [1852-60]
NB Mr 13 1847-Je 1849
NBHi My 19,Je 23 1829;67-73;84-85;86-92
NGe Jl 5 1862
NN 1821;Ja-My 1825[30-32]-Mr 26,Je 22-24,26, D 4 1833;My 17,Je 7,Ag 9 1834;S 1,O 8 1836;O 11 1837-Je 1842;43-Je 1846;Je-D 1848; Jl 1849-Je 1854;55-56;58-59[My,Jl-S,D 1861] Ja 24,F 20,Mr 12,My 16,S 30 1862;Jl 9,21,S 17 1863;Je 22 1864;Mr 13,Ap 7-8,11-15,18-28, Jl-D 1865;67-73;O 1881-1923
NNHi 1821-63;N 11 1864-[65]81-90
NNMC Ap 6 1821;O 10 1885
NNMT 1834-38;40-45;47-48;F-D 1849
NNS 1821-27;32-Je 1846
NNUnC Ap 9 1841
NSchU My 12 1842;D 20 1827;Ja 8, 1828;D 20 1830;F 9,Ag 12 1831;My 19,S 19,26,29,O 16, 18-19,29,N 1-3,5,7,14,17,22-23,28-29,D 1,3-4,14-15,17-19 1832;33-Je 23,S 27-28 1836
NT Ja 10 1835-54
NhD F 11 1839;O 12 1844;Je 19 1874
NjHi [1821-24]-59
NjR [1833;43;48;76]
OClWHi D 24 1840;Ag 18 1841;Jl 12 1862;D 3 1864
PBf N 15 1881
PEHi Je 14 1856
PEL [1846]-52
PHi 1831
PPM 1827;31-37
RW Ap 26 1861
TJT Ja 2 1878
VU O 9 1905
WHi Jl 28 1824;Ap 21 1826;Mr 26 1827;D 30 1841
—w,sw ed *See* Weekly commercial advertiser

GLOBE and emerald; or, Saturday's journal of literature, politics and the arts. w My 27 1824-Je 3 1826||?
My-D 18 1824 as Emerald; or, political, literary and commercial recorder
IaDH Jl-D 1825
MWA Je 19,Jl 31,Ag 28,S 25,D 25 1824-[My 1825-Je 1826]
N 1824-Ap 16,Jl 9-O 15 1825; Ja 14,28-F 1826
NBHi D 18 1824
NNHi Jl 31 1824-25

GOLDEN dollar. w D 1851?-
DLC F 21 1852

GOTCHNAG. *See* Hayastani gotchnag

GRANT and Colfax campaigner. w Ag 26-1868||
Campaign paper
NNHi Ag 26-S 2 1868

GRAPE-SHOT. w Jl 1-N 11 1848||?
Campaign paper
CSmH S 16 1848
CtY Jl 1 1848
DLC Jl-O 1848
DDE Jl 7 1848
NN N 4 1848
NNHi Jl 13-27,Ag 12,26-S 9,30,O 14-28 1848

Daily GRAPHIC. d Mr 4 1873-S 23 1889||
CL Jl 19 1881
CLM Ap 13 1882
CSmH Ap 20 1882
CaQMM Ap 20 1881
Ct D 16 1875;F 17 1881
CtSp My 11 1877;S 20 1881;My 29 1882;Jl 18 1884;Jl 24 1885;F 19 1889
CtY 1873-Je 1884
DLC complete
DDE [1873-78]-[81]
DC Mr 7-My 29,S 15 1873-[74-75]Ja 1876
ICHi Ap 24,S 6,10 1873;Mr 27 1879-Ja 2,Jl 19-O 1880;Je 30 1882
ICM [My 1880-F 1883]My 15 1884;S 6 1885; Je 10 1879;Ap 20 1881;F 19 1884
ICN [Mr-O 4 1877]
ICU 1873-Je 29 1878;81
IU Je 19 1876
IaDH 1873-N 1 1878
IaHi [1883]
InI S 18 1874
KHi Je 9 1875;S 25 1878;S 24,D 11 1885
KyLo Mr-Je 1873
M Je 1875
MB complete
MBAt Mr 8 1873-Jl 1887
MHi F 16 1874;Je 1 1875;S 23 1880
MNF 1873-F 1877
MWA [1873-79]-O 4 1882;Mr 30,Ag 25,S 13, 18 1883;Ja 19-21,F 8-9,14,Ap 8,Ag 16,S 29, O 9,14,27,N 21,D 12 1884;F 23,Mr 25,Ap 10, 14-15,Jl 28,S 22,O 1,5-7,20,22,N 4-5,10-11,16 1885;Mr 27,O 27 1886;F 26 1887;Je 13,Jl 31 1888;Ja 29,Ap 29 1889
MdBP complete
MiG My 5 1883;Mr 12,29,Ap 14 1884;F 10,19-20,27,Mr 14,26,28,Ap 8,Jl 18,25,Ag 22,26,S 10, O 13 1885
MiU-C [1873-75;85]
MoS 1873-O 1876;My 1878-89
MsU [1887-88]
N Mr 1873
NBHi 1873-Je 1874;82-F 1886
NIC complete
NN complete
NNC 1873-Je 1884
NNHi 1873-O 1878;N 1879-F 1882
NNY-H Mr 8 1873-O 1882
NbHi Ag 13,S 6,23-24 1879;Mr 17 1882;Ap 8 1885;N 10 1887
NcD [1873;80-82]
NcU F 23,Je 2 1876;Ja 26,D 17 1878[81]F 3, 21-23,25 1882
NhD Mr 16,Ag 21 1874
NjCHi Je 6 1889
NjFHi Je 27 1878
NjR [1873-83;85]
OC 1877-89
OCHi My 12-Je 5 1875
OClWHi [Ag 1873-75]-[81-83;86-88]
OCon 1873-O 1874
OOxM Je 15 1876;S,D 16 1879
P 1873-F 1879
PCarlHi D 23 1878;F 17-D 1879;F 17-D 1880
PHi My 27 1874
PLaL My 11 1876
PMcC Je 22 1877
PMilC Ja 2 1879
PPiHi My 10 1875;N 27 1882[85]
PPot S 25 1885
PWaHi D 13 1876
PYHi D 23 1878
T Mr 3,Je 30 1874
TxGR Je 21 1877
TxU Mr-O 1873
Vt 1873-O 1875;Mr 1876-O 1877;Ja-F 1878
WHi 1873-Mr 2 1875;My 1880-Ag, D 1883

Weekly GRAPHIC. w Ja 24- 1874||?
NB Ja-Je 13 1874

Weekly GRAPHIC. w 1882-83||?
MB Ap 1 1882-Mr 24 1883
MWA My 26 1888

New York evening GRAPHIC. d S 15 1924-Jl 7 1932||
M N 21 1928
MWA S 15 1924;Jl 7 1932
NN S 15-O 1924
PPeS N 7 1928

GREEN banner. w O 3 1835-
DGU 1835-Ap 22 1837
NCH O 31 1835;S 17,O 1836-Ap 29 1837
NNH 1835-O 1 1836

GREENWICH VILLAGE weekly news. ir O 10 1931-Jl 1933||?
Ag 25-S 10 1932 as Magazine of Greenwich Village and the Greenwich Village weekly
NN-J 1931-Je 1933
NN-M 1931-Jl 1933

GUARDIAN. w 1871-Ja 1873||
United with Westchester clarion to form Westchester clarion and the guardian, later North New Yorker and Westchester clarion

GUIDE (Al-Dalil). w 1905?-14||?
In English and Arabic
NN 1910-13

Daily HALF-CENT. d S 15 1853-
DLC S 29 1853
MWA S 19 1853
N S 15 1853
NNHi S 22 1853
RW O 25 1853

New-Yorker HANDELS-ZEITUNG. w,sw F 21 1855-Jl 14 1917||
F-Ap 4 1855 as New-Yorker geschaefts-bericht; Ap 10-My 22 1855 New-Yorker geschaefts-bericht; handels zeitung
sw Jl 20 1887-Ja 14 1888
In German
DLC 1858;65-Mr 1868;71-[74-75]
NBHi 1858;65-69;73-75
NN 1855-Ja 1 1856;59;65-1917

New-Yorker HANDELS-ZEITUNG. d
In German
NN Ag 31 1857-58

HARLEM life. *See* Harlem local-life

HARLEM local. w,sw 1870-74||?
United with Harlem local reporter to form Reporter and Harlem local, later Harlem reporter and Bronx chronicle
w 1870-73?

HARLEM local-life. w 1890-1925||?
1890-1901? as Harlem life; 1902? Harlem local; 1903?-05? Harlem local and life
NN Ja 2,Jl 25,S 12-26,O 10-N 14,28,D 12-26 1903;Ja 9,23-Je,Jl 9-Ag 20,S 3 1904;Jl 22 1905; S 26 1908;Ja 9-Ap 17,My-Je 1909
NNHi Ja 4 1902;N 26 1904

HARLEM local reporter. *See* Harlem reporter and Bronx chronicle

HARLEM reporter. w 1905-07||?
NN 1905;Ap 25 1907

HARLEM reporter and Bronx chronicle. w,sw 1873-1933||?
1873-Mr 19 1904 as Harlem local reporter (187?-88? Reporter and Harlem local)
sw 1874?-1907?
NN D 26 1903;08-Ja 1,22 1910;11
NNHi D 28 1889[90-93]-[96-93]Ap 1 1899;F 2 1901;Mr 1 1902

HAWK and buzzard. *See* Spy, and New York and Brooklyn Saturday courier and enquirer

HAYASTANI gotchnag. w D 15 1900+
1900-19 as Gotchnag
In Armenian
pub 1900+

HEBREW. *See* Ha-Ivri

HEBREW world. w 1889-97||?
DLC S 1890-Je 1891

NEW YORK (*Continued*)

NEW YORK CITY—*Continued*

HEINT. d Ja 1-F 21 1920||
In Yiddish
NN 1920

New York HERALD. 1802-17 *See* Evening post

New-York morning HERALD. d F 2 1829-S 11 1830||
Formed by the union of National advocate and New York statesman. Merged with New York standard
DLC 1829-Ja 1830
LNC My 6 1835
MWA Mr 6,Ap 6,Ag 17 1829;Ja 8,13,Jl 1 1830
NNHi F-Jl,N 19,30-D 5,10,19,25,30 1829-F,Mr 3,8-9,20,Ap 22,24,26,29,My 8,11,28 1830
NjHi Je 16 1830
NhD F 10,12,19 1829
WHi F-S 11 1830
—sw ed *See* New York standard and statesman

New York HERALD. d My 6 1835-Mr 18 1924||
1835-S 19 1840 as Morning herald (Ag 31 1835-My 20 1837 Herald). United with New York tribune to form New York herald-New York tribune, later New York herald-tribune
Suspended from Ag 12-31 1835
For F-S 1920 *See* Sun
A Ag 1851-Jl 1856;My 1860-Ag 1861;F 1862-Ap 1863;Ap-D 1864[66]-[69;87;95]1900-02[15]
ArHi Je 12 1846;N 1 1848;Ja 13 1849;Ap 15 1865;S 24,O 1 1881
ArU Je 1861-80
AzU 1852[60]-[68-69;71]98-[1900-01]03-[07-08]
C 1848-Mr 16,Ap 13-N 4 1852;Jl 6 1853-54;87-89
CClP [Mr-Ap 1865]
CL Jl 15 1864;Ap 15 1865
CLM Mr 5 1861;Ap 10,15-16,20,My 6,24 1865;F 28,O 28 1872;Ja 26,Mr 23 1874;Je 28 1875;S 20-25 1881;My 10 1882;Mr 7,N 12,25 1888;Je 15 1901
CP Ap 15,26 1865;Ap 30 1889
CSf My-D 1906
CSmH Jl 12 1846;Jl 14 1847;Ja 9 1848;N 9 1857;O 27,D 20 1859;Ap 4,Je 17 1861[My-D 1862]-Ag 1863;Ja 22 1864;Ja-S,D 30 1865;Ja 19 1866;F 2,Mr 2 1919
CSt Mr 16 1854;65-Je 1900[01-02]
CSt-H [1914-17]-19
CU O 7,N 25 1837;Ap 15 1865(facsimile);Ja-Je,S,N 1866-95;Jl 1897-Ag 1902
CU-B D 20 1862;Ap 15 1865
CaB 1881-98
CaM 1884-1905
CaQMF 1864-65;71-76
CoBoC Ap 15 1865;Jl 31 1887
CoD My 20,27,Je 17-18,Jl 11,22,29,Ag 10,13-14,29,N 16,20,27,D 16,31 1861;Ja 6-F 6,Mr 8,10,12-14,20,Ap 2,10 1865
CoHi N 14 1861;F 26,Mr 10-12,15-16,21 1862;Ap 15,19-20,22,26,My 14 1865
Ct [1835]Ag 26 1837;N 3 1852;Ag 28 1855;Ja 28 1856[61]My 5 1862;D 17 1863[64-65]Je 17-18 1875;Ag 26 1882;D 11 1887
CtD Ap 16 1865
CtDe Ap 15 1865
CtN Ap 15 1865
CtNlC Ap 17,24 1865
CtSp Je 1 1840[42;46]S 2 1858[65]
CtSta 1861-65
CtY My 11 1837;S 30 1841;N 30 1842;Ap 10,16,18,N 1,D 4 1846;My 10 1849-Je 1878[79-1905]-24
DLC Mr 10 1836-My 1837;Ap-D 1839;Mr 5,24,Ap 19,My 12,25,Je 1,Jl 14 1841;O 4 1842[43-47]-1924
DeWI Ap 15-My 9 1865
FU Ap 15 1865
GAA My 28 1871
GAtCo Ja 5 1840
GDE O 6 1836;O 31 1850
GMM [N 3 1838-Ap 24 1839]85
IC Ap 14,16-22,24-26,29-My 9,11 1865
ICM O 17 1870;D 16 1871;Ja 4 1872;Ap 12 1875[77]Ja 24,Mr 21 1878[79-Jl 1882]F 19,My 14 1884;Ap 5 1885;O 26 1887;Mr 10 1888;D 22 1889;O 18,N 11,29 1891;Mr 21 1894;D 15 1901;My 21,O 29 1903
ICN [My 24 1855-Ag 1857;O 1858-59]-[65]-[Ja-Jl 26 1867]69-78;O 1879-1900
IF F 23 1857;O 11 1859;Jl 24-O 1860[61-F 1862]Mr 7,My 3 1865
IP Ap 15,O-D 1865;Ja-Je 1884;O-D 1886;O 1887-Je 1888
IU [Ja 5-Je 1848]52;My 1853-Ag 1854;55-Ag 1856;57-58;Jl-D 1859;Jl 1860-Mr 1883;Jl 1884-1900;N 6-D 1909;Ja 28-31,Mr 2-Ap 26 1910
IaA Ap 15 1865
IaDH 1848-Je 1854;55-95;Ap 1896-Ag 16 1898;N 1900-Je 1901;08-14
IaGG Jl 27 1861;S 5 1862
In 1890-Ap 1897
InI [1890-95]
InLHi S 3 1862
InMovHi Ap 15 1865
InNcHi Ap 13 1865
KyLo 1869-76
LNC My 6 1835;Ap 17,My 7,Ag 25 1861;My 31,D 20 1862;My 12,Je 27 1863;Ap 15 1865
LNH My 15 1863
LU 1853[My 7, 1854-O 8 1858;59-60]-[62]-Mr,O 1-24,26-D 2,4 1865;Ja-Mr 23,25-Ap 3,5-26 1866;F 16,19,24-25,27-28,Mr 1-3,11,24-28,30,Ap 3,5 1869
MAtt D 27-28,30-31 1862;Ap 15 1865;Ap 5 1891;Ag 5 1894;Ap 12,23,26,My 3,Ag 13,23 1898;S 8,14,19 1901;My 27 1902;Jl 21-23,26 1903;Mr 16 1917
MB Ja-Mr 1844;Ja-Mr 1854[Ap 1857-64;79-85;Jl 1887-90]
MBAt My 6 1835;Ja 23 1836[38-39]D 3 1845;Mr 1,S 13 1846;Ja 1 1847;61-1907
MBeHi 1842
MCheHi Ap 15 1865
MHi Je 11,Ag 20 1839;Ja 30 1840;My 25,Je 19,S 6,9 1841;Jl 7,Ag 2 1843;My 19 1846;S 3 1849[52-58]Ja 28 1859-[60-75]
MMarHi Jl 12 1861-Ap 15 1865
MNF 1861-64;Ap 4-D 1865
MNaHi My 16 1860;My 24 1862
MSaE F 22 1862
MWA My 6(facsimile)S 8,D 21 1835[Mr 12-D 1836]37;Je 11,Ag 9 1838;S 25(extra)O 10,17 1839;Mr 11-12,My 15,26,S 17,21 1840-Ap 26 1843[44]-[Jl 1845-46]-[48-49]-[Ap-D 1860]-1909;F 14 1914;My 15 1918;Mr 1 1922;Ap 10 1923
MdBJ S 17 1860-Ap 20,My 3,Ag 31 1861-62;Jl 1863-Je 1864;65-66;Jl 1868-S 29 1878
MdBP Jl 1852-53;Jl-D 1854;Ag 18-21 1858;Mr 1859-60;Ap 21,Jl 1,9,11,19,29-Ag 4,7,9,23,S 8,13,23,O 10-11,14,24-25,28,30-N 1,16-18,21-26,D 1-2,6,8,21,23 1861-Je 1865;66
MdBSa Ap 15 1865
MdHW Ap 1865
MdHi 1861-65;67-Je 1868
MeAu My 6 1835;Ap 15 1865
MeBa Ap 15,20 1865
MiAlH Ap 15 1865
MiG F 18 1862;Ap 15,17 1865
MiGh Ap 15 1865;Ap 28 1897
MiU [1849]53-[55]-[57]-[60-61]-[64-67]70-[74]-[76]-[78]-80[82]-84;86-[1906]-[19]20
MiU-C [1835;37;39;41-47;49-58;61-65;75-77;79-80;82-85;89;91-92;94;98]
MnHi [Jl 4 1847-58]-77
MnS 1853-Je 1854;F-D 3 1862
MnU Ag 19 1858;61-Je 1865;90-1905
Mo Jl 1867-Je 1868
MoCaT Ap 15 1865
MoHi Ap 15 1865
MoS Jl-D 1855
MsHi 1847-64
MsU 1887[88]
N My 6 1835(reprint)Mr 10-D 1836;N 1 1837;Je 5 1838-Mr 22,Ap 4-N 2,D 19 1839;Je-D 1840;Ap 10,My 12,Jl 22 1841;42-45;Jl 29 1846;47-My,Ag 1898-[1903-08]Jl 1909-Ap,Jl 1911-24
NB 1850;My 1852-Mr,Jl 1869-Mr,Jl 1870-S 1871;72-Ja 1920
NBHi Jl 20 1835;61-92
NBrM Ap 15 1865
NBu O 1878-Mr 1900
NBuG S 9 1840;S 20 1856;Ja 25,27,30-31,Ap 23-24,My 2-11 1861;D 5 1862;S 5 1863;Jl 4,22 1864;Mr 30 1872
NCH Ja-Mr 1862
NChM Je 1862-Je 1866
NEh Je 9 1836;F 27 1840
NGe Je 19-20,Jl 4 1862
NHuHi My 6 1835;My 20 1837;S 7 1850;Mr 5 1861;Ja 11,Ap 15-16 1865
NMi Mr 7-S 10 1840
NN My-Ag 12,D 21 1835;Mr 10-Ap 2,9,12-30,My 4-11,S 15 1836[Ja-O 1838;Je-D 1839]F 4,S 21 1840-[42]-Jl 6,Ag 5 1844-Mr 1870[71]-Mr,Je 1872-1924
NNC 1860-65;Ap-S 1866;Jl 16 1870-Mr 1871;Ap 19 1875
NNCC S 1914-16
NNCU [Ja 26 1864-66;Jl 1867-Je,O 1885-Ja 1920]
NNCom 1840-[Ag 1911-S 1914]-24
NNHi My-Ag 12[S-O,D]1835;Mr 10 1836-[38-39]-[41]-43;Je 17,23 1845-46;My 26,S 13,O 10,N 2,18,D 5 1847-1924
extras:Ap 7,21 1848
NNMC My 6 1835;Ag 31 1835-Ja 1 1836;Jl 13 1837;Je 1 1847;F 25,Ap 30,Jl 24 1853;O 11,N 9 1857;Ja 22,Mr 24,Ap 13 1861;Ja 1 1862;My 9,D 5 1864;Ap 15-16 1865;Ap 19 1875;Jl 3,S 20,S 27 1881
NNMT 1855-67;96-97;Ap 1898-F 1899;1900-19
NNRa Ap 3,My 10 1856;S 18 1857;Ag 6,18,S 2 1858;Je 26,O 12-14,O 27 1860;N 2,D 29 1861;Je 24 1862
NNS Jl-D 1862;Ja-Je 1864
NNUnC My 6 1835;Jl 22 1837
NNiU F 6-S 25 1875;84
NPV Mr 1843-O 1847;48-F 1913
NRU D 1-27,29 1860;Ja 23,25 1861;N 12,14 1863;Jl 4,6 1865;D 31 1866;88-Je 1893;96-Je 1908
NSchU Mr 9,My 3,Je 3,19,27,Jl 6,Ag 14,O 2 1842
NShi Ap 16 1865
NSm My 15 1878
NSyU Ag 1,14,S 3-4,O 3 1861;62-65
NbHi Ap 15 1865;Jl 11,21,S 7-8,13,D 4,18 1866;Ja 10 1867;Mr 29,Ap 3-4,25,Je 6 1868;F 16 1870;D 7 1878;F 19 1879;O 22,24-31,D 1884-87;Jl 5 1889;Jl 17 1892;My 27 1898;S 18 1901;Ag 23,O 23-30,D 4,6-7,9-11,16-19,26 1906
NcAsS Ap 15 1865
NcD My 6 1835;N 1,9,14 1836;Ja 6,12 1837;D 31 1840;Ja 14,Jl 14 1841;Mr 10 1844;O 14 1845;48;Je 19 1849;D 30 1850[51]-[Ja-Ap 1853;Ap-Je 1855]Ag 20,22,S 3,25,27,O 26 1856;Ja-Mr,O-D 1857;Ja 4-5,7-16,My 3-8,10,19,Je 9,11,N 28,D 3,24 1859-1918
NcGrW Ag 10 1870
NcU Mr 17,Je 21,Jl 12,14,19 1845;Ap 26 1848;O 26 1858;Je 18,Jl 28,Ag 4,S 6,19,D 25 1859[Ja,Je 1860-My 1861;62]Je 1 1863[64-Je 1865]O 4 1867;Ja 3 1868;Ag 21 1873;Ja 16,O 20 1874;Je 2 1875;My 31 1876;Mr 29 1877;Ag 24 1878;S 5,24 1879;S 4,27 1881;Jl 13,Ag 21,S 14 1882;My 1 1885;N 25 1887;Je 19 1893;Je 24 1898;D 10-11 1907
NhD [1861-Je 1865]
NjHi Mr 14 1838
NjJ 1860-65;S 1871-Mr 1872;Jl 1874-Je 1879;Ap 16-O 1898
NjN S 9 1861;Ap 26,My 4,11,Ag 11,18,20,22,S 1-2,4,6,9,11,15,18-20,24 1862;Ja 6 1863;Ap 28,My 14,22,28 1865;Jl 29-30 1866
NjNb Jl 1859-62;82
NjO Ag 5-6,14,S 20 1861;Ap 15 1865;My 1,Je 20 1889
NjP 1861-91[96-98]-[1901-05]-[20]-[24]
NjR [1837-38;40;43]45-[56;58;60-66;70;72-77;80-81;84-85;87]-[93;1901;03]
NjWdHi Je 18(supp)1864
OC Jl 1844-53;55-1924
OCHi Mr 10,Ap 24-My 19 1838;My 18 1839;Ap 15 1865;Ap 19 1875;S 20 1881
OCl [1855;60]-[66]-[68;77;81]-91;1902-15
OClWHi Ag 24 1837-Mr 10 1838;My 30 1840
OHi My 12 1851;S 15 1859-Ap 23 1860;F 28 1861-Ap 24 1865;S 17 1867-Mr 1877
OOxM Ag 14 1883;Mr 19 1887
OrU [1857-58;60-65;68-73]
P [1860-71;80]
PArdL Ap 15 1865
PAtM Ap 15 1865
PBL [1864]-71
PBf Ja 12 1861;Ja 12-13,Ap 12,15(extra)1865
PBr Ap 16 1865
PEHi Jl 8 1856;Ap 15 1865
PEL N 8 1860-My 2 1864
PErW Ap 15 1865
PHi [1850]-53;60-67;82-[86]-[91]-1909
PHsHi N 30 1860;Ja 5 1861;Ap 15 1865
PLaF Ag 12 1858-Mr 20 1875;N 3 1918
PLaHi Ap 17-S 1865
PLewL S 12,O 22,N 9 1861;Mr 19,S 11 1862
PLhT Mr 5 1861
PMcC Ag 10 1876
PMe Ap 15 1865
PMilC Ap 10 1876;D 6 1878[79]
PMilHi N 4 1852;91
PNoHi Ap 15(extra)1865
PP Ap 25 1846[47-51]Ja 31,S 10 1852;Ap 5,S 25 1857[61-62]-Je 1865;Jl 1 1866;Jl 26-27 1872;Je 23 1873;O 7 1878;Ja 23,Mr 14,27,Ap 3,9,D 21 1879;Ag 9 1885[98]O 6 1917;Mr 24 1918
PPFfHi My 15 1861;Ap 21 1865
PPGr Ap 19 1865
PPL [1842;47;49-52;57;61]62[64-65;72;78]
PPM F 1841-42;61-1900
PPeS Ap 15 1865;Jl 6 1868
PPi F 7 1861-F 1864
PPiHi Jl 13 1861;Jl 4,S 12,D 12 1863;Ap 15,Jl 1 1865;Mr 4,Je 20 1897;S 30 1899;Ag 9 1923
PSF S 27 1881
PSuHi Ap 15 1865
PToHi [1858]Ap 16 1865
PW Ap 15 1865
PWCl [1841-42]
PWaHi Ap 15 1865
PWbW [1852]-55;Ja 26,F 1 1861;F 11 1862;Ap 15,24 1865;66-67;Jl 2 1899
PWcHi My 5 1854;Ja 19,23-24,F 25,D 1 1865;Ja 12 1896
PWcT Ja 12 1896
PYHi S 23,26 1881
REdH Ap 15 1865;Ap 19 1875
RP Ap 15 1865
RW N 3 1836;My-D 1861;My 1862-Ap 1863
ScNC Ap 15 1865
T Ap 15 1865
TC Ap 15 1865
TJT Ja 7 1917
TKL Ap 15 1865
TU Jl 3 1851;F 9 1856;O 24 1860
Tx Ag 5 1859;O 23,D 8,11 1860;My 22,Jl 30 1861;Ap 15,19 1865;O 13 1871;Jl 1904-18
TxCoE Ap 15 1865
TxGR Mr 15 1861;Ap 15(facsimile),D 16(supp)1865;Ap 19 1875(facsimile);D 21 1879(reprint);My 1,N 21 1884;S 17 1893;Ja 21,S 12,16 1900
TxH D 29 1880;O 28,N 1,3-4,6-10 1884
TxU Ja-Je,O 1860-Je 1865
V 1843;45;58-85
VAsR Ap 15 1865
VHi S-D 1862;76-Mr 1877
VLyR Ap 15 1865
VNo [D 30 1855-56]
VRC O 1859-62;Ap 7,My 1863-Je,O 5 1865;My 12 1867
VU [Ap 21-D 1853]My 18,D 16-21,23-25,28,31 1861[Ja-Ag 1862]Ap 15 1865;S 8 1892;My 5 1895;Ag 23 1896;N 24,D 1 1901;O 2 1902;O 29 1907;S 13,21-22,27 1908[Mr-D 1910;Mr 1911-12;Ap 1913-24]
VtBeM Ja 7-D 13 1865
VtMiS [1861-82]-96
WHi My 6 1835(facsimile)Je 4 1836-My 1837;My 30,Ag 18 1840;O 15 1844-Mr 19 1845;My 9-D 1849;O 14,16 1850;51;D 30 1855-Ap 26 1896;N-D 1898
WaPS O 1920-F 1921;Mr 1 1922
WvU 1861-65
—w ed *See* California herald; Dollar weekly herald

Sunday HERALD. w Je 14- 1835||
NNHi Je 21 1835

Weekly HERALD. w D 3 1836-96||?
Title varies slightly
A Je 1846;Ag-D 1854
CL S 26 1840-D 19 1846;47-48
CP Ap 15-26 1865
CSmH Ap 22 1865
CoHi S 1 1860;N 14 1861;F 26,Mr 10,15-21 1862;Ap 15-26,My 14 1865
CtSp N 21 1840;N 26 1842
CtTo Ap 29 1865
DLC My 1837-Ap 21 1838[39-40]-[43]-Ag 5 1854;55-57;61-62[68;70;72]O 31 1885-O 1886
GDE Je 24 1848
GU O 25 1860;O 20 1895
IA Ag 27 1863;Ap 15 1865;O 1869-Ap 1873
IAls Ap 15 1865
IC 1844-Jl 1847[Mr-D 1848]
ICHi Ap 26 1862-D 22 1866
ICU S 24 1881
IG Ap 15-26 1865
IHi [Je 15 1856-Ap 1865]
IU Ag 24 1839;Jl 18,Ag 15,29,O 24 1840;My 15 1841
IaHi [1878;82-84;87-92]
In Je 1843-89
InI Ap 15 1865;F 1876-Ap 2 1878[81-89]
InRE N 26 1856
InU Ap 15 1865
KHi [Mr 1844-S 8 1866]
LNH Jl 14 1849
MB [D 1839-S 1860]
MBAt [1838-39]Ag 17,S 21-28 1844;N-D 13 1845;46-47;Je 10 1848
MHi D 19 1840;My 15 1841[61-62]Ap 29 1865
MWA Mr 25[N 1837-39]-[56-57]My 1,Je 5,Ag 28,S 18 1858;Ja 15,S 3 1859;D 1 1860;Jl 18 1861[62-Je 1865]Jl 7 1866;Mr 1882-My 1885
MeBa Ap 10 1841
MiG F 1841-42;Mr 18 1843-Ap 13 1844
MiU-C [1838-39;41-45]-[51-55;57;60-65]
MnHi Ap 11 1840;O 29 1842;O 8 1853
MoS 1847-56
MsHi 1847

NEW YORK (*Continued*)

NEW YORK CITY—*Continued*

Weekly HERALD. 1836-96‖?—*Continued*
N F 15-D 17 1840;Ap 10 1841;42-48
NBHi 1840[41]-49;N 1860-63
NBuG Jl 9 1859;N 1-15,D 27 1862;Ja 17-30,F 14,27-My 9,23-30,Ag 8-15,S 12-26,N 21-D 5,26 1863-Ja 1,23,F 6,Mr 5,19-My 7,21 1864;Ag 28 1869
NCanHi Je 28,Ag 9,23,N 22 1845
NN 1836-38;Mr 16 1839-[47]Mr 25,Je 24 1848; 49-Mr 1852[53]54;58-64;Ap 15 1865;68-70
NNCom D 1836-55
NNHi N 18 1837;F 29 1840[Mr-Je 1841]-Ap [Je 1842-F]Je 20 1846;D 2 1848;53-54
NPyC D 28 1839-S 19 1840
NSchU Mr 5,My 7 1842
NUHi My 15 1847
NbHi Ap 15 1865
NcD N 11 1837;Mr 6,Ap 10-12 1841;N 12-26 1842;Je 24,Ag 26 1843;Ag 31 1844;Ag 23 1845 [46-47]48;F 3 1849[52-53]D 15-22 1855;My 24, Je 14-21,Jl 5-12,26-S 6,20,O-D 20 1856;Ap 23 1859;Ja 12 1861;Ja 7 1865;D 4 1869[70]Ja 7 1871;Ja 5,Je 29 1878;Ap 7,S 15 1883;Jl 17,N 6 1886
NcU Mr 19 1842;Jl 13 1844;Ag 23 1845;Ja 12, Je 14,N 3 1856;N 5 1859;Ja 19 1884
NhD Mr 30 1844
NhM Jl 16 1853-Ja 21 1854
NjFHi Je 14 1847;Ap 15 1865(reprint)
NjH N 27 1864;Ap 29,Mr 7 1865;Ag 8 1885
NjHi [1836-52]55-Mr 1879;80-81
NjNb 1853-62
NjR [1844;47-48]56-57[95-96]
OC N 30 1844-Je 20 1846;F 20-D 1847;N 27 1852-N 12 1853
OCHi Je 13 1838-S 12 1840;D 14 1844;O 4,D 6 1845;Ja 10 1846
OCl F 28 1885
OClWHi D 1837-Ap 7 1838;D 22 1839-Ag 1840; Je 12,D 3 1841;D 31 1848;Ag 23 1860;Ap 18, My 30 1863;Ap 1864-Mr 17 1866;S 30 1876; Ag 1 1885
ODW Ap 9 1864
OHi Ag 19 1861;My 13 1866
OrHi 1846
P Je 10 1840;Je 8 1844
PLaF My 29 1841-S 16 1843
PPCHi [1888-89]
PPL Ap 4 1840[41]-N 23 1844
PPiHi Ap 19 1862
PWcHi O 18 1845
RPB S 2 1837[50-52]
RW My 29 1841
TJT Ja 8 1887
Tx Ap 7 1866;D 3 1870;D 27 1871
TxDM [Mr-D 1847]
TxGR My 23 1861
TxHuS My 7,O 17 1863;Ap 20 1864
TxU [My 31 1841-S 15 1845]Mr 1852-Je 1854 [Ja 13 1855-59]
Vt [Je 12 1841-Mr 5 1872]
WHi Ag 1 1840;Je 26 1841-Je 1842;Ag 24 1844-Ag 1845;O 24 1846;S 25,N 27 1847;O 14 1848-49;S 1850-54;56-59;F 27 1864;Ap 22 1865

Evening HERALD. d My 22 1837-Mr 30 1839‖
My-Jl 11 1837 as Evening chronicle
DLC 1837
MWA F 2 1839
NN Je 14 1837;Ja 4,10,22,F 27,Ap 5,12,23-24,My 22,28,Je 7-8,14,16-18, 25,30,Jl 7,Ag 15,D 21 1838
NNHi 1837

New York HERALD. sw Ja 10 1838-70‖?
Title varies slightly
CtHT Ap 16-17,20 1865
CtY N 5 1852
ICHi Mr 5,19 1841;Ja 1,Je 24 1847;Mr 19,Ap 11 1848;Je 16 1860;D 5 1861;Mr 14,21,Ap 18, 25,Ag 23 1862;Mr 9,Ap 11,Jl 14-19,D 2 1863;Ap 15,Ag 19 1865
MeBe 1840-O 1841

HERALD. *See also* California herald; Dollar weekly herald; Herald for Europe

New York HERALD and general advertiser. tw 1836-39‖?
DLC Ja 23 1839
OCHi Jl 23(extra)1839
OClWHi S 15 1838

HERALD for Europe. ir,w My 31 1846-79‖
Issued every steam packet day
CSmH Jl 15 1846
CtY Ag 20 1846
MiU-C My 11 1847
NN 1846-Ja 14 1848;49-54;Jl-D 1862
—d ed *See* New York herald

EL HERALDO. w My 6 1916-
In Spanish
NN 1916-Jl 17 1918

New York HERALD-TRIBUNE. d Ap 10 1841+
Ap 22 1842-Ap 9 1866 as New York daily tribune; Ap 10 1866-Mr 18 1924 New York tribune; Mr 19 1924-My 30 1926 New York herald-New York tribune
A [1851]Mr 29 1856-[69]-[88;94]1900-02
AzU [1841-1907]
C 1887-89;Jl-D 1890;O 1903-Je 1905
CClP [1862;64-66]Je-O 21 1904
CL Mr 4 1861;S 23 1862;72-Ap 1884;Ag 8 1885
CSf Ap 1906-33
CSmH My 14 1846;My 20,Jl 13 1861;Je 27,Jl 31,Ag 26 1862;Ag 11 1864;Ap 22 1865;My 29 1867[86-Je 1913;17-21]
CSt [1861;67;93-97;1900-01;04]09-[11]
CSt-H [1914-16]-[18-19]
CU Ap 10-Ag 7 1847
CaM 1884-86
CaNSa 1906-08
CaO 1895+
CaOLU 1855-Mr 1861;Mr 1863-F 1865
CaOTL 1889[91]-[94;1909]Jl 1913
CaQMF 1864-65
Ct Ag 8 1846;Ag 1847-[S 1854-58;60]Ap 1861-Ap 1869;Je-D 1870;72-N 1887;88-O 1907;24-Ja 1928
CtAn [1861]-65[96]-98
CtB O 1884-1914
CtDe Ap 10(supp)1841
CtHCo 1856-66
CtHi 1843;Jl-S 1,O-D 1861;Mr 4 1862-64;67-79; 81-90;S-N 1891;92-Mr 1912
CtNh Ap 1877-Ap 1882
CtSp D 21 1841[42]Je 10 1846[56]Ja 13 1857 [58]My 26 1861;Ja 3 1863[74;76]Je 27 1882;D 25 1883;F 16 1884[85]O 29 1886[87-89]94+
CtTo S 1856-92
CtW Jl 1856-S 1886;87-F 1930
CtY 1841-Ap 9,N 29 1842;F 3,23,Mr 18,20,O 31,N 8,D 16,30 1843;N 26 1845-1924
DLC 1841+
DeWI N 5 1855-Ap 9 1856[62-63]Ap 15-My 9 1865;Jl-D 1874;77;97-1915
IB Jl 13 1861-68
IBa Ja 7 1854-55
IC Mr 22 1842;Ag 12 1844;Je 15,Ag 11,S 22,D 1 1847;My 1,D 14 1848;Ap 14 1849;Ap 10-D 1850;S 16 1851;Mr 13[Ap 16 1852-Mr 9 1853]Je 15,Jl 18,20,22,26-27,Ag 1861-64;Ap 15,17,20,26 1865;Ja-O 13 1866;Ja 21-Je 1873;Jl 1885-Mr 1886
ICHi [Ja-My 1847]Ag 13,28 1850;Ja-Je 1857; D 10 1860;Ja 12,Ap,S 26,O 13 1865;O 9-17,19, 27,N 21 1871
ICJ 1841-Ap 6 1842
ICM My 20 1868;N 17,D 14,16 1871;N 6-7 1872[F]Mr 1 1876;Je 6 1877;My 10 1878[Je-Jl 1880;Ja-Je 1882]My 14 1884; Je 20,O 28,D 14 1885;D 16 1887[Je-D 1891;Ap]N 23,27 1892;Ja 10,My 28,Jl 16 1893;D 22(supp)1897 [Ag 1903]
ICN [1858-Ap 18]D 15-16,18 1859-[64-65]68-S 14,O 1870-S,N 1871-Je,S,D 1872-Je,N 1-14 1873;Ap 1,Je-Jl 1874;Ja,Ap-My,N 1875;Ap-My,Jl,S 1,23 1876-86;Ja-F,Ap-My,Jl,S 1 23 1876-86;Ja-F,Ap,Je 1891+
ICU Mr 9 1848;O 12-14 1850[54-F 13 1857;Jl 1858-Ja,Mr-D 1859]-Je 11,S 1863-[64-65]-1901
IF O 20 1853-N 16 1854;Je 21,23,Ag 28,O 2 1856;F 19,S 9,11 1858;Mr 8,31,Ap 8,Je 16,Ag 11,30,O 5-6,D 14 1859;Ap 24,My 23,Je 20,O 15 1860[61]Ja 8,F 15,20-21,26,Mr 4 1862;Mr 7,Ap 15,19,My 4,6 1865
IHi [1850-89]
IP Ag-N 1858;59-Je,O 1865-Ap 1866;Ap 1868-Ja,Je-S 1870;O 1872-Ja,Jl 1873-F,Jl 1874-Ap 1875;Je 1890-Ap 1904
IU Mr 22,Jl-Ag 24,N 29 1842;My 14 1847;Ag 14 1848;Ap 10-19,My 3-4,10-11,Je 22 1850[Je 19 1851-52]Ap 28 1854-Ap 1855;S-D 1858;O 8 1860-Ag 1868;Ap 11-Je 2,N 1 1872[Mr-O 1873; 74]-Ja 20 1875;84-1919;Mr 1920-S 8 1921;D 16 1925+
IaAS 1861-65
IaDH Ap 10 1841;Je 1876-O 1879;Ag 1892-1915
IaHi Jl 1878-Mr,Jl 1879-81
IaU O 14 1845-F 21 1849;Je 2-D 1 1856[57]61-Je,S 1864-65;69-97;1900-O,D 1907;F 1913-Je 1914;Jl-D 1915;F, My-D 1916
In Je 1844-N 1892
InGoE [1856-61]
InI 1842-63;F 1876-83;91-95
InNcHi [F 13-D 18 1878]Ja 1 1879
InRE Jl 24 1855-Ap 4 1857
InU [1842-52]
KHi [My 13 1846-Ap 9 1850]-1930 extra Jl 18 1879
KU Ja 3 1853-Ap 29 1865
LNM My 10-D 1870
LU My 1850-Je,Ag 1865-67;Jl 1868-Je 1876;N 1877-86
M 1890+
MB Ap 10-S 24 1850;Ap-S 1851[Ap 10 1852-Je 1884]Ja-Je 1885[86-90]Jl 1895+
MBAt D 1841[42]O 15 1844+
MBeHi 1860-65
MBr 1900-12
MCam Ap-Je 1895;Ap 1896-98
MHi Mr 15 1843;Je 15 21,N 7,12-13,16,21,D 2 1844;My 16,20,22-25,Je 12 1846;Ap 10 1850-Mr 1851;Ag 26 1854[56]F 2,24 1857[My 20 1858-Mr 14,Ag 15 1859-62;64-65]D 7 1872;Ap 19,Je 18 1875;N 21,29 1879
MMarHi Ap 26 1865
MMel 1861-65
MNF [O 11 1860-61;Mr 13-D 23 1862;Ja 5-My 8 1863;My 14-D 1864;Ap 15-My 10 1865]
MNS [S 1932+]
MNb Je 1862-S 1894;Mr 1911-13
MPi 1849;52
MSaE F 26 1847;F 2,S 14,26-29,D 1849[F 1850-S 1851]Jl 15 1854;Ag 3,N 14 1857[58]O 26 1859;S 14 1860;D 7 1861;S 13 1862
MWA [Ap 10-D 8 1841]Ja 5,12,Mr 12,22,Ap 14,Jl 1,Ag 11,O 8,19 1842;Ja 12,18,F 22,Mr 3,15,My 13,19,Ag 9,D 6 1843[44]F 7,Ap 17,My 27,30,Jl 7,N 15,18,D 2 1845[Ja-Jl]Ag 6,31 1846-[Jl-D 1847]Ja 1,5,7,10(supp)[Je 29-D]1848-1914
MWiC 1900-04;Ja-Ap,S 1906-10
MdBJ Mr 29-S 24 1878;Ja 7-D 23 1879;80;Ja-Mr 10 1885
MdBP Mr 30,My 4-25,Je 22,Jl 6-20,Ag 10-S 28,O 12-N 30 1844;Ja 15-F 5,19-Mr 11,25,Ap 8-Jl 1,15-S 2,16-O 7,28,D 2-9,23 1848;Ja 6-Mr,Ap 14-My 5,26,Je 9-14, 28-O 6,20-N 10,24-D 8,29 1849;54-[61]Je 6,25,Jl 19,21,Ag 18,N 1,13 1862;Ap 29-30,Je 1-27,O 1-7 1863;64-72
MdHi Ja 5-Ag 10 1850;N 1871-Ja 1872[85]
MeBB Jl 1890-Je 1913
MiAC [1880-90]
MiU Ja 29,My 21 1844[50-51;60]-[85]-88[93]-[95;1906]-[13-14]24+
MiU-C [1841-42;44-46;50-52;54;58;60-66;69;72; 76;78-82;84-85;87-88]-92[96-97]
MnHi [1860-72;76-1912]
MnM Ap 1892-Ap 1908
MnS Mr 27-D 1861
MnU Ag 1 1849[50-51;54;56;59-70]83-1912
Mo Jl-D 1867;S 1868-Jl 1870
MoS Ja-S 1857;Ja-F 9,23-Mr 18,Ap-D 1859; 76;79-Mr,O 1883-99
MoSW 1881-1901
MsHi 1864
N Ap 13-My 1,8-22,26,Je 1,17,S 3,11,O 5-14,18-19 1841[43-46;48-49]52;Ja 22,O 1 1853;Ja-Ap,Je 16,S-D 1854;F 28 1855;S 1856+
NB N 25 1857-58;D 1860-S 1861;80-81
NBHi 1843-46;48-1914;24—
extra:Ap 9 1874
NBP 1892-1929
NBi Je 7 1859-Ap 14 1860;Ap 13 1861-Je 1865
NBu 1861;Mr 1862-70;F-Je,S 1871-72;Ap 1900-S 1913
NBuG N 1841-Je 1854;55-S 1862;S 27 1866;Ag 1 1867;Ja 31 1868;S 1871-Je 1874;75-76;O (extra)1888
NCH 1866-68;Ja,Jl 1877;Mr-Je,N 1879-Mr 1880;95-O 1896
NChM 1860-66
NCcr O 1858-D 25 1874
NCcrt D 9 1842-D 9 1843
NDe Ap 1918+
NHe Je 27 1929+
NHerHi Ap-Ag 26 1854
NHf N 1847-52
NHuHi Ap 10(supp)1841;Ja 1919
NI Je-N 1841
NIC My 8 1848-[61]-1903
NLi [1842-48]
NN 1841-Jl 12 1848;49+
NNC O 18,28 1843;Je 6 1846-50;Jl 1851-52;Ap 11 1853-N 8 1854;57+
NNCC 1841;45-46;Mr 1848-60;Ap 1861-64;Jl 1865-91
NNCU 1841-Ap 9 1842;Jl 1864-66;Jl 1867-O 1919
NNCom 1846-My 1859;Mr 1861-[My 1910-S 1915]+
NNFo 1934+
NNHi 1841-[49]-[58-59]-My 1862;My 2 1865; Je 5,Jl 18,S 28,N 5 1866;Ag 11,20,S 3,5,7 1870;Jl 15 1871;Ja 11,D 4 1872;O 13 1873[98]; Mr 19 1924+
extras:O 29 1842;Mr 2 1843;My 8,D 25 1847
NNMT 1841-Ap 1846;47-48 My 18 1857-60;67-69
NNRa Je 16 1865
NNRo 1894-Ap 1920
NNS O 15 1841-Je 1846;50-52;Jl 1853-1913
NNUT [1853]Jl-D 1854;65-76
NNUnC Ap 1850-52;61-1913
NOH Ja 19 1863
NOsC S 19 1836;63-Ja 14 1865
NPV Mr 14 1851-Ap 9 1853[F 1861-Je 1914;S 8 1931+]
NPo Jl 1861-62
NSchU Ag 11 1841-Ap 9 1870;Ap 10 1871-Ap 9 1875;Ap 10 1876-83
NSyU D 21 1849[61-62]63[65-72]-1918
NT S 8 1846-47
NUHi 1853-55;62-67;80-87
NcD 1841-[44-45]-86;Jl 1887-O 1903;04-09;Ag 1927-My,Jl 1928-[Ja-Mr]My-S 1929;S 1930+
NhD Ag 13 1845;Ap 10,N 9,25 1848;Jl 11,O 29-31,N 6 1850;Ag 28,S 13 1851;Ja 7,My 11,13 1853;D 1860-Ap 1865;D 5 1872;Ag 15 1874[Ja-F]Mr 6,11,My-O,D 1875;Ap-Je 1876;D 21 1881;88-Je,S 1908-09
Nj Ap 10 1850-Ap 9 1867
NjCH Ap 22-O 1851
NjHi 1841;43-Je 1844[49]Je 1850-My 1852;57-Mr 1879[80-81;88-93]94[1917;19;32]
NjJ O 1866-67;S-D 1873;My-Ag 1874;75-Ap, S 1876-Je 1879
NjN [1846-52]N 4 1864;Ap 10 1865;Je 26 1869
NjO [1860-65]
NjP [1850-52;59-71]
NjR [1841;44;47;49;52-53]-[56]59-[62-63;65;68-77;81;83-84]+
NjU 1929+
OC Ap 10 1845-49;Ag 22 1853-Je 1933
OCl [1861]62[69]71-[77-78]80-[90]-[1915-16]-[18]
OClWHi Ap 10 1841;F 22,O 22 1842;Ap 4,Ag 28 1843;44-46;Ja 17 1848;S 6 1849;F 1851-52; F 15,Je 27,Ag 4 1856;S 15 1857;Ja 21,Ap 7 1859;F 1860-Ap 1896;S 14-20 1901;Mr 19 1924
OHi Jl 1850-Ja 2 1854;My 1855-Je 1858;Jl 1859+
OXG Ag 28 1933+
OrU Jl 1841[Jl-D 1843;Ap 3-D 3 1844;45-46; 58-73]
P 1841-1917
PAg 1860-62;Jl 1894-My,Ag 1896-S 1903
PAlHi 1860-61
PB Jl 14 1870-Ja 1871
PBL 1851
PBf [1857]Ja 4,11,25,F 8,Mr 14-21,Ap 18-25 1860[61-64;68-69]Ap 22,Je 1-2,S 27-28,N 17 1881
PE Mr 18 1861-S 12 1862
PEHi [1856-57]F 2 1868;Je 23 1871
PEr [1899-Mr 1900]
PFr Ja 31 1858-Ag 1868
PHi 1854-65;82-1909
PHsHi Ap 10(supp) 1860-Ja 15 1861[65]Ap 11 1891;Ja 23 1901
PJR [Mr 31 1864-Je 1865]
PLaF [1852]-[58]-73;S 28,O 19 1930;F 8,16, My 17,Ag 16 1931;Ag 27 1933[34]
PLaHi 1860-F 4 1864
PLaN Ap 12 1853-[56-77]
PLewL [1861-62;67-69;71]
PMe Jl 2 1861
PP Ja 12 1843;O 4,6-8 1847;Ap 10 1849-Ap 9 1852;Ja 22-23,My 16,29 1855-56;Mr 9-12,D 25 1857;Ja 15,20,F 6,8,27,Mr 4,Ap 9,Jl 9,17, 29-30 1858[59-60]-65;My 1872-[86]-Ap 13 1895;1929+
PPF 1858-[68]
PPL [1847;49-52;55-56;61-65;72]-[86]-[95]
PPM O 1842-43[55-56]-Ag 1860;61-[1901-02]-07;10-[28]+
PPeS F 14 1857;Ag 18,S 1 1860;O 31 1863[66-67;69-76]N 7 1928
PPi 1859-1909;17+
PPiHi Ja 11,Je 11,Jl-D 1861;Jl-D 1862;O 24,N 12 1918;Ja 17 1919
PPot Mr 20 1857[58-61]Je 7 1862;Ja 19,Jl 8, N 9 1863;Ag 8 1871
PStP [1851]-[53;55]-[58]62-[64]-[69;71;79]-[82;97-98]-1915
PToHi Ap 10 1841
PU 1860;D 1861-62;Mr-My 1863[91-92;94]
PWbW [1842-46]Je 2,S 1,O 20 1855[56]F 14, Mr 28,S 19 1857[58-61]Jl 4 1863[76-77]85+

NEW YORK (*Continued*)

NEW YORK CITY—*Continued*

New York HERALD-TRIBUNE. 1841+—*Cont.*
PWcHi Mr 20 1857;D 11,18,25 1858;59[60]Ag 8 1871
RPo 1861;66-70
RW [1841-Jl 24 1885]
TC Ap 8 1844-[Ja-Ap 24 1846;48]Ja-S 1850 [My 9-D 1861]-S 1875
Tx Mr 26 1844;Jl-S 1856[Mr 26 1861-Ap 12 1865]
TxHuS Ja 23,My 11,16,Je 4 1864
TxU [Ja 5 1856-Mr 1858]O 19-D 1859;61-Ag 1866;My 4 1931-Mr 1932
VNo [D 29 1855-56]
VRC Ja 30 1861;My 13,Je 4-5,Jl 1,5,7,9,16,21 1862[My 5-N 9 1863;64]My 30 1865
Vt 1850;61-62
VtMiS [1854-75]-[77]1901-12
VtU [Mr 22 1842-77]
WHi N 1841-O 24 1845;My 28 1846;S 11,28,O 6,N 4,23 1848[Mr 3 1849-Ag 3] S 2 1850-S,O 10,11 1851; 53-Je 13 1854;Ap 4 1857-My 18, Ag 25 1858-61;My 1862+
WM 1856-1933
WaPS Jl 2,9 1879;Ag 19 1896;My 8 1920[24]N 19,21 1932
WaS 1848-Je 1853;54-1916
—evening ed *See* Evening tribune
—Index.
CtY 1875-1906
ICN 1875-80;82-96;98-99;1901-05
MoS 1876-77;79-94
NB 1875-1906
NBHi 1875-99;1901-06
NIC 1876-88;90-91;93;95-99
NN 1875-1906
NNUT 1879;81;84
WHi 1875-1906

New Yorker HEROLD. Morgenblatt. d 1845?-N 30 1919‖
1845?-56? as New-Yorker staats-demokrat; 1857?-76? New Yorker demokrat; 1877?-78? New Yorker allgemeine zeitung; 1879?-1913? New Yorker zeitung
In German
DLC Ap 15,17-21,N 1 1865;Jl 5 1879-80
MBAt Ap 17 1865
MWA My 27-28 1856[O 18-N 23 1860]Ja 19 1863
NN 1916-19
PScrHi D 3 1867;Ap 11,D 5 1871
WHi [S 20-D 5 1860]

New Yorker HEROLD. d 1880-D 1 1934‖
1914?-N 30 1919 as New York herold. Abend zeitung; D 1 1919-21? New Yorker herold und New Yorker staats-zeitung. Abendblatt. United with New Yorker staats-zeitung und herold
In German
MB [Mr 7-My 11 1918]
NN [1907;O 1908-10]16-34
NNSh complete
WHi S 30 1930
—w ed *See* Revue

Der Täglicher HEROLD (Yiddish) *See* Warheit

A HET (The week). w
In Hungarian
PPiHi [Mr 15 1924-S 5 1925]

HLAS lidu. d 1886-1921‖?
In Bohemian
NN [1905]

Al-HODA. d 1897?+
In Arabic
IU 1918-D 17 1919
KHi Jl 27 1915

HOME news. [Bronx ed] w,sw,tw,d 1906+
1906-24? as Bronx home news
w 1906-12?; sw 1913?-15?; tw 1916?-21?
NN D 28 1916;Ja 7,11,18-25,30-Mr 15,O 1917-Mr 1918
NNHi Ap 28 1910
—East Harlem and Yorkville ed
NN Ja-Mr,Jl-D 1918;Jl-D 1919
—Harlem ed
NN Jl-S 1918;Ap-D 1919
—Harlem and the Heights ed
NN O 1917-18
—Washington Heights ed
NN Ap-D 1919

HUDSON'S exchange shipping list. tw Jl 23 1835-Mr 15 1836‖?
MWA Jl 30,N 21,D 5 1835;Mr 15 1836
NN Mr 5 1836

HUMORIST, or, real life in New York. d My 23-Jl 11 1834‖?
InNh Jl 1 1834
NNHi Je 27,Jl 11 1834

IBERIA. d O 15 1894-
In Spanish
NN O 15-16,20-N 13 1894

L'IDÉE. w Ag 9? 1856-
In French
DLC N 15 1856

IDISCHE welt. *See* New Yorker morgen blatt un Idische welt

IDISCHER journal (Jewish journal). w 1899?-Ap 20 1906‖
In Yiddish
NN My 26 1899-1902
—d ed *See* New Yorker abend post

INDEPENDENT press. d -O 10 1835‖?
NNHi O 1,3,10 1835

L'INDICATEUR. tw N 2 1839-Ja 9 1840‖?
In French
DLC Ja 9 1840

INTERNATIONAL journal. *See under* Boston

IRISH advocate. w Jl 6 1850-
NNHi Jl 6-13 1850

IRISH-AMERICAN. w Ag 12 1849-1915‖?
DGU Jl 25 1857-58
DLC F 1862-F 10 1866
IU O 14 1899;Ja 6 1900
MB Ag 24 1861;Je 1866-[Ja-S 21 1867;Ap 12-D 6 1873;Ja 10-D 12 1874]Ja-F,Ap 17 1875
N Jl 15 1871
NN 1849-1903;06-Jl 4 1915
NNHi D 13,27 1851;F 7 1852
NjR S 14 1861
OHi 1912-13
PLewL My 17 1862
PPCHi [1855-61;63;71;79-82;85-90;93-97;1900;15]

IRISH citizen. w O 19 1867-72‖?
IU 1867-O 9 1869
NN O 19 1867-O 10 1868
NNHi O 19 1867-Jl 1872
NNIHi 1867-N 18 1871

IRISH nation. w 1881-85‖?
NN N 13 1881-N 3 1883

IRISH volunteer. w 1843?-
CSmH N 7 1846
NNHi Je 19 1847

IRISH world and American industrial liberator. w 1870+
1870-D 14 1878 as Irish world
Jl 1876 is centennial supp
A 1900-18
CL Ja-Mr,Je 28-D 1879;Ja 17 1880-Jl 23 1881
CLM O 29 1892
CU-B Ap 26,My 10 1919
CaSMuS S 24 1904-S 17 1914
Ct Ja 28 1922
CtY 1915+
DLC Ap 8,My 13-Je 3,Ag 5 1876
ICU Ap 13 1878
IU S 1875-Ag 15 1885;1920+
KHi [Jl 1876-S 1929]
MB 1923+
MiU Jl 1876
N Ag 28 1886
NN N 1870-[71]-My,Je 14,Jl 19 1879[S-D 1880]-Ag 1882;S 1883-Ag 1884;Ag 23-D 1885; Jl-Ag 14,31 1886;Ag 20-D 1887;Ja-Ag,N 23 1889;91-93;95+
NNHi Jl 1876
NNIHi 1900-12
NbHi Ja 2,30,Je 19 1875;Jl(supp)1876;My 19-Je 23,Jl 7-21,Ag 4,25-O 6,20-27,N 10-D 1-22 1877;Ja 5,19-F 2,16,Mr 2,Ap 6,20,My 18,Je 8,29,Jl 13,S 21,O 12-19,D 7 1878;Ja 18,Jl 5 1879
NcD Ja 1 1916
OO [1879-1911]
OkHi [1911-16]
PDoHi O 13 1888
PP Ap 1921;Jl 26 1924[30]+
PPCHi [1880]-[90]-[99-1901;05-06;10;12]-[33]
PPot S 13,N 8 1884
WHi 1889-95;97-1904

IRISHMAN. w Jl 12- 1824‖?
MWA Je 19 1824

IRISHMAN and foreigners' advocate. d 1835‖?
MWA Jl 15,20 1835

ISKRA. d Jl 18 1921-
In Russian
NN [1921]

Al-ITTIHAD. *See* Union 1921-22

Ha-IVRI. (Hebrew) w 1891-Ja 24 1902‖
Suspended from Jl 29 1898-Je 7 1901
DLC 1895-1901
NN Ap 11 1892-1902

JAPANESE times. w,sw 1911+
Title varies slightly
w 1911-17
In Japanese
IU Ag 1917+
NN My 5,Je 2,16-30 1906;Jl 13-20 1907;Ja-Jl 1913;My 1914-N 1918;19+

JAPANESE-AMERICAN. w,sw 1900+
1900-S 13 1902 as Japanese American weekly news; S 20 1902-22? Japanese-American commercial weekly
In English and Japanese
Ct Je 10-Ag 15 1931
CtY [1907-22]+
DLC D 1901-S 13 1902;03-11;14-22
IU 1917+
MWA O 14-17 1931
MiU [1924]+
NN 1906-12;15-25
NNC 1916-[18-21]
TxU Je 17 1931-32

JEFFERSONIAN. d Jl 28 1834-36‖?
Ct [1834-36]
CtY Jl 30,Ag 4,O 8,28,30,N 1834-[Ja-F]S 21 1835
DLC N 22 1834-Ap 6 1835
InNh Jl-Ag 19 1834
MWA [Mr 6-My 6]Jl 14 1835;Ja 1 1836
NN O 8 1834
NNHi N 13,D 11 1834;Mr 3,Ap 17,My 31 1835
TU N 22 1834;Ja 14 1835

New York JEWISH abend-post. *See* New Yorker abend post

JEWISH daily bulletin. d O 15 1924+
pub 1924+
ICU Ag 29 1930+
MB 1925
MoCoB Jl 15 1929-My,S 1932-My,S 1933+
NNJHi 1924+
OCH 1924+
PP [1928]-F 1930
PPiHi Jl 1931+
TxGR F 23 1925+

JEWISH daily forward (Vorwärts). d 1897+
In Yiddish
pub 1897+
CtY My 11 1898
DLC Je 1927+
KHi N 10 1914
M Je 28 1933
MdBE S 1933+
MnU [D 1927-28]-[31]-34
NN Jl 1900+
PP [1927]+
PPJ 1904-34

JEWISH gazette (Jüdische gazetten). w 1874-F 24 1928‖
In Yiddish and Hebrew
MWA Jl 6 1881;Ag 27 1886
NN Ag 22 1890-1928
NNJ 1916-19
—d ed *See* Jewish daily news

Daily JEWISH herold. *See* Warheit

New York JEWISH illustrated journal. w? O 22 1887-
NIC 1887-Je 14 1888

JEWISH journal. *See* Idischer journal

JEWISH morning journal and the Jewish daily news (Morgen journal-tageblatt). d Jl 2 1901+
1901-Ap 29 1928 as Jewish morning journal (Morgen journal)
In Yiddish
pub 1907+
DLC 1910+
IU Mr 1918-Ap,S 2 1928+
M Mr 28 1928
NN 1906+
VU D 4 1907

JEWISH nation. *See* Dos Yiddische folk

JEWISH daily news (Jüdisches tageblatt). d Jl 1885-Ap 29 1928‖
United with Jewish morning journal to form Jewish morning journal and the Jewish daily news
In Yiddish and English
DLC Jl 1916-28
KHi Ag 29 1899;O 22 1906;Ja 29 1926
MnHi Mr 17-Jl 22 1898
NN 1906-28
NNJ [1888-89;92-94;96;98-1928]
TxGR N 25 1915
—w ed *See* Jewish gazette

Daily JEWISH press. *See* Tägliche presse

New York JOURNAL. w,sw,d Ag 21 1824-
w 1824-Ag 22 1826;sw Ag 25-D 20 1826
NN Ag 22,S 12-O 6,N 1-15,20,29,D 9-20 1826

New York evening JOURNAL. d F 1? 1829-Je 9 1832‖
F-S? 1829 as Evening journal. United with New York American advocate to form New York advocate and journal
CSmH Ag 14 1830
DLC Ja 23,26,28 1830;N 19 1831
MWA Mr 25,My 11,Ag 26-27 1829;S 23,N 8,10 1830;My 27 1831;My 23 1832
N [N 1830-Ap,Je-O 1831]
NIC F 6-Je 20 1829
NNHi O 1829-Mr 1830;Jl 7 1831

New York evening JOURNAL. For the country. sw 1829?-Je 12 1832‖
United with New York American advocate for the country to form New York advocate and journal for the country, later New York advocate and journal
MWA Ja 27,Je 12 1832
N My 27 1831

Weekly JOURNAL. w 1850-
MWA Ap 27 1850;Jl 22 1866
—d ed *See* Merchants' day book

Morning JOURNAL. 1882-95 *See* New York American

New York evening JOURNAL. d S 28 1896+
ArHi S 14 1897
CL Ap 1904-Jl,S 1910-Ja 1927
CLM F 1,4 1924
CSt-H [1914]-19
Ct F 4 1903;O 19 1906;D 6 1907
DLC S 25 1897-98
GAtCo S 4,27,O 9,11 1896;N 6 1900
ICM N 17 1900
IU O 15-D 1923
KHi [1898-1919]
MAtt Ap 19 1898
NHuHi Ja 9 1919
NKenHi Ap 17 1912
NN O 1906+
NNHi Mr-D 1898
NcD Mr 5 1897;Ag 11 1917;My 2,6-7,9,15-16 1919
NjJ Ap 20-O 1 1898
PMe Jl 4 1898
PYHi S 14-16 1901
VU My 28 1898;F 9 1909
WHi S 9 1896-Ap,N 1898-[99;1901]O 13 1913-14
—LONG ISLAND and Brooklyn ed.
NN F 1923-Ja,Mr-D 1925

*New York evening JOURNAL and patron of industry. d N 1 1809-D 31 1821‖
1809-Ap 18 1817 as Columbian; Ap 19 1817-Je 30 1821 New York Columbian. United with New York statesman (Albany) to form New York statesman and evening advertiser, later New York statesman (New York City)
DLC 1821
MWA Ja-D 19 1821
NBHi Jl-D 1821
NIC 1821
NNHi 1821

New York JOURNAL of commerce. sw S 6 1827-92‖?
CSmH Jl 4 1829;S 9 1837;Jl 13 1861
DLC O 12 1833-40;Ap 1841-43;Ag 28 1852;O 8 1856
GU Ag 14 1833-34
MWA Mr 13-27,Ap 28 1829;F 5 1831;Je 16 1832;Ja 1-Mr 5,N 5 1834;Ap 20,N 27 1844;Ap 27(supp)Ag 3 1850;Ap 5 1882
MiG Ap 18 1828
MiU-C [1830;35;37-39;44]

NEW YORK (*Continued*)

NEW YORK CITY—*Continued*

New York JOURNAL of commerce. sw 1827-92—*Continued*
NBuG S 10,24 1856;66-[86]87;89-90;Ap 1891-Ap 6 1892
NN 1827-33;Ap 19-Je 18,Jl-D 1834;46-56
NR Je 6 1834-36
NSchU Ap 19,O 29 1832;Jl 24 1833;S 17 1842
OC Ja 23-D 1828
OCHi [Ag 25 1841-O 14 1848]

Weekly JOURNAL of commerce. w S 5 1828-1902||?
1828-Je 1843? as New York mercury; Je 1843?-73? Mercury and weekly journal of commerce Jl 25 1828 is specimen ed
CSmH Ag 18 1830;Jl 25 1861
Ct [N 16 1831-Je 1835]
DLC Jl 25 1828(specimen number);S 1829-Ap 11 1833;60-61;63;65-66;68;71-[76]-80
ICHi S 1829-32
ICM N 1- 1880
MBC 1839-49
MH-BA 1828-S 1 1830
MWA 1852-55;My 10,24 1860;D 1 1864
MiU N 1 1843
N F 9(extra)1832;33-34
NBuG Ag,O 17-24,N 14-D 5,19-26 1847;Jl 16 1859;Mr 24,S 29 1860;F 9-D 1861;F 1-15,Mr 1-8,O 1862-63
NCH N 27 1834;Ag 1835-40;Jl 1841-57
NHuHi 1828-Ag 1830
NN 1832;47-58[Mr 1860-F 1861;Mr-D 1863]64; Je 1865-Ap 1868;81-90;Ja-Je 7 1893
NNHi 1828-Ap 1831;F 19(extra)My 16-Jl 4,25, Ag 8,S 23,O 10,N 14-D 1832;Je 22 1843;O 28 1847
NSchU Mr 31 1842
NcD [1840]52;N 25 1858;D 8 1859[60-61;68]73-78;O 1898-F,O 1899-Ja 1900
NjNH 1828-31;36-43;S 20 1857
OCHi N 20 1845-Ja 1847
P-M D 6 1838;Ja 10 1839;Ja 16,Mr 12,Jl 2 1840
PEL S 1830-Ag 1831
PPAp [1830-31]
PToHi O 18 1855-O 16 1856
RPB [1830-31]
WHi S 1829-32[F 27 1834-S 23 1841]F 3 1842;N 4 1847

JOURNAL of commerce, Jr. d 1851-D 30 1865||
CSmH Ag 1 1856;Mr 26,30,Jl 1,4,8-11,15,17,23, 25,29,31,Ag 3,19-20,31 1861;Ja 6 1862
CtY O 1851-F 11 1857;My 26,Ag 4 1864
DLC Ja 3 1856;My 26 1859;Ap 2 1864;F 9-D 1865
FMaS S 20-N 3 1860
GU D 25 1860
MSaE [Jl-D 1861]
MWA O 1? 1851;Ja 29,Jl 10,Ag 13 1852;Ap 15 1857;Ap 20 [Je-D 1861]-[Ag,O-D 29 1865]
MeBa My 29 1863
MiU-C [1852-63]
MsHi 1858-61
N Mr 17 1855
NBuG O 1852-65
NcU Ja 9,29,F 5,9,Mr 20,23,28,Ap 12,15 1861
PBL Ja-Jl 24 1857

JOURNAL of commerce and commercial. d S 1 1827+
1827-Je 10 1893 as New York journal of commerce(My-D 1840 New York journal of commerce of gazette) Je 12 1893-D 31 1926 New York journal of commerce and commercial bulletin
S 27 1927 is centennial ed
pub 1928+
CL S 27 1927
CSt [1917-18;22]-[24;26]+
CU Ap 1-26 1904;06+
Ct Je-Jl 1929[31]
CtHi Jl 16 1835-48
CtNw My 15 1839
CtY 1833-42;66-Je 1891;92+
DA 1908+
DC 1897+
DLC Ag 29,N 15 1828;Mr 24,S 16,O 17,D 22,28 1829;Je 10,Jl 5 1831;S 25 1832;S 18 1833;D 18 1835;37-50 Jl-D 1867;82+
ICHi O 26 1865;O 10 1871
IEN [Jl 1917;Mr 1918]Mr-Ap,Jl,N 1920-Ja,F 12-Mr 17 1921;Ag 1924+
IEN-C Ag 1922-Ap 24,My 21 1923+
IU 1902+
LU N 1929—
M D 28 1928;N 2 1932;F 15 1933
MB Ja 31,F 19,Ap 13,S 20 1831;My 8 1832;Ja 25,Ap 10,25 1833;D 27 1834;My 26,Jl 11 1835; My 26,Je 1,D 26 1842;Ja 30 1843;Ap 1850-Jl 1854;S 17 1857;60-Ag 1861;63-68;71-72
MBAt Mr 1 25,29,My 10,20 1828;Je 27,29,Jl 1-2 1829;Ja 7,Jl 29 1830;31-33;35;69-70
MH-BA 1916-Mr,Jl 1927+
MHi Ag 2 1831;Ag 21 1832;Ap 18 1863
MSaE D 30 1829;S 20 1837;Ja 3,13 1838;My 29 1852;O 12 1857;O 11 1860
MWA Jl 17 1829;Jl 27,S 29,N 8 1830;My 12,Je 9,18,Jl 20 1832;33;Ja 22,Ap 19,D 9 1834;35;Ja 25-26,30,F 1-6,20,25,Je 14,D 27,29 1836;37-42; Ja 11-12,26-28,Ap 18,29 1843;Ap 29,Jl 2,17,31, S 21,30,O 2,D 9 1844;Ja 7(extra)[Ap 23-D 3]1845;Ja 23,My 13,Je 11 1846;D 18 1850 [Ja-O 4 1851]Ja 1,Jl 17 1852;Ja 1,12,My 31 1853;Mr 30 1854;Ag 1 1856;N 11 1857;Ja 28,S 1 1858;N 19-21 1859;Jl 5,9,11,N 29,D 10-11,16, 20, 26 1861;Ja 2,Mr 7,11-12,My 10,Jl 5,Ag 14-15,S 23,D 2 1863;My 21,S 30,D 3 1864;Je 27, Jl 14,O 9-10 1865;N 27-28 1866;F 5-7,16,Ap 22 1870;F 10 1872;F 10-Ag 8,O 17 1874-[Ja-My 1875]O 7,N 2-4 1876;Ja 14,24,D 12 1878;Mr 3-5 1879;O 3 1881;Ap 14 1882;Ag 24 1883;Ja 3 1888;My 2,Je 12 1893-94
MdBJ F 15 1933
MiD 1930+
MiG O 12 1836
MiU [1917]+
MiU-C [1835 38;40-42;59;1903]
MnHi D 27 1834;F 24 1862;Ag 20 1863
MoSW O 1931+
MsHi 1877

N 1857-73;Jl 1913+
NB 1862-63
NBHi Mr 28,Ap 4 1829;79-92
NBuG Ag 13,15,D 23,25-27 1851;F 4-7,17-21, 24,Mr 20,My 8,25,Je 24,Jl 1-3,S 7-11,14-16 1852;F 26,Jl 5,28,N 25 1853
NCH N 1827-Ag 1835
NIC O 30 1905+
NN 1827-59;D 2 1862-Ja 8 1863;S 13 1870+
NNC-B S 1921-24;Mr 1925+
NNHi S 22 1829;N 30 1832;N 1837-S 12 1839; Je 27 1848;My 19 1849;61-82
NNMC Jl 26 1856;Ag 28 1873
NNSt Je 1917+
NSyU F 23,Ap 22 1861;Ja 11,18 1862;Ag 6 1864
NT [N 14 1836-40]
NUHi 1831-34
NcD [1823;35-42;47;64-65;79]
NcU D 15 1858;S 1 1859;My 11,Je 5,O 20,24,27 1860;F 1,Mr 12,Ap 8,10,13,15,17,22,My 16,24 1861
Nj 1852-57
NjHi 1828-F 1829;My 1831-35;My-D 1840;My 1841-Ap 1847;Ap 19 1865
NjN Ap 25 1865;1917+
NjN-B [1917+]
NjR S 7 1839;Ag 23 1858[1928]+
OC Ja 3-Ap 1829;N 1874-Je 1878 80-Je 1881
OCHi [Ag 21 1832-Je 15 1833]
OCl 1930+
PEHi F 5 1868
PP F 13 1852;Ap 1-29 1916[19]+
PPCo 1931—
PPM 1863-Je 1865
PScrHi Ja 3 1910
PU 1901-[11]-14;S 1921+
RPB S 6 1830;Mr 20 1848;My 18 1850;O-D 5 1851
RW F 11,18-19 1847;F 14 1858
Tx 1905-08
TxGR S 29 1927[F 3 1928+]
TxU [Ja-My 1861]Ja-Ag 27 1909;12-34
V 1845
VNo [S 6 1827-Ag 29 1828]
VRC F 22,Ap 15 1861
WHi Jl 25 1835;Je 21 1836;Ag 11 1841;Jl 21 1843;My 16 1861-63;Jl 1865-Je 1866;Ja-Je 29 1867;1907+
WaS Ap 1920-F 1923
WaSp 1932+
WaU [1909]-Ja 15,Ap 7 1917-26

JOURNAL of finance. d S 10 1890-1904||?
DLC 1890-93;Ap 6-D 1899;1901

JOURNAL of the day. d 1870?-
MiG My 6 1871

JOURNAL of the people. tw
PP Jl 22 1847

JÜDISCH... *See also* Yiddish

JÜDISCHE gazetten. *See* Jewish gazette

JÜDISCHES tageblatt. *See* Jewish daily news

JUGOSLOVENSKI svijet. *See* Svijet

JURAB-UL Kurdy. sw,tw,d 1907-13||?
sw 1907-11?; tw 1912?
In Arabic
NN N 1 1911-My 1913

JUSTICE news. d,w O 22 1928-
1928-F 9 1929 as Justice daily news(d)
In Chinese
IU 1928-Ap 8 1933

KAWKAB America. w,d 1892-1909||?
w 1892-97?
In Arabic and English
CtY Je 10,Jl 1 1892
KHi Ap 22 1892-F 28 1896

KHLIEB i volia. w F 26 1919-
In Russian
CSt-H [1919]
DLC Mr 5 O 23 1919

KLEIN'S weekly news. w F 14-N 8 1913||
F-Je 7 1913 as Klein's weekly
NN complete

LADIES' morning star. *See* Morning star 1836

LANG, Turner & Co's New York gazette and general advertiser. *See* New York gazette and general advertiser

La LATTA. w Ja 9 1909-
WHi Ja-Ag 28 1909

New York LEADER. w Mr 18 1854-71||?
Title varies slightly
CoD F 9 1861-67
DLC Je 3 1854;Jl 16 1859-Je 14 1862
ICHi Ap 22 1865
MBAt Ap 22 1865
MWA Mr 11-25,Ap 8,My 13,Je 3,S 16-23 1854; N 23 1856;My 25,O 12 1861;My 6, Jl 15 1865
N Ap 15 1854 Ag 20 1864;Mr 4 1865
NN F 13 1853-F 5 1859;N 23-30 1861;64-F,D 1868-69:71
NNHi Ap 8 1854;F 14 1857-70
extras:F 6 1860;My 25 1867
NSyU S 22 1860
NcD S 23 1854;Ag 22-29 1857
NjR Ag 8 1857
OClWHi Ja 14 1865
OHi N 11 1854
P-M O 14 1854
TU O 7 1854
WHi F 14 1857-F 12 1861

Sunday LEADER. w My 27 1855-
NN 1855-F 7 1857

Evening LEADER. d 1871|?
NN Mr 4-My 6 1871

New York LEADER. d My 30 1908-N 12 1923||
1908-S 1923 New York call (title varies slightly)
CSt-H 1915-[22]
Ct F 17 1909
CtY [1911]Mr 31 1913
DLC Jl 1912-23

KH D 10 1916;F 13,Mr 9[Je 11-Ag 8]1921
MnHi 1917-F 10 1920
MoSC Mr 1913-Ag 1917
N Jl-N 1917;Ja-Ap 1918
NN 1908-[F-Jl]N 1911-23
NNC Jl 1911-Je 1912
NNRa complete
NPV Mr 1909-15
NjP [1919]-22
PHi Ap 5 1915
PP [1912]-18
PU [1909-10]11
TxU D 1914-17;Mr-Ap 1918;Ja-F 1919;20-23
WH 1908-S 1923
WaPS [D 1916]

New York evening LEDGER. d Ja? 1846-
NNHi Ja 27 1846

Ha-LEUMMI. (Nationalist) w D 14 1888-Je 14 1889||
In Hebrew
CtY complete
NN complete
NNJ complete

New-Yorské LISTY. d 1875—
In Bohemian
IU D 12 1917+
NN [1906-07]
PP [1928]+

Nedělní New-Yorské LISTY. w 1889+
In Bohemian
IU D 16 1917-Ag 9 1925
NN [1917-18]+

LOG CABIN. w My 2 1840-N 20 1841||
New York weekly tribune issued for S 13 1841
Suspended from N 9-D 5 1840
Also dated in Albany
Campaign paper
CoHi My 30 1840
DLC complete
extras:Jl 4,Ag 29 1840
DeHi My 2,S 11 1841
ICHi Je 13,Ag 22,S 26,N 9 1840
ICU Jl 4,Ag 1-8,22-S 19,O,D 1840-F 13,27-S 11 1841
IU Jl-D 24 1840;Ja 16,My 22 1841
IaDH My-N 9 1840
IaU My 9-N 9,D 26 1840
KHi Je 13,Ag 22,S 12,O 24 1840;Ja 16 1841
MB complete
MH complete
MHi Je 27,Ag 15-22,S 5 1840
MWA My-N 9 1840;Mr 6,My 11,22 1841
MiG D 1840-My 15 1841
MiU [1841]
N complete
NBu My-N 9 1840
NCort complete
NIC complete
NN complete
NNHi My-N 9 1840
extras:Jl 4,Ag 22,29 1840
NNMC complete
NRiH My 9 1840-N 13 1841
NhD Ag 29-S 5,19,O 3,24-31,N 9 1840;Ja 23 1841
NjFHi Ag 29(extra)1840
NjHi My 2,Jl 11,Ag 8,O 3 1840
OCHi complete
OO complete
P Je 6 1840
PHi complete
PP [1840]
PWbW [1840]
PWcHi Je 20-27 1840
Vt Jl 11 1840;S 11 1841
VtBr My-N 9 1840
WHi 1840[41]
—*See also* New Yorker

LOYAL. *See* Nomotages

McINTYRE'S telegraph... *See* New York telegraph, McIntyre's bank note and prices current

MACKENZIE'S gazette. *See under* Rochester

MAGAZINE of Greenwich Village... *See* Greenwich Village weekly news

MAGYAR banyászlap. *See under* Detroit, Mich.

New York MAGYAR hirlap.
In Hungarian
PPiHi [D 15 1923-Ag 19 1926]

MAGYAR ujsag. d Je 14 1932-
In Hungarian
PPiHi 1932-O 14 1933

Evening MAIL. d O 11 1841-
MWA O 11 1841

Evening MAIL. d S 21 1867-Ja? 1924||
1867-81 as New York evening mail; 1882-F 13 1904 Mail and express. Merged with Evening telegram, later New York world-telegram Ap 27, 29-30 1889 are Centennial of Washington Inauguration eds
CClP Je 2 1898
CP Ap 29-30 1889
CtY Ag 8 1881;Ap 29-30 1889;S 14 1901
DLC 1867-Je[S-D]1874;Jl 15 1875;F 12 1876; Mr 4(supp)Ap 27,29-30 1889;Ag 14 1895-Mr 1899;S 17 1901
GU O 11 1879;S 8 1891
ICM D 17 1881;Ap 29 1885;Ap 26 1887;My 3,Je 26-28,Ag 18 1888;Ja 4 1889;Ag 19,O 29,N 3-4, 14 1891
KHi Mr 4,Ap 27,29 1889;Jl 4 1891[Ap 1897-Ap 1900]O 5 1901
MWA S 26,30,O 2 1867;Ja 3,My 2 1868;S 2 1871;F 16,My 10 1872;Mr 4,11,My 16 1874;Ag 19 1876;Mr 16 1877
MWo Ag 30 1890
MiG Ap 27-30 1889;Ap 27(extra)1897;O 9 1909
MnHi Ap 27,29-30 1889
N D 9 1874
NB O-D 1904;Ja-Je 1906
NBHi 1870-73

NEW YORK (*Continued*)

NEW YORK CITY—*Continued*

Evening MAIL. 1867-1924||—*Continued*
NCorL Ap 27,29-30 1889
NHuHi Ja 7 1919
NN 1867-1904;06-Ja 1924
NNHi F 5 1874;98
NNMC Mr 4 1889;S 14 1901;S 25 1909
NcD Ap 2 1888
OClWHi Ap 29-30 1889
OHi O 1886-88;Ag 1895-My 23 1896
PArdL Ag 3 1923
PBf N 15 1881
PDoHi S 21 1901
PEHi F 3-4 1868
PPiHi Ap 29-30 1889;S 30 1899
PSuHi Ap 27-30 1889
VU Ap 29-30 1889;Ag 24 1892
WHi My 2 1868;98-S 5 1903
—**Index.**
NN 1891

Saturday evening MAIL. w 1871?-1916||?
1871-81 as Weekly mail;1881-1904? Weekly mail and express
CSmH Je 28 1913
ICM My 16,Jl 11-18,Ag 1-8,22-S 19 1888
KHi O 31 1888
MWA F 7,28 1872;F 26,Jl 23 1873;Mr 12 1884; Ap 29-My 1 1889;F 25,Ag 19(extra) 1891;S 1898-Mr 1906
NNHi Ja 19,F 9,S 28,N 16 1907;Jl 4,N 28 1908
NcD Mr 30 1887[Mr-Je 1891]
OClWHi Ja-Ap 9 1898
TJT O 23 1889

MAJOR DOWNING'S advocate and mechanics' journal. tw,sw,d Mr 12-N 1 1834||?
Mr-Jl? 1834 as Major Downing's advocate tw Mr-Jl? 1834;sw Jl 9- 1834
Ct Ap 12 1834
DLC Mr-Je 23 1834
NBHi My 8 1834
NN Jl 9-N 1 1834
NNHi Mr 26,My 26,Jl 26,S 30 1834

MAN. d F 18 1834-Jl 17 1835||?
Ct S 19 1834
CtY S-O[D 1834-Mr 5]Ap 20-Jl 17 1835
InNh My-Ag 1834
LNH Ap 6-9 1835
N My 17-S 10,O 9,22,28,30,N 4-6,8-12,14-15,19, 21,26-28,D 17,19,22 1834
NN F-Ag 29,D 5,20 1834;Ja 1-2,5-Mr,My 5,Je 27 1835
NNHi 1834-Jl 6 1835
NjR F 20 1834
PDoHi [Je 1834]
WHi F-My 16,Je 14-S 2 1834;Ja-Jl 17 1835
—**w ed** *See* Young America

New York MECHANIC. d Jl? 1834-
NNHi Jl 21 1834

MECHANIC. d Ag 24? 1835-
NNHi Ag 25 1835

MECHANICS' gazette. sw My? 1822-Je 4 1823?||
NNHi Je 8 1822;Ap 26,My 3-7,14-Je 4 1823

El MENSAGERO semanal. w Ag 19 1828-Ja 29 1831||
Ag 19 1828 as El Mensagero semanal de Nueva York
Ag 26 1828-Mr 1829 pub in Philadelphia, Pa.
In Spanish
NN Ag-N 8,22 1828-Ja 3,24-Je 20,Jl 11-25,Ag 15-O 17,N 7-21,D 5-12,26 1829;Ja 9-Ag 14,28-O 23,N 20 1830-31

MERAAT ul-Gharb. (Mirror of the west) tw,d 1899+
d 1913?-Jl 12? 1932
In Arabic and English
IU S 5 1917-[33-34]+
NN S 12 1910-Ag 1924

***MERCANTILE advertiser.** d F 15 1792-Mr 31 1838||?
Follows New-York packet (not in this list). 1792-93 as Diary; or, Loudon's register; Ja 1 1794-F 1795 Diary; or, evening register; F-My 1795 Diary and universal daily advertiser; My 1795-Ja 1796 Diary and universal advertiser; F 1 1796-Mr 19 1797 Diary; Mr 20 1797-S 13? 1798 Diary and mercantile advertiser; N 13? 1798-Ap 19 1833 New-York mercantile advertiser; Ap 21 1833-F 21 1838 Mercantile advertiser and New-York advocate
Suspended from S 13-N 13 1798?
CSmH Ag 16 1830
Ct [1826-28;30-31;33]
CtY Je 12 1833
DLC 1821-26;D 1 1828;Jl 27,S 25,N 2-3,27 1829; Ja 12,Ap 7 1830;F 9,Je 2 1831;O 10,D 6 1832; D 24 1835;F 22 1838
MBAt F 9 1821;Ap 24 1822;Ja 27,Mr 15 1830
MWA S 12,D 31 1821;Ap 8-9,25 1823;S 20,29,O 1-2,N 18 1824;Ja 19,F 28 1825;My 13 1826;Jl 1 1828;F 24,Mr 13,N 12 1829;Mr 15 1830;Ja 14 1831;F 6,Je 15 1832;Ap 22-N 27 1833;N 26 1836;O 4,16 1837
MiU-C [1821]
MnHi Mr 15 1830
NN Mr 2,9,Ap 5-6,16,N 11 1825
NNHi 1821;S 17 1823;Ja 13,Ap 20,Je 19 1824;D 29 1830;Ja 30 1832;Ap 22-O 19 1833;Ap 22 1834-O 22 1835
NNMC Ja 16 1835
NNMT 1834-38
NjHi Ja 1 1821[23-26]O 9 1827[S,N 1828;My 1829-34]
RW Ag 30 1824
—**sw ed** *See* New York advocate and journal

MERCANTILE advertiser. w 1845||?
MWA N 11 1845

New York MERCANTILE journal. w 1863-89||?
Title varies slightly
ICHi O 11 1865
MWA Ja 23 1864;S 27 1865;Jl 6-13 1871;Mr 11 1876
N O 16 1865
NcU Mr 2-9,30 1858;Ag 7,28 1875
TxU My 10 1865-S 23 1869

New York MERCANTILE journal, financial recorder and railroad gazette. tw 1854?-
MWA My 4 1852
N O 2 1855;F 7 1856
P-M S 16 1854

MERCHANTS' day book. d Ag 5? 1849-
WHi Ag 11 1849
—**w ed** *See* Weekly journal

MERCHANTS' intelligencer and New York weekly record of general information, business and amusement. w -My 1834||?
United with Constellation to form Constellation, with which the Merchant's intelligencer is incorporated, later Constellation
MWA F 28,Ap 11,Je 6,S 12 1833

MERCHANTS' ledger and market reporter. w 1847-
1847-S? 1848 as Merchants' ledger and statistical messenger; N 1- 1850 Merchants' ledger
DLC N 28 1850
MWA Je 11 1853
NN N 1 1848
NNHi Ja 13 1855
NhD F 5 1853
PP Mr 18 1854

MERCHANT'S telegraph. d Ja 24-Je 14 1828||?
CSmH F 23 1828
MBAt F 22,My 20 1828
MWA Ap 1,4 1828
NNHi Ja-Ap 1828
NjHi Je 14 1828

MERCURIO de Nueva York. w 1828?-31||?
In Spanish
CSmH O 4 1829
DLC My 17 1828;Je 25 1831

New York MERCURY. 1828-43 *See* Weekly journal of commerce

Daily MERCURY. d 1893-N 1897||?
MWA Ja 17 1893
NNHi Ja 17-O 28 1893

Sunday MERCURY. *See* Morning telegraph

Le MESSAGER franco-américain. w,sw 1859-83||?
w 1859-68?
In French
DLC Je 12-Jl 4,Ag 1-8,O 31,N 14-D 5,26 1867; Ja 9 1868
MWA O 20 1871;F 16 1879
PP My 7 1876
TNV S 1870-71

Le MESSAGER franco-américain. d Ja 5? 1860-83||?
In French
CaQMF 1864;70-72
DLC F 1862-70;73-83
LNF N 9-18,D 3-6 1879;My 22-Je 19 1880
MWA Ja 15 1863;Mr 28,Ap 18,My 24,Je 18,25 1866
NN F 23 1872
NNHi Ap 16-D 1863

New York weekly MESSENGER and young men's advocate. w Je 4 1831-F 10 1836||?
1831-Ag 8 1832 as Badger's weekly messenger
CtY Ag 22 1832
DLC F 18 1835
DeHi S 18 1833
MWA Jl 1831-Jl,N 13 1833;Je 11 1834;Mr 25,Jl 22,Ag 5,S 9,23-30,N 18,D 2 1835;F 10-17,Ap 6,27,Je 29,Ag 3,S 14 1836
N O 30 1833;My 13,Ag 19 1835
NN 1831-Jl 11 1832;34-Ja 14 1835;F 8 1837
NNHi Je 4,Ag 3 1831;Ag 1 1832;D 11 1833
PPL Je 19,Jl 17-S 4,18-O 2,16-N 20,D 4,18 1833-Ja 22,F-Ap 2,O 15 1834;Ja 28,F 11,Ap-Jl 1835

MILITANT. *See* New militant

Evening MIRROR. d O 7 1844-
Je 3-14 1845 as New York daily evening mirror
CtNc 1844-Ap 7 1845
CtY My 22 1848
DLC 1844-F 1 1845;D 26-27 1848;Mr 9 1849-O 6 1856
MB My-Jl 2 1846;Ja 5-My 1856
MWA O 16,N 22 1844[F 10-N 15 1845]Ap 30,S 7,O 7,D 5 1846;O 7 1847-Ap 6,Je 12 1848;Mr 7-N 28 1851;Ja 3,23,Ap-My,Ag-S,D 16,31 1852-[54]-[Ja 22-F 22 1858]
MiU-C O 2,25 1851
NB O 7 1856-Ap 6 1857
NHuHi My 31 1856
NN 1844-47
NNHi 1844-Ap 6 1854
NNS 1844-Je 1846
OClWHi Ja 1 1854
PPL Jl 15 1847
RPB [1853]-56

Daily MIRROR. d Je 24 1924+
NN Je-Jl 1924
WaPS F-Mr 9 1929

New York MIRROR advertiser. w
NNMC N 27 1830

MIRROR of the west. *See* Meraat ul-Gharb

Al-MOHAJER. (Emigrant) sw 1902?-13||?
In Syrian
NNC O 30 1912-Ag 2 1913

MONITOR. *See* Aristocratic monitor

MONITOREN. w 1878-
In Swedish
IRA 1878

MORGEN journal-tageblatt. *See* Jewish morning journal and the Jewish daily news

New Yorker MORGEN BLATT un Idische welt. sw,d D 1 1899-Ap 19 1905||
1899-Ja 1 1905 as Idische welt
sw 1899-Ja 15 1900?
In Yiddish
NN D 1 1899;Ja 15 1900;Je 27 1902-05

MORGEN FREIHEIT. *See* Morning freiheit

MORGEN-JOURNAL. *See* Deutsches journal

MORRISANIA gazette. w Jl 31-O 30 1874||
DLC complete
NNHi complete

Daily MUSEUM. d D 1858-
P-M D 21 1858;Ja 1 1859

NARODNAIA gazeta. w Mr 21 1918-20||
In Russian
CSt-H 1918-19
DLC 1918-Ag 14 1919
IU 1918-Ag 14 1919
NN 1918-19

NARODNI list. d 1898-1922||
In Croatian
NN 1908-[11]-18;20-21

Al-NASR. *See* Syrian eagle (Brooklyn)

***NATIONAL advocate.** d D 15 1812-Ja 31 1829||
Not to be confused with New York national advocate. United with New York statesman to form New York morning herald
CSmH Jl 24 1827
DLC 1821-28;Ja 31 1829
DeHi D 13 1828
MBAt Ap 5 1822;Je 4(extra)1828
MWA 1821-24;My 13,28,Jl-D 1825[Ag 17 1827-N 13 1828]
MiU 1821-[25]-[28]
MiU-C [1821]
MnHi Ag 4 1826
N 1822;N 3,D 21 1824;Mr 11-12 1825
NN Ap 25 1821;Ag 7 1828
NNHi Ja 1-13,F 22-Mr 3,5,Jl 3 1823-[24]-My 13 1825
NSchU O 2 1827
NcD Ja-O 10,N 22,27,29,D 18,20,22 1821;Ja-Je 1828
NjR Ag 21 1823
WHi 1823-Ja 17 1825

New York NATIONAL advocate. d D 16 1824-Jl 17 1826||?
Not to be confused with National advocate
Ct [1826]
CtHi Mr 6-Je 24 1826
DLC Ja 14 1825-Jl 17 1826
GU [Jl-D 1825]
MWA D 30 1824;Ja 31-F 1,Mr 9 1825
N F 3,Mr 12,D 20 1825-Jl 4 1826
NBHi My 28 1826
NN My 12,16,18-20,22,26 1826
PDoHi F 4 1825

New York NATIONAL advocate. w 1824-26||?
MWo Jl 22 1825
NGl N 1 1825
PHHi D 28 1824-Je 6 1826

***NATIONAL advocate, for the country.** w,sw Ja 1813-Ja 1829||
w 1813-Ja 1814
CSt [1827-28]
Ct D 20 1825[26-27]
CtY My 3,31 1825;Jl 29,S 2,12 1828;Ja 9 1829
DLC Ja 30,F 24,Mr 2-9,My 21,28-Je 11,Jl 9 1824
MBAt O 12 1821;Ja 11 1822
MWA Mr 23[Jl 31-D 25]1821;Jl 22 1823;My 11,N 19 1824;F 15,Jl 15 1825[Ja-Ap 1826]Ja 12,19,Mr 9,My 8,Je 12,Jl 20,27 1827
MeBt 1823-26
N 1821;Ap 25 1826;Ja 5 1827
NN F 2,14-16,Mr 16,30,Ap 24,Ag 7,14,S 7,D 21,28 1821;Ja 8,18,22,F 12,26 1822;Mr 8,Ap 22-29,Jl 26,N 4,11-29,D 9 1825;Ja 10 1826
NNHi [1822]F 13,Mr 16 1824;Ja 27,F 10,Mr 17 1826
NUHi Ja 16,F 6 1824
NcD N 27 1827
NjHi Ja 9,30 1821;My 7 1822;My 13 1823;S 30 1825;S 29 1826
NjR [1823-25]
PBL Ja 9-Je 8 1821
PDoHi S 26,D 29 1826
PHHi D 28 1824-Je 6 1826
WHi My 1 1821;22-23;N 11 1828

NATIONAL banner. w S 22 1838-
MWA S 22 1838

Daily NATIONAL democrat. d 1851?-
MWA N 4,D 2 1852;F 3[Je 23-S 26]1853;D 30 1854
N Je 28 1853
NhD My 6,D 20-21,24 1853
P-M S 15 1854

New York NATIONAL democrat. 1855-56 *See* New York weekly news

NATIONAL herald. (Ethnikos kerux) d Ap 2 1915+
In Greek
pub 1915+
IU D 6 1917+
MWA O 30 1915
PP [1928]+

NATIONAL herald. m Jl 1915+
pub 1915+

NATIONAL journal. w 1876-82||?
MWA Jl 12 1879
N F 25 1882

NEW YORK (*Continued*)

NEW YORK CITY—*Continued*

NATIONAL union. w D 20 1823-F 5 1825||?
Suspended from N 6 1824-F 5 1825
DLC 1823-N 6 1824
MBAt F 5 1825
MWA O 20 1824
N Je 2-Jl 7,31-Ag 21,S 18,O 30-N 6 1824;F 5 1825
NBHi 1823-N 6 1824
NNHi Ag 28,O 9,23 1824
NcD 1823;Ja 10-17,Ap 3,My 15,Jl 10,Ag 24,N 6 1823
NjCHi Jl 10-N 6 1824

NATIONALIST. *See* Ha-Leummi

NATIVE American and democratic citizen. d O 17 1835-
Ct O 17,N 10,17 1835
NNHi O 19 1835

NATIVE American democrat. d O 14 1835-
NNHi O 14 1835

NEGRO world. *See* Ethiopian world

NEIE warheit. d Mr 14-N 19 1925||
In Yiddish and Hebrew
NN complete

NEUE arbeiter-zeitung. w F 8 1873-75||?
1873-O 17 1874 as Arbeiter-zeitung
In German
NN F 14,28,Ag 22 1874-Mr 13 1875
WHi 1873-Mr 13 1875

NEUE volkszeitung. w D 17 1932+
Follows New Yorker volkszeitung
In German
pub 1932—
NN 1932+
NNRa 1932—
NjR [1934]+
WHi 1932+

Die NEUE zeit. w Ap 14? 1855-
In German
MoS Ap 21 1857-Ap 3 1858
Tx Jl 21 1855

Die NEUE zeit. (New era) w D 14 1912-
In Yiddish
NN 1912-F 1916

NEW leader. w Ja 19 1924+
Title varies: New leader and American appeal
DLC D 1927-Je 6 1931;33+
ICJ D 1927+
IEIC D 1931+
IU [D 1927-31]+
IaDa Current 3 months
KHi D 31 1927
MnHi D 1927+
MnU [1928-30]
MoSC 1930-31
NN 1924+
NNRa 1924+
NPV D 1931+
PP 1928+
TxH Ap 12 1930+

NEW militant. w N 15 1928+
1928-D 8 1934 as Militant
CSt [1928]
CSt-H 1928+
NN 1928+
NPV D 15 1934+
OCl [1931]—
TxH D 15 1934+
WaU 1928-Mr 1935

NEW weekly telescope. w S 4 1830-
CSmH Ja 15 1831
DLC S 4 1830
MWA O 30 1830

NEW world. w O 26 1839-
MWA O-N 2,16-D 7,21 1839[40-S 18]D 18 1841;F 12 1842;Ja 15 1848

NEW ERA. *See* Democratic republican new era

NEW ERA. (Yiddish) *See* Die Neue zeit

NEW ERA and American courier. *See* Weekly democratic republican new era and American courier

Sunday morning NEWS. w My 17 1835-O 1 1844||?
My 8? 1836-My 7 1837 as New York Sunday morning news
Ct [1835-36]
DLC 1835-My 8 1836;My 22 1842
IaDH O 25-D 1 1840
MWA My 17,Jl 12,Ag 2 1835;Mr 6,27,Je 12, S 18,O 2-9,D 25 1836 [My 20 1838-39]-Ja 19, F 2,16-Mr 8 29,Ap 12-Ap 26 1840;My 22 1842
N F 26 1837
NCanHi My 23 1841
NN 1835-F 16 1840
NNHi Jl 3,O 9,N 13-20 1836;D 10 1837;O 1 1844
NcU D 18 1836
OClWHi Ap 11 1841
P-M Jl 30 1837
PPL 1835-Mr 3 1840
RPB My 31 1835

Daily NEWS. d S 2 1837-
CU 1837-Ja 8 1838
Ct D 21 1837
NNHi 1837

New York morning NEWS. d Ag 21 1844- S 8 1846||?
DLC Ag 22-23,S 28 1844;Ja-S 8 1846
MWA N 2,5 1844;D 25 1845;Ap 24 1846
MiU-C S 6 1844
NN S 27 1845
NNHi 1844-S 8 1846

New York weekly NEWS. w S 7 1844-S 5 1846||?
InI Ap 25 1846
MWA D 14 1844
N N 30 1844-S 5 1846

NBuG 1844-Ag 1845
NN 1844-D 20 1845;Ja-F 7,21-28,Mr 14-Ap, My 9-S 5 1846
OClWHi Ag 22 1846
TJT Jl 26 1845

New York weekly NEWS. w 1855-86||?
1855-Je 14? 1856 as New York national democrat; Je 21?-N 1856 New York weekly news and national democrat
CSmH Ag 12 1865;Ap 20,Jl-N 2,16-D 21 1867; Ja 4-18,F-My 9,23-Je 1868
Ct N 10 1860
DLC Jl 12-O 4,18-N 8,22-D 13,27 1856;Ja 10-17 1857;Ja 15,29 1859
GAA D 30 1865
IHi Je 30 1866
IaHi Mr 1881-My 1882
LNH S 10,24,D 10 1864
MWA F 12-19 1859;O 24,D 5 1863;Ja 16 1864; Ap 14 1866;Jl 19 1871
MeBa D 31 1864
MiG Ja 7,Ap 7 1860;Ja 19,F 16,Mr 2,My 25, Jl 20,Ag 10 1861
MoS My 31 1856-Ag 15 1857
N My 3 1856;Ja 17,Mr 7,21,My 23,Je 30,Jl 25, O 10-17,22,D 26 1857;F 6,D 25 1858;Ja 15,Ag 6,20,S 17 1859;Jl 7,Ag 11-18,S 1,15-22 1860; Ja 12,Ap 3 1861;Je,Jl 18,S 12,O 3-10,N 7, 28 1863;Ja 16 1864
NBuG My 9-16,Jl-Ag 1857
NNHi S 8-15,29,O 27-N 3,17-D 8 1855[Ap 1856-F 1857]S 21,N 30 1864
NSyU 1855-57
NcD [1865-67]
OClWHi Jl 1857-D 11 1858;Ja 29 1859;Ja 14, F 11,25 1860;Mr 30,Jl 27 1861;S 26 1863-My 5 1866
OHi Mr 3 1861

New York NEWS. For the Pacific coast. 1855?-
Steamer ed
CSmH Ap 5 1859
DLC Ja 20 1859

New York daily NEWS. d Ap 1855-1906||?
CoD D 4 1863
CtY Je 28-S 2 1861;O 10 1863;Ap 9 1864;Jl 29 1868
DLC O,D 1856;Ja-Je 1858;O 31 1864
DeWI [1863]
IC Ap 17,26 1865
ICHi Ap 15,S 27,O 3 1865
KHi Ap 15 1865
LNC Je 20,24-25 1861;Ja 16-20,F 10 1865
LNH [Ag-D 1864]
MBAt Ja 4 1864[Ap 3-Jl 5 1865]
MWA Jl 2,O 16,N 3,6,10,D 5 1855;O 16,30 1856;Jl 9 1860;F 19,My 17,20,Je 13-19,24-25, 28-Ag 21,29 1861;Je 4,15,23,Jl 9,13,16-17,20-23,Ag 3,18 1863;Ag 12-13,29,S 17,O 22 1864; Ap 4,My 3,6,27,Ag 1,S 23 1865;Ap 16,My 22 1866;Ap 1 Jl 8 1868;Je 23 1882;Ag 6 1885;S 1898-Mr 1906
MWiC Je 22 1861
N O 14 1865-Jl 12 1871
NB 1855-F 17 1857
NBuG F 19 1857
NN Ap 24 1855-Ag,D 12 1856;58-S 14 1861; Je 15-Jl 1863;64-Je 1866;Jl 25,Ag 19,S 5,10,20 1867;Jl 27 1869;Ja-Mr,Jl-S 1872;Jl 20 1874; 1902-Ag 1905
NNHi [Ap 1855-Ap 1856;57]Ja 25 1859;S 28 1860-Ap 1861;Jl 14,N 6 1863;Mr 18,Je 10 1865;F 13 1866[68-70] Ag 23 1884;N 1 1905
NSyU O 3-5,27,D 15 1859;F 21-22,Ap 20,25, Je 28,Ag 3,S 25,O 9,25 1860;61;63-66
NcD F 1 1864;S 23,N 8 1865;Ag 10 1866
NcU D 8 1865
NjHi F 20 1872
NjR Jl 22 1861
OClWHi Mr 31 1858;Ag 11 1861;N 12 1863;O 15 1864-Je 7 1865
OHi Je 22-Ag 26 1861;N 2 1863
PToHi O 1856-Ag 27 1857
PWcHi Mr 1865
TxU [S-D 1863]
V My 23-S 14 1861;Ja-Ap 1864;N 6 1870-Ap 1871
VRC Je 8,Jl 21,N 15 1864;Ap 26,Jl 3,Ag 16 1865
WHi Mr 10,20 1857;Ag 24,27-31,S 6 1861

Semi-weekly NEWS. sw O 3 1865-
MWA O 3 1865
VU N 24,D 8,19 1865;Ja 16,23,Mr 3,27,Ap 3-6,13,24-27,My 4-15,Je 1,19,29 1866

New York Sunday NEWS. w 1866-
DLC Je 2 1867
MB My 5 1867;Je 29 1873
NjWdN F 6 1887
PPeS Jl 5 1868

New York NEWS. w S 13 1913+
Negro
pub 1913+
NN D 30 1915;Ja 20,F 3,Mr 16,Ap 5,20,My 18,Je-Jl 6,20-Ag 10,S 14-N 16,30 1916;17-18; Ja 30 1919-23

Daily NEWS. d Je 26 1919+
Je-N 18 1919 as Illustrated daily news; N 19 1919-O 4 1920 News
Sunday issues as Sunday news
pub 1919+
CL S-N 1921
CLM F 4 1924
DLC 1919+
KHi Jl 29 1923
NN 1919-[Je-Jl 1921]+
NNHi 1932+
NcU 1930+
PP N 10-18 1929;D 4,8 1934
PPeS N 7 1928
VU Ja 29 1930
WaPS F 20-Mr 20 1929

NEW YORK and Richmond county free press. w 1831?-
WHi N 2 1833-Ap 26 1834

NEW YORKER. w Mr 22 1834-S 11 1841||
Followed by New York tribune
Ct Mr 29 1834;Mr 8 1841
CtY 1834-Mr 13 1841
DLC 1834-[37-S 8 1838]
IC Mr 22,N 29,D 27 1834[35]Ja,Mr 12,Jl 23-N 1836
IHM [N 29 1834-41]
IU S 29 1838
MWA Mr 22 1834;Je 20,Jl 18-25,Ag 22 1835; Ja 16,Mr 12,My 28 1836 Ap 29 1837;Ap 7,My 19 Je 2 1838;Mr 30,Ap 20-My 25,Je 8-Jl,S 14 1839;My 16 1840
NN complete
NcD [1834]35[39-40]41
NcU My 10 1837
PCarlHi [1834]-[36]
VtBr S 12 1835;Ap 9,Jl 2 1836;Mr 11 1837;D 1 1838;Mr 23 1839-Je 20,Jl 4,18-O 24,N 1840-Ap 17 1841
—campaign ed *See* Log cabin

NEW YORKER. [quarto] Mr 26 1836-S 11 1841||
CSt complete
Ct S 22 1838-Mr 1840
CtY 1836-Mr 1841
DLC complete
ICHi Je 10 1837
ICU [1836]-S 1838;Mr 1839-41
IU complete
KyLo Ap 1837-Mr 1838
MB complete
MHi Mr-S 1836;Mr 1837-S 1840
MNF 1836-S 1837;Mr-S 1838
MSaE Je 18 1836
MeB S 1836-Mr 1840;Mr-S 1841
MiD-B 1836-S 1837;Mr 1838-Mr,S 1840-41
MiU 1836-Mr 1837;Mr-S 1838;Mr-S 1839;Mr 1840-41
MnHi Mr 1837-41
MoU [S 1838-Mr 1839]-Mr 1840
N 1836-S 1840;Mr-S 1841
NAubHi S 23 1837-My 19 1838;Mr 20-S 1841
NB complete
NBHi complete
NBuG Mr 1840-Mr 1841
NCH Mr 1837-S 1839
NCor D 1 1838
NIC 1836-Mr 1837;S 22 1838-S 1839;Mr 1840-Mr 1841
NN complete
NNC [1836]-Mr 1839
NNHi 1836-Mr 20 1841
NRU Mr-S 1839
NjJ S 23 1837-S 15 1838;S 21 1839-41
NjN 1836-Mr 1839
NjP Jl 1837-Mr 13 1841
OHi 1836-Mr 14 1840
OO [1836-41]
OU S 1840-41
OrU Mr-S 1836;Mr 1837-S 1838;Mr 1839-Mr 1841
P [1836-40]
PScrHi Jl 30 1836
PW [1837-38]
VtBr Mr 20-S 1841
WHi complete

NEW-YORKER. d 1849?-
DLC Mr 25,Ap 12,18,23,My 23,30,Je 6,Ag 7 1851
MWA Jl 19,23 1851

Weekly NEW-YORKER. w Mr 1 1851-
MWA Je 21 1851

New York NINTH. w
NNHi Jl 31 1862

NOAH'S weekly messenger. *See* Sunday times and messenger

NOMOTAGES. (Loyal) w Ap 5 1919-20||?
In Greek
NN 1919-Jl 10 1920

NORDISKE blade. *See under* Brooklyn

NORDLYSET. *See under* Brooklyn

NORDSTJERNAN. w,sw S 21 1872+
sw 1911?-My 28 1920
In Swedish
pub Jl 1874+
IRA 1872+
IU D 1917+
KHi Jl 12-Ag 16 1888
MnHi [1881-84]+

NORTH New Yorker and Westchester clarion. [Morrisania] w 1872-75||?
1872-Ja 17 1873 as Westchester clarion; Ja 24 1873-74? Westchester clarion and the guardian
MWA Ja 24 1873;O 30 1875

NORTH-ENDER. [Harlem] w N 23 1867-
CaOTA F 15 1868
NGe 1867-Jl 4 1868
NNHi 1867-Jl 4 1868

NORTH SIDE news. w 1897+
NN Ap 29 1899-My 10 1908;Mr 7 1909-Mr 6 1910
NNHi F 24-Jl 21,O 13 1907-[Ja-Je,D 1908]My 23,O 10 1909;Mr 3 1912;S 29,O 13-20 1918;Ap 27 1919
NNHu [1930]-Jl 10 1932;34+

Daily NORTH SIDE news. d 1902+
NNHi D 21 1902;D 20 1903;D 9 1908;Mr 26,My 27 1910,D 21-22 1912;S 20 1917;S 4,O 9,21-22, D 23 1918;Mr 24,Ap 5,12,18-19,21,26,Jl 3,Ag 8,S 2 1919
NNHu [1933-34]+

NOTICIOSO de ambos mundos. w 1836-
In Spanish
DLC 1836-38;Je 15-29,Ag 10 1839;O 22-N 1842; Mr 4,My 13,27-Je 3,24-S 16,30,O 14-N 10 1843
supp:N 5 1842
NN 1836-43
TxGR Ag 12-D 1859

NEW YORK (*Continued*)

NEW YORK CITY—*Continued*

NOVEDADES. sw,d 1877-97||?
sw 1877-81?
In Spanish
CLM F 9,Je 29,Jl 10 1878;Jl 6,D 23 1881
DLC Ja 27 1891
MWA Mr 12 1890

NOVOE Russkoe slovo. d 1910+
1911-Ag 19 1920 as Russkoe slovo
In Russian
pub 1920+
CSt-H 1932-33
DLC Ja 29 1918-Ag 28 1919;Ap 27 1920+
IU S 1917-Ap 2,O 24 1921-S 12 1924
NN Ap 1917-18;Ja-Je 1920
PP [1930]+

NOVY mir. d,tw,w 1911+
tw Ag 9 1914-Ap 1926(d D 12 1914-18?)
In Russian
CSt-H 1926[31]33
DLC S 1917-Je 1918;Ap-S 1919
IU S 19 1913-14[S 1917-Je 21 1918]
NN Ap 1911-19[F-Je 1923;Jl-D 1924]26-Ap 1927[Ja-Ap 1928]29+

Il NUOVO mondo. *See* La Stampa libera

NY tid. w 1905+
1905-Jl 1921 as Svenska socialisten; Jl 1921-Mr 1922 Facklan
1905-Mr 1931 pub in Chicago
In Swedish
ICJ Mr 1922+
IRA 1909;13-20
IU Ag 30 1917+
MnHi [Mr 13 1912-23]+

OCEAN news. w
NNHi Ag 15 1857

OESTERREICHISCH-UNGARISCHE zeitung. (Austro-Hungarian gazette) w 1881-1912||?
In German
NIC S 1902-S 1903

OLD countryman. w O 10 1829-48||?
1829-S 23? 1835 as Old countryman: and English, Irish, Scotch, Welsh, and colonial mirror; S 30 1835-Ja 11 1843 Emigrant and Old countryman
1829-Jl 1 1830 pub in Boston
CSmH Ag 26 1830;My 21 1845
CtY O-N,D 9 1830-Jl 14,27-O 6 1831;My 6,Je 3 1835
DLC O 28 1835-N 1837;Ja 31,Ap 11-18 1838;N 6 1839;D 2 1840;Ja 18 1843
GAtCo F 8 1840
MB O 10 1829
MWA D 31 1829;Je 3,Jl 1 1830; Ag 11 1831-Ja 12 1832;Ja 1 1834;O 19 1836;Ja 13-27,F 10, 24,Mr 24,Ap 28 1841;Jl 13,N 30 1842;S 13 1843
MsHi 1833-36
N Ja 19-D 1832
NIC S 2 1840;Ja 20,My 19 1841;S 25 1847-D 16 1848
NNHi Mr 15-22 1843
NRU O 1830-Ja 12 1832
OHi N 8 1832;Ag 28 1834;F 24 1836-37;41-F 1842;43-F 19,D 3 1845
PLewL My 22-N 6 1833

OMNIBUS. w Ag 3? 1844-
MWA Ja-F 13,27,Mr 13,My 1,15 1847
NNHi Ag 31 1844
P-M Ag 8 1846
WHi Ja 9 1847

OMNIUM advertiser. d? F 1837?-
N Mr 1 1837

Sunday PACKET. w 1838-39||?
CtY Jl 7 1839

New York PACKET. w Jl 27?-N 16 1845||?
NNHi N 2-16 1845

Evening PAPER. *See* Abend blatt für die arbeiter zeitung

New York PATHFINDER. sw,w 1847-70||?
sw 1847-O 1850
DLC Mr 23,Jl 27 1848-D 20 1852
MWA Jl 1862;S 12 1863;My 1868
NNHi Je 3(extra)1849;My 30 1850
NcD D 9 1850
NcU Ja 21 1857
P-M My 31-Je 1849
RW D 11 1851
WHi Je 1,19 1848

PATRIA. w,sw 1892-98||?
w 1892-96?
In Spanish
CtY O 22 1892-98
DLC Ap 3,Ag 27,S 20 1892;Ap 28 1894;My 23,Jl 20,Ag 10,S 25(extra)28,O 9 1895;Ja 22,F 12,24,D 12 1896;Ap 10,Je 16-19 1897;Ap 27,N 26 1898
MB [Mr 26 1892-D 10 1898]

New York PATRIOT. sw My 1823-24||?
InI My 5 1824
MBAt S 10,O 4-11,N 22,D 29 1823;Mr 22-26,Ap 29 1824
MWA S 3 1823
N Je 14,Jl 16,Ag 2,S 6 1823-Ja,F 7,18-21,Mr 3,10,17-My 1,S 13,25,N 12-17 1824
NNHi S 20,N 8,29,D 17 1823;Ja 10,24,31,My 1-6,S 11,25 1824
PLewL My 8 1824

New York PATRIOT and morning advertiser. d My 28 1823-D 31 1824||?
1823-O 16 1824 as New York patriot
CtY Ag 3 1824
DLC 1824
MWA Jl 10,O 26,30,N 24 1824
N N 1,18 1828
NNHi Ag 27-29,O 8-9,27,N 17 1823;Ap 19-20, My 6,O 18 1824
NNS 1823-Ja 1 1824
NcD N 13 1823;Mr 24,Ap 24,O 20,N 18 1824
WHi Je 21 1824

*PATRON of industry. sw Je 28 1820-Je 30 1821||
United with Columbian to form New York evening journal and patron of industry
CtY 1821
DLC F 3-Ap 14,25,Je 2,13,20 1821
MBAt Ja 3 1821
MWA Ja-Je 1821
PPL [1821]
T F 7,Ap 11 1821

PAUL PRY. w D 1838?-
DLC Ag 31 1839-F 1840
MWA My 1 1839
NNHi Mr 23 1839-Ag 1840

PELHAM BAY herald. w S 30 1933-N 17 1934||
Followed by East Bronx herald
NNHu complete

PENNY weekly dispatch. *See* New York dispatch

PENNY daily gazette. d Jl-Ag? 1834||
United with American whig to form Constitution
NNHi Jl 28 1834

PENNY daily gazette. d Jl 1839-
CtY Ag 4 1839

PENNY post. w D 18 1832-Mr 12 1833||?
NN Mr 12 1833
NNHi Ja 23 1833

New York PENNY post, and weekly gazetteer. w F 24 1851-
MWA Mr 10 1841

PENNY press. d S 8-O 1 1841||?
DLC O 1 1841
NNHi S 8 1841

Weekly PEOPLE. w Ap 5 1891+
Follows Workmen's advocate (not in this list) 1891-Je 17 1900 as People
CSt-H [1913-20]-Mr 1924
CU Ap 1911+
CU-B Ap 1922-Mr 24 1923
Ct My 17 1913;S 7,N 9 1918
CtY [1893-1900]Ap 1910-Mr 1913
DL Ap 1912+
DLC Ap 1897-Mr 1901;Ap 1904-Mr 1906
ICJ 1891+
ICU [1900-27]
IU 1891-Mr 1892;Ja 8-15,Ap 16 1893-D 17 1899; 1900-O 12 1907;N 1920-My 10,S 27 1924+
KHi Ag 11 1895
M 1903-Ap 1913
MB 1891+
MH Ap 1901+
MoS Ap 1897-Mr 1909
NN [1899-1900]-Mr 1910
NNC [1891-1912]
NNHi My 1892-Mr 1898
NPV Ap 1902-My 21 1904
OU [1915-24]+
PP F 1934+
PPi Ap 1899+
WHi Ap 24 1892+

Daily PEOPLE. d 1900-13||?
NN [F 1903-My 11 1906]Ag 24 1908
NNC Jl 1900-Je 1904
WHi Jl 1900-S 1907

PEOPLE'S advocate. w 1826?-
OCl D 29 1830

PEOPLE'S advocate. sw Jl? 1833-
N O 19 1833

New York PEOPLE'S organ. w 1840?-
P-M D 24 1853

PEOPLE'S own. w Ag 9? 1848-
DLC D 16 1848

PEOPLE'S rights and organ of the National reform association. sw 1844||?
DLC My 22,25 1844
NN Jl 10 1844
NNHi Ag 10 1844
Tx My 4 1844

PERSIAN American courier. w 1915-21||?
Ap 16 1919-Je 13 1920? as Assyrian American
In Persian
IU S 12 1917-Je 1920

PICK. w F 21 1852-
CaQMM Mr 13 1852-F 12 1853
MMarHi Mr 19 1853
MWA Jl 3 1852;Ja 22 1853
NNC 1852
NNHi [Ag 28 1852-53]
PDoHi Je 19 1852
PPFfHi Mr 5 1853

New York PILOT. w Mr 1830-
CSmH S 1 1830
MWA N 24 1830
NNHi O 20 1830

PINE and palm. *See under* Boston, Mass.

PISZKAFA (Poker). w
In Hungarian
PPiHi [Je 28 1923-O 21 1926]

New-York PLANET. d My 4 1840-My 10 1841||?
DLC My 4,N 18 1840;My 5,10 1841
MWA My 7 1840

Daily PLEBEIAN. d Je 27 1842-My 12 1845||
Merged with New York morning news
DLC Jl 2,S 16 1842
IU F 21 1845
MWA [Je-O 1842]Ja 5,23-24,D 2,23 1843;Ja 13,Mr 2,16,23,30,N 4 1844
N Jl-D 1842
NN Ag 26 1844
NNHi Ap 15 1843;S 28 1844;Ja 18 1845
NNS complete
OClWHi O 10 1843;My 17,Jl 29,N 8 1844
WHi Jl 9 1844

New York weekly PLEBEIAN. w 1842-45||?
IU Ag 3 1844
MnHi N 9 1844
NN N 11 1843-D 7 1844

PLOUGHBOY. w Ja 16 1833-
Ja-Jl? 1833 as American ploughboy
N Ja-Mr 6,N 13 1833-Jl 2 1834
NN Jl 10 1833

POKER. *See* Piszkafa

POLITICIAN. w Ap 4 1901-08||?
DLC Ap-Ag 22 1901
NN [1901;03-04]

POMEROY'S democrat. *See* Pomeroy's illustrated democrat (Chicago)

El PORVENIR. ir Ap 15 1863-
In Spanish
DLC Ap-S 2,19-24,O 24 1863-F 3,20-Mr 19 1864

*New York POST. d N 16 1801+
1801-O 16 1832 as New-York evening post; O 17 1832-N 15 1920 Evening post; N 16 1920-Mr 28 1934 New York evening post
A 1872-77
C N 1887-F 23 1889;Je 17 1915-Ap 8 1924
CL Ja-Je 1913
CSmH Je 10 1829;Mr 12 1867;S 19-26 1923
CSt [1891]-93[96]
CSt-H [1914]-[16]-[19]
CU Jl,S 1914-Ja,Mr 1915-Mr,Je-N 1916;Ja-Ap, Je 1917-Ag 1918
CoD Ap 15 1865
CoHi N 7 1883
Ct [1831-33;35;Je 17 1915-Je 1918;27+]
CtDe My 3 1856
CtHi Jl 24 1827-28;35-70
CtW N 11 1861-63
CtY Ag 23 1824-Ap 6 1825;Jl 8,O 3-4,D 28 1826;F 11-12,18,24,Mr 3,6,10,Ap 21 1829;N 17 1830;My 14 1836;Je 21 1837-Je 1839;40-42;Jl 1843-46;48;Ja-Je 1850;Ja-Je 1851;52-Je 1856; 57-59;N 7 1860;Ap 13-D 23 1861;Ap 23-D 3 1862;Ag 10 1864;Ja-Je 1868;70-86
DCE Ap 1918-19
DLC 1821-[27-30]32;34-36[38-40;44]50-Ap,Jl 1900-02;Mr-Ap,Jl 1905+
IC Ja 9-Je 1873
ICHi Ap 17,21-22,26,28,S 28 1865;S 21 1912
ICM My 1,Je 8 1884;Ap 29 1885;O 22,N 20, 23 1891;O 28 1903
ICN Jl 3-D 1879;D 8 1917-N 1918;Ja 8 1919-S,N 1923+
ICU Jl 2,6,S 20-22 1881;Jl-D 1895;Je 23 1928+ (Saturday ed only)
IF Ap 15 1865
IU O 4 1855;1909-[S-D 1922]-F 11,D 16 1924-Je 23 1925;26+
In Je 1915-Je 1918
InI N 6 1874-F 9 1877
InU 1904;06;21[32-33]+
KHi D 3 1859;Jl 18 1864;F 26,Mr 5-12 1878, Mr 16 1918;F 5,19 1927
LSfD Je 5 1883;S 7 1896
M F 15 1869+
MB O 9 1867-Jl 7 1871
MBAt 1821-32[53]56-1921
MBr 1872-77
MHi F 23 1836
MWA 1821-23;Ap 23(photostat)Jl,D 31 1824; Ja 31,F 4,Mr 4,My 6,N 2-3,5 1825;Mr 10-11 1826;Je 13,O 30 1827;28-38;Ja 3,Ap 2-3,20 1839;Ja 9,N 7 1840;Ja 7,S 10 1841;F 16,S 16 1842;Ap 9,27 1844;Jl 1 1848[Mr 6-D 1849]-[1851-S]N 10 1852;My 3,S 11 1855;F 6,Mr 15,24,Jl 2 1856;Ag 27 1857;My 26,Jl 23 1859;D 8 1860[My 14-N 7 1861;Mr 11-S 1862;63-Je 1865]-Mr 1903;Mr-Ap,Jl 1905-Jl,S 1906-Je,Ag-D 1907;S 1908-13;F 1914-Mr 14,Je 1922-F,Ap-D 1924
MeU My 8 1821
MiU [1861]-[65]1909-[14-15;25]+
MiU-C [1823;28-30;32-33;35-36;51;64-65;71;76; 86;95;98-99;1906;14]
MnU [1864-65]Je 1915-Jl 26 1918;D 1933+
MoHi N 16 1901;My 23 1911;Ag 13 1920
N N 11 1830-Je,Jl 14-O 17 1831;O 30 1833; 92-94;1911;My-D 1912;Mr 1913-33
NAlU Ap 1925-My 1927
NB Jl-D 1904
NBHi 1821-1901
NN 1821-61;Jl 1862-65;67+
NNC 1831;37-48;61-67;69-84;Jl 1907;13-24
NNCom 1893-Jl 1900
NNHi 1821-[33]F 22 1834[35-36]O 11 1837-S 10 1839;Mr 19-S 10 1841;52[57]-66;98 extras:Ap 2 1828;F 25 1830;Ap 8 1839
NNMC F 24,S 18 1826;Mr 12-14 1888;My 1 1893
NNMT 1847-48
NNRa Ap 27 1906-Mr 1907
NNS 1821-Je 1902;06+
NNSt Ap 1913+
NPV 1900-Je 1919
NSchU N 20,22 1823;Jl 1,19,21,D 20 1825;F 28,Jl 1,N 27 1826;Ap 13,23,Je 6,8,27,Ag 4,6, 8-9,11,25,S 12,18,26,O 5-6,16,23,25-26 1827;Ja 18,21,F 4 1828;S 13,O 21 1831;Jl 30,O 12 1832
NSyU Mr 18 1857;S 8,24 1860;Ap 19,My 3,10, 17,31,Jl 19 1862;Jl 23,D 10 1864
NcD D 19 1821;Ja 16,Mr 12,Ap 29,My 11,29, Ag 14,29,O 11 1822;Ja 12-15,17-31 1828;My 29 1862;S 12 1863;Jl 23,25,Ag 18,N 20 1868;Je 22 1869;O 3 1884;O 1903-10;Ap-Je 1911;1923-F 26 1924;Jl 2 1926
NcU My 25 1876
NjCHi N 16 1901
NjHi [1821-30]-33[73-79]81-86[88]-[90-91]-94; F-Mr 1932
NjN Ja 7,28,F 8,Mr 27,My 8 1862
NjO My 9 1861
NjP Ap-O 15 1898
NjR [1828;31;35]Jl 1889-95;98+
OC N 8 1874-Je 23 1882
OCl 1911-[15]-[18]
OClWHi Jl 10 1844;F 16 1850;Mr 9 1861-Jl 6 1866;Mr 1 1869-O 1873;Jl 2,S 20 1881;Ag 8 1885;Jl 6 1891;S 30 1892;Ja 27 1894;Mr 18 1901;My 23,N 29 1911;Je 19 1912;Ag 26 1914; Ap 24 1915;O 18 1919

NEW YORK (*Continued*)

NEW YORK CITY—*Continued*

*New York **POST.** d 1801+—*Continued*
OHi Ap 12 1855;Ap 23,25,D 6,10,21,27 1861;Ap 23 1868;1912-Ag 1922
P My 12 1831;1907-Je 1917
PAg [1896]-[99-1902]
PBf N 16 1881
PEHi F 3-4 1868
PEL 1821-Jl 1 1828
PHi 1821-30
PLaF D 31 1918;Ja 4 1919;Ag 21 1920
PMeA [1924]
PPi Jl 13 1894-1909[12]O 1913-27
PPiHi S 13 1872;N 11 1918
PU N 16,18 1901
PWCl D 31 1846;Mr 18,Ap 8,Jl 7,29,O 14 1847
RPB 1821-67
RW N 25 1824
Tx O 1917-Je 1918
WHi Ja-Je 27 1821;24-Mr 24 1829[My 15-N 14 1845]Mr 18 1847-Ap 12 1848;49-Ag 18 1882;98-1919;S 17 1920-Je 1921
WaPS [1910-12]Ja 1913[24]
—**Editorial** index.
MoS 1913-14
NN 1913-17
—**Literary** review index. w S 9 1922-F 24 1923‖
NN complete

***Evening post.** sw Ja 2 1802-1919‖?
1802-N 15 1817 as New York herald; N 19 1817-Ap 2 1840 New York evening post for the country; Ap 6 1840-Mr 26 1850 Evening post for the country
CaOTA Je 9 1829
Ct Ja 26 1835-37
CtHi 1829-32
CtY Ja 30,Jl 1821-23;F 18 1825;28-30;57-58;61-65
DLC Mr 28 1829-O 17 1846[S-O]-D 1848;F 16 1856;My 1863-Ap 11 1865;Jl 4 1873
IaDH Jl 12 1897-S 1900
IaFd Ag 8 1857-Ap 1858;Ap 6 1859-D 1 1877
MBAt F 5 1822;Ag 29 1826;Ap 14 1865
MHi Mr 13,Ag 31 1849;Mr 26 1850
MSaE D 5-7 1830;Ja-N 1831;S 16-D 26 1853[54-58]-Mr 1859
MWA Ap 24,Ag 28[O 9 1821-22]Mr 4 1823;Je 1,Jl 16,Ag 6,S 24,N 5 1824;D 13 1825;Ja 17,F 7,17,My 9,Jl 14,Ag 11,S 1,D 29 1826[Ja 19-N 2 1827;Mr 14-D 16 1828;Ja 23-Ag 18 1829]Ja 22-28,My 7 1830;S 13 1831;F 17,S 6 1832;My 19 1834;N 10-14 1836;Mr 12 1838;Jl 18 1839;My 7,28 1840;N 30 1847;Mr 29 1850;Mr 16,Ap 11,Je 6,S 7,17 1852-S 16 1853;Jl 4 1854;Ag 16,23-27 1856[58]Ja 8-12,19-22 1859;Ap 25 1860[Ja-My]-D 1861;Jl 4 1862;Ja 20,F 24,My 19[Jl 7-D 11 1863;F 5-N 4 1864;65-66]Ja 8,F 22,Mr 1-5 1867;S 8-11,O 16 1868;Je 29 1869
MiG Ap 24-D 1874;N 17 1876
MiU [1834]-[37]55-56[59]81-[87-88]-[1906-07]
MiU-C Ja 25 1828[52;61]
MnHi Ap 10 1834[57-67;69;75-76]
N Mr 1822-[25]-Mr 9 1830;Je 16 1834-Ap 9 1835[39-43]
NBHi Ag 5 1828
NN Ja-My 1821;Jl 1825;D 5 1828;My 1834-Ap 6,D 1-4,26 1840;Mr 10,20,24,31,Ap 14 1841;My 6 1843;Ap 14 1849;50-Ap 1851;Ja 21 1853-57;Ag 14-N 1861;N 1887-1901
NNHi [1821]-[23]-[Ja-Jl 1825]O-D 1832;D 29 1834[38]-[49-50]-86
extras:O 27,29 1840
NSchU Jl 2 1832;Mr 2,Jl 30;Ag 10-13 1842
NcD S 7 1861;N 24-27,D 4 1890[Ja 19-Ap 1891]
NcU [N 1874]-F 9 1877
NhD N 6 1827;D 1 1840
NjFHi Ag 11 1826
NjR [1823]24[39;61-65]
OCHi F 11,Mr 10-20,Ap 10-17,24-28,My 19 1868-79
OClWHi F 2,Jl 12 1860;Ja-N 13 1861;Mr 18-Jl 15 1862;Ja 2,9,N 7 1863;Ja 1,My 17 1864;Mr 30,Ap 13 1869;Ja 28 1870
OHi 1821-My 13 1823
PBL Ja 30,F 6-20 1821
PEL 1821-[28]
PToHi Ag 24 1861;Ag 13 1867;Jl 17 1868;Je 2 1874
VtU Jl 1860-61

New York **POST.** w O 9 1841-1913‖?
Title varies slightly
CaQMS [1857-70]
CtY Ja 22 1868
DLC O 9 1841;O 23 1846-51;Ag 11 1853;Ja 20 1859
IC O 13 1853-O 5 1854
KHi My 24-O 1888;Jl 11 1889
MBAt Mr 29 1865
MHi Jl 30 1850;Jl 22 1851;My 27,Je 8 1861[63]Je 23,Ap 7,Mr 14 1865;My 24,Je 15 1866;N 28 1868;N 16 1901
MWA D 2 1847;Je 8,Jl 6,27 1848;N 18 1852,Mr-N 1854;My 1855-My 22 1856;61[62]-S 20,N 8,22 1871-Mr 13 1878
MdBJ Ap 30-My 21,Je 18-25,Jl 9,23-Ag 6,20-N 19 1842;D 19 1845;My 22,Jl 24-31,O 30,N 13 1846
MeBa [1861-F 1867]
MiU O 9 1841;52-54
MiU-C Jl 19 1876
N Je 1848-Je 21 1849
NCanHi Mr 17 1843
NN Ja 11,Mr 29,D 27 1847;O 28 1852-54;Ag 8-15 1861;Ap 19 1865;My 1888-1901
NcD N 4 1847;Mr 10 1897
NjR D 2-16 1847
OCHi Ag 21 1851-Ag 1852
OClWHi Ja 27 1859-Ag 2 1860;Mr 28,My 2 1861;N 13 1862;N 4 1863
P 1907-09
TxU [Je 1907-N 15 1913]
WHi [O 14 1874-Ap 4 1877]S 18 1895-97[Je 14-N 15 1905]

Morning **POST and family gazette.** d 1833‖?
Ct [1833]
NNHi Ap 1 1833

New-York **POSTSCRIPT.** sw Jl? 1830-
CSmH Ag 24 1830

PRAVDA. *See under* Olyphant, Pa.

PRAVOE dielo. (Right cause) w Ag 5 1922-Mr 13 1926‖?
In Russian
DLC 1922-Mr 13 1926

La **PRENSA.** w,d 1913+
w 1913-17
In Spanish
pub 1913+
CLv [1927-30]
CSt-H [1931]-33
CU-B Mr 25,O 27 1916;Je 17,O 12 1921 Ja 14,16,18,20,24,26,28,31,F 28-Mr 25 1922;Ap 16-Jl 2,S 20 1927-Ap 1928
CoAT Mr-D 1933
Ct [1919]
CtY My 21-22 1919;O 11 1923
DPU current year only
FTS N 12,15,17,19 1932;Ja 5,7,My 31 1933
IU Jl 19-Ag 19 1919;22-Ja 12 1933
IaGG current year only
KHi My 1-3 1919
LNT-M Mr 21,S 20 1930
M N 10 1930
MWA My 15-16 1919;My 18 1936
MeBa S 9-16,30 1916
McP [1922-24]-27
NIC Je 9 1931-D 20 1932
NN Jl 29 1916+
NNiU 1873-74
NSW S 18 1933+
OkU [1921-22]-[24-25;34]
PP Je 7 1926[28]-[32]
WHi Mr 25 1916;D 19 1924
WaPS [1916-29]

New York Saturday **PRESS.** w O 23 1858-
O-N 1858 as Saturday press
CtY Ag 12 1865-Ja 6 1866
DLC O 30 1858-D 1 1860;65-66
MB O 7 1865
NN F 13(extra)1861;Ag-S 23,N 4,25-D 1865;Ja 13-F 17 1866
NbHi S 1 1858
PHi [1858]-D 15 1860;Ag 1865-Je 2 1866

Evening **PRESS.** d 1868-70‖?
NN Ap 17 1869

New York **PRESS.** d D 1 1887-Jl 2 1916‖
1887-Ap 1 1896 as Press. United with Sun to form Sun and New York press, later Sun
CP Ap 30 1889
CU-B Jl 13 1890
CtY D 4 1891
DLC D 16 1887-1916
GAtCo Ag 22 1896
ICM My 19 1893[Jl-S 1894]
IaDH Ja 8 1893
KHi Ag 14 1894
MWA D 1,23 1888;Ap 7,28-My 2 1889;Ap 9 1890;My 5 1893;98-Ap 1906;S 1912-16
MiG S 14,17-18 1901
MnU [My 30 1891-Ja 16 1893]
N Mr 1913-16
NAubHi Ja 28 1893
NB O 1902-Je 1904;Ja-Je 1906
NN complete
NNHi 1898
NbHi F 29,Ag 30 1888;Ag 6 1889;Jl 13 1890;Je 15,Ag 15,28,30,S 1-2,5-6,8,10-11,13,17-21,24-25, 27-28,O 4-5,11,13 1892;Ja 24,28,F 26 1893
NcD Ap 25-27 1894;Ja 21 1897
NjPa Ap 1903-S 1912;13-Je 1916
PArdL Ap 7 1908
PBloHi Ag 23 1888
PMe Je 4-6 1898
PPot S 7 1883;D 2 1895
VtMS [1888-1904]
WHi Jl 2-N 1888;Jl 2 1891-Je 1894
—**BROOKLYN** ed.
NN Mr 26,30-Ap 7,9-17,19,22-23,25-27,30-My 4,16 1888

New York **PRESS.** w D 15 1887-99‖?
NN 1887-Ap, O-D 1896;Ap-N 3,D 1897[98]

New Yorker **PRESSE.** d Je 23 1873-76‖?
In German
DGU 1873-S 29 1876
NNiU 1873-74
—**SONNTAGSBLATT.** w Je 22 1873-
DGU 1873-74

Tägliche **PRESSE.** (Daily Jewish press) d My 16?-S 2 1898‖?
In Yiddish
NN My 17-S 2 1898

New York **PRICE current.** d Ja 2- 1902‖
DLC Ja-Je 1902
—**morning** ed *See* New York commercial

Le **PROGRÈS.** d Ja 1909?-
In French
NN Ja 4-6,10-15,F 3-4,7-12,24-Mr 30 1910

Le **PROGRÈS.** w Ja 1909?-
In French
NN Ja 2,F 6,27-Mr 1910

PROGRESSIVE democrat. w S 19?-D 5 1846‖?
DLC N 21-D 5 1846
IaDH S 19 1846

El **PROGRESSO.** *See* La Epoca de New York

Il **PROGRESSO italo-americano.** d 1880+
In Italian
pub 1895+
DLC My 1932-S 25 1934
IU D 8 1917-19
KHi Jl 18 1889
NHe Ja-Ap 1931
NN 1886;Ja-Je 1888;Jl-D 1889;Jl 1890-92;F-D 1893;Jl-D 1894;My 1907-Ag 1912;13-15;Jl 1919+

PUBLIC advertiser. w N 7? 1840-
N 7-D 19 1840 as Spirit of seventy-six
DLC D 12,26 1840

Le **PUBLIC canadien.** w
In French
CaQMS [Ja 3 1867-Ja 1868]

RANNEE utro. d D 28 1932-
CSt-H 1932[33]

RASSVET. d 1918-My 15 1926‖
United with Russkiĭ vestnik (Chicago) to form Russkiĭ vestnik-rassvet, later Rassvet (Chicago)
In Russian
DLC F 21 1925-26

New York **RECORDER.** d F 18 1891-O 11 1896‖
CLM Ag 16 1891
DLC complete
ICM N 13,25 1891
KHi My 3 1891
MWA complete
NN F,Je 22 1891-96
NcD F 1 1894
TJT O 10 1896
WHi N 1891-Je 1894

Sunday **RECORDER.** w Mr 22 1891-O 11 1896‖
1891-S 6 1896 as New York recorder
MWA complete

RECRUIT. w Je-O 24 1848‖?
Campaign paper
ICHi Ag 1 1848
NEh Jl 25 1848
NNHi Ag 8-15,S 19,O 24 1848
WHi S 19 1848

El **REDACTOR.** tm,w 1826?-D 31 1831‖?
tm 1826?-30
In Spanish
CSmH S 10 1830
DLC Ja 21 1828;31
MB [Mr-O 1828]
MWA Ja 10 1829

REFORM. w,sw,d Mr 5? 1853-
w Mr-Ap 30 1853;sw My 4-O 12 1853
In German
WHi Mr 12 1853-Ap 20 1854

REFORMER. sw O 2 1839-
DLC O 9 1839

New-York **REFORMER, farmers', mechanics', and working men's champion.** sw S 1830-
CSmH S 10 1830

REPORTER and Harlem local. *See* Harlem reporter and Bronx chronicle

New York **REPOSITORY.** d F 28 1931-F 7 1933‖
pub to retain Associated Press morning franchise but never circulated
MWA Mr 7-8,14-17 1931;F 7 1933
NN complete
NNMC F 28 1931
—**evening** ed *See* New York world-telegram

REPUBLIC. w 1843-45‖?
IU F 20,My 24 1844
MdBJ My 11 1844
NNHi Mr 9-16,Ap 13 1844

REPUBLIC. d Ja 21 1844-F 1 1845‖?
DLC Ja 30,Mr 11 1844
MWA F 12,Ap 15,My 2 1844
NNHi [Mr 9-Jl 15 1844]

Evening **REPUBLIC.** d S 9 1869-
N S 11,21,24 1869
NNHi S-D 6 1869

REPUBLIC. d O 5 1874-
CtY O-D 14 1874
MWA O 20,23,N 24-D 14 1874
NBHi O-D 14 1874
NN O-D 31 1874

New York **REPUBLICAN.** w Ag 23? 1856-
KHi N 22 1856

New-York **REPUBLICAN.** w Mr 26 1871-74‖?
DLC Jl 22-Ag 12,O 21 1871
KHi D 23 1871;Ag 28 1872
MWA N 18 1871
N 1871-Mr 25 1872

REPUBLICAN campaign. 1880‖?
Campaign paper
N S 23 1880

New York **REPUBLICAN, medicinal gazette and general advertiser.** w O 5? 1848-
DLC N 30 1848

REPUBLICAN sentinel. sw Je? 1821-D 28 1822‖?
DLC O 27 1821
MBAt D 5-8 1821;N 30 1822
MWA [Ap 20-D 1822]
NN D 8 1821

Le **REVEIL.** w 1825-26‖
Followed by Le Propagateur louisianais (New Orleans, La.)
In French

REVUE. w 1847?-1921‖
1847?-78? as Der Beobachter am Hudson; 1879?-93? New Yorker revue und beobachter am Hudson. United with Sonntagsblatt des New-Yorker staats-zeitung to form Sonntagsblatt staats-zeitung und herold
In German
MWA O 28-N 18 1860
NNSh 1865-1921
Tx My 24 1857;Ja 27,F 3-17,Mr,Ap 14-28 1861
—**d** ed *See* New Yorker herold

RIGHT cause. *See* Pravoe dielo

RIVISTA italo-americana. *See* L'Eco d'Italia

RODNAIA riech'. d 1913-18‖
In Russian
DLC Ja 6-O 23 1918

NEW YORK (*Continued*)

NEW YORK CITY—*Continued*

ROSSIYA. w,d Ap 16 1933+
w 1933-Ja 1935
In Russian
CSt-H 1933+
DLC 1933+

ROUGH and ready. w 1847||
Campaign paper
DLC O 23 1847

RUSSIAN problem. w F 28 1920-
Ct 1920
DLC Mr 6-27 1920

RUSSKAI͡A gazeta. (Russkaya gazetta.) w,sw N 29 1931-Mr 11 1934||
sw Ja 10-Ap 10 1932
In Russian
CSt-H 1931-33
NN complete

RUSSKAI͡A vecherni͡ai͡a pochta. w Ap 5 1931-
In Russian
CSt-H 1931

RUSSKAI͡A zemli͡a. w 1915-
In Russian
DLC Jl 29 1915-S 12 1916

RUSSKAYA mysl. d D 9 1923+
In Russian
IU F 2-My 25 1924
NN 1923+

RUSSKAYA zemlya. d 1913?-16||
In Russian
NN Jl-D 1916

RUSSKII emigrant. d 1912-15||?
In Russian
DLC Ja 31-Jl 17 1915

RUSSKII golos. w,tw O 25 1907-10||?
w 1907-Je? 1910
In Russian
DLC 1907-Ja 27,F 10,24,Mr 9-16,My 10,24,Je 7,15-21,Jl 5-8 1910

RUSSKOE slovo. *See* Novoe Russkoe slovo

RUSSKY golos. d F 1 1917+
In Russian
pub 1917+
CSt-H 1927-28;31-32
DLC 1918;Ja 28 1921;Je 16 1922;24-Mr 9 1926; 33+
NN 1917-Je 1918;Jl 1922+
PP [1928]-Mr 23 1933

SATURDAY. . . *See under* next important word; e.g., New York Saturday press is alphabeted under Press

As-SAYEH. w,sw,d 1912+
d Ap 7 1928-Ja? 1930;w F? 1930-31?
In Arabic
IU S 17 1917-Ja 10,F 20 1930-F 19 1931

SCOTSMAN and Caledonian advertiser. My 16 1874-
CaOTA My 16 1874

SEIT. *See* Zeit

La SEMANA. w Ap 10 1906-
In Spanish
NN 1906-My 27 1908

New York daily SENTINEL (for the country). tw 1829-
DLC Mr 7/8 1831
MWA N 9,12-13 1830;O 11 1831;Mr 9 1833
NjR 1831

New York daily SENTINEL. d,sw F 15 1830-Mr 11 1833||?
sw My 15-Je 30 1832
CSmH Ag 4 1830
Ct Ap 28 1830
DLC D 7-8,10,15,18,22-23 1830;O 2 1832
PEL Ja 21 1831
WHi F 15 1830-32
—w ed *See* Young America

New York SENTINEL and working man's advocate. *See* Young America

SERBIAN daily. *See* Srpski dnevnik

New York SHAMROCK. w Jl? 1822-
DLC Jl 17-24 1824
N Ja 15 1825
NNHi O 6 1823
NjHi Ag 21,S 7,O 21,D 16 1822

SHIPPING and commercial list and New York price current. *See* New York commercial

SI͡EN otechestva. *See* Carpatho-Russia

Evening SIGNAL. d O 12 1839-42||?
CtW 1839-Ap 13 1840
CtY Ja 9 1840
DLC 1839-Ap 18 1840
MWA 1839-F 20,Jl 30,N 6(extra)1840
NNHi 1839-O 17 1840
OClWHi Ag 18 1840
WHi Je 1,3,Ag 4 1840;Ap 5 1841

SLOVAK v Amerike. d,sw 1899+
sw 1899-1913?
In Slovak
pub 1905+
IU D 1917-O 24 1927

SOBER second thought. w Je 8-N 30? 1844||
Prospectus My 18 1844
Campaign paper
DLC O 5(extra)1844
MWA My 18,Ag 10,O 26 1844
MoSM O 12 1844
NN Jl 13-Ag 24,S-O 5,26 1844
NNHi Je 22 1844
NjFHi Jl 13 1844
NjR My 18 1844
Tx O 26 1844
WHi S 21 1844

SOCIALIST call. w Mr 23 1935+
NNRa 1935+

SONNTAGSBLATT. . . *See under* next important word; e.g., Sonntagsblatt staats-zeitung und herold is alphabeted under Staats-zeitung

Der SOZIALIST. *See* Vorwärts 1885-94

New York SPECTATOR. *See* Weekly commercial advertiser

SPIRIT of '76. d Ap 19? 1835-
Title varies: Spirit of '76 and commercial register; Commercial register and spirit of '76
Ct [1835]
MWA [Jl 29-O 6 1835]
N Je 22 1835
NNHi [Ap 22-O 8 1835]
NcD S 26 1835

SPIRIT of seventy-six. 1840 *See* Public advertiser

SPLIFINCATOR. w Jl 16? 1836-
NN Ag 13,S 3 1836
NNHi Ag 27 1836

New-York SPY. w
CSmH My 24 1828

SPY, and New York and Brooklyn Saturday courier and enquirer. w F 19? 1826-
1826-32? as Hawk and buzzard; Ag 18 1832-D 1834? Ely's hawk and buzzard; or, New York and Brooklyn courier and enquirer
MWA S 1-15,29 1832;Ag 31-S 21 1833
MnHi Mr 7 1835
NN Ap 29 1826
NNHi D 14 1833

SRPSKI dnevnik. (Serbian daily) d 1911+
In Serbian
CSt-H [1932]

New-Yorker STAATS-DEMOKRAT. *See* New Yorker herold. Morgenblatt

New-Yorker STAATS-ZEITUNG. w D 31? 1834-1919||?
Title varies: Wochenblatt der New-Yorker staats-zeitung; New-Yorker staats-zeitung wochenblatt
In German
pub D 21 1836-D 13 1837;D 18 1839;42;46;48-50
ICHi [1875-76]-Ja 20 1877
IEN S 1908-F 1909
MWA Ap 20 1836
MiG Ag 16 1856
NN 1856;62-65;67-1907
OCl 1902-11
WaPS 1916-19

New-Yorker STAATS-ZEITUNG. tw 1836?-
In German
pub Ag 12 1842-D 18 1843

New-Yorker STAATS-ZEITUNG. Abendblatt. d 1892-N 30 1919||
1892-Mr 9 1914 as Abendblatt der New Yorker staats-zeitung. United with New Yorker herold. Abend zeitung to form New Yorker herold und New Yorker staats-zeitung. Abendblatt, later New Yorker herold
In German
DLC Jl-D 1897
NN S 27 1892-S 1918[Ja-F]-N 1919

Sonntagsblatt STAATS-ZEITUNG und herold. w Ja 3 1848+
1848-1921 title varies: New-Yorker staats-zeitung. Sonntagsblatt; Sonntagsblatt der New-Yorker staats-zeitung
In German
pub 1848+
DLC 1864-73;75-86
ICHi D 24-31 1876;Ja 21 1877
IU S 1917-18
N F 17-Mr 16,Ap 6,Jl 27 1836;Mr 12 1876
NN 1859;63-69;71-85;87-1902;Jl 1903-06
PU 1884-89
TxCoE N 18 1889;Ja 7,F 4,Ap 29,Jl 29 1900
TxF O 1926+
WHi Je 24-N 4 1855;S 6,D 13 1914

New Yorker STAATS-ZEITUNG und herold. d Ja 1 1853+
1853-D 1 1934 as New-Yorker staats-zeitung (D 1 1919-21? New-Yorker staats-zeitung und herold. Morgenblatt)
In German
pub 1853+
CSt F 1912-N 1921;Ja 1922
CtY Mr 1915+
DLC S 14 1886+
IC Ja 21-Je 1873
IEN Mr 27-N 1909;10-My 1911;F-D 1916;Je-Ag,N 1919-Jl,S 1920-21
IU O 16 1884;Ag 27 1917-Je 1918
MiU 1892-[94-95]-[99]
NBuG S 1914-Ja 12 1921
NN Jl 1863-64;66+
NNHi 1870-O 1907
NjP Jl 26 1914-Ag 1920
NjR S 24 1885
OC N 1874-82
PPeS [O 1915-Ja 1916]
TxU Ap 1916-20;D 16 1915
TxU Ap 1916-20;Mr 1922-26
WHi N 5 1860;D 16 1915
WaPS 1918-[20]-Ja 9 1921

La STAMPA libera. d N 16 1925+
1925-N 29 1931 as Il Nuovo mondo
In Italian
pub 1925+
DLC 1930-N 1931
WHi Ag 8 1934

New York STANDARD. d 1827-My 5 1834||
1827-S 12? 1830 as Standard. Followed by New York times (1834-)
CSmH S 14 1830
Ct D 14 1831;F 6(extra)1832
DLC 1832-34
MB My 8 1832
MBAt D 24 1830
MWA F 5,21-22,S 7,9 1831;Ja 18,S 28,N 7,22,26, 28-30,D 12 1832[Ja-My 13 1833]Ap 21,25 1834
MiU My 17(supp)1832
MiU-C D 12 1832
NNHi complete
NNMT D 7 1833-34
NNS 1832-33
NSchU Ag 22,S 15,22,24,N 23,D 4 1832
NhD Ag 1,9,13-21,27-29,31,S 11 1832
NjR F 14 1831
P-M S 22 1832

New York STANDARD. d S 1 1840-
DLC D 15 1840;Ja 19,F 1-2 1841
IU S 28 1840;Ap 20,27,Ag 17 1844
IaDH N 15 1840
MB D 28,31 1842
MHi N 6 1840
NN S 28,O 23 1840
NNHi N 8,17 1842
NNS 1840-My 9 1843
NSchU O 19 1842

New York STANDARD. w D 16 1843?-
DLC My 25 1844
NjR D 16 1843;Jl 6,S 8 1844

New York STANDARD. d O 14? 1850-
CSmH O 15 1850
MB O 31-N 29 1850

New York STANDARD. d Ap 30 1870-Jl 10 1872||
DLC complete
MB My 7,Jl 2,6-7,9 1870;Jl 13 1871
NBHi complete
NN My 2 1870-Je 29 1872
PPL My 3-Jl 30 1870

New York STANDARD and statesman. sw Ja 3 1822-My 6? 1834||
1822-F 1823? Statesman and advertiser for the country; Mr 1823-Ag 24? 1828 Statesman; Ag? 1828-Ja 31 1829 New York statesman (for the country) F 2 1829-S 14 1830 New York statesman
CSmH Ap 27 1830
CSt [1829]
Ct [1830-31]
CtY F 12,Jl 2,A 20 1830
DLC F 7,Ap 4 1822;Ap 28,Je 2,S 10 1823;F 13, My 3,Jl 2,N 5 1824[27]Ap 5,My 3,Je 10,N 15 1831;Ap 3,Je 5,Ag 10 1832
IU Ja 5 1823
MB [1822-23;Jl-N 16 1825;Ap-N 21 1826;27-F 19 1828]
MBAt My 22 1823;D 28 1824;F 29,S 10 1828
MHi Mr 9 1822;Mr 8 1824
MWA Ja 11-15,F 18,Ap 18-29,Je 10,Jl 22,Ag 5 1822;Ja 2-6,Jl 25,S 30 1823;Ap 13 1824-29; Ja 1,8-15,22,Mr 9,Ap 2,O 19,D 3-7 1830;Ja 4,N 8 1831;F 28,Ap 13,My 15 1832;Ap 29 1834
MeB N 14 1823-My 6,O 18-D 1825;Ja 13 1826-Ag 7 1827
MiU-C F 3 1826
N 1824-27[F 29-Ag 20]S 20-N 12 1828;Je 11 1830;O 29 1833;Mr 24 1834
NCorL S 16 1825
NHuHi Ja 13 1826;S 14 1828
NN Ja 3 1822;Ja 16 1823;Ag 6 1824-Ja 22,Mr-Ag 16,N 15-18 1825;Ja 13-17,Mr 31-S 5,N 17 1826;Ja 8-Jl 23 1830
NNHi Mr 3,10,17,Ap 3-10,17-21,28-My 1,19,28, Je 2-19,26 1823;Ja 23,D 17 1824-27;Je-Ag 20, 27-D 1828;Jl 21 1829;Je 1830-S 13 1831;S 1832-F 25,Mr 25,Ap 15 1834
NSchU [My-D 1831]Ja 3,10-13,31,F 14,17(extra) Mr 9,Ap 3,10,My 4-8,Je 8,Ag 5,N 2,D 2 1832
NT 1822-Ja 24 1832
NcD 1825[26]-28
NhD [F 11-D 1822]-[24]-26[Mr 1831-Mr 2 1832]Mr 15 1833
NjHi Ja 5,Jl 1823-24;D 2 1825;Jl 18 1826;Jl 10,S 21,O 9 1827
NjR Ag 23 1831
P-M Ja 28 1822
PEL Mr 18 1831
WHi Mr 3 1826;Mr 28-My 1834
—d ed *See* New-York morning herald

Evening STAR. d S 25 1833-Ag 29 1840||
United with New York times and commercial intelligencer to form New York times and evening star
DLC O 8 1833;Ap 15 1839
InI Ja 10 1834-Jl 14 1837
MBAt O 7 1835
MWA O 10 1833;My 3 1834;Ja 28,Mr 17,N 7,D 17-21,23,28-30 1835;Ja 12-13,25-26,29-F 2,5-8, 19,24,26,Mr 18,My 6,O 10 1836;F 16,Ap 26,O 3,D 21 1837;Ja 5,Mr 9,Je 14,N 17-D 1838;Ap 2,6 1839
MiG D 3 1864
N O 11 1833;Jl 5 1836;Ja 30,F 1,6,Mr 18,23-Ap 28 1837
NBHi O 1833-35
NN S 25 (photostat)S 26 1833-Mr 1834
NNHi S 27 1833-S 24 1834;S 26 1836-40
NNMT N 1833-40
NNS 1834;Je 6 1837-40
OC N 1833-N 1835;Jl 1836-Mr 1837
RPB Je 12 1834-Ap 4 1835
WHi Ja 5 1836-S 14 1837;Ja 25-D 1838

Evening STAR, for the country. sw 1833-40||?
United with New York times and commercial intelligencer to form New York times and evening star
Ct O 29 1833
GAtCo Jl 2 1839
ICU Mr 8 1836
MWA Ja 10,F 14-18,25 1834;Ap 3-14,21,My 5, Je 16,23-26,S 25,D 1,25 1835;Mr 22-25 1836
N Ap 13 1838
NN N 19 1833-My 13,20-30,Je 6-13,20-24,Jl 1-11,18,25-29,Ag 5-15,22-O 17,24-D 12,19-30 1834;Ja 2,9-F 20,27 1835
NNHi S 26 1837-S 24 1839
OClWHi Ag 3 1838
P-M D 1 1838
PBL D 17,24 1833-[Ja-Ap 1834;Ja-Mr 1835]
PEL S 26 1833-S 26 1834
PWCl Ag 1835;Jl 17-28 1840

NEW YORK (*Continued*)

NEW YORK CITY—*Continued*

Morning STAR. d Mr 21-My 1 1834‖?
MWA Mr 21,24-My 1 1834
NNHi Mr 29,Ap 22-24 1834

Morning STAR. d Ap 23 1836-
Ap-S 17 1836 as Ladies' morning star
NN My 2 1836
NNMC My 9 1836
PHi Je 10 1836-Ja 19 1837
WHi Ap-S 6,17 1836

Morning STAR. d Ap 12 1842-
DGU Ap 12-30 1842

Evening STAR. d S 15? 1845-
MWA S 18 1845

Morning STAR. d F 25 1848-
MWA Je 15 1849;Ja 26 1852
NN O 1848-[49]-Mr 8 1850

New York STAR. d 1868-Ja 1891‖
Title varies slightly. Followed by Daily continent
DLC My 14,21 1871;S 22 1885-91
ICM Je 14 1880;S 26 1886
MB Ap-Je 1888;Ja-Je 1889[Ja-Je 1890]
MWA My 11 1868;Mr 24-Je 1878;79-Mr,Jl 1880-Mr 1882;S 15 1885-S 1886;Jl 6,N 21,D 8-11,18-19 1887;Ja 3,F 27,Mr 16 1888
N N 2 1880;Ap 1-26,Jl-S 1881;O 25 1882
NBHi 1870-76
NN 1878-91
NcD [Je-Jl 1889]Ap 15 1890
NcU S 4 1884
NjR S 30 1881
OHi S 15 1885-S 15 1886
WHi O 6-7 1871

New York STAR. w 1885-90‖?
MWA O 26 1900
NN Ja 18-Ag 9 1885

STAR. [Uptown ed]
NNHi [My,N-D 1887]

New York STAR. w 1898-99‖?
NN Ap 9,23-Jl 9,23-Ag 20,O 8-D 3 1899

New York evening STAR and American advertiser. d S 16 1865-
MWA S 16 1865

New York STAR EAGLE. w F 1 1936+
MWA F 1 1936

New York STATESMAN. d Ja 2 1822-Ja 31 1829‖
Formed by the union of New York statesman (Albany) and New York evening journal.
1822-F 1823 as New York statesman and evening advertiser. United with National advocate to form New-York morning herald
Ct [1824-26]Ag 31 1830
CtY My 16 1822
DLC 1822-26;Mr 28,S 18 1827;My 13,Jl 7,Ag 16 1828;Ja 31 1829
DeHi D 4 1828
MBAt My 13 1822;Ja 27,S 16 1824;O 5,11 1827;N 17 1828
MHi Mr 8 1824;Mr 17-18,Ap 4,15 1825;My 3,5,S 4 1827
MWA Jl 31,S 12,O 26 1822;Ja 28,Mr 28,S 10,O 10 1823;Ap 16,Ag 9-12[S-D]1824; Ja 10,26,F 5,Mr 10,14-15,22,Ap 8,30,Je 11,N 5 1825;Ag 5 1826;D 27 1827 Ap 8 1828;Ja 27 1829
MiU-C Jl 23 1822
N Je 4,Jl 3,Ag 5,O 11,24,N 22,25 1823;Ag 26,28,S 5,21,O 7,26,28-29,N 1-18 1824;Mr 10-12,15,22,24-25,Ap 1,7-19,Je 10-Jl,Ag 5,8,O 31 1825;Ja 24,N 10 1826;F 9,Je 2,O 15,N 2,9-17 1827
NI 1822-23
NN Mr 11,O 21,N 5,8 1825;Ap 11,My 19,Jl 8,O 25,30 1826
NNHi Jl 1822-29
NNS 1822-23
NhD My 8-9,S 9,19 1822;Ag 12 1823;F 18 1824;Ja 7,Ag 23,O 17 1825;Mr 16 1826;O 11,N 8 1828;Ja 27 1829
WHi N 25 1824;O 21 1825;Mr 17 1826

STATESMAN and advertiser for the country. *See* New York standard and statesman

SUBTERRANEAN. w My 27 1843-N 27 1847‖?
For O 12-D 21 1844 *See* Young America
CSmH Jl 11 1846
DLC Ja 30 1847
NN My 24 1845-My 22 1847
NNHi Ja 27,F 24,1844;My 24 1845-N 27 1847

SUBTERRANEAN and the working man's advocate. *See* Young America

SUBURBAN news. w
MWA Je 24,S 9,23 1865;F 21 1867
P-M O 25-N 1 1866

SUBURBAN reporter. w Ja 28 1864-
MWA My 26 1864
NNHi Ja-Jl 22 1864

SUN. d S 3 1833+
Ap 13-S 28 1840 as New York sun; Jl 3-30 1916 Sun and New York press; F-S 1920 Sun and New York herald
S 2 1933 is 100th anniversary ed
A 1883-[85]-[87-88]-[90]1900[01]02
C S 19,D 22,24-25,27 1834;F 8 1887-89
CL S 3 1833
CSt S 2 1933
CSt-H [1914]-[17]-19
CU-B S 3 1833
Ct [1834-37]76-O 1907;11-Je 1913;O 12 1914
CtY S 3 1833(facsimile)Ja-Je 1835;Mr 7 1837;Je 17-O 3 [N-D]1839;S 10(extra)1841;Mr 21 1842;Ag 7 1843;Ag 23 1846;My 1,Je 1,Jl 26,28 1848;Ag 18 1862;63-67;70-86;F 14 1891+
DLC 1833-Ag 1835;39;Ap 27,29,Jl 14 1843;Ja 14 1845-50;Jl 9 1851;O 29 1861;Ap 26 1865;Ja 31 1868;F 14 1870;S 1871-F 1901;02+
FSaHi Ap 25 1865
GDE S 2 1933
ICHi Mr 11,My 10,14,31,Je 4,11,16,Jl 12-13,21,Ag 4,11-12,O 11,D 13 1836;O 10 1871;S 26 1881;F 12 1909
ICM N 27 1877[F-Ap 1878]D 10 1880;Jl 18,S 6,N 14 1881;My 14 1884;Je 4,15,17,O 28 1885 [91-My 1892]My 18-19 1893;N 3 1894;S 2 1933
ICN Mr 3 1863-65;69-70;Jl 1871-72;Jl 1873-N 1874;Ja-N 1875;76-78
ICU Mr 11-D 1834
IaDH Jl 1894-1914
InMovHi 1901
InNh [Mr-Ag 1834]
InU S 3 1833;1932+(Sunday ed only)
KHi [1833-1912]O 15 1920;Ap 24 1926
M S 11 1928;S 2 1933
MB [1842-90]
MBAt S 3 1833(facsimile)Ap 11(extra)1841;Ap 17-18,24 1865;My 1 1889;1914-S 1920;S 2 1933
MMarHi Ap 15-26 1865
MWA S 3 1833(facsimile);Mr 29,Ap 4,10,My 29,Je 5,20 1834;Ja-Je 1835;Ag 12,O 11 1836;O 30,D 6 1837;My 7,Ag 22 1838;Je 10,Jl 29 1839;Ja 9,Ap 1,O 24 1840;Ja 16,F 16,Ap 13,Jl 7 1841;Ja 24 1842;F 4,7,24,Je 21 1843;Ap 11-12 1844;Mr 24,My 3-5,Je 28,N 4 1845;Je 8 1847;Ja 13 1851;Ja 1,F 2,Ag 20,O 18 1852;S 5 1853;O 16 1854;My 7 1856;Ag 6 1857;Je 27-29 1861;N 27,D 19 1862;Ja 1,Ag 6,S 24,O 26-27 1864;Ja-Je 1865;Ap 28-30,Ag 30,S 11,O 10-12 1866;S 25,O 19 1867;Ja 27,Ag 26 1868;Ja 14 1869 Ja 25,Ap 19,N 12,D 12 1872;Jl 28 1873;N 20 1875;Ja 21,S 21,O 9,26 1876;Mr 3,Ap 1,My 31,Je 4 1877;Ja 20,Jl 19 1879;S 3 1883;Je 3 1886;My 1 1889;My 30 1892;Jl 5,O 31 1894;Ja-Je 1895;Ja-Je 1897;98[Ap 17-Je 1 1899]S 11 1901;Jl 18 1905;Ap 1 1913;Ja 14 1928
extras:D 19 1835;D 5 1838;S 10,D 26 1839;Ja 20,Mr 18,D 7 1840;Ja 6,Ap 11 1841;My 19,D 8 1842;Ap 13 1844;My 9 1845;Je 13,N 29 1846;S 10 1848
MiU [1885;1914-15]-[18-19]20
N S 3(reprint)N 14 1833;Mr 24,Ap 21,Je 7 1834;D 19(extra)1835;S 3 1839;Jl 19 1843;55;57-59;61-80[83]-[88]89;Ap-S 1890;Ja-Je 1892;O 1896-S,N 22 1920-Mr,Jl 1923
NB Ja 6-Je 1835;42-44
NBHi Ja 28-Je 5 1834;68-92
NBuG D 11 1933-Ja,Mr-N 1934
NCH 1881-F 1913
NHuHi S 3 1833;S 2 1933
NN 1833-Ja 1,Jl 4 1836;Je 1 1837;Ja 26,O 5 1838[39] Ag 11 1849[64]66[67]+
NNC [1886-1909]S 2 1933
NNCom 1870-Ja 1920
NNHi [1833]-Ag 1835;Ja 15-D 1836;Mr 25,Ap 18,My 6,N 14 1837;My 24 1838;F 25 1839;D 7 (extra)1840 Je 23 1841;Ja 22,Je 17 1842;Je 24,Jl 31 1845;O 18 1849;N 3 1859;My 30 1863;Ap 15,19 1865;Je 13,O 20 1868;Ag 20 1873;S 26,O 18 1881;Ag 9 1885;My 5,8,Je 5-6,9 1886
NNMC Ap-Ag 1834;Ja 5-Je 1835;O 24,D 13 1854;D 7 1872;S 2 1933
NNMT S 2 1933
NNRo Ap 22-Ag 1898
NNY-H S 2 1933
NRU 1896-Je 1908
NSaN S 3 1833(facsimile)F 14-D 1834
NSyU 1882-1913;S 2 1933
NbHi S 3 1833;O 29 1868;S 8 1877;Ja 28 1887;F 22,Mr 6,11,Jl 17 1888;D 1 1889;F 21,Jl 19,S 26 1891;Jl 3,17,Ag 7,21 1892;Mr 30,Je 17 1893;Ap 4,S 11,15[O-N]1894;Je 15 1895;Ap 20,N 1-8 1896;Ag 22 1907
NcD S 3 1833(reprint)Ap 11 1841;Ag 23-S 23 1870;Ja 8 1872;S 22 1878;Ja 6,Mr 8,10,Ap 21,My 1,O 30 1879;Mr 28 1886;N 27 1887;My 24,31 1896;Jl 4 1897;S 18 1901;Ag 31 1915;Ja 4-5 1916;My 4,21 1918;F-Mr 1932;S 2 1933
NcU [1876]-84;F 11-12,Jl 1885-Je 1886;Jl 5 1889;Jl 25 1890;99-1903
NhD Ag 26 1835;Ag 8 1870;Jl 18 1872;Jl-D 1886;88-Je 1898;Ja-Ap 1899;My,Jl 1899-1902;04-F 1913
NjBa Ap-Ag 1898
NjHi 1836-92;F 1898-99[1917-19]
NjJ My 2-N 1 1834;74-85;Ap 1901-Mr 1903;04-Je 1916
NjM Jl 24 1914-S 1919
NjN S 3 1833 My 1 1865
NjR S 3 1833(facsimile)[34-35;51]N 3(extra) 1859[77-78;83]
OC 1879-80
OHi 1887;Je 1890-Ja 1920;Jl 1929+
P Ja 20 1907-Je 1917
PBL Mr 21,28 1839;My 1 1844[Ja 31-F 24 1845]Je 6 1846
PHi 1882-1909
PPL [1889-90;92]
PPi [1884]-1916
RW [S-D 1833]D 3 1836;O 17 1837;Ja 20 1871
Tx My 10 1851;S 2 1933
TxGR S 2 1933
V D 8 1873-Je 1874
VtMS [1877-1900]
WHi Ja 13-S 2 1834;Ja 3-Je,Ag 20,O 6 1835;48;Jl 1877-My;O 1879-Mr 28,Jl-D 1880;83-90;O 1892-Je,N-D 1898;S 27 1900-Mr 11[Ap 6-My 15 1901]O 1902-Je 17,S 22 1903-My 6,S 23 1904-My,O 2 1905-Je 15,S 22 1906-Ap 22,S 20 1907-My 28 1908;F 4[O 14 1909-D 19 1910]N 13 1913-14
WaPS Mr 1913-19;My 1920-F 1921;N 26 1927

Weekly SUN. w F 1836-94‖?
Title varies Sun weekly; New York weekly sun; Dollar weekly sun
CSto Mr-D 1881
CoHi N 8 1851
CtY [F 1845-N 1846]Ap 24 1847
DLC D 15 1838-[N-D 1840]-Ap 9 1842;Ap 1 1843;O 17 1846;Je 2 1849;F 16-Mr 1,15-22 1876;Ap 17 1878
GColS [1881-82]
ICM D 31 1884
ICU Je 11 1884;Mr 13 1889
IU Mr 22 1845;Ag 29 1846
IaHi Mr 1876-F 1881
KHi Je 29 1844-Mr 21 1846;N 4 1874;S 23 1877[Jl 1881-Ag 2 1882]
MWA Je 5 1836;My 19 1838[Ja 9-O 15 1841]Jl 1 1843;F 24,N 23 1844;Je 28 1845;Ap 18,Je 6,Ag 8 1846;O 1847-O 1848[F-D 1850]Jl 5 1851;Ja 10 1852;Jl 22,S 2,16-23 1854;Ja-Je 1865;S 11(extra)1872;Jl 15 1885
N F 17 1844;S 25 1847;S 5 1883
NN D 9 1843;Jl 26 1845;Ja-Je 1873
NNC 1877-Ja 16 1878
NNHi Ja 14,Mr 4 1843;Je 5 1847;48-49;D 17 1853-Je 10,S 30 1854-My 5 1855;Je 17 1862
NSchU Mr 9-26 1842
NUHi Mr 9 1844
NbHi S 22 1869;D 13 1871;N 4,D 9 1874;S 20 1876;F 19 1879
NcD Mr 30 1870[74]-F,O 5 1875;F 2,Mr 8,My 10,24-31 1876;Mr 7-21,Ag 1 1877;F 27,Mr 20,Ap 24 1878;Mr 5,S 24,O 15-N 5 1879;D 15 1880;F 9-16,D 14 1881;N 29 1882[83]Mr 12 1884;Jl 15,O 28 1885;Jl 24 1886;F 15,Ap 25 1888;Ag 30,S 13 1893;S 19 1894
NcU Ag 16 1882
NhD My 26-Jl 14 1875;F 2 1876
OClWHi Je 15 1844;Ap 11 1863;Ap 3-14 1865;Jl 1873-Ap 19 1876;F 13-D 1878;Jl 1880-Je 15 1881;82-O 22 1884
PP O 1 1876;Ja-Je 1889;Jl-D 1890;Ja-Je 1892
TxH Je 5 1872
VU O 28 1874;S 22-29 1875 S 8,D 1 1880
WHi S 22 1862;Ap 25 1865;D 29 1875;Ap 1876-D 14 1881;S 3 1883;Ja-Je 1892;94

Semi-weekly SUN. sw -1873‖?
NN Ja-Je 1873

Evening SUN. d Mr 17 1887-S 30 1920‖
CSmH [Ja 29 1917-Je 23 1920]
CSt-H [1917]-19
DLC My 1917-20
IU N 5-D 1909;Ja 27-31,Mr-Ap 25 1910
MWA N 17 1887;My 1 1889
NBHi 1887-92
NN F 1915-20
NNC 1913-19
NNHi My 1 1890
NNSt F 1912-Ap 1918
NcD My 16 1888
OClWHi Ap 16 1887
PJR Je 17 1889;Mr 29 1914;My 31 1915;Ja 28 1919
VU O 9 1905;S 29 1908

SUNDAY. . . *See under* next important word; e.g. Sunday times and messenger is alphabeted under Times

SVIJET. d 1908+
1908-23? as Jugoslovenski svijet
In Croatian
IU N 6 1917-Ap 1918;Mr 23,O 9 1935+
NN 1917+

SYLVESTER'S reporter, counterfeit detector, New York prices current and general advertiser. w 1830-49‖?
Title varies: S. J. Sylvester's reporter and counterfeit detector; etc.
GAtCo Je 23 1840
MWA D 2 1830;F 3 1831;My 16 1832;O 17,D 26 1833;My 29,S 18 1834;Jl 26,O 11(extra) 1847
MdBJ D 29 1845
MiU-C S 24 1849
N Mr 24,Je 22,Jl 13 1831;D 25 1837
NN O 1 1838;N 27 1848
NSchU D 26 1833;Mr 28,My 23-30,Jl 4,Ag 1 1842
NcD F 1 1832
P-M O 3 1832
WHi Mr 16 1840

TÄGLICH. . . *See under* next important word, e.g., Der Täglicher herold is alphabeted under Herold

TAGEBLATT (Yiddish). *See* Jewish daily news

Evening TATTLER. d Jl 8 1839-Ag 1842‖?
F-My 17 1840? as Dispatch and tattler
DLC Ag 27 1839;F 18 1840
MHi N 21 1840;Ag 19 1841
MWA S 3 1839;Mr 3,N 23 1840;Mr 23-24,Je 21 1841;Je 9,24-25 1842
N Ag 8 1840
NN Jl-S 21 1839;Ap 29[My-Jl]1840-[Ap-S 1841]
NNHi Jl-O 11 1839;Mr 7 1840;Ap 5 1841;F 15 1842
NSchU Je 3,Ag 11 1842
P-M Jl 29 1840
—w ed *See* Brother Jonathan

New York TATTLER. w Jl 7 1866-
CtY Jl-S 8 1866

Daily TATTLER. d N 7-21 1896‖
CSmH complete
OClWHi N 9-18 1896

Evening TELEGRAM. *See* New York world-telegram

TELEGRAM codzienny. d 1913-25‖?
In Polish
IU D 4 1917-Je 20,Jl-Ag 1925
NN [1915]-23

Morning TELEGRAPH. w,d My 12 1839+
My-O 20 1839 as Sunday morning visitor; O 27 1839-N? 1897 Sunday mercury
w 1839-N? 1897
pub [1900-10]+
CSmH S 6 1840
CSt-H [1917-19]
DLC 1841;61;67,69;70,72;77;89-90;1910+
ICHi Ap 16 1865
IU Mr 31 1844
KHi Jl 4 1841
M [Jl 1933]
MB 1848;Mr 19-Ap 1859;69;Ja-Jl 1871
MWA 1839-O 17 1841;Jl 30,N 26 1843;Mr 31-Ap 14,28-My 5,Ag 25 1844;Ag 9 1846;D 12-19 1847;N 19,D 10 1854;Ja 14,28,Mr 4,25,Ap 29,S 16 1855;60-61;S 13 1863;My 26,Je 16 1867;F 13 1870;D 19 1880;S 1898-S 1901;Ja-S 1902;Ja-Je,N 1903-Mr 1906;D 4 1928
MnHi Ja 28 1860;My 15 1864
NBuG N 1862-My 22 1864
NN Ag 27 1843;Ap 10 1859-Je 10,N 13 1870

NEW YORK (*Continued*)

NEW YORK CITY—*Continued*

Morning TELEGRAPH. 1839+—*Continued*
NNHi Jl 4 1841;Ja 16-23 1842;Ja 2 1848;S 12 1852;Ap 20 1862;Ja 24 1869;98
NcD Jl 14 1861
NjHi [1876-78;81-85;89-90;92]
NjNh [1876-92]
NjR Jl 4 1841;Ap 7 1861;Ja 2 1876
NjVi 1888-91
OClWHi Ap 12 1863
OHi Ja 9 1858;Ja 7 1860;S 7,14 1901
VU Ja 9 1887
WaPS [1921;23-25]
See also Daily mercury

TELEGRAPH. 1842?-
NcD S 22 1842

Daily TELEGRAPH. d D 25 1845-D 23 1846||?
1845-D 18 1846 as Morning telegraph
NNHi 1845-D 23 1846
P-M Ap 16 1845

Daily TELEGRAPH. d O 6 1885-
NN O 6 1885

New York TELEGRAPH, McIntyre's bank note and prices current. w F 12?-O 15 1840||?
F? 1840 as McIntyre's telegraph and weekly advertiser; Mr 4-My? 1840 New York telegraph, McIntyre's gazette and general advertiser
DLC My 6,O 15 1840
GAtCo F 19 1840

THERMOPYLAE. tw,d 1900?-07||?
tw 1900?-06?
In Greek
NN N 16 1906-Ja 2 1907
VU N 11 1907

THIRD AVENUE journal. w S 25? 1879-
NjR D 25 1879

New York TIDNINGEN. w 1901-
In Swedish
IRA [1901-02]

TIMES. d Ap 27 1826-
MBAt Jl 3 1826-Je 8 1827
MHi O 20 1826
N 1826-S 22 1827
NN 1826-Ap 26 1827
NjHi [1827]

New York TIMES. d My 12 1834-
Follows New York standard
CtSp F 12 1839
DLC 1834-36
GDE D 25 1835
MWA 1834-Ja 1,14,25-26,29-F 1,5,10,17,22,27,Mr 19,Ap 21 1836
NCH Jl 24,O 14-28 1834
NN Mr 20 1835
NNHi [Ag-D 1834]-O 20 1837
NNMT 1835-37
NNS My-D 12 1834
NT Ja 13 1835-36
NjHi [1834-37]

New York TIMES. sw My 16 1834-
WHi [1834-Mr 13 1840]

Weekly TIMES. w Mr 21? 1840-
N Ap 18 1840
NFre O 31 1840;Ap 10 1841
WHi Ap 11 1840

Sunday TIMES. w Jl 1841-Jl 1843||?
United with Noah's weekly messenger to form Sunday times and Noah's weekly messenger, later Sunday times and messenger
MWA S 26,O 17,N 21-28 1841;F 13 1842
NNHi Mr 20 1842
NSchU Ag 14 1842

Daily TIMES. d Ja 5-F 16 1846||
United with Evening gazette to form Gazette and times
NNHi complete

New York evening TIMES. d S? 1851-
DLC O 23,31,N 24 1851;Ap 26,Jl 31,S 16 1852
MWA S 18 1851;D 2 1852;My 25,S 9 1854;Mr 16,S 19,O 3-4 1855;S 8 1857
NN Je 8 1854;F 17-My 1857
NNHi D 23 1853
NcD [1853-54;56]
NhD [N 1852-Jl 1853]S 5 1854;My 27 1857
OC F 27 1854

New York weekly TIMES. w S 1851-95||?
CSto F 23-D 1881
IA F 1860;F 1863-65;F 1870
ICU D 23 1854;Ja 20 1855-56
IEN 1888-94
IHi [F 27 1858-Je 18 1859]
IU Ja 8-15,F 5,19,Ap 9 1873
KHi Ag 18 1866[Ag 11 1880-O 11 1882]
KyLo Ap 11 1868-Mr 15 1871
MB [S 27 1851-S 18 1852]My 28,O 15 1853[N 1854-68]
MWA O 30-N 6 1852;Jl 9,Ag 13,27 1853;S 1 1855;Mr 28 1863;F 17 1866;D 11 1869;Ap 30 1873;My 10 1876;F 23 1881;Jl 16 1884;Jl 29 1885
MdBJ S 15 1855-Ja 3,D 12,26 1857-Ja 2,Ag 14-28 1858
MeBa S 28 1881
MiU-C [1857;65]
MnS N 1851-O 1852
N [1856-58]
NBuG F 14 1857;Jl 23 1859
NCor Ja 24 1872-Ja 8 1873
NN O 18 1851-S 8 1860;66-90
NNC 1851-My 1858
NNHi My 13-S 2,16-N 18 1854
NbHi Mr 13 1869;My 8,Jl 10 1872;Ag 1,O 31 1877;O 9 1878
NcD My 7,Jl 30 1853;Je 12 1858;Je 16 1866;N 8 1871;S 4 1872;Ag 9 1876
NhD Mr 12-Ap 23,Jl 4,Ag 22,S 3,D 10 1853;Ja 14,28,F 11,Ap 1,Je 17-Jl 1 1854;Mr 7,28-Ap 4, Je 27,Jl 11-25,O 10,24-D 12 1863;Ja 9-F 13,Mr 5,Ap 9-My,Je 18,Jl,Ag 13-27 1864
NjHi Ag 13,27 1853
NjP 1851-65
OCHi Ap 2,Je 18 1853
PPeS N 19 1873;S 21-28 1881
PToHi My-D 1854;S 21 1881
Tx D 4 1869
Vt 1864
WHi Ja 29 1853-Mr 18 1854;F 6 1864

New York TIMES. d S 18 1851+
1851-S 12 1857 as New York daily times
pub 1851+
A Ja-Je 1865[66-67;72-74]83-84[86-89;1917]-[33]
ArAH 1933+(Sunday ed only)
ArCH 1923+
ArMA S 1932-33 (Sunday ed only)
ArMoA 1934+ (Sunday ed only)
ArP 1931;33+ (Sunday ed only)
ArU 1915-26;Mr 1927+
AzU [1851-54]-[56-67]O 17 1914+
C F 4 1887-F 23 1889;N 8 1918+
CCh 1927+(Sunday ed only)
CClP Ap 16 1865;Ap 9 1885;D 31 1911+
CL Ap 13 1861-Jl 10 1865;Je 1913+
CLJ [1929-33]+
CLM Ap 15,28 1865;S 20 1881;Jl 29 1885;F 23 1890;F 13 1897;O 5 1901;Mr 5 1904;S 13 1931
CLO O 9 1920+
CLSU Mr 1922+
CLU 1927+
CLb Jl 1914+
CMiC 1921-[Je 1922]+
CO Mr 1919+
CP O 1925+
CPa current 2 years only
CPo N 1927+ (Sunday ed only)
CRed F 1907+
CRiv 1913+
CSf S 1891-Ap 1893;Jl 1913+
CSmH [Je 17 1861-N 1865;73-96;1906-13;16-25]
CSt [1860-65]73-[84;92;96;1900]+
CSto 1914+
CU S 19 1851-[My 1865]N 1902-Ap 1904;08+
CU-B D 30 1852;Ja 1 1853
CaB Jl 1913+
CaM 1918+
CaOKU 1915-Ap 1923;S 1928+
CaOLU [1861-64]
CaOOA S 1915-17
CaOOR 1929+
CaOTL Jl 1913+
CaQME 1930+
CaQMM 1914-20;F 1933+
CaSRR [1935]+(Sunday ed only)
CaSU [1918]+
CoAT [1925+]
CoCC 1908-F 1913;My 1917+
CoD Mr 5 1861-85;Jl 1914+
CoLo 1932-33(Sunday ed only)
CoS 1930-33(Sunday ed only)
Ct N 1851-[66;68-69;D 22 1871-89]Ap 20 1901; 03-04;11+
CtAn [1855]
CtB 1913+
CtHC F 1934+
CtHT Ap 18 1865
CtHi 1851-64
CtN 1862-Je 1865;1934
CtNh 1913;F-Je 1914
CtNlC Ap 20 1865;1926+
CtSo D 31 1861
CtSp [1859]61-66;Ap 30 1870[74;76]O 1 1880[81; 84;88]Ap 19 1912[13]+
CtSta Ja 17 1913+
CtW Jl 1 1862;63-S 1866;67+
CtWb My 9-S 4 1854;56-Ja 15 1857;1922+
CtY 1851+
DA 1932+
DCE 1913+
DL 1933+
DLC 1851+
DeWI S 18 1860-[62]1916+
FDe 1932+
FDeS 1929+
FJ 1917+
FL 1929+
FO Ap 1932+
FTS [1929;Mr-Ag 1930;Jl-F 1932]F 1933+
FTa F 11 1917+
FU O 25,N 3,10,17,24 1918;Mr 14 1919+
FWpR O 1930+
GA Jl 1927+
GDE [1925]+
GU S 14 1872;Je 30 1879;Je 7 1924;27
I 1916-Ja,Mr 1919+
IAC [1933-34]+
IB 1924+
IC 1872-89;O 1890-Mr 1892;93-Je 1901;N 1917+
ICHi N 5,D 6 1858;D 7,20-21,26 1860;O 21,N 2 1861;Mr 10,Ag 1 1862;Mr 7,Je 1863-Je 1865;Je 7 1866;Mr 5 1881
ICM Je 20,22,27 1880;Ja 10,F 3,5,8 1882;Ja 23 1883;My 14,N 20 1884[85]S 19 1886;F 24,D 16 1887[Ag-D 1891;Ap 1892]My 12 1893;N 11 1914;S 17 1933
ICN 1851-Je 1878;O 29 1880-F 12 1881;D 12 1882-Mr 1899;Ag 1917+
ICU S 23 1851;Je 16 1854;O 27 1858;61-Je 1866;Mr-My,Jl-S,D 1868-70;F 1871-Ja,Mr,My 1872-Jl 1873;1913+
IEN 1917+
IEN-C Ap 1927+
IEuC Jl 1921-S 1922;Je 1923+
IF Ap 19 1865;Ja 7 1916-S 1,24,O 23 1919-29 [33-35]
IG D 17 1917+
IHi [Ap 23 1861-F 28 1919]
ILP 1914-18;O 1925-30
IMaW current 2 months only
IU 1860-Ap 1865;1916+
IaAS [1917]+
IaCfT N 1916-Ap,S 1917-Je,N-D 1918;Mr-O 1919;Jl-O 1920;Ap-My,Jl 1923-30; current year
IaD Ap 1916+
IaDH 1860-65;1914+
IaDa 1914-20;25+
IaFP current 16 months only
IaGG Ag 1919+
IaMu Sunday ed current year only
IaSc current 3 years only
IaU O 19 1854-65;1916-[19]+
IdU-S F 1922+
In F 1867-Ja 1868;S 1913-Jl 1935
InCr My-Je 1927
InEv 1926+
InFw 1916-26
InI 1876-Ja 1878[Ag-N 1880]Jl 31-N 19 1917; N 1919-Ja,Mr 1925+
InLP 1917+
InT 1913-21
InTI Je 28 1913+
InU 1854-55;57-81;96+
KEmT F 1918+
KHK 1930-My 1933
KHi D 1854-F 1856;N 22 1861-[S 6 1865-Ap 1889;1913-25]31+
KHu S 1929+
KPT 1928+
KU O 1913-25;Jl 1926+
KWi 1917+
KyLo Mr 26 1861-Je 3 1867;D 5 1869
KyU Ag 1913+
LBL My 15 1932+
LNH 1917+
LNaS My 1915+ (Sunday ed only)
LU [1860-Je 1861]Ap-Je,O 1862-Je 1863;64 [65]1918;Ap 1927+
M 1866-68;1914+
MAd current 3 years only
MB [Jl 1851-59;62-63;68-Mr 1870;Ap 1876-90] 1914+
MBAt Ag 21 1858;O 1859-76;S 18 1926
MBHe My 1928+
MBr 1913+
MCam 1918
MFra 1863-66
MH 1853-[58]-[70]-[81;93-96;98-1910;13]-[18]-[20]+
MH-BA Mr 1921-Ap,Je 1936+
MHi Ap 1854-Mr 1855;O-D 6 1856;Jl 9 1857;F 12 1858;Ja 25 1861-[63-O 1864;65-66]Ag 27,O 21 1876;Ja 5 1877;My 5 1883;Ap 28-My 1 1889
MMarHi Ap 26 1865
MNF Ap 1913+
MNS 1908+
MNb 1914-26;28+
MPi Je 1876-Mr 1877;Jl 1881-S 1895;1927+
MW 1913+
MWA O 23[D 3 1851-F 14]Mr-Ag,O 9,25 1852-95;Jl 1897-98;S 18 1901(supp)S 18,O 26 1905; Mr 30-Ap 6,O 26 1907;My 1914-O 1918;Jl 30 1924;25+
MWa F-D 1887
MWiC 1857-Ag 1859;Ap 1861-62;Ja-O 20 1864; 71;73-Ag 21 1878;79-Ag 14 1882;83-1900;11+
MdBE My 1920+
MdBJ S 1914+
MdBP F 1860-Je 1865;S 1908-O 1911;12;Mr-D 1913
MdChW S 15 1923+
MdFH O 1922+
MdU 1931+
MeBB Jl 1913+
MeBa Ap 1914+
MeBi 1918+
MeLB 1932+
MeU Jl 1922-23;Je-N 15,D 1930+
MeWC 1922+
MiAC [1931;33]34
MiAdT current 5 years only
MiD S 1913+
MiDN S-N 1917;F 1918+
MiElS Jl 1917-[21-23]30+
MiG S 19 1859;N 20 1861;1915+
MiHoM 1924+
MiK 1860-61;63-64
MiS Jl 1904+
MiU [1861-62]-[66;71-72]-88[98;1901;03]-[06;12-13]-[26]+
MiU-C [1854]-59[67-68]-72;79-88
MnD 1929+
MnHi [1854-57;Ap 1865]
MnS 1918+
MnU [1856]61-64;My-D 1865[96]Ja-My 1913;Jl 1914+
MoCaT 1933+
MoCon 1932-33
MoFuW S 5 1930-Je 3,S 8 1931-Je 2,S 7 1932-Je 2,S 10 1933+
MoJo Mr 1914-My 1922
MoK My 1913+
MoKS 1929+(Sunday ed only)
MoMaryT 1927+
MoP Ja-N 1933
MoS 1851+
MoSM S 1915-19;current 6 years
MoSW 1916-17;Jl 1918+
MoSj 1922-23
MoSpD 1934+
MoU 1915+
MoWeW S 1930+(O 1932+ Sunday ed only)
MsSM 1917+
MsU [1916-18](Sunday ed only)
N 1851-98;Je 1901+
NAlU F 1932+
NAnnS 1851-91
NAub N 1860-65;N-D 1915;30+
NAubT 1860-70
NB 1859-60;Ja 5,Ap 11 1861-S 1901;Ja-Je 1902; 03-04;My,O 1905-Je,S 1906-Ap,Je 1910+
NBHi 1851-92;1913+
NBP 1915-18;30+
NBi N 8 1852-Ap 16 1863;Jl 1913+
NBu 1853-S 1870;71-72;O 1913+
NCH Jl 1862-Je 1865;Jl 1914+
NChM Mr 1856-57;D 4 1865-72
NCor 1852-Ap 1855;F 4 1865-D 7 1867
NCort S 18 1852-Mr 1853
NFu current 2 years only
NGenH O 1930+
NGr 1915;18;24+
NHe 1931+
NIC 1851+
NIl 1928+
NLer current year only
NMam O 18 1930+
NMi 1914-Ag 1920
NN 1851+
NNC S 18 1851(facsimile)[52-53]54;61-1904; 07+
NNCC 1863;My-Je 1865;Ja-Ap 1866;My-O 1870;Ap-S 1898;1922-23;30+

NEW YORK (*Continued*)

NEW YORK CITY—*Continued*

New York TIMES. d 1851+—*Continued*
NNCU D 20 1899+]
NNCom S 1852-[1911-15]+
NNFo Ag 1923+
NNHi 1851-My 1868;D 7 1875;F-D 1898
NNMT 1861-Je 1864;1921+
NNMu 1913+
NNPr Ap 1934+
NNQ [1927-29]+
NNRa 1915-22
NNRo 1880-1921
NNS 1853-73;Jl 1913+
NNSt My 1913+
NNUnC 1914+
NNY-H 1873;99-1904;08-09;14+
NNr D 1912+
NOHi S 18 1851
NOL [1851-66]
NPV [Ja 23 1861-N 1865]1913+
NPw 1908-Je 1918
NR 1928—
NRU Ja 1-4,7-Ap 2,12,16,Ag 6,8 1861;Jl 4,7 1863;Jl 27,29 1864;Ja 2,4,Ap 3,5,Jl 15,18-31 1865;1916—
NSk 1931+
NSyU S 20 1859;F 6,Je 25,Ag 9,S 8,10-11,15, 24-27,O 10,30,N 5,20,D 17 1860[61]Je 17,O 12 1864;Ja-D 1914;F 1915-Mr,My 1917-[22-24]+
NT [1852-Ap 1891]
NWpG [F 10 1930-Je 14 1934]
NbHi Ap 10 1873;Je 12 1874;F 14 1877;My 26 1889;O 2 1890;Ja-S 1891;Ja-Mr,Jl-Ag 1892; Ja-Mr 1893;Ja 2 1899;Ag 18,S 5,8-9,11 1907 [Je-D 1913]-Mr 21,23-26 1924
Nc S 1917+
NcD S 18 1851(reprint) O 29,N 8,D 22 1852 [53-54]-58;58;Jl 18,O 12,N 21,D 28,31 1860;Ja 5,F 26,Ap 15-17,Jl 1861-Mr 2 1869;S 27,N 20 1873;Ja 20-21,F 8 1875;Mr 4-5 1881;Jl 20,O 23-24 1882;S 18,O 14 1883;Jl 21-Ag 8 1885;Ja 22,26 1886;Ja 20 1887;My 3 1889;Ap 14-17,22, 24-26,28-29,My 18 1891;Je 1892+
NcEloC 1918-30
NcRS 1914—
NcSC 1925+
NcU 1860-Je 1873;Ja-Je 1874;Ag 16-17,31 1875; O 24 1879;S 4 1880;Jl 18 1886;Je 23 1906;14-F 1920
NcWaC 1852-1927
NdHi Jl 1913-F 1915
NdU 1920—
NhD N 11,16 1852;Ja 1 1853[54-58;60]Mr-Ap 1908;13+
NhM My-Ag 1914[15]-[18]+
NhU 1930+
Nj Jl 1913+
NjBl Ap 1917-19
NjCHi F 25 1865-Jl 22 1867
NjFHi S 1852-My 1853
NjH Ap 1,29 1865;Jl 24,Ag 9 1885
NjHi [1851-94;98;1918]
NjJ 1859-60 72-Je 1879;1913+
NjM O 1919+
NjN D 28(supp)1859;Mr 1(supp)Je 5,29 1860; Ap 15,S 9,O 10-11,21,25-26,29,N 2,11-12,18,30, D 3-4,11,13,31 1861[62]S 21,O 31,N 7-9,D 2 1864;Ja 20,F 21,25,Ap 10,15-17 1865;S 1913+
NjNb Ap 1923+
NjO [1861-63]
NjP 1851-My 1855;56-57;Ap 11 1861-Ap 1866 [98]1913+
NjPa Jl 1912+
NjR 1851-S 1854[58;60-62;64-67;75-77;81-82;84; 86;88;94-95;1901;13]Je 1914+
NjU 1929+
NmSA S 10 1929+
NmU O 14 1920+
Nv 1914-20
NvR [1930-32]+
OAU 1925+
OAk D 1921—
OAkU 1921-Ja 15,F 16 1929+
OC 1851-53[D 7 1860-Jl 8 1861]81-Mr 1883; 1913+
OCHi Ag 11 1914-Ag 1919
OCU Jl 1914-Mr 1921;27+
OCl [1853-54;58;67;1911]-[14]+
OClWHi Ja 27 1854;Ja 26 1856;Ap 30 1859;F 13 1860-Ap 1896
ODW 1914-O 1918;19+
OGrD Jl 9 1931+
OHi 1851-My 3 1853;Ag-N 9 1854;Ap 20 1861-Je 1911;14+
OOxM Jl 1 1876;1925+
OkCO [1918]—
OkDS 1933+
OkEdC [1932-33]+
OkEr [1932]— (Sunday ed only)
OkOOk 1926+
OkP 1932+ (Sunday ed only)
OkPW 1927-[29-30]+ (Sunday ed only)
OkShO [1932]+
OkStO [1919]-[21-24]-[31]+
OkT [1928]-[31]+
OkTaN [1929-33]+
OkU [1916]-[18-20]-[22-29]-[33]+
OrCA O 1913+
OrP 1916+
OrU Je 2 1852;Jl 11 1853;My 4 1859;62[1904-07]-[10]-[13]-[15]-[17-18]+
P 1855+
PA 1929+
PAg 1860;Ap 1861-S 1862;Ap 1897-S 1899;1900-S 1903;Ag 1915+
PArdL Ap 17 1865
PAtM Ja 4 1858;Ap 15-My 5 1865
PBL Jl 1853-Je 1855;My 1858-O 1859;F 1860-Ap,N 10 1861-63;66-71;76;Jl 1913+
PBf Jl 8 1863[1929+]
PBfG 1930-31
PBmC [1914]-36]
PEHi F 4-5 1863
PEr Jl 1915+
PHi 1882-1909
PHsHi D 10 1863-Ap 8,16 1865
PJR Mr 1925-D 23 1928
PLaF 1862-Je 1863;64+
PMeA 1916-[24-27]+
PMilA Ja 27 1860[61;72]
PP 1854-63;S 13-O 21 1864;Ap 4,10,14-16,18-20 1865;Je 28 1873;My 12,O 6 1875[79]-[97]S 20 1914;F 2 1917+
PPCHi Ap 1861-64;84-1934
PPCo [1913]-[17]+
PPL [1861]-63;85-1934
PPM 1862-Je 1863
PPi My 9 1854-57;S 1858-N 1896
PPiHi S 18 1851;S 21 1854[61]Jl 1,11 1864;Ja 1,S 15,18,25 1901;Ja 18,O 1,15,N 1-2,5 1918; My 8,Jl 7 1919;Mr 5 1921;Ag 3-4,8-11 1923;F 4,7 1924,Mr 5 1925
PStP [1863;64-66;79-80;1902-03;07-08]
PToHi Ag 11 1854-Jl 1860[81]
PU 1861-66;1915+
PW [1914]+
PWaHi Ap 17,19-20 1865
PWbW Ja 20 1858[60]-[65-66]S 10 1867;Ag 14,16 1868[73]Ja 5,Ap 16,S 5 1874[78]Mr 9 1879;F 13,Ap 8 1883[88]+
RNR 1914-19;28+
RP N 1860-Mr,O-D 1864;Ag 1914-Ja,Mr 1918-19
RPB F 14 1852;Ja 11,F 23 1854;58;60[61]-[63]-65;71;76-92[1914]-[19]+
RWo Jl 1915-Je 1917
TBrK Ja 21 1926+
TC 1873;1921+
TMG Jl 1927+
TMaM O 1927+
TMuT 1934+ (Sunday ed only)
TN [1860-61]
TNF Jl 31 1931+
TNV [1914-17]+ (Sunday ed only)
TSS My-D 1864;1935+
TU N 5 1860;Ag 30 1861;Mr 24,Ap 17,Je 27,Jl 26,Ag 14,16,21,N 15,27,D 5 1862;Ja 16,F 18,Ap 23-24,My 1,30,Je 1,Ag 11,O 27,N 11,D 25 1863; Ja 28,F 2,22,S 7-8,N 23 1864;1921+
Tx Je 4 1864;Jl 9 1865;Je 29,Ag 8 1875;My 30 1884;Ap 24 1910;Jl 1913-O 1919;Ja-F,My-Jl 1920;Ja,N-D 1921;F,Ag 1922;F-Jl,S,N 1923+
TxAS 1916+
TxB 1929+
TxBroH Ag 22 1926-F 11 1934
TxCA Mr 1918+
TxDM 1916+
TxDeN F 1919+
TxF O 1903+
TxGR Je 1 1864(supp)D 31 1905+
TxH S 7 1917+
TxHR Mr 1914+
TxHnS Ag 20 1865;Mr 1926+ (Sunday ed only)
TxLT O 1925+
TxU Ja 21 1861-65;Ja 27 1868-76;Ap 1905+
TxWB 1924-O 1932
UPB N 1924;Ja-Ag,N 1925-Je,S 1929+
UU Ap 1921+
V 1851+
VHH 1929+
VHaH Ja-Mr 1917;S 17-30 1919;Ja 22 1926+
VNo [N 1914-18;Je-S,N 1920-F 1921]
VRC O 23,D 4,9-10,12 1861[F 15-S 18 1862]My 5,8,18,28,Je 26,Jl 1,6,15 17-18,S 11,18,O 6,17,24, D 2 1863[64]Mr 6,Je 2 1865
VSbC 1911-Je 1914;O 1928-N 1935
VU Je 9-10,12,17-18,23-25 1862;Mr 1915+
Vt Ja-Jl 1863;My 2-Jl 1864
VtBeM Ap 10 1860-My 15 1866
VtMiS [1873-1900]
VtU 1916+
WAL Ja-Je O 1919-Ja,Ap 1926+
WHi S 18 1851(facsimile)53-Jl 1879;Ja 24 1882-Ja 28,O 1890-Je 1897;Ap 11-D 11 1898;O 18 1901;F 4-Ap 3 1907;S 21 1908-Je 24 1909;10+
WM 1914+
WMJ Jl 1913+
WO 1929+
WaPS Je 25 1870;S 20 1881;1916-[19-21]-[23-25]-[27]-[29]+
WaS O 1913+
WaSp Jl 1913+
WaSpS D 1933+
WaU N 1934+
WaWW 1916+
Wv 1916-23
WvU 1916+
—Index. m,q,an 1913+
1913-29 quarterly with annual compilation; 1930— monthly with annual compilation
CCh 1927+
CL 1913+
CLU 1921+
CO 1913+
CPo 1913+
CSf 1913+
CU 1913+
DL 1913+
DLC 1913+
ICN 1913+
MWiC 1913+
MdBE 1913+
MdBJ 1913+
MiG 1913-16;22+
MoS 1913+
NB 1913+
NBHi 1913+
NN 1913+
NPV 1913+
NjBl Ap 1917-Mr 1920
TxHR 1913+
WM 1913+

Semi-weekly TIMES. sw 1855?-95||?
Title varies slightly
Ct Ap 1862;64-Ja 8 1865[66]-Je 1867;F-D 1868; Jl 1869-70;Ja-Je 1872;73-75;Jl 1876-Ap 16 1878;Jl-D 1879;82-Je 1883;84;Jl-D 1885
CtHT 1861-76
CtY [1859-60]66-67
IC Ja-My,Jl 1857-58
ICU [1857-59]60[66]S 20 1881
KyLo Mr 24-27 1868;My 3-6 1870;Mr 30 1872
MB Mr 26-30 1872;O 1 1880
MBr 1863-78
MHi Ap 1855-S 1859
MWA Mr 15,My 6,Jl 19 1864;Ap 18-25 1865;D 10 1869;O 31,N 21 1871
MdHi O 15-D 1872
MnHi Ap 18,25 1865
NN Ja-Ap 26,My-D 1861;Ap 18 1865
NbHi F 4 1873;F 12 1878
NcD O 30 1866
NhD Ag 30,S 6-23,30-N 15,22-D 6,13-23 1864 [Ja-N 1865]
OClWHi Je 5 1860;Ja 5 1866;S 5 1876
OrP Mr 24 1863-64
PLewL D 10 1869
PPeS My 30 1876
PToHi 1855;Ja-N 1859;Ja-O 1860
VU O 9 1866
Vt 1856;61-62;64;67-68;73-74
VtMiM [1860-65]
WHi O 13,N 27,D 22-29 1863;Ap 18-21 1865;N 26 1869

Evening TIMES. 1906 *See* Die Abend zeitung

Sunday TIMES and messenger. w 1843-92||?
-Jl 1843 as Noah's weekly messenger; Jl 1843-75? Sunday times and Noah's weekly messenger
DLC F 22 1846
IU N 5 1843;F 9 1845
MWA Mr 31,My 5 1844;My 18-25,Ag 3,S 14 1845;Ap 5,Jl 19 1846;Ap 4 1847;S 23 1849;Jl 28 1850-Jl,D 14 1851;S 3-17,N 26 1854;S 16 1855; Ap 27,My 11 1856;Mr 18,Jl 1 1860;Mr 31 1861;Ag 13 1865;F 27 1870;S 20-D 13,27 1874 [Ja-N 1875]Mr 12,O 1 1876;F 18,Ag 12 1877;D 8-15 1878
MiU-C My 25 1845
N D 5 1875
NN Jl 26 1846;My 20 1866
NNHi 1847-52;Ap 23,Jl 30 O 1 1854;Jl 6 1856; Ja 9-Jl 17,S 1859-Mr 4,25,Je 17,Jl 22,N 18,D 1860-61;My 25,Jl 6,27,Ag 17-S 7 1862[63]64[67] Ja-My,S,O 11,25-N 22 1868-Mr 2 1873;Ag 1,15-22,S 5,19 1875;Ag 9 1885
NNMC Ja 25 1863
NjFHi S 1848-52;N 20 1863

New York TIMES and weekly register. w Ja 12 1822-
WHi Ja 12 1822

New York TIMES and evening star. d Mr 14 1838-O 21 1841||
Mr-O 20 1838 as Times and commercial intelligencer; O 22 1839-Ag 29 1840 New York times and commercial intelligencer. Merged with Commercial advertiser, later Globe and commercial advertiser
DLC 1838;Jl-D 1839;Jl-D 1840
MWA Mr 14,21,Ap 16,20,My 29 1838;My 2,D 12 1840;Je 10 1841
N S 1839-40
NNHi My 7 1838-41
NNMT 1839-41
NNS D 25 1839-Ag 20 1840
P-M Ag 2 1838;Ag 26 1839

New York TIMES and evening star. sw 1838?-41||?
1838?-Ag 1840 as New York times and commercial intelligencer for the country
GAtCo Ja 21 1840
MB Jl 19,29,N 15,D 14 1839-Ja 24 1840
MBAt D 11 1840
MWA Mr 29,Je 14 1839
N D 7 1839;Mr 17 1840
NN N 16 1838
NcD O 2 1840;Ja 5 1841

Der TOG. *See* Day

TOMPKINS SQUARE news. ir
NNR Je 1917;Ja-Ag 1918;F-Mr 1919

Ha-TOREN. w,m Je 1913-D 1921||
w Mr 3 1916-Mr 18 1921
In Hebrew
DLC complete

New York daily TRANSCRIPT d 1859-66||?
MWA F 13 1862;D 19,28 1865;F 12,Ap 12 1866

New York daily TRANSCRIPT. Extra D 10 1864-Ja 23 1865||
Extra sheets, with lists of men liable to the draft
DLC complete
NN complete
NNCU [1864-65]
NNHi complete
OClWHi complete

TRANSCRIPT and wasp. d Mr 10 1834-Jl 25 1839||?
1834-Jl 24 1839 as New York transcript (title varies slightly)
C [Ap 19-D 1834]
Ct Mr 26 1834;Ag 27[S 1835;35-37]
CtHi Jl 1837-[38]
CtSp N 5 1838
CtY My 28,Jl 7,11,Ag 23,S 12,O 1,3,7,16 1834-Ja,Mr 24-Ag 11 1834 [?]
DLC My 23-O 1834;Ap 9-D 11 1835;Jl 25 1839
GAtCo S 10 1838
InNh [Mr,Ap 22-Ag 1834]
MWA S 25-O 1834;Ja 16,F-Ag 22 1835;Ja 15, Ap 28,My 12-13,Je 8,28,Jl 25,30-Ag 1,18,S 5, 17 1836;O 4-5 1838
N Ag 1834-Ja,Mr 17-My,Jl 8-37[Ag 24 1835-Ap]-Jl 1836
NN My 27,S 20,O 8-D 1834;Ja 2,F 9 1835-Ap 1836;Ag 2,7-11,18-19,21,23,25-31,S 5,7-12,15-16, 20-21,23-O 2 1837;Ap 13,Je 23 1838;F 21,Mr 26 1839
NNC F-Ag 22 1835
NNHi Ap 7,My 14,Je 23-S 23 1834;F 1835-Mr 17,Ap 2,13,Je 6,8,13,Jl 21 1836;Ap 27 1837;My 4,Je 9 1838;Ap 18 1839
NSchU Je 17,23 1836
NcD [F 12-Je 18 1835]
NjFHi O 4 1834-Ja 1835
NjHi Je 11 1834-Ja,Ag 1835-Ap 1836
NjR [1835;37-38]
RP Mr 5-Ag 21 1835
RPB S 21 1835
WHi 1834-Ag 9 1836

New York TRIBUNE. d 1841-1924 *See* New York herald-tribune

NEW YORK (*Continued*)

NEW YORK CITY—*Continued*

New York TRIBUNE. w S 18 1841-1906‖?
Follows New Yorker. Title varies slightly
CL 1849-50;O 8 1859-Ja 3 1863
CLM Je 27 1888
CLSU Ja 20 1844-D 23 1854[Ap 14 1855-Ap 9 1873]
CP S 21 1881
CSmH S 13 1845-S 5 1846;Ap 22 1865;My 29 1867
CaOLU 1852-53
CaQMS [1850-69]
CoD Ja 30 1878-Ja 17 1883
CoHi Jl 4 1846;My 31 1857
Ct [1843-46]-My 1850;52-59;F 4 1865;Je 5 1872;F 15 1888
CtHC 1841-S 9 1843;46-N 1847
CtHi 1841-Mr 1842;46;Ap-D 1854
CtW My-D 6 1893
CtY 1841-47;N 18 1848;Ap 1850-Ja 11 1851
DLC 1841-[61]64;66-72
DeHi S-O 1841
DeWI N 22-29 1882
IA Jl 12,1864;71-My 1873
IC O 23 1841;Mr 5 1842;S 1844-Mr 1845;S 15 1849-S 13 1851;Ag 1859-Je,Ag 25 1860
ICHi 1841-46;Ja 30,My 1,Je 26,Jl 24 1847;Mr 9,My 4,18-Jl 20,Ag-N 9,23-D 14,28 1850-Mr 8 1851;O 1859-62;My 14 1864;Mr 25 1865
ICM F 23 1881;Ag 23 1893
ICU 1841-O 23 1852;S 1853-Ja 12,Mr 9 1870-F 21 1877;Ja 16 1878-Ja 8 1879;83-Ap 17 1889;S 24-D 1890
supp:Ap 3 1878
IF N 2 1850;O 11 1851-Jl 23 1853
IHi [S 11 1847-Ag 1868]
ILeM Mr 24-D 1860
ISal Ap 10 1841
IU 1841-S 9 1843;Ja-Ag,S 8-22,N 24 1849-50;Ja 11-18,F-N 22,D 27 1851;D 24 1859;Ap 27,My 28 1861;N 21 1866;S 30 1868;Je 23,Jl 14,Ag 18,D 8 1869;Mr 6,O 30 1872;Ap 12 1893
IaDH D 25 1847;Mr 25 1854-56;Ja 14 1880-Ja 4 1882
IaHi 1858-72
IaK 1852-Je 1853
IaOs 1870-91
In Jl 1843-My 1875
InEv My 17 1851-Mr 1853
InRE Mr 17 1849[52-53]S 23 1854[55-57]Mr 20 1858;Ap 14 1860;Ag 10 1861
InT 1841-S 7 1844
InU 1878-80
KHi F 6 1858;My 3 1862
KM S 13 1845-Je 2 1847;50-O 1851;Ap 12 1853-S 1 1854
KU Ja 24-My 2 1877
LU 1851-53
MB [N 27 1841-N 18 1843;Mr 24 1849-Ag 1853;56-71;F 1897-Ap 1898]
MBAt S 18,O 23,N 13-D 18 1841;Mr-My 7,21-S 10,24-D 10,24 1842-S 6 1845
MHi N 23,D 21 1844;My 16,30 1846;54-57[62] Ja 24 1863;Mr 4 1874
ML 1862-85
MSaE Ja 18,F 1-8,Mr 15,My 3-10,S 6,O 18-23 1845;47[Ja-S 1848;Ja-Ag 1849]Ag 31 1850[O-D 1853]-[Ja-O 1862]O 14 1865;Ag 7 1867;Ja 26,F 2,16-23,Mr 9 1870
MWA 1841-[63]-[67-69]-[73]Ja 14 28,Mr 11,Ap 1 1874;O 18 1876;Je 20,D 5(supp)1877[78-79]Je 28-Jl 5 1882
MWo My 18 1861
MdU Ja 16 1878-80
MeBa S 1851-Ag 1852;Je 1854;N 10-17,D 1855;O 11 1862;D 10 1879-Ja 7 1880;81-84;89;91;93-F 14,Mr 28-Ap 4,O 17 1894;D 16 1896-Ag 11,25,D 8-22 1897
MiBcS O 5 1844[45-47]48
MiG Mr 16 1850-F 1853;Ap 22-29 1865
MiU [1862]63[74]-76;80-85;87-1906
MiU-C [1841-43;45-46]-[52-53]-[55-57]-[60-68;70-71]
MnM 1844-48;72-77;79-86;89-91
MnS 1841-My 18 1844;N 24 1855-F 6,Je 11 1859-Je 1864
MnU [1844-55]-[57-59]N 17 1860[61]-63;D 31 1864[65;71-72]
MoS Mr 1854-F 10 1855
N 1841-Ag 1852;F 26,Ag 5,S 1853-Ja 20 1855
NAubHi 1841-Ap 12 1845
NBuG N 30 1844;D 20 1845-[Ja-Jl 1846;Mr 1847-52]-54;Ja 27-F 3 1855;Je 26 1858;My 19 1860;Ja 3 1863;Ja 2 1864;Ja 30,Mr 6,Ap 24,Je 12,Jl 17,Ag 28,O 2,D 4 1867;F 5-12,Mr 11,Ap 29,O 28,D 16 1868;My 8 1872;S 17 1873;Je 21 1876;D 11 1878;O 15,29,D 31 1879;S 8 1880;N 2,D 20 1882;F 28,N 7,28 1883
NCanHi 1841-S 14 1844;D 27 1845-Jl 4 1864;D 4 1872;Ap 24,S 21-28,O 12 1881
NCort S-N 1841;D 10 1842;F 22 1845-Je 20 1846
NHf N 1847-52
NHor 1880
NN S 18,O 16 1841-S 9,N 18 1843[My,S]N 1844-[45]47-[54]56-O 1863[64-66]O 8 1868;D 4 1872;74[75]D 1877-S 18,O 30-D 1878;O 1879-83
NNC D 25 1842-60
NNHi N 25 1843-Ap,D 19 1846-48;Jl 13-20 1850;My 1851-Ag 1853;Ja 6 1866
NNMC Ja 21 1843
NNUnC 1841-S 10 1842
NNY-H Je 1880-My 1881
NPV 1842-51
NR 1841-S 2 1843
NSchU S 18 1841;Je 25,S 3 1842
NSyU 1850;53-[55]-57[61-63;68-69]
NbHi S 18,O 16 1841-S 7 1844[Mr 27-S 1 1849] 58-67;Je 3 1868[69]-F 2,16,Mr 2,16-23 1870;F 22-Mr 22,My 10,Je 14,Jl 26,Ag 9,S 6,D 20 1871;Ja 24 1874;D 5 1877;Mr 27 1878-Mr 14,Ag 1,N 7 1883;Jl 1884-Mr 3 1886;Ja 19 1887;My 1 1888;Ap 15 1891;Ja 27 1892-F 1,15,Mr 15,29-Ap 19,My 31 1893;Ja 10,24,F 14-Mr 7,Ap 11,Je 20,Jl 4 1894[Mr 25-D 16 1896]Ja 6,Mr 11,Jl 21 1897;Mr 9 1898;My 1899;Ja 24 1901
NcD F 3,Mr 30 1844;Je 27 1846;Mr 6,1847;48;F 24,S 8 1849-Ag 1850;O 23 1852;N 15 1856-Ja 3 1857;F 27 1858;Jl 12,Ag 2-9,23,S 6-1862;Mr 28,N 28,D 15 1863[Ja-O 1864]F 12 1868;S 22 1875;S 11 1878-Ja 1,F 12 1879
NcU D 25 1852[53]Jl-S,O 12,26-N 16 1861
NdHi D 22 1860-S 1861
NhD [1842]My 29 1852;Mr 5 1853;Mr 17 1855;N 28 1857;Mr 13,Ap 3,My 1,Ag 28,O 2,N 6,D 18-25 1856;Ag 27 1859;S 15 1860;My 11-18,Je 1,15,Ag 17,S 7,D 28 1861
NhK 1850-52
NjHi 1850-51
NjN [1846-47]
NjR [1858;71]80[81]
NjWdHi Ag 6 1879;Ap 12,26,My 3 1882
OC N 1849-D 18 1852;78-D 22 1880
OCHi N 1848-N 17 1849;S 16 1854-O 10 1857
OCX S 13 1845-N 2 1846
OCl 1851-52;S 1853-S 1854;59
OClWHi S 18 1841-56;Mr 28-My 16 1857;My 12 1860-Ja,Jl 26 1862;Ja 10,F 21 1863;Ap 9,S 27 1864;F 4,Ap 22-29 1865;Ap 7 1866;D 1 1869;Ja 18,D 6 1871;D 4 1872;Ag 1,N 28 1877;My 1 1878;O 8 1879-Ap 1880;O 18 1882;Jl 24 1885;Mr 10 1897
OCon 1848-51
OHi N 18 1841-Je 1860;N 20 1867-74
OOxM Je 1850-51
P Jl 1843-71
PAtM S 1844-Ag 1862
PBr D 4 1872
PDoHi [1841;59-76]O 3 1888
PEr [D 11 1841-D 6 1851]
PHi [1844-45]
PLaHi 1864-65
PLaL [1880]
PLaN Ap 1850-52
PLhT Ag 20,S 24 1859[60]Jl 27 1861
PNoHi Mr 3 1866
PP Ap 10 1846;Mr 1857-Ap 1861;F 22,Ag 16,30,S 20-27 1862;Ja 3-10,24 1863;Ja 16 1864-Jl 18,Ag-D 12 1864;Ja 16,Ap 3,17-24,My 1,29,Je 3,O 10,D 19-26 1867;F 21-Ap,Je 3,17,Jl 1-8,22,Ag 12,26-O,N 25-D 2,23 1868[69-78;84]-Ja 8,22 1890;Ap 15,D 30 1891-[93]
PPeS F 14 1857;Ag 18,S 1 1860;O 3,11 1863;Mr 10 1866;D 15 1869-Ja 12 1870;S 18 1872
PPiHi 1862-Je 17 1865
PScrHi F 7 1863;Mr 11 1865
PScrWi Ap 18,21-28 1865
PToHi O 21 1843-O 5 1844;Mr 11-Jl 1854
PU [1841-48]
RPB [1844;46;48-53]
T S 23 1876
TJT O 1848-Ag 1851
TN [1859]-[61]
TxU 1841-N 16 1844;Ja 23 1847-Ag 1853;Jl 21-D 17 1854;Ag 15 1866-My 15 1867;F 15 1871-F 4 1872
Vt [1856-67]
VtMiM [F 19 1842-F 7 1846]
VtMiS 1847-49;56;58;61-63;68-69
VtU 1841-70;84-90
WHi 1841-59;Ja 14,My 1860-Ja 5 1861;62-[Ap 8 1866-D 4 1872]

Evening TRIBUNE. d S 1 1843-
CLM Ap 15 1865
DLC Je 25 1849
NN [Je 1846-Ap 1847]Ap 25,My 10,24-26 1848;Ap 7,Jl 9,S 29 1849
NcD [1849-50]
NjN Mr 11,My 12,Ag 21 1862;Ja 5 1863
—*See also* New York herald-tribune

New York semi-weekly TRIBUNE. sw My 17 1845-99‖?
Titles varies slightly
CMa Mr 7 1856-57
CSmH My 14 1867;S 24 1870
CSt Jl 1892-93
CU Je 1856;Je 11 1858-66;76;85-87
CU-B Je 20-27 1856
CaOLU 1859-62
CaOT Ag 10 1855-Ag 12 1856
Ct [1846-48]-[51-54]-[61-66]O 1867-Ja[Mr 1868-69] Ag 19,S 3 1870[72;Ap 30-D 6 1878] Mr 24 1880;N 16,D 7 1887;Ja 25,Mr 7 1888;D 29 1891[92]Mr 11 1893
CtHi Ap-D 23 1854
CtW My 15 1855-Je 1 1858
CtY My 18 1858-Ag 1862
DLC [1848-50]-[64]Ja-My,Jl 1868-[73]F 10 1874-D 3 1875[77]-86;88-Je 1899
GDE [1874]-[76]
GU S 14 1872;Je 30 1879;Je 7 1924
IA F 1869-70
IC Ag 1 1846;Mr 20[Ap 14 1847-51]-D 12 1854;Ap 12 1861
ICHi Jl 1847-F 13,20-23,My 1-18,25-Ag,S 4 1850; Mr 8 1851-68
ICM [Ja-Ag 1852]Je 5 1855;F 1,Mr 19-22,Ap 2 1861;Ja 11 1878
ICN [1858]-Je 12,D 1859-Je 25 1872
ICU Jl 15 1853-[57-59]-Mr 9 1860;Mr 9-D 7 1877;81-82;Ap 19 1889-S 19 1890
IF [1856-58]-60
IHi [My 13 1851-D 9 1887]
ILeM O 21 1859-S 25 1860;Jl 1861-My 26 1868;Je-D 1869
IU 1861-97
IaDH Ja-Je 1889;Ja-O 1890
IaDeL S 1855-Mr 24 1857
IaFd Ja 18 1861-F 4 1862
IaGG F 27,My 25,O 16 1855;F 27,Mr 18,Je 6,Jl 1,Ag 22,S 27,O 7,N 7-11 1856;D 1883-84
IaHi 1851-53;Jl 1854-Je 1856;57-58
In Ag 1846-Ag 1877[79-88]
InEv D 30 1853-F 12 1856
InI Ag 10 1852-[53-55]-Je 1866;Ap 15 1873-75
InRE S 10,O 8,15 1872
KHi [1846-99]
KU Je 1877-85
LNM My 15-D 1870
MAm D 1850-51
MB [Ap 1853-Ap 1855;72]
MHi Ap 1851-55;Mr 20 1863;Ap 18-My 12 1865
MNF F 9-D 1864
MSaE F 28,Ag 8,D 5,12,19-22 1846;O 30,N 3-6,13-24,D 1-4 1847;O 26 1850;F 27,Mr 16 1858;N 2-9 1860
MWA O 1 1845;Ja 10,F 4 1846;S 6-9 1853;N 2 1855-56;Mr 10 1857;My 18,Jl 20 1858;S 6 1859;S 14,O 9 1860;O 11,N 15 1861;Ap 15,My 2 1862;Ja 6,F 13 1863;Ja 30,D 7 1866;F 1 1870;O 8 1878;O 7-10,21-28,N 4,14,28 1884
MdHi My 23-D 1873;My-N 1 1874;Ja-Jl 1881
MeAuC 1857
MeBB 1860-Mr 22,S 3-13 1861;Ja 24,Ap 4 1862;65-My 26 1868
MeBa D 6 1872;Je 14-21,Jl 5-8,22-29,Ag 5-9,19-O 25,N 15 1881;Jl 7,N 3,10 1882;D 23 1884-88;90;Ja 2-5 1894
MeWC 1862-65
MiAC [1877-99]
MiU Je 3 1845;78-79
MiU-C [1856;61-64]
MnHi [1846-47;50-51;75-77]
MnM 1860-61;63-65;84[85]87-[89]
MnU Ap 12-D 1853;Ja 4-7 1859;Ag 17 1860;S 19 1862;Ap 18 1865;91;93-[96]
MoS S 1856-S 1857
NBuG Ja 14 1853;D 29 1854[55-Je 1864;67-89] Ja 3 1890[91-93]
NCH 1857
NCanHi Ap 18-My 5 1865
NCoo 1861
NN O 1850-[S-O 1851]-[53-58]-61;Ag 8 1862 [63-65]O 30 1868;Ja 8,19 1869;D 3-6 1872;73-[75]D 11 1877;79[S-O 1884]F 10 1893-Jl 10,Ag 7 1894-F 12 1895
NNHi My 16 1846-My 24 1848;My-Je,Ag 1860-Mr 1861;Ag 21 1866
NNY-H D 1877-78;Je 1879-My,D 1880-My 1881
NbHi O 22,N 22 1861;Je 9,22 1866-Je 12,N 24,D 15 1868;Ja 1,Mr 19,Ap 20,My 4,25;Ag 17,31,N 19,26,D 21,28-31 1869;F 9 1870;Ag 29 1871;My 7-10,Ap 30 1872;Ap 26 1873;Ja 29,F 22,Je 4 1878;Jl 22,Ag 1,29 1879;Ap 15 1891;Ja 24 1893
NcD [Jl-D 1848]-My 22 1850;F 27 1858;F 7,Mr 4 1862;Ja 19 1877;S 10,D 10,31 1878;Ja 17,Ag 29,O 31 1879
NcU D 18 1855;Jl 15,O 17 1856[68]-F 19 1869;S 9 1879
NhD Jl 5 1859[F 28-N 21 1860]S 1,O 19,N 16,30,D 7 1861;Ap 11-My 2,9-Je 20,27-Ag 5,12,19-30 1862;Ja-F 6,13-27,Mr 6-10,17-Ap 3,14,21-My 5 1863
OCHi D 18 1857-59;66-D 12 1882
OClWHi N 15 1853-My 1869;Je 10 1879-Ja 4 1881
ODW Ap 29-Jl 12 1853
OOxM 1852[53-56]
OY Ag 6 1875-80
OkHi 1880[94-95]
P Ag 27 1858;68-71
PEHi Ag 8 1856
PEr [D 12 1851-D 13 1867]
PLaHi [1864]65
PLaN Ap 1864-65
PLewL D 10 1868
PPeS D 7 1866-D 7 1869;Ja 11 1870-Ja 14 1876
PScrWi My 5 1865
PToHi O 24 1846-47;F 12-My 10 1848;49[52] Mr 18 1853;N 19 1858-O 1860
VtU [My 31 1845-77]
WHi My 25 1850-S 17 1852;54-55;Je 20-N 7 1856;Mr 22 1861;Ja 24 1862-D 3 1867;F 25 1870-Mr 3 1871
WMa Ja 23 1880-Ja 21 1881

New York TRIBUNE. tw 1899-1909‖?
Ct Ja 21 1900
ICU 1903-[1905]06
MiU 1907-08

TRIBUNE for California. ir,w 1850?-
CU-B N 5 1852;Mr 5,21 1853
NEh Ja 27 1855
NN Ja 27 1855

New-York TRIBUNE for Europe. ir
"pub on the departure of each Mail Steamer for Liverpool"
CSmH S 25 1850

TRIGLOT. sw D 1829-
CtY D 26 1829

TRUE national democrat and morning star. d 1849?-
MWA Ap 29 1854
NNHi Ap 10 1854

TRUE sun. d Ja 22-26 1835‖?
NNHi Ja 22 1835

TRUE sun. d Mr 20 1843-Jl 31 1848‖?
pub by striking compositors of the Sun
DLC Jl 14 1843
MWA S 28 1844;Ja 5,D 2,29 1846;Ja 5,N 10 1847
MdBG D 15 1845
NN S 20 1843-Mr 19 1844;Mr 21-S 19 1845;Ja 20-My 4,Jl 9,21,23,Ag 9 1847-Ap 21,Je 7,Jl 31 1848
NNHi Ag 12 1845;Mr 19 1847
—w ed *See* Dollar weekly true sun

Weekly TRUE SUN. w 1843-48‖?
MWA Jl 1 1848

New York TRUMPET. d Mr?-Ap 20 1841‖?
DLC Ap 5,17,20 1841

TRUTH. d Je?-Ag 27 1834‖?
NNHi Ag 4,27 1834

TRUTH. d My 3 1841-
DLC My 3 1841

TRUTH. d 1879-84‖?
Title varies
DLC S 20 1881
MWA My 18,O 27,30,N 2 1880;Ja 15,Jl 28,S 26,N 26 1881;My 25,Je 8,Jl 13,15,1882;Ap 8,N 24-26 1883;Mr 1 1884
NN [Jl-D 1880]-Ja 7 1884
NSyU Ap 28 1881
NjHi S 26,N 19 1882
NjR O 30 1880
PWcHi O 27 1880
TJT Ja 19 1884
WHi Ja 6 1882

TRUTH. 1894-1919 *See* Warheit

TRUTH teller. w Ap 2 1825-55‖?
CSmH S 11 1830;45-Ja 1850
CtY 1825-D 14 1833
DGU 1825-Ap 1840
DLC 1825-[29]31-32;38-39

NEW YORK (*Continued*)

NEW YORK CITY—*Continued*

TRUTH teller. w 1825-55||?—*Continued*
InNU 1825-26
MiU Mr 2,16 1833
MiU-C [1834-35]
MoSU [N 24 1849-52]
MoScR 1835
N Ap 9-16,Jl 16,Ag 6,20-O 8,29,D 24 1825;Ja 7,F 4,O 7-21,N 4,18-25 1826;My 26,Jl 7,Ag 4 1827;My 30-Je 6 1829;O 12 1833[34-39]
NN 1825[26]-33
NNHi My 24 1828;O-N 19 1831;Jl 14 1838-43; Jl 1844-Ag 9 1845;Jl 8-15 1848
NNIHi 1825-28;D 24 1831-My 14 1836
NcD 1855
NcU Ja 12 1839
OHi My 21 1831
P Ag 11 1832
PLaHi N 21 1840

TSEIT. *See* Zeit

TURNER'S New-York shipping and commercial list. *See* New York commercial

UKRAINIAN daily news. *See* Ukrains'ki shchodenni visti

UKRAINS'KI shchodenni visti. (Ukrainian daily news) d 1919?+
In Ukrainian
CSt-H [1923]
PP 1932+

UNCLE SAM. w Ag 7 1841-
MWA S 18 1841

UNCLE SAM. w S 2 1876-
Campaign paper
MWA O 7 1876

UNION. d Ap 21-Jl 6 1836||?
Ct Je 9 1836
NN Ap 21-Jl 6 1836

UNION. d Jl 23 1842-Mr 17? 1843||
United with New York aurora to form New York aurora and union, later New York aurora
MWA O 28-31 1842
NNHi O 7,D 6 1842;Mr 3,7,13 1843

UNION. w O 14 1865-
Campaign paper
MWA O 21 1865

UNION. (Al-Ittihad) w My 28 1921-Mr 25 1922||?
In English, Arabic and Syrian
NN 1921-Mr 1922

UNION shield. w O 7- 1848||?
Campaign paper
RPB O 7,21 1848

New York UNIONIST. w Ap 17?- 1852||?
Campaign paper
NN My 22 1852
—d ed *See* Evening day-book

New York UNIVERSE. w 1846-
1846?-49 as Weekly universe
CoHi Ja 5 1850;N 8 1851
DLC Ap 1 1854
IU Mr 3 1849
KHi O 23 1852
MWA My 19-O 6 1849;Jl 1853-[54]-F 24 1855
NN N 13 1847
NcD Je 16 1849;My 13-Je 10 1854
OC Je 7 1851

UNSER kamf. bw F 1 1932-N 1933||
In Yiddish
NN 1932-33

UP-TOWN news. w 1884?-89||?
NNHi Ap 26 1884;F 5,19,Mr 12,26,My 28-Je 11,25 1885;Ag 14,28-S 4,O 2-23,N-D 11,25 1886;Ja 1,22,F 5,26-Ap 2,30,My 28-Je 4,18-25 1887

UP-TOWN news. d 1885?-89||?
NNHi Jl 2,19,30,Ag 27,S 3,10-11,O 15,N 5,13,19, D 10,17,24,31 1885-F 18,24-Mr 15,25,Ap 1,5-7,9-10,12-14,16-17,21,My 14,28,Je 8,15-16,19,21-24,28-30,Jl 3,6-10,12-14,16,31 1886

UTRO. d Ja 2-Mr 14 1922||?
In Russian
CSt-H Ja-Mr 14 1922
DLC Ja-Mr 14 1922
NN Ja-Mr 14 1922

VEREINIGTE STAATEN zeitung. w S 1-N 3 1900||
Campaign paper
In German
DLC complete

Sunday morning VISITOR. *See* Morning telegraph

Daily VOICE. d O 19 1886-
IC O 19-22,24-N 3 1886
MWA O 19-22,25-N 1,3 1886
NBu O 19-22,25-N 1,3 1886
OClWHi O 25-29 1886

VOICE of the worker. *See* Empros

Der VOLKSADVOCAT. w 1887?-1924||?
In Yiddish
NN Jl 27 1888-Je 12 1895;D 30 1904-24
WHi Ag 10,N 16 1888;Je 28,Jl 5 1895
—d ed *See* Warheit; Day

VOLKSSTIME. w Mr 29-S 20 1912||
In Yiddish
NN complete

Der VOLKS-TRIBUN. w Ja 5 1846-
In German
CSmH D 5 1846

New Yorker VOLKSZEITUNG. d Ja 8 1878-O 12 1932||
Followed by Neue volkszeitung
In German
DLC Jl 1881-88
ICJ My 25 1897-Je 1902
MB F 21 1903
NN 1894-Ag 1918;Ja-Ap 1919;O 1920-32
NNRa 1878-[84]-[1932]
PU F 21 1903
WHi My 1 1886;N 11-14 1887;O 22 1889-99;Ap 14 1902-O 12 1932
—w ed *See* Vorwärts

Sonntagsblatt der New Yorker VOLKSZEITUNG. w 1878?-1928||?
Title varies slightly
ICJ My 30 1897-Je 1902
IU My 27-Je 3,Ag 19,S 23,O 7-21,N 4,18,D 1906-Ja 13,27-F,Mr 10,31,My 12,26 1907
WHi 1889

VOLUNTEER. ir O 13- 1854||?
Campaign paper
N O 13,30 1854

VOLUNTEER. w Jl 28 1860-
NNHi Jl 28 1860
NSyU Ag 4 1860

VORWÄRTS. w 1878-O 15 1932||
1878-My 1897 as Wochenblatt der New Yorker volkszeitung
In German
ICJ Je 23-S 22 1888;Je 27-Ag 8,N 7 1891;F 20-Je 18 1892;Je 1897-1902;06-[26]-32
IU Ja 31 1903-Ag 18,D 1906-O 12 1907
KHi Jl 23-D 1 1888
NIC [1893-1907]
NN 1911-Ag 1918;Ja-Ap 1919;O 1920-32
NNRa 1878;80-1932
—d ed *See* New Yorker volkszeitung

VORWÄRTS. w Ja 3 1885-94||?
1885-91? as Der Sozialist. Merged with Wochenblatt der New Yorker volkszeitung, later Vorwärts
In German
CtY [1885;92-93]
ICJ 1885-Ap 5 1890
ICU [1893-94]
IU [1893-94]
KHi Ag 15 1888-F 1889
NN 1885-[83] -94
WHi 1885-89[92]94

VORWÄRTS. (Yiddish) *See* Jewish daily forward

VOZ de la America. tm D 1865?-
In Spanish
DLC Ja 20,Mr 1,10,21,31,My 11,21,Je 11 1866; supp Ap 21,My 1,23 1866

VOZROZHDENIE Rossii. w My 2 1926-
In Russian
DLC My 2-22 1926

WALL Street journal. [Evening ed] d N 1882-O 31 1934||
1882-Jl 6 1889 as Dow Jones letters
Je 27 1932 is fiftieth anniversary ed
pub complete
CL D 1918-Ja,Mr 10 1919-34
DA 1928-34
EHi S 27 1910-S 1928
MH-BA Ja-Mr 1907;O-D 1911
MN Jl 1905-07;Je 1908-Ja 3,5,Mr-O 1909;Ja-My,S 1910-Ag 1911
NNHi Je 27 1932

WALL STREET journal. [Morning ed] d Ja 1 1899+
pub 1899+
CL D 1917+
CLO Mr 9 1927+
CSt 1903-[12]+
CaB 1928+
CaQMR 1930—
C: S 9 1918 35+
CtY 1912+
DA O 1934+
DLC My 1902+
FDeS 1929-34
IC 1914-Mr,Jl 1920-F,My 1927-28
ICJ D 29 1915-[17]-[20]+
ICM Je 18 1903;Ja 13 1909
ICU O 1913-14;Mr 1915-Je 1918;19-S 1920;21+
IEN Jl 1925+
IEN-C Jl 2 1928+
IU Ag 19 1905+
IWW Ag 1934-F 1935
IaDa current 6 months
IdU Je 1921+
InI Je 1914-17 19;Jl 1924-26;32+
InSb 1930+
InU O 1924+
LNH [1928-30]
LU D 1929-O 1930;Ja-Je,O 1931-Mr 1933
M [N 29 1928-Ja 7 1931]
MH-BA [1902]Jl 1903-06;Ap 1907-S 1911;Ap 1912+
MdBe Mr 1931+
MiD 1924+
MiU [1905]+
MnU 1912-O 1919;F 1920+
MoFuW O 15 1933+
MoS [1924+]
MoSW Ap 7 1908+
NIC 1910-16[22,24+]
NN Je 13,19 1900+
NNC-B N 1931+
NNSt 1914+
NcD 1908-[10-15]Ja 4,Ap 17,20-30,Jl 13 1928;Ja 4,Ap 17,20 1929+
NcFS 1925+
OAU N 1927+
OCl O 1919+
OHi F 1923-Ag 1929
OkStO [1929]+
OrCA [1930]+
OrU [1927-28]+
PP [1913]-[17-18]+
PPN 1917-[19]-[26]-[34]
PU [1908-09]12-14;23+
PWaHi [1921]
TNV [O 1931-34]+
TxGR D 10 1907 Jl 1930+
TxLT 1934+
WHi Jl 1903-11;Ap 2 1928
WaPS F 19,Mr 18 1915;My 17 1917;Mr 16 1922;Ap 17 1928;N 26 1929[30;33]
WaSp 1923+

WALL STREET journal. [Pacific Coast ed] d O 1 1929+
pub 1929+

WALL STREET journal and real estate gazette. w? 1851?-
IU O 18 1851
P-M O 28 1854

WALL STREET daily news. d 1879-1907||?
NN Jl 15-16 1879;Ag 13 1884;Je 3 1885;My 19 1893[Ap-Je 1894;S-O 1905]F 19-N 15 1907
WHi [1879-N 16 1907]Ap 2 1928

WALL STREET news. d 1893?-My 30 1930||
1893?-Ap 12 1910 as Wall Street summary; Ap 13 1910-Jl 20 1924 Financial America. Merged with Wall Street journal
CSt N 1926-Ag 1929
ICJ 1909-30
IU 1908-Je 19 1920;Ja 9 1926-30
KHi Jl 23 1925
MiU 1908-30
NN 1905-09;D 29 1911-S,N 26 1919-Ag 1924;25-30
NNSt 1914-[16-17]-Ap 1918
RW S 8-9 1880
WHi Ap 2 1928

WALL STREET reporter. w Mr 10 1843-Ap 27 1850||?
DLC Ag 25 1848
InI Ag 21 1845
MWA My 12 1843;O 19(extra)1844;Je 30 1845; N 18(extra)1846;Ap 27 1850

WALL STREET summary. *See* Wall Street news

WARHEIT. (Truth) d Ag 23 1894-F 28 1919||
1894-N 10 1905 as Der Täglicher herold (English title: Daily Jewish herold). United with Day to form Day and the Warheit, later Day
In Yiddish
IU D 6 1917-Je 1918
NN 1894-Ap 13 1899;N 11 1905-19
WHi [Jl 31-Ag 27 1907]
—w ed *See* Volksadvocat

New York WASHINGTONIAN. w Mr 19? 1842-
NNHi My 21 1842

New York WASHINGTONIAN, reformer, crystal fount, and olive plant. w 1843-
Title varies slightly
NcD Ap-My 13,27-Je 10,24 1843

WASHINGTONIAN daily news. d N? 1842-
DLC D 22 1842
WHi F 10 1843

WASHINGTONIAN weekly news. w 1843||?
P-M Ap 22 1843

WESTCHESTER clarion. *See* North New Yorker and Westchester clarion

WESTCHESTER county journal. (Morrisania) w 1852-72||?
NNMC Jl 31 1852

WESTCHESTER gazette. (Morrisania) w Ag 9 1850-56||
1850-Mr 1851 pub in West Farms; Ap 1851-My 29 1852 in Mott Haven
NEh Ag 9 1850
NNMC S 3 1853
WHi Ag 8 1851-Jl 1852

WESTCHESTER globe. w 1889?+
NNHu [1891;1930-31]+

WESTCHESTER globe. d 1933||?
Campaign paper
NNHu 1933

WESTCHESTER globe. d 1935||?
Campaign paper
NNHu 1935

WESTCHESTER independent. w 1885+
NNHu [1891-92;1930-31]+

WESTCHESTER sentinel. *See* Bronx sentinel

WESTCHESTER times and New York weekly advocate. (Morrisania) w 1865-95||?
1865-87? as Westchester times (1881?-82? Westchester times and East Chester news) 1888?-89? Westchester times and the New York people; 1890?-91? Westchester times and New York people and weekly advocate. Merged with New York advance, later Bronx record and times
NN N 20 1874
NNHi F 3-10 1865;F 14 1873,Ap 30 1875;F 1878-[90-91]Ja 15 1892;Mr 24,Ap 15,Ag 5 1893;My 25 1895
NNMC My 26 1888
—d ed *See* New York advocate

WESTCHESTER union. (Morrisania) w 1872?-76||?
N My 2 1874

New York WHIG. d My 10 1831-My 10 1832||
NNHi D 30-31 1831;Ja 3-20,22-27,29-F 13,15-26,Mr 1-20,22-Ap 19,22-My 2,5-10 1832

New York WHIG. sw My 10 1831-My 13 1832||
MWA Jl 15,Ag 2,S 20-27,O 21-23,N 25-D 2,9-27 1831
NN D 30 1831;Ja 13 1832
NNHi My 22-N 13 1832

New-York WHIG. w My 11 1831-F 1 1834||?
DLC My 18,Ag 3 1831
MB My 18 1831-Je 20 1832
MWA S 5,O 3 1832;Ag 28,S 11 1833;Ja 4,F 1 1834
MiU [1831-32]
N O 12 1831;S 19,O 17,D 19-26 1832;Ap 24,O 16 1833
NN [Ag-O 1831]-Mr 6 1833
NNHi O 7,D 28 1831;N 21 1832-Jl 3 1833
NjHi 1831-Jl 10 1833

NEW YORK (*Continued*)

NEW YORK CITY—*Continued*

New York daily WHIG. d D 26 1837-Mr 18 1840‖
Merged with New York gazette and general advertiser
CtY Ap 7 1838
DLC Ap 4(extra)1838;Je 7 1839
MWA Mr 27,D 10 1838;My 4 1839
NN [Ja-Ap]My 30,Je 19,28 1838
NNHi [Ja-S 1839]Mr 18 1840
NNMT F 19-N 1838;39
P-M Ag 2 1838

New York weekly WHIG. w Mr 3 1838-
DeHi Mr 9 1839
MBAt My 4 1839
MWA My 5-12 1838;Ja 26,Jl 6 1839

WHIP. w My 6? 1839-42‖?
GAtCo Ag 3 1839
IU My 13-20,Jl 6,27 1839

WILLIAMSBRIDGE courier. w 1889-97‖?
NNHi N 1889-N 16 1896

New York daily WITNESS. d Jl 1871-79‖?
MHi Ja 24,F 25-Ap 5 1876
MWA Mr 4 1873;Je 8 1876;O 17 1878-My 28 1879
NjR O 19 1878
P-M My 11 1876
PCA [1873-77]
WHi Mr 7 1876

WOCHENBLATT. . . *See under* next important word; e.g., Wochenblatt der New-Yorker staats-zeitung is alphabeted under Staats-zeitung

WöCHENTLICH. . . *See under* next important word; e.g., Wöchentlicher New Yorker democrat is alphabeted under Democrat

Daily WORKER. w,d Ja 24 1922+
1922-Ja 12 1924 as Worker(w)
1922-Ja 23 1927 pub in Chicago
pub 1923+
DL Je 1924+
DLC F 1922+
IU Ap 25 1929+
MnHi 1927+
NBuG Jl 1922-Ap 1931
NNC [Ja 22 1924+]
NNC-B 1928+
NNRa 1924+
NPV Jl 22 1932+
WaU Jl 29 1927+

WORKER'S age. w,sw Ja 23 1932+
sw 1933?
NNC 1932-D 15 1933
WaU F 16 1935+

WORKING MAN'S advocate. *See* Young America

WORKMAN'S paper. *See* Arbeiter zeitung

WORLD. w 1860-93‖?
Title varies slightly
DLC My 19,Jl 14-28,N 3,D 8 1864;Ja 25,Mr 1,29,Je 14,D 8 1865
ICM Mr 7 1877[O 1878-Mr 1883]
ICN Ja 17-S 1863;64-65;69-78
IU Mr 30,Ap 13 1861
IaDH 1878-80
MWA O 13 1860;Mr 30 1861;O 18,D 13 1862-[63]Ja 21-F 4,Mr 3-10,My 19-26,Jl 21 1864
MiU-C [1861-64]My 26 1880
N [1860-61]Ja 7 1864[70]
NN Jl 1860-75
NRU Jl-D 1875
NbHi F 9-16,Mr-Ap 6,My 4-11,25,Je 15-Jl,Ag 17,31,S 14,O 12-N,D 14-21 1870;Ja 4,My 24 1871;N 24 1875;Je 6,S 12,N 21,D 26 1877;My 15 1878;Ag 13 1879;Ja 20 1886;O 10 1888;Ap 17,N 12 1889;D 28 1892
NcD D 29 1860;Je 22,Jl 13,Ag 10,S 7-14,28 1870;D 4 1872;F 26,Mr 26,My 28,Jl 16 1873 [74-75]F 16,Je 28-Jl 5,Ag 2 1876;Ap 18 1877 [Ja-Je 1878]D 29 1880;Mr 8 1882;Mr 14 1883; Ja 7 1885;Je 15,Jl 20,Ag 3 1887;S 12 1888;Mr 6,Jl 17 1889;Jl 15 1891;Ja 27,Jl 13-Ag 1892
NhD D 14,28 1861-Mr,Ap 12-Jl 19,Ag-D 6 1862
OClWHi S 21 1861;Ja 21 1863;Mr 17 1864
OHi Ag 11 1860
PP 1861[83]-Ap 1884
PPL 1886-87[89]
PSuHi [1872-74;89]
TKL O 2 1887
VU Ag 13 1879;My 12,Je 30-Jl 7 1880;F 23 1881

WORLD. d Je 14 1860-F 27 1931‖
Jl 1861-O 17 1863 as World, morning courier and New York enquirer. United with Evening telegram and Evening world to form New York world-telegram
Ja 1 1901 is Harmsworth ed
A 1867[69-70]-[83]-[98]1924
C F 5 1887-89;Jl 1890-96;Ja-Je 1898
CSmH S 25,27,29-30,O 14-15,17-18,N 7,12,26,D 12,15-17,26 1862;Ap 15,O 19 1865;S 19 1867
CSt My 1928-[29]30
CSt-H [1914-15]-[19]
CU Ag 1914-My,Jl-O,D 1915;F,Ap 1916-Ja,Ap 1918-N 1919
CaOLU 1861
CoD Je 20-D 1861;Ja 3-4,F 14-22,Mr 1,7,18, Ap 26,My 1,Je 9 1862;Ap 3,8,15,17-18,20-21, 23-26,28-My 8 1865
Ct O 18 1860;F 11-12 1862;Ja 2 1865;Jl 4,Ag 11 1886;F 20 1887
CtY 1860-97;F 27 1931
DLC complete
IC Ap 17,19-22,24,26 1865[Ja 10-Je 1873]Jl 14 1885-Mr 1886
ICHi 1860-Ja 6 1862;F 18,Ap 15,17-19,24,26,S 26,O 2,6,N 23-24 1865;O 10 1871;My 2 1893
ICM S 23 1870;N 4,13,D 14,21 1871;Mr 27,N 6-7 1872;S 28 1874[75-78]Je 23 1879[Je-Jl 1880;81-85]Ap 7 1886
ICN Ja 2-S 1863;64-65;69-78(Sunday ed only)
ICU Je 15 1860;61[62-65]-D 11 1866;67[68]-F, Ap-D 1873;N 3 1880;Jl 3-6,S 20,24,26-27 1881; N 8 1884;Mr 10 1888;N 9 1898
IEN-C Jl 1930-31
IF Ap 15 1865
IHi [D 5 1860-My 25 1865]
IU Ap 20,My 4,22,Jl 24 1861;Ap 16 1864
IaDH Jl 17-D 1860;Jl 1872-73;Jl 1874-Je 1875; Jl 1878-Je 1879;Jl-D 1885;Ap-S 1887;Ja-Mr,O 1888-90;Mr 1891-Mr,My 1894-1914
IaGG Je 26,Jl 4 1862
KHi [1862-1918]Jl 4,7 1920;Jl 4 1927
LNC O 29 1862;Ap 11 1863
LNH Je 6 1863;My 7 1864
LSfD My 9 1863
M 1928-F 1931
MB Ag 4,O 3,22,N 21 1860-[65-67]-73;79;Je 1883-86;88-90
MBAt 1860-76
MBr 1860
MHi [1861-63]Jl 7 1865
MNS O 5 1876-Je 1877;78-79;Jl 1880-81;N 1892-Ap 1902
MWA [Je 14-Jl 14]Ag 24 1860-95;Jl 1897-98; Ja 1 1901;O-D 1903;F 26-27 1931
MWiC [Ag-S 1861]Ja 16-17 1863[Mr-Je,Ag-N 1868]Mr 30 1869
MdBJ Mr 15-20 1861
MeBa My 31 1862
MiG S 10-11 1863;Ap 17-18,22 1865;F 21 1878; Mr 17 1893;S 15,17(extra)1901
MiU [1860]-63[83;95;98]-[1901]
MiU-C [1860-66;68-70;80-81;85;87-91;93-95;98-99]
MnHi Jl 18 1861-S 1862
MnU Jl 1862-Je 1864[84-85]91-97
MsHi Ap 30 1864
N 1860-[68-Je 9 1870]Mr-Je 1873;Ja-Mr 1874 [76]Ap-Je 1877;Jl-D 1878;Jl 1880-81;Ja-Je 1883;Jl-D 1884;Jl-S 1885;Je-S 1886;O-D 1887; 90-F 1891;Jl-Ag 1892;Ja-Je,O 1893-[94]1911-N 1922
NB 1860-Je,O-D 1861;Ap 1862-Mr 1864
NBHi 1860-62;66-92
NBuG Je 27-Jl 25 1863;My,Ag-N 1871;72-Je 1880;81-O 1894
NCH 1861-O 9 1862
NMi S 22 1863-Ag 1865
NN 1860;F 1861-1931
NNC Ja 3-Ap 1869;Ja-Ag 1870;71-Ap 6 1873; Ja-Je 1876;80-1931
NNCU [N 6 1860-My 7 1880]
NNCom 1863-[N 1910-My 1915]-31
NNHi 1860-86;O 21 1888;My 19,Je 2 1889;My 4 1890;S 4 1892;98
NNMC Ja 1,Ap 3 1861;Ap 29-30 1889;F 26-27 1931
NNRo 1894-My 1920
NPV D 1927-31
NRU Jl 14 1860;Jl 10,12 1861;My 28,Je 2 1862; D 29,31 1863;My 18,23 1864;Ja 2,4 1865;Mr 31 1883
NSyU Ag 9,S 8,15,25-26,O 10-11,30,N 5-15,23-24,28-30,D 11-15,17,19,21,27-29 1860;Ja 4,7-10, Ag 24,S 21,27-28,O 3,5,N 9,30 1861
NUHi 1868-69
NcD [Ag 22 1860-Je 1862]D 29 1863[64-65]Jl 17,O 8,D 12-21,24 1866-[67-69]Ja 24,26-27,31, My 18,Ag 31 1870;73-82;F 2 1883;Ja 23 1885;F 8,12,25,Mr 4,28, Je 1,S 27 1886;Ap 20 1887;My 7,Ag 13,29-31,S 2-10,12-15 1893;O 10 1894;D 19 1895;Jl 22,30,O 9 1896;Je 8 1897;O 8 1898;Ja-Mr 1904;Ja 24 1905;S 9,11-25 1921;N 5 1930;F 27 1931
NcU D 25 1870;Ja 27 1876-Ap 19 1878;Ag 24,S 2 1880;My 18 1883[N-D 1886]N 20 1919
NhD Ag 20 1886
NjHi Ag 5 1861;65-Jl 1878
NjJ 1866;68;S 1871-S 1873;74-S 1875;Ap 20-O 1 1898
NjO [1860-61]
NjR [1861;64-68;73-76;78-79;85;88-89;92;94]
NjU 1929-[31]
OC N 1874-82
OClWHi D 3 1860-N 6 1861;S 17 1862-Ap 24 1879;F 10 1886;Mr 5 1889;S 4-O 27 1892;Ja 18,My 7 1893;My 20,22 1898;F 26 1899;My 25 1916
OHi 1861-Ja 14 1862;F 19,Mr 7,D 5 1863;Je 9, Ag 2,4 1864;F 10,Ap 5,Jl 9 1865;F 1868-93; 1912-31
OOxM 1860-74
OrP D 28 1861-63
P Mr 1885-S 1910
PBf Ap 18 1861;N 15 1881
PDoHi [F 11 1865-F 2 1901]
PEHi Jl 7 1863;F 5 1868
PEL D 17 1861
PHi 1863-Je 1865;82-1909
PP Ja 12 1863-Jl 6 1865;Mr 9 1867;Mr 5-6,N 1 1873[74]-[76-77]F 9 1879;F 23 1881;O 14,26 1893;O 27 1904;My 30 1910;28-31
PPL [1861]63;Mr 9 1865[66]Mr 5-6,N 1 1873 [77]F 9 1879;F 23 1881
PPM My 1865-Je 1897;F 1903-O 1904
PPeS S 6,13,O 4,18 1864;Je 6 1865
PPot F 3 1862;N 3 1886;O 7 1894;Jl 26 1896
PStP [1866-83;89]90
PSuHi [1872-74;89]
PWCl [1864]Ja 2,Mr 11 1865;O 14 1868
PWbW [1862]-[68-75]
PYHi [1901]
RP Jl 20 1861-[Je 1865]
RPB Mr 1868-69
TJT N 2 1896
TM My 7 1893
TSS Ap-Ag 1861;62;S-D 1863
TxU 1864-Ag 12 1865
V D 7 1870-Ap 1871
VHi Ja-Mr 1863;64
VRC [My 5-D 1863;F 15 1864-65]
Vt Jl 1860-61;Ja 4 1862;O 18 1871-72;78
WHi 1861-Mr 8 1899;N 13 1913-Ja 1 1914;18-31
WaPS [1917-19;23-24;26] (Sunday ed only)
—Brooklyn ed.
ICM Ap 16,22 1888;Je 7,O 23,28,N 11,15 1891
NBHi Je 3 1886

New York WORLD. sw,tw 1861-1924‖?
Title varies: Twice-a-week world
sw 1861-94?
Ct Ja 3-7,14 1862
DLC Jl 12 1863-64
GAtCo Je 17-22,S 18-21 1896;Mr 5 1897
ICN F 13 1863;My 26 1865;Ap 9,23-Jl 23 1869; Ag 16 1870-78
IaHi Ap 1897-S 1901
In 1882
KHi N 23 1900
MWA 1862-S 6 1867;Ap 28 1874
NN Mr 19,My 10,24,31,Je 7,25,Jl 2,19,30-Ag 2,9 1861
NbHi Ja 24 1865
NcD O 9 1896;Je 14 1897;Je 28,Jl 5-7 1899;Mr 3 1900;Mr 29 1907;D 30 1908;Mr 5-10 1909;Ja 31,Ap 22 1912
OClWHi My-Ag 1862;63-N 1864
VHi 1861-65;Jl 1866-67
VU S 26 1877;O 16,N 20 1903;Ap 22,My 30-Je 1,13,S 28,N 16 1904;Ja 20,Mr 13[Je 1905-07]-Ja 10,17-27 1908;Mr 12,Je 14,Ag 30-S 1,10,O 4,13-15,27-29 1909[F 16 1912-S 8 1913]S 30,O 19,D 28 1914-Ja 6,13,Mr 15,My 19-24 1915;My 3 1916;Mr 8-Ap 3,10-12,My 3-8,17,Je 26,Jl 1-8,15-22,29 1918;My 7,Je 18,O 1 1924

WORLD. w 1864‖
Campaign paper
PPeS S 6-13,O 4,18 1864

Evening WORLD. d O 10 1887-F 26 1931‖
United with World and Evening telegram to form New York world-telegram
Ap 30 1889 is centennial extra
CP Ap 30 1889
CoHi Ap 30 1889
DLC Ap 30 1889;F 26 1931
ICM D 5 1891;Jl 22 1892;Mr 26,Ap 16,30,My 12-13 1893
IU N 6-29,D 4-31 1909;Ja 27-31,Mr 1-7,14,18-26,29-Ap 23,26 1910
MWA Je 23 1924
NN O 10 1887-Jl 1927
PPeS N 7 1928

WORLD peace echo. *See* Ethiopian world

New York WORLD-TELEGRAM. d 1867+
1867-F 26 1931 as Evening telegram
CSt [1931]
DLC Ja-F 1870;N 5(extra)1872;S 20(extra) 1881;F 27 1931+
ICM Mr 14 1888
KHi [S 1884-S 1887]
M Jl 30 1930;F 28 1931
MWA F 24,Jl 9 1868;Ap 25 1870;Mr 2,Ag 5,N 28 1871;Ap 25,My 12,Je 13,O 3 1876;Je 25,O 17 1877;Ja 18-20,Jl 8,16,18-19,D 9 1879;Jl 21 1880;Ag 1 1883;F 14,Jl 23,30,Ag 8 1885
N Jl 12 1871;Ag 8 1885
NHuHi Ja 6 1919
NN Jl 20,Ag 14,16,S 24 1867-S 1868;69-71;F 1872-S 1877;78-Ja,Mr 1901-My 14,Ag 1904-Jl, S 1910-Mr 1924;Ap 22 1930+
extra:Ap 2 1917
NNMC Mr 9,Ap 30 1889;Ap 27 1892;F 27 1931
NcU S 7 1881
NjR Ap 3 1874;Ja 16 1880;S 20-21,24 1881;Jl 23 1885;D 26 1893-96
NjU 1931+
OClWHi S 25 1876;Jl 25,S 22-23,O 1 1881
OHi 1931+
PBf Jl 6 1881
PDoHi 1870[76]Ag 8 1885;Je 8 1907
PNhF Ag 6 1886
PP 1928+
PPeS S 25,N 7 1928
RW Je 3 1889
WHi Ap 2 1928;F 27 1931+

Weekly YANKEE. w 1843?-D 29 1849‖?
DLC N 20 1847-49
MWA Ja 1[S 1847-Je 24 1848]Ag 18 1849

Dos YIDDISCHE folk. (Jewish nation) w 1908-31‖?
NN F 26 1909-29

New Yorker YIDDISCHE volkzeitung. w Je 25 1886-D 20 1889‖
In Yiddish
MiU Ja 20 1888
NN complete
WHi 1886-D 13 1889

Der YIDDISCHER Kaempfer. w 1912?-
In Yiddish
IU Ap 20 1917-Ag 30 1918

YIDDISCHER. . . *See also* Jüdischer; Idischer

YOUNG America. w,sw O 31 1829-51‖?
1829-Mr 22 1845 as Working man's advocate (Je 9-Ag 14 1830 New York sentinel and working man's advocate; O 12-N 9 1844 Subterranean united with the Working man's advocate; N 16-D 21 1844 Subterranean and the working man's advocate)
Suspended from 1836?-Mr 16 1844
sw Je 9-Ag 14 1830
Ct F 26 1831[35]Ag 24 1844
DLC O 31 1821;Ag 14 1830[Mr 16 1844-Mr 22 1845]
InNh 1829-Je 5 1830
KHi Mr 23 1844-Mr 22 1845;Ap 29-S 23 1848
MSaE S 11 1847
MWA Ag 28 1830;Ja 21,My 12 1832;Je 1,Jl 6 1844;Ja 10 1846;My 12 1849
NN [1830]F 5 1831;N 24-D 1,29 1832-Ja 12,26, F 9-Mr 9 1833[34-Ja 16 1836]
NNHi Je 23 1830;N 2 1844;F 8 1851
NSyU F 19,Mr 11 1848
OHi 1829-S 22 1832
RPB My 17 1845
VU D 8 1832
WHi [1833-36]
—d ed *See* Man; New York daily sentinel

YOUNG Hickory banner. w Ag 10-S 28 1844‖
Campaign paper
DLC complete

YOUNG MEN'S advocate. w F 23 1832-F 7 1833‖?
NNHi F-Ap 5,19,My 10-Jl 19,Ag-S 20,O 25-N 15,29 1832-F 7 1833
NjHi N 29 1832
VRB 1832-F 7 1833

NEW YORK (*Continued*)

NEW YORK CITY—*Continued*

ZEIT. d Ag 29 1920-Ap 26 1922||
In Yiddish
NN 1920[21-22]

New Yorker ZEITUNG. w 1845?-98||?
1845?-76? as Wöchentlicher New Yorker demokrat; 1877?-78? New Yorker allgemeine zeitung
Tx F 18,S 1 1860;F 9-My 18 1861

New Yorker ZEITUNG. d *See* New Yorker herold. Morgenblatt

NEWARK

ARCADIA weekly gazette. *See* Newark gazette

COURIER. w Jl 2 1846+
pub Ja 14 1869+
MWA F 22 1883
N F 8 1877
NNe 1911+

Newark GAZETTE. w Ap 6 1887-Mr 25 1908||
1887-Ag 1 1906 as Arcadia weekly gazette. United with Newark union to form Newark union-gazette
NNe complete
NNeU complete

Newark UNION-GAZETTE. w,sw Ag 24 1872+
1872-Mr 1908 as Newark union
w 1872-S 1929
pub Ap 1908+
NCanHi Ja 15 1916
NNe Ap 1908-My 14 1910;11+
VU My 26,Ag 25-S 1 1883

WAYNE standard. w Je 1838-41||
MBAt Je 5 1841

NEWBURGH

Daily DEMOCRAT. d
NNHi F 1 1868

FAMILY visitor. sm N 23 1839-
N [1839-Ag 15 1840]

Newburgh GAZETTE. w Je 7 1823-
MWA 1823-My 1824;O 24 1829;D 19 1835
N O 19 1833
NMi 1831-32
NNHi Je 26 1840-42;N 7 1855[Jl 1856-57]-[59-60]

Newburgh HIGHLAND chieftain. *See* Newburgh journal

Newburgh HIGHLAND courier. *See* Newburgh journal

Newburgh JOURNAL. w,sw 1833-1909||
1843-50? as Highland courier; 1851-My 1861 as Newburgh highland chieftain; Je 8 1861-My? 1887 as Newburgh weekly journal
w 1833-My? 1887
MWA D 23 1827;My 25 1839;S 11 1852;Je 1862-Jl 6 1864
NN F 16 1861
NNHi Mr 1848-F 1850;Jl 23 1859-My,Jl 1862-Jl 1864;Mr 10-17 1869;D 27 1871;Mr 5,26 1873;O 3 1878;O 2-9 1879;S 23-O 7 1880;N 9, D 7 1882;Ja 25,Mr 29,Je 21,S 20,N 15,29,D 13-27 1883;Ja 8,22-Mr 5,26,Ap 9-23,My-Je 11, 25 1885;Ap 7,S 27,O 14 1887;F 9 1892
NjR My 6 1874

Newburgh daily JOURNAL. d 1862-1916||?
KHi O 18-19 1883
MWA S 2 1870;Ag 22 1879;Ja 10 1882;O 20 1883;My 29 1884
N [Mr-D 1868]S 13 1869
NN Je 13,26-Jl 2,5-O 11,14-17,21-22,26,28,N 4 1867
NNHi Jl 5 1862-63;65-66;F 7 1867;68[69-73] Ap 6,22,O 12 1874;Mr 15 1875[76-81]Jl 3,6,N 7 1882[83-84]Ap 18,S 15 1885;F 2,S 14 1886; O 22,D 4 1888;Ap 11,O 16 1889;Ja 7 1890;N 2 1892
extras:D 14 1866;S 26 1879

Newburgh NEWS. d S 5 1885+
pub 1885+
CLM My 28 1932
N My 20 1913+
NNHi [Ag-D 1856]Je 24 1859;Ag 11,O 5 1860; Je 22,Ag 5 1861;S 15-16,18-19 1885;Mr 16,31, S 21 1887;F 20 1888;N 1 1892;Je 29,O 21 1896;Ap 8,23,My 4 1907

ORANGE county patriot. *See under* Goshen

ORANGE telegraph. w 1829-
CSmH S 9 1830

*POLITICAL index. w Ap 17 1806-
DLC Ja-F,Mr 13-Ap 1821
MWA Ja 11[Mr 22 1825-D 19 1826]F 13 1827
NNHi My 31 1825;My 6-13,Jl 15,D 23 1828

Newburgh weekly PRESS. w 1867-69||
NNHi 1867-My 6 1869

Newburgh PRESS. d 1888-1904||?
Title varies: 1888-94? as Newburgh evening press
NNHi My 7 1891;N 2 1892

Newburgh weekly REGISTER. w 1829-
1829-75? as Newburgh weekly telegraph
MWA S 11 1862
N O 31 1833;N 8 1838-Jl 1 1847
NNHi Ap 1836-My 14 1840;D 5 1844;S 2 1847; S 16,O 31 1850;N 17,D 1 1853[54]Mr 22 1855; Mr 27,My 15 1856;My 12 1859[62-66]Ja 2 1867[69-72]-Je 10 1874;D 13 1882;Je 27,Jl 11, S 12,D 5-19 1883[84-85]N 23 1887-88;N 13,D 4,18 1889;Ja 1,Mr 5 1890

Newburgh daily REGISTER. d 1860-1907||
1860-75? as Newburgh morning telegraph
O 18 1883 is centennial ed
MWA Je 22 1863
NNHi Je 3-4,Jl 26,O 2 1869;Mr 11,Ap 9,Ag 29,S 29 1870;My 1 1873;Ap 22 1874;F 1 1877; Mr 12 1878;Ag 30 1881;O 18 1883;Ja 16,O 28 1884;F 25,S 14-17,O 10 1885;S 16 1886;Ap 14, S 19 1887;Ja 7,F 17,My 17,Ag 15 1888;Je 29 1896;Ap 3 1900;Ap 5,9,24 1907

Newburgh TELEGRAM. w 1889-1916||?
NNHi Ag 27 1910

Newburgh TELEGRAPH. *See* Newburgh register

Newburgh TIMES. w 1856-
NNHi Ja 29 1858;Ja 11,18,F 2,29 1860;Ja 30 1863

NEWCOMB

ADIRONDACK news. w Ag 25 1893-96||?
NHi Ag 25 1893

NEWFANE

Newfane GAZETTE. w 1918-25||?
NBarR Mr 2 1918-Ja 27 1923

NEWPORT

Newport ADVERTISER. *See* Frankfort register (Frankfort)

Newport JOURNAL. w 1894-1916||?
NHerHi 1896-1900

Newport PATRIOT. w F 10 1824-
Title varies: Newport patriot and record of the times
DLC Mr 24-31,Je 2-9,Jl 28,N 12 1824
MWA O 22 1824

Newport REGISTER. *See* Frankfort register (Frankfort)

NEWTOWN. *See* ELMHURST

NIAGARA FALLS

Niagara Falls GAZETTE. w,sw My 17 1854-95||?
w 1854-87?
MWA N 1 1876

Niagara Falls GAZETTE. d 1881+
EHi O 31 1888
N Mr 1913+

NIAGARA herald. w O 1855-
NSyU My 25 1861

Il RISVEGLIO italiano. (Italian awakening) w
N 1920+
In Italian
pub 1920+

TRANS-CONTINENTAL. d My 24-Jl 4 1870||
pub on the Pullman hotel express, between Boston and San Francisco
CSmH complete
MnHi My 24 1870

NORTH TONAWANDA

Evening NEWS. d 1880+
N O 26 1917-19
NNt Jl 1905+

NORTHPORT

Northport JOURNAL. w 1885+
pub My 1885-My 1886;1917+

SUFFOLK county journal. *See* Bay Shore journal (Bay Shore)

Northport WEEKLY. w N 16 1878-
NHuHi D 28 1878

NORWICH

ANTI-MASONIC telegraph. *See* Chenango telegraph

CHENANGO free democrat. w Ja 1 1849-
NNo O 20 1849;D 13 1850;S 19,N 21 1851

CHENANGO telegraph. w,sw Ap 8 1829+
1829-Mr 1835 as Anti-masonic telegraph. Title varies: Chenango semi-weekly telegraph
w 1829-94
pub 1829-60;66+
DLC Je 17-25,Jl 22,Ag 5-15,26-S 16,O,N 25-D 2,23 1829-Ja 6 1830;Ja 19 1831;Ag 28 1839
KHi S 13 1855
MWA Jl 1 1840;Je 27 1866;Jl 13,Ag 3 1876
MeHa S 19 1860
N 1829-Mr 1831;Ap 1833-Mr 1834;Je 10 1846; My 1913+
NIC D 31 1851
NNo 1829+
NSchU D 1 1841

CHENANGO union. w 1847+
pub 1847+
DLC Mr 13 1861
N Ap 5 1854
NIC O 15 1851
NN O 27-N 3,24 1847;S 26 1849;My 25 1870
NNo O 9 1861+
NSyU Je 17 1886

*Norwich JOURNAL. w N 14 1816-
N Ja 5 1826;N 26 1828;O 17 1833
NN Jl 26 1826
NNo Ja-D 19 1821;D 25 1822-D 17 1823;S 10 1828-S 1,N 3 1830

LITERARY independent. w
NNo S 13-N 1858;Ja 14-21,F 2 1859

OMNIOGRAPHER. tm Ap 15? 1849-
DLC Ap 17 1849

PEOPLE'S advocate. w Jl 7 1824-
DLC N 24 1824

Norwich POST. w N 11 1881-84||
NIC 1881-F 29 1884
NNo N 25 1881;Ja 27 1882

Norwich SUN. d Mr 17 1891+
1891-Mr 15 1904 as Morning sun
pub 1891+
N F 17 1892-94;F 1899-Jl 1902
NNo 1891+

Sunday TIMES. w 1874-75||
NNo S 26,O 17,D 5,26 1874-Ja 2,16,30-F 13,Mr 6-27 1875

NORWOOD

COMMERCIAL advertiser. w 1873-76||?
N Je 17,Ag 26 1875

Norwood NEWS. w Mr 1878+
pub [1878]+

NUNDA

INDEPENDENT gazette. w N 12 1841-
NSchU D 10 1841

LIVINGSTON democrat. w 1868-75||?
NHor Mr 22 1873-Mr 14 1874
NMmE Mr 18 1871

Nunda NEWS. w O 1 1859+
pub 1859+
MWA My 12 1866
NMi D 2 1902

Nunda TELEGRAPH. w 1850-
NN D 19 1850

Nunda TIMES. w Ja-Jl 1852||
NN Jl 24 1852

NYACK

JOURNAL-NEWS. d My 6 1889+
1889-Ag 24 1928 as Nyack evening journal; Ag 31 1928-O 5 1932 Rockland county evening journal
pub 1927+
—w ed *See* Rockland county journal

Nyack daily NEWS. d 1922-O 5 1932||
United with Rockland county evening journal to form Journal-news

ROCKLAND county journal. w Jl 1850-1916||?
MWA D 5 1857;N 16 1907
NNHi Ap 22 1865;Ja 9 1869;D 14 1872;F 8 1873
—d ed *See* Journal-news

OGDENSBURG

ADVANCE. d 1861-
MWA Je 2 1863

BOY'S daily journal. *See* Republican-journal

Ogdensburg JOURNAL. *See* Republican-journal

NORTHERN light. w Jl 7 1831-34||
N Ag 23 1832

REPUBLICAN-JOURNAL. d My 1 1855+
1855-56? as Boy's daily journal; 1857?-1915? as Ogdensburg journal
ICHi Ag 15 1864
MBAt Ap 17-18 1865
MWA Je 25 1869;Ag 9 1870;Mr 17 1873;Ja 13 1876
N Ja 13 1865;Mr 12 1913-14;Je 1916+
NOg 1855+
—w ed *See* St. Lawrence republican

*ST. LAWRENCE gazette. w D 1815-30||
Merged with St. Lawrence republican
CSmH S 7 1830
ICU Jl 11 1826
N N 23 1824
NNHi Ap 18 1826-Ap 10 1827

ST. LAWRENCE republican. w Ja 4 1831-1915||?
Title varies slightly
DLC Jl 4 1837;S 13 1853;Jl 25 1854;O 23 1855
MWA Jl 6,Ag 17,S 7 1852;N 29,D 13 1853-N 20 1855;O 10 1871;O 8 1872;F 5 1879
N Mr 22,Ap 12,S 13-20 1831;O 15 1833;D 15 1835;N 20-D 4 1838;Ja 1 1839;Je 23 1840;F 22 1853
NN Jl(extra)1837
NNHi Ag 30 1853;Ap 1 1873
NOg 1843-54
NhD Jl 30 1839
—d ed *See* Republican-journal

OLD FORGE

ADIRONDACK arrow. w Je 3 1926—
pub 1926+

OLEAN

To 1836? as Hamilton

Olean ADVERTISER. w My 9? 1866-
MWA F 21 1867
N Ag 29 1867

Olean ADVOCATE. *See* Olean times

ALLEGHANY mercury. *See* Olean times

CATTARAUGUS union. *See under* Salamanca

Olean DEMOCRAT. w 1879-1909||
NOl 1880-1909

NEW YORK (*Continued*)

OLEAN—*Continued*

Olean evening HERALD. d 1881-N 1924‖
United with Olean times to form Olean times-herald
NOl complete
NOlT 1883-1924

Olean JOURNAL. w
IaDH S 16 1852-O 12 1855

Olean TIMES. w 1835-1911‖?
1835? as Alleghany mercury; 1836?-37? Olean advocate
NOl O 6 1860-Jl 6 1861;97-1911
OClWHi Jl 11 1866

Olean TIMES-HERALD. d 1879+
1879-N 1924 as Olean times. Title varies slightly
My 15 1935 is Diamond jubilee ed
NOl 1897+

ONEIDA

Oneida DEMOCRATIC union. w O 15 1856+
1856-Mr 1863 pub in Hamilton
pub 1906+
MWA F 5,19,Mr 19-26,O 22,N 5 1863;S 14 1876
N O 22-N 1856;Ja 21,F 4 1857
NNo 1906+
NOHi 1862-65;S 3 1868;72-91

Oneida DISPATCH. w,sw 1854-1931‖?
sw 1888?-1904?
N Jl 9 1864
NOHi 1863;65-92
OClWHi Je 30 1866

Daily Oneida DISPATCH. d 1926+
NOHi 1926

Oneida FREE PRESS. w 1880-96‖?
NOHi Ap 3 1880-86

Oneida SACHEM. w O 11 1851-
1851-Je 3 1854? as Oneida telegraph
MWA Mr 31 1855
N 1851-Je 3 1854;O 23 1858
NNHi F 7 1861
NOHi 1851-52;54-56;Ap 24 1858

Oneida TELEGRAPH. *See* Oneida sachem

ONEONTA

Oneonta COMMERCIAL. w 1872-76‖
NOn D 16 1874;Ja 1-6,My 6,Ag 5 1876

Saturday CRITIC. w 1894-99‖
NN Jl 11 1896[97-My 1898;Jl-O 1899]

DOLLAR newspaper. w Jl 23 1874-
NOn [1874]

Oneonta HERALD. w F 9 1853+
Title varies: Oneonta herald and democrat; etc.
pub 1873+
N S 28 1877
NOn 1853-90

Oneonta weekly JOURNAL. w
NNHi F 25 1841
NOn Je 3 1841

Oneonta LIBERAL. w 1872-74‖
NOn My 23,Ag 29 1874

OTSEGO democrat. w Mr 13 1847-73‖
NOn Mr 20 1847;Ap 16-30,Jl 2,23,Ag 20,S 10,O 1-8,29-N 5,19,D 1870-Ap 1 1871;Ja 13,27-F 3, 17-24,Mr 9,23,Je 8,29,Jl 13,Ag 31,S 7-21 1872; Ja 11-18,F 8,Mr 8,29,Ap 18,Je 13,27,S 26 1873

Oneonta PRESS and Otsego county democrat. w 1876-1921‖?
1876-98? as Oneonta press
MWA Mr 5 1885
NIC Mr 5 1885
NOn Mr 13 1884-Jl 2 1885;Ja 28 1886-N 19 1891

Oneonta SPY. w 1887-1903‖?
NOn Ap 2 1887-91

Oneonta daily STAR. d Je 19 1890+
pub 1890+
N Mr 1913+
NDm 1890-Ap 19 1910;17+

SUSQUEHANNA independent. w 1868-69‖
NOn Jl 31 1868-My 28 1869

ONONDAGA

Onondaga JOURNAL. w 1821-S 1829‖
United with Syracuse advertiser (Syracuse) to form Onondaga standard, later Syracuse post-standard (Syracuse)
N N 16 1825
NCorL D 8 1824;O 5,19 1825;Jl 19,S 27,O 4 1826;Ap 122 1829

Onondaga REGISTER. *See* Onondago register and Syracuse gazette (Syracuse)

ONTARIO

WAYNE county mail. w Je 7 1901+
pub 1901+

ORISKANY FALLS

Oriskany Falls NEWS. w 1880-1918‖
NOrHi complete

Oriskany Falls TIMES. w S 1932-My 17 1934‖
Merged with Hamilton republican (Hamilton)
NOrHi complete

ORLEANS

Orleans REPUBLICAN. w? 1842?-
MBAt Ap 19 1865

OSSINING

To 1901? as Sing-Sing

CITIZEN-REGISTER. d 1902+
1902-04? as Citizen

HUDSON RIVER chronicle. w 1837-84‖?
MSaE N 13 1838;Ap 2 1839;O 17 1843
N 1837-Ap 14 1880
NN Ja 9 1838(photostat);O 1 1839
NNHi Ja 9 1838;Ag 22 1854;My 15 1855-Jl 8 1856;F 10,My 12,N 3-10,D 1-8,29 1857;Je 1 1858
OClWHi S 20 1876

REPUBLICAN. w Ap? 1857-1912‖?
Follows Republican (Peekskill)
CU Je 5-19 1862
MBAt Ap 20 1865
N My 7 1863
NNHi [Ap 1857-N 1858]Ja 13-20,Je 9 1859;Jl 12 1860;F 25 1864;Mr 22,Jl 12,Ag 9,S 13 1866
OClWHi Jl 19 1866
WHi Mr 8 1866

UNION. w
NN O 15 1864

*WESTCHESTER herald. w Ja 15 1818-57‖
1818-O 6 1829 as Westchester herald and farmers' register; O 13-D 1829 Westchester herald and gazette; 1830-33 Westchester herald and Putnam gazette
1818-43 pub at Mt. Pleasant
CSmH Ap 25 1826;Ag 18 1829
DLC D 15 1829;Ja 5,26 1830;O 10,N 2 1852
MWA 1821-23;N 18 1828;Ag 11,O 20 1829-[30-Mr]Je 14,Ag 2 1831;Je 5,Ag 21 1832;Ja 1,F 4 1834;S 22 1835;My 2,Je 6,S 12-19 1837;Ap 24, S 11,O 23,N 6-13 1838;Mr 26 1839;Ja 14,F 4,25-Mr 3,24,Ap 7,S 1,29-O 6 1840[41]-[43-44] Mr 4,Ap 29,My 13,Ag 5,N 25 1845;Ja 6,20,Mr 10,O 27-N 17 1846;Ap 6-13,N 23 1847[Ag-D 5 1848]Ja 23,Mr 20[Je 25-D 1849]-[51]-56
N O 29 1833
NNHi 1821-27;Ag 26,N 1828-N 13 1832[34]My 5,Ag 11,D 1 1835[36-40]-[45-49]-Ja 13,27 1857
OClWHi My 30-Je 13 1855

WESTCHESTER sentinel. w Ag 10 1866-
NEh Ja 19 1867

OSWEGO

Oswego ADVERTISER. tw,d 1836-
N Jl 30 1836
OClWHi O 21 1841

Oswego ADVERTISER and times. *See* Oswego times

Oswego COMMERCIAL advertiser. w D 16 1829-66‖?
Follows Oswego democratic gazette. United with Oswego commercial times to form Oswego commercial advertiser and times, later Oswego times
DLC D 23 1829;Ja 21 1830
MnHi Je 21 1865

Oswego daily COMMERCIAL advertiser. d 1864?-66‖?
United with Oswego commercial times to form Oswego commercial advertiser and times, later Oswego daily times
NOs Mr 1864-Mr 1866

Oswego COMMERCIAL herald. w 1837-43‖
WHi Je 15 1840

Oswego COMMERCIAL-TIMES. *See* Oswego daily times

Oswego DEMOCRATIC gazette. w F 1827- 1829‖
1827-Jl 8 1829 as Oswego gazette and advertiser. Followed by Oswego commercial advertiser
DLC Mr 2 1827;Je 24,Jl 22,Ag 5,S 16 1829

Oswego morning EXPRESS. d 1881-82‖
Merged with Oswego daily times
NOs Ag 1881-N 1882

FREE PRESS. w F 17 1830-
CSmH Ag 25 1830
MWA Mr 14 1832
N My 30-Je 6,N 28 1832

Oswego GAZETTE and advertiser. *See* Oswego democratic gazette

Oswego morning HERALD. d 1878-79‖
NNHi My 31 1879
NOs Ag 1878-Ag 1879

Oswego OBSERVER. w F 1835-N? 1836‖
N N 30 1836

ONTARIO post. w 1917-19‖
IU Mr-Jl 26 1919

OSWEGO county whig. w Ja 3 1838-
DLC Je 13 1838;My 15 1844
N Ja 10 1838
NOs 1839-D 4 1843

*Oswego PALLADIUM. w,sw O 7 1819+
Title varies slightly
w 1819-98?
pub 1852+
DLC Ja 29 1834
MWA N 8 1837;Ap 30,N 26 1852
N 1837;Jl 4,N 25 1838
NOs 1820+
NOsC 1886+
NSyU S 29 1830
NUHi Mr 9-16 1824
NjWdN D 4 1833
P-M Jl 2 1845
WHi Je 22 1847-Je 12 1849

Oswego daily PALLADIUM-TIMES. d 1851+
1851-Ap 21 1925 as Oswego daily palladium
pub 1925+
DLC 1898
ICM F 13 1893
MWA Je 12 1851
N Jl 15 1896;Ap 21 1925+
NN My 2,21,Je 3,7,18 1867
NOs 1854-Je 1856;Ja-Je 1857;58-Je 1859;91; 1924+
NOsC Ap 1925+
NjR [1933]

PILOT. w
WHi Je 20 1840

Oswego morning POST. d 1882-83‖
NOs N 27 1882-Ap 2 1883

Oswego daily PRESS. d Ap 14 1870-71‖
DLC Ap 8 1871

Oswego REPUBLICAN. w Mr 22 1825-27‖
N Mr-Ap 6 1825

Oswego TIMES. w,sw 1837+
Title varies: Oswego advertiser and times; Oswego times and express; Oswego times and journal; etc.
w 1837-89?
pub 1837+
NOs F 17 1854-56
NOsC 1886+
WHi D 18 1856

Oswego daily TIMES. d 1846-Ap 19 1925‖
1846?-66? as Oswego commercial times; 1867?-Je 1873 Oswego commercial advertiser and times. Title varies: Oswego times and express; etc. United with Oswego daily palladium to form Oswego daily palladium-times
pub 1847-1925
DLC 1898-Je 1900
MBAt Ap 15-18 1865
MWA N 29 1852
N Je 28 1862;1913-25
NOs Ap 11,Je 30 1848-Je 1854;57-Je,Ag 1860-Ap 1865;Ja-Je 1867;Je 1872-92;1924-25
NOsP complete
NSyU My 28,Je 12,Ag 16,S 21,O 24 1861
OClWHi Mr-My,Jl 1870-Jl 1871;F 16 1872
WHi Jl 26 1864

UNION herald. w My 6 1836-
ICHi My 20,Je 3,17-Jl 8,22-O,N 9 1836-My 3 1837
OClWHi O 28 1836

OTSEGO. *See* COOPERSTOWN

OVID

Ovid BEE. w F 21 1838-73‖
Followed by Ovid independent, later Ovid gazette and independent
CtSo Jl 22 1845
DLC Mr 14 1838
N Ap 12 1854
NOrG 1838-59;61;67-73

Ovid EMPORIUM. w
NSchU Jl 12 1832

Ovid GAZETTE. 1817-18 *See* Waterloo gazette (Waterloo)

Ovid GAZETTE. w 1894-1900‖?
United with Ovid independent to form Ovid gazette and independent

Ovid GAZETTE and independent. w 1873+
Follows Ovid bee. 1873-1900? as Ovid independent
pub 1896-97;1907;09-23;25+

Ovid GAZETTE and Seneca county register. w Ja 5 1830-
Follows Seneca republican
CSmH S 7 1830

SENECA republican. w Jl 4 1827-29‖
Followed by Ovid gazette and Seneca county register
DLC D 19 1827
MWA Ja 9 1828

OWEGO

Owego ADVERTISER. *See* Owego times

Owego BLADE. w Ja 1 1880-Ap 23 1887‖
NOwHi complete

Daily BLADE. d N 4 1882-Ap 23 1887‖
NOwHi complete

*Owego GAZETTE. w Je 1814+
Follows American farmer (not in this list). F-N 1839 as Owego and Tioga county gazette
CSmH Ag 4 1840
Ct [1828-29]Ja 20 1837
MWA Jl 24 1821;Ag 24 1824;F 5 1828;Je 3 1841
N F 1 1825;S 25 1827;Mr 20 1913+
NIC 1864;D 1 1870;My 28 1891
NNHi S 30,D 2 1823
NOwHi [1821-60]+
P-M Je 28 1832;S 6 1854
PEL Ap 6 1831

Owego daily RECORD. d D 20 1886-1910‖
NIC complete

SOUTHERN tier times. *See* Owego times

NEW YORK (*Continued*)

OWEGO—*Continued*

Owego TIMES. w Mr 25 1836+
1836-Je 1853 as Owego advertiser; Jl 1853-Je 1855 Southern tier times
MWA S 21 1871
N My 15,29 1845;O 29 1863
NIC S 9 1858;Je 9,Jl 21 1859
NNHi Je 11 1863;F 20 1873
NOwHi [1836-60]+
P-M N 6 1845
PAtM Mr 6 1862
PWbW Mr 29 1855

TIOGA county record. w 1871-1907||?
NIC 1885;87-1907

OXFORD

CHENANGO republican. *See* Oxford republican

*Oxford GAZETTE. w D 7 1813-
United with Chenango republican to form Chenango republican or Oxford gazette, later Oxford republican
NOx 1821-Mr 26 1823

Oxford PRESS. w 1899-1905||?
NOx N 24 1899-1902

Oxford REPUBLICAN. w Je 30 1826-47||
1826-32? as Chenango republican (title varies slightly)
CSmH S 8 1830
CtY Jl 9 1834
DLC Ja 7 1829;Mr 31 1830
N D 1 1826;S 7 1827;O 16 1833;My 10,Jl 5 1837
NN O 6 1826
NNo Je 5 1840-D 3 1841;43-S 25 1845
NOx D 10 1828-S 20 1830

Oxford REVIEW. w N 12 1909-Ja 1 1915||
United with Oxford times to form Oxford review-times
KHi Ja 1 1915
NOx complete

Oxford REVIEW-TIMES. w 1836+
1836-1914 as Oxford times
pub 1910+
KHi Ja 22 1915
N O 23 1845
NOx O 6 1841+
RW My 15 1861

Oxford TIMES. *See* Oxford review-times

OYSTER BAY

Oyster Bay GUARDIAN. w F 10 1899+
pub 1899+

PAINTED POST

Painted Post TIMES. w 1870-78||
MWA S 20 1871;Je 13 1877
N [1873-Mr 1873]

PALMYRA

Palmyra COURIER-JOURNAL. w 1838+
1838-My 23 1929 as Palmyra courier
pub [F 1846-O 23 1891]1917-18;26+
MWA N 24 1852
NSyU F 14,Mr 21,O 10-17 1849;F 6 1850

Palmyra FREEMAN. w Mr 11 1828-29||
Followed by Lyons countryman (Lyons)
MBAt S 2 1828
NjHi Mr 18,Je 10 1828

Palmyra HERALD. w Mr 21 1821-S 1823||
Follows Palmyra register. 1821-Je 12 1822 as Western farmer. Followed by Wayne sentinel
N 1821-Mr 12 1823

REFLECTOR. m 1828-30||
NNHi D 22 1829-Ap 19,My 1830-Mr 19 1831

*Palmyra REGISTER. w N 26 1817-Mr 7 1821||
Followed by Western farmer, later Palmyra herald
N Ja-Mr 1821
NjHi Ja 3 1821

WAYNE county journal. w Jl 7 1871-My 30 1929||
United with Palmyra courier to form Palmyra courier-journal
NPalC [D 21 1871-D 7 1882]Ja 9 1901-29

WAYNE sentinel. w O 1 1823-
Follows Palmyra herald
CSmH Jl 2 1830
Ct Je 19 1835
DLC Mr 17,31,Ap 14,28,Je 2,O 13,N 10 1824;D 26 1832
IU Mr 13,My 1-8,22 1844
MWA O 13 1824;Ja 26 1842;N 10 1852
N 1823-S 15 1852
NCorL Ag 10 1827
NPalC F 18 1852
NSchU Je 15,Jl 13,27,Ag 17,31-S 7,21 1842
PErW O 10 1828
PWbW Je 10 1831

WESTERN farmer. *See* Palmyra herald

WESTERN spectator. w Je 9 1830-31||
Subtitle varies: . . . and public advertiser; . . . and Wayne advertiser; . . . and Anti-masonic star. Merged with Anti-masonic enquirer (Rochester)
CSmH Ag 11 1830
MWA S 8 1830
N [N 1830-Jl 19 1831]
NCH Ja 25-Ap 19 1831
NSchU Je 30 1830

PANAMA

Panama HERALD. w S 10 1846-48||
OClWHi N 26 1846

PATCHOGUE

Patchogue ADVANCE. w 1871+
pub 1885+
NPa 1931+
NRc Mr 21 1874

ARGUS. w 1884+
1884-87 as Suffolk democrat; 1888-94? Suffolk county argus
pub [1910+]
NPa 1931–
NRiHi F 16 1895
NcD N 3 1887

ISLAND news. w Jl 1 1932+
pub 1932+

SUFFOLK county argus. *See* Argus

SUFFOLK democrat. *See* Argus

SUFFOLK herald. w Ag 14 1858-
N Ja 23-30 1863
NBHi 1858-Ap 1865
NEh S 4 1858;O 11 1861
NRc Ag 3-10,D 2 1864
NSm Jl 1-8,O 28 1863;Mr 3 1865

SUFFOLK daily island news. d 1923+
Title varies slightly
NShi F 23 1934

PAWLING

Pawling CHRONICLE. w 1890+
DLC F 18-Mr 11 1933
NPV Je 27-Jl 4,S-D 19 1935
NPawM Je 9 1923+

PEARSALLS

QUEEN'S county review. w Mr 7 1882-
NBHi Mr-N 2 1882

PEEKSKILL

Peekskill BLADE. w Ja 15 1878-1909||?
CSmH [1878-99]
KHi S 27 1881
NNHi S 27 1881

COLUMBIAN chronicle. w 1825-
Title varies
MWA F 21 1826
MN Jl 19 1825(photostat)
MNHi Jl 19 1825(photostat)

Peekskill CRITIC. w 1890-93||
United with Peekskill messenger to form Messenger-critic
CSmH O 27 1892;N 2 1893

HIGHLAND democrat. w Mr 10 1840+
1840-N 30 1841 as Westchester and Putnam democrat
pub [1850-62]+
CSmH [My 28 1859-Ja 7 1899]
MWA O 29,N 26 1859;Ap 14,Jl 28 1860
N Ja-N 1861
NNHi 1840-N 24 1842;F 20,Je 15 1909

HIGHLAND eagle. w S 18 1851-58||
CSmH S 18 1851;F 14 1852;Mr 5 1853;Ag 1 1857;Mr 17,My 15 1858

MESSENGER-CRITIC. w Je 27 1861-1920||
1861-93 as Peekskill messenger
CSmH Je 27 1861;Ja 2 1862;O 1 1863;Mr 19 1874;Je 15 1876;Jl 26 1877;Mr 7 1878;N 20 1879;F 19 1880;Ag 11 1881;Jl 13,S 28 1882;Ja 25,My 31,N 29 1883;S 4 1884;Jl 30 1885;My 1886;O 20 1887;D 12 1889;F 7 1890;Ap 10 1891;Ja 15 1892;F 17 1893;Mr 9 1894;Jl 12 1895;Ap 3 1896;D 17 1897;Jl 22 1898;O 27 1899
OClWHi Jl 5 1866

REPUBLICAN. w My 27 1830-Mr 1857||
Follows Westchester gazette.
Title varies; Westchester and Putnam republican. Followed by Republican (Ossining)
CSmH O 28 1830;N 6 1832;Je 25 1839;N 12 1844;Je 2 1846;Ja 13 1851;Ag 2 1853;S 18 1855;Ag 28 1856;F 19 1857
N O 15 1833
NN Ag 15 1843

SENTINEL. w F 5 1833-
N F 26 1833(photostat)
NNHi F 26 1833(photostat)

Evening STAR. d My 1922+
pub 1922+

WESTCHESTER and Putnam democrat. *See* Highland democrat

WESTCHESTER and Putnam gazette. *See* Westchester gazette

WESTCHESTER and Putnam republican. *See* Republican

*WESTCHESTER gazette. w O 1808-30||
Title varies: Westchester gazette and Peekskill advertiser; Westchester and Putnam gazette. Followed by Westchester and Putnam republican later Republican
NN Ap 21 1821

PELHAM

Pelham SUN. w 1910+
pub 1920+

PENN YAN

BUNKER HILL club. w
NCH Ap 24,Je 8-O 16 1840;Ja 8 1841

CHRONICLE-EXPRESS. w D 16 1824+
1824-31 as Yates republican; 1831-32 Penn Yan enquirer; 1832-37 Western star; 1837-39 Democratic whig; 1839-56 Yates county whig; 1856-1925 Yates county chronicle
pub 1824-28;O 12 1831-Mr 13 1833;41-45;52-83;86+
CSmH Ag 3 1830
KHi Ja 5 1887
MWA Jl 30 1839;Jl 19 1855;S 21 1871
MiK Je 19 1832-33
N O 15 1833;Jl 7 1853;My 1913-24
NNH Je 25,Jl 2,Ag 6 1863;My 22 1873
NPy 1852-57;59-63;67-70;73-76;78-79;93-1908
NPyC Ag 17-N 8 1855
NPyCl 1847-53;55-66;68-74;76-77
NPyD N 23 1831-S 5 1832
NPyF 1828;30
OClWHi Jl 12 1866;F 11 1925
P-M O 3 1832

*Penn Yan DEMOCRAT. w My 1818+
1818-19? as Penn Yan herald
pub 1908+
CSmH S 7 1830
IU O 12 1841
MWA S 4 1827;Jl 1 1828;My 3 1918
N O 20 1835;Ap 27 1917-19
NNaR D 17 1822
NhD My 30 1848
PEL O 22 1835
PW My 31 1842

DEMOCRATIC whig. *See* Chronicle-express

Penn Yan ENQUIRER. *See* Chronicle-express

Penn Yan EXPRESS. w 1865-D 25 1925||
United with Yates county chronicle to form Chronicle-express
KHi [Ag 27 1884-N 18 1891]
NPyC 1874-1925

GORHAM new age and Rushville chronicle. w 1902-25||
Merged with Chronicle-express
Also dated in Gorham and Rushville
NPy 1905-25

Penn Yan HERALD. *See* Penn Yan democrat

Penn Yan daily TELEGRAPH. d 1846||
NN Mr 9 1846

WESTERN star. *See* Chronicle-express

YATES county chronicle. *See* Chronicle-express

YATES county whig. *See* Chronicle-express

YATES republican. *See* Chronicle-express

PERRY

AMERICAN citizen. w 1836-39||
Followed by American citizen (Rochester) 1836 pub in Warsaw
NSyU N 27 1839

COUNTRYMAN. *See* Free citizen

Perry DEMOCRAT. w 1841-53||
NMmE F 11 1848
WHi Ap 13 1849

FREE citizen. w 1843-Ag 1847||
1843 as Countryman; 1844-45 Impartial countryman
MWA S 25 1845
NPy 1843

FREEMAN'S register. *See* Perry register

IMPARTIAL countryman. *See* Free citizen

Perry RECORD. w Ja 1 1894+
pub 1894+
TxGR Ag 27 1925

Perry REGISTER. w Ja 3 1840-
Running title: Freeman's register
DLC Ja 3 1840
NCanHi Ag 14 1840

SILVER LAKE sun. w D 7 1865-73||?
NPe 1865;67;69-70;72
OClWHi Je 15 1866

WYOMING times. w My 1855-
N O 21,D 9 1859

PERSIA

FREEMAN and messenger. w 1839-Ag 5 1843||
N Ja 21 1841-43

LODI banner. w Ja 17 1844-Ap 13 1844||
Ja-F 14 1844 as People's advocate and Lodi banner. Followed by Springfield express (Springfield)
DLC F 24 1844
N complete

PEOPLE'S advocate and Lodi banner. *See* Lodi banner

PETERBORO

MADISON county advertiser. *See under* Morrisville

PHELPS

To 1834? as Vienna

Phelps CITIZEN. w 1832+
pub Ja 20 1887+
N Jl 22 1880

Phelps JOURNAL and Vienna advertiser. w F? 1833-45?
Title varies: Journal and advertiser. Followed by Western atlas
N O 16 1833
NSchU Mr 9 1842

NEW YORK (*Continued*)

PHELPS—*Continued*

WESTERN atlas. w 1846-
Follows Phelps journal. . .
N Ja 2 1847
NCanHi O 8 1853
NNHi N 14 1846-N 6 1847

PHILADELPHIA

Philadelphia ADVANCE. *See* North country advance

NORTH country advance. sm,w 1904+
1904-11? as Philadelphia advance
sm 1904-10?
pub S 15 1905+

PHOENIX

Phoenix REGISTER. w 1857+
pub 1926+

PIERMONT

Piermont CHRONICLE and Rockland county democrat. w S 25 1857-
MWA D 4 1857

PINE BUSH

Weekly CASKET. w
NNHi D 7 1867

PINE HILL

Pine Hill OPTIC. w Mr 17 1892-1918||?
DLC Mr 17 1892

PINE PLAINS

Pine Plains HERALD. w F 1 1859-1927||
United with Pine Plains register to form Register-herald
MWA S 29 1865
NNHi O 28 1859;S 26 1862

REGISTER-HERALD. w Ap 7 1882+
1882-1927 as Pine Plains register
pub 1882+
NNHi D 16 1887;O 13 1893
NSchU 1882+

PLATTSBURG

Plattsburg AURORA. w 1827-
1827-29? as Aurora Borealis
CSmH Jl 7 1830
NNHi O 21 1830
WHi Ag 18 1830

CLINTON county democrat. w Ja? 1869-
N O 26 1869

CLINTON county whig. w D 19 1839-
DLC My 23 1840
MWA N 6 1852
NhD D 26 1840

DEMOCRATIC press. w Mr 21 1833-
N O 17 1833

NORTHERN intelligencer. w My 7 1822-29||?
United with Aurora Borealis to form Plattsburg aurora
MWA S 10,O 15 1822;N 23 1825
N Ag 27 1822-Ap 29 1823;Mr 16 1825

Plattsburgh daily PRESS. d 1894+
pub 1902+
N Je 1923+

*Plattsburgh REPUBLICAN. w,d Ap 13 1811+
1811-O 1813 as Republican
w 1811-1914?
pub [1871]1900+
DLC My 11 1844
MWA N 19 1825;N 17,D 15 1827;N 27 1852
N 1821-28;N 6 1830;Ag 1833-1913[16-17]29+
NChaF Je 2 1821
NHi N 3 1832;O 24 1836;My 15 1841;O 29 1842;S 13 1862
NN Mr 30-Ap 6,20,My 11-Jl 20,Ag-S 14,28-O 19,N,D 14 1822-Ja 18,F,Mr 8-Jl,Ag 9-O 11, 25-N 8,22,D 6,20 1823-Mr 20 1824
NNHi Ja 29 1829;S 13 1845;My 8 1847;Ap 12 1873
VtMS 1895-My 3 1902
WHi My 22 1830

Plattsburgh SENTINEL. w,sw 1856+
w 1856-1912?
pub 1864+
MWA S 17 1875
N S 29 1872
NNHi D 22 1859;Ap 18 1873

Plattsburgh TIMES. w F 5 1827-
N F 12 1827

Plattsburg TIMES.
Campaign paper
NHi F 1 1897

PLEASANTVILLE

Pleasantville JOURNAL. w Ja 1887+
pub 1914+

POOLVILLE

Weekly PIONEER. w Jl 10 1879-Ja 29 1880||
N complete
NPoo complete(photostat)

PORT BYRON

Port Byron GAZETTE. w 1849-
MWA My 30 1864
NhD Ap 20,My 25 1854

Port Byron HERALD. w O 8 1844-
NAubHi N 12 1844-Ja 27 1846
WHi Ap 22 1845

Port Byron TIMES. w 1851-70||?
ICHi F 10 1860

PORT CHESTER

Port Chester ENTERPRISE. w 1884-1914||?
Ct S 1884-S 1889

EXPERIMENT. w 1848-
CSmH Je 16 1849

Daily ITEM. d Mr 2 1899+
NPc [My 1918+]

Port Chester JOURNAL. w N 1868-1914||?
Ct F 1872-N 1874;75-Ag 1883
MWA Jl 4 1872;F 6 1873;F 17 1887
NPc 1868-1904;Ap-S 1905;Je-Mr 1906;08-11

Port Chester MONITOR. w 1864-
MWA D 2 1865

NINETEENTH century. w Mr 25 1846-
MWA N 11 1846

PORT HENRY

CHAMPLAIN VALLEY review. w Je 28 1934+
pub 1934+
NHi 1934+

ESSEX county news. w 1907+
pub 1907+

Port Henry HERALD. w 1873-88||?
NHi 1874-75;83

Port Henry INDEPENDENT. w Ja 12-Jl 1861||
NHi F 23 1861

MORIAH enterprise. w My 1- 1896||
NHi My 15,29 1896

Port Henry TIMES. w O 1933+
pub 1933+
NHi 1933+

PORT JEFFERSON

Port Jefferson ECHO. w 1892-Mr 1931||
United with Port Jefferson times to form Port Jefferson times-echo

INDEPENDENT press. w 1865-73||?
NRc S 16 1869;F 3 1870;Jl 20 1871;Ap 12 1872

LONG ISLAND leader. w Ap 12 1873-80||?
Merged with Port Jefferson times, later Port Jefferson times-echo
MWA Je 2 1877
NRc Ap-D 20 1873;Ja 17-Mr,S 2 1874

LONG ISLAND news letter. w F 22 1884-87||
NN [S 1884-Mr 1887]

LONG ISLAND star. w
NRc S 7 1870

Port Jefferson TIMES-ECHO. w D 14 1878+
1878-Mr 1931 as Port Jefferson times
pub 1906+
NBHi Je 26 1924-32
NNQ My 11 1934+
NRc Mr 8,N 8 1879

PORT JERVIS

Evening GAZETTE. d Ap 22 1869-D 12 1924||
United with Port Jervis union to form Port Jervis union-gazette
NPj 1869-74;76-80;84-1900;02-24
NjR F 23 1905;Ag 3 1911
PMilC D 15 1877;Jl 13 1878;F 13 1879;Je 3 1887

Port Jervis weekly GAZETTE. w 1869-1924||
NNHi Ap 4 1873;Mr 1 1889
NjR N 14 1918
PMilC S 14 1877;F 7 1879

TRI-STATES union. w,sw N 7 1851-1924||
DLC N 4 1852;O 5 1866
MWA Jl 25 1889
NPjU complete
P-M My 18 1854
PMilC [1879]
PMilHi Mr 9 1854

Port Jervis UNION-GAZETTE. d 1872+
1872-D 12 1924 as Port Jervis union
pub 1872+
NPj 1882+
NcD F 9 1898
PHsHi Ag 4 1876

PORT ONTARIO

Port Ontario AURORA. w 1837-39||
Ct Ja 20 1838
MiU-C D 30 1837

PORT RICHMOND

Papers published in Port Richmond are listed under Staten Island

PORT WASHINGTON

INDEPENDENT enterprise of Port Washington and Sands Point. w Ja-D 1923||
NPw complete

Port Washington NEWS. w Ja 1914+
NPw 1914+

PLAIN talk. sw 1911-14||
PLaL complete

Port Washington POST. w Ja 1928+
NPw 1928+

PORTVILLE

Portville AUTOGRAPH. w 1895-1908||
NPo 1900-08

Portville REVIEW. w 1907+
NPo 1909+

POTSDAM

Potsdam COURIER and freeman. w 1851+
Title varies: Potsdam courier; Potsdam courier and journal
MBAt Ap 19 1865
MWA N 18 1852;Ag 26 1880
N N 8 1851
OClWHi Je 26-Ag 21 1856
WHi My 21 1852

Potsdam HERALD-RECORDER. w 1878+
1878-F 1905 as St. Lawrence herald
pub 1879+
MWA Mr 6,O 16 1903

PATRIOT. w Ap 14 1830-
CSmH Je 30 1830

Potsdam RECORDER. w 1886-1905||
United with St Lawrence herald to form Potsdam herald-recorder
MWA My 25 1895

ST. LAWRENCE herald. *See* Potsdam herald-recorder

POUGHKEEPSIE

Poughkeepsie AMERICAN. w D 6 1845-53||?
1845-46 as American. United with Dutchess democrat to form Dutchess democrat and Poughkeepsie American, later Dutchess democrat
DLC N 4 1852
MWA D 19 1846;D 11 1847;S 16 1852
NN D 6,20 1845;46-N 1847
NNHi 1845-48;O 19 1850
NP 1845-N 1848
NPV D 9 1848

AMERICAN mechanic. *See under* Rhinebeck

BRANCH. w S 1835-
NHi Jl 16 1836

Poughkeepsie CASKET. w 1836-
Ct Je 2 1838

CLAY club and tariff advocate. w My 1 1844-
NNHi My-O 1844

COUNTRY journal. . . *See* Poughkeepsie journal

Sunday COURIER. w D 15 1872+
pub S 28 1873+
NN N 16 1879
NNHi [Je-D 1883;F-My 1884]N 19(supp)1883
NP 1873+

DEMOCRATIC American. w
NNHi Ag 18 1849;Ap 27,Jl 27 1850

DUTCHESS county democrat. w N 16 1905-N 5 1906||
United with Poughkeepsie weekly enterprise to form Dutchess democrat and enterprise
NPS complete

DUTCHESS democrat. w O 6 1853-Ag 5 1856||
O 6 1853?-Mr 31 1854 as Dutchess democrat and Poughkeepsie American. United with Poughkeepsie telegraph to form Poughkeepsie telegraph and Dutchess democrat, later Poughkeepsie news-telegraph
NN Ja 3 1856
NP [1854-56]

DUTCHESS democrat and enterprise. w 1883-1915||?
1883-O 1906 as Poughkeepsie weekly enterprise
N Jl 1885-Je 1886

DUTCHESS enquirer. w S 29 1829-
CSmH Ag 18 1830

DUTCHESS intelligencer. *See* Intelligencer and republican

*DUTCHESS observer. w My 10 1815-26||
United with Republican telegraph to form Republican telegraph and observer, later Poughkeepsie news-telegraph
DLC My 4-11,Je 1-22,Jl 6-13,Ag 1825
MWA D 12 1821;D 3 1823;My 12 1824
NNHi O 6 1824
NP [1821-F 22 1826]

DUTCHESS republican. w Ag 1831-S? 1833||
United with Dutchess intelligencer to form Intelligencer and republican

DUTCHESS true American. w 1828-
NPV Ja 30 1828

Poughkeepsie EAGLE and news-telegraph. w,sw 1835-Je 1 1933||
Follows Intelligencer and republican. 1838-1917 as Poughkeepsie eagle (1844-49 Poughkeepsie journal and eagle)
w 1835-88
DLC Ap 17 1841;F 17 1844;F 1 1851
MWA Je 10 1835;D 16 1843;Ja 11 1845;Jl 24 1852;Je 2 1860
N Ja 20 1838;Ap 10 1841;Mr 19 1842;Je 10 1843;46-49;N 20 1858;S 27 1862
NN F 11 1871

NEW YORK (*Continued*)

POUGHKEEPSIE—*Continued*

Poughkeepsie EAGLE and news-telegraph. w,sw 1835-1933||—*Continued*
NNHi F 24 1836;Mr 16 1839-My 7 1842;Ap 23 1843-48;My 3,S 21,N 9 1872;Ja 24,My 2,Ag 1, S 5,N 28 1874;S 15-22 1877;Ja 19 1878;S 20 1881;Ag 19 1882;S 18 1886
NP 1844-[N 23 1850-D 19 1874]
NPV 1861-1907
NSyU O 21,N 11 1848;F 24 1849
NjR Mr 16 1839;O 1899
OClWHi Ap 10 1841;Ag 12 1865
P-M N 23 1836
WHi [Jl 23 1864-S 29 1866]

Poughkeepsie EAGLE-NEWS. d D 4 1860+
1860-Ap 12 1915 as Poughkeepsie daily eagle
pub 1931+
MBAt O 3,N 9 1864;Ap 17-18,26 1865
MWA [Ap-N 1861;Ja-Ap 1862;Jl-N 1863;Mr-D 1864]Ap 30 1878
N Mr 14,D 4 1862-Je 1863;Ap 29 1864;Mr 21, Ap 26 1865
NP [1860+]
NPV [1860-Ag 1932]+
NbHi S 1(supp)1866
OClWHi Ag 16 1865

EMPIRE locomotive. w
NNHi Mr-Ap,My 13,27-Je 3,24,S-O 14 1846

Poughkeepsie evening ENTERPRISE. w Ag 6 1883-S 29 1917||
United with Poughkeepsie evening star to form Poughkeepsie evening star and enterprise
N Jl 1884-Mr 1914
NP complete

Poughkeepsie weekly ENTERPRISE. *See* Dutchess democrat and enterprise

Poughkeepsie FREIE PRESSE. w Ap 25 1908-
In German
NPV Ap-Je 13 1908

Poughkeepsie GAZETTE. w Ja 9 1859-
NNHi 1859-Jl 18 1860

HERALD of reason and common sense, and advocate of equal rights and free discussion. w
NNHi Ja 10,F,Mr 14,21 1835

INTELLIGENCER and republican. w Ap 30 1828-34||
1828-S? 1833 as Dutchess intelligencer. Followed by Poughkeepsie eagle, later Poughkeepsie eagle and news-telegraph
CSmH S 8 1830
DLC F 25,Jl 29,S 9,23-30,O 28,D 30 1829;Ja 19 1831
MWA Je 15 1831;F 13 1833
N O 15 1833
NNHi N 16 1831
NP 1828-34

*Poughkeepsie JOURNAL. w Ag 11 1785-1844||
Title varies: Country journal and Poughkeepsie advertiser; Country journal and Dutchess and Ulster county farmer's register; Poughkeepsie journal and constitutional republican; etc. United wtih Poughkeepsie eagle to form Poughkeepsie journal and eagle, later Poughkeepsie eagle and news-telegraph
CSmH S 8 1830
CtY My 15,Je 12-19,Jl 3,31,Ag 28-S 4,O 23,N 27 1833
DLC S 16,O 28 1829;Ja 6,27 1830
MWA F 9 1825
N N 15 1826;S 26 1827
NNHi My 7 1823;My 11 1836;O 10,N 28-D 12 1838;F 20 1839[40-43]Ag 20 1845-Ja 5 1848
NP 1821-[26-44]
NSchU S 22 1824;Ap 6,20,Ag 3,31 1842

Poughkeepsie JOURNAL and eagle. *See* Poughkeepsie eagle and news-telegraph

Poughkeepsie daily NEWS. d My 4 1868-82||
United with Poughkeepsie daily press to form Poughkeepsie news-press
CtY O 11 1880
ICM Ag 13 1881
N Mr 6,Jl 3 1869;Ja 4,N 21 1870
NP 1868-Jl 21 1871;72-Ap 18 1881

Poughkeepsie NEWS. w Jl 30 1871-83||
United with Poughkeepsie telegraph to form Poughkeepsie news-telegraph

Poughkeepsie NEWS-PRESS. d My 3 1852-Ap 12 1915||
1852-82 as Poughkeepsie daily press. United with Poughkeepsie daily eagle to form Poughkeepsie eagle-news
MWA O 2 1858;Mr 3,N 10 1859;Mr 7 1860;N 13-14,16,D 27 1861;F 17 1862;S 23 1869
NN Jl 24,Ag 31 1852;Ja 21,Mr 11,15,S 3 1853;S 30,N 2 1858;Ag 30,S 20,26,30,O 2 1859; S 22 1860
NP [1852-83]-1915
WHi D 15 1860

Poughkeepsie NEWS-TELEGRAPH. w My 5 1824-1917||
1824-Ap 1826 as Republican telegraph; My 1826-Ap 21 1831 as Republican telegraph and observer; Ap 28 1831-Je 23 1883 Poughkeepsie telegraph (Ag 1856-N 22 1859 Poughkeepsie telegraph and Dutchess democrat). United with Poughkeepsie eagle to form Poughkeepsie eagle and news-telegraph
CSmH Ag 4 1830;Mr 23 1831
DLC Mr 16 1836;Ap 12 1837;Ja 22 1851
MWA Jl 13 1825;Jl 12 1826;Ap 30 1828;My 13 1829;O 16 1844;N 30 1852;S 25 1869
N O 11 1843;S 25 1844;Ja 7 1846;S 20,O 18 1873; N 6-13 1875;Je 10,O 14 1876;F 17,Mr 10 1877; My 4 1878;D 27 1879;My 1,15 1880;Mr 5-12 1881
NN Jl 22 1851;N 17 1857
NNHi O 24,N 10 1824;Ja 1,F 26 1840;D 20 1843; 44-Ag 15,S 24 1845;48;N 2 1852;My 6,Je 17,N 18-25 1856;Ap 26 1873
NP [1824-26]-[30-31]-1916
NPV N 19 1827[Mr 10 1847-Mr 20 1855]
NSchU Ag 10,24 1842
NjR [1845-49]
OClWHi F 10 1866

NORTHERN light. w Ag 9 1848-
N Ag 16 1848

Daily POUGHKEEPSIAN. d Jl 1 1863-
MWA Jl 14,16,21,S 12,18 1863;F 18,Mr 16-21, My 9 1864
NPV Jl 9 29 1863

Poughkeepsie daily PRESS. *See* Poughkeepsie news-press

*REPUBLICAN herald. w Ag 28 1811-23||
NN D 4 1822
NP 1821-S 23 1823

REPUBLICAN telegraph. *See* Poughkeepsie news-telegraph

Poughkeepsie evening STAR and enterprise. d Ap 24 1889—
1889-S 1917 as Poughkeepsie evening star
pub 1921+
NP 1889+

Daily evening TELEGRAPH. d N 28 1854-
MWA N 28 1854

Poughkeepsie TELEGRAPH. w *See* Poughkeepsie news-telegraph

PRATTSBURG

Prattsburg ADVERTISER. w O 11 1867-O 24 1872||
NPrH O-N 22,D 20 1867;Ja 3,F 21-Je 12,26,Jl 17,Ag 14,O 2,23,N 20-27,D 25 1868,Ja 22-29,F 12-Mr 19,Ap-My 21,Je 4 1869;Jl 15 1870;My 25,Jl 13,N 30 1871-Ja 11 1872;Ja 25-Ap 18,My-O 3,O 24 1872

PRATTSVILLE

Prattsville ADVOCATE. w 1846-58||
DLC O 2,23 1847
MWA N 25 1852
N Mr 30 1854
NNHi Ja 23 1847;Jl 1,15,Ag 12,26 1848

Prattsburg ARGUS. w Ja 2 1878-
NPrH Mr 6-13 1878

Prattsville NEWS. w 1855+
NNHi Ja 22 1861;D 10 1862;Mr 22 1873

Prattsburg NEWS. sw My 3? 1864-
NPrH My 6 1864

Prattsburg NEWS. w D 12 1872-D 2 1920||
NPrH complete

PULASKI

Pulaski ADVOCATE. w Ja 15 1840-
DLC F 20 1840;Jl 22 1841

Pulaski BANNER. w S 29 1830-34||
1830-31 pub in Richland?
CSmH S 29 1830
Ct Jl 30 1832
NN O 2 1832

Pulaski DEMOCRAT. w S 25 1850+
1850-Jl 14 1853 as Northern democrat
pub 1850-54;59-61;67+
N S 23 1852;Ag 12 1869
NN S 9 1852
WHi Mr 21 1861;O 4 1866

NORTHERN democrat. *See* Pulaski democrat

RICHLAND courier. w F 25 1847-F 20 1850||
NN F 23 1848-50
NPuD complete

PUTNAM

Monthly STANDARD. m Ja 1 1875-
NHi My 1 1875

QUEENS VILLAGE

QUEENS review. w 1922+
pub 1922+

RANDOLPH

CATTARAUGUS sachem. w Je 13 1851-52||
IaDH 1851-Je 4 1852

Randolph HERALD. w Mr 1842-44||?
PW Ag 1 1842

Randolph REGISTER. w 1865+
pub 1879+

Randolph REPORTER. w Jl 1852-Jl 5 1858||
1852-57 as Randolph whig
PW F 18 1858

Randolph WHIG. *See* Randolph reporter

RAVENA

COEYMAN'S herald. w 1877-1907||
United with Ravena news to form News-herald
NRaN complete

NEWS-HERALD. w 1872+
1872-1907 as Ravena news
pub 1872+

RED CREEK

Red Creek HERALD. w Mr 15 1894+
pub 1894+

RED HOOK

Red Hook JOURNAL. w Ap 29 1859-1916||
NPA complete
OClWHi Ag 4 1871

RENSSELAER

To 1899? as Greenbush

Rensselaer EAGLE. w 1873-1923||?
1873-92? as Evening star; 1893?-1902? Star-eagle
Dated also at Bath-on-the-Hudson
N Ag 1906-Je 1914

GREENBUSH guardian. w Ag 7 1856-
N Ag 7 1856

Rensselaer PRESS. w O 11 1872-79||?
N Ja 18,Mr 8-Ap 26 1873

RURAL folio. w Ja 3 1828-
CSmH Ag 31 1830
N F 14,Mr 13,Ag 29 1828

Evening STAR. *See* Rensselaer eagle

STAR-EAGLE. *See* Rensselaer eagle

Rensselaer TRANSCRIPT. w Jl 20 1928+
pub 1928+

RHINEBECK

Rhinebeck ADVOCATE. w Je 11 1844-
DLC Je 11 1844
NNHi Ag 13 1844

AMERICAN mechanic. w 1849-54||?
Merged with Rhinebeck gazette
1849 pub in Poughkeepsie
N F 15,S 25 1851;Je 9,N 24,D 1 1853;Je 1,Jl 13 1854

Rhinebeck GAZETTE. w Ap 28 1846+
Title varies slightly
pub 1846+
DLC Ap 1 1862
N F 8 1872;F 12-19 1874;Je 3,N 18 1875;Je 8,Jl 20-Ag 3,O 12,26,N 23 1876;Ja 18,F 15 1877;Mr 27,D 4 1879;Ja 8,Mr 25 1880
NGL Mr 1,15 1930

Rhinebeck TRIBUNE. w 1869-72||
N Ja 7,N 4 1871;Ja 13,F 17,Ap 13,Je 1,Ag 31 1872
NNHi F 19 1870

RICHFIELD SPRINGS

Richfield Springs DAILY. d 1888-1920||?
pub only during the summer months
pub 1888-1917

Richfield Springs MERCURY. w 1866+
pub 1885+
ICM My 28 1881;Mr 1,O 11,25 1888-Ap 11,My 9,Je 6*,27,Ag 8,S 26,O 24 1889

RICHLAND

PULASKI banner. *See under* Pulaski

RICHMOND HILL

ILLUSTRATED advertiser.
NBHi S 1873;Ag 1874

LONG ISLAND news. sw 1920+
pub 1927+

Richmond Hill RECORD. w S 8 1900+
pub 1903+
NNHi 1900-N 7 1903
NNQ 1909-18;21-[28]+

RICHMONDVILLE

Weekly PHOENIX. w S 1879+
pub 1879+
N [My 10 1882-N 1889]

RIDGEWOOD

Papers published in Ridgewood are listed under Brooklyn

RIPLEY

Ripley REVIEW. w 1882+
pub Je 1914+

RIVERHEAD

COUNTY review. w S 11 1903+
pub 1903+
N Mr 1913-21
NEh 1923-29
NRiHi Jl 19 1928+

Weekly GAZETTE. *See* Suffolk county gazette

Riverhead NEWS. w Mr 3 1868+
1868-My 16 1895 as Riverhead weekly news
pub 1892+
MWA Ja 14-16 1903(extras)
NBHi Ap 21,D 29 1868;93-1926
NRc F 23 1869
NRiHi Mr 3 1868;My 23 1895
NSm Je 8 1889;Mr 8 1890;Mr 21,O 3 1891;Jl 2,16-Ag 5 1892;Ja 28,Mr 4-11 1893;F 26 1898; Mr 5 1904;Ap 12 1918

NEW YORK (*Continued*)

RIVERHEAD—*Continued*

SUFFOLK county gazette. w S 7 1849-55||
Title varies: Suffolk gazette: Suffolk weekly gazette; Weekly gazette
1851-54 pub in Sag Harbor
NBHi D 14 1850
NHuHi Jl 16 1852
NRiHi S 7 1849
NSm O 12 1849;Ja 11,Ap 5 1851;Ag 2,S 17 1852;Ag 12 1853;F 24 1854;Je 8 1855

SUFFOLK county monitor. w S 21 1865-
NBHi S 21 1865
NRiHi O 26 1865;F 29 1866

SUFFOLK union. w Jl 15 1859-D 20 1862||
NBHi complete
NRiHi Jl 15 1859
NSm Mr 16,Ap 13 1860;D 20 1862

ROCHESTER

Daily ABENDPOST. d 1851+
1851-81? as Rochester beobachter; 1882?-F 1902 Rochester abendpost und beobachter
In German
pub Mr 1902+

Rochester ABENDPOST. w Ap 10 1852+
1852-79? as Beobachter am Genesee; 1880?-1902? Wochenblatt
In German
N Ag 25 1855
NCanHi Je 20 1857

ABRUZZO-MOLISE. *See under* Pueblo, Col.

Rochester daily ADVERTISER. 1826-56 *See* Rochester times-union

Morning ADVERTISER. 1833-34 *See* Democrat and chronicle

ALBUM. w O 1825-28||
Merged with Rochester telegraph
Ct Mr 6 1827
MWA Je 12 1827;Ja 15 1828
NR O 9 1827-Jl 22 1828
NRU S 19,O 31 1826
PPL [Je 27-Ag 8 1826]

Rochester daily AMERICAN. d D 23 1844-D 4 1857||
United with Rochester daily democrat to form Rochester democrat and American, later Democrat and chronicle
Ct N 24 1846;F 23 1847
DLC Ag 9-D 1850
ICN Ja-Je 1864[65]
MWA D 19,24,27 1844-Je 1845[Ja-Je 1848]-[49-50]-[Jl-D 1855]-57
N O 6 1847
NCanHi Je 27,Jl 2 1857
NNHi 1844-57
NR [Ag 13-D 6 1847;Ja 27-Ap 1 1848]
NjR N 25(extra)1847
WHi N 30,D 7,31 1846;F 18,20 1847

Rochester weekly AMERICAN. w 1844-D 5 1857||
United with Monroe democrat to form Rochester democrat and American, later Democrat and chronicle
MWA D 2 1852

AMERICAN citizen. w Ja 5 1841-
Follows American citizen (Perry)
DLC F 16,N 16 1841
NCanHi D 14 1841;O 4,N 8-15 1842
NIC 1841-42
NNHi My-D 1842

Rochester daily AMERICAN democrat. *See* Democrat and chronicle

AMERICAN revivalist and Rochester observer. w 1827-33||
CtY S 29 1832-S 28 1833
N N 24 1832

ANNUNCIATION. w Ap 4 1850-51||
NRU Ap 4,Je 20 1850;Ja 1,My 14,O 6 1851

ANTI-MASONIC enquirer. w F 12 1828-F 1834||
Follows Rochester balance. United with National republican to form Monroe democrat, later Democrat and chronicle
CSmH S 7 1830
DLC Jl 8-22,Ag,S 9-29,O 28,N 11 1828;Ap 21-My 12 1829
MWA Ja 20 1829;My 20 1832
N 1828-O 1831;O 15 1833
NN Ja 10,F 7 1832
NNHi Ag 21 1832;O 8 1833
NR S 15 1829-33
NRU Ap 8-My,S 29-O 21 1828;F 10-My 5 1829

Rochester BALANCE. w 1827-Ja 28 1828||
Followed by Anti-masonic enquirer
N D 10 1827
NRU Ja 14-28 1828

Rochester BEOBACHTER. *See* Daily abendpost

BEOBACHTER am Genesee. *See* Rochester abendpost

CATHOLIC courier. w O 5 1889+
1889-Mr 8 1929 as Catholic journal; Mr 15 1929-Ja 5 1933 Catholic courier and journal
pub 1889+

CATHOLIC journal. *See* Catholic courier

Rochester daily CHRONICLE. d S 12 1868-N 30 1870||
United with Rochester democrat and American to form Democrat and chronicle
CtY My 16 1870
IHi Je 18 1869
NR complete

Rochester semi-weekly CHRONICLE. sw 1868-70||
United with Rochester semi-weekly democrat to form Rochester semi-weekly democrat and chronicle
OHi Mr 2,D 17 1869

CLAY bugle. w My 11-N 2 1844||
CtY My 11-Je 15,Jl 13-Ag 4 1844
NR complete
NRU complete

Rochester morning COURIER. d Ja 4 1830-
DLC Ja 5,8,12-13,22 1830

Rochester COURIER. w Ap 20 1848-
Merged with Rochester advertiser, later Rochester times-union
MWA F 16 1866
NRU Ap 27-My 4 1848

Rochester daily DEMOCRAT. *See* Democrat and chronicle

Rochester DEMOCRAT and American. *See* Democrat and chronicle

DEMOCRAT and chronicle. w Mr 1834-1913||?
Formed by the union of Anti-masonic enquirer and National republican. 1834-57? as Monroe democrat
Title varies: Rochester weekly democrat; Rochester democrat and American; etc.
DLC D 22 1840;F 25,Ap 8,Jl 1,22-29,Ag 12-S 2,O 14-21,N 25,D 23-30 1863
ICHi O 13 1871
ICM S 28 1877;F 9,Je 3 1878
MHi Ag-N 2,16 1864-Ja 11,25-F 1,15-22,My 3,O 11 1865;Je 10 1868;Ja 27,F 17,S 29 1869
MiG Je 26 1889
MiU-C F 15 1842
N S 11(extra)1834;F 16,Je 28,Ag 9,D 6 1836; Ja 24,My 30 1837;Ja 23,Mr 13 1838;Ja 12 1841
NCanHi O 1 1862;Ap 19 1865
NN D 1 1835;Ap 4 1849;Ja 18 1850;My 15 1860; My 3 1877
NNHi N 17,D 29 1835;D 6,20 1836;Ja 24,Ap 4 1837;Mr 20-27,Jl 24 1838;Jl 23,Ag 27 1839;Ja 7 1840;My 4,25 1841;Ja 18,O 11 1842;Ja 17,F 7 1843;Ap 16,Je 25,N 19 1844
NR My 19 1846-54
NRU Ap 22,S 4,O 16 1834;Ja 27 1835;N 15 1836;D 4 1838;My 31 1842;N 19 1844
NbHi Ap 23 1872
OClWHi D 26 1838;D 17 1863;D 10 1874;F 23 1876;O 15 1899;My 7 1910
TJT Mr 24 1886;N 7 1900
VU O 4 1905
WHi D 13 1836;My 20,Jl 10 1845;O 28,N 18-25 1852;Ja 27 1853;O 19 1854

DEMOCRAT and chronicle. d Ja 1 1833+
1833-F 16 1834 as Morning advertiser; F 17 1834-D 4 1857 Rochester daily democrat; D 5 1857-N 3 1870 Rochester democrat and American (title varies slightly)
pub D 1870+
DLC Ja 2 1833;F 10 1834;D 23 1840;F 4 1850-Ag 1853;F 6,Jl 3 1860;63;Mr 16 1864;65-O 1866;67;98-1902
ICHi Ja 27,F 1,11 1838
ICN Ja-Je 1864;65
MBAt Ap 17-18 1865
MHi N 7 1864;D 21-22,31 1868
MWA Ag 28 1835;F 26 1842;N 12 1852;Mr 9 1860;Ap 18 1865;O 26 1871;N 5 1872; Ja 21 1873;Je 19(supp)1880;D 22 1881;Je 9,25 1884; My 18,30,O 17 1885
MiU D 14 1845
MnHi N 8 1861;Jl 3 1865
N Mr 11 1860;Je 28 1862;O 1 1872;Ap 19 1873; 1914+
NAub current 2 years
NN Ag 1 1836
NNHi 1836-[38]Jl 3 1863;F 26,Ap 8,My 1 1873
NR F 17 1834-Ag 28 1837;D 1838-Je 1854;Ja-Je 1855;56-Je 1858;59-60;Jl-D 1861;64-Je 1877; O 1878+
NRU F 16,My 20 1833
OClWHi D 16 1863
PP 1934+
VU My 25 1883
WHi F 20,Ag 1 1839;D 21 1840;Ap 9,Je 1,4 1841;Ja 3 1842;Je 21,Jl 25 1843;My 3,Je 3,Jl 10,15,18 1844;Ja 8 1847;O 24 1848;F 19,27,Mr 1,3 1849;Jl 11-13 1850;Ja 1 1856

Rochester semi-weekly DEMOCRAT and chronicle. sw 1861-87||?
1861-70 as Rochester semi-weekly democrat
OClWHi D 15 1863

DEMOCRATIC clarion. w Je 1-N 23 1844||
NRU complete

Rochester DEMOCRATIC press. w S 1 1860-
NSyU S 15 1860

Rochester evening EXPRESS. 1859-82 *See* Post express

Rochester morning EXPRESS. d O 17 1866-Jl 31 1867||
NNHi Mr 29,Ap 2 1867
NR complete

Rochester weekly EXPRESS. *See* Rochester post-express

FLAG of freedom. w Ap 15 1840-
NRU Jl 15 1840

FREDERICK Douglass' paper. w D 3 1847-Ag 1863||
1847-Ap? 1851 as North Star
Ct D 11 1857
CtY F 1 1856;F 17 1860
DLC Je 26,Jl 24-31,Ag 21,S 4,23-30,O 9,23-30,N 13,D 11-25 1851;Ja 8-F 13,Mr 4-18,Ap-My 20, Je 17,Jl 1,Ag 13-20,O 1-15,N 5,19,D 24 1852-Ja 14,F 4,18-25,Mr 11-18,Ap 1,15,My,Jl 15-29, Ag 19,S 30,N 25,D 9 1853;Mr 24,S 8,29,N 17, 24,D 8,22 1854;F 9,Mr 16,Ap 27-My,Ag 10,31,S 21 1855;F 1,29-Mr 7,21,Je 6,27,S 26 1856;Je 19 1857;Jl 22,Ag 30 1859;Je 8 1860
KHi F 2 1849[1852-Je 1854]
MB 1847;F 1848-49
MHi N 24,D 22 1848
MWA F 13,27,Ap 1851;Ag 27,O 29,N 12 1852;F 1854-Mr,Ag-O 12,N 30 1855;Ja 18,Jl 4 1856;N 13,D 4 1857;F 12,My 6,S 24,D 31 1858[Ja-My 13 1859]
MdBJ S 25 1851-Ja 15,F 12-Ap 22,My-Jl 1,16-Ag 13,27 1852-Mr 18,Ap-Je 3,17-24,Jl 15-S 23,O 28,N 18-D 16 1853;Ja 6-20,F 3-17,Mr 3-17,Mr 31-My 5,19-O 13,N 10-D 22 1854;Ja-Jl 6,20-O,N 9-D 14 1855
MeBa Ap 25 1856
MiU [1847-48]
N Jl 23,O 29 1858
NIC 1847-Ja 5 1849
NNHi Ag 11,D 15 1848;Je 20-27,S 12 1856;O 29 1858;N 11 1859;Mr 16,30,Ap 27,My 11-18, Je 15 1860
NOHi 1854
NSyU F 11-18 1848;D 8-15 1854
NUHi Mr 10 1854
PWcHi Je 16,D 1 1848
VHaH Je 10 1852
WHi [F 24 1854-F 23 1855]Jl 8 1859

Rochester FREEMAN. w Je 12 1839-
MBAt Ag 7 1839
MWA Je 26 1839

Rochester GAZETTE. *See* Rochester republican

Rochester HERALD. w S 27 1838-
NRU O 4 1838

Rochester HERALD. d Ag 5 1879-F 26 1926||
ICM N 16 1912
KHi N 27 1910
MWA Je 22 1880
N O 8 1913-Jl 1922
NR complete
OClWHi D 15 1900
WHi D 5,29 1883;Ap-D 1896

Rochester weekly HERALD. w Jl 4 1888-D 27 1901||
NR 1888-O[D 1897-D 22 1899]1900-01

JEWISH ledger. w S 27 1924+
pub 1924+

JOURNAL American. d Je 25 1922+
1922-Jl 15 1923 as Rochester journal; Jl 16 1923-28? Rochester journal and post express
pub 1922+
OClWHi Ag 3 1923

LABOR herald and citizen. w O 31 1913+
pub 1913+

LEVEL. w Ag 1 1835-
ICHi O 31 1835
NRU Ag 22,S 26-O 10 1835

LIBERAL advocate. w Jl 3 1832-
NRU Jl 3 1832;N 27 1833;Ap 6,Je 7-21 1834

MACKENZIE'S gazette. w My 12 1838-D 23 1840||
1838-F 16? 1839 pub in New York City
CaBVR 1838-My 4 1839
CaO 1838-F 15 1840
CaOTU complete
CaQMF N 10 1838-My 4 1839
DLC My 25 1839;O 31 1840
MB [1838-40]
MWA D 1 1838;O 12 1839
NGe 1838-Ap 12 1839

Daily MAGNET. d Je? 1849-50||
NRU Ag 6 1849

Rochester MERCURY. w Ja 2-My 29 1827||
Merged with Rochester republican
ICHi My 22 1827
MWA Ja 2,F 6,My 29 1827
N complete
NRU Ja 23 1827

MONROE democrat. w Jl 15 1828-
DLC Ag 5-S 2,O 14 1828

MONROE democrat. 1834-57? *See* Democrat and chronicle

MONROE republican. 1821-27 *See* Rochester republican

MONROE republican. w Je 28 1928+
pub 1928+
NR 1928+

MONROE weekly and American democrat. *See* Democrat and chronicle

NATIONAL reformer. w S 28 1847-
Also dated in Auburn
NNHi [O-D 1847]Mr 18,Ap 8 1848
NR My 25-N 16 1848
NRU D 7 1848

NATIONAL republican. w 1831-F 11 1834||
United with Anti-masonic enquirer to form Monroe democrat, later Democrat and chronicle
N Ja 28,F 11 1834
NNHi Je 14 1831
WHi Ja 27 1833

Rochester evening NEWS. d Ap? 1849-
NRU Je 13,15,Jl 24 1849

NORTH STAR. *See* Frederick Douglass' paper

Rochester OBSERVER. bw,w Ja 6 1827-32||
bw Ja-Je 23 1827
CSmH Ag 13 1830
CtY F 22-Mr 1832
MWA Mr 20 1829
NAubT 1828-31
NN Ap 3 1829
NR [Ja-Je 23]F 17 1827-S 19 1832

PAUL PRY. sm,w Mr 27 1828-
Suspended from Ag 28 1828-My 9 1829
sm 1828
N My 22 1828-Ag 29 1829
NRU Ap 24 1828

ROCHESTER—*Continued*

Rochester evening POST. d 1841-N 1843||
Jl 3-S 23 1843 as Rochester evening post and working man's advocate
MBAt Ap 30 1842[43]
NNHi Je 1841-42
NR Mr 8-D 1842
NSchU Ag 23 1842

Rochester POST-EXPRESS. w 1859-1903||?
1859-80? as Rochester weekly express. Followed by Farm stock journal (not in this list)
MWA N 9 1871
NNHi Ja 5 1860;Mr 23 1865;F 27 1873
NR N 1860-O 24 1861;62;68-75
NRU S 20-27,O 18-D 13,27 1866;Ja 10-Mr,Ap 11-D 1867
OClWHi O 15 1863

POST EXPRESS. d Ja 24 1859-Jl 14 1923||
Ja 24-Je 8 1859 as Rochester daily times; Je 9-D 29 1859 Rochester daily express; D 30 1859-My 3 1882 Evening express. United with Rochester journal to form Rochester journal and post-express, later Journal American
Ct Je 15 1900;Ja 8-9 1901;Ap 14 1909
DLC D 9 1864
ICM Ag 17 1877;O 24 1881
MBAt Ap 15-18,20 1865
MWA [O 16-N 21 1860]Jl 23,Ag 30,S 11,18-19 1862;Je 7 1884;Mr 3 1885;Ap 3 1888
MiG Je 4 1889
N My 26 1914-Je 1922
NCanHi Je 10 1865
NNHi Ja 25,29,F 1-2,9,11-12,Mr 11,Jl 14,N 4,15 1859;Mr 24,Ap 4,D 22 1860[61]F 19,21-22,Mr 12,Ag 14 1862;My 8(extra)1864;Mr 17,20-21,Ap 10,15,20 1865;Mr 29-30 1867;Ag 22 1872;My 1,O 14 1873
NR Ja 24-Ap 5,Je 9-My 3 1882
NRJ Je 9 1859-My 3 1882
NSyU S 14 1861
OClWHi O 3 1890
VU My 21 1883
WHi My 4 1895

*Rochester REPUBLICAN. w Je 1816-84||?
1816-Mr 6 1821 as Rochester gazette; Mr 13 1821-Jl 31 1827 Monroe republican
CSmH D 29 1829
Ct [1829-37]
DLC D 25 1825-26;Ja-F,Mr 18 1828;Jl 14-21, Ag 4-11 1829;N 30 1830;Ja 11 1831;32-Ag 20 1833;Ja 14 1834-D 22 1835;Mr 15 1836;37-39;N 4 1852
ICHi Jl 12 1825;Ag 21,O 9,D 4 1832;F 16 1836; F 13 1838;S 21-28 1841
ICN Ap-Je 1864;35
IU S 11,O 2 1838
MWA Ag 28,D 18 1827;Ja 1,F 26,Ap 1,My 6 1828;N 25 1852;Mr 29 1860
N O 29 1833;Jl 7,N 17 1835;Jl 12 1836
NN O 31 1826;Ap 22 1834;F 10,D 1 1835;Je 27 1837;Jl 6 1876
NNHi Mr 13 1821-[22]-Ap 1823;Jl 26 1825-Jl 24,D 18 1827;Jl 1829-Je 1830;Jl 24 1832-Je 18, O 15,N 5 1833;My 6 1834;35;O 25 1836;O 18(extra)N 22,D 18,20-27 1825;My 9,D 13 1826
NR Ja-F 13 1821;Ag 1825-Ag 1 1826;D 29 1829-32;36-37;My 1839-44;46-49
NRU Ap 10,14,Je 26,Ag 28-S,N 24,D 18 1821; N 4 1822[23-N 1 1825]Jl 4,18-S,O 10 1826-Jl 1827;Je 10-Jl 22,O 7-14 1828;Mr 31-Ap 7,Ag 11-S 15,29-N 3 1829;S 18 1832;O 6 1834;Je 2 1835;Ag 30-S 20,O 1836-Ja 8,29-F,Mr 26-Ap 9 1839;Ja 21,Jl 14 1840-Ja 12,26,Mr 2-9,30,Ap 27-Je,Jl 20,Ag-S 8,28,O 12-19,N 2,16-30,D 14 1841-F 1,Mr 1,15-Ap 12 1842;N 30 1847
NSchU Mr 1 1842
NhD Je 22 1841
OClWHi Je 19 1873;My 28 1874
WHi Ja 1 1822;Ap 4 1861

Rochester SOCIALIST. w 1907-
WHi D 14 1907-Mr 27 1908

La STAMPA unita. w 1906+
In Italian
pub My 8 1920+

Rochester daily SUN. d Ap? 1839-
NR [Je 11-D 31 1839]
NRU Je 22,29 1839

Daily SUN. d
NNHi Ja 8-Jl 15 1879

*Rochester TELEGRAPH. w,d Jl 7 1818-Ja 4 1829||
Merged with Rochester daily advertiser, later Rochester times-union
DLC D 6 1825;D 8 1826;Ag 28 1827;Ag 28,30 1828
ICHi D 3 1822;Jl 8,22 1823
MBAt Ja 16 1821
MWA Jl 22 1823;Ja 4,Jl 12-19,N 1 1825;Ja 15 1828
N Jl 27,O 26 1821;Jl 26 1825;D 1 1826
NNHi 1821-22;Jl 15,29,S 9,20,D 2 1823;O 26 1824;F 16 1828
NR 1821-S 6 1825[Je 28-N 26 1828]
NRU F 7-14,My 16,Ag 15 1826;D 11-15 1827; Ja 15,My 20 1828
WHi F 15 1825

Rochester daily TIMES. 1859 *See* Post-express

Rochester TIMES. w 1872-78||?
NNHi Mr 2 1873;F 22(supp)1874

Rochester TIMES-UNION. d O 25 1826+
1826-D 12 1856 as Rochester daily advertiser; D 15 1856-Mr 11 1918 Rochester union and advertiser
Suspended from N 23 1834-Je 30 1835
pub D 15 1856+
CSmH Je 21 1830
CtY Ag 20,31,S 1 1832
DLC O 5(reprint)1826;Ja 5,Je 17,20,S 1,16,O 30,N 2,12,26-28 1829;Je 1846-48;60;Ap 17,21 1865;89;My 1898-Ap 1899
ICHi Ja 31 1838;O 25 1856;N 3 1865
ICM Ag 15 1877;Je 3 1878;F 20,D 16 1879;F 12,S 5 1881;O 8 1883
ICN [Ja-Je 1864]65
KHi Mr 23 1888
MBAt Ap 15,18,20 1865
MWA O 25,D 16 1826;Jl 4 1828;S 26 1844;N 27 1852;Jl 1,N 25 1857;Ap 1 1858;Jl 24 1862; Mr 23 1888
MiU-C O 25 1826
N 1826-38;N 24 1842;O 6 1847;Ap 1913-S 21 1918
NBrM O 25 1826
NCanHi O 25(reprint)1826;Ap 15,17-18 1865
NN O 25(photostat)1826;Jl 5-6 1876
NNHi O 25(facsimile)1846-Mr 5 1827;S 23,28 1861;Mr 7,10 1862;Ag 22 1872;F 8,My 2 1873
NR [Je 18 1828-F 10]Jl 17 1829-Ap,N 1831-Je, N 1832-My,O 1833-Ja 1,S 20 1834-52;O 15 1853-Je 1854;Ja-Je 8,Ag 3-D 8 1855;56+
NRU O 25 1826;Ja 6,N 1 1827;S 1829;Jl 25 1831;Ja 18 1833;Mr 18 1834
NSyU Mr 2 1849;My 4,Ag 6,24,S 7,14,21,O 11,N 13 1861
OClWHi O 26 1826
RW D 12 1826
WHi D 13 1861;My 17 1864;N 2 1867

TRUE democrat. w F 13 1838-
DLC F 13 1838

TRUE Jeffersonian. d S 18-N 17 1840||
NRU O 16 1840

Rochester daily UNION. d Ag 16 1852-D 13 1856||
United with Rochester daily advertiser to form Rochester union and advertiser, later Rochester times-union
MWA O 30 1852;Jl 26 1855
NR complete
NRT complete

Rochester semi-weekly UNION and advertiser. sw
DLC S 11-14,25-28,O 12,23 1860

Rochester UNION and advertiser. d *See* Rochester times-union

L'UNIONE; formerly Abruzzo-Molise. w Ja 7-Ap 8 1927||
Merged with L'Unione, Pueblo, Col.
In Italian
IU complete

WESTERN weekly American. w Ja 4 1845-
NCanHi N 22 1845

WESTERN New Yorker. w
NNHi D 31 1841-42
WHi Je 27,Jl 11-18,S 26,O 23 1843;Jl 14 1847

Rochester daily WHIG. d Jl 8-N 1840||
Campaign paper
NRU N 10 1840
WHi Ag 14 1840

WOCHENBLATT. *See* Rochester abendpost

WORLD as it is and general advertiser. w Ag 7 1835-
NNHi F 20 1836
NRU Ap 2-Je 11,Jl 2 1836
OClWHi Jl 16 1836

ROCKAWAY BEACH

WAVE. 1893+
pub 1896+
NNQ 1910-18;20-25;27+

ROCKTON

Rockton ENTERPRIZE and Mohawk Valley news. w Ja 5 1839-
MWA My 10 1839
NEh Jl 5 1839

ROCKVILLE CENTRE

HERALD. w 1908-16
NRc D 31 1915-16

LONG ISLAND news and owl. *See* News-owl

NASSAU daily review. *See under* Freeport

NEWS owl. w 1909+
1909-D 26 1919 as Owl; Ja 2 1920-D 27 1923 as Long Island news and owl; Ja 3 1924-Mr 19? 1931 Long Island news owl
pub 1926+
N Mr 29 1917-18
NRc D 11 1909;Ja 11,F 15-S 1910;11-Jl 12 1917;18+

OWL. *See* News-owl

PICKET. *See* South side observer and Nassau post

SOUTH SIDE observer and Nassau post. w Je 16 1865-D 31 1920||
1865-O 1870 as Picket; 1871-Jl 19? 1918 South side observer
MWA Je 16,30,Jl 21 1865;My 11 1866
N Jl 27 1917-18
NBHi Je-Ag 4 1865;82-1916
NRc 1913-N 5 1920
NRcN complete

ROME

Rome semi-weekly CITIZEN. w,sw Ag 25 1840-1901||?
1840-86? as Roman citizen
w 1840-Je 13 1888
DLC D 15 1840;Ja 12 1841;O 20 1846
MWA O 13 1852
N S 8 1852;O 18(extra)1854;My 31 1867
NNHi Ap 25 1873
NRom Jl 1840-My 9 1842;Ap 1844-Je 3,D 1845-Je 2,Jl 9 1848-52;D 1855-57;D 1858-67;72-75; 76-79;82-83;Je 1884-Jl 1885;86-1901
NhD O 19 1841
P S 3 1844
WHi Ap 16 1844

DEMOCRATIC sentinel. *See* Rome sentinel

Rome EXCELSIOR. w 1853-
MWA N 27 1852;F 11 1854
N Ag 5 1854

ONEIDA observer. *See* Utica observer (Utica)

ONEIDA republican. w Je 1828-29||
Merged with Rome republican
CSmH D 30 1829
DLC O 28,D 30 1829

Rome REPUBLICAN. w My 25 1825-31||
Followed by Rome telegraph
N O 26 1825;My 30,Je 27,Jl 4,Ag 15 1827

Rome REPUBLICAN. w,tw 1881-1912||?
w 1881-94?
NRom N 1881-95;N 30 1899-N 22 1890

ROMAN citizen. *See* Rome semi-weekly citizen

Rome SENTINEL. w 1838-1924||?
Follows Rome telegraph. 1838-45 as Democratic sentinel
pub N 8 1842-Mr 20 1846;Ap-D 1847;Mr 28 1849-Mr 20 1850;Ja 30 1861-D 19 1881
DLC O 23 1850
MBAt Ag 2 1842
MWA Ap 11 1843
N Ag 19 1845;Jl 15 1873
NNHi Ap 19 1842;F 4 1873
NRom Ja-N 19 1851;Jl 15 1852-Jl 12 1853;Ag-D 1855;D 8 1863-Jl 3 1881
NhD Je 16 1840
OClWHi Ja 2 1866

Daily SENTINEL. d Jl 15 1852-57||?
pub 1852-Jl 31 1855
N F 2,Ap 1,Je 8,Jl 29,N 21 1854;Ja 16,N 13, 17,23 1855;N 28 1856;F 5,Mr 16,My 4,13,Ag 8,O 13,20,N 5-6 1857

Rome daily SENTINEL. d D 19 1881+
Ag 6 1930 is Mohawk Valley historical and progress number
pub 1881-Je 12,D 19 1883-85;87-93;96+
N Mr 1914-Jl 1922
NNY-H Ag 6 1930
NRom 1881+
NJH Ag 6 1927

Rome TELEGRAPH. w 1832-38||
Follows Rome republican. Followed by Democratic sentinel, later Rome sentinel
N Ja 1 1833
NRom Jl 8 1834-Ag 7 1838

RONDOUT. *See* KINGSTON

ROSCOE

ROCKLAND review. *See* Sullivan county review

SULLIVAN county review. w 1892+
1892-1909 as Rockland review
pub 1892+

ROSENDALE

PEOPLES press. w
NRosM My 18 1853-My 15 1857

Rosendale STAR. w 1895-99||?
DLC O 31 1895
NNHi D 4 1897

ROSLYN

Roslyn NEWS. w 1878+
NEh 1926+

NORTH HEMPSTEAD gazette. w D 1846-50||
Followed by Plaindealer
NBHi O 5 1848

ONCE-A-WEEK. w
NBHi 1863-64

PLAINDEALER. w Ja 12 1850-55||
Follows North Hempstead gazette
Also pub for Glen Cove
NBHi 1850-Ja 4 1854

ROUSES POINT

Rouses Point ADVERTISER. w Ja 1852-58||
MWA D 1 1853
NChM S 15 1853;Je 15-22,D 2 1854;F 24,Mr 17 1855;O 4 1856;D 5-12 1857

NORTH countryman. w 1928+
pub 1928+

TRAVELERS companion and business directory. w Ap 23 1855-
NChM Je 12 1855

ROXBURY

DELAWARE times. *See* Roxbury times

Roxbury TIMES. w 1879+
1879-89? as Delaware times
pub 1900+
IU S 4 1890
N S 16 1880
NRo 1935+

RUSHVILLE

Rushville CHRONICLE. *See* Gorham new age and Rushville chronicle (Penn Yan)

RYE

Rye BUDGET.
In manuscript
NN Jl 11,13 1832

Rye CHRONICLE. w N 11 1905+
NRy [1905-N 3 1906]F 1922+

NEW YORK (*Continued*)

SACKETS HARBOR

BLACK RIVER journal. *See under* Watertown

COURIER. w 1832-
N O 17 1833

FREEMAN'S advocate. w
DLC N 27 1828
MWA F 15 1827
NN O 19,N 2 1826

JEFFERSON farmer. w Mr 1848-
1848-52 as Sackets Harbor observer
WHi Ap 16 1852

JEFFERSON republican. w F 1821-
MWA Je 28 1822

Sackets Harbor JOURNAL. w O 10 1838-51||
DLC O 17 1838

Sackets Harbor OBSERVER. *See* Jefferson farmer

SAG HARBOR

AMERICAN eagle. *See under* Huntington

CORRECTOR. w,sw Ag 3 1822-D 30 1911||
w 1822-O 1834
CSmH Je 26 1830
MWA Ag 2 1823;S 6 1828;Ap 22 1871
N N 19 1825
NBHi [My 1822-F 1841]59-96
NEh 1822-Ap 1823;Mr 14 1829[34]F 7 1857
NN Ja 20 1836[Ap-D 1854]Ja,F 27 1855
NNHi F 10,24 1844
NRc F 20 1869;Je 22 1872
NRiHi N 13 1830
NSh 1856-1911
NSm O 26,N 9,16-23,D 14 1822-Ja 4,18-F 1,22 1823;N 2 1861

Sag Harbor EXPRESS and the news and the corrector. w Jl 14 1859+
1859-Ap 10 1921 as Sag Harbor express
pub 1922+
MWA Ag 17 1871
NBHi 1859-1922
NEh [Mr-D 19 1867]Ag 25 1870;Je 8,29,Ag 31, N 4,16-23 1871;Jl 4,Ag 22,N 7 1872[73]Mr 19, Ap 23,My 14,28-Je 18,Jl 2,D 31 1874;Ja 28,F 25-Mr 4,Ap 1,29-My,Je 17,N 11,D 30 1875
NNHi O 11 1860;Jl 16 1863;My 1,D 4 1873;Ag 1 1899
NRc Je 27 1872
NSh 1859+
NSm Mr 27 1862;Ja 7-14 1864;F 16 1865;Je 19 1890;Ja 15-22,Ap 30 1891;S 5,19,O 1895;Ja 31 1901;Ja 23-30 1902;Ag 20 1903;Ag 12 1909
NSo 1899-[1907]+
P-M S 17 1863

Weekly GAZETTE. *See* Suffolk county gazette (Riverhead)

REPUBLICAN watchman. *See* Watchman of the Sunrise trail (Mattituck)

SUFFOLK county gazette. *See under* Riverhead

ST ALBANS

INVESTIGATOR. w
MWA Ap 16 1829

St. Albans LEADER. w F 1931+
pub 1934+

ST. GEORGE

Papers published in St. George are listed under Staten Island

ST. JOHNSVILLE

St. Johnsville ENTERPRISE and news. w Je 10 1898+
1898-Je 26 1918 as St. Johnsville enterprise
pub 1898+
Ct D 26 1934+
M D 6 1933
N S 16 1931+
NHi 1930+
NNHi S 21 1932+
NSa 1907+
OClWHi Ja 29-My,O 1930-33
PDoHi My 3 1933

St. Johnsville HERALD-TIMES. w 1885-87||
1885 as St. Johnsville herald
NSaE Ap 9 1886

INTERIOR New Yorker. *See* St. Johnsville times

St. Johnsville NEWS. w O 7 1891-Je 26 1918||
United with St. Johnsville enterprise to form St. Johnsville enterprise and news
N Ja 4 1893
NSaE 1892-96

Weekly PORTRAIT. *See* St. Johnsville times

St. Johnsville TIMES. w 1875-84||
1875-76 as Interior New Yorker; 1877-83? Weekly patriot. United with St. Johnsville herald to form St. Johnsville herald-times
NSaE Jl 21 1875;Jl 5 1878;Ja 17 1883

SALAMANCA

CATTARAUGUS county republican. w 1867+
1867-1931? as Cattaraugus republican
pub 1867+
N Ap 24 1913+

CATTARAUGUS republican. *See* Cattaraugus county republican

CATTARAUGUS union. w 1856?-1914||
Some years dated also at Little Valley and at Olean
NOl 1910-14

Salamanca REPUBLICAN-PRESS. d Ap 24 1904+
pub 1904+

SALEM

Salem AXIOM. w D 11 1885-1907||
Merged with Salem press
NSalC Ag 26 1892

COUNTY post and North star. *See* Washington county post (Cambridge)

NORTHERN post. *See* Washington county post (Cambridge)

Salem OBSERVER. w Ja 1822-
NFeH D 5 1840

Salem PRESS. w My 21 1850+
Jl 1885-1909? as Salem review-press
N 1850-77;S 3-10 1880;S 1 1882;D 1886-98
NFeH 1887-97
NSal 1852-53;58-60;73-85;1914-16;18-31
NSalC [1856]My 1862-Ap 10 1866[72;80-81]
OClWHi Mr 9 1900
WHi Ja 8-15 1867

Salem weekly REVIEW. w D 8 1877-Je 1885||
United with Salem press to form Salem review-press, later Salem press
N 1877-Ap 10 1880
NSalC Ja 5 1881;O 1 1882

Salem REVIEW-PRESS. *See* Salem press

WASHINGTON county post. *See under* Cambridge

***WASHINGTON register.** w N 1803-30||
MWA S 20 1826
N Ja 11,F 15,Ap 12 1821
NFeH D 28 1825
NHi N 22 1821

SALINA

Papers published in Salina are listed under Syracuse

SANDY CREEK

Sandy Creek NEWS. w 1870+
pub 1885+
NSc Ja 25 1934+

SANDY HILL. *See* HUDSON FALLS

SANGERFIELD

CIVIL and religious intelligencer. *See* Sangerfield intelligencer and Madison and Oneida counties gleaner

***Sangerfield INTELLIGENCER and Madison and Oneida counties gleaner.** w N 18 1816-35||
1816-25 as Civil and religious intelligencer
CSmH S 15 1830

SARANAC LAKE

ADIRONDACK enterprise. w,sw,tw,d 1894+
w 1894-1913;sw 1914?-19?;tw 1920?-26?
N N 11 1925-F 5 1926

Daily ITEM. d Je 25 1918-
NChaF Jl 1918

SARATOGA SPRINGS

OLD settler. *See under* Keeseville

Morning POST. d? D 1856-
N Jl 2-N 28 1857

Daily Saratoga POST. d Je 1869-
MWA Ag 17 1869

Saratoga daily REGISTER. d
pub in July and August only
N 1882;87;89

Saratoga REPUBLICAN. w Ja 5 1844-
Title varies slightly: Republican and sentinel
DLC N 5 1852
IU O 16 1846
N Ja 12-D 20 1844
NHi F 12 1847;N 17 1848
NN F 13 1846

Daily Saratoga REPUBLICAN. d Je 24 1844-
pub summer months only
N 1844-Ag 1845;Je 21-S 15 1847

SARATOGA county exchange. w F 6 1839-
GAtCo Jl 23 1839

SARATOGA county press. w 1857-
Follows Saratoga whig
N F 6 1857-Ja 28 1859

SARATOGIAN. w,sw 1852-1905||?
w 1852-99?
MBAt Ap 27 1865
N 1856-D 7 1876;D 13 1877-Je,D 1885-N 1890

SARATOGIAN. d Je 25 1855+
pub 1901+
CtW S 20 1893
DLC Ap 30 1887-98
ICM My 21-30 1883
MWA Ag 16 1856;Ag 4-12 1864;Ag 16 1869; Ag 29 1879;S 22-23 1882
N 1855-Je,S 9 1872-Je,S 8 1873-Je,S 15 1874-Je,S 16 1878-My 15,S 15 1879-S 14 1889;Mr 1913+
NNHi Ap 30 1873
OClWHi Ag 30 1874
OOxM My 16-22 1879

Semi-weekly SARATOGIAN. sw My 10 1868-
N 1868-Je 27 1869

***Saratoga SENTINEL.** w My 26 1819-47||
Merged with Saratoga republican
CSmH S 29 1829
CoD [Ap 30 1839-O 27 1840]
Ct [1828;31-38]
CtY S 18 1832
DLC D 14 1830;Ap 12 1831;O 9 1832;O 13 1840;Je 29 1841
GAtCo Jl 9 1839
MWA 1821-Ap 1834;Je 11 1839
N N 24 1824;O 24-31 1826;D 18 1827;O 27,N 10 1829
NChaM Ja 31 1832
NHi [1836-39]Ap 19 1842[45-47]
NN N 25 1828;S 22 1829
NNHi F 7,Mr 28-Ap 23 1821;O 29,D 31 1822;O 21 1823;O 10-24 1826;F 13,Jl 24 1827-28;O 5,19-26 1830;S 8 1840
NSchU F 8,Ap 5 1842
NhD O 2 1838

Daily Saratoga SENTINEL. d 1841-47||
Merged with Saratoga republican
MWA Je 6-Ag 29 1842;Jl 30 1845
N Je 6-Ag 27 1842
NNHi Je-Ag 1842

Saratoga SUN. w S 16 1870-1906||?
DLC Je 28 1883
MWA Mr 4 1876
N Mr 25 1871;Je 23 1873

Saratoga WHIG. w F 26 1839-56||
Followed by Saratoga county press
DLC F-N 5 1839
MWA Mr 12-19,S 24 1839;Jl 13 1841;D 15 1846
MiU Ag 18 1840
N 1839-F 1843;Je 16 1846;Ag 22 1851-F 1 1856
NSchU F 8 1842

Daily Saratoga WHIG. d Je? 1844-
DLC Ag 22 1844;Ag 9 1851
MWA Ag 12 1846;Jl 24 1847;Ag 28 1852;Jl 6 1853
N Je 28-S 24 1853
WHi Ag 10 1848

SAUENEMIN

Sauenemin HEADLIGHT. w 1904-My 1932||
United with Cullom chronicle to form Chronicle-headlight

SAUGERTIES

Saugerties TELEGRAPH. w O 28 1846+
1846-O 26 1850 as Ulster telegraph
DLC O 2 1847;Ap 7 1849
N [Mr 29 1851-Mr 14 1889]My 24 1894;Ja 16, Mr 6 1896;Ja 28 1897
NNHi Ja 22,F 5 1848;Ap 11 1873;Mr 21 1878;N 17 1881
NSau 1846-O 1850
OClWHi Je 1 1866
RW Jl 3 1863;Ap 21 1865

ULSTER palladium. *See under* Kingston

ULSTER telegraph. *See* Saugerties telegraph

SAVANNAH

Savannah TIMES. w Ap 7 1894+
pub N 1908+

SAYVILLE

SUFFOLK citizen. w 1919+
pub Je 1923+

SUFFOLK county news. w 1885+
pub 1888+
N F 8 1918-D 26 1919

SCARSDALE

Scarsdale INQUIRER. w Jl 1 1901+
pub 1901-07;N 15 1919+

Scarsdale SUN. w,d Ap 13 1928+
w 1928-32
pub 1928+

SCHAGHTICOKE

Schaghticoke SUN. w Jl 20 1894+
pub 1894+

SCHENECTADY

Daily ANCIENT City. d Ag 10-N 29 1852||
N S 4-O 12,26 1852
NSchU complete

***Schenectady CABINET.** w My 26 1810-57||
Follows Western budget (not in this list). 1810-23 as Cabinet; 1831-Je 1837 as Schenectady cabinet: or Freedom's sentinel; Jl 1837-Je 1839 Freedom's sentinel
CSmH S 8 1830
Ct Je 10 1835
DLC F 20 1833
MWA Ap 17 1822;Ag 19 1823;F 3,Ap 20,O 19,N 9 1824
N 1821-Je,O 2 1822;Ag 5-19,S 16 1823;Mr 23, My 18 1824;Ja 4,Mr 23 1825;My 9,Jl 4,O 17 1827;Je 15 1831;O 3 1832;My 8 1833;Ap 23,Je 3 1834;My 25 1836;F 15,Mr 15,My 24,Je 14, 28 1837-My 14,N 26 1839[40-56]Ap 14 1857

NEW YORK (*Continued*)

SCHENECTADY—*Continued*

*Schenectady **CABINET.** w 1810-57||—*Cont.*
NN N 1 1826
NNHi D 11 1822-Ja 1,Ag 11,O 7 1823;O 26 1824;D 12 1827;Ja 2 1828;My 13 1829;O 17 1832;O 2 1849
NSch 1852-53;56-My 5 1857
NSchHi Ja 10-17,31-F 7,Mr 28-My 9,Je 20-27, S 5,26,O 24 1821;Ja 2,23,F 13-20,Mr 20,Ap 3-10,My 15,Ag 14,S 4,O 2-9,D 11 1822-Ja 1,29,O 14,N 11 1823;24-Mr,Ap 19-Je,Jl 12 1826-Ja 5,19-F 9,Mr-Ag 3,S 14-28,O 12 1831[32-33]-Ap 9,My 28,Jl 23-30,Ag 20-27,N 12 1834-[35;F 10-D 1836]-Mr 1,15-Je 21,D 5 1837;Ja 2,16 1838-Mr 12,Ap 16,30,My 14 1839-45;Jl 1846-My 5 1857;My 25 1858
NSchU Jl 1822-D 23 1823;Jl 1824-Je 1825;D 12 1827;Ag 6,D 10 1828;Je 17 1829-Mr,Je 15-29 1836;O 5,N 9 1841;F 15-22,Mr 1,Ap 5,Ag 2 1842;F 14 1843-O 1849;50-53
NjHi [1821-23]F 17 1824;Je 1,O 26,N 30 1825

Schenectady **CITIZEN.** w My 20 1910+
pub 1910+

Schenectady **DEMOCRAT.** w Ja 3 1854-N 1 1860||
United with Schenectady reflector to form Schenectady democrat and reflector, later Schenectady reflector
NNHi Ja 10,17,Mr 20 1860
NSch Mr 31-My 9 1857
NSchHi [Mr 1857-59]60

Schenectady **DEMOCRAT** and reflector. *See* Schenectady reflector

FREEDOM'S sentinel. *See* Schenectady cabinet

FREEMAN'S banner. w Jl 13-N 2 1848||
N complete

GAZETA tygodniowa. w Mr 1908+
In Polish
pub 1923+

Schenectady **GAZETTE.** w 1869-1913||
NSchHi My 29,Je 19,Jl 17,Ag 21,S 25,O 17,N 20,D 25 1874;Mr 5,26,Ap 9,23,Je 25-Jl 2,Ag 20-27,O 15-22,D 24-31 1875;Mr 3,Ap 28,Je 23,Jl 7,S 1,N 24-D 1 1876;Ja 19,F 2,Jl 13-20, Ag 31-S 7,N 2 1877;Ja 4,F 1,22,Jl 12,S 20-27,N 22 1878;F 7,Jl 4,25,Ag 29,O 24 1879;Ja 2 1880

Schenectady **GAZETTE.** d 1893+
pub 1914+
N Ja-Je,Ag 12 1911+

Schenectady **HEROLD-JOURNAL.** w Mr 25 1910+
In German
pub 1910+

Schenectady **LEADER.** w 1905+
NN [S-O 1914]-Ja,F 12,Je 26 1915

MOHAWK sentinel. w 1824-25||
MWA Ag 4 1825
N N 3 1825
NNHi Je 2 1825
NSchU Je 24 1824-Je 16 1825

Schenectady daily **NEWS.** d Ap 11 1859-Je 15 1861||
N [My 26-S 16 1859]
NNHi Jl 16,19,21 1859;Ja 4 1861
NSch 1859-Ag 16 1860
NSchHi [1859-61]
NSchU Ap 12 1859-Ap 11 1861
NSyU Jl 11 1860;My 25 1861

Schenectady **REFLECTOR.** w D 30 1834-1903||?
Follows Schenectady whig. 1834-Ja 1841 as Reflector and Schenectady democrat; O 25 1860-My 9 1867 Schenectady democrat and reflector
DLC Ja 20 1835
MWA Ja-Je 17 1836;Jl 26 1839
N F 3 1835;Ja 27,D 29 1837;Mr 23,D 28 1838 [39-Ja 22 1841]F 18,Ap 1,S 30 1842;N 24 1843[44]-Ja 10 1845;Je 4,Ag 27,O 8 1847-Jl 14, Ag 25 1848;Ag 29 1851[52]-59;62-65;68-69;N 30 1871;74
NCH 1834-Ja 1837
NHi 1834-O 12 1860
NN Mr 28 1845
NNHi 1834-Je 1836;D 18 1862;Ja 18,My 21,D 17 1863;Ap 14,Je 30,Jl 21,Ag 11,O 6,27 1864;F 23,Mr 16,Jl 6 1865;F 15,My 17 1866
NSch 1838-39;41-44;47-N 20 1862;63-66;68-70; 73-85
NSchHi 1834-[37-38]-Ja 11,25-Mr 8,22-29,Ap 12,Ag 9,23,S 13-20,N 1-22,D 20-27 1839;Ja 24, Mr 27,Ag 2-16,N 6,20-27,D 11-18 1840[41-42]-[44-45]-[48]-My 4,Je 1,22-Jl 13,S 7,O 19,N 8 1860-Ag 10,31-S 7,28-O 5,N 2,D 1865-N 8 1866; Ap 4,18-My 23,Jl 25-Ag 1,S 12,26 1867;Ap 2,O 22 1868;70;72-73
NSchU 1834-Jl 1836;38;41-80
NSyU Ag 31 1860

Schenectady **REPUBLICAN.** w S 1857-
MWA D 9 1865
N Ap 23,My 7-14 1858;My 20,Ag 15 1863;64;Ap 22,O 21 1865;66
NNHi Ag 15 1863
NSch 1859-N 9 1867

SCHENECTADY county whig. *See* Schenectady whig

Schenectady and Saratoga **STANDARD.** *See* Saratoga and Schenectady standard (Ballston Spa)

Evening **STAR** and times. *See* Schenectady union-star

Schenectady evening **TIMES.** d Ja 3-Je 1 1861||
United with Evening star to form Evening star and times, later Schenectady union-star
NSchHi F 12,My 21,24 1861
NSchU complete

TRUE blue. w S 3 1868-70||?
N S 3 1868;S 8 1870

Schenectady daily **UNION.** d O 28 1865-Ag 5 1911||
United with Schenectady daily evening star to form Schenectady union-star
ICM Je 28 1893
MWA Ja 1866(extra)
N D 5 1865;F 1,Mr 1,20,23,O 28 1866;My 19-20 1868;Jl 11 1872
NSch complete
NSchS 1900-11
NSchU 1868-Je 1870

Schenectady weekly **UNION.** w D 20 1865-1906||?
MWA Ja 4 1866

Schenectady **UNION-STAR.** d Je 1855+
1855-Ag 6? 1911 title varies: Morning star; Evening star; Evening star and times; Schenectady daily evening star
pub 1900+
ICM F 19,21 1881
N Je 9,11,S 21,D 28-29 1855;Mr 29,Ag 5 1856; Jl 8 1857;Ja 7,Ag 21,S 27 1858;Je 27,O 11 1859;Ag 14-17 1860;S 4,O 15 1861;F 21-Mr 3 1862;Ag 17,O 11 1864;Ap 15,Je 17,30 1865;S 18 1866-My 1867;My 2,Je 30 1868
NNHi O 2,D 5 1858;Ja 27-28,F 12,Mr 15,17,Je 13,N 11,17,30,D 28 1859;F 23 1865
NSch N 18 1863;1911+
NSchU F 21 1855-57;Mr 1858-My 1883
OClWHi D 9 1865

Schenectady **WHIG.** w O 30 1830-D 23 1834||
1830-31? as Schenectady county whig. Followed by Reflector and Schenectady democrat, later Schenectady reflector
Ct [1830]
N O 30,N 9 1830;D 27 1831;Jl 17,O 6,N 1832-D 23 1834
NSchU Je 7,S 27 1831;O 28,D 2-16 1834
P N 13 1832

SCHENEVUS

Schenevus **MONITOR.** w D 1865+
pub [1898]Ap 1929+

SCHOHARIE

DEMOCRATIC republican. *See* Schoharie republican and county democrat

Schoharie **FREE PRESS.** w Je 9 1830-32||
CSmH Ag 4 1830

*Schoharie **OBSERVER.** w O 28 1818-24||?
N Ja 16-23,My 30,S 5 1821
NNHi Ja 9 1822;O 2 1823
NjHi [1821-22;24]

Schoharie **PATRIOT.** *See* Schoharie union

*Schoharie **REPUBLICAN** and county democrat. w 1819+
1819-1904? as Schoharie republican (D 6 1854-Je 1858 Democratic republican)
CtY O 3 1861
MWA Ag 31 1852;S 7 1865
N 1828;S 1829-D 4 1832;Ja-Ag 1834;39-40;Ja 10 1843-82;Ap 12 1888
NN Jl 11 1827
NNHi Ag 26 1829

Schoharie **UNION.** w F 15 1838-98||?
1838-N 12 1863 as Schoharie patriot
MWA Ag 26 1852;Je 23-30 1853;Je 29 1865
N My 17 1838;Ap 18,S 26,O 24 1839;D 16 1842; O 28 1847;F 27 1851;N 17,D 15 1853;Ap 13,S 21-28 1854;N 29 1855;Mr 6,Ap 3,My 1,Je 5,Jl 3,Ag 7,28,S 4,O 2,N 6 1856;Je 4-18,O 29 1857;N 5,D 8 1859-82;Ap 12 1888;89-F 6 1890
NNHi S 20 1838
NSch 1865-70;73-N 1874

SCHROON LAKE

Schroon Lake **PRESS.** w Je 28 1935+
Issued during summer months only
pub 1935+

SCHUYLERVILLE

Schuylerville **HERALD.** w D 12 1844-
Title varies
DLC Mr 28 1845
NN D 30 1846
P-M Ag 1 1845

SARATOGA county American. w D 1857-
NNHi Jl 3 1862

SARATOGA county standard. *See* Schuylerville standard

Schuylerville **STANDARD.** w 1871+
1871-75? as Saratoga county standard
pub 1912+
NjR S 12 1874;O 18 1877

STANDARD. d O 6-31 1877||
N complete

SCOTIA

Scotia **JOURNAL.** w N 11 1926+
1926-F 15 1928 as Scotia news
pub 1926+

Scotia **NEWS.** *See* Scotia journal

SENECA FALLS

AMERICAN weekly reveille. *See* Seneca Falls reveille-standard. . .

Seneca Falls **DEMOCRAT.** w 1839-49||
MBAt Ap 8 1841

Seneca **FREE SOIL** union. w S 5 1848-
NCanHi O 3,31,N 24 1848

HARRISON banner. w My 12 1836-
OClWHi My 19-S 15 1836

Seneca Falls **JOURNAL.** w 1829-32||
Merged with Seneca farmer
CSmH Ag 25 1830

Seneca Falls **REVEILLE**-standard and Seneca county commercial. w Ja 13 1855+
1855-70? as American weekly reveille
MWA S 15 1855;Ja 26 1856
N Ja 20 1871;S 8 1876;My 11 1877
OClWHi Je 24 1865

SENECA county courier-journal. w Je 4 1839+
1839-1901? as Seneca county courier
DLC Je 4 1839;Ap 14 1841;Ag 11 1848
MWA Je 5 1862;Mr 26 1863;Ap 20 1865
N F 18 1840;S 2 1852
NCanHi N 25 1853
NN S 14,N 2 1865;Mr 8,Ap 5,20 1866
NNHi My 8 1873
NSchU Jl 6,20 1842
NWat 1879-87
WHi Ap 2 1846

SENECA county press. w 1912+
pub 1912+
Ct N 2 1921

SENECA farmer. w 1822-33||?
Title varies: Seneca farmer and Seneca Falls advertiser; Seneca farmer and Waterloo advertiser
1822-31? pub in Waterloo
CSmH S 8 1830
DLC D 3 1828
MWA O 27 1824
N O 23 1833
NWat 1823-24;26-31
P-M O 10 1832

SETAUKET

LONG-ISLAND star. w 1867-
NBHi 1868-70
NRc S 20-27 1867
NSm S 13 1867

SHARON SPRINGS

Sharon Springs **GAZETTE.** w Mr 1 1873-79||?
N Mr 1,My 17 1873;Je 20 1874

SHERBURNE

Sherburne **HOME** news. *See* Sherburne news

Sherburne **NEWS.** w Mr 2 1864+
1864-65 as Home news and weekly advertiser; 1865-68 Sherburne home news
CtY Ag 30 1873;S 5 1874
MWA Ag 2 1866;S 2 1876
NNHi Ap 5 1873
NShe 1864+

SHERMAN

CHAUTAUQUA news. w 1875+
pub Ap 15 1932+
CtY [1933]
NShem D 17 1879-1918

Weekly **RECORD.** w
NWavS Jl 31-D 4 1872

SHERRILL

Sherrill **SENTINEL.** w
NSher 1929-30

SHORTSVILLE

ENTERPRISE. w F 1 1883+
pub 1883+
NNaR N 26 1887

SIDNEY

DELAWARE county times. w 1870-78||?
MWA S 15 1876

Sidney **ENTERPRISE.** w 1895+
pub 1895+
NSi 1916+

Sidney **RECORD.** w 1882+
pub 1882+
NSi 1910+

SILVER CREEK

Silver Creek **NEWS.** w 1906+
NWe D 3 1931

SING-SING. *See* OSSINING

SKANEATELES

Skaneateles **COLUMBIAN.** w 1831-53||
DLC Jl 11 1838;Ag 6 1841
MWA S 12 1838;Je 9 1842
N O 30 1833;Ag 4 1842
NAub 1837-53
NNHi My 30,N 21,D 12 1832;Mr 20 1833;Ja 17-Ap 4 1838
NSk 1833-50
P-M Mr 28 1832

NEW YORK (*Continued*)

SKANEATELES—*Continued*

Skaneateles DEMOCRAT. w 1840-Ap? 1926||
United with Skaneateles free press to form Skaneateles press
MBAt Ap 20 1865
MWA D 3 1863;Je 29 1865
N Ag 19 1842;N 28 1845
NSk 1843-80
NSkP complete
WHi Mr 8 1844-Ap 25 1845;Ap 10 1846-Ap 13 1849

Skaneateles FREE PRESS. w 1874-1926||
United with Skaneateles democrat to form Skaneateles press
NSk complete
NSkP complete

Skaneateles PRESS. w Ap 19 1926+
Formed by the union of Skaneateles free press and Skaneateles democrat
pub 1926+
NSk 1926+

SMITHTOWN BRANCH

MESSENGER. w 1887+
pub 1887+
NSm F 16 1907;Ap 4 1908;Ag 7 1909;My 12 1911;Ap 21 1922+

Smithtown STAR. w Mr 14 1930+
pub 1930+
NSm 1930+

SMYRNA

CHENANGO tribune. w 1881-84||
NNo complete
NNoS Mr 12 1881-84

Smyrna CITIZEN. w 1875-76||
MWA Ag 26,N 4 1876
NNo O 30 1875-N 25 1876
NNoS complete

SODUS

RECORD. w Ap 7 1897+
pub 1897+

SOUTH NEW BERLIN

South New Berlin BEE. w 1897+
pub 1897+

SOUTHAMPTON

Southampton PRESS. w My 29 1897+
NRiHi D 31 1931+
NSo [1897]+

SEA SIDE times. *See* Southampton times

Southampton TIMES. w D 10 1891+
1891-1920? as Sea side times
NSm N 30 1893
NSo [1895]-1900;02+

SOUTHOLD

LONG ISLAND traveler. w 1871+
NBHi 1885-1933
NNHi Ja 6 1876;O 10 1878
NRiHi Ap 18 1872-98;Ap 28 1932+
NShi S 9 1899

SPENCER

Spencer NEEDLE. w Ja 1 1888+
pub 1888+

SPENCERPORT

Spenceport STAR. w N 15 1889+
pub 1889+

SPRING VALLEY

ROCKLAND county leader. w Ja 5 1893+
pub 1928+

SPRINGVILLE

Springville EXPRESS. w 1844-
Follows Lodi banner (Persia)
N My 18 1844-Jl 22 1848

Springville HERALD. w My 1850-66||?
United with Springville journal to form Springville Journal and herald, later Springville journal
MWA My 19 1855
N Ap 30 1859

Springville JOURNAL. w 1867+
1867-1921 as Journal and herald
pub 1867+
NSp Mr 1867-68;Jl 1869-S 1870[1909-34]

LOCAL news. *See* Springville news

Springville NEWS. w 1879+
1879-95? as Local news
pub 1895+
NSp [1911-34]

STAMFORD

Stamford MIRROR-RECORDER. w My 28 1851+
1851-75 as Bloomville mirror (Bloomville); 1876-1905 Stamford mirror
pub N 3 1851;Mr 24 1854;S 14 1852;Mr 8 1864; F 7 1865;66+
CSmH My 13 1856
MWA N 6 1860;Je 20 1865;My 21 1889
N 1853-81;Je 21,Ag 20,D 31 1887;Mr 12 1924+
NNHi 1861-62
NSchU [1851]66-78;88+
NSt 1851-1905;27+
NStM N 3 1851;Mr 24 1854;S 14 1852;Mr 8 1864;F 7 1865;66-75
NStV 1856-1901

Stamford RECORDER. w 1894-1905||
United with Stamford mirror to form Stamford mirror-recorder
NSt My 5 1894-Ap 11 1896
NStM 1895-1905

STAPLETON

Papers published in Stapleton are listed under Staten Island

STATEN ISLAND

Staten Island CHRONICLE. (Stapleton) w 1855-
MWA Mr 26 1858
NSyU Mr 4 1857

DEMOCRAT-HERALD. (Tompkinsville) w 1880-1916||?
1880-Mr 27 1908 as Richmond county democrat
NN O 24 1908-Mr 1909

GAZETTE and sentinel. w My 10 1882-1889||
Formed by the union of Richmond county gazette and Richmond county sentinel
NN Jl-S 1883
NSM complete

Staten Island INDEPENDENT. w O 21 1893-O 23 1894||
Merged with Staten Island news
NSM complete

Staten Island JOURNAL. w
NSD Jl 25,O 17 1865

LITTLE corporal. w S 17 1853-
NSD S 24 1853
NSM S 17 1853

NEW YORK and Richmond county free press. w 1832-36||
NSM My 11-O 19,N 2 1833-O 4 1834
WHi N 1833-Ap 1834

Staten Island NEWS. w 1893+
Title varies: Staten Island news and independent; etc
NN [N 1906-07]

NEWS-LETTER. (St. George) w 1896-1903||?
NSM D 5 1896-N 6 1897

Staten Island REPUBLICAN. w,sw 1876-1900||?
CtY Jl 13 1895

RICHMOND argus.
NSM Mr 1-D 1 1902

RICHMOND county advance. w,d Mr 27 1886+
w 1886-1917
pub 1886+

RICHMOND county democrat. *See* Democrat-herald

RICHMOND county gazette. w F 12 1859-My 3 1882||
United with Richmond county sentinel to form Gazette and sentinel
CSmH Ag 3 1864
MBAt Ap 19-26 1865
NSM Ja 22 1859-82

RICHMOND county herald. w,sw 1880-1910||?
w 1880-1907?
NN [Je 1907-Ag]S 1908-Mr 27 1909

RICHMOND county mirror. bw Jl 1837-Jl 1839||
not pub S 9 1837
N 1837-Ja 1839
NBHi 1838-39
NNHi S 2-16 1837;Ag 4,25-S 1,O 13 1838
NSM complete
NhD Jl 13 1839

RICHMOND county republican and Saturday morning advertiser. w O 27 1827-1831||
1827-30 as Richmond republican
NSHi complete
NjR N 20 1830
OClWHi My 23 1829;Jl 31 1830

RICHMOND county sentinel. w 1880-My 3 1882||
United with Richmond county gazette to form Gazette and sentinel
NSM complete

RICHMOND county standard. w Ag 9 1881-1900||
NSM 1881-94;1900

RICHMOND republican. *See* Richmond county republican. . .

SEPOY. w F 12 1859-Je 15 1859||
NSHi complete

Staten Island STAR. w 1877-1914||?
NN S 4 1885;O 24,31,N 14-D 12 1908;Ja 2-Ap 3,17-My 29 1909
NjR N 21 1896

STATEN ISLANDER. w Ag 7 1847-
DLC D 29 1860;Ja 5,My 25 1861
NSM S 11 1847;S 15 1852;Ja 23 1856-57

STATEN ISLANDER. sw 1889-Jl 1928||
N S 24 1892
NN 1906-Ja 3 1927
NSM 1891-1921

TIMES-TRANSCRIPT. *See* Staten Island transcript

Staten Island TRANSCRIPT. w,sw 1881+
1881-89? as Westfield times; 1890?-99 Staten Island times; 1899-Je 22 1907 Staten Island transcript; Je 29 1907-29? Times-transcript
pub 1931+
NN N 10 1906-N 1907;Jl 3,N 6,20,D 1908-Je 18 1909
NSM 1927+

Staten Island UNION. w
NBHi D 21 1865;Ja 4-11,F 15,Mr 1,15-Ap 1866

Staten Island WORLD. w 1901-Ja 31 1920||
NSM 1901-05;07-20

STONY BROOK

INDEPENDENT press. w Ag 17 1865-
NBHi N 2 1865;Ja 21 1867
NRc My 10 1866
NSm Mr 14 1867;Je 17,Ag 19,N 11 1869

SUSPENSION BRIDGE

Papers published in Suspension Bridge are listed under Niagara Falls

SYRACUSE

Syracuse ADVERTISER. w 1826-S 1829||
United with Onondaga journal (Onondaga) to form Onondaga standard, later Syracuse post-standard
MWA Ap 23 1828
NSyU 1828[29]
OClWHi Ag 29 1827

Syracuse AMERICAN. w My 23 1832-
N S 12 1832

Syracuse ARGUS. w 1831-33||
Follows Onondaga register and Syracuse gazette
DLC D 14 1832

CARSON league. *See under* Albany

CENTRAL City daily courier. *See* Syracuse daily courier

CENTRAL New Yorker. w 1850-
NSyU D 11 1851

Weekly CHRONICLE. w Ja 1 1853-56||
Merged with Syracuse journal
MWA Je 11 1853

CONSTITUTIONALIST. w Ag 7 1833-35||
Follows Onondaga republican. Followed by Onondaga chief
MWA Ap 22,My 27 1835
N O 23 1833

CONSTITUTIONALIST and free trader. w Jl 19 1862-
Title varies slightly
MWA S 19 1863
NSyU Jl 19,N 8-15,D 13 1862

CORRIERE di Syracuse. w O 26 1907+
1907-Ja 17 1913 as Risveglio coloniale
In Italian
pub 1907+

Syracuse daily COURIER. d O 1856-99||?
Title varies: Syracuse daily union and courier; Central City daily courier
ICM My 3 1884
MWA D 19 1870;S 20 1871;Ag 22 1876
MnHi Mr 1 1862
N Ja 22 1858;N 4 1859;S 20 1860
NBuG O 19 1860
NN My 10 1862
NSyU S 15 1859[60-61;77-81]84-96

Syracuse weekly COURIER. w,sw O 1856-99||?
N 1858-89 as Onondaga weekly courier (title varies slightly)
w 1859-89
N Ag 8 1868
NSyU Je 8 1861

Syracuse evening DEMOCRAT. d
NNHi O 7 1848

DEMOCRATIC freeman. *See* Syracuse weekly star

FREE SOIL campaigner. w 1848||
Campaign paper
NSyU Jl-N 1848

Syracuse GAZETTE and general advertiser. w Ap 1823-28||
1823? as Onondaga gazette. United with Onondaga register (Onondaga) to form Onondaga register and Syracuse gazette
MWA Jl 30 1828
N F 13 1828

La GAZZETTA di Syracuse. w 1906+
In Italian
IU Mr 8 1918-29

Syracuse HERALD. d 1877+
Title varies: Evening herald
pub 1887+
DLC S 2 1878-My 16 1885;Jl 1898-1905;My-Ag 1908;My-Ag 1909
MWA Ap 2 1918
N Ja-Mr 1904;Jl 1913-Jl 1922
NCortHi Ja 24 1901
NN O 16 1877
NNHi Ag 26,31,S 27,D 31 1881;S 20 1882
NSyU [1878]

L'INDIPENDENTI di Syracuse and Risveglio coloniale. w 1907?-18||?
In Italian
IU 1917-N 22 1918

NEW YORK (*Continued*)

SYRACUSE—*Continued*

Syracuse weekly JOURNAL. w,sw Mr 20 1839-1905||?
1839-44? as Western state journal
w 1839-99?
Ct My 14 1851
CtY Ap 26 1848
DLC Ap 3 1839
MWA My 22 1839;Ap 15 1840;S 14 1878
N Ag 7,D 18 1839;Ap 8 1840
NSchU Ja 19 1842

Syracuse daily JOURNAL. d Jl 4 1844+
CtY D 8 1859
KHi Jl 19 1852;S 20 1890
MBAt Ap 17,20 1865
MWA O 9 1845;Je 15,25 1847;Mr 4 1850;N 25 1852;O 15-19,22-N 2,10,16-21 1860;Jl 23 1862; D 11 1865;N 13 1869;Ja 24 1870;O 11 1879
MWiC O 12 1865
MoHi Mr 1 1854
N Je 28 1862
NCort F 15 1864
NCortHi S 18 1879
NNHi F 26 1877
NSyU Mr 16 1857;Ja 2,Je 1 1861;62-63;66-79
P-M Mr 30 1852
PScrWi Ap 27 1865

LIBERTY intelligencer. w Ag 27 1846-
MWA F 26 1846

ONONDAGA chief. w 1835-
Follows Constitutionalist
Ct Jl 12,O 4 1837
MWA Je 21 1837
NSyU 1835-37

ONONDAGA weekly courier. *See* Syracuse weekly courier

ONONDAGA democrat. w Ap 4 1846-48||
Merged with Onondaga standard, later Syracuse post-standard
MWA N 14 1846
NNHi F 19 1848

ONONDAGA gazette. *See* Syracuse gazette and general advertiser

*ONONDAGA register and Syracuse gazette. w S 28 1814-30||
1814-28 as Onondaga register (Onondaga). Followed by Syracuse argus
CSmH S 8 1830
CtY F 17 1830
DLC O 21,D 23 1829;Ja 13 1830
MWA S 8,O 27 1824;Jl 7 1830
N O 20 1824;F 17 1830
NNHi O 20 1824
NSyHi 1821-30

ONONDAGA republican. w Mr 3 1830-33||
Followed by Constitutionalist
CSmH S 1 1830
MWA Je 9 1830
NSyU Mr 24 1830-F 9 1831
P-M O 10 1832

ONONDAGA sentinel. w 1845-50||
N D 11 1847

ONONDAGA standard. *See* Syracuse post-standard

PATRIOT express. w O 20 1838-
OClWHi N 24 1838

PEOPLE'S union. w O 24 1861-
NSyU O-N 1 1861

Syracuse POST. d Ag? 1894-98||?
United with Syracuse daily standard to form Post standard?
IaDH Jl 10 1894
KHi N 30 1894
NN F 2 1895

Syracuse POST-STANDARD. w,sw S 16 1829-1906||?
Formed by the union of Onondaga journal (Onondaga) and Syracuse advertiser. 1829-73? as Onondaga standard; 1874?-98? Syracuse standard
w 1829-89?
pub [1833-36;45]51
CSmH S 8 1830
Ct O 25 1837
DLC S 16 1829;S 4 1839;Jl 16 1845;Ag 12 1846
IU S 4 1844
MBAt Ag 16 1843
MWA Je 26,Jl 10 1833;My 17 1837;N 14 1838; Jl 17 1839;Ja 1 1840;Ag 25 1841;Ag 28 1844;O 18 1848;F 25 1857
MWiC D 31 1845
N N 4 1829;Ap 20 1831;D 26 1832;O 16 1833; D 10 1834;D 20 1837;Ag 5 1840;Mr 8,Je 14 1843;N 16 1859;D 18 1867;Mr 11 1868
NN My 19(extra)1847;O 5 1852
NNHi O 21 1829;F 24 1836;N 29 1843;Ja 30 1867
NSyU 1829-31;34-35;37;39-44;46-51

POST-STANDARD. d 1854+
1854-98? as Syracuse daily standard (title varies slightly)
pub 1854+
ICHi Ja 22 1868
MBAt Ap 17-18 1865
MWA Je 4,Ag 13 1852;O 28 1869;Je 20 1871; Ag 22 1876;O 11 1887
N O 19 1934
NAub current 2 years only
NChM O 17 1865
NFu current 2 years only
NN D 6 1856;Jl 20,27,N 3 1864;F 11,Ap 29,D 30 1865;Jl 21 1868
NSc 1934+
NSk 1933+
NSyU 1850-58[Ap-N 1861;Jl-N 1862]
TJT My 13 1890

Syracuse REVEILLE. w 1848-49||
N Jl 2 1849
NSyU complete

RISVEGLIO coloniale. *See* Corriere di Syracuse

LA RUCHE. w S 13 1851-
In French
N S 20 1851

SALINA herald. w O 1826-
1826-27 as Salina sentinel
CSmH My 19 1830

SALINA sentinel. *See* Salina herald

Syracuse STANDARD. *See* Syracuse post-standard

Syracuse weekly STAR. w F 8 1844-O 1853||
1844? as Democratic freeman
CSmH Je 14 1844
DLC N 13 1852
MWA Mr 4 1848;My 29 1852
NN N 13 1852;Ja 1 1853

Syracuse daily STAR. d 1845-53||
MWA D 15 1851;Mr 30,Ag 25 1852;Jl 26 1853
N F 28 1849
NSyU S 27 1847

STATE league. w Ag 1858-
MnHi S 27 1862
NNHi Jl 13 1861

SYRACUSEAN and mechanics' and farmers' advocate. N 26 1841-
DLC D 10 1841

Syracuse daily UNION and courier. *See* Syracuse daily courier

WESTERN state journal. *See* Syracuse weekly journal

TARRYTOWN

Tarrytown ARGUS. w 1867-1920||?
CtSp O 9 1897;Mr 25,Ag 5 1905;My 4 1907

KNAPSACK.
PScrG F 26 1862

Daily NEWS. d 1912+

Tarrytown PRESS-RECORD. w 1887+
CtSp Jl 1910
NN F 25 1910-12
WHi Je 13 1894

TICONDEROGA

ADIRONDACK eagle. w 1878-
NHi Ja 28 1881

Ticonderoga SENTINEL. w F 7 1874+
pub 1898-1906;08-09;30+
N 1909-S 1917
NHi [1874]-[81]-85[89;91]-[21]25+
PScrHi My 26 1932

TICONDEROGAIN. w 1881-F 1884||?
Merged with Ticonderoga sentinel
NHi Mr 9 1883

TOWN topics of the Champlain Valley. w Jl 1932-Je 1933||
NHi complete

TIOGA VILLAGE

TIOGA county gazette and general advertiser. w
PEL O 2 1830

TOMPKINSVILLE

Papers published in Tompkinsville are listed under Staten Island

TONAWANDA

Tonawanda HERALD. w 1874-1903||?
CtY O 3 1889

TOTTENVILLE

Papers published in Tottenville are listed under Staten Island

TROY

Troy ADVOCATE. w
WHi Ja 19,31,F 16,Mr 9,30-Ap 6,28-My 9 1903

Troy AMERICAN. sw O 13? 1823-
DLC F 14 1834

AQUARIAN. w Ap 2 1843-Jl 27 1844||
N complete

Troy daily ARENA. d O 18 1859-
IU 1859-O 17 1860
NT 1859-Ap 1861

L'AVENIR national. . . O? 1871-75||?
Follows Le Protecteur Canadian (St. Albans, Vt.)
1871-72? pub in St. Albans, Vt.
In French
MWA Ja 18-N 23,D 19 1872-Ja 16 1873

*Sunday BUDGET. w Je 20 1797-Ap 1927||
1797-1825? as Northern budget. United with Troy observer to form Troy observer-budget
1797-My 8 1798 pub in Lansingburg
CLM Mr 10-17 1901
CSmH S 10 1830
Ct [1826-28;30-38]
DLC 1827-28;F 15 1853;90-F 6 1898
IU Ag 4 1840
InRE Ap 26 1836
MWA Je 20 1826;S 14,D 25 1827;Ja 15,Ap 8, Ag 5 1828;Ja 4,S 6 1831;Jl 31,S 4 1838;Ag 31,O 12 1841;Ja 4 1842;Ag 2 1850;Ja-Je,Ag 19,24,N 30 1852;Ja 18-25 1853;O 10 1854;Ap 9 1871;Ag 22 1870;Mr 13 1876

MnHi F 19 1833
N 1833-My 17 1836;O 1837-39;Jl 1840-42;49
NNGe Jl 1840-43
NNHi My 13,Jl 15 1823;Ag 17 1824;Ja 14,Ap 8-My 20,Je 3-17,Jl 1-8,22-29,Ag 12,S-N 11, 25-D 23 1834;Ja 20,F-D 1835;S 16 1840;Ja 17 1844;Mr 24 1875
NSchU Jl 29,Ag 3 1842
NT 1821-1925
NTO 1880-1927
P-M D 5 1854
Vt [Ja 2- 1843-Je 17 1848]

Troy daily BULLETIN. d D 6 1841-
MWA F 22 1842
NT Ja 21 1842

CALDERS cornucopia. w
MBAt S 15 1831
MeU O 4,N 1-8,29 1832;Ap 4 1833

CHRONICLE. w Ap 4 1835-
NNHi Ap 4 1835

COMMERCIAL advertiser. d Mr 28 1848-
NT Mr-D 1848

DEMOCRATIC press and Lansingburgh advertiser. *See* Lansingburg democrat

FAMILY journal. w 1844-
Title varies: New York family journal; Fisk's family journal
MWA N 4 1848;D 3 1852;Ap 3 1853
NT D 10 1852-53
WHi S 30 1848-Ap 4 1851;Ap 1852-My 4 1861

*FARMERS' register. w Ja 25 1803-
1803-N 10 1807 pub in Lansingburgh
CSmH S 7 1830
MWA F 2-,My 25,Jl 13,Ag 3 17,31-S 14,O 12-26 1824;Ja 11,Mr 1-8,Jl 19,O 11 1825;My 8-15,29,Je 19,Jl 3-10,24,Ag 21,D 18 1827;F 19 1828
N Ap 22 1823;Jl 20,Ag 2,S 28-O 5,19,D 21 1824;Ja 11,Mr 8,Je 21,S 13-20,N 15 1825;Je 5,Jl 31,S 11-O,N 20 1827
NN O 17 1826
NNHi Jl 15,N 5 1822;Ja 21,Jl 22-Ag 5,S 23, O 7-14,S 1-,D 30 1823
NT S 21 1824
NJHi [1821-26]

FISK'S family journal. *See* Family journal

FOWLER. w Mr 23 1824-
NNHi My 11 1824

Saturday GLOBE. w Je 25 1927-
NT Je-Ag 13 1927

Troy Sunday HERALD. w Ap 13 1890-
NT Ap 20 1890

LANSINGBURGH weekly chronicle. sw,w Ap 6 1864-
1864 as Semi-weekly chronicle (other slight changes)
N Ap 9 1864-Jl 4 1866
NT 1864-O 17 1866

LANSINGBURGH courier. w D 24 1875-1909||
N D 24 1875 D 24 1880;Ja 7 1881;My 16 1885; Jl 24,O 16,30,N 27 1890;Ja 19,Ap 20 1893
NT 1875-Jl 11 1894

LANSINGBURGH democrat. w Ja 13 1838-Ap 6 1861||
1838- as Democratic press and Lansingburgh advertiser. Followed by New advertiser
MWA Jl 23 1857
N 1838;Ag 21 1851;O 1852-Ap 6 1861
NT 1838-D 5 1840;F 7 1844-61

*LANSINGBURGH gazette. w S 18 1798-My 12 1883||
Follows American spy (not in this list)
Title varies: Rensselaer county gazette; State gazette; Lansingburgh state gazette
CSmH S 7 1820
DLC Ja 22 1828;Jl 28-Ag 4,25,S 8 1829
MWA Jl 13 1824;F 19 1863
N Ap 10,My 8,29,Je 19,Ag 14,28,S 11,25,N 13,27-D 4 1821;Ja 15,Jl 2,S 10,24,O 22,D 3,24 1822;23-24;Ja 11,F 22,Mr 8,O 25,N 25 1825;O 23,D 11 1827;N 5 1833;Ag 5 1834;F 3,My 10, Jl 7 1835;N 13 1837;D 3 1838;Jl 6-13 1843
NHi Jl 16 1822-F 22 1844
NNHi 1821-22;F 17 1829;Mr 28 1873
NT 1821-83
NjR Ja 29 1822

LANSINGBURGH times. w Jl 13 1887-1904||?
NT 1887-My 1895

Troy morning MAIL. d 1837-40||
Title varies slightly. Merged with Troy daily whig, later Troy morning record
DLC O 19,D 18 1837
MWA F 3,My 18 1840
N N 15 1837-N 4 1840
NT Ag 19 1837-40

NEW advertiser. Lansingburgh) w Ap 13 1861-
Follows Lansingburgh democrat
N Ap 20 1861
NT Ap 13-Jl 12 1861

NEW YORK family journal. *See* Family journal

NEW YORK state journal. w S 9 1835-
N 1835-Je 15 1836
NT 1835-S 7 1836

NEW YORK state republican. w Ja 9 1849-
NSyU O 9 1849
NT 1849-51

Troy evening NEWS. d N 9 1860-Mr 18 1861||
NChM complete

Troy NEWS. w Ag 21 1864-
N Ap 16 1865
NNHi S 11,N 6,27,D 4 1864[65]Ja 21,28,My 27 1866
NT 1864-Ag 13 1868

NORTHERN budget. *See* Sunday budget

NORTHERN watchman. *See* Troy watchman

NEW YORK (*Continued*)

TROY—*Continued*

Troy OBSERVER-BUDGET. w 1875+
1875? as Trojan observer; 1876?-Ap 1927 Troy observer
pub 1897+
NcD Je 20 1920

*Troy POST. w S 1 1812-Jl 1823||
Followed by Troy sentinel
OClWHi Mr 20 1821

Troy daily POST. d O 1 1843-53||?
Followed by Troy daily traveller
DLC Ag 11-D 1846
MWA S 16 1853
N Ja 6,Jl-Ag 8 1846;Ja 2,My 31 1847
NNHi [My-D 1849]
NSyU Ag 12,N 3,8,13 1848
NT Ap 1846-51

Daily Troy PRESS. d Mr 14 1833-34||
DLC Jl 19 1833
N Mr 14,Je 28-O 10,16 1833;Ja-Je 1834

Troy daily PRESS. d Ag 8 1863-Je 30 1911||
United with Evening standard to form Standard-press
CtY D 7 1892
DLC D 7 1876;Je 19,22 1883;Ap 21 1892
ICM O 16 1891
MWA Ag 18-19 1870;Ag 26 1876
N Ag 29,31,S 5 1863;Jl 2,O 14 1864;Ja 23,S 6 1865;Mr 11-27 1868;Mr 16,Ap 6,Ag 17 1869;Ja 13-F 10,Mr 24,Ap 21,Ag 22 1870;Ja 24 1871;O 24 1873;N 16 1896-F 1897
NNHi S 12,26,O 3,17,N 28,D 5 1863;Ja 2,23,F 13,17,Mr 26,Ap 2,9,16,23,My 14,21,23-24,26-28, 30-31 1864;My 2 1873
NT complete
OClWHi My 20 1865

Troy RECORD. w,sw Jl 1834-1903||
1834-Ag 1880 as Troy whig; S 1880-96 Troy telegram
w 1834-96
MWA N 10 1835;Jl 7,D 8 1840[41-Ap 5 1842]
NT Je 20 1896-Je 1903

Troy morning RECORD. d Jl 1 1834+
1834-Ag 28 1880 as Troy daily whig; Ag 30 1880-81? Troy morning telegram and whig; 1882?-96 Troy daily telegram
MWA S 23 1834;N 11 1835;Ja 19 1837;Jl 14 1840;Ap 8 1842;N 4 1862;N 30 1863;My 16 1867;Ag 19-22 1870;S 25 1876;Je 9 1880
N [1835]Jl 1836-46;48-82;85+
NNGe 1842
NNHi N 16 1854;62-63;F 21,Mr 7,My 13,Ag 3, N 25 1865
NT 1834-Ag 1880;81-86;Jl 1887-91;96+
NTR 1834-Je 1839
NhD O 1 1841;N 5 1845
OClWHi Ap 6 1861
P-M Ap 24 1855
PHi [Jl-O 1834]
WHi Ja 4 1843

Troy RECORD. [evening ed] d D 6 1899+
NT 1899+

RENSSELAER advertiser. w O 1 1863-
N My 5 1864
NT 1863-My 5 1864

RENSSELAER county gazette. *See* Lansingburgh gazette

RENSSELAER county post. w S 22 1846-
N 1846-S 14 1847
NT 1846-Ja 2 1849

Troy REPUBLICAN. w Jl 1 1828-30||
Ct N 25 1828
DLC My 19,Jl 28,Ag 25,S 15,N 24 1829
NNHi Je 2 1829
NT 1828-Ja 5 1830

Troy REVIEW. sm Ja 4 1826-D 20 1827||
NBHi Ja 4 1826
NT complete

Troy SENTINEL. sw Jl 15 1823-D 28 1832||
Follows Troy post
CtY Ja 28 1831
MWA Jl 6,S 24,O 15 1824;Ja 4-7,Jl 12,N 29 1825;Je 12,O 16 1827;Ja 29 1828
DLC Jl 16,Ag 6,S 21,N 2-5 1824;D 2 1825;Mr 18,Jl 1 1828;Jl 17,31,S 15-18,O 6,27,D 1,26-29 1829;Ja 15,22-26 1830;F 21 1831;N 13 1832
N 1823-Jl 3, S 18 1827
NN O 13,27 1826
NSchU 1824-Ag 5,D 27 1825-Ja 19 1827
NT complete
NcD My 4 1824
NhD F 23 1827
NjHi N 28 1823;N 25 1828
OClWHi S 19 1828

Daily Troy SENTINEL. d My 1 1830-Ag 1831||
CSmH Je 28 1830
MWA S 27 1830

STANDARD-PRESS. d O 17 1877-1915||?
1877-1911? as Evening standard
N S 26 1881;Mr 1913-Ja 1915
NT 1894;96-99

STATE gazette. *See* Lansingburgh gazette

Troy TELEGRAM. *See* Troy record

Troy daily TIMES. d Je 25 1851+
pub 1851+
DLC Mr 6,My 5 1862;O 12 1864
IC Ap 30 1889
IU F 23 1863
M Ag 17 1931
MBAt Ap 15,20 1865
MWA Ag 18 1852;Ap 12 1856;Jl 25 1864;Ag 18,20 1870;D 10 1872;Mr 29,D 9 1873;F 22 1877;D 11 1878;S 4 1900;Ap 15 1916
N 1851-F 15 1935
NNHi My 8 1854;Mr 17 1860;D 31 1861;Je 31,S 12,17,22-23,N 1,12,D 15,20 1862[63-66]My 3
NT 1851-Mr 1903
OClWHi Mr 22 1866
P-M D 5 1857
WHi Jl 27 1863-65

Troy TIMES. w,sw 1856-1917||?
w 1856-98?
CtY Ap 23 1870
DLC Ja-Je 1866;Ja-Jl 1879;Ja-Je 1880;Jl-D 1885;88;Jl-D 1889;Ag 1890-Je 1891;Ja-Je 1892
ICM Je 4 1891
N Je 1856-Jl 1859;Ag 1863-F 1871;72-Je 1881; 1911-17
WHi Ag 1863-65

Troy semi-weekly TIMES. sw Ap 1906-D 1932||
pub complete
DLC Ap-Je 1901;Jl 1902-Mr 1903
NT complete

Troy daily TRAVELLER. d 1854-Ja 26 1856||
Follows Troy daily post
NT O 2 1854-Ja 1855

TROJAN. d D 23 1834-Mr 31 1835||
N Ja-Mr 1835
NNHi complete
NT 1834-Mr 27,31 1835

TROJAN observer. w *See* Troy observer-budget

Troy daily UNION. d My 18 1861-
NSyU My 28 1861
NT My-Jl 1861

Troy WATCHMAN. sw F 22 1830-32||
1830-31? as Northern watchman
CSmH Ag 24 1830
ICHi 1830-Ja 14 1832
MBAt My 3 1831
MWA Ja 9 1832

Troy WHIG. *See* Troy record

TRUMANSBURG

Trumansburg ADVERTISER. w
Title varies slightly
Ct F 1 1837
NIC Je 26 1839-Je 17 1840

FREE PRESS. w 1885-D 27 1890||
United with Trumansburg sentinel to form Trumansburg free press and sentinel
NIC 1889-90

Trumansburg FREE PRESS and sentinel. w 1866+
1866-75? as Tompkins county sentinel; 1876-90 Trumansburg sentinel
NIC Mr 30 1881-1924

Trumansburg NEWS. w S 7 1860-F 18 1864||
N D 6 1861
NIC 1860-Ag 1861;N 28 1862-64

TOMPKINS county sentinel. *See* Trumansburg free press and sentinel

TUCKAHOE

SPY. w
NNHi D 30 1914-Mr 6 1915

TULLY

Tully TIMES. w Ja 1 1883+
pub 1883+

TURIN

Turin GAZETTE. w Mr 17 1881-86||
N Mr 17 1881;Mr 19 1885;F 18 1886
NJR Je 12 1884

LEWIS county democrat. *See* Lowville herald (Lowville)

UNADILLA

HOME and abroad. *See* Unadilla times

Unadilla TIMES. w 1855+
1866-75 as Home and abroad
pub 1897+
MWA S 14 1876
NSyU My 23 1861

UNION

Union ENDICOTT news. *See* Endicott times (Endicott)

Union NEWS. *See* Endicott times (Endicott)

Union NEWS-DISPATCH. *See* Endicott times (Endicott)

UNION SPRINGS

Union Springs ADVERTISER. w Ap 1865+
pub 1880+
NAuW Ja 15,29 1885
NN F 27 1873

CAYUGA tocsin. *See under* Auburn

CENTRAL New-Yorker. w Je 1 1865-
MWA Jl 13 1865

UNION VILLAGE. *See* GREENWICH

UTICA

AMERICAN citizen. w Je 8 1830-
CSmH Ag 3 1830
MWA Ag 3 1830
N Je 8 1830

L'AVVENIRE. w 1900-05||?
In Italian
NU [O 1900-D 2 1905]

CAMPAIGN. Ag 30 1879-
NUHi Ag 30 1879

CENTRAL independent. w Ja 1855-
1855-57 as Ilion independent (Ilion). Merged with Utica herald
NHerHi Ja-D 17 1857
NU 1858

CENTRAL New York demokrat. *See* Utica deutsche zeitung

CENTRAL news. w 1845-
Title varies: Central Washington news
MWA S 1 1848
N F 4 1848
NSyU N 19 1847;Ja 28,F 25,Mr 10 1848

CENTRAL Washington news. *See* Central news

La COLONIA. w 1914-29||
1914-27 as Il Pensiero italiano
In Italian
IU S 8 1928-Ap 20 1929
NU [Jl 1914-Je 23,S 1928-Ap 20 1929]

*COLUMBIAN gazette. w Mr 21 1803-Je 1825||
Follows Columbian patriotic gazette (Rome) (not in this list). United with Utica sentinel to form Utica sentinel and gazette
N Ap 16 1822;F 4-11 1823;Ag 31,S 14 1824
NN Je 26 1821
NUHi 1821-25

Utica DEMOCRAT. w Ag 1 1836-52||
1836-S 3 1839 as Democrat. Merged with Utica observer
MWA Ag 31 1841
N D 12 1837;S 11 1838;S 1839-Ag,N 8 1842;My 9 1843-S 2 1845
NCH S 13-20 1836
NU [S 13 1836-S 5 1837;S 11 1838-S 3 1839] Mr 17 1846

DEMOCRATIC rasp. w Jl 24-N 9 1840||
NCH S 12,O 2,N 9 1840
NU complete

DEMOCRATIC sledge hammer. Ag 21- 1840||
NU Ag-O 29 1840
NUHi S 11 1840

Utica DEUTSCHE zeitung. w,sw 1853+
1853-54? as Central New York demokrat; 1855-71? Oneida demokrat
sw 1853-54?;65+;w 1854?-64
In German
NU 1901+

Utica evening DISPATCH. d 1899-1900||
United with Utica morning herald and daily gazette to form Utica herald-dispatch
CLM F 14 1900

Y DRYCH. (The mirror) w 1851+
In Welsh
CLM Ap 6 1893
CSmH D 1 1860
MWA D 28 1865;Mr 25 1869;My 16 1878;Ap 8 1880[F 17-Je 9 1881]Ap 6,Jl 6 1882;O 4,D 20 1883;O 23 1890;Ja,N 26 1891;Je 23,Jl 7,N 10 1892-[93-1901]-Mr 1 1917;Ap 1 1926
IU O 25 1917-[25]+
NU [N 15-D 1902]-Jl 1918;Ja 29 1920;Mr 24 1921
NcD Mr 29 1900;Ag 20-O 8 1903;Ap 28-My 5,26,Je 9-23,Jl 7-21,Ag-S 8,O 13,D 22 1904;Ag 17,S 14,N 30 1905;F 27 1908

ELUCIDATOR. w My 7 1826-My 1834||
United with Sentinel and gazette to form Oneida whig
CSmH S 14 1830;F 21 1832
N [Mr 20 1832-Ap 1 1834]
NCH Jl 10,Ag 7,S 18-25,O 16,N 13,D 4 1832
NNHi 1830-31
NU D 17 1833
NUHi 1829-My 20 1834
P-M F 19 1833

EQUALIZER. w 1850||
Campaign paper
NCaz S 7-N 2 1850

FIFTY cent weekly. w
NUHi D 17 1859

FREE trader. w
NCaz S 17 1846-My 6 1847

FRIEND of man. w Je 1836-42||
Follows Standard and democrat. Followed by Liberty press
CtY Jl 6 1841
DLC [1836]
MiU N 17 1836;Ja 12,Ap 26,My 3 1837
N Ja 15,Je 3,S 9-16,O 7,21,N 4-11,D 1 1840;Ja 5-12,26-F 2,16 1861
NIC 1836[37-40]-Ja 1842
NN [1836-37]38;O 16 1839-O 7 1840;F 2,16,Mr 2,16,Ap 6,My 4-11,Jl 13,S 28 1841
NSyU F 14,S 26 1838;Ag 13(extra)D 3(extra) 1840
NhD Je 22 1841
OHU-M Ap 17 1839;D 1 1840
OO 1836-40
WMeno [1841-42]

Utica daily GAZETTE. d F 1842-Ja 29 1857||
United with Oneida morning herald to form Utica morning herald and daily gazette, later Utica herald-dispatch
DLC F 7,D 31 1851;Ja 13 1853
IU O 13 1849
MWA D 1 1852
N My 20 1846[48-55]
NSchU Je 8,Jl 27-Ag 3 1842
NSyU Ja 25 1849
NU F 3 1842-Je 1855
NUHi F 3 1842-57
WHi N 13 1851;F 2 1852

Utica weekly GAZETTE. w
Follows Oneida whig
NChM Je 26-Jl 3 1855

NEW YORK (*Continued*)

UTICA—*Continued*

Utica Saturday GLOBE. w My 21 1881-1924||
CLM Ja 25 1890
CtY O 20 1894
ICM Mr 30 1889;F 14 1891
KHi Mr 2 1895
MWA Je 7 1884;Je 8-22 1889
NChM Ag 8 1885
NEh Mr 3 1888
NFre Ja 5 1900
NU Mr 2 1895;Je 1898-F 9 1924
OHi S 14-21 1901
PPeS Je 8 1889
TxGR S 29 1900

Utica weekly HERALD and gazette and courier. w 1847-99||?
Title varies: Utica weekly herald; Utica weekly herald and gazette
MWA Je 6 1876

Utica HERALD-DISPATCH. d 1847-Ap 1922||
1847-57 as Oneida morning herald; 1858-Mr 1907 Utica morning herald and daily gazette. United with Utica daily observer to form Utica observer-dispatch
CaQMM F 28 1882
CtY 1867-73
DLC Mr 28 1849-O 1850;Ap 17 1865;S 20 1881; 98
ICM [Je-S 1881]N 12 1883;Je 5 1884
ICN Mr 3-O 22 1857
IU Ja 5 1861
KHi Mr 11 1862;Ap 17 1873
MBAt Ap 17,19 1865
MWA N 8 1852;Jl 27 1857;[O 17-N 22 1860]F 20,Mr 4 1861;S 20 1862;Jl 17 1863;Ap 7 1864; My 17 1871;Ja 10,30 1873;N 19 1874;Ag 21 1876;Je 26 1877;Je 25,D 11 1878;Ap 1,29 1884; Ja 30 1888
MnHi O 11 1861[62]Ag 31 1863
N My 22 1851;S 1913-Je 1918
NCH S 25,D 25 1849;F 5 1853;61-63;75-84;Mr 3-D 1886;Ag 1895-S 1896
NChM Ap-My 1865
NNHi Jl 17 1863;O 26 1868
NSyU O 6,12,21,28,N 9,14-15 1848;Ja 25,Mr 23 1849;Ap 18,30,My 29 1861;O 31 1862
NU 1847-Ap 1853;D 22 1898-1922
NUHi Ja-Je 1847;53-54;57-91
NUO F 1920-Ja 1922
OClWHi O 31 1864;Ja 25,Je 28 1865;Jl 6 1880; Ap 17 1882 F 13 1884;O 11 1889;Ap 15 1896
—w ed *See* Utica Sunday tribune

Utica INTELLIGENCER. w Ja 31 1826-31||
Title varies slightly
CSmH Ag 31 1830
Ct [1826]
DLC Jl 7,Ag 4,S 15,O 27 1829;Ja 26 1830
MWA O 31 1826
N Mr 7-14,My 2,Ag 8,O 31,D 5 1826;Je 19,Jl 10,S 4-11,25,N 13 1827;F 12-19,Mr 11,Ap 1, My 13,27,Je 10,Jl 1,Ag 26,O 7,28 1828;Ja 20,F 3-10,Ap 21,My 19,Ag 18-25,O 27,N 17-D 1 1829;Ja 19-26,F 9,Ap 27,Ag 24,O 26,N 9,30 1830;Ja 25-F 1 22,Mr 15-29,My 10,O 11 1831
NCH Mr 25,S 9,O 21 1828
NNHi 1826-F 13 1827;N 17 1829-Ja,F 9,Mr-O 5 1830
NU [1827-30]

Utica JOURNAL. w 1894-1907||
1894-D 7 1902 as Utica Sunday journal
NU [O 1894-O 1906]-Mr 3 1907
NUHi 1896-97

LEVER. w O 21 1831-My 22 1832||
WHi O 28 1831

LIBERTY press. w 1843-49||
Follows Friend of man
MBAt S 26,O 10,24 1843
NN Ap 26,Ag 30 1845
NNHi Ag 13,N 9 1844;My 31,Je 14,28,Jl 19,Ag 16,N 1 1845;F 14,N 19 1846;F 4 1847
NSyU Ag 1-8,22,S 19-26,O 24-31,N 14,D 5 1843;N 29 1845;Mr 2-16 1848

LA LUCE. The light. w 1901-21||
In Italian and English
NU [N 16 1901-Ja 22 1921]

MECHANIC'S press. w N 4 1829-30||
Merged with Utica intelligencer
N F 20 1830
NUHi N 14 1829-Jl 24 1830

MLOTEK duchowny. w? -Je 7 1912||
In Polish
NU O 27 1910;11-12

MODEL worker. w Jl 14 1848-
MdBJ Jl 21 1848-Ap 6 1849
NIC Jl 14-Ag 11,S 22 1848
NNHi 1848-Ap 6 1849

Utica daily NEWS. d Ja 1- 1842||
NSchU Ja-F 16,Ap 23 1842
NUHi Ja-Mr 1842

*Utica OBSERVER. w Ja 7 1817-1916||?
1818-30 as Oneida observer
1818-19 pub in Rome
CSmH S 7 1830
Ct [1826-38]
DLC S 28 1824;Ap 19 1831;D 18 1832;D 10 1833;Ap 29 1834;Je 9 1835
MBAt My 1 1827
MWA S 5 1826;D 4 1827;Mr 11 1828;D 7 1830; Ja 12 1836;My 16 1837;N 30 1852
N S 21 1824-Ap 18 1826;Ja 16,Jl 3,24,Ag 21 1827;Jl 22 1828-33;Je 29 1841;Ja 24,F 28 1843 [46-49]
NU Mr 8,Jl 19 1831;O 8 1834;Ag 13 1839-F 14 1843
NUHi F 20 1821;Ag 26 1828;O 13 1834;Ag 16 1836;37;F 9 1841;Je 24 1845;73-74
NUO O 1825-Ja 1827;F 10 1836-37;72-1916
OCl S 18 1901
WHi Jl 19(extra)1832;N 2(extra) 1847

Utica OBSERVER-DISPATCH. d 1848+
1848-Ap 1922 as Utica daily observer (title varies slightly)
pub Ap 23 1858+
CLM D 13 1890
CSmH Ag 16 1831
Ct [D 1854]
CtY Ap 19 1866;My 26 1871;N 30 1872
DLC 1866-68;Je 23 1883;98
ICM Ag 23,S 20,24,27,O 6-7 1881;D 24 1883
KHi Mr 7 1891
MWA Ag 10 1852;Ap 26 1865;Je 26 1877
MnHi Ag 13 1861;N 22 1862;Ja 10,D 26 1863;Jl 22,N 7 1865:Ag 17 1866
N [1848-50;54-55;57]N 2 1864;Ja 19,Mr 16 1867[69]F 17,25,Ap 12,My 2,Je 2 1870;Mr 8,N 23,25 1871:F 21,Je 26 1872;D 15 1873;Mr 19 1875;Je 26 1877;Ag 5 1881;My 1913+
NCH Ap 15,D 8 1859;61-64
NN Ap 21 1829;O 23 1833;O 31(extra) 1861
NNHi Ja 23 1885
NSyU Ap 20,My 25,30,Je 29,Ag 10 1861;Ag 3 1864
NU S 12 1867;Ap 24 1868;Jl 19 1870;D 15 1873; Je 30 1874,Jl 1875-79;Ap 1880+
NUHi S 18,O 8 1834;Ap 22 1835;Ag 29 1863;My 20,24,Ag 29,N 1 1879;Ja 12,24,26,S 7,15,O 30 1880
OClWHi Ap 14 1883;Ja 9 1891
WHi Ja 9 1871

ONEIDA chief w Je 28 1844-
NU S 13 1844

ONEIDA democrat. w My 21 1833-34||
Ct Je 25-Jl 2,Ag 13 1833
N O 29 1833
NU Jl 15 1834
WHi My 21,S 3-10,O 22,N 19,D 10,31 1833;Ja 9,21,F 11-25,Mr 11-18,My 20-Je 10,N 18,D 2 1834

ONEIDA demokrat. *See* Utica deutsche zeitung
ONEIDA morning herald. *See* Utica herald-dispatch
ONEIDA observer. *See* Utica observer

ONEIDA whig. w My 20 1834-O 15 1853||
Formed by the union of Elucidator and Sentinel and gazette. Followed by Utica weekly gazette
CtY Je 2 1835;Ag 2 1842
MWA Ja 31 1837;S 3 1844
N S 22 1835 Mr 9,Je 29 1841;N 1 1842;My 12 1846
NSchU Ag 9 1842
NSyU Ja 23,F 27,Mr 20 1849
NU 1834-Je 1846
NUHi 1834;D 13 1836;D 27 1842
OClWHi Mr 31-Ap 21 1835;Ap 13 1841

Il PENSIERO italiano. *See* La Colonia

Morning POST. d O 1 1834-
NU O 9-10 1834

Utica daily PRESS. d Mr 13 1882+
pub Mr 19 1883+
Ct Je 24 1907
MWA Ap 8 1884;O 29 1886
NCH Mr 19 1883-Mr 11,S 14 1893-Jl 19,S 13 1895+
NI 1927+
NU 1882+
NUHi O 1884-1919

Utica daily REPUBLICAN. d O 22 1877-
NU [1877-F 7 1879]
NUHi 1877-F 25 1879

Utica SENTINEL and gazette. w 1821-My 1834||
1821-Je 7 1825 as Utica sentinel. United with Elucidator to form Oneida whig
CSmH S 7 1830
DLC S 28,N 16,30-D 7 1824;N 18(extra)1828;Ja 8(extra),Je 30-Jl 14,Ag 4,S 1,15-29,O 27 1829
MWA D 27 1831
N D 24 1822;Ja 28,Mr 18,Ap 22,Ag 5-12,D 9,30 1823;Mr 2,Ap 6,O 5,26,N 9,D 20-28 1824;F 8 Mr 15,Je 21,Jl 26,Ag 30,S 13-20,N 1,15 1825; Ap 25 1826;Ja 19,F 13 1827;My 16 1828;Ag 4,S 1-8,29 1829;Ag 10,31,S 14 1830
NN N 18(extra)1828;Ja 8(extra)1829;Jl 31 1832
NNHi Jl 15-22 1823;Ap 20 1824-[25-My 1826]
NU Je 14 1825-Je 8,Ag 10 1827;Je 10 1828-34
NUHi 1826-32;34
WHi Ja 7 1834

Utica SENTINEL and gazette. sw
MWA Ag 1 1826;N 6 1827
N N 17 1826;S 13 1827
NCH Je 18,Jl 2,16,Ag 6 1822;Je 7 1823;F 3 1824;Ap 22,25,29,My 2,Je 3,6,24,Jl 29 1828
NN Je 13,O 20,27,N 3-7 1826
NUHi My 25,D 4 1821;Ap 22 1823;Je 1 1824; Ja 11,My 10 1825

La SENTINELLA. Mr 21 1915-
In Italian
NU 1915

Utica daily SIGNAL. d N 12 1849-
NUHi N 12 1849

SLOWO polskie. w 1910+
In Polish
NU S 25 1911-14;22+

STANDARD and democrat. w O 25 1833-42||
1833-35 as Oneida standard. Followed by Friend of man
1833 pub in Waterville
DLC F 7 1834
MWA Ja 2 1835;F 12 1836
N N 1 1833
OClWHi N 13 1835
WHi O 30 1835;Je 22,F 5 1836

Utica morning TELEGRAM. d 1920-Ja 11 1922||
NU Jl 1920-22

Utica evening TELEGRAPH. d My 1 1851-66||
IHi Ap 15,20 1865
MWA [O-N 1860]N 3 1862
MnHi Mr 4 1862;My 14 1864
N Jl 26 1858;My 11,Jl 27,29 1861[Ap-O 1862;Je 1864-Ag 1865]

NN O 19,D 7 1864
NNHi My 14 1853
NSyU Ap 20,Ag 14 1861
NU [F 15 1854-D 10 1859;61-My 12 1863;My 2 1864-Jl 1866]
NUHi N 4 1852-Je 1853;Mr 4 1858-65

TIMES. w 1914-15||?
NUHi Jl 4 1914

La TRIBUNA. w F 24 1912-
In Italian
NU F-Mr 8 1912

Utica Sunday TRIBUNE. w My 6 1877-Ap 30 1922||
NCH 1888-90;92
NU complete
NUHi N 2 1879
NUO My 1921-22
OClWHi Ap 28 1878
—d ed *See* Utica herald dispatch

TRUE democrat. w O 11 1879-
NUHi N 1 1879

Utica daily UNION. d O 12 1895-D 31 1896||
NU complete

UTICANIAN. d,tw Ap 13 1842-
d Ap-Jl 1842
NNHi Ap-Ag 4 1842

WASHINGTONIAN. w
NSchU F 25 1842

WASHINGTONIAN news. w 1845-
DLC Ja 8 1846
N Ap 30 1847

Utica WEEKLY. w
NUO 1863-65

WESTERN recorder. w 1824-33||?
CSmH S 7 1830
CtY Ag 12-18,S 16 1828
DLC F 23,Mr-D 14 1830;31
N Mr 16 1824;Ja 11 1825-26;Ja 26 1830[Ja 25-D 1831]O 16 1832;O 14 1834
NCH 1825-27;29-31;33
NN My 6,27 1834
NSchU Ja 9 1826
NU S 1825-30;Ap 5 1831;32
NUHi F 3,Ap 13,27,My 11,25 Je 8,22,Jl 20,Ag 3,31,S 14,O 12,26,N 9,23,D 7,20 1824;Ja 11-18, Mr 22,My 10,Jl 5,19-26,Ag 9-23,S 13-20,O 18 1825;26;Ag 21 1827;Mr 4 1828;S 22 1829;Ja 4-11,25-F 1,Mr 8-15,29,My 3,Ag 30-S 6,O 18,N 1-15 1831;F 14 1832;Je 4 1833

WHITESTOWN gazette. w?
NU F-D 1903

VALATIE

ROUGH notes. w 1854?+
Follows Kinderhook sentinel (Kinderhook)
Title varies: Kinderhook rough notes 1854-98? pub in Kinderhook
pub O 1934+
DLC N 11 1875-My 13 1892
MWA Jl 19 1907
N Jl 9 1886

Valatie weekly TIMES. w 1854-
N Ja 15 1856

VALLEY STREAM

Valley Stream MAIL and Gibson herald. w 1925+
pub 1925+

Valley Stream RECORD. w N 1921+
pub 1921+

VAN BUREN HARBOR

Van Buren TIMES. w
Ct F 21,Ag 5,S 16 1837
NFre Ag 19 1837
NJ 1836-37
NWe Mr 14 1837

VAN ETTEN

VALLEY breeze. w S 11 1891-1913||?
NVe 1891-Jl 18 1913

VERNON

Vernon COURIER. w Jl 1835-40||
N N 27 1838

VICTOR

Victor HERALD. w 1881+
pub [1881-98]+
NN Jl 11,25,Ag 29 1919

VIENNA. *See* PHELPS

WALDEN

CITIZEN-HERALD. w 1888+
1888-1909 as Citizen
pub 1919+
NWal [1914-18]+

Walden HERALD and recorder. w 1870-1909||
United with Citizen to form Citizen-herald
NNHi Ag 11 1875

WALTON

Walton BLADE. w
NWa 1856-59

NEW YORK (*Continued*)

WALTON—*Continued*

Walton CHRONICLE. w 1869-1916||?
Title varies: Walton chronicle-times
NWa 1871-97

Walton REPORTER. w 1881+
pub [1887-89]+
NDe Ap 1918+

WAPPINGER'S FALLS

CHRONICLE. w 1870+

WARRENSBURGH

Warrensburgh NEWS. w 1878+
pub 1878+
N 1917+
NLg 1910+
NWar 1917+

WARSAW

AMERICAN citizen. *See under* Perry

Warsaw SENTINEL. w My 20 1830-
CSmH Ag 12 1830

WESTERN New Yorker. w 1841+
pub 1841+
CaOTA My 12 1864
MWA D 13 1853;S 21 1865;Mr 6,O 9 1879
N S 14 1852
WHi O 22 1868

WYOMING county mirror. w 1848-
MWA F 18 1851;Je 29 1859
WHi Ap 25 1848

WYOMING county times. w 1872+
pub 1872+
N O 18 1917-19;My 24 1923+

WYOMING democrat. w Mr 23 1863-
MWA Ap 6 1863;S 22 1871

WARWICK

Warwick ADVERTISER. w Ja 1866+
pub [1866-79]+
NNHi S 30,O 14-21 1880;O 13 1881

WASHINGTONVILLE

ORANGE county courier. w 1928+
pub [1929-33]+

ORANGE county record. w 1899-1926||?
NNHi Ap 10 1901

WATERFORD

ANTI-MASONIC recorder. w My 20 1829-
CoD Je 17 1829-O 27,D 24 1829
NNHi Jl 28,S 29,O 20,D 1 1829

Waterford ATLAS. w D 1 1832-
DLC D 18 1833;F 5 1834
IU S 30 1835
N F 20 1833

DEMOCRATIC champion. w Ap 1840-
NHi O 27 1840

Waterford MESSENGER. w Ap 1 1865-
N Ap 1 1865

NEW YORK state journal. w 1836-
IU Ap 19 1837

Waterford REPORTER. w 1822-
CoD O 4-11,25,N 8 1825
MBAt Jl 29-Ag 5 1828
MWA Ag 9 1824;N 27 1827
N S 14 1824
NNHi N 11 1823;S 1825-O 17,31 1826;My 1827-My 6,Ag 26 1828;extra S 9 1828
NhD S 14 1824

SARATOGA recorder and anti-masonic democrat. w Je 8 1830-
CSmH Ag 31 1830
NNHi O 12-N 9 1830

Waterford SENTINEL. w My 18 1850-
IU My 25 1850;Ja 17,F 7,Mr 7-21 1863;D 28 1871
MWA Je 4 1864
N Jl 25 1857-66

Waterford TIMES. w Je 19 1901-N 3 1920||
N complete

UNION. w My 9 1832-
DLC N 14 1832

WATERLOO

*Waterloo GAZETTE. w My 28 1817-
1817-18? as Ovid gazette (Ovid)
DLC F 21 1821
NWat Ja 31-Mr 7,Je 20-Ag,S 19,O 17-24,N 14-D 12 1821
NjHi [Ja-Mr 14 1821]
OClWHi Jl 1 1824

Waterloo OBSERVER. w 1826+
1831?-57? as Seneca observer
pub 1892+
CSmH Ag 25 1830
MWA Ja 19,Mr 9 1831;Je 19 1844
N Ap 20 1831;D 19 1832;F 13,O 16 1833;O 21 1835;S 2 1852;Mr 30 1854
NN Je 11 1857;Je 2 1880
NWat 1839-40;73-81;83-95;97-98;1901-04;07-10
P-M Jl 9 1845

Waterloo REPUBLICAN. w 1822-
NWat 1822-23

SENECA county news. w 1878+
pub 1878+
N Je 1923+
NWat 1879-89;93-98;1901-08

SENECA farmer. *See under* Seneca Falls

SENECA observer. *See* Waterloo observer

WATERTOWN

ANTI-MASONIC sun. w Je 15 1830-
CSmH S 7 1830

BLACK RIVER journal. w 1844-46||
Dated also at Sackets Harbor
DLC Mr 25 1845
NhD Ag 26,S 2,D 16 1845

DEMOCRATIC standard. w 1833-35||
Follows Watertown freeman. Merged with Watertown eagle
N O 30 1833

Watertown morning DISPATCH. d Ag? 1872-79||?
N O 15 1872;Ja 13,F 15 1873;Ap 16,N 20,D 4 1874;Ja 11,F 4,25 1875;Mr 1 1876

Watertown EAGLE. w Mr 6 1832-35||
DLC S 25 1832
N O 8 1833

Watertown FREEMAN. w Ja 22 1824-33||
1824-29? as Freeman's advocate. Followed by Democratic standard
DLC My 21-28,O 29 1824;D 25 1832
MWA O 15 1824;O 5 1830
N O 29 1824
NhD Ja 4-11,25,Mr 5,O 1,1824

JEFFERSON county union. w 1855-
Follows Watertown Jeffersonian
NSyU Ap 26 1861
OClWHi Ap 12 1861

Watertown JEFFERSONIAN. w 1838-55||
Title varies slightly. Followed by Jefferson county union
DLC O 23 1852
MWA Jl 15 1839
N S 3 1844
NhD Ap 23 1844;O 28 1845;My 26 1846;F 26 1847;My 18,Jl 20,O 5 1849;O 5 1850;Ap 12 1851
WHi Je 13 1840

NEW YORK daily reformer. *See* Watertown daily times

NEW YORK reformer. w *See* Reformer and times

Watertown daily NEWS. d F? 1861-
MnHi My 20,22,24 1861
N Je 17 1861;O 9 1862
OClWHi My 9 1872

NORTHERN New York Journal. w Ag 18? 1846-
1846-47? as Northern state journal
MWA Ag 18 1847
N Jl 20 1853
NhD S 16 1846

NORTHERN state journal. *See* Northern New York journal

La PHARE des Lacs. w My 1859-
In French
CSmH Ap 28 1865
MWA Mr 15 1861
NN Ap 14 1865

REFORMER and times. w,sw Ag 1850-1924||?
1850-52? as Watertown reformer; 1853?-66? New York reformer
w 1850-93?
N Ja 29 1857;S 16 1858;S 3 1863;D 21 1865;Ja 11 1866
NNHi [Je-Jl 1859]-Ag 13 1863
NhD F 10 1853

Watertown REGISTER and general advertiser. w 1828-35||
Title varies slightly
CSmH S 8 1830
DLC N 30 1831
KHi Ag 21 1841
MWA My 28 1829
N O 16 1833

Watertown RE-UNION. w,sw? 1866-1917||?
w 1866-97?
N O 8 1868;Ja 27,Ap 14 1870

Watertown SPECTATOR. w Ja 1847-49||
NhD Mr 9 1847

Daily Watertown STANDARD. d D 1 1893-1929||
KHi Mr 28 1895
NWatrP 1893-1929

Watertown daily TIMES. d 1861+
1861-70 as New York daily reformer
pub 1861+
ICM S 22 1882;Ap 19 1888
MWA Jl 10 1876
N F 20 1874;D 31 1875;D 20 1883;F 26,Mr 22,27 1886
NBuG O 31 1877
NSc 1934+
OClWHi Jl 14 1864

WATERVILLE

ONEIDA standard. *See* Standard and democrat (Utica)

Waterville TIMES. w 1855+
pub 1858-68;70+
MWA Ag 2 1866;Ap 27 1871
N F 8 1884

WATKINS GLEN

Through Mr 1852 as Jefferson

DEMOCRATIC citizen. w 1843-50||
Follows Chemung democrat (Montour Falls)
NNHi F 9 1843;Ja 18 1844;Ja 17,Ap 11 1845

Watkins EXPRESS. w Ja 28 1864+
pub 1864+
OClWHi Jl 26 1866

Watkins INDEPENDENT. w 1866-
CtY F 7 1868

INDEPENDENT freeman. w Je 14 1850-51||
Followed by Jefferson eagle
NNHi Je 22,Jl 26,Ag 9,S 27,D 20 1850

JEFFERSON eagle. w 1851-52||
Follows Independent freeman
NNHi N 27 1851;Ap 1 1852

Watkins REPUBLICAN. w Je 3 1854-My 1863||
NNHi Je 3 1854;My 12,O 25 1855;F 8,O 2 1856;F 19,26 1857

Watkins REVIEW. w Mr 14 1896+
pub 1896+
N Ag 22 1923+
NIC 1896-[1901-02]

WAVERLY

Waverly ADVOCATE. w,sw S 17 1852-1901||
Title varies: Waverly and Athen democrat w 1852-96?
KHi Ap 21 1865
MWA Jl 22 1864
NIC 1852-53;58-68
NNHi Ag 16 1867;F 23 1869
NWav Jl 1854-1901

Waverly ENTERPRISE. *See* Waverly free press and Tiogo county record

Waverly FREE PRESS and Tioga county record. sm w O 15 1867-1914||?
1867-O 1876 as Waverly enterprise; N 22 1876-1906? Waverly free press
sm 1867-70
NIC [1886-93]95-1905;07-09;11-14
NWav N 14 1902-D 16 1904
NWavS 1871-Ja 8 1875;N 22 1876-Mr 15 1879; My 1882-92
NWavSm N 22 1876-1914

Waverly LUMINARY. w O 1851-
NWavSm N 1851-Ap 1852

Daily REVIEW. d 1876-82||
NWavSm O 1881-F 1882

Waverly SUN-RECORDER. w 1908+
1908-10? as Waverly sun
pub 1932+
M F 18 1932
OClWHi F 18 1932-33

TIOGA county tribune. w Ap 27 1882-96||?
1882-93? as Waverly tribune
NWavSm 1882-Ap 19 1883

Waverly TRIBUNE. *See* Tioga county tribune

WAYLAND

Wayland REGISTER. w 1889+
pub 1913+

UNION advertiser. w 1873-1905||?
N Je 21 1890

WEBSTER

HERALD. w 1899+
pub Ja 25 1907+

WEEDSPORT

CAYUGA chief. w 1877+
pub 1877+

Weedsport SENTINEL. w 1866+
NNHi F 16 1871-O 17 1872

WELLS

HAMILTON county democrat. w
NHerHi O 7 1892-D 29 1893

HAMILTON county journal. *See* Wells journal and republican

HAMILTON republican. w 1862-73||
United with Hamilton county journal to form Wells journal and republican
NHi Je 2 1868

Wells JOURNAL and republican. w 1870-87||?
1870-73 as Hamilton county journal

WELLSVILLE

ALLEGANY county reporter. w,tw,sw 1836-1930||?
sw,tw 1895-1920?
NWel 1897-1902

Wellsville FREE PRESS. *See* Genesee Valley free press

GENESEE VALLEY free press. w 1852-74||?
Title varies: Wellsville free press
OClWHi Ja 21 1863
P-M Ag 23 1854

Wellsville daily REPORTER. d 1880+
NKenHi D 2 1930
NWel 1897-1906

NEW YORK (*Continued*)

WEST FARMS

Papers published in West Farms are listed under New York City

WEST MENDON

HONEOYE standard. w
NNHi O 26,D 21 1837

WEST NEW BRIGHTON

Papers published in West New Brighton are listed under Staten Island

WEST SENECA

West Seneca BULLETIN. w Je 10 1904-09||?
N Je 24 1904

WEST TROY

West Troy ADVOCATE. w O 1837-
Title varies: West Troy advocate and Watervliet advertiser
N O 9 1837-Mr 28 1849
NN S 23,N 18 1857;Ag 28 1861

ALBANY county democrat. w 1860-84||?
MWA F 23 1867
MnHi O 12 1865
N Mr 28(supp)1868

NEW YORK palladium. w N 5 1829-
CSmH Ag 3 1830
DLC N 12 1829

WEST WINFIELD

Winfield STANDARD. w Ag 23 1859-76||
1859-70 as Standard bearer
N Mr 28 1860 S 25,O 16 1861
NHerHi 1858-D 21 1870;73
NHi Ag 10 1859

STANDARD bearer. *See* Winfield standard

West Winfield STAR. w Ag 18 1892+
NHerHi 1892-1908
NRom 1900

WESTBURY

Westbury TIMES. 1915+
pub 1927+

WESTCHESTER

Papers published in Westchester are listed under New York City

WESTFIELD

AMERICAN eagle. w 1831-38||
Follows Chautauque phenix
OClWHi My 7 1833

CHAUTAUQUE phenix. w 1829-31||
Follows Western star. Followed by American eagle
CSmH Jl 27 1830
MWA My 17-24 1831
N Ja 27-F 3 1830
NFre 1829;D 28 1830
NJ 1829-31

LAKE SHORE enterprise. w 1868-71||
NWe O 2 1869;Mr 12 1870;Ap 8 1871

Westfield MESSENGER. w Ag 6 1841-51||
Followed by Westfield transcript
DLC Ag 6-13 1841
NFre 1841
NJ 1841-50
NNHi Mr 9 1842
NWe Je 8-Jl 13 1842;Mr 8 1843;Mr 27,My 1,Ag 28 1844;Mr 5,Ap 9,N 10-17 1845;Jl 26,Ag 23,N 24,D 22 1847;Mr 1,Ap 12 1848;Mr 20,Ap 10,My 15,22,Jl 31-Ag 14 1849
P-M Ap 16 1845

PANTHEON. sm Je 8 1830-
CSmH Je 8 1830
NFre Je 23,Jl-Ag,S 15 1830
NJ 1830-31

Westfield RECORD. w 1897-98||?
NWe Jl 13 1897

Westfield REPUBLICAN. w Ap 25 1855+
pub 1855+
CtY [1933]
MWA Je 22 1864;N 15 1865
N S 1917-19
NWe 1855-Mr 1862[63-70]73-Mr 1885;87+

Westfield TRANSCRIPT. w 1832-57||?
Follows Westfield messenger
NWe Ja 15 1852;Je 2 1853;Ag 24 1854;F 22,My 5 1855

WESTERN argus. w 1857-58||
Followed by Dunkirk press and Western argus (Dunkirk)
NWe Ja 5,F 16 1858

WESTERN star. w Je 3 1826-28||
Followed by Chautauque phenix
MWA F 8 1828
N Je 3-Jl 29 1826
NJ complete

WESTHAMPTON BEACH

HAMPTON chronicle. w 1907+
pub 1907+
N S 1917-19
NRiHi Je 1931+

WESTPORT

Westport COURIER. w S 20 1849-
Suspended from Mr 15-Ap 26,O 8-N 15 1850
N 1849-My 9 1851
NNHi O-N 1 1849;Ja 18,F 8-22,Mr 8,Je 7,21, Ag 9 1850

ESSEX county times. *See* Westport patriot and Essex county advertiser

Westport PATRIOT and Essex county advertiser. w O 19 1833-D 7 1848||
1833-My 1 1845 as Essex county times (Ag 4 1841-Jl 1843 Essex county times and Westport herald). Followed by Essex county reporter (Elizabethtown)
N O 23 1833
NHi O 9 1833-O 8 1834;Ag 4-11,S 1 1841;Mr 22,My 17,31,Je 14-21 1843;Ap 17,Je 6,Ag 1 O 31 1844;Mr 19 1846-48
NNHi O 9 1833-O 8 1834;41-48
NhD Ag 29 1841;S 7 1842

WHITE PLAINS

EASTERN state journal. *See* Home news and eastern state journal

HOME news and Eastern state journal. w 1845+
1845-1918 as Eastern state journal
pub 1845+
MBAt Ap 14 1865
MWA Ag 20 1852;Je 15 1860;My 17,31,Ag 2,D 13,D 6 1861;Ja 31,Ap 11,My 9 1862;F 22 1867; F 7 1873
N Ap 23 1875
NNHi O 6,27,N 17,D 29 1854[55-56]-[58-61;63-70]71;73-[75-77]-[79-95]
WHi Je 30 1865

Evening RECORD. d O 30 1902-19||?
NNHi O-D 5 1902

White Plains daily REPORTER. d O 20 1917–
pub 1917+
NWp N 1925+

WESTCHESTER county times. w S 11 1930+
pub 1930+
NMam My 15 1931+

WESTCHESTER news. w O 14 1871-Ja 24 1931||
MWA F 8 1873
NWpL complete

WESTCHESTER spy. w My 11 1830-48||
CSmH S 7 1830
DLC Je 3 1848

WHITEHALL

AMERICAN sentinel. w Je 1855-
N Je 30 1855

AMERICAN star. w 1857-
NHi Ja 1 1858

Whitehall CHRONICLE. w Je 1840-1922||?
1864-70 as Washington county chronicle. Merged with Whitehall times
DLC Mr 14-21 1845
MWA Ap 2,D 24 1841;N 19 1852
N D 23 1864;Ja 13 1865;Ja 4 1866;S 18-25,O 9 1868;Ja 1,Ag 13 1869;Ag 5 1876;F 10 1877
NFeH S 30 1842;Ja 22 1847;S 14 1855;Ja 20 1877
NHi Ap 6 1860;N 5 1870[76]Ag 11 1877[78]89-[94]Jl 20 1906
WHi Ag 26,O 28 1853;O 27 1854;F 16 1855

Whitehall DEMOCRAT. w 1844-
MWA N 5,26 1852
NHi F 2 1848;My 31 1850
NN Jl 17 1845

Whitehall EMPORIUM. w 1822-28||?
NN S 14 1824

LION. w Mr 4 1858-
NHi Mr 25 1858

NORTH STAR. w Jl-D 1834||
United with Northern post to form County post and north star, later Washington county post (Cambridge)
NFeH D 17 1834

Whitehall REPUBLICAN. w O 9 1827-
CSmH O 9 1827
Ct [1828-29]
MWA F 3 1829
N O 9 1827
NN Ag 5 1828

Whitehall evening TELEGRAPH. tw Ap 1847-
NFeH Ap 7 1847;Ap 5 1848

Whitehall TIMES. w 1860+
pub [1873-77;88-98;1919-24;26-27]29+
N F 20 1864;Ag 30 1871;O 13 1875;Ag 2 1876;F 14 1877;S 22 1880;S 21,N 9 1881;D 27 1882;Ag 3 1887;N 2 1893;Ja 23 1896
NHi N 30 1861;S 12 1863;F 5,S 3 1873[75;80]N 12 1884;O 17 1888;N 6 1890[93]F 10 1898
NNHi N 28,D 5 1888
NSyU N 12 1864
NWh [1873-85]

WASHINGTON county chronicle. *See* Whitehall chronicle

WASHINGTON county news. w Mr 7 1871-73||?
N Mr-My 20 1871
NHi [1871-73]

WHITEHALLER. w Ja 1849-
NHi Mr 16 1849

WHITESBORO

ONEIDA county gazette. w 1901-D 31 1908||
NU [1904-Ja 1905]-08

WHITESTONE

Whitestone HERALD and College Point news. w,sw My 24 1871+
1871-1930 as Whitestone herald
pub [1871+]
NNQ 1910+

WHITNEY POINT

NIOGA reporter. *See* Whitney Point reporter

Whitney Point REPORTER. w 1873+
1873-80? as Nioga reporter
pub Ap 1897+
NLi 1920;26+
OClWHi O 25 1878

WILLIAMSBRIDGE

Papers published in Williamsbridge are listed under New York City

WILLIAMSBURG

Papers published in Williamsburg are listed under Brooklyn

WILLIAMSON

Williamson SENTINEL. *See* Williamson sun and sentinel

Williamson SUN and sentinel. w 1878+
1878-Jl 30 1925 as Williamson sentinel
pub F 1885+

WILLIAMSVILLE

AMHERST bee. w Mr 20 1879+
pub 1879+

WINDHAM

Windham JOURNAL. w 1857+
N N 15 1859;My 11 1865;Jl 20 1871;D 23 1875; Ag 17,N 2 1876;Ap 18 1878;Ja 23,Mr 30,Jl 17 1879;Ja 10 1880;Ag 31 1882;Jl 26 1883[86] Ja 27,Je 2 1887;Ag 31 1893;My 20-27 1915

WINDSOR

Windsor STANDARD. w 1878–
pub 1878-1902;10+

WOLCOTT

LAKE SHORE news. w O 8 1874+
pub 1874+

WOODHAVEN

Woodhaven ADVERTISER and literary gazette. d 1853||
NBHi Ag 6-13 1853

LEADER-OBSERVER. w 1909–
pub 1911+

WOODSIDE

Woodside HERALD. w O 1927+
pub 1934+

WORCESTER

Worcester TIMES. w 1876+
pub 1876+

WYOMING

Wyoming REPORTER. w 1885+
pub 1930+
NWy 1896;98;1900-14

YONKERS

CLARION. w 1862-N 1863||
United with Yonkers examiner to form Yonkers statesman

Yonkers EXAMINER. w F 1856-N 26 1863||
United with Clarion to form Yonkers statesman
N N 4 1858
NNHi S 4 1856
NY Ja 29 1857-63

Yonkers GAZETTE. w 1851-1923||?
Title varies: Gazette. Journal for Westchester, Rockland and Putnam counties
CSmH D 23 1865
DLC My-D 16 1865
MBAt My 1865-My 19 1866
MHi My 1865-Mr 24 1866
MWA [S 16-D 1865;Ja 13-Mr 17 1866]N 4 1876
NN O 22,N 19 1887-Ja 7 1888
NNHi My 1865-My 5 1866;Mr 26 1870
PHi My 1865-Ap 28 1866
WHi My 1865-Ap 1866

Yonkers HERALD. d 1889-Mr 14 1932||
United with Yonkers statesman to form Herald-statesman
NY 1900-32

NEW YORK (*Continued*)

YONKERS—*Continued*

HERALD-STATESMAN. d N 10 1883+
1883-Mr 14 1932 as Yonkers statesman (O 3 1921-Je 12 1924 Yonkers statesman news)
pub 1883-O 3 1921;Je 12 1924+
MWA O 31 1895
NY 1883+

Daily **RECORD.** w,d S 1912+
1912-F 1932 as Sunday record(w)
pub 1912+

Yonkers **STATESMAN.** w D 3 1863-99||?
Formed by the union of Clarion, and Yonkers examiner
pub 1874-99?
N Ja 26 1871
NN F 16 1865;Ap 28,Je 2 1870;N 9,30 1871;Ja 4,25 1872;O 31 1895
NNHi Ja 28,F 18-25,Mr 3 1864
NY complete

Yonkers **STATESMAN.** d *See* Herald-statesman

WESTCHESTER news. w My 6 1853-Ja 1856||
1853 pub in New Rochelle
MWA [1853]Ja 20,F 24-My 3,24,Ap 7,Jl 2 1854
NNrS 1853-Ap 28 1854

YORKTOWN HEIGHTS

Yorktown **HERALD.** w Je 1 1924+
pub 1924+

NORTH CAROLINA

AHOSKIE

HERTFORD county herald. w 1905+
pub [1915-16]+
NcD N 11 1910

HERTFORD herald. w 1905-06||?
NcD Mr 30,Jl 13 1906

ALBEMARLE

Albemarle **CHRONICLE.** *See* Chronicle (Concord)

Albemarle **ENTERPRISE.** *See* Stanly news-herald

Albemarle **NEWS.** *See* Stanly news-herald

PIEDMONT press. *See* Stanly news and press

Albemarle **PRESS.** *See* Stanly news and press

STANLY enterprise. *See* Stanly news-herald

STANLY news and press. w,sw 1919+
1919-21? as Piedmont press; 1922-28 Albemarle press
w 1919-28
pub 1919+
NcAl 1929+

STANLY news-herald. w,tw,sw 1891-1928||
1891-97? as Stanly news; 1898-1911? Stanly enterprise; 1912-17? Albemarle enterprise; 1918-19? News. United with Albemarle press to form Stanly news and press
w 1891-1917?;tw 1918-19?
NcAl 1928
NcAlP [1901-09]-28
NcD Ja 19 1893;S 25,30,N 25 1919;Je 7 1921;D 1 1922

ASHEBORO

BULLETIN. w 1905-20||?
Nc 1914-15

COURIER. w 1876+
Early years as Asheboro courier
pub 1876+
DLC Je 1 1881
Nc 1903-12;14-[18]-[21]+
NcD O 7 1879;O 1 1884;Mr 3 1892;D 30 1920
NcU My 22 1885;O 25 1894;O 17 1895;My 28, Je 18,S 10-17,N 26 1896;S 2-9 1897;Mr 30-Ap 20,My 4,Ag 17 1899;Ap 16 1903;Ja 2 1904;S 13,N 15-D 1917;Ja-Mr,Ap 11 1918;N 10 1921; S 28,D 7 1922[23-24]-Ag 11,O 13-N 3,17 1927

NORTH CAROLINA bulletin. w F 15 1856-
NcGrW Jl 12,Ag 9 1856

RANDOLPH herald. w Ap 14 1846-
NcD Ap 21 1846-Ap 13 1847
NcU Jl 5 1848

RANDOLPH regulator. w F 2 1876-79||
NcD Mr 14 1877
NcGrW Mr 1,S 20 1876
NcU 1876-Ja 24 1877

RANDOLPH tribune. w Je 1924+
pub 1924+

SOUTHERN citizen. w D 31 1836-
1836-Ja? 1840 as Southern citizen and man of business
DLC N 27 1840
NcD F 4,N 25 1837[38-40;44]
NcU 1836-37;F 8 1839-Ja 24 1840

ASHEVILLE

Asheville daily **ADVANCE.** d 1883-87||?
NcAsS D 30 1887
NcD Ag 20 1885
NcU F 22,Je 14,20,Jl 7,D 19 1885[S-N 1886]Ja 4,Ap 28 1887

Asheville **ADVOCATE.** w 1915+
1915-23? as Labor advocate
NNC [1931-33]
NNC-B 1931+

BLUE RIDGE republican. w 1926+
pub [1926+]

Asheville **CITIZEN.** w,sw F 3 1870-1918||?
1870-D 30 1880? as North Carolina citizen
sw N 1894-1910?
DLC Je 2 1881
Nc Mr 28,My 9 1872;78-81;Jl 1882-[84-85]-[89]-O 18 1901
NcD Jl 17 1873;My 6 1886;Ap 21,Ag 25,D 1,15 1887;Ja 5,F 9 1888
NcHi Ap 11,25 1872
NcU Mr 31 1870;Ja 4 1872;My 14,O 12,N 2 1876;F 15,Mr 1-8,Ap 19 1877;Ag 14 1879[Jl-D 1881;Ag-D 1883;F-O 1884]
TKL Ja 4 1872

Asheville **CITIZEN.** sw 1882-84||?
1882? as North Carolina citizen
NcU [1882]Ja 2,20-24,F 7,17 1883;D 20 1884

Asheville **CITIZEN.** d 1885+
1895? as Asheville daily citizen
Sunday issues as Asheville citizen-times
S 9 1912 is historical and trade ed
DLC Mr 1932+
Nc F 1889-95;Ag 1-17,D 19 1896-My 18 1897; 1902-Mr,My 1903-Ap,Ag 30 1921+
NcAs 1908+
NcAsS O 2 1885;Jl 29,30;Ag 1 1886;Je 3 1893; Jl 15,D 15,19 1899;My 13 1902;Ap 25 1910;Ap 12 1914;N 12 1916;My 26 1918;My 8 1919;S 20 1920;Mr 18,25,S 23,D 26 1928;F 22 1931;D 25 1932
NcD D 20 1885;Ap 24(supp)Je 15 1886;Mr 9 1887;Ja 29,Mr 13 1888;Ag 23 1895;My 24,S 20 1903;S 29 1912;Ja 2,F-[My]1925
NcHi N 28 1895;Ag 5 1898;Mr 13 1902;N 30 1921;Ap 19 1930
NcU [1885-89]Je 17,S 23 1896;Jl 3,6 1897;Jl 8,Ag 23 1898;O 8 1903
TU My 2 1886;Mr 23 1912

Asheville **CITIZEN-TIMES.** *See* Asheville citizen; Asheville daily times

Asheville **DEMOCRAT.** w O 10 1889-S 25 1892||?
Nc 1889-S 1892
NcAsS D 5,19 1889

Asheville daily **GAZETTE.** *See* Asheville daily times

HIGHLAND messenger. *See* Asheville messenger

Asheville semi-weekly **JOURNAL.** sw 1878-81||?
NcD Ap 2 1879

Evening **JOURNAL.** d 1888-91||?
NcAsS D 7,11 1889
NcU My 18,Jl 13,15 1889

LABOR advocate. *See* Asheville advocate

Asheville **MESSENGER.** w Je 5 1840-
1840-46? as Highland messenger (Ag 1842-Ja 1843 Messenger)
DLC Je 13,O 30 1840;Mr 19 1841-Jl 15,Ag-O 7,28,N 18-D 16,30 1842;Ja 13-27,F 10-Ap 21, My-Je 1,16-Jl 7 1843;Ja 6 1848
ICHi Ja 31,Mr 14 1845
MoS 1840-Je 16 1843
NcAsS Ap 10 1846
NcD [1841-44]S 27,N 22,D 27 1849;Mr 6,Je 19,Jl 24,Ag 7-14 1850;Ag 27 1851
NcHi Mr 20 1846
NcU Je 10,S 30 1842;F 6 1844;Je 6 1845;Ag 23,O 29 1849;Ap 17,My 29,O 23,D 11 1850;Mr 12,Ap 16-30,Jl 23,Ag 6,N 12,26 1851;Ap 21,My 26,O 27 1852
NhD My 28 1841

Asheville **NEWS and western farmer.** w 1849-
1849-62? as Asheville news
DLC Jl 28 1853
ICHi O 28 1852
Nc F 23 1854-59;62;Mr 28,My 9 1872
NcHi Mr 12 1868
NcU My 18,Jl 27 1854[69]
T Je 14 1855

NORTH CAROLINA citizen. *See* Asheville citizen

Weekly **PIONEER.** w Je 1866-79||?
1866-69? as Asheville pioneer
DLC D 1,15-22 1870;F-D 19 1874;N 24(supp) 1870
Nc Je 8 1871-Je 1872
NcD Ag 15 1872
NcU O 17,N 7 1867;F 13,Mr 12 1868;My 20,Ag 26-O 7,23-N 6 1869

Asheville **REGISTER.** w 1892-1906||?
1892-1903? as Register (1895?-96? State register) 1904?-05? Asheville Saturday register
NcAsS Mr 31 1894;S 27 1895;Jl 21 1899;Ap 5, 26-My 3,Jl 19,Ag 2 1902;Ja 10 1903
NcD N 4 1905

Asheville **SPECTATOR.** w Ja 19 1853-
NcD My 11 1853;Je 19,Jl 17 1856
NcU Mr 2,Ap 27,My 18,Jl 13,N 2,D 14 1853;F 14 1856;Ag 19 1858
TKL Mr 22 1854

STATE register. *See* Asheville register

Asheville daily **SUN.** d Mr- 1888||?
Nc My 31,Je 7-Ag 5 1888
NcU Jl 6 1888

Asheville daily **TIMES.** d Ja 1892+
1892-1902 as Asheville daily gazette; 1903-F 19 1916 Asheville daily gazette-news
Sunday issues as Asheville citizen-times
DLC Je 19 1900-F 1932
Nc N 23 1897-Je 1901;02;Ag 1909+
NcAsS My 17,Je 7-8,D 3 1892
NcD O 13 1897;S 27 1899;F 3 1902;Jl 9 1910; Ap 5 1915
NcGrW Ag 15 1900
NcHi Jl 16 1916
NcU Jl 3 1892
WaPS Ja 9-13,16 1930

WESTERN expositor. w Ja 30 1873-77||?
NcU Ap 10 1873
TU S 4 1873

AULANDER

Aulander **ADVANCE.** w 1923-26||
United with Windsor ledger to form Ledger-advance, later Bertie ledger-advance (Windsor)
NcWdL complete

AYDEN

Ayden **DISPATCH.** w 1914+
pub [1917-Mr 1920]+

BAKERSVILLE

ROAN MOUNTAIN republican. w My 27 1876-80||?
NcD Jl 8,S 24,O 7 1876;F 3 1877;Mr 12 1879

BATTLEBORO

Battleboro **ADVANCE.** w 1870-73||?
NcD Jl 5 1872

BEAUFORT

CARTERET county telephone. w 1881-85||?
NcD D 23 1881;D 12-19 1884

Beaufort **EAGLE.** w Ap 26? 1876-
NcD Jl 29,O 7 1876
NcU My 17,31,Je 14,Ag 17 1876

Beaufort **NEWS.** w 1912+
pub 1917+
Nc F 1925+

OLD north state. w,sw D 24 1864-
w 1864-Ja 1865
DLC Ja 7-21,F 10-Mr 25,Ap 8-15 1865
NN Ap 1 1865

Weekly **RECORD.** w 1886-88||?
Nc Ja 13 1887-N 23 1888
NcD N 4-18 1887

BENSON

Benson **REVIEW.** w 1911+
pub 1913+

BESSEMER CITY

DISPATCH. *See* Journal

JOURNAL. w 1912-18||?
1912-13? as Dispatch
Nc Mr 8-D 20 1912

BOONE

WATAUGA democrat. w 1888+
Nc [Ag-D 1888]-[92-93]-[95]-[99;1901-05]07-[09]-15;18-N 16 1922;23+

BREVARD

FRENCH BROAD hustler. *See* Hendersonville news (Hendersonville)

Brevard **NEWS.** *See* Transylvania times

SYLVAN VALLEY news. *See* Transylvania times

TRANSYLVANIA times. w Ja 1 1896+
1896-1908 as Sylvan Valley news; 1908-31 Brevard news
pub 1896+
Nc 1907;09-11

BRYSON CITY

SWAIN county herald. w Ja 1889-90||?
Nc 1890

Bryson City **TIMES.** w 1895-96||?
Nc [1895]96

BURGAW

PENDER star. w 1895-97||?
NcD My 14,O 29,N 26,D 10 1896;Ja 6,20,F 11, 25,Mr 11,S 23-O 14 1897

NORTH CAROLINA (*Continued*)

BURLINGTON

Burlington CITIZEN. w 1908-30||?
1908-24? as Burlington journal; 1925? Burlington herald.
Nc F 28-D 19 1923

Burlington HERALD. *See* Burlington citizen

Burlington JOURNAL. *See* Burlington citizen

Burlington NEWS. w,sw 1887-1930||?
United with Burlington daily times to form Daily times-news
w 1887-1924
Nc [Ja,Je-D 1900]
NcD My 23 1888;S 6 1905;N 4 1920
NcU Ap 13 1904

STATE dispatch. w My 1908-17||?
Nc N 18 1908-12
NcU O 7 1908

Daily TIMES-NEWS. d 1922+
1922-30? as Burlington daily times
pub 1931+
NcEloC F 1927+

CARTHAGE

Carthage BLADE. w 1886-D 1911||
United with Moore county news to form Moore county news and Carthage blade, later Moore county news
Nc Ag 10 1887-97;1902-07

CARTHAGINIAN. w Ja 3 1878-79||?
NcD Ja-Mr 7,21,Ap 4-11,My 9-Je 13,Ag 29 1878

MOORE county news. w 1904+
1912-18? as Moore county news and Carthage blade
MWA Ap 11 1918
Nc 1920-Ja 7,D 16 1926+
PHsHi Je 24 1920

MOORE gazette. w 1881-85||?
DLC F 17 1881
NcD Je 10 1881;My 14,Jl 31,S 11,O 16,D 25 1884-Ja 2 1885
NcU O 25 1883

MOORE index. w O 9 1879-80||?
NcD N 27,D 18 1879;F 12,Mr 18 1880

CHAPEL HILL

COLUMBIAN repository. w Je 18 1836-
NcD Je 18,Jl 2-9,28,S 15,O 8 1836
NcU Je 18,Jl 16 1836

HARBINGER. w Ag 27 1833-
NcD O 29 1833;Ja 16,30,Ap 3-10,My 1,Jl 5,26-Ag 2 1834
NcU S 10-17,N 5-12 1833;Ja 2,Mr 13,Jl 19 1834

Chapel Hill LEDGER. w Ap 18 1878-80||?
1878-Jl 1879 as Weekly ledger
DLC My 11-18,Jl 20,D 21 1878;F 1-8,Mr 1-8, Je 7,21-Jl 5,26,O 18,N 8-15 1879;Ap 24 1880
NcU [1878-S 1880]

Chapel Hill LITERARY gazette. w Ap 1857-
NcU Je 13,Jl 25 1857;F 27,Je 25,Jl 17 1858

Chapel Hill NEWS. w O 12 1893+
NcD Je 14,Ag 2-23,N 15 1906
NcU O 19,30,N 16-23,D 14-21 1893;Ja 4-11,25 1894;N 4 1898;N 2 1899;Je 16 1904;Ja 30 1908

Chapel Hill WEEKLY. w Mr 1 1923+
Nc Mr 1927—
NcU 1923+

CHARLOTTE

Tri-weekly BULLETIN. tw 1840-81||?
DLC Ja 8 1881
NcD My 30,Je 8 1865
—w ed *See* Charlotte weekly courier

Evening BULLETIN. d My 17 1859-78||?
1859-68? as Daily bulletin
DLC F 24-25,Mr 6,My 9,16,25,D 22 1863;Ja 18,F 24,Jl 7 1864;F 25-26,Mr 2-4,7,21,23-24,26, 28,30,Ap 2,4-5,11 1865;Je 8 1881
MH Ja 3,Mr 10 1865
Nc N 23,D 28 1863;Mr 23(supp)1868
NcD My 17 1859;S 1 1860;My 9-10 1862;My 10,O 3 1863;S 25 1864;Ja 13 1868
NcHi Jl 19 1861
NcU [1859-64:69]
OClWHi D 2 1863

Daily CAROLINA observer. *See* Daily Charlotte observer

Daily CAROLINA times. d 1854-70||?
Nc Jl 11 1864 Je 15 1869
NcD N 4 1862
NcU N 19 1866;F 7 1867[My-N 1869]

CATAWBA journal. 1824-27 *See* Journal (Salisbury)

Weekly CATAWBA journal. w 1859-
Nc Je 10 1862
NcD Je 30 1863;Mr 24,Ag 30 1864
NcU Ja 24-31 1860

Evening CHRONICLE. d My 25 1903-My 7 1914||
United with Charlotte news to form Charlotte news and evening chronicle, later Charlotte news
Nc 1909-Mr 1914
NcD Jl 25 1907;N 17 1909;O 6,D 2,11 1911;Ag 10,N 26 1912

Charlotte daily CHRONICLE. *See* Charlotte observer 1886+

Charlotte weekly COURIER. w 1865-81||?
DLC Je 3 1880;Ja 13 1881
—tw ed *See* Tri-weekly bulletin

Charlotte DEMOCRAT. w Jl 10 1852-O 7 1897||
1852-D? 1870 as Western democrat; O 1881-F 1 1884 Charlotte home and democrat; F 8 1884-Jl 8 1887 Charlotte home-democrat. United with Mecklenburg times to form Times-democrat
DLC [1857]F 14,Ag 22-S 4,O 17 1865;Jl 20 1874;Ja 17 1876;Mr 21,23 1879;Jl 9,O 15 1880; Ag 5 1881;Ja 12 1883
MH F 7 1865
MWA D 17 1861;Mr 12 1862
Nc F 24 1854-Ja 5,F 9 1855-64;Ja 10,31-F 21, Mr-Ap 4,S 1865-[68]-My 22,Ag 12 1873-76;78-97
NcD Ja 29,Mr 12,D 31 1861;F 5,Jl 29 1862;N 10 1863;F 12,Ap 2-9,O 1,N 19 1867[68-73;80-86] Ag 5,26,O 7,D 2-16 1887;F 10,Ap 20,My 4,Ag-S 7,21,O 19 1888[89-90]Ap 17,Je 26,Ag 7-14 1891;Ja 15,S 30 1892
NcHi Ja 28 1853;Jl 22-29 1873;Jl 6 1894
NcU O 7 1856;F 24 1857;My 7 1861;Mr 17 1863;Mr 20,Je 19,D 18 1866;Ja 8,Mr 19 1867; F 4,18 1868[69;71-72]S 21-O 5 1874;Ja 11 1878;Je 3,Jl 15 1881;Mr 10 1882;F 23 1883;Jl 1885-[97]

Charlotte HOME and democrat. *See* Charlotte democrat

HORNETS' nest and true southron. w Jl 7 1849-
1849-50? as Hornet's nest
DLC S 7 1850
NcD S 1,15,O 27 1849;Ja 12 1850;Jl 12,Ag 30 1851
NcHi Ag 11 1849;D 7 1850
NcU Jl 7 1849[50]Ja 4,Ap 26 1851

Charlotte JOURNAL. w 1831-
DLC N 7 1839;Mr 26,D 10 1840;Jl 29-Ag 5,19, S 16-30,O 28,N 18,D 16-23 1841[42]Ag 1 1844;Ja 24-31,D 19 1845;Jl 10 1846;Mr 18, Je 24,S 16 1847;O 9 1850
NcD [Ag 1835-37]-[44-45]-51
NcU My 2 1839;Je 4 1840;Jl 25,Ag 8 1845;My 23 1851

Daily JOURNAL. d Ag 22 1882-Mr 25 1883||
United with Daily Charlotte observer to form Journal-observer, later Daily Charlotte observer
NcD complete

JOURNAL-OBSERVER. *See* Daily Charlotte observer

MECKLENBURG Jeffersonian. w Mr 9 1841-
DLC 1841-Jl 1842;Ap 13 1843;Ag 16,D 13 1844; Ja-F 14,Mr-Je 13,27-Jl 11,25-Ag 22 1845
Nc S 26 1845
NcD Mr 16 1841-Mr,Ap 5,Ag 9 1842[43-45]My 8,Je 19,S 4,18 1846;F 5,19 1847;Ap 19,Jl 12 1848
NcHi Jl 5 1844
NcU Je 28 1842;S 5 1843;O 18 1844;F 7-14,Mr 7,28,Jl 18 1845;O 23 1846;Ap 11 1849

MECKLENBURG times. 1888-96 *See* Times-democrat

MECKLENBURG times. w 1924+
Nc 1927[28]+

MINERS' and farmers' journal. w S 27 1830-
DLC O 11,N 15 1830[Mr 10 1831-O 11 1834]
NcD O 11-18,N 15 1830[31-32]-[My-S 1835]-S 1836
NcHi N 22 1830;N 27 1832
NcU Mr 28 1832
P-M S 13 1834

Charlotte NEWS. d 1888+
1888-91? as Daily news; My 8 1914-16? Charlotte news and evening chronicle D 23 1898 is Western North Carolina ed; F 21 1917 Textile, industrial and educational ed
pub [1888+]
Ct My 17-23 1931
MWA F 21 1917
MdBJ F 21 1917
Nc Jl 3 1899+
NcD Ag 5 1889;My 21 1892;D 23 1898;My 21 1903;Ag 16,N 11 1907[08]Ja 19,My 18 1909;Ap 11 1912;Je 28 1913;My 18 1915;F 1917;F 9-Ap 14,21-My 15,18,20,31 1925;Mr 17 1929
PWp F 21 1917
VU F 16-18 1915
—sw ed *See* Times-democrat

NORTH CAROLINA whig. w Ja 21? 1852-
DLC F 25,Mr 11,Ap 21,Ag 25,N 24,D 15-22 1852;F 2,Ap 20-27,My 18,Je 15,29-Jl 13 1853;F 7,Jl 13,N 21-28 1854;Je 26,O 9,30 1855;Jl 15 1856;Ap 14 1857[59-60]Je 25 1861;Ja 7,F 11, Mr 4,Ap 22,My 20-Je 3,17-Jl,S 30,O 21 1862; Ja 27-F 3 1863
MWA Ap 27,Jl 6 1853;Ap 14 1857;Mr 27 1860
NcD Ja 21,F 1852-N 4,D 2,16-23 1862;Ja 27-F 10,Mr 3 1863
NcHi Je 20,Jl 13,S 19,N 21 1854;Je 26 1855
NcU Ap 7,S 15 1852;Je 22-29,N 1 1853[54-55]Jl 15,O 28 1856;N 22 1859;Ja 3,24,F 21-28 1860

NORTH CAROLINIAN guardian. d?
NcD My 30 1867

Daily Charlotte OBSERVER. d Ja 25 1869-Je 30 1886||?
1869-72? as Daily Carolina observer; Mr 27-O 13 1883 Journal-observer
DLC Ap 4-7,9-11,13-14,My 4 1876;Jl 2,28 1880
Nc [1873-74]Ja 2-6 1875;F 1879-[84]
NcD [1873]F,Ap 1,My 1874-Mr 26,O 1883-Je 1886
NcGrW F 9 1882
NcHi Ag 24 1869;My 22 1875;Ag 20 1879;Ag 27-28,31,S 7 1881
NcU [My-O 1869]Jl 13 1873[75-76]-Je 17 1877;N 27 1878;O 16 1879;Je 30,S 24,26,29,O 6,N 4 1880

Weekly Charlotte OBSERVER. w 1869-Je 1886||?
1869-Mr 20 1883 as Weekly observer; Mr 27-D 1883? Weekly journal-observer
NcD Je 7 1883;Ja 15-Je 18 1885
NcU Ap 8 1876;N 6(supp)1879

Charlotte OBSERVER. d 1886+
1886-F? 1887 as Charlotte daily chronicle; Mr? 1887-Mr 1892 Charlotte chronicle; Ap 1892-Jl 10 1897 Daily Charlotte observer; Jl 11 1897-Ap 2 1916 Charlotte daily observer
Ct My 17-23 1931
DLC Je 26 1900-02
GAtCo Ap 24,N 7 1898
KHi S 21 1925
MWA My 18 1925
Nc Je 28 1892-Je 1894;S 7 1901+
NcD F 1,O 9 1887;F 12-14,19,Mr 3,14,O 6,N 25 1888[Mr 1893-98]-N 22 1928;29+
NcEloC 1933+
NcGrW Ja 28 1900;Jl 20 1902;F 9 1906
NcHi Jl 25,Ag 8 1897;Ag 24 1900;Jl 30 1914; Mr 4 1917
NcU [1889]D 19-20 1891;F 25 1892;F 9,16 1895;F 17,Ap 18,N 12 1897;Ja 1,My 5,21 1898; 99-1901;Jl 1902-09;Ap 1910+
OClWHi Ag 17 1905
P-M Ja 16 1913
T S 30 1930-D 6 1931
VU F 17-18 1915;Je 2 1929;Jl 12,S 15,29,O 2-3,7 1934
WHi My 18 1925;D 10 1934

PEOPLE'S paper. w 1894-1905||?
NbHi Ja 23,F 20 1901
Nc 1898-1903
NcD Ja 24 1896

Daily SOUTH CAROLINIAN *See under* Columbia, S.C.

SOUTHERN home. w 1870-S 1881||
United with Charlotte democrat to form Charlotte home and democrat, later Charlotte democrat
DLC N 10-17 1873;F 8,Je 28 1875;My 27 1881
Nc [1873]-[75-78]-[80-81]
NcD 1871;Ja 29 1872;73-Mr 13,Jl 3,D 4 1876
NcHi Mr 22,My 10,Jl 5 1875;My 7 1877
NcU [1870-73]Je 21-Jl 19,Ag 2 1875;79-My 14,Je 4,18,S 3,O 8,22 1880;Jl 15 1881

TIMES-DEMOCRAT. w,sw 1888-1922||?
1888-O 1897 as Mecklenburg times
w 1888-96?
Nc 1889-O 7 1897
NcD D 27 1894;Ja 17 1895;Jl 22 1901
—d ed *See* Charlotte news

UNION republican. w D 1867-
NcD Ap 1 1868
NcGrW Ap 14 1868

WESTERN democrat. *See* Charlotte democrat

YADKIN and Catawba journal. *See* Journal (Salisbury)

CHINA GROVE

Papers published in China Grove are listed under Salisbury

CLINTON

CAUCASIAN. *See under* Raleigh

NEWS dispatch. w 1908-23||?
Nc [N 1909-10]-17

SAMPSON democrat. *See* Sampson independent

SAMPSON independent. w 1892+
1892-Mr 20 1924 as Sampson democrat
Nc 1920[21]+
NcD O 20 1892;O 18-N 15,22 1894[95-97]Ag 8 1901
NcU Ap 28 1898
OClWHi O 10 1912

SAMPSON news. w F 19 1930+
pub 1930+

CONCORD

CAROLINA flag. w 1860-
MWA Mr 11 1862

CHRONICLE. w,sw 1907-17||?
1907-My 1913? as Albemarle chronicle (Albemarle)
w 1907-My 1913?
NcD My 9,N 7 1912[13-Mr 1917]

OBSERVER and Kannapolis star. w 1914+
1914-30? as Concord observer
NcD My 17-31,Jl 12-19,Ag 23 S 6,29 1917;Ap 18,Ag 1,N 21 1918

Concord REGISTER. w 1875-86||?
DLC S 17 1880
NcU Ja 8 1876

Concord STANDARD. w 1888-1903||?
Title varies: Standard
Nc Ja 14 1888-[93]94;Jl-D 1895;Ag 1896-[98]-1901
NcD D 14 1893;D 29 1898

Concord TIMES. w,sw 1883-D 30? 1929||
1883-90? as Times
w 1883-N 3 1903
Nc N 19-26,D 10-24 1885;86-Je 22 1892;Jl 29 1893-1929
NcD F 27-Mr 6,19-Ap 2,16 1891;Jl 28 1892;Jl 11,25-Ag 1 1901;F 6,Jl 31 1902;Ap 22,S 16,D 1 1903[04-19]Ja 19 1925
NcHi Ja 4 1889
NcU Jl 15 1886

Concord daily TRIBUNE. d 1900—
1900-10? as Evening tribune
pub [1907-Je 1922]+
Nc Jl 1904+
NcD Ap 1 1901;S 7 1905[16-19]Ja 7 1925;My 31 1932

COOLEEMEE

Cooleemee JOURNAL. w 1908+
NcD F 26,Ap 16,N 5,26 1909;Jl 22 1910;O 22 1915;Ag 25 1916;Mr 15 1923

NORTH CAROLINA (*Continued*)

DALLAS

GASTON current. w 1885-N 1887||
United with Weekly Lincoln press (Lincolnton) to form Salisbury press (Salisbury)

DANBURY

OLD constitution. w Je 3 1870-
NcD Je 17 1870

Danbury REPORTER. w Je 8 1876+
1882-95 as Reporter and post (Je 1884-92 Danbury reporter-post)
DLC Ag 26 1880
Nc 1910-O 16 1912;Ap 30 1913-15;22+
NcD Je 8,Jl 20,O 19 1876[77-90]Je 25 1891;O 11-18 1894[1904-06]Ap 1 1907;S 20 1911;O 9 1912;Ap 29 1914
NcU Jl 21 1881;Ag 13 1885;Jl 29 1886

DUNN

CENTRAL times. w F 28 1891-95||?
Nc 1891-Ag 19 1894;95

COUNTY union. w 1890-99||?
Nc 1896-99

DEMOCRATIC banner. w 1881-1903||?
Nc 1901-D 13 1902

Dunn DISPATCH. w,sw Ap 1 1914+
w 1914-19?
pub 1914+
NcD Ja 16 1918

HARNETT courier. w 1888-90||?
Nc Ag 1888-Ag 21 1889

Dunn SIGNBOARD. w 1887-89||?
Nc S 1887-Ag 15 1888
NcD Ja 19 1888

STATE'S voice. Ja 15 1933-Ag 15? 1935||
Followed by Robeson voice (Lumberton)
Nc 1933-Ag 15 1935

DURHAM

CAROLINA tribune. *See under* Raleigh

DURHAM county republican. w Jl-O 1884||
NcD Jl 15-S 23,O 1884

Durham GLOBE. w 1872-96||?
1872-Je 1895 as Durham weekly globe
NcD O 15 1889;Jl 11 1895-Je 4 1896

Durham daily GLOBE. d 1888-Jl 1895||
Nc Ag 6 1891-94
NcD O 6,12,15 1889;Je 11,Jl 24,O 30-N 6,D 23 1890;Je 28,O 8,12,26 1892;Ja 9,My 18 1893; F 2,Je 8,12,O 19 1894
NcU Ag 4 1894;Jl 25 1895

Durham morning HERALD. d 1894+
1894-O 4 1919 as Morning herald
Sunday issues as Sunday herald-sun
pub 1901-Ag 1920;21+
Nc [1895-96;98] Jl 1899-Je 1901;02-Mr,O 1915-Mr 1922;Ap 1923-D 16 1925
NcD N 26,D 19 1894;Mr 24,Ap 8,N 13,19 1896; Mr 4,My 4-5,Jl 25,Ag 29 1897;O 30 1898;N 12, D 9 1902;Ag 6 1903;Jl 31 1904;Ja 13-15,20,22, D 1,30 1905;Jl 26 1906;Je 2,4-6 1907;13-15;17-[27]+
NcDu [1922+]
NcU Jl 12 1896;Je 6 1897;F 6 1898;F 12 1899;D 31 1904

Sunday HERALD-SUN. *See* Durham morning herald; Durham sun

***Durham RECORDER.** w,sw F 8 1820-1911||
1820-Ja 1896 as Hillsborough recorder (1880-Ap 1895 Durham recorder)
1820-79; My 1895-Ja 1896 pub in Hillsboro
Suspended from Ap 19-My 3, 17-Je 26? 1865
sw 1908; 11?
DLC Mr 10,Ap 28,My 19-26 1824;Jl 8-15,29 1829;O 10,28 1832;N 5 1840;S 1 1842;45[Mr 1846-Mr 1847]Mr 8,29,S 13 1848-49;O 16,30 1850;Ap 6 1853;My 16 1855[60-62]-My 10 1865;Jl 8 1880
MWA Jl 27 1825;Ag 5 1863
NNHi D 25 1872
Nc F 22 1854-S 20,D 1861-Ap 5,S 20 1865-[68]O 31 1877-78;Ag 11 1887-[88]-Mr 1893 [95]96;1907-11
NcD N 26,D 10 1828;Ag 11 1830;Mr 9,Jl 25 1831;N 13 1835;N 4 1836;S 19 1839;F 24,Mr 24 1842;D 21 1843;Mr 28-Ap 11 1844;Ag 28 1845; Je 1 1853;S 27,O 11 1854;O 3 1855;Ap 16 1856; My 1 1861;F 17 1864;Ap 28,S 29,O 20 1869; [70-71]-Ja 3,F,Ap 3 1872;S 24 1873;Jl 15 1874; Je 29 1881;My 13,27-Je 3 1885;My 9 1888;N 19 1890;Ja 19 1899;D 6 1900
NcHi F 3 1833;Ja 30-F 6,Je 9,S 18 1835;D 1 1836;S 12 1839;Ag 3 1843;Ja 25 1844;Ja 14,Je 10 1847;Ja 17 1849;My 5,S 29 1852;N 6,D 26 1860;My 1 1861;S 20 1865;D? 1874;Jl 28 1875
NcU [Ja-F]S 1821-Jl 24,Ag 21 1822-Jl 1823;N 17,D 1,16 1824;Ap 6-13,27-My 4,18,Je-S 14 1825;Mr 7 1827;Mr-D 3 1828;Ap 8-D 9 1829 [34-36]37;Mr 9 1838-N 13 1839[40]-N 1841[42-43]-[51]-Je,Ag 25 1852-[53-56;58] Mr 2, Ap 6,S 14,N 30 1859;Ja 23,25,F 1860-Mr, Jl 26 1865;Ap 25,My 23,Je 27,Ag 29,S 5,19 1866;My 22-29,D 13 1867;Ja 8,22,F 12,Ap 15,Je 17 1868[69]F 2,Mr 16,My 18,Jl 20,O 26 1870;My 3 1871;My 28 1873;Mr 4-11, Jl 1-15,29 1874;Ag 25-S 1 1875;Ja 22 1879;Mr 17 1880;Je 29 1881;N 29 1882;Jl 15,29,S 17 1885;Ja 6,Jl 14,Ag 4 1886;N 2 1887[D 1895-F 1897]F 9 1899;Ap 16 1900
REdH N 12 1828

Durham RECORDER. d 1886-88||?
1886-N 1887 as Durham daily recorder. Merged with Durham daily globe
NcD My 7 1886;Ap 25,My 14,16,N 15,26[D] 1887;Ja 3,9-12,F 3,6-9 1888
NcU Jl 27 1886;Ja 26 1888

Daily REPORTER. d 1884-85||?
NcD Je 5 1885
NcU S 9,25-26,O 17 1885

Durham SUN. d F 26 1889+
1889-1911 as Durham daily sun
Sunday issues as Sunday herald-sun
pub [Mr-N 1910;My-S 1911]13-Je 1915;23+
Nc 1889-F,Ag 30 1894-F 1898;Jl 1910-S 1917
NcD Mr 1-2,Je 28,S 6 1889;Jl 18 1890;Ap 5,7, N 28 1892;Ja 9,13,My 19-20,Ag 3-4 1893;F 1, Mr 30,Je 12,D 15 1894;Ap 22,26,My 16,Ag 2, O 25 1895[96]Ja 30,F 15,19,Jl 24 1897;F 26 1898-Ag 1904[Ja 1905;Mr 1911-My 1913;Mr-My 1925]
NcU Ag 4 1894[96-97]F 10-11,Mr 17-18,Jl 25 1898;Ap 14 1899

TOBACCO plant. w Ja 1872-92||?
Title varies slightly
NNHi D 18 1872
Nc S 15 1886-88
NcD F 14 1872;Ap 28,S 8 1875[76-81]-Ap 5 1882;Mr 19,Jl 9-16 1884;My 13-Je 3,Jl 15-22, Ag 5-12,O 14 1885;Ap 13-27,O 26,N 23,D 7-21 1887;F 1,Je 22 1888
NcU Ap 28 1875;S 21,O 26 1887;Ja 25 1888

Daily TOBACCO plant. d Je 1888-Ag 1889||?
Merged with Durham daily globe
NcD 1888-Ag 2 1889

EDENTON

ALBEMARLE bulletin. w 1850?-
NcD S 3 1851

ALBEMARLE observer. w 1910-28||?
Nc Je 19 1914-15

ALBEMARLE sentinel. w Jl 6 1839-
DLC Jl 6 1839
NcHi Jl 6 1839
NcU N 2 1839;My 9 1840;N 20 1841

AMERICAN banner. w Mr 20 1856-
NcD O 23 1856
NcU My 8-15,Ag 7,O 2,18 1856

CAROLINA miscellany. *See* North-Carolina miscellany

Edenton CLARION. w 1879-81||?
DLC Jl 10 1880
NcU Jl 23,S 10 1881

EXPRESS. w Ag 1857?-
NcU N 2 1859

FISHERMAN and farmer. w 1886-1901||?
Nc [Ag-D 1887]-[93]-[98]-1901
NcU Jl 11,S 19 1890

***Edenton GAZETTE.** w Ja 1 1806-
1806-F 10 1807? as Edenton gazette and North-Carolina advertiser; 1814-26? Edenton gazette and North-Carolina general advertiser; Jl-Ag 1830 as Edenton gazette and farmer's palladium
DLC Ja 26 1827;F 21-27,Mr 27,Ap 22,Je 3,Jl 8, Ag 19 1830;Mr 3,23,Je 29,Ag 3,24 1831
MWA F 26 1821;My 8 1827
NcD Jl 31 1827
NcHi Ja 26 1827;F 21-27,Mr 27,Ap 22,Je 3,Jl 8,Ag 19 1830;Mr 3,23,Je 29,Ag 3,24 1831
NcU Jl 29 1822;Mr 13 1827

NORTH-CAROLINA miscellany. w Ja 31 1832-
1832? as Carolina miscellany
DLC Mr 7 1832
NcHi Mr 7 1832
NcU F 20-27 1833

Edenton SENTINEL and Albemarle intelligencer. w My 1 1841-
DLC My 1 1841
NcD N 6 1841

ELIZABETH CITY

ADVANCE. w,sw 1911-20||?
w 1911-F 1913?
Nc 1912-14[18]-N 19 1920

Elizabeth City ADVANCE. d My 1916+
Nc [1916]-[18]+

ALBEMARLE register. w Je 23 1874-75||?
NcU Ag 25-S 1 1874;Ap 20 1875

ALBEMARLE southern.
VRC O 19 1860

DEMOCRATIC pioneer. w 1850?-
Nc F 21 1854-Ag 16,O 18-N 1859
NcD S 2 1851;S 6 1853;Je 24,Ag 26 1856;Ja 13 1857

ECONOMIST. w F 19 1872-1905||?
1891-94? as Economist-falcon
NcD My 7,Je 30 1872;O 22 1878;Mr 20 1888;D 15 1893;S 7 1900;F 27 1903
NcHi F 26 1889
NcU Jl 9-16 1872;Ap 29 1884;Jl 13 1886;O 15,N 5 1889[90]-Ja 13,F 10,24,Ag 30 1891;Ag 3,17,D 7 1894;Ag 23-30 1895;My 8-15,D 18 1896;Mr 5,My 7,Je 11 1897;S 8,D 16 1898;Mr 23,My 4, Je 8-15,Ag 24 1900

FALCON. w Mr 31 1876-90||
United with Economist to form Economist-falcon, later Economist
Nc [1887]-90
NcU Jl 28 1881;Jl 7,D 12 1884;F 27-Mr 6,Ap 3,S 4 1885;Mr 19 1886;S 20 1889;O 24,D 12 1890

HERALD of the times. w 1823?-
InSHi S 5,D 29 1835;Ja 30,Ap 30 1836
NcU Ag 22 1835

INDEPENDENT. w Je 1908+
pub 1919+
Nc F 1919+

INTELLIGENCER and Nag's Head advocate. w O 13 1840-
DLC D 8 1840;Ja 26 1841

NORTH CAROLINA advocate. w Jl 31 1832-
DLC Ja 15 1833
NcHi Ja 15 1833

NORTH CAROLINIAN. w Jl 1 1869-1903||?
DLC Ag 25 1880
Nc 1871-[75]-N 1876;Je 22 1887-88;My 22 1889-[98]-[1903]
NcD S 23 1869;Ag 31 1871;F 29 1872;D 24 1879;Jl 13,D 14 1892;Ap 25 1894;My 22 1895;F 12,My 6 1896
NcU 1879[70-72]Jl 20 1881;Jl 14 1886

OLD north state. w 1841-
Nc Jl 22 1854
NcU N 12 1853;S 23 1854
NhD My 25 1841

Elizabeth-City STAR and North Carolina eastern intelligencer. w 1821-
1821-24? as Elizabeth-City star
DLC D 13(extra)1823;My 15-Je 5,Jl 10,N 16 1824;Mr 11 1829;Ja 16 1830;N 9 1832
InSHi [1822-33]
MWA F 18,Je 3 1826
Nc F 11 1826-N 1827
NcHi D 13 1823;My 15-Je 5,Jl 10,O 16 1824: Mr 11 1829;Ja 16 1830;N 10 1832

TAR HEEL. w Ag 1901-10||?
Nc 1902-03;09-10
NcD F 8-15 1907
NcU N 23 1906[07-08]Ja 15,Ap 9,Jl 9,23 1909

Weekly TRANSCRIPT. w Ap? 1867-
MBAt Jl,Ag 14,28-S 4 1867

ELIZABETHTOWN

BLADEN journal. w 1907+
pub [1928+]

ELKIN

Elkin TRIBUNE. w 1911+
pub 1918-20;23+

ELM CITY

Elm City ELEVATOR. w 1901-05||?
Nc 1902

ENFIELD

PROGRESS. w 1905+
NcD Ja 3,Jl 19,Ag 30,N 29 1906;Je 14,Jl 5,O 11 1907;Ap 10 1908

Enfield SENTINEL. w 1880-81||?
DLC D 2 1880
NcU Jl 21 1881

FAISON

DUPLIN journal. w Je 1901-06||?
NcD Jl 19-Ag 9,23 1901;Mr 27,N 20 1902

FAYETTEVILLE

CAROLINA observer. *See* Fayette observer

COMMUNICATOR. w 1848?-
NcU Ap 16 1850

Daily COURIER. d F 23 1860-
NcD F 23,Je 7,Jl 4,14 1860

Weekly COURIER. w F 25 1860-
DLC Mr 10,24-31,Ap 21,My-Jl 14,28-Ag 4,S O 9-16 1860
NcD F 25-Ap 14,My 12-S,O 9-16 1860

EAGLE. w Ag 12? 1868-75||?
Nc N 2,30,D 21 1868;Ag 16 1869;F 24 1870
NcD [Ag 12 1868-69]S 29 1870[71]Ja 11-18, Mr 28 1872; F 6,O 9-23 1873;Jl 2,N 12,D 10-17 1874;Ap 29,My 13 1875
NcU S 10,24,O 22-29 1868;My 27-Je 17,Ag 12,S 2,N 4,D 9 1869;Ja 20-27,Ap 21,My 19,Je 16,Ag 18,S 29-O 6,27 1870;Je 28 1871

EAGLE. sw Ag 24 1868-73||?
NcD [1868]Ja 11 1869;S 21,N 2,12,D 3,7-14 1872[Ja-S 1873]
NcU O 22-26,D 7,31 1868;Ja 11 1869

EAGLE. d Jl 16? 1872-
NcD Jl 17,28,Ag 8,10,18,27,30-31,S 10,13 1872
NcU Ag 22 1872

Fayetteville EXAMINER. w Ap 22 1880-83||?
DLC D 30 1880
NcD My 13,O 14 1880;N 2 1882;Ja 11-F 1 1883
NcU Ap 22 1880;F 10,Mr 31,O 13,D 1 1881

***Fayetteville GAZETTE.** w F 1820-
NcU F 14 1821;My 15,29 1822

Daily GAZETTE. d
NcD N 11 1874

Fayetteville INDEX. w 1909-17||?
Nc F 17 1909-16
NcD Je 3,S 23,N 18 1914

Weekly INTELLIGENCER. w F 10 1864-
NcD F 10,Mr-My 10,24-Je 14,28-Ag 16 1864

MESSENGER. w Ap? 1887-N 30 1888||
Nc O 14 1887-88

NEWS. d Jl? 1865-
NcD S 5,O 27 1865

NORTH CAROLINA (*Continued*)

FAYETTEVILLE—*Continued*

Fayetteville NEWS. w Mr 13? 1866-
1866-Ja 8 1867 as Fayetteville news; Ja 15-Mr 1867 Weekly news
NcD My-Je,Jl 31 1866-Ag 5 1868

NORTH CAROLINA argus. *See under* Wadesboro

NORTH CAROLINA gazette. w Ag 14 1873-78||?
GColS [1876-77]
Nc N 1? 1874
NcD S 25-O 2,30 1873;Mr 5,My 7,D 17-24 1874 [75-79]Ja 22-29 1880
NcGrW O 2 1873
NcU 1873-Ag 6 1874;Je 10,Ag 15 1875-77;Ja 24-31,Mr 7,My 30,Jl 18,S 5 1878

NORTH CAROLINA journal. w My 17 1826-N 28 1838||
CSmH My 19 1830
Ct [1827 36-38]
DLC 1826-D 12 1827;S 9,O 21-28,N 18,D 2 1829;Ja-F 17,Mr 10-31,Ap 14,28-Jl 14,28-S 1, 15-23,O 6,20-N 3,24-D 22 1830;Ja 19 1831;Mr 12 1834-N 1838
MWA D 9 1835
N O 9 1833
Nc O 23 1833
NcD Ja 17-24,O 3,D 26 1827;S 16,O 28 1829; Ja 6,20-F 3,S 15,D 22 1830;Mr 30,Ag 3 1831; S 12,O 17 1832
NcHi Mr 17,O 21,N 18,D 12 1826;O 21,N 18, D 2 1829;Ja 13,F 10-17,Mr 10-31 1830;Mr 12 1834;N 28 1838
NcU O 4 1826;D 12 1827;Mr 5,Je 4 1828[29;31-32]

NORTH CAROLINA minerva. . . *See* Raleigh minerva (Raleigh)

NORTH CAROLINA telegraph. w -1826||
United with Richmond family visitor to form Visitor and telegraph, later Southern religious telegraph (Richmond, Va.)

NORTH CAROLINIAN. w Mr 2 1839-
DLC Mr ? 1839-N 14 1840;Ap 17 1841;Ap 22, Jl 15,Ag 26 1843;Ag 10,31-S 7,N 30,D 28 1844;D 27 1845;Ja 10-Ap,My 9,Je 27,O 24-N 7 1846;Ja (-20,F 17-Mr,Je 30,S 1,15-D 1855
Nc F 27 1847;F 19,Je 11 1853;My 31 1856;Mr 14 1857;F 20 1858;F 23 1861
NcD My 16,Je 27-Jl 4,Ag 15,O 17,D 19 1840; Je 19,O 2 1841;Ja 8-15,Ap 16,Je 11,S 3,N 5 1842;Mr 25,Je 29,S 16 1843[45-Ap 1861]
NcHi Je 25 1842
NcU Mr 9 N 2 1839;Mr 6 1847;D 14 1850;D 6 1856

Daily NORTH CAROLINIAN. d 1859?-
Title varies: North Carolinian
Nc Je 11 1860
NcD My 24,Je 1859;F 1,Mr 13-14,Ap 9 1860 [64]Ja 27 1865

***Fayetteville OBSERVER.** w Je 20 1816-65||
1816-31? as Carolina observer (Ja-O 1823 Carolina observer and Fayetteville gazette)
CSmH S 2 1830
Ct F 24 1851
CtY Mr 13 1823
DLC D 9 1824;Ja 22 1833;N 14 1838;N 10 1840; Ja 6 1841;Jl 20 1842;Ag 3 1863;Ja 18-25 1864
KyU F 26 1833
MWA My 19 1825;Jl 19 1826;D 31 1829;Ap 22, N 4 1830
Nc Mr 4 1824;25-[27-29]-44;Ag 27 1850;51-Jl 18,Ag 8-15 O 3,17-D 19 1864
NcD 1823-24;D 30 1834;Mr 18,Ap 22,Jl 22,S 16,D 23 1840;Mr 10,Jl 14 1841[42-44]N 30 1847 [48-Ag 1850 Ag 26 1851;Ja 6 1852;Je 27,D 24 1853;D 3 1855[56-58]-N 1863[64]-F 13 1865
NcGrW Mr-Je 1,Jl-N 2,16-30 1857;Mr 15-29, My 24,Je-Jl 12 1858
NcHi D 9 1824;Ja 22 1833;F 13 1858[61-65]
NcU Je 24,Ag 12 1824;Mr 1-8 1827;Ag 28 1828; Ja 7 1830;Jl 27 1831;Ja 13 1835;Je 10 1840;Ja 31 1844;F 5 Mr 5,My 7,Jl 16,S 10, D 2 1845; Ag 4 1846;47 [48-53] D 24 1855; Ja 28,F 14, Mr 3,N 13,D 29 1856 [57-58] 59; Je 11,Jl 16 1860;My 16,Je 17 1861
P-M Je 30 1836

Fayetteville OBSERVER. sw Jl 3 1851-65||
Nc 1851-Ap 2,Jl 1856-S 1861[62;Ja-Ap 4 1864]
NcD Jl 2 1853;Jl 17 1854;Ja 10,F 21,Mr 3,O 2 1856;Je 8, Ag 13,O 12 1857;Mr 11,N 4,18 1858;F 14 1859;My 21 1860-My,O 9,16,N 6, 18,D 29 1862 F 9,19,My 14,Jl 16,23,Ag 3,D 21 1863;Ja 18,F 22,Mr 10,N 7 1864-Mr 9 1865
NcGrW My 23-26 1864
NcU [1854]O 12 1857;Ap 28,My 2,Je 6,Jl 25 1859;Ja 9,Mr 8-12,Je 25-28,Jl 23,Ag 6 1860 [62-64]Ja 9,16,Mr 2 1865
OClWHi Mr 10-Ap 18 1864
TxU F 2-13 1855
WHi F 13 1865

Fayetteville OBSERVER. w,sw 1883-1919||?
1885? as Observer and gazette
sw 1889?
DLC Ag 28 1884;Jl 5 1894
Nc My 31 1888-[89-90]-1919
NcD [1883-84]Ja 29-F 5,Mr 5,Ap 2,My 28 1885;N 4 1885;My 5 1887;Je 27 1889;Mr 10 1892;S 16,30 1897;O 18 1900;Je 24,S 2 1914
NcHi Je 21,Ag 30 1883;O 15 1885;Mr 31 1887; F 2,My 3 1888;O 31 1895;My 6,Jl 28 1897; F 15 1899;Ag 23,O 10 1900;Mr 18 1904;Ja 17-24,N 2-13 1905
NcU F 8 1885-Je 1906;D 1907-18

Fayetteville OBSERVER. d 1896+
Title varies slightly
pub 1922+
Nc N 6 1924—
NcD S 21 1900;D 3-9 1901[02-Je 1903;26]
NcHi O 19 1923
NcU F 1896-Ap 1919

PEOPLE'S advocate. w 1922+
pub 1922+
NcD My 27,O 14,N 11,D 2 1926

STATESMAN. w Ap 5 1873-74||?
NcD [1873-Ag 8 1874]

SUN. w S 26 1883-85||?
NcD O 3,31 1883;S 16,O 7,N 25 1884;Mr 25,Ap 29 1885

Daily TELEGRAPH. d Ja 1865-
MWA Mr 4 1865
NcD Ja 26,Mr 1,4,7,9 1865

WIDE AWAKE. w 1875-
NcD Jl 19,S 19,D 20 1876

FRANKLINTON

DISPATCH. w Jl 21 1887-88||?
Nc 1887-Jl 5 1888
NcU S 2 1887

FUQUAY SPRINGS

Fuquay GOLD LEAF. w 1914-19||?
VU My 28-N 12,26-D 24 1915;Ja 14-My 19 1916

GASTONIA

Gastonia GAZETTE. w,sw,tw,d 1880+
w 1880-1901?; sw 1902-16?; tw 1917-19?
O 1 1907 is Gaston county industrial ed
pub 1880—
NcD S 8 1905;O 1 1907

GATESVILLE

GATES county index. w 1932+
pub 1932—

GOLDSBORO

Goldsboro ARGUS. w,sw 1884-1915||?
1884-Mr 11 1909? as Goldsboro weekly argus
sw Mr 15 1909-14?
Nc [Ap 1892-95]-[1904-05]07-[11]12[14]15
NcD Ja 10 1889

Goldsboro daily ARGUS. d 1885-S? 1929||
United with Goldsboro news to form Goldsboro news-argus
Nc My 17 1890-Mr 1891;Ag 1892-[93-96]-[1901-04]-[06-08]-[13]-16
NcD S 6 1909
NcHi O 13 1892
NcU My 1 1889;Ja 12 1892;Ja 1 1897;F 23, Je 1,N 17 D 1,15 1898

CAROLINA messenger. *See* Goldsboro messenger sw

CAUCASIAN. *See under* Raleigh

EASTERN CAROLINA republican. *See* North Carolina republican

Goldsboro HEADLIGHT. w,sw S 9? 1887-1920||?
sw 1905
Nc [N 25 1887-88]-[1901-02]03

Goldsboro MESSENGER. sw 1867-Je 1887||?
1867-Mr 1877 as Carolina messenger
DLC O 4 1880
Nc S 9 1872-N 23,D 30 1878-[85]-Je 13 1887
NcD O 21 1880;O 23 1884;Mr 12-16,My 28 1885; My 31 1886
NcHi Jl 23 1877;Mr 15,Je 22 1882
NcU F 15 1870;D 3 1885

Goldsboro daily MESSENGER. d 1868?-70||?
DLC S 6 1869
NcD Ap 1,27,Jl 12 1869
NcU [My-N 1869]

Goldsboro MESSENGER. w *See* Semi-weekly Wilmington messenger (Wilmington)

NEW ERA. w 1852?-
NcD O 27,N 24 1853;Mr 15 1854;F 13 1855

Goldsboro daily NEWS. d 1865-
Nc D 2 1865
NcHi Ag 30,O 3,25 1866

Goldsboro NEWS. w Jl 18 1865-74||?
NcHi Ag 30 1867
NcU O 17 1865;D 17 1867[Je-N 1869]

Goldsboro NEWS-ARGUS. d 1922+
1922-S 22 1929 as Goldsboro news
NcD F 21 1895;Ap 8 1935

NORTH CAROLINA republican. w 1847-
1847-Ja 1850 as Republican; F 1850-My? 1851 Eastern Carolina republican; My? 1851-52? Republican and patriot
1847-Mr 11 1851 pub in New Bern
Nc [F-D 1851]
NcD Ap 21-My 12,26-Ag 3,17-25,S 22-D 22 1847;48-F,Mr 18-My 6,Jl 10 1851-Mr,Ap 27, My 18-N 8 1852;My 24-Ag,S 21-O 1853
NcHi Je 21 1848
P-M S 19 1854

NORTH CAROLINA telegraph. w 1848-
1848-F 1850 as Goldsboro telegraph
NcD Ja 3,31,F 28,Mr 17-Ap 4,My 9,23-30,Jl 4,Ag 8 1850;Je 10-17 1852;F 24 1853;Jl 13 1854;My 23 1855
NcU D 18 1851

Goldsboro PATRIOT. w Ap 14 1849-
NcD Jl 28,Ag 11 1849

REPUBLICAN. *See* North Carolina republican

Daily ROUGH notes. d
NcD My 4 1861
OClWHi F 25 1861

Daily morning STAR. d Je 1867-
NcD Jl 10 1867

Daily STATE journal. d 1858-
DLC D 20 1864
MBAt Ap 5 1864
NjR N 6 1864

SÜDLICHE post. d O 1 1869-
In German
NcU O 1,23,N 27 1869

Goldsboro TELEGRAPH. w *See* North Carolina telegraph

Weekly TRANSCRIPT and messenger. *See* Semi-weekly Wilmington messenger (Wilmington)

Goldsboro TRIBUNE. tw
MH My 8 1862

GRAHAM

ALAMANCE gleaner. w F 9 1875+
pub My 15 1880+
DLC Mr 7 1881
Nc N 23 1875;Jl 27 1916
NcD D 7 1875;Ap 24 1882;N 18,D 30 1915;My 11 N 2 1916;F 29,Jl 5,O 18 1917;Ap 11,My 16-23,Jl 18,S 5-12 1918
NcU 1875-F 1878;N 4 1886;N 8 1888

GREENSBORO

To 1844? as Greensborough

BEACON. w O 1879-81||?
DLC Je 8 1880
NcHi Jl 20 1880

CAROLINA beacon. w My 25 1836-
NcD [1836]Ja 13 1837

CAROLINA patriot. *See* Greensboro patriot

Daily INDUSTRIAL news. *See* Greensboro daily news

LITTLE ad. w My 12-Jl 1860||
NcD complete
NcU Je 2,23-30,Jl 21 1860

NEW north state. w 1871-84||?
DLC Jl 1,22 1880
Nc [1874]-[76]78-81;Jl 1882-[83-84]
NcD N 1872-73;Jl 15,D 18 1874;D 18 1879;N 18 1880[81]Ja 26,F 9,My 4,Je 22-29 1882;Ap 17,Jl 31,S 18 1884
NcU O 31 1872;Je 6 1878;Mr 5 1879

Morning NEWS. d 1887||?
Nc Ja 25-S 5 1887

Greensboro daily NEWS. d C 8 1905+
1905-Jl 17 1909 as Daily industrial news
Ag 5 1917 is industrial ed
DLC Jl 1921+
MWA Ag 5 1917;Jl 2 1919;Ag 6 1922;D 28 1924
Nc 1905-08;Jl 18,30 1909+
NcD 1905-Ja 29,S 1909-Je,N 17,19,21,24,27 1926 [Mr]-Jl 1927;28+
NcEloC [1924]+
NcGuC Je 1929+
NcHi Mr 25 1917;N 11 1918;Mr 8 1925
NcHic [1927+]
NcU 1905-08;Jl 18 1909-O 1922;23+
PWp Ag 5 1917
WHi Jl 1 1931

Greensboro NORTH state. w S 1885-92||?
1885 as North state
NcD D 17 1885-Ap 15,Je 3,24-Jl 1,15-29,O 7, 21 1886;Ap 28,Ag 4,S 8,22,O 27,D 15 1887;S 1888-S 10 1891
NcGrW Jl 8 1886;Ja 17 1889
NcU Jl 15 1886;D 15 1887

Greensboro PATRIOT. w,sw 1826+
1826 as Patriot; 1827-My 16 1829 Patriot and Greensborough palladium; My 23 1829-42 Greensborough patriot (1837-Ja 1839 Carolina patriot) 1843 Greensboro patriot; 1857-58 Patriot and flag; Je 11 1868-Ja 1869 Patriot and times
w 1826-1913?
CSmH Ag 4 1830;N 5 1863
DLC O 11 1828;My 23,Je 6,27,Ag 1-8,S 19-26, O 24,N 28,D 12,30 1829-Ja,D 4,15 1830;D 1 1840;Ja 30 1847;Ja 26 1850-Ag 7 1852;Mr 10, Ag 18 1864;Ap 10 1865;Je 9,Ag 20 1880
ICM Jl 18 1900
MBAt Mr 17-Ap 7 1864
Nc F 18 1854-[56]-60;My 1 1862[64]Mr 30 1865[67]Je 15 1871-Je 25 1873;77-[80-81;87-88]-Ap 18 1889;99-1903;17-[27-28]+
NcD Jl 26 1828;F 24,O 20,D 22 1827;Jl 5,O 25 1828[29-34]N 11 1835[36]D 19 1837[38-Ja 1839]-[42-43]45[46-50]Ja 29 1853;Mr 18 1854; F 10,S 14 1860;Ap 18,30-Je 1861;Mr 20,Ag 21 1862;My 20,N 20-D 3 1863;Ag 11 1864;Mr 2 1866;Ap 12 1867;Mr 1868-77;S 1882-Jl 7 1885; O 22 1886;Je 22 1888[91-F 1893]94-1902;O 28, D 30 1903;S 14 1904
NcGrW Jl 17 1862
NcU My 12 1827;Ap 6 1831;Ag 22 1832;Je 16 1840;My 20,Je 17,Ag 5,S 16,N 4,D 9 1843[44-45]-F,Mr 14,28 1846;D 16-23 1848;Ag 4 1849; D 25 1852;Je 18-Ag 13 1853;Ja 14,Mr 11 1854 [59]Ag 10 1860;Ja 10 1861[64]Ag 19,S 30,D 23 1865[66-69]Jl 28 1875;Jl 13 1881;Jl 16 1886;Jl 21 1909
NhD Je 8 1841

Greensboro PATRIOT. d My 1880-83||?
NcD O 13 1880;Ap 4-5,7-11,13 1881

Daily evening PATRIOT. d 1888||?
Nc Je 20-N 8 1888

Greensboro daily RECORD. d N 17 1890+
GAtCo Jl 3 1896
ICM Mr 22 1900
Nc My 29 1891;Ag 20 1902-Mr 1916;My 1923+
NcD Je 27 1896;S 6 1905;Ap 5 1915;N 22 1919
NcU Ap 8 1892;F 15,My 4,Je 8 1898;Ap 30 1904;F 28 1908

NORTH CAROLINA (*Continued*)

GREENSBORO—*Continued*

Greensboro REGISTER. w 1867?-
NcU Jl 7-21,Ag 1,18-S,O 13-27,N 10-24 1869

REPUBLICAN. w F 17 1870-71||?
NcU Mr 17-Ap 7,28 1870

REPUBLICAN gazette. w Ag 12 1869-
NcU Ag 26,S 16,26,O 21-N 4 1869

Daily SOUTHERN citizen. d Je 1864-
NcGr Jl 24,O 20 1864
NcU Ag 12,16 1864

SOUTHERN telescope. w Ja 6- 1837||?
Merged with Greensboro patriot
NcD Mr 10,S 29,O 13,N 10 1837

Twice-a-week TAR HEEL. w,sw N 9 1905-07||?
1905-06? as Weekly tar heel (w)
Nc 1906
NcD 1905-My 3,N 1906[Mr-O 1907]

Greensboro TELEGRAM. d Jl 3 1897-1911||?
1897-1900? as Greensboro evening telegram
Je 15 1905 is industrial ed
InNcHi N 8 1908
Nc [1897-98]-[1901]Ag 13 1910-S 9 1911
NcD Jl 31 1897-Ja 27 1898;Jl 22,25,27 1901;O 29 1902;Je 15 1905
NcHi Je 30 1900;Ap 8 1909

TEXTORIAN. w O 1927+
pub 1927+

TIMES. sw,w Ja 1856-Je 11 1868||
United with Greensboro patriot to form Patriot and times, later Greensboro patriot
sw My 1861
MWA Jl 16 1857;Mr 3,17 1860
NcAsS 1859
NcD 1858-N 1861;F-Je 4 1868
NcHi Mr 10 1860
NcU Ja 16 1858;Jl 2 1859;Jl 21,S 8,N 3 1860;F 9 1861

TOPIC. w 1869-
NcU My 26,Je 16 1869

WATCHMAN and harbinger. w S 1863-
NNHi N 6,27 1863
NcGr Ap 22 1864

WAY of the world. w Ja 5 1862-
NcD Mr 15,29-Ap 19 1862;Je 1863-[Ja-Je 2 1864]
NcU Ja 16,Ap 30,S 10 1863

Greensboro daily WORKMAN. d 1883-93||
1883-90 as Daily workman. Merged with Greensboro daily record
NcD N 30,D 10 1889;Ja 13,16,N 27-29,D 1-6 1890;F 7-Mr 4,28,Ap 10-11,14-24 1891
NcHi Ja 23,25 1889;F 5-7, 9-11 1891
NcU Jl 28,Ag 3,S 21,25 1885;N 28 1889;F 4 1892

GREENVILLE

CAROLINA home and farm and eastern reflector. sw,w 1882-1919||?
1882-1911? as Eastern reflector
sw O 1897-1910
Nc O 19 1887-[1906]-15
NcHi F 26 1901
NcU Jl 14 1886;Ja 20 1892;D 6 1893;O 9 1895; Mr 8,My 20 1896;N 12 1897;My 17-27,O 14, 28,D 2,13,20,30 1898;Ja 6-13,20,Mr 7,14,O 3 1899;N 30 1900;F 14 1902;Je 16 1903;Mr 29,Ap 19,My 31,Je 7,14 1904
—d ed *See* Daily reflector

EASTERN reflector. *See* Carolina home. . .

Greenville EXPRESS. w 1877-81||?
DLC Jl 8 1880
NcU Jl 21 1881

KING'S weekly. w,sw,tw,d Ja 11 1894-1908||
1904-05? as King's dollar daily
sw Ag 1898-1901;tw 1902-03;d 1904-05?
Nc [F 1894-95]-[98]-1902
NcD Ag 18 1899
NcHi Ja 7-14,F 4 1898
NcU Ja-N 15 1895;D 3,17 1897;98[99]1901

Greenville daily NEWS. d 1917-21||?
Nc [Je-D 1917]-21

Daily REFLECTOR. d 1894+
NcHi Ag 21 1920
NcU My 12,16,18,24 1898
—w,sw ed *See* Carolina home and farm and eastern reflector

HALIFAX

FREE PRESS. *See* Tarboro southerner (Tarboro)

Halifax MINERVA. w Ja 24 1829-
DLC Ja 24,Mr 5 1829;F 25 1830
NcHi Ja 24,Mr 5 1829;F 25 1830

ROANOKE advocate. *See* Roanoke republican

ROANOKE republican. w 1829-
1829-32? as Roanoke advocate; 1833?-42? Roanoke advocate and state rights banner
CSmH Ap 29 1830
DLC Mr 4-11,My 6-13,S 30-O 2 1830;F 24,Mr 24 1831;Jl 5,N 15 1832;My 11 1842
NcD F 19,Mr 4,Jl 29 1840;Mr 1 1843
NcHi Mr 4-11,My 6-13,Ag,S 30,O 21 1830;F 24,Mr 24 1831;Jl 5,N 15 1832
NcU My 11 1853;F 7 1855

HAMLET

MESSENGER. w 1907-19||?
United with Hamlet news to form Hamlet news-messenger

Hamlet NEWS-MESSENGER. w 1918+
1918-19? as Hamlet news
pub [1918+]

HENDERSON

BORDER review. w Mr 1 1879-80||?
United with Tobacconist to form Tobacconist and review
NcD O 10 1879
NcU My 24 1879

Henderson daily DISPATCH. d 1914+
pub 1914-24
NcD Ag 29 1916;F 9,Je 3,20,S 30 1918;D 29 1919;D 8 1933
NcHe 1925+

Henderson GOLD LEAF. w,sw 1881+
sw 1914?-24?
pub 1911+
Nc D 23 1886-1911
NcD My 31 1883;Ap 17 1890;S 19 1907

Henderson INDEX. w 1866-70||?
NcD Jl 3 1868;Ja 26,F 9 1869
NcU My 21-Je 4,18,Jl 30,Ag 20,S 2,17-24 1869;F 11,Mr 4 1870

Semi-weekly INDEX. sw 1868?-
NcD Ap 9 1869

Henderson NEWS. w Ap 1 1887-88||?
Nc F 10-D 13 1888
NcU Jl 22 1887

Henderson PIONEER. w My 16 1866-
MWA D 18 1866
NcU My 30 1866; My 1-8,Je 27-Jl 3,17,S 12 1867

TOBACCONIST and review. w 1876-81||?
1876-80? as Tobacconist
DLC F 2 1881
NcHi My 11 1881

TRIBUNE. w 1873-76||?
NcD [Mr-D 1874]-Ap 7 1876

HENDERSONVILLE

COTTAGE visitor. w 1867-72||?
NcU Jl 16,30,Ag 13-20,S 3-17,O 8-29,N 10-17 1869

FRENCH BROAD hustler. *See* Hendersonville news

HENDERSON county advertiser. w My 28 1874-76||?
ICHi O 1 1874

INDEPENDENT herald. w My 20 1881-82||?
NcAsS Jl 22 1881
NcU Jl 22 1881

Hendersonville NEWS. w 1891-1927||
1891-1919 as French Broad hustler (1913-15 Western Carolina democrat; or, French Broad hustler) United with Hendersonville times to form Times-news
Nc 1906-11;13-18
NcHen 1915-19;21-27

Henderson TIMES. w 1862?-
NcHi Ja 14 1864

Hendersonville TIMES. 1886-97? *See* Western Carolina times.

TIMES-NEWS. d 1924+
Follows Western North Carolina times. 1924-27 as Hendersonville times
Nc 1924+
NcHen 1928+

WESTERN Carolina democrat. *See* Hendersonville news

WESTERN courier. w 1877-81||?
NcD Je 20 1878

WESTERN North Carolina times. w,sw Ap 1 1886-1923||?
1886-97? as Hendersonville times. Followed by Hendersonville times (d) later Times-news
w 1886-1922?
Nc [1914]15;18-23
NcU O 21 1886;O 1 1896

HERTFORD

EASTERN courier. w 1895-98||?
Nc [F 20-D 1895]-97
NcU D 15 1898

PERQUIMANS record. w 1890-96||?
Nc O 22 1890-[93-94]
NcD Ap 1 1891

HICKORY

CAROLINA eagle. w 1871-72||?
NNHi D 19 1872
NcD Ja 11 1872

Hickory DEMOCRAT. w,sw 1899-1919||?
sw My 20- 1915?
Nc Jl 1906-15

Hickory MERCURY. *See* Times-mercury

PIEDMONT press. *See* Hickory press

Hickory PRESS. w 1870-1904||?
1870-87? as Piedmont press; 1888?-95? Press and Carolinian
DLC Jl 10 1880
GAtCo Jl 28-Ag 4,S 1-15,N 10,D 8 1892;Ja 5 1893
Nc Ag 1887-[98]
NcD Ap 14 1877;S 1 extra 1888
NcHi O 11 1900
NcU S 10,N 25 1873;Jl 16,Ag 13 1874;O 2 1875;D 15-22 1877;Ag 14 1886;N 7 1889;Ja 9-16 1890
VU Ja 9 1890

Hickory daily RECORD. d S 11 1915+
pub [1915-27]+
Nc Je 1916+
NcD Ja 19 1922
NcHic [1927+]

Hickory TIMES. w 1896-97||
United with Hickory mercury to form Times-mercury
GAtCo O 22 1896

TIMES-MERCURY. w,sw Ap? 1891-1925||?
1891-97 as Hickory mercury
w 1891-1921?
GAtCo D 2 1891;Mr 9,Ap 6,Je 29,Ag 24-31,S 14-21 1892
Nc Ag 11 1897-98;Mr 22 1899-[1903;08]-12
NcD Ag 10 1898;Je 29 1906
NcU Mr 16 1898-Ap 4 1900

WESTERN Carolinian. w 1878-87||?
United with Piedmont press to form Press and Carolinian, later Hickory press
DLC Jl 2 1880

HIGH POINT

High Point ENTERPRISE. d 1904+
1904-08? as Daily enterprise
pub [1914-18]+
Nc [Ja-Mr 1908]09-S 1918
NcD Je 10-11 1914;Ja 20 1935
NcHpC S 15 1932+

ENTERPRISE-HERALD. w,sw 1879-1912||?
1879-1909? as High Point enterprise
sw Ja 6-S 28 1904
Nc 1900-[04]-D 9 1908
NcU Jl 16 1886

High Point REPORTER. w Ja 12 1860-
NcU Ap 20,My 4,D 13 1860

REVIEW. w 1909-25||?
Nc [1914]-21
NcD My 27,S 30,O 14,N 4 1915

HILLSBORO

To 1874? as Hillsborough

NORTH CAROLINA democrat. w My 1848-
NcD My 16 1849;Mr 7 1850

ORANGE county observer. w 1878-1918||?
DLC Mr 19 1881
Nc S 10 1887-O 1891;92-94
NcD Ap 23,D 1887-Ja 14,F 4-11 1888;Ag 10 1895
NcHi Ag 31 1889;Ja 10 1891;S 3-17,D 10,24 1896[97]-Mr 1898
NcU [1880-85]-[89-92]-[95-96]-[99-1908;17]

Hillsborough PLAINDEALER. w N 1860-
NcD Mr 6 1861

Hillsborough RECORDER. (1820-79; 95-96) *See* Durham recorder (Durham)

Hillsboro RECORDER. w Ag 18 1887-88||?
NcD D 8 1887;Ja 12 1888

HOKEVILLE

Hokeville EXPRESS. w F 28 1855-
NcU Je 27 1855

HOLLY SPRINGS

CAPE FEAR enterprise. w 1899-1912||?
Nc 1900
NcD Jl 22 1899;Ap 26-My 3 1901

JONESBORO

Jonesboro LEADER. w 1888-92||?
Nc F 29 1888-F 24,Mr 23,Ap 14-My 14 1892

JONESVILLE

Jonesville EXPRESS. w? 1858?-
NcU Je 4 1858

KANNAPOLIS

INDEPENDENT. w Jl 1927+
pub Jl 1933+

Kannapolis STAR. w 1915-30||?
United with Concord observer (Concord) to form Concord observer and Kannapolis star (Concord)

KELLY

Kelly MESSENGER. w
Nc [O 1895-O 1898]

KERNERSVILLE

EASTERN CAROLINA news. *See* Forsyth news

FORSYTH news. w 1905-16||?
1905-08? as Eastern Carolina news
Nc [My 1908-09]-11

NEWS and farm. w 1881-93||?
Nc O 1887-Jl 6 1888

KINGS MOUNTAIN

Kings Mountain HERALD. w 1903+
pub N 1913-O 1925;32+

NORTH CAROLINA (*Continued*)

KINSTON

AMERICAN advocate. w 1855-
MWA Ap 24 1856;Ap 30,Ag 13 1857

Kinston FREE PRESS. w,sw,d 1882-1924||
sw 1896-1910;d D 1896
Nc Mr 5 1888-94;Ap 18 1895-1901;F 19-D 1902
NcD D 7 1882;Ap 3 1884;S 1892-[93-94]Je 27, Jl 15,D 12-13 1896;Ag 18 1897[99-Ja 1900;Ag-N 1901-02]supp Ja 30 1897
NcHi S 12 1889

Kinston daily FREE PRESS. d 1898+
Title varies slightly
pub Ap 1 1924+
Nc [Ap 1898-99]-1904;O 1929+
NcD Ap 28[My]1898;O 28 1901
NcU Ja 3 My 14 1908;D 21 1909;D 14 1911;Ag 3 1916;Mr 31 1917[18-19]O 6 1920

Kinston JOURNAL. w D 20 1878-82||?
DLC Jl 1880
NcU 187-Mr 1882

LA GRANGE

La Grange VIDETTE. w Ja 1 1875-
NcD F 25 1875

LASKER

PATRON and gleaner. *See* Roanoke-Chowan times (Rich Square)

LAURINBURG

Laurinburg EXCHANGE. w 1882+
D 15 1932 is 50th anniversary ed
NcD D 15 1932
NcU Jl 15 1886

SCOTCHMAN and observer. w Je 3 1873-
NcD Jl 25 1873

LEAKSVILLE

DAN VALLEY echo. w Ap 16 1885-87||?
NcD Ap 15,My 8 1885;Ap 15 1886[87]extra O 16 1886

Leaksville HERALD. w Ag 25 1860-
NcU O 19,N 23 1860

Leaksville NEWS. w Ap 1 1924+
pub 1924+
VU Ap 1 1924

TRI-CITY daily gazette. d 1919-24||?
Nc [Jl 1919-20]-Mr 1922

LENOIR

CALDWELL messenger. *See* Lenoir topic

NEWS-TOPIC. w,sw S 23 1898+
1898-Ap 1919 as Lenoir news
sw 1906?-D 2? 1920;23?
pub 1898+
Nc My 1915+
NcL 1898+
NcU S 14 1906;D 24 1907;O 20,D 8 1908;Je 13 1911;Ja 16 1912;Ap 8 1913;Ja 11,Ap 21-25,Je 2, O 24 1916;Ja 5,19,Mr 15,S 4 1917;Ja 4,Mr 22, Ap 5,O 18,D 20 1918;Ja 17 1919

Lenoir TOPIC. w,d S 25 1875-Ay 1919||
1875-N ? 1876 as Caldwell messenger. United with Lenoir news to form News-topic
d Je 12-Ag 11? 1884
DLC Ag 26 1880
MWA Mr 28 1888-S 17 1890
Nc S 29 188-[99-1900]-[02]-05;08-19
NcD Mr 23-30,Ap 6,20,My 11,D 4 1904[05-Jl 1907]
NcHi Mr 28 1888-Ag 1889
NcL complete
NcLN 1875-23
NcU 1875-[73]-Je,N 3 1898
WHi S 23 1885-Ag 12 1891

LEXINGTON

DAVIDSON county news. *See* News (Thomasville)

DISPATCH. w,sw 1882+
1885?-N 12 1902 Davidson dispatch
w 1882-O 22 1919
pub 1890+
Nc Ap 1888+
NcD D 6 1883[84]Ja 25 1888;My 15 1889;My 14 1891;O 6 1892;S 19 1894;Ja 23 1895;Mr 2,23, Ap 13 1898[99-1905]D 19-26 1906;Ja 16-23 1907;Mr 11,S 23-O 7,28-N,D 9 1908;D 6-20 1916[17-19]
NcHi Ja 10 1900
VU S 1 1915

Lexington and Yadkin FLAG. w Ag 1855-
NcU Ja 11 1856

Lexington HERALD. sw,w Je 4 1915-18||?
sw 1915-F 11 1916
NcD [1915-16]F 22 1917

NORTH state. w My 1904-08||?
Nc 1906-07
NcD N 23-30 1904[05-Mr 1908]

LILLINGTON

HARNETT county news. w Ja 1 1919+
pub 1919+
NcD S 2 1920
NcU 1919-33

LINCOLNTON

CAROLINA republican. w S 5 1848-
DLC S 5-12,27-O 4,30,D 16,29 1848;F 6,20-Je 8,22-29,Ag-O 5,19-26,N 8-D 7,21 1849
NcD F 6-27,Mr 13,Ap 17,My 11-18,Jl 6 1849
NcU Ap 10,My 18 1849;Mr 29 1850;My 15 1851; Ja 27 1853

LINCOLN county news. w,sw 1894+
1894-1906? as Lincoln journal (w)
pub 1908+
Nc 1907+
NcD Mr 24 1899;S 20 1910
NcU Mr 24,Jl 22 1899

LINCOLN courier. ir 1844-
DLC My 2,Jl 24,Ag 8,22,S 12,O 3,N 19-26,D 22 1846;Ja 16,28,F 20-27,Mr 13,27-Ap 3,17,29,Je 4-12,24,Jl 7-15,28,Ag 11,28,S 25,O 9,N 6,D 2 1847;Ja 1,20,Mr 15-30,Ap 29,My 26-Je 2,24-Jl 7,28,Ag 25-S 8,23,O 3,14,28,N 25,D 15,30 1848;Mr 31,Ap 14,Mr 5-19,Je 2-16,30,Jl 20-Ag 4,18-N,D 8-22 1849;F 15 1851
NcU Jl 30-Ag 6 1845;My 10 1851

LINCOLN courier. w 1867?-
MBAt My 31-Je 7,S 5,14 1867

LINCOLN courier. w 1883-95||?
Nc N 9 1888-95
NcD F 7 1890;Ja 4 1895
NcU S 16,30 1887

LINCOLN democrat. w 1894-98||?
Nc 1896

LINCOLN journal. *See* Lincoln county news

Weekly LINCOLN press. w 1883-N 1887||?
United with Gaston current (Dallas) to form Salisbury press (Salisbury)
NcU D 5 1884

LINCOLN progress. w 1873-82||?
DLC S 28 1880
NcHi My 17,31 1873

LINCOLN republican. w 1837-
DLC Ja 23,F 26,Mr 25,Je 10,O 14 1840;F 17-24,Mr 10,24-Ap 21,My 26-Je 2,23,Jl 7,21-S 8,22-O 6,20-N 17,D 1841-My 1842
NcD S 1 1841

LINCOLN transcript. w? Je? 1836-
NcHi D 10 1836

WESTERN whig banner. w S 1839-
NcD Je 27,Jl 18 1840
NcU My 9 1840

LITTLETON

COURIER. w 1892-95||?
1892-94 as Littleton courier
NcD S 1,N 10,D 15 1892;My 25 1893
NcHi S 22-29,N 13,D 1 1892;Je 1 1894

NEWS REPORTER. w 1896-1925||?
NcD [1897]Ja 16,28 1898;Mr 24,Ag 4,S 1,N 17 1899[1900-05]D 20 1907;F 28,Ap 24,My 29,O 23 1908[10-11]Jl 4-18,D 12,26 1913[14]-O 6, N,D 1-8 1916[17-My 14,Ag 1917-[18-Jl 1920]
NcHi Jl 17,O 12-26,D 14-21 1900;Ja 18,F 22, Mr 22,Ap 12,26-My 3,Je 28,Ag 9-16,30-S 6, D 13 1901;Mr 7,Je 20 1902;F 20 1903;F 12,Ag 5 1904;Ap 28 1905

TIMES-HERALD. w 1905-09||?
1905-Ja 1906? as Littleton times
NcD N 15,D 7 1905[06-09]
NcHi O 18 1906

LOUISBURG

FRANKLIN courier. w 1871-77||?
NcD Je 9 1876
OClWHi Ap 12 1872;73-Ja 2 1874

FRANKLIN times. w 1870+
pub 1870+
DLC Mr 18 1881
Nc [1888]-[1903]+
NcD N 6 1879;N 29 1880;S 7 1883;S 7 1894
NcU Jl 22 1881

Weekly NEWS. w
Nc F 10 1855

NORTH CAROLINA times. *See* Raleigh times w 1847-

Louisburg UNION and North Carolina miscellany. w
Nc Mr 18,Jl 27 1847

LUMBERTON

Lumberton ARGUS. sw 1900-05||?
Nc Ap 1904-05
NcD Jl 28 1905

ROBESON voice. 1935+
Follows State's voice (Dunn)
Also dated in Red Springs

ROBESONIAN. w,sw 1870+
w 1870-1903
pub Je 19 1900+
DLC S 25 1880
NNHi N 27 1872
Nc [1897]1904+
NcD Je 8 1870;My 23-30,Je 13 1872;Ag 27 1873; Mr 25 1874;S 8 1875;Mr 21 1878;Je 17 1885

MADISON

Madison ENTERPRISE. w 1873-74||?
NcD Je 4,25 1873;Mr 4,Ap 29 1874

MAGNOLIA

Magnolia ADVERTISER. 1872-73||?
Nc My 17 1872

Weekly RECORD. w
N Ap 12 1877

MAIDEN

Maiden NEWS. w N 13 1923+
pub 1923+

MARION

Marion RECORD. w 1892-95||?
Nc 1895

MCDOWELL news. sw 1924+
pub Jl 1928+

MESSENGER. w 1897-98||?
Nc [1897-98]
NcD Ap 30 1897

MARSHALL

MADISON county record. *See* News record

NEWS RECORD. w,sw 1901+
1901-11? as Madison county record
w 1901-29?
pub O 1924+
Nc [1902]-[14]15;22+

MARSHVILLE

Marshville HOME. w 1892+
1892-1912? as Our home
pub 1929+
NcU Ag 16 1898

OUR home. *See* Marshville home

MAXTON

SCOTTISH chief. w 1886+
1886-91? as Maxton union; 1892?-93? Union and Scottish chief
pub Mr 1928+
Nc Mr 19 1889-Jl 14 1891;Ag 11 1892-[93-94]-
NcD D 1 1898
[96]-Ag 1898

UNION and Scottish chief. *See* Scottish chief

MEBANE

Mebane LEADER. w 1909-21||?
Nc 1911-15

MILTON

Milton CHRONICLE. sw,w Ag 3 1841-84||?
sw S 1869
DLC Ag 3,18 1841;D 9 1880
NcD Mr 22 1844;N 1 1849;Ap 4-11,My 16,Je 5,Jl 4,Ag 1-8 1850;F 12 1857;My 24 1861;Ja 20 1875;My 27-Je 3,Jl 1,15-22,Ag 5-12 1880;Mr 10 1881
NcHi Jl 7 1853;My 16 1854 O 10 1855;My 21 1858;Je 28,N 22 1861;My 16 1862;N 4 1864
NcU F 6 1846;Ag 28 1847;Ap 17 1851;Mr 10 1859;Ap 12 1861;My 27,Jl 3,Ag 19,S-O 6,14, 28 1869;Jl 21 1881
VRC N 14 1862;F 13,Ap 10-17 1863;Ja 27 1864

Milton GAZETTE and Roanoke advertiser. w 1823-
DLC F 26,Ap 22 1824;F 28,Ag 28 1828
Nc Ag 28,S 11-18 1830;F 13,Mr 16 1831
NcD Ag 21 1830
NcHi F 26,Ap 22 1824;F 28,Ag 28 1828
NcU Mr 1 1827;Je 5 1830

Milton SPECTATOR. w O 1831-
DLC N 7 1832
NcD N 30 1831;O 24-31 1832;S 27 1836
NcHi N 7 1832;Ja 29 1839
NcU Jl 11 1837

Milton SPECTATOR. w 1853-
DLC Jl 12,S 6,O 4-18 1854

MOCKSVILLE

Mocksville COURIER. w 1906-09||?
Nc F 22 1906-[07]
NcD S 13 1906

DAVIE record. w Mr 15 1899+
pub 1899+
Nc 1908;10;12+
NcD F 9 1905;Ap 5 1916

DAVIE times. w 1879-1905||?
NcU [1881-82]Ja 5 1883[84-86]Ag 12,O 7 1887;My 18,Je 8,Ag 3-17,S 7-14,28,N 23 1888 [89]D 19 1890;Ja 15 1892

Mocksville HERALD. w 1910-16||?
Nc 1912

MONROE

ENQUIRER. sw 1873+
1883?-89? as Monroe enquirer and express; 1890? Register-enquirer
pub 1928+
DLC My 19 1881
NcU Jl 7 1877;Jl 16 1886

Monroe EXPRESS. w 1876-82||?
United with Enquirer to form Monroe enquirer and express, later Enquirer
NcU Jl 22 1881

NORTH CAROLINA (*Continued*)

MONROE—*Continued*

Monroe JOURNAL. w,sw F 21 1894+
w 1894-Mr 1914
pub 1914+
Nc Mr 17 1903-[21]-[26]+

REGISTER enquirer. *See* Enquirer

MOORESVILLE

Mooresville ENTERPRISE. w S 8 1898+
pub [1898-1921]+
Nc 1910-16;18+

MOREHEAD CITY

CARTERET county herald. w 1900+
1900-Ap 1926 as Morehead City coaster
pub 1921+

Morehead City COASTER. *See* Carteret county herald

MORGANTON

BLUE RIDGE blade. w F 14 1876-83||?
DLC Jl 10 1880
NcU F 14,Ag 8,O 10 1876;S 7-14,O 5-19,N 9 1878[79]F 21,Mr 20,D 25 1880;F 26-Mr 19, Ap 16,30,My 14 1881

BURKE county news. *See* Morganton news-herald

FARMER'S friend. w Jl 1897-98||?
Nc [1898]
NcU Mr 16,My 25 1898

Morganton HERALD. w Mr 6 1885-N 1901||
1885-89 as Morganton star. United with Burke county news to form Morganton news-herald
GAtCo S 1 1892;Mr 14-28,Je 20 1895
Nc N 1889-1901
NcD Jl 21 1898
NcMorN [1885-1901]
NcU Ap 10 1885;Jl 16-23,Ag 6 1886;Ap 28 1890;S 24 1894

Morganton NEWS-HERALD. d,w 1899+
1899-N 22 1901 as Burke county news
d 1916?
pub [1899+]
Nc 1899-1900;N 29 1901-[03]+
NcD Jl 18,20-21 1916;extra Jl 19 1916
NcMor Mr 1927+

Morganton STAR. *See* Morganton herald

MOUNT AIRY

Mount Airy NEWS. w 1880+
1880-94? as Yadkin Valley news
pub 1887+
DLC N 27 1880
NcD S 25 1886;O 4 1890;S 18,O 2,16,30-D 18 1891;Ja 8 1892;F 18 1897;Ap 6 1899
NcU Jl 23 1881;Jl 17 1886;My 28 1887

SURRY weekly visitor. w 1872-82||?
DLC Jl 16 1880
NcD Je 6 1874

Mount Airy WATCHMAN. w 1875-78||?
NcD N 24-D 1 1877

YADKIN VALLEY news. *See* Mount Airy news

MOUNT OLIVE

Mount Olive TRIBUNE. w 1904+
pub [1914-24]+

MURFREESBORO

ALBEMARLE enquirer. w 1875-81||?
1875-79? as Murfreesboro enquirer
DLC S 2 1880
Nc 1877-[Ja-Je 1879]
NcD S 11 1879
NcU Jl 21 1881

ALBEMARLE southron and union advocate. w Ja 4 1860-
NcD Ap 5,My 17,Jl 26 1860

CITIZEN. w 1858-
MeBa Ag 1859-D 1 1860
NcD Ag 30 1860

Murfreesboro ENQUIRER. *See* Albemarle enquirer

Murfreesboro INDEX. w 1885-1909||?
Nc Ap 29-S 9 1887;Ap 27 1888-Je 8 1894; 95[96]

NORTH-CAROLINA chronicle. w Mr 16 1827-
DLC Mr-Je,Jl 21(extra)1827
NcU Mr 16 1827

MURPHY

CHEROKEE herald. w D 1873-80||?
NcD Je 24 1874

NASHVILLE

GRAPHIC. w 1895+
pub 1904+
Nc [1900-08]-18;20+

Nashville REPUBLICAN. sw 1825-
NcU Ja 8 1830

NEW BERN

To 1870? as Newbern; 1871?-80? New Berne

CAMPAIGN anti-radical. w? 1870||?
NcU Jl 30 1870

CAROLINA sentinel. *See* Newbern sentinel

COMMERCIAL news. d Ap 3 1866-81||?
Ap-O 19 1866? as Daily Newbern commercial; O 20 1866-Ap 25 1867 Newbern daily journal of commerce; Ap 26 1867-Jl? 1881 Newbern journal of commerce; Ag-S 13? 1881 Daily commercial news
DLC O 20-N 3 1866;Ja-D 12 1867;Ag 21 1875
MBAt Ap 3-4,6,9,11-17,19,21,O 23 1866;Mr 29 1867
Nc [S 17-D 1881]
NcD S 17 1867;D 23 1869
NcHi My 14 1866;Ja 8 1867;Jl 4,S 5,N 12 1871;Ap 18,28 1872;Ag 13,S 20 1881
NcU S 3,O 23,D 13 1866[69]S 27 1867;N 5 1870;My 24,Je 7-9 1871;Mr 17,22,Jl 20,Ag 29,31,S 14 1872;Jl 26 1873;Ja 2 1874[Ag-N 1875]S 14 1881
—w ed *See* Newbern journal of commerce

Daily DELTA. d
Nc Ap 5-19,My 3-Je 28,Jl 6,19 1859

New-Bern DEMOCRAT. d 1879-80||?
NcHi Jl 9-10,12 1879

EASTERN CAROLINA republican. *See* North Carolina republican (Goldsboro)

Newbern ENQUIRER. w 1860?-
NcD Je 12 1860

Daily HERALD. d Ja 1868-
NcAsS Ja 26 1868

New Bern weekly JOURNAL. w
Nc [F 1854-56]

New Bern weekly JOURNAL. w,sw 1878-1915||?
United with Semi-weekly sun to form Semi-weekly sun-journal
w 1878-Ag 10 1897
Nc Ap 1887-Mr 1889;Ap 1892-S 9 1915
NcD Ag 2 1888;Je 27 1889;Ap 29 1897[1908-My 1909]
NcHi O 26 1882;O 15 1891
NcU [1882]-[Ag 10 1897-Jl 1898]

New Bern daily JOURNAL. d 1882-1915||?
1882-95? as Daily journal. United with Sun to form Sun-journal
NcD O 27 1885;Jl 3 1887;D 15 1889;Ja 23,S 15 1892[F-Je 1908]F 2,9 1909
NcHi Jl 23 1882;Mr 30,N 17 1883;Je 30,Jl 4,D 11,18 1885;Ja 5,Ap 16 1886;F 12 1887;D 16 1888;Ap 18,23,Jl 7,12,S 7,18-22,24,N 22,D 1 1889;Ja 14 1891;Mr 4,O 1 1892;S 11 1893;Ap 17 1896
NcU D 8 1882;Ap 5 1883-Ap 3,O 5 1884-S,O 27 1885-Mr 6,Ap 1886-Mr,Ap 24-S 1888;Ap-S 1889;Ap 1890-99

Newbern JOURNAL of commerce. w 1866-76||?
1871? as Weekly journal of commerce
MBAt O 30-N 6,20-D 4,18 1866-Ja 4,18-Mr 1,22,Ap 5,Ag 16 1867
NcD N 18 1871
NcHi F 23 1869;N 18 1871;Ja 17,F 14-28,Mr 21-Ap 11 1874;Ja 22 1876

Newbern daily JOURNAL of commerce. *See* Commercial news

Daily LIBERAL. d N 1872-73||?
NcHi D 1 1872

NEW ERA and commercial advertiser. w
Nc [Ag 1858-Mr 1859]

NEWBERNIAN. 1843-50 *See* Newbernian and

NEWBERNIAN. sw,w 1874-83||?
sw 1874-77?
DLC Jl 3 1880
NcD Jl 12-Ag 2,30,O 18 1879;Ap 24 1880;Jl 23 1881
NcHi My 16,30,Jl 17 1874;Ag 11-18,O 20 1877; Ja-F 1878;F 21,S 6,20-21,O 8,11-12,N 2,D 4 1880;Ja 29,Je 25 1881
NcU O 14 1874-[Ja-F 1875;Ag-D 1876]-Mr 1877;Jl 10 1880;Jl 23 1881

NEW BERNIAN. d 1916-31||
Merged with Sun-journal
Nc 1928-31

NEWBERNIAN and North Carolina advocate. w Je 24 1843-
1843-O 1 1850 as Newbernian
DLC Je 24 1843
GDE O 1 1850
NcD S 14,O 26 1847;Ja 18,F 29 1848;Ap-Ag,S 25-D 4,25 1849-[50]S 2,D 2 1851;Ja 6,N 9 1852
NcHi F 4 1845;Je 22 1847
NcU Ap 30,Je 4 1844;Je 17 1845;Jl 28 1846;My 23,Ag 1 1848;D 11 1849;Ag 27 1850

NORTH CAROLINA sentinel. *See* Newbern sentinel

NORTH CAROLINA times. *See* New Berne times

Daily NUT SHELL. d Ja 1874-83||?
DLC Jl 5 1880
Nc My 25 1877
NcD F 25,Mr 1,6 1875
NcHi Je 22 1875;F 1,Mr 15 1876;Jl 24,Ag 16, O 29 1877;Jl 18,Ag 9,12-13 1878;D 1 1879;S 6 1880;Je 16,D 1 1883
NcU Ja 18,Mr 21 1876;S 12 1877

PEOPLE'S advocate. w Mr 20- 1886||?
Negro
NcU Jl 31 1886

Newbern daily PROGRESS. d S 1858-
1858-61? as Daily progress
CSmH Ap 19 1862
CtHT Ap 12,My 22 1862
CtY S 1859-N 23 1865
DLC Mr 22,26,Ap 2,16,19,23-24,My 21,26-27,Je 20,Ag 27,N 12,D 3,20 1862
ICHi D 16 1862
MBAt Ap 29,My 1-2,7-9,S 24 1862
MH Ap 24 1862-F 4 1863
MHi [1862-Ja 1863]
MLei Jl 31 1862
MWA F 26,Ap 26,29-My 1,Jl 14,Ag 4,18,22[S 1862-Ja 16 1863]
MiU-C Ap 16 1862
NNHi Mr 18,26,Ap 19 1862
NcD S 6 1860;My 9,Je 4 1862
NcHi F 11 1861
NcU O 14,16 1858;F 16,25,Jl 5,7,S 8,O 6,22,N 12,28 1859;Ap 2,My 11,Je 25,Jl 3,17,O 1,10,D 26 1860;Jl 26 1861;N 29 1862;My 13,Jl 6,18-19, Ag 31 1865
PLewL My 16,20-Je 3,6,9,11,19-20,23-25,27-28, Jl 9 1862

Newbern weekly PROGRESS. w 1858-
Title varies slightly
CSmH Mr 18 1862
DLC Ag 9,30,D 20 1862
MBAt My 3,17 1862
MH Mr 18-Ap 19 1862
MHi Ap 26-My 3,Ag 23 1862;Ja 10-17 1863
MSaE Je 14-21,Jl-Ag 23,S 20,O 11-N 1 1862
MSte Ap 16 1862
MWA Mr 18,My 3-17,31-Je 7,28-Ag 23,S-N 22,D 13 1862-Ja 10,24-31 1863
NIC Ap 19 1862
NcD D 6 1859;Ap 21 1862
NcHi Ap 16 1862
OClWHi Ap 26 1862
PHi Je 7 1862
PLewL Mr 18,Ap 9 1862

Newbern PROGRESS. sw
MBAt Mr 22-26,Ap 12-19 1862;Ja 31-F 4 1863
MHi [1862]Ja 21-24,31 1863
MWA Mr 22-Ap 9,16-23 1862
NBHi Mr 22 1862
NN Mr 26 1862
NcD Mr 22,Ap 5,16 1862
OClWHi Mr 29-O 1862

REPUBLICAN. 1847-50 *See* North Carolina republican (Goldsboro)

New Bern REPUBLICAN. w Ap 27? 1867-
MH [My 1867]

New Berne daily REPUBLICAN. tw,d My 2 1867-
1867-O 3? 1868 as New Bern republican (tw)
MBAt [1867;My 14-D 1868]
MH O 13 1868-Ja 13 1869
NcD O 3 1868

REPUBLIC-COURIER. w 1867-74||?
United with New Berne times (w) to form New Bern weekly times and republic-courier
NcD Mr 29 1873
NcHi Ja 4 1872;N 29 1873
NcU N 25,D 9 1871-Ja 13,F 3,17 1872;N 1873-My 1874

*Newbern SENTINEL. w Mr 21 1818-
1818-O 26 1822 as Carolina centinel; D 7 1822-Jl 12 1828 Carolina sentinel; Ag 9 1828-D 21 1836 North Carolina sentinel
DLC 1821-S 6 1823;Ja 24 1828-D 19 1829;Ja 2-16,My 1,29,Je 12,Jl 17-24,O 10-16 1830;Ja 13 1836-O 7 1837
GDE O 28 1835
MH 1821-Je 5 1824
MWA My 23,Je 29 1822
N O 18 1833
NcD My 15,N 20 1824;N 24 1827;F 28,Jl 11-25 1829;S 6 1833;Mr 1,Je 14,Ag 19-O 7 1837
NcHi [1821-30;36-37]
NcU Ag 17 1822;O 2 1824;Ag 5 1826

Newbern SPECTATOR. w 1828-
1828-32? as Newbern spectator and literary journal; 1833? Spectator
DLC Ja 2-9,23,N 20 1830;Mr 12,Ap 16 1831;O 12 1832;O 16 1840;Ap 3-10,Je 26,Jl 10-O 16, 30,N 20 1841;Ja 8-15,F 19,Jl 23-30,Ag 20-S 10 1842
MWA Ap 10 1841
NcD N 4 1831;S 4 1835;Ja 13,O 13 1837;My 16, Ag 1-8,29,S 26 1840
NcHi Ja 2-9,23,N 20 1830;Mr 12,Ap 16 1831; O 12 1832;Ag 9 1833
NcU D 9 1831;D 21 1832;Ag 9 1833;My 17 1839;N 7 1840;My 22,Je 5,O 9 1841
OClWHi My 1 1841

SUN-JOURNAL. d Jl 3 1907+
1907-15? as Sun
Nc 1907-O 21 1908;Jl 6-S 1914;31+

Semi-weekly SUN-JOURNAL. sw 1907-19||?
1907-15? as Semi-weekly sun
Nc S 13-D 1915
NcU S 26 1917

New Berne TIMES. w,sw,d Ja 1864-75||?
1864-Ap 25 1865 as North Carolina times; Ap 26-My 1865 North Carolina daily times; My-S 6 1865 Daily North Carolina times; S 7 1865-Mr 13 1866 New Berne daily times; Mr 15-Ap 28 1866 New Bern daily times; My 1-Ag 16? 1866 Newbern daily times; Ag 21-O? 1866 Newbern weekly times; O? 1866-Mr 1873 New Berne daily times
w Ja? 1864;sw F-D? 1864;w Ja 7-28 1865;sw Ja 31-Ap 25 1865;d Ap 26 1865-Ag 16? 1866;w Ag 21-O? 1866;d O 1866-75?
DLC Ja 9,23,Mr 30-S,D 2,15 1864;Ja 7-O 21 1865;Ja-O 19 1866;F 1871-Mr 1874
MBAt S 9 1864;Ap 14,Je 24,Ag 14 1865-[Ja-O 1866]Ja 14,17,Ag 10,S 1,14 1869
MDeHi Je 25 1864
MWA Ja 16,Je 15,22,29,Ag 2,N 26,S 29 1864
MnHi Ja 2 1864
N Ap 27,Je 25 1864
NN Je 18,22-25 1864;S 9 1866
NcD F 24 1864;D 7 1865;Ag 28,S 15 1866;Je 14 1872;S 28 1873;Jl 14 1874

NORTH CAROLINA (*Continued*)

NEW BERN—*Continued*

New Berne TIMES. w,sw,d 1864-75||?—*Cont.*
NcHi [Ja 26-N 7 1865]My 6,12-13,19,Je 4 1866; Je 4 1869;D 4 1872
NcU Mr 9-30,Ap 9,16-30,My 14-18,Je 1-8,Jl 20, Ag 16,20,S 16,N 26,D 8,24 1864;Ja 7-14,F 10,28-Mr,Ap 14-25,My 2-12,Je 7,17,S 30,O 17,19,N 3,D 5 1865[Je 27-O 19 1866;My 26-N 1869]Mr 29-Ap 8,22-S 21 1873
OClWHi Je 11,29 1864
PPGr Je 22 1864

TIMES. w 1926+
Suspended from Ap-N 1934
pub 1930+

New Bern weekly TIMES and republic-courier. w 1868-?6||?
1868-7-? as New Berne times
NcD Jl 23 1874
NcU My 1,Jl 24,Ag 7,21-S 4,18 1873

UNION. w
Nc [1857-Jl 1858]

NEWLAND

AVERY advocate. w Ag 28 1927+
pub 1927+

NEWTON

CATAWBA county news. *See* Catawba news-enterprise

CATAWBA news-enterprise. w,sw My 1903+
1903-Ag 12 1919 as Catawba county news
w 1903-? 1905
Nc 1903-Mr 17,D 24 1910+
NcD S 6 1905[06-F 1909]
VU Ap 11 1916;Ag 24,S 4,28,O 16,N 2-6,13-17, 23-30 1917;Ap 4,12,19,Ag 27,N 5-7,19-22,29-D 3,13 1918

Newton ENTERPRISE. w,sw 1879-Ag 5 1919||
United with Catawba county news to form Catawba news-enterprise
w 1879-My 13 1915
CtY S 26 1912
DLC Ag 25 1880
GAtCo Ja 6,My 6,27-Jl 1,S 9 1892;S 8 1905
Nc S 15 1887-[98]-1916
NcD D 7 1900[18]
NcU Jl 23 1881

NORLINA

Norlina HEADLIGHT. w Jl 24 1914+
pub 1914+
Nc 1914-15;Mr 1924+
NcD [1914-Jl 1920]

NORTH WILKESBORO

CARTER'S weekly. *See* Wilkes journal

North Wilkesboro HUSTLER. w,sw 1896+
1896-99? as Hustler
sw 1914-20?
Nc 1914
NcD My 26 1899

PATRIOT-JOURNAL. w,sw 1906+
1906-N 21 1932 as Wilkes patriot
1906-25? pub in Wilkesboro
w 1906-29?
pub 1917+
NcD Je 19,Jl 3,17 1913

WILKES journal. w,tw 1917-N 1932||
1917-24 as Carter's weekly. United with Wilkes patriot to form Patriot-journal
w 1917-30?
Nc 1920-30
NcNwP complete

WILKES patriot. *See* Patriot-journal

NORWOOD

SOUTHERN vidette. w 1885-93||?
Nc 1892

OXFORD

Oxford BANNER. sw 1911-13||?
Nc F-D 16 1911

DAY. d 1889-92||?
Nc 1890

Oxford EXAMINER. w Ja 1830-
CSmH My 29 1830
DLC O 4 1832;My 17 1838
MoCaT Ag 9 1832

Oxford FREE LANCE. *See* Granville free lance

GRANVILLE free lance. w 1876-82||?
1876-My 3 1878 as Oxford free lance
DLC Je 25 1880
Nc Ja 11 1878;Ag 8 1879
NcD [1881]Ja 20,Jl 7,N 10,D 1 1882
NcU Ja 22,F 1,Mr 8-Ap 5,My 3-17 1878

GRANVILLE whig. sw 1850?-
NcD Ap 27,My 25,Je 12,26,Jl 3 1850

LEISURE hour. w F 4 1858-
NcU 1858-Ja 1859

Oxford MERCURY and district telegram. w Jl 1841-44||
1841? as Oxford mercury and citizen of Granville
DLC Ag 12,S 16 1841
NcD O 20,D 1,15 1843[44]

PUBLIC ledger. w,sw 1888+
Title varies slightly
w 1858-1911?
pub [1920+]
Nc My 1890-[98]-O 6 1905;F 12 1916+
NcD N 29-D 6 1900;Jl 16,30-Ag 6,20 1903[04-05]-[07]My 15 1908;Ap 18,S 9,D 19-23 1914
NcU Ag 9 1900;F 1 1907

TORCHLIGHT. w D 22 1873-88||?
1881-84 as Oxford torchlight
DLC F 8 1881
Nc O 23 1877-My 8 1885[86]-Je 1888
NcD Ap 14,Je 9 1874;My 29 1877;O 28 1879;Je 29,O 12 1880;Je 7 1881;Ag 21,O 30-N 6 1883;D 1884;O 12 1886;Ja 25,F 8,Ap 26,D 6-21 1887;Ja 4,F 8,Mr 14 1888
NcU F 17,Mr 24 1874;Jl 13,27 1886

PITTSBORO

CENTRAL reflector. w 1832-
NcHi Je 7 1833

CHATHAM citizen. w 1894-1905||?
Nc 1897-99
NcU Mr 28 1900

CHATHAM record. w S 19 1878+
DLC Ag 19 1880
Nc 1878-Jl 1920;21+
NcD O 10 1878;Mr 27 1879;N 3 1881;Je 2 1882
NcHi F 10 1898;O 15-22 1931
NcU 1878-Ag 1,N 21 1917;F 13 1918;Ag 1919-Jl 1920

COMMUNICATOR. w Je 2 1847-
NcHi Ag 18 1847

Pittsboro HOME. w 1883-89||?
Nc O 13 1887-F 7 1889
NcU Ap 16 1885

PLYMOUTH

Plymouth BANNER. w Ja 1856-
MWA F 15 1856
NcU O 31 1856

Plymouth NEWS. w O 12 1849-
NcD O 12 1849;D 11 1850

OLD flag. w My 19 1865-
DLC My 19 1865

ROANOKE cresset. w Je 18 1859-70||?
NcU O 29 1859;F 9,My 27 1861

POLKSTON

Weekly ANSONIAN. w Ap 16 1874-78||?
NcD Ap 23 1874
NcU Ap 5 1876

RALEIGH

Daily AD VALOREM banner. d Ja 1861-
NcD Ja 19(extra)F 23,Ap 5 1861
NcU F 11,15,21,26,Mr 18 1861

Weekly AD VALOREM banner. w Ja 31? 1861-
NcD F 21,Ap 25 1861

Raleigh AMERICAN. d
Nc [Ja 31-My 13 1920]

AMERICAN signal. w? Je? 1856-
NcD Jl 9 1856

CAROLINA beacon and metropolitan omnibus. w Ap 7? 1840-
DLC Ap 21 1840

CAROLINA era. *See* Era

CAROLINA Jeffersonian. w Jl 16 1924-25||?
Nc 1924-25
NcU Jl 16 1924

CAROLINA tribune. w Ap 1926+
Also dated in Durham
Negro
pub Jl 1935+

Daily CAROLINIAN. d O 17 1871-72||?
Followed by Daily news, later News and observer
DLC O 24 1871
NcD O 18,20 1871
NcU [1871-F 14 1872]

CAUCASIAN. w 1882-1913||
Merged with Union republican (Winston-Salem)
1882-93? pub in Clinton; 1894?-95? in Goldsboro
GAtCo My 26,N 3 1898
NbHi S 12(supp)19 1895
Nc F 28 1889-[98]-N 1901[03]-12
NcD Mr 13 1884;My 11,Je 22-29,S 28,D 7 1893; Mr 29 1894;Mr 14,S 12-19,O 24 1895;Ja 30, My 21,Je 4,25-Jl 16,Ag 27,O 22,D 3 1896;Je 24 1900
NcHi Ag 31 1893;S 12 1895;Je 11,Ag 13 1896
NcU N 22 1894;Ag 27(supp)S 17 1896;Je 17-24,S 30-O 7,28-N,D 9-23 1897[98;1909-11]Ja 30 1913

Daily CHRONICLE. *See* State chronicle

Daily CONFEDERATE. d 1861?-
DLC F 27,29,Mr 2-3,5,8,10,23,Ap 29,Ag 9 1864; Mr 7-8,10,13-22,24,28-30,Ap 4,6-7 1865
LNC Ap 6 1865
MBAt Mr 22-23,26,30 1864
MH Ja 7 1865
MWA F 13 1865
NN D 17,20 1864
NNHi Jl 26 1864
Nc Mr 9,21,24,Ap 2,4,6,My 7,Je 14,23,Ag 17, 30-S 1,O 17,31,N 3,11 1864;Mr 25 1865
NcD Ja 26,F 20,Ap 8,My 4,23,Je 23,Jl 15,Ag 16,N 22,D 30 1864;Ja 2,F 17,Mr 2 1865
NcGrW My 28 1864
NcH My 4,Je 9,11 1864;Ja 10,F 23 1865

NcU F 20,26,29[Mr-S]O 5,N 3,D 13 1864
OClWHi Mr 9-Ap 28 1864;Ap 6 1865
VRC Ja 29-30,F 3,13,19-20,Mr 4,My 18,Ag 18-19,24-26,S 5,9-10,12,D 6,8-9 1864
WHi Ap 7 1864

CONFEDERATE. w F 3? 1864-
Nc F 24-Mr 23,Ap 6-Ag 17,S 14-21 1864;Ja 11-F 22,Mr 1 1865
NcU My 4,18-25,Je 15-Ag 3,24,S 7-14,28-O 5 1864

CONFEDERATE tri-weekly. tw
NcHi Mr 28/29 1864

Daily CONSERVATIVE. d Ap 16 1864-
DLC Ap 26,28-29,Ag 1,26,1864;Mr 2-4,7,10,17, 28-29,31,Ap 7-8,10-11 1865
MBAt Ap 25-27 1864
Nc Jl 16,19,21 1864
NcD Jl 19 1864
NcHi Je 11 1864
NcU Ap 16,22,25,28[My-Jl]Ag 15,25,S 23,O 10,14,21-22,N 23,D 13-14 1864;Ja 13,25-27,30,F 8-10,14,21,24-25,27,Mr 1,4,27-28,Ap 7-8,My 10 1865
OClWHi Ap 7 1865
P-M F 23 1865

Weekly CONSERVATIVE. w Ap 20 1864-
DLC Jl 6-13 1864;Mr 22 1865
MBAt Ap 20 1864
Nc Ap-My 4,18,Je-Ag 3,17-O 5,19-26,N 9-30, D 14-21 1864;Ja-Ap 5 1865
NcD Jl 6 1864;F 1,Mr 29 1865
OClWHi Ap 12 1865
VRC Ag 17 1864;Mr 22 1865

Daily CONSTITUTION. d -Ag 14 1875||
NcD Jl 5-Ag 1875

Tri-weekly CONSTITUTION. tw Ap? 1876-
NcD Je 17,Jl 12 1876

Daily CONSTITUTION. d 1876?-
Nc Ag 9 1876

Weekly CONSTITUTION. w Ag 31 1876-
DLC O 26 1876
NcD S 28,O 19-26 1876
NcU O 12 1876

CONSTITUTIONALIST and people's advocate. w N 15 1831-
1831-? as North Carolina constitutionalist and state rights' advocate; 1832?-O 15 1833 Constitutionalist, people's advocate and state gazette; O 22-N 1833 North Carolina constitutionalist, people's advocate and state gazette
DLC N 15 1831;Ja 22-D 20 1833
N O 8 1833
NcD N 21 1832
NcU N 14 1832;F 12 1833
VU F 12 1833

COURIER-JOURNAL. w 1933?+
Nc 1933+

Daily evening CRESCENT. d Mr- 1874||?
Mr 1874? as Evening crescent
NcD Ag 21 1874
NcHi Jl 10 1874
NcU Mr 27 1874

DEMOCRATIC press. *See* State journal

DEMOCRATIC signal. w Je 7 1843-N 15 1844||
Nc O 27 1843
NcD O 27,N 17,D 8-15 1843[44]
NcHi S 22 1843;O 11 1844
NcU Je 7,29-N,D 8-22 1843;Ja-My,Je 14,28-O 18,N 1,15 1844

ENTERPRISE. w F 5 1866-
NcD F 5,Mr 5 1866
NcU Ap 9 1866;F 11,18 1867

Tri-weekly ERA. tw Je 6 1871-76||?
1871-N 1 1872 as Carolina era
DLC N 28 1871;Ja 25,F 6,Mr 16,My 7,11,Jl 2, 11,Ag 15,31,S 10-12,17-O 8,12-19,N 1,8-18,D 4 1872
NcD 1871-Je,Jl 11,23-25,O 17,N 22,27,D 2-4 1872;My 21,Je 6,Jl 16 1874
NcGrW Je 15,O 1871
NcU [Jl 13 1871-D 16 1872]Ja 14-16,Ag 10,S 7,O 5 1876

Weekly ERA. w Je 8 1871-77||?
1871-O 1872 as Carolina era; N 1872-Mr 1874? Era; Mr 1874? Weekly era and examiner
DLC S 9 1871;Ap 10 1873
NcD [1871]-[73-74]Ap 22,My 13,Jl 15-29 1875; F 3,Ag 24,S 14-21,D 4,18 1876
NcGrW Je 22 1871
NcU Je 8,22,Jl 1 1871

Daily ERA. d O 21 1872-73||?
DLC O 21,23,25,N 6 1872;Mr 1,3,6 1873
NcD N 25,29,D 6,14,17 1872;Ja 9,15 1873
NcU O-N 16,19-23,25-26,29-30,D 2-4,6-8,10-24, 30 1872-Mr 8 1873

Daily EXAMINER. d Ja?-Mr? 1874||
United with Era to form Weekly era and examiner, later Weekly era
NcD Mr 7 1874

EXTRA standard. sm Mr 12 1841-
DLC Mr 12 1841
NcD My 14,Je,Jl 30-Ag 1841
—w ed *See* Weekly standard

GAZETTE. w 1870-71||?
MWA F 4 1871

GAZETTE. bw,w 1883-97||?
bw 1883-92?
Negro
Nc D 9 1893
NcU D 16 1893;My 19 1894;O 31,N 21 1896-Ag 7 1897

HALE'S weekly. w 1879-
NcD O 7,N 4,D 9 1879;Ja,F 24-Mr 2,30 1880
NcU Ja 13,Ap 27 1880

NORTH CAROLINA (*Continued*)

RALEIGH—*Continued*

HARBINGER. w 1902-05||?
NcU My 16,30-Je 6,Jl 4,S 5,N 7 1903;F 20 1904

HAYSEEDER. w 1893-98||?
NcD O 22 1896;F 3 1898
NcU O 29 1896;O 14-N 4,18,D 2 1897;F 17 1898

HOLDEN record. w Mr 12-Ap 16 1868||
DLC Mr 19-Ap 16 1868
MWA complete
Nc complete
NcD Mr 19 1868
NcU Mr 19-Ap 16 1868

INDEPENDENT. w Jl 4 1843-
NcU D 5 1843;F 22,Ap 30 1845

INTELLIGENCER. w Je 7 1890-
1890? as North Carolina intelligencer
Nc Ap 15 1891
NcD O 15,N 26,D 24 1890;Ap 1 1891
NcHi O 15 1890
NcU Ja 7,F 25,Ap 29 1891

JOURNAL of freedom. w S 30 1865-
MBAt S-O 1865
MH S 30 1865
NcHi O 7 1865
NcU O 7-21 1865

LIVE giraffe. w
Nc Ag 6,S 3 1857
NcD N 18-25 1858;F-Ap 1859

LIVE giraffe. w F 4 1869-
NN F 11 1869

*Raleigh **MINERVA.** w Mr 24 1796-
1796-Ap 1799 as North-Carolina minerva and Fayetteville advertiser; My 7 1799-1800 North-Carolina minerva and Raleigh advertiser; 1880-Ap 1803 North-Carolina minerva; My 1803-05 Minerva; or, Anti-Jacobin; 1805-N 23 1809 Minerva
1796-Ap 1799 pub in Fayetteville
Nc Ja 7-21 1821

NATIONAL. w Ag 14 1878-79||?
NcD Ag 21,S 25,O 16,30-N 5,15 1878

NATIONAL democrat. sw S 8 1860-
NcD S 8,O 17 1860
NcU S 29 1860

NEWS and observer. d Mr 1 1872+
Follows Daily Carolinian. 1872-Ag 1876 as Daily news; S 1876-S 11 1880 Raleigh news; Jl 2 1893-Ag 11 1894 News-observer-chronicle
pub 1916+
DLC N 5-11,14,19 1876;80-Ag 1919;Mr 1920+
GU Ap 19 1925
M F 20 1929
Nc 1872-75[Mr 1876]Mr 21 1878+
NcAsS D 7,11 1889;My 3 1893;Ag 14 1904;Ap 11 1905;Ag 1(supp)O 3 1909
NcD S 20 1872[73-80]Ja 6,S 20 1881;F 21,Mr 1-2,5,11,15-16,21,23,My 30,Je 9,13 1882;My 17, Je 9,13,29,N 1,12 1883[84]Ja 3,26,F 6,Mr 13, 15,28,Ap 24,Je 4 1885[86-90]-[92-97]-[1926]+
NcEloC F 1924+
NcGrW Ap 26 1875
NcGreE D 1923+
NcHi Ap 9,Ag 19,21 1873;O 25,D 19 1874;My 16,22,Je 21 1875;Jl 7,O 31 1876;Ja 15 1878;N 30 1880;My 26-27,Je 1-2,10,Jl 17,S 13,18 1881; Je 25 1882[84-85]F 25 1886;Ja 13,18 1887;Ja 27,F 21-22,Mr 16,D 4 1888;F 17,Mr 10,Jl 21 1889[92]Ag 9,29 1895;Ja 11,Je 16,24 1896;N 24 1897;O 15,20,D 11,14 1898;F 26,Jl 16 1899; Ap 8,Je 26,Ag 22,O 9,N 15,D 21 1900;F 3,Je 20 1901;S 24 1903;My 11,Je 2 1904;Ja 30 1907; Ap 26 1916;N 11 1918;supp D 1874
NcRS 1925+
NcU [1872-78]Mr 6,9,Je 12,S 12,N 23 1879; Je 17,22,D 28 1880[81]Mr 6,My 26 1882;F 3,Ap 21 1883[85]O 22,D 10,28,31 1886;F 15, Mr 15,My 17,Ag 14,D 6 1887;Ja 17,26,31,F 2,Mr 6,Je 23 1888;My 24,Je 2,18,Ag 9,S 17,D 16 1889;My 5 1891:Mr 4,Je 26,O 18-19,N 3,D 23 1892;Ja 20,22 1893[94-96]-[98]1900-S 1910; 11+
NcWaC 1909+
PP 1934+
VRC F 3 1884
WHi Mr 1915+

NEWS and observer. w 1872-1917||?
1872-Ag 1880 as Weekly news; Ag 5 1892-1909 North Carolinian
GAtCo S 30 1892;Mr 7 1895;Ap 14,My 12,O 6 1898;N 29 1900;D 6 1906
Nc Ag 5-19,D 1892-1902;Ap 23 1903-15.
NcD Ja 19,S 27 1876;Mr 12,26 1877;My 17 1881;Mr 20-27,Jl 10 1883;Mr 10 1885;My 18 1886;S 13 1887;Mr 5 1889;Ag 26,S 15,O 21,N 4,18-25 1892;Ja 13,Mr 3,S 15,O 20,N 10,D 1-14 1893;Ja 25-F 1 1894;Mr 14 1895;Ja 11, 25,F 8,My 17 1900;F 28 1901;My 14 1903;S 12-19,D 26 1907
NcHi Ag 5-12,O 7-14,N 4,D 16-20 1892;Ja 20, O 13 1893;Jl 12 1894;Ap 12 1900;My 1 1902
NcU [1874;76]Je 11 1877;D 3 1878;Ja 18,F 5,Mr 23,Ap 7,N 24 1881;Ja 6,Mr 4,Je 10,S 3 1882;D 1883-[91-92]-Ag 14 1894;Ja 23,F 6 1895[96]F 18-25 1897;99[1900]My 16-Je 6,20-27 1901;My 1 1902;Ap 28,O 13 1904

NORTH CAROLINA constitutionalist. . . *See* Constitutionalist and people's advocate

NORTH CAROLINA intelligencer. *See* Intelligencer

NORTH CAROLINA minerva. *See* Raleigh minerva

NORTH CAROLINA standard. *See* Standard

***NORTH CAROLINA star.** w N 3 1808-
1808-15 as Star; 1816-N 20 1834 Star and North Carolina state gazette; N 27 1834-F 1850 Raleigh star and North Carolina gazette; N 29 1848 Raleigh star and North Carolina gazette
Ct [1827-28]Ap 2 1829[31]Je 4 1835
DLC D 31 1824;D 13,27 1827;Mr 27,Ag 14 1828;Ja 8-F 5,Jl 2-9,30,Ag 13-20,S 3-17,N 5-12,D 3,9(extra)24 1829-Ap,Je-D 1831;Je 21 1833;Jl 10-17 1839;F 5,N 4,D 30 1840[41]Ja 1,Mr 13 1844[50]
ICHi Je 24 1830
MBAt Mr 29 1822
MWA S 7 1821;My 14 1824;Ja 8,22-F 5,Jl 2-9,30-Ag 6,27-S 17,N 19-D 3,9(extra)24 1829; Ja 14,Mr 18 1830;My 12 1831
N O 11 1833
Nc Ja 25 1822;23-24;26-My 3 1827;28-31;33-37; 39-[41-43]-[51]52
NcD Jl 27 1821;D 29 1826-Ja 3,Ag 14,D 4 1828; D 10,31 1829-31;F 10,Ap 6,Je 15-22 1832; D 27 1833-35;Ap 14,S 15,29,N 24 1836;Ja 19,F 2 1837;Ja 24,O 3,D 5 1838;Je 26-Ag 21,S 11-18,O 2,23-30 1839[40-44]D 23 1846;N 29 1848 [Ag 1849-Ag 1850]Je 4,Jl 9,S 17 1851;S 21 1853;Ag 8 1855;extra:Ja 25 1840;supp:F 6 1850
NcHi Mr 27 1828[29]Ja 14 1830;Ag 5 1840;Ja 10 1843;Ja 13,F 17,Ap 7,28,Jl 7,N 10 1847;Mr 1,22,Ap 12,N 22 1848
NcU S 21 1821;Mr 29 1822;24-25;Mr 9,My 31, Je 21,Jl 19 1827;F 7,My 22,Jl 4,24 1828;Je 18, Jl 23 1829;Je 10-24,Jl 1-15 1830;My 18,D 14 1832;Ja 21-28,F 11,Mr 1836-[37-38]39;Ja 22 (extra)Je 10 1840;Ja 27,My 19,S 29,O 7,N 17-24,D 22 1841;Ja 12,Ap 6,27,Ag 3,N 2 1842;F 15 1843;O 16 1844;Je 2-9,Jl 21-28 1847[49]-Je 18 1856
WHi S-N 10,D 2-23 1831;Ja,Je 29-Jl 1832
—tw ed *See* Tri-weekly star

Semi-weekly **NORTH CAROLINA star.** sw 1850-
NcU F 2-12 1853

NORTH CAROLINA times. 1849 *See* Raleigh times

NORTH CAROLINIAN. d Ja 30 1868-72||?
Nc Ja-Mr 21,Ap 6-11 1868
NcHi Ja 30,F 14,17,23,25,29,Mr 1,4 1868

NORTH CAROLINIAN. w
Nc Ap 8-15 1868
NcD N 17,28,D 28 1871

NORTH CAROLINIAN. 1892-1909 *See* News and observer w

OBSERVER. d N 16 1876-S 11 1880||
United with Raleigh news to form News and observer
DLC F 24 1877-80
Nc complete
NcD [1876-Je 1877]-[Jl 1879-80]
NcU [1877-80]

OBSERVER. w N 23 1876-S 12 1880||
United with Weekly news to form News and observer
Nc 1876-F 1,20,Mr 27 1877-78
NcD Ja 2-9 1877;O 7,21,N 11,25-D 9,30 1879;Ja 13-F 10,Mr 9,23 1880
NcHi D 9,19 1877;Ja 15,25,Ap 30 1878;Jl 9 1879
NcU 1876

Morning **POST.** d D 1 1897-1905||?
Nc 1897-N 12 1905
NcAsS S 1 1901
NcD Ja 30 1898-N 13 1905
NcHi Jl 8 1900;My 11,14 1904
NcU Ap 5,11,My 18-21,23,25-26,28-29,S 1 1898; Ja 18,F 15,Mr 2,11,24,S 14,N 5,D 10 1899; Ja 27,29,F 3,Mr 25,Ap 8,Je 7,Jl 11 1900 [01]O 24 1902;Ja 8-9,18,20,30,F 28,Mr 3,Ap 24,30,N 18,D 27 1903;Ap 17 1904;Je 11 1905

Raleigh **POST.** w 1898-1905||?
NcD Jl 13 1899[1900]

Daily **PRESS.** d 1894-Jl 1895||?
United with Evening visitor to form Press-visitor, later Raleigh times
NcD My 20,Jl 9 1895

PRESS-VISITOR. *See* Raleigh times 1879+

Daily **PROGRESS.** d 1859?-
CSmH Ap 19 1865
DLC Ap 19,29 1864;Ap 19,My 27,Jl 6 1865
LNC Ja 21 1865
MBAt S 8,19-21 1864[Ap 17-D 1865]Ja 2,10,20, F 5 1866
MH D 2 1862
MWA N 6,9,12,16,18 1863;Ap 15,17-18 1865
NNHi Ja 25 1864
NbCR Ap 15,19 1865
Nc Mr 20 1863-Ap 1864
NcD N 17,19,21,D 25,31 1862;Ja 2,9-10,Jl 31, Ag 18,O 13,29,N 28 1863;My 10,26,Je 5,S 15 1865;Mr 10,N 27-28 1866;Ap 3-4,Ag 13,S 10,O 5,N 27 1867
NcGrW Ja 27,D 14 1863
NcHi Ja 14,D 9 1863;D 13 1864
NcU Je 6,9,11,17,Jl 20,29,Ag 3,9,11 1863;F 19, Mr 1,9,26,Ap 6-7,Je 13,Jl 6-8,Ag 29,S 19,O 21,D 21 1864;Mr 10,12,16,19,23,Je 7,22,Jl 6,D 4 1866;Mr 13,19,Ap 10,S 24 1867
OClWHi Mr 11-Ap 21,Ag 8-S 16 1864;Ap 22,28 1865
ODW Ap 18 1865
PHi N 20 1863;My 10 1865
WHi Ap 7 1864

Weekly **PROGRESS.** w Mr 6? 1864-
Nc Ap 4 1865
NcD Mr 13-S 13 1864;N 29-D 1866;Ja 10-F 14,28,Ag 8 1867
NcU Ap 25,Jl 19,Ag 2 1864;Mr 17 1866
WHi Ap 5 1864;Mr 28 1865

Semi-weekly **RECORD.** sw Mr? 1865-
NcD S 2 1865

RECORD. d Je 2? 1865-
MBAt Je 8 1865
NcU Je 3,9-10,13-14,16,26,Jl 6 1865

*Raleigh **REGISTER.** w,sw O 22 1799-
1799-N 1800 as Raleigh register and North-Carolina weekly advertiser; D 1800-24? Raleigh register and North-Carolina state gazette (D 28 1811-D 19 1823 Raleigh register and North Carolina gazette) 1825?-40? Raleigh register and North Carolina gazette; 1841?-50? Weekly Raleigh register and North Carolina gazette; 1851-Je 1867? Weekly Raleigh register
1864 pub in Petersburg, Va.
sw N 22-D 13 1804
Ct [1826]
CtY Mr 3 1852
DLC 1821-N 14 1823;Ag 27 1829;Ja 14,28,D 9 1830;D 22 1835;Jl 6,20,S 14 1839;F 18 1842;Mr 31 1843;Mr 1844-D 18 1846;F 21 1849;My 21,Jl 23 1856;Ja 12,F 16,Ag 17,S 14 1859;Mr 13 1861;Jl 5,S 24,O 22 1867
GAtCo Jl ?, Ag 7 1840
ICHi D 30 1833
MBAt D 2 1828;F 10,13,Je 23 1829
MHi S 21,N 23 1821;Ja 4,F 8,N 29 1822;N 25 1823;S 14 1824;D 2 1825;Ja 5,Jl 17 1827
MWA S 1822;Ja 17 1823;Je 3 1825;My 4,S 14,D 1832-Ja 4,25-F 22,Mr 5,26,Ap 23-30,D 24 1833;Ja 21-Mr 4,Ag 26-S 16,O 7,N 18,D 16 1834;Ja 20-Ap 7 1835;D 3 1856;Jl 5 1867
N Mr 21-Ap 4,18 1823;Ja 22 1828
NNHi Mr 16 1832;Ag 5(extra)1837;Jl 11 1849
Nc 1821-27,29-N 10 1831;N 16 1832-O 1839;F 22 1854-S 9,O 17-23,N 13-27 1863;extra Ja 7 1832
NcD 1821-23;Ja 30,Jl 9 1824;Ap 7-14 1831;Jl 6,O 26 1832;O 22 1833;D 1 1835;N 13 1837;S 17,D 10,24 1838[39]Ap 24,My 8,O 9 1840;Ja 8,Je 11,S 24,O 8 1841;F 18,S 19 1842;Ja 12,My 31,Je 28,Jl 19,S 13-20 1844;Jl 5 1848;Jl 11 1849;F 20,Ag 21,O 23 1850;Je 4 1851;Ja 5-12, Ap 20 1853[54-61]F 12,Mr 5 1862;My 13 1863
NcHi S 28,O 26 1832;O 22 1833;F 4,Ap 15-22,Jl 1,15,O 21-28,N 11 1834;Je 2,Ag 11,S 15,N 10,D 8,29 1835-Ja 12,26,F 9,23-Mr 1,15-22,Ap 12,26-My 3,Jl 5,N 15 1836;Ja 10,Jl 3,17,N 13 1837; Ja 1,Ap 30,S 10 1838;S 14 1839;Mr 31 1840;D 12,29 1843;Ag 11,D 22 1849;S 7 1850;Jl 27 1853; Ag 2 1854;Ja 17 1855;S 8 1858;Ag 3,S 7,D 14 1859;Ag 29,N 14 1860;My 15,O 9,23 1861;Mr 26-Ap 2,Ag 20 1862;Ap 15,29,Jl 15 1863;Mr 4,Ap 2,23 1868;extra Ag 1837
NcU Je 7 1822;F 17,D 31 1824;Mr 8 1825;Mr 24,Jl 14,O 13 1826;Ja 30,F 20-27,My 18,Jl 21 1827;F 5,Je 20 1828;My 19 1829;Ja 4,25 1830;My 4,S 7,O 5-12,26 1832;Ja 18,F 8,Ap 9,Je 4,Jl 9 1833-[35]-O 1840;Ag 16,26 1842;Ja 31,F 21,Mr 18,Je 6,27,S 26 1845;Ja 2,25,F 25,Jl 14,Ag 21,S 25 1846;Ja 15,O 13 1847;F 28,Ag 15 1849[50]-57[60]62-Ja 7,21-Mr 4,Ag 9 1863;Jl 5,S 3,24 1867;F 27,Ap 9-16 1868
TKL O 27 1852;Ap 27 1853

Raleigh **REGISTER.** sw N 18 1823-
1823-O 1848 as Raleigh register and North-Carolina gazette (D 12 1823-24? Raleigh register and North Carolina state gazette) 1852-54? Semi-weekly Raleigh register
CSmH Jl 1 1830
DLC 1823-Ja 14,28,Jl 29 1830;Mr 17,24,Je 2,Ap 14,O 31 1831;N 9 1832;D 22 1835;O 16-23 1840;Je 22-D 1841;S 9,D 2,9-20,30 1842[43]F 13,Jl 2,9,Ag 16,S 24,O 29 1844;D 23 1845;Je 25,Jl 9,Ag 11 1847;Mr 3,O 27,D 22 1849;F 11 1852;D 6,16-20 1854;Ja 12,F 16,Ag 17,S 14 1859;Mr 13 1861;S 10-13,N 26 1867
MH Jl 5 1867
MWA D 21 1824;Jl 21 1826;D 5 1843
NNHi D 23-27 1825;S 27 1841
Nc 1825-N 11 1830;40-O 24 1849;51-54;D 18 1858;Ja 1,15,22,Mr 9 1859[60-62]Ja 17,F 4,11, 21 1863;67
NcD 1823;O 1,N 16,23,D 28-31 1824;Ag 16 1825; Jl 11,N 24 1826;S 11,D 14,25 1827-Ja 4,My 9 1828;Jl 13,27-Ag 10,17,S 7-10 1829;S 30 1830 [40-42]-[44-49]Ja 30,Mr 13,My 11,Je 8,22 1850;O 6,27,N 3,D 1,15,22,29 1852;Je 25-29,Jl 6,13-16,O 26,N 9 1853;D 13,23 1854;N 15,D 31 1856;F 9,Mr 23,Ap 6,My 1,Ag 17,S 7 1861;F 22 1862
NcHi Mr 22,Jl 23 1844;Ja 3 1845;Ja 5,F 19,Ap 23,My 14,S 8,N 10 1847;F 19,Mr 15,Ap 12,My 27,Je 14,21,Jl 10,26 1848;Mr 21,N 7 1849;Jl 26,D 24 1856;Mr 24,My 15,D 8,22 1858[59-60] 61[Ja-Ag 1863;Jl-D 1867]Ja 3,10-17,28,F 12, 19 1868
NcU Ag 10-13,27-S 4,O 1-12 1829;My 15-19,26, Je 16[N-D]1840;Mr 15 1842;Ja 23,F 23,My 3,D 6 1844;Je 6,O 10 1845;Jl 14,D 22 1846[47-48]-[56-57]-[59-61]O 19 1863[67]F 28-Mr 7, 23 1868
WHi Je 25 1824

Daily **REGISTER.** d 1848?-
Nc N 19 1850-Ja 1851
NcD Ja 11,17,24 1851

Raleigh **REGISTER.** w,sw 1877-78||?
w 1877?
NcD N 1-8,D 6,20-27 1877;Ja 10-31,F 14-Ap 10 1878

Raleigh **REGISTER.** w F 27 1884-Ja 6 1886||
Nc [Mr 1884-85]
NcD complete
NcHi Ja 6 1886
NcU complete

Weekly **REPUBLICAN.** w Je 22 1867-
MBAt Je 29 1867
MWA Jl 20 1867

Raleigh **REPUBLICAN.** d My? 1874-
NcD Jl 3,16 1874

Weekly **REPUBLICAN.** w Je 4? 1874-
NcD Jl 2 1874

REPUBLICAN touchstone. w Mr 13 1840-
DLC Mr 13 1840

NORTH CAROLINA (*Continued*)

RALEIGH—*Continued*

Raleigh SENTINEL. d Ag 8 1865-F 27 1877||
1865-Jl 21 1876 as Daily sentinel.
Merged with Observer
DLC Ag 8,N 18,D 14,16 1865[66]Ja 30,Mr 1, Je 7,Jl 15,18,22,31,Ag 2,6-7 1867;Ja 13,F 19, Mr 16,Ap 2,Ag 19,S 22-24 1868;Ja 6 1869;F 8 1871;Jl 3 1874-77
MWA Ap 13-16,Je 26(extra)Ag 22 1866
Nc 1865 Je 1866;67-[70]-Je 1871;72-[D 1876]
NcD S 1,C 25,N 29,D 13,18 1865[66-68]Ap 25, Je 29,N 3 26 1869;F 1,Jl 30 1870[71-73]Ja 14-15,Jl 30,O 14 N 30 1874;Ja 19 1875;Mr 16,22-24,28,30-31,Ap 3,Jl 13 1876
NcGrW Ap 28 1869
NcHi [1865-72]F 28,Ap 18,D 23-24 1873;N 19 1874;Je 24,Ag 26,D 20 1875
NcU 1865[66]-N 1871;72-[74-N 1876]

Weekly SENTINEL. w Ja 25? 1866-76||?
1866-Mr 4 1867 as Sentinel
ICM F 1- 1876
Nc 1866-Jl 2 1867;Ag 30 1870
NcD [1866-67]Jl 7 1868;Mr 16,Je 8,22-Jl 6,Ag 3,N 16 1869;Ja 18,D 20 1870;Ja-Ap 4,Jl 4 1871;Ap 16 1872;My 27 1873;Ja 5,N 15,30,D 8-22 1874[75-Jl 11 1876]extras:Ja 25,F 8 1867
NcHi Mr 10 1868;S 19 1871
NcU Je 1- 1867;D 5-19 1871
VU My 3 1870

Semi-weekly SENTINEL. sw 1866-76||?
DLC Je 5 1867;Mr 5,Ap 16,S 3-7,O 8 1870;My 17,Jl 19,N 22 1871
Nc Ag 18 1866;S 12 1868
NcD D 1 1867[68-69]-[Ja-My 1872]F 1 1873
NcHi Ap 10 1872
NcU [1860]-[70;72]
VRC My 25,O 15 1867

Raleigh SIGNAL. w D 30 1886-92||?
Nc 1886-D 22 1887
NcD N 10 1887;F 16,My 24,Je 28,S 13,27-O 11,25-N 1,15-22,D 6-13 1888;F 21-Mr 7,28,Ap 18-25 1889;O 27 1892
NcHi F 21 1889;S 26 1891;O 27 1892
NcU Mr 10 1887;Mr 22,My 10 1888;Ap 14-21 1892

SOUTHERN weekly post. w 1851?-
DLC S 10,O 3,N 26 1853
MWA Ag 25 1855
NN O 8 1853(photostat)
Nc S 17 1853
NcD D 10 1853;Ag 19,S 2,23 1854
NcU D 13,27 1851;Ja 24-Ap 10,N 13,D 11 1852[53-55]

SPIRIT of the age. w 1849-65||?
DLC F 19 1852
MWA My 27 1857
NNHi F 20 1861
Nc Mr 3,30 1852;Mr 30,S 28 1853;Ja 4,Je 14 1854;Je 13 1860;O 16-23 1861;S 15-1862[My-D 1863]F 15-29,Mr 28 1864
NcD [Jl-D 1852]-[55-60]Ja 30 1861;N 12 1864; Ja 7,F 4 1865
NcU Mr 21,Ap 11,My 30,Jl 25,Ag 21,O 10,N 14 1851;Ja 9,Mr 10-17,Ap 28 1852;F 16,Mr 9, 23,My 4,25,D 7 1853;My 17,31,Je 28,O 11 1854; Ag 29 1855;Ja 2,Mr 26,Ap 30,Je 4,25,Ag 15,O 29,D 24 1856 Ja 7,F 18,S 30,N 25 1857[58]Jl 20 1859;N 7-14,28-D 12 1860;Ja 23,F 13,Ap 3, 17,Je 12,26-Jl 3,Ag 10,S 11-25 1861;S 29 1862; Mr 16 1863

SPIRIT of the age. w 1867-96||?
NcD D 5 1874;N 23 1881;Ja 23,Ag 12 1882;Mr 19,Jl 30,S 24 1884;Ja 22 1890;Je 27 1894
NcU F 27,O 9 1875;Ap 8 1876;Ag 11 1886

Weekly STANDARD. w,m,sm N 7 1834-70||?
1834-O 23 1850 as North Carolina standard; O 30 1850-Ag 11? 1869 Weekly North Carolina standard (N 17 1858-F 1867 Weekly standard)
m Mr-Ap 1864;sm Ap 1864
Ct S 9 1837
CtY My 19 1863-Jl 22 1864
DLC 1835-[41-43]-[50]N 12-29 1851;My 26,O 27 1852;My 25 1853;Jl 9,30,Ag 20,D 31 1856 [57]Ja 27,Je 16-23 1858;O 9 1861;Jl 18,Ag 13 1862[63]-Ja 20,Je 22 1864;Ap 17 1867
GU 1834-41
MBAt O 7,21 28 1863;Ja 6,Ap 6,Je 1 1864
MWA Ja 4 1837;Jl 14,S 8,N 17,D 1841[Ja-N 1842]F 22-Ap 5,My 10,31 1843;Je 2 1847;My 21 1862;Ag 26,S 9 1863;Ja 10 1866
Nc 1834-[36 -[38-39]-[43-44]-[46-49]-[51-54]-[62-63]-Ap 5 1865[66]-69
NcD Ag 20 1835;N 1836-[38-40]-[43-45]-O 1850[51-52]-[63-64]Ja 4 1865;66-[68-S 1870] extras:Je 22 1839;Jl 10,12,29 1864supp:F 5 1868
NcGrW O 30 1850;Mr 25 1857;O 6 1858[60]Ja 30,My 29,Jl 17-24 1861[Ja-N 1862]-Ap 22,Ag 19 1863;Ja 6-20,F 10,Ap 6,My 18-25,Je 8,22-29,Ag 10 1864;Jl 27,S 21 1870
NcHi D 15 1835;My 20 1840;Je 9,D 15,29 1847; F 16,Ap 12,Je 28 1848;F 14,Mr 14 1849;My 17-24 1854;S 14 1861;Ja 8,D 31 1862;Ja 30,Je 24,O 21 1863;Ap 6,Je 29,Jl 20,Ag 31,S 14 1864-Ap 5 1865
NcU Jl 10,O 22,N 12,26,D 15 1835[36-37]-[42]-[48]-[56]-[61-64]N 13 1867;Mr 25 1868 [69]
NhD My 26 1841
TKL Ja 20 1835
TxU O 27 1847-O 23 1850
VRC Ap 11 1865
—*See also* Extra standard

Semi-weekly STANDARD. sw,tw N 2 1850-70||?
1850-Ja 3 1852 as North Carolina standard; Ja 7 1852-D 27 1853 Semi-weekly North Carolina standard
tw during legislative sessions as Tri-weekly standard

CSmH Ag 31 1853
DLC D 14 1850[52]Ja 1-8,29,Mr 9 1853-60;Ja 31,F 21,Ap 27,Je 5-8,Jl 10,Ag 21,D 7 1861;N 7 1862;Ja 6,My 22,Je 5,Jl 7,14-17,24,Ag 11 1863; Jl 12(extra)1864;Ja 10 1865
MBAt F 23 1864;My 30 1868
MWA Jl 14 1852;Mr 16,Je 8 1853;Ja 14 1854;O 25 1856;Ja 6,Mr 9 1859;My 19 1860;D 5 1862; Jl 21,O 23,N 3 1863;Ag 2 1864;Jl 3,Ag 18 1866;Ap 20-25,Je 4-6,13,29,Jl 18-20,27,Ag 3, 10,S 10,21 1867
MnHi S 29 1852
NNHi D 15 1860
Nc N 6 1850-Ap,O 1851-[55;59]-[61-Je 19 1863] Ap 20 1864;Ja 27 1865;Mr 26 1867-Ja 11 1868
NcD 1850-[57]-[59]-[Jl-Ag 1861]-[63]
NcGrW Ja 29,D 28 1859[Ja-Ag 1861,S 1862-Mr]N 24 1863;F 12,Mr 3,Ap 29,My 17-20 1864;My 8,N 22 1866;F 26,Mr 9 1867;My 21,Jl 7 1868
NcHi [1858-67]
NcU [1850]-[56-57]-[60-64]Mr 28 1865[66-67] Ja 7,My 5,30,Je 25-27 1868
OCHi F 24 1865
OClWHi N 23 1859;60;Ap 20 1864
TxU N 1850-N 18 1854

Daily STANDARD. d,tw Ap 17 1865-70||?
O 4 1865-Mr 17 1866 as Daily North-Carolina standard; Mr 20 1866-Ja 1868 Tri-weekly standard; Ja 14-S 23 1868 Daily North Carolina standard; S 23 1868-Ag 16 1869 North Carolina standard
tw Mr 20 1866-Ja 1868
CoHi Ap 18 1865
DLC Ap 21[Je 29-D 1865]-Ag 25 1866;Ja-D 17 1867;Ja 14 1868-70
MBAt [Ag 1865-F 1866;My-S 1869]
MWA Ap 21 1865;F 27 1866;Mr 30,S 19 1868; D 3 1869;Mr 19,My 2,12 1870
NBHi My 9 1865
NN Ap 20 1865
NbCR Ap 19 1865
Nc [1865]-Mr 16 1866;Mr 30 1867;Ja-Ap 1868; 69-70
NcD 1865-[Mr-Je 1866]Mr 28,30,Ap 6,Je 16,S 7,D 19,31 1867-Ap,Jl 9,14,23-31,Ag 25 N 14, 25,D 1,8 1868[Ja-Je]N 17,22,D 16,18 1869;F 1,Mr 15,Ap 14,Je 25 1870
NcGrW Ag 26 1868;Mr 23 1869;My 13,Je 18,N 26,D 15,17 1870
NcHi [1865-Mr 16 1866]
NcU [1865-Mr 1866;68-69]-Je,S 1 1870
NjR Ap 17 1865
OClWHi F 3-Ap 27,Jl 15-D 25 1868
ODW Ap 17-18,29 1865

Tri-weekly STAR. tw N 1850-
DLC Ja 4,21 1851
NcD Ja 2-4,F 8 1855
NcU N 26 1850-Ja 4,9-28,Mr 5,Je 16,N 19 1851

STAR. w *See* North Carolina star

Weekly STATE chronicle. w S 15 1883-Je 30 1893||?
1883? as State chronicle. United with News and observer to form North Carolinian, later News and observer (w)
GAtCo S 27 1892
Nc F 25 1886;O 27 1887-Ja 24 1890
NcD S 15,D 1 1883;Ja 12,My 10 1884;My 8,29, Jl 2-23,Ag,D 3 1885;F 4,18,My 6,Je 25,Jl 2-9,S 2,D 9 1886;Mr 10-17,31,Ap 14-21,D 8-22 1887;Ja 5,F 2-10,O 19-N 2,23 1888[89]-Je 9 1891;Ap 5,My 10,31,Ag 30,S 13 1892
NcHi Ja 23 1885;S 23,D 16 1886[87-88]Ap 15, My 31,Jl 26,Ag 2,N 1,15 1889;F 21,Jl 9,Ag 13,S 3,N 12 1890;Ja 21,Ap 8,18,D 4 1891[92]
NcU N 10 1883;My 31-Je 7,28 1884;Ja 10,Jl 1885-Ja 24 1890
VU Mr 30 1888

STATE chronicle. d Mr 6 1890-Je 1893||
1890-O 29 1891 as Daily state chronicle; O 8 1890 Daily chronicle. United with News and observer to form News-observer-chronicle, later News and observer
GAtCo Jl 26 1892
Nc complete
NcD [1890]Ja 9,O 30 1891[92]Ja 1-11,18,Mr 3,Ap 1-2 1893
NcHi O 8,N 16 1890;Ja 7-9,14-15 1891[92]Ja 12-13,18 1893
NcU complete

STATE journal. w My 21 1859-64||?
1859-N 21 1860 as Democratic press
CSmH Jl 10,Ag 7 1861
Nc N 28 1860-O 1861[62-63]Ja 12-19 1864
NcD 1859;Mr 5,S 26-O 3,N 21,D 8 1860;Ja 2, F 27,Mr 20,My 22,N 6 1861;Je 25,Jl 9,23 1862; Jl 22 1863
NcHi Ap 17,My 15,Je 5-19,S 25,O 16-23,N 20 1861;Ja 29,Mr 29 1862
NcU Ap 30,O 10,D 12 1860;Ja 2,Mr 1861-Ja 7,Mr 13 1863

Daily STATE journal. d 1859?-
1859?-N 1860? as Democratic press
DLC D 17 1862
MWA N 6 1863;F 5 1865
Nc N 22 1862
NcD N 17 1862;Ja 9,N 28 1863
NcGrW D 10 1863
NcU Je 19,Jl 12,14,21,Ag 4,7,21,27,S 22,O 10, 18,23 1860;Ap 22,Jl 8,16 1863;My 19,28,S 20, 28-29,O 4,N 2,4,D 15 1864
VRC N 18-19,27-28,D 2-3,6,8,13,15-17,22-25 1862;Ja 1,3,5,10,12-13,15-17,19,F 3,6-7,9,Mr 17-18,Ap 11,13,21-24,N 4,6,10-13,16-19,27,D 31 1863;Ja 14,18-20 1864

STATE journal. sw D 1 1860-S 1863||
DLC Je 5,22,N 30 1861:Ja 1,18,D 17 1862
Nc D 1 1860;Ja 18 1862
NcD D 12,22 1860;Ja 12,30,F 6,13,Mr 30-Ap 6, 13-17,My 1,S 21,D 11 1861
NcU D 5-22,29 1860[Ja-N 1861]
WHi Jl 16 1862

STATE journal. w D 1879-82||?
DLC Je 15 1880
NcD D 23 1879;Ja 7,F 17,Ap 13-20 1880;S 7 1881;Jl 27 1882
NcU S 14 1881

STATE journal. w F 7 1913-20||?
NcHi Ag 17 1917
NcU 1913-My 8 1914;15-18
NcWaC Ap 25 1913-D 13 1918

Raleigh daily TELEGRAM. d F 1- 1871||
Title varies slightly
NcD Je 3 1871
NcGrW F 13,Ap 5,Je 11 1871
NcU [F 5-Ag 8 1871]

Raleigh weekly TELEGRAM. w Mr 15?1871-
NcD Ap 5 1871

Daily TELEGRAPH. twice daily Je? 1862-
NcHi Je 20 1862

Raleigh TIMES. w 1847-
1847-49? as North Carolina times
1847-Jl 1848? pub in Louisburg
Nc Ag 5 1848
NcD Ag 19 1848;Ag 31,S 14-28,O 19,N 2-16,30 1849;Ja 25,Mr 1-22,Ap 12-19,My 10,31,Je 14, Jl 5,Ag 2-9,O 18 1850
NcHi My 13,Je 24-Jl 1 1848;Je 15 1849
NcU Jl-Ag 19,S 2,N 11-18,D 1,15 1848;49-My 23 1851;Ja 16,30,F-Ag 13 1852

Raleigh TIMES. d 1879+
1879-Jl? 1895 title varies: Evening visitor; Daily evening visitor; Raleigh evening visitor; Ag? 1895-S 1897 Press-visitor; O 1897-S 1900 Times-visitor; O 1900-Je 1901? Raleigh times and evening visitor; Jl 1901-04? Raleigh times; 1905-07? Raleigh evening times; 1908? Evening times; 1909?-11? Raleigh daily times
Ja 11 1929 is inaugural ed
pub 1924+
CLM Ja 11 1929
Ct Ja 11 1929
DLC Je 11 1881
ICM My 23 1914
M Ja 11 1929
Nc O 31 1879-N 21 1881;My 24 1890-Mr 27,My 20 1892-95;Ag 1896-[98]-My 1 1919;My 1920+
NcD My 6,Je 5,S 4,O 2,23,30,N 13-14,17,D 23, 30 1879;Ja 11,14,28,N 1 1880;N 12 1881;Ap 26,Je 22 1882;Jl 28,N 19,D 18 1883;Mr 29,Jl 3 1884;Ag 16 1887;Mr 1,My 6,Jl 6-10,12-15 1889;O 2 1890;Ap 27,My 10 1894;O 19 1896;Ag 8 1898;F 4 1899;Mr 21,O 24 1900;Jl 27 1901; Ja 5,Jl 18,S 14 1905[06]My 11,Jl 27 1907;S 25,28-29,D 11 1908;Jl 17,25,Ag 18,S 11,28 1911; O 9 1912;Ap 8,28,Je 13,S 28,O 31 1914;Je 8 1915 Ap 21 1916;Ja 3 1920 Ja 11 1928;Ja 11 1929
NcHi Jl 17 1885[1906]Ja 2 1907;N 11 1918
NcRS 1925+
NcU N 9 1894;F 14,Mr 27,Ap 26,D 26 1895[96-S]D 1-2 1897;Mr 5,My 2-,24-26,S 8 1898;F 1,Mr 23,Ap 6,Je 2,Jl 25,N 11,30,D 11 1899;Ag 16,S 19,D 22 1900;Mr 16,Jl 1,Ag 31,S 17-18 1901;Ag 8,S 6,26,29 1902;Ap 27,Jl 1,16,24,Ag 28,S 2,O 13,N 6,D 18 1903;My 12-13,Je 18,Ag 2,8,22 1904;D 29 1905[06-07]F 6,11-12,14,Mr 17,Ap 16,O 1,N 3 1908[Ja-Ap 1909]
NjR Ja 11 1929
WHi Ja 11 1929

Tri-weekly TOPIC. tw F? 1875-
NcD Ap 3 1875

Raleigh daily TRIBUNE. d Ja 1897-98||?
Nc Ja 10-Mr 1897
NcD Ja 14,21,My 7-8 1897
NcU Mr 7 1897

UNION herald. w 1919+
Nc 1919+

Evening VISITOR. *See* Raleigh times

WE KNOW. w F 10- 1872||?
NcD F 17 1872

WHIG clarion. w My 10 1843-N 7 1844||
Suspended from My 10-31 1843?
MoSM Jl 24 1844
NcHi D 13 1843;Ja 3 1844
NcU My 10,31-D 20 1843;Ja-My 15,Je 12-N 1844

RED SPRINGS

Red Springs CITIZEN-NEWS. w Jl 1902+
1902-31? as Red Springs citizen
NcD S 25 1902+

Red Springs COMET. w 1892-93||?
Nc Mr 1892-F 9 1893

ROBESON voice. *See under* Lumberton

REIDSVILLE

Reidsville DEMOCRAT. w
Nc [S 28 1887-Je 13 1888]

ENTERPRISE. w N 1874-
NcD Ja 2 1875

Reidsville NEWS. w 1875-79||?
NcD N 27 1875;Mr 3,17,Ag 31 1877;D 19 1879

RECORD. w My 1872-74||?
NcD S 13 1872

Reidsville REVIEW. w,sw,tw F 27 1889+
w 1889-S 15 1899;sw S 19 1899-1923?
Nc 1889-98;Mr 9 1899-[1917]-[26]+
NcD D 11 1900;My 20 1925

Reidsville TIMES. w 1876-92||?
MWA Jl 19 1889
Nc O 18,N 29 1883[84-Ap 19 1889]
NcD Mr 27 1879

NORTH CAROLINA (*Continued*)

REIDSVILLE—*Continued*

WEBSTER'S weekly. w,sw 1875-1913‖?
1875-89? as Webster's dollar weekly
w 1875-1909?
DLC My 24 1881
Nc My 24 1894-[98]-1913
NcD D 21 1880;My 30,Jl 4,O 10 1882;Ja 30,O 23 1883;D 16 1884;Je 10,Jl 29,Ag 12 1890;Ja 26-F 16,Ap 19,My 3,Jl 12 1892;S 14 1893;Jl 9-Ag 20,S 3-10,D 10 1896;Ap 15 1897;Ja 5-12, Ag 11 1898;Jl 13,N 9 1899;F 1-8,22,Mr 29,D 12 1900;F 4-11,N 3 1904;My 18-O 12 1905;F 15,Je 14,28,Jl 26,Ag 23-S 6 1906;Ap 11,25,N 14 1907[08]N 18 1910;My 2,Ag 29,S 8 1911;Ap 14 1914;supp Ag 18 1899;Mr 15 1900
NcHi Jl 2 1896
NcU Mr 3,Ap 7,28,My 26-Je 2 1898;Ap 9 1903

RICH SQUARE

PATRON and gleaner. *See* Roanoke-Chowan times

ROANOKE-CHOWAN times. w 1892+
Follows Gleaner (not in this list)
1892-S 1899 as Patron and gleaner
1892-96 pub in Lasker
Nc My 21,Je 21 1894+
NcD S 22-N 1892;Jl 13-20 1893;Ag 2 1894[95-97]-[99]-[1901-06]-[08-12]Mr 6,Ag 21 1913[15-16]S 13 1917[18-22]

RIDGWAY

Ridgway PRESS. w O 29 1869-70‖?
NcU N 12,26 1869

ROCKINGHAM

BEE. w 1874-82‖?
1874-79? as Pee Dee bee
DLC Ag 21 1880
NcD Ap 5 1879;Ja 17,31 1880

PEE DEE bee. *See* Bee

PIEDMONT dispatch. w D 18 1915-N? 1917‖
United with Rockingham post to form Rockingham post-dispatch

Rockingham POST. w Ja 18 1909-N 1917‖
United with Piedmont dispatch to form Rockingham post-dispatch

Rockingham POST-DISPATCH. w D 1 1917+
Formed by the union of Rockingham post and Piedmont dispatch
pub 1917+
Nc 1933+
NcD Ja 12-19,F-Mr 1,15,Ap 12 1928

RICHMOND county journal. w 1931+
pub N 8 1931+

RICHMOND rocket. *See* Rockingham rocket

Rockingham ROCKET. w 1881-98‖?
1881-85? as Richmond rocket
NcD Jl 9,Ag 6 1885;F 25,Mr 11-18,Ap 8-29,Je 3,Jl 8 1897
NcU Jl 15 1886

SPIRIT of the south. w F 4 1873-93‖?
DLC Mr 12 1881
Nc N 26 1887-88;91-D 3 1892
NcD [1873]My 9 1874;S 25 1880
NcU Jl 23 1881;Jl 17,Ag 7 1886

ROCKY MOUNT

Rocky Mount HERALD. w 1934?+
Nc F 9 1934+

ROXBORO

Roxboro COURIER. w Ja 1883+
1883-95? as Person county courier
Nc 1887-[1905-07]-17
NcU S 23,O 14 1885;S 7 1898

PERSON county courier. *See* Roxboro courier

PERSON county times. w 1929+
pub 1930+

RUTHERFORDTON

Rutherford BANNER. w Jl 22 1881-93‖?
1881-86? as Mountain banner
Nc [S 9 1881-F 1883]
NcD Ap 11 1884
NcHi Jl 6 1883;Ap 27 1884;N 17 1887
NcU Ag 12 1881;Jl 15 1886

CAROLINA gazette. w 1836-
NcHi My 18 1837
NcU Ag 11 1836

Rutherford ENQUIRER. w 1858?-
NcD Mr 6 1860

Rutherfordton INTELLIGENCER. w My 13 1841-
DLC My 13,Je 3 1841
NcD O 28 1841
NcHi S 14 1842;Ap 26 1843
NcU Mr 17 1842

MOUNTAIN banner. w Je 21 1848-
Nc Ag 24,O 4,D 6-13 1848;F 21,N 7 1849;Jl 30 1850
NcD Ap 9 1850
NcU O 4 1848;Ja 3 1849

MOUNTAIN banner. 1881-86 *See* Rutherford banner

NEW régime. w F 5 1876-
NcD F 12 1876

NORTH CAROLINA spectator and western advertiser. w F 19 1830-
CSmH Ag 13 1830
DLC Ja 21 1832;O 18 1834
ICHi Ag 13 1830
MWA Ap 23 1830
NcHi [Mr 26 1830-Mr 10 1832]O 18 1834
TKL F 28 1835

RUTHERFORD county news. w 1926+
pub 1926+
Nc 1933+

Rutherford STAR. w 1867-Je 11 1871‖
MBAt Ag 26 1869
NcU Jl 1,15-Ag 5,S 25,O 16-23,N 6-13,27 1869

WESTERN North Carolina republican. w 1843-
NcU Jl 29 1847

WESTERN star of liberty. w 1836-
NcHi My 19,D 8 1840
NcU My 12,Je 9 1840

WESTERN vindicator. w Mr 2 1868-73‖?
Nc Je 26 1871
NcD Mr 23,Ap 13,N 30 1868
NcGrW Jl 22 1872
NcU [My-N 1869]Ap 7 1873

SALEM

Papers published in Salem are listed under Winston-Salem

SALISBURY

Salisbury BANNER. w 1853-
NcD Ag 14,S 4 1860
NcU N 3 1854;F 3 1857;Ja 5,D 1 1858;Ja 5,My 25,N 29 1859;Ja 10,Je 19,S 25,O 23,D 25 1860; F 19,Mr 5,My 7,17,Je 21,Jl 12-19,O 4-11 1861

Salisbury BANNER. sw 1854?-
DLC Ja 5 1859
NcD Ja 15 1859;My 28 1861

Salisbury BANNER. tw 1866?-
NcD O 16 1867

CAROLINA watchman. w Jl 28 1832+
Ja 10 1868-Ja 1869 as Watchman and old north state
Suspended from Je? 1865-Ja 8 1866;from Ja 1869-S 15 1871
pub Ag 1931+
DLC Ja 19 1833;Jl 12 1834;N 12 1836;Jl 15 1837;D 11 1840;Mr 13,My 29,Ag 14 1841;Ja 15 1842;My 4 1844;N 28 1850;Jl-D 1852
Nc F 24 1854-[60-61]-64[66]67;S 22 1871-73;Je 1874-[76]-S 13 1894
NcD [1832-34;36-40]N 20 1841;Ja 8,F 19,Ap 30, S 10 1842;My 6,Je 10,Jl 22,S 16,O 21,D 30 1843;Ja 27,F 10-17 1844;Ja 1 1847;Ap 17 1851; O 14 1852;O 6 1857;D 11 1868;O 21 1875; Ap 28 1881;Mr 15 1883;My 22,N 13 1884;D 10 1885;N 4 1886;O 10 1889;Mr 27 1890;Jl 2,Ag 13-20,O 8-22 1891;F 28,Ag 18,O 13 1892;Ja 5, F 23,Ap 6,Ag 3,N 16-23 1893;S 6,20 1894; Ag 8,O 31,D 12 1895;Mr 6,Ap 9-My 7,S 24 1896;Ja 28,Je 10,Ag 12,O 28,D 16 1897;F 17,S 1 1898;Ja 4-11,25,D 15 1904[05-19]
NcHi Ja 19 1833;Jl 12 1834;N 12 1836;Jl 15 1837;D 4 1846;S 14 1848;Ap-My 3,S 20 1849; S 5,N 28 1850;F 15 1851;Ap 29,My 13 1852; Ja 26 1854;Jl 2,Ag 2 1855;N 18 1856;My 5 1857;Jl 6 1858;F 5,My 21,O 29,N 19,D 17 1874[76-78]
NcU O 13 1832;Jl 5-12,Ag 23 1834;Ja 3 1835; N 12-19 1836;Ap 1,Jl 15 1837;Mr 29,Ag 1839-Ap 10 1841;Jl 31 1842-Jl 22 1843;My 1844-53;Ja 26,Je 22,Ag 3 1854;My 31 1855-My 24 1859;Jl 31-Ag 7,21 1860;My 9,Jl 11,N 24 1861;My 12,Je 30,Ag 11,S 29,N 10 1862;Ja 26,Ap 20,My 4,25,Je 8-15,Jl 13,Ag 3,S 14,N 29 1863;Ja 25,F 15,29-Mr 7,Ap 23,O 6-13 1864; Ja,F 13,Ap 12 1865;66-[69]Mr 18 1870[71]-[74]-90
OClWHi F 28,Jl 10 1840;Ap 3 1865

Daily CAROLINA watchman. d Je 1864-
NNHi S 5 1864
NcD D 23 1864
NcU Je 14,20,23,27-29,Jl 7,12-13,15,18,25,Ag 11-12,16,18,22,26,30,S 3,5,12,15,17-18,23,27-28,30,N 7-8 1864

CHINA GROVE record. *See* Rowan record

EXAMINER. tw Je 1869-72‖?
NcU [Je 9-N 1869]

FARMER'S journal. w Je 26 1846-
NcU Jl 31,N 27 1846;F 19,Je 22,Jl 23 1847

Salisbury GLOBE. w,sw 1887-1905‖?
1887-Ja 1900 as Salisbury truth; Ja-Jl 1900 Salisbury truth-index; Jl 17 1900-03? Salisbury semi-weekly truth-index
sw Jl 17 1900-03?
NcD Jl 25-Ag 1 1889;N 19,D 10 1891;S 8,N 3, 24 1892;Mr 30,S 14 1893;N 14 1895[96-1904] Ja 4,F 8-15,Mr-Je,Ag 9-30 1905

Daily HERALD. d S? 1891-96‖?
NcD O 23,N 30-D 1 1891;S 9,12 1892[93]My 2,10,23,Je 20,26,29,Jl 6 1895;Ap 21,My 16,Je 15 1896

Salisbury HERALD. w *See* North Carolina herald

Salisbury daily INDEX. *See* Salisbury daily truth-index

JOURNAL. w O 4 1824-
1824-27? as Catawba journal; 1828?-33? Yadkin and Catawba journal
1824-S 1828 pub in Charlotte
CSmH Je 22 1830
DLC 1824;O 2 1827;Mr 17,Ag 11,S 8,22,N 17, D 1,15 1829;Ja 5-12,26 1830;Ja 14 1833;F 10-17 1834
MBAt Jl 22-29 1828
MSaE Ja 20 1834
MWA D 21 1824;My 3 1825;Mr 25 1828;N 17 1829
NcD Jl 24 1827;Mr 3 1829;Ag 3 1830
NcHi 1824;O 2 1827;Je 5-12,26 1830;Ja 14 1833; F 10-17 1834
NcU 1824-Ap,My 20 1828;Ja 5,Jl 29,Ag 17, N 9 1830[Jl 1832-33]

Weekly JUBILEE. w Jl 17 1852-
NcU S 4,O 26 1852

LITTLE adder. w Je 1- 1860‖?
NcD Je 8-29,Jl 13-20 1860
NcU Je 8,22-Jl 6 1860

Salisbury NEWS. w Ag 31 1878-79‖?
NcU Ag 31 1878

NORTH CAROLINA herald. w N 7 1855-96‖?
1855-87 as Salisbury herald
NcD N 6 1889;Ja 15 1890;Je 17,Jl 22,S 2 1891;N 8 1893;My 29,O 23,N 13 1895;Ja 29,Ap 22-29,Jl 1,22 1896
NcU N 14,D 26 1855;Ja 9,My 21 1856;F 25, Mr 11 1857;O 26 1887;S 12,26,O 17 1888;Ja 2-9,23,F 6-20,Mr 6-20,Ap 24,My 29 1889;D 10 1890;Ap 15 1891
—d ed *See* Daily herald

OLD north state. tw 1866-
NcU My 7 1866;N 5,16 1867;F 1,8,Mr 5,Ap 2 1868

OLD north state. w 1866-S 15 1871‖
For Ja 10 1868-Ja 1869 *See* Carolina watchman
DLC Ja 30 1871
NcD Ja 8,F 26,Ap 2 1869
NcGrW Ja 13 1871
NcHi N 12 1869;Ja 28,O 21 1870

Salisbury evening POST. d Ja 8 1905+
pub [1905-11]+
NcD [1905-18]N 16 1922;Mr 19,26,29,N 26 1924; Ja 5,19-20 1925
NcSC 1925+

Salisbury weekly POST. w F 1 1905-10‖?
NcD F 1,Jl 26 1905;F 28,Jl 4,18,S 12,O 31-N 14,28 1906

Salisbury POST. sw *See* Yadkin Valley herald

Salisbury PRESS. w D 1887-88‖?
Formed by the union of Gaston current (Dallas) and Weekly Lincoln press (Lincolnton)
NcU My 4,Je 1-22,Jl 27-Ag 3,24-31 1888

ROWAN record. w 1908-31‖?
1921-28? as China Grove record
NcD [1909-19]N 26 1920;Ja 1 1925

ROWAN whig and western advocate. w O 30 1852-
NcU O 30 1852;Mr 4 1853;Je 29 1855

Salisbury evening SUN. d F? 1897-1905‖
1897-D 2 1904 as Salisbury daily sun
NcD My 10,D 3,6,25 1897[98-S 1905]
NcU N 19 1897

Salisbury weekly SUN. w Mr 4 1897-Ja 1905‖
Merged with Salisbury globe
NcD [1897-1901]Ag 3,O 29 1902;F 4,10,Je 24-Jl 1,15,O 7 1903;Mr 30,Ap 20,O 19,N 23 1904

TRIBUNE. w Je 18 1872-
NcU Jl 2,30,S 10 1872

Salisbury daily TRUTH-INDEX. d O? 1899-
1899-Ja 1900 as Salisbury daily index
NcD [D 1899-Ap 13 1901]

Salisbury TRUTH-INDEX. w *See* Salisbury globe

WATCHMAN and old north state. *See* Carolina watchman

***WESTERN Carolinian.** w Je 13 1820-44‖
Ct [1826-27]
CtY S 9 1828;My 2 1831
DLC 1824-29;N 28,D 19 1831;Mr 5 1832;F 15-D 20 1834[39-42]
MWA Ap 12,Je 21,D 20 1834;Ja 8 1841
N Jl 15,29,Ag 12-19 1823
NNHi Mr 19 1822
Nc Je 10 1823-O 1824;Mr 8,22-My 10,31 1825
NcD Je 10 1823-Je 1 1824;S 25,N 13-20,D 18 1827-[F 1828-N 1833]Ja 13-20,Mr 29-Ap 5,26,Je 7 1834;D 5 1835;O 8 1836;O 11 1838; Mr 18,Ap 1 1842
NcHi [1825-26]Je 6 1835
NcU 1821-My 6,Je 17,Jl 8,Ag 26-S 2,16 1823; Ja 20,F 24,Mr 30,Ap 13,My 4,Je 1,Jl 13,D 28 1824;Ja 18,Mr 1,Ap 19 1825;Ja 31,Ap 11,Jl 25,O 10 1826;Ap 10,My 8,Jl 3 1827;Ja 15, My 6,27,Je 17,Jl 29-Ag 5 1828;Jl 21-S 8 1829; Ja 5,F 16,Ap 20,S 6,O 26,N 30 1830;Ja 18, Je 13 1831-Je 4,Jl 16,Ag 13-S 3,O 1,29,D 10 1832[33]Mr 1834-F,Ap 18-My 2,23-Je 6,20, Jl 11,25,N 14,28 1835;Ja 16,F 6,D 10 1836; My 13,O 6 1837;F 23,Mr 30,Je 15 1838-My 7,Je 4-11,D 10 1841-S 16 1842
TxU Mr 1835-[36-F 2 1838]

Evening WORLD. d S 1895-
NcD S 12,O 28,N 23 1895[96-97]F 18 1898

Weekly WORLD. w S 17 1895-
NcD O 15,D 10 1895;My 19-26,Ag 11 1896

YADKIN and Catawba journal. *See* Journal

YADKIN VALLEY herald. sw 1905-19‖?
1905-Mr? 1912 as Salisbury post;Ap? 1912-S 1913 Semi-weekly post
NcD Ag 16,S 20,O 29 1907;S 8,O 9,16,D 4-8 1908;F 19,Je 1,18,O 22,29, 1909[10-12;F 1918-19]

SANFORD

CENTRAL express. *See* Sanford express

Sanford EXPRESS. w 1886+
1886-90? as Central express
Nc [Ag-D 1888]-[94]-97
NcD D 20 1912;D 3 1920;O 28,N 25 1921;Mr 17,Ap 28 1922

NORTH CAROLINA (*Continued*)

SANFORD—*Continued*

Sanford HERALD. sw 1900+
pub D 1930+
Nc 1933+

SCOTLAND NECK

Scotland Neck COMMONWEALTH. w,sw,d Ag 2 1882+
Title varies slightly
w 1882-1915?;d 1918?-29?
pub [1882-1903]20+
Nc 1896-[98]-[1902]-[15]-[21]+
NcD D 21 1882;Ap 19 1900;O 3 1907;Ag 6 1908
NcHi Ap 14 1921

DEMOCRAT. w 1884-89||?
Nc F 1887-95
NcD S 3,17-24 1886;O 29 1888;Je 20 1889
NcU Jl 15,30 1886

SELMA

JOHNSTONIAN-SUN. w 1916+
1916-28? as Johnstonian
pub 1928+

Selma NEWS. w 1887||?
Nc Ap 14-N 3 1887

SHELBY

Shelby AURORA. w 1877-1910||?
DLC Ja 13 1881
NcD D 13 1883;S 12 1889;My 8 1890; Mr 14 1895;S ? 1904;D 14 1906

CLEVELAND star. w,sw,tw 1892+
w 1892-1905; sw 1906-24?
Nc 1898-Je 3 1903; 04-15;17-S 21 1923;24+

NEW ERA. w 1885-89||?
Nc 1887[88]-Jl 5 1889

SILER CITY

CHATHAM news. sw 1924+
pub 1926;29+

Siler City GRIT. w 1904-22||
NcRoP Ap 1909-D 1 1917

SMITHFIELD

Smithfield HERALD. w,sw 1882+
w 1882-1913
pub Je 29 1882;O 26 1889;My 11,O 19 1893;N 5 1896;Mr 1901+
Nc O 30 1885-[90]-[97]-[1903]-[13-14]+
NcD O 30 1903;Jl 22 1921

JOHNSON county news. w 1921+
NcBeR 1928+

SNOW HILL

GREAT sunny south. w 1889-1900||?
Nc [1898]

GREENE county standard. *See* Standard laconic

STANDARD laconic. w 1896+
1896-1906? as Greene county standard
Nc [My-D 1906]-15
NcD N 11 1910

SOUTHERN PINES

PILOT. D 1920+
pub 1920+

PINE knot. w 1886-88||?
Nc S 25 1886-Je 9,Jl 21-28 1888

SOUTHPORT

Southport HERALD. w Ap 19 1905-09||?
NcU Ap 19 1905;F 20,Mr 12-19,Ap 2,23-My 7, 21-Je,Jl 9 1908;Ja 21-28 1909

Southport LEADER. w F 1889-97||?
Nc F 27 1890-96
NcD S 28,O 26,N 9-16 1893
NcU Je 22 1893;Ja 21 1897

Southport STANDARD. w Jl 30 1897-1905||?
NcU Ag 5,26 1897;Mr 8-22,Ap 5,26,Je 14 1900; Ja 17,My 16,Je 6 1901;Mr 20 1902;Ja 15 1903; F 2-16 1905

SPARTA

ALLEGHANY times. w 1925+
pub F 1933+

SPENCER

Spencer CRESCENT. *See* Spencer news

Spencer NEWS. w,sw Ap 17 1908+
1908-15? as Spencer crescent
sw Jl 1908-Ag 12 1909
pub 1908+
NcD [1908-09]Ja 7 1910;N 24 1911;Je 26 1914; Mr 21 1930

STATESVILLE

Statesville AMERICAN and tobacco journal. w 1858-86||?
1858-85? as American
DLC Jl 10 1880
NNHi D 2 1872
NcD N 29 1879
NcU Ap 16 1867;Je 1-8,Jl 5-19,Ag 2,23-S 6,O, N 22 1869;Jl 13,Ag 3 1886

CAROLINA mascot. *See* Statesville sentinel

IREDELL county mascot. *See* Statesville sentinel

IREDELL express. w 1857?-
DLC F 9 1865
NcU N 20 1862;F 19 1863
OClWHi Ap 13 1865

LANDMARK. w,sw 1874+
1874-79? as Statesville landmark
w 1874-Je 20 1895
pub [1874-79]+
DLC Jl 23 1880
Nc S 12 1889-Jl 1892;94+
NcD Ap 12 1875;Je 1 1883;Jl 11-18,Ag 1 1889; My 22 1890;O 19 1893;D 11 1914;Je 16 1916
NcU S 19,O 24,N 21,D 12 1874;Ag 2,16-23,N 1,13,25,D 4,18 1875;F 15,Je 27,Jl 18,Ag 8,S 24,O 10,N 24,D 15 1876;Ja 19,F 14 1877;D 1 1883;D 12 1884;My 27 1886;Ap 19,My 6,10,13, 17,25,Je 7,10,21,Ag 2 1898;S 26 1899

Evening MASCOT. d 1908-Jl 1909||
Nc Ag 17 1908-Je 1909

Statesville MASCOT. w *See* Statesville sentinel

Statesville SENTINEL. w,sw,tw 1893-1923||?
1893-1901? as Mascot; 1902?-04? Carolina mascot; 1905?-Jl 8 1909 Iredell county mascot
w 1893-1916?(sw 1904?-10?)tw 1919?-21?
Nc Ap 22 1897-[98]-1901;10-[12]-17
NcD [S 1908-09]Ja 3-6 1910
NcU Ap 7 1898
—d ed *See* Evening mascot

STONEWALL

PAMLICO enterprise. w 1882-84||?
Nc [Je 1882-F 1884]

SYLVA

JACKSON county journal. w 1904+
Nc 1913-15;18+

TARBORO

Early years as Tarborough

CAROLINA banner. w 1889-91||?
Nc 1889-Ja 9 1891

ENQUIRER. w S 30 1871-D 20 1873||
United with Tarboro southerner to form Enquirer-southerner, later Tarboro southerner
NcU complete

ENQUIRER-SOUTHERNER. *See* Tarboro southerner

FARMERS' advocate. w 1891-92||?
Nc Ap 8 1891-D 7 1892

FREE PRESS. *See* Tarboro southerner

Tarboro MERCURY. w 1859-
NcD Ag 9,N 9 1859
NcHi Ap 3 1861
NcU My 22 1861

NORTH CAROLINA free press. *See* Tarboro southerner

NORTH CAROLINIAN. w N 1827-70||?
NcU N 12-19 1869

Tarboro PRESS. *See* Tarboro southerner

Tarboro SCAEVOLA. w My 12-D 29 1837||
Merged with Tarboro press, later Tarboro southerner
NcU complete

Tarboro SOUTHERNER. w My 28 1824+
1824-Ag 18 1827 as Free press; Ag 25 1827-N 22 1833 North Carolina free press; N 29 1833-34 Tarborough free press; 1835-47 Tarboro' press; 1848-51 Tarborough press; 52-Ag 1867? Southerner; 1874 Enquirer-southerner; Ja 8-22 1875 Southerner-enquirer; Ja 29 1875-Mr 8 1903? Tarborough southerner
1824-Jl 1826 pub in Halifax
pub [1860-65]1923+
CSmH S 11 1829
CtY F 15 1831
DLC Ap 10 1832;40-My 15 1841;S 28 1844[69]Jl 8 1880;Jl 21 1881
MWA Jl 9 1842-Mr 2 1844
Nc [1869]-N 1870;Jl 1871-Je 1872;F 10 1887-[98-99]-1910;Mr 1919+
NcD Ag 28 1832;Mr 21 1840;Je 4-11 1845;Ja 30 1847;My 30 1867;My 27 1869;Je 23 1870;Mr 13 1879;Ja 31 1884;My 26 1887;Ja 25 1900
NcHi S 2 1825;My 30 1867
NcU S 17,D 3 1824;Ag 22-29,S 12-O 23,N-D 4,18 1829-59;N 30 1861;Ap 5 1862;N 21 1863 [66]-S 1870;72[73]-78;D 22 1881;82-83;85;89-90;Ja,N 15,D 1 1898[1900]Ja 3,Mr 14-21,Ap 1901-My 8 1902

Daily SOUTHERNER. d 1889+
pub 1923+
Nc Mr 6 1919+

TAYLORSVILLE

ALEXANDER county journal. w Ja 1886-90||
Nc S 15 1887-F 1890
NcU My 17 1888

Taylorsville INDEX. w 1890-93||?
Nc My 1890-My 7 1891

THOMASVILLE

DAVIDSON county news. *See* News

NEWS. w 1890-1903||?
1890-98? as Davidson county news
Some years dated also at Lexington
Nc 1897-98

NEWS-TIMES. w,sw 1903+
1903-25? as Times; 1926-31? News and times
sw 1903?
pub 1931+
Nc 1906-Ja,Jl 10 1907-15;18-19
NcD Ja 25,F 22 1918

TROY

MONTGOMERIAN. *See* Montgomery herald

MONTGOMERY herald. w 1893+
1893-1904 as Trojan?; 1905-23 Montgomerian;
pub 1929+
Nc 1908-12;14-15;Jl 13-D 1918

MONTGOMERY vidette. w Ja 7 1886-91||?
Nc [D 1887]-91
NcU Jl 15 1886

TROJAN. *See* Montgomery herald

TRYON

POLK county news. w 1895+
Je 19 1924 is National publicity ed
Nc [S 27 1897-99]-[1901-03]-[09]-11;14-15;18-26
TxGR Je 19 1924

VASS

CAPTAIN. w Ag 31 1932+
pub 1932+

PILOT. w N 26 1920-32||?
NcU 1920-D 4 1925;F 1926-N 1932

WADESBORO

ANSON times. w 1880-86||?
Follows Pee Dee herald
Nc Ja 5,F 17 1881-[84-O 1886]
NcD [O-D 1881]-[83-86]

ANSONIAN. sw,w 1906-19||?
1909-10?
Nc My 14 1907-08

Wadesboro INTELLIGENCER. *See* Messenger and intelligencer

Wadesboro MESSENGER. w 1887-Je? 1888||
United with Wadesboro intelligencer to form Messenger and intelligencer

MESSENGER and intelligencer. w,sw 1881+
1881-Je 1888 as Wadesboro intelligencer
sw 1910-O 8 1914
Nc Ap 12 1888-[98]+
NcD N 18 1882;Mr 17 1883;N 4 1909
NcU Jl 15 1886

NORTH CAROLINA argus. w Ja 3? 1848-76||?
1854-57? pub in Fayetteville
DLC Ag 7 1852
Nc 1859-Ap 1861[62-63]-F,Mr 31 1864-Mr 2,30 1865
NcD N 14 1848;My 15,O 2,D 11 1849;Mr 2,Jl 13 1850;Ag 28 1852;F 8,D 15 1854;Ag 31,S 8 1855[53-57]D 9,23 1858;Ja 13 F 24-Mr 10 1859
NcHi Ag 7 1862
NcU F 23 1856;Ap 25,My 15 1857;S 23 1858;My 27,Je 17,Jl 1-15 1869

PEE DEE herald. w 1870-80||?
Followed by Anson times
DLC Ag 18 1880
Nc F 20-D 1878;Jl-D 1879
NcD Je 2 1875

PEE DEE star. w My 13 1854-
DLC My 27,Je 17-24,Jl 8-Ag 19,S 9-16,30 1854

WALNUT COVE

STOKES record. w O 5 1932+
pub 1932+

WARREN PLAINS

PEOPLE'S paper. w Ag 16 1895-97||?
NcD D 20 1895;Ja 3,F 14,Je 12,O 16 1896

WARRENTON

CENTENNIAL. w F 4- 1876||?
NcD F 4,My 12-19,Ag 11,25,N 17 1876
NcU D 3 1876

Warrenton GAZETTE. w 1872-97||?
DLC Ja 25 1881
Nc [O-D 1887]-[92-94]95[97]
NcD D 13 1873;Ag 7,O 9,23 1874;Jl 9,O 15 1875[76-79]Ja 23,Je 4-11 1880;Je 24-Jl 8,O 28 1892;Ja 26 1893
NcHi My 17 1873;D 22 1876;F 20 1880;My 4 1883;S 20 1892;Ap 19 1895;F 28 1896;Ja 22,N 5 1897
NcU N 9,23-D 7 1872[73]Je 1874-[77-78]-[83]-N 7 1884

INDICATOR. w Ja 9 1867
Nc 1867-Jl 24 1868
NcU 1867-My 1868

LIVING present. w Ja 1869-
NcU My 21-28,Jl 16-30,Ag 26-S 3,17,29-O 1,22 1869

Warrenton NEWS. w 1850?-
DLC Mr 24 1853
NcD F 26-Mr 5 1858;S 21 1860;Mr 22 1861

Semi-weekly NEWS. sw 1851-
MWA F 20 1857
NcD F 5 1856

NORTH CAROLINA (*Continued*)

WARRENTON—*Continued*

Warren NEWS. w N 1 1878-82||?
NcD N 22-29 1878;F 7,Mr 14,Ap 11,Jl 11,Ag 1,22-29 1879;F 20,Mr 5,19 1880;F 24 1882
NcHi D 17 1880

Warren RECORD. w,sw N 17? 1892+
1892-1916 as Record
sw Ja 30 1917-20
Nc 1900-[16]+
NcD D 15 1892;Ja 19 1893;Ja 26,N 30 1894;My 17 1895[96-1911]Jl 4-11 1913;14-S,O 20,N 1916-[Ap 1917-Mr 1920]
NcHi Mr 3,31 1893;Mr 29,Ag 30 1895;Ja 15,F 12 1897;Ap 1,Ag 26, 1898;F 1,Mr 31,Ap 21,My 19,O 13,27 1899;Ag 17,D 21 1900;Ja 4,18,F 15, Ap 5,My 10,Jl 12-Ag 9,30 1901;Je 6 1902;Ja 8, Ap 3,My 8 1903

Warrenton REPORTER. w,sw O 1824-
1824-35? as Warrenton (North Carolina) reporter
sw 1824-25?
DLC O 22 1824;Jl 8,O 4-11,18 1825;F 24 1831
N O 10 1833
NcD N 1 1832;My 30 1840
NcHi My 9 1835
NcU Mr 2 1827

WASHINGTON

*AMERICAN recorder. w Ap 21 1815-
DLC 1821-23;F 27,Ap 2,16,My 7,Je 4 1824
MWA My 27 1825
NcHi [1821-Je 4 1824]

Washington DISPATCH. w 1857?-
MBAt D 3 1861

EASTERN intelligencer. w F 9 1869-70||?
NcU Je 1,15-Jl 6,20-Ag 3,17-24,S 14-21,O 26-N 9 1869

FREEMAN'S echo. w 1828-
MWA Jl 11 1829

Washington GAZETTE. w 1872-1906||?
1900-05? as Gazette-messenger
Nc [S-D 1889]-96
NcD Ag 29,O 3 1889;N 6 1890;My 18 1893; Ap 5-12 1894;Ja 23-30,Mr 5,My 7,Jl 2-9 1896; Ja 14, F11 1897;Jl 16 1904

Washington GAZETTE. d 1877-99||?
United with Washington messenger to form Gazette-messenger, later Washington messenger
NcU Ag 25 1887;Ja 21 1892;O 24 1895;Ja 27 1898

GAZETTE-MESSENGER. d *See* Washington messenger

Washington HERALD. w 1828-
CSmH Jl 24 1827

Washington MESSENGER. d 1894-1908||?
1894-99 as Evening messenger; 1900-05? Gazette-messenger
NcD Mr 4,S 17,O 6 1896;Je 15 1897
NcHi F 3 1898;Mr 5 1900
NcU D 21 1896;Ag 18,D 20-21,23 1897[Ja-My 1899]Ja 13,16,23-24,F 14,Mr 28,Ap 8,10 1902; N 23 1903[04]
—w ed *See* Washington gazette

NEW ERA. w My 28 1862-
DLC Je 11 1862
MBAt Je 11 1862
MHi [1862]
MWA Je 11 1862

Washington daily NEWS. d 1909+
pub 1915+
Nc 1910[11]-20
NcU My 20 1918

NORTH CAROLINA conservative. w Ag 24 1867-
NcU F 5 1868

NORTH CAROLINA times. w 1855?-
DLC Ja 25 1860
NcD O 8 1856

NORTH STATE press. w Je 1877-82||?
DLC Jl 6 1880
NcD My 6 1879
NcU Mr 2 1880
NjR N 12 1878

NORTH STATE whig. w 1834-
1834-My 15 1839 as Washington whig; My 22 1839-42? Washington whig and republican gazette
DLC F 23-D 21 1842;F 1850-51;Ja 21 1852; Ja 12-O 1853
NcD Jl 29 1840;My 5 1841;N 30 1842;Ag 3,N 2, 23,D 21 1843;Mr 21,My 30,Je 27,Jl 18 1849; Jl 9 1851
NcU Ag 1-8,O 17 1835;F 6 1838;F 12,Mr 5, Ap 30,My 22 1839;O 6,N 17 1841;Ja 19,Jl ?, N 2,30,D 14 1842;Ap 20-27,N 30 1843;Mr 21-Ap 4,My 30,Je 27-Jl 4, Ag 1 1844;Ap 17, My 29,O 16 1845;Jl 29,D 9 1846;F 24,Je 23 1847;Ja 12,O 18 1848;Jl 31,D 8 1852;O 11 1854

Washington PROGRESS. w 1886+
pub 1930+
Nc My 17 1887-[1906]-24
NcU My 9,26 1897;D 3,21 1898[99]Mr 8 1900; Ap 18 1901;Mr 12,26 1903

REPUBLICAN. w Mr 12 1839-
DLC Mr 19 1839
NcD Jl 23 1839

ROUGH and ready. w S 15-N 15 1848||
DLC O 14 1848

STATESMAN and third congressional district advertiser. w Ag 22 1834-
DLC S 26 1834
NcU F 7 1835

UNION advance picket. My 15 1862-
OClWHi My 15 1862

WHAT next. w D 9 1875-
NcU Mr 18 1876

Washington WHIG. *See* North state whig

WAYNESVILLE

CAROLINA mountaineer. *See* Waynesville mountaineer

Waynesville COURIER. w,sw 1888-1916||?
United with Carolina mountaineer to form Mountaineer and courier, later Waynesville mountaineer
sw 1902-03?
NcD F 26,Mr 10,26 1897

Waynesville MOUNTAINEER. w 1914+
1914-16? as Carolina mountaineer; 1917?-18? Mountaineer and courier; 1919?-20? Mountaineer courier; 1921-31? Carolina mountaineer and courier
pub 1921-25;32+
NcD Ap 25 1935

WELDON

N.C. republican and civil rights advocate. w My 15- 1884||?
Negro
NcD My 22 1884

Weldon PATRIOT. w Ja 1850-
1850-52? as North Carolina patriot
NcD Ag 10 1859
NcU S 9 1852;F 2 1859

ROANOKE news. sw,w My 1867+
sw 1867-Ja 16 1878
pub 1883+
DLC N 4 1874;F 3 1881
MWA O 22 1873
N N 20 1879
Nc Mr 9 1872-73;Mr 11 1874-Mr 6 1875[Mr-Ag 1876;Je 1877-Ag 4 1878]
NcD D 14 1867;O 23 1869;Ag 24 1870;Mr 20, My 11,25 1872;My 28 1873;Ja 3,Jl 25,N 18 1874[S-D 1877]Ja 2,12-16 1878;Je 28 1883;S 23 1886;Ag 25 1887;Je 19,Jl 3,17 1890;Je 24 1897
NcU [My-N 1869]Ja 21-25 1871;Ja 12 1875; Ja 12 1876;Jl 14 1881
NcWe [1924+]
OClWHi Ag 13 1870-F 17 1872;Ag 9 1873-Ja 1874

WENDELL

GOLD LEAF farmer. w 1911+
pub Mr 1923+

WILKESBORO

INDEX. w 1879-81||?
DLC Jl 22 1880
NcU Jl 21-28 1881

Wilkes PATRIOT. *See* Patriot-journal (North Wilkesboro)

WILLIAMSTON

DEMOCRATIC banner. w Ag 7 1856-
NcD Ag 7,S 4-11,O 16-23 1856;My 7 1857

ENTERPRISE. w,sw 1898+
w 1898-1920?
Nc [1901-02]-18;23+
NcHi My 9 1913

Williamston EXPOSITOR. w Mr 3 1866-
NcU Mr 17 1866;Ja 16 1867

Williamston MERCURY. w Mr 1 1859-
NcD Ap 5,20-Je 15,Jl 6-20 1859

WILMINGTON

Wilmington ADVERTISER. w Ja 1835-
DLC N 5 1840;Ap 22 1841
GAtCo Jl 9 1840
NcD Jl 14,Ag 11,S 22,N 10 1837
NcU My 14,Je 25 1840
NhD Je 25 1840

Wilmington ADVERTISER and merchants' and farmers' gazette. w D 1832-
DLC Ja 2 1833

CAPE FEAR. d O 1876-
Nc [O 17-D 1876]
NcD O 27 1876

*CAPE-FEAR recorder. w My 13 1816-
CSmH Jl 21,Ag 25 1830
Ct F 22 1826
DLC S 6 1823;Mr 7 1827;Ja 14,Jl 1,15-22,S 23-30,O 28 1829
MHi D 8 1821;O 16-23 1824
MWA Ag 2 1823;Ap 13 1825
N N 15 1826
NcD My 11 1831
NcHi Ap 11 1827
NcU Ap 14 1821;F 2 1822;Ap 4 1827;Ja 18 1832
WHi Ap 11 1827

CAROLINA farmer and morning star. *See* Weekly star

Wilmington CHRONICLE. w 1839-
1839-40? as Wilmington weekly chronicle
DLC N 18 1840;Mr 6 1844
MWA S 16 1840
NN Ja 25 1843
NcD Jl 15 1840
NcU Je 3 1840;S 12 1849

Tri-weekly COMMERCIAL. tw 1846-
DLC Jl-D 1852;Ag 2-16 1856
NcHi N 13 1852
NcU Mr 17-S 15 1846;Mr 14,24,29 1851-52;Mr 1853-[56]
T Mr 21 1851 (extra)

Weekly COMMERCIAL. w Ag 1847-
DLC Jl-D 1852
NcD Je 30-Jl 7,28 1854;Ja 2-9, 1857
NcU Je 2,Ag 25 1848-[50]-Ag 13 1852;Ja 8-15 1857;Ja 8 1858

Wilmington DEMOCRAT. w O 1877-78||?
NcD N 8-15,D 13-20 1877;Ja 10 1878
NcU Mr 23,My 4 1878

Daily DISPATCH. d O 9 1865-
Nc [N 11 1865-Je 13 1867]
NcD 1865-[66-F]Je 18 1867
NcU Ja-Jl 25 1867

DISPATCH. w Ja? 1866-
NcD Ja 4 1867

Evening DISPATCH. *See* Wilmington news

Wilmington EXPOSITOR. w Ja 1866-
NcU Ja 16 1867

Daily Wilmington HERALD. d 1851-
1851-55? as Daily herald
DLC Je 22,S 11-D 1865
MBAt [Jl 1865-Mr 22 1866]
NNHi Je 15 1865
NcD Ap 21 1856;My 22 1858;S 1 1865
NcHi Ap 21-22 1856
NcU Jl 27 1854;N 1,30 1855;Ap 22-23 1856;N 23 1857;Jl 16 1860-My 1,9 1861[Je-S 1865]

Wilmington HERALD. w,sw 1851-
w 1851-52?
MWA Ag 4 1852
NcD Mr 4 1852;O 29 1853

Wilmington HERALD. d 1865-
NcD N 8,15,D 13,20 1877;Ja 10 1878

Sunday morning HERALD. w 1865?-
MBAt F 18-25 1866

HERALD of the union. d F 28 1865-
CLM Mr 3 1865
MBAt Mr 6,21 1865
MWA Mr 4,My 5 1865
NBHi Mr 14 1865
NcU F-[Ap-My]-D 15 1865;Ja-Mr 22 1866
OClWHi Mr 22 1865

Weekly INTELLIGENCER. w 1864?-
NcD F 8 1865

Wilmington JOURNAL. w S 21 1844-95||?
CtY Ag 15 1851
DLC O 2-9,23-N 13,27? 1846-[48]-52;S 7-14 1855;56-Ag 1857;Ja 10 1867;N 5 1880
Nc 1844-S 12 1845;S 15 1848-S 2 1853;F 17 1854-O 9,N 20,D 4-11 1862;63-Ja 12 1865;F 8 1866-76
NcD O 1845-S 4 1846;Ja-Mr 6,20-My 1,15-29, Je 12-19,Jl 10-Ag 14,28-O 9,N 20,D 1862-63; Ap 28,S 22 1864;F 8 1866-F 4 1870
NcHi My 28 1847[62-Mr 5 1863]
NcU 1844-S 12 1845;S 18 1846-S 8 1848;N 1851-My,S 9 1853-Ag,N 1859-O 9,N 20 1862-Ja 12 1865;F 8 1866-F 7 1868;My 28 1880;Ja 13 1893;Ap 13 1894
NjP [1862-Ja 12 1865]
PNoHi N 24 1864
TxU 1862-S 17 1863
—d ed *See* Daily journal; Daily review

Daily JOURNAL. d S 8 1851-78||?
Title varies slightly
DLC Mr 8 1853-Ag 18 1856;Mr 20 1857-[58]-60;Ap 5,O 6 1862;Mr 21-23,25-26,29,Ap 5,Je 3,S 17 1864;Mr 26-Je 28 1866;F 19 1867[69] Mr 8,My 11,22,Ag 13 1870; Ap 30 1872;Je 4,6 1876
MBAt Ap 21 1862;F 19,Ap 5 1864[Ap 1866-Ag 1867; F 1868-69]
MWA N 29 1852;Jl 13 1857;Ap 24 1862;N 5 1864;F 14,Mr 4,My 5,15 1868
NBHi Mr 10-12 1864
NNHi F 2 1863;F 2-3 1864;My 1 1873
Nc S 6 1852-S 3 1853;Ap 4 1854-S 5 1855;S 7 1857-S 5 1861[Jl-N 1863;Mr-D 1864]-S 28 1876
NcD S 1853-Ap 3 1854;S 6 1859-S 5,N 30,D 20-21 1860;Mr 23,Ap 29,My 13,N 11,18 1861; Ap 2,9,O 2 1863;My 20 1864;F 15,20,Je 24,N 13 1866-S 27 1870;O 23 1872
NcHi D 12 1861;F 18 1862;F 10,My 26-27 1863;My 25,D 31 1864;Ja 3 1868;Ap 14,N 6 1869;O 19,21,N 10,D 7 1870[71]My 30 1872;Ap 22,O 22-23,31 1875
NcU S 9 1851-S 4 1852;S 9 1853-S 5 1854;S 10 1855-S 4 1856;Ag 21,S 9 1857-Ag 1858;S 14 1860-[S-D 1862]- [Ja-F] S 28 1865-[O-N 1866]-Je 1872;73-Je[D]1876;Ja 24-25,30,F 6 1877
NjP Jl 17 1863-Ja 19 1865
OClWHi D 11-12 1863;N 30 1864
PMedD F 7 1865
PPL F 6 1864
VRC Ag 22 1863
WHi S 9 1856-S 2 1857;S 24 1858-Ag 1859

LIBERALIST and Wilmington reporter. w? 1827?-
CSmH S 8 1829

Semi-weekly Wilmington MESSENGER. w,sw 1867-1907||?
1867-73? as Goldsboro messenger; 1874?-89? Weekly transcript and messenger; 1890?-96? Wilmington messenger
1867-87 pub in Goldsboro; 1888-90? dated in Goldsboro and Wilmington
w 1867-96?
DLC O 1 1880
NcD Ap 4,D 12,26 1879;O 21 1880;Ag 26,D 16 1881;Je 13,Ag 1 1884;S 17 1886; Ap 29,N 17 1887;N 29,D 6-13 1888;F 28,Je 27 1889; D 3 1901
NcU Ap 9 1880;Jl 22 1881;D 19 1884;Mr 5 1886

NORTH CAROLINA (*Continued*)

WILMINGTON—*Continued*

Wilmington MESSENGER. d Je 1887-1908||?
Nc Je 2?,Jl 7 1887-O 9 1894;O 29 1905-Mr 1908
NcD Ja-Je,S 21,28,D 1890-Ap 25 1891[S-O 1894;Ja-Mr 1895]O 3-9 1896[Ap-S 1897]Ap 15 1898;Ap ?,S 14 1901;My 5-Ag 1903
NcHi My 17 1889;Ap 27 1890
NcU [1887-My 1891;Ap 1892-1900]Mr 2,9,S 14, N 14 1901;Jl 1 1902;O 23 1903;Ap 26,My 14, 31,Ag 16,S 2,25,D 17,22-23 1904;Je 2,23 1905; Ja 9-11,Ap 15,29,S 23,O 25,30,N 3,D 2 1906; Ja 9,23,Jl 10,Ag 2,S 8,N 8 1907;F 11-12 1908
NcWiS 1888-1908

Wilmington NEWS. d O 1895+
1895-F 12 1923 as Evening dispatch; F 13?-O 23 1923 Wilmington news; O 24? 1923-S 29 1929 Wilmington news-dispatch
Sunday issues as Sunday star-news
pub 1895+
Nc 1908-15
NcD Ap 5 1915
NcU My 20,N 7,9-10,12 1898[1917-18]Ja 19,F 14,Jl 25,S 24,N 21 1919

Daily NORTH CAROLINIAN. d
NcD D 17 1864[Ja-F 1865]
NcU [D 1? 1864-F 20 1865]

PEOPLE'S press and Wilmington advertiser. w Ja? 1833-
Ct [1833-34]
N O 9 1833

Evening POST. d,tw,sw Ag 5? 1867-75||?
Title varies slightly
d Ag-D 3 1867;tw D 7 1867-Ap? 1868; d Ap?-My 3 1868;sw My 7 1868-Je? 1869; d Jl-D 1869?;sw 1870?-My? 1872; d Je? 1872-75?
MBAt [1867-O 14 1869]
Nc [1867-72]-Ag 7 1874
NcD Jl 19,O 18 1868;D 16 1869;Ja 27,Ag 11 1870;Mr 7,My 12 1872;Jl 13 1874;Jl 24,28-31, Ag 3-4 1875
NcU [Ag-O 1867;Ap-N 1869]Ag 14 1874

Wilmington POST. w 1867-84||?
Title varies slightly
DLC Mr 25 1875-D 21 1883
Nc [Ap 1875-81]
NcD Je 14-23,Jl 19-26,Ag 9-16,30,S 20 1872; D 17-25 1874[75-76]O 26 1877;N 10 1878[79-81]Ja 29,F 12,Ap 23,My 21,O 12-19 1882;Ja 25-F 1,15-22 1884
NcU O 12 1879;Ap 18 1880;Jl 10 1881;Ap 6 1882

Wilmington daily RECORD. d
Nc Ja 21-My 3 1861

Saturday RECORD. *See* Union labor record and Carolina farmer

Daily REVIEW. d O 7 1875-95||?
1875-76? as Evening review
DLC Jl 6 1878;My 18,N 9 1880;N 6 1890
NNHi Mr ?? 1877
Nc [1875-8?]
NcD D 14,?? 1875[76]My 9 1879
NcHi Mr 31,Ap 11,14,Je 5 1877;Ja 9,28,31,F 5,Jl 6,O 2 1878;Ap 24 1879;Ap 15,24,My 15, 18,27 1880;Ja 5 1881;Ja 14,My 6 1882;Ap 9,O 3,16 1883;Je 3,O 24 1884;Je 5,S 24,O 5,N 23 1885[87-90]
NcU D 13 1876-[86]-90;Ja 3,F 6,Mr 16,24,Ap 13,Je 11 1891;My 12,Je 24 1893;Mr 20,My 23-24,Jl 16 1894;My 24,N 8-9 1895
—w ed *See* Wilmington journal

Wilmington morning STAR. d S 23 1867+
Title varies slightly
Sunday issues as Sunday star-news
pub 1867+
DLC My 1? 1868;Mr 23 1871-Mr 22 1872;Jl 1875-1902;24-Ag 1927
MBAt N 25,7,9-14,16-22,28-D 5,7,10-11,14,18 1867;Ja 7,10-11,15,F 11,Ap 14-15 1868;D 12, 16-17,19,28-29 1869
NNHi D 20 1872;Mr 2 1873
Nc [Mr 27 1873-81]O 25 1908+
NcD 1867-S 22,29,D 31 1868;Ja 5,29,Mr 23 1869-[70]-[71-75]-Mr 22,Jl 9 1889;Mr 23 1890-S 22 1893;Mr 23 1894-S 22 1896;S 23 1897-Mr 22,S 23 1898-S 22 1900;Mr 23 1901-S 1903;Je 10 1913;My 3 1914;My 28-29,Je 1 1926
NcU 1867-Mr 31,Ap 12 1868[69]-[My-D 1872]-F 16,Mr 2,9,My 14-18 1873;Mr 21,Ap 8,13,O 14,2?,N 5 1875;F 27,Ap 14,D 5 1876;Mr 25,Ap 3,S 5,O 13,D 21 1877[Ja-My 1878]Ja 1,Je 12,S 16,D 18 1879[F-Jl 1880]Ja 5,Ap 16,Jl 14-15,Ag 5,S 29,O 11 1881;F 22,Mr 5,15,Ap 2,Je 27 1882;Ap 17,My 10 1883;Ap 25,O 26,D 3 1884;Mr 14,My 29,Je 14,Jl 29,Ag 6,O 11,N 12 1885[86-88]-[90-93]Ja 4-5,Jl 24 1894;Ja 6 1895;Mr 21 1896;Ap 3,20 1897;Ag 18,N 10,13 1898;N 1 1899[Jl-Ag 1901]Je 2 1903;Mr 3 1906;F 17 1907;My 16-17,O 30,N 22,26,29,D 1,20 1908[09-12]F 21,Mr 29,My 4,11, Je 6,13,Jl 18,Ag 24,S 3,N 9 1913;My 14 1914; D 8 1915;My 28,Je 20 1916[17-19]F 29,Mr 21,My 23,Je 23,S 20,26,O 10,N 3,5 1920 Ja 31, Mr 27,My 4,Je 13,26,Jl 19,O 15,21 1921
VHi Ap 29 1917

Weekly STAR. w 1867-1913||
1868-69 as Carolina farmer and morning star; 1870? Carolina farmer and morning star; or, the weekly star
pub complete
DLC Jl 2 1880
Nc My 1875-[85]-[1904]
NcD N 1869-O 1871;Je 5 1874[77-80]S 30 1881; Mr 31,Ap 21 1882;S 28-O 5 1883;F 29,Mr 14, Je 6,S 5 1884;Mr 20 1885;Jl 23,Ag 6 1886;Je 28 1889;Jl 18-25,Ag 8 1890;Mr 20 1891;Jl 15 1892;Ag 18,N 10,D 29 1893-[95-99]-[1903-05]
NcHi My 22 1891

Sunday STAR-NEWS. *See* Wilmington news; Wilmington morning star

Wilmington SUN. d 1878-79||?
NcU D 29 1878;Ap 24 1879

Weekly TRANSCRIPT and messenger. *See* Semi-weekly Wilmington messenger

UNION labor record and Carolina farmer. w N 20 1915+
1915-20 as Saturday record; 1921-24 Union labor record
pub 1915+
WaPS [1924-26]

WILSON

Wilson ADVANCE. w 1870-99||?
N? 1897 is industrial ed
DLC Ag 20 1880
NNHi Ap 19 1878
Nc N 3 1887-[96-99]
NcD F 8 1884;Je 30 1887;N ? 1897
NcU Jl 22 1886;Ap 28 1887;Je 14 1888;Ag 13 1896

Wilson LEDGER. w 1858?-
NcD N 13,27 1860-F 1861

LITTLE jewel. w My 6 1875-
NcU My 13 1875

Wilson MIRROR. w 1882-95||?
Nc S 13 1887-94
NcAsS N 13-26,D 25 1889

NORTH CAROLINIAN. sw Ja 1865-
NcD Ja 13,Ap 13 1867;Ja 15 1868
NcU Mr 23 1867

PLAINDEALER. w F 1868-76||?
NcU Je 8-Jl 6,20-27,Ag 17,31-S 7,21-28,O 12-N 9 1869

Wilson TIMES. w,sw 1895+
w 1896-O 4 1906
pub 1896+
Nc Jl 3 1896-[98-99]-1901;F 1903-14

Wilson TIMES. d 1902+
pub 1902+

Daily TOPIC. d Mr 1876-
NcU Mr 23 1876

WINDSOR

ALBEMARLE times. w Ja 1873-76||?
NcD F 26 1875
NcU O 16 1874

BERTIE ledger-advance. w 1884+
1884-1926 as Windsor ledger; 1926-28? Ledger-advance; 1929? Ledger
pub 1929+
Nc O 1887-[97-99]-1901[03-04]-[08]12-15;Ag 23 1933+
NcD Ja 1-22,F 12-Mr 12 1890;F 25 1904;F 17 1910;Ap 2 1914;Mr 16 1916
NcHi Je 23,O 27 1910;Je 1 1916

Windsor HERALD and Bertie county register. w My 1832-
NcU O 4,N 1 1833

Windsor LEDGER. *See* Bertie ledger-advance

WINSTON

Papers published in Winston are listed under Winston-Salem

WINSTON-SALEM

AMERICAN advocate. w Je 23 1870-71||?
MH Je 23 1870

BUSINESS guide. w -1907||?
Nc 1902-06

Weekly CHRONICLE and farmers' register. w 1832?-51||?
1832?-Ja 1836? as Farmers' reporter and rural repository
NcD N 10(reprint)1832;F 13,Ap 2,16,My 14-21,Je 4,18-25,Jl 16,30,Ag 27-S 17,O 1-8,D 17-24 1836;Ja 21,F 4 1837

FARMERS' reporter and rural repository. *See* Weekly chronicle and farmers' register

Winston-Salem JOURNAL. d Ap 3 1897+
Sunday issues as Journal-sentinel
pub 1920+
Nc 1902-[05-06]+
NcD D 9,11,15-20 1910[Ja-F 1911]Ag 9 1912; Ap 4 1915;D 24 1916;Ja 22 1918;Ja-My,Je 18 1925;Jl 24 1935
NcHi O 11 1898
NcWin [1911-28]+

JOURNAL-SENTINEL. *See* Twin City sentinel; Winston-Salem journal

Winston LEADER. w 1879-85||?
DLC O 5 1880
Nc Ja 21 1879-84

NATIONAL republican. *See* Union republican

PEOPLE'S press. w F 8 1851-92||
Merged with Western sentinel
DLC Jl 8 1880
Nc [O-D 1873]-[84-85]-92
NcD Ap 30 1853;Je 24,Jl 29-Ag 12,S 23,O 7 1859 Ag 10 1860;Mr 29,My 3,24 1861;Je 20,Jl 11-Ag 22 1862;Ap 24 1868;Mr 26 1869;F 11 1870 O 6 1872;My 4 1882;D 16 1886;Mr 31,Je 30 1887;My 3,Ag 30 1888;Ag 21 1890;Mr 10 1892
NcHi [F 28 1852-D 1 1892]
NcU F 5 1858;Jl 8 1859;S 6 1861;Mr 21 1862;O 6 1864;My 4 1865;Je 22 1866;Je 5,N 20 1868 [69]Jl 11 1876;Ja 10 1878;My 13 1879;My 27,Jl 8,S 2-9,23-O 7,N 18 1880;S 22,D 8 1881;My 4-11 1882;Ja 25 1883;Ja 15,Ap 30,Ag 27 1885;F 18,Mr 27,Ag 5,S 9,D 16 1886;S 13 1888;Ja 4 1892
VRC Ag 20 1863

TWIN CITY daily. *See* Twin City sentinel

TWIN CITY sentinel. d My 4 1885+
1885-D 1890 as Twin City daily
Nc Jl 18 1892+
NcD Ja 30,F 17,Mr 30,Ap 3-7 1888;Je 5-7,9,N 28,D 1-6 1890;Ag 23 1892;N 4 1897
NcHi Mr 7,S 27,N 6,D 24 1890[91]F 16,24,Ag 7,29,O 14 1892[93-1900]Ap 27 1906
NcU S 19 1892;Jl 21,27,O 16,23,N 5,D 21 1894 [95-96]F 22 1897;Je 2,Jl 25 1898;Ja 16,My 24, 27-28 1902
NcWin [1909-28]+
—w,sw ed *See* Western sentinel

UNION republican. w Ja 10 1872+
1872? as National republican
DLC Jl 8 1880
Nc Jl 1896-[98]-[1904]-[20]+
NcD Mr 13 1879;Je 17 1880;D 2 1886;Ap 17,S 11,O 2-9 1890;F 5,Jl 2,N 3,D 24 1891;Ja 28,F 11-25,Ap 28,My 12,D 1,22 1892;S 14-21,D 14 1893;Mr 22 1894[96-1900]-N 1901;02-Je 1909; Ja 27 1910[13-16]F 22,Mr 8,Jl 17 1917;Je 24 1920
NcGrW Jl 10 1879
NcHi Jl 17 1879;N 26 1885 S 13 1894;Ap 18 1895
NcU F 28 1872;Jl 21 1881;Jl 15 1886;Mr 29 1900;Je 27 1918

WESTERN sentinel. sw,w 1855-1925||?
w 1855-1909
DLC F 3 1881
MBAt S 8,22-29,O 20-N 3,17,D 15 1865;Ja 12,F 9-16 1866
Nc Ja 11-My 10 1861;62-Mr,S 22 1865-67;77-S 1898
NcD N 16 1860;My 15 1863;Mr 31 1870;Ap 22 1880;Ap 27 1889
NcHi F 25,Je 24 1859;Jl 8 1875;Je 11 1891;D 29 1892
NcU Je 24,S 16,D 2 1859;Je 22,O 5 1860;Ap 19 1861;My 9,Ag 29-S 5,N 14 1862;Ja 2,Mr 13 1863;N 10,D 1-8 1864;Ja 19 1865;D 20 1866 [69]O 1 1874;Mr 25,Ap 22,O 14,N 18,D 2,23 1875;Ja 13,Mr 9,Ap 20 1876[77-81]O 12 1882 [83-89]Ja 14-21,Jl 7 1892
T F 25 1864
—d ed *See* Twin City sentinel

YANCEYVILLE

CASWELL messenger. w F 25 1926+
pub 1926+

RUBICON. w F 14 1840-
NcU My 16 1840

ZEBULON

Zebulon RECORD. w 1925+
pub 1926+

NORTH DAKOTA

ABERCROMBIE

Abercrombie HERALD. w 1894-1909||?
NdHi N 5 1903-D 22 1905

Abercrombie MESSENGER. w 1912-18||?
NdHi O 29 1915-N 3 1916

Abercrombie weekly NEWS. w 1909-10||
NdHi [Ap 1909-10]

ADAMS

Adams BUDGET. w Ag 18 1905-13||
Ag 18-O 20 1905 as Sarles budget (Sarles)
NdHi 1905-Ag 15 1913

Adams ENTERPRISE. *See* Park River republican and Adams enterprise (Park River)

Adams STANDARD. w 1912-26||
NdHi O 22 1915-N 5 1926

ALEXANDER

MCKENZIE county chronicle. w 1903+
NdHi Ja 23 1908+

ALKABO

Alkabo GAZETTE. w 1915-19||
NdHi Ap 9 1915-O 1919

ALMONT

Weekly ARENA. w D 21 1910-14||
1910-Ag 2 1913? as Almont arena
NdHi 1910-Ag 2,D 20 1913-Je 12 1914

AMBROSE

Ambrose HERALD. w Mr 24 1927+
pub Mr 1934+
NdHi 1927+

Ambrose NEWSMAN. w 1906-F 27 1914||
Merged with Ambrose tribune
NdHi Ja 10 1908-14

NORTH DAKOTA (*Continued*)

AMBROSE—*Continued*

Ambrose TRIBUNE. w 1908-21||
NdHi Ag 6 1909-F 17 1921

AMIDON

FARMERS press. w 1915-24||
Merged with Slope county post
NdHi O 1917-Jl 1924

SLOPE county news. w *See* Slope county post

SLOPE county post. w 1910+
1910-Ag 1 1924 as Slope county news 1910-Ap 23 1912 pub in Chenoweth
pub 1915+
NdHi Ja 27 1911+

ANAMOOSE

Anamoose PROGRESS. w 1899+
NdHi My 1905+

ANETA

Aneta PANORAMA. w S 1896+
pub 1896+
NdHi D 24 1903+
NdU S 17 1896;My 1897-99;Ja-My,Je 13-Ag, S 12,1901-Ag 18,S-O 13,27-D 22 1904;Ja 5 1905;Jl 12-19,D 27 1906;F 14-S 5,19,O 3 1907-My 7 1908

ANTLER

AMERICAN. w My 27 1905-Jl 24 1919||
NdHi complete

ARNEGARD

Arnegard CALL. See McKenzie county farmer (Watford City)

MCKENZIE county farmer. *See under* Watford City

MCKENZIE county leader. w
NdHi Ap 17 1931+

ARTHUR

Arthur NEWS. w Jl 27 1917-24||?
NdHi 1917-1922

ASHLEY

Der DEUTSCHE republikaner. w 1899-1911||?
In German
NdHi F 18 1904-My 1907

Ashley TRIBUNE. w 1900+
In German and English
pub 1900+
NdHi D 1903+

BAKER

Baker HERALD. w 1913-15||
NdHi Ap 9 1914-Jl 22 1915

BALDWIN

Baldwin BULLETIN. w 1915-18||
NdHi Ag 10 1916-My 1918

BALFOUR

Balfour LEADER. w 1902-05||
NdHi N 1903-N 1905

Balfour MESSENGER. See Drake register (Drake)

Balfour STATESMAN. w 1900-23||?
NdHi D 31 1903-D 22 1910

BANKS

Weekly PRESS. 1909-10||
NdHi My 7 1909-O 15 1910

BANTRY

Bantry ADVOCATE. w 1905-27||
NdHi Ja 17 1908-Je 30 1927

BARLOW

Barlow ENTERPRISE. w 1907-12||?
NdHi Jl 18 1907-10

BATHGATE

PINK paper. w 1886-1916||
NdHi Mr 29 1905-N 15 1916

BEACH

Beach ADVANCE. w 1908+
pub Ag 1911-[12]-15;17+
NdHi Mr 19 1909-34

GOLDEN Valley chronicle. w 1905-16||
NdHi Ja 10 1907-D 13 1916

GOLDEN Valley progress. w 1913-21||
NdHi Je 13 1913-S 30 1921

Beach REVIEW. w 1931+
pub O 1933+

BELDEN

INLAND representative. w 1907-09||
NdHi N 23 1907-Je 19 1909

BELFIELD

Belfield HERALD. w
NdHi F 4 1932-Mr 9 1933

Belfield REVIEW. w N 27 1908+
1908-Jl 2 1920 Belfield times
pub 1908+
NdHi 1908-[N-D 1912]-[S 25 1931-Ja 6 1933]+

Belfield TIMES. *See* Belfield review

BENEDICT

Benedict BANNER. w F 27 1908-20||?
NdHi 1908-Ap 15 1920

BENTLEY

Bentley BULLETIN. w D 2 1910-19||
NdHi 1910-Mr 7 1919

BERG

INLAND call. *See* McKenzie county farmer (Watford City)

BERLIN

Berlin RECORD. w 1909-12||
NdHi Je 17 1910-Ap 5 1912

BERTHOLD

Berthold TRIBUNE. w Ap 1902+
pub 1903-My,O 19 1926+
NdHi Ap 27 1905+
NdMC Ap 1931-Je 3 1935

BERWICK

Berwick POST. w 1901-08||
In Englih and German
NdHi Mr 12 1904-Mr 27 1908

BEULAH

Beulah INDEPENDENT. w 1913+
pub D 1914+
NdHi 1915+

BINFORD

Binford TIMES. w 1903-30||
NdHi Ap 27 1905-F 13 1930

BISBEE

• Bisbee GAZETTE. w 1892+
NdHi Ap 20 1905-[Ja-O]-[D 1908-N 1910]+

BISMARCK

BURLEIGH county farmer. *See* public opinion

BURLEIGH county farmer press. w,sw 1901-21||
1901-Ja 16 1919 as Palladium
NdHi 1904-F 17 1921

Bismarck CAPITAL. w,sw O 5 1922+
w 1922-Ag 1928
pub 1922+
NdB O 1931+
NdHi 1922+

DAKOTA freie presse. w 1916+
1916-Je 1927 as Nordlich; Je 1927-N 16 1928 Eureka rundschau; N 23 1928-N 4 1932 Dakota rundschau (Winona, Minn)
In German
pub 1927+
MnHi Mr 9 1920+
NdHi O 14 1920-[24]-Je 8, D 21 1927+

DAKOTA rundschau. *See* Dakota freie presse

DAKOTA settler. *See* Public opinion

EUREKA rundschau. *See* Dakota freie presse

FARMER-labor state record. *See* North Dakota state record

Weekly HERALD. w 1882-83||
NdHi D 6 1882[F 14-S 21 1883]

Bismarck INDEPENDENT. w S 22 1904-
NdHi S 22-N 3 1904

Saturday evening JOURNAL. d 1885-86||?
MnHi [1886]

LEADER. w Jl 4 1933+
NdU 1933+
NdVS Jl 1934+

NORD Dakota herold. *See under* Dickinson

Das NORDLICHT. *See* Dakota freie presse

NORTH Dakota non-partisan. w 1923-28||
MnHi D 24 1924-Ag 29 1928

NORTH Dakota state record. w S 16 1920+
1920-Ag 20 1925 as Farmer labor state record. O 20 1927-Ap 21 1933 merged with Bismarck capital
NdHi 1920-O 13 1927;Ap 28 1933+
WHi Ag 3 1922;Ap 17,D 11 1924

PALLADIUM. *See* Burleigh county farmers press

PUBLIC opinion. w 1885-Ja 15 1920||?
1885-F 12 1887 as Burleigh county farmer; F 19 1887-89? Dakota settler; 1890?-Ap 4 1912 Bismarck settler; Ap 11 1912-O 9 1913 Bismarck times; O 16 1913-Ja 28? 1915 State news
NdHi F 19 1887-[F 1895-1904]-Ja 15,O 7 1915-Ja 15 1920
NdU Jl-D 10,24-31 1891;Ja 14-21 1897

Bismarck SETTLER. *See* Public opinion

Der STAATS-anzeiger. w Ag 1906+
In German
pub 1913+

STATE news. *See* Public opinion

Bismarck TIMES. *See* Public opinion

Bismarck TRIBUNE. d 1873+
pub [1873-1919]+
CSmH Jl 6(extra)1876
DLC 1882+
KHi O 12 1890-Ag 8 1898
MWA Jl 31 1885
NdB O 1931+
NdHi [D 1882-N 1883]Je 30 1885-[Ja-Je 1887]-[92]-[1903]+
NhD Springtime 1883
OClWHi Jl 31 1914;Ap 7 1934
SdHi N 1904-Jl 1911
WHi 1917-21;Ap 7 1934

Bismarck TRIBUNE. w Jl 11 1873-1919||?
CU-B My 7 1880;My 27-Ag 5 1910
DLC F 25 1878-D 9 1881
KHi D 1887-Ja 7 1916
MnHi 1873-F 1885
N S 22-29 1875
NbHi Jl 26-D 1901;Ag 1902-18
NdHi Ag 13 1873;My 12 1875;1885-[90-94]-[96-97]-[Ja,Mr 1915]-D 12 1919

BOTTINEAU

BOTTINEAU county herald. w 1899-Jl 1929||
1899-Mr 29 1918 as Bottineau county news; Ap 5 1918-Mr 10 1927 Farmers advocate
Merged with Bottineau courant
NdHi 1904-[Jl 1907-Ap 1908]-Mr 10 1927

BOTTINEAU county news. *See* Bottineau county herald

Bottineau COURANT. w Jl 1885+
1885-94 as Bottineau pioneer
pub [1885+]
NdHi D 18 1903+
NdU F 1 1907

FARMERS advocate. *See* Bottineau county herald

Bottineau PIONEER. *See* Bottineau courant

BOWBELLS

Bowbells BULLETIN. w 1903-15||
Merged with Bowbell tribune
NdHi Jl 28 1905-Ap 1915

Bowbells TRIBUNE. w 1899+
pub 1889-1901;04-[23]+
NdHi Ap 28 1905-[Jl 1907-Je 1908]+

BOWDON

Bowdon BANNER. w 1930||
NdHi Mr-Ag 1930

Bowdon GUARDIAN. w 1900-22||
NdHi Ap 21 1905-S 1922

BOWMAN

BOWMAN county leader. w N 15 1917-28||?
1917-Jl 1923 as Farmers leader; Ag 1923-Je 18 1924 Farmer-labor monitor
NdHi 1917-26

BOWMAN county news. *See* Bowman citizen

BOWMAN county pioneer and Bowman citizen. w My 16 1907+
1907-Ap 30 1917? as Bowman county pioneer My 16-Ag 8 1907 pub at Twin Butte
pub O 1918+
NdHi 1907+

Bowman CITIZEN. w 1907-17||?
1907-Ja 5 1911 as Bowman county news
NdHi Mr 1908-Ap 1917

FARMER-labor monitor. *See* Bowman county leader

FARMERS leader. *See* Bowman county leader

BRADDOCK

Braddock NEWS. w 1904-Jl 24 1919||
NdHi Ap 6 1905-[My-D 1908]-[Ja-F 1914]-19

BRINSMADE

Brinsmade NEWS. w
NdHi S 2 1926-Je 21 1928

Brinsmade STAR. w My 31 1906-N 6 1924||
NdHi 1906-[N 1919-F 1923]-24

BROCKET

Brocket INDEPENDENT. w
NdHi Je 27 1912-Mr 1914

Brocket NEWS. w Ag 27 1908-12||?
NdHi 1908-D 9 1910

BUFFALO

Buffalo EXPRESS. w 1893+
NdHi Ap 27 1905+

NORTH DAKOTA (*Continued*)

BUFORD

Buford TRIBUNE. *See* Fairview tribune (Fairview)

BURNSTAD

Burnstad COMET. w 1910-20||
NdHi My 13 1910-Ja 1 1920

LOGAN county farmer. w
NdHi Ja 20-D 23 1920

BURT

Burt ECHO. w 1911-19||
NdHi My 26 1911-Ag 8 1919

BUXTON

Buxton OUTLOOK. *See* Traill county news (Hillsboro)

CALIO

Calio NEWS. w 1912-15||?
NdHi N 23-S 1915

CALVIN

Calvin TIMES. *See* Western Cavalier county independent

WESTERN Cavalier county independent. w 1907-27||
1907-23? as Calvin times. United with Sarles advocate to form Western Cavalier county advocate (Sarles)
NdHi Ja 9 1908-[My 1912-15]-22;S 11 1924-S 1 1927

CANDO

Cando RECORD. w O 1 1889+
For 1906-13 *See* Towner county democrat and Cando record
pub 1889+
NdHi O 25 1889-[O 25 1890-S 4 1903]+

TOWNER county democrat and Cando record. w 1903-D 11 1913||
1903-05 as Towner county democrat. Followed by Cando record
NdCR 1906-13
NdHi My 1905-13

CARPIO

Carpio FREE press. w 1911-18||
NdHi D 15 1911-Mr 1 1918

HARTLAND herald. w 1912-17||
NdHi My 1913-D 7 1917

Carpio weekly NEWS. w 1902-13||
NdHi My 22 1902-F 6 1913

CARRINGTON

FOSTER county independent. w Ag 8 1883+
1883-My 14 1914 as Carrington weekly independent
pub [1883-1908]+
NdHi Je 29 1905+

Carrington weekly INDEPENDENT. *See* Foster county independent

Carrington RECORD. w 1898-1921||
NdHi Ag 1905-My 1921

CARSON

Carson PRESS. w My 6 1908+
NdHi 1908+

CASSELTON

CASSELTONIAN. *See* Casselton reporter

Casselton COURIER. *See* Casselton reporter

DAKOTA blizzard. *See* Casselton reporter

Casselton EYE. w 1889-1906||
NdHi Ap 26 1905-Ja 24 1906

NORTH Dakota republican. *See* Casselton reporter

Casselton REPORTER. w 1880+
N 22 1884-Ap 25 1885 as Casselton courier; My 2 1885-D 28 1888 Dakota blizzard; Ja 4 1889-My 18 1894 North Dakota republican; My 25 1894-O 11 1895 Casseltonian
pub N 22 1884+
ICM Ag 18 1881
NdHi Mr 18 1904+

CAVALIER

Cavalier CHRONICLE. w N 1890+
pub 1890+
NdHi F 26 1904-[Ja 15 1921-Jl 1925]+

PEMBINA county news. w 1922-23||
NdHi Je 1922-Ja 12 1923

CAYUGA

Cayuga CITIZEN. w 1910-20||
NdHi Ja 26 1911-Jl 1920

SARGENT county sentinel. w 1922-23||
NdHi D 29 1922-S 13 1923

CENTER

Center REPUBLICAN. w J 12 1903+
pub 1903+
NdHi My 1905+

CHARBONNEAU

Charbonneau HERALD. w 1904-18||
1904-F 20 1914 as Tagus mirror (Tagus)
NdHi Ap 14 1905-Je 15 1918

CHARLSON

MCKENZIE county journal. w 1907-21||
NdHi N 1907-My 1921

CHENOWETH

SLOPE county news. *See under* Amidon

CHRISTINE

Christine EAGLE. w 1902-06||?
NdHi Ap 28 1905-D 26 1906

CHURCHS FERRY

Churchs Ferry SUN. w O 9 1886+
pub 1886+
NdHi 1905+

CLEVELAND

STUTSMAN county leader. w 1903-25||
NdHi Je 14 1906-[Ja-F 1914]-Jl 1925

COAL HARBOR

TIMES. *See* Underwood times (Underwood)

COGSWELL

Cogswell ENTERPRISE. w N 3 1903+
pub 1906+
NdHi 1913+

COLUMBUS

Columbus REPORTER. w Jl 1906
pub F 1920+
NdHi Ja 10 1908-[1921-27]+

CONWAY

Conway CITIZEN. *See* Lankin weekly reporter (Lankin)

COOPERSTOWN

Cooperstown COURIER. *See* Griggs county sentinel-courier

GRIGGS county sentinel. w 1898-Mr 13 1913||
United with Cooperstown courier to form Griggs county sentinel-courier
NdHi Mr 20 1905-13
NdJC 1908
NdMC [1909-My 1910]

GRIGGS county sentinel-courier. w 1883+
1883-Mr 1913 as Cooperstown courier
NdHi Mr 24 1904-Mr 13,Ap 1913+

COURTENAY

Courtenay GAZETTE. w 1897-Ag 17 1922||
NdHi N 12 1903-[Ap 27 1916-F 1918]-22
NdJC 1904,09;16

Courtenay HERALD. w 1928+
NdHi Jl 1929-Je 1932

Courtenay REVIEW. w
NdHi Mr 22-My 1923

CRARY

Crary PUBLIC opinion. w 1902-19||
NdHi D 30 1903-19

CRETE

PRAIRIE press. w 1908-33||
NdHi Mr 20 1909-33

CROSBY

DIVIDE county farmers press. w 1903+
1904-Ja 26 1917 as Crosby review
pub 1903+
NdHi Mr 10 1905-Ja 1917;Mr 14 1919+

DIVIDE county journal. w 1902+
1902-05? as Flaxton eagle (Flaxton); 1906?-My 5 1916 Crosby eagle
pub 1917+
NdHi Je 1905-My5,19 1916+

Crosby EAGLE. *See* Divide county journal

Crosby REVIEW. *See* Divide county farmers press

CRYSTAL

Crystal CALL. w 1890-1928||?
NdHi N 1903-26

DAVENPORT

Davenport NEWS. *See* Red River Valley register (Fargo)

Davenport RECORD. w 1923-31||?
NdHi Ag 1925-27

DAWSON

Dawson LEADER. w 1906-21||?
NdHi Ja 25 1906-[Ja-F 1907]-Ag 1913;N 26 1919-Ap 15 1921

Dawson PRESS. w 1911-19||
NdHi Je 15 1911-Jl 17 1919

Dawson TIMES-STANDARD. w 1888-99||?
1888-96 as Dawson times
Ct Jl 16 1891

DAZEY

Dazey COMMERCIAL. *See* Commercial citizen

COMMERCIAL citizen. w My 26 1911-24||?
1911-Ag 9 1918 as Dazey commercial
NdHi 1911-N 11 1921

Dazey HERALD. w 1906-09||
NdHi D 21 1906-Ap 9 1909

DEERING

Deering ENTERPRISE. w 1904-21||
NdGrH O 1904-Jl 31 1921
NdHi Ja 18 1908-Jl 28 1921

DE LAMERE

De Lamere MISTLETOE. w 1900-16||
NdHi N 19 1903-N 9 1916

De Lamere NEWS. *See* Independent reporter (Forman)

DENBIGH

Denbigh PROMOTER. w 1902- ||
NdHi Mr 31 1905-N 3 1911

DENHOFF

DAKOTA staats zeitung. *See* State press (McClusky)

Denhoff VOICE. w 1903+
NdHi My 11 1905-Ap 7 1933
NdMeG 1910

DES LACS

Des Lacs VALLEY observer. w 1903-20||
NdHi N 1904-[N 1911-13]-N 4 1920

DEVILS LAKE

Devils Lake DEMOCRAT. w D 11 1884-85||?
MnHi D 11-18 1884

Devils Lake FREE press. w 1892-1906||?
1892-1903 as Free press. Merged with Devils Lake inter-ocean
NdHi S 8 1892-[My,Ag 1893-O 1894]-[F,My-Je 1895]-[My 1896]-[Jl 1897]-[F,Ag,D 1898]-[Ja-Ap]-[Ag 1899-Ap 1901]-Ja 22 1903;04

Devils Lake INTER-OCEAN. w 1883-1914||
Merged with Devils Lake world
NdHi N 27 1903-D 25 1914

Devils Lake JOURNAL. w 1904-20||?
NdHi Je 9 1905-18

Devils Lake daily JOURNAL. d D 3 1906+
pub 1906+
NdHi N 9 1909-[1914]-[Ag-D 1916]+

Devils Lake daily WORLD. d 1911-20||
NdHi Je 5 1911-[14-18]-[Ja-Mr]-Je 1920

Devils Lake WORLD. w 1911—
pub O 23 1923+
NdHi 1911+

DICKEY

Dickey REPORTER. w 1902-22||
NdHi My 1905-Je 16 1922

DICKINSON

Die DEUTSCHE zukunft. w,sw 1908-11||
In German
NdHi My 8 1908-Mr 24 1911

NORD Dakota herold. w N 29 1907+
1907-Je 18 1909 pub in Bismark; Je 25 1909-13 in Mandan
In German
MoSC [Ap 11 1924-Mr 1927]-[Ap 1928-Mr 1929]-Ap 1929
NdHi 1907-[16;18-19]-[22-24]-[30-My 15 1931]+

Dickinson POST. sw,w Mr 10 1906-D 30 1910||
1906-Ap 23 1908 as Post. United with Dickinson recorder to form Recorder-post
NdHi Ap 30 1908-10

NORTH DAKOTA (*Continued*)

DICKINSON—*Continued*

Dickinson PRESS. w Mr 1883+
pub 1883+
NdD 1926+
NdHi N 7 1903+

Dickinson daily PRESS. d
NdHi My 1931-32

Dickinson RECORDER. *See* Recorder-post

RECORDER-POST. w 1892-1927‖
1892-1910 as Dickinson recorder. Merged with Dickinson press
NdHi D 1903-08;11-27

Der VOLKSFREUND. *See under* Richardton

DODGE

Dodge DISPATCH. w 1916-21‖
NdHi Mr 3 1916-21

DOGDEN

Dogden JOURNAL. w 1917-19‖
NdHi 1918-O 23 1919

Dogden NEWS. w 1907-24‖
NdHi Ja 16 1908-N 17 1922

Dogden OBSERVER. w 1907-10‖
NdHi Ja 9 1908-My 26 1910

DONNYBROOK

Donnybrook COURIER. w 1901+
pub [1901]+
NdHi D 1903+
NdMC D 1931-Ap 1935

DOUGLAS

Douglas HERALD. w 1906-22‖
NdHi D 20 1907-Ag 10 1922

DRAKE

Drake NEWS. w 1903-20‖
NdHi Jl 21 1905-[Je 1907-O 8 1915]-Mr 4 1920

Drake REGISTER. w F 1 1906+
1906-Ag 12 1920 as Balfour messenger (Balfour)
NdHi 1906+

Drake TELEGRAM. w 1908-10‖
NdHi Ja 23 1908-Ag 4 1910

DRAYTON

Drayton ECHO. *See* Red River Valley leader

RED River Valley leader. w 1888+
1888-F 13 1925 as Drayton echo
pub 1888+
NdHi 1904-[Je 1907-15]+

DRISCOLL

Driscoll NEWS. w 1906-14‖
NdHi Ja 8 1908-Jl 14 1914

DUNN CENTER

Dunn Center JOURNAL. w 1915+
NdHi Je 17 1915+

SPRING Valley times. *See* Dunn Center times

Dunn Center TIMES. w 1913-20‖
1913-Ja 17 1919 as Spring Valley times
NdHi Mr 1914-Ja 17,31 1919-My 28 1920

DUNSEITH

Dunseith HERALD. 1884-1904?. *See* Rolette county herald (Rolla)

Dunseith HERALD. w 1924-25‖
NdHi Mr 6 1924-Jl 23 1925

Dunseith MAGNET. w 1902-19‖
1902-N 21 1907 as North Dakota magnet
NdHi Jl 13 1905-Jl 17 1919

NORTH Dakota magnet. *See* Dunseith magnet

EDGELEY

Edgeley MAIL. w 1887+
NdHi Ap 21 1905+

EDINBURG

Edinburg TRIBUNE. w 1900-19‖
NdHi My 12 1905-Ag 15 1919

EDMORE

Edmore HERALD-NEWS. w 1901+
NdHi N 1903-[Ja 8 1920-Je 13 1929]+

EGELAND

Egeland ENTERPRISE. w F 1906+
pub 1915+
NdHi My 24 1906+

ELGIN

GRANT county news. w 1910+
1910-Mr 15 1923 as Shields enterprise (Shields); Mr 22 1923-26 Elgin news
pub 1926+
NdHi Je 1911+

Elgin NEWS. *See* Grant county news

Elgin TIMES. w 1911-20‖
NdHi N 22 1912-N 12 1920

ELLENDALE

DICKEY county leader and Ellendale commercial. w 1882+
pub [1882+]
MnHi D 22 1882
NdHi Mr 23 1905-[D 1914]+

NORTH Dakota record. w 1894-1916‖
NdHi Ja 13 1904-Je 29 1916

EMERSON

DUNN county settler. *See under* Manning

ENDERLIN

Enderlin INDEPENDENT. w Je 6 1894+
1895-1910 as Ransom county independent
pub My 1920+
NdHi Mr 17 1904-O 1910;Ja 12 1911+

RANSOM county independent. *See* Enderlin independent

EPPING

Epping BULLETIN. w 1906-12‖
NdHi Ja 16 1908-My 9 1912

EPWORTH

Epworth EXAMINER. w 1910-14‖
NdHi Mr 11 1910-Mr 13 1914

ESMOND

Esmond BEE. w 1900-19‖
NdHi Ap 29 1905-S 29 1919

FAIRDALE

Fairdale TIMES. w 1905-20‖?
NdHi My 1906-N 12 1920

FAIRMOUNT

Fairmount NEWS. w 1894+
pub 1931+
NdHi Jl 27 1906+

FAIRVIEW

Fairview TRIBUNE. w 1900-18‖?
1900-Ag 29 1913 as Buford tribune (Buford)
MnHi Ag 24 1900-D 20 1901
NdHi Ja 15 1904-Ag,S 12 1913-Ja 18 1918

FARGO

Fargo ARGUS. d 1879-98‖
United with Morning call to form Morning call and argus
Pub simultaneously in Fargo, and in Moorhead, Minn.
Je 7 1894 special Fire anniversary ed
DLC Jl 1882-85
ICM My 28,Ag 11-12 1881;D 25 1883;My 14 1884
MnHi Ja 3 1888; Je 7 1894
NdFF [1879-98]
NdU 1889-Je 1890

Sunday ARGUS. *See* Sunday call and argus

Fargo BLADE. w 1911-33‖
NdHi Ja 29 1916-33

Sunday CALL and argus. w 1881-1909‖?
1881-98 as Sunday argus
ICM Ag 21 1881;My 13 1883
MWA Ag 9 1885
NdU 1889

Morning CALL and argus. d 1898-1910‖?
1898 as Morning call. Merged with Fargo daily news
MnHi [1903-04]-09
NdHi F 18 1904-Mr 18 1909

CO-OPERATORS' herald. w 1913-21‖?
NdHi O 3 1913-Jl 7 1916

Fargo daily COURIER-NEWS. d Jl 1 1908-Ap 17 1923‖
1908-D 16 1910 as Fargo daily news. Followed by Fargo daily tribune
DLC Je 1920-23
MnHi 1911-[18-23]
MoSC Ap 17-O 19 1919
NN Jl-O 3 1919;Ap 9 1920-23
NdFA S 1910-23
NdFF D 23 1910-23
NdHi Ag 8 1908-23
WHi Ap 1917-23

DAKOTA. *See* Fram

Fargo EXPRESS. *See* Fargo times. 1874-81

FJERDE juli. w 1889-F 24 1897‖?
United with Dakota to form Fjerde juli og Dakota, later Fram
IaDeL Ag 19,S 23-30 1896;Ja-F 1897

FJERDE juli og Dakota. *See* Fram

FOLKETS ven. w 1895-97‖
Dated also at Moorhead, Minn.
IaDeL S 30-N 4,18-D 16 1896

Fargo FORUM. d (morning ed.) My 13 1925+
Follows Fargo daily tribune
pub 1925+
ICM Ag 25 1929
NdFA 1925+
NdHi 1925-[S-D 1930]+

Fargo FORUM and daily republican. d evening ed. N 17 1891+
1891-96 as Daily forum
pub 1891+
DLC D 3 1891;98-1912 [Jl,D 1916]+
MnHi [1901-24]
MoSC Je-O 21 1919
NdFA 1906+
NdHi O 7 1903-[Je 1907-Jl 1908]+
WHi D 12 1922+

Fargo FORUM and republican. w 1891-1913‖?
1891-96? as Fargo forum
NdHi O 16 1903-[08]-13

FRAM. w 1879-1918‖?
1879-83? as Red River posten; 1884?-85? Norske Amerikaner; 1886?-89? Fargo posten; 1890?-F 24 1897? Dakota; Mr?-Ap 27 1898 Fjerde juli og Dakota
In Norwegian and Danish
IaDeL Je 25,S 3 1890;Ap 6-13 1892;Mr 13 1895;S 16 1896-[1917]
MnHi [1899-1918]
NdHi Ja 24 1885-87;Ag 1905-17
WHi O 16 1895-Mr 11 1898

INDEPENDENT. *See* Rural independent

INDEPENDENT review. *See* Rural independent

Fargo JOURNAL. w 1904-07‖
NdHi Mr 17 1905-Mr 15 1907

Fargo MIRROR. w 1875‖
United with Fargo express to form Fargo times

Fargo daily NEWS. *See* Fargo daily courier-news

NON-PARTISAN leader. w,sw S 25 1915-O 31 1921‖
WHi complete

NORD Dakota tidende. w Ag 14 1919-23‖
Suspended from D 1920-O 1921
1919-21 pub in Grand Forks
In Norwegian and Danish
MnHi 1919-20;D 29 1921-Jl 26 1923
NdHi [1919-22]

NORMANDEN. w 1886+
1886-My 7 1932 pub in Grand Forks
pub 1886+
IU D 18 1917+
IaDeL [Jl 1896-98]-[1901-02;My 1904-My 1908;09-13] 16-24;26;29
MnHi [1907-F 19 1926]+
NdHi N 4 1903-[18-19]-[21-24]+
WHi F 15 1899+

NORSKE Amerikaner. *See* Fram

NORTH Dakota democrat. *See* Red River Valley record

NORTH Dakota leader. w F 16 1918-26‖?
Suspended from O 29 1921-My 20 1922
ICJ 1919-N 18 1922
IU 1919-O 22 1921
MnHi Mr 9 1918-O 22 1921
MoSC 1918-D 21 1919
NdHi 1918-[N 1921-My]-D 1922

NORTHERN Pacific mirror. w S 12 1874-75‖
Merged with Fargo times
NdHi O 14,31,N 21 1874;F 27,Ap 24,My 15 1875

Fargo POST. w 1905-20‖
1905-Ap 7 1917 as Search-light
NdHi S 15 1906-Je 24 1920

Fargo POSTEN. 1886-89. *See* Fram

RED River posten. *See* Fram

RED River Valley record. w 1911-20‖
1911-Jl 26 1919 as North Dakota democrat
NdHi Ja 11 1912-N 25 1920

RED River Valley register. w My 26 1911-20‖
1911-N 13 1919 as Davenport news (Davenport)
NdHi 1911-F 6 1920

Daily REPUBLICAN. sw,d S 5 1878-96‖
United with Daily forum to form Fargo forum and daily republican. (evening ed)
ICM My 16 1884
MnHi [1881-84]
NdFF [1878-96]

Fargo REPUBLICAN. w 1878-94‖?
United with Fargo forum to form Fargo forum and republican
ICM My 14 1884
OClWHi D 5 1883

RURAL independent. w,m Mr 3 1919-24‖?
1919-21 as Independent; 1922-23? Independent review
MnHi [1919-21]
NdHi Ja-Jl 1924

SEARCH-light. *See* Fargo post

Die STAATS presse. w 1902-07‖?
In German
NdHi N 1903-S 23 1906

STATE democrat. *See* State record

STATE record. w 1922-25‖?
1922-24 as State democrat
NdHi My 24 1923-N 1924;F-N 1925

Fargo SUN and Saturday evening journal. w 1889-98‖?
1889-96? as Fargo sun
MnHi [1898]

NORTH DAKOTA (*Continued*)

FARGO—*Continued*

Fargo TIMES. w Ja 1 1874-81||
1874 as Fargo express. Merged with Fargo republican
ICHi F 1 1879 (special ed)
MWA N 3 1877
MnHi [1879-81]
NdHi Ja 1-8,Mr 12-19,Ap 9,30,My 7,21-Jl 9,Ag 6,S 3-10 1874;S 18 1875;F 1,O 25 1879

TIMES. w 1930+
NdHi Ja 22 1931-32

Fargo daily TRIBUNE. d Ap 18 1923-My 12 1925||
Follows Fargo daily courier-news. Ap 18-30 1923 as Fargo daily tribune and courier-news. Followed by Fargo forum (morning ed)
DLC complete
NN 1923-Mr 14 1924
NdFA complete
NdFF complete
NdHi complete
WHi Ap 18-Je 24 1923

VESTEN. w 1888-89||
United with Posten to form Posten und vesten, later Fram
NdHi Je 23 1888-My 22 1889

FESSENDEN

STAATSZEITUNG. w
In German
NdFeW S 1 1897-O 28 1898

WELLS county farmer. w Je 13 1918-Ap 26 1934||
Merged with Wells county free press
NdHi complete

WELLS county free press. w 1897+
NdHi My 12 1905+

WELLS county news. w S 12 1895-O 1908||
Merged with Wells county free press
NdFeW complete
NdHi Ap 27 1905-08

FINGAL

Fingal HERALD. w Je 20 1898+
pub 1915+
NdHi Ap 27 1905-[S 1913-F 6 1914]+

FINLEY

Finley BEACON. *See* Steele county press

Finley GOLDEN slope. *See* Steele county press

NORTH Dakota times. w Ag 1928-Ag 1934||
NdFiT complete

STEELE county farmers press. *See* Steele county press

STEELE county observer. w 1919-22||
NdHi S 11 1919-Ag 31 1922

STEELE county press. w 1896+
1896-98 as Finley golden slope;1899-My 29 1919 Finley beacon; Je 5 1919-29 Steele county farmers press
pub 1896+
NdFiT 1896+
NdHi N 1903+

FLASHER

Flasher HUSTLER w 1903-19||
NdHi Je 16 1905-Ja 17 1919

Flasher TRIBUNE *See* Morton county news (Mandan)

FLAXTON

Flaxton EAGLE. *See* Divide county journal (Crosby)

Flaxton TIMES. w 1902+
pub 1902+
NdHi Ap 28 1905+

FORBES

FARMERS sentinel and Forbes republican. w Mr 22 1906-O 3 1929||
1906-My 1907 as Forbes republican; Je 1907-Ja 3 1918 Forbes republican and tribune
NdHi complete

Forbes REPUBLICAN. *See* Farmers sentinel and Forbes republican

Forbes REPUBLICAN and tribune. *See* Farmers sentinel and Forbes republican

Forbes TRIBUNE. w 1906-07||
United with Forbes republican to form Forbes republican and tribune, later Farmers sentinel and Forbes republican
NdHi Mr-My 1907

FORDVILLE

Fordville CHRONICLE. w S 4 1912-Ag 15 1919||
NdHi complete

TRI-COUNTY sun. w My 17 1922+
pub 1922+
NdHi F 1923+

FORMAN

Forman INDEPENDENT news. *See* Sargent county news

INDEPENDENT reporter. w 1919-23||
1919-F 4 1921 as De Lamere news (De Lamere)
NdHi 1920-S 27 1923

Forman NEWS. w 1895-O 13 1911||
United with Sargent county independent to form Forman independent news, later Sargent county news
NdHi 1904-11

SARGENT county independent. *See* Sargent county news

SARGENT county news. w 1888+
1888-O 12 1911 as Sargent county independent; O 20 1911-My 10 1918 Forman independent news
pub Je 1921+
NdHi Mr 1905+

FORT RICE

FRONTIER scout.
MWA Jl 13-20,Ag 10,24-31 1865
MnHi Jl 22, Ag 17 1864; Je 15 1865
NN O 12 1865 (photostat)

SLOPE advocate. w 1911-13||?
NdHi My 13 1911-Ag 15 1913

FORT YATES

SIOUX county pioneer-arrow. w O 1914+
1914-O 4 1929 as Sioux county pioneer
pub 1914+
NdHi N 27 1914+

FORTUNA

Fortuna LEADER. w 1905-20||?
1905-13? as Stady leader (Stady)
NdHi Ag 5, D 3 1909;10-My 2 1913;N 16 1914-16

FOXHOLM

Foxholm NEWS. w
NdHi S-D 1915

FRYBURG

BILLINGS county pioneer. w O 9 1913+
1913-Ag 8 1919 as Fryburg pioneer
NdHi 1913+

Fryburg PIONEER. *See* Billings county pioneer

FULLERTON

Fullerton INDEPENDENT. w 1915-19||?
NdHi Je 13-S 5 1919

GARRISON

Garrison ADVANCE. w N 17 1915-Jl 31 1919||
NdHi complete

McLEAN county independent. w 1903+
pub [1913-Dec. 24 1920]+
NdHi Ag 17 1906+

Garrison TIMES. *See* Underwood times (Underwood)

GASCOYNE

Gascoyne ADVANCE. *See* Mineral Springs tribune (Mineral Springs)

Gascoyne GAZETTE. w Ap 7 1915-N 7 1917||
NdHi complete

Gascoyne NEWS. w 1918+
NdHi O 3 1918+

GILBY

Gilby CHRONICLE. w 1913-20||?
NdHi Ja 4,S 18 1918

GLADYS

WILLIAMS county review. w 1908-11||?
NdHi Ap 1909-Jl 28 1911

GLEN ULLIN

Glen Ullin NEWS. w D 1902+
pub 1902+
NdHi Ja 29 1904+

GLENBURN

Glenburn ADVANCE. w Jl 28 1903+
Jl 28-O 16 1903 as Glenburn tribune
pub 1903+
NdHi My 19 1905+

GOLDEN VALLEY

Golden Valley AMERICAN. w My 3 1912+
1912-16 as German American (Krem)
NdHi 1912-D 22 1916;Ap 13 1917+

GOODRICH

Goodrich weekly CITIZEN. w N 19 1903+
pub 1923+
NdHi 1903-[N 1917-Ja]-[Ap,My]-[S 1918-Ja]-[Mr,Ap]-[Je 1919-S 1922]-[23-N 1927]+

GRACE CITY

Grace City GAZETTE. w 1916-
NdHi Mr 2 1916-S 24 1919

GRAFTON

Grafton NEWS and times. w May 26 1881+
1881-O 19 1883 as Acton news
pub 1881+
NdHi N 13 1903-[Ap 1926-28]+

Grafton POSTEN. w F 14 1905-F 5 1909||
In Norwegian
NdHi complete

WALSH county record. w 1889+
pub 1889+
NdHi O 14 1903+

WALSH county republican. w 1901-Mr 11 1911||
1901-S 4 1908 pub in Park River. Merged with Grafton news and times
NdHi Ap 27 1905-11

GRAND FORKS

Grand Forks AMERICAN. d S 30 1918-Mr 31 1920||
MnHi [1918]-20
NdHi complete
NdU complete

Grand Forks COURIER. w 1904-05||
Merged with Weekly times, later Weekly times-herald
MnHi complete
NdHi Ap-D 1905

Grand Forks HERALD. d Je 13 1879+
Title varies slightly: Grand Forks daily herald, etc. Je 26 1904 is Silver anniversary ed
pub 1879+
CoU S 1906-10
DLC Ap 1914+
MWA Jl 19 1884
MnHi [1918-20]Mr 8 1932+
NdG 1904-Mr 1916
NdGP D 1911+
NdHi N 3 1903-[Ja-Je 1908]—
NdU Ag 16 1884;Ap 6,My 16 1885;Ag 7 1903; 1906-S 1918;19+
WHi 1917-19

Grand Forks INDEPENDENT. w 1915-17||?
NdHi D 2 1915-N 8 1917

NORD Dakota tidende. *See under* Fargo

NORMANDEN. *See under* Fargo

NORTHWEST news. w 1887-98||?
NdG 1887-96
NdU D 25 1895

Grand Forks daily PLAINDEALER. *See* Evening press and daily plaindealer

Grand Forks weekly PLAINDEALER. *See* Grand Forks weekly press

Grand Forks weekly PRESS. w Ap 6 1882-1907||?
1882-Mr 10 1904 as Grand Forks weekly plaindealer
NdU 1882-N 17,D 1887-N 15 1888;90-O,D 1902-Mr 10 1904

Evening PRESS and daily plaindealer. d N 13 1882-Mr 1908||?
1882-Mr 11 1904 title varies: Grand Forks daily plaindealer; Grand Forks plaindealer; Daily plaindealer
DLC Ag 20 1890-Mr 1908
NbHi D 12 1890
NdHi 1882-[Ja-My 14 1887]-[Je 29 1889-N 1903]-Je 17 1907
NdU Jl 1890-O 1902;03-05
OClWHi My 17 1899

Grand Forks PROGRESSIVE observer. w 1911-17||?
NdHi Ja 5 1911-F 24 1917

RED River Valley citizen. w O 7 1926+
Follows Reynolds enterprise (Reynolds) 1926-29? pub in Reynolds
NdHi 1926-32

Grand Forks TIDENDE. *See* Minneapolis tidende (Minneapolis, Minn.)

Evening TIMES. d Ja 1906-Mr 30 1914||
Merged with Grand Forks herald
DLC Ag 1906-14
NdGH complete
NdHi 1906-[Jl 8 1907-Je 1908]-14
NdU D 14 1906

Weekly TIMES-HERALD. w 1903-16||
1903-O 19 1911 as Weekly times
MnHi [1906-11]-16
NdHi 1906-16

GRANDIN

Grandin CHRONICLE. w 1892-1907||?
NdHi N 1903-05

GRANO

Grano TRIBUNE. w Jl 13 1905-Ag 16 1918||
NdHi complete

GRANVILLE

Granville HERALD. w Ap 15 1904+
1904-Ag 11 1916 as Herald
pub 1904-Ap 1909;Ap 1918+
NdHi 1904-Ag 11 1916;17+

Granville RECORD. w 1900-O 8 1909||
Merged with Granville herald
NdHi D 18 1903-08

NORTH DAKOTA (*Continued*)

GRASSY BUTTE

Grassy Butte ADVERTISER. w 1916-17||?
NdHi My 24 1916-Ag 29 1917

Grassy Butte NEWS. w 1918-22||
NdHi My 16 1918-Ja 12 1922

GRENORA

Grenora EXAMINER. w 1905-23||
NdHi Jl 14 1916-D 27 1923

Grenora GAZETTE. w 1916-17||?
NdHi Ag 10 1916-Mr 8 1917

Grenora NEWSMAN. *See* Williams county newsman

WILLIAMS county newsman. w 1911?+
1911?-My 21 1926 as Grenora newsman
NdHi Mr 13 1925+

GWINNER

Gwinner GAZETTE. w 1905-08||
NdHi 1906-08

PRAIRIE press. w 1908-33||
NdHi 1911-33

HALLIDAY

DUNN county promoter. *See* Halliday promoter

Halliday PROMOTER. w Je 12 1913+
1913-Ap 3 1914 as Dunn county promoter
NdHi 1913+

HAMILTON

NORTH Dakota independent. w 1901-18||?
NdHi Ap 21 1905-Jl 19 1918

HAMPDEN

Hampden GUARDIAN. w 1908-
NdHi S 15 1909-F 14 1917

Hampden NEWS. w 1917-24||?
NdHi Jl 18 1917-22

HANKINSON

Hankinson NEWS. w 1890+
NdHi N 1903+

HANNAFORD

Hannaford ENTERPRISE. w My 24 1904+
pub 1904+
NdHi Ag 1905+

HANNAH

MOON. w 1896-Ag 29 1919||
NdHi Jl 14 1905-19

HANSBORO

Hansboro NEWS. w 1909-21||
NdHi 1910-Ja 14 1921

Hansboro PIONEER. w 1906-08||
NdHi Mr 9 1906-08

HARVEY

Harvey HERALD. w 1893+
NdHi Ap 27 1905+

Harvey JOURNAL und Die Deutsche rundschau. w Ja 21 1915-D 27 1918||
Merged with Harvey herald
In English and German
NdHi complete

HASTINGS

Hastings HERALD. w 1923-26||
NdHi My 11 1923-S 10 1926

Hastings TIMES. w 1908-19||?
NdHi O 9 1908-Jl 9 1919

HATTON

Hatton FREE PRESS. w Ja 1905+
pub 1906+
NdHi Ap 12 1906+

VESTERHEIMEN. *See under* Crookston, Minn.

HAVANA

Havana HERALD. w 1923||
NdHi Ap 25-Jl 4 1923

Havana RECORD. w 1905-08||?
NdHi Ap 19 1907-Je 26 1908

Havana UNION. w 1910-25||
NdHi Ja 14 1915-Je 25 1925

HAVELOCK

AMERICAN German. w 1915-18||
In English and German
NdHi D 24 1915-Mr 22 1918

HAYNES

Haynes GAZETTE. w Mr 7 1908-Je 1909||
United with Haynes register to form Haynes register-gazette
NdHi complete

Haynes REGISTER-gazette. w 1908-20||
1908-Je 24 1909 as Haynes register
NdHi Mr 18 1909-D 9 1920

HAZELTON

EMMONS county republican. w 1885-20||
NdHi F 16 1905-Mr 11 1920

Hazelton INDEPENDENT. w My 24 1923+
pub 1923+
NdHi 1923+

HAZEN

MERCER county star. *See* Hazen star

Hazen STAR. w 1912+
1912 as Mercer county star
pub D 1913+
NdHi My 12 1916+

HEBRON

Hebron HERALD. w 1898+
1898-Ap 7 1916 as Die Wacht am Missouri
1898-F 9 1906 pub in New Salem
pub 1908-11;14-21;S 1925+
NdHi Je 23 1905+

Hebron TRIBUNE. w 1909-19||
NdHi Mr 1911-Ag 1 1919

Die WACHT am Missouri. *See* Hebron herald

HETTINGER

ADAMS county record. w Je 6 1907+
pub 1907+
NdHi 1907+

Hettinger JOURNAL. w 1913-19||
NdHi Ja 4 1913-Jl 31 1919

Hettinger TRIBUNE. w 1926-28||
NdHi Ja 14 1926-28

HILLSBORO

AFHOLDS basunen. w 1886-96||
1886 as Folkets röst. Followed by Folkets avis
In Norwegian
IaDeL [1890;92;95-96]

Hillsboro BANNER. w 1880+
pub 1882+
NdHi D 18 1903+

FOLKETS avis. w 1899-1902||
Follows Afholds-basunen. Merged with Statstidende
In Norwegian
IaDeL Mr 4,Jl 1,D 16 1899-Mr 24,Ap 19-26 1900;Mr 30 1901
WHi 1899-1901

FOLKETS röst. *See* Afholds basunen

FREMTIDEN. w 1906-09||
In Norwegian
NdHi [Je 26 1907-Mr 3 1909]

STATSTIDENDE. w My 1897-1910||
In Norwegian
IaDeL My 25-Je 1897;O 24 1899-Je 3 1902[F 9 1904-N 10 1909]
NdHi Ja 12 1904-Ja 12 1910
WHi 1899-1902

TRAILL county blade. w 1905-11||?
NdHi Ap 27 1905-Je 13 1907

TRAILL county news. w 1915-21||
1915-18 as Buxton outlook (Buxton)
NdHi Mr 1916-N 15 1918;Ja 30 1919-Jl 21 1921

HOPE

Hope PIONEER. w Ap 1882+
pub [1884+]
MnHi D 22 1882

HUDSON

Hudson HERALD. *See* Oakes times (Oakes)

HUNTER

Hunter HERALD. w 1894-1926||
NdHi Jl 13 1905-Mr 18 1926

Hunter TIMES. w 1928+
NdHi Je 28 1929+

HURDSFIELD

Hurdsfield BANNER. w 1907-13||?
NdHi N 22 1907-N 14 1913

Hurdsfield HERALD. w Je 23 1916-Je 7 1919||
NdHi complete

INKSTER

Inkster ENTERPRISE. w 1907-27||
NdHi Ap 1914-27

TIMES-vidette. w 1896-1908||?
NdHi Ap 6 1905-N 8 1906

JAMESTOWN

Jamestown ALERT. *See* Jamestown sun

Jamestown daily CAPITAL. d 1882-Jl 5 1918||
Merged with Stutsman county press
NdHi Jl 1896-[97-Je 1903]-18

Jamestown CAPITAL. w. *See* Stutsman county press

NORTH Dakota capital. *See* Stutsman county press

STUTSMAN county democrat. *See* Stutsman county record

STUTSMAN county press. w F 24 1882-
1882-S 13 1889 as Jamestown capital; S 21 1889-Jl 12 1918 North Dakota capital
DLC 1882-F 3 1883;90-Ja 12 1893
NdHi Jl 1887-[Jl 1890-Je 1891]-[Jl 1892-Je 1896]-[Jl 1897-N 1903]-F 4 1921

STUTSMAN county record. w S 1904+
1904-Mr 4 1926 as Stutsman county democrat
pub 1904+
NdHi Je 22 1905+

Jamestown weekly SUN. w Jl 4 1878+
1878-F 17 1882 as Jamestown alert; F 24 1882-Je 25 1925 Jamestown weekly alert
pub [1879-80]
DLC 1878-Jl 21 1882
NdHi 1904-D 23 1926

Jamestown SUN. d 1881+
1881-Je 30 1925 as Jamestown daily alert
pub [1881+]
MdHi Ja 13 1904+

JUD

Jud LEADER. w 1907-19||
NdHi Ja 9 1908-Je 26 1919

KATHRYN

Kathryn RECORDER. w O 1 1908+
pub D 13 1928+
NdHi 1910+

Kathryn weekly STAR. w 1902-08||
NdHi Je 9 1905-[Ja-Mr 1906]-Jl 1908

KENMARE

Kenmare JOURNAL. w 1900-O 9 1919||
Merged with Ward county press, later Northwest press (Minot)
NdHi N 19 1903-19
NdMC Ja-Ap 6,20-Je 1,15-22,Jl 6,Ag,S 14-O 5,N-D 21 1916

Kenmare NEWS. w 1899+
NdHi Ag 1905+
NdMC Ag 10,D 1910;Ja 11 1912

KENSAL

Kensal JOURNAL. w 1902-15||
1902-07? as North Dakota state journal
Merged with Kensal progress
NdHi My 1905-S 1907;Mr 19 1908-N 4 1915

NORTH Dakota state journal. *See* Kensal journal

Kensal PROGRESS. w Mr 3 1916-My 30 1929||
Merged with Medina citizen (Medina)
NdHi complete

Kensal TIMES. w Ja 16 1930+
pub 1930+
NdHi Ja 30 1931+

KERMIT

Kermit NEWS. w Jl 26 1906-11||
Jl-D 13 1906 as Kermit republican; D 20 1906-Je 6 1907? Republican
NdHi D 20 1906-Je 6 1907;09-F 3 1911

Kermit REPUBLICAN. *See* Kermit news

KILLDEER

Killdeer HERALD. w F 25 1915+
pub 1915+
NdHi Ap 1915+

Killdeer TRIBUNE. w 1914-21||
NdHi 1917-F 11 1921

KINDRED

Kindred TRIBUNE. w Ap 19 1899+
N 3 1905-Je 19 1926 as Tribune
pub 1910+
NdHi F 24-O 1905;Je 26 1908+

KNOX

Knox ADVOCATE. w 1899+
pub [1899+]
NdHi Ap 27 1905-[Jl,O-N 1905]-[Ja 1907]+

Knox INDEPENDENT. w 1903-05||
NdHi D 9 1904-Ap 28 1905

KRAMER

BOTTINEAU county record. *See* Lansford journal (Lansford)

NORTH DAKOTA (*Continued*)

KREM

GERMAN American. *See* Golden Valley American (Golden Valley)

MERCER county star. w 1912-16||
NdHi S 20 1912-My 5 1916

KULM

Kulm MESSENGER. w 1897+
NdHi Ag 1905+

LaFOLLETTE

LaFollette FORUM. *See* Plaza pioneer (Plaza)

LAKOTA

Lakota AMERICAN. w 1902+
pub 1912+
NdHi Mr 19 1904+

Lakota HERALD. w 1902-06||
NdHi Mr 24 1905-Ag 10 1906

NELSON county observer. w 1888-1922||
NdHi D 11 1903-Ag 31 1922
NdLA Je 17 1920-Jl 20 1922

LA MOURE

La Moure CHRONICLE. w N 15 1883+
1883-Ap 25 1885 as La Moure progress; My 2 1885-D 21 1888 La Moure progress and chronicle; D 28 1888-Mr 19 1917 La Moure county chronicle; Mr 26 1917-Mr 13 1918 La Moure county chronicle-echo; Mr 20 1918-D 27 1932 La Moure county chronicle
pub 1883+
NdHi N 1903+

La Moure ECHO. w 1908-Mr 15 1917||
United with La Moure county chronicle to form La Moure county chronicle-echo, later La Moure chronicle
NdHi My 1909-17

LA MOURE county chronicle. *See* La Moure chronicle

La Moure PROGRESS. *See* La Moure chronicle

LANGDON

CAVALIER county farmers press. w 1885-1921||
1885-Ap 15 1920 as Courier-democrat
NdHi Ja 28 1904-Ag 18 1921

CAVALIER county republican. w 1888+
pub 1898+
NdHi D 17 1903+

COURIER-democrat. *See* Cavalier county farmers press

LANKIN

Lankin weekly REPORTER. w Ag 15 1907-18||?
Ag 15-O 10 1907 as Conway citizen (Conway)
NdHi O 10 1907-O 25 1918

LANSFORD

Lansford JOURNAL. w 1905-22||
1905-Je 9 1909 as Bottineau county record (Kramer)
NdHi Jl 16 1909-D 8 1922

Lansford LEADER. w My 1925+
pub 1925+
NdHi O 22 1925—

Lansford TIMES. w 1903-10||
NdHi Ap 28 1905-D 16 1910

LARIMORE

Larimore PIONEER. w Ja 1 1881+
pub 1881+
NdHi 1882;F 22 1883-F 14 1884;87-F 1899;F 1901+

LARSON

Larson LEADER. w 1908-D 23 1910||
NdHi Ja 3 1908-[Mr-D 1909]-10

LAWTON

Lawton REPUBLICAN. w 1909-26||
NdHi O 1909-Ap 30 1926

LEEDS

Leeds NEWS. w 1888+
pub [1888+]
NdHi O 29 1903-D 20 1928

LEITH

Leith INDEX. w 1911-23||
NdHi O 20 1911-F 16 1923

LEONARD

Leonard JOURNAL. *See* Leonard leader

Leonard LEADER. w 1910-26||
1910-24? as Leonard journal
NdHi S 10 1915-O 9 1919[D 17 1925-26]

LIDGERWOOD

Lidgerwood BROADAXE. *See* Richland county farmer (Wahpeton)

Lidgerwood JOURNAL. w 1923-25||
NdHi Ap 26 1923-S 25 1925

Lidgerwood MONITOR. w S 1 1900—
pub 1900—
NdHi N 19 1903+

LIGNITE

BURKE county bulletin. w 1911-13||
NdHi Ja 12 1911-Ap 24 1913

LINTON

EMMONS county advocate. w 1901-10||?
NdHi Ap 20 1905-08

EMMONS county free press. w Ja 28 1915-31||
Merged with Emmons county record
pub 1916-31
NdHi complete

EMMONS county record. w Je 10 1884+
1884-98 as Winona times (Winona)
pub 1884+
NdHi Ap 28 1905-[20]+

LISBON

DAKOTA clipper. *See* Ransom county gazette

Lisbon FREE press. w My 1882+
1882-93 as Lisbon star
pub [1893-1901]+
NdHi N 1903+
NjR Ap 8 1898

RANSOM county gazette. w 1883+
1883-85? as Dakota clipper
pub My 1910+
NdHi Mr 25 1909+

Lisbon STAR. *See* Lisbon free press

LITCHVILLE

Litchville BULLETIN. w Mr 1900+
pub 1900+
NdHi Ap 1905-[15]+

LUCCA

Lucca LEDGER. w
NdHi O 12 1905-Jl 5 1906

LUVERNE

Luverne LEDGER. w 1913-17||
NdHi D 19 1913-S 7 1917

McCLUSKY

McClusky GAZETTE. w S 28 1905+
1905-Ja 7 1909 as McLean county gazette
pub 1905+
NdHi 1905+

INDEPENDENT. w 1908-11||
NdHi 1909-Je 1 1911

McLEAN county gazette. *See* McClusky gazette

NORD Dakota staats zeitung. *See* State press

SHERIDAN post. w 1913-17||
NdHi Ja 17 1913-Ap 14 1917

STATE press. w 1906-12||
1906-N 20 1908 as Dakota staats zeitung (Denhoff); N 27 1908-S 1 1911 Nord Dakota staats zeitung
In German and English
NdHi Je 13 1907-S 13 1912

McCUMBER

McCumber HERALD. *See* Rolette record (Rolette)

McGREGOR

McGregor HERALD. w 1914-22||
NdHi Ja 22 1914-22

McHENRY

FREE press. w 1903-10||?
NdHi Ap 27 1905-08

McHenry TRIBUNE. w 1899-Ag 1 1929||
NdHi Ap 27 1905-[S 22 1921-Ap]-Ag 1 1929

McKENZIE

McKenzie GAZETTE. w S 5 1907-Ap 22 1923||
1907-10? as Moffit messenger (Moffit)
NdHi 1907-N 3 1910;S 12 1912-20

McVILLE

McVille JOURNAL. w Je 14 1906+
pub 1906+
NdHi Ap 25 1907-[Je 1908-O 1910]+

MADDOCK

Maddock STANDARD. w 1900+
pub 1900+
NdHi 1904+

MAKOTI

Makoti HERALD. w 1913-16||
NdHi Ja 23 1914-Mr 9 1916

Makoti SENTINEL. w 1916-27||
NdHi Je 8 1916-[Jl 9 1919-21]-F 17 1927

MANDAN

DEMOCRAT. w 1908||?
NdHi Ap 30-O 22 1908

FARMER-labor. w
NdHi S 30-D 7 1922

INDEPENDENT. *See* North Dakota oil journal

MORTON county farmers press. w 1904-22||
1904-18 as Mandan republican
MnHi [1919-20]
NdHi Ap 14 1905-My 2 1912;My 1918-O 6 1922

MORTON county news. w Ap 21 1921+
1921-32 as Flasher tribune (Flasher)
pub Ja 12 1933+
NdHi 1921-32

Mandan NEWS. *See* North Dakota oil journal

NORD Dakota herold. *See under* Dickinson

NORTH Dakota oil journal. w 1892-1929||?
1892-1908 as Independent; 1909-Jl 21 1927 Mandan news
NdHi My 12 1904-08;Ja 15 1909-[S 26 1913-15]-Jl 21 1927

Mandan PIONEER. w 1881-1930||
Merged with Mandan daily pioneer
Ja 1882 is special emigration edition
pub complete
MnHi Ja 1882
NdHi 1885[86-90]-[98-O 1903]-[17-18]-30

Mandan daily PIONEER. d 1882+
1882-90 as Daily pioneer
Suspended from 1891-Mr 1914
pub Ap 1914+
NdHi 1885-90;My 1914+

Mandan REPUBLICAN. *See* Morton county farmers press

Mandan TIMES. w 1882-1907||
NdHi Ap 1904-Mr 9 1907

VOLKSZEITUNG. w Je 9 1926-27||?
In German
MnHi 1926-Je 1 1927

MANNHAVEN

Mannhaven JOURNAL. w 1900-07||
Follows Stanton pilot (Stanton)
NdHi My 1905-My 31 1907

MANNING

DUNN county news. w Mr 5 1908-Je 19 1919||
NdHi complete

DUNN county settler. w 1907-18||
1907-16 pub in Emerson
NdHi Ja 21 1910-Ag 29 1918

MARION

Marion SENTINEL. w 1900+
pub [1900+]
NdHi My 20 1905+

MARMARTH

Marmarth MAIL. w D 20 1907+
NdHi 1907+

MARTIN

SEARCHLIGHT. w 1904-19||
NdHi Je 8 1905-S 25 1919

MAX

Max ENTERPRISE. w 1906+
pub 1931+
NdHi 1908-[23-24]+

MAXBASS

Maxbass MONITOR. w 1905-Jl 18 1919||
NdHi Je 1907-19

MAYVILLE

GOOSE River farmer. w 1890-D 31 1908||
United with Mayville tribune to form Mayville tribune-farmer, later Traill county farmer
NdHi 1903-08

PEOPLES press. *See* Traill county tribune

TRAILL county tribune. w S 1882+
1882-F 11 1915 as Mayville tribune; F 18 1915-Je 13 1918 Mayville tribune-farmer; Je 20 1918-22? Peoples press; 1923? -Mr 28 1929 Mayville tribune
pub 1889-Ja 23 1919;23+
NdHi D 31 1903-Ja 23 1919;23+

Mayville TRIBUNE. *See* Traill county tribune

VESTERHEIMEN. *See under* Crookston, Minn.

MEADOW

Weekly STAR. *See* Upham star (Upham)

NORTH DAKOTA (*Continued*)

MEDINA

Medina CITIZEN. w 1904+
S 23 1920-21? as Stutsman county citizen
NdHi Mr 1905-Je 1925;Jl 11 1929+
NdJ 1911-18
NdJC 1905-08;10-11

Medina NEWS. w 1920-21||
NdHi D 8 1920-My 25 1921

STUTSMAN county citizen. *See* Medina citizen

MEDORA

BAD lands cow boy. w 1884-86||?
DLC N 27,D 18 1884;Ja 29 1885;N 25 1886
MWA N 25 1886
NN N 13,27,D 18 1884;Ja 29 1885;N 25 1886 (photostats)
NdHi N 27 1884
WHi N 13,27,D 18 1884;Ja 29 1885;N 25 1886 (photostats)

BILLINGS county herald. w 1906-Ag 8 1919||
Merged with Billings county pioneer
NdHi 1908-19

BILLINGS county pioneer. w 1913+
pub 1913+

MERCER

Mercer TELEGRAM. w D 26 1907-Je 30 1919||
NdHi 1907-[Ja 19 1917-Ap]-Je 1919

MERRICOURT

Merricourt VALLEY news. w My 8 1907-09||?
NdHi 1907-08

MICHIGAN

NELSON county arena. w O 6 1905+
S 15 1916-Mr 7 1919 as Michigan arena
pub Mr 21 1919+
NdHi 1905+
NdU 1905-My 1 1908

NELSON county independent. w 1892-1905||
NdHi N 1903-Ag 4 1905

MILNOR

SARGENT county teller. w 1883+
pub [1883-1900]+
NdFoC 1883-Jl 20,Ag 10-My 9 1884;My 14 1886-Ja 22,F 11-Ap 22 1887
NdHi Ap 20 1905+
NdLiF 1892-1901

MILTON

Milton GLOBE. w 1888+
NdHi O 15 1903+

MINERAL SPRINGS

Mineral Springs TRIBUNE. w 1910-17||
1910-14? as Gascoyne advance (Gascoyne)
NdHi Mr 1915-S 27 1917

MINNEWAUKAN

BENSON county farmers press. w 1884+
1884-Je 19 1919 as North Dakota siftings
NdHi Ag 11 1905+

NORTH Dakota siftings. *See* Benson county farmers press

MINOT

DAKOTA state journal, messenger and northwest press. w 1908-34||?
1908-Ag 8 1918 as Messenger
MnHi [1919]
NdHi O 14 1915-32

DEMOCRAT. w 1908-15||
NdHi D 10 1908-O 8 1915

ICONOCLAST. w 1912-16||
NdHi My 24 1912-Jl 21 1916

MESSENGER. *See* Dakota state journal

Minot MIRROR. w 1895-96||
NdMN Jl 1895-N 1896

Minot daily NEWS and daily optic-reporter. d D 28 1903+
1903-My 6 1914 as Minot optic; My 7 1914-N 25 1916 Minot daily optic-reporter
pub 1903-My,S-D 1905;F 1906-Jl,S,N 1908;Ja-Mr,O 1909-Ag 1910;Ja 8-Ag 1911;N 1913;Ja, Mr,My 1914-15;F,Ap,Je 1916-Mr,My 1920+
NdHi Mr 22 1904-13;My 7 1914+
NdM [1903+]
NdMC Ag 10 1929-S 6 1930

NORTHWEST press. w Ag 28 1919-27||
1919-S 13 1923 as Ward county farmers press
NdHi 1919-S 29 1927

Minot OPTIC. *See* Minot daily news and daily optic-reporter

Minot daily OPTIC-REPORTER. *See* Minot daily news and daily optic-reporter

Minot weekly OPTIC-REPORTER. w 1898-1918||?
1898-1914? as Minot weekly optic
pub 1898-1902;06-O 1911
NdHi 1905-O 1916

Minot POSTEN. w 1906-09||
In Norwegian-Danish
NdHi Ja 9 1908-F 25 1909

Minot daily REPORTER. d O 5 1905-My 6 1914||
1905-Ag 1906 as Ward county reporter. United with Minot optic to form Minot daily optic-reporter, later Minot daily news and daily optic-reporter
pub 1905-Ag 1906
NdHi O 17 1905-14
NdMN 1905-1907;Mr-S,N 1908-Ap;Je;O 1909-Ja 1914

WARD county farmers press. *See* Northwest press

WARD county independent. w Ap 1 1902+
pub 1902+
NdHi Mr 23 1904-[05-Je 7 1906]+
NdMC F 21 1909[Ja-S 1910]Ja 16 1914[Ja-N 1915]Ja-My 27 1917

WARD county reporter. w 1886-1914||
United with Minot weekly optic to form Minot weekly optic-reporter
pub Ja-O 1895;Ja-O 1896;98-O 1912;My 1913-Ja 1914
NdHi Mr 24 1904-Je 5 1913

WARD county reporter. d *See* Minot daily reporter

WORK. w Je 11 1936+
NdHi 1936+

MINTO

FOREST River journal. *See* Minto journal

Minto JOURNAL. w Je 1882+
1882 as Forest River journal
pub 1900+
NdHi S 28 1905+

MOFFIT

Moffit MESSENGER. *See* McKenzie gazette (McKenzie)

MOHALL

INDEPENDENT. w
NdHi Ap 5 1905-F 8 1906

Mohall NEWS. w 1901-My 7 1914||
United with Mohall tribune to form Mohall tribune-news
NdHi D 25 1902-14

RENVILLE county farmer. w N 14 1917+
1917-Jl 16 1919 as Renville county nonpartisan; Jl 23 1919-Ag 2 1928 Renville county farmers press
NdHi 1917+

RENVILLE county nonpartisan. *See* Renville county farmer

RENVILLE county farmers press. *See* Renville county farmer

RENVILLE county tribune. *See* Mohall tribune-news

Mohall TRIBUNE-news. w 1902-20||
1902-Ag 1914 as Renville county tribune
NdHi N 26 1903-Ag,S 10 1914-Ap 15 1920
NdMC Ja-Je 1908;Ja 1909

MONANGO

Monango JOURNAL. w 1908-20||
NdHi Mr 26 1908-F 13 1920

MONTPELIER

Montpelier MAGNET. w Je 15 1914+
NdHi 1914+

MONTROSE

WILLIAMS county plainsman. w N 27 1908-Ja 2 1919||
NdHi complete

MOTT

HETTINGER county dynamo. w 1905-
NdHi N 9 1905-O 18 1906

Mott PIONEER press. w Mr 9 1907+
pub [Ap 1907+]
NdHi 1907+

Mott SPOTLIGHT. w 1912-19||?
NdHi My 2 1912-N 1917

MOUNTAIN

Mountain NEWS. w
NdHi Jl 7 1910-Ag 15 1919

MUNICH

Munich HERALD. w 1905-20||
NdHi Jl 27 1905-O 7 1920

NAPOLEON

Napoleon HOMESTEAD. w Je 11 1886+
pub 1886-O 12 1934
NdHi Mr 17 1905+

LOGAN county argus. w
NdHi O 28 1932-Ag 18 1933

NECHE

Neche CHRONOTYPE. *See* Chronotype express

CHRONOTYPE express. w 1897+
1897-1928 as Neche chronotype
pub 1897+
NdHi 1897+

NEKOMA

Nekoma NEWS. w 1907-16||
NdHi 1911-S 27 1916

NEW ENGLAND

HETTINGER country herald. w D 19 1907+
pub 1907+
NdHi Ja 30 1908+

New England POST. w 1911-12||?
NdHi F 16 1911-Ap 12 1912

RAINY Butte sentinel. w Je 17 1887-My 30 1890||
NdHi complete

NEW LEIPZIG

New Leipzig SENTINEL. w 1911+
pub 1911+
NdHi Je 30 1911+

NEW ROCKFORD

EDDY county provost. *See* Farmers provost

FARMERS provost. w 1901+
1901-F 28 1918 as Eddy county provost
pub 1901+
NdHi Ap 28 1905+

New Rockford STATE center. d Ag 29 1916-N 1920||
Merged with New Rockford transcript
NdHi complete

New Rockford TRANSCRIPT. w S 13 1883+
1883-Ag 20 1920 as Transcript
pub 1883+
NdHi Ap 28 1905+

NEW SALEM

Der DEUTSCHE pionier. w 1905-13||
In German
NdHi 1905-Ja,Je 22 1907-Ap 5 1913

New Salem HERALD. w 1903-06||
NdHi Ap 29 1905-Mr 17 1906

New Salem JOURNAL. w My 1907+
pub [1907+]
NdHi Ja 17 1908-[S 22 1909-S 1911]-[D 19 1919-O 5 1923]+

Die WACHT am Missouri. *See* Hebron herald (Hebron)

NEWBURG

Newburg SUN. w 1908-12||
NdHi Ag 6 1908-Ja 18 1912

NOME

MIRROR. w
NdHi [1905]

Nome TRIBUNE. w 1905-23||?
NdHi Mr 1908-O 1921

NOONAN

Noonan MINER. w 1906+
1906-12 as Noonan republican
NdHi 1909+

Noonan REPUBLICAN. *See* Noonan miner

NORMA

Norma GAZETTE. w 1914-15||
NdHi Ja 8 1914-Je 10 1915

NORTH LEMON

LEMON tribune. w 1908-17||?
1908-11 as State-line herald; Ja 1912-? Lemon herald
NdHi Ap 3 1908-Jl 5 1917

NORTHWOOD

Northwood GLEANER. w 1888+
Follows Northwood headlight
pub D 1899+
NdHi N 1903+
WHi O 23 1912+

Northwood HEADLIGHT. w 1884-87?||
Followed by Northwood gleaner

NORWICH

Norwich ITEM. w 1903-18||?
NdHi My 19 1905-[09-17]-Ag 14 1918

OAKES

Oakes JOURNAL. w 1907-19||
NdHi Ja 15 1908-S 4 1919

Oakes REPUBLICAN. *See* Oakes times

Oakes TIMES. w 1883+
1883-86? as Hudson herald (Hudson); 1887?-Ja 18 1906 Oakes republican
pub [1883-Ja 6 1916]+
NdHi Ja 25 1906+

OBERON

Oberon REPORTER. w 1895-1907||
NdHi O 8 1903-My 23 1907

NORTH DAKOTA (*Continued*)

OMEMEE

Omemee HERALD. w 1899-1918||
NdHi Ja 15 1904-F 1 1918

ORISKA

Oriska POST. w 1907-10||
NdHi F 28 1908-Je 17 1910

Oriska SENTINEL. w 1911-13||
NdHi Mr 15 1911-Ja 23 1913

OSNABROCK

Osnabrock INDEPENDENT. w 1901-20||
Merged with Cavalier county farmers press (Langdon)
NdHi Ap 13 1905-[N 12 1908-Ap 1 1909]-Ap 15 1920
NdU Ja 24 1907

Osnabrock RECORD. w 1920-25||
NdHi Ap 22 1920-Ap 30 1925

OVERLY

Overly NEWS. w 1916-19||
NdHi Ap 28 1916-Jl 11 1919

PADDINGTON

WILLOW Lake wave. w
NdHi Ja 15-Jl 23 1909

PAGE

CASS county tribune. w 1921-23||
NdHi Jl 8 1921-My 4 1923

Page RECORD. w 1900-19||
NdHi Mr 24 1905-O 19 1919

PALERMO

Palermo INDEPENDENT. w 1916-19||
NdHi N 2 1916-Jl 24 1919

MOUNTRAIL county herald. w 1910-17||
NdHi Je 16 1910-N 29 1917

Palermo STANDARD. w 1902-13||
NdB Ja 9 1908-13

PARK RIVER

Park River GAZETTE. *See* Walsh county press

Park River GAZETTE-NEWS. *See* Walsh county press

Park River HERALD. w 1914-19||
NdHi Ag 20 1914-Ag 15 1919

Park River NEWS. w 1897-1901||
United with Park River gazette to form Park River gazette-news, later Walsh county press

Park River REPUBLICAN and Adams enterprise. w 1905-11||?
1906-S 17 1908? as Adams enterprise (Adams)
NdHi Je 28 1906-S 17 1908

WALSH county farmers press. *See* Walsh county press

WALSH county press. w 1883+
1883-1901? as Park River gazette; 1902?-My 2 1919 Park River gazette-news; My 9 1919-My 20 1926 Walsh county farmers press
pub 1909+
NdHi My 15 1903-[21]-[28-34]+

WALSH county republican. *See under* Grafton

PARSHALL

Parshall LEADER. w 1914-19||
NdHi 1915-Je 19 1919

Parshall PLAINSMAN. w 1919+
pub F 1920+
NdHi D 17 1919+

Parshall POST. w 1913-16||
Merged with Parshall leader
NdHi N 1914-Ja 20 1916

PEKIN

Pekin BUDGET. w 1912-26||
NdHi O 11 1912-O 8 1926

PEMBINA

Pembina NEW era. w Ap 26 1929+
pub [1929+]

Pembina PIONEER-express. w Ag 7 1879-1928||
1879-82? as Pembina pioneer. United with Neche chronotype (Neche) to form Chronotype express (Neche)
pub complete
MnHi 1879[80]
NdHi complete
NdNC complete

PENN

Penn HUSTLER. w
Merged with Churchs Ferry sun (Churchs Ferry)
NdHi Je 19 1905-15

PERTH

Perth JOURNAL. w 1898-1908||?
NdHi Ja 8-D 17 1904

PETERSBURG

Petersburg RECORD. w S 28 1905+
pub [1923-Jl 1931]+
NdHi 1905+

PETTIBONE

Pettibone SPECTATOR. w 1913-19||
NdHi S 11 1913-S 26 1919

PINGREE

Pingree PATRIOT. w 1904-23||
1904-F 5 1908 as Stutsman county patriot
NdHi F 9 1905-[Ja-O 7 1909]-Jl 5 1923

Pingree RECORD. w 1924-29||
NdHi D 4 1924-Ja 30 1929

STUTSMAN county patriot. *See* Pingree patriot

PLAZA

Plaza JOURNAL. w 1921||
NdHi Ap 28-D 8 1921

Plaza PIONEER. w Mr 1 1906+
Mr-Jl 19 1906 as LaFollette forum (La Follette)
NdHi 1906+

PROGRESSIVE west. w 1909-12||
NdHi Mr 31 1909-Mr 23 1912

PORTAL

INTERNATIONAL. w Ap 1 1900+
pub 1910+
NdHi D 1903-[O 21-D 1904]+

PORTLAND

Portland REPUBLICAN. w S 1894+
pub [1894+]
NdHi My 26 1904+

POWERS LAKE

Powers Lake ECHO. w Mr 1 1905+
1905-N 9 1909 as Vanville echo (Vanville)
pub Mr 1910—
NdHi Ja 20 1911+

RALEIGH

GRANT county leader. w Je 2 1911-21||
1911-18 as Raleigh herald
NdHi 1911-Mr 22 1918;19-21

Raleigh HERALD. *See* Grant county leader

RAWSON

Rawson TRIBUNE. w 1914-17||
NdHi Je 25 1914-O 11 1917

RAY

Ray PIONEER. w 1903+
pub Jl 1932+
NdHi Jl 14 1905-[27-My]-[N 1928-My 1932]+

Ray RECORDER. w 1907-10||?
NdHi Mr 22 1907-08

REEDER

ADAMS county times. *See* Reeder times

Reeder TIMES. w 1907-Ja 27 1911||
1907-Ap 9 1909 as Adams county times. United with Western call to form Western call and times
NdHi Mr 13 1908-11

WESTERN call and times. w F 1 1908+
pub 1908+
NdHi 1908-32

REGAN

Regan ADVANCE. w 1918-20||
NdHi Mr 21-[O 17 1918-Mr 13]-[My,S-D 1919]-Ag 19 1920

Regan HEADLIGHT. w 1913-18||
NdHi Ap 3-[My,Jl,Ag,N 1913]-[Ap,My,Jl-S, N 1917]-Ja 3 1918

REGENT

Regent TIMES. w Jl 8 1910+
pub 1910—
NdHi 1910+

REYNOLDS

Reynolds ENTERPRISE. w 1891-S 1926||
Followed by Red River Valley citizen (Grand Forks)
NdHi D 17 1903-[06-Mr 11 1909]-26

RED River Valley citizen. *See under* Grand Forks

RED River Valley sun. w 1906-07||
NdHi Ap 5 1906-S 12 1907

RHAME

FARMERS review. *See* Rhame review

Rhame REVIEW. w 1908+
N 7 1918-19 as Farmers review
NdHi Mr 18 1909+

RICHARDTON

Richardton NEWS. w 1905-11||
NdHi Ag 11 1905-N 3 1911

STARK county star. w 1926-27||
NdHi Ap 21 1926-Ag 4 1927

Der VOLKSFREUND. w 1903-24||
1903-09 pub in Dickinson
In German
MoSC [Mr 1921-Je 1924]
NdHi Mr 17 1905-[Je 1907-08]-21

WESTERN star. w 1917||
NdHi Mr 10-O 6 1917

ROBINSON

MCLEAN county independent. w
NdHi My 26 1905-Ag 15 1906

Robinson TIMES. w 1913-18||
NdHi F 1915-O 10 1918

ROCKLAKE

Rock Lake RIPPLES. w 1905-10||
NdHi Je 1907-D 23 1910

ROGERS

Rogers CITIZEN. w 1913-18||
NdHi My 1913-Ag 16 1918

ROLETTE

Rolette RECORD. w S 28 1905+
1905-N 14 1907 as McCumber herald (McCumber)
NdHi 1905-[My 11-N 22 1923]+

ROLETTE county examiner. w 1905-16||
NdHi S 1906-Jl 7 1916

ROLLA

ROLETTE county herald. w 1884-1916||
1884-1904? as Dunseith herald (Dunseith)
NdHi Ap 20 1905-16

TURTLE Mountain star. w S 1 1888+
pub S 1894+
NdHi Ag 10 1905+

ROSEGLEN

Roseglen JOURNAL. w 1917-20||
NdHi Je 15 1918-Ag 7 1920

ROSS

Ross PROMOTER. w 1906-08||
Merged with Mountrail county promoter (Stanley)
NdHi Ag 24 1906-08

Ross VALLEY news. w 1904-18||
NdHi complete

RUDSER

WILLIAMS county leader. w 1906-09||
NdHi Je 1907-Jl 29 1909

RUGBY

Rugby FARMERS news. w 1917-21||
NdHi O 18 1917-Ja 20 1921

OPTIMIST. w 1900-16||
NdHi D 18 1903-F 11 1916

PIERCE county globe. w 1925-29||
NdHi Mr 26 1925-S 26 1929

PIERCE county press. w Ap 6 1922+
NdHi 1922+

PIERCE county tribune. w Jl 1888+
pub [Jl 1888+]
NdHi Ja 16 1904+

Der STAATS anzeiger. w 1905-13||
In German
NdHi Ap 11 1907-Jl 24 1913

RUSO

Ruso RECORD. w Je 7 1907-22||?
NdHi 1907-N 24 1922

RUSSELL

Russell SENTINEL. w 1905-17||
NdHi Je 1905-Mr 22 1917

RUTLAND

Rutland LEADER. w 1906-11||
NdHi Ap 23 1908-O 20 1911

NORTH DAKOTA (*Continued*)

RYDER

Ryder JOURNAL. w 1911-16‖
NdHi 1912-F 24 1916

Ryder NEWS. w N 12 1903+
NdHi 1903+

SAINT JOHN

Saint John LEADER. w 1913-18‖
NdHi O 16 1913-O 25 1918

Saint John TRIBUNE. w 1906-09‖
NdHi Mr 19 1908-Jl 22 1909

SAINT THOMAS

Saint Thomas TIMES. w 1882-1927‖
NdHi O 16 1903-S 22 1927

SANBORN

Sanborn ENTERPRISE. w D 16 1881+
pub [1881+]
NdHi Ap 27 1905+

SANDOUN

Sandoun ENTERPRISE. *See* McLeod enterprise

MCLEOD enterprise. w 1904-07‖
1904-05 as Sandoun enterprise
NdHi Ag 18 1904-Je 6 1907

SANGER

Sanger ADVANCE. w 1916‖
NdHi O 26-D 14 1916

SANISH

Sanish PILOT. w 1915-17‖
NdHi Ap 23 1915-S 7 1917

Sanish SENTINEL. w My 1 1915+
pub 1915+
NdHi My 5 1915+

SARLES

Sarles ADVOCATE. *See* Western Cavalier county advocate

Sarles BUDGET. *See* Adams budget (Adams)

WESTERN Cavalier county advocate. w O 1 1905+
1905-Ja 8 1927 as Sarles advocate
pub 1905+
NdHi Ja 16 1908+

SAWYER

Sawyer CLIPPER. w 1903-08‖
NdHi Je 13 1905-08

Sawyer TELEGRAPH. w 1911-20‖
NdHi S 21 1911-Ja 29 1920

SCHAFER

Schafer RECORD. w 1906-19‖
NdHi Je 1907-S 18 1919
NdWaM 1909-Ag 7 1919

SCRANTON

BRIQUETTE. w D 6 1907-21‖
1907-Ag 30 1917 as Scranton register
NdHi 1907-O 20 1921

Scranton REGISTER. *See* Briquette

Scranton STAR. w Je 19 1924+
pub 1924+
NdHi 1924+

SELFRIDGE

Selfridge JOURNAL. w My 23 1918+
pub Je 1918+
NdHi 1918+

SENTINEL BUTTE

BILLINGS county republican. *See* Sentinel Butte republican

Sentinel Butte REPUBLICAN. w 1904-Jl 31 1919‖
1904-12 as Billings county republican
NdHi 1913-19

Sentinel Butte REVIEW. w 1922-32‖
NdHi 1924-32

SHARON

Sharon REPORTER. w D 9 1904+
NdHi 1904+

SHELDON

Sheldon ENTERPRISE. *See* Sheldon progress and Sheldon enterprise

Sheldon PROGRESS. w 1896-My 26 1905‖
United with Sheldon enterprise to form Sheldon progress and Sheldon enterprise
pub complete
NdHi Ja 8 1904-05

Sheldon PROGRESS and Sheldon enterprise. w 1885+
1885-My 19 1905 as Sheldon enterprise
pub 1885+
NdHi My 26 1905+

SHERBROOKE

STEELE county tribune. w 1887-My 1919‖
Merged with Steele county press (Finley)
NdHi D 17 1903-19

SHERWOOD

Sherwood JOURNAL. w 1903-D 12 1907‖
United with Sherwood tribune to form Sherwood tribune and journal, later Sherwood tribune
NdHi Mr 31 1905-My 23 1907

Sherwood TRIBUNE. w 1904+
D 12 1907-13? as Sherwood tribune and journal
pub 1905+
NdHi Ap 1905+

SHEYENNE

Sheyenne STAR. w Ap 1897+
pub 1897+
NdHi Ag 1905+

SHIELDS

Shields ENTERPRISE. *See* Elgin news (Elgin)

SILVA

Silva JOURNAL. w 1916-18‖
NdHi Mr 17 1917-Ag 10 1918

SOURIS

Souris MESSENGER. w 1901-18‖
1901-O 4 1907 as Souris republican
NdHi D 18 1903-Je 21 1918

Souris REPUBLICAN. *See* Souris messenger

SPRING BROOK

Springbook EAGLE. *See* Spring Brook news

Spring Brook NEWS. w 1904-13‖?
1904 as Springbrook eagle
NdHi Jl 5-S 19 1904;Jl 18 1905-08

STADY

Stady LEADER. *See* Fortuna leader (Fortuna)

STANLEY

MOUNTRAIL county independent. w 1910-16‖
NdHi Ap 1914-Jl 20 1916

MOUNTRAIL county promoter. w O 1907+
pub [1907+]
NdHi Ap 16 1909+

Stanley SUN. w 1902+
NdHi Ap 28 1905+

STANTON

MERCER county farmer. w 1914+
1914-Jl 12 1918 as Stanton post
NdHi Jl 1915+

MERCER county republican. w 1887-1920‖
Merged with Hazen star (Hazen)
NdHi Je 14 1907-Ja 29 1920

Stanton PILOT. w 1883-89‖
Followed by Mannhaven journal (Mannhaven)
NdHi Ja 30 1889

Stanton POST. *See* Mercer county farmer

STARKWEATHER

Starkweather TIMES. w S 1902+
NdHi N 1903+

STEELE

Steele weekly HERALD. w Mr 10 1883-86‖?
NdHi Mr 10 1883

KIDDER county farmers' press. w 1911-D 20 1928‖
United with Steele ozone to form Ozone and Kidder county farmers' press
NdHi Jl 24 1919-28

OZONE and Kidder county farmers' press. w 1885+
1885-1928 as Steele ozone
NdHi O 8 1892-[Jl 12 1895-98]+

STERLING

BURLEIGH county farmer. *See* Public opinion (Bismark)

Sterling STAR. w 1908-11‖
NdHi Jl 3 1908-11

STIRUM

Stirum CITIZEN. w 1923-24‖
NdHi Ja 31-My 23 1924

STREETER

Streeter HERALD. w 1908-19‖
NdHi Mr 19 1909-19

Streeter INDEPENDENT. w 1927‖
NdHi Je 23-N 2 1927

TRI-COUNTY journal. w 1929-30‖
NdHi Je 18-O 29 1930

SUTTON

Sutton REPORTER. w 1913-31‖
NdHi My 8 1913-31

SYKESTON

Sykeston NEWS. w Mr 25 1904+
1904-Je 11 1915 as Sykeston tribune; Je 18-Jl 30 1915 Wells county news
pub 1904-Ag 6 1915;Ja-F,S 1918+
NdHi 1905+

Sykeston TRIBUNE. *See* Sykeston news

WELLS county news. *See* Sykeston news

TAGUS

Tagus MIRROR. See Charbonneau herald (Charbonneau)

TAPPEN

Tappen JOURNAL. w 1913-19‖
1913-14? as Leader-journal
NdHi Ag 15 1913-D 6 1919

TAYLOR

Taylor REPORTER. w S 23 1910-Ja 3 1919‖
NdHi complete

THOMPSON

Thompson NEWS. w
Merged with Reynolds enterprise (Reynolds)
NdHi D 17 1903-Jl 22 1904

Thompson TRIBUNE. w
NdHi Jl 3,O 16 1919

THORNE

Thorne RECORD. w 1905-07‖
NdHi N 23 1906-O 4 1907

TIOGA

Tioga GAZETTE. w 1903+
NdHi 1904+

TOLLEY

Tolley JOURNAL. w D 23 1904-20‖
1904-Jl 16 1909 as Mouse River journal
NdHi 1904-Ag 27 1920

MOUSE River journal. *See* Tolley journal

TOLNA

Tolna TRIBUNE. w 1906-25‖
NdHi Jl 12 1906-Jl 30 1925

TOWER CITY

MESSENGER. *See* Tower City topics

Tower City TOPICS. w 1880+
1880-81? as Messenger
pub [1880+]
NdHi F 1904+

TOWNER

MCHENRY county independent. *See* Mouse River farmers press

MOUSE River farmers press. w F 15 1890+
1890-Je 7 1895 as McHenry county independent; Je 14 1895-Ag 26 1910 Towner news and stockman; S 2 1910-My 29 1918 Towner news-tribune
pub 1904+
NdHi N 13 1903+

Towner NEWS. *See* Mouse River farmers press

Towner TRIBUNE. w 1905-Ag 19 1910‖
United with Towner news and stockman to form Towner news-tribune
NdHi Je 15 1906-10

TRAVARE

DAKOTA sun. w 1884-87‖?
MnHi [1885]
NdHi Ja 8 1885

TURTLE LAKE

MCLEAN county journal. w N 25 1925+
pub 1925+
NdHi 1925+

Turtle Lake WAVE. w 1903+
NdHi Ja 10 1908+

NORTH DAKOTA (*Continued*)

TUTTLE

Tuttle REPORTER. w 1913-15||
NdHi Ap 25 1913-Ap 23 1915

Tuttle STAR. w Ag 25 1915-Ap 26 1923||
NdHi complete

Tuttle TIMES. w O 4 1923+
pub 1923+
NdHi 1923—

TWIN BUTTE

BOWMAN county pioneer. *See under* Bowman

UNDERWOOD

Underwood JOURNAL. w O 16 1903-14||
1903-Mr 1904 as McLean county miner (Washburn); Ap 1904-O 1907 Underwood leader; N 1907-Ag 5 1910 Underwood miner
NdHi 1903-O 9 1914

Underwood LEADER. *See* Underwood journal

Underwood MINER. *See* Underwood journal

Underwood NEWS. w Jl 28 1932+
pub 1932+

Underwood REPORTER. w 1929-30||
NdHi S 5 1929-S 18 1930

Underwood TIMES. w O 5 1904-22||
1904-Ag 30 1905 as Times (Coal Harbor); S 6 1905-D 11 1914 Garrison times (Garrison)
NdHi D 18 1914-N 2 1922

UPHAM

Upham CHRONICLE. w Jl 26 1928+
NdHi 1928-[Ag 8 1929-Jl 20 1933]+

Upham LEADER. w 1925-26||
NdHi S 3 1925-Ap 15 1926

Upham STAR. w My 6 1905-18||
1905-Mr 1906 as Weekly star (Meadow)
NdHi 1905-O 25 1918

VALLEY CITY

Valley City ALLIANCE. w 1883-1907||?
1883-1900? as Farmers' alliance
NdHi Ap 13 1905-Je 1907

BARNES county citizen. w 1915-30||?
NdHi Jl 1915-O 1 1925

Valley City COURIER. *See* Peoples opinion

FARMERS' alliance. *See* Valley City alliance

GOOD will messenger. w Ap 24 1928+
pub 1928+

NORTH Dakota citizen. w
Merged with North Dakota patriot
NdHi D 10 1903-Ja 7 1904

NORTH Dakota patriot. w 1884-1930||?
NdHi 1904-[N 1916-F 1917]-[Mr 1922]-Jl 19 1923

NORTHERN Pacific times. *See* Valley City times-record

Valley City morning PATRIOT. d 1907-12||
NdHi N 10 1907-12

PEOPLES opinion. w Ap 17 1913+
1913-N 28 1918 as Valley City courier
pub D 1922+
NdHi 1913-[Ag,D 1920]+
NdVS [Jl 1921-23]+

Valley City TIMES-record. w 1879+
1879-80? as Northern Pacific times; 1881?-86? Valley City times
pub 1879-[81-82]+
MnHi Je 12 1879-F 1884
NdHi 1904-[Ja,Ap 1905]-Ap[D 1913-16]-N 9 1922
NdVS 1901-14

Valley City TIMES-record. d 1906+
Title varies slightly: Evening times-record; Daily times-record
NdHi F 17 1910+
NdV 1933+
NdVS 1909+

VAN HOOK

Van Hook JOURNAL. w 1914-
Merged with Van Hook tribune, later Van Hook reporter
NdHi Ag 20 1914-Jl 14 1916

Van Hook REPORTER. w N 12 1914+
1914-Ag 11 1922 as Van Hook tribune
pub 1916+
NdHi 1914+

Van Hook TRIBUNE. *See* Van Hook reporter

VANVILLE

Vanville ECHO. *See* Powers Lake echo (Powers Lake)

VELVA

Velva JOURNAL. w 1900+
1900-O 12 1916 as McHenry county journal
pub 1900+
NdHi Ap 27 1905-Ag 17,O 19 1916+

MCHENRY county journal. *See* Velva journal

VERONA

Verona ADVANCE. w
NdHi Ag 8 1907-S 24 1909

Verona weekly INDEPENDENT. w
NdHi O 7 1909-N 10 1910

Verona STANDARD. w
NdHi Ja-Ag 1911

VILLARD

Villard LEADER. w Mr 6 1886-N 23 1889||
NdHi complete

WABEK

Wabek MESSENGER. w
NdHi Ag 24 1917-Je 7 1918

WAHPETON

Wahpeton GAZETTE. *See* Wahpeton globe

Wahpeton GLOBE. w 1879-Ag 12 1927||
1879-1903? as Richland county gazette; 1904?-My 1907 Wahpeton gazette; Je 1907-S 15 1921 Globe-gazette. United with Richland county farmer to form Richland county farmer-globe, later Richland county farmer
NdHi D 1903-27

Wahpeton GLOBE. w 1886-My 30 1907||
1886-1902? as North Dakota globe. United with Wahpeton gazette to form Globe-gazette, later Wahpeton globe
NdHi N 1903-My 1907

GLOBE-GAZETTE. *See* Wahpeton globe 1879-1927

INDEPENDENT press. w 1879-1920||
1879-Ja 9 1919 as Wahpeton times
NdHi Ap 13 1905-Ja 15 1920
WHi N 21 1912-Ja 15 1914

NORTH Dakota globe. *See* Wahpeton globe. 1886-1907

RICHLAND county farmer. w,sw 1887+
1887-1918 as Lidgerwood broadaxe (Lidgerwood); 1919-Ag 11 1927 Richland county farmer; Ag 16 1927-32 Richland county farmer-globe
pub Ag 16 1927+
NdHi Ap 27 1905-Jl 20 1918;19+

RICHLAND county farmer-globe. *See* Richland county farmer

RICHLAND county gazette. *See* Wahpeton globe

Wahpeton TIMES. *See* Independent press

WALCOTT

Walcott REPORTER. w Je 1900+
pub 1900+
NdHi N 24 1904+

WALES

Wales PROGRESS. w 1913-18||
NdHi O 13 1913-Je 28 1918

WALHALLA

Walhalla MOUNTAINEER. w 1896+
pub [1927+]
NdHi O 28 1903+

WARWICK

Warwick NEWS. w 1914||
NdHi F 6-S 25 1914

Warwick weekly SENTINEL. w 1906-19||?
NdHi 1908-[S 1909-Jl 1910]-Jl 24 1913
NdJC 1914-15

Warwick weekly TRIBUNE. w
NdMC [Ap 17 1913-N 1916]

WASHBURN

Washburn LEADER. w My 10 1883+
1883-85 as Washburn times
pub [1883+]
NdHi S 16 1893-[D 1894]-[Ag-N 1895]-[Jl 1896]-[Ja-My 1899]-[D 1901]-[Jl 1902-O 1903]+
NdMC [Ja-N 1906]Ja 4-11 1907

MCLEAN county miner. *See* Underwood journal (Underwood)

Washburn TIMES. *See* Washburn leader

WATFORD CITY

MCKENZIE county farmer. w 1909-Ap 19 1928||
1909-D 11 1913 as Inland call (Berg); D 18 1913-My 13 1915 Call (Arnegard); My 20 1915-Ag 23 1917 Arnegard Call (Arnegard). United with Watford guide to form McKenzie county farmer and Watford guide
NdHi F 10 1910-28
NdWaM Ja 1921-28

MCKENZIE county farmer and Watford guide. w Mr 11 1915+
1915-Ap 19 1928 as Watford guide
pub 1915—
NdHi 1915+

WATFORD guide. *See* McKenzie county farmer and Watford guide

WERNER

DUNN county spotlight. w O 22 1915-24||
1915-Ap 11 1919 as Werner record
NdHi 1915-Ap 11,My 30 1919-F 1 1924

Werner RECORD. *See* Dunn county spotlight

WESTBY

Westby NEWS. w
NdHi Ap 18 1913-Mr 24 1922

WESTHOPE

MOUSE River standard. *See* Westhope standard

Westhope REVIEW. w 1903-My 21 1904||
Merged with Westhope Standard
pub O 31 1903-04

Westhope STANDARD. w My 3 1901+
1901-Je 3 1904 as Mouse River standard
pub 1901+
NdHi N 27 1903+

WHEATLAND

Wheatland EAGLE. w 1884-1908||
NdHi N 19 1903-08

Wheatland NEWS. w 1909-
NdHi My 8-N 25 1909

WHEELOCK

Wheelock TIMES. *See* Wildrose mixer (Wildrose)

Wheelock TRIBUNE. w 1904-13||
NdHi Ap 13 1905-Je 5 1913

WILLIAMS county mixer. *See* Wildrose mixer (Wildrose)

WHITE EARTH

White Earth RECORD. w 1902-20||
NdHi Ap 14 1905-[12-15]-Ja 2 1920

WILDROSE

Wildrose MIXER. w 1902+
1902-N 2 1907 as Wheelock times (Wheelock); N 9 1907-Ag 2 1917 Williams county mixer (Wheelock and Zahl)
pub 1912+
NdHi Jl 15 1905-[O 1909-Ag 11 1911]+

WILLIAMS county plainsman. w N 27 1908-Ja 2 1919||
NdHi complete

WILLISTON

AMERICAN liberal. w
NdHi Ag 17-O 26 1926

Williston GRAPHIC. *See* Williams county farmers press

Williston HERALD. w 1899+
pub 1917—
NdHi Je 1905+

Williston daily STATE. d
NdHi F 25-D 1907

Williston weekly STATE. w 1907-15||?
NdHi My 23 1907-Ap 4 1912

WILLIAMS county farmers press. w 1895+
1895-My 15 1919 as Williston graphic
NdHi Ap 27 1905+

Williston WORLD. w 1906-08||
NdHi Je 8 1907-D 18 1908

WILLOW CITY

Willow City EAGLE. *See* Willow City review

NORTH Dakota eagle. *See* Willow City review

Willow City REVIEW. w 1886+
1886-Jl 1927 as North Dakota eagle; Ag 1927-?1930 Willow City eagle
NdHi 1904-O 9,D 1930+

WILMOT

ROBERTS county record. w Ja 1? 1884-87||?
NdHi Ja 8 1885

WILTON

Wilton NEWS. w 1899+
pub 1914+
NdHi Ap 28 1905+

WIMBLEDON

Wimbledon NEWS. w Ag 1895+
pub [1895+]
IU Mr 31 1922-Ap 1925
NdHi Je 30 1905-[1909-Mr 1912]-[O,D 1914]+

WING

Wing STATESMAN. w 1912-19||
NdHi Je 12 1912-Jl 3 1919

WINONA

Winona TIMES. *See* Emmons county record (Linton)

NORTH DAKOTA (*Continued*)

WISHEK

Wishek NEWS. w 1902+
pub D 1917+
NdHi N 20 1903+

WOLFORD

Wolford MIRROR. w 1906-23||
NdHi Mr 1906-23

WOODWORTH

Woodworth RUSTLER. w Mr 1 1912+
pub 1912+
NdHi Mr 28 1912+
NdJC 1918

WYNDMERE

Wyndmere ENTERPRISE. w 1907-09||
NdHi O 5 1907-D 16 1909

Wyndmere HERALD. w 1900+
1900-My 23 1923 as Wyndmere pioneer
NdHi O 29 1915+

Wyndmere PIONEER. *See* Wyndmere herald

YORK

York CITIZEN. w 1915-20||
NdHi F 4 1915-Jl 8 1920

York DISPATCH. w 1911-13||
NdHi My 5 1911-Ap 18 1913

York LEDGER. w 1898-1910||
NdHi S 10 1904-F 10 1910

York NEWS. w
NdHi Mr 29-Je 28 1928

ZAHL

WILLIAMS county mixer. *See* Wildrose mixer (Wildrose)

ZAP

Zap ENTERPRISE. w 1916-26||
NdHi O 20 1916-Ag 12 1926

OHIO

ADA

Ada HERALD. m,sm,w Je 20 1885+
1885-Ag 18 1916 as University herald
m 1885-90?; sm 1891?-92?
pub 1885+
OHi 1885-My 1888;1900-01[03-05]-Je 11,N 1920-Ag 20,O 1926-O 4 1929

Ada RECORD. w 1872-1919||?
OHi Ja 2 1901;F 28 1906-19

UNIVERSITY herald. *See* Ada herald

AKRON

AMERICAN democrat. *See* Free democratic standard

Akron daily ARGUS. d Mr 2 1874-79||?
OCHi D 2-3,5,7 1874
OClWHi Mr 2 1874;D 20 1877;O 8 1878;Je 16, 26 1879

Akron BEACON journal. d D 6 1869+
1869-90 as Akron daily beacon; 1891-Je? 1897 Akron beacon and republican
Je 18,25 1925 are centennial eds
pub 1895+
ICM Je 2 1881;Je 9 1883
MWA F 5 1927
OAk D 17 1869+
OClWHi Ja 11 1879;S 20-21 1881;Ja 19 1882;Je 24 1885;F 4 1888;Ag 10 1895;Je 27 1907;Ap 13 1908;F 6 1913-33
OHi 1890-96;Ja-My,D 6 1898-D 5 1899;Je 7 1900-D 5 1902;Je 6 1903-D 5 1904;Je 6 1905-F,O-D 1916;F-Ap 23 1917;Je 1918+
—w ed *See* Summit county beacon

Akron BUZZARD. w 1844||?
CSmH Je 25 1844

Akron CITY times. *See* Akron weekly times

Die Akron COLUMBIA. w 1869+
1869-Jl 1920 as Die Akron Germania
In German
IU O 16 1884

Die Akron COLUMBIA. tw 1887-1925||?
1887-Jl 9 1920 as Die Akron Germania
In German
OHi Ja 1 1901[19-25]

Akron daily DEMOCRAT. *See* Akron evening times

Akron EAGLE. *See* Free democratic standard

FREE democratic standard. w Ag 10 1842-
1842-D 14 1848 as American democrat; D 21 1848-Je 1849 Akron eagle; Jl 5-N 1? 1849 Akron free democrat
CSmH Ja 16 1845
ICHi O 19 1842
IU Mr 1,S 13 1843[44]Ap 17 1845;Ag 16 1849
MWA Ja 13 1853
MnHi 1849-F 1851
OClWHi 1842-D 21 1848;49-F 1851;52-54
OHi 1849-O 1850

Sunday GAZETTE. *See* Sunday morning republican

Die Akron GERMANIA. *See* Die Akron Columbia

HERALD. w 1901-21||?
1901-Mr? 1919 as People
OHi F 1916-O 1919
WHi D 5-12 1902

Akroni HIRLAP. *See* Akroni Magyar hirlap

Evening JOURNAL. d 1896-Je 1897||?
United with Akron beacon and republican to form Akron beacon journal

Akroni MAGYAR hirlap. w 1912+
1912-30? as Akroni hirlap
In Hungarian
PPiHi [1923]-[31]

NEW republic. d Mr 26- 1894||?
WHi Mr 26-27,31,Ap 3,10,Je 20 1894

Daily NEWS. d 1882-83||?
MWA Ja 28 1883

PEOPLE. *See* Herald

Akron PRESS. *See* Akron times press

Sunday morning REPUBLICAN. w 1878-D 27 1891||?
1878-87? as Sunday gazette; 1888?-89? Sunday telegram
IU F 16-Je 8,29-Jl 20 1879
OAk 1891
OClWHi Ag 24 1879

Akron REPUBLICAN. d O 1888-D 31 1890||
1888-S 1889 as Daily telegram
United with Akron daily beacon to form Akron beacon and republican, later Akron beacon journal
OAk My-D 1890
OHi 1888-Je 1890

Daily STANDARD. d 1854-
OClWHi S 21 1854

SUMMIT county beacon. w,sw Ap 15 1839-1910||?
1839-Mr 11 1857 as Summit beacon
w 1839-97?
MWA D 22 1852;F 1 1866
OAk 1877-Ap 11 1901
OClWHi D 9 1840;Ja 6 1841;F 2 1842;N 15 1843;Ag 21 1844;D 6 1848;F 16 1857;D 15 1858;D 7 1859;Ap 16 1863;Ag 19 1864;Ap 20 1865;My 2 1888;My 13 1897
OHi Mr 1849-68;71-85;87-90;92;94-96;Ap 21 1898-Ap 13 1899;Ap 18 1901-Ap 14 1904
WHi D 10 1856;Ap 29 1857;F 23 1859
—d ed *See* Akron beacon journal

SUMMIT county journal. w 1865-67||
Merged with Summit county beacon
OClWHi Ja 10 1867

SUMMIT democracy.
OClWHi O 20 1855;N 11 1858

TELEGRAM. *See* Republican

Akron weekly TIMES. w Ja 1868-1914||?
1868-D 29 1892 as Akron city times; Ja 5 1893-99? Akron times-democrat; 1900?-D 27 1906 Weekly times-democrat
MWA Ap 5,Jl 26 1876
OAk 1869-99;1904-09
OClWHi 1913-S 12 1914
OHi 1873-78;82-92;94-97;99-1902

Akron evening TIMES. d Ap 21 1892-Mr 15 1925||
1892-1902? as Akron daily democrat; 1903?-My 2 1906 Akron times-democrat.
United with Akron press to form Akron times press
OAk 1892-Ap 20 1900;03-Je 1912;Mr 1921-25
OAkU 1916-My 1917;My 1918-Ja 1921;F 1922-25
OClWHi Je 27 1907
OHi Ap 22 1892-1902;F 1914-F,O-D 1916;F-Ap 1917;Je 1918-25

Akron TIMES PRESS. d 1893+
1893-Mr 15 1925 as Akron press
NN Mr 12 1923
OAk Mr 1921+
OHi Ap,Jl 1915;Mr 16 1925+

ALLIANCE

FREE press. w? 1857?-
OClWHi Je 25 1862;Jl 29 1863

Alliance LEADER. d 1892-1914||?
United with Alliance daily review to form Review and leader, later Alliance daily review

Alliance LOCAL. *See* Alliance review

MONITOR. w Jl 14 1866?-77||?
1866? as Saturday monitor
MWA F 14 1866;F 21 1867
OHi S 8 1866

Alliance REVIEW. w,sw 1868-1914||?
1868-74? as Alliance local; Mr 14 1888-98? Alliance standard review
w 1868-94?
OAl 1875-78;81;83;86
OHi 1884;87-90;95;97;1901;05;Ja-Je 1908;09-14

Alliance daily REVIEW. d 1888+
1915?-26? as Review and leader
OAl Jl 1924+
OAlMU 1931+
OClWHi Jl 28 1906;Je 7 1932
OHi F 11-S 16 1890;99-1904;06-27;Mr-Ap,O 1928-Je 1930;33

Alliance STANDARD. w 1879-Mr? 1888||
United with Alliance review to form Alliance standard review, later Alliance review

Alliance STANDARD review. *See* Alliance review

AMHERST

To 1872? as Amherstville; 1873?-1922? North Amherst

Amherst FREE PRESS. w Jl 31 1875-79||?
OCHi [F-D 1876]
OClWHi 1875-Je 1879

Amherst NEWS-TIMES. w Ag 7 1914+
1914-My? 1919 as Amherst weekly news
OClWHi 1914-My 1,S 1919-My 8 1924

Amherst TIMES. w 1917-My? 1919||
United with Amherst weekly news to form Amherst news-times

AMHERSTVILLE. *See* AMHERST

ANDOVER

Andover CITIZEN. w 1881+
OClWHi N 27 1883;Ap 22 1884;S 13 1888;Mr 14 1889;My 22 1890;O 26 1894;My 10 1895;Ag 5 1898;N 2 1900;Ja 8 1901-My 2 1902;Mr 19 1909-Jl 12 1918
OHi Ja 4 1901

Andover ENTERPRISE. w 1872-75||?
OClWHi S 10-17 1873;N-D 1874;Ap-My 23 1875

Andover REVIEW. w 1878-79||?
OClWHi Ja9 1879

ANTWERP

Antwerp GAZETTE. *See* Paulding county republican (Paulding)

ASHLAND

Ashland DEMOCRAT. w Ap? 1846-
OClWHi S 9-O 8 1846;Ja 21,F 4 1847

Ashland GAZETTE. sw,w 1887-1902||?
United with Ashland times to form Ashland times gazette
sw 1887-1900?
OAshT Mr 1898-Mr 21 1899

Evening GAZETTE. *See* Ashland times-gazette

OHIO globe. w? 1835?-
OClWHi My 11 1836

OHIO union. *See* Ashland press

Ashland PRESS. w 1846-1920||?
1846-47? as Ashland standard; 1848?-67? Ohio union; 1868?-71? States and union; Ja?-Ag 1? 1872 Ashland union
DLC N 3 1852
MWA S 22 1852
NNHi O 20 1853
OAshT 1861-62;Ag 8 1872-1920
OClWHi Jl 8 1847;Je 1850-My 21 1851;Ap 11-18,Jl 5,18-25 1860;Ja 16-23,F 6,Mr 6-13,O 2-9 1861;F 19-26,Ap 9,30-My 14,28 1862;F 18-25, Ap 1-16,N 4-18 1863;Mr 30,Ap 27,My 11,Jl 6,Ag 17-24 1864;Ja 4-11,Mr 29-My 10,S 13-N 8 1865;F 1866;F 5,Je 22-Jl 1,O 7 1868;Ag 11 1869;F 2 1870;F 24,D 19 1872;Ap 8 1875;S 24 1885;F 1886-Ja,Jl 31-Ag 21 1907;My 4 1910;Ag 4 1915
OHi My 26-Je 16 1852;My 25 1853-60;63-64;F 15 1865-67;76-Je 24 1897;98-1901;03-19
WHi N 16 1876-Ap 13 1877

Ashland STANDARD. *See* Ashland press

STATES and union. *See* Ashland press

Ashland TIMES. w Jl 14 1853-1918||?
1905?-08? as Ashland times-gazette
pub 1853-Ag 2 1855;Jl 28 1859-Jl 12 1866;Jl 30 1868-D 18 1873;Jl 19 1877-Jl 13 1882;O 1883-1904
MWA Jl 13 1865
OClWHi Ag 5 1858;D 18 1879
OHi 1853-Jl 13 1854;Jl 17 1856-Ja 5 1888;90-1901;03-17

Ashland TIMES-GAZETTE. d 1901+
1901?-02? as Evening gazette
pub 1919+
OAsh My 1930-O 1931

Ashland UNION. *See* Ashland press

OHIO (*Continued*)

ASHTABULA

Ashtabula BEACON. d 1888+
1900?-08? as Ashtabula beacon-record. United with Ashtabula star to form Ashtabula star-beacon
OClWHi Ag 1 1900;S 4 1908
OHi Ja 1 1901

Ashtabula CITIZEN. w Ja 2 1879-
OClWHi Ja-My 1879

DEMOCRATIC free press. w Ja 20 1834-35||
OClWHi F 15,Ap 12,My 10,31-Je 7,Ag 9 1834

DEMOCRATIC standard. *See* Sunday standard

Ashtabula JEFFERSONIAN. w O 8 1870-71||
OClWHi 1870-O 4 1871

Ashtabula JOURNAL. w Je 15 1826-
Follows Ashtabula recorder. 1826-27? as Western journal and weekly advertiser; 1828?-Je 6? 1829 Western journal
CSmH Jl 31 1830
CtY Ag 6,23-30,S 13,N 22-29 1828
MWA Ag 5 1829
OClWHi Je 20 1826;O 11-N 1 1828;Ja 10-24, N 14 1829-Mr 12 1831

LIBERTY herald. *See under* Warren

Ashtabula NEWS. w Je 7 1873-96||
MWA Jl 19 1876
OClWHi 1873-Mr 1881;Mr 9 1896

Ashtabula RECORD. d 1897-99||?
United with Ashtabula beacon to form Ashtabula beacon-record, later Ashtabula beacon

Ashtabula RECORDER. w 1823-26||
Followed by Western journal, later Ashtabula journal
InI N 20,D 22 1824
MWA S 27 1823;Jl 17 1824
OClWHi Ap 21,My 21,Je 13,Jl 2-9,23,Ag 20, S 10,N 22,D 13 1823;Ja 3,17,Mr 6,27,Ap 10-Je 19,O 9,N 27 1824;Ja-Mr 1825

Ashtabula REPUBLICAN. w
OClWHi S 30 1831

Ashtabula SENTINEL. *See* Ashtabula county sentinel (Jefferson)

Sunday STANDARD. w N 1876-1923||?
1876-N 28 1919 as Democratic standard
OClWHi 1913-Ja 14 1923
OHi Ja 4 1901

Ashtabula STAR-BEACON. d 1914+
1914-15? as Ashtabula star
OClWHi O 19-26 1928

Ashtabula TELEGRAPH. w 1846-1911||?
1850-D 31 1853 as Ashtabula telegraph and Lake county advertiser
IDa 1855-56
MWA Jl 21 1876
NNHi My 1,Je 27 1863;My 3 1873
OClWHi 1852-82;My 28-Je 4,Jl 16 1902;F 18 1903
OHi Jl 9 1864;Ja 4 1901;Ja-Ag 15 1906;Ja-O 9 1907;My 28 1909-S 1911

WESTERN journal. *See* Ashtabula journal

ASHVILLE

PICKAWAY county news. w 1896+
OClWHi Je 23 1921
OHi Ja 5 1901

ATHENS

ATHENS county gazette. w 1889-1909||?
OHi D 30 1897-1909

ATHENS county journal. *See* Athens journal

ATHENS county republican. w 1881-82||?
OHi Je 21,Jl 26,Ag 9 1882

Athens HERALD. w S 27 1882-93||
United with Athens messenger to form Athens messenger and herald, later Athens messenger
OHi S 27,O 18,D 13 1882;Jl 4,25,Ag 8 1883;Mr 26,O 15 1884;Mr 11,Je 16,O 28,D 9 1886;87-93

HOCKING VALLEY gazette and Athens journal. *See* Athens messenger

Athens JOURNAL. w,sw Ja 6 1870-1911||?
1870-74? as Athens county journal
w 1870-1908
OClWHi 1886
OHi Je 30 1870;N 2 1871;Ag 15 1872;My 16-23 1878;F 9 1882;D 28 1888;89-1910

Athens MESSENGER. w My 22 1830-1909||?
1830-S? 1837 as Western spectator and Athenian chronicle; S 16 1837-42? Hocking Valley gazette and Athens journal; 1843?-D 11 1862 Athens messenger and Hocking Valley gazette; 1894-1905? Athens messenger and herald
DLC D 11 1830;N 3 1832;Ja 26 1839;S 28 1840
MWA F 25 1842;O 24 1861
NdHi F 9 1839;Ja 27 1843;Mr 20 1862
OCHi My 22,S 11,N 20 1830;Ap 16,My 7-21,O 29,D 3 1831;Ja 7 1832;S 21 1833;Ja 11 1834
OClWHi N 11 1837;F 7,28 1840
OHi Ja 18 1850;Ja 3 1855;O 1856-S 1858;Jl 1, 29,D 30 1859;F 17,Ap 6-13,Jl 27 1860;Ap 25 1861;62-Je 1864;Ap 6-13 1865;Je 7 1866;F 21, Mr 21 1867;68-1903;05
TxU O 1858-S 21 1860

Athens MESSENGER. d N 1905+
pub [1905+]
OAU D 1905-N 24 1915;Mr 1926+
OClWHi S 28 1917
OHi Je 10 1909-15,17

Athens MIRROR and literary register. w Ap 16 1825-
DLC Je 27,Jl 11-18,Ag 1,S,O 24 1829
IU S 15 1825
MWA N 4 1826;Ja 25 1827
OCHi Ap 23,Jl 2-9 1825[26]Ja 11,F 1,Mr 22, 22,My 24,S 14,28-O 5,20,N 10,24 1827;Mr 1,15-22,My 3,17,Ag 23-S 13,27,O 11 1828;My 23,Je 6-13,Jl 11-25,S 5-12 1829;F 13,Mr 20-27,My 15 1830
OClWHi F 14 1829

WESTERN spectator. . . *See* Athens messenger

AURORA

Aurora EXAMINER. w My 1? 1870-
OClWHi My 15,Je 1 1870

BAINBRIDGE

OHIO spectator. w Ja 8 1846-
WHi Ja 8,31,My 30,Je 6,Jl 28 1846

BARNESVILLE

Barnesville ENTERPRISE. w,sw 1866+
sw 1922?-30?
OClWHi O 2 1890;Ag 18,S 15 1892;D 17 1923
OHi Ja 3 1901

Barnesville WHETSTONE. w 1894+
pub 1894+

BATAVIA

CHRONICLE of the times. w 1826-35||?
1826-S? 1829 as Spirit of the times
CSmH Ap 24 1830
DLC N 22 1828;Jl 11-18,Ag 1,S 5,N 14-28,D 26 1829;Ja 9 1830;Ja 8 1831;N 3-10 1832
FDsB 1827-28
MWA Ja 23 1824
OCHi N 28 1829

CLERMONT courier. w Mr 19 1836+
DLC My 9 1836;My 9 1840;Je 28 1882
IU S 9,N 18 1843
MWA Ag 10 1844
MsHi Mr 11,Ap 1 1843
OCHi D 24 1847
OClWHi 1836-Mr 18 1837;My 29(extra)1872
OHi Ja 2 1901;09-18
WHi Jl 10 1846

CLERMONT sun. w 1828+
1828-44? as Ohio sun (1833? Ohio sun and Clermont advertiser)
CSmH S 1 1830
DCHi Ag 18 1830
IU N 6 1833;O 29 1834;Mr 16 1835;O 24 1836; O 30 1837;Ag 21 1838;O 26 1840;N 1 1841;S 8,22,D 1 1843;Ja 12-F 23,Mr 8,29-Ap 12 1844
MsHi S 10 1834
N O 9 1833
NN Je 11 1834
OClWHi Ap 22 1829;D 1840-My 24 1844;F 22, My 18 1854;Mr 1855-Je 4 1857;Je 17 1858-60
OHi My 31 1844-My 1846;Ag 19 1852-57;S 20 1876-1925;27

OHIO farmer and western horticulturist. w Ja 1 1835-
OHi 1835-D 1 1839

OHIO sun. *See* Clermont sun

SPIRIT of the times. *See* Chronicle of the times

WESTERN patriot. w Je 5? 1824-
DLC Je 12,N 20 1824;Jl 23 1825
InI D 11 1824
MWA S 4 1824

YANKEE DOODLE. w 1856?-
OClWHi D 18 1858;Ja 8 1859

BEDFORD

COUNTY intelligencer. w D 2 1897-98||?
OClWHi 1897-F 10,My 19-N 10 1898

Bedford GAZETTE. w 1899||?
United with Bedford news register to form Bedford news register and gazette, later Bedford news register
OClWHi My 11,Ag-O 1899

Bedford HERALD. w 1922-26||?
OClWHi Ap 10 1924;F 5-12,Ap 2 1925

Bedford NEWS register. w 1891+
1900?-01? as Bedford news register and gazette
pub 1913;15;20;23;27;29+
OCl Jl 1929+
OClWHi D 1891-Ja 1,N 11 1892-Mr 3,Je 30, S 8 1893;Jl-D 1895;Ap 8 1897;F 16-N 23 1899; Ja 25,Je 6 1900;O 3 1901;Ja 26,F 2 1922;F 11,Ap 1,15 1926;N 3,D 8 1932;Ja 5-12,F 16 1933
OHi Ja 31 1901

Bedford TIMES. w 1926+
OCl Jl 1929+

BELLAIRE

Bellaire daily INDEPENDENT. d 1879-1918||?
OHi Ja 1 1901;Mr 10 1914-F 1916

Bellaire daily LEADER. d 1913+
pub 1913+
OHi Je 30 1925

PROGRESS. w 1893-95||?
WHi [Jl 1894-Mr 16 1895]

BELLE CENTER

HERALD-VOICE. w 1896+
1896-N 1902 as Belle Center herald
OHi Ap 1897-Mr 18 1898;1901;F 1902-[10-F 2 1930]31+

Belle Center VOICE. w 1900-N? 1902||
United with Belle Center herald to form Herald-voice

BELLEFONTAINE

Weekly EXAMINER. w 1830+
1830-33? as Bellefontaine gazette; 1834?-52? Logan gazette; 1853?-71? Logan county gazette
DLC Ap 11,S 19,N 28 1840
IU N 22 1833;N 30 1840;N 20 1844;N 27 1847; D 17 1852
MWA S 3 1852
OClWHi Mr 28 1840-43;My 4 1844;Je 10 1921
OHi Ja 21-Je 1860;D 8 1865-Ap 7 1871;Je 1873-96;D 30 1898-1911;13

Bellefontaine GAZETTE. *See* Weekly examiner

Weekly INDEX-REPUBLICAN. w 1859-1924||
1859-1905 as Logan county index. Merged with Weekly examiner
OHi 1880-N 5 1885;F 1888-1907;09-13

LOGAN county gazette. *See* Weekly examiner

LOGAN county index. *See* Weekly index-republican

LOGAN gazette. *See* Weekly examiner

Bellefontaine PRESS. w 1858-76||?
MWA D 23 1869
OHi D 16 1869-71

Bellefontaine REPUBLICAN. w Ap 20 1855-1905||
United with Logan county index to form Weekly index-republican
DLC S 16 1864-Ja 20 1865
IU D 7 1855;D 11 1857;D 10 1858;D 7 1861;D 5 1862;supp O 29 1861
OClWHi Ja 24 1879
OHi 1855-Ja 4 1862;Ja 25 1867-O 1873;O 1875-F 6 1880;Ap 14 1882-1904

Bellefontaine REPUBLICAN and Logan register. w Je 1830?-
CSmH Jl 10 1830

WESTERN Aurora, and farmers' and mechanics' advocate. w Jl 4? 1835-
DLC Ag 22 1835

BELLEVUE

Bellevue GAZETTE. w Ag 6 1867-1919||?
OClWHi 1913-Ag 7 1919

Bellevue INDEPENDENT. w My 11 1861-
OClWHi My-N 1861;F 8,Ap 26,My 17,Je 21, Ag 9,N 1 1862

BEREA

Berea ADVERTISER. w Je 20 1868-1908||?
1868-Ap 10? 1869 as Advertiser; Ap 17 1869-77? Grindstone City advertiser; 1878?-79? Republican and advertiser
OClWHi F 20 1879;F 5 1886

Berea ENTERPRISE. w 1898+
OClWHi Je 20 1902;Je 24 1932

GRINDSTONE CITY advertiser. *See* Berea advertiser

Berea NEWS. w,sw F 20 1924+
w 1924-O 1933
pub 1924+

REPUBLICAN and advertiser. *See* Berea advertiser

BERLIN HEIGHTS

Berlin CALL. w 1912+
OClWHi 1913+

BETHEL

Bethel JOURNAL. w S 14 1898+
pub O 1927+

BLANCHESTER

STAR-REPUBLICAN. w Mr 1 1870+
1870-1900? as Blanchester star
pub 1912+

BLUFFTON

Bluffton NEWS. w 1875+
pub 1890+
OHi Ja 3 1901

BOWLING GREEN

Bowling Green DEMOCRAT. *See* Wood county news

Daily SENTINEL-TRIBUNE. d 1890+
1890-1906? as Daily sentinel
OHi Ja 2 1901;Jl 1914-F 1916
—w ed *See* Wood county sentinel-tribune

Evening TRIBUNE. d 1892-1906||?
United with Daily sentinel to form Daily sentinel-tribune
OHi Ja 2 1901
—w ed *See* Wood county tribune

WOOD county democrat. *See* Wood county news

OHIO (*Continued*)

BOWLING GREEN—*Continued*

WOOD county news. w 1876+
1876-81? as Bowling Green democrat; 1882?-1930? Wood county democrat
OHi Ja 4 1901;O 8 1909-My 10 1918

WOOD county republican. w D 18 1918+
pub 1918+

WOOD county sentinel-tribune. w 1867-1926||?
1867-1906? as Wood county sentinel
N Jl 6 1876;F 18 1886
OHi Ja 3 1901

WOOD county tribune. w 1889-1906||?
United with Wood county sentinel to form Wood county sentinel-tribune
OHi Ja 3 1901
—d ed *See* Evening tribune

BRADFORD

Bradford SENTINEL. w,sw 1884+
Title varies slightly
Dated also in Covington
w 1884-93?
pub 1884+
OHi Ja 2 1901

BRIDGEPORT

BELMONT farmer. w D 27? 1846-
OHi 1847-Je 20 1848

BROOKLYN

Papers published in Brooklyn are listed under Cleveland

BRYAN

Bryan DEMOCRAT. w,sw 1863+
w 1863-1905?
pub 1909+
IU N 23 1871
MWA D 3 1863;Ag 24 1876
OBr 1884+
OBrC 1864+
OClWHi Je 23 1864;Ap 15 1869
OHi Ja 3 1901;Mr-Ag 17 1906;Jl 1907-19;F 1920-O 9 1925

Bryan PRESS. w 1854+
1854?- as Williams county gazette
pub Je 1889+
IU Ag 12,N 11 1858;F 10 1859
NbHi Ja 17 1878
OBr 1884+
OBrC 1854+
OHi Ja 3 1901;Mr 1906-Mr 1908;Je 18 1914-F 1916

WILLIAMS county gazette. *See* Bryan press

BUCKEYE CITY

CITIZEN. *See under* Danville

BUCYRUS

CRAWFORD county forum. *See* News-forum

CRAWFORD county news. w,sw,tw 1873-1900||?
1873-76? as Independent democrat (Crestline). United with Crawford county forum to form News-forum
w 1873-79?; sw 1880?-98?
ODa My 14-D 1875
OHi Ja 1 1901
OOxM My 8 1874

Bucyrus DEMOCRAT. w 1839?-
OClWHi S 22 1841

DEMOCRATIC republican. tw? 1840?-
OClWHi Je 9-11 1840

Daily FORUM. d 1891-1922||
United with Bucyrus telegraph to form Bucyrus telegraph-forum
OHi Ja 1 1901;My-Je,D 1915-F 1916

Bucyrus JOURNAL. w Ja 6? 1853-1908||?
DLC 1853;56-61
MWA Je 30 1853;Mr 4(extra)1870;Mr 10(extra)1871
OClWHi My 12 1853
OHi Ap 22 1865;Ja 4 1901

NEWS-FORUM. w,sw Ap 12 1845-1922||?
1845-50? as People's forum; 1851?-1900? Crawford county forum
w 1845-1900?
O 4 1921 is special historical ed
DLC O 22-29 1852
IU Ap 12 1845
MWA Ag 27 1852;S 5 1862
OClWHi My 24,Je 28 1850;Jl 28 1854;70-S 14 1872
OHi N 12 1858;F 27 1906-Jl 21 1922
—d ed *See* Daily forum

PEOPLE'S forum. *See* News-forum

Bucyrus TELEGRAPH-FORUM. d 1887+
1887-1922 as Bucyrus telegraph
pub 1887+
OHi Ja 1 1901

BURTON

GEAUGA leader. w D 18 1874+
Ja 3 1922-D 30 1924 as Geauga county leader
OClWHi 1874-Ja 22,My 14 1875-Ap,D 8 1876-[90]-[92-93]+

Burton INDEPENDENT. w D 29 1883-84||?
OClWHi 1883-84

CADIZ

DEMOCRAT sentinel. w 1893-1932||
1893-S 1910 as Harrison county democrat; O 1910-N 1911 Cadiz democrat. Merged with Cadiz republican
OHi 1897-99;1901-17

DEMOCRATIC sentinel. *See* Cadiz sentinel

DEMOCRATIC whig standard and public advertiser. w F 6 1844-
OClWHi 1844-F 8 1845

HARRISON county democrat. *See* Democrat sentinel

HARRISON county organ. *See* Cadiz organ

HARRISON news. *See* Cadiz news

HARRISON republican. *See* Cadiz republican

HARRISON telegraph. w 1821?-
DLC O 16 1824;F 10,Ag 2,S 6 1828;Ja 2,F 11, S 18 1829;Ag 4 1830;Ja 1 1831;N 3 1832
IU My 24 1834
InI S 25 1824
OClWHi My 22,O 16 1824
OHi Ap 24,Jl 3,O 2,30 1826

LIBERTY courier and register of facts. w Ap? 1844-
OHi My 8,Je 12,Jl 10,31 1844

Cadiz NEWS. w 1896-1917||?
1896-N 1916 as Harrison news. Merged with Cadiz republican
OHi 1897-N 1916;Ja-Ap 5 1917

Cadiz ORGAN. w 1836?-
1836-O? 1837 as Harrison county organ
DLC D 14 1837
MWA O 5 1837
OClWHi F 6-13 1840

Cadiz REPUBLICAN. w Je 4 1840+
1840-F 1845 as Harrison republican
pub 1868+
DLC Jl 9 1840;N 14 1850;Je 23 1932
MWA Je 30 1853
OClWHi Jl 16-O 22 1862;O 28-D 2 1863;Je 22 1864;D 19 1907;Ja 18 1917;O 1918+
OHi Je 25 1840-Je 1843;44-O 1845;Ja 1-15 1846;52-1917;S 22,O 27 1927;Jl 1929+

Cadiz SENTINEL. w 1833?-N 1911||
1833?-43? Cadiz sentinel and Harrison county farmer (title varies: Sentinel and sun); 1852?-63? Democratic sentinel. United with Cadiz democrat to form Democrat sentinel
DLC O 27-N 3 1852
IHi O 6 1837
IU Ag 19 1841
MWA D 22 1852
OClWHi F 13,Jl 16 1840;Ag 14,28 1844;Ag 26 1846;N 3 1847;Je 17,S 30,O 28-D 23 1863
OHi Mr 21 1844-Ap 1 1846;Ap 10 1850-68;70-1911

CALDWELL

CITIZENS' press. *See* Caldwell press

Caldwell JOURNAL. *See* Republican journal

NOBLE county leader. w My 3 1899+
pub 1899+
OHi 1899-Ap 14 1915;Ap 18 1917-Ap 10 1918

NOBLE county republican. w 1858-97||?
United with Caldwell journal to form Republican journal
OHi S 1880-S 2 1886

Caldwell PRESS. w 1871?-1933||?
1871?-72? as Caldwell spectator; 1873?-Ap 1884 as Citizens' press. Merged with Republican journal
OClWHi N 2 1910
OHi S 1880-My 10,S 1883-Ag 1886;S 15 1887-S 1901;06;08-D 12 1912;Jl 1914-18

REPUBLICAN journal. w 1884+
1884-97? as Caldwell journal
OHi Ja 3 1901;Ag 1904-Jl 3 1907;Jl 15 1908-Jl 12 1922

Caldwell SPECTATOR. *See* Caldwell press

Caldwell STAR. w 1851-61||
1851-52? as Democratic courier (Sarahsville)
MWA Ag 9 1852

CAMBRIDGE

CLARION of freedom. w? 1844?-
OClWHi S 10 1847

GUERNSEY county times. *See* Weekly Guernsey times

GUERNSEY Jeffersonian. *See* Cambridge Jeffersonian

Weekly GUERNSEY times. w S 18 1824-1915||?
1824-D 31 1903 as Guernsey times (Ja 3 1835-D 29 1839 Guernsey times and farmers and mechanics advocate; Ja 4 1840-D 31 1842 Guernsey county times); 1908?-11? Republican press and Guernsey times
DLC Ag 8 1828;Jl 18-25,Ag 8,O 3,31,D 5 1829; Ja 8 1831
MWA My 11 1827;Jl 17 1841
MiU-C D 1839
NjR Ag 19 1826
OClWHi 1824-Ja 1828;My 1830-S,D 10 1836-Ag 14 1846;Ja 7 1848;49-Ja 20,My 24 1855-59; 62-90;92-93;95-Jl 1905
OHi Ja 18 1840-My 1842;N 2,D 14 1844;D 24 1863;Ja 3 1901
PPL N 15-22 1850
—d ed *See* Cambridge times

Daily GUERNSEY times. d 1883-84||?
OClWHi Mr 14,S 3,D 15,19 1883;Mr 27-28 1884
OHi N 6 1884

Cambridge JEFFERSONIAN. w 1843-1917||?
1844-My 16 1872 as Guernsey Jeffersonian
OCHi F 24,Mr 2,16,My 11-18,Je 8,Ag 26 1876
OClWHi Je 7-14,Jl 5,Ag 9 1848;Mr 28,S 17, O 10 1850;Ja 16-My 15 1851;52;F 24 1853;Ja 13 1859;Je 17 1864;N 10 1865;66-Ap 1873;Ag 26 1880;Ap 13 1882;Jl 30 1885
OHi Ja 7 1886;Ja 3 1901

Daily JEFFERSONIAN. d 1892+
OClWHi Jl 31,S 29 1913
OHi Ap 1914-My 1 1915;Jl 1919-My 25 1920;S 3,O 4 1921

LITTLE joker. Ja 1 1863-
OClWHi Ja 1 1863

REPUBLICAN press. w 1885-1907||?
United with Weekly Guernsey times to form Republican press and Guernsey times, later Weekly Guernsey times
OHi Ja 3 1901

REPUBLICAN press and Guernsey times. *See* Weekly Guernsey times

Cambridge TIMES. d 1899-1919||?
Merged with Daily Jeffersonian
OClWHi Ap 7 1899-Jl 9 1905
OHi Ja 1 1901

CAMDEN

PREBLE county news. w Ap 1902+
pub 1902+
MWA Ag 19 1933
OHi 1930+

CANAL DOVER. *See* DOVER

CANAL WINCHESTER

Winchester TIMES. w 1871+
pub 1871+
OClWHi Je 24 1891
OHi Ja 2 1901

CANFIELD

DEMOCRATIC union sentinel. *See* Mahoning sentinel

Canfield weekly HERALD. *See* Mahoning Valley news

MAHONING county herald. *See* Mahoning Valley news

MAHONING county news. *See* Mahoning Valley news

MAHONING dispatch. w Ap 4 1861-
OClWHi Ap 11 1861-N 6 1862;Ja 8-Je 1863

MAHONING dispatch. w Ap 1877+
pub 1877+
CtY Jl 21,Ag 4 1933
OClWHi Ap 23-30 1897;Ap 1902-Mr 20 1914
OHi Ja 4 1901;Mr 11-D 1932;Mr 11-D 1933
OY Ja 22 1897-Mr 1900;N 1927+

MAHONING herald. *See* Mahoning Valley news

MAHONING index. w My 20 1846-
OClWHi Ag 25,D 29 1847;Ap 26,Je 14,Ag 23, S 13-O 4,18 1848;Ag 8 1849;Ap 19-My 17,Je 28-Jl 5,Ag 9-16,O 4-18 1850;O 10 1851
OY 1846-My 12 1847

MAHONING sentinel. w Mr 26 1852-66||
Mr-N 23 1852 as Democratic union sentinel; N 30 1852-Ap? 1860 Republican sentinel
Dated also in Youngstown
Suspended from O 23 1861-Jl 10 1862
MWA D 21 1852;S 24 1861
OCfD 1857-58
OClWHi S 29 1854;D 25 1857;Ja 2,16,F 6,My-Jl 10 1861;Je 27-D 5,26 1866
OY 1852-Ap 12,My 9 1860-F 1861

MAHONING VALLEY news. w Ap 4? 1861-77||?
1861-Ja 22 1863 as Mahoning herald; Ja 29-D 16 1863 Mahoning weekly herald; D 30 1863-My 1869 Canfield weekly herald; Je 1869-71? Mahoning county herald; 1872?-75? Mahoning county news
OY My 1861-[70-71]74

NATIONAL union. w 1866-72||?
OClWHi S 25,O 22 1866
OY O 1866-S 1867

REPUBLICAN sentinel. *See* Mahoning sentinel

CANTON

Canton daily DEMOCRAT. *See* Canton daily news

DEMOCRATIC transcript. w Ap 8 1853-
OClWHi N 4 1853
OHi 1853-Ja 24 1855

Der DEUTSCHE Americaner. w 1852?-
In German
MWA S 2 1852

FOCUS. w
WHi [Mr 22 1894-Ap 20 1895]

FULTON telegraph. w Ap? 1841-
DLC Jl 3 1841

Canton daily NEWS. d Ap 1 1884-Jl 3 1930||
1884-Mr? 1888 as Canton daily democrat; Ap? 1888-N 19 1912 News-democrat (O 1903-Ag 17 1910 Morning news). United with Canton evening repository to form Repository and news
My 30 1926 is industrial ed
OCa 1890-Je,Ag 1892-Je,Ag 1900-30
OClWHi 1884-Mr 1888;Ja-N 12 1889;D 30 1923;Mr 22 1925
OHi 1901-30
PYHi S 20 1901
—w ed *See* Stark county democrat

OHIO (*Continued*)

CANTON—*Continued*

NORTH CANTON Sun. w N 2 1922+
pub 1922+

OHIO repository. *See* Canton repository

Canton PRESS. w 1835?-
DLC Jl 22 1837

***Canton REPOSITORY.** w Mr 30 1815-1913||?
1815-N 5? 1868 as Ohio repository (1825?-40? Ohio repository and Stark county gazette); N 12 1868-Je 5 1874 Canton repository and republican
CLM O 7 1870
CSmH Jl 20 1830
DLC Ag 23 1827;Ja 3 1828;Jl 31,S 4-11,O 23 1829;Ja 1-8 1830;Ja 6 1831;F 22 1838;F 14 1839;N 5 1840
ICHi O 1846-Mr 6 1850
IU Ag 4 1842
InRE O 28 1870
MWA Ag 25 1852
NbHi Mr 18 1869;My 8 1874
OClWHi O 21,D 24 1824;Ja 28 1825-Ja 5 1827; Jl 3 1829;O 22 1841;Ag 19 1863-Mr,S 20 1865; Jl 4,O 17 1866-Ja 9,Jl 10,D 25 1867
OHi Je 20 1828;Ap 21 1852-79;S 24 1880;81-82; 84-86; 88;90-99;1901-04;06-09
OOxM Mr 22,Je-Jl 19,Ag 16,30,S 13-20 1833; Ja 10-F 1,Mr 7-14,28,Ap 11-Je 1834
P-M Ag 7 1845
WHi Ag 28 1829;Ja 6 1842

REPOSITORY and news. d 1878+
1878-Jl 1 1930 as Canton evening repository
DLC Ja-Je 1898
ICM D 27 1884
MoBoH F 1897
OCHi Je 17 1882
OCa 1889+
OClWHi N 3 1900;S 19 1901;Ag 5 1923
OHi 1911;Ap 27 1912-Je,Ag 1914-F,My 1917-Mr 1918;Jl 1919+
PYHi S 19-20 1901

STARK county democrat. w,sw 1834-1911||?
w 1834-Mr 11 1899
DLC Jl 22 1835;Mr 28,Jl 1854-D 16 1846;O 27 1852
GAtCo Je 22 1840
IU Ap 12 1844
KyLo D 17 1838
NNHi N 3 1852
OClWHi Mr 7 1844;My 24 1848-S 11 1850;52-My 19 1858;60-66;68-72;75-79;Jl 29 1880;81-N 1882;Ap 1884-87;Ja-Ag 13 1891
ODW Je 26,O 2 1867;D 12-19 1872;Mr 20 1873
OHi My 25 1840-My 24 1841;Je 23 1852-Mr 1857;Je 15 1859-D 14 1871;Je 12 1873-78;80-81;83-93;95-1908
—d ed *See* Canton daily news

STARK county republican. w N 12 1858-N 5 1868||
United with Ohio repository to form Canton repository and republican, later Canton repository
MWA F 15 1866
OCa complete
OClWHi D 25 1861-My 17,S 7,O 19,N 9-16,D 7 1865;O 4,N 8 1866
OHi My 20 1859-68

Der VATERLANDSFREUND und geist der zeit. w 1829?-
1829?-33? as Der Vaterlands-freund
In German
ICHi O 5 1833
IU Ag 2 1844

Der WESTLICHER beobachter und Stark county anzeiger. w D 21? 1820-
In German
DLC Jl 6 1821
MdBG Ap 6,20 1821

CARDINGTON

Cardington INDEPENDENT. *See* Morrow county independent

MORROW county independent. w 1866+
1866-71? as Cardington republican; 1872?-88? Cardington independent
OClWHi D 17 1868
OHi 1889-1921

Cardington REPUBLICAN. *See* Morrow county independent

CAREY

Carey TIMES. w 1873+
1873-86? as Wyandot county times
pub S 19 1888+

WYANDOT county times. *See* Carey times

CARROLLTON

CARROLL chronicle. *See* Carroll journal

CARROLL county chronicle. *See* Carroll journal

CARROLL county union. *See* Free press-standard

CARROLL democrat. w Ja 1856-
1856-58? as Citizen democrat
OClWHi Jl 24 1856;F 5 1857;Jl 8-22 1858;F 26,Jl 13 1859

CARROLL free press. *See* Free press-standard

CARROLL journal. w 1871+
1871-94? as Carroll county chronicle; 1895? Carrollton chronicle; 1896?-Ap 18? 1935 Carroll chronicle
pub Ap 25 1935+
OClWHi N 10 1873
OHi Ja 4 1901;Mr 1906-08

CARROLL union press. *See* Free press-standard

Carrollton CHRONICLE. *See* Carroll journal

CITIZEN democrat. *See* Carroll democrat

Carrollton COURIER. w Ap 1 1863-
MWA Ap 8 1863

DEMOCRATIC crisis. w Mr 8? 1844-
OClWHi Mr 29,Je 21,Ag 30 1844

FREE press-standard. w S 20 1834+
1834-1905? as Carroll free press (title varies: Carroll county union; Carroll union press; etc.)
Jl 29 1915 is centennial ed
DLC D 11 1840
OClWHi 1834-O 8 1841;Ja 1,Mr 14 1845;Ap 26 1855;Ag 21 1856;Ja 8 1857;My 4 1859;Mr 26 1862-64;Mr 4 1868;Je 2 1869;N 24 1880;N 28 1883-Ja 1 1890;F 2 1898;Jl 29 1915
OHi S 18 1835-S 9 1836;N 12 1852;Je 22 1906-Je 1916

Carrollton GAZETTE. w 1832-
DLC D 14 1833
OClWHi Ja 26 1833-S 6 1834

JEFFERSONIAN. w Jl 1837-
OClWHi O 12,26 1837;S 19,O 3-10,21,N 7 1839; Ja 16,My 14,Jl 30 1840;Je 30,N 17 1842

NEW era. w? 1849?-
OClWHi O 1 1849

OHIO picayune. w Jl? 1846-
MWA N 5 1852
OClWHi O 30,N 26 1846;Je 4 1847;Je 2 1848; Ap 19 1850,S 19 1851;F 27 1852

REPUBLICAN-STANDARD. w Ap 21 1881-1905||?
1881-97? as Carrollton republican. United with Carroll free press to form Free press-standard
OClWHi Ap 1881;F 11 1897-F 9 1900
OHi Ja 4 1901

CARTHAGE

CARTHAGENIAN. w? 1840?-
OClWHi Je 18 1840

CEDARVILLE

Cedarville HERALD. w 1880+
OHi Ja 5 1901
OXG D 29 1933+

CELINA

Celina DEMOCRAT. w 1895-1920||?
OHi 1898-1902;04-18

Celina JOURNAL. w 1868-74||?
1868-F 2 1871 as Workingman's journal
OHi D 16 1869-Ja 1 1873

MERCER county observer. w 1874-1925||?
OHi Ag 27 1885;Mr 18 1886-1918

MERCER county standard. w 1848+
1848-68 as Western standard
FTaM My-Ag 1849
MWA D 16 1852
OCHi Jl 13-27,Ag 10-24,S 21 1876
OClWHi Ap 22 1852-Mr 9 1876
OHi Ap 22 1852-Mr 8 1866;Mr 14 1872-Mr 7 1878;Mr 11 1880-S 15 1881;Mr 1884-1906;08-17

Daily STANDARD. d 1904+
pub 1924+

WESTERN democrat. w 1874-76||?
OClWHi Ap 12-Je 10,O 7 1875

WESTERN standard. *See* Mercer county standard

WORKINGMAN'S journal. *See* Celina journal

CENTERBURG

Centerburg STAR w? Je 7 1849-
OClWHi Je-S 13 1849

CENTERVILLE

Centerville RECORDER. w? 1832?-
OClWHi O 24,D 15 1832

CHAGRIN FALLS

Chagrin Falls EXPONENT. w,sw Ja 1 1874+
sw My 3 1927-Je 27 1930
pub 1874+
OCl Jl 1929+
OClWHi F 24 1876;S 5 1878;Ja 27 1881;F 10-24 1887;Ja 21 1892[96]Je 23,S 1 1898;My 10 1900;Je 13,27,Ag 15-29 1901;S 1909+
OHi Ja 3 1901

CHARDON

DEMOCRATIC record. *See* Geauga county record

FREE democrat. *See* Geauga republican-record

GEAUGA county record. w D 23 1886-D 30 1921||
1886-D 31 1887 as Geauga record; Ja 7-D 29? 1888 Geauga democratic record; 1889-91? Democratic record. United with Geauga republican to form Geauga republican-record
OClWHi 1886-88;F 2-9,My 11,Jl 6,N 9 1889;F 1,Mr 15,29,My-D 1891;Ap 22-Jl 1 1892;93-Ap 5 1894;S 12,O 21,D 19 1895;Ap 2,Je 25 1896[97-1901]-03;Jl 8-D 1904;Ag 1905-21
OHi Ja 3 1901;03-18

GEAUGA democrat. *See* Geauga republican-record

GEAUGA democratic record. *See* Geauga county record

GEAUGA freeman. *See* Geauga republic

GEAUGA record. *See* Geauga county record

GEAUGA republic. w My 22 1840-Ja 17 1854||
1840-N 1842 as Geauga freeman; D 1842-D 18? 1849 Geauga republican and whig
Followed by Cleveland daily express, later Cleveland morning express (Cleveland)
N Ag 13 1842
NN My 6 1843
OClWHi My 23,Je 6,S 26,N 7 1840;Ja 16,My 1,Je 19,Jl 3,Ag 7-21 1841;F 19,Ap 2,30,Je 11-Ag 6,O 15-29,N 12 1842;Je 17,S 9,O 28 1843; Ja 13,F 3,17-24,Ap 13,D 7,21 1844;Ja 28,D 2,17 1845;Je 9-16;Ag 11,N 17,D 7,22 1846;Mr 16,My 20,Je 15,S 28-O 5,N 23-29,D 28 1847;F 1,Mr 28,Ag 8 1848;F 27,Ap 17,My 29,O 23,D 25 1849-54
OHi D 2,16 1845;Mr 26-D 1850
P-M D 16 1845

GEAUGA republican and whig. *See* Geauga republic

GEAUGA republican-record. w D 22 1849+
1849-53 as Free democrat; 1854-65 Jeffersonian democrat; Ja 3 1866-D 27 1871 Geauga democrat; Ja 3 1872-D 29 1921 Geauga republican
MWA Ag 10 1852;Ag 12 1876
N Ap 21 1865
NN O 26 1852
OClWHi 1849-94[96]Ja 6,F 17-Ap 14 1897;Je 22-29 1898;F 13 1901-07;Je 24 1908+
OHi 1857-60;62-65;O 31 1866;68-71;73-80;95-1918

JEFFERSONIAN democrat. *See* Geauga republican-record

Chardon SPECTATOR and Geauga gazette. w 1833-35||
Merged with Toledo gazette (Toledo)
CSmH Je 28 1834
OClWHi Ag 1833-N 1835

Chardon TIMES. w S 7 1872-75||*
1872 as Western Reserve times
OClWHi 1872-Ag 23 1873

WESTERN Reserve times. *See* Chardon times

YOUNG hickory and eagle spread. w Je 26-1844||?
Campaign paper
OClWHi Je 26 1844

CHICAGO JUNCTION. *See* WILLARD

CHILLICOTHE

Chillicothe ADVERTISER. w,sw Ap 21 1824-1924||?
Follows Friend of freedom. 1824-Je 1829 as Chillicothe times; Je 30 1829-F? 1830 Ohioan and Chillicothe advertiser; Mr 6? 1830-Je 4? 1831 Chillicothe evening post
sw 1910?-19?
CSmH Je 26 1830
DLC 1824-Je 8 1825;Ag 25 1829;My 1 1841;Ja 18-25 1836
IU Jl 28 1824;Jl 7 1829;Ap 24,O 2 1830;Ag 22,S 5,19-O 1840;Ag 9(extra)1843;Ag 31,S 14,O 19 1844[My 1846-47;F 13-N 1850]-F 7,Ap 18,My 9-16,D 5 1851;Ja 9-16,F 6,Mr 11,Je 18 Jl 2 1852;Ja 21 1853;Jl 22-Ag 5,S 30 1892
MWA Je 16 1824;Ap 13 1845;D 24 1852
NN Ja 25-F 1,My 11 1826
OChH Jl 1831-Je 1832
OClWHi Ap-Je 23,O-D 8 1824;F 2,Ap 13,Je 29 1825;29-Ja 2,Mr 27-D 1830;Ja 15,Mr 5,Ap 16-23,My 21,Jl 16,Ag 6,S 10 1831-My 1 1846; O 15 1847;Ap 6,Ag 10,O 18 1849-Je 14,Ag 9-16,S 13 1850;Ja 24,Mr 7,Jl 25 1851;Je 4 1852; F 11-Ap 8,Je 29,Ag 26-D 9 1853;Ja 20-Ap 14 1854;57-60;Jl 26,D 20-27 1861;Ja 24,Mr 21 1862-Ap 1863;Ag 10 1865-My 24 1866;F 25 1869-71;73-O 12 1876;77-S 17 1879;80-N 21 1890[91-Ja 19 1894]1905;Ja 12-19,Mr 26 1918; D 29 1919;My 31-Jl 1921
OHi 1824-Ap 20 1825;S 17 1831;S 30(extra) 1843;Jl 1852-Jl 1886;88-S 1895;Ja 4 1901
WHi Ap 2 1842;D 19 1862;Ja 16-23 1863;Ap 22 1864;O 12 1865;D 14 1866;My 14 1868
—d ed *See* Chillicothe news-advertiser

Chillicothe morning ADVERTISER. d
OClWHi Mr 16 1855
WHi O 18 1855

ANCIENT metropolis. w Ag 6 1845-
IU Ag 20 1845;S 29,N 17,D 15 1846;Ja 19,Mr 30,Ap 13,27-My 4,Ag 10,27 1847-Ap 21,D 25 1848;N 12 1849;Ja 1,Je 24 1850;O 28 1852
MWA O 29 1845;O 8 1847;Jl 30 1852
MiU-C O 6 1847
OCHi 1845-Jl 1848
OClWHi Ag 13-S 10,O 8,29,D 31 1845-Ap,Jl 8-O,D 8 1846;Ja 5-12,Ap 13,My 18-25,Ag 1847-Ja 1,15,29,Mr 19-26,Ap 16-Jl 9,N-D 17 1849;Ja 14-Mr,My 6,Je 10,Jl-Ag,O 5,19,D 7 1850;Mr 20,Ap 4,My 9-23,D 16 1851;Ja 23,My 9 1852
WHi [S 17 1845-F 11 1848]

Daily ANCIENT metropolis. d O? 1849-
IU N 14,D 4-5,10,12-24 1849[Ja-N 1850]Jl 31,S 10 1851;Mr 12,15,22,My 26,Je 22 1852; Mr 30,S 26,O 3,8,19 1853;Ja 20,28,F 13,20,Mr 11 1854
MWA D 23 1852
OClWHi N 14,20,D 14,28 1849-Ap,Je 8,Jl 7,Ag 16-17,O 12,D 11,15,23,27-28 1852;53-F 21 1854
WHi [My 20 1851-Je 26 1857]

OHIO (*Continued*)

CHILLICOTHE—*Continued*

BUCKEYE. w Jl 1 1834-
IU Jl 29 1834
OClWHi Jl 8,Ag 5-12 1834

CAMP PRENTISS register. N 11 1861-
OClWHi N 11 1861

CHILLICOTHEAN. w Jl 28 1826-
Ct [N 1826-Ja 1829]
CtY S 1,15 1826;Jl 12 1828
DLC Jl 31 1827;Ja 26 1828
IU S 1 1826
N Ag 18 1826;N 3 1827
NNHi D 12 1828
OClWHi Ag 1826-D 12 1828
OHi [Ag-O 11 1828]
WHi O 25 1828

CITY observer. O 16 1852-
OClWHi O 16 1852

Daily evening DISPATCH. d O 1849-
OClWHi O 12-N 6 1849

FLAG of the union. w Ag 17 1861-
IU Ag-O 5 1861
WHi Ag-O 5 1861

FOUNTAIN. sw F 1 1847-
OClWHi 1847-Ja 15 1848

FRIEND of freedom. w F 4- 1824||
Followed by Chillicothe times, later Chillicothe advertiser
DLC F 4,18-25 1824
MWA F 4,18 1824
N F 1824
OHi F 18,25 1824
WHi F 4 1824

Chillicothe GAZETTE. d D 1841-
OClWHi D 17 1841-Mr 14 1842
—w ed *See* Scioto gazette

Chillicothe GAZETTE. tw 1841-
pub during sessions of legislature
DLC D 15 1841
IU F 14 1842
NN D 17 1841-Mr 14 1842
WHi D 17 1841-Mr 9 1842
—w ed *See* Scioto gazette

Daily GAZETTE. *See* Scioto gazette

Chillicothe daily HUSTLER. d S 1 1890-
IU S 1,10,19-20,22,24 1890
OClWHi S 1-17 1890

Chillicothe INTELLIGENCER. sw D 6 1842-D 8 1843||
DLC complete
NN complete
OClWHi D 9 1842-N 21 1843
WHi complete

Chillicothe INTELLIGENCER. w D 10 1842-
NN 1842-D 9 1843

Chillicothe LEADER. w My 12 1883-D 30 1893||
United with Scioto gazette to form Leader-gazette, later Scioto gazette
OClWHi 1883;My 10 1884-85;Jl 31-Ag 7,O 23 1886;87;My 12 1888-My 4,Ag 24 1889;My 10 1890-My 2,N 21 1891;My 14 1892-93
OHi F 2 1889

LEADER-GAZETTE. *See* Scioto gazette

LOG CABIN herald. w Mr 9- 1840||?
Campaign paper
IU Mr 16,Jl 28,Ag 17 1840
OClWHi Mr 30,S 28,O 19-26 1840
WHi Ap 20,Je 22 1840

NATIONAL express. S 6 1878-80||?
IU S 6 1878
OClWHi Ag 13,D 17 1880

Chillicothe daily NEWS. d Mr 1880-S 30 1899||
United with Chillicothe advertiser to form Chillicothe news-advertiser
IU Je 30,Jl 27,29-Ag 13 1892
OChN 1896-99
OClWHi Ap 14-20 1880;S 10 1886-87;Je 15 1897
OHi F 2 1889;S 27 1895
—w ed *See* Ross county register

Chillicothe NEWS-ADVERTISER. d 1896+
1896-S 30 1899 as Chillicothe advertiser
My 20-21 1903 are centennial eds; N 16 1931 is 100th anniversary
pub O 2 1899+
MWA N 16 1931
OChH 1900-07
OHi My 20-21 1903;N 16 1931
WHi N 16 1931
—w ed *See* Chillicothe advertiser

Der OHIO correspondent.
In German
MWA S 4 1852
OClWHi Ap 5,Je 28 1851

OHIOAN and Chillicothe advertiser. *See* Chillicothe advertiser

PLEDGE of honor.
IU Je 5 1847

Chillicothe evening POST. *See* Chillicothe advertiser

ROSS county register. w 1868-1909||?
IU Ag 6 1892
MWA Jl 2 1870;Jl 12 1873
OClWHi [1869]-72;Ap 1873-75;78-84;Jl 1885-O 1886;87;N 3,17 1888;1905
OHi Ja 1 1901;Mr 1906-Ap 20 1909
WHi Ag 27-S 3 1870
—d ed *See* Chillicothe daily news

***SCIOTO gazette.** w,sw Ap 25 1800-1925||?
Ag 1815-F 15 1821 Scioto gazette and Fredonian chronicle; F 21 1821-F 15 1827 Supporter and Scioto gazette; Ap 23 1834-Ap 15 1835 Scioto gazette and independent whig; 1894-Ap 28 1900 Leader-gazette
w 1800-1907?
CSmH S 1 1830
DLC 1821-26;Mr 8 1827;Mr 25,S 2-9,30,O 21 1829;Ja 6 1830;O 24 1832;Ap 3 1833;My 7 1834;N 5 1840
ICHi 1821-F 21 1828;Ja 18 1832
IU Ja 4,18-F 15 1821;N 8 1823;Ja 6 1825[Mr 1827-31]Mr 14-28,Ap 11-18,Ag 8,D 5 1832;Mr 19,Ap 2-16,My 21,O 1-8,N 12-D 1834;Ja 28-F 4,18,Mr 4-11,25,Ap 15-29,My 27-Je 10,O 14 1835;F 17,Mr 9,30-Ap 13,My 11,Je 8,29, Ag 3-10,31,S 14-21,O 13 1836-[Ja-N 1837] O 18-25,N 8-15,29 1838-Ja,F 14-Ap 18,My 2-9 1839;N 12 1840;Mr 31 1842;S 12 1844;My 31 1848;Ja 17,Ap 4,O 3,N 14,D 12 1849-Ja 2,Mr 20-27,Je 12,Jl 3,Ag 14 1850;My 7,Ag 6 1851;D 18 1855;Mr-Ag 6,S 1867-Ja 14 1868;Mr 29 1882;Mr-Ap 19 1888;Jl 18,Ag 1-15,S 12, 26-O 10,D 5 1890[My-D 11 1891]Ap 15,Jl 29-Ag 6 1892[Mr 22-N 8 1893]My 23 1903;Ja 16 1904;My 6 1905
InI Je 26 1848
MBAt D 12 1821;N 22,D 27 1823;Mr 18 1824
MH [1829-93]
MWA My 31,Jl 19 1823;My 20 1824;Ja 25,Mr 15 1827;F 14-28 1828;D 29 1830;My 11,D 21 1831;F 1 1832[Ap 22-D 1835]-39;S 16 1846; S 29 1847;D 20 1848;My 16 1849;Ag 10 1852; Ap 28 1900
MiU-C S 29 1847
N D 30 1825-Ja 1826;Jl 16 1846
NN Ja 25-F 15,Ag 1,O 3-10 1821;N 6-13,27 1822;F 8,Mr 29,Ap 26,My 10,Je 14,Jl 5-19,Ag 16 1823;D 15-29 1825;Ja-Ap 20,Je 22-Jl 13,Ag 1826[27-Jl 1829]38;Ap 15 1841-Mr 1847;Ap 1848-Mr 17 1852
NNHi Jl 9,O 1,N,D 10 1840-F 4 1841;Ja 9 1863;Ap 16 1873;Mr 8 1888
OCl Ag 27 1840
OClWHi Ja 3,17,Ap 18,My 30,Je 20,Jl 4,18, Ag-N 14,D 12 1821;F 27,Ap 17,My 29,Je 19, Jl 10-N 1822;23-O 6 1825;Ja 26,Ap 27,My 25, Je 29,Jl 13 1826-Mr 17,N 2 1852;Mr 15 1853-Mr 6 1855;My 27,Jl 29-Ag 12 1856;O 13 1857-O 16 1860[66]-[72-73]-Ja 1,D 31 1879-86;F 3, Ap 14,28,My 12,O 20 1887;Ja 12,26-F 2,Mr 15,Ap 12,Je 21 1888;Ap 27 1889;S 19,N 14-21 1890;S 4-11,O 2-9 1891;My 13-20,S 23 1892 [93-96]O 23 1897;Ap 28 1900;Ja 27 1911;Ja 4, N 11 1918;Je 10 1921
OHi O 30 1822;Jl 26 1823-O 1825;Mr 1827-Mr 1830;Ag 27 1840;N 14 1844;F 2 1889;Ap 22 1899-1900
OOxM Ap 1,29 1829;N 14 1832-[33]Ja 15,F 5 1834
WHi O 10 1821-Ja 1822;Ap 20 1826;Je 24 1829; Ap 1831-N 1837;41-Mr,N 3 1847[Mr 28 1849-D 20 1859]

Daily SCIOTO gazette. d D 1 1849-57||?
IU S 19-20,N 24 1851;Ja 6,F 2,21,D 21 1852; Mr 10,O 31,D 31 1853;Ja 17,23-24,F 9,15,Mr 8-9,11 1854;Ja 15 1855
MWA S 15 1851;Ja 5-13,16-19,27-29,F 2-3,11, 14,17-18,21,Je 29,Ag 26,D 4,18,29 1852;Mr 2, 8,10,15,18,23,26,S 7,24 1853;My 22,Je 26,Ag 16,O 14 1854
NN 1849-F 1854
OClWHi 1849-O 12 1857
WHi D 21 1849-[56-S 28 1857]

SCIOTO gazette. d N 28 1892+
1892-99? as Daily gazette
My 21 1903 is centennial ed
IU N 28 1892;Mr 20-21,23-24,27-29,Ap 24,27, My 2-3,9,11,15-16,22,24,26,Je 1,Ag 17 1893
OClWHi 1893;Mr 30 1909;N 28 1913;O 31 1916; O 17 1917;My 21-23,Jl 3,5,8 1918;Ja 1920
OHi Ja 1,5 1901;My 21 1903;Ap 1914-F 1916; Jl-N 1919;Ja-Ap 1920

SCIOTO VALLEY post. w 1872-Jl 1876||
OClWHi 1873-Jl 14 1876

SHARP stick. w 1844||?
IU S 14,O 4 1844
OClWHi S 1 1844

STAR of liberty. w S 12 1834-
OClWHi S 12 1834
WHi S 17-O 4 1834

***SUPPORTER.** w O 6 1808-F 14 1821||?
United with Scioto gazette to form Supporter and Scioto gazette, later Scioto gazette

SUPPORTER and Scioto gazette. *See* Scioto gazette

Chillicothe TIMES. *See* Chillicothe advertiser

TRUE democrat. w Ag 2 1843-Jl 30 1845||
IU Je 5-19,S 11,O 23 1844
OClWHi 1843-Jl 1845
OHi Ja 8 1845

CHIPPEWA LAKE

Chippewa CROAKER. w Je 18 1886-
OClWHi Je-Jl 2,16,30 1886

CINCINNATI

ABEND post. d 1877-80||?
In German
OC Mr 1877-80

Tägliche ABEND-PRESSE. d 1877-1919||?
In German
OHi Ja 1 1901[19]
—morning ed *See* Cincinnatier freie presse

ADVERTISER. 1846 *See* Cist's advertiser

***ADVERTISER and journal.** w,sw,d Je 23 1818-Ap 1 1841||
Je-Jl 1818 as Inquisitor and Cincinnati advertiser; Ag 4 1818-22? Cincinnati inquisitor advertiser; 1823-D 12 1829 Cincinnati advertiser; D 19 1829-S 28 1838 Cincinnati advertiser and Ohio phoenix; O 1838?-Ap 13? 1839 Daily advertiser and journal. Followed by Daily Cincinnati enquirer, later Cincinnati enquirer
w 1818-22; sw 1823-S 28 1838
Ct O 15 1828
DLC Jl 31,S 4-18,O 2 1824;Je 8 1825;Je 28 1826;Ja 3,Je 6 1829-30;33-39
IU S 30 1840
InRE Ag 3-6 1836
MWA D 30 1826;F 24 1827
N Jl 13 1825
NNHi Je 25-Jl 5,30-Ag 9,S 3-13,O 8-11,29-N 1,D 10-20 1828;F 4-7,18-21,Mr 17-Ap 4,22-My 2,27-30,Je 17-20,Jl 8-18,Ag 19-22,S 16-19,30-O,N 18-21,D 9-12,23-26 1829;F 3-6,17-20,My 1 1830
OC 1826;Ag 22[O-D]1827
OCHi D 1821-25;Ag 1-4,29,S 15,22,29,O 10,N 3 1827;28-Ap 12 1837;N 5 1838;31-41
OClWHi N 26 1834;Ag 1 1836
OHi 1821-Ap 2 1822;23-F 18 1826
TxU Ap 12-O 4 1838;Ja 22 1840-Mr 1841
—campaign ed *See* Friend of reform. . .

Cincinnati ADVERTISER and western journal. tw 1838-41||?
IU Jl 22 1840
OCHi D 23 1840
OClWHi F 19,Je 24 1840

Cincinnati AMERICAN. sw F 22 1830-32||
CSmH Ag 23 1830
IU Mr 8,Ag 23 1830
MWA 1830;Mr 27 1832
OC 1830-F 21 1831
OCHi F-D 16 1830;31-Ja 27,F 3,Mr-Ap 10 1832
WHi My,Je 10,17,24-Jl 1,N 11-D 2,9-30 1830

Cincinnati AMERICAN (for the country). w F 25 1830-32||
DLC N 22 1830
IU F-Mr 4,18-25,Ap 8-15,29-Je,Jl 15-22,Ag 5, 19,30,S 13-O 18,N,D 13,27 1830-Ja 10,24-31,F 14-21,Mr 5-12,Ap 2-23,My 28-Ag 6,20,O 1,22-29,D 24 1831;Ja 7,21-28,Ap 7-21,My 4 1832
MWA Je 4 1831;F 4 1832

Cincinnati AMERICAN. d O 24 1912-13||?
OC O-D 1913
OCHi O-N 2 1912;My 8-10,14-27,29-Je 1,3 1913

AMERICAN republic. w S? 1863-
MWA D 6 1863
WHi Mr 20 1864

AMERICAN republican bulletin. d 1842?-
MWA D 10,17 1844

Cincinnati ANZEIGER. w 1880-1901||?
In German
IU My 31 1895
OC 1881-1901
OHi Ja 1 1901
WHi D 16 1900;F 18,Mr 3,Ap 2-8 1901

Die ARBEITER von Ohio. w
In German
NN F 24-Mr 3 1877

ARTIST and artisan daily. d O 7 1845-
OClWHi O 7-18 1845

Daily Cincinnati ATLAS. d N 1 1843-
O 1849?-50? as Daily chronicle and atlas (other variations slight)
CP Ja-Je 1849
DLC 1843-My 4 1844
IU O 11 1845
InRE N 11 1844
MWA D 25 1844;Mr 13 1847;S 9 1852
NN 1843-My 1844
NNHi D 3 1844
OC 1843-D 15 1846;Jl 1848-Je 1849;Ja-D 3 1850;Ja-Je 30 1854
OCHi N 3 1843-My 4 1844;My-O 1845
OHi Jl 2 1847-Je 12 1848

Weekly Cincinnati ATLAS. w Ja 1844?-
Title varies slightly
KyLoF Ap 19 1847
MWA O 3,31,N 14 1844;Ja 22,F 12-19,Mr 12, Ap 2,16,My 21,Ag 6,O 8 1846
WHi S 11 1851;Ap 29,N 11-18 1852

BANNER of reunion. w Jl 4 1861-
NNHi Jl 4 1861

BROWNLOW'S Knoxville whig. [Cincinnati ed] w
DLC Ja 30-F 13,My 21-Je 1864

Cincinnati morning BULLETIN. d Ag? 1844-
MWA Ag 30 1844

CAMPAIGN and tariff advocate. w My 11-1844||?
MiU My 15 1844

CAMPAIGN gazette. w Ag 27- 1868||?
OHi Ag 27 1868

CAMPAIGN times. S 20- 1855||?
OClWHi S 20 1855

Cincinnati CAMPAIGNER. w Je 24-S 30 1848||?
OClWHi Jl-S 30 1848
OHi S 30 1848

CHILD'S newspaper. sw Ja 7 1834-
OClWHi Ja-S 2 1834

Cincinnati CHRONICLE. w S 24? 1836-49||?
1836-Ap 1? 1837 as Cincinnati chronicle and literary gazette. Merged with Cincinnati atlas
DLC O 1839-S 1840;N 20-D 1841[42]
IU Jl 4,25-Ag 1,15-O 3,17-31,N 28,D 12,26 1840;Ja 16-F 6,20-Mr 13,My 22-29,Je 12-S,O 9,23,N 6-13,27-D 4,25 1841-Ja,F 12-Ap,My 14-Je 4,18-Jl 2 1842

OHIO (*Continued*)

CINCINNATI—*Continued*

Cincinnati CHRONICLE. w 1836-49||?—*Cont.*
MWA D 12 1840[41]-Ja,F 19,Ap 23 1842;D 23 1843;Ag 31 1844
N Mr 14 1840
NNHi My 14-Ag 1847
OC D 17 1836-Ap 1,22 1837-S 1842
OCHi O 1837-S 1839
OClWHi F 20,Mr 20,D 3 1836;F 11 1837
TxU [F 25-S 1837]38-S 1839
WHi S 24 1836-S 1839[Ap 17 1846-Jl 12 1849]

Daily Cincinnati CHRONICLE. d N 28 1839-S 1849||?
1839-O 5 1840 as Daily chronicle. United with Daily Cincinnati atlas to form Daily chronicle and atlas, later Daily Cincinnati atlas
CP Je-N 1841
DLC N 28 1839;N 30 1840;Je-N 1843;D 13 1844;Ap 18-Je 21 1849
IU 1839-My 1840;S 7 1841
NN Je-N 1840;Je 1842-My 1844;48-Je 1849
OC 1839-My 1844;47-My,Jl 1848-Je 30 1849
OCHi 1839-My 1844;F 22 1845-46
OHi 1839-N 1840;Je-N 1841;Je-N 1842;Je 1843-My 14,Jl 29 1848-S 28 1849
TxU D 3 1839-O 6 1843;Ja-My 1844

Cincinnati daily CHRONICLE. d Mr 9 1868-Ap 29 1871||
1868-N 30 1869 as Cincinnati evening chronicle. United with Cincinnati times to form Cincinnati times and chronicle, later Cincinnati times-star
DLC Je 1869-71
MH 1869
MWA D 28 1868;O 19,30 1869
OC Mr 10 1868-71
OCHi complete
OClWHi N 29 1870
OHi Ap 2 1870
OOxM N 5 1868;Ja 15,N 25 1869;Ag 13,N 21 1870
TxU 1868
WHi My 11 1869;S 6 1870

Cincinnati weekly CHRONICLE. w Mr 18 1868-71||?
United with Cincinnati weekly times to form Cincinnati times-chronicle, later Cincinnati times-star
OC 1869
WHi Mr 18 1868

Daily CHRONICLE and atlas. *See* Daily Cincinnati atlas

Cincinnati CHRONICLE and literary gazette. w D 30 1826-Ap? 1835||
1826-N 1827 as Saturday evening chronicle; N 1827-28 Saturday evening chronicle of general literature, morals and the arts. Merged with Cincinnati mirror (not in this list)
CSmH My 15 1830
Ct [1828]Ja 3 1829[31-32;34-35]
DLC D 21 1833
ICN 1830
ICU F 17-Ap 7,21-28,My 19,N 15 1827;F 16,N 15,D 27 1828;Jl 18,O 24 1829
IU Ap 7,28,Ag 18 1827;My 17-Je 7,Jl 12-Ag 9,30,O 4 1828
InVi 1826-D 29 1827;Ja-Jl 5 1828
MWA Jl 14,D 1,22 1827;Je 7,Ag 23 1828;Mr 14 1829;Jl 17 1830;F 26,D 10 1831;32
NN Ag 22 1829
NNHi 1830
OC 1828-30
OCHi 1826-Ap 11 1835
OClWHi F 14,Mr 21,My 9,Je 7 1829
OHi My 1827-Mr 1835
OOxM F 21 1829[Ja-Je 1833]
TxU 1827-33
WHi Ag 18 1827-28;S 19-26,O 24-31 1829;Je 19-26,N 6-13 1830;Ja 15 1831-32

CIST'S weekly advertiser. w F 9 1844-Ap 29 1853||
F-S 1844 as Western general advertiser; O 1844-Mr 15? 1844 Cist's advertiser; Jl?-N 18? 1846 Weekly advertiser
CtY Ja 8 1845-Je 1846;My 17 1847-51
DLC Ap 9 1845-Je 1846
ICU Ja 14-Je 1846;Mr 22 1847-F 1850
IU 1845-Ja 15,F 5,19-Je 1846;My 1847-F 1850;Mr 13-F 6 1852
In Mr 1847-53
InU Ap 12 1847-Ja 21 1852
MB [Ap 11 1845-53]
MWA D 1844-Ja 22,Jl 30,D 17 1845-[Ja-Jl 1846;Ap 12-Je 22 1847]-F 1850;Jl 11 1851;F 13 1852-53
MiU-C [1847-48]
NBHi 1847-53
NN F 19 1845-Je 1846;Mr 22 1847-Mr 14 1848;Mr 13 1850-F 6 1852
NbHi Ap 5-19,My 3-17,Je 1,22-Ag 24,S 21-O 19,N 9-16,D 1847;Ja 11-18,F 15-22,Mr 14-Ap 4,My 2,Je 7 1848
OC Ja 29 1845-Je 1846;Mr 29 1847-53
OCHi F 16-Ap,D 18 1844-Je 1846;Mr 22 1847-F 1850
OCU F 19 1845-Ja 14 1846;Ap 12-19,Je-Jl 6,20-27,Ag 10,31-S 14,N 16,30,D 14 1847-Ja 4,18 1848;Ja 31-Mr 14 1849
OClWHi Ja 29 1845
OHi D 18 1844-Ja 21 1853
TxU My 24 1844-Je 1846;Mr 21 1848-53
WHi Ag 21-Je 1846;Mr 22 1847-53

CIST'S daily advertiser. d Je 22? 1846-53||?
1846? as Morning advertiser
DLC Jl 1,9,11,18,20,Ag 3-5,11,14,27 1846
IU Jl 24 1846
MWA Jl 1,O 29,D 13 1846;Mr 29,Ap 13,D 10 1847;Ja 31-F 1 1848
MiU-C Ap 6,10 1848
OClWHi D 6-9 1847;D 10 1852-F 25 1853
TxU Mr 16 1847-Ap 15 1848

CITIZEN. w Jl 5 1851-
DLC Jl 12 1851
MWA Ag 23 1852

Daily evening CITIZEN. d 1852-
MWA Ag 25 1852

Daily CLAY champion. d S 3- 1844||
DLC S 6 1844
MoSM S 3 1844

COLORED citizen. w 1863-69||?
Negro
MWA My 19 1866

Cincinnati daily COLUMBIAN. d 1853-
1853-Jl 1855? as Columbian and great west
IU S 8 1854
OC Je 19 1854-Je 28 1855;Jl 21-S 10 1856
OHi Ap 16-Je 12 1856
WHi Jl 22,Ag 3-4 1854

COLUMBIAN. w *See* Dollar weekly Columbian

Cincinnati COMMERCIAL. d *See* Commercial tribune

Cincinnati weekly COMMERCIAL. w S 1845-82||?
1845-62 as Dollar weekly commercial
ICU Je 5 1867
IHi Ap 3 1862
InNcHi N 3 1875
KHi O 28 1874
KyLo Ap 15 1868-Ap 17 1872
MWA Mr 27,Je 12 1851;F 5 1852;N 15 1855
OC 1868-N 1869;70
OCHi Mr 1846-Ag 1862;63-70;72
OClWHi My 29 1862;O 3 1877;N 10 1880
OHi Mr 27 1851;Mr 29 1860;Ag 1 1861;F 26,Ap 23,My 27 1863[65]Je 19 1867
OOxM Jl 9 1868
Tx S 24 1846-S 13 1848;Ap 24 1851-Ap 15 1852

COMMERCIAL daily advertiser. *See* Cincinnati daily whig

Cincinnati COMMERCIAL gazette. *See* Commercial tribune

Cincinnati COMMERCIAL herald. w Mr 14? 1843-
DLC Mr 28 1843

Cincinnati COMMERCIAL register. d D 30 1825-Je 1833||?
United with National republican and Cincinnati mercantile advertiser to form Daily Cincinnati republican and commercial register, later Daily Cincinnati republican
Suspended from Je 1826?-28
MWA Ja 23 1827
OCHi 1825-My 20 1826

COMMERCIAL tribune. d O 2 1843-D 3 1930||
1843-Ja 3 1883 as Cincinnati commercial (title varies slightly) Ja 4 1883-Je 15 1896 Cincinnati commercial gazette; Je 16 1896-F 13 1898 Cincinnati commercial tribune. Merged with Cincinnati enquirer
A Jl 1886-88;Ap-O 1892;Ja-Ag,N 1893-Je 1894
ArHi Je 18 1864
CtY D 21 1860;Mr 2 1863-Je 15 1896
DLC Ag 4-D 1845;My 11-D 1846;F 26 1847;Mr 14 1849;61-1930
IC D 5 1860-62;64;Ja-Je 1873;My 1 1889
ICHi Ja 5 1841;N 8,12 1861;Ja 27-Ag 20,N 6,22 1862;Ja 6 1863;Je 13 1864[Mr-N 1865]Ja 4-5,D 20 1883;My 28 1884
ICM S 9 1876;F 18,Je 22 1880;My 23,D 23 1882;Mr 20,Ag 7 1887
ICN O 23 1865-86
ICU O,N 16,D 4 1843-S 1844;N 1849-Ap 6 1850;Ap 22 1851-D 2 1854;S 1855-Ap,O 1870-Mr,Jl-D 1871;Ap-Je 1872;73-S 1874;O-D 1876;F-Mr,N 13,20,D 12 1879;80;Jl 1881-Mr 1882;Ap 1885-Je,O 1888-Je 1890;94-S 1903;04-O 1913;14-Je,O 1916
IU F 16 1847;Ja 9,Jl 3,7,10,18,21-22-25,29,31,Ag 15 1857;Je 4 1858[Ap 5 1860-D 6 1861]-[63]-[65]-67;My 23 1869;Ja 5,Ap 1870-Je,O 1877-79;Ja 3-4 1883
In Ja-N 1858;60-61;63-Mr 1874
InI [Ag 1858-Je 1865;66]-[68;70-72]Jl-S 1877
InLHi Ap 25 1866
InNcHi Je 16 1895
InRE D 5-6 1835;My 1878
InU [1849-50;58-My 1860]Jl 1862-64;O 23 1865-[66-72;76;78]79[82-84]1921;23-27
KHi Jl 4 1876[80-Ja 1 1893]extra Je 26 1880
KyLo Ja-S 1867
MBAt [1863]65-66;68-76
MH My 5 1860;Ap 25,My 1,S 24 1862;64-65
MWA Mr 17-Ag 16 1845;F 16 1846-O 15 1847;Ap 1848-Ap 6 1850;O 15 1852;O 13,30,N 16,D 30 1857;F 15,Ag 19,S 12,N 22-24 1859;Je-N 1860[F 13-D 1861]62[Ja 8-My]Jl 1863-65;Ap 1866-Je,O 1872-Ap,D 2 1873;Ap 5,S 2,D 4 1875;Mr 24,Ap 16,Je 30,S 20,N 21 1876;S 30 1877;My 16 1878;F 5 1879-Je 1896;98
MiU-C [1862;67]
MnHi N 4 1863
MnU 1861-Mr,My 1867-Ag 1870;71-78
MoS S 1861
N F 16 1860;N 7 1861;O 6,D 14 1863;Ja 29 1864;Jl 1,S 25 1865;F 18 1868;Ag 19 1871
NN Ap 12-D 1861;Jl 1862-S,N-D 1865
NcD Ap 20,S 17 1861;S 18 1862;Mr 6 1865;N 19 1869;F 14 1870;Ap 26 1871;F 6 1878;Ja 14,Mr 7,Ap 30 1888;Ja 17,19,28,F 2,13,Mr 30,Ap 27 1889
NjP [Ap 19 1861-Ap 1865]
NjWdHi D 5 1865
OC Ja 5-Ag 4 1852;58-1930
OCHi 1843-S 28 1844;F 11 1845-S 1874;75-1930
OCl Je 13 1871-N 21 1881
OClWHi Ag 7 1858;My 19,Ag 28,N 23 1859;Ap 12,My 18,Ag 13,27,30,N 6 1860;61-63;Jl 1864-65;Ja 27,Je 18-Jl 1866;Jl 4,D 4 1867;Mr 18,25,Ap 8 1868;My 1869-Ap 25,My 19 1870;Jl 25 1873;Ag 18,26,N 23 1875;Je 14,Jl 4 1876;Mr 2 1877;S 29-O 26 1878;Mr 23,D 11-12,21 1879;Je 21 1880;Ag 5,S 25,27 1881;Ja 21,29,F 7,My 27 1882;D 27 1884;My 16-18 1885;F 16,My 15,O 17 1886;Mr 12 1887;Ap 8-9,My 1-2,Je 16 1889;S 20 1890;Ja 12,N 24 1891;Je 12 1892;My 18,Je 18,1893;Ag 18 1894;Ja 16,S 5-10 1898;Mr 18 1899;Jl 1 1900
ODa O 1862-Mr,Jl-D 1863;S-D 1866;Ja 18-S 28 1881
ODW My 1860-My 23 1861
OHi Ap 28-Ag 16 1845;Jl-N 9 1850;Mr 4 1851-F 19 1852;Ag 12 1854-55;Jl 1856-Je 1872;73-1930
OMM Ap 8 1858;Jl 16,S 14(supp),O 3,8,N 16 [D 1860-61]F 7,24,Mr 10,12,29,Ap 15,Je 14,O 17,N 13,28 1862;F 4,Mr 3,My 1,15,S 8-9,O 23,N 10,18,D 7 1863;Mr 5,14,16,Je 24 1864[N 1880;Je 1881;83]Mr 4-Ap 20 1884;Je 2-19,S 12-25 1885[86;93-94;Mr 19-Ap 1,My 2-S 1895 [96-Je 6 1899]
OOxM N 12,D 11,13-14,17 1850;Ja 3,23,F 6,8 [Ag]1851;Je 27 1864;Ap 12,15 1865;Ap 25,Jl 3 1866;67-F 1888
P My 10 1880-1917
PAg O 1861-S 1862
PBf [Ag-O 1863]
PPiHi Jl 4 1861;Ag 9 1885
THi Jl 9 1863
TKL Ja 6 1865
TU Mr 27-28 1855;Ap 20 1865
TxU O 4 1849-Ap 6 1850;Ap 14 1851-Ja 1854;O 5 1855-Je 1856;Jl 1857-83
WHi N 7 1856;O 27 1858;D 11 1860-Ja 12,Ap 6,15,19,Ag 19 1861-Ag 3-1878;79;S 7-D 1880;F 2-Ag 1881;Jl-D 1882;Ap 1884-N 4 1885;86;Ja-Ap 1888;90-91;94-O 2 1895;F 6-Je 9 1896
—w,sw ed *See* Cincinnati weekly commercial; Cincinnati gazette

COMMONER. w S 26 1865-S 7 1872||
1865-S 12 1868 as Cincinnati west and south
DLC S 21 1867-68;S 17 1870-72
NcD D 18 1865
OC 1865-Je 6 1869
OCHi S 21 1867-S 11 1869
OOxM F 19,O 1,N 12-19,D 8-10,31 1866[67-S 12 1868]
WHi S 21 1867-S 12 1868

COON-SKINNER. w? 1842||?
Campaign paper
CU O 18 1842

Cincinnati daily COURIER. d 1860?-
DLC D 30 1860

Täglicher Cincinnati COURIER. d 1869?-74||?
In German
OC 1871-Mr 1874

DAY star. w 1841?-
InU [1843-46]
OClWHi F 18 1845-46

Cincinnati DEMOCRATIC intelligencer and commercial advertiser. *See* Cincinnati daily whig

DEMOCRATIC standard and whig of '76. w Mr 20- 1846||?
OClWHi Mr-N 10 1846

DEMOKRATISCHES-tageblatt. d 1849-
In German
DLC Ja 28 1851-52
MWA S 14 1852
OClWHi My 3 1851;Ja 1-10,Ap 1,My 13-D 1852

DEMOKRATISCHES wochenblatt. w My 1850?-
In German
DLC My 1 1851

Der DEUTSCHE beobachter. w
In German
KHi Je 20 1888-Ja 1889

Der DEUTSCHE Franklin. w 1834?-
In German
DLC My 30 1835

Der DEUTSCHE patriot. w
In German
P-M O 12 1832

Der DEUTSCHE republicaner. *See* Cincinnati republicaner

DEUTSCH-UNGARISCHER bote. w 1905-18||?
In German
IU Ja-My 23 1918

DISPATCH and democratic union. d Je 1848-
1848-S 2 1850 as Cincinnati daily dispatch
DLC Je 27 1848
IU O 1 1849
OCHi Jl 21-N 2 1850
OClWHi Jl 20 1850
OHi Jl 29 1848
OOxM [Je-D 1848]-Je 4 1849
—w ed *See* Dollar weekly dispatch and democratic union

DOLLAR. w Jl 18 1878-
MWA Jl 18 1878

DOLLAR weekly Columbian. w 1846?-
1846?-F 1850 as Columbian; Mr 1850-Jl? 1855 Columbian and great west
DLC Je 1 1850;F 23 1856
IU [1854]Ja 7,Mr 3,My 5,Je 2,Jl 7,O 27,D 1 1855;Ja 5,Mr 8-Ap 5,My 10-17,Jl 5-19,Ag 2 1856
MWA O 20 1849;Mr 30 1850
OHi 1850-Ja 11 1851;My 1853-Ap 1855
PPL N 30-D 7 1850
WHi Ag 10 1850-F 5,19,Mr 12,O 2 1853;F 10 1855

DOLLAR weekly commercial. *See* Cincinnati weekly commercial

OHIO (*Continued*)

CINCINNATI—*Continued*

DOLLAR weekly dispatch and democratic union. w Ap 1848-
Ap-Jl? 1848 as Saturday evening news and dollar weekly dispatch; Ag? 1848-S 1850? Dollar weekly dispatch
DLC N-D 7 1848;Ag 1 1850
MWA Je 24 1848
NbHi Ap 8-My 6,20-27,Jl 8-15 1848
OCHi Ag 1-8,29-S 26,O 10-31 1850
—d ed *See* Dispatch and democratic union

DOLLAR weekly message. *See* Weekly message

DOLLAR weekly nonpareil. w 1849?-
MWA D 23 1852
OCHi Mr 25-Ag 1852
—d ed *See* Cincinnati daily nonpareil

DOLLAR weekly times. *See* Cincinnati weekly times

ELEVATOR. w N 20 1841-
OHi N 27 1841-Ap 23 1842

EMANCIPATOR. w F 24 1877-
OCHi Mr 24-31,Je 30,Jl 21-Ag 4 1877

Cincinnati EMPORIUM. w F 12 1824-29‖?
United with National crisis to form National crisis and Cincinnati emporium
DLC Mr 1824-Ag 1826
MWA [Mr 1824-Ap 1826]
NcD D 23 1824
OC Ag 10-17,31 1826
OCHi F 19 1824-F 3 1825
OMM O 21,D 9 1824;O 13 1825;Jl 20-27 1826
OOxM Je 22 1829
WHi 1824-F 3 1825

Cincinnati ENQUIRER. d Ap 10 1841+
Follows Advertiser and journal; N 27 1843-My 25 1844 Enquirer and message; My 27 1844-Ja 18? 1845 Daily enquirer and message (other variations slight)
pub 1865+
A O 15 1877-85;Ap 1886-Je,S 1898-1902
C F 4 1887-89;Jl-D 1890
CLM D 29 1878
CtW My 9 1893
DA [F 1921-Jl 11 1923]
DLC [S-D 1844]-[46]Ja 15 1847-49;Ja-S 23 1851;My 9 1852-Je 1854;55-Ag 1856;N 5 1858; D 1869+
ICHi Je 9-10,Jl 2,S 1,N 14,21 1861;F 13,17,29, Mr 3,9,16,20,22-24,Ap 5-6,8,12,19,21,My 15-16, 23,25,N 21 1865
ICM Ag 14 1877;Je 20-21 1880;Ja 22,My 23 1882;Je 20 1883;F 21 1885
ICU [1861]-[64]-[69]-72;S 1873-S 1876[77-79] Je 19,21-25,O 26,N 3 1880;S 19-20 1881;Je 22 1892;Jl-Ag 1896;1903-My 1908;17-N 1929;Ja-Ap 1930;Ja-Jl 1931
IHi Jl 10,28 1896
IU S 6 1841;Ag 12 1848;Je 10,Jl 26,Ag 7-8,14, 26,S 12,20,22,30,O 2-3,N 13 1863;F 5,Je 1,3, 16-17,Ag 12,16,31,S 2-3,9,11,18,28,O 1,14,26,N 2 1864;My 27 1865;Ap 15-28,My 6,31,Jl 17,S 12,14 1866;S 20,O 21 1869;Ap 18 1871;Ag 9 1885;Je 26 1896;Ag 6 1909;O 17 1913;N 16-18 1915
IaK S 1852-Mr 12 1853
In My 1856-Mr 1874
InI D 29 1841
InTI [Ag 1863-F 1866]
KHi [Je 1880-Ag 1890]
KyU Ap 10 1841
LNH Ap 13,22-23,My 8,10-13,26-28 1864
MBAt Ap 17-19 1865
MWA Ap 10(facsimile)1841;D 7 1852;S 11 1859;Ja 4,22,F 5,Mr 5,Ap 8,11,S 23,O 9 1862; F 5,Mr 18,25,My 1,30,S 26 1863;Ja 13 1866; Ap 14 1869;N 21 1876;Ja 27 1877;N 4 1880; Ag 1 1898;O 4 1902;S 9 1917-21
MnU My 1918-Mr,Je 2 1919-Mr,N 1920-Ap,Jl-N 1921
MoS Ag-S 1861
N Ja 23,N 1 1864
NcD [1861-66;70;78;83;88]
NcU Ap-Je 1877
NjR O 11 1867
OAU 1862
OC Ap 10 1841(facsimile)S 16 1852-My 22 1853;54;Jl 1855-Jl 20,S 11-D 1856;Ap 28 1857-Jl 1858;59-65;69+
OCHi 1841-1921
OCU 1924+
OCl Ap 10 1841
OClWHi F 24 1842;Ja 10 1843;F 15 1844;S 25-26 1845;My 27,Je 24 1848;Je 30 1849;Je 19, Jl 23 1851;Mr 8-D 1853;S 8 1857;O 26 1860; Ja 1,Ap 11,Je 25,Jl 23-O 1862;Ja-O 24 1863; Jl 22 1865;Ja 17,N 6 1876;O 10 1877;Mr 2 1878;Ja 9,F 8,Jl 12,S 7,11-12 1879;Je 22,24 1880;Jl 9-S 27 1881;D 2 1882;Ja 9,21,Ap 6,Je 23 1883;Jl 22 1887;Je 26 1888;Mr 5,Je 2,11 1889;Ja 11 1892;Jl 10 1896;S 5-10 1898;Ag 29, 31 1899;Je 14 1900;S 7 1901
ODW D 11 1844-Ap 1 1846;Ap 2-Ag 1847;My 26-S 15 1852;Ja-Ap 26 1857;Ag-D 1858;Mr 2 1861-65;Je 2 1889;Je 1933+
OHi N 29 1846-N 25 1851;S 13 1856;59-62;Jl 1863+
OOxM Ag 12-15,17-22,24,26,28-29 1851;My 7 1853;Ap 30,My 7 1865;Ja 15,N 5,D 30 1869; Ja 7 1870;Ja 2,Ag 1,S 11,O 6-8,10-13 1871;F 7,21-22,O 6 1872;Ja 1,Mr 19,Je 1873-F 1888; Ap 1931+
OXG D 1932+
P My 17-Je 26 1880
Tx [Je 21-N 15 1862]Ag 14 1863;Ja 14,26 1864: Je 18 1866;Mr 20 1867;D 4 1868;Ja 6,S 28,D 8 1870;F 1,24,Ag 9 1871;Ap 24,D 23 1872;Mr 22 1873
TxGR My 27 1928
TxU Ap 1846-Mr 1847
WHi Ag 12,28 1862;My 30,Je 9 1863;Ap 30,Ag 11,S 8 1865;D 29 1885;1915-Mr 1919

Cincinnati weekly ENQUIRER. w Ap? 1841-1921‖?
N 1843-Ja 1845? Enquirer and message (other variations slight)
CoU 1905-Ag 1907
DA 1914-Ja 5 1921
DLC My 8,Jl 10,D 11 1844;S 24 1846;Ap 15-My 20,Je 3-10 1847;Ja 20 1848
ICU D 18 1861;F 12 1862
IU Jl 28,Ag 11,25-31,S 29,D 8-15 1841;Ja 26-F 9,23-Mr 2,30-Ap 6,27,Je 1,15,O 8,D 21-28 1842;Mr 8-15,Ag 2,S 6,20,O 4,N 1,21,22(extra),29,D 6 1843;F 14-21,Mr 6 1844;Mr 6,Ap 3 1861;O 22,N 5 1862;O 5 1864;S 10,O 15,N 26 1866;Jl 15,Ag 12-S 16,30,O 14-21,N 25 1897; F 10-My 19,Je 9 1898;Ag 28 1902
IaHi Mr 1879-Mr 3 1880;F 1896-F 1897
InMovHi 1882
InNcHi N 27 1878
KHi O 17 1883;N 10 1904;N 15 1906
KyU Jl 5 1882
MWA D 23 1852;N 19 1857;F 19,Mr 19,Je 2, Ag 18,S 3,O 15,N 5-12 1862;Ja 14,Ap 15,My 20-27 1863
MnHi D 9 1844
NbHi F 20 1861;F 4 1863;Ja 5 1876;Ap 18,O 24 1877;F 7 1891;O 22 1896
NcD [1861-62;68-69;79-80;84;88]
NcU S 15(supp)1886
NhD N 13 1844
OC Mr 25 1858;D 4 1867
OCHi Ag 13 1845-[S-O 1851]Ja-S 2 1852;Ja 1 1873
OClWHi Jl 6 1842;F 29 1843;Ap 28,My 19 1859;F 12-D 10 1862;Ja 28-F 4,18,Ap 1,O 7 1863;Ap 29,Je 3,18 1868
OHi My 17 1859;Ja 19,Ag 1 1860[S 12 1866-S 1867]S 18 1872[82-83]O 8 1896;Ja 3 1901
TU-J My 28 1879
Tx Jl 30 1846
TxU [Ag 20 1852-54]Mr 21 1866-O 16 1867
VU Ag 14,D 4 1867;Mr 11,Ap 8,My 27 1868;F 3,Ap 7,D 15-29 1869[70-76]-Jl 1878[80-85]
VtBr Jl 16 1857
WHi O 19 1854;Mr 2 1864;N 15 1865
WaPS [1916]S 25 1917

Cincinnati daily EXPRESS. d
NNHi Je 27-D 1831
OCHi Mr 3 1838

Daily FOCUS. d Mr 1 1841-
DLC Mr 1 1841

Wecli FONETIC advocat. w 1848?-
Ct F 5 1853
MWA Ag 2,S 27 1851;Je 26 1852

FREE nation. w F 2 1861-
DLC D 7 1861
MWA F 9,D 7 1861
NcD D 7 1861

FREEMAN. d Mr 12 1856-
OCHi Mr 12,14,18-19,22,Ap 1 1856

Cincinnatier FREIE PRESSE. d 1874+
In German
IU Ja 18 1906;F 16 1907
OC Ag 1874-1918
OHi Ja 2 1901;Ag 24 1918-N 5 1920

Der FREISINNIGE. w 1842-
OCHi Jl 18 1844

FRIEND of reform and corruption's adversary. w? 1828‖
Campaign paper
T Mr 22-O 22 1828
—d ed *See* Advertiser and journal

***Cincinnati GAZETTE.** w,sw D 4 1804-1913‖?
1804-Ap 6 1809 as Liberty hall and Cincinnati mercury; Ap 13 1809-D 4 1815 Liberty hall; D 11 1815-O 1857? Liberty hall and Cincinnati gazette (title varies slightly)
sw Mr 9 1819-Je 15 1827;90?
CSmH Ap 15 1825;Ag 29,O 27 1826
DLC 1821-My 22,Je 1-22 1827;Ap 12 1832;F 4, Je 16,30,Jl 7,Ag 11-S 15,29 1836;Ag 24 1837; Je 6,20-27 1839;Ap 23 1840;Ap 30 1857;Mr 19 1862;Ap 27 1864
ICN Ag-D 1863
ICU Mr 24 1821;N 17 1826;Ja 30,Ap 27 1827 [36]-[41]-Ag 21 1845
IU S 8 1821-F,Ap 18 1823-My 22 1827;F 14 1828;N 28 1850;78-81
In Jl 1841-F 1844;F 1850-O 1856;Ag 1858-72
InI Ja 8 1835
InNcHi Ja 28 1847;N 15 1849;Ja 19 1854
InRE O 26 1837;Ja 4 1838;Ja 10 1839;Ag 13 1840;D 1 1857
MWA 1821-22;Ag 1-8 1823;Ja 16 1824;Mr 25, Je 14,Jl 19 1825;Je 5 1831;O 22 1840;Mr 25 1841;Mr 30,Je 14 1849;Mr 20 1851;Jl 22 1852; Je 11,O 8 1857;Mr 29,Ag 16 1860;62-63;65-66; 68-70;72-73;75
MiU-C S 30 1863
MnHi Ap-My 3 1865;D 5 1866[70]
N D 27 1822
NN O 6(supp)1826;Ja 30,S 24 1840;Ja 5 1881
NNHi Mr 23 1827;Ja 19,F 9,23 1827;Jl 26 1838; O 31 1839;Ja 9,My 14,Jl 9,S 24,O 8 1840-F 4 1861;F 2 1860;Ja 28-F 2 1870;Mr 14 1873
NcD [My 1838-Ap 1839]Je 21 1865
OC 1821-My 14 1824;D 1826-29;Jl 1835-37;F 11 1841;Mr 30 1848-51;F 12-D 1873;75;78-81
OCHi Jl 21 1821-25;Mr 24 1826-Ja 15,F 26[Ap 1829-Je 3]S 1830-S 1833;My 15 1834-Mr 22, My 24 1838-Je 21 1855;57-77;82;Ja,Ap 26,My 31,Jl 1893-95;1911-12
OClWHi O 15 1824;26-27;D 19 1833-37;D 5 1844;My 5 1845;Ja 29,Mr 19,N 5 1846;Ap 15 1852;Je 26 1861;F 24 1864;Ap 30,My 14-28 1879;S 21 1881;F 15 1882;Ap 4,Ag 22 1883
ODa 1825;S 10-D 24 1827;Je 27-D 24 1828;S 27 1830-Je 1831;Ja-Je 1834;Jl 1838-Je 1839;41; Je 27-D 1842;Je 26-D 1843;Je 26-D 1845;Ag 12 1861-Je 23 1862
OHi 1821-27;Mr 17 1830-O 18 1832;33;36-N 3 1837;Ap 2,10 1838;Ag 20 1840;Ag 11 1853;O 2 1856;Ap 23 1857;D 27 1860;Ag 26 1863;Jl 12 1865
OOxM S 17,D 3 1824;Mr 25,My 20,Je 10,Ag 5 1825;Jl 26 1827;Mr 27,Ap 10,My 1,O 2,N 7, 27-D 4,25 1828[29]O 20,D 1831-Ap 5 1832
PPiU-D My 9 1833
Tx N 27 1845
TxU Ja 2-N 20 1822;Ap 22 1852-Ap 14 1853
VU Ja 6 1874
WHi [F 18 1825-N 7 1826;S 17 1829-30]Ja 6 1842[Ja 11 1844-47]Mr 21-Ap 11 1850;Ag 4 1869
—d ed 1883-1913 *See* Commercial tribune

***Cincinnati gazette.** w Jl 15-D 1815‖
United with Liberty hall to form Liberty hall and Cincinnati gazette, later Cincinnati weekly gazette

Cincinnati daily GAZETTE. d Je 25 1827-Ja 3 1883‖
Title varies slightly. United with Cincinnati commercial to form Cincinnati commercial gazette, later Commercial tribune
CL Jl 19,31,Ag 16,N 16 1861;O 27 1863
CMlC D 2 1863
CPo D 4 1856
CSmH Ag 18-19 1830
CtY Ja 17-D 1863;D 7-13 1877
DLC D 27 1828-29;33-Je 1837;Mr-D 1841;O 28 1845;Mr 29 1849-52;62-65;F-N 3 1866;67-83
IC Jl 4 1864;F 5-Je 1873
ICHi [S 1864-N 1865] F 12 1868;
ICN Ag-D 1863;F-D 1873
ICU Ja-Je 1835;Ja-Je 1837;38-40;Ja-Je 1845; Ja-Je 1862;Jl-D 1863;66-Je 8,Ag 1866; Jl 1868-70;F 1873-75;Jl-D 1876
IHi My 21 1861;S 20 1881
IU N 3 1842;Ap 5,Ag 27,S 26,O 1-2,4,12,24,N 1,D 1,12,22,29 1860[61-62]Ja 5-6,8-9,14,20,Mr 25,My 11,18,Je 12,17,Jl 11,15,D 12 1863;Ja 14,Mr 12,Je 28-D 1864;Ap 30 1866;69;71;Jl 1872-F 4 1873;S 2 1878-Ap,S-D 1879;81
In D 1841-56;60-75
InI 1857;N 8 1858-59;Ja-Je 23 1861;62-63;Ap-Je 1876
InNcHi [1860]-[62]D 3 1873
InRE F 9 1858;Ap 10,15,19-20,28,Jl 1,6,Ag 1-2 1865
InTi [N 1861-F 1866]
InU 1849;Jl 1850-Mr,My 1876-83
N N 7 1861;Ap 25,My 8 1864
NEh Mr 4,Je 18 1840
NN Je 26 1828-29;S 27 1830-Mr 1831[Ja-Mr] Ap 3,Je 22-S 7 1838;Mr 1839-42;44-45;50-O 21 1854;Jl-N 1855;56-S 1859;60-Je 1864;65-S 1868;69-81
NNHi Je 5(extra)1857; Ap 28 1860;Jl 22 1862-Je 1867;S 4 1868;My 2 1873
NcD O 16 1840;S 6,9 1861
OC Je 26 1827-Je 25 1831;32-Je,Jl 21,27,D 5 1835;36-83
OCHi D 25 1827-83
OClWHi Ag 6 1828;F 21 1835;Je 16-S 28 1836; F 11 1839;D 11 1846;Je 30,Jl 11 1856; Ap 1861-Je 1865;Je 24-S 28 1867;F 3 1868;F 1869-My 1873;F 9 1874;Je 4, Ag 7,S 30-O 1 1875; Je 13,N 11 1876; F 17,Mr 10,S 24 1877;F-N 1878;S 27-O 1,N 10 1881;Ja 3 1883
OHi 1828-Je 12 1830;O 3 1833-83
OMM Jl 30 1861;N 30 1863-[Ja-Ag 1865]
OOxM D 29 1828-Je 25,D 28 1829-Je 25 1831; Ap 6 1832-O 2 1833 [Ja-My 1837] S 19-D 1838;O 29, D 6,14,23 1850 [51] O 28-29 1864; F 21,Ap 13-15 1865;Ap 28 1866;My 22 1868; Ap 13,Ag 9,N 2,5,D 9 1869; Je 30,D 28,31 1870;Ja 2,Je 30,Ag 1,10,O 4,6-7,10-13,N 22 1871;F 21-22,Mr 13,S 19,23,27 1872;Ja 1,3,F 24-25,Mr 18-19,My 10 1873-83
P My 12-Jl 2 1880
PHi Je 15 1861-Ap 26 1865
PPM 1837-My 1840;62-66;Jl-D 1867
TKL O 31 1864
TNV S 17 1867-68;70
TU Jl 17 1869
TxU D 28 1829-Je 24 1830;Je 27-D 1831;O 25 1833-51; Ja-S 11 1862;Jl 1863-76
WHi [Je 25 1857-D 27 1860]Ap 4,My 2,29-Ag 2,O 10 1861; S 25,D 19 1862;63-66;F 22,Ap 14,S 30,D 1876-Je 1877;Ja-Ap,S-D 1880

Cincinnati tri-weekly GAZETTE. tw
DLC My 11 1850;Ja 11,18 1851
IU D 30 1843
MWA O 14 1856
NN Jl 8 1854;Ap 14 1857

Cincinnati semi-weekly GAZETTE. sw 1865-82‖?
Title varies slightly
DLC O 8 1880
MWA O 5 1866;68-82
OCHi 1867-70
OClWHi Mr 10 1868
OMM Ag 3-10 1866
WHi Jl 1867-F 1878

Daily GAZETTE (for the country). tw
DLC Je 25 1827-28;Jl 22 1829;Ja 9,12,21 1830; Ja 15 1831;Ja 10 1832
MWA O 26/27 1827

Cincinnati weekly GLOBE. w D 16 1846-
1846-S 14 1848 as Cincinnati weekly herald (Mr 24 1847-Ja 12 1848 National press and Cincinnati weekly herald)
MWA O 18-N 1 1848
OCHi 1846-48
OHi 1847-48

Cincinnati weekly GLOBE. w 1881?-
OClWHi Ja-Ag 22 1883

GREAT west. w My 6 1848-F 1850‖
United with Columbian to form Columbian and great west, later Dollar weekly Columbian
IU My 6 1848
OHi 1850

HAMILTON county democrat.
OClWHi Je 15 1840

HAVERSACK. w O 11 1862-
OHi O 11,25 1862

OHIO (*Continued*)

CINCINNATI—*Continued*

Cincinnati HERALD. w Ap 13 1833-
OOxM Ap 27-My 11,Je 1,Jl 3 1833

Cincinnati morning HERALD. d Ag 29 1843-
DLC 1843-Ag 29 1844
IU S 14 1847
OC O 5 1843-Jl 1844;Ja-N 27 1845
OCHi Ag 30 1843-S 1 1845;46-My 1 1847
OClWHi F 28 1844;D 17,22 1847;Ja 4 1848
VtBr Ja 12 1844

Cincinnati weekly HERALD. 1846 *See* Cincinnati weekly globe 1846

Cincinnati HERALD. d Mr 1900-
OCHi Mr 28-29,Ap 1-2 1900

Cincinnati weekly HERALD and philanthropist. w Ja 1 1836-46||?
1836-O 11 1843 as Philanthropist
Ja-Ap 3 1836 pub in New Richmond
Ct Ja 1 1836
CtY [Jl 3 1835-40]-S 11 1844
DLC 1836-Je 9,N 17 1841-O 15 1842;My 24 1843-N 1846
ICU [My 5 1836-F 17 1847]
IU Ja 28 Mr 3,Je 16 1840;F 3-10,Jl 7,D 22 1841
KHi Jl 7,D 29 1841
MWA Mr 11,Ap 8 1836
MdBJ 1836-43
MiU 1837
N Mr 27-D 25 1838
NIC F 26 1836;F 1837-Ja 1838;O 28 1840
NNHi S 15 1846
NSyU Mr 30,S 10 1842
NcD My 13 1840
OCHi [Ja-Ap 8 1836]-D 9 1846
OClWHi 1845-46
OHi My 26 1836;N 7 1837;F 13 1838-Je 1842; My 31 1843-My 21,Je 18 1845
OMM Jl 29,O 14 1836[37-40]Ja 13,27,F 17, Mr 17 1842;Jl 16,Ag 27,N 12,D 14,28 1842-F 1,15,Mr 8,Ap 19-26 1843
OO [1844]
PSF Ap 23-30,S 3,N 12 1845;S 2,O 7,D 1,16 1846
WHi 1838-41

HILLTOP news. [Mount Healthy] w N 1 1919+
1919-Ap 30 1930 as Hilltop weekly
pub [1919-33]+

Der HOCHWAECHTER. w Jl 3 1845-
In German
IU 1845-Jl 17 1846

Cincinnati HOME journal. w? 1855?-
ICHi My 19 1855

INDEPENDENT press. w Je 24 1826-
InVi S 9-D 16 1826
OCHi Je-D 16 1826

INDEPENDENT press and freedom's advocate. w Jl 4 1822-N 13 1823||
Jl 4-O 1 1822 as Independent press
ICN S 26-N 7,N 21-28 1822;Ja 9-16,F 20-Mr 6,20-Ap 10,24-My 1,15,29-Je 12,26,S 11,25-O 16 1823
IU Ja 9 1823
N D 26 1822-Ja 9 1823
NNHi Ap 2- 1823
OC Jl 18 1822-Ja 2 1823
OCHi Jl 11 1822-23
OHi O 30 1823

INQUISITOR and Cincinnati advertiser. *See* Advertiser and journal

JEWISH daily world. *See under* Cleveland

Cincinnati morning JOURNAL. d Ja 4-Ap 28 1883||
United with Cincinnati news to form Cincinnati news and journal
OCHi complete
OOxM complete

Cincinnati JOURNAL of commerce. w 1865-95||?
DLC N 1866-Je 1867
ICHi N 4 1865
MWA Ap 17 1869

Cincinnati weekly LEADER. w
OClWHi Jl 15 1865

LIBERTY hall. *See* Cincinnati gazette. 1804-1913

Cincinnati LIVE stock record. d 1897?+
DA S 1915-[14-Je 1923]+

MAGNET. w Mr 12 1827-
DLC Mr 12 1827
KHi Je 9-Ag 1827

MECHANICS advocate. w O 29 1831-
OCHi O 29 1831;Ja 21,Mr 10 1832

MERCANTILE daily advertiser. d S 4 1826-30||?
United with National republican and Ohio political register to form National republican and Cincinnati daily mercantile advertiser, later Daily Cincinnati republican
OC S-N 1826

MERCHANTS and manufacturers bulletin. w 1869-82||?
Followed by Merchant and manufacturer (not in this list)
KHi F 29 1872
MB F 17 1870-Mr 14 1872

Cincinnati evening MERCURY. d F 1 1849-
OCHi F 2-Jl 14 1849

Daily MESSAGE. d 1841?-N? 1843||
Title varies slightly. United with Cincinnati enquirer to form Enquirer and message, later Cincinnati enquirer
IU Ag 22 1843
MWA Je 6 1842
OCHi Ag 1 1843

Weekly MESSAGE. w 1842-N? 1843||
1842? as Dollar weekly message. United with Cincinnati weekly enquirer to form Enquirer and message, later Cincinnati weekly enquirer
DLC O 29 1842
IU S 9 1843
OCHi D 17 1842-N 11 1843

Daily MICROSCOPE. d 1840?-
IU Ja 17 1842
OClWHi O 23 1841-Ja 1 1842

Cincinnati tägliche MORGEN-POST. d 1877-78||?
In German
OC Mr-O 13 1878

NASH journal. w D 6 1926-N 28 1927||
WHi complete

NATIONAL banner. w S 1864-
ICHi O 16 1865
N Mr 12 1865
OCHi Ap 16 1865

NATIONAL crisis and Cincinnati emporium. sw,w My 24 1824-
1824-Ag 1826 as National crisis
w 1824-25?
CtY S 15(supp)1824
DLC Je 14,D 16 1824;Ag 20,27 1827;Ag 4,11 S 8 1828
ICU Ag 8 1825
InI F 23 1826
MWA D 27 1824;Ja 31,F 28,My 9 1825;Mr 1,Je 7 1827;Ja 17 1828
NN Je 7 1824;D 12 1825;Ja 19-F 12,20-23, Mr 2,6,13-30,Ap 10,17-27 1826
NNHi F 26 1827
OC D 16(extra)1824;Je 15-19 1826[27]
OHi Ja 17 1825
WHi S 5 1825

NATIONAL patriot. w
PCA [1853-54]

NATIONAL press and Cincinnati weekly herald. *See* Cincinnati weekly globe 1846

NATIONAL republican. . . *See* Republican 1823-42

NATIONAL union. w 1862-69||?
WHi Jl 25 1865

Daily NEWS. d Ja 1838-
OCHi Ja 23 1838

Saturday morning NEWS. w My? 1838-
MWA O 27 1838

Daily NEWS. d F 8 1839-
DLC F-Je 8 1839
MWA Mr 11,Ag 11 1840
OClWHi F 9 1839
WHi [F 8 1839-Je 1840]

Evening NEWS. d Mr 1845-
Mr-Je? 1845 as Daily evening news
OCHi Je 12,25,27,Ag 1 1845

Sunday NEWS. w My 1846-
DLC S 6 1846

Cincinnati weekly NEWS. w 1883||?
CaOTA Je 6 1883
OClWHi O 24 1883

Saturday evening NEWS and dollar weekly dispatch. *See* Dollar weekly dispatch and democratic union

Cincinnati NEWS and journal. d D 2 1882-Je 7 1884||
1882-Ap 29 1883 as Cincinnati news. United with Sun to form Sun, Cincinnati news journal, later Sun
OC complete
OCHi complete
OHi complete
OMM [Ja-Mr 5 1883]
OOxM 1882-Mr 1884

Cincinnati daily NONPAREIL. d 1847?-
MWA S 30 1852
OC N 1851-My 1852
OCHi My-O 1851
—w ed *See* Dollar weekly nonpareil

Cincinnati OCCASIONAL. d Ag 5 1858-
OCHi Ag-D 17 1858

OHIO organ. *See* Ohio Washingtonian organ

OHIO organ of temperance reform. w 1852?-
Early issues as Organ of temperance reform
MWA S 24,O 8 1852
WHi S 9 1853

OHIO union. d S 13 1845-
DLC [S 1845-Je 1846]

OHIO volksfreund. d 1841?-
In German
CtY D 25 1841

OHIO volksfreund. sw Ap 1841-
In German
OCHi Ap 21 1841

OHIO Washingtonian organ. w 1845-
1845-47? as Ohio organ
OClWHi D 31 1847
OHi Jl 14 1848

ORGAN of temperance reform. *See* Ohio organ of temperance reform

OUR village news. *See* Suburban news

PARTHENON. w S 16 1826-
KHi N 3 1827
MWA S 16-23,N 25-D 2 1826;Ja 6-19,F 2-15, Mr 3-22 1828

Cincinnati daily PATRIOT. d 1843-
IU N 30 1843

Weekly PATRIOT. w Mr 1 1853-
DLC 1853-F 25 1854
MWA Jl 30 1853

PENNY paper. *See* Cincinnati post

PENNY post. *See* Cincinnati post

PENNY press. *See* Cincinnati daily press

PEOPLES advocate. w 1834||?
DLC Je 14 1834

PEOPLE'S paper. d Ag 1843-
OC [Ag 21 1843-D 18 1845]
WHi N 21 1843-Mr 9 1844;Ja-F 15 1845

PHILANTHROPIST. *See* Cincinnati weekly herald and philanthropist

Daily evening POST. d My 1835-39||
IU My 25 1835
NNHi N 12 1838
OCHi My 11 1835-36;My 6 1837-D 21 1839
TxU O 2 1838-Mr 2 1839
WHi F 4-D 12 1837

Cincinnati POST. w Ja 8-S 3 1842||?
Ja-Jl 30 1842 as Cincinnati post and anti-abolitionist
MWA [F-S 3 1842]
NNHi Ja 8 1842
OCHi Mr 26 1842

Cincinnati POST. d Ja 3 1881+
1881-82? as Penny paper; 1883? Penny post; 1884?-S 1 1890 Evening post
pub 1883+
DLC S-D 1897;Jl-D 1898
In Mr 1895-O 1896
OC 1888+
OCHi S 20 1881;F 17 1883
OClWHi Je 5 1897;F 7-19 1908
OHi My 4,6,8 1886;Ap-D 1892;S 9,24,N 4 1896; F 22-Ag 16 1898;S 15 1901;Ap-D 13 1918;Ap 1920-Je 1932
OOxM Je 13 1885
VU My 12 1904;Je 13 1930

Cincinnati daily PRESS. d F 22 1859-
F-Jl 16 1859 as Daily press; Jl 18 1859-F? 1860 Penny press
IU [Mr 16 1860-S 3 1862]
InRE Jl 3 1860
MWA Je 19,S 29 1860;Mr 4,Ag 13,O 9-10 1861;Mr 15,Jl 3 1862
MoHi Ag 8 1860
OC F-Ag 20 1859;S 1860-Ag 1861
OCHi F-Jl,Ag 22 1859-F 21,Je 1860-My 1862
OClWHi S 1861-F 21 1862
OHi F-Jl 1 1859;Je 30 1860-Je 28 1861

PRESS and advocate. w
NNHi Ap 24 1823

Cincinnati PRICE current. d O 1853?-
OCHi O 1853-59

Cincinnati daily PRICE current. d 1913?-D 13 1915||
DA 1913-15

PRICE HILL news. w My 25 1928+
pub 1928+

QUEEN CITY. d Ag? 1841-
DLC Ag 20 1841
TxGR O 2(extra)1847

RAIL splitter. w Ag 1-O 27 1860||
Campaign paper
OCHi complete

Cincinnati RECORD. d N 23 1906-
OCHi N-D 2 1906

Daily REPORTER. d My 18 1850-
OClWHi My 18-29 1850

Daily Cincinnati REPUBLICAN. sw,d Ja 1 1823-42||?
Follows Western spy and literary cadet. 1823-30 as National republican and Ohio political register; 1831-Jl 10 1833 National republican and Cincinnati mercantile advertiser; Jl 11 1833-38? Daily Cincinnati republican and commercial register; 1839? Cincinnati daily republican
sw 1823-30
CSmH Ag 31 1830
DLC Ja 1,7,17,Mr 4,18-28,O 24-N 7,18,D 2,9 1823;Ja 9,31-F 6,24,Mr 5,16,26,30,Ap 9,30,My 28-Je 4,18,O 12-15 1824;Ja 27,Mr 13,20,Jl 7,14,21-24,Ag 7-11,S 1,29,O 2,20-23,N 20,D 25 1829;30;F 26,Ag 15 1833;Ag 15 1839;O 31 1840;42
ICU Mr 16 1824
IU O 10 1831;Ag 27 1832;Jl 13,S 6-7 1841;Ja 13,N 3 1842
InI Je 7 1832
MWA My 30,Je 24,Jl 18 1823;Ja 4-7,25-28,F 15 1825;Ap 25 1826;F 23,N 30,D 7 1827;O 25 1832;O 5 1836;Ja 3,My 18 1839;Ja 12 1841
MdBJ N 9 1842
N Mr 14,21,28,S 2,N 4 1823;Ja 23,F 24-27,Je 4,15,Jl 23,Ag 3,S 17-21,O 1 1824;Jl 19-22,29 1825
NN Ap 9-18 1826
NNHi Je 3,Jl 4,Ag 4 1823;Ja 6,Jl 27,Ag 17,O 19,N 5 1824
NjR N 30 1827;S 30-O 1 1831
OC [Mr 12 1824-27;Mr 25-Ap 6,O 26 1831-Jl 9 1833;My 4-D 25 1835]Mr 11 1837;S 7 1840-Ag 1842
OCHi 1823-24;26-Ja 8 1830;O 12 1832[35-38]F 5 1839[O 1840-Ap 1842]
OClWHi 1823-26;S 21 1827;F 19,S 23,D 12 1828;Ja 5-12,22,N 30 1830;Ja 22,Jl 7 1831-Jl 4,17 1833-O 17 1835
OHi 1823-26;O 6 1831;Jl 11 1833-D 20 1837;Ja-Mr 25 1839
OOxM Ag 22,S 5-12,26,O 10-D 2 1823;F 20-27, Mr 26,Ap 2,30,My 14 1824;27-Ja 18 1828
TxU 1823-S 26 1831;Ap 10 1832-Jl 10 1833;34-35;Jl 2 1836-Jl 18 1837
WHi 1823-Je 2,S 1 1826;My 18,Je 8,22,S 7,21, 28,O 26,D 7,21 1827;Ap 25 1828;S 11,25,N 6 1829;Mr?(extra)1836

OHIO (*Continued*)

CINCINNATI—*Continued*

Cincinnati weekly REPUBLICAN. w 1823?-42||?
1823?-30? as National republican and Ohio political register; 1831?-38? Weekly Cincinnati republican and commercial register
Ct [1826-28]
DLC My 27 1840
InI D 10 1834
MWA F 13 1824;Mr 23 1827;F 8 1828;Ag 27 1830;Jl 23 1834
N D 12 1823
OC O 10 1838
OClWHi S 29-O 7,21 1841
OHi Je 9 1841
OOxM Jl 31-Ag 7,21-28,S 11,25,O 9,N 13-D 4 1833;Ja 1-8,29-F,Mr 19-Ap 2,16-Jl 2 1834
P Jl 16 1834

Cincinnati REPUBLICAN. [country ed] tw
-Jl 1833? as National republican and daily mercantile advertiser
DLC Je 8/9 1831;Mr 7/8 1836

Cincinnati daily REPUBLICAN. d S 15 1852-
MWA S 15 1852

Cincinnati semi-weekly REPUBLICAN. sw 1852-
MWA O 6 1852

Cincinnati REPUBLICAN. w Je 1914-17||?
1914-My 10 1915? as Cincinnati republican gazette
OCHi Ja 11,F 22-Mr 1,15,Ap 12,My 10,D 6 1915;Mr 27 1916;Ja 1-15 1917

Cincinnati REPUBLICANER. d S 1842-
1842? as Der Deutsche republicaner
In German
DLC O 1850-Jl 1851;52-54;Ap 23,28,30 1855;58
IU [N 30 1858-Mr 23 1861]
OCHi O 3 1842;Ag 17 1843
OClWHi D 3 1850;Ap 29 1854

Cincinnati REPUBLICANER. w 1842?-
1842? as Der Deutsche republicaner
CSmH Ap 17 1845
IU [Mr 1860-Mr 1861]
MWA S 4,N 20 1852
OCoC [Mr 1844-N 1846]-S 18 1847

Cincinnati SATURDAY night. w 1872-84||?
CoHi My 15 1875

SHIRES' commercial advertiser. w 1857?-
OC Je-D 25 1858

Der SONNTAGSMORGEN. w 1867?-1907||?
In German
DLC Je 8 1873-My 1875
IU Jl 14 1867;Je 27 1869;Ja 30,Ap 17,My 29 1870
WHi Je 16 1867-68;Je 12 1870-Je 4 1871;Je 1875-Ap 1906
—d ed *See* Cincinnati volksfreund

SPIRIT of the times. *See* Cincinnati times-star

Morning STAR. sw 1841-
OCHi F 19 1842

Cincinnati daily STAR. d Ja 4 1872-Je 26 1880||
1872-F 26 1874 as Evening star; F 27 1874-Jl 12 1875 Star. United with Cincinnati times to form Cincinnati times-star
DLC complete
IU complete
NN Ja-Je 1872
NbHi Je 27,Jl 1,10,29-30,Ag 6,10,27,S 1 1878
OC 1872-Je 1879;80

Cincinnati weekly STAR. w Mr 14 1872-80||?
IU 1872-73
MWA Ap 8 1875
NN 1872-F 17 1887
NbHi D 4 1876
OC 1872-79

Morning STAR and western temperance journal. w 1841-
1841-Ap? 1842 as Morning star
OCHi Je 7,Ag 22-S 13 1842
OClWHi Ja 1 1843
OHi Ap 19 1842
PCA My 24 1842

Daily STRAIGHTOUT. d 1844||?
Campaign paper
MoSM Ag 6 1844

SUBURBAN news. w 1880+
1880-81? as Our village news; 1882?-84? Walnut Hills news
ICM O 6 1882

Daily SUN. d 1838?-
NEh Jl 8 1839
OC My 14 1839

SUN. d 1842?-
IU F 3 1844
OCHi S 8-D 23 1843

SUN. d 1852?-
MWA S 13 1852

Cincinnati SUN. w D 16 1869-70||?
In English and German
DLC 1869-Ag 26,S 30 1870

SUN. d Ja 1-F 22 1879||
OCHi complete

SUN. d Je 5 1884-87||?
Je 8-9 1884 as Sun, Cincinnati news journal
OC Je 8-Jl 1884;N 16 1885-F 1 1887
OCHi Je-Jl 1884;Je 27 1886
OOxM S 17 1886

Daily SUNBEAM. d N 27 1848-
OCHi 1848-F 1 1849

TÄGLICH. . . *See under* next important word: e.g., Tägliches Cincinnatier volksblatt is alphabeted under Volksblatt

Morning TELEGRAM. d Ap 1885-89||?
1885-D 22 1888 as Evening telegram
OC [O 19 1885-N 4 1886;Ap 19 1887-D 22 1888]-F 7 1889
OCHi Jl 23 1885
OOxM S 30 1887

THISTLE. w N 18 1822-
OHi N 18 1822

Cincinnati weekly TIMES. w 1844-1901||?
1852?-65? as Dollar weekly times; My 1871?-Jl 1873? Times and chronicle
CtY My 21 1857;64
DLC Mr 27 1851;Mr 8 1855
ICU N 20-D 18 1856;Ja 1-22,F 5-19,Mr 26,Ap 9-My 7,21-Je 4,18-Jl,S 17 1857;F 4 1858
IHi Ap 20 1865
IU Ap 20,My 4,Jl 6,20-Ag 3,17-O 19,N 2 1876; F 8-15 1877
KHi 1879-1901
MWA Jl 6 1844;D 2 1852;Mr 31 1853;Ap 20 1854;F 1855-[56-My 7 1857]Ap 10 1873
MWiC My 26 1853
MiU-C Mr 1-8 1855
MnHi N 29 1855
NN F 16 1865;Jl 15 1880-88
NNHi F 18 1869;Ap 3 1873;My 8 1879
NbHi Jl 20 1871;F 17,N 16,D 21 1876;N 8-15 1877;O 31 1878;F 13 1879
NcD [Je 1855-Ja 1856]Ap-Je 6 1861;D 21 1865;N 20 1879
OC [Jl 13 1854-N 22 1855]74;78;Jl 15 1880-86; 89
OCHi N 25 1852;Mr 17,Jl 1853-My 3 1855
OClWHi Jl 19,Ag 2,23-30,O 11,D 6,20 1855;Ja 3,F 14 1856;Ap 11 1861;Ag 21-27,N 27 1862; D 3,17-24 1863;Jl 6 1865;My 28 1868;Mr 18, Ap 1,15,Je 24 1869;70-72;N 23 1876;My 24-31,Ag 16,30,S 13,N 1,29 1877[78]
OHi Ag 1853[F-My 1856]My 15 1860-Mr 7 1851;Ap 24,O 3 1861;Mr 12 1868;Mr 20 1873; Mr 21 1878
P-M Jl 20 1854;My 12,Jl 12,26 1855
PLHt Ag 8 1861
PPL N 21 1850
TU My 17 1855
TxU Ja 11-My 10 1855;Ja 17 1864
VU D 2 1869;Mr 25 1875;F 3 1876
WHi O 6,N 17 1853;N 23 1854;Mr-Ap 9 1857; Mr 10,31 1863;S 29 1885

Cincinnati TIMES-STAR. d Ap 25 1840+
1840? as Spirit of the times; 1841?-Je 26 1880 Cincinnati daily times (My 1871-Jl 12 1873 Cincinnati times and chronicle; other variations slight)
pub 1842+
CoHi Mr 23 1842
CtY Ja 21 1864-65
DLC Ag 19 1840;N 1 1842;Ja 18 1849;S 7 1860; Ja-Je 1862;O 10,12 1863;My 1871-98
GAtCo S 30 1880
ICHi My 18 1840;Ap 7,S 27,O 19 1865
ICM Je 21 1880
ICU Mr 22 1862;Ap 19 1864;Jl 1871-Je 1873;Jl 1874-Je 1879;Ja-Je 1880;S 11 1884
IU O 16 1840;F 13 1851[60-61]Ja 3,25,F 26,Mr 17,19,Jl 3-4,17,S 12-13,O 3 1862;Ja 31,My 9 1863;Jl-D 1873;Je 28 1880-89;Jl 1890-92;94-Je 1896
KHi D 3 1855;N 18 1877;Je 25 1880;F 17 1884; N 3 1904
MBAt O 22 1864
MSaE N 30(supp)1861
MWA Ag 25 1852;Jl 6 1860;Ap 26,Ag 5,30 1861;Ja 27 1862;O 22 1864;Jl 24 1872;F 25 1933
MiU 1876-[80]81
N Ap 25 1865
NN [1886]
NNHi Jl 14 1862;F 17 1869
NbHi N 14 1877
NcU O 13 1875
OC D 4 1845-48;S 2 1860-Je[S 21 1863-64]-Je 1865;My 1871-Je 1878;79+
OCHi Ap-O 27 1840;My 1 1841;My 2 1843;N 16 1852-53;56+
OClWHi Ja 11 1842;Mr 1,O 22,N 11 1862;S 18 1863;Ap 11,S 5 1864;Ap 25-27 1865;Ag 25 1869;S 4-5 1872;D 5 1877;F 13 1878
OHi [Je 1861-Ag 1862]Mr 7,19,Ap 11,My 9 1863;F 14,23,Mr 6,18,Ap 3-4,7,My 3 1865;86+
OOxM Ap-O 27 1840;D 10 1850;Ja 14,21,F 10-11[Ag]1851;Ap 30 1866;Ja 15,F 9,D 20 1869; Mr 29 1870[71]Je 13,Jl 8 1873;Je 11-12,18 1874;N 30-D 1 1877;S 9 1882;Je 11,21,N 1883-85
PPL N 20 1850
TxU O 1862-N 1864;65-[Jl-D 1870]-76;Jl 2-D 1877
WHi O 28 1840-O 26 1841[My 12 1856-O 9 1867]My 12 1919-20

TRAIN ligue. ir Ja 1- 1874||
Campaign paper
DLC Ja 1,F 2,Mr 15 1874

Evening TRANSCRIPT. d N 23 1834-
DLC N 23 1834

Cincinnati TRIBUNE. d Ja 4 1893-Je 15 1896||
United with Commercial gazette to form Commercial tribune
MWA D 10 1895
OCHi complete
OClWHi D 10 1895
OHi complete

Cincinnati TRIBUNE. w Ja 4 1893-Je 15 1896||
OC complete

TRUE blue and castigator. w Ja 16? 1832-
Campaign paper
MWA Mr 12 1832
NNHi My 7 1832
OC F 27-Mr 5,19,Ap 23,My 7,Je 4 1832

TRUE sun. 1843?-
IU N 21 1843

TYPE of the times. w 1848?-
KHi 1854-Ag 1855
MWA O 13 1855
OHi N 25 1854

Cincinnati weekly UNION. w Jl 4 1866-
OClWHi Jl 11 1866

Cincinnati UNION. w 1907+
Negro
OHi O 1918-S 23 1923

Cincinnati daily UNIONIST. d D 24 1853-
OClWHi 1853-Mr 13 1854

VISITER. d My 3 1841-
DLC My 3 1841

Das VOLKSBLATT. w Mr 7 1836-
In German
MWA O 19 1837;S 9 1852;O 11(extra)1854
MnHi Mr 7 1836
OCHi Ag 22 1839;Mr 16 1843[Ap 8 1847-S 2 1852]
OClWHi Mr 3,24 1864;Ag 31,S 28,N 22 1865
TxU Ja 26 1854-D 20 1855

Tägliches Cincinnatier VOLKSBLATT. d My 7 1836-D 5 1919||
Title varies slightly
In German
DLC F 4 1839;Mr 4 1840;O 1 1841;D 31 1845; Ja 16-D 26 1846;Jl 27 1847-54;Ja 5-N 1858;Mr 6 1866-O 1869;Ap 1882-O 1886;S 17 1888-Ag 1889;Ja-My 1890;98
IU My 8 1885;Mr 11,25,My 27 1894;N 30 1905; Ja 18,D 3 1906;Mr 3 1907;S 16,30 1910;N 30,D 7 1911;Ja 10,Mr 5,Jl 16 1913;D 2 1915;F 22-Je 29 1918
MWA Mr 30 1860;Ag 24 1876
OC Jl 12 1872-1918
OCHi My 7 1836;F 15,Mr 26-28,30,Ap 1 1839 [43-Jl 1846]Ja 30 1879;D 5 1919
OClWHi O 15 1850-Ja 14,My 18-D 1852;Ag 13 1853
OHi Ja 1 1901[D 1918-19]
WHi S 2-D 1889;Je 2 1890-Mr 1891
—Sunday ed *See* Westliche blätter

VOLKS-BÜHNE. 1841?-
In German
OCHi Je 28 1843

Cincinnati VOLKSFREUND. d O 12 1850-1908||?
Title varies slightly
In German
DLC 1850-O 11 1863;O 13 1864-Je 1893
IU Je 4 1861;F 16 1881;Mr 5 1906
MWA D 29 1852;Mr 27 1866
NcD O 12-D 28 1871
OC Jl 1872-Je 11 1908
OClWHi Ja-O 10 1854;O 14-D 1856;Ja 4,Ag 16 1857;O 12 1858;Ja 9 1859;O 12 1861;O 13 1865-Mr 25 1866
WHi F 16-O 11 1866;Ag 7 1869-Ap 15 1908
—Sunday ed *See* Der Sonntagsmorgen

Cincinnati VOLKSFREUND. w Mr 3 1853-1907||?
Title varies slightly
In German
DLC 1853-F 21 1856;F 26 1857-F 16 1860;F 19 1862-F 11 1863;F 15 1865-F 7 1866;F 13 1867-F 5 1868;F 9 1870-F 1 1871;F 1874-Ja 1876
ICHi N 18 1865
MWA Mr 21 1866
OCHi Ja 3 1855;Ja 10,24-F 7,21,Mr 13-27,Ap 10-24,Jl 24-31,O 2,16 1856
OHi Ja 1 1901
WHi F 18 1863-F 18 1865;F 12 1868-F 13 1869; F 17 1872-Ja 1873;F 1876-D 25 1907

WAGON boy. w? 1840||
Campaign paper
DLC S 30 1840

WALNUT HILLS news. *See* Suburban news

Cincinnati WEST and south. *See* Commoner

WESTERN fountain. w
OHi O 5 1850

WESTERN general advertiser. *See* Cist's weekly advertiser

WESTERN journal. w? -S 28 1828||
United with Cincinnati advertiser and Ohio phoenix to form Daily advertiser and journal, later Advertiser and journal

WESTERN police gazette. w 1849?-
MWA Mr 29 1851

WESTERN shield. w 1833?-
MWA Jl 19 1834
OC Ap 5 1834

*WESTERN spy and literary cadet. w S 1 1810-D 28 1822||
1810-Ja 9 1819 as Western spy; Ja 16 1819-Ap 22 1820 Western spy and Cincinnati general advertiser. Followed by National republican and Ohio political register, later Daily Cincinnati republican
MWA N 30 1822
MiD-B [1821]
NN N 10 1821
NjHi N 30 1822
OC 1821-Mr 9 1822
OCHi 1821-22
OHi 1821-22
OOxM O 20-N 17,D 15 1821;F 16-Mr 2,16-23,O 12,N 23-D 7 1822
TxU 1822

WESTERN statesman. w Jl 23 1842-
DLC Jl 23 1842
IU N 5 1842
MWA S 24 1842
MdBJ Jl 30 1842

WESTERN steamer. d Ag 10 1840-
DLC Ag 11 1840

WESTERN tiller. w Ag 25 1826-
MWA Mr 16 1827
OCHi 1826-Ag 3 1827
OHi 1826-Ag 3 1827

WESTERN token. 1848?-
OClWHi Ap 3 1848

OHIO (*Continued*)

CINCINNATI—*Continued*

WESTERN transcript. 1844?-
ICHi Ap 17 1845

WESTERN world. w? 1849?-
OClWHi My 13 1849

WESTLICHE blätter. w N 5 1865-1919‖?
In German
IU Ap 22 1866;Ja 12,Mr 15-22,Je 28-Jl 12,26, Ag 16 1868;Ap 11-18,Je 20,Ag 1,S 5-19,O 10-31,N 14 21 1869;Ja 16-23,My 29-Je 5,Jl 3-17 1870;Mr 4 1906;F 10-17,Mr 22 1907;Je 11-18,Jl 9,N 26 1911
OC 1865-F 1868;Jl 14 1872-1918
OHi Ja 5 1901
WHi S-D 1889;Je 1890-Mr 1891
—d ed *See* Tägliches Cincinnatier volksblatt

Der WESTLICHE merkur. tw Mr? 1840-
In German
DLC Mr 7 1840

Cincinnati daily WHIG. d 1829-39‖
1829-F 1834? as Commercial daily advertiser; Mr 1834-Ap 15? 1835 Cincinnati democratic intelligencer and commercial advertiser; Ap 16 1835-Mr? 1839 Cincinnati daily whig and commercial intelligencer
DLC N 15 1829;N 2 1832
MWA Mr 2,26,31,O 23-24,29 1829;Ja 22-23,27-F 23,Mr 1-2,5-6,17-18,28-Ap 1,14-15,21-22,My 20,N 3 1830;F 20,Jl 27 1836
N F 23 1837
OC N 17 1831;O 30 1832
OCHi Jl 15 1829;Mr 1834-Mr 23,Je 19[Ag-N] 1839
TxU [Ap 16 1835-Mr 23 1839]

Cincinnati weekly WHIG and commercial intelligencer. w 1829?-39‖?
InRE Je 27 1836
OClWHi Ag 1,D 6 1836;O 10 1837

WORLD we live in. w 1860?-
MWA Je 20 1860

Cincinnati ZEITUNG. d 1886-O 20? 1901‖
In German
ICHi Je 2 1897-O 20 1901
NN My 27,Je 6,10,S 1-4,24,O 2,12,D 11 1888;Ja 17,D 18 1889;F 6-7 1891;F 19 1892;Ja 21,Je 7,12 1895
OC Jl 1887-Ja, Jl 1899-O 20 1901
OHi Ja 1 1901
WHi Ap 1- 1900

CIRCLEVILLE

Circleville DEMOCRAT. *See* Circleville watchman 1844-1927

Circleville DEMOCRATIC guard and Pickaway and Fayette pilot. *See* Circleville watchman 1844-1927

DEMOCRATIC herald. *See* Circleville herald 1870-1909

DEMOCRATIC whip. w? S 21? 1843-
IU S 28,O 5 1843

Circleville HERALD. . . 1830-32;39-61 *See* Circleville union-herald

Circleville HERALD. w 1870-1909‖?
1886?-1905? as Democratic herald
MWA Ag 25 1876

Circleville HERALD. d 1894+
1894-1928 as Daily union-herald
pub 1919+
—w ed *See* Circleville union-herald

INDEPENDENT American and Circleville herald. *See* Circleville union-herald

OHIO observer. w Ag 21? 1833-
N O 2 1833

OLIVE branch. . . *See* Circleville union-herald

***Circleville UNION-HERALD.** w Ag 10 1817+
1817-Ag 5? 1826 as Olive branch; Ag 12? 1826-D 25 1829 Olive branch and Pickaway herald; Ja 2 1830-D 29 1832 Circleville herald and Ohio olive branch; Ja 5 1833-D 3 1837 Independent American and Circleville herald; Ja 5 1839-61 Circleville herald; 1861-Ap? 1870 Circleville union; My? 1870-76 Circleville herald and watchman; 1928?-30? Union-herald and watchman
pub 1910+
DLC Jl 8 1826;Mr 15,Ag 9,23 1828;Mr 21,Jl 4,S 12,O 24 1829;Ap 24,O 23 1830;S 11 1863
ISh Ja 30 1830
IU Ja 31 1829
MWA Ag 15 1825;Je 30 1827;O 30 1830;D 24 1852;O 6 1910
N F 14 1823;Jl 30,Ag 13 1825
NN Mr 6 1847
NNHi My 22,Je 5-12 1863
OCl D 23 1826
OClWHi Ag 16 1828-Jl 6,O 23 1833-My 2 1840; 41-D 2 1842;51-64;N 24 1875;O 24 1877;Mr 9 1881;O 3 1916;Je 9-27 1921
OHi D 22 1827;Mr 14 1829
WHi My 22 1863

Daily UNION-HERALD. *See* Circleville herald 1894+

Circleville WATCHMAN. w? 1838?-
IU F 10(extra)1843;F 22,My 4,Je 22 1844

Circleville WATCHMAN. w Ag 2 1844-1927‖?
1844-D 29 1845 as Circleville democratic guard and Pickaway and Fayette pilot; Ja 2 1846-D 28 1849 Watchman; Jl? 1862-N 1870 Circleville democrat; D 1870-1926? Circleville democrat and watchman. United with Circleville union-herald to form Union-herald and watchman, later Circleville union-herald

IU S 20,O 18 1844;My 23 1845
KHi Ag 23 1895
MWA D 23 1852
OClWHi Ag 9 1844-S 9 1857;Ag 10 1859-1911; Je 30 1921
OHi Ap 19 1850-My 12 1916

CLEVELAND

Cleveland daily ADVERTISER. d Jl 4 1836-
1836? as Daily advertiser
Ct Jl 5 1836
OClWHi Jl 5-D 2 1836;F 17,Mr 21 1837-Mr 22 1838

Cleveland ADVERTISER. w *See* Weekly plain dealer

Cleveland ADVOCATE. [Newburg] w 1873-96‖?
1873-83? as South Cleveland advocate
OClWHi My 24-O 1884;Ja 1,My 8-15 1886[87] F 25,Mr 17,Ap 21-Jl 14 1888;Ja 12,F 18,N 16 1889;F 18 1893

Cleveland ADVOCATE. w 1914-23‖?
Negro
OHi Je 1917-D 18 1920

ALL around the clock. [Newburg] w 1873-74‖?
OClWHi N 14 1873

AMENDMENT herald. w Je 30? 1883-
OClWHi Jl 14,Ag 4,O 18 1883;Ag 7,S 25 1884; F 26-Mr 12,Ap 9-23 1885

AMERICA Roumanian news. w,sw,d,tw 1905+
1905-27? as America
w 1905-09?;sw 1910?-16?;d 1917?-33?
In Roumanian
OHi [Mr 1918-N 2 1922]
PP [1928]+

AMERICAN. d 1899+
In Bohemian
IU 1918+
OHi Ja 11 1918+

AMERICAN liberal. w D 20 1854-
MWA D 20 1854;Ja 3-10,F 21 1855

AMERICAN union. w 1888-91‖?
DLC D 28 1888;F 2,9,Mr 30 1889

Clevelandska AMERIKA. *See* Ameriška domovina

AMERICKÉ dělnické listy. w D 1908+
In Bohemian
pub 1909+
OHi Je 17 1918+

AMERIŠKA domovina. sw,tw,d 1908?+
1908?-18? as Clevelandska Amerika
sw 1908?-15?;tw 1915?-Ag 2 1929
In Slovenian
IU 1918;F 26 1919+
OHi [Mr 1919-N 1920]

Clevelander ANZEIGER und deutsche presse. w 1871-93‖
1871-76? as Wochenblatt des Clevelander anzeiger; 1877-91? Clevelander anzeiger. United with Wächter am Erie to form Wächter und anzeiger
In German
OClWHi F-S 1876;77-78;Jl 1880-89;91-Ag 1893

Clevelander ANZEIGER und deutsche presse. tw,d 1872-S 1893‖
1871-D 31 1872 as Cleveland anzeiger; Ja 2 1873-D 30 1876 Täglicher Clevelander anzeiger. Ja 2 1877-D 31 1891 Clevelander anzeiger. United with Wächter am Erie to form Wächter und anzeiger
tw 1871-72
In German
MWA Ap 28 1876
OClWHi Ag 1872-O 1 1893

Daily ARGUS. d 1885-86‖?
OClWHi Mr 4 1885-F 27 1886

AXE. w Ap 23-N? 1840‖
Campaign paper
KHi Je 11 1840
MWA My 21 1840

BALD eagle. sw N? 1838-
OClWHi D 21 1838-Ja 15 1839

BEE. w? D? 1838-
OClWHi D 25 1838

Die BIENE. w 1873-86‖?
In German
OClWHi My 30-D 1875;78-80

Die BIENE. tw Ag 8 1873-79‖?
In German
OClWHi 1873;Ap-S 5 1874;Mr 20-N 25 1875;Ja 27-Mr 14 1876

BROOKLYN news-times. w 1919+
1919-26? as Brooklyn news
OCl Jl 1929+

Cleveland CALL and post. w F 22 1921+
1921?-29? as Cleveland call
Negro
pub 1932+

CAMPAIGN dealer. w 1848‖
OClWHi My 31-N 23 1848

CAMPAIGN dealer. w 1852‖
OHi Ag 19 1852

CAMPAIGN dealer. w 1856‖
OHi O 31 1856

CAMPAIGN plain dealer and popular sovereignty advocate. Je 30- 1860‖
OClWHi Je-N 17 1860

CAMPAIGNER and tariff advocate. w My 8-? 1844‖
DLC My 15-22 1844
MWA My 11 1844
MdSM My 22 1844
OClWHi My 15-22 1844

CLEVELAND HEIGHTS dispatch. w 1902+
pub [1902+]
OCl Jl 1929+

CLEVELAND HEIGHTS press. *See* Heights press

Daily CLEVELANDER. d 1855?-
OClWH Ja 3-N 18 1856

COLLINWOOD citizen. w 1900-20‖?
OClWHi 1913-14

Cleveland COMMERCIAL. w N 1851-
MWA S 9 1852
OClWHi O 13-N 3 1853;Ag 11 1855

Cleveland COMMERCIAL. 1922 *See* Cleveland times

COMMERCIAL bulletin. d Ag 29 1901-My 1910‖?
OCl 1901-My 1910

COMMERCIAL gazette.
OClWHi Mr 28,Ap 28 1861

COMMERCIAL intelligencer. d 1838?-
IU Mr 8 1838

Cleveland CORRESPONDENT. w S 14 1908-12‖?
In German
OClWHi 1908-Mr 4 1911

CUYAHOGA county news-ledger. w 1886-1915‖?
1886-1907? as Cuyahoga county news
OClWHi S 14 1895;F 18 1899

CUYAHOGAN. [Brooklyn] w 1881-1905‖?
OCl Ag 3 1885
OClWHi S 14 1895;F 20 1897;Ja 15-22,Ag 17-31 1901 F 11,25 1905

DEUTSCHE-ungarisches volksblatt. *See* Siebenbürgisch amerikanisches volksblatt

DEUTSCHE presse. d 1889-D 31 1891‖
United with Clevelander anzeiger to form Clevelander anzeiger und deutsche presse
In German

Cleveland evening DISPATCH. w Jl? 1864-
MWA Ag 11 1864

EAGLE-EYED news-catcher. d Ap?- 1841‖?
OClWHi My 10,14,17,28 1841

EAST CLEVELAND signal. w 1901+
pub [190-+]
OCl Jl 1929+

EAST CLEVELANDER. w 1909-10‖?
OClWHi My 21,S 11,D 11 1909

Uj ELŐRE. d 1904+
1904-21 as Előre
1904-Mr 1931 pub in New York City
In Hungarian
IU D 10 1917-[18-21]+
WHi O 23 1909-Mr 24 1911

ENAKOPRAVNOST. d 1918+
In Slovenian
pub 1920+

Cleveland ENTERPRISE. *See* West county advocate

EUCLID BEACH news. w Ag 15? 1908-32‖?
pub only Apr-S each year
OClWHi Ag 22 1908;S 15 1911;Je 14-Jl 5,19, Ag 2,16-30 1913;My 30-S 14 1914

EUCLID observer. *See* Northeast observer

EXAMINER. w 1884?-95‖?
OClWHi Jl 4-11,Ag 1-8 1891;Ap 30-D 1892;F 18 1893;Ja 13,27-F 3,24-S 1894

Evening EXPRESS. [Ohio City] d Ag 1852-
MWA S 1 1852

Cleveland morning EXPRESS. d Ja 1854-
Follows Geauga republic (Chardon) 1853-54? as Cleveland daily express
OClWHi Ap 21-D 1854:Ja 22-Je 1855

FAMILY visitor. w,bw Ja 3 1850-58‖?
1851?-52? pub in Hudson
w 1850?
ICHi 1850-My 10 1853
NcD Mr 27,D 23 1851-F 17,Mr-Ap 6,My 4 1852
OHi 1850-O 5 1852

FOAIA poporului. [People's news] w,sw,tw 1912-28‖?
tw 1912-20?;sw 1921?-24?
In Roumanian
MnHi Je 29 1928

Daily FOREST CITY. d Ap 1852-O 15 1853‖
United with Morning true democrat to form Daily Forest City democrat, later Cleveland leader
MWA O 15 1852
OClWHi Mr 19,Je 10,Jl 1 1852;Mr 10,Ap 4,My 28,Jl 15,Ag 13-O 1853

Weekly FOREST CITY. w My? 1852-O? 1853‖
United with True democrat to form Weekly Forest City democrat, later Cleveland weekly leader
MWA O 20 1852;Jl 6 1853

FOREST CITY democrat. *See* Leader

FREIE PRESSE. w 1883-1903‖?
In German
KHi Jl 14 1888;Ja 5 1889

GARFIELD HEIGHTS record. w 1927+
pub 1927+
OCl 1930+

Cleveland GATHERER. w 1850?-
IU D 3 1842
WHi N 2(extra)1842

Cleveland daily GAZETTE. d 1836?-39‖?
Merged with Cleveland herald
OClWHi S 6 1836-37

OHIO (*Continued*)

CLEVELAND—*Continued*

Cleveland weekly **GAZETTE.** w Ja 4 1837-39‖?
United with Cleveland herald to form Herald and gazette, later Cleveland herald
OClWHi Ja-Mr 22 1837

Morning **GAZETTE.** [Ohio City] d 1852?-
MWA Jl 27 1852

GAZETTE. w Ag 25 1883+
Negro
pub 1883+
DLC Ja 13 1900;Ap 6-13 1901
M Mr 15 1930
OHi Ja 5 1901;My 1918+

Cleveland **GERMANIA.** w 1846-53‖?
MWA Ag 5 1852

Cleveland daily **GLEANER.** d N 1859-
OClWHi D 2 1859

GLENVILLE times. w 1888+
1909?-32? as Cleveland-Glenville times
OCl Jl 1929-30

GRIP. *See* Cleveland star

HARPOON. w Ag 28? 1852-
MWA N 27 1852

HEBREW observer. w 1888-1900‖
United with Jewish review to form Jewish review and observer
OClJ complete

HEIGHTS press. w 1919+
1919-22? as Cleveland Heights press
pub 1919+
OCl S 1921+
OClWHi F 17,Mr 26,Ap 21,Jl 2 1922;My 28 1926;S 16,N 4 1927;S 1932-33

*Cleveland **HERALD.** w O 19 1819-Mr 1885‖?
1819-38 as Cleveland herald; 1838-O 4 1843 Cleveland herald and gazette. United with Cleveland weekly leader to form Cleveland weekly leader and herald, later Cleveland weekly leader
CSmH Jl 29 1830;O 27 1831
CtY Je 27,S 5 1828;Ag 16 1838
DLC 1821-25;My 5,D 8 1826-Ja 12[F-D 1827]-30;Je 9,O 27,N 17,D 22 1831;Ja 12,26,F 23,Mr 1-15,Ap 12 1832;N 9 1833;Mr 22 1834;Mr 25, Ap 1,Je 24[Ag-N 1837]Jl-D 12 1838;Ja 9, 30,F 27,Mr 13,27,Ap 10,24,My 8,15,Je 5,D 10-24 1839[40;42-50]
ICHi O 21 1871
ICN [1864-65]
KyU Ja 6,20-Ag 4,D 1,15-22 1841
MWA D 25 1821;N 14 1822;My 29,Ag 14,O 2, D 4-18 1823[24]F 23,O 26-N 2,16-23,D 7,21 1827[28-O 21 1830]My 27 1840;Ja 4 1843;S 21 1859;My 6 1865;F 22 1873
N O 26 1833
NN F 6 1823
NNHi Je 1 1847
OCl S 23 1825-O 6 1826;33;47-48;76;78-84
OClWHi 1821-Je 1832;Je 8 1833-N 8 1834;Ag 1 1835;O 29 1836;Mr 25 1837-[54]-My 21 1856;F 1857-Ja 17 1874[75]76[79]Mr 5,Jl 9-30,O 1 1880;Ap 1,Ag 26-N 1881;Ja 20,Ap 28-D 1882
OHi O 23 1823;My 4 1827

Cleveland **HERALD.** d My 30 1835-Mr 14 1885‖
United with Evening news to form News and herald, later Cleveland news. Title varies slightly
CU-B S 26-27 1881
Ct My 26 1831;Ag 11 1841;S 16 1863
DLC My 18 1840;Ja 30 1843;Ap 6 1850-52;Ag 28-29 1871;My 31 1878
ICHi Ag 24,28 1861
ICM My 25-28 1881;Ag 18 1883
IHi [My 13-Jl 23 1862]
IU My 14,Je 20(supp)1822
KHi My 6 1865;S 26 1881
MWA S 5 1845;Ag 25 1852;Mr 20,My 8 1855; Jl 2[O 16-N 21]1860;Jl 23,Ag 27,30,S 2,18 1862;Ap 17 1865;N 22 1876;D 6 1880
MnHi Mr 19 1846;S 25 1881
NBuG Je 16-17 1870
OCl 1850-[53]-85
OClWHi My-N 1835;Ap 16 1836-81;Jl 1882-85
ODW D 7 1869;Mr 8,10-14,19 1873
OHi F 17 1841-85
OOxM Mr 16 1882
WHi Mr 8-9 1864;Ag 31,S 9 1865;Ag 10 1866;Ja 8 1868;Jl 27 1869

Tri-weekly Cleveland **HERALD.** tw 1851?-85‖?
DLC Ap 30,My 4,14,18 1867
MWA N 15 1860
OCl Ag 13 1861
OClWHi Je 25 1857;O 21 1858;Je 14 1860;F 25,N 26 1864;F 7,Ap 11,15,Ag 5 1865;My 21,O 8 1867;F 10 1876-My 5 1877;Je 11 1878;Je 5, 17,Ag 12 1880;Mr 31 1881
ODW Ap 29 1865

Cleveland morning **HERALD.** d 1861-Mr 15 1885‖
United with Cleveland leader to form Cleveland leader and morning herald, later Cleveland leader
CL O 17 1864;S 12 1865
DLC Jl 22,27,29 1863;Ja-Jl 7 1866;Ja-N 22 1867
MWA My 12 1866;Je 16 1876
NbHi Ap 28 1865
OCl O 3 1862;Ap 28 1865;Jl 3 1881;Mr 15 1885
OClWHi Ja 1,Je 13,O 24 1864;Ja 10,F 25,Ap 28-29 1865;Ja 28,F 4 1867-Jl,N 24,D 26 1870; 71-N 1873;Ap 20,27,My 20-21,Jl-D 9 1874;D 4 1875;Ja 1,S 27 1876;Je 8-9,25,Jl 4,S 14,N 3, 29 1877[80]-82;D 11 1883;Ja-Je,S 9 1884;Mr 15 1885

Clevelander **HEROLD.** w,d Mr 2 1901-08‖?
w 1901-Ap? 1906
In German
OClWHi 1901-My 1,Jl 31 1906-Ag 24 1908

HLAS. w 1905-21‖?
In Slovak
IU D 1917-S 28 1921
OHi Je 1918-Je 1921

HLAS. d,tw 1916-29‖?
1916-Ja 2 1925 as Denny hlas (d)
In Slovak
IU D 5 1917-N 1927
OHi [Je 1918-24]-N 1927

INDEPENDENT news-letter. w 1827?-
CSmH Ag 10 1830
Ct S 13 1828;F 25 1829
DLC My-D 1829
MWA Mr 18 1829

JEDNOSC polek. w Ap 5 1923-
In Polish
OHi Jl 19 1923-Ag 1931

JEWISH independent. w Mr 9 1906+
pub 1906+
NNJ 1906+
OCl 1906-13;16+
OHi Ag 16 1918-Je 1928
OU [1911-23]-[Je-O 1931]-[D 1935+]
TxU [Jl 14 1922-D 16 1927]
WHi Ja 7,14-28,Mr 17-D 1916;F 23-Ag 17 1917;Ja-O 18 1918

JEWISH review and observer. w 1892+
1892-1900 as Jewish review
pub 1892+
NN Ap 1898-D 16 1921;Je 19 1925-Je 5 1931
OCl 1907+
OHi Ja 4 1901
TxU Jl 14 1922-27
WHi 1916-Ag 3 1918

JEWISH daily world. d N 1907+
also dated in Cincinnati
In Yiddish and English
pub 1907+
IU D 12 1917-Je 1925

Cleveland **JOURNAL** weekly. w Jl 8? 1837-
OClWHi Jl 13-S 21 1837

Cleveland **JOURNAL.** w 1903-12‖?
Negro
OClWHi Mr 28 1903-Ap 9 1910;Ap 22,Ag 19 1911

JUTRZENKA. w 1893-1923‖?
In Polish
OHi Ja 31 1901;Je 1918-My,Jl 1921-Jl 1923

KEPES vilaglap. w 1915-16‖?
In Hungarian
PPiHi [1915-16]

LAKEWOOD courier. w 1896+
pub [1896+]
OCl Jl 1929+

LAKEWOOD herald. w D 1909-15‖?
1909-12? as Lakewood independent
OCl 1909-N 1911

LAKEWOOD independent. *See* Lakewood herald

LAKEWOOD post and West Shore post. w 1924+
1924-29? as Lakewood post
OCl Jl 1929+

Cleveland weekly **LEADER.** w 1846-1904‖?
1846-O? 1853 as True democrat; N? 1853-Mr? 1854 Weekly Forest City democrat; Mr? 1885-91? Cleveland weekly leader and herald
Early issues pub in Olmsted Falls
DLC S 15 1852;Ag 1880-82;Mr 1889-96
MWA Mr 15,O 18-N 1 1848;Ja 21,Je 10,Jl 15 1857;F 17 1866
OCl Jl 25,Ag 15 1885
OClWHi Ap 21-28,O 13-D 1847;Je 28,N 22 1848[49]-53;Mr 29,My 3,O 11 1854-S 1855;56-62;D 23-30 1865;Mr 26 1870;N 2 1872;Ja-Je 12 1875;Jl-D 1876;78-80;Jl 1883-88;Mr 16-30, Jl 1889-99;Jl 1900-Ap 1904
OHi S 30(extra)1852;D 20 1873;D 5(supp) 1860
TJT S 15 1900

Cleveland **LEADER.** d Ja 13 1847-Ag 31 1917‖
1847-D 31 1851 as Daily true democrat; Ja 1 1852-O 14 1853 Morning true democrat; O 15 1853-Mr 15 1854 Daily Forest City democrat; Mr 16 1885-91? Cleveland leader and morning herald. Merged with Cleveland plain dealer
Jl 19-26 1896 are centennial eds
CL My 26,Jl 9,30 1864;S 26 1881
CoU 1901;S 1906-My 1910
Ct Jl 22 1896
CtY Jl 22 1896
DLC Ap 15 1865;Jl 11 1874-Je 29 1880;Ja 6 1895;98-Ap 1899;S 14 1901
ICHi Mr 13,Ap 29 1865;Jl 22 1896
ICM S 2 1879
IU S 20,22-27 1881;Ag 6 1909
InRE Ja 12 1875
KHi S 20-D 1881;S 17 1886;Jl 22 1896
MBAt Ap 15,17,28 1865
MWA Mr 8 1854[F 2-Ap 1855]My 7 1864;Je 30,Jl 8 1873;Ja 7,Ag 25 1876;Ag 11 1877;N 25 1894;S 8 1901
MiU Jl 19-Ag 19 1896
MnHi Jl 8-N 26 1863;Ap 28 1865[66]S 20,26 1881;Jl 24 1885;S 14 1901
NNHi Jl 11,Ag 26 1863
NcD My 26 1895;My 3 1896;D 27 1898
NbHi Ap 15 1865
OCHi [Jl-N 17 1847]
OCl Jl 1850-1917
OClWHi 1847-S 14,O 15 1853-Mr 4,Je 1854-57;Ag 16 1858-My 1890;S 14 1892;Ja 4,9,22,31, Jl-D 1894;My 8 1895;Ja-Ag 20 1896;97-Jl 1898;S 1899-S 20 1901;Je 13 1902;Mr 6,29,Je 1904;05-17
OHi F 4 1858-78;Jl 12 1879-1917;supp My 16 1864

OOxM Ag 19 1851;Mr 16 1882
TJT Ap 17 1886
WHi Jl 16 1861;My 31 1865;Jl 26 1869;My 27 1886;Jl 22 1896

Cleveland tri-weekly **LEADER.** tw -1904‖?
Mr 1885?-91? Leader and herald
OClWHi O 20 1858;O 13-D 1860;F 23,Jl 1 1861;My 19,O 28 1862;Mr 24 1864
WHi F 2 1856

LEMKO. w 1928?+
In Ukrainian
CSt-H [1932]+

Cleveland **LIVE STOCK** news. w,d 1896?+
d 1913?-D 9 1929
IU Jl 1919-S 29,O 2-9 1922;D 10-31 1923;Ja 2-Jl 1924;Ap-Jl 1,D 24 1925-Jl 16,D 16 1926+

MAGYAR banyászlap. *See under* Detroit, Mich.

Cleveland daily **MAIL.** d Jl 4 1881-
OClWHi Jl 5-S 8 1881

Cleveland **MESSENGER.** w My? 1836-
OClWHi N 16-23 1836;Mr 8 1837

MONITOR. w,d 1891+
1891-Je 30 1923 as Polonia w Ameryce (w) Jl 1 1923-D 31 1929 Monitor Clevelandski
In Polish
pub S-D 1893;Je 30 1923+
OHi Je 13 1918-Je,S 29 1923+

Daily **NATIONAL** democrat. d Ja 3 1859-
DLC 1859-60
OClWHi Ag 18,20,S 11 1859

Weekly **NATIONAL** democrat. w Ja 5 1859-
OClWHi Jl-N,D 28 1859-My,Jl 13-O 1860;F 15 1861
OHi Ag 17 1859;O 12,26 1860

NEUE heimat. *See* Siebenbürgisch amerikanisches volksblatt

NEW Sunday morning times. w 1874?-82‖?
1874?-80? as Sunday morning times
ICM Jl 29 1877
OClWHi O 15 1871;N 28 1875;Jl 20 1879;O 24 1880;Jl 3 1881
WHi S 19 1875;Jl 30 1876

NEWBURG CITY news. sm
OClWHi S 10 1910-11

Cleveland **NEWS.** d 1868+
1868-Mr 14 1885 as Evening news; Mr 15 1885-1905? News and herald
S 19-26 1928 are Cleveland achievement eds
DLC Jl 14,18,22 1885;Mr,Ap 10,13-14,17-20,22, 26-27 1886
KHi Ja 1 1891;S 27-29 1920
M S 19-26 1926
MBAt S 19,23,26 1926
OCl F 19,S 20,24,27 1881;Ap 14 1882;Je 23 1885;Jl 1905+
OClWHi [F 1869-My]Jl 11 1871-N 1873;O 11 1876;Jl 1878-80;Jl 2,4 1881;Ag 28 1883;Jl 23 1885;Ap 3 1886;Ja 20-26 1888;91-Je 1895;Ag 26 1896[98]Jl 2 1900;S 14,21 1901;Ja-Je 1903;F 12 1909;F 17 1911;O 1912-O 17 1914;15-32
OHi Ja 1 1901;Mr 1918-My 19,O 12 1920+
T S 19-20,23,26 1928
WHi D 19 1868;Mr 13 1877;Je 3 1886;S 26 1926

NORTHEAST observer. w 1907+
1907-Je 1931 as Euclid observer
pub 1896+
OCl Jl 1929+

OHIO American. [Ohio City] w S 19 1844-48‖
Merged with True democrat, later Cleveland weekly leader
KHi S 26-O 24 1844
MWA Mr 27,Ap 17-24,Je 12 1845;Ap 15,O 21,N 18-25 1846;Ja 6,20,F 10,Mr 24 1847

OHIO CITY argus. *See* Ohio transcript and farmers register

OHIO transcript and farmers register. [Ohio City] w My 26 1836-39‖
1836-Je? 1838 as Ohio City argus
DLC O 3 1838
MnHi My-O 13 1836
OClWHi My 26,Ag-O 20 1836;Ja-F,Je 1837-Je 7 1838

Cleveland, **OHIO** western intelligencer. *See* Ohio observer (Hudson)

PARMA citizen. w 1923+
pub 1923+
Oct 1930+

PENNY PRESS. *See* Cleveland press

PEOPLE'S forum. w 1894-
WHi Ag 1894-Ag 22 1895

PICTORIAL world. w Ap 17 1875-
MWA Ap 17 1875

Weekly **PLAIN DEALER.** w Ja 6 1831-1904‖?
1831-41 as Cleveland advertiser
Ct [1835-38]
DLC [1847-52;55;61;65]Mr 21 1878
IU S 13 1843;Ag 6 1909
InLoHi N 16 1832
InNcHi Je 11 1873;Ap 5 1883
MWA S 30 1841;Je 18,Jl 2,D 10 1856
NNHi N 3 1852
NcD My 1 1896
OCHi S 14 1901
OCl Ag 2 1831;My 16 1833;Ja 13 1847;Mr 12 1856;86-98;1900-04
OClWHi 1831-Ja 2,Mr 14,N 9-16 1832;Ja 23, Mr 28-Ap 11,My 23-30,Ag 29 1833;Je 26,S 1834-38;Ap 8 1839-Mr 19,O 8 1840;42-66;71-74;Jl 3 1884;Ag 9 1885;87-88;95-97;Jl 4 1898; 99;1901-02
OHi 1850;54-58;F 7 1860
P-M F 7 1855
WHi Mr 26 1862

OHIO (*Continued*)

CLEVELAND—*Continued*

Cleveland tri-weekly PLAIN-DEALER. tw 1843?-52||?
DLC Mr 18 1878
MWA Mr 16,N 6 1852
OHi Je 22 1866

Cleveland PLAIN DEALER. d Ap 1845+
1845-D 31 1886 as Cleveland daily plain dealer
My 23 1916 is Diamond jubilee number
Ct N 29 1925-Ap 1 1928
DLC Ap 17 1845;Ap 1848-Mr 1849;Ap-S 1850; Ag 1851-[Jl-D 1855]-Je 1857;Ja-[Ag-D] 1858;60-Je 1861;Jl 1862-Je 1863;Mr 16 1885-88;Jl-D 1892;Jl 1893-Je 1895;96;Jl 1897+
ICU 1917-O 1921;22-27;35+
KHi Je 4,13 1894;Jl 31 1918;S 27-29 1920
MWA Je 27 1851[Ap-D 1853]Ja-Je 1857;Ja-Je 1861;S 8 1901;My 23 1916;S 27-29 1933
N Jl 3 1847
OCl Jl 1880-[81]Mr 16 1885+
OClWHi 1845+
ODW Je 1933+
OHi Ja 16 1866+
OXG D 1933+
VU Mr 2,Ap 3 1917;S 28-29,O 2,7 1934
WHi Ap 28 1908;17+
WaPS O 20 1915;S 25 1917;D 19,21-22 1922

Evening PLAIN DEALER. d 1846?-1905||?
O 1893-96 as Evening post
DLC Ja-Je 1886;Jl-D 1890
OCl 1850-68;72-[80]-[86]-[93]-[95]-[1905]
OClWHi S 12 1894;S 11,29 1896
OHi Ja 1 1901

POKROK. w 1867-79||?
In Czech
NNHi Ap 10 1870

POLONIA w Ameryce. *See* Monitor

Sunday POST. w 1875-78||?
United with Sunday morning voice to form Sunday voice and post, later Voice
OClWHi Ap 8,Je 4 1876;Je 9 1878

Cleveland POST. d O 4 1879-
OClWHi 1879-Ja 17 1880

Evening POST. *See* Evening plain dealer

Cleveland PRESS. d N 2 1878+
1878-85? as Penny press
CtY F 26-Mr 3 1934
DLC S 1897+
IC Ap 30 1889
KHi S 27-28 1920
MoS Ap 26-N 1879
NcD F 26-Mr 3 1934
OCHi Jl 4 1895
OCl D 15 1879;N 1895+
OClWHi N 2,D 31 1878;Je 4,6,27 1879;Ap 21 1880-Mr 1907;D 29 1908;Ja 7 1909;Ap 1913+
OHi D 31 1900;Ap 1918-My 1920;Ap 28 1926+
VU Ap 3 1917

RADNICKA borba. w 1905?+
In Slavonian
PP [1934]+

Cleveland RECORDER. d S 9 1895-1910||?
Followed by Legal news and recorder (not in this list)
OCl 1895-97
OClWHi N 1895-97;Jl-Ag 1898;Jl 1899-Jl 1901; Ag 1902-Je,O-D 1904;F,My-O,D 1905-06
OHi Ja 2 1901
WHi Mr 2 1896-S 1897;Jl-D 1899

Cleveland REPUBLICAN. w My 2 1844-
DLC My 2 Jl 18 1844
OClWHi My 2,Jl 18 1844

RESERVE battery. w Jl 20- 1848||?
Campaign paper
DLC Ag 10-23,S 7,21,O 5-12 1848
MWA Ag 10-S 7,21,O 5-12 1848
OHi Jl 20,N 2 1848

Cleveland daily REVIEW. d Jl 2 1857-61||
OClWHi 1857-Ja 26,My 22 1860;My 9 1861
OHi Ja 25-Je,N 9 1858

Cleveland semi-weekly REVIEW. sw Ag 10 1858-
OClWHi Ag 10-27 1858;Ja 20 1860

Sunday morning REVIEW. w Ap 18-D 1858||?
OClWHi Ap-D 18 1858

ROBITNIK. w,d 1914-19||?
w 1914-16?
In Ukrainian
NN 1917-Jl 1918;19

ROCKY RIVER call. w 1915+
pub [1915+]
OCl Jl 1929+

ROMANUL. d,w,sw,m 1903-33||?
d 1903?-N 27 1917;w N 29 1917-29? (sw My 19 1918-Ap 4 1923)
1920-28? pub in Youngstown
In Roumanian
IU S 1917-Ap 15 1928
NN Mr 16 1924
PP [1928-29]

SCOTT soup bowl. w Jl 8- 1852||?
Campaign paper
OHi Jl 29 1852

SENTINEL. w 1879-86||?
ICHi Ag 7,21-28,S 25,O 16-23 1886
OOxM S 18 1880

SHAW observer. [East Cleveland] sm
OClWHi S 25 1930-My 14,O 1931-[33]

SIEBENBÜRGISCH amerikanisches volksblatt. w 1905+
1905-14 as Neue heimat; 1914-Je 8? 1917 Deutsch-ungarisches volksblatt
In German
pub 1907+
OHi 1919+

SLOVENSKÁ ozvena v Amerike. w Ja 12 1928-
In Slovak
IU 1928-31
OHi 1928-31

SOUTH CLEVELAND advocate. *See* Cleveland advocate

SOUTH END news. w 1922+
OCl O 23 1925-O 14 1927;Jl 1929+

SOUTH EUCLID citizen. w F 20 1924+
pub 1924+
M Ag 20 1932

Cleveland STAR. w,d 1886-92||?
1886-Ag 1889 as Grip; S-D 1889? Daily grip (d
OCl Mr 1886-89;91

SUBURBAN news and herald. w D 3 1914+
1914-F 18 1915 as Suburban news
pub 1914+
OCl Jl 1929+

Cleveland Sunday SUN. w 1880-84||?
United with Cleveland voice to form Sun and voice, later Voice
S 25 1881 is Garfield ed
MiU S 25 1881
OClWHi Jl 3,24-31,S 11,25-O 2 1881;My 14,Je 4,18,Jl 2 1882;Ag 24,S 21 1884

SUN and voice. *See* Voice

SVET. d F 22 1911+
In Bohemian
pub 1911+
IU D 18 1917+
OHi Mr 10 1918-Ja 1,Mr 21 1921+

SZABADSÁG. w,d N 12 1891+
w 1891-1905?
In Hungarian
pub 1891—
IU D 6 1917-Ap 14 1933
OHi Ja 3 1901
PP [1928]+
PPiHi [S 23 1914-Ap 1919;22]-[29-Jl 1930]+

Cleveland weekly TIMES. w S 10 1845-48||
Merged with Cleveland plain dealer
DLC S 24-D 24 1845;Ja 7,F 18,Ap 29,My 13-Je 17,Jl 1-8,29,Ag 26,S 9,O 21,N 11,D 2-16 1846;Ja 13 1847-D 20 1848
OClWHi 1845-D 9 1846;Mr 1847-F 7 1849

Daily Cleveland TIMES. d O 13 1847-48||
Merged with Cleveland plain dealer
OClWHi O 13,15,D 11 1847

Sunday morning TIMES. *See* New Sunday morning times

Cleveland TIMES. d Mr 2 1922-Mr 3 1927||?
1922 as Cleveland commercial; 1923-25? Cleveland times and commercial. Merged with Cleveland plain dealer
MWA Mr 2 1922
OCl 1922-F 1927
OClWHi 1922-Mr 3 1927
OHi Ap-S 2 1922;Ap 1925-F 1927

Cleveland TRIBUNE. w 1883?-96||?
1883?-88? as Sunday tribune
OCl O 10 1886
OClWHi Ap 6 1884;S 7 1889

Cleveland TRIBUNE. w
OClWHi Je 8,Ag 24,N 9 1912-Mr 1 1913

TRUE democrat. *See* Cleveland leader

Az UJSAG. [Hungarian news] w 1920-31||?
In Hungarian
PPiHi Mr 1924-S 25 1931

La VOCE del popolo italiano. w,d 1904+
w 1904-22
In Italian
IU [D 8 1917-My 11,Je 8 1918-D 20 1919]

VOICE. w O 15 1871-1903||?
1871 as Sunday voice; 1872-D 29 1878 Sunday morning voice; Ja 5-D 1879? Sunday voice and post; 1880?-D 26 1896 Cleveland voice (1885?-95? Sun and voice); 1897? Sunday voice and Clevelander; 1898? Sunday voice
KHi O 2 1881
MWA S 25 1881;D 2 1894
OClWHi O 15 1871;N 10 1872;Mr 30,Je 1 1873[74-76]Jl 8 1877-Je,Jl 21 1879;80-82;85-88;Mr 4 1889;My 11 1890;My 31 1891;Jl 30 1893;Jl 4,S 16-23 1894;Je 6,D 21 1895-N 4 1899

WÄCHTER am Erie. sw Ag 9 1852-
OCl Ag 9 1852
OClWHi 1853;50-93

WÄCHTER und anzeiger. w Ag 9 1852-99||?
1852-S 1893 as Wächter am Erie
MnHi Je 8-D 15 1859
OHi Ag 9 1852

WÄCHTER und anzeiger. d S 17 1866+
1866-S 1893 as Wächter am Erie
Ag 9 1902 is Cleveland golden jubilee number
IC Ag 9 1852;Ag 9 1902
IU Ag 25 1917-My 21 1918
MWA Ap 28 1876;Ag 25 1924
NcD Mr 9 189-
OCl 1899+
OHi Ja 1 1901[19-N 3 1922]
PScrHi Ag 5 1890;F 15 1897;F 18 1906

WEST and South. w 1865-
NcD D 18 1865

WEST county advocate. w 1907?-Mr 26 1932||
1907-Ja 18 1930 as Cleveland enterprise
OCl 1912-14;16-32
OHi N 30 1911

Cleveland WHIG. w,sw Ag 1834-
w 1834-F 1835
CSmH D 10 1834
MWA O 28 1835

WIADOMOŚCI codzienne. d 1915+
In Polish
pub O 11 1916+
IU 1918-28;Mr 1929+
OHi Je 11 1918+

Cleveland daily WORLD d Ag 29 1889-Je 1905||?
Merged with Cleveland news
DLC Ap 1890-S 1894;N 1895-Mr 1896
NN O 1895-S 1896
NcD D 20 1893
OCl [1895]-[97]-1905
OClWHi Ap 1890-1905
OHi Ap 1895-Mr 1896;F 25 1899-F 1902

COALTON

Coalton TIMES. *See* Wellston telegram (Wellston)

COLLINWOOD

Papers published in Collinwood are listed under Cleveland

COLUMBIANA

Columbiana INDEPENDENT. w Ja 8 1898-1901||?
OClWHi Ja 8,S 1898-Ag 1899
OHi Ja 5 1901

INDEPENDENT register. w 1870-98||?
OClWHi S 6 1877
OHi O 1881-O 4 1883;O 8 1885-S 1887;S 1891-S 1893

Columbiana LEDGER. w 1858?-
OClWHi F 7 1862

Columbiana LEDGER. w 1889+
pub 1926+
OHi Ja 2 1901

TRUE press. *See* Leetonia reporter 1875+ (Leetonia)

COLUMBUS

Daily ADVERTISER. d
OHi D 6 1833

Columbus evening BULLETIN. d Ag 22- 1860||
OHi Ag-O 12 1860

Evening BULLETIN and United States republican. sw
WHi Mr 1-4,11-14,25-Ap 7 1830

CAMPAIGN statesman. w 1848||
WHi Ap 8-N 11 1848
—d ed *See* Ohio statesman

Daily CAPITAL CITY fact. *See* Daily evening express

Sunday CAPITAL-TRIBUNE. w F 17 1878-91||?
1878-85? as Sunday capital
IU Ap 10(supp)1887
OCo 1878-F 6 1881
OHi My 26 1878

Columbus CITIZEN. d Mr 1 1899+
pub 1899+
OCo 1899+
OHi 1899-F,Je 1900+

COLUMBIAN. *See* Ohio columbian

CRISIS. w Ja 31 1861-71||?
CSmH 1861-Ja 21 1863
DLC 1861-Ja 1865
ICHi 1861-Ja 23 1862;Ag 12,S 9 1863
ICN 1861-Ja 1865
ICU 1861-Ja 20 1869
IHi [1861-64]
IU 1861-Ja 24 1866
In O 1862-64
InU 1861-Ja 20 1864
KHi 1861-Ja 20 1869
LNH 1861-Ja 1865
MB 1861
MWA 1861-Ja 20,Mr 23,O 12,D 28 1864;Ja 4,F 15,Ap 5-12,Je 21,Jl 5-12 1865;Ja 31 1866-Ja 19 1870
MnHi 1861-Ja 1865
MnU 1861-Ja 20 1864
MoScR 1861-63;65
N D 24 1862;Ja 21,F 18 1863;Ap 6 1864;Jl 5 1865
NN 1861-[63-65]
NSyU Ag 13 1862;D 30 1863;F 10 1864
NcD Je 3 1863;Jl 20,D 7 1864
OC 1861-Ja 20 1864
OCHi 1861-Ja 1865
OCo 1861-Ja 18 1871
ODW 1861-Ja 23 1869
ODa Mr 11 1863-Ja 18 1871
OHi 1861-My 1871
OO [1862-66]
OT Ja-O 1861;Ja 29 1862-Je 21 1863
OU 1861
PAg 1861-Ja 1868
TxU 1861-Ja 1865
WHi 1861-Ja 1866

Columbus DEMOCRAT. d 1878-80 *See* Columbus news

Columbus DEMOCRAT. w 1875-80 *See* Columbus press

Columbus DEMOCRAT. w 1915-20||?
OHi S 16 1916-S 8 1917

DEMOCRATIC call. w S 13 1894-97||?
OClWHi S 1895-Ag 1896
OCo 1894-Ag 1896

OHIO (*Continued*)

COLUMBUS—*Continued*

Columbus evening DISPATCH. d Jl 1 1871+
Sunday issues as Sunday journal dispatch
DLC 1898;Ag 1918+
M Ja 10 1934
MWA Jl 1(facsimile)1871;Ap 12 1876;Je 5 1910
OClWHi Mr 16 1874;Ja 29-30 1875;S 1 1877;S 11-15 1879;S 26 1881;Je 4-8 1897
OCo 1871+
ODW 1926-27
OHi Jl 1(facsimile)1871;Jl 22-N 1872;73+
VU Ap 3 1917
WHi Ap 10 1895

Columbus DISPATCH. w 1874-1900‖?
1874-84 as Dollar weekly dispatch
TxU [Jl 1877-Ja 17 1878]

DOLLAR weekly dispatch. *See* Columbus dispatch

DOLLAR statesman. w S 29 1849-Ja 10? 1852‖
WHi 1849-Ja 10 1852
—d ed *See* Columbus news

Daily evening EXPRESS. d Jl 4 1851-Je 1864‖
1851-S 28? as Daily Capital City fact
MWA Ag 29 1852
OHi 1851-Je 4 1864
OOxM Ja 6-My 1 1862
—w ed *See* State capital fact

Weekly Columbus EXPRESS. w 1894-1917‖?
In German
OHi 1894-95;97-1917

EXPRESS und westbote. d O 1 1891-1918‖?
1891-Ag 1 1903 as Columbus express
In German
OHi 1891-Ag 19 1918
—Sunday ed *See* Der Ohio sonntagsgast

EXTRA Ohio statesman. w Ap 4- 1840‖
Campaign paper
InRE O 17 1840
MWA O 10 1840
NNHi S 5 1840
OCHi Ag 29-O 3,17-24 1840
See also Ohio statesman

Daily Columbus FREEMAN. d 1841?-
DLC S 30 1841
IU D 29 1841;Ja 3-5,7-8,11-13,16,22 1842
OClWHi O 2 1841;Ap 9,Je-Jl 1842

Columbus FREEMAN. w 1841?-
IU Mr 5 1842
MdBJ Jl 23 1842

Columbus GAZETTE. 1817-25 *See* Ohio state journal. w

Columbus GAZETTE. w 1849-86‖
1849-56 as Swan's elevator
MWA Ag 28 1852;S 9 1859
OClWHi Je 9 1871;Jl 19 1872;Jl 2 1880
OCo Ag 9 1856-62;Ja 27-My 1883
OHi Ja 24 1852-My 20 1854;Ag 9 1856-Jl 1869; Je 17 1870;Je 9 1871;Ag 2 1872
TxU Ja 23 1857-64
WHi D 13 1851

Columbus Sunday HERALD. w 1875-83‖?
OClWHi S 2 1877;S 14 1879

Columbus HEROLD. w My 1 1920+
In German
pub [1920-32]+

INDEPENDENT press. w? 1838?-
OClWHi D 24 1838

JEWISH chronicle. w Mr 29 1918-20‖?
OHi 1918-Ja 10 1919

Columbus daily JOURNAL. *See* Ohio state journal d

Sunday JOURNAL dispatch. *See* Ohio state journal; Columbus evening dispatch

MAGICIAN. w Jl 4- 1836‖?
IU Jl 18,O 3-24 1836
OHi Jl-Ag 22 1836

MAGYAR banyászlap. *See under* Detroit, Mich.

Columbusi MAGYAR ujsag [Columbus Hungarian news]. w
In Hungarian
PPiHi [Ag 29 1930-Je 19 1931]

Daily MAIL. d N? 1843-
IU D 1 1843

Columbus daily MONITOR. w,d Ag 7 1915-17‖
1915-Jl 8 1916 as Columbus Saturday monitor (w)
OClWHi 1915-Jl 5 1917
OCo 1916-Mr 1917
OHi 1916-Je 1917

NATIONAL enquirer. w My 24 1827-
Suspended from My 24-Je 21 1827
DLC F 23 1828
IU My-O 13,N-D 1827;N 1828
MWA My 24,Je 21 1827
N My 24 1827
OHi Jl-S 1 1827;S 4 1828

Daily NEWS. d Mr 31 1845-
IU Mr 31 1845

Columbus NEWS. d Ag 11 1847-Ag 3 1911‖
1847-N 1878 as Daily Ohio statesman (My 23 1854-F 24 1855 Ohio statesman and democrat) D 1878-Mr 13 1880 Columbus democrat; Mr 15 1880-S 1888 Daily times; O 1888-F 25 1898 Columbus press (title varies slightly) F 26 1898-Jl 10 1909 Columbus press-post (title varies: Columbus press-post; Evening press; Columbus evening press; Columbus daily press)
CSmH Ja 6 1881
DLC 1847-Jl 6 1849;Mr 4-D 1853;55-Mr 2 1861;98
ICHi Ap 24,My 30 1865
In [My 23-S 15 1854]
MWA Ap 19 1854;Je 15 1855
N Jl 4,Ag 20,25,S 16,O 10,21,27,29 1863
NNHi Ap 1853-My 22 1854
OCHi Ja 28,F 25,Mr 21-22 1848;Jl 27-28 1849; Je 19-20,Jl 3,25,D 12-13,26 1850[Ja-Mr 1851] 57-65
OClWHi Ja 9,Mr 30 1879;Jl-D 1883
OCo N 1847-48;Ja-N 1850;Je 20 1851-My 22 1854;F 1862-Ja 1867;68;Jl-Ag,N-D 1894;My-Je,S-O 1895;Mr 1898-O 1899;Ja-F,My 1900-O 1901;My-Je,N-D 1902;Mr-D 1903;My-Ag 1904;Ja-My 1905;Ja-Je 1908;Ja-F,S-O 1909; 10
OHi D 1878-Ag 3 1911
OOxM Ja 7-My 1 1862
TxU [1847-51]
WHi N 1847-S 1848;F-Je 1849;50-51;Jl-D 1852
—w ed *See* Columbus press; Dollar statesman
—sw,tw eds *See* Ohio statesman
—campaign ed *See* Extra Ohio statesman
—family ed *See* Dollar statesman

Sunday morning NEWS. w 1867-1900‖?
MWA N 15 1874
OHi Jl 17 1870-N 1884

OHIO columbian. w Ja 6 1853-56‖
1853-54? as Columbian. Merged with Ohio state journal
DLC Ja 10 1855-Mr 1856
MWA F 10 1853;Ag 29,S 19,O-D 12 1855;Ja 9, F 6-13,Mr 19 1856
OCo 1853-F 1 1854
OHi 1853-F 6,Je 11 1856

OHIO confederate and old school republican. *See* Old school republican and Ohio state gazette

OHIO coon catcher. w Ag 17-N 16? 1844‖
Campaign paper
DLC Ag-N 2 1844
IU S 28 1844
MeBa [Ag-N 16 1844]
MoSM Ag 31 1844
OC Ag-N 16 1844
OHi Ag 24-N 16 1844

OHIO freeman and Columbus herald. sw Mr? 1841-
MWA Ap 3 1841
NN Ap 3 1841

***OHIO monitor.** w,sw My 16? 1816-36‖
Jl 28 1821-25? as Ohio monitor and patron of industry. Merged with Western hemisphere, later Columbus press
sw during sessions of legislature
CSmH Ag 25 1830
Ct [1834-36]
DLC Je 23-30,S 1,O 6,N 3 1821;Ja 31,F 7,Mr 13,Ap 2-10,24,My 22 1824;Ag 18 1827;Mr 8,S 10 1828;Mr 18,Jl 8,22 1829;Ja-D 22 1831;33-S 26 1836
ICHi Jl 27 1830
IU Jl 28-Ag 18 1821;Jl 13-Ag 2,S 7,21,N 23 1822;Ja 5-12,26 1828;F 21-Mr 3,O 5,N 23,D 7-15 1831;Ja 2,16,Ap 11-25,My 9,23,Je 13-Jl 11,Ag 1,22,O 10,D 13 1832;F 4,21,Mr 13,Ap 17-24,My 8-15,29,Je 19,Jl 3,D 2,12-23,30 1833-Ja 9,20-F 6,13-17,27,Mr 5 1834;Mr 10 1836
extras: Jl 6,13 1822;O 17 1832
land extras:Jl 20,27,Ag 3,17 1822
MWA Ja 13,F 17,Mr 17-Ap 14,My 26,Jl 7,O 27 1821;Ag 2,10-17,N 2-9 1822;F 15-Mr 1,15,S 27-O 18,N-D 6,20 1823-[26-27]-Je,D 1832[Ja-Mr 20 1833]Jl 2,23 1834;Ja 25,F 12 1835
N Jl 23 1825;O 30 1833
NcD Je 21,N 6-13 1828;Mr 25,Ap 1,15-22,My 6 1829
OClWHi Jl 7,S 28,D 8-15 1821;22;F 8,Mr 15-29 1823;Je 17 1835;Ag 22 1836
ODW S 8 1821-N 23 1822;F 1829-My 15 1830
OHi Mr 24,Jl 28 1821-S 1823;My 21 1825;Jl 1826-My 15 1833
WHi [1821-O 23 1824]

OHIO people's press. w My 25 1836-
IU My 25,N 9 1836
MWA N 2 1836
OClWHi My-N 9 1836
OHi My-N 9 1836

OHIO political register. w -S 1837‖
United with Ohio state journal and Columbus gazette to form State journal and political register, later Ohio state journal

OHIO populist. *See under* Greenville

OHIO press. sw,d Ja 23 1846-48‖?
Title varies slightly
d during sessions of legislature
CSmH D 11 1846
DLC 1846-My 1848
IU D 14-17 1846[F 1847-My 1848]
MWA Ja 21,F 10 1848
OCHi F-N 1846
OClWHi D 21 1847-F 24 1848
OHi 1846-Je 1848

OHIO press. tw F? 1846-
OClWHi Ap 25-D 8 1846

OHIO register and antimasonic review. w,sw 1830-33‖
sw during sessions of legislature
DLC Jl 11 1833

Der OHIO sonntagsgast. w 1878?-1917‖?
In German
OHi Mr 18 1882-90;Jl 1891-1917
—d ed *See* Express und westbote

OHIO staats-zeitung und volks-advocat. (Ohio state gazette and people's advocate) w? 1839-
In German and English
DLC My 22,O 13 1840

OHIO standard. w 1848?-51‖
NSyU Ja 10,F 7 1849
OCHi Jl 25,Ag 22-29,O 17 1850

OHIO state bulletin. w,sw Jl 29 1829-31‖?
sw during sessions of legislature
CSmH S 1 1830
DLC Ag 26 1829
IU Jl 14 1830
MBAt S 15 1830
OHi 1829-Jl,Ag 25 1830-Mr 4,15 1831
WHi [Ag 1829-Ag 18 1830]Ja-Mr 4 1831

OHIO state bulletin. w? My 1 1839-40‖
DLC My 1, 1839
ODW Mr 28 1840
OHi 1839-Mr 1840

OHIO state courier. w? My 16 1835-
IU My 16 1835

OHIO state democrat. w Jl? 1853-54‖?
OClWHi S 10 1853

Daily OHIO state democrat. d D 12 1853-My 1854‖
United with Daily Ohio statesman to form Ohio statesman and democrat, later Columbus news
IU F 27 1854
MWA Mr 27 1854
OCo 1853-My 22 1854
OHi 1853-My 22 1854

OHIO state gazette. w 1827-Je 11 1828‖
IU O-D 12 1827;Ja 2-9 1828
MWA D 26 1827
OHi Ja 9-Je 1828
WHi F 20 1828
—sw ed *See* Ohio state journal

***OHIO state journal.** w,sw Jl 17 1811-Je 17 1904‖
1811-F 1817 as Western intelligencer; F 20?-N 1817 Western intelligencer and Columbus gazette; D 1817-S 15 1825 Columbus gazette; S 22 1825-S 1837 Ohio state journal and Columbus gazette (Je 19-D 4 1828 Ohio state journal and gazette) O 1837-Ap 11 1838 State journal and political register;Ap 18 1838-Mr 12 1839 Ohio state journal and register (other variations slight)
w 1811-94? (sw during legislative sessions D 12 1827-41)
1811-N 1817 pub in Worthington
CSmH S 2 1830
Ct F 2 1831
CtY S 2 1830
DLC 1825-28;Ja 21,Jl 9,Ag 6,S 3,O 1,29,D 19 1829-Ja 13, 23,Ag 19,D 11,22 1830-Ja 1,15 1831;S 29 1832;Ja 4 1834;N 27 1840;Mr 30-S 24 1841;D 25 1875
ICHi S 18 1828-Mr 1837
IU Je 28,Jl 12 1821;Je 6,20,Jl-Ag 1822;S 22,O 1825-Ja 5 1826 (photostat) [27] Ja 5-12,30-F 9,21,Mr 6,My 1, 22,N 6-13,27-D 1828;Mr 19, Ap 23-Ag,S 10-17,O 8-N 12,D 10-30 1829[31] S 12 1832
extras: Je 5,Ag 29,S 5 1822;N 23 1826;Je 8 1835
InI My 10 1859
MWA F 15 1821;Ja 19 1826;F 22,Mr 15 1827; Ap 14,My 26,N 24,D 5-8,12-15,22-29 1832;Ja 2-23,30-F 6,13,20-25 1833;O 1837-N 1849;Ja 22-N 26 1850;F 1852-O 9 1860;Ap 9 1861
N S 23 1824;Jl 7,D 1 1825;O 12 1833
NN D 20-27 1821;F 12 1824;D 8,22 1825-F 9 1826;D 29 1841;Ja 5,F 23,Mr 9-Je 15,29,Jl 13 1842-F 7,D 25 1844-Ja 1,15,Jl 9,23 1845-Ja 10,24-Ap 22,My-Je 3,Jl 22-S,O 14 1846-N 1849;Ja 22-N 1850;N 29,D 27 1851;F 1852-53
supps: O 7,14,21,N 4 1851;Mr 29 1853
NNHi S 16 1824;F 12 1831;D 26 1832;Ja 5,9, 19,F 9 1833
OCHi 1825-32;Ap 1835-Mr 1836[Ap-S 1839]Ap 1,O 7 1840
OClWHi Mr 29 1821 D 12 1822-Ja.D 4-18 1823;Ja 8-Mr 4,D 9,23, 25 1824-Ja,O 27 1825; Mr 30 1826-[27-28]-37;N 28 1838-S 1840;D 1841-N 1844;Je 10 1846;S 15,O 13 1847;Mr 26 1850-Mr 1852;Jl 30,S 1861-Ja 14 1862; 66-N 9 1867;71-72;N 25 1891
OCo 1821-N 14 1822
ODW O 6,12,20,N 3,24,D 1-5,12,19,26 1837;Ja 12,19-Mr 2,9,16,O 24 1838
ODa My 11 1842;Je 26,Jl 10-31,Ag 14-O 2,16-N 13,D 11 1844;Ja 8(supp)1845
OHi Ja 10 1822-Je 17 1904
OOxM Ag 17,O-N 2 1826;F 1,My 10 1827[Jl 1828-Jl 1829] D 10,21-28 1831[32-Jl 12 1834]
TJT O 19 1900
TxU N 15 1873-F 2 1878
WHi F 15 1821-D 18 1823;D 1826;Ja 11-Ap 5 1827;S 18 1828;Ap 30 1829-Je 1831
—w ed 1827-28 *See* Ohio state gazette

OHIO state journal. d Jl 10 1837+
Jl-S 1837 as Columbus daily journal; O 1837-Ap 10 1838 Daily journal and register; Ap 11 1838-Mr 15 1839 Journal and register (other variations slight) Sunday issues as Sunday journal dispatch
DLC Mr 11-D 1849;F 28 1850-52;N 19 1858-Je 1859;Ag 1861-65;Ja-Jl 13 1867;76;O 11 1898+
ICU Ap 3 1845
IU O 14 1837
IaDH O 26-27 1852
KHi Ap 29 1865
MBAt Ap 17 1865
MWA Mr 30 1841;Mr 8 1844;N 29,D 27 1851; O 13-20,23-24,26-27,30-31,N 10-17,20 1860;Je 8 1871;N 22 1876;Ja 21,Jl 7 1898
MiU Jl 2 1841
N Jl 26 1861;Ja 19 1863
NN Ja 3 1852;D 27 1853
NNHi My 16,Je 24,Jl 18 1863
NjWdHi D 28 1865
OAU Ag 1925+
OCHi D 11 1840-D 4 1841;57-61
OCl N 23 1875
OClWHi D 1839-Mr 21,S 10 1840-Mr 1841;F 1-3 1843;Mr 8 1844;Ja-N 1845;F 5,10,D 1846-F 8,Ag 11 1847-Je 1848;Ja 22,Jl 3,D 6 1850; 57;N 19-D 15 1858[59] Mr 1 1860;Ap 16,Jl 1 1861;F 19,Mr 4,Ap 14 1862-[69]-[75]-[82]-[84]-[86]-[91]-[95-96]-[98]Ag 31 1899[1900-01]Je 3 1903;16-33

OHIO (*Continued*)

COLUMBUS—*Continued*

OHIO state journal. d Jl 10 1837+—*Continued*
OCo S 22 1825+
ODW My 9-16 1838;Je 4 1889;1910-11;Ja 1920; 23+
ODa D 1843-Jl 1846
OHi 1837+
OOxM F 1 1873;Ja 30-F 8,10-14 1916
TxU Jl 1859-Je 23 1860
WHi Mr 28-D 1851;Ap 3,6,Jl-D 1852;Ag 26 1862;Je 3 1867;Ja 30 1868;1917-20

OHIO state journal. w
Title varies slightly
MWA My 13 1839;O 31 1860
OClWHi Mr 24-D 9 1840;Ap-S 1841;Je-D 1844;F 2-Ag 10 1847;Mr 15,Je 26,Jl 12 1860

OHIO state tribune. w,sw Ap? 1843-45||
Ap?-D 2? 1843 as Columbus herald(w) D 1843 Ohio state tribune and Columbus herald
sw during sessions of legislature
IU S 2,30-O 7,N 11,D 2-16 1843;Ja 17,24-F 14 1844

OHIO state tribune. w? 1846?-
NSyU Ja 29,F 19 1848

OHIO statesman. sw,tw,d Ap 20 1838-
Title varies with frequency
sw(tw during sessions of legislature) 1838-My 21 1839; tw(d during sessions) My 24 1839-
DLC 1838 40;F 4 1845-Ag 1847
IU Je 22 1841;Ja 29,F 14,Ag 10 1842;O 11 1844
MWA Ag 14,28,O 17 1844;Je 13 1845;My 8 1846
OCHi [Je 1840-D 3 1841]-Ja 14 1842;F 6,D 7 1844;F 8 1847
OCo Ap-N 1844
ODa Ap 2-,Jl 3-O,N 13 1844;Mr 18(extra)1845
PNoHi My 3 1845
TxU F 10 Ag 4 1847
WHi D 3 1838-Mr 15 1839;D 4 1843-Jl 23 1845

Daily **OHIO statesman.** *See* Columbus news

OHIO statesman. w *See* Columbus press

Daily **OHIO sun.** d Jl 4 1906-09||
OHi 1906-My 5 1908

OHIO temperance advocate. w? 1834?-
IU Je 1835

OHIO torch. w O 1928-
O 5 1929 is anniversary ed
Negro
OHi O 5-12 1929

OLD school republican and Ohio state gazette. w,sw Ap 6 1839-44||
1839-Jl 1841 as Ohio confederate and old school republican
sw during sessions of legislature
DLC Ap 19 1839;Ag 25,S 29 1841;43-44
ICHi Mr 10 1842
IU Ap 19 1839;Mr 4 1840;D 17 1841
MB Ja 18,F 11,Je 9-16 1842;Ja 20-24,F 3 1843
OC Ja 26 1841
OCHi 1839-Ap 8 1841
OClWHi Mr 17 1839-Ap 4 1840
OHi complete

"OLD Zack." w Je 24-N 4? 1848||
Campaign paper
OHi Jl-N 1848

PALLADIUM of liberty. w D 27 1843-
NhD My 22 1844
OHi 1843-N 13 1844
WHi F 7 1844

PEOPLE'S press. w My 12- 1859||
OHi My-O 13 1859

Daily **POLITICAL tornado.** d O? 1840-
Campaign paper
DLC O 28-29 1840
MWA O 31 1840

Columbus morning **POST.** d D 4 1888-F 25 1898||
United with Columbus evening press to form Columbus press-post, later Columbus news
For Ag 2 1892-Ag 9 1895 *See* Columbus news
NhD F 27 1891
OCo Mr 2-Ap,Jl-Ag,N 2 1897-98
OHi 1888-91 Ap-Jl 1892

Columbus **PRESS.** w,sw My 1 1833-97||?
1833-Je 1837 as Western hemisphere; Jl 1837-N 1878 Ohio statesman (title varies with frequency) D 1878-Mr 1880 Columbus democrat; Mr 1880-S 1888 Columbus times
sw during sessions of legislature 1833-54?
Ct [1835-37]F 2 1838
DLC Mr 9 1836;37-N 1839;F 3,N 17-D 21 1847; Mr 27-Jl 3,O 30-D 1849
IU My 1-22,Je,Jl 10-17,31-Ag 14,28-O 2,16-N,D 11-25 1833[34-36]-My 10,24-31,Je 14-21 1837
MBAt Jl 19 1843
MWA D 14 1840;Je 23 1841;F 8 1842;F 6 1844;S 16 1851;Ja 31 1854;Je 28-Jl 5,Ag 2-9,S 6,O 4-11,N 15-22,D 1871;D 23 1872
MdBJ Ag 10 1842
MnHi O 16 1844
N O 30 1833
NNHi Ja 18 1853-My 23 1854;Jl 9,23 1860
OCHi D 6-10 1839;Ja 14,Mr 24 1840;D 14 1847-Ag[N-D]1852;Ja 6,20-My 4 1852;Ja 18-My 23 1853
OCo D 1841-Mr 7,Jl 25 1842-Mr 13 1843;D 1844-Je 1845
OHi Ag 1833-Je 1837
OOxM Ag 7,21-S 18,O 2 1833;Ap 23-My 7 1834
PNoHi My 3 1843
TxU [Jl 1838-Mr 15 1844]-N 16[D 15 1846-47] Ja 25 1848-O 23 1849;Ja 8-Mr 19,Jl 23-O 8 1850;My 11-Je 4,N 9 1852-Mr 1854;Ag 13-N 12 1860
WHi Ap 16 1834-F 13,N 11 1846-Ag 1849;Ap 1850-N 2 1852;Ja 7-My 1853;Ap-N 17 1864;Ja 12-D 21 1865

Columbus **PRESS.** d *See* Columbus news

Columbus **RECORD.** w 1879-1900||?
OClWHi O 5 1893
CHi 1886-Ag 1894

REPUBLIC. w 1839?-
OCo S 1843-Jl 1845

Columbus **SENTINEL.** sw,w Mr 15 1831-35||
Merged with Ohio state journal and Columbus gazette, later Ohio state journal
sw during sessions of legislature
Ct [1833-34]
DLC D 7 1832;Ap 15 1833
IU Ja 3,17-24,F 14,Mr 15-Ap,Jl 19-Ag 7,17-30,S 12,O 4,N 1,15 1832
InI Mr 18 1835
MWA Ja 27,D 11 1832
N O 10 1833
OCHi S 1831-Ja 1832
OClWHi N 15 1831;Jl 19 1832;Je 20 1833-F 4,Mr 3 1835
OHi 1832-Je 25 1834
OOxM [F 1833-Je 1834]
PEL Ja 21 1834
WHi Mr 15-Jl 5 1831

Daily Columbus **SENTINEL.** d S 10 1872-
OHi S-N 11 1872

Daily **STANDARD.** w D? 1848-
OHi D 7 1848-F 26 1849;O 10 1850

STATE capital fact. w 1851?-
MWA Jl 31 1852
—d ed *See* Daily evening express

STATE journal and political register. *See* Ohio state journal w

STRAIGHT out Harrisonian. w My 1- 1840||?
Campaign paper
DLC My 1 1840
OCHi My-O 9 1840
OHi My-O 2 1840
WHi Je 26 1840

Columbus **SUN.** w 1892-95||?
WHi Ja 19 1895

SWAN'S elevator. *See* Columbus gazette

TAX killer. w My 16- 1846||?
Campaign paper
OHi My-O 10 1846

Columbus **TELEGRAM.** w O 30 1883-87||?
OHi 1886-N 19 1887

Columbus **TIMES.** 1880-88 *See* Columbus press

Daily **TIMES.** *See* Columbus news

Columbus **TIMES.** w 1911-20||?
OHi 1914-15

TRI-COMMUNITY news. [Gahanna, New Albany and East Columbus] w Ap 10 1931+
pub 1931+

UNION league. w 1863?-
ICHi S 29 1864
WHi Je 11-Jl 11,25-Ag 8,22-S 12,26-O 10 1863

WEEK. w 1910+
OCo O 1914-S 23 1916;Mr 31 1917-S 20 1919
OHi Mr 29 1913-Mr 1922

Der **WESTBOTE.** w,sw O 2 1843-1918||?
w 1843-95?
In German
IU [Je 8 1865-S 19 1867]
OHi 1843-Ag 17 1871;72-Jl 1881;84-87;89-95;D 31 1896-1901;Ag 1903-Ag 20 1918

Der tägliche **WESTBOTE.** sw,tw,d 1853-Ag 1 1903||
Title varies with frequency. United with Columbus express to form Daily express und westbote
sw 1853-84;tw 1884-Je 1893?
MWA Ag 23 1876
NN Jl 27 1861
OHi 1872-90;92;Jl 1893-Jl 2 1900;01-03

WESTERN hemisphere. *See* Columbus press

WESTERN intelligencer. *See* Ohio state journal w

WESTERN statesman. w 1825-
Ct Ap 4 1827
IU Ja 13,Jl 25,Ag 15 1827
MWA Ja 24 1827
N Ag 3,17,31-S 21 1825

WHIG battering-ram, or straight out revived. w? 1844||?
IU S 27 1844

CONNEAUT

To 1834? as Salem

Conneaut **ADVANCE.** w 1913-17||?
1913-14? as Ashtabula county advance
OHi Mr 23 1914-Ja 20 1915

Salem **ADVERTISER.** *See* Conneaut gazette

ASHTABULA county advance. *See* Conneaut advance

ASHTABULA county gazette. *See* Conneaut gazette

BUCKEYE democrat. d Ap? 1857-
CSmH Ap 17 1857

Conneaut **GAZETTE.** w 1831-Ap 1843||
1831-32? as Salem advertiser; D 12 1840-Je 12? 1841 Ashtabula county gazette
Suspended from Je 12-S 11 1841
DLC N 1,D 21 1832
MWA F 6,N 20 1841
MiU-C [1833-37]
NjR F 13,Mr 13 1841
OClWHi Ja 25-Ag,S 13-N 22,D 20 1832[33-34]S 11-18,O 16,N 13 1835;N 25 1836;F 10,My 18 1837;Ap 19 1838-Je 12 1841[42]
OCon My 15 1835-Je 12,S 11 1841-Ap 6 1843

Conneaut **HERALD.** *See* Conneaut news-herald

MEDIUM and reformer's companion. w? 1856?-
CSmH Jl 12 1856

Conneaut evening **NEWS.** d D 22 1897-D 31 1906||
United with Conneaut daily post-herald to form Conneaut news-herald
OClWHi D 22 1897
OCon 1903-06

Conneaut **NEWS-HERALD.** w,d 1882+
1882-Ap 5 1895 Conneaut herald (w) Ap 11 1895-Ag 5 1896 Conneaut daily herald; Ag 6 1896-N 20 1897 Conneaut post-herald; N 22 1897-1906 Conneaut daily post-herald
OClWHi 1890-[95]-Ag 6 1896;97-1906[17]
OCon Ja 17 1890-Je 1909;10+
OHi Ja 4 1901

Conneaut evening **POST.** d 1892-Ag 5 1896||
Merged with Conneaut daily herald to form Conneaut post-herald, later Conneaut news-herald
OClWHi Ag 5 1896

Conneaut **POST-HERALD.** *See* Conneaut news-herald

Conneaut **REPORTER.** w Ja 1844-1900||?
DLC 1844-56;61-63
MWA D 2 1863;S 21 1864;F 22 1866;N 9 1876
OClWHi 1844-[64-65]-[67]-[70]-[73]-Ja 9 1879;80-1900
OCon F 1848-1900

CORTLAND

Cortland **GAZETTE.** w My 13 1876-87||?
OHi 1876-79;82-Ja 5 1883

COSHOCTON

Coshocton **AGE.** w 1826-Je? 1914||
1826-O 1? 1845 as Coshocton spy; O 8 1845-49 Democratic whig; 1849-52 Coshocton republican; 1852-61 Progressive age. United with Coshocton weekly times to form Coshocton weekly times age
CSmH My 12 1830
DLC N 13 1874
MWA D 1 1827;Jl 29 1829;Ag 25 1852;S 13 1854;Ag 13,S 17 1856;O 21-28 1875
MiU-C O 8,D 17 1845;Ja 14,Ap 1,15 1846
OClWHi My 4 1826;Je 25 1828;N 10,D 1 1830; D 11 1833;My 6,Je 10,Jl 1,O 28,N 11,D 2 1835;Ja 23 1839;F 6 1840;Ag 23 1843;F 20,D 11 1851;D 22 1852;D 26 1855;D 10 1856;Mr 28,S 20 1860;Jl 4 1861;Ja 30,My 28 1864;S 30 1875;S 7 1878
OHi My 19 1830;Jl 25 1855;Mr 24-Ap 7,Ag 25 1858;Ap 22 1865;O 12 1866;68-Jl 7 1909;Ja 4,D 19 1912

Coshocton **AGE.** d 1899-1914||?
United with Coshocton daily times to form Coshocton daily times age
OHi My 24 1900-Ag 1903 Ja-Ap,S 1905-Je 1907;Ja-Mr 24,Jl-D 1908;Jl 1909-Mr 14 1914

COMMONWEALTH. *See* Democratic standard

Coshocton **DEMOCRAT.** *See* Coshocton weekly times age

DEMOCRATIC standard. w 1879-1901||?
1879-80? as Commonwealth; 1881?-83? Democratic standard-commonwealth. United with Coshocton democrat to form Coshocton democrat and standard, later Coshocton weekly times age
OHi Ap 8 1882-1901

DEMOCRATIC whig. *See* Coshocton age w

PROGRESSIVE age. *See* Coshocton age w

Coshocton **REPUBLICAN.** *See* Coshocton age w

Coshocton **SPY.** *See* Coshocton age w

Coshocton weekly **TIMES AGE.** w Ap? 1840-1917||?
1840-1901? as Coshocton democrat; 1902?-06? Coshocton democrat and standard; 1907?-Je? 1914 Coshocton weekly times
ICHi N 3,D 1 1852
MWA O 20,D 15 1852;N 15 1854;Mr 20 1861
MiU-C Ja 6 1841
OClWHi O 24 1840;Je 23 1841;F 9,N 2-9 1842; Mr 27,N 20 1844;D 10 1845;D 16 1846;D 1,27 1847;D 27 1848;Ja 1,D 1 1850;D 21-28 1853;D 19 1854;O 31 1855;D 28 1859;My 3 1865
OHi D 14 1842[S-D 1856]S 16 1857-S 18 1861; S 1863-1901;07-Jl 1 1909

Coshocton daily **TIMES AGE.** d 1904-17||?
1904-Je? 1914 as Coshocton daily times. United with Coshocton tribune to form Coshocton tribune and times age
OHi My 1909-Ag 1916;Ja-O 1917

Coshocton **TRIBUNE** and times age. d 1909+
1909-17? as Coshocton tribune
My 3 1931 is historical ed
OClWHi My 3 1931
OHi My 5 1918-21;F 1922-Ag 1 1923;28;30+

COVINGTON

BRADFORD sentinel. *See under* Bradford

Covington **GAZETTE.** w 1870-1907||
United with Weekly tribune to form Covington tribune-gazette
OHi Ja 3 1901

Covington **TRIBUNE-GAZETTE.** w 1897+
1897-1907 as Weekly tribune
pub [1886+]
OHi Ja 3 1901

OHIO (*Continued*)

CRESTLINE

Crestline ADVOCATE. w 1869+
pub 1869+
OHi Ja 3 1901;Ag 3-12 1923
OOxM My 2-9 1874;Jl 4 1879

INDEPENDENT democrat. *See* Crawford county news (Bucyrus)

WATCHMAN and reporter. w Ap 4 1856-
OHi My 23 1856

CUYAHOGA FALLS

AMERICAN eagle. w? 1840||
DLC O 13 1840
OClWHi O 13 1840

OHIO review. *See* Cuyahoga Falls review

Cuyahoga Falls REPORTER. w 1870+
MWA Mr 15 1879
OClWHi 1900;S 10 1908+
OHi Ja 4 1901

Cuyahoga Falls REVIEW. w N 30 1833-
1833-37? as Ohio review
Ct [1834-37]
DLC N 24 1838
MWA O 30,N 20 1835;My 13,Je 3 1836
OClWHi 1833-D 12 1834;Ja 19,Mr 30,Ap 27-My 4,N 24 1838

TRUE American. 1841?-43||
OClWHi Ag 26 1841

WESTERN horizon.
OClWHi N 7 1838

DAYTON

ASHLANDER. w My 23? 1844-
MWA Jl 18-25 1844

Dayton tri-weekly BULLETIN. tw S 1 1848-50||
ODa 1848-Ap 17 1850

Dayton weekly BULLETIN. w O 7 1848-
OCHi 1848-O 1849
OClWHi Ag 3 1849

Daily CITY item. d 1852-
MWA D 27 1852

Daily DAYTONIAN. d 1846-
ODa N 6 1846

COON dissector. w My 7- 1844||?
Campaign paper
MWA S 6 1844
MoSM Ag 30 1844
ODa My-N 22 1844
OHi My-N 22 1844
OOxM Jl 12 1844

Dayton daily DEMOCRAT. d 1874-76||?
United with Dayton daily herald and empire to form Dayton democrat, later Daily times
MWA O 4 1876
OClWHi N 8,10 1876
ODa Ja-Je 1875

Dayton DEMOCRAT. 1877-89 *See* Daily times

DEMOCRATIC herald. *See* Weekly empire and democrat

DEUTSCHES journal. w 1849-
In German
MWA S 4 1852

Tri-weekly Dayton EMPIRE. tw S 1848?-
OClWHi Ag 17,S 28,O 14,N 30 1848

Evening EMPIRE. *See* Daily times

Weekly EMPIRE and democrat. w 1826?-90||?
1826?-29 as Miami herald and Dayton republican gazette; 1830-34? Dayton republican; 1834?-37? Democratic herald; 1838?-41 Democratic herald and workingmen's press; 1842-47? Western empire; 1848? Western empire weekly; 1849-O? 1874 Weekly empire
Ct Ja 2 1827[35-37]
DLC Mr 10 1836
ICHi Mr 3 1836
IU Ja 24 1832;O 5 1838;S 7,21-O 5,N 16 1843;F 15 1844
MBAt Jl 14 1842
MWA Je 12 1827;Ap 19 1831
OClWHi F 1,Je 6,Ag 1,S 12 1844;S 2,16-23,O 7-14 1847;Ja 13-20,F 24,My 1,29 1848;Je 6-13,Jl 4 1849;Ja 16 1850;Jl 13,Ag 10-S 21,O 12-N 9,23,D 1861-62
ODa Ja 13 1842-Ag 12 1847;Ja 7 1865;77-81;83-87
OHi 1874-F 1890
P-M Ag 12 1828
—d ed *See* Daily times

Dayton FORUM. w My 16 1913+
Negro
pub [1920+]
OHi Je 1918-O 24 1919

Dayton weekly GAZETTE. w 1850?-
MWA O 4 1851
ODa D 17,31 1859

Dayton GAZETTE. d 1850-
Title varies slightly
MWA S 30 1852
ODa N 6 1850-51;53-S 23 1859
WHi My 14 1851

GRIDIRON. w Ag 1822-Ap 24 1823||
OClWHi S 26-O 10,24-N 1822;Ja 23,F-Mr 6 1823
ODa S,O 10-31,N 14 1822-Mr 6,20-Ap 1823

GROSS-DAYTONER zeitung. d 1866+
1866-Ag 1 1914 as Daytoner volks-zeitung
In German
IU D 1917+
ODa 1876;78-Je 1882;83-98;Je 1899-Je 1909;10-12;Ap 1913+
OHi 1919-29

Dayton daily HERALD. d 1878+
1879-80? as Evening record
KHi Je 22 1907
OClWHi D 8 1897;Ja 15 1912
ODa Jl 1882-91;Jl 1893-95;Jl 1896-1902;Je 1903-Je 1904;Jl-D 1905;Ap-Je,O 1906+
OHi S 15 1908-10;F 1911-Mr 1913;S 1918-Ja 1920
VU Ap 5 1917

Evening HERALD. *See* Daily times

Daytoni HIRADO [Dayton herald]. w
In Hungarian
PPiHi [Ap-Je 12 1931]

Dayton JOURNAL. w,sw N 30 1826-1904||?
Follows Miami republican and Dayton advertiser. 1826-N 27 1827 as Ohio national journal and Montgomery and Dayton advertiser; D 4 1827-57 Dayton journal and advertiser
w 1826-99?
DLC Ag 20 1827;Mr 17,Jl 14,S 1,22-29,O 30,D 1 1829;Ja 5,19 1830;N 17 1840;O 19 1858;O 16 1860;F 18 1862
MWA Je 21 1853;F 13 1866
OCHi Ag 24(extra)1842
OClWHi S 7-13 1842
ODa Mr 13 1832;Ag 14 1838;D 14 1841;My 10 1842-F 5,My 10 1853-Ap 10 1860;61-My 5,Jl 7,28 1863-Jl 20 1869
OHi S 27(extra)1842
OOxM N 13-D 4,18 1832[33-Jl 1834]
PDoHi Ja 29 1827
WHi Ap 25 1865

Daily Dayton JOURNAL. d D 16 1840-Je 11 1841||
ODa D 16 1840(facsimile)

Dayton daily JOURNAL. d My 6 1847+
Title varies slightly
DLC O 13,15 1863;N 8 1864;D 13 1869;98
IU Mr 31 1914
MBAt Ap 17 1865
MWA Ag 28 1852;Je 23-24,27,Jl 2 1862;My 6-7 1863;D 10 1864;Ja 14 1903
OClWHi S 7 1849;N 25 1866;S 26 1871;Ap 25,My 31,S 11,24 1873;Ag 30,O 1-2 1874
ODa O 18 1848;Ja 18-D 1850;D 3 1851-53;Ap 26 1854-N 24 1856;Ja 16 1857-[My 7-Jl 27 1863]-D 18 1868;Ja 27 1869-Jl 1870;71;Ap 1872-Je,Ag-N 15 1889;Ja-Je 1894;1900;Ja 21 1903-Je,O 1905-Mr,Jl 1908-12;Mr 25 1913+
OHi F 1864-Jl 27 1865;66;68-69;F 6 1870-Je 1877;78-Je 1882;83+
OXG D 1933+
WHi My 7 1863

Dayton JOURNAL and advertiser. tw,d 1827-d 1840?
DLC Je 16 1841
IU O 4 1831;Ag 29,S 4,O 1 1843;My 13,Ag 26(extra),S 10 1844;N 18 1846

Dayton daily LEDGER. *See* Daily times

Dayton weekly LEDGER. w 1863?-68||?
ODa D 1867-68

LOG cabin. bw Mr 21- 1840||
Campaign paper
DLC Ap 18,Je 13,Ag 8,S 18 1840
IU Ag 8 1840
MWA My 2,Jl 25 1840
MiD-B Mr-O 23 1840
MnHi S 18 1840
MoSM Mr 21 1840
OCHi Je 27 1840
OClWHi Je 13,S 18 1840
ODa Mr-O 23 1840
OHi Je 27,S 18,O 23 1840
PP My 2 1840

MIAMI herald and Dayton republican gazette. *See* Weekly empire and democrat

MIAMI republican and Dayton advertiser. w S 2 1823-S 7 1826||
Followed by Ohio national journal and Montgomery and Dayton advertiser, later Dayton journal
DLC My 4,18,Je 8,O 12 1824
ODa Ag 8 1826

MIAMIAN and manual of *American* principles. w F 17 1843-
CSmH N 23 1844
DLC [1843-Je 1844]
IU F 17-24,Ag 19-S 2,16-O 7,28,D 2,16-23 1843;Ja 13-20,F 3,Mr 9,30-Ap,My 11-18,Ag 31-S 7,21,O 5,19 1844
MWA S 7 1844

Evening MONITOR. *See* Dayton daily news

NEW nation. w Ag 1 1903-
1903-Ja 1904 as Ohio socialist
WHi 1903-My 28 1904

Dayton daily NEWS. d 1887+
1887-89 as Evening monitor
MWA F 29 1919
OClWHi Mr 11-12,17-28 1904;My 7 1908;My 24 1911;Ap 4,16 1913
ODa 1888-1902;Jl 1903-S 1907;Ja-Mr,O 1908-Mr,Jl 1910+
OHi Ag 22 1898-1902;Jl 1903-N 1916;17+
OOxM N 1909-Ap 1911
VU Ap 6 1917;Ap 6 1930
—Morning ed *See* Daily times

OHIO national journal and Montgomery and Dayton advertiser. *See* Dayton journal

OHIO socialist. *See* New nation

OHIO watchman. *See* Dayton watchman; or farmers' and mechanics' journal

Saturday PEOPLE. w 1876-85||?
MWA D 17 1881
OHi Ja 20 1877-S 1880

Dayton evening PRESS. d 1892-1904||?
DLC Ja-Je 1898

Evening RECORD. *See* Dayton daily herald

Dayton REPUBLICAN. *See* Weekly empire and democrat

THAT same old coon. w 1844||
Campaign paper
DLC Ap 12 1844
MWA My 25,Je 8-N 16 1844
MoSM Jl 13 1844
OCHi S 21 1844
OClWHi Je 8,Jl 6,20,Ag 10-S 14 1844
ODa Ap 12-N 16 1844

Daily TIMES. d 1849?-97||?
1849? as Evening empire; 1850?-Jl 9 1867 Dayton daily empire; Jl 10? 1867-N 1869? Dayton daily ledger; D 1869?-Ap 4 1874 Evening herald; Ap 5? 1874-76? Dayton daily herald and empire; 1877?-89 Dayton democrat
Suspended from My?-S? 1863
DLC N 6 1852
MWA S 9, 15 1852;F 27,Mr 26 1861
NSyU Ag 17 1864
OClWHi S 12,28,O 23 1849;Je 25 1873
ODa F 7 1851-52;Ja 28 1853-Ag 6 1858;Ap 5 1859-Ap,My 5,Je-S 29,O 16,19-20 1860;O 1862-My 4,Ag 21 1863-N 24 1865;Jl 10 1867-N 29,D 22 1869-N 2 1870;71-Je 1893;94-Je 25 1896
OHi Ja 25 1864-N 25 1869;F 5 1870-97
—evening ed *See* Dayton daily news
—w ed *See* Weekly empire and democrat; Dayton weekly ledger

Daily TRANSCRIPT. d D 24 1840-
Title varies slightly
DLC D 24 1840
ODa Ja 10-O 21 1850

Dayton TRANSCRIPT. sw Ja 1841-
My 14-N 2 1844 Dayton transcript and Ashland whig
DLC F 1 1845
IU Ja 13 1844;Ja 7 1846
MWA Ja 15 1842
OC Je 1 1850
OCHi Je 12 1841;O 1843-Mr 1846
OClWHi O 9 1841;Je 6 1846;S 1,22 1847;S 12,Jl 18 1849
ODa Je 12,Ag 25,S 4,22,O 2,16 1841;Ja 12 1842-Ja 14 1843;S 21 1844;F 15,22,Mr 8,15,26,Ap 5,23,My 7-10,N 22,D 3 1845-O 7 1846
OHi S 13 1845

Tri-weekly Dayton TRANSCRIPT. tw
ODa Ag 7 1850

Daytoner VOLKS-ZEITUNG. *See* Gross-Daytoner zeitung

*Dayton WATCHMAN; or farmers' and mechanics' journal. w N 27 1816-N 21 1826||
1816-D 18 1821 as Ohio watchman
IU Je 4,Jl 9 1822
MWA Ag 20 1822;F 15,Ap 19-26,Je 21,Jl 5,19 1825;Je 13 1826
ODa 1821-D 7 1824

WESTERN empire. *See* Weekly empire and democrat

Dayton WHIG and Miami democrat. w 1832?-
IU F 22 1834
N O 12 1833
OOxM F 2,Mr-Ap 13,27,My 11,Je 1-15,29-Jl 20,Ag 3,17-O 5,19-N 2,16-23,D 1833;Ja 11-F 1,15,Mr 1,29,Ap 19-26,Je 21,Jl 5-19 1834

DEFIANCE

Defiance BANNER. w Je 16 1838-
DLC Je 16 1838

Defiance BANNER. w 1849?-
MWA Ag 12 1852

Defiance CRESCENT-NEWS. d 1888+
1888-99? as Defiance crescent
OHi Ja 1 1901;S 2 1919+

Defiance DEMOCRAT. w,sw 1844-1919||?
sw 1910?-14?
DLC Ag 7 1844
MWA D 25 1852;Ap 6 1861
OCHi F 28 1873
OClWHi D 1873-Jl 1880;S 10 1885
OHi Mr 3 1855;Ja 3 1901

DEMOCRATIC times. w N 5 1881-84||?
OClWHi 1881-O 20 1883
OHi O 28 1882-O 20 1883

Defiance daily EXPRESS. d 1894-1919||?
OHi S-D 1919

Der HEROLD. w 1881-1920||?
In German
OHi 1919-Ja 22 1920

Evening NEWS. d 1892-99||?
United with Defiance crescent to form Defiance crescent-news

DEGRAFF

Degraff BANNER. w 1871-79||?
PLaL Ap 12-19,D 20 1878

DELAWARE

Delaware daily CHRONICLE. d 1878-84||?
OHi Jl-D 1884

COLUMBIAN advocate and Franklin chronicle. *See* Semi-weekly gazette

DELAWARE county journal and Ohio state gazette. w
OHi Jl 21 1831-Ja 20 1834

OHIO (*Continued*)

DELAWARE—*Continued*

DELAWARE county news. w D 1 1864-
OHi 1864-Jl 13 1866

Delaware DEMOCRATIC herald. w Ag 23 1866-1902||?
1866-85 as Weekly herald. United with Weekly journal to form Weekly journal-herald
OClWHi Ap 22 1880;Je 18-25 1891
OHi 1866-Ja 16 1873;74-87;89-90;92-O 1897;98-99

DEMOCRATIC standard. w O 30 1845-
1845-O 21? 1847 as Loco foco
MWA S 9 1852
OClWHi Jl 27 1854
OHi 1845-Mr 1 1849;Mr 1851-N 1864

FRANKLIN chronicle. *See* Semi-weekly gazette

***Semi-weekly GAZETTE.** w,sw Ja 7 1820-1930||?
Ja-My? 1820 as Columbian advocate and Franklin chronicle; Je? 1820-N 1821? Franklin chronicle; O 1821?-Ap 9 1823 Delaware patron and Franklin chronicle; Ap 16 1823-My 6 1830 Delaware patron (Je 14-N 8? 1827 Delaware patron and Marion and Crawford advertiser) My 13 1830-Ag 16 1834 Ohio state gazette; Ag 23-D 20 1834 Ohio gazette; D 27 1834-D 14 1855 Olentangy gazette (other variations slight) 1820-N 1821? pub in Worthington
w 1820-D 9 1886
pub [1860-1930]
CSmH Ap 22,S 2 1830
DLC F 16 1821;F 26-Mr 4,Ap 8,My 6,Je 3 1824;D 6 1827;Ag 6,N 26-D 3 1829;N 8 1832; Ap 11 1833;D 18 1841
IU My 27,Jl 10 1822
MBAt Ja 20 1825
MWA O 1 1821;Ja 31 1828;Ag 27 1852
OClWHi Ja 3 1821;Jl 30 1823;N 22 1832;N 30 1839;Ap 17,O 16,D 25 1840;Ja 1 1842;Ja 17 1845[48-52]-[54-55]Ja 29,Mr 21-Ap 4 1856;S 24 1858;Ag 19 1859;Ag 9 1861;Ja 3,F 28 1862;O 30,N 27 1863;Ag 19 1864;Ja 6,Ap 21, My 5,Je 9-23,Jl 7 1865;Ap 13 1866;My 9 1873
ODW Ag 26 1830-O 4 1834;Mr 28 1835-1927
OHi 1821-[D 27 1834-O 20 1838]40;Mr 14 1851-1914

Delaware GAZETTE. d Ja 10 1884+
pub 1884+
ODW 1884-1919;21+

HARRISON flag. bw,w Ap 25-O 26? 1840||
Campaign paper
bw Ap-Jl 1840
MWA Je 22 1840
OClWHi Ag 31 1840
OHi Ap-O 26 1840

Delaware daily HERALD. d 1892-1902||?
United with Daily journal to form Daily journal-herald
OHi Je 1,15-Jl 1895;Ja 1 1901

Weekly HERALD. *See* Delaware democratic herald

Daily JOURNAL-HERALD. d Ap 11 1900-29||?
1900-02? as Daily journal. Merged with Delaware gazette
OHi 1900-Ap 1927;O 1928-Mr 1929

Semi-weekly JOURNAL-HERALD. w,sw Ap 19 1900-29||?
1900-02? as Weekly journal; 1903-N 1911 Weekly journal herald. Merged with Delaware gazette
w 1900-N 1911
OClWHi Je 20,28 1921
OHi 1900-26

LOCO foco. *See* Democratic standard

OHIO state gazette. *See* Semi-weekly gazette

OLENTANGY gazette. *See* Semi-weekly gazette

Delaware PATRON *See* Semi-weekly gazette

PEOPLE'S advocate and Delaware and Sandustky advertiser. w? 1827?-
DLC F 20 1828

Delaware SIGNAL. w S 23 1873-86||?
ODW 1873-F 1886

DELPHOS

NORTHWESTERN whig. w Je? 1853-
MWA D 31 1853

Delphos ORACLE. w 1849?-
MWA D 22 1852
PPL Mr 19 1851

DELTA

FULTON democrat. w 1851?-
MWA D 16 1852

DENNISON

TUSCARAWAS chronicle. *See* Uhrichsville chronicle (Uhrichsville)

DESHLER

Deshler FLAG. w N 17 1876+
pub 1900+

DOVER

To 1915 as Canal Dover

Dover CITIZEN. w 1851-
MWA Je 30 1853
OClWHi O 6-13 1853

IRON VALLEY reporter. w 1872-1903||?
OClWHi Mr 25 1882
—d ed *See* Daily reporter

IRON VALLEY times. w Ap 9 1857-
OClWHi Ap 9 1857;D 1 1859

Monthly Dover NEWS. m
OClWHi F 1 1862

OHIO democrat and Dover advertiser. *See* Ohio democrat and times (New Philadelphia)

Daily REPORTER. d 1903+
OHi 1915-F 1916
—w ed *See* Iron Valley reporter

Dover TELEGRAPH. 1838?-
OClWHi My 23 1838

DRESDEN

Dresden HERALD. w 1848?-
MWA D 15 1852

EAST CLEVELAND

Papers published in East Cleveland are listed under Cleveland

EAST COLUMBUS

Papers published in East Columbus are listed under Columbus

EAST LIVERPOOL

East Liverpool GAZETTE. *See* Potter's gazette

Evening NEWS review. *See* Evening review

POTTER'S gazette. w,d 1871-90||?
1871-76? as East Liverpool gazette
w 1871-89?
NNHi D 14 1872
OClWHi N 25 1876-N 15 1877

Evening REVIEW. d 1885+
1890?-1903? as Evening news review
1924?-27? Review-tribune
OHi Mr 11 1914-F 1916

Morning TRIBUNE. d 1902-23||?
United with Evening review to form Review-tribune, later Evening review
OHi Ap 6 1914-F 1916

EAST PALESTINE

Daily LEADER. d My 1 1915+
pub 1915+
OHi 1915-Ap 1926
—w ed *See* Reveille echo

REPUBLICAN reveille. *See* Reveille echo

REVEILLE echo. w N 7 1886-1922||?
1886-90? as Palestine reveille; 1891?-F 1894? Republican reveille
OHi 1886-N 7 1888;N 25 1891-O 1892;N 15 1893-F 21,Mr 8 1894-Ap 6 1922
—d ed *See* Daily leader

VALLEY echo. w Ap 12 1878-F 1894||?
United with Republican reveille to form Reveille echo
OHi 1878-Ap 9 1885;Ap 22 1886-Ap,Jl 12 1888-Mr 23 1893

EATON

DEMOCRAT. w Ap 18? 1840-
OClWHi S 26 1840

Eaton DEMOCRAT. w,sw S 15 1843+
1902?-09? as Preble county democrat; 1927?-32? Eaton semi-weekly news
sw 1917?-34?
CSmH D 17 1846
Ct D 20 1923
MWA N 17 1843;F 19 1857-Jl 5 1934
NNHi D 19 1872
OClWHi S 5 1850
OHi [O 1843-46]-S 1847;Je 1848-Ag,O 1856-58; F 11 1867;72-77;81-86;O 13 1887;F 2,Ap 19,Je 21 1888;Ja 17 O 17 1889;My 24,Je 5 1890;O 15 1891;N 16,D 7 1893;Ja 3 1901;My 12 1927;28-32

DEMOCRATIC citizen. w 1852-
OHi S 28 1854-S 1857

DEMOCRATIC press. w Ag 23 1860-
OHi Ag 30 1860-Ap 1865

Eaton HERALD. w 1898-F 27 1918||
United with Eaton register to form Register herald
OHi F 28 1906-18

Eaton semi-weekly NEWS. *See* Eaton democrat

PREBLE county democrat. *See* Eaton democrat

REGISTER herald. w 1820+
1820-F 1918 as Eaton weekly register (1834- Eaton register and Preble county gazette)
Suspended from F 8-Mr 8 1827
pub 1860+
CSmH Jl 1 1830
DLC Ja 31,F 7,My 15 1834
KHi [D 31 1830-Mr 1853]
MWA Je 4,Jl 23 1825;Je 24,N 11,D 9-16 1826; Mr 8 1827;Ja 28 1829;N 16 1843;F 1,Ap 4 1844;F 28 1850;Jl 7 1853;Jl 31-Ag 7 1862
NNHi My 2,Ag 2,15-29 1861;My 1 1873
OClWHi Ag 9 1838;O 5 13-2;62-[65]Ja 28 1920
OHi [My 28 1825-Jl 21 1836;F-D 1839]-41[Jl 25-O 10 1844]Ap 18 1847-48[Mr 1849-Jl 7 1853]F 1854-1907;Jl 1914-15;Mr-Je 1918;27-32

Eaton REPUBLICAN. w O 1 1841-
DLC O 29 1841

ELDORADO

Eldorado BEE. *See* Eldorado news

Eldorado NEWS. w 1898-193-||?
1898-1927? as Eldorado bee
OHi 1908-27

ELMIRA

Elmira NEWS. w F 6 1914-
OHi F 13-S 4 1914

ELYRIA

Elyria ASTONISHER. w? 1878?-
OClWHi Ag 24 1878;N 1 1878

BUCKEYE sentinel and Elyria advertiser. *See* Elyria courier

BUDGET. Je 13 1860-
OClWHi Je 13 1860

Elyria CHRONICLE. d Jl 6 1901-Je 1919||
Title varies slightly. United with Evening telegram to form Elyria chronicle-telegram
OClWHi [1901-F 3 1909]
OHi Ap 6 1914-F 1916;Ap-My 1918

Weekly CHRONICLE. w 1901-13||?
OClWHi [Mr 1902-Mr 18 1904]

Elyria CHRONICLE-TELEGRAM. d S 13 1898+
1898-1901 as Elyria daily reporter; 1902-Ap 1907 Elyria reporter; My 1907-13 Evening telegram; 1914-Je 30 1917 Elyria telegram
pub My 1907-Je,Ag 1911-Jl,S 1914-15;F 1916-Jl 1918;19+
OClWHi [1898]-[1902-Ap 1907;08]+
OEly 1929+
OElyC Mr 1907-Je,Ag 1911-Jl,S 1914-15;F 1916-Jl 1918;Ja-Je 1919
OHi Mr 1914-F 1916;My 1 1918;Ap 27 1926+

Elyria CONSTITUTION. *See* Elyria democrat

CONSTITUTIONALIST. *See* Elyria democrat

Elyria COURIER. w Jl 24 1829-Mr 1854||?
1829-Mr? 1832 as Lorain gazette; Ap?-Jl 5? 1832 Elyria times; Jl 12 1832-Je 12 1844 Ohio atlas and Elyria advertiser; Je 19 1844- 1846 Buckeye sentinel and Elyria advertiser. Merged with Independent democrat, later Elyria republican
Suspended for a few months in 1846
CSmH Ag 20 1830;O 28 1831
CtY N 12 1844
DLC Jl 16 1830;My 8,Jl 10 1834;O 20 1840;D 21 1842
MWA S 18 1834;S 22 1852
MnHi Jl 4 1833
NN O 14 1831;S 4 1834
OClWHi Jl 24,S 4,O 8,30 1829;Ja 15,Mr 5,26, My 14-28,Jl 16,O 22,N 12-26 1830;Ap 8,Je 17,Jl 1,Ag 12-N 14 1831;Jl-S 20 1832;O 10-D 19 1833;Jl-Ag,S 11,O 30-N 13,D 11-18 1834;F 26,Ag 13 1835;Jl 27,N 23 1836;F 15,Mr 19,S 27-O 5,18 1837[38-39]Mr 24 O 20-27 1840 [41;43]Je 26-Jl 2 1844;Ja 28,Mr 4,Ap 22,Jl 22 1845;N 1846-My 9,Ag 1,S 5-12,O 3 1848;Ap 24-Je 26 1849;Je 1850-F 10 My 25 1852-Ja 1854
P-M D 27 1832

Elyria DEMOCRAT. w O 2 1866-1916||?
1866-Mr 18 1875 as Lorain constitutionalist (Je-D 1869 Constitutionalist) Mr 25 1875-S 8 1887 Elyria constitution
OClWHi Mr 25 1875-Ja 13 1916
OEly S 15 1887;S 13 1888;Ja 7 1891;Ja 10 1895;98;1900;Ja 1 1903;04;Ja 7 1909;Ja 6 1910
OElyC 1890;96;1901-02
OHi Ja 3 1901;Mr 22-My 17 1906

INDEPENDENT democrat. *See* Elyria republican

INDEPENDENT register. 1833-
OClWHi D 1 1833

INDEPENDENT treasury. w O ?? 1841-
OClWHi N 18 1841-N 9 1842

LORAIN argus. *See* Lorain county argus

LORAIN constitutionalist. *See* Elyria democrat

LORAIN county argus. w 1848-
1848-52? as Lorain argus
MWA O 13 1852;F 15 1854
OClWHi F 15,Mr 7,21,O 24,N 1? 1848;Ap 3,S 18 1849;Mr 12 1850;Ja 20,F 4-18,Mr 11-25 1851;F 10,Mr 23 1852;F 23-Mr 2,My 4,25 1853; Ag 30-S 20,O 4 1854;Mr 2? 1855

LORAIN county eagle. w Mr 4 1857-
OClWHi 1857-Mr 15 1860;My 6 1861
OEly Mr 23 1858

LORAIN county reporter. *See* Elyria reporter

LORAIN gazette. *See* Elyria courier

LORAIN republican. w O 2 1834-
1834?-38? as Elyria republican (1835?-Je? 1837 Elyria republican and working men's advocate
Ct [1835-37]
OClWHi O 9 1834[O 1835-S 1836]F 22,Je 21,Jl 18,23 1837;Ap 25 1838;D 1842-Ja 11,Ap 26 1843-D 11 1844

OHIO (*Continued*)

ELYRIA—*Continued*

LORAIN standard. w 1835?-
OClWHi Ap-N 3 1840

OHIO atlas and Elyria advertiser. *See* Elyria courier

OLD TIP'S broom. w 1840||
Campaign paper
DLC Je 4 1840
OClWHi Je 4 1840

PEOPLE'S banner. w Jl 14 1838-
OClWHi Jl-O 6 1838

Elyria REPORTER. w 1890-1907||?
1890-98? as Lorain county reporter. Merged with Elyria republican
OClWHi 1892-[94-97]-[99]-1901;F 13,27,Mr 20 1902[03-06]F 28 1907

Elyria daily REPORTER. *See* Elyria chronicle-telegram

Elyria REPUBLICAN. 1834-38 *See* Lorain republican

Elyria REPUBLICAN. w Ag 5 1852-1918||?
1852-Ja 1877 as Independent democrat. Merged with Elyria telegram, later Elyria chronicle-telegram
MWA Ag 18 1852;Jl 1 1863;F 7 1866
OClWHi 1852-F 1 1854;D 1855-93;S 1894-S 5 1895;96-97;S 1,O 20-N 3,D 8 1898-[1900]-03;Jl 21 1904;05-06
OEly 1859-60;63-65;68;70;73;75;79;81;83-84;89; 98-1900;03-04;08
OElyC 1862;66;71;76;82;86-87;92;94;97-1917
OHi Ja 3 1901
WHi Jl 14 1869

Evening TELEGRAM. *See* Elyria chronicle-telegram

Elyria daily TELEPHONE. d Ap 26? 1886-87||?
OClWHi [Ap 27 1886-87]

Elyria TIMES. 1832 *See* Elyria courier

Elyria TIMES. w 1880?-
OClWHi O 11 1881;Ja-F 21 1882

EUCLID BEACH

Papers published in Euclid Beach are listed under Cleveland

FINDLAY

ADVANCE guard. w 1896-99||?
WHi [Ag 21 1896-Ag 17 1899]

Findlay daily COURIER. d F 1887-D 31 1932||
United with Morning republican to form Republican-courier
OFiR F 28 1888-F,Ap 1890-97;99-Je 1907;08-32
OHi Ap 1914-F 1916

Findlay COURIER. w *See* Hancock courier

COURIER-UNION. *See* Hancock courier

DEMOCRATIC courier. *See* Hancock courier

HANCOCK courier. w 1836-1913||
1836-S 1845? as Findlay courier; S 23 1845-51? Democratic courier; 1905?-06? Courier-union
DLC Ja 10 1837
MWA S 1 1852
OClWHi S 23 1845;Ja 23 1879
OFiR D 10 1874-N 18 1880;93-1911;13-14
OHi [1846-N 1848]Ja 27 1855-56;Je 13 1860; Ja 25 1861-Je 5,O 9 1863;My 31,Ag 23 1866; My 2 1867;Ag 13 1868;Ja 1 1901
—d ed *See* Findlay daily courier

HANCOCK Jeffersonian. *See* Weekly Jeffersonian

HANCOCK journal. w
PPL N 29 1850

HANCOCK populist. w 1894||?
WHi O 5-26,N 30-D 7 1894

HOME companion. *See* Weekly Jeffersonian

Weekly JEFFERSONIAN. w,sw Je 8 1854-1920||?
1854-55? as Home companion; 1856?-70? Hancock Jeffersonian; 1871?-1904? Weekly Jeffersonian; 1905 Republican-Jeffersonian
sw 1905-07
DLC D 13 1861-S 16 1864
OCHi D 21 1866-S 4 1868
OClWHi S 4(extra)1868
OFiR 1854-Je 21 1855;N 24 1865-O 19 1866;69-Ap 1875;Je 1876-86;My 1888-N 1903;05-11
OHi D 4,18 1857;Ja 22 1858[59-60]Je 14 1861-My 1863;My 6 1864;Je 18 1869;Je 30 1871;Ja 3 1901
—d ed *See* Republican-courier

Evening JEFFERSONIAN. d N 1880-1910||?
OFiR D 24 1880-85;F-N 1886;F-N 1887;88-1901;03-10

Findlay REPUBLICAN. w,sw 1879-D 30 1904||
1879-Ja 1897 as Weekly républican. Merged with Weekly Jeffersonian to form Republican-Jeffersonian, later Weekly Jeffersonian
w 1879-Ja 1897
OFiR Ja 31 1889-Ja 1895;F 1896-1904

REPUBLICAN-COURIER. d Jl 5 1886+
1886-1932 as Morning republican
pub 1886-Je 1889;Jl 1890-96;Ap 1897-98;Mr 22-D 1899;Ap 1900+
DLC 1898
OHi Ja 5 1901;Mr 14-N 1914;F 1915-F 1916;Je 25 1926+

REPUBLICAN-JEFFERSONIAN. *See* Weekly Jeffersonian

Findlay UNION. w N 1890-1904||?
United with Hancock courier to form Courier-union, later Hancock courier
OFiR N 26 1891-N 17 1898

WESTERN herald. w 1845?-
MWA Ap 29 1845

FORT LARAMIE

Fort Laramie PROGRESS. w My 20 1915-
OHi 1915-Je 14 1917

FORT RECOVERY

JOURNAL. w 1890+
pub F 6 1917;32+

FOSTORIA

Fostoria DEMOCRAT. w Jl 8 1875-1912||
pub complete
DLC F 4 1886
—d ed *See* Fostoria daily times

Fostoria DISPATCH. d 1887-Ap? 1897||
United with Fostoria daily review to form Daily review-dispatch, later Fostoria daily review

Fostoria DISPATCH. w 1887?-Ap? 1897||
United with Fostoria review to form Fostoria review-dispatch, later Fostoria review

Fostoria weekly NEWS. *See* Fostoria review

Fostoria REVIEW. w,sw 1860-F 8 1917||
1860-65 as Fostoria weekly news; Ap 23? 1897?-Jl 1908? Fostoria review dispatch
sw My 1898-99
pub Mr 8 1867-68;Mr 1869-My 6 1870;Mr 1876-78;80;82-S 1893;Ap 1895-1917
OHi S 25 1863;Ja 3 1901

Fostoria daily REVIEW. d N 21 1892+
Ap 19 1897-Jl 24 1908 Daily review-dispatch
pub N 23 1892+
OHi Ja 1 1901;Ag 3-12 1923

Fostoria daily TIMES. d Ag 1890+
pub 1890+
—w ed *See* Fostoria democrat

FRANKLIN

Franklin CHRONICLE. w 1876+
1876-86? as Valley chronicle
MWA O 28 1909
NjFHi Ag 21-28 1913
OClWHi O 5 1905;Jl 5-19,S 13,27,O 11-18 1906;Ja 10-17 1907;O 28 1909;Ja 29 1911;Ja 4 1912
OHi Ja 3 1901

Franklin NEWS. w 1895-1923||?
OClWHi Ja 27,S 29 1903;Jl 29 1904;Ja 27,My 26,Je 23,O 13 1905;F 2,16,Mr 16-23,O 12-19 1906;O 18,N 8,D 4-12,28 1907-Ja 3,17-24,F 7, 21 1908;F 26,Mr 19,O 1,15,29 1909;Ja 20 1910; Ja 20-Mr 3,Jl 14 1911;Ja 26,Ag 27 1912;Je 6, D 25 1913;Ja 2 1914;Ja 18,S 20 1918;Ja 3 1919
OHi Ja 4 1901

OHIO argus and Franklin gazette. w 1831?-
MWA F 25 1837

Franklin TIMES. w My 15? 1841-
DLC My 22 1841

VALLEY chronicle. *See* Franklin chronicle

FREEPORT

Freeport PRESS. w O 1 1880+
pub 1923+
OHi Ja 4 1901

FREMONT

To 1848 as Lower Sandusky

Fremont COURIER. w 1859-1923||?
In German
NNHi D 12 1872

Fremont DEMOCRATIC messenger. *See* Fremont messenger

Fremont weekly FREEMAN. w 1849?-
MWA Ag 28 1852

Fremont weekly HERALD. w
OClWHi Mr 1870-Ag 18 1871;Jl-S 17 1875;F-N 1878

Fremont weekly JOURNAL. w Jl? 1837-1925||?
1837-Ap 1839? as Lower Sandusky times; My 1839?-Ja 1853? Lower Sandusky whig
CL Ap 3,S 25 1863;Jl 29 1864;Je 23,O 13 1865
DLC My 11,D 7 1839;S 22 1865-O 12 1866
MWA F 19 1853;F 23 1866
OCHi S 9 1837;My 1839-[Mr 1840-41]
OF 1858-63;68-72;75-80;86-88
OHi O 23 1857;S 21,O 5 1877;Mr 8 1878;Ja 4 1901

Fremont MESSENGER. w,sw 1842-1925||?
1842-1900? as Fremont democratic messenger
w 1842-94?
OClWHi N 9 1876
OHi Ja 1 1901

Fremont daily MESSENGER. d 1896+
OHi S 1919-Ja 1926;Je 1932-F 13,S 1933+

Fremont daily NEWS. d My 4 1887+
pub 1887+
OF [1887-1902]+
OHi Ja 1 1901;S 1919-Ag 1922;Je 1932-F 13 1933

Fremont NEWS. w,sw 1888-1927||?
sw 1896?-1919?
OClWHi O 31 1911
OHi Mr 1906-S 1915;F-Jl 1916

SANDUSKY democrat. w 1838?-
1838?-52? as Sandusky county democrat
MWA My 18 1842;Ag 14 1852
NN Ap 8,My 6 1840
OClWHi Je 29 1840;Mr 3 1862
OHi Je 1858-My 1860
WHi N 30 1842

Lower Sandusky TIMES. *See* Fremont weekly journal

Lower Sandusky WHIG. *See* Fremont weekly journal

GAHANNA

Papers published in Gahanna are listed under Columbus

GALION

Galion INQUIRER. w 1876-1906||?
1876-S 22? 1877 as Republican free press
OGI 1876-77
OHi Ja 4 1901

Galion INQUIRER. d 1893+
1893-1906? as Evening inquirier
pub 1893+
OG N 5 1912+

REPUBLICAN free press. *See* Galion inquirer

Weekly REVIEW. w 1865-81||?
United with Galion sun to form Galion sun-review
MWA F 21 1867

Galion SUN-REVIEW. w,sw 1872-1908||?
1872-81? as Galion sun
w 1872-93?
OHi Ja 1 1901

Weekly TRAIN. w Mr? 1856-
OHi Jl 18 1856

GALLIPOLIS

BUCKEYE and Gallipolis journal. *See* Gallipolis journal

Gallipolis BULLETIN. w D 18 1867-1919||?
OClWHi 1867-69;Ag 1871-[1913]-17
OHi Ja 4 1901

Gallipolis DISPATCH. w? 1838?-
OClWHi S 2 1846

GALLIA courier. w 1849?-
MWA D 22 1852

GALLIA free press. *See* Gallipolis journal

GALLIA gazette. *See* Gallipolis journal

GALLIA phoenix. *See* Gallipolis journal

GALLIA tribune. *See* Gallipolis tribune

***Gallipolis JOURNAL.** w N 1818-1913||?
1818-Mr? 1825 as Gallia gazette; Mr 31 1825-Mr 1831? Gallia free press; Ap-1831? Gallia phoenix; 1831?-Jl 3? 1834 Gallipolis weekly journal and Gallia and Meigs public advertiser; Je 10?-D 1834? Buckeye and Gallipolis journal
DLC F 9 1827;N 26 1840
IU Ag 28,S 11,O 2-9 1834
MWA F 9 1827;Ag 19 1852;Mr 12 1857;Ag 29 1861;Ap 10 1862
OCHi F 16 1832;F 14 1833
OClWHi Ap 7 1825;D 4 1829;Jl 29,D 30 1841; F 3,17,D 15 1842;45-[51;54]57-61
OHi Ap 7 1825;F 16 1832;Ja 2 1901
WHi D 25 1834;My 8 1862

Gallipolis daily JOURNAL. d Mr 17 1892-1913||?
IU Mr 17,Ag 4 1892
OGal 1899-1900
OHi Ja 2 1901
VHi My 17 1902

Gallipolis LEDGER. *See* Gallipolis tribune

LOCOMOTIVE. *See* Gallipolis tribune

Gallipolis TRIBUNE. w 1871-1930||?
1871? as Locomotive; 1872?-81? Gallipolis ledger; 1882?-89? Gallia tribune
OGal D 1890-1902;04
OHi 1899-1919;Mr 30-D 1923

Gallipolis daily TRIBUNE. d 1894+
pub Jl 1895+
OGal 1899-1900;03;05-Je 1908;09-Je 1913;14-21; 23+

GAMBIER

Gambier weekly ARGUS. w 1874-81||?
OHi Ap 18 1878

Gambier OBSERVER. w My 28 1830-38||?
Followed by Gambier observer and western church journal (not in this list)
OClWHi 1830-O 2 1835;N 15 1836-N 15 1838
OHi 1830-32;S 13 1833-N 8 1837

GARRETTSVILLE

Saturday ITEM. w 1885-90||?
OClWHi Ja 29,F 12,S 10 1887;Ap 7-14,28-My 5 1888;F 16 1889;S 20 1890

OHIO (*Continued*)

GARRETTSVILLE—*Continued*

Garrettsville JOURNAL. w Jl 10 1867+
KHi F 7 1876
OClWHi O 23 1867;F 3 1869;D 15 1870;Ap 27, My 23 1871;F 1 1872;D 10 1873;D 12 1878-[79]-Ap 7,S 22-29 1881[82]Jl 11,S 12 1883;Ap 10,Jl 31 1884;Ap 8,29 1886;F 24 1887;Ap 19 1888;Jl 25,D 12 1889;F 27,Jl 3,N 5 1890;S 22,D 1,22 1892-Ap 6,27,Je 29 1893;My 24,Jl 26 1894 Je 20,Jl 18,Ag 28,S 12-18 1901;O 13 1904;Je 15 1905;O 25 1906;N 14 1907;Jl 2,S 3,N 26 1908;13+
OHi 1927-My 22,Je 5,19,Ag 14 1930+

WESTERN pearl. sm Ja 1 1836-
N Ja,Mr-My 1 1836
OClWHi Ja 1-15 1836

GENEVA

ASHTABULA county democrat. w My? 1853-
Title varies: Ashtabula democrat
OClWHi D 26 1853;Ap 10,O 2,23 1854
WHi My 29 1854

Geneva weekly FREE PRESS. w 1876-1901||?
OClWHi 1899-1901

Daily FREE PRESS. d 1900+
1902?-20? as Daily free press-times
OClWHi Ja 26,Jl 23 1903;O 17-26 1904;N 13,D 14 1908;Ja 31 1910;F 1913-Je 1921
OGe Mr 1901-F 1902;My-O 1911
OHi Ja 3 1901

Geneva TIMES. w D 20 1866-1901||?
United with Daily free press to form Daily free press-times, later Daily free press
MWA Ag 17 1876
OClWHi 1866-67;Ag 27 1868;69-88;F 16 1898
OGe 1868;71-Je 19 1879;81-87;89-1900
OHi Ja 2 1901

GENOA

Genoa ENTERPRISE. w 1871-73||?
NNHi D 14 1872

GEORGETOWN

*BENEFACTOR and Georgetown advocate. w 1820-
1820-22? as Benefactor
1820 pub in Levanna
DLC Mr 13 1824
OClWHi Je 20 1822;O 25 1824
OHi My 10 1821

BROWN county democrat. w 1855-S? 1859||
United with Democratic standard to form Southern Ohio argus, later Brown county news
MWA Jl 22 1858
OClWHi Ag 30 1855;58-S 1 1859

BROWN county democrat. w 1883-88||
United with Brown county news to form News democrat

BROWN county news. w 1837?-88||
1837?-S? 1859 as Democratic standard (O 1850-O 1854? Democratic union) O? 1859-Jl 6 1864 Southern Ohio argus. United with Brown county democrat to form News democrat
IU Ag 22 1843
MWA N 22 1843;Mr 6 1851;F 3 1853;O 6 1859;Ap 5 1865
OClWHi Jl 20 1838;N 2 1841;Je 28,Jl 26,O 4,N 1,15,29 1842;Je 20,N 14-28 1843;Ap 2,N 12 1844;N 20,D 25 1845;Jl 9,D 17 1846;N 27 1849;Je 11,Jl 16-O 1850;Ja 16 1851-O 1854;Ag 26 1858-Ag 3 1859-Ag 12 1863;Ja 27-F 3,Ap 20,S 21,N 23 1864-Ag 2 1865;O 10 1866;N 6 1867;F 1868-F,O 13 1869;Ja 19,D 21 1870; Jl 26,S 28 1871;Mr 27 1872;S 9 1874
OHi O 31 1839;Ag 1840-F 1845;64-65;N 28 1877-D 15 1886

CASTIGATOR. *See* Ripley bee (Ripley)

DEMOCRAT and journal. w S 8 1849-O? 1850||
1849-Mr 1850 as Western literary journal. United with Democratic standard to form Democratic union, later Brown county news
OClWHi My 9,D 13-19 1850

DEMOCRATIC standard. *See* Brown county news

Georgetown GAZETTE. w 1880-1926||?
OHi O 1905-S 15 1920

INDEPENDENT American. w N 9 1854-
ICHi My 24 1855
MWA F 22 1855
OClWHi 1854-N 6 1856

Weekly NATIONAL union. w 1863?-
1863? as National union
OClWHi N 19 1863;F 23 1865;Mr 21-29 1866; F 20 1867

NEWS democrat. w 1888+
Formed by the union of Brown county news and Brown county democrat
OHi Ja 3 1901;04-S 1911;O 1912-S 1913;O 1914-S 1915;O 1916-S 1918;O 1919-S 1920

POLITICAL examiner. *See* Ripley bee (Ripley)

SENTINEL. w 1874-82||?
OClWHi F 15 1877

SOUTHERN Ohio argus. *See* Brown county news

TRUE Jeffersonian. w D 11 1856-
MWA Je 11,Jl 23 1857
OClWHi 1856-N 1857

UNION. w N 29 1860-
MWA Ja 17 1861
OClWHi 1860-N 13 1861
OHi Ap 25 1861

WESTERN aegis. w Je 19 1827-
IU D 23 1828;Ja 6,27 1829
MWA Je 15,Mr 18 1828
OHi Je 26 1827-F 2 1829

WESTERN literary journal. *See* Democrat and journal

GERMANTOWN

AMERICAN republican. w 1845?-F 12 1857||
1845?-Ap 27 1854 as Western emporium; My 4 1854-Ag 16 1855 Twin Valley locomotive. Followed by White Cloud Kansas chief (White Cloud, Kansas) later Weekly Kansas chief (Troy, Kansas)
Suspended from Ag 16-S 13 1855
KHi Ap 19 1850-57
MWA My 7 1852
OC Mr 21 1851
PP D 6 1850

TWIN VALLEY locomotive. *See* American republican

WESTERN emporium. *See* American republican

GIRARD

Girard NEWS. w Ap 1 1927+
pub 1927—
OHi S 22 1927-33

GLENVILLE

Papers published in Glenville are listed under Cleveland

GLOUSTER

Glouster PRESS. w S 1896+
pub 1898+
OHi Ja 3 1901

GRANVILLE

Granville INTELLIGENCER. *See* Licking bee

LICKING bee. w 1848?-
1848?-My 1853? as Granville intelligencer
MWA O 28 1852;Je 23 1853
OClWHi My 2 1849;Ag 26 1853
WHi Jl 10 1851

Granville TIMES. w Je 11 1880+
Suspended from 1920-24
OClWHi Je-Ag 20,N 19 1880;My 27,Ag 19-26,S 23,N 25 1881;S 1 1882;Je 27,N 7 1884;Mr 26,Je 18-25 1886;Mr 4 1887;My 18 1888;Je 20 1889;My 3 1890-O 13 1892;My 17 1894;Ja 4,Je 16 1900;Ja 3,Je 27 1901;Je 1902-O 17 1918;D 1924+
OGrD 1880-My 1886;N 1930-O 19,N 2-9,23 1933+
OHi F 18 1892-O 22 1896;Ja 3 1901

WANDERER. w F 8? 1822-
NN Je 13 1823
OCHi My 17-S 6,N 8 1822-S 1823
OClWHi My 10,Ag 1822;O 24 1823;Ja 16 1824

GREENFIELD

Greenfield BLADE. w 1852?-
MWA D 24 1852

Greenfield INDEPENDENT. w S 16 1920-22||?
OHi 1920-D 7 1922

TAYLOR'S illustrated newspaper.
OClWHi Mr 5 1857

GREENSPRING

Greenspring ECHO. w 1895+
OClWHi Mr 3 1921;O 22 1925
OHi Ja 3 1901

GREENVILLE

Greenville daily ADVOCATE. d 1893—
pub 1893+
MWA My 4 1895
OClWHi D 20 1894;My 4,Jl 6 1895
OHi Jl 8-O 1900;O 7,D 31 1912;Je-Ag 1917;N-D 7 1923;Ag 1924;My 1925;Ja,Mr 1926-Je, Ag-N 1927;28+
WaPS D 30 1918[19]
—w ed *See* Democratic advocate

Greenville COURIER. w 1875-1918||?
1875-95? as Greenville Sunday courier
OHi 1877-84;90-92;Ja 5 1901;14-Jl 6 1918

DARKE county democratic advocate. *See* Democratic advocate

Greenville DEMOCRAT. w 1864?-1927||?
OClWHi Ag 1-8 1894
OHi Je 16 1869-Mr 18 1908;Je 30-D 1909;Jl 13 1910-N 5 1921;Ap 1923-25;Ja-My 1927

DEMOCRATIC advocate. w 1883+
1883-93? as Darke county democratic advocate
OHi [Ag 30 1883-O 21 1886]Ja 19 1888-O 1891; 92-O 4 1894;95-98;Ap 15 1909-Je 1915;26-29
—d ed *See* Greenville daily advocate

Greenville JOURNAL. w 1832-1918||
MWA N 5 1896
OClWHi N 5 1896;Ap 19 1900-01
OHi Ja 3 1901;Mr 1906-Je 1918

Daily NEWS-TRIBUNE. d My 31 1921-29||?
1921-Ap 1923 as Greenville daily news
OHi 1921-Mr,My 1923-F 1929

OHIO populist. w 1894-96||?
1894-95 pub at Columbus
WHi Je 8,29-N 16 1894;Ag 6,20 1896

Greenville TELEGRAPH. w 1851?-
MWA O 22,N 19 1852

Daily TRIBUNE. d 1890-Ap 1923||
United with Greenville daily news to form Daily news-tribune
OHi Ja 1 1901;S-D 1914;F-Mr,O 1915;Ja-F 1916;Je 1919-23

WESTERN statesman and Greenville courier. w My? 1832-
DLC O 27,N 3 1832

GROVEPORT

COMMONWEALTH. w 1896?-
WHi [Ap-Ag 19 1899]

HAMILTON

Hamilton ADVERTISER. *See* Hamilton intelligencer

BUTLER county democrat. w S 1861-1922||?
1861-Mr 10 1870 as True telegraph
OClWHi N 6 1862-O 20 1864
OH O 1870-72;74-75;78;82-84;86-91;93-96;98; 1901-02;04-05;07-09
OHi [1882-84]
OOxM S 18 1879;My 31,D 16-27 1883[Ja-Je 1884]Ap 21,D 15 1887[Ap 1888-91]-[94]-[96]-[1901-04]-[06-13]-[15-22]

BUTLER county press. w Ap 22 1900+
pub My 1913+
OHi My 10 1918-Ap 18 1919
WHi D 11 1903

BUTLER county telegraph. *See* Hamilton telegraph

CIVILIAN.
Ct Ag 10 1830

DEMOCRACY untrammeled and Butler county investigator. [Rossville] w S 20- 1849||?
OClWHi S 20 1849
OHi S-O 4 1849

Hamilton daily DEMOCRAT. *See* Hamilton journal-news

FREE soil banner. w Ag 21 1848-
OClWHi Ag-O 14 1848
OHi Ag 21,28,S 4,O 10,21,N 4 1848

Hamilton GAZETTE and Miami register. *See* Hamilton intelligencer

HARRISON democrat. w F 4-O 20 1840||
Campaign paper
DLC F 4 1840
OHi F-O 20 1840

HICKORY club. [Rossville] w 1838||?
Campaign paper
OOxM O 23 1838

*Hamilton INTELLIGENCER. w Je 22 1814-My 1862||
1814-O 5 1819 Miami herald (Mr 29 1816-S? 1817 Philanthropist); O 12 1819-N 4? 1821 Hamilton gazette and Miami register; N 11 1821-Ja 3 1825 Hamilton intelligencer and advertiser; Ja 10 1825-N 10 1826 Hamilton advertiser; N 17 1826-O 26 1827 Hamilton Ohio advertiser; Ja 4 1838-F 1840 Hamilton Ohio intelligencer. Merged with Butler county telegraph, later Hamilton telegraph
Suspended from O 26 1827-Ag 1828
Ct F 23 1827;Jl 26 1831
DLC Ja 20,F 10,Mr 2,23-Ap 13,My 18-25,Je 8-15,O 11 1824;Ag 26,S 23 1828;Mr 31,Je 30-Jl 7,Ag 4,25-S 1,N 17,D 29 1829;Ja 5,Jl 20,Ag 10,D 28 1830;Mr 5,O 30 1840
IU Ag 31 1843;Ja 16,30,Mr 5,Ap 2,30,My 21,Je 20,Ag 8 1844
MWA Ja 19 1827;Ja 12 1834;O 4 1838;S 20 1849
OCHi [N 12 1831-Ja 18 1834]
OClWHi 1821-Ja 3 1825;N 28 1839-Je 22 1843; My 29 1845-Ja 18,S 6 1849;My 9,Ag 1 1850;Ja 2 1854;My 13 1852-Ja 9 1862
OHi 1821-O 1827;Ag 16 1828-N 2 1837;38-Ja 10 1856
OOxM D 15,29 1823-N 22 1824;Ag 16-O 7 1828; N 12 1831-N 2 1833;My 23 1850-My 13 1852

Hamilton JOURNAL-NEWS. d 1886+
1886-97? as Hamilton daily democrat; 1898-Jl 1907? Hamilton evening democrat; Ag-D 1907 Hamilton democrat-sun; 1908-31? Hamilton evening journal
DLC 1898
OH 1886-88;Ja-Je 1897;1917-Je 1918;Ja-Mr, My 1919-33
OHi Ja 1 1901;Mr-Je,S 1906-Jl 22,O-D 1916; S 1921;Ap-My 1922

MIAMI democrat. [Rossville] w Ja 10 1850-
OClWHi Ja 10,S 17 1850-O 7 1851
OHi 1850-O 21 1851

MIAMI echo. w D 5 1842-
OHi 1842

MIAMI herald. *See* Hamilton intelligencer

MURRAY'S weekly volunteer. w Ap 11 1821-
1821-Ap 22 1822 as Volunteer
MWA Je 13,Jl 4-11,25 1821;My 11 1824
OCHi 1821-D 14 1825
OClWHi Ag 26-O 21 1822;Mr 24,Ap 7,Ag 11-D 15 1823
OHi O 6 1823

OHIO (*Continued*)

HAMILTON—*Continued*

Hamilton daily NEWS. d 1879-Mr 1898||
1879-1888? as News. United with Hamilton daily republican to form Daily republican-news, later Hamilton daily news
DLC D 22 1879-Je 1888
OClWHi Ap 27 1880;N 18 1883;Ap 29,My 8,O 28 1885;O 3 1888;My 17 1893

Hamilton daily NEWS. d 1892-1931||?
1892-Mr 19 1898? as Hamilton daily republican; Mr 21? 1898-1918? Daily republican-news. United with Hamilton journal to form Hamilton journal-news
DLC 1898
OClWHi My 17 1893;Ap 18 1921
OHi Ja 1 1901;Ap 7 1914-F 1916;Jl 1919-My 9 1925
OOxM O 1909-O 1914;Jl 1915-Je 1916;23+
—w ed *See* Hamilton telegraph

Hamilton OHIO advertiser. *See* Hamilton intelligencer

OHIO independent press. w Ag 5? 1830-
Ct S 9 1830

Hamilton OHIO intelligencer. *See* Hamilton intelligencer

PHILANTHROPIST. *See* Hamilton intelligencer

Daily PRESS. [Rossville] d Ap 21? 1851-
OHi Ap 22-23,26 1851

Hamilton daily REPUBLICAN. *See* Hamilton daily news 1892-1931

ROSSVILLE advertiser. sw Ap 20 1849-
OHi Ap-Ag 10 1849

SCOTT battery. w Je 13- 1852||
Campaign paper
OHi Je-S 14 1852

Hamilton evening SUN. d 1902-Jl? 1907||
United with Hamilton evening democrat to form Hamilton democrat-sun, later Hamilton journal-news
OClWHi My 28-29 1903

Hamilton TELEGRAPH. w N 2 1827-1919||?
1827-Mr 4? 1831 as Western telegraph and Hamilton Ohio advertiser; Mr 11 1831-Mr 2 1832 Hamilton telegraph and Butler county advertiser; Mr 9 1832-F 11? 1847 Western telegraph and Butler county advertiser (title varies slightly) F 18 1847-My 1862 Butler county telegraph
Mr 9 1832-Ja 1834 pub in Rossville
DLC D 18 1879-S 1887
IU S 5 1834;Ag 9 1838
InI D 23 1841
MWA N 2 1827
N S 27 1833
NjFHi S 27 1850
OCHi [Je 1828-Ag 13 1830;Jl 22 1831-Ag 9 1833]-Ja 1834
OClWHi N 28 1834;F 13,D 18 1835;Ag 26,D 9 1836;Ap 21,My 26,Je 23,O 1837;N 7 1839;O 29 1840;O 1841-Ag 3 1843;O 10 1844;Mr 13, Ag 21,N 13-20,D 25 1845;F 19-26,Ap 30,Je 18,Jl-Ag 20 1846;Ap 29,Jl 15 1847-N 6 1851; Mr 18,N 11 1852-O 24 1861
OH O 1862-81;O 1894-S 1895
OHi D 5 1867;Ja 3 1901
WHi Ap 23,O 8 1863;Mr 10,24-Ap 14,My 5,Ag 4 1864;F 7 1867
—d ed *See* Hamilton daily news 1892-1931

TRUE telegraph. *See* Butler county democrat

VOLUNTEER. *See* Murray's weekly volunteer

WESTERN telegraph and Hamilton Ohio advertiser. *See* Hamilton telegraph

HARLEM SPRINGS

JACKSONIAN.
OClWHi O 21-22 1845

RURAL tiara.
OClWHi Je 25,Jl 9 1845

HARRISON

Harrison ADVOCATE. *See* Harrison news

Harrison NEWS. w 1868?-
1868?-D 9? 1871 as Harrison advocate
In Ap 22-N 16,D 16 1871-D 27 1872

HAYESVILLE

Hayesville JOURNAL. w Jl 9? 1875-90||?
OClWHi Ag 6,N 18 1875;Ja 27,O 12-19,D 21 1876;Ja 15 1885

HILLSBORO

To 1879? as Hillsborough

AMERICAN citizen. 1854?-
OClWHi N 18 1854;N 7 1857;Mr 6,Ap 3,Jl-Ag 21 1858

Hillsboro DISPATCH. w,sw F 26 1898-1922||?
1898-F 17 1900 as Dispatch
w 1898-1907?
OClWHi N 8 1910;Ag 15 1911;F 11 1913
OHi 1898-Ja 10 1922

Hillsboro GAZETTE. *See* Hillsboro press-gazette

Daily evening GAZETTE. d My 19- 1883||?
OHi My-D 11 1883

Saturday HERALD. w 1880-F 1885||?
United with Highland news to form News-herald
OClWHi Mr 9 1881;F 25-Ag 5 1882;Ja 19 1884
OHi Jl 29 1882-F 7 1885

HIGHLAND democrat. w D 7 1865-
OClWHi 1865-Jl 1866

HIGHLAND news. *See* News-herald

Hillsboro MAIL. 1871-73||?
OClWHi Ja-O 1873

NEWS-HERALD. w Ap 21 1837+
1837-44? as Ohio news; 1845?-F 1885? Highland news
DLC Jl 10,O 23,N 20 1840;Jl 8 1842;extra N 4 1840
IU S 13-20 1839;O 22 1841;F 11-18,O 28-N 4 1842;Ag 16-S 15,29-O 13,N 24-D 8 1843;Ja 12,F 2,23-Mr 8 1844;F 21,Ap 4-11 1851
MWA D 24 1852
NNHi My 21 1863;Ap 10 1873
OClWHi 1837-Ap 17 1840;Je 7,Jl 30 1844;Jl 1845-Je 1846;51-F,Je-Ag 1855;Ap 24,Ag 28 1856-F 17,Jl 21 1859;Jl 12 1860-Ja 10 1883; D 8 1910
OHi My 14 1852-84;Ap 1886-1901;04-14;16-23; 32
OOxM Je 25 1874

OHIO news. *See* News-herald

PEOPLE'S press. w N 7 1923-O 1926||?
United with Hillsboro gazette to form Hillsboro press-gazette
OHi 1923-O 1926

***Hillsboro PRESS-GAZETTE.** w,sw Je 18 1818+
1818-51? as Hillsborough gazette and Highland advertiser; 1852?-79? Hillsborough gazette; 1880?-O 1926? Hillsboro gazette
w 1818-1932?
Ag 27 1920 is historical ed
CSmH S 4 1830
DLC S 19 1829;N 3 1832;F 11 1851
IU Je 21 1821;My 16,Je 6 1822;N 9 1833;Ag 31 1838;My 6,N 11 1842;Ag 25,S 15,O 6 1843;Ja 19-26,F 9,23-Mr 1,S 13,27,O 18 1844;D 7 1849;Ap 22,30(extra)1851
MWA Je 16 1827;My 13 1875
OClWHi Jl 21,Ag 4 1827;S 20 1828;O 28-N 4 1829;O 23-30 1830;Jl 9 1831;N 17 1832;O 19-N 2 1833;My 16,30,O 24-N 21 1834;O 16 1835;Je 24,O 14-N 11 1836;My 19,Je 23,Ag 11 1837;Ja 19-S 21 1838;Ja-Je 7 1839;O 23-29 1840;D 29 1848;N 1849;51-S 12 1854;Ja 19-28,Ap 1855-F 1857;Ja 29 1858-F 8,S 12 1860-64;D 20 1866-D 8 1881[82-83]Ja 17 1884;S 13 1907;S 8 1916;Ag 27 1920
ODa My 11 1855-N 13 1857
OHi Ap 11 1860-Mr 6 1861;79-D 24 1924
WHi D 8(extra)1853

HUBBARD

Hubbard ENTERPRISE. *See* Hubbard news

Hubbard NEWS. w 1877+
1877-1925 as Hubbard enterprise
pub S 1926+
OClWHi O 25 1894;O 10 1895;F 1913-O 18 1917
OHi O 1927-33

HUDSON

Hudson CITIZEN. w 1914-16||?
OClWHi Je 25-Jl 2,30-Ag 13,S 3 1914;F-Mr 4 1915

FAMILY visitor. *See under* Cleveland

INDEPENDENT. w 1895-1920||?
1895-1908? as Hudson independent
OClWHi O 1897-98;1900-Ja 18 1901;Ja-O 1902; Ap 8,22 1904;Jl 1905-07;Mr 20 1908;Ag 27 1919-S 17 1920
OHi Ja 4 1901

INDEPENDENT register and family visitor. w 1850?-
CtY N 22 1853
ICHi N 22 1853
MWA [Je 7-D 20 1853]

OBSERVER and telegraph. *See* Ohio observer

OHIO observer. w Jl 20 1827-Je 20 1855||
1827-D 27 1828 as Cleveland, Ohio western intelligencer; Ja 3 1829-D 30 1830 Hudson, Ohio western intelligencer; Ja 6 1831-D 28 1833 Observer and telegraph. Merged with Cleveland journal (Cleveland)
1827-28 pub in Cleveland
CSmH S 2 1830
Ct Ja 21 1836
CtY D 16 1830;Ja 20,F 3,17-24 1831;Jl 23 1840; Ap 16 1845;Jl 15 1846
ICHi O 14 1830;O 16 1834-35
IU Mr 16,My 11,Je 22,Ag 10 1843
MBAt Je 11 1840;Ja 19,My 18,Jl 13,S 21,O 19,N 9 1843
MWA Jl 21 1852;F 8-D 1854
NNHi Mr 7 1855
NSchU Ap 14 1842
NhD Ap 23,My 7,Je 11,Jl 9,Ag 13,S 10,O 8, N 12,D 17 1840;Ja 7,F 11,Mr 11,Ap 3,My 13, Je 10,Jl 8,Ag 12,N 18,D 2,16 1841;Ja 13,F 17-24,Mr 10,Ap 14,My 12,Je 9,Jl 14,Ag 11,S 22,O 13,N 10,D 15 1842;Ja 19,F 9,Ap 13,My 18,Je 15,Jl 13,Ag 17,O 12,26,N 16,D 14 1843; F 8,N 12 1844
OCHi [Ap 23-N 12 1840]Je 8 1843;N 20,D 4,25 1844;Ja 29,F 19 1845
OClWHi 1827-37;Ap 16 1840-Je 20 1855
OOxM [Ag 27 1835-My 1837]
P-M Je 9 1831;Je 14 1854

Hudson, OHIO western intelligencer. *See* Ohio observer

HURON

Huron COMMERCIAL advertiser. w 1837?-
DLC S 3 1839;Je 1,22 1841
OClWHi Mr 19 1839-Mr 8 1842

Huron weekly NEWS. w Jl 5 1853-
MWA Jl 5 1853

Huron weekly TIMES. w 1874-78||?
OClWHi S 18 1875;Ja 6 1876

IRONTON

Ironton DEMOCRAT. w N 20 1874-78||?
OIB 1874-D 20 1877

HEROLD der union. w My 3? 1861-
In German
NN Je 7 1861

Semi-weekly IRONTONIAN. w,sw 1878-1927||?
1878-92? as Saturday Irontonian; 1893?-96? Weekly Irontonian. Merged with Ironton evening tribune
w 1878-96?
OClWHi Je 14 1921
OHi Mr 1906-Mr 1914;16-Ag,O 1917;Je 1918-S 1919;Jl-Ag 1921

Morning IRONTONIAN. d 1888-1925||?
Merged with Ironton evening tribune
OHi Mr 13 1914-F 1916;Ag 1919-25

Ironton JOURNAL. w S 4 1867-78||?
OIB 1867-71

Ironton REGISTER. w,sw Ag 1 1850-1925||?
w 1850-1910?
MWA S 23 1852;Jl 27 1854;O 27 1864
OClWHi 1850-Jl 22 1852;Je 7,Jl 5 1855;S 3 1857;D 2 1858;Je 14 1860;Ag 25 1864
OHi Ja 3 1901;Ja 1 1903
OIB 1850-1900
WHi Jl 4 1861

Weekly REPUBLICAN. w 1880-1907||?
OHi Ja 5 1901

Ironton daily REPUBLICAN. d 1889-1901||?
DLC 1898
OHi Ja 1 1901

Ironton evening TRIBUNE. d Ja 2 1926+
OHi 1926+

JACKSON

DEMOCRATIC herald. *See* Jackson herald

Jackson EXPRESS. w 1857-64||?
1857-61? as Iron Valley express. Followed by Democratic herald, later Jackson herald
IU Ap 12 1860
OHi F 26 1858-Ag 15 1861;Ag 14 1862-N 1864

Jackson HERALD. w,sw O 17 1866+
Follows Jackson express. 1866-My 13 1868 as Democratic herald; My 20 1868-F 14 1894 Jackson herald; F 21 1894-F 15 1900 Semi-weekly herald
w 1866-F 14 1894
OClWHi 1866-Mr 20 1867
OHi 1868-69;73-74;83;My 13 1886-F 7 1889; F 12 1890-F 15 1902;03-12;14;16-23;26-33

IRON VALLEY express. *See* Jackson express

Jackson JOURNAL. *See* Jackson standard-journal

Jackson STANDARD. w 1847-Jl 26 1888||
United with Jackson journal to form Jackson standard-journal
MWA D 23 1852
NNHi My 21,Je 11 1863
OClWHi My 15 1873
OHi Mr 31 1853-70;73-88
OJS complete

Jackson STANDARD-JOURNAL. sw,w Jl 5 1882-D 29 1925||
1882-Jl 25 1888 as Jackson journal. United with Jackson sun to form Jackson sun-journal
w 1882-My 30 1905
OClWHi 1916-17
OHi 1882-1921;23;25
OJS complete

Jackson SUN-JOURNAL. w,sw 1887+
1887-1925 as Jackson sun (1900?-1918 Semi-weekly sun)
w 1889-99?
pub 1887+
OHi 1895-96;1901-16;18-23;26-29;31-32

JAMESTOWN

GREENE county journal. w 1870+
OXG D 1933+

JEFFERSON

ASHTABULA county sentinel. w,sw Ja 1 1832-1911||?
1832-1900? as Ashtabula sentinel. United with Jefferson gazette to form Gazette and sentinel, later Jefferson gazette
1832-52 pub in Ashtabula
sw O 25? 1878-84?
CP Ap 15,Jl 29 1858;Ja 4 1860
CSmH S 19 1835;Jl 20 1839;F 27 1841;Mr 26 1842
DLC O 27 1832;Ja 10-D 1856;O 6 1859;61;F 5 1862;Ag 2,S 13,27-O,N 8-15 1865
ICU Je 26 1845
IU F 23 1854
InLHi Je 14 1847
KHi Mr 21 1860
MBAt Ap 19 1865
MWA F 8-22,Mr 21-28,O 10,30,D 26 1840;Ag 19,S-O,N 11-25,D 9-30 1843;Mr 23,Je 22,Ag 31,D 14 1850;Ja 11 1851;Jl 10,31,Ag 28,S 18-25,O 9-16 1852[Ja 27-D 1853]D 31 1857[Ja-Jl 11]D 26 1860;O 9,D 4 1861;Jl 9 1862;F 21 1866;Ag 3 1876
N Mr 22 1847
NNHi N 4 1843;Ap 18 1860;S 2 1863
NjR [N 28 1840-46]
OClWHi 1832-Ap 21 1910
OHi Ja 15 1853-59;D 31 1862-63;Je 22 1864;Ja 3 1901
WHi 1860;Ja 2,16,F 27,Ap,O 2-9,N 6-13,27-D 4,18 1861-63;Ja 20,Ap 27 1864;Mr-D 1868

OHIO (*Continued*)

JEFFERSON—*Continued*

ASHTABULA republican and farmers and mechanics advocate. w? 1830-
1830-3-? as Ashtabula republican
IU F 27 1832
OClWHi O 21,D 19 1831;Ja 9-N 2 1832

ASHTABULA sentinel. *See* Ashtabula county sentinel

DEMOCRAT. 1853?-
OClWHi Je 6 1853

Jefferson GAZETTE. w,tw,sw N 3 1876+
1912?-18? as Gazette and sentinel
w 1876-1904?;tw 1919?-30?
OClWHi Ag 26,D 2 1881;S 3-10,24-O 8,22 1897; Jl 12 1902;My 5,Ag 4-14 1904;Jl 20-22,O 31,D 2-14 1906;Mr 19,N 17 1906[07-08]-33
OHi Ja 4 1901;Je-Jl 12 1921;D 1925-O 14 1926;Mr 17 1927

OHIO luminary and Ashtabula pioneer. w N 12 1828-30||?
1828-Jl? 1830 as Ohio luminary
CSmH S 11 1830
MWA My 8,Je 5 1830
MiU-C Ja 8 1830
OClWHi D 10 1828;F 11,N 13 1829;Ap 17 1830

KALIDA

Kalida SENTINEL. w 1855?-
MWA Ap 9 1863

Kalida VENTURE. w 1840?-
MWA Ag 27 1852
OClWHi S 23 1845

KENT

Kent BULLETIN. w,sw O 3 1866-1908||?
Follows Saturday review (not in this list). 1866-67 as Commercial bulletin (other variations slight: Saturday bulletin; Saturday morning bulletin)
DLC 1868;73;Mr 21 1874;77
OClWHi Ap 13-D 1867;Ja-Je 1875;My 1876-1902
OHi Ja 4 1901

COMMERCIAL bulletin. *See* Kent bulletin

COURIER-TRIBUNE. w,sw O 28 1886+
1886-D 25 1928 as Kent courier (w)
pub 1886+
OClWHi O 1912-33

Kent NEWS. w O 30 1867-69||?
OClWHi N 1867-Ap 18 1868

Kent TRIBUNE. w 1916-28||
United with Kent courier to form Courier-tribune

KENTON

Kenton DEMOCRAT. w Mr 7 1857+
1857-80? as Hardin county democrat
OClWHi 1857-My 1 1858;N 9 1876
OHi 1912-18

Kenton daily DEMOCRAT. d 1893+
OHi Jl 1918+

DEMOCRATIC expositor. w 1851?-
MWA Ag 25 1852

DEMOCRATIC news. *See* Graphic-news-republican

GRAPHIC-NEWS-republican. w,sw 1885-1919||?
1885-87? as Democratic news; 1888?-89? Kenton news; 1890?-1911? Graphic-news
sw 1885?
OClWHi Je 10 1885
—d ed *See* Kenton news-republican

HARDIN county democrat. *See* Kenton democrat

HARDIN county weekly republican. w Ja 19 1847-1911||?
1847-92? as Kenton republican (My 20 1853-D 27 1866 Hardin county republican)
United with Graphic-news to form Graphic-news-republican
IU D 24 1852;D 23 1853;D 15 1854;N 9,D 14 1855
MWA Ag 11 1852;Ag 11 1854;F 15 1866
NNHi My 22,Je 5,Ag 28 1863
OClWHi 1847-F 2 1848;50-Ja,O 1864-66;F 1867-Ja 23 1868
OHi Mr 11 1853-F 8 1856;F 12 1858-Ja 1863;Ja 21 1875-77;80;85;93

Kenton NEWS. w *See* Graphic-news-republican

Kenton NEWS-REPUBLICAN. d 1889+
1889-95? as Kenton news

Kenton REPUBLICAN. *See* Hardin county weekly republican

KINGSTON

Kingston BLADE. w Ap 9 1887-99||?
IU Ap 9-16 1887

KINGSVILLE

Kingsville TRIBUNE. w 1883-1904||?
OClWHi Ag 5 1887;N 1897-O 1900;01-[03]-Ja 1904
OHi Ja 4 1901

KINSMAN

Kinsman NEWS. w My 14 1897-1907||?
OClWHi My 14 1897
OHi Ja 4 1901

KIRTLAND

Kirtland ADVERTISER. My? 1844-
OClWHi My 10 1844

ENSIGN of liberty. Ap? 1847-
OClWHi Ap 11 1847

NORTHERN times. w Ap 3? 1835-
Ct O 2-9 1835

Evening and morning STAR. Je 1832-
OClWHi 1832-Jl,D 1833-S 1834

LAKEWOOD

Papers published in Lakewood are listed under Cleveland

LANCASTER

AMERICAN Lancaster gazette. *See* Lancaster gazette

BUCK EYE. w 1840||?
Campaign paper
DLC S 5 1840

BUENA VISTA. 1848||?
Campaign paper
DLC Jl 25 1848

Lancaster daily EAGLE. d Ap 7 1890+
OHi 1890+
—w ed *See* Ohio eagle

FAIRFIELD county democrat. w,sw 1890-1926||?
w 1890-99?
OHi Ap 15 1908-09

Lancaster GAZETTE. w,sw 1826-1910||?
1826? as American Lancaster gazette; My? 1827-Je 14 1831 Lancaster Ohio gazette (N? 1829-Ap 19 1831 Lancaster gazette) Ap? 1832-34? Gazette and enquirer; 1839?-44? Lancaster gazette and express (other variations slight)
sw 1883?-98?
Ct My 9 1833
DLC S 16-30,O 21 1828;N 1 1832
IU Jl 19-26 1832;Ja 24-F 7,Mr 21,Ap 4,My 30 1833;S-O 13,D 15 1843-Mr 8,Ap 5,My 3-10,Ag 23,O 11 1844
InRE S 14 1887
MWA Ag 7 1827;Ap 1 1858
N D 17 1847
OClWHi D 22 1829;N 30 1830;Je 3 1842;Je 30 1843;O 7 1880
OHi Ag 1826-33[F 1834-N 1844]My 10-N 11,D 27 1850-Mr 11,My 1852-F 1856;O 1-15 1857;Mr 11 1858-Mr 1 1860;Mr 1861-Jl,D 30 1875-N 1910
OOxM [O 18 1832-O 24 1833]
WHi S 29 1864

Lancaster daily GAZETTE. d 1895+
1895-1900 as Evening gazette
OHi 1910;Mr,O-D 1918;Ap-D 1919;Ja-Mr,My 8 1919+

INDEPENDENT democrat.
IU O 6 1843

LITTLE magician. 1840||?
Campaign paper
OClWHi S 9 1840

***OHIO eagle.** w 1812+
1831?-33? as Ohio eagle and Fairfield advertiser
CL Ag 20 1831
CSmH My 1 1830
DLC O 5 1843;O 21 1852
ICHi Ag 29 1850
IU My 9 1822;F 1(extra)Ag 31 1843
MWA Ja 3,Mr 21 1829
NcD My 4,Jl 8-20 1822;D 31 1825
OClWHi Mr 7,S 5,O 3,N 14 1844
OHi My 30 1850-F 1856;Mr 1858-Jl 1875;76-1915
WHi Je 1 1833
—d ed *See* Lancaster daily eagle

Lancaster OHIO gazette. *See* Lancaster gazette

Lancaster TELEGRAPH. w Ap 28? 1850-
MWA D 14 1852
OHi Je 4 1850

LAURELVILLE

BORDER news. w 1879+
pub 1900+

LEBANON

AMERICAN democrat. w? 1829?-
CSmH Ag 14 1830

DEMOCRATIC citizen. *See* Warren democratic citizen

Lebanon GAZETTE. w 1877-93||?
United with Western star to form Western star and the Lebanon gazette, later Western star
OHi 1884-F 9 1893

Lebanon PATRIOT. w 1868+
OHi Jl 8 1869-My 4 1893;95-O 8,N 22 1913-16

REPUBLICAN-RECORD. w 1899-1905||?
1899-Ag 15? 1903 as Warren county record
OHi 1902-Ag 15,S 30 1903-O 1905

SOBER second thought. w 1846-
OClWHi Ap 16 1847
PDoHi N 27 1846

STAR and gazette. *See* Western star

THOUGHT and eagle. w 1848||?
OClWHi S 29-O 6 1848

UNION volunteer. w Mr? 1867-
OHi N 5 1867

WARREN county record. *See* Republican-record

WARREN democratic citizen. w Jl? 1852-63||?
1852-D 25 1863 as Democratic citizen
MWA D 8 1852
OClWHi Ag 25 1859-Ag 8,N 20 1862-My 1 1863

***WESTERN star.** w F 13 1807+
1823?-S 5 1825 as Star and gazette; S 15 1825-Je 28? 1828 Western star and Lebanon gazette; F 23 1893-Ja 12? 1899 Western star and the Lebanon gazette
CSmH Ag 21 1830
DLC Ag 23 1825-26;Ag 13 1827;Je 28,Ag 16 1828;Mr 14-21,Je 27,Jl 11,Ag 1,S,N 21 1829;Ja 2-9,23,D 11 1830;O 30 1840
IU Jl 9,23-30 1821;My 25 1822
MWA Je 9 1827;Ap 23 1847;My 4 1849;D 17 1852;N 2 1876
OC S 12 1856
OClWHi Ag 16 1823-24;29-Jl 20 1832;S 14,O 30 1835-39;Ja 31,Jl 17 1840;F 5 1841;Ag 30 1844;Mr 19 1847;O 10 1907;Mr 19,My 14,Je 11 1908;Ap 22 1909;O 19 1911;N 1913-Ap 9 1914
OHi Ag 25 1827;Ja 4 1866;Jl 25 1867-Jl 8 1869; 71-1916;O 1919+
OOxM Ap 23,D 1-8 1827;Ja 19-F 2,Mr 1-8,22-My 3,Je 14,28,Jl 19,Ag 2-16,30-S 12,O 10-N 7,21 D 13,27 1828;Ja 24,F 7-21,Mr 14-21,Ap 4-18,Je 6,Jl 11-25,Ag 1 1829
WHi F-O 17 1828;N 21 1829

LEESBURG

Leesburg BUCKEYE. w 1885-1913||?
OHi F 17 1899-1912

Leesburg CITIZEN. w D 18 1913+
pub 1913+
OHi 1914-26

DEMOCRAT and advocate. *See* Highland democrat and workingman's advocate

Leesburg ENTERPRISE. w My 21 1872-73||?
OClWHi My 21 1872

HIGHLAND democrat and workingman's advocate. w Jl 4? 1832-
1832-F? 1833 as Highland democrat and railroad advocate; Mr?- 1833? Democrat and advocate
IU S 15-22,N 17 1832;Ja 12,26,F 27,Mr 13-20, Ap 3 1833;Mr 27 1834

LEETONIA

Leetonia DEMOCRAT. *See* Leetonia reporter 1875—

Leetonia REPORTER. w Ja 4 1872-77||?
OHi 1872-Ja 4 1873;Ja 21 1876-77

Leetonia REPORTER. w Jl 14 1875+
1875-Mr 18 1882 as True press; Mr 25 1882-Je 1889 Leetonia democrat
1875-Je? 1881 pub in Columbiana
OHi 1875-Je,Ag 13 1881-Je 1890;Jl 1892-Ja 4 1901;02-10;12-29

LEVANNA

BENEFACTOR. *See* Benefactor and Georgetown advocate (Georgetown)

LEWISBURG

Lewisburg LEADER. w 1897+
OClWHi D 27 1928-Ja 3 1929

LIMA

ALLEN county democrat. *See* Times democrat w

ALLEN county republican. w 1874-91||
United with Lima gazette to form Allen county republican-gazette
OHi 1889-91

ALLEN county republican-gazette. w,sw 1854-1917||?
1854-91 as Lima gazette
w 1854-92
OClWHi Ap 28 1880
OHi 1892-1901;03-07;10-F 1916

Lima ARGUS. w 1841-
1841-43? as Porcupine
IU My 4 1844

Lima GAZETTE. *See* Allen county republican-gazette

Lima daily NEWS. d 1897+
1920-28 as Lima news and times-democrat
S 20 1931 is hundredth anniversary of Allen county ed
pub 1884+
CL S 20 1931
OHi Ap-Je 1914;Ag 17 1926+

PORCUPINE. *See* Lima argus

Lima REPORTER. w S 24 1844-
ODa 1844-O 19 1847

Lima REPUBLICAN. *See* Lima morning star

OHIO (*Continued*)

LIMA—*Continued*

Lima SENTINEL. w 1894-95||?
WHi S 29 1894-Mr 16 1895

Lima morning STAR. d 1882-1932||?
1882-91 as Lima republican; 1892-1924 Lima republican gazette; 1924-30? Lima morning star and republican gazette
OHi Je 24 1926-F 1929

Lima STAR. sw 1915-24||
United with Lima republican-gazette to form Lima morning star and republican-gazette, later Lima morning star

TIMES-DEMOCRAT. w,sw 1853-1911||?
1853-93 as Allen county democrat (w)
OHi 1874-76;Ja-O 1878;88-1902;05-S 1908;09-11

TIMES-DEMOCRAT. d 1884-1920||
1884-90? as Lima times. United with Lima daily news to form Lima news and times-democrat, later Lima daily news
OHi Ja 1 1901;Ja 10 1911-16

LISBON

To 1895 as New Lisbon

AURORA. w Mr 15 1832-
DLC Je 30-Jl 7 1849
MWA Jl 16 1845;Ag 1 1846
OClWHi 1832-Ja 1837;Mr 1838-Ja 5 1839;40-Jl 10 1847;49-F 16 1850;Je 1851-F 1855
OHi Ap 24 1841
PShH [1839-42]

BUCKEYE state. w,sw S 23 1852+
w 1852-1915?
OClWHi O 1852-S 17 1874;76-97;99-1909;11-15;17-18
OHi Ap 9 1857;Ja 4,Mr 28 1858;65-Je 20 1872;Ja 28 1875-78;S 18 1879-1920
OLiC 1929+
—d ed *See* Evening journal

CABIN democrat. Je 26- 1840||?
Campaign paper
IU Je 26 1840

COLUMBIANA American and New Lisbon free press. *See* Western palladium

COLUMBIANA republican. w? 1827?-
OClWHi S 26 1827

FREE discussion. w
OClWHi Mr 1837-F 1838

New Lisbon GAZETTE. w 1824||?
WHi Mr 12 1824

Lisbon JOURNAL. w Ap 19 1867-1901||?
OClWHi 1867-Ja 1 1877;78-Mr 12 1888
OHi 1867-Ap 4 1870;Ja 7 1901

Evening JOURNAL. d Ja 11 1909+
OLiC 1929+
—sw ed *See* Buckeye state

***OHIO patriot.** w,sw 1809-1923||?
1828-30? as Ohio patriot and New Lisbon gazette; 1835?-39? Ohio patriot and farmers and mechanics shield
w 1809-D 13 1894
CSmH O 29 1825;Jl 17 1830
DLC Ag 21 1840;43-47;O 15 1852
IU Jl 8 1842
MWA D 6 1828;Ag 22 1829;Ap 7,D 29 1832
OClWHi 1821-S 1830;Je 11-25,O 22 1831-My 25,N 22 1833;Ap 10 1835-Ag 23 1839;F 21,Ap 9,Ag 21,N 13 1840-O 1849;Ap 5,S 6 1850;S 5,15 1851;Mr 1852-F 1856;My 28 1858-My 15, D 4 1868;Mr 10 1871;D 1873-N 6 1890;Ja 15, F 12 1891;Je 27 1903;S 23 1921;Mr 24 1924
OHi Je 14 1821;My 20 1870-My 2 1873;N 25 1880-O 1900;Ja 1 1901;19
TKL Jl 24 1840

REPUBLICAN leader. w 1891-97||?
DLC S 10 1891-S 1 1892
OClWHi Ja 21 1897

TINY buffle.
OClWHi Jl 25,Ag 1 1840

WESTERN palladium. w Je 27 1827-54||
1827-28? as Columbiana American and New Lisbon free press. Merged with Buckeye state
DLC Ag 29 1827;N 29 1828;F 21-28,Mr 14-21, Je 27,Jl 18,Ag 8,S 5,19 1829
IU F 24 1842
MWA Je 27 1827
OClWHi S 12 1827;F 9,23-Mr 1 1828;Jl 4 1829; Ja 5,19,F 30,S 14,N 16 1838;Mr 1,Ap 26-My 2,Jl 26 1839;40;Ja 28,Jl 8 1841;Ag 4 1842;S 19 1844;F 5 1846;F 3 1848;Ap 4,Jl 4 1850;Ap 3,Ag 28 1851;F 19,Ap 29,Jl 1 1852;Ja 25 1855
OHi D 6 1828;Ag 6 1831;Jl 8 1841;Je 29 1843; D 5 1844;Ap 8,Je 3 1847;My 16 1850;Ag 10 1854

LITHOPOLIS

BUCKEYE news. w 1902+
OCwT 1902+

LODI

Lodi REVIEW. w 1886+
OClWHi Mr 25 1915
OHi Ja 3 1901

LOGAN

DEMOCRAT-SENTINEL. w Jl 3 1886+
1886-Mr 15 1906 as Ohio democrat
OClWHi Ap 4 1907;F 21 1924
OHi Jl 10 1886-1900;02-13;Je 1914-15;17;21-22

HOCKING county sentinel. *See* Hocking sentinel

HOCKING republican. w Jl 2 1903-08||?
OHi Jl 16 1903-05;07-08

HOCKING sentinel. w 1842-Mr 15 1906||
Title varies: Hocking county sentinel. United with Ohio democrat to form Democrat-sentinel
DLC O 28 1852
ICHi N 4 1852
InRE Ag 7 1873
MWA O 14 1852
OClWHi Je 26 1844;Ja 4-11,F 8-15,Mr 1 1849; Ja 3 1850;Ja 2 1851;Mr 17 1859-60;My 19 1864-Ag 20 1868;Ap 27-D 1871;73-76;N 28 1878;Je 18-Jl 9 1891;Jl 19 1900
OHi Ag 1850-Ag 14 1856;Mr 22 1860-My 5 1864;Ag 27 1868-81;Ap 20 1882-Ap 12 1883; 84-95;98;1900-03;F 1904-06

HOCKING VALLEY gazette. *See* Republican gazette

HOCKING VALLEY journal. *See* Journal-gazette

HOCKING VALLEY republican. w 1839?-
DLC Ap 15 1840

HOCKING VALLEY republican. w 1852-Ja 1861||?
1852-55 as Morning star. United with Republican press to form Logan record and monitor
MWA D 24 1852

JOURNAL-GAZETTE. w,tw,sw 1891-1916||?
1891-Jl 23 1895 as Hocking Valley journal
sw 1913?;tw 1914?-15?
OHi Ja 13 1892-D 3 1895;96-1910

OHIO democrat. *See* Democrat-sentinel

Logan RECORD and monitor. w Ja 24 1861-
Formed by the union of Hocking Valley republican and Republican press
MWA Ja 24 1861

Logan REPUBLICAN. w 1869-83||?
United with Hocking Valley gazette to form Republican gazette
OHi S 1871-82

REPUBLICAN gazette. w 1877-Jl 18 1895||
1877-83? as Hocking Valley gazette. United with Hocking Valley journal to form Journal-gazette
OHi N 28 1877-F 12 1879;80-Je 1883;84-93;95

REPUBLICAN press. -Ja 1861||?
United with Hocking Valley republican to form Logan record and monitor

Morning STAR. *See* Hocking Valley republican 1852-61

LONDON

BUCKEYE union. *See* Madison county democrat

London semi-weekly ENTERPRISE. w,sw 1872+
1872-90 as London enterprise (w)
OHi Ja 26 1887-88;D 1889-1911;13-14

MADISON chronicle. *See* Madison press

MADISON county democrat. w,sw,tw F 18 1857+
F-O 28? 1857 as Buckeye union; N 4? 1857-Mr 13 1862 National democrat
w 1857-D 4 1901;tw 1917?-18?
InDG 1857-Ja 7 1858
OClWHi Je 10 1921
OHi 1858-66;68-69;71-82;D 12 1883-1915
WHi Je 16 1864

MADISON county republican. w 1886-1904||?
1886-S 1896 as London vigilant
OHi 1888-D 12 1893[94-95]-My 22 1901;F 8 1902-04
—d ed *See* Daily nickle plate

MADISON county union. *See* Madison press

MADISON patriot. w 1832-
DLC F 7 1834
IU O 30 1832
WHi N 29 1833;Ap 11,Jl 18,Ag 15 1834

MADISON press. w,sw Ag 12 1843+
1843-F? 1851? as London sentinel; Mr? 1851-F 1854 Madison reveille; Mr 1854-My 1863 Madison chronicle; Je 4 1863-O? 1870 Madison county union; O 27 1870-1916? London times
w 1843-1916?
DLC Ag 19,D 9 1843
MnHi Jl 5 1860
NhD Mr 21-28 1877
OClWHi O 28 1915
OHi Je 1850-F 22,Mr 8 1851-F 1854;Mr 1856-F 18 1858;63-64;67-68;70-O 22 1873;75-N 1880;81-86;O 14 1887-1915;S 1919+

MADISON reveille. *See* Madison press

NATIONAL democrat. *See* Madison county democrat

Daily NICKLE PLATE. d 1889-1904||?
OHi Ja 1 1901;Ja 4 1902
—w ed *See* Madison county republican

London SENTINEL. *See* Madison press

London TIMES. *See* Madison press

London VIGILANT. *See* Madison county republican

LORAIN

CHRONICLE telegram. *See* Lorain journal and times-herald

Daily DEMOCRAT. *See* Lorain Ohio news

Lorain evening HERALD. *See* Lorain times-herald

Lorain JOURNAL and times-herald. d 1919+
1919-My 1921 as Chronicle telegram; Je-Jl 1921 Lorain chronicle telegram; Ag 1921-Mr 20 1922 Lorain evening journal; Mr 21 1922-D 20 1932 Lorain journal
OClWHi S 8 1928-33
OHi D 9 1928+
OL F-[N 1921-22]-[24-25]-O,D 1926-[28]-Ja, Mr-Ap,My 22 1929+

MAGYAR hirnok. w 1913-24||?
In Hungarian
PPiHi D 15 1921-Mr 1924

Lorain daily NEWS. *See* Lorain Ohio news

Lorain OHIO news. d S 29 1900-18||?
1900-S 29 1903 as Daily democrat; S 30 1903-Mr 21 1918 Lorain daily news
OClWHi Ap 22,N 8 1905;F 19 1906;O 12,22 1907;F 22,Mr 7,Jl 14 1918
OHi Ja 2 1901
OL 1900-Ag 10 1918

Lorain POST. w 1894-1918||?
In German
OClWHi Mr 30 1905
OHi D 27 1900-Ja 3 1901

Lorain TIMES. d 1894-My? 1901||
United with Lorain evening herald to form Lorain times-herald

Lorain TIMES-HERALD. d 1894-D 20 1932||
1894-My 4 1901 as Lorain evening herald. United with Lorain journal to form Lorain journal and times-herald
OClWHi 1895-Ag,N 1906-Mr 1907;S 15 1921
OHi Ja 2 1901
OL Ap 1903-S 1908;09-O,N 20-23,D 1914-My, Jl 1919-My,Ag 1920-Je,Ag 1925-O,D 1927[28-29]-32

Lorain es VIDEKE. w 1913-
In Hungarian
PPiHi [D 23 1925-O 1931]

LOUDONVILLE

Loudonville ADVOCATE. *See* Loudonville times

Loudonville DEMOCRAT. w 1879-1919||?
United with Loudonville advocate to form Loudonville times
OClWHi Mr 31 1887
OHi Ja 3 1901

Loudonville INDEPENDENT. w 1870-74||?
OClWHi Ag 19,D 22 1870

Loudonville TIMES. w 1872+
1872-1919? as Loudonville advocate
OClWHi O 7 1874;N 3,D 16 1875;Je 1,D 6 1876[78]F 12 1881;Ja 12,Ag 10 1883;My 9 1884;Ap 9,Je 11 1891;Ap 14 1892;Je 22,D 14 1893;Ag 29 1895

LOWELLVILLE

Lowellville JOURNAL. w Ja 1928+
pub 1928+

LOWER SANDUSKY. *See* FREMONT

McARTHUR

McArthur DEMOCRAT. *See* Vinton record

McArthur DEMOCRAT-ENQUIRER. w Ja 24 1867+
1867-Ja 15 1873 as Democratic enquirer; Ja 22 1873-Ja 9 1884 McArthur enquirer
pub D 1905-D 10 1907;26-Ja 2 1927;34+
OHi 1867-1923

DEMOCRATIC enquirer. *See* McArthur democrat-enquirer

McArthur ENQUIRER. *See* McArthur democrat-enquirer

McArthur JOURNAL. w Ag? 1857-
OHi D 24 1857-Ja 15 1863

MINERAL region herald. w 1855?-
OHi Ap 17-My 1856

McArthur PLAIN DEALER. w 1887-91||?
IU Ag 18-25,S 15,29 1887;O 11,N 15 1888

McArthur REGISTER. w Ap 23 1863-
MWA Je 2 1864
OHi 1863-O 1865

McArthur REPUBLICAN. w Ap 13 1850-
1850-Ag 15 1852 as Vinton county republican
MWA D 24 1852
OClWHi N 25 1853
OHi 1850-D 9 1853
WHi Jl 29-Ag 5 1853

REPUBLICAN tribune. w 1894+
1894-F 29 1912 as Vinton county republican
OHi Mr 22 1894-1908;10-23;26
OMcD 1915

McArthur TRIBUNE. w Je 18 1908-F? 1912||
United with Vinton county republican to form Republican tribune
OHi 1908-10

VALLEY democrat. w Ap 6?- 1864||?
MWA My 25 1864
OHi Jl 1 1864

VINTON county democrat. w 1879-Ja 1884||
United with McArthur enquirer to form McArthur democrat-enquirer
OHi Ag 11 1881-N 1883

VINTON county flag. *See* Vinton record

VINTON county republican. 1850-52 *See* McArthur republican

OHIO (*Continued*)

McARTHUR—*Continued*

VINTON county republican. 1894-1912 *See* Republican tribune

VINTON record. w Ag 26 1852-98||?
1852-Ag 26 1853 as Vinton county flag; S 2 1853-28 1865 McArthur democrat
MWA N 4 1852;Jl 22 1853
OClWHi 1873-75
OHi 1855-Mr 2 1882;Mr 8 1883-91;Mr 1892-95

McCOMB

HANCOCK county herald. *See* McComb herald

McComb HERALD. w 1881+
1881-1927? as Hancock county herald
OHi [My 1895-Mr 14 1900]

McCONNELLSVILLE

McConnellsville DEMOCRAT. *See* Morgan county democrat

McConnellsville weekly ENQUIRER. w
OHi Jl 11 1862

Weekly HERALD. w 1844+
Follows Ohio whig standard and Morgan county democrat. 1844-O 24 1845 as Independent; O 31 1845-68 Morgan herald; 1869- McConnellsville herald
DLC F 16-Mr 1 1844
IU My 24 1844
MWA Jl 1 1853;Ag 25 1876
OClWHi 1856;59-60[My 1862-63]64;66-69
OHi S 1845-84;Je 16 1932+
TxU Ap 1855-Mr 21 1856;Mr 26 1857-Mr 1858

INDEPENDENT. *See* Weekly herald

MORGAN county democrat. w 1871+
1871-86 as McConnellsville democrat pub 1871+
OHi Ja 4 1901;Je 19 1914-15;Jl 1929+

MORGAN herald. *See* Weekly herald

MORGAN sentinel and McConnellsville gazette. w 1827?-
MWA F 13 1828

MUSKINGUM VALLEY. w 1836?-
WHi Je 17 1841

OHIO whig standard and Morgan county democrat. w 1839-43||
Followed by Independent, later Weekly herald
DLC Ap 2 1841
OClWHi S 9 1841

MADISON

Madison GAZETTE. w Ja 3 1872-78||?
1872-73? as Independent press
OClWHi 1872-Ap 23 1873

INDEPENDENT press. *See* Madison gazette

Madison REVIEW. w,sw 1899-1911||?
w 1899-1906?
OClWHi D 10 1909
OHi Ja 4 1901

MANCHESTER

Manchester GAZETTE. w Ag 1 1867-76||?
OHi 1867-Jl 15 1869

PEOPLES' intelligencer. w 1851?-
MWA Ja 26 1853

MANHATTAN

Manhattan ADVERTISER. w Jl 13 1836-
DLC Jl 13 1836
OClWHi Ag 16 1837;Ag 1 1838
OT Ag 22 1838-D 16 1840;Mr 3,28 1841
PWCl Jl 15-22 1840

MANSFIELD

Mansfield GAZETTE and Richland farmer. w 1823-32||
Title varies: Mansfield gazette. United with Western herald to form Ohio spectator, later Richland shield and banner
CSmH S 1 1830
DLC Mr 24 1825;Ag 23 1827;Ja 2,Mr 19,Ap 2,My 14 1828;Jl 1,O 21 1829
OHi D 17 1828

Mansfield HERALD. w O 20? 1838-93||?
1838? as Richland herald and democratic advertiser 1839?-50? Richland Jeffersonian
DLC N 3 1853;O 31,N 28 1855
MWA Ag 4 1852;F 14 1866
NN S 19 1855;F 6 1856
NNHi F 18 1845
NSchU Je 8 1842
OClWHi D 28 1839;Mr 28-Ap 4 1840;Ja 24, My 1 1844;Je 24,O 28 1846;S 29 1870;Jl 15 1875;N 20 1879;F 26 1880
OHi 1873-74;77-84;N 19 1885-N 11 1886;Ja 31 1889-90

Mansfield daily JOURNAL. d S 13 1924-26||?
MWA S 13 1924

Mansfield NEWS. w,sw 1885-1912||?
1886?-87? Mansfield news and Ohio liberal (other variations slight)
sw Ag 1894-Ap 24 1900
OHi 1891-F 1912

Mansfield NEWS-JOURNAL. d 1885+
1885-S 20 1932 as Mansfield news
DLC 1898
OHi Mr 1912-My,S 1918-21;F 1922-N 1923;O 1924+
VU Mr 2 1917

OHIO liberal. w Ap 9? 1870-
OClWHi Je 18,Jl 2,Ag 20 1870

OHIO liberal. w 1872-85||?
United with Mansfield news to form Mansfield news and Ohio liberal, later Mansfield news
OClWHi S 13 1876
OHi 1883-84

OHIO spectator. *See* Richland shield and banner

Morning PENNANT. w Ap 23 1844-
IU Ap 23,My 27,Ag 20-27,S 17 1844

RICHLAND democrat. w 1860?-
NN Jl 13 1861
NNHi Ja 26,F 23,Mr 9,Ap 27,My 4,Jl 27,Ag 3,24,O 12 1861;Mr 29,Jl 5,O 25 1862

RICHLAND herald and democratic advertiser. *See* Mansfield herald

RICHLAND Jeffersonian. *See* Mansfield herald

RICHLAND shield and banner. w,sw 1830-1913||?
1830-32 as Western herald; 1832-41? Ohio spectator; 1841?-51? Shield and banner
sw D 15 1896-1900
DLC Je 8 1833;Mr 18,Je 24 1841;O 20-27 1852
MWA Ag 25 1852
OClWHi Mr 22 1848;Ag 31 1859;S 11 1875;S 24 1881;S 23 1882
OHi 1877-78;My 17,N 8-15 1884;85-1912
—d ed *See* Mansfield shield

Mansfield SHIELD. d 1888-1918||?
OHi N 9-10 1892;Ja 2 1901;Jl 7 1913-16
—w ed *See* Richfield shield and banner

SHIELD and banner. *See* Richland shield and banner

WESTERN herald. *See* Richland shield and banner

MANTUA

OHIO watchman and liberal enquirer. sw 1835?-
CSmH Jl 8 1837

MARIETTA

AMERICAN friend. *See* Marietta gazette

BUCKEYE newspaper.
OClWHi Ag 21 1845

Der Marietta DEMOCRAT. w 1857?-
In German
OClWHi Jl 18-25 1858

DOLLAR weekly news. w 1884-86||?
OMMu F 13 1884
—d ed *See* Daily news

***Marietta GAZETTE.** w Ap 24 1813-42||
1813-Je 19 1823 as American friend; Je 26 1823-33? American friend and Marietta gazette; 1833?-41? Marietta gazette and Washington county agriculturist. Merged with Marietta intelligencer, later Marietta register
Suspended from F 26-Ap 9 1814;from Ja 12-Mr 15 1816;from Mr 6-My 8 1818
CtY Jl 27 1839
DLC Ag 1,S 19-26,O 24 1829;N 2 1832;N 14 1840
IU My 24 1822;O 17 1840
MBAt Mr 13 1824
MWA F 4 1860
OCHi [1821-Ap 1833]S 26 1835;Mr 30,O 26 1839;Mr 14,Ag 22,S 12 1840
OClWHi Ag 9 1822;Ja 18 1823;24[25-26]Ag 1, 15 1827;28[29]Ja 9,Jl 31 1830[32]F 2-16 1833
OHi S 26 1827-My 11 1833
OMMu [1824-31]-Ja 12,23,Mr,Ap 20,Jl 7 1833; Ap 6 1839;Je 20 1840;Ap 10 1841;Ag 27,O 15-29 1842;Je 4 1859
PEL Jl 22 1824

HOME news. w Ja 1? 1859-
OMMu Je 4 1859

Marietta INTELLIGENCER. tw 1851-
OMM [1852]Mr 4-6,22,Jl 10-12,24,29,N 13,D 23 1856;My 19,O 1 1857;F 16,O 16,N 11,30, D 4 1858;Ja 27,Je 30,D 17 1859;F 23,Mr 6,Ap 21,My 5,Je 28-30,Jl 14,Ag 14,S 27,O 9,20-23,N 8 1860

Marietta INTELLIGENCER. w *See* Marietta register

Marietta JOURNAL. w? N? 1866-
OMMu D 1 1866

Marietta daily JOURNAL. d 1902-19||?
OHi Jl 1914-O 1919
OMMu Ap 7-8 1909;Ap 19 1912

Marietta daily LEADER. w,sw,tw,d 1881-S 8 1906||?
Title varies slightly. Merged with Marietta daily register to form Daily register leader, later Marietta register
w 1881-89;sw 1890-Ag 25 1894;tw Ag 28 1894-Ap 2 1895
OHi F 21 1882-Ja 25,F 20 1883-O 1 1897;98-Je 1906
OMMu F 19-26 1884;Jl 28 1885;Ap 3-10,My 3,Je 12-19,Jl 17-31 1888;Ap 23 1889;Ap 9 1890;Ap 8,My 13 1891;S 15 1901;Je 14,26-27 1902;Ja 26 1904

MARIETTIAN. w 1870-72||?
IU Ap 27 1872

Marietta MINERVA. w S 3 1823-
MWA Jl 23 1824
OMMu S 3 1823;Ap 9,My 21-28,Je 18,Jl 2,Ag 20-27,O 15 1824

Daily NEWS. d My 5 1883-
OMMu My 5 1883
—w ed *See* Dollar weekly news

PRESIDENCY. 1828||?
OClWHi S 8-15 1828

Marietta REGISTER. w,sw,tw,d Ag 29 1839-1927||
1839-My 1862 as Marietta intelligencer; S 10 1906-O 13 1923 Daily register leader (other variations slight) Merged with Marietta daily times
w 1839-N 29 1883; sw D 4 1883-O 18 1889; tw O 19 1889-Je 5 1894
D 18 1901 is centennial ed
DLC Ag 29 1839
IU D 28 1843;Ja 18,F 15,29,Ap 25,My 16-23,O 17,N 7 1844;F 27 1851
MWA D 22 1852;My 27 1880;O 6 1881
OClWHi D 2 1841;Je 6 1844;My 14 1846;Ap 9,28 1857;Ag 17-S 1 1858;Jl 20 1859;Jl 25 1862;D 4 1863;My 5,O 6 1881;Jl 16 1886;Jl 16-20 1888;Ap 5 1894-O,D 1904-N 1906;N 16 1910;Ag 10 1912
OHi 1839-Ag 20 1840;52-60;62;64;66-79;81-Ap 1927
OMM 1839-[S 1844-52]Mr 30,My 25,S 14,D 21 1853;D 27 1854;Ap 25,Ag 15,N 8 1855[56]F 11,Jl 22-29,Ag 26,S 9,D 16 1857;F 24,Mr 31, Ap 14,N 10 1858;F 2,Mr 2-9,Ap 13,Je 22,N 2,D 7 1859[60-My 21,Je 27 1862-N 1863]-[65-69]-[72]-O 16 1888[Mr 20-D 6 1926]-My 14 1927
OMMu Ag 14 1851;Jl 21 1852;Ag 18 1858;Ap 27 1859;O 1884;F 15-19,Mr 4,O 7 1885;O 8 1886;F 15,Je 10-14,Ag 9,S 6,27,O 18,N 22,29, D 6,20 1887[Ja-Jl 1888]F 12 1889;F 8 1895[F-Ag 1898]O 22-26 1900;Ap 9,Ag 17,S 6-21 1901;Ja 11-16 1902;S 1 1903;Ja 27 1904;F 13, 25,Mr 21,Ap 7 1905;Ap 20 1906;F 12,Mr 18, Ap 7 1909;Mr 14 1913;N 9 1918
PWCl Jl 7 1842
—tw ed *See* Marietta intelligencer

Marietta REPUBLICAN. w D 1849-
MWA Je 30 1853;Ap 26 1861
OClWHi 1849-N 21 1856;Ag 27,S 17 1858;Ag 16,O 18 1861
OHi Ap 25 1850-53;Mr 16 1854-57;61-N 5 1863
OMMu Mr 28 1850

Marietta TIMES. w 1864-1918||?
OClWHi O 21 1867;Ap 12 1888
OHi O 1864-67;69-1900
OMMu Je 16,N 24 1887;F 9,Mr 8,22,Ap 12,My 31,Je 7,Jl 19,Ag 2,23,O 18 1888
WHi My 5 1870

Marietta daily TIMES. d 1898—
pub Ap 9 1913+
OHi 1901-23;D 1927+
OMM My 16-21,23-25,31-D 1927;Mr 2,5-6,12 1928
OMMu Ap 7 1930;D 8 1931

Marietta and WASHINGTON county pilot. w 1826?-
MWA Je 7 1827;O 24 1829
OClWHi D 2 1829
OMMu D 19 1829

WASHINGTON democrat. w Mr 10? 1840-
WHi Mr 17-N 21 1840

Marietta ZEITUNG. w 1868-1904||?
In German
IU O 16 1884
NNHi D 27 1872

MARION

BUCKEYE eagle. w My 22 1844-
Title varies: Marion buckeye eagle
DLC S 25 1844
ICHi S 4 1844
MWA D 23 1852
OClWHi Jl 24 1844
OHi 1844-My 9 1849

Marion DEMOCRATIC mirror. w 1842?-
1842?-44? as Democratic mirror
ICHi N 5 1852
IU F 25,Ag 12,O 28(extra)D 16,30 1843;Ja 13-F 3,17,Mr 2,23,My-Je 8,Ag 17 1844;N 27 1847;D 4 1861
MWA Jl 29 1853
OClWHi [Ag 22 1846-D 6 1847]D 15 1848;Je 22,Jl 27,Ag 31,S 28,O 26 1849[50]Ja 10 1851
OHi N 7 1889

Marion INDEPENDENT. w,sw 1857-95||?
w 1857-83?
MWA Ap 9 1863;Ja 6 1876
NNHi My 14,Je 4-11,Jl 2 1863;Jl 17 1873

MARION county whig. w 1842?-
OClWHi Ja 7 1843

Marion daily MIRROR. *See* Marion tribune

PEOPLE'S advocate and Marion and Sandusky advertiser. w Ja? 1829-30||?
CSmH D 17 1829
DLC Je 25 1829

Marion PHENIX. w My 27?1830-
CSmH S 2 1830
OCl D 4 1830

Marion REPUBLICAN. sw,w 1896-1905||?
1896-97? as Republican transcript
sw 1896?
OHi Ja 2 1901

OHIO (*Continued*)

MARION—*Continued*

Marion STAR. d 1884+
pub 1884+
KHi Jl 5 1922
M Ag 20 1932
MiG Ag 3,11 1923
OClWHi My 20 1898;Je 1 1926
OHi Jl-D 1914;F 1915-F,O 1916-Ja 22 1917;Jl 1919+
VU Ap 3 1917

Marion TRIBUNE. d 1892-1922||?
1892-1911? as Marion daily mirror
MWA N 3 1906
OHi Ja 1 1901;My 1914-Mr 1916

MARTINS FERRY

Evening TIMES. d 1891+
pub 1917+
OHi Ja 1 1901

MARYSVILLE

ARGUS and Union county advertiser. w? 1845?-
IU N 24 1847

Marysville TRIBUNE. w 1849+
IU N 25 1851;D 15 1852;D 14 1853;D 12 1855; D 16 1857;D 12 1860;D 4 1861;Ja 6 1863
MWA D 15 1852
OClWHi Jl 11 1860;My 20 1863
OHi Ap 8 1863;O 23 1867;Mr 20 1870;Ja 5 1901

Evening TRIBUNE. d 1898+
OHi Jl 1919-Ap 1920

UNION county democrat. w 1863-
OHi Mr 9 1864

UNION county journal. w,sw Je 6 1874+
w 1874-Je 1918
pub 1874+
OClWHi F 20 1908

UNION gazette. w? 1842?-
OClWHi F-My 4 1844

UNION journal. w My 17 1843-
OClWHi My-Ag 16 1843

UNION press. w 1859?-
OHi My 1 1861;Ap 9 1862;Mr 4 1863

UNION star. w 1839?-
DLC Mr 26 1840;My 21 1841
OClWHi Ag 15,S,O 10-31,N 16 1839-O 1841

MASON

DEMOCRATIC citizen. w? 1862?-
ICHi Je 10 1864

MASSILLON

Massillon weekly AMERICAN. w 1869-91||?
MWA Mr 16 1870;F 11,Mr 4,Ap 29-My 13 1874;O 27,D 29 1875;Mr 22,My 10,Je 28,Jl 12 1876;Je 6,27 1877;O 23 1878;Ap 23,O 22 1879
OClWHi Mr 16 1870;Ag 28 1881

COXEY'S daily. d O 21 1895-
KHi O-N 6 1895
WHi O 29-N 6 1895

Massillon GAZETTE. w? 1839?-
IU N 16 1842

Massillon GLEANER. w 1886-1908||?
OHi Ja 4 1901;Mr 1906-Je 1908

Massillon INDEPENDENT. w,sw Jl 3? 1863-1911||?
w 1863-95?
CLM Jl 3 1878
MWA Je 16,Jl 28 1869;Ag 23 1876;F 21,Je 27 1877
MiU-C Je 16 1869
OHi S 4 1863

Evening INDEPENDENT. d 1887+
S 9 1926 is centennial ed
OClWHi [S 15 1909-Je 9 1910]
OHi Ja 1 1901;Ap-Ag,O 1914-F 1916;S 9 1926

MINERS' independent and wage earners' tribune. w 1889-94||?
1889-94 as Miners' independent
WHi Je 1889-Mr 6 1890

Massillon NEWS. w 1849?-
MWA D 9 1852
OClWHi Ja 31,Ap 11 1851

Massillon REPUBLICAN. w? 1837?-
OClWHi D 9 1837

SOUND money. w Je 6 1895-97||?
AEvC F 14 1896
KHi 1895-F 20 1897

Massillon TELEGRAM. w? 1847?-
OClWHi Ja 12,Mr 15 1848

MAUMEE

Early years as Maumee City

Maumee ADVANCE-ERA. w F 1896+
1896-1901? as Maumee advance
pub Mr 5,19 1896;My 8 1908;S 17 1909+
OHi Ja 5 1901[Je 1915-O 1918]19-Je 24,D 30 1921-F,S 1925-Jl 1929;Ja-Jl 18,N 21 1930-32

Maumee ADVERTISER. w 1873-
OMauA My 21 1874;F 18-25 1875

Maumee EXPRESS. w Mr 25 1837-
Title varies: Maumee City express
MWA Je 10 1837;Ja 20,S 8 1838
OHi 1837-Mr 1839

Maumee LYRE. w Jl 22 1893-
OMauA Jl 22 1893

MAUMEE RIVER times. w 1840-
CU-B Ja 21 1843;O 5 1844;D 20 1845;O 2 1847
MWA N 27 1852
OHi O 31 1841
OMauA Mr 15 1845;Ag 28 1847;O 8 1853;F 25 1854;Je 14 1855
WHi O 9 1852

MAUMEE VALLEY news. w 1925+
pub 1925+

Maumee NEW era. w 1872-1901||?
United with Maumee advance to form Maumee advance-era
OHi Ja 4 1901
OMauA O 26 1894

NORTH-WESTERN democrat and Lucas county landmark. w My 22? 1852-
MWA Ag 28 1852

MAUMEE CITY. *See* MAUMEE

MEDINA

CONSTITUTIONALIST. w
P-M Je 28 1843

Medina DEMOCRAT. w 1849?-
OClWHi N 20 1851;Jl 23 1852;Mr 12,N 8,D 27 1853-Ja 10 1854

Medina DEMOCRAT. w 1875-81||?
OClWHi D 9,23 1875;Ja 13-22,Mr 2,23,Ap 6 1876

DEMOCRATIC watchman. w? 1844?-
CSmH Jl 31 1844

MEDINA county gazette. w,sw 1835+
1835-43? as Constitutionalist; 1843?-53 Democratic whig; 1853-65? Medina gazette
w 1836-Ag 25 1921
pub 1870+
DLC S 13 1854-Jl 25 1855
MWA Ag 25 1852;D 29 1865
MnHi N 25 1836
OClWHi O 14-21,N 3-11 1836;Ag 26,O 14 1840; Ap 9 1845;Je 16 1847;Mr 14-21 1849;Ja 5 1852;O 5 1853;Ja 28,S 20,O-D 13 1854[55]Mr 26,N 5 1856;Je 1857-61;Ap 5 1862;63[Ja-N 5 1864]-[66-67]-Ja 1 1869;Jl 13 1877;80;Je 6 1890;O 8 1896;Ap 1909-[14]+
OHi Ja 3 1901
P-M Jl 18 1855

MEDINA county republican. w Jl 25? 1867-
OClWHi S 5,O 10,31,N 28,D 13-20 1867;Ja 17-24,F 21-28 1868

Medina MIRROR. w 1849?-
OClWHi 1854-55
P-M Jl 3 1854

OHIO free press. w? 1832?-
1832?-34? as Ohio free press and Medina county advertiser
OClWHi O 29,N 17 1832;N 5 1833;N 1 1834;Je 11,25 1836

Medina SENTINEL. w 1884+
OClWHi Mr 10,My 19 1916+
OHi Ja 3 1901;14-15

WATCHTOWER. w S 1838-42||
OClWHi 1838-Mr 23 1842

MIAMISBURG

Miamisburg BULLETIN. w 1867-95||?
OMia complete

Miamisburg NEWS. w Ap 1 1880+
pub 1880+
OHi Ja 3 1901
OMia 1898+

MIDDLEBURY

PORTAGE journal. w 1825-
F 28-O? 1827 as Portage journal and weekly advertiser
DLC My 14,28,S 18-25,O 23 1828
MWA Ap 30 1828
OCl [Mr 29 1826-O 1827]
OClWHi Jl 19 1826;D 22 1827;My 14,28,S 18,O 23 1828

MIDDLEFIELD

GEAUGA independent. w 1884-85||?
OClWHi Ja 8-15,F 19,Mr 19-26,My 7 1885

Middlefield MESSENGER. w Ag 13? 1885-1902||?
OClWHi S 10 1885;Mr 26 1891;My 7,D 10 1896;Ja 21,Mr 4,Ap 22 1897;Ag 21 1902

Middlefield NEWS. w 1910-11||?
OClWHi Ap 14,S 15-29,N 18 1910;N 10 1911

Middlefield TIMES. w Ap 1 1903-08||?
OClWHi Ap 1 1903

Middlefield TIMES. w 1912+
1912-Ja 17? 1917 as Western Reserve times
OClWHi F 12 1913-[16]-[24-25]-[27]-[30-31]+

WESTERN RESERVE times. *See* Middlefield times 1912+

MIDDLEPORT

HERALD. w 1876-F 1894||?
1876-84? as Meigs county herald. United with Meigs county republican to form Republican herald, later Republican
OHi 1880-85;Jl 1886-93

MEIGS county herald. *See* Herald

MEIGS county news. *See* Republican

MEIGS county republican. *See* Republican

REPUBLICAN. w N 22 1871-1918||?
1871-75? as Meigs county news; 1876?-F 1894? Meigs county republican; Mr 1894?-Ja 24 1902 Republican-herald
MWA Mr 18 1875
NbHi 1871-N 13 1872
OClWHi F 28 1872;N 8 1876;Ag 7-14 1878;Ja 21,F 11 1880;Mr 18,Jl 26 1891;Ag 16 1893
OHi 1877;79-82;84-86;88-93;Mr 1894-1904;06-12;14-17

MIDDLETOWN

BUTLER county signal. w 1874-1906||?
1874-1900? as Middletown signal
OMi Ja-N 1881;N 25 1882-D 1 1883;91-93;96-98;1900;03-04
—d ed *See* Middletown news signal

Middletown EMBLEM. w Ap 26 1851-
MWA D 17 1852
OHi 1851-Je 10 1853
PCA D 10,24 1852

Middletown HERALD. w 1851?-
OHi Ag 19 1853-54

Middletown JOURNAL. d 1891+
OHi Ja 2 1901;O-D 1916;My 1920-N 23 1925
OMi 1913+

Middletown MAIL. w Ap 20 1839-
DLC Ap 27 1839
OHi My 18,Je 1-22,Jl 1839-Ap 18 1840

Middletown daily NEWS. d 1905-06||?
United with Middletown daily signal to form Middletown news signal

Middletown NEWS signal. d 1888-1929||
1888-91? as Daily signal; 1892?-1906? Middletown daily signal
OHi Ja 1 1901
OMi 1890-91;93;96;98;1901-03;05-29

Daily SIGNAL. *See* Middletown news signal

Middletown SIGNAL. w *See* Butler county signal

MILAN

Milan ADVERTISER. w 1870-1904||?
OClWHi Ag 25 1894
OHi Ja 5 1901

Milan FREE PRESS. w Ja? 1830-
CSmH Jl 6 1830

Milan FREE press. w 1851?-
MWA S 18 1852

Milan LEDGER. w 1889+
OMilT D 15 1912+

Milan TRIBUNE. w S 22 1843-51||?
OMilT 1843-Ap 1 1851
OT 1843-Ap 1851

WESTERN intelligencer. w Ap 1? 1834-
MWA Je 3 1834

MILFORD CENTER

OHIOAN. w Ap 17 1888+
IU Ap 17 1888
OHi Ja 3 1901

MILLERSBURG

COSMOPOLITE. w 1838?-
DLC F 1 1840

HARRISONIAN democrat. w Ap 27- 1840||?
DLC Ap 7 1840

HOLMES county farmer-hub. w,sw 1828+
1828-1926 as Holmes county farmer (title varies: Holmes county farmer and free press)
sw 1932?
ICHi Je 16 1864
MWA D 2 1852
OClWHi Mr 1 1866;My 2 1867;Ap 22 1869;Jl 20,N 9 1876
ODW Jl 12 1866;Je 27 1867
OHi F 26 1857-F 3,Mr 17 1859-Ja 9,F 16 1890-Jl 1926

HOLMES county hub. w Je 21 1844-1926||
1844-Ag? 1856 as Holmes county whig; Ag 12 1856-95? Holmes county republican; 1896?-1922? Millersburg republican. United with Holmes county farmer to form Holmes county farmer-hub
Suspended from 1864-70
MWA D 9 1875
OClWHi My 8-29,Je 19 1862-Ap 20 1865
OHi 1844-Mr 13,Je 10 1847-Ap 1853;56-Ap 17 1862;Ag 25 1870-Ag 13 1874;Ag 19 1875-Jl 1895;96-1911

HOLMES county republican. *See* Holmes county hub

HOLMES county whig. *See* Holmes county hub

Millersburgh JOURNAL and standard of liberty. w Ag 14 1838-
WHi 1838-Ag 6 1839

Millersburg REPUBLICAN. *See* Holmes county hub

MINERVA

Minerva weekly COMMERCIAL. w 1868-78||?
DLC Ag 12 1876

Minerva KODAK. w 1892-98||?
United with Minerva news to form Minerva news-kodak, later Minerva news and Clay City times

OHIO (*Continued*)

MINERVA—*Continued*

Minerva NEWS and Clay City times. w 1884+
1884-1910? as Minerva news (1899?-1905? News-kodak)
pub 1918+
OHi Ja 1 1901

MINSTER

Minster POST. w Mr 1 1895+
pub 1898+

MONROEVILLE

Monroeville SPECTATOR. w 1870+
OClWHi F 12 1913-S 21 1932
OHi Ja 2 1901

MONTPELIER

Montpelier ENTERPRISE. w 1880-1923||?
United with Montpelier leader to form Montpelier leader-enterprise
IU Jl ? (extra)1893
OHi Ja 3 1901

Montpelier LEADER-ENTERPRISE. w 1889+
1889-1924? as Montpelier leader
KHi Ap 1-22 1897
OHi Ja 3 1901

MOUNT EATON

ANTI-MASONIC mirror. w? 1828?-
CSmH Jl 2 1830

MOUNT GILEAD

DEMOCRATIC messenger. *See* Union register

MORROW county republican. w 1905-19||?
OHi 1906-19

MORROW county sentinel. w 1848+
1848-60 as Whig sentinel
pub 1850+
OHi F 1869-Je,S 1882-1921
MWA Jl 27 1853;Ja 25 1866;Ap 8 1886

UNION register. w 1848+
1848-63? as Democratic messenger
pub Ag 1 1855;Ja 23,O 12 1856;O 22 1863;Jl 12 1876+
MWA Ag 19 1852
OClWHi S 13,D 13 1848;Ja 17-24,F 7-14,Jl 4,Ag 1 1849;Ap 24-My 15,Je 26,Jl 10,Ag 21 1850;S 24 1924;S 12 1928
OHi 1869-1921

WHIG sentinel. *See* Morrow county sentinel

MOUNT HEALTHY

Papers published in Mount Healthy are listed under Cincinnati

MOUNT PLEASANT

Weekly HISTORIAN. w O 6 1823-
WHi O 6 1823

JEFFERSON gazette. w 1825?-
DLC Jl 7 1826

*PHILANTHROPIST. w S 8 1817-
OClWHi N 10 1821-Ap 1822

MOUNT VERNON

AMERICAN standard and Knox county advertiser. w? 1824?-
OClWHi O 29 1828

Daily BANNER. d 1898-Ag 10 1935||
United with Daily republican news to form Republican news-daily banner
OHi D 19 1898-D 16 1899;Ja 2 1901
OMv 1914-Je 1915

DAY-BOOK. w Jl? 1833-
N O 3 1833

Mount Vernon DEMOCRATIC banner. w,sw O 14? 1837-1923||?
1837-N 1853 as Democratic banner; D 11 1886-87 Knox county democrat; Ja-Mr 1888 Mount Vernon tribune
w 1837-97?
Ct O 21 1837-Mr 17 1838
DLC D 3 1850
ICU Jl 31 1843
IU S 5-12,26-O 10,N 21(extra)1843;F 20-27, Ap 23-30,My 14,Ag 27 1844
MWA Ag 17 1852
MnHi N 1847-S 9 1851
NNHi Mr 12,Je 11,Ag 13,O 15 1861
OClWHi D 22 1837;Mr 3-10 1838;Jl 13 1839[40-42]Ja 3,F 21 1843[44]D 24 1850;Ap 13,27 1852; N 10 1857;O 26,D 14 1858;Ja 1 1861;N 21 1863;S 24 1864;Ap 22,My 27 1865;Jl 4,N 10 1876;Ja 8 1885
OHi Ja 10 1843;N 1847-63;Ap 22 1865-Ap 20,D 1867-71;73-80 83-89;91-1911
OMv Ap 27 1852-94
TxU D 1853-F 1867

Mount Vernon GAZETTE. w 1826?-
DLC N 2 1833
OClWHi S 31 1831;N 15,D 13 1833;Ja 3,17,O 4,N 29 1834

KNOX county democrat. *See* Mount Vernon democratic banner

KNOX county semi-weekly express. sw 1861?-
OClWHi Ag 22 1861

KNOX county news. sw 1894-98||?
United with Mount Vernon republican to form Mount Vernon republican-news, later Knox county republican-news

KNOX county republican. w? Ap? 1840-
OClWHi S 26,O 24 1840

KNOX county republican-news. w,sw,tw O 6 1841-1921||?
1841-Ja 3? 1846 as Republican times; Ja 10? 1846-Ag 1848 Times; S 1848-Ag 3 1852 Ohio times; Ag 10 1852-O 10 1854? Ohio state times; O 17 1854?-98 Mount Vernon republican; 1899?-1900? Republican-news
w 1841-84?;tw 1898?
DLC D 21 1850
MWA Ag 31 1852
MnHi S 9 1856
OClWHi O 6,29,D 3,15 1841;F 8,Ag 2-8,O 4 1842;S 19 1843;Ja 30,Ag 13 1844;Ag 25 1846;F 18 1851;Ag 10 1852-O 10 1854;Ap 3 1855;D 25 1860;Mr 30-Ap 6,My 25-Je 1,Ag 3,O 23 1869; Je 24 1921
OHi Je 1845-O 10 1854;Jl 17 1855-My,O 1857-O 1865;O 18 1870-O 21 1873;75-79;D 10 1884-89;91-D 3 1892;93-1916
OOxM Ja 20 1846-Ap 6 1847
—d ed *See* Republican news-daily banner

KOKOSING tribune. *See* Tribune

Mount Vernon NATIONAL. w? 1858?-
OClWHi Ag 19 1858

Mount Vernon NEWS. *See* Republican news-daily banner

NORTON'S daily true whig. d Mr 22 1853-
MWA Jl 2 1853
OHi 1853-S 21 1854

OHIO times. *See* Knox county republican-news

Mount Vernon REPUBLICAN. *See* Knox county republican-news

REPUBLICAN news-daily banner. d 1894+
1894-97? as Mount Vernon news; 1898?-Ag 10 1935 Republican-news
pub 1894+
OClWHi Ag 5 1897
—w ed *See* Knox county republican-news

REPUBLICAN times. *See* Knox county republican-news

TIMES. *See* Knox county republican-news

TRIBUNE. sw,w 1884-88||
1884? as Kokosing tribune
sw 1884-87?
OClWHi Mr 12 1884

Mount Vernon TRIBUNE. 1888 *See* Mount Vernon democratic banner

Mt. Vernon TRUE whig and Chippewa war club. w Ag 9 1848-
1848-51? as Mt. Vernon true whig
MWA S 1 1852
OClWHi Jl 3,S 4,18 1850;Ag 18 1852
OHi Ag 15 1848-51;Ag 11 1852-Mr 1855
WHi Jl 21 1852

Mount Vernon WATCHMAN and Knox county advertiser. w? 1836?-
OClWHi Jl 22 1837

WESTERN Aurora and Mt. Vernon gazette. w? 1826?-
DLC N 28 1829

WESTERN home visitor. w Ag 5 1852-
MWA Ag 28 1852
OClWHi Ag 5 1852;Ja 22,Ap 16,Je 25,N 26,D 31 1853

NAPOLEON

DEMOCRATIC northwest. *See* Northwest-news

HENRY county signal. w 1865+
OHi Ja 3 1901;N 1919-Ag 19 1920

NORTHWEST-NEWS. w S 8 1852+
1852-65? as Northwest; 1866?-My 28 1898 Democratic northwest
pub 1863+
DLC O 22 1852
ICHi D 3 1852
MWA S 8 1852;Ag 24 1865;O 2 1869
OClWHi 1852-O 20 1858;Ap 20 1859-65;Ap 12-D 20 1866;My 16 1867-N 19 1868
OHi Ja 3 1901

NEVADA

Nevada ENTERPRISE. *See* Nevada news

Nevada NEWS. w Ja 12 1872-1931||?
1872-1909? as Nevada enterprise
OClWHi Ja 12 1872

NEW ALBANY

Papers published in New Albany are listed under Columbus

NEW CONCORD

CLARION of freedom. w 1844?-
DLC Mr 24,S 22 1848
OClWHi D 31 1847

NEW LEXINGTON

Weekly AMBROTYPE. w 1855?-
OHi Ap 28-S 15 1858

DEMOCRATIC herald. *See* New Lexington news

DEMOCRATIC organ. w 1853?-
OClWHi Mr 15 1854

New Lexington HERALD. *See* New Lexington news

MINERAL region news. *See* Perry county republican

New Lexington NEWS. w,d 1867+
1867-1928? as New Lexington herald (1873?-74?; O 1887-S 6 1888 Democratic herald) 1929? Herald-tribune; 1930?-31? New Lexington sentinel; 1932? Perry county sentinel; 1933?-34? Perry county news
w 1867-1934?
OClWHi Je 16 1921
OHi N 18 1870-N 10 1871;73-74;D 1880-S 1889; O 1891-N 11 1926

PERRY county democrat. w S 11 1879-80||?
OHi 1879-N 18 1880

PERRY county news. *See* New Lexington news

PERRY county republican. w 1856?-73||?
1856?-69? as Perry county weekly; 1870?-Ag 22 1872 Mineral region news
OHi Ap 1861-62;Ap 1864-D 2 1869;Mr 18 1870-Mr 6 1873

PERRY county sentinel. *See* New Lexington news

PERRY county tribune. w 1871-1928||?
1871-1924? as New Lexington tribune. United with New Lexington herald to form Herald-tribune, later New Lexington news
OClWHi Mr 30,Ap 20-27 1876
OHi Mr 1873-77;My 1879-S 1889;Ap 1891-1912; 14-15;17-19;23-24

PERRY county weekly. *See* Perry county republican

New Lexington SENTINEL. *See* New Lexington news

New Lexington TRIBUNE. *See* Perry county tribune

NEW LISBON. *See* LISBON

NEW LONDON

New London RECORD. w 1870+
OClWHi [D 15 1870-82]-[87]-[89-91]-[93]-[1902]-[08]-[13-14]
OHi Ja 3 1901

New London TIMES. w 1868-70||?
OClWHi Jl 19 1869;F 24,Ap 14 1870

NEW MADISON

New Madison HERALD. w 1894+
OHi D 1907-Ag 1923

NEW PHILADELPHIA

ADVOCATE of Tuscarawas. *See* Tuscarawas advocate

ADVOCATE-TRIBUNE. w 1893-1930||?
1893-1910? as New Philadelphia tribune
OClWHi D 19 1923
OHi Ja 2 1901;Jl 1914-15;F-My 1918

FARMERS' and mechanics' friend. w? 1838?-
OClWHi O 5 1838

OHIO democrat and times. w Ag 1 1839-1925||?
1839-Ja 13 1842 as Ohio democrat and Dover advertiser (Canal Dover); Ja 20 1842-1910? Ohio democrat
MWA Ja 26,Ag 17,S 21 1843;S 12 1844;F 11, My 6-13,Je 17,Ag 5,S 30-O 7,N 4-11,25-D 2 1847;Jl 13 1876
OClWHi Ag 5-12 1841;My 5,N 17 1842;43-Ja 9,F 20 1845;Ja 29,Ap 9,Je 25 1846-Ja 18,Ap 1849;51-D 6 1861;D 18 1863-D 8 1865;Ap 12 1875
OHi S 19 1839-Ja 12 1843:44-Ja 9 1845;63;Ja 3 1901;03-Je 1909;10-Jl,S 1918-25

Daily TIMES. d 1903+
S 25 1929 is historical ed
OClWHi Ag 21 1922;Ag 24 S 24 1923;S 25 1929
OHi Mr-My 1915;Ja-F 1916;20+

New Philadelphia TRIBUNE. *See* Advocate-tribune

*TUSCARAWAS advocate. w Ag 24 1819-1910||?
1819-O 1834? as Tuscarawas chronicle; O 25-D 1834 Advocate of Tuscarawas; 1840?-41? Advocate. United with New Philadelphia tribune to form Advocate-tribune
IHi S 15 1837;Ap 21 1865
IU S 1 1848
MWA F 27 1827
NN Ag 16 1823;Jl 5 1825;D 30 1831;S 29-O 13 1835;Mr 16 1837
OClWHi 1834-O 13 1836;O 13 1837;My 1,O 30 1840;Ag 20 1841;Ja 28 1842;N 17 1843;S 26 1845;D 22 1848;My 27,Ag 5,S 23,D 30 1859; 60-64;Ap 20 1866-1902
OHi Ja 4,F 8-15,Mr 29,Ap 13 1833;Je 30 1837; N 2-9,23 1838;Mr 8 1844;My 20 1864

TUSCARAWAS chronicle. 1819-34 *See* Tuscarawas advocate

TUSCARAWAS chronicle. 1865- *See* Uhrichsville chronicle (Uhrichsville)

NEW RICHMOND

CLERMONT independent. w 1869-87||?
United with New Richmond news to form Independent-news
DLC N 6 1885

INDEPENDENT-NEWS. w 1881-1919||?
1881-87? as New Richmond news
OClWHi Ja 2-9,23-31 1913;Ja 2-9 1914

OHIO (*Continued*)

NEW RICHMOND—*Continued*

New Richmond **NEWS.** *See* Independent-news

LUMINARY. w Ap 30? 1823-
OCHi Je 25 1823

PHILANTHROPIST. *See* Cincinnati weekly herald and philanthropist (Cincinnati)

NEW SALEM. *See* SALEM (COLUMBIANA COUNTY)

NEW STRAITSVILLE

New Straitsville **RECORD.** w 1901-My 20 1910‖?
ONS [F 1901-02]-[04-06;08-10]

NEW WASHINGTON

New Washington **HERALD.** w 1881+
pub F 1914+
OHi Ja 4 1901

NEWARK

Newark **ADVOCATE.** w,sw D 28 1820-1914‖
1820-36? as Advocate
sw 1900?-1907?
pub [1828-76]-1914
DLC D 1 1832;D 12 1840;O 27-N 3 1852;O 28 1870;71-Je 7 1872;Ap 24 1874-Ja 18 1878
IU O 22 1836
MWA F 22 1827;S 1 1852;My 19 1858
MnHi S 23 1857
OClWHi Ap 22 1824-Je 15 1826;Mr 22,S 6,O 4 1827;My 29 1829;Ag 18 1832-Ag 13 1836; Ag 18 1838-Ag 17 1839;My 15 1841;Mr 31 1858;Ja 19 1859;Ja 14 1861[Mr 28 1862-O 14 1864; Ja 13,F 24 1865[67;69-70]Mr 1 1878;Ap 18 1879;S 3 1880;N 7,19 1884;Mr 5,29,N 6 1889;N 4 1890;N 9 1892;Je 30 1896;Jl 9 1910
OHi Ag 24 1850-Ag 16 1854[60-61]My 11 1866-F 12,Ap 1869-S 22 1871;Ag 22 1873;74-Ag 3 1875;76-Ag 3 1877;80-90;93;95-96;98-1901;;03-07

Newark **ADVOCATE and American tribune.** d 1882+
1882-1927 as Newark advocate
O 26 1921 is centennary ed
OClWHi Je 9-13 1913;O 26 1921;O 20 1927;Ap 20,24-25 1934
OHi 1912-14;Ja-Ag 1927;O 1929-O 27 1930

Newark **AMERICAN-TRIBUNE.** w,sw D 20 1827-1927‖
1827-Ja? 1852 as Newark gazette (title varies: Newark gazette and mercantile advertiser; Newark gazette and farmer's journal); F? 1852-Je? 1855 Newark weekly times; Jl? 1855-56? North American; 1857?-Jl 16 1863 Newark North American; Jl 24 1863-67? True American; 1868? American and wool grower; 1869?-97? Newark American
w 1827-94?
ICHi D 23 1864;N 19 1869;D 19 1873
IU F 1 1844;My 11 1848
InRE Ja 31 1873
MWA D 20 1827;Mr 25-Ap 1,29 1829;Ja 8,S 25 1852;Ap 23 1859;Ap 10 1863;Jl 12,S 6 1867; Mr 27[Ap 24-S 11]N 6 1868[F-Je,N 19 1869-N 1871]Ja 5-12,Jl 12-26,O 11 1872[Ja-Jl 18]D 19 1873;Ja 1,F 12,Ap 2,S 24,N 19-26 1875;S 14 1877
MiU-C D 7 1842
NN Jl 7 1876
OCHi Ja 3 1873;Mr 19 1880;Ag 17 1883
OClWHi F 9 1831;Jl 30 1834;Ap 1 1835;Ag 10 1836;S 4 1839;Ag 31,O 10 1842;F 16 1843-[45-46]-Ja 1 1852;Jl 18-25 1856;D 28 1859;Je 28 1860;F 6,Ap 10,Ag 28-S 1862[Jl 16 1863-Je 1864]Mr 17-Ap 7,My 12,Je 2-9,O 6 1865;Je 14,Jl,Ag 9-16,S 6,O 1867-[69]-[71-73]Ap 10 1874;Ag,S 17 1875;Ja 21,F 11 1876;Jl 12 1878; O 10,D 5 1879;O 8,D 17 1880;Jl 18-Ag 5,S 30 1881;Ag 3 1903
OHi Je 23 1855[Jl 1859-62]O 20,N 18 1864; Mr 24,Ap 14,O 20 1865;Ap 13,27,S 19,O 31,D 7 1866;Ja 16-23,Mr 15 1867[Ap 1868-Ap 1870] O 3-10,31,N 28 1873;F 22,Mr 15 1877;99;Ja 30 1900-08
OOxM Ap 16,My 6-13,Je 10,24,Jl 8 1829
P-M Ja 15 1864
TxU S 10 1850-Ja 24 1851

Newark **AMERICAN-TRIBUNE.** d 1887-1927‖
1887-97? as Newark American. United with Newark advocate to form Newark advocate and American tribune
OClWHi Mr 11 1892;Je 11 1894
OHi 1901-Ap,Jl 1911-Je,Ag 1914-Je 1918;My-Jl 1922;Jl-D 1925;D 14-31 1926

Newark **BANNER.** *See* Newark tribune

Newark **CONSTITUTIONALIST.** w 1837?-
Title varies slightly
DLC N 17 1837
IU Ja 15 1842;Mr 30,Ap 13,My 11-25,Je 15,Ag 10,24,O 12,N 2 1844
OClWHi N 20 1838;Ap 26,Ag 30 1839;O 3 1840

DEMOCRATIC rasp. 1840‖?
Campaign paper
OClWHi Je 29,S 14 1840

Newark **EXPRESS.** *See* Newark leader

Newark **GAZETTE.** *See* Newark American-tribune

KICKAPOO. w 1844‖?
OClWHi Je-O 1844

Newark **LEADER.** w 1895+
1895-1916 as Newark express (In German)
pub 1927+

LICKING county herald. w 1844?-
MWA Ag 19 1852

LICKING county republican. *See* Newark tribune

LICKING Ohio democrat. w? 1836?-
OClWHi O 5 1836

LICKING record. w Je 14? 1864-
OHi N 29 1864

NEWS-ISSUE. *See* Newark tribune

NORTH AMERICAN. *See* Newark American-tribune

OHIO laborer. w S 17 1842-
OClWHi 1842-Ja 14 1843

OHIO tribune. *See* Newark tribune

Newark **PASTORAL.** w? 1880?-
OClWHi Ag 21-S 4,18 1880

Newark weekly **TIMES.** *See* Newark American-tribune

Newark **TRIBUNE.** w,sw 1874-97‖?
1874-87? as Newark banner; 1888? News-issue; 1889?-91? Licking county republican; 1892?-93? Ohio tribune. United with Newark American to form Newark American-tribune
sw 1889?-91?
OClWHi Mr 8 1876;O 13 1880;D 10 1889

TRUE American. *See* Newark American-tribune

NEWBURG

Papers published in Newburg are listed under Cleveland

NEWCOMERSTOWN

Newcomerstown **NEWS and index.** w S 15 1898+
1898-Ap 4 1928 as Newcomerstown news
Ag 19 1914 is anniversary ed
pub 1898+
OClWHi Ag 19 1914
OHi Ag 19 1914

Newcomerstown **INDEX.** w 1878-Mr? 1928‖
United with Newcomerstown news to form Newcomerstown news and index
OHi Ja 3 1901

NEWTON FALLS

Newton Falls **HERALD.** w 1882+
OHi My 8 1930-33

NILES

Niles **INDEPENDENT.** w 1876-1922‖?
1876-90? as Trumbull county independent
OClWHi Mr 24 1876

Niles daily **NEWS.** d 1890-1923‖?
OHi Ja 2 1901;Jl 1912-F,Ap-Ag 1916
ON S 12 1908-Je 21 1923

Niles evening **REGISTER.** d 1922-23‖?
ON 1923

Niles daily **TIMES.** d Ag 11 1924+
OHi S 21 1927-33
ON 1924+

TRUMBULL county independent. See Niles independent

NORTH AMHERST. *See* AMHERST

NORTH BALTIMORE

Weekly **BEACON.** w 1884+
pub 1884+

NORTH CANTON

Papers published in North Canton are listed under Canton

NORTH FAIRFIELD

North Fairfield **GAZETTE.** w Ap 30? 1856-
OClWHi [1856-60]Ja 3,31,F 14,28,Mr 28-Ap 4 1861

NORWALK

Norwalk **CHRONICLE.** w 1875-1913‖?
OClWHi My 14,O 8 1891;Je 23 1897
OHi Ja 3 1901;Mr 8-D 1906;Mr-Je 22 1911;12-Ag 13 1913

Norwalk **EXPERIMENT.** w Ag 20 1835+
1835-D 28 1847 as Experiment; Ja 4 1848-D 26 1885 Norwalk experiment; Ja 2? 1886-D 20 1887 Experiment and news; Ja 6 1888-94? Experiment news
MWA Ag 17 1852
NN N 24 1841
OClWHi Ag-S 23 1845;Ag-S 1,29 1846-Ag,S 28 1847-S 17 1850;S 23 1851-[55-56]-[59]-N 17 1862[Ja-N 1863;Ja-N 1864]My 20 1878-Ap 1889;F 11 1913-O 1916
OHi Ja 2 1901

FIRELANDS news. *See* Huron county news

Norwalk evening **HERALD.** d 1897-Ja 1913‖?
United with Daily reflector to form Norwalk reflector-herald

HURON county news. w 1883-1927‖?
1883-84 as Firelands news; 1884-85 Sunday news For 1886-94 *See* Norwalk experiment
OClWHi F 14 1913-O 1916
OHi Ja 3 1901

HURON reflector. *See* Norwalk reflector

Sunday **NEWS.** *See* Huron county news

Norwalk **REFLECTOR.** w,sw F 2 1830-1913‖?
1830-D 27 1853 as Huron reflector
w 1890?-1912?
MWA My 29 1849;S 10,24,O 29 1850;Je 3,Jl 1 1851;Ag 24 1852
N F 16 1847
NjR [S 10 1844-45;47;49-53;61-62;64]
OClWHi 1830-Ja,O 10 1832;Je 11,N 5 1833;N 4 1834;F 1836-Ja 1838;F 1840-[72]-94;O 25 1913
OHi Je 12 1864;Ja 1 1901;06-Ap 14,Je 2 1908;D 1912
P-M D 2 1845
PEL Ja 18-25,D 12 1831;Ja 30,Ap 23 1832
WHi Jl 19 1864

Norwalk **REFLECTOR-HERALD.** d S 22 1882+
1882-Ja 25 1913 as Daily reflector
pub 1913+
KHi F 14 1893
OClWHi 1882-S 21 1886;Mr 22 1887-94

Norwalk **REPORTER and Huron advertiser.** w 1828?-
CtY S 6 1828
MWA D 22 1827
OClWHi O 24 1829

OAK HARBOR

EXPONENT. *See* Ottawa county exponent

OTTAWA county exponent. w Ap 7 1871+
1871-80? as Exponent
pub 1882+
OClWHi Je 9-23 1871
OHi Ja 5 1901

OAK HILL

Oak Hill **PRESS.** w 1907+
OHi My 22 1919-33

OBERLIN

LORAIN county news. *See* Oberlin news-tribune

Oberlin **NEWS-TRIBUNE.** w,sw Mr 7 1860+
1860-D 1873 as Lorain county news; 1874-Mr 1930 Oberlin news
w 1860-D 25 1896;sw Ja 1 1897-S 16 1904
pub 1860+
CLM Je 29 1900
MWA F 14 1866;Ja 28 1875
OClWHi My 8,Ag 5 1861;Mr 4,S 30 1863;Ja 10,D 12 1866;Ap 8-15 1868;O 5 1871;Ag 20,N 19 1874;Ag 12 1875;Jl 13,N 18,D 30 1876;79-90;Ap 30 1891-[92]-[95]-[1919-20]
OHi Ja 4 1901;Mr 1906-S 23 1908

OHIO American. S 19 1844-
OClWHi 1844-S 11 1845

TRIBUNE. w 1894-Mr 1930‖?
United with Oberlin news to form Oberlin news-tribune
OClWHi My 9,Je 6 1902[03]-[06]D 13 1907;16-19

WILSONIAN. F 15- 1916‖?
OClWHi F 15,Mr 15,Je 1,Jl 15 1916

OHIO CITY (CUYAHOGA COUNTY)

Papers published in Ohio City are listed under Cleveland

OLD WASHINGTON

Early years as Washington

GUERNSEY Jeffersonian. *See* Jeffersonian

JEFFERSONIAN. w 1843?-
1843?-44? as Guernsey Jeffersonian
IU My 18,Ag 30,S 20,N 8 1844
OClWHi Ja 3,Ap 26,My 22,Jl 3,Ag 7 1844;My 1846-Ap 1848

Washington **REPUBLICAN, and Guernsey** recorder w 1826?-
DLC Je 27,Jl 18,Ag 1,29,S 12-O 3,24 1829
MWA Mr 3 1827
OClWHi O 6 1829

OLMSTED FALLS

TRUE democrat. *See* Cleveland weekly leader (Cleveland)

ORWELL

Orwell **NEWS** letter. w 1890+
1890-D 30 1914 as News letter
OClWHi F 12 1913-17

OSBORN

BATH township herald. *See* Tri-county herald

Osborn **HERALD.** *See* Tri-county herald

TRI-COUNTY herald. w 1923+
1923-25? as Bath township herald; 1926?-29? Osborn herald
OXG D 1933+

OHIO (*Continued*)

OTTAWA

Ottawa GAZETTE. *See* Putnam county gazette

PUTNAM county gazette. w 1881+
1881-1927? as Ottawa gazette
OHi Ja 4 1901;Ag 1914-15

PUTNAM county sentinel. w Jl 1 1854+
pub 1915—
OHi [S 14 1865-Je 1877]Jl 1879-Mr 20,Je 19 1884-Je 17 1886;F 3,S 1 1887;Je 20 1889-My 22 1890;Je 13 1895-D 9 1897;Ag 17,S 7,21,O 12 1899;Ag 1914-15

OXFORD

Oxford CHRONICLE. w Mr 22 1834-
DLC Mr 22,Ap 5 1834
OHi Mr-Ap 19 1834

Oxford CITIZEN. w 1855-Ag? 1892||
United with Oxford news to form News-citizen, later Oxford news
MWA Ag 29-S 5 1857;Ja 10,My 17 1863
OClWHi Ap 22 1865
OHi F 28-Mr 7,21,Ap 18,O 24-31 1857
OOxM N 22 1856;O 31 1857;Ap 2 1870;Je 3-10,24,Jl 15-Ag 12,S 2 1875;Ja 22 1885-Ap 16 1891

Oxford FORUM. w Ap 18 1913-15||?
OOxM 1913-O 9,N 27 1914-F 12,Ap 9-Jl 2,16-Ag 13 1915

Oxford FREE press. w Ap 7 1932+
1932-33? as Oxford press
OOxM 1932+
OOxW O 1933+

Oxford HERALD. w S 24 1909-13||?
OOxM 1909-Mr 21 1913

Oxford NEWS. w 1886-1909||?
Ag 27 1892-Mr 23 1893 as Oxford news-citizen
OOxM Ja 15 1887;S 28 1889-S 20 1895;S 25 1896-S 23 1898[1902]D 2 1904;Ja 17 1908;F 5,S 10-17 1909

Oxford NEWS. w Mr 22 1928+
OOxM 1932+

Oxford PRESS. *See* Oxford free press

Oxford TOWN. w N 4 1926-30||?
OOxM 1926-27

PAINESVILLE

Painesville ADVERTISER. *See* Painesville republican 1868-1906

Painesville COMMERCIAL advertiser. *See* Press and advertiser

Painesville DEMOCRAT. w Je 30 1880-93||?
w 1880-92?
OClWHi 188?-Je 14 1890

Painesville FREE press. w Jl 14 1852-
MWA Jl 14 1852
OClWHi Jl 25-Ag 5 1852

GEAUGA gazette. w Ag 19 1828-
Ct My 24 1831
DLC Ag 19 1828;Mr 10 1829;Mr 15 1831
MWA S 30 1828
OClWHi 1828-S 15 1829;N 29 1831;Ja 24-S 22 1832

GRAND RIVER record. w D 11 1852-53||
OClWHi D 18 1852;Ja 15,F 5,Mr 5,Ap 9,My 7,21,Jl 2,16,Ag 6-20;S 3-10,N 5-12 1853

Painesville GRAPHIC. w 1882?-83||?
United with Painesville advertiser to form Advertiser-graphic, later Painesville republican
OClWHi F 3,Mr 10 1883

Painesville daily JOURNAL. d Jl 15 1892-
OClWHi 1892-D 1 1894;Mr 11-Ap 3 1895

LAKE county advertiser. *See* Painesville republican 1868-1906

LAKE county herald. w,sw 1899-1927||?
1899-1916? as Lake county weekly herald
sw 1917?-27
OClWHi Je 7 1901;O 7 1904;Jl 30,O 22 1908; Ja 10 1922

NORTHERN Ohio journal. w Jl 15 1871-96||?
1871-D 28 1872 as Painesville journal
OClWHi 1871 Ja,Jl 9 1895-F 18 1896

PATRIOT'S friend. w? 1838?-
OClWHi Ja 13 1839

Painesville PRESS. w N 16? 1859-Mr? 1860||
United with Painesville commercial advertiser to form Press and advertiser
DLC D 28 1859
OClWHi D 28 1859-60

PRESS and advertiser. m,w Je 16 1855-N 1861||?
1855-Mr 10 1860 as Painesville commercial advertiser. Merged with Painesville telegraph
m Je-Ag 1855
DLC Je 30 1855-S 19 1857;58-Mr 17,Ap 3,24,Ag 15,O 31-N 21,D 19 1860;Ja 16,F 27 1861
MWA O 24,N 14 1860
OClWHi Je 16,30,Jl 28,Ag 21,S 29 1855-My 2,Ag 1860-N 13 1861
PPiHi Ag 14 1861

Painesville REPUBLICAN. w N 17 1836-51||?
Ct [1836]
DLC N 24-D 1,15-29 1836;F 23,Mr 16,My 25-Je,Jl 13,27,Ag 10,27,S 14,N 2-16,D 7-21 1837 [38-39;Mr-My 1840]
MWA My 16 1839
OClWHi 1836-Jl 14 1841

Painesville REPUBLICAN. w 1868-1906||?
1868-83? as Painesville advertiser; 1884?-88? Advertiser-graphic; 1889?-98? Lake county advertiser; 1899? Painesville republican and Lake county advertiser. United with Painesville telegraph to form Telegraph-republican, later Painesville telegraph
DLC Ap 24 1869
OClWHi 1868-Je 1869;Ja-O 1870[71]Mr 30 1872;N 29 1873;Ap 25 1874;O 13-20 1877[79-82]F 8-15,Mr 7-14,D 5 1884;Ja 9,F 12,Mr-O 1886;Ja 20,F 3,Mr 23 1888;Mr 22,D 20 1895; Ag 13-O 15,D 17 1897;Ja 7,Ap 8 1898;99;D 27 1900-F 14 1901;Mr 2 1905
OHi Ja 3 1901

Daily REPUBLICAN. d N 1898-D 31 1906||
Merged with Evening telegraph to form Telegraph-republican, later Painesville telegraph
OClWHi D 13 1898;99;Jl 5,21 1900;Ja-Jl 1901
OHi Ja 2 1901

Painesville TELEGRAPH. w,sw Jl 16 1822-1918||?
Titles varies: Painesville telegraph and Geauga free press; Telegraph; Painesville telegraph and Geauga county whig; Telegraph-republican; Painesville telegraph and Painesville republican
w 1822-N 15 1905
CSmH Je 15,Ag 24 1830;N 8 1831
DLC [1822-41]42[44-47]-[51]-[55-57]-[71-72]-[96]
ICHi Ag 17 1830
MWA Jl 20 1830;S 26,O 8 1839;S 15-22,D 15 1841;Ag 25 1852;D 21 1853-O 18 1854;N 7 1855
N Mr 16 1842
NN N 8 1831:Ap 2 1840
NNHi My 16 1855;Ja 23 1873
OCHi Ja 2 1901
OCl My 8 1884
OClWHi 1822-Je 8 1909;F 11 1913-Jl 1916
P-M Ja 3,F 7 1855
WHi Je 8 1855

Painesville TELEGRAPH. d Jl 21 1892+
1892-D 31 1906 as Evening telegraph; Ja 2 1907-15? Telegraph-republican
Jl 15 1922 as centennial ed
pub 1933+
OCHi Jl 1919-O 3 1921;Jl 15 1922
OClWHi Jl 21 1892;My 12,O 24,N 14 1893;Ja 26,F 15,22,My 28,Je 20,28,Jl 6 1895;Jl-N 1897; Mr-Ap 16,Je 14 1898-Ja 4,Ap 25-D 1904;Jl 19-D 8 1905;My 1906-08;Ap 1 1912;Mr 16 1914;Ag 1916-33

PARMA

Papers published in Parma are listed under Cleveland

PATALASKA

Patalaska STANDARD. w Mr 11 1886+
pub 1886+
OHi Ja 3 1901

PAULDING

Paulding GAZETTE. w 1864?-
MWA S 29,O 27 1864

Paulding GAZETTE. 1879-87 *See* Paulding county republican

Paulding INDEPENDENT. w 1860?-
MWA Mr 28,Ap 11 1861

PAULDING county republican. w 1866+
1866-78 as Antwerp gazette (Antwerp)
1879-87 Paulding gazette
CHi Ja 3 1901
CPA 1866+

PEEBLES

ADAMS county news. *See* Peebles news-reporter

Peebles NEWS-REPORTER. w O 9 1890-1905||?
1890-92? as Adams county news; 1893?-1903? Peebles news
OHi O 16 1890-Ja 7 1892

PEMBERVILLE

Pemberville LEADER. w 1884+
pub Ap 26 1889+
OHi Ja 4 1901

PERRY

Perry FORUM. w O 13 1899-1900||?
OClWHi 1899-Mr 9 1900

Perry JOURNAL. w F 12 1904-05||?
OClWHi 1904-F 24 1905

PERRYSBURG

DEMOCRATIC post. w S 2? 1845-
CU-B O 21 1845

FOREST CITY visitor. w 1855?-
CU-B Ap 5 1856

Perrysburg JOURNAL. w 1834?+
1834?-37? as Miami of the lake; 1838?-Mr? 1853 Ohio whig and Perrysburg commercial advertiser
CU-B Ap 20 1839
DLC Ag 26,O 23 1834;Ag 18 1838
ICHi Mr 9 1836
MWA Mr 31 1835;Je 20 1853;Ja 12 1866
OPe Je 20 1853-Ap 14 1855;Je 23 1859+

MIAMI of Lake Erie. w My 28? 1844-
CU-B Ag 23 1845
DLC S 17 1844

MIAMI of the lake. *See* Perrysburg journal

NORTHWESTERN democrat. w My 22? 1852-
MWA Jl 31,S 11,D 25 1852
OClWHi Je 25 1853

OHIO whig and Perrysburg commercial advertiser. *See* Perrysburg journal

REPUBLICAN. w? My 25? 1841-
CU-B N 9 1841

STAR. w 1844?-
CU-B Jl 19 1851

WOOD county packet. w Ag 22? 1838-
CU-B N 7 1838
MWA F 20 1839

PETTISVILLE

Pettisville PROGRESS. w F 6 1914-
OHi F 13-S 4 1914

PIKETON

HICKORY sprout. w? 1844||?
Campaign paper
IU Ag 29,O 2 1844
OClWHi Ag 22 1844

Piketon JOURNAL. *See* Republican herald (Waverly)

PIKE county democrat. w 1851?-
MWA D 16 1852

PIKE county press. w? 1861?-
IU N 14,D 19 1861

PIKE county tocsin. *See* Republican herald (Waverly)

PIKETONIAN. w? 1845?-
IU O 30 1845

SCIOTO VALLEY times. w? 1854?-
IU D 28 1854

Weekly SCIOTO VALLEY union. *See* Waverly democrat 1856-1915 (Waverly)

Piketon SUN. w 1886-88||?
IU Ja 1 1887

Weekly Piketon UNION. *See* Waverly democrat 1856-1915 (Waverly)

PIONEER

ALLIANCE. *See* Tri-state alliance

BORDER alliance. *See* Tri-state alliance

TRI-STATE alliance. w 1879+
1879-81? as Border alliance; 1882? Alliance
pub 1905+

PIQUA

Piqua daily CALL. d 1883+
Mr 26-Ap 5 1913 are flood editions
MWA Mr 26-Ap 8 1913
OClWHi Mr 18 1916
OHi Je 27 1892;O 19 1896;Ja 1 1901;Mr 4 1905;Mr 26-Ap 7 1913;Je-Jl 1914;Mr-My,Jl 1915-F 1916;My-Jl 1922;Je 9-13,23-Jl 11 1924; My 15,19 1926;My 20-Je 4,10-18 1927
OPi D 1911+

Piqua COURIER and enquirer. w Mr 14 1835-
1835-38? as Western courier and Piqua enquirer
FTaM 1835-36;My 1837-Mr 1847
MWA N 25 1837
NEh Ag 24 1839
OClWHi O 6,D 1 1838
OHi 1835-Ap 11 1840

Piqua DEMOCRAT. *See* Miami leader-journal

Piqua daily DISPATCH. d 1886-1901||?
Title varies slightly. United with Piqua daily leader to form Leader-dispatch
OHi Jl 27 1892;D 18 1895;O 21,28 1896;1900-Ja 1 1901

Piqua ENQUIRER. *See* Piqua journal

*Piqua GAZETTE and register of news, agriculture arts and manufactures. w Ag 24 1819-
1819-22? as Piqua gazette
DLC Mr 5,Ap 30,Je 4-11 1825;Je 20,Jl 11,Ag 1,29,S 26 1829
IU Je 6,Jl 4 1822
MWA Ap 30 1825
OHi [1821-Ag 1834]

Piqua INTELLIGENCER. w Jl 18? 1841-
DLC Ja 2 1841
OHi O 31,D 12 1840;Ja 30,F 13 1841

Piqua JOURNAL. w 1849-1901||?
1849-64? as Piqua enquirer
OHi S 11,N 20 1862;F 5,Jl 2,S 24 1863;F 11, Ap 2,Je 2 1864;Ja 7 1869;My 4,17 1871;O 1-8 1874;Je 24 1875;Mr 2 1876;F 8,O 11 1877;Ap 10,Je 1879-My 24 1883;Ja 3 1901
WHi Jl 27 1865

LEADER-DISPATCH. d Ag 1888-1919||?
1888-1901? as Piqua daily leader
OHi Ag 14 1888-Ag 6 1889[O 1896]Ap 6 1897; Ja 1 1901
—w ed *See* Miami leader-journal

MIAMI county democrat. *See* Miami leader-journal

MIAMI county helmet. w 1874-1911||?
1874-1909? as Miami helmet
CLM Ja 19 1893
OHi S 18,N 6 1884;Ja 3 1901

MIAMI democrat. *See* Miami leader-journal

OHIO (*Continued*)

PIQUA—*Continued*

MIAMI democratic enquirer. w S 14? 1831-
PLewL D 28 1831-Ja 4 1832

MIAMI leader-journal. w 1863-1911||?
1863-70? as Piqua democrat; 1871?-72? Miami county democrat; 1873;-82? Miami democrat; 1883?-1901? Miami leader
OHi Je 29 1876-Jl 21 1877;My 18,Jl 27 1878-Jl 24 1882
—d ed *See* Leader-dispatch

MIAMI VALLEY register. *See* Piqua weekly register

Piqua weekly REGISTER. w 1841-
1841-42? as Miami Valley register
IU Jl 30 1842
MWA D 24 1852
NN Ag 15 1862
OHi Jl 25,O 3 1846;Mr 24 1849;Ja 12 1855;Ja 25 1858;Ag 1,S 18 1862

Piqua REGISTER. sw
OHi O 16 1847;Ap 4,My 5,Je 13,Jl 25 1849;Jl 13 1850

Piqua REGISTER. tw
MWA Ja 3 1851;Ja 29 1852
OHi Mr 4 1852;Ag 6 1853;D 24 1854

WESTERN courier and Piqua enquirer. *See* Piqua courier and enquirer

PLYMOUTH

Plymouth ADVERTISER. w 1853+
NNHi O 25 1853-O 6 1855
OHi Ja 5 1901

POMEROY

Pomeroy BANNER. w My 9 1867-69||?
1867-Ap 1868? as Star spangled banner
OHi My 16 1867-Ap 1868

Pomeroy CRESCENT. w 1869-71||?
OHi 1870-71

DEMOCRAT. w S 13 1888+
1888-F? 1891 as Pomeroy democrat
pub 1927+
OHi 1889-1917

INDEPENDENT. sw 1903-10||?
OHi Jl 1908-10

Pomeroy JOURNAL. w 1879-84||?
In German
OHi 1880-81

Pomeroy LEADER. w Ag 1 1895-1917||?
OClWHi Ag 8 1907
OHi 1895;97-1917

MEIGS county news. w
OHi 1873;76

MEIGS county press. w
OHi Mr 20 1867-69;71

MEIGS county telegraph. *See* Pomeroy tribune-telegraph

MEIGS county times. *See* Pomeroy tribune-telegraph

MOSQUITO. w D 7 1883-85||?
OHi 1883-Ja 2 1885

Daily NEWS. *See* Evening tribune

STAR spangled banner. *See* Pomeroy banner

Pomeroy weekly TELEGRAPH. *See* Pomeroy tribune-telegraph

TRIBUNE. w Ap 13 1887-93||?
United with Pomeroy telegraph to form Pomeroy tribune-telegraph
1887-N 5? 1890 pub in Racine
OClWHi Ag 17 1892
OHi 1887-93

Evening TRIBUNE. d 1910+
1910-26? as Daily news
OHi 1911;Jl-D 1922;My-Ag 1925;31+

Pomeroy TRIBUNE-TELEGRAPH. w O 20? 1843+
1843-48? as Meigs county times; 1848?-84? Meigs county telegraph (1860?-66? Pomeroy weekly telegraph) 1885-93? Pomeroy telegraph
IU F 7-14,27-Ap 3 1844
MWA D 21 1852;D 14 1858;My 26 1864
NbHi D 23 1856-57
OClWHi N 3,15-22 1843;Ja 3,31,Ap 10,S 11,O 25,N 13 1844;Ap 19,Ag 9 1848;Ja 9 1850;F 13,Mr 6,Jl 3-10,N 11,D 23 1851;F 3 1852;Jl 5 1853;N 7,28 1854;Mr 13-Ap 9 1855;Je 24,S 25,O 10 1856;Je 1 1858;My 10 1859;Ag 7 1860;Jl 5-12 1861;S 2 1874;O 9,23-30,N 20,D 11 1878;Mr 5,Ag 20-27 1879;Ag 18 1880;Mr 2-23,My 25 1881;Ag 16,30,O 11,D 6 1882;Mr 28,Ag 15,S 5 1883;Ja 2,Mr 19,Ap 2,Ag 20 1884;F 8,Mr,My 13 1885;My 19,Ag 18 1886;Ag 17 1887;D 19 1888;Ag 20,D 24 1890-Ja 7 1891;Ag 17 1892;Ja 17 1893
OHi Ap 17-D 1851;53;F 13 1856-O 22,D 10-17 1884;85-86;88-1915;17-24;31+

PORT CLINTON

Port Clinton DEMOCRAT. *See* Ottawa county news

OTTAWA county herald. w 1902-24||?
United with Ottawa county republican to form Port Clinton republican-herald
OHi Mr 1906-S 19 1913;14-Ag,O 1917-My 1918

OTTAWA county news. w 1865+
1895?-1930? as Ottawa county news-democrat (1909?-18? Port Clinton democrat)
pub 1865+
OClWHi N 10 1876
OHi Ja 4 1901;Mr 1906-30

OTTAWA county republican. *See* Port Clinton republican-herald

Port Clinton REPUBLICAN-HERALD. w 1887+
1887-1924? as Ottawa county republican
OHi Ja 4 1901

PORTSMOUTH

Portsmouth BLADE. w,sw 1876-1913||?
1876-79 as Valley blade
w 1876-89?
IU Je 11 1881
OHi 1890-95;97-1900

Portsmouth daily BLADE. d 1886-1913||?
OClWHi O 20 1903
OHi O-D 1898;Ja 2 1901;03-Mr 1904;09-12

Portsmouth CLIPPER. w F? 1845-47||?
United with Portsmouth tribune to form Tribune and clipper, later Portsmouth tribune
IU D 7 1846
OHi F 16 1847

Portsmouth CORRESPONDENT. w 1858-1913||?
In German and English
OHi 1894-1908

Portsmouth COURIER. *See* Portsmouth tribune

Portsmouth DEMOCRAT. w
IU Jl 3,16-23,Ag 6-20,S-O 22 1844

DEMOCRATIC enquirer. *See* Portsmouth inquirer

Portsmouth Daily DISPATCH. d N? 1849-
OClWHi D 21 1849
OHi Ap 26 1853-N 14 1854
WHi Jl 20 1850

GAZETTE and Lawrence advertiser. w Jl 30 1824-
MWA S 2,16 1825
OHi 1824-O 1825

Portsmouth INQUIRER. w 1848?-
1848?-49? as Democratic enquirer
IU Mr 27 1849;D 15 1854
MWA Jl 1 1853
OHi Ap 8 1850-Mr 1853;D 1854-Jl 13 1855

OHIO pennant. w Ag 25 1855-
OHi 1855-Je 13 1856

Portsmouth PRESS. w 1889-1903||?
OHi 1897-O 3 1903

Portsmouth REPUBLICAN. w 1852-76||
United with Portsmouth tribune to form Portsmouth tribune and republican, later Portsmouth tribune
OHi Mr 7,Ap 11,Jl 18-25 1867;Jl 24 1868-Ag 7 1869

SCIOTO county democrat. *See* Valley sentinel

***SCIOTO telegraph and Lawrence gazette.** w Mr 4 1820-
Mr 4-S 28 1820 as Scioto telegraph
IU Je 30 1821
OHi Ja-S 1 1821

SCIOTO tribune. *See* Portsmouth tribune

SCIOTO VALLEY post. w Je 9? 1840-
IU Je 16,30-Jl 7,21-28,Ag 18 1840;S 5,25,O 3-24 1843

SCIOTO VALLEY republican. w 1852?-
IU Ja 7(extra)24-F 1,22,Mr 8,22-Ap 5 1854;Ja 14 1860
MWA Je 23 1853

SPIRIT of the times. *See* Portsmouth times

Morning STAR of Portsmouth. d 1914-15||?
OHi Ja 30-D 1915

TEMPORARY advertiser. w F? -Ap 6 1826||
OHi F 24-Ap 6 1826

Portsmouth TIMES. w 1852-1922||?
1852-My 4 1858 as Spirit of the times
IU D 29 1857;N 30 1858;Ap 14 1860;Jl 23 1892
OC D 5 1885
OHi 1857-Je 1860;Jl 25 1863-Ag 1869;Mr 18 1871-94;N 9 1895-1904;Ap 9 1910-17

Portsmouth daily TIMES. d 1894+
OClWHi O 20-21 1903;Je 15 1917;Je 9-10,12-13,23,29 1921
OHi Ja 2 1901;Ap-Je 1914;F 8-Mr,Ag 14 1915-F 7 1916;18;Jl 1919+

Portsmouth TRIBUNE. w Ja 1 1831-1904||?
1831-35? as Portsmouth courier; 1836-38? Scioto tribune; 1848-53? Tribune and clipper; 1877-80? Portsmouth tribune and republican; 1881?-82? Tribune-republican
DLC N 3 1832
IU Ag 23 1836;Ja 6,Mr 11,Ap 1,22,My 13,S 30,N 4,D 19 1837[38]Ag 25,O 13,N 10 1843;D 15 1853;D 12 1855;Ja 2 1856
MWA D 24 1879
NNHi 1839-Ja 15 1841
OC Je 20 1850;My 12,S 24 1851
OHi 1831-F 1 1832;Ag 2-9 1839;My 1850-Ag 17 1853;My 14 1855-60;Jl 1872-N 1890;91-92;97;Mr 1898-1903
WHi N 12 1862

Daily evening TRIBUNE. d 1851?-
1851?-52? as Daily tribune and clipper
IU D 23 1853
MWA S 20 1852
OHi Ag 14 1853-O 1855

VALLEY blade. *See* Portsmouth blade

VALLEY sentinel. w D 1897-1917||?
1897-98? as Scioto county democrat
OHi Ja-F 1898;Ja-N 1899;1901-03;Ap 13 1910-Je 6 1917

WÄCHTER am Ohio. w
In German
NN O 1860-Ag 1861

WESTERN times. w Ap 18 1826-
DLC Jl 4-11,S 19,O 24 1829;Jl 22,D 16 1830
ICHi Ja 13 1831
MWA Ap 27,D 14-28 1826;F 22,Ap 5,My 24 1827
OHi 1826-My 11 1830

RACINE

TRIBUNE. *See under* Pomeroy

RAVENNA

BUCKEYE democrat. w My 21 1838-F 14 1839||
OClWHi complete

CAMPAIGN democrat. w Ag 6- 1855||?
MnHi Ag-O 15 1855
OHi Ag-S 10,O 4 1855

CAMPAIGN democrat. w Mr 17- 1876||
OClWHi Mr 17 1876

CENTENNIAL gazette. Mr 17 1876-
OClWHi Mr 17 1876

COUNTY democrat. *See* Ravenna evening record

Ravenna DEMOCRAT. *See* Portage county democrat

DEMOCRATIC press. *See* Portage county democrat

GRAPHIC. sw D 1 1893-95||?
OClWHi 1893-Ag 16 1895

HICKORY flail and fusion thresher. w Ag 22- 1855||?
OClWHi Ag-O 4 1855

HOME companion and whig. *See* Ravenna evening record

INDEPENDENT press. *See* Reformer

Ravenna weekly JOURNAL. w 1909-10||?
OClWHi S 17 1909-Mr 18 1910

OHIO star. w Ja 6 1830-Ap 1854||
United with Home companion and whig to form Portage county democrat, later Ravenna evening record
CSmH S 1 1830
DLC [1830-31]S 27 1832;Jl 19 1838;D 6 1843
IU Jl 27 1842
MWA F 17 1830;Je 30,Ag 18 1852
MnHi 1834-D 19 1839;D 1842-D 8 1852
N Ap 5,Je 21,Jl 12,Ag 2,16,S 6,20,O 4,18,D 6,20 1832;Ja 17,Ap 18,N 14,D 18 1833
OClWHi 1830-Mr 22 1854
P-M D 6 1832;D 18 1834

OHIO watchman. m,sm N 1834-37||?
1834-Ja 1835 as Watchman
m 1834-36?
OClWHi 1834-36;My 13-Jl 20 1837

PEOPLE'S advocate. w Ag 3 1838-
MnHi Ag-O 16 1838
OClWHi Ag-S 7 1838

PORTAGE county democrat. 1854-76 *See* Ravenna evening record

PORTAGE county democrat. w S 3 1868-1927||?
1868-1901 as Democratic press
OClWHi 1868-Je 1901
OHi Ag 19 1891-Ag 16 1893;Ag 19 1897-Ag 15 1901

PORTAGE county republican. w 1878-Mr 1 1882||
Merged with Republican-democrat, later Ravenna evening record
OClWHi Je 13-20,Jl 11,N 21,D 4 1879;Ja 9,Mr 5,Je 18,Jl 16-S 3 1880;D 2 1881

Weekly PORTAGE county sentinel. w Je 5 1845-62||
1845-54 as Portage sentinel
MWA Jl 27 1853
OClWHi 1845-F 15 1862

PORTAGE county whig. *See* Ravenna evening record

PORTAGE sentinel. *See* Weekly Portage county sentinel

Ravenna evening RECORD. w,sw,tw,d Ag 30 1848+
1848-Ag 1852 as Portage county whig; S? 1852-Mr 29 1854 Home companion and whig; Ap 5 1854-My 3 1876 Portage county democrat (1870? County democrat); My 10 1876-83? Republican-democrat; 1884?-Mr? 1928 Ravenna republican
w 1848-Ja 27 1916;sw F 1916-18?;tw 1919?-24?
DLC N 7 1855
MWA S 8 1852;Ja 7,F 25 1857;O 16 1861
MnHi Ap 1854-S 20 1882
N S 19-26,O 17 1877
NNHi F 11 1841;Je 10 1863
OCHi 1848-Mr 23 1859
OClWHi Ap 18,Ag 29 1849-Je 2 1898;Je 22 1899;Je 12 1902;Ap 16 1908-33
OHi F 13 1895-F 1 1912;F 1914-Mr 9 1916;Jl 12 1920-21;F 1922-26;S 8-N 1927[Ja 12-My] 1928-My 1 1930;My 6-D 1931
P-M Mr 28 1855
WHi Je 22 1899

REFORMER. w Ap 25 1855-
1855 as Independent press; 1856 Independent press and reformer
DLC My 1 1857
OClWHi 1855-My 1 1857

Daily REPUBLICAN. d Je 19 1886-
OClWHi 1886-Je 18 1887

Ravenna REPUBLICAN. w,sw,tw. *See* Ravenna evening record

WATCHMAN. *See* Ohio watchman

OHIO (*Continued*)

RAVENNA—*Continued*

WESTERN courier. w Ap 23 1825-38||
1825-Ap? 1826 as Western courier and western public advertiser; 1831?-Ja 5 1837 Western courier and Portage county democrat
CSmH Ag 19 1830
DLC Je 2,Jl 24,Ag 28,S 11-25,O 23,N 13,27,D 25 1829;Ja 13 1831;Ja 10 1833
ICHi My 10 1828-Je 6 1829
MBAt Jl 5 1828
MWA D 1 1827;F 16,Mr 15 1828
MnHi 1825-Ap 15 1826[27-30]
MoHi My 12 1827-My 3 1828;My 1836-Ap 1837
OClWHi Ap 23 1825;Ja 10 1833;O 16 1834;S 10 1835;Ap 6,My 11 1837;Jl 12-19 1838
OHi Ap 30 1825-Ap 1,My 27 1826-Ja 15 1830; My 1833-O 1837
P-M [1830]

WESTERN RESERVE cabinet and family visitor. w Ja 1 1840-F 21 1843||
ICHi N 20 1841
MnHi complete
OClWHi Mr 1840-43

REPUBLIC

LITERARY casket. w S 17? 1850-
OHi Ja 28 1851
OOxM O 22 1850

REYNOLDSBURG

NEWS gazette. w 1906+
OCwT 1910–

RICHMOND

OHIO clipper. w? F? 1850-
OClWHi Jl 2 1850

RIPLEY

Ripley BEE. w 1824+
1824-D 3 1833 as Castigator; D 10 1833-37? Castigator and democratic expositor; 1837?-44? Political examiner
1827?-44? pub in Georgetown
pub 1926+
CSmH Jl 6 1830
DLC My 16 1839
IU S 4 1844
MWA F 20 1827;Ag 11 1829;D 11 1852;Mr 7 1861
OCHi Jl 10 1833-O 1834
OClWHi Je 2 1825-Jl 11 1826;N 1 1838;Ja 23,Je 26 1847;Jl 13 1850;My 24 1851;S 15,O 5 1855;60-[72-73;75]Mr 29,S 20 1876;Ja 24 1877; N 20 1878;Ag 14 1912
OHi Jl 1832-Jl 3 1833;Ag 5 1848;Je 1850-My 22 1852;S 3 1859;S 25 1872;Mr 27 1878-Ap 1880;Ja 2 19—;1906-S 1918;19-20

FREEDOM'S casket. w? My 25? 1844-
IU Je 15 1844

Ripley HERALD. w? My 13? 1852-
OClWHi My 2 1852

INDEPENDENT press. w Ag 2? 1867-
MWA Mr 6 1868
OClWHi D 13 1867-My 1 1868

OHIO VALLEY times. *See* Ripley times

SCOTT battery. w? 1852||
Campaign paper
MWA Ag 24 1852

Ripley TELEGRAPH. w 1839?-
IU Ag 26,S 30 1843;F 3-10 1844

Ripley TIMES. w 1875-81||?
1875? as Ohio Valley times
OClWHi Ja 13,Mr 21,Je 2 1875
OHi N 1879-81

ROCK CREEK

Rock Creek SIGNAL. w 1893-1917||?
OClWHi F 22-Mr 8,22-29,Ap 12 1917
OHi Ja 3 1901

ROCKFORD

Rockford PRESS. w Je 1883+
pub 1883+

ROCKY RIVER

Papers published in Rocky River are listed under Cleveland

ROSSVILLE

Papers published in Rossville are listed under Hamilton

ST. CLAIRSVILLE

*BELMONT chronicle. w Ag 1818+
1818-F? 1834 as Belmont journal; Mr? 1834-Jl? 1836 Belmont journal and enquirer
CSmH Ap 4(extra)1847
DLC S 14 1833;F 3,Mr 29,Jl 20 1834;Ag 13 1836;S 2 1838;Ja 5,Je 1 1841;50
MWA D 17 1852
NN Ap 4(extra)1847(photostat)
OCHi O 13 1848-O 4 1855
OClWHi Jl 31-O 23 1838;Ja 3 1851
OHi My 23,S 19,O 17 1835;37-O 1863;64-1906

BELMONT journal. *See* Belmont chronicle

Saint Clairsville GAZETTE. w 1824+
Mr 1849?-67 as Saint Clairsville gazette and citizen
CSmH F 13 1830
DLC Ag 2 1828;Mr 29,Ap 19,My 10 31-Je 7,23 1844
IU Ag 31,S 21 1839;My 9 1840;N 24-D 1843; F 2-16,Ap 26,My 24,Je 7,Ag 2-16,30,S 20-27,O 11 1844;Ja 17 1845
MWA Mr 3 1827;Ap 4 1861
OClWHi Ag 23 1844
OHi S 17 1825-Je 1829;30-F 1849;51-F,S 3,O 15 1857;Jl 15,D 30 1858;Mr 1859-78;80-93;95-1901;03-06;10-15;Mr 1916-17

INDEPENDENT republican. w 1854?-
OHi Mr 1856-62

NATIONAL historian and St. Clairesville advertiser. w F 1826-
CSmH Jl 17 1830
DLC N 29 1828;Je 27,Jl 18-Ag 15,S 12-19,N 21 1829;Ja 2,Ag 14,D 25 1830;Jl 30 1831
MWA My 12,Ag 4 1827
NN My 30 1829
NNHi Jl 30 1831-Je 22 1833
OClWHi F 7 1829
OHi F 1827-Jl 6 1833

SAINT MARYS

Evening LEADER. d 1902+
pub F 1926+
KHi S 21 1926
OHi O 1914-F 1916

SENTINEL. w 1842?-
IU Ag 30,S 13-27,D 20 1843;Ja 17,F 7-14,28, Ap 3-17,My 15-22,Ag 21,D 25 1844

SAINT PARIS

Saint Paris DISPATCH. w 1881-84||
United with New era to form Era-dispatch, later Evening news-dispatch

DISPATCH. 1902 *See* Evening news-dispatch

ERA-DISPATCH. *See* Evening news-dispatch

NEW era. *See* Evening news-dispatch

Saint Paris NEWS. w 1888?-1902||?
United with Dispatch to form Saint Paris news dispatch, later Evening news-dispatch
OHi Ja 4 1901

Evening NEWS-DISPATCH. w,sw,d 1871+
1871-84? as New era; 1885?-1901? Era-dispatch; 1902? Dispatch; 1903?-Mr 1934? Saint Paris news-dispatch
w 1876-Mr 1934(sw 1886?)
pub 1871+
OClWHi Ap 30-My 7 1908

SALEM (ASHTABULA COUNTY). *See* CONNEAUT

SALEM (COLUMBIANA COUNTY)

ANTI-SLAVERY bugle. w Je 20 1845-61||?
DLC Ja 3,17-31,F 14,Ap 3,My 22-Je 5,Jl 10,S 25,N 6-13,D 4,18 1852;Ja 8,29,Je 4 1853;Ag 26,O 28,D 9,30 1854;S 1-8,O 6 1855;Ja 10,F 14,Je 20,O 17-24 1857;O 1 1859;F 18,Mr 31 1860;My 4 1861
KHi Ja 7 1860
MB Ag 17,S 1 1850;Jl 26,O 25 1851[F 12 1853-D 16 1854;F 17-Ap 21 1855;Jl 16 1857-Ja 1860]
MHi Ap 27-My 4,Ag 1850;My 20 1860;F 16 1861
MiU Mr 30 1850
MnHi Mr 14 1857
NIC 1845-61
NN [1849]-[51]
NcD F 19 1859
OCHi Ag 2 1856
OClWHi 1845-Ja 19 1861
OHi 1845-Ag 4 1847; S 15 1848-S,O 25-N 1,22,D 20 1851[52-Ja 1857]
OO 1845-[50-51;53-56]
OSa 1845-S 6 1851
PSF O 9 1846
PWcHi My 4 1850
TN [1845-Jl 1849]
TxU 1845-O 1849

COLUMBIANA county republican. *See* Republican era

Salem ERA. w 1873-89||?
United with Salem republican to form Republican era
OClWHi Jl 5 1876

Salem GAZETTE and public advertiser. w 1825?-
OClWHi My 3,Ag 13,N 19,D 23-31 1825; Je 24 1826
OHi Jl 8 1826

HOMESTEAD journal. *See* Republican era

Salem daily NEWS. d Ja 1 1889+
pub 1889+
OClWHi Je 15,19,22-23,25-26 1906;Jl 12 1921
OHi Ja 2 1901
OSa 1902-04;06-10;12-16;18-22;Jl-S 1923;Ja-Ag 1924;25-My,Jl 1931+

REPUBLICAN era. w,sw Ap 1842-1919||?
1842-Je 16 1847? as Village register; Je 23 1847?-Ap 4 1855 Homestead journal; Ap 11 1855-Je 17 1857 Columbiana county republican; Je 24 1857-89? Salem republican
sw N 7 1883-Je 10 1885
DLC D 6 1842;Je 24 1843
MWA Mr 2 1852
MoHi D 28 1859
OClWHi Ap 23,Jl 26,Ag 16 1842;Ag 1-8 1843; Ap 23,Je 4-11,Jl 21,S 10-17,N 26,D 24 1844; Mr 25,Jl 1-8,Ag 5,O 28,N 25,D 16 1845[46-50]-[52-53]Mr 8,Jl 5,19,O 18 1854;Mr 21,My 9, Ag 29,N 14,D 26 1855[56-57]-[59-60]Je 6, Ag 14,S 18-25,N 13,D 3 1861[63-65]Je 13,N 27-D 5 1867;F 5,26,Mr 18,N 25 1868;Mr 31-Ap 7,Je 9,30 1869[70-77]Je 10 1880;Mr 9,Je 1 1882;Ap 10,N 17 1883;Mr 12-19,Ag 16,30,N 1 1884;Je 17-24 1886
ODW F 28,N 6 1872;Ja 16-30,F 13 1873
OHi Ja 3 1901
OSa My 3,O 11,N 29 1842[43-45]Ja 27,Ag 11-18 1846;47-89;1902-03

VILLAGE register. *See* Republican era

SALINEVILLE

Salineville REVIEW. w Ja 6 1910-14||?
OHi 1910-11

SANDUSKY

BAY CITY weekly mirror. w D 13 1842-57||
1842-53 as Sandusky democratic mirror
MWA Ag 31 1852
OClWHi D 13 1842;N 19 1850
OHi My 30 1854[Ja-Je 1855]My 31-Jl 12,26-Ag 2 1856
—d ed *See* Sandusky daily mirror

Der BAYSTADT demokrat. *See* Der Sandusky demokrat

CLARION. *See* Register

COMMERCIAL register. *See* Register

Sandusky DEMOCRATIC mirror. *See* Bay City weekly mirror

Der Sandusky DEMOKRAT. w 1856-1919||?
1856-73 as Der Baystadt demokrat
Ag 1 1906 is goldenes jubiläum ed
In German
MWA Ag 30 1878
NN Ag 1 1906
OHi Ja 2 1901[18-19]

Halbwöchentlicher DEMOKRAT. sw 1861-
In German
NN Je 18 1861

ERIE county news. w Ap 23 1863-70||?
United with Sandusky weekly journal to form Weekly journal and Erie county news, later Sandusky weekly journal and local
OHi 1863-F 9 1865

INTELLIGENZ-BLATT. w 1851-61||?
In German
MWA Ag 21 1852

Sandusky weekly JOURNAL and local. w Ag 16 1866-D 22? 1904||
1866-Mr 1887 as Sandusky weekly journal (1871?-78? Weekly journal and Erie county news) United with Sandusky weekly star to form Sandusky weekly star-journal
OClWHi 1880-84;Mr 1887-N 1888;N 19-D 1896
OHi 1876;78;88;98-99;1901

Sandusky evening JOURNAL and local. d Ja 1 1885-1904||
1885-Mr 2 1887 as Sandusky daily journal (other variations slight) United with Sandusky daily star to form Sandusky star-journal
Suspended for several weeks in Ja 1887
OClWHi Mr 1886-O 3 1888;O 4 1889-Ap 4 1891;Ap 1892-Mr 1893;Ap 1894-Mr 1904

Sandusky LOCAL. w N 18 1882-Mr 1887||?
United with Sandusky weekly journal to form Sandusky weekly journal and local
OClWHi 1882-N 14 1885
OHi N 22 1884-86

Daily LOCAL. d Ap 2 1883-Mr 2 1887||
United with Sandusky daily journal to form Sandusky evening journal and local
OClWHi 1883-Ap 1,O 5 1886-87

Sandusky daily MIRROR. d 1849?-54||?
MWA S 3 1852
—w ed *See* Bay City weekly mirror

PARTERRE. w?
MWA Je 26? 1822

Weekly REGISTER. w Ap 24 1822-1911||?
1822-48* as Sandusky clarion; 1848?-51? Sandusky weekly register; 1851?-57? Weekly commercial register
pub 1875-1911
CtY Je 5 1822[47-51]
DLC My 31 1852-Je 9 1855;My 14 1859
ICHi F 24 1844;Mr 8,29,Mr 10-17,Je 8 1847
MBAt My 1 1822
MWA D 22 1827;My 28 1834;O 25 1852;F 3 1866
N Je 6 1829
NNHi O 30 1822
OCHi Je 5 1830
OClWHi 1822-My 20 1836;Ja 9,23 1830;O 10 1832;N 7 1840;Ap 23 1841;Ja 28,Ap 1,S 2-16,O 21 1843;Ag 3 1844;My 31 1852-Je 9 1855;Mr 5 1864;Ag 12,29 1865
OHi My 26 1824-My 1826;Ja 14 1874-Ag 11 1875;Mr 8 1876-81;83-84;F 18 1885-86;F 1887-93

Sandusky REGISTER. d 1843+
1843-Ap 23? 1848 as Clarion; Ap 24 1848-My 23? 1851 Daily Sanduskian; My 27 1851-O 13 1857 Daily commercial register (other variations slight)
pub Mr 1865+
DLC My 27 1852-My 25 1855;Ja-Je 25 1856
ICU Ap 24 1848-My 26 1856;57-Je 1858;S 13 1859-My 7 1862;Je 24 1864-Ap 25 1867
MWA Jl 9 1853;Mr 23,My 1,Ag 28 1876
N Je 29 1857
NNHi Je 2,4,6,8-11,13-18,21,23,25,28,30-Jl 1 1859
OClWHi Mr 15 1859;Mr 27,My-Je 9,Ag 12,O 19 1865;O 2 1867;70-Je 1872;Ja-Je 21 1873;74; Jl 1875-Je 1878;80-D 3 1893;My 1894-Ag 1897;Ja-Ap,S 1898-1903;My 28-29 1908;Jl 1910-Jl 16 1918;D 31 1922
OHi My 27 1851-72;Jl 1873-74;Jl 1898+

OHIO (*Continued*)

SANDUSKY—*Continued*

Sandusky tri-weekly REGISTER. tw 1852?-1905||?
DLC F 10 1855
MWA F 8 1853
NNHi My 14-17,21-31 1859
OClWHi F 10 1855;F 8 1862

REPUBLICAN standard. w Ap 28? 1831-
ICHi Je 4 1831

Daily SANDUSKIAN. *See* Sandusky register

Sandusky STAR-JOURNAL. d 1898+
1898-1904? as Sandusky daily star
pub 1898+
OClWHi Jl 5 1910-Jl 18 1918
OHi N 29 1911 -15

Sandusky weekly STAR-JOURNAL. w 1898-1911||?
1898-D? 1904 as Sandusky weekly star
OHi 1902-08;10-11

Sandusky TRIBUNE. w 1879-80||?
OClWHi Je 28 1879

SARAHSVILLE

DEMOCRATIC courier. *See* Caldwell star (Caldwell)

NOBLE county democrat. w Jl? 1857-
OHi O 3 1857

SARDINIA

Sardinia NEWS. w 1905+
pub Jl 1915+

SCIO

Scio weekly HERALD. w 1879-1920||?
OClWHi My 25 1888
OHi Ja 31 1895-My 13 1905;06-N 16 1908

SEBRING

Sebring TIMES. w,sw 1907+
sw 1907-14?
pub O 1920+
OClWHi F 21 1913-O 1 1915
OHi S 30 1927-33

SEVILLE

Seville DEMOCRAT. w? Ap? 1868-
OClWHi Ag 6 1868

Seville NEWS. w Ap 23- 1914||
United with Seville weekly times to form Seville times-news
OClWHi Ap 23-My 7 1914

Seville TIMES-NEWS. w 1871-1916||?
1871-1914 as Seville weekly times
OClWHi 1915-F 1917
OHi Ja 3 1901

SHAKER HEIGHTS

Papers published in Shaker Heights are listed under Cleveland

SHAWNEE

Shawnee JOURNAL. w Ja? 1878-
OHi Mr 14 1878-Ja 3 1879

SHELBY

Daily GLOBE. d Ap 24 1900+
Ag 2 1934 is centennial ed
pub 1900+
OHi Ag 2 1934

Shelby MIXUPTION. w? Jl 4 1869-
OClWHi Jl 4 1869

Shelby PAPER. w? 1864?-
OClWHi Je 15 1865;Mr 13 1866

Shelby TIMES. w 1876-1901||?
OOxM My 10 1884

SHERRODSVILLE

NEW standard. w N 23 1894-97||?
1894-D 25 1896 as Sherrodsville standard. United with Carrollton republican to form Republican-standard (Carrollton)
OClWHi 1894-F 5,Ap 20 1897

Sherrodsville STANDARD. *See* New standard

SHREVE

To 1874? as Shreve City

HOME mail. *See* Shreve news

HOME mirror. *See* Shreve news

Shreve JOURNAL. *See* Shreve news

Shreve City MIRROR. *See* Shreve news

Shreve NEWS. w 1868+
1868-72? as Shreve City mirror; 1873?-74? Home mirror; 1875?-81? Shreve journal; 1882?-83? Home mail
pub O 27 1927+
OClWHi Ap 8 1873-Mr 24 1874

SHREVE CITY. *See* SHREVE

SIDNEY

DEMOCRATIC spark. w Je 21? 1844-
OClWHi O 18 1844

Sidney daily JOURNAL. d 1908-28||?
OHi 1915-F 1916

Sidney JOURNAL. w *See* Weekly republican

Sidney daily NEWS. d 1892+
pub 1892+
OHi Ja 1 1901;Mr-D 1914
—w ed *See* Shelby county democrat

OHIO argus and Sidney aurora. *See* Weekly republican

Weekly REPUBLICAN. w 1832-1927||?
1832-1909 as Sidney journal(Ag 5? 1839-54? Ohio argus and Sidney aurora)
CLM S 27,O 25 1889
DLC D 9 1839;N 28 1840
MWA D 30 1839
OHi D 25 1841;Jl 26-Ag 9 1845;F 19 1869-1913
WHi My 20 1864

SHELBY county democrat. w Ja 1 1849+
pub Ja 28 1876+
MWA D 24 1852;Jl 22 1853
OHi 1869-1913
—d ed *See* Sidney daily news

VALLEY sentinel. w 1880-86||?
OHi O 27 1881-N 16 1882;Ja 18 1883-Je 17 1886

SOMERSET

Somerset ADVOCATE. w 1866-69||?
OClWHi Ja 9 1868
OHi My 1867-F 1869

DEMOCRATIC union. w 1857?-
NN My 22 1862
OClWHi Ag 11 1858
OHi Ap 21 1858-65;My 1866-O 1867

FLAG of '76. w S 24 1842-
DLC D 22 1843
OClWHi S 24 1842;Mr 8 1844
OHi 1842-Ag 16 1844

OHIO courier and Perry democrat. w? 1836?-
Ct Ag 10 1837

PEOPLE'S advocate. *See* Somerset post

PERRY county democrat. w S 14 1849-
MWA D 1 1852
OClWHi D 13 1849;Je 13,27 1850;Ja 9 1851
OHi 1849-Jl,O 1851-O 1853

PERRY record. *See* Somerset post

Somerset POST. w 1822-
- 1822 as Western world and political tickler; 1822-25? Perry record; 1826?-28? Perry record and Ohio whig; 1829?-31 People's advocate; 1832-50? Western post(title varies slightly)
DLC O 13 1832;O 31 1840
MWA Ag 3 1827;O 31 1828;D 22 1852
OClWHi Ap 27 1833-Je 1 1852;Ag 16 1854-Jl 18 1855
OHi F 24 1843;F 28 1850-Ap 4 1855
WHi S 2 1825

Somerset PRESS. w 1873+
OClWHi Je 8-15,29 1921
OHi O 10 1873-77;My 1879-S 1889;O 1891-98

Somerset REVIEW. w Ja 29 1857-
OClWHi 1857-O 7 1858
OHi N 12 1857

Somerset TRIBUNE. w S 6 1871-
OHi 1871-F 1873

WESTERN post. *See* Somerset post

WESTERN world and political tickler. *See* Somerset post

SOUTH EUCLID

Papers published in South Euclid are listed under Cleveland

SPENCERVILLE

Spencerville JOURNAL-NEWS. w 1879+
1879-1901? as Spencerville journal
pub 1905+

Spencerville NEWS. w 1897-1901||?
United with Spencerville journal to form Spencerville journal-news
OHi Ja 3 1901

SPRINGFIELD

Springfield weekly ADVERTISER. w 1866-76||?
NNHi D 6-20 1871;F 5 1873
OCHi S 16 1869;Je 22 1870-Je 17 1872
OClWHi 1870-71

CHAMPION City daily times. d Mr 3 1886-S 22 1888||
United with Springfield daily republic to form Springfield daily republic times, later Springfield daily news
IU Ap 10 1886
OHi 1887-Je 1888
OSHi complete

CHAMPION city weekly times. w F 17 1887-
OHi F 24 1887-S 20 1888
OSHi 1887-D 2 1892

Springfield daily DEMOCRAT. d 1888-My? 1905||
United with Springfield press-republic to form Springfield daily news
MoHi N 20 1891
OHi O 13-28 1896;Ja 2 1901

DEMOCRATIC expositor. w My 27? 1853-
MWA Jl 8 1853;Ap 28 1854

DOLLAR nonpareil. *See* Mad River Valley news and Clark county journal

FARMER. *See* Springfield weekly republic

FARMER'S advocate. *See* Springfield weekly republic

FARMERS' chronicle and Clark advertiser. w Ja 3-Je? 1833||
United with Western pioneer to form Pioneer and chronicle, later Springfield weekly republic?
DLC Ja 10 1833
IU Ja 10,31-F 7,21,Mr 7-21 1833

Springfield weekly GAZETTE. w 1872-1906||?
OHi Ap 1905-07

Springfield daily GAZETTE. *See* Springfield times d,w

Springfield GLOBE. d 1882||?
United with Springfield daily republic to form Globe republic, later Springfield daily news

Springfield GLOBE. w 1882||?
United with Springfield weekly republic to form Globe republic, later Springfield weekly republic

GLOBE republic. d *See* Springfield daily news

GLOBE republic. w *See* Springfield weekly republic

MAD RIVER democrat and advocate. w 1838?-
OHi O 10 1839

MAD RIVER VALLEY news and Clark county journal. w Ap 14 1854-
1854-Mr 24 1858 as Dollar nonpareil
OSHi 1854-N 22 1862
—d ed *See* Springfield daily news

Springfield daily NEWS. d Jl 24 1855+
1855-Mr 23 1858 as Daily nonpareil; Mr 24 1858-D 31 1866 Springfield evening news and journal; Ja 1 1867-S 22 1888 Springfield daily republic (1884 Globe republic); S 24 1888-S 7 1900 Springfield daily republic times; S 8 1900-My 30 1905 Springfield press-republic
Sunday issues as News-sun
DLC Mr 7 1873
NN Ap 11 1915
OCHi Ag 22 1863
OClWHi Ag 9 1880;O 17,21 1915
OHi 1865;67-78;81-83;1901-Je,O 1902-Mr,Jl 1904-Je 1911;12-14;Ja-Mr,S 1918-N 1921;22+
OSHi 1855-My 1905
VU Ap 4 1917
—w ed *See* Mad River Valley news. . .; Springfield weekly republic

NEWS-Sun. *See* Sun; Springfield daily news

Daily NONPAREIL. *See* Springfield daily news

OHIO press. w? 1858?-
OClWHi Ap 12 1860

OLD soldier. 1840||?
Campaign paper
OClWHi Mr 7 1840

PIONEER and chronicle. *See* Springfield weekly republic

Springfield daily PRESS. d S 19 1899-S 7 1900||
United with Springfield daily republic times to form Press-republic, later Springfield daily news
OSHi complete

Springfield PRESS-REPUBLIC. *See* Springfield daily news

*Springfield weekly REPUBLIC. w F? 1819-1905||?
1819-20? as Farmer; 1821?-25? Farmer's advocate; 1826?-Ag? 1839 Western pioneer (Je?-Ag? 1833 Pioneer and chronicle) 1884 Globe republic
CSmH Jl 17 1830
DLC My 30,Je 20-27,Jl 11,25,S 12,26,O 24,D 26 1829;Ja 2,23,Jl 17-24,Ag 14 1830;N 3 1832; Ag 23-30 1839;D 11 1840
IU Ja 22,D 17 1831;F 4 1832
MWA S 17 1823;D 26 1827
N Mr 30 1833
OClWHi O 1 1841;Ja-My 8 1872;Ag 12 1880
OHi Jl 1888-90;92-94;96-98;Ja 10 1901
OOxM [N 10 1832-Jl 5 1834]
OSHi Ag 22 1829-My 1905

Springfield daily REPUBLIC. *See* Springfield daily news

Springfield REPUBLIC. tw 1849?-84||?
MWA S 30 1852
OHi Ag 19 1861-Ag 19 1864

Daily REPUBLICAN gazette. *See* Springfield times d,w

SUN. d 1894+
1901? as Daily morning sun. Sunday issues News-sun
O 5 1930 is sesqui-centennial ed
OHi Ja 1 1901;S 1918-Ag 1919;D 16 1928;O 5,10 1930

Springfield TIMES. d,w 1878-Ap 1914||?
1878-Jl 21 1905 as Springfield daily gazette; Jl 22 1905-Je 15 1908 Daily republican gazette; Jl 19 1908-F 10 1909 Springfield times and the republican gazette; F 11 1909-Jl 17 1910 Springfield morning times and the republican gazette
Jl 20-D 7 1910 merged with Sun
d 1878-F 1911
OClWHi Mr 10 1881
OHi Ap-D 1905;Jl 1906-Mr 1909;Mr 1910-F 1911
OSHi Jl 1906-Je 1910
—w ed *See also* Springfield weekly gazette

Springfield TIMES. w 1895-98||?
OHi 1897-98

OHIO (*Continued*)

SPRINGFIELD—*Continued*

TIPPECANOE calumet and war chief. w? 1836||?
Campaign paper
OClWHi Ag 4 1836

TIPPECANOE calumet and war chief. w 1840||?
Campaign paper
OClWHi Ap 7-14,My 5-12,Ag 11,S 1-15,N 18 1840

WESTERN pioneer. *See* Springfield weekly republic

STEUBENVILLE

AMERICAN union. w My 31 1837-
IU F 18 1840
MWA D 22 1852
OClWHi Mr 6 1841;O 8 1842;Ja 15,Jl 2 1846;Ja 28,F 11 1847;Jl 1858-D 10 1862
OHi 1837-My 7 1839;My 1850-Ag 24 1859

Steubenville **COURIER.** w? 1863?-
ICHi Ag 24 1864

Steubenville weekly **GAZETTE.** w S 1 1865-1919||?
Title varies slightly
OClWHi 1865-69;Ag 27 1897
OHi 1870-O 20 1897;98-1903;F 1904-17

Steubenville daily **GAZETTE.** d 1873-1925||
OChH 1876-1900
OClWHi Ag 26 1897
OHi Ja 1 1901;Mr 1914-F 1916;S 1919-Ap 1920
WHi N 18 1886

Steubenville **GERMANIA.** w Ag 11 1876-1918||?
In German
OHi 1876-77;Ag 10 1878-Ag 2 1879;80-86;88-99;1901-16

HARRY-OF-THE-WEST. w? 1844||
Campaign paper
IU Mr 30 1844
OClWHi Mr 30 1844

*Steubenville **HERALD.** w Je 7? 1806-1925||?
1806-16 as Western herald; Ja 3 1817-F 8? 1844 Western herald and Steubenville gazette
DLC 1821-O 1825;26;Ag 24-31 1827;Mr 22-29 1828;29-Ja 23,My 22 1830;Ja-Ap 20 1843
ICHi Je 9 1842
ICU F 28,Mr 5 1825
IU Mr 10,Ap 14,Je 9,24-Jl 21,Ag-S 14 1827;N 8,22-29,D 13 1828;Ja 10,24,Mr 21-28,Ap 18,My 9-23,Je-Jl 1..25-Ag 8 1829;N 2 1831;Ag 22 1832;Ag 17-S 21,O 5-12,N 2,16,30,D 28 1843;Ja 18,F 8,Ap 25,Je 13-20,Jl 25,Ag 29,S 19,O 10-17 1844
MBAt My 11 1822
MWA Ja 27,Fe 2,23 1827;F 9,S 6,27 1828;Mr 14-21 1829
NNHi N 3 1821
OClWHi [1822]Ag 21 1830-33;F 27 1861;F 19 1862;D 31 1862;64-65;Ja 17 1879
OHi Mr 15 1823-N 13 1824;Je 1850-Je,Jl 25 1855-61;66-S 1873;74-1917
OOxM Ap 14 1827;Jl 24 1833-Je 1834
WHi O 27-N 3 1821

Steubenville **HERALD-STAR.** d 1847+
1847-98 as Steubenville daily herald (title varies slightly)
DLC 1868
MWA D 24 1852
OClWHi N 21,23 1865;S 4 1911
OHi Ja 1 1901;Jl 1914-F 1916;My-Jl 1922;Je 19 1928+
WHi Mr 26,28 O 22 1850;S 11 1851;N 8 1886

LOG CABIN farmer. w 1840||
Campaign paper
DLC Ap 30,My 7,S 24 1840
MWA Jl 2 1840
MdHi Ap-O 29 1840
OClWHi My 7,Je 11,25,S 15 1840

Steubenville daily **MESSENGER.** d 1850?-
MWA D 17 1852

Steubenville daily **NEWS.** d 1871-73||?
MWA Jl 26 1873

Steubenville weekly **NEWS.** w 1871-73||?
OHi 1872-O 3 1873

OHIO republican ledger. w 1826?-
1826?-29? Steubenville republican ledger
CSmH Ag 25 1830
MWA S 24 1828;Ja 7 1829
OClWHi F 27 1828

PLOW and hammer. w 1839?-
OClWHi O 1 1840

Steubenville **REPUBLICAN ledger.** *See* Ohio republican ledger

Steubenville morning **STAR.** d 1889-98||
United with Steubenville daily herald to form Steubenville herald-star

TRUE American. Ja 4 1855-
OClWHi 1855-61

Steubenville morning **UNION.** d 1852?-
MWA D 25 1852

WESTERN herald. *See* Steubenville herald

STRASBURG

Strasburg **RECORD.** w My 8 1907+
pub 1907+
OHi 1928+

STRUTHERS

Struthers **JOURNAL.** w 1928+
OHi Ap 11 1928-33

TIFFIN

ADVERTISER-TRIBUNE. d My 3 1886+
1886-Ja 6 1933 as Daily advertiser
pub 1886+
OClWHi My 9 1901
OHi Ja 2 1901;Je 1914-Ja,Je 1915-F 1916;D 12 1919-22
—w ed *See* Seneca advertiser

Tiffin **FAMILY newspaper and whig.** w 1848?-
MWA S 24 1852
NNHi Ja 30 1852

Tiffin **GAZETTE.** *See* Seneca advertiser

Evening **HERALD.** *See* Tiffin tribune

INDEPENDENT chronicle and Seneca advertiser. *See* Seneca advertiser

PLOW and hammer. w 1889-93||?
WHi [S 17-D 3 1890]Ja-My 24 1893

SENECA advertiser. w,sw Ag 4 1832-D 26 1919||
1832-Ap 19 1834 as Seneca patriot; Ap 26 1834-N 1835 Independent chronicle and Seneca advertiser; N 1835-F 1838 Tiffin gazette, Mr? 1838-Ap? 1842 Tiffin gazette and Seneca advertiser
sw 1891?-1900?
DLC My 10 1834;N 28 1840
IU Ag 20(extra)1842;D 22-29 1843;My 3,17-24, Ag 16 1844
MWA Mr 28 1835;S 3 1852
OCHi F 19-26,Mr 26,Jl 30,N 5,19 1847;Je 16-23,Ag 25,N 10 1848;S 6 1850
OClWHi My 3 1844;Ap 17 1846;O 13,D 5-15 1848;D 4 1857;Ap 20 1865;Ja 30 1879;Ap 12 1892
OHi My 31 1850-Ap 1854;O 19 1855-O 16 1863; My 1867-Ap 22 1869;My 1872-D 11 1919
PPL N 8 1850
—d ed *See* Advertiser-tribune

SENECA patriot. *See* Seneca advertiser

Tiffin weekly **TRIBUNE.** w 1848-1918||?
MWA O 10 1856
NbHi S 18,Jl 25 1872
OCHi N 1868-69
OClWHi My 2 1872
OHi O 11 1861-O 11 1866;O 22 1869-Ag 18 1903;04-18

Tiffin **TRIBUNE.** d 1877-Ja 1933||?
1877-86? as Evening herald; 1887?-N 7 1921 Tiffin daily tribune and herald. United with Daily advertiser to form Advertiser-tribune
OClWHi Ap 23 1878
OHi Ja 2 1901;20-25
WHi Mr 6 1886

TIRO

Tiro **WORLD.** w Ag 1 1911+
pub 1911+

TOLEDO

AMERYKA-ECHO. w 1888-1927||?
1888-89? as Gwiazda; 1890?-1903? Ameryka
In Polish
OHi Ja 2 1901
OT 1888-93;95-96;99-1900;03-04
PPCHi [1890]-[92-93]

AMERYKA-ECHO. d,w 1915?+
d 1915?-33?
In Polish
IU D 4 1917-O 24 1922

Toledo evening **BEE.** d 1876-Je 7 1903||
United with Toledo daily news to form Toledo news-bee
KHi S 16 1886
OClWHi Ag 21 1890
OHi Jl 1898-1903
OT Jl-D 1890;Jl 1891-Je 1897;98-99;Je 13 1900-03
WHi S 3-4,N 19,D 1,31 1888;Ja 1,F 1,9,Mr 2,4,25 1889

Toledo weekly **BLADE.** w 1836-1923||?
1840-52 as Toledo blade
DLC D 9 1840,O 28-N 4 1852;N 28 1867
ICN 1865
IU F 4 1842;D 25 1856;O 14 1858;My 17 1860
KHi Jl 24-O 15 1879;S 16 1886;D 5 1895;O 1 1896;F 1 1906
MWA Ja 6 1853;Jl 4 1867[Jl 1868-69]N 23 1876;S 5,19,O 3 1878;O 26 1882;D 12 1889 Ja-O 1890
MiU-C [1868-69]
MnHi N 3 1870
N S 2 1842
NbHi O 15,N 5,16 1868;Jl 8 1869
NcU [1870]My 23,Je 6 1872
OClWHi 1877-N 20 1879;F 17-D 1881;Ja 12-19,Ag 24,N 23 1882;F 1-8 1883[85-86;98]O 29 1903;Ap 1914-Ap 1,D 9 1915;S 14,O 19 1916
PLhT Ja 2 1868
PPL Mr 17-24,Ap 7-14 1870
PWC N 5 1868
TJT Ja-Mr 14,Ap-N 7 1878;Ap-My 8,D 18-25 1879;N-D 1877;Ja 1 1880;Ap-Je 1881;Mr-Je 1893;D 23 1897
WHi Jl 12 1844;Mr 10 1870-Mr 2 1871;Mr 1884-Mr 1886;S 4 1888;Jl 1892-96

Toledo tri-weekly **BLADE.** tw 1846-81||?
CU-B D 29 1847
OClWHi S 4 1846;O 1 1866

Toledo **BLADE.** d 1848+
Title varies slightly
pub 1848—
CL F 11 1864
CU-B Ag 31 1848;S 6 1851;Mr 3 1864;Jl 26 1866;Ap 25 1870;S 14,17-18 1901
DLC Jl-D 1866;68-72;Jl 1873-Je 1874;98
ICN 1865
MBAt Ap 15,18,20 1865
MWA N 29 1852;My 12 1860;Jl 8 1867;My 11 1869;Ja 2 1875;Ag 18 1876
MiU 1892-96[98-99]
MiU-C Ag 6 1868
OCHi Ja 2 1875
OClWHi F 23 1861;Mr 27 1864;O 3 1866;Jl 30,O 15 1868; Mr-D 1870 Ja 26,Ag 24 1871; Je 13 1872-[73-74]-N 23 1876;Mr 22 1879;F 5,Ap 1 1880;Ag 31 1908
OHi Je 1 1850;S 28 1854;O 27 1856-65;S 24 1868;73;Jl 1890-Je 15 1916;17-S 1918;Jl 1919+
OMauA Ag 21,O 7 1848
OT My 1837-F,My 1846-N 1849;Je-D 1850; 52-72;My 24 1875-O 1876;81+
VU D 6 1877
WHi F 3 1868

Toledo **COMMERCIAL.** w 1849-96||?
1849-52 as Toledo commercial republican; 1880?-82? Toledo telegram; 1883?-84? Commercial telegram
Suspended from 1858-62
OHi Mr 13 1880;N 1 1883
OOxM O 31 1872
TJT Mr 4 1886

Toledo tri-weekly **COMMERCIAL.** tw -1878||?
OClWHi O 8 1866

Toledo **COMMERCIAL republican.** d *See* Toledo times

Sunday morning **COURIER.** *See* Toledo Sunday journal 1893-1908

Sunday **DEMOCRAT.** w 1875-80||?
OClWHi O 1 1876

EGYETERTES. *See under* Homestead, Pa.

Toledo **EXPRESS.** w,d 1853?-1917||?
1853?-D 26 1856 as Ohio staats-zeitung (w)
In German
MWA Ag 22 1876
OT 1854-My 1857;O 9 1871-77;Jl 1878-S 1879; 80-Je 1882;83; O1889-Je 1890 Jl 1891-Je 1895; 96-Je,O 1910-11;O 1912-Mr 1913

Toledo **EXPRESS.** w 1853+
In German
NN 1903 (goldenes jubiläum ed)
OHi Ja 2 1901;Jl 1803-09;Jl-S 1910[18-19]
OT 1867-73

Toledo **FREIE presse.** d 1887-90||?
In German
OT Jl 1888-Je 1889

Toledo **GAZETTE.** w 1835?-
OHi Mr 12,25,Jl 2,30,N 12 1836

GWIADZA. *See* Ameryka-echo

Toledo **HERALD.** w S 14 1841-44||
1841-N 1843 as Toledo register
DLC S 14-21 1841
IU Ja 11 1842
OT S 14 1841-My 8 1844

INDUSTRIAL news. w 1878-95||
1889-90 as Industrial news and household companion
WHi O 10,24,N 21-D 5 1885;F 13 1886-Mr 21,Je 13 1889
—d ed *See* Toledo news-bee

Toledo Sunday **JOURNAL.** w 1868-99||?
United with Sunday morning courier to form Sunday courier-journal, later Toledo Sunday journal
KHi S 1886
OClWHi Ag 27-S 3 1876
OT Ag-S 3 1876

Toledo Sunday **JOURNAL.** 1893-1908||?
1893-98? as Sunday morning courier; 1900?-08? Sunday courier-journal
OHi Ja 6 1901
OT My-D 1907

KURYER katolicki. *See* Kuryer Toledoski

KURYER Toledoski. w 1900-26||?
1900-D 25 1924 as Kuryer katolicki
In Polish
IU Mr 14 1918-Ja 14 1926

Toledo **NATIONAL.** w 1877-
NcD Ja 26 1878

Toledo **NEWS-BEE.** d 1888+
1888-Je 7 1902 as Toledo evening news
DLC 1914+
IU Je 26 1896
OHi Ja 1901;Je 8 1903+
OT Ap 1912-Mr 1913;D 1919-Jl,O 1920-Ap, Jl 1924+
—w ed *See* Industrial news

Toledo **NON-PARTISAN.** w Ap 22 1899-1900||?
Ap-S 9 1899 as Toledo Saturday night
OHi Ap-N 1899
WHi Ap 29-S 9,O 7,28 1899

NORTHERN Ohio democrat. d 1876||?
DLC O 8,N 1 1876
OClWHi S 18,O 4,8,N 1,8,15 1876
OT [My 14-D 10 1876]

OHIO staats-zeitung. *See* Toledo express d

Toledo **REGISTER.** *See* Toledo herald

Toledo weekly **REPUBLICAN.** w 1847?-
MWA N 1 1852

Sunday morning **REVIEW.** sw,w 1875-79||?
Title varies slightly
sw 1876?-77?
MWA D 16 1877

Toledo **SATURDAY night.** *See* Toledo non-partisan

SOCIALIST. *See* Workingman's paper (Seattle)

Toledo **TELEGRAM.** d *See* Toledo times

Toledo **TELEGRAM.** w *See* Toledo commercial

OHIO (*Continued*)

TOLEDO—*Continued*

Toledo **TIMES.** d 1849+
1849-58 as Toledo commercial republican; 1862-99 Toledo daily commercial (1880?-82? Toledo telegram; 1883-84? Commercial telegram; other variations slight)
Suspended from 1858-62
pub 1914+
CU-B N 24,28 1855;S 20-21 1881;S 14,16 1901
DLC O 23,N 2 1852;Ja-Ap 1898
ICHi Jl 1 1865
KHi Ap 6 1872;S 19 1886;Ja 16 1887
MWA Ag 28 1852;S 8 1874
NN S 26 1881
NNY-H 1871-Je 1873
NcU Ja 31 1876-Ja 1878
OClWHi O 10 1866;O 1,3 1879;Ag 21 1890
OHi 1866-75;Ja 29 1892-Je 1899;Ja 1 1901;My-S 1914;Je 19 1926-27
OT My 24 1875-F 1877;Jl 1890-Je 1892;Jl 1898-Mr,Jl 1899-Mr 1900;Ja-Je,Ag-O 1918;Ja-Je,Ag 1919+
WHi F 22-23 1878
—w ed *See* Toledo commercial

Toledo es **VIDEKE.** w 1922-26||?
In Hungarian
PPiHi [D 13 1923-D 23 1925]

TORONTO

Toronto **TRIBUNE.** w 1879+
pub 1879+

Toronto daily **TRIBUNE.** w 1890+
pub 1890+
OHi Ja 1 1901

TROY

Troy **DEMOCRAT.** w 1880+
OHi Ja 3 1901
—d ed *See* Daily news

HERALD. w S 27 1845-
MWA S 27 1845

MIAMI reporter. w My 19? 1827-
MWA Je 16 1827

MIAMI union. w Ja 1 1865+
pub 1865+
OHi Ja 6,S 15,O 13-20,N 17-24 1877;O 11 1879; Ja 3 1901
WHi Je 18 1887
—d ed *See* Daily news

MIAMIAN. w 1839-
DLC My 18 1840

Daily **NEWS.** d 1909+
pub My 1914+
—w ed *See* Troy democrat; Miami union

Troy **OHIO** times. *See* Troy times

Troy **TIMES.** w 1830?-71||?
1830?-34? as Troy Ohio times
DLC Jl 17,Ag 21 1833;36-70;Je 15-22,Jl 20-Ag 10 1871
MDeHi Ag 30 1849;Ja 10 1850
MWA Je 23 1853
NNHi Je 18 1834
NbHi Mr 25 1847-Mr 8 1849
OClWHi D 25 1845-49
OHi Ag 19 1831-33[47-49]51;53-57;62-68
OTr Je 20 1838-Ja 1 1840;O 8 1845;Ap 16 1846-N 18 1847;Mr-D 18 1848;F 22,D 1849-My 16,D 5 1850
WHi Ag 3,31 1865

UHRICHSVILLE

Uhrichsville **CHRONICLE.** w S 1? 1865-1930||?
1865-99? as Tuscarawas chronicle
Early years dated also in New Philadelphia and Dennison
ICHi O 19 1871;O 15 1875
MWA D 28 1865
NcD Ja 7 1891
OClWHi O 5-12,N 2 1865;Ja 18-25,F 15-22,My 17,S 17 1866
OHi Ja 2 1901

TUSCARAWAS chronicle. *See* Uhrichsville chronicle

UNION VILLAGE

DAY star. ir
N D 26 1846
OClWHi Ja 16,30,F 13,Mr 4,20,Ap 12,21,My 5,26,Je 15,Jl 1 1847

UPPER SANDUSKY

Daily **CHIEF.** d F 17 1896+
pub 1899+
OHi 1896-F 15 1897

Weekly **CHIEF.** *See* Wyandot chief

DEMOCRATIC pioneer. *See* Wyandot union-republican

Die **GERMANIA.** w Je 12 1886-95||?
In German
OHi 1886-My 9,Ag 22-D 1895

Daily **UNION.** d 1890+
1900?-02? as Wyandot daily union; 1903?-16? Wyandot union-republican
OHi S 1919-F 1926;My 1929+
—w ed *See* Wyandot union; Wyandot union-republican

UNION. w *See* Wyandot union

WYANDOT chief. w,sw Ag 16 1879-1905||?
1879-87 as Weekly chief
w 1879-87
OHi Je 1880-My 14 1881;82-85;Ag 1886-Jl,O 25 1887-99
—d ed *See* Daily chief

WYANDOT county republican. *See* Wyandot union-republican

WYANDOT democrat union. *See* Wyandot union

WYANDOT pioneer. *See* Wyandot union-republican

WYANDOT daily republican. d 1902||?
United with Wyandot daily union to form Wyandot union-republican, later Daily union
—w ed *See* Wyandot union-republican

WYANDOT union. w 1857-1902||?
1857?-80? Wyandot democrat union; 1881?-82? Union. United with Wyandot county republican to form Wyandot union-republican
w 1857-85?
OHi N 13 1884

WYANDOT union-republican. w,tw 1845-1917||?
1845-53? as Democratic pioneer; 1853?-66? Wyandot pioneer; 1867?-1902? Wyandot county republican
w 1845-1912?
MWA D 24 1852
OHi My 4 1854;Jl 11 1889;Ja 3 1901
—d ed *See* Daily union; Wyandot daily republican

Wyandot union-republican. d *See* Daily union

URBANA

BUCKEYE democrat. w 1875||?
United with Urbana union and patron to form Union-democrat, later Champaign democrat

CHAMPAIGN democrat. w,sw Ap 26 1855+
1855-61? as Ohio state democrat; 1862?-74? Urbana union (1872? Democratic plaindealer) 1875? Urbana union and patron; 1876?-79? Union-democrat
OHi 1855-Mr 18 1858;Ap 1879-Mr 22 1883;My 1887-1909;S 21 1901-13

CHAMPAIGN republican. w Mr 17-D 28 1893||
United with Urbana citizen and gazette to form Citizen and gazette and Champaign republican
OHi 1893

Urbana daily **CITIZEN.** d 1883+
1893?-1909? as Urbana daily times-citizen
ICHi O 29 1889
OHi S 11 1893-D 10 1895;Jl-O 1914;15-16

CITIZEN and gazette and Champaign republican. w,sw Ap 24 1838-1914||?
1838-47? as Western citizen and Urbana gazette; 1848?-93 Urbana citizen and gazette
DLC Ap 24 1838;S 1 1840;D 27 1842
ICHi S 25 1836;N 16 1841;Je 3 1845;Ag 8 1851;Je 10 1875;F 14 1898
IU N 23 1847
MWA Ag 20 1852
NNHi Je 11-18,Jl 16-30 1863;Mr 27 1873
OClWHi Mr 3 1841
OHi Ap-My 20 1848;Ap 20 1849-Mr 1863;Mr 30 1865-Mr 14 1872;Mr 19 1874-Mr 15 1888; Mr 13 1890-93;95-My 1914
P-M D 16 1845
PLewL Ja 28 1840

COUNTRY collustrator and Mad-River courant. w 1831?-
1831? as County collustrator
DLC O 25 1832
ICHi O 19,D 7 1833;F 1,Je 7-14,O 25 1834
IU N 9 1833
NNHi Jl 7 1831

Urbana daily **DEMOCRAT.** d 1914-27||?
OHi Ja 12 1914-16;Je 1919-Ag 1920

DEMOCRATIC plaindealer. *See* Champaign democrat

MAD-RIVER courant. w 1820?-31||?
United with Country collustrator to form Country collustrator and Mad-River courant
DLC Jl 25,Ag 1,O 24 1829;Ja 9,D 4 1830;Ja 16 1831
IU Ap 29,Je 3,Jl 29,O 1,22,D 9 1824;N 21 1828
MWA Mr 2 1827
OClWHi Ap 6 1827

OHIO state democrat. *See* Champaign democrat

Urbana daily **TIMES.** d Mr 14-S 9? 1893||
United with Urbana daily citizen to form Urbana daily times-citizen, later Urbana daily citizen
OHi Mr-S 9 1893

Urbana daily **TIMES-CITIZEN.** *See* Urbana daily citizen

Urbana **UNION.** *See* Champaign democrat

WESTERN citizen and Urbana gazette. *See* Citizen and gazette and Champaign republican

UTICA

Utica **HERALD.** w 1878+
pub 1906-16;23+
OHi Ja 3 1901

VAN WERT

BUGLE. *See* Van Wert bulletin

Van Wert **BULLETIN.** w 1844-1932||?
1844-58? as Bugle; 1859?-68? Ohio weekly bulletin
w 1844?-89?
OHi Je 15,Ag 10,31 1864

Van Wert daily **BULLETIN.** d 1887+
OHi Jl 1919-F 1920

Van Wert **DEMOCRAT.** w 1849?-
MWA D 8 1852

Van Wert **DEMOCRAT.** w 1897-1903||?
United with Van Wert times to form Van Wert times-democrat
OHi Ja 1 1901

OHIO weekly bulletin. *See* Van Wert bulletin

Van Wert daily **TIMES.** d 1904+
pub 1904+
OHi Mr 13 1906-Mr 1911;12-Ag 1914;Jl-D 1919

Van Wert **TIMES-DEMOCRAT.** w,sw 1866-1914||?
1866-1903? as Van Wert times (w)
OClWHi Ap 28-Jl 14 1870
OHi Ja 4 1901

VERMILLION

Vermillion **BUGLE.** S 9 1876-
NN O 7-20,N 1876-F 9 1877
OClWHi 1876-Ja 1877

WADSWORTH

Wadsworth **BANNER-PRESS.** w 1885+
1885-Je 1906 as Wadsworth banner (1891? Wadsworth banner and enterprise)
pub O 1907+
OClWHi D 4 1903;F 27 1913-Je 12 1919
OHi Ja 4 1901

Wadsworth **ENTERPRISE.** w My 4 1866-90||
United with Wadsworth banner to form Wadsworth banner and enterprise, later Wadsworth banner-press
OClWHi Ap 21 1870;Ap 1878-F 1879;Mr 22-29,Ap 12-My 3,17,Jl 19-26 1882
WHi F 1876-Ap 1879

Wadsworth **NEWS.** w S 1924+
pub Ja 24 1929+

WAKEMAN

INDEPENDENT press. w 1876-1915||?
Early issues as Wakeman independent press
OClWHi Jl 8 1876;F 15 1913-Ja 1915

Wakeman **WORLD.** w Ja 30 1915-17||?
OClWHi 1915-Ja 1917

WAPAKONETA

AUGLAIZE county democrat. w 1848-1918||?
ICHi Jl 22 1864
OClWHi S 20 1857
OHi Ja 3 1901

AUGLAIZE county republican. w 1881-1928||?
1881-1927? as Auglaize republican
CLM F 12,26-Mr 12 1891
MWA D 15 1852
OHi Ja 3 1901

AUGLAIZE republican. *See* Auglaize county republican

WARREN

Warren daily **CHRONICLE.** d Ap 14 1883?-Ap 26 1924||
United with Warren daily tribune to form Tribune chronicle
OClWHi Ap 14 1883;84-Je,S 17-O 9 1886;87-93; Jl 1894-97;Jl 4 1898;99;Jl-D 1903;O 19,28 1907;Ag 29,N 2 1910;11;Mr 18-19 1912;N 11 1913;22-24
OHi Ja 1 1901;S 1919-24
OW 1884-1903
OWT 1884-88;1923-26

Warren **CONSTITUTION.** w Jl 15 1862-84||?
MWA Je 4,18 1867
NNHi S 9 1862;Jl 14,N 17-24 1863;Ja 5,F 2, Mr 29,O 25,N 29 1864;Mr 14,Ap 11,My 9,30-Je 6,Jl 18,S 19,N 14,D 5 1865;Ja 2,30-F 6,Mr 13-20,Ap 3,17,My 1,15 1866[67]F 18,Ap 28,My 12-19 1868;My 17 1870
NjHi Jl 2 1867
OHi 1862-Je 1870;72-75;77-78;83-84
OClWHi 1862-Ag 2,O 18 1864;Ja 24-F 7,Ap 4, My 23,Je 13-20,Jl 11,Ag 15 1865;Jl 10 1866-Ap 9 1867

LIBERTY herald. w S 14 1843-
Dated also in Ashtabula
DLC N 20 1844
MWA O 16-23,N 27,D 1-26 1844;Ja 16-30 1845
OClWHi S 21 1843-D 20 1845;Ja 17,F 21 1846

MAHONING VALLEY review. w 1887-92||?
OClWHi Ap 24-Je 1889;Jl 16,D 17-23 1891;Ja 7-14,28,F 18-25,Mr 31,Ap 21-Jl 1892

Evening **MERCURY.** w Ap 7? 1843-
OY Je 2,Jl 21-28 1843

Warren **NEWS-LETTER.** *See* Trumbull democrat

Warren **RECORD.** w Ja 14 1876-84||?
OClWHi 1876-78
OHi 1876-81

REPUBLICAN argus. w
OClWHi Ag-O 1836

SHARP-SHOOTER. w 1856||?
OHi Ag 1 1856

TAXPAYER'S guardian. w 1887-89||?
OClWHi O 24 1888-Ap 17 1889

OHIO (*Continued*)

WARREN—*Continued*

Warren TRIBUNE. w Ag 14 1876-1918||?
Title varies slightly
Je 1 1898 is centennial ed
OClWHi D 13 1876-Ja 18,Mr 8 1877;Ag 1878-Jl 1879;Mr 29 1881;Ap 20 1886-Ap 19 1887;O-N 1892;Ap 4,S 1-8,N 10,D 1 1893;Mr 23,Je 29,O 5-11 1894;Ja 25,Jl 26 1895-Jl 10,Ag 21,O 16 1896;Jl 2 1897[98-1902]-[04-05]-[07;09]S 22-29,O 20 1910;Je 8 1911;Ja 25,F 22 1912;Jl 22 1915 My 15 1916
OHi Ag 1876-Jl 1879;Jl 27 1880-Jl 16 1889; 93-99;1901 03-15

TRIBUNE chronicle. d 1891+
1876-Ap 28 1924 as Warren daily tribune
MWA S 10 1921
OClWHi N 26-27 1895;Je 20 1908;F 13-O 22 1913
OHi O 1900-Ja 1 1901;Ja-Mr 14 1925

TRUMBULL county whig. *See* Western Reserve transcript and whig

TRUMBULL democrat. w 1830?-62||?
1830-31? as Warren news-letter; 1832?-38? Warren news-letter and Trumbull county republican. Merged with Western Reserve chronicle
Ct [1836-37]
DLC Jl 26 1836;Jl 13,Ag 31 1841
ICHi Ja 12 1836
MWA Ag 28 1852;F 11 1854;Ag 14,S 25 1856;Jl 9,30 1857;Je 14 1860
N O 15 1833
NNHi Mr 12,Ag 20,S 24,N 5,19 1853;Ja 7,Ap 15,Ag 26 1854[55-60]Ja 31,Ap 4,O 10,D 26 1861
OClWHi My 11 1830-D 19 1836;Ja 31,Mr 7,Ap 4,My 16,Je 20,S 12,O 12 1837;Ja 9,F 6,27,Mr 27,Ap 24,S 11,O 16 1838;F 12 1839;Je 16 1840; Jl 13,Ag 31 1841;Ag 16 1842;Jl 28 1845;D 14 1846;Mr 8,Jl 12 1847;Je 1849-My 1850;Je 18, Ag 20 1853;Mr 24,Ap 28,O 13 1859;Ja-Ag 9 1860;Ja 24,Ap 18 1861-Ja 1862
OHi My 2 1831;Je 1850-My 1853;Je 1854-Ap, Je 14 1860-My 1861
OWT Je 1853-My 1854

TRUMP of fame. *See* Western Reserve chronicle

*WESTERN RESERVE chronicle. w Je 9 1812-1918||?
1812-S 27 1816 as Trump of fame; 1854?-55? Western Reserve chronicle and transcript
Je 9 1912 is centennial ed
CSmH N 3 1831
Ct S 4 1872
CtY My 9 1826(facsimile) Ag 28-S 4,D 4 1828
DLC Mr 5,My 23 1824;Mr 12,Jl 23,Ag 6-13,27, S 17,D 3 1828;Ja 21,Jl 22,Ag 19,S 23 1830;O 4 1832;D 27 1842
ICHi My 16-23,Ag 8,N 7 1833;Ap 23 1835
IU O 6 1831
MBAt O 4 1823 F 13,Je 25,Ag 27,D 31 1824 [26-27]
MWA Jl 14 1821;Ja 25 1827[49;52]Mr 28 1866; Je 9 1912
MnHi Ap 25 1850
NN N 10-17 1831
NNHi F 26,Mr 12-19,Ap 2,Jl 23,O 1,N 19 1862; F 4,Mr 11 1863;F 3-10,Mr 9,Je 8,Jl 6,O 5,N 2,23 1864;Ja 4,Je 7,S 13,27,O 25 1865;Mr 21,Ap 4,My 9 1866;Je 24,Ag 28-S 11,N 6-13,D 4-11 1867;F 19,Mr 13,D 23 1868
OClWHi 1827-43;Je 11 1844-51;Ag 4 1852;Ja 19,F 9-16,Ap 4 1853-Ja 3,Ap 4,25 1855-Mr 14,Jl 12 1861-1906;Mr 1912-Jl 1921
OHi O 18 1827;38;43-44;48-F 16 1853;Ag 23 1854-64;Ag 23 1865-Jl 1870;Ag 1871-85;87-89; 91-96;98-1914
OW Ag 23 1873-79;82-1904
OWT 1835-42

WESTERN RESERVE democrat. w Mr 30 1883+
OClWHi 1883-Mr 10 1904:09-22
OHi 1885-99;Ap 12 1900-15

WESTERN RESERVE transcript and whig. w O 23 1848-54||
1848-O 17 1851 as Trumbull county whig. United with Western Reserve chronicle to form Western Reserve chronicle and transcript, later Wester Reserve chronicle
DLC Je 17 1852-F 1854
MWA S 9 1852
OClWHi 1848-O 17 1851;F 5,Mr 18,Ap 1,Je 17 1852-F 1854
OHi Je 28 1850-Ag 16 1854
OY N 25 1852-53

WASHINGTON (FAYETTE COUNTY)
See WASHINGTON COURT HOUSE

WASHINGTON (GUERNSEY COUNTY)
See OLD WASHINGTON

WASHINGTON COURT HOUSE
Early years as Washington
(Fayette county)

Washington AURORA. w 1838?
IU Mr 16,Ap 20-My 4,18-Je 8,Jl 18,N 15-29 1839

CIRCULATOR. w Ja? 1838-
DLC D 15 1838
IU Je 30,Ag 11,S 15-22,D 22 1838;F 2-16 1839

CYCLONE-republican. w Ap 25 1888-N 30 1905||
1888-Ja 9 1889 as Cyclone; Ja 16 1889-D 29 1904 Cyclone and Fayette republican. United with Fayette county record to form Record-republican
OClWHi complete
OHi 1888-1904

DEMOCRATIC signal and literary compiler. w 1838?-
IU Je 11 1841

FAYETTE advertiser. *See* Washington daily news

FAYETTE county herald. w D 11 1858-1910||?
1858-N 29 1860 as Washington herald. Merged with Ohio state register
S 13 1885 is cyclone ed
DLC 1858-N 29 1860
IU N 6 1862
KHi Ja 26 1882
OClWHi 1858-N 1864;N 29 1866-N 19 1868; Je 30 1870;Je 1 1876;N 13 1879-N 3 1881
OHi My 10 1866;Mr 14 1867-N 14 1872;My 29 1873-Ap 8,N 4,D 30 1880-Mr 17 1881;S 13 1885
—d ed *See* Washington Court House herald

FAYETTE county record. *See* Record-republican

FAYETTE democrat. w Ap 11? 1840-
IU My 9,22-Je,Jl 24-Ag 21,S 16-30,Ag 14-28 1840
OClWHi Ap 18 1840

FAYETTE democrat. w 1888?-99||?
1888-94? as Fayette register-democrat
IU Ap 27 1888

FAYETTE new era. *See* Ohio state register

FAYETTE register-democrat. *See* Fayette democrat 1888-99

FAYETTE republican. w Mr 14? 1840-
IU Je 13-Jl 4 1840

FAYETTE republican. w 1879-Ja 1889||
United with Cyclone to form Cyclone and Fayette republican, later Cyclone-republican
OClWHi S 14 1881-Je 22 1886

FREEDOM'S advocate. w 1829-
DLC D 19 1829

GENIUS of liberty. w Ag 2? 1834-
IU Ag 9,O 18-25,N 8 1834;Ja 9,Ap 18,30,My 21,Je 11,Jl 2 1836

Washington Court House HERALD. d 1885+
pub Ag 1910+

Washington Court House HERALD. w *See* Fayette county herald

HERALD and Fayette county register. w O 6? 1832-
IU O 13-27,N 17-D 1 1832;N 29,D 27 1833;Mr 7,Ap 25, My 23,Je 11,25,Jl 9-30,O 1-8,N 6-20 1834;Ja 8,Ap 2,16,My 14,Jl 2,S 24 1835;Ja 7 1836
OHi N 17 1832

Washington daily NEWS. d Jl 26 1907-17||?
1907-13? as Fayette advertiser; 1914?-Je 23? 1917 Daily news-advertiser
OClWHi N 12 1909;Ja-Je 23,25 1917
OHi 1907-Jl 17 1908

OHIO state register. w 1849-1927||?
1849-Mr? 1855 as Fayette new era; Mr 15 1855-Je 1864; Washington register; 1871-D 24 1874 Register and peoples advocate
IU O 9-16 1862
OClWHi Ja-Mr 17 1853;55-F 1861;N 2 1871; F 1899-1908
OHi Ja 27 1859;Mr 8 1866-74;Ja 1 1880;1903-17
—d ed *See* Washington evening register

PEOPLE'S palladium. w Ag 26? 1831-
ICHi Ja 28 1832
IU S 23 1831;Ap 21,Je 2-16,30-Jl 14,28-Ag, S 8-15,29 1832

RECORD-REPUBLICAN. w,sw 1901+
1901-D 5 1905 as Fayette county record w 1901-Ag 15 1907
OClWHi Ag 18 1904-D 5 1905;07;09;Mr 11, Je 21 1921
OHi D 1905-06

Washington evening REGISTER. d My 7 1900-
OClWHi My-Jl 14 1900

Washington REGISTER. w *See* Ohio state register

WASHINGTONIAN. w Ag 8 1840-
DLC Jl 10,Ag 7 1841
IU Ag 8-D 5,19-26 1840;Ja 16-Ap 10,My 1-8, 29,Je 12,26,Jl 10-24 1841;Ja 13,27-F 10,Ap 13 1844
OClWHi D 5 1840;Ja 9 1841

WATERVILLE

Waterville CHRONICLE. *See* Waterville times and chronicle

Waterville TIMES and chronicle. w 1914+
1914-24? as Waterville times; 1925? Waterville chronicle
OMauM 1925+

WAUSEON

DEMOCRATIC expositor. *See* Fulton county expositor

FULTON county expositor. w,sw Ja 1 1875+
1875-1928? as Democratic expositor sw 1918?-20?
OClWHi N 9 1876
OHi 1875-Ja 2,Jl 1914-20;23-26;28-29

FULTON county tribune. w 1883-1925||?
OHi 1902-24

NORTHWESTERN republican. *See* Wauseon republican

Wauseon REPUBLICAN. w 1854+
1854-93? as Northwestern republican
OClWHi Mr 15 1884
OHi D 11 1873-N 13 1891;92-Ja 10 1902;Ja-S 13 1929

Wauseon SENTINEL. w 1856?-
MWA Je 12 1857

WAVERLY

Waverly COURIER. w D 12 1889-Ap 1896||
United with Waverly watchman to form Courier watchman, later Waverly democrat
OHi 1890-93

Waverly DEMOCRAT. w 1856-1915||?
1856-57? as Weekly Scioto Valley union; 1858?-61 Weekly Piketown union; 1867-Ap 9? 1896 Waverly watchman; Ap 16 1896-1906 Courier watchman
1856-61 pub in Piketon
IU D 3 1857;Ja 5,D 27 1860
OHi 1867-91;93-95;Ap 16 1896-F 23,Ap 1899-1904;S 20 1905-14

Waverly DEMOCRAT and Pike and Jackson advertiser. w Je 15? 1832-
Je?-O? 1832 as Waverly democrat
IU S 7-21,O 12,N 2,D 21 1832

Waverly NEWS. *See* Republican herald

PIKE county republican. *See* Republican herald

REPUBLICAN herald. w Ap 10? 1845+
1845-Jl? 1847 as Pike county tocsin; Ag? 1847-57? Piketon journal; 1858-Ap 6? 1893 Pike county republican (Mr? 1881-82? Republican); Ap 13 1893-O 1914 Waverly news
1845-57? pub in Piketon
pub 1879+
IU O 16 1845;Ja 1,28,Mr,Ap 9,O 15 1846;Ja 21-28,Ap 15,My 13,27,Je 31,Jl 8,S 30-O 14,N 18,D 23 1847;Ap 13,27,Je 8,29,Jl 13,Ag 31,S 28,D 7-14 1848;My 3,S 27,D 13 1849;F 15,Mr 7-14,Ap 4,18,My 9,Ag 8,22,O 17-24 1850;My 16 1851;F 24,Mr 10-17,Ap 7,21,Ag 11,S 8,22,O 13 1853;F 23,Mr 16-23,Ap 4 1854;N 12,D 6 1855; Ja 1 1863;S 5 1884;N 25 1887
OHi S 24 1868-S 14 1871;S 19 1872-81;83-92;Ap 13 1893-1917
WHi N 27 1845;Ja 8,Je 11 1846

Waverly WATCHMAN. 1867-96 *See* Waverly democrat 1856-1915

Waverly WATCHMAN. w S 15 1912+
pub 1912+
OHi 1913-17

WAYNESVILLE

MIAMI gazette. w 1860?+
Title varies: Miami gazette and Harveysburg reporter; Miami gazette and Waynesville news
OClWHi Ja 30 1907
OHi S 10 1879;Jl 21 1880;Ja 2 1901

MIAMI visitor. w 1849?-
MWA S 8 1852

WEINSBURG

Der DEUTSCHE in Holmes. w
MWA D 9 1852

WELLINGTON

CHEESE CITY courier. w N 10 1894-96||?
OClWHi 1894-96

Wellington ENTERPRISE. w,sw S 19 1867+
1900? Wellington enterprise and observer w 1867-Ap 15 1919
OClWHi S-O 15 1867;F 4 1868;Mr 7 1872;Ja 2,S 10,O 9 1884;89-93;Jl 1894-99;Ja 10,Jl 25 1900;Ag 28 1901;Ap 9 1902;04-08;Jl 1910-Mr 10,S 1927-34
OHi Ja 2 1901

Wellington JOURNAL. w Mr 11? 1852-54||?
MWA S 23 1852
OClWHi Ap 1,Ag 12 1852

OBSERVER. w 1898-99||?
United with Wellington enterprise to form Wellington enterprise and observer, later Wellington enterprise
OClWHi N 15 1898-Je,O-D 1899

WELLSTON

Wellston REPUBLICAN. *See* Wellston telegram

Wellston SENTINEL. w 1883-1920||?
OHi 1895-1916

Daily SENTINEL. d Ja 7 1901+
OHi 1901-Je 19 1905;06-Je 1908;09-10;12-Je 1914;Jl 1915-22;24-34

Wellston TELEGRAM. w 1889+
1889 as Coalton times (Coalton) 1890-92 Welston republican
pub 1893;Ag 1898+
CHi Ja 1 1901;15-16;18-20;22-33

WELLSVILLE

Wellsville COMMERCIAL advertiser and farmers and mechanics register. w? 1837?-
OClWHi Je 18 1839
PPiHi D 22 1835

Wellsville NEWS. d N 23 1926+
pub 1926+
MWA F 5 1932

OHIO (*Continued*)

WELLSVILLE—*Continued*

Wellsville PATRIOT. w 1845?-
MWA D 14 1852;Ap 2 1861
OHi F 15 1853;D 12 1854

Evening RECORD. d 1898-1903‖?
United with Daily union to form Union-record, later Wellsville union
OHi 1902-03

Wellsville STANDARD. d 1892-95‖?
OHi My 1892-93

UNION. w S 3 1863-1912‖?
OClWHi 1863-Ag 20 1868
OHi F 11 1882-My 1884;Je 12 1885-Je 8 1888; Je 27 1890-My 3 1898;Je 1903-11

Wellsville UNION. d,tw 1886+
1886-1903? as Daily union; 1904? Union-record
d 1886-1918
OHi 1891-98;N 1899-1904;08-13

WEST ALEXANDRIA

West Alexandria RECORD. w Ja 27 1905-12‖?
OHi 1905-Je 3 1910

TWIN VALLEY echo. w Mr 3 1898+
OHi [1898-1901]-N 1924;25-31

WEST LIBERTY

West Liberty BANNER. w D 21 1882+
pub 1882+
OHi Ja 3 1901

MAC-A-CHEEK press. *See* West Liberty press

West Liberty PRESS. w 1858-69‖?
1858-66? as Mac-a-Cheek press
ICHi Ja 14 1860
OHi 1860-Mr 1861;O 1865-S 21 1866

WEST MILTON

West Milton RECORD. w 1892+
pub Ap 1902+
OHi Ja 2 1901;S 25 1918+

WEST UNION

ADAMS county democrat. w Jl 11? 1844-
IU Ag 22-29 1844
MWA Ja 26 1852
NNHi Ap 30 1858
OClWHi D 23 1847;D 31 1859
OHi D 24 1846-O 1851;52-O 7 1859

ADAMS county new era. w 1877-1909‖?
1877-82? as New era
OHi Je 16 1893;Ja 19 1894;Ag 26 1898;Ja 4,F 1 1901;S 5 1902

ADAMS county news. w Ap 26 1928+
OHi 1928;S 12 1929+

ADAMS county record. w 1902-1920‖?
OClWHi Ag 11-18 1910
OHi N 26 1903;S 6,O 25 1906;Ag 11 1910; Ag 31 1911;D 25 1913-O 1914;Jl 12 1917

COURIER of liberty. *See* West-Union register

DEMOCRATIC union. w F 17 1860-
OClWHi Ap 11 1862-N 6 1863;Mr-My 5 1865
OHi 1860-O 13 1865

FARMERS chronicle and advocate of internal improvement and domestic manufactures. w Je 17 1823-
Je 17 1828-Jl? 1829 Village register and advocate of internal improvement and domestic economy; Ag? 1829-Ja? 1830 Village register and Adams county anti-masonic investigator
DLC D 9 1823;Ap,My 11,Je 1-15,Jl 20-27 1824; Ja 19,Jl 16 1829
IU Ag 25,D 22 1828;Ja 12,26 1829
MWA My 16 1826
OCHi 1823-Je 20 1826
OClWHi S 30 1823;Ag 28 1824;Ja 4 1825;Ag 13 1829;F 18 1830
OHi [Mr 23 1824-Jl 7 1828]
PPiU-D [1823-My 1828]-Ap 2 1829;D 14 1830; F 24,Mr 31,My 19 1831

West Union FREE press. w 1835?-
OHi S 21 1838

West Union INTELLIGENCER. w 1841?-
IU F 2(extra)1844
OClWHi N 27 1845
OHi D 14 1842;N 2 1843;Ag 25 1844;O 30 1845-Mr 14 1849

JUVENILE journal. w 1825?-
OHi O 29 1825

NEW era. *See* Adams county new era

PEOPLE'S defender. w Ja 16 1866+
MWA My 19 1932
OClWHi My 19 1932
OHi Mr 2-9,Ap 20-27,Je 15,29-Jl 20 1866;D 21-28 1882;F 9,Je 14 1888-Ap 17,Jl 1890-1927; Ap 12-26 1928;S 1929+

PEOPLES intelligencer. w Ap 24 1851-
OHi 1851-Je 9 1852

*POLITICAL censor. w Mr 1815-
PPiU-D F 1 1821;Ap 18,Jl 18 1822;F 25 1823

West-Union REGISTER. w F 21 1831-
F-Ap 1831? as Courier of liberty
OHi 1831-Ap 1832
PPiU-D N 5,19 1831;Mr 3,My 5,19,Je 2,Jl 13 1832;Ap 19,My 10-17,31,Jl 12-26,Ag 23 1833; Mr 8,O 21 1834

West Union REPUBLICAN. w 1839?-
OHi N 15 1839;N 24 1841

West Union SCION. w 1853-1902‖?
1853-58? as Scion of temperance; 1859?-68? Scion
MWA S 19 1862;Mr 25 1864;Ap 21 1865;F 2 1866
OClWHi Je 1853-Ap 14 1854;D 7 1855;F 15 1856-Ja 16,Mr 1857-N 12 1858;D 8 1859-[60] Je 28,O 11,N 8 1861;Mr 21 1862-O 14 1864;Ja-Je 16,O 20 1865-F,Ag 9 1867-O 23 1868;N 29 1883;Ja 17 1884;Ja 22 1885;N 20 1902
OHi Je 24 1859;N 13 1863;F 25 1875;Ag 10 1876;Mr 1 1877;Ag 15 1878;S 11 1879;Je 15 1893;Ja 4,18 1894;N 20 1902

VILLAGE register. *See* Farmers chronicle

WEST UNITY

West Unity CHIEF. *See* West Unity reporter

West Unity EAGLE. *See* West Unity reporter

West Unity REPORTER. w Mr 20? 1878+
1878-Ag? 1885 as West Unity eagle (title varies slightly) S? 1885-Je? 1890 West Unity chief
IU Ap 1878-F 16 1916
OHi Ja 2 1901

WILLIAMS democrat. w O 16? 1852-
MWA D 18 1852

WESTERVILLE

Westerville BANNER. *See* Public opinion

NEMESIS. w Je 27 1860-
OHi Je 27 1860

PUBLIC opinion. w 1869+
1869-78? as Westerville banner; 1879?-84? Westerville review
pub 1890+
MWA Ag 25-S 1 1876
OClWHi O 24 1929
OHi [1888;96-97;1900;03;05;08;10]

Westerville REVIEW. *See* Public opinion

WHITEHOUSE

Whitehouse STANDARD. w 1925+
OMauM 1925-34

WILBERFORCE

OHIO standard and observer. *See under* Xenia

WILLARD

To 1918 as Chicago Junction

Willard TELEGRAPH. w 1912-19‖?
1912-18 as Chicago Junction telegraph
OClWHi Je 1916-O 6 1919

Willard TIMES. w 1883+
1883-1918 as Chicago times
pub 1883+
OClWHi F 20 1913-N 7 1919

WILLIAMSBURG

*FARMER'S friend. w F 1820-
IU Jl 21-Ag 4 1821

WESTERN herald. w F 18? 1848-
MWA Ap 15 1848

WILLIAMSPORT

Williamsport NEWS. 1886+
OClWHi Je 30 1921
OHi Ja 4 1901

Williamsport's RAG-BABY. Ag 11 1888-
IU Ag 11 1888

WILLOUGHBY

CITIZEN. w Ag 3- 1904‖?
OClWHi Ag-O 19 1904

DISTRICT gazette. w S 1875-79‖?
1875-78? as Willoughby gazette
OClWHi My 19 1876;Je-Jl 13,S 21 1878;D 10 1879
OHi S 17(extra)1878

Willoughby GAZETTE. sm,w O 1 1868-70‖
sm 1868?
OClWHi O 4,N 4 1869;F 1,Mr 15 1870

Willoughby GAZETTE 1875-78 *See* District gazette

INDEPENDENT. w Ap 18 1879-1920‖?
1879-1911? as Willoughby independent
OClWHi 1879-Mr 11,My 27,Jl 22 1904;Ja 27, Mr 17 1905-Mr 2 1911;F 1913-My 1920

LAKE county republican herald. w,sw 1892+
1892-1927? as Willoughby republican
sw S 20 1927-F 28 1933
OClWHi Je 27 1919-28;30+
OHi Ag 5 1921;Ap 15 1930-32

Willoughby REPUBLICAN. *See* Lake county republican herald

WILMINGTON

Wilmington ARGUS. w N 11? 1824-
1824-27? as Western argus
DLC Ag 25 1827;Ja 9,Mr 13-20 1829
IU N 18 1826
InLHi Je 8-N 4 1826
OClWHi N 25 1824;Ja 20,S 29 1827;Je 7,Ag 30, O 11 1828

Wilmington BANNER. w Ag 17? 1848-
OClWHi Ag 31-S 14,28,O 12,N 2-9,23-D 7,28 1848-Ja,F 8,22-Ag 16 1849

CLINTON county democrat. w 1880+
OClWHi S 8 1880;S 23 1881;Ag 31 1883;F 8, Mr 21 1884;Je 9 1921
OHi 1888-89;My 1899-Ap 1900;Mr,Ja 3 1901;Mr 1906-N 1907;08-09;F 1910-S 1918;24

CLINTON democrat. w Ag 14? 1863-
OClWHi O 23 1863-Ap 1864

CLINTON republican. w 1838-1913‖
1838-39? as Western whig. United with Wilmington journal to form Journal-republican
DLC S 19 1840;N 13 1847-Ja 1850
IU Ag 19,S 2,16,N 11 1843[44]
NNHi My 15 1863
OClWHi Mr 13,Ap 10 1841;Mr 28 1846-70;Jl 31 1873;O 25 1877;Ap 28 1881
OHi N 17 1870-N 17 1881;92
OOxM S 25 1873-79

CLINTONIAN and farmer's repository. w N 26 1829-
1829? as Clintonian
CSmH Ap 31[!]1830
DLC N 26 1829

CONSTITUTIONAL republic. w? My 14? 1831-
OClWHi Je 18 1831

DEMOCRAT and herald. w 1832?-
Title varies: Democrat and railroad advocate
IU Je 7,21 1833
OClWHi Ap 19,My 10-24,Je 7 1833;Ja 23 1835; Ja 8,Ag 5 1836;37-38;Ja 11-25;Ap 1839-40

DEMOCRATIC advocate. w O 22 1852-
OClWHi O-D 2 1852

DEMOCRATIC star. w My 24? 1844-
OClWHi My 31-Ag,S 13,O 25-N 1 1844

Weekly EMPYREAN. w Ja 2 1850-
MWA F 14 1851
OClWHi Ja 2-16,F 1-8,Mr 8-Ap 5,My 1850-Jl 18,Ag 30 1851

FARMERS' herald. w? Ja 4? 1833-
OClWHi Ja 17 1833

GALAXY. 1821?-
IU My 27 1822
OClWHi Je 24,S 16 1822

Wilmington weekly GAZETTE. w 1870?-
OClWHi Mr 30,S 7 1871

HERALD of freedom. w O 31 1851-
OClWHi 1851-Ja,Mr 2 1855

Wilmington INDEPENDENT. w F 9 1855-
OClWHi F-My 4,Je-S 7,21-O 5,26-N 2,16 1855
OHi F 9,23-Mr 2,16-Ap 1855

INDEPENDENT. w Mr 23- 1872‖?
OClWHi Mr 23 1872

JOURNAL-REPUBLICAN. w 1868-1919‖
1868-1913 as Wilmington journal. United with Wilmington daily news to form Wilmington news journal
OClWHi Jl 1868-Mr 24,O 13 1869;F 23,Ag 31, O 5 1870;Je 1 1871;F 8 1872;D 15 1880;S 21 1881;Mr 26 1884-1917
OHi O 20 1871-Ja 1874;Ap 19 1877-Ap 1881;Mr 26 1884-Ag 1919
OOxM O 16 1873-79;Ja 14,28,F 18 1880

Wilmington NEWS journal. d 1915+
1915-19 as Wilmington daily news
OClWHi D 15 1916-Je 1919;Ap 24 1924
OHi O 14 1915-18;Ap-D 1919;Ja-Je 1925;26-28

PEOPLE'S advocate. w 1832?-
IU Je 8,Jl 5 1833

PEOPLE'S press. w My 29? 1847-
OClWHi Je 26,Jl 31-Ag 7,24,S 4 1847

Wilmington SPECTATOR. w 1823?-
DLC F 14,Mr 6,27,Je 3 1824
OOxM F 7 1824

TANNER and type. w
OClWHi S 18,26,O 3,10 1868

Wilmington WATCHMAN. w Ja? 1856-
OClWHi O 17 1856;My 15,Je 19,O 30 1857;Mr 19,Je 11,N 5 1858;Mr 4,Jl 1859-Jl 11 1861;Mr 13,D 25 1862

WESTERN argus. *See* Wilmington argus

WESTERN whig. *See* Clinton republican

WOODSFIELD

Woodsfield HERALD. w Ja 1 1858-
OHi [Ja-N 5 1858]

MONROE county republican. sw D 7 1899+
pub 1899+
OHi N 25 1912-N 15 1917;N 1918-S 23,N 12 1923-N 6 1924

MONROE courier. w 1905-12‖?
OHi 1911

MONROE democrat. *See* Monroe gazette

MONROE gazette. w 1873-1910‖?
1873-Jl 18 1879 as Monroe democrat
OClWHi N 3-10 1910
OHi Jl 30 1875-Jl 1 1897;Jl 1898-Jl 1902

Woodsfield REPUBLICAN. w My 25? 1860-
OHi S 14-28 1860

SPIRIT of democracy. w 1844+
OClWHi Je 24 1848;Jl 8 1863
OHi 1863-Ja 1891;F 1892-Ja 1893;F 1894-Ja 6 1901;Ja 12 1911-17

OHIO (*Continued*)

WOODVILLE

Woodville **NEWS.** w N 24 1924+
pub 1924+

WOOSTER

AMERICAN eagle. w O 11 1851-
OHi O 11,N 1-15,29-D 13,27 1851

Daily evening **DEMOCRAT.** d 1876?-
OClWHi Je 11-18 1879

Wooster **DEMOCRAT.** w *See* Wayne county democrat

DEMOCRATIC times. *See* Wayne county democrat

Der **DEMOKRAT.** w 1851?-
In German
MWA Ag 25 1852

JACKSONIAN. w 1881-1904||?
OClWHi D 27 1894-95

Wooster **JOURNAL** and democratic times. *See* Wayne county democrat

Wooster daily **NEWS.** d 1905-Ja 1920||?
United with Wooster daily republican to form Wooster daily record
OClWHi Jl 14-D 1905;D 10 1909
OHi Je-D 1919

OHIO citizen and farmers' register. w My 1? 1830-
CSmH Jl 3 1830
MB [Je 19-D 18 1830]

OHIO oracle. w Ap 28? 1826-
DLC O 3 1828;My 15 1829
OClWHi O 27 1826;Mr 23,Ap 27,Jl 13 1827

Wooster daily **RECORD.** d 1888+
1888-Ja 25 1920 as Wooster daily republican (title varies slightly)
OClWHi Jl 1888-My 1889;Je 3 1919;D 20 1921
OHi Je 1919-O 1920;Je 9 1928-Jl 1929

Wooster **REPUBLICAN.** w,sw -1918||?
sw Ap 5-D 27 1877
DLC Je 16 1859
OClWHi Ag-D 1852;My 19-Je 9 1853;54-N 1856;57-95;1900-08
OHi N 1 1855;Ag 20 1874;Jl 1 1875

Wooster **REPUBLICAN.** w
ODW F 15 1872

Wooster **REPUBLICAN.** w
WHi Je 16 1853-D 29 1859;Ja 2 1862-D 31 1863;Ja 4 1876-D 28 1876;Ja 3 1878;D 25 1879

Wooster daily **REPUBLICAN.** *See* Wooster daily record

REPUBLICAN advocate. w Ag 30 1826-
MWA Ja 26,Ap 26 1828
OClWHi Ag 30 1826;Ag 4-11,S 15 1827;Ja 5, Mr 29,Ag 23,N 22,D 22 1828;N 7 1829;My 15 1830-Ap 9,Je 18-O 8 1831;Je 9-16 1832;Ap 13 1833;My 31-Je 7,28 1834-Ap 11 1835
WHi My 1837-Ap 26 1838

Wooster and Wayne **SPECTATOR.** w -1825? as Wooster spectator
OClWHi My 10 1823-My 1824;Ja 8-Ap 2,My 14-Je,S 10,D 24 1825;Ja 14-F 1826

WAYNE county democrat. w,sw My 15? 1833-1916||?
1833? as Democratic times; 1834?-Ag? 1840 Wooster journal and democratic times; S? 1840-48? Wooster democrat
w 1833-1912?
DLC D 11 1833;Ja 29-F 5,Ap 2 1834;S 9-16 1840
MWA D 23 1852
OClWHi N 5 1834;Ap 28 1836-54;Mr 22 1855-Mr 13 1856;57-Mr 7 1861;Mr 13 1862-N 17 1864;65-Ja 4 1866;Ja 1,F 20,Mr 12 1868-76;79-1911
OHi D 6 1849;Jl 4 1867;Je 3 1869;D 3 1880;N 9 1881;N 10,12 1884;Mr 21 1888;Ja 29,N 27 1890;Ja 2 1901
WHi Mr 21 1850-Mr 13 1851;Ag 1852-Mr 7 1861;Jl 1862-Mr 3 1864;Mr 11 1869-F 18 1880
—d ed *See* Daily evening democrat

WAYNE county standard. w 1844?-
OClWHi F 26 1846

WESTERN telegraph. w 1833?-
ICHi Ja 14 1836
OClWHi Ap 26 1837

WORTHINGTON

COLUMBIAN advocate and Franklin chronicle. *See* Semi-weekly gazette (Delaware)

Worthington **NEWS.** w Ap 9 1925+
pub 1925+

WESTERN intelligencer. *See* Ohio state journal w (Columbus)

XENIA

BACKWOODSMAN and Greene county courant. w Mr 25? 1830-
CSmH Ag 12 1830
OCHi My 20 1830

CLINTONIAN and Xenia register. w O 19 1825-
N O 27 1825-Mr 23,Jl 12-S 20,O 13 1826
NN O 19 1825

Xenia **DEMOCRAT.** w -1872||?
United with Xenia news to form Xenia democrat-news

Xenia **DEMOCRAT-NEWS.** w 1872-D 31? 1894||
1872-73? as Xenia enterprise; 1874-77 Xenia news. United with Xenia herald to form Xenia herald and democrat-news
OHi Jl 17 1875-82;F 16 1884-94
OXG Ja 9-30 1875;S 15 1877

DEMOCRATIC spark. w? 1839?-
IU Jl 10 1840

Xenia **ENTERPRISE.** *See* Xenia democrat-news

FARMERS' record and Xenia gazette. w Ja? 1829-
DLC Mr 12,26,Jl 23-Ag 13,S 10,O 29,D 3,24 1829

Xenia **FREE PRESS.** *See* Ohio free press

Xenia **GAZETTE.** w,sw 1868-1920||?
Ag 10 1888-Je 17 1902 Xenia semi-weekly gazette and torchlight (other variations with frequency)
w 1868-My 25 1883
pub Ag 9 1878-Ag 1 1879;Ag 1880-Ag 19 1881;Ag 22 1882-Ag 21 1883
DLC Ja 17-Je 9 1899
OHi 1870-1912
OXG Ag 18 1868-Ja 21,Ag 1873-Ag 18 1882; Ag 24 1883-Je 17,Ag 1902-Jl 8 1905

Evening **GAZETTE.** d N 21 1881+
1881-Mr 18 1918 as Xenia daily gazette (1888?-1902? Xenia daily gazette and torchlight)
pub N 23 1881+
M Jl 5 1932
OClWHi Ap 6 1911
OHi N 1915-Jl 1916;S 1928-Ag 1929
OXG Mr 12 1932+

GREENE county gazette. w D 24 1835-
InRE My 26 1836
OXG 1835-Mr 1837

GREENE county journal. w? 1863?-
ICU O 1863-F 19 1864

GREENE county torch-light. *See* Semi-weekly torchlight

Xenia **HERALD** and democrat-news. w 1891+
1891-Ag 22 1907 Xenia herald (1895-Ja 1896 Xenia herald and democrat-news)
OClWHi Mr 6 1924
OHi 1895-1924

Xenia **NEWS.** w 1854?-
DLC Ag 19 1859

Xenia **NEWS** 1874-77 *See* Xenia democrat-news

OHIO free press. w O 15 1831-
1831-S 1 1838 as Xenia free press; S 8-N 1838 Free press
DLC D 1 1832;My 22 1841
OHi 1831-Mr 11 1843
IU N 22 1834
MWA Ap 20 1839

OHIO interior gazette. w? 1823?-
DLC S 21 1824

OHIO people's press. w My 24 1826-Ap 1840||?
Title varies: People's press and impartial expositor; Ohio people's press and political expositor; Ohio people's press and farmer's repository; Ohio people's press and Xenia gazette. United with Greene county torch-light to form Ohio people's press and Greene county torch-light, later Semi-weekly torchlight
DLC Ap 26,Jl 26,Ag 23 1827;D 9 1828;Ja 1 1829
IU S 27,D 9 1828
MWA My 3 1827
OCHi My 24 1827-D 9 1828
OXG 1826-F 14 1828;29
WHi Je 21 1826

OHIO people's press and Greene county torch-light. *See* Semi-weekly torchlight

OHIO standard and observer. w 1897-1903||?
Also dated in Wilberforce
Negro
DLC Ja 27 1900

PEOPLE'S press and impartial expositor. *See* Ohio people's press

Xenia **REGISTER** and patron of industry. w 1825?-
MWA Ja 17,F 14 1827

Xenia daily **REPUBLICAN.** w,d 1878-1926||?
1878-Ap 13 1880 as Xenia sunlight; Ap 20 1880-My 1881 Xenia weekly sunlight; Je-Ag 1881 Xenia weekly sunlight and Greene county republican; S 1881-Ap 10 1883 Xenia republican and weekly sunlight; Ap 17 1883-1912? Xenia republican
w 1878-1912?
OHi N 1879-O 13 1903;04-08;10-12;Ja 29 1914-Jl 1915

Xenia **SUNLIGHT.** *See* Xenia daily republican

THOMAS JEFFERSON. w 1844||?
NN Jl 18 1844

Semi-weekly **TORCHLIGHT.** w,sw S 1838-Ag 8 1888||
1838-My 8? 1839 as Greene county torch-light and Xenia advertiser; My 16? 1839-Je 15? 1843 Greene county torch-light (My 1840?- Ohio people's press and Greene county torch-light); Je 22? 1843-Ag 15 1883 Xenia torch-light. United with Xenia semi-weekly gazette to form Xenia semi-weekly gazette and torchlight, later Xenia gazette
w 1838-Ag 15 1883
DLC My 9 1839;Jl 18 1850;My 29-Je 5 1861
ICU Jl 1,15,29,Ag 12-S 2,16,O 7-14,D 30 1841-Ja 20 1842;Jl 31,O 23,D 4,18 1845-[46-D 19 1850]
MWA Ja 12,D 9 1839;S 8 1852
NNHi Jl 22 1863;Ap 9 1873
OClWHi F 1,Mr 26,Jl 4 1844
OHi N 12 1840-62;69-83;85-88
OXG My 23 1839-Ja 12 1843;Jl 1844-Je 18 1846;Je 22 1848-Je 13 1850;52-58;60-64;66-86
WHi S 12 1838-S 3 1840;Ap 12-19,D 20 1854

Daily **TORCHLIGHT.** d My 6 1884-88||?
United with Xenia daily gazette to form Xenia daily gazette and torchlight, later Evening gazette
OXG 1884-86

Xenia **TRANSCRIPT.** w F 16? 1833-
N O 26 1833
OClWHi D 28 1833

TRUE American. w F 14? 1855-
OClWHi My 2,Je 6,Jl 18-Ag 8,22-S 5,19-O 10,31-N 7,28-D 5 1855

WESTERN cornet and Xenia gazette. w S 21 1827-
DLC Ag 8 1828
MWA D 21 1827

YELLOW SPRINGS

Yellow Springs **NEWS.** w 1894+
MWA Ag 9 1934
OHi Ja 4 1901

YOUNGSTOWN

AMERIKAI Magyar hirlap. w 1912+
In Hungarian
OY 1920+

CITIZEN. w Je 24 1915-25||?
OY 1915-Je 11 1925

CITTADINO italo-americano. w 1902?-33||?
In Italian
OY 1920-D 23 1933

DEMOCRATIC union sentinel. *See* Mahoning sentinel (Canfield)

MAHONING county register. *See* Semi-weekly telegram

MAHONING courier. *See* Miner and manufacturer

MAHONING free democrat. *See* Semi-weekly telegram

MAHONING register. *See* Semi-weekly telegram

MAHONING sentinel. *See under* Canfield

MAHONING vindicator. *See* Youngstown vindicator

MINER and manufacturer. w 1865-N 1874||
1865-72? as Mahoning courier
OY Ag 23 1865-My 1869;Ja 31 1873

Daily **MINER** and manufacturer. d Je 1873-N 1874||
OY Ag 4 1873

NEW star. w My 28 1879-82||?
OY 1880[82]

Youngstown evening **NEWS.** d Jl 16 1877-Ja 20? 1882||
United with Youngstown daily register to form Youngstown daily news-register, later Youngstown telegram
OClWHi S 10 1880;Mr 15,Ap 30 1881
OY Ja 15-Jl 13 1878

Youngstown **NEWS.** w 1878-Ja 18 1882||
United with Youngstown register to form Youngstown news-register, later Semi-weekly telegram
OY 1881-Ja 4,18 1882

Youngstown daily **NEWS.** d Ap 6-N 30 1885||
United with Youngstown daily news-register to form Youngstown evening telegram, later Youngstown telegram
—w ed *See* Sunday morning

NEWS-REGISTER. *See* Telegram

OHIO republican. w 1847?-N 16 1852||
United with Democratic union sentinel to form Republican sentinel, later Mahoning sentinel (Canfield)
DLC O 15 1852
MWA S 5 1849
OClWHi Ja 19,Ap 26,Jl 12,Ag 9,S 13-27,O 18-N 1 1848;Mr 7,28,Jl 4,Ag 1,22,S 5,19 1849;Ap 26,My 10-17,Jl 5,Ag 16 1850;F 7,Ag 15 1851
OY My 21-Je,Jl 9-N 16 1852

OLIVE branch and new county advocate. w Ag 25 1843-45||?
DLC My 17 1844
IU S 1,15-22 1843;Ja 12-F 2,Mr 15,Ap 5 1844
OClWHi My 17 1844
OY Ag 25-S 1,15-N,D 8,22 1843-Mr 7 1845

REGISTER. *See* Telegram

REPUBLICAN sentinel. *See* Mahoning sentinel (Canfield)

ROMANUL. *See under* Cleveland

Youngstown **RUNDSCHAU.** w Ag 1874-1916||?
In German
IU D 2 1915
OHi Ja 3 1901
OY Ja 18 1884-1908

Youngstownske **SLOVENSKÉ** noviny. w 1910+
In Slovenian
OY 1920+

SUNDAY morning. w Ap 1882-N 29 1885||
United with Youngstown news-register to form Weekly telegram, later Semi-weekly telegram
—d ed *See* Youngstown daily news

OHIO (*Continued*)

YOUNGSTOWN—*Continued*

Semi-weekly TELEGRAM. w,sw,tw D 31 1852-1913‖?
1852-Ja? 1855 as Mahoning free democrat; F?-Ag? 1855 True American; Ag? 1855-Mr 1865 Mahoning county register; Ap 1865-F? 1875 Mahoning register; Mr? 1875-S 1880? Register and tribune; O 1880?-Ja 1882 Youngstown register; Ja 1882-N 30 1885 Youngstown news-register (other variations with frequency)
w 1852-92?;tw 1897?-98?
OClWHi Ja 7 1853;D 18 1855-[56-57]S 6 1860; My 23 1861;O 16-23 1862;Ja 1,29,F 12-19 1863;S 17 1874;S 3,D 9 1880;Je 30 1881
OHi Je 2 1864;92-95;Jl 1897-O 1898;99-1903; 06-09
OY 1852-Ja 3 1855;F 21 1856-57;Ja 21,F 1858-65;67-D 5 1872;73;Je 1874-F 18 1875;80-Jl,S 15-N 10,D 8,22 1881-F 14,Mr 14 1883-D 2 1885;87-Mr 23,S 19 1898-F 13 1913

Youngstown TELEGRAM. d D 1874-Jl 2 1936‖
1874-Ja 20? 1882 as Youngstown daily register; Ja 21 1882-N 30 1885 Youngstown daily news-register; D 1 1885-91? Youngstown evening telegram. United with Youngstown vindicator to form Youngstown vindicator and the Youngstown telegram
OClWHi F 1 1879;S 10 1880;Jl 2 1881;D 25 1883;S 11 1886;My 2 1895;Jl 4 1896;98;O 17,D 17,D 4 1914
OHi Ja 2,Mr 1901-S,D 1915-32
OXG Ja-Mr 1899;1903-36
OY O 14 1881-[Ja 1882]

Daily TIMES. d Ag 24 1903-04‖
OY Ag-D 22 1903

Youngstown TRIBUNE. w F 18 1874-F? 1875‖
United with Mahoning register to form Register and tribune, later Semi-weekly telegram

TRUE American. *See* Semi-weekly telegram

Youngstown VINDICATOR. w,sw Je 1869-1916‖?
1869-75 as Mahoning vindicator
w 1869-1901
OY [Je 1870-My 1871]-Ja 16,Ap-D 1874;80-Je 20 1910

Youngstown VINDICATOR and the Youngstown telegram. d S 23 1889+
1889-Jl 2 1836 as Youngstown vindicator
KHi My 23,Jl 17,31 1918
OClWHi F 1913+
OHi Ja 2 1901;Mr-Ap,Je,Ag-O,D 1914-Mr 11 1916;My-Jl 1922;Ag 3-12 1923;O 14 1926+
OY Mr-Ap 16,D 1903+
PP O 15 1928;34+

ZANESVILLE

Zanesville AURORA. *See* Zanesville signal

Zanesville CITY times. w S 4 1852-75‖?
MWA O 2 1852
OClWHi Jl 27 1861;S 30 1869;Ja 17 1873
OHi [1852-Ag 1855;56-Jl 1858]

Daily COMMERCIAL aurora. d Ja 11 1854-
PPiHi Ja 11 1854

***Weekly COURIER.** w D 30 1812-1913‖?
1812-Je 1820 Zanesville express and republican standard; Je 1820-Ja 1823? Express and public advertiser; Ja 11 1823-45? Ohio republican; 1845?-62? Weekly Zanesville courier; 1863? Zanesville courier and gazette
DLC N 22 1823;Je 27,D 26 1829;Ag 7 1830;O 6 1832;N 28 1840
IU Mr 16 1833;S 16-O 7,28-N 4,D 16 1843;Ja 6,20-F 10,Mr 2,Ap 27,My 25-Je 1,S 28,O 19 1844
KHi Jl 28 1882
MWA My 24,O 25 1823;Ja 24 1824;F 19 1825; F 24 1827;Mr 21 1829;Je 11 1831;Ja 21 1832; Ja 14 1853
OClWHi Ja 21 1837;Ap 18 1840;S 11 1841;F 19 1858;My 22 1863;Jl 4 1873;Ag 18 1875;Ap 20 1877;D 10 1880;Ag 1,S 12 1907;Ja 7,Ap 15, O 1909-O 13 1910
OHi [1823;32-34;36-37]Je 7 1845;Je 18 1852;My 27 1853;Ag 31 1855;My 23 1856;F 16-D 14 1893;96-1905;07-Jl 10 1913
OOxM [Jl 20 1833-Mr 1 1834]
WHi Ap 19 1823;Mr-Ap 3,Je 19-26,Jl 10 1830

Zanesville COURIER. tw Mr 31 1846-72‖?
1846-47 as Tri-weekly courier
OClWHi 1846-Mr 24 1849
OHi [Ap 16 1846-Ap 19 1851]
WHi F 8,O 20 1849

Zanesville COURIER. d Ag 7 1847-1915‖?
MWA S 1 1852;F 19 1863
OClWHi Mr 18 1863;Ja 2 1867;Je 26 1873;N 5,7-8 1877;S 16 1904;Ja 21 1915
OHi Ag-N 5 1847;D 22 1852-Jl 1853;O-D 1855; Ap 23 1860-68;70-75;Jl 1876-Ja 1915

Daily DEMOCRAT. d 1879?-
OHi O 31 1879

DEMOCRATIC union and Zanesville advertiser. *See* Zanesville signal

Daily EXPERIMENT. d Mr 9 1846-
OCHi Mr-S 1 1846

Zanesville EXPRESS and republican standard. *See* Weekly courier

Zanesville GAZETTE. w 1831-62‖?
United with Weekly Zanesville courier to form Zanesville courier and gazette, later Weekly courier
DLC O 17 1832;N 4 1840
IU O 12 1831;Mr 20-Ap 3 1833;My 8-15,N 27 1844;Ag 6 1845
MWA S 1 1852
MnHi Ag 4 1841
OClWHi Mr 16 1831;Ap 25-Jl,O 21 1835-Mr 17, N 15 1848;Je 2 1857
OHi My 8 1844;Ap 30 1845;47-50[My 1851-Ap 1856]

HARRISONIAN. w Ja 22- 1840‖?
Campaign paper
DLC Ja 29,Ag 26 1840
IU O 28 1840
OClWHi Ja 29,Je 17,Jl 29-Ag 5,O 7,22 1840

MUSKINGUM democrat. 1844-
DLC O 25 1844

***MUSKINGUM messenger and democratic republican.** w N 18 1809-37‖
1809-21? as Muskingum messenger (D 8 1810-Ap 1 1812 Muskingum messenger and Ohio intelligencer)
DLC N 3 1832;Jl 20 1833
IU My 28,O 15 1831
MWA Jl 29 1823;Mr 18,Jl 15,Ag 12,O 21 1826; Ja 27,F 24,Mr 10,My 19,Jl 27 1827;N 1 1828
NBHi Je 18 1822
NNHi F 5 1822
OClWHi Mr 28 1829;Mr 22,Ap 19,O 4 1834;D 15 1835;Ja 16 1836
PDoHi Mr 31 1827

OHIO family journal. w Ja 18? 1865-
OClWHi F 8-Mr,Jl 12 1865

OHIO republican. *See* Weekly courier

OHIO signal. *See* Zanesville signal

Weekly RECORDER. w 1884-Ja 1885‖?
United with Daily morning times to form Daily times recorder

Zanesville SIGNAL. w Jl 26 1834-1905‖?
1834-F 1836 as Democratic union and Zanesville advertiser; Mr 5 1836-63? Zanesville aurora; 1864? Ohio signal
Ct Jl 16 1836
DLC Ag 2 1834;N 3 1852
IU Mr 16,S 21 1838;Jl 10 1840;S 24 1841;Ja 4-18,F 1,15-22 1844;My 1 1845;Ja 4(extra) 1844
MWA Mr 12 1836;Je 22 1853;S 11-18 1874
OClWHi Ja 19 1849;Ap 14 1852;Ag 27 1858;Je 17 1859;Je 23 1871;Je 27 1873;Ag 20 1875;Je 1 1878
OHi [Jl 14 1848-O 5 1849]Ag 31 1865-77;F 1880-99;1903
WHi D 12 1867

Zanesville morning SIGNAL. d 1865-69‖
OHi Ja 10-Je 12 1866;F 25 1867-Ag 1869

Zanesville daily SIGNAL. d 1882+
Sunday issues as Sunday times signal
pub 1925+
MWA N 7 1889
OClWHi N 6 1918
OHi Mr 21 1882-S 1904;05-S 1909;Ja-Mr,O 1910-Mr,Jl 1920-24

Daily TIMES recorder. d 1877+
1877-Ja? 1885 as Daily morning times
pub 1925+
OClWHi Ag 21 1878;F 12 1880;Jl 23,27 1885; My 26 1914;My 22 1918
OHi Ja 1,Jl 1885-Je 1887;88-Je 1890;Jl 1891-Mr,Jl 28 1896-Je 1901;Ja-Mr 20,Jl 10-S 14 1902;03-06;Ap 1907-Je,O 1919-24

Sunday TIMES-SIGNAL. *See* Zanesville daily signal; Daily times recorder

Evening VISITOR. w Ja 30 1837-
1837 as Zanesville evening visitor
OClWHi Ja 30,Ap 1837-Jl 14 1838

WESTERN recorder. w? 1839?-
OClWHi Mr 25 1842

OKLAHOMA

ACHILLE

Achille PRESS. w 1913-23‖?
OkHi 1913[14;16;19-22]

ADA

Ada BULLETIN. w,sw S 1920+
sw Mr 15 1921-Ap 28 1923
pub 1920+
OkHi [1920-21]-[23-24]

Ada morning BULLETIN. d D 1 1920-23‖?
OkHi [1922-23]

Ada DEMOCRAT. w 1900-10‖?
1900-06? as Ada weekly star
OkHi [1904-07]-[10]

Ada ENTERPRISE. *See* Pontotoc county enterprise

INDIAN arbiter. *See* Oklahoma statesman

Ada weekly NEWS. w 1901+
OkHi [1904-05]+

Ada evening NEWS. d 1904+
OkHi [1904;06;20]+

OKLAHOMA statesman. w O 5 1905-06‖?
1905-O 1906 as Indian arbiter
OkHi [1905-06]

PONTOTOC county enterprise. w My 1910-11‖?
1910-My 1911 as Ada enterprise
OkHi 1911

PONTOTOC county farmer. w F 3 1916-D 30 1920‖?
Merged with Ada bulletin?
OkAdB 1916-20
OkHi 1916-20

Ada REPUBLICAN. w 1910‖?
OkHi [1910]

SOUTHERN republican. sw S 14 1906-
OkHi [1906]

Ada weekly STAR. *See* Ada democrat

STAR democrat. w 1912-19‖?
OkHi [1913]-[19]

ADAIR

Adair AMERICAN. w 1913-14‖?
OkHi [1913-14]

Adair CITIZEN. w 1915?+
OkHi 1915-[23]+
pub S 26 1923+

Adair LEDGER. w 1904-N 1912‖?
F-Je 1905 as Adair weekly ledger. United with Big Cabin sentinel to form Big Cabin sentinel and Adair ledger (Big Cabin)
OkHi [1904-05]

ADDINGTON

Addington ADVERTISER. w 1909‖?
OkHi [1909]

Addington FREE LANCE. w 1905-06‖?
OkHi [1906]

Addington JOURNAL. w 1904‖?
OkHi [1904]

AFTON

Afton ADVANCE. *See* Afton climax

Afton AMERICAN. w 1908+
OkHi [1909]+

Afton CLIMAX. w,sw 1895-1908‖?
1895-97 as Afton advance
w 1895-1907?
OkHi [1905]-[08]

Afton DEMOCRAT. w 1907-09‖?
OkHi [1908-09]

METEOR. w 1901?-05‖?
1901?-03? as Afton pioneer
Also dated in Frisco
OkHi [1905]

Afton NEWS. w 1892-95‖?
OkHi [1894-95]

Afton PIONEER. *See* Meteor

AGRA

Agra NEWS. *See* Queen City times

QUEEN CITY times. w 1904-18‖?
1904- 1906 as Agra news
OkHi [1904-06]-[18]

ALBION

Albion ADVOCATE. w 1910-23‖?
Title varies: Albion union advocate
OkHi [1910]-[13-14]-19[21]-[23]

KIAMICHI VALLEY reporter. w 1907-10‖?
OkHi [1908]

Albion UNION advocate. *See* Albion advocate

ALEX

Alex TRIBUNE. w 1907+
OkHi [1907-08]-[11]-[13]-[30-31]+

ALFRED. *See* MULHALL

ALINE

Aline CHRONOSCOPE. w 1900+
1900 as Chronoscope (Cleo) 1925-28 Aline review
pub 1901+
OkHi [1904]-[06]-[11]-[16]-[18-19]-[25]-[28]+

Aline REVIEW. *See* Aline chronoscope

ALLEN

Allen ALTRUIST. w Jl 25-O? 1912‖
United with Allen hustler to form Allen altruist and Allen hustler, later Allen democrat
OkHi [1912]

Allen ALTRUIST and Allen hustler. *See* Allen democrat

OKLAHOMA (*Continued*)

ALLEN—*Continued*

Allen DEMOCRAT. w D 29 1905+
1905-Je 4 1920 as Allen hustler (O 24-D 5 1912 Allen altruist and Allen hustler)
pub 1920+
OkHi [1904-09]-[12]-[15;19-21]-[26]-[28]

Allen HUSTLER. *See* Allen democrat

Allen NEWS. w
OkHi [1915]

ALTUS

Early years as Frazer; 1901?-02? Leger

JACKSON county chronicle. w 1927+
OkHi [1930]+

LEGER news. *See* Altus weekly news

LEGER plaindealer. w 1897-1902||?
1897-S? 1901 as Altus plaindealer
OkHi [1898;1901-02]

LEGER times. *See* Altus times-democrat

Altus weekly NEWS. w 1900-21||?
O 3 1901-Je 30 1904 as Leger news
OkHi [1900]-[21]

OKLAHOMA democrat. w 1907-Jl 26 1917||
United with Altus times to form Altus times-democrat
OkAlT [1908]-[17]
OkHi [1907-08]-17

Daily OKLAHOMA democrat. d 1908-12||?
OkAlT [1908-09]

Altus PLAINDEALER. w 1897-1901 *See* Leger plaindealer

Altus PLAIN DEALER. w 1922-27||?
OkAlT 1923-[27]
OkHi 1923-[27]

Altus daily TIMES. d
pub 1909-[11]

Altus TIMES-DEMOCRAT. w,d 1900?+
1900?-Ag 4 1904 as Leger times; Ag 11? 1904-Jl 26 1917 Altus times
w 1900?-S 16 1927
pub [1901]-14;18-19;27+
OkHi [1903-04]-[27]+

ALVA

Alva CHRONICLE. w 1893-95||?
OkHi 1893-[95]

CONSTRUCTIVE socialist. w 1910-13||?
1910? as Woods county socialist
OkHi [1910-13]

Alva COURIER. w,sw 1896-Ja 1908||?
Title varies slightly. United with Alva review to form Alva review-courier
sw F 19 1902-Je 14 1903
OkHi 1899-[1902]-[08]

Alva daily NEWS. d 1908-10||?
OkHi [1908]

Alva PIONEER. w 1893-1919||?
OkHi 1893-[1911]

Alva daily PIONEER. d Je 24 1901-19||?
Title varies slightly
OkHi [1905-06;11]-[19]

PROHIBITION agitator. w
OkHi [1906]

Alva daily RECORD. w,d Jl 10 1902+
1902-F 18 1921 as Renfrew's record; F 25 1921-31 Alva record
w 1901-31
pub 1902+
OkHi [1902]+

RENFREW'S record. *See* Alva daily record

Alva REPUBLICAN. w 1889-97||?
Merged with Alva courier
OkHi [1894]-[97]

Alva REVIEW-COURIER. d 1906+
1894-F 6 1908 as Alva review
KHi Je 13 1918;Ag 21 1919;N 28 1921
OkHi [1894-96;99]-[1903-04]-[07-08]-14

Alva REVIEW-COURIER. w 1906+
1906-08? as Alva review
pub 1915+
OkHi [1919]-[22]+

WOODS county socialist. *See* Constructive socialist

AMBER

Amber PRESS. w 1909-10||?
OkHi [1909-10]

AMES

Ames ENTERPRISE. *See* Ames review

Ames LEDGER. w 1931+
pub 1931+
OkHi [1931-32]+

Ames REVIEW. w 1903-21||
1903-S 18 1914 as Ames enterprise
OkHi [1909-13]-[21]

AMORITA

Amorita HERALD. w 1910-19||?
OkHi [1910]-[19]

Amorita NEWS. w 1908-10||?
OkHi [1908]-[10]

ANADARKO

Daily AMERICAN-DEMOCRAT. w,d 1911+
1911-Jl 1 1915 as Anadarko American; Jl 8 1915-33? American-democrat
w 1911-33?
pub 1920+
KHi My 17 1922
NN Ag 12 1915
OkHi [1911]+

CADDO county democrat. *See* Anadarko democrat

CADDO county record. w 1923-25||?
OkHi [1923-25]

CADDO county times. w Ag 1901-04||?
OkHi [1901-02]-[04]

Anadarko daily DEMOCRAT. d S? 1901-14||?
Title varies slightly
OkHi [1901-04]07-[09-10;14]

Anadarko DEMOCRAT. w 1901-Je 1915||?
1901-Jl 1906 as Weekly democrat; Ag 1906-08? Caddo county democrat. United with Anadarko American to form American-democrat, later Daily American-democrat
OkHi [1904-09]-[13]15

LIFE. *See* Oklahoma life (Oklahoma City)

Anadarko daily NEWS. d 1933+
Title varies slightly
pub 1933+
OkHi 1933+

PLAINDEALER. w Ag 4 1904-
OkHi [1904]

Anadarko RECORD. w
OkHi [1901-02]

Anadarko evening TRIBUNE. d 1901-02||?
OkHi [1901-02]

Anadarko TRIBUNE. w Ag 2 1901+
OkHi [1901-04]05[07]+

ANTLERS

Antlers AMERICAN. w Ja 5 1910+
1920? as Antlers American-news-record
pub [1910-20]+
KHi Je 6 1918
OkHi 1910[11]-[18]+

Antlers DEMOCRAT. w 1900-01||?
OkHi [1900-01]

KIAMICHI VALLEY news. *See* Sandy Land torch

Antlers NEWS-RECORD. w 1903-Ja 16 1920||
1903-N 1908? as Antlers news. United with Antlers American to form Antlers American-news-record, later Antlers American
OkHi [1904-05]-[07]-[09]-[18-20]

Antlers RECORD. w 1906-N 1908||?
United with Antlers news to form Antlers news-record
OkHi [1907]

SANDY LAND torch. w 1924-31||?
1924-29? as Kiamichi Valley news
OkHi [1925]-29

APACHE

APACHAN. w 1909-11||?
OkHi [1909]-[11]

Apache REVIEW. w 1901+
1901-34? as Week's review
OkHi [1902-05]-[25-26]

WEEK'S review. *See* Apache review

Apache WORLD. w 1904-07||?
OkHi [1904-07]

APPALACHIA

Appalachia OUT-LOOK. w 1905-06||?
OkHi [1905-06]

APPERSON

Apperson AMERICAN. w 1921-25||?
OkHi [1923]-[25]

ARAPAHO

Arapaho ARGUS. *See* Custer county clarion

Arapaho ARROW. *See* Arapaho bee

Arapaho BEE. w Ap 29 1892+
Ap-O? 1892 as Arapaho arrow; N?-D 24? 1892 Arapaho citizen
KHi My 27 1917
OkHi [1892-93]-[1932]+

Arapaho CITIZEN. *See* Arapaho bee

CUSTER county clarion. w Ja 20 1893-1907||?
1893-98? as Arapaho argus
OkHi 1893[94]-[96;1901]-[07]

CUSTER county news. w 1900-06||?
OkHi [1902-06]

Arapaho JOURNAL. w 1906-18||?
OkHi [1908-16]

ARCADIA

Arcadia GAZETTE. w 1911?-14||?
OkHi [1911]-[14]

Arcadia NEWS. w 1909-10||?
OkHi 1909

Arcadia OBSERVER. w 1915-16||?
OkHi [1915-16]

Arcadia REVIEW. w Ja 1917-18||?
OkHi [1918]

Arcadia STAR. w 1904-08||?
OkHi [1904]-[08]

ARDMORE

Ardmore morning ADVERTISER. *See* Ardmore morning democrat

ALLIANCE courier. w 1888-96||?
1888-92? as Ardmore courier
OkHi [1893-96]

Daily ARDMOREITE. d O 25 1893+
Some Sunday issues as Sunday Ardmoreite-press
pub 1893+
KHi Jl 26 1923
OkHi [1894]1901-[19]+

Weekly ARDMOREITE. w 1894-1928||?
Ap 25 1922-Mr 31 1927 as Ardmore statesman and weekly Ardmoreite
OkHi 1922-[27]

AVALANCHE. w
OkHi [1908]

CARTER county citizen. *See* Ardmore democrat

CHICKASAW chieftain. *See* State herald

Ardmore CHIEFTAIN. *See* Ardmore chronicle d

Ardmore CHRONICLE. w 1889?-98||?

Ardmore CHRONICLE. d F 29 1892-97||?
1892-96? as Ardmore chieftain; 1897? Daily state herald
OkU F 29 1892

Daily COURIER. d My 9 1905-
OkHi [1905]

Ardmore COURIER. w *See* Alliance courier

Morning DEMOCRAT. d 1906-09||?
OkHi [1907-09]

Ardmore DEMOCRAT. w Ap 3 1930+
1930-Ag 13 1931 as Carter county citizen
pub 1930+
OkHi [1930-31]+

Ardmore morning DEMOCRAT. d 1934+
1934? as Ardmore morning advertiser
pub 1934+
OkHi 1935+

FARMERS union advocate and union review. *See* Union advocate-review

INDIAN TERRITORY sun. *See* Ardmore sun

Ardmore daily PRESS. d 1921?-Ap 15 1927||?
Merged with Daily Ardmoreite
Some Sunday issues as Sunday Ardmoreite-press
OkHi [1921]-27

STATE herald. w My 11 1889-96||?
1889-Ag 1890 as Oklahoma chief (Oklahoma City) S 1890-94? Chickasaw chieftain. Merged with Ardmore chronicle
OkHi Ja 19,Ap 27 1890[93-96]
OkU My 25 1890

Daily STATE herald. *See* Ardmore chronicle

Ardmore STATESMAN. w 1906-Ap 18 1922||
United with Weekly Ardmoreite to form Ardmore statesman and weekly Ardmoreite, later Weekly Ardmoreite
OkHi [1908]-22

Ardmore STATESMAN and weekly Ardmoreite. *See* Weekly Ardmoreite

Ardmore SUN. w 1901-10||?
1901-07? as Indian Territory sun
Negro
OkHi [1904-05]

UNION advocate-review. w 1905-10||?
1905-D 3? 1908 as Union review; D 10 1908-Ag 5 1909 Farmers union advocate and union review
OkHi [1905-07]-[10]

UNION review. *See* Union advocate-review

WESTERN world. *See under* Oklahoma City

WORLD. w Je 8 1907-
OkHi [1907]

X-RAY. w
OkHi [1914]

ARNETT

ELLIS county capital. w 1908+
OkHi [1908-09]-[22]+

ELLIS county statesman. w 1924+
pub 1924+

Arnett LEADER. w 1905-Mr 1 1918||?
OkHi [1905-06;11-12]-[15-16]-18

ASHER

Asher ALTRUIST. *See* Asher record

Asher CLIPPER. w 1908-09||?
OkHi [1908-09]

Asher RECORD. w 1901-07||?
1901-O 5 1906? as Asher altruist
OkHi [1904]-[06-07]

SOUTH POTTAWATOMIE progress w 1911-18||?
OkHi [1911]-[16]

ASHLAND

Ashland NEWS. w 1911-12||?
OkHi [1911-12]

OKLAHOMA (*Continued*)

ATOKA

ATOKA county gazette. w 1926-30||?
OkHi [1927]-[29]

ATOKA county Jeffersonian. w 1908+
1908-S 1 1911? as Atoka miracle
OkHi [1909-11]-[13]-[17]-[28]

BRANDING iron. *See* Indian champion

Atoka CHOCTAW champion. w 1898||?
In English and Choctaw
OkHi [1898]

Atoka DEMOCRAT. w F 2 1905-Je? 1909||?
F- 1905? as Atoka news. United with Indian citizen to form Atoka democrat and Indian citizen, later Indian citizen-democrat
OkHi [1905-08]
OkShO [1908]

Atoka DEMOCRAT and Indian citizen. *See* Indian citizen-democrat

Atoka INDEPENDENT. w Jl 27 1877-78||?
In English and Choctaw
OkHi [1877-78]

Atoka INDEPENDENT. 1886-89 *See* Indian citizen-democrat

INDIAN champion. w F 23 1884-D 28 1885||?
F-Mr 15? 1884 as Branding iron
In English and Choctaw
NN N 1 1884;F 7 1885
OkHi [1884-85]

INDIAN citizen-democrat. w 1886+
1886-F 1889? as Atoka independent; Mr 2 1889-Je 10? 1909 Indian citizen; Je 17-Ag 5 1909 Atoka democrat and Indian citizen
Early years in English, Choctaw, and Chickasaw
NcD Ja 11 1894
OkHi [1886-89]-[1931]+
OkShO O 3 1907;S 3,O 22 1908
TxU Jl 3,Ag 28 1902[Je 30-S 15 1904]

Atoka MIRACLE. *See* Atoka county Jeffersonian

Atoka NEWS. *See* Atoka democrat

Atoka RECORD. w
OkHi [1912]

Atoka VINDICATOR. w Mr 2 1872-Ja 6 1877||
1872-Mr 20? 1875 as Vindicator (New Boggy). United with Oklahoma star to form Star-vindicator (McAlester)
OkHi [1872-73]

AUGUSTA

FREE homes. w 1900-03||?
OkHi [1900]01

HEADLIGHT. *See under* Carmen

WOODS county news. *See* Alfalfa county news (Carmen)

AVANT

Avant DERRICK. w 1909-11||?
OkHi [1909]-[11]

Avant HUSTLER. *See* Osage county hustler

Avant NEWS. w 1919-25||?
OkHi [1924-25]

OSAGE county hustler. w 1913-19||?
1913-My 25 1917 as Avant hustler
OkHi [1913-14;16]-[19]

AVARD

Avard TRIBUNE. w 1904-Jl 26 1918||?
OkHi 1904-[15]-18

AYLESWORTH

Aylesworth LEADER. w
OkHi [1914]

BACONE

Bacone INDIAN. bm 1929?+
NNHu [1929;33-34]+

BARNSDALL

To 1921? as Bigheart

Barnsdall AMERICAN. w 1920-23||?
OkHi [1922-23]

BIGHEART chronicle. w 1908-12||?
OkHi [1908]-[12]

BIGHEART star. w 1906-07||?
OkHi [1906-07]

BIGHEART times. *See* Barnsdall times

Barnsdall TIMES. w 1919+
1919-21 as Bigheart times
OkHi [1920]+

BARTLESVILLE

CRITERION. w 1919?-Ja 9 1920||
United with Independent and Dewey world to form Criterion and independent, later New era and independent
OkHi [1919-20]

CRITERION and independent. *See* New era and independent

Bartlesville daily ENTERPRISE. d Ag 3 1905+
pub 1905+
KHi O 3 1909;Ag 5 1919;Ag 1,9 1921;D 5,7 1922;O 16 1926
OkHi [1905;12]-[16;18]+

Bartlesville ENTERPRISE. w *See* Washington county sentinel and weekly enterprise

Weekly EXAMINER. w Mr 8 1895+
1895-Ap 11 1903 as Bartlesville magnet
pub 1912+
KHi 1895-Ap 11 1908
OkHi [1900]-[03]-[09]

Morning EXAMINER. d 1907+
pub 1907+
KHi My 5 1916;Ap 14 1918;Ja 16 1920;Jl 13 1929
OkHi [1909]+

INDEPENDENT and Dewey world. *See* New era and independent

Bartlesville MAGNET. *See* Weekly examiner

NEW ERA and independent. w Mr 13 1906-21||?
1906-Ag 1914 as Dewey world; S 4 1914-Ja 9 1920 Independent and Dewey world; Ja 16- 1920 Criterion and independent
1906-Ag 1914 pub in Dewey
KHi D 31 1915
OkHi 1907-[12]14-[19-20]

Bartlesville daily NEWS. d 1906-10||?
OkHi [1906-07]

Bartlesville weekly NEWS. w 1909-10||?
OkHi [1909-10]

WASHINGTON county sentinel and weekly enterprise. w Ap 8 1904-19||
1904-D 8 1911 as Bartlesville enterprise; D 15-22 1911 Washington county sentinel, Bartlesville weekly enterprise and Dewey sentinel
pub 1904
OkHi [1904]-[06]-[17-19]
—d ed *See* Bartlesville daily enterprise

BEAVER

Beaver ADVOCATE. *See* Herald-democrat

BEAVER county democrat. w 1892-1912||?
OkHi [1893-94;1906-07]-[12]

DEMOCRAT. w N 11 1915-Jl 26 1923||?
United with Beaver herald to form Beaver herald and democrat, later Herald-democrat
OkHi [1915]-23

HERALD-DEMOCRAT. w 1887+
1887-91? as Territorial advocate; 1892-Ja 24 1895 Beaver advocate; F 7 1895-Jl 26 1923 Beaver herald; Ag 2 1923-Jl 10 1924 Beaver herald and democrat
pub 1895+
KHi Jl 12 1928
OkHi 1893-[95-96]-[99;1904]+

Beaver JOURNAL. w 1903-11||?
OkHi [1904-05]-[07]

SOUTH and west. w 1894-97||?
OkHi [1894-95]-[97]

TERRITORIAL advocate. *See* Herald-democrat

BEAVER CITY

Beaver City TRIBUNE. w 1888-90||?
1888-89? as Benton county banner (Benton)
OkHi Je 19 1886;My 30 1890

BEGGS

Beggs HUSTLER. w
OkHi [1911]

Beggs INDEPENDENT. w,sw 1901+
1901-F 9 1906? as Standard
sw Jl 19 1921-N 23 1923?
OkHi [1904-07]09-[23]-[32]+

STANDARD. *See* Beggs independent

BENNINGTON

Bennington TRIBUNE. w 1903-22||?
OkHi [1903]-[08;10]-[17;20-22]

BENTON

BENTON county banner. *See* Beaver City tribune (Beaver City)

BERLIN

Berlin HERALD. w 1906||?
OkHi [1906]

Berlin VENTURE. w 1899-S 19 1901||?
OkHi [1901]

BERWYN

Berwyn LIGHT. w 1905-12||?
OkHi [1905]-[07-08]

BESSIE

OKLAHOMA vorwärts. w 1900-16||?
1900-03? pub in Weatherford; 1904?-S 10 1915? in Cordell
In German
OkHi 1902-[16]

WASHITA breeze. w 1904-06||?
OkHi [1904-06]

BETHANY

Bethany TRIBUNE. w 1925+
pub 1925+
OkHi [1926-27]-[31]+

BIG CABIN

Big Cabin MONITOR. w S 10 1914-
OkHi [1914-15]

Big Cabin SENTINEL and Adair ledger. w 1911-13||?
1911-N 21? 1912 as Big Cabin sentinel
OkHi 1911-13

BIGHEART. *See* BARNSDALL

BILLINGS

Billings NEWS. w S? 1899+
1899-D 27 1901 as Red Rock Valley news
pub [1900]+
OkHi [1900]+

RED ROCK VALLEY news. *See* Billings news

BINGER

Binger JOURNAL. w 1902+
OkHi 1903[04]-[18]-[22]-30

BIXBY

Bixby BULLETIN. w F 24 1905+
pub 1905+
OkHi 1905-[08]-[10-11]-[13]-25[27]

Bixby JOURNAL. w 1906-09||?
OkHi [1907-09]

BLACKBURN

Blackburn FLASH-LIGHT. w 1902-08||?
OkHi [1904-05]-[08]

Blackburn GLOBE. w My 31 1895-96||?
OkHi [1895-96]

Blackburn NEWS. w 1908-12||?
OkHi [1908]-[12]

BLACKWELL

1894? as Parker

BLACKWELL ROCK record. *See* Blackwell record

Blackwell EAGLE. w 1893-94||?
OkBlT 1893
OkHi [1893-94]

KAY county democrat. w 1894||?
OkHi [1894]

KAY county sun. *See* Blackwell sun

Blackwell LION. w 1894-
OkHi [1894]

Blackwell daily NEWS. d D 22 1899-1922||?
Title varies slightly
OkHi [1904;07]-[22]

PARKER independent. w O 11 1894-
OkHi [1894]

PARKER times-record. *See* Times-record

Blackwell RECORD. w S 16 1893-F 22 1894||?
S-N 16 1893 as Blackwell Rock record. United with Blackwell times to form Times-record
OkHi 1893-94

Blackwell SUN. w 1895-1924||?
1895-My 1897? as Tonkawa register (Tonkawa) Je 1897?-F 14 1900 Kay county sun; Ag 1 1910-My 8 1924 Blackwell weekly sun
OkBl 1895-1923
OkHi [1895-1902]-[24]

TIMES-RECORD. w N 1 1893+
1893-F 22 1894 as Blackwell times; Ap 19-My 10 1894 Parker times-record
OkBlT 1894+
OkHi [1893]-[95]-[1924]

Blackwell morning TRIBUNE. d 1915+
1915-Ja 11 1919 as Blackwell daily world?
pub 1919+
OkHi [1916-17]-19[22]+

Blackwell daily WORLD. *See* Blackwell morning tribune

BLAIR

Blair MESSENGER. w 1924-28||?
OkAlT 1926-[28]

ORIENTAL progress. w 1904-18||?
1904-14? as Blair progress
OkHi [1907]-[10-12]-[18]

Blair PROGRESS. *See* Oriental progress

BLANCHARD

MCCLAIN county news. *See* Blanchard news

Blanchard NEWS. w 1907+
1907-13? as Blanchard record; 1914?-19? McClain county news?
pub 1909+
OkHi [1907]-[09-10]-[14]-[16-19]

Blanchard RECORD. *See* Blanchard news

BLISS. *See* MARLAND

BLUEJACKET

CRAIG county gazette. w 1902-S 30 1920||?
1902-N 19 1909 as Bluejacket news; N 26 1909-10? Bluejacket gazette
OkHi [1905-07;09-11]-[14]-[20]

OKLAHOMA (*Continued*)

BLUEJACKET—*Continued*

Bluejacket GAZETTE. *See* Craig county gazette

Bluejacket NEWS. *See* Craig county gazette

BOISE CITY

CIMARRON courier. w Jl 1907-
OkHi [1908]

CIMARRON news. *See* Boise City news

Boise City NEWS. w 1898+
1898-Jl 13 1930 as Cimarron news
1898-1911 pub in Kenton
pub [1898-1926]+
OkHi [1899-[1911]+

Boise City TRIBUNE. w 1907-11||?
OkHi [1908]-[11]

BOKCHITO

Bokchito BULLETIN. w N 1902-04||?
OkHi [1904]

Bokchito NEWS. w Ja 11 1906-20||?
1906-11 as Bokchito success
OkHi 1906[07-08;11-13]-[15-16]-[18]-[20]

Bokchito SUCCESS. *See* Bokchito news

Bokchito TIMES. w Mr 23- 1905||?
OkHi 1905

BOKOSHE

CHOCTAW herald. w 1906-09||?
OkHi [1906]

Bokoshe CHRONICLE. w D 17 1904-
OkHi [1904-05]

Bokoshe ENTERPRISE. w 1911-18||?
OkHi [1911-13]14

BOLEY

BEACON. w
Negro
OkHi [1908]

Boley PROGRESS. w 1905-26||?
Negro
OkHi [1905-06;08-09]-[11;15;26]

BOOKERTEE

Bookertee SEARCHLIGHT. w
Negro
OkHi [1919]

BOSWELL

Boswell NEWS. w 1902+
KHi O 20 1917
OkHi [1910-12;14;20]+

SUBMARINE. w 1912-15||?
OkHi [1913]-[15]

BOTSFORD

Botsford TRIBUNE. *See* Temple tribune (Temple)

BOYNTON

Boynton AMERICAN. *See* Boynton eagle

Boynton EAGLE. w F 1903-07||?
1903- 1905 as Boynton news; 1905- 1906 Boynton American
OkHi [1904-07]

Boynton INDEX. w 1910+
OkHi [1910]+

Boynton JOURNAL. w 1908-09||?
OkHi [1909]

Boynton NEWS. *See* Boynton eagle

BRAGGS

Braggs BUGLE. w 1912-13||?
OkHi [1912-13]

Braggs JOURNAL. w 1908-10||?
OkHi [1909-10]

Braggs LEDGER. w 1914||?
OkHi [1914]

BRAMAN

Braman LEADER. w 1902+
pub [1902]+
KHi Ag 4 1922;Ap 15 1927
OkHi [1904]-[08-09;11]-[13-14;17]+

Braman STAR. w 1899-1904||?
OkHi [1901]-[04]

BRIDGEPORT

Bridgeport GRIT. w 1907-11||?
OkHi [1907]-[10]

Bridgeport NEWS. w 1901-07||
1904?-05? as News-tribune. United with Hinton record and Lookeba light to form Hinton record, Bridgeport news and Lookeba light, later Hinton record (Hinton)
OkHi [1904-07]

Bridgeport NEWS. w 1921?-27||?
OkHi [1921]-[27]

Bridgeport SENTINEL. w 1910-14||?
OkHi [1911]-[13]

Bridgeport TRIBUNE. w 1903||?
United with Bridgeport news to form News-tribune, later Bridgeport news

BRINKMAN

Brinkman COURIER. w 1911-17||?
OkHi [1911-13]

Brinkman NEWS. w
OkHi [1910]

BRISTOW

Bristow ENTERPRISE. w Ja 1904-Mr 24 1917||?
1904-13? as Territorial enterprise. United with Bristow record to form Bristow record and Bristow enterprise, later Bristow record
OkHi [1904]-[08-09]-[13]-17

Bristow RECORD. w,sw O 20 1899+
My 31 1917-Ap 22 1922 as Bristow record and Bristow enterprise
sw Ag 6 1931-F 27 1933
pub 1899+
OkHi [1904-07]-[16-17]-[26]+

Bristow daily RECORD. d Ap 24 1922+
pub 1922+
OkHi [1923]+

Bristow SHOPPER. w 1927+
pub Ap 1927+

TERRITORIAL enterprise. *See* Bristow enterprise

BRITTON

NORTH STAR. w 1909-10||?
OkHi [1909-10]

OKLAHOMA county post. *See* Britton progress

Britton POST. *See* Britton progress

Britton PROGRESS. w 1916+
1916-N 16? 1928 Britton post; N 23 1928-N 11 1930 Oklahoma county post
pub 1930+
OkEdB [1931]+
OkHi [1925-26]+

Britton weekly SENTINEL. w 1908-14||?
OkHi [1908-09]-[14]

BROKEN ARROW

Broken Arrow DEMOCRAT. w 1905-Mr 29 1918||
United with Broken Arrow ledger to form Ledger-democrat, later Broken Arrow ledger
OkHi [1905]-18

Broken Arrow LEDGER. w 1903+
Ap 4 1918-S 3 1925 as Ledger-democrat
pub 1903+
OkHi [1904]-[06-07;10]+

TULSA county journal. w
OkHi [1911-12]

BROKEN BOW

Broken Bow DEVELOPER. w 1911-13||?
OkHi [1911-13]

Broken Bow NEWS. w 1912+
pub 1912+
OkHi [1913-16]-[19-22;33]+

BROMIDE

Bromide HERALD. w 1911-17||?
OkHi [1911-13]

BRULE

Brule POST. *See under* Buffalo

BUFFALO

Buffalo BUGLE. w Ap 1905-13||?
OkHi [1912-13]

HARPER county democrat. w Ap 19 1907-My 16 1924||
United with Buffalo republican to form Harper county journal
OkBfH 1921
OkHi [1907]-24

HARPER county journal. w 1908+
1908-My 15 1924 as Buffalo republican (S 10 1908-F 17 1911? Buffalo republican and post)
pub 1921+
OkHi [1908;10]+

POST. w Je 9 1905-S 3 1908||?
United with Buffalo republican to form Buffalo republican and post, later Harper county journal
1905-06? pub in Brule
OkHi 1905-[07-08]

Buffalo REPUBLICAN. *See* Harper county journal

BURFORD

MOUNTAIN PARK eagle. *See under* Mountain Park

BURLINGTON

Burlington RELIANCE. w 1906-08||?
OkHi [1906-07]

BUTLER

Butler HERALD. w 1905+
OkHi 1905-[24;26]+

Butler NEWS. w 1904-05||?
OkHi [1904-05]

Butler NEWS. w 1909-11||?
OkHi [1909]-11

BYARS

Byars BANNER. *See* News and advertiser

Byars BOOSTER. w
OkHi [1910]

NEWS and advertiser. w 1902-14||?
1902-11 as Byars banner
OkHi [1904-06]-[08-09]-[11-14]

BYRON

Byron PROMOTER. w 1911-20||?
OkHi [1911]-[15]-[18-19]

Byron REPUBLICAN. w 1900-12||?
OkHi [1900]-[04-08]-[11]

CACHE

Cache CLARION. *See* Cache register 1908-14

Cache JOURNAL. w N 1902-05||?
OkHi [1904]

Cache REGISTER. w 1905-07||?
OkHi [1905-07]

Cache REGISTER. w 1908-14||?
Jl 10 1908-10? as Cache clarion; 1910?-11 Cache clarion and Indiahoma news
OkHi 1908-[10]-[14]

CADDO

Caddo FREE PRESS. w 1878-81||?
CU-B Je 27-Jl 4,25,Ag 22,S 27-O 11,25-D 6,27 1878;Ja 10,24-31,F 21-Ap 11,25-My 2,16-23, Je-Ag 15 1879
OkHi [1878-79]

Caddo HERALD. w 1895+
pub 1895+
OkHi [1904;10]+

OKLAHOMA star. *See* Star-vindicator (McAlester)

CALERA

BANNER-LEDGER. w 1896-1904||?
1896-1902? as Sterrett banner
1896- 1904? pub in Sterrett
OkHi [1904]

CHOCTAW ledger. w 1902||?
United with Sterrett banner (Sterrett) to form Banner-ledger

Calera NEWS. w 1910-11||?
OkHi [1911]

Calera NEWS. w 1917-25||?
OkHi [1917]-[25]

CALUMET

Calumet CHIEFTAIN. w 1908+
pub 1908+
OkHi [1908]+

Calumet weekly CRITERION. w 1908-12||?
OkHi [1908]-[10]-[12]

CALVIN

Calvin ENTERPRISE. *See* Hughes county enterprise

HUGHES county democrat. w Mr 22 1907-
OkHi [1907]

HUGHES county enterprise. w 1902+
1902-Mr 24 1916 as Calvin enterprise
OkHi [1904]-[06]-[08-09]-[31-32]

Calvin NEWS. w 1908-12||?
OkHi [1908-11]

CAMARGO

Camargo COMET. w 1912-19||?
OkHi [1912;15]-19

CAMPBELL. *See* GORE

CANADIAN

CANADIAN VALLEY news. w 1910-14||?
OkHi [1910-12]

Canadian ENTERPRISE. w 1904-10||?
OkHi [1907-08]

CANEY

CHOCTAW news. *See* Caney news

DEMOCRAT and leader. w 1914-17||?
1914-15? as Caney leader
OkHi [1914-15]

Caney LEADER. w 1909-12||?
OkHi [1910;12]

Caney LEADER. 1914-15 *See* Democrat and leader

OKLAHOMA (*Continued*)

CANEY—*Continued*

Caney NEWS. w 1901-08||?
1901-Ag 4? 1905 as Choctaw news
OkHi [1904]05[07-08]

CANTON

CANADIAN VALLEY record. *See* Canton record

Canton RECORD. w 1905+
1905-20? as Canadian Valley record
pub 1905-15;21+
OkHi [1905]-[21]-[26-29]+

CANUTE

Canute BANNER. w F 1903-05||?
OkHi [1904-05]

Canute LEADER. w 1907-10||?
OkHi [1907-09]

CAPITOL HILL

Papers published in Capitol Hill are listed under Oklahoma City

CAPRON

Capron HUSTLER. w 1903-20||?
OkHi [1904]-[14;16]

CARLTON

Carlton JOURNAL. w 1903-08||?
OkHi [1907]

CARMEN

ALFALFA county news. w 1898-1912||?
1898-D 25 1907 as Woods county news
1898-1901 pub in Augusta
OkHi [1899]-[1901]-[03]-[12]

HEADLIGHT. w 1900+
1900-01? pub in Augusta
pub 1900-[28-29]+
OkHi [1900-01]-[16;20]22-[29]

RURAL industrialist. w
OkHi [1907]

Carmen SUNLIGHT. w 1914?-15||?
OkHi [1914-15]

WOODS county news. *See* Alfalfa county news

CARNEGIE

Carnegie DEMOCRAT. w 1909-12||?
OkHi [1911]

Carnegie HERALD. w 1903+
pub [1903-17]+
OkHi [1904-05]-[21]+

CARNEY

Carney weekly CITIZEN. w 1930+
pub My 16 1930+

Carney ENTERPRISE. w 1902-18||?
OkHi [1904-05]-[18]

NEW ERA. w 1919||?
OkHi [1919]

CARRIER

Carrier MONITOR. w Je 11 1903-06||?
OkHi 1903-[06]

CARTER

BECKHAM county advocate. w 1913-14||?
OkHi [1913]

Carter EXPRESS. w 1910+
OkHi [1910]+

CARTHAGE

Carthage ENTERPRISE. w 1907-11||?
OkHi [1910-11]

CARWILE

Carwile JOURNAL. w 1898-1903||?
OkHi [1899]-[1903]

CASHION

Cashion ADVANCE. w 1900-08||?
KHi N 22 1900
OkHi 1901[02;04]-07

CITIZEN. w 1909-10||?
OkHi [1909]

INDEPENDENT. w 1908+
OkHi [1908-09]-19;23+

CASTLE

Castle NEWS. w
OkHi [1908]

CATOOSA

CATOOSAN. w 1905-08||?
OkHi [1905-07]

CEMENT

Cement COURIER. w 1902+
OkHi [1904]-[12-14]-[16-21]+

CENTRAHOMA

To Je 1907 as Owl

COAL county register. *See* Centrahoma register

OWL. w F 16 1906-
OkHi [1906]

OWL tribune. w Ja 13 1905-
OkHi [1905]

Centrahoma RECORD. w 1916||?
OkHi [1916]

Centrahoma REGISTER. w Mr 15 1907-09||?
1907-08? as Coal county register
OkHi [1907]

CENTRALIA

Centralia REGISTER. w 1903-23||?
1903-18? as Centralia standard
OkHi [1904]-18[23]

Centralia STANDARD. *See* Centralia register

CESTOS

Cestos NEWS. w 1908-12||?
OkHi [1911]

Cestos REPORTER. w 1902-08||?
OkHi [1904]-[06-07]

CHANDLER

DEMOCRAT. *See* Lincoln county democrat and telegram

LINCOLN county democrat and telegram. w 1892-1901||?
1892? as Sac and Fox warrior; - 1893? Democrat-warrior; 1893?-97? Democrat
OkHi [1893-95;99]-[1901]

LINCOLN county republican. w 1901+
1901-N 27 1919 as Chandler tribune
pub 1901+
OkHi 1903;05-[17]+

Chandler NEWS. w 1891-My 1909||?
United with Chandler publicist to form Chandler news-publicist
KHi N 20 1896-O 22 1903
OkHi [1893]-1900;02-09

Chandler NEWS-PUBLICIST. w 1894+
1894-My 14 1909 as Chandler publicist (title varies slightly)
OkHi [1894]-[1902-03]-[05]-[09]-27;29+

Chandler daily PUBLICIST. d N 1901-06||?
OkHi [1903]-[05-06]

Chandler PUBLICIST. w *See* Chandler news-publicist

Chandler REVIEW. w -1913||?
OkHi [1911;13]

SAC and Fox warrior. *See* Lincoln county democrat and telegram

Chandler TELEGRAM. w 1897||?
United with Democrat to form Lincoln county democrat and telegram

Chandler TRIBUNE. *See* Lincoln county republican

WESTERN world. *See under* Oklahoma City

CHANT CITY. *See* McCURTAIN

CHATTANOOGA

Chattanooga NEWS. w 1906-29||?
OkHi 1923-[29]

CHECOTAH

Checotah ENQUIRER. w O 1896-1912||?
OkHi [1909-10]

MCINTOSH county democrat. w N 1907+
OkHi 1913-[15]34+

Checotah TIMES. w 1902-25||?
OkHi [1925]

CHELSEA

Chelsea COMMERCIAL. w Ap 1895-1907||?
OkHi [1901;03;07]

Chelsea HERALD. w 1918||?
United with Chelsea reporter to form Chelsea reporter and Chelsea herald, later Chelsea reporter

Chelsea REPORTER. w 1894+
1919? as Chelsea reporter and Chelsea herald
pub [1894-1926]+
OkHi [1905]10;35+

CHEROKEE

ALFALFA county news. w 1925+
pub [1932]+
OkHi [1925]

Cherokee MESSENGER. w 1902+
Title varies slightly
pub 1902+
OkHi [1905]-[18-19]-[21]+

Cherokee REPUBLICAN. w 1901+
pub 1901+
OkHi [1907]08[10]-[27]+

STATE journal. w My 10 1907-09||?
KHi S 6 1907
OkHi [1907-08]

Cherokee WARRIOR. w 1906?-07||?
OkHi 1906[07]

CHEYENNE

ROGER MILLS county news. w 1930+
pub [1930]+

ROGER MILLS sentinel. w 1907-O 1918||
United with Western star to form Cheyenne star and Roger Mills sentinel, later Cheyenne star
1916-My 30 1918 pub in Strong City
OkHi [1907]-[09-11]13-[16]-18

Cheyenne STAR. w 1901+
1901-04 as Western star; O 24 1918-My 2 1929 Cheyenne star and Roger Mills sentinel
OkHi [1904-05]-[17]+

Cheyenne SUNBEAM. w 1893-1905||?
Title varies slightly
OkHi [1894-95]1901-03;05

WESTERN star. *See* Cheyenne star

CHICKASHA

Chickasha DEMOCRAT. w Mr 1901-04||?
OkHi [1902]

Chickasha daily EXPRESS. d D 28 1899+
Title varies slightly
pub [1899]+
OkCO 1919+
OkHi [1900]-[02]-[04-09]-[15]+

Chickasha EXPRESS. w *See* Grady county express

GRADY county express. w My 21 1892-1928||?
1892-1903? title varies: Chickasha express; Weekly express
OkHi [1893-95;1902-05]06
OkU My 28 1892

GRADY county star. *See* Chickasha star

Chickasha daily JOURNAL. w,d 1903-12||?
1903-Ag 1906? as Chickasha journal (title varies slightly) S 1906?-Je 29 1907 Chickasha journal and star
w 1903-Ag 1906?
OkHi [1904-08;11]

Chickasha LEDGER. w O 11 1907-
OkHi [1907]

NEW STAR and Chickasha telegram. *See* Chickasha star and telegram

Chickasha RURALIST. w
OkHi [1916-17]

Chickasha STAR. w 1900+
Some years called Chickasha weekly star; Je 5 1908-My 7 1915 as Grady county star
pub 1900+
KHi Ag 12 1921
OkHi [1906;08]12+

Chickasha STAR and telegram. d S 1898-Ag 29 1906||?
1898-F 28 1905 as Chickasha telegram; Mr 2-Ap 29 1905 New star and Chickasha telegram. United with Chickasha journal to form Chickasha journal and star, later Chickasha daily journal
OkHi [1904-06]

Chickasha TELEGRAM. *See* Chickasha star and telegram

Chickasha VOICE. w Ja 19 1906-
OkHi [1906]

WASHITA VALLEY gazette. w
OkHi [1915]

CHOCTAW

Choctaw COURIER. w Ap 10 1908-14||?
OkHi 1908-[09]-[14]

Choctaw NEWS. w 1894-98||?
OkHi [1894-96]-98

CHOTEAU

Choteau HERALD. w Mr 16? 1906+
pub 1906+
OkHi [1906-07;10]-[13-16;21]-[23-24]+

CLAREMORE

CHEROKEE vindicator. *See* Claremore courier

Claremore COURIER. w O 14 1898-1900||?
1898-My 12 1899 as Cherokee vindicator
OkHi [1898-1900]

Claremore MESSENGER. w 1895+
OkHi [1901-02]-[20]-[23]-[31]34+

Daily MESSENGER. d Ag 1899-
OkHi [1900-01]

NATIONAL. w Mr 26 1895-
OkHi Mr 26 1895

OKLAHOMA (*Continued*)

CLAREMORE—*Continued*

Claremore PROGRESS. w 1893+
Ja 6 1911-D 28 1916 as Claremore progress and Rogers county democrat; Ag 30 1923-D 31 1931 Claremore weekly progress
KHi Mr 1? 1918
OkHi [189?-95]-[97]-[1901-02]+

Claremore daily PROGRESS. d 1909+
OkHi [1930]—

ROGERS county news. w 1909-12||?
OkHi [1909-12]

STATE herald. w F 8 1905-
OkHi [1905]

CLARITA

Clarita ENTERPRISE. w 1910-12||?
OkHi [1910-12]

CLARKSVILLE

Clarksville ECHO. w S 1904-
OkHi [1905]

Clarksville SENTINEL. w Ja 27 1904-
OkHi [1904]

CLAYTON

OKLAHOMA standard. w 1891-94||?
OkHi [1893-94]

CLEARVIEW

Clearview PATRIARCH. w 1911-17||?
Negro
OkHi 1911-[13-14;16]

CLEO SPRINGS

To 1920? as Cleo

Cleo CHIEFTAIN. w 1895-1921||?
OkHi [1900]-03;05[06]08-16

CHRONOSCOPE. *See* Aline chronoscope (Aline)

Cleo EAGLE-CHIEF. w Mr 1- 1894||?
OkHi [1894]

Cleo JOURNAL. w 1902-08||?
OkHi 1905[06-08]

CLEVELAND

Cleveland AMERICAN. w 1910+
1910-19 as Cleveland leader
pub 1921+
OkHi [1910]-[31-[33]+

Cleveland ENTERPRISE. w 1903-18||?
OkHi [1905]06;09-[18]

JORDAN VALLEY journal. w Ja 5 1894-95||?
OkHi [1894]

Cleveland LEADER. *See* Cleveland American

TRIANGLE. w 1898-1908||?
OkHi [1899]-[1908]

CLINTON

Clinton daily CHRONICLE. d 1910-11||?
OkHi [1910-11]

Clinton CHRONICLE. w *See* Custer county chronicle

CUSTER county chronicle. w,sw 1899+
1899-Ag 18 1927 as Clinton chronicle (1907? Clinton chronicle and Clinton journal; Ja 15 1920-My 10 1923 Clinton chronicle and Clinton messenger)
sw My 3 1921-D 29 1922
pub Ag 25 1927+
KHi Ag 18 1911-Ag 21 1913;Ag 24 1925
OkHi 1904-[06-07]-[11]-[13]-[29]
—d ed *See* Clinton daily chronicle; Clinton daily news

CUSTER county news. *See* Clinton news

Clinton JOURNAL. w Ja 1905-06||?
Early issues as Washita journal. United with Clinton chronicle to form Clinton chronicle and Clinton journal, later Custer county chronicle
OkHi 1905[06]

Clinton MESSENGER. w 1914-Ja 8 1920||?
United with Clinton chronicle to form Clinton chronicle and Clinton messenger, later Custer county chronicle
OkHi [1915]-[17-18]-20

Clinton NEWS. w 1906?-17||?
1906?-Jl 3 1909 as Custer county news
OkHi [1906]-[16]

Clinton daily NEWS. d 1923+
pub 1923+
OkHi [1929]+
—w ed *See* Clinton news; Custer county chronicle

Clinton SUN. w My 23- 1912||?
OkHi [1912]

Clinton TIMES. sw,w 1909-24||?
w Ag 23 1923-My 1 1924
OkHi [1910-11;23-24]

Clinton TIMES-TRIBUNE. w,sw 1930+
1930-O 29 1931 as Clinton tribune
w 1930-O 29 1931;Ja 3-D 26 1935
OkHi [1930-31]+

Clinton TRIBUNE. *See* Clinton times-tribune

WASHITA journal. *See* Clinton journal

CLOUD CHIEF

Cloud Chief BEACON. *See* Cordell beacon (Cordell)

Cloud Chief BULLETIN. w,m
Mr 1912-S 1914 as Gernert's bulletin
w Mr 2-D 8 1915
OkHi 1912-[15]-[17]

GERNERT'S bulletin. *See* Cloud Chief bulletin

Cloud Chief HERALD. *See* Herald-sentinel (Cordell)

Cloud Chief SENTINEL. w -Mr 1893||?
United with Cloud Chief herald to form Herald-sentinel (Cordell)

COALGATE

COAL county register. w 1907?-10||?
United with Coalgate record to form Coalgate record-register

Coalgate COURIER. w Jl 6? 1899+
pub 1909+
OkHi [1899-1906]-[08-09]+

Coalgate INDEPENDENT. *See* Coalgate record-register

Lehigh-Coalgate LEADER. *See* Lehigh leader (Lehigh)

Coalgate NONPAREIL. w D 1 1893-95||?
KHi Ag 10 1894
OkHi [1893-95]

Coalgate RECORD-REGISTER. w 1893+
1893-94? as Twin Cities independent; 1895?-1907? Coalgate independent; 1907?-10? Coalgate record
pub 1908+
KHi S 12 1913
OkHi [1906-08]-[10-11]14;16-[18;20]-27

TWIN CITIES independent. *See* Coalgate record-register

COLBERT

Colbert TIMES. w Je 1917-19||?
OkHi [1917-18]

COLDWATER

Coldwater STAR. w Mr 23 1905-07||?
OkHi [1905]-[07]

COLEMAN

Coleman COURIER. w 1911-12||?
OkHi [1911-12]

Coleman NEWS. w
OkHi [1913]

COLLINSVILLE

Collinsville NEWS. w 1899-1918||?
OkHi [1902]-[05]-[07]09[10-11]-15[18]

Collinsville NEWS. d,sw,w 1916+
1920? as Collinsville news-star
d 1916-19?;sw 1920?-22?
pub 1920+
OkHi [1920-21;27]+

ROGERS county voice. w
OkHi [1913-14]

Collinsville STAR. w 1912-20||?
United with Collinsville news to form Collinsville news-star, later Collinsville news
OkHi [1913]-20

Collinsville TIMES. w,sw 1904-16||?
sw My 13 1910-O 30 1914
OkHi [1910-14]-[16]

COLONY

Colony COURIER. w 1909-17||?
OkHi [1909]-17

Colony ENTERPRISE. w 1919-21||?
OkHi [1919]20

COMANCHE

AMERICAN. w 1908-17||?
OkHi [1908]-16

Comanche NEWS. w 1899-1908||?
OkHi [1905-07]

Comanche REFLEX. w 1901-33||?
OkHi [1904-13]-[15-16]-[20]-[33]

COMMERCE

KING JACK. w 1917-21||?
OkHi [1919]-[21]

COPAN

Copan LEADER. w 1910-22||?
OkHi 1910-[15-17]

CORDELL

Cordell BEACON. w 1897+
1897-1900 as Cloud Chief beacon (Cloud Chief)
pub [1897]+
OkHi [1899-1900]-[02]-[05]-[07]-[09]+

HERALD-SENTINEL. w 1892?-1917||
1892?-Mr 1893? as Cloud Chief herald
1892?-1900 pub in Cloud Chief
OkHi [1893-94]-[98;1900;04-05]-[19]

INDIAHOMA union signal. *See under* Shawnee

Cordell MESSENGER. w 1893-1900||?
OkHi [1899-1900]

Cordell NEWS. w 1901-05||?
OkHi [1904-05]

OKLAHOMA vorwärts. *See under* Bessie

STATE republican. w F 15 1906-07||?
OkHi [1906-07]

CORN

WASHITA county enterprise. w 1919+
pub 1927+
OkHi [1920]+

CORNISH

Cornish NEWS. w 1909-14||?
OkHi [1909-11]-14

Cornish-Ringling TIMES. w
Also dated in Ringling
OkHi [1916]

COSMOS

PIONEER. *See* Morton county pioneer (Rolla, Kansas)

COUNCIL HILL

Council Hill EAGLE. w Jl 27 1905-
OkHi [1905-07]

Council Hill TIMES. w 1913-
OkHi [1914-16]

COVINGTON

Covington ADVOCATE. w 1908-
OkHi [1908]

Covington LEADER. w 1905-
OkHi [1906]

Covington RECORD. w 1916+
OkHi [1916;19;21]-[34]

Covington RECORDER. w Ap 21 1904-
OkHi [1904]

COWETA

Coweta COURIER. w 1903-11||?
OkHi [1904-05]-[11]

Coweta MESSENGER-DEMOCRAT. w 1909-12||?
OkHi [1911]

Coweta STAR. w 1912-Ag? 1918||
United with Coweta times to form Coweta times-star
OkHi [1912]-[17-18]

Coweta TIMES-STAR. w 1905+
1905-Ag 29 1918 as Coweta times
OkHi [1905]-19;21+

COYLE

CIMMARON VALLEY clipper. w 1900+
pub [1900]+
OkHi [1900]-[03]-[08]+

CRAWFORD

Crawford BLADE. w 1906-09||?
OkHi [1907]-[09]

CRESCENT

Crescent City COURIER. w Ja 12 1894-
OkHi 1894[95]

LOGAN county news. w 1902?+
pub 1902+
KHi F 16 1928
OkHi [1904]-[06;08]-[10]17;19+

Crescent City TIMES. w Ag 22 1895-
OkHi [1895-96]

CROSS

Cross RESIDENT. w 1893-95||?
OkHi [1893-95]

CROWDER

To 1904 as Juanita

Crowder City ADVERTISER. w 1894-1904||?
1894-1901? as Farmer's union advertiser
OkHi [1902;04]

FARMER'S union advertiser. *See* Crowder City advertiser

Crowder City GUARDIAN. w 1905-16||?
OkHi [1905-06]-[09]-[14-16]

CURTIS

Curtis COURIER. w 1900-27||?
KHi N 22 1917
OkHi [1904]-[27]

OKLAHOMA (*Continued*)

CUSHING

Cushing CITIZEN. w 1907?+
KHi Mr 17 1921;Ag 2 1923
OkHi [1912]-[22-24]-[30]+

Cushing DEMOCRAT. w 1906-12||?
OkHi [1906]-[08-09]-[12]

Cushing HERALD. *See* State herald

Cushing INDEPENDENT. w 1901-17||?
OkHi [1901]-[03-04]-[13]-17

SEARCHLIGHT. w D 1 1909-
OkHi [1910-12]

STATE herald. w Jl 5 1895-1906||?
1895-Ap 1904 as Cushing herald
OkHi [1895]-[98]-[1902-06]

CUSTER CITY

CUSTER courier. w 1900+
pub [1900-34]+
KHi N 23 1916;F 8 1917
OkHi 1903-[11-17]+

Custer City JOURNAL. w 1906-08||?
OkHi [1906]-08

CYRIL

Cyril ADVOCATE. w 1911-14||?
OkHi [1912-13]

Cyril ENTERPRISE. w 1914-17||?
OkHi [1914-17]

Cyril EXPRESS. w 1908-10||?
OkHi [1909-10]

Cyril PIONEER. w
OkAnN [1932]-33
OkHi [1931]-32

DACOMA

Dacoma ENTERPRISE. *See* Dacoma mascot

Dacoma HERALD. w 1923+
pub [1923]+

Dacoma MASCOT. w 1912?-21||?
1912?-N 9 1917 as Dacoma enterprise
OkHi [1912]-[17]-[20]

Dacoma NEWS. w 1909-11||?
OkHi [1909]-[11]

DARLINGTON

CHEYENNE and Arapaho carrier pigeon. sm 1911-12||?
NN My 15 1911

CHEYENNE transporter. sm D 5 1879-86||?
KHi D 26 1881-Jl 12 1886
OkHi [1880]-[86]

DARROW

Darrow PRESS. w 1904-08||?
OkHi [1905-07]

DAVENPORT

Davenport DISPATCH. w 1925+
pub 1931+
OkHi [1931]-[33]+

Davenport LEADER. *See* Davenport new era

Davenport NEW ERA. w 1904-18||?
1904-09 as Davenport leader
OkHi 1904-05[08-09]-13;15-[18]

DAVID

David PROGRESS. w S 1894-96||?
OkHi [1894-96]

DAVIDSON

Davidson NEWS. w 1909-28||?
OkHi [1910-12]-18[21]27[28]

Davidson POST. w 1904-10||?
OkHi [1904-10]

Davidson TRIBUNE. w 1903-09||?
OkHi [1908-09]

DAVIS

Davis ADVERTISER. *See* Davis news

Davis NEWS. w My 8 1894+
1894? as Davis advertiser
pub [1898]+
OkHi [1894-95]1901[08]+

Davis PROGRESSIVE. w Je 14 1894-
OkHi [1894-95]

DAWSON

Dawson GAZETTE. w
OkHi [1907]

DEER CREEK

Deer Creek ANCHOR. w 1909-12||?
OkHi [1909]-12

Deer Creek NEWS. w 1914-19||?
OkHi [1914]-[18]

Deer Creek TIMES. w 1900-08||?
OkHi [1900-01;04]-[08]

DELAWARE

Delaware EAGLE. *See* Delaware news

Delaware NEWS. w 1912-24||?
1912-15? as Nowata county republican; 1916?-20? Delaware register; 1921?-22? Delaware eagle
OkHi 1923[24]

NOWATA county republican. *See* Delaware news

Delaware REGISTER. w 1910-12||?
OkHi [1910-12]

Delaware REGISTER. 1916-20 *See* Delaware news

DEPEW

Depew INDEPENDENT. w 1909+
pub 1909+
OkHi [1909-10]-15[17]-[22-23]

DEVOL

Devol DISPATCH. *See* Devol review

Devol REVIEW. w 1909-24||?
1909-22? as Devol dispatch (1918? Devol review; 1919? Review-dispatch)
OkHi [1909-13]-[16;18-19;23]

DEWAR

Dewar NEWS. w My 7 1914-25||?
1914-My 15 1924 as Dewar telegram
OkHi [1914]-[25]
OkHnN 1920-24

Dewar TELEGRAM. *See* Dewar news

DEWEY

Dewey GLOBE. *See* Dewey news

Dewey NEWS. w 1911-34||?
1911-33? as Dewey globe (title varies slightly)
KHi N 28 1913
OkHi [1911-13]19-24

Dewey SENTINEL. w 1909-N? 1911||
United with Bartlesville enterprise to form Washington county sentinel, Bartlesville weekly enterprise and Dewey sentinel, later Washington county sentinel and weekly enterprise (Bartlesville)
OkHi [1909-11]

Dewey WORLD. *See* New era and independent (Bartlesville)

DILL CITY

Dill City NEWS. w 1908-10||?
OkHi [1908-10]

Dill City TIMES. w
OkHi [1911-12]

WASHITA county standard. w
OkHi [1912]

DILWORTH

Dilworth NEW ERA. w 1916-18||?
OkHi [1917-18]

DOAKSVILLE

CHOCTAW intelligencer. w Je 6 1850-Ja 7 1852||
In English and Choctaw
DLC complete

CHOCTAW telegraph. w 1849-
In English and Choctaw
DLC My 3-D 20 1849
PPeS S 6 1849

DOBY SPRINGS

MONITOR. w 1907-11||?
OkHi [1907]08

DOUGLAS

Douglas NEWS. w 1904-06||?
OkHi [1904]-[06]

DOUTHAT

INDEPENDENT. w
OkHi [1917]

DOVER

CHEROKEE chieftain. *See* Kingfisher county beacon

KINGFISHER county beacon. w 1892-94||?
1892-Ag 24 1893 as Cherokee chieftain
OkHi [1893]

Dover NEWS. w 1901-18||?
OkHi [1904-05]-[08;10]-[15]-[18]

DOWNS

Downs DEMOCRAT. w 1894-97||?
OkHi [1894]-[97]

DRUMMOND

Drummond HERALD. *See* Messenger

MESSENGER. w 1903-19||?
1903-F 20 1908? as Drummond herald
OkHi [1904]-[07-08]-[19]

DRUMRIGHT

Drumright DERRICK. w 1913+
OkHi [1913]-15

Daily DERRICK. d 1914+
Title varies slightly
OkHi [1916]+

Drumright NEWS. w 1914+
OkHi [1915]-[17-18]-[21;24]-30

Daily NEWS. d 1916-18||?
OkHi [1917-18]

Drumright TIMES. w
OkHi [1924]-[26]

DUKE

Duke BOOSTER. w 1911-12||?
United with Duke times to form Duke times-booster, later Duke times
OkHi [1911-12]

Duke GAZETTE. w
OkHi [1910]

JACKSON county tribune. w 1923+
pub [1923-26]+
OkHi [1923-24]

Duke TIMES. w 1908-23||?
1912? as Duke times-booster
OkHi [1908-11]-[13]-[15-16]-[19-20]-22

DUNCAN

Duncan AMERICAN. w Jl 1933+
OkHi [1933]+

Duncan BANNER. w 1892-1930||?
OkHi [1893-95;1905-07]-25;27;29

Duncan daily BANNER. d 1921+
1922?-23? as Duncan daily banner and eagle
pub 1921+
OkHi [1921]-[23;26]

Duncan EAGLE. w,sw 1894+
w 1894-N 6? 1935
OkHi [1906-10]+

Duncan JUSTICE. w Ja 11- 1907||?
OkHi [1907]

OKLAHOMA socialist. w 1910||?
OkHi [1910]

DURANT

Durant ADVERTISER. w 1912+
1912-30? as Saturday morning advertiser
pub N 4 1912+

BLUE county democrat. *See* Bryan county democrat

BRYAN county democrat. w 1904+
1904-07 as Blue county democrat; 1932?-33? Southeastern Oklahoma citizen and Bryan county democrat
pub 1910+
KHi Ap 25 1918
OkHi [1904-05;32-33]+
—d ed *See* Durant daily democrat

Durant daily DEMOCRAT. d 1901+
1901-10 as Durant daily news
pub [1910]+
OkHi [1905-06;11-12;14-15;17;20]-27

Durant EAGLE. *See* Durant weekly news

INDEPENDENT farmer. w Ja 12 1905-06||?
OkHi 1905-[06]

Durant weekly NEWS. w 1893+
1893-1900? as Durant eagle; 1901? Times-eagle
pub [1893]+
OkHi [1904-06;13]-[16;30]+

Durant daily NEWS. *See* Durant daily democrat

SOUTHEASTERN Oklahoma citizen and Bryan county democrat. *See* Bryan county democrat

Durant STATESMAN. w 1906-08||?
OkHi [1906-07]

Durant TIMES. w 1896-1900||?
United with Durant eagle to form Times-eagle, later Durant weekly news

TIMES-EAGLE. *See* Durant weekly news

DURHAM

Durham DISPATCH. w
OkHi [1907]

DUSTIN

Dustin DISPATCH. *See* Dustin news

DUSTONIAN. *See* Dustin news

Dustin NEWS. w 1904-24||?
1904-12 as Dustin dispatch; 1912-19 Dustonian
OkHi [1904-07;11-12]-[17;19]-[24]

OKLAHOMA (*Continued*)

EAGLE CITY

Eagle City RECORD. w S 1905-
OkHi [1905-06]

EARLSBORO

BORDER signal. w Je 19 1896-
OkHi Je-Ag 21 1896

Earlsboro ECHO. w Jl 9- 1903||?
OkHi [1903]

Earlsboro MESSENGER. w 1912-15||?
OkHi [1912]-[14]

Earlsboro TIMES. w Mr 1904-
OkHi [1904]

ECTER

BEAVER county republican. w 1906-10||?
OkHi [1906]-10

EDMOND

Edmond BOOSTER. w 1925+
pub 1925+
OkHi [1929]+

Edmond DEMOCRAT. w 1892-O? 1893||
United with Edmond Oklahoma sun to form Edmond sun-democrat, later Edmond sun
OkHi [1892-93]

Edmond ENTERPRISE. w 1901+
pub [1931]+
OkHi 1901-[09-10]-[13-14;21]+

Edmond NEWS. w 1894-95||?
OkHi [1894-95]

Edmond OKLAHOMA sun. *See* Edmond sun

Edmond REPUBLICAN. w 1893-99||?
OkHi [1894;97]

Edmond SUN. w Jl 18 1889+
1889-O 20 1893 as Edmond Oklahoma sun; O 27 1893-1900? Edmond sun-democrat
pub 1908+
KHi Ag 28 1890-My 1 1900
OkHi [1893]-1900[04-05]-[16]-27;29+
OkU Jl 18 1889

ELDORADO

Eldorado COURIER. w 1903+
pub [1903-29]
OkHi [1904]-[15]-[21]+

Eldorado DEMOCRAT. w O 18 1906-12||?
OkHi [1906;11-12]

ELGIN

Elgin CHIEF. w 1905-07||?
OkHi [1905]-[07]

Elgin ECHO. w
OkHi [1908-09]

FARMERS champion. *See* Fletcher herald (Fletcher)

Elgin NEWS. w 1905-
OkHi [1908]

Elgin TRIBUNE. w
OkHi [1909-10]

ELK CITY

BECKHAM county news. *See* Elk City daily news

Elk City DEMOCRAT and statesman. w 1901-10||?
1901-06? as Roger Mills democrat; 1907? Elk City democrat
OkHi [1901-02]-07[09]10
—d ed *See* Elk City daily news

Elk City JOURNAL. w 1924+
pub 1924-25;33+
OkHi [1932-33]
—d ed *See* Elk City daily news

Elk City daily NEWS. w,sw,d 1907?+
1907?-12? as Beckham county news; 1913? Elk City news; 1914-S 1929 Elk City news-democrat
w 1907?-S 1929(sw D 1924-My 1925)
OkHi [1914]-[29]+
—w ed *See* Elk City democrat and statesman; Elk City journal

Elk City PRESS. w Ja 1915-26||?
1915-16? as Southwestern news and leader; 1917?-25? Elk City southwestern press (1919?-21? Elk City press)
OkHi 1916[17]19-[24-26]

Elk City RECORD. w 1901-13||?
OkHi [1904]-[13]

ROGER MILLS democrat. *See* Elk City democrat and statesman

SOUTHWESTERN news and leader. *See* Elk City press

Elk City SOUTHWESTERN press. *See* Elk City press

Elk City morning TIMES. d 1932+
OkHi [1933]+

ELMER

Elmer DISPATCH. w 1911-13||?
OkHi [1911]-[13]

Elmer RECORD. w 1907-
OkHi [1908-10]

ELMORE

Elmore DEMOCRAT. w 1906-08||?
1906-07? as Elmore record
OkHi [1906]-[08]

Elmore GAZETTE. w
OkHi [1910-11]

Elmore RECORD. *See* Elmore democrat

EL RENO

El Reno AMERICAN. w 1896-1906||?
1896-Jl? 1901? as El Reno news; Jl 25 1901?-04? American-news
pub 1896-1901
OkHi [1896]-[1901]-[03]04;06-07

El Reno AMERICAN. d,w 1901+
1901-10? as El Reno daily American(d)
pub Ag 28 1901+
DLC 1904-10
OkHi [1901]03-08]12+

El Reno evening BELL. d 1897-F 1903||?
1897-1901? as El Reno supper bell. United with El Reno daily globe to form El Reno daily globe and El Reno evening bell, later El Reno daily globe
OkHi 1900-02

CANADIAN county courier. w N 1889-93||?
Merged with El Reno democrat
KHi Mr 23 1892-N 2 1893
OkHi [1893]

CANADIAN county democrat. w O 1931+
pub 1931+

CANADIAN county republican. w 1894-98||?
Title varies: El Reno republican
OkHi 1894-[97]

Der COURIER. w D 22 1893-
In German
KHi 1893-My 25 1894
OkHi [1893-94]

El Reno DEMOCRAT. w Ja 1891-1914||?
1891-F 1893 as Oklahoma democrat; D 21-28 1905 El Reno democrat and globe
KHi D 28 1893-Ag 15 1907
OkHi [1891-93]-[96]-1900;03;05-08;10-[13]

El Reno daily DEMOCRAT. d O 10 1901-O 1 1929||?
United with Peoples press to form El Reno daily tribune
OkErT 1901-28
OkHi [1904-06;09;15]21-29

El Reno EAGLE. w 1889-96||?
1889-90? pub in Reno City
OkHi [1893-96]

El Reno daily EAGLE. d Jl 1893-96||?
OkHi [1893-95]

El Reno daily GLOBE. d 1893-1905||?
F 12-Mr 31 1903 as El Reno daily globe and El Reno evening bell
OkErT [1894]-97
OkHi [1894]1904-05

El Reno weekly GLOBE. w 1893-D? 1905||?
United with El Reno democrat to form El Reno democrat and globe, later El Reno democrat
OkHi [1894]-[1905]

El Reno HERALD. w Je 20 1889-97||?
Je 20 1889- 1890 as Reno herald (Reno City) 1894? Oklahoma herald
KHi [O 8 1890-Ja 16 1891]
OkHi [1891-92;94-95]-[97]
OkU Je 20 1889

El Reno daily HERALD. d 1892-94||?
OkHi [1892-94]

Weekly INDUSTRIAL headlight. w,sw S 7 1894-96||?
1894-F 1895? as Populist platform; Jl-1895? Semi-weekly industrial headlight(sw)
OkHi [1894-96]

El Reno MINSTREL. w Je 2 1893-
OkHi [1893]

El Reno NEWS. *See* El Reno American

OKLAHOMA democrat. *See* El Reno democrat

OKLAHOMA herald. *See* El Reno herald

OKLAHOMA volksblatt. w 1898-1912||?
In German
OkHi 1908-10

OKLAHOMA volksblatt. d
In German
OkHi [1911]

PEOPLE'S press. d,sw,tw 1910?-O 1 1929||?
United with El Reno daily democrat to form El Reno daily tribune
d 1910?-12?;sw 1913?-23?
OkHi 1911[12]

POPULIST platform. *See* Weekly industrial headlight

REPUBLIC. w 1907-10||?
OkHi 1909

El Reno daily REPUBLICAN. d Ja 1 1896-
OkHi [1896]

El Reno REPUBLICAN. w *See* Canadian county republican

El Reno evening STAR. d 1896-99||?
OkHi [1896]-98

STATE tribune. w
OkHi [1907]

El Reno SUPPER bell. *See* El Reno evening bell

El Reno daily TRIBUNE. d O 2 1929+
Formed by the union of El Reno daily democrat and People's press
pub 1929+
OkHi 1929+

ENID

To 1894? as North Enid

COMING events. *See* Enid events

Enid DEMOCRAT. *See* Garfield county democrat

Enid EAGLE. w S 21 1893-1908||?
Title varies slightly
OkHi 1893[94]-[97]-[99]1904-03;07[08]

Enid daily EAGLE. d S 1901+
pub [1917;28]+
OkE [1924]+
OkHi [1906;08]-[13]-[26]-29-30]+

Enid ECHO. w Ja 3 1900-06||?
OkHi 1900-[04]-[06]

Daily ENTERPRISE. d S 18 1893-94||
OkHi [1893-94]

Enid EVENTS. w O 19 1893+
O 19 1895-Ap 17 1902 as Coming events
pub 1893+
OkHi 1893-[1900]+

GARFIELD county democrat. w,d S 19 1893-N 1908||?
1893-Ap 24 1894 as West Side democrat; My 2 1894-N 23? 1895 Daily tribune-democrat; N 30 1895-My 1897? Enid democrat. United with Enid wave to form Enid wave-democrat, later Enid weekly news and Jacksonian
d My 2 1894-N 23? 1895
OkHi 1893-My 8 1897;99-1908

GARFIELD county press and Enid wave-democrat. *See* Enid weekly news and Jacksonian

JACKSONIAN and Garfield county press. *See* Enid weekly news and Jacksonian

Enid morning NEWS. d D 11 1893+
1893-Ap 25 1908? as Enid daily wave; Ag 1-S 30 1917 Enid daily morning news; D 2 1917-F 18 1923 Enid daily news
pub [1924]+
OkE 1893-[1909;12]+
OkHi 1893-[96]97;99[1900]01[05-06]-08[10]+

Enid weekly NEWS and Jacksonian. w 1893-Jl 5 1918||?
1893-N 1908? as Enid weekly wave; D 5 1908?-F 9 1911 Enid wave-democrat; F 16 1911-F 23 1912 Garfield county press and Enid wave-democrat; Mr 1 1912-Ap 19 1918 Jacksonian and Garfield county press
OkHi 1894[95]97-98;1900;02-04;D 1908-Jl 5 1918

OKLAHOMA staats-zeitung. w 1906?+
Follows Die Enid post? 1906?-15? as Enid staats-zeitung
In German
OkHi 1906-11[13]14;18+

Die Enid POST. w 1902-05||?
Followed by Enid staats-zeitung, later Oklahoma staats-zeitung
In German
OkHi 1902-03[05]

Enid STAATS-ZEITUNG. *See* Oklahoma staats-zeitung

Enid STATE tribune. w My 17-S 4 1900||
OkHi [1900]

Enid daily TIMES. d
OkHi [1920;27-28]

Enid TIMES. w
OkHi [1925-26]

TOWN builder. w
OkHi [1907]

Enid TRIBUNE-DEMOCRAT. w 1894-95||?
1894? as North Enid weekly tribune (North Enid)
OkHi [1893-94]

Daily TRIBUNE-DEMOCRAT. *See* Garfield county democrat

Enid daily WAVE. *See* Enid morning news

Enid weekly WAVE. *See* Enid weekly news and Jacksonian

WEST SIDE democrat. *See* Garfield county democrat

ERICK

Erick ALTRUIST. w 1904-14||?
1904-Ap 4 1907 as Greer county republican
OkHi [1904]05[07-08]-[10-11]-[14]

BECKHAM county democrat. w Ja 1907+
Ja 5-D 27 1928 as Erick democrat
OkHi 1909-[12-17]-[20-21]-23;26+

Erick DEMOCRAT. *See* Beckham county democrat

Erick ENTERPRISE. w 1901-05||?
OkHi [1904]05

GREER county republican. *See* Erick altruist

ESCHITI

Eschiti BANNER. w 1907-09||?
OkHi [1907-08]

EUFAULA

Eufaula DEMOCRAT. w 1906-19||?
1906-D 26 1913 as Eufaula republican
OkHi [1906-09]-[12]-[16]

OKLAHOMA (*Continued*)

EUFAULA—*Continued*

INDIAN journal. w,d My 11? 1876+
1876-Mr? 1877;O 1878-Mr 23 1887 pub in Muskogee
d S 30-O 20 1876;O 1878;O 1880;S 1881;1902?
pub 1907+
DLC My 25,Jl 13 1876
MWA Ja 16 1878
MnHi Ja 26 1888
OkHi [1876-92;94-95;98]1902[03-05]-[16-17;19]-[33]+
OkMP 1887;89
OkU O 9 1878;O 1 1880;S 15 1881
WHi Jl 6 1895

Eufaula REPUBLICAN. *See* Eufaula democrat

Eufaula weekly STAR. w 1925||?
OkHi [1925]

FAIRFAX

Fairfax BANNER. w
OkHi [1910-11]

Fairfax CHIEF. w Jl 29 1904+
1904-Ag 17 1923 as Osage chief
pub [1908]10+
OkHi [1904-09]11-[15]-[21-22]-24

OSAGE chief. *See* Fairfax chief

OVER-LAND. w
OkHi [1912]

FAIRLAND

Fairland HERALD. w Ap 4-Ag 29 1913||?
United with Fairland news to form Fairland news-herald, later Ottawa county democrat
OkHi [1913]

Fairland NEWS. *See* Ottawa county democrat

OTTAWA county democrat. w My 12 1905+
1905-Ag 29 1913 as Fairland news; S 5 1913-34? Fairland news-herald
OkHi [1905]-[07-08]-[17]

FAIRVIEW

Fairview ENTERPRISE. w 1903-Ja 1919||?
United with Fairview leader to form Fairview leader-enterprise
OkHi [1914]-[17]

Fairview LEADER-ENTERPRISE. w 1907-21||?
1907-Ja 23 1919 as Fairview leader
OkHi [1908]-[15-16]-[21]

MAJOR county democrat. w 1914-24||?
1914-My 31 1922 as Northwestern press
OkHi [1921-22]

Fairview NEWS. w D 10 1930+
pub 1930+

NORTHWESTERN press. *See* Major county democrat

PEACE pipe. w
OkHi [1922]

Fairview REPUBLICAN. w 1900+
OkHi [1904]+

FALLIS

Fallis GAZETTE. w 1913-14||?
OkHi [1913]

Fallis STAR. w 1903-06||?
OkHi [1903]-[05-06]

FARGO

Fargo JOURNAL. w S 23 1903-12||?
OkHi 1908-12

Fargo REPORTER. w 1909||?
OkHi 1909

Fargo REPUBLICAN. w 1909-18||?
OkHi [1911]-[18]

SOUTHWESTERN news-digest. w
OkHi [1912]

FAXON

Faxon LEADER. w 1905-12||?
OkHi [1907-11]

Faxon SIGNAL. w 1913-18||?
OkHi [1914]-[18]

Faxon weekly STAR. w Mr 10 1904-06||?
Title varies slightly
OkHi [1904-06]

FAY

Fay FORUM. w 1911-14||?
OkHi [1912-13]

Fay MAGNET. w 1908-09||?
OkHi [1908-09]

FITZHUGH

Fitzhugh HERALD. w
OkHi [1914]

FLETCHER

ADVOCATE. w 1905-09||?
OkHi [1905]-[08-09]

Fletcher ENTERPRISE. w
OkHi [1915]

FARMERS champion. *See* Fletcher herald

Fletcher HERALD. w 1910+
1910-F 1 1922 as Farmers champion
1910-21? pub in Elgin
pub 1922+
OkHi [1912]-[17]21+

Fletcher TIMES. w
OkHi [1904]

Fletcher TIMES. 1910-15 *See* Comanche county times (Lawton)

Fletcher TRIBUNE. w 1915-17||?
OkHi [1915-16]

FORAKER

Foraker FREE PRESS. w
OkHi [1912]

Foraker SUN. w Ap 20 1906-14||?
1906-10 as Foraker tribune
OkHi [1906]-[10]-[14]

Foraker TRIBUNE. *See* Foraker sun

FORGAN

Forgan ADVOCATE. w 1927+
OkHi [1927]-[34]

Forgan ENTERPRISE. w 1912-N 4 1915||?
OkHi [1912]-N 4 1915

FORT COBB

CADDO county record. w 1902-23||?
1902-22? as Fort Cobb record (title varies slightly)
OkHi [1904-08]-[10]-[12-13]-[16]-[18-19;21-23]

Fort Cobb EXPRESS. w 1923+
pub [1923]+
OkHi [1924]-[33]+

Fort Cobb RECORD. *See* Caddo county record

FORT GIBSON

CHEROKEE tomahawk. ir
In English and Cherokee
KHi Mr 13 1865

Fort Gibson DEMOCRAT. w 1906-08||?
OkHi [1907-08]

Fort Gibson GAZETTE. w 1915-16||?
OkHi [1915-16]

Fort gibson INDEPENDENT. w 1921+
pub 1921+

INDIAN arrow. *See* Tahlequah arrow (Tahlequah)

Fort Gibson NEW ERA. w 1911-22||?
OkHi [1910]-16;21[22]

Fort Gibson POST. *See* Muskogee county republican (Muskogee)

Fort Gibson TIMES. w 1922?-23||?
OkHi [1922]

FORT TOWSON

Fort Towson ENTERPRISE. w 1905-20||
OkHi [1908]-[20]

Fort Towson NEWS. w 1918+
OkHi [1929-31]

FORT WASHITA

CHICKASAW intelligencer. w 1854-55||?
NbHi Ag 26 1854

FOSS

Foss ENTERPRISE. w 1901+
OkHi [1904]-[10-11]-[17;19]-[29]-[32]-[34]

FOYIL

Foyil City BREEZE. w
OkHi [1912]

Foyil City LEADER. w 1903-11||?
1903- 1908 as Statesman; 1908-09? Rogers county democrat; 1910? Rogers county leader
OkHi [1907-11]

ROGERS county democrat. *See* Foyil City leader

ROGERS county leader. *See* Foyil City leader

STATESMAN. *See* Foyil City leader

FRANCIS

Francis BANNER. w Ja 5 1901-
OkHi [1901]

Francis BULLETIN. w S 1 1905-
OkHi [1905-06]

Weekly FRANCISCAN. w Je 17 1903-06||?
OkHi [1904-05]

Francis HERALD. w 1921-27||?
OkHi [1924]

WIGWAM. w O 1907-21||?
OkAdB 1909-[13]
OkHi [1907]-[09]-[13-14]-[17-21]

FRAZER. *See* ALTUS

FREDERICK

Frederick ENTERPRISE. *See* Frederick star

FREE PRESS.
OkFP 1903

FREE PRESS. 1920-23 *See* Frederick press

Frederick LEADER. w O 8 1904?-28||?
OkHi [1907-09]-[16]19-[21-22]

Frederick LEADER. d 1917+
KHi Mr 17 1924
OkHi [1920]-[22]+

Frederick PRESS. w 1920+
1920-My 29 1923 as Free press
pub 1920+
OkHi 1922+

Frederick STAR. w,sw 1902-19||?
1902-F 13 1914 as Frederick enterprise (title varies slightly) F 20 1914- 1917 Tillman county enterprise
sw 1917-Jl 1918
OkFP 1902-18
OkHi [1904]-[06]-[19]

TILLMAN county enterprise. *See* Frederick star

FREEDOM

Freedom BOOSTER. w 1915-17||?
OkHi [1916]-17

Freedom CALL. w 1922+
1922-25? as Cimarron call
pub [1922-25]26;34+
KHi S 8 1927

CIMARRON call. *See* Freedom call

Freedom EXPRESS. w 1906-14||?
OkHi [1906]-[08]-[14]

FRISCO

Frisco HERALD. w O 24 1889-91||?
KHi 1889-Ap 16 1891

METEOR. *See under* Afton

GAGE

Gage BANNER. *See* Ellis county republican

ELLIS county advocate. w 1918-23||?
OkHi [1918]-[20-21]-[23]

ELLIS county republican. w Ja 3 1906-Je 26 1913||
1906? as Gage banner
OkHi [1906]-[10-11]-13

Gage RECORD. w 1901+
1909?-22? as Republican record
OkHi [1904-05]-[08-10;13]-[20]

REPUBLICAN record. *See* Gage record

GARBER

Garber SENTINEL. w 1899+
pub 1899+
OkHi [1901]-[28]

GARVIN

AMERICAN socialist-democrat. w
-Ag 4 1910 as American socialist
OkHi 1910

Garvin GRAPHIC. w 1903-19||?
OkHi 1904-[06-09]-11[15]-[17-19]

Garvin PIONEER. w 1908-12||?
Negro
OkHi [1908-10]

GATE

GATE VALLEY star. w 1906-22||?
OkHi [1906-08]-19

GEARY

BLAINE county star. *See* Geary star

Geary BOOSTER. w 1912-15||?
OkHi [1912]-15

Geary BULLETIN. w 1899-1913||?
OkHi [1899]-[03-05]-13

Geary JOURNAL. w 1902-Ja 9 1919||
Title varies slightly. United with Geary times to form Geary times-journal
OkHi [1904]-[09-13]-19

Geary STAR. w 1927+
1927-29? as Blaine county star
pub 1927-30;32+
OkHi 1928+

Geary TIMES-JOURNAL. w 1912+
1912-Ja 9 1919 as Geary times
OkHi 1916-[21]-[24-31]+

GERONIMO

Geronimo ADVOCATE. w Ap 5 1906-12||?
OkHi [1906-08]-12

GIBSON

NEW county hub. w 1908-09||?
1908? as Looney record (Looney)
OkHi [1908-09]

OKLAHOMA (*Continued*)

GLENCOE

Glencoe MIRROR. w 1900+
OkHi 1901-[02;04]-07[09]-[18;20]+

GOLTRY

Goltry EAGLE. w 1915-17||?
OkHi [1916-17]

Goltry LEADER. w 1921+
pub [1926]+
KHi F 10 1922
OkHi [1931]+

Goltry NEWS. w 1901-14||?
KHi Ja 20 1911-S 1913
OkHi [190-]-[09]-[14]
OkJV 1904-[1906]

GOODNIGHT

Goodnight NEWS. w Ap 12? 1906-
OkHi [1906-08]

GOODWELL

Goodwell NEWS. w 1908-17||?
OkHi [1908-10]

GOODWIN

Goodwin ENTERPRISE. w 1906-07||?
OkHi [1906-07]

GORE

To 1908? as Campbell

CAMPBELL register. w S 14 1906-08||?
OkHi [1906-07]

CITIZEN. w 1912||?
OkHi [1912]

GOTEBO

To 1905? as Harrison

Gotebo GAZETTE. w Ag 1901-23||?
1901-Mr 1 1907 as Harrison gazette
OkHi [1902-03]-[14-15;19]-[26]

HARRISON gazette. *See* Gotebo gazette

GOULD

HARMON county news. w 1909-12||?
OkHi [1911-12]

Gould RECORD. w 1910-20||?
OkHi [1916]-[1-]

GRACEMONT

Gracemont GRAPHIC. w Ap 13 1906-11||?
OkHi [1906]-[11]

Gracemont HERALD. w 1913-19||?
OkHi [1914-15]-[17;19]

Gracemont NEWS. w 1931+
pub [1931]+

GRAND

CANADIAN VALLEY echo. w 1902-07||?
OkHi [1904]-[07]

DAY county progress. w 1895-1908||?
1895-1900? as Day county tribune
OkHi [1902]-[04-05]-[07-08]

DAY county tribune. *See* Day county progress

GRANDFIELD

Grandfield ENTERPRISE. w 1906+
OkHi [1908-09]-[1-]-[17-18]+

GRANITE

Granite ENTERPRISE. w My 11 1900+
pub 1900+
NcD Je 4 1907
OkHi [1900-01]-[05-06]-12;15+

GRAY

BEAVER county republican. w 1905?-18||?
OkHi 1915-[18]

GREENFIELD

Greenfield BOOSTER. w
OkHi [1911-12]

Greenfield HUSTLER. w 1913-21||?
OkHi [1913]-[17]-[19-21]

GROVE

DELAWARE county news. w 1909-O 2 1914||?
OkHi 1910-[11-12]-14

Grove MESSENGER. *See* Grove sun

Grove SUN. w 1900+
1900-03? as Grove messenger
pub 1900+
OkHi [1904-07]+

GUERTIE

Guertie NEWS. w Ag 31 1905-06||?
OkHi 1905-[06]

GUTHRIE

Evening DEMOCRAT. d 1889-90||?
1889-Ja? 1890 as Daily state herald
KHi Ja 16-N 13,17 1890
OkU Ja 16 1890
—w ed *See* Oklahoma state herald

Guthrie DEMOCRAT. d Je 1 1892-
OkU Je 1 1892

FARMERS' union advocate. w 1906-
OkHi [1910]

Guthrie FEDERAL. w 1901-
OkHi [1901]

Guthrie GETUP. *See* Guthrie republican

Guthrie daily LEADER. d 1892+
pub 1892+
CoU 1899;1905;S 1906-09
KHi Jl 13 1897-99;N 16 1907
OkG 1906+
OkHi [1893]-[98]-[1917]+
—w ed *See* Oklahoma leader

Guthrie weekly NEWS. w Ap 22 1889-94||?
KHi N 25 1889

Guthrie daily NEWS. d My 23 1889-94||?
KHi [Ap 9-My 21 1890]
OkHi [1889;93-94]

OKLAHOMA capital. *See* Oklahoma state capital

OKLAHOMA enterprise. w 1908-12||?
OkHi [1908-09]

OKLAHOMA guide. w 1892-1923||?
Negro
OkHi [1900]-[12]-[17]-[22]

OKLAHOMA leader. w 1892-1932||?
OkHi [1896;1900]01[11]
—d ed *See* Guthrie daily leader

OKLAHOMA optic. d My 6?- 1889||?
Merged with Guthrie daily news
KHi My 20-Ag 10 1889

OKLAHOMA populist. w Ap- 1893||?
OkHi [1893]
WHi Ag 10 1893

OKLAHOMA representative. w N 15 1891-97||?
OkHi [1894]-97

OKLAHOMA safeguard. w 1894?-1915||?
Negro
OkHi 1905-06

Weekly OKLAHOMA state capital. w Mr 30 1889-1911||?
Mr 30 1889-90? as Oklahoma capital
KHi 1889-Je 12 1897
OkHi 1895-1900[02-03]-07;09
OkU Mr 30 1889

OKLAHOMA state capital. d Ap 22 1889-Mr 28 1911||?
Title varies: Daily Oklahoma capital; Daily Oklahoma state capital
DLC Ag 21 1890-95;97-Mr 1911
KHi My-S 7 1889;S 11 1893-Ap 20 1898
OClWHi S 23 1890
OkG 1904-11
OkHi [1891;93]-[96]-[1901]-[07]-11

OKLAHOMA state herald. w 1889||?
KHi O 14-N 1889
—d ed *See* Evening democrat

OKLAHOMA state journal. *See* West and South

OKLAHOMA state register. w 1898+
KHi O 22 1925
OkG 1912+
OkHi [1900]+

PEOPLE'S elevator. w
OkHi [1922-23]

Guthrie REPUBLICAN. w Ap 29-N? 1889||
Ap-Ag as Guthrie getup. Merged with Guthrie weekly news
KHi [Ap-N 14 1889]
OkHi Ap-My 5 1889
OkU Ap 29 1889

SOUTHWEST world. w Mr 3 1900-03||?
OkHi [1900]03

Guthrie weekly STAR. w 1907?-12||?
OkHi [1912]

Guthrie daily STAR. d 1908?-12||?
OkG [1912]
OkHi 1912

Daily STATE herald. *See* Evening democrat

Twice-a-week SUN. sw 1911-14||?
OkHi [1913]

WEST and South. w 1890-92||?
1890-N 1891 as Oklahoma state journal
KHi 1891-Jl 7 1892

WESTERN world. *See under* Oklahoma City

GUYMON

Guymon DEMOCRAT. w 1907-19||?
OkGuP 1909-18
OkHi 1907[08;15]-19

Guymon HERALD. *See* Panhandle herald

PANHANDLE herald. w,d 1891+
1891-Ja 22 1925 as Guymon herald
w 1891-D 25 1932
pub 1925+
KHi N 3 1921
OkHi [1904]+

Guymon daily NEWS. d Jl 1 1934+
pub 1934+

TEXAS county news. w Jl 2 1930+
pub 1930+

Guymon TRIBUNE. w 1921-26||?
OkGuP 1921-23
OkHi [1921]-26

HAILEYVILLE

HEADLIGHT journal. w 1902-05||?
OkHi [1904-05]

Haileyville HERALD. w 1919-Jl 7 1921||?
My 20 1920-Jl 7 1921 as Herald
OkHi [1919]-21

NEW STATE. w 1905-10||?
OkHi [1905]-[07]-09

Haileyville SIGNAL. w 1909-1-||?
OkHi [1909]

HALLETT

Hallett HERALD. w 1907-18||?
OkHi [1907-09]-[13-14]-[18]

HAMBURG

Hamburg BLADE. w Je 8 1906-07||?
OkHi [1906-07]

HAMMON

Hammon ADVOCATE. w 1910+
pub 1923+
OkHi [1911]-[19]

BOOSTER. w
OkHi [1913]

Hammon NEWS. w 1910-12||?
OkHi [1910-12]

HARDESTY

Hardesty HERALD. w 1891-1901||?
OkHi [1893]-[95-96]

Hardesty TIMES. w My 3- 1890||?
KHi [My 31-Ag 16 1890]

HARRAH

Harrah ENTERPRISE. w 1906||?
OkHi [1906]

Harrah HERALD. w 1925+
pub 1930+
OkHi [1925]+

Harrah NEWS. w 1907-16||?
1907-08? as Harrah tribune; 1909? Harrah news and tribune
OkHi [1907]-[09-11]-[16]

Harrah TRIBUNE. *See* Harrah news

HARRISON. *See* GOTEBO

HARTSHORNE

Hartshorne CRITIC. w 1901-05||?
OkHi [1904-05]

Hartshorne NEWS. w S 29 1911-12||?
OkHi [1911-12]

OKLAHOMA sun. *See* Hartshorne sun

PITTSBURGH county republican. w 1919-22||?
OkHi [1921-22]

Hartshorne SUN. w O 1895+
Mr 1-N 22 1923 as Oklahoma sun
pub [1901]02;04-05;08+
OkHi [1895;1904]-[08-10]-[32]+

HASKELL

Haskell JOURNAL. w 1904-09||?
OkHi [1905]

Haskell NEWS. w 1909+
OkHi [1910-11]-33

HASTINGS

FREE LANCE. w O 28 1904-05||?
OkHi [1904-05]

Hastings HERALD. w 1912-22||?
OkHi [1912-14]19-[21]

Hastings NEWS. w 1902-12||?
OkHi [1904-07]09-12

HAWORTH

Haworth HERALD. w 1912-23||?
OkHi [1912]-[21]

HEADRICK

Headrick LEADER. w 1906-12||?
OkHi [1907]-[12]

HEALDTON

Healdton HERALD. w Ag 2 1917+
pub 1917+
OkHi [1930]+

OKLAHOMA (*Continued*)

HEAVENER

Heavener DISPATCH. w 1910-D 6 1917||?
United with Heavener ledger to form Heavener ledger-dispatch, later Heavener ledger
OkHi [1916]17

Heavener LEDGER. w 1904+
D 1917?-19? as Heavener ledger-dispatch
pub 1920+
KHi O 14 1926
OkHi [1908-10]-19

HELENA

Helena FREE PRESS. w 1903-08||?
OkHi [1903]-[08]

Helena HERALD. w 1903-06||?
OkHi [1903]-06

Helena STAR. w 1905+
pub 1930+
OkHi [1905-06;08-09]-[15]-[29]+

HENNESSEY

Hennessey CLIPPER. w N 21 1889+
KHi Je 13 1890-O 1903
OkHi [1892-93]-96;98+
OkU N 21 1889

Hennessey COURIER. *See* Kingfisher times (Kingfisher)

Hennessey DEMOCRAT. w 1893-Ja 25 1895||?
United with Hennessey press to form Press-democrat
OkHi [1893]-95

EAGLE. w My 9 1901-04||?
OkHi 1901-[02]-[04]

Hennessey KICKER. w 1893-99||?
KHi F 26 1896-Ja 5 1900
OkHi 1896-[98]99

PRESS-DEMOCRAT. w Jl 27 1894-1914||?
1894-Ja 26 1895 as Hennessey press
OkHi [1894-96;1900]-13

HENRYETTA

Daily FREE-LANCE. w,d N 27 1902+
Title varies slightly
w 1902-Ja 31 1916?
pub 1902+
OkHi [1903-09]-[20-21]+
OkHn 1925+

Henryetta NEWS. w 1924?+
pub 1924-27
OkHi [1925-27]-[31-32]+
OkHn [1933]+

Henryetta RECORD. w 1905-09||?
OkHi [1908-09]

Henryetta STANDARD. w 1910-24||?
OkHi [1906;11]-[23]24
OkHn [1910]-[23]

Henryetta daily STANDARD. d 1923-24||?
OkHi [1923-24]
OkHn [1923-24]

HEWITT

CARTER county record. w 1911-14||?
OkHi [1913]

CARTER county record. w
OkHi [1931]

HINTON

Hinton NEWS. w 1910-
OkHi [1913]-[16]

Hinton RECORD. w 1902+
1904?- 1907 as Hinton record and Lookeba light; 1907-Ap 3 1908 Hinton record. Bridgeport news and Lookeba light
OkHi [1904]-[07-08]-[33]+

HITCHCOCK

Hitchcock CLARION. w Ja 1908+
pub [1908]+
OkHi 1908[09]-20;22-[28]

VANGUARD. w N 1901-06||?
OkHi [1904-06]

HOBART

CHIEF. *See* Democrat-chief

Hobart daily DEMOCRAT. d 1903-Ap 1909||
United with Hobart daily chief to form Hobart democrat-chief
OkHi [1906-07]

Hobart DEMOCRAT. w 1903-Ap 8 1909||?
United with Hobart weekly chief to form Weekly democrat-chief
OkHi [1906;08]

Weekly DEMOCRAT-CHIEF. w 1901-Ap 20 1928||
1901-Ap 8 1909 as Hobart weekly chief
OkHi 1902[03]-[06;08]-28
OkHo [1926-28]

Hobart DEMOCRAT-CHIEF. d 1903+
1903-Ap 1909 as Hobart daily chief
OkHi [1913;19]-[22;28]-[34]+
OkHo 1917-[19-20;28]+

Hobart GAZETTE. w Mr 1926-Ap 4 1927||?
OkHi [1926]
OkHo [1926]27

KIOWA county review. w 1924+
OkHi [1924]-[28]
OkHo [1926]27

KIOWA county star. w 1932+
pub 1932+
OkHi [1934]+
OkHo 1932+

Hobart NEWS. w *See* Hobart republican

Hobart daily NEWS-REPUBLICAN. *See* Hobart daily republican

Hobart daily POINTER. d 1902-
OkHi [1904]

Hobart weekly POINTER. w 1902-06||?
OkHi [1904-05]

Hobart REPUBLICAN. w 1901||?
United with Hobart news to form Hobart news-republican, later Hobart republican

Hobart REPUBLICAN. w 1901-20||?
1901? as Hobart news; 1902?-06? Hobart news-republican
OkHi [1901-02]05-[20]
OkHo [1918-20]

Hobart daily REPUBLICAN. d 1903-20||?
1903-06? as Hobart daily news-republican?
OkHi [1904]-08[19-20]
OkHo 1917[18]-[20]

HOFFMAN

Hoffman HERALD. w 1906-09||?
OkHi [1906]-[08-09]

Hoffman OBSERVER. w
OkHi [1915]

HOLDENVILLE

Holdenville DEMOCRAT. w 1907-31||?
OkHi [1908]-12;16-28;30[31]
OkHlN [1907]11-31

HUGHES county tribune. w 1901+
Early years as Holdenville tribune
OkHi [1904]-[07-08;12-14]-22[25]-[30]+
—d ed *See* Morning tribune

Holdenville daily NEWS. d 1927+
pub 1928+
OkHi [1931]+

Holdenville TIMES. w 1896-1910||?
OkHlN [1900]02-09

Morning TRIBUNE. d 1935+
OkHi 1935+

Holdenville TRIBUNE. w *See* Hughes county tribune

UNION signal. w Ap 1907-08||?
OkHi [1907]

HOLLIS

HARMON county tribune. w 1910-22||?
Title varies: Hollis tribune. United with Hollis post-herald to form Hollis post-herald and Harmon county tribune
KHi [My-D 11 1919]
OkHi [1910]-[14]-[16;18]-[20-22]

Hollis HERALD. w Je 1904-F 2 1906||?
United with Hollis post to form Hollis post-herald, later Hollis post-herald and Harmon county tribune
OkHi [1904]-06

Hollis POST-HERALD and Harmon county tribune. w Je 29 1905+
1905-F 1 1906 as Hollis post; F 8 1906-Ag 24 1922 Hollis post-herald
OkHi [1905-08]-27;31+

Sunday TIMES. w 1920+
Title varies: Saturday times
OkHi [1920-22;32]-[34]+

Hollis TRIBUNE. *See* Harmon county tribune

HOMESTEAD

Homestead NEWS. w 1901-
OkHi [1901]-06

HOMINY

Hominy HERALD. w
OkHi [1910-11]

Hominy JOURNAL. w 1921+
pub [1922]+

Hominy NEWS. w Jl 28 1905+
N 1 1907-D 27 1917 as Hominy news-republican
OkHi 1905-[07-10;12]-[32;34]+

OSAGE eagle. w
OkHi [1910]

HOOKER

Hooker ADVANCE. w 1904+
pub 1904+
OkHi 1904+

FARMERS voice. w 1909-
OkHi [1909]

HOWE

Howe EAGLE. w
OkHi [1908]

HERALD. w D 7 1906-
OkHi [1906;17]

WESTERN star. w S 5 1902-
OkHi [1902-04]05

HUGO

CHOCTAW county democrat. w 1921?-23||?
United with Hugo Husonian and Choctaw herald to form Husonian-democrat
OkHi [1921-22]

CHOCTAW herald. w 1906-20||?
United with Hugo Husonian to form Hugo Husonian and Choctaw herald, later Husonian-democrat
OkHi [1910]-[13]-19

Hugo daily HUSONIAN. *See* Hugo daily news

HUSONIAN-DEMOCRAT. w,sw 1902+
1902-D 30 1920 as Hugo Husonian; Ja 6 1921?-23? Hugo Husonian and Choctaw herald
sw 1919?
OkHi [1906;08-09;11]-[16]-[19-21]

Hugo daily NEWS. d 1907+
1907-16? as Hugo daily Husonian
KHi Jl 11,D 19 1924;Ja 14 1927
OkHi [1914-16;33]+
—w ed *See* Husonian-democrat

SOUTHEAST Oklahoman. tw,sw,w 1920+
tw 1920?;sw 1921?-22?
pub 1921+

HUNTER

Hunter ENTERPRISE. w 1901+
OkHi [1904-05]07[08]-[11]-[23]

HURLEY

Hurley LEADER. w 1907-08||?
OkHi [1908]

HYDRO

Hydro JOURNAL. w N 3 1904-05||?
OkHi 1904[05]

Hydro REVIEW. w 1901+
pub 1926+
OkHi [1904]-[21]+

IDABEL

BEACON-TIMES. w 1911?-My 1915||?
-1911 as McCurtain county beacon
OkHi [1911]-13

DEMOCRAT-RECORD. *See* McCurtain democrat

Idabel GAZETTE. w,sw My 1905+
1905-06? as Signal; 1907?-31? McCurtain gazette
w 1905-10
pub 1907+
OkHi [1905;07-11]-[15]-[23-24]+

MCCURTAIN county beacon. *See* Beacon-times

MCCURTAIN democrat. w,sw 1908?+
1908?-19 as Democrat-record; 1919-Ap 14 1922 Idabel news
sw Ap 18-N 1922
OkHi [1910]-[19]-[25-26]-32

MCCURTAIN gazette. *See* Idabel gazette

Idabel NEWS. *See* McCurtain democrat

SIGNAL. *See* Idabel gazette

INDEPENDENCE

Independence COURIER. *See* Custer courier

CUSTER courier. w Je 1900-02||?
1900-Ag 1 1902? as Independence courier
OkHi [1900]-02

Independence HERALD. w Je 1904-
OkHi [1904]

INDIAHOMA

Indiahoma ADVOCATE. w 1905-11||?
1905-Ja 21 1910 as Junction advocate (Junction)
OkHi [1909-10]

Indiahoma CHAMPION. w 1910-12||?
OkHi [1910]-[12]

INDIAHOMAN. w 1913-15||?
OkHi [1913-15]

INDIANOLA

Indianola ENTERPRISE. w 1903-09||?
OkHi [1905-06;08-09]

Indianola HERALD. w
OkHi [1911-12]

OKLAHOMA clipper. w
OkHi [1913-14]

Indianola PRESS. w Jl 1903-04||?
OkHi [1904]

INGERSOLL

Ingersoll ENTERPRISE. w 1901-10||?
1901-09 as Ingersoll review
OkHi [1904]-[06-10]

Ingersoll MIDGET. w 1912-14||?
OkHi [1912-14]

Ingersoll REVIEW. *See* Ingersoll enterprise

INOLA

Inola NEWS. w 1921-26||?
OkHi [1921-24]-[26]

Inola REGISTER. w 1905-20||?
OkHi [1906]-[18]

OKLAHOMA (*Continued*)

IVANHOE

Ivanhoe INDEPENDENT. w 1915-18||?
OkHi [1916]-[18]

Ivanhoe NEWS. w 1911-15||?
OkHi [1913-15]

JAY

DELAWARE county chieftain. *See* Jay record

DELAWARE county journal. w Ag 1931-
OkHi [1932-33]

Jay RECORD. w 1921+
1921-Je 25 1930? as Delaware county chieftain
KHi Mr 28 1923
OkHi [192]-[30]-32

JEFFERSON

Jefferson REVIEW. w 1897-1919||?
1897-1902 as Jefferson rustler
OkHi [1897]-[1902]-06

Jefferson RUSTLER. *See* Jefferson review

JENKS

Jenks ENQUIRER. w 1915-18||?
OkHi [1915-16]-[18]

Jenks NEWS. w 1918+
OkHi [1919-23]

Jenks TIMES. w 1933+
OkHi [1933-34

JENNINGS

Jennings HUMMER. O 27 1904-06||?
OkHi [1904-06]

Jennings NEWS. w 1900+
pub [1900-01]
OkHi [1900]-[19-21]-31;33+

JET

Jet NEWS. *See* Jet visitor

Jet VISITOR. w 1901?+
1901?-03 as Jet news
pub [1901]+
KHi Mr 23 1916
OkHi [1904]—

JONES

CANADIAN VALLEY news. *See* Oklahoma county news

OKLAHOMA county news. w 1901+
1901-Ap 30 1915 as Canadian Valley news
OkHi [1904-10]+

JUANITA. *See* CROWDER

JUNCTION

Junction ADVOCATE. *See* Indiahoma advocate (Indiahoma)

KANSAS

CHEROKEE hummer. w Mr 16 1906-
OkHi 1906[07]

DELAWARE tribune. w 1910-11||?
OkHi 1910[11]

KAW

Kaw City DEMOCRAT. w 1912-O 11 1917||?
United with Kaw City review to form Review-democrat, later Kaw City news
OkHi [1912]-17

Kaw City NEWS. w 1915+
1915-O 12? 1917 as Kaw City review; O 19 1917-18? Review-democrat; 1919?-22? Star-democrat
pub 1923+
OkHi 1917[18]

Kaw City REVIEW. *See* Kaw City news

Kaw City STAR. *See* Kaw City tribune

STAR-DEMOCRAT. *See* Kaw City news

Kaw City TRIBUNE. w 1902-13||?
1902-Ag 19 1910 as Kaw City star
OkHi [1902]-[13

KELLYVILLE

CREEK county leader. w 1927||?
OkHi [1927]

KEMPTON

Kempton NEWS. w
OkHi [1910]

KENDRICK

Kendrick DISPATCH. w 1905-06||?
OkHi [1905-06]

Kendrick NEWS. w 1927+
OkHi [1927-29]-33

Kendrick REVIEW. w 1904-11||?
OkHi [1909]-[11]

KENEFIC

To 1915 as Kenefick?

Kenefick DISPATCH. w 1910-19||?
OkHi [1910]-[13]

KENTON

CIMARRON news. *See* Boise City news (Boise City)

KEOKUK FALLS

Keokuk KALL. w Ja 28 1899-
OkHi [1899]

KEOTA

Keota RECORD. w 1913-15||?
OkHi [1915]

KETCHUM

Ketchum NEWS. w
OkHi [1923]

Ketchum TELEGRAM. w
OkHi [1913]

KEYSTONE

Keystone NEWS. w 1905-08||?
OkHi [1908]

KIEFER

Kiefer CHRONICLE. w 1913-18||?
OkHi [1915-18]

Kiefer DEMOCRAT. w 1923-26||?
OkHi [1925-26]

LAW and order journal. w
OkHi [1909-10]

Kiefer NEWS. w
OkHi [1907]

Kiefer SEARCHLIGHT. *See* Creek county republican (Sapulpa)

KIEL. *See* LOYAL

KILDARE

Kildare JOURNAL. w 1894-98||?
OkHi [1894]-98

SOONER. w S 14 1893-Ja 10 1894||?
OkHi [1893-94]

KINGFISHER

Kingfisher COURIER. *See* Kingfisher times

Kingfisher weekly FREE PRESS. w 1889+
1889-1907 as Kingfisher free press; 1907-Je 19 1913 Kingfisher weekly star and free press
KHi Je 25-D 1891
OkHi [1891]+

Kingfisher daily FREE PRESS. d 1909-23||?
OkHi [1913]-[23]

Kingfisher JOURNAL. w Mr 20- 1890||?
OkU Mr 20 1890

Das Kingfisher JOURNAL. w Ja 5 1893-
In German
OkHi [1893-95]

KINGFISHER county news. w 1926-27||?
OkHi 1927

Daily MIDGET. d 1908-13||?
OkHi [1908-10]-[13]
OkKT [1912]

NEW world. w 1889-91||?
KHi Je 1889-Je 6 1891
—d ed *See* Kingfisher daily world

Kingfisher NEWS. *See* Kingfisher times

Kingfisher REFORMER. w Ag 31 1893-1905||?
OkHi [1893]-[95;97]-[1905]

Kingfisher daily STAR. d 1902-07||?
United with Kingfisher free press to form Kingfisher weekly star and free press, later Kingfisher weekly free press
OkHi [1902-05]-[07]

Kingfisher weekly STAR and free press. *See* Kingfisher weekly free press

Kingfisher TIMES. w N 20 1889+
1889-Ag? 1890 as Hennessey courier (Hennessey) S?- 1890 Kingfisher courier; 1891? Kingfisher news
pub 1901+
KHi Ja 9-Ag 16,S 13-N 22 1890;S 18-N 19 1891
OkHi [1892-93]-[1918;24]+

Kingfisher daily TIMES. d
OkHi [1892-93]

Kingfisher daily TIMES. d 1915-
OkHi [1917-18]-[20-21]

WESTERN world. *See under* Oklahoma City

Kingfisher daily WORLD. d Mr 19- 1890||?
OkU Mr 19 1890
—w ed *See* New world

KINGSTON

MARSHALL county messenger. *See* Red River dairy farmer

RED RIVER dairy farmer. w 1902-30||?
1902-N 9 1928 as Marshall county messenger; N 16-D 28 1928 Red River dairy farmer and Marshall county messenger
OkHi [1904-05]-[08]-[23-24;26]-30

KINTA

Kinta ENTERPRISE. w 1905-07||?
OkHi [1905-06]

Kinta JOURNAL. w 1911-14||?
OkHi [1913-14]

KIOWA

Kiowa BREEZE. w Mr 29 1901-07||?
KHi Mr-D 6 1901[Ag 12 1902-Ja 1903]
OkHi [1904]-[06-07]

Kiowa CHRONICLE. w 1906+
OkHi [1906]-[12-14]-[18]

Kiowa SENTINEL. w 1903-07||?
OkHi [1904]-[06-07]

KNOWLES

FARMER'S news. w 1907-20||?
OkHi [1908]-[10]-12[19-20]

KONAWA

Konawa CHIEF. *See* Konawa leader

Konawa LEADER. w N 25 1904+
1904-Je 23? 1905 as Konawa chief; Je 30? 1905-23? Konawa chief-leader
pub [1925]+
OkHi [1904-10;17-19]-[23;25]-33

Konawa TIMES. w 1907||?
OkHi [1907]

KREBS

Krebs ADVERTISER. w My 19 1910-
OkHi [1910]

Krebs BANNER. w 1906-08||?
OkHi 1906[07-08]

Krebs CYCLONE. w F? 1899-1901||?
1899-1900? as Krebs eagle
OkHi [1900]

Krebs EAGLE. *See* Krebs cyclone

OKLAHOMA miner. w 1912-22||?
OkHi [1912-17;19-22]

KREMLIN

CHEROKEE cosmos. w F 9 1894-
OkHi [1894]

Kremlin JOURNAL. w 1908-21||?
OkHi 1910-21

Kremlin NEW ERA. w 1903-09||?
OkHi [1904]-[07-08]09

OKLAHOMA sun. w D 8 1905-
OkHi [1905-06]

KUHN

IMMIGRANT guide. w 1910-13||?
OkHi [1910-13]

KUSA

Kusa INDUSTRIAL. w N 11 1915-20||
OkHi [1915-18]-[20]

LAHOMA

Lahoma NEWS. w 1898-1929||?
1898-Ap 6 1923 as Lahoma sun
OkHi [1900]-[03-04]-[29]

Lahoma SUN. *See* Lahoma news

LA KEMP

CITIZEN. w 1908-10||?
OkHi [1909-10]

CITIZEN. w 1916-17||?
OkHi [1916-17]

La Kemp MIRROR. w 1909-14||?
OkHi [1909-11;13]

LAMAR

Lamar NEWS. w 1907-12||?
OkHi [1907;09]-[12]

LAMBERT

MESSENGER. w 1904?-05||?
OkHi [1904-05]

Lambert NEWS. w
OkHi [1914-16]

LAMONT

Lamont DISPATCH. w N 15 1900-06||?
OkHi [1900]-[06]

LAMONT VALLEY news. *See* Valley news

Lamont RECORD. w 1906-10||?
OkHi [1906]-[10]

OKLAHOMA (*Continued*)

LAMONT—*Continued*

VALLEY news. w 1903+
Title varies: Lamont Valley news
OkHi [1905;11]-[18]+

LANGSTON

To 1900? as Langston City

Langston City HERALD. w My 2? 1891-1902||?
Negro
DLC Ja 27 1900
KHi N 14 1891-Mr 2 1893
OkHi [1896-97]

LIVING age. *See* Western age

WESTERN age. m,w 1904-09||?
1904? as Living age
Negro
OkHi [1905-09]

LAVERNE

BEACON light. *See* Laverne tribune

LEADER-TRIBUNE. w 1912+
1912-O 12 1917 as Laverne leader
pub 1912+
OkHi [1912]+

Laverne TRIBUNE. w 1912-O 12 1917||?
1912-16 as Beacon light. United with Laverne leader to form Leader-tribune
OkHi [1914]-[16]17
OkLvL 1912-17

LAWTON

COMANCHE county booster. w
OkHi [1914]

COMANCHE county times. w 1910-16||?
1910-Jl? 1915 as Fletcher times (Fletcher) Ag 6- 1915? Fletcher times and Comanche county times
OkHi [1910-13]-[15-16]

Lawton CONSTITUTION. w,sw Ja 1 1902-14||?
1902? as Lawton weekly enterprise; Ap 25?-Je 27 1907 Lawton constitution democrat; Jl 4 1907-09? Lawton constitution-state democrat
sw Ap 26 1909-Ap 25 1910
OkHi 1903[04]06-[15]

Lawton CONSTITUTION. d 1902?+
1902? as Lawton enterprise; Ap 1907?-08? Lawton constitution-state democrat; 1909?-10? Constitution democrat
pub 1907-[10-18]+
OkHi [1904;06;15]-[33]+
OkL 1921+

DEMOCRAT. *See* State democrat

Lawton ENTERPRISE. *See* Lawton constitution

FLETCHER times and Comanche county times. *See* Comanche county times

MINERAL kingdom. *See* Oklahoma farm news

Lawton NEWS-REPUBLICAN. w 1900-14||?
1900-Ag 20 1903 as Lawton news
OkHi 1902-06

Lawton NEWS-REVIEW. d,w D? 1900+
1900-My 28 1903 as Daily news; Je? 1903-10? Daily news-republican; 1911?-14 Daily news and star; 1915-23 Lawton daily news
d 1900-23?
pub 1923+
KHi My 3 1922
OkHi [1904-05;07]-[16]-[18]-[23]+

OKLAHOMA farm news. w O 24 1903-07||?
1903-04? as Mt. Sheridan miner (Meers) 1905? Mineral kingdom
OkHi [1903-05]-[07]

Daily REPUBLICAN. d 1901-03||?
United with Daily news to form Daily news-republican, later Lawton news-review
OkHi [1902]

Weekly REPUBLICAN. w Ag 1901-Ag 20 1903||?
United with Lawton news to form Lawton news-republican
OkHi [1903]

Lawton weekly STAR. w,sw 1907-09||?
Title varies with frequency. Merged with Lawton news-republican
sw 1907?
OkHi [1907]-[09]

Lawton daily STAR. d 1908-10||?
United with Daily news-republican to form Daily news and star, later Lawton news-review
OkHi [1911]

STATE democrat. d 1901-Ap 1907||?
Title varies: Democrat. United with Lawton constitution to form Lawton constitution-state democrat, later Lawton constitution
OkHi [1904-05]

STATE democrat. w Jl 1901-Ap 11 1907||?
1901? as Lawton democrat. United with Lawton constitution to form Lawton constitution-state democrat, later Lawton constitution
OkHi [1904]-[06-07]

WILSON'S weekly democrat. w 1908-11||?
OkHi [1908]-11

WORKING man. w
OkHi [1910]

LEEDEY

Leedey HERALD. w 1904-16||?
United with Leedey times to form Leedey times and herald, later Leedey times
OkHi [1912-13]-[16]

Leedey NEWS. w 1933+
OkCaR 1933+

Leedey TIMES. w Je 1904-32||?
1917?-23? as Leedey times and herald?
KHi S 9 1926
OkHi [1911]-31

LEGER. *See* ALTUS

LEHIGH

Lehigh LEADER. w 1891-1912||?
Early years as Lehigh-Coalgate leader
KHi Ja 27 1893
OkHi [1904]-[08-09]-[12]

Lehigh NEWS. w 1888-F 1889||?
United with Atoka independent to form Indian citizen, later Indian citizen-democrat (Atoka)

Lehigh NEWS. w 1913-21||?
OkHi [1913-14]-[20]

LENAPAH

Lenapah NEWS. w 1903-07||?
OkHi [1904-06]

Lenapah POST. w 1910-20||?
OkHi [1911]-[13]-[17-18]

LENORA

Lenora LEADER. w 1902-11||?
OkHi [1904]-[09;11]

Lenora NEWS. w
OkHi [1914;16]

LEWIS

AGITATOR. w
OkHi [1908]

LEXINGTON

CLEVELAND county leader. *See* Lexington leader

Lexington LEADER. Je 4 1891-1923||?
1891-1902? as Cleveland county leader
OkHi [1891-92;94-95;97;99-1900]01[04-06;08]-[23]

Lexington NEWS. w 1929-31||?
OkAnN [1929]-31

SOUTHERN democrat. w D 10 1892-93||?
OkU D 10 1892

Lexington SUN. w 1931+
pub [1931]+
OkHi [1931]+

Lexington TRANSCRIPT. w S 26 1889-
OkU S 26 1889

YOU ALL'S doings. w 1899-1902||
OkHi [1900]01

LIMA

Wewoka and Lima COURIER. *See under* Wewoka

LINDSAY

Lindsay NEWS. w 1902+
pub 1906+
OkHi [1904-05;08]+

LOCO

Loco TIMES. w My 11- 1906||?
OkHi [1906]

LOCUST GROVE

Locust Grove TIMES. w 1913-27||?
OkHi [1919]-[23-24]-[27]

Locust Grove TIMES. w 1929-32||?
OkHi [1930-31]32

LONE WOLF

Lone Wolf ECHO. *See* Kiowa county news

KIOWA county news. w 1902+
1902-08? as Lone Wolf echo
OkHi [1904]-[08-11]-[13]-[15]-[29]

Lone Wolf TIMES. w
OkHi [1910-11]

LONGDALE

Longdale LEDGER. *See* Longdale news

Longdale NEWS. w 1903-18||?
1903-Ja 4 1907? as Longdale ledger
OkHi [1903]-[07]-[09]-[18]

Longdale TIMES. w 1908-10||?
OkHi [1909-10]

LOOKEBA

Lookeba INDEX. w 1909-16||?
OkHi [1909]-[16]

Lookeba LIGHT. w 1903||?
United with Hinton record to form Hinton record and Lookeba light, later Hinton record (Hinton)

Lookeba NEWS. w 1925+
pub [1925]+

LOONEY

HARMON county news. w Ja 7 1910-
OkHi [1910]

Looney RECORD. *See* New county hub (Gibson)

LOVELAND

Loveland HERALD. w 1909-10||?
OkHi [1910]

LOYAL

To 1917? as Kiel

KIEL herald. w 1909-10||?
OkHi [1909-10]

KIEL press. w 1900-04||?
OkHi [1900]-[04]

KIEL record. w
OkHi [1915-16]

LUTHER

Luther REGISTER. w 1899+
OkHi [1904]-[11]+

McALESTER

To My 10 1907 as South McAlester

McAlester CAPITAL. w 1893-S 3 1908||?
1893-1906? as South McAlester capital. United with Pittsburg county news to form McAlester news-capital
OkHi 1894[95]-[97]-1906;08

Daily CAPITAL. d Ag 18 1896-S 2 1908||
Title varies slightly. United with McAlester daily news to form McAlester news-capital
DLC O 7 1901-03;05-Je 1906
OkHi [1896-97;1902;07]08

CHOCTAW gazette. w 1902?-
OkHi [1903]

CHOCTAW herald. *See* McAlester news-capital

McAlester DEMOCRAT. w 1905+
1905-Mr 20 1930 as McAlester guardian
pub [1914]-[22-23]+
OkHi [1917-19]+

McAlester DEMOCRAT. w 1910-12||?
1910-11 as Weekly herald-democrat
OkHi [1910-12]

McAlester GUARDIAN. *See* McAlester democrat. 1905+

Weekly HERALD-DEMOCRAT. *See* McAlester democrat

INDIANOLA herald. *See* McAlester news-capital

McAlester MESSENGER. w 1902-05||?
OkHi [1904]05

McAlester NEWS-CAPITAL. w 1891+
1891- 1898? as Choctaw herald; - 1898? Indianola herald; 1899?-Ja 1900? South McAlester review; F 1900-06? South McAlester news; 1907?-S 3? 1908 Pittsburg county news
OkHi [1898-1900]-05;S 10-D 1908

McAlester NEWS-CAPITAL. d 1902+
1902-S 2 1908 as McAlester daily news (title varies slightly)
DLC 1909-16
OkHi [1907]+
WHi 1917-19

OKLAHOMA star. *See* Star vindicator

PITTSBURG county news. *See* McAlester news-capital

Weekly REGISTER. w 1911-12||?
OkHi [1911-12]

REPUBLICAN. w 1895-1906||?
OkHi [1904;06]

SOUTH MCALESTER capital. *See* McAlester capital

SOUTH MCALESTER news. *See* McAlester news-capital

SOUTH MCALESTER review. *See* McAlester news-capital

SOUTH MCALESTER wasp. *See* McAlester wasp

STAR vindicator. w Ja 14 1874-Ja 11 1879||?
1874-Ja 16 1877 as Oklahoma star
1874-D 9? 1876 pub in Caddo
CU-B O 26 1878
DLC D 8 1877
ICN Ja 26 1878
OkHi [1874-79]
OkU S 14 1876

McAlester weekly TRIBUNE. w 1910-14||?
OkHi [1911]-[13-14]

McAlester WASP. w 1904-08||?
1904-06? as South McAlester wasp
OkHi [1904]

OKLAHOMA (*Continued*)

McCURTAIN

To 1905? as Chant City

McCurtain AMERICAN. w N 1903-04||?
OkHi [1904]

HASKELL county news. w 1907-18||?
OkHi [1910-12]-13[18]

SANS BOIS news. w O 6 1904-05||?
OkHi [1904-05]

McGEE

CHICKASAW news. *See* Stratford chronicle and Chickasaw news (Stratford)

McGee NEWS. *See* Stratford chronicle and Chickasaw news (Stratford)

McCLOUD

McLoud DEMOCRAT. w 1914||?
OkHi [191-]

FREE PRESS. w
OkHi [1912]

McLoud NEWS. w Ag 17-N 28 1895||?
OkHi [1895]

McLoud OBSERVER. w 1896-1919||?
1896-190? as McLoud sunbeam
OkHi [1904-05]-[10]-[12]-[14-18]

McLoud PRESS. w
OkHi [1914

McLoud STANDARD. w 1903-05||?
OkHi 1904[05]

McLoud SUNBEAM. *See* McLoud observer

MACOMB

To 1914? as McComb

McComb HERALD. w D 28 1904-18||?
OkHi [1911-12]-[15-18]

McComb LEADER. w
OkHi [1908-09]

Macomb TRIBUNE. w 1919-21||?
OkHi [1919]

McQUEEN

McQueen BOOSTER. w My 27 1910-
OkHi [1910-11]

MADILL

Madill DEMOCRAT. *See* Marshall county democrat

Madill HERALD w
OkHi [1907]

MARSHALL county democrat. w 1906-Ap 16 1909||?
Title varies: Madill democrat. United with Madill news to form Marshall county news-democrat, later Madill record
OkHi [1907-09]

MARSHALL county news-democrat. *See* Madill record

Madill NEWS. *See* Madill record

Madill RECORD. w,sw 1896+
1896-Ja 1906? as Madill news; F 1906?-Ap 1909 Madill twice-a-week news (title varies slightly) Ap 23 1909-D 1916 Marshall county news-democrat
sw F 1906?-My 4 1909
pub D 1916+
KHi F 9 1922
OkHi [1904-08]-[13-19]+

Madill SENTINEL w
OkHi [1906-07]

SOCIALIST herald w
OkHi [1912]

Madill TIMES. w Ja 5 1911-16||?
OkHi 1911-[14-15]

Madill daily TRIBUNE. d 1934+
pub 1934+

MANCHESTER

Manchester JOURNAL. w 1893-1928||?
OkHi [1893]-[95]-1902-[28]

Manchester JOURNAL. w 1932+
pub [1932]+

TRI-COUNTY index w 1904-05||?
OkHi [1905]

MANGUM

GREER county democrat. w 1896-S 1916||?
1896-Ap 4 1901 as Greer weekly sun; Ap 11 1901-13 Mangum sun-monitor. United with Mangum star to form Mangum star and Greer democrat, later Mangum daily star
OkHi [1900-01]-16

GREER county monitor. w 1890-Ap 1901||?
United with Greer weekly sun to form Mangum sun-monitor, later Greer county democrat

GREER county news. w 1927-29||?
OkHi [1927]-[29]

GREER weekly sun. *See* Greer county democrat

Mangum MIRROR. sw 1917||?
OkHi [1917]

Mangum daily STAR. w,sw,d O 1887+
1887-1929 as Mangum star (S 14 1916-My 10 1917 Mangum star and Greer democrat)
w 1887-1929 (sw Mr 10-D 30 1920)
OkHi [1899-1900]-[02]04+

Mangum SUN-MONITOR. *See* Greer county democrat

MANITOU

Manitou FIELD-GLASS. w Je 11 1903-12||?
OkHi 1903-[09-12]

Manitou MONITOR. w
OkHi [1907]

Manitou NEWS. w 1915-17||?
OkHi [1915-16]

TILLMAN county democrat. w 1911-14||?
OkHi [1913-14]

MANNFORD

Mannford ENTERPRISE. w 1907-09||?
OkHi [1907]

Mannford HERALD. w 1910-
OkHi [1910-11]

MANNSVILLE

Mannsville HERALD. w 1910-13||?
United with Tishomingo leader to form Tishomingo leader and Mannsville herald, later Tishomingo leader (Tishomingo)
OkHi [1910-13]

Mannsville MONITOR. w 1914-17||?
OkHi [1914]-[17]

Mannsville NEWS. w Jl 1 1904-09||?
OkHi 1904-[07-09]

MARAMEC

CAPTAIN Maramec. *See* Maramec monitor

Maramec MONITOR. w 1903-12||?
1903-Mr 2 1906 as Captain Maramec; 1908?-10? Captain-monitor
OkHi [1904]-12

Maramec NEWS. w 1912-29||?
OkHi [1912-14;17;19]

MARBLE CITY

Marble City ENTERPRISE. w D 1903-06||?
OkHi [1904-06]

Marble City NEWS. w 1910-12||?
OkHi [1910]-[12]

MARIETTA

Marietta HERALD. w 1925-
OkHi [1925]-[32]

LOVE county news. w 1907-
OkHi [1908]-[11-12;19]

Marietta MONITOR. w 1895+
1895? as Marietta star
pub 1906+
OkHi [1896-98;1904-10]+

Marietta STAR. *See* Marietta monitor

MARLAND

To 1919? as Bliss

BLISS breeze. w 1902-Mr 1908||?
United with Ponca City democrat to form Ponca City democrat and Bliss breeze, later Ponca City democrat (Ponca City)

BLISS news. w
OkHi [1917-18]

Marland-Red Rock RECORD. w 1923-26||?
OkHi [1925-26]

MARLOW

Marlow MAGNET. w 1893-95||?
OkHi [1893]-[95]

Marlow REVIEW. w,sw 1896+
sw Mr 1 1928-D 29 1929
pub [1900-28]+
OkHi [1905]-[09]+

MARSHALL

Marshal TRIBUNE. w 1902+
pub 1902+
OkHi [1904]+

MARTHA

Martha weekly NEWS. w Je 30 1911-13||?
OkHi [1911]-[13]

MAUD

Maud DEMOCRAT. *See* Maud messenger

Maud daily ENTERPRISE. d 1923+
OkHi [1932-33]+

Maud MERCURY. w 1904-05||?
OkHi [1904-05]

Maud MESSENGER. w 1906-11||?
1906-09 as Maud democrat
OkHi [1906-09]-[11]

Maud MONITOR. w F 1904+
OkHi [1905-07;09-11]-19;2-[28]

MAY

May BUGLE. w S 4 1913-23||?
OkHi 1913[14]-[16;19-21]-[23]

May MONITOR. w 1905-07||?
OkHi [1905-07]

May RECORD. w 1912-17||?
OkHi [1916-17]

MAYSVILLE

BOOSTER. w 1910-12||?
1910-11? as Maysville friend
OkHi [1911-12]

Maysville FRIEND. *See* Booster

Maysville NEWS. w 1907+
1909-10? as Maysville news and Chickasaw banner
Dated also in Wynne Wood
pub 1916+
OkHi [1907-12]-[15]17-[24;2?]+

MEDFORD

CHALLENGE. w Mr 1904-
OkHi [1904]

GRANT county journal. w 1928+
pub [1929]+
OkHi [1928]+

GRANT county socialist. w
OkHi [1912-13]

Medford JOURNAL. w 1893-95||?
OkHi [1893-95]

Medford MASCOT. w O 3 1893-94||?
1893- 1894 as Medford monitor
OkHi 1893[94]

Medford MONITOR. *See* Medford mascot

Medford PATRIOT-STAR. w,sw S 1893+
1893-Ag 28 1913 as Medford patriot; S 4 1913-Ja 29 1914 Medford patriot and Medford star
pub 1911+
OkHi 1895+

Medford STAR. w 1893?-Ag 28 1913||?
United with Medford patriot to form Medford patriot and Medford star, later Medford patriot-star
OkHi [1904]06-13

MEEKER

Meeker HERALD. w 1903-33||?
OkHi [1904-06]-[18]

MEERS

MT. SHERIDAN miner. *See* Oklahoma farm news (Lawton)

MERIDIAN

Meridian EAGLE. w 1905-
OkHi [1905]

Meridian SUN. w N 30 1911-13||?
OkHi [1912-13]

MIAMI

Miami DISTRICT news. *See* Miami daily news-record

Miami ENTERPRISE. tw 1913-14||?
OkHi [1913-14]

HERALD. w 1895-Ja 27 1904||?
Title varies slightly. United with Miami record to form Miami record-herald
OkHi [1901]02

LIVE wire. w 1910-15||?
Merged with Ottawa county republican
OkHi [1910]-[15]

Miami daily NEWS-RECORD. w,d 1900+
1900-17? as Miami republican; 1918?-N 30 1923? Miami district news
w 1900-05?
KHi Ag 11 1924
OkHi [1904-06]23+
—w ed 1908-17 *See* Ottawa county republican

OTTAWA county beacon. w 1908-10||?
OkHi [1908]

OTTAWA county republican. w 1908?-17||?
OkHi [1916]
—d ed *See* Miami daily news-record

Miami RECORD-HERALD. w 1897-N 30 1923||?
1897-Ja 1904 as Miami record
KHi Ja 27 1922
OkHi 1905-23

Miami daily RECORD-HERALD. d 1917-N 30 1923||
United with Miami district news to form Miami daily news-record
OkHi [1918]-23

Miami REPUBLICAN. *See* Miami daily news-record

OKLAHOMA (*Continued*)

MILBURN

Milburn MIRROR. w Je 9 1904-05||?
OkHi [1904-05]

Milburn NEWS. w 1905-29||?
OkHi [1907;09;11-12;19]

MILL CREEK

Mill Creek HERALD. w 1915-21||?
OkHi [1920-21]

Mill Creek NEWS. w 1908-15||?
Suspended 1912?
OkHi [1908-14]

Mill Creek TIMES. w 1900-07||?
OkHi [1905-07]

MILLERTON

Millerton PROGRESS-NEWS. w 1905-11||?
1905-09? as Millerton progress
OkHi [1908-10]

MINCO

Minco HERALD. *See* Minco minstrel

Minco MINSTREL. w Jl 4 1890+
N 3 1916-S 16 1921 as Minco herald
KHi O 1890-My 15 1896
OkHi [1893-94]-[96-97;1902;04]+
OkU Jl 4 1890

MOORE

CLEVELAND county courier. w 1894-96||?
OkHi [1895-96]

CLEVELAND county times. w 1931-33||?
1931- 1933 as Moore times
OkHi [1931]-[33]

Moore ENTERPRISE. w Jl 22 1904-05||?
OkHi [1904-05]

Moore MESSENGER. w 1908-14||?
OkHi [1908-09]-[14]

RECORD. w 1902-03||?
OkHi [1903]

Moore STAR. w
OkHi [1933-34]

Moore TIMES. *See* Cleveland county times

MOORELAND

Mooreland LEADER. w 1903+
pub 1903+
KHi My 22 1914
OkHi [1904]+

MORRIS

Morris ENTERPRISE. w
OkHi [1906-07]

Morris NEWS. w Je 1905+
1905-10 as Morris star
pub [1910]+
OkHi 1909[10]-[16]-33

Morris STAR. *See* Morris news

MORRISON

Morrison HOMECROFTER. w 1908-11||?
1908-Ap 1910 as Morrison new era
OkHi [1908]-[11]

Morrison NEW ERA. *See* Morrison homecrofter

Morrison SUN. w 1903-07||?
OkHi [1903]-[07]

Morrison TRANSCRIPT. w 1912+
OkHi [1912]-[25-26;30]-33

MOUNDS

Mounds ENTERPRISE. *See* Tri-county news

Mounds MONITOR. w 1901-05||?
OkHi [1903-05]

Mounds SIGNAL. *See* Tri-county news

TRI-COUNTY news. w 1905-21||?
1905-10? as Mounds enterprise; 1910?-16? Mounds signal
OkHi [1905]-[08]-[10-11]-14;16-[21]

MOUNTAIN PARK

Mountain Park EAGLE. w 1901-03||?
1901-02? pub in Burford
OkHi [1901-02]

Mountain Park HERALD. w Ja 1904-23||?
1904-My 10 1906 as Mountain Park lance
OkHi [1904-08]-[23]

Mountain Park LANCE. *See* Mountain Park herald

Mountain Park NEWS. *See* Otter Valley news (Snyder)

MOUNTAIN VIEW

Mountain View PROGRESS. *See* Mountain View times

Mountain View REPUBLICAN. w 1903-06||?
OkHi [1904;06]

SOUTHWESTERN progress. *See* Mountain View times

Mountain View TIMES. w 1899+
1899-1902? as Southwestern progress; 1903?-07 Mountain View progress; 1907-N 7 1919 Tribune-progress
OkHi [1900-01]-[06-07]-[25]

Mountain View TRIBUNE. w 1907||?
United with Mountain View progress to form Tribune-progress, later Mountain View times
OkHi 1907

TRIBUNE-PROGRESS. *See* Mountain View times

MULDROW

Muldrow PRESS. w 1898-1914||?
OkHi 1904-[14]
OkSlD [1911]-14

Muldrow REGISTER. w 1890-94||?
MWA O 6,20 1892

Muldrow SUN. w 1915-34||?
OkHi [1916-17;20]-[25]26;28-[30]
OkSlD [1922]23;28;30-32

MULHALL

To 1891? as Alfred

ALFRED monitor. *See* Mulhall monitor

Mulhall CHIEF. w 1891-95||?
OkHi [1893-94]

Mulhall ENTERPRISE. w Ja 1893-1911||?
OkHi [1894]-1911

Mulhall MONITOR. w Ap 10 1890-91||?
1890-F 1891? as Alfred monitor
KHi 1890-F 19 1891

STATE journal. w 1902-26||?
Title varies slightly
OkHi [1903]-[18-20]-[22]-26

MUSKOGEE

Early years as Muscogee

Muskogee CIMETER. w 1910-30||?
Negro
OkHi [1904-13;15-21]

Muskogee COMET. w Je 16 1904-
OkHi [1904]

Muskogee DEMOCRAT. d Mr 5 1904-F 28 1906||
United with Muskogee evening times to form Muskogee times-democrat
OkHi [1904]-06
OkM [1904]-[06]

GULICK'S weekly review. w 1908-16||?
OkHi [1911-12;14]

INDIAN journal. *See under* Eufaula

Muskogee LANTERN. w 1902?+
1920?-26? as Watchman-lantern
Negro
pub [1927]+

Muskogee MONITOR. w 1906-11||?
OkHi [1910]

MUSKOGEE county democrat. w 1903?+
pub 1912+
OkM [1909-10]

MUSKOGEE county republican. w 1896-1912||?
1896-Ap 28 1910 as Fort Gibson post (Fort Gibson) My 5 1910-11? Muskogee county republican and Fort Gibson post
KHi F 14,Ag 15,O 31 1907
OkHi [1897-98]-[1900;03-04;08-12]

NEW state tribune. w 1897-1909||?
1897-1904? as Muskogee times
OkHi [1906]-09

Muskogee daily NEWS. d 1923?-26||?
OkHi [1925-26]
OkMP [1924]-[26]

Muskogee PHOENIX. w,sw F 16 1888+
sw S 13 1894-95?
pub 1888+
KHi Ag 23 1906
OkHi [1893]-[95-96;98-99]1901[02]

Muskogee daily PHOENIX. d Ag 25 1901+
pub 1901+
DLC D 6 1903+
KHi Jl 4 1906+
OkHi [1904]-[16-18]+
OkM [1907]-09;12+
WHi 1917-19
—morning ed *See* Muskogee times-democrat

PIONEER. w 1898-1907||?
Negro
OkHi [1905]

Muskogee daily PRESS. d D 2 1912-
OkHi [1912-13]
OkMP [1912-13]

Muskogee weekly PRESS. w
OkHi [1912]

Muskogee daily PRESS. d
OkHi [1926]

Muskogee weekly PRESS. w
OkMP [1926]

Muskogee REPUBLICAN. d,w 1905-12||?
d 1909- 1910?
Negro
OkHi [1910]

Daily SEARCH-LIGHT. d 1905-06||?
Negro
OkHi [1905]

Muskogee STAR. w 1912||?
Negro
OkHi [1912]

TATTLER. w 1915-17||?
OkHi [1916-17]

Muskogee TIMES. *See* New state tribune

Muskogee TIMES-DEMOCRAT. d S 1 1896+
1896-F 28 1906 as Muskogee evening times (title varies slightly)
pub [1914]+
KHi Je 18 1925
OkHi [1896-98;1906]+
OkM [1900]-03;06+
—evening ed *See* Muskogee daily phoenix

WATCHMAN-LANTERN. *See* Muskogee lantern

MUSTANG

Mustang ENTERPRISE. w 1905-14||?
OkHi [1906;09]-[14]

Mustang MAIL. w F 28 1902-N 1905||?
United with Yukon sun and Yukon weekly to form Yukon sun, Yukon weekly and Mustang mail, later Yukon sun (Yukon)
OkHi 1902-[05]

MUTUAL

OKLAHOMA enterprise. w 1901-18||?
OkHi [1905]-18

PERSIMMON VALLEY index. w F 28 1907-
OkHi [1907]

NARDIN

Nardin INDEPENDENT. w 1912-23||?
OkHi [1912]-[23]

Nardin STAR. w 1896-1911||?
OkHi [1900]-[08]-11

Nardin STAR. w 1923-25||?
OkHi [1923]-[25]

NASH

To 1911? as Nashville

Nash NEWS. w 1905+
Ag 4 1905-D 1 1911 as Nashville news
OkHi [1905]-[21]

NASHVILLE. *See* NASH

NAVINA

Navina LEADER. w 1910-13||?
OkHi [1910-11]

NELAGONEY

Nelagoney NEWS. w 1919-23||?
OkHi [1921]-[23]

NEW BOGGY

VINDICATOR. *See* Atoka vindicator (Atoka)

NEW WILSON. *See* WILSON

NEWALLA

Newalla NEWS. w Ja 25 1912-14||?
OkHi 1912-[14]

Newalla weekly RECORD. w Ag 1906-
OkHi [1906-07]

NEWKIRK

Newkirk DEMOCRAT. w S 16 1893-1901||?
United with Newkirk herald to form Democrat-herald, later Newkirk herald-journal
OkHi [1893]-[95-98]-[1901]

DEMOCRAT-HERALD. *See* Newkirk herald-journal

Newkirk daily EAGLE. d 1916-22||?
OkHi [1917]-[22]

Newkirk HERALD-JOURNAL. w 1899+
1899-1901? as Newkirk herald; 1901-Ap 26 1928 Democrat-herald
pub 1928+
OkHi 1902+
—d ed *See* Daily reporter

KAY county populist. *See* Oklahoma daily socialist

OKLAHOMA daily socialist. w,d 1894-1905||?
1894-1901? as Newkirk populist (title varies: Kay county populist) 1902?-03? Oklahoma socialist
w 1894-1903?
OkHi 1894[95-96;1901-05]
WHi Ag 28 1902;Ap 9 1903

OKLAHOMA state guide. *See under* Ponca City

Newkirk POPULIST. *See* Oklahoma daily socialist

Daily REPORTER. d 1916+
pub 1919+
KHi Ap 17 1928
—w ed *See* Newkirk herald-journal

OKLAHOMA (*Continued*)

NEWKIRK—*Continued*

REPUBLICAN news journal. w N 24 1893-Ap 1928||?
1893?-95? as Newkirk republican; 1896?-98? Newkirk and Kay county republican. United with Democrat-herald to form Newkirk herald-journal
KHi 1893 N 6 1908;Ap 8 1910;Mr 15 1912;My 3 1918
OkHi [1893-95]-[1918]-[28]

SOONER. w 1893-94||?
OkHi [1894]

Newkirk TIMES. w 1893-96||?
Merged with Newkirk democrat
OkHi [1893-96]

NINNEKAH

Ninnekah TIMES. w N 7 1906-09||?
OkHi [1907-09]

NOBLE

CLEVELAND county leader. w 1892-
OkHi 1893

Noble weekly JOURNAL. w O 13 1904-06||?
OkHi [1904-06]

Noble NEWS. w
OkHi [1906]

Noble NEWS. w 1911-12||?
OkHi [1911]

Noble PICAYUNE. w 1895||?
OkHi [1895]

RECORD. w F 20- 1902||?
OkHi 1902

Noble STAR. w
OkHi [1906]

NORMAN

Norman ADVANCE. *See* Democrat-topic

CLEVELAND county democrat-news. w,sw 1924-N 24 1932||?
w 1929?
OkHi 1929-32
OkNT [1928]-32

CLEVELAND county enterprise. w Ag 5 1892-1920||?
1892-O 7 1910 as Peoples voice
KHi N 1917-D 12 1918
OkHi [1892-93]95-[1920]
OkU Ag 5 1892

CLEVELAND county times. w S? 1931+
pub S 1931+

DEMOCRATIC-TOPIC. w,sw,d Jl 11 1889-O 25 1917||?
1889-Ap 1892? as Norman advance; Ap 27 1892-Mr 7 1894 Democrat; Mr 10 1894-Ap 22 1897 State democrat
w 1889-S 1917(sw Ap 27 1892-Mr 7 1894; D 5 1911-Ag 16 1912)
OkHi [1890]94-95;97-[99]-1917
OkU Ap 27 1892

Norman daily INDEPENDENT. d D 29 1908-10||?
OkHi 1909[10]

Norman JOURNAL. w 1898||?
OkHi 1898

OKLAHOMA call. w 1893-94||?
OkHi [1894]

PEOPLES voice. *See* Cleveland county enterprise

STATE democrat. *See* Democrat-topic

TERRITORIAL topic. w Ag 1 1889-Ap 23 1897||
United with State democrat to form Democrat-topic
1889-S 21 1889? pub in Purcell
KHi O 9 1890-Ja 22 1891
OkHi [1890;93-95]-[97]
OkU Ag 1 1889

Norman TRANSCRIPT. w Jl 13 1889-1917||?
Suspended from Jl 20-N 9 1889
pub [1907-08]
KHi O 25 1890-O 25 1917
OkHi [1889]-[1902-04]-17
OkU 1889-[97]

Norman TRANSCRIPT. tw,d 1913+
tw Ja 2 1921-D 5 1922
pub [1915-17]+
KHi S 17 1923
OkHi [1914]+

NORTH ENID. *See* ENID

NOWATA

Nowata ADVERTISER. *See* Nowata times

CHEROKEE air. *See* Nowata times

Nowata daily STAR. d 1909+
pub 1914+
OkHi 1922+

STAR-TIMES. w 1904+
1904-23? as Nowata star (title varies slightly)
OkHi [1904-05;10-11]-19

Nowata TIMES. w 1894-1923||?
1894-1901? as Cherokee air; 1902?-14? Nowata advertiser. United with Nowata star to form Star-times
OkHi [1904-06]-[1 20]-[23]

NUYAKA

Nuyaka NEWS. w 1921||?
OkHi [1921]

OAKWOOD

Oakwood NEWS. w 1908-16||?
OkHi [1911]-[14-15]

OCHELATA

OCHELATAN. w 1905-07||?
OkHi [1905]-[07]

Ochelata OUTLOOK. w 1908-11||?
1908-F 3 1910? as Ochelata weekly progress (title varies slightly)
OkHi [1908-11]

Ochelata weekly PROGRESS. *See* Ochelata outlook

OIL CITY

Oil City DERRICK. w My 1911-Ag 7 1913||
OkHi complete

OILTON

Oilton GUSHER. w 1915+
OkHi [1915-16;20]-[25-27]

OKARCHE

Okarche TIMES. w O 11 1892+
pub [1892]—
OkHi [1893]-[95;1901]+

OKEENE

Okeene DEMOCRAT. w S 15 1916-18||?
OkHi [1916]-18

DEUTSCHER anzeiger. w Je 3 1904-05||?
In German
OkHi [1904-05]

Okeene EAGLE. w S 26 1894-1917||?
OkHi 1894-[1900]-[08;10]-[13-14]-17

Okeene LEADER. w 1906-26||?
OkHi [1906-08]-[13]-[15]19-[26]

Okeene RECORD. w 1901+
pub 1919+
OkHi [1919]+

OKEMAH

Okemah HERALD. sw Je 9 1933+
OkHi [1933]+
OkOk [1933]—

Okemah INDEPENDENT. *See* Okfuskee county news

Okemah LEADER. w Mr 1904-
OkHi [1904-05]

Okemah daily LEADER. d 1925+
pub [1926-27]+
OkHi [1932]+
OkOk [1928-29]+
—w ed *See* Okemah ledger

Okemah LEDGER. w Ja 31 1907-32||?
Merged with Okfuskee county news
OkHi [1907]-29
—d ed *See* Okemah daily leader

OKFUSKEE county news. w S 9 1904+
1904-14 as Okemah independent (title varies slightly)
pub 1907+
KHi Ja 26 1922
OkHi [1904]-[14]+
OkOk 1934+

SLEDGE hammer. w 1912-14||?
OkHi [1913-14]

OKLAHOMA CITY

Oklahoma City ADVERTISER. w 1931?+
pub 1931+

AMERICAN guardian. w,d 1914+
1914-Mr 27 1931 as Oklahoma leader (title varies slightly)
d Ag 16 1920-Jl 23 1923
pub 1931+
CSt [1931-32]
CSt-H [1930-32]
CU-P F 17 1933—
KHi Je 25 1926;Ag 19 1927
MWA Jl 3 1931
NNC F 1932-S 8 1933
NNC-B F 1932+
NNRa 1931-33
NPV Jl 1931-F 10 1933
OkHi [1918]-33
OkOOk 1920+
PP Ag 26 1932
PUn [1932-33]
WHi F 20 1925-Ag 18 1933

Daily BEACON of Capitol Hill. d Mr 5 1934?+
pub 1934+
OkHi 1934+

BLACK dispatch. w 1915+
Negro
pub 1915+
OkHi [1916-17]+

BULL moose. w 1912||?
OkHi [1913]

CAPITAL American. w 1925-
OkHi [1925-27]-31

CAPITAL democrat. w 1908-13||?
OkHi [1910-11]

CAPITAL siftings. w 1911-13||?
OkHi [1912-13]

CAPITOL HILL beacon. w,sw 1905+
1905-18 as Capitol Hill weekly news (Ja 3 1910-Ja 29 1911? Capitol Hill weekly news-Oklahoma fairdealer) Ja 3 1919-21? Capitol Hill news-republican; 1922?-23? Oklahoma republican
pub 1926+
OkHi [1905]-[11-12]-[14-17]-[22]-[25-27]+

CAPITOL HILL epoch. w
OkHi [1927]

CAPITOL HILL weekly news. *See* Capitol Hill beacon

CESKY Oklahoman. w 1905-09||?
In Bohemian
OkHi 1907-[09]

Oklahoma City EXAMINER. d N 15 1910-
OkHi [1910]

FAIRDEALER. sw 1909||?
United with Capitol Hill weekly news to form Capitol Hill weekly news-Oklahoma fair-dealer, later Capitol Hill beacon
OkHi [1909]

FREE pointer. *See* Oklahoma City daily pointer

Evening FREE PRESS. d N 15 1910-Ag 29 1911||
OkHi complete
OkOOk complete

Evening GAZETTE. d My 21 1889-My 25 1893||?
My-Jl 23 1889 as Oklahoma gazette. United with Oklahoma daily press to form Oklahoma daily press-gazette
KHi Jl 26 1889-Je 1894
OkHi My 2,9 1890
OkU 1889-93

Sunday GLOBE. w 1889-
KHi [1893-Ap 2 1898]

GRIT. w Ja 6 1906-12||?
1907? as Oklahoma grit
OkHi [1906-07]

HARLOW'S weekly. w Ag 17 1912+
pub 1912-[15]+
OkHi 1912+
OkU 1917-19;24+
OkWeS 1926+

INDUSTRIAL democrat. w 1909-
OkHi 1910

JACKSONIAN democrat. w S 25 1913-
Title varies slightly
OkHi [1913-14]

Oklahoma City JOURNAL. d Je 3 1889-91||?
United with Daily times to form Oklahoma times-journal, later Oklahoma City times
—w ed *See* Oklahoma journal

LIFE. *See* Oklahoma life

NEWS. *See* Oklahoma news

NEWS-STATE tribune. w -1911||?
OkHi 1910[11]

OKLAHOMA advance. w
OkHi [1922]

OKLAHOMA champion. w Ja 1896-1900||?
United with Weekly Oklahoman to form Weekly Oklahoman and champion, later Weekly Oklahoman
OkHi 1896-[1900]

OKLAHOMA chief. *See* State herald (Ardmore)

OKLAHOMA citizen. w 1925?-
OkHi [1926]-32

OKLAHOMA democrat. w 1890||?
OkHi [1890]

OKLAHOMA eagle. w
OkHi [1906]

OKLAHOMA free daily pointer. *See* Oklahoma City daily pointer

OKLAHOMA gazette. *See* Evening gazette

OKLAHOMA grit. *See* Grit

OKLAHOMA guide. w 1898-1903||?
Negro
KHi O 1898-Jl 1 1903

OKLAHOMA journal. w My 9 1889-91||?
My 9 1889 as Oklahoma times (not to be confused with Oklahoma City times). United with Oklahoma City times to form Oklahoma times-journal, later Weekly times-journal
OkHi [1890-91]
—d ed *See* Oklahoma City journal

OKLAHOMA leader. *See* American guardian

OKLAHOMA life. w 1902-09||?
1902-06? as Life
1902-Ja 1906? pub in Anadarko
OkHi [1903-08]

OKLAHOMA news. d O 1906+
N 1-D 30 1916 as News
pub 1906+
KHi 1920-Ap 17 1929
OkHi 1906[07-08;15]+
OkOOk 1912+

OKLAHOMA pioneer. w 1883?-1915||?
In German
OkHi [1893]-[95;1910-12]
OkU My 11 1889

OKLAHOMA post. w 1901-07||?
Title varies: Oklahoma Saturday post
OkHi [1901-02]-[07]

OKLAHOMA post. d 1906-07||?
OkHi [1906-07]

OKLAHOMA press. *See* Sunday press-record

OKLAHOMA (*Continued*)

OKLAHOMA CITY—*Continued*

OKLAHOMA daily press-gazette. d Ja 25 1893-Jl 5 1894||?
Ja-My? 1893 as Oklahoma daily press
OkHi 1893-94
OkOOk Ja 27 1893-94
—w ed *See* Sunday press-record

OKLAHOMA republican. 1895-96 *See* Weekly republican

OKLAHOMA republican. 1922-23 *See* Capitol Hill beacon

OKLAHOMA standpatter. w
OkHi [1914]

OKLAHOMA daily star. *See* Oklahoma City daily star

OKLAHOMA state. w 1894-
OkHi [1894-95]

OKLAHOMA state capital. w
OkHi [1916]

OKLAHOMA times. My 9 1889 *See* Oklahoma journal

OKLAHOMA times-journal. d *See* Oklahoma City times

OKLAHOMA times-journal. w *See* Weekly times-journal

OKLAHOMA tribune. w 1907-11||?
OkHi [1907-10]

OKLAHOMA volksblatt. w 1893-1907||?
In German
OkHi [1903]-07

Daily OKLAHOMAN. d Ja 14 1894+
F 10-Mr 1 1894 as Evening Oklahoman
pub [1894]95[98]+
DLC Ja 25 1898+
KHi Jl 1895-Mr 1897;N 16 1907;Ap 22 1909; N 15 1911;Jl 25-29 1915;Je 6 1921;N 3 1922
OkCO 1918+
OkDS 1933+
OkEdC [1932-33]+
OkHi 1894[95]-[1905-06]+
OkP 1932+
OkShO [1932]+
OkSt [1927-33]+
OkStO [1920]+
OkU 1918[19-21]-[29]+
OkWeS [1928]+
VU D 27 1926-Ja 1,3,5-8,10-11,D 26,29-30 1927; Ja 3-4,6-7,9-11 1928;D 18 1929
WHi 1917-21
—evening ed *See* Oklahoma City times

Weekly OKLAHOMAN. w,sw 1894-S 7 1911||?
1901?-Je 25 1903 as Weekly Oklahoman and champion. Followed by Oklahoma farmer-stockman (not in this list)
sw N 27 1903-Ag 12 1904
OkHi [1894;1900]
OkOOk 1895-[1904]09-11

Saturday evening OPTIMIST. w
OkHi [1910]

Oklahoma City daily POINTER. d Ja 18? 1906-21||?
Title varies: Oklahoma free daily pointer; Free pointer; Oklahoma City pointer
OkHi [Ja 20-D 1906]-[08-09]-[11;13-15;18-19;21]
OkOOk [1917]-19

Weekly PRESS-GAZETTE. *See* Sunday press-record

Sunday PRESS-RECORD. w 1891-95||?
1891-92? as Oklahoma press; 1893?-94? Weekly press-gazette
OkHi [1895]
OkOOk 1893
—d ed *See* Oklahoma daily press-gazette

RECONSTRUCTIONIST. w
OkHi [1921-22]

Weekly REPUBLICAN. w N 1 1895-
1895-Ap 1896? as Oklahoma republican
OkHi [1895-96]

Daily REPUBLICAN. d Ap 1896?-
OkHi Je 21 1896

SOCIAL democrat. w 1912-
OkHi [1913]

SOUTHWESTERN commercial news. w Jl 28 1910-
OkHi [1910]

Oklahoma City daily STAR. d N 4 1894-95||?
Title varies: Oklahoma daily star
OkHi 1894[95]

STATE capital. w
OkHi [1911-12]

Oklahoma City TIMES. d Je 30 1889+
1889-91? as Daily times; 1891?-Je 29 1895 Oklahoma times-journal; Jl 1 1895-Mr 25 1906 Daily times-journal
pub [1901]+
KHi 1890-Ja 27 1900;Je 4-O 14 1911
M Jl 16 1930
OkHi [1889;91;93]-[95-96]1900+
OkP 1932+
OkSt [1927-31]-[33]+
OkStO [1928]+
OkU [1918-20]-[24]-[26-27]-[29]-[31]+
OkWeS 1930+
—morning ed *See* Daily Oklahoman

Weekly TIMES-JOURNAL. w D 29 1888-Mr 27 1908||
1888-91? as Oklahoma City times; 1891?-98? Oklahoma times-journal
F-Je 1889 pub in Purcell
KHi S 3 1897
OkHi D 29 1888;Mr 13,Ap 29 1889[91-93;95-99;1901-02]-04;06;08
OkOOk [1901]-04;08
OkU D 29 1888

TRUTH. w
OkHi [1909-10]

WESTERN world. w 1902-04||?
Also dated in Guthrie, Shawnee, Chandler, Kingfisher and Ardmore
Negro
OkHi [1903-04]

OKMULGEE

CAPITAL news. w 1900-07||?
OkHi [1904]05

Okmulgee CHIEFTAIN. w,sw 1901-19||?
sw My 10 1904?-Je 30 1905?
OkHi [1904-05]-[07-08;10-15]-[17-18]
OkOm [1906-07]
OkOmT 1901-[06]
—d ed *See* Okmulgee daily times

Okmulgee CHIEFTAIN. d,tw 1905?-13||?
d 1905?-07?
OkOm [1905-13]

Okmulgee DEMOCRAT. d,w 1910+
1910-32 as Okmulgee daily democrat(d)
OkHi [1913]-[16;20]-32
OkOmT [1910-11]-[32]

Okmulgee DEMOCRAT. w *See* Mid-Continent oil and farm news

Okmulgee daily HERALD. d 1908-11||?
OkHi [1911-12]

MID-CONTINENT oil and farm news. w,sw 1900-25||?
1900-11? as Okmulgee democrat
sw N 16 1901-Mr 17 1910
OkHi 1906[07]-[10-11]
OkOm [1903;05-13]
OkOmT 1902[06]-[12-13]15-23
—d ed *See* Okmulgee democrat

Okmulgee daily TIMES. d 1918+
Sunday issues as Sunday times-democrat
pub 1920+
M Ag 25 1929
OkHi [1920-21]+
—w ed *See* Okmulgee chieftain

OKTAHA

Oktaha AMERICAN. *See* Oktaha news

Oktaha CALL. w 1910-12||?
OkHi [1911-12]

Oktaha DEMOCRAT. w 1906-07||?
1906? as Oktaha independent
OkHi O 26 1906;Ja 18 1907

Oktaha INDEPENDENT. *See* Oktaha democrat

Oktaha LEADER. w
OkHi [1909-10]

Oktaha NEWS. w O 1904-05||?
1904-O 6 1905 as Oktaha American
OkHi [1905]

Oktaha PRESS. w
OkHi [1912-13]

OLUSTEE

Olustee DEMOCRAT. w 1907-25||?
OkHi [1907]-[09]-[25]

Olustee OUTLOOK. w 1903-08||?
OkHi [1904]-[08]

OOLOGAH

Oologah ENTERPRISE. w 1912-13||?
OkHi [1912]13

Oologah STAR. w 1902?-04||?
OkHi [1904]

OPTIMA

OPTIMIST. w 1907-18||?
OkHi [1915]-[17-18]

ORLANDO

Orlando CLIPPER. w 1906-34||?
OkHi [1906]-[33-34]

Orlando weekly HERALD. w 1892-1901||?
OkHi [1893-94]-[98-99]-1901

OSAGE

To 1912? as Osage City

Osage City HERALD. w 1909-12||?
1909-10 as Osage City news
OkHi [1909]-[12]

Osage City NEWS. *See* Osage City herald

OWASSO

Owasso LEDGER. w 1903-05||?
OkHi [1904-05]

OWL. *See* CENTRAHOMA

PADEN

Paden HERALD. w 1911-16||?
OkHi [1911-13;16]

Paden NEWS. w 1908-09||?
OkHi [1908-09]

OKLAHOMA clipper. w
OkHi [1914]

Paden PIONEER. w 1903-06||?
OkHi [1904-06]

Paden PRESS. w
OkHi [1908-09]

Paden weekly SUN. w 1916-28||?
OkHi [1919]

PALACE

Palace weekly PIONEER. w 1905-07||?
United with Woodward county democrat to form Woodward county democrat and Palace weekly pioneer, later Woodward county republican (Woodward)
OkHi [1905-07]

Palace PROGRESS. w 1907-08||?
OkHi [1907-08]

PAOLI

Paoli LEADER. w
OkHi [1911]

PARKER. *See* BLACKWELL

PAULS VALLEY

CHICKASAW enterprise. *See* Pauls Valley enterprise

Pauls Valley DEMOCRAT. w 1904+
1904-06 as Pauls Valley sentinel
pub [1911]-15;31+
OkHi [1904]-[06-07;09-10]-16[19]+

Pauls Valley ENTERPRISE. w Ja 15 1887+
1887-F 11 1904 as Chickasaw enterprise; F 18-Ap 14 1904 Chickasaw enterprise and Valley news
pub 1904+
OkHi [1893]-[95;1901-02]+

GARVIN county herald. w 1906-10||?
OkHi 1909[10]

Pauls Valley REPUBLICAN. w
OkHi [1906-07]

Pauls Valley SENTINEL. *See* Pauls Valley democrat

VALLEY news. w 1895-F 1904||?
United with Chickasaw enterprise to form Chickasaw enterprise and Valley news, later Pauls Valley enterprise

PAWHUSKA

Pawhuska daily CAPITAL. w,d Ja 1904-Ap 4 1925||?
Title varies slightly. United with Pawhuska daily journal to form Pawhuska daily journal-capital, later Daily journal-capital
w 1904-19
OkHi [1904]-[11-12]-[19]-25
OkPwJ 1919-25

Pawhuska daily CAPITAL. d 1906||?
OkHi [1906]

INDIAN herald. *See under* Vinita

Daily JOURNAL-CAPITAL. d 1904+
1904-Ap 4 1925 as Pawhuska daily journal; Ap 7-S 1 1925 Pawhuska daily journal-capital
pub 1925+
KHi Je 12 1927;Jl 25 1928
OkHi 1923-[30]+
OkPw 1925-[33]+
—w ed *See* Osage journal

OKLAHOMA free press. w
OkHi [1912-13]

OSAGE county news. w 1919+
pub 1919+
OkHi [1919]+
OkPw [1924]+

OSAGE journal. w,sw 1898+
sw O 6 1921-My 30 1922
pub 1906+
OkHi 1901-[03-04]-[25]
—d ed *See* Daily journal-capital

PEOPLES tribune. w O 26 1906-07||?
OkHi [1906-07]

Pawhuska POST. w
OkHi [1911]

WAH-SHAH-SHE news. w 1893-95||?
OkHi [1894-95]

WORLD WIDE war. w 1915-17||?
OkHi [1915-17]

PAWNEE

ANSWER. w My 23- 1894||?
OkHi [1894]

APPEAL. w 1894-95||?
OkHi [1894-95]

Pawnee COURIER-DISPATCH. w S 7 1899+
1899-F 26 1903 as Pawnee county courier; O 3 1918-D 13 1928 Pawnee courier-dispatch and times-democrat
pub [1921]+
KHi Ja 25 1923
OkHi [1900-01]-[03]+

Pawnee DEMOCRAT. w -Ap 1894||?
United with Pawnee times democrat to form Times-democrat

OKLAHOMA (*Continued*)

PAWNEE—*Continued*

Pawnee DISPATCH. w 1894-F 27 1903||?
United with Pawnee county courier to form Pawnee courier-dispatch
OkHi [1895-96;1900]-03

PAWNEE county courier. *See* Pawnee courier-dispatch

PAWNEE county outlook. w Ag 29 1907-08||?
OkHi [1907-08]

PAWNEE C county republican. w D 1893-95||?
OkHi [1894-95]

Pawnee weekly PIONEER. w S 21 1893-
OkHi S 21 1893

Pawnee SCOUT. w S 22 1893-94||?
OkHi [1893-94]

TIMES-DEMOCRAT. w 1893-S 26 1918||
1893-Ap 13 1894 as Pawnee times democrat. United with Pawnee courier-dispatch to form Pawnee courier-dispatch and times-democrat, later Pawnee courier-dispatch
OkHi 1893-95[1900]-18

PAYNE

OKLAHOMA hawk. *See* Payne county news (Stillwater)

PECKHAM

Peckham DEFRICK. w 1915-17||?
OkHi [1916-17]

LEADER. w Je 13 1902-04||?
OkHi [1902-04]

PERKINS

Perkins BEE. w 1893-94||?
OkHi [1893-94]

Perkins EXCELSIOR. w 1894||?
OkHi [1894]

Perkins JOURNAL. w 1892+
OkHi [1893-95]-[96-97;1900]-[16-17]-22[30]-[32-33]+

PAYNE county democrat. w Je 8 1894-96||?
OkHi [1894-95]

PEOPLE'S press. w 1905-07||?
OkHi 1905-[07]

PERRY

Perry DEMOCRAT. d 1893-96||?
Title varies slightly
OkHi [1893-96]

DEMOCRAT-PATRIOT. w N 1893-98||?
1893-F 11 1897 as Perry democrat (title varies slightly)
OkHi [1894-95 -[97]98

Daily ENTERPRISE-TIMES. d? 1893-1913||
1893-N 30 1895 as Perry daily enterprise
OkHi 1895-[98-1900]-[07]-[09]-[11]-[13]

Perry ENTERPRISE-TIMES. w S 7 1894-1917||?
1894-N 22 1895? as Perry enterprise
OkHi [1894-95 1905;07;09;13-14]

Perry JOURNAL. w S 16 1893+
1893-Ja 31 1924 as Noble county sentinel
pub 1893-1903;05-[23]+
KHi S 14 1899;Mr 22,Je 21,O 31 1924
OkHi [1895]-[13]-[1911]-[24;27]-[29]
OkPeJ 1893-1903;06-23

Perry daily JOURNAL. d 1914?+
pub [1919]+
KHi Jl 22 1925-F 9,Ag 23 1926;Jl 3 1928
OkHi [1929]+

Perry daily NEWS. d 1907-09||?
OkHi [1907]-[09]

NOBLE county news. w 1901-05||?
OkHi [1904-05]

NOBLE county patriot. w Ap 23 1896-F? 1897||
United with Perry democrat to form Democrat-patriot
OkHi [1896]97

NOBLE county sentinel. *See* Perry journal

OKLAHOMA neuigkeiten. w 1902-23||?
In German
OkHi [1906-08]-[23]

Perry REPUBLICAN. w 1893-1924||?
KHi D 29 1921
OkHi [1899]-[1924]
OkPeJ 1901;05;07-23

Perry RUSTLER. w N 25 1893-
OkHi [1894]

Perry daily TIMES. d 1893-N? 1895||
United with Perry daily enterprise to form Daily enterprise-times
OkHi [1893]-[95]

Perry weekly TIMES. w 1893-N 21? 1895||
United with Perry enterprise to form Perry enterprise-times
OkHi [1895]

PERSHING

Pershing AMERICAN. w
OkHi [1920]

Pershing GAZETTE. w 1920-22||?
OkHi [1921]

PICHER

KING JACK. *See* Tri-state tribune

TRI-STATE tribune. w 1923?+
1923?-31? as King Jack
pub 1932—

PIEDMONT

Piedmont NEWS. w Ja 30 1909-
OkHi 1909-10

Piedmont POST. w 1905-06||?
OkHi [1905-06]

Piedmont PRESS. w O 30 1903-05||?
OkHi [1903]-[05]

PITTSBURGH

Pittsburgh ENTERPRISE. w 1904?-13||?
OkHi 1910-[13]

Pittsburg HERALD. w 1915-31||?
OkHi [1921-22]

PLAINVIEW

BEAVER county republican. w 1911-12||?
OkHi 1911[12]

POCASSET

Pocasset POST. w 1907-11||?
OkHi [1908]

PONCA CITY

CHEROKEE STRIP guide. *See* Oklahoma state guide

Ponca City COURIER. w N 23 1893-1923||?
KHi 1893-F 1919[F 12-Ap 1]Jl 8-29,S 23 1920
OkHi [1893]-[98-99]1909-[19]-[21]-[23]

Ponca City daily COURIER. *See* Ponca City news

Ponca City DEMOCRAT. w S 30 1893-1913||?
1893-Mr 15 1895 as Ponca democrat; Ap 2 1908-My 6 1909 Ponca City democrat and Bliss breeze
OkHi [1893]-[98]-[1905]-[15]
OkPU 1893-1905[09]-16

Ponca City DEMOCRAT. d 1912-18||
United with Ponca City daily courier to form Ponca City news
OkHi [1915]-18
OkPN [1918]

Ponca City NEWS. d O 4 1897+
1897-1918 as Ponca City daily courier
pub 1919+
KHi [1897-N 1 1900]N 24 1910
OkHi [1897]-1908[19]+
OkP 1932+

OKLAHOMA state guide. w My 19 1893-95||?
My-S 1? 1893 as Cherokee Strip guide
My-S 1? 1893 pub in Arkansas City, Kansas; S 8? 1893-94? in Newkirk
KHi S 27 1893-My 5 1895
OkHi [1893-95]

Ponca TOMAHAWK. w Ja 8 - 1895||?
OkHi [1895]

POND CREEK

CHEROKEE sentinel. w N 1? 1893-
KHi [1894-S 1895]
OkHi [1893]-[95]

DEMOCRATIC voice. w D 1893-
OkHi [1894-95]

Pond Creek ECHO. w O 13 1893-
KHi 1893-Je 1894
OkHi 1893[94]

Pond Creek FREE-PRESS. *See* Grant county republican

GRANT county news. w 1893-F 28 1918||?
D 23 1893-Ag 3 1895 as Pond Creek news. United with Grant county vidette to form Vidette-news, later Pond Creek herald
OkHi 1893[94-95;97-98]-[1903;05]-18

GRANT county republican. w Ja 9 1901-05||?
1901? as Pond Creek free-press
OkHi 1901-[05]

GRANT county vidette. *See* Pond Creek herald

Pond Creek HERALD. w 1895+
1895-1923? as Grant county vidette (Mr 7- 1918? Vidette news)
OkHi [1897-1900]-18;24-33
—d ed *See* Pond Creek daily vidette

L county republican. w O 21 1893-
OkHi [1893]

Pond Creek NEWS. *See* Grant county news

Pond Creek TRIBUNE. w 1893-96||?
KHi N 16 1893-Ja 16 1896
OkHi 1893-[95]

Pond Creek daily VIDETTE. d Mr 11 1901-05||?
OkHi [1901]-[05]
—w ed *See* Pond Creek herald

VIDETTE news. *See* Pond Creek herald

PORTER

Porter ENTERPRISE. w 1903-13||?
OkHi [1904-05]-[09-11]

Porter NEWS. w 1922+
OkHi [1922]-[29]

PORUM

Porum JOURNAL. w 1906-23||?
1906-09? as Porum press
OkHi [1906-08;10-11]-[19]-[21]

Porum PRESS. *See* Porum journal

POTEAU

Poteau JOURNAL. w 1902?+
OkHi [1904-07]-[18]-25;29+

LE FLORE county sun. w 1900+
1900-23? as Poteau weekly sun
pub [1929]+
OkHi 1909-[14-15]-[18]-[31]

Poteau NEWS. w Je 1897+
pub 1897+
OkHi 1926-28

Poteau weekly SUN. *See* Le Flore county sun

PRAGUE

Prague NEWS. w 1902-17||?
OkHi [1904]-[10]-[12-13]-[17]

Prague NEWS-RECORD. w 1903+
1903-09? as Prague patriot; 1910?-N 27 1930 Prague record
OkHi [1904]-[07-09]-17[20]+

Prague PATRIOT. *See* Prague news-record

Prague RECORD. *See* Prague news-record

PRYOR

To 1908? as Pryor Creek

Pryor CLIPPER. w 1899-1920||?
1899-1908? as Pryor Creek clipper
OkHi 1901[02-04]-20

Pryor JEFFERSONIAN. w Ap 22 1932+
pub 1932+

MAYES county democrat. w 1913+
pub 1926+
OkHi [1919]+

MAYES county new deal. w 1908+
1908-Je 1 1933 as Mayes county republican
pub 1933+
KHi Ap 6,My 20 1922
OkHi [1910-11]+

MAYES county republican. *See* Mayes county new deal

PRYOR CREEK. *See* PRYOR

PURCELL

Purcell ENQUIRER. w F 7 1895-96||?
OkHi 1895[96]

MCCLAIN county news and Purcell republic. w 1909-13||?
1909-Je 1913 as Purcell republic
OkHi [1909]-13

Purcell REGISTER. w N 23 1887+
pub 1916+
KHi Ap 10 1891-98;Ja 19 1922;Ja 25 1923
OkHi 1887[88;90]-[97]-[1918-20]+
OkU N 23 1887

Purcell REPUBLIC. *See* McClain county news and Purcell republic

TERRITORIAL topic. *See under* Norman

TIMES. *See* Weekly times-journal (Oklahoma City)

Purcell TRIBUNE. w 1902-07||?
OkHi [1903-04]-[06-07]

PURDY

ISONOMY. w Je 18- 1904||?
OkHi [1904]

PUTNAM

Putnam PIONEER. w 1904-11||?
OkHi [1907-08;11]

QUAPAW

Quapaw MINING herald. w 1917-20||?
OkHi [1919]

Quapaw WORLD. w
OkHi [1917-18]

QUAY

Quay TIMES. w 1917-19||?
OkHi [1918]

Quay TRANSCRIPT. w 1904-
OkHi [1904]

QUINLAN

Quinlan ADVANCE. w 1913-19||?
OkHi [1913]-19

Quinlan MIRROR. w 1903-13||?
OkHi [1904]-[10]-[13]

Quinlan REPORTER. w 1921-23||?
OkHi 1922[23]

OKLAHOMA (*Continued*)

QUINTON

Quinton PIONEER. w 1903-16||?
OkHi [1904;07]-[16]

Quinton TIMES. w 1912+
OkHi [1912]-[24]-33

RALSTON

Ralston EXPONENT. *See* Ralston independent

FREE PRESS. w 1900-09||?
OkHi [1900]-[02-06]-[09]

Ralston INDEPENDENT. w 1905-15||?
1905-Ap 14 1910? as Ralston exponent; Ap 21-D 1910? Ralston new era
OkHi [1905]-[10]-[13]-[15]

Ralston NEW ERA. *See* Ralston independent

Ralston REFLECTOR. w 1903-04||?
OkHi [1904]

Ralston TRIBUNE. w 1916-
OkHi [1916]-[18]-[20-21]

RAMONA

Ramona HERALD. *See* Washington county herald

Ramona STAR. w 1905-06||?
OkHi [1905-06]

WASHINGTON county herald. w 1903-30||?
1903-29? as Ramona herald
OkHi 1904-[06;08;10]-[16-17;20-21;24-25]

RANDLETT

COTTON county times. w
OkHi [1912]

Randlett ENTERPRISE. *See* Randlett progressor

Randlett NEWS. w 1919-22||?
OkHi [1919]-[22]

Randlett PROGRESSOR. w 1907-18||?
1907-12 as Randlett enterprise
OkHi [1911-12;15-18]

RAVIA

Ravia GAZETTE. w D 23 1905-07||?
OkHi [1906-07]

Ravia HERALD. w 1908-09||?
OkHi 1908[09]

Ravia weekly NEWS. w 1910-
OkHi 1910[11]

Ravia TRIBUNE. 1902-05||?
OkHi [1904-05]

RED FORK

Red Fork DERRICK. w 1902-10||?
OkHi [1903-07;10]

TRI-CITY record. w
OkHi [1920]

TRI-CITY weekly. w
OkHi [1921]

RED OAK

Red Oak HERALD. w My 14 1909-
OkHi [1909]

Red Oak NEWS. w 1911-16||?
OkHi [1911]-[13]

RED ROCK

Red Rock CHIEFTAIN. w 1919-23||?
OkHi [1919]

Red Rock OPINION. w Ag 1 1903-12||?
OkHi [1903]-[08-09]-12

Red Rock RECORD. w 1913-18||?
Title varies slightly
OkHi [1913-14]-[17-18]

RENFROW

Renfrow TRIBUNE. w 1900-16||?
Title varies slightly
OkHi [1904]-[06]-[16]

RENO CITY

Reno EAGLE. *See* El Reno eagle (El Reno)

Reno HERALD. *See* El Reno herald (El Reno)

REYDON

Reydon REVIEW. w 1932?+
pub 1932+

RICHMOND

POST. w 1911||?
OkHi [1911]

RINGLING

Ringling EAGLE. w 1909+
1909-S 1 1921? as Ringling news (1917?-18? Western oil news)
pub [1918]20+
OkHi 1915-18[20]21;24+

Ringling NEWS. *See* Ringling eagle

Cornish-Ringling TIMES. *See under* Cornish

WESTERN oil news. *See* Ringling eagle

RINGWOOD

Ringwood LEADER. w 1901-18||?
OkHi [1904]-[06-07]-[18]

Ringwood RECORDER. w 1921+
OkHi [1922]-25;27-[32]

Ringwood TIMES. w My 19- 1904||?
OkHi [1904]

RIPLEY

Ripley BULLETIN. w 1913-17||?
OkHi [1913]-[17]

Ripley MAIL. w 1909-12||?
OkHi [1909-12]

Ripley NEWS. w Ja 19 1900-02||?
OkHi [1900]

Ripley RECORD. w 1918-28||?
OkHi [1919]-28

Ripley TIMES. w 1900-07||?
OkHi [1900]-[04]-[07]

ROCK FALLS

OKLAHOMA war chief. *See under* Caldwell, Kansas

ROCKY

Rocky weekly ADVANCE. w 1906-08||?
OkHi [1906]-[08]

Rocky NEWS. w 1914?-25||?
OkHi [1914-16;19]-[25]

Rocky RECORD. w 1908-13||?
Title varies slightly
OkHi [1911-12]

ROFF

BLUE VALLEY farmer. w 1902-30||?
1902-04? as Roff enterprise; 1905?-29? Roff eagle
OkHi [1904-05]-[17]

Roff EAGLE. *See* Blue Valley farmer

Roff ENTERPRISE. *See* Blue Valley farmer

ROLL

Roll GRAPHIC. w
OkHi [1907-08]

ROOSEVELT

Roosevelt RECORD. w Mr? 1902+
OkHi [1904-07]-[18]-31

ROSSTON

GENERAL. w
OkHi [1923-24]

Rosston NEWS. w 1917-23||?
OkHi [1917-19]

RUSH SPRINGS

Rush Springs GAZETTE. w 1893+
1893-94? as Rush Springs light; 1895?-1928 Landmark; 1928-29 Sterling gazette
pub 1928+
OkHi [1893-95;1904-06]-[15]-[19]23[24-25;31]32

GRADY county town and farm. w
OkHi [1910]

Rush Springs HERALD. w 1912-13||?
OkHi [1912-13]

LANDMARK. *See* Rush Springs gazette

Rush Springs LIGHT. *See* Rush Springs gazette

Rush Springs RECORD. w
OkHi [1909]

Rush Springs RECORD. w 1922-24||?
OkHi [1922-23]

STERLING gazette. *See* Rush Springs gazette

RYAN

Ryan ENTERPRISE. w 1903-06||?
OkHi [1905]

Ryan LEADER. w 1906+
OkHi [1909;13]-[15;19]

Ryan RECORD. w 1893-97||?
OkHi [1894]

Ryan RECORD. w
OkHi [1909]

TIMES-DEMOCRAT. w 1905-06||?
OkHi [1905-06]

SALINA

GRAND VALLEY times. *See* Salina post

Salina HERALD. *See* Salina post

Salina HUSTLER. *See* Salina post

Salina NEWS. w 1921-Ja 4 1924||?
United with Salina herald to form Salina news-herald, later Salina post
OkHi [1921]-24

Salina NEWS-HERALD. *See* Salina post

Salina POST. w Ap 11 1913-32||?
1913-27? as Salina herald (Ja 1924?-25? Salina news-herald) 1927?-29? Grand Valley times; 1929?-Ag 15 1932? Salina hustler
KHi N 13 1925;F 3 1928
OkHi [1913]-[18-19;26-27]-[29]
OkPrJ 1928-32

SALLISAW

Sallisaw AMERICAN. 1925-My 1929||?
United with Sequoyah county democrat to form Democrat-American
OkSlD 1926-28

CHEROKEE republican. *See* Democrat-American

DEMOCRAT-AMERICAN. w Ja 1906+
1906-12 as Cherokee republican; 1912-13? Sallisaw new era; 1914?-My 24 1929 Sequoyah county democrat
pub 1916+
KHi Ap 22 1921
OkHi [1906-07;11-13]-[16]-[18]+

Sallisaw GAZETTE. *See* Star-gazette

Sallisaw NEW ERA. *See* Democrat-American

OKLAHOMA progressive. w
OkHi [1912-13]

SEQUOYAH county democrat. *See* Democrat-American

SEQUOYAH county times. w 1932+
pub 1932+

Sallisaw STAR. w 1895-1907||?
United with Sallisaw gazette to form Star-gazette
OkHi [1902-03]

STAR-GAZETTE. w S 24 1898-1916||?
1898-1907? as Sallisaw gazette
OkHi [1909]-[16]
OkSlD O 1898-99;1902-16

SALT FORK

Salt Fork BANNER. w 1903-
OkHi [1904]

SAND SPRINGS

Sand Springs LEADER. w 1914+
KHi D 16 1926
OkHi [1914]-[17]-[21]-[23;31]+

Sand Springs REVIEW. w,sw 1912-14||?
sw My 15-Jl 31 1914
OkHi 1914

SANDS CITY

FARMER'S news. w 1907-08||?
OkHi [1907-08]

SAPULPA

COUNTY democrat-news. *See* Democrat-news

CREEK county courier. w 1905-12||?
OkHi [1910]-[12]

CREEK county republican. w 1907-21||?
1907-S 29 1911 as Kiefer searchlight (Kiefer)
OkHi [1908-09]-[21]

Sapulpa DEMOCRAT. w 1901-11||?
Title varies slightly
OkHi [1906-09]
OkSpH 1901-06

Sapulpa evening DEMOCRAT. d 1907-14||?
Title varies slightly
OkHi [1907;10]12[13-14]

DEMOCRAT-NEWS. w 1910?+
1910?-23? as County democrat-news
pub 1922+
OkHi [1921-23]+

Sapulpa HERALD. d 1914+
pub [1914]+
OkHi [1914]+
—w ed *See* Oklahoma farmer and laborer

Sapulpa LIGHT. w 1897-1912||?
OkHi [1904]-[07]

Sapulpa evening LIGHT. d 1908-13||?
Title varies slightly
OkHi [1908]-[12-13]

OKLAHOMA farmer and laborer. w 1909-16||?
pub 1911-14
OkHi 1911-[13-15]
—d ed *See* Sapulpa herald

Sapulpa SIGNAL. w 1903-05||?
OkHi [1904-05]

SASAKWA

Sasakwa LIFE. w 1911-20||?
OkHi [1911]-[13-15;19]20

Sasakwa NEWS. w 1932?+
pub 1932+

SAVANNA

Savanna NEWS. w 1915-17||?
OkHi [1916]

OKLAHOMA (*Continued*)

SAWYER

Sawyer TIMES. w D 21 1911-12||?
OkHi [1912]

SAYRE

AGITATOR. w O 31 1913-14||?
OkHi [1913-14]

Sayre CITIZEN. w 1910||?
OkHi 1910

Sayre DEMOCRAT. w F 20-Ap 29 1920||?
OkHi [1920]

Sayre ENTERPRISE. *See* Western star

Sayre HEADLIGHT. w,sw 1899+
1899-My 15 1902 as Sayre venture; 1927? Sayre headlight-journal
sw Ag 25 1930-Ag 6 1931
OkHi [1901-02]-[12;19;30]+

Sayre JOURNAL. w 1923-27||?
United with Sayre headlight to form Sayre headlight-journal, later Sayre headlight
OkHi 1923-[27]

Sayre STANDARD. w 1904-21||?
OkHi [1904]-[07]-17[20-21]

Sayre STAR. w 1923-24||?
OkHi [1923]24

Sayre VENTURE. *See* Sayre headlight

WESTERN star. w O 1901-03||?
1901-Jl 17 1903 as Sayre enterprise
OkHi 1902-03

SCULLIN

Scullin ADVOCATE. w 1906-08||?
OkHi [1907]

SEILING

Seiling GUIDE. w 1901-09||?
OkHi 1902-[09]

Seiling MESSENGER. w 1906-18||?
OkHi [1906]-[18]

SEMINOLE

Seminole morning NEWS. d 1927-32||?
OkHi [1928-29]-[32]
OkSeP 1927-32
—w ed *See* Seminole county news

Seminole PRODUCER. d 1927+
pub 1927+
OkHi 1931+
—w ed *See* Seminole county news

Seminole morning REPORTER. d S 1934+
OkHi 1934+

SEMINOLE county news. w 1907+
Suspended from 1929?-32?
pub [1932]+
OkHi 1908[09-11]-[27]-[29;32]+
—d ed *See* Seminole morning news; Seminole producer

SENTINEL

Sentinel LEADER. w 1904+
1904-F 4 1910 as Sentinel news-boy
pub [1925]+
OkHi [1904]+

Sentinel NEWS-BOY. *See* Sentinel leader

SWORD of truth. w 1912-14||?
OkHi [1912]-14

SHAMROCK

Shamrock BLARNEY. *See* Creek county democrat

Shamrock BROGUE. *See* Creek county democrat

CREEK county democrat. w 1914+
1914-16? as Shamrock brogue; 1916? Shamrock blarney
pub D 20 1914+
OkHi [1916]-[30]

SHARON

Sharon NEWS. w 1921+
pub 1921+

SHATTUCK

ELLIS county news. w 1914+
1914-Ag 9 1917 as Ellis county socialist
KHi Ja 25 1923
OkHi [1915]-[30]31

ELLIS county socialist. *See* Ellis county news

HOMESTEADER. *See* Shattuck republican

Shattuck MONITOR. w 1905-24||?
OkHi [1911]-[24]

NORTHWEST Oklahoman. w,sw 1930+
sw My 1-D 28 1934
pub Jl 1930+
OkHi [1931]+

Shattuck REPUBLICAN. w 1903-11||?
1903-My 9 1907 as Homesteader; My 16-1907? Square-dealer and homesteader; 1908?- 1910 Square-dealer
OkHi [1905]-[10-11]

SQUARE-DEALER and homesteader. *See* Shattuck republican

SHAWNEE

Shawnee daily CAPITAL. d 1896-
OkHi [1897]

Shawnee CHIEF. w F 1895-97||?
OkHi [1895]

Shawnee daily CHIEF. d 1895-99||?
OkHi N 16 1895;F 24 1896

CONSTITUTION. w Ap 20 1906-
OkHi [1906]

COUNTY democrat. w 1931?+
OkHi [1931]+

FARMERS union advocate. w 1907-D 1908||?
United with Union review (Ardmore) to form Farmers union advocate and union review, later Union advocate review (Ardmore)
OkHi [1908]

Shawnee HERALD. w 1901+
1904? as Herald democrat; 1912?-16? Shawnee transcript; 1917?-19? Pottawatomie county transcript
OkHi [1901-04]07[12;14-15]-[18]-[27;29]

Shawnee HERALD. d 1902-11||?
1904? as Herald democrat. United with Shawnee news to form Shawnee daily news-herald, later Shawnee morning news
OkHi [1902-04]-11

INDIAHOMA union signal. w 1905-08||?
Mr-O 1905 pub in Cordell
OkHi [1905]-[07]

Shawnee NEWS. w 1895-98||?
1895-Ja 4 1896 as Weekly news
OkHi [1895-96]

Shawnee morning NEWS. d 1902+
1902-11? as Shawnee news; 1912-Jl 31 1919 Shawnee daily news-herald
OkHi [1903-04]-[06]-[30]+
OkShO [1932]+
OkStO [1902-06;08;11]
—evening ed *See* Shawnee evening star

OKLAHOMA clipper. w 1913-16||?
OkHi [1915-16]

OKLAHOMA union messenger. w 1906-07||?
OkHi [1906-07]

POTTAWATOMIE county transcript. *See* Shawnee herald

POTTAWATOMIE times-record. *See* Shawnee times-record

Shawnee QUILL. w Jl 4 1895-1904||?
OkHi [1895]-[97]

Shawnee daily QUILL. d 1901-04||?
OkHi [1904]

Shawnee Saturday REVIEW. w 1918-19||?
OkHi [1919]

Shawnee SENTINEL. w Mr 5- 1914||?
OkHi [1914]

Shawnee STANDARD. w 1901-10||?
OkHi [1909-10]

Shawnee evening STAR. d 1930+
OkHi [1930]+
—morning ed *See* Shawnee morning news

Shawnee STATE journal. w 1906-07||?
OkHi [1906-07]

Shawnee TIMES-RECORD. sw,w 1927?+
Some years as Pottawatomie times-record
sw 1927?-31?
OkHi [1931]+

Shawnee TRANSCRIPT. *See* Shawnee herald

UNION gazette. w Ap 1907-
OkHi [1907]

WESTERN world. *See under* Oklahoma City

SHIDLER

Shidler REVIEW. w 1927+
pub 1927+
OkHi [1932]33

SIBONEY

Siboney NEWS-LETTER. w Ap 27 1906-07||?
OkHi [1906-07]

Siboney SENTINEL. w Ja 29 1904-
OkHi [1904]

SPOKESMAN. w N 2 1905-
OkHi [1905-06]

SKEDEE

HUSTLER. w Jl 15 1904-05||?
OkHi [1904-05]

SKIATOOK

Skiatook NEWS. w 1911+
OkHi [1911]-33

Skiatook SENTINEL. w 1905-12||?
OkHi [1905]-[11-12]

SMITHVILLE

MCCURTAIN county American. w Ap 27-1907||?
OkHi [1907]

SNYDER

KIOWA county democrat. w N 2 1905+
S 1 1910-O 19 1911 as Swanson county democrat
pub 1905+
OkHi [1905]-[07-08]-[12]+

OTTER VALLEY news. w D 26 1901-05||?
1901-04? as Mountain Park news (Mountain Park)
OkHi 1902-[05]

OTTER VALLEY socialist w 1914-18||?
OkHi [1915]-[18]

Snyder SIGNAL-STAR. w D 1902-30||?
1902-03? as Snyder signal
OkHi [1903]-[30]

Snyder STAR. w 1903||?
United with Snyder signal to form Snyder signal-star

SWANSON county democrat. *See* Kiowa county democrat

SOPER

CHOCTAW county democrat *See* Soper democrat

Soper DEMOCRAT. w 1911+
1911? as Soper enterprise; 1912?-13? Choctaw county democrat
pub [1911-13]+
OkHi [1911]+

Soper ENTERPRISE. *See* Soper democrat

Soper HERALD. w 1906-10||?
OkHi [1907-08]-[10]

SOUTH CANADIAN

South Canadian BAZOO. *See* Monitor

MONITOR. w O 1894-97||?
1894- 1895 as South Canadian bazoo
OkHi [1895]

SOUTH COFFEYVILLE

South Coffeyville TIMES. w 1909-11||?
OkHi [1909-11]

SOUTH McALESTER. *See* McALESTER

SPARKS

Sparks REVIEW. w D 19 1902-08||?
1902-D 16 1904 as Sparks visitor
OkHi 1902-[04]-[06-08]

Sparks VISITOR. *See* Sparks review

SPEERMORE

ADVOCATE. w Ag 25 1905-19||?
OkHi [1905]-[18]

PUMPKIN roller. w Mr 3 1905-
OkHi [1905]

SPENCER

Spencer NEWS. w Ap 4- 1903||?
OkHi [1903]

Spencer SIFTINGS. w 1908-14||?
OkHi [1908-09]-[13-14]

SPIRO

Spiro TIMES. w 1920+
pub 1921+

Spiro TRIBUNE. w 1905-18||?
OkHi [1905-08;10;12;17-18]

STECKER

Stecker SUN. w
OkHi [1909]

STERLING

COMANCHE county farmer. w 1902-04||?
OkHi 1903[04]

Sterling NEWS. *See* Oklahoma ledger

OKLAHOMA ledger. w 1904-22||?
1904-11 as Sterling news
OkHi [1909-15]-[22]

Sterling STAR. w 1901-06||?
OkHi 1902-03

STERRETT

Sterrett BANNER. *See* Banner-ledger (Calera)

CHOCTAW ledger. w 1902||?
United with Sterrett banner to form Banner-ledger (Calera)

Sterrett NEWS. w 1910||?
OkHi [1910]

Sterrett SUN w 1906-07||?
OkHi [1906-07]

STIGLER

Stigler BEACON. *See* Haskell county news

HASKELL county leader. w
OkHi [1911]

OKLAHOMA (*Continued*)

STIGLER—*Continued*

HASKELL county news. w 1903-My? 1930‖
1903-23? as Stigler beacon. United with State sentinel to form Stigler news-sentinel
OkHi [1906]-[09-11;29]30

HASKELL county tribune. w 1931+
pub [1931]+
OkHi [1933]

Stigler NEWS-SENTINEL. w 1904+
1904-My 6 1930 as State sentinel
OkHi 1909-[16-18;20]-[28-29]+

STATE sentinel. *See* Stigler news-sentinel

STILLWATER

Stillwater ADVANCE. w S 1 1892-Ag 31 1905‖
1892-1900? as Payne county populist. United with Stillwater democrat to form Advance-democrat, later Payne county news
OkHi [1893-95;1900]-05

ADVANCE-DEMOCRAT. *See* Payne county news

COMMON people. w O 1 1903-04‖?
OkHi [1903-04]

Stillwater CONDOR. w F 16- 1894‖?
OkHi [1894]

Daily DEMOCRAT. d 1902-06‖?
OkHi 1903[04-06]

Stillwater DEMOCRAT. w *See* Payne county news

EAGLE-GAZETTE. *See* Stillwater gazette

FARMERS fact and fancy. w S 28 1904-
OkHi [1904-05]

Stillwater GAZETTE. w,sw 1889+
Ja 5 1894-F 14 1895 as Eagle-gazette
sw F 7 1905-Mr 16 1906
pub 1893+
OkHi 1893-1908;10+
OkSt [1927-29]+
OkStO [1914]18-28;30+

Stillwater MESSENGER. w O 12 1894-
OkHi 1894[95]

OKLAHOMA eagle. w 1892-D 29 1893‖
United with Stillwater gazette to form Eagle-gazette, later Stillwater gazette
OkHi D 29 1893

OKLAHOMA hawk. *See* Payne county news

OKLAHOMA standard. w Ag 3 1889-90‖?
KHi 1889-Ap 12 1890
OkU Ag 3 1889

OKLAHOMA state. d Ja 1898-
Title varies slightly
OkHi [1898]

OKLAHOMA state. w 1898-
OkHi [1898]

OKLAHOMA state sentinel. *See* Payne county news

PAYNE county news. w,sw Mr 15 1890+
1890-92? as Oklahoma hawk; 1892?-98? Oklahoma state sentinel; 1898?-S 27 1928 Stillwater democrat (S 7 1905-F 26 1925 Advance-democrat)
1890? pub in Payne
sw O 2 1928-Ag 1929
pub 1892+
KHi [Mr-Ag 23 1890]
OkHi [1893-94]96-97[1900]-[03;05]+
OkStO 1892+

PAYNE county populist. *See* Stillwater advance

PAYNE county republican. w 1892-
OkHi [1893]

PEOPLE'S press. w 1904-12‖?
1904-07 as People's progress
OkHi 1906[07]-[12]

PEOPLE'S progress. *See* People's press

Stillwater daily PRESS. d 1908+
pub 1925+
OkSt 1928+
WaPS [1923;25]

STILWELL

ADAIR county democrat. w 1900+
1900-D 2? 1910 as Stilwell standard; D 9 1910-Ap 6 1928 Standard-sentinel
OkHi [1901-02;04-08;10-11]-[31]-[33]

ADAIR county gleaner. w 1916+
1916-22? as Adair gleaner
OkHi 1920-[24-26]

ADAIR county republican. w 1900-15‖?
OkHi [1913]-[15]

ADAIR county sentinel. w 1904-D? 1910‖
United with Stilwell standard to form Standard-sentinel, later Adair county democrat
OkHi [1909-10]

ADAIR gleaner. *See* Adair county gleaner

NEW ERA. w Je 23- 1906‖?
OkHi [1906]

Stilwell STANDARD. *See* Adair county democrat

STONEWALL

Stonewall weekly NEWS. w 1903-23‖?
OkHi [1904-05]-[08]-[10-13]-[15]-23

STRATFORD

CHICKASAW news. *See* Stratford chronicle and Chickasaw news

Stratford CHRONICLE and Chickasaw news. w 1902-07‖?
1902-06? as Chickasaw news (title varies: McGee news) 1902-06? pub in McGee
OkHi [1904;06-07]

Stratford LEADER. w 1908-23‖?
1908-17? as Stratford tribune
OkHi [1908]-16;20-[23]

Stratford STAR. w 1923+
pub 1923+

Stratford TRIBUNE. *See* Stratford leader

STRONG CITY

Strong City HERALD. w 1912-27‖?
OkHi [1912-14;16]-[19]21-[25]

ROGER MILLS sentinel. *See under* Cheyenne

STROUD

Stroud DEMOCRAT. w O 7? 1919+
OkHi [1910-11]-[29-30]-[32]

LINCOLN county journal. w 1906-10‖?
F? 1907-09? as Lincoln county journal-Stroud star
OkHi [1906]-[10]

Stroud MESSENGER. w 1898+
OkHi [1899]-[1903]+

Stroud STAR. w 1898-F 15 1907‖
United with Lincoln county journal to form Lincoln county journal-Stroud star, later Lincoln county journal
OkHi [1900]-[02-03]-[06]07

TUSHKAHOMMAN. w Mr 5 1935+
NNHu 1935+
PP Ag 27,N 26 1935+
WHi Ag 27,S 24 1935+

STUART

Stuart EDUCATOR. w 1907-09‖?
OkHi [1908-09]

Stuart ENTERPRISE. w N 10 1911-15‖?
OkHi [1911-12]-[14-15]

Stuart STAR. w 1919-23‖?
OkHi [1919]-[21]

SUGDEN

Sugden CLARION. w N 1906-14‖?
1906-10? as Sugden signal; 1911-12? Socialist signal
OkHi [1907;13-14]

REASONER. w
OkHi [1910]

Sugden SIGNAL. *See* Sugden clarion

SOCIALIST signal. *See* Sugden clarion

SULPHUR

Sulphur DEMOCRAT. w 1900-S 2 1926‖
1900-06? as Sulphur journal; 1909? News-democrat? United with Sulphur times to form Sulphur times-democrat
OkHi [1904]-[06-10]-[14]-26
OkSuT 1908-26

Sulphur JOURNAL. *See* Sulphur democrat

MURRAY county record. w
OkHi [1909-11]

NEW century. w 1911-13‖?
OkHi [1911]-[13]

Daily NEWS. d 1933+
pub 1934+

NEWS and Murray county times. w 1906-09‖?
1906-07? as Sulphur news. United with Sulphur democrat to form News-democrat, later Sulphur democrat?
OkHi [1906;08-09]

NEWS-DEMOCRAT. *See* Sulphur democrat

Sulphur POST. w Ap 1903-14‖?
OkHi [1904-05;11]-[14]

Sulphur TIMES-DEMOCRAT. w 1912+
1912-S 2? 1926 as Sulphur times
pub 1912+
OkHi 1922[23;28]+

SUPPLY

FORT SUPPLY republican. *See* Supply republican

Supply REPUBLICAN. w 1902-28‖?
1902-D 4 1911 as Fort Supply republican
OkHi [1904]-[07-11]-[25-26]

SWEETWATER

Sweetwater BREEZE. w 1909-11‖?
OkHi [1909-11]

TAFT

Taft ENTERPRISE. w 1910-14‖?
Negro
OkHi [1911]

TAHLEQUAH

Tahlequah ARROW. w F 10 1888-F 21 1920‖
1888-S? 1894 as Indian arrow; S 19?-D? 1894 Arrow-telephone; Ja? 1895-96? Arrow. United with Cherokee county democrat to form Arrow-democrat, later Cherokee county democrat-star
F-Mr? 1888 pub in Vinita; Ap? 1888-Ag 8 1889 in Fort Gibson
MWA S 10 1898-Ag 1899;S 13 1902-S 3 1904
OkHi [1888-89;94-96;98-99]-[1912]16-20

ARROW-DEMOCRAT. *See* Cherokee county democrat-star

CHEROKEE advocate. w S 26 1844-Mr 3 1906‖
Suspended from S 28 1853-Ap 26 1870; from Ja 1875-Mr 4 1876
In Cherokee and English
CoU 1899-Mr 1906
CtY N 30 1887
DLC 1844-S 1853;Mr 25,Ag 5,D 9 1876;D 1877-Mr 1879;O 26 1887
ICN [Ja-N 6 1887]Ja 1-8 1890
supp:N 7 1889
IHi D 24 1904
KHi S 11 1845;Jl 27 1881-97;Ag 13 1904;Mr 25 1905
MWA S-O 19,N 9-21,D 5 1844;Ja 2-9,23-30,Ag 21,S 25,D 4 1845;49-S 1853;O 21 1876;F 11 1905-F 10 1906
N N 23 1887
NN Mr 27 1845[46-48]Ap 23,Ag 13 1849;Ja 7,21-28,F 11-18,Ap 22-29 1850;Jl 22 1851[Ja-Ag 1853]Ap 22 1870;O 10 1874;Ja 12,My 18 1883;My 29-Je 1889;Mr 3 1900
NcU Ja 15-22 1846
NhD Ag 9 1902;O 3 1903
OHi Ap 18 1896
OkHi My 1 1845;O 29 1846;D 9 1847;Je 5,Ag 14 1848;Ja 15 1849[70-76]-[78-79]-[83-1900]-06
OkM N 25 1893[99]Jl 28 1900
OkTa 1884;89;91-92
OkTaN [1878-83;86-87]88;90[91]-[94-99;1903-05]
OkU [1873;76;78-81;83;89-93;95-1906]
TxU O 1844-S 1846;83;87[Ag 1902-D 24 1904]
WHi O 22 1870(photostat);Ap 29 1871;D 18 1885[Mr 27-D 18 1889]F 19 1890;O 26 1891

CHEROKEE county democrat-star. w 1912+
1912-O 31 1930 as Cherokee county democrat (F 27 1920-N 3 1927? Arrow-democrat)
pub [1926;29-30]+
KHi Mr 26 1925
OkHi 1912-[14]-[27;29]+
OkTa 1931+

CHEROKEE telephone. *See* Telephone

Tahlequah CITIZEN. w 1931?+
OkHi [1932]33

Tahlequah COURIER. *See* Indian sentinel

DEMOCRATIC leader. *See* Tahlequah leader

Tahlequah HERALD. w,sw 1902-12‖?
sw 1902-07?
OkHi [1909-12]

INDIAN arrow. *See* Tahlequah arrow

INDIAN sentinel. w 1891-1901‖?
1893? as Tahlequah courier
KHi Ag 10,24 1892
OkHi [1891;93;97]-[1900]
TxU Ja 11 1901

Tahlequah LEADER. w 1904‖?
OkHi [1904]

Tahlequah LEADER. w 1921-23‖?
1921-22? as Democratic leader
OkHi [1921-23]

REPUBLICAN STAR. w 1923-O? 1930‖
United with Cherokee county democrat to form Cherokee county democrat-star
OkTaC [1929-30]

Tahlequah SUN. w 1909-19‖?
OkHi [1910-12;14]15

Tahlequah TELEGRAM. w 1913-17‖?
OkHi [1913-14;16-17]

TELEPHONE. w 1886-S 1894‖?
1886-93? as Cherokee telephone. United with Indian arrow to form Arrow-telephone, later Tahlequah arrow
TxU N 9 1893

TALALA

Talala GAZETTE. w 1908-14‖?
OkHi [1908]-[10]

Talala TOPIC. w 1903-
OkHi [1904]-[07]

TALIHINA

Talihina AMERICAN. w 1905+
1905-18 as Talihina tribune
pub 1909+
OkHi [1905-06]-[09]-[11-13]15-[18-19]-[21]

CHOCTAW news. *See* Talihina news

Talihina DEMOCRAT. w 1910?-12‖?
OkHi [1910]-12

KIAMICHI VALLEY democrat. w 1914-
OkHi [1916]-[18]

Talihina NEWS. w 1892-1901‖?
1895?-98? as Choctaw news
OkHi [1894-95]

Talihina NEWS. w
OkHi [1909]

Talihina TRIBUNE. *See* Talihina American

OKLAHOMA (*Continued*)

TALOGA

Taloga ACCIDENT. w 1892-
OkHi [1892-93]

Taloga ADVOCATE. w 1895-Mr? 1921||
United with Taloga times to form Taloga times-advocate
OkHi [1895;1900]-[02]-[18-21]

Taloga TIMES-ADVOCATE. w 1898+
1898-Mr 24 1921 as Taloga times
KHi My 17 1923
OkHi [1900]-[10]-14[16-17]-[28-29]

Taloga TOMAHAWK. w 1893-94||?
OkHi [1893-94]

WESTERN Oklahoma. w 1895-97||?
OkHi [1896-97]

TAMAHA

Tamaha BANNER. w 1906-07||?
OkHi [1906-07]

TANGIER

Tangier CITIZEN. w 1904-08||?
OkHi [1904]-[08]

TECUMSEH

COUNTY democrat. w Ja 1894-1931||?
KHi F 15 1924
OkHi 1894-97;99-1901[04]-[20]-[30-31]

Tecumseh HERALD. w 1891-97||?
OkHi [1893]-[97]

Tecumseh LEADER. w 1894-99||?
OkHi [1894]-[97]-[99]

Tecumseh LEADER. d Ap 1897-
OkHi [1897]

NATIONAL citizens' unionist. w
OkHi [1897]

Tecumseh OIL record. w 1928-31||?
OkHi [1929-30]

Tecumseh REPUBLICAN. w 1892+
OkHi [1893-94]-[99-1900]

Tecumseh STANDARD. w 1901-Je 1909||?
OkHi [1904-06;08]09

TEMPLE

Temple TRIBUNE. w 1902+
1902? as Botsford tribune (Botsford)
pub 1902+
OkHi 1905-[12]

TERLTON

Terlton ENTERPRISE. w 1912-16||?
OkHi 1913-[14]-[16]

Terlton TIMES. w 1908-10||?
OkHi [1909-10]

TERRAL

Terral TIMES. w 1893-94||?
OkHi 1893[94]

Terral TIMES. w
OkHi [1910]

Terral TRIBUNE. w 1905-08||?
OkHi [1907-08]

TEXHOMA

Texhoma ARGUS. w 1908-18||?
OkHi [1911-12]-14

Texhoma TIMES. w 1904+
pub 1915+
OkHi [1907]-33

TEXMO

Texmo TIMES. w 1904-11||?
OkHi [1904-05]-10

TEXOLA

Texola HERALD. w 1902-21||?
OkHi [1904-05]-07[09-10]

Texola TRIBUNE. w 1925+
OkHi [1925-26]

THOMAS

Thomas NEWS. w
OkHi 1927

Thomas TRIBUNE. w Ag 1902+
pub 1902+
OkHi [1904]-26;28+

TIPTON

Tipton PROGRESS. w 1918-22||?
OkHi [1920]-[22]

Tipton weekly TIMES. w 1913-17||?
OkHi [1913]15[16-17]

Tipton weekly TIPS. w 1909-14||?
Title varies slightly
OkHi [1909-10;14]

Tipton TRIBUNE. w 1922-
OkHi [1922-25]

TISHOMINGO

CHICKASAW capital. w 1901-My 12 1910||?
United with Johnston county democrat to form Johnston county capital-democrat
OkHi [1904-06]-[08-10]

JOHNSTON county capital-democrat. w 1903+
1903-07 as Tishomingo news; 1907-My 12? 1910 Johnston county democrat
OkHi [1904]-[06-07]-[09]-12[20]-[33]+

JOHNSTON county democrat. *See* Johnston county capital-democrat

JOHNSTON county socialist. w 1910-12||?
OkHi [1911-12]

Tishomingo LEADER. w 1913?-18||?
1914? as Tishomingo leader and Mannsville herald
OkHi [1914]

Tishomingo NEWS. 1903-07 *See* Johnston county capital-democrat

Tishomingo NEWS. w
OkHi [1916-17]

TONKAWA

Tonkawa CHIEFTAIN. w 1904-15||?
1904-05? as Tonkawa enterprise
OkHi [1904-05]-[07;10-11]-[14]15

Tonkawa ENTERPRISE. *See* Tonkawa chieftain

Tonkawa NEWS. w,sw 1898+
1898-99? as Salt Fork Valley news
w 1898-Ap? 1925
pub 1907+
KHi N 28 1918
OkHi [1900-01;04-05]+

Tonkawa REGISTER. *See* Blackwell sun (Blackwell)

SALT FORK VALLEY news. *See* Tonkawa news

Tonkawa WEEKLY. w Mr 16- 1895||?
OkHi [1895]

TRIBBEY

Tribbey PROGRESS. w 1911-13||?
OkHi [1911-13]

TRYON

LINCOLN county leader. w 1926+
pub 1926+

Tryon MERCURY. w 1895-98||?
OkHi [1895-96]-98

Tryon NEWS. *See* Tryon star

Tryon STAR. w 1903-13||?
1903-05? as Tryon news
OkHi [1904-05;07]-13

TULSA

AMERICAN Saturday night. w 1917+
pub 1917+

Tulsa CHIEF. *See* Tulsa county chief

Tulsa DEMOCRAT. w 1895-1919||?
1895-98? as New era
OkHi 1901-[04]-[12]-[18]
OkTT 1900-04

Tulsa DEMOCRAT. d *See* Tulsa tribune

Tulsa GUIDE. w 1906-07||?
Negro
OkHi [1906]

INDIAN republican. w,sw 1893-1907||?
1893-95? as Tulsa review
sw 1894?
OkHi [1894-95;1902-04]-[06]07

INTER-STATE post. w 1904-06||?
OkHi [1904]

NEW ERA. *See* Tulsa democrat

OIL and gas journal. w 1904?+
OkHi [1910;12]-[17-18]

OKLAHOMA constitution. w 1904-06||?
OkHi [1906]

OKLAHOMA critic. w 1917?-18||?
OkHi [1917]

Tulsa weekly PLANET. w
OkHi [1912]

Tulsa POST. d 1910-11||?
OkTT [1910]11

Weekly PROGRESS. w
OkHi [1905]

Tulsa daily REGISTER. d 1926-28||?
OkHi [1927-28]

Tulsa REVIEW. *See* Indian republican

Tulsa STAR. w 1912-21||?
Negro
KHi Ag 1 1913
OkHi [1913]-[15-19]-[21]

Tulsa STAR. d
Negro
OkHi [1916]

Tulsa evening SUN. d 1914||?
OkTT [1914]

Tulsa TIMES. w 1904-Jl 6 1906||?
OkHi [1905]06

Tulsa morning TIMES. d 1916-19||?
OkHi [1919]
OkTT 1917-19
WHi Ja 14 21,28,F 4 1917

Tulsa TRIBUNE. d 1904+
1904-D 5 1919 as Tulsa democrat; D 6-31 1919 Tulsa tribune-democrat
pub [1904]-[20]+
MnU O 22 1931
OkHi [1904;11]+
OkSt [1930]-32
OkT [1927]+
WHi 1917-F 1920

TULSA county chief. w 1904-16||?
1904-09? as Tulsa chief
OkHi [1904]-[11;16]

TULSA county journal. w 1911-12||?
OkHi [1912]

WEST Tulsa news. w 1922+
pub 1922+

Tulsa daily WORLD. d 1905+
pub 1905+
DLC 1911-[16]+
KHi My 21 1921;Je 25,N 6 1922;Je 5 1924
NN N 12 1923
OkHi [1905-06;10-11]+
OkOOk 1924+
OkStO [1923-25;27]+
OkT [1927]+
OkTT [1908]+
PP O 16 1928;F 8 1929

TUPELO

Tupelo TIMES. w 1904-12||?
OkHi 1904;06-[12]

TUSKAHOMA

Tuskohoma ITEM. w
OkHi [1911]

TUTTLE

GRADY county news. w 1914-28||?
1914-F? 1928 as Tuttle news
KHi Mr 31 1927
OkHi [1921]-[28]

Tuttle NEWS. *See* Grady county news

Tuttle STANDARD. w 1907-10||?
OkHi [1907]-[10]

Tuttle TELEGRAM. w 1911-12||?
OkHi [1911-12]

TIMES. w Mr 17 1905+
Title varies slightly
OkHi 1905+

TYRONE

Tyrone MERCURY. w
OkHi 1899

Tyrone OBSERVER. w 1904+
pub 1904+
OkHi 1909-[11-13]-[18-19]-33

UNION CITY

Union City ADVOCATE. w 1901-02||?
OkHi [1902]

Union City ALERT. w 1908-14||?
OkHi [1908]-11;13[14]

Union City CLIPPER. w Ja 25- 1890||?
OkU Ja 25 1890

Union City LEADER. w 1894-98||?
OkHi [1894-95]

VALLIANT

McCURTAIN record. w 1908-10||?
OkHi [1908-10]

Valliant NEWS. w 1905-07||?
OkHi [1905-07]

Valliant TIMES. w
OkHi [1910-11]

Valliant TRIBUNE. w 1911+
pub [1911-31]
OkHi [1911-12]-[14-15;17;19]-[34]

VERA

CHEROKEE times. w 1906||?
OkHi [1906]

Vera MONITOR. w
OkHi [1911]

Vera RECORD. w
OkHi [1913]

VERDEN

Verden NEWS. w Jl 14? 1905+
pub 1923+
OkHi [1905-08;10]-[14]16-[18-19]-33

VIAN

Vian AMERICAN. w 1925||?
OkHi [1925]

Vian PRESS. w 1907-33||?
1907-17? as Sequoyah county democrat
OkHi [1909-10;12;14-16]-[18]-[20]-[23]-[25]-29
OkSlD 1924;29-33

SEQUOYAH county democrat. *See* Vian press

OKLAHOMA (*Continued*)

VICI

Vici BEACON. w 1911+
pub 1911+
OkHi [1912-13;19-21]-[29]-33

Vici VISITOR. w
OkHi [1906]

VINITA

CHEROKEE champion. w Mr 20 1895-
OkHi [1895]

Weekly CHIEFTAIN. w S 22 1882-1912||?
1882-D 25 1902 as Indian chieftain; Ja 1 1903-Ag 31 1905 Vinita weekly chieftain
CU-B Ja 9 1890
DLC Ag 1885-F 2 1888
KHi Je 15 1883-D 11 1902;03-Je 1908;S 27 1912
NN O 22 1884;O 14 1886
OkHi [1883]-[1904-05]09-12
TxU S 29 1907

Vinita daily CHIEFTAIN. d O 3 1898-1913||?
OkHi 1898-[1902]-[04-06]-[08]-[11]-[13]

CRAIG county democrat. w 1930+
pub 1930+
OkHi [1932]33

CRAIG county gazette. w 1920-Je 27 1929||?
OkHi [1920]-[29]

Vinita GLOBE. w 1891-95||?
1891-92? as Vinita world
OkHi Jl 18-25 1891[95]

HERALD. d 1915||?
United with Morning sun to form Vinita evening sun-herald
OkHi [1915]

INDIAN arrow. *See* Tahlequah arrow (Tahlequah)

INDIAN chieftain. *See* Weekly chieftain

INDIAN herald. w 1875-80||?
1875-77? pub in Pawhuska
DLC Ag 15 1877
NN Mr 3 1877

Vinita weekly JOURNAL. w 1907-19||?
Title varies slightly
KHi My 29 1919
OkHi [1910-11]-19

Vinita daily JOURNAL. d 1918+
KHi Ap 17 1924
MWA O 15,N 4,23 1931
OkHi 1919+

Vinita LEADER. w 1895+
KHi N 23 1922
OkHi [1895-97]99-[1919;29]+
OkWcW 1914

Vinita REPUBLICAN. w D 6 1899-1906||?
KHi F 22 1900
OkHi [1899;1902]-[05-06]

Vinita evening SUN-HERALD. d 1913-19||?
1913-15? as Morning sun
OkHi [1914-15]-[19]

Vinita WORLD. *See* Vinita globe

VINSON

Vinson NEWS. w
OkHi [1909]

WAGONER

Weekly COURIER-SAYINGS. w 1911-S 30 1915||?
1911-Ap 16 1914 as Wagoner county courier. Followed by Wagoner county democrat?
OkHi [1911-15]

Wagoner ECHO. w Jl 28 1904-
OkHi [1904]

INDEPENDENT speaker. w 1910-12||?
OkHi [1911]

Wagoner NEW ERA. w 1904-05||?
OkHi [1904-05]

RECORD-DEMOCRAT. w O 1 1892+
1892-S 16 1909 as Wagoner record; S 23 1909-Jl 1 1920 Wagoner county record
OkHi [1894-95;99-1901;04-06;09]+

Wagoner weekly SAYINGS. w 1896-Ap 16 1914||?
United with Wagoner county courier to form Weekly courier-sayings
OkHi [1904-05]-[14]

Wagoner TRIBUNE. w 1920+
pub [1921]+
KHi My 19 1927
OkHi [1920-21;26]-33

WAGONER county courier. *See* Weekly courier-sayings

WAGONER county democrat. w O 7 1915-Jl 1 1920||
Follows Weekly courier-sayings? United with Wagoner county record to form Record-democrat
OkHi 1915-20

WAGONER county record. *See* Record-democrat

WAINWRIGHT

Wainwright AMERICAN. w Je 1905-
OkHi [1905]

Wainwright ENTERPRISE. w 1911-12||?
Title varies slightly
OkHi [1911-12]

LEADER. w
OkHi [1910-11]

WAKITA

Wakita HERALD. w 1897+
Title varies slightly
KHi S 22 1927
OkHi 1902-[08]-33
WyToT 1898-1908

WALTER. *See* WALTERS

WALTERS

To 1917? as Walter

COTTON county democrat. *See* Walters herald

COTTON county enterprise. *See* Walters herald

Walters DEMOCRAT. *See* Walters new era

Walters HERALD. w,sw 1907+
1907-Ja 15 1914 as Walter journal; Ja 22 1914-Ap 8 1920 Cotton county democrat; Ap 15 1920-Ja 20 1922 Cotton county enterprise
sw My 4 1920-My 6 1921
pub 1922+
KHi Ap 29 1920
OkHi [1907-08]-[23;28]30+

Walter JOURNAL. *See* Walters herald

Walters NEW ERA. w 1901-Ap 8 1920||
1901-S 30 1904 as Walter democrat. United with Cotton county democrat to form Cotton county enterprise, later Walters herald
OkHi 1904-[07]-20

Walter RECORD. w F 15 1906-
OkHi [1906]

WANETTE

Wanette ENTERPRISE. w 1911-18||?
OkHi [1911]-[16]-[18]

FREE PRESS. w
OkHi [1913]

Wanette JOURNAL. w 1903-
OkHi [1904]

MESSENGER. w 1905-Ap 1913||?
OkHi [1910]-[13]

Wanette NEWS. w 1919-23||?
OkHi [1919;21-23]

Wanette PRESS. w
OkHi [1913-14]

Wanette STANDARD. w 1903-11||?
1904-07? as Wanette winner
OkHi [1904]-[06-08]-[11]

Wanette TIMES. w 1905-06||?
OkHi [1906]

Wanette WINNER. *See* Wanette standard

WANN

Wann PROGRESS. w,sw 1905-17||?
sw N 27 1914-Mr 26 1915
OkHi [1910-11]-[16]

WAPANUCKA

Wapanucka PRESS. *See* Wapanucka world and press

Wapanucka WORLD. w 1920-23||?
OkHi [1921]

Wapanucka WORLD and press. w 1901-29||?
1901-28? as Wapanucka press
OkHi 1902-[17]20-24

WARNER

Warner TIMES. w 1910-12||?
OkHi [1911-12]

WASHINGTON

MCCLAIN county democrat. w 1909-13||?
OkHi 1909-[10;13]

Washington PROGRESS. w
OkHi [1914]

WATONGA

BLAIN county herald. w 1894-96||?
OkHi [1894-96]

Watonga HERALD. w 1902-29||?
OkHi [1904-05]-29

Watonga REPUBLICAN. w O 18 1892+
pub 1916
KHi F 27 1919
OkHi [1893-99]-1902;04+
OkWtF 1894-1916

Watonga RUSTLER. w 1892-97||?
OkHi [1893]-[96-97]

WATTS

Watts JOURNAL. w 1930+
pub 1930+

Watts WATCHMAN. w 1912||?
OkHi [1912]

WAUKOMIS

CHEROKEE republican. w Ag 3- 1894||?
OkHi [1894]

FARMERS elevator. w Ap 24 1903-
OkHi [1903]

OKLAHOMA hornet. w My 31 1899+
pub 1899+
OkHi [1899]-[1901]-20;31-33

Waukomis WIZARD. *See* Waukomis world

Waukomis WORLD. w 1894-96||?
1894-95 as Waukomis wizard
OkHi [1894-96]

WAURIKA

Waurika DEMOCRAT. w 1906-Ag 31 1911||?
1906-N 11? 1909 as Waurika herald. United with Waurika news to form Waurika news-democrat
OkHi [1908]-11

Waurika HERALD. *See* Waurika democrat

Waurika NEWS-DEMOCRAT. w 1902+
1902-S 1 1911 as Waurika news
KHi Ja 16 1920
OkHi [1904-12]+

Waurika PRESS. w
OkHi [1908]

Waurika TELEGRAPH. w S 21 1905-
OkHi [1905]

WAYNE

Wayne GAZETTE. w 1909-10||?
OkHi [1909-10]

Wayne IGNITOR. w
OkHi [1911]

WAYNOKA

Waynoka DEMOCRAT. w 1909-14||?
1909-F 16 1912 as Waynoka tribune
OkHi 1909-[14]
OkWyW 1913

Waynoka TRIBUNE. *See* Waynoka democrat

WOODS county enterprise. w 1900+
pub 1900+
KHi Je 25 1926
OkHi [1900]-[02]-[05;08;11]13+

WEATHERFORD

Weatherford BOOSTER. w 1899-1923||?
1899-1909 as Custer county republican
OkHi 1900-[23]

Weekly CHRONICLE. w 1899-1903||?
OkHi [1900]-03

CUSTER county republican. *See* Weatherford booster

Weatherford DEMOCRAT. *See* Weatherford news

Weatherford NEWS. w 1899+
1899-1922? as Weatherford democrat (1901? Oklahoma democrat)
KHi Mr 30 1899
OkHi [1901;04-07]-[13]

OKLAHOMA democrat. *See* Weatherford news

OKLAHOMA vorwärts. *See under* Bessie

WEBBERS FALLS

Webbers Falls MONITOR. w 1900-03||?
OkHi 1901

Webbers Falls RECORD. w 1906-12||?
OkHi [1908]-[11-12]

WELCH

Welch WATCHMAN. w 1903+
pub 1909+
KHi O 29 1924;D 15 1926
OkHi [1904]-[13]+

WELEETKA

Weleetka AMERICAN. w 1902+
OkHi [1904]-[12;20]-33

DEMOCRAT. *See* State democrat

STATE democrat. w 1906||?
Title varies: Democrat
OkHi [1906]

WELLSTON

Wellston LEADER. w 1911-12||?
OkHi [1911]12

Wellston NEWS. w 1894+
pub [1900]-[12]-[18]+
OkHi 1899-[1906;08-11]-[17]-33

WEST TULSA

Papers published in West Tulsa are listed under Tulsa

WESTVILLE

ADAIR county democrat. w 1904-11||?
1904-07 as Westville American
OkHi [1904-05;07]-[10-11]

Westville AMERICAN. *See* Adair county democrat

OKLAHOMA (*Continued*)

WESTVILLE—*Continued*

CHEROKEE wigwam. w 1901-04||?
OkHi [1904]

Westville RECORD. w 1912+
pub [1919]+
OkHi [1912]-[18]

WETUMKA

Wetumka GAZETTE. w My 2 1907+
pub 1908+
KHi Ap 26 1917
OkHi [1907]-[09-10]-[16]-[18]-[23]+

Wetumka HERALD. w 1901-02||?
United with Wetumka news to form Wetumka news-herald

Wetumka NEWS-HERALD. w 1902-07||
1902? as Wetumka news
OkHi [1905-07]

WEWOKA

Wewoka CAPITAL-DEMOCRAT. w 1901+
1901-Je 28 1917 as Seminole county capital
OkHi [1904]-[09]-[22]-[29]
—d ed *See* Wewoka times-democrat

Wewoka and Lima COURIER. w
OkHi [1913-14]

Wewoka DEMOCRAT. w 1906-Je 28 1917||
United with Seminole county capital to form Wewoka capital-democrat
OkHi [1906-07]-[09-10]-[12]-17

Wewoka HERALD. w 1905?-07||?
OkHi [1905-07]

SEMINOLE county capital. *See* Wewoka capital-democrat

Wewoka TIMES-DEMOCRAT. d 1926+
1926-27? as Wewoka daily times
pub 1928+
OkHi [1926-27;29]+
—w ed *See* Wewoka capital-democrat

WHEATLAND

Wheatland weekly WATCHWORD. w 1908-14||?
OkHi [1908]-[14]

WILBURTON

Wilburton GAZETTE. *See* Latimer county democrat

LATIMER county democrat. w 1899-Ap 2 1915||
1899-D 26 1913 as Wilburton gazette. United with Wilburton news to form Latimer county news-democrat
OkHi [1904]-15

LATIMER county news-democrat. w 1898+
1898-Ap 2 1915 as Wilburton news; 1927?-33? Wilburton news-democrat
pub [1900-25]+
OkHi [1904-05]-[07-08]-[15]-33

Wilburton NEWS. *See* Latimer county news-democrat

WILLOW

Willow TIMES. w 1916-18||?
OkHi [1916-18]

WILSON

1918?-19? as New Wilson?

Wilson daily DEMOCRAT. d 1921-25||?
OkHi [1923-25]

Wilson DEMOCRAT. w,sw 1923-27||?
Title varies slightly. United with Wilson post to form Wilson post-democrat
sw F 9-Ap 3 1926
OkHi [1923-25]-27

Wilson GAZETTE. w 1914-23||?
1914-17? as Wilson news; 1919? Wilson good roads gazette
OkHi 1915-[17;19-20]-[23]

Wilson GOOD roads gazette. *See* Wilson gazette

Wilson NEWS. *See* Wilson gazette

Wilson POST-DEMOCRAT. w 1924+
1924-27 as Wilson post
OkHi [1923]-[30-31]

WISTER

Wister INFORMER. w 1904-05||?
OkHi [1904-05]

Wister NEWS. w 1906-12||?
OkHi [1906-09]-[12]

Wister RECORD. w 1914-16||?
OkHi [1914]-[16]

WOODVILLE

Woodville BANNER. w 1911-15||?
OkHi [1911-12]-[15]

Woodville BEACON. w 1905-07||?
OkHi [1905-07]

Woodville STAR. w
OkHi [1908]

WOODWARD

Woodward BULLETIN. *See* Woodward news-bulletin

Woodward daily DEMOCRAT. d 1907-
OkHi [1909-10]
OkWoW [1909-10]
—w ed *See* Woodward county republican

Woodward DISPATCH. w 1900-09||?
OkHi [1900]-[03]

Woodward daily DISPATCH. d
OkWoW [1909]

Woodward JEFFERSONIAN. w 1893-95||?
OkHi [1893-95]

Woodward NEWS. w Je 1 1894-Jl 30 1909||
United with Woodward bulletin to form Woodward news-bulletin
KHi Ag 31 1894-1909
OkHi complete
OkWoN [1903-09]

Woodward NEWS-BULLETIN. w,sw F 14 1896+
1896-Jl 30 1909 as Woodward bulletin
sw My 5-26 1933
pub [1900]-[27]+
KHi Ag 1909-Ag 19 1910;D 5 1924
OkHi [1900]-[27]-[32-33]

Woodward daily PRESS. d 1923+
pub 1923+
KHi Ag 16 1923;Ja 11 1926
OkHi [1930]+

Woodward STAR. w Ag 29- 1896||?
OkHi [1896]
OkWoN [1896]

WOODWARD county democrat. *See* Woodward county republican

WOODWARD county journal. w 1932+
pub 1932+

WOODWARD county republican. w 1905+
1905-07? as Woodward county democrat; 1908?-09? Woodward county democrat and Palace weekly pioneer; 1909?-32? Woodward democrat
pub 1910+
KHi F 16 1912
OkHi [1907]-[09]-[16-18]-[32]
—d ed *See* Woodward daily democrat

WYANDOTTE

OTTAWA county courier. w 1907-11||?
OkHi [1908-09]-11

WYNNE WOOD

Wynne Wood BEACON. *See* New era farmer

CHICKASAW banner. w 1906?-08||?
1906?-08? as Republican. United with Maysville news to form Maysville news and Chickasaw banner, later Maysville news (Maysville)
OkHi [1907]08

FIELDS' state gazette. *See* Wynne Wood gazette-new era

Wynne Wood GAZETTE-NEW ERA. w 1906+
1906-14? as Fields' state gazette; 1915?-F 26 1931 Wynne Wood gazette; Mr 5-1931? Wynne Wood gazette and new era farmer
pub 1913+
OkHi [1910]-13[21]-[23]+

NEW ERA farmer. w 1902-F 26 1931||?
1902-F 7 1929 as Wynne Wood new era (1925?-26? Wynne Wood beacon). United with Wynne Wood gazette to form Wynne Wood gazette and new era farmer, later Wynne Wood gazette-new era
OkHi 1903-[25]-[31]

NEWS. *See* Maysville news (Maysville)

Wynnewood REPUBLIC. w 1892-1901||?
OkHi [1895]

REPUBLICAN. *See* Chickasaw banner

WYNONA

Wynona ARGOSY. w 1919-20||?
OkHi [1919-20]

Wynona ENTERPRISE. w 1909-12||?
OkHi [1909]-[12]

Wynona FREE PRESS. w 1923-25||?
OkHi [1924-25]

Wynona RECORD. w 1919-22||?
OkHi [1920-22]

YALE

Yale DEMOCRAT. w,tw 1908-24||?
1908-N 25 1914 as Payne county farmer
tw Mr 24 1919-Jl 6 1922
OkHi [1908]-[14]-[24]

PAYNE county farmer. *See* Yale democrat

Yale RECORD. w 1902+
pub [1903-21]+
KHi D 29 1927
OkHi [1904-05]-[20-21]-[30]+
OkY 1926+

YEAGER

Yeager RECORD. w 1905-07||?
OkHi [1905]-[07]

YUKON

CANADIAN county courier. w Ap 23 1891-92||?
KHi 1891-Mr 3 1892

Yukon REGISTER. w Jl 2 1892-94||?
OkHi N 4,D 16 1893;Ap 13-27 1894
OkU Jl 2 1892

Yukon SUN. w 1899+
Mr 15 1901-N 24 1905 as Yukon sun and Yukon weekly; D 1 1905-Je 28 1907 Yukon sun, Yukon weekly and Mustang mail
OkHi [1901]-[09-12]-[16-17;19;21]+

Yukon WEEKLY. w 1893-Mr 1901||?
United with Yukon sun to form Yukon sun and Yukon weekly, later Yukon sun
OkHi [1894]-[96-98]99

OREGON

ALBANY

Albany DEMOCRAT. w,sw,w Ag 1 1865-1929||
Follows Oregon democrat. 1865-Ap 13 1900 as State rights democrat
sw 1913-23
pub 1866-1929
CU-B [1868]-Je 5 1869;70-[79]80;Mr 24 1882;Ja 19 1884;86-87
Or N 13 1924-Ja 2 1926
OrHi Mr 14 1873;Ja 23 1874;Ag 4 1893-[1900-01]Ag 1904-Ag 3 1917;Mr-D 1925;Jl 17 1926-Ja 1927
OrU D 30 1865;F 3 1866[Je 1904-05;Ja-Ag 1907]15

Albany DEMOCRAT-HERALD. d 1887+
1887-Mr 2 1925 as Albany democrat
pub 1887+
CU-B [Ja-N 1876]
Or [1923-24]
OrA 1922+
OrHi Jl 1926+
OrU [1915-18]-[20;23-24]-[27]+

GREATER Albany. w Ja 17 1929+
Follows Halsey rural enterprise (Halsey)
OrA Ja 13 1933+
OrU [1929-31]+

Albany HERALD. w N 28 1879-1920||?
CU-B [1880;D 29 1881-My 18 1882]
OrHi Ja 16 1880 S 25 1885-O 9 1888;Ag 1893-Jl 1897;D 1898-Ja 17 1901;Jl 9 1903
OrU [1905-06;08-09]

Albany HERALD. d 1885-Mr 7 1925||
United with Albany democrat to form Albany democrat-herald
CU-B [1888-89]-F,Ap 1891
OrA Mr 15 1912-24
OrHi F 17 1905
OrU [1911]20-[21]-[24]-F 1925

Albany INQUIRER. *See* Oregon State democrat

Albany JOURNAL. w Mr 12 1863-Mr 1868||
Suspended S 1866-Mr 1867
OrHi Ap 9 1864[65]Ja 19,F 16 1866
OrU [1864-65]F 23 1866

LINN county advertiser. w F 13? 1878-
CU-B Ag 14-28 1878

OREGON democrat. *See* Oregon state democrat

OREGON state democrat. w 1859-64||
1859-Ja 1861 as Oregon democrat; F 1861-Ap 10 1862 Albany inquirer. Followed by State rights democrat, later Albany democrat
CU-B Je 25 1864
OrHi [1860-64]

PEOPLE'S press. w 1895-1902||?
OrHi Jl 28 1899-Ag 1901

Albany REGISTER. w S 12 1868-80||?
CU-B [O-D 1868]-[71]-[73]-Ag 31 1877;N 21,D 12-26 1879-80

STATE rights democrat. *See* Albany democrat

ALBINA

Albina COURIER. w 1887-93||?
CU-B O 19-D 7 1889;Ag 9-23 1890

ALOHA

Aloha NEWS. w Mr 17 1927+
pub 1927+
OrHi 1928+
OrU 1927+

OREGON (*Continued*)

AMITY

Amity STANDARD. w 1910+
pub 1917+
Or 1926+
OrU [1913-15]-16;20-[22]+
WaPS Jl-S 9 1932

Amity VALLEY times. w 1891-1904||?
OrHi Je 1901-My 1904

ANTELOPE

APPEAL. w F 26 1903-05||?
OrHi 1903-Ag 10 1905

Antelope HERALD. w 1892-1925||
OrU [1904]

ARLINGTON

Arlington BULLETIN. w 1883+
Or [1924]-[26-28]+
OrU 1926-[33]+

Arlington INDEPENDENT. w 1899-1901||?
OrHi O 12 1900-My 3 1901

Arlington RECORD. w 1892-1912||?
OrHi [O 26 1900-Jl 27 1911]
OrU [1903-04;06-09]

Arlington TIMES. w 1887-92||?
CU-B Ja 25,Jl 5 1889;Ja 9-16,Jl 19 1890

ASHLAND

Ashland AMERICAN and Ashland register. w
OrU [1927]

LITHIA City news. w 1934+
Friday ed of Ashland tidings
pub 1934+

Ashland RECORD. w 1888-1919||
1888-1911? as Valley record. Followed by Pacific record-herald (Medford)
CU-B D 26 1889;Ja 2-16,Mr 6-20,Ap 17 1890
OrHi S 14 1899;F 27 1900;01-Ag 30 1911
OrU F 27 1902

Ashland REGISTER. sw 1925-28||?
OrU [1928]

Ashland TIDINGS. w,sw,w Je 17 1876-1926||
sw 1893-1919
pub complete
CU-B O 7-D 23 1876;Je 16 1877-[79-N 5 1880; 86]Je 3 1887;Ja-Je 1888;89-90;Jl 21 1893
Or Jl 12 1878
OrAs (1913-18)
OrHi Ag 2,30 1878[1893-95]-[1912-17]-26
OrU [1893-94;1901-07]-[09]-11;13-[15]-[17]-[20-22]-[24]
MWA D 21 1888

Ashland TIDINGS. d S 1 1919+
pub 1919+
OrAs [1913-18]
OrHi 1919+
OrU [1924-25]-[28]+
—Friday ed. *See* Lithia City news

TOWN talk. *See* Ashland tribune

Ashland TRIBUNE. sw 1896-1906||?
1896-1902? as Town talk
OrU Ag 16 1902

VALLEY record. *See* Ashland record

ASHWOOD

Ashwood PROSPECTOR. w 1901-04||?
OrHi Ag 17 1903
OrU [1904]

ASTORIA

ASTORIAN. d *See* Astorian-budget. d

ASTORIAN. tw,w Jl 1? 1873-1919||?
tw 1873-Ja 1874
CU-B [Jl 1873-Ja,Jl 1874-Jl 1877]-78;F 7,Ap 4,Je 6 1879-80;Ja 14 1881[Mr-S 1882]O 23-30 1886[87]
OrHi S 13 1873;Jl 9 1874[75-76]-78;Jl 1881-Ap 1886;Je 13 1892

ASTORIAN-BUDGET. d My 1 1876+
1876-Ag 1930 as Astorian
pub 1876+
CU-B O 13 1877-[My 1878-79]80;My 15,Jl 19-D 1881;88-N 28 1891
OrAt 1876+
OrHi [1876-78]-[82-86]D 1903-30
OrU [1904-Je 1906]26+

Astoria BUDGET. d 1892-Ag 30 1930||
United with Astorian to form Astorian-budget
OrAt complete
OrHi Jl 1920-Ap 1927
OrU [Ap-Je 1911;15-18]-[22-23]-30

Astoria BUDGET. w 1892-1920||?
OrHi 1904;17-20

Astoria HERALD. w 1890-1908||?
1890-95 as Sunday herald
OrP F 26 1893
OrU [1901]-02-[03-05]

Sunday HERALD. *See* Astoria herald

Astoria MARINE gazette. w Ag 9 1864-66||?
CSmH My 14 1866
CU-B Ap 16,Je 25 1866
MWA D 20 1864
OrHi Ag 30 1864[65-66]

Astoria daily MESSENGER. d 1931+
OrU [My 28-S]O 1931-[33]
WaPS [F 17-My 1931]

Astoria daily NEWS. *See* Astoria news-herald

Astoria NEWS-HERALD. d 1894-1906||?
1894-1904? as Astoria daily news
OrHi 1902[03]

Astoria daily PIONEER. d 1887-89||?
CU-B My 23 1888
OrHi S-O 1887;Je 26 1888;F 18 1889

Astoria RAPPORT. m 1914-
In Swedish
IRA 1914-18

Astoria TIMES. w 1922-23||?
OrHi [1922]

Astoria TRANSCRIPT. w 1882-89||?
OrHi [1886-89]

ATHENA

Athena PRESS. w Ja 1 1887+
pub Je 1889+
OrHi Ag 21 1903
OrPe 1927+
OrU 1926-[30]+

AUMSVILLE

Aumsville weekly RECORD. *See* Aumsville star

Aumsville STAR. w 1911-30||
1911-Ag 31 1923 as Aumsville weekly record
Or 1918-[24]Ja 8 1925
OrHi F 1915-Ag 11,S 6 1923
OrU [1927-30]

AURORA

Aurora BOREALIS. w 1900-07||?
Follows Three sisters (Barlow)
Followed by Aurora observer

Aurora OBSERVER. w 1911+
Followed Aurora Borealis
OrU N 12 1925-[30]+

BAKER

BAKER county record. w 1925-30||?
OrU My 19 1927-[30]

BAKER county reveille. *See* Baker reveille

BEDROCK democrat. w My 1870-F 1 1929||
CU-B Ap 22 1871-76;Ja 1878[79]-80[82]F 13-27 1884;88-[91]
OrHi [1894-95]96-O 11 1897

Baker DEMOCRAT-HERALD. d 1887+
1887-F 1 1929 as Baker democrat
CU-B Ag 16 1889
OrB S 1929+
OrHi O 26 1906-Ag 1929;My 1930+
OrU [Jl 1908-25]-[28-29]-[32]+
—w ed. *See* Bedrock democrat

Baker City HERALD. w 1873-75||?
CU-B N 4 1874-[S 29-D 1875]

Baker HERALD. w 1893-1921||?
OrHi Ag 17 1893;N 28 1901;Ag 14,18,19,1903

Baker HERALD. d 1901-F 1 1929||
United with Baker democrat to form Baker democrat-herald
OrHi 1901-O 1906;07-Ja 1909;10-[17]-22
OrU [1910;12-23]-[25]-[28-29]

OREGON republican. sw 1896-1902||?
OrHi Je 7 1901-My 28 1902

RECORD-COURIER. w 1901+
1901-O 22 1931 as Haines record
1901-33? pub in Haines
pub 1926+
OrU [N 1925-27]+

Baker REVEILLE. w O 20 1880-91||?
1880-90 as Baker county reveille
CU-B [N 10 1881-87]
OrHi Mr 4 1889

BANDON

Bandon RECORDER. w 1883-Je 27 1916||
CU-B Ja 3,O 3 1890
OrHi Je 13-D 1901;03-16
OrMnH 1915
OrU [1901-11;13-16]

Bandon WESTERN world. w 1912+
OrU S 1915-16[18]+

BANKS

Banks HERALD. w 1910-23||
Merged with Beaverton review (Beaverton)
OrHi N 17 1916-N 29 1923

BARLOW

THREE sisters. w 1892-95||?
Followed by Aurora Borealis (Aurora)
OrHi Mr 8,My 10 1894

BAY CITY

Bay City CHRONICLE. w
OrHi My 15-Ag 14 1924

Bay City TRIBUNE and western watchtower. 1891-92||
1891? as Bay City tribune
CU-B Ja 28,My 12 1892

BEAVERTON

Beaverton ENTERPRISE. w Mr 17 1927+
pub 1927+
OrHi 1928+
OrU 1927-[31]+

Beaverton OWL. w 1911-14||?
OrHi N 13 1912-My 16 1914

Beaverton REVIEW. w 1922+
pub 1922+
OrHi D 1924+
OrU 1926+

Beaverton TIMES. w 1912-25||?
OrHi Mr 30 1916-N 27 1925
OrU [Ag 1915-16;18-19]-22

BEND

Bend BULLETIN. w Mr 20 1903-Ja 7 1932||
pub complete
OrHi Mr 27 1903-Mr 8 1911;Mr 13 1912-32
OrU 1915

Bend BULLETIN. d D 6 1916+
pub 1916+
OrBd Je 1921+
OrU 1916-[31]+

CENTRAL Oregon press. d 1918-19;21-Ag 1926||
Title varies: Bend press; Bend daily press. Merged with Bend bulletin
OrBd F 1922-26
OrU [1926]

DESCHUTES echo. w
OrHi Ap 30-Je 25 1904

Bend PRESS. w 1915-24||?
OrBd [My 27 1921-Ap 24 1924]

BLY

Bly BULLETIN. w 1929+
OrU 1930-Jl 1931

BROWNSVILLE

Brownsville TIMES. w 1888+
pub 1888+
CU-B Ag 8-20 1890
OrHi My 30 1903-S 1918
OrU [1901-07;13-14]-16[19]-[21-23]-[27]-[33]

BURNS

EAST Oregon herald. *See* Burns times-herald

Burns FREE press. w 1930+
OrU Ap 23 1931+

HARNEY county news. *See* Burns news

HARNEY Valley items. w 1884-1904||?
CU-B Ag 21-28 1889
OrHi N 30 1901-N 23 1904
OrU [1902]

Burns NEWS. w 1894-1929||
1894-1926 as Harney county news. Merged with Burns times-herald
OrU [1913-14]-[19;25]-[27]-29

Burns TIMES. w 1891-96||
United with East Oregon herald to form Burns times-herald

Burns TIMES-HERALD. w 1887+
1887-96 as East Oregon herald
CU-B Ag 1,15-22,O 31,D 12,26 1889
OrHi Je-N 1901;Ap 9 1904
OrU [1930]-[33]

CANBY

CLACKAMAS county news. *See* Canby herald. 1915+

Canby HERALD. w 1906-16||?
1906-Mr 11 1909 as Canby tribune; Mr 18 1909-12? Canby tribune and Willamette valley irrigator; 1913-14 Canby irrigator
OrU [1909-11;13]14

Canby HERALD. w 1915+
1915-22 as Clackamas county news; 1923-25 Canby herald-Clackamas county news
OrHi Ag 28 1924-F 1925
OrU [1915]16;19-[21]-[24]27-[30-33]

Canby IRRIGATOR. *See* Canby herald. 1906-16

Canby TRIBUNE. *See* Canby herald. 1906-16

CANYON CITY

BLUE Mountain eagle. w 1900+
Follows Long Creek eagle (Long Creek)
pub 1900+
OrHi [1909]Ja 7-14 1910;Ag 23 1929+
OrU [1901-04]-[06]-[12;14-15]-[20-21]+

CITY journal. ir N 9 1868-70||?
Followed by Grant county news
OrCaB N 9 1868;Ap 17,Je 28,Jl 12,26,S 6 1869

GRANT county news. w Ap 12 1879-1908||
Follows City journal, Grant county times, and Grant county express. Merged with Blue Mountain eagle
1903-08 pub at John Day.
CU-B My 10 1879-80;My 6 1882;Jl 15,S 9,D 16 1886;Ap 28,N 10 1887-N 7 1889
OrCaB [1879-1908]
OrHi Ag 20 1903
OrU [1904-07]

CARLTON

Carlton SENTINEL. w 1907-31||?
OrU 1926-N 1931

OREGON (*Continued*)

CENTERVILLE

HOME press. w 1888-89||?
CU-B Mr 15-29 1889
OrHi Mr 2 1888

CENTRAL POINT

Central Point AMERICAN. w 1925+
pub N 1931+
OrU 1926

Central Point HERALD. w 1906-17||?
OrHi Ap 26 1906-Je 28 1917

Central Point STAR. w 1928-31||?
OrU [Ap 5 1929-S 5 1930]

CLATSKANIE

Clatskanie CHIEF. w 1890+
OrU 1917-[20-21]-[25-26]-[31-32]+

CLOVERDALE

Cloverdale COURIER. w 1905-18||
OrU [1916-17]

CONDON

Condon GLOBE-TIMES. w 1891+
1891-Ap 4 1919 as Condon globe
pub 1891+
OrHi 1901-Mr 6 1902;Mr 12 1903-Mr 3 1904;Mr 30 1905-Mr 15 1906;Mr 22 1907-F 1908
OrU [1919-20]21[24-25]-[31-32]+

Condon TIMES. w 1900-Ap 4 1919||
United with Condon globe to form Condon globe-times
OrCoG complete
OrU [1901;11]-[13-15]-18

COQUILLE

Coquille BULLETIN. w 1894-1904||?
Title varies: Coquille city bulletin
OrHi Je 7 1901-Jl 1 1904

COOS county courier. w 1927+
OrU 1929+

Coquille HERALD. w 1882-1926||?
1880 as Coquille city herald
CU-B S 11 1883[84-90]O 10 1893
OrCqV [1882-1926]
OrHi S 11 1894-Ja 1901;My 28 1901-D 2 1902;My 14 1904-Jl 8 1904[08-17]
OrU 1902-[03;05-10]26

Coquille VALLEY sentinel. w 1904+
Title varies: Sentinel-herald
pub 1904+
OrH 1918+
OrU [1915]17-[18-20]-[30]-32

CORNELIUS

Cornelius NEWS. *See* West Washington county news

PEOPLES searchlight. w 1890-95||?
IU My 15 1895

WEST Washington county news. w 1928-29||?
1928 as Cornelius news
OrU [1928]

CORVALLIS

BENTON county courier. w O 11 1906-25||
1906-Mr 11 1915 as Benton county republican. Merged with Benton independent, later Benton county herald
OrHi 1906-Jl 26 1924
OrU My 21 1912

BENTON county democrat. *See* Benton democrat

BENTON county herald. w 1904+
1904-Jl 28 1932 as Benton independent
Or 1931+
OrCA [1927-32]+
OrU 1926+

BENTON county reporter. w
OrHi O 11 1906

BENTON county republican. *See* Benton county courier

BENTON democrat. w 1871-78||?
Title varies: Benton county democrat; etc.
CU-B Mr 21 1872;Je 28,Jl 12,Ag 23,O 25 1873;Jl 18 1874;Ag 6 1875[77]-N 1878
OrCA [1872-73]
OrU Jl 20 1871

BENTON independent. *See* Benton county herald

BENTON leader. w F 24 1882-92||?
CU-B My 19 1882;O 24-N 14,D 1884;Ja 16-23,Ap 9,30-My,Jl 30,Ag 27-S 3,O 29-N 12,D 17 1885-Ja 1 1886;S 26 1890

Corvallis CHRONICLE. w O 14 1886-87||
CU-B Ja 14-My 27 1887

DEMOCRATIC crisis. w F 2-Mr 2 1859||
Follows Occidental messenger. Followed by Oregon weekly union
OrHi complete

Corvallis GAZETTE-TIMES. w,sw,w 1862+
1862-1908 as Corvallis gazette (F 1899-Ap 1900 Union gazette)
sw My 1901-08
pub 1915+
C O 17 1868
CU-B Ap 21-N 10,D 1-8,22 1866;67-Ja 14 1871;72-80 Ag 19,N 4 1881;F 17-Ag 4 1882;S 5-12,26-O 10,N-D 5,19 1884-[85-87]-N 1888;89 [90]91;Ja 8,22 1892
Or [1918]-[21]
OrCA [1879-85;89-97;99-1908]
OrHi [1868-70]Je 27 1874[76-77;93]-[95-96]-[98-1901;03-08]12-[16]+
OrU D 1872-Ap 1873[76]78-[80-83]84[89-93;95-99]1901[03]-[08;13;16-17]-20
WaU D 26 1868[1869-Jl 1870;Ap 29 1871-76]

Corvallis GAZETTE-TIMES. d 1909+
pub 1915+
OrCA [S 1918-25]+
OrU [1909-14]-[16-21]24-[31]+

OCCIDENTAL messenger. w Je 1857-58||
Followed by Democratic crisis
OrHi [1857-58]

OREGON statesman. *See under* Salem

OREGON weekly union. w Mr 9 1859-63||
Follows Democratic crisis
CU-B N 25 1861
OrHi 1859-[61]

OREGON union. w Jl 1897-F 1899||
United with Corvallis gazette to form Union-gazette, later Corvallis gazette-times
OrCA complete
OrU [1897-98]

Corvallis TIMES. w,sw F 1888-Jl 2 1909||
United with Corvallis gazette to form Corvallis gazette-times
w 1888-92
CU-B Mr 5-12 1889
OrCA [1900-07]
OrHi Mr 11 1905-Je 1909
OrU [1900-02]-[04-05]-[07]

UNION gazette. *See* Corvallis gazette-times. w

COTTAGE GROVE

BOHEMIA nugget. w 1897-1910||?
OrHi O 1904-Ja 1 1908
OrU [1901-05]-06

ECHO-leader. *See* Cottage Grove leader

LANE county leader. *See* Cottage Grove leader

Cottage Grove LEADER. w Je 15 1889-Ag 27 1915||
1889-90 as Cottage Grove leader; 1891-95 Echo-leader; 1896-1903 Cottage Grove leader; 1904-Ap 22 1905 Lane county leader
CU-B S 21-28,O 5 1889;Ag 2-23 1890
OrHi O 1904-Ja 7 1905;Ap 20 1907-Jl 1912;N 11 1914-15
OrU [1901-06]07[13]-15

Cottage Grove SENTINEL. w 1889+
pub 1889+
OrHi S 24,O 8-22 1909
OrU [1914-15]-[19]-[21]-[26]+

WESTERN Oregon. w,sw 1905-09||?
OrHi N 2 1905-[09]

CRANE

Crane AMERICAN. w Ag 18 1916+
pub 1916+
OrU 1926+

CRESWELL

Creswell CHRONICLE. w 1910-18||
OrU 1914-O 1915[17]

DALLAS

LIBERAL republican. w Mr 5 1870-74||?
CU-B 1870-[71]-D 6 1873;Ap 18 1874

POLK county itemizer-observer. w 1875+
1875-Je 1 1927 as Polk county itemizer
pub [1882]-[1927]+
CU-B [S 1875-80 Ja-S 3 1882]
OrHi Jl 3-23 1887[93-1910]-O 15 1914
OrU 1931+

POLK county observer. w 1888-Je 1 1927||
United with Polk county itemizer to form Polk county itemizer-observer
Or [1926-27]
OrDP 1892-[1912-24]
OrHi My 16 1902-Ap 15 1904;Je 10 1910;Ag 23 1913-Ag 11 1914;Je 26 1924-F 4 1926
OrU [1901-03]23-26

POLK county signal. w Mr 23 1868-69||
C D 15 1868
CU-B Ap 6,My 4-19,Je,Jl 13-20,Ag 3-10,31,S 14-21,O 5-12,22-D 22 1868;Ja 5-12,26-F 2 1869

POLK county times. w My 1 1869-F 12 1870||
CU-B [1869-70]

Morning STATE journal.
P-M N 20 1863

DALLES. *See* THE DALLES

DAYTON

Dayton HERALD. w 1883-1906||?
1886-89? as Yamhill county herald
CU-B Mr 7-21,Je 27,Jl 11-18,Ag 22,O 17-N 7,D 5-12 1889;Ja 15-F 6,Ag 15,29 1890
OrHi Ag 1893-O 1906

Dayton NEWS. w N 19 1891-92||?
CU-B F 26,Mr 11,Ap 15-29,My 13-20 1892

Dayton TRIBUNE. w 1912+
OrU [1912-14]-[16-20]-[27]29[32]+
OrHi Ag 28 1924+

YAMHILL county herald. *See* Dayton herald

DELAKE

BEACH resort news. w 1927+
OrU [F 28-D 1930]-[32-33]

DONALD

Donald RECORD. w 1916-18||?
OrHi [1917-18]

DRAIN

ECHO. w 1886-90||
CU-B Jl 5,Ag 23,S 20,N 8,22 1889-Ja 3,17-24,S 19 O 3-10,24-31 1890

Drain ENTERPRISE. w 1922+
OrHi 1922+

Drain NONPAREIL. *See* North Douglas herald

NORTH Douglas herald. w 1901-15||?
1901-14 as Drain nonpareil
OrHi [1909-14]-S 24 1915
OrU [1903-S 1905]

Drain WATCHMAN. w Ja 1898-1901||?
OrHi [1900-01]

DUFUR

Dufur DISPATCH. w D 12 1891+
Suspended 1892-My 1 1896
pub [1891+]
OrHi Je 22 1910+
OrU [1904-05;25-26]-[28]-[33]

EAST PORTLAND

Papers published in East Portland are listed under Portland

ECHO

ECHO'S echoes. w 1909-13||?
OrEcN 1912-My 15 1913

Echo ENTERPRISE. w
OrEcN O 16 1914-F 11 1915

Echo NEWS. w Ag 8 1913+
pub 1913+
OrHi Ag 1916-Jl 1925
OrPe 1927+
OrU 1917-[19]+

Echo REGISTER. w 1901?-09||?
OrHi S 17-O 1 1901[09]

ELGIN

Elgin RECORDER. w 1891+
pub 1891+
OrHi [1903-16]Je 25 1917-Ja 5 1922
OrU [1929]-[31]

ELLENSBERG

GOLD Beach gazette. w 1885-90||
CU-B Mr 15-22,Ap,Jl 5,19-Ag 2,S 6-13,N 8,22-D 20 1889;F 21,My 16,Ag 29,O 24-31 1890

EMPIRE CITY

COOS county argus. Mr 22-D 27 1879||
CU-B [1879]

ENTERPRISE

BORDER signal. *See* Enterprise signal

Enterprise NEWS-RECORD. w,sw 1899-Ag 17 1911||
United with Wallowa chieftain to form Enterprise record-chieftain
w 1899-1907
OrHi S 14 1907-11

Enterprise RECORD-CHIEFTAIN. w 1884+
1884-Ag 24 1911 as Wallowa chieftain
1884-92 pub at Joseph
pub 1901+
CU-B Ja 23,F 20,Jl 31,Ag 14,O 9,23-30 1890;Ag 12 1892
OrHi O 16 1896;1911+
OrU 1913[14;17 24]-[28]+

Enterprise SIGNAL. w 1888-92||?
1888-90? as Border signal
CU-B Jl 5-12,Ag 2,S 27 1889

WALLOWA chieftain. *See* Enterprise record-chieftain

WALLOWA county reporter. w 1911-21||
OrHi Ag 1917-F 10 1921

ESTACADA

CLACKAMAS county news. w D 1 1904+
1904-Ag 20 1908 as Estacada news; Ag 27 1908-F 17 1916 Estacada progress; F 24 1916-27? Eastern Clackamas news
OrHi D 1-15 1904;05-N 12 1925
OrU [1916-17]-[27-29]

OREGON (*Continued*)

ESTACADA—*Continued*

EASTERN Clackamas news. *See* Clackamas county news
Estacada NEWS. *See* Clackamas county news
Estacada PROGRESS. *See* Clackamas county news

EUGENE

COOS Bay news. *See under* Marshfield
DEMOCRATIC herald. *See* Eugene guard
DEMOCRATIC register. *See* Eugene guard
DEMOCRATIC review. sw 1862-
1862-S 16? 1865 as Eugene City review
CU-B Ag 12 1865;Jl 2,12-Ag 17 1867

Eugene GUARD. w 1858-1910||
1859-My 8? 1862 as Democratic herald; Mr 15-S 30 1862 Democratic register; N 1 1862-S 16 1865 Eugene City review; S 23 1865-Mr 30 1867 Democratic review (Salem)
pub [1876-90]-1910
Or O 24 1868-O 9,23-D 18 1869
OrHi [1862-S 16]O 16 1865-Mr 30 1867
OrU Ap 18 1863[68-76;1901-07]Ja-Ap 1910
CU-B Jl 27 1867-77;Jl 13 1878-80;86;Mr 11-Ag 7 1907

Eugene daily GUARD. *See* Eugene register-guard

Eugene City HAWKEYE. w 1873-Je 1874||
OrU My 30 1874

LANE county citizen. w
OrHi Jl 11-D 29 1900

Eugene morning NEWS. d Mr 5 1931+
pub 1931+
DLC 1931+
OrE Ja 15 1932+
OrU 1931+

OREGON register. sw,w 1884-1918||?
1884-1911? as Eugene register
sw 1884-94
OrER complete
OrHi [N-D 1899]Ap 15-O 21 1904;17-My 2 1918
OrU [1901-Je 1902]-04

OREGON state journal. w Mr 12 1864-My 29 1909||
Follows State republican
CU-B N 25 1865-[81]-1905;Ja 27,N 24 1906;S 7,N 30 1907-09
ICU Ap 9-My 7,Jl 16-Ag 6,N 1864;Ag 5-12,S 2-16,O 8-21 1865;Ja 6-13,N 10-D 8 1866;Ja 5-19,My 18-Jl,Ag 10-17,S-D 21 1867;Ja 4,18-F 1,22-29,Mr 8-21,My 23-Ag 6,22 1868-78;90-1908
Or complete
OrHi complete
OrU [1864-68:72-79]-[83]-[99-1900]-09
WaU [Ap 17 1869-1908]

PEOPLE'S press. w 1858-62||?
OrHi [1859-60]

Eugene morning REGISTER. d 1899-N 17 1930||
United with Eugene daily guard to form Eugene register-guard
OrE 1919-30
OrER complete
OrHi [My-Jl 1917]
OrU complete

Eugene REGISTER. w *See* Oregon register

Eugene REGISTER-GUARD. d 1890+
1890-N 17 1930 as Eugene daily guard
pub 1890+
OrE 1919+
OrHi O 1933+
OrU Je 6 1891;N 3,D 8 1906[10-14]-[26]+

Eugene City REVIEW. *See* Eugene guard

STATE republican. w Ja 1 1862-Mr 5 1864||
Followed by Oregon state journal
CSmH Mr 22 1862
CU-B Je 7 1862
OrHi [1862]

FALLS CITY

Falls City NEWS. w 1904-18||
OrU 1915-16[18]

FLORA

Flora JOURNAL. w 1900-18||?
OrHi Je 20 1902-Ag 21 1903

FLORENCE

SIUSLAW oar. w Je 8 1928+
pub 1928+
OrU [1928]+

SIUSLAW pilot. w 1913-15||?
OrU [Mr 12-D 1913]-15

WEST. w 1896-Ja 7 1921||
OrFS 1898-1921
OrHi Je 1901-Ap 27,My 11 1917-21
OrU [1901-20]

FOREST GROVE

AURORA. w
OrHi Ap 27,My 20,N 7 1882

Forest Grove EXPRESS. w 1916-18||?
Merged with Washington county news-times
OrHi Ap 6 1916-S 19 1918

Forest Grove INDEPENDENT. w Ja 5? 1873-74||
CU-B N 15 1873-O 15,D 3 1874
OrP Ag 30 1873

Forest Grove PRESS. w 1909-14||?
Merged with Washington county news-times
OrHi Mr 1912-Mr 19 1914

Forest Grove TIMES. *See* Washington county news-times

WASHINGTON county news. w 1903-Je 1910||
United with Forest Grove times to form Washington county news-times
OrHi [My 22 1903-Jl 20 1905]

WASHINGTON county news-times. w 1887+
1887-Je 1910 as Forest Grove times
CU-B [Ja 8 1892-Mr 15 1894]
OrHi Ap 24,My 15 1891;Je 29 1899-1906;D 24 1908-Je 24 1909;Jl 7 1910+
OrU [1908]09;19-[26]+

FOSSIL

Fossil JOURNAL. w S 1886+
pub 1886+
OrHi Je 20-27 1902;Ag 30 1929-32
OrU [1928]-[30]-[32]

FREEWATER

Freewater TIMES. w 1902+
pub 1910+
OrHi [1903-05]
OrPe 1927+
OrU [1928]+

GARDINER

PORT Umpqua courier. *See under* Reedsport

GARIBALDI

Garibaldi NEWS. *See* Rockaway news

ROCKAWAY news. w 1922+
1922-31 as Garibaldi news
OrU 1926-[28]-[33]

GERVAIS

Gervais STAR. w Je 8 1890+
pub N 11 1919+
OrHi Je 4 1901-[10]-Je 11 1926
OrU [1901-04]-[06-07]-08;13-[15]-[22]-[28]+

GLENDALE

Glendale LOG. w 1902+
1902-N 25 1926 as Glendale news
OrGC 1902-N 1926
OrHi Ag 18 1916-S 2 1926
OrU 1915-[17-18]-[20-24]-26[28-31]+

Glendale NEWS. *See* Glendale log

GOLD BEACH

CURRY county reporter. w 1915+
1915-22 as Gold Beach reporter
pub 1915+
OrHi Ag 22 1918+
OrU [1918-23]-[27-28]+

Gold Beach REPORTER. *See* Curry county reporter

GOLD HILL

Gold Hill NEWS. w 1897+
pub 1906+
OrU [1911-13]15[16;26]-[29-30]+

GRANTS PASS

ARGUS. w
OrHi S 17 1885-Ja 8 1886

Grants Pass BULLETIN. w 1924+
1924-27 as Southern Oregon spokesman
OrU 1926[27]-[32]+

Grants Pass COURIER. d 1910+
pub 1910+
OrHi D 12 1929+
OrU [My 1919-20]-[22-23]-[26-29]+
—w ed. *See* Rogue River courier

Grants Pass HERALD. w 1904-05||?
OrHi O 12 1904

OREGON observer. w 1884-1926||
OrGC 1885-1926
OrHi [1901-Ja 20 1926]
OrU [1904-05]15-27

PACIFIC outlook. w 1895-1911||?
OrHi O 23 1909-O 17 1911

ROGUE River courier. w Ap 3 1885-1929||?
OrGC 1897-1929
OrHi [1893]N 16 1899-Mr 26 1926
OrU [1915]-Ag 30 1918[28]29
TJT Mr 16,Ap 13 1899;S 1 1905
—d ed. *See* Grants Pass courier

SOUTHERN Oregon spokesman. *See* Grants Pass bulletin

GRASS VALLEY

Grass Valley JOURNAL. w Ag 1897-F 1931||
United with Sherman county observer (Moro) to form Sherman county journal (Moro)
OrHi Je 1901-O 11 1918
OrMoS [1904-05]15-31
OrU [1904]-[06-07]-[10-11;13]-[15]-[18]24-31

GRESHAM

BEAVER state herald. w 1905-F 24 1911||
1905-Jl 20 1906 as Multnomah record. Followed by Gresham outlook
OrHi Jl 1906-11
OrP 1906-11
OrU [1908-11]

MULTNOMAH record. *See* Beaver state herald

Gresham OUTLOOK. sw Mr 3 1911+
Follows Beaver state herald
pub 1911+
OrHi Mr 1912+
OrP 1911+
OrU [1911-17]-[19]-[27]-[29]-[31]+

HAINES

Haines RECORD. *See* Record-courier (Baker)

HALFWAY

PINE Valley herald. w 1910-32||?
OrU [1918-19]-[21]-[28;32]

HALSEY

Halsey ENTERPRISE. *See* Halsey rural enterprise

Halsey JOURNAL. w 1932+
OrU [1932]+

Halsey RURAL enterprise. w 1912-Ja 17 1929||
1912-25 as Halsey enterprise. Followed by Greater Albany (Albany)
OrHi Ap 10 1913-O 16 1919
OrU [1917]-29

HARRISBURG

Harrisburg BULLETIN. w 1900+
1918-19 as Harrisburg bulletin-commonwealth
OrHi Ag 1901-Jl 1902;Jl 1932+
OrU [1917-19]-[21]-[23]+

COMMONWEALTH. w 1913-17||
United with Harrisburg bulletin to form Harrisburg bulletin-commonwealth, later Harrisburg bulletin
OrHi F 19-O 15 1915
OrU [1916]

DISSEMINATOR. w 1882-86||
OrHi [1882-83]D 1-18 1885;Ja 1,Ap 30 1886

NUCLEUS. w 1876-80||
CU-B S 3-D 24 1880

HELIX

Helix ADVOCATE. *See* Helix view point

Helix HERALD. w 1906-07||?
OrHi Ap 26,My,Je 14 1907

Helix VIEW point. w 1912+
1912-24 as Helix advocate
OrPe Jl 1933+
OrU [1929-30]+

HEPPNER

Heppner GAZETTE-TIMES. w,sw Mr 30 1883+
1883-F 15 1912 as Heppner gazette
sw Mr 1892-99?
CU-B [My 1889-D 11 1894]
OrHi [1893-98]-1908;10-Mr 1915;Ap 1920+
OrU [1901-03;17]-[20]-[22]+

MORROW county record. *See* Heppner record

Heppner RECORD. w O 23 1890-96||?
1890-91? as Morrow county record
CU-B O 30 1890

Heppner TIMES. w N 18 1897-F 15 1912||
United with Heppner gazette to form Heppner gazette-times
OrHi N 25 1897;Ag 2 1903

HERMISTON

Hermiston HERALD. w 1906+
OrPe 1927+
OrU 1917[21]-[24]-[31]+

HILLSBORO

Hillsboro ARGUS. w 1894+
pub Mr 28 1895+
Or Ag 12 1926+
OrHi 1928+
OrU 1925+

Hillsboro DEMOCRAT. w 1891-92||
CU-B S 30-O 7 1892

Hillsboro INDEPENDENT. w 1873-1932||
1873-82 as Washington county independent
Merged with Hillsboro argus
CU-B O 30 1874-[75]-Ja 1877;Ja-Je 1888
OrHbA [1873-1932]D 18 1874;O 14 1875;
OrHi D 26 1884[89-My 11 1906]N 27,D 18 1908[09]My 1910-Ap 9 1926
OrU [1901-05;17]-31

WASHINGTON county democrat. w 1889-90||?
OrHi [1889-90]

WASHINGTON county independent. *See* Hillsboro independent

HOOD RIVER

ENTERPRISE. w 1914-
OrP Mr 27 1914

OREGON (*Continued*)

HOOD RIVER—*Continued*

Hood River GLACIER. w 1889-N 3 1933||
Merged with Hood River news
OrHi [1889;97;99]1901-26
OrHrN [1894-1930]
OrU [1901-02]03;16[17]-[20]-[24-25]-[32]33

Hood River NEWS. w 1905+
pub 1915+
OrHi O 7 1905-16;Ja 14 1917+
OrU O 1915-[17-18]-19[21]-[26]-[32]+

HOULTON

COLUMBIA herald. w 1913-19||?
OrHi Je 12 1914

COLUMBIA register. w 1904-06||?
OrHi Ap 29 1904-Je 1 1906

HUBBARD

BEAVER state news. w 1906-13||?
OrHi S 13 1907-My 23 1912

Hubbard ENTERPRISE. w 1914+
OrHi Mr 9 1917+
OrU 1919-[20-21]-[23]-[26-28]30-[31]-[33]

Hubbard HERALD. w
OrHi Ag 8 1912-F 20 1913

HUNTINGTON

Huntington COURIER. w 1930-31||
OrU [Mr 5-O 1 1931]

Huntington HERALD. w 1891-1912||?
OrHi D 18 1897

INDEPENDENCE

Independence ENTERPRISE. w 1894+
1905-09 as West Side enterprise
pub My 1920+
OrHi Ja-S 12 1901;D 1902-N 1903;F 21 1908-My 1910;My 26 1911-Mr 1913
OrU [1909-10]24-[27]+

Independence MONITOR. w 1912-18||?
OrHi Ag 1913-Jl 6 1918
OrU [Ag 1912-My 1914]

POLK county post. w 1918-21||?
OrHi Mr 26 1918-D 16 1921

RIVERSIDE. w Ja 24 1879-D 31 1880||
CU-B [My 9 1879-80]
OrHi N 19 1880

WEST side. w 1883-1902||?
United with Independence enterprise to form West side enterprise, later Independence enterprise
OrHi Ap 28-D 28 1900

WEST side enterprise. *See* Independence enterprise

IONE

Ione INDEPENDENT. w 1912-31||?
OrU 1925-[28]-Je 19 1931

IRRIGON

Oregon IRRIGATOR. w 1904-12||?
OrHi [1905-06]

JACKSONVILLE

DEMOCRATIC news. w My 1 1869-1871||
Follows Jacksonville reveille. Followed by Democratic times
CU-B [1869]-O 22 1870
OrHi [1869-70]

DEMOCRATIC times. w,sw,w Ja 7 1871-1907||?
Follows Democratic news
sw 1895-1901
CU-B 1871[72-73]-[78-80;82;84-86]-[88]-91
OrHi Ap 18 1879;Mr 17 1893;1894-[1896-1901]-Ag 15 1907

Jacksonville HERALD. w Ag 1 1857-
CSmH O 10 1857
MWA Jl 17 1858

OREGON intelligencer. w N 7 1862-64||
Followed by Oregon reporter, later Southern Oregon press
CU-B Ap 25 1863
OrHi [1864]

OREGON reporter. *See* Southern Oregon press

OREGON sentinel. w N 24 1855-88||?
1855-58 as Table Rock sentinel
CU-B 1864[65]-[71]-[79]80[84-85]86
MWA Mr 22-29,O 25 1856
Or Ja 5,Ag 9 1856[58-59;61-69]
OrHi D 6 1856[60-63;66]-69[71-73;77-78]-80;My 31,Ag 2 1884;S 5-12 1885
OrP [1861]-[69;72]-[77]

Jacksonville POST. w 1889+
pub 1930+
OrHi My 30 1908-Jl 12 1918

Jacksonville REVEILLE. w N 15 1867-Ap? 1869||
Follows Southern Oregon press. Followed by Democratic news
CU-B [1868-Ja 2 1869]
OrHi [1868]

SOUTHERN Oregon press. w Ja 1865-Ag 21 1867||
1865-66 as Oregon reporter. Followed by Jacksonville reveille
C My 5 1866
CU-B Jl 21 1866;Jl 13,27,Ag 10 1867
OrHi [1865-67]

TABLE Rock sentinel *See* Oregon sentinel

JEFFERSON

Jefferson REVIEW. w Ja 18 1890+
CU-B O 4-11 1890
OrU [1901-05]-[07-10]14-[17-20]-[22;24-25]-[27-28]-[30]-[33]

JOHN DAY

EAST Oregon ranger. *See* John Day Valley ranger

GRANT county news. *See under* Canyon City

John Day VALLEY ranger. w Mr 14 1930+
1930-Mr 6 1931 as East Oregon ranger. Follows Long Creek ranger (Long Creek)
OrU 1930-[32-33]+

JORDAN VALLEY

Jordan Valley EXPRESS. w 1909-25||
OrU [1924]

JOSEPH

Joseph HERALD. w 1895+
1895-1899 as Wallowa herald; 1900-02? Silver Lake herald
OrHi 1901-My 2,D 12 1902-Jl 16 1909
OrU [1920-21]-[25]30-[32]+
WaPS [1919]

SILVER Lake herald. *See* Joseph herald

WALLOWA chieftain. *See under* Enterprise

WALLOWA herald. *See* Joseph herald

JUNCTION CITY

Junction City BULLETIN. w 1898-1901||?
OrHi F 28-Jl 18 1901

Junction City PILOT. w 1888-90||?
CU-B Ag 16-S 20,N 21-D 5 1889;Ja 2 1890

Junction City REPUBLICAN. w 1878-80||
CU-B Mr 3,17-My 5,19,Je-Jl 2 1880

Junction City TIMES. w 1891+
pub 1893+
OrHi 1908;Ja 24 1917-Ag 15 1918
OrU [1917-18]-19;25+

JUNTURA

Juntura TIMES. w 1913-19||?
OrHi My 7-21 1915

KLAMATH FALLS

Klamath Falls EXPRESS. w 1892-1926||?
OrHi D 1909
OrU [1901;03;07-10]26

Klamath Falls evening HERALD. d 1906+
pub [F 1908+]
OrK [1909;17-18]-[22-26]-[30]+
OrU [1914-15]20-[22-25]-[28-29]-[31]+

KLAMATH basin progress. w F 23 1928+
Follows Malin progress (Malin)
pub S 1931+
Or 1928-F 21 1929
OrU [1928]30-[33]

KLAMATH county courier. w 1926+
OrU [1928]-30;Ja-Ag 4 1932

Klamath NEWS. d N 1923+
pub N 1923+
OrK [1927]+
OrU [1927]-[29]-[31-32]+

Klamath REPUBLICAN. w 1896-1914||
OrHi [1909-10]
OrKN Jl 1899-1914
OrU [1904;06-11]-[14]

Klamath Falls NORTHWESTERN. d 1912-15||?
OrU [1913-15]

Klamath STAR. w 1884-96||?
1884-94 as Klamath county star (Linkville)
CU-B Mr 1-22 1889
OrHi [1895]

LA GRANDE

BLUE Mountain times. w Ap 18 1868-
CU-B Jl 25-Ag 1,S 12-O 10,24-31,D 19 1868
OrHi My 2 1868

La Grande CHRONICLE. d 1890-1909||
1890-91? as Grande Ronde chronicle
OrHi S 18 1891;Mr 18,Ap 8,My 3 1892;D 14 1894;Ag 17 1903;N-D 31 1909

La Grande DISTRICT news. w 1924-Ag 28 1931||
Merged with La Grande observer, later La Grande observer-star
Or [1929]-31
OrU [1926]-[28]-31

EASTERN Oregon observer. *See* La Grande observer

La Grande GAZETTE. w 1875-98||?
CU-B [O 26 1878-Ap 24 1880]
OrHi My 20-27 1892

GRANDE Ronde chronicle. *See* La Grande chronicle

MOUNTAIN democrat w Mr 20 1870-71||
CU-B Ag 7,S 10,O 8,N 6 1870;Ja 24,F 8-15,Mr 1-15,29,My 14 1871
OrHi Jl 9 1870

La Grande evening OBSERVER. d 1898+
pub 1898+
OrHi D 6 1930+
OrL 1928—
OrU [1908-17];1918;1924-[27-30]+
WaPS Mr 22,O 17 1917;Jl 19-20,22,1918

La Grande OBSERVER-STAR. w 1898-D 5 1930||
1898-N 3 1905 as Eastern Oregon observer; N 10 1905-13 La Grande observer
OrHi Ja-O 23 1903;S 23 1904-13;O 16 1914-30

La Grande STAR. w 1890-1914||
United with La Grande observer to form La Grande observer-star
OrHi Ja-O 9 1914

LAFAYETTE

Lafayette COURIER. w Ja 23 1866-80||?
CU-B [F 13 1866-Ag 1868]Ap 27,N 29[D 13 1872-O 5 1877]

OREGON register. w 1881-Ja 1889||?
United with West Side telephone (McMinnville) to form McMinnville telephone-register

Lafayette VISITOR. w 1913-14||
OrHi Ap 25 1913-Ap 17 1914

LAIDLAW

Laidlaw CHRONICLE. w 1905-11||?
OrHi N 23 1906[08]

LAKEVIEW

Lakeview HERALD. w 1895-1915||?
1895-1901 as Lake county rustler. Merged with Lake county examiner 1915
OrHi Ja 27 1910-Ja 28 1913
OrU [1901;08]-[10-11]

LAKE county examiner. w 1880+
CU-B N 17 1883;Je 21-Ag 23,S 6,20-O,N 8,22-D 1884;My 23 1885;D 18 1886;Ap 28 1887;Mr 7-21,Je 13,Jl 11,Ag 29-S 19,O 24-31,N 21-D 5 1889;Ja 2-9,Ag 21,O 2-16 1890
OrHi Jl 27 1893-N 21 1901;Ag 14 1902-S 29 1904;[1908-10]
OrU [1901-04];[1906-10];1912-[15]-[17-19]-[21-22]-[27-28]+

LAKE county review. w
OrU [1913]

LAKE county rustler. *See* Lakeview herald

LAKE county tribune. sw,w 1928+
Follows Silver Lake leader and Lake county tribune (Silver Lake)
OrU [1928-31]+

STATE line herald. w S 1878-83||?
Merged with Lake county examiner
CU-B [Mr 22 1879-S,D 1880]Mr 18 1882
Or N 18 1878

LEBANON

Lebanon ADVANCE. w 1891-98||
United with Lebanon express to form Lebanon express-advance, later Lebanon express

Lebanon CRITERION. w 1898-Jl 31 1924||
Merged with Lebanon express
OrHi Je 23 1919-24
OrU 1918-[15]-[21]-24

Lebanon EXPRESS. w 1887+
1887-98 as Lebanon express; 1899-1908? Lebanon express-advance
pub 1887+
OrU [1901]-[04;06]17+

LINN county advocate. w 1897-1913||?
OrHi F 8 1912-Ja 25 1913

LEXINGTON

BUDGET. w 1888-90||
CU-B Ja 2,16-23 1890

Lexington WHEATFIELD. w 1905-07||?
OrHi S 28 1905-S 19 1907

LINKVILLE

KLAMATH county star. *See* Klamath star (Klamath Falls)

LONG CREEK

Long Creek EAGLE. w 1884-1900||
Followed by Blue Mountain eagle (Canyon City)
OrCaB [1884-1900]
CU-B O 18-N 1 1889;Ja 24,Ag 29,S 12,O 3,17-24 1890;Jl 15-22,Ag 5 1892

Long Creek RANGER. w 1900-Mr 7 1930||
Followed by East Oregon ranger, later John Day Valley ranger (John Day)
OrU [1927]-[29-30]

LOSTINE

Lostine LEADER. w 1897-1902||?
OrHi My 30-Jl 14 1902

McMINNVILLE

CAMPAIGN. d Ap 3-Je 11 1886||
OrHi complete

McMinnville COURIER. w 1866?-69||?
CU-B S 1868-Ag 1869

McMinnville NEWS. w 1901-04||
United with Yamhill county reporter to form McMinnville news-reporter

OREGON (*Continued*)

McMINNVILLE—*Continued*

McMinnville NEWS-REPORTER. w,sw N 22 1870+
1870-Ag 2 1872 as West-side; Ag 8 1872-1904 Yamhill county reporter
w 1870-N 11 1887;sw N 1887-88;w 1889+
pub S 1911+
CU-B [D 13 1870-Ag 8 1872]-[75-79;86]-[88-N 1889]
OrHi N 21 1878;Ap 25 1879;N 19 1885;D 29 1899-D 14 1900;1901-N 1913;N 30 1916-O 11 1917
OrU D 10 1880;Ap 1 1881;Ag 17 1882[1901-07]-[10-11]26+

McMinnville TELEPHONE-REGISTER. sw,w Je 15 1886+
1886-Ja 1889 as West Side telephone
pub 1889+
OrHi Je 15-D 10 1886;Ag 10 1893-Ja 1894; 1900+
OrU [1901-04]-[08-13]-[19]-[27]+

WEST-side. *See* McMinnville news-reporter

WEST Side telephone. *See* McMinnville telephone-register

YAMHILL county reporter. *See* McMinnville news-reporter

MADRAS

Madras PIONEER. w 1904+
pub 1904+
OrHi S 8 1904-Ag 10 1905;[N 1909-10]
OrU 1915-[18-19]-[25]-[28]-[32]+

MALIN

Malin PROGRESS. w 1924-F 9 1928||
Followed by Klamath Basin progress (Klamath Falls)
Or [1926]-28

MARSHFIELD

COAST mail. w 1879-1906||
CU-B 1887;Jl,Ag 14-21,S 11-O 4,16,30-N 6,D 18 1890
OrHi My 25 1901-Je 1906

COOS Bay news. w 1872-1917||
1872-N 1877 pub at Eugene
CU-B [My 1874-78]-[80-87]-My 4 1892
OrHi [1893-1901];Ag 6 1907-O 30 1917
OrU 1909-[10-12]-17

COOS Bay times. d 1906+
pub 1907+
OrM 1924+
OrU [Ap-S 1918;26]-[29-30]-[32-33]

Marshfield evening RECORD. *See* Southwestern Oregon news

SOUTHWESTERN Oregon news. d,w 1911+
1911-20 as Marshfield evening record; 1920-29 Southwestern Oregon daily news
d 1911-29
pub 1920+
OrM 1924+
OrU Ja-Mr 1920[22]-[25-29]-[32]+

MAUPIN

Maupin TIMES. w 1914-30||
OrU 1926[27]-Jl 1930

MEDFORD

CLARION. w 1921-24||
OrU [1922]-[24]

Medford ENQUIRER. w 1894-1903||
OrHi F 9 1900-Jl 31 1903

JACKSON county news. w 1924-O 15 1926||
Followed by Medford daily news, later Medford news
OrMe 1924-My 1926
OrU [1925]-26

Medford MAIL-TRIBUNE. w Ja 1889-1931||
1889-1909? as Medford mail
CU-B Ag 15 1889

Medford MAIL-TRIBUNE. d N 6 1909+
pub 1909-[27-29]+
OrHi [1909-12]14+
OrMe 1913+
OrU [1909]-[11-12]-14[16-18;22-23]-[25]-[30]+

Medford NEWS. d,w 1926+
Follows Jackson county news. 1926-33 as Medford daily news
d 1926-Ap 1933
Or [1926-27]+
OrMe O 1926-Ap 1933
OrU [1927-29]-[31-33]

PACIFIC record-herald w 1920-33||
Follows Ashland record (Ashland)
OrU 1929-32[33]
WaPS [Mr 25 1926-29]

Saturday REVIEW. w 1909-12||?
OrHi Je 11-N 26 1910

SOUTHERN Oregon eye. w
OrHi [1899-1900]

SOUTHERN Oregonian and Jacksonville times. sw 1902-09||?
1902-07 as Southern Oregonian
OrHi Ap 5-Jl 16 1902;S 4 1907-Ag 28 1909

Medford SUCCESS. w 1902-03||?
OrHi O 31 1902-Ap 28 1903

Medford SUN. w 1911-D 27 1925||
Sunday edition of Medford mail-tribune
pub complete
OrMe complete
OrHi Ag 4 1918-25
OrU [1911;14]-[17]-25

Medford TRIBUNE. w 1896-1909||
United with Medford mail to form Medford mail-tribune

METOLIUS

JEFFERSON county record. w 1915-23||?
OrHi Ja 25 1917-Ap 21 1923
OrU 1916-[19]21-23

MILL CITY

Mill City LOGUE. *See* Western stamp collector

WESTERN stamp collector. w Ag 1927+
1927-F 2 1933 as Mill City logue
pub 1927+
OrHi 1928+
OrU [1926]-[28-29]-[33]

MILTON

Milton EAGLE. w Ja 1887+
pub 1887+
CU-B F 3 1888;N 15-29 1889;Ag 1-15 1890
OrHi 1901-Ja 19,F 2 1917+
OrPe 1927+
OrU [1914]-[17]-[21]-[24]-[26]-[32]+

MILWAUKIE

Milwaukie PRESS. w 1916-19||?
OrHi O 5 1916-Ap 12 1917

Milwaukie REVIEW. w 1922+
pub Ap 16 1926+
OrU 1926+

WESTERN star. w N 21 1850-My 29 1851||
Followed by Oregon weekly times (Portland)
OrHi complete
OrP N 21 1850

MITCHELL

Mitchell SENTINEL. w 1904-25||
OrHi F 11 1915-S 3 1925

WHEELER county chronicle. w 1929+
OrPrC 1929+
OrU [Mr 27 1930-31]+

MOLALLA

Molalla PIONEER. w 1913+
OrU 1919-[20;23]-[31]+

MONMOUTH

Monmouth DEMOCRAT. w F 27 1890-91||?
CU-B Ag 21 1890

Monmouth HERALD. w S 4 1908+
pub 1908+
Or [1918]-[21]-[23]-[25]-[32]+
OrHi 1908+
OrU [1908]-[12]17-[18]+

POLK county observer. w 1888-89||?
OrMnH Ap 7 1888-F 15 1889

MONROE

Monroe LEADER. w 1911-16||
United with Monroe monitor to form Monroe leader-monitor

Monroe LEADER-MONITOR. w 1916-19||?
1916-17 as Monroe monitor
OrU 1917

Monroe MONITOR. *See* Monroe leader-monitor

MONUMENT

Monument ENTERPRISE. w 1904-10||
OrHi Je 23 1910

MORO

Moro BULLETIN. w
OrHi Je 5-N 13 1902

Moro LEADER. w 1895?-99||?
OrMoS [1895-99]

SHERMAN county journal. w N 8 1888+
1888-F 1931 as Sherman county observer
pub [1893]+
OrHi 1903-09
OrU [1917]-[30]32+

SHERMAN county observer. *See* Sherman county journal

MOSIER

Mosier BULLETIN. w 1909-17||?
OrU S 1915-D 1916

MOUNT ANGEL

Mount Angel NEWS. w 1921+
OrU [1926]+

MULTNOMAH

Multnomah CITIZEN. w 1929-31||
OrHi Jl 19 1929-F 6 1931

Multnomah PRESS. w 1921+
Some issues as Multnomah community press
OrBeE 1923+
OrU O 1925-[27]-[32]+

MYRTLE CREEK

Myrtle Creek MAIL. w 1903+
OrHi Ag 18 1916+
OrU [1928-29]

MYRTLE POINT

Myrtle Point ENTERPRISE. *See* Myrtle Point herald

Myrtle Point HERALD. w 1893+
1893-1917 as Myrtle Point enterprise; 1917-Mr 22 1928 Southern Coos county American
OrHi 1907-[16]-O 25,D 6 1917-D 2 1926;Mr 29 1928+
OrU [1904;07-08]16[17]19-[21-22]+

SOUTHERN Coos county American. *See* Myrtle Point herald

WEST Oregonian. w 1889-95||?
CU-B O 20 1894

NEHALEM

Nehalem ENTERPRISE. w 1909-15||?
OrHi O 14 1910-D 18 1914
OrU [1911]

NEWBERG

Newberg ENTERPRISE. w 1902-18||
OrHi F 22 1912-Jl 4 1918
OrU 1914-16

Newberg GRAPHIC. w 1888+
pub D 1888;O 20 1904+
CU-B N 16-30 1889;Ja 11,Ag 22,O 24-31 1890
OrHi N 24 1899;1901-O 14 1909;O 20 1910-O 10 1912;O 12 1916+
OrP [D 1888-Mr 1921]
OrU [1891-92;97]-[99-1901]-[03-04]-[08]17-29 [31]+

Newberg SCRIBE. w 1931+
pub 1931+
OrU 1932+

NEWPORT

Newport JOURNAL. w 1925+
OrU Mr 4 1925-[27]-[32]+

Newport NEWS. w 1886-88||
CU-B Ag 16,O 18,N 1,15-29 1888

YAQUINA Bay news. w 1892+
OrHi F 28 1901+
OrU 1919-[29]-[33]

YAQUINA republican. w 1888-90||
CU-B Ag 28 1890

NORTH BEND

COOS Bay harbor. w Ja 14 1905+
pub 1905+
OrU [1907-12]-13[15-16]18-[25]+

NORTH POWDER

North Powder NEWS. w 1902+
pub 1907+
OrBR 1917+
OrU [1928]+

NORTH YAMHILL

Papers published in North Yamhill are listed under Yamhill

NYSSA

GATE City journal. w 1904+
pub 1904+
OrU [1918]-19[23-25]-[1930-33]

OAKLAND

Oakland ADVANCE. *See* Oakland tribune

Oakland OWL. *See* Oakland tribune

Oakland TIMES. d
OrHi S 26 1881;Mr 6 1882;F 19 1884

Oakland TRIBUNE. w 1900+
1900-Ap 15 1910 as Oakland owl; Ap 22 1910-19 Oakland advance
pub 1921+
OrHi Ap 15-O 21 1904;Ap 13 1906-Ag 14 1914
OrU 1928+

UMPQUA call. w Ap 18 1874-
CU-B My 9-S 26 1874

OCEANLAKE

LINCOLN county press. w 1929+
OrU [O 10 1929-31]

ONTARIO

Ontario ARGUS. w N 1895+
1895-N 1900 as District silver advocate
pub 1913+
OrO 1926+
OrHi [Je-D 1909];Ja 7,F 24,1910;O 8 1914
OrU 1914-15;1917-[18-19]-[23]-[29]+

OREGON (*Continued*)

ONTARIO—*Continued*

Ontario DEMOCRAT. w 1901-18||
OrHi Mr 22-Je 28,Jl 5 1902
OrU [1912]-[16]-[18]

DISTRICT Silver advocate. *See* Ontario argus

OREGON CITY

Oregon City BANNER-COURIER. w,sw 1883+
1883-Jl 8 1919 as Oregon City courier (1901-02 Oregon City courier-herald)
pub 1905;07-08;12-17;22+
CU-B Jl 12-19 1889;Ja 3,17 1890
OrHi [My 11 1894-98;1901-06;08;10-19]+
OrOr Jl 1930+
OrU Ja-F 20 1890;Ja-F 14 1891[1901-05;07-13]-16;Jl 8 1919+

CLACKAMAS county banner. w 1916-19||
Combined with Oregon City courier to form Oregon City banner-courier
OrHi Mr 22 1918-O 22 1919

CLACKAMAS county record. w
OrHi Ja-Jl 1903

CLACKAMAS democrat. w Je 4 1879-80||
CU-B [Ja 22-N 11 1880]

Oregon City COURIER. *See* Oregon City banner-courier

Oregon City COURIER-HERALD. *See* Oregon City banner-courier

Oregon City ENTERPRISE. w O 27 1866+
Title varies slightly
pub 1866-87;1889-1902;1906+
CU-B 1866-N 7 1878[81-82]86[87-Ag 1889]
MoHi Ja 1 1892
OrHi O 27,N 3 1866;Mr 30,S 21 1867;My 16 1868;My 16 1873;Je 24 1886[91-96]-N 7 1902; 03-04;D 4-25 1908;[09-10]13-28
OrP O 27 1866-O 31 1868
OrU Je 23,Jl 28,Ag 4 1876;Ja 18 1877;My 26 1887;My 3 1888;My 23,S 26,1889;F 13 1890 [1904]-[06-07]
WaU [Ja 9-F 13,Jl 31 1869-Ja 4 1877]

Oregon City ENTERPRISE. d 1911+
1911-33 as Morning enterprise
pub 1911+
CSmH N 6 1929
OrOr 1931+
OrU [1915]N 4 1916;23-[24]-[28]-29

OREGON argus. w Ap 21 1855-My 1863||
Merged with State republican (Eugene)
CU-B O 12 1861;N 22 1862
MWA Jl 28 1855
OrHi 1855[56]58-[62]63
OrU [1855-63]
WHi Ja 22 1859

OREGON free press. w Ap 8-D 16 1848||
MWA Ap 29-My 6,Je 3,Jl 1,15 1848
NNHi complete
OrHi Je 10,Jl 8,Ag 26,S 9 1848

OREGON spectator. sm,w F 5 1846-Mr 1855||
First newspaper on Pacific Coast. Suspended Mr 1852-Ag 1853
sm 1846-Ag 1850
C Mr 1854-Mr 10 1855
CSmH [1846-47,My 8 1851]
CU-B 1846-Ja 20 1848
MHi F 5,Jl 9 1846
MSaE 1846-Ja 7 1847
MWA F 10,24,My 4 1848;N 21 1850;My 12 1854
NN F 5,Jl 4 1846(photostat)
NNHi 1846-[48-50]Ja 9,30,Je 12-19 1851
NhD My 30 1850
OrHi 1846-[48-54]
OrP 1846-Ja 21 1847;Ag 8 1850
OrPM 1846-Ja 20 1848
P-M Jl 21 1864
Wa 1846-S 1850
WaU 1846-Ja 20 1848

OREGON statesman. *See under* Salem

Oregon City PRESS. sw 1892-99||?
OrHi [1898-99]

PRODUCERS call. *See under* Portland

Oregon City STAR. d
OrHi S 24-27,N 30 1906;My 17-18,Je 3 1907

OSWEGO

Oswego REVIEW. w 1921+
1921-29 as Western Clackamas review
OrU [1928]-[31]+

WESTERN Clackamas review. *See* Oswego review

PENDLETON

EAST Oregonian. w,sw 1875+
w 1875-81
CU-B [F 12-D 1876]-O 13 1877;78;Jl 11 1879-80;Je 11,O 1,D 31 1889;Ag 12 1890;S 11,O 9-D 1891
N O 10 1884[Mr-O 1885]Ag 3 1886;Ja 28 1887;S 20 1889
OrHi [1882-84;88-90;92-93;96-1909]+
WaPS O 24 1918[19]Ja 28 1921[23]N 27 1930

EAST Oregonian. d 1887+
CU-B F 28,Mr 1,4,Je 10,12-13,26-27,D 28,30-31 1889;Ag 8 1890
OrPe [Ja 1923+]
OrU [1901-02]08-[09-14]-[18-19]-[23]-[27]+

EASTERN Oregon weekly tribune. *See* Oregon weekly tribune (The Dalles)

Pendleton INDEPENDENT. *See* Pendleton tribune

Pendleton LIVE wire. *See* Pendleton tribune

Pendleton TRIBUNE. w Ja 3 1878-1920||
1878-79? as Pendleton independent; My 15 1910-13 Pendleton live wire
CU-B Ja-Ap 1878;Ja-Je 1888;89-[90]
OrHi Ap 24 1879;F 9,N 27 1888;N 18 1889;My 23 1890;S 19 1892[97-98;1900-01]O 1908-[17]-20
WaPS [1919-20]

Pendleton evening TRIBUNE. d 1894-1923||
OrHi [1893;1900-01]
OrPe [1922-My 1923]
OrU 1917-[18]-[20-22]

PHILOMATH

BENTON county review. w 1905+
OrHi [1915]
OrU [Ja-My 1908;17]-[19]-[23]-[32-33]

CRUCIBLE. w 1877-81||?
CU-B My 15 1879

PILOT ROCK

Pilot Rock RECORD. w 1903-1932||
OrHi [1909]
OrU O 9 1925-[26-27]-29[32]

PORT ORFORD

Port Orford NEWS. w 1926-Mr 21 1933||
Or [1926]-[30]-33
OrU 1926-[27]-[32-33]

Port Orford POST. w My 27 1880-82||?
CU-B Je 10,Jl 15-22,Ag 12-19,S 2,16-N 11,25-D 16,31 1880

Port Orford TRIBUNE. w 1892-1925||
OrHi My 21 1901-F 2 1921
OrU [1901-03]

PORTLAND

Portland daily ABSTRACT. *See* Journal of commerce

Portland ADVERTISER. d My 31 1859-62||
MWA Ag 5 1859;Ja 24 1860
OrHi [1859-61]
—w ed. *See* Oregon advertiser

ADVOCATE. w S 3 1903+
Negro
pub [1903+]
OrU 1924-[30-33]

ALBINA courier. w 1887-94||
OrHi F 15 1890;Ag 12 1893 Je 23 1894

Portland AMERICAN. w 1904-O 10 1917||?
1904-Je 30 1917 as Oregon deutsche zeitung
In German and English
OrHi O 2 1916-O 10 1917

BEE. d 1875-79||?
CU-B My 25 1877[My 15-N 13 1878]
OrHi N 2 1875-D 31 1879
OrU Jl 5,Ag 29,S 6,18,N 18 1876;Mr 6,My 1,3 1877

BEE. w 1875-79||?
OrU Je 15,Jl 6 1876

BONNEVILLE dam record. w D 9 1933+
OrHi 1933+
OrP 1933+

Evening BULLETIN. d Ja 6 1868-S 21 1872||?
OrHi [Jl 8-29 1868]S 16 1872
OrP [Ja 18 1871-S 21 1872]

BULLETIN. d 1870-D 31 1880||
1870-N 10 1872 as Morning bulletin
CU-B Ag 4,25 1870[Je 30 1871-Ja 6,My 1872-73]-[75-80]
OrHi Ag 4 1870-D 24 1874;Je 19 1877[78]Ap 27 1879;F 11 1880
OrP Ja 18 1871-Ja 16 1875
OrU Ja 16,My 22,Je 16,O 10,14,16,22,N 3 1874

BULLETIN. w Jl 29 1871-82||?
CU-B Ja 18,F 22,Mr 8-15 1873
MB Ja 27 1872-S 13 1873
OrHi S 24 1880
OrP Jl 29 1871-Ap 3 1875

BULLETIN. d 1916(?)-F 14 1917||
Merged with Daily record-abstract, later Journal of commerce
OrP Jl 1 1916-17

CAMPAIGN herald. *See* Oregon herald. w 1866-73

Portland CHRONICLE. w 1877-1906||?
OrHi [Jl]1894-My 22 1896;F 19 1897-Ag 20 1904

COLUMBIA staats-zeitung. *See* Oregon staats-zeitung. w

Portland COMMERCIAL. sw 1853-
OrHi [1853]

Portland COMMERCIAL. d S? 1868-69||?
CU-B D 11,28 1868;Ja 12-13,Ag 8,O 21-22 1869

COMMERCIAL reporter. *See* Journal of commerce. w

Portland COMMERCIAL review. w Mr 1 1890+
pub 1890+
OrHi S 1925-Ag 1926

CRITERION. w Je 3-Ag 6 1898||
OrHi complete
OrP complete

DEMOCRATIC era. w Ap 21 1871-72||?
CU-B Ap 28,D 21 1871;F 15-O 24 1872
OrHi 1871-Ap 11 1872

DEMOCRATIC standard. w Jl 19 1854-59||
Suspended Ja 4-F 1859
CSmH Je 18 1857;Ag 5 1858
MWA Ag 30,S 27,N 8 1854;Je 18 1857;My 20 1858;F 16 1859
NNHi Je 18 1857
NjHi Je 5 1856
OrHi [1854-59]
OrU [D 1857-N 1858]
P-M Jl 26 1854

Portland DISPATCH. d 1889-93||?
OrHi Je 17 1891
OrP 1891-O 7 1893

Portland DISPATCH. w 1891-Ag 28 1902||
OrHi Je 20 1901-02
OrP Je 15 1893-Jl 11 1895;96-1902
OrU [1901-02]

Portland daily EXAMINER. d 1889-91||?
OrHi Ap 6 1891
OrP [O 20 1890-My 30 1891]

Portland daily EXAMINER. d 1912-14. *See* Oregon building record

FIREBRAND. w 1895-97||?
KHi N 24 1895;S 1896-S 1897

FREIE presse. w 1885-94||?
In German
KHi S 13-O 25 1888

Evening JOURNAL. d 1875-76||?
OrHi Ap 20 1875-Ja 3 1876

Portland evening JOURNAL. *See* Oregon daily journal

JOURNAL of commerce. sw Ap 3? 1853-
NNHi Ap 6-20 1853
OrHi Ap 9,13-16,Je 7 1853

JOURNAL of commerce. w Mr 4 1872-
1872-81? as Commercial reporter; 1882?-84? Commercial reporter and journal of commerce
CU-B Ap 1,O 18,D 1872;Jl 29,Ag 19,S 2,23,O 14,28-D 2,16-30 1875;Ja 21-28 1876;Ja 30 1880
MWA My 30-Je 7 1853

JOURNAL of commerce. d 1908+
1908-Je 1 1916 Portland daily abstract; Je 2 1916-O 1 1925 Daily record-abstract
pub Je 1916+
MWA D 10 1908
OrHi 1908-[09]D 30 1916-O 17 1917;O 1925+
OrP Ag 21 1908-Je 1 1916;F 15 1917+
OrU [Ja-Mr 1920;22]-[27-29]+
Wa S 1933+

LANTERN. w 1893-1921||?
CU-B Mr 30 1897
OrHi D 23 1897-D 1 1899;Je 5 1903
OrP [1905-17]

MARKET examiner. w
WaPS [1919]Ja 6 1920

Sunday MERCURY. w 1879(?)-1921||?
Follows Weekly Salem mercury (Salem)
CU-B Je 22-Jl 6,D 28 1889;F 8 1890
OrHi Jl 8-29 1883

MONTAVILLA sun. sm,w Mr 12-Je 18 1915||
sm Mr 12-26 1915
OrHi complete

MONTAVILLA times. w 1921+
pub 1921+
OrU [1926-29]31-32

MOUNT Scott herald. w 1910-25||?
OrHi 1915-Ag 1925
OrU 1916-[17-19]-20[22]

MOUNT Scott news. w Ja 4 1906-14||?
OrHi 1906-D 19 1907;Je 30 1910-Ja 30 1914

NACHRICHTEN. w 1887+
In German
pub 1887+
IU S 27 1917-Mr 7,S 1918-19
OrHi O 11 1917-19

Portland NEW AGE. w 1896-1907||
Negro
OrHi Ap 7 1900-My 4 1907
OrP [1905-07]

NEW Northwest. w My 5 1871-87||
CU-B Ag 11 1871-[79-80]F 10,Mr 31,Ap 21 1881
N O 20 1881;F 16 1882
OrHi My 5 1871-[76]-[78]-87
OrU S 30 1874;Je 21,28,1878;Jl 29 1886
WaU [1876-Mr 1877]Ag 30,D 27 1883;Ja 10 1884

NEWS. d Ap 18 1859-60||?
First daily in Oregon
MWA F 26 1860
OrHi [1859-60]

Weekly NEWS. w Ap 29 1873-74||
OrHi S 4 1874

Portland daily NEWS. d My 28? 1873-
CU-B [Je 3-Jl,O 17 1873]-S 30 1874

Portland daily NEWS. d Ja 1 1883-88||?
1883-Je 21 1884 as Northwest news
CSmH Ja-Ap 1883
MWA Mr 5 1883
OrHi 1883-87
OrU My 29 1886

NEWS-TELEGRAM. d 1906+
1906-My 5 1931 as Portland news
pub 1906—
Or My 6 1931+
OrCA My 6 1931+
OrHi 1908+
OrU [1926]

Portland NEWSPAPER union. w
WaPS [1916;18-19]Ag 19 1922

OREGON (*Continued*)

PORTLAND—*Continued*

NORTHWEST herald. w My 27 1899-1900||?
OrHi Je 10 1899
OrP My 27,S 16,O 21 1899

NORTHWEST news. *See* Portland daily news

OREGON advertiser. w Ja 1 1861-62||
OrHi Ja 19 1861;F 22 1862
—d ed. *See* Portland advertiser
—Steamer ed. sm Je 6 1859-
MWA Je 6 1859

OREGON argus. w 1856?-
OClWHi Mr 9 1861

OREGON building record. d 1912-Je 1 1916||
1912-14 as Portland daily examiner. United with Portland daily abstract to form Daily record-abstract, later Journal of commerce
OrP [F 1912-16]
OrU [Ap 1912-14]

OREGON deutsche-zeitung. w Ag 1 1868-84||
Follows Oregon pionier
In German
CU-B Ag 1 1868-[Ag,S-N 1871;F-My,Ag 1872]-Jl,O 6 1877;My 11 1878-N 13 1880
OrPN D 24 1868;F 20 1869

OREGON deutsche zeitung. w 1904-17. *See* Portland American

OREGON free press. Ap 8 1848-
CSmH Ap 8 1848

OREGON herald. d Mr 17 1866-73||
CU-B Jl 14 1866;S 3-5,O 2,13,29,N 7 1867;Mr 25,Je 14,D 29 1868;Ap-D 1870;My 28 1873
OrHi [1866-69;71]S 24 1872;My 8 1873
OrP [Mr 17 1866-Mr 16 1872]
Wa D 10 1867

OREGON herald. w 1866-1873||
Ap 11 1868 as Campaign herald
C D 17 1868
CU-B Ag 31 1867;Ja 4,Jl 18,Ag 8 1868-Ap 23 1869;Je 4-18,Jl 2,23-S 10,24-N,D 10 1870-Ap 1,S 23 1871;D 14,28 1872-F 1,22-Mr 22,Ap 19-My 3,17 1873
OrHi [1866-72]

OREGON daily journal. d 1902+
1902-03? as Portland evening journal
pub 1902+
DLC Jl 1903+
MoS S 8 1907
NcD D 11 1905
OrCA 1920-[27]+
OrHi Mr 11 1902+
OrP [1902-03]+
Or N 1906+
OrU [1907]-09;[1911]+

OREGON journal. sw,w 1902-31||?
OClWHi Jl 11 1912
WaPS S 20 1914,Mr 14 1919,Mr 26 1921,N 6 1923,Ag 4 1924[25;30] Ap 19 1931

OREGON news. d 1902+
In Japanese
IU D 1917-Ap 8 1927

OREGON pionier. w 1866-68||
Followed by Oregon deutsche-zeitung
In German
CU-B Je 8 1867-My 23 1868

OREGON posten. w 1908-Ja 1936||
United with Svenska journalen (Seattle, Wash.) to form Svenska posten (Seattle, Wash)
In Swedish
IRA 1909-17;22
MnHi D 1908-[20;24]Ap 1928-36
OrPL complete
OrU Jl 1929-36

OREGON siftings. w 1884-89||?
OrHi N 19-26 1887

OREGON staats-zeitung. w 1879-99||?
1879-85 as Oregon staats-zeitung; 1886 Columbia staats-zeitung; 1887-89 Portland-staatszeitung
OrHi Jl 31 1893-My 4 1899

OREGON staats-zeitung. d 1886-99||?
1886-94 as Portland staats-zeitung

OREGON weekly times. w Je 5 1851-64||
Follows Western star (Milwaukie)
CSmH Jl 24 1851;F 4 1854
MWA D 25 1852;F 26 1853;O 13 1855;My 8,22,Jl 10-24 1858;Ja 15 1859;Mr 3 1860
NNHi S 18-N 6,27 1852;Ja-My 14,28-Jl 9,30-Ag 6,N 12-D 3 1853;Ja 9 1856
OrHi 1851-N 6 1858[59-62]

OREGON daily times. d D 18 1860-1864||
CU-B D 21 1863
OrHi Je 15-D 31 1863

OREGON vindicator. w 1879-90||
CU-B Jl 5-19 1889;S 19 1890

Weekly OREGONIAN. w D 4 1850-1922||
pub D 6 1851-1922
CLM D 4 1850;O 30 1888;S 21 1902
CSmH Ap 17,My 22,Je 5 1852;Ja 5 1856
CU-B F 7 1852;D 1853-Ap 14 1855;Ja 5 1856;N 27,D 1858-My 19 1860[64-65]-[70-71]-Je 1880[S 1881-N 3 1882;88;90-S 5 1891]
IaDH Je 1905-14
MB My 17 1889-My 16 1890
MWA D 4 1850;My 15,Je 6,Jl 17-24,Ag 7 1858;Ja 22,F 12,1859;F 25 1860;My 24 1889-My 16 1890
MnU My 17 1889-My 16 1890
NNHi D 4 1850;Ja 25-Je 21 1851;D 1852-Jl 9,30 1853;Ag 11-25,O 27 1855;Ja 12 1856;Ap 26 1873
NcD Ag 8 1890
OClWHi Ja 2 1863
Or Jl 1885-1906[14]-[18]
OrHi [1850-52]-[54]-[58-65;81]
OrP D 4 1850(photostat[D 1852-N 19 1853;Je 1854-N 8 1862;N 21 1863-N 9 1867
OrU Je 26,N 29 1863
PWCl F 22 1851
TxGR Ja 1 1920
WHi O 20 1855;Ja 16-Ag 21 1858;My 17 1889-My 16 1890;96-Ja 17 1902
WaU Ja 20 1872-N 1872

Morning OREGONIAN. d F 4 1861+
Ja 2 1905 is Lewis and Clark centennial no.
D 4 1925 is 75th jubilee no.
pub 1861+
C O 15 1868;Jl 1890-Je 1891;Jl 1904+
CL D 4 1850;D 4 1925
CSt My 12 1892
CU-B [F-D 4 1861;62-63]-Ja,Mr 1868-80;Ja 6,12,Je 19,Ag 31 1882;Jl 4 1883-Mr 1,Ap 1890-[92-1904]D 12 1925-D 15 1927
CoAT 1925-31
DLC Ag 6 1862-Ja 6 1863;Jl 1874+
ICU 1935+
IHi F 4 1911
IdU 1918+
MWA My 20 1862;Ap 27 1866;Ja 7,26,Je 12 1876;Ja 2 1888;Ja 1,S 16 1889;Ja 1,S 22 1890;Ja 2 1905;Ja 1,D 4 1925
MiG Ja 2 1905
NNC D 4 1850(reprint)
NbHi N 14 1902-D 10 1904;Ja 1 1913
NvR 1932+
OClWHi Ag 9 1881;F 4 1911;Jl 12 1912;Ja 2 1915
OHi 1923+
Or 1895+
OrCA 1918[19]+
OrHi [1861-74]-[88;92-93]95[96-98]+
OrP F-My 4 1861;F 1865+
OrU [1866-68;70-75;84-91;97-1900;04-06;08-09]-[15]+
P Jl 8 1890-Je 1917
PU Jl 4-O 10 1889
TxGR Ja 1 1907
WHi D 7 1907+
Wa N 12 1867;Je 16 1875;Je 19 1879;My 1906+
WaPS D 5 1850;Jl 16 1886;Mr 5 1887;O 13-14 1894[1904-19;21-27]-[29]+
WaS 1906+
WaU 1874-S 1 1881;Ap 22,S 7-8,O 8 1899;Ag 12,S 2,O 7,14 1900;Ap 28,Ag 27,D 28 1901;05+

Sunday OREGONIAN. w 1881-1927||?
CU-B Ja 1 1882;O 12 1884[Ja-Je 1888]F 1889-D 20 1891;My 1,Ag 2,N 6 1892;D 7 1897;D 13-27 1925;Ja 10 1926-D 11 1927
OClWHi Jl 7 1912

PACIFIC express. w 1885-90||
CU-B Ap 11-18,My 2,S 1889;Ja 2-23 1890
OrHi My 10 1888

PENINSULA herald. w 1912+
pub 1920+
OrHi Jl 4-D 20 1913
OrU 1922-[25]-[28]-[31]

PEOPLE's party post. w 1894-96||?
OrHi D 6 1894-Mr 19 1896

PEOPLE'S press. w 1907-17||?
OrP [N 1912-Ja 1913]

Portland PLAINDEALER. d 1862-
OrHi My 23 1862

POLARIS. w 1881-83||
OrHi Mr 1882

POPULIST voice. w 1893-95||?
OrP Mr 25 1893

PRODUCERS' call. w 1922-31||?
1922 pub in Oregon City
OrU [1922-23]

Daily RECORD-ABSTRACT. *See* Journal of commerce

Portland daily RECORDER. d -Je 1 1916||
United with Portland daily abstract and Oregon building record to form Daily record-abstract, later Journal of commerce

Portland REVIEW. w 1891-96||?
OrHi Ag 5 1893-Je 17 1896

ST. JOHNS review. w 1904+
OrU 1929-[31]+

SANDY Road news. w 1925-30||?
OrU D 3 1926-D 30 1927

SATURDAY eye. w 1900||?
OrHi Je 7-D 8 1900

SELLWOOD bee. w 1906+
pub O 6 1906+
OrHi Je 10 1910+
OrU 1923-31

Portland STAATS-ZEITUNG. *See* Oregon staats-zeitung

STANDARD. d Jl 29 1876-84||?
1876-Ap 1877 as Evening standard
CU-B Ag 4,30 1876-78;[F-D 1879]-Je 4,11,22-S 29,N 19-D 1880;N 2-7,11-18 1881
NN D 20 1881
OrHi 1876-Ag 31 1877[78-81]82;84
OrP [S-D 1879],F 24 1880

STANDARD. w Ja 15 1876-84||?
CU-B Ap 21 1876-[83]-Ja 11 1884
OrP Ja 15 1876-D 26 1884

La STELLA. w O 20 1922+
In Italian
WaPS [1924]-[27-33]

SUN. w
OrHi Mr 8 1884-O 21 1887

SUN. d O 15 1894-Ag 3 1895||?
OrHi O 15 1894-Ag 3 1895

SUNNYSIDE gazette. w Mr 27 1915+
1915-18? as Sunnyside Portland gazette
pub 1915+
OrU 1925-[28]-[33]

SVENSKA posten. *See under* Seattle, Wash.

Portland TELEGRAM. d 1877-My 5 1931||
1877-1911 as Evening telegram. United with Portland news to form News-telegram.
CU-B 1878[79]80;O 29 1881;Je 22 1883;Ap 19-21 1887;Mr-Je, D 22 1900;D 14 1903;Ag 12, 16,S 19-20,N 7-8,14-18,D 8,15 1904;My 29-31,Je 10-17 1905;Ja 9,Ap 18-19 1906;My 1,Je 13,Ag 3 1907;Ap 9,N 28,D 2 1908;Je 25,Jl 8,Ag 9,12 1910;Ja 2,25,F 11,Mr 31,Ap 6,24,My 23,25-26,29,Je 10,13,Jl 3,5-7,N 2,13 1911;F 12,Je 19,S 18 1912;Ja 3,F 15,Ap 18,Je 13-14,S 11,19,O 25,D 1,16 1913;1922-F 1931
OClWHi Jl 11 1912
Or 1913-My 4 1931
OrCA [1909];[1922-23]-[30]-My 5 1931
OrHi Jl 15 1886-My 5 1931
OrP [Ja 1913-My 5 1931]
OrU Ap 1882;D 23 1898;D 25 1899;[1922]-[27]-[29-30]-31
WaPS [1917-25;28-29]F 9 1931

Portland TIMES. d D 18 1860-64||
C O 11 1861
OrHi [1860-62]

TOWN topics. w 1898(?)-1918||?
OrHi Mr 14 1902;D 21 1918

Portland TRANSCRIPT. w
IaDH Jl 1848-Ap 1849

La TRIBUNA Italiana. w 1911+
In Italian
OrU 1926-32

Morning TRIBUNE. d 1896-98||?
OrHi My 1-31 1898

Portland daily UNION. d Ja-My 1864||
OrHi F 24 1864

WORLD. w D 25 1885-1901||?
CU-B Ag 1 1889;F 19,Ag 19,S 2-23,D 10 1892-Ja 7 1893
OrHi 1885-D 15 1887;My 3 1888
WHi Ap 9 1886

POWERS

Powers PATRIOT. w Ap 26 1918-Ap 13 1923||
OrHi complete

PRAIRIE CITY

GRANT county journal. w 1900+
1900-14 as Prairie City miner.
OrHi Ap 16 1914
OrU [1916;19]-[23-26]-[31-32]+

Prairie City MINER. *See* Grant county journal

PRINEVILLE

CALL. *See* Central Oregonian

CENTRAL Oregon enterprise. *See* Central Oregonian

CENTRAL Oregonian. w 1885+
1885-Jl 8 1920 as Central Oregon enterprise; Jl 15 1920-21 Call
pub 1915+
OrHi [1921]+
OrU D 1919-[Jl 15-D 1920]22+

CROOK county journal. w 1895-Jl 7 1921||
United with Call to form Central Oregonian
OrHi Je 1901-21
OrPrC 1898-21
OrU [1901-12]-15[17-21]
WaPS Ja 15 1920-21

Prineville NEWS. w 1885-1917||
1885-95 as Ochoco review; 1896-Jl 30 1914 Prineville review
CU-B Mr 9-23,Jl 27-Ag 10 1889;Ja 11-25,Ag 9-30,O 1890
OrHi N 27 1902-Ja 4 1916;Ja 16,F 13 1917
OrPrC 1885-98
OrU [1901-14]

OCHOCO review. *See* Prineville news

Prineville REVIEW. *See* Prineville news

RAINIER

Rainier GAZETTE. w 1893-1905||
OrHi D 17 1901-D 12 1902;D 30 1904-Je 16 1905

Rainier REVIEW. w 1905+
OrHi D 12 1924+
OrU [1917]-[19]+

REDMOND

OREGON hub. w,d 1909-14||?
OrHi O 28,N 11 1909;Ja 26-27 1910

Redmond SPOKESMAN. w 1910+
OrU [1917-20]-[23-24]-[26]+

REEDSPORT

PORT Umpqua courier. w 1913+
1913-N 10 1917 pub at Gardiner
pub [Ap 22 1921+]
CU-B My 20 1921-My 1922
OrHi Ap 24 1915+
OrU [1919]-[26-27]+

OREGON (*Continued*)

RICHLAND

EAGLE Valley news. w 1900-19||?
OrHi Ja 25 1917-Jl 10 1919

RIDDLE

SOUTH Umpqua news. w 1910+
1910-18 as Riddle tribune
OrHi Ag 17 1916-Ag 8 1918
OrU [1913-17]

Riddle TRIBUNE. See South Umpqua news

ROGUE RIVER

Rogue River ARGUS. w 1911-Ag 17 1916||
OrHi My 1915-16
OrU [Ja-Ag 1916]

ROSEBURG

Roseburg CHIEFTAIN. w S 4 1931+
OrU 1931+

DOUGLAS independent. w 1876-D 27 1884||
CU-B Je 15 1878-84
OrHi Ja 20 1883

Roseburg ENSIGN. See Umpqua ensign

Roseburg EXPRESS. w N 17 1859-
MWA D 22 1859

Roseburg NEWS-REVIEW. sw,w 1868-1928||?
1868-1906? as Plaindealer; 1907?-20 Umpqua Valley news
sw 1901-15?
pub 1873-87[90-1920]
CU-B Jl 22 1870[72-74]-78;Jl-D 1879;Jl-D 1880[86-Ap 1888;89;91]
Or Mr 25 1870;F 2 1872
OrHi [1883;85;87]Ag 1893-[96]-N 18 1912;13-N 1916
OrU N 4,O 28 1876[1901-14]-Ap 1 1920;21 [22;24]-28

Roseburg NEWS-REVIEW. d 1909+
1909-Mr 25 1920 as Roseburg evening news
pub [1909+]
Or 1920-[22]-[25]-[27]+
OrHi Ja 12 1917-19;Ap 1920;24+
OrU 1926+

PANTOGRAPH. w Ag 10 1872-73||
Follows Umpqua ensign?
CU-B 1872-Ag 2 1873

PLAINDEALER. See Roseburg news-review. w

Roseburg REVIEW. w,sw O 26 1877-Ap 1 1920||
1877-80? as Western star. United with Umpqua valley news to form Roseburg news-review
CU-B [D 14 1877-80;85-S 1889]
Or [F 23 1914-20]
OrHi [1893]98-1909;11-20
OrRN [1890-1920]
OrU 1900-[01-08]-[10-15]-19

Roseburg REVIEW. d 1898-Mr 1920||
United with Roseburg evening news to form Roseburg news-review. d

SPOKESMAN. w 1906-07||?
OrHi Je 1 1906-D 26 1907

UMPQUA ensign. w Ap 30 1867-72||
1867-70? as Roseburg ensign. Followed by Pantograph?
CU-B 1867[68]-[Ja-Je 1871]F 24 1872

UMPQUA valley news. See Roseburg news-review

WESTERN star. See Roseburg review

SAINT HELENS

COLUMBIA county news. w 1896-1902||?
OrHi Ap 27 1900-Ja 3 1902

COLUMBIAN. w 1880-86||
CU-B [Mr 10 1882-F 4 1886]

Saint Helens MIST. See Saint Helens sentinel-mist

Saint Helens SENTINEL. w 1926-Mr 30 1933||
United with Saint Helens mist to form Saint Helens sentinel-mist
OrU 1929-33

Saint Helens SENTINEL-MIST. w 1881+
1881-Mr 30 1933 as Saint Helens mist
OrShA [1900-33]
OrU [1917-19]-[21-24]-[27]+

SALEM

AMERICAN unionist. See Oregon unionist

CAPITAL chronicle. w Ag 31 1867-
CU-B Ag 31-O 19,N 2,16 1867-Ja 4,18,Mr 9 1868

CAPITAL journal. w 1887-1917||?
OrU [1901-08]

CAPITAL journal. d Mr 1 1888+
pub 1888+
CU-B O 16-17,19 1889;S 27,O 1 1890
Or 1907-13;22+
OrCA 1925+
OrHi F 14 1890[1907]-My 13 1912
OrU [1903;05-06;09-12]-[14-15]-[18-19;27-28]-[30]+

CAPITAL press. w 1928+
1928-D 9 1932 as Hollywood press
Or [1928-31]+

Salem CHRONICLE. d N 19 1867-
CU-B N 20-21,D 14 1867;Ja 28 1868

Weekly DEMOCRATIC press. w F 9 1869-Je 11 1870||
CU-B My 15 1869
OrHi Ap 24 1869;Ja 8,Je 11 1870

DEMOCRATIC review. See Eugene guard (Eugene)

McMAHAN'S wasp. w Ap 29 1894-
CSmH Ap 29 1894

Salem MERCURY. d 1869-71||?
CU-B S 10,16,21,23,29,O 4 1870;Ap 22,25 1871

Weekly Salem MERCURY. w Ag 25 1869-79||?
1869-Je 15 1870 as Willamette Valley mercury; Je 22-Ag 31 1870 Willamette mercury; S?-N 12 1870 Weekly Oregon mercury; N 19 1870-Ja 30 1872 Salem mercury. Followed by Sunday mercury (Portland)
1869-Ag 1870 pub at Corvallis
CU-B Ag 25 1869-[71]-76;Jl 6 1877
Or O 15,29-[N 19 1870-Ag 15 1873]
OrHi D 31 1870[71]N 23 1877

OREGON arena. w 1864?-65||?
CU-B Ag 21 1865

OREGON argus. w 1855?-63||?
CU-B Ag 17 1863

OREGON democrat. w
OrHi Mr 22 1894

OREGON free press. w 1896-1912||?
OrHi Je 24 1910-D 2 1910

OREGON literary vidette. See Oregon vidette

Weekly OREGON mercury. See Weekly Salem mercury

OREGON statesman. w Mr 28 1851-1928||?
1851-Je 4 1852 pub at Oregon City; Ap 14-D 8 1855 at Corvallis. Ja 1867-S 10 1869 merged with American unionist, later Oregon unionist
CSmH Ap 23 1853
CU-B S 28 1863-66;S 17 1869-[71-73]-[78]-D 10,31 1880[Ap 11-D 1884]-Mr 6 1885[86]-My 4,D 21-28 1888
DLC Je 21 1853-59;N 1863-S 1866;S 17-D 17 1869;Ja 28 1870-72
MWA F 26 1853;O 13,N 3,24,D 8,25 1855;Ja 8,22,F 12-26,Ap 8,My,Je 24 1856;Je 1 1858;F 28 1860
NNHi Je 13-20,N 8-15,29 1851
CClWHi Ap 7-14 1857;D 8 1863
OrHi Mr 28 1851-[60-66]Ag 1869-[71;74-77;79; 81-82;86;89]Mr 17 1903-Mr 11 1904
OrP Mr 28 1851-66;D 9 1892
OrSB 1851-63
OrU [Ag 26 1867-Ag 17 1868]
P-M My 7 1853;O 10 1854
WHi Ag 3 1858

OREGON statesman. d Jl 19 1864+
Merged with American unionist, later Oregon unionist
pub 1885+
C D 16 1868
CSmH Ap 15 1865
CU-B [Jl 20-N 1864;Mr 29 1868-74]-[79-80;Ap 5-Je 14 1884]86-F 11,Mr 1888-Ja 13,S 24 1889-Je,Ag-N 1890;91;Ja-Mr 22 1907;Ag 4 1927-My,Ag 31,S-O 13 1928
DLC Ap 18 1899+
MWA Ja 7,F 1,Ap 14,Je 9,14 1876
Or Ag 19 1881;Je 4 1882;94+
OrHi [1864]Ag 3 1869-72[75;77;80-81;84-85,89-90;93-94;99]S 17 1904+
OrU [1869-72]D 30 1875;Ja 22 1891;Je 25 1897[1914]-[16-17;25-26]-[28;Ag 12 1933+]

OREGON unionist. w Ag 27 1866-S 10 1869||
1866-Ag 7 1869 as American unionist
CU-B Ag 27-S 3[O 1866-S 10 1869]

OREGON vidette. w Mr 1879-88||
Mr 1879 issued as monthly as Oregon literary vidette
CU-B F-Ap 1879
OrHi Mr 1879;Ap 1880[83-85;87-88]

Salem evening POST. d 1896-
Or Mr 1896

Salem daily PRESS. d Ap 14 1870-
Or Ap 15-Je 9 1870
OrU My 10 1870

Salem daily RECORD. d Je 10 1867-68||?
CU-B O 23 1867
OrHi 1867-[68]
OrU [1867-68]

RECORD. w 1867-69||?
CU-B O 7-28,N 11-D 16,30 1868-Ja 20,F 3,Mr 2-9,30-Ap 20,My-Jl 13 1869
OrHi O 7 1867-Jl 13 1868

RECORD. d Ap 17 1874-78||?
CU-B 1874-Jl 17 1875;My 4-N 9 1878
OrHi [1878]

Salem morning REGISTER. d
OrHi Ag 18-O 19 1909

Salem SENTINEL. w 1897-1903||?
OrHi D 18 1897-Ja 1 1898;Ap 27 1901-Ja 27 1902

TALK. d 1878-86||?
CU-B Ja 6 1879[80]
OrHi My 24-25 1880

VOX populi. w D 18 1851-Ja 16 1852||
Four numbers only issued
OrHi D 18 1851;Ja 9-16 1852

WILLAMETTE mercury. See Weekly Salem mercury

WILLAMETTE Valley mercury. See Weekly Salem mercury

Salem WORLD. d 1927-28||
Or O 20 1927-Jl 30 1928

SANDY

CLACKAMAS county news. w
OrU [1928]

Sandy NEWS. w 1914-18||?
OrHi Mr 11 1915-S 14 1917

SCIO

Scio PRESS. See Santiam news

SANTIAM news. w 1889-191?||
1889 as Scio press
OrHi O 9 1903-S 12 1904
OrU [1889]

Scio TRIBUNE. w 1912+
pub S 1921+
OrU [1925-26]+

SCOTTSBURG

UMPQUA weekly gazette. w My 6?-D 9 1854||?
CSmH D 9 1854
MWA D 2 1854

SEASIDE

Seaside SIGNAL. w 1903+
pub 1905+
OrHi [1908-09]My 24 1917+
OrU [1917]-[25-26]-[29]-[31]-[33]

SHERIDAN

NEW sun. See Sheridan sun

Sheridan SUN. w 1901+
1904-07 as New sun
OrHi Je 7 1901+
OrU D 1919+

SHERWOOD

Sherwood JOURNAL. w 1914-16||?
OrHi Ja 2 1914-Jl 16 1915

Sherwood VALLEY news. w 1911+
1911-16 as News-sheet; 1917-22 Tualatin Valley news
OrU 1926-[28]+

SILVER LAKE

Silver Lake LEADER and Lake county tribune. w 1907-28||
1907-20 as Silver Lake leader. Followed by Lake county tribune (Lakeview)
OrHi [S 10 1909-10]
OrU O 22 1915;16[19;25]-[28]

SILVERTON

Silverton APPEAL-TRIBUNE. w 1880+
1880-Ag 1 1930 as Silverton appeal
CU-B [1885-87]Je 29-Jl 20 1889;Ja 4-18 1890
OrHi My 1904-Ap 1910;My 9 1913-O 14 1921
OrU [1901;04-05;14]19+

Silverton TRIBUNE. w 1914-Ag 1 1930||
United with Silverton appeal to form Silverton appeal-tribune
OrU 1926-29

SPRAY

Spray COURIER. w 1903-22||?
OrHi F 18 1915-S 14 1916

SPRINGFIELD

LANE county news. See Springfield news

Springfield NEWS. w 1902+
1911?-17 as Lane county news
OrHi F 4 1915-Ag 15 1918
OrU [1913;18]-[32]+

STANFIELD

Stanfield STANDARD. w 1909-28||
OrHi O-[D] 1909;Ja 7,Mr 4 1910;N 13 1925-S 1926
OrU Ap 31 1925-26

STAYTON

Stayton MAIL. w 1894+
OrHi F 8 1912-Jl 10 1919
OrU [1904]-[06-08]26+

Stayton STANDARD. w 1915-17||
OrHi F 14-21 1917

SUMMERVILLE

ANNOTATER. w Jl 19 1889-N 1 1890||
CU-B O 11,N 8,29,D 6-13 1889;Ja 10,F 21 Mr 7,Jl 4,S 12-O 10,24-N 1 1890

SUMPTER

BLUE Mountain American. w 189?-1918||
OrHi O 27 1900-D 19 1912;13-N 8 1917
OrU [1904]-[07]

Sumpter NEWS. w F 26 1897-99||?
OrHi F 26 1897

OREGON (*Continued*)

SUTHERLIN

Sutherlin STAR. w N 5 1920-22||?
OrU N 5 1920-N 11 1921

Sutherlin SUN. w Jl 29 1910+
Suspended 1921-22?
pub 1910+
OrU 1917-[19-20]23+

SWEET HOME

NEW era. w 1929+
OrU 1930-[31]-[33]

THE DALLES

The Dalles daily CHRONICLE. d D 15 1890+
pub 1890+
OrU [1911;14-23]-[25-27]-[29]+

The Dalles CHRONICLE. w 1890+
pub 1890+
OrHi Ag 18 1903;Ja 21 1915+
OrU [1901-06]

INLAND empire. w Jl 6 1878-79||?
CU-B D 28 1878;My 24,Je 14-21,Jl 26 1879
OrHi D 28 1878;Mr 5 1879

MOUNTAINEER. *See* The Dalles times-mountaineer

The Dalles OPTIMIST. w 1906+
pub 1920+
OrHi Je 19 1906-Jl 1918
OrU 1929-Je 3 1932

OREGON weekly tribune. w Mr 11 1874-77||?
1874-75? as Eastern Oregon weekly tribune
1874-S 4 1875 pub at Pendleton
CU-B [1874-S 5,D 25 1875]-Jl 7 1877

TIMES. w Ag 24? 1879-D 28 1880||
United with Mountaineer to form The Dalles times-mountaineer
CU-B [Ap 27-D 1880]

The Dalles TIMES-MOUNTAINEER. w F 6 1860-1904||?
1860-Je 17 1882? as Weekly mountaineer
CU-B [Jl 16 1865-67]-N 1870;N 18-D 23 1871;F 17,Mr 2,Jl 27 1872-[75-77]Jl 3 1879;80;85-87;Mr 23 1889;F 1 1890[Jl-D 1891]
NN Ja 15-22,F 12-Ap 16,30-Jl 9,23-Ag 20,S-O 8,N 5-19,D 1881-Je 17 1882
OrHi [1861-62;67-73]Ag 28 1875;Ag 12 1893-S 1904
WHi O 12-19 1860
Wa O 6 1883
WaU [Jl 30 1869-73]75-77[S 18 1879-N 11 1880]N 25-D 9 1882;Ja 6-13,Mr 24[My 19 1883-Ap 12]My 17-31 1884;D 31 1887-Jl 7,Ag 4 1888-[F 9 1889-N 8 1890;Je 20 1891-Ag 1 1891]Ap 30,My 14-O 8,N 12,D 24 1892[F 4-Ag 12 1893]

The Dalles TIMES-MOUNTAINEER. d 1862-66;89-1902||?
1862-66 as Mountaineer
CU-B [Je 23 1865-Je 11 1866]
MSaE N 20 1862
OrHi N 1865-Je 4 1866

WASCO county sun. w 1880-93||?
CU-B 1889-D 2 1891
OrHi Mr 21-28,Ap 11 1883

TIGARD

Tigard SENTINEL. w Ag 1 1924+
OrBeE 1924+
OrHi 1924+
OrU 1925-[29-33]

TILLAMOOK

Tillamook HEADLIGHT. w Je 8 1888-Mr 1934||
United with Tillamook herald to form Headlight-herald
CU-B Ag 16-23 1889;Ag 11 1892
OrT [1919-20]-34
OrU [1904-08]-[11]-[13]-15;17-[20]-[27-28]-34

Tillamook HEADLIGHT-HERALD. w Ag 1 1896+
1896-Mr 1934 as Tillamook herald
OrHi My-D 1900;Ap 11 1901-Ap 1902;Ap 28 1903-Ap 19 1905;O 8 1907-09;Ap 1917+
OrT [1919-20]+
OrU [1901-02;04-08;23]-[28]+
WaPS Ap 28-My 5 1921;Je 11,12 1931

Tillamook HERALD. *See* Tillamook headlight-herald

Tillamook INDEPENDENT. w 1902-04||?
OrHi D 31 1902-Ja 7 1903

WESTERN watchtower. w 1889-90||
United with Bay City tribune (Bay City) to form Bay City tribune and Western watchtower (Bay City)
CU-B Ag 2,16 1890

TOLEDO

LINCOLN county leader. w 1893+
OrHi Jl 17 1903+
OrU [D 1919-20]-[27]-[29]+

YAQUINA post. w
OrHi Je 15-D 21 1901
OrU [1901-02]

TURNER

Turner TRIBUNE. w 1915+
OrU [1922]24-[30-31]

UMATILLA

Umatilla ADVERTISER. tw My? 1865-69||
CU-B D 6 1865
OrHi O 1 1865

COLUMBIA press. w D 21 1866?-68||?
CU-B Jl 27,Ag 17-O,N 16-30,D 14-21 1867;F 29-Mr 7,21-28,Ap 11-25,My 9,23-30,Je 20,Jl 18,Ag 8-29 1868

INDEX. w Ap 6 1866-
CU-B Ap 27 1866

UNION

EASTERN Oregon republican. w 1888+
Title varies: Weekly republican: etc
CU-B Jl 31,Ag 21,O 2-16 1890;Jl 14-28 1892
OrHi Ag 3 1901-Jl 13 1907
OrU [1901]-[03-05]
WaPS [1918-19]

GRANDE Ronde sentinel. *See* Mountain sentinel

MOUNTAIN democrat. *See* Mountain sentinel

MOUNTAIN sentinel. w My 2 1868-86||?
1868-70? as Grande Ronde sentinel; 1871? Mountain democrat
1868-77? pub at La Grande
CU-B My 2,Ag 1,O 2,17-31,N 27,D 19 1868;Ja 16,Mr 17,D 25 1869;Ja 15,29,F 12-19 1870;N 22 1873;Ja 31 1874[75-O 23 1880]
OrHi [1872-77]Ap 9 1881;Jl 3 1886

OREGON scout. w 1884-1918||?
CU-B [1889-90]Ja 21-Je 2,23,Ag 4-S 15,29-O 16,30,N 17 1892-[93]F 22 1894

Weekly REPUBLICAN. *See* Eastern Oregon republican

VALE

Vale DEMOCRAT. w 1901-02||?
OrHi Je 29 1901-Mr 15 1902

MALHEUR booster. m 1908||?
OrHi Jl-D 1908

MALHEUR enterprise. w N 1909+
pub 1909+
OrHi Ja 15-22,Jl 1910+
OrO 1927+
OrU 1916-[20]22+

MALHEUR gazette. w 1889-1908||?
CU-B Ag 14-28 1890
OrHi Ag 14 1902-N 14 1907

NEW atlas. w 1888-90||
CU-B S 5,19,O 10,N 28,D 12 1889;F 6,Ag 9,23,S 27,O 25 1890

OREGON Oriano. w 1905-1911||?
OrHi Ja 17 1906-D 16 1910;Ja 6-13,D 23-30 1911
OrU S 19 1908

VERNONIA

Vernonia EAGLE. w Ag 1922+
pub 1922+
OrU [1926]+

WALDPORT

PACIFIC herald. w 1915-26||?
1915-20? as Waldport watchman
OrHi Je 25 1917;D 1925-Ap 1 1926

Waldport TRIBUNE. w Je 16 1926+
pub O 16 1926+
Or Je-Ag 1926
OrU 1928[29]+

Waldport WATCHMAN. *See* Pacific herald

WALLOWA

Wallowa NEWS. w 1899-1907||?
OrHi S 28 1900-F 21 1902;My 29 1903-Mr 29,Ap 19 1907

Wallowa SUN. w 1907+
OrHi F 4 1915+
OrU [1912-14]-[24]-[26]-[28]+

WARRENTON

CLATSOP county argus. w 1914-28||?
OrU 1925-[27-28]

Warrenton NEWS. w Jl 21-D 8 1932||
OrHi complete

PORT Oregon tribune. w 1896-1902||?
OrU [1901-02]

WASCO

Wasco NEWS. *See* Sherman county news

Wasco NEWS-ENTERPRISE. *See* Sherman county news

OBSERVER. w 1888-90||
CU-B S 20,O 4 1889;Ja 3,Ag 15 1890

SHERMAN county news. w 1891-1931||?
1891-1909 as Wasco news; 1910-Ag 19 1927 Wasco news-enterprise
OrU [1904;06-07]24-26;Ag 19 1927-[28]29

WEST LINN

AMPLIFIER. w
WaPS [O 26-D 21 1931]

WEST SALEM

West Salem CLARION. w
OrHi Mr-S 4 1931

WESTON

Weston LEADER. w D 21 1878+
pub 1895+
CU-B D 21 1878[80;85]Ja 14-21,F 4 1890;Ag 12 1892
OrHi Ap 13 1888;Ag 21 1903
OrPe 1927+
OrU [1908]-[12-13]15-[16]+

WHEELER

NEHALEM valley reporter. *See* Wheeler reporter

Wheeler RECORDER. w 1930+
OrHi S 17,24,O 1 1931
OrU [1930-33]

Wheeler REPORTER. w 1910+
1910-15 as Nehalem Valley reporter
OrHi D 26 1913-14;Ag 27-S 10 1931;My 1933+
OrU 1929-[31]+

WILLAMINA

Willamina TIMES. w Ag 19 1909+
pub 1929+
OrU [1928]-[30]+

WOODBURN

Woodburn INDEPENDENT. w 1887+
pub 1897+
CU-B Ag 31-S 14,N 30 1889;Ag 30 1890;S 1 1893
OrHi S 1894-Ja 1896;F 19 1903-N 1909;D 1910+
OrU [1904-05]-[07]-08;17-[29]-[31]

Woodburn TRIBUNE. w 1911-14||?
OrHi Jl 14 1911-Mr 6 1914

WOODS

OCEAN wave. w 1896-1903||?
OrHi [1901-02]

YAMHILL

NORTH Yamhill leader. w S 3 1891-94||?
CU-B Ja 15,29-F 5,Mr 4,Ap 8-15 1892

NORTH Yamhill record. *See* Yamhill record

Yamhill RECORD. w 1894-1929||
1899-1909 as North Yamhill record
OrHi [1899]-[1901-03;06-12]My 1 1919-F 19 1929
OrU [1901-03]

YONCALLA

Yoncalla TIMES. w 1911-14||?
OrU [1911]

PANAMA CANAL. *See Canal Zone*

PENNSYLVANIA

AARONSBURG

Der CENTRE berichter. *See* Millheim journal (Millheim)

DEMOKRATISCHER berichter und Center county anzeiger. *See* Millheim journal (Millheim)

ABBOTTSTOWN

DEUTSCHES wochenblatt.
In German
TxU Ag 3 1848

YELLOW jacket. w D 11 1839-
DLC D 25 1839
PYHi Jl 1840

ALBION

ERIE county enterprise. w 1877-80||
PEr Ap 10 1879

ALIQUIPPA

Aliquippa GAZETTE. sw 1922+
1922-Ja 27 1928 as Woodlawn gazette
pub 1922+
PA 1922+

NEWS-STANDARD. sw
PA [1920-21]

WOODLAWN gazette. *See* Aliquippa gazette

WOODLAWN news. w 1921-
PA [1921]-[23]

WOODLAWN times. sw
PA [1923]

ALLEGHENY

Papers published in Allegheny are listed under Pittsburgh

ALLENTOWN

Early years as Northampton

Der ANTI-FREIMAURER und Lecha county patriot. *See* Der Lecha Allentown patriot

Allentown morning CALL. d 1889+
1889-94 as Morning critic
pub 1889+
MWA Ja 8 1916;My 19 1928
P Mr 30 1920+
PP Jl 14 1928+

Allentown CHRONICLE. d Mr 3 1870-75||
United with Lehigh Valley daily news to form Chronicle and news, later Chronicle and news and item
MWA Ag 12 1871
PAlC complete

CHRONICLE and news and item. d 1866+
1866-75 as Lehigh Valley daily news; 1876-1921 Chronicle and news
pub [1870]+
MWA Je 9 1870
NN Ag 14 1880
PAlC [1871]-[75]
PAlHi [1866]-[74]

Daily CITY item. d Ja 1 1878-1921||
United with Chronicle and news to form Chronicle and news and item
MWA Ap 24 1880
PAlC complete

Weekly CRITIC. w My 26 1883-88||
PAlC [D 7 1883-88]

Morning CRITIC. *See* Allentown morning call

Allentown daily DEMOCRAT. w,d Ap 26 1837-1919||?
1837-79 as Lehigh bulletin; 1879-1906 Allentown democrat
w 1837-1906
MWA My 17 1837;Mr 10 1880
NjR F 28,S 5,D 12 1850;Ag 5,19 1852
OClWHi Je 13 1866
P Ja 27 1879-1918
PAlC [1852]-1912
PBL [1839-40]
PDoHi [1867-68]Mr 5 1873

Evening DISPATCH. d Mr 8? 1866-
MWA Mr 15(extra)1867

*Allentown FRIEDENSBOTE. w S 28 1812-1916||?
Title varies: Der friedens-bote und Lecha county anzeiger; Der friedens-bote und Lecha, Northampton, Bucks and Montgomery counties anzeiger; etc.
In German
DLC Jl 25 1838;Ja 18 1865
MWA S 18 1834;Jl 31 1878
NNHi Ag 12 1840
P-M Mr 6 1828
PAlHi 1841[42]-49;54-58;60-[85;95;1908]-16
PE [1822]-24;34-35
PPeS [1821-37;39-40;45;47;51;59-62;66;77-79;83;88;90;95-96]

HARRISONIAN of Lehigh. w Ap 23 1840-
DLC Ap 30 1840

Allentown morning HERALD. d
PAlC N 1919-Mr 1920

LECHA bote. d,tw 1868-86||
1868-77 as Stadt und land bote(d)
In German
PAlHi 1868-72;75-[81-82;85]86

Der LECHA Allentown patriot. w 1827-72||
1827-41 as Der Anti-freimaurer und Lecha county patriot; 1841-48 Der Lecha patriot und Northampton demokrat; 1848-59 Der Lecha patriot. Merged with Lehigh register
In German
PAlCh [1838;40;46;48;51;53-68]
PPHi [1841]-[49]-[69]
PPeS [1834-35]-Ja 21 1836[37]Mr 7,Ap 25 1838;My 10,Jl 5 1854;Ja 6,F 17 1858

LEHIGH bulletin. *See* Allentown daily democrat

LEHIGH herald. w
P N 20 1828

LEHIGH journal and Northampton and Lehigh counties advertiser. w 1838-
DLC D 25 1839

LEHIGH register. w O 1846-1912||?
Title varies: Lehigh register and patriot
MWA Ap 24 1861;Ja 23 1866
NbHi Ag 18 1869
P 1889-1912
PAlC 1846-[59]
PAlCh [1866-72]-[74]75[80;84;86;89]92-[95-97]1901
PPeS Je 6 1883;D 1 1886

LEHIGH reporter. w 1846-
MWA Ja 19 1847
PHi [1846]-Ja 24 1848

LEHIGH republican and Mauch Chunk farmer's and mechanick's register. w 1825?-
Title varies slightly
DLC My 7 1829
MWA Jl 27 1826

LEHIGH VALLEY daily news. *See* Chronicle and news and item

LEHIGH VALLEY review. w 1909+
PPeS S 25 1931

Allentown RECORD. d 1921-23||?
PAlC 1921-22

STADT und land bote. *See* Lecha bote

Allentown STAR. w N 4 1824-
NjHi N 11 1824
P-M Jl 28 1825

*Der UNABHÄNGIGE republikaner. w Jl 27 1810-1916||
Jl 24 1812-Ap 8 1814 as Der Unabhängige republikaner und Lecha county freiheits freund
In German
CtY O 7 1840
DLC Je 13 1838
MWA Ap 20 1842
P D 18 1828;O 3 1829;Ap 25 1830
PAlHi 1821-65;67;1900
PPeS [1821]O 6 1825;Je 21 1827;S 7 1836

WELT-BOTE. d N 25 1854-1916||
In German
PAlHi 1857-1916
PNazHi [1866]
PPiHi S 14-O 12,N 2,16-23,D 7-21 1887
WHi S 18 1900

ALTOONA

Evening CALL. *See* Altoona mirror

DEMOCRATIC call. *See* Altoona mirror

Altoona MIRROR. d Je 13 1874+
1874-N 1878 as Evening mirror; D 1878-Jl 1880 Democratic call; Jl 1880-85 Evening call
pub [1874-75]-[79]Mr 5,8,17 1880;Mr 15 1882 [88]+
P [1903]-[21;27]-[35]
PArdL Ag 3 1923
PP [1923]+

Altoona SUN. w 1866-92||?
PLaL Je 13,S 5 1873

Altoona TIMES. d 1886-1920||
United with Altoona tribune to form Times-tribune, later Altoona tribune
P Jl 1903-20
PAltHi 1886-90
PHHi F 3 1897;Mr 9 1917

TIMES-TRIBUNE. *See* Altoona tribune 1873+

Altoona TRIBUNE. w Ja 3 1856-1920||
NcD Ja 3 1856
PAltHi 1858-67;74-91;94-95;97-1901

Altoona TRIBUNE. d Ja 2 1873+
1920 as Times-tribune
Suspended from 1875-78
P Jl 1889+
PAltHi 1874-75;78-1902
PEbHi D 23 1893

AMBLER

Ambler GAZETTE. w 1882+
Follows Fort Washington times (Fort Washington)
pub 1896+

Ambler NEWS. w Mr 28 1935+
pub 1935+

AMBRIDGE

Ambridge daily CITIZEN. w,sw,tw,d Jl 1904+
1904-11 as Ambridge economy citizen
w 1904-My 14 1912;sw My 14 1912-S 17 1923; tw S 17 1923-Mr 4 1929
pub 1904+
PAmL 1927+

Ambridge ECONOMY citizen. *See* Ambridge daily citizen

Greater Ambridge LEADER. w O 7 1932-Je 9 1933||
PAmC [1932-33]

NEWS-HERALD. sw,w 1906+
sw Jl 23 1926-My 29 1930
pub 1906+

ARCHBALD

Archbald CITIZEN. w My 3 1894+
pub 1894+
OClWHi Ap 1-8,29-My 6 20-Je 3,17 1916
PScrHi My 28 1936

ARDMORE

Ardmore CHRONICLE. w N 1889+
Title varies: Lower Merion Ardmore chronicle
pub 1891+
PNoHi 1904-18

LOWER MERION Ardmore chronicle. *See* Ardmore chronicle

MAIN LINE journal. w
PArdM [1935-36]

MAIN LINE daily times. d N 1930+
pub 1930+
PP 1931+

MAIN LINER. w Ja 1920+
pub 1926+
P 1932+
PP N 21 1930+

ASHLAND

Ashland ADVOCATE. w Ap 1864-1920||?
MWA D 17 1879
P Jl 1889-Je 1907

Ashland NEWS. w,d 1896+
w 1896-1909
pub 1896;98-99;1901;06;09+

ATHENS

ATHENIAN. w 1852-S? 1854||
Followed by Athens gazette (1854-56)
PAtM O 5 1853;Je 21 1854

Athens DEMOCRAT. S 1855-
WHi S 18,25,O 2 1855

Athens GAZETTE. w O 6 1854-56||
Follows Athenian
PAtM Jl 11 1856
WHi 1854-S 12 1856

Athens GAZETTE. w Ap 1870-D 1918||
PAtM Ja 1 1875;Mr 9 1876;Ap 20 1877;S 30 1880-Ag 21 1913
PToHi [1897-98]

Athens GLEANER. w Mr 16 1870-O 1874||
PAtM 1870-[73]
PWbW [1870-73]

Athens SCRIBE. w Ag 5 1841-D 1842||
Title varies slightly
DLC Ag 26 1841
PAtM [1841-42

AUSTIN

Austin REPUBLICAN. w 1898-1945||?
PEIJ [1898-99]

AVONDALE

Avondale and Landenburg EXPRESS. w 1892-
PWcHi Jl 18 1896;S 25 1897

Avondale HERALD. w Ap 17 1896+
PWcHi Jl 17 1896;O 27,N 24 1899;S 28,O 5 1900;Ap 18 1902
PWcL [1896]-[1915;17]-[19-21]

Avondale STAR m O 1894-Mr 17 1896||
PWcL [1894]

BALA-CYNWYD

NEWS of Bala-Cynwyd. w 1923+
pub 1923+

BARNESBORO

Barnesboro STAR. w Jl 1 1904+
pub 1904-[16]+

BEAVER

*Beaver ARGUS. w S 1 1818-Jl 1930||
S 11 1818-Ag 21 1843 as Western argus; Ag 21 1843-S 17 1873 Beaver argus (Jl? 1853-59 Beaver county argus);S 24 1873-Ap 1903 Argus-radical. Merged with Beaver times
CSmH Ap 16 1825;Jl 9 1830
DLC My 30,Jl 11,Ag 8-S 5 1855
MWA Ja 31 1866
OClWHi S 2 1823;My 23-S,O 31,N 14,28 1855
OHi Jl 13-20 1864
P Jl 1889-D 12 1912
P-M N 21 1828
PBeT 1821-30
PBf Jl 11 1860-61
PPiHi Je 21 1833-39;42-Jl 1843[45-46]
PPot N 29 1857
WHi My 2,Ag 29,S 26,O 24 1855

PENNSYLVANIA (*Continued*)

BEAVER—*Continued*

BEAVER county argus. *See* Beaver argus

BEAVER county patriot. w Je 1841-O 1843||
PBL [1843]
PBf My 3 1861

BEAVER RIVER gazette. w F 11 1834-
DLC F 11 1834

GLOBE-STAR. *See* Star

RADICAL. w N 1868-S 17 1873||
United with Argus to form Argus and radical, later Beaver argus
DLC Mr 15 1872

Beaver REPUBLICAN. w Je 1826-My 1835||
CSmH Ag 12 1830
PBL My 28 1834

STAR. w,sw 1877-1908||
1887-My 5 1892 as Globe-star
w 1877-92
P Jl 1889-[1908]

Beaver TIMES. w 1874-1911||?
pub [1874-99]
PBfT 1875-78
PJ My 10 1877

Beaver daily TIMES. d Ap 27 1899+
pub 1899+
P 1927-32
PA 1930+

WESTERN argus. *See* Beaver argus

BEAVER FALLS

Early years as Brighton

BEAVER county enterprise. *See* Beaver Falls tribune

BEAVER county palladium. w 1840-41||
Follows Beaver Falls chronicle (Rochester)
DLC S 19 1840;F 26,Mr 12,Jl 30 1841
PPi [Ag 29 1840-S 23 1841]

BEAVER VALLEY news. w -1928||
United with Beaver Falls tribune to form News tribune

Beaver Falls COURIER. *See* Beaver Falls tribune. 1875-1906

Evening JOURNAL. d Je 1888-92||
P Jl 11 1889-Je 1891;92

NEWS-TRIBUNE. d 1884+
1884-1928 as Beaver Falls tribune
P Jl 1891+
PBeC 1899

Beaver Falls REVIEW. w 1897+
PBeC 1907

Beaver Falls TRIBUNE. w 1875-1906||?
1875-79 as Beaver Falls courier; 1879-80 Beaver county enterprise
P Ap 1892-1900
PBf N 15 1879

Beaver Falls TRIBUNE. d *See* News tribune

BEAVER SPRINGS

Weekly HERALD. w Mr 1887-Mr 1923||
Merged with McClure plain dealer (McClure)
PMiR 1893-1916
PPCHi My 4,25,Je 8,29 1905

BEDFORD

DEMOCRATIC inquirer. *See* Bedford inquirer

*Bedford GAZETTE. w S 21 1805+
S 21 1906 is centennial ed
pub 1821+
DLC Jl 2,16-23,O 15 1824;Mr 21 1845
MWA Je 29 1827-Je 17 1831
P S 1834-Jl 3 1893;Jl 1894-1912;18+
PBL F 13,O 9 1835[36]
PBedI 1850-61;67-75;87-89
WHi N 15 1844;N 5 1847;Mr 3 1854;N 5 1852;D 18 1857;Ap 6 1860;S 21 1906

*Bedford INQUIRER. w Je 12 1813+
1813-O 12 1827 as True American; O 12 1827-Ag? 1834 Democratic inquirer; Ag? 1834-N 24 1842 Democratic inquirer and farmers' and mechanics' advertiser; Ja? 1850-F 16 1854 Democratic inquirer; F 16 1854-N 20 1857 Inquirer and chronicle; 1884?-88? Republican and inquirer
pub 1850-52;54-61;64-77;79+
CSmH S 3 1830
DLC O 29 1824;Je 27-Jl 4,26-Ag 15,S 19,O 3 1828
MBAt Ap 14 1865
MWA 1847-Ja 4 1850
NNHi My 15 1863;Ap 4 1873
P Ag 12 1831-D 6 1833;88-1912;Ag 12 1931-N 13 1932
P-M Ja 20 1828
PP My 17 1899-1912
PWcT Ag 31 1866
WHi O 12 1827-Jl 1831;N 25 1836;D 1842-46

REPUBLICAN and courier. *See* Bedford inquirer

REPUBLICAN and inquirer. *See* Bedford inquirer

TRUE American. *See* Bedford inquirer

BELLE VERNON

Belle Vernon COURIER. w Je 4 1877-Je 13 1878||
PChaW [1877-78]

ENTERPRISE. w 1886+
pub 1886+
PUn [1902;04]-Mr 10 1905

BELLEFONTE

CENTRAL press. *See* Bellefonte national

CENTRE county democrat. *See* Centre democrat

CENTRE democrat. w 1827+
1827-33 as Centre county democrat
pub 1835-[37;40]-[45]79-1913;15+
Ct [1832-37]
MWA D 21 1858
N O 26 1833
P-M F 26,My 21,D 10 1831;F 10 1832;N 12-19, D 31 1834;F 18,Ap 1,22,O 3 1835;Ap 8,14,Ag 18 1838;Ap 12 1839
PBL S 14 1830;Jl 6 1833;D 10,31 1834[35]D 15 1838;F 16,Je 4-11 1839[43;45]S 16 1846;Jl 17, Ag 16,O 27 1848
PBelC [1893-94]1908-09;12-19
PHHi Mr 26 1896
PStP 1879-93

CENTRE herald. w My 16 1878-
IGa My-D 12 1878
PStP 1878

COMET. w
P-M Je 13 1857

DEMOCRATIC watchman. w Ja 1 1855+
1876-82 as Bellefonte watchman
pub 1855+
DLC Jl 21 1871
MWA Ja 3 1868
P Ap 1861-63;Jl 1889+
PBelB [1857-59]
PBelC [1893]-1907;10-19
PJsJ [1856-60]
PPL Ap 23 1856
PStP 1876-[1925]

DEMOCRATIC whig. w 1840-58||
Merged with Central press, later Bellefonte national
DLC My 22,Je 5 1841;Ag 31 1844
PBL Ap 23 1842;O 8 1845
PBelB N 18 1843;Ag 27 1845;F 14,Jl 18 1855;N 5 1856
PStP [1841]-[43]
PSuHi S 9 1846;F 10 1847

KEYSTONE gazette. w 1885+
pub [1885]-[1905-06]-[16]18;20-27;29+
P Je 28 1889-Je 1912
PBelC [1893]-1915
PStP 1886-93

Bellefonte NATIONAL. w S 1858-70||
1858-66 as Central press. Merged with Bellefonte republican
KHi Ap 21 1865
MWA Mr 2 1866;Ja 28 1870
P Ap 25 1861-63
PMarH My 15 1863;Ap 21 1865

*Bellefonte PATRIOT. w My 18 1818-
Title varies slightly
CSmH Ag 26 1830
DLC N 1 1832;Je 13 1833

Bellefonte REPUBLICAN. w Ja 6 1869-1931||?
MWA Ja 6 1869;Ag 23 1876
P Jl 1889-Ja 29 1931
PBelB Je 16 1869
PBelC 1910-11;16-19
PStP 1876-93

Bellefonte WATCHMAN. *See* Democratic watchman

BELLEVUE

CITY and suburban life. w S 6 1901+
1901-08 as Suburban life
pub 1901+

SUBURBAN life. *See* City and suburban life

BENTON

Benton ARGUS. w 1892+
pub [1910]+

INDEPENDENT weekly. *See* Milton record (Milton)

BERWICK

Berwick ARGUS. *See* Enquirer

Berwick CITIZEN, and democratic watchman. w My 6 1852-53||
MWA D 2 1852

COLUMBIA gazette. *See* Enquirer

Berwick CONSERVATOR. w Je 13 1840-
Follows Independent ledger
DLC Je 20 1840

ENQUIRER. w 1824-49||
1824-32 as Columbia gazette; 1832-34 Berwick gazette; 1834-37 Berwick argus; 1837-43 Berwick sentinel. Followed by Star of the North (Bloomsburg)
DLC Jl 2 1846
MWA Ap 6 1843
PBL My 18 1837;D 27 1838[42-43]S 5 1844
PBerH [1843-44]
PBloHi Ap 25 1835

Berwick ENTERPRISE. w,d 1900+
1900-04 as Berwick weekly enterprise(w)
pub [1917]+
PBerR [1900]-[04-05]Mr 29,Ap 1 1911

Berwick GAZETTE. 1832-34 *See* Enquirer

Berwick GAZETTE. w Mr 25 1882-86||?
PWbW Ag 21 1886

Berwick INDEPENDENT. w 1871-1907||
1871? as Pennsylvania independent. Merged with Berwick enterprise
PWbW 1871-79

*Berwick INDEPENDENT American. w My 2 1818-
MWA Je 2 1821

INDEPENDENT ledger. w 1834-40||
Followed by Conservator
PBerH [1839-40]

PENNSYLVANIA independent. *See* Berwick independent

Berwick SENTINEL. *See* Enquirer

BERWYN

ANTI-MASONIC examiner. w O 28 1829-Ag 30 1831||
PCoaH Ag 30 1831

CHESTER county leader. w Ja 11 1935-
PDowN Ja 11-My 31 1935
PWcHi Mr 22-29 1935

Berwyn HERALD. w 1889-1905||?
PWcHi [1893]-95;My 3,Je 7 1901;Ap 24 1902

BETHANIA

Bethania PALLADIUM. w Je 8 1832-
ICHi Jl 6 1834
MWA Ag 1832-O 25 1833
PLaHi [1832-33]Jl 4-11,25 1834

BETHANY

REPUBLICAN advocate. *See* Wayne county herald

WAYNE county free press, and Bethany and Honesdale advertiser. w
DLC Ja 7 1840

*WAYNE county herald. w Mr 7 1818-
1818-22 as Wayne county mirror; D 1822-N 29 1829 Republican advocate; Ja 12 1830-Mr 1833 Wayne enquirer
NjHi Jl 4-11,S 26 1823;Ap 30 1824
PBL Mr 3-17 1830;Mr 10-17 1831
PHsHi F 17 1830
PWbW Mr 5 1824

WAYNE county mirror. *See* Wayne county herald

WAYNE enquirer. *See* Wayne county herald

BETHLEHEM

AMERIKANSZKI szlovencov glasz. w Ap 20 1921+
In Wendish
pub 1921+

Die BIENE. Ein volksblatt. sm Ja 3 1846-48||?
Title varies slightly
In German
PBL [1846]
PE 1846-47;Ja 15,F 12,D 16 1848
PHi 1846-47
PPeS [1847-48]

Bethlehem GLOBE. d 1894-O 19 1925||
United with Bethlehem times to form Bethlehem globe-times
PB 1918-25
PBG complete

Bethlehem GLOBE-TIMES. d 1867+
1867-O 19 1925 as Bethlehem times
pub 1927+
KHi [Ap 8 1893-Je 12 1918]
MWA O 26 1869;Je 13(supp)1877;D 24(supp) 1891
NNHi O 9 1873;Je 11 1880
P 1927-32
PB Je 1892;1927+
PBG 1867+
PEC 1905-[09]
PMcC Mr 31,Ap 3 1876

Bethlehem HIRADO (Bethlehem Hungarian news). w Ap 20 1923+
In Hungarian
pub 1923+
PPiHi [1926-27]

Bethlehem HUNGARIAN news. *See* Bethlehem hirado

Morning PROGRESS. [South Bethlehem] d 1871-74||
MWA Jl 2 1874

SOUTH BETHLEHEM star. d Ja 1877-1903||?
Title varies: Morning star; etc.
KHi [Ap 21 1894-My 25 1898]
MWA F 20,Mr 8 1877

Bethlehem TIMES. *See* Bethlehem globe-times

Der VATERLAND freund. w
In German
MiU-C F 1 1849
PE My 10,Je 7 1849

BIRDSBORO

DISPATCH. w 1885+
pub 1915+

Birdsboro weekly RECORD. w 1878-80||
PPot Ap 23 1880

BLAIRSVILLE

APPALACHIAN. *See* Blairsville record

CITIZEN and Blairsville advocate. *See* Blairsville record

CONEMAUGH republican. w F 19 1830-
CSmH S 3 1830

PENNSYLVANIA (*Continued*)

BLAIRSVILLE—*Continued*

Blairsville daily COURIER. d My 5 1894-Jl 1 1904||
1894-Je 1 1896 as Blairsville evening courier
PBlD 1894-99

Blairsville COURIER. w *See* Blairsville dispatch

Blairsville DISPATCH. w,sw My 5 1905+
1905-20 as Blairsville courier(w)
pub 1905+

Blairsville ENTERPRISE. w,tw Ap 9 1880-N 17 1918||
P Jl 20 1889-1912
PBl 1880-[95]98-1918
PBlD 1895-1918

NEW ERA. *See* Blairsville press

Blairsville PRESS. w D 1864-Ja 21 1870||
1864-D 1866 as New era. United with Register and American (Indiana) to form Indiana progress (Indiana)
PBlD 1865-66
PIP 1866-Ja 7 1870

Blairsville RECORD. w 1826-66||
1845-46 as Citizen and Blairsville advocate; My 1846-N 1855 Appalachian; N 1855-57 True American. Merged with Indiana weekly register, later Register and American (Indiana)
CSmH My 20 1830
Ct [1835-38]
P Ap 28 1852
P-M N 25 1830;Mr 5 1834
PBL S 11 1844[45-46]
PBl [1834-35]46-49[D 1858-F 25 1863]

TRUE American. *See* Blairsville record

BLOOMSBURG

COLUMBIA county register. w O 5 1826-44||
1826-Ap 1828 as Bloomsburg register
CSmH S 7 1830
PBloHi Ja 12 1830;D 31 1833;Ja 14 1834
PLewL S 2 1828
PToHi Mr 4 1843

COLUMBIA county republican. w Mr 1 1857-1917||?
P Je 17 1889-Je 12 1912
PBloHi S 8 1887;F 21,My 16-23 1889
PWbW S 24 1863;O 31 1867;S 20 1879

COLUMBIA democrat. *See* Bloomsburg democrat

COLUMBIAN. w My 5 1866-1909||?
PBloE Jl 12 1867-1908
PBloHi S 11 1868-1905
PToHi O 18 1895

Bloomsburg DAILY. *See* Daily sentinel

Bloomsburg DEMOCRAT. w Ap 29 1837-69||
1837-66 as Columbia democrat; 1866-67? as Democrat and star. Merged with Columbian
DLC O 10 1840;F 28 1846;N 6 1852;O 15(extra) 1862
MWA N 20 1852
PBL O 28 1837;Ap 1 1843
PBlo 1837-66
PW Jl 2 1842
PWbW Ag 24 1839

DEMOCRATIC sentinel. w S 1870-1918||
P Jl 1884-Je 1885;Jl 1889-1912
—d ed *See* Daily sentinel

Bloomsburg JOURNAL. w 1876-87||
PBlo 1880-[82]

Morning PRESS. d 1902+
pub 1908+
P 1927-Je 1932
PBlo 1913+
PBloHi [1902;15-16;19;21;23]

Bloomsburg REGISTER. *See* Columbia county register

Daily SENTINEL. d 1892-1918||
1892-1908 as Bloomsburg daily
P 1892-Jl 1912
PBlo [1892]-[1901]
PBloHi [1904;08-09]-[18]
PDC N 4 1898;Jl 23,O 13,N 10 1899
—w ed *See* Democratic sentinel

STAR of the North. w F 1 1849-F 1866||
Follows Enquirer (Berwick). United with Columbia democrat to form Democrat and star, later Bloomsburg democrat
IU Je 10 1852
MWA Mr 22(extra)1849;Ap 11 1850;F 27 1851; N 18 1852
PBloM [1849]-[51]

BLOSSBURG

Blossburg ADVERTISER. w 1885-1917||
Follows Blossburg register
P Je 1889-Je 3 1910
PBlosH [1910;12-17]
PBlosM [1888]

Blossburg HERALD. w 1912+
pub [1913]-[27]+
KHi S 4,18 1924

Blossburg INDUSTRIAL register. *See* Blossburg register

Blossburg REGISTER. w Ja 1 1870-85||
1879-81? as Blossburg industrial register. Followed by Blossburg advertiser
P 1879-S 1881
PBlosM [1871;75-76]79-81

BOYERTOWN

Boyertown BANNER. *See* Berks county democrat

BERKS county democrat. w 1858-Ap 3 1930||
1858-66? as Boyertown banner; 1867?-1904 as Boyertown democrat. Merged with Boyertown times
1858-75 in German; 1876-85? in German and English
PBoT D 13 1867-1930
PPeS My 10,Jl 5 1928

Boyertown DEMOCRAT. *See* Berks county democrat

Boyertown TIMES. w Ag 10 1927+
pub 1927+

BRADDOCK

Evening HERALD. d 1893-1907||
United with Braddock daily news to form Braddock news-herald
PBra complete
PPiHi F 1900-Ja 1901

Evening JOURNAL. d O 1905-08||
PPiHi D 1 1905-08

Braddock NEWS-HERALD. d 1887+
1887-Je 15 1907 as Braddock daily news
PBra 1892+
PPiHi 1894-Je 15 1907
PUn Je 11 1900
WHi D 21 1895

Braddock TRIBUNE. w 1884-1902||?
P Jl 13 1889-Je 10 1890;Jl 1891-Je 1893;Jl 1894-Jl 1895

BRADFORD

Daily BREEZE. d S 1878-Mr 19 1879||
Merged with Bradford daily era
P D 31 1878-79

Bradford morning CALL. d
PBrS 1886-87

Bradford daily ERA. d O 1877+
1877-87 as Bradford era
pub 1877+
MWA My 25 1883
P Mr 1879-Jl 1887[89]-[1912]
PBr 1877+
PPi 1878-83

Bradford weekly ERA. w 1888-1916||?
P Je 27 1889-Je 27 1912

Bradford Sunday HERALD. w 1895+
pub 1922+

Bradford MINER. *See* McKean county miner (Smethport)

Bradford NEW ERA. w,sw Ag 28 1875-76||?
w 1875
MWA 1875;My 24 1876

Bradford daily RECORD. d 1891-1908||
United with Bradford evening star to form Bradford evening star and daily record
PBrS complete

Bradford evening STAR and daily record. d 1879+
1879-1908 as Bradford evening star
pub 1890-97;1908+
P F 1927-Mr 1933

BRIDGEPORT

Weekly MONITOR. w Je 21 1889-Ja 21 1907||
1889-94? as Union monitor (Brownsville); 1894?-1901? Bridgeport monitor. United with Brownsville clipper to form Clipper monitor (Brownsville)
PBro Jl 13-20,S 7 1894
PUn N 25 1893;Ja 17,F 3 1899;F 2 1900;Jl 11 1902[03-05]

BRIGHTON *See* BEAVER FALLS

BRISTOL

BUCKS county gazette. w Ag 14 1873-1926||
OClWHi Mr 16 1882
PBriC [1872]-[84;88]-[1926]

BUCKS county independent. w 1920-32||
PBriC [1921]-[32]

Bristol daily COURIER. d O 3 1910+
pub 1910+

Weekly COURIER. w 1912-13||
pub complete

BROOKLINE

HAVERFORD township news. w 1928+
pub [1928]+

BROOKVILLE

DEMOCRATIC republican. *See* Brookville republican

GAZETTE. *See* Brookville republican

Brookville GRAPHIC. w 1876-79||
1876-N 30 1877 as Jefferson county graphic
NN O 6 1876-[77-78]

JEFFERSON county graphic. *See* Brookville graphic

JEFFERSONIAN. *See* Brookville republican 1832-39

JEFFERSONIAN democrat. w 1878+
P Jl 31 1889+

Brookville REPUBLICAN. w 1832-Ap 1839||
1832-34 as Gazette; 1834-36 Jeffersonian; 1836-37 Democratic republican. Followed by Clarion democrat (Clarion)
MDeHi D 22 1836
NNHi D 1 1836;Mr 7 1838
PBL Je 12,Jl 31 1834;F 12 1835

REPUBLICAN. w Ag 10 1859+
P 1928

BROWNSVILLE

AMERICAN observer. w 1825-26||
Merged with Genius of liberty (Uniontown)
DLC Ja 31 1826

CLIPPER monitor. w Je 1 1853-Jl 1 1928||
Follows Brownsville free press. 1853-Ja 21 1907 as Brownsville clipper. Merged with Brownsville telegraph
OCHi My 1 1878
OClWHi Ap 4 1866
P Je 1889-1912
PBro My 29,S 11 1884;F 18 1886;Ap 23,D 20 1888;F 7-21 1889[93-94]Je 29,S 12 1895;O 12,D 14 1899;F 1 1900;Mr 7,Je 22,Ag 25 1911;S 20, D 20 1912;My 30-Je 1913;Je 12,Jl 3 1914;O 29 1915;Ja 5,My 18 1923
PUn [1894;1905]

FAYETTE and Green Jacksonian galaxy. w Ag 4 1827-
PUn Ag 11 1827

FAYETTE journal. w Mr 27 1838-
DLC Ap 3 1838

Brownsville FREE PRESS. w Ap 15 1840-My 25 1853||
Followed by Brownsville clipper, later Clipper monitor
DLC My 6 1840

INTELLIGENCER. w 1831-
CSmH Ag 3 1833
MoHi Mr 13 1832

Brownsville TELEGRAPH. d Ja 27 1915+
PBro [1927]+

THREE towns. *See* Uniontown news (Uniontown)

Brownsville TIMES. w,sw S 3 1857-
w 1857-Je 1861
MWA [S 24-D 17 1857]Ja 14 1858-Je 12,Jl 16-O 25 1861
VRC Mr 14 1860

UNION monitor. *See* Weekly monitor (Bridgeport)

WESTERN observer. w N 19? 1838-
DLC Ja 23 1839

*WESTERN register. w 1817-
Title varies: Western register and Brownsville gazette
MWA Mr 3 1823
PUn My 5-19 1821

BRYN MAWR

HOME news. w 1877+
Ag 22 1890-My 1893 as News and home news
pub Jl 8 1881+
PNoHi [1882]-88
PP F 3,My 25 1928[30]+

NEWS and home news. *See* Home news

BUTLER

AMERICAN citizen. *See* Butler citizen

BUTLER county citizen. *See* Butler citizen

BUTLER county whig. w Je 24 1846-
NNHi Ag 1846-My 1851
PPi 1846-Ap 11 1855

Butler CITIZEN. w,d D 9 1863-1920||?
1863-72 as American citizen; 1873-83? Butler county citizen
w 1863-1909?
MWA Ja 10 1866
P Je 28 1889-Je 1919
PPiHi 1863-D 4 1867

DEMOCRATIC herald. *See* Butler herald

Butler EAGLE. w 1870-1908||?
PPiHi [N 16 1870-Je 1906]

Butler EAGLE. d 1902+
P 1927+

Butler HERALD. w Mr 14 1823-1917||?
1823-My 1842 as Butler repository; My 1842-61 Democratic herald; 1861-72 Union herald; 1872-99 Zieglers democratic herald
CSmH S 3 1830
DLC Jl 23 1824;Je 18-25 1828;O 27 1852
N Jl 16 1824
P N 14 1835-Ap 21 1838;Jl 12 1839-Je 1896;Jl 1897-1912
PBL Mr 14,O 10,D 5-12 1835;My 14-21 1836; Ag 4 1847
PKiK [1829]
PPiHi Mr 25 1825
PW Jl 18 1840;Mr 3 1841

Butler INTELLIGENCER. w
P Je 15 1833-D 11 1841

Butler REPOSITORY. *See* Butler herald

*Butler SENTINEL. w O 7 1820-
DLC Je 28,Jl 12,26-Ag 23,S 20,N 1 1823
OClWHi N 11 1826

UNION Herald. *See* Butler herald

PENNSYLVANIA (*Continued*)

BUTLER—*Continued*

WESTERN sentinel and democratic press. w My 29 1830-
CSmH Jl 31 1830

ZIEGLERS democratic herald. *See* Butler herald

CALIFORNIA

MONONGAHELA VALLEY spirit. w
VRC Ag 25,O 4,D 13,27 1860;Ja 10-24,F 14-21,Mr 7-21,Ap 4-11,25-My 2,16,30,Je 13,Jl 4,Ag 6,O 1 1861;F 5 1862

CAMBRIDGE SPRINGS

To 1897? as Cambridgeboro

ENTERPRISE-NEWS. w,sw 1892+
1892-1921? as Enterprise
w 1892-1900?
pub 1910+

CAMP EDWARD

KNAPSACK. w
P F 26 1862
PScrG F 26 1862

CANONSBURG

Canonsburg HERALD. w 1872-1906||
1888-92 as Local herald
CtY Ja 14 1881
P Jl 1889-Ag 23 1906
PCanN F 2 1876
PCanP [1872]-[88]

LOCAL herald. *See* Canonsburg herald

Canonsburg NOTES. w 1875-1905||?
1875-85? as Rural notes (title varies slightly)
pub O 3 1891;O 13 1893
P F 1880-N 16 1882
PCanB F 2 1876

Canonsburg daily NOTES. d Ap 11 1894+
pub 1894+
P Mr 29 1909-18

RURAL notes. *See* Canonsburg notes

CANTON

Canton SENTINEL. w My 1871+
pub 1910+
PToHi [1904;20-27]

CARBONDALE

ADVANCE and Jermyn advocate. w My 23 1857-1918||?
Follows Carbondale transcript and Lackawanna journal. 1857-89? as Advance; 1890?-99? Advance and advocate
MWA D 19 1857
PCar 1857-[79;82-83]-[86]

Carbondale CRITIC. w My 1879-
PCar [1879]-[82]

Carbondale DEMOCRAT. *See* Lackawanna citizen

Carbondale GAZETTE. w My 5 1842-46||
N Ag 11 1842
PCar [1842]-[46]

Carbondale JOURNAL. d Ap 1838-41||
P-M D 8 1838
PCar [1838]-[41]
PHi D 8 1838-D 3 1840
PWbW D 20 1838

LACKAWANNA citizen. w 1845-Ap 1 1854||
1845-49 as Carbondale democrat; 1849-50 Lackawanna citizen and Carbondale democrat
MWA O 8,22 1852
PCar [1845]-[53]
PWbW My 21 1852

LACKAWANNA journal. *See* Carbondale transcript and Lackawanna journal

Carbondale LEADER. w,sw,tw,d Je 1872+
w 1872-84?;sw 1885?-86?;tw 1887?
PCar [1872]-[82;84]-1932
PScrHi O 26 1883;Mr 12 1936

Carbondale TRANSCRIPT and Lackawanna journal. w 1849-57||
1849-51? as Lackawanna journal. Followed by Advance and Jermyn advocate
MWA N 26 1852
PCar [1849]-[51;53]-57
PScrHi O 26 1849
PWbW My 28 1852;N 11 1853

CARLISLE

Carlisle ADVISER. w 1821-25||?
Title varies slightly
MiU [Jl 14 1824-Je 29 1825]
PWcHi [1824-25]

Carlisle AMERICAN. w Mr 1855-63||?
Merged with Carlisle herald, later Volunteer-herald
OHi Jl 20 1864
PCarlHi [1855]-F 25 1863

AMERICAN democrat. w 1847-
DLC Jl 10 1851-53
PHHi Je 7 1849

***AMERICAN volunteer.** w S 15 1814-D 1909||
United with Carlisle herald to form Volunteer-herald
DLC Jl 25 1839-[Mr-My,N-D 1852;F-Je,D 1853; Ag-N 1854;F-My,N 1855-Mr 1858]
MWA Mr 11 1824;S 12 1833-Mr 3 1836
NcD Ja 16 1840;Ap 28 1842[47-48]S 25 1851
NhD D 25 1845
P O 8 1835-Ja 8,Je 15 1848-Je 7 1849;Je 9 1853-63;Je 22 1865-Je 13 1867;Je 17 1869-Je 8 1871;My 27 1885-1909
P-M F 19,Ap 9,My 7 1835;N 7 1839;Jl 19 1855

DEMOCRATIC republican. w Ja 20 1824-Ja 2? 1830||
Follows Carlisle whig. Title varies slightly. United with Carlisle gazette to form Carlisle republican
MWA Ap 28 1824;Mr 5 1829
PCarlHi 1824[29]

Carlisle EXPOSITOR and people's advocate. w Ja 12 1830-D 1 1836||
1830-Jl 16 1832 as Expositor, and people's advocate. United with Carlisle herald to form Carlisle herald and expositor, later Volunteer-herald
DLC Ja 12 1830
MWA Ja 30-Mr 19,Ap 9-S 24,O 22-29,N 12-19 1832;F 18 1833

Carlisle GAZETTE. w Ja 1823-Ja 12 1830||
United with Democratic republican to form Carlisle republican
MnHi [1826]-29
N F 22,Mr 15-Ap 12,D 27 1826
NjR O 25 1826
P D 16 1829
P-M Jl 8 1823;Ap 11,D 12 1827;Ja 16 1828
PCarlHi [1823-24]Ap 1 1829;Ja 6 1830
PShH D 3 1828

Carlisle GAZETTE. w Ag 1897-N 1 1900||
PCarlHi 1897[98-99]1900

Daily GAZETTE. d O 25 1899-O 18? 1900||
PCarlB 1899
PCarlHi 1899-Ja 19 1900

Carlisle evening HERALD. d S 20 1886-D 31 1919||
1886-D 18? 1909 as Carlisle daily herald
P S 20 1886-S 19 1888;89-95;98-1901;05;Ag 16 1909-19

Carlisle HERALD. w *See* Volunteer-herald

HERALD and mirror. *See* Volunteer-herald

LOCAL mirror. *See* Carlisle mirror

Carlisle MIRROR. w,sw F 23 1875-Mr 10 1881||
F-Ag 3 1875 as Local mirror(w) United with Carlisle herald to form Herald and mirror, later Volunteer-herald
w F-Jl 1875
P 1875-Ja 14 1879
PCarlHi 1875-78

PENNSYLVANIA statesman. sw
NhD Ja 3 1846

PENNY stranger.
DLC S 3 1842

Carlisle REPUBLICAN. w Ja 21 1830-
Formed by the union of Carlisle gazette and Democratic republican
CSmH Jl 22 1830
DLC Ja 21 1830;Ag 11 1835-Ja 4 1838
MWA Ag 12 1830
PBL S 11 1833;S 1,D 17 1835;My 5 1836;Ag 30 1838
PCarlHi 1830-[38]

Evening SENTINEL. d D 13 1881+
1881-S 11 1889 as Daily evening sentinel
P Je 1899+
PCarlHi 1881-[90]-92[94]-1932
—w ed *See* Valley sentinel

VALLEY sentinel. w,sw My 1874-1924||?
w 1874-Jl 1908
P Jl 1889-Je 25 1912
—d ed *See* Evening sentinel

Carlisle VOLUNTEER. d 1900-19||?
Title varies: Evening volunteer; Carlisle daily volunteer; etc.
P My 21 1905-Je 1909

***VOLUNTEER-HERALD.** w Je 30 1802-D 25 1919||?
1802-1909 as Carlisle herald (title varies: . . . and general advertiser; . . . and Cumberland and Perry advertiser; . . . and expositor; Herald and mirror)
CSmH S 9 1830
DLC F 22 1827;Mr 20,Je 26-Jl 3,24-31,S 18 1828;S 3-18,O 1,N 26-D 10,31 1829-Ja 14,1830; O 19 1842;Ag 14-21 1844;Jl 9 1851;Mr 24,Jl 7-21,Ag 18,S 8-15,O 6,N 10,D 8,22-30 1852;Ja 26-F 2,16-23,Mr 30,My 25-Je 1,22-29,N 30 1853;Ja 25,Ag 30,S 13 1854-N 5,D 3-17 1856; Mr 25-Ap 1 1857;F 10 1858
MWA Ag 22 1822;N 25 1840;Mr 23 1853;Ja 10 1855;Ap 14 1858;Je 5 1865;S 16 1864
MiU-C Ap 24(supp)1838
N Ja 17,N 13 1844
NcD D 22 1852
NhD Ja 19 1842
P 1860-1919
PCarlHi [1829;31-33;36]-[39-40]-51;53[65]68-86 [91]92
PYHi [1854]-[56]

Carlisle WHIG. w 1822?-23||
Followed by Democratic republican
PCarlHi [1822-23]

CARNEGIE

CHARTIERS VALLEY signal. w 1898-1907||
1898-1904? as Valley signal. United with Carnegie item to form Carnegie signal-item

Carnegie ITEM. *See* Carnegie signal-item

Carnegie SIGNAL-ITEM. w 1873+
1873-1907 as Carnegie item
PCarn 1895+

Carnegie UNION. w 1891+
pub 1920+
PCarn 1894+

VALLEY signal. *See* Chartiers Valley signal

CARROLLTOWN

Carrolltown NEWS. w 1879+
1879-83? as Northern Cambria news
pub 1902+
PEbHi [1879]O 29 1881

NORTHERN Cambria news. *See* Carrolltown news

CATASAUQUA

COUNTRY merchant. bw 1870-72||
Followed by Catasauqua dispatch
PCatD complete
PCatH complete

Catasauqua DISPATCH. w 1872+
Follows Country merchant
MWA Je 5 1875

Catasauqua HERALD. w Ap 28 1858-Jl 19 1861||
PCat complete

VALLEY record. w Ag 1870-97||?
NcD D 14 1871
P Jl 11 1889-Je 1897
PMcT Mr 18 1875

CATAWISSA

Catawissa NEWS item. w My 16 1878-1932||
PCataV [1878]-[1932]

CENTRE HALL

Centre REPORTER. w 1868+
pub 1868+
PBelC 1894-1909
PBloHi D 9 1915
PLewL Ap 30 1896
PStP [1868-69;72-73;80;83]85-1912

CHALFONT

BUCKS county daily news. d 1921-24||
PDoHi [1921]-[24]

BUCKS county news. w 1925+
1925-32 as Chalfont news; 1932-33 Bucks county news digest
pub [1933]+
PChalP [1925-33]

Chalfont NEWS. *See* Bucks county news

CHAMBERSBURG

CUMBERLAND VALLEY sentinel. w 1840-52||
1840-Ag 7 1846 as Chambersburg times. Merged with Valley spirit
PPFfHi Jl 14 1845
WHi Ap 27,My 11-18,29-Jl,Ag 14 1846-Mr 1850

DEMOCRATIC chronicle. w
P 1880-82

Semi-weekly DISPATCH. sw Ap 19 1861-63||
Merged with Repository and transcript, later Franklin repository
DLC 1861-My 6 1862
P 1861-My 6 1862

***FRANKLIN repository.** w Ap 21 1796-My 14 1931||
Ja-Mr 1840 as Franklin repository and Chambersburg whig; Ap 1840-My 1841 Chambersburg repository and whig; Je 1841-43? Repository and whig; 1843?-55 Franklin repository and whig; 1855-63 Repository and transcript
CSmH Ag 3 1830
DLC Ap 24,N 6 1827;Ja 15,Je 24,Ag 12-19,S 16-23,O 7-14,28,N 18,D 2 1828;Jl 14-21,S 8,29, N 24,D 29 1829-Ja 5,26 1830;O 2,N 6 1832;F 7-14,N 26 1840;My 8 1845;Ja 18 1854
MWA O 17 1844;Jl 11 1855;Ja 20-27 1858
N Ap 22 1847
NNHi F 17,Mr 16 1824;Jl 5,29,Ag 9 1825;Je 24,D 30 1828[29-32]O 28 1834;N 25 1868;F 10 1869;N 16 1870;Mr 12 1873
NjR S 16 1834
P 1821-S 1 1842;90-1912;S 1925-31
PBL 1840-[42]
PChP 1840-46;50-[55-57]-59[61-63]
PHi 1854[64]65
PPiHi D 10 1840
PToHi Ap 23 1862
WHi O 17 1844

FRANKLIN repository. d 1883-1931||
P 1928-My 14 1931

***FRANKLIN republican and Chambersburg advertiser.** w My 1817-34||
DLC Mr 20 1827;Jl 7-14,28-Ag 11,S 15-29,N 3,D 8 1829;Ja 12,26 1830;Ja 11 1831
MWA Je 11-18 1822
PBL S 25 1832
PChP [1825;27-28;31-33]

FRANKLIN review. w My 1895-96||?
Merged with People's register
P S 26 1895-Je 25 1896
PChP 1895-My 1896

FRANKLIN telegraph. w O 2? 1831-
DLC N 6 1832
OOxM Mr 27,Ap 10-My 1832

PENNSYLVANIA (*Continued*)

CHAMBERSBURG—*Continued*

Chambersburg GAZETTE. w Ja 12? 1829-40||
CSmH S 7 1830
PChP [1829-37]

Chambersburg daily HERALD. d 1878-86||
Merged with Valley spirit
PChP [1881-82]

Saturday LOCAL. w 1876-78||
Merged with Franklin repository
PChP N 25 1876-78

Weekly MESSENGER. w
DLC 1841-S 14 1842;S 20 1843-Mr 20,Ap 3-17, My 8-15,Je 12,26,Ag 21,O 9 1844-S 5 1850
P S 1834-Jl 10 1844

OLD flag. w Jl-N 1864||
PChP Jl 21-28,Ag 25-N 3,17 1864

PEOPLE'S register. w N 1877-1925||
P Jl 1890-1925
PChP 1897-1923

PUBLIC opinion. w Jl 1869-1912||?
Merged with People's register
pub 1869-[76-77]-[79]-[82-83]-[92]
NNHi S 12 1871;Ja 7 1873
P N 22 1883-D 13 1912

PUBLIC opinion. d 1901+
pub S 1902+
P Je 3 1931+

***Der REDLICHE registrator.** w 1813?-
In German
DLC N 4-11 1828

Chambersburg REPOSITORY. *See* Franklin repository

SPIRIT and times. *See* Valley spirit

TILT-HAMMER. w Jl 29 1840-
Campaign paper
DLC Ag 19 1840
OClWHi O 14 1840

Chambersburg TIMES. 1840-46 *See* Cumberland Valley sentinel

TIMES. w 1858-
MsHi O 19-26 1860

VALLEY spirit. w Jl 8 1847-1930||
1847-62 as Valley spirit and Cumberland and Franklin county democrat; 1862-63 Spirit and times. Merged with Public opinion
P 1879-1912
PCh 1847-82

VALLEY spirit. d 1878-1930||
P My 10 1887-Je 24 1896
PChP 1878-84;86;1903[08]10-13
PHHi O 10 1873;Jl 14 1897

Chambersburg WHIG. w 1834-40||
United with Franklin repository to form Repository and whig later Franklin repository
P Ja 23 1835-Ja 24 1840
PChP Je 1834-39

CHARLEROI

Charleroi MAIL. d Je 5 1900+
pub O 1905-16[08]-13[21;23]+

L'UNION des travailleurs. w 1900-S 14 1916||
In French
IU [Ap 16-S 14 1916]
IaHi [1901-Je 1903]
NNC [1900-16]
WHi Mr 1901-S 7 1916

CHARTIERS

Chartiers UNION. w 1888-90||?
PCarn [Je 8 1888-O 17 1890]

CHESTER

Chester ADVERTISER. w
PCHi Ja 18 1868

Chester ADVOCATE. *See* Delaware county advocate

Chester BUG. w 1850-
PCHi My 18 1850

DELAWARE county advocate. w 1869+
1868-71 as Chester advocate; 1871-74 Chester advocate and Delaware county item
pub [1868]-1905:29+
PCHi Je 5 1869;Ap 29,Jl 8 1876;N 4 1922

DELAWARE county democrat. w Ag 1867-1916||?
P Je 27 1889-1912
PCHi Je 3,S 23 1871

DELAWARE county republican. *See* Chester republican

Chester NEWS. d 1872-1901||
1872-99 as Chester evening news
NjR Ap 1879
PCT [1872-74-76-79]81-[84-85]-[87-89]-[92]-[95-96]-[1901]

POST BOY or Delaware county union. *See* Upland union

PUBLIC press. w 1929?+
PCHi [1929]-[35]

Chester REPUBLICAN. w,d Ag 30 1833-1923||
1833-95? as Delaware county republican(w) 1896?-99? Delaware county morning republican. Merged with Chester times
MWA F 20 1857
MnHi [1862-63;65-66]
NbHi S 12 1862;Ag 23 1872;Ag 2 1878
OClWHi Mr 5 1869
P-M N 13 1836
PCC Ag 30 1919
PCHi N 29 1835[37-39]Je 18 1841;Ja 27 1843;F 28 1845[46-63;65-70;72;75;95]Mr 17 1895;Ag 4 1900;S 7 1901;O 2 1916;Ap 11 1917
PCT [1833-37;40]-67;94[95]-[1900]-[23]
PWcP Mr 17 1876

Chester TIMES. d S 1876+
pub S 7 1876+
P Jl 1889—
PCHi [1883;1901]Je 27 1902;Ap 11 1917;S 7 1926;Ja 9 1932
PP [1928]+

***UPLAND union.** w N 8 1817-F 19 1861||
1817-26 as Post boy or Delaware county union
Suspended from Mr 30 1852-58
DLC Ag 22 1837
MWA Ap 1 1823
MiU-C N 11,D 23 1834;Mr 28,N 14 1837
P Ag 1834-My 16 1843
PCHi S 7 1830;S 18 1832[38-52;60]
PMedD Ag 17 1824

Weekly VISITOR; or, Delaware county gazette. w 1828-
CSmH Ag 27 1830
DLC Jl 4-Ag 22,S 5,19-O 3 1828;O 20 1832
MWA Mr 1 1831
PCHi Jl 16 1830

CHRISTIANA

Christiana LEDGER. *See* Local ledger

LOCAL ledger. w Ja 3 1883+
1883-1915? as Christiana ledger
pub 1883+

CLAIRTON

Clairton CRUCIBLE. w 1902-06||?
PPiHi O 1902-06

Clairton PROGRESS. w 1917+
pub N 1917+

CLARION

Clarion DEMOCRAT. w Ap 1 1839+
Follows Brookville republican (Brookville) 1839-O 1840 as Strattanville clarion republican
pub [1876]+
MWA D 14 1863-S 16 1865
P Je 27 1889+
PBL Ag 7 1847
PClK [1894]-[1929]
PW Jl 30 1840;S 9 1841;Jl 14 1842

Clarion JACKSONIAN. w,sw 1873-N 28 1901||
w 1873-O 3 1895
PClK [1893]-[1901]

Clarion REPUBLICAN. w 1869+
1880-99 as Clarion republican gazette
NNHi My 9 1873;Jl 7 1876
P Je 11 1889+
PClK [1893]-1928

STRATTANVILLE clarion republican. *See* Clarion democrat

CLAYSVILLE

Claysville RECORDER. w Je 1888+
pub 1888+

CLEARFIELD

BANNER. *See* Clearfield republican

COUNTRY dollar. *See* Clearfield republican

Clearfield DEMOCRAT. w S 7 1833-39||?
United with Banner to form Democratic banner, later Clearfield republican
N O 26 1833
P-M Je 28,Jl 12 1834;F 28 1835

DEMOCRATIC banner. *See* Clearfield republican

PENNSYLVANIA banner. *See* Clearfield republican

Clearfield PROGRESS. d 1912+
pub 1912+
P Ap 1927+

RAFTSMAN'S journal. w Je 1854+
P S 1862—
PSuHi F 10 1858

Clearfield REPUBLICAN. w 1827+
N 1827-34 as Pennsylvania banner; 1834-36 Republican and pioneer banner; 1836-Ja 1839 Banner; Ja 1839-Je 21 1849 Democratic banner; Je 21 1849-F 15 1851 Country dollar
CSmH F 13 1830
DLC Jl 4 1838;N 4 1840
MWA Ap 3 1861
MnHi [1839-42]
P Jl 1889-Je 1910
P-M Mr 17 1832;Mr 21 1833;Je 8 1837
PLewL Jl 6 1839;Jl 19 1844;S 18 1847

CLYMER

Clymer HERALD. w 1911-13||
PBaS [1911]-[13]

COALDALE

Coaldale OBSERVER. w O 1 1910+
pub 1910+

COALPORT

Coalport STANDARD. 1885-Mr 1934||
United with Houtzdale citizen to form Citizen-standard (Houtzdale)

COATESVILLE

ANTI-MASONIC examiner and Chester county recorder. w 1829-Ag 1831||
United with Anti-Masonic register (West Chester) to form Anti-Masonic register and Chester county examiner, later Register and examiner
PPiHi D 7 1830

CHESTER VALLEY union and Chester county times. w,sw Je 6 1863-1909||?
1863-1907? as Chester Valley union
w 1863-86?
MWA Ap 11-18 1868
PCHi Ap 2 1887[94-95]Jl 22 1896
PCoaW [1873-79]Ap 23 1881;F 15 1899
PWcT 1894[95]
WHi Ag 21 1869
—d ed *See* Daily union

GENERAL advertiser and journal of the times. w My 1836-38||?
PCHi Ap 16,D 3 1836

Coatesville RECORD. d O 9 1908+
pub [1908]+
KHi D 1 1926
P 1908+
PCoaH N 11 1911;N 11 1918
PCoaW [1908-09]F 21 1928
PP [1928]+

Coatesville weekly TIMES. w My 1879-1928||
P 1883-1923
PCHi Je 15 1882;Ap 16 1887;Jl 18 1896;Ja 28 1905
PCoaC 1884-1928
PCoaH D 14 1889;Ja 7 1928
PCoaW F 3 1883;My 6 1893;My 23,Ag 24 1895;S 10 1898;N 13 1909;My 1 1926;Ap 30 1927;Ja 7 1928
PPot Je 11-18 1892

Daily UNION. d D 1901-13||
PCHi D 26 1901[02]
PCoaW D 2 1901;Je 21 1902;My 28 1906;Ag 19,S 11 1909;Je 8,14 1911;F 1 1913
—w ed *See* Chester Valley union. . .

COLLEGEVILLE

INDEPENDENT. w Je 4 1875+
1875-81 as Providence independent
1875-Ap 5 1883 pub in Trappe
pub 1875+
PPeS Mr 15 1883

COLUMBIA

Weekly COURANT. w 1838-1916||?
1838-39? as Pennsylvania courant and Columbia and Marietta advertiser
DLC Ja 4 1840
NjR [Ag 21-N 20 1839]
PColN [1914]-[16]
PLaHi [1871-72]80-85
PPCHi [1887-88]

Columbia DEMOCRAT. *See* Columbia independent

Columbia HERALD. w D 3 1867-1911||?
MWA Ag 4 1870
NN O 24-D 5,19 1872-Mr,Ap 17-Je 1873
PLaHi Ag 4 1870[73]-75
PPCHi [1888]

Columbia INDEPENDENT. w 1872-1912||?
1872-89 as Columbia democrat
P Je 1891-D 25 1912
PLaHi [1872]

Columbia daily NEWS. d 1888+
pub [1895-97]-[1902-03]-[12]+
P S 28 1888

PENNSYLVANIA courant. *See* Weekly courant

PENNSYLVANIAN. w N 1 1822-
MWA N 15 1822
NN N 22 1822

PROTECTOR. w Mr 22 1843-
MWA My 17 1843

Columbia SPY. w Je 17 1830-1919||?
Title varies: Columbia spy and literary register; Columbia spy and York and Lancaster county record; Columbia spy and Lancaster and York democrat
CSmH Je 24 1830
DLC Je 23,Ag 25 1831;N 9 1832;My 2 1840;Jl 4 1846
MWA Jl 1833-Jl 1834;My 9 1835
N O 19 1833
NNHi Je 16 1831;Ja 12 1832;Je 20 1834
P Jl 13 1889-1912
P-M O 13 1831
PBL [1840-44]
PLaHi Jl 29 1830[31-33]-[35]N 19,D 3-10 1836[37]My 30,Ag 15 1840[43]D 7 1844;Ap 12 1845[46-48]Ap 27,D 7 1850;Je 19,Jl 3,Ag 7 1852;Ap 16,My 7 1853;Je 10,15,D 21 1861[62] Ja 10,Mr 21 1863;S 24 1864[65-67]-S 4 1869
PPL N 23 1850

CONNEAUTVILLE

AMERICAN republican banner. w 1853-
OClWHi Je 9 1855;Ja 5,Mr 15-29-Ap 5,19,My 17 1856

PENNSYLVANIA (*Continued*)

CONNEAUTVILLE—*Continued*

Conneautville COURIER. w N 14 1847+
1864-70 as Record and courier
MWA N 19 1862
OClWHi F 9 1876;F 14 1877;Ap 18,My 2 1878;F 20,Jl 24 1879
P Jl 1889-1912
P-M S 12 1849
PMe Mr 26 1886

CRAWFORD county record. w
United with Courier to form Record and courier, later Conneautville courier
PMe S 20 1862

CRAWFORD statesman. w
PMe Ag 25 1838;My 4 1839

RECORD and courier. *See* Conneautville courier

ROUGH and ready. w
P-M S 6 1848

Conneautville WHIG banner. w F 18? 1852-
MWA D 24 1853
OClWHi Ag 6 1853;Mr 11,Jl 1,22,Ag 12 1854

CONNELLSVILLE

COURIER. w Jl 1879-Je 28 1929||
1879-Jl 12 1888 as Keystone courier; Je 19 1888-F 6 1903 Connellsville courier
pub [1879]-[1929]
DLC 1911-28
P Jl 1889-Je 1912
PBro Ja 6 1881
PCo [1898]-[1929]
PUn Je 19 1896

Daily COURIER. d N 10 1902+
pub [1902]+
PCo 1902-[28]-[31-33]+
PUn [1895-96]98-[1904-05]

Connellsville ENTERPRISE. w Jl 6 1855-
DLC 1855-Je 10 1859

FAYETTE monitor and Youghioghenian. *See* Monitor

KEYSTONE courier. *See* Courier

MONITOR. w 1870-Ap 1899||
Ap 12 1870-95 as Fayette monitor and Youghioghenian; 1895-97 New Monitor
PUn [1894-97]

NEW monitor. *See* Monitor

Connellsville NEWS. w 1898-1920||?
PUn Mr 24 1898;Jl 1 1909

Daily NEWS. d My 11 1898-1929||
PCo [1904-11;13-16]20-[28-29]

PATRIOT. Jl 4 1891||
PUn complete

CONSHOHOCKEN

Conshohocken RECORDER. w,sw 1869+
w 1869-S 1895
pub [1879-83]-86;S 24 1887;89+
PNoHi [1882-99]

CONYNGHAM

MOUNTAINEER and Susquehanna and Lehigh advocate. Je 15 1833-
DLC Je 15 1833

CORAPOLIS

RECORD. w 1906+
pub 1906+

CORRY

Corry daily BLADE. d 1869-74||?
MWA D 3 1873
—w ed *See* Corry telegraph

Corry weekly HERALD. w 1877-S 1900||
P Jl 1889-My 1900

Corry City NEWS. w O 22 1863-
MWA O 22 1863

Corry PETROLEUM telegraph. *See* Corry telegraph

Corry TELEGRAPH. w 1865-1916||?
1865-66? as Corry petroleum telegraph
PEr My 27 1880
PPiHi Ag 10 1865
WHi Je 15 1865
—d ed *See* Corry daily blade

COUDERSPORT

DEMOCRATIC republican. *See* Northern democrat

HIGHLAND patriot. *See* Northern democrat

NORTHERN democrat. w Ja 1 1839-59||
1839-Ap 1842 as Potter pennon; Ap 1842-Ap? 1843 Democratic republican; My 26 1843-F? 1851 Potter pioneer; F? 1851-F? 1854 Potter county union; F? 1854-58 Highland patriot
PCtA S 12 1855
PCtC [1843-44]

PEOPLES journal. *See* Potter county journal

POTTER county journal. w 1848+
1848-83 as Potter journal (1853-61 Peoples journal; D 20 1872-Je 24 1874 Potter journal and news item)
MWA Ag 6 1857;D 26 1865
P Jl 1889+
P-M Je 7 1855
PCt 1848-75;82+
PCtHi 1848[49-50]-[72]+
PCtT [1867]-72

POTTER county union. *See* Northern democrat

POTTER enterprise. w My 1 1874+
pub [1897-98;1900-01;03-04;08-15]-[18]+
P Jl 17 1889-1912
PCtHi [1911]-[34]

POTTER journal. *See* Potter county journal

POTTER pennon. *See* Northern democrat

CROSS FORK

Cross Fork NEWS. w 1897-1906||?
PCtHi [1904]-[06]

DALLAS

Dallas POST. w 1888+
pub [1888-1928]+
PWbW 1897-1902

DANVILLE

Danville DEMOCRAT and tariff advocate. w 1840-Ja 1864||
Merged with Montour American
DLC My 27 1842
MWA Ja 13 1843;O 29 1852
PBL S 13 1844
PBloHi D 19 1856
PDA O 9 1863
PShH F 23 1844;O 18 1848

GEM. w 1885+
PD [1885]-[1902]
PDC [1894-99]

Danville INTELLIGENCER. w 1828-1907||?
CSmH Jl 3 1830
MWA O 29 1852
MoHi Ja 15,29 1836
NjR Ag 14 1840
P N 18 1828;Jl 8 1904-Je 15 1907
PBL S 4 1835;Ja 24 1840;Mr 21 1845;Ag 20 1847
PD Jl 15 1828-[61]N 24 1905
PDA D 26 1862[63-65]
PDC [1894]-[97-1903]O 27 1905[06-07]
PDM Jl 9 1836;My 2,26 1837;Mr 9 1838;Ap 3 1840;N 18 1864
PDN [1872-73;77]-79[84-85]
PEL Jl 10 1835
PSuHi My 24 1839

MONTOUR American. w D 11 1855-1920||?
1855-59 as Montour American; 1859- Montour herald
P Je 11 1889-Je 1910
PBf Ag 7 1879;O 26 1893
PDA O 22 1864;Ag 1867;Ag 6 1868;Ag 26,S 2 1869;My 25 1876
PDC [1894-96]-[98]-[1900-03]O 26 1905;Mr 21 1907[10-11]
PDN [1871-72]74;76-79;86;88-90[1900-01]09-16

MONTOUR county democrat. w 1895-1930||?
PDC [1898-99]Mr 2 1900;N 9 1906

MONTOUR herald. *See* Montour American

Weekly NATIONAL record. w Mr 16 1876-1901||?
1876-Mr? 1878 as Danville record
PD F 2-9,23 1878

Morning NEWS. d 1897+
pub [1899]-[1902-05;09-11]-[14-16]-[19]-[33]
P [1923]+
PBf [1911]-18

Danville RECORD. *See* Weekly national record

REPUBLICAN press. w 1821-
PWbW S 5,N 21 1821

SUN. d N 5 1883-1902||?
PDC F 10 1897
PDN 1894

*WATCHMAN. w 1820-28||
PD Mr 16 1826
PWbW S 27,N 8 1821

DARBY

PROGRESS. w 1888+
PP [1932]+

DELAWARE WATER GAP

MOUNTAIN echo. w 1878-99||?
pub Je-O only
KHi Jl 27 1889
PMilHi Ag 26 1882

DELTA

Delta HERALD-TIMES. w N 1878+
1878-Mr 9 1894 as Delta herald (title varies slightly)
pub 1878+
MdHi-H 1918
P [1932]33

DENVER

Denver PRESS. w,sw My 24 1890+
w 1890-1906
pub My 24 1890;D 24 1906+

DONORA

Donora AMERICAN. *See* Donora herald-American

Donora HERALD. d 1916-27||
United with Donora American to form Donora herald-American

Donora HERALD-AMERICAN. w,d 1901+
1901-27 as Donora American(w)
pub 1901+
CtY [Jl-Ag 1933]
OClWHi D 1923-D 12 1924

DOWNINGTOWN

Downingtown AMERICAN. *See* American republican (West Chester)

AMERICAN republican. *See under* West Chester

AMERICAN spectator and people's friend. w
PWcHi [1834]

Downingtown ARCHIVE. w 1872+
1872-87? as Chester county archive
pub 1910+
MWA Jl 8-29,Ag 12-19 1876
MiU-C Je 22 1876
PWcHi Ap 8 1876;Mr 15 1879;Mr 12 1887[93-95]Ja 4 1896
PWcT [1893]-[96]

CHESTER county archive. *See* Downingtown archive

CHESTER county democrat. w Ap 20 1830-Ja? 1833||
Follows Independent journal. United with American republican to form American republican and Chester county democrat (West Chester)
CSmH S 7 1830
Ct [1830-31]
MWA D 14 1830;Ja 31 1832
P Ap 27 1830
PBL [1830]31
PHi Ap 20 1830;Ja 22 1833
PWcHi [1830-33]
PWcLa 1830-[33]

INDEPENDENT journal. w Ag 29 1827-30||
Followed by Chester county democrat
Ct Ag 29 1827[28-29]
MWA S 25,N 6,D 4,18-25 1827;Ja 15,F 5,Jl 8,O 14 1828;Ja 27-F 3,Mr 3-10,Ap 7-14,My,Je 9-16,Jl 14-28,Ag 18-25 1829
PBL [1829]30
PHi [1827]-[29]
PWcHi [1827]-[29-30]
PWcLa [1829]30
PWcT [1827]-[30]

Downingtown NEWS. w My 1929+
pub 1931-[34]
PP [1930]-[34]
PWcHi Mr 22 1935

REPUBLICAN standard and democrat journal. w 1835-36||
Title varies
PCoaW Ag 25 1835
PWcT [1835]

TEMPERATE zone. *See* American republican (West Chester)

DOYLESTOWN

BUCKS county bauer. *See* Der Morgenstern

BUCKS county democrat. *See* Doylestown democrat

BUCKS county express and reform. w Jl 4 1827-1917||?
1827-31? as Doylestown express; 1831?-66 Bucks county express; 1866-69? Express and reform
In German
P-M N 25-D 9 1873
PDoHi [1827-28]F 1847;S 2 1856;Ja 17 1860;Jl 30 1861
PNoHi Jl 31 1860
PQZ S 4 1860

*BUCKS county intelligencer. w Jl 7 1804+
1804-Ag 3 1818 as Pennsylvania correspondent and farmers' advertiser; Ag 10 1818-22? Correspondent and farmers' advertiser; 1823?-24 Pennsylvania correspondent; 1824-27 Bucks county patriot and farmers' advertiser; 1827-43 Bucks county intelligencer and general advertiser
Ct S 19 1825
DLC D 8,29 1824;Jl 17 1826;Je 30 1828;N 4 1840
ICHi S 23 1835-Ja 13,27-Ap 6 1836;Mr 22,Ap-Je 14,28-Ag 16,30-S 6 1837;Mr 21-28,Ap 11-My 2,16-Ag 1,15-S 5,19 1838
MWA F 28 1825;D 24 1832;N 1854-Ap 17 1855;Je 23 1868
N S 3 1827
NN My 11 1852
NbHi N 1854-Ap 17 1855;Ja 22 1861;O 31 1865;Ja 16,S 1,O 20 1868;D 30 1876;O 26 1888;Ap 12,My 10,24-31,Je 21 1890-1900;03-[Ja-O 12 1905]-F 1,Ag 30-S 6,27-O 4,18,N 1-15 1906[07]
NjR Ag 27 1822
P Jl 1889-1912;18+
PBL Ap 28 1834;S 30 1835
PBuE S 8 1847
PChalK Ag 3,N 30 1858;Ap 17,Je 26 1860
PDoHi 1821-24[27]-90
PFgR F 14 1825
PHi 1890-[98]
PNaK [1861-77]
PNeB O 26 1836
PNhE Je 13 1831
PNhF N 16 1836;N 2 1842;Mr 19 1845
PNoHi Je 18 1827;N 24 1828
PNoT 1863-64[66]-72
PPFfHi S 30,N 18 1862;Je 16,Ag 25 1863;Mr 7,Ap 25 1865
PSoP O 19 1829;Mr 30 1836
PWcHi Ag 20-27 1822
—d ed *See* Doylestown intelligencer

*BUCKS county messenger. w Je 28 1819-Ap 2 1821||
United with Bucks county democrat to form Doylestown democrat
MWA Ja 2,16-Ap 2 1821
PDoHi Mr 26,Ap 2 1821

PENNSYLVANIA (*Continued*)

DOYLESTOWN—*Continued*

BUCKS county weekly mirror. w 1869-1917||?
DLC D 6 1873
PDoHi Ja 15 1876;Ja 11 1887

BUCKS county patriot and farmers' advertiser. *See* Bucks county intelligencer

BUCKS county political examiner. *See* Political examiner. . .

BUCKS county republican. w Jl 28 1829-32||
Follows Political examiner
MWA O 20 1829
PDoHi [1829]-[32]

CORRESPONDENT and farmers' advertiser. *See* Bucks county intelligencer

***Doylestown DEMOCRAT.** w S 17 1816-1919||?
1821 as Bucks county democrat
Suspended from S 27 1820-Ja 2 1821
CSmH S 7 1830
Ct [1827-28;31]
DLC My 22 1832;Ja 6-13,F-Mr 3,17-24,Ap 7-21,My 5,19-Je 2,16-Jl 21,Ag 11-18,S-O 6,20,N-D 1847;O 24 1848;O 19,N 2 1852
MWA Ap 10-My 15,29-O 9 1821;Je 2 1829;F 16 1864;Mr 28 1876;Mr 5 1878
NbHi Ja 11-Mr 22 1853;Je-S 6,N 1 1859;Ja-Mr 13,Ap 10-Ag 7,21-S 4,18,O-N 6 1860;Ja 8,Ap 23,Jl 9,N 5,D 10 1861;S 30-O 7 1862;Je 30,Ag 18,N 10 1868;Je 25 1889-99;1902-03;Jl 21 1904;My 11,Jl 6,N 30 1905;Jl-Ag,S 13,O 11,25 1906
NcD N 17 1847
NhD Ag 10 1842;D 24-31 1845
NjHi S 20-27,O 4 1825;My 2,30 1826
NjR Ap 11 1826;Mr 17-24 1868
OClWHi Ja 17 1860;O 20-27 1863
P Jl 1864-Je 1865;Jl 1889-S 1894;N 1895-S 1899;Jl 1900-Je 1912
PBL [1834-35]Ja 29,F 12,My 20 1840;S 4 1844
PBuE My 2 1838
PChalS Ja 2,F 27 1866
PDoHi 1821-29[34]-60
PEL D 12 1832;Je 3 1834
PHolP [1845-46]
PNeB O 3 1865
PNeBr 1823
PP [1861]-34
WHi Ag 17 1852

Daily DEMOCRAT. d 1890-1921||
PChalS Ja 1 1895;Ja 2 1899;Mr 8 1902
PDoHi [1890-1905;07-21]

DEMOCRATIC standard. w Ap 19 1859-Ap 1 1861||
NbHi N 1 1859;Ja 3-10 1860
PDoHi Jl 12 1859

Doylestown EXPRESS. *See* Bucks county express and reform

INDEPENDENT democrat. *See* Doylestown watchtower

Doylestown daily INTELLIGENCER. d 1886+
Jl 7 1929 is Anniversary ed
MnU Jl 7 1929
P F 1928-32
PDoHi [1886-89;92-1932]
PP [1930]+
—w ed *See* Bucks county intelligencer

JACKSON courier and democratic advertiser. w
DLC Ap 8 1835-F 3 1836

Der MORGENSTERN. w Ag 11 1835-89||?
1835-43 as Bucks county bauer. Title varies slightly
In German
DLC My 10 1843
MWA Ag 22 1876
PDoHi Ap 27 1841[43-62]
PPeS S 20 1837;Mr 19 1845;S 6 1864;Ja 21 1868;Mr 10 1874

PENNSYLVANIA correspondent. *See* Bucks county intelligencer

POLITICAL examiner and Bucks county advertiser. w N 24? 1827-Jl 1829||
1827-D 1 1828 as Bucks county political examiner. Followed by Bucks county republican
DLC Jl 7,Ag 4,18,S 15-29,N 3-17 1828
MWA Ja 14 1828
NjHi D 1 1828
PDoHi [1827-29]
PLewL 1829
PNeB N 10 1828

REFORM von Bucks. w 1866||
United with Bucks county express to form Express and reform, later Bucks county express and reform
In German
PDoHi Ag 21 1866

Daily REPUBLICAN. d N 1 1893-1909||
PDoHi 1893-[1901]-[03]-[09]
PNhF Jl 14 1895

Doylestown SPY. w 1853-54||
PDoHi Jl 16,30,S 17 1853;Mr 14 1854

Doylestown WATCHTOWER. w F 1847-53||
1847-52 as Independent democrat
PDoHi [1848]-[53]

DREXEL HILL

ARONIMINK beaver. *See* Upper Darby township review

UPPER DARBY communities review. *See* Upper Darby township review

UPPER DARBY press. w 1926+
pub 1926+

UPPER DARBY township review. m,w Jl 4 1929+
1929-Je 5 1930 as Aronimink beaver; Je 5 1930-Ap 9 1931 Upper Darby communities review
pub [1929]+

DU BOIS

Du Bois COURIER. w,d 1879+
w 1879-88
P Jl 1884-Je 1885;Jl 1889-Je 1903

DUNDAFF

INVESTIGATOR. w F 18 1830-
CSmH S 2 1830
NjHi Je 24 1830
PEL F 25 1830;F 10 1831

NORTHERN Pennsylvania. w 1828-33||
MnU Jl 13 1832
P-M Jl 20 1832
PCar [1832]-[35-36]
PWbW [Je 15 1832-O 3 1834]

Dundaff REPUBLICAN. w 1828-
CSmH S 1 1830
PCar 1828-[32]
PEL O 13 1830;O 6 1836

DUNMORE

DUNMOREAN. w 1912+
pub [1912]+
PScrHi Ap 4 1936

Dunmore PIONEER. w 1886-98||
Title varies slightly
PHsHi D 17 1887;Ag 17 1889;Ag 1898
PScrHi Ja 5 1893

DUQUESNE

OBSERVER. w 1892-1911||
1892-97? as Tri-town tribune. United with Duquesne times to form Times observer, later Duquesne times

Duquesne TIMES. w D 9 1904+
1912-19? as Times observer
pub 1904+
P 1904+
PDu 1904+

TRI-TOWN tribune. *See* Observer

DUSHORE

Dushore GAZETTE-HERALD. w 1887-1912||
1887-1905? as Sullivan gazette
P Jl 11 1889-1912
PSulR 1887-95

REPUBLICAN news item. w 1906?+
PSulR 1922+

SULLIVAN democrat. w 1851-
PSulR 1851-62

SULLIVAN gazette. *See* Dushore gazette-herald

SULLIVAN review. w 1878+
pub 1878+
P 1920-23;26+

EAST BERLIN

East Berlin NEWS-COMET. w 1893+
1893-1926? as East Berlin news; 1927?-30? East Berlin and Biglerville news
PEaK 1900-30

EAST BRADY

East Brady REVIEW. w N 27 1885+
pub 1885-[92-98]+

EAST GREENVILLE

PERKIOMEN weekly ledger. w N 28 1890-1912||?
PPT 1890-1912
PPeS F 20,O 28 1892;Jl 31 1896;Ap 14 1899
PPeT N 28 1890

EAST LIBERTY

Papers published in East Liberty are listed under Pittsburg

EAST STROUDSBURG

JEFFERSONIAN republican. *See* East Stroudsburg press and Jeffersonian

East Stroudsburg PRESS and Jeffersonian. w Ja 15 1840-1923||?
1840-53 as Jeffersonian republican; 1853-1910? Jeffersonian (Stroudsburg)
DLC Je 23,O 6 1841
MWA Ja 17 1861
P Ap 11 1889-D 19 1912
PEHi Jl 23 1857
PESS 1840-[50;53]-99[1919]-21;23
PHHi F 13 1873
PMcC Je 28 1877
PMilC Jl 2,16 1908
PStrR [1844]-[50;53]-[75;77-79]
PWbW S 30 1852

Morning SUN. d D 12 1925+
pub 1925+
PP 1934+
PScrHi D 1 1934

EASTON

ALT Northampton. w F 9 1841-Ap 12 1843||?
PE 1841-[43]

AMERICAN free press and Northampton farmer. *See* Easton semi-weekly free press

Easton ARGUS. w,sw 1827-1916||
F 15 1827-Je 17 1830 as Pennsylvania argus; Je 17 1830-F 10 1853 Easton democrat and argus. Merged with Easton express
w 1827-90
MWA D 15 1831;D 13 1832
NN Mr 29 1832;Ag 21,O 9,D 11 1834
NhD Ag 17 1848
NjHi Ag 15 1828;Ja 7 1836
P Jl 1889-1913
PE 1827-[43-44]-[57]-[1906-07]-[13]-[16]
PEHi Jl 28 1864;My 3 1880
PRHi Jl 13 1827

Easton daily ARGUS. d 1879-D 29 1916||
DLC 1898
KHi My 5 1890

Der BEOBACHTER. w Mr 22 1860-Ap 18 1861||
In German
DLC complete

Sunday CALL. w My 6 1883-My 27 1923||
PE [1883]-[1923]
PEHi Ap 3 1921

Easton CENTINEL. *See* Easton sentinel

CORRESPONDENT und demokrat. *See* Der Northampton correspondent

DELAWARE democrat and Eastern gazette. w My 4 1827-N 21 1828||
United with Pennsylvania argus to form Easton democrat and argus, later Easton argus
Ct [1827]
DLC Jl 17 1828
MWA Ag 16 1827;Ja 10,Mr 13 1828
NjHi O 15,N 1 1827
PE complete
PRHi Jl 12 1827

Easton DEMOCRAT and argus. *See* Easton argus

Easton morning DISPATCH. d My 16 1874-Ag 28 1875||
1874-F 15 1875 as Eastern morning dispatch
PE [1874-75]

EASTERN morning dispatch. *See* Easton morning dispatch

EASTONIAN. w,d 1850-57||
w 1850-Mr 1854
PE [1850]-[52]Ap 2 1854;My 26 1855;Jl 31 1857

EXPOSITOR. w Ag 19-N 18 1822||
PE [1822]

Easton EXPRESS. d N 1855+
Title varies: Easton daily express; Evening daily express; Daily express; Daily evening express
pub 1926+
MWA O 20(supp)1873;My 11 1886
NN O 20 1873
NbHi O 6 1876;Je 21 1877
NjHi [F 22-Jl 19 1872]
P 1926+
PE N 5 1855-59[61-62]65-[67]-[90]+
PEHi S 7 1861;O 6,17,D 28 1864;My 3 1880;Ag 8 1885
PEL 1876[77]-85
PHi [1856]-[64;66-67]

Easton semi-weekly FREE PRESS. w,sw 1852-1926||
1852-57 as Northampton farmer; 1857-59 American free press and Northampton farmer; 1859-80 Easton free press
w 1852-80
NbHi Ja 16 1868;N 2 1877
NjHi D 21 1865
P-M F 15 1854
PE [1854-55;57]-[59]-74;Ja 12 1876[77-78]-[1911]-13
PEHi Ap 27 1865;Jl 26 1866;Mr 4 1869;F 17 1870;S 2 1890

FREE PRESS. d S 25 1866-S 1926||
Title varies: Evening free press; Daily free press; Easton daily free press. Merged with Easton express
MWA F 17,D 24 1877
P Jl 1889-Je 1890;92-Ja 1926
PE complete
PEHi S 6,N 9 1869;Jl 22 1874;Ja 20 1875;Je 27 1876;Ja 30 1878;Ag 14 1884;Mr 30 1921

JEFFERSONIAN and Northampton, Bucks, Pike, Wayne, and Lehigh telegraph. w Jl 28 1831-
DLC S 8 1831
PE Jl 28 1831

***MOUNTAINEER.** w Ja 7 1820-Ag 17 1821||
PDoHi Ap 13 1821
PE [1821]

Daily NEWS. d Ag 11 1834-
PE Ag 11 1834

Der NORTHAMPTON correspondent. w Ja 25 1806-1902||
1860-75 as Correspondent und demokrat. Merged with Easton argus
In German
PE 1861-[88-89]-93;95-[99-1900]-02
PEHi [1821]-[34]S 14 1843;S 14 1848[64-65]F 9-16 1870[71]Ja 21,N 27 1872
PPeS Je 14 1839

NORTHAMPTON county journal. w Ap 11 1828-S 16 1868||
1828-Jl 1840 as Northampton whig; Jl 1840-D 4 1850 Whig and journal; D 4 1850-Ja 5 1859 Easton whig
CSmH Jl 13 1830
DLC Ag 15-22 1828
MBAt Ap 26 1865
NjR Jl 7 1852
PE [1828]-[68]
PEHi [1840]Ag 5 1846

PENNSYLVANIA (*Continued*)

EASTON—*Continued*

NORTHAMPTON democrat. w Ag 20 1834-35||
In German
PE Je 3 1835

NORTHAMPTON democrat. w,sw Ap 28 1882-1915||?
Merged with Easton argus
w 1882-99?
PE Ap 28 1882
PEC [1905]-[09]

NORTHAMPTON farmer. w? Jl-N 1835||
Campaign paper
PBL S 23 1835

NORTHAMPTON farmer. 1852-57 *See* Easton semi-weekly free press

NORTHAMPTON messenger. w 1840-41||
United with Easton centinel to form Easton sentinel and Northampton messenger, later Easton sentinel
PBL [1841]

NORTHAMPTON whig. *See* Northampton county journal

PENNSYLVANIA argus. *See* Easton argus

***PENNSYLVANIAN.** w Je 16 1815-N 1824||
1815-D 12 1823 as Spirit of Pennsylvania
NjHi Ag 9 1822;O 22 1824
PE [1821]-[23-24]
PWbW D 7 1821

PLAIN DEALER. w Ag 24 1878-
PE Ag 24,S 28 1878

REPUBLICAN star and general advertiser. w
MWA N 12,D 1822-D 23 1823[F 10-Je 1824;Mr 22 1825-Ag 15 1826]Ag 12-26,S 23-O 14,N 4,18-25 1828

REPUBLIKANISCHE presse. w F 15 1827-F 5 1830||
In German
PE [1827]-[30]

*Easton **SENTINEL.** w Jl 1 1817-1917||
1817-34 as Easton centinel; 1841-43 Easton sentinel and Northampton messenger
KHi O 16 1906
N Ag 19(extra)1825
NjHi [Mr 23-N 16 1821]Ja 11,Ag 23,N 1 1822; Je 6,Jl 11 1823[24]O 7,28 1825;My 19,S 29 1826;N 30 1827;Ja 11,F 8 1828;Je 12-19,S 18 1829
PBL D 20 1833;My 30,N 12 1834[35;41-43]My 30,Je 13 1844;D 24 1846[47-48]
PE 1821-[44;49]-51;My 1854;60-[68]-[71]-79[88-89]97-99[1902]-[17]
PEHi 1824-25
PHi Ag 10 1821
PMilA Jl 14 1833
PMilD Mr 24 1824
PRHi Jl 14 1826
PWbW Ap 13-20 1821

SPIRIT of Pennsylvania. *See* Pennsylvanian

Easton **TIMES.** d,sw,w Ap 18 1858-Je 6 1861||
Ap 19 1858-Je 11 1859 as Morning times (d);Je 13? 1859-Ap 25 1861 Easton times (sw)
DLC S 1859-61
NjR Jl 22 1858
PE Ap 19 1858;Je 11,Ag 18 1859;Ja 14,S 17 1860

TRUE democrat. w 1874||
PE O 29 1874

Der **UNABHANGIGE demokrat.** w 1843-60||
Title varies slightly. United with Der Northampton correspondent to form Correspondent and democrat, later Der Northampton correspondent
In German
PE [1848]-60
PEHi 1847[48;53]Mr 9,My 11 1854;F 22,My 17,Je 21 1855;Ag 26 1857;N 3 1858;F 2 1859;My 21,Ag 8-15 1860

WEYGODT gridiron. Ag 11 1826||
PE complete

Easton **WHIG.** *See* Northampton county journal

EBENSBURG

ALLEGHANIAN. w 1853-71||
Followed by Cambria herald, later Mountaineer-herald
PEbHi O 5 1854[59]-[68-69]
PEbM S 1859-[70-71]
PJ Mr 30 1865

CAMBRIA freeman. w Ja 1867+
DLC S 6 1878
P Jl 1889-Je 1932
PEbHi 1867-82;85-1903
PWayHi O 13 1870

CAMBRIA herald. *See* Mountaineer-herald

DEMOCRAT and sentinel. w 1852-66||
1852-53 as Mountain democrat
MWA Je 1 1854;Jl 30 1862
PEbHi 1857-66
PJR Ja 27,S 9 1857

DEMOCRATIC journal. w 1838-
DLC Jl 5 1838
PEbHi Ag 29 1839

MOUNTAIN democrat. *See* Democrat and sentinel

MOUNTAIN sentinel. w 1844-53||
United with Mountain democrat to form Democrat and sentinel
PEbHi Je 4,S 11 1845
PJR [1845-48]

MOUNTAINEER. w 1836?-60||?
PEbHi [1858]-[60]
PJ Jl 25,Ag 22 1838;Ap 4 1860
PJR [1838-39]Ap 19 1843

Ebensburg **MOUNTAINEER.** w 1891-98||
United with Cambria herald to form Mountaineer-herald
PEbHi Jl 21 1892;D 29 1894

MOUNTAINEER-HERALD. w 1871+
Follows Alleghanian
1871-98 as Cambria herald
pub 1871+
NNHi O 17 1872
P 1931+
PEbHi 1898-[1916]
PJR S 3 1903;Ag 13 1913

Ebensburg **SKY.** w Jl 1831-
DLC N 8 1832
MWA S 26 1833
PEbHi [1831]-37
PHi Mr 22 1832
PJR S 2 1835

EDINBORO

Edinboro **INDEPENDENT.** w F 1880+
P Jl 18 1889-1912

ELDRED

Eldred **EAGLE.** w 1878+
pub 1878+

ELIZABETH

Elizabeth **BLACK DIAMOND.** *See* Elizabeth herald

Elizabeth **HERALD.** w Ag 1873+
1873-74 as Monongahela Valley messenger; 1874 Elizabeth black diamond
P Jl 1889-Je 1912
PClaP 1873+
PPiHi S 19 1874-1931

MONONGAHELA VALLEY messenger. *See* Elizabeth herald

ELIZABETHTOWN

Weekly **CHRONICLE.** w 1869+
pub 1919+

ELKLAND

Elkland **JOURNAL.** w Ap 4 1876+
pub [1890-92;94-96;1907-10;17]+

EMLENTON

HOME news. *See* Emlenton news

Emlenton **NEWS.** w,sw 1885+
My 14-N 1886 as Home news
sw My 14 1886-89
pub [1885]+

Emlenton **TIMES.** w 1875-76||
DLC Mr 2,Jl 27 1876

EMPORIUM

CAMERON county press. *See* Press-independent

Emporium **INDEPENDENT.** w 1867-1921||
United with Cameron county press to form Press-independent
P [1904]-12

PRESS-INDEPENDENT. w 1866+
1866-1921 as Cameron county press
P Je 13 1889-D 20 1928

EPHRATA

Ephrata **REVIEW.** w F 10 1873+
1873-83 as Saturday review
pub 1873+
PLaHi [1903-04]

ERIE

Erie **ADVERTISER.** w Ap 1 1876-93||?
PEr [1879]-89

Erie **CHRONICLE.** w 1840-
MWA O 27 1840[41-Mr 1 1842]Ja 3 1854

CONSTITUTION. w O 12 1853-
MWA D 21 1853
OClWHi Jl 16 1856;Ap 1,Ag 19,O 21,N 25 1857[58]

Erie City **DISPATCH.** w 1851-Ja 1895||
United with Erie gazette to form Dispatch-gazette, later Erie gazette
MWA D 5 1863;F 13 1864
OClWHi Ap 15 1865
PEr 1863-Ja 10 1895
PErW My 3 1856;Ja 1,F 4 1862

DISPATCH-GAZETTE. *See* Erie gazette

Erie **DISPATCH-HERALD.** d 1861+
1861-Ja 21 1922 title varies: Erie morning dispatch; Erie daily dispatch
DLC Ja 18 1865(facsimile)
ICHi O 3,18,N 6 1865
MWA O 17 1868;Jl 23 1872;Ag 25 1876;Mr 24 1884
OClWHi Ap 27 1865
P [1889]+
PEr [1864]+
PErW Ag 15 1866;Ap 29 1870
WHi Ag 16 1869

*Erie **GAZETTE.** w Ja 15 1820-1901||?
Ja 17 1895-Mr 11 1897 as Dispatch-gazette
CSmH S 9 1830
DLC Je 18-25,S 3-17,O 1,D 24-31 1829;O 22 1840
ICHi Jl 15 1830;O 5,N 16 1865
MWA Ap 10 1823;Mr 9-16,30 1826;F 15,S 13 1827;Mr 6-20,Ap 3 1828;Ja 6,F 4,25,Mr 11 1830;Mr 1-8,Jl 5 1832;Mr 13,N 13 1834;Je 4,S 10,O 22 1835;Ja 14,Mr 3,My 5,Jl 28,Ag 25 1836; F 23,My 4-11,Je 8,Jl 6,Ag 10,S 21,O 26 1837; Mr 8,22,Ap 5,26,My 17,Je 28 1838;Jl 22 1847;S 27 1860;F 1 1866
NFre Ap 12,Je 7-14,S 6,27,N 8 1832;Mr 7,28,Jl 18,O 17 1833;Ja 16 1834
NcD Mr 30 1826
OClWHi Je 10 1841;Je 10 1858;Je 14 1860;F 21 1861;S 26 1872;S 12 1895
P Jl 1889-O 31 1901
PBL [1821]-[32]-37;40[41]48-[58]
PEr 1895-99
PErC [1826]Jl 24-31 1828;D 17,31 1829;Mr 4-11 1830;Je 30 1831;Ag 23 1832;My 30 1833;Ag 23 1838[47]Ag 14 1851;O 21 1852;S 21,O 5 1854;Ap 20 1884;Ja 3-10 1886;Je 14 1888
PErW Ja 29 1829;N 10 1831;Ja 31 1833;Ag 20 1835;S 8 1842

Erie Sunday morning **GAZETTE.** w Mr 16 1875-94||
Mr-Je 1875 as Saturday evening gazette
PEr complete

Erie Sunday **GRAPHIC.** w My 2 1880-D 1896||
United with Erie Sunday messenger to form Erie Sunday messenger-graphic
PEr [1892-93]

Erie weekly **HERALD.** w 1878-1905||?
PErW F 26 1884;S 4 1886;S 29 1888

Erie evening **HERALD.** d Jl 20 1878-Ja 21 1922||
United with Erie daily dispatch to form Erie dispatch-herald
PEr [1890-1922]

Erie **JOURNAL.** d 1896-98||
PEr [1896]-[98]

Erie Sunday **MESSENGER-GRAPHIC.** w F 1894-1910||?
1894-96 as Erie Sunday messenger
PEr [1898]-[1910]

Erie evening **NEWS.** d 1892-1903||?
PEr N-D 1894

Erie **OBSERVER.** w,sw 1830-Je 1898||
w 1830-Ja 1895
Ct [1833-35]
DLC D 15 1832
MWA O 29 1831
N O 12 1833
NNHi Ap 28 1832;Ja 15 1873
OClWHi Ap 30 1836;My 8 1847
P Je 1889-98
PBL Jl 6 1833[34-35;37]Ap 14 1838[43-44]Ap 12,My 17 1845;Jl 22 1848
PEr [1830-60;62-80;84]1930-32
PErC F 1 1834
PErW S 30 1848;Mr 15 1856
PMe [1855]-[59]
PNc [1840]-[43]
PW S 14 1833;My 30,Jl 11,Ag 1 1840;Mr 6,O 30 1841

Erie Sunday morning **POST.** w 1902-04||
PEr [1902]-[04]

SLEDGE. w Jl 14 1840-
PW Jl 28 1840

Erie **TAGEBLATT-WOCHENSCHRIFT.** d O 1 1884+
1884-1930 as Erie tageblatt
In German
PEr [1899-1920]

Erie daily **TIMES.** d Ag 12 1888+
PEr 1891+
PPiHi Mr 31 1933

TRUE American. w 1854-
MWA My 28 1858

ZUSCHAUER und sonntagsgast. w 1852-99||?
1852-53 as Erie-zuschauer; 1854?-81? as Zuschauer am Erie; 1882-92? Zuschauer in der neuen heimath
In German
MWA D 23 1853;Ag 24 1876
MnHi [1866]

EVERETT

BEDFORD county press. *See* Everett press

Everett **PRESS.** w 1868+
Mr 1868-Ja 1881 as Bedford county press
P Jl 1889-Je 1910

FALLSTON

BEAVER FALLS union and Beaver county advocate. w Ja 13 1838-
PPi [1838-Mr 2 1839]

FARVIEW

Farview **ECHO.** ir
PHsHi [1920-24]
PScrHi [1922]Ja 1924;Je 1 1933

FAYETTE CITY

Fayette City **JOURNAL.** w 1899+
pub [1905]+
PUn D 25 1903;Ja 15,Ag 26 1904;Mr 5 1905

PENNSYLVANIA (*Continued*)

FOREST CITY

Forest City NEWS. w D 8 1887+
pub 1887-95;97+
PScrHi Je 6 1935

FORT WASHINGTON

Fort Washington TIMES. w D 1881||
Followed by Ambler gazette (Ambler)
PAmbG complete

FRACKVILLE

Frackville LEDGER. w 1898+
PSheN 1898+

Frackville STAR. w 1892-1908||?
PFraM 1892-93

FRANKFORD

Papers published in Frankford are listed under Philadelphia

FRANKLIN

DEMOCRAT and arch. w Jl 1845-
Formed by the union of Venango democrat and Democratic arch
PW Jl 30 1845

DEMOCRATIC arch. w Jl 11 1842-Je 1845||
United with Venango democrat to form Democrat and arch
PW Jl 11 1842

DEMOCRATIC republican. w
DLC Mr 9 1829

Franklin GAZETTE. w
DLC My 13-27 1844

Franklin daily HERALD. d 1904-My 4 1919||
United with Evening news to form Franklin news-herald
PFr [1904-05]-[09]-19

INDEPENDENT press. w 1876-84||
United with Venango citizen to form Venango citizen press
PFr complete

Franklin INTELLIGENCER. w Ag 5 1834-42||
DLC Ag 5 1834
MWA S 19 1837
NNHi N 22 1836;F 27 1838
PFr [1834]-[39]
PW Je 16 1835

Daily LEADER. d 1900-03||
PFr F 1900-[03]

Franklin NEWS-HERALD. d F 1878+
1878-My 5 1919 as Evening news
P 1927-My 1933;Mr 1935+
PFr 1882+

VENANGO citizen-press. w F 1855+
1855-84 as Venango citizen
MWA Je 17 1869;Ag 17 1876
P Je 27 1889-1912
PFr 1884+

VENANGO democrat. w 1823-Je 1845||
Title varies: Venango democrat and Western register; etc. United with Democratic arch to form Democrat and arch
CSmH Jl 6 1830
Ct S 26 1837
PBL S 29 1835;N 15 1839;Ap 21 1840;Ap 5 1843;Je 10 1845
PLewL F 2 1833
PPot S 12 1837
PW Ag 11 1835;Jl 7 1840;Ag 24,N 30 1841;Ap 5,Je 7 1842

*VENANGO herald. sw S 1820-28||
Merged with Venango democrat
PW Ap 25,My 2,9 1822

VENANGO spectator. w 1849-1916||?
MWA D 22 1853;My 2 1855
OClWHi S 21-N 23 1864
P Jl 1889-1912
PFr D 1849-93
PMe 1880-81

Franklin VINDICATOR. w 1902-16||?
PFr [1903]-16

FREEBURG

CENTRAL courier. *See* Freeburg weekly courier

Freeburg weekly COURIER. w 1866-Ja 12 1934||
1866-Ja 1868 as Central courier. Merged with Middleburg post (Middleburg)
PDoC Ja 9 1889
PFreB 1868-1934
PMiC [1892-1900;03-05;12-14;26]
PMiCo 1930-34

FREELAND

PRESS. w 1893+
PFrlF [1895]-1927
PFrlJ [1927]-33
PHazS 1930+

FREEPORT

COLUMBIAN, and Freeport, Leechburg and Warren advertiser. w
DLC F 2 1841

Freeport JOURNAL. w My 1876+
P Ja 17 1879-86;88-Je 1893;Jl 1894-Je 1912; 18;20[32]+

GALETON

DISPATCH. *See* Leader-dispatch

LEADER-DISPATCH. w 1893+
1893-1902? as Dispatch
PCtHi [1923]D 29 1927

GALLITZEN

Gallitzen ITEM. w 1906+
PEbHi S 11 1931;D 10 1935
PPiHi S 11 1931

GERMANTOWN

Papers published in Germantown are listed under Philadelphia

GETTYSBURG

ADAMS centinel. *See* Gettysburg star and sentinel

ADAMS sentinel. *See* Gettysburg star and sentinel

ANTI-MASONIC star. *See* Gettysburg star

*Gettysburg COMPILER. w S 16 1818+
1818-My 18 1857 as Republican compiler; My 18 1857-Ap 27 1868 Compiler
pub 1821+
CSmH Jl 3 1830
DLC O 9,30 1832;Ja 11 1847-48;69
MWA N 22 1865
NjR Ag 1837-S 17 1839
OOxM Ag 20,O 22,N 26 1828;F 4,Mr 18,Ap 29,My 20-Je Jl 14 1829
P Jl 1889-Ag 1919
P-M O 27-N 3 1829
PBL Jl 24 1832;F 24,Jl 2 1835;S 9 1844
PGC [1893;1902-03]+
PYHi Ja 23 1900
TxU F 4 1850

PEOPLE'S press. w Ja 9 1835-Ja 15 1836||
PGT 1835[36]

REPUBLICAN compiler. *See* Gettysburg compiler

Gettysburg STAR. w 1827-My 29 1867||
1827-N 3 1830 as Anti-Masonic star; N 3 1830-Ja 23 1831 Anti-Masonic star and republican banner; Ja 23-O 4 1831 Star; O 4 1831-Ap 10 1832 Star and Adams county republican banner; Ap 10 1832-My 23 1849 Star and republican banner; My 23 1849-62? Star and banner. United with Adams sentinel to form Gettysburg star and sentinel
CSmH Ag 14 1830
Ct Ap 24 1827
DLC S 17 1863
MHi N 16 1835;Mr 14 1836
MWA O 24 1836;Ag 15 1856;Ap 27 1865
PDoC Ja 3 1832;Ag 20,O 15 1833[35-36]Jl 19 1861;Ja 8,O 15 1863
PGS 1827-[30-32]-[40;45]-[67]
PYHi [1839]40

*Gettysburg STAR and sentinel. w N 12 1800+
1800-F 1 1826 as Adams centinel; F 8 1826-My 29 1867 Adams sentinel
pub 1821-67;73+
CoHi My 15 1882
DLC Jl 9,Ag 13-20,S 24,O 8,N 5-12,26 1828;Jl 22,S 9-23,O 7,N 3 1829;O 2 1832;N 30 1840
MWA My 24 1852
M Jl 28 1824
MNHi N 1832-O 1834;Jl 21 1871;F 12 1873 extra:D 6 1832
NjHi [1821-Mr 9 1825]
OClWHi O 10 1827
OOxM Mr 18,Ap 29,My 27-Je 10,Jl 15 1829
P D 1841-N 1843;Jl 9 1889-1921
PGC 1893+
PPCHi Jl 12 1852
PYHi 1841[43]-45
TxU S 11,O 2 16,N 6 1868
WHi N 1828-O 1829

STAR and sentinel. d My 5 1914-Ag 31 1917||
PGS [1914]-[17]

Gettysburg TIMES. d Ja 1 1904+
pub 1909+
P O 3 1927-32

GIRARD

COSMOPOLITE-HERALD. w 1867+
1867-86 as Cosmopolite; 1886-1910 Girard cosmopolite
NBuG Je 25,S 24,N 26,D 3-10,24-31 1869;Ja 13 1871
NNHi Ap 3 1873;Ag 3,S 7 1876
P Jl 1889-1912
PEr [1879-80]

GLASSPORT

Glassport TIMES. w Ja 30 1930+
PClaP 1930+

GLEN ROCK

ITEM. w 1870+
P S 1879-F 17 1882
PYHi Je 18 1897

GLENSIDE

EAST MONTGOMERY county news. w F 7 1923+
1923-31 as Glenside news
pub 1923+
PP 1932+

Glenside NEWS. *See* East Montgomery county news

GREAT BEND

PLAINDEALER. w Ag 1 1874+
1874-84? as Great Bend reporter
pub 1888+

Great Bend REPORTER. *See* Plaindealer

GREENCASTLE

CONOCOCHEAGUE herald. *See* Echo-pilot

ECHO-PILOT. w 1849+
1849?-53 as Conococheague herald; 1853-55 Franklin intelligencer; 1855-57 Franklin gazette; 1857-60 Ledger; 1860-66 Pilot; 1866-S 1893 Valley echo
P F 1863-Je 1864;Jl 1895-1912
PUn Ja 13 1863

FRANKLIN gazette. *See* Echo-pilot

FRANKLIN intelligencer. *See* Echo-pilot

LEDGER. *See* Echo-pilot

PILOT. *See* Echo-pilot

Greencastle PRESS. w Ap 1878-1912||
P Jl 1889-S 13 1912
PGrT [1897]-1908

VALLEY echo. *See* Echo-pilot

GREENSBURG

AMERICAN herald. *See* Greensburg herald

Greensburg CLIPPER. w Ja 3 1896-1909||?
1896-Ap 1901 as Latrobe weekly clipper (Latrobe); My 1901-02? Westmoreland clipper
PGrT 1901-04
PPiHi My 21-28 1897

Greensburg DEMOCRAT. w N 18 1853-64||
United with Westmoreland republican and farmers' chronicle to form Democrat and republican, later Westmoreland democrat
P D 30 1853-D 1 1857
PPiHi F 22 1855

DEMOCRAT and republican. *See* Westmoreland democrat

FARMERS' register. *See* Westmoreland democrat

FRANK COWAN'S paper. *See under* Pittsburgh

Greensburg GAZETTE. *See* Greensburg herald

*Greensburg HERALD. w Ag 22 1811-72||
1811-F? 1832 as Greensburg gazette (Ap 25 1828-F 1 1828 Greensburg gazette and farmers' and mechanics' register) F 1832-N 8 1850 Westmoreland intelligencer; N 8 1850-F 5 1856 Intelligencer; F 5 1856-N 1857 American herald. United with Greensburg tribune to form Tribune-herald
CSmH D 16 1825;S 10 1830
DLC Jl 24 1827;Je 26-Jl 3,17-Ag 14,S-O 2,30,N 20-27 1829;Ja 1-8,22-29 1830;N 13 1840
MWA Ap 3 1829
NjP 1821-S 20 1822
OClWHi Mr 8 1839
P D 1823-Ag 1827;F 8 1833-Ja 1834;N 8 1850; Ja 16 1861
PGrT [1828]-[30]-[33]-[44-50]
PPiHi My 13,O 28 1856;Je 13,S 18 1859;My 13 1863;S 13 1864;O 24 1866;Je 24 1868

INTELLIGENCER. *See* Greensburg herald

NEWS record. d Ja 21 1915-N 6 1924||
PGrT 1915[16-17]-[19]-[24]

PENNSYLVANIA argus. w My 25 1832-1922||?
Title varies: Pennsylvania argus and farmers' and mechanics' advocate; Pennsylvania argus and Westmoreland democrat
DLC N 2 1832;O 21 1852
P Jl 1889-S 1912
PBL Ap 3 1835;Ja 30 1840;Jl 29 1842;S 20 1844; O 24 1845
PBf F 2 1881
PGrL [1834-35;37]-54;64-66[72]-74[76]-78[80]-86[90]-[1911-12]
PGrT [1832-34;68]-70;72[80]-82[84]-[90;1907]-12
PMilC F 22 1872
PPiHi Je 28 1839;F 7,Mr 27 1856;Ja 22,Mr 12,Jl 9 1857

Greensburg PRESS. d 1881-1908||
1881-91? as Evening press
PGrT [1881]-[91;97]-1908
PPiHi Ap 1 1889

Greensburg PRESS. w 1881-1923||?
Title varies: Weekly press; Greensburg press and tribune-herald; etc.
P S 1887-1912
PGrT 1881-1923
PJ My 25 1899

Greensburg daily RECORD. d Ap 1 1886-93||?
PGrT [1886]-90

Greensburg and Indiana REGISTER. *See* Westmoreland democrat

Morning REVIEW. d Ap 1903+
pub 1908+

Greensburg SENTINEL. w 1840-
DLC Jl 30 1841

Greensburg morning STAR. d Mr 20 1901-O 31 1903||?
1901-Jl 1902 as Morning star
PGrT [1901]-[03]

Daily TRIBUNE. d F 4 1889+
pub 1889-[92-94]-[96]+
P 1927+

PENNSYLVANIA (*Continued*)

GREENSBURG—*Continued*

TRIBUNE-HERALD. w Jl 22 1870-1908||
1870-F 8 1872 as Greensburg tribune. United with Greensburg press to form Greensburg press and tribune-herald, later Greensburg press
P 1875-Je 1903
PGrT 1870-[1908]
PPiHi D 26 1894

WESTMORELAND clipper. *See* Greensburg clipper

*WESTMORELAND democrat. w My 24 1799+
My 24-N? 1812 as Farmers' register; N 26 1812-Ap? 1818 Greensburg and Indiana register; Ap 25 1818-Ag 1828 Westmoreland republican; Ag 1828-64 Westmoreland republican and farmers' chronicle; 1864-69? Democrat and republican
pub [1871-81]+
MWA Ja 12-26,F 23-Ap 6,20-My 18,Je 1,15-29, Jl 13-S 21,O 5,19-26 1821;Je 8 1864
P My 24 1899
P-M Ja 1 1869
PGrT 1821-[24]
PJ My 24 1899;My 21 1902
PPiHi D 25 1835;S 6 1839;S 22 1842;F 11 1863; Ja 31 1866-Ag 21 1867;Ag 28 1868-Ag 1869;S 1870-71;76-80;82-83;Ag 28-N 8 1884;My 13 1891-94;96;1901-05
WHi Jl 13 1821

WESTMORELAND intelligencer. *See* Greensburg herald

WESTMORELAND republican. *See* Westmoreland democrat

GREENVILLE

ADVANCE-ARGUS. *See* Record-argus

EXPRESS. *See* Record-argus

GAZETTE and national republican advocate. w Jl 31 1832-
DLC O 9 1832

INDEPENDENT press. *See* Record-argus

Evening RECORD. d N 1 1897-1923||
United with Advance-argus to form Record-argus

RECORD-ARGUS. w,d 1848+
1848-52 as Express; 1852-56 Independent press; N 22 1856-62 Times; 1862-71 Rural argus; O 1871-N 1877 Shenango Valley argus; N 1877-1923 Advance argus
w 1848-1923
P Jl 1889-1912;28+

RURAL argus. *See* Record-argus

SHENANGO VALLEY argus. *See* Record-argus

TIMES. *See* Record-argus

GROVE CITY

Grove City HERALD. w 1903-Ap 24 1926||
1903-S 1 1922 as Mercer county herald. United with Grove City reporter to form Grove City reporter-herald
PGcR [1906-10]D 27 1912;D 26 1913[22]-24[26]

MERCER county herald. *See* Grove City herald

Grove City REPORTER-HERALD. w,sw 1879+
1879-99 as Grove City telephone; 1900-Ap 1926 Grove City reporter
w 1879-Ap 1926
pub [1884]-[99]1926+

Grove City TELEPHONE. *See* Grove City reporter-herald

HALIFAX

Halifax HERALD. w F 28? 1844-
MnHi O 3 1844

HAMBURG

Hamburg ADVERTISER. w Jl? 1863-
MWA Ja 21 1865

Hamburg BERICHTER. w Jl 21 1871-73||?
In German
MWA Jl 21 1871

ITEM. w Ap 22? 1875+
pub 1902+
MWA Ap 1 1876
PHam 1918;20-[22]-32

Hamburger SCHNELLPOST und allgemeiner demokratischer anzeiger. w My 1841-98||?
In German
MWA S 1 1863;S 16 1873

HANOVER

Hanover ADVANCE. w 1891-94||?
United with Hanover citizen to form Weekly record

Hanover CITIZEN. *See* Weekly record

DEMOCRAT and farmers' and mechanics' advocate. w
PYHi Ja 6 1843

*Hanover GAZETTE. w Ap 4 1805-64||
ICHi Mr 6 1828
MWA Je 4 1829
PHHi [1838]-[41]
PTHi Ap 5 1837;Mr 11,Ap 29 1846;Je 30 1858
TxU Mr 21 1850

*Hanover GUARDIAN. w Ag 1818-
DLC F 13 1828

Hanover HERALD. w Je 1872-1915||?
PYHi Jl 1 1876;S 24 1881;S 30 1905

Evening HERALD. d 1894-1904||
United with Hanover daily record to form Record-herald
MWA N 26 1897

Das Hanover INTELLIGENZ-BLATT und öffentlicher anzeiger für York und Adams counties. w 1824-26||
In German
PYHi Ap 7 1824-Ap 13 1826

Weekly RECORD. w 1861-1924||
1861-94? as Hanover citizen
PYHi 1900

RECORD-HERALD. d 1892-1929||?
1892-1904 as Hanover daily record
PYHi Mr 4 1915

Hanover SPECTATOR. w 1844-92||
PYHi N 10 1848[56]Mr 21 1872[75-76]N 5 1885 [87]

HARLEYSVILLE

Harleysville NEWS. w 1886-1912||?
PPeS F 17 1892;D 5 1894;N 10 1897

HARRISBURG

Harrisburg daily AMERICAN. d D 6 1850-53||?
Merged with Harrisburg telegraph
MWA Ag 2 1851
P D 27 1850-Ap 25 1851
PHHi [1851]
PP F 11 1851

AMERICAN standard. w
PHHi Ap 28 1852

Der AMERICANISCHE bauer und Pennsylvanische democrat. w
In German
NNHi Ap 3 1829

ANTI-MASONIC inquirer. *See* Republican and anti-Masonic inquirer

ANTI-MASONIC state democrat. w D 2? 1835-Mr? 1837||
United with Pennsylvania intelligencer to form Pennsylvania intelligencer and state democrat, later Pennsylvania intelligencer
MWA [Ja-Ag 1836]Ja 31,Mr 7-14,28 1837

Harrisburg ARGUS. w N 24 1827-31||?
DLC Ja 5-12,F 23-D 1828;Mr 4(extra)Jl 4 1829;Ja 21,F 1,Ap 16,My 21,N 20,D 10 1845;Ja 28,Mr 18,Ap 15,My 20,Je 3-10,Jl 1-8,22-29,S 2-9,O 7,N 4-11,25,D 9-30 1846;Ja 13-20,F 3-10,Mr 3,24,Ap 8-15,My 6-13,Je 3-10,Jl 8,Ag 26,S 16,O 28,D 16 1847;Ja 13 1848
MWA N 24 1827;F 16,Mr 22,Je 7-21,Jl 5-12,S 6-13,27-O 11,25-N 8 1828;Ap 4,25 1829
P 1827-Jl 4 1829
PBL [1827-29]
PHHi [1827]-Mr 26 1831

Harrisburg ARGUS. w Mr 23 1843-48||
DLC Ap 6 1844
NhD Je 3,Jl 8,Ag 26,N 4,25,D 23 1847;Ja 6-20, F 10-Mr 2,23,Ap 6 1848
NjP 1843-45
PBL [1843-44;46]Ag 12,S 5 1847;Ja 20 1848
PHHi Ja 21 1845;Ja 29 1846;Jl 1,S 30,D 23 1847

BOMB-SHELL. w -N 1 1848||
Campaign paper
MWA N 1 1848

BOROUGH item. d Ja 2 1852-
Title varies: Item; etc.
DLC D 9 1853
PHHi [1853;55]

Morning CALL. *See* Commonwealth

*Harrisburg CHRONICLE. w,sw My 31 1813-42||
1813-Ag 17 1818 as Chronicle or Harrisburg visitor; Ag 24 1818-Ja 27 1820 Chronicle, and Harrisburg advertiser
sw during sessions of legislature
CSmH D 6(extra)1838
DLC Ja-My 1821;Je 1833-My 1824;N 12 1832-N 3 1834;D 19-26 1838;Ag 7 1839;N 18 1840;Ag 23,S 13-20 1842
MWA [1821-25]Ag 26 1876
MoHi Ap 7 1834
N Ag 1 1825
NNHi Ap 1823-N 19 1824
NcD [Je-S 1822]-[Ap-My 1823]Ap-[N-D]1824-Mr 1825;Ja-[Ap]-[N-D]1834-[36-Je 1838]
OClWHi S 13 1880
P 1821-Je 17 1840
P-M Mr 28 1822;Ja 27 1823;Ag 9-23 1824;Ag 11 1828;Ag 17 1829
PBL [1833-34]
PEL Ja 3 1833
PHHi 1821-42
PHi [1821-22]
PLewL D 15 1827;Ja 12 1828;Mr 19,30 1829;D 2 1833
PPiHi D 12 1838
PPot D 5 1838
PToHi [1837-39]
PWbW 1829-34

CLAY bugle. w Ja-O 1844||
Campaign paper
DLC Mr 21 1844
MWA S 12 1844
MoSM Jl 25,S 12 1844
NNHi F 8,29,Mr 21,My 15,Je 12,Ag 8,S 19 1844
P [1844]
PPot Ap 4,8,Ag 8 1844
PRHi [1844]

COMMONWEALTH. w 1822-24||
sw during sessions of legislature
DLC D 13 1823;F 17,Mr 5,Ap 20,My 18 1824
MWA O 13 1823
NN N 25 1823
PBL [1822-24]
PHHi D 31 1822

COMMONWEALTH. w Jl 29 1843-
NjR Jl 29 1843

COMMONWEALTH. d 1885-99||
1885-98 as Morning call
P Ja 12 1885-88
PHHi S 17 1885[97]-[99]

Sunday COURIER. w 1903+
1903-11 as Courier
pub 1903+
P Mr 29 1908-Je 1912

DAUPHIN county journal. w 1877-87||
United with Pennsylvanische staatszeitung to form Pennsylvanische staatszeitung and Dauphin county journal
In German
P 1883-87
PPoU 1877[81]-87

DEMOCRATIC state journal. w Mr 28 1832-Ja 25 1837||
United with Pennsylvania reporter to form Pennsylvania reporter and democratic state journal, later Pennsylvania reporter
Ct [1835]
P Mr 1835-37
PBL Je 13-20,Jl 11 1835

DEMOCRATIC union. w,sw Je 7 1843-Ag 1855||
Formed by the union of Pennsylvania reporter, Keystone, and State capitol gazette. United with Pennsylvania patriot to form Patriot and union, later Patriot
sw during sessions of legislature
DLC Ap 16,Ag 27,N 19,D 10 1845[Ja-Ap]Je 3,24-Jl 8,22-29,Ag 12,S 9,30,O 28,N 4,25-D 1, 16-30 1846;Ja 13 1847-D 13 1848;O 27 1852
MWA My 12,Ag 11 1852
NcD Je 3 1846[47]Mr 15-22 1849
NjR F 27 1847
OClWHi Jl 9 1845
P 1843-N 1849;Mr 23,27 1850
P-M Mr 9-23 1850
PBL complete
PEL 1843[44]
PScrG Jl 6 1844
PW O 5 1844

Der Tägliche DEMOKRAT. d
In German
PHHi Ja 5-D 29 1863

EVERY Saturday night. w Ja 1879-82||?
P My 31 1879-D 23 1882

Harrisburg daily HERALD. d D 1853-Ag 1858||
Merged with Harrisburg telegraph
P 1853-N 1855;Ag 25-D 12 1856;F 8,Ag 1858
PHHi [1855]D 25 1857[58]

HOME journal. *See* State journal

Harrisburg INDEPENDENT. *See* Star-independent

Daily INTELLIGENCER. d Ja 5? 1841-
DLC Ja 8 1841
NNHi Ja 12-Mr 9 1847

INVESTIGATOR. w
PHHi Je 25-N 5 1852

IRON gray. w Jl 15 1838-
1838-39? as Iron grey and Cumberland and Dauphin democratic signal
Also pub in Mechanicsburg
CSmH Mr 21 1840
MWA S 9 1838
PBL S 8 1838[39]Ja 25-F 1,My 2 1840

ITEM. *See* Borough item

KEYSTONE. w,sw Ag 24 1836-Je 1843||
United with Pennsylvania reporter and State capitol gazette to form Democratic union
sw during sessions of legislature
DLC 1836-My 1843
MWA Jl 26 1837;Jl 17 1839
MnHi N 9 1842
NNHi [S 1836-Je 1838]
NcD Ag-O 5,19-N,D 7-10,17-21,28 1836
NcU Jl 15 1840
NjR [F 22 1839-42]
OClWHi F 15 1839
P 1836-My 1843
P-M S 5 1838
PE 1838-43
PHi [1836]-[40]
PLaN [1840-41]
PMiltS 1836-38
PPot Ag 29 1838;Ag 28,O 16 1839
PToHi [1842-43]
PWbW Mr 28 1838

Daily KEYSTONE. d 1841-
NcD My 2,21-23,Jl 10 1845

KEYSTONE. w,sw Je 13 1848-
sw during sessions of legislature
DLC N 3 1852
MWA 1848-My,N 11-18 1851;Mr 27,Ap 21,My 12,N 17 1852
NjR [1851]
P 1848-Je 1850;Je 1851-Ag 1858

LOG CABIN rifle. w Je 6 1840-
Campaign paper
DLC Je 6,Jl 11-18 1840
MWA Jl 4 1840
NNHi Je 20 1840

MAGICIAN. w Je 27-O 26 1840||
Campaign paper
CSmH Ag 29 1840
MWA complete
PBL O 19-26 1840

Evening MERCURY. d 1871-74||?
P 1874
PHHi [1871]-[74]

PENNSYLVANIA (*Continued*)

HARRISBURG—*Continued*

*Harrisburger **MORGENRÖTHE.** w Mr 12 1799-N 5 1840||
1799-Ag 4 1800 as Unpartheyische Harrisburg morgenröthe zeitung; Ag 11 1800 Die Harrisburger morgenröthe zeitung
In German
P 1821-40
P-M Mr 1 1824;Mr 16 1837
PHHi O 4 1832

Harrisburg evening **NEWS.** d 1895-97||?
Title varies slightly
PHHi F 2,Jl 2,7 1897
PLewL O 28 1895

Evening **NEWS.** d F 15 1917+
pub [1917]+
P 1928-Je 1932;D 31 1933

OLD warrior. w F 22-O 26 1844||
Campaign paper
DLC F 22-Mr 16 1844
MWA My 25 1844
MoSM Jl 27,Ag 17 1844
P complete
PHHi My 11 1844

***ORACLE of Dauphin.** w O 20 1792-N 17 1827||
1792-Ja ? 1808 as Oracle of Dauphin, and Harrisburgh advertiser
Ct Mr 11 1826
DLC O 16,30 1824;My 27,Je 10,24 1826-Ap 21, Ag 11-25,S 8-15,N 10-17 1827
MWA Ap 6-13 1822
NNHi [F-O 1821]Mr 30-Ap 6 1822[23-Ag 1824]
NjHi Mr 2 1822;Ap 10 1824
P 1821-27
P-M Je 28 1823;Ja 8-15,F 12 1825
PBL N 15 1823;F 21,D 25 1824[25-26]Jl 14-21 1827
PHHi 1821-[25-27]
PWbW Ap 17 1824

PATRIOT. w Mr 4 1854-1904||
1854-Ag 1855 as Pennsylvania patriot; S 1855-69 Patriot and union
sw during sessions of legislature
CaOTA Ja 22 1863
DLC O 21,N 4,D 9,30 1854-Ja 6,30,F 3,Mr 3-10,31-Ap 7,O 6,N 10,24 1855[56;F-D 3 1857]Ja 20-Ap 22 1858
MWA Ag 18 1855
NNHi S 26 1832
P O 7 1854
P-M Ap 18,My 13 1861;Je 30 1863
PBL [1854-58]
PHHi D 23-30 1869
PToHi 1856-58;60-[62]
WHi Ag 30 1860-Ag,S 19 1861

PATRIOT. d 1857+
Title varies: Pennsylvania patriot; Daily patriot and union; Morning patriot; Daily patriot
pub 1868+
DLC My 17 1850;Jl 1872-Je 1873;Jl 14 1874+
MBAt Ap 19 1865
MWA Ja 22,F 5 1863;Mr 16,Jl 12 1864;F 25 1869;O 4 1876
NbHi Mr 6,16 1863;N 1 1870
OClWHi Jl 2-Ag 21 1866
P D 1858+
P-M N 5 1862;O 22 1866
PBL [1863-64]
PHHi S 9 1857;O 25,D 31 1858;S 12 1860;F 27,Mr 22 1862;Mr 18,D 29 1863;Ap 11 1864; Je 11,15 1865;Ja 8 1867;Ap 8-9 1869;S 24 1872; 74-1909;12
PLewL Ja 14 1863
PMcT [1875]
PPeS Mr 6-13 1862
PToHi 1859
Tx D 31 1872

***PENNSYLVANIA intelligencer.** sw,w D 5 1820-50||?
Follows Harrisburg republican (not in this list). 1828-34 as Pennsylvania intelligencer and farmers' and mechanics' journal; 1837-Je 1839 Pennsylvania intelligencer and state democrat; Jl 3 1839-My 28 1840 united with Pennsylvania telegraph to form Telegraph and intelligencer. See note under Harrisburg telegraph
CSmH S 7 1830;O 1 1831
Ct [1827]
CtY D 7 1837
DLC 1821-26;Ap 3,13,My 1-N 6 1827;Ja-D 22 1828;Je 30-S 22,N 3,23-D 3 1829;Ja 18,28 1830; Ja 20 1831;N 1-8 1832;Ja 7 1836;S 22 1842;Jl 12 1849
IU 1829-F 4 1830
MBAt My 25 1824
MWA Mr 26 1822;F 25,O 3 1823;O 8(extra) 1825;N 24 1826;S 11,25-O 9,23-N 6 1827;28-30; Je 7 1832;Ag 29 1833;Ja 9 1834;My-Je 8 1837; D 7 1838;Ja-F 9 1844
MiU-C Mr 10 1828
MnHi Jl 6,Ag 24 1843;Je 7 1844
N Mr 20 1834
NNHi [Ap 1823-Mr 1824;Ap-N 1827;28-Mr 1831;Ja-Je 1838]
NcD Ap 1824-Mr 1825;Jl 1,D 4 1828;Ja 4-7,Ap 9 1831-Mr 1832;Ja-Mr 6,My 29-[D]1834;Ap 14 1835-[Ja]-[Mr]-[S-D]1836-Ap 3 1837;O 29 1840
NjHi Ap 26,Je 7,Ag 9 1832
NjR Ja 31 1850
OCHi Jl 23 1835
OClWHi Mr 17 1828;My 7 1831;Ap 26 1832
OOxM N 11,25 1828;Ja 8,19-29,F 5-12,26,Mr 9 1829
P 1821-S 1844;My 26 1846
P-M Ag 10 1821;F 20,O 31,D 1823-F 20,Mr 7 1824;D 5 1826;Ja 2,S 25 1827;Ja 1,S 23 1828; My 17,O 4 1832;Mr 31 1838
PAtM My 15 1825
PEL [1832]-[34]
PEr 1825-[28]
PHHi 1821-[27-28;38-40;43-44]
PHi 1821[22]
PIW [1821-24]
PLewL [1826-27]
PPiHi D 15 1826
PPot O 25 1822;Ap 1 1823;Je 3,N 2 1824;Ja 1 1829;Jl 16 1831;O 26,D 14,28 1838;Ag 15 1839
PW My 8 1827

PENNSYLVANIA patriot. *See* Patriot

PENNSYLVANIA reporter. w,sw N 20 1827-Je 2 1843||
1827-Ja 12 1836 as Pennsylvania reporter and democratic herald; Ja 15-Ag 4 1836 Reporter and state journal; Ag 11 1836-Mr 1 1839 Pennsylvania reporter and democratic state journal. United with Keystone and State capitol gazette to form Democratic union
sw during sessions of legislature
Ct Ap 2 1835
DLC 1828-D 4 1840
MBAt F 5 1828
MWA N 20 1827;F 26,Ag 22-29 1828;N 11 1831; Ap 25,D 2 1834
N O 11 1833
NNHi [1827-Je 1838]
extras:O 7,21 1828
NSchU D 16 1834
NcD Ja 11,29,Mr 28,Ap 8-11 1828;Ap 1831-Ap 1 1834;35[Ja-Ap]-[D 1836]
extra:D 13 1836
NhD N 6 D 25 1845;Ja 8,Ap 28,Je 23 1846
OClWHi My 31 1839
P complete
P-M O 30 1829;O 3,D 19 1834;Ja 13 1835;N 20 1840
PBL [1827-30]-[33-38]-My 19 1843
PHHi [1827-29]S 25 1840;Ja 23,F 3 1846
PHi [1827]-29
PLewL [1828-30]
PMilC Ap 22 1831
PPot D 26 1828;Ag 31-S 7,D 11 1838;Ag 31,O 12 1839
PSuHi Je 5 1835;Je 22 1839
PW Mr 8 1831;Mr 15 1833

PENNSYLVANIA state sentinel. *See* Daily state sentinel

PENNSYLVANIA statesman. w Ag 11-N 3 1860||
Campaign paper
MWA Ag-S 8,22-N 3 1860
PPiHi [1860]

PENNSYLVANIA telegraph. d 1831-57? *See* Harrisburg telegraph

PENNSYLVANIA telegraph and legislative register. d Ja 8 1840-Ap? 1841||?
1840 as Daily telegraph and intelligencer
Prospectus is dated D 21 1839
DLC D 21 1839;Ja 8,Jl 22 1840
NjR F 1 1841

PENNSYLVANIAN. w Ja 10 1824-Ja 3 1825||
DLC complete (scattered numbers are photostats)
NcD S 18,N 27 1824
P complete
PBL [1824]
PPot F 7 1824
WHi complete

PENNSYLVANISCHE staats-zeitung and Dauphin county journal. w My 1843-1916||
1843-86 as Pennsylvanische staats-zeitung
In German
P 1843-N 1848;S 20 1890
P-M S 10 1845
PHHi [1886-1916]
PPoU 1888-1907

PENNY advertiser. sw Jl-O 1843||
P complete

REPORTER and state journal. *See* Pennsylvania reporter

REPUBLICAN and anti-Masonic inquirer. w My 1828-Mr 26 1831||
1828-Jl 4? 1829 as Anti-Masonic inquirer. United with Statesman to form Statesman and Anti-Masonic republican
DLC Jl 11,25-Ag 15,S 5-12,26-O 3,24,N 14-28,D 26 1829-Ja 23 1830
NNHi Jl 11 1829-31
P complete
P-M Ja 2 1830
PBL [1830-31]
PBro Mr 17 1830
PEL S 5 1829
PHHi [1831]
PLewL S 19 1829

SIGNAL. w 1841-
PBL O 27 1841-[42]

Harrisburg evening **STAR.** d Ag 1889-Ag 1891||
United with Harrisburg independent to form Star-independent
P complete

STAR-INDEPENDENT. d 1876-1917||
1876-91 as Harrisburg independent. Merged with Harrisburg telegraph (evening)
DLC Ja-Je 1838
P Ag 27 1889-F 16 1917
PHHi [1876]-1911
PHT [1877]-[1917]

STARS and stripes. w
P Jl 23,Ag 6-27,S 17,O 1-29 1856
PBL Jl 16 1856

STATE capitol gazette. w Jl 1839-Je 1843||
United with Keystone and Pennsylvania reporter to form Democratic union
MnHi O 21 1842
P complete
P-M Je 18-25 1841
PBL [1839-43]
PHHi O 16 1839

Daily **STATE guard.** d 1867-69||
DLC Je 25 1868
P-M My 27 1869
PPoU D 2 1867-Je 15 1869

Daily **STATE journal.** d O 3 1870-N 6 1873||
MWA Mr 3 1873
P complete

STATE journal. w Ap 1882-D 1885||
1882-Ag 11 1883 as Home journal
Negro
P My 1883-85

Daily **STATE sentinel.** d 1859-60||?
Some issues as Pennsylvania state sentinel
OClWHi Ag 11 1860
P My 14,O 22 1859;Jl 7,Ag-O 1860
PBf N 5 1859

STATESMAN and anti-Masonic republican. sw Jl 7 1828-S 1831||
1828-Mr 1831 as Statesman. Followed by Pennsylvania telegraph, later Harrisburg telegraph
DLC Jl 7-16,Ag,S 10-O 1 1828;D 16-19,26 1829;Ja 27 1830
NcD [Ap]-[S 1831]
P complete

Harrisburg **TELEGRAM sun.** w 1883-96||?
Title varies: Sunday morning telegram
MWA Jl 4 1886
P Je 9-16 1889;Jl 1 1894
PHHi F 19 1893

Harrisburg **TELEGRAPH.** w,sw,d S 7 1831-1904||
Follows Statesman and anti-Masonic republican. 1831-57? as Pennsylvania telegraph (Jl 3 1839-My 28 1840 Telegraph and intelligencer; N 9 1853-D 6 1854 Pennsylvania telegraph and whig state journal)
w 1831-90?;d,sw during sessions of legislature
DLC Ap 1832-33;F 26 1834-F 6,Mr 30 1836-Je 3,D 21 1838;Jl 3,N 21-28,D 19 1839-Ja 2,8,17-F 11,Jl 22,D 2 1840;51-O 1853
MWA 1832-[34-38]-Jl 3 1839;My 28[Jl 22-D] 1840;F 27,Ap 28 1841-[45-46]-[48-50;Ja 27-Je 1851]Ja 10,24-F 4,Mr 17,Ap 28,S 15 1852;S 28, N 9-16,D 14,28 1853-[54]F,Mr 3,27,Ap 24 1857
MiU-C Ja 14 1846
MnHi Ag 30 1843;Mr 19 1845
NNHi F 2 1836
NcD S 21 1831-Mr 1832;D 26 1839;Ja 24,F 11 1840
NhD Je 29 1847
NjR F 1 1841
OClWHi Je 11 1840;O 30 186-
P 1831-Ap 1833;Jl 1834-S 14 1858;F 2 1870;Jl 1879-My 1887;Jl 25 1890
P-M Ag 17 1836;F 21 1846;Ja 23 1857
PAltHi 1837-38
PBf [1860]
PEL Mr 19 1832
PErW Ap 11 1845
PHHi [1831-34;38-55;59;61-62]N 4 1863[64-65] Jl 15-23 1873;O 6 1897
PJR Je 3 1846
PLaN 1840-41
PLewL My 8 1833
PLhT Ap 6 1864
PPiHi Ja 28 1861
PPot F 25 1854
PShH Jl 29 1840
PYHi Ap 15,18,21 1865
WHi Ap 1864-65

Harrisburg **TELEGRAPH. [evening]** d Ja 8 1856+
1856-D 17 1857 as Harrisburg daily telegraph; D 19 1857-64? Pennsylvania daily telegraph (title varies: Harrisburg daily telegraph; Daily telegraph; Evening telegraph etc.)
S 7 1931 is centennial ed
CL S 7 1931
CtY S 7 1931
DLC 1835
IHi S 7 1931
MWA [1857]My 21 1862;63;Je 10 1864;Jl 6-D 1865;F 8,My 28 1866-67;S 7 1931;Ja 25,27,F 2,8-9 1934
MiU S 7 1931
MnU S 7 1931
NNHi Jl 27 1871
NbHi Ja 19 1859;F 22 1861
NcD Jl 1 1858
NjR S 7 1931
OClWHi D 1 1864;Mr-Jl 11 1881
P D 1857+
P-M Mr 21 1857;Mr 10 1865
PHHi My 9,Jl 4 1862;Jl 8,12 1865;Mr 7 1866; Jl 15 1873;Ap 9,24 1909;Ag 11 1914;S 3 1916; My 13,Ag 14 1920
PLewL My 16 1862
PPeS S 21 1867;My 20 1911
PWcHi [1882[83]
T S 7 1931
VU S 7 1931
WHi F 1864-65;S 7 1931

Morning **TELEGRAPH.** d 1933+
pub 1933+

Daily **TIMES.** d 1853||
Merged with Harrisburg telegraph
NNHi N 3-D 22 1853
PHHi [1853]

UNPARTHEYISCHE Harrisburg morgenröthe zeitung. *See* Harrisburger morgenröthe

Der **VATERLANDS wächter.** w 1832-75||?
In German
MWA F 22 1833
OClWHi D 5 1864
P Ap 12 1833
PHHi Ag 20 1844;S 19,D 24 1853
VtBr Ja 26 1838

WATCHMAN. w Je 12-O 19 1841||
Campaign paper
P complete

WHIG state journal. d 1850-Ap 26 1854||
Merged with Harrisburg telegraph
P Ap 1851-54
PHHi Ag 5 1851

PENNSYLVANIA (*Continued*)

HARRISBURG—*Continued*

WHIG state journal. w Ja 1851-N 1 1853||
United with Pennsylvania telegraph to form Pennsylvania telegraph and whig state journal, later Harrisburg telegraph
MWA Jl 29 1852
P Ap 1851-53

HASTINGS

NORTH CAMBRIA news. w 1902+
pub 1902+

Hastings TRIBUNE. w 1889-96||?
PEbHi 1894-96
PJR O 9 1896

HATBORO

PUBLIC spirit. w 1873+
Dated also in Jenkintown
pub 1875+
MdBJ O 7-14,28,N 18 1882
P D 11 1880-Je 1882
PDoC [1911]-[32]
PP D 17 1931-[36]

HATFIELD

Hatfield INVINCIBLE. *See* Hatfield times

Hatfield TIMES. w 1893+
1893-99? Hatfield invincible
pub 1920+

HAWLEY

Hawley FREE PRESS. w
PHsHi F 24,Jl 16 1865

Hawley TIMES. w 1874+
PHawB [1884-87]-[96-99]-[1918-19]+
PHsHi F 9 1877;Ap 21 1916;Ag 9 1918
PMilC Ag 21 1885
PScrHi D 18 1874;Je 30 1876;S 18 1924

HAZLETON

Daily BULLETIN. d F 25 1879-83||
Title varies slightly. Merged with Hazleton sentinel, later Standard-sentinel
P [1879-80]-[83]
PConE [1879]-[81]
PHazL [1879-82]83
PHazM [1880-81]
PHazSs [1878-79]

INDEPENDENT democrat. *See* Plain speaker

MOUNTAIN beacon. w 1877-82||?
PHaz [1877-79]

Daily NEWS. d 1870-75||
Merged with Hazleton sentinel, later Standard sentinel
PHaz [1874]
PHazSs [1873-74]

PLAIN speaker. w 1880-93||?
1880-85? as Independent democrat
PHazSs [1880]-[84;86;90]
PWbW Jl 22 1881

PLAIN speaker. d F 6 1882+
PHazSs 1882-1933
PP [1930]+

Hazleton SENTINEL. w Ja 1865-93||?
MWA D 6 1866
PHazSs 1881-89
PNuL D 12 1867

Hazleton SENTINEL. d *See* Standard-sentinel

SLOVAK citizen. *See* Slovensky obcan

SLOVENSKY obcan. (Slovak citizen) w Jl 12 1912+
In Slovak
pub F 23 1923+

Daily STANDARD. sw,d Mr 25 1885-O 27 1917||
1885-Mr 23 1892 as Semi-weekly standard (sw). United with Hazleton sentinel to form Standard-sentinel
pub [1885]-[90;92-93]-[1909]-[13]-[15-16]17
P Jl 1889-1917

STANDARD-SENTINEL. d 1869+
1869-O 27 1917 as Hazleton sentinel
pub 1895+
KHi D 1 1926
P 1918;Jl-Ag 1921;28+
PWbW Ag 1879-Jl 1880

L'UNIONE Italiana. w 1920+
In Italian and English
pub 1921+

Hazleton VIGILANT. w O 1 1903+
pub O 1 1903;D 31 1910;22-33

HERNDON

Herndon NEWS. w D 11 1908+
pub 1908+
PSuHi My 9,30 1928

Herndon STAR. w Je 29 1898-S 1918||
Merged with Herndon news
PHeN complete

HOLLIDAYSBURG

Hollidaysburg BEACON light. w Ja 1843-My 1845||
Merged with Democratic standard
PBL [1843-45]
PHoHi 1843-44

BLAIR county radical. w 1845-69||?
1846-66 as Blair county whig; 1866-68 Radical and Blair county whig
MWA D 13 1853;F 3 1866
PHoR [1849]-[52]

BLAIR county whig. *See* Blair county radical

CANAL and portage register. *See* Hollidaysburg register

DEMOCRATIC standard. w My 1 1845-1920||?
Title varies slightly
OClWHi Je 24 1863
P Jl 1889-Je 1891;Jl 1892-Je 1907;Jl 1908-12
PBL Mr 18 1842;45-[48]-[58]
PHoHi Mr 1 1854
PP N 28 1849

RADICAL and Blair county whig. *See* Blair county radical

Hollidaysburg REGISTER. w O 26 1836+
1836-S 1838 as Canal and portage register
DLC D 23 1840
MWA D 7 1853
PHoHi 1836+
PJR [1838-39]

Hollidaysburg STANDARD. w 1838-Ja 1843||
PHoHi 1839-43

HOLMESBURG

Papers published in Holmesburg are listed under Philadelphia

HOMER CITY

INDIANA county farm journal. *See* Indiana county journal

INDIANA county journal. w S 14 1926+
1926-N 21 1929 as Homer City journal; N 28 1929-31 Indiana county farm journal
pub 1926+

Homer City JOURNAL. *See* Indiana county journal

HOMESTEAD

MESSENGER. d 1889+
pub 1930+
PCC 1924
PHom 1889+

HONESDALE

Honesdale CITIZEN. *See* Wayne county citizen

Honesdale DEMOCRAT. w 1844-64||?
MWA My 5 1852
PHsHi O 15 1844;O 27 1847;O 9 1856;F 13 1862
PHsWi [1844-64]
PScrHi F 21 1861

INTELLIGENZBLATT. w
In German
NN Ap 6 1861

PETE'S national express. w
PHsHi [1847]

REPUBLIC. w 1864-68||
PMilaS Ap 20 1865

WAYNE citizen. *See* Wayne county citizen

WAYNE county citizen. w,sw,tw Je 1868+
1868-75? as Wayne citizen; 1875?-1908 Honesdale citizen
w 1868-1907?;sw 1908?-28?
pub [1870-71;73;1908]+
P My 28 1889-1912;17+
PHsC 1924+
PHsHi Jl 9 1869;Mr 20,Ag 14 1873;O 12 1876; S 22 1881;N 21 1889;O 26 1893;Ag 9 1894; My 30 1907[11-12;19;29-31]
PHsS 1870-[80]-[92]-1908[14]-22
PHsT F 6 1890;F 25 1892;F 23 1893;F 21 1895; F 13 1896;F 11 1897;F 3,Mr 31 1898;F 23 1899;F 22 1900;F 21 1901;F 16-23 1905;F 22, Mr 6 1906;Ap 18,Jl 25 1907[08]Mr 1,Ap 1 1911;F 28 1912;Mr 27 1914[16]
PHsWi 1864-1908
PMilaS S 24 1874;Mr 18 1886;O 30 1928
PP [1932]+

WAYNE county free press. w Ja 1 1838-43||
PBL [1842]

WAYNE county herald. w,sw O 5 1832-My 9 1913||
Title varies slightly
w 1832-1906
pub [1870]-93
DLC Jl 19-26 1833;My 21,Jl 16,D 17 1839
MWA D 2 1852
P Jl 1904-Jl 1 1910
P-M My 3 1833
PBL Mr 1 1843;Ap 12 1845
PE Je 4 1839
PHsHi [1833-34]-[36;39-40]Mr 4,O 14 1847;Ja 5 1848;Ag 11 1853;S 5 1861;F 13 1862;O 1 1863; Ja 28 1869[72]Ja 23 1890;Ja 2 1912
PHsS 1893-[1913]
PHsT F 3,Mr 24,Ap 14 1898;F 20,N 6,18 1902; F 26 1903;Mr 3,Ap 17,N 3 1908;F 16 1909
PMilC S 7,21-28 1871;F 13 1873
PMilHi Jl 21 1842
PW N 16 1844
PWbW F 20 1834

WAYNE independent. w,sw F 7 1878+
w 1878-90?
pub [1878]-[91]-[1914]+
Ct S 24 1918
PHsHi [1897]-[1912;17-18]+
PHsS 1878-[80-92]-1923
PHsW [1878]-[89]
PMilaS S 29 1881;Jl 5 1883;My 30 1894;My 7 1921
PScrHi Ag 10 1929

HONEY BROOK

Honey Brook GRAPHIC. w F 15 1879-1919||?
PHnM [1911]-14
PWcHi Ap 1 1887;Ap 18 1902

Honey Brook HERALD. w My 10 1928+
pub [1928]+

WAYNESBURG press and Chester, Berks and Lancaster advertiser. w 1833-34||
PWcHi Ja 8,29 1834

HOUTZDALE

CITIZEN-STANDARD. w 1882+
1882-99 as Houtzdale observer; 1900-Mr 1934 Houtzdale citizen
pub 1882+
NN S 12-26,O 10 1895-F 23,Mr 9-16 1899

Houtzdale OBSERVER. *See* Citizen-standard

HOWARD

Howard weekly HORNET. w 1894-97||?
PStP [1896]

Howard HUSTLER. w 1898-1915||
PHwR [1911-15]
PStP [1905-06]-11

HUGHESVILLE

Hughesville ENTERPRISE. *See* Hughesville mail

Hughesville MAIL. w Je 19 1874+
1874-83 as Hughesville enterprise
pub [1874]-[79]
P N 1900-12
PWp [1877-78;80]

HULMEVILLE

Hulmeville BEACON. w 1873-77||
Followed by Delaware Valley advance (Langhorne)

DELAWARE VALLEY advance. *See under* Langhorne

HUMMELSTON

Hummelston SUN. w 1871+
pub Jl 1913+
P Jl 26,N 29 1872

HUNTINGDON

ADVOCATE and sentinel. w 1835-
MWA Jl 13 1836
PBL [1836]-[38-39]F 19,Ap 29 1840

Huntingdon COURIER and anti-Masonic republican. w Je 2 1830-My 20 1835||
CSmH S 15 1830
NjHi Jl 21 1830
P-M Je 28 1833
PHi 1830-[33]
PHuJ [1830-32]-[34]

DEMOCRATIC watchman. w 1841-
PBL Jl 21,Ag 11,S 8-15,N 11 1841[1842]

***Huntingdon GAZETTE.** w F 12 1801-
CSmH S 15 1830
DLC F 5 1824
MWA D 7 1831
P 1821-Jl 10 1823;33-My 13 1835
PHuJ 1821;24-[39]

Huntingdon GLOBE. w N 1843-1921||?
DLC D 27 1843
NbHi Ja 13 1874
P Ja 12-D 13 1870;Jl 1889-1912
PBL Ja 10,Mr 6,Ap 3,Je 5 1844
PHuJ [1843;50]-[77]78;80-1918

HUNTINGDON county republican. w S 15 1869-70||
S-N 1869 as Republican
P Ja 5,D 3 1870

Huntingdon JOURNAL. *See* New era journal

JOURNAL and new era. d 1907-21||
1907-17? as New era
P N 1906-13
—w ed *See* New era journal

MESSENGER. w
PHuJ [1846-47]-[49]

Huntingdon MONITOR. w Ja? 1863+
Suspended from My 14-Jl 2 1863
P Ja 12-D 13 1870
PHoHi Mr 16 1870
PHuJ [1874]-1912

NEW ERA. d *See* Journal and new era

NEW ERA journal. w,sw S 1835-1912||?
1835-1904 as Huntingdon journal
w 1835-1910?
DLC D 12 1838;S 1,N 17 1841
MWA Je 26,N 13,27-D 1844[Ap 30 1845-47]Jl 18 1848;Mr 29 1854;Ap 4 1866
P O 1838-41;D 14 1858-D 1 1870;Ja 12 1889-1912
PBL [1845]
PE O 3 1838;Je 5 1839
PHuJ 1836-[38-40]42-1909
PMcC F 11 1876
—d ed *See* Journal and new era

Daily NEWS. sw,d Mr 1874+
1874-1927? as Semi-weekly news(sw)
P Je 1889+
PEbC Je 7 1901
PHuJ 1874-79;89-96

REPUBLICAN. *See* Huntingdon county republican

PENNSYLVANIA (*Continued*)

HUNTINGDON—*Continued*

*REPUBLICAN advocate. w Ag 10 1820-
InPeHi 1833-35
P-M Ja 14-21 1826
PHoHi Ja 12 1828
PHuJ [1825]-34

STANDING-STONE. w Je 11 1853-
1853-Jl 8 1854 as Standing-stone banner
WHi 1853-Ja 5 1855

UNION. w
PHuJ 1859-[61]

INDIANA

*AMERICAN and whig. w 1814-30||
1814-25 as American; 1826-28 American and republican gazette
DLC Je 11 1827
PIP [1827-28]
PIWa Je 18 1824

CLARION of freedom. *See* True American

Indiana DEMOCRAT. w My 7 1862+
pub 1862—
MWA My 25 1876
P D 26 1889-1930
PIC 1893-1932

Indiana DEMOCRAT and farmers and mechanics weekly advertiser. w
PBL Ap 22 1840

DEMOCRATIC messenger. *See* Indiana messenger

Indiana ENQUIRER. w Jl 1 1830-
CSmH Ag 5 1830

FREE PRESS and Indiana and Jefferson advertiser. w Mr 11 1830-Ja 1834||
CSmH S 2 1830
PIT [1830]-[33]

Indiana evening GAZETTE. d Ag 24 1903+
pub 1903+
P Ap 1927—
—w ed *See* Indiana county gazette

INDIANA county gazette. w Ag 13 1890-Ja 1 1913||
—d ed *See* Indiana evening gazette

Indiana MESSENGER. w Ag 20 1856+
1856-F 20 1861 as Democratic messenger
pub 1856+
PIC 1893-1932

PATRIOTA. w,sm Ag 8 1914+
In English and Italian
w 1914-28
pub 1914+

Indiana PROGRESS. w 1870+
Formed by the union of Blairsville press (Blairsville) and Register and American
pub 1870+
NNHi D 19 1872
P Ap 21 1897+
PIC [1893]-1932

REGISTER and American. w 1834?-70||
1834?-66 as Indiana weekly register. United with Blairsville press (Blairsville) to form Indiana progress
NNHi F 4 1862
PBl O 14 1835[52]-[58]Je 1860-Ja 1870
PBlaG S 21 1858
PKiK [1852]

Indiana TIMES. w 1878-1926||?
P Je 26 1889-1912

TRUE American. w 1840-66||
1840-54 as Clarion of freedom. United with Indiana weekly register to form Register and American
PIP D 18 1844
PIWa [1847]My 10 1853;F 14,Mr 28,O 17 1854

Indiana and Jefferson WHIG. w Jl 9 1821-28||
United with American and republican gazette to form American and whig
MBAt Ja 9 1822
P F 13 1826
PIP My 15 1822

IRWIN

Irwin CHRONICLE. *See* Republican standard

REPUBLICAN standard. w 1881+
1881-85? as Irwin chronicle; 1886-1901 Irwin standard
pub S 2 1882,N 24 1883[86;93-95;1901;11-12;25]+

Irwin STANDARD. *See* Republican standard

JEANNETTE

Jeannette DISPATCH. *See* News-dispatch

Jeannette NEWS. sw 1914-18||
United with Jeannette dispatch to form News-dispatch

NEWS-DISPATCH. w,sw,tw,d 1889+
1889-1918 as Jeannette dispatch
w 1889-1914;sw 1914-20;tw 1920-22
pub [1889-1915]+

WESTMORELAND journal. w 1902-14||
PJeL N 12 1902-Jl 1914

JENKINTOWN

Jenkintown JOURNAL. w D 6 1935+
pub D 6 1935+

OLD YORK ROAD post. w Mr 17 1932+
Mr 17 1932 as Old York Road press
pub [1932]+

OLD YORK ROAD press. *See* Old York Road post

PUBLIC spirit. *See under* Hatboro

TIMES-CHRONICLE. w My 1894+
My-D 1894 as Jenkintown times
pub 1894-1926;28+

YORK ROAD times. w Ap 5 1935+
pub 1935+

JERMYN

Jermyn PRESS. w 1890+
pub 1890+
PScrHi Ap 3 1936

JERSEY SHORE

ANTI-MASONIC advocate. w 1832-
PLewL F 14 1833

Jersey Shore HERALD. w 1864-1912||?
pub 1866-74
P S 11 1889-D 5 1912
PJsK Ag 27 1864;D 14 1870;Mr 10 1880;Ja 26 1881;F 23 1887;Ja 4 1888;F 14 1900

Jersey Shore HERALD. w 1903+
pub 1925+

NATIONAL vidette. *See* Jersey Shore vidette

Jersey Shore NEWS LETTER. w Je 29 1854-
PJsJ 1854-56

Jersey Shore REPUBLICAN. w 1846-57||
PJsJ 1846-52
PJsK N 16 1848;Jl 20 1853
PWpP Mr 26 1856

Jersey Shore VIDETTE. w 1865-1915||?
Early title: National vidette
P Jl 11 1889-1912
PJsJ Jl 9,S 17-24 1868
PJsK Mr 23 1871

WEST BRANCH courier and Jersey Shore advertiser. w Ja 8 1827-30||
PWp 1827-[29]

JOHNSTOWN

ALLEGHENY MOUNTAIN echo and Johnstown commercial advertiser and intelligencer. w Ag 15 1849-61||?
1849-50 as Mountain echo and Cambria transcript; 1851-53 Mountain echo
MWA Ag 31,O 19,N 2,16-D 7,21 1853-Ja 18,F-Je 7 1854
PJ O 26 1853;Jl 25 1860
PJR Je 1 1853;Ja 24 1855
PJT [1853]-55
WHi My 17 1854

CAMBRIA gazette. 1841-53||
PJR Ag 16 1841;D 17 1845;Ja 14 1846

CAMBRIA transcript. w Ag 17 1848-49||
MWA Ag 17,S 22 1848
PBL Ag 26 1848
PJ Ag 17 1848;Ag 29 1849

CAMBRIA tribune. *See* Johnstown tribune

Johnstown DEMOCRAT. w Mr 1863-1916||
pub complete
MWA My 4 1870
NNHi D 25 1872
P Jl 1889-Je 1912
PBl 1863-Ja 25 1865
PEbHi O 7 1863;N 1 1865;D 19 1890;D 25 1895;Jl 14 1897;N 2 1899
PJ Ap 27 1870;O 6 1900
PJR Ja 8 1865;Mr 14 1866;Mr 2 1870;S 24 1881[95-97]

Johnstown DEMOCRAT. d Ag 1888+
pub 1888+
PEbCo 1928+

Johnstown DEMOCRAT and Cambria and Somerset advertiser. w 1835-36||
MWA Ap 26 1836
PBL [1835]
PJ Ap 26 1836

DEMOCRATIC courier and tariff advocate. w S 2 1843-48||
MWA S 9 1846
PJ [1846-47]

DEMOCRATIC sentinel. w S 13-N? 1844||
MWA S 13,O 4 1844
PJ S 20 1844
PJR S 20 1844

ECHO and voice. *See* Voice and echo

Johnstown FREIE PRESSE. w 1871-1921||?
In German
PEbHi Ja 9 1901
PPeS N 13 1889;S 4 1895

FULTON county democrat. w 1843-
DLC Ap 1 1845

FULTON county republican. w 1839-
CtY Ja 15 1845
DLC Mr 5 1845

Johnstown HERALD. w
CtY Jl 17 1827;Ap 20 1830;Ap 12,26,Jl 12 1831;O 21 1834
NNHi S 18(extra)1832

Weekly HERALD. w,sw 1885-99||?
w 1885-94
PJT [1888]-[99]

Daily HERALD. d 1891-99||
PJR [1891]-[94]
PJT 1891-[99]

MOUNTAIN echo. 1849-53 *See* Allegheny Mountain echo

MOUNTAIN echo. 1870-93? *See* Voice and echo

NATIONAL democrat.
PEbHi O 3 1857

Johnstown NEWS. w Mr 3 1848-
MWA Jl 7 1848

NORTHERN banner and Montgomery democrat. w 1836-
DLC Jl 26 1838

SKY. w 1831-38||
PEbHi [1831-37]
PHi [1832]

Johnstown TRIBUNE. w D 16 1853-1917||
1853-S? 1864 as Cambria tribune
pub complete
DLC Ap 15,O 21 1864-S 25,D 1868-F,Ap 11 1873-Jl 10 1874
MWA Je 3 1854;Ap 22 1870
OClWHi Je 14 1889
P complete
PEbHi 1853-[64]Ap 22 1870;F 19,D 20 1889;D 22 1893;94-1915
PJR [1889]Ap 24 1896

Johnstown daily TRIBUNE. d 1873+
pub 1873+
MWA Ap 25 1876
P Jl 5 1889-Je 1912;Ap 1927+
PEbCo 1928+

VOICE and echo. w 1870-78||?
1870-73? as Mountain echo; 1874? Echo and voice
PJR Mr 13 1873[75-76]

KANE

Kane REPUBLICAN. d 1893+
pub 1893+

KENNETT SQUARE

Kennett ADVANCE. w,tw Ag 4 1877-1909||?
PKM [1883-86]
PWcHi [1877]-[83;86]-96;98[99]D 19 1903;My 14 1904[05]

Kennett Square FREE PRESS. w Jl 31 1855-58||?
MWA S 11-18,O 2,16,D 11 1855
PK [1855]
PWcT [1855]

Kennett LEADER. w Ja 14 1871-73||
1871-Mr 2 1872 as Weekly leader
PWcT 1871-[73]
WHi S 9,D 9 1871

Kennett NEWS and advertiser w Ja 1877+
PKY [1877-78;98-99]
PWcT [1893]-[95;1934-35]

KERSEY

Kersey weekly HERALD. *See* Saint Mary's weekly herald (St. Mary's)

KINGSTON

WYOMING republican and farmer's herald. w 1832-39||
NN Ap 11 1838
NjR N 15 1837
PWbW [1832-39]

KITTANNING

ARMSTRONG county democratic press. *See* Kittanning free press

ARMSTRONG democrat. 1834-64 *See* Armstrong republican

ARMSTRONG democrat and sentinel-times. w 1864+
1864-80 as Democratic sentinel; 1880-1921 Armstrong democrat and sentinel
pub 1881+
DLC Ag 4 1865
P Jl 11 1889-Je 1896;Jl 1897-Je 1910
PKiF F 1878

ARMSTRONG republican. w Je 1834-1902||
1834-64 as Armstrong democrat
MWA Jl 10 1863
P Je 26 1889-Je 1892;Jl 1893-Je 1902
P-M S 10 1834
PBf [1881]
PKiHa [1834]-55
WHi N 19 1840

*COLUMBIAN. w 1819?-Ap 1831||
Title varies slightly. United with Kittanning gazette to form Kittanning gazette and Columbian, later Kittanning free press
MWA S 11 1830
PHi [1830]

DEMOCRATIC sentinel *See* Armstrong democrat and sentinel-times

Kittanning FREE PRESS. w Ap 1825-1930||?
1825-40 as Kittanning gazette (My 1831-39? Kittanning gazette and Columbian); 1840- Armstrong county democratic press; -64 Kittanning free press; 1864-95? Union free press
DLC D 26 1839
MWA Ja 11 1866
P Mr 1878-Ag 1880
P-M S 4 1833
PBL F 18,Mr 18 1835
PHHi N 20 1833
PKiR Jl 21 1846
PPiHi Jl 7 1840;D 18 1845

Kittanning GAZETTE. *See* Kittanning free press

PENNSYLVANIA (*Continued*)

KITTANNING—*Continued*

MENTOR. w D 17? 1862-64||
MWA Jl 16 1863

SIMPSON'S leader-times. d My 1 1909+
1909-My 1 1921 as Simpson's daily leader
pub 1909+
P 1927+

Kittanning weekly **TIMES.** w 1882-My 1 1921||
United with Armstrong democrat and sentinel to form Armstrong democrat and sentinel-times
PKiL 1882-[1921]

Kittanning **TRIBUNE.** w 1896+
pub 1896+

UNION free press. *See* Kittanning free press

KNOXVILLE

Knoxville **COURIER.** w 1883+
Jl 13 1892-O 1 1902 as Knoxville courier and Tioga county independent
pub [1889-95;1902]-[05]-[17]+

KULPSVILLE

TOWAMENSING item. w Ja 13 1885-91||
PNoHi [1885-86]-[88-89;91]

KUTZTOWN

AMERICAN patriot. *See* Kutztown patriot

Der **GEIST der zeit.** w Je 1 1841-64||
In German
DLC My 11 1843
MWA F 6 1845

Kutztown **JOURNAL.** w F 2 1870-1909||
In German
PPeS F 27 1879
PRHi [1872-79]

Kutztanner **NEUTRALIST.** w Je 12 1833-41||
In German
PRHi [1833-37]

Kutztown **PATRIOT.** w 1874+
1874-87? as American patriot
In German and English
pub 1889+
PRHi [1874-75]

LANCASTER

Lancaster **ADLER.** w O 26 1826-
Ct Mr 3 1827
P-M F 15 1832
PB D 16 1826
PLaHi D 9 1826;Ja 19 1831;S 31 1832
PPeS Ja 1829

Lancaster **ADVERTISER.** w S 11 1930+
pub 1930+

AGE and Lancaster weekly gazette. w 1841-
1841? as Age
DLC Ja 1 1842
MWA Mr 15 1842
PLhT Jl 17 1841;Ag 22 1842

AMERICAN press and republican. w 1843-Jl 1859||?
1843-45 as Workingman's press; 1846 American press. Merged with Lancaster inquirer
DLC 1846-D 23 1848
MWA Jl 21 1849
NNHi N 20 1843;Ap 27,Je 29,Jl 27 1846
PLaHi Ag 19 1844;F 10 1845

Lancaster **AMERICAN republican.** w Ap 29 1830-46||
1830? as Republican and anti-Masonic opponent. United with American press to form American press and republican
CSmH My 6 1830
DLC Jl 4 1846
PLaHi Ap 29 1830;F 13 1833;N 28 1846

AMERIKANISCHE staatsbothe. *See* Neue unpartheyische Lancaster zeitung und anzeigs-nachrichten

ANTI-MASONIC herald, and Lancaster weekly courier. w Je 26 1828-Ap 3 1834||
1828-29 as Anti-Masonic herald. United with Lancaster examiner to form Lancaster examiner and herald, later Lancaster examiner and new era
DLC Ja 31,Je 19,N 6 1832
MWA D 18 1829
NjHi D 12 1828;Je 26,Jl 3 1829;F 24,Jl 23 1830
P 1829-Ag 1832
PHHi Jl 24 1829
PLaHi [1828-30]

Lancaster **BEOBACHTER.** w Ap 13 1832-Ap 4 1834||
United with Der Volksfreund to form Der Volksfreund und beobachter
Specimen number issued Ap 24 1830
In German
DLC complete
PLaHi Ap 24 1830

BUCK EYE. w Jl 11 1840-
DLC Jl 11 1840
P-M Jl 31 1841
PLaHi Jl 11 1840;Jl 24 1841

CONSTITUTION. ir 1860-
PLaHi S 6 1860

Lancaster **DEMOCRAT.** w 1831-
N O 24 1833
PLaHi N 7,D 19 1833;F 25 1834

Lancaster **DEMOCRAT.** w 1844-
PBL [1844-46]
PLaHi D 25 1844;Ja 15,Ap 16 1845;D 16 1846
PLaN [1845-46]

Der **DEUTSCHE porcupein und Lancaster anzeigs-nachrichten.** *See* Neue unpartheyische Lancaster zeitung und anzeigs-nachrichten

Lancaster daily **EXAMINER.** d Jl 1 1872-1920||
1877-80? as Lancaster daily examiner and express. United with New era to form Examiner and new era, later Lancaster new era
DLC Ag 19 1873;S 10 1879
NcD O 3 1900
PHHi S 21 1909
PLaHi S 9,N 18 1874;O 13 1875[77]Je 16 1881[82;89;94]-1913
PLaL [1876-79]
PLaN 1872-[76]-[82-83]-[98]-[1915]-[20]
PP S 8 1910
WHi Ap-O 1896

Lancaster **EXAMINER and new era.** w,sw Ap 15 1830-1922||
1830-Ap 3 1834 as Lancaster examiner; Ap 10 1834-76 Lancaster examiner and herald (Title varies: Examiner and herald; Examiner and democratic herald); 1877-1920 Lancaster weekly examiner and express
w 1830-90?
CSmH Jl 29 1830
DLC 1830-Ap 3 1834;Ja 7 1836;Mr 8,22-Ap 19,Jl 5,S 20-O 4,25-N 8 1838;F 28,Mr 7-14,S 19 1839;Ja 29,O 7 1840;Ja 31 1844;Ja-Je 1847;Jl 4 1849
MBAt Ap 19 1865
MHi N 12-19,D 10 1835;Ja 28,F 18,Mr 10,31,My 12 1836
MWA Ap 19 1832-Mr 7 1833;Ap 17 1834-Ap 2 1835;F 11,My 26,Jl 21,Ag 18-25,D 22 1836;Ja 5,Jl-Ag 3,N 23 1837;Mr 21,O 10 1839;Ap 15-22 1840;O 10 1860;My 7 1862
MnHi S 28 1842
N F 18 1846
NNHi My 27,D 9 1830;Je 30 1831;Ap 17,Ag 14 1834
NSchU Jl 27-S 7 1842
NcD Ag 11 1831;O 10 1833;F 24 1847
NjHi My 27,O 14 1830
OClWHi Mr 24 1866
P O 27 1858-64;Je 25 1884;Jl 9 1889-1916
PBL Ja 10,F 7 1839;Mr 25 1840
PLaF 1856-[70]95;97-1908;10-11
PLaHi Ap 15 1830-34;Mr 16 1842;S 1 1847;Jl 17,S 25 1850[60]-66;S 21 1881
PLaL D 17 1856[57]Ja 25 1871
PLaN Ap 15 1830-39[44]-1922
PPot Jl 31 1867;Ag 28-S 4 1868

EXAMINER and new era. 1920-23 *See* Lancaster new era

Weekly **EXPRESS.** w F 10 1843-D 30 1876||
1843-Mr 20 1853 as Saturday express; Mr 27 1853-N 1856 Saturday evening express. United with Lancaster examiner to form Lancaster weekly examiner and express, later Lancaster examiner and new era
MBAt Ap 15 1865
MWA F 15 1845;Ap 10 1847;Jl 2 1848
PLaHi Ap 24 1856;O 25 1862;D 2 1865;Ja 20, Je 2 1866
PLaN [1850]-[56]
PLewL [1852-56]

Daily evening **EXPRESS.** d N 3 1856-D 30 1876||
United with Lancaster daily examiner to form Lancaster daily examiner and express, later Lancaster daily examiner
DLC My 6 1858-My 2 1859;61-63;My 27 1868
MBAt Ap 15,18 1865
MWA D 2 1859;Ag 23 1866
NNHi Ja 13 1857;My 20,Je 23,Jl 20 1863;My 25 1870;Mr 29,My 16,O 7 1873
NjCHi S 23-24 1859
OHi 1861-62
P 1860-65
PLaF [1861]62[73]
PLaHi [1856]-[59-60]-76
PLaN complete
PLhT [1863]

FATHER Abraham. w 1868-70||
NNHi Je 11 1869;My 20 1870
PDoHi S 24 1869
PLaHi O 2 1868;Jl 1 1870
PLaL [1868-70]
PNoHi Jl 30 1869

***FREE PRESS.** w My 10 1819-25||
Merged with Political sentinel
DLC Jl 26-Ag 2,N 15 1824
MWA Ja 4,Ag 16,N 15 1821-N 3 1823
P-M S 26 1822
PDoHi Ap 25 1825
PHi [1821]-[23]
PLaHi D 20 1821[22]-[25]

Daily **FREE PRESS.** d
PLaHi Je 1,6 1855

Lancaster **FREIE PRESSE.** d 1882-1903||
In German
P O 1882-My 1884;Jl 11 1888-Je 1891
PLaHi [1882-83]85-[91]-[1903]

*Lancaster **GAZETTE.** w 1817?-50||?
Title varies: Lancaster gazette and farmers' and mechanics' register; Lancaster gazette and farmers' register
CSmH S 7 1830
DLC D 20 1825;D 15 1829
MWA Ap 1,29,My 13-20 1823;S 25 1827;Ag 26 1828
NNHi S 1-8,O 27,N 27 1829
P Jl 19 1825
P-M F 18 1823
PLaHi Ja 1 1822[23-25]O 16 1827;Mr 18 1828; Ja 20 1829;Mr 2,Je 15 1830;Je 29 1850
PLewL F 24 1829

Semi-weekly **GAZETTE.** sw Ag 19-D 23 1840||
WHi complete

Daily **GAZETTE.** d D 28? 1840-
DLC D 30 1840

GRAPE shot. w Jl 15 1848-
CSmH S 9 1848

GREELEY banner. w 1872-
PLaHi Je 5,25 1872

Lancaster **HERALD.** w 1829-
N My 21-28,Jl 16,S 10-17,D 24 1833;Mr 11-18 1834

HEROLD und zeitschrift. w
In German
PLaHi 1885-[87]

Lancaster **INDEPENDENT.** w O 20 1935+
pub 1935+
PLaF 1935+

INDEPENDENT whig. w 1853-57||
United with Lancaster union to form Independent whig and Lancaster union, later Lancaster union
DLC Ap 18 1854

INLAND daily times. d 1853-S 1858||
1853-My 19 1857 as Inland daily
DLC O 22 1855-My 6 1858
NN Ap 28 1855
P F-D 1854
PLaHi My 30,S 17 1853[54-55]F 14 1856;My 22 1857;Ag 6 1858

INLAND weekly and campaign banner. w 1855-58||
1855 as Inland weekly. Merged with Lancaster union
DLC Mr 3 1855
MWA My 31,N 1 1856
PLaHi N 15 1856

Lancaster **INQUIRER.** w Ja 1859+
MWA Ap 11 1863
NNHi My 16,Je 20-27,Jl 18-25 1863;Mr 29 1873
P Jl 1889-Je 1912
PLaHi O 12 1867;S 6 1873;83;1906;08-13;16-18
PLaN 1870;77-[1921]
PPCHi Ja 27,Jl 22,Ag 29,D 8,9,14,30,31 1863;Ja 4,8,F 2,13 1864

*Lancaster **INTELLIGENCER.** w,sw Jl 31 1799-1922||?
Title varies slightly: Intelligencer and weekly advertiser; Intelligencer and journal; etc.
Mr 9 1895 is centennial number
w 1799-1889?
A Ap 1857-Ap 1869
DLC [Ja 12-Ag 1847]-48
ICHi Mr 9 1895
IaDH Mr 9 1895
MBAt Mr 9 1895
MWA F 22,Mr 4,25-Ap 8,My 27,Je 17,Jl 8,S 2 1823;O 4 1825;O 20 1829;N 30 1852;D 8 1863; My 31 1864;Mr 9 1895
N N 15 1865;S 12 1866
NNHi D 4 1838;D 5 1843;My 25 1870
NSchU Jl 26-S 6 1842
NbHi N 18 1868
NhD Mr 9 1895
OClWHi Mr 9 1895
P 1821-22;F 1823-F 1824;Mr 1825-26;F 1827-Ja 1828;Jl 1833-52;Jl 1889-1920
PBL 1853[54]-[58]
PBf Jl 30 1837
PHi 1821[22]
PJsJ Jl 14 1886
PLaF 1893-99;1901-[10]11
PLaHi [1821]-[26]Ap 20 1832;Ag 25 1835[38-39]Mr 24 1840;My 18-25 1841;Mr 22,Je 14 1842[50-53;64]-69;71-73[81]-87
PLaN 1821-[23;27]-[29]38-[45;47]-1920
PNc [1821]23-[25]
PP 1822[23]Mr 9 1895
PPL N 6 1849;S 3 1850
TU Mr 9 1895
WHi Mr 9 1895

Lancaster **INTELLIGENCER-JOURNAL.** d Ag 29 1864+
1864-Ap 15 1928 as Lancaster intelligencer; Ap 17? 1928-29? Lancaster intelligencer and news journal
CtY Ag 1 1868;Mr 9 1895
KHi D 1 1926
MdHW F 7 1843
NN Jl 12 1876;Jl 21 1888;Mr 9 1895
P 1909+
PLaF [1893]-[98]-1911;Je 10 1915;Ag 26 1916; Mr 4 1921;Ja 19 1922;Je 24,28 1924[27]Je 22 1929;Mr 13 1934;Mr 2 1936
PLaHi [1864]-[81;84-86]-1932
PLaN 1864+

*Lancaster **JOURNAL.** w,tw,sw Je 1794-O 1839||
United with Lancaster intelligencer to form Intelligencer and journal, later Lancaster intelligencer
tw Ag 23 1815-Ja? 1819;sw Ja 20 1819-Ja 3? 1820
DLC N 24 1826
MWA Ja 5 1821;Jl 26,S 13,N 29 1822[Ja-Jl 1823]Ap 23 1824;Ja 19 1827
P 1821-25;28
PBL [1821-22]
PLaHi 1821-38
PLaN 1821-[34]
PPiU-D Jl 11 1823-Je 24 1825

Morning **JOURNAL.** d Jl 1 1909-Mr 6 1915||
United with Morning news to form News-journal
PLaHi [1909]-[15]
PLaN [1909]-[13]14

LANCASTRIAN and chronicle of the times. w Ja 1848-O 1855||
DLC Ap 20 1853-Ap 12 1854
MWA Mr 15 1848
P 1848-Ja 1855
PLaN F 21 1849

PENNSYLVANIA (*Continued*)

LANCASTER—*Continued*

Die LATERNE. w 1870-D 31 1903||
In German
MWA N 27-D 4 1875
P 1887-1902
PLaHi N 6 1897

MILL BOY. w My 1-N 1 1844||
Campaign paper
MWA Je 3 1844
MoSM Ag 3,S 28 1844
P-M O 5 1844

*NEUE unpartheyische Lancaster zeitung und anzeigs-nachrichten. w Ja 3 1798-
1798-99 as Der Deutsche porcupein und Lancaster anzeigs-nachrichten; 1800-21? Amerikanische staatsbothe (title varies slightly)
In German
PLaHi My 4 1831

Lancaster NEW ERA. d Ap 28 1877+
1877-1920 as New era; 1920-Jl 1923 Examiner and new era
DLC 1877-Ap 1896;98
NNC Je 22 1929
P 1877+
PHHi F 3 1897;Je 22 1929
PLaF 1877-85[89]-92;94-[1902]-[11]Ag 3-4 1914; N 17 1915;Je 14 1916;S 14 1918;My 6,20 1919; Je 7,9,N 26 1920;Ag 23 1923;F 8 1924;36+
PLaHi 1877-[1920-23]-32
PLaN 1877-[1920-23]+
PP [1928]-[30]
PPeS Je 22 1929
PStP 1879-98

Semi-weekly NEW ERA. w,sw My 5 1877-1920||
1877-Ap 28 1894 as Weekly new era. United with Lancaster examiner to form Lancaster examiner and new era
OClWHi D 5 1891
P 1877-Ap 1878
PLaF 1877-[1913-16]-20
PLaHi 1877-[82-84]My 1894-[99-1900]-[02-04]-[06;08;10-11]
PLaN 1877-[1910-11]-[14-15]-19
PStP [1878]-[87]91-[1911]

Sunday NEWS. w S 1923+
P Je 1928-Je 1932
PLaF Je 22,Jl 20,O 19 1924;S 13 1925;My 15 1932
PLaHi 1923-34
PLaN 1923+

Daily NEWS and chronicle. d
PLaHi [1847-48]

NEWS-JOURNAL. d Ja 25 1890-Ap 14 1928||
1890-Mr 6 1915 as Morning news. United with Lancaster intelligencer to form Lancaster intelligencer and news journal, later Lancaster intelligencer-journal
P Ja 23 1890-1919
PLaF [1892;96;1905]14;Ja 22, N 5 1924
PLaHi 1890[91-92]-[98-99]-[1902]-[05]-[12-13]15-[22]-28
PLaN [1890]-[93]96-[99-1900]02-28

OLD guard. w Mr 27 1839-40||
Merged with Examiner
DLC Mr 27 1839
PBL [1839]
PLaHi [1840]

*PENNSYLVANIA gazette. w Ag 12 1817-
PLaHi Mr 27 1824

PENNSYLVANISCHE staats-zeitung. w
In German
PHHi Je 28 1866-Je 1 1868

PLAINDEALER. w My 1 1840-O 25 1844||?
Campaign paper
MWA Ag 9 1844
P-M S 24 1841
PLaHi [1840]-[44]
PLaN [1844]

POLITICAL sentinel and Lancaster literary gazette. w N 18 1826-30||
DLC S 5 1827;Jl 1-22,Ag 12,S 9-O 7,28,D 3 1829;Ja 13 1830
MWA Ag 15,S 5 1827
NNHi 1826-N 6 1827;Mr 5 1828
PLaHi [1826]-[28]
PLewL Jl 7,21 1830

PUBLIC register and American citizen. w D 1853-
1853-Je 1854 as Public register
PLaHi S 30 1854;Mr 10 1855

Lancaster REPORTER. w O 3 1827-29||?
MBAt Jl 31 1828
MWA Jl 9 1829
P O 30,D 25 1828
PLaN 1827-28

REPUBLICAN and anti-Masonic opponent. *See* Lancaster American republican

REPUBLICAN telegraph. w N 12 1825-26||
MWA N 19 1825
P-M Ap 22 1826
PBL D 24 1825
PDoHi My 6 1826
PLaHi [1825]26

Morning REVIEW. d 1874-75||
PLaF [1874-75]
PLaHi Je 24 1874

STANDARD of liberty and Lancaster county democrat and public advertiser. w D 3 1830-
DLC D 24 1830
MWA Mr 11 1831
PLaHi Je 10,S 23 1831

Lancaster weekly TIMES. w 1852-
PLaHi Ap 14,Ag 18 1858

TRIBUNE and public advertiser. w Ap 11 1846-
DLC Jl 4 1846

*Lancaster UNION. sw,w 1818-64||
1818-34 as Union(sw);N 1834-48 Lancaster union; 1851-57? Independent whig and Lancaster union. Merged with Lancaster examiner
DLC [1847]
MWA O 24 1843;F 19 1850
P D 1851-Ja 3 1853
PBL Jl 29 1834
PLaHi [1821-22;34]-[39]Jl 13 1841;O 10 1843; Ja 26 1847;F 29 1848;Jl 16 1850;O 31 1854[55] Je 10,O 21 1856;My 19 1857[58-60]D 4,18 1861[62]

*Der VOLKSFREUND und beobachter. w Ag 9 1809-1910||
1809-Ap 1 1834 as Der Volksfreund. Title varies slightly
In German
KHi Ja 26-29,Mr 1 1833
MWA Ag 21 1821;My 16,D 26 1826;D 22 1829; Mr 9,My 11,25 1830;Mr 3 1840;N 14 1843;My 21 1844;Ag 12 1851
OOxM Mr 10 1829
PLaHi Ap 27,Je 15 1824;My 31 1825[26-27]N 2 1830[35]-[37]My 13 1845;D 22 1846[50-51] Mr 30 1852;S 26,O 31 1854[55]Ja 5 1858;S 15 1863;Je 8 1870;My 29 1872;Ap 26 1876

*Der WAHRE Amerikaner. w N 10 1804-
Title varies slightly
In German
DLC My 11 1843
MWA Ja 5 1822
PLaHi D 22 1821[22]Ag 23 1833;Jl 5 1841
PLaN 1848-49

WASHINGTONIA. w
PLaHi Jl 31 1834
PLewL [1824]

WORKINGMAN'S press. *See* American press and republican

LANDISBURG

*PERRY forester. w Jl 12 1820-
DLC F 21 1828
WHi S 20 1821

LANGHORNE

Langhorne and Hulmeville BEACON. *See* Delaware Valley advance

DELAWARE VALLEY advance. w S 6 1877+
Follows Hulmeville beacon (Hulmeville). 1877-79 as Langhorne and Hulmeville beacon
1877-My 7? 1925 pub in Hulmeville
pub 1884-[1901-05]+
PDoHi [1877-79;1913-15;28]-[34]

Langhorne LEADER. w 1912-24||
PDoHi [1914]
PLanA [1912-14;16-24]

LANSDALE

MONTGOMERY county presse. *See* Stimme des volkes. . .

NORTH PENN reporter. w,tw,d O 27 1870+
1870-F 1923 as Lansdale reporter; Mr 1923-Ja 1927 North Penn review and Lansdale reporter
w 1870-F 1923;sw Mr 1923-Ja 1927
pub 1879+
MWA D 22 1930;Jl 27 1932;My 25 1933
PPeS D 26 1882;O 27 1887

NORTH PENN review. tw Ja 2 1916-Ja 7 1918||
United with Lansdale republican to form Lansdale republican and North Penn review
PLansN complete

Lansdale REPORTER. *See* North Penn reporter

Lansdale REPUBLICAN and North Penn review. w,tw Ja 3 1884-F 1923||
1884-1917 as Lansdale republican. United with Lansdale reporter to form North Penn review and Lansdale reporter, later North Penn reporter
w 1884-1917
PLansN complete

STIMME des volkes und Montgomery county presse. w Ag 6 1860-78||?
1860-75? as Montgomery county presse
1860-62? pub in Norristown
In German
MWA Ja 22 1861
PDoC My 24 1863;Jl 23 1880
PPeS D 13 1864;Je 13 1865[75]Mr 28 1876

LANSFORD

Lansford LEADER. w 1893+
P Je 17 1897-1912

Lansford evening RECORD. d 1920+
pub 1920+
PLfH 1926-[28]
—w ed *See* Summit Hill and Lansford record

SUMMIT HILL and Lansford record. w 1879-1920||
pub [1879-1920]
PMc [1890-94]
—d ed *See* Lansford evening record

LAPORTE

REPUBLICAN news-item. w 1883-1918||?
1883-My 1896 as Sullivan republican
P Je 28 1889-Mr 1896[98-1912]

SULLIVAN county democrat. w 1851-61||
MWA N 16 1852;D 2 1863
P-M Ag 26 1859
PLewL Ap 12 1853

SULLIVAN republican. *See* Republican news-item

LATROBE

Latrobe BULLETIN. d D 19 1902+
pub [1902]+

Latrobe weekly CLIPPER. *See* Greensburg clipper (Greensburg)

LAWRENCEVILLE

Lawrenceville HERALD. w 1881-1906||?
1901?-04? as Lawrenceville new herald
DLC My 10 1884-Ja 10 1885

Lawrenceville NEW herald. *See* Lawrenceville herald

Lawrence SENTINEL. w 1840-
PWeT [1841]

LEBANON

Lebanon ADVERTISER. w Jl 4 1849-1901||
MWA My 12 1852;Mr 20 1861
NjR [S-D 1849;Ja-F 1855]
P 1849-My 23 1901
P-M Jl 7,21 1858;S 21 1859,D 31 1862
PLewL Je 4 1862

Daily ADVERTISER. d Jl 1 1884-Jl 11 1885||
P complete

*Lebanon COURIER and semi-weekly report. w O 15 1819+
1819-1907 as Lebanon courier
pub 1908+
DLC Mr 21 1872;Ap 20 1887-93
MWA Jl 13 1836;N 22 1837;D 7 1842;My 29 1857;N 21 1861
MnHi Ag 10,24 1842;Ag 9-16 1843
NjR Mr 13 1847;O 6 1849;O 13 1854
P [1836;41;47;49-58;61-64;67;69;71;76;79;85]Je 26 1889+
P-M My 9 1838;N 13 1839;Ja 11 1843;My 15-22 1844;Ja 22 1845;Ja 9 1852;My 22 1857;O 25 1860;Ja 1 1869
PBL [1834-35]
PLeHi [1844-89]-[91]-[95-98]1900-[03;09]
PPot My 21 1845

Libanon DEMOKRAT. *See* Der Pennsylvanier

Der FREYMÜTHIGE Libanoner. *See* Libanoner morgenstern

LIBANON county demokrat. *See* Der Pennsylvanier

*Der Libanoner MORGENSTERN. w Ja 1 1807-37||
1807-N 30 1808 as Der Freymüthige Libanoner
In German
MWA Ag 29 1834;N 26 1836
NjR N 26 1830
P 1821-D 14 1834
P-M 1821-D 14 1839
PLeHi Ag 14 1824;O 21 1825;S 13 1829;S 21,N 19 1832;Mr 10 1836

Lebanon daily NEWS-TIMES. d S 14 1872+
1872-1925? as Lebanon daily news
pub 1872+
P Je 18-26,Jl 15 1889;My 5 1902
PLeHi [1874-77]-[80-82;89]-[91]1928+

Der PENNSYLVANIER. w 1827-N 1880||
1827-44 as Libanon demokrat (1831-32 Libanon county demokrat); 1845?-Ap 1865 Lebanon demokrat. Followed by Die Lebanon volks-zeitung
In German
MWA S 21 1832;D 7 1838;N 29 1844;Ag 31 1849;S 12 1861;Je 6,Jl 18,Ag 22 1866;O 23,D 9 1868;Ja 2,23,F 20 1873;O 31 1877
P Jl 22 1831;D 5 1834;F 15 1839-46;My 17 1850-Ap 7 1854;Mr 27 1862
P-M Ja 1 1862;Jl 23 1863;Ja 1,Ap 7 1864;Ja 1 1868;Ja 1 1869

PENNSYLVANISCHE beobachter. *See* Wahrer demokrat

Evening REPORT. d N 1 1889+
P N 1890+

Lebanon REPUBLICAN. w 1826-
MWA My 22 1827
P D 21 1824;Mr 15 1827
P-M Jl 18 1826;Ap 24 1827;Ja 29,Mr 18 1828

Lebanon daily TIMES. d F 1876-1925||?
United with Lebanon daily news to form Lebanon daily news-times
P Jl 15 1889
PHHi Jl 4 1876
PLeHi [1876]-92;94-96;1900-05
—w ed *See* Lebanon Valley standard

Der UNPARTHEYISCHE berichter. *See* Wahrer demokrat

Lebanon VALLEY standard. w N 4 1871-1920||?
MWA N 11 1871
P N 4 1871
PLeHi [1874]-79;84-85
—d ed *See* Lebanon daily times

Die Lebanon VOLKS-ZEITUNG. w N 1880-1908||
Follows Der Pennsylvanier
In German
P Je 1889-Ja 1 1908

PENNSYLVANIA (*Continued*)

LEBANON—*Continued*

*Der WAHRE demokrat. w Ja 1 1816-99||?
1816-26 as Der unpartheyische berichter; 1827-35 Der Pennsylvanische beobachter; 1837-63? Der wahre demokrat und volks-advokat
In German
MWA Ag 8 1835;Jl 2,30 1836;F 19 1841;O 16 1846;Ag 3 1849;My 31 1865
NjR F 27 1829
P Ja 12 1822-Mr 7 1828
P-M Jl 20 1822;S 27 1823
PLeHi Je 9 1842[43]Jl 5 1844

LE RAYSVILLE

Le Raysville UNION. w Ag 25 1865-
PToHi N 17 1865

LEWISBURG

BUFFALO VALLEY news. w
PLewB [1909-11]

Lewisburg CHRONICLE. w S 1843-1912||
1843-My 1849 as Lewisburg and Union county general advertiser; My 1849-58 Lewisburg chronicle and West Branch farmer; 1859-Ja 1865 Union county star and Lewisburg chronicle
CSmH Ap 15(extra)1865
MWA O 22 1858;Ja 27 1860
P D 1877-Je 29 1912
PHi 1851-59
PLewB 1847-51[67;71-73;75;82;84-89;91-99;1902-04;06-08;10]
PLewC 1893-95
PLewJ 1847-52;57-65
PLewL [1843]44[47-48;54;57]Ja 8-23,Ag 1858-[59;65]O 18-D 1867;My 27,Je 10,Jl-D 16 1870; 71-74;77-[86-91;95-96]
PLewT N 5 1859[61-64]Mr 17 1865;My 18,Je 8,Ag 3,D 28 1866;D 4 1868;Ag 19 1870-[71-77; 79]
PLewW 1853-57
PSuD 1857-65

Lewisburg DEMOCRAT. w 1835-
Title varies slightly
Ct Jl 15 1835
PLewL 1835[36;52]-54

INDEPENDENT press. w S 4 1841-42||
DLC S 4,18 1841;Ja 15,Jl 26 1842
PLewL complete

Lewisburg JOURNAL. w My 1 1830-
CSmH Jl 17 1830
PLewL [1833-34]

Lewisburg JOURNAL. w 1865+
pub [1871]-86;1919;22;24-31
P Jl 1889+
PLewB [1896-97;1901-04;06-17;19;21]
PLewC [1895;1901-02]-[09]11-14;16;18-[23-31]
PLewL 1830-32;91-[95]-[97;1930-33]
PSuHi D 13 1865

LOCAL news. *See* Lewisburg Saturday news

Lewisburg Saturday NEWS. w 1882+
1882-83 as Local news
pub 1882-1933
P 1883-Ap? 1888;Je 24 1928+
PLewB [1889-90;97;1900-01;10-13;15-18]
PLewC [1893]-1911;13;15-[27]-32
PLewL [1888-89]93;95[96;1930-33]

PEOPLES advocate. w 1838-41||
PLewL [1838]-[41]
PShH N 10 1838

Lewisburg STANDARD. w 1837-39||?
Title varies slightly
PBL [1838-39]
PLewL [1837]-[39]

*UNION county star. w 1814-58||
United with Lewisburg chronicle and West Branch farmer to form Union county star and Lewisburg chronicle, later Lewisburg chronicle

UNION hickory. w F 17 1829-30||
F-Ap 1829 pub in New Berlin
PLewL [1829-30]

UNION weekly whig. w 1851-52||
PLewL [1851-52]

LEWISTOWN

Lewistown DEMOCRAT. w 1835-
PBL O 7,D 5 1835;F 13 1836

Lewistown DEMOCRAT and sentinel. w 1845-1922||?
Follows Lewistown republican. 1845-79 as True democrat
MWA Ja 8 1845-54;60-[62-65]
NNHi My 2 1878
P 1855-57;59-64;67-79;Je 1889-1912
PBL [1845-58]

*Lewistown GAZETTE. w 1811+
1811-34 as Juniata gazette
CSmH Jl 22 1830
Ct Ja 1 1829;Jl 21 1835
DLC N 3 1832
MWA Jl 5-12 1825;S 18,N 6 1828;Mr 19,Ap 23,Jl 16 1829;Ja 7,Mr 25,Ap 15 1830;Jl-Ag,S 13-27,O 11-20,N 17,D 15-22 1832;Ja 5-19,F 2-9,23-Mr 2,16,30-Ap 1833;D 1 1834
P Ag 1889-Je 1912;18-23
PHHi Je 1 1916

JUNIATA gazette. *See* Lewistown gazette

MIFFLIN county gazette. w Mr 11? 1841-
MWA O 28,N 11 1841
P-M My 27,D 16 1841;Ja 27 1842

MIFFLIN eagle and Lewistown intelligencer. w 1817-32||?
1817-27 as Mifflin eagle
Ct [1826]Ja 29 1832
P Je 29 1826-D 15 1831
P-M Ag 27 1829
PLewL Mr 15,O 1 1828

Lewistown REPUBLICAN. w Ag 1832-O 16 1844||
Title varies slightly. Followed by True democrat, later Lewistown democrat and sentinel
Ct O 12 1833[34-35]
CtY S 25 1844
DLC My 29 1844
GAtCo Mr 18 1840
MWA F 23,My 25,Ag 6,D 7 1833;Ja 18[Mr 15 1834-F 1835;Je-D 1836]Ja 10 1837[40-N 10 1841]Mr 30,My 11,O 15 1842[My 24-D 1843] Ja 10[My 15-O 23]1844
P F 1840-44
PBL [1832]34-[36]-[39-40]

SENTINEL. d 1903+
pub 1903+
P Jl 1889-1912;Ap 1927-Je 1932

TRUE democrat. *See* Lewistown democrat and sentinel

LEWISVILLE

ULYSSES sentinel. w Ag 25 1881-Jl 25 1918||
PCtHi [1881]-[1918]

LIGONIER

Ligonier AMERICAN. w My 12 1906+
pub 1931+
PPiHi 1906-07;My 15 1908-Je 21 1913

Ligonier ECHO. w S 15 1888+
pub 1888+
P 1888-1917;20+

LITITZ

Lititz EXPRESS. m,w 1877+
Ap 1877-Ag 1881 as Sunbeam
pub [1877]+
P Je 7 1905
PPeS My 5 1916;Jl 17 1930

Lititz RECORD. w S 1 1877+
pub 1877+

SUNBEAM. *See* Lititz express

LITTLESTOWN

ADAMS county independent. w 1888+
PGCo [1894]+
PLiA 1888+

LIVERPOOL

Liverpool MERCURY and peoples advertiser. w 1831-36||
DLC N 2 1832
PBL [1835]

Liverpool SUN. w 1881-1924||
United with Newport news to form News-sun (Newport)
P O 1881-S 1889

LOCK HAVEN

CLINTON county whig. w N 19 1839-
DLC N 9 1842
PLhT S 1 1841

CLINTON democrat. w,sw 1841-S 28 1923||?
w 1841-1901?
MWA O 16 1862;Je 9 1864
P Jl 1889-Je 1899;Jl 1900-Je 1912;18
PBL D 9 1843;Ag 26 1845;S 8 1846[47]
PJsK Ag 29 1848
PLhT [1842;44-45;56]-D 22 1864
PSaS 1861-62

CLINTON republican. w Mr 1863-1923||
MWA Ja 3 1866
P Je 26 1889-Je 1912;20-S 1923
PLhT Ap 4,Je 27 1863;My 11 1864;My 24 1865; Ag 8 1866;My 18 1868;Ja 19 1870-[71;75;94; 98;1902;04-05]

Lock Haven weekly EXPRESS. w Mr 1882+
pub 1882+
P O 1923-Je 1932

Lock Haven PRESS. w 1861-
PLhT F 13,Mr 20 1862

LOGANTON

COUNTY journal. *See* Sugar Valley journal

SUGAR VALLEY journal. m,w 1898-1918||
1898-1904 as County journal
m 1898-99?
PLoK Je 7 1901[17-18]

LUMBERVILLE

DIARIST. w?
PNhE Jl 27 1849
PNhF Jl 27 1849

LYKENS

Lykens REGISTER. w 1865-1903||
1865-70? as Upper Dauphin register
P Jl 1895-Ja 23 1903

UPPER DAUPHIN register. *See* Lykens register

McCLURE

McClure PLAIN DEALER. w Ap 19 1905+
Title varies slightly
pub 1905+
PMiC [1909;11;13;22;25]
PMiCo 1932+

McCONNELLSBURG

FULTON democrat. w Je 1 1850+
Je- 1870 as Jackson democrat
pub 1872+
P Jl 1889+

FULTON republican. w 1851-1921||?
OCon Ja 10 1863-Je 1865

JACKSON democrat. *See* Fulton democrat

McDONALD

McDonald RECORD-OUTLOOK. w 1895+
1895-1932 as Record
pub 1901+
PWaHi [1899]-1901

McDonald TELEPHONE. w,sw 1895-97||
PWaHi [1896-97]

McKEES ROCKS

GAZETTE. w 1892+
pub 1892+

McKEESPORT

INDEPENDENCE. *See* Samastatnost

Daily NEWS. d Jl 1 1884+
pub 1884+
PMK 1923+

PENNSYLVANIA posten. w 1893-97||
In Swedish
IRA [1896-97]

SAMASTATNOST. (Independence) w O 25 1929+
In Slovak
pub 1929+

McKeesport STANDARD. w
InI N 8 1856-My 12 1860

SVENSKA veckobladet. w 1890-1919||
In Swedish
IRA complete
MnHi [1907-19]
PMN [1886]-[1914]

McKeesport TIMES. d 1871-1914||?
PMN [1886]-[1914]

MACUNGIE

Macungie PROGRESS. w 1880-1911||
PMacK [1880]-[1911]

MAHANOY CITY

Mahanoy City RECORD. w,tw 1871-81||?
1871-77? as Mahanoy Valley record(w)
MWA Je 22 1876

RECORD-AMERICAN. tw,d 1877+
1877-95? as Tri-weekly record(tw);1895?-1918? Daily record
pub 1919+
P Jl 1889-Je 1894

SAULE. (Sun) sw 1888+
In Lithuanian
pub 1909+
IU D 11 1917-O 7 1932

SUN. *See* Saule

Mahanoy VALLEY record. *See* Mahanoy City record

MALVERN

Malvern ITEM. w 1878-1908||?
PWcHi D 2 1879;O 17 1885[87]S 29,O 6 1888; S 13,27 1890;O 10,24 1891;O 22 1892[93-94]Jl 18 1896;My 3 1901

Malvern STAR. w Mr 20 1901-F 1906||?
PWcHi [1901]

MANAYUNK

Papers published in Manayunk are listed under Philadelphia

MANHEIM

Manheim weekly PLANET and Rapho banner. w 1846-
MWA Je 13 1848
NNHi Ag 3 1847

Manheim SENTINEL and advertiser. w Ja 3 1846+
pub 1846+
MWA D 4 1863

MANOR

EAGLE herald. w
PP [1932]-34

MANOR VALLEY news. w 1890-99||?
PPiHi Ap 1891-D 22 1893

PENNSYLVANIA (*Continued*)

MANSFIELD

Mansfield ADVERTISER. w 1872+
1872-Ja 21 1875 as Valley enterprise
PMa [1875-78]80;83-[1906]-11[29]+

Mansfield ITEM. w 1873-94||
PCarn [D 26 1873-76]

Mansfield UNION. w
PCarn [Je 8 1888-O 17 1890]

VALLEY enterprise. *See* Mansfield advertiser

MARCUS HOOK

Marcus Hook HERALD. w N 19? 1896-97||?
MWA Je 5 Jl 3 1897
PWcHi D 12 1896

MARIENVILLE

Marienville EXPRESS. w D 5 1890+
pub 1922+
PTioC 1894+
PWS [1890]

MARIETTA

Marietta ADVOCATE and farmers and mechanics intelligencer. w 1832-Ja 22 1835||
P [D 28 1833-35]
PLewL My 9 1832

ANT. w Ap 15 1840-
DLC Ap 22 1840

Weekly ARGUS. w Ag 20 1844-47||
DLC My 28 1844
PLaHi [1844-45]

MARIETTIAN. *See* Marietta register

Marietta PIONEER. w 1826-34||
Title varies slightly
DLC Jl 4,17 1828;Jl 10-17,S 11-18,O 2,30-N 6,27,D 25 1829
P S 26 1826-Jl 1834
PLaHi S 21 1827;Mr 21 1828

Marietta REGISTER. w 1854-1909||?
1854-70 as Mariettian
PLaHi [1870]

Marietta TIMES. w N 26 1876+
pub 1876-98;1901-29;31+

MARION CENTER

Marion Center INDEPENDENT. w 1881+
pub 1881-1927;31+

MATAMORAS

PIKE county times. w 1928+
pub 1928+
PMilHi [1930-31]

MAUCH CHUNK

CARBON county democrat. *See* Mauch Chunk democrat

CARBON county gazette. *See* Mauch Chunk coal gazette

CARBON county transit. *See* Mauch Chunk courier

CARBON democrat. *See* Mauch Chunk democrat

Mauch Chunk COAL gazette. w,sw 1845-1914||?
1845-52? as Carbon county gazette; 1853?-69 Mauch Chunk gazette
w 1845-98?
MWA N 25 1852;Je 26 1856
NjR Jl 24 1856
P Je 1889-My 1912
PMc 1845-52;55-64[68]-[70-71]-[74]87-88;93-1911
PMcC N 5 1875;F 4,Je 27 1876
PMcT [1869]-82
—d ed *See* Mauch Chunk times-news

Mauch Chunk COURIER. w Mr 1829-45||?
1829-32 as Lehigh pioneer and Mauch Chunk courier; 1843-44 Carbon county transit
Suspended from N 1834-N 1835
CSmH Je 3 1830
DLC D 17 1829;Ap 23 1832
MWA N 8 1830
NSchU F 14 1842
PEL F 23 1833
PHaC [1829-30;34-36]-38
PMc [1829-30]-[35 35;38-43
PMcT [1829-30;35]-[39]

Mauch Chunk DEMOCRAT. w 1847-1910||
1847-73 as Carbon democrat; 1874-81? Carbon county democrat
MWA N 17 1849-N 20 1852;Ap 4 1863
P Je 1889-Ag 1910
PMc [1847]-[49]-53;Ag 1867[71]-[73]-[79]90-92;95-1909
PMcC [1876]Je 21,Jl 23 1877
PMilC F 1 1872;F 13 1873
PWbW Ap 27 1850
—d ed *See* Mauch Chunk daily news

Mauch Chunk GAZETTE. *See* Mauch Chunk coal gazette

LEHIGH pioneer and Mauch Chunk courier. *See* Mauch Chunk courier

Mauch Chunk daily NEWS. d 1893-1926||
United with Mauch Chunk daily times to form Mauch Chunk times-news
PMc 1913-23;25-26
—w ed *See* Mauch Chunk democrat

Mauch Chunk TIMES-NEWS. d 1883+
1883-1927 as Mauch Chunk daily times
pub [1883]-[91]96[1904]07-[09]-[15-16]-[21]-[33]
P Je-D 1912;My 1927-Je 1932
PMc 1913-23;26+
—w ed *See* Mauch Chunk coal gazette

MAYFIELD

Mayfield NEWS. w 1929+
PScrHi Ap 10 1936

MEADVILLE

CRAWFORD county whig journal. *See* Crawford journal

CRAWFORD democrat. *See* Meadville democrat and messenger

CRAWFORD journal. w Ja 13 1848-1918||
1848-Je 1850 as Democratic whig journal; Je 1850-52 Gazette and whig journal; 1852-Jl 15 1855 Crawford county whig journal
MWA O 30,D 25 1855;F 24,Je 23,S 1,15-22,O 13-20 1857;Ap 27 1858;My 21,N 20 1867;Mr 20 1879
NNHi Ap 17 1855;Je 2 1863;Mr 6 1873
P O 6 1863;Jl 1889-1912
PMe 1848-64[83]-97;99-1908
PMeA [1869]-1908
PMeT 1866-68;73;75;77-83;1911-12;15-18

*CRAWFORD messenger. w Ja 2 1805-O 3 1835||
Followed by Crawford democrat, later Meadville democrat and messenger?
DLC N 25 1823;Jl 23 1824;Jl-Ag 21,S 18-O 1, 30-N 13 1828;Jl 23,S 3,17,O 1 1829;D 16-24 1830
MWA Ap 15,Je 10 1823;Ja 20 1825;Ag 23 1827; S 11 1828;Mr 3 1831
OOxM Ap 30,Je 4,Jl 2,16 1829
P Mr 26 1829-35
PMe F 24 1824;S 7 1826;My 28 1829;F 25,D 9 1830
PMeA 1821-33
PMeR 1821-31

CRAWFORD statesman. w Jl 27 1836-41||?
1836-Ja 17 1837 as Statesman; Ja 24 1837-Ja 20 1838 Statesman and Crawford county free press; Ja 27 1838-39 Crawford statesman and independent free press; 1839-My 1840 Crawford statesman and people's free press
MWA Mr 25 1837
PE Je 1-8,N 30 1839
PMe 1836-S 23 1841
PW Jl 31 1840

Meadville DEMOCRAT and messenger. w 1834-1903||
Follows Crawford messenger? 1834-Je 9 1884 as Crawford democrat (title varies: Crawford democrat and Northwestern advertiser; Crawford democrat and Meadville courier) Je 9 1884-Mr 18 1897 Meadville messenger and Crawford democrat
DLC [1847]N 13 1860
MWA F 5 1856;Ag 11 1857
P O 1835-Ap 1847
PEL D 7 1839
PMe O 22 1835;S 17 1836[37]-[59;61]-[80]-[84] 88-1903
PMeA 1834-37
PPiHi O 27 1857;N 16 1858;Ja 25 1859;O 9 1860[Mr 1861-Je 1866]
PW Jl 1840;Je 7 1842

DEMOCRATIC messenger. w 1879-Je 9 1884||
United with Crawford democrat to form Meadville messenger and Crawford democrat, later Meadville democrat and messenger
PMe [1880]81
PMeT 1880-83

DEMOCRATIC whig journal. *See* Crawford journal

Meadville GAZETTE. w F 28 1844-Je 1850||
1844-Ap 13 1847 as Meadville gazette and farmers' advocate. United with Democratic whig journal to form Gazette and whig journal, later Crawford journal
DLC Mr 27 1844
ICN Ap 13 1847-Ap 1850
MWA Ap 11 1848
PMe 1844-48

Meadville GAZETTE. w 1886-1907||
P Je 1889-F 1 1907

GAZETTE and whig journal. *See* Crawford journal

Meadville INDEX. w O 30 1877-Mr 30 1881||
1877-Ap 7 1880 as Index. Merged with Meadville republican
MWA D 18 1878
PMe 1880[81]

Meadville daily MESSENGER. d 1903-My 6 1920||
PMe 1903-[10]12-20

Meadville MESSENGER and Crawford democrat. *See* Meadville democrat and messenger

Meadville MONITOR. m
PPCHi Ap 1896-Mr 1897

Meadville REPUBLICAN. w My 1860-Mr 1885||
Follows Spirit of the age? United with Tribune to form Tribune-republican
MWA Je 30 1870
MnHi D 7 1861;Jl 19 1862
NNHi Mr 6 1869;Ap 11 1873
PEHi N 16 1861
PPiHi N 16 1861

Evening REPUBLICAN. d Je 1865-Mr 1885||
United with Meadville daily tribune to form Daily tribune-republican
MWA S 20 1876
PMe Mr 11 1865;71-81

SATURDAY night. w 1889-90||
PE Je 1-8,N 30-D 7 1889
PMeA complete
PMeT complete

SPIRIT of the age. w Ag 27 1853-My 18 1860||
Followed by Meadville republican?
MWA D 17 1853
NNHi N 16 1855
OClWHi D 3 1853;S 2,30-N 1859;F 3-17,Mr 2-16 Ap 27-My 18 1860
PMe D 3 1858

Meadville morning STAR. d Je 1891-Ap 1909||
Merged with Daily tribune-republican
PMe D 19 1893;Je 27 1895;D 13 1906;F 18 1907
PMeA 1907-[09]

STATESMAN. *See* Crawford statesman

TRIBUNE-REPUBLICAN. w Ap 11 1884-1910||
1884-Mr 1885 as Tribune
pub 1885-1910

Daily TRIBUNE-REPUBLICAN. d Ap 11 1884+
1884-Mr 1885 as Daily tribune
pub 1884+
MWA My 11 1888
OClWHi My 11 1888
P Jl 1889+
PEHi My 12 1888
PMe [1898]-1906[09]-26
PMeA 1884-98;1907-[09;21-32]+

MEANSVILLE

BRADFORD settler. *See* Northern banner and Bradford democrat (Towanda)

SETTLER. *See* Northern banner and Bradford democrat (Towanda)

MECHANICSBURG

CUMBERLAND VALLEY journal. w N 13 1856-72||
P 1856-N 12 1857
PYHi 1856-N 12 1857

Mechanicsburg FREE PRESS. w My 30 1891-1905||
P Je 1894-Je 1902

Mechanicsburg weekly GAZETTE. w N 13 1856-N 12 1857||
DLC complete
P complete

IRON gray. *See under* Harrisburg

Saturday evening JOURNAL. w O 1878-1928||
PMecL 1894;1924[25]-28

Daily JOURNAL. *See* Daily local news

Daily LOCAL news. d 1900+
1900-D 14 1923 as Daily journal
pub [1905-10]-20[23]+
P N 20 1901-12

MEDIA

DELAWARE county American. w 1858-1917||?
MWA F 17 1869
P Je 26 1889-1912
PMedD F 22 1860;F 6 1861;F 19 1862;F 4 1863;Ja 22 1868;Ja 13,30 1869;Ja 15 1870
PSF S 28 1881
PWcHi Jl 4-11,S 19,D 19 1866;F 28 1877

DELAWARE county record. w 1878-1924||?
PCHi Mr 23 1878;F 12 1916

DELAWARE county republican. w
PMedD Ag 30 1833[35]

Media NEWS. w 1930+
pub Mr 1932+

UNION, and Delaware county democrat. w My 25 1852-
MWA O 12 1852
PCHi [1852]

MERCER

DEMOCRATIC register. w 1858-
MWA F 14 1861

Mercer DISPATCH and republican. w 1857+
1857-58 as Mercer county dispatch; 1858-87 Mercer dispatch (Ap 1864-65 Whig and dispatch)
pub O 19,N 2 1859;Ap 11,Ag 29 1860[61-64]Ap 21,Je 2 1865;F 28 1868;Ja 6 1871[74]-81;83 [86]-88;90-91;93+
MWA F 6 1861
P Je 12 1889-1912;18+

Mercer GAZETTE. w 1825-27||?
Merged with Western press
DLC S 15 1827
PW My 16,Je 6 1826

INDEPENDENT democrat. w O 13? 1850-
MWA Ja 28 1853
OClWHi My 13 1851
PMerD Mr 12 1853;S 25,O 30 1854;Ap 7 1855

Mercer LUMINARY. *See* Mercer county luminary

MERCER county dispatch. *See* Mercer dispatch and republican

MERCER county luminary. w Ag 2 1830-Jl 3 1850||
1830-33 as Mercer luminary
CSmH Ag 16 1830
DLC F 6 1833
PMe Ja 6,Je 17,Ag 19 1846
PMerD [1837-39;47]
PPi Jl 28 1847-Je 6 1849

PENNSYLVANIA (*Continued*)

MERCER—*Continued*

MERCER county whig. w Je 15 1844-64‖
United with Mercer dispatch to form Whig and dispatch, later Mercer dispatch and republican
PMerD 1847;49-53;60

*WESTERN press. w F 22 1811-1919‖?
1827-29? as Western press and Mercer county gazette
DLC S 12 1829;Ja 1 1831
MWA Jl 22 1823;Ja 27 1854;My 24 1861
OClWHi Ja 4 1834
P N 15 1828
PMerD N 11 1823;Mr 17 1825;O 11 1828;D 22 1849;O 5 1855;O 19,28 1861;N 27 1896;Ap 9 1897;Ag 26,O 7,D 9 1898;D 29 1905;Ag 27 1909;Mr 31,N 3 1911
PNc [1836]-[39]
PPiHi D 7 1821;Ap 14 1838
PW N 15 1834;Ag 13 1836;Ap 29,Jl 1842;Je 4 1852

WHIG and dispatch. *See* Mercer dispatch and republican

MERCERSBURG

Weekly JOURNAL. w 1846+
pub 1857+
DLC Ap 14 1846;Ag 4 1847
MWA Ap 10 1863
PE Ja 21 1848

MEYERSDALE

Meyersdale COMMERCIAL. w Mr 1878-1917‖?
P Je 1889-1912

MEYERSTOWN

Die Meyerstaun GAZETTE und wahrer republikaner. w 1849-
In German
PNoHi O 7 1853

NEUTRALE wachter. w
In German
P-M Ja 4 1844

MIDDLEBURG

Middleburg NEWS item. *See* Snyder county news

Middleburg POST. w 1864+
pub F 1868+
P Ag 1879-1912;17+
PHHi O 5 1899
PLewL [1880]
PMiCo 1929+
PMiR [1870]-1916

SNYDER county news. w 1888-Jl 13 1916‖
1888-99 as Middleburg news item. Merged with Middleburg post
PMiC [1888-99;1901-02;04-05;07-11;13-15]

SNYDER county tribune. w 1856-69‖?
1856-60? as Weekly tribune
MWA Ap 11 1860;Ja 3 1866

SNYDER county volksfreund. w 1852-73‖?
1852-69? as Volksfreund
In German
MWA O 10 1860
PMiHi O 6 1853;Ag 31 1854[55-57]My 12,Je 23,Jl 21,O 30,N 13,D 15 1858;Ja 21,Ap 13 1859;F 15,My 30,D 12 1860

Weekly TRIBUNE. *See* Snyder county tribune

VOLKSFREUND. *See* Snyder county volksfreund

MIDDLETOWN

DAUPHIN journal. *See* Journal

Middletown EMPORIUM and Portsmouth weekly advertiser. w 1850-
DLC O 30 1852
MWA N 6 1852
PHHi My 2 1850;Ap 17 1851

JOURNAL. w 1854+
1854-90 as Dauphin journal
NNHi Jl 27 1871;F 6 1873
PHHi D 25 1856;My 13 1858;Ja 14 1864

Daily JOURNAL. d 1890+
PPot S 13 1894

Middletown PRESS. w Jl 16 1881+
pub [1881+]
PHHi [1881]-[1909]Je 9 1917

MIDLAND

Midland weekly NEWS. w 1928+
pub [1928]+

MIFFLINBURG

Mifflinburg TELEGRAPH. w Je 10 1862+
pub 1877+
MWA Je 17,Ag 12-19,S 9,23,O 14-21,N 4-11,25,D 9-16 1862;Ja 20-27,Mr 10,31,Ap 14-21,Je 2,25,Ag 13,S 10-24,D 10 1863;F 18,Mr 24-Ap,My 19,Jl 21,Ag,N 24 1864;Mr 30,My 25,Jl 20 1865;F 22 1866;Jl 1 1869;Mr 17,N 24 1870;My 25,Je 8-15,O 19,N 16,30 1871;Ja 25,F 8,Ap 11 1872;Ja 15,F 12,Mr 26 1879
P Je 12 1889+
PLewB [1883;89;1901;08;11]
PLewC 1893-1927;30-31
PLewT Je 25,S 17,N 19 1862;Ja 7,F 4,Mr 25,Ap 22,Ag 13,O 18,N 5-12 1863;Jl 7 1864[73-74]78

UNION county press. w Mr 7? 1858-62‖
MWA Ja 25,O 17 1860
PLewT D 5 1860;Mr 12,Ap 2-9 1862

UNION county star. w
P Jl 17 1856-Ja 15 1857

MIFFLINTOWN

DEMOCRAT and register. w 1846-1912‖
1846-48 as Pennsylvania register; 1848-O 1867 Juniata register (1852-58 Tuscarora register)
DLC Ag 27 1839
NNHi Je 21 1823
P My 1849-O 1851;D 1852-Mr 1 1855;Je 1889-D 19 1912

*Mifflin EAGLE. w 1817-
NNHi Je 21 1823

JUNIATA free press. w 1831-
MWA D 19 1832-Ja 2,30-F 13,Mr 20,Ap 24,Je 19 1833
PBL Je 17 1835

JUNIATA herald. w F 1880-1912‖
P Jl 1889-D 18 1912

JUNIATA journal. My 28 1835-
DLC My 28 1835

JUNIATA register. *See* Democrat and register

JUNIATA republican. w 1866-O 1873‖
United with Juniata sentinel to form Juniata sentinel and republican

JUNIATA sentinel and republican. w D 9 1846+
1846-O 15 1873 as Juniata sentinel
pub 1873+
MWA Ap 10 1861;Ja 31 1866
OCon My 1857-Ap 20 1859

JUNIATA telegraph and peoples advocate. w My 15 1831-
MWA Je 1 1831
P My 15-N 30 1831

JUNIATA tribune. w 1876+
pub 1928+
P 1920-Je 1932

JUNIATA true democrat. w Je 1860-O 1867‖
United with Juniata register to form Democrat and register

PENNSYLVANIA register. *See* Democrat and register

SPIRIT of the times and democratic press. w 1836-
P-M O 20 1842

TUSCARORA register. *See* Democrat and register

MILFORD

Milford DISPATCH and Pike county press. w Jl 1827+
1827-28 as Eagle of the North; 1828-31 Northern eagle and Milford monitor; 1847-52 Pike county democrat; 1852-78 Milford herald; 1878-1926 Milford dispatch
pub [1852;55-56]-[62-63]-77
CSmH Jl 23,Ag 27 1830
DLC D 19 1851;F 9,Mr 1,O 25-N 1 1852;F 25 1854
NNHi S 14 1869
P Jl 1889+
PHsHi Ja 26,F 23 1852
PMilA [1856-61]
PMilC 1870+
PMilHi My 11 1832[52]F 16 1853;Jl 29 1854[64]D 18 1866;71-78
PP Ag 5 1873
PWbW D 1 1827;F 8,22-29,Mr 14-Ap 4,18,My 2,23,Je 6 1828

EAGLE of the North. *See* Milford dispatch and Pike county press

Milford HERALD. *See* Milford dispatch and Pike county press

JEFFERSONIAN republican. w
DLC Ja 20 1842

NORTHERN eagle and Milford monitor. *See* Milford dispatch and Pike county press

PIKE county democrat. *See* Milford dispatch and Pike county press

PIKE county press. w 1895-1926‖
United with Milford dispatch to form Milford dispatch and Pike county press
P Jl 8 1904-D 18 1923
PMilHi 1895-1903

MILFORD SQUARE

Der BUCKS county patriot. *See* Patriot and reformer

*PATRIOT and reformer. w 1804?-90‖
1804?-77 as Der Bucks county patriot; 1878-80 Der Bucks county patriot and reformer and agriculturist; My 6 1880-81 Bucks county patriot
In German
PDoHi [1821-90]
PPeS D 21 1876;Ja 11,F 8,22 1877;F 28,My 16,Ag 8,S 26,O 31 1878;F 13 1879

MILLERSBURG

Millersburg HERALD. w Ja 1875-1918‖?
PHHi [1877]-1909
PLaL Jl 23,Ag 6,1875;My 10 1878

Millersburg SENTINEL. w 1864+
PHHi [1884]-1907;N 2 1917;N 28 1919

Millersburg TIMES. w Mr 16 1932-Ja 4 1933‖
PMillH complete

MILLHEIM

DEMOKRATISCHER berichter. *See* Millheim journal

Millheim JOURNAL. w 1827+
1827-47 as Der Centre berichter; 1847-71 Demokratischer berichter und Center county anzeiger; 1871-80 Demokratischer berichter
1827-71 pub in Aaronsburg
pub 1895+
P Jl 1889-D 19 1912
P-M Je 6-13 1889
PStP 1877-93

MILLVILLE

Weekly TABLET. w 1887-1919‖?
PBloHi [1887-89]

MILLWOOD

Der WAFFENLOSE waechter. w 1871-
In German
PLaHi Ag 21,O 3 1871;F 1872[1873]Je 1877

MILTON

Milton weekly ARGUS. *See* Milton record

Morning BULLETIN. d S 14 1912-F 28 1914‖
PMiltS [1912]-[14]

Milton DEMOCRAT. w Ap 1852-59‖
PMiltS S 29 1852
PSuHi Ap 5 1856

Milton ECONOMIST. w 1884-89‖
United with Milton weekly argus to form Milton record
PSuHi Je 25 1887

Milton LEDGER. w 1838-44‖
PLewL Ag 4 1838
PMiltS S 30 1843;Jl 24,O 29 1844
PSuHi Ap 17 1844

*MILTONIAN. w S 21 1816-My 17 1933‖
United with Milton evening standard to form Standard and Miltonian
KHi D 19 1884-[N 1905-Ag 10 1906]-S 6 1923
MWA Mr 15-29 1823;Jl 3 1830;D 3 1852
NcU My 3,Ag 25-S 6,O 14 1867
P F 8 1823;Jl 1889-Je 1932
P-M Ap 16 1825;Je 7-14 1889
PEL Jl 12 1834
PLewB [1909-17;19]
PLewL 1823[24]-[26-27]-[30-34;50;85]
PLhT My 21 1880
PMiltS 1834-35[37-64]67;69;71-72;74-[79]-93;1906-29;33
PShH [1839-44]
PSuHi My 1 1828;O 18 1833;Je 23 1836;N 16 1839
PWbW Je 9 1848

NORTHUMBERLAND county herald. w 1868-
PMiltS D 15 1869

Milton RECORD. w Ap 1 1874-95‖
1874-S 1877 as Independent weekly (Benton); O 1877-89 as Milton weekly argus
PMiltS N 26 1880
PSuHi 1894

STANDARD and Miltonian. tw,d 1890+
1890-1900 as Standard(tw);1900-My 17 1933 Milton evening standard
pub 1890;94;98-[1904]-[11]-[20]-[24]+
PLewB [1908-18]

STATE'S advocate. w F 23 1826-38‖?
DLC Mr 30-Ap 6 1826;Je 26,Jl 10,31-Ag 14,S 25 1828
MWA 1826-Je 25 1829
P Mr 1826-F 2 1829
P-M S 8 1831
PJsS 1826-[29]
PLewL N 24 1831

WEST BRANCH farmer and true democrat. w 1834-37‖?
PSuHi [1836]

MINERSVILLE

Minersville BULLETIN. w 1850-
MWA N 24 1852;N 22 1856

SCHUYLKILL republican. *See under* Pottsville

MONESSEN

Friday evening CALL. w 1908-26‖
United with Monessen news to form Monessen news-call
PMoN [1924-25]

Monessen daily INDEPENDENT. d 1902+
pub Je 11 1902+

Monessen NEWS-CALL. w 1899+
1899-1926 as Monessen news
pub 1899+

MONONGAHELA

DEMOCRAT-SENTINEL. w O 1891-92‖
P 1891-Je 1892

PENNSYLVANIA republican. d 1881+
pub 1881-88;90-[1903-04]-12[14]+
PWaHi [1886;92]
—w ed *See* Monongahela Valley republican

Monongahela RECORD. w Mr 1876-91‖
1876-83? as Valley record
P Je 1889-F 5 1891

PENNSYLVANIA (*Continued*)

MONONGAHELA—*Continued*

Monongahela TRIBUNE. w F 12- 1891||?
P F-Je 1891

VALLEY record. *See* Monongahela record

Monongahela VALLEY republican. w 1848-1907||?
pub 1851-58;61-62;64-66;69;71-79
P Ja 20 1874-Je 12 1883
PWaC 1896-97
PWaHi [1881-93]
—d ed *See* Pennsylvania republican

VALLEY sentinel. w O 11 1860-
MWA D 20 1860

MONROETON

Monroeton ENTERPRISE. w Mr 1887-1917||
Suspended 1891-1900
MWA S 20 1888
PMonR [1904]-[10]
PToHi Ag 10 1904

MONTROSE

CANDID examiner. w 1825-28||
PScrHi [1825-26]

Montrose DEMOCRAT. w 1844-1927||
1844-48 as Northern democrat. United with Independent republican to form Montrose independent
MWA N 11 1852
P [Je 1889-1923]
PEL 1845
PToHi 1846;51
PWbW F 23 1848;55-62

DEMOCRATIC volunteer. *See* Montrose volunteer

*Montrose GAZETTE. w F 20 1816-25||
1816-My 9 1818 as Susquehanna centinel
PWbW 1821-N 1825

Montrose INDEPENDENT. w Ja 4 1855+
1855-1927 as Independent republican
MBAt Ap 18 1865
MWA Ap 14 1863;Ja 5 1874
NNHi My 26-Je 16,Ag 18 1863;My 5 1873
P [S 1889-1934]
PHsHi Je 21 1864
PScrHi [1928;31-32]
PWbW 1855-64

INDEPENDENT volunteer. *See* Montrose volunteer

NORTH star. w Je 1840-41||
United with Montrose volunteer to form Volunteer and North star, later Montrose volunteer
PEL Je 11,D 31 1840

NORTHERN democrat. *See* Montrose democrat

PEOPLE'S advocate. w 1846-48||
PToHi [1846]

Montrose REGISTER. *See* Susquehanna register and northern farmer

SPECTATOR and freeman's journal. w 1836-
DLC D 12 1839
MWA O 31 1839
PPiHi Je 15 1837-Je 7 1838

SUSQUEHANNA centinel. *See* Montrose gazette

SUSQUEHANNA register and northern farmer. w 1826-55||?
1826 as Montrose register; Ja 5 1827-31? Susquehanna register; 1831 Susquehanna register and northern Pennsylvanian
CSmH Jl 9 1830;Ja 15 1835;D 6 1838;Jl 11 1839;Ag 31 1843;D 7 1848
DLC Ag 14 1839
MWA D 2 1852
NN Mr 21 1839
NPhN Ja 10 1839-40
NjR Ap 6 1848
P N 21 1828
P-M N 2 1832
PAtM F 26 1830
PEL N 21 1828;35-37;40;42;45
PPiHi Je 15 1837-Je 7 1838
PToHi D 23 1831;38;O 1 1840;Jl 8 1841;43;46;51
PWbW [1826-31]

Montrose VOLUNTEER. w N 1831-44||
1831-32 as Independent volunteer; 1832- Democratic volunteer; -1838 Independent volunteer; 1841-My 1843 Volunteer and north star
MWA Ja-F 10,My 11,Je 1 1832
P-M Ag 8 1833
PBL D 4 1834
PEL 1836-37;40;42
PPiHi Je 15 1837-Je 7 1838

MORTON

DELAWARE county observer and Morton chronicle. w Je 17 1880+
Title varies: Delaware county observer
pub [1880]+

MOUNT CARMEL

Il CORRIERE Tirolese. *See under* New York

Mount Carmel ITEM. w,sw,d Ja 7 1888+
w 1888-Ja 9 1896;sw Ja 16 1896-O 1902
pub 1888+

MOUNT JEWETT

Mount Jewett ECHO. w 1922+
pub 1922+

MOUNT JOY

Mount Joy BULLETIN. w Je 1 1901+
pub 1901+

Mount Joy STAR and news. w 1873-1917||?
1873-78? as Mount Joy star
MWA D 19 1913
PLaHi [1873]-76;94

MOUNT OLIVER

HILL TOP record. w My 3 1904+
pub 1904+

MOUNT PLEASANT

Mt. Pleasant JOURNAL. w Je 5 1873+
pub 1882+
PPiHi O 8 1874
PUn Ap 21 1896;F 12 1897

Mount Pleasant REGISTER. w
DLC Je 20 1838;D 18 1839;N 11 1840
PP S 11-25 1839

MOUNT UNION

Mt. Union HERALD. *See* Shirleysburg weekly herald (Shirleysburg)

Mount Union TIMES. w 1873+
P Je 1889-1912
PHuJ 1874-[77]
PJ Ja 17-24 1884

MUNCY

Muncy LUMINARY. w Ap 10 1841+
Title varies: Muncy luminary and Lycoming county advertiser
P Je 14 1889+
PHuJ Ag 21 1847
PJsJ Ja 16 1866
PSuHi O 5 1858
PWp Ja 21 1865

Muncy TELEGRAPH. w Ap 1831-41||
MiU-C N 5 1836
PWp [1835-36]

NANTICOKE

BULLETIN. w 1932+
pub Mr 1932+

Nanticoke TRIBUNE. w 1883-91||?
PWbW 1887-91

NARBERTH

OUR town. w O 15 1914+
pub 1914+
PHar 1914-[24]29+
PP [1914]-Mr 1915;D 18 1931

NAZARETH

ABEND zeitung. w 1835-39||
In German
P-M S 7 1838
PNazHi [1837]-[39]
PFeS F 2 1838

Nazareth ITEM. w 1891+
pub 1891+

NEW ALBANY

Albany weekly MIRROR. w Ja 28 1895-1919||?
PToHi Ja 28 1895

NEW ALEXANDRIA

New Alexandria PRESS. w D 23 1930+
pub 1930+

NEW BERLIN

AMERICAN flag. w N 2 1851-
PLewL N 2 1851

SPIRIT of the Age. w 1835-
PLewL S 11 1835
PNc [1835]

Die STIMME von Union, Northumberland, und Centre counties advertiser. w 1822-
In German
PLewL O 23 1823
PSuHi D 5 1822

TELEGRAPH and anti-Masonic reporter. *See* Union telegraph and anti-Masonic argus

UNION annalist. w S 7 1823-
PLewL S 7 1823;F 21 1824

UNION anti-Masonic telegraph. *See* Union telegraph and anti-Masonic argus

UNION county free press. w 1833-
PNoHi F 8 1833

UNION county star. w
KHi [F 24 1853-F 9 1854]

Der UNION demokrat. w
In German
MWA F 11(extra)1846
PNorG [1847]-[52]

UNION hickory. *See under* Lewisburg

UNION star. w 1840-
pub [1846]-[49]
DLC My 31 1844
PLewL [1840]D 20 1844;Mr 7 1850
PPiHi Ap 30 1841

UNION telegraph and anti-Masonic argus. w 1827-
1827-29 as Union telegraph; 1829-30 Telegraph and anti-Masonic reporter; 1830-32 Union anti-Masonic telegraph
NjHi S 9 1829;F 5,My 21,Ag 13 1830
PLewL [1827-30]Mr 11 1831;Je 29,Jl 13 1832
PNc [1832]

UNION times. *See* Selinsgrove times (Selinsgrove)

NEW BLOOMFIELD

PEOPLES' advocate and press. w Je 1853+
1853-S 1868 as Peoples' advocate and Perry county democrat press
pub 1853+
MWA Ap 3 1861
P Jl 1889+

PERRY county democrat. w O 1836+
pub 1836+
DLC Jl 4 1844
P Je 12 1889+
PHi [1841]-[47]

PERRY county freeman. w Je 21 1839-O 1905||
1839- Perry freeman. Merged with Peoples' advocate and press
MWA S 29 1853;Jl 3 1862;Je 2 1864
P Jl 1895-Je 1898
PHHi F 15 1882

PERRY county standard. *See* Perry standard

*PERRY forester and public advertiser. w 1820-
MWA N 18 1830
P N 15 1827;N 13 1828

PERRY freeman. *See* Perry county freeman

PERRY standard. w S 1841-48||
1841-Ag 15 1844 as Newport standard (Newport); Ag 22 1844-45 Perry county standard
MWA D 27 1843;N 13 1845
PBL S 5 1844;F 6,Ag 19 1847
PHi [1844]-46

NEW BRIGHTON

BEAVER county press. w Mr 24 1871-Ja 14 1874||
PMe Mr 14 1873

BEAVER VALLEY news. w,d My 22 1874-1928||
United with Beaver Falls tribune to form News tribune (Beaver Falls)
w 1874-Ja 1883
PBeC 1874-1906
PBf [1877;79;83]

New Brighton TIMES. w O 21 1857-65||
PBf F 7-14,Ap 4,Je 17,28 1861
PPi O 9 1862-Ja 21 1864

NEW CARLISLE

New Carlisle EAGLE and whig advocate. w My 7 1844-
DLC My 7 1844

NEW CASTLE

New Castle COURANT. *See* New Castle herald

New Castle DEMOCRAT. w 1874-O 1921||
1874-82 as Paragraph
P Jl 18 1889-1912
PNcC 1886-[97-98]-[90]92-1921

FREE PRESS. w 1908-13||
WHi Jl 25 1908-Jl 26 1913

GAZETTE and democrat. w 1843-74||?
OClWHi Jl 14 1871
PNc [1872]-[74]
PNcC 1873-74
PPi Jl 16 1846;Ja 7,Mr 18-My 13,27 1847-Je, Ag 9 1849

New Castle GUARDIAN. w 1870-95||
1870-89 as Lawrence guardian. United with New Castle courant to form Courant-guardian, later New Castle weekly herald
P Je 27 1889-95
PNc [1870]-[79]82-[93]
PNcC complete

New Castle weekly HERALD. w 1857-1906||
1857-96 as New Castle courant; 1896-1901 Courant guardian
P Je 1889-1906
PNcC 1870-1905
PPiHi Je 30 1865

New Castle daily HERALD. d 1887-1924||
1887-96 as New Castle courant; 1896-1901 Courant-guardian
P [1889]-[1924]
PNc [1911;23-24]

New Castle INTELLIGENCER. w Ag 13 1836-
OClWHi Ag 25 1836;My 4,25-Je 1 1837

LAWRENCE guardian. *See* New Castle guardian

LAWRENCE journal. w 1849-74||
MWA F 13 1864
PNc [1849]-62;64-66
PNcC [1849]-[58;60-61]64-67;70-[74]

New Castle NEWS. w,d 1880+
w 1880-1912
pub [1880]+
NjWdHi O 12-15 1927
P 1927+
PNc [1917-18]
PNcC 1891-1900;03-04;06-12

PARAGRAPH. *See* New Castle democrat

New Castle REGISTER. w N? 1826-
DLC Mr 9 1827

PENNSYLVANIA (*Continued*)

NEW CUMBERLAND

FREEMAN'S advocate and Cumberland, York and Dauphin advertiser. w D 25 1839-
DLC Ja 1,D 26 1840

NEW HOLLAND

ANTI-MASONIC herald. w
P Ja 30 1829-Ag 28 1832

New Holland CLARION. w Ja 18 1873+
pub 1873+
PLaHi 1873-88;91-1903

NEW HOPE

New Hope MONITOR. w 1881-82||
PDoHi Jl 21 1882
PNhF Je 18 1881

New Hope NEWS. w 1892+
pub 1913+
PDoHi 1903-09;12;14

NEW KENSINGTON

DISPATCH. w,sw,d N 21 1891+
w 1891-1915;sw 1915-19
pub [1891]+

NEW OXFORD

New Oxford ITEM. w 1879+
pub 1888+
PGCo [1893-94]

NEW WILMINGTON

New Wilmington GLOBE. w Mr 6 1880+
pub [1880-81]92-93;97-1916;20+
PNcC 1889-[91]

NEWPORT

NEWS-SUN. w,sw N 18 1868+
1868-D 23 1924 as Newport news
sw 1914-F 10 1928
pub 1868+

Newport STANDARD. *See* Perry standard (New Bloomfield)

NEWTON

CLAY trumpet. w 1844||
Campaign paper
PDoHi Ag 20 1844

Newton ENTERPRISE. w Mr 1868+
pub Mr 19 1868+
PDoHi [1868-1915]
PNeB Mr 3 1877
PP [1931]-34

Newton JOURNAL. w 1842-50||?
Ag 16-S 14 1842 as Literary chronicle and working man's advocate; S 20 1842-44 Newton journal and working men's advocate; 1845-46 Newton journal and native American; 1846-48 Newton journal and dollar weekly
MWA Ja 23 1849
PDoHi 1845-46;Ja 25,Mr 28 1848;50
PNeB [1842]-[45]

LITERARY chronicle and working man's advocate. *See* Newton journal

NEWVILLE

ENTERPRISE. w 1871-86||
United with Star of the Valley to form Star and enterprise, later Valley times-star

STAR of the Valley. *See* Valley times-star

Newville TIMES. *See* Valley times

VALLEY times. w My 1882-Ap 2 1914||
1882-N 12 1885 as Plainfield times (Plainfield). United with Star and enterprise to form Valley times-star
P Jl 1901-04;06-07;Jl 1909-Je 1910
PNewT complete

VALLEY times-star. w 1858+
1858-86 as Star of the Valley; 1886-1914 Star and enterprise
pub S 1865-78;97-[1907;14]-[20;27]+

NORRISTOWN

CLAY flag staff. w My 8- 1844||
Campaign paper
MoSM Jl 31,O 30 1844
PNoHi Ag 7 1844

Norristown FREE PRESS. w D 15 1829-F 1 1837||
United with Norristown herald and Montgomery county advertiser to form Norristown herald and free press, later Norristown weekly herald
pub [1831]-[33]-[37]
CSmH Ag 17 1830
MDeHi S 19 1832
MWA Mr 29 1831
NjHi N 2 1830
NjR F 13 1833
P-M O 10 1832
PDoHi 1833
PNo [1829]-[37]
PNoHi [1831]-[34]

Norristown GAZETTE. *See* Norristown herald and Montgomery county advertiser

Norristown weekly HERALD. w F 1 1837-1920||?
Formed by the union of Norristown herald and Norristown free press. 1837-O 3 1887 as Norristown herald and free press (title varies slightly)
pub 1837-1916
DLC N 11 1840;S 21(extra)1864
MWA Ja 11 1866
NjR F 22 1837
OClWHi N 23,D 2 1865
P Jl 1889-1912
PDoHi F 23 1865;Jl 11 1876;F 12,Je 25 1878
PNo 1837
PNoHi [1841-43]-1906
PPeS [Ja-Jl 1844;45]Ja 14,Mr 4,Je 3 1846;Ag 4,S 8,O 6 1847[48-53]Ja 11,F 1,Mr 15,Ap 5 1854[55-62]Ap 14,My 5,O 20 1863;O 4,18-25 1864;Ja 3,Ap 20,Jl 13,Ag 24,N 9,D 28 1865; S 6 1866;Ja 31,Ap 25,My 16,Je 13,Jl 11 1867; Ja 30 1868;Mr 16 1871;O 24 1872;S 19 1876;Ap 30,S 10 1878[79]Ja 13,N 9 1880;Ja 9,F 13,27 1882;Ag 6,O 1-15,N 5 1883[84]Ag 16 1886
PPot Jl 10,O 16 1839;Jl 14 1847;Ap 28 1849;Ja 2,Jl 17 1850;D 18 1860
VU Ag 12 1869

Semi-weekly HERALD. sw F 4 1865-N 10 1866||
PNoT complete

Norristown daily HERALD. d D 20 1869-D 31 1922||
Title varies: Daily herald; Norristown herald. United with Daily times to form Norristown daily herald and The Norristown times, later Times-herald
pub 1869-79[83]85-1922
P N 9 1871
PDoHi Ja 14 1876
PHHi Jl 22 1873
PNoHi D 21,29 1869[70]Mr 8-9 1871;D 10 1872; My 7,13,18 1874[76]Ja 5 1878[1912]-17
PP [1912]
PPeS My 20,31,Je 20,Ag 13 1887;Mr 5,N 14-15 1890;S 25 1908
PPot [1884;90]Je 6 1891
VU Je 11 1870

*Norristown HERALD and Montgomery county advertiser. w Je 1 1799-F 1 1837||
1799-My 30? 1800 as Norristown gazette; O 10 1880-Je 23 1830 Norristown herald and weekly advertiser. United with Norristown free press to form Norristown herald and free press, later Norristown weekly herald
DLC Jl 9,23-Ag,S 24,O 8,N 5-19 1828
NjR S 30,D 2 1835
P Ag 1822-F 23 1825
PNo [1835]
PNoHi 1821-34
PNoT 1821-34
PPeS D 5 1827;D 10 1828
PPot Mr 23 1825

Norristown daily HERALD and The Norristown times. *See* Times-herald

INDEPENDENT. w Je 8 1865-75||?
PNoHi 1865-Mr 28 1872

MONTGOMERY county presse. *See* Stimme des volkes and Montgomery county presse (Lansdale)

MONTGOMERY sentinel. w 1830-31||
Merged with Norristown register and Montgomery county democrat
PBL [1830-31]

MONTGOMERY watchman. w 1849-O 12 1857||
*1849-50 as Watchman. United with Norristown register to form Norristown register and Montgomery watchman, later Norristown register and Montgomery county democrat
PHi [1849]-[51]
PNoHi Ag 21 1850[51-57]
PSuHi Ap 15 1849
PWcHi [1851-53;55-57]

NATIONAL defender. w Ag 1856-1900||?
MWA Ag 9 1864-Ag 10 1869;Je 15 1880
PDoHi N 10 1874;S 16 1884
PNoHi Ag 12 1856-[68]-[77]80-Jl 14 1896
PPeS O 16 1866;My 21 1867;D 7 1869;My 12 1874;Mr 18 1879
PShH O 26,N 16 1858

OLIVE branch. *See* Norristown republican

Daily REGISTER. d 1875-1917||
Title varies: Norristown register; Norristown daily register; Norristown morning register
P 1913-[17]
PDoHi S 20,26,O 3 1881
PNoHi O 5 1875;Ap 19,Je 14 1876;Jl 7 1877[86]-1917
PPeS Ap 5 1883;Ja 3 1885;Mr 14 1913
PPoT Je 24 1880;Mr 4 1885;S 29 1886;N 5 1890

Norristown REGISTER. d 1880-1917||?
P 1913-Je 1917

*Norristown REGISTER and Montgomery county democrat. w S 22 1803-1914||?
Title varies: Norristown register; Register; Weekly register; Norristown weekly register; Norristown register and Montgomery democrat; Norristown register and Montgomery watchman
DLC 1847-48
MWA S 3 1828;Jl 20 1852
N O 16 1833
NjHi My 9,30,Jl 4,25 1821;Jl 9 1823;My 12,Jl 7,N ,17-D 1 1824;Ag 24,N 9 1825;Mr 22,Ap 12,My 24,Ag 16,S 6,N 8 1826
NjR O 22 1828;Ap 27,Ag 24 1831;N 18 1835
P N 12 1827;N 26 1828;O 1889-1912
PBL [1833-36;38;40;53]-[58]
PDoHi Ag 23 1870;O 14 1879;Ja 4 1881
PHi [1843]-[49;54]-[57-58]-[65]70-[72]
PNo [1822]-[27]
PNoHi [1832]-[46-49]-[54-55;57]-[66]78-[81]87-[1901]
PPL Je 6,O 31 1849;My 21 1850
PPeS N 7 1827;Ja 18,Jl 12 1843;Je 3,Jl 15,O 14,D 9 1846;Je 23,Jl 28 1847[48]Ag 22-29,D 12 1849[50-54]D 11 1855;Mr 4,Ap 8,Je 3,D 30 1856;Ja 13,F 10,Mr 10,Jl 28 1857;D 7 1858; Ap 26 1859;Mr 6,Ap 10 1860;D 3 1861;Mr 25-Ap 15,29,Je 3,17,Jl 1-15,Ag 5 1862;S 18 1866; Ja 22,Mr 19-26,Ap 30-My 7 1867;Mr 10 1874; Jl 27 1875;Mr 12 1878;S 23 1890
PPot Ap 27 1825;Mr 1 1826;My 12 1841;My 3 1843;My 12 1844;Mr 26 1845;Jl 10-17 1860
VU N 15 1880

Norristown REPUBLICAN. w 1841-O 11 1864||
1841-Mr 17 1857 as Olive branch (title varies slightly); Mr 26 1857-My 3 1861 Norristown republican and Montgomery, Bucks and Philadelphia advertiser; My 10 1861-Mr 21 1862 Republican democrat. Merged with Norristown weekly herald
MWA O 28 1851
NNHi Jl 3 1863
PDoHi Ap 7 1847;N 30 1852
PNoHi [1851-52]-[64]
PNoT [1854-55]-62

Norristown REPUBLICAN. sw N 13 1866-My 18 1869||
PNoT 1866-Ja 1869
PWcHi D 8 1866

REPUBLICAN democrat. *See* Norristown republican. w

Weekly TIMES. w N 19 1881-D 29 1906||?
pub 1882-1906
PDoHi Je 30 1882;Ap 11 1885;Ap 11 1886
PPeS S 13 1884;O 25,N 8 1890

TIMES-HERALD. d N 10 1881+
1881-1922 as Daily times; Ja-Ap 13 1923 Norristown daily herald and The Norristown times
pub 1881-1901;06+
P 1927+
PDoHi [1884-85]
PP [1928]+
PPeS My 15 1889;O 19 1929;F 8 1930
PPot [1886]O 22,N 5 1890;N 7 1894

WATCHMAN. *See* Montgomery watchman

NORTH EAST

North East BREEZE. w My 1 1893+
pub [1907]+
CtY [1933+]

NORTH LEBANON

LEBANON VALLEY times. w Ap 4 1867-
MWA Ap 4 1857

NORTH WALES

North Wales RECORD. w 1855-
PDoHi O 17 1855

North Wales RECORD. w Jl 1874+
pub [1874]1907+
PPeS F 27 1875;F 20 1886;Ag 21 1915

NORTHAMPTON. *See* ALLENTOWN

NORTHUMBERLAND

PUBLIC aspect. w 1832-
PLewL F 28 1833

PUBLIC press. w O 1872-Je 1917||
PNorG [1872]-[1917]
PSeHi Ap 20 1877

Northumberland UNION and Susquehanna navigation register. w 1832-
PLewL O 9 1833
PNorG My 8 1833

OAKDALE

Oakdale TIMES. w 1895+
P Jl 1899-Je 1907

OIL CITY

Oil City BLIZZARD. d My 22 1882+
pub [1882]+

Oil City DERRICK. d S 1871+
pub 1871+
CaB S 11 1871
IHi Je 25 1874
KHi S 20 1905-Je 1912;Ja 9 1922
MWA S 29 1882
NN O 24 1922-S 5 1923
NNHi My 9 1873;Ap-Ag 4 1887
P Jl 1889-1912;28+
PBr S 20 1881;Jl 1 1882
PP Ag 27 1907[31]+
PPi Ja 14 1876-1929

Oil City DERRICK. w 1885+
DLC Jl 1889-1927;35+

Oil City REGISTER. w 1863-
OClWHi Mr 19 1863-N 1864

Daily evening TELEGRAPH. d 1872-Ja 15 1873||
MWA Ja 13,15 1873

OLYPHANT

Olyphant GAZETTE. w 1887+
pub 1887+
PScrHi Ja-Je 1936

NEW life. *See* Nove zhittia

NOVE zhittia. (New life) sm,w 1912+
In Ukrainian
DLC Mr 21,Ag 16,S 1,16,D 16 1921;Ja 1 1922
PP D 1924[27]+

PENNSYLVANIA (*Continued*)

OLYPHANT—*Continued*

PRAVDA. w,sw 1902-23||
1904-06 pub in New York City
w 1902-Jl 1914
In Russian
DLC Je 27-N 10 1922
NN 1902-17

Olyphant RECORD. w 1892+
PScrHi Ag 27 1935

ORWIGSBURG

Die FREIHEITSPRESSE. *See* Die Stimme des Volks

Orwigsburg NEWS. w Jl 27 1889+
pub 1927+
MWA Jl 27 1889

Die STIMME des volks. w 1823-58||
1823-27 as Die Freiheitspresse
In German
MWA N 25 1824;N 11 1836;F 3 1838;O 10 1840;Ap 1 1852
P 1833-58
PPL N 23 1850
PPoC 1843-4-;51-52
PPoHi 1834-37;40-43;46-50

Orwigsburg TIMES. w 1875-78||?
NbHi S 14 1878

OSCEOLA MILLS

Osceola LEADER. w 1888+
P Je 21 1889-D 20 1912

OVAL

OVAL ledger. w Ag 8 1890-1923||
PWp Ag 8 1890;Jl 27 1899
PWpCo 1907-23

OXFORD

Oxford PRESS. w F 14 1866+
pub [1866-67]1909-[35]+
MWA F 14 1866
PWcHi F 19 1873;Ap 20 1887;D 24 1896;F 25 1897;Ja 5 1899-1905]
PWcT [1873]-[75]
VU Jl 14 1886

PALMYRA

Palmyra RECORD w O 1 1900+
pub 1933+

PARADISE

Paradise HORNET. w 1821-
MWA O 12,N 16 1822;Ap 19,My 24,Je 14,O 11, N 8 1823
P-M My 19 1821
PHi My 19 1821-[22]
PLaHi [1821]-23
PWcHi O 12 1822

WASHINGTONIA. w 1824-
PLewL [1824]

PARKESBURG

CHESTER county times. w Ja 4 1879-1906||?
United with Chester Valley union (Coatesville) to form Chester Valley union and Chester county times (Coatesville)
PPaS 1879-86
PWeT 1894-95

Parkesburg HERALD. w
PWcHi O 9 1875-Ag 6 1887[94-95]S 15 1899;O 9 1903

Parkesburg weekly NEWS. w F 9 1901-06||?
PWcHi Mr 23,Ap 27,My 25 1901

Parkesburg POST. w Ja 4 1935+
PWcHi F 8 1935

Parkesburg PRESS. w 1901-12||?
PWcHi Jl 13 1901;S 13 1902;My 20,N 7 1903

PARKINSON'S FERRY

MONONGAHELA patriot. w 1834-
PPiHi Ap 21 1835

PATTON

Patton COURIER. w N 1893+
pub 1893+
PEbHi My 6 1895

PENNSBURG

Der BAUERN freund und Pennsburg demokrat. w 1828-1907||?
1828-58 as Der Bauern freund; 1858-62 Bauern freund und demokrat
1828-58? pub in Sumneytown
In German
MWA N 10 1852;Ag 29 1876
PDoHi Ag 9-16 1864;F 28-Mr 7,Ap 4 1866;Mr 13 1867
PNoHi O 22 1828;F 20,Mr 27 1833;Ap 22 1857-96
PPeS Ag 6 1828-Jl 7 1858;D 3 1861;Ap 27 1864;S 3 1866;Jl 24,Ag 6 1867;Ja 20,Mr 31,Ap 21,O 27 1869;Je 28,Ag 30 1871;D 2 1874;Je 13,D 15 1875;Mr 15 1876;D 18 1877-[78-81]Ja 10-17 1882;Mr 20 1883;O 28,N 11-18 1884[85] Jl 6,O 5 1886;My 15,Jl 5 1888;F 12 1889;N 4-11 1890;D 6 1892;Mr 1 1899;Ap 30,Ag 27 1901

Pennsburg DEMOKRAT. w Ap 1857-58||
United with Der Bauern freund to form Der Bauern freund und Pennsburg demokrat
PPeS N 11 1857

PERKIOMEN VALLEY press. w Ja 10 1874-1904||?
OClWHi N 9 1880
PNoHi 1874-76;91-92;97

TOWN and country. w Ap 1899+
pub [1899]+
MWA Je 30 1900
PPeS [1899]-[1936]+

PERKASIE

CENTRAL news. w Je 9 1881+
pub 1881+

PHILADELPHIA

ABEND. . . See under next important word: i.e Abend gazette is alphabeted as . . . gazette

ADVANCE. *See* Twenty-first ward advance

Philadelphia ADVERTISER and city gazette. w Mr 30 1830-
CSmH Je 8 1830
DLC Ap 27 1830
PP My 4 1830

Weekly ADVOCATE. *See* Colored American (New York City)

AGE. w 1841-
FLhT Jl 17 1841;Ag 27 1842
PNoHi Ja 7 1837

AGE. 1863-74 *See* Illustrated new age

ALEXANDER'S express messenger. w Ja 4 1837-N 1 1843||?
Follows Salmagundi. 1837 as American weekly messenger; 1838-F 1844 Alexander's weekly messenger. United with Saturday gleaner to form Family messenger and national gleaner
DLC Ap 18,O 24 N 14 1838
IU S 19 1838
MWA 1837[38]-Ja 16,Ap 10,D 4 1839;O 14-21,N 4,18-25,D 9-30 1840;Ja 6,20-F 3,17-Mr 3, Ap 14,My-Je 9,S 1,29 1841;Je 1,S 14,O 5,N 9 1842;Mr 1,Jl 19-Ag 2,S 13,N 8 1843;Ja 17-24 1844;F 5,My 7,D 3 1845
MeBa Ja 17-31,F 21-28,Mr 14,Ap 18,My 2,16, Je 6,27,Jl 11-25,Ag 8-29,S 19,O 3-10,31-N 7 28,D 19 1838
MiU-C D 6 1837;Ja 3 1838
N My 27,Je 17 1840;Je 19 1844
NN Ja 1846
NNHi Je 24 1840;S 22,N 10 1841;Mr 2,16-23 1842
NSchU Mr 9 1842
NcD Jl 31 1839
NjR Mr 15 1837;Ja 3 1838;My 22 1839;S 30 1840[42-46]
OClWHi Mr 8 1837-Ja 2,16 1839;Ja 15-29,My 20-27 1840;My 21 1845;O 14,D 2 1846
OHi 1838-39
P-M S 17 1845
PAtM Ap 14 1841
PBL F 22,My 10,24,Ag 2 1837;F 13 1839
PDoHi Ap 8 1841
PHi 1837-38;Ja-N 1843
PNoHi N 13 1839[45]46
PWcHi F 23 1842;F 8,Jl 19 1843
TKL Mr 8 1837
WHi F 7 1844-N 1 1848

ALEXANDER'S pictorial messenger. w Ja 6 1847-N 1848||
ICHi S 27 1848
NNH Mr 15-22 1848
PHi O 25 1848
PNoHi [1847-48]
TxU D 8 1847-N 1 1848

ALL DAY city item. *See* Philadelphia evening item

Die ALTE und die neue welt. w Ja 24 1834-44|?
Title varies slightly
In German
IU 1834-44
NNHi My 9,Jl 11,25,Ag 1,15-S 5,19,O 24 1840; Ap 17,O 2,30 1841;S 16 1843;F 17 1844
PPG 1834

AMERICA. d,tw 1911+
d 1911-N 23 1913
In Ukrainian
pub 1927+
CSt-H [1932]
IU D 1917+
PP N 19 1927+
PPiHi [1931-32]

AMERICAN advocate. d 1844-45||
Followed by Native eagle and American advocate
DLC Jl 13 1844-Ja 14 1845
NN [Jl 1844-Ap 1845]
PE Mr 21 1845

Saturday AMERICAN and temperance advocate. w S 21 1844-
MWA N 9 1844
NcD F 1845-Mr 14 1846

AMERICAN banner and national defender. w Ap 13 1850-56||
1850-54? as American banner
dated also in Camden, New Jersey
MWA D 16 1854
NN S 27 1856
NNHi Ap 26 1851-Ap 17 1852
NjCHi Ap 24 1852-My 7 1853
OHi Ag 26 1854
P-M D 16 1854
PBuE [1855-56]
PHi Ap 13,My-Ag 10,24 1850-Ap 10 1852
PShH Mr 10 1855[56]

AMERICAN centinel. *See* American sentinel

AMERICAN citizen. w Mr 29 1845-46|
CtY 1845-Ap 18 1846
MWA Je 25 1846
NIC O 18 1845;Ap 4 1846
PNoHi Je 18,D 17 1846

AMERICAN Saturday courier. w My 1831-N 8 1856|
1831-Mr 4 1848 as Saturday courier (D 19 1835-Mr 13 1841 Philadelphia Saturday courier) Mr 11 1848-Mr 1 1851 McMakin's model American Saturday courier. Merged with Evening bulletin
Ct D 28 1833;Ap 4 1835;My 25 1839;Ja 2 1840
CtSp O 29 1836
CtY Mr 29,N 1 1834;Ja,F 13-Mr 26,S 24-O 1,29 1836;Ap 1,Ag 5-12,S 2 1837 Mr 19 1842-My 25 1844
DLC Jl 13,S 14 1833;D 20 1834;Mr 26 1836-Mr 17 1838[39-46]S 18 1847-Mr 1,S 27 1851-F 1852
GAtCo Ap 11 1840
ICHi D 25 1841;Ja 22,Mr,O 15,N 12,D 10-17 1842;Ja 6-13,F 17,My 11,Je 22,Ag 3,24,S 7,21-28 1844;My 24,Jl 19,Ag 16 1845;S 9 1848;My 19,Ag 4,S 15,O 13 1849;Ap 6 My 4 1850;Ap 17, Je 26 1852;Ja 7,My 20 1854;Je 2,16 1855
ICU Je 4 1842;Ap 1 1848;Ja 5 1850
IHi [Je 19 1841-O 8 1842]
IU Jl 24 1832;S 8 1838;S 11,O 2 1841;Mr 5,My 28 1842;Ag 31 1844;My 31 1845;D 11 1847;Ap 14 1849
In Ap 1843-Mr 1847
MBAt S 3 1831
MHu Je 15 1839;Je 10 1843;My 1 1847;Jl 31,D 18 1852
MWA My 28,Jl 16 1831-56
MeBa N 4 1843;Je 1,29,Ag 24,O 12,D 14 1844 [Ja-N 1 1845;F 21-D 1846]-Ja 9,30-F 20 1847
MiU-C [1832-34;37;41;43-46;48]
MoHi D 26 1846
MsHi 1833-35;39-41
N Jl 25,D 5 1835;My 8,Je 25,O 29 1836;S 9 1837;Ap 28 1838-F,Ag 29 1840;Ag-N 1841;F 9 1846;My 13 1847;Jl 8 1848;Ag 27 1853
NBuG D 10 1836-My 6,20-Ag 5,19,D 23 1837; 38-39
NEh Jl 26 1834
NFre D 14 1839
NHuHi Je 26 1841
NN Ja 28 1832;Je 10 1837-Mr 14 1840;O 14 1848;Jl 9 1853
NNHi 1833[34-37]D 8 1838;Je 15 1839;My 1-8, Jl 31 1841;Jl 16,Ag 27 1842[Ja-Ap,D 1843-Ag 1844]Ja 10 1846;Ja 2 1847;My 20,Jl 8,Ag 12,S 23,O 14,D 16-23 1848;Ja 6,F 3,24 1849;Ja 18,O 4,D 1851-53;O 14 1854;55[F-Je 1856]
NSchU Ap 16-30,Jl 2 1842
NUHi D 16 1837
NcAsS Mr 11 1848
NcD [1832-34;37-38;42-Ag 1848]My 21-28,Jl 16, Ag 20,O 22,N 5 1853;F 4 1854
NcU O 14 1837;Ja 26,F 16,My 25,S 28,N 2 1839;F 1,Jl 11,Ag 15,29,O 10-N 7,D 19 1840; Ja 23-30,Ap 3,Je 5,Jl 10,S 25,O 9-30 1841;Ja 17 1846;Je 28-Jl 5 1851
NhM F 10 1849-Je 26 1852
NjHi D 17 1836
NjR [1834,41-43;46-47;50-53;55]
NjWdHi N 25 1848
OC O 29 1842;Je 26 1847
OClWHi [Ap 21-O 6 1832;F 16-N 2 1833]S 6 1834[35]-O 1836;Ja 13,Ag 25 1838;Mr 23,Jl 27,D 28 1839;Je 13,N 7 1840;Ag 21,O 5 1844; Ja 21 1845;D 26 1846[47-49]Ja 23,Ag 3 1850 [51]
P-M Ja 8 1853
PBL S 3 1831;D 14 1833[36-40]N 22 1845
PCarlHi Ap 6,Jl 20 1850
PCt [1841]-[43]
PDoHi S 14 1833;S 26,O 24 1835;Jl 2,Ag 20 1836;Mr 10 1838[49]
PHi S 1832-Mr 1 1851;52
PLaF [1832]
PLhT F 14 1846
PMe Mr 13 1841
PNoHi [1850-52]-56
PP My 26 1832;N 25 1843;My 25 1844;F 1,Je 21 1845;Ja 30 1847
PPL Ap 22 1834;37-Mr 16 1839;Mr 19 1842-Ag 1844;Mr 15 1845-Mr 14 1848;Mr 10 1849-Mr 1 1851
PShH O 1-8 1836
PW Jl 29 1837
RPB Mr-D 1832;Ag 16 1834;Ja 11 1842-D 15 1849
RW Je 4,Ag 23 1834
TKL Mr 8 1834
TU My 31 1851
Tx Mr 13,Ag 21,O 16 1847;Ja 8,Mr 8,Ap 22, My 13-20,Je 10 1848
TxU F 1851-Mr 1852
WHi Ja 7 1832[Ja 23 1836-38]F 23,O 12-19 1839;S 16 1843
—quarto ed See Philadelphia mirror

AMERICAN eagle and Philadelphia county democrat. d Jl 25? 1836-
DLC Jl 27 1836

AMERICAN weekly messenger. *See* Alexander's express messenger

AMERICAN pioneer and fireman's chronicle. w Mr 5 1830-Je 15 1833||?
1830-F 1831 as Pioneer; Mr-D 1831 American pioneer and military chronicle
PHi 1830-F 1832
PP [Mr 1831-Ja]Je 15 1833

*AMERICAN sentinel. d Ag 26 1816-D 31 1846||
1816-20 as American centinel and mercantile advertiser. Followed by Cumming's evening telegraphic bulletin, later Evening bulletin
CSmH Ag 27 1830
DLC N 1,3,9,18 25,30,D 9,11 1824;Ap 1,Je 6,S 15 1825;Ap 15,N 9 1826;N 26 1827;Ja 14-15, 17-18,Mr 1,S 9,12,17-18,24 1828;29-30;Ja 13, 18-21,24 1831;32-46
MBAt N 12 1827;Ja 20,F 9,Mr 21,S 8,D 23,28 1829;Ag 26,D 31 1830

PENNSYLVANIA (*Continued*)

PHILADELPHIA—*Continued*

*AMERICAN sentinel. d 1816-46‖—*Continued*
MHi N 7,D 21-22 1821;Ja 1,Jl 24-25,O 22,N 14-15,D 6 1823;Ja 12,F 16,Mr 12,17,Ap 3,21, My 4,9 1827
MWA Ap 30 1824;Ag 23,D 28 1830;F 4 1831; My 27 1846
MiU-C F 15 1823
N O 21 1833
NcD [Jl 1829-Ja,D 1830;N 9 1832;Ap-My,Ag 1845-Ag 1846]
NjCHi Ag 26 1841-Ag 25 1842
OClWHi F 4 1841;Mr 16 1842;Je 25-26 1845
P complete
P-M Mr 20 1833
PCHi [1831]
PDoHi [1830]
PEL [1825]32
PHHi [1845]
PHi 1827-31
PHsHi [1838]
PP Jl 6 1838;Ja 14,Ap 10,21,My 29 1846
PPL [1822;24-26]-29;32-[35]-[39]-Mr 12 1841
PW My 6 1838
PWHi [1821;29]
PWbW Ap 7 1836
PWcHi Je 1 1822
PWeT Mr 22-25 1836

*AMERICAN sentinel. tw Ag 25 1816-
1816?-20? as American centinel and mercantile advertiser
MWA Ja 10-12,Je 18,N 14 1821[Mr 6-D 1822] Ja 3,8,13-17,29,F 5-7,21,Ap 11,Je 11,O 31,N 7,10,19,D 3,10 1823;Mr 8,My 14,D 1 1824;My 4 1825;Ap 9,Ag 24,S 19,O 26,N 12 1827;Ja 16,F 4,Mr 2,Ap 3-6,15-29,Je 19 1829;Mr 3,31, Ap 5 1830;D 8,15 1834;Jl 22 1836;Ja 25,Mr 8 1837

*AMERICAN sentinel. w Ap 13 1818-41‖?
Ct [1826-27]Mr 23 1829;D 2 1837
MWA S 14,O 19 1822;Ja 17 1825;Ja 30,Mr 13,Ap 10,Ag 7,N 27 1826;Je 18,Jl 16,S 10,O 1, N 26,D 31 1827;Mr 24,Ap 28,O 27 1828;Jl 11 1829;O 2 1830;N 26,D 17 1831;F 18-25,Mr 24 1832;D 7 1833
NjHi [1821-22;24;26-30;32]
NjR [1823-25;30-31;33-35]

AMERICAN statesman and spirit of the age. d Mr 27? 1840-
DLC Ap 17 1840

AMERIKANISCHER correspondent. *See* Der Philadelphiaer telegraph und Deutscher wochenblatt

ARTHUR'S home gazette. w S 7 1850-55‖
ICU O 26-D 14 1850;Ja 11,25-F 1,Mr 1,22-Ap 19,My 31-Je 7,21-Jl 12,26-Ag 2,16-23,S-N 8, 22-29 1850
MWA S 14 1850-Ag 1852[Ja-S 1853]Ja 21,F 11,Mr 4-11,Je 10 1854
MnHi 1851[52]
NcD [My 1851-54]
NhM D 24 1853;Ja 28 1854
OCHi S 14-N 16 1850;My 31,N 1851-[Ja-Je] S 10 1852-[Jl-S 1833]S 16-D 23 1854
OClWHi S 25 1851;Je 19,O 23,N 27 1852
PBL Ap 3,My 1-15 1852

ATKINSON'S Saturday evening post. *See* Saturday evening post

Philadelphia Sunday ATLAS. w N 7 1858-My 5 1861‖
PHi N 18 1860
PPL complete

*AURORA. d O 1 1790-Ap 25 1835‖
1790-N 1 1794 as General advertiser(title varies) N 8 1794-N 22? 1824 Aurora. General advertiser; N 22? 1824-Mr 1828 Aurora and Franklin gazette; Ap 1828-29 Aurora and Pennsylvania gazette
Suspended from 1830-Je 1834
CSmH Jl 25 1827
DLC 1821-24;Ja 17 1825-26;Ap 14 1828-29
DeHi [1821]D 23 1822
MBAt Ja 23,D 3 1821[22]Mr 1 1825;F 6 1828
MHi N 20-21 1821;Ja 16 1822
MWA 1821-22;Ja 3 1823;D 8 1827;Ag 1 1829
NN Mr 11 1826;Ap 14 1828-29
NNHi N 1 1822;Jl 7,12,O 17 1823;F 12,Ap 21,Jl 12,31 1824;D 8 1825;N 28 1829
NcD O 8 1829
OHi Ja-O 1 1821
P Ap 8 1827-29
PBL S 17 1823
PDoHi Ag 24 1825;Jl 14 1826;Ap 2 1827
PEL F 12 1828
PHHi Jl 4 1834-35
PHi 1821-22; Ap 14-S 1828;Jl 1834-Ap 18 1835
PP Ag 2-3 1821;Ag 20-21 1827
PPFfHi 1821-22
PPL 1821-29
PRHi Jl 13,27 1826
PU Jl-D 1823
WHi O 10,N 21 1822

*AURORA. tw,sw Je 14 1797-
1797-Mr 7 1800 as Bache's Philadelphia aurora; Mr 10-N 5? 1800 Philadelphia aurora; N 7 1800-My 30 1817 Aurora for the country
Suspended from 1830-Je 1834
tw 1797-1822
DLC My 15,Je 30 1824
IU O 19-23 1824
MWA [N 15 1822-Mr 10]Ag 16,N 29 1823;Ap 14,Jl 14,O 13 1824;O 19 1829
NN 1834-Ap 1835
NcD F 14-21,28,Mr 6,20-27,Ap 24,28,My 5, 12,19,26,Je 9-12,28,Jl 28,Ag 4 1824
OClWHi O 15 1823

*Weekly AURORA. w Je 19 1810-
1810- as Aurora weekly
Suspended from 1830?-Je 1834
DLC Ja-F 12 1821
DeHi 1821;N 4 1822
MWA O 24 1821
NNHi [1821]Ja,Mr 25-Ap 15 1822
OHi 1834-Ap 1835

BACHE'S Philadelphia aurora. *See* Aurora

BICKNELL'S reporter, counterfeit detector, and prices current. sm,w Jl 31 1830-Je 30 1857‖
Title varies: Bicknell's counterfeit detector and Pennsylvania reporter of bank notes, broken banks, stocks; etc.
sm 1830-Ja 17 1831
IU Jl 14 1840;D 12 1843;Mr 19 1844
InI D 22 1835
MWA My 9,D 5 1831;Ja 13,28-F 4,18,O 21,D 30 1834;F 10 1835;S 10,D 10,31 1839;Mr 3,Jl 14,Ag 4,25,N 24,D 1,22-29 1840;Ag 3,24-31 1841;Jl 27 1852
MdBJ N 1 1842
NjHi N 22 1830
OClWHi F 2 1835;Jl 1,19,S 20,O 1,N 1,D 1 1836;Ap 1,Je 1,O 1,N 1,D 1 1837[40-41]F 15 1842;Mr 7 1843
OOxM D 17 1832;Ja 7,21,F 11,Mr 4,18-25,My 13,Je 10,24 1833
P-M Ja 30 1832
PBL D 23 1833-Ap 15 1834;O 27 1835;My 23 1837;Jl 21 1840
PLewL [1830-34]
PPAm Ap 1 1834
PPM Jl 31 1830-Ja 17 1831;Jl 30 1832-57
PShH Jl 21 1840
PW My 4-11 1833

Die BIENE. Ein volksblatt. sw Ja 3 1846-D 18 1847‖
In German
PHi complete

BLANCHE'S Sunday press. w O 9 1853-
D 11-18 1853 as Sunday press
MWA D 11 1853-O 15 1854

BLUE book. ir Jl 4 1856-
Campaign paper
PHi Jl 4 1856

Philadelphia BREVITIES. *See* Philadelphia briefs

Philadelphia BRIEFS. w Jl 20 1932-Je 27 1934‖
PP complete

Saturday BULLETIN. w N 1827-Ja 5 1833‖
Merged with Saturday evening post
CSmH S 18 1830
Ct Mr 28 1829
MWA [O 11 1828-Jl 4 1829]Mr 6-20,My 15 1830;O 1,15-D 3,31 1831-32
NNHi My 8 1830
NcD Jl 14,O 6,N 24,D 22 1832
PDoHi Ja 17,Mr 14,28 1857
PPL My 15 1830-N 17,D 1832
PW D 11 1830

Evening BULLETIN. d Ap 12 1847+
Follows American sentinel. Title varies: Cummings' evening bulletin; Cummings' evening telegraphic bulletin; Daily evening bulletin
pub 1847-1911;Ap 1912;Jl 1913+
CL O 11 1854
CPo [1876]
CtY F 11 1854;D 31 1863
DLC Ap 13 1847-48;My 13-24,28,Je 13 1849;My 22 1858;Ja-My,Je 10,Jl 19,S 7,N 13,16 1861; 62-64;Ap 15,17 1865;Je 20 1872;S 29 1874;Jl 4 1876;Je 19,N 22 1878;D 16 1879;Je 5-7,N 23 1880;Mr 4-5,My 11,Jl 2-5,S 6,19-20,24,O 19 1881;Je 30,O 23-28,N 8 1882;94;1910+
DeWI Ap 15-24 1865
ICHi Jl 1 1869
ICM F 2 1881;Mr 2 1884
ICU Ap 12 1847(facsimile)
IU Jl 1,6,12,15,22,25 1861;F 20,Mr 13,My 14,Je 7, 18,20,28 1862
KHi Ag 8 1885
MBAt Ap 17-18,20 1865
MHi D 31 1853;Ag 19 1854;Ap 11,Jl 24,Ag 6 1860
MWA My 16,Jl 9,O 14,N 3 1851;F 19,27 1852; Ja 9,My 28 1857;D 29 1860;Mr 1,9 1861[F-Je 13,O 1862-Ap 1863]O 29 1864;Mr 21 1865;N 24 1866;Ap 15,Je 10 1868;Mr 12 1869;F 28,Mr 20,Je 21 1873;N 13 1874;Jl 1,4 1876;My 9,23, 30,Je 12,20,25-26 1879;Ap 4 1881;Mr 2 1883;S 6 1884;Ja 27 1893
MiU-C [1862-63;65]
MnHi O 12,D 29,31 1860;D 6,24 1862[63]
MnU My 7(extra)1864
N N 18 1863
NN D 10 1849;Ag 12 1854;Ap 17,22 1865;F 24(supp)1873
NNHi Jl 3 1856;Ap 26 1858;D 16 1859;O 13,N 7, D 18 1860;Ja 12,F 22,Mr 4,Ap 13,15,My 15 1861;Ag 9,23 1862;Ap 3,10,15 1865;My 16,26,O 14,N 4 1868;Mr 4,Jl 1 1869;S 3 1870;Ja 30,O 11 1871
NbHi My 22 1865
NcD D 7,21 1848
NjCHi Ap 9,Je 2 1864;F 17-18,23-25,Mr 7 (extra)19 1898;S 9,11,13,18 1901;F 24 1905
NjR Mr 5 1861;Ap 21,26 1865;S 1 1866[76]
NjWdHi Je 21,Jl 6 1865;My 2,Je 2 1898;Je 11 1927
OCHi Ap 12 1847(facsimile)
OClWHi Ja 22,Mr 4,Ap 13-27,My 1,Je-D 1861; Ja 17,Mr 11,Ap 8,My 12,19,Je 3,6,19,S 15,21,O 2 1862;Mr 31,Ap 3-4,18,26,My 5 1865;N 24 1866;F 28-Mr 17 1860
OOxM My 15 1872;Je 16-18 1875
P Je 1850-S 1865;1927-Je 1930
P-M Jl 6 1854;F 3,Jl 16 1855;Ap 15 1865
PBL [1848]-[50]-55;Ap 10 1856-My 8 1858
PBf [1881]
PCHi S 4 1862[97-98;1901;14]
PDoHi [O 26 1863-O 10 1908]
PHHi [1930]-32
PHi Jl-N 1857;60-66;82-1917
PLaHi My 10 1876
PLaS [1918]
PNoHi [1851]Ap 3,13 1865;My 8 1869
PP [1847]-[55]-[59]O 10-11 1860;F 1,20,22-23, Ap 10,12-13,My 2-3,11 1861;Jl 6-7,O 9 1863;O 12,20,N 9 1864;F 21,24,Ap 6-7,13,15,21,27,My 2-3,11 1865;Mr 30 1868;Jl 22 1869;Mr 29 1894 [1901;12]-[18-19]-[24-25;27]+
PPFfHi Ag 9 1851;Ag 18 1863;Ap 14 1865
PPL Jl 16,Ag 5-6 1847[50-51]F 19,Mr 20 1852; 53;55-56[63-64]65;O 30 1874;Ja 18 1875;Mr 8 1876;F 5 1878
PPM [1861-Ap 1896]1903-04
PPeS S 15,18 1862;Ja 13 1923;N 7 1928;N 9 1932
PPiHi [S 1898-Mr 1899]
PPot [1856]Ag 24 1859[84;86]
PWcHi S 22 1862;My 6 1867
PWcT My 16 1867[1918]
Tx Mr 4 1869
VRC My 29 1862;S 17 1864
WHi Jl 2 1851;61-65;Mr 6 1873;S 14 1901

Philadelphia evening BULLETIN. For the country. sw O 30 1850-54‖?
MWA S 8 1852;F 8 1854

Philadelphia Saturday BULLETIN and American courier. w N 15 1856-
ICHi Mr 28 1857
MWA S 3 1851;N 15,29,D 13 1856;Ja 3-17 1857
NNHi D 1856-Ja 10 1857

BUSINESS journal and traveller. *See* United States journal

BUSYBODY and Philadelphia whip. sw Ap 9 1840-Je 25 1842‖?
PHi Je 25 1842

Evening CALL. d S 17 1883-S 8 1900‖
ICM My 27 1885
MB [N 23 1883-O 21 1884]
PCHi Mr 14 1888;N 2 1900
PP complete
PPiHi [Ap 12 1898-Mr 1899]

Weekly CALL. w D 1883-95‖?
MB [Je 7-N 1 1884]
MWA D 22 1883
NcD D 22 1883
Whi Ja 7 1889

CAMPAIGN age.
Campaign paper
OClWHi S 8 1864

CAMPAIGN dial. d Je 19 1862-64‖
1862-Ag? 1864 as Dial
CSmH S 8 1864
NjP S 8-N 5 1864
PHi Je 19 1862-Mr 26,My 25,S 12 1863;S 8 1864

CENTRAL North Philadelphia news. *See* North Philadelphia press

CHAT of North Penn. w F 16 1928+
1928-33 as Chat
pub 1928+
PP Je 12 1930+

CHESTNUT HILL and Mount Airy herald. w O 1924-D 27 1929‖
Merged with Germantown bulletin
PP Ag 30,S 13-D 27 1929

CHESTNUT HILLS times. w F 11 1931-Je 23 1932‖
PP complete

Daily CHRONICLE. d Ap 7 1828-My 1834‖
CSmH Ag 12 1830
Ct O 22 1833
DLC 1828-Je 1832;Ja-Mr,Jl-S 1833
DeHi N 11 1828
DeWI N 1 1831
MBAt N 8 1828;N 2 1829;F 22,Jl 1 1830
MHi S 26,28-29,O 10,N 12,D 24 1829;F 15 1832
MWA Jl 5 1828;Mr 14,18,Ap 1,7,24,My 26,Je 20,Jl 7,14 1829;Ja 12,S 22 1830;F 5 1831;Jl-D 1832
MdHi Ja 4-N 9 1833
N O 16 1833
NN Mr 24 1829;N 8 1830
NNHi Ap 7,O 6 1828;Ja-Je 1829;S 10 1830;31
NcD [Jl-Ag 1828;Je 1829-Ja 1830]My 23 1832
OCHi Mr 17 1834
PBL [1828;31-34]
PDoHi Je 2,D 31 1829;Ja 7,14 1830
PEHi [1831]
PHi 1828-Je 1829;31-32;O 1833-Ap 19 1834
PNhE Ap 30 1830;F 11 1831
PPCHi [1833-34]
PPL [1828]-33
PPM 1828-Je 1830;Jl 1832-Je 1833
PRHi Je 2,D 31 1829;Ja 7,14 1830
PU 1829;Ja 2-Je 1830

Saturday CHRONICLE. w 1836-42‖
Title varies: Saturday chronicle, philanthropist and mirror of the times; Saturday chronicle and mirror of the times.
Merged with Saturday evening post
CtY Je 25 1836
DLC Jl 20 1839
ICHi Mr 14 1840
MB O 29,N 12 1836;Ap 8 1837-Ap 1842
MWA Je 23 1836;F 20 1841
NcU Ja 2,F 6,27 1841;F 12,Mr 5-12,Je 4,Ag 13,O 1,29 1842
OClWHi D 29 1838
P Ja 9 1841-S 3 1842
PBL [1836-40]N 20 1841;Mr 5 1842
TKL F 26 1842
WHi Je 25 1836

Daily CHRONICLE. d My 4 1840-47‖
1840-41 as Daily chronicle and general advertiser
CSmH Ag 13 1846
CtY O 28 1840
DLC My 25 1840; Je 1(extra)1841;Ja 11,Ap 15,O 16 1845
MHi My 11,S 4 1841
MWA 1840-My 3,Ag 14 1845;Ap 22,My 26 1846
MiU N 4 1841
NN Ja 31[Ag-N 1842;F-Ap,Je-O 1843;Mr-My]O 16 1845;F 28,Mr 5,Je 3 1846

PENNSYLVANIA (*Continued*)

PHILADELPHIA—*Continued*

Daily CHRONICLE. d My 4 1840-47||—*Cont.*
NSchU D 21 1841
NcD Ap 7 1843
NjR [1840;43]
OClWHi O 31 1840;O 10 1844
PHoHi 1840
PLewL Ap 29 1844

Philadelphia evening CHRONICLE. d 1866-N 28 1877||
United with Evening herald to form Chronicle-herald, later Herald
NNHi N 11 1876
PHi O 9-10 14,N 9-10,16-18 1874;My 30 1876
PP D 6 1876

CHRONICLE and advertiser. w Ja 2 1869-O 22 1931||
PHi 1869;71-88;90-O 2 1891
PP 1889;S 2,23 1892;Mr 10 1893;Je 11-O 22 1931

CHRONICLE-HERALD. *See* Herald

CITIZEN soldier. sw 1843-44||
United with Home journal to form Home journal and citizen soldier
PDoHi 1843[44]

CITY item. w *See* Weekly item

Evening CITY item. *See* Philadelphia evening item

CITY register and daily advertiser. d My 1823-O 1824||
Merged with Freeman's journal
DLC Jl 16 1824
MWA Jl 26,N 10 1823;S 17 1824

CLAN-NA-GAEL. w
In Gaelic
MWA Ag 5-12 1888
WHi F 25 1888

COHEN'S lottery journal and general register. w
PToHi Je 14 1826

COLORED American. *See under* New York City

COLUMBIAN observer. d Ap 1 1822-Je 30 1825||
DLC O 25,27,29 1823;My 21,24,Je 14,Jl 7,Ag 1824-Mr 15,Ap 22,25,My 7,Je 20 1825
MWA Ja 10,F 3,5,12,16,18,Mr 17 1825
NjR Je 3 1824
PPL Ja-Je 1825

COLUMBIAN observer. w,sw,tw Ap 6 1822-Jl 28 1825||
Followed by National chronicle
w Ap-Jl 1822;sw Ag-N 1822
DLC Jl 21,23,26,28 1825
ICHi Ag 4,S 15 1824
MWA Ap 12,S 29,O 3 1823;F 14,Mr 14,30-Ap 1,6,My 6-9,Jl 6 1825
N Ap 6-20,Je 8 Ag,S 25,O 5,12,D 5,10-14,26,31 1822[Ja 7-My 9]O 23,N 8 1823;Je 30,N 1 1824;Mr 28,Ag 6-8 1825
NNHi Je 1,N 8 1822;My 21-Je 3,13,Ag 11,S 12 1823;Ap 16,My 5,Jl 30-31,Ag 2,17,S 25,D 13 1824
WHi N 2 1822

COLUMBIAN star. w F 2 1822-D? 1829||
PHi 1827-Je 1829

COMMERCIAL herald and Pennsylvania sentinel. d Jl 1827-40||
1832-Jl 1837 as Commercial herald. Merged with North American
DLC D 25,31 1832;D 18(extra)1835[My-Je 1836]
MWA Ag 16 1834;D 2 1835;Mr 12 1839
P Ag 12 1834-My 12 1840
PEL 1833-[37]
PP [F 1838-S 1839]Ap 17-18,28,My 5,13 1840
PPL 1838;Ja 10,Je 15 1839
PPi [Ap 24 1833-Mr 21 1836]
PWeT [1834]

COMMERCIAL intelligencer. d D 1830-N 20 1834||
P D 1833-34

COMMERCIAL list and maritime register. w,sw My 26 1827-N 14 1931||
1827-O 17 1829 as Philadelphia price current; O 24 1829-Ja 21 1835 Philadelphia price current and commercial advertiser; Ja 24 1835-D 30 1848 Commercial list and Philadelphia price current; Ja 6 1849-52? Commercial list and trade and statistical register; 1853?-D 25 1922 Philadelphia commercial list and price current
sw O 24 1829-Ja 21 1835
CSmH S 1 1830
CtY 1847-50
DLC Ja 29,Jl 11,O 24-31,N 18-28,D 2-9,26 1829-D 15 1832;Jl 7 1860;O 1863-D 23 1865;My 14 1870-74;O 24 1931
MBAt F 6,10 1830
MSaE Ja 20 1842
MWA Ap 2 1842;Ag 14 1852
MnHi O 24 1829-O 23 1830
NNHi 1858;61-62
NcD Ja 2-16,Je 9 1830;Ja 19,F 23,Ap 16,Je 16-18 1831;Mr 5,23,Je 4,Jl 30 1832
OC O 1844-Ja 1846
PHi 1827-32;35-50
PP Ja 13 1838;70-88;90-N 1922;My 19 1923-31
PPL 1847;Ap 21 1849[50-51]N 27 1852
PPM O 24 1829-O 23 1830;47-48;F 28 1857-59
PU 1853-56;60;62-82

COMMONWEALTH. w My 23 1874-F 28 1880||
DLC D 25 1875;Ja 22,My 13,Ag 12 1876;F 3 1877
PHi 1874-[77]
PPL [1874-80]

COMMONWEALTH and independent democrat. w
PBL N 1 1837

Weekly CONSTITUTIONAL union. *See under* Washington, D.C.

Daily CONSTITUTIONAL union. *See* Evening union (Washington, D.C.)

Philadelphische CORRESPONDENT. . . *See* Philadelphiaer telegraph und Deutscher wochenblatt

COUNTRY gazette of the United States. *See* United States gazette for the country

Saturday COURIER. *See* American Saturday courier

CUMMINGS' evening bulletin. *See* Evening bulletin

CUMMINGS' evening telegraphic bulletin. *See* Evening bulletin

Philadelphia DAY. d N 4 1869-81||?
MWA Ap 6 1876
PCHi N 27 1869
PDoHi O 7 1876
PHi N 4 1869
VU My 4,7,9-10,25,27,Je 1 1870

DEMOCRAT. w Jl 30 1834-
PHi S 3 1834

DEMOCRATIC and commercial register. tw
PBL Ja 19,F 4 1837

DEMOCRATIC argus. d O 23 1843-Ja 22 1844||
PHi 1843-Ja 22 1844

DEMOCRATIC herald and champion of the people. sw Ja 1 1835-
Ct [1835-36]
IU Ja 21-24,F 21,Mr 4 1835
PBL F 4,O 17 1835
PHi F 4 1835

DEMOCRATIC keyhole. w Mr 10-Ap 14 1934||
PP Mr 21,Ap 14 1934

DEMOCRATIC leader. w Ag 21 1862-
MWA O 10 1862;Ja 3-17 1863
NbHi Ag 21,O 3 1862
PHi Je 26 1863

DEMOCRATIC news. w N 1 1934-O 21 1935||
PP N 1 1934;O 14-21 1935

*DEMOCRATIC press. d Je 29 1807-N 30 1829||
Merged with Philadelphia inquirer
CSmH Jl 23 1827
Ct [1826-27]
CtY Ag 5-6,O 14-15 1828
DLC 1821-N 4 1829
MBAt My 23 1822;Ja 12,Ap 6 1824;Ja 11 1828; Mr 3 1829
MDeHi Ap 26 1826
MHi Mr 21-22,D 6 1822;Ap 15 1823;Ap 4 1825; F 14 1826; Ja 9,F 13 1827
MWA Ja 24,F 3-4,8,25,Mr 18 1825[Mr 27-D 28 1827;Ja 14-N 10 1828]
MiU-C Ja 21 1825
NNHi D 22 1823;Je 22,Jl 10,D 14 1824;Ap 25,27,My 15 1829
NcD My 5,18 1827
P Ag 29 1821;Je 24,26 1826
PBL [1823]
PDoHi [1821;24-28]
PNoHi D 5-6 1822;S 1-2 1825
PPL [1821]-[23;25]-28
PPM 1827
PPot [1829]
PWbW S 8 1821
PWeT Mr 20 1822[24]
WHi Ja 1 1824;Mr 13 1825;Ap 12 1826

Weekly DEMOCRATIC press. w Ap 8 1826-N 26 1829||
Merged with Philadelphia inquirer
MWA N 17,D 1 1827
NjR [1825;28]
OOxM O 17 1826;Je 9,23 1827;Ag 30 1828;F 7 1829
PDoHi [1827]-[29]
PLewL N 29 1828
PPM 1826
PPot Ap 22 1826
VU Mr 24 1827

*DEMOCRATIC press for the country. tw Mr 27 1807-N 30 1829||
Merged with Pennsylvania inquirer, later Philadelphia inquirer
DLC D 13 1823;My 27,Jl 10,O 1,18,N 25,D 24 1824;S 14 1825;Ja 21,29 1828[Je 30-N 14 1829]
MBAt Ap 16-17 1822;D 28-29 1824;Ja 20-21,F 26-28 1825
MWA Jl 11,N 12 1823;Mr 5,Ap 7,My 7,14,N 30,D 15 1824;Je 15 1825;Ja 8,Je 25-Jl 2,N 14,23,26-28,D 7 1827;Ap 25,O 8,24 1828
NjR [1821;24]
P [1826]
PHi 1821-Je 24 1824;25-29

DEMOCRATIC standard. tw My 10 1836-
MWA My 10,17,Je 9 1836

DEMOCRATIC union. w
PHi [1843]-45

Philadelphia DEMOKRAT. d,tw Ag 11 1838-My 8 1918||
Title varies: Philadelphia demokrat; Der demokrat; Philadelphia demokrat und anzeiger der deutschen; Philadelphier demokrat. United with Morgen gazette to form Gazette-democrat
D 21 1907 is jubilee ed
tw Ja-Jl 23 1842
In German
DLC S 24 1839;My 4 1843
NN O 17-18 1872;D 21 1907
PPG 1838;Ag 22 1840;42;Ja-Je 1844;S 1847-88; Jl 1889-1902;Jl 1903-04;Jl 1905-07
PPL Ap 11-12,21,28,My 2 1856
PPeS D 21 1907
PPot S 9 1848
PU 1887

Der DEMOKRAT. w *See* Vereingten staaten zeitung

DEUTSCHE national-zeitung. w 1838-
In German
MB S 28 1839-F 29 1840
MWA My 4 1839

DIAL. *See* Campaign dial

Sunday DISPATCH. w My 14 1848+
1921-Jl 20 1924 as Philadelphia dispatch
pub 1848+
DLC Je 4 1848;My 1854-Ap 1860:Ap 28 1861-Je 22 1884
ICU D 1856-Ja 4,F 1-15,Mr 8-15,Ap 5-12,26-My 3,17-31 1857;Jl 3 1881
IU Ja 9,F 13,Jl 31-Ag 7,S 13,D 4-11,25 1859; Ja 6,20-Mr 10,O 27,N 10-D 1 1861;Jl 13,D 14-28 1862;F 15 1863
InU 1860-Ap 3 1862;Ap 1862-65
MWA My 14 1848-My 4 1884;My 10 1885-My 11 1887
MdBJ 1867-Mr,My 1869-D 8 1872
MiU-C [1851-52;54;62-64]-[67-69]-[73]-[75-77]-[83]
NN Ag 18 1861[Ja-F,My-Je,Ag,O 1862-F 1863] F 7 1864;Ja 22 1865;N 23(supp)1873;Jl 9 1876
NcD N 16 1879
NhM S 20 1857
OHi Ja 30,N 20 1859
P Je 1890-Je 1912
PCHi Ag 2 1857
PP Je 1848-84;Ag 31 1917;D 25 1918;Je 4 1922; Ja 4 1924;Ap 4 1926;S 11 1927+
PPCHi [1869]
PPFfHi Mr 27 1853;Mr 8 1863
PPL 1848-82;My 7 1905-08
PPM 1848-My 7 1882
PPeS N 17 1861;N 9 1862
PU 1867-69
WHi N 15 1863

DOLLAR weekly news. w Mr 1847-Mr 1869||?
OClWHi N 30 1850
PMe Ja 16,Jl 31 1861
PPL Mr 18 1869
PShH O 28 1858;Je 30 1859;My 31 1860;My 9 1861

DOLLAR newspaper. *See* Philadelphia home weekly

DOLLAR weekly Pennsylvanian. w Jl 9 1832-D 1861||
1832-N 25 1854 as Pennsylvanian
DLC Ag 26 1848
IU My 29 1841;Mr 9 1844
MWA S 10 1836;My 29 1841;Jl 5 1845
MdBJ Je 6 1846
MiU-C My 14 1839
MnHi My 29 1841;O 7 1852
NNHi O 11 1856
OClWHi Ag 9 1834;S 28 1844;Ag 6 1845;Je 17,Jl 1,29-Ag 2 1845;S 6,27 1856
PCHi [1854-55]
PPeS Jl 24 1841
PPot [1856]
PU [1854]-Ap 6 1861
WHi Jl 12-N 6 1856

Philadelphia ENQUIRER. *See* Philadelphia inquirer

ERIN. sw Ag 1822-
DLC Ja-O 25 1823

EXCHANGE and trade register. w Mr 9 1842-
MWA Jl 20,S 13-20,O 19-26,N 16,D 7 1842
PBL [1842]

EXPERIMENT. d Ap 1? 1834-
DLC Ap 8 1834

Daily EXPRESS. d Ag 1-S 4 1832||
MWA Ag 6 1832
PPL complete

Evening EXPRESS. d S 26 1874-78|
PCHi [1875]
PHi O 8,10,12,N 18 1874
PP O 9 1876
PPL S 26,D 14 1874

FAIR play. w N 6 1936+
pub 1936+
PP Ja 28 1937

FAMILY messenger and national gleaner. w N 8 1848-
Formed by the union of Alexander's express messenger and Saturday gleaner
IC 1848-Jl 17 1850
MWA N 15-D 13 1848;Ja 10-31 1849
NNHi D 20 1848
NjR Mr 7 1849
PNoHi [1849-51]
WHi 1848-Ja 3 1849

FEDERAL gazette and Philadelphia daily advertiser. *See* Philadelphia gazette and daily advertiser

52nd and Girard avenue news. *See* Northwest news

FINANCIAL bulletin. d
NN Mr 29-Ap 6,My 7-N 12 1907;My 4 1908;Ja 23,Mr 31 1909

Philadelphia FINANCIAL journal. d Ag 11 1895+
1895-Ap 23 1901 as Philadelphia financial news; Ap 24 1901-Ap 28 1929 Philadelphia news bureau
pub Ag 1898-Jl 1903;04+
PP Jl 31,D 21 1920;Ja 21,Mr 14,24 1921[24]Ja 21, N 7, 14 1925;My 4,Ag 10-11,O 15,N 25,D 4 1926;Mr 9,14 1927;My 15 1928+

Philadelphia FINANCIAL news. *See* Philadelphia financial journal

FITZGERALD'S City item. d *See* Philadelphia evening item

FITZGERALD'S City item. w *See* Weekly item

Daily FOCUS. d S 1837-40||
DLC N 13 1837;F 15-D 1 1838
PBL Jl 12 1838
PHi My 21-N 1838

FORNEY'S weekly press. *See* Weekly press

FORNEY'S war press. *See* Weekly press

PENNSYLVANIA (*Continued*)

PHILADELPHIA—*Continued*

Daily FORUM. d S 7 1842-44‖
1842 as National forum;Ja-Je 3 1843 Philadelphia national forum
DLC 1842-Jl 1 1843;O 10 1844
MWA My 30 1844
NN O 12 1843;O 10,28 1844
NcD S 8 1842
PBL [1843-44]
PHi Mr-D 1843
PNhF S 26 1842

Weekly FORUM. w 1843-
MWA D 28 1844
PBL F 18 1843

FRANKFORD dispatch. w Je 22 1877+
pub 1902+
PPFfHi 1914+
PP N 10 1922;N 11 1927,Ja 6 1928; F 8 1929+

FRANKFORD gazette. w Ap 1868+
1868-73? as Weekly gazette (Holmesburg) 1874?-76? Frankford and Holmesburg gazette;1891-1915? North Philadelphia gazette
ICHi My 15-Jl 17,31-Ag 21,S-O 9,23-N 6,20 1875-Ja 22,F 5-12,26,Mr 4-18 1876
NNHi F 6 1869;Ja 17 1873
PP Je 1926+
PPFfHi Jl 1-8 1876;S 24 1909+

FRANKFORD herald. w 1854-1915‖?
PP Je 9 1894;My 11 1901
VU Mr 29-Je 28 1884

FRANKFORD news-gleaner. w O 18 1882+
pub 1920+
PP [1926]+

***FRANKLIN gazette.** d F 23 1818-N 19 1824‖
United with Aurora. General advertiser to form Aurora and Franklin gazette, later Aurora
DLC 1821-24
MBAt Mr 21 1822
NcD Jl 15,28,O 1,18,23-N 8 1824
OCHi O 29 1823
PBL [1821-24]
PDoHi [1821-23]Ja 9,Ap 8 1824
PHi 1821-23
PP [Mr 1823-24]
PPM Ja-My 4 1821
WHi Ja-N 12 1824

FRANKLIN gazette. w Jl 21 1825-
MWA D 1 1825
N Ag 4 1825
NNHi Ja 19 1826

***FRANKLIN gazette for the country.** sw My 27 1819-N 1824‖
MBAt F 28,D 22 1821
MWA O 30 1821[Ja 30-D 18 1822]Ja 1,Ag 6 1823
NN Mr 29-Ap 2,S 6-8,24-O 15 1823
NjR Ja 29 1823
PLaHi [1821]-[23]
PP [1821-F 1823]
PPot D 21 1822
WHi 1821-N 1822;Mr 15-D 1823

FREEMAN and Irish-American review. w 1889-91‖
MnHi [1890-91]
PPCHi [1889]-[91]

***FREEMAN'S journal, and Columbian chronicle.** sw,tw F 20 1805-N 1824‖
1805-N 1808 as Freeman's journal for the country
tw 1805-My 1808
MWA Ja 16,Mr 22,My 20,Jl 3,Ag 30 1822;Jl 2 1823;O 11 1824

***FREEMAN'S journal and Philadelphia mercantile advertiser.** d Ja 24 1775-Ja 6 1827‖
1775-Je 13 1804 as Pennsylvania evening post (title varies). Followed by National palladium and freeman's journal
DLC N 25 1824
MHi Mr 3 1821;N 24 1823;Ap 7 1826
MSaE Mr 5 1822
MWA My 13 1825
NIC Ja-S 17 1821
NjHi My 13 1824;S 1825-Ag 1826
PDoHi [1821-26]
PPF 1821
PPL Mr 1825-Ja 6 1827

FREEMAN'S journal for the country. *See* Freeman's journal, and Columbian chronicle

FREIE arbeiter stimme. *See under* New York City

Philadelphia FREIE PRESSE. d Ja 1 1849-D 31 1887‖
1849-D 31 1859 as Die freie presse
In German
MWA My 12 1858;Ag 24 1876
PPG complete
—w ed *See* Sonntags-blatt der freien presse

Philadelphia FUGGETLENSEG. (Independence) w N 1923+
In Hungarian
pub 1926+
PP Ap 1928+
PPiHi [1926-O 1931]

Saturday GAZETTE. w Ap 19-My 24 1823‖?
PHi My 24 1823

Saturday GAZETTE. w O 12 1844-D 9? 1853‖
Follows Philadelphia Saturday museum. 1844-Mr 17 1849 as Neal's Saturday gazette;Mr 24 1849-S 28 1850 Mammoth Saturday gazette. Followed by Graham's Saturday mail, later Saturday evening mail
MWA 1844[Ja-My 24]Je 21 1845-[46]-O 7,N 4,25 1848;49 [50-O 1 1853]
MiU-C [1844;47]
NNHi N 21 1846;My 15 1847;Ap 27 1850
NcD [1846;My 15 1847-Ja 25 1851]
NhD 1844-O 10 1846
NjR S 2 1849;Mr 16,Jl 20 1850;Ap 3-10 1852;Jl 16 1853
OC Ja 11 1845
OClWHi Ap 11 1846;Ap 24 1847;My 6-13 1848
OHi Je 17 1848
PBL F 13,Mr 6 1847[48-49]
PHi 1845;Jl 6 1850
PP 1844-O 4 1845
PWcHi [1845]
TU Ag 24 1850
VU Ag 14 1847

Philadelphia GAZETTE (Abend ausgabe). d Ja 25 1879-Je 15 1908‖
1879-Ja 24 1880 as Philadelphia neue zeitung;Ja 26 1880-Ap 11 1890 Philadelphia gazette. Merged with Philadelphia demokrat
In German
PPDe 1879-[90-91;94-95]-[1901-07]

***Philadelphia GAZETTE and daily advertiser.** d O 1 1788-N 3 1845‖
1788-93 as Federal gazette (title varies); 1803-Mr 17 1823 Relph's Philadelphia gazette and daily advertiser
CSmH S 1 1830
Ct [1831]
CtY Ap 6 1843
DLC S 12 1823;Jl 27,Ag 4,9,S 29,O 13,30,N 2,D 4 1824;O 1827-Ap 12,S 10,D 31 1828[Jl 17-D 18 1829]Ja 7,11-12,15,18 1830;Ja 18 1831;Ja 2-Je 1832;Jl 25 1834;N 22 1837;N 6 1840;Ap 5 1841;Ag 4-D 12 1842;S 16 1845
DeHi D 5 1822
MBAt Je 12-13 1822;Ja 9,Mr 22 1828;Mr 2,My 30,O 29 1829
MHi O 18,N 19 1821;N 18,D 6,12 1823;Ap 15 1824;My 14,D 23 1825
MSaE D 17 1823
MWA Je 12,Jl 3,S 19,D 27,29 1821;F 21 1822;23-27;Jl 15-17,24,O 9,N 20 1828;29-30;F 25 1832;D 7-9 1833;Mr 28,Je 22,D 7,9,12 1836;My 16,20 1840
MiU-C [1824-26;28]
MnHi Mr 21 1845
N O 16 1833;D 9 1842
NN D 11 1823;O 15 1825;O 14 1826;Ja 12,20,F 1,Mr 9 1827;Ja 14-15,D 22 1829;S 15,O 5 1842
NcD N 7 1832
NjCHi D 3 1836
NjR 1828[31]
OCHi F 19 1836
P Mr 1834-My 3 1836
PHi 1821;33;Jl 1844-45
PP 1821-45
PPM 1821-22;26-27;Jl 1828-29;My 25 1831
PPiHi Ap 17,My 8 1828

GAZETTE-DEMOCRAT. d Ap 12 1890+
1890-N 26 1892 as Morgen gazette; N 28 1892-My 8 1918 Philadelphia Morgen gazette
In German
pub Je 1892+
PP Je 1927+
PPG Ja-F 15 1914
PPeS My 6,8 1922
—w ed *See* Pennsylvanische staats-gazette
—Sunday ed *See* Philadelphia sonntags-gazette

GAZETTE of the United States. *See* United States gazette

GENERAL advertiser. *See* Aurora

GERMANTOWN bulletin. w O 1928+
Title varies slightly
pub 1928+
PP S 12 1929+

GERMANTOWN chronicle. w,d N 7 1868-73‖
w 1868-N 13 1869
DLC N 7 1868-N 13 1869;N 6 1872-My 5 1873
PP 1868-N 5 1872;Ap 6-N 6 1873

GERMANTOWN courier. w D 4 1936+
pub 1936+

GERMANTOWN guide. *See* Guide

GERMANTOWN news. w O 1898+
pub D 1931+
PP D 31 1914;Mr 4 1917;Jl 31 1919[Je 1925-O 1927]33+

GERMANTOWN independent gazette. *See* Independent gazette and Germantown guide

GERMANTOWN social. m Ag 1876-Jl 1877‖
PHi complete

GERMANTOWN telegraph. w Mr 17 1830-1930‖?
Mr-My 19 1830 as Village telegraph; Ja 12 1831-39 Germantown telegraph and Philadelphia and Montgomery advertiser
CSmH Jl 14 1830
DLC My 19 1841;76-Ja 1 1879
MWA S 11 1833;O 6 1858;Mr 9,Jl 13,S 21 1859;F 29,Ap 18,Je 27,Ag 1,N 21 1860;F 25 1863;D 28 1864;Ag 30 1876;O 15-22,N 19-26 1879;88;Ja 2-16,30,Mr 27,My 22-29 1889
NjR Mr 23 1831
NjWdHi N 26 1873
OClWHi My 10 1865
P Jl 1889-Jl 1912
PBL Ag 17 1842
PDoHi [1852-81]Mr 6 1883
PHi Mr 17 1830-Ag 15 1883
PNoHi Je 27 1849
PP Mr 26,Ap 9,My 7-14,Jl 1851-S 15 1852;O 12,N 9 1853;Ja 1854;N 17 1858;S 21 1859;Jl 15 1863;Jl 19 1865;Jl 22 1868;F 25 1874;D 8 1875-S 4 1889;Ja 12 1890;Ag 3-10,O 26-N 2,D 23 1892;Ja 4 1893;Je 14 1908;Ap 1-22 1927;D 27 1929;Je 12 1930+
PPL Mr 17 1830-57;Mr 13 1861-Mr 1 1865;Mr 11 1868-F 1875;Mr 16 1881-Ag 15 1883;D 12 1888-Ap 17 1889
PPeS Je 11 1851;F 11-18,Jl 7 1852[53-59]F 15, Mr 7-14,Ap 18-25,Jl 18 1860;Ag 14 1861;Ja 29,D 10 1862;Ja 21,Ap 22,Je 24-Jl 1,O 4 1863;Ja 6,Je 15-22,Ag 24,S 7,O 19,N 9,D 21 1864;Ap 5,Je 28,Ag 30,N 22,D 20 1865;O 16-23 1872;F 7 1877[78-86]
PWcHi Mr 21 1902
TJT N 25 1874

GIRARD avenue news. *See* North central bulletin

Saturday GLEANER. w Ja 2 1847-O 1848‖
United with Alexander's express messenger to form Family messenger and national gleaner
DeU Ja 15,Ap 22 1848
MWA [Ja-D 18 1847;Ja-O 7 1848]
NjR Ag 26 1848
PLhT Je 12 1847
PPL Ja 9-Ap 3 1847

GLOBE. w -D 18? 1824‖
United with Emerald to form Globe and emerald (New York City)

Daily GLOBE. d O 6-N 23 1868‖
PCHi O 10 1868
PHi complete

GRAHAM'S Saturday mail. *See* Saturday evening mail

GRAPHIC news. *See* Tabloid

GREENBACK herald. w Jl 4- 1875‖
Jl 4-25 1875 as People and anti-monopolist; Ag 1-22? 1875 People
PHi Jl-O 1875
WHi S 5,19 1875

GROONG. w S 15 1919+
In Armenian
pub 1919+
PP My 27 1932+

GROTJAN'S Philadelphia public sale report. *See* Philadelphia public sale report

GRUND'S Pennsylvanischer deutscher. w
In German
CtY Mr 13 1841
DLC O 10,31 1840
NNHi F 13 1841
PShH Ag 1 1840

GUIDE. m,sm,w D 21 1871-D 2 1926‖
1871-N 21 1872 as Germantown guide; N 30 1872-S 5 1873 Weekly guide. United with Germantown independent gazette to form Independent gazette and Germantown guide
m 1871-Ag 1 1872;sm Ag 15-N 21 1872
PP D 1875-O,D 1876-Je 23,Ag 25 1877-My 14,Jl 22,N 30,D 21 1878;Ap 1879-[82]-Je 23 1888;F 22 1905;My 12,Ag 15,S 5 1914;15-[19]Jl 3 1920;S 9 1922[Je-D 1924;Je-D 1925] 26
PPFfHi Ap 19,Je 21,Ag 30 1913;My 16,Je 6,20, Jl 4 1914;N 4 1916

Saturday GUILLOTINE. w D 3 1820-Ja 5 1830‖?
PHi Ja 5 1830

GWIAZDA (Star). w Ag 14 1902+
In Polish
pub 1902+
PP Ag 5 1926;D 29 1927+

Saturday morning HERALD. w N 10 1827-
MWA N 17,D 8,22 1827
NjHi Ja 12 1828
P Ja 10 1835-37

HERALD. d Ag 27 1866-1913‖
1866-1911? as Evening herald (N 29 1877-85? Chronicle herald; 1885?-88? Daily herald)
MWA Ap 6 1876;Mr 9 1877
NcD My 23 1879
PCHi F 25 1868
PP S 22 1881
PPoHi D 27 1884-D 15 1885
PPot [1884]
PU 1866-69
Tx Mr 24 1869

Philadelphia HEROLD. w Ja 6 1894+
1894-Ja 10 1925 as Vereins und logen zeitung
In German
pub N 25 1911+
PP D 31 1927+

HOME journal and citizen soldier. w 1843?-
1843-O? 1844 as Home journal
MnHi [1851]
NNHi N 20 1844
NhD Ja 24-F 21,Mr 13-Ap 10,My 15-29,Je 26-S 11,25 1844-Ja 8,F-Mr 5,Ap 2-9,My 21 1845
P-M My 1 1843

Philadelphia HOME weekly. w Ja 25 1843-68‖
1843-D 21 1864 as Dollar newspaper; D 28 1864-D 20 1865 Home weekly and household newspaper
CtY [1844;47]-52
DLC Mr 4(sup)1844;Ap 30,Je 11,Jl 23,N 19-26 1845;Jl 8,S 23 1846;Mr 24,Ap 28,O 27 1847;S 26 1849-D 19 1866
IC Mr 29 1848-Mr 19 1851
ICU Ja 21 1846-Ja 10 1849;Ja 14,Mr 11,Ag 5,O 7,21,D 1857;63-65
IU Ap 16 1845
InNcHi Je 16 1852
KHi Ja 4 1860
MB D 27 1865-D 11 1867;Je 3,24,Ag 19 1868
MWA [1845]-[57-60]Ja 9,30,Mr 6,Jl 24,Ag 7, 21,N 6 1861;Ja 29,Mr 12,Ap 2 1862;Ap 8-15 1863;D 27 1865-D 5 1866;F 20 1867;F 19(supp) 1868
MiU [1859]
MiU-C O 8 1851;N 2 1853
MnHi F 19,N 5 1862;Ap 6,Je 29 1864;Je 13 1866
NIC O 17 1855
NN F 21,O 24 1855

PENNSYLVANIA (*Continued*)

PHILADELPHIA—*Continued*

Philadelphia HOME weekly. w 1843-68||—*Cont.*
NNHi Mr 12 1845;F 9 1848;Mr 28,My 30,Je 13,27,Jl 13-Ag 1,S 5-12,N 14 1849;Ag 1850-64; My 8-22,Je,Ag 7,28 1867
NcD [1848-56]
NhD F 7 1844
NjCHi Ap 23-O 15,N 5,19-D 17 1845
NjWdHi Je 3,D 28 1846;My 3 1854;Ag 7 1861
OClWHi F 12-19 1845;Ja 21 1846;47-Ja 10 1849;50-[54]-[60-62]Ja 18 1865
OHi Mr 27 1850;F 26 1862
P F 8-15,Mr 7,S 5,N 28,D 12 1860-[Ja-Jl 3 1861]Jl 2-23,S-N 19,D 3-17 1862;Ja 2-8,Mr 14, 25,Ap 8-15,My 27,Jl 3-10,S 9,D 23 1863
PCHi D 28 1853
PDoHi 1850-51;53-[55]56
PEbHi D 29 1847
PHHi [1847]-[49]
PHi [Mr 14 1849-D 22 1862]
PLhT F 27 1850;S 1-8 1858;N 21 1860
PNhF N 4 1846;S 8 1847
PNoHi [1847]Jl 11,O 17 1855;Mr 7 1860;Ja 8 1862
PPFfHi My 9 1860;S 9,30 1863;Mr 30 1864;Ja 18 1865
PP Mr 26 1851;F 9 1853;Mr 5 1862
PPL S 17 1845;D 27 1848[51-52]Jl 20,S 21-28, D 21 1853;O 4,D 13 1854;Ap 9,Jl 23 1856;Jl 22,Ag 12,O 21 1857[58-61]Ja 15,F 19 1862
PPeS Ap 30,Je 25 1845;F 18-25,Mr 11,Ap 9 1846
PToHi Ja 7 1846;Mr 7 1855;F 11,25 1856;Ja 28 1857
PU Ja 21 1846-Ja 7 1852;O 5 1853;Ja 11 1854-D 21 1864
PWcHi Jl 15,S 10 1845[47-49]N 20-27 1850[51; 54]Mr 7,O 31 1855;F 27 1856;Ja 28,N 25 1857
VU Jl 3 1844:N 21-28,D 12,26 1849;F 13,Mr 20-Ap 3,My,Je 23,Ag 28-S 4 1850;Jl 21-Ag 4,18-S 1,22-O,N 10-17,D 29 1852-Ja 5,26,F 23,Mr 23-My 25,Je 29,Ag 10-O 5,N 2-23 1853;Ja 4,F 1,Ap 26-My 24,Je 14-28 1854;S 17,O 22,N 5-19 1856;Ap 15-22,My 13-20,Je 3-17,Jl 1,S 9-N 4,D 9 1857-Ap 21,Je 9-16,30 1858

HOSPITAL register. w F 14 1863-Ap 1 1865||
1863? as West Philadelphia hospital register
DLC Ag 29-O 17,31-D 1863;Ja 9-Jl 2 1864
DSG complete
MBM [1864]
NIC [1863-64]
NNHi S 5 1863
NjP Ag 29 1863-65
NjWdHi [Mr-Ap,D 1864-65]
OClWHi 1863-Mr 1864
PHi complete
PPot Ja 9,My 14,28,Je 11,Jl 9,Ag 3,S 3-10,O 1,N 5,D 10 1864

HY SIRD. w,m Ap 14 1926+
w 1926-N 1935
In Armenian
pub 1926+
PP 1928+

IDISHE welt (Jewish world) d F 1 1914+
In Yiddish and English
pub 1914+
IU D 4 1917-Jl 11,O 20 1921+
NN 1922+
PP O 5 1926;Je 10 1927+

ILLUSTRATED new age. d Mr 25 1863-Mr 12 1875||
1863-Je 10 1866 as Daily age; Je 11 1866-Mr 8 1874 Age
DLC* Jl 29 1863-Je 29 1867;68-Je 1870;Ap 7 1873
DeU Je 7 1864
ICHi S 28 1865
MWA S 26 1863-Mr 24,Jl 8,Ag 22 1864;N 30 1865;F 24(supp)1873
N Je 1 1865
NNHi Ap 18-19,21 1865;Ap 30 1866;S 3 1868;My 3 1873
NcD Ja-Je 1865;Mr 29 1870
PCHi My 15 1868
PDoHi Ap 5 1865;My 4 1872
PHHi N 2 1865
PHi Jl 1863-65;Ag 18,21 1873
PP 1863-Jl 1864
PPCHi S 16 1869
PPFfHi Jl 16,27,31 1866
PPL Mr 25,My 2,5-Ag 6,8-S 18,20-N 26,28 1863;D 31 1864[Ja-O 20 1865]Mr 25-Ap 9,13,18-My 10 1867;Mr 28-Je 1,3-Jl,Ag 2-O 21,23 1869-74;Ja 30 1875
PPM Mr 1863-Je 1870;71-75
PPeS Ag 19 1865;O 8 1868
PU Mr 25 1863-Mr 2 1874
PWcHi Mr 5,O 31 1868
VU O 15 1870;S 27 1873
WHi Je 1863-Jl 1865

ILLUSTRATED new age. w Je 6 1863-Mr 12 1875||
1863-Jl? 1874 as Philadelphia weekly age
DLC Ap 9 1864
NbHi Ja 3 1868
OClWHi Je 27 1863
PPot O 1 1866
PWcHi S 26 1863;Mr 13 1869

INDEPENDENCE. *See* Philadelphia fuggetlenseg

INDEPENDENT. d S? 1843-
DLC N 3 1843

Philadelphia INDEPENDENT. w My 10 1931+
pub [1931]-34
PP 1935+

*INDEPENDENT balance. w Ap 16 1817-
DLC 1821-Ap 17 1822;O 16 1824;S 6,N 1,D 6 1828;O 31,N 14 1829;D 22 1832
MBAt F 5 1823
MWA Je 6 1821
NN Ja-My 1821
PHi Ja 10,31,Mr,Ap 11-25 1821;S 17 1825
PLewL O 8-29 1825
PPL Ag 22 1829
PPiHi Mr 31 1827
V O 20 1822

INDEPENDENT democrat and protector of American industry. w Jl 26 1834-
PNo Jl 26 1834

INDEPENDENT gazette and Germantown guide. w 1882-My 17 1928||
1882-D 2 1926 as Germantown independent gazette
PP D 9 1926-28

INDEPENDENT weekly press. w D 5 1835-
PPL D 5 1835

Philadelphia INQUIRER. d Je 1 1829+
1829-Je 1830 as Pennsylvania inquirer; Jl 1830-Je 1 1834 Pennsylvania inquirer and morning journal; Je 2 1834-D 31 1841 Pennsylvania inquirer and daily courier; Ja 1 1842-Ap 1 1860 Pennsylvania inquirer and national gazette
pub 1829+
ArHi Ap 28 1852
CSmH S 9 1830;Mr 30(supp)1850;Mr 1861-Je 1862
Ct My 19 1866
CtNlC Ap 18 1865
CtSp Ap 18 1865
CtT Mr 5 1861
CtY Ja 3-N 7 1842;61-Je 1867
DLC [Je-D 1829]Ja 5,23,25,29-30 1830;N 9 1832; My 25 1833;F 18 1836;F 26-27,Mr 5,8 1838;Mr 10 1845-52;Ja 14 1857;Je 16(extra)1860;Ja 29, Mr 4(extra)12,Ap 8 1861-S 13 1865;Ja-N 3 1866;67;70-81;Jl-D 1882;Jl-D 1884;Jl 1885-87; Jl-D 1888;Jl 1889-91;Jl 1892-94;S 1897-Mr 1899;Jl 1900—
DeU [1860-65]Jl 5 1866;Mr 12 1875[76]Je 4,20 1878
DeWI [1865]S 29 1901
GAtCo Je 15-16 1840
GU Ja 19 1913
ICHi Ap 5 1862;Ap 5,24,My 24,S 27 1865;O 11-12 1871
ICM Je 9 1881;Je 22 1882;Je 5,Ag 19 1884;Je 6 1896
IEN Ap 16 1934+
IHi O 16,D 20 1860;My 23,29-31,Je 3,8,11-15,18-20,Jl 4,15,17 1861;Ja 6-11,13-18,20,22-25,27-29 1862;Ap 3-4,6-11,13,18,20-24,28-29 1863;Ap 4, 18-22,25,My 10,12-13,15-20,22-26,Je 12 1865
IP 1861-63
IU Ap 19,23,Jl-Ag 9,21,23,S 21,N 18,D 5 1861; Ja 11,15,21,31[F 11-25]Mr 4[8-S 11]16,18,22,O 15,17 1862[My 18-D 1863]
IaDH O 1860-S 1861;62-Je 1865
InRE Ja 31 1855
KHi [Ap 18-My 4 1865]
LNC My 17 1862
LNH Ap 20 1865
MB O 2,N 30 1860;Ja 15,31,Jl 31 1861;Jl 9,31,N 5 1862;Ja 16-17,Ap 24,28,My 5,O 20 1865;N 4 1868;Ja-Je 1877;Ja 19 1882;Ja 19 1892
MBAt D 28 1829;D 24 1830;Jl 4,N 29,D 3,27 1845;N 28,D 9,25 1846[47-48;50]-76;Ap 11-24 1899
MHi S 25-26,O 2,5,8-10,17,N 7,D 3 1829[30-32]O 15,N 21,D 11 1861;Mr 5,8,My 24 1862;Ja 14,F 11-13 1863;Mr 19 1866
MMarHi F 22-Ap 20 1865
MSaE [1861]-68
MWA N 9,D 25 1830;Ja 6,S 30 1831;Ja 19,Ap 5 1832;Ag 17 1833;D 9 1845;F 16 1848;Mr 6 1851;N 30 1852 D 26 1853-[Ja-Ag 12 1854]S 2 1857;Mr 2,5,My 1861-Je,Jl 7,Ag 18,30,S 27,N 27,D 4,20,27 1863;F 6,Mr 12[Je 18-Jl]Ag 15,C 12,N 5 1867;F 29,Mr 10[Jl 14-Ag 25]O 1,27,D 17,25 1868;My 3,20,Je 1,26 1869-[Ja 2-20]O 10,26 1871;N 12 1872;Jl 7,D 12 1873;Jl-D 1874; F 19,My 17,O 30 1876;Mr 24 1877;Je 7 1884;Ag 5,19 1886;F 20 1888;Mr 25 1890;Ap 21 1831;F 11-12 1892;F 16 1894;Mr 2 1899
MiG O 20 1856
MiU [1892-93;1901-02]-[04]-[08]
MiU-C [1861-63;65-66;68;81;90]
MnHi Jl-S 1862
N Je 19-20,O 11 1833;Mr 9 1837;D 12,24 1862;O 12 1872
NBuHi 1861-65
NN [Ap 1860;Ja-F 1862]-[Ja]-D 1863;Ja[F] 1865-Ja 8 1866
NNHi My 1 1830;Jl 21 1831;O 10 1834;My 12, 19,Je 9,11,30,O 12 1860;61-65;O 26 1868;O 10-11 1871;Ap 1 1873;Mr 12 1874;Ap 19(extra)20 1862
NbHi Jl 29 1861;Mr 4,My 28,N 8 1862;Ja 12 1863;S 5,O 10 1864;Ja 27,Ap 4,My 5,O 17 1865;Mr 17 1887;N 16 1893;My 16 1895;Ag 25, 30,S 9-12,15,17-18,21-22 1907
NcD S 13 1854[58;61-67;95;98;1904]
NcU [Jl 6-S 3 1861;Je-O 15 1862;Ag 1863;Ja-O 1864]Ag 13 1865;Ap 5 1866;Ja 24,Jl 17 1867
NjCHi D 16 1831;Mr 3 1837;D 20 1844;Ja 29 1845;Jl 1861-62;Jl-D 1863;Ap 15 1865-Jl 22 1867
NjFHi Ja 15 1869
NjR Mr 16 1836;Mr 29,My 16 1837;D 11 1845 [60-62;65]
extras: Ap 15,Mr 4 1861
supps: Ap 28,30,My 12,19,Je 9,11,14,16,20,28,30, Ag 25,O 13 1860
NjWdHi [1861]S 3-4,13,16 1862;My 4 1863;Ap 14,Ag 29 1864;S 15-16 1887;O 24 1898;Je 5 1927
OCHi Ap 24 1865
OCl My 24 1862-Mr 1863
OClWHi Jl 10,N 7 1860-Je,S 1-4,8,15 1863;Ja-Ag,S 27,O 3,18 1864;Ap 4,10,17-29,My 9-10,16, Je 12,Jl 7,O 12 1865
OHi Jl 6 1861-My 23 1865
OOxM Je 16-19 1875;Jl 6 1876
P Jl 30-Ag 7 1829;D 20 1833-Ag,N 21 1839;Je 12 1840;Mr 20 1844;Ag 22 1850;Mr 1861-O 1 1864;Ap 24 1865;O 5 1881+
PArL My 12 1862;Je 1 1926;Je 9,15,29,N 7 1928;Jl 2,S 1,N 9 1932;Ja 6,8 1933;F 7,N 17 1934;F 14,Mr 28 1935
PBL S 12 1832
PBf My 20 1861
PBloHi Ap 18-20 1865;My 2,Je 1-2,7 1889-[1923]
PCC Ap 22,25-26,28-29,Jl 24 1861;Je 1 1929
PCHi [1861]Jl 4 1876;Ag 28 1878;S 7-8,11-20 1901
PCarlHi F 21 1909
PDoHi S 6 1859[S 5 1861-Jl 5 1866]Mr 11 1902;O 4-11 1908
PE [1834-35]
PEHi Ap 25 1865
PEL D 25 1830-Ja 1831
PHHi Je 11 1860;Ap 17 1865;F 3 1897;Ag 14 1898
PHi Je-D 1834;42-43;50;52;60-1917;Ap 16 1934+
PHoHi O 28,31 1864
PLaF D 20,31 1897[98]Mr 19 1936+
PLewL [1861-62]
PLhT N 8 1862;Ag 29,S 11 1863;Ap 19,25,My 13 1865
PNeB Je 11,22,Jl 23,S 28,N 7,D 28 1861
PNoHi [My-D 4 1861]-Ap 1862;F 1,Ap 10,17-26,28-29,O 19 1865
PP Je 1 1829;40-Je 1842;My 7 1846;60-Mr 1862;Ap 14-D 1863;F 20,O 3,D 27 1864;Mr-N 1865;F 23-24,Jl 20 1866;Ag 31 1867;Mr 31,My 6 1868;Ja-Je 1870;Ag 1871;F 21 1874;Ja-Mr, My 1875-Ja,Mr 1876-Mr,Je 4 1878;Ja-S 1881; Ja-Je 1883;Ag 11 1884;Jl 1889-Je 1890[92-93] 94;96;Mr 2,O 4-5 1899[1901]Ja 15 1907;O 4-11 1908;Jl 1913-Jl 1917;Je 1924-Mr 1925;26+
PPCHi Je 5 1834;Jl 9 1835
PPFfHi F 20,Ap 17,21,24,My 20 1865;N 29 1867
PPL 1829-38;D 14 1839[Ap-Jl 1840]Ja-Je 1841; 44;46;Jl-N 1847;Ja-O 1848 49;Jl-D 1850;Jl 1852-55;Ap 1856-Je 1862;63-71;Mr 1872-Ag,O 1875-Je 1876;77-Je 1880;81-88;Mr 1889-1925
PPM Ap-D 1831;Ja-My 1833;41-Je 1849;57;My 1860-Ap,S 1862-68;F 1869-Ap 1878;81-Je 1897; Mr 1902-Ag,N 1903-Ag,N 1906-F,My-Je 1907; Mr-Ap 1908;10-Je,Ag 1913-Je,S 1916-Ap,Jl 1920-My,D 31 1921-Ja,Ap,D 31 1922-O,D 31 1928+
PPeS My 19 1860;Ja 21-Ap 3,9-17,Jl 18,22,26,S 13,22-O 11 1862;Ap 17,19-22,24-Je 17 1865;Je 26,N 20 1890;My 15 1897;N 8 1928;O 24 1929; Mr 9 1930;N 9-13 1932
PPiHi Ja-Je 1862;N 19 1863;My 13 1864
PPoHi Jl-S 16 1865
PPot Ap-D 1830;O 16 1839;O 26 1849;D 9 1851;Je 5,17,27,S 14,O 12,N 6,16,20 1861[Ja-Ap 1862]Ap 7,S 5,O 3 1863;Je 14,N 21 1864 [Ap 10-Ag 4 1865]N 1 1869;Jl 26 1870; S 28 1871;N 3 1886;S 17 1887;Jl 5 1888;Je 24-26 1890;Je 11 1892;Mr 5 1893[96]
PSC Ap 21-22,24-29 1865
PSF S 27 1881
PShH Ag 14,S 12 1874
PSuHi Ap 20 1865;N 12 1872[74;76;1931]
PU 1862-S 1865;Ap 16 1934+
PW Mr 21,28,Ap 4,7 1840;Jl 7-D 1862
PWcHi Ja 7,14,21,F 18 1832;N 7 1837;Je 10 1860[61-62]Mr 12,Ag 15,D 2 1863;Jl 5,27,D 28 1864[65]Mr 14,My 22 1866;Ja 1 1867;F 10 1869;Je 29 1913
PWcT N 16,23 1861;My 17,Je 3,9-10,12,Ag 16,S 16,O 4,N 8 1862;D 28 1864;N 23 1865;Mr 14,My 22 1866;S 14,19 1901
RPB 1860-66
TxU 1861-65
V Ap 1860-63
VRC D 28 1861;F 7,Ap 18,My 31,Jl 4,31,Ag 29,S 2 1862;N 5 1863;My 13 1864;Ap 30 1865
VU Ag 16,18-22 1862;Ag 27,S 26-27,30,O 2-3,8 1934
WHi 1846[My 2-D 1860]-N 1869;Mr-Jl 1870;Ja-Je,N 7 1871;73-74;O 25-27 1882;D 16 1894;S 3 1901

Philadelphia INQUIRER. tw 1829-
1829-41 as Inquirer; 1842-Ag? 1860 Pennsylvania inquirer and national gazette for the country
DLC Ag 13,15 1829[Jl 1838-Je,N 19,21,23,30 1839;Ja 14 21,23,F 4,8,15,18 1840;46
MBAt F 1845-D 7 1848[50]
MWA D 28 1829;Mr 26,Je 7 1830 Ja 20,25,F 8 1842;Mr 8,S 6 1860;Ja 1 1861;Jl 1866-Je 15 [29-N 7]1867-Je 24 1869
N Ag 6,18-19 1842;My 25,S 2 1844

Philadelphia Saturday INQUIRER. w 1829-
1829-43? as Pennsylvania inquirer and morning journal
MB S 16 1830;Jl 15 1831[Ap 16-D 1842;Ja-D 22 1849]
MWA D 25 1830;Ja 11,N 1 1845
PBL D 6 1845
PPL Ag 15,S 19,O 31-N 7,21-D 5 1846;Ja 9-Mr 13,27-Ap 3 1847

Daily INTELLIGENCER. d D 1 1832-33||
MWA Jl 17 1833
N O 13 1833
PBL [1833]
PHi 1832-Ag 1 1833
PPL D 10 1832-Ap 23 1833

IRISH republican shield and literary observer. w
DLC Ag 18-D 27,N 10-17,D 1-8 1832;Ja 12,F 2,Mr 8,O 16,23 1833
MeU Ja 12 1833
NcD S 8-22,O 6 1832
PP S 15 1832

Philadelphia evening ITEM. d F 1846-1915||
Title varies: City item; Fitzgerald's city item; Evening city item; All day city item
DLC S 10 1870-84;My-Ag 1885;86;My-D 1887; 89-Je 1891;92-1912
KHi O 14 1876
MWA Ap 6,Je 6,25 1876
NNHi My 2 1873
PCHi N 19 1870
PDoHi S 29 1875;Ja 23 1876[94-95]
PP 1900-12
TJT O 8 1900

Weekly ITEM. w S 25 1847-97|
Title varies: City item; Fitzgerald's city item
DLC 1847-S 14 1850;78-86;F 1887-Je 1888;90-97
IaHi Mr 1896-Mr 1897
MWA Ag 12 1848;Ja 5 1850;O 16 1852
PMcC [1876]
PP Mr 24 1848-S 15 1849

PENNSYLVANIA (*Continued*)

PHILADELPHIA—*Continued*

Philadelphia Sunday ITEM. w S 1847-N 30 1930‖
Title varies: All day city item. Sunday ed; Sunday item
CLM D 22 1889
DLC Mr-D 1874;S 1877-87;89-1912
MWA S 8 1878
OClWHi Ag 9 1885
PBL D 11 1847
PP Ja-Je 1897;1900-12;My 1928-30
TJT Mr 6 1898

JACKSON star, and daily orb. d Mr 1834-
MWA My 30 1834

JEDNOSC. w Ja 1916+
In Polish
pub 1925+
PP O 1929+

JEWISH exponent. w O 1887+
pub 1887+
PHi Mr 4 1910
PP Ja 3,D 12,26 1890-Ja 1891;Ap 22,My 6 1892;1912+

Philadelphia JEWISH morning journal. d Ja 1 1901+
In Yiddish
pub 1913-Ap 1922;24;30+
PP Jl 24 1932+

Philadelphia JEWISH times. w Ap 1925+
pub Ap 30 1926-Ja 6 1928;29+
PP Mr 11 1928+

JEWISH world. *See* Idishe welt

Morning JOURNAL. d Ja 1-Je 30 1830‖
Merged with Pennsylvania inquirer, later Philadelphia inquirer
CSmH Ja 4 1830
DLC Ja 1,26 1830
MWA Mr 1,Ap 13 1830

Saturday morning JOURNAL. w Ja-Je 1830‖?
NNHi Ja 30-Mr 6,27,Ap 10-24(extra)Ap 28 1830

Philadelphia evening JOURNAL. d My-N 1842‖
N S 26 1842
NN My 4,Ag 27-31,S 3,6-8,24,26,28-N 18,21-28 1842

Philadelphia evening JOURNAL. d Ap 12 1856-Jl 2 1863‖
CSmH Jl 4(extra)1863
CtY Jl 2 1858
DLC My 15 1856;Mr 20 1858;Ja 18 1859;Ap 25 1863
DeWI Ap-Jl 1863
MWA Ap 12 1856;My 19 1857;Jl 19 1860;Ap 30,D 31 1862-Ap 27 1863
NNHi Jl 5(extra)1863
NjWdHi Jl 5(extra)1863
OClWHi Ap 15 1861;Je 1 1863
PHi 1856-O 11 1859;Ja 28-Ap 11,O 12 1861-Ap 11 1862
PP D 1 1862;Jl 2 1863
PPeS Ap 29 1856
PPot My 11,Je 12 1857;Mr 25,27,29 1858;Jl 28, 30-Ag 1 1860
TU S 26 1860
WHi Ap 15 1863

JOURNAL. w Ja 30 1930+
pub 1930+
PP Ag 1932+

JUSTICE. *See under* Wilmington, Del.

KENSINGTON bulletin. w Ja 1922+
PP O 25 1929-Je 23,S 8-O 27,N 24 1933

KENSINGTON critic. w Mr 1894+
pub 1927+
PP Ag 13 1932+

KENSINGTON news. w Ja 18 1934+
pub 1934+
PP D 27 1934+

KENSINGTONIAN. w Ja 1925-Jl 24 1936‖
PP Mr 1935-36

Daily KEYSTONE. d 1844-Jl 21 1847‖
United with Spirit of the times to form Spirit of the times and daily keystone, later Spirit of the times
DLC [Mr-Jl 1845;46]Ja 14,22,F 4-6 1847
MWA Ap 22 1846
NN D 21 1844
PBL [1845-46]
PHi N 24 1844

KEYSTONE. w Jl 20 1867-Jl 11 1868‖
PHi complete

KNAPSACK. d O 24-N 4 1865‖
CSmH complete
OClWHi O 25 1865

LAWNDALE press. w O 28 1922+
pub 1922+
PP Mr 24-31 1935

Weekly LEDGER. *See* United States and dollar newspaper

LIBERA parola. w Ap 20 1917+
In Italian
pub 1917+
PP My 28 1932+

LOGAN times. w Ja 1914-My 26 1933‖
PP N 5,19-26 1920;O 16,N 26 1925[26-O 1928] Jl 19 1929-30;Je 5,19-D 4 1931;F-My 1932; My 26 1933

McMAKIN'S model American Saturday courier. *See* American Saturday courier

Saturday evening MAIL. w D 16 1853-
Follows Saturday gazette. 1853-F 3 1855 as Graham's Saturday mail
MWA [Ja 21-D 1854]Ja 13,F 3,Jl 21,N 30 1855
NNHi Je 3-17 1854
P-M Je 3,Jl 15 1854
PLhT Ap 15 1854
WHi• Ja 7 1854

Philadelphia MAIL and universal, literary and general advertiser. m O 1829?-
Title varies: Philadelphia mail
DLC My 30 1830
MBAt My 20,Je,S,D 1830;N 1831;Ja,Jl 1832;My 1833
NN D 1830
NNHi Ja,Jl 1832
P-M Jl 1832
PHi Ap 20,D 1830
PW N 1831

MAMMOTH Saturday gazette. *See* Saturday gazette

MANAYUNK courier. w Ja 1-Mr 18 1848‖
PHi complete

MANAYUNK review. w Ja 4 1900+
pub 1900+
PP 1934+

MANAYUNK sentinel. w N 5 1870-Ap 26 1917‖
Follows Our once-a-week visitor. 1870-Ap 30 1871 as Sentinel. Title varies slightly
PHi 1870-S 24 1891
PP complete

MANAYUNK star and Roxborough gazette. w F 5 1859-Ag 9 1862‖
PHi complete

MECHANIC'S free press. *See* Philadelphia times, mechanics free press and working man's register

El MENSAGERO semanal. *See under* New York City

Philadelphia MERCURY. w S 29 1827-
DLC 1827-Ja 19 1828
MWA Mr 29 1828
N S-N 24 1827
NNHi [D 15 1827-Mr 21 1829]
P-M D 27 1828
PBL F 14,Ap 11 1829
PLewL F 23 1828

Sunday MERCURY. w F 23 1851-91‖?
My 11 1851-Ag 27 1852 as Upham's Philadelphia Sunday mercury
DLC Ja 29-Jl 2 1854;Ap-Jl 1861;N 12 1862;Mr 8,22,Ag 30 1863;Ja 10,Ap 24 1864-My 14 1865
ICHi Ag 20,S 3,24 1865
ICU D 18 1864-D 3 1865
IU O 1860-D 8 1861
MWA Ja 29-Mr 12 1854;My 4,Je-S 7 1856;N 9 1862;Mr 29-Ap 5,19-26 1863;O 15,29 1865;S 13 1868;Ja 8 1871;Ag 6 1876
NcD Ap 14 1861
NjCHi S 25 1881
NjR Ja 27 1861
OHi Ja 30 1859
P 1866-69;71-76
PCHi Ja 28 1872
PDoHi My 17 1868
PP O 28 1855;F 1 1857;Je 13 1858;F 6-7,My 22,N 20 1859;Jl 19-26,S 20 1868
PPFfHi Ap 24 1853
PPL Ap 20 1856
PPeS Ja 18 1891
VU O 20 1867
WHi Ap 5 1891

Philadelphia MERCURY and evening journal. d 1842-44‖
NN O 11 1843;My 23 1844
PBL Ap 13 1843
PWeT Mr 25-28 1844

Saturday evening MESSENGER. w My 3-Je 28 1856‖
PPL My 24,Je 28 1856

Philadelphia MIRROR: quarto edition of the Philadelphia Saturday courier. w Jl 2 1836-Jl 24 1837‖?
Jl-Ag 15 1836 as Philadelphia mirror
DLC 1836-Je 26 1837
MWA 1836-Je 26 1837
MiU-C [1836-37]
NN Ja-Jl 1837
NNHi Jl 16 1836-Jl 24 1837
TxU Ag 8 1836-Jl 24 1837

Il MOMENTO. w Ag 1917-My 3 1919‖
In Italian
PP S 29,O 6,D 8 1917;F,Mr 16-Ap 27 1918;Ja 11-25,F 15-My 3 1919

MOORE'S Philadelphia price current or trade news and shipping list. w D 14 1833-Ja 17 1835‖
D 14 1833 as Philadelphia price current or trade news and shipping list. United with Philadelphia price current and commercial advertiser to form Commercial list and Philadelphia price current, later Commercial list and maritime register
DLC My 31 1834
PHi complete

MORGEN gazette. *See* Gazette-democrat

Philadelphia Saturday MUSEUM. w D 10? 1842-O 5 1844‖
Followed by Neal's Saturday gazette, later Saturday gazette
MWA F 4 1843;Ja-O 5 1844
MiU-C S 14 1844
NcU Mr 4,18,Ag,N 1,Ag 5 1843
WHi Je 10 1843-Ja 20,Mr 2 1844

NATIONAL argus. d F 15 1851-N 10 1861‖
Title varies: National daily argus; National evening argus
DLC N 6 1852;O 6-D 1853;O 4 1858
MWA Jl 9,O 30 1851;Ap 23-24,My 17,29,N 29 1852
NNHi F 17 1855
PBL Ja 23 1852
PPL F 15,My 10 1851;Mr 20 1852;Mr 6,19,Ap 9 1856

NATIONAL atlas and Tuesday morning mail. w Jl 31 1836-38‖
Jl-S 1836 as National atlas and Sunday morning mail
NNHi 1836-Ja 23 1838

NATIONAL banner, and Philadelphia literary gazette. w Ag 17 1833-
DLC S 14,O 12 1833
MWA [Ag 17 1833-Ja 3 1835]

NATIONAL chronicle. d 1822?-
N S 12,14 1825

NATIONAL chronicle. tw Ag 15 1825-
Follows Columbian observer
MWA Ag 15,29,S 7,O 10,14-17 1825
PBL S 23,O 28 1825

NATIONAL enquirer. *See* Pennsylvania freeman

Philadelphia NATIONAL forum. *See* Daily forum

*NATIONAL gazette. sw,tw Ap 5 1820-Ja 1 1842‖
1820-O 2 1841 as National gazette and literary register. United with Inquirer to form Pennsylvania inquirer and national gazette for the country, later Philadelphia inquirer
sw 1820-N 31 1822
CtY 1821-35;Ag 22 1837;Ja 27 1838
DCU 1822-29
DGU O 10 1821-F 6 1836
DLC 1821-Ap 3,S 1828-Ag 1831;F 28 1832-O 12 1833;Ja 16 1834-Je 18 1835;Ap 9 1836-My 28 1839
DeHi Ja 1,D 31 1825
ICHi Mr 15 1825
ICU 1824-26[31]S 13,20-25,O 2-11,16-N 8,13-D 11,15-20,25 1832[33-O 2 1834]
IP Jl 10 1822-Mr 1824
LU Ag 9 1828-S 1841
MB 1821-Mr 1829
MBAt 1821-S 1841
MH 1821-26;28
MHi [1821-D 21 1822]26
MNF 1824;27-28[31]
MNb 1824-27
MSaE Ja 12 1822;F 12 1823;D 1825[26-28]
MWA 1821-32;F 26,Jl 18,S 5,D 12 1833[34-Ag 15 1835]F 25 1836;Ja 12-14,F 2,21-23,Mr 7, 16,Ag 15-19,O 14,28,N 7,25-28,D 5,16-19 1837[F 20-S 25 1838]Je 25,Ag 22,29,S 5,O 8,15-17,D 8-10 1840;Ja 7,14-16,F 9,Mr 16,Je 12-15,19,Jl 3,7,13-29,Ag 3,7-S 14,18-21,25-O 2,7 1841-42
MiU 1821[22-29]30[32-34;40]
MoS F 28 1828-S 10 1829
MsHi F 3,12 1825;Mr 24 1827
N [1821]-[28]
NBHi N 7 1829
NIC 1821-22;24-Mr 9 1826
NN Ja 6,O 13,17,N 10 1821[22-24]-[29-30]F-Je 1831;32[35]
NNHi Ap 1823-Ap 5 1831;Mr 1,My 18,Jl 26,S 18,N 20 1832-N 19 1833[O 10-D 1837]-S 16 1839
NSchU Ap 26 1825-Ap 13 1826
NcD [1821-37;40]
NcU 1821-[26-Mr 1 1827]Mr 5-7,Ap 13 1833;Jl 3 1841
NhD 1823-Mr 1824;My 24 1831-Ap 17 1832;Ag 20 1833-S 27 1834
NhED F 8 1823;Mr 25-D 1824
NjCHi [1821-25]
NjHi 1825-Mr 1828
NjP My 14 1831-My 12 1835
NjR [1821-22]Je 27-D 1826;31-33;35-O 22 1836
NjVi 1832-33
OC My 27 1827-Mr 28 1828
OCHi Mr 18 1833-Je 1840
OClWHi Ap 1 1823;Ag 23 1824;26;Jl 1830-31; 37-40
OHi My 25,O 19,26 1822;O 26 1825;Ap 12 1827
P 1821-Je 1824;25-42
PEL 1822;32-40
PP D 5 1823;N 16 1824
PPH [1821-40]
PRHi 1825[26-27]
PU 1821-32
RW Ag 26 1824
THi Mr 1825-28
TKL Je 23 1831
TNV D 1823-24
TxU 1821-Mr 1835;Ja-Je 1836;37-40;Je 17-D 1841
V 1821-25;27-40
WHi 1821-[32]

*NATIONAL gazette. d N 1 1820-41‖?
1820-My 29 1841 as National gazette and literary register. United with Pennsylvania inquirer to form Pennsylvania inquirer and national gazette, later Philadelphia inquirer
CSmH Ag 7 1827
CtY My 2 1835-Ap 29 1837
DLC 1821-22;Mr 1823-41
ICU Ja 21 1825-27
MB [1821-24]Mr 29 1825-27[30]F 19,Mr 29,Ap 26,28 1831;Mr 7,My 7,O 24 1833;Ap 15,S 27 1834[My 28 1835-Mr]Ag 16 1836[D 18-28 1841] Ja 1 1842
MBAt [1827-28]F 18,Mr 12,18,Je 18,Jl 3,D 15 1829;Ja 1,Ap 2,26(supp)D 11 1830;F 9,14-15, 19,24-25 1831;Ja 14(supp)1835;O 6-D 30 1841
MHi 1821-Ap 1831;D 3,11,22 1832[34]Ap 9,My 2 1835;My 20 1837;Ja 9 1840
MSaE Ja 3 1822
MWA Ja-Ag,N 1821-Ap 16,My 26 1835-[40-My]Je 23-24,O 6 1841
MiU-C [1831-33;35-38]
NN F 11 1825;Ap 17,Je 1,9,N 4,18,23 1826;N 22,D 3 1827;Ja 7 1829;Ja 4 1831;O 22 1832;F 22,Ap 20 1833;N 25,27,D 3-4,6 1834-Ja 9,12-13,15-20,26,28-F 2,4-10,12-16,20,23 1835;Jl 12, Ag 28,O 14,N 24 1837;Ja 10,Ag 23,27-28 1838; Jl 16,S 6,19,25 1839;Ap 13,25 1840

PENNSYLVANIA (*Continued*)

PHILADELPHIA—*Continued*

*NATIONAL gazette. d 1820-41||?—*Continued*
NNHi Ja-Mr,O 16 1821-25;27-30;Jl 26 1831[Ap 29-S 22 1834]
NcD [1821-41]
NhD 1823-Ap 1 1824;My 24 1831-Ap 17 1832[Ag 20 1833-S 27 1834]
NjR [1821;24-25]-28[35;37;41]
P 1821-[24]-Ja 1 1842
PAtM [1831]
PBL Mr 8 1821;Mr 22,Jl 1825-[26-37]
PCarlHi D 20 1823[24]27;Ag 16,19,21 1828;Mr 24,Ap 7,28,My 3,Jl 12,17 1838[39]
PDoHi [1822-Jl 14 1827]
PNhE O 1 1825;F 16,Je 14 1826;D 20 1828;D 8 1829;F 19 1830
PP Jl 28 1825;27-29;D 30 1837[38-S 1839]40-41
PPA 1835-41
PPFfHi O 18 1825
PPL D 13 1822-Ja 4 1840
PPM 1821-39
PPi [D 15 1827-Mr 7 1829;Ap-D 1830;F 21 1833-Je 10 1836
PPiHi Ja 18 1821;Mr 10 1829-Ap 1 1830;31
PPiU-D 1822-24;Je 16 1825-My 3 1826;27-30
PSew Ja-O 1839
PToHi [1841]
PU 1821-34;Jl 16,S 6,25 1839
PWcHi Ag 20 1822;F 5,Je 30 1829[32]Ja 27 1835]
PWcT [1840-41]
ScCa 1823-41
TxU Jl 7 1826-27

NATIONAL palladium and freeman's journal. d Ja 8 1827-Ap 8 1828||
Follows Freeman's journal. . .
CSmH Jl 25 1827
Ct [1827]
DLC S 19,N 26 1827;Ja 14,16,18 1828

NATIONAL reviewer. w O 25 1826-
MWA O 25 1826

NATIONAL union. w Jl 14 1838-
DLC Jl 14 1838

NATIONAL union. w S 24 1864-
PPot S 24 1864

NATIONAL whig. w S 9 1839-
DLC S 9 1839

NATIVE American. d Ap 11 1844-Jl 26 1866||
DLC My 24,28 1844
MWA Ap 11-N 1844
NN My 8-18,28.Jl 9-20,O 9,21,N 19-20 1844; My 5 1845
NNHi Ap 15-N 9 1844
PBL Ag 20,S 6 1844
PHi Ap 23,Ag 12 1844
PPCHi [Je-Jl 1844]

NATIVE American sentinel. w Ag 2-N 29 1845||
PHHi complete

NATIVE eagle and American advocate. d D 1 1845-46||
Follows American advocate
CSmH O 7 1845
DLC Je 26-27,D 5 1845
MWA complete
NN N 8 1845;N 14,16,D 1 1846
PBL My 30,Jl 31,Ag 8 1845
PWcHi O 10 1846

NEAL'S Saturday gazette. *See* Saturday gazette

Philadelphia NEUE zeitung. *See* Philadelphia gazette (Abend ausgabe)

NEW ERA. w S 23 1865-Je 9 1866||
PHi complete

NEWS. w Jl 4 1829-
N Jl-D 1829
NNHi 1832-Ap 27 1833

Philadelphia daily NEWS. d Ja 1830-69||
Title varies: Daily news; Daily news and chronicle; etc.
DLC My 18 1846;Ag 14 1847-F 15,Je 8, 9(extra)10 1848[Mr 12 1849-50]53-Je 1868
IU Jl 1862-65
InNh Jl 29-Ag 9 1834
MWA Jl 7 1856;D 26 1864
NN Ap 24 1865
NjR [1851;53;57]
NjWdHi Ap 2 1851
OClWHi Mr 6 1850
PBL [1839]O 2-3 1848;N 30 1849;Jl 10 1850 [52]
PCHi My 22 1868
PHi Je 23 1865
PLaF [1848]
PLaHi [1847-48]
PNoHi Ap 11 1859;Mr 1,5 1865
PP O-D 3 1849
PPFfHi D 29 1849;Ag 24,S 19,28,O 4,10 1860; My 17 1861
PPL Mr 25,D 10 1851;Mr 15 1869
PPot My 17 1850 Ja 27 1860
PShH Ag 28 1848;Ag 27,S 14 1858
PSuHi Ap 3 1858
PWcHi [1848;50-52]

Evening NEWS. d 1879-1924||
S 20 1881 has extra ed on the death of President Garfield
CL S 20 1881
CtY D 3,24,27,29 1880;Ja 7 1881
DLC O 3 1885
MWA O 3 1885
NjCHi S 20,23-24 1881
OClWHi N 3 1880-F 14 1894
PCHi O 3 1885
PHi Ja 3 1910
PLaF My 20 1915
PP [My 1914-F 1915]
PPot [1884]Jl 25 1885;N 6 1888

Sunday NEWS. w 1884-90||
PPot O 17 1886

Philadelphia daily NEWS. d Mr 31 1925+
pub 1925+
PP Je 1927+

Philadelphia Saturday NEWS, and literary gazette. w Jl 2 1836-Ja 5? 1839||
United with Atkinson's Saturday evening post to form Atkinson's evening post and Philadelphia Saturday news, later Saturday evening post
CtY Jl 9,23-O 15,29,N,D 10 1836-Ja 21 1837
DLC Ja 7 1836;Mr 24 1838
MWA 1836-Je 4,O 7 1837;Je 16,Jl 7,28,O 27-N 3 1838
N F 25-Mr 4,N 25,D 23 1837
NN Ag 25 1838
NNHi [Ap 1838-Ja 1839]
NcU Je 3 1837;Je 14,D 15 1838
OClWHi Ap 22 1837
P D 31 1836-Ag 11 1838
PHi Ja 20 1838

Philadelphia NEWS-BUREAU. *See* Philadelphia financial journal

NORTH AMERICAN. d Mr 26 1839-My 17 1925||
1840-O 20 1845 as North American and daily advertiser; Jl 1847-Ap 15 1876 North American and United States gazette. Merged with Public ledger
CSmH Ap 26(supp)1847
CtY Jl 8,S 7,N 12 1839;D 29 1840;O 28 1862-Je 29 1867
DLC complete
ICHi Mr 12 1861;S 25-26,O 31 1865
IaDH Jl 1853-Jl 1859;60-Jl 1866;67-68
KHi S 20 1884;S 16 1887;Je 29 1913
MBAt Ap 15,18 1865
MSaE 1861-65
MWA My 25-26,N 14 1840;Ap 30(supp)O 7,N 28-D 2,5-8,13-14,16-17,22-23 1846[Ja-S 10 1847]Ja 12,My 10,25,29 1848;F 14 1851[F-S 1861;62]-Ap,S 1865-[67;My-D 1868]69;71-Jl 15 1872;F 24,Mr 13,Jl 4,N 29,D 27 1873;Ag 2-3 1875;D 2 1876;Mr 5 1878;F 7 1882;S 20 1884;Jl 2 1885;Je 10 1889
MiU Mr 16-D 1841[49]-[52]53[56;69;76-77]
MiU-C 1861;68]
MnHi Jl 4 1862;Ap 15,20 1865
MnU [1918-21]
N Ag 4 1842
NFre Mr 3 1847
NN 1855-64;66-67;S 15 1887
NNHi Je 28 1847;Ap 19-20 1865;My 15 1873;Ja 7 1879
NbHi 1839-87
NcD [1840;44-48;51-52;56;59-60;64;74;1914;16]
OHi Ap 10 1859;Je 30 1862
P My 23 1840-S 2 1842;47-55;O 26 1868;Ja-Je 1885;1900-25
P-M Ap 17,19 1865
PAg Je 1849-My 1851
PBL [1839]-[41;44-45]My 1846;Jl 13-14,16 1852
PCHi D 30 1861;Je 10-11 1864;S 20 1884;S 15 1887;S 11,19 1901
PDoHi S 8-17 1901;O 4-11 1908
PHi Mr 26 1839-79;85-1925
PLaF Je 11 1916;Ap 7 1917
PLaN [1847]48
PLhT Ag 9 1863;Ap 27 1864;My 17,24 1865;S 29 1867;My 19 1869
PP Mr 26 1839-Je 1845;46;Je 1847-1925
PPA Jl 1847-88
PPL O 2,14 1839[40-41]Ap 1 1842;Mr 1846-1925
PPM Jl 1847-Je 1853;54-Je 1856;57-Je 1860;61-Je,S 1903-Je,N 1904-Je,S 1905-06;Mr 1907-Ap 1908;O 1909-Ag,N 1913-O 1915;Mr-Je 1916; Mr-O 1917;18-25
PPeS O 2 1872;Ap 5 1897;S 14 1901;Ja 15-18, 20-21 1908;F 4 1924
PPi F 6 1877-Ap 1878
PPot Ap 12 1866;S 15 1887;N 7 1888;Jl 4 1890
PU 1853;55;F 1857-Mr,My 1858-N 1859;F-Ap,S-D 1860;F-Ap,Jl 1861-82
PWbW Jl 21 1841;Ja 28 1854;D 8,12,14,18 1860;Jl 30,O 25 1862
TNV [1843-44]
Tx Jl 10 1873;My 16,21 1874
TxU D 11 1855-Je 1856
WHi O 23 1849;S 15 1887;S 7 1901;N 14 1913-15
WaPS [1916]-Ja 6,8-11 1917

NORTH AMERICAN. tw Ap 11? 1839-
MWA Jl 25 1839;Je 18 1844;Ap 12 1861-Je 1865;My 31 1873-Je 1882

Weekly NORTH AMERICAN. w 1839-
MWA My 27 1842
P [1840]-[42]
PBL Ap 2-D 31 1839

Weekly NORTH AMERICAN. w Mr 3 1847-70||?
1847-52 as North American for town and country
DLC My 10 1848
MWA Mr 24-31,Ap 14 1847;Je 2 1852;F 11,D 2 1863;Ap 20 1864 Mr 1,Ap 5,Je 28 1865;Ja 17 1866;S 11 1867;Je 24,Ag 26 1868;F 24 1869
NjR F 13 1850
OClWHi N 9 1852;D 7 1853;62-Mr 1869
PBL My 11 1846
PDoHi Ap 5 1848;F 28 1849;My 31 1854
PLhT Ag 19 1863;Ap 27 1864;My 17-24 1865;My 19 1869
PPeS O 15 1862;Ag 3 1864

NORTH central bulletin. w D 1924-Je 3 1932||
1924-Ap 1932 as Girard avenue news
PP S 1929-32

NORTH PHILADELPHIA gazette. *See* Frankford gazette

NORTH PHILADELPHIA globe. w O 31 1929+
pub 1929+
PP N 1929+

NORTH PHILADELPHIA press. w 1925-Mr 24 1932||
1925-N 25 1931 as Central North Philadelphia news
PP Je 11 1931-32

NORTHEAST news. w My 30 1927+
pub 1927+
PP Ag 23 1935+

NORTHWEST news. w Jl 30 1935+
Jl-D 10 1935 as 52nd and Girard avenue news
pub 1935+

Philadelphia OBSERVER. w My 6 1825-Ap 18 1839||?
1825-Ap 14 1836 as Philadelphian
CtY N 26 1830-O 3 1833
DLC Jl 21 1826;D 13(extra)1832;F 6-13 1834
DeHi Ap 24 1834
MiU [1825-26]
N Ap 19 1838
NNHi Ja-S 1834
NjR [Ag 10 1827-My 8 1829]
OOxM [1835]-N 17 1836
P Jl 6 1827-38
P-M Mr 3 1836
PHi 1828-D 16 1831;S 21 1837;S 28,N 17-24 1838;Ap 18 1839
PPL Ja 13,Je 9,30,S 1-8,O 13,N 10-19,D 15 1826;27-O 1830;31[Je 1836-Ap 1838]
PPPHi Ap 21-Ag 10 1837;Ja 12 1839
WHi Jl 30,D 10 1835;F 11 1836

Philadelphia OBSERVER. w D 6 1863-Ja 10 1864||
PHi D 13 1863

OLNEY times. w Ja 4 1910+
1910-S 13 1929 as Suburban times and review
pub Ja 4 1910;S 20 1929+
PP F 1929+

ONCE-A-WEEK. *See* Our once-a-week visitor

L'OPINIONE. d Ja 6 1906+
In Italian
pub 1906+
PP Je 1927+

Daily ORB. d Ap? 1834-
DLC Jl 15 1834
InNh Ag 1834

OUR daily fair. d Je 8 1864-S 11 1865||
Complete file consists of 13 numbers Je 8-21 1864 and S 11 1865
CSmH complete
NNHi Je 8-9 1864
NjCHi Je 8-21 1864
NjP complete
PDoHi Je 8-21 1864
PWcHi complete
PWcT Je 15-16 1864

OUR once-a-week visitor. w Mr 24-O 27 1870||
Mr 24-31 1870 as Once-a-week. Followed by Manayunk sentinel
PHi complete

PALMETTO flag. Mr 30-Ap 6? 1861||
MWA Mr-Ap 6 1861
NBHi Mr 30 1861
OClWHi Ap 6 1861
PHi Ap 16 1861

PATRIOT and shield. (Frankford) w
-1826* as Patriot
DLC Mr 22,Je 29 1832
NNHi F 26-Jl 1826

PATRYOTA. w N 21 1889+
In Polish
pub 1912;22;24-28;30+
IU D 1917-O 17 1919
PP Je 1927+

PENNSYLVANIA enquirer. *See* Philadelphia inquirer

PENNSYLVANIA freeman. w Ag 3 1836-Je 29 1854||
1836-Mr 8 1838 as National enquirer
DLC D 31 1836[Ja-Ag 1837]My 5,17-24 1838;My 21,O 1,D 3 1840;Ag 1 1844;Ja 9-16,30-F 5,20, Mr-Ap 17,My 1,22,Je 12-19,Jl 3,24-Ag 7,S 4,O 9 1851;O 20 1853-Je 1854
ICU Je 1843
IaGG F 6 1840
MB My 24(supp)1838
MHi S 3 1846;Ja 7 1850;Ap 3 1851
MiU Ag 13,O 22 1846;Ag 16,S 16,O 7 1847;Ja 13,Je 8,Ag 10 1848;Ja 4,D 27 1849;Ja 1,15,O 30 1852
NIC 1836-41
NNHi [Mr 29 1838-39]-41
NSyU O 15-22,D 3 1840;Ap-Je 1842
OHi N 19-D 10 1836;O 19,D 9,14 1837
P 1847
PDoHi [1839-54]
PHi 1836-S 3 1840;46-53
PNoHi [1840]Mr 25 1847;Jl 17 1851
PP F 1844-54
PPL 1836-O 5 1839;S 10 1840-O 1842;44-53
PSF D 10,24 1836-[38]F 15 1854
PWcHi My 31 1838[39]Je 11,S 9,N 26 1840;Je, Ag 1842[44-45]-[53]
PWcT [1838]-[54]
WHi S 14 1837-S 6 1838;Ag 11 1842

PENNSYLVANIA gazette. d O 1 1827-Ap 12 1828||
United with Aurora and Franklin gazette to form Aurora and Pennsylvania gazette, later Aurora
MBAt Ja 7,F 4,15,Mr 14 1828
MWA Ja 7-8,Mr 31 1828
NN Ja-Ap 12 1828
P O 6 1827-Ap 8 1828
PHHi F 16-Ap 1828
PPL complete
PPoU complete
PWeT Mr 28,31-Ap 1 1828

Saturday PENNSYLVANIA gazette. w O 6 1827-29||
O-D 1 1827 as Pennsylvania gazette
CtY Mr 28 1829
DLC 1827-F 16 1828
MWA My 10-17,Jl 19,S 20-27,O 18 1828;My 16 1829
PHHi F 16-My 17 1828
PLewL Mr 4 1829

PENNSYLVANIA (*Continued*)

PHILADELPHIA—*Continued*

PENNSYLVANIA inquirer. *See* Philadelphia inquirer

PENNSYLVANIA evening post. 1775-1804 *See* Freeman's journal and Philadelphia mercantile advertiser

PENNSYLVANIA sentinel. d 1830-Jl 1837||
United with Commercial herald to form Commercial herald and Pennsylvania sentinel
PBL Jl 8,10 1837

PENNSYLVANIA statesman. d N 1851-Ja 12 1852||
MWA N 5 1851
P Mr 7 1851
PPL Ja 12 1852

PENNSYLVANIA township banner. w 1831-
MWA Je 23 1832;Je 1 1833
PNoHi S 15 1832
PWcHi Jl 14,S 1,O 20 1832

PENNSYLVANIA whig. sw Ag 13 1831-O 3 1832||
DLC My 23,O 27 1832
IU N 12 1831
NN D 31 1831
NNHi Ag 22 1832
NjHi Ap 28,My 9 1832
PHi 1831-Ag 8,O 3 1832
WHi [S 14 1831-Je 20 1832]

Morning PENNSYLVANIAN. d Jl 9 1832-Ap 2 1861||
Title varies: Pennsylvanian; Daily Pennsylvanian; Philadelphia daily Pennsylvanian
DLC D 11 1832;Ja 24,F 26,Mr 11,17,25,27-29,31 1833-[Ja-Je 1845]Je 1850;51;Jl 1852-Mr 1861
MHi S 29,O 4-6,10-11,22-23,D 8 1832
MWA Ja 19,Mr 15,Ap 20,My 9,Ag 28 1833;Ja-Je 6 1836;37;Ja-Je,D 9 1840;Jl 7-D 1841;Ap 4,My 21,23,26,Je 9[Jl-D]1845;My 21-23,Je 4, 27,Jl 1,4[Ag 24-D 24]1846;Jl 26,S 22,O 6 1847; Je 10,N 6,9 1848;Je 1,Jl 3,17 1849;Ag 19,22;S 5-6,N 21 1851;Mr 24,My 18,20-21,25-27,31-Je 3,8-9,Ag 17,N 2,D 1 1852;53[Ja-Je 1854]-[Ja-My 25]Jl 7 1855;Ja-Je 1856;Ja-Je,O 22 1858-Mr,Ap 22-My 7 1859;Ja-Je 1860
MiU [1847-48;53;56-57]
N O 25 1832;O 31 1833;Mr 19 1834
NN My 24 1851
NNHi Ja 6 1844;O 15 1847
NSchU [Ap 1833-Ap 19 1834]
NcD [1839;47-48;50;54-55;57-Je 1859]
NjHi Je 16 1837
NjR My 9-10 1834
OClWHi Ap 1 1856;Jl-D 1860
OHi O 5 1860
P 1833-Jl 1858
P-M My 18 1852
PAtM D 6-8,13 1851
PCHi [1839]-[41-45]-[47-54]Jl 25 1855
PDoHi Je 28 1833;Je 25 1834
PE 1843
PHi 1833-[61]
PJsK O 22 1856
PNeBr 1831
PP O 10 1832;D 7 1833;40-[42]
PPFfHi Je 24,Jl 1,3,14 1845
PPL 1832-S 1834;35-38;Mr 25 1839-N 1845;46-53;Je 13 1854-N 1857;58-Je 1859
PPi N 13 1846-Mr 5 1853
PPot [1832]-[34]-[38-40]-55;58[59]Jl 3 1860
PToHi [1846-47;49]Jl-D 14 1857;F 12-D 6 1858; My 14 1859-Je 1 1860
PU 1846-61
PW Mr 6-9 1844;Mr 7,9-12 1846
PWeT Ap 3-6 1838;Mr 30-Ap 2 1840
TNV 1842[46]

PENNSYLVANIAN; for the country. tw Jl 9 1832-
DLC [Mr-Ap,D 1833-F,Ag 1834]
IU N 4,21 1837
MWA O 27 1836;Jl 16 1840
N Jl 24-25 1833
NcD Jl 13-20,S 7,O 3 1839

PENNSYLVANIAN. w 1832-54 *See* Dollar weekly Pennsylvanian

PENNSYLVANISCHE staats-gazette. w,sw Mr 28 1896-S 24 1917||
sw N 10 1909-Jl 6 1915
pub 1896-Mr 1898;Jl 1907-17
—**d ed** *See* Gazette-democrat

PEOPLE and anti-monopolist. *See* Greenback herald

PEOPLE'S advocate. sw Jl 9? 1823-S 1838||?
Followed by Morning star and people's advocate
MWA Ag 30 1823
PBL Ag 3,S 4 1838
PDoHi Jl 30,Ag 2,N 12 1823
PE S 8 1838

PEOPLE'S omnibus. w O 23 1852-
WHi O 23 1852

PHILADELPHIAN. 1825-36 *See* Philadelphia observer

PHILADELPHIER demokrat. *See* Philadelphia demokrat

PHILADELPHISCHE correspondent. *See* Philadelphiaer telegraph und Deutsche wochenblatt

PIONEER. *See* American pioneer and fireman's chronicle

Morning POST. d
CtY Ap 18 1836
NN Ja 17 1845
PBL Je 7 1845

Philadelphia morning POST. Jl 4 1863||
IF complete
MBAt complete
MiG complete
P-M complete
PHHi complete
PPot complete

Philadelphia POST. d O 7 1867-78||?
1867-Ja 8 1871 as Morning post
DLC O-D 13 1867;Je 9-10 1869
MWA 1867-D 15 1868;Je 16,Jl-D 1869;Jl-D 1871
NNHi N 9(supp)1867;Ja 30 1871
NcU [1877-Je 1878]
PCHi Ap 20 1869
PPL O 8 1867-O 15 1872
PPM D 14 1867-Je 1871
PPiHi O 26 1869

POST. w My 5 1930-Jl 18 1931||
PP My 5,O 22 1930-31

Saturday evening POST. *See* Saturday evening post

***POULSON'S American daily advertiser.** d O 1 1800-D 28 1839||
Follows Claypoole's American daily advertiser (not in this list). Merged with North American
CSmH Jl 2 1829
Ct [1827]
CtY F 8 1831
DLC 1821-39
MBAt Ap 14 1824;My 2 1827;Ag 6 1828;S 7,22 1829
MHi Ja 10,12 1824;F 27,My 11,14,O 29 1825;Ja 31,F 22 1826
MSaE Je 11 1823
MWA 1821-23;O 29 1824;O 29 1825;F 23 1830; Ap 25,Jl-D 1832;Ja 2 1836;Ja 15 1839
MiU 1821-32
MiU-C [1821-22]
N Ja 26 1825;D 29 1826;31-34
NN Ja 17,31,F 19,Mr 8,30,Ap 4,My 22,O 11 1821;S 6,N 19,D 4,30 1822;S 9,N 5-6 1823;S 23 1824;Jl 23 1825;F 27,Mr 25,Ap 2,4,8,10,My 19,Jl 31,D 17,19 1829;Ag 13,18,S 8 1830;Ja 23,F 28,Ap 8,24,28,My 4,S 2-3,7,14,21 1835;F 15-16, Jl 2 1836;Ag 10 1837
NNHi D 8 1825;Mr 3 1826[Ja 29-Jl 5 1827]Ja 9 1832;N 23 1833;My 1 1834;Ap 14,S 4 1835
NcD [1821-22;24;26-27;29-33]
NjCHi Jl 3 1821;F 23 1822
NjFHi O 26 1822
NjHi Ja 11,F 4,Ap 19 1821;Jl 18,Ag 8,S 12,O 24,N 7 1822;Ja 8,F 12,Ag 19,O 24 1824;S 27 1827;Mr 22,My 3 1832
NjR [1821;23;36]
OCHi Ja 19 1836;N 15 1838
OClWHi F 15 1830
OOxM Jl 14,21,Ag 4,11,25,S 4 1828;F 2,Mr 2,9,Ap 20.27,My 18,Je 8,15,Jl 13,Ag 10 1829[O 1831-Jl 1834]
P 1821-22;O 12 1832;D 11 1834
P-M O 2 1832
PBL My 9 1837
PDoHi [1821-28]
PEHi My 30 1823
PHi 1821-39
PNhE Ja 16 1822
PP 1821-Jl 18 1824;25-My 4 1828;D 14 1833;S 13 1838;Je 28,Jl 1 1839
PPA 1830-39
PPL 1821-23;Ja-S 1825;O-N 1827;D 1-13 1830; Ja 2-16 1834;F-D 1835;F-My 8 1836;My-D 1837
PPM 1821-29
PPiU-D [1831]
PPot Ag 19 1822
PU 1821-29
PWcHi Je 1,29,Jl 30 1822;Ja 18 1833

PRAVDA. sw Mr 11 1902+
In Russian
pub 1902+
CSt-H 1930;32-33
IU D 4 1917-N 10 1922;23+
PP N 1927+

Sunday PRESS. 1853 *See* Blanche's Sunday press

PRESS. d Ag 1 1857-O 1 1920||
1880-Ja 31 1885 as Philadelphia press. United with Public ledger to form Public ledger and Philadelphia press, later Public ledger
A Ja-Je 1868;72-77;84-Je 1886;S-O 1892;O-D 1918
C F 5 1887-89;Jl-D 1890
CSmH F 7 1861;Ja 21 1867
Ct My 18 1866
CtY Mr 10 1863-65;73
DCHi Jl 5 1876
DLC complete
DeWI Ap 15-My 8 1865;F 21 1886
IC Ja-Jl 14 1873;My 1 1889
ICHi N 14,1865;Jl 4 1876
ICM Jl 31 1883;Ap 1 1885;Je 8 1886;N 6 1887; My 29 1888;Jl 12 1891
IF D 15 1881
IU Jl 2 1860-Ag,O 23 1861-My,Je 27-S 4,23-O 6 1862;Ja-Mr 18 1863;My 8 1866
IaDH 1889-Je 1890;O 1891-O 1907
IaHi [1861]-Ag 1864
InI Ja 27-Je,Jl 4-S,O 2-D 1876
KHi Ja 5 1878-Je 1880
MB Ag 12,17,O 19-21 1857;My 24,Je 21,26 1858; F 7 1863
MBAt Ap 18-19,24 1865;Ap 11-24 1899
MWA Ag-D 1857;F 1858-Ja,Mr-N,D 20 1861; Ja-Je,O 6,14-15,21,N 3 1862[Ja 5-Ap]Je 1863-64;F 4,Ag 17 1866;Mr 27,Je 20 1867;F 24,My 29 1868;My 23 1871;Mr 5,11,Ap 11,My 9 1873; Jl 17 1875;Ja-[Jl-N]1876;D 16-23 1879;82-Je 1895;98
MiG Jl 5 1876
MiU 1858-[66]-[70]-[75]-[77]-79;81[1900]-05
MiU-C [1872;76;82-83]
MnHi Mr 30-N 14 1861[Je 13 1862-Ap 10 1865] Ag 29,S 12 1870
NN Ag 1857-Jl 1858;59-Je 1863;Ap 21-24 1865; N 25 1874;My 10-11,Je 8,S 23,N 9-10 1876
NNC N 1881-Ag 1888;Ja-F,S 1889-O,D 1890-Mr 1912;13-Jl 1914
NNHi Je 25,N 30 1860;Jl 5,D 30 1861[Mr 1862-F,Ap 1863-Ja,Mr 1864-77]Ja 2-3,O 10,D 3 1878;Ap 5,D 17 1879;Jl 4 1876
NbHi F 26,Ap 13-16,18-23,25-26 1859;My 16,O 29 1861;O 21 1863;D 6 1865;Ag 23 1867;D 14 1869;Ap 9 1873;Ja 27 1877
NcD [Ag 1857-Jl 1858]59-Je 27[Ag-D]1860;61; Ja 3 1862;Ja-Je 1863;Ja-Jl 1864[65-Jl 1876]
NcU Mr 7 1860;My 11,14,Je 18,Jl 2,16,23,Ag 7,27,S 24 1864;Mr 27 1879
NhD Je 26 1861
NjR [1858;63;66]Jl 5(supp)1876[81;1901]
NjWdHi My 7 1859[65]S 1881;S 4-5 1885;Jl 30 1911;F 25 1917
NjWdN O 12 1866
OClWHi D 24 1859;Ja 2,24,Ap 1,19,24,My 1,3, 8[Ag-D]1861-[Ja-Je 1863]64[Ja-O 1865]Ja-Je 1866;Jl-D 1867;Je 7 1872;N 3 1880;Ap 8 1890; Ja 18 1892
OHi Ja 26 1860;87-1920
OOxM My 15 1872;Je 16-19 1875;Jl 5-6 1876
P complete
PBf Je 12 1867;Mr 10 1879[81]
PBloHi My 22 1880[85]Je 2-3 1886[87-89;1916]
PCHi Jl 10 1861;Je 7 1864;S 25 1881;O 22,25-26 1882;Ap 27 1887;Mr 15 1888;Mr 4-5 1897;S 16,19 1901
PDoHi N 19 1857[62-89]S 14 1901[08]
PEHi Ag 28 1869
PEr 1899-1920
PHHi Ja 1 1874;Ap 7,24 1880;F 3 1897;F 23 1909;Ja 1 1912
PHi 1857-69;My 13 1876-Je 16 1877;82-1916
PHoHi My 24 1865
PLaF [1857]-73
PLaL Ag 13 1867;F 7,Je 17 1876;77;My 8-9,Je 18 1878;Ap 14,D 30 1888;Ja 15 1893
PLhT Ag 13 1861;My 17 1880
PMcC Je 18,22 1877
PMe Ja 7-Je 26 1861;O 19 1863;Ag 4 1864
PNhF Ag 1,S 9 1886;My 9 1887;Ag 16 1895;N 7 1897
PNoHi 1858-[66]D 14 1868;Ja 15,Ap 2 1869;Jl 4 1876
PP 1857-Mr 21 1868;69-Je 14 1905
PPFfHi Ap 12 1859;My 16,Je 20 1863
PPL Ap 1863-1912
PPM 1857-O 1904;15-20
PPeS F 2,Mr 21 1860;S 2 1861-Ag,O 4 1861;F 12,Mr 12 1863;S 12,D 8 1866;Je 23,O 18 1884 [89]Mr 15 1890;D 4 1897
PPi 1858-Ja 1877;My 1878-1920
PPoU 1876
PPot Ap 6 1863;Jl 5 1871;Ja 1 1873;Je 7-10 1880[84-88]F 15 1891
PRHi [1859]
PSHi S 8 1864-69[89]90
PSuHi S 8 1864-D 14 1869[89]90
PToHi [1858;61-62]
PU Jl-D 1861;O 16 1865-Je 1867;Ja-Je 1868; 69-Je 1870;74-82
PWaHi [1857-58]Ja 28 1893
PWcHi N 13 1857;Ja 9,Ag 25,S 30,D 8 1858;Ja 28,Mr 12 1859;Ap 25 1861;N 21 1863;S 19 1864[65-66]F 24,My 13 1867;O 2 1868;My 16,S 22 1871;F 11,N 3 1873;Jl 15,17 1875[76]Ja 1 1877;Je 20 1878;O 22 1882;Jl 24 1885;S 6,17,21 1886;Mr 14 1888;Ap 17 1896;O 27 1899
TKL Jl 5 1876
TU Jl 4 1876
Tx O 6 1868;Ja 1-2,12-14,Mr 4 1869;D 8 1870; Mr 4 1871;F 7-8,N 11,15 1872
TxU 1864-Je 1865
VU Ap 20 1878;Ag 13 1884;D 7 1889;Je 25 1899
WHi 1857-Mr 21 1863;N 18 1863;O 10 1864;Mr 4 1868;Ag 18 1869;Jl-D 1871;Jl 3-5,11,S 28-29 1876;S 14 1901

Weekly PRESS. w Ag 15 1857-1905?
1857-N 9 1861 as Weekly press; N 16 1861-N 4 1865 Forney's war press; N 11 1865-76? Forney's weekly press
CMa Ja 23 1858-Je 25 1859
CtY Jl 30 1864-65;72
DLC Mr 20 1858;F 18,Ap 14-28,Ag 18 1860;Jl 19 1862
ICHi D 19 1857-D 11 1858;My 1859-Je 1863
IHi Ap 22 1865
IU S 19,D 19-26 1857;Mr 13,Ap 10-Je 19 1858
KHi Ag 10-O 1857;S 10 1859;Jl 1-8 1880;Ag 2,4 1885
MWA Ap 11-18 1863;Ap 29,N 25 1865;Ag 6 1870;Ap 11 1888
MiU 1860-63
N Je 11 1859;Jl 8 1876
NN Ap 22 1865
NNHi Ap 29-My 13 1865;Jl 7,S 8-15 1866;O 10-17,N 7 1868;Mr 13 1869;Ap 30 1870;Ap 19 1873;Ja 1 1876
NbHi Je 1 1860;Mr 14 1868
OClWHi O 26 1857;Ja 8,29,F 12,Mr 5-19 1859; Jl 8 1876
P 1874-77;Mr 11 1888-D 18 1889
PBf Mr 18 1865;Mr 21 1866
PCHi My 13 1876
PJsK Ag 15 1857
PLhT Jl 5 1862;S 30 1876
PPeS O 19-26 1867;N 21 1868;Ja 9,23 1869;Jl 9 1870;O 12,26 1872;O 19 1878
PPiHi N 21 1857;Ag 30 1862
PToHi 1860-Ag 3 1861
PWcT D 1861-N 8 1862
TJT Mr 28 1874
TxU O 22 1860-N 4 1865
WHi Ja 23 1858-Ja 15 1859
—**California edition.** sm O 20 1857-
CSmH N 5 1857-Ja 20 1859

Philadelphia PRICE current. . . 1827-35 *See* Commercial list and maritime register

Philadelphia PRICE current. . . 1833 *See* Moore's price current . . .

PUBLIC ledger. d Mr 25 1836-Ap 14 1934||
Title varies: Public ledger and daily transcript; Public ledger and Philadelphia press; Public ledger and North American. Merged with Philadelphia inquirer
pub complete
CSmH Jl 2 1846
CU Mr 25 1836

PENNSYLVANIA (*Continued*)

PHILADELPHIA—*Continued*

PUBLIC ledger. d 1836-1934||—*Continued*
CoHi Mr 25 1836
CtHT Mr 25 1836
CtY Mr 25 1836;Ag 8,13,S 6 1839;N 21 1843;Ap 24 1893;Ap 27 1894
DLC 1836-Mr 27,S 28 1838-Mr 28 1839;My 26,O 31,D 7 1840;S 30 1841-S 24 1850;Ja 17 1854-56;Je 27 1857;59-79;Jl 1880-Je,O 1891-92;94-Je 1896;98-1934
DeHi Je 30 1860
DeWI Mr 25 1836;My 2,N 20 1840;Ap 15-My 5 1865;Ag 29 1873
FSaHi Mr 25 1836;Ap 24 1865
GAtCo Ja 24 1839
IC Ap 30-My 1 1889
ICHi Mr 25 1836;S 21,O 2 1865
ICM S 23 1876;F 20 1880;S 5(supp)1885;F 5 1894
ICN Mr 9-Ap 9,11-D 4,6-20,22,25,27 1863-Ja 1, Jl 4,6-D 26,28-31 1864;D 11 1917-18;Ja 14 1919-Ja 4 1920
ICU Mr 25(facsimile)1836;S 24 1864-Mr 24 1865;Mr 27-S 25 1866;Mr 26 1867-Mr 24 1871; Mr 25-S 22 1874;N 3 1880;Jl 4-8,S 20,27 1881; F 12 1923
IEN 1914-O,D 1918-Ja,Ap-O,D 1919-F,Ap-Jl, S-O 1920;Ja-F,N-D 1921;Mr,My-Jl 1922;My 1-18,20-Ag 11,13-30,D 1923;Mr-Ap,S,N 1924-Ja,Ap 1925-Ja 1928;Ap 1934
IHi Ap 15 1865
IP 1861-65;O 1872-76;95-Ap 1902;S 29 1910
IU N 6 1909-Ja 1,28-F 1,Mr 2-Ap 26 1910
IaDH S 1839-Ja 1840
InNcHi S 11 1839
KHi Mr 25 1836
KyU Mr 25 1836
LSfD Ag 4 1838
M [F 22 1931-Ja 8 1934]
MB D 3 1861-62
MBr 1914-28
MHi Mr 31 1858;N 22 1860
MWA [1836-Jl 1 1837]38;41-Ap 1899;1900-02;F 1903-Ap,S 1904-05;S 1908-My,Ag 1913-My 16, Jl,S 1919-Mr,Je 1921-Ap 14 1934
MWo Ag 10 1839
MdBJ O 6 1843
MdHi 1836-S,D 14 1840-44;S 1845-S 1848;Mr 1849-S 1850;S 26 1851-Mr 1852;S 1854-Mr 1855; Mr 1856-Mr,S 26 1859-S 1864
MeBa Mr 25 1836
MiG Mr 25 1836
MiU [1862-63]-[65-66]-[68]69;71-79
MiU-C [1836-37;80;98]
MnHi Mr 25 1836(reprint)N 18 1853;Mr 25 1886
MnU Mr 23 1836(facsimile)F 12,14-15,17 1862; Jl 5 1863;Ja 27,My 9,Jl 31,S 20 1864;Ap 7 1865
MoS Mr 25 1836;Jl 18-D 1855
NBHi Mr 25 1836
NN 1836-40;Mr 29 1841-D 1844]-Je,Jl 31-[O-D]1845-[48]-57;Ja-Mr 1865;My 10,S 21 1876; D 5 1898;My 18 1925
NNHi Mr 25 1836;My 10,Ag 16 1838;N 14 1849; Ap 16 1850;Ap 14,My 2,Jl 18 1856;Mr 13,S 21,28,O 6,14 1857;Ag 6,S 2 1858;O 19-21;D 3,17 1859;F 3,Mr 27 1860;F 19,22-23,25,Ap 20,My 4,Je 12 1861;Je 24,27,29,Jl 1-3,6-9 1863;Ap 15 1865;My 7 1873;Je 30 1876 extras:F 29 1844;Jl 6,7 1863
NPrH Mr 25 1836
NSchU O 15 1841;Jl 15-16 1842
NcD [1838;41-49;51-52;57-59;61-63;65;68;71-77; 94-95]
NjCHi Mr 25 1836,O 15 1839;Jl 18 1848;Mr 25-S 22 1853;Ja 19,21 1857;S 2 1858;Jl 6 1863;Jl 22 1864;Ag 3,30,S 5,10,14,20,23 1870;Ja 31,F 2,Mr 2,4,Jl 22 1871;S 11 1901
NjHi Mr 25 1833
NjN Mr 25 1836
NjR [1836;43;51-53;61;63;69;85;97-1901]
NjWdHi Mr 25 1836;Ja 4 1838;S 25 1846;My 7-Jl 6 1863;Ap 17 1865;Jl 30 1874[98]Jl 4 1913; D 15 1927
NjWdN D 17 1863
OCl Mr 25 1836
OClWHi Mr 25 1836;D 3 1850;Ap 19,Ag 8-S 4,6-7,9,11,18,21 1861;Je 23,Jl 6 1863;Ja 29,Ap 22-23 1864;Ja 19 1865;Jl 30 1893
OHi Mr 25 1836;Ap 18-21 1865;1921-23;N 1924-O 1925;Ja-Ap,N-D 1926;Mr 4-Je 1927;N-D 1928
P My 18 1844-S 1861;62-76;Jl 1889-1934
PAg [1851]
PArL Mr 25 1836;Jl 6 1863;F 4 1924;Ap 5 1935
PAtM Mr 25 1836
PBL Mr 25 1836;My 18 1837[38]My 10,15 1839 [42-43;45-46]-[58]
PCC Mr 25 1836;Mr 25 1915;D 7 1924;Mr 1 1925
PCHi Mr 25 1836;Ag 21 1853;O 1 1878;Mr 13,D 15 1888;Ap 22 1893;F 15 1899;F 22 1900;S 14, 20 1901;Ag 11-12 1902;O 10-12,18 1908;Ap 25,N 6 1909;My 10 1910;N 10,D 1,15 1912;Jl 4 1913; Ap 14-15 1934
PCarlHi Mr 25 1836;Jl 13 1913
PChalK Ag 21,S 16 1848
PDoHi Mr 25 1836[55-1908;18]
PEHi Mr 25 1836
PEL [1842-43]76
PHaC Mr 25 1836
PEr [1920]-31
PHi 1836-Jl,S-N 1838;39-55;57;60-93;95-97;99-1917;25-34
PLaF O 27 1912;Jl 4 1913[14;16-20;24-25;33-34]
PLaHi [1837]-39[41]-30;Ja 11 1909
PLaN [1848-49]
PLewL Ap 30 1844
PMcT [1875]
PMe Mr 25 1836
PNoHi Mr 25 1836[37-38]F 18,Mr 23,S 3,O 12 1839;Mr 16,N 3 1840[41]Ja 27,Jl 6 1863;D 7, 9,16,31 1868[69]Ag 7 1879
PP 1836-S 23 1853;54-S 22 1855;Ja-S 19 1856; Mr 24 1857-S 18 1858;Mr 25 1859-S 20 1862;Mr 1863-Je,S 24 1891-1934
PPA Mr 25 1836;87-1931
PPFfHi Mr 25 1836;Jl 9 1850;My 3 1853;N 1 1860;Jl 24 1885
PPL 1836-Ap 1932
PPM F 23 1841-D 9 1843;44-Je 1868;70;91-S 1894;95-S 1897;98-N 1905;Mr 25 1906-Ja,My 25-Jl 25 1907;Ja-Jl 1908;10-19;F 1920-Je,S 1925-34
PPeS Mr 25 1836;O 25 1862;D 6 1865;Mr 28 1870;N 8 1873;N 24 1890;Ag 25,O 12 1919[20] F 20,Mr 5 1921;N 18 1924;Ag 12 1928
PPi S 1920-Ag 1928
PPiHi [Mr 1897-My 1916]
PPct Mr 25 1836;Jl 26,Ag 28 1858;Jl 10 1860;N 7 1888;My 28 1895
PPotW Mr 25 1836
PU Mr 1845-Mr 1846;Ap 1847-S 22 1851;Jl 1852-64;Mr 25 1865-S 1875;Mr 1876-Mr,S 1877-Mr 1879;98-1900;S 1902-34
PWaHi Mr 25 1836
PWcHi Mr 25 1836;My 6 1837[43]Ap 18 1846;O 22 1847;Ap 10,Jl 8 1848;Ja 9 1849;My 21,Ag 7,22,D 20 1850;Mr 13,O 18 1851;Je 21,Jl 2 1852; O 12 1854;Jl 21 1856;Jl 15 1863;My 16 1867;96-97;99;Je 7 1902;D 27 1903[04]F 18 1906;O 8 1908[11]14-18
PWcT [1867]S 11 1900;S 14,18-19 1901[18]
PYHi Ap 3 1865
TKL Mr 25 1836
TxU [O 28 1837-Jl 9 1838]39-Mr 25 1848;S 24 1849-My 23 1850
VLyR Mr 25 1836
VRC D 16 1861;My 1 1862
VU S 21 1867;Jl 24(supp)1885;Ap 14 1934
WHi Mr 25 1836(reprint)N 20 1847;Je 4,Jl 12, Ag 14-15,31 1849;S 11,24 1850;Jl 22-23,30-31, Ag 20-21,25,S 12,15-18,20,O 18-23 1851;Mr 29 1852;N 5 1856;63;Ag 17,20 1869;D 10 1872-Ag 7 1873;N 1900-My 18 1901;O 1902-My,S 21 1903-Ap,O 1904-My,O 1905-Je 11,S 21 1906-Ap 20,S 21 1907-My 16,S 22 1908-F,My-Je 21 1909;15-23

Evening PUBLIC ledger. d S 14 1914+
pub 1914+
DLC 1923+
NNC 1914-19
NjWdHi Je 11 1927
PArL [1917;25;28-29;32-34]
PP 1914+
PPeS N 7 1928
WaPS D 3-9 1916[Ja 1918]D 5 1930

PUBLIC record. *See* Philadelphia record

***Philadelphia PUBLIC sale report.** w My 11 1812-Ap 28 1827||
1812-S 10 1825 as Grotjan's Philadelphia public sale report
DLC My-O 1 1825
MHi [1822-25]
MWA Mr 11,25 1826
PHi S 8 1823;My 1825-27
PPL Ja 28 1826-Ap 21 1827

QUAKER CITY. w D 30 1848-50||
OClWHi F 9,Mr 16 1850
PHi 1848-49

QUAKER CITY brevity. *See* Tabloid

RAG BABY. w Ag 16-N 13 1879||?
Campaign paper
MWA Ag 16 1879
WHi Ag 16 1879

Philadelphia RECORD. d My 14 1870+
1870-Ap 30 1877 as Public record; My 1 1877-O 11 1879 Record
pub 1870+
CSt-H [1914]-[18]
CoU 1901
DA 1923+
DLC 1872-86;S 21 1891+
IC Ap 30-My 1 1889
ICM My 19 1893
MWA My 24 1873;Je 1 1877(facsimile)My 15 1886;Mr 6 1889
MiU 1899-[1901]
NNHi Mr 25 1893
NcD F 13-15,D 30 1895;Ja 2,Mr 30,Ap 4,17 1896;Ja 14-17,20,Ap 21 1902
NjCHi Je 1-17 1889;S 6,11,13-14,16-18,20-21,23-25 1901
NjHi Jl-Ag 1914;15-16
NjWdHi Je 1 1877;Mr 16 1917[20]F 20 1921
P 1885+
PArL Ap 15 1904
PCHi [1881-82;1901]Ja 16 1910
PDoHi [D 31 1881-1910]
PHHi Mr 26 1885;F 3 1897
PHi 1870-N 13 1873
PLaF [1933]+
PNoHi Je 1 1877
PP 1870-My 13 1871;N 1877+
PPCHi Ag 12 1888;Ag 9 1895;N 4 1896
PPR 1870+
PPeS My 2-Je 27 1920;N 6-8,My 14 1932
PUn My 2-Je 27 1920
PWcHi Ja 7 1906;My 16,Je 13 1909;Ja 8 1911
WHi Ap 1875-Je 17 1876

Philadelphia daily REGISTER. d S 5 1847-S 4 1854||
Title varies: Daily register; Philadelphia evening register
DLC F 3-Ap 23 1853;F-My 1854
MWA Ja 26 1854
NNHi 1853
PCHi Ag 11 1854
PHi S-N 1 1851

RELPH'S Philadelphia gazette and daily advertiser. *See* Philadelphia gazette and daily advertiser

Daily REPUBLIC. d
DLC O 10,N 7,9,16,23,D 9,22 1848
NNHi O 31 1848
PBL [1848-49]
PLaHi [1848]
PWcHi [1848]

Sunday REPUBLIC. w 1867-84||?
MWA Je 27 1869;F 6,Je 18,Ag 6 1876
P O 22 1876-O 10 1880

SALMAGUNDI: and news of the day. bm Ja 2-D 23 1836||
Followed by American weekly messenger, later Alexander's express messenger
MWA Jl 7-O 5,N 9-23,D 16,28 1836
NjR Ja 2 1836
PPL Ag 3 1836

SATURDAY evening post. w Ag 4 1821+
1831-Ja 5 1839 Atkinson's Saturday evening post (Ja 5-S 21 1833 Atkinson's Saturday evening post and bulletin); Ja 12-N 2 1839 Atkinson's evening post and Philadelphia Saturday news; O 8 1842-S 23 1843 United States Saturday post and chronicle; S 30 1843-Ag 9 1845 United States Saturday post
After My 13 1871 the notices of marriages and deaths were omitted, seeming to indicate that the editors no longer considered this a local newspaper
Holdings after 1871 are not included in this list. For holdings after this date *See* Union List of Serials
Ct Jl 2 1836
CtSp O 22 1842;My 20,S 23 1843
CtY S 27 1823;Mr 20 1824;Je 25,Ag 13,O 22,D 31 1825
DLC Ag 18 1821-25;Jl 8 1826-Mr 29 1827;28-33;35-36;39-40;O 14 1848-63;Je 24-Ag 26 1865; Ja 6-Ag 4 1866;Ap-Jl 18 1868;Ag 8 1869-71
DeHi F 21 1824;27[28-29;32-35]Jl 9 1836
DeU N 28 1857
DeWI O 18 1823;Je 14 1828
GAtCo F 23 1839
ICU Jl 16 1825
IHi [S 16 1837-Je 1840]N 13 1852
IU My 7,Ag 20 1836;S 9 1843
MB 1827-28;D 1-8 1832;Ja 7 O 8,29,D 24-31 1842;Je 24,Ag 12,O 7 1843;Mr 9 1850;Mr 26 1853;Mr 3 1855;S 26 1857;My 21,Ag 27 1859; 60
MDeHi Jl 1,Ag 19 1848
MSaE 1829-37
MWA Ag 1822-37;D 8 1838;39[40]-43;O 12-26, D 7,21 1844-[45-46]O 2,D 18-25 1847[48]Mr 10 1849;S 7,O 19,D 28 1850-[52]Ap 16 1853-My 5, Jl 28 1855;56-60;Ja 26[Je-D 21 1861;Ja 11-My 24 1862]Ap 4-11 1863;Ja 16 1864;Ap 4 1868;My 28 1870;O 21 1871
MiG Ja 28 1854
MnHi O 11 1834
MoS [1824-25;28-29]
MoSU 1830
MsHi Jl 16 1836-Jl 1839;Ag 31 1850
N My 11 1822-24;O 19 1833[Ap 26 1834-D 12 1835]O 6,N 3 1855[60-61]
NN My 12 1832;Jl 3 1847
NNHi D 25 1824;F 27 1827-N 1828;D 29 1832 [Ja-S 1839]Ja-Jl,S-D 1855
NbHi Je 17-24 1848;Ja 24,F 7,21,Mr 14-Ap 4,Je 13,O 3,17-24 1857;Jl 13 1861
NcD 1824-26;Ja 5,Ap 20 1833;S 27,D 20 1834;Je 27 1835;35[37-60;69-71]
NcU My 2 1835;Ag 14 1847
NjCHi Ja 31 1857
NjFHi Je 27 1835
NjHi Je 2 1827;N 15 1828;Ja 10,N 21 1829;Ja 9 1830
OClWHi Jl 16 1825;Ag 11 1827-Ag 1 1829;O 23, N 20 1830;My 26 1832;Mr 30 1839;Ja 16 1842; Ap 18 1846;S 18,O 16 1847;Ja 1,My 6,Jl 8,N 4 1848;Ap 7,Je 30 1849;F 9,Mr 16-23,Jl 27 1850[51;53]Ja 14,O 28,N 18 1854[55;58-61]Ja 11,Mr 22,Jl 12 1862[63]
OHi N 23 1844
OOxM O 1 1825
P-M S 14 1844;S 16 1854
PAg F 1823-30
PBL [1833-34]Ap 30,Ag 20 1836;D 15 1838[39-40]D 18 1841;F 5 1848
PCHi Mr 21 1835;N 5 1870
PDoHi Mr 26 1842
PE 1831-32
PFgR My 25 1867;My 22 1869
PHHi [1830]-[34;48]
PHi 1822-37
PJsK O 29 1859
PLaHi D 11 1824;25[26;33-34]Mr 16 1839
PLaN [1827]-[30]
PLewL 1832[33]O 25 1834
PLhT Ap 16 1842
PMe S 14 1850;Ja 19 1856
PNoHi My 17 1851;Jl 16 1853
PPCHi F 28 1835
PPFfHi [1821]-24
PPL [1823-24]-[27]31-32;Jl 20 1850 Ag 30,D 31 1851;F 21,Ag 7,O 23,N 27 1852[53-63]69[78]-[81]
PPM [1821]-24;Ja 1 1832[39]
PPeS Ag 1 1857
PPi O 14 1826-32
PPiHi Je 23 D 8 1832;Jl 12 1834;O 23 1858
PPitE Ag 28 1847
PSuHi Ag 18 1863
PToHi Jl 2 1842
PWCl [1854]
PWcHi N 28 1829;Ap 17-24 1830;S 10,D 1831 [32]Ja 5 1833[60-61]
PWcT Mr 10 1850;Ja 19 1856
RW D 24 1842;Je 22 1844
TKL Mr 16 1833
VU Ap 9 1842;S 21 1844

SCHWABISCHER merkur. w S 5 1885-Jl 14 1888||
1885-Mr 10 1888 as Philadelphia schwabische merkur
In German
PPG complete

SCOTT'S weekly paper. w Ag 15 1846-55||
DeU D 25 1852;Mr 26 1853
NjR F 17 1849
OHi S 6,D 6 1851;Ja 3 1852
PPL Ja 8 1853

SENTINEL. *See* Manayunk sentinel

SONNTAGS ausgabe des tageblatts. *See* Philadelphia sonntagsblatt

PENNSYLVANIA (*Continued*)

PHILADELPHIA—*Continued*

Philadelphia SONNTAGSBLATT. w S 7 1879+
1879 as Sonntags-zeitung des tageblatts; 1880-1921 Philadelphia sonntagsblatt; 1922-Jl 20 1930 Sonntags ausgabe des tageblatts
PPG 1890-Jl 1900;01-08;My 1909-S 1911;12-16; Jl 1917-24;Ap 1925-Mr,Jl 1926-S 1928;Jl-S 1929
—d ed *See* Philadelphia tageblatt

SONNTAGS-BLATT der freien presse. w Je 20 1858-83||?
PHi 1858-Je 10 1860
PPG Je 19 1859-Je 10 1861
—d ed *See* Philadelphia freie presse

Philadelphia SONNTAGS-GAZETTE. w N 27 1892-1918||?
pub [1892-96;98-1901;04-06;08]-[17-18]
—d ed *See* Gazette-democrat

SONNTAGS JOURNAL. w D 3 1876-1917||
PPG D 9 1888-N 21 1909

SONNTAGS-ZEITUNG des tageblatts. *See* Philadelphia sonntagsblatt

SOUTH PHILADELPHIA. w Ag 31 1929+
pub 1929+
PP 1929+

SOUTHERN monitor. w Je 6 1857-60||
DLC Ja 23 1858-My 26 1860
MWA My 8 1858
PHi 1857-My 1858
PLewL Je 6 1857

SOUTHWEST chronicle. *See* West Philadelphia chronicle

SPIRIT of '76. d Je 21 1837-
MWA Je 22 1837

SPIRIT of the times. d Je 10 1838-51||?
N 3 1845-O 7 1846 as Times; Jl 22 1847-D 25 1849 Spirit of times and daily keystone
CSmH Jl 17 1846
DLC Je 11 1838;F 25 1840;Jl 13 1841;O 29,N 4,7,11,15,27,D 4,12,16,18,20,24,28 1844;Mr 6 1845-48
IU My 26 1841;My 20 1845
MHi Jl 31,Ag 15,S 13-14,O 1,9 1839
MWA Mr 4 1840;Mr 16 1841;Ja 20 1844;Ag 22 1845;My 27 1846;Je 1 1847;Je 10 1848;N 5 1850
MnHi Ag 7 1840
NN [Ag-N 1842;F-O 1843;44;F-Je]N 15 1845; F 28,Mr 3,5,Jl 30,Ag 11,S 17 1846
NcD My 12,Jl 20,Ag 19 1846[Mr 1847-My 1848]
NjR Mr 30,Jl 9 1849
OClWHi Jl 13 1840
P Je 29 1838-N 1849
PDoHi O 7 1848
PHi Je 23 1838[39]Ja 25 1840[43-44]Je 30 1845;O 20,22,26,28 1847[48]N 11 1850
PLaHi 1839-41;Ag 25 1847
PNoHi [1839-41]
PP Jl 29,Ag 26 1839;My 27,Je 27 1841;F 25 1848;O 31 1849
PPL Jl 22 1847;49[50-51]
PWcHi F 26 1844
WHi Ap 9 1845;Ag 14 1849

SPY, and Philadelphia county courier. w Je 30 1827-
DLC N 10 1827

SPY and spirit of the age. w Jl 6-D 28 1833||
NNHi complete
PHi complete

Daily STANDARD. d Ja 5 1840-41||
DLC Ja 6-7 1840;F 12 1841

Weekly STANDARD. w 1840-43||
United with Temperance advocate to form Temperance advocate and standard

Philadelphia STANDARD.
NNiU 1875

Evening STAR. d Ap 2 1866-O 2 1900||
DLC 1866-Je 1898;D 19 1899
MWA S 11,N 13 1876;Mr 8 1877
N Je 1,8 1876
NNHi My 24 1873;Ag 6 1885
NcD Ag 14 1894;My 3,17 1895
NjN O 12 1875;O 12 1877
NjWdHi D 2 1882
PCHi Je 4 1867
PEHi Ag 31 1867
PEbHi My 1 1866
PP S 12,N 1 1866[67-68;70-82]
PPL [1867]-[75]-[78;81-83]-89[91-93]-[95]-[1900]
PPot [1884-86]
PU Je 30 1867-Je 1894

STAR. 1902+ *See* Gwiazda

Evening STAR. d,sw D 9 1908+
d 1908-O 21 1933
pub 1908+
PP Mr 12 1931+

Philadelphia evening STAR and daily advertiser. d 1835-
Ct Jl 15-16,N 11-12 1835
NCanHi Ag 31 1840
NjHi Mr 8 1836
PBL [1835]Ja 1,My-Je 15 1836
PHi My 4 1839
PPot [1839]

Morning STAR and people's advocate. d O 2 1838-
Follows People's advocate
DLC O 3 1838
PBL N 26 1838
PPL D 6 1838

STAR SPANGLED banner. tw F 22 1834-
CSmH Ag 2 1834
DLC F 22,My 23 1834
NjR Ap 1 1834

SUBURBAN press. w F 7 1929+
pub 1929+
PP 1929+

SUBURBAN times and review. *See* Olney times

SUN. d 1829?-
CSmH Ag 14 1830
P D 15 1831
P-M F 12 1835
PDoHi N 29-D 6 1832
PLaHi O 1 1829
PLewL Ag 11 1831;O 25 1832

SUN. w D 15 1830-
DLC F 3-D 1 1831;F 16,D 13 1832-Ap 4,Jl 4-O 10 1833;Ja 9,23,F 6 1834
NNHi Ag 16,S 20,O 11,17 1832
OClWHi Je 6,Jl 25-Ag 1,15-22,O 10,21 1833
P D 15 1831
PHi O 3-D 3 1833

SUN. d 1841-57||
CSmH S 5 1846;S 1 1853
DLC My 7 1849-50
MWA Ag 1844-Jl 3 1845;Ap 22 1846;Ap[My]S 11[D 1851-Ja]Ap 27-28[My]1852;53-Je 1855; Mr 1 1877
MdBJ O 16 1856
NN S 16-23 1843[My-D 1844]Ja 25,My 5-6,8, O 16 1845;Ap 15,Ag 4-5,24,S 3,5,12,17,23,O 28,N 2 1846;Je 3,10 1848
NSyU Ja 20 1845
NjCHi Je 1 1844;My 22-23,25-26 1860;D 4 1871; O 31 1873
NjR Jl 3 1852;F 5 1855
OHi N 22 1844
PBL [1844-48;52]
PCHi Jl 4 1856
PHi 1845-Je 1857
PNoHi [1844]D 13 1845;Je 8 1847
PPFfHi O 8 1852;O 30 1856
PPL O 8 1847[49]-51
PPPHi [1845-48]-52[57]
PShH My 18 1843
WHi S 16 1853

Weekly SUN. w 1841?-
CtY My 13 1844
P Je 10-Ag 24 1847

SUN. d 1877-83||
DLC F 1877-83
NcD F 12-17,Mr-D 1877;F 1878-80;82-83

TABLOID. w Mr 31 1933-F 2 1934||
Mr-S 15 1933 as Quaker City brevity; S 29 1933 Graphic news; O 6-27 Tabloid news
PP complete

TABLOID news. *See* Tabloid

Philadelphia TAGEBLATT. d N 19 1877+
In German
pub 1927;O 1928-Je,O 1929+
NN N 20 1877;Mr 8,17,Jl 25,Ag 9,11,O 7,N 26 1879;Jl 21,S 23 1880;Ja 21 1895
PP Ag 3,9,21-29 1917;Je 1927-43
PPG 1877-N 18 1890;Ap 1891-Jl 1899;Ap-Jl 1900;01-08;My 1909-S 1911;12-16;Jl 1917-25; Ap 1926-S 1928;Jl-S 1929
WHi Ap 29,D 18,28 1896
—w ed *See* Philadelphia sonntagsblatt

TAGGARTS' Sunday times. w D 6 1863-1901||
1863-N 29 1874 as Sunday morning times; D 6 1874-S 18 1881 Philadelphia Sunday times; S 25 1881-N 16 1884 Taggarts' Philadelphia Sunday times; N 21 1887-Je 10 1900 Taggarts' times. Merged with Public ledger
DLC D 27 1863;Ja 10-Ap 17 1864;Je 18 1865;N 1 1874
MBAt Ap 23 1865
MWA Je 11 1876;Je 5 1892
MnHi Ap 23 1865
NNHi D 19 1886
OClWHi Je 4 1865
PCHi S 18 1870;N 12 1893
PDoHi Mr 30 1890
PHi N 14 1869-97
PP Ap 30 1865;Jl 19-26,S 20 1868
PPL N 14 1869-S 4,N 13 1870-Ja 20 1901
PPM S 11-N 1875;76-N 19 1882;N 25 1883-O 1900
PPeS Ap 23 1865

Evening TELEGRAPH. d Ja 4 1864-Jl 1 1918||
Merged with Public ledger
CtY Ap 15 1865
DLC My 28,Je 3,18,20,25,30,Jl 1,5,11-13,22,30 1864;Ap 3,7,10 1865;F 13 1871;Ap 20,Jl 3,N 11 1872;F 26 1873[Ap 16-N 9 1874]F 6 1875;Jl 4-5 1876;Jl 1879-80;Jl 2,4,S 19-20 1881;N 2,8 1882
DeWI [1865]
MBAt Ap 20 1865
MWA N 11 1864;Ap 15,24 1865;Ap 13 1866; Jl 27 1867;Ap 1 1868;D 4(supp)1871;Mr 31 1874;Je 27,Jl 1,15,N 8 1876;D 16 1879;N 16 1887
MiU-C Ap 1,10,20 1865
NN Ap 22,26 1865
NNHi Je 4 1864;Ap 3,10 1865;O 14,N 4 1868;Ja 8,Je 10,S 3 1870;Ja 30,O 11 1871;Je 1 1872; My 5 1873;S 9 1874;N 8 1876
NbHi O 7,N 7,14 1864;Ja 12,20,Mr 7,Ap 4-7, 10-11,My 30 1865;Mr 1,13 1868
NcD S 19 1874;F 13 1880
NjR Mr 3,Ap 25,29,My 1,15,17,19-20,22 1865; Ag 24 1892
OClWHi Ap 4,Jl 21 1865
OHi D 6 1864
OOxM Je 17-18 1875;Jl 5 1876;N 9,13 1877
P-M Ap 10,15,17 1865
PCHi Ap 15 1868
PDoHi [1901;08]
PHHi [1914]
PHi Ja-Je 1864;D 1865-1916;Je-O 1917
PLaHi [1876]
PMcC [1876-77]
PNoHi S 20 1869
PP 1864-67;Jl 1868-Je 1871;S 1872;73-76;F 1877-N 2 1896;F 1897-1910;F 1911-S 1917
PPL 1873-96
PPeS O 9 1872;S 19 1901
PPiHi [1897-98]
PPot O 6 1868[70;86;93]
PWcHi Ap 20-22,25-26,N 14 1865;My 8 1867 [71;76;97;1901;04;08]
WHi 1865[N 30 1870-S 29 1871]My 4 1872;S 2,14 1901

Philadelphiaer TELEGRAPH und deutscher wochenblatt. sw Ja 5 1825-D 31 1831||?
1825-29 as Amerikanischer correspondent; 1830 Philadelphische correspondent und allgemeiner deutscher anzeiger
In German
MnU Ja 8-N 23 1831
PHi Ag 19 1829-Ag 7 1830;F 16-D 14 1831

TEMPERANCE advocate and standard. sm,w 1841-45||
1841-Jl 1 1843 as Temperance advocate and literary repository. United with Sunday American to form Sunday American and temperance advocate
MWA Mr 16 1844
NNHi Ag 14 1841-Jl 1 1843
PPFfHi Ja 20 1844
PWcHi Ja 1 1842

Philadelphia TIMES. w Mr 27 1830-
Ct [1834-35]
DLC Mr 27 1830

TIMES. d 1845-46. *See* Spirit of the times

Daily morning TIMES. d Ap 9 1855-57||
DLC Ag 9,11,14,16,S 18,22,25,O 1 1855
MWA Je 8,18 1855;Je 19 1856
NCanHi Ap 25,27 1857
NNHi Ag 20 1856
OClWHi F 14 1856
PEHi [1857]
PHi O 12 1857
PPL F 28,Ap 19,My 7 1856

Philadelphia weekly TIMES. w My 16 1857-
MWA My 16,Jl 18,Ag 1,22-S 5 1857

Sunday morning TIMES. 1863-74 *See* Taggarts' Sunday times

Philadelphia TIMES. d Mr 13 1875-Ag 11 1902||
Jl 1 1892-My 31 1902 as Times. Merged with Public ledger
A Jl-Ag 1894;96-F 1899
CLM D 3 1893
DCHi D 17 1879
DLC Ja-My 2,11,Jl 4-5 1876;Ja 8 1879;Je 30 1883;Jl 1885-Je 1886;Mr 14,Jl 1891-Ap,S 1894-95;Mr 1897-1902
DeWI F 3,Je 9 1889
IC Ap 30-My 1 1889
ICHi Jl 3 1876
ICM F 12 1884;Ja 17 1885;Ag 28,D 5 1887
InI My 1876-Je 17 1878
MWA Ap 14,My 17,Je 8,24,S 21,O 12 1876;O 16 1885;Mr 5 1889;Je 10 1892;Ja 1 1896
NN Ja 1 1876
NNHi N 11,25,29 1876
NbHi Ap 17-24,My 8-15,Je 5,19,Jl 3,17-24 1880;Jl 13 1884
NcD S 9 1876;Je 28 1877;Ag 5 1878;Je 24 1883; Mr 26 1887[O 1898;My 1899]
OClWHi D 17 1879;S 21 1881;Jl 24 1885;N 1 1896
OHi S 15-17 1887
P complete
PHi 1876-84;1901-02
PP My-Ag 1876;77-Mr 12 1883;S 15 1887;Je 27,S 12,D 16 1889;Ja 18 1891;F 12,Mr 9,Ag 17 1892;Ja 28,D 20 1893;Jl-S 1901
PPM 1875-Je 1879;80-90;Ja-Mr 1901;Ja-Mr 1902
PPeS O 12 1886;Mr 6 1890;My 15 1897
PPot S 20 1881;N 5 1884[85-88;94]
PU 1875-Ap 12 1883;93-95
PWcHi Jl 4 1876;O 5 1881;O 22 1882;S 17 1887;Mr 3 1889[90]Ag 25 1893;F 23 1896[97; 99]S 11 1900
Tx Mr 20,Ag 27,31 1877;O 25 1894
VU S 26,29-30,O 5,25-N 4,6-11,13-17,20-24 1876; My 11 1877
WHi O 24 1900-Ap 12 1901

Weekly TIMES. w Mr 3 1877-D 1896||
Ct 1877-78
FU [Ja 15 1886-Ja 8 1887]
GU Ap 13 1878
KHi Mr 3 1877;S 24 1881
LNC Je 2 1878[80-F 1886]
MB 1877-F 23 1878
MHi 1877-F 21 1880
NNHi My 25 1878[My 1879-Ap 1880]
NcD Ap 7 1877
NcU Je 10,N 11,D 30 1882;Mr 13 1884;O 3,N 7-14,D 26 1885;Ja 9-16,F 6 1886
NjP 1877-F 17 1883
P 1877-Mr 1879
PSuHi [1877]
WHi [Mr 8 1884-F 1885]

Evening TIMES. d Jl 15 1908-Ap 14 1914||
PP complete

Philadelphia TIMES, mechanics free press and working man's register. w Ja 2 1828-O 17 1835||?
1828-Ap 23 1831 as Mechanic's free press. Title varies slightly
CSmH S 11 1830
Ct [1830-31]
N N 2 1833
NCanHi S 11,25,O 9,30,N 13,27,D 11 1830
OC F 8 1834
PHi Ap 12 1828-Ap 23 1831;O 18 1834;O 17 1835
PPL 1830-Ja 1 1831
PPM Ap 12-O 18,D 13 1828-Mr 21,Ag 1829-30
WHi My 18 1833

TIOGA news. w 1904+
pub Je 15 1922+
PP D 1930+

PENNSYLVANIA (*Continued*)

PHILADELPHIA—*Continued*

Daily TRANSCRIPT. d S 1835-S 1836||
United with Public ledger to form Public ledger and daily transcript, later Public ledger
Ct Mr 19,21 1836
DLC Je 7 1836

Sunday TRANSCRIPT. w O 19 1856+
pub Ag 1903+
DLC Ja 11 1863;S 26 1869
IU S 1926+
M Ap 8 1928
MWA Je 28 1857;Ap 10,D 11 1864;Ag 6 1876
NN Ap 23 1865
NNHi Ap 16-23 1865
P Mr 27 1864
PP My 15 1859;Jl 5,19-26,Ag 30,S 13-20 1868; Je 16,O 29 D 29 1929;D 28 1930;Jl 12 1931+
PPFfHi F 14 1869
PPeS S 7 1862
TxU Ag 22 1926-33
WHi Mr 9 1862;F 26 1933
WaU Ag 7 1927;Ag 26,S 2 1928;S 8 1929+

Sunday TRIBUNE. w S 13 1874-S 5 1875||
PP complete
PPL 1874-Ja,F 14,Je 20-S 1875

Philadelphia TRIBUNE. w N 2 1884+
Negro
pub 1884+
PP N 28 1925-Je 1927+
TNY O 10 1929-My,Ag 14,S 18-O 1930

Die TURN zeitung. w O 24 1850-O 18 1855||
In German
PPG N 1854-55

TWENTY-FIRST ward advance. (Manayunk) N 9 1887-1909||?
1887-1908? as Advance
PHi N 9 1887-S 23 1891

UNION (1819-23) *See* United States gazette

UNITED STATES and dollar newspaper. w 1837-O 1 1842||
1837-Ap 1841 as Weekly ledger. Merged with Saturday evening post
DLC My 1839-Ap,O 9,24(extra)1841
InRE Ja 5,Ag 31,S 14,28,N 30,D 21 1839;Ja 4,18,Mr 14,28 Je 20,S 5 1840;Mr 20-27,Ap 10 1841
MWA O 30 1841;Je 18,S 3,O 1 1842
MiU O 9 1841
NcD Ap 11-18 1840
OClWHi D 19 1840

UNITED STATES business journal. *See* United States journal

***UNITED STATES gazette.** sw,d Ap 15 1789-Je 30 1847||
1789-F 18 1804 as Gazette of the United States (subtitle varies); Mr 9 1818-Mr 31 1823 Union. United States gazette and true American. Merged with North American
Suspended from S 18-D 11 1793
sw 1789-S 18 1793
CSmH S 6 1830
Ct F 27 1828
CtY F 1(extra)1831;N 7 1842-Je 1846
DLC Ag 9 1823;Jl 9,12,Ag 5,7,O 2,14,N 26,D 2,11,17,22 1824;Ja 21,Mr 18 1826;29;Ja 1,27, Ap 27 1830;Ja 6,D 8,10,15 1831;[32-Mr 1834] Mr 15 1841;42-D 14 1844
DeWI Ap 11 1838
MB O 5 1831;D 6 1832;My 14,28 1834;Ap 16, My 29,D 21 1835;My 31 1842;F 8 1843;D 3 1846
MBAt Mr 22 1828;Je 23,S 9 1829
MHi Mr 16 1821
MWA My 1821-[22;F 4-Mr 19 1823;Ja 10-Mr 14 1825]Ja 4,F 21 1826;Ag 6 1827;F 18,20,Jl 4,11 1828;Jl 16,S 10 1829;D 18 1830;Jl 15,25 1831;D 12 1832;Jl 9,Ag 6,D 16 1833;Ja 11 1834; S 6 1837;Ag 6 1840;D 16 1841
MiG Ap 9 1838
NN Jl 24,Ag 12 1826
NNHi Jl 29,D 16 1823;My 13,Jl 10 1824;Ag 21 1826-Ag 1827;S 19 1828;Ap 28(extra)1830; D 21 1833;S 10 1840
NcD Ja 10[Jl-Ag]1829
NjCHi D 19 1829
NjR [1827]
OCHi S 13 1842
P 1821-47
P-M Je 19,Ag 27 1821;Jl 20,23 1830;Ja 19 1832
PB Je 15 1842
PBL [1822-33]36-[42]44-45]
PDoHi [1821-22]
PE Je 30 1838
PEL [1833-34]
PHi 1821-Je 1827;28-41;Jl 1842-Ap 16 1846
PHoHi 1833-38
PLewL [1829-31]
PNhE F 19 1823
PNo S 1 1835
PP Ap 1821-22;Jl 1823-26;Jl-D 1827;Jl 1828-30;41-Je 1842;Jl-D 1845;Ja-Je 1847
PPA 1835-47
PPAm Mr 22 1834
PPL 1821-47
PPM 1824;Mr 1844-47
PPiHi [N 9 1830-Jl 20 1836]
PPot O 25 1857
PShH Jl 30 1842
PSuHi Mr 13 1832;Mr 6 1833;Ap 2 1834
PWbW Je 29,Ag 10 1821;D 31 1824;D 30 1825; Ap 28,My 5 1826;Ja 29 1828;Ap 19 1834;Mr 9 1836;F 1 1837
PWcHi My 30,Ag 10 1822;Mr 20 1833;Mr 27 1835;Ap 19,Ag 4 1839
PWeT Mr 19,24,26-27 1832
T [1821]
WHi Jl-D 1839;Jl 1841-Je 1842

Weekly UNITED STATES gazette. w 1843-46||?
DLC Ap 12 1845
NjR D 5 1846
PJR Ap 3 1847
PToHi 1845-46

***UNITED STATES gazette for the country.** sw Ag 10 1801-47||
Ag 10-S 11 1801 as Gazette of the United States; S 14-N 2 1801 Country gazette of the United States; N 6 1801-F 17 1804 Gazette of the United States for the country; Mr 11 1818-Mr 1823 Union. United States gazette and true American for the country
DLC N 19 1822;My 13,Je 17,27,Jl 4,25,S 6,O 17,21,24,N 4,25,D 6 1823;F 6,Ap 13,16,30,Ag 24-31,O 26,D 7,10,14,17,21 1824-[25-Mr]D 5 1826;Ja 5,My 25,Je 12,S 7 1827;Mr 18,Ap 8-Jl 15,22,29,S 23 1828;Ja 20,Mr 31,Je 16,Jl 7,28 Ag 4,28,N 27,D 18 1829;N 22 1831-Je 1833;Ja-Ap 12 1834
ICHi F 4 1823
MHi D 22 1823;Ja 16,20,F 17 1824
MWA Ja 26,F 6 1821;Ap 9,Je 4,7,11,25-28,Ag 30-S 3 1822;F 25 1823;Ja 20,F 3,Mr 23,Jl 20 1824;F 15,Mr 15-18,Ap 12,Jl 22,Ag 2 1825; Mr 3,Ap 14 Je 9,Jl 11,Ag 4,O 10,31 1826;Ja 12, My 11,O 9,N 9,D 4-7 1827[Ja-S 12]N 25 1828; Ja 27,Mr 21,Ag 18,N 17 1829;F 19,Mr 23-26, Je 1 1830;31-[Ja-My 4,O 12-D 1833]-Ap 4 1835;Mr 19 1836;Ag 1 1840;Je 12,Ag 28 1841;N 15 1843;Mr 21 1846
MdHi 1821
MiU-C [1823;28;30-33]
MNHi [1821]
MjHi N 27,30 1821;Ag 3,N 26 1824;Ag 19 1825; My 19,Jl 31 1829
OCHi 1821-[O 1825-F 1826]-[D 1828-30]31[33-Ap 1842]
OClWHi O 5 1822;Ap 11 1827;F 14 1829
OOxM [1821]-Ap 5 1822;23;25-39
OY My 25 1827-30
P 1821-Je 30 1847
PBL 1822
PDoHi 1821[22]
PEL [1833-34]
PHoHi 1833-38
PLaHi 1821-O 18 1822
PSuHi [1832-34]
PWbW 1823-27
WHi Ap 9 1822-23

UNITED STATES journal. d D? 1854-69||
1854-56 as Business journal and traveler; 1856-57 United States journal and traveler; 1857- United States business journal
MWA S 5 1857
PPL Ap 12 1856,My 1 1869

UNITED STATES journal. w 1854-72||?
DLC Je 17,Jl 22,S 16,N 11 1865;Ja 20,F 10, Mr 17,Ap 7,My 12,Ag 25,D 8 1866;Mr 9,Ap 20,Je 1,D 28 1867;Mr 7,Ap 21,Je 20,Jl 18,S 5,O 10,D 12 1868;Ja 21,F 6,27,Ap 10,My 1,Ag 21 1869;Mr 5,My 7,Je 11 1870;Ja 14,Mr 4,My 13,Jl 1,Ag 5,N 4,D 2 1871;Ja 6,F 3,My 4,Je 1,Jl 6,S 14 1872

UNITED STATES Saturday post. *See* Saturday evening post

UPHAM'S Philadelphia Sunday mercury. *See* Sunday mercury

VEREINGTEN staaten zeitung. w 1843-1907||?
1843- as Der Demokrat (title varies)
In German
PPG Ag 24 1856-Je 1857;Ja 12 1879-Je 1907
PPeS Mr 9 1843
PU Ja 15-D 2 1888;89

VEREINS und logen zeitung. *See* Philadelphia herold

VILLAGE telegraph. *See* Germantown telegraph

Die VOLKS-STIMME. w My 1 1925-30||?
In German
NNRa Je 24 1925-28
PPG 1925-Mr 1930

WEST PHILADELPHIA chronicle. w Je 20 1929+
1929-Ag 1934 as Southwest chronicle
pub 1929+
PP 1929-Je 13 1934[35-Jl 1936]

WEST PHILADELPHIA hospital register. *See* Hospital register

WEST PHILADELPHIA Saturday star. w 1860-72||?
MWA Ja 5 1861

WEST PHILADELPHIA times. w My 1924+
pub 1934+
PP D 30 1927+

WEST PHILADELPHIA tribune. w N 16 1933-F 23 1934||
PP complete

WORLD. d Mr 30-O 9 1839||
DLC Mr 5,S 3 1839
PP Ag 19,26 1839
PPL Jl 12,Ag 10,29,S 6,19,O 9 1839
PWcHi [1839]

Sunday WORLD. w F 6 1876-1907||?
PCHi My 25 1902
PDoHi Jl 3 1881
PP S 25 1881
PPot Je 8 1884

PHILIPSBURG

Philipsburg weekly JOURNAL. w O 17 1868+
pub 1881—
PPhA 1868;77
PStP 1876-93

Philipsburg daily JOURNAL. d Ap 2 1888+
pub 1888+

Philipsburg LEDGER. w 1883+
PStP 1884-[94-95;97]

PHOENIXVILLE

Phoenix ADVERTISER. w 1902-08||?
PWcHi [1902]

Phoenix GAZETTE. w
PWcHi N 24 1846

INDEPENDENT. w 1856-88||
MWA Ap 4 1863
PPot Ap 22 1865[81]
PWcHi Mr 4 1865;D 16 1871;Ap 1 1887;Je 1 1888

MESSENGER. w Ja 14 1871-1910||
Title varies slightly
P Jl 1889-Je 1910
PNoHi Ap 16 1904
PPhoF 1871
PPhoN [1873-74]
PWcHi Mr 19 1887[93]
PWcT [1893]-[95]

PENNSYLVANIA guardian and Phoenix gazette. w
PWcHi Ap 13 1861

Phoenixville PIONEER. w D 29 1846-F 21 1849||?
PWcHi [1847]

Weekly REPUBLICAN. w 1888-89||
PPhoF [1888-89]
PWcHi Je 8 1888

Daily REPUBLICAN. d 1888+
pub 1902+
PK Mr 18 1896
PP F 6 1928[34]+
PPeS S 9 1929
PPhoF 1888+
PPot Je 4 1904
PWcHi O 3 1880;Ap 5 1889[93]-[95]N 10,17 1902
PWcT [1893]-[95]

PITCAIRN

EXPRESS. w 1893+
pub S 6 1893+

PITTSBURGH

Pittsburgh ABEND-ZEITUNG. w
In German
PHHi F 2-D 17 1864;65

Daily ADVOCATE and advertiser. d 1832-
1832-33? as Pennsylvania advocate (title varies slightly)
DLC O 2 1833;Ag 12 1834;D 2 1840
MWA My 14,23 1840
OClWHi Ja 18,21,23,Jl 16,O 19,D 6 1836[37-F 1838]F 21,Mr 20,Je 26,Jl 25 1839[41-42]Ja 20,Jl 14-18 1843
PPi O 18 1839-N 6 1840
PPiHi O 1837-Je 1840

Weekly ADVOCATE and emporium. w Ag 13 1832-
1832-33? as Pennsylvania advocate. Title varies: Advocate and statesman; etc.
DLC N 10 1832
OClWHi Ag 13,N 10 1832;Ap 27,My 18,Je 17,Jl 2,11,S 3 1833
PAg 1838-39
PPiHi 1841-Ja 7 1842

ALLEGHENIAN. w Ja 1846-96||
P Jl 1890-Je 1896
PAg Je 1886-N 1888;S 1889-90;92-Je 1893
PPiHi Ag 9 1885
PPiW 1846-47

ALLEGHENIER und Pittsburger sonntagsbote. *See* Der Sonntagsbote

ALLEGHENY democrat. w Je 22 1824-F 1841||
Title varies: Allegheny democrat and farmers' and mechanics' advertiser; Allegheny democrat and workingman's advocate. United with Pittsburgh mercury to form Pittsburg mercury and Allegheny democrat, later Weekly mercury and manufacturer
Ct D 5 1826[27-31]Ap 24 1832;N 19 1833
DLC Ap 12 1825;Jl 29 1836
MWA Je 24 1828
OClWHi Jl 14 1837
OHi F 22 1825
P 1824-31
P-M Ag 25-S 1,22 1829
PAg 1838-39
PBL [1833-34;36]F 3 1837
PPiHi Ag 14 1827;N 29 1833-Je 21 1836
PPiU-D O 12 1824-Je,O 4,18-25,N 22,D 6 1825; F 14 1826
PPitE O 30 1841
REdH N 11,Ag 19 1828

ALLEGHENY daily enterprise. d Ag 29 1850-
PAg Ag 1851-Ag 1852
PPiHi 1850-Ag 28 1851

ALLEGHENY morning express. d Jl 1844-
DLC Jl 30 1844

ALLEGHENY evening mail. d 1873-83||?
DLC S 2 1873
MWA My 12 1876
PBf Jl 13 1881

ALLEGHENY evening record. d 1896-99||
P 1896-98
PAg S 1896-F 1899

ALLEGHENY evening times. d
PAg Ja-O 5 1866

Pittsburgh AMERICAN. w 1839-
WHi Mr 29-D 27 1854

Pittsburgh daily AMERICAN. d 1840-
Title varies: Daily American and general advertiser
DLC N 28 1840
OClWHi N 7 1842
PBL [1844-45]
PPiHi Ap 7-Ag 24 1841;S 10 1846
WHi My 5 1852
—w ed *See* Saturday evening visitor (1834-42)

PENNSYLVANIA (*Continued*)

PITTSBURGH—*Continued*

AMERICAN manufacturer. w Mr 6 1830-S 3 1842‖
United with Pittsburgh mercury and Allegheny democrat to form Weekly mercury and manufacturer
CSmH My 1 1830
Ct O 12 1833;Jl 6,D 20 1834[35-36]O 28 1837
NcD N 19 1831
PPi F 27 1841-42

Morning ARIEL. d 1845-
DLC Je 2-S 22 1845
PBL [1849]

Daily AURORA. d Je 22 1843-
DLC Je 26 1843
PBL [1843]
PPi [Je 24 1843-My 21 1844]

Pittsburgh weekly AURORA. w Ag 24 1844-
NN Ag 24 1844

Pittsburgh CHRONICLE-TELEGRAPH. w 1841-1901‖?
1841-84 as Pittsburgh weekly chronicle
DLC Ap 15 1865;Ag 24 1867
ICM N 16 1880
OClWHi D 23 1865
OOxM F 13 1872
P 1874-My 1883
WHi Mr 14 1863-65

Pittsburgh CHRONICLE TELEGRAPH. d Je 26 1841-Ag 1 1927‖
1841-84 as Pittsburgh morning chronicle (title varies: Morning chronicle; Evening chronicle; etc.)
Ct [1835]
DLC Je 26-30,Jl 7 1841;My 3,20-23,25,Ag 13,D 10,27 1845[Ja-S 1846]Ag 29 1894
MBAt Ap 15,18-19 1865
MWA Ap 20 1846;N 29 1852;S 22 1876;My 16 1879;S 16 1880
OClWHi [1842]Ap 19,21,Ag 2-3,9 1843;Ja 13 1845;N 2 1859;Ag 6,D 21 1861;N 26 1870
OHi Jl 28,31,Ag 2,N 24 1856
P S 21 1863;74-My 1883
PAg Mr 1843-S 11 1845;97-99
PBL Ap 11 1844
PBf Ja 12 1880;Ja 5 1881;S 20,O 5 1883[84]
PPi F 16 1841-Ap,Ag 1844-Je 1849;S 1850-Mr 1855;F-Ap 1856;F 1858-Jl 1863;F 1864;Ja 1868-S 1883;84-1927
PPiHi S 11 1841;Ja 8 1842;D 28-29 1857[61-65] Mr 27 1868;Ag 30,S 14 1873;Ja 28 1874;N 9 1876;Jl 2,S 20,D 31 1881;S 14 1882[84-85]D 31 1886;N 11 1887[88-89]O 21,N 9 1892;N 4 1896;F 19,Mr 28,Ap 22 1898;F 19,Mr 28,Ap 22 1901;Ap 19 1912;Ap 8,N 11,17 1914;F 23,30,N 23 1915;S 20 1916;N 11-12 1918
PUn Mr 21 1864
WHi Mr 2 1863-65

CITIZEN'S press. tw D 11 1838-
DLC Jl 23 1838

Pittsburgh COMMERCIAL. w 1861-77‖
1861-O 1866 as Saturday morning commercial
NNHi O 11 1871;F 22,Je 2 1873
P Jl 1874-F 14 1877
PAg O 1863-O 1868;69-76
PPi [N 10 1866-76]

Pittsburgh COMMERCIAL. d S 7 1863-F 15 1877‖
United with Daily Pittsburgh gazette to form Pittsburgh commercial gazette, later Pittsburgh gazette-times
DLC 1867-75
MWA F 6(extra)1874;Ap 12 1876
N O 26 1864
NN Jl 6 1876
NcU N 11 1865
OClWHi Jl 26,28 1866;Mr-O 1870;Ja 20 1871
ODW S 11 1868;N 27 1871;Ja 9 1873
OHi Ja 22 1867;N 13 1873
P F 19 1873;Jl 1874-77
PAg 1863-74;Jl 1875-76
PPi 1863-F 10,My 30-Jl 1864;Ap 3,10 1865;Ja-Je 1871;72;N 2 1875
PPiHi 1863-[64-65]-75
WHi Ag 7 1865

Pittsburgh COMMERCIAL gazette. *See* Pittsburgh gazette times

Daily COMMERCIAL journal. d 1845-61‖
Title varies: Daily commercial journal and spirit of the age. United with Daily Pittsburgh gazette to form Daily Pittsburgh gazette and commercial journal, later Pittsburgh gazette-times
DLC O 9-D 19 1845;Ja 15 1846-50;52-My 29 1853
OClWHi Ja 13 1851;Ja 31,F 3,11 1852
PAg Ja-Ap,N 1850-My 1851;Ja-Ag 1852
PPi Ap 23 1846-Ap 1849
PPiHi D 20 1845-46;N 16 1847-N 7 1848;S 19-20 1849;Ja-Je 1850;51-[55-56]-58

COMMONWEALTH and Pittsburgh manufacturing and commercial advertiser. w S 28 1827-
MWA N 2,D 22 1827
PPiHi D 27 1828
PSew Ja 19-26,Ap 25,My 17,Je 14,Jl 18,Ag 2,23,S 6-13,D 20 1828;Ja 3-10 1829

CONSTITUTIONALIST. w D 4 1839-
DLC D 4 1839

Der Pittsburger COURIER. w 1842-
In German
MWA D 21 1853

Pittsburgh COURIER. w 1910+
Negro
pub 1924+
P Mr 25 1911-12
TNF 1933[34]+

Pittsburgh CRITIC. d 1875-83‖
DLC S 1 1878
PPiHi Jl 9,19(extra)29-30,Ag 2(extra)13 1876; My 13(supp)1883

Der Täglische DEMOKRAT. d
In German
PHHi Ja 5-D 29 1863

Der Pittsburgher DEMOKRAT. w
PHHi Ja 9 1864-65

Pittsburgh DISPATCH. d F 8 1846-F 14 1923‖
Title varies: Pittsburgh daily dispatch; Daily dispatch
CoU 1899;1903-04;06-10
DLC Jl 9 1874-Mr 23 1897;98-1923
IC Ap 30 1889
MWA Ap 20 1846;Mr 12 1860;My 14 1879;Ag 25 1883;F 8 1907
N D 8 1862;My 27,S 29 1863
NN Jl 6 1876
NcU Je 11 1875
NjR N 26 1858
OCHi S 24-25,27 1888
OCl Mr 5 1889
OClWHi S 22 1881;O 8 1893;S 5-22 1894;F 8 1896;O 1 1899
OHi Jl 1898-1922
P N 1881-1922
PAg 1895-1901;03-23
PBL Mr 21,24 1846[47]F 1 1849
PBf [1879-84]
PDC S 27 1898
PEbHi D 25 1887;Ag 18 1889;D 20 1896;F 5,12 1899
PHHi F 3 1897
PPi Ag 9 1847-50;55-Ja 1863;Ja-Je 1864;Je 1892-1923
PPiHi [F 1861-My 1863]O 16 1869;F 1 1877;F 28 1878[S-N 1881]F 28 1882;S 9 1883[84-90]F 19 1891[92-93]D 26 1895;96-1921
PPitE [1907-09]
PSew Je 11 1898-Ja 2 1899
PUn Ja 20,Jl 7 1863
PWaHi Mr 3 1860;O 10 1921
VU S 27 1905
WHi 1864-65;F 8 1896

Pittsburgh weekly DISPATCH. w 1853-1922‖?
NN Jl 8 1876
TJT O 11 1900

Saturday DOLLAR chronicle. w
PPi Ag 27 1859-61

DOLLAR weekly leader. w 1868-77‖?
PPi [1873-Mr 1875]
PPiHi O 10 1874

DRUID. sm 1907-F 15 1933‖
1907-Je 15 1918 as Welsh-American
pub complete
IU Jl 1918-S 1 1930;D 1932-33

EAST LIBERTY tribune, d,w 1901+
1901-13 as Pittsburgh herald(d)
pub 1916+
PPiHi N 23 1928

FRANK COWAN'S paper. w My 22 1872-75‖
1872-F 1874 pub in Greensburg
DLC 1872-Jl 31 1875
NjR My 22 1875
OClWHi Ag 1872
PPiHi N 28 1874

FREEMAN. w 1836-
PBL D 13,27 1836-Ja 3 1837

Der FREIHEITS freund. w 1834-Ja 1901‖
In German
PAg Jl-S 1894;95-Mr,O 1896-97
PPi Jl 1852-Je 1866;73-90

Der FREIHEITS freund. d 1844?-Ja 1901‖
United with Pittsburger volksblatt to form Volksblatt und freiheits freund
In German
MWA Ag 24 1876
PPi D 10 1844-Ap 1847;Jl 1850-51;Jl 1852-Mr, Jl 20 1853-1901

FRIEND. w Ap 10 1833-
OClWHi Ja 9 1834;Mr 19,Je 25 1835
PPi Ja-Je 11 1835
PPiHi S 25 1834
PPiW 1834-35
PSew 1833-Jl 2 1835

***Pittsburgh GAZETTE.** w Jl 29 1786-1876‖
Title varies: Pittsburgh gazette and manufacturing and mercantile advertiser; etc.
CSmH Je 25 1830
Ct S 22 1837
DLC 1821-N 1 1822[Mr-D 1827]Ja 11,S 19 1828[Mr 1829-Ja 1830]Mr 26,Jl 30 1841;D 19 1844;Ja 2,F 6 1845;Mr 21 1849-52;Mr 9 1868;S 17-18 1873
ICM S 8 1874
MWA Ap 3-10 1829
N Ag 5,D 2 1825
NN Jl 25 1876
NNHi Ap 18 1850;Ap 6 1852;F 12 1869;My 30 1873
NjP S 23 1825-S 18 1829;N 19 1830-Mr 15 1833
OCHi [F-Ag 10 1827]
OClWHi D 24 1828;Jl 12 1833;Ag 7 1835;Mr 29 1844;Je 12 1847;O 23 1874
OHi N 10 1853-Ja 4;F 15 1855;Ap 24 1868;D 11 1869
OOxM My 25 1872
P N 14 1828
PAg 1838-39;O 1844-S 19 1845;S 19,O 1869-Mr 2 1872
PBf Mr 15,My 17 1855;Ap 24 1856;64
PPL [1826]
PPiHi Ja,D 27 1822;F 1823-S 16 1825;Ag 17 1827;S 22 1829-Mr 13 1835;41-Ja 7 1842;O 31 1845;D 16 1863
WHi Ap-N 1864;65;S 23 1867

Pittsburgh GAZETTE-TIMES. d Jl 31 1833-Ag 1927‖
1833-1905 title varies: Daily Pittsburgh gazette; Pittsburgh daily gazette and advertiser; Daily Pittsburgh gazette; Daily Pittsburgh gazette and commercial journal; Pittsburgh commercial gazette. United with Daily post to form Pittsburgh post-gazette
DLC F 15 1923-27
MB S 20 1881[Mr 29-O 21 1884]
MWA Ag 31 1835;My 4 1852;O 27 1875;My 13-16,Ag 16 1879;Jl 29 1886;Je 10 1887;Jl 26 1911
N S 24 1863
NN Jl 6 1876
OClWHi S 1 1862;Ap 4 1879;Jl 23 1885;Jl 29 1886;S 10-15 1894;D 4 1897;Ag 28 1899;My 9, Ag 30,N 29 1900
P 1880-Jl 1927
PAg 1833-34;Mr-D 1839;45-46;O 1847-Mr,O 1848-Mr,O 1849-N 20 1850;51;Ja-Je 1854;Je 20 1855-Je 1856;Ja-Je 1858;59-Je 1860;61-62; 65-Je 1866;Ja-Je 1869;O 1870-71;Jl-D 1873; Jl 1874-Je 1876;Ja-F 1877;N 1901-Jl 1927
PBL F 28 1834[37]Jl 28 1842
PBf [1861;79-84]
PBro Jl 28 1853
PHHi F 3 1897
PHi [1833]-[35]
PMe O 21 1859;Je 3-4 1898
PLaL F 26 1875
PP My 5 1846;Ja 13 1848;Mr 24,Ap 13 1907
PPi 1833-Jl 1834;Ja-Ap,N 1836-Je 1837;Ja 15, 17-30 1838;O 17 1839-[41]-1927
PPiHi 1833-40;Ap 12-Ag 1841;F 8 1845;48-Ag 1863;My 5 1864;Ag 9-10 1865;71-73;Jl 18 1876; F 20,Ag 21 1877;My 17 1879;Jl 4 1881;F 27 1882;Je 14 1883;F 7,N 6 1884[85-90]My 3,Je 11 1892;S 30,D 12 1899;D 28 1900[01]Mr 26 1914; Ja 1,O 28 1916;Jl 17 1919-27
PUn Mr 14,Ag 12 1863;Jl 29 1886
PW Ap 17 1865
WHi Ap-N 29 1864;65;Jl 29 1886;F 11-Ag 7 1901;O 1902-My,S 21 1903-My 9,O 1904-Je 15 1905;15-Ag 1 1927

HARRIS' intelligencer. *See* Pittsburgh intelligencer

HARRY of the West. w Ap 15- 1844‖
DLC Ap 15 1844
MoSM Je 26 1844
OClWHi Je 28 1844
PDoHi O 12 1844

Morning HERALD. d D 8? 1840-
OClWHi D 11 1840

Pittsburgh HERALD. 1901-13 *See* East Liberty tribune

Pittsburgh HERALD and weekly advertiser. w Ap 30 1841-
DLC Ap 30-My 14 1841

HOME news. [West End] w
PCarn D 26 1873-76

HRVATSKI glasnik. *See under* Chicago, Ill.

HUNGARIAN herald. *See* Magyar hirado

HUNGARIAN people. *See* Magyarsag

HUNGARIAN world. *See* Magyar vilag

Der IDISCHE post. (Jewish post) w Ap 28 1903-Jl 2 1909‖
In Yiddish
NN complete

INDEPENDENT republican. w
DLC Jl 15,D 3 1829

Pittsburgh INTELLIGENCER. w Jl 30 1836-43‖?
1836-41 as Harris' intelligencer, commercial reporter and general advertiser
DLC N 28 1840;N 20 1841
ICU Jl 29 1843
OClWHi Ag 6,S 3 1836;Ap 11 1840;O 30 1841
PBL [1841-42]
PPiHi Jl 10,N 27 1841;Ja 5 1842

IRON CITY and Pittsburgh weekly chronicle. w N 27 1841-
NNHi Ja 14 1852
OClWHi Ag-S 3,14-24 1842
PPi 1841-N 19 1842;53-Jl 26 1854
PPiHi D 11 1841;Ja 8 1842

JEWISH criterion. w 1895+
PPiHi S 20 1901;31-32

JEWISH leader. w 1887+
In Yiddish and English
pub 1921+
PPiHi Ja 29 1932+

JEWISH post. *See* Der Idische post

JEWISH volksfreund. w 1889-1923‖
1889-Je 1922 as Der Volksfreund
In Yiddish and Hebrew
IU D 1917-Jl 14 1922
NN 1892-1923

Pittsburgh evening JOURNAL. d
NNHi My 11,Jl 10,23 1863;O 12 1871

JUSTICE. w 1911-F 28 1914‖
WHi O 11 1913-14

Pittsburgh Sunday LEADER. w 1865-79‖
MWA S 30 1866
NbHi Ja 26 1879
OHi Ja 16 1870
PPi D 26 1869-Je 19 1870

Pittsburgh LEADER. d O 18 1870-F 14 1923‖
DLC S 4 1873
MWA D 3 1881
NcU Ag 8 1875
OCHi S 23 1888
PAg Ja-Mr 1871;Ja-Mr,O-D 1874;Jl-D 1875;Jl-S 1876;95-98
PBf [1880-82]Jl 24 1884

PENNSYLVANIA (*Continued*)

PITTSBURGH—*Continued*

Pittsburgh LEADER. d 1870-1923‖—*Continued*
PPi Ja-S 1873;Ja-Mr,Jl 1874-Mr 1875;N 1895-1923
PPiHi O 18 1870;Jl 20,22 1877;Ja 17 1878;S 20,25,N 7 1881;Jl 23,Ag 8-9 1885;D 12 1886;Jl 1, N 11 1887;S 23-24 1888;Je 2-3,5 1889;S 12 1894;N 3 1897;Ag 27,D 5 1899;S 8,16-20 1901;O 27 1915
PUn O 18 1870

MAGYAR hirado. (Hungarian herald) w,sw 1907-Je 30 1925‖
w 1907-S 14 1920
In Hungarian
IU D 13 1917-25
PPiHi My 16 1918[Jl 13 1923-25]

MAGYAR vilag. (Hungarian world) w 1914+
In Hungarian
PPiHi [O 1931-Ap 9 1932]

MAGYARSAG. (Hungarian people) w 1925+
In Hungarian
PPiHi [Ag 21 1925-N 1931]F 12 1932+

*Weekly MERCURY and manufacturer. w S 26 1811-Jl 26 1845‖
1811-F 24 1841 as Pittsburg mercury; Mr 1841-42 Pittsburgh mercury and Allegheny democrat
DLC D 1825-Ja 18 1826
OClWHi N 30 1829
P-M N 9 1832
PPi 1821-Je 15 1824;Jl 1826-Je 3 1828;35-45
PPiHi D 2 1829;Ap 1830-N 1832;Ag 3,S 14 1836;Mr 1841-Ja 5 1842[44-45]

Sunday MESSENGER. *See* Der Sonntagsbote

MISSISSINEWA war club. w? Mr? 1844-
DLC Ap 6 1844

MOUNT WASHINGTON news. w 1903+
pub 1911+

NARODNA slovo. (National word) w 1915+
In Ukrainian
PPiHi D 17 1931-Mr 24 1932

NÁRODNÉ noviny. (National news) w 1908+
In Slovak
pub 1908+
IU 1915+
PPiHi F 23 1932+

NATIONAL news. *See* Národné noviny

NATIONAL word. *See* Narodna slovo

NEW world. w Ja 6 1922+
In Greek
pub 1922+

Pittsburgh daily NEWS. d Mr 16 1896-Ja 8 1901‖
DLC Mr 20 1896-Je 17 1898
PAg 1896-99;Jl-D 1900
PHHi F 3 1897
PPi complete
PPiHi F 10 1899

OAKLANDER. w Ap 20 1911-
PPi 1911-Mr 14 1928

OHIO VALLEY budget. w
WHi Ap 28-My 5,19 1888;F 23 1889

OLD Granny. w Ag 22 1840-
Campaign paper
DLC Ag 29 1840
MWA S 16 1840

PENNSYLVANIA advocate. *See* Advocate

PENNY press. *See* Pittsburgh press

PITTSBURCZANIN. w 1920+
In Polish
PPiHi 1925+

Daily PITTSBURGHER. d 1839-
DLC F 13 1840
PPi Ja-O 1840

Weekly PITTSBURGHER and Allegheny democrat. w 1840-F 24 1841‖
United with Pittsburgh mercury to form Pittsburgh mercury and Allegheny democrat, later Weekly mercury and manufacturer
PPiHi 1841

Pittsburgh POST-GAZETTE. d S 10 1842+
1842-Ag 1 1927 title varies: Pittsburgh morning post; Daily morning post; Daily post
S 10 1917 is 75th anniversary ed
pub 1842+
DLC Mr 7-D 1845;Ja 11 1847-48;O 28,N 2,9 1852;Ag 8 1870;My 29 1878;My 1893+
ICHi Ja 9 1861
IU Mr 16 1847
M S 10 1917
MBAt Ap 17-18,20 1865
MWA S 10 1842(facsimile);N 30 1852;S 27 1873;S 10 1917
MoHi S 10 1842;S 10 1917
NGL Mr 6,13 1927
NN S 10 1842
NNHi O 30 1852
OClWHi S 10 1842;Ag 2,10 1847;Jl 23 1861;Ja 27 1869;Ag 1 1872;N 8-9,11 1876;S 12 1894
OHi Je 7 1856;Jl 23 1862;1912-33
P F 4 1846;74;O 1885-S 1887;F 15 1923+
PAg Ap 1894-Mr 1895;Jl-S 1899;Ap-Je 1901; Ap-Je 1902;O 1904-Mr 1907;Ag 1927+
PBL [1852-53]-[55]
PBf Je 27 1857
PJR O 1 1864
PMe S 1842;Ap 28 1898
PP S 16-17 1852[1927]-Ja 2,7 1933
PPi 1842+
PPiHi S 10 1842;50-Mr 1852;53-54;56-Je 1859; 60-62;71-Je 1873;F 7 1884;Jl 22 1887;Je 3 1889;Jl 5 1890;N 9 1892;D 5-6 1899;S 14,20 1901;Ag 26 1914;Ag 10 1923;Ag 1927+

PPitE S 10,18 1842
PWayHi [1897]-[1900]
TxU Ap 7 1858
WHi S 13 1862;O 1905-Je 18 1906;S 10 1917;Ag 1927+

Pittsburgh PRESS. d Je 23 1884+
1884-Jl 5 1888 as Penny press
pub 1884+
DLC Ag 4 1885;89-98;Je 1926+
IEN N 16 1934+
PAg Ja-Je 1886;O 1894-1900
PHHi F 3 1897
PP D 15 1928-[29]+
PPi 1884+
PPiHi Je 26 1884;Jl 21,23,Ag 4,6-8 1885;Ag 13,N 18,D 27,29,S 1 1886;Mr 7,S 16,28,N 7,9-11 1887;F 20 1891;My 7,N 3 1898;S 14,18 1901; Mr 31 1914

PROGRESSIVE. w Mr 15 1915+
pub 1915+

Pittsburgh RECORDER. w 1822-
OClWHi [1823-27]
PPiW 1822

REPUBLIC. d 1866-
DLC Jl 13 1867
PPiHi S 12 1868

Pittsburger REPUBLIKANER. d 1854-78‖?
In German
MWA Ag 22 1876

RUSSIAN messenger. *See* Russkiĭ vfestnik

RUSSKIĬ vfestnik. (Russian messenger) w 1917+
In Russian
CSt-H 1933+
PPiHi My 12 1932+

SLOVENSKY svet. w 1926+
In Slovak
pub 1927+
PLatS 1926+

Der SONNTAGSBOTE. (Sunday messenger) w 1878+
1878-1910? as Alleghenier und Pittsburger sonntagsbote
In German
PPCHi N 9 1918;F 15 1919
PPiHi N 1931+
PScrHi Ag 19 1911
WHi S 8 1901

SPECTATOR. w Jl 10? 1827-
OClWHi 1828-Ja 1 1829

SPIRIT of liberty. w 1842-47‖?
Followed by Saturday visitor
MWA Mr 25 1843
MiU Jl 13 1845
OClWHi Jl 8 1843[44]
PPi Jl 23 1842
PPiHi Je 5 1846

SPIRIT of the age. d 1843-44‖?
United with Daily commercial journal to form Daily commercial journal and spirit of the age, later Daily commercial journal
DLC Ap 24 1843
NN My 17-18,22-25,Je 17 1844
OClWHi My 13 1844
PPiHi Ja 26-27 1844

*STATESMAN and Pittsburgh public advertiser. w My 9 1818-36‖?
1818-D 1826 as Statesman
DLC 1821-26[Mr 1829-Ja 1830]O 3 1832;Ja 6 1836
MBAt D 25 1824
MWA Ap 15 1829
N Jl 16,Ag 6 1825
OClWHi Mr 13 Je 26,Jl 24,O 2 1833;N 5 1834; Ja 20 1836
OHi Je 9 1834
P-M N 14 1827;Ja 15,Jl 22-Ag 13 1828
PEL Jl 31 1833
PPiHi Ja 3 1824;Mr 5 1825;O 14 1826;Ag 11 1827;Jl 6 1831
PPiU-D Ap 8 1823;F 12,Je 25,Jl 2,S 10,D 24 1825[My 1828-O 1829;F 1830-Ap 13 1831]
PSew O 29 1825;Jl 16,O 8,N 5-12,D 3,17-24 1828;29;Mr 9-16 1831;32;Ja 16,Ag 7,21-S 4,O 30,D 11 1833;34

Daily SUN. d 1842-
PBL [1844]
PPiHi My 25 1842

Weekly SUN. w 1842-
PBL My 11 1844

Pittsburgh SUN. d Mr 1 1906-Ag 1 1927‖
United with Pittsburgh chronicle telegraph to form Pittsburgh sun-telegraph
DLC Je-Jl 1927
PPi complete
PPiHi complete

Pittsburgh SUN-TELEGRAPH. d Ag 2 1927+
Formed by the union of Pittsburgh sun and Pittsburgh chronicle telegraph
pub 1927+
DLC 1927+
P 1929-Mr 26 1933
PAg 1927+
PPi 1927+

Pittsburgh TELEGRAPH. w 1847-84‖
United with Pittsburgh weekly chronicle to form Pittsburgh chronicle-telegraph
PPi My 27 1847-Mr 22 1848;Ap 17 1875-Ag 21 1880

Pittsburgh TELEGRAPH. d Ap 16 1873-84‖
Title varies: Pittsburgh evening telegraph. United with Evening chronicle to form Pittsburgh chronicle telegraph
DLC O 16,D 4 1874;N 26 1875;Ja 20 1876
MWA Ap 21 1876;My 16 1879
P 1875-Mr 6 1880

PAg O-D 1879
PBf [1878-83]
PBro Jl 29 1873
PPi complete
PPiHi S 26 1881

Pittsburgh weekly TIMES. w Ja 15 1831-38‖?
DLC Jl 22 1835;Ag 17 1836
MHi O 21-N 4,18 1835;Ja 27 1836
N Ap 25 1832
NjP 1831-Ja 9 1833
PPi N 8 1837-N 21 1838

Pittsburgh TIMES. d 1879-Ap 30 1906‖
United with Pittsburgh commercial gazette to form Pittsburgh gazette-times
DLC My 25 1894;96-98
PAg 1895-1906
PBf S 1 1880;O 15,24 1881;Mr 1 1882;Jl 19 1884
PPi F 1880-1906
PPiHi F 7 1884[Jl-Ag 1885]D 29,31 1886;Ja 11, My 14 1887;Je 5,7 1889;Je 1 1892;Ja 28 1893; N 4 1896;D 5 1899

TRINACRIA. w 1900+
In Italian
IU D 8 1917-O 23 1925
PPiHi N 1931+

TRUE press. w
PPi Jl 7 1858-Ja 7 1861

Daily UNION. d 1852-
DLC 1857
ICHi N 5 1852
PBL [1852]-[58]
PPiHi Mr 3 1854;Ja 21,D 10 1857

Weekly UNION. w Je 5 1852-
MWA N 13 1852

Pittsburger UNION zeitung. w
In German
PHHi Ja 9 1863-D 28 1865

UNIONE. w 1890+
In Italian
PPiHi N 1931-O 1932

Saturday evening VISITOR. w Jl 12 1834-42‖?
MWA N 3 1838;Jl 17 1841
OClWHi Jl 12-19 1834[35-36]Mr 18,D 30 1837; Jl 21,Ag 11 1838;Mr 23,My 1839
PPi [1836-38]Mr 16 1839;O 9 1840;Jl 23 1842
—d ed *See* Pittsburgh daily American

Saturday VISITOR. w D 18 1847-
Follows Spirit of liberty. 1848-50 as Pittsburgh Saturday visitor
CLM N 19 1853
MWA N 24 1849;Je 22-D 7 1850[F 15-D 6 1851; Ja 17-Ag 18 1852]
MnHi D 20 1847-48;F 9 1850-Ja 11 1851
NSyU D 25 1847
OClWHi Ag 11 1849-Ja 17 1852;O 29 1864
ODW S 20 1851
PPi F 26 1848;49-Ja 28 1854

VOLKSBLATT und freiheits freund. d 1859+
1859-Ja 1901 as Pittsburger volksblatt
In German
pub 1898+
KHi D 1 1926
P Je 25 1889-1914;16-18
PAg Ag 1894-S 1899;F 1901+
PPi F 1901+
PPiHi Ag 12 1869

Der VOLKSFREUND. *See* Jewish volksfreund

Y WASG. w 1873-88‖?
In Welsh
MWA D 22 1883

WASHINGTON banner. [Allegheny] w N 18 1841-
PPiHi F 5,S 17,O 1 1842

WELSH American. *See* Druid

WESTERN emporium. [Allegheny] w Ap 30 1838-
Title varies slightly
DLC Ap 30 1838
MWA Je 12 1839

WESTERN journal. w 1827-
OOxM Ag 23,O 18 1828

ZAJEDNIČAR. w 1905-20‖
In Croatian
IU Je 1915-Jl 28 1920

PITTSTON

Pittston COMET and Wyoming Valley journal. w 1870-77‖
1870-73 as Comet
PWbW [1872]

DOLLAR weekly news. *See under* Wilkes-Barre

Pittston GAZETTE. w Ag 1850-1900‖
Title varies: Pittston gazette and Susquehanna anthracite journal; Pittston gazette and Luzerne anthracite journal; Pittston gazette weekly
pub 1866-1900
MWA N 5 1852;Jl 25 1856
P Jl 1889-Je 1900
PSuHi Jl 28 1858
PWbW 1850-74
PWcHi Jl 21 1854

Pittston GAZETTE. d Je 1882+
pub 1898+
P [Mr 1913-S 1921]
PScrHi My 29 1929;Ag 2 1930
PWbW [1903+]

PLAINFIELD

Plainfield TIMES. *See* Valley times (Newville)

PENNSYLVANIA (*Continued*)

PLYMOUTH

Plymouth STAR. w 1869-99||?
PWbW [1883-97]

Plymouth TRIBUNE. d 1883-93||?
PWbW 1891-93

VIENYBE. *See under* Brooklyn, N.Y.

POINT MARION

Point Marion NEWS. w Jl 12 1928+
pub [1928]+
PUn Jl 12-26 1928

PORT ALLEGHENY

Port Allegheny ARGUS. *See* Reporter-argus

REPORTER-ARGUS. w 1902+
1902-18 as Port Allegheny argus
pub 1918+

PORT CARBON

Port Carbon GAZETTE. w 1831-32||?
United with Schuylkill county advocate (Pottsville) to form Schuylkill advocate and Port Carbon gazette (Pottsville)
MWA Ag 22 1832

PORTLAND

Portland ENTERPRISE. w 1874+
PEC 1907-08

POTTSTOWN

Pottstown ADVERTISER. w 1873?-79||
PPot Mr 30 1878;Ja 1 1879

*Der ADVOCAT und bauern anzeiger. w Jl 19 1820-F 7 1827||
1820-My 11 1825 as Der Advocat
In German
PPotM complete

AMERICAN star. w Mr 3,1829-
CSmH Ag 31 1830
DLC Mr 3,17-24 1829
PPot N 15 1831

BERKS, Chester and Montgomery ledger. *See* Montgomery ledger

BLADE. w D 13 1890+
pub 1893-94;96-1910[13]+
PPot 1890

Pottstown daily CHRONICLE. d 1879-
PPot [1879-80]
PPotW [1879]

Pottstown GAZETTE. w 1834-
PPot O 29 1834

Pottstown HERALD. w Ap 3 1896-
PPot Ap 3 1896;Ag 6 1897

Pottstown morning HERALD. d Ag 7 1933+
pub [1933]+

Pottstown JOURNAL. w Ap? 1839-N 10 1843||
DLC Ja 8 1840
PNoHi Je 2 1841

Pottstown JOURNAL. w Ja 29 1881-85||?
PPot [1881]Ap 4 1885

LAFAYETTE aurora. w Ja 29 1825-
PNoHi 1825-[27]

Daily Pottstown LEDGER. d O 1 1873-1924||
pub [1874]-1919
P Jl 1889-Je 1912;O 1917-Mr 1920
PNoHi [1873-74]
PPeS Mr 14 1876;Ap 23 1880
PPot O 1 1873;Ag 25 1874;Jl 4-5 1876[80-82]Jl 14 1883;Ap 26,D 13 1890;Ja 28,F 6,9 1895

Pottstown MERCURY and news. d S 29 1931+
1931-Mr 4 1933 as Pottstown mercury
pub 1931+
PP [1932]+
PPeS Ap 21,N 10 1932

MONTGOMERY ledger. w N 10 1843-1906||?
Title varies: Montgomery ledger and Berks and Chester advertiser; Berks, Chester and Montgomery ledger
MWA My 28 1867
P Jl 1889-1912
PNoHi [1853]-62;65-[73]
PPeS S 30 1862;Jl 26 1864;Je 19,Ag 14 1866; Mr 16,Je 8 1875[79-80]N 22 1881;Ap 4 1882;F 26,D 9-23 1884[85]
PPot Jl 17 1844;Ag 22 1849;D 17 1851;O 30 1855;F 21 1865;Jl 10 1866;Jl 11 1876;Mr 10 1885;Ja 10 1888
PPotM [1858]-[61-64;66]-[69-72]

*MONTGOMERY republican. w Mr 4 1820-
DLC Ag,S 23,N 4-11 1828;D 24 1829
PPotM [1828-29]

Pottstown daily NEWS. d 1887-Mr 4 1933||
United with Pottstown mercury to form Pottstown mercury and news
pub 1889-1933
PNoHi Ap 4 1911
PPeS F 16 1933
PPot D 14 1881;Ag 27,D 13 1890;My 19 1893;F 20 1895

REPUBLICAN. w 1877-
PPot Jl 21 1877

Weekly SALESMAN. w N 30 1912-S 27 1913||
PPotB [1912-13]

Pottstown TARIFFITE and democratic guard. N 22 1843-
DLC N 29 1843;F 14 1844
PPot Je 25 1845

*TIMES and farmers' advertiser. w Jl 1 1819-
1819-My 11 1825 as Pottstown times; My 18 1825-Jl 5 1826 Times and farmers' advocate
MWA O 15 1823;Mr 1 1826
PNoHi [1821]
PPot O 22 1823;Jl 27 1825
PPotM [1821]-[27]

POTTSVILLE

AMERIKANISHER republikaner. w 1855-1909||?
In German
MWA Jl 19 1861
NNHi N 22 1872
PPoHi S 26 1862-S 23 1864;Je 16 1865-N 7 1873;75-92

ANTHRACITE gazette and Schuylkill county advertiser. w 1844-
DLC My 1,Je 12-26,Jl 10-24,Ag 7-14,S 18,O 2-16,N 6,20-27,D 18 1847
MnHi Ag 3 1844
PPi [O 1845-F 5 1848]

Evening CHRONICLE. d 1875-1923||?
NNC [F 28-Mr 12 1876]
PPoHi [1875-1921]

DEMOCRATIC press. w 1845-
Merged with Pottsville emporium
MWA N 26 1846

DEMOCRATIC standard. w 1857-
MWA Ag 16 1862

DEMOKRATISCHE freiheits-presse und Schuylkill Columbia und Northumberland counties anzeiger. 1837-56||
In German
MWA S 7 1838
PPoHi 1838-[47;49]-[51;54-55]

Wednesday DOLLAR journal and Pottsville general advertiser. w My 23 1855-
MWA O 24 1855

Pottsville EMPORIUM. w 1838-Ja 15 1854||
Title varies slightly. United with Mining register and Schuylkill county democrat to form Mining register and Pottsville emporium
DLC Je 20 1840-Ag 17 1844;Ja 9 1847-D 21 1848
MWA F 7 1850;N 18 1852;D 15 1853
MnHi O 5 1844;My 31 1845
OClWHi Jl 19 1845
PBL [1838;40-41]Ap 30 1842[45-47]My 11 1848
PP F 18 1843;Je 18 1850
PPL N 15 1849
PPoHi My 11 1838-[40]43-44
PShH D 3,24-31 1842;O 23 1858
PSuHi N 21-28 1857

Pottsville GAZETTE. w 1834-
PBL [1835]

HERALD of freedom and advocate of the Illinois rail splitter. w
PPoHi Ja 18 1860

JEFFERSON demokrat von Schuylkill county. w 1855-
In German
MWA Mr 22 1862
PPoHi [1855]56

Pottsville JOURNAL. d S 1 1869+
1869-N 16 1909 as Miner's journal
pub 1926+
ICM Je 22 1877
MWA My 22 1871
P Je 1889-1918
PPi Jl 1889-D 12 1891
PPoHi 1869-[81-82;84]-[86-87]-[90]-[98-99]-[1902-03;11]14-[22]
—w ed *See* Miner's journal

MINER'S journal. w Mr 17 1825-1909||?
Title varies: Miners journal and Schuylkill coal and navigation register; Miners journal and Pottsville general advertiser
CL F 19 1848
CSmH S 11 1830
DLC 1834;Mr-D 1839;41-43;45-53;55-My 11 1875
MB Jl 18,Ag 1,O 17 1835;Ja 16,F 13-27,Ap 9 1836;Je 3,Ag 19 1837
MWA Mr 31 1825-Mr[Ap 15-O 21]1826-S 8,O 20-27 1827;O 30 1830;Ja 5,F 16 1833;N 22 1834; Ap 18,Je 27,S 12 1835;Ja 13,Mr 24 1838[Mr 23-Je 22 1839]My 2 1840;48-D 15 1849;Mr 10(supp)1860;Mr 10 1866;Mr 7,Je 20 1868-[69]-N 5 1875;D 1 1876;F 8,Mr 22 1878;Jl 25,D 12 1879
MnHi S 9 1843;Je 1 1844
NNHi Jl 25 1857;Je 27 1863;D 12-19 1868;Ja 1869;My 12,Je 7,Ag 28 1873
NcU Ja 13 1855
NjR Je 5 1852
OClWHi Ja 9 1858
PBL [1836-37]
PHi 1825-[33]41-50
PLewL Je 1 1833
PP S 26 1857
PPL [1825-29;31-33]Ja 4-11 1851
PPi N 9 1839-Ag 8 1845;Ja 10 1846-47;56
PPoHi [1830]-[36;38]-62;64-97
PPoU [1825]-[28]
PPot My 19 1860
PShH [1838]-44

MINER'S journal. d *See* Pottsville journal

MINING register and Pottsville emporium. w Ja 1850-
1850-Ja 15 1854 as Mining register and Schuylkill county democrat
DLC O 30-N 6 1852
MWA D 14 1850;F 28 1852;O 12 1861
PP My 21 1853
PPL F 22 1851

Pottsville morning PAPER. d O 27 1922+
pub 1922+
PCC Jl 26 1926
PNoHi Jl 28-29 1926

Pottsville REPUBLICAN. d O 1884+
Title varies: Pottsville evening republican
pub O 28 1884+
P Je 7 1889;N 1909-Mr 1933;35+
PDoHi [1920]
PEr Jl 28 1926
PHHi O 7 1914
PP [1927]+
PPeS Jl 28 1926
PPoHi 1907-21
PWp O 7 1914
—w ed *See* Schuylkill republican

SATURDAY night review. w 1889-1918||?
PPoHi [1901-[03]

SCHUYLKILL advocate and Port Carbon gazette. w Ja 5 1831-
1831-32? as Schuylkill county advocate
CSmH My 18 1831;F 15 1832
MWA Mr 2,Jl 15 1831;F 13 1833

Schuylkill county advocate. *See* Schuylkill advocate and Port Carbon gazette

SCHUYLKILL republican. w 1872-1920||?
1872-84 pub in Minersville
pub [1872]-[74]-81[87]-91
MWA D 17(supp)1879
P Je 13 1889-Je 1910
PPoHi [1886]87[92]-[94]-1911
PPoR [1872]-[74]-81
—d ed *See* Pottsville republican

Pottsville STANDARD. w 1859-1907||?
MWA Ag 25 1866
P Jl 30 1870
PPoHi 1872-[74-76]

PROVIDENCE

Papers published in Providence are listed under Scranton

PUNXSUTAWNEY

MAHONING VALLEY spirit. *See* Punxsutawney spirit

Punxsutawney NEWS. w O 21 1885+
1885-88? as Punxsutawney Valley news
MWA Ag 7 1889
P Jl 10 1889+

Punxsutawney PLAINDEALER. w Jl 13 1868-71||
PMiltS Ag 6 1869-O 5 1871

Punxsutawney SPIRIT. w,d 1873+
Je 1873-76 as Mahoning Valley spirit(w)
pub 1873+

Punxsutawney VALLEY news. *See* Punxsutawney news

QUAKERTOWN

Quakertown FREE PRESS. w Ag 13 1881+
pub 1881+

PATRIOT and reformer. w 1882-88||
In German
PDoHi [1882-86]
PPeS F 23,Ag 31,D 14 1882;Ja 10-24,F 7,Mr 20 1884;F 12,Je 18,O 1,15,D 31 1885;O 14,N 18,D 2 1886;Ja 5 1888
PQF [1886]87

QUARRYVILLE

POST. *See* Quarryville sun

Quarryville SUN. w,tw,sw 1885+
1885-O 1891 as Post
w 1885-Ap 1903;tw My 1903-My 1907
pub 1891+

READING

*Reading ADLER. w Ja 3 1797-Mr 22 1913||
1797-Ja 10 1797 as Der Unpartheyische Reading adler; Ja 17 1797-1800 Der Unpartheyische Readinger adler; 1801-68 Readinger adler
A preliminary no. was issued N 29 1796 as no. 1
In German
MWA 1821-S 12 1826;27-1913
MiU-C F 4,Mr 18 1845;Ag 29 1876
P O 6,20 1829;N 13 1883;85-Je 1912
P-M O 20 1829
PB S 2,O 28 1867
PLewL Mr 5 1839
PNoHi 1830-32
PPeS Ja 30,N 6 1821;Mr 11 1823;F 14 1826; Mr 9 1830;My 22 1832;Ja 30,F 27 1838;Ap 18 1865
PPot S 4,O 16 1821;N 9 1824
PRHi 1821-97

ALT Berks - Der stern im Osten. w Ja 28 1840-44||?
In German
PHi 1842-44

BANNER von Berks. w D 1864-1909||
In German
P Je 5 1888
PPoU 1864-[67]
PRHi D 1 1864-88

*BERKS and Schuylkill journal. w Je 8 1816-1910||
CSmH S 11 1830
DLC Ap 14 1827;Ja 12 1828;D 5,26 1829;Ja 2,D 25 1830;D 22 1832;N 14 1840
IU My 28 1825-[26]-My 19 1827;My 17 1834-My 9 1835;My 12 1838-Ap 1844
MWA My 3 1823;Ag 15 1829;Mr 4 1854;D 4 1869
NNHi S 8 1849;Jl 25 1863;Mr 1 1873

PENNSYLVANIA (*Continued*)

READING—*Continued*

*BERKS and Schuylkill journal. w 1816-1910||
—*Continued*
P [Ag 18-25,O 25 1821;Je 1822-F 1837]D 27 1862;Ja 3-10 1863;Mr 18,Ap 22-29 1865
PBL [1821-22;33-34]
PPeS S 18,O 30 1880;Jl 9,S 24 1881;Jl 25 1885; Ap 1886
PPoU [1826]-28
PPot Ag 15 1821[22]Mr 20,My 29,Jl 3 1824
PRHi 1821-97;1902;04-10
PRN [1821-24]

BERKS county free press. *See* Democratic press

BERKS county press. *See* Democratic press

Reading CHRONICLE. w 1822-36||
My 1822-23 as Chronicle of times and Berks and Schuylkill advertiser; 1823-33 Chronicle of times. Merged with Berks county press, later Democratic press
CSmH Jl 2 1823
MWA My 31 1825;O 20 1829
N O 22 1833
P S 17 1823;D 24 1824-D 8 1835
PAlCh [1825]
PBL [1828]
PPoU [1822]-[24;29-30]
PPot [1822;24]Jl 1 1828;Je 23 1829
PRE [1828]-[31]

DEMOCRAT. w 1868-69||
PRHi Ap 22 1868-S 30 1869

Reading DEMOCRAT. w 1894-99||
PRH [1894-97]

DEMOCRATIC press. w Ap 24 1830-N 1865||
1830-34? as Berks county free press; 1835- Berks county press
CSmH S 11 1830
MWA Mr 5 1844;S 24 1861
NhD D 4 1849
P Mr 31 1835-Ap 14 1840
PHHi Je 10 1845
PPL Jl 14 1846
PShH Je 30 1854

Der Readinger DEMOKRAT. w O 4 1826-F 1835||
In German
MiU-C O 10 1827

Evening DISPATCH. d 1863-68||?
United with Daily times to form Times-dispatch, later Reading times
MWA S 11 1868

Reading EAGLE. d Ja 28 1868+
pub 1868+
DLC 1898
MWA Ja 28 1913;Ja 28 1914;Ja 28 1915
OHi O 11 1876
P Jl 1932+
PHHi D 22 1909
PPeS S 3 1873;Ja 28-29 1874
PPot My 28 1895
PR 1904-[06]33+
PRHi [1906;23]
PRT [1929]-33

Reading EAGLE. w 1878-1927||?
pub [1878]-91;1919-26
P N 13 1883;95-[1912]
PPeS Je 23 1917;Ja 11 1919;N 6 1920;Ag 11 1923;Ja 15,F 9 1924

FATHER ABRAHAM. w,ir 1864-
PPeS Ag 30-N 8 1864
PPot S 18 1866
PRHi Ag 1-N 15 1864

GAZETA Readingska. w 1909+
In Polish
pub 1909+

Reading GAZETTE and democrat. w 1840-78||
1840-48 as Reading gazette
DLC O 30 1852
MWA Jl 5 1851;My 22 1852;S 21 1861
NhD D 8 1849;Mr 16 1850;Je 26 1852
NjR Je 24 1843
P Ap 22 1843-Ja 1848;56-Ap 1858
PPeS Ja 24 1874
PPot Ap 22 1865
PRE [1840]-78
PRHi 1850-78
PSuHi S 25 1858

HERALD-TELEGRAM. d S 1881-1923||
1881-98 as Morning herald; 1898-1920 Evening herald
PPeS Jl 4 1887
PR 1882

JACKSON democrat. w Ap 26 1826-
DLC Ap 26 1826

JEFFERSON democrat. w 1838-48||
United with Reading gazette to form Reading gazette and democrat
DLC S 15 1840
PPL Ag 10 1847

Weekly LEADER. w 1860-61||
PRHi [1860]

Der LIBERALE beobachter und Berks, Montgomery und Schuylkill counties allgemeiner anzeiger. w S 10 1839-My 10 1864||
In German
PHi complete
PPeS Ja 5 1841;N 25-D 16,30 1856-F 10 1857

Reading daily NEWS. d 1880-1914||
United with Reading times to form News-times, later Reading times
PRHi [1885-86]

Reading NEWS. w 1881-1909||
PRHi 1881-1907

NEWS-TIMES. *See* Reading times

PEOPLE'S advocate. w
PWbW Ag 22 1832

Die Reading POST. d 1868-1912||?
In German
MWA Ag 26-28 1876

REPUBLIKANER von Berks. w Ja 6 1869-F 1 1899||
Merged with Kutztown journal (Kutztown)
In German
PPeS O 14 1869

Daily REVIEW. d 1894-99||?
PRHi [1895]-[97]

SPIRIT of Berks. w 1876-81||
PR 1876-80
PRHi [1873]-81

STARS and stripes. w F 1918-Je 13 1919||
PRHi complete

Reading TELEGRAM. d 1887-1920||
United with Morning herald to form Herald-telegram
PPeS N 11 1918
PR [1904]-[06;19]

Reading TIMES. d Jl 1858+
1858-70 as Daily times; 1870-81 Times-dispatch; 1881-1914 Reading times; 1914-23 News-times
pub [1924]30+
InRE Ag 10 1877
MWA D 6 1864;Mr 6,Ag 30 1878
P Jl 1889-Je 1897;Jl 1898-1918;20+
PPeS N 3 1880;Ja 1 1885;N 7 1888
PPot N 3 1880;S 20-21 1881
PR 1859-60;S 3 1861-Ag 1862;1904[05]
PRHi [1858]-83;85-[1914]-[23]
PShH Mr 1 1859

Reading TRIBUNE. d 1923-26||?
PRHi 1923-[26]

Der UNPARTHEYISCHE Readinger adler. *See* Reading adler

Der WAHREN democrat. w
In German
P-M Ja 1 1862;Ja 1 1864;Ja 1 1865;Ja 1 1866

*Der WELT bothe und wahre republikaner von Berks, Schuylkill und Lebanon counties. w 1810-
In German
MWA F 6 1822;Ag 6 1823;D 26 1827
P-M Mr 20 1822
PPeS D 4 1822;N 24 1824

RENO

Reno TIMES. w N 30 1865-
MWA N 30,D 21 1865-Ja 4,Mr 15-29,Ap 12 1866

RENOVA

Evening NEWS. d S 21 1883-Ag 1913||?
PNarD [1883-84]
PReK 1884-89

Renova daily RECORD. d O 4 1907+
pub [1907]-[34]+

RIDGEWAY

Ridgeway ADVOCATE. w 1871-1932||
1871-82? as Elk county advocate
P 1898-1912;17-My 5 1932

ELK county advocate. w 1850-
MWA N 20 1852;Je 2 1855

ELK county advocate. w N 25? 1868-
MWA Mr 5 1869

ELK county advocate. 1871-82 *See* Ridgeway advocate

ELK county democrat. w Ag 1869-1924||?
1869-98 as Elk democrat. Merged with Ridgeway advocate
P Jl 11 1889-1912

ELK democrat. *See* Elk county democrat

RIEGELSVILLE

Riegelsville STANDARD. w 1885-86||
PDoHi [1885-86]

ROCHESTER

BEAVER FALLS chronicle. w O 12 1839-Ag 25 1840||
Followed by Beaver county palladium (Beaver Falls)
DLC Je 4 1840
PPi Jl 23,Ag 8 1840

ROCKDALE

Rockdale HERALD. w O 15 1898+
pub [1898]-[1901]-[09;11]-[15]+

ROCKLEDGE

BREEZE. w F 3 1934+
pub 1934+

NORTHEAST breeze. w Ag 4 1927+
pub 1927+

ROYERSFORD

Weekly ADVERTISER. w F 22 1890+
pub [1890]+

SAINT CLAIR

SPLINTERS. w 1894-1909||?
PPoHi [1897]-[1903]

ST. MARY'S

ELK county gazette. w S 24 1867+
P 1928-Je 1932
PPiHi Ja 19 1933+

ELK enterprise. w 1905-15||?
P Ja 19 1905-12

Saint Mary's weekly HERALD. w 1887-1904||
N 1891-Je 24 1899 as Kersey weekly herald (Kersey)
P Je 30 1889-Je 1904

KERSEY weekly herald. *See* St. Mary's weekly herald

SALEM

VILLAGE register. w
PShH [1842]-[44]

SALISBURY

SOMERSET county star. w 1865-
PPiHi 1903-Ag 1 1929

SALTSBURG

Saltsburg PRESS. w S 5 1875+
pub 1886+

SANDY LAKE

Sandy Lake BREEZE. w O 1902+
pub 1902+

Sandy Lake NEWS. w F 4 1876-Je 16 1898||
PSanB [1876;78]-93[96]-[98]

SAYRE

Evening TIMES. w 1891+
pub 1921+

VALLEY record. d 1905-07||
Merged with Evening times
PToHi My 8-9 1905

SCHUYLKILL HAVEN

Schuylkill Haven CALL. w 1891+
pub 1910+
P 1892-1912

SCHWENKVILLE

Schwenkville ITEM. w S 7 1877+
1877-My 20 1881 as Weekly item
pub 1877-[80]98-1903;05;07-12;14-15;18+
NN My 19-Jl 7 1882
PNoHi 1877-81;Ja 5,F 2 1883;Ag 26 1887;D 21 1888
PPot F 15 1878
PPeS [1880]F 25,Je 24,S 23-30 D 2,16 1881[82] Ja 5,F 2,Mr 9,Jl 6,Ag 3 1883;S 13,O 24,N 7,D 12-19 1884[85]Mr 4 1915;D 10 1931;Ap 21 1932

SCOTTDALE

Scottdale INDEPENDENT-OBSERVER. w 1879+
1879-1926 as Scottdale independent
pub [1879+]

OBSERVER. w 1900-26||
United with Scottdale independent to form Scottdale independent-observer
PScI complete

SCRANTON

Scranton CITY journal. *See* Scranton journal

COUNTY mirror and Lackawannian. [Providence] w 1845-
PScrHi Mr 10 1847
PWbW Mr 14 1846

DOLLAR weekly news. *See under* Wilkes-Barre

Sunday morning FREE PRESS. w Je 9 1872-1901||?
MWA F 18 1877
N S 22 1872
NbHi F 16 1879
POlG [1877]78[80-81]
PScrT [1878]-[95]

HERALD of the union. w Ap 3 1853-59||
1853-56 as Lackawanna herald (title varies slightly)
CtY [1853-56]
PScrWi Ja 21 1858

Scranton JOURNAL. w 1867-84||?
1867-75 as Scranton City journal
PScrHi O 27 1883

LACKAWANNA democrat. w 1882-84||
PScrHi complete

LACKAWANNA herald. *See* Herald of the union

LACKAWANNA register. w Je 4 1863-69||
MWA Je 9 1864
P Ja 12-19,F 9-16,Mr 9,30-Ap 6 1869
PScrG Ap 15 1865
PScrHi 1863-Je 6 1867
PWbW [1865-67]

Il MINATORE. (The Miner) w 1912+
In Italian
pub O 1928+

MINER. *See* Il Minatore

PENNSYLVANIA (*Continued*)

SCRANTON—*Continued*

NARODNA wola. (People's will) sw 1913+
In Ukrainian
CSt-H [1933]
IU D 6 1917+
NN Mr 19 1918-24;26
PPiHi D 31 1931-Mr 1932

Scranton Sunday morning NEWS. w 1878-1901‖?
PWbN D 25 1880-81

Scranton evening NEWS. d 1882‖
PWbN Jl 12-N 11 1882

Scranton daily NEWS. d Ag 1913-16‖
PHsHi My 25 1915
PScr [1913-15]

Scranton daily NEWS and Hyde Park advertiser. d 1861-62‖
PScrHi Mr 28,Ap 3 1861

PEOPLE'S will. *See* Narodna wola

PROVIDENCE register. w 1876-1917‖
1876-99? as Register (Providence)
PHsHi F 3 1917
PScrHi S 30 1911

Weekly REGISTER. w 1863-69‖
NNHi S 16 1869

Scranton REPUBLICAN. w 1856-1915‖
MWA Je 2 1864;Mr 16 1883
NbHi D 18 1872;Ja 5 1875
PScrG S 26 1862
PScrHi O 6 1859;S 8 1862;Mr 27 1865
PWbW 1856-64;66-69

Scranton REPUBLICAN. d N 1 1867+
1910-Mr 1915 as Tribune-republican
pub 1867+
DLC 1898-Je 1901
ICM Jl 20 1893
MWA My 19 1869
NNHi Jl 13 1871;Mr 19,My 6,Jl 24,N 29 1873
P Je 20 1891+
PHHi F 3 1897
PHsHi S 10 1869;S 30 1916;Ag 9 1929
POlG [1872-73]75
PScr 1871-[98]-[1900]-[11-12]-[14-15]-[26-27]+
PScrHi Ap 5 1867;O 13 1869[83;85]-[1914;18-19]
PWbW 1877;Jl-D 1879;82;Mr-O 1883;84;Mr 31, My-D 1895;1908-14

SCRANTONIAN. w 1897+
pub [1897]+

SLOVAK defense. *See* Slovenská obrana

SLOVENSKÁ obrana. (Slovak defense) sw 1913+
In Slovak
IU F 17 1933+

Scranton SUN. d 1926-32‖
PDaH [1926-32]
PScrHi [1927-32]
PScrT 1929-[32]

Scranton TIMES. d 1870+
Title varies: Scranton evening times
pub [1895]-[1934]+
P Je 1891+
POlG [1873-74;76-77]-[79]-[81]-[85]
PP 1928+
PScr 1893-96
PScrHi 1872-87[91;1902;16-19;25;27-29;32]
PScrWi 1874-[78]

Scranton TRIBUNE. d F 1891-Ja 31 1910‖
United with Scranton republican to form Tribune-republican, later Scranton republican
P complete
PScr [1892]-1909
PScrHi O 8 1904;Mr 24,O 18 1909

TRIBUNE-REPUBLICAN. *See* Scranton republican

Scranton TRUTH. d Ap 1885-Mr 1915‖
Ct Je 5 1909
ICM Jl 15,19-20 1893
P Je 1904-F 1915
PScr [1893-94]
PScrHi 1885-87;Mr 4 1889;Ja 5 1905;Ap 8,O 18 1909;S 27 1911;My 30 1912
WHi Je 2-D 1896

Scranton WOCHENBLATT. w 1863-1918‖
In German
PScrHi 1865-[1918]
PScrW 1865-[1918]

SELINSGROVE

JOURNAL-TIMES. *See* Selinsgrove times

SNYDER county tribune. w 1854+
pub 1854+
P D 20 1877+
PMiC 1888;94;96;98;1900;02;04-05;07-10;23-27
PMiCo 1930+
PSuHi My 30 1889;Ap 15 1926

*Selinsgrove TIMES. w 1815+
1815-22 as Union (New Berlin); 1822-52 Union times; 1852-58 Journal-times
pub 1859+
CSmH S 10 1830
P N 12 1828;Ja 25 1833-Ja 6 1843
PHi [1847]
PLewJ [1832]
PLewL [1824]-[28]-[31-34;36;41;44-45;1930-33]
PMiC [1925;27-28]
PMiP [1850]-[54]
PMiR 1893-1916
PNc [1832]-[35]
PPL Ag 17 28 1847
PPiHi My 24 1833;Ap 17 1835
PSuHi Ag 1 1862[1918]24

UNION times. *See* Selinsgrove times

SELLERSVILLE

Sellersville HERALD. w Ja 1897+
pub 1897+

SEWICKLEY

HERALD. w S 1 1903+
Title varies: Weekly herald; Sewickley herald
pub 1903+
PSew S 9 1903+

Sewickley VALLEY. w 1895-1912‖
PSew Ap 2 1910-My 30 1912

VALLEY gossip. m D 1880-D 1881‖?
PSew 1880-81

SHAMOKIN

ADVERTISER. *See* Shamokin weekly times

Shamokin DISPATCH. *See* Shamokin news-dispatch

Shamokin HERALD. w 1862-1918‖?
P Je 28 1889-Je 1894
PShH Ag 24-S 7 1865;F 18,Jl 29 1875[82]-[89]

Shamokin daily HERALD. d 1887+
pub 1897+
P Je 1889-Je 1894

Shamokin daily NEWS. d 1893-S 17? 1933‖
United with Shamokin dispatch to form Shamokin news-dispatch
pub 1893+

Shamokin NEWS-DISPATCH. d 1886+
N 21 1886-S 18 1933 as Shamokin dispatch
pub [1886]-[89]1922+

Shamokin weekly TIMES. w 1872-89‖
Ja-Je 13 1872 as Advertiser
PSchN [1880]-[83-84]-[87]-99

SHARON

Sharon EAGLE. w 1875-1913‖?
1875-85? as Mercer county eagle
P Je 1889-Je 1910

MERCER county eagle. *See* Sharon eagle

SHARPSBURG

Sharpsburg and Etna HERALD. 1878+
pub 1895+

SHARPSVILLE

Sharpsville ADVERTISER. w 1870-78‖?
OClWHi F 14 1877

SHEFFIELD

Sheffield OBSERVER. w Je 1902+
pub 1902+
MWA Ap 14 1921-26
OClWHi Ap 14,28,My 12,26,Je 16 1921-26

SHENANDOAH

Shenandoah weekly HERALD. w 1870-1907‖?
Title varies slightly
MWA Je 13 1872;D 17(supp)1879
P Jl 1889-99
PMcC D 29 1876;Je 15 1877
PPoHi [1870-83]
PShH [1876-77]

Evening HERALD. d 1885+
P Je 1889-S 21 1907
PPoHi [1890-94]

NEWS budget. w 1892+
pub [1892]+

SHICKSHINNY

MOUNTAIN echo. w 1873+
pub 1916+
PWbW [1882-83]

SHINGLEHOUSE

OSWAYO VALLEY mail. w 1886+
PCtHi [1923]-[30]

SHIPPENSBURG

CHRONICLE. w F 4 1875-S 1 1927‖
1875-D 19 1884 as Democratic chronicle. United with Shippensburg news to form News-chronicle
P 1880-My 1888;1918-27
PShiN [1879]-1927

DEMOCRATIC chronicle. *See* Chronicle

FREE PRESS. w Ap 18? 1833-
DLC N 28 1833;F 20,Je 26 1834

Shippensburg HERALD, and Cumberland and Franklin county weekly family visitor. w Je 26 1839-
DLC Ap 24 1839
MWA Jl 10 1839

INTELLIGENCER. w S 19 1833-
DLC S 19 1833

NEWS-CHRONICLE. w,sw Ap 26 1844+
1844-52 as Weekly news; 1852-Ag 31 1927 Shippensburg news
w 1844-Ag 1927
pub 1849-[51-52]-N 1862;S 21 1867[79]+
NNHi Mr 16 1861-Jl 5 1862
NcD Ja 12-19 1927
P 1871-Ja 5 1916;18-Je 1932

VALLEY sentinel. w 1864-73‖?
MWA Ag 24 1866

SHIRLEYSBURG

Shirleysburg weekly HERALD. w 1874-77‖
1874-75 as Mount Union herald (Mount Union)
PPhJ [1876-77]

SKIPPACK

MONTGOMERY transcript. w 1888+
PPeS [N 1894+]

Der NEUTRALIST. w 1848-Jl 27 1898‖
Title varies slightly
In German
PDoHi Jl 21 1863
PNoHi Ag 22 1848;Jl 3,24,S 25 1849;My 11 1858;Ja 13 1863;Ap 3 1864;My 15 1866;Ja 8 1879;D 19 1888
PPeS N 30 1852;My 3 1853;D 4-11 1855;Ja 15, Jl 22,O 28 1856;F 17 1857[58]Ja 25 1859;F 28 1860;Ap 23 1861;Ap 15,O 14,D 16 1862;Ag 4 1863;Ap 12,Jl 5,Ag 23,S 20,O 25 1864;Ap 25, My 2,Ag 8,O 17-24 1865;Ja 16,F 6-13,N 6 1866;D 4 1872;Ag 23 1876;Mr 14,Ap 11 1877; Ja 2,Ap 3,My 15,N 20 1878[79-80]S 21-28 1881;Ag 16,S 6 1882;Ap 2 1884;F 4,N 4 1885;D 29 1886;Ja 12 1887;Ag 5 1891;Ja 6 1892;S 6 1893;D 5 1894;N 13-20 1895;Ja 29,S 23 1896;F 10,17,Mr 17,Ap 14 1897;Mr 9 1898

SLATINGTON

Slatington NEWS. w S 2 1868+
pub 1868+

SLIPPERY ROCK

Slippery Rock SIGNAL. w Jl 1 1925+
PGcR 1925+

SMETHPORT

MCKEAN citizen. w Je 15? 1854-
MWA My 5 1855

MCKEAN county democrat. *See* McKean democrat

MCKEAN county journal. w
PW Ap 30 1836

MCKEAN county miner. w Mr 12 1858+
1858-63 as Bradford miner (Bradford); 1863-68? Miner
pub 1861+
MWA Je 27 1863
P Jl 1889-1912;18-32
PBr My 19,Ap 9 1858

MCKEAN democrat. w 1860+
1860-64? as McKean county democrat
pub 1875+
MWA Ap 14 1864

MCKEAN miner. *See* McKean county miner

MCKEAN yeoman and Elk county advertiser. w
PBr My 29 1847

MINER. *See* McKean county miner

Forester and Smethport REGISTER. w Ap 21 1832-
DLC N 22 1832
MWA Jl 28 1832
PAtM Ag 24 1833
PHi [1832-33]

SETTLER. w O 12 1839-
DLC N 23 1839
PBr Ag 13 1840;Je 11 1842
PW Jl 2 1840;Jl 8 1842

SOMERSET

Somerset DEMOCRAT. w Jl 4 1853+
P Jl 10 1889-1912

Somerset HERALD. w,sw 1827+
Title varies: Herald-republican; Herald and whig
w 1827-1929?
CSmH S 14 1830
MWA Mr 29 1854
NjHi D 9 1828;Ap 27 1830
P O 27 1829;Je 1890+
PEbHi F 18 1880;S 27 1881
PJR Je 22 1927;Je 12-19 1929
WHi Ag 1 1843

Somerset daily HERALD. d 1929+
PPiHi D 5 1931-Ja 8 1932

MEYERSDALE commercial. w 1878-1912‖?
P [1889]-1912

Somerset PATRIOT. w
P Jl 17 1833

Somerset weekly VISITOR. w 1846-
MWA N 20 1850
P Jl 16,D 3 1851
WHi Ja 26 1853

PENNSYLVANIA (*Continued*)

SOMERSET—*Continued*

*Somerset WHIG. w O? 1813-50||?
Merged with Somerset herald
CSmH Ag 18 1830
DLC Ag 8 1827;F 27 1828;Jl 1-22,Ag 12,S 2-9,23-30,O 21,N 5,25 1829;Ja 6 1830
OClWHi Ap 18,My 16,O 8 1838
P O 1 1828
P-M F 1,15,O 4 1826;S 2,23 1829;D 16 1845

SOUDERTON

GERMANIA gazette. *See* Souderton independent

Souderton INDEPENDENT. w Ag 16 1878+
1878-Ap 9 1881 as Germania gazette
1878-Ap 9 1881 in German
pub 1878+
PP My 12 1883
PPeS Jl 1 1932

SOUTH BETHLEHEM

Papers published in South Bethlehem are listed under Bethlehem

SPANGLER

Spangler TIMES. w 1924+
pub 1924+

SPARTANSBURG

Spartansburg SENTINEL. w 1895-1924||?
P Ag 29 1902-D 20 1912

SPRING CITY

INTERBOROUGH press. w O 10 1913+
pub [1917]+

Spring City SUN. w 1872-Ja 10 1907||
PSprI [1887]-[1901]03-11
PWcT [1894]-[96]

SPRINGTOWN

Springtown weekly TIMES. w 1885-1918||
NcD O 26 1889
PSpF complete

STATE COLLEGE

CENTRE daily times. w,d 1898+
My 2 1898-Mr 1934 as State College times (w)
pub 1898+
PStP My 12 1898;My 1923[34-35]+

State College TIMES. *See* Centre daily times

STEELTON

Steelton ADVOCATE-VERDICT. w 1887-1907||?
1887-99? as Steelton advocate
PHHi [1889-90]

Steelton ITEM. w 1875-85||
PHHi [1879]-85

Steelton PRESS. w 1890-1912||
Negro
P Jl 1903-12

Steelton REPORTER. w My 1882-1912||
P Je 1889-1912
PHHi [1882]-[1907]

STRASBURG

Strasburg BEE. w 1851-
PLaHi F 14,Ap 24 1852;Je 11 1853

Strasburg HERALD. w 1858-61||
PLaHi Ap 16 1859;F 4 1860

Strasburg NEWS. w N 3 1898+
pub 1898+

STROUDSBURG

JEFFERSONIAN. *See* East Stroudsburg press and Jeffersonian (East Stroudsburg)

MONROE democrat. w S 6 1836-Je 26 1918||
United with Stroudsburg times to form Stroudsburg times-democrat, later Monroe record and times democrat
DLC O 26,D 21 1839
MWA S 17 1846;D 2 1852
P Je 27 1889-Je 1912;17-18
PMilO F 1 1872;F 3,N 17 1875
PStrR [1864-65]-[70-71]-[78-79]-[83]87-[99; 1907]-18

MONROE journal. w 1880-82||?
PStrR [1880]-[82]

MONROE record. w Mr 5 1908-Jl 1 1920||
United with Stroudsburg times-democrat to form Monroe record and times democrat
pub 1908-19

MONROE record and times democrat. w Jl 20 1888-1926||
1888-Je 1918 as Stroudsburg times; Jl 1918-Je 24 1920 Stroudsburg times-democrat
pub Jl 1920-26
P 1917-23
PStrR 1888[89-92;97]1902-20

Morning PRESS. d Mr 19 1913-Je 1 1929||
United with Record and times democrat to form Record and morning press, later Record
PStrR complete

RECORD. d Ap 2 1894+
1894-Ag 1907 as Stroudsburg daily times; S 1907-F 1917 Daily times and democrat; F 23 1917-Je 1920 Times-democrat; Jl 1920-Je 1928 Record and times democrat; Jl 1929-Ja 1930 Record and morning press
pub 1894-99[1901]04;06-[14]+

Daily RECORD. d Je 3 1909-Jl 1 1920||
United with Times-democrat to form Record and times democrat, later Record
PStrR complete

Stroudsburg TIMES. w *See* Monroe record and times democrat

Stroudsburg daily TIMES. *See* Record

TIMES-DEMOCRAT. d *See* Record

TIMES-DEMOCRAT. w *See* Monroe record . . .

SUGAR GROVE

ADVERTISER and home journal. w Ag 9 1873-77||
PSugW [1873-77]

Sugar Grove INDEPENDENT. w Mr 28 1878-79||?
PSugW [1878-79]

Sugar Grove JOURNAL. m Mr 31 1849-
PSugW Mr 31,O 24 1849;F 29,Mr 19 1853

Sugar Grove NEWS. w 1884-89||
PSugW [1885-89]

WARREN county item. w
PSugW [1891 97-1900]

WARREN county record. w 1902-06||?
PSugW [1902]Mr 24 1904

SUMMIT

CRUSADER. w Ja 1852-53||
CSmH Ja 27 1853
PJR Mr 3 1853

SUMMIT HILL

Weekly INTELLIGENCER. w 1874-76||
PMcC [1876]

SUMNEYTOWN

Der ADVOCAT und Montgomery county anzeiger. w Ap 27 1827-Ap 27 1829||
In German
PPot complete

Der BAUERN freund. *See under* Pennsburg

SUNBURY

AMERICAN. w S 1840-S 1916||
1840-48 as Sunbury American and Shamokin journal; 1848-Ap 1879 Sunbury American; Ap 1879-Ap 1880 merged with Sunbury gazette as Sunbury gazette-American
MWA D 3 1864
P D 1877-D 15 1882
PBL S 7-14 1844
PShH [1840-44]
PSuD [1871]-86;1906-[16]
PSuE [1840-43]-[52;66;69]
PSuHi [1840;44;56;58-62;67]1899;1901[02;04-10]
PSuS 1887-92

BEACON. w Mr 15 1830-
CSmH My 17 1830

Sunbury DAILY. d O 6 1872+
Suspended from 1876-79
pub 1890+
P N 1926+
PSuHi [1873]S 28 1881[1903;05;07-12]Jl 11 1922; F 7 1925;S 1 1927

Sunbury GAZETTE. w 1838-Mr 1883||
Title varies: Sunbury gazette and miner's register; Sunbury gazette-American; Sunbury gazette and Northumberland county republican. Merged with Sunbury news
NcU S 7-14 1861;O 17 1863;My 7 1864;Ap 17,O 12,N 8,23 1867;Mr 14,My 16,Je 6-13,Ag 1,21,S 12-O 24,N 7 1868;Ja 2-9,23-F 13 1869
P F 19 1848;Ag 1879-82
PBL S 7 1844;O 25 1845
PSuE [1860]61
PSuHi [1846;49;54;61-62;67-68;80]
PSuY [1827-33]-[38]-[40-41]-[43-46;49-57]58[65-67;76-77]Ap 11 1879-Ap 2 1880[81]-[83]

GAZETTEER. w 1824-33||
P-M S 3 1831
PLewL [1824-26]
PSuHi My 15,19 1825;My 15 1827;My 1 1828

Sunbury ITEM. d 1892+
1892-Ag 28 1904 as Sunbury evening item; Ag 24 1904-My 31 1927 Sunbury daily item
pub [1894]+
PLaF S 2 1925
PSuHi Jl 26 1907;D 3 1910;My 23 1911;Je 16 1928;Jl 7 1931

MID-DAY bulletin. Ja 12 1900-N 22 1901||
PSuS complete

Sunbury NEWS. w 1881-92||?
pub [1883]-[86]
P 1881-O 1888;Mr 1889-My 19 1892
PSuHi [1881]-[83]O 12 1888;D 13 1890

*NORDWESTLICHE post. w N 13 1818-
In German
MWA 1821-Jl 24 1822
PSuHi Jl 15 1827

NORTHUMBERLAND county democrat. w 1861-Ap 26 1923||
NcD Ag 16,S 20,O 11,N 15-22 1861
P Jl 1889-1912
PSuD 1861-74;80-91;99-1923
PSuE My 15 1861-Mr 7 1862
PSuHi Ag 4 1865;D 20 1867;Je 2 1902

NORTHUMBERLAND county republican. w S 2 1900-01||
PSuS [1900-01]

*PUBLICK inquirer. w Ja 1820-
PMiltS S 27 1821[22]

SUSQUEHANNA

Tri-weekly JOURNAL. w,tw 1868-1906||?
1868-Ap 1888 as Susquehanna journal(w)
P [1889]-[1906]

Evening TRANSCRIPT. d 1886+
pub 1886+

SWARTHMORE

Swarthmore NEWS. w 1891-1928||
1891-1914? as Swarthmore
PSC [1927-28]

SWARTHMORE. *See* Swarthmore news

SWISSVALE

HOME news. *See* Swissvale independent

Swissvale INDEPENDENT. w 1923+
1923-30? as Home news
pub 1930+

TAMAQUA

Evening CALL. d
PTC [1914]15

Tamaqua COURIER. w,sw,tw,d 1869+
1869-73? as Saturday courier
w 1869-92;sw 1893-98;tw 1899-1900?
pub [1874]-92[94]-[1900]+
PMcC Ja 22 1876

TARENTUM

Evening TELEGRAM. d 1914-22||
PTaV complete

VALLEY daily news. d Je 27 1904+
pub 1904+

TERRE HILL

Terre Hill TIMES. w Ja 3 1892+
pub 1892+

TIDIOUTE

Tidioute JOURNAL. w 1867-73||?
PW Ja 5 1872

Tidioute NEWS. *See* Tidioute press

Tidioute PRESS. w 1874-1927||?
1894-1918? as Tidioute news
PWC 1894-1910

TIOGA (Philadelphia county)

Papers published in Tioga (Philadelphia county) are listed under Philadelphia

TIOGA (Tioga county)

ARGUS. w 1892+
pub 1910[11]+

TIOGA county express. w 1873-85||?
PTiA [1874-76]-[80]

TIONESTA

DEMOCRATIC vindicator. w Ag 6 1885-Ap 27 1932||
Merged with Forest republican
P [1904]-12
PTioC 1894-1932
PTioF complete

FOREST county bee. *See* Forest republican

FOREST press. w 1867-78||
PTioF [1867]-[78]
PTioH F 5 1867-F 1,11 1868-O 5 1878

FOREST republican. w My 4 1868+
1868-F 24 1869 as Forest county bee
pub 1868—
P Jl 1889+
PTioC 1894+

TITUSVILLE

Titusville COURIER. w 1911-12||
P [1911]12

Titusville GAZETTE and Oil Creek reporter. *See* Titusville weekly herald

Titusville weekly HERALD. w Ja 20 1860-1911||
1860-63? as Titusville gazette and Oil Creek reporter; 1864?-65 Petroleum reporter and Creek gazette
CaOTA Jl 22 1864
DLC Ag 17 1882
OClWHi Ja 29 1863
P Jl 1889-1911

PENNSYLVANIA (*Continued*)

TITUSVILLE—*Continued*

Titusville morning HERALD. d Je 14 1865+
Ag 22 1934 is Diamond jubilee of oil ed
DLC Ag 31 1881
MWA Ap 19,Je 15 1880
NcU My 18 1880;Mr 26,28-29 1881
NhD Ag 22 1934
PMe Ag 22 1934
PW [1934]
Tx Ja 17 1873

PETROLEUM reporter and Creek gazette. *See* Titusville weekly herald

Titusville morning STAR. d 1869-
NcU My 27 1869;D 27 1879

Titusville WORLD. w 1880-1903||
P [1901]-[03]

TOWANDA

BANNER and democrat. *See* Northern banner and Bradford democrat

BRADFORD argus. w F 6 1834-1916||?
DLC F 6 1834
KHi Ap 6 1839
MWA Ag 15 1840-Ag 21 1843;S 3 1862
NN N 1 1834;Mr 12 1836;Ag 20 1857
P Jl 1889-1912
PAtM F 3 1838[40]-[52;55]-[64;66]-[77-78]-[1916]
PToHi 1834-[36]-39;42-45;48-49;51;56;62-65[75;93]-[97]1900-16
PWbW F 4 1841;Mr 17 1855

BRADFORD herald. w
PAtM Ag 3 1859
PToHi [1859]-[61]

BRADFORD porter. *See* Reporter-journal and Bradford republican

BRADFORD reporter. *See* Reporter-journal and Bradford republican

BRADFORD republican. w,sw 1875-1903||
United with Reporter-journal to form Reporter-journal and Bradford republican
sw My 1892-O 1896
P My 1889-[92;97]-1903
PToHi [1876-81;84]-[90;93]-[1903]

BRADFORD settler. *See* Northern banner and Bradford democrat

BRADFORD star. w Ap 26 1894-Ap 29 1920||
P Ag 1895-1912
PToF [1900]-[05]
PToHi [1894-96]-[1912-13]-[20]
PToR [1894]-[97]

BRADFORD times. w Jl 23 1856-
MWA Ag 13 1856

Towanda BUSINESS item. w 1871-75||
PToR [1873]-75

DEMOCRAT. w 1835?-Mr 1837||
United with Northern banner to form Northern banner and Bradford democrat
PAtM Ja 15-Mr 15 1835

Towanda JOURNAL. w My 14 1873-84||
United with Bradford reporter to form Reporter-journal, later Reporter-journal and Bradford republican
PToHi F 14 1874;Jl 6 1881
PToR [1873-74]-84

NORTH BRANCH democrat. w D 6 1850-Ja 1852||
PAtM D 28 1850;Ja 10 1852
PToHi Ag 23 1851

***NORTHERN banner and Bradford democrat.** w S 5 1818-43||
1818-23 as Settler; 1823-Mr 2 1833 Bradford settler; Mr 9 1833-Mr 1837 Northern banner; Mr 1837-D 1841 Banner and democrat
1821-30 pub in Meansville
Ct S 22 1825[26]My 8 1828[30-31]Ap 21 1832[33-36]O 14 1837;Mr 3 1838
DLC D 14 1839
MWA Ag 11 1821-Jl 20 1822;Mr 16 1826;Ja 25 1827;Ja 21,F 25 1830
N F 17-Ap 7 1825;N 8 1827
P N 27 1828
PAtM [1821;23-26]29;31;O 11 1834
PToHi [1823-29]-[32-33]-[37]N 30 1839;Ja 16, Ap 24,S 2 1841[42]
PW Ag 8,O 10 1835
PWbW Mr 23 1822;Mr 9-16 1826[27]Ja 31,Mr 13,My 8 1828;Mr 25 1830;Mr 12,Ap 20 1832
PWcHi Mr 16 1826

PEOPLE'S daily advocate. d 1911||
PToHi [1911]

REPORTER-JOURNAL and Bradford republican. w Je 4 1840-Ap 29 1920||
1840-Ap 2 1844 as Bradford Porter; Ap 10 1844-84 Bradford reporter; 1885-Ap 29 1920 Reporter-journal
DLC Je 4,18 1840;Jl 28 1841;My 1,S 18 1852;F 13 1873-Mr 25 1876
N Ap 21 1887
NNHi Ap 5 1843
P [1845]-[52]1904-Je 1912
PAtM Jl 5 1843[52]-[60;63-64]
PBL [1844-55]
PScrHi O 25 1883
PToF [1899]-1910
PToHi [1840]-[56-57]-[75;80]-[82-83]92-[1903-04]-[17-20]
PToR [1842]-[51-52]-[54-55]-[62]-[79;82]-1918
PW [1842]
PWbW Ap 5 1860
WHi [Je 16 1855-D 15 1859]

Towanda REPUBLICAN. w D 1826-Jl 1829||
Title varies slightly
PAtM F 14,Je 18 1828
PToHi F 7 1828
PWbW Ap 23 1828

Towanda daily REVIEW. d 1879+
pub [1879-80;83]+
P 1927-Je 1932
PToHi [1879]Ag 12,15,S 13 1881;N 20 1882;Mr 23,Ag 15 1883;Ag 11 1899;My 12 1903

Towanda weekly REVIEW. w Ap 10 1883-N 1896||
PToR 1887-92

SETTLER. *See* Northern banner and Bradford democrat

TOWER CITY

VALLEY echo. w D 1882-Ag 1910||
Merged with West Schuylkill herald
PTowW [1882-84]-91;93-94[97]-[99;1903-04]

WEST SCHUYLKILL herald. w My 1898+
pub 1898+

TRAPPE

INDEPENDENT. *See under* Collegeville

PROVIDENCE independent. *See* Independent (Collegeville)

TREMONT

WEST SCHUYLKILL press. w 1877+
PPCHi S 26 1891

TROY

ANTI-MASONIC democrat. w Jl 17 1830-
CSmH S 18 1830
P-M S 3 1831

Troy BANNER. w My 28-N 1846||
PToF complete
PWeT complete

DEMOCRATIC analyzer. w 1839-
KHi My 23 1840-N 22 1842
NIC Je 1840-Mr 1842
NSchU Mr 31 1842

Troy GAZETTE-REGISTER. w 1863+
1863-Ja 1905 as Northern tier gazette
pub 1905+
PToHi [1897-98;1920]-30

NORTHERN tier gazette. *See* Troy gazette-register

Daily REGISTER. d 1884||?
PToHi [1884]

Troy TIMES. w Je 14 1862-
MWA Ag 16 1862

TUNKHANNOCK

NORTH BRANCH democrat. w 1854?-61||
Followed by Wyoming democrat
PScrHi S 1,O 27 1858
PTuM 1854-60
PWbW Mr 26 1856;Jl 1857-Ja 5 1861

Tunkhannock REPUBLICAN and new age. w Ag 1 1868+
1868-Ja 1904 as Tunkhannock republican
pub 1904+
P Ag 1889-1912;30+

WYOMING county herald. w
PWbW S 25 1844-S 16 1846

WYOMING county record. w S 25 1844-
DLC O 16 1844
PToHi F 11 1846
PWbW S 23 1846-Ja 9 1850

WYOMING county whig. w 1849-52||
MWA N 4 1852
PWbW 1850-52

WYOMING democrat. w 1849-
MWA N 2 1852

WYOMING democrat. w 1861+
Follows North Branch democrat
pub Ag 7 1867+
P Jl 26 1889-F 1922
PMilC F 12 1873
PTuM 1861-[67]

WYOMING patrol and republican standard. w
P-M Je 28 1842
PBL Mr 22,Ap 5 1843
PTuM [1842]-[47]
PWbW My 18 1846;My 3 1848

TYRONE

Tyrone daily HERALD. d 1887+
pub 1887+
P Jl 1889-Je 1919

Tyrone STAR. w 1858-
MWA Jl 21 1860

UNION CITY

Union City TIMES-ENTERPRISE. w,sw 1870+
1870-1911? as Union City times
w 1870-1901?
PEr Ja 15-Mr 25 1880

UNIONTOWN

AMERICAN standard. *See* News-standard

Uniontown DEMOCRAT. *See* Jeffersonian democrat

Uniontown weekly DEMOCRAT and Fayette county advertiser. w Ag 1827-N 11 1854||
1827-44 as Pennsylvania democrat (title varies slightly)
CSmH F 1 1849
DLC Ag 29 1827;Jl 9,30-Ag 20,S 17,O 1,D 3 1828;Jl 1-8,22-Ag 5,S 9-16,O 1,N 4,18,D 2 1829; Ja 6-13,27,D 6,20 1830;Ja 3 1831;O 31 1832; Ag 25 1840
OCHi S 2 1847
OClWHi Jl 17 1839
PBro Ap 29 1828;Mr 26 1834[43]Ja 9,F 6 1844
PPiHi O 18 1830;O 2 1833;My 31 1849
PUn S 26 1827;F 8,My 8 1855
PWaHi Mr 31 1833

DEMOCRATIC daily. d O 14 1897-
PUnR O-N 3 1897

DEMOCRATIC shield. w 1835-
MiU Jl 6 1836
MoHi Ag 12 1835

FAYETTE county republican. w Je 6 1878-Mr 21 1879||
United with American standard to form Republican-standard, later News-standard
PPiHi complete

Evening GENIUS. d My 1900+
P 1900+
PUnC 1929-33
PUnR 1900-08

***GENIUS of liberty.** w F 22 1805-1917||
Subtitle varies: . . . and Fayette advertiser; . . . and American telegraph; . . . and American observer; . . . and Fayette and Greene advertiser; . . . and democratic shield advertiser
CSmH My 31 1830
DLC S 11(extra)1835
IU O 26 1840
MBAt N 6 1821
MoHi S 26 1831
NNHi Je 7 1825
OClWHi My 17 1837
OHi O 9 1827
P Je 27 1889-1912
PBL Ag 29,S 12 1844
PPi Ap 25 1872-1900
PPiHi Ja 16(extra)1835;D 26 1838
PUn [1821;26-27;30-33]Jl 7 1842;Ja 14 1847[52-54;60;63-67;70;73-74;76;78-79;81-84;86-87;90-1900;02-05]
PUnR Ja 31 1861-1917

HARRISONIAN and weekly conservative. w Mr 4 1840-
DLC Mr 11 1840

Morning HERALD. d Ja 8 1907+
pub 1907+
MWA O 9 1907
PUn 1929+

INDEPENDENT. w 1920+
Ja 15 1920-Ja 1922 as Week end special
pub 1920+
PUn [1932-33]

JEFFERSONIAN democrat. w 1878-1900||
1879-90? as Uniontown democrat
PUn [1893;95-1900]

NATIONAL. w Jl 31-N 1879||
PUn Jl-O 23 1879

Uniontown NEWS. w 1862-O 30 1893||
1882-84 as Three towns (Brownsville)
United with Republican-standard to form News-standard
PBro [1883]
PUnN 1882-84
PUnR 1886-[91]

NEWS-STANDARD. w N 18 1854+
1854-Mr 21 1879 as American standard; Mr 28 1879-O 30 1893 Republican-standard
pub [1868]-[80-81]+
MWA F 29 1872
P 1874
PPiHi Mr 27-S 1879;Mr 25 1880-Je 9 1881
PUn My 8 1855;81-1906
PUnR 1871-[80-81]-1908
PWaHi N 22 1855

Evening NEWS-STANDARD. d D 17 1888+
1888-O 1893 as Evening news
pub 1888+
MWA N 14 1907
PUn 1888-90;1929+
PUnR 1890[94]-1904

Morning NEWS-STANDARD. d Ap 4 1896+
pub 1896+
PUn 1896-1906
PUnC 1925;29-33
PUnR 1896-1908;25-33

PENNSYLVANIA democrat. *See* Uniontown weekly democrat and Fayette county advertiser

PEOPLE'S tribune. w Je 8 1893-1913||
PUn 1895-[98]-1905;09
PUnR [1905]-08

Daily RECORD. d Ag 14 1913-Ja 14 1915||
PUn [1913-14]

REPUBLICAN-STANDARD. *See* News-standard

WEEK END special. *See* Independent

WESTERN enterprise. w 1896-
PUn Jl 17,31 1896

UPPER DARBY

Upper Darby CHRONICLE. w 1930+
PArdM [1935]+

Daily CHRONICLE. *See* 69th Street news

Weekly NEWS. *See* 69th Street news

Upper Darby PRESS. w 1925+
PP N 1931+

PENNSYLVANIA (*Continued*)

UPPER DARBY—*Continued*

69TH STREET news. w N 20 1933+
1933-O 8 1934 as Daily chronicle; O 11-D 27 1934 Weekly news
PArdM 1933+

VALLEY VIEW

VALLEY citizen. w 1929+
pub [1929]+

VANDERGRIFT

Vandergrift NEWS. w,d N 16 1905+
w 1905-N 14 1927
pub [1905]+

VERONA

Verona-Oakmont LEADER. w 1908+
pub 1916—

WARREN

ALLEGHENY mail. *See* Warren mail

Warren BULLETIN. w My 11 1836-S 2 1839||
PW [1836-39]

Warren morning CHRONICLE. d 1917-19||
PHHi Ap 7 1919
PW 1917-18

CONEWANGO emigrant. w Jl 24 1824-26||
PW Jl 30,D 3 1824;Jl 8,O 21 1825

Warren evening DEMOCRAT. d 1897-1900||
Merged with Warren evening times, later Warren times-mirror
PW [1897]1900

Warren weekly DEMOCRAT. *See* Warren weekly times

DEMOCRATIC advocate. w S 2 1839-Mr 25 1847||
PW [1839-44;47]

Warren GAZETTE. w F 18 1826-31||
1826-Mr 1829 as Warren gazette and farmer's and mechanics herald
DLC N 20 1828
PSugM My 11 1826;F 22 1828
PW [1827;29]

HICKORY club. w Jl 13-N 1844||
PW Jl 27,O 5 1844

Warren LEDGER. w My 1 1849-Ap 27 1897||
CSmH D 24 1862
MWA Ap 3 1861
P Je 28 1889-97
PW 1849-[63;69;73-74]-[97]

Warren MAIL. w 1849-1917||
Jl 25 1849-N 20 1849 as Allegheny mail
P Jl 1889-Je 1912
PSugW Ja 3 1882;N 6 1883
PW [1848-52]-1917
WHi S 18 1849;My 13 1865

Warren weekly MIRROR. w,sw O 1 1882-1919||?
w 1882-1902
P My 22 1897-1913
PW 1891-1910

Warren morning MIRROR. d 1886-1928||
1886-1920 as Warren evening mirror. United with Warren evening times to form Warren times-mirror
PW 1892-1928

PEOPLE'S monitor and Warren democrat. w 1838-45||
DLC S 11 1838
N D 6 1842;Je 5 1845
PSugM Ja 22 1839
PW [1840-42]

Warren STANDARD. w My? 1847-Mr 6 1849||
PW [1847-49]

Warren weekly TIMES. w 1893-1914||?
1893-1900 as Warren weekly democrat
PW 1893-1910

Warren TIMES-MIRROR. d 1900+
1900-28 as Warren evening times
P Jl 1929+
PW 1901-[28-29]+

Warren TRIBUNE. d D 1923-Je 1928||
P 1927-28
PW complete

UNION. Je 8 1831-33||?
CSmH Ag 31 1830
PSugM Jl 26 1832

VOICE of the people. w Ag 27 1829-Ja 6 1836||
MWA Ja 31 1832
P N 26 1829
PW [1829-34]

WARREN county democrat. w Mr 30 1836-
PW Ap 13 1836

WASHINGTON

ADVANCE. *See* Washington observer

CHAMPION of whig principles. w
MoSM Jl 31,S 2,O 23 1844

COMMONWEALTH. w My 1848-Ap 1 1858||
United with Washington weekly reporter to form Washington reporter and commonwealth, later Washington reporter
MWA My 19 1852
PWayHi D 25 1850

DEMOCRAT. w Ap 3 1878-93||
P Je 1889-91
PWaHi [1878]-[90]

Washington DEMOCRAT. d 1892-1920||
P 1892-Ap 1905
PWaC 1894-1904
PWaHi 1892;Ja 10 1920

DEMOCRATIC eagle. w S 10 1827-
N S 10 1827
NdHi D 1 1827
WHi Je 28 1828

Washington EXAMINER. *See* Washington review and examiner

Washington daily NEWS. d 1914-19||
P Ap 1914-18

Washington OBSERVER. m,w S 18 1871+
1871 as Advance monthly(m); 1872-Mr 4 1874 Weekly advance
w 1872-O 1889
pub 1872+
P Ap 22 1881-84;D 1887-S 18 1902
PWaC 1894-99;1903+
PWaHi 1887-[90-92]95[96;1901]

OUR country. w 1835-40||
Merged with Washington examiner, later Washington review and examiner
PBL N 1 1837

Washington PATRIOT. w
CtY My 17 1845
NSyU O 30 1847
PWaHi N 29 1845[46]D 22 1848

PETROLEUM exchange. w O 21 1889-N 12 1890||
P My 20-O 1890
PWaHi [1889-90]

Washington RECORD. d 1904-13||
P 1905-13

*Washington REPORTER. w,sw,tw Ag 15 1808-N 1900||
Title varies: Reporter; Washington weekly reporter; Washington reporter and commonwealth; Reporter and tribune; etc.
w 1808-83;sw 1883-97
pub 1821-23;29+
CSmH S 6 1830
CtY Ag 11 S 15 1828
DLC O 30-N 6 1832;My 6 1834;F 13 1836;N 28 1840;N 20 1841;Ja 16 1847
IaHi Ja-My 21 1821
MWA My 26 1852;Jl 23 1858;Ja 24 1866
NhD Jl 24,N 20 1850;Ja 1-15,29,Mr 19,Ap 9,Je 11,Jl 2 1851-Je 30,O 27,D 8,22 1852;Mr 2,16 1853
OClWHi My 28 1821;Ag 29 1840
OHi Ag 7 1826
P 1877-78;81-88;90-92;94-1902;04-05;07-18
PBL My 20 1834
PBf [1867]
PPiHi Ag 15 1908;S 28 1910
PUn Ag 3 1893;Ag 15 1908
PWaC [1894]1902[04-05]
PWaHi D 4 1826;Jl 7 1828;F 13 1836;My 26 1858;Ja 12 1859[60-69;78-83]S 19 1896
PWcHi 1910
WHi Je 4 1824;Ag 15 1908

Washington REPORTER. d Ag 4 1876+
MWA Ag 15 1908;Je 30 1923;Ag 15 1933
P 1877-78;80-83;90-92;94-1902;04-05;07-18
PP Ag 15 1908

Weekly REVIEW. w O 9 1851-65||?
United with Washington examiner to form Washington review and examiner
PWaHi 1859-Je 1865

*Washington REVIEW and examiner. w My 28 1817-92||
1817-65? as Washington examiner (title varies slightly)
DLC Ap 9 1825;Ag 4,S 29 1832
IU O 30 1841
NNHi D 20 1828
OClWHi Ag 18 1838;S 3,O 1 1842;O 8,24 1846
OHi N 8,16 1823
P Jl 1890-Je 1892
P-M Je 20 1834
PBL [1834-35]
PBf Mr 6 1867
PPiHi My 27 1822;N 15 1828
PWaHi N 17-24 1827[40]-[44]N 18 1845[51]-56 [64]-77

SPY. w Ag 5 1848-
OClWHi S 2 1848

Saturday evening SUPPER TABLE. w My 30 1885-1900||
P Mr 1889-Je 1899
PWaHi [1888-89]

Washington TRIBUNE. w 1856-60||
United with Washington reporter and commonwealth to form Reporter and tribune, later Washington reporter
OClWHi F 4 1858

WATERFORD

Waterford LEADER. w 1878+
pub 1900+

YOUNG'S Waterford dispatch. w 1852-
MWA D 24 1853

WATSONTOWN

RECORD and star. w 1870-1926||
1870-84 as Watsontown record
PWatF [1877-78;82]-[84]-[1926]

WATTSBURG

Wattsburg CHRONICLE. w 1878-80||?
PEr Je 3 1880

WAYMART

FAIRVIEW echo. m
PHsHi [1920]-[24]

WAYNE

NEWS and Delaware county citizen. w 1888-90||
PLFT [1890]

SUBURBAN and Wayne times. w 1885+
pub [1906]+
PP [1931]+

WAYNESBORO

BLUE RIDGE zephyr. d 1894-1909||
Merged with Waynesboro record
PWaynR 1897-[1904]-[08-09]

HERALD. d 1901-18||
United with Waynesboro record to form Record-herald
pub complete

Waynesboro KEYSTONE gazette. w 1875-1900||?
Merged with Village record, later Waynesboro record
P Jl 18 1889-N 1900
PWaynR [1882]-[91]

Waynesboro PRESS. d 1919-28||
PWaynR complete

Waynesboro RECORD. w Mr 13 1846-1920||?
1846-N 1900 as Village record
pub [1851-54]-[56]-[58]-[60;62]-[68-69;71-73;75]-[80;82]-[89;94]96-[1900]
P Je 29 1900-12
PWaynR [1903-04;08-09]

RECORD-HERALD. d 1900+
1900-18 as Waynesboro record
pub 1901-[05;07-09]+

VILLAGE record. *See* Waynesboro record

WAYNESBURG

*DEMOCRAT-MESSENGER. w,sw 1813+
1813-1914 as Waynesburg messenger
pub Ap 28,N 3 1821;O 17 1829;Ag 14 1832;Jl 13,S 18 1840;F 25 1843;O 17 1844;O 26 1847;Ag 8 1848;O 24 1853;Jl 9 1856;Ap 7 1875[86]1916+
P Jl 19 1889-1914;20-28
P-M Ag 20 1825
PPiHi Ap 18 1866-68;Ap 14 1869;O 27 1880
PUn Jl 8 1830
PWayC 1896-97[1918-20;24-30]
PWayHi N 30 1822;Je 14 1823;O 15 1825;Ap 29 1830;S 26 1837;O 24 1844;My 8 1849;Mr 17 1869;Je 1 1870;N 24 1903;Jl 31 1914

Waynesburg EAGLE. *See* Waynesburg republican

GREENE county democrat. w Ja 1 1881-1914||
United with Waynesburg messenger to form Democrat-messenger
DLC My 26 1846
P Jl 19 1889-1914
PPiHi Ap 1 1882
PWayHi Je 17 1910;My 2 1913

GREENE county republican. *See* Waynesburg republican

GREENE county whig. *See* Waynesburg republican

INDEPENDENT. w 1872-1912||
1872-F 18 1904 as Waynesburg independent
PWayC [1896-97]
PWayHi [1896;1903]-[05]Mr 15 1916;Jl 4 1917

Waynesburg MESSENGER. *See* Democrat-messenger

Waynesburg REPUBLICAN. w 1833+
1833-66 as Greene county republican (1838-53 Greene county whig; 1853-56 Waynesburg eagle)
pub Ja 24 1855;Jl 30 1856;My 29 1860;Mr 19,O 8 1861;F 9,N 30 1864[70]-[75-79]-[89-97;99]-[1905]+
MWA N 24 1875;F 16 1876
P Jl 11 1889-1912;31-Je 1932
PPiHi Ag 11 1863;O 4 1864[My 1866-Ag 1868] Mr 17 1869;O 1 1879;S 1,N 17 1880;My 11 1933
PWay 1896-97[1918-20;24-30]
PWayHi S 3 1833;Ap 13 1852-Ag 3 1853;N 1 1854;S 7,O 26 1858;Ag 26 1862;Ag 16 1865;S 5-6 1877

ROLLING ball.
DLC S 3 1840

Waynesburg daily TIMES. d 1901-13||
PWayHi Mr 24 1902;F 17,N 16 1904;Mr 7-8,O 26 1905;S 30,N 16 1907;Ja 3,Mr 8 1908;Mr 25-27,S 25 1909;O 12 1910;My 20 1914

WEATHERLY

Weatherly HERALD. w 1880+
pub [1881]+
PMc 1888-94

WELLSBORO

Wellsboro ADVERTISER. w 1849-54||
MWA N 26 1852
PWeT [1849-54]

AGITATOR. w 1854+
1854-Ja 9 1867 as Tioga county agitator
pub [1854]-[56-57]+
KHi [Ap 29 1858-Ap 23 1913]
MWA Ag 6 1862;My 25 1864
NNHi Jl 1,29 1863
P Jl 1889-1912;16-28;31+
PMaT 1872-94
PWe [1874-1915]
PWeT [1857;59-60;62;65-66;69-70,72;1928-30]+
PWpHi Ag 20 1862

PENNSYLVANIA (*Continued*)

WELLSBORO—*Continued*

Wellsboro weekly DEMOCRAT. w Je 30 1838-79||?
1838- as Democratic star
DLC Je 30,Ag 18 1838
KHi Ap 28,O 27 1858;My 4 1859;S 26 1860

DEMOCRATIC star. *See* Wellsboro weekly democrat

GATE keeper. w 1909-12||?
PWeM [1909]-12

Wellsboro GAZETTE. w 1874+
pub 1874+
P Je 20 1889-1912

REPUBLICAN-ADVOCATE. w Jl 1884-1919||
P Jl 1906-12
PWeM 1905-07

TIOGA banner. *See* Tioga county banner

TIOGA county agitator. *See* Agitator

TIOGA county banner. w N 26 1846-
1846-51? as Tioga banner
KHi Jl 13 1848-Ja 16 1851;Mr 18 1863
PToF 1846-[48]
PWeT 1846-[51]

TIOGA county phoenix. w 1827-
1838-46 as Tioga phoenix and Potter county gazette
CSmH Jl 31 1830
PHi Ag 25 1827[30-32]
PWeA [1833-35]
PWeT [1846-47]

TIOGA eagle. w
PToHi S 25 1844
PWeT Ag 23 1838[40-50;52-56]

TIOGA phoenix and Potter county gazette. *See* Tioga county phoenix

TIOGA pioneer. w 1825-27||
PWeG 1825-27

WEST CHESTER

*AMERICAN republican and Chester county democrat. w,sw Je 7 1808-98||
1808-Jl 25 1809 as Temperate zone; Ag 1809-Ag 3 1813 Downingtown American republican; Ag 3 1813-N 18 1833 American republican
1808-Ap 2 1822 pub in Downingtown
w 1808-Jl 1876
DLC Ap 19,Ag 1,26 1826;N 6 1832;47-48;N 9 1852
MWA S 24 1823;S 30 1828;N 9 1830[F 19-S 10 1833]S 23 1834;F 17,My 26,Je 23,Ag 18 1835;Mr 13 1838;Jl 23 1839;D 26 1843;Ja 28 1845;Jl 29,N 18 1851;Ja 12,F 23,Ag 3,O 12,D 14 1869;Ag 23 1870;D 2(supp)1873;My 12 1874
NNHi My 19 1863
OClWHi N 5 1823
P-M Ap 13 1825
PBL [1833-35]Mr 12 1844;S 22 1846[47]
PCHi Jl 20 1869
PHi [1821]33-[41]
PPot My 20 1851;My 24 1853;Ap 24 1855;N 10 1868
PWcHi [1821-22]-[32-47]48[53-55]-[62-66]-76
PWcLa [1821-22]-24;28-30;35-37
PWcT 1822-31;33-[35]43-52;66-[98]

AMERICAN star. w My 1839-Ag 23 1841||
DLC D 15 1840
PWcHi F 14 1840;Jl 20 1841

ANTI-MASONIC register. w S 30 1829-Ag 31 1831||
United with Anti-Masonic examiner. . . (Coatesville) to form Anti-Masonic register and Chester county examiner, later Register and examiner
CSmH S 8 1830
MWA Mr 2,Ap 6,Je 15-Ag 1831
N complete
NjHi O 20 1830

CHESTER and Delaware federalist. *See* Record

CHESTER county chronicle. sm 1863-64||?
PWcHi F 13 1863[64]

CHESTER county democrat. w S 11 1879-98||
P Je 28 1889-Mr 1898
PWcHi 1879-[89-90]-[96]Ja 27,Mr 31 1898
PWcT 1879-S 5 1895

CHESTER county times. w Ap 25 1857-Ja 1 1863||
Merged with American republican and Chester county democrat
NNHi Jl-D 1861
PPot My 23 1857
PWcHi Ja 23 1858;Ja 21 1860[61-62]

CHESTER county village record. *See* Record

INDEPENDENT herald and free American. w Ja 1 1854-57||?
1854-Ap 24 1856 as Independent herald
MWA Jl 7 1855;D 6 1856
PWcHi F 9 1854;D 8 1855;Jl 12,O 4 1856[57]

JEFFERSONIAN. w 1842-1910||?
Title varies: Jeffersonian and democratic herald; etc.
DLC O 26,N 6 1852
MWA Mr 5 1850;D 5 1863
OClWHi 1862
PBL F 14,Ap 18 1843;N 4 1845
PCHi Je 23 1863;F 1 1868
PPL [1847-48]
PPot D 26 1842;Je 24 1845;F 25 1854
PWcHi D 10 1844[45-59]-65[67]-[71-72]-[76-78]-[80;83-84;93-94]-96
PWcL 1843-[48]-[53]-[58]-1910
PWcLa [1848]-[50]
VU My 18,Je 27 1878;Ap 24,O 23 1880;N 4 1882

LITERARY casket and general intelligencer. w Mr 1829-N 1830||?
CSmH S 7 1830
PK [1830]
PWcHi Je 22 1830

Daily LOCAL news. d N 19 1872+
pub 1872+
CLM Ja 28 1889;Je 12 1890
DLC Ja 15 1899
MWA O 10,30-N 8,11-12,14,17-19,D 3,16 1873;F 23,Mr 24,Ap 1,9,My 18,Ag 1,5,12-15 1874;O 25 1889;My 21-22,26,29-31,Je 4 1890
MiU-C My 26 1890
NN N 18 1922
NjWdHi [1907-11]
P N 19 1872;Ap 1923-Je 1932
PCoaW N 9 1872[73]F 5 1874;Mr 10 1877;S 5 1885;Ag 4 1886;Mr 21 1890;Ap 11,S 4 1894;Mr 29 1898;S 7 1900;S 20 1901;N 11 1905;My 22-23,28 1906;O 6 1909
PNoHi [1880]
PP S 30 1887;Ag 30 1894
PWcHi 1872-[76-77]-[80]-1934
PWcT [1872-99]
VU O 15-20 1883;N 11-12,15 1884;N 8 1886

NATIONAL republican advocate and literary gazette. w 1830-Ap 8 1834||?
MWA D 11 1832
PK [1830]-[32]
PNoHi Mr 12 1833
PWcHi O 18 1831;F 28 1832

*RECORD. w,sw Je 8 1809-1918||?
1809-17 as Chester and Delaware federalist; 1818-1913 title varies: Village record; or, Chester and Delaware federalist; Village record and general advertiser; Village record and register and examiner; Chester county village record; Village record
sw 1880-1910?
CSmH Je 23 1830
CtY Mr 5 1823
DLC 1821-Jl 23 1823;Jl 28,Ag 4,N 17-24,D 1,29 1824;My 18,Jl 20 1825-28;Jl 1-22,Ag 12,S 9-16,O 7,28,D 2,30 1829;Ja 13,Ag 11 1830
MWA 1821-25;Jl 26 1826-My 2 1832;My 31 1864
MiU-C [1831]
MnHi [1863-65]
N Je 12 1822;25-27;Ap 1835-F 1841
NNHi 1821-Ja 18 1826;Mr 28,N 7 1828
extras:F 11,My 5 1824
NjHi Mr 5 1844
OClWHi Ap 25 1827;S 28 1861;S 27 1862-63
OOxM Ap 1,My 6,Je 10,Jl 15 1829;Je 29,O 19 1831-My 23 1832
P 1821[22]Je 22 1889-1912
PBL [1821-22]Ja 13 1830;N 16 1831;Jl 2 1834
PDoHi [1821]Ap 2 1823
PHi 1821-27
PPL [1821;26]
PPeS Ag 31 1847
PPot Ag 29 1821;N 17 1822;O 30 1835;Ja 22,Mr 14 1850;My 29 1858;Jl 30 1867;D 1 1874
PWbW 1821-Mr 19 1834
PWcHi 1821-[27-28]-[32;34-35]-38[55]-[1920]
PWcM [1821-26]
PWcT [1821-51;78-95]
WHi O 9 1860-N 1 1862

REGISTER and examiner. w S 7 1831-54||
Formed by the union of Anti-Masonic register (West Chester) and Anti-Masonic examiner (Coatesville). 1831-O 20 1835 as Anti-Masonic register and Chester county examiner
MWA S-O 5,19 1831;O 2 1832;Mr 15,29,Ag 16,S 13,D 20 1836;Ja 10,24-31,Mr 7,Jl 4 1837;Ap 17,Jl 24,N 6 1838;Ap 2,Jl 16-23,Ag 20-S 3 1839;Je 30,Jl 21,Ag 25,O 27 1840
MiU-C [1831]Mr 7 1837
N 1831-O 4 1836;O 20 1840-50
PBL Jl 1 1834
PLewL Ja 29 1833
PPiHi F 25 1834
PPot N 5 1835
PWcHi [1831-54]

Morning REPUBLICAN. d 1878-1914||?
NcD Ag 29 1892
PWcHi [Ap 27 1881-My 25 1892]-95;99-[1904;12]-[14]
VU N 11,13-14 1884

TEMPERANCE advocate and journal of the times. w S 8 1831-My 1835||
PWcHi D 21 1833;Ap 4 1835

Daily VILLAGE record. d 1878-94||
PWcHi complete

VILLAGE record. w *See* Record

WHIG. w Ap 15 1834-My 1835||
DLC Ap 15 1834
PWcHi [1834-35]

WEST GREENVILLE

INDEPENDENT press. w 1852-
MWA D 21 1853

SHENANGO VALLEY times. w
WHi F 15 1860

WEST GROVE

INDEPENDENT and Chester county mirror. w 1884+
pub 1926+
PWcHi Mr 17 1884;Ja 25,Mr 15 1894;Je 11 1896

WEST NEWTON

West Newton PRESS. *See* West Newton times-sun

West Newton TIMES-SUN. w 1878+
1878-86 as West Newton press; 1886-93 Youghiogheny times; 1893-1904 West Newton times
pub [1878-79;86]-88;1907-[34]+

YOUGHIOGHENY times. *See* West Newton times-sun

WEST PHILADELPHIA

Papers published in West Philadelphia are listed under Philadelphia

WESTFIELD

Westfield FREE PRESS. w 1878+
1878-99 as Free press
pub [1889]-93;95-96[98]-1900;02-03;05-12;20+
PWfR 1880-89

Westfield INDEX. w 1873-78||?
PWfF [1873]

WHITE HAVEN

White Haven JOURNAL. w N 19 1879+
pub 1879+
PWbW F 1889

White Haven RECORD. w Ap 20 1923+
pub [1923]+

WILKINSBURG

Wilkinsburg PROGRESS. w 1921+
PWi 1927+

WILKES-BARRE

Wilkes-Barre ADVOCATE. w 1832-Ap 13 1853||
1832-O 4? 1837 as Anti-Masonic advocate. United with Record of the times to form Record
MWA N 10 1852
P My 27,O 7 1840
P-M Mr 4 1840;S 4 1843
PWbW O 11 1837-Ap 22 1840;D 1843-53

ANTI-MASONIC advocate. *See* Wilkes-Barre advocate

BAYONET. d 1886||
PScrHi [1886]
PWbW My 18,22,26-29 1886

BRATSTVO (Slovak news). w 1898+
In Slovak
pub 1900+
IU D 13 1917-[21]+

COURIER-HERALD. w 1894+
pub 1932+

DEMOCRATIC expositor and Luzerne miner's and farmer's journal. w Mr 2-D 27 1854||?
PWbW [1854]

DEMOKRATISCHER wächter. *See* Wächter

DOLLAR weekly news. w 1878-1903||?
1878-84? as Dollar news-dealer; 1885?-1902 News-dealer
Dated also in Pittston and Scranton
PHsHi Ag 22 1881
PWbT [1884-87;92]-[1902]
PWbW [Je 17 1882-99]

Wilkes-Barre GORNIK. (The miner) w 1893+
In Polish
pub 1920-22;31+

Sunday INDEPENDENT. w N 4 1906+
pub [1906]-08[10]+

INDEPENDENT republican. w 1855-69||
PWbW [1855]56;60[61-62;66-69]

Wilkes-Barre LEADER. w Ja 22 1876-Ja 9 1879||
United with Luzerne union to form Union-leader
PWbW complete

Wilkes-Barre LEADER. d O 1 1879-D 31 1906||
1879-84 as Daily union leader. United with Daily times to form Times-leader
DLC Ap 1885-Mr 1887;O 1888-Je,O 1894-Mr,Jl 1895-97;Ap 1898-Mr,Jl 1899-Je 1900
P complete
PWbT [1881-90;98-1903]-06
PWbW complete

Sunday morning LEADER. w Ja 1885-1904||?
P N 22 1885-Mr 26 1893
PWbT [1885-86;88;90]
PWbW 1885-1902

*LUZERNE democrat. w Je 22 1810-52||
1810-31 as Susquehanna democrat. United with Republican farmer to form Luzerne union, later Union-leader
CSmH Jl 9 1830
DLC 1847-D 13 1848
MWA Ag 4,D 1,15 1826;My 25 1827;D 1 1852
N O 16 1833
NjHi My 11,Jl 27 1821;S 13,N 22 1822;S 5 1823;O 1,D 17,31 1824;F 11-18,My 6-13,S 16,N 4 1825;Je 9 1826
P-M Mr 19 1834
PPL Je 11 1884;F 4,My 4 1835;Ap 16 1845
PToHi S 15 1826
PWbW 1821-34[F 1847-52]

LUZERNE leader. w 1877-78||
United with Luzerne union to form Union-leader

LUZERNE union. *See* Union leader

MINER. *See* Wilkes-Barre gornik

Sunday morning NEWS. w 1877||?
PScrHi [1877]

PENNSYLVANIA (*Continued*)

WILKES-BARRE—*Continued*

Wilkes-Barre NEWS. d 1884+
1884-1901 as Wilkes-Barre news-dealer
N 1903
P N 1884-S 1893;Ap-Je 1898
PHHi F 1897
PWbW N 1884-1920

Wilkes-Barre Sunday NEWS. w S 22 1885-1902||
1885-1901 as Wilkes-Barre Sunday news-dealer
PWbN 1889-1902
PWbT [1880-81;83]-[87]93-98
PWbW 1882-90;Jl 1891-Je 1892;Ja-Je 1898;F-Je 1900

NEWS-DEALER. w *See* Dollar weekly news

RECORD. w,sw 1852-1919||
1856-1911 as Record of the times (subtitle varies)
MWA Jl 23 1856;D 18 1861;N 5 1862;S 21 1888; Ag 2 1889
NNHi Je 2-Ag 5 1863;My 7 1873
NbHi Jl 2-3 1878
P Ap 1853-Je 1899
PWbW Ap 20 1853-My,Jl 22-D 1919
PWcHi Mr 4 1857

Wilkes-Barre RECORD. d 1873+
1873-79 as Record of the times
DLC Ap-S 1887;Ap 1888;Je,O 1892-Mr,Jl 1893-Je,O 1894-Je 1900;S-O 1901
MWA S 13 1883;N 28 1884;F 21 1885;Mr 6 1886;F 8,O 3,D 10 1887;F 13,My 12 1888;Ja 29 1889
MiU 1898
NjHi S 13 1884
P My 1884-Mr 1887;Je 1889+
PHsHi Ap 23 1881
PWbT [1878]
PWbW 1873+

RECORD of the times. *See* Record; Wilkes-Barre record

REPUBLICAN farmer and democratic journal. w 1828-52||
United with Luzerne democrat to form Luzerne union, later Union-leader
DLC Ja 22 1840
MWA Jl 8 1840;N 17 1852
NN Ja 3 1838;Mr 6 1839
P F 18 1835-Mr 1847
UScrHi D 2? 1848
PWbT [1832;42]-[52]
PWbW [1828-52]

SLOVAK news. *See* Bratstvo

SPECTATOR and freeman's journal. w
PWbW Je 11 1836-Je 7 1838

SUSQUEHANNA democrat. *See* Luzerne democrat

Wilkes-Barre TELEPHONE. w 1880-1901||?
PWbW 1884-98

Wilkes-Barre TIMES. w 1894-1904||
PWbT [1894-1901]
PWbW complete

TIMES-LEADER. d 1889+
1889-1906 as Daily times
pub [1893;1902-06]+
P Ap 1893-Je 1899;1907+
PP [1928]-Ja 9 1934
PWbW [1903]—

Wilkes-Barre TRANSCRIPT. w
PToHi Jl 25 1846

TRUE democrat. w S 30 1852-
MWA N 25 1852
PWbW S 30 1852;Jl 13,27-O 12 1853

UNION-LEADER. w 1852-1908||?
1852-Ja 9? 1879 as Luzerne union
MWA Mr 15 1876;N 14 1884
NjR Mr 28 1860
P Ja 19 1853-59;79-[87]
PDoHi S 8 1859
PWbT 1883-1907
PWbW [Ja 1? 1853-O 23 1878]Ja 17 1879-82

Daily UNION leader. *See* Wilkes-Barre leader

WÄCHTER. w 1841-1931||?
1841-1909? as Demokratischer wächter (subtitle varies)
In German
MWA D 2 1852;Je 8 1864
PWbW Jl 11 1844-1920

WOODWARDS weekly review. w
PScrHi D 14 1878-F 15 1879

***WYOMING herald.** w S 18 1818-
MBAt Ag 1 1828
P-M D 31 183-
PBL Ja 14 1835
PScrHi N 6 1829
PWbW 1821-Mr 20 1833

WYOMING republican and farmers herald. w
PWbW [Ap 18 1832-39]

WILKINSBURG

Wilkinsburg PROGRESS. w 1921+
PWi 1927+

WILLARDSBURG

NORTHERN banner. w
P-M Ag 14 1825

WILLIAMSPORT

Daily BANNER. d 1874-Je 2 1881||
PWb [1880-81]
PWpS [1879]-81

Sunday BREAKFAST table. w Mr 7 1879-95||
PHHi Je 21 1890
PJsK 1881-[86]
PLaHi Ja 10 1891
PPot Je 21 1890
PWp 1879-94
PWpCo Ja 28 1885

Evening BULLETIN. d Ag 3 1868-N 15 1869||
United with Daily gazette to form Daily gazette and bulletin
—w ed *See* West Branch bulletin

DEMOCRATIC banner. w Je 13 1874-Je 2 1881||
United with Weekly sun to form Williamsport sun and banner
PWp [1874-76]
PWpCo Ag 25,D 5 1878;Je 12,Jl 30 1879;Ag 26 1880;My 12 1881
PWpS [1879-81]

Williamsport EMPORIUM. w 1841-
PLhT [1842]
PWp Ap 2-9 1842

FREEMAN. w 1839-
PLhT Jl 18 1840;Je 3 1841

***GAZETTE and bulletin.** w 1801-1912||
1801-Je 1837 as Lycoming gazette; Je 21 1837-69 Gazette and chronicle
pub [1822-25]55;Jl 1869-[82-84]-[88-90]-[98-99]
CSmH S 1 1830
MWA F 18 1828;Jl 14 1830
NNHi N 27 1821
P 1889-97
P-M Ja 5 1831;Ag 1 1832;S 10 1834
PBL Ja 12 1831;Ag 14 1833;Ja 20 1836;Ap 22 1843;My 4,N 2 1844;Ja 11,My 10 1845;My 31 1847
PJsJ Ap 25 1855;Jl 1869;My 3 1873;Je 1882
PLewL [1824]N 21 1827;Ag 19 1843;Mr 9 1844; N 21 1855
PLhT [1842;44]
PPL Ag 25 1847
PPot O 24 1872
PSuHi Ag 4 1858
PW Mr 25 1835
PWeA Ja 1 1822;Mr 22 1823;Mr 3,O 20 1824;F 16,Mr 2,My 11 1825
PWp [1821-26]-38;40-[42-67]68;70-81;85-1912
PWpCo N 15 1826;Ja 6 1842;Jl 1869-[82-83]-86; Mr 10 1888;Jl 16 1889

Daily GAZETTE and bulletin. d Ap 10 1857+
1857-Ap 3 1869 as Daily gazette
pub 1916+
ICM Je 3 1878
MWA Je 7 1894
NcU Ag 31 1876
P Je 1889+
PWp N 22 1869+
WHi Je 29 1895

GRIT. w 1882+
pub 1882+
P Jl 20 1930-Je 1932
PPeS Je 6 1920
PWp [1884]-1931
PWpCo My 27 1894;Ja 17 1897;My 20 1900
TJT D 13 1891;O 28 1900;Jl 7 1901;My 3 1903;N 11 1904
VU Ja 23 1910

INDEPENDENT. w 1876-78||?
PWp Ag 22 1878

INDEPENDENT press. *See* Williamsport press

JACKSON democrat. w 1846||
PBL My 26 1846
PJsJ [1846]
PWp S 15 1846

LYCOMING chronicle. w S 26 1829-Je 1837||
United with Lycoming gazette to form Gazette and chronicle, later Gazette and bulletin
MWA S 26 1829;Ja 20 1836
P O 5-12,N 23 1831;F 22 1832
P-M O 5-12,N 23 1831;F 22 1832
PBL Ag 14,28,O 2 1833
PHHi S 25 1833
PLewL Mr 30-Ap 6 1836
PWp 1833-[37]

LYCOMING democrat. w Je 4 1851-52||
PWp S 4 1852

LYCOMING gazette. *See* Gazette and bulletin. w

LYCOMING ranger. w 1873-74||?
PW [1873-74]
PWpHi 1873-74

LYCOMING standard. w 1865-73||?
DLC Ja 25 1871
PWp O 5 1870;F 12 1873

Evening NEWS. d 1894-1912||
Merged with Daily sun
PWp Ag 16 1894-N 18 1912

NEWS-MIRROR. w Jl 16-S 16 1933||
PWp [1933]
PWpCo [1933]

NORTHERN Pennsylvania. w D 23 1843-44||
PWp D 23 1843

Williamsport PRESS. w 1852-69||
1852-58 as Independent press
PWp O 15 1856;S 11,O 30 1858;S 17,O 1 1859 [61]N 3 1869

Daily REGISTER. d 1872-74||
PWp [1874]

Williamsport REPUBLICAN. w My 18 1889-94||
PWp Je 3 1889;My 5 1892

Williamsport morning STANDARD. d Ap 20 1868-
PWp 1868[69]S 11 1872

Daily SUN. d 1872+
Ap 27 1895 is Centennial ed
pub 1872+
P 1926-Ap 1933;F 1935+
PWp 1923+
WHi Ap 17 1895

Williamsport SUN and banner. w,tw Jl 8 1870-1923||
1870-80? as Sun and Lycoming democrat; 1880?-Je 2 1881 Weekly sun
w 1870-94
pub [1870-72]-[84]-1923
P Je 27 1889-1916
PWp [1871]-[73-79;81]-1923
PWpCo [1870]-[94]

Sunday TIMES. w Ap 4 1875-78||?
PWp Ag 22 1875

Williamsport TIMES. d 1893-99||?
P Jl 2-6 1895
PWp [1894]Ja 12 1897
PWpC Je 1 1895

WEST BRANCH bulletin. w 1860-N 22 1869||
United with Gazette and chronicle to form Gazette and bulletin
MBAt Je 17 1865
MWA F 24,Ag 4 1866
NNHi D 5 1868
PWcHi Je 11 1864;D 2 1865;Ja 13 1867
PWp Ja 5,Je 5-12,O 17-19 1860;My 18,S 7,O 19 1861;63-68
—d ed *See* Evening bulletin

WEST BRANCH democrat. w 1837?-
MWA Jl 2 1863
PJsJ Jl 16 1863
PWp Jl 26,O 18 1851;My 19 1863; Ap 19 1865
PWpCo O 1860-S 1861

WILLOW GROVE

Willow Grove GUIDE. w Jl 16 1925+
pub 1925—

WRIGHTSVILLE

Wrightsville STAR. w 1854+
1854-69? as York county star
PYHi Mr 18,Ap 15,N 8 1858

YORK county star. *See* Wrightsville star

WYALUSING

Wyalusing HUSTLER. w Ag 24 1898-Mr 1899||
PToHi [1898-99]

Wyalusing ROCKET. w 1887+
PToHi [1897-98;1903]-[13-30]

WYCOMBE

Wycombe HERALD. w 1899-1922||
PWyW [1899]-[1922]

YARDLEY

Yardley REVIEW. w 1908-24||?
PDoHi D - 1913
PLanA [1908-17]-24

YELLOW SPRINGS

LITERARY casket and general intelligencer. w Ap 14 1829-
NjHi Ap 2- 1829
PPL [1829-30]
PPiHi Je 2,Jl 21,S 22 1829;Ja 5,F 2 1830

YORK

AGE. d Ja 1883-97||
1883-90 as Democratic age
P Jl 1889-Ja 31 1897
PYG 1883-Ja 31 1897
PYHi N 7 1883;94

AMERICAN eagle. w 1855-
OClWHi Ja 30 1857

CARTRIDGE box. w Mr 5 1864-Jl 8 1865||
pub at U.S. Army General Hospital
MWA complete
PYHi complete
WHi Ap 23,D 24 1864;Ja 7 1865

York DAILY. d O 5 1870-Ag 30 1918||
United with York gazette to form Gazette and daily
DLC 1876
MWA D 29 1882
P 1878
PYD Jl 1 1874[76-77]
PYG [1871]-[73-74]-[76-77]-[89]91-93;95-1918
PYHi [1871]-76;1903
—w ed *See* York weekly

DEMOCRATIC age. *See* Age

DEMOCRATIC press. w,sw 1839-1901||
Title varies: Democratic press and people's advocate; York democratic press
w 1839-99
MWA Ja 28,Mr 17 1876
PBL O 23 1839[40]S 20,N 22 1844;My 28 1845; Jl 21 1846
PYG Jl 8 1839-[62;65]-[98]
PYHi [1845]-[53;97]-1901

Die DEUTSCHE York gazette. w 1822-28||?
In German
PYG [1822-23;26]-[28]

Weekly DISPATCH. w Je 7 1864+
1864-76 as True democrat
MWA F 16,Ap 27 1869
NNHi S 8 1868;F 4 1873
PYD 1864-[79]82-[88;92]-[99-1904]-05
PYHi 1864[65]-[68]-75;97-1900

PENNSYLVANIA (*Continued*)

YORK—*Continued*

Evening DISPATCH. d My 29 1876+
N 22 1877-Je 17 1878 as Dispatch and record
pub 1876+
KHi D 1 1926
PYG [1915-24]+
PYHi 1876[77-1915]
WHi Ap 11-D 1896

*Die York GAZETTE. w O 16 1795-
Suspended from 1805-21?
In German
MWA N 7 1845
PPeS Je 16 1876

*York GAZETTE. w,sw My 18 1815-1905||?
Title varies: York gazette and public advertiser; etc.
w 1815-93
CSmH Jl 6 1830
Ct [1828-29]
DLC My 27 1828-S 15 1829;31-D 18 1832;Ja 15, F 19,Ag 27,S 24,O 1,15-22,D 2,10 1833;Ja 21,Mr 25 1834;Mr 13,27-Ap 3,24-My 8,S 11-18,O 9, 23-30,D 11,25 1838;Ja 22-29,F 12-Mr 19,Ap 30, N 19,D 24 1839;Ja 21,F 18 1840;47[48]
MWA Ap 10 1821;O 23 1827
N F 12 1850
NNHi O 1835-Je 1838;Jl 25 1871;Ap 8,18 1873
NcD My 24,S 27 1831
ODW S 25 1838
PBL Ap 21 1835;Je 27 1837;F 27,Mr 26,S 10 1844;Je 10 1845
PYG [1821;23-24]-[26]27[29-33]35-90;94;98-1902; 04
PYHi [1822]-[24]-[26;28]-[30-32]-[34-35;50-55; 58]-[63]66-69

GAZETTE and daily. d 1887+
1887-Ag 1918 as York gazette
pub 1887-[96]
DLC 1898
P O 21 1897-1918;20-23;25+
PYHi 1894+

INDEPENDENT republican and York recorder. *See* York recorder

ITEM. w 1870-
P S 5 1879-[82]

PENNSYLVANIA republican. w Mr 16 1830-83||
1830-S 25 1832 as York republican and anti-Masonic expositor
CSmH S 14 1830
DLC D 6 1830;Ja 25 1831-[O 1832-Ap 1834]Ap 4-18,My 9,S 26-O 3,17-24 1838;Ja 6,27,Mr 6, Ap 17,N 20 1839;F 19,D 2 1840;F 21 1858;Je 27,Jl 18 1860
MWA S 28 1830;Jl 31,Ag 14 1832;Ja 14,F 4 1852;Jl 1-8 1863
PYHi [1832-34]-[44]-[48]-[52]

PENNSYLVANIAN. w Jl 19 1851-1910||?
PYHi My 4 1867;N 16 1872;F 6,22,S 6 1873;Ag 15 1874

PEOPLE'S advocate. w
PYD [1851-52]
PYHi [1849-51]-[54-55;57-61]

Evening PRESS. d O 1897-1906||
P 1898-D 13 1906
PYG O 11 1897-Ja 13 1906
PYHi D 24 1901[02]

*York RECORDER. w,d Ja 29 1800-Mr 9 1830||
Mr 28-Jl 24 1821 Independent republican and York recorder; Jl 31 1821-Mr 19 1822 York recorder and independent republican. Merged with York republican, later Pennsylvania republican
w 1800-Jl 24 1821
DLC 1821-30
MWA 1822-D 23 1823;Je 24,Jl 8-15,Ag 26-S 2 1828
NNHi Ap 12,19 1825
NcD F 24,Mr 1824-Mr 11 1828;Jl 14,28,S 8-22,O 6,N 3,D 1,29 1829;Ja 12-26 1830
PYHi [1821-30]

York REPUBLICAN and anti-Masonic expositor. *See* Pennsylvania republican

Der REPUBLIKANISCHE herold. w Ap 9 1828-Mr 12 1830||
In German
DLC complete

SPHERE. m Ap 1911-17||?
PYHi [1911-12]-[14-15]

TRUE democrat. *See* Weekly dispatch

York WEEKLY. w 1876-1903||
PYD [1880]-1903
—d ed *See* York daily

YORK county farmer. w D 23 1831-34||
PYHi [1831-32]-[34]

YORK SPRINGS

York Springs COMET. w 1873-1930||?
TxU N 9 1882-My 3 1883

YOUNGSVILLE

Youngsville EXPRESS. w Je 30 1849-N 1853||
PW [1849-53]

ZELIENOPLE

CONNOGUENESSING VALLEY news. *See* News-beacon

NEWS-BEACON. w O 1878+
1878-Ag 1 1932 as Connoguenessing Valley news
pub 1900+
P Jl 11 1889-Je 1891

PHILIPPINE ISLANDS

Ceded to the United States by Spain on April 11 1899

ALBAY

El BUSILIS de Albay. w Je? 1900-
A manuscript newspaper issued by the revolutionary party in Albay, Luzon
DLC D 30 1900;Ja 20,F 10,Mr 3-17 1901

APARRI

Aparri NEWS. w Mr 2? 1900-
KHi Ja 12 1901

BACOLOD

El IMPARCIAL. w? 1905-
CU-B Ap 24 1906

La LIBERTAD. tw 1899?-
DLC Jl 4 1899-Jl 22 1900

La IGUALDAD. d 1902-
DLC [Ap 27-O,D 8-21 1906;F 8-25,Mr 15-18, Ap-My,Je 7-8 1907]

BARASOAIN

ANG kaibigan nang bayan. d N 1 1898-99||?
Some issues pub in Malalos
In Tagalog
DLC D 13 1898
KHi [N 6 1898-F 14 1899]

BAYAMBANG

La INDEPENDENCIA. *See under* Manila

CABANTUAN

GACETA de Filipinas. *See under* Malolos

CEBU

Cebu CHRONICLE. sw 1909-19||?
In English and Visayan
DLC Ap-D 1910
PPCHi D 1 1909
PWaHi N 3-24,D 1 1909

Cebu COURIER. w Je 29 1907-08||?
DLC Ag 30 1907-D 28 1908

El IMPARCIAL. sw 1899-
DLC O 18,25,N 15 1900

La JUSTICIA. w Mr 5 1899-
DLC Ap 16,Je 25,Jl 2 1899

El NACIONAL. w Je 14 1899-
DLC Ag 2-9,26 1899

El NUEVO dia. d 1900-02||
DLC Ap 1-3,5,16-19,21,28-30 1902

PROGRESS. w My 4 1930-33||
DLC My 4-15,N 23 1931-N 27,D 4 1932-D 3 1933

El PUEBLO. w Mr 28 1900-
DLC Ap 11,18-Je 19,Jl 4-7 1900

ILOILO

El ECO de Panay. w,d 1887-98||?
ICN Mr 8 1887

El TIEMPO. d 1900-22||?
DLC D 12 1903-Je 29 1908

Iloilo TIMES. sw S 5 1901-
CPo Jl 3 1902

MALABON

La INDEPENDENCIA. *See under* Manila

MALOLOS

ANG kaibigan nang bayan. *See under* Barasoain

GACETA de Filipinas. ir My 17 1899-
Also pub in Cabantuan and Tarlac
CtY Jl 29-S 24,O 1 1899

El HERALDO de la revolución. *See* Heraldo Filipino

El HERALDO Filipino. sw S 29 1898-99||
1898-Ja 22 1899 as El Heraldo de la revolución
CtY 1898-Ja 8,19-22 1899
DLC 1898-Mr 23 1899
KHi 1898-Mr 23 1899
NbHi O 16 1898;Ja 12,F 2,9 1899

MANDALOYAN

La REPÚBLICA filipina. *See under* San Fernando (Pampanga)

MANILA

El Adelanto. d Mr 17 1904-07||?
DLC 1904-Jl 1905;Ja 3-20,Mr,My-Jl,S-D 1906

Manila AMERICAN. d O 15 1898-S 1907||
1898-Ja 1901 as American; F-Je 1901 New American. United with Cablenews to form Cablenews-American
CSmH Je 16 1899
CSt 1898-Je 1899
CU-B N 29-30 1898;Mr 29-30,My 13,16 1899
CoBoC Jl 16 1899
CoHi O 25 1898-99
DLC [1898-99]-1905;My-Ag,S 1906-07
KHi [D 1898-S 3 1899;My 16-Je 13 1907]
MWA F 8,Mr 10-11 1899;F 2 1901;Je 24 1902;D 23-24,29 1903-Ja 1,5-8,15-21,F 3-6,9-10 1904
MnHi O 21,N 26,D 28 1898;Ja 22,F 1,7-9,12,15-17,19,21,23-25 1899;My 29 1903
NN D 20,23-24,30 1899[1900;04-05]
NNHi Ap 15-16,18 1899
NbHi Mr 9,24 1899
NcD Ap 7 1900
NdFC Ja 1,8,18,29,F 5,8,10,Mr 25,D 20 1899
NdHi [O 15 1898-Mr]Ap 19,21,Jl 21 1899
OHi Jl 27 1899;D 26 1900;Ja 29,F 2,My 3,Jl 17 1901
PPiHi Jl 7,11-12 1899
PScrHi Je 11 1899
PUn O 27 1898
WHi F 17 1899;Ap 29 1900;Ag 19,22,29 1901
WS D 16-19 1899
WaU [1898-D 7 1899]

AMERICAN soldier. *See* Soldier's letter

El AMIGO del pueblo. d Je? 1893-
KHi S 14 1893;Ja 24 1895

ANG kapatid ñg bayan. d Je 1899-1914||?
In Tagalog
DLC Jl 4,15,S 21,26 1899;Ag 13 1903-Je 11 1904
WHi Ja 13 1900
—Spanish ed *See* El Grito del pueblo

ASEMBLEA Filipina. d O 14 1907-
DLC O 18-N 11 1907

BOLETIN oficial de Filipinas. *See* Gaceta de Manila

Manila daily BULLETIN. d F 1 1900+
CCIP O 7 1929-Ja,Ap,S 1930
DLC Ag 1900-O 1901;F-[My-O]1903;F 1906-[My-N 1907]
ICN Ag 5 1906
KHi Je 25 1913
MBAt N 3 1907
MWA F 15 1903;F 1919;N 21 1921;F 1 1930
OCl [1925-26]-[28]

CABLENEWS-AMERICAN. d Ag 1902-20||
1902-Ap 9 1905 as Manila cablenews; Ap 10 1905-S 1907 Cablenews. Merged with Philippines herald
DLC Ag 8-9,13,23,28,S 4-5,22,O 18,30-31,N 3,D 2 1902;Ja 12,F 3-4,9-10,12-O 3,25,27-31,N 3,D 30 1903;Ja 21 1904-Ag 1920
KHi [N 28 1905-Ja 10 1906;My 16-Ag 2 1907] Ag 16 1911
PWaHi N 2,D 19 1909

El CATOLICO filipino. d D 13 1898-99||?
KHi D 13-24 1898

El COMERCIO. d 1869-1925||?
DLC S 15,O 17,22,26,N 4-5,24 1898;Ja 19,F 8, 10,15-16,Mr 7,11,16,Ap 8,My 3,9-10,24,27,Je 2,6-9,14,Ag 16,21,23-24,S 19 1899;S 14 1901 [Ag-D 1903]-Mr,Ag 3-19 1905;Ja 10,23-26,F 1,3,5-9,14-17,Ap 3-4,10-11,14,16,21,23-25,Je 18-23,25-26,28,30 1906-Mr,My-S 1908
KHi My 23 1883[F 26 1889-O 1897]

COURIER. d Ap 15 1899-
In English and Spanish
DLC Ap 15 1899

Manila CRITIC. w S 26? 1901-
N 3 1907 is anniversary ed
KHi F 1 1902;N 3 1907
MnHi F 7 1903

La DEMOCRACIA. d My 16 1899-1917||
In Spanish and Tagalog
CU-B N 9 1901;Ag 9,14,S 28 1906;Mr 19,22-30,Ag 4,D 4 1915;Ap 7-14,18-20,23-27 1917
DLC Je 6,10,Jl-D 7 1899;Ap 20 1901-S,N 1902-F,Mr 15-23,Ap 1904-[Ja-Mr]My 1905-Ap 1917
KHi Ag 11 1899

DIARIO de Filipinas. d 1901?-
DLC O 10 1901-F 21 1902

DIARIO de Manila. 1848-52 *See* Gaceta de Manila

DIARIO de Manila. d 1860-99||
Suspended F 19-My 16? 1898
DLC Ag 12,18 1898
ICN Mr 6-Jl 1872
KHi N 7 1898-My 16 1899
NbHi My 16,Ag 16 1898

PHILIPPINE ISLANDS (*Continued*)

MANILA—*Continued*

El ECO de Filipinas. d Ap 1 1887-
1887-90 as La Opinión
KHi [F 19-Je 18 1890]S 20 1891;S 17-O 27 1893

El ESPANOL. d D 28 1894-98||?
NbHi Ag 25 1898

FILIPINAS. w? 1900-
CU-B N 20 1901

El FILIPINO libre. d Je 1899-1900||?
DLC Jl 4,9,11,13,16,S 12,14,20-21 1899
WHi Mr 8 1900

La FRATERNIDAD. d 1900-
CU-B N 16 1901
DLC S 13-14,16 1901

FREE PRESS. w Ja 20 1907-
KHi Ja-Mr 17 1907

FREEDOM. sw,tw,d O 15 1898-1906||?
Title varies: Manila freedom. Merged with Manila times
sw 1898;tw 1899
CLM N 23 1898;F-My 26,Jl 4,31,Ag 5,12 1899
CU-B N 5,12,30 1898;Mr 28,30,My 17,25,30,Je 1 1899
CoBoC Jl 10 1899
CoHi Mr 2,Jl 4 1899
DLC O 22-29,N 19-23 1898[F-D 1899]-O,N 5-6,9,11-12,20-22,27,D 13 1902;Ja-Jl 1,11-30,Ag 8-27 1903
KHi D 10 1898-S 2 1899
MWA N 23 1898;F 16,Ap 18,Je 11,Jl 4 1899;My 27,Je 5,17,24,Jl 1 1902
MnHi O 22,26,N 2-5,D 31 1898;Ja 21,F 9,11,25,Je 24-25 1899
NN Jl 14,D 25 1899;Jl 16 1900
NNHi O 19,O 29,N 22 1898;Je 19,Jl 14-15 1899
NbHi D 31 1898;F 11,16,My 21 1898
NcD My 1 1899
NdFC [Ja-Ag 1899]
NdHi [1898-Ag 12 1899]
PNoHi F 16 1899
PPiHi Jl 6 1899
WHi F 25,My 19-20 1899;S 24 1900
WS D 8-25 1899
—United States ed. bm My 1 1899-
MWA My 1 1899

FUERZA. w Ag 12 1906-
CU-B Ag 12-19 1906

GACETA de Manila. d 1848-Ag 8 1898||
1848-52 as Diario de Manila; 1852-60 Boletin oficial de Filipinas
MBAt D 16 1849;Ja 30 1851
NbHi Ap 23,My 1,4,6,8,10,Je 9,Jl 2,5-7,19,Ag 6,8 1898

GACETA oficial. w 1902+
In Spanish
DLC 1904-16;Jl 1920-23;32;34-S 1935
—English ed *See* Official gazette

El GRITO del pueblo. d Ag 1899-1914||?
CU-B N 9 1901;Ag 30 1906
DLC S 20,22-24 1899;Ag 12 1903-Jl,Ag 4,18,S 1 1904;Ag 1 1905;D 1906;Ja 3-4,26,29-31 1907
—Tagalog ed *See* Ang kapatid ñg bayan

La ILUSTRACION del Oriente. w O 7 1877-
Follows El Oriente
ICN O 7-28,N 11-18,D 1877-F 17 1878
TxU 1877-Ap 7 1878

La INDEPENDENCIA. d S 3 1898-N 11 1899||
Also pub in Malabon, San Fernando and Bayambang
DLC S 23-24,O 5-6,11-12,N 3,7-8,12,15-16,D 20 1898;Ja 10-11,13,15,17-18,20,26,Je 19,O 9 1899
KHi [S 7 1898-Mr 20 1899]
MB complete
MnHi N 21,D 29 1898;Ja 14(extra)19(extra) 1899
NbHi Ja 4,15,21,28,Mr 27-29 1899
WHi Ag 18 1899

La INDEPENDENCIA. d
DLC Jl 21,24-26,28,30,N 1906-Je 28,Jl 1,5-22 1907

INSULAR daily press. d Jl 16-Ag 29? 1899||
DLC Ag 9,23,26 1899
KHi Jl 19-Ag 29 1899
NbHi Ag 21-26 1899

KON leche. w S 24 1898-
MnHi O 1,N 12,26 1898

La LECTURA popular. w Ap 1890-Mr 1892||
KHi My 30 1890

LIBERTAS. d 1898-1917||?
DLC S 7,11,13-14 1901;Ag 11 1903-Mr,Ag 3-17,S 4,6,9,11-15 1905
NN Ag 23,25,30,S 1,3,5 1902
PPCHi D 26,28 1911
WHi Mr 5 1900

La LUZ. w Ag 5 1906-
CU-B Ag 5,S 15 1906

LUZON life. w Ap 28 1901-
KHi My 5 1901

El MERCANTIL. d Ap 7 1902-30||?
DLC Ja-N 1903;Mr 1904-09
NFre Jl 31 1917
WHi My 31 1902

El MOTIN. w O 2 1898-
MnHi O 9 1898

NEW AMERICAN. *See* Manila American

NEW ORIENT. w,ir O 15? 1898-
DLC D 2 1899
KHi Ja 21 1899
OHi N 25,D 16,30 1899;Ja 6,F 10 1900

El NOTICIERO de Manila. d N 18 1895-1904||?
1895-Mr 1896 as El Noticiero
DLC S 7 1901-My,Ag 18-20,25-28 1902
WHi Mr 2 1900

La OCEANIA española. d 1877-99||
Followed by El Progreso
DLC Ag 17 1898
KHi [My 2 1892-Ja 27 1898]
MnHi Ag 13,17 1898

OFFICIAL gazette. d Ag 23 1898-
MnHi Ag 20,23-24 1898

OFFICIAL gazette. w S 10 1902+
DLC 1902+
ICN 1902-05
NN 1902+
NNC 1902+

La OPINION. *See* El Eco de Filipinas

El ORIENTE. w O 3 1875-
Followed by La Ilustración del Oriente
ICN 1875-Mr 26 1876

Manila OUTPOST. w N 12 1898-
KHi N 12 1898

La PATRIA. d S 16 1899-1903||?
In Spanish and Tagalog
DLC Ja 20-D 30 1903

PHILIPPINES free press. w Ja 20 1907+
In English and Spanish
DLC 1907+
MiG 1925+
MnU Ja 10 1931-Ja 7 1933

PHILIPPINES herald. d Ag 8 1920+
C S 21-N 12 1920;Ja 11 1921-Ja 29 1922
CU [Ap 1923-Ja,O 1924-Ag 1927]-[28-29;Je 8-9,Jl 19,O 15-D 1930]+
Ct F 3 1923
DLC 1920+
ICU Ja 27 1922-My 1924;My 1925+
MWA F 3 1923
MiU 1928-[30]+
PP 1921;Ja 17,19-20 1922
TxGR F 3 1923
Vt O 29 1921
WHi Mr 19 1921-Ja 29 1922;F 3 1923

El PROGRESO. d Je 1 1899-1904||
Follows La Oceanía española
DLC Jl 19 21,Ag 1,3,15,S 24 1899;1900-Mr 4 1904
NN D 23 1899

El RENACIMIENTO. d S 1901-10||
Followed by La Vanguardia
CU-B D 31 1901;Je 9,Jl 20-21,Ag 22 1906,Ja 4 1907
DLC Ja 18 1902;Ag 17 1903-Mr 1908
KHi S 11 1905-Je 13 1906
WHi N 9 1904
—English ed d O? 1908-
MWA D 4 1908

La REPÚBLICA filipina. *See under* San Fernando (Pampanga)

El RESUMEN. d Jl 10 1890-
KHi [1890-Mr 17 1893]

SOBERANIA nacional. d Je 18 1906-07||?
CU-B Je 18 1906

SOLDIER'S letter. w S 10 1898-99||?
1898-Ja 1 1899? as American soldier
C D 5-18 1898
CU-B N,D 12-18 1898
CoHi D 18 1898
DLC S 24-O 1898
KHi N 19 1898-Ja 1 1899
MBAt 1898-Ja 1 1899
MnHi S 10,24-O 8,N 5-12,26 1898-Ja 1 1899
NbHi O 8,N 12,D 5,18 1898-Ja 1 1899
NdHi S 10,24-O 15,N 5,19-26,D 12 1898
PWaHi S 24 1898

La SOLIDARIDAD. m Je 1906-
CU-B Jl 27 1906

Sunday SUN. w 1900-06||?
KHi Jl 4,D 25 1903;Jl 4 1904;Ag 6 1905

TALIBA. d 1910+
In Tagalog
MeBa Ap 4 1911
—Spanish ed *See* La Vanguardia
—morning ed *See* Tribune

TATLONG Bitwin. d Ag 1 1906-
CU-B Ag 1-2 1906

Manila TIMES. d O 11 1898-Mr 14 1930||
C Jl 18 1901-Je 29 1902
CSt complete
DLC O 12 1898;Ja 19,F 18,Mr 1,25,Ap 8,10,17,21-22,24,Je 6-8,12,Jl 1899-[Ap 1900-Ap]Jl-S,D 1901;Ap 26 1902-Ap 1907;S 1923-30
ICN F 13 1902
KHi [F 3-Ag 1899]Je 29 1900[D 12 1905-Je 1909]-Ag 11 1910;Ag 31 1911
MWA Mr 10,Ap 20 1899;My 11,D 25 1900
MiU 1904[05]
MnHi N 5 1898;F 7 1899;Ap 17 1900;O 20 1901-Ja 19 1902;My 27,29,S 3-4,14 1903;F 17,Mr 3,17 1918
MnU Mr 28-Ag 16 1901
NN D 20-21,29 1900;Ja 15,Ap 5,15[Ag 1900;01-03]11-30

NdHi N 9,16,21 1898;Ja 3,10,16,F 15,Mr 6,18,Jl 21 1899
OHi F 21,My 18,27,D 25 1900;Ja 27,F 5,S 4 1901;Je 7;10,Ag 21 1902;Mr 21,Ap 6,30 1903
PWbW O 16 1900
TxU F 23 1920-F 1928
WHi Ap 29 1901

Manila TIMES. [Evening ed] d
NN [1900-02]
NbHi Je 26 1899;My 17 1900

Manila TIMES. w 1907-23||?
CU-B D 16 1910;Ag 18-S 15,O,N 17-D 1911;Ap 26-Jl 1912
DLC Jl 1908-Je 1913
KHi [O 16 1908-Mr 19 1911]
MiG 1913-D 23 1923
MoHi Mr 1 1912
NN [1908-10]

TRIBUNE. d 1899-
DLC O 6,16,26,N 4,18,D 10,27-31 1899;Ja 17,23 1900
WS D 20,22 1899

TRIBUNE. d Ap 1 1925+
CSt [1925]+
DLC Ap-O 16 1930;Jl 21 1932+
MiU [1926-27]28
—afternoon ed *See* La Vanguardia

UNCLE SAM. w O 15 1898-
CU-B N 5,26 1898
DLC O 15,29 1898
MBAt O 29 1898
MnHi N 5 1898
NbHi O 15 1898
NdHi O 15,D 3 1898

La UNION. d Ag 1 1900-
DLC Ag 1-23 1900

La UNION iberica. d Ja 1899-
KHi F 11 1899
MnHi F 6-7 1899

La VANGUARDIA. d 1910+
Follows El Renacimiento
DLC 1930-Mr 1932
MeBa Ap 4 1911
—Tagalog ed *See* Taliba
—morning ed *See* Tribune

VIDA Filipina. d F? 1906-
CU-B S 11,22 1906
DLC N 2 1906-07

La VOZ Española. d Jl 4 1888-1898||
1888-Mr 4 1892 as La Voz de España
DLC Ag 1-6 1898
MnHi O 11(extra)1898

NUEVA CACERES

An PARABARETÁ. sw,w Ap 3 1899-
Prospectus issued F 15 1899
DLC F 15,Ap-Jl 28 1899

La PAZ. w 1902-11||?
In Spanish, English and Bicol
DLC Je 21,Jl 2-16 1902

SAN FERNANDO (PAMPANGA)

El IMPARCIAL. sw Je 21 1907-
Half of paper printed in Tagalog as Ing Emangabiran
DLC Je 27,N-D 1907

La INDEPENDENCIA. *See under* Manila

Ing EMANGABIRAN. *See* El Imparcial

La REPÚBLICA filipina. d S 15 1898-99||?
1898? pub in Mandaloyan
Early issues also dated in Manila
CU 1898-Ja 1899
DLC S 15-O 21,N 3-D 4,6,21-25 1898;Ja 28-29,Mr 3 1899
KHi S 16 1898-Mr 1899
MB 1898-Ap 26 1899
MnHi S 27 1898
NN Ap 27 1899
NbHi S 15-17,29,D 3 1898;F 12,15,21,25,Mr 1-2,4,12,16,21 1899

SEBU. *See* CEBU

TARLAC

GACETA de Filipinas. *See under* Malolos

VIGAN

La NUEVA era.
DLC Je 1905-Mr 1907

ZAMBOANGA

MINDANAO herald. w N 25 1903+
DLC Mr 1905-N 6 1909
MWA Mr 6 1909;Ag 13-20 1927;Ja 18,S 27-O 4 1930

PUERTO RICO

Ceded to the United States by Spain on April 11 1899

AGUADILLA

El JIBERO. w? 1866-
CU-B Ag 18 1866

ARECIBO

La CAMPANA. d 1911-
MWA Mr 26 1913

La DEMOCRACIA. w Ag 24 1873-
CU-B Ag 24,O 12,26 1873

El DUENDE. d 1904-13‖?
MWA Mr 18 1913

BAYAMON

EL BALUARTE republicano. w? 1913-
MWA Mr 30 1913

CABO ROJO

El COCUYO. tm S 1873-
CU-B N 10-30 1873

HUMACAO

La ABEJA. w? 1879?-
CU-B Ja 2 1881

La JUVENTUD. tm Je? 1880-
CU-B D 20 1880

MAYAGÜEZ

AMERICA. d Ag 1898?-
DLC Ag 27 1898
NN O 12-13 1898

El AVISADOR del comercio. d S 1863-
CU-B N 5 1863

La BANDERA Americana. d 1898-1920‖?
1898-1900? as La Nueva bandera
DLC Je 6 1899-Je 2 1900
MWA Ap 3 1913

El COMPILADOR industrial. w 1855-
CU-B O 31 1863

El CREMATISTICO. d F 18 1896-
DLC F 18 1896

DIARIO del oeste. d 1909+
MWA Mr 31 1913

El ECO del pueblo. w 1872-
CU-B Ja 3-10 1874

El IMPARCIAL. d 1887-1900‖
DLC Ag 2 1898;Je 6 1899-Je 1 1900

El LIBERAL. d Je 12 1886-
DLC Je-D 30 1886

La NUEVA bandera. *See* La Bandera Americana

La RAZON. w 1871-
CU-B Ag 5,15 1873

El REPUBLICANO. tw Je 27 1899-
DLC Je,Jl 4-8 1899

EL SEMANARIO mayaqüesano. w 1850-
CU-B Ag 11 1852

La UNION obrera. *See under* San Juan

La VOZ de la patria. d 1901-23‖?
MWA Mr 17 1913

PONCE

El AGUILA de Puerto Rico. (Puerto Rico eagle) d 1902+
DLC S 2 1905-F 1913
LNT-M [O 1927-Je 1931]
MWA Ap 5 1913
NcD 1923[24]-27[Jl-D 1928]-[30]-Je 1931

CORREO de Puerto Rico. d 1898-99‖?
—**English ed** *See* Porto Rico mail

La CRONICA. d 1876-
CU-B Ja 11 1881
DLC Jl 22 1879

El DEBATE. d D 5 1899-
DLC D 6 1899

La DEMOCRACIA. d 1890-99‖
DLC Mr 24 1898;F-D 1899

El DERECHO. ir My? 1873-
CU-B Ag 12,17,22 1873

El DIA. d 1909+
LNT-M O 4 1932+
MWA Ap 3 1913
NN [S-D 1917]
NcD My 19 1923-Ja 12 1925

El DIABLILLO-ROJO. w N 2 1873-
CU-B N 9-16,30 1873

El ECO del comercio. w 1861-
CU-B O 31 1863

La ESTRELLA solitaria. d 1898-1900‖?
DLC [1898]

El FENIX. w 1855-
DLC O 13 1855-D 23 1858

HERALDO de trabajo. w 1878-
CU-B Ap 5,Jl 28 1880

El NACIONALISTA de Ponce. d 1923-27‖?
CU-B Mr 13,Ap 24-My 15,29,O 3,N 7,D 1925-Ja 9,Jl 24,Ag 28,N 20,D 18 1926;Ja 15,29,Je 11 1927

El NOTICIERO. d 1912-14‖
DLC Ja 24-28,F 2,24-Mr 2 1914
MWA Ap 3 1913

La NUEVA ERA. d Jl 30 1898-1901‖?
DLC Ag 19,O 29,N 25-26,28,D 2,31 1898;Je 9-10,12,Ag 4-5,S 18,O 19,24,N 21,23,25,28,D 6-7,14-16,21 1899;F 28 1900
WHi Jl 30 1898

LA PEQUEÑA Antilla. *See* La Propaganda

El PONCEÑO. w 1852-
CU-B My 14 1853
DLC Mr 25,Ap 22,Jl 8 1854

PORTO RICO American. tw F 4 1899-
DLC F 4 1899

PORTO RICO mail. d O 1898-99‖?
DLC O 22 1898
—**Spanish ed** *See* Correo de Puerto Rico

La PROPAGANDA. d 1895?-1900‖?
1895?-98? as La Pequeña Antilla
DLC My 14 1898;N 10,22,D 9 1899

PUERTO RICO eagle. *See* El Aguila de Puerto Rico

La VANGUARDIA. d N 1899-
DLC N 21,23,28,D 1-2,5,10,12,14,21 1899

SAN JUAN

El AGENTE. tw 1873-
CU-B N 2,4 1880

La ARANA. w? Ja 1902-
NjR F 16 1902

BOLETIN instructivo y mercantil. *See* Boletin mercantil de Puerto-Rico

BOLETIN mercantil de Puerto-Rico. sw,d 1839-1919‖?
Title varies: Boletin instructivo y mercantil; etc.
CSmH O 23 1859
CU-B My 19,Je 26 1841;D 4 1844;D 2 1846
DLC My 16,Ag 5 1857;Mr 28,Ap 27 1864;Ag 1-3,15-S 5,15-16,18-22,25,O 11-12,18,31,N 28,D 13-16,18-23 1899;Ja 12 1900-Ag,O 1901-Je,S 1902-My 4 1907
MWA My 24 1843;Mr 28 1913

CORREO dominical. w
NcD Ag 15,S 5,O 3,31-N 21,D 5-19 1926;27[Ja-S 1928]

La CORRESPONDENCIA de Puerto Rico. d 1890+
DLC D 20 1892;Je 1899-1903;Jl 1904+
MWA Ap 4 1913
NcD Jl 1911-[16-21]-N 1932
NjR F 16 1902

La DEMOCRACIA. d 1890+
DLC 1905+
NcD 1922-23;25-Je 1933

DIARIO de Puerto Rico. d 1900?-
DLC Ap 5-7,9-11,23 1900

El DUENDE. w Mr 4? 1866-
DLC O 7 1866

El FOMENTO de Puerto Rico. tw 1864-
DLC O 6 1864

GACETA de Puerto-Rico. tw,d 1832-99‖
1832?-58 as Gaceta del gobierno
tw 1832?-96
CU-B [1833;41]
DLC 1836;41-46;48-51;53-97;99
NN 1836[41]-[43]-[46]48[49;51]-[53;55]-[57-61]-[63-67]-[71-77]-[80-86]-[90]-[94]-[96-98]99

GOVERNMENT of Porto Rico official gazette. sm Ja 15 1909-Ja 1 1914‖
1909? as Official gazette of Porto Rico
In English and Spanish
DLC Ja-Mr 1909;Mr 1910-Ja 1,Mr 1913-14
NN Ja-Mr 1909;10-14

EL HERALDO español. d 1894-1914‖?
MWA Ap 3 1913

El IMPARCIAL. d 1918+
NcD N 1 1921[22-26]-[29-30]-N 2 1932

El MUNDO. d 1919+
DLC 1929+
NcD Ja 20-21,23,25,F 13-14,My 17-18,20,O 12 1922[My 1923-28]My 14 1931-32

San Juan NEWS. tw,d N 9 1898-Ap? 1905‖
1898-Ap 1899(tw) in English; 1900+(d) in English and Spanish
DLC Ag 19-S 5,O 11-12,31-N 1,D 16,19 1899; 1900-04
MdBSa Ag 16 1899
MiU [1902]-04
NbHi S 8-11,15,17,19 1901
NhD Jl 4 1899
NjR F 6-7 1902
WHi 1898-1904

El PAIS. d 1895-1905‖?
DLC My 30-N 24 1899

OFFICIAL gazette of Porto Rico. *See* Government of Porto Rico official gazette

El PAIS. d
NcD S 22-O 5,N 3-14,16-D 7,15-31 1932

PORTO RICO journal. d D 25? 1903-
DLC D 26,29 1903

El PREGONERO. d Ag? 1898-1902‖?
DLC O 16,18-19 1898

El PROGRESO. tw 1870-
DLC Mr 31 1872

La PROVINCIA. ir O 1871-
CU-B N 4,12 1871

PUERTO RICO progress. w D 8 1910+
DLC 1910-N 12 1912;D 10 1913-33

El TERRITORIO. d 1899?-
DLC My 30-D 21 1899

El TIEMPO. (Times) d 1907+
In Spanish and English
CtY S 23-24,26 1910;Ja 5 1914
DLC Ja-Je 1908;13-Je 3 1931
MWA Mr 1,18,Ap 9 1913
MiU 1926+
NFre Ag 15 1917
NN Ja-[Ap-Jl]-D 1912;Jl 1916-N 1918;19-Je 3 1931
NcD 1913-29;Mr-N 1930;Ap 15-My,Je 3 1931
WHi Ja 15 1918

TIMES. *See* El Tiempo

La UNION obrera. d 1902+
1902-18? pub in Mayaguez
MWA Ap 2 1913

La VOZ del obrero. w 1903+
MWA Mr 30 1913

RHODE ISLAND

APPONAUG

WARWICK city herald. *See under* Warwick

ARCTIC

PAWTUXET VALLEY daily times. *See under* West Warwick

AUBURN

CRANSTON CITY times. *See under* Cranston

Weekly MESSAGE. w Ja 25 1894-95‖
RHi F-Ag 10 1895

BARRINGTON

Warren and Barrington GAZETTE. *See under* Warren

BLOCK ISLAND

Block Island BUDGET. *See* Mid ocean

MID OCEAN. w,sw,tw Jl? 1885-1915‖?
1885? as Block Island budget
w 1885?;tw during season only
Ct Ag 31 1889
MWA Jl 30 1889
RHi Jl 1889-S 5 1906
RPS Ag 8 1885

Block Island WIRELESS. d Jl 9 1903-
RHi Jl-Ag 29 1903

BRISTOL

Bristol GAZETTE and family companion. w S 14 1833-S 2 1837‖
Followed by Bristol phenix, later Bristol phoenix
DLC N 2-9,23-D 7,21 1833-Ja 11,25-F 15,Mr 22-29,O 25 1834;Ja 3-10,F 7,21,Ap 11,Je 20,Ag 22,S 19,D 26 1835;F 27,Ap 2,My 14,28,Je 18,Jl 16,30,Ag 20,D 24 1836;Ja 7-21,F 18,Mr 4-18, Ap 1-8,22-My 6,Je 3,24-Jl 15 1837
MWA Ja 3 1835
RBrC complete
RBrP complete
RHi D 13 1834;Ag 22 1835;Ja 23 1836
RNHi Je 11 1836
RWa My 24,Je 28-Jl 12,26 1834

Bristol PHENIX. *See* Bristol phoenix

Bristol PHOENIX. w,sw S 16 1837+
Follows Bristol gazette and family companion. 1837-Mr 6 1869 as Bristol phenix
w 1837-N 1894
pub 1837+
DLC Mr 28 1840;Ja 11 1845;N 8-15 1851[52-54]S 29,N 24 1860;Mr 9 1861

RHODE ISLAND (*Continued*)

BRISTOL—*Continued*

Bristol PHOENIX. w,sw 1837+—*Continued*
MWA D 30 1837;Ja 18 1840;S 7 1844;Ja 11 1845[51]-Jl 8,D 5(extra)1854;Jl 14,Ag 18,S 8, 29-O 13 1855;D 3,6 1856[My 26-D 1860]-My 1861;O 25 1862;O 31 1868;Je 1 1878;Mr 16,Ag 31,S 28 1897;Ja 5-19 1912
MiU-C Mr 16 1897;Ja 5 1912
N N 5 1853
NCor Mr 1858-My 13 1871
NjFHi Jl 27 1861
RHi Mr 20 1841;Jl 1847;50+
RNHi Jl 4 1840;Mr 6 1841;Je 25 1853;91-93;95-1907
RPB O 6 1860;Mr 1 1861;Ap 22 1865
RW S 14 1839;Ja 28 1854

A VOZ da colonia. *See under* Providence

BURRILLVILLE

Papers published in Burrillville are listed under Pascoag

CENTRAL FALLS

L'ESPERANCE. sw Mr 26 1891-99||?
In French
RHi 1891-Mr 22 1899

Central Falls JOURNAL and wage earners advocate. w My 25 1895-1901||?
1895-Jl 21 1900 as Central Falls journal
RHi Ap 15 1899-Jl 21 1900;Je 2 1901

La JUSTICE. w Ap 5 1906-
In French
RHi 1906-Mr 1910

Weekly VISITOR. w O 1 1869-Ja 2 1891||
United with Pawtucket record to form Record visitor (Pawtucket)
MWA N 1869;F 18-25,My 13-20 1870;Jl 28-Ag 4,S 15 1871;Mr 16 1883
RHi complete

CRANSTON

Cranston CITIZEN. w 1915-20||?
REdH [N 1915-Ja 1916]

Cranston CITY times. w My 7 1895-D 23 1927||
1895-1920? pub in Auburn. United with Cranston news to form News-times, later Cranston news
REdH O 19 1911-27
RHi complete

Cranston LEADER. w Je 13 1889-
RHi 1889-F 6 1890

Cranston NEWS. w Jl 1 1922+
1928? as News-times
pub 1925+
REdH 1922+
RHi 1922+

EAST GREENWICH

GREENWICH enterprise. w 1888-89||?
RHi 1888-O 1889

KENT county atlas and East Greenwich observer. w My 18 1850-Je 25 1853||
1850-Ag 28 1852 as Kent county atlas
1850-Jl 3 1852 pub in Phenix
MWA D 11 1852
RHi complete

KENT county news. w O 17 1913-N 13 1914||
MWA O 17,31-D 24 1913;Ja-F 6 1914
RHi complete

East Greenwich NEWS. w Ap 21 1927-Je 28 1934||
United with Rhode Island pendulum to form Rhode Island pendulum and East Greenwich news
RHi complete

Weekly PENDULUM. . . *See* Rhode Island pendulum and East Greenwich news

RHODE ISLAND circle. Washington county weekly. w My 8-D 25 1925||
RHi complete

RHODE ISLAND pendulum and East Greenwich news. w My 27 1854+
1854-Je 14 1856? as Weekly pendulum and general advertiser for Kent and Washington counties; Je 21 1856-Je 30 1934 Rhode Island pendulum
1857-My 17 1878 also dated at Wickford
MWA S 16,N 25 1854;Mr 10,31 1855;D 4 1858; Ja 28,D 29 1876;S 15 1882;N 16 1911
REg 1914+
RHi 1854-Je 14 1856;Jl 20 1857-Je 8 1861;Je 1868-1909;S 14 1911+

EAST PROVIDENCE

East Providence EAGLE. w Je 14 1882-1910||
RHi 1882-F 1910

LEADER. w O 31 1930-S 11 1931||
RHi complete

East Providence MIRROR. w 1897-1906||?
RHi Ap 14 1899-My 1901

O POPULAR. w Ap 2 1914+
In Portuguese
RHi O 1933+

East Providence RECORD. w O 31 1885-O 18 1889||
Merged with Olneyville times, later Providence county times (Olneyville)
Ag 27 1887-O 18 1889 pub in Providence
RHi complete

RHODE ISLANDER. w 1884-1919||?
1884-Jl 24 1891 pub in Olneyville
MWA F 17[Je 23-D 1900]Ja,Ap 27,Je 1901-Ja 4,18-25 1902;05-Ja 13,27,F 3 1906;Ja-Je 1911
RHi Jl 31 1891-Jl 21 1893;Je 8-O 19 1895;Ag 1896-1911
RW Jl 31 1891-My 6 1892;Jl 15 1897-O 5 1901

East Providence STANDARD. w 1929-30||
RHi complete

GEORGIAVILLE

WOONASQUATUCKET weekly union. w F 23 1894-95||
RHi 1894-F 15 1895

HARRISVILLE

BURRILLVILLE news. *See under* Pascoag
BURRILLVILLE star. *See under* Pascoag

HOPE VALLEY

Hope Valley ADVERTISER. w Ja 6 1876+
1876-80 as Wood River advertiser; My 3 1883-Ap 26 1894 Sentinel advertiser
pub 1876-82;My 1883+
MWA Jl 18 1878
OClWHi Je 3 1886
RHi 1876-82;My 1883-Je 1885;86-93;Mr 1,My 1894+

Hope Valley FREE PRESS. w Jl 1891-Jl 6 1904||?
RHi Jl 11 1900-Jl 6 1904

SENTINEL advertiser. *See* Hope Valley advertiser

WOOD RIVER advertiser. *See* Hope Valley advertiser

KINGSTON

RHODE ISLAND advocate. w N 4 1831-
DLC O 5 1832
MWA D 30 1831;F 24,Mr 16-Ap 20,Je 1,Jl 27,Ag 17 1832
RHi 1831-N 23 1832

LONSDALE

BLACKSTONE VALLEY argus. w D 2 1882-84||
RHi 1882-Jl 12 1884

NARRAGANSETT

Narragansett Pier BREEZE. w S 1 1917-Ap 27 1918||
RHi complete

Narragansett HERALD. w Ap 21 1876-1901||?
1876-Ap 13 1877 as Narragansett herald and Hopkinton gazette and North Kinston courier
RHi 1876-98

SEASIDE topics. w Je 24 1905+
RHi Jl 8-Ag 1915;Ag-S 6 1917

Daily TIMES. d 1880?-1910||?
RHi Je 24 1896-S 9 1910
RNHi Je 19-S 7 1895;99-1900;02-03

Narragansett TIMES and Washington county advertiser. w
DLC Ja 24,F 28,Mr 6 1868

NEWPORT

Newport daily ADVERTISER. d N 16 1849-
Suspended Ap 1-29 1850
MWA N 22 1849
RHi 1849-Ap 1 1850
RNHi 1849-S 13 1850

Newport ADVERTISER. w Ja 2? 1850-D 8 1864||
1850-D 10 1851 as Newport weekly advertiser
DLC Ap 10 1850-64
MWA S 15 1852;F 17,Je 16(extra)1858
NNHi N 2 1852
NcD Ja 25 1854-[55]Ag 26,N 11 1857;58-59
OClWHi Ap 1863-Mr 1864
P-M Ap 21 1852;Ag 16 1854
RHi Ap 10 1850-Mr 1863;Ap-D 1864
RNHi [Ap 10 1850-64]

Newport ADVERTISER. w 1880-82||
RNHi [1882]

L'ALBA. w 1910+
1910-18? pub in Providence
In Italian and English
IU Ja 23,Je 19-26,Ag 1920-Ap 1923;Jl 1924-Ja 17,Ap-O 1931[32+]
M N 1 1930
RHi S 20 1913-O 1917;S 20 1919+
RNHi Ja 3 1913
RPB F 12 1927

ANTI-MASONICK Rhode Islander. w Ap 29 1829-
MWA S 23,N 4-11 1829
RHi Ap 29,My 20,Je 17-24,Ag 26,S 23,N 18-25 1829
RNHi Ap-N 1829

Newport ENTERPRISE. ir Mr 1 1886-S 23 1897||
MWA Mr 22 1886;D 22 1887;O 1890-S 1891
RHi complete
RNHi O 1891-97

FREEDOM'S advocate. w O 1 1830-
RNHi O-N 1830

FRESHEST advices. *See* *Newport mercury and weekly news

GLEANER. w Ag 11 1849-
RNHi Ag 11 1849

GUARDIAN of liberty. *See* Rhode Island republican

Newport daily HERALD. d D ? 1847-
RNHi D 8 1847-N 3 1848

Newport HERALD. d Mr 23 1892+
MWA Ja 1,My 21 1910
RHi 1892-1910;F 6 1911-18;20+
RNHi 1892+

HERALD of the times. w Ap 7 1830-56||
Ap 1846?-49? as Herald of the times and Rhode Islander
CtY 1830-50;S 18 1851;Ja 6 1852;Ja 20,F 3,17-24,Mr 24-31,My 26 1853;N 9 1854
DLC Ja 18 1838;N 5 1840[Mr-D 1841]Ja 3 1850;Mr 31 1853
MWA Ap 12,S 13 1832;Ap 1834-35;S 7,N 2 1837;D 5 1839;F 27,Jl 16 1840;My 5,Je 10,S 30 1841;My 28 1846;Mr 28 1850;Je 10 1852
N Je 30,Jl 14 1836
NNHi N 13 1834;Ap 25 1850
P-M O 8 1832
RHi Mr-D 1841;50-Mr 10 1853
RNHi 1830-55;Ap 17 1856
RNR [1830-48]
RPB [Ap 14 1830-O 1831]
RW Mr 21 1833;F 21,23,Je 15 1837
WHi Ja-O 16 1856

Newport JOURNAL and weekly news. w 1867-Ap 27 1928||
1867-S 30 1877 as Newport journal. United with Newport mercury to form Newport mercury and weekly news
MWA S 21 1871
RHi 1874-1928
RNR 1867-76;88;91

Newport weekly JOURNAL and Rhode Islander. w
RHi Ja 1,S 24,N 12,D 10 1857

Newport evening MERCURY. d Jl 4 1853-F 15 1854||
RHi O 8 1853
RNHi complete

*Newport MERCURY and weekly news. w Je 19 1758+
1758-Ja 23? 1759 as Newport mercury; or, the weekly advertiser; 1759-Ap 28 1928 Newport mercury (N 6 1775 Occasional paper; N 13-27 1775 Freshest advices)
Suspended from D 4 1775-Ja 5 1780
pub 1821+
CSmH S 4 1830
Ct N 7 1835
CtY S 7 1822;My 26,Ag 11,S 1 1832;N 9 1833; 49-Je 1851; F 10,Mr 24,Ap 14,My 12,26,Je 9, 30 1855;59-63
DLC 1821-78;Mr 19 1881-Je 12 1886;98+
MH Ag 30,O 25 1856
MSaE Jl 26 1823
MWA 1821-60[Ap 12-D 1842]-79;D 31 1881-[84]-[87]-Je,D 13 1890;91-1930
MiU [1842]-[45]58-62
MiU-C [1823;25;30-40]-[42-49]-[51]-[57]-[60-61; 63-71]-[74-76;83;86;91-1904]-[07]09-10[12-13]
NN Ag 14 1824;Je 12 1858
NNHi Jl 26,N 8,D 13 1823;Ag 28,S 11-18,D 18 1824;Jl 5 1828;D 28 1833;Ja 12 1850;Mr 8, O 4 1873;My 31,Je 21,N 15-22,D 6 1879;Ap 24 1880;Ap 15 1882
NNS F 1901-My 10 1902
NbHi Je 12 1858
NcD O 20 1849;Je 12 1858
NjHi [1821-28]
PWbW 1899+
RHi 1821+
RPB Mr 11,Ap 22 1865[79-82]
RW O 31 1868
—d ed *See* Newport daily news

Newport daily NEWS. d My 4 1846+
pub 1846+
CtY S 3 1877
DLC O 26 1849-Ag 26 1852
MWA My 4(supp)Je 15,27,Jl 3 1846;D 1 1852; N 24 1854;Jl 4 1855;Ja 18 1856;Ag 23,D 2 1859;Ja 24,Ap 18,20,24,Je 14,20,Jl 22(extra) 1861;Jl 8 1864;Ag 17 1866;Ap 10,17 1868;Je 7 1871;Je 17 1875;Je 29 1878;Ap 7,Je 18,S 20 1880;Ja 17,N 11 1884;Mr 12,21,Ap 22 1885; Ag 18 1886;S 29 1887;Ap 17 1888;Ja-Ap 10 1891
MiU-C N 8 1875
NNHi My 4 1846(supp)Ap 19 1873;Je 25-26 1889
RHi O 25 1850;Jl 15 1854;F 22 1859;My 29 1863;64+
RNHi My 4 1846(reprint)[48-Jl 2 1849]-54;Jl 1855-O 15 1856[Je 12 1857-Ap 1 1876]77;88-91; Ja 1892
RW My 4 1846;S 6 1859;My 4 1893
WHi My 4 1846(reprint)
—w ed *See* Newport mercury and weekly news

Newport weekly NEWS. w
MWA Ap 1 1859

Newport daily OBSERVER. d Je 7 1886-Je 30 1894||
1886-My? 1888 as Season; Je?-Ag 31 1888 Newport daily observer and the season
DLC Je 13 1889
MWA Jl-D 1893
NNHi Je 26-27 1889
RHi Je-S 1886; Je 16 1888-94
RNHi Jl 1890-94

OCCASIONAL paper. *See* Newport mercury and weekly news

QUILL. w O 17 1878-Ja 2 1879||
RNHi complete

RHODE ISLAND gazette. w S 27 1834-
DLC O 4-11 1834

RHODE ISLAND (*Continued*)

NEWPORT—*Continued*

*RHODE ISLAND republican. w O 3 1800-Ap 21 1841||
1800-S 26 1801 as Guardian of liberty. Followed by Rhode Islander
Suspended Je 26 1806-Mr 22 1809
Ct [1833-38]
CtY 1832-39
DLC 1821-D 13 1827;29-30;Ja 3,S 11,O 9,21,D 11-25 1832;O 9 1833-41
MB S 26 1821;My 26-Je 9 1825
MBAt My 7 1828
MHi [1832-1833]S 23 1835
MSaE Jl 16 1823;Ap 10 1839;Ap 1 1840
MWA [1821-O 23 1822;23-N 11 1824;Ja-Ap 1825]F 16,Je 22,Ag 17,S 22 1826;Ja 4,My 10 1827;Ap 17,My 15,O 23 1828;F 12,Mr 12-19,O 8,D 3,24 1829;My 13 1830;Je 9,21 1831;Ja 10 1832;Ag 6-20,O 15 1834-O 12,N 23 1836;F 8-15, Mr 1,Je 14 1837[Mr 21-D 5 1838]My 27 1840; Mr 5(extra)1841
N Ag 4,18 1825
NNHi Ag 22 1821;Ap 2 1823;Ja 29 1824;Ja 31-F 14,Mr-My 8 1832;S 17 1833
NcD Mr 5 1823;37
RHi 1821-41
RNHi 1821-35;O 26 1836-41
RNR [1821-35]

RHODE ISLANDER. w My 4 1841-Mr 4 1846||
Follows Rhode Island republican. United with Herald of the times to form Herald of the times and Rhode Islander, later Herald of the times
DLC My 4,19-26 1841;Mr 16 1842;Mr 18-My 1845
MWA S 22 1841;Je 29 1842;S 13 1843;Ag 28 1844
NNHi Mr 22 1843
RHi Ja 12-D 1842;D 24 1845
RNHi complete
RWa Ja 7 1846

SEASON. *See* Newport daily observer

TEA TRAY.
RHi O 10 1866
RNR Ag 10 1866

WORKINGMAN'S journal. w My 31 1853-
Prospectus Mr 8 1853
DLC Je 7 1853
MWA Mr 8,Je 7 1853

NORTH SCITUATE

LITTLE Rhody. *See under* Scituate

OLNEYVILLE

Olneyville HERALD. *See* Olneyville news herald

Olneyville NEWS herald. w My 18 1928-Mr 10 1932||
1928-Jl 2 1931 as Olneyville herald
RHi complete

PROVIDENCE county times. w S 3 1887+
1887-Ap 27 1909 as Olneyville times
MWA Ja 3-10,O 17,31 1913;S-D 1914;Ja 8 1915
RHi 1887-Ag 1909;F 1911+

RHODE ISLAND citizen. w Ja 4 1884-85||
RHi 1884-Ag 7 1885

RHODE ISLAND citizen. w Ag 1 1890-95||?
RHi 1890-Jl 24 1891

RHODE ISLANDER. *See under* East Providence

Olneyville TIMES. *See* Providence county times

Olneyville TRIBUNE. w S 2 1893-96||?
RHi 1893-Ag 1894

PASCOAG

BURRILLVILLE gazette. *See* Burrillville news gazette

BURRILLVILLE news. w Mr 23 1892-93||
United with Burrillville gazette to form Burrillville news gazette
1892-Ja 1 1893 pub in Harrisville
RHi 1892-Mr 17 1893

BURRILLVILLE news gazette. w F 12 1880-D 28 1894||
1880-93 as Burrillville gazette. Merged with Pascoag herald, later Pascoag herald and news gazette
RHi 1880-Ja 1893;94

BURRILLVILLE star. w Ap 30 1895-
Dated also at Harrisville
RHi 1895-Ap 21 1896

Pascoag HERALD and news gazette. w Ap 2 1892-Ap 12 1918||
1892-Mr 30 1905 as Pascoag herald
F 24 1905 is historical ed
MWA Je 30 1894;F 24,Ap 7,21,Je 2,N 10 1905
NcD Je 30 1894
RChT complete
RHi 1892-1909;11-18
RPas complete

Weekly WORLD. w Ja 28 1932-D 21 1933||
RHi complete

PAWTUCKET

Pawtucket CHRONICLE and Rhode Island and Massachusetts register. w N 12 1825-Ap 19 1839||
1825-Ja? 1827 as Pawtucket chronicle, and manufacturers' and artizans' advocate. United with Pawtucket gazette to form Pawtucket gazette and chronicle
Ct [1826-27]
DLC Ja 4,O 7 1826;Ja 19 1828;Jl 18-Ag 8,22,S 5,19,O 3,24-31,N 28,D 6,26 1829;Ja 1-9,23 1830
MWA D 17 1825;Ja 14,D 16-23 1826;Ja 20,Mr 17,Ap 14,My 19,Jl 28,S 29-O 6,20,N 3,D 1827; Ja-S 13 1828;29-32;Ag 1-8,S 26,D 12 1834;S 4 1835;Ap 22 1836;39
MiU-C [1828;30]
N Mr 21 1834
NNHi N 12 1825
NcD Ap 10-D 1830
OClWHi S 19 1829
PEL Ja 23,F 20 1830
RHi N 11 1826-38
RPa complete

Pawtucket GAZETTE and chronicle. w Ag 3 1838-1914||
1838-Ap 26 1839 as Pawtucket gazette
ICHi F 20 1846
MWA My 1839-41;Jl 27 1849-89;O 3-17 1890; 91-99;1903-09;O 11 1912
MiU-C [1850]52[53-64]-[70-71]-[78-79]
NNHi Ja 22 1841;Ja 24 1873
NcD Mr 7 1856
NjR [Jl 22 1853-Jl 14 1854]
RPB Ag 31 1860;Ap 21 1865
RPa My 1839-92
RW F 26 1875
WHi Mr 24 1854;O 3 1890

Pawtucket HERALD and independent inquirer. w S 3 1828-Ja 20 1830||
Followed by Providence free press and Pawtucket herald (Providence)
DLC F 18,Ap 15-22 1829
MWA D 17 1828
RPB complete

Le JEAN-BAPTISTE. w 1874+
In French
IU [D 14 1917-Ag 23 1918]
MWA Je 30 1933
RHi 1897-F,Jl 17-Ag 11 1933

Pawtucket OBSERVER. w 1860-
RPB Ag 30,S 13 1860

Pawtucket evening POST. *See* Sun

REAL ESTATE record. *See* Record visitor

RECORD visitor. m,w Ap 1 1886-91||
Ap-My 1886 as Real estate record; Je 1886-D 30 1890 Pawtucket record
m Ap-My 1886
RHi 1886-Ja 7 1891

Pawtucket SUN. w Ja 31 1883-Ja 21 1888||
RHi complete

SUN. d D 11 1893-97||
1893-N 5 1897 as Pawtucket evening post
RHi 1893-D 11 1897
RPA 1893-D 10 1896

Pawtucket TIMES. d Ap 30 1885+
N 12 1886-Mr 26 1890 as Pawtucket evening times
pub 1885+
Ct Je 30 1922
DLC 1898+
MAtt Jl 11 1902; Ja 9 1905
MWA S 21-22 1886;S 29 1890;My 10,15 1905; Mr 31 1906;My 21-D 1913
RHi Ap 30 1886-S 24 1892;Mr 27 1893+
RNHi Mr 26 1891-Mr 1910
RPA S 26 1895+

Evening TRIBUNE. d S 15 1888-1900||?
S 29 1890-S 14 1895 as Pawtucket tribune
RHi 1888-S 14 1895;N 30 1896-Ag 17 1900

PHENIX

Daily GLEANER. d Jl 1 1892-93||?
RHi 1892-93
—w ed *See* Pawtuxet Valley gleaner

Phenix weekly JOURNAL. *See* Village journal

KENT county atlas. *See* Kent county atlas and East Greenwich observer (East Greenwich)

PAWTUXET VALLEY gleaner. w 1876-1906||?
RHi My 19 1877;78-1902;05-06
RPB Jl 19 1879-81
RW S 16 1892
—d ed *See* Daily gleaner

VILLAGE journal. w N 1 1860-
1860-61? as Phenix weekly journal
RHi 1860-O 24 1861;My 15 1862
RPS Ap 4 1861

PORTSMOUTH

PRUDENCE ISLAND beacon. w
RHi Jl 31-S 4 1926

PROVIDENCE

ADVANCE. w,m Jl 6 1906+
w 1906-N 1914
Negro
RHi N 16 1906+

Daily ADVERTISER and American. d Jl 20 1829-Ja 31 1833||
1829-Je 5 1830 as Providence daily advertiser; Je 6-D 31 1830 Daily advertiser
CSmH Ag 14 1830
DLC [1829-Ja]N 19,D 4,7 1830;O 2 1832
MWA [1829]Ja 30,F 16 1830-31;N 23 1832; Ja 4-8 1833
MiU-C [1829-30]
RHi 1829;Je 1830-Mr 3 1832
RW Ag 22 1829-Jl 16 1830
—sw ed *See* Rhode Island American and gazette
—w ed *See* Microcosm, American and gazette

L'ALBA. *See under* Newport

Providence ALLEHANDA. w 1891-92||
In Swedish
IRA [1891-92]

AMERICAN. *See* Rhode Island American and gazette

AMERICAN citizen. d
RHi My 14,29 1855

Providencer ANZEIGER. w 1884-Jl 1918||
In German
IU S 15 1917-Jl 6 1918
RHi 1889-1912

BANGS'S trumpet. w O 18 1856-O 3 1857||
Followed by Evening telegraph?
MWA complete
RHi complete

BEACON. w N 11 1823-
Suspended Jl 31-S 25 1824
MWA Ja 3-24,Je 19,Jl 10,D 4 1824[25-O 1826] S 17,O 8,29 1827
MiU-C [1826]
NNHi Jl 2 1825;Ja 14 1826
RHi 1823-F 11,Mr 11,O 28 1826
RPB Ja 17 1824-F 11 1826
RW S 23 1826

BEACON light. w Mr 11- 1829||?
RHi Mr 11 1829

Weekly BULLETIN. w Mr 15 1861-
RHi Mr 29 1861

Evening BULLETIN. d Ja 26 1863+
pub 1863+
DLC S 23 1863
IHi Ap 27 1865
InRE S 30 1885
MAtt S 8 1896
MSaE Ag 1 1866
MWA Ja 26(facsimile)S 23 1863;My 7,19 1864;Ap 15,27,My 2,Ag 1,S 20 1865;S 8 1866; Ja 26,Ag 24,S 4 1869;Ja 29,D 22 1870;S 16 1871;Jl 26 1873;Ja 15,S 25 1879;Ja 16,N 5 1880;Mr 14,30,Ap 4 1881;F 4 1882;Ja 24 1883; Je 12,23-25 1886;F 20 1888;S 30 1890;N 27, D 29-30 1891;D 1,22,30 1893;Ja 5,10,13,17,29 1894;My 29 1905;Ja 25 1913
MiU-C [1891-92;1903]
NN S 30 1865
NNHi F 4 1865;My 1 1873;N 8,17 1876
NbHi F 11-12,Ap 13,15,17,20,22,My 22,26,Je 3,Jl 3,O 14 1865
NcD Je 20 1878(supp)Je 16 1885
OClWHi Jl 23 1863;Ap 15 1865;S 15 1881
RA Ja-N 11 1863
REdH Ja 26,S 23 1863;S 12-13,16-17 1901
RHi Ja 26(facsimile)S 23 1863;My 7 1864-65; 68-69;D 7 1870;S 7,11-13 1872;74-Je,S 1911+
RP Ja 26(facsimile)1863;My 1864-Ap 1865; 1916+
RPB [1863-D 16 1865]Ja 26(facsimile)1863
WHi Je 25 1886
—morning ed *See* Providence journal
—sw ed *See* Manufacturers' and farmers' journal
—w ed *See* Rhode Island country journal

CADET and statesman. w,sw Ap 22 1826-Jl 18 1829||
1826-Ap 14 1827 as Literary cadet and Saturday Evening bulletin; Ap 18 1827-Ja 7 1829 Literary cadet and Rhode Island statesman. United with Rhode Island American and Providence gazette to form Rhode Island American, statesman and gazette, later Rhode Island American and gazette
w 1826-Ap 14 1827
CtY F 3,My 16,S 12 1827
DLC 1826-Ja 24,Mr 11,Jl 18 1829
GMM N 25 1826-[27-Ap 15 1829]
MB 1826-Ap 14 1827;Ap 12 1828
MSaE [Je 1826-Ap 1827]Ap 11 1829
MWA 1826-Jl 15 1829
NN complete
NNHi 1826-Ap 7 1827
NcD 1826[27]-[29]
REdH Je 10 1826-Ap 12 1828
RHi complete
RPA 1826-F 11 1829
RPB Mr 31 1827
RW Je 11 1828

Evening CALL. d Ap 30 1889-90||?
RHi N 19 1889-Ja 11 1890

Campaign JOURNAL. sw 1861||?
RHi Ap 1 1861
RPB Mr 21-25 1861
RW My 22 1861

CAMPAIGN post. sw 1856||?
RHi S 23-O 10 1856

CHRISTIAN monitor and weekly register. w My 26 1821-N 13 1824||
My-Jl 7 1821 as Religious intelligencer; Jl 14 1821-My 16 1823 Rhode Island religious intelligencer; My 23 1823-My 14 1824 Religious intelligencer and evening gazette
MWA complete
MiU-C [1821-22]D 12 1823;N 13 1824
NcD [My-Jl 1821]-Ap,My 10-17,N 1,D 6 1822
RHi Ag 22,O 10 1823;Ap 30,Jl 3 1824
RPB My 23 1823-My 14 1824
RW Ja 11 1822

Daily evening CHRONICLE. d Mr 30 1842-Ja 13 1844||
United with Daily transcript to form Daily transcript and chronicle, later Daily evening transcript
DLC F 15 1843
MH My 14,16,Je 28 1842
MWA [My 3 1842-N 6 1843]Ja 1-5,8-10,12-13 1844
NcD Mr 29-Ap 3,5-7,25 1843
RHi 1842-S 29 1843
RPB [Ap 26 1842-43]
—w ed *See* Narragansett chief

Providence evening CHRONICLE. d O 10 1874-
RHi O 10 1874

Saturday CHRONICLE. w 1878-79||?
KHi O 12 1878

RHODE ISLAND (*Continued*)

PROVIDENCE—*Continued*

CHRONICLE and American. *See* Rhode Island American and gazette

CHRONICLE of the times. sw S 28 1831-My 1832||
United with Rhode Island American and gazette to form Chronicle and American, later Rhode Island American and gazette
RHi S 28 1831

Providence **CITY gazette and literary subaltern.** d,w F 1 1833-34||
F-N? 1833 as Providence city gazette(d)
Ct [1834]
MWA My 25,Je 11 1833
N O 25 1833
RHi F-O 21 1833;Mr 7 1834
RPB My 30-O 21,D 6 1833-Mr 1834

CLARK'S counterfeit expositor and weekly miscellany. w 1831?-
RHi F 5 1831

COLD water gazette. w Mr 21- 1840||
MWA Ap 11 1840
NcD Ap 11 1840
RHi Mr 21-28,Ap 11 1840

COLUMBIAN phenix. *See* Providence patriot

Providence **COMMERCIAL advertiser.** d My 27-Jl 25 1834||
DLC My 29 1834
MWA My 29,31,Je 7,11,19-20, 24-25,28-Jl 2,7, 14,18,21-22 24-25 1834
RHi complete

CONSTITUTIONAL union. sw? 1861-
RHi Ap 3-5 1861
RPB Mr 13 1861

Il CORRIERE del Rhode Island. w 1904-25||?
In Italian
RHi 1917-D 19 1924;Ja 9,Ap 17-24,My 22 1925

COSMOPOLITAN. *See* Echo

Morning **COURIER and general advertiser.** d Je 6 1836-
MB Ja 30(supp)1838
MWA Jl 13-15,O 31,N 21 1839
RHi Je 13, S 16 1836;Ap 10,Je 6,Ag 15,O 17, N 21,28 1837;Mr 25,O 15 1839
RPA Ag 8 1838-Ja 27 1840
RPB 1836-[D 17 1839-Ja 24 1840]

Morning **COURIER and general advertiser.** sw Je 7 1836-
DLC Ap 20,29,Je 5-15,O 12 1838;Je 4,Jl 2, O 18 1839;Ap 14 1840
MNb N 1839-N 1840
MSaE Ap 9 1839
MWA N 10 1837;Ag 10,S 4-7,O 26,N 9 1838;F 26,Ap 16,23-30,My 7-17,24-S 3,10,D 31 1839; F 18,My 12 1840;41
NNHi Jl 30 1839
RHi F 18-D 1840;42;F 14,Ag 11,18,S 15,My 6 1843;Ja 13 1844
RPA Ja 31-S 1840
RPB 1836-Ja 15 1847

Le COURRIER. w 1906-07||?
In French
RHi My 1906-Ap 1907

DAY STAR. d
RHi Mr 5 1849-F 9 1850

Weekly **DEMOCRAT.** w Ag 27 1870-
RHi S 10 1870

DEMOCRATIC republican. sw Mr 5 1845-N 7 1846||
MWA Jl 23 1846
RPB Jl 9-12,S 10 1845
—d ed *See* Providence daily gazette

Providence Sunday **DISPATCH.** w My 24 1874-91||?
Title varies: Sunday dispatch
DLC 1874-My 14 1876
MWA Je 3 1877,Jl 21 1878
RHi 1877-79;81-84;O 31 1886;Ag 20 1890-Ag 1891

Providence daily **DISPATCH.** d S 6 1886-My 11 1889||
Title varies: Evening dispatch; Providence evening dispatch
RHi Jl 7-S 5 1887; F 12 1889

Providence morning **DISPATCH.** d 1887-89||
MWA N 1 1888
RHi F 12 1889

EAST PROVIDENCE record. *See under* East Providence

ECHO. w Mr 16 1876-F 15 1879||
1876-Ja 11 1879 as Cosmopolitan. Merged with Parrott
MWA Ja 11 1879
RHi complete

L'ECO del Rhode Island. *See* Italian echo

ELMWOOD sector. *See* Elmwood times

ELMWOOD times. w My 2 1924-
My-Jl 11 1924 as Elmwood sector
RHi My 23 1924-My 7 1926

Sunday **EXAMINER.** w S 17 1933-My 6 1934||
S 17 1933 as Sunday mirror
RHi complete

Providence **EXPRESS.** d Mr 16 1842-Ap 29 1843||
CSmH My 3 1842
DLC O 11 1842
MAtt S 24 1842
MWA Mr-Je 27,S 13 1842-[Ap 1843]
MiU-C [1842]
NcD Ap 12 [My-Je] 1842
RHi complete
RPB [1842-43]

EXTINGUISHER. w 1840||
RPB O 7 1840

FINANCIAL news. sw Je 7 1890-91||?
MWA D 1890-O 3 1891
RHi 1890-O 3 1891

FOLKETS röst. w 1894-96||?
In Swedish
IRA [1896]

Providence **FREE PRESS and Pawtucket herald.** w Ja 28 1830-31||?
Follows Pawtucket herald and independent inquirer (Pawtucket)
CSmH My 6 1830
RHi D 23 1830
RPA 1830-Ja 20 1831
RPB Ja-Ag 19 1830

FREMONT flag. S 10 1856||
RHi complete

FRIEND of man. w D 17 1842-D 9 1843||
CtSp complete
RHi complete
RPA complete

GASPEE torch light. w Ag 7-O 29? 1840||
DLC Ag 27 1840
MWA Ag 14-O 1840
NcD O 29 1840
RHi S 4,O 2,29 1840
RPB Ag 7 1840

*Providence **GAZETTE.** w,sw O 20 1762-O 8 1825||
1762-Ja 10 1795 as Providence gazette and country journal; Ja 12 1811-F 22 1817 Providence gazette and country journal; Mr 1 1817-19 Providence gazette and moral, political and commercial register. United with Rhode Island American to form Rhode Island American and Providence gazette, later Rhode Island American and gazette
Suspended My 11 1765-Ag 9 1766
w 1762-1819
CtY 1821-O 1 1825
DLC 1821-[24-25]
MBAt D 17 1823;Mr 17 1824
MSaE F 12 1823
MWA 1821-25
MiU [1821]-[23-25]
N Ja-N 14 1821
NN 1821[22]-[Ja-Jl 1825]
NNHi [1821-23]Ja 7,21-28,F 21 1824
NcD [1821-Ag 10 1825]
NjR [1821-F 6 1822]
PPL [1824]
RHi 1821-25
RPB 1821-25
RW Ag 6 1823

Providence daily **GAZETTE.** d Ap 20 1844-N 7 1846||
DLC [1845-46]
MWA Ja-Jl 1,24,Ag 13 1845;O 29 1846
RHi complete
RPB Jl 20 1844[Mr 29 1845-Je 20 1846]
—sw ed *See* Democratic republican

Providence weekly **GAZETTE.** w Mr 6 1867-73||?
United with General advertiser to form General advertiser and Providence weekly gazette
MWA F 17,Ag 25 1870
RHi 1867-69;Mr 1870-F 1871;F 29-N 9 1872

Saturday evening **GAZETTE and ladies toilet.** w 1828-
GMM Ja 24-Jl 18 1829
MWA Ja 24,Mr 14 1829
REdH F 28 1829
RHi My 9,Je 20 1829

GENERAL advertiser and Providence weekly gazette. w D 4 1847-91||?
1847-73? as General advertiser
DLC F 14 1863
MWA D 18 1847;Mr 23 1850;Ja 25 1851;D 25 1852;My 19 1855;Ja 9-16,Ag 7 1858;Jl 7 1860; My 18-Je 1,29,Jl 6-20 1861;N 14 1868
MiU-C Je 29,Jl 20 1861
RHi D 11 1847;My 20 1848;Ag 24,S 21 1850;S 6 1856;Ja 17 1857;My 1873-Je 1884
RPB Mr 16 1850

GOSPEL messenger and Providence and Worcester journal. w N 28 1840-
1840-Ja 8 1842 as Gospel messenger
MWA Jl 10-N 20 1841
RHi 1840-Ja 6,F 25 1843

HERALD. w 1828 *See* Republican herald

Providence morning **HERALD.** d Mr 18 1850-My 21 1873||
1850-My 11 1867 as Providence daily post
Suspended My 11-21 1867
DLC F 1854-Je 1863;Ja-Je 1864;Ja-Je 1865;66-67;Ja-N 27 1869
MBAt Ap 17 1865
MWA 1850;My 6,9,Jl 1851-My 11,Jl 1867-73
MiU-C [1855;57]-[59-63;65-66;68]
NIC Jl-D 1858;Jl-D 1860
NN Mr 11 1853;Ja 18,30,F 9 1854
OClWHi Ag 6 1862
RHi 1850-Mr 17,Jl 23-24,S 2,12,15,19 1856;57-73
RPA Jl 1851-56
RPB Ap 3 1852;S 16-19,23,O 5 1854[58-My 11 1867]-73
RW [Mr 11 1852-Jl 14 1863]
—sw ed *See* Republican herald
—w ed *See* Rhode Island weekly post; Republican herald and Rhode Island gazetteer

Daily evening **HERALD and commercial intelligencer.** *See* Republican herald

Providence **HEROLD.** w O 21 1897-99||
In German
RHi 1897-O 15 1898

INDEPENDENT. *See under* Woonsocket

INDEPENDENT citizen. w Ja 5 1889-98||
RHi 1889-Ja 1 1898

INDEPENDENT gazette. w Ja 7 1843-
MWA Ja-Mr 1843
MiU-C Ja 19,F 2 1843
RHi Ja 19 1843

INDEPENDENT inquirer. *See* Rhode Island country journal

INDICATOR. w My 10 1883-88||
S 13 1884 as Indicator and society journal; My 1 1886 Providence indicator
RHi 1883-87;Je 9 1888

INVESTIGATOR and general intelligencer. w O 11 1827-Ja 9 1829||
United with National philanthropist (Boston) to form National philanthropist and investigator (not in this list)
DLC D 4 1828
MWA Ja 17,My 29,O 23 1828
N O 11 1827
RHi complete

ITALIAN echo. w O 2 1897+
1897-1929 as L'Eco del Rhode Island
In English and Italian
RHi 1897+

ITALIAN review. w Mr 29 1924-D 19 1925||?
RHi 1924-D 19 1925

Evening **ITEM.** d Ag 2-N 22 1886||
Merged with Providence star
RHi complete
RPB complete

Providence **JEWISH chronicle.** ir Mr 14 1919-20||?
Followed by Jewish review
RHi Mr-O 24 1919

JEWISH herald. w S 1929+
RHi N 14 1930+

JEWISH review. w,ir F 20 1920-N 20 1931||
Follows Providence Jewish chronicle. 1920-S 22 1922 as Rhode Island Jewish review
MWA Mr 19,Ap 2,O 15 1920
RHi complete

Providence **JOURNAL.** d Jl 21 1829+
1829-Je 4 1830 as Providence daily journal and general advertiser; Je 5 1830-F 9 1920 Providence daily journal
Jl 23 1929 is centenary ed
pub 1829+
CL Jl 23 1929
CSmH Ag 26 1830;Jl 19 1842
Ct Ap 13 1877;N 30 1925
DLC [1829-Ja 1830]Ja 18 1831;O 6 1832[My-D 1836]Ag 16,O 9,N 7,20 1837;Mr 26,My 1,S 6 1838;Je 4 1839;D 5 1840;F 17 1841;Ja-N 12 1842;Ja-Jl 1843;S 11 1849;Ja 7 1850-Jl 1853;F 10,22 1854;55-56;S 1-14,N 1857;58+
ICHi N 3 1865
ICN Mr 1863-Je 1864
IHi F 4-6,Mr 4,7 1924;Jl 23 1929
M [Ja 28 1929-D 4 1933]
MBAt Je 4 1830;Ap 15,19 1865;Je 24 1886;Jl 23 1929
MHi Ag 18,S 4 1832[36-38]S 27 1851;S 1 1853; S 23 1863;Jl 23 1929
MNaHi D 14 1864;Ja 12 1865
MSaE Jl 25-26,Ag 5,11,O 27,N 19,25,D 27 1864[65-69]S 26,28-30 1881
MWA Jl 23,27,Ag 7 1829[30-Ja]Ap 6,Je 15, 17,Ag 16,N 25 1831[32]Mr 11,Jl 15 1833;N 1,3-4 1834[35-O 4 1836]Mr 22,Je 2,Jl 3,8, Ag 7-8 1837;F 23,O 4,8-9 1838; Ap 8-D 1839 [S-D 1840]-95;D 25 1896;Jl 1897-98;Ja 19 1900;S 14 1901;My 31,O 20 1902-[Ja-N 11 1903]Ag 17 1905;O 1908+
MeBa Ja 25 1844
MiU Ag 1860-Je 1866;Ja-Je 1872;Jl-D 1874
MiU-C [1830;35;39;42-61]-[63-65]-[67-73]-[75-76]-[80-99;1901-03;10]
N O 14 1833;F 3 1855
NIC 1862-Je 1864;Ja-Je 1865;66-70
NN 1858-80
NNC Jl 23 1929
NNHi Ag 7 1869;My 2,O 6 1873
NbHi N 4-11 1900
NcD My 18-21,26Je 28 1842;D 11 1844;Ja 15, Mr 22,My 12 1845;Jl 13,D 21 1850[51-52]Ap 7 1853[54]Ja-Ap,Je-D 1857;F 1858;Ja-N 18 1859;Ap-O 1860;Ja-O 1861;N 1863;Ja-F,Ap-Je,S-O 1864;Jl-D 1865[67-69;72]O 2 1873[74-75]-[80]-Je 1881[82]Mr 1-4,Ap 1883-[84]-[86-87]
OClWHi S 7 1860;Mr 29,Ap 15-25,My 19,27 1865
OHi 1933+
PP Je 17 1841
REg 1915+
RHi Jl 23 1829-Mr 3 1832;33+
RP Ja-Je 1836;Jl 1838-45;Ja-Je 1853;S 1857-Mr 1858;59-Je 1874;S 1884-S 1893;My-D 1897; My 1898-Ap 1899;S 1900-Ag,O-D 1901[My 1902-Ap 1904]+
RPA Jl 17 1846-1910
RPB [O 21 1829-38]+
RW [Je 22 1841-S 14 1872]
VU O 10 1905
WHi My 15 1864;Je 24 1886;S 21 1918-19; O 14 1920+
—evening ed *See* Evening bulletin
—sw ed *See* Manufacturers' and farmers' journal
—w ed *See* Rhode Island country journal

Providence weekly **LEDGER.** w 1890-92||
RHi F 22 1890-S 1892

La LIBERTA. w 1901-09||
In Italian
RHi Jl 1902-D 23 1909

LITERARY cadet. . . *See* Cadet and statesman

RHODE ISLAND (*Continued*)

PROVIDENCE—*Continued*

LITERARY subaltern. sw,w Ja 1 1829-N 22 1833||?
United with Providence city gazette to form Providence city gazette and literary subaltern
sw Ja-Je 1829
CtY Jl 17 1829-D 7 1832
DLC Ja 6,Mr 17,N 20,29 1829;30;Ja 21 1831
GMM 1827-D 7 1832
MTaHi 1829-31
MWA [1829]Ap 23,Je 4(extra)Jl 30,Ag 20, S 24,N 19 1830;Ap 6-13 1832
N O 21 1831
PEL F 11 1831
RHi Ap 24 1826-N 22 1833
RPB Ja 6 1829-N 22 1833

LOOKOUT. *See* Rhode Islander

Evening **MAIL.** d S 29 1884-N 5 1885||
RHi complete

***MANUFACTURERS' and farmers' journal.** sw Ja 3 1820-D 31 1907||
1820-Ap 27 1848 as Manufacturers' and farmers journal and Providence and Pawtucket advertiser
pub complete
CL O 20 1825;Jl 23 1827
Ct [1826-30]
CtSp Jl 23 1829
CtY 1836;44-47
DLC [F-N 1824]Mr 24,Ap 4,N 24 1825-36; Mr 8 1838-39;S 20 1841;D 6 1849;Ag 28 1865
ICN Jl 13 1863-Je 1864
MH Ag 4,11,S 18,O 20,D 15 1823;Ap 17 1828; Ja 20 1840;D 10 1846;Jl 1 1861;O 19 1899
MHi Ja 1,D 6 1824;F 1-8 1827 [36-38;48-50] Ap 23 1863
MSaE Jl 30 1821
MSob 1823
MWA Jl 23 1821[Je 13-D 1822]-[30-31]-Ja 17,Jl 25,D 2 1833;34-38;O 24 1839;40-69;Ja 3-13 1870;Ja-F 1872;Mr 18 1875;S 18 1876
NGL Jl 22 1833
NN S 6 1840;Ap 12 1841;F 24 1851;S 18 1871; Jl 6 1876
NNHi D 27 1824;42-43;Mr 20 1873
NcD Ja 22 1824;Mr 28,Jl 30 1829;Jl 12,Ag 19,O 21,N 4,18,D 6 1830;Jl 10,Ag 4 1834;F 18 1836;Jl 18[N 1864-65]Je 15 1885
NhD O 17 1839
OClWHi Ag 31 1829
PDoHi S 25 1826
PPL Ja 1-15,22-F 8 1821
RHi 1821-D 19 1879;81-92;94-1907
RP 1861-64
RPB Ja 5,Mr 13 1826[33-42]O 16 1843[45-46]O-N 1853;Je 26 1854
RW [Je 24 1824-F 15 1841]
—**evening ed** *See* Evening bulletin
—**morning ed** *See* Providence journal
—**w ed** *See* Rhode Island country journal

Weekly **MESSENGER.** w Jl 7-N 24 1855||
MWA N 24 1855
RHi Jl 14 1855

MICROCOSM, American and gazette. w Je 10 1825-Mr 29 1834||?
1825-30 as Microcosm; Ja 1 1831-F 2 1833 Microcosm and weekly American
Ct [1827]
CtY F 20 1829
DLC Je 24,Jl 1-8 1825[F 1831-My 1832]Ja 11, 25 1834
MB 1825-Je 1 1827
MH Je-Jl 14,D 3,16-22 1826;Jl 27 1827
MWA 1825- [28-Je 4]S 30,O 29,D 10 1831;Ja 14,Je 30,O 6-13,N 10-D 1832;Ja 19 1833-Mr 1834
MiU-C [1825-27]
N 1825-Je 2 1826
NNHi Jl 9,D 3 1831;F 18 1832
NSchU Ag 26,S 23,O 26,N 4-18,D 30 1825;Ja 6,F 24,Mr 10-17,31,Je 23,S 1,22 1826
NcD 1825-Ag 17,D 28 1827;Mr 7,Ap 4-11,S 26 1828;F 20-Mr 13 1829;Mr 4-11 1833;Mr 1 1834
RHi 1825-26;S 1827-S 18 1830;F 9 1833-Mr 29 1834
RPA F 9 1833-Mr 29 1834
RPB 1825-27;30-32
WHi Ap 17,Je 5 1830
—**d ed** *See* Daily advertiser and American
—**sw ed** *See* Rhode Island American and gazette

Morning **MIRROR.** d My 1849-54||
Je? 1849 as Rowe's mirror; D 1849 Evening mirror
MWA My 3 1850;F 27,D 2(extra)1851;D 7 1852
RHi Je 1849-51;Ap 7 1852;Ja 7,F 16-17 1853
RPB 1849-51;D 30 1854

Sunday **MIRROR.** *See* Sunday examiner

NARRAGANSETT chief. w My 28 1842-Ja 13? 1844||
Followed by Weekly transcript
DLC 1842-My 20 1843
MWA Jl 9-Ag 6,S 3,N 12 1842;Ap 1-8 1843
—**d ed** *See* Daily evening chronicle

Daily **NATIONAL union.** d Mr 1863-
RPB Ap 2 1863

NEW AGE. w N 20 1840-Ap 1843||?
1840-Mr 12 1842 as New age and constitutional advocate
Suspended Je 28-S 19 1842
MWA 1840-Mr 1,4(extra)8(extra)19,Ap 16,Je 11,25 1842
MiU-C [1840-42]
NN D 3 1841;F 25 1842
RHi 1840-Ap 21 1843
RPB [1840-Mr 12 1842]-Ap 28 1843

NEW AGE and constitutional advocate. sw Mr 18-Je 28? 1842||
MWA Ap 5,15,26-My 6,Je 14,28 1842—
RPB [Mr-Je 28 1842]

NEW ENGLAND family visitor and literary journal. w Je 7 1834?-
RPB Jl 19 1834

NEW world. w Mr 18 1870-
RHi Mr 18 1870;F 24 1871

Providence daily **NEWS.** d My 1834-Ag 1836||
Follows Evening star. Title varies slightly
DLC [1834-Mr 1835]
InNh [Ag 1834]
MWA S 18,N 6,10 1834-F 27,Je 15 1835
N Jl 28 1834
NNHi Jl 3 1835
RPB Je 11 1834

Providence evening **NEWS.** d? O 7 1856-
MWA O 7 1856

Evening **NEWS.** d O 1 1884-Mr 7 1885||
Follows Providence evening press. Merged with Providence star
MWA complete
RHi 1885

Providence **NEWS.** d 1891-1906;18-29 *See* News-tribune

Weekly **NEWS democrat.** w 1891-Mr 1909||?
1891-My 10 1906 as Weekly news
RHi 1892-Je 7 1906
—**d ed** *See* News-Tribune

NEWS democrat. d *See* News-tribune

NEWS-TRIBUNE. d S 21 1891+
1891-D 10 1929 as Providence news (My 11 1906-Mr 20 1909 as News democrat; Mr 22 1909-Ap 29 1918 Evening news and news democrat)
Ja ? 1896 is industrial ed; Je 20 1936 tercentenary ed
pub D 11 1929+
CtY Ja ? 1896
DLC Ag 25 1897-98
M F 11 1931
MWA D 18 1893;Ja 29 1896;Je 20 1936
RHi 1891+
RP 1914-15
—**w ed** *See* Weekly news-democrat

PAPER. w D 1- 1888||
RHi D 8 1888

PARROTT. sm,w F 16 1878-79||?
sm F-N 9 1878
RHi 1878-Mr 8,Jl 15 1879

***Providence PATRIOT and Columbian phenix.** w,sw My 11 1802-
1802-F 21 1807 as Providence phenix; F 28 1807-Ja 9 1808 Phenix; Ja 16 1808-Ja 12 1811 Columbian phenix; Ja 19 1811-Ja 8 1814 Columbian phenix; or, Providence patriot; Ja 15 1814-Ja 7 1815 Providence patriot. Columbian phenix
sw Ja 2 1819-Je 25? 1832
CSmH S 18 1830
Ct [1826;28-31]Ag 2 1834
CtSp Mr 30 1825
DLC 1821-26;28-34
MBAt Mr 16 1822
MSaE Jl 19 1823
MWA 1821-[30-31]Ja 14-18[Ap 21-O 20 1832] Mr 23[My 1833-Ag 1834]S 22 1843
MiU-C [1821-28;30]
N 1821-27;O 19 1833
NNHi [1821-Ap 1823]27
NcD F 17,28,Ag 18 1821;Jl 28,N 13 1824[26-27]-[29-30]F 5 1831;Ag 3,17 1833;Ja 4,F 1,Mr 29 1834
PDoHi Ap 21 1827
REdH D 1 1821;Ag 29 1827;N 12 1828
RHi F 28,S 29,O 24-27,N 24 1821;Ja 21 1822-25;Jl 12 1826;27-32;Ap 25 1835
RPB [1821-25]
RW Mr 5 1828
WHi 1823-Je 25 1825

PENNY post. w Ja 4 1834-35||?
DLC Ag 23 1834
MWA My 24-31 1834
MiU-C [1834]
NN Ja 4 1834
NNHi Jl 12 1834
RPB Ja-Ag 16 1834

PEOPLE. w D 5 1885-88||
RHi 1885-My 1888
RPB [1886]
WHi O 16 1886

PHENIX. *See* Providence patriot and Columbian phenix

PILGRIM. d N 19 1872-
REdH N 19-20 1872

PLAIN speaker. m Ja 30 1841-
MWA Ja 30,Mr-Je,D 1841
RHi 1841
RPB Ja 30 1841

PLAINDEALER. d Mr 14- 1855||
MWA Mr 14,Ap 20 1855
RHi Mr-My 4 1855

Providence daily **POST.** *See* Providence morning herald

Providence evening **PRESS.** d Mr 14 1859-S 30 1884||
O 7 1861-Je 11 1864 as Evening press. Followed by Evening news
CtY Je 21 1877
DLC 1859-Je 24,S 14 1865-S 13 1867;S 13 1869-Mr 12,S 14 1870-Mr 13 1871;S 14 1872-S 13 1876
MBAt Ap 15,17 1865
MWA complete
MiU-C [1859-73;75;84]
NN N 19 1863;Ag 6 1864;Ag 21 1879
NcD F 18,Mr 10,14,My 17,Jl 5 1860[Mr-S 1863;Mr-S 1865]Mr 14 1866-S 12 1868;Mr 14-Ag 1870;Mr 14-S 13 1871;Mr 19-S 13 1872;Mr 14 1877-84
OClWHi O 2 1860;Jl 11 1863;Ap 14,My 26 1865
RHi complete
RPB [1859-68;70-81]
RW F 23 1860;Mr 21,27,Ap 22,30 1861;S 10 1869
WHi O 1861-O 4 1865;extras[Ap 13 1861-Ap 16 1865]
—**morning ed** *See* Providence star
—**w ed** *See* Rhode Island press

Providence **PUBLIC ledger and daily commercial advertiser.** d Ja 1 1831-
RHi Ja 1-3 1831

RELIGIOUS intelligencer. *See* Christian monitor and weekly register

RELIGIOUS messenger. *See* Rhode Island religious messenger

Sunday **REPUBLICAN.** *See* Rhode Island republican

REPUBLICAN gazette. w F ? 1856-
RHi Mr 6 1856

REPUBLICAN herald. w,sw,d Ag 30 1828-D 28 1852||
Ag-S 13 1828 as Herald; F 5-Jl 3 1840 Daily evening herald and commercial intelligencer
w Ag-S 13 1828;d F 5-Jl 13 1840
DLC 1833;35-Je 26 1841;N 5 1842;Ag 31 (extra)1843;Mr 26 1845-50
MSaE F 27,Mr 13 1839
MWA D 15-22 1832;Je 26,Jl 6 1833[Ap 9 1834-Jl 2 1836]Ag 5 1837;F 19(extra)My 16, O 31 1838[Ap 13-D 1839]Ja 1840;41;N 12 1842-Ja 1,15-29 1851[My 22-D 4 1852]
MiU-C [1834;38-39;43]
REdH Ag-D 20 1828
RHi 1829-52
RPA Mr 18-Jl 3,D 8 1840-D 11 1852
RPB [1832-52]
—**d ed** *See* Providence morning herald

REPUBLICAN herald and Rhode Island gazetteer. w Ag 3 1828-My 21 1873||
1828-68? as Republican herald (Ja 1 1853-My 18 1867 Republican herald and post)
Ct [1830-31]
DLC Je 29 1844
MBAt Jl 30 1831
MWA N 15 1828;Jl 4 1829;Jl 24,S 4 1830;Jl 21-28,S 29 1832;Ja 31 1835[Je 11 1836-37]Je 2,16,Jl 21,O 13,D 1-15 1838[My 11 1839-41] D 17 1842[My-D 1843]Ja 13,F 17,Mr 16,O 5 1844;Mr 29,S 7,O 4 1845;Jl 25,O 24 1846; Je 12,D 4 1852[F 10 1855-N 1858]Ja 29,F 5,My 21,S 17,D 3-24 1859;F 11,My 5,Je 2 1860[Jl 26-D 1862]-S 1863;Mr 12,Ag 6,20, O 8 1864;Mr 18,Jl 8,D 9,30 1865;Ap 7,28,Je 2 1866;Ja 12-26,My 4,Je 15-22,O 26 1867;F 15, Ag 1 1868;S 11 1869;S 2,O 28-N 4,18,D 23 1871;Jl 20,S 21,O 26,N 2 1872
MiU-C [1867]
NN F 6 1847;N 23 1850
NNHi D 27 1834-S 17 1836[Ap 1839-Mr 1840] Ap 29 1854
NbHi Mr 8 1834
NcD F 4 1843;D 25 1844-Jl 2 1845
OClWHi S 29 1847;Je 6 1863
P-M Jl 1 1854
RHi D 20 1828;D 12 1829;D 10 1836;Jl 20,D 21 1839;O 10 1840;Ag 1841;Ap 27 1842;Jl 22-29 1843;Je 14 1845;Ag 28 1847;Mr 11-18 1854; D 28 1861-[Mr 25 1865-Ag 4 1866]
RPB [1829-43;46-54]Je 23,S 8 1860;Ap 9 1864
—**d ed** *See* Providence morning herald

***RHODE ISLAND American and gazette.** sw O 1 1808-F 1 1833||
1808-O 17 1809 as American; O 20 1809-23 Rhode Island American and general advertiser; 1824-O 7 1825 Rhode Island American; O 11 1825-Jl 17 1829 Rhode Island American and Providence gazette; Jl 21 1829-D 28 1830 Rhode Island American, statesman and Providence gazette; My 8 1832 Chronicle and American
Ct [1827]
CtSp S 22 1826
CtY S 8 1829
DLC 1821-25;Jl 7,S 8-15,O 13-D 1826;N 20 1829;Mr 10,Je 26-30,Jl 7,17 1829;My 4 1830;Ja 14,F 25,My 27 1831;F 3-7,17-21,28,Mr 6,Ap 27,My 1,11,Je 15,Jl 17,S 4,O 16 1832
MB S 10-O 20 1824;Mr 30 1825-Ag 17 1827
MBAt D 2 1823;28-Je 26 1829;30-O 28 1831
MH Jl 21 1829[30]Ap 20 1832
MSaE Je 3 1823;Ja 2 1824
MTaHi 1828-Jl 17 1829
MWA 1821-32
MiU-C [1821-23]-[27]-[30-32]
N Ja 4 1825;My 5,Jl 7 1826;N 23 1827;F 12, Ap 15-18,25,Jl 8,O 17,D 12-16 1828;Mr 20,Jl 17,31 Ag 7,D 11-15 1829;F 2,Mr 26,30,Ap 23,Jl 13 1830
NHuHi My 3 1825
NN Ag 17 1824;Ap 12 1825;Jl 8 1831
NNHi O 5 1821[Jl 1823-S 1825]D 11 1827
NcD 1821-Jl 1829;Jl 2,9,16,D 21 1830;Mr 15 1831
PDoHi Ap 26 1825
PP Ja-O 2 1821
REdH S 5,16,N 21-27 1828
RHi 1821-33
RPA 1821-33
RPB 1821-33
RW [1824;26-31]
WHi Ja 18 1825
—**d ed** *See* Daily advertiser and American
—**w ed** *See* Microcosm, American and gazette

RHODE ISLAND constitutionalist. ir Mr 12-1834||?
MWA Ap 7 1834
RHi Mr-Ap 7 1834

RHODE ISLAND (*Continued*)

PROVIDENCE—*Continued*

RHODE ISLAND country journal. w Ag 28 1823-O 3 1397||
1823-My 19 1825 as Independent inquirer and commercial advertiser; My 26-Ag 25 1825 Independent inquirer; S 1 1825-Ag 27 1830 Independent inquirer and Rhode Island journal; S 3 1830-47? Rhode Island country journal and independent inquirer
pub 1833-97
Ct N 23 1836
CtY S 10 1830;Jl 6 1833;42-43
DLC Ja 29,Ap 22,My 6-13,Je 3,Jl 15 1824; My 5 1825;O 21 1836;Jl 6 1849;N 5 1852
IC Jl 16,29,Ag 26 1859-F 21,Mr 23,Jl 27-Ag 3,S 14 1860
ICN Ag 1863-Je 1864
MB 1823-Ag 18 1825
MHi S 7 1832;O 21,N 11,D 30, 1836-Ja 13, Ap 14,My 5, Je 23,Jl 21 1837;My 4-11, Je 15 1838
MSaE O 16 1823;My 12 1825;Mr 22 1867
MTaHi 1823-Ag 1825
MWA 1823-Ag 25,S 22 1825;26-Je 21,Ag 23 1827;Ag 21,S 11 1828;Ag 15,S 11,D 4 1829[30] Ap 14,Ag 11 1837; My 27,Jl 1-21,S 9 1842;Ja 5 1844;Mr 21 1845;S 3 1847;S 6 1850;F 13,Mr 5 1852;Mr 3 1854;F 16,Mr 16,Je 22 1855;Je 13,Ag 1 1856;Ap 16 1858 S 14 1860;My 31,Ag 30 1861;N 4 1864;S 8,22 1871;S 16 1881;Jl 1889-92
MiU-C [1823;25-26]Ag 4 1864
NN 1823-S 1 1825;Ap 17-My 1,22 1828;Jl 7 1876
NNHi O 30 1840;O 20 1848;Ap 20,Je 1,29 1849-[F-Je 1850]
NbHi My 19 1825;My 20 1842
NcD Ja 19,Ag 31 1826;F 22 1827
OOxM Je 18 1828
RHi 1823-Ag 1825;Ap 3-10,My 15,Je 5-12,26-Jl 3 1828;30[My 1833-Mr 1885]
RPA S 20 1827-Jl 23 1830
RPB [1823-25;D 1832-Ag 12 1836]Ap 9 1847;N 15 1861;Ap 21 1865
RW Mr 1 1827[F 16 1833-S 9 1842]
—morning ed *See* Providence journal
—evening ed *See* Evening bulletin
—sw ed *See* Manufacturers' and farmers' journal

RHODE ISLAND democrat. w Je 14 1879-94||?
MWA 1879-80;93;Ja-F 17,Mr 10-17 1894
NcD Je 14,Jl 26 1879
RHi 1879-Ja 5,F 10-Ag 1894

RHODE ISLAND examiner. w S 22 1911-14||?
MWA S 22 1911
RHi Ja-D 18 1914

RHODE ISLAND free democrat. w O 7 1852-
DLC O 21,N 11 1852
MWA D 16 1852
RHi O-D 2 1852

RHODE ISLAND freeman. w 1853-57||?
MWA Mr 11 1853
NIC F 1854-F 1855
RHi Ap 1-8,29 1853;D 22 1854

RHODE ISLAND Jewish review. *See* Jewish review

RHODE ISLAND lantern. w Ja 29 1870-73||?
MWA F 5-12 1870
NcD F 5 1870
RHi Ja-Mr 5 1870

RHODE ISLAND pendulum. *See* Rhode Island pendulum and East Greenwich news (East Greenwich)

RHODE ISLAND philanthropist. w Ap? 1833-
RHi Jl 17 1833
RPB My 15 1833

RHODE ISLAND weekly post. w 1850-52||
United with Republican herald to form Republican herald and post, later Republican herald and Rhode Island gazetteer
RHi Ja 11-F 1,15 1851;N 27,D 25 1852
RPB F 8 1851
—d ed *See* Providence morning herald

RHODE ISLAND press. w O 22 1859-D 27 1886||?
MWA Je 29 1861;N 5 1864;71-86
MiU-C [1861;71-74;76;82-86]
OClWHi Mr 10 1866;Jl 13 1867
RHi O 22 1859;Ja 14 1863-86
RPA Mr 28 1874-Mr 11 1876
RPB Mr 19 1860[62-65]Ag 16 1879-Jl 1881
—morning ed *See* Providence star
—evening ed *See* Providence evening press

RHODE ISLAND religious intelligencer. *See* Christian monitor and weekly register

RHODE ISLAND religious messenger. w Jl 2 1825-28||?
1825-Mr 18 1826 as Religious messenger
MWA Jl-D 10 1825[26-27]Ja 4,18,F 8,22,Mr 14 1828
MiU-C F 25 1826 Mr 16 1827
RHi S 3 1825;Je 10-17,N 10,D 29 1826;Ja-Mr 16,Ap 27 1827-Ja 4,F 29,Mr 14 1828
RW D 31 1825

RHODE ISLAND republican. w
MB My 5 1840

RHODE ISLAND republican. w S 26 1888-91||?
1888-91? as Sunday republican
RHi D 1890-D 6 1891

RHODE ISLAND telegram. w S 13 1934+
RHi 1934+

RHODE ISLAND temperance journal and family visitor. w Ja 6- 1871||?
MWA Ja 13 1871

RHODE ISLAND weekly tribune. w 1853?-59||?
1853?-Ap? 1855 as Weekly tribune: My-D 1855? Rhode Island weekly tribune and temperance advocate
MWA Ap 20 1855
RHi My 3,D 29 1855;Jl 3,D 4,25 1858;F 12,O 15 1859
—d ed *See* Providence daily tribune

RHODE ISLAND wochenblatt. Beilage zur New England staaten zeitung. (Boston) w Je 1881-83||?
1881-Ap 7 1883 as Rhode Island wochenblatt
In German
MWA Jl 23 1881-D 15 1883

RHODE ISLANDER. w Ap 11 1924-Jl 7 1933||
1924-Ap 27 1927 as Lookout
MWA My 1 1925;S 30 1927
RHi complete

ROWE'S mirror. *See* Morning mirror

Providence daily SENTINEL. d Jl 21 1846-Jl-N 18 1846 as Daily sentinel
MWA S 22,24-29 1846
RHi 1846-F 5 1847
RW O 13 1846

La SENTINELLA. w Ja 1921-Ag 27 1926||
In Italian
RPV Mr 1922-D 19 1925

SPIRIT of Roger Williams. m D 1837-
RPB Jl 1838

Evening STAR. d Ap 3-My? 1834||
Followed by Providence daily news
RHi Ap 3-4 1834

Providence evening STAR. d Ap 20? 1847-
RHi Ap 22-My 11 1847

Providence STAR. d D 6 1869-Mr 6 1887||
1869-D 31 1872 as Morning star; Ja 1 1873-N 22 1886 Providence morning star
Ct Ag 8 1885
DLC S 16 1883
IHi S 20 1881
MAtt D 18 1872
MWA 1869-N 22 1886
MiU-C [1869-72]-[76]-[82]-[86]
NcD 1869-D 5 1871;73-D 5 1878;79-81;Je 6 1882-85;Jl 17-N 22 1886
NjR Jl 12 1870
RHi 1869-N 22[D]1886
RPA 1869-D 5 1876
RPa Ja-Je 5 1884
RW S 20 1881;N 3 1885
TxGR Ja 2 1887
WHi S 18 1871
—evening ed *See* Providence evening press
—w ed *See* Rhode Island press

Daily SUN. w,d D 5 1874-77||?
1874-N 18 1876 as Sun (w)
MWA D 5 1874;My 6,D 21 1876;F 1 1877
RHi 1874-F 10 1877

Sunday TELEGRAM. w 1876-F 1906||
MiU-C [1893-94;1903]
RHi 1877;79-D 10 1882;Ja 6-29 1884;85-1906
—d ed *See* Evening tribune

Evening TELEGRAM. 1880-1906 *See* Evening tribune

Weekly TELEGRAM. w Ja 30 1899-1905||?
RHi 1899-1903;Jl 1904-05

Providence evening TELEGRAM. d Ap 20 1931-
RHi Ap 20 1931

Evening TELEGRAPH. d Mr 1-Jl 3 1858|
Follows Bangs's trumpet?
MWA complete
NcD [Ap 16-Jl 1858]
RHi complete

TEMPERANCE advocate. w 1852-Ap 26 1855||
United with Weekly tribune to form Rhode Island weekly tribune and temperance advocate, later Rhode Island weekly tribune
MWA Jl 24 1852
RHi Ap 24,My 29 1852;Ja 14-28,F 11-Mr 11, Ap 1 1854;Ja 27-F 17 1855

TIDEN. w D 8 1888-91||
In Swedish
RHi 1888-N 1890

Providence daily TIMES. d Jl 1852-
MWA Jl 28 1852
RHi N 1 1852

Providence weekly TIMES. w D 22 1859-
MWA My 23-Je 13 1861
RHi 1859-D 6 1860
RPB S 12 1861

Providence evening TIMES. d F 13? 1877-78||
RHi F 14-Mr 5 1877

Providence TIMES. w O 3 1876-79||?
RHi 1876-N 8 1879

TOWN and country. w Ja 5 1875-79||
MWA My 1,S 19 1877
RHi 1875-Je 25 1879

Daily evening TRANSCRIPT. d 1841?-Mr 8 1858||
1841-43? as Daily transcript; 1844-Ap 13 1847 Daily transcript and chronicle; Ap 14 1847-Ag 31 1848 Daily evening transcript; S 7 1848-My 9 1849 Daily evening transcript; and free soil advocate
DLC F 2 1844;Ja 29,Mr 30 1846
MWA [1844]-Ag 7 1847[48]Mr 20 1856
MiU-C [1842-43 45;47]
NN My 16,Jl 23,O 17,D 30 1856;My 19 1857
NcD My 30 1845[46]-[My 1847]S 27 1848
RHi Ja 17 1844-46;My 24 1847-Mr 16 1850; Je 18-D 19 1855;56-57
RPA Ja-Je 1845;56
RPB [1849]

Weekly TRANSCRIPT. w Ja 27 1844-
Follows Narragansett chief
MWA Ag 22 1846;F 19 1848
RHi 1844-Ja 17,Ap 25 1846;D 25 1847-Je 1848

Sunday TRANSCRIPT. w 1879?-85||?
1879?-84? as Sunday morning transcript
RHi S 28,N 2 1879;Jl 18,D 26 1880-84

Providence TRAVELER. Mr 16 1912||
RHi complete

Providence daily TRIBUNE. d Je 13 1853-O 4 1859||
DLC Ja 20,F 20(extra)1854
MAtt N 23,D 29 1854
MWA Ja 20,F 20,Mr 24(extra)1854;Ja 30,N 5 1855;Mr 4,Jl 23 1856;57-58;F 10,23(supp) 1859
NN Ja 20 1854;Jl 27 1859
NcD Ja-Je 1857;Ja-Je 1858
P-M Ap 26 1855
RHi complete
RPB 1853-S 22 1855;Ap 16 1858-59
RW Mr 29,My 30,O 18 1854;F 20 1855

Evening TRIBUNE. d Ap 5 1880-D 10 1929||
1880-Mr 10 1906 as Evening telegram; Mr 12-Ag 15 1906 Evening tribune and telegram. United with Providence news to form News-tribune
DLC S 1902-29
IHi Mr 4 1924
MWA Je 23 1886;Jl 23 1907
RHi complete
RP Jl 1906-N 1929
RPB Jl-D 1882
RPNt Mr 12 1906-29
—w ed *See* Sunday telegram

Morning TRIBUNE. d Jl 4 1906-Je 28 1908||
RHi complete
RP complete

Weekly TRIBUNE. *See* Rhode Island weekly tribune

TRIBUNE of the people. w N 18 1845-Mr 31 1846||
MWA N 18 1845;F 28 1846
RHi complete
RPA complete

TRUE union national advocate. ir Mr ?-Ap 1864||
OClWHi Ap 5 1864
RPB Ap 2 1864

Providence VISITOR. w O 1875+
1875-F 2 1884 as Weekly visitor (some issues as Sunday visitor)
pub 1885+
IU Mr 22 1918+
MB Ag 21-O 2 1880;Ja 8,29,Mr 5 1881
MWA Ap 6 1878;Je 21 1879;Ap 7 1911
PPCHi [1886-95;97-98;1901-03;05-08;10-14;18; 20-22;31;33]
RHi O 1876-S 16 1910;11+
RP Ap 19 1912

A VOZ da colonia. w Mr 11 1926+
1926-Mr 1928 pub in Bristol
In Portuguese
RHi 1926+

WIDE awake. ir 1860-
RPB D 20 1860

Wschód. w Jl 3? 1904-
In Polish
RHi S 4 1904

YANKEE times. My 24 1862-
RPB My 24 1862

SCITUATE

LITTLE Rhody. w F 6 1891-96||?
F-Mr 27 1891 pub at North Scituate
RHi 1891-95

SHANNOCK

Shannock SENTINEL. w 1881-Ap 26 1894||?
United with Hope Valley advertiser (Hope Valley) to form Sentinel advertiser, later Hope Valley advertiser (Hope Valley)

TIVERTON

NEWPORT county sentinel. w N 14 1925+
RHi 1925+
RNHi 1925-Jl 8 1927;N 22 1928;D 24 1931

WAKEFIELD

Wakefield ADVERTISER. 1851?-
RPS Ap 19 1851

NARRAGANSETT times. w My? 1855+
D 2 1864-Mr 22 1889 as Narragansett times and Washington county advertiser
pub 1855+
DLC Ap 21 1865;O 3 1873;Ap 24,Je 10 1876
MWA Je 11-D 1859;65[66-68]Ap 15,My 6 1870; Je 30 1871;O 3 1873;Mr 3-24,Je 10,S 15 1876; Mr 2 1877;Je 21,S 13 1878;F 7 1879;F 25,D 16 1881;My 19 1882;N 27 1885
MiU-C [1859;65-68]
RHi Je 9,Jl 7,21,D 15 1855;Ja-Ap 1856;Je 11 1859-Jl,Ag 21 1863;Ap 1889-Je 19 1891;Je 30 1893-1915;S 8 1916+
RNHi Je 27 1890-Je 19 1891;Je 30 1893-Je 22 1894
RPd Jl 16 1880-Je 20 1890;Je 26 1891+

SOUTH county journal. w Je 12 1858-Je 4 1859||
Merged with Narragansett times
MWA complete
MiU-C [1858-59]
RHi Je 8,22 1858-59

RHODE ISLAND (*Continued*)

WARREN

BRISTOL county item. w S 27 1906-12‖?
MWA Ap 11 1907
RHi 1906-S 1909;My 12 1911-O 1912

CLARION; or, Bristol county advertiser. w N 29 1823-N 20 1824‖
DLC D 13 1823-O 1824
MWA complete
RHi Ja 10-N 20 1824
RWa complete

CONSTITUTIONALIST. w? 1834‖
United with Northern star to form Northern star and constitutionalist, later Northern star

Warren and Barrington GAZETTE. w,sw My 19 1866+
1866-Mr 29 1907 as Warren gazette; Ap 5-Ag 30 1907 Warren gazette and Barrington call
Also dated in Barrington
w 1866-1916?
pub [1907+]
MWA Jl 14 1866;My 18 1867-Ap 1868;Ja 8, My 1869-Ap 1870;Ja 2-16 1885;Ap 16 1886
NcD S 21 1867
RHi 1866+
RNHi 1891-1902;04-07
RWaC 1888+

NORTHERN star. w F 25 1826-Jl 13 1855‖
Follows Telegraph. 1826-30 as Northern star and Warren and Bristol gazette; 1830-34,S 9 1837-Je 23 1849 Northern star and farmers' and mechanics' advocate; 1834-S 2 1837 Northern star and constitutionalist
CSmH S 18 1830
Ct [1826]
DLC Je 1826-F 4 1829;Ja 16,F 20 1830-F 12, Mr 5 1831;Jl 2 1836;D 5 1840;Ap 17,Je 12-D 1841[43]
MWA Mr 18,My 20,S 30 1826;F 10,Mr 31,O 6 1827;Ag 29,O 17,N 21-28 1829;Mr 28 1835 [Mr 12 1836-37]Ja 6,20,F 3,24,Mr 3,My 19,D 1 1838;Mr 30,Ap 20,Jl 13,Ag 3 1839;Ja 18 1840; Mr 6,Ap 10,S 11,D 22?(extra)1841;Mr 12, S 9,O 1-8,29 1842;Ja 14,Ap 8-22,My,Je 10-D 1843;F 24,N 9 1844[Ja 11-Ag]O-N 8,D 27 1845;Ja 3,24[My 16 1846-47]-Ja 6,20,F 24, Je 16,30 1849;Ja 26 1850-51;Ja,Mr 27,Je 12, Jl 3-10,S 4 1852;Ja 22 1853-54;F 10-Jl 1855
NNHi [1826]-F 16 1828
NcD O 14-21,N 4 1843[48;50-Ja 1852]Ap 30 1853;F 4,My 27,Jl 8-22,Ag 26,S 9 1854;Jl 13 1855
RHi 1831-Ja 3 1833;Ja 24 1835-55
RNHi My 17,Je 14-21 1834
RPB S 13 1834;Ag 9 1851;Ja 31 1852
RWa 1826-F 17 1827
RWaT F 1841-Ja 21 1843

RHODE ISLAND telegraph. sw Jl 18 1855-Jl 18 1857‖
MWA Jl 18 1855;N 1 1856;Je 27 1857
NjFHi Jl 30 1865
RHi complete
—w ed? *See* Warren telegraph

TELEGRAPH. w F 23 1825-F 15 1826‖
Followed by Northern star and Warren and Bristol gazette, later Northern star
DLC My 25-D 14 1825
MWA Mr 9 1825-26
NcD My 11,Jl 13 1825
RWa F 23 1825;Ja 18 1826

Warren TELEGRAPH. w F 7 1857-Jl 27 1861‖
MWA Ja 1,22,Mr-Ap 23,My 14 1859-61
NcD My 21,Jl 30-Ag 6,S 3 1859
NjFHi Ap 21 1860
RHi F 21 1857;58-F 2 1861
—sw ed? *See* Rhode Island telegraph

WARWICK

Warwick CITY herald. w Jl 13 1932-Mr 9 1933‖
Jl-S 29 1932 as Warwick city times
O 1932-Ja 12 1933 pub in Apponaug
MWA S 8 1932
RHi complete
RPB Jl-S 1932

Warwick CITY times. *See* Warwick city herald

WASHINGTON PARK

NEIGHBORHOOD news. w
REdH S 1930-My 1 1931

WATCH HILL

Watch Hill LIFE. Jl 12 1894-Ag 31 1912‖?
RHi Jl 1899-S 7 1901;Ag 3 1904;Jl 26 1905;Ag 4-10 1907
RW 1894-S 2 1908

SEASIDE topics. w Jl 9 1904+
1904-Je 17 1905 as Watch Hill topics
RHi 1904-Je 17 1905;Je 28 1913-S 10 1931
RW 1904+

Watch Hill TOPICS. *See* Seaside topics

WEST WARWICK

PAWTUXET VALLEY daily times. d Jl 20 1892+
1892-Ag 14 1925 pub in Arctic
MWA Mr 17 1894
RHi 1892-Jl 19 1906;Jl 8 1907-09;11+

WESTERLY

AMERICAN federalist. w S 15 1883-S 17 1887‖
1883-Mr 4 1884 as Rhode Island telephone; Mr 15 1884-Jl 9 1887 Westerly news and Rhode Island telephone
1883-87? also dated in Wickford
RHi complete

CALL. w 1885-87‖
RHi D 31 1886-87

Westerly ECHO and Pawcatuck advertiser. *See* Literary echo

Westerly ENTERPRISE. m N 1867-
MWA O 1869
RHi 1867-O 1868

Westerly HERALD. d Ap 1 1899-Mr 29 1901‖
RHi complete
RW complete

Westerly JOURNAL. w Je 19 1888-93‖?
RHi 1888-Ag 1891
RW 1888-Jl 20 1890

LITERARY echo. w Ap 3 1851-Mr 18 1858‖
1851-Je 15 1854 as Literary echo and Pawcatuck advertiser; Je 22 1854-Ap 19 1855 Westerly echo and Pawcatuck advertiser. Followed by Narragansett weekly, later Westerly Narragansett weekly
MWA Ap 29,My 13,Jl 8,N 4,D 30 1852;Ja 13, 27-F 10,24-Mr 10,24,D 29 1853;Ag 31 1854;N 13 1856;F 26 1857
NcD Jl 5,19 1855;Ag 21 1856
RHi Je 12,O 30-N 6 1851;Ap 8 1852-Ap 19 1855;Je 14,Jl 5,26,Ag 10,30,S 20-27 1855;Ja 24 1856
RW complete

Westerly NARRAGANSETT weekly. w Ap 29 1858-Mr 16 1899‖
Follows Literary echo. 1858-Mr 21 1878 as Narragansett weekly. Merged with Westerly daily sun
MWA O 21-28 1858[59-62]-F 12,Mr 5-19,Ap 2-9 1863;S 22 1864;S 7 1865;My 30 1867-F 6,S 3-10,24,O 1-15 1868;S 23-D 9,23 1869;Ja 6,20,F 3-10,Mr 3-24 1870;Ap 18 1872;D 11 1873;Mr 3 1881
MiU-C [1859;61]
NcD N-D 2 1858;N 27 1862;Je 20 1872
RHi Jl 8 1858-My 12 1883;Ag 4 1887;91-94;Mr 19 1896-99
RPB N 8 1860
RW complete
WHi Ag 4,18-S 1 1859

Westerly NEWS. w Ag 7 1895-
RHi Ag 7 1895

Westerly NEWS. w N 24 1916-19‖
RHi 1916-S 19 1919

Westerly NEWS and Rhode Island telephone. *See* American federalist

RHODE ISLAND telephone. *See* American federalist

Westerly daily SUN. d Ag 7 1893+
MWA Ja 27-Jl 5 1911;Ap 14,My 5 1931
RHi 1893+
RNHi Ag 1907-Ag 1909
RW 1893+

Westerly TIMES. w Ag 31 1901-Je 29 1935‖
RHi complete
RW Ag 1 1908

Westerly daily TRIBUNE. d S 6 1888-My 19 1898‖
CtY F 3-My 3 1894
RHi S 18-O 22 1889;Jl 24 1894-98
RW complete

WICKFORD

Weekly PENDULUM. . . *See* Rhode Island pendulum and East Greenwich news (East Greenwich)

RHODE ISLAND pendulum. *See* Rhode Island pendulum and East Greenwich news (East Greenwich)

RHODE ISLAND telephone. *See* American federalist (Westerly)

Wickford STANDARD. w Ag 4 1888+
MWA supps:D 8 1888-Ja 5 1889
RHi 1888-Jl 1908;Ag 1909+

WASHINGTON county advocate. w Ag 12 1830?-
N Mr 4,18,Ap 15 1831
RHi Ag 26 1831

WOONSOCKET

Woonsocket CALL and evening reporter. d My 31 1892+
1892-N 15 1908 as Evening call; N 16 1908-F 28 1917 Evening call and evening reporter
M [1931-Jl 15 1933]
RHi 1892+
RWo Ap 1928-S 1934

CAMP Kettle. 1861?-
OClWHi Ja 25 1862

Le COURRIER de Woonsocket. w Ag? 1880-84‖?
In French
MWA O 7 1880

L'INDEPENDANT de Woonsocket. d F 4 1935+
Follows La Tribune
In French
pub 1935+
IU 1935+
RHi 1935+

INDEPENDENT. w Jl 17 1843-
1843-Jl 13 1844 pub in Providence
DLC Mr 9 1844
MAtt Jl 27 1844
MWA Jl-O 1843;Mr 9,O 19 1844
NN My 13 1844
OClWHi Mr 16 1844;Ja 11-18 1845
RHi 1843-N 1844;Ja 4 1845

Woonsocket PATRIOT. w Ja 1833-1904‖?
Ap 15 1854-Mr 10 1876 as Woonsocket weekly patriot and Rhode Island state register (My 22 1855-F 8 1856 Woonsocket patriot) My 15 1885-Ag 6 1886 Woonsocket patriot and New England news
DLC N 15 1844
MNaHi Jl 6 1860
MWA O 5 1833;N 13 1835;Jl 29,S 2,O 28,D 9-16 1836[37]-43;Mr 22,N 1 1844;Ja 17,My 30,Ag 1 1845;F 20 1846;Ja 2 1852;S 15 1854-My 18,Je 16,Ag 4 1855;56-[59]-62;N 20,D 18 1863;64-68[My 1869-71]-97[Mr 18-D 2 1898;F 10-D 1899]My 25-O 5,D 21-28 1900;Ja 11-18,F 15,Jl 5,Ag 30 1901-[02-03]-F 5 1904
MiU-C [1857-68;71-92]
NN D 18 1840
NcD F 9 1855;F 1856-[57]58;Ag 12-26,N 18 1859;Mr,Ap 27 1860;O 11 1861;Jl 21 1865;Ja 18 1867;My 3 1872;Mr 28 1873;Mr 3 1876;Ja 4,18 1878
NjR Ag 11 1848
P-M Ja 23 1845;Je 2 1854;Je 23 1855
RHi Jl 13,D 21 1838;S 29 1843-S 12 1851;Ap 16 1852;53-96;98-Ag 12 1904
RPB N 4 1864;Ap 21-28 1865
RWo Jl 1856-77;80;86
TJT Mr 26 1875
WHi N 24 1864;My 19,Ag 11 1865

Woonsocket PATRIOT. sw 1855‖?
RHi My 22-25 1855

Woonsocket daily PATRIOT. d Ap 3 1876-Mr 16 1881‖
Merged with Woonsocket evening reporter
MWA S 27,O 14 1876
RHi 1876-81
RWo 1876-80

Le PROGÈS. w Je 24 1898-Je 27 1913‖?
Merged with La Tribune
MWA Ja 4,19,F 16 1912;Ja 10-24,F 7,Je 27 1913
RHi 1898-1911;Jl 1912-Je 27 1913

Woonsocket evening REPORTER. d O 1 1873-N 14 1908‖?
1873-Mr 18 1876 as Woonsocket daily reporter. United with Evening call to form evening call and evening reporter, later Woonsocket call and evening reporter
MWA Je 13 1885;Ap 24 1889
RHi 1873-N 14 1908
RWo 1873-Mr 1874;79-83

RHODE ISLAND advocate. w O 9 1835-
MWA O 9,30,D 11 1835;Ja 1-8,F 5,Mr 4,25 1836
RHi 1835-Mr 4 1836

RHODE ISLAND state register. w 1833-Ap 1854‖
United with Woonsocket patriot to form Woonsocket patriot and Rhode Island state register, later Woonsocket patriot

Woonsocket SENTINEL and Thomasonian advocate. w F 16 1842-Mr 22 1843‖
RHi complete

La SENTINELLE. d,w Ap 4 1924-29‖?
d Ap-N 8 1924
In French
NhMA 1924-F 14 1929
RHi 1924-28

Evening SUN. d Ja 2 1899-
RHi Ja-Mr 17 1899

La TRIBUNE. d Ap 6 1895-D 24 1934‖
Followed by L'Independant de Woonsocket
In French
IU O 20 1917-34
RHi 1896-1934

VALLEY republican. d Ap 26- 1886‖
RHi Ap-Ag 4 1886

SOUTH CAROLINA

ABBEVILLE

Abbeville BANNER. *See* Press and banner and Abbeville medium

INDEPENDENT press. w Je 3 1854-N 2 1860||
United with Abbeville press to form Abbeville press and banner, later Press and banner and Abbeville medium
NcD F 1 1856
ScAP complete

Abbeville MEDIUM. w,sw 1871-
United with Abbeville press and banner to form Press and banner and Abbeville medium
sw 1921-24
NcD Je 11,D 10 1873;N 15 1876
ScAG 1871-O 1 1879;94-1904
ScAR O 3 1879-Ja 1889;1905-10

Abbeville MESSENGER. w O 1 1884-F 8 1887||
ICM Jl 22 1885
ScAP complete

PRESS and banner and Abbeville medium. w, tw,sw 1844+
1844-N 2 1860 as Abbeville banner; N 9 1860-1924 Abbeville press and banner
w 1844-1920;tw 1921-26
pub Mr 1847-S 2 1848[50-57]-F 16,N 9-D 21 1860;61;Ja 16-O 2 1863;Ag 17-D 1 1865;66-Ag 23 1867;S 29 1869-97;99-1909;12;14;16;18-21; 23+
CtY Ag 11 1853
ICM Jl 22 1885
KHi Ja 28,My 4 1925
MWA Jl 2 1852;F 6 1866;Ap 10 1868
NcD Ag 19 1848;O 12-19 1850;S 26 1851;My 7 1852;Ap 9,S 3-10,O 15 1869;Ja 14-21 1870;76-S 1878;Ja 1,Mr 12 1879-[80]-87;F 14 1917;My 4,Ag 5,S 2,O 14 1925;F 11,My 10,D 23 1926; Ja 20,Mr 7,21,31,Je 20,S 29,N 10 1927;Jl 12-19,O 22 1928,F 18 1929;Ag 28,S 25 1930
NcU Je 9 1869

AIKEN

Aiken COURIER-JOURNAL. *See* Aiken journal and review

Aiken daily JOURNAL. d 1871-73||
NNHi Ap 2,30-My 1[Jl-D]1872-F 21 1873

Aiken JOURNAL and review. w 1871+
1871-73? as Aiken journal; 1874-79? Aiken courier-journal
MWA Mr 31 1880
NNHi [Je-Ag,O 1873]-Je 13,Ag-O 1874;Ap 25, N 29,D 20 1882;F 28-Mr,My-Ag 22,N 28-D 5 1883;Ja 2-9,23-30 1884;O 30-N 13,30-D 4 1889; Ap 30,Jl 9,O 22 1890

Aiken PRESS. w Jl 4 1867-
MBAt Jl 25-Ag 1 1867
MWA Jl 4,S 5,19 1867

Aiken RECORDER. w,sw 1881-1910||?
w 1881-1905
NNHi D 19 1882;Ja-Je,O 2,N 6-13 1883;S 25, O 30-N 7 1888[D 1889-O 1890]

RESORT life. w 1929+
pub 1929+

Aiken STANDARD. w My 1915+
pub 1915+

Aiken TRIBUNE. w N 25 1871-76||
DLC 1871-75
MWA Ja 30 1875
NNHi [1872-76]

ALLENDALE

ALLENDALE county citizen. w 1919+
pub 1919+
KHi O 17 1924

ANDERSON

Anderson APPEAL. w Mr 26 1866-
MBAt My 30,Je 13 1866

BLEASE'S weekly. w 1925-27||?
Ct D 10 1925

Anderson GAZETTE. w 1844-
1855? as Gazette and advocate
DLC D 20 1844;Mr 22,Je 21 1854;Je 13 1855
MWA Mr 20 1861
NcAsS Je 3-10,Jl 15-N 4 1847
NcD N 14 1855;S 7 1859

HIGHLAND sentinel. w S 5 1840-
1840 pub at Calhoun
DLC N 26 1840;Ja 7,Ap 15-My 13,Je 17,Jl 15-O,N 12-19,D 1841;Ja,F 10,24-Mr 10,Ap 7,My 26,Je 9,Jl 14 1843
NcD O 3 1840

Anderson INDEPENDENT-TRIBUNE. d 1924+
1924-25 as Anderson independent
KHi Ja 4,6,22 1925

Anderson INTELLIGENCER. w Je 22 1865-1917||?
MBAt O 12-19 1865
MWA S 13 1866
NN O 1896(souvenir ed)
NcD Je 24 1866

Anderson JOURNAL. w 1876-96||?
NNHi Ap 23-My 7 1890

Anderson daily MAIL. d O 6 1899+
pub 1899+
KHi Ja 6,13 1925

SOUTHERN rights advocate. w My 26? 1852-
MWA Jl 7 1852
NcD Jl 28 1852;F 1 1854

Anderson TRIBUNE. d 1915?-25||
United with Anderson independent to form Anderson independent-tribune
KHi D 19 1924;Ja 21 1925

TRUE Carolinian. w 1856-
NcD Je 18 1857

BAMBERG

BAMBERG county times. w Ap 1888+
pub 1900+
KHi D 18 1924;Ja 22-29 1925

Bamberg HERALD. w 1891+
pub 1900+
KHi Ja 15,29 1925

BARNWELL

PALMETTO sentinel. *See* Barnwell sentinel

PEOPLE-SENTINEL. w N 1 1877+
1877-Ag 1878 as People; S 1878-My 1925 Barnwell people
pub 1877+
KHi Ja 22 1925
ScU N 1-8,D 6,20 1877-Ja,F 14-21,Ap 11-My 9,23,Je 6-18,Ag 8 1878;S 8 1898-Ag 1899;S 8 1904-06;S 1907-Ap 9,S 1908-Jl 22,S 1909-My 5,19-S 1 1910;S 1911-F 6 1913

Barnwell SENTINEL. w 1852-My 1925||
1852-60? as Palmetto sentinel. United with Barnwell people to form People-sentinel
DLC Mr 22,My 24,Je 7,Jl 5-12,26,D 13-20 1862; Je 13,Jl 4,S 12 1863;Ja 10,F 10,Ap 28,Je 2 1866;Ap 20,My 4,Ag 3,31,O 12,N 23 1867;Mr 14,Jl 18,Ag 29,O 31 1868
MBAt Jl 6,Ag 24,S 14,O 12-19,N 2-9,23-30,D 14 1861;S 24,O 22,D 3,17-24 1864
MWA Je 23 1852;O 17 1868
NcD Je 30,Jl 14-21,Ag 11-25,S 8,O 13-27,N 10-17,D 22 1866;N 7 1868

BATESBURG

SUMMERLAND headlight. w Mr 14 1924-25||
KHi O 24,D 19 1924;Ja 23 1925

TWIN-CITY news. w 1923+
pub 1923+

BEAUFORT

BEAUFORT county times. w Ap 22 1871-72||?
MWA Ag 26 1871
NNHi D 21 1872

CAMP kettle. ir S 21 1861-
DLC S 12,D 5,30 1861;Ja 25,My 1 1862

CRESCENT. w 1872-80||?
NcU S 25,O 23 1879

FREE south. w Ja 10 1863-64||
CtHT Mr 7,21,Je 13-20,O 1,15 1863
DLC Ja 17,O 17,N 14,D 19 1863-Ap 9,My 21-Je 18,Jl 2-16 1864
MBAt Ja-D 12 1863;Ja 23,F 6,20-Mr 5 1864
MH Ja 10-17,31-F 7,28,Mr 21-Ap 4,25-My 9, 23-30,Jl 14,Ag 29-S 5,O 31,N 14,D 19 1863;Ja 9-30,F 13,27-Mr 12,26-29,My 12-21,Jl 2,30,Ag 13,S 10,O 1,N 12-19 1864
MHi [1863-64]
MSaE Ja 10 1863;Mr 26,Ap 16 1864
MWA Ja 10,Mr 7,21,Je 27,D 26 1863;Ja 9,23-30,Mr 12 1864
MnHi Ja-F,My 23 1863
NNHi Ja 9,30,F 13,27-Mr 12,26,Ap 16,30-My 21,Ag 13,S 10,24-O 1,22 1864
OClWHi [1863-Mr 1864]
OHi My 9 1863
P-M Ja 10 1863;My 21 1864
PHi Ja 17,31,F 7 1863
PPGr My 2 1863
PPL [1863-Je 1864]
PWcHi My 14,Ap 18,Je 13,Ag 22 1863

Beaufort GAZETTE. w 1897+
KHi O 23,D 25 1924;Ja 22 1925
MWA Jl 7 1922

PORT ROYAL standard and commercial. *See* Beaufort tribune and Port Royal commercial

Beaufort REPUBLICAN. w O 2 1869-O 16? 1873||
United with Port Royal commercial to form Port Royal commercial and Beaufort county republican (Port Royal)
DLC O 12 1871-O 16 1873
MBAt N 6,20 1869

SEA ISLAND news. w 1879-88||?
NNHi D 16 1882;Ap 28 1883

SOUTHERN standard. *See* Beaufort tribune and Port Royal commercial

Beaufort TRIBUNE. w 1874-76||
United with Port Royal standard and commercial to form Beaufort tribune and Port Royal commercial
MWA N 22 1876

Beaufort TRIBUNE and Port Royal commercial. w 1872-78||?
1872-73 as Southern standard; 1874-76 Port Royal standard and commercial

BELTON

Belton JOURNAL. w 1914-25||
KHi Ja 22 1925

Belton NEWS. w 1925+
pub 1925+

BENNETTSVILLE

Bennettsville JOURNAL. w 1866-70||?
NcD D 24 1869

MARLBORO county herald. w S 3 1931+
pub 1931+

PEE DEE advocate. w My 26 1885+
pub 1896+

PEE DEE argus. w 1888-92||?
NcD Mr 26 1891

BISHOPSVILLE

LEE county messenger. w 1901+
KHi D 25 1924

BLACKVILLE

BARNWELL journal. w
DLC Jl 24,N 27 1869

BRANCHVILLE

ENTERPRISE. w 1927+
pub 1927+

CALHOUN

HIGHLAND sentinel. *See under* Anderson

CAMDEN

Camden and Lancaster BEACON. w
ScU Mr 15 1831-O 6 1832

Daily BULLETIN. d My 9 1864-
NcD My 10-14,18-19,21-27,Je 1,Jl 8,19-20,30, Ag 4 1864
ScU My 9-16 1864

Camden CHRONICLE. w 1888+
KHi Ja 23 1925

Camden COMMERCIAL courier. w
ScU My 1837-Je 16 1838

Camden CONFEDERATE. w O 31 1861-65||?
Ja?-S 1864 as Camden weekly confederate
DLC N 30 1864
NcAsS Mr 21,My 16,Ag 3,S 5,O 31-D 5,19 1862;Ja 9,30-F 13,27,Mr 13,27-My 15,29,Je 12, 26-Ag 7,28-S 4,26,O 16,23,N 20 1863;Ap 27, My 11-Je 8,22,Jl 6-27,Ag 10-24,N 16 1864
NcD N 7 1862;Ja 16,Ap 10,24-My 8,Jl 10,O 9-16 1863;My 4,N 9,D 7 1864;Ja 11 1865
ScU N 1861-D 11 1863;Ap 6,Je 8-15,O 26-N 2,16 1864;Ja 4-11,F 8 1865
VRC F 6 1863

Camden CONFEDERATE. d Jl-D 1864||
United with Camden daily journal to form Journal and confederate, later Camden daily journal
ScU Jl 22,Ag 1,10,12,31,S 6,21-28,30-O 20,26, 31-N 1,D 1,7-8,13,19,29 1864

Camden JOURNAL. w 1826-91||?
Title varies slightly: Camden journal and southern whig; Camden weekly journal; etc.
CSmH Je 6 1829
Ct Ag 20 1831;N 9 1842
DLC S 29 1832;Ja 6,20-F 17,Mr 3,17-24,Ap 7, 21,My-Je 9,23-Jl 7,28 1841;Je 1 1842
ICU Ap 1840-Ap 1842
MWA F 24 1827;Je 2 1841;Jl 3 1852
N O 26 1833;Ap 29 1880
NBuG S 4 1860
NNHi Je 18 1861
NcD Ag 22-S 19 1835;F 22 1840;Je 30 1849;F 1,Mr 5-8,26,Ap 2,12-16 1850;Mr 1-15,29-Ap 5 1853;Jl 24 1855;My 29 1860;Mr 19,Ap 30 1861; F 26,Mr 11-Ap 8,22,My 6,27,Je 3-10 1864;F 10,Ap 1,Jl 7,28,Ag 18,N 3-10,D 1 1865;Je 1,Jl 20 1866
NcU S 9 1846;Ja 13,Mr 3 1847;Jl 5 1850
NhD Mr 24 1841
OCHi O 25 1843
OClWHi Mr 30,Ag 14 1866
ScU Ja 21 1826-28;Mr 13 1830-Mr 18 1837;D 1839-42;48-50;52-[54-55]F 24,Mr 31 1857;My 15-29,Jl 10-17,Ag,S 18-N 13 1860;Ap 29,My 20 1864;Ag-S 1,22,N 10,24,D 8,22 1865[66-68] 69;O 1870-[71-74]Jl 12-19,O 23 1877-78
TxU Je 8 1842-47
VtBr S 5,N 18 1840;Ag 18 1841;Ag 4 1842

Camden daily JOURNAL. d Jl 1 1864-
Mr-My 1865? as Journal and confederate
DLC [Jl-D 1864]
NNHi Jl 1 1864
NcD [Jl]-[S-O]-D 1864
OHi Jl 13,21,Ag 2,30,O 21,25,29,31,N 7,10,18 1864
ScU Mr 31-My 12 1865

Tri-weekly JOURNAL. tw Ja 1? 1865-
Mr-My 1865 as Journal and confederate
NcD Mr 31,Ap 24,My 3-5,19,26,Je 12 1865
OClWHi F 13 1865
ScU Ja 13,My 31-Je 2,7 1865

KERSHAW gazette. w 1873-87||?
NNHi Jl 22 1874
ScU F 10 1874[My-Jl 1876;S 1879-Je 1880]N 30 1882-S 4 1884

SOUTHERN chronicle. w
Sub-title varies: . . . and Camden gazette; . . . and Camden aegis; . . . and Camden literary and political register
DLC Ap 7,28,My 12-Je 2,Ag 4,O 20 1824
ScU Mr 14 1822-Ag 13 1825

SOUTH CAROLINA (*Continued*)

CAMDEN—*Continued*

SOUTHERN republic. w
NcD Je 21-Ag 22,S 12-O 10,24 1851

WATEREE messenger. w O 7 1884+
pub 1884+
KHi O 25 1924;Ja 6-13,27 1925

CHARLESTON

Charleston ADVERTISER. w D 22 1877-
NcD D 29 1877-My 1878

Charleston ADVOCATE. w F 16 1867-68||
MWA Ap 6 1867;S 5 1868

AFRO-AMERICAN citizen. w 1899-1900||?
Negro
DLC Ja 17 1900

Sunday BUDGET. w 1887-91||
MWA Ag 31 1890
NcD F 12,D 23 1888
ScCC Je 30 1889
ScCL S 13 1888-Je,O 1889-O 7 1891
—d ed *See* World

Daily Charleston BULLETIN. *See* Daily morning chronicle

Saturday BULLETIN, and independent literary and domestic journal. w
DLC Ag 18 1838

*CAROLINA gazette. w Ja 4 1798-S 29 1840||
Ct [1831;34-35]
DLC 1821-N 1822;N 29 1823;S 8-29 1840
MB Ja 18 1837-Je 26 1838
MBAt 1829;Ja 18 1837-[38]-40
MWA D 20 1823;Mr 27 1824;My 21,Je 11 1825; S 26 1828;S 20 1830
NcD Jl 14 1821
ScCL 1821-24;1827-28;O 16 1838-40
ScU 1821
TxU 1821;Jl-D 1822

Daily morning CHRONICLE. d Ja 27 1873-74||?
Ja-My 11 1873 as Evening bulletin; My 12-31 1873 Daily Charleston bulletin
NcD Ja-Je 1873

*CITY gazette and commercial daily advertiser. w,sw,tw,d F 15 1783-1840||
1783-F 1784 as South-Carolina weekly gazette; Mr 1784-Ja 14 1786 as South-Carolina gazette and public advertiser; Ja 18 1786-O 1787 Charleston morning post and daily advertiser; N 1787-Je 1810 City gazette and daily advertiser (1804-Je 1806 City gazette); Jl 1810-20? City gazette and commercial advertiser
w 1783-F 1784; sw Mr 1784-Jl 10, N 23 1785-Ja 14 1786; tw Jl 12-N 1785
CSmH Ag 14 1827
CtY N 1 1828;Je 5 1830;F 18 1832
DLC Ja-Je 1821;22-28;Je 18,Jl 11,31,Ag 4,S 5,N 20 1829;30;N 15 1831;Jl-D 1832
MBAt F 5 1823;D 3,16 1828;Ag 17 1830
MHi [1823-26]
MSaE N 7 1831
MWA My 11,Je 8,12,N 22 1822;Mr 14-15,Ap 8-9,19,23,D 12 1823;Ja 24,Mr 12,20,24,Ap 22, 29,My 25-26,Je 4,16,Jl 19,Ag 14,N 12,D 13 1824;Ap 8 1826;F 23,S 18 1827;Ag 4,D 4,12, 27 1828;Ja 1,27,N 2,4,8,13,D 16,30 1830;D 3 1831;N 5,D 24 1832
N N 27 1824
NNHi Jl 1822-Je 1823;Ja-Je 1825
NcD Mr 26,Ap 4-Je 1821;Ja 4-Ap 1 1822
NjR Je 8 1822;F 21 1833
OC [Je 18 1830-Je 1831]
PEL Je 1 1831
ScCC 1821;23-25;27-28;Jl 1829-Je 1831;32-Ap 1833
ScCL 1821-33
ScU Jl 1-2,4,7-Ag 8,17-N 6,8-D 22,24-30 1823; Ja 1,3-Ap 16,19-Je 1824
TxU 1821-28;30-Je 1832
WHi 1822-Je 1826;Ja-Je 1827;Ja-Je 1828;29-31

Charleston COMMERCIAL advertiser. sm 1874-75||
ScU Ja 15 1875

COMMERCIAL journal and Charleston wholesale prices current. w
MWA O 30 1841;Ja 15,F 5,26,O 15 1842

Charleston daily COURIER. *See* News and courier

COURIER letter sheet review of the market and prices current. w
Title varies slightly
MHi [1836]Mr 23 1839
MWA N 3 1833;Mr 23,29,O 1,26,N 23,D 21 1839-[Ja-Je 13]O,N 14,D 19 1840;Ap 24,N 20,D 18 1841;O 1 1842;Ja 28,O 21 1843;D 20 1850

Daily DEMOCRAT. d O-N 1877||?
NcD N 19,23-24 1877

DEUTSCHE zeitung. w,sw O 4 1853-1918||?
N 22 1913 is Jubilee ed
In German
DLC 1853-S 1859;72-1900;05-17
IU O 18 1860-Ja 23,F 14-S 26 1861
NcD Ap 21 1884
ScCL N 22 1913

Charleston EXAMINER. sw Jl 15 1837-
Ct Jl 15 1837
MWA Jl 15,Ag 2 1837
NhD Ag 2 1837

FREE PRESS. w Mr 28 1868-
MBAt Ap 4-11 1868
MWA Ap 4 1868

GAZETTE. d
WHi Je 18-Jl 25 1832

GAZETTE. w 1867-69||
CSmH Je 6 1868
NcU S 12 1868;O 23 1869

Evening HERALD. d D 12 1878-
NcD D 12 1878

HOWARD'S prices current. w 1830-
MWA F 11,Mr 24 1832

Charleston INDEPENDENT. w D 2? 1875-
NcD Je 24 1876;O 17 1884

IRISHMAN and southern democrat. w 1829-32||?
My 23-Ag 22 1829 as Irishman and Charleston weekly register; Ag 29 1829-My 15 1830 as Irishman
CSmH Jl 17 1830
MH Ag 18 1832
NNHi My 23-Ag 22 1829;My 29 1830-My 14 1831

Charleston JOURNAL of commerce. d 1876-78||
MWA Je 29,N 4 1876
NcD Je 28,N 13,D 22,25 1876;Ja 4-5,9,11-13, 16-18,23-24,27 F 5-10,15,17-Mr 5,Ap 10(extra) 1877
NcU My 11 1876
ScCL [N-D 1876;Mr-Ap,Jl-S 1877]-Je 1878
TxU 1877

Charleston MERCURY. d Ja 1 1822-N 1868||
1822-23? as Charleston mercury and morning advertiser
Suspended from F 1865-N 19 1866
CSmH Ag 13 1827;D 20(extra)1860
Ct [D 1826-33;35-37]
CtHT My 26,Je 10,15,21,30,Jl 4,7,Ag 12 1864
CtY N 3,21,D 27 1860[61-65]
DHU-M Ap 25 1825
DLC Mr-D 1822;Je 15,Jl 16,24,Ag 3,S 22,O 26,N 12,18-20,26,D 6,13,18,21 1824,O 11 1826; Ag 21 1827;Ja 10,15,D 5 1828;Mr 21,Je 18-19,23,26,Jl 7-8,10-11,18,25,29,31-Ag 1,7,13-14,S 3,18,25-26,N 27,D 15,21 1829;Ja 20,23,D 1,3,8-9,29,31 1830;Jl 13 1831;Ja,F 18 1833;D 30 1836;O 19 1837;Ag 25 1838;Jl 12,O 6 1840;Ap 21-22,S 7 1841;F 3,7,15 1842;F 21,24,27,Jl 15-16,18,21,D 8 1843;Mr 28 1844-Ja 20,24-25,29,31-F 14,16-17,19,21-22,24,27-Mr 8,10,12-14,16-17, 19-26,Ag 3,D 8 1849;Ap 27,S 7,19,21,30,O 26-27,D 25 1850;N 1 1851;O 29 1852;N 19,D 10,26 1853;Ja 2,Ap 14,17 1854;Ja 1,Ap 6 1855;56-F 21,Mr 5,29,Ap 10,15-16,30,My 2,27,29-30,Je 8, 13,15,18,Jl 6,Ag 2,6,26,29 1861-64;Ja 4-7,9,11, 13,16-20,24,28,F 12 1865;N 19,22,24,26,D 6 1866;67
GU [Jl-D 1839]-[41]Ja 20-21,Ap 16-17,28-29, My 5 1851
ICHi Jl 8,S 16,O 7,N 4,25-D 16 1858[Ja-O 1859]Ja 7 1865
ICN Ap 8,14,17-18,20-23,My 2,4,6 1863;N 4 1864
ICU Mr 29,Je 15,Jl 6 1861;Ja 25,Mr 6,10,Ap 3, 10,18,My 27,Ag 6,9,S 20,N 18,20,22,25,D 8-9, 13,20,29 1862[63-64]Ja 6-12,14,18,21,24 1865;D 4 1866
IP Ja 7-Je 27 1860
IU Je 15,Jl 24,26,N 21 1860[61-63]My 12,14,Je 2-3,7,13,16,Ag 4,22,24,29,31 1864
LNC N 20,D 13 1860;F 1,My 30 1861
MB Ap 10 1848;Ap 30,N 19,21 1860;Mr 1-29 1861
MBAt Ap 1,My 9,15,17 1822;Mr 13,Jl 25,Ag 15,D 9,23 1828;S 18-19 1843;57-60;Ja 1-24,26-F,Ap 1-11,15-29,My 2,4,7-18,21,Je 15 1861;Ja 17,Ap 21,Je 9,21,Jl 1,19 1862[F 17-N 26 1863; Mr 17-D 17 1864]Ja 30-31,F 2,7 1865;Je 26 1867;Je 17 1868
MH [1856-57]Ag 20 1861;Ag 5,O 31,N 5,22,24, 26,D 7 1864;Ja 5,16,19-20,24,31,F 2,11 1865
MHi [1860-65]
MWA [Mr 20-D 16 1822]D 17 1824;Ja 24,Jl 25 1825;F 24,D 24 1827;Jl 29,Ag 13,N 29 1828;D 31 1830;F 5 1831;D 9,14-16,21 1833;My 22 1840;Jl 31 1844;N 13 1845[46-47]Ap 27,Jl 5,N 27 1852;N 22 1856[Ap 18-Jl 16 1860]N 4 1861;Ap 1,11 1862;Ja 3,Je 8,11,O 21 1863;Ag 2,4,12-13,18,23,25 1864;Jl 8(supp)11 1868
MiU-C [1861-64]
MnU F 11 1823;Ag 2,O 4 1825;Ja 7 1826
N O 7 1833
NN Ap 30 1832;D 20(extra)1860;My 8,10,28,D 16 1862;Ja 12,29-30,F 5,13,20-21,24-28,Mr 12, 18,Ap 11,My 16,18,30,Je 3,9,19,Jl 9-10,14-15, Ag 25-26,31-S 1,11,N 27-28 1863;F 15,My 18, 21,O 8,11,N 14,16 1864;Ja 19 1865
NNHi Jl 12 1831;Ap 17-20 1850;My 3 1855;Ap 7,18,Je 7,O 22,31,N 13,D 12 1861;Jl 19 1864
NSyU Ap 24-26,28,30-My 2 1860
NcAsS Ag 23 1862;Ag 1-24,26-30 1863
NcD F 19 1830;Mr 26,N 18,22,29,D 1-4,9,19,25 1845;Je 20 1846;Ja 27,Ag 2 1847[48]Ja 4 1853; Ja 2 1854;O 15 1856;Ja 14,Mr 26,S 25,D 1,20 1858;Ap 9,N 26 1859[60-64]Mr 11,D 14 1867; supp N 1 1860
NcU Ap 23,25,28,30,My 2-3,D 18 1860;Je 8 1861;My 15,Je 7,Jl 19,D 18 1862;Ap 15,20,S 12,D 17 1863;Ap 11,16,D 12,20 1864
NhD Ap 8 1841;Ag 12-14 1851
NjP Jl 1822-23
OClWHi Ap 17,19 1861;Ag 12 1862[Mr 1863-F 1865]D 1 1866;Ag 1,12 1867;My 31,Jl 22 1868
OHi My 22 1828;D 21 1858-D 20 1859;60-My 18 1861;Ja 8 1864
P Mr 18 1862
PPL [1861]Ap 11 1863
PPiHi [1860-61]
ScCC Jl-D 1827;Jl 7-N 23 1830;31-32;Jl 1833-[34]35;Jl-D 1837;Ja 18-My 1838;39;Ja 13-Je 29 1840;41[42]-Je 1845;46-48;Jl 2 1849-Je,O 3-D 16 1854;55-Je 1856;Ja-Je 1857[58]59;Jl 11-17 1862
ScCL 1823-Je 1827;28;Jl 1829-64;Ja 3-F 11 1865;N 1866-67;F-N 1868
ScCoCR S 1 1856;Mr 13,Jl 4,O 9,N 13,20,29,D 29 1860[61]Ja 31,F 14-15,Mr 8,24,My 15,Je 18,30,Jl 9,S 3,6,8,11,15,O 1,8,16,23,31,N 1,4-5, 11-12,19-20,22,26,29,D 3,6,8,10,15-18,24-25,29 1862[63]64
ScU Ap 1851-Je 1852;53;Ja-N 1861;62-D 17 1864
TKL O 16 1860
TSS Ag 16 1861
TU Jl 17 1848
V Jl 18,27 1861;O 3,27 1862
VRC Ap 1-3,6 1850;N 6-7 1854;Jl 5,8-24,26-O 27,29-N 24,26-D 26,28 1859-[63]64;Ja 3-7,9-14, 17-21,23-28,31,F 2-5 1865;N 19-24,26-29,D 1,3, 5,7-8,10-15,17-22,24-25,27-29,31 1866-Mr 8,10-Ap 1,3-Je 9,11-N 1,3-17 1868
WHi My 25 1825;Jl 14-16 1828;S 21 1835-36;Ja 4-Ap 20,N 1841-Ap 28 1842[Jl 3 1848-Ja 28 1865]

Tri-weekly MERCURY. tw 1827-68||
1827-57 as Charleston mercury (country ed); 1858-O 5 1861 Charleston mercury (tw)
CLM Mr 29 1832;Ja 17 1839;Ap 26 1842
CSmH D 6 1864
CtY S 25 1860-My 14 1861
DLC [1827-28;31;35;38-39;42-65;67-68]
ICU [N 6 1860-Ag 10 1861]Ja 25,F 25,Mr 6,10, Ap 3,18,My 27 1862;My 28-29,S 26-29 1863;D 4 1866
IU Ja 12-14,N 27-29,D 20 1860[61]
LSfD Je 4,Ag 3,10,29 1861
MBAt [1861]Ap 22,Je 19,S 4 1862;F 5,Ap 28, My 2,Jl 18,D 22 1863[64]
MWA Je 3/4 1831;O 26/27 1832;D 18/19 1833; Ja 4/5 1838;O 20/21 1854;D 8/9 1856;Ja 16/17 1857;Ap 21,28,My 1-3,17 1860;Je 22 1861;My 31 1862;Ag 9,S 10,D 6 1864[Ja-Ap] Je-Jl 7,Ag 20-27,S 1-22,26-N 14 1868
MiU Mr 29 1862
NNHi [F-D 1862]F 17-19,Mr 4,17,Ap 9,Jl 21,S 19,N 27 1863;F 24(extra)1868
NcD [Ap 1844-52]N 28/29-30/D 1,23/24,30/31 1853;Mr 15/16,Ap 12/13,N 8/9 1854;F 5/6,Je 18/19 1855;F 11/12,Ag 20/21,O 8/9 1856[O 1858-64]
NcU S 22,29,O 25,N 13,17,D 22,27 1838;F 5,Ap 18 1839;My 5,18,Je 13 1840;O 4 1842[43-51]Ja 22,F 19,My 15,25,O 28,N 30 1852;Ap 16,19,My 5 1853;Je 19 1862
OCHi [1861-Jl 1862]Je 13,Jl 11-16,Ag 20 1863
OClWHi Ap 24 1862
OHi Mr 23,28 1861
PHi Mr 15 1860-Mr 14 1861;Ap 12 1862-Mr 17,27,S 11,N 13,D 9 1863;Ja 1,3 1864
PPL O 20 1859;Ja 19-24,29-Mr 12,21-29,Ap 4-18,30-Je 18 1859
ScCC F 27 1862
ScCoCR F 1-11,20,21,Mr 4,11,18-22,Ap 8,26,My 1,20-31,Je 6,7,19,26,Jl 4,10,17-19,26,Ag 21,28 1862[63]Ja 5-7,Mr 12 1864
TSS Ag 15 1861
WHi [S 12 1861-F 13 1862]

MERCURY prices current and commercial journal. d
MHi Je-D 28 1860;F 1 1861
MWA Ja 1,F 5-Je 3,17-Jl 8,O 6-28,N 24 1848; Ja 5,F 2 1849;N 15,D 6 1850;Ja 14,N 4-11,D 2-30 1853;Ja 6-F 17,Mr 3-10,31-Ap 7 1854

Daily MERIDIAN. d My 4 1844-
DLC My 4 1844

Charleston MESSENGER. w O 13 1894+
pub 1894+
M S 13 1930
OCHi D 18 1860[F-S]O 23,N 5,D 5 1861;Ja 1,25,My 16 1862;Ag 19 1863

METEOR
Colonial Dames supplement to News and courier
ScCo Ap 6 1895;O 5 1903;My 31 1904;D 25 1931

MONITOR. w 1888-89||?
NcD My 26 1888

NEW ERA. w 1880-84||?
NcD Ap 3,24 1880;N 19 1881[82-My 1884]

Charleston evening NEWS. d O 1 1845-61||
CSmH Ag 10 1846
CtY My 4-30 1861
DLC Ja 10,28,Mr 4,My 7,16,Je 6 1861
ICU My 19-20,Je 10-11,Jl 9,14,17 1846
MWA D 11 1845;Jl 8,N 26 1852
NNHi S 10,O 5 1858;Ja 3,21,24-25,28,Mr 4,Ap 15,Je 1,3,S 6 1859;Mr 7 1860
NSyU Ap 27-30 1860
NcD My 29-30 1846;Ap 2 1850;Ja 30 1852;D 11 1858
NcU Ap 26,My 3 1860
P-M S 29 1846
PPL Mr 29-30 1858
ScCL O 1845-46;Jl 1847-Je 1849;50-Je 1853;54-56
VRC O 8,N 22,D 6,8,22,27 1859;Ja 5,21,30,F 8,19,Mr 2,16,Je 14,Jl 3,22 1861
WHi My 29 1852

Weekly NEWS. w 1852-
DLC Mr 12 1853-Ag 14 1856
MWA Jl 10 1852
NcU Ja 29 1853
ScCL Je 26,Jl 31 1852

Charleston NEWS. tw N 14? 1852-
MWA N 27 1852;Ap 9 1859

Charleston daily NEWS. d Ap 14 1865-Ap 5 1873||
United with Charleston daily courier to form News and courier
DLC Ag 21-23,26-31,S 2,8-16,20,23-25,27-28,O 10-12,18-19,21,26,N 2,4,9,15,17,D 6,9,12,16,30 1865;Ap 25 1866-O 1867;Ja 18,21-22,28,31,F 18, 20,24,Mr 11,Ap 6,Jl 8,10-11,28,Ag 11 1868;69
IU Ag 6 1868
KHi Ap 29,My 11-12 1869
MBAt Ag 17,19-24,26-31,S 2,8-13,16,N 25,D 2, 19,21,23,27,30 1865;Ja 11,13,22,23,25-29,31-F 5, 14-15,24,Mr 23 1866[S 1867-69]
MWA Mr 15 1867;F 27,Ap 6-7[Jl 11-N 12]1868; Ap 21 1870;Ja 3,5 1871;Mr 26 1872
N Je 23 1868
NNHi Ja 24 1866
NcD S 3,27 1866;Ag 29 1867[68]My 20,28,Je 1 1869[70-72]Mr 5 1873
NcU Ja 16 1866
OClWHi O 13 1870
PP [F 17-Mr 20 1860]

SOUTH CAROLINA (*Continued*)

CHARLESTON—*Continued*

Charleston daily NEWS. d 1865-73||—*Continued*
ScCC S 12-15,O 12-14,29,31[N]1868
ScCL F 27,Jl 1866-Ap 5 1873
ScCN complete
ScU [Je-D 1866]F 15,My 29-30,Je 22,S 19 1872;Ja-Ap 6 1873
VRC My 23-S 14,16-N 25,27-29,D 1-13,15 1866-73
WHi Mr 22,Ap 2-4,7,9-11,13 1866

Charleston tri-weekly NEWS. tw Ja 1868-Ap 7 1873||
United with Charleston tri-weekly courier to form News and courier
MWA Jl 28-Ag 8 1868;F 21 1871
NcD F 29,Ag 11 1868;F 5 1870

Sunday NEWS. 1879-1926 *See* News and courier w

***NEWS and courier.** d Ja 10 1803+
1803-Ja 1852 as Charleston courier; Jl 1852-Ap 5 1873 Charleston daily courier
pub 1856+
A 1841-48;96-1902
C Jl 2-D 1840
CSmH Ag 3 1827;Ag 13 1853;Ag 15 1863
CoU 1900;05-My 1910
Ct [1833]Je 12-13 1845;D 7 1889
CtHT Ap 18 1861;Je 20 1863;Je 13,18,29,Jl 2,6,8,Ag 5,O 28,31 1864;Ap 25,27-28,My 5 1865
CtY D 17 1839-Jl 21 1846;Mr 23 1860-O 22 1866;1903(special ed)
DLC 1821-Je,O 6,N 24 1832;33-Ja 13,19-20,24-26,30,F 2-4,22 1865-72;Jl 16 1873+
DHU-M Ag 13 1836
GAtCo S 10-11 1838
GDE [1850]
GU 1832-[37-Je 1838]Ap 29 1907
ICHi F 16,26 1875;S 1 1876
ICM Mr 5 1885;Ja 31 1889
ICN D 11 1917-My 20 1920
IHi Ap 19 1861
IU Ja 3,Ap 24,Jl 31,S 3,D 25 1861;My 21 1863;My 6 1909
KHi Ap 15 1865;Ja 26 1925
LNC Je 24 1861
LNH S 11-12 18-O 5,7-D 7 1895
M 1903(special ed)
MB Ap 25 1839[F 1860-My 17]N 13 1865
MBAt My 15-18 1822;Ap 7 1828;Ja 17 1829;Jl 2 1832-35;Jl-D 1837;Jl 1838-Je 1839[40]Mr 18,My 8,Ag 20 1841[42]-Je 1843;My 15,Jl-D 1844;Ja-Je 1854;Ja-Je 1855;Jl 29-Ag 3,6-10,13-16,20-24,27-S 14,18-N 15,19-D 9,11 1861-[62]-[65]-69
MH Ap 20,My 6 1863;Ja 25,28,F 3,8-9,14,Mr 22-23 1865;Mr 31,My 14,20,24,28,Jl 27,Ag 20,26,S 1-4,7,9-11,14-15,17-18,22-25,27-29,O 6,8,N 1,D 23 1875;Jl 24 1885;Jl 12 1917
MHi F 21,Je 30,Ag 20,D 18 1824;Ap 23 1825;N 24 1832;N 27 1835[60-64]Ap 29 1865;Jl[O 1875-Ap]O 31,N 7,9-11,29,D 1,5-6,15,22 1876;Ja 1[Mr 1877-81]Ap 20 1904
MSaE Jl 28 1831;Je 21 1843
MWA S 23 1823;Mr 24,29,Je 1,N 29 1824;Ap 27,My 3 1825;F 24 1827;Ap 29,My 27,Jl 4,N 26,D 2 1828 Je 8,Jl 8,S 5,18,26,O 30,N 27 1829;Ja 19-20,23,S 23,N 2,4,8 1830;Je 7,14,21 1831;D 10,14 1833;Je 7 1834;Ag 19,O 16 1839;Ja 8,N 30 1840;Jl 29-30,Ag 22 1844;Ja 13 1848;Je 30,Jl 5,N 19,27 1852;S 26,D 21 1857;Ap 20,26,28-My 3,8-9,12,15-16,D 29 1860[Ap 15-D 1861]Ja 1,4,9,13,15-16,20-21,29,31,F 4,12-13,21,28,My 14,27,Jl 4,O 21,D 27 1862;F 19,Mr 27,Ap 3,14,Je 8,13,17,22,26,Ag 11,17-18,24,O 13,27 1863;Ja 1-19,F 1,Mr 21,My 4,Je 29,N 16 1864;F 27,Ap 5-6,17,20,Jl 11-12 1865;Ap 7,D 8 1866;Ag 1,D 9 1867;Ap 9 1868;Mr 1(supp)21 1870;Ap 21 1871;Je 20(supp)1873;Ap 20,Je 29,Jl 20,22-29,S 8,O 4,D 4 1876-Je 1895;96-Je 1897;98-Je,S 30 1902-Jl,D 1903-06;Jl 1908-My,Jl,D 1914-21;Ja 2 1922;D 30 1924+
MiU Ap 17 1865
MiU-C [1861-64]
N Ja 24 1826;Ja 12,Ag 6 1847;N 11 1859[Mr-N 1861]Je 29 1863
NBHi D 3 1864;Mr 10,Ap 15 1865
NCanHi Jl 1 1852
NN S 29 1825;Ap 23,My 4 1860;Ap 17,My 16,Jl 24,O 12,N 9,22 1861[62-64]Ja 5-6,Ap 15 1865
NNC 1903(special ed)
NNHi Ap 8 1834;N 25-26 1842;D 21 1860;My 6,14,Je 22,N 7,11,D 13 1861;D 9,16 1862; F 7,S 19 1863;Mr 1,9,Ap 14-15 1865;Ap 14 1873
NSyU Ap 24-My 2 1860
NcD N 9 1839;Ja-Je 1845;Ja 1 1848;49-[51]-[54]-58;Mr 21 Ap 26,My 2 1861[62]-[64]Mr 17,Ap-Je,N 13 1866;67-[73-77]-79;Je 3,Jl 15,S 29 1880;My 12 1881[82-83]F 15,O 18 1884[85-87]Ja 18,23,My 5 1888;Mr 13-16,O 9,17 1889;Je 19 1890;O 5 1891;Je 12,Ag 5,S 6 1892[95]F 15-18,N 21 1897;My 12,Jl 9,Ag 10,O 27,N 1 1899;Je 30 1900;Je 28,Ag 6,24,S 16,D 19 1901;Ag 23 1904;D 1 1905;F 6 1906[13-14]Mr 1-4,6-7,9-11,13-31,C 1-2,4-25,28-31 1916
NcU F 4 1856 F 13 1860[61-64]D 25 1869;F 1876-Je 1877;Ag 13,O 17,25,N 3,11,14,21-22,26 1879;Je 5,O 11 1880;My 11 1899
NhD Ap 9 1841;Jl 25 1846;Ja 5 1864
NjR Ap 15 1865
OCHi N 3 1860 Mr 29,Je 15,D 25 1861;Ja 1,F 21,28,Ap 18,My 16,Jl 4,D 27 1862;Ja 3,Mr 7,Ap 3 1863
OClWHi Mr 19-22,25 1833;Ja-Je 1854;59-60 [Ap-D 1861;Je 1862-Jl,N 1864]Ja 12,Ap 15 1865
OHi D 17 1823;Ap 29,My 20,Je 27-29,Jl 14 1863;Ap 11,13-14,My 3,9,S 17-N 1 1864
OOxM Ap 19-20 1880;S 1 1883
P S 30 1861;Jl 1890-Je 1917
PEL Ap 7 1831
PHi N 12]14 1863;F 15,17,21 1865
PPL [1860]Je 1 1861[62-63]Je 26,Jl 12-13 1865; Je 1866
RPB Ag 11 1835
ScC 1931+
ScCC 1821-[23]-25;Jl 1826-Je 1831;32-33;Ja-Je 27,D 29 1834-Je 1835;Ja 4-Je 28 1836[37;39]-[42]Jl 4 1844-Je 1852;Jl 1853-Je 1854;55;Ag-D 1856;Jl 31 1857-S 24 1859;Mr 14-18,20,22-31,Ap 3-6,12,14,17-22,24-29,My,Je 1865;Jl 10,14,21 [Ag]S,N 14-17,D 10(supp)1868;Ja 1869[Ja-F, Ap]My 16-17 1870[Ag 1874]S-O 18 1886;Je 25-Jl 1 1889
ScCL Jl 1852+
ScCoCR Mr 13,Je 7,12,Jl 17,Ag 4,7,10,18,S 1,6,18,O 4,7,N 29,D 4,7 1861;Ja 10,17,24,27,29,F 4,Mr 17 1862;S 17 1863;Je 23,27,Jl 1,11,21,Ag 27,29,S 4 1864
ScGF 1880-90
ScRW 1898+
ScU 1824[Ag-D 1833]-34;Ap 1851-52;Ja 10,Je 24,Jl-D 1853;S 11 1854 Je 2 1859;My 9,Ag 9,N 21,D 21,28 1860[Ap 13 1861-My 1862]-Jl,Ag 3,21,29 1863-[64]F 11,My 26,Jl 15,S 29,O 18 1865;67+
T N 20 1840
TKL Je 23 1887
TSS N 21,D 27 1860;Ap 26,Je 15,Ag 21,26-28,S 9,18,23,27,O 4-5,N 15,D 25,31 1861;Ja 1,11,18,F 21,28,Mr 6,My 16 1862;80-S 20 1884;85-Je 1887;Ag-D 1889;Jl-S,O 2-D 1890;S 4-O,N 2 1893-F,Mr 2-Je 29 1895;Je 2-30,Jl 2-Ag,S 2-O,N 2 1897-98;My 2-Ag 1899
Tx My 11 1861
TxU 1829-32;Ja-Je 1835;36-Je 1837;39-Mr 1846;47-53;Jl 1854-60;Jl-Ag 29 1861;62;F 3 1863-Je[S 1864-Ja 24]Mr 6 1865-1905;08-Mr 1910;N 16 1912-My 12 1913;17-53
V Jl 24,Ag 4 1861;My 28 1862;F 6,My 13 1863
VP 1854
VRC Ap-My 7,9-Jl 3,6-Ag 26,28-N 20 1856;57-[64]Ja 7,21,26,F 1-4,6-11,13,15-16 1865;Ap 7-18,20-22,24-My 29,31-Jl 9,11-D 17,19 1873-75;F 24 1876;Jl 13 1885;Jl 22 1886
WHi Jl 1839-42;Jl 1843-Je 29 1844;Jl 1845-51;Jl 1852-53;Jl 1855-56;Jl 1857-Je 1858[Ap 23 1862-N 12 1863]64-65;Je 6 1866-68;Jl-D 1869;Jl 1885-Je 1892;O 26 1912+
—**Colonial dames supp** *See* Meteor

***NEWS and courier.** tw 1809-82||?
1809-54? as Charleston courier; 1855?-Ap 5? 1873 Charleston tri-weekly courier
CLM Jl 22 1862
DLC Ap 19,My 8/10,27/28,Je 3/4,Jl 1/2,15/16 1824;Je 10/11 1831;Ag 28 1834;Je 24/25,Ag 21/22,26/27 1844;S 29 1849;D 20 1855;Ag 26-My 1,10-12,Je 2,Jl 12,N 10 1860-F 7 1865;F 20 1868;N 25 1869
IU Ja 12-14,26,O 6,11,16,23,30,N 24-29,D 20 1860[61]
IaRE My 11 1861
MBAt D 17 1861;Ja 15,F 12,Ap 23 1863;Ja 2,7-8,12-28,F 2-6,11-18,23,27-Ap 3,8-22,27-Ag 5,10-12,17,21-N 2,6-D 23,28 1869-71
MWA N 1 1822;Jl 26/28 1823[F 14/16-Jl 22/23] D 25/28 1824[Ja 15/17-Ap 23/25]Jl 6 1825;O 31 1826;D 27/28 1827;O 10/11 1828;Ag 23/24 1830;S 5/6 1834;Ag 1839-[44-51]-O-N 1852]F 21 1854;Ja 23,Ag 19,28,S 14,21,25,30,O 9,19 1858;My 10 1859;My 1,O 18,27,N 1,6,24 1860;Ja 12-17,Mr 23,Ap 11,16,Je 25,Jl 2,20,Ag 8-N 14,19-D 24,28 1861-[62-Je 1863]Ja 19,Ap 7,My 5,12,24,Je 4,Jl 12,Ag 4,30,S 13,O 18-22,N 10-15,19-26,D 8,13-15 1864;F 12 1867;Ap 29 1876
MiU-C [1861-62]
NBHi O 31 1831
NN Je 14,17 1862;Ap 23 1863
NNHi S 26 1861
NcD Ja-F 1841;Mr 18/19 1842;Ja 5/6,S 23/24 1844;Ap 14/15,26/27 1848;Mr 9 1858;Jl 21 1859;My 26 1860;Ja 23 1862;F 25,Ap 2 1864;D 10 1867;F 11,S 10 1868;Ja 13-18,23-27 1872;N 13 1875
NcU Jl 13 1854;O 16 1860
NjR F 22-23 1841
OCHi N 24 1852;Ja 30,Jl 1,O 21,D 30 1854;D 15 1855;Mr 15,My 27 1856;Jl 14,N 29,D 8 1859;Mr 27,Ap 26,Je 7,16,N 8-17,27 1860-Ag 20 1863
OClWHi Ja 31 1861
OHi Jl 21 1859
PHi F 19 1861
ScCoCR Ja 6 1863
ScU Jl 16 1853;Ap 22,My 31-Je 14 1856;Ja 17 1857;Ap 26-My 1,10,Je 12-Ag 1861
TSS [S 1860-62]
TxGR Ap 18,Je 27 1863;Ja 5-7,12 1865[68-69]Ja 13,25,29,F 1-5,15-19,Mr 29,Ap 9,21,26 1870;F 16 1871
WHi S 2 1862

NEWS and courier. w,sw 1870?-1912||
1870-73? as Weekly news
w 1870?-Mr 1898
MB My 26 1875-Je 1877
MWA Ap 26 1876
NcD [My-D 1879]Ja 7,F 4-18,Mr 31,Ag 4 1880;Je 1,D 21 1881[82-84]O 13,N 3,D 1 1886;Ja 4,Ag 8 1888;Ap 17-24,Je 12 1889;Ja 13 1892;S 29 1897;O 14,25-28,N 4 1899
TJT O 17 1900
TxU Je 22 1892-N 15 1912
VRC Ja 3,17 1883
WHi 1896-O 5 1912

NEWS and courier. w N 23 1879+
1879-Ag 29 1926 as Sunday news
A Jl 1897-Ja 1914
MWA Ag 30 1885;Mr 27 1904-06;Jl 1908-My,Jl 1914-21;25+
NcU S 17 1882;F 25 1883;My 24,Ag 16,O 4 1885;My 9,Je 13,S 26 1886;Mr 20,Ap 10,My 15,O 23 1887;Ap 21 1889;Jl 13 1890;Ja 18,D 13 1891;F-Ap 3,17,My 15,Je 5 1892;D 20 1901;Je 26 1904;D 20 1914
OOxM Ap 18 1880
TxU 1913-14
VU Jl 1 1906

Charleston OBSERVER. w Ja 6 1827-
DLC Ja 20,F 3-10,24-Ap 21,My 5-12,Je 2-16,30-Ag 18,S 8-D 1,15-29 1827;Ja 26,F 9-16,Mr 15-Ap 5,My 3,17-31,Je 14-28,Jl 12,26-Ag 2,16-S 6,20-N 1,15-22,D 6-13,27 1828-Ja 3 1829;O 27,N 10 1832;Ag 24-31,S 21,D 8-29 1839;Jl 16 1842-O 1843
GAtCo Jl 21 1838
GDE [1833-38]
ICHi Ag 7 1830;D 7 1833
KyLo D 28 1838-Ja 19 1839
MDeHi Mr 22 1828
MWA My 5 1827
NNHi 1828-Ag 6 1831[Mr 1832-33]-36
NcD Je 3 1837;Ag 3 1839
NhD Ap 3 1841
OOxM [Ap 18 1835-38]
PHi Jl-S 2 1843

PALMETTO flag. sw,tw S 12 1851-
NcD S-O 25 1851

Charleston evening POST. d O 1 1894+
pub 1894+
A N 1914
KHi D 26 1924
NcD D 5 1901
ScCL My 5,13 1899;Ag 1900+
T Ap 10 1930
TxGR N 24 1914
VU N 24 1914

Charleston morning POST and daily advertiser. *See* City gazette and commercial daily advertiser

PRICES current. w
MHi Ag 2,O 1 1827;Ag 25 1828;O 1,N 10,D 29 1832;My 11 1835

RAMBLER. tw 1843-
N Ja 6 1844
ScCL D 1843-Mr 1844

Weekly RECORD. w D 16 1865-
MBAt D 30 1865-Ja 6,27-Mr 10,24 1866

Charleston RECORDER. w Ja 30 1886-90||?
MWA Ja 30 1886
NcD N 6 1886;Ag 27 1887

Charleston daily REPUBLICAN. d Ag 19 1869-Jl 12 1872||
1869-S 8 1871 as Daily republican. Suspended from S 8 1871-F 19 1872
DLC 1869-F 20,26,Ap 11-12,Je 22,Jl 5-6,9,12 1872
MBAt Ag 25-S 1,4,7,9-16,18,21-22,24-25,28-O 1,4-5,13-15,18-19,23,26,28-30,N 4,6-10,13,16,19,22,24-D 2,4-28,30 1869
MWA S 22(supp)O 8(supp)15(supp)N 29(extra)1870;Ja 4 1871
NcD O 21,23 1869[70-71]Je 12 1872

Charleston REPUBLICAN. w 1869-72||?
NNHi Ap 1872

Charleston REPUBLICAN. d C 1876-77||?
NcD O 20,25 1876

SOUTH-CAROLINA weekly gazette. *See* City gazette and commercial daily advertiser

SOUTH-CAROLINA gazette and public advertiser. *See* City gazette and commercial daily advertiser

SOUTH CAROLINA leader. w O 7 1865-
CtY N 25 1865
DLC O 28,N 25,D 23 1865;Ja 6-13,27,F 24,Mr 24,Ap 7,21,O 20 1866;Mr 23 1867
MBAt O 7-21,D 9-23 1865;Mr 31,My 12 1866
MH O 7-14 1865
MWA O 7,D 16 1865

SOUTH CAROLINA republican. *See under* Columbia

Daily SOUTH CAROLINIAN. d
LNC Ap 8 1866
MBAt [N 17 1865-Ap 23 1866]
WHi F 13,Ap 12,Jl 25,O 11 1866

SOUTH CAROLINIAN. tw 1871-73||
NcD O 24 1872;Ap 1 1873

SOUTH CAROLINIAN. d F? 1872-73||
MWA Ap 5,19,25 1872
ScU N 6 1872-Je 1 1873

SOUTHERN free press. w Ja 16? 1830-
CSmH My 15 1830
IaDH Mr 6-N 13 1830

***SOUTHERN intelligencer.** w 1819?-
MWA Jl 27 1822
NcU S 11 1824[25]Ja 14-21,F 18,Mr 11 1826
NjHi [1822-My 1825]

SOUTHERN medium and impress of the times. sw 1839-
DLC Ja 8 1840

***SOUTHERN patriot.** d Jl 1814-48|
1814-Ag 10 1825 as Southern patriot and commercial advertiser
CSmH Ag 15 1827
Ct Ag 18 1831
CtY My 3,O 29 1828
DLC 1821-26;Jl 1827-Je 1829;Ja-Jl 2 1830;Ja 12-Je 1831;Jl-D 1832[Mr 6-Je 1833]-N 28 1842;Jl 1844-Jl 2,8-9,14,31,O 2,N 28-29,D 1,4,8,12,17-19 1845;Jl-D 1846
GU [F 23 1838-My 2 1839]
MBAt Ja 21,Mr 30,Ap 4 1822;F 18 1829;Ag 20,S 8,17,N 13 1830
MHi Je 30,D 7-8,10 1824;F 17 1826;N 21,29-30 1832;Jl 17 1846
MWA Jl 10,13 1821;My 23,O 2? 1823;N 10 1824;Ap 30,D 9 1825;F 23 1827;Je 20,Jl 10 1829;D 20,23,27 1833;N 14 1834 D 30 1837;Je 13 1839;My 16 1840;Ja 4 1842
MoSM Jl 3 1845-Je 1846
NCanHi Ja 15 1824
NCorL Ap 12 1823
NNHi N 12 1832
NcD Jl-D 1823;F 24,Jl 1824-[25]-S 16,O 23 1826;Jl-O 9 1827;Ja-Je 1830;N 26-27 1832;Jl-D 1837[Ja-Je 1840]
NhD Mr 26 1841
P-M N 9 1847
ScCC 1821-22;24;26;28;Jl 1829-35;Jl 1841-44
ScCL 1823;25;Jl-D 1827;Ja-Je 1829;30-Je 1838;39-Je 1840;Ja-Je 1841;45-48
ScU Ja-Ap 15,17-Ap 1824;Jl 1826-Je 1827

SOUTH CAROLINA (*Continued*)

CHARLESTON—*Continued*

*SOUTHERN patriot (for the country). tw Ja 21? 1815-
DLC Mr 20 1833
N O 10-11 1833
NcD Jl 10/11 1832

SOUTHERN standard. *See* Charleston standard

Charleston daily STANDARD. d 1851-Je 1858‖?
1851-Ag 1853 as Southern standard
CSmH Ag 31 1853
MWA Jl 7,Ag 4 1852
NcD D 10(extra)1853;D 5,12,26 1856
VRC N 21 1854[N 1855-D 2 1856]F 14 1857

Charleston STANDARD. w,tw Ag 30 1851-Je 25 1858‖
Follows Sun. 1851-S 1853 as Southern standard
MH Jl 7-[N 1861-Jl 24 1852]
NcD Jl 11/12 1851;Ja 21/22,D 10(supp)S 29 1855;O 23,D 3,5,12,26 1856
ScCC F 25 1854
ScCL Jl 1852-55
ScU Ja 31,F 9 1856
VHi Jl 1851-53;Jl-D 1854;Jl 1855-Jl 1857

STATE rights and free trade evening post. d O 1 1831-
Ct [1831-32]
MWA N 14 1833
N O 8 1833
ScCC 1831-Je 29 1833
ScCL 1831-My 9 1834

SÜDLICHER correspondent. sw Je 29 1869-71‖?
In German
DLC 1869-70

SUN. w S 30 1850-Je 1851‖
Followed by Southern standard, later Charleston standard
ScCL O 1850-Ja 1851
VHi 1850

SWAMP angel. *See under* Morris Island

*TIMES. d O 6 1800-
O 6-N 16 1800 as Times and political and commercial evening gazette. N 17 1800-Mr 15 1801 as Times, city gazette and merchants' evening advertiser
ScCL Ja-Jl 1821

TRANSCRIPT. d 1836?-
DLC Jl-D 1841
MWA D 4,12,15 1845
NhD Ap 8 1841

WORLD. d 1888-91‖?
NcD Mr 13,15 1889
ScCC Je 25-29,Jl 1 1889
ScCL F-Ap,S 13 1888-O 7 1891
—Sunday ed *See* Sunday budget

WORLD and Sunday budget. *See* Sunday budget

Charleston ZEITUNG. w S? 1852-
MWA My 12 1853

CHERAW

CAROLINA sun. *See* Cheraw sun and monitor

Cheraw CHRONICLE. w 1896+
KHi Ja 15-22 1925

FARMER'S gazette. *See* Cheraw gazette

Cheraw GAZETTE. w
ICHi Ja 5 1836
ScU N 17 1835-N 8 1836

Cheraw GAZETTE. w N 15 1839-
1839-47? as Farmers' gazette (title varies slightly)
DLC D 20 1839;N 4 1840;Ja-F 21 1843;N 23 1847
ICHi Mr 11 1845
MWA Jl 6 1852
MdBJ Ag 2 1842
NcD Jl 15 1840;D 1 1841;S 28 1853
NcU Je 24 1840;Ap 27 1847
ScU 1839-F 14 1843;F 6 1856

Cheraw INTELLIGENCER and southern register. w Je 5 1823-Mr 10 1826‖
United with Pee Dee gazette to form Pee Dee gazette and Cheraw intelligencer, later Pee Dee gazette and Cheraw advertiser
CtY Je 12-Jl 17,31-Ag 14,28-S 11,D 5 1823;Mr 5-19,Ap 9-My 21 1824
DLC complete
MWA complete
ScCL Mr 5 1824;My 27 1825

PEE DEE gazette and Cheraw advertiser. w 1821-33‖?
1821?-My 16 1826 as Pee Dee gazette and Cheraw intelligencer; My 23-Je 2 1826 South-Carolina spectator
DLC Ag 10 1824;Mr 21-D 1826;Ag 13 1833
ICHi D 3 1833
MWA My 16 1826;O 29 1833
NNHi Je 2 1826
NcU Ap 3 1835
PDoHi Jl 21 1826

SOUTH-CAROLINA spectator. *See* Pee Dee gazette and Cheraw advertiser

SOUTHERN radical. w Ag 22 1828-
DLC Ag 22-29 1828

Cheraw SUN and monitor. w 1880-84‖?
1880-82? as Carolina sun
NcU Ag 11 1881

CHESTER

Chester BULLETIN. w 1879-89‖?
1879-82? as State bulletin
NcD Ja 4 1882

Chester LANTERN. sw 1898-F 1915‖
NcD Ap 27 1900
ScChN complete

Chester NEWS. sw 1913+
pub 1913+
KHi O 21 1924;Ja 13,23 1925

PALMETTO standard. w 1850-
MWA Je 30 1852
NcD Ja 16 1850

Chester REPORTER. w,sw 1869+
pub Jl 1906+
KHi O 6 1924;Ja 1,20,22 1925
NcD Ag 5 1881;Ap 12 1883;Ag 18 1887

Daily SOUTH CAROLINIAN. *See under* Columbia

Chester STANDARD. w 1850?-
NcD F 3,D 22 1859;F 27 1862

STATE bulletin. *See* Chester bulletin

CHESTERFIELD

ADVERTISER. w 1880+
pub 1915+

CLINTON

Clinton CHRONICLE. w Ja 1 1902+
pub [1902+]
KHi Ja 22 1925
ScCliP D 3 1920+

Clinton weekly GAZETTE. w 1888-1917‖?
NcD S 26 1889

CLOVER

Clover HERALD. w N 8 1928+
pub 1928+

COLUMBIA

Columbia BANNER. w
NcD O 28,D 16 1857
ScU My 24 1853

CAROLINA free press. w Ja 31 1930+
pub 1930+

CAROLINA planter.
NcD Je 10 1840

Daily CAROLINA times. d Mr? 1854-56‖?
MWA Ap 21 1854
NcD D 9 1856
ScU Ja-Je 1856

Weekly CAROLINA times. w 1855-
NcD Jl 26 1855
NcU Je 4 1857
P-M O 12 1855
ScU Mr 17-Ap 3,17-My 22,Je-Jl 10,24-Ag 7,21 1866

Tri-weekly CAROLINA times. tw
-Jl 1857 as Carolina times
NcD Ag 11/12,29/30,O 24/25,31/N 1,5/6, 12/13 1856;My 8/9,Je 15/16,Jl 8/9,Ag 15,29-S 1,17,29,O 17,22,N 24,D 8 1857

COURANT. w
MB [My 26-Ag 18 1859]

Columbia FREE PRESS and hive. *See* Columbia hive

Columbia GAZETTE. *See* South-Carolina state gazette and Columbia advertiser

Weekly GLEANER. w 1864-75‖?
ScU Ag 18 1869-70;Je 21,Ag 26-30,S 20-O 4,N 22 1871
—d ed *See* Phoenix

Tri-weekly GUARDIAN. tw 1860?-65‖?
1860?-63? as Tri-weekly southern guardian
DLC Mr 14,My 30,Je 15,D 22 1861;My 15 1862; Ag 11 1863
NcD D 20 1860;Je 27 1861;F 8 1862;Mr 18/19, Ap 24/25,O 23/24 1863;D 5/6 1864;Ja 13/14,F 1/2 1865
ScCoCR Ag 8 1862
VRC F 6 1861

Columbia HIVE. w F 5 1831-
Follows Edgefield hive (Pottersville). 1831-Ja? 1832 as Columbia free press and hive
Ct [1834-36]
DLC S 29 1832;Je 28 1834
MWA F 12 1831
N O 5 1833
TxU 1831-Ja 28 1832

Columbia MONITOR. w
NNHi S 7,D 7 1883

Evening NEWS. d Ja 1 1895-97‖?
ScU Ja 24-O 4 1895

PALMETTO leader. w Ja 10 1925+
pub 1925-29;31+

PALMETTO-STATE banner. w N 2 1846-
DLC F 6 1849
MWA Je 8,Jl 6 1852
NcD Ja 26 1847;Ag 30,D 18 1849;Ja 8 1850

PALMETTO-STATE banner. d 1850-
MWA Jl 6,Ag 2 1852

PEOPLE'S recorder. w 1893-1905‖?
Dated also in Union
Negro
DLC Ja 13,27 1900

Tri-weekly PHOENIX. tw Mr 21 1865-75‖
DLC S 29 1866;N 13,23 1869
NN Mr 21-25,30-Ap 10 1865
NcD [Mr-My 9 1865]S 19 1867;D 3 1869;F 18, My 4,16,S 5,12 1871;Ap 6 1872;Ap 17 1873;Ag 13,S 17 1874;Ja 12,Je 12,17,29 1875
ScCL Mr 21,23,28,Ap 1,8,My 4-5 1865

Daily PHOENIX. d Mr 21 1865-78‖
Mr-My 13 1865 as Columbia phoenix; My 15-Jl 2 1865 Columbia daily phoenix
DLC N 10 1869
LNC Jl 6 1866
MBAt O 24 1868
MWA Ap 8,My 24 1865;F 25 1866;O 8 1876
NNHi N 22,D 3,11 1865;F 17 1866;Mr 5 1873
NcD [Ap-S 1865]F 3,Jl 6,20,S 25,O 28 1866;S 12 1867;O 22 1870[N 1871-72;74]My 27 1876; Ap 10 1877;N 3 1878
P-M Jl 22 1865
ScU 1865-Jl 25 1875
—w ed *See* Weekly gleaner

PORTFOLIO. w 1855?-
MH Ja 31,F 8 1865
NcD Ja 20-D 1864
TxU Je 1 1864

Columbia RECORD. d 1891+
1891-1913 as Daily record
Ap 8 1913 is South Carolina water power ed; O 22 1916 Textile industrial ed
pub 1915+
KHi [S 10 1924-O 18 1925]
MWA O 22 1916(special ed)
MdBJ O 22 1916
NcD O 13 1899;F 1,N 5 1913;O 22 1916;S 1929; F,Ap-My,Jl,O 1930-Ja,Mr,Ag-O 1931;Mr-My, Jl-O,D 1932-Ag 1933;F 1934
ScU Ap-Je 1910

Columbia daily REGISTER. d Jl 28 1875-D 3 1898‖
Title varies: Columbia register; Daily register; etc.
MWA O 9(supp)1876;D 14,21 1887
NN Jl 30 1884-Jl 26 1885
NcD N 6,D 19 1876;Ap 11,My 20 1877;F 19,21, 27,O 5-6 1878;O 7 1880;Mr 26 1881;Jl 28 1883-Jl 1884;S 4 1886;Jl 28 1889-O 5 1892;Jl 28 1893-D 5 1895
NcU S 28 1879;Ja 31 1880;Jl 27 1881
ScCoCS Jl 28 1883-Jl 27 1884;Jl 28 1889-O 28 1895
ScU complete
WHi S 10-D 1895

Columbia REGISTER. w,sw 1875-98‖?
w 1875-F 1894
NcD Ag 1892-[94]-Jl 1896
NcU My 5 1880
ScCoCS Jl 1883-Jl 1884;Ag 1892-Jl 1896

Daily REPUBLICAN. d Ag 8? 1868-
MBAt Ag 14,17-18,26-28 1868
MWA S 5,7 1868

SOUTH CAROLINA advocate. w
NhD Mr 25 1841

SOUTH-CAROLINA gazette and Columbian advertiser. *See* South-Carolina state gazette and Columbia advertiser

SOUTH CAROLINA legislative times. d
NN N 26-D 19 1855
NcAsS N 26-D 19 1855
ScNC D 7-19 1855

SOUTH CAROLINA republican. w O 10 1868-79‖?
1868-Ag 1869 pub in Charleston
IU O 31 1868
MBAt O 10-31,N 14-21,D 12-19 1868
MWA O 10-24,N 28 1868-[70]
N O 31 1868
NcD S 18 1869

*SOUTH-CAROLINA state gazette and Columbia advertiser. w F 28 1794-1830‖
Title varies: Columbia gazette; State gazette; South-Carolina state gazette and general advertiser; South-Carolina gazette and Columbian advertiser; South-Carolina state gazette and Columbian advertiser; State gazette and Columbian advertiser. United with Southern times to form Southern times and state gazette
CSmH Je 6 1829
CtW Ja 20 1824
CtY Ag 16-23,S 6-13,O 25,N 29 1828
DLC Ja 9-30,F 20-Je 5 1821;Jl 27 1824;O 11 1828;Je 27-Ag 8,S 12-26 1829
MBAt N 26,D 27 1828
MHi Ja 1-8,N 29 1822;Jl 22,N 28,D 19,30 1823-Ja 13,S 9 1824;F 12 1825
MWA D 8 1824;Ap 30 1825;F 28,Je 20 1829;O 13 1855
NcD D 15 1824;Ja-Jl 3 1830
ScU Ja 20-Mr 10,24 1827-28

SOUTH-CAROLINIAN. sw,w N 20 1838-
sw during sessions of the legislature
DLC N 20 1838;Mr 28-Ap 4,My 30-Je 6,Jl 4, Ag 1,15-29,S 12,26,O 17-24,N 7,21-30,D 7-11, 18-21 1844;Ag 27 1846-Mr 16 1849
MWA Jl 4 1844;Jl 8 1852
NN Ag 1 1844
NcD S 28 1838;F 18 1841;Mr 21,Ap 18,25,S 29,O 20 1848;Ja 2 1852
NcU Mr 1,Ap 12 1839;My 22 1840;N 11 1841;O 12,N 10,D 1 1842
WHi O 4,25,D 3-6 1839;Ja 24,Ag 7,S 3 1840;S 2,D 13-16 1841

SOUTH CAROLINIAN. tw 1849-65‖
Title varies: Tri-weekly Carolinian; Tri-weekly South Carolinian
DLC Ap 10 1849-Mr 1851;Ja 1,Je 5,16 1860;Ja 3,8,15-17,29,F 2,12-19,Mr 7,12-14,19-23,28-29, My 2,7-9,14-16,23-Je 1,5-8,25,Jl 23,N 6 1861; Ap 26,S 25 1862;D 31 1863;Ja 12,My 5,14 1864
MWA Jl 3,N 25 1852;S 15 1857;My 5,14 1864
NcD D 20 1849;F 7 1850;D 2 1851;Ja 15 1853; Mr 21,Ap 18,My 4,S 2 1854;Mr 14,Jl 7,26,N 1-3,24,D 15 1855;O 4,16 1856;Je 27,Jl 4,S 22, O 17,N 28,D 12 1857;Mr 12,N 22 1859;Je 2, Jl 28 1860;Je 13 1861;Ja 4,25-28 1862;D 31 1864;Ja 7 1865
OClWHi My 14 1861;Ap 21,26,My 5-7,14 1864
ScCoCR Ja 10 1863
ScU F 19-Mr 11,Jl 22,S 18,24,O 23 1851[Ag 1863-Ja 10 1865]
TxU O 6 1864
WHi Mr 16,My 5-7,14 1864

SOUTH CAROLINA (*Continued*)

COLUMBIA—*Continued*

Daily SOUTH CAROLINIAN. d 1850?-67||?
Mr 14 1865 pub in Charlotte, N.C.; Ap 29-30 1865 in Chester, S.C.
DLC 1851-Ag 1862;Je 25,Jl 23-25,Ag 7,N 6 1861;Ja 5,8,F 28,Mr 11-13,Ap 26,Ag 20,S 25,O 8 1862;Ja 31,My 8,15,30-31,Je 4,10-11,19-20,24, 27,Jl 8,15,17,Ag 21,O 31,D 4,31 1863;Ja 3,10, 12,F 6-7,23-24,Mr 6-8,25 My 6 1864;F 3,Mr 14,Ap 29-30 1865
FGS Je 5 1864
MBAt F 26-27 1861;Ap 5-6 1864
MH Ja 31-F 1,12 1865
MHi O 2,6-7,11-12,14-15,22 1864
MWA Jl 7 1852;Mr 6 1856;Ap 25 1861;Ja 10 1865
NNHi D 20 1860;Jl 24 1863
NcD N 25,D 3 1852;S 21,O 17,N 4 1853;N 29, D 4-5,11 1854;F 1,D 2,9,13,20 1856;D 22 1858; Ap 13-15 1861;Ja 1,19,Mr 19,Je 28,Ag 7,15-16 1862;Je 28,Jl 28,O 13,D 22,26 1863;64;Ap 13 1865;O 4,7 1866;F 24 1867
NcU Ja 31,D 22 1858;Ap 23 1861;Ag 1 1863
OClWHi O 20 1861;F 14 1863;Mr 15-Ap 27,Jl 31,O 13-14 1864
P O 14 1864
PHi O 11,21 1864
PPL S 29 1863
ScCL S 29 1858
ScCoCR O 9 1864
ScNC Ap 19 1865
ScU S 24,N 3-18 1851[52-Mr 1853]Mr 5,My 2 1863[F 19-D 1864]Ja 12 1865
TKL Je 7,12,O 7 1864
V My 9,13,Je 7,10 1863;Je 12,14,23,Jl 24,26 1864
VRC [N-D 1855]-[Ja-N 1 1864]

SOUTH CAROLINIAN. d
TxU Ja 1-Je 30 1906

SOUTHERN chronicle. w 1840-
DLC N 26 1840;Je 16-30,Jl 14-Ag 11,25-O 6, 20-28,N 17-D 1841;Ja 4-18,F-My 10 1843
NcD F 14 1844
NhD Mr 31 1841
ScNC Jl 7 1841-45;Jl 29 1846-Je 16 1847
ScU Jl 1840-Je 1841;Jl 10 1844-45
TxU Jl 1846-Je 23 1847

Daily SOUTHERN guardian. d 1857-F 15 1865||
DLC F 11-14,My 7,25,Je 5,Jl 23,30 1861;Ja 9-10,F,Mr 3,Ap 21,30,My 16,20,Ag 5,18,O 17,N 29,D 24 1862;Jl 15-16,Ag 17-18,20,D 21,25 1863;Ja 1,28,F 8-11,O 31-N 4,7,9-15,18-26,29-30,D 3,5,7,9-13,15-17,21,23-24,28 1864
MBAt Je 24 1862;Ap 27,Jl 2,8,Ag 12,28,S 9, 21-25,28-O 1,30,N 19,D 2,10,21 1863;Ja 14-15, 28,F 2,11,18,29,Mr 19,22,31,Ap 4-5,22-23,30,My 9,14,Je 17,Ag 11,31,S 13,19,O 21 1864
MH Ja 23,25,27,31,F 3-4,8,13 1865
MWA F 15 1865
NNHi D 9 1862;Ja 21,My 14,Je 29,D 29 1863;N 21-22,D 8,13-14,19,23 1864 Ja 4,7,13,29,F 1 1865
NcD N 27,D 20 1858;Je 1 1860;F 18,Je 12,26,Jl 7,S 9,O 3,N 26 1862;Ja 19,F 19-22,26,Mr 23, My 18,Jl 16,Ag 3-6,8-21,29 1863;My 16 1864
NcU My 2 1861;F 20,24-26,28,Mr 3-7,10-15,17-18,Ap 8 1862;O 6 1864
OClWHi My 19 1863
PHi S 28 1863
PPL O 21,23 1862
ScCL Ap 15 1861;N 8 1864
ScCoCR F 5 1862
ScU F 10,Ap 11,S 1-21,23-28,30-O 1,6-22,24-N 16,19-29,D 5-7,10,18-22,28-29,31 1863;Ja 1,4-9, 12,16-25,28,F 1,4-11,Je 4,28-D 1864;Ja 2 1865
TKL Ag 26 1863
V Je 6-7,9,14-15,Jl 23,25-26 1864
VRC S 29 1862;O 3,6,D 9 1863[64]Ja 2,4-7,9-14,16-18,21,23,25-29,31,F 2-4,7-11,15 1865
WHi S 23,O 13,N 5,11,24,D 6,13,20,22 1862

Weekly SOUTHERN guardian. w 1857-65||?
NcD Jl 16 1863

Tri-weekly SOUTHERN guardian. *See* Tri-weekly guardian

SOUTHERN times and state gazette. w,sw 1830-
CSmH Ag 19 1830
IU D 20 1830
NcD Mr 9 1832;N 28 1837;S 7 1838
NhD Ag 18 1837
P-M Ap 29 1830
ScNC Jl 10 1835-37
ScU Ja 29 1830-F 4,26-My,O 8 1831;My 25 1832

STATE. d F 18 1891+
O 3 1914 is Industrial ed
pub 1891+
A 1904-O 1916;F-O 1917;18-Ag 1919;Je 1920-Mr 1921
Ct O 3 1914
DLC 1898-My 14 1899;My 30 1901+
IC O 3 1914
IaDH 1907
KHi Jl 8 1901;Ap 12 1912;Ja 29 1913;Ap 6 1919;S 19 1920[24-My 1929]
MWA Mr 21 1936
MoS O 3 1914
MsSM D 24 1913;Ap-Je 16 1914
NbHi 1909;Ap 1910-Ap,Je 1916-Ja 16 1917
NcD [1891]-[93-94]-[96]-Je 1898;Jl 1899-Mr,Jl 1900-01;Ap-Je,O-D 1902;Mr-S 1903;Ja-S,O 16, N 20 1904;Ja-Ap 7 1905;06-Je,O 1907-Mr,Jl-O,D 1908-S 1909;10-S 1912;Ja-Mr,Jl 1913-Ap, Jl 1916+
PEr O 3 1914
PWp O 3 1914
ScCCl 1933+
ScCo S 10 1902[03;10;21;26]Ap 1927-Mr,Jl 1928+
ScCoC 1932+
ScD O 1920-Mr 1930
ScGF 1930+
ScHC 1930+
ScUn D 1919-32
ScRW 1898+
ScSW 1931+
ScU F 22 1892+
TxGR O 3 1914
TxU 1906-[Ja-Ag 12 1908]
VU Ag 26,S 27,29,O 2,6-7 1934
WHi 1917-19

STATE gazette. *See* South-Carolina state gazette and Columbia advertiser

Daily TELEGRAPH. d 1847-51||
DLC F 9 1849
NcD Je 30,Jl 2 1851
ScU O 19 1847-48;Ja 29-O 13 1849;Ap 15-O 15 1850[F 26-Jl 9 1851]

TELEGRAPH. tw
NcD N 19/20 1849;Ap 1/2,5/6,8/9,My 31/Je 1 1850

***Columbia TELESCOPE.** w D 19 1815-
Title varies: Telescope; Columbia telescope and South Carolina state journal; etc.
sw during sessions of the legislature
CSmH S 3 1830
Ct F 28 1826
CtY D 20(extra)1832
DLC N 23 1824;Jl 20 1827;Jl 11 1828;Mr 13,Je 26-Ag 14,28-S 11,25-O 16,30-N 20,D 1829-D 20 1831;33
ICHi F 25 1837
ICU N 14 1828
MBAt Ja 4 1828
MWA D 13 1827;Je 26,S 4,25,O 16,N 20,D 1,4, 24 1829;Ja 1,22,Je 4,25,Ag 6,S 3,N 29,D 3,7 1830;Ja 7,F 18 1831;Ag 13,D 13 1833
N Jl 6,13 1827
NNHi Jl 3 1835
NcD N 23(extra)D 13 1832;N 27 1839
NcU Mr 15,D 13 1833;Ag 2-9 1834;My 2,S 12, N 7 1835;Ja 16,F 13,Mr 5,19,Ap 9-16,30 1836; O 27 1838
NjR Ag 14 1824;Ag 29 1826;Mr 19 1830
PLewL F 13 1829
ScU 1829;S 11 1832;Jl 7,21,S 1,15,29 1838
VHi [Je 1830-Ja 1836]

Columbia semi-weekly UNION. sw 1869-74||?
NcD Je 4-8,Jl 20-Ag 6,31-S 17,24,O 5 1874

UNION-HERALD. d 1870-77||
1870-71 as Daily union; 1872-My 23 1873 Columbia daily union
A Ja-Jl 1875
CtY O 5 1876
DLC 1872-My 23,O 20 1873;74-Jl 1875;Jl 1876-Mr 9 1877
MWA F 14 1872;S 9 1876
NcD Ja 6 1871[My 1873-O 1874]Ja 19,Mr 3,D 31 1875;Ja 5 1876

CONWAY

FIELD. w 1903+
KHi D 18 1924
NcD My 11 1914

HORRY herald. w Ja 1886+
pub 1886+
KHi Ja 22 1925

HORRY news. w 1809-78||
NcD D 24 1869

HORRY progress. w 1883-85||?
NNHi Ap 11 1883

HORRY telephone. w 1878-82||?
NcU Jl 28 1881

DARLINGTON

Darlington FLAG. w 1851-
MWA Jl 1 1852

NEW ERA. w Jl 18 1865-
DLC Jl 18-25,S 26,D 6 1865
MBAt Jl 25-S,O 10,31,N 14-28,D 19 1865-Ja 9,30-Mr 27 1866
NN Jl 18,S 26-O 3,17 1865
NNHi Jl 18-25,Ag 8,S 5-19,O 3-10 1865

NEW ERA. 1903-05? *See* News and press

Darlington NEWS. w 1875-1908||?
United with New era to form News and press
NcU Jl 28 1881

NEWS and press. w 1903+
1903-05? as New era; 1906?-08? Darlington news
KHi O 9 1924;D 25 1925
ScD 1921+

Darlington SOUTHERNER. w 1860-83||?
MWA F 10 1865;S 3 1875
NNHi O 13 1865
OClWHi Mr 13 1861

DENMARK

EDISTO news. w 1911+
pub 1911+

DILLON

Dillon HERALD. w Ap 1894+
pub 1904+
KHi O 23 1924

DUE WEST

Due West TELESCOPE. 1850-
CtY My 10 1861
MWA My 7,Jl 23 1852;Ja 2 1857
NcD Jl 13 1860

EASLEY

Easley PROGRESS. w 1902+
pub 1920+
KHi Ja 21 1925

EDGEFIELD

Edgefield ADVERTISER. w F 11 1836+
Follows Carolinian
pub [1836-92]+
KHi Ja 21 1925
MBAt Jl 17-31 1867
MWA N 10 1852;My 27-Je 10,Jl 22-29,Ag 26-S 2,16 1868;F 12 1936
NcD Jl 20 1842;My 31 1843;My 28 1848;My 16, Je 27 1849;My 29 1850;Je 19 1851;F 19 1868; Ja 27 1869;Je 13,Ag 8 1875 Ja 30,F 27-Mr 6 1879
NcU Ap 21 1847
NhD Mr 25 1841
ScCoCR Ap 9,D 24 1862-Ja 7 1863
ScE 1836-1928
TSS 1836-Ja 21 1848

CAROLINIAN. w Mr 14 1829-F? 1836||
Followed by Edgefield advertiser
DLC Mr 21,My 30,Ag 1 1829
NcD O 9 1830

Edgefield CHRONICLE. w 1881-1925||
KHi O 9 1924;Ja 8 1925
ScE complete

FLORENCE

Florence NEWS. d 1922+
pub 1922+

Florence OBSERVER. d 1931+
pub 1931+

Florence PIONEER. w 1873-76||
NcU Mr 29 1876

Florence daily TIMES. d 1894-1925||
KHi Ja 14,22 1925

FORT MILL

CATAWBAN. *See* Fort Mill times

Fort Mill TIMES. w 1892+
1892-Mr 1893 as Catawban
pub 1900+
KHi D 18 1924

FOUNTAIN INN

Fountain Inn TRIBUNE. w Ja 24 1911+
pub 1911+

GAFFNEY

CHEROKEE times. sw 1922-29||?
KHi N 24 1924;Ja 5 1925

Gaffney LEDGER. tw F 16 189-+
pub 1894+

GEORGETOWN

Georgetown GAZETTE. sw O 12 1823-
DLC Ja 9,F 17-19,My 7,25-28 O 19,N 12,D 3 1824
MWA Ja 26 1827
NcD Ja 4 1825
ScCL O 18 1825-O 13 1826

HARVEST. sw Ja? 1828-
MWA O 17,D 19 1828

HARVEST. w
MWA D 12 1828

Georgetown INQUIRER. w 1880-89||?
NNHi My 30 1883

Georgetown TIMES. sw,w 1865+
1877? as Georgetown semi-weekly times; 1878-80? Times and comet; 1921? Times-index
sw 1896-1910
pub 1922+
KHi N 21,D 26 1924;Ja 23 1925
MBAt Jl 17 1867
NNHi Ap 24 1873;Je 16-Jl 7 1883;Ja 19-F 2, 16-23 1884
NcD Ap 11 1896

***WINYAW intelligencer.** sw,w O 1817-
sw 1817-Jl 1833
DLC Jl 21-24,S 18,N 13 1824;Ag 12,D 27 1826; 29-Ja 1 1831;O 6 1832
MWA Ap 9,20,My 11 1825;F 21,Mr 3 1827;D 30 1829;Ap 21 1830;Ap 6 1831
NcD Jl 11-16,23,30 1833-Ja 21 1834
ScCL 1825;27;32-Je 1833

WINYAW observer. w 1841-
MWA Ap 20 1844
NhD Mr 31 1841

GREENVILLE

Greenville DEMOCRAT. w 1891-94||?
ScCL F 15 1893-My 2 1894

Greenville ENTERPRISE. w 1854-Je 11 1873||
1854-F 6 1870 as Southern enterprise. United with Greenville mountaineer to form Enterprise and mountaineer, later Piedmont and mountaineer
ICHi F 2 1865
MWA Je 23 1869
NcD O 23 1867;Ag 18,S 8,N 17 D 8 1869[71-72]F 19,Ap 16 1873
ScCL My 19 1854-Jl 21,D 1859-D 20 1860;O 10-31 1861;63;69;F-D 21 1870;71-72
WHi Ag 30 1871-73

Daily ENTERPRISE. d
ScCL Ag 5-D 14 1876

ENTERPRISE and mountaineer. *See* Piedmont and mountaineer

SOUTH CAROLINA (*Continued*)

GREENVILLE—*Continued*

GREENVILLE county observer. w 1928+
pub 1928+

LANCASTER news. w
ScU F 9-D 21 1853;Ja 18-F 8,Ap 1854-F 6 1861

Greenville MOUNTAINEER. *See* Piedmont and mountaineer

Greenville NEWS. d 1874+
Title varies: Greenville daily news
pub 1901+
CtY F 27-28 1916
KHi D 28 1924
MWA Ag 31 1881
NcD F 26 1875;D 1 1878;Ja 28 1880[Jl 1899-Je 1900]My 11 1913(exposition ed);Ja 13,20,F 3, 24 1929;Ag 10,S 7,28,O 5 1930;Ja 31,O 30 1932; D 17 1933
NcU F 21 1878
ScU [Je 17 1900-01]-Ag 24,S 27,30 1902

PATRIOT and mountaineer. *See* Piedmont and mountaineer

Greenville PIEDMONT. d 1902+
pub 1919+
KHi D 26 1924
—w ed *See* Piedmont and mountaineer

PIEDMONT and mountaineer. w,sw Ja 10 1829-1911‖
1829-1901 as Greenville mountaineer (Mr 1857-61? Patriot and mountaineer; D 1866-71 Mountaineer; Je 18 1873-92 Enterprise and mountaineer)
sw 1896-1908
A Mr 12 1836-Ap 5 1844
DLC Ja 10,Je 27-Jl 4,Ag 29 1829;N 26,D 10-17 1830;O 20,N 10 1832;Ja-Ap 2,16,30-My 14 1841;Ja 23 1864
MWA D 4 1840;Je 17 1852
NcD Ja 25 1850;Mr 12,N 12 1857;Mr 21,Ag 22 1861;Mr 12 1863;My 31,Je 4,D 13 1866;Mr 19 1868;F 1,22 1871;Jl 31,S 18 1872;Je 18,O 1 1873;Ag 5,O 7,N 25 1874;O 31 1877;Je 12,Ag 7 1878;D 15 1880;O 19 1881;Ja 31,Ag 1 1883;F 20 1884;O 12 1892;Ja-My 20 1896;Mr 10 1897 [O,D 1901]Ja 3,14 1903[04]N 15 1905[Ja-Jl 4 1906]
NcU Ag 14 1856
NhD Mr 26 1841
ScCL Mr 24 1832;Ja 12,N 9 1833;Ja 14,Mr 25 1837;Ja 26,S 21,N 2 1838;N 20 1840;Jl 8,Ag 12,N 18,D 23 1842;D 22-29 1843;O 4 1844;Je 27 1845;O 23 1846-D 14 1849;75-91
TKL F 7 1835
WHi Je 18 1873-N 13 1878;Ja 8 1879;Mr 2 1881;Jl 5 1882
—d ed *See* Greenville piedmont

Greenville REPUBLICAN. w Ag? 1826-
DLC Ag 30 1828
MDeHi My 3 1828
MWA F 24 1827

SOUTHERN enterprise. *See* Greenville enterprise

SOUTHERN patriot. w F 28 1851-F 1857‖?
United with Greenville mountaineer to form Patriot and mountaineer, later Piedmont and mountaineer
DLC 1851;O 28-N 4 1852
MWA Je 3,17 1852
NcD Mr 21,Jl 11,Ag 15 1851;Ja 22 1852;Je 2 1853
P-M S 2 1852
ScCC N 1 1855
ScCL 1851-F 17 1853

GREENWOOD

INDEX-JOURNAL. d N 7 1897+
1897-Ja 19 1919 as Greenwood index
pub 1897-1905;07+
KHi Ja 6,9,12 1925
VU N 11 1918

Greenwood JOURNAL. d My 1895-Ja 19 1919‖
United with Greenwood index to form Index-journal
ScGrI [1915-19]

NINETY SIX guardian. w 1878-79‖
ScGrI complete

GREER

Greer CITIZEN. w 1917+
pub [1917+]

Greer TRIBUNE. w 1924+
pub 1924+

HAMBURG

Hamburg GAZETTE. w F 19? 1823-
MWA Jl 23 1823;Jl 21 1824

Hamburg JOURNAL. sw Ap 18 1840-
DLC Ap 18,My 9 1840
NhD Mr 27 1841

Hamburg REPUBLICAN. w 1845?-
MWA Jl 9 1852

VALLEY pioneer. w S 12? 1854-
NcD Ja 3 1855

HAMPTON

HAMPTON county guardian. w 1879+
KHi F 6 1921;N 19 1924;Ja 7 1925

HARTSVILLE

Hartsville MESSENGER. w 1892+
KHi D 18 1924;Ja 8 1925

HEATH SPRINGS

AGE-HERALD. w O 7 1932+
pub 1932+

INMAN

Inman TIMES. w 1920+
pub 1921+

JOHNSTON

Johnston HERALD. w 1923+
pub 1923+
KHi D 19 1924;Ja 23 1925

KERSHAW

Kershaw ERA. w 1888+
pub Jl 4 1891+
KHi Ja 21 1925

KINGSTREE

COUNTY record. w Mr 1885+
pub 1896+

LAKE CITY

Lake City NEWS. w 1901+
pub 1901+
KHi Ja 23 1925
ScKC Mr 1928+

LANCASTER

CAROLINA review. *See* Lancaster review

Lancaster CITIZEN. sw 1916-24‖?
KHi My 28 1923

Lancaster JOURNAL. w
DLC O 8 1862

Lancaster LEDGER. *See* Lancaster news

Lancaster NEWS. w F 10 1852+
1852-1907 as Lancaster ledger
pub [1912-20]
DLC D 9-16 1863;Ja 13,F-Mr 2,My 31,Je 14, Jl 26-Ag 9,S 10-20,O 4-11,25,N 15 1864;Jl 24 1867
KHi O 24 1924;Ja 9 1925
MWA Jl 7 1852
NcD D 7 1859;Mr 27 1861[62-Jl 1863]Ja 20, Mr 2,15-22,Ap 12,26 1864;F 20,Ap 10,Jl 24-31, Ag 14 1867;My 26 1875;Ag 21,N 13,27 1878
NcU Ag 10 1881

Lancaster REVIEW. w 1878-1904‖?
1878-79 as Carolina review
NcD N 8,13,27 1878;Ja 8,22-F 19 1879

LAURENS

Laurens ADVERTISER. w Ag 5 1885+
pub Jl 1886+

Laurensville HERALD. w N 26 1845-1933‖
1845-48 as Laurensville weekly herald
KHi Je 10-O 14 1881
MWA Je 25 1852
NcD 1845-S,O 22 1847;Ap 14 1848;Je 22,N 30 1849;53-55;D 7 1860
PP O 12 1849
PPL N 22 1850

LEXINGTON

DISPATCH-NEWS. w 1870+
1870-1920 as Lexington dispatch
KHi Ja 21 1925
NcD Ja 31,Ag 7,N 6 1872
NcU Ag 3 1881

Lexington FLAG. w F 12 1857-
NcD Mr 12,Ap 23,Ag 20,S 10-17,O 29 1857; Ag 19 1858;D 15 1859;My 10,S 13 1860

Lexington TELEGRAPH.
NcD My 31 1855;Ap 8 1856

MCCORMICK

ADVANCE. w Mr 19 1885-89‖?
ICM 1885-Jl,S-O 1886;Mr 3,Ap 21 1887

McCormick MESSENGER. w My 1902+
NcD O 9 1930

McCormick NEWS. w 1887-94‖?
ICM D 22 1887;My 31,S 27-N 15,D 13 1888;Ja-Ap 11 1889

MCELWEESVILLE

REPUBLICAN whig democrat. w Ap 13 1841-
DLC My 8,Ag 21 1841
NhD Ap 13 1841

MANNING

CLARENDON banner. w 1859?-
DLC My 29 1860;F 12,My 7,Je 2,Jl 9-16,30-Ag 6,20-27,O 1,N 5,26 1861;Ap 22,S 9 1862;My 10 1864
MWA Ag 20 1861
NhD F 19 1861

CLARENDON press. w 1867-79‖?
NcD Je 25 1868;O 10 1878

MARION

Marion STAR. w 1846+
pub 1875+
NNHi S 2 1868;O 25 1871;Ap 9 1873
ScM 1852-56;75+

MONKS CORNER

BERKELEY democrat. w 1913+
pub 1913+

MORRIS ISLAND

SWAMP angel. ir
Pub "semi-occasionally" by Federal soldiers stationed on Morris Island in Charleston Harbor
CtHT My 26 1864
MBAt My 19 1864
NNHi My 19-26 1864
PPGr My 26 1864
WHi My 26 1864

MOUNT PLEASANT

BERKELEY gazette. w Je 1882-95‖?
1882-Ja 1883 as Berkeley county gazette
NcD [1882-83]-Je 1884

MULLINS

Mullins ENTERPRISE. w My 17 1897+
pub 1897+
KHi Ja 15 1925

NEWBERN

NORTH CAROLINA times. sw
NN Je 18-22 1864

NEWBERRY

Newberry HERALD and news. w,sw 1865+
1865-84? as Newberry herald
w 1865-1921
pub 1920+
KHi Ja 23 1925
MBAt Ja 23 1867
NcD My 1 1884
ScCoA 1920

Newberry OBSERVER. sw Ja 1 1883+
pub 1883+

RISING sun. w 1856-
MWA D 12 1860
NNHi S 28 1859
ScNH Mr 1859-Mr 1860

Newberry SENTINEL. w 1850-
MWA Je 30 1852

ORANGEBURG

Orangeburg DEMOCRAT. w Ja 3 1879-S 22 1881‖
United with Orangeburg times to form Orangeburg times and democrat
NcU Ag 4 1881
ScU complete

EDISTO clarion. w 1877-78‖?
1877-Je 21 1878 as Tax-payer
ScU O 12 1877-Je 21,Jl 5-Ag 9,O 11-18,D 12-20 1878

Orangeburg NEWS. w 1867-Mr 11 1875‖
United with Orangeburg times to form Orangeburg times and news, later Orangeburg times and democrat
ScU D 21 1867;68-Mr 6 1875

Orangeburg evening NEWS. d S 28 1904-17‖?
ScU 1904-S 27 1911

Orangeburg NEWS. w Ja 1931+
pub 1931+

SOUTHRON. w
ScU Ap 30-My 7,21-Je 18,Jl 2 1856;Mr 9 1859; Jl 6,F 13-Mr 14,28-Ap 11,N 14 1860

Orangeburg SUN. w 1894+
KHi Ja 14 1925

Daily TAX-PAYER. d Ja 7-Je 21 1878‖
Merged with Edisto clarion
ScU Ja 7 1878

TAX-PAYER. w *See* Edisto clarion

Orangeburg TIMES and democrat. w,sw,tw,d 1867+
1867-S 1881 as Orangeburg times (Mr 20 1875-S 22 1877 Orangeburg times and news)
w 1867-1907; sw 1908-Ja 1 1909; tw Ja 5 1909-20
pub 1874+
KHi N 25 1924;Ja 6,15,22 1925
NcD F 13 1901
ScU F 14-D 4 1872;73-1911

PAGELAND

Pageland JOURNAL. w 1910+
KHi Ja 14 1924

SOUTH CAROLINA (*Continued*)

PENDLETON

*Pendleton MESSENGER. w Ja 16 1807-
1807-12? as Miller's weekly messenger
CSmH Je 30 1830
DLC 1821-N 22 1826;Mr 11,Jl 8-15,Ag 26,D 30 1829;D 1,15 1830;Ja 5 1831;N 6 1840
GAtCo Mr 6 1840
MWA F 21 1827
NBuG S 15 1832
NcU N 30 1838;Ja 18 1839;My 15-22 1840;N 25 1842
NhD Ap 2 1841
OCHi D 4 1833
ScU F 8 1826-Mr 11,Ap 7 1848
WHi Ja-Ap,Ag 8 1821-Je 11 1823;Mr 24-N 24 1843

MILLER'S weekly messenger. *See* *Pendleton messenger

PICKENS

KEOWEE courier. *See under* Walhalla

Pickens SENTINEL. w S 1871+
pub 1875+
KHi N 20 1924;Ja 22 1925

PORT ROYAL

Port Royal COMMERCIAL and Beaufort county republican. w 1870-74||
1870-O 16? 1873 as Port Royal commercial. United with Southern standard to form Port Royal standard and commercial, later Beaufort tribune and Port Royal commercial (Beaufort)
DLC O 30 1873-Ap 1874

NEW SOUTH. w Mr 15 1862-66||
Suspended from Mr 29-Ag 16 1862
CoHi O 4 1862
CtHT Mr 15,Ag 28,N 1 1862;F 14,Ap 9,S 19, O 8 1863
DLC Mr 15-O 4,18-N 22,D 6-20 1862;Ja 17-F 14,Mr 5,28,Ap 4-18,My 2,30-Je 20,Jl 25-O 3, 17-31,N 14-21,D 5,19 1863-Ja 23,F 20-27,Mr 12,26,Ap 9,30,My 21,Jl 30-Ag 6,D 10 1864;Mr 18 1865
IHi N 28 1863
KHi [Jl 18-N 14 1863]
MBAt Mr 15-22,Ag 23-O 4,N 8,22 1862;S 5-12 1863;Mr 12,N 5 1864;Ap 5,Jl 8,Ag-O 14,D 16 1865;Mr 10,My 5,Je 2,16 1866
MHi [1862-65]
MWA Mr 15-22,Ag 23-N 8,22-D 1862;Ja 17-Mr 21,Ap-My 16,Je 6,20,Jl 4,Ag 15-29,S 12-O 3, N 28-D 5 1863;Ja 9-16,F 27-Mr 5,19-26 1864; F 18,Mr 25,Ap 22,Jl 15,S 9 1865;Je 9 1866
MiU-C My 2-9 1863
MnHi [1863]
N Ap 25 1863
NBHi Mr 15 1862;Mr 12 1864;Mr 11 1865
NN Ag 30-S 20,O 18-N 1,15 1862-Ja 3,17-F 14,Mr-Ap 4,18-My 2,30-Ag 8,S 12 1863;Ja 2-9,23,Ap 2 1864
NNHi Ja 17-24 1863
NcD Ag 23-S 13,O 4,25-N 8 1862;Ja 31-F 7, Mr 5,28-Ap 4 1863;F 20-27 1864
NjN O 25,N 15 1862
OClWHi Ja 15-22[Ag 23 1862-Jl]-N 21,D 19 1863;Ja 2,F 27,Mr 12,Ag 6 1864
OHi S 6-13 1862;Ag 19 1865
PAtM Ag 15 1863
PDoHi [Ap 18 1863-S 10 1864]
PHi O 18-25,N 22 1862;Ap 22 1865
PWcHi S 20-N 15 1862[63]Ja 17-S 5 1864
PYHi O 4 1862
RP Mr 5 1863
RW Je 27 1865
ScCL Ag 23 1862
WHi Ag 29 1863

PALMETTO herald. w Mr 3 1864-
CtHT Ap 14,O 6-13 1864
DLC Mr 17,24,31,O 13 1864
MBAt Mr 10-17,Ap 7 1864
MHi Mr-Ap 7,Je 9,Jl 21 1864
MSaE Je 16,S 22,D 1 1864
MWA Mr 3-17,31,Ap 18(extra)My 26 1864
NBHi Mr 10,24-31 1864
NN Mr 17,31,Ap 14 1864
NNHi Mr 17-24,Ap 14,28,My 12,Je 2,Jl-Ag 4,18,S 8,29-O 6,20,N 3-10,24 1864
OClWHi Mr 10,31,My 12 1864
P D 22 1864
PDoHi [Je 23-D 29 1864]
PHi Mr 10-My 12 1864
PWcHi Mr 3 1864
TxU Mr 10,Ap 21 1864

POTTERSVILLE

EDGEFIELD hive. w 1824?-Ja? 1831||
Followed by Columbia free press and hive, later Columbia hive (Columbia)
CSmH Jl 16 1830
MWA Ap 7 1827,O 29 1830

SOUTH CAROLINA republican. w 1825-
MWA Mr 3 1827

RIDGELAND

JASPER county record. w F 1924+
pub 1924+

ROCK HILL

HAMPTON herald. *See* Rock Hill herald

Rock Hill HERALD. w,sw,d 1876+
1876-79 as Hampton herald; 1880-N 1911 Weekly herald
w 1876-97;sw 1898-N 1911?
pub [1880-1900]+
KHi F 4 1924;Ja 13,24 1925
NcD Ja 28 1886

INDIAN land chronicle. w 1857-
DLC Mr 11 1859

Rock Hill MESSENGER. w 1896-1919||?
Negro
DLC Ja 26 1900

Rock Hill RECORD. sw 1902-29||?
KHi Ja 22 1925

ST. GEORGE

DORCHESTER county record. w Mr 1927+
pub 1927+

DORCHESTER eagle. w 1899+
pub 1899+
KHi Ja 23 1925

ST. MATTHEWS

CALHOUN times. w 1907+
KHi Ja 15 1924

SENECA

Seneca JOURNAL. w 1881-
NcU Ag 19 1881

Seneca JOURNAL. w Ap 1903+
pub 1903+

SPARTANBURG

CAROLINA spartan. *See* Spartanburg journal and Carolina spartan

CAROLINA state news. w Mr 1931+
pub 1931+

Spartanburg EXPRESS. w 1854-
DLC My 23 1866
NcAsS Ja 11 1860
NcD Ag 21 1856
ScGa [1858]
ScU Ja 4 1860-Ap 23 1862

Spartanburg HERALD. w 1872-1920||?
NcU Jl 27 1881
ScU Mr 2 1875-F 25 1880

Spartanburg HERALD. d 1890+
pub [1905-18]+
KHi O 26 1924
M Mr 12 1930

Spartanburg JOURNAL. d S 1904-11||
United with Carolina Spartan to form Spartanburg journal and Carolina Spartan
ScSJ [1904-11]

Spartanburg JOURNAL and Carolina spartan. d D 22 1843+
1843-44 as Spartan; 1844-1911 Carolina spartan
pub [1843-1918]+
DLC D 22 1843;Ja 31 1844;O 20 1864
KHi Ja 2 1925
MWA Jl 1 1852;D 1 1853;Ag 23 1855
NcD D 27 1845
NcU N 24 1858;N 19 1879;Jl 27 1881
TU F 6 1844

SPARTAN. *See* Spartanburg journal and Carolina spartan

Spartanburg SUN. d 1924-25||
KHi O 22 1924;Ja 22 1925

TEXTILE tribune. w 1926+
pub 1927+

SUMMIT

Summit COURIER. w 1876-79||?
NcD Je 6,27 1877;F 6,Ap 3,24 1878

SUMTER

Sumter BANNER. w 1846-
MWA Je 22 1852
ScU N 6 1846-[47-My 1855]

BANNER of freedom.
MnHi Ap 10 1865

BLACK RIVER watchman. *See* Watchman and southron

Sumter DISTRICT reporter. m 1885-86||?
ScU F 1885-Ja 1886

Sumter GAZETTE.
A S 1831-Ag 1833

Sumter HERALD. w 1897+
KHi D 25 1924;Ja 21 1925

Sumter daily ITEM. d O 15 1894+
1894-1931 as d ed of Watchman and southron
pub 1915+
KHi [Ja 22 1924-Ja 13 1925]
NcD Ag 27-28 1908

SOUTHERN whig. w
DLC Ja 12 1833

SPIRIT of the times. w 1881-84||?
NNHi Ap 19 1883

TRUE southron. w Je 1 1866-Jl 26 1881||
United with Sumter watchman to form Watchman and southron
ScSuI S 1866-O 1876
ScU complete

WATCHMAN and southron. sw,tw,w Ap 27 1850-Ja 1 1932||
1850-Je 1 1855 as Black River watchman; Je 6 1855-Jl 26 1881 Sumter watchman
tw 1856?-O 19 1863; sw O 27 1863-
DLC Ja 2 1861;N 10 1862;D 22 1863;Ag 17 1864
MBAt Jl 1 1868
MH D 7 1864
MWA Jl 3 1852;O 19 1876
NcD Ag 3 1864
PPL Ag 10-17,O 19,N 2 1864
ScSuI [1860-72]1915-32
ScU 1850-60[Ap 1861-N 1862]-Je 8,S 14,N 9-16 1864;S 20 1865-S 13 1873;N 29,D 27 1877-Je 12 1879;N 11 1880;Ag 1881-1904
—d ed *See* Sumter daily item

TIMMONSVILLE

Timmonsville NEWS. w 1928+
ScKC 1929+

UNION

Unionville JOURNAL. w 1851-
MWA Jl 2 1852
NcD D 31 1852;Mr 9,Je 22,Ag 3,N 16 1855; Ja 15 1858

PEOPLE'S recorder. *See under* Columbia

Union PROGRESS. sw,w F 4 1900-32||?
sw 1900-11
KHi D 17 1924;Ja 21 1925
ScUn 1907-24

Union TIMES. w,d F 21 1850+
1850-1920? as Weekly Union times
w 1850-1920
pub 1850+
NcD Jl 19-26,S 27-O 4 1867;D 18 1868;Ap 4-11,25 1873;Ap 2 1875;Jl 16 1886
NcU Jl 29 1881
ScUn 1922+

WALHALLA

Walhalla BANNER. w 1857-
NcD Jl 27 1859

KEOWEE courier. w 1849+
1849-56? pub in Pickens
pub 1885+
KHi Ja 14,D 9 1925
MWA Jl 29 1880
NcD O 27 1855;F 5 1859;Ja 28 1860;Ag 24 1861; F 17 1881;Ag 24 1900;Ag 23 1933
NcU Jl 28 1881
ScCoCR Jl 30 1875
ScU Ap 25 1857-Je 16,Ag 11 1860-Ag 3 1861; S 23,O 14-28,N 11,25 1865-[68-71]-[86-87]-90

WALTERBORO

COLLETON and Beaufort sun. w 1859-
MWA D 25 1860

COLLETON democrat. *See* Press and standard

PRESS and standard. w 1877+
1877-89? as Colleton democrat; 1881?-89 Colleton press
pub 1906+
DLC Mr 11 1931

WESTMINSTER

TUGALOO tribune. w Jl 1909+
pub 1909+

WILLISTON

Williston WAY. w S 1921+
pub 1921+

WINNSBORO

FAIRFIELD herald. w 1849-76||
United with Winnsboro news to form News and herald
MWA Jl 1 1852

NEWS and herald. w,tw 1863+
1863-76 as Winnsboro news
tw 187?-1903
KHi O 24 1924;Ja 23 1925
NcD Je 6 1885

Daily REGISTER. d 1851-
MWA Jl 1 1852
NcD My 10,N 9 1853

YORK

To 1916? as Yorkville

Yorkville COMPILER. w 1840+
NcU Je 1 1840
NhD Mr 26 1841
ScYE Je 1840-My 1841

ENCYCLOPEDIA; a weekly newspaper. w O 8 1825-O 28 1826||
NcD complete
ScYE complete

Yorkville ENQUIRER. w,sw Ja 1855+
w 1855-94
pub 1855+
DLC Ag 15 1867
NNHi Mr 23 1865;Mr 27 1873
NcD Je 11 1857;Ap 12-My 17,O 4-11,N 1 1860; Mr 2 1864;O 12 1865;Ja 4-18,F 6,My 3 1866; Ag 1,15,N 28-D 19 1867[68-70;72-88]Ag 28,O 9 1889;Ja 21 1891;Ja 13,F 17-24,O 12 1892; Mr 8,Jl 27 1893;My 23,Je 13 1894[95;99]
NcU S 20 1855;Mr 6 1856;D 6 1860;Jl 28 1881

York ENTERPRISE. w 1888-92||?
NcD Ag 28,N 6-13 1889;Ap 2,N 5 1890;Ja 13 1892

FARMER'S miscellany. *See* Yorkville miscellany

SOUTH CAROLINA (*Continued*)

YORK—*Continued*

Yorkville **MISCELLANY.** w 1844-
1844?-50? as Farmer's miscellany
NcD Je 15 1846;Ag 2 1851
ScYE 1851-54

PEOPLE'S advocate. w 1825-
NjR D 4 1828

PINCKNEY whig. w 1833-
NNHi Ag 28 1834
NcU Ag 16,D 6 1833

PIONEER and South-Carolina whig. w Ag 16 1823-
Title varies: Pioneer and Yorkville advertiser; Pioneer and commercial register
DLC N 29-D 6 1823;F 7,21,Ap 3,17-24,My 22, Je 5 1824;Jl 4,18-Ag 9,S 5,19,O 24,D 11 1829;Ja 2-9 1830;Ja 8 1831
MWA Je 8 1827
ScYE 1823-Jl 31 1824

REMEDY. w S 30? 1852-
MWA Mr 11 1852

Yorkville **YEOMAN.** w 1893-1902||?
NcD F 24,Ap 7,28,D 8 1899

YORK district chronicle. w
NcD Jl 2 1858

SOUTH DAKOTA

ABERDEEN

AMERICAN. w Ja 1904-16||
SdHi 1904-Je 1916

Aberdeen morning **AMERICAN.** d 1906+
pub D 7 1906+
DLC N 15 1927+
SdA Je 1906-Ja 23 1909
SdHi Je 7 1906+

DAKOTA democrat. w 1890-1916||?
1890-1902? as State democrat; 1903?-09? Democrat
SdHi Ag 1890-Ag 1902;Mr 1903-Je 1917

DAKOTA free press. w
SdHi My 7 1903+

DAKOTA freie presse. w 1874-1925||
1874-My 1909 pub in Yankton
In German
SdHi Je 1904-F 1925

DAKOTA pioneer. *See* Saturday pioneer

DEMOCRAT. *See* Dakota democrat

JOURNAL. d 1920-22||
SdHi Ap 1921-22

NEUE deutsche presse. w 1910-18||
In German
SdHi S 1910-Ja 1918

Weekly **NEWS.** w 1885-1919||
Merged with American
SdA 1886-88
SdHi Je 1904-Je 1919

Aberdeen **NEWS.** d 1886+
pub N 26 1886+
SdA 1903-Ja 23 1909
SdHi My 20 1903+

NORTHWEST square deal. d 1920-21||
SdHi My 1920-Mr 1921

Saturday **PIONEER.** w 1881-90||?
1881-89? as Dakota pioneer
CLM Mr 8 1888
MWA Mr 22-29 1883
SdA Ja 25-Mr 21 1890

REPUBLICAN. w 1881-90||?
SdA 1886-88

STATE democrat. *See* Dakota democrat

ADA

ADVOCATE. w 1908-14||?
SdHi D 1908-Je 1912

AGAR

ARGUS. w 1910-15||?
SdHi Mr-D 1913

ENTERPRISE. *See under* Onida

ALCESTER

UNION. w 1891+
pub 1895+
SdHi My 1903-Jl 1908;My 8 1913+

ALEXANDRIA

HERALD. w Ja 1 1879+
pub 1886+
SdHi 1886-88;93;95;98;1901;03-18

JOURNAL. w 1887-1915||
SdHi My 1903-O 1915

ALPENA

JERAULD county journal. *See* Journal

JOURNAL. w 1883+
1883-87? as Jerauld county journal
pub 1898+
SdHi O 1903-D 7 1917;Jl 1922+

ANDOVER

GAZETTE. *See* Journal (Webster)

ARDMORE

AMERICAN. w 1909-30||?
SdHi My 1915-Je 1926

ARLINGTON

SUN. w 1885+
pub 1901+
SdHi My 8 1903-Je 1918;Jl 1922+

ARMOUR

CHRONICLE. w 1882+
1882-92? as Douglas county chronicle; 1893?-1917? Chronicle-tribune
pub 1890+
SdHi Ap 30 1903+

DOUGLAS county chronicle. *See* Chronicle

HERALD. w 1889+
SdHi Jl 1 1904+

ARTESIAN

COMMONWEALTH. w 1901+
pub 1901+
SdHi Mr 17 1904+

SANBORN county advocate. w 1881-1914||?
Merged with Commonwealth
SdHi Ap 15 1904-D 1909

ASHTON

CHRONICLE. w 1894+
1894-1904? as Spink county chronicle
SdHi 1894+

SPINK county chronicle. *See* Chronicle

AURORA

TIMES. w 1884-1914||
SdHi S 17 1903-Mr 1914

AVON

CLARION. w 1901+
pub F 7 1901+
SdHi Ap 13 1905-Je 1911

BALTIC

Baltic-Crooks **BOOSTER.** w 1920+
1920-26 as Baltic weekly globe
MnBvV 1920-26
SdHi Jl 1930+

Baltic weekly **GLOBE.** *See* Baltic-Crooks booster

MINNEHAHA. w 1901-18||?
SdHi O 1907-Ap 1908

BELLE FOURCHE

BEE. w 1891+
pub 1895
SdHi Mr 17 1904+

NORTHWEST post. w,d 1902+
w 1902-34
SdHi Jl 23 1914+

BERESFORD

NEWS. w 1883-1926||
SdHi Ap 21 1904-Je 1926

REPUBLIC. w 1896+
pub 1896-1900;02-23;25+
SdHi My 14 1903+

BIG STONE CITY

HEADLIGHT. w 1884+
1884-95 dated also at Ortonville, Minn.
SdHi My 21 1903+

BISON

COURIER. w 1909+
SdHi Jl 1915+

BLUNT

ADVOCATE. w F 17? 1883+
MWA Ag 11 1883
SdHi Jl 1883-Jl 1885;My 1903+

BONESTEEL

ENTERPRISE. w 1922+
pub 1922+

GREGORY county news. w 1898-Je 1908||
1898-99? as Tribune-independent. United with Tripp county news to form Gregory county news and Tripp county news, later News (Dallas)
SdHi Ap 1904-Je 1905

TRIBUNE-INDEPENDENT. *See* Gregory county news

BOWDLE

PIONEER. w 1883+
MWA My 29 1888
SdHi Jl 1904+

BRADLEY

GLOBE. w 1887-1926||?
SdHi O 8 1903-Ap 1926

BRIDGEWATER

McCOOK county democrat. w 1884-1920||
SdHi Mr 1904-O 1920

TRIBUNE. w 1892+
pub 1913-20;27+
SdHi My 1903+

BRISTOL

DAY county news. w 1913+
SdHi Ap 1915+

BRITTON

DAKOTA daylight. *See* Marshall county journal

DAYLIGHT. *See* Marshall county journal

MARSHALL county journal. w 1883+
1883-84? as Daylight; 1884?-89? Dakota daylight; 1890?-96? South Dakota daylight
SdHi S 24 1903+

MARSHALL county sentinel. *See* Sentinel

SENTINEL. w 1888+
1888-1914? as Marshall county sentinel
SdHi S 17 1903+

SOUTH DAKOTA daylight. *See* Marshall county journal

BROOKINGS

BROOKINGS county press. w 1879+
SdHi 1879;F 1880-F,Ap 1881-89;Jl 23 1903+

INDIVIDUAL. w 1891-1906||
SdHi Ap 1903-Je 1906

Daily **PRESS.** d
SdHi Je-S 1886

REGISTER. w,sw 1890+
w 1890-93?
pub 1890+
SdHi My 1903+

SOUTH DAKOTA home messenger. w 1913-17||
SdHi O 1913-Je 1917

BRUCE

HERALD. w 1903-31||?
SdHi Je 1903-Je 1930

BRYANT

HAMLIN county news. w 1897+
SdHi Ag 1903+

BUFFALO

HARDING county era. w 1909-16||
SdHi D 1914-Mr 1916

TIMES-HERALD. w 1910+
1910-20? as Times
pub 1917+
SdHi 1934+

BUFFALO GAP

GAZETTE. w 1909+
Follows Republican
pub 1909+
SdHi 1909+
WaPS [1919]

REPUBLICAN. w 1889-1908||
Followed by Gazette
SdBgG Ag 13 1889-1908
SdHi Ap 1905-08

BURKE

GAZETTE. w 1904+
SdHi Je 28 1917+

SOUTH DAKOTA (*Continued*)

CAMP CROOK

RANGE gazette. w 1907+
SdHi Ap 1915+

CANISTOTA

CLIPPER. w 1901+
SdHi N 17 1904

CANOVA

HERALD. w Je 30 1899+
pub 1903+
SdHi My 8 1903+

CANTON

ADVOCATE. w 1876-97||?
1876-My 1877 as Lincoln county advocate
NbHi Jl 9,S 12 1878
SdHi Ap 26 1876-Ap 12 1883
WHi Mr 3-10 1881

DAKOTA farmers' leader. *See* Farmer's leader

FARMER'S leader. w 1889-1930||?
1889-1919? as Dakota farmers' leader
SdHi My 1903-Je 1916;Ag 1919-30

LINCOLN county advocate. *See* Advocate

SIOUX VALLEY news. w Ag 15 1872+
NN Ag 15-22,S 26-O 10,N 2-9,D 21-28 1872;Ja-F 1,15-22,Jl 12 1873
NNHi F 22 1873
NbHi Ap 23 1878
SdHi Ap 24 1903+

VISERGUTTEN. w 1895+
1895-O 17 1918 pub in Story City, Iowa
In Norwegian
IU 1918+
IdDeL [1896-98]-[1902-Je 1903;18-19]-[27]
MnHi Jl 29 1926[30;33]+
SdHi Ap 1915-16
WHi S 26 1929

CARTER

NEWS. w 1910-16||
SdHi Ap 1915-16

CARTHAGE

NEWS. w 1882+
pub 1882+
SdHi S 1903+

CASCADE SPRINGS

GEYSER. w 1891-93||?
SdHi Jl 1891-Ag 1892

CASTLE ROCK

HOMESTEADER. *See* Castle Rock press and Moreau news

Castle Rock PRESS and Moreau news. w 1911-28||
1911-F? 1917 as Homesteader
SdHi Mr 29 1917-Je 1928

CASTLEWOOD

HAMLIN county republican. w 1888+
1888-91? as Republican
pub 1888+
SdHi Ag 26 1904+

REPUBLICAN. *See* Hamlin county republican

CAVOUR

CLARION. w 1904-12||
SdHi Ap 1911-Je 1912

PRESS. w
SdHi Ap-S 1882

CENTERVILLE

CHRONICLE. w 1883-1908||
1887?-98? as Chronicle-index
SdHi Ap 1903-Ja 1908

JOURNAL. w 1887+
pub 1887+
SdHi Ap 1903-Je 1917;O 26 1918+

CENTRAL CITY

REGISTER. *See* under Lead

CHALKBUTTE

NEWS. w 1910+
pub 1916+

CHAMBERLAIN

DEMOCRAT. *See* Leader

LEADER. w Je 4 1882+
1882-1927 as Democrat
pub 1911+
SdHi Ag 26 1915+

MISSOURI Valley news. w
SdHi My 1903-F 1904

REGISTER. w Je 23 1881+
pub 1881+
SdHi Jl 7 1904+

CHANCELLOR

NEWS. w 1903+
SdHi Ap 1904-Je 1906

CLAREMONT

TRIBUNE. w 1902-05||
SdHi O 1903-Mr 1905

CLARK

CLARK county courier. w 1881+
pub 1888+
SdHi My 14 1904+

CLARK county pilot. *See* Pilot-review

PILOT-REVIEW. w 1883-1924||?
1883-85? as Clark county pilot
SdHi Ap 1904-07

CLEAR LAKE

COURIER. w 1891+
pub 1920-23;30+
SdHi 1892+

DEUEL county advocate. w My 1883+
pub 1887+
SdHi Ja 1890+

COLMAN

ARGUS. w F 23 1901+
pub 1901+
SdHi Ap 14 1904-

COLOME

TIMES. w Mr 6 1909+
pub 1909+

COLTON

COURIER. w 1901+
pub 1901+

CORSICA

GLOBE. w 1884+
pub 1884+
SdHi S 1903+

CRESBARD

BEACON. w 1906+
pub O 11 1916+
SdHi 1928+

CROOKS

Crooks COUNTRY visitor. 1921-26||
United with Baltic weekly globe to form Baltic-Crooks booster (Baltic)
MnBvV complete

CUSTER

CHRONICLE. *See* Custer county chronicle

CUSTER county chronicle. w 1880+
1880-1931? as Chronicle
pub 1880+
CU-B Ja 31,Ap 24 1880
SdHi Je 1904-Mr 1908;My 1915+

DALLAS

DEMOCRAT. w
SdHi Jl 1916-Je 1919

GREGORY county news. *See* News

NEWS. w 1907+
1907-Je 1908 as Tripp county news; Jl 1908-21? Gregory county news (title varies slightly)
pub 1927+
SdHi Ap 1907-Je 1908

TRIPP county news. *See* News

DAVENPORT

CHEYENNE Valley news. w 1910-12||
SdHi Ja 1911-Ja 1912

DEADWOOD

BLACK HILLS news. d Jl 1? 1879-
CU-B Jl 8,12,16 1879

BLACK HILLS news. w Ja 1 1880-
CU-B Ja 1 1880

BLACK HILLS pioneer. *See* Deadwood pioneer-times

BLACK HILLS times. w Ap 5 1877-96||?
United with Black Hills weekly pioneer to form Deadwood pioneer-times
CU-B F 26 1881
DLC My 27 1877
MnHi [1877]

BLACK HILLS daily times. d My 10 1877-96||?
United with Black Hills daily pioneer to form Deadwood pioneer-times
CU-B F 26 1881
ICHi Je 30 1877
MWA N 23 1877
MnHi [Je 1877-79;80]

BLACK HILLS weekly and Whitewood plaindealer. d,sw,w 1906+
1906-26? as Telegram; 1927?-31? Black Hills weekly and Deadwood telegram
d 1906-24?;sw 1925?-28?
pub 1930+
MWA Je 23,Jl 28 1933
SdHi N 23 1908-Jl 1924;Jl 1928+

Daily CHAMPION. d Je 1? 1877-
ICHi Je 29 1877

INDEPENDENT. d 1890-1903||?
MWA N 29 1897
SdHi O 1892-D 1902

INDEPENDENT. w 1890-1903||?
SdHi Mr 1892-Je 1898

LANTERN. w 1905-10||
WHi N 25 1909-Je 2 1910

Deadwood PIONEER-TIMES. d 1876+
1876-87? as Black Hills daily pioneer; 1888?-96? Daily pioneer
pub 1877+
CU-B [1878-F 12]Ag 26,28,S 3,O 16-17,N 19 1880;Ja 10,Mr-Jl 1882
MWA N 16 1879;Je 28 1924;Jl 8 1929;S 24 1933
SdHi Jl 1902-19;My 24 1922+

Deadwood PIONEER-TIMES. w Je 8 1876+
1876-87? as Black Hills weekly pioneer; 1888?-96? Weekly pioneer
CU-B S 11 1880
ICM D 27 1879
MnHi 1876-[79]
NN My 10 1883

TELEGRAM. *See* Black Hills weekly and Whitewood plaindealer

DELL RAPIDS

Dell Rapids EXPONENT. w 1879-87||?
WHi F 26,Mr 19,26,Ap 2,23 1881

Dell Rapids JOURNAL. w 1871-73||?
NNHi F 5 1873

TIMES. *See* Tribune

TIMES-TRIBUNE. *See* Tribune

TRIBUNE. w 1885+
1885-1907? as Times; 1908?-20? Times-tribune
SdHi Ap 15 1904+

DELMONT

RECORD. w Ap 15 1897+
pub 1919+
SdHi S 1903+

DE SMET

KINGSBURY county independent. w 1890-1929||?
SdHi My 1904-S 1911

KINGSBURY county news. *See* News

NEWS. w 1880+
1880-90? as Kingsbury county news; 1891?-97? News and leader
pub 1880+
SdHi My 22 1903+

DIANA

Diana MONITOR. w Ag 11 1882-85||?
1882-N 9 1883 as Miner sentinel (Miner); N 16? 1883-84? Diana sentinel
MWA 1882-Ag 1 1884
SdHi 1882-My 1884

Diana SENTINEL. *See* Diana monitor

DIRKSTOWN

LYMAN county record. w 1903-06||
SdHi Ag 1903-Je 1 1906

DOLAND

TIMES-RECORD. w 1882+
pub 1887+
SdHi My 1903-Je 1918;Jl 1936+

DRAPER

LYMAN county republican. w 1903-11||
1903-Ap 1905 pub in Presho; My-D 1905 in Mussman
SdHi My 1904-Je 1911

DUPREE

LEADER. w 1910-24||
SdHi Jl 1910-Je 1924

ZIEBACH county news. w Ap 27 1911+
pub 1911+
SdHi Je 1936+

EAGLE BUTTE

NEWS. w 1910+
SdHi Je 1936+

EDGEMONT

EXPRESS. w 1891-1928||
SdHi Ap 1904-O 1912;Je 1915-Jl 1928

TRIBUNE. w Ja 4 1923+
pub 1923+
SdHi 1923+

SOUTH DAKOTA (*Continued*)

EDGERTON

CHARLES MIX county news. *See under* Geddes

EDSON

PRESS. w 1911-13||?
SdHi F 1911-F 1912

EGAN

EXPRESS. w 1878+
SdHi Je 1880-89;91-98;1902-F 1924
WHi Ap 21 1881

ELK POINT

LEADER-COURIER. w 1889+
1889-1913 as Union county leader
pub 1912+
SdHi My 1903+

Elk Point TRIBUNE. w 1880-81||
WHi Mr 8 1881

UNION county courier. w 1871-Je 1913||
United with Union county leader to form Leader-courier
NNHi Ap 2 1873
SdEL complete
SdHi My 1903-13

UNION county leader. *See* Leader-courier

ELKTON

RECORD. w 1884+
SdHi S 11 1903+

EMERY

ENTERPRISE. w 1890+
pub 1890+

ESTELLINE

BELL. w 1883-90||?
SdHi Ag 1883-Ag 1885

HAMLIN county republican. *See* Tribune

JOURNAL. w 1916+
pub 1916+

TRIBUNE. w 1892-1917||
1892-95? as Hamlin county republican
SdHi O 1903-N 1917

ETHAN

ENTERPRISE. w 1901+
SdHi Mr 1904+

EUREKA

NORTHWEST blade. w 1884+
SdHi My 1901-Je 1918

POST. w 1890-1912||
SdHi My 1902-Je 1912

Die Eureka POST. w 1890-1912||?
In German
SdHi Ap 1904-Je 1907

Eureka RUNDSCHAU. *See* Rundschau und das nordlicht (Winona, Minn.)

EVARTS

STATE journal. *See under* Glenham

FAIRFAX

ADVERTISER. w 1902+
pub 1902+
SdHi Ap 1915-N 1916

REVIEW. *See* Sun-review

SUN-REVIEW. w 1892-1907||
1892-1903? as Review
SdHi My 1902-Je 1907

FAIRVIEW

EAGLE. w 1902-25||
SdHi N 1905-My,O 1906-Jl 1908

FAITH

FAITH. w 1911-12||
SdHi F 1911-Je 1912

GAZETTE. w My 1910+
pub 1910+
SdHi Jl 1915-Je 1916;Jl 1936+

INDEPENDENT. w 1927+
pub 1927+

FAULKTON

ADVOCATE. w S 17 1898+
pub 1898+
SdHi My 1903-Je 1919

FAULK county republican. *See* Record

FAULK county times. w 1882-1901||?
SdHi D 1882-D 1894

RECORD. w 1886+
1886-93? as Faulk county republican; 1894?-1905 Republican-record
SdHi Ap 15 1904+

REPUBLICAN-RECORD. *See* Record

FLANDREAU

HERALD. w 1882+
SdHi My 1903+

MOODY county enterprise. w 1878+
pub 1878+
SdHi My 1903-Je 1920
WHi Mr 3,17,Ap 7 1881

FOREST CITY

PRESS. w S 20 1883-1919||
ICHi S 20 1883
SdHi O 1903-My 1908;Jl 1911-Je 1919

FORESTBURG

MINER county mercury. w
SdHi Je-N 1880

FT. PIERRE

FAIRPLAY. w 1890-1912||
SdHi My 1903-Je 1912

TIMES. w 1915+
SdHi Jl 1915+

FORT RANDALL

INDEPENDENT. ir 1865-
CSmH N 29,D 20-27 1865;Ja 20,Mr 28 1866
DLC D 5 1865
MWA N 23,D 20 1865

FRANKFORT

NEWS-MESSENGER. w 1903+
SdHi Je 1903-Je 1918

FREDERICK

BROWN county news. w 1930+
pub 1930+
SdHi Jl 1931+

FREE PRESS. w 1882-1930||?
SdHi S 1903-Je 1925

FREEMAN

COURIER. w 1896+
pub 1901+
SdHi Ap 28 1904+

FULTON

ADVOCATE. *See* Hanson county advocate

HANSON county advocate. w 1901-24||
1901-22? as Advocate
SdHi Jl 1913-Jl 30 1924

GANN VALLEY

CHIEF. w 1888+
1888-1914? as Dakota chief
pub 1888+
SdHi My 1903+

DAKOTA chief. *See* Chief

GARDEN CITY

TRIBUNE. w 1902+
pub 1929+

GARRETSON

NEWS. w Jl 2 1903+
pub 1903+
SdHi 1903+

SOUTH DAKOTA vindicator. w 1898-1905||
SdGN 1903-04
SdHi Ap 1904-S 1905

GARY

DEUEL county news. w
SdHi Ja-Ap 1901

INTERSTATE. w S 1878+
pub 1905-07;10+
SdHi S 1 1886-Je 25 1931;Jl 1936+

GAYVILLE

OBSERVER. w 1904+
SdHi N 1905-Mr 1906

GEDDES

CHARLES MIX county news. w 1884+
1884-98? pub in Edgerton
pub 1884+
SdHi O 1903+

RECORD. w 1903-13||?
SdHi My 14 1903-Mr 6 1908

GETTYSBURG

HERALD. w 1883-1915||
SdHi Jl 3 1913-My 20 1915

POTTER county news. w 1894+
pub 1894+
SdHi O 22 1903+

GLENHAM

STATE journal. w 1901-14||?
1901-Mr 1908 pub in Evarts
SdHi Ap 1904-Je 1913

GOVERT

ADVANCE. w 1911+
SdHi Je 1 1928+

GRAND RIVER

PRESS. w 1908-10||
SdHi Ja 17 1908-My 13 1910

GREGORY

ROSEBUD democrat. w 1906-21||
SdHi Jl 1913-Mr 1914

TIMES-ADVOCATE. w 1904+
1904-08? as Times
pub 1904+
SdHi F 18 1908+

GROTON

INDEPENDENT. w 1881+
pub 1881+
SdHi My 14 1903+

HARRISBURG

JOURNAL. w 1900-15||?
SdHi My 1904-Ja 1912;My-N 1915

HARRISON

GLOBE. w 1884-1906||
SdHi S 24 1903-Je 8 1906

HARROLD

JOURNAL. w 1908+
1908-10 as Pioneer
pub 1908+
SdHi S 1908+

PIONEER. *See* Journal

HARTFORD

HERALD. w 1892+
SdHi My 1903-Je 1913

HAYES

STANLEY county homestead. w 1904-15||?
SdHi S 30 1904-Je 1911

HAYTI

HAMLIN county herald-enterprise. w 1907+
1907-29? as Hamlin county herald
pub 1907+

HAZEL

NEW ERA. w 1904-08||
SdHi Ja 22 1904-Ja 10 1908

HECLA

BROWN county journal. *See* Journal

JOURNAL. w 1913+
1913-22? as Brown county journal
pub Jl 20 1922+

STANDARD. w 1893-1915||
SdHi O 8 1903-My 6 1915

HENRY

INDEPENDENT. w 1884+
SdHi My 1903-Je 1908;Ja 1920+

HERREID

PRAIRIE picayune. w Jl 25 1888+
pub 1888+
SdHi Jl 1904+

HETLAND

NEW ERA. w 1901-16||
SdHi Mr 1904-Mr 1916

HIGHLAND

HERALD. w 1906-08||
SdHi Mr 1906-1908

HIGHMORE

HERALD. w 1882+
SdHi Mr 17 1904+

HYDE county bulletin. w 1885-1928||
SdHi Ap 1904-Fe 1914;D 1921-Je 1928

NONPAREIL. w 1930+
pub 1934+
SdHi Jl 1931+

SOUTH DAKOTA (*Continued*)

HILL CITY

HARNEY PEAK mining news. *See* Hill City news

Hill City NEWS. w 1890+
1890-1921? as Harney Peak mining news
SdHN 1922+
SdHi Ap 1904+

HITCHCOCK

NEWS-LEADER. w 1886+
1886-1906 as News
SdHi Ap 1904-Je 1906;Mr 1911-Je 1917;Jl 1936+

HOLABIRD

HYDE county news. w 1909-14||?
SdHi Mr 1913-Je 1914

HOT SPRINGS

Hot Springs daily HERALD. d 1891-95||?
MWA D 6 1892

HERALD. w *See* Times-herald

MINNEKAHTA herald. *See* Times-herald

STAR. w 1886+
pub 1904+
SdHi Je 5 1904+

STAR. d 1929+
pub 1929+
SdHi Jl 1936+

TIMES-HERALD. w 1889-1926||
1889-91? as Minnekahta herald; 1892?-98? Herald
SdHi Ap 1904-Ap 1909;Mr-Je 1926

HOVEN

REVIEW. w 1919+
pub 1933+

HOWARD

ADVANCE. w 1881-1906||
SdHi S 1881-82;Ap 1904-F 1906

FARMER. *See* Miner county pioneer

MINER county democrat. *See* Miner county pioneer

MINER county pioneer. w 1882+
1882-84 as Farmer; 1885-1918? Miner county democrat
pub 1890+
SdHi D 1882-Ja 1884;My 1903+

SPIRIT of Dakota. w 1897-1909||
SdHi Je 1905-Je 1905;O 1907-F 1909

HUDSON

HUDSONITE. w S 1 1900+
pub 1900+
SdHi Ap 1904+

HUMBOLDT

JOURNAL. w 1903+
pub 1903+

HURLEY

HERALD. w 1883+
1883-1930? as Turner county herald
pub 1883+
SdHi My 1883-Je 1918

TURNER county herald. *See* Herald

HURON

DAKOTA Huronite. w 1881-1908||
pub 1881-85
SdHi 1882-My 1896;Jl 1905-My 1908

Huron weekly HERALD. w 1884-1915||
1884-Je 1909 as Herald-democrat
SdHi Ap 1904-Mr 1915

HERALD-DEMOCRAT. *See* Huron weekly herald

HURONITE. d 1886+
pub 1886+
SdHi 1886+

JOURNAL world spirit. *See* State spirit

SOUTH DAKOTA news. w 1919-24||
SdHi Je 1919-Ap 1924

STATE spirit. w 1903-19||
Ap?-My 14 1903 as Weekly world; My 21 1903-Ja 1908 Journal world; F-D 1908 Journal world spirit
SdHi Ap 1903-Je 1919

TRIBUNE. d 1881||?
SdHi Je-D 1881

Weekly WORLD. *See* State spirit

INTERIOR

INDEX. w 1907-28||
SdHi Mr 1920-Je 1928

IONA

PIONEER. w 1902-05||
SdHi Ja 1904-Je 1905

IPSWICH

DAKOTA tribune. *See* Tribune

EDMUNDS county democrat. w 1889-1927||
Merged with Tribune
SdHi F 23 1905-Je 22 1927
SdIT complete

SOUTH DAKOTA tribune. *See* Tribune

TRIBUNE. w 1883+
1883-87? as Dakota tribune; 1888?-1910? South Dakota tribune
pub 1883+
SdHi Ap 14 1904+

IRENE

TRI-COUNTY news. w 1899+
pub 1903+
SdHi My 27 1915+

IROQUOIS

CHIEF. w 1888+
pub 1888+
SdHi My 22 1903+

ISABEL

NEWS. w Jl 3 1910+
pub 1910+
SdHi Jl 6 1911-Je 13 1917;Jl 1922+

JAVA

HERALD. w 1903+
SdHi S 1903+

KADOKA

PRESS. w 1908+
pub 1908-15;19+
SdHi N 1908+

KENNEBEC

ADVOCATE leader. w 1903+
1903-Je 1923 as Prairie sun; Je 1923-25? Lyman county advocate
1903-05 pub in Lyman
SdHi Jl 1903-Je 1908;Je 1922+

LYMAN county advocate. *See* Advocate leader

PRAIRIE sun. *See* Advocate leader

KEYSTONE

RECORDER. w 1900-11||?
SdHi Ap 15 1904-Je 25 1909

KIMBALL

BRULE county news. w 1931+
pub 1931+
SdHi Je 1936+

BRULE index. *See* Index

GRAPHIC. w Ap 4 1882+
pub 1882+
SdHi My 1903+

INDEX. w 1882-1905||
1882-1901? as Brule index
SdHi Ap 30 1903-Je 22 1905

LAKE ANDES

CHARLES Mix county courier. w 1885-1927||
1885-N 1917 as Courier (Wheeler)
SdHi O 1903-Je 1912;Jl 1913-Je 1918;Jl 1919-Je 1927

WAVE. w Je 20 1902+
pub 1902+
SdHi Je 5 1917-Je 21 1918

LAKE CITY

JOURNAL-TIMES. w 1915+
1915-Je 1923 as Journal
SdHi Mr 1915-Je 1923;Je 1924-Je 1926

LAKE PRESTON

TIMES. w Ag 1881+
pub 1880+
SdHi S 24 1903+

LAMRO

ADVOCATE. w 1910-11||
SdHi F 1910-Je 22 1911

LEAD

BLACK HILLS blade. w
SdHi Je-O 1904

BLACK HILLS world. d
SdH My 1-31 1901

CALL. d Ag 12 1894+
pub 1900+
SdHi N 24 1894+

REGISTER. w 1876?-1912||?
1876?-1905 pub in Central City
SdHi Jl 1905-Je 1911

Daily TRIBUNE. d 1881-1907||?
MWA F 3 1887

LEBANON

INDEPENDENT. w 1892+
pub 1894+
SdHi S 24 1903+

LE BEAU

Le Beau LEADER. w My 31 1883-Mr 11 1886||
C Je 1883-86

PHENIX. w 1907-11||?
SdHi Je 1908-Je 1910

LEMMON

Lemmon LEADER and Grand Valley herald. w 1907+
1907-Je 1929 as Grand Valley herald (Meadow)
pub 1929+
SdHi 1907+

TRIBUNE. w Ap 1917+
pub 1918+
SdHi Mr 10 1921+

LENNOX

INDEPENDENT. w 1885+
SdHi Ap 9 1915-Je 30 1927,Je 1936+

LEOLA

BLADE. *See* McPherson county herald

MCPHERSON county herald. w 1886+
1886-90? as Blade; 1891-93? Northwest-blade
SdHi S 24 1903+

NORTHWEST-BLADE. *See* McPherson county herald

LESLIE

PIONEER. w 1904-05||
SdHi Je 30 1904-Je 29 1905

LESTERVILLE

COURIER. w 1929+
pub 1929+
SdHi Je 1931+

LEDGER. w 1901-21||
SdHi Ap 9 1915-Ap 30 1921

LETCHER

CHRONICLE. w 1892+
pub 1931+
SdHi 1915+

LILY

LEADER. w 1914-20||
SdHi Je 1918-My 1920

LOYALTON

RECORD. w 1920-22||
SdHi Jl 1920-My 1922

LYMAN

PRAIRIE sun. *See* Advocate-leader (Kennebec)

MADISON

LAKE county leader. w 1880+
pub 1880+
WHi Mr 19,26 1881

LEADER. d 1890+
pub 1890+
SdHi My 1903+

OUTLOOK. w 1891-1915||
SdHi My 26 1903-Je 25 1915

SENTINEL. w 1879+
MWA Mr 4 1881
SdHi Ap 1904+
WHi Mr 4-11 1881

SENTINEL. d 1893+
SdHi Ap 1904-Je 1918;Je 1936+

SIGNAL. w
SdHi Jl 1905-Jl 1906

MANILA

PRAIRIE pioneer. w
SdHi Ap-N 1915

MARCUS

WHITE OWL oracle. w 1908-Ja 1930||?
1908-My 1918 pub in White Owl
SdHi My 1915-Ja 1930

MARIETTA

EAGLE. w 1907-11||
SdHi Je 1907-Je 1911

MARION

RECORD. w 1900+
SdHi Jl 1909-Je 1912

SOUTH DAKOTA (*Continued*)

MARTIN

BENNETT county booster. w 1911-18||?
SdHi Ap 1915-Je 1916

BENNETT county news. w 1930+
pub 1933+

BENNETT county review. w 1927-28||
SdHi Ja-N 1928

MESSENGER. w 1912+
SdHi Jl 1922+

MARVIN

MONITOR. w 1911-24||
SdHi Ap 8 1915-Je 24 1924

MEADOW

GRAND VALLEY herald. *See* Lemmon leader and Grand Valley herald (Lemmon)

MELLETTE

TRIBUNE. w 1881+
SdHi F 1900+

MENNO

HUTCHINSON county herald. w 1882+
pub 1895+
SdHi Jl 1883+

MIDLAND

MAIL. w 1908+
pub 1908+
SdHi F 1912+

WESTERN star. w 1904-12||
SdHi Je 1 1904-Je 27 1912

MILBANK

ADVANCE. *See* Herald-advance

GRANT county news. w 1902-14||
1902-N 1906 pub in Twin Brooks
SdHi O 1905-Je 1914

GRANT county review. w Ag 19 1880+
MnHi S 30 1880+
SdHi 1880

HARRIS' graphic. w S 20 1887-
MnHi 1887-[88]

HERALD-ADVANCE. w 1882+
1882-87? as Index; 1888?-89? Advance
pub 1882+
SdHi My 1903+

INDEX. *See* Herald-advance

MILLER

GAZETTE. w 1884+
pub 1885+
SdHi Mr 16 1904+

HAND county press. *See* Press

PIONEER-PRESS. *See* Press

PRESS. w 1882+
1882-94? as Hand county press; 1895?-1906? Pioneer-press
SdHi D 1906+

SUN. w 1902+
SdHi Ap 13 1904-F 1 1908

MILWAUKEE JUNCTION

Milwaukee HERALD. w
SdHi D 1882-Ap 1883

MINER

Miner SENTINEL. *See* Diana monitor (Diana)

MISSION

TODD county tribune. w 1920+
SdHi Mr 17 1921+

MISSION HILL

HISTORIAN. w Mr 17 1910-12||
MnHi 1910-11
NdHi 1910-Mr 8 1912
SdHi 1910-Je 30 1912

MITCHELL

CAPITAL. w 1879-1918||
SdHi Jl 1903-Je 1918

CLARION. w 1901-16||
SdHi Ap 14 1904-Je 29 1916

DAVISON county gazette. *See* Gazette

GAZETTE. w 1881+
1881-89? as Davison county gazette
pub 1889+
SdHi Mr 1906+

REPUBLICAN. d 1883+
pub 1883+
SdHi S 1903+

SOUTH DAKOTA leader. w Mr 16 1918-24||?
MnHi 1918-[22-23]

MOBRIDGE

NEWS. w 1908-18||
SdHi 1909-Je 1918

TRIBUNE. w 1907+
pub 1910+
SdHi Ap 1918+

MONTROSE

HERALD. w Jl 1886+
pub 1886+
SdHi Mr 25 1904+

MORRISTOWN

WORLD. w 1909+
pub 1909+
SdHi Ap 1915-Je 1918;Je 1935+

MOUND CITY

MONITOR. w 1918+
pub 1918+

MOUNT VERNON

NEWS. w 1893+
pub 1901+

MURDO

COYOTE. w 1904+
SdHi 1904+

PIONEER. w 1906-11||
SdHi Jl 1906-Je 1907;Jl 1908-Je 1911

MUSSMAN

LYMAN county republican. *See under* Draper

NEW UNDERWOOD

TIMES. w 1916+
SdHi Je 6 1922+

NEWARK

STATE line news. w 1906-23||
SdHi Ap 6 1911-Je 30 1918;Ja 22 1920-Je 1923

NEWELL

BUTTE county courier and reclamation news. w 1911-22||
1911-16? as Reclamation news
SdHi Je 1915-Je 1916;Jl 1917-Je 1918

RECLAMATION news. *See* Butte county courier and reclamation news

VALLEY irrigator. w O 2 1907+
pub 1907+

NISLAND

BUTTE county press. w 1910-31||?
SdHi Ap 1915-Je 1929

NORTHVILLE

JOURNAL. w 1898-1922||?
SdHi Ap 14 1904-Je 28 1918

OACOMA

GAZETTE-LEADER. *See* Lyman county argus-leader

LYMAN county argus. w 1895-Je 1907||
United with Gazette-leader to form Lyman county argus-leader
SdHi Ag 1904-07

LYMAN county argus-leader. w 1893-1924||
1893-98? as Lyman county leader; 1899?-Je 1907 Gazette-leader
SdHi Ap 1904-Ja 1924

LYMAN county leader. *See* Lyman county argus-leader

OELRICHS

ADVOCATE. w 1911+
SdHi Ap 1915+

OKATON

JOURNAL. w 1906-24||?
1906-Je 1910 pub in White River
SdHi Ag 1906-Je 1919

OKOBOJO

TIMES. w 1884-1929||
SdHi Ap 14 1904-Ja 1929
SdNW My 1885-My 1890;Je 1899-My 1900;My 1907-My 1916

OLDHAM

REGISTER. w 1898+
pub 1917+
SdHi Ap 26 1904+

OLIVET

HUTCHINSON herald. w 1886?-98||?
In English and German
SdHi Ja 1888-D 1889

LEADER. w 1896-1916||?
SdHi Mr 17 1904-Je 27 1912

ONIDA

ENTERPRISE. w 1919+
1919-26? pub in Agar
SdHi S 19 1919+

SULLY county watchman. *See* Watchman

SULLY news. w 1911-13||
SdHi Je 1912-Ja 1913

WATCHMAN. w 1883+
1883-93? as Sully county watchman
pub 1883+
SdHi Ap 1904+

ORAL

ANGOSTURA messenger. w 1917-19||?
WaPS Je 12,Jl 17-Ag 7 1919

ORIENT

ARGUS. w 1901+
pub 1922+
SdHi Mr 1904+

OWANKA

BEE. w 1908-26||
SdHi Ja 27 1921-Je 24 1926

PARKER

KING'S Parker press-leader. *See* Turner county tribune

NEW ERA. w O 28 1875+
pub 1875+
SdHi Ap 1904-My 1907;F 1913-Je 1930;Je 1935+

PRESS. *See* Turner county tribune

PRESS-LEADER. *See* Turner county tribune

TURNER county tribune. w 1884+
1884-1904? as Press; 1905?-23? Press-leader (1907?-10? King's Parker press-leader)
SdHi Ag 1903+

PARKSTON

ADVANCE. w 1883+
pub 1904+
SdHi S 10 1903+

PEEVER

PILOT. w 1904-18||
SdHi Je 1904-Je 1911;Ap 1915-Je 1918

PHILIP

BAD RIVER news. w 1906-12||
SdHi N 15 1906-Je 30 1912

PIONEER. w 1917-20||
United with Review to form Pioneer-review
SdHi Ap 1917-Je 1920

PIONEER-REVIEW. w 1907+
1907-20 as Review
SdHi Je 1907+

REVIEW. *See* Pioneer-review

PIERPONT

SIGNAL. w 1899+
pub 1901-11;14+
SdHi Mr 18 1904-Ap 1 1908;Jl 9 1914+

PIERRE

CAPITAL City spirit. w 1910-12||
SdHi Je 2 1910-Je 27 1912

CAPITAL-JOURNAL. w 1880+
1880-87? as Dakota journal; 1888?-97? Journal
pub 1892+
NhD Ag 8 1889;N 13 1890
SdHi D 11 1880-O 1882;Je 1890-O 1894;O 1901-Ap 1905

CAPITAL-JOURNAL. d F 20 1890+
F-D 7 1890 as Daily capital
pub 1891+
DLC Ag 20 1890-96
KHi F 28 1890-Je 20 1898
SdHi Je 1890+

DAKOTA journal. *See* Capital-journal

Daily DAKOTAN. d 1903+
pub 1903-18;24+
SdHi N 1903-Je 1918;24+
WHi 1917-Ag 14 1918

Weekly DAKOTAN. w 1903-13||
SdHi D 3 1903-Ap 10 1913

FREE PRESS. w 1883-1918||
ICM D 23 1884
MnHi 1890-95
SdHi D 1883-My 1884;My 1888-My 1895;O 1903-Je 1918

SOUTH DAKOTA (*Continued*)

PIERRE—*Continued*

FREE PRESS. d 1884-91||
Title varies: Evening free press; Daily free press
SdHi Mr 31 1884-Mr 14 1891
JOURNAL. *See* Capital-journal
NEW ERA. w 1907-09||
SdHi complete
RUSTLER. w
SdHi 1902-04
SIGNAL. w 1880-91||
MnHi [Je 1889-91]
SdHi Je 1880-My 1883
SOUTH DAKOTA messenger. w 1910-14||
SdHi Jl 1 1912-O 1914
STATE journal. w
SdHi Ap 1904-Je 1912
STATE register. w
Merged with Capital-journal
SdHi 1899-Ja 1902
Daily STATE spirit. d
SdHi Ja-Mr 3 1905

PLANKINTON

SOUTH DAKOTA mail. w 1889+
pub 1889+
SdHi S 25 1903+

PLATTE

ENTERPRISE. w 1900+
SdHi Jl 1915+
EPITOME. *See* Tribune
TRIBUNE. w,d 1900+
1900-Je 1909 as Epitome
w 1900-30?
SdHi Ag 1904-Je 1916

POLLOCK

CAMPBELL county progress. w 1902+
1901-04? as Progress
pub 1925+
PROGRESS. *See* Campbell county progress

PRESHO

HERALD. *See* Lyman county herald
LYMAN county herald. w 1903+
1903-19? as Post; 1920?-21? Herald
SdHi Jl 1904-Je 1919
LYMAN county republican. *See under* Draper
LYMAN county settler. w 1905-13||
SdHi Jl 5 1906-Je 28 1913
POST. *See* Lyman county herald

PUKWANA

PRESS-REPORTER. w 1883+
1883-1901 as Press
pub 1925+
SdHi 1915+

QUINN

COURANT. w 1907-25||
SdHi N 1922-Je 1925
TIMES. w 1926+
SdHi Je 1936+

RAMONA

TIMES. w 1889+
pub 1922+
SdHi Je 1927+

RAPID CITY

BLACK HILLS booster. w 1915-18||?
SdHi Mr 1915-Ja 1917
BLACK HILLS weekly democratic. w 1886-89||
SdHi Jl 1886-Jl 1889
BLACK HILLS journal. w 1878-1930||
pub complete
SdHi 1878-O 1886;90-94;My 1903-Je 1930
BLACK HILLS union and stock review. w 1889-1911||?
1889-F 1904 as Black Hills union
SdHi Ag 1889-Je 1892;95-F,Jl 1904-Mr 1907;Jl 1909-Je 1911
GATE CITY guide. w 1908+
pub 1909+
SdHi Jl 1910-Ag 1911;34+
JOURNAL. d 1885+
pub 1885+
SdHi F 1886+
REPUBLICAN. d 1884-92||
SdHi 1889;My-Ag 1890;N-D 1892
Saturday REPUBLICAN. w 1884-99||?
CtY Ag 20(supp)1885
SdHi Ag 1884-Je 1888;98
WORLD. w
SdHi My 1901-My 1902

RAVINIA

REGISTER. w 1916-20||?
SdHi Jl 13 1916-Je 26 1919

RAYMOND

GAZETTE. w 1883-89||
SdHi D 1883-O 1889

REDELM

RECORD. w 1917-25||
SdHi Mr 1917-Je 1925

REDFIELD

JOURNAL-OBSERVER. w,d 1882+
1882-91? as Journal
w 1882-1934
SdHi My 1903+
PRESS. w 1885?+
SdHi My 1903-F 1923

REE HEIGHTS

REVIEW. w 1911+
pub 1911+

RELIANCE

LYMAN county democrat. w 1908-10||
SdHi S 1908-Mr 1910
LYMAN county record. w 1903-26||?
SdHi Je 5 1906-Je 30 1919;F 1924-Je 1926

REVILLO

Weekly ITEM. w 1897+
SdHi Ap 28 1904-Je 1913

ST. LAWRENCE

HAND county news. w 1907+
SdHi S 1907-Ap 1909

SALEM

PIONEER register. w 1879+
pub 1892+
SdHi Ap-N 1904;O 1907-Je 1918
WHi Ap 29,My 20 1881
SPECIAL. sw,w 1885+
sw 1885-93?
SdHi My 1903+

SCOTLAND

CITIZEN-REPUBLICAN. w 1877-1921||
1877-87? as Dakota citizen; 1888?-94? Citizen
SdHi O 8 1903-Je 30 1921
DAKOTA citizen. *See* Citizen-republican
JOURNAL. w 1895+
SdHi 1904-Je 1926

SELBY

WALWORTH county record. w 1885+
pub 1885+
SdHi Ap 16 1904+

SENECA

JOURNAL. w 1902+
SdHi D 1902-Je 1929;35+

SIOUX FALLS

ARGUS-LEADER. sw,w 1880-1915||?
1880-F 1885 as Argus
sw 1903-Ja 1906
SdHi O 1903-Mr 1915
Daily ARGUS-LEADER. d Mr 4 1885+
Title varies: Sioux Falls argus-leader; Argus-leader
DLC Ag 22 1890—
IaSc current 6 months
MnHi [1920-24]
SdHi 1900+
CATARACT. w
SdHi Mr 1904-N 22 1906
DEMOCRAT. ir Jl 2 1859-
MnHi Jl 2,Ag 5,26-N 8 1859;F 18 1860
DEUTSCHER-HEROLD. w 1890-1918||?
1890-99? Süd Dakota nachrichten; 1900?-07? Nachrichten herold
In German
SdHi Jl 1903-Jl 1918
DISPATCH. w 1910-11||
SdHi N 1910-S 1911
FARMER-LABOR news. w O 9 1919-28||?
1919-23? as Labor news
MnHi [D 11 1919-25]
SdHi Je 1923-Je 1924
FREMAD. w My 17 1894-Ag 15 1935||
Followed by Weekly news
In Norwegian
pub complete
IU D 6 1917-F 13 1930
IaDeL [S 1896-Jl 1918]
SdHi S 10 1903-35
WHi S 1898-Ag 15 1935
Sioux Falls INDEPENDENT. w 1873-79||?
OCH S 8 1877
JOURNAL. w
SdHi My 1903-Je 1918;Jl 1921-Ap 1924
JOURNAL. w 1928+
1928-F 1930 as South Dakota journal
SdHi Ag 1929+
LABOR news. *See* Farmer-labor news
Sioux Falls LEADER. w 1883-86||
United with Sioux Falls argus to form Argus-leader
CL Ap 1885-Ap 7,21-My 12 1886
NACHRICHTEN herold. *See* Deutscher-herold
Weekly NEWS. w Ag 22 1935+
Follows Fremad
WHi 1935+
Sioux Falls PANTAGRAPH. w 1872-80||?
NN [My]-[S-N 1872;Ap 1873-N 1875]Ja 19 1876
NNHi Ag 27 1873
Sioux Falls POSTEN. w 1907-My 30 1916||
In Norwegian
IaDeL [O 29 1908-16]
SdHi D 31 1908-16
WHi N 28 1912-16
Sioux Falls PRESS. d 1883-Ja 1 1928||
Merged with Sioux City tribune (Sioux City, Iowa)
DLC Mr 1924-27
PU [1889]
SdHi Ap 1900-28
WHi Mr 1917-28
PUBLIC. w
SdHi Je-N 1911
SOO critic. w 1903-11||
SdHi O 16 1903-Je 30 1911
SOUTH DAKOTA journal. *See* Journal
SOUTH DAKOTA state forum. w 1893+
pub 1903+
SdHi Ap 15 1904-Mr 20 1908,Jl 30 1913-N 5 1915
SÜD DAKOTA nachrichten. *See* Deutscher-herold
SYD DAKOTA ekko. w 1889-Ag 30 1906||
In Norwegian
IaDeL 1893-[1901-06]
WHi O 16 1895-1906
Sioux Falls TIMES. w 1871-81||
WHi Ap 19 1881

SISSETON

BANNER-NEWS. w 1893-1909||?
1893-Ap? 1903 as Inter-empire; My? 1903-06? Roberts county banner
SdHi My 1903-F 1907
COURIER. w 1915+
pub 1915+
SdHi 1915+
INTER-EMPIRE. *See* Banner-news
JOURNAL-PRESS. w 1930+
pub 1930+
SdHi 1930+
POSTEN. w 1902-12||?
In Norwegian
SdHi D 6 1904-Je 30 1912
ROBERTS county banner. *See* Banner-news
ROBERTS county record. w 1910-13||
SdHi Je 1911-Je 1913
STANDARD. w My 28 1892-1928||?
MnHi My 28,Jl 9,O 8 1892;Ja 17 1896;Je 10-24 1898
SdHi D 1904-N 1921;Je 1922-28

SOUTH SHORE

REPUBLICAN. w 1898-1918||
SdHi O 1903-Ap 1918

SPEARFISH

ENTERPRISE. w 1903-17||?
SdHi Ja 1 1910-Je 1915
QUEEN CITY mail. w 1889+
SdHi S 1903-Je 1905;Ja 1921+

SPENCER

NEWS. w 1892+
1892-99? as Populist
pub 1933+
SdHi Je 1907-My 1908;Je 1914-Je 1928
POPULIST. *See* News

SPRINGFIELD

TIMES. w 1869+
pub 1869+
NNHi Mr 20 1873
SdHi Mr 9 1905-07;F 1914-Je 1926;Je 1927-Je 1928;Je 1936+

STICKNEY

POSTAL card. w 1906-18||
SdHi Ap 1915-Je 1918

STRATFORD

NEWS. w 1903+
pub 1931+

SOUTH DAKOTA (*Continued*)

STURGIS

ADVERTISER. w 1887-98||?
SdHi [Jl 19 1887-O 1 1891]

BLACK HILLS press. w 1896+
SdHi Ap 1915+

BLACK HILLS tribune. w 1929+
pub 1929+
SdHi Je 1936+

Weekly RECORD. w 1883+
pub 1883+

SUMMIT

INDEPENDENT. w 1912+
pub 1912+
SdHi Ap 15 1915+

SIGNAL. w 1892-1914||?
SdHi Ag 1901-Je 1910

SWEENEY

PIONEER. w
SdHi Je 1905-Je 1906

TERRY

BALD MOUNTAIN news. *See* News-record

NEWS-RECORD. w 1896-1912||?
1896-1901? as Bald Mountain news
SdHi 1899-Je 1901;O 1903-Ag 1910

TIMBER LAKE

TOPIC. w 1911+
SdHi My 1915+

TORONTO

HERALD. w 1897+
SdHi F 5 1897-Je 1919;Jl 30 1922+

TRIPP

LEDGER. w 1892+
pub 1892+
SdHi Ap 1915+

TWIN BROOKS

GRANT county news. *See under* Milbank

TYNDALL

BON HOMME county register. w 1885+
1885-1926? as Register
SdHi S 1903+

REGISTER. *See* Bon Homme county register

TRIBUNE. w 1881+
SdHi Ap 21 1904+

VALLEY SPRINGS

REPORTER. w 1921-25||
SdHi Je 1922-Je 1925

VIDETTE. w 1891-1912||
SdHi N 1907-Je 1912

VEBLEN

ADVANCE. w 1900+
1900-04? as Advance-republican
pub 1930+
SdHi Ap 1904-Mr 1906;Je 1936+

ADVANCE-REPUBLICAN. *See* Advance

VERMILLION

CLAY county register. w 1872-76||
NNHi Jl 17 1873
SdHi S 1872-Mr 1876

DAKOTA republican. w Ag 31 1861+
pub 1875+
DLC Ap 5-12,My 24,Je 7-14,N 22 1862;Ja 10, 31,F 14,28,Mr 7-21 1863;Ag 27-S 10 1864;Ja 4-11,25-F 29,Mr 14-28,Ap 11,25,My 16-23,Je 20-Jl 4,18-30,Ag 13-S 17,O 8,21-N 12,D 19-26 1868;Ja 16-Je 5,19-26,Jl 10-17,21-S 4,O 23-N 6,20,D 4 1869;Ja 29 1870-Ja 28,O 14 1875
N Ag 31 1861
NNHi Ap 17 1873
NcD [Ap 1870-Ap,S-O]-D 1874
SdHi Ap 30 1903+

PLAIN talk. w 1884+
pub 1884+
SdHi Ap 30 1903-Je 27 1918;Je 1936+

VIBORG

ENTERPRISE. w 1898+
pub 1898+

VIENNA

STANDARD. w 1900-18||
SdHi My 1915-Je 1918

VIVIAN

WAVE. w 1904-18||?
1904-My 1905 pub in Westover
SdHi Ap 1904-My 1912;Ag 1913-Je 1918

VOLGA

TRIBUNE. w 1882+
pub 1915+
SdHi S 1904+

VOLIN

ADVANCE. w Ag 26 1909+
pub 1909+
SdHi Ap 1915+

TIMES. w 1904-08||
SdHi S 22 1904-Ja 23 1908

WAGNER

CHARLES MIX new era. w 1900-14||?
SdHi Mr 3 1905-Je 30 1912

POST. w 1912+
SdHi Jl 5 1912+

WAKONDA

MONITOR. w 1891+
pub 1888
SdHi Ap 30 1903+

WALL

EASTERN PENNINGTON county courant. *See* Pennington county courant

PENNINGTON county courant. w 1907+
1907-24? as Record; 1925?-32? Eastern Pennington county courant
pub 1932+
SdHi Ap 1915-F 1917;Je 1927+

RECORD. *See* Pennington county courant

WARNER

Weekly SUN. w 1883-90||?
SdHi Ag 18 1883-Ag 24 1888

WASTA

GAZETTE. w 1907+
SdHi Jl 1911+

WATERTOWN

CONKLIN'S Dakotian. w 1887-90||
SdHi N 1889-Je 1890

COURIER-NEWS. *See* News

DAKOTA news. *See* News

HERALD. w 1903+
pub 1904+
SdHi My 1903+

NEWS. w 1879-92||?
1879-84? as Dakota news; 1885?-88? Courier-news
ICHi F 18 1882
ICM F 18 1882
SdHi Je 1879-Je 1884

Saturday NEWS. w 1903-20||?
SdHi F 14 1908-Je 1919

PUBLIC opinion. d 1887+
pub 1887+
SdHi Mr 1887-Mr 1889;My 1903+

SÜD DAKOTA staats-zeitung. w Ap 29 1891-92||
In German
MnHi complete

TIMES. w 1896-1914||
SdHi Jl 6 1905-Je 25 1914

WAUBAY

CLIPPER. w My 1890+
pub 1903+
SdHi O 22 1903+

WEBSTER

DAY county herald. *See* World

JOURNAL. w 1883+
1883-1926 as Gazette (Andover)
pub 1926+

REPORTER and farmer. w 1881+
pub 1884+
SdHi S 1903+

WORLD. w 1883-1917||
1883-96? as Day county herald
SdHi S 24 1903-Je 28 1917

WENTWORTH

CITY bond. *See* Dakota letter

DAKOTA letter. w 1883-87||?
1883-84 as City bond
SdHi Jl 1883-85;D 1886-Ja 1887

ENTERPRISE. w 1900-19||?
SdHi Ap 1904-F 1912;Ap 1915-Je 1919

PROGRESS. w 1923+
pub 1934+
SdHi 1936+

WESSINGTON

TIMES-ENTERPRISE. w 1882+
1882-Ap? 1909 as Times
pub 1905+
SdHi Mr 1909+

WESSINGTON SPRINGS

DAKOTA sieve. *See* Independent

INDEPENDENT. w 1891+
1891-Je 1906 as Dakota sieve; Jl 1906-20 Jerauld county review
SdHi My 1903-Je 1915;31+

JERAULD county review. *See* Independent

REPUBLICAN. w 1883+
1883-1915 as True republican
MWA N 9 1916
SdHi My 1903+

TRUE republican. *See* Republican

WESTOVER

WAVE. *See under* Vivian

WESTOVER. w
SdHi Ap 1904-Je 1905

WHEELER

COURIER. *See* Charles Mix county courier (Lake Andes)

WHITE

CHIEF. w 1891-1901||?
1891-My 6 1892 as Record
SdHi My 1891-Ja 1901

LEADER. w 1900+
pub 1906+
SdHi Jl 1912-Je 1913;Jl 1916+

RECORD. *See* Chief

WHITE LAKE

AURORA county standard. w 1903+
pub 1925+
SdHi O 1903+

WAVE. w 1892-1921||
SdHi Ap 1904-Je 1918;Jl 1919-My 1921

WHITE OWL

White Owl ORACLE. *See under* Marcus

WHITE RIVER

JOURNAL. *See under* Okaton

WHITE ROCK

JOURNAL. w 1899-1931||
SdHi Ap 1904-Je 1911;Ap 1915-Je 1931

WHITEWOOD

Whitewood PLAINDEALER. w 1890-1932||?
United with Black Hills weekly and Deadwood telegram to form Black Hills weekly and Whitewood plaindealer (Deadwood)

WILLOW LAKE

NEWS. w 1888+
1888-91 as News-rustler
SdHi My 1903-S 1911;Ap 1915+

NEWS-RUSTLER. *See* News

WILMOT

ENTERPRISE. w 1917+
pub 1917+
SdHi Jl 1917+

REPORTER. w 1886-1908||
SdHi Jl 1886-Mr 1908

REPUBLICAN. w 1894-1918||
1894-1915 as Roberts county republican
SdHi Ap 1904-Je 1 1918

ROBERTS county republican. *See* Republican

WINFRED

DISPATCH. w 1904+
SdHi Jl 1906-Je 1934

PUBLIC ledger. w 1884-D 1888||?
1884-My 1885 as Witness
SdHi Ag 1884-88

WITNESS. *See* Public ledger

WINNER

ADVOCATE. w 1910+
SdHi Jl 1911+

Daily JOURNAL. d 1917-18||
SdHi 1917-Je 1918

TRIPP county journal. w 1911+
pub 1911+

WITTEN

TRIPP county index. w 1907-17||?
SdHi Jl 1909-My 1912

WOKAMA

LEADER. w 1907-12||
SdHi Jl 1908-Ja 1912

SOUTH DAKOTA (*Continued*)

WOLSEY

BEADLE county herald. *See* Herald

HERALD. w 1903+
1903-24 as Beadle county herald
SdHi My 1903+

WOOD

MELLETTE county pioneer. w F 1912+
pub 1912+
SdHi Ap 1915+

WOONSOCKET

NEWS. w 1884+
SdHi S 1904-D 1909

SANBORN county herald. w 1898-1917||
United with Times to form Sanborn county herald-times
SdHi My 1903-Je 1917

SANBORN county herald-times. w 1882-1924||
1882-1916? as Times
SdHi S 1905-Je 1924

TIMES. *See* Sanborn county herald-times

WORTHING

ENTERPRISE. w 1892-1930||?
SdHi O 1903-Jl 1908

YANKTON

ANPAO, the Daybreak. m Ja 1878-82||?
In Sioux language
CU-B Ap 1878-Mr 1879;Je 1880
ICHi Je 1882
ICN Jl 1880

DAKOTA freie presse. *See under* Aberdeen

DAKOTA herald. w,sw 1872-1918||?
w 1872-Je 1903
NN [Ja-Ag,D 1873]Ja 27,F 17,Je 30,N 3 1874 [Mr-D 1875]-S 8 1877
NNHi Ap 8 1873
SdHi S 1900-S 1901;S 1903-Ap 1913

DAKOTA union. w Je 21-D 6? 1864||
United with Weekly Dakotian to form Union and Dakotian, later Yankton press and Dakotan
DLC Je 21-Ag 23,D 6 1864
WHi Je-Ag 23 1864

Weekly DAKOTIAN. *See* Yankton press and Dakotan

Yankton PRESS. w Ag 10 1870-N 12 1873||
United with Union and Dakotian to form Yankton press and union and Dakotian, later Yankton press and Dakotan
DLC Jl 19 1871-73
MnHi Mr 1[Ap-D 1871]-[73]
N Ja 10 1872
NNHi Ap 16 1873
WHi complete

Yankton PRESS and Dakotan. w 1861-1928||?
1861-N 12 1864 as Weekly Dakotian; N 19 1864-N 12 1873 Union and Dakotian; N 20 1873-Ap 4 1884 Yankton press and union and Dakotian (Other slight changes)
DLC Ap 1862-D 17 1864;D 28 1867;D 1873-Jl 13 1876;Je 1877-Ja 9 1896;Ja 14 1897-99
MH D 8 1866
MWA Ja 14-28,My 6,27 1865;O 1 1893
MnHi Jl 27 1861[N 23 1873-80]
NNHi My 8 1873
NbHi Je 20 1861
SdHi N 1873-1928
SdY 1873-1928
WHi Je-S 14 1861;Je 1862-S 24,N 19 1864-Ja 12 1871;N 20 1873-Mr 1875

Yankton PRESS and Dakotan. d Ap 26 1875+
1875-89 as Daily press and Dakotian
N D 15 1875
NbHi S 7,N 5 1876;O 8 1877
NdHi 1875-[Mr-Ap 1878]-1902
SdHi 1875+
SdY 1875+
WHi 1875-Jl 1902

PUBLIC opinion. w 1921+
SdHi My 1921+

UNION and Dakotian. *See* Yankton press and Dakotan

TENNESSEE

ADAMSVILLE

MCNAIRY county appeal. w 1926+
TU [D 1934]+

ALLARDT

Allardt GAZETTE. w 1891-95||
United with Fentress county news (Jamestown) to form Fentress county gazette, later Fentress county news (Jamestown)
T N 12 1891-Ja 7,N-D 8,22 1892-Ja 19,F 2-23,Ap 13-My 18,Je 1893-Jl 5,S 27-N 1 1894;Ja 10-Mr 21 1895

ALLENTOWN. *See* HAMPTON

ASHLAND CITY

Ashland City TIMES. w Ja 1890+
pub 1897+

ATHENS

ATHENIAN. w 1882-1930||
United with Athens post to form Post-Athenian
T Ap 1 1926
TKL Jl 1,S 30-O 7,21,D 2 1887;Ap 6 1894

HIWASSEAN and Athens gazette. w 1826-32||?
CSmH Ag 12 1830
DLC O 25 1832
MWA Jl 19 1832
T [1827]
TKL F 20 1828

HIWASSEE patriot. w Ja 22 1839-Mr 9 1841||
Early numbers pub in Madisonville
NcU My 14 1840
TC Ja 29 1839-41

McMINN county herald. w 1929+
pub 1931+
TU F 28 1935

NEWS. w 1874-77||?
DLC O 14 1876
TKL N 18 1876

POST-ATHENIAN. w 1848+
Follows Post (Knoxville). 1848-1930 as Athens post
DLC Jl 26,S 6 1861
MWA Ja 6,27,F 3,17,My 19,D 15 1854;F 9,23, Mr 9,Ap 13,27,S 14,O 5,D 21 1855;My 9-16 1856;F 6,Ap 10,My 8,Je 5,Jl 17-24,N 13,D 11 1857;Ap 25 1884;Je 19 1885
NNHi My 4 1860
NcD F 15,Ap 19-Jl,Ag 16,30-S,O 18,N 29,D 20 1861;Ja 31,F 14-28,Mr 14-My 16,30-Je,Jl 18-25,Ag 8-29,S 19,O 3,D 5,26 1862; Ja 16-F 6,27-Mr 6,20,Ap 3,17,My 1-8 1863
OCHi Mr 1 1861;Mr 21 1862;Jl 17 1863
OClWHi Ja 3,F 7-14,Mr 7,Ap 11-18,My 9,30-Je 6,20-27,Jl 11,Ag 8,22,O 17-24,D 5,19 1862; F 13-20,Ap 24,My 22-30,Ag 14 1863
OHi O 3 1862
T D 19 1873-74
TKL D 10,24 1862;Je 26 1868;D 3 1869;D 7 1883;Ja 19,D 21 1894
TU [1849-69]
Tx Ag 21 1863
WHi Je 1854-O 1 1858

Daily POST-ATHENIAN. d 1931+
TU [1934]

Athens REPUBLICAN. w Jl 12 1867-69||
MBAt S 6 1867;Ja 9-23,F-My 14,28-Jl,Ag 13-27,S 10-O 1,15,29,D 17 1868;Ja,F 11,Mr-Ap 1, 15-Je,Jl 22-29,Ag 12,28-S 11,O 2 1869
MWA Jl 12,26,S 13,27 1867

TENNESSEE journal. w 1833?-38||?
DLC My 24 1833;Ja 18,F 4,Je 11 1834
TKL Jl 25,Ag 22 1838
TU [My 20,D 16 1835;S 14,O 12 1836;N 15 1837]
TxU Je 6 1838

Athens UNION post. w S 17 1863-
DLC S 17 1863

WATCHMAN. w Ja 1?-Jl 9 1842||
MWA Jl 9 1842

BELLS

CROCKETT county sentinel. w 1873+
TU [1934-35]

BENTON

POLK county news. w 1907+
T [1933]

BOLIVAR

Bolivar BULLETIN. w 1865+
1887 as West Tennessee star
pub [1865+]
ICHi S 28,O 19 1865
NcD N 9 1934
TBC 1865+

Bolivar FREE PRESS and farmers herald. w Mr 8 1834-35||?
DLC Mr 29 1834
TKL Ja 21 1835
TU [Jl 8 1835]

Bolivar PALLADIUM. w D 2 1829-30||?
CSmH My 21 1830
DLC D 2 1829

UNION banner. Jl 31 1862-
IHi Jl 31 1862

WEST TENNESSEE star. *See* Bolivar bulletin

BRISTOL

Papers published in Bristol are listed under Bristol, Virginia

BROWNSVILLE

Brownsville BEE. *See* States-graphic

DISTRICT herald. w D 4 1838-
DLC D 11 1838;O 31 1840
NcU My 12 1840

INDEPENDENT American. w 1860-
WHi D 20 1860

SOUTHERN atlas. w 1859-60||?
DLC Jl 18 1860

Brownsville STATES. w 1870-80||?
United with Brownsville bee to form States and bee, later States-graphic

STATES and bee. *See* States-graphic

STATES-DEMOCRAT. *See* States-graphic

STATES-GRAPHIC. w 1868+
1868-79? as Brownsville bee; 1880?-86? States and bee; 1887?-90? States-democrat
TU D 28 1934+

BURNS

NEW idea. w S 1 1905+
pub S 1905+
T N 9,16 1922;Mr 1923-Je 1924;25-O 1926;Ja 7,Ap 23,D 17 1931

CAMDEN

Camden CHRONICLE. w 1890+
TU D 21 1934+

CARDIFF

Cardiff HERALD. w 1890-91||
TKL Ja 21 1891

CARTHAGE

Carthage COURIER. w Jl 3 1913+
pub 1913+
TU F 1,Je 14 1934

REPUBLICAN. w Ja 1 1842-44||?
DLC Ja 1 1842;O 4,N 29 1844
TCaC F 2 1844

TENNESSEE republican. w 1824-25||?
DLC My 25 1825
InI D 20 1824

CELINA

BILL FISKE'S bugle. w O 26 1910+
pub 1910+

CLAY county courier. w 1928-
T S 1928

CENTERVILLE

HICKMAN county news. w 1892+
pub [F 8 1884-F 12 1886]1920+
TU [1931-34]

HICKMAN county pioneer. w 1878-93||?
T 1878-80[83;85]

CHARLOTTE

Charlotte NEWS-BANNER. w 1930+
TU Jl 31 1931[34-35]

CHATTANOOGA

Chattanooga ADVERTISER. w 1850-62||
Merged with Chattanooga gazette
CSmH D 22 1859
DLC O 28 1852
MWA Ja 3 1857
OClWHi F 13 1862
TC Ja 24 1861
TKL Mr 18 1858

Chattanooga ADVERTISER. tw 1852-
MWA S 4,6 1855

Daily AMERICAN union. d F 19 1866-68||?
DLC Je 26,N 20 1867;F 27 1868
MBAt F 19-23,26-28,Mr 2-9,14-16,20,31,Ap 7, 10-14,18,21-22 1866
MWA Ag 9 1866;D 25 1867
MnHi D 22 1866
OClWHi My 11-12 1866
TKL F 27 1867
WHi Ap 27,My 1 1886

CHEROKEE courier. w 1934+
T F 7,Mr 8,Je 7,S 25 1934

Chattanooga COMMERCIAL. w 1874-87||
TC 1878-[80]-83;O 27 1885-[86-87]
TKL Ag 18-24 1878
TU S 24 1882

Chattanooga daily COMMERCIAL. d 1884-87||
Title varies slightly
TKL [S 18 1873-S 1876;Je 30-D 1 1887]
TU Ja 22 1887

TENNESSEE (*Continued*)

CHATTANOOGA—*Continued*

CRABTREE'S Saturday press. w 1890-1906||?
1890-Ag 5 1905 as Chattanooga press
TC Ag-N 1891;94-Ja 13 1906

Chattanooga daily DISPATCH. d 1877-
DLC O 11 1877

Chattanooga GAZETTE. w 1838-64||?
1838-39 as Hamilton county gazette; 1862?-63? Gazette and advertiser
MWA My 10,Jl 12 1856
OCHi Ja 4-11,25 1862
OClWHi Ja 25 1862
TC F 16 1849;Je 14 1850;Ja 20 1855;Ja 22 1861; F 6 1862
TKL My 18 1844

Chattanooga daily GAZETTE. d F? 1864-66||?
CtY Ap 4,My 27,Je 7,23,25,26,30,Ag 20,26,27, S 19 1865
DLC Jl 12 1864;Mr 10 1865
ICHi S 15,O 7,N 8 1865
KHi Ap 26 1865
MBAt Mr 31,Ap 19,My 11 1864;Mr 2,S 23,O 6,14,25-29,N 1-2,5-8,10-11,15-22,24-28,30,D 2 1865;Ja 26,28 1866
MWA F 27(extra)Mr 17 1864;Ag 24,N 29 1865
MnHi Mr 5 1864
OCHi Mr 20 1864
OCl Jl 8,10 1864
OClWHi [Mr-Je 1864]-F 10,Mr 28,S 2 1865
OHi My 31 1864;Jl 6-O 20 1865
TU Ja 8 1861
WHi Mr 24,Ap 9,Je 9,17,19,25,30,Ag 7,30,S 1, 18,O 15 1864

HAMILTON county gazette. *See* Chattanooga gazette

HAMILTON county herald. w 1914+
pub 1930+
GU Ag 14 1925
T Mr 23 1923
TU [1931;34]+

HAMILTON vindicator. w Ag 28 1852-
MWA S 18 1852

Chattanooga HERALD. d,w 1872||
d Je?-D 5 1872
GU Je 17 1872
TKL Ag 9,S 3,20,O 8,N 4,28,D 5,12 1872

JUSTICE. w Je 11? 1887-88||?
Negro
MWA D 24 1887

Chattanooga NEWS. d Jl 2 1888+
1888-89 as Chattanooga evening news
pub 1889+
NcD My 12 1903;My 27-30 1913
T My 1901-Je,O 1918+
TC Jl 1889-My 17,Je 30 1890-Je 27 1896;Ja-Mr,Jl 1907-Je 1909;10-Mr,Jl 1911-Mr,O 1912-Mr,Jl 1917-Je 1919;21+
TCU 1922-31
TU [1931]+

Chattanooga NEWS. w *See* Weekly news and farm journal

Weekly NEWS and farm journal. w 1888-1912||?
1888-1905? as Chattanooga news
NcD D 19 1901;Ap 28 1910

Chattanooga PRESS. d 1890-96||?

Chattanooga PRESS. w *See* Crabtree's Saturday press

Chattanooga daily REBEL. d Ag 1 1862-
Title varies slightly
Jl 1863-Ap 1865 pub ir in Marietta, Ga.; Griffin, Ga.; Selma, Ala.
CLM Ag 9 1862
CSmH Je 28 1863
CtY F 7-Mr 7 1863
DLC [S 10 1862-Je 20 1863] Mr 23,26,Ap 1, Je 9,S 17,N 21,23 1864;Ja 7,F 6,Ap 27 1865
GDE Ag 26 1864
ICN Ap 19 1865
LNC Ag 9 1862;D 23 1864
MBAt D 31 1862;Je 25,Jl 30 1863;Mr 18,22, 27,Ap 21-22,Je 10,14,18-19 1864
MH [Je 18-S 17 1864]Ja 16 1865
MWA Ag 9,D 17 1862;Ap 12,Je 28 1863;Ap 1 1865
MnHi [Je 10-D 1863]
MsHi Ag 9 1862;Ap 1 1864
NN Ag 9 1862;Jl 22 1863
NNHi Je 26 1863; Ja 20,N 19 1864;Ja 10,13-14 1865
NbHi Ag 9 1862
NcD Ag 9 1862;My 8-9,12-13,16 1863;F 23, S 8 1864;Mr 15 1865
OCHi S 26,N 6 1862[Ja 20-Ag 1863]
OClWHi [Ag-N 1862;Mr-Jl 1863]Ag 31 1864
PPGr Ag 1862
PPiHi Ag 9 1862
T Ag 9 1862;Ap 3,Je 9,21,26,28 1863;F 24,Mr 15,26,28 1865
TC Ag 9 1862;Je 28 1863
TKL Ap 1,My 1,Je 2-3,Jl 3,Ag 4 1863
TU Je 28 1863
TxGR Ag 9 1862
TxU D 25 1862
WHi Ag 9 1862(reprint)Jl 24 1863;Ag 26 1864

Chattanooga REPUBLICAN. w Mr 18 1888-93||?
Merged with Chattanooga press
MWA Ap 13 1890
TC 1888-92;Ja 14-Mr 11 1893

SOUTHERN press. w My 27 1871-
MWA Je 24 1871

Chattanooga daily TIMES. d D 15 1869+
A Jl 1900+
CtW My 1 1890
DLC 1898-S,N 1918+
GU O 22 1896
IC My 1 1889
ICHi Jl 4 1890
KHi S 18-21 1895
MBAt D 30 1869
NN Je-Jl 1925
NcD Je 29 1880;Je 17 1881;Jl 4 1890;S 25 1898;My 27-30 1913
NjN Ap 20 1864
P D 17 1912
PCA Jl 15-17 1897
PDoHi S 7 1870
PHi [1895]
PP S 18-22 1895
T F 27 1873-74;Jl 1875+
TC F 17 1870;S 7 1871;Jl 2,S 13-15,17,O 12 1878;O-D 1879;Jl 1880-Je 1883;84-Mr 1894; S 18-22 1895;Ja-Mr,O 1898-1900;02-Je 1904; 05-Mr 1907;08-Mr 1913;14+
TCN 1907+
VU O 18 1886;My 18,25 1889;Ag 25,27,S 27, 29,O 2,6-7 1934
WHi S 18 1889;S 18-21 1895

Chattanooga Sunday TIMES. w 1881-1916||?
TKL Ag 30 1885;Ap 3 1892;D 30 1894;My 31 1896

CLARKSVILLE

Clarksville CHRONICLE. w Jl 14 1830-88||
United with Clarksville tobacco leaf to form Clarksville leaf-chronicle
DLC O 4 1834;O 29 1840
ICHi O 13 1865
MWA Ap 25,Je 27 1856;Ja 12 1866
NNHi Ag 15 1856
PDeH My 23 1856
TClaL 1858-88
TKL Mr 18 1847

Clarksville JEFFERSONIAN. w Mr 18 1843-67||?
DLC Mr 25,Ap 15,My 6 1843;O 30 1847
NNHi My 25 1844-N 14 1855;My 2 1860
TClaL 1865-67
WHi Ap 25 1860

Clarksville LEAF-CHRONICLE. sw 1888-1919||
Formed by the union of Clarksville tobacco leaf and Clarksville chronicle. 1888-95? as Tobacco leaf chronicle
pub complete

Clarksville LEAF-CHRONICLE. d 1888+
Formed by the union of Clarksville tobacco leaf and Clarksville chronicle. 1888-95? as Tobacco leaf chronicle
Ag 31 1933 is "Century and a quarter ed"
pub 1888+
GSD Jl 21 1896
NcD Ag 31 1933
NcU Jl 15 1905
T D 1922-23

ROUGH and ready. tw My 21 1847-
IU My 21 1847

Clarksville STAR. w 1890+
pub 1925+

TENNESSEE watchman. w Ja 13 1821-
DLC [1821-Ja 3 1824]
MWA Je 21 1822

Clarksville TOBACCO leaf. w,sw 1869-88||
Title varies: Clarksville semi-weekly tobacco leaf. United with Clarksville chronicle to form Clarksville leaf-chronicle
w 1869-79?
DLC F 19 1873-O 7 1874
GAtCo Ag 31 1883;F 15,29,Mr 14 1884;S 25, N 10,20-24 1885[Ag-N 1886]F 4-15 1887
T S 8 1875-Ag 24 1876

TOBACCO LEAF-CHRONICLE. See Clarksville leaf-chronicle

CLEVELAND

Cleveland BANNER. w,sw,d 1854+
1854-55 as Cleveland dipatch; 1906-16? Journal and banner
w 1854-1909, 17-23;sw 1910-16
MWA S 13 1854;F 8 1855;D 12 1856;Je 5 1857
NcD My 24-31 1861;Mr 14 1862
OClWHi O 11 1866
T [1934]
TC Ag 28 1862
TCl 1865-85;91-93;1902-14;18-21
TKL Ap 2 1880
TU Je 25 1868;Ja 7 1887[1934]+
TxU Ap 25 1862

COMMERCIAL republican. w 1872-74||
T Ap 25-My 16,29-N 13,27 1873-Ag 1874
TKL Jl 10 1873;Jl 30 1874
TU Ap 4 1873

Cleveland DISPATCH. *See* Cleveland banner

EAST TENNESSEE herald. w S 5 1856-
MWA O 17 1856

Cleveland HERALD. w Jl 14 1876+
pub 1913+
MWA S 1 1876;N 22 1877
TKL O 27 1876;Je 12 1879;Je 24,N 18 1881
TU N 25 1932;Ap 14-21,S 29 1933;Ja 19 1934

Cleveland JOURNAL. w 1891-1906||
United with Cleveland banner to form Journal and banner, later Cleveland banner

JOURNAL and banner. *See* Cleveland banner

Cleveland TRIBUNE. w 1929-30||?
T F 14-My 2,23 1930

CLIFTON

WAYNE countian. w 1915+
T Ap 28 1922

CLINTON

ANDERSON county news. w 1905+
TU [1933-34]+

Clinton COURIER. w Ag 31 1933+
TU S 28 1933

Clinton weekly GAZETTE. w 1887-1903||?
MWA Mr 30 1888

TRIBUNE. w Ap 30? 1875-
TKL O 8 1875

UNION pilot. w 1868-69||
MWA N 20 1869

COLUMBIA

Columbia BEACON. w N 18 1846-48||?
DLC N 25 1846-F 18 1848
TKL Ja 15 1847
TxU My 28,Je 11 1847

CHRONICLE. w
DLC Ag 1 1846

COLUMBIAN. w
DLC Ap 21 1825

CURRENT. w 1892-
DLC My 26 1892

DEMOCRATIC herald. w
DLC Jl 7-O 27 1855
TxU Ap 17 1852

Columbia HERALD. w 1850+
pub 1900+
DLC Je 23,Jl 14 1871-Ja 5,F 23-Mr 8,22-Ap 5,19-My 3,17-24,Jl 19,O 18,N 1-8,D 6-20 1872
MWA My 12 1866
T Je 22 1861;Jl 23 1869-Jl 10 1874;O 4 1892; 1921+
TU 1915+
TxU Ap 17 1852;F 2,Mr 16 1861

Daily HERALD. d O 3 1899+
pub 1899+
T Ja 1 1934

MAURY county herald. w Ag 11 1865-
ICHi S 30 1865

MAURY democrat. w 1888+
T N 7 1921;Mr 20-O 23 1924;Ap 30 1925;Ap 21-S 1927;Jl 3-10,31-O 9,23-D 18 1930;Ja-Mr 1931
TU [D 1934]+

MAURY intelligencer. w 1848-
T [Ap 26-Ag 16 1849]
TxU Ap 8,22 1852;Ag 31 1854

MAURY press. w 1860-61||?
T F 1860,Ap 4 1861
TxU My 16 1860

Columbia MIRROR. w
TxU Je 3 1856

Columbia OBSERVER. w Je 19 1834-45||?
DLC Je 26,Jl 11,Ag 8,S 19-O 2,15-20 1834; Je 5 1835;N 19 1840
MBAt S 12 1844
MWA Jl 19 1838;Jl 8 1841;Ap 27,My 18,Je 1, 15-22,Jl 20 1843
TKL Ja 9 1845
TU [Ap 27 1836;O 29 1837]
TxU My 21 1846

Columbia REVIEW. w 1819-22||?
T Jl 27 1822

SENTINEL. w S 4? 1863-
DLC F 6 1864
OClWHi F 20,27 1864

SEVENTH BRIGADE journal. w Ap 1 1862-
OClWHi Ap 15 1862
WHi Ap 8 1862

TENNESSEE democrat. w 1835-50||?
DLC N 12 1835;O 6(extra)1836;S 13 1838; Ag 3,14,28 1844
NcU Ap 30 1840;Ja 13,Mr 10,S 8 1842
TKL Jl 23 1846;S 19 1850

WESTERN mercury. w
CSmH Jl 20 1830
DLC Ja 10 1829;Ap 17 1832;Je 17 1833(extra)
NNHi D 20 1828

COOKEVILLE

PUTNAM county herald. w 1903+
1927-29 as Putnam county herald and Upper Cumberland news
TSE 1932+
TU Mr 30 1922;D 20 1934+

UPPER CUMBERLAND news. w 1923-27||
United with Putnam county herald to form Putnam county herald and Upper Cumberland news, later Putnam county herald
T Ja 31 1923

COVINGTON

Covington LEADER. w 1886+
pub 1914+
T Ja 12 1922
TM Je 26 1924
TU [1930]+

CROSSVILLE

Crossville CHRONICLE. w 1886+
pub 1886+
T Ja 26 1928
TSE 1932+
TU D 1 1932

Crossville TRIBUNE. w Ja 5-Ap 6 1878||
TKL F 23,Ap 6 1878

TENNESSEE (*Continued*)

DANDRIDGE

AMERICAN statesman. w N 13 1856-
MWA D 25 1856;Ja 30 1857

Dandridge BANNER. w 1928+
T My 25-S 17,O 8-22,N-D 24 1931;32
TU [1929+].

Dandridge HERALD. w N 9? 1854-
MWA Je 8 1855

Dandridge weekly NEWS-VISITOR. w 1892-1900||?
1892-94 as Dandridge weekly news
TKL Je 22 1894

REPUBLICAN banner. w Ap 19 1882-87||
Suspended from N 20 1883-Mr 20 1884
MWA O 25 1882
TU 1882-My 19 1887

Dandridge WATCHMAN. w O 17 1877-79||?
DLC D 12 1877
TKL Je 12-19,Jl 3,D 25 1878;Ag 6,20 1879

DAYTON

Dayton HERALD. w 1880+
pub Mr 12 1925+

DOVER

STEWART county times. w 1921+
pub 1922+
T Ja 29 1926
TU [D 1934]+

DRESDEN

Dresden DEMOCRAT. *See* Dresden yeoman

Dresden ENTERPRISE. w 1882+
pub 1903+
TU Ja 29 1932;S 14 1934

TENNESSEE patriot. w Ja 21 1839-
DLC F 4,S 25 1839
MWA O 16 1839

WEST TENNESSEE democrat. *See* Dresden yeoman

Dresden YEOMAN. w 1871-79||
1871-76? as West Tennessee democrat;
1877?-78? Dresden democrat
TDrE 1875

DUNLAP

TRIBUNE. w O 10 1889+
pub 1889+

DYERSBURG

NEAL'S state gazette. *See* Weekly state gazette

Weekly STATE GAZETTE. w O 1865+
1865-96? as Neal's state gazette
pub Mr 15 1905+
T O-N 10 1932
TU-J Ja 10 1885

Daily STATE GAZETTE. d O 15 1928+
pub 1928+

ELIZABETHTON

Elizabethton NEWS. w O 21 1926+
pub 1926+
T Ag 13 1931
TU S 28 1933;Ja 11,D 20 1934;Ja 20-Mr 3 1935

Elizabethton REPUBLICAN and manufacturers advocate. w Ap 21 1838-
DLC My 12 1838
MWA N 24,D 8 1838

Elizabethton STAR. d 1927+
T O 1 1928

TENNESSEE whig. *See* Knoxville whig and chronicle

ERWIN

MAGNET. w,d,sw 1891-1928||?
w 1891-1925;d 1926
T N 15 1923

Erwin NEWS. w 1924-
MWA Jl 16,25,Ag 22 1924
T N 21 1924

Erwin RECORD. w 1927+
TU [1933-34]

ETOWAH

Etowah ENTERPRISE. w Ja 7 1907+
pub 1907+
TSE 1932+
TU F 1 1934[35]

FAYETTEVILLE

Fayetteville EXPRESS. w 1873-86||?
T Mr-Jl,D 22 1880

IMPARTIAL compiler. w
T F 25 1827

INDEPENDENT yeoman. w 1833?-35||?
DLC Jl 31 1834
TKL F 13 1835

LINCOLN county news. w 1903+
TU [1930+]

LINCOLN journal. w
TH 1858-60

Fayetteville OBSERVER. w D 17 1850+
pub 1850-60;66+
TU D 1 1932[D 1934]+

STANDARD. w
T Mr 9 1858

STANDARD of the union. w 1836-
MWA N 3 1837

WESTERN cabinet. w O 2 1829-30||?
CSmH Ag 21 1830
DLC O 9-16 1829

WESTERN freeman. w 1828-33||?
T Ja 1 1833

FRANKLIN

FEDERAL knapsack. w Mr 7 1863-
OHi My 2 1863

HOME press. w 1852||?
T My 18-Je 3 1852

INDEPENDENT gazette. w
T N 24 1821;Ja 5,26,Mr 30-Ap 6,My 3,Je 8,Jl 20, S 14,28-O 19,N 2,16 1822;F 22,Mr 8,29, Ap 28,My 9-Je 20,Jl 4,18,N 7-14,D 5,19 1823; N 28,D 26 1823-Ja 9,23,F 13 1824

REVIEW-APPEAL. w Ap 20? 1831-
1831-40 as Western weekly review; 1830?-71? Weekly review; 1872?-90? Review and journal
Ct Ap 19 1833
DLC Je 28 1833;39;Ap 10 1840;Jl 2 1841
ICHi O 7,28 1865
MWA Ap 27 1832;S 19 1856
N F 17 1837
T Ja 13-Ap 20 1832;My 3-9 1834
TFW 1934+
TU [Ag 29 1912]
TxU My 9 1834-My 1836;Je 9 1837-56

WESTERN balance. w 1827-30||?
CSmH Ap 7 1830
DLC Ag 3-10 1827;Ja 30,Je 19,N 20 1829

WESTERN weekly review. *See* Review-appeal

WILLIAMSON county news. w My 1897+
pub 1897+
TU [1931-32]

FRIENDSHIP

TRI-COUNTY news. w 1912+
TU D 20 1934+

GAINESBORO

JACKSON county sentinel. w 1898+
TSE 1932+
TU [D 1934]+

GALLATIN

Gallatin COURIER. w
TxU Mr 20-Ap 17 1861

Gallatin EXAMINER. *See* Examiner-Tennessean

EXAMINER-TENNESSEAN. w 1860+
1860-1905 as Gallatin examiner
ICHi O 21,N 11 1865
NNHi Ag 19 1871
T Ja 20 1872 supp 1879
TxU F 11 1860-F 9 1861

Gallatin JOURNAL. w Ag 17 1827-
DLC S 20 1828;F 24,Mr 3 1829
MWA S 21 1827
T Mr 28 1828

REPUBLICAN sentinel and Sumner, Smith and Jackson intelligencer. w Ja 14 1840-
DLC Ja 28,Ap 28 1840

SUMNER county news. w 1898+
pub 1900+
TU [D 1934]+

SUMNER county republican. w Je 13 1868-
MBAt Je 13,Jl 4-11,25-Ag 15 1868

Gallatin TENNESSEAN. w 1872-1905||
United with Gallatin examiner to form Examiner-Tennessean
T S 2 1893

Gallatin UNION and Sumner advertiser. w 1834-43||?
1834-39? as Gallatin union
MWA My 30 1834
IU F 21 1840
T Ap 27 1838-Ja 10 1840;O 7 1841;Ap 7 1843

GREENEVILLE

Greeneville AMERICAN. w Ja?-D 2? 1874||
United with National union to form Greeneville union and American
DLC D 2 1874

AMERICAN economist and East Tennessee statesman. w 1823-25||?
DLC Ag 16 1823;Ap 17,My 1,Je 3,Jl 15,29 1824;O 8,22-N 5,D 3,17-24 1825
MWA Ap 30 1825
TKL Jl 15 1824

Greeneville DEMOCRAT. w 1858-
TKL Je 22 1859

Greeneville DEMOCRAT-SUN. w 1879-1928||?
1879-1920 as Greeneville democrat

Greeneville DEMOCRAT-SUN. d *See* Greeneville sun

EAST TENNESSEE miscellany. w S 21 1842-
DLC N 23 1842

EAST TENNESSEE news. w 1892-99||?
ICM My 11 1893
TKL My 5 1892

Greenville INTELLIGENCER. w Ag? 1874-76||?
DLC O 1 1874
NcD Mr 22 1875
TKL Ag 6 1875

NATIONAL union. *See* Greeneville union and American

NEW ERA. w Je 24 1865-85||?
DLC Jl 8,S 2,30-O 7,D 23 1865;Jl 7,S 15 1866;F 14 1867;Ja 12,Ag 4 1871;Je 21 1877
ICHi S 9,23-30;O 14,28-N 4 1865
OHi Ag 12,S 16 1865
TKL Je 15 1871

Greeneville SENTINEL and reporter. w D 14? 1870-73||?
1870-72? as Greeneville sentinel
TKL Je 8 1871

Greeneville SPY. w 1850-
DLC S 18 1851;My 20 1852 Je 1 1854
TKL Ap 17 1851;Ag 5 1852

Greeneville SUN. w 1891-1920||
United with Greeneville democrat to form Greeneville democrat-sun

Greeneville SUN. d 1918+
1921-31? as Greeneville democrat sun
sesqui-centennial ed Ag 11 1933
DLC Ag 11 1933
T Mr 3,My 30-31 1923;D 19 1929
TU Ja 17,20,22 1934

Greeneville UNION and American. w D 19 1866-75||?
1866-74 as National union
DLC Mr 7 1867;D 3 1874;D 23 1875
MWA My 18 1870
TKL Ag 17 1870

HAMPTON

To 1892? as Allentown

ALLENTOWN times. w Jl 29 1891-
TJT 1891-Ja 13 1892

HANSONHURST

Hansonhurst WEEKLY. w
TM Ag 2,30 1923

HARRIMAN

Harriman daily ADVANCE. d 1890-97||?
TKL Ja 26-27,Mr 3 1894

Harriman weekly ADVANCE. *See* Harriman record

Harriman RECORD. w 1890+
1890-1900 as Harriman weekly advance
pub 1919+
NN F 2 1893
NcD O 11,25 1894;D 26 1895
TU Ag 21 1928[32-34]+

Harriman TRIBUNE. w 1891-94||?
TKL My 10 1894

HARRISON

UNCONDITIONAL.
DLC Jl 16 1867

HARTSVILLE

Hartsville GLOBE. *See* Hartsville times

Hartsville SENTINEL. *See* Hartsville times

Hartsville TIMES. w Ja 11 1878-1912||
1878-87 as Hartsville sentinel; 1888-93 Hartsville globe; 1894-97 Vidette. Followed by Vidette 1913+
THV [1878-87;97-1912]

VIDETTE. w Ag 16-24 1862||
OCHi Ag 24 1862
THV Ag 16 1862

VIDETTE. w 1894-97. *See* Hartsville times

VIDETTE. w D 12 1913+
Third paper of this name. Follows Hartsville times
pub 1913+

HELENWOOD

SCOTT county call. w Mr-N 1887||?
TKL S 2,23-30,N 11 1887

HOHENWALD

LEWIS county herald. w 1894+
pub Mr 1920+
T S 18,D 18 1924;Ap 9,Ag 13 1925;Ja 28 1926

HUMBOLDT

COURIER-CHRONICLE. w 1886+
1886-Ja 10 1902 as Humboldt courier
pub [1908-19]+
TU Je 14 1934
TxU [Ag 27 1915-Je 16 1916]

SOLDIER'S budget. w Jl 24 1862-
OClWHi S 22 1862
WHi Jl 24,Ag 14-23,S 4,15-22 1862

TENNESSEE (*Continued*)

HUNTINGDON

Huntingdon ADVERTISER. w Jl 5 1839-
DLC Jl 5 1839

CARROLL county democrat. w 1888+
TU Mr 23 1934

TENNESSEE republican. w 1870+
pub 1920+
DLC Ap 7 1871
TU My 1 1931

HUNTSVILLE

CUMBERLAND chronicle. w 1889-1917||?
TKL O 6 1894

JACKSON

CENTRAL democrat. w
TxU S 1 1853

DISTRICT intelligencer and southern statesman. w
DLC My 15,Jl 10 1841

DISTRICT telegraph. w N 30 1837-39||?
DLC Jl 24(extra),Ag 16 1839
ICHi Mr 30 1838

FORKED deer blade. w 1883-
IU S 24 1887

Jackson GAZETTE. w 1824-30||?
Follows Pioneer
CSmH Ag 7 1830
DLC O 30 1824;My 28[S 10 1825-28]
MWA O 15 1825;N 29 1828
WHi My 29 1842-My 1826[Je 1828-D 4 1830]

PIONEER. w 1822-23||
Followed by Jackson gazette
DLC S 9 1823
NcU Ja 28 1823

Jackson REPUBLICAN. w 1842-
Ap 18 1845-46? as Republican
DLC Jl 22 1842;S 20,D 20 1844;45-F,O 16,N 6-20,D 4,18 1846;D 3,17 1847;Ja 7,21,F 4-11, Mr 3-10,24 1848
NcU S 2 1842
TDrE 1848

SOUTHERN statesman. w 1831-33||?
T F 5 1831-Ja 12,F 23-Je 8,22-S 21 1833

Jackson SUN. w 1873-1906||?
1879?-95? as Tribune and sun
MWA Ja 4 1884
T Je 9 1876;F 9 1877;Ja 24 1879

Jackson SUN. d 1888+
1888-95? as Jackson tribune and sun
pub 1914+
T Je 6-Jl 27 1923
TU N 5 1933

Jackson TRIBUNE. w 1869-70. *See* Whig and tribune

Jackson TRIBUNE and sun. *See* Jackson sun

TRUTH teller and district sentinel. w Ap 25 1834-
DLC Jl 11 1834

WEST TENNESSEE plain dealer. w
TxU Mr 8 1872

WEST TENNESSEE whig. O 7 1842-65||?
DLC O 7,28 1842;Mr 9,My 4-11,25-D 7,21 1849
ICHi O 7-N 4 1865
MWA Ag 31 1855
T O 29 1847
TKL My 28 1847
TM N 23 1849
TxU N 23 1849

WHIG and tribune. w 1869-78||?
1869-70? as Jackson tribune. United with Jackson sun to form Tribune sun, later Jackson sun

JAMESTOWN

FENTRESS county gazette. *See* Fentress county news

FENTRESS county news. w 1891+
1896-1916 as Fentress county gazette
T [1895-96]-[1900-02]-[05-06]-[14-16]
TSE 1932+
TU F 26 1931

MOUNTAIN courier. w 1930-33||?
T Ap 29 1932

JASPER

Jasper HERALD. *See* Valley herald

VALLEY herald. w 1873-90||
1873-80? as Jasper herald
TKL D 6 1878

JEFFERSON CITY

DANDRIDGE banner. w S 5 1928+
pub 1928+

JEFFERSON county standard. w 1926+
pub [1926-32]+
T O 13,N 17 1932;Ja 12 1933
TJeD S 1932+
TU Ja 25,Jl 26 1934

JOHNSON CITY

Johnson City CHRONICLE. d Jl 3 1921+
Sunday ed as Chronicle staff-news
pub [1921]+
T [1923]

COMET. w Mr 22 1884-1919||?
TJT 1884-1912
TKL My 26 1887
TU D 21 1899

ENTERPRISE. w 1883-91||?
T Ag 4 1883

STAFF-NEWS. d 1891+
1891-1923 as Johnson City staff
Sunday ed as Chronicle staff-news
T Ja-My 1926
TJT F 20 1896;Ja 25 1907;O 20 1908;S 19,O 10,25,29,N 21 1912;N 27,D 3,20 1921
TU F 26 1909
WHi O 31 1923

TENNESSEE republican. w 1906-
TJT My 10,24,Je 14 1906

JONESBORO

ADVANCE. w
TJT Je 15 1911-F 1913;O 17-24,N-D 5 1918;Jl 24 1919;Ja-Mr 18,Ap 22,O,N 1920;Ja 27,Je 22 1921;O 19-26 1922;Ap 4-11 1923;De 17 1924; Je 17 1925;Ap 28-My 4 1926;Ag 24-S 7 1927; Ap 25,Je 6 1928

Jonesboro ECHO. d O 30 1884-
TKL O 30 1884

Jonesboro EXPRESS. w 1860-63||?
T Ja 25, 1861
TKL My 31 1861;Jl 1 1863

FARMER'S journal. w N 25 1825-28||?
DLC N 25-D 16,20 1825; F 24,D 21 1826;S 15 1827
T Je 9 1827
TKL S 27 1828

HERALD and tribune. w Ag 26 1869+
DLC O 7 1869;Jl 28 1870
MBAt Ag 26,S 30 1869
T N 3 1870;N 1 1876
TJT Ja-Mr 1886;O 1894-Mr 1895;Jl 21,N 1897-Je 15 1898;Ap 19-N 1899;1908;Ja 13-20,Mr 3,17 1909;Mr 8-22 1911;Ja 17-Mr 20 1912;D 10 1913-Mr 1914;D 29 1915-F 9,Ag 30-S,N 1 1916;Jl 31-D 1919;Mr 25 1920;Ag 6 1924; Ap 7,Ag 18-S 1,29-O 13,27-N,D 1,15-22 1926
TKL F 6 1873;D 15 1881;N 17,D 1 1887
TU [1889-1906;30;34]+
TxU Mr 10 1870;My 2 1872;My 25 1876;N 2 1882

Jonesboro JOURNAL. w 1875-83||?
TxU S 8 1875;Ag 8 1878
VU Jl 18 1878

OLD HICKORY. Je 1 1846-
DLC Je 1 1846

RAILROAD journal. w Ap 6 1850-54||?
NcU F 1,My 10,Ag 31,O 18 1851;F 11,D 23 1854
T My 21 1853
TKL Ap 13,27-My 4,Ag 3,S 21-O 5,26 1850

TENNESSEE patriot. w 1872||?
T Ap 27 1872

TENNESSEE sentinel. w 1835-45||?
DLC Jl 31 1841;S 28 1844;Jl 19 1845
T O 19 1844
TKL My 8,18 1841;Ja 25 1845

Jonesboro TIMES. w 1877-78||?
TJT O 18 1878
TKL O 18 1878
TxU N 8 1878

Jonesboro UNION. w Je? 1860-
MWA My 4 1861

UNION flag and commercial advertiser. w My 19 1865-72||?
DLC S 25 1868;Ap 8,Jl 22-29 1870
ICHi O 13-27 1865
OClWHi O 19 1866
MBAt Jl 16 1869
MWA O 19 1866;F 18(extra)1870
T Ja 26 1872
TKL D 22 1865;Ap 5,16,S 6 1867;My 29,O 9 1868;Ag 11 1871;N 15 1872
TU My 11 1866;D 17 1869
TxU D 15 1865

WASHINGTON republican and farmer's journal. w Ag 5 1832-36||?
DLC N 4 1832;Ja 12 1833;F 1 1834
NcD Ag 27 1836
TKL D 26 1835

Jonesboro WHIG. *See* Knoxville whig and chronicle

KINGSPORT

Kingsport TIMES. d 1916+
TU [1934+]

KINGSTON

Weekly CYCLONE. w S 10 1881-
TKL O 8-15,N 5,19 1881

Kingston EAGLE and gazetteer. w 1855-
MWA Ap 26 1856

EAST TENNESSEAN. w Jl 29 1865-1906||
ICHi O 7-21 1865
NcU Ap 17 1879
T Jl 13 1876
TKL Je 2 1868;Ap 13 1876;O 9 1879

Kingston GAZETTE. w Mr 30 1854-55||?
TKL 1854-Ap 7 1855

INDEPENDENT. *See under* Knoxville

ROANE county banner. w 1928+
pub 1933+
TU [1931-32]

ROANE county herald. w 1877-78||?
TKL Ap 11-18,My 2,16,30,Je 13-20,Ag 1,15,O 10,24 1878

ROANE county republican. w 1880-96||?
TKL S 15,O 3 1887

VALLEY news. *See* Independent (Knoxville)

KNOXVILLE

ADVERTISER and commercial reporter. w 1869-72||
1869-Ag 1870 as Tennessee advertiser
DLC S 2 1872
OClWHi [Ag 1870-Ap 1871]

Knoxville weekly AGE. w Ap 2 1874-1877||
1874-Jl 1 1875 as Grange outlook; Jl 8-S 20? 1875 Living age and outlook; S 27? 1875Jl 1876 Living age and grange outlook. United with Knoxville tribune to form Knoxville tribune and age, later Knoxville tribune
DLC [1874-Jl]N 9 1876;F 15,Mr 8 1877
TKL O 22 1874;Ja 21,F 4,Mr 25,My 6,Ag 19 1875;Ja 13,Mr 23 1876
TU My 20,Ag 12 1875

Daily Knoxville AGE. d 1875-77||
1875-76 as Age
Ja 4 1877 incorrectly titled Weekly Knoxville age
DLC Ag 2 1876;Ja 4,Mr 10 1877
MWA S 4 1875;S 2 1876
TKL S 28,N 16 1876

AMERICAN campaigner. w Ap 21-N 17 1856||
Campaign paper
MWA Ap 21,My 12,26,Je 23,Jl-Ag 4,25,S 8-15, O,N 17 1856
T S 29 1856
TxU Ag 18 1856

AMERICAN statesman. *See* Knoxville statesman

AMERICAN whig and Knoxville enquirer. w D 31 1828-My 6 1829||
Follows Enquirer. Followed by Western chronicle
DLC D 31 1828
IU D 31 1828-Ja 7,Mr 18,Ap 22-My 6 1829
MWA Ja 14,F 11-25,Mr 11,25-Ap 1,My 6 1829
TKL F 4 1829

ARGUS and commercial herald. w Je 27 1839-D 4? 1844||
Followed by Standard, later Knoxville standard
DLC Je 27,Jl 30 1839;Ja 21-D 23 1840;S 4 1844
MWA Jl 18,O 1 1839
NcU My 19 1840;F 22 1843
TH Je 1839-Je 1840;Je 1841-Je 1842

ARMY mail bag. w Ja 31? 1864-
Suspended Ap 18-My 23 1864
Ja 31?-Ap 11 1864 pub in Lexington, Ky.?
MBAt My 30-Je 6 1864
MWA My 30-O 8 1864

BROWNLOW'S Knoxville whig. *See* Knoxville whig

Knoxville daily BULLETIN. d Je 6 1863-64||?
DLC Je 12,S 5,7,12,14,16,O 13,15,17 1863
MBAt Je 6,12,Jl 15 1864
MWA Je 10 1864
OClWHi S 8,14-16,21,30,O 7 1863,Je 17 1864
TKL Je 30,Jl 8 1864

Knoxville weekly CHRONICLE. w Ap 6 1870-Mr 24 1875||
United with Brownlow's Knoxville whig to form Knoxville whig and chronicle
DLC Ja 4,My 18 1870;Ja 25,F 22,Ap 19-26, My 24,O 25 1871;Ja 24,Je 19,Ag 7,S 11,N 27 1872;Mr 29,Je 11,Jl 2,30,Ag 20-27 1873;F 25,My 13,Je 17,Jl 15-22,S 2 1874;Ja 6 1875
MWA Ja 8-22,F 5,19,D 10-17,31 1873-Ap 22, My 6,20,N 25-D 23 1874;75
TKL Ap 12 1871-Mr 24 1875
TU [1870-71]-Mr 25 1874

Knoxville daily CHRONICLE. d My 1870-86||
DLC My 11,Je 10,12,S 4,O 7,20,23 1870;71-Je 25,Ag 27 1873;Mr 4,Ag 13(extra),S 11,O 7,D 23 1874;Ap 4,28,Jl 15,O 16,N 14 1875;F 23,S 27,N 17 1876;Je 9,Ag 9,D 8 1877;Jl 30,O 24 1878-Je 30,Ag 5,S 3 1886
MWA Je 4 1870;Ja 15 1873;Je 2 1874
TC O 30 1883
TKL Ap 6 1870-S 4 1886
TU 1870-[72-78;80-86]

Knoxville daily COMMERCIAL. d Ja 1866-67||?
CtY Ja 23-24,29,F 19,21,23,26,28,Mr 1-3,5-7,22-23 1866
DLC Mr 12,My 10,Ag 4 1866
NcD Ap 28 1866
OCHi F 5,7,19 1866
T My 8, 1866
TKL Ag 1,S 5,O 10,17,D 12 1866;Ap 3,Je 22,26 1867
TU My 5 1866

Weekly COMMERCIAL. w Ja 23? 1866-67||?
DLC Mr 13,Ap 24,O 2,30 1866
MWA My 17 1867
N Je 26 1866
TKL Mr 13 1866

Daily DISPATCH. d Jl 1879-81||
DLC Ag 1,16,O 3,18 1879;Jl 15,Ag 2,6,19,S 26,29,O 5,10 1880;Ja 7,Ap 8,Jl 15,27 1881
T Mr 24 1880
TKL Ag 4,9,S 20,O 2,10,17,N 11,17 1879;N 25,27 1880
TU Ap 17 1880

DOLLAR plebian. *See* Knoxville plebian

Daily EAST TENNESSEAN. d F 27 1862-
OClWHi F 27 1862

EAST TENNESSEE news. w 1906+
Negro
TU D 14 1912;Ap 29 1926;My 19 1932;F 1,N 29,D 20 1934

TENNESSEE (*Continued*)

KNOXVILLE—*Continued*

ENQUIRER. w Jl 21 1824-D 24 1828||
1824-N 15 1826 as Knoxville enquirer. Followed by American whig and Knoxville enquirer
DLC N 10 1824;Mr 17 1825-28
IU O 15,29-D 3,17-24 1828
MWA My 1,30-S 5,O 10-N 7,21,D 12 1827-F 6,Mr,Ap 9,23,My-O,N 19-26,D 10 1828
MiU-C [1828]
OHi Jl-D 1827;Ap 16-N 1828
TKL O 13 1824-Ag,S 26,O 24,N 14,28 1827;F 20-Mr 12,26,Ap 16,My 14,Jl 9 1828

FLAG of the union. w Ag 1- 1844||
Campaign paper
MWA O 24 1844
TKL Ag 13,O 3 1844

Knoxville daily FREE PRESS. 1867-68 *See* Daily press and herald

Weekly FREE PRESS. w Jl 4 1867-68||
United with Knoxville messenger to form Press and messenger
TKL Ag 22 1867

Knoxville FREE PRESS. d Ap 30 1896-
TKL My-O 1926
TU [1896-97]

GRANGE outlook. *See* Knoxville weekly age

Knoxville HERALD. d O 27 1867-O 1 1868||
United with Knoxville daily free press to form Daily press and herald
MWA D 11,25 1867
TKL O 31 1867-68

HOLSTON journal. w D 10 1862-
DLC Jl 16 1863
NcD Ja 29,F 12-19,Mr 5,19,Ap 9-23,My 7 1863
OClWHi F 26,Mr 12,My 7,Je 11-18,Jl 30-Ag 6 1863
TKL Ag 13 1863
TU Ja 29 1863

INDEPENDENT. w Je 2? 1873-75||
1873-Je? 1874 as Valley news (Kingston); Jl ?-D 1874 Independent (Kingston)
TKL F 17,Ap 28,Je 2,O 6,N 10,D 8-15 1874; F 26,Ap 9,My 12,Je 11,Ag 6 1875
TU Ap 28 1874

Knoxville INDEPENDENT. w S 1 1894+
DLC O 4 1896;Jl 23,N 6 1898
TU Ja 26,Mr 10,31,S 29 1934

***Knoxville INTELLIGENCER.** w 1817-Jl 14 1823||?
DLC Mr 27-Ap 9,23-My 7,28-Ag 6,S 10-D 24 1822;Ja 22,F 17,Mr 10,27-Ap 28,My 12-26,Je 9-23,Jl 14 1823
TKL Mr 27 1822-Jl 4 1823

Knoxville JOURNAL. d F 26 1885+
Jl 1 1898-F 9 1925 as Knoxville journal and tribune (title varies slightly)
pub 1898+
DLC 1898-Ag,N 1918+
IU N 8 1894
M Mr 24 1929
MWA S 27 1898
T Jl-D 1896;1920+
TC Je 15 1889
TKL F 26 1885-N 2 1886;Je 1887-97;Jl-D 1898; Ap 1899-Mr,Jl-D 1906;Ap-Je,O-D 1907;Jl-S 1908;09-Mr 1916;17-24+?
TMaM 1923—
TU [1887-1920]-[22;33]34
VU Je 26 1903

Knoxville Sunday JOURNAL.
Ct S 16 1934
WHi S 16 1934

Weekly JOURNAL and tribune. w 1885-1922||
1885-97 as Weekly journal
NcD Ag 10 1904

LITTLE tattler.
TxU My 24 1856

LIVING age and grange outlook. *See* Knoxville weekly age

MAGNET. w 1888-
DLC D 30 1888

Knoxville MERCURY. tw 1856-
MWA Ja 6,F 5,7,Ap 18 1857

Knoxville MESSENGER. *See* Press and messenger

MESSENGER of peace. *See* Press and messenger

NEGRO world. w N 17 1887-95||?
Negro
DLC Ag 10,N 24 1888;F 2 1889;My 7 1892
IU F 3 1888
OClWHi F 28 1891
TKL O 15,N 26 1887

Knoxville NEWS-SENTINEL. d 1881+
1881-1926 as Knoxville news
T Mr 1899-S 1907
TKL N 21 1921+
TU F 18,Jl 27 1925[27-35]+

Knoxville PLEBIAN. w D 23? 1849-
1849-50 as Plebian; My 3 1851 Dollar plebian
MWA Jl 29,O 21-28 1850;My 3 1851;Jl 3,N 6 1852
TU Mr 25 1850

Daily morning PLEBIAN. d D 14? 1851-
MWA D 20 1851;Ja 2,23 1852

POST. w Ap 22 1841-48||
My 17 1842-Ap 11 1843 as Knoxville Tennessee post. Followed by Athens post, later Post-Athenian (Athens)
DLC Ap 22,My 1 1841;F 23 1842
MWA My 15 1841;Ap 20 1842-[43]Ja 10,24-F, Mr 19-26,Ap 9,My 28,Ag 27,O 22,N 12,D 11 1844
MiU-C [1842-44]
THi Ap 1840-Ap 1843
TKL My 17,Ag 30 1842;Mr 21 1843,F 7,S 10,N 1844

Daily PRESS and herald. d Je 1867-76||
1867-Ap? 1868 as Knoxville daily free press (title varies slightly). Followed by Knoxville tribune
DLC F 14,My 19,Jl 8,N 19 1868;Je 5-6 1869;F 12 1870;Mr 1 1871;Ag 20 1872
MBAt N 23 1869
MWA D 25 1867;My 22-23,Jl 12,16,22 1868;D 19 1871
OClWHi F 13,Mr 26 1868
TKL O 4 1867;O 3 1868-Mr 25,O 31-D 1876
TU D 9 1869;Ap 16 1871;My 30 1873;Ap 1 1875

PRESS and messenger. w 1866-76||
1866-68 title varies: Messenger of peace; Knoxville messenger
DLC F 17 1869;N 23 1870;O 15 1873
MWA My 9 1867;Ja 8-22,F 26,D 10-31 1873; Ja 14-28,F 11-My 6,20,O 21,D 2-23 1874;Ja-Jl 14,Ag 11-D 15 1875
TKL 1868-75
TU [1868-69;72]

***Knoxville REGISTER.** w Ag 13 1816-N 20? 1863||
D 25 1839-41? as Knoxville register and weekly times
CSmH Ag 18 1830
Ct [1830-31 34-35]
CtY Mr 15 1860
DLC 1821-D 23 1826;28-30;S 7,21,N 23 1836;S 4 1839;F 23 1842;Ag 28 1844;N 12 1845;Jl 29 1846;Je 30 1847;Ja 19-D 19 1850;Ja 8 1852;Ja 24,Je 12-19 1856;Mr 17 1859;Jl 8 1862
MBAt Ja 7 1822
MWA D 12 1823;Mr 26 1824;F 11-Mr 4,Ap 15 1825;Ag 16,30 1826;Je 6,25(extra)S 12,N 7-14,28 1827;F 13,Mr 12-19,S 10 1828;F 18,Je 3, 17-Jl,Ag 12,S 23,O 14-21,D 2,30 1829-Ja 6, 20,Mr 3,Je 30,N 3 1830;Ag 1 1832;D 4 1833;Mr 5,19-My 7,21,Je 4-11,Jl 16,30,Ag 13-S 3,D 13 (extra)31 1834;F 4,Mr 4,25,Ap 15,My 6-13,23 (extra)Je 10,D 2 1835;O 12 1836;F 1-8,Ap 19, My 3,31-Je 21,Jl 5,19-Ag 9,30,O 11-18 1837;F 28,Je 27,Ag 8 1838;Ja 2,Ap 17-24,Jl 23(extra) S 18,O 8,22 1839;Ja 15-22,F 5,19,Mr 11-25,Ap 8,22,Je 3,17-Ag 19 1840;Mr 17,My-Je 2,16,S 15 1841;O 5,N 2 1842;Ag 9,N 1 1843;Ag 28,S 11,O 2 1844;My 14 1845;F 4 1846;Ja 13 1847;F 23,Mr 15,Je 14,O 25 1848;F 28 1849;O 24,N 14 1850;Ja 9,Mr 13-20,My 29(supp)1851;Ja 8, Je 2,O 4,6 1852;Jl 1,4,25(extra)Ag 26,S 14 1853;Ap 26,Jl 26,31,Ag 11,16,28,O 16,27 1854; Ja 24,My 10,24,Jl 19-26,Ag 16-23,S 6-13,D 13 1855;Mr 6,24,Ap 10,24,My 15,Je 26,Jl 3,31-Ag 7,S 25,O 16,N 27-D 4,18-25 1856;Ja 8,29,Ap 2, 16,My 7,Je 4-18,Jl 9,Ag 6-13,S 24-O 1,22,N 26 1857;F 3-17,Mr 10-17,31,Je 2,23,N 17 1859; Mr 10 1863
MiU-C My 23(extra)1835;Je 18 1857
NcD Ap 24 1833;Ja 20 1847;Ag 30 1855
NcU Ap 6 1831;O 28 1835
OCHi [D 1860-O 3,D 26 1861-My 8 1862]
OClWHi S 27 1860
OOxM Ap 29 1829;Je 22 1850
P-M D 21 1836
T F 21 1827 F 23,S 26,D 12 1850;Ag 6 1852;F 14,Mr 14-21,Ap 4 1855;O 7 1858
TH Mr 1830-F 1834;My 1849-Jl 1850
TKL Jl 30 1822;Jl 29 1825[26-29]D 4 1833;Ja 1-8,Jl 2 1835;Mr 16,Jl 13,O 19,N 2 1836;F 8, Mr 8 1837;My 30 1838;D 25 1839-D 16 1840; D 21 1842-D 10 1845;Ja 14,F 4,Je 24,Ag 19 1846[Mr-D 1847;My-D 1848]Ja 24,My 30 1849; F 2,Mr 2,30 O 3,N 28,D 19 1850;Ja 16,Mr 20, Ap 3,My 15,Ag 14,O 16 1851;Mr 10,Jl 1852; Je 22,Jl 25,D 28 1853;S 1 1854;My 1855-Je 17 1858[My-D 1861]
TU [1823-24]-[29;35-37;46-50;52-56;61-63]
Tx D 30 1858
TxU O 29 1845;Je 10,Ag 5,D 16 1846;Ap 14 1847

Daily REGISTER. d Ja 1861-63||?
1861 as Knoxville daily register
CtHT Je 26 1863
CtY N 8-D 14 1862;Ap 19-Jl 15 1863
DLC Jl 5,S 26,O 19,N 9,30,D 12,16 1862;Ja 4,23,My 12 1863
MBAt My 12 Je 23,S 15-16,19,25,28,30,O 6-10, 12-14,17,19,21-22,24-25,27,29-N 1,3 1863
NcD Mr 18,Ap 19,30[My-Ag]S 26 1862;Mr 13-14,Je 26 1863
OCHi [My 29 1861-Ag 27 1863]
OClWHi F 28 Je 5,10,Jl 11,S 20,O 5,23,29,N 21 1861[62-Ag 26 1863]
OHi My 23,Jl 22,Ag 14 1862
T Ap 3 1862;Mr 4,17-18,21,24,27 1863
TKL F 12 1862

Knoxville REPUBLICAN. w S 14 1831-34||
Followed by Uncle Sam
DLC O 24 1832
MWA Jl 11,D 26 1832
OOxM O 24 1832-F 19 1834
TKL N 23,D 28 1831;Ja 25,F 15 1832
TU Jl 17 1833

REPUBLICAN. w 1879-82. *See* Republican chronicle

Knoxville REPUBLICAN. w Je 23 1891-94||
DLC Jl 21, 1891;My 13-20,O 7,28,N 11 1892; F 16-23,Mr 16-30,Ap 20,Je 14,28,Jl 5,O 18 1894
TC O 23 1891;S 22-29 1893
TKL [1891-92]-N 8 1894
TU 1891-94

REPUBLICAN banner. w Ja 25 1894-
DLC F 8-15 1894

REPUBLICAN chronicle. w Ja 1 1879-S 1 1886||
1879-Mr? 1883 as Republican
DLC Ja 8,My 26,O 6,N 17 1879;Ag 16-23,S 13 1880;Ja 24,Ap 5-12,My 10,Je 7,S 6,27,N 22 1881; O 5(extra),10-17 1882;Mr 5,Ap 30,Jl 16 1884;My 20-27,Jl 29,S 30,O 21 1885;Ja 27,F 3,24,Mr 17,My 12,Ag 18,S 1 1886
MWA Ja 1 1879
TC Mr 29 1880
TKL F 23 1880;82-S 1 1886
TU N 10-D 1879;Mr 29,Ap 26,My 17 1880;Je 14,S 20,N 15,29 1881;Ag 1,22-29 1882;My 30 1883;F 13,Mr 19,Ap 16 1884

REPUBLICAN leader. w Ap 5-N 1 1894||
DLC [Ap-N 1894]
TKL Ap-Ag 9,23-30,S 13-O 11,25-N 1894
TU [1894]

Knoxville SENTINEL. d D 20 1886-1926||
United with Knoxville news to form Knoxville news-sentinel
MWA Mr 2 1893
TKL F 1887-Je 1888;Jl-D 1889;Jl-S 20 1891; 93-Je 1895;Ja 7-Mr 25 1896;Jl-S 1898;Ja-Mr 1899;1900-04;O-D 1905;O-D 1906[09]-O 1926
TU [1892-1916]F 26 1925;Ap 13 1926
TxGR Ja 31 1916

Knoxville weekly SENTINEL. w, sw S 10 1887-1916||?
w 1887-91?
DLC S 10 1887
P-M D 17 1912
TKL Je-D 1892

Daily SOUTHERN chronicle. d Je 28-Ag 26 1863||?
CtY Jl 11,18 1863
NcD Je 30 1863
OCHi [Je-Ag 1863]
OClWHi [Je-Ag 1863]
TKL Jl 14 1863

SOUTHERN citizen. w O 17 1857-
KHi O 31 1857
MWA Ja 21,F 4,Mr 18,Je 3 1858
TKL My 13 1858

SOUTHERN commercial gazette. w O 1888-
DLC N 2,9,D 11 1888
TKL O 19,N 2-9 1888

SOUTHERN herald. w F 5 1896-
DLC Mr 19 1896

Knoxville STANDARD. w D 11 1844-56||?
Title varies slightly: Standard; Standard and reformer
DLC D 18 1844;Mr 26 1845-Ap 11 1848;Ja 10-S 20 1855;Ag 27 1856
MWA Ap 14,S 29-O 13,N-D 8,22 1846[47]My 15-22,Je 5 1849;Ap 4,My 9,Ag 2,16-23,S 13 1855;Ap 17,My 1,Je 21-28,Ag 9 1856
T Ja 1 1845;N 4 1848
TKL Ja 5 1847

Knoxville STATESMAN. w D 14? 1852-
1852- 1854 as American statesman
DLC Ap 20 1853;Ja 7-Ap 29,My 19-D 2 1854
MWA My 18,Je 1,29,Jl 23 1853;Ag 5 1854
TKL Jl 6 1853

TENNESSEE advertiser. *See* Advertiser and commercial reporter

Knoxville TENNESSEE post. *See* Post

TIMES. sw My 14 1839-O 30? 1840||
Merged with Knoxville register
DLC My 14-21 1839;Ag 4,O 30 1840
MWA My 14,Ag 27 1839;Ap 3-7,24,My 13,Jl 24,Ag 28,O 13 1840
TKL My 1839-My 15 1840

Sunday TOPIC. w 1885-87||
DLC D 20 1885;F 7,Ap 11,25,Je 27,Jl 24,Ag 8, 22-29 1886;Mr 13,Ap 10,24 1887

Knoxville TRIBUNE. w My 1846-1860||
Merged with Knoxville register
DLC F 24 1847;N 29 1848
MWA Jl 7,S 1 1847;Ap 19,My 3,Je 7 1848
T Je 9-16,S 29-O 13,N 3-10,24,D 15,29 1847; Ja 25,F 9,23,Mr 15-29 1848;S 13,Ap 11 1849
TKL S 2 1846;S 29 1847;Ap 26,S 5,N 15 1848
TU [1847;49]
Tx Mr 15 1848

Knoxville weekly TRIBUNE. w 1876-97||
Follows Knoxville press and herald. United with Weekly journal to form Weekly journal and tribune
DLC Jl 20 1876;Ap 12,O 18,D 20 1877;Ja 31, O 10 1878;Ap 17,Ag 21-28 1879;S 8 1880;Ap 6,N 9 1881;Je 28 1882
MWA N 9 1876;Jl 4 1879
WHi Ap 23 1884-Ap 28 1886

Knoxville TRIBUNE. d 1876-98||
Follows Daily press and herald. Title varies: Knoxville daily tribune; Knoxville daily tribune and age. United with Knoxville journal to form Knoxville journal and tribune, later Knoxville journal
DLC N 8,25 1876;F 20,Ap 25,Je 14,16,Ag 20 1877;Ja 9,19,F 6,Mr 16,My 5,18-19,N 28,D 8 1878; Jl 25,Ag 17,S 5,9 1879;F 7,Je 30, Ag 28,31,S 5,O 12,N 18 1880;F 12,S 21 1882; Ja 14,N 16 1883;N 27 1885;Je 19 1889;N 7 1893;Ap 27 1898
MWA N 25 1888;Ag 16 1896
NcD Je 29,Ag 10,17 1890;O 18 25,N 8 1891;Mr 15 1895
T [1895-98]
TJT F 16 1898
TKL Je-Ag 1876;77-O 1879;Ag 1880-Jl 1883;87-N 1894 95;Ap 1896-Je 1898
TN 1891-[95]-[97-98]
TU [1879;82-87;93-97]

Tri-weekly TRUE American. tw Jl 18?-Ag 9 1856||
Merged with Knoxville standard
MWA Jl 30 1856

Daily TRUE republican. d 1871-
DLC Ap 10,My 12 1871

TENNESSEE (*Continued*)

KNOXVILLE—*Continued*

TRUE republican. w 1871-
TKL Je 6,Jl 10 1871

UNCLE SAM. sw Ap-My? 1834||?
Follows Knoxville republican (1831-34)
DLC My 10 1834
TKL Ap 26,My 3 1834

VEDETTE. w My 16? 1840-
Campaign paper
MWA Je 18,Jl 13,Ag 1-8 1840

WATCHTOWER. w My 6? 1840-
Campaign paper
MWA Je 17?,Jl 15?, Ag 19? 1840
TC S 2? 1840

WESTERN chronicle. w My 13 1829-30||?
Follows American whig and Knoxville enquirer
CSmH Je 3 1829
DLC My 13,Jl 1-8,29-Ag 5,S 2,30,N 27 1829; Ja 6,20 1830
IU Mr 20 1829
TKL O 27 1830

Tri-weekly WHIG. tw Ja 4 1859-
CSmH Je 20 1861
DLC Ja 4-D 29 1859;F 21,Je 11 1861;Jl 12, 19 1867
MWA D 6 1859;Ap 5,N 1 1860;F 9,Mr 7,My 23 1861
OCHi Ja 24 1860[Ja 22-Jl 1861]
TKL N 24 1859
TU [1860-61]

Knoxville WHIG. d F 2 1869-70||
O 12-D 1869 as Knoxville daily whig
MBAt [F 11-D 1869]
MWA O 26 1869;Ag 10 1870
NcD Ag 3 1870
TU 1869-70

Knoxville WHIG and chronicle. w My 16 1839-Mr? 1883||?
1839-My 1840 as Tennessee whig (Elizabethton); My 1840-N 3 1841 Whig (Jonesboro); N 10 1841-My 11 1842 Jonesborough whig (running title My 28-N 3 1841 Jonesborough Tennessee whig); My 18 1842-My 12 1849 Jonesborough whig and independent journal; My 19 1849-Ap 7 1855 Brownlow's Knoxville whig and independent journal; Ap 14 1855-O 26 1861 Brownlow's weekly whig; N 11 1863-F 21 1866 Brownlow's Knoxville whig and rebel ventilator; F 28 1866-Ja 27 1869 Brownlow's Knoxville whig. United with Republican to form Republican chronicle
Suspended between O 26 1861-N 11 1863; F 1872-Mr 3 1875
CSmH Mr 23 1861
CtHT N 11 1863;Ja 9,Mr 5,Ap 9-16,27,30-My 7 1864
CtY Ja 26-Je 15 1861;N 11-18 1863;Ja 9-Jl 29,,S 3,14-D 1864;Ja 25,F 22,Ap 5 1865
DLC 1839-Ap 19,My 19 1849-O 26 1861;N 11 1863-S 15,O 20,D 8,22 1869[70-71;75-82]
ICHi Ap 9,Ag 17 1864;N 8 1865
IHi Mr 16 1861;Ap 19 1865
IaGG [N 11 1863-Je 18 1864]
MBAt Jl 10 1844;Ap 2,Jl 9,S 28,O 26 1864;O 18 1865;Ja 17,31-F 21,Mr-Je 6,20-Jl 11,25,Ag 8-S 12,26-O 3, 17-31,N 28 1866-Ja 16,30-F,Mr 13,27-My,Je 12-Ag 21,S 4-11,25 1867-Ja 22,F-Ap,My 13-27,Je 10-S 23,O-N 11,25 1868-Ja 13,27-F 3 1869
MWA Je 13-20 1839;F 20,My 6,N 25-D 2 1840;My 28-Je 2 1841;F 28,Ap 10,My 1,Je 26,Jl 17-24,Ag 28,S 11 1844;Ap 2,30 1845; Ja 28,F 18,Mr 18,Ap 1,My 6,N 4,18 1846; Ja 20,Mr 24,Ap 7-14,My 5,Je 2,Ag 25,S 15, O 6 1847;O 26 1850;Mr 15,S-D 1851[Ja 24-O 1852;Ja-S 17 1853]S 30 1854;Ja 27,Je 16-Jl 7,S 1,N 10,D 15 1855;Ja 12,Mr 22-29,Ap 12-26,Je 7,Jl 5,O 25,D 6 1856;Ja 10-24,Mr 28,My 2,23,Je 6,20-Jl 4,18,Ag 1-8,N 14-21 1857;O 23,D 11 1858;Ja 8-15,29,Ag 13 1859; Mr 17 1860;Mr 16,Ap 6,Ag 10 1861;N 11 1863-Je,Jl 23,Ag 10-17,S 28,N 16 1864;Ja 11, 25,Ap 26,My 24 1865;Ag 22,O 10,N 28,D 19 1866;F 20,Jl 3 1867;Ja 29-F 5,Ap 29,Jl 8,Ag 19 1868;Ja 13 1869;Mr-D 22 1875
MiU-C O 26 1850[63-64]
MnHi Ja 9 1864
N Je 27 1866
NBHi Ja 9 1864
NN Mr 22 1843;N 11-18 1863;Ja 23 1864;Ap 19,My 17,31 1865
NNHi Ap 26 1865
NcD Je 17 1846;F 28,Jl 17 1852;N 10 1860;Je 1 1861;N 11 1863;F 20 1864
NcU Ag 18 1849;Mr 29 1851;My 28 1853;O 26 1861
OCHi My 26,S 22 1855;Ap 19-26,My 17,N 22 1856;Mr 21,My 30,Je 13-20,Jl 25,D 19 1857; My 25,Ag-O 1861;N 11 1863;Ap 9 1864
OClWHi N 11-18 1863;Ja-Je,Ag 10-17,S 28, N 16 1864;Ja 4-11,Mr 1 1865;Jl 4 1866;F 19 1868
T Je 15 1861;Mr 22,Ap 5 1843;My 6 1845;S 1 1847;My 18 1862;Ja 23 1864;Mr 29 1865
TKL Jl 18 1839;Ap 16 1840;My 12 1841;D 21 1842;F 15 1843;Je 25,Jl 23,Ag 2,O 7 1845[Je 1849-51]Ja 10-24,Jl 3,N 13-20,D 11 1852;My 26 1855;Mr 15,My 24,Je 7 1856;D 12-19 1857; Ja 1,My 21,Ag 13 1859;Ja 5,Je 2,D 15 1860 [My-O 1861]N 11 1863[64-65]F 7,21(supp), My 23,Je 20,Jl 25 1866;Je 22,26 1867;Mr 11, Je 10;S 16,O 14 1868;F 24,Je 10,Jl 9,21,S 30, O 13 1869;S 18,N 8 1870;Ap 1875-Mr 2 1883
TN [1863-65]
TU Jl 21 1844;Jl 14 1847;Jl 28 1849;N 20 1850;Ag 14 1858;Ag 25,S 29 1860;F 14,Mr 5-12,S 21 1864;My 16-17 1865[69-70]75-[82]
Tx S 16 1854
TxU Mr 5 1864
VU N 13 1844
WHi N 24 1847;Jl 5 1848;Jl 5,Ag 9,D 6 1851; F 21,My 29,Je 12-19 1852;Ap 27 1861;N 11 1863;Ja 30,F 20 1864-Ap 7 1865

Evening WORLD. d Ap 7 1910-
TKL Ap-N 16 1910

LAFAYETTE

MACON county times. w 1919+
TU D 20 1934;35+

LA GRANGE

WESTERN whig and La Grange herald. w 1837-
MWA Mr 22,Jl 5,N 29 1839

LAWRENCEBURG

DEMOCRAT-UNION. w 1884+
1884-1932 as Lawrence democrat
T F 2 1921[22]-[25]-[28]
TU [1931-32]33

Weekly MESSENGER. w Ja 30 1852-
TKL F 13 1852

MIDDLE Tennessean. w 1849-
MWA Mr 21 1851

Lawrence PRESS. w S-D 1854||?
TKL S 8-O 7,N 4-18,D 2-23 1854

Lawrenceburg PRESS. w 1873-85||
MB Je 21 1882-N 5 1885
MWA Je 1882-D 18 1884[Ja 8-N 5 1885]

TENNESSEE patriot. w Ag 15 1853-
MWA O 3 1853

Lawrenceburg TIMES. w 1846-47||?
TKL F 4,Je 3 1847
TxU Mr 4,Ap 15,29,Je 10 1847

Lawrenceburg UNION. w F 26 1886-1932||
United with Lawrence democrat to form Democrat-union
TKL Ag 4 1892
TU F 3 1921[31-32]

LEBANON

Lebanon BANNER. w 1900+
pub 1931+
T My 31 1923;O 4 1928
TU [1931-34]

Lebanon CHRONICLE. w Mr 29 1839-
DLC Mr 29-Ap 5,My 17 1839

DEMOCRAT. w 1888+
pub 1888-91;96;98;1900;03;07-08;14-15;23-24;26-27;29+

Lebanon HERALD. w 1853-88||?
ICHi O 28 1865
MBAt O 21 1865
MWA Jl 8 1880

PATRIOT. w
NOHi Ap 3 1847

Lebanon RECORD. w Ag 15 1868-69||
MBAt S 19-O 10,24-31,N 14 1868;F 20,Mr 13, My 22-Je 5,19,Jl 3-10,31-Ag 7 1869

LENOIR CITY

LEADER. w S 18 1895-
TKL S 18 1895

Lenoir City NEWS. w Je 1 1905+
pub [1905-Jl 16 1926]+
TU D 20 1934+

LEWISBURG

DEMOCRATIC mirror. w
NNHi Ag 5 1838

MARSHALL gazette. w 1871+
T Ja 27 1922

Lewisburg TRIBUNE. w Ag 3 1899+
pub 1899+

LEXINGTON

Lexington PROGRESS. w 1884+
TU [1931]+

Lexington REPUBLICAN. w Ja 4 1894+
pub 1894+
T Ja 28 1927;D 25 1931

LINDEN

PERRY countian. w 1924+
T D 5,19 1924[Ja-D 11 1925]
TSE 1932+

Linden TIMES. w 1880-83||?
T [F-D 1880]

LIVINGSTON

Livingston ENTERPRISE. w 1891+
T [F-S 1928]My 1929
TSE 1932+
TU D 21 1934;35+?

LOUDON

Loudon FREE PRESS. w N 18 1852-55||?
MWA S 23,D 16 1853;F 3 1855
TKL F 14 1855

Loudon INDEPENDENT. w S 25 1878-
TKL O 30 1878

Loudon JOURNAL. w Jl 20 1872-Ag 12 1881||?
DLC My 17 1878
MWA Mr 30 1877;My 2 1878
TKL Jl 20-27,Ag 31 1872[73]F 11,My 9,Ag 15,28,N 6 1874;Ja 22,Mr 12,My 14 1875;Mr 2,Ap 27,D 14 1877[78-79]Je 25 1880;Ag 12 1881
TU Jl 26 1873;F 14 1874;Ap 26 1878;My 23 1879

LOUDON county herald. w 1928+
TU Ja 18-25 1934

Loudon ORION. w F 1? 1856-
MWA S 27,O 18 1856

REPUBLICAN farmer. w 1872-82||
MWA N 10 1881
TKL F 2 1882
TU F 2 1882

Loudon TIMES. w Je 6 1874-78||?
DLC Je 6 1874;S 11 1875
MWA Ag 12 1876
TKL Je 13-20,Jl 4-11,Ag 15,S 26,O 3 1874;Ag 21 1875;Ja 22,Mr 4,Ap 29,My 20 1876
TU Je 13,Ag 15 1874

LYNCHBURG

MOORE county news. w 1928+
TU Ap 30 1931

MCEWEN

McEwen SUN. w 1926+
T Ap 28 1926;Jl 30 1931;D 1 1932

MCKENZIE

McKenzie BANNER. w 1892+
TU Ja 29 1932

MCMINNVILLE

CENTRAL gazette. w 1832?-48||?
DLC O 26,N 16 1840;Je 17 1842;My 19 1843; Jl 26,D 20 1844[45-Mr 1848]
T Je 23 1838

McMinnville ENTERPRISE. w 1866-70||?
T [My-D 14 1867;F 5-Je 11 1870]
VU Mr 19 1870

McMinnville NEW ERA. w 1855-1906||?
MWA S 12 1872;N 30 1882

PEOPLE'S paper. w F 16-Mr 2 1861||?
TKL Mr 2 1861

SOUTHERN standard. w 1879+
pub 1926+
T [1926]F 4 1927
TSE 1932+

WARREN county times and McMinnville new era. w 1903+
TSE 1932+

MADISONVILLE

HIWASSEE patriot. *See under* Athens

MANCHESTER

Manchester GUARDIAN. *See* Tullahoma guardian (Tullahoma)

Manchester TIMES. w 1881+
IU F 12 1892
T [Jl 1932]
TSE 1932+
TU Ap 12-19,Je 22,S 28 1933

TRUE patriot. sw 1862-63||?
DLC Ap 4 1863
WHi Ap 11 1863

MARTIN

Martin MAIL. *See* Weakley county press

WEAKLEY county press. w Ja 1 1886+
1886-N 1920 as Martin mail
pub D 1920+
T S 14 1923;Ap 4 1924
TU [1930-31]+
TU-J S 1927+

MARYVILLE

ADVOCATE. w N 19 1853-
MWA N 19 1853

BLOUNT county democrat. w My 22 1879-82||?
TC Mr 17 1880
TKL Jl 31 1879;Mr 7 1880;Ag 12,O 26 1882
TU Mr 17 1880

EAST TENNESSEEAN. w Je 1 1855-
MWA Je 8,O 26 1855;Je 13 1856

Maryville ENTERPRISE. w O 1906+
pub Jl 1912+
TMaM 1922;25+
TU Jl 14 1932;34+

INDEPENDENT. w 1873-76||?
TKL Ja 26,My 17 1876

Maryville INDEX. w F 27 1878-79||
TKL Je 26,Jl 3,17,31,S 4,18 1878;F 5,Mr 12 1879
TMa [1878-79]
TU N 5 1879

Maryville MONITOR. w Mr 1872?-
DLC N 1872
MWA Ap 1872;Je 1873

TENNESSEE (*Continued*)

MARYVILLE—*Continued*

Maryville REPUBLICAN. w 1867-78||?
DLC D 6 1873
TKL N 2 1867;Je 27 1868;Ap 4,25,My 2,30, Ag 1,15 1874;F 13,Mr 6 1875
TU Ap 4,My 2 1874

SOLDIER'S gazette. w 1870-
DLC My 7,Ag 26,D 8 1870

Maryville TIMES. w,sw 1884+
T 1923
TKL O 5,N 2-9 1887;D 20 1893
TMaM 1924+
TU Ja 8 1934+

MEMPHIS

Memphis ADVOCATE and western district intelligencer. w Ja 18 1827-33||
1827 as Memphis advocate
DLC F 8 1827;O 30 1832
T Mr 1 1827;Ja 26 1828
TN [1828]

AMERICAN eagle. *See* Memphis weekly eagle and enquirer

Memphis APPEAL. tw
Title varies: Memphis daily appeal (for the country); Memphis tri-weekly appeal
DLC 1849[50] Mr 22,Jl 5,Ag 23[N 1853-Mr 1854]Ja 4,My 10,31,S 13 1855;My 24,Je 26,Jl 4,O 16 1856;Ap 16,28,D 3 1857;Ja 30 1858
MWA S 1855;Ap,O 11 1856;D 1861-Ja,F 27, Mr,Ap 5-12,17-26,My 1,8,15-17 1862
NcU O 8 1861
TM Jl 30 1844-F,Ap 8-Je 7,Jl 17-N 11 1856; Mr-Jl,S-D 1849

Memphis evening APPEAL. d D 1 1926-Je 30 1933||
TM complete
TxGR Jl 11 1931-D 17 1932
—morning ed *See* Memphis commercial appeal

Weekly APPEAL-AVALANCHE. w,ir 1840-Je 30 1894||
Follows Western world and Memphis banner of the constitution. 1840-N 8 1890 as Memphis weekly appeal. United with Memphis weekly commercial to form Memphis weekly commercial appeal
Je 6 1862-N 5 1865 pub ir in Hernando, Grenada, Jackson and Vicksburg, Miss.; Atlanta, Griffin and Macon, Ga.; Montgomery and Selma, Ala.
A D 17 1864
DLC Ap 7,My 26 1843;Ja 11-F 1,15,Mr 1-8, 29-My 17 1849
ICM F 13 1839
LSfD D 15 1862
MWA Mr 6,20,O 2 1861;Mr 12 1862
MnHi N 11 1864
NcD Jl 2 1862;Mr 9 1865
OCHi My 22 1861
PHi [1863]
PLaHi Ag 3,5,8,18 1864
TM Ag 18 1842-Ap 1847;My 4 1853;58;D 21 1859-D 5 1860-76;Ap 26 1882-D 16 1885;Mr-D 1886;92
TMC 1842-94
TU Ap 25 1867

Memphis APPEAL-AVALANCHE. d My? 1847-Je 30 1894||
1847-N 8 1890 as Memphis daily appeal. United with Memphis commercial to form Memphis commercial appeal
C Jl 4-D 1890
CSmH Je 13 1863
CtHT Je 27 1863
CtY O 12-N 14 1863
DLC D 17 1847;Mr 7-N 24 1848;49[50;53-55]-N 1860;F 8,12-13,18,27,Mr 15,31,D 22 1862; Je 19,S 12,15,20,O 14,N 4,D 3,5,10 1863[70]-[73-84;86-87;90]-94;extraS 1 1870
GSD My 19,21,23,Je 10,15,25,N 3 1864
ICHi N 19 1865
ICM Ja 9,Mr 26,28 1878;My 18 1879;D 24 1882
InNcHi Je 10 1863
LNC D 24 1862;Ja 1,Ap 13-14,16,18,My 4,8, Je 9-12,16,21-22,26,29,Jl 4,6,9-10,13,20,25,Ag 3, 15,17-20,31,D 3,10,12,20 1863;O 19 1864;Ja 3, 22 1865
MB N 1860-Je 4 1862
MBAt Ja 10-11,F 9-11 1862[Ap 9 1863-Jl 3 1864]
MHi [1863]
MWA O 2 1861;Ap 3,Je 6,21,Jl 16,18,21,23,28, Ag 1,8,11,15,18,20,S 25 1862;Ap 28,N 24 1863; Mr 11 1864;Jl 29 1869;Ap 29 1892
MsU 1887[88-89]90
NNHi Jl 23,S 5 1861;N 12 1863
NcD F 1 1862;Ap 17,Je 12,29,Jl 27 1863;My 7 1864;Jl 13 1872;My 15,Jl 3 1873; Ap 8,18,My 2,Je 4,N 22 1870 Jl 28,S 26 1880;N 18 1881; Jl 21,Ag 12,S 20 1882
OCHi Ag 29,O 8,25,D 10,15,18,22,24 1861-Ap 17 1862;Je 13,18-27,30,Jl 13-18,21,28-29,31,N 30 1863;Ja 9 1864
OClWHi [Mr-Je 1862]
OHi Mr 27 1863
P Jl 1890-Ja 17 1903
PHi S 22,28,30,O 1,5,9,O 18,26 1863
PLaHi Ag 3,6,8,18 1864
T Ag 15 1864;Mr 5 1865;Mr 1874-79;81-[88-90]-Ap 1894
TKL Mr 7-8,Je 27,O 1 1872;Mr 23,My 6 1873;My 9 1879;O 18,29,N 24 1887
TM Jl 27 1847-Ag 4 1848;Ja-Je 1851;Ja-Je 1853;Jl 1854-My 4 1855;Ja-Ag 20 1856;Je 28 1857;Ap 15 1858-59;S 19 1860-Je 1864; 67-[70-71]-[73-74]-[78-79;84;86]-[88]-[90-92]-Je 1874
TMC complete
TMS Ja 13 1875-Je 1893
Tx My 9 1883
TxGR Jl 9 1862
TxU [D 11 1861-Mr 19 1862]
WHi D 1 1863;My 10 1864;O-D 1870;Ja-Mr 1872;Ja-Mr 1873;Ap-Je 1874;O-D 1875;Jl-S 1876;Jl 1877-S 1878;Ap-D 1879;Ap-Je 1880; O 1881-Je 1882;Ja-S 1883;Ap-Je 1884;85-Mr 1886

Memphis daily ARGUS. d 1859-66|
Title varies slightly
DLC F 17-19,21-22,Mr 1,My 6,8 1862;S 20 1864
GAtCo O 17 1865
ICHi O 3,14,27,N 19 1865
ICU Ja 19 1864
ME [O 15 1861-Je 1862]
MBAt F 4,11,20 1862[Ja 26-My 13 1866]
MWA Jl 31 1861
MnHi Ag 30 1860
NNHi Je 6 1862
P-M Je 17 1862
PHi F 11 1862
TM S 21-O 25 1860;Ja 5-Ap 10 1861;My 3-Je 21 1862;Ap 21-N 11 1865;F 3-D 2 1866

Memphis AVALANCHE. d Ja 12 1858-N 8 1890||
1858-Mr 4 1866 as Memphis daily avalanche. United with Memphis appeal to form Memphis appeal-avalanche
For Ap 1862-65? *See* Memphis bulletin
DLC 1858-60; Jl 17 1861;66-Ap,Jl 1869-Ap 1870; Jl 1874-90
ICHi [S-O]-D 1866
ICM My 17,S 27,D 25 1881
KHi Je 20 1862
MB O 1861[Ja-Je 1862]Jl 16 1867
MBAt N 28 1860;Ja 25 1866;D 17,19-20,23 1868-[69]
MWA O 14-15 1858;Mr 30 1860;My 15-18,Jl 30 1867;D 4 1871;Jl 18 1873;S 1 1882;Jl 28 1887
MsU [1887-88]
NN Je 5 1862
NcD Ap 26 1861;F 7 1872
NcU S 13 1868
OCHi Ap 2,4 1859;F 3,7 1862
OClWHi Jl 21-D 1858;Ja 3,6-11 1859[Ag-S]-D 1860;N 30 1861[Mr-Je 1862]Ap 3 1866;Mr-Jl 1867
OOxM N 14 1873
P [1890]-1903
PHi My 21 1862
T [1872-86;89-90]
TKL Ap 12 1862;Je 5 1872;Mr 22 1873;Je 2 1881;N 11,17,27-28 1887
TM Ja 21-O 3 1861;Ja 28-Je 1862;N-D 1867; Mr 4-N 10 1868;F 6-S 1 1869;Jl 1870-D 6 1872;Ja 1873-76;Jl-D 1879;Jl 15 1880;S-D 1887; My 8 1889-N 8 1890;N 1894-Ja 26 1895
TMS 1875-85;87-90
Tx My 25,Je 1 1884
TxU My 24 1860
WHi Ag 10 1859-Ja 1860;S-D 1866

Memphis weekly AVALANCHE. w Ja 19 1858-N 1890||
United with Memphis weekly appeal to form Weekly appeal-avalanche
CSmH D 11 1860
DLC 1858-60;Ja 30 1868
LNC N 19 1861
MBAt Ja 21 1862
NcD My 30 1867
WHi F 1859-60

Memphis tri-weekly morning BULLETIN. tw Ag? 1855-
DLC Jl 23-24,Ag 20,D 10 1856;Jl 23,Ag 22 1857;Je 8 1858; Mr 20-Ap 10,20-22,My 15,24, Jl 1,13 1859;Ja 2 1860
MWA Ag 14,D 11 1856;Ja 11-17 1857

Memphis BULLETIN. d S 1 1855-D 31 1868||
Title varies: Memphis daily morning bulletin; Memphis daily bulletin
Ap 1862-64 replaces Memphis daily avalanche
ArHi Mr 14 1865
DLC 1855-Ja 28,O 28 1860-Mr 14 1861
GAtCo D 12 1866
IP Jl 26 1862
MBAt Ap 20 1861;Ja 3 1865;Ja 13,15,26,F 4 1866[Ap-D 1868]
MWA Ap 15 1856;Je 2-3,O 15 1857;Ap 30,O 7 1859;Je 23 1863;Ap 2 1864;My 27 1867
NcD S 4,O 7 1862
OClWHi Mr 1 1863;Mr 10 1865
OHi F 26 1863
PHi N 4 1868
T My 7 1856;Ap 18 1861
TKL Je 25 1868
TM N 9 1855; Mr 3 1859;Ja 25 1860;Jl 4 1862-Je 1865;67
Tx D 15 1860

Weekly Memphis BULLETIN. w S 5 1855-61||?
DLC Je 12 1857;S 3 1858;F 28 1861
IU Mr 14-27,Ap 24-Je 5 1861
MWA F 24 1860
NcD Mr 14 1856
TxU Ag 26 1856

Daily CAMPAIGN review. d S 26 1864-
DLC S 27,O 7,19-21 1864

Weekly COMMERCIAL. w
TxU F 13,Mr 20,My 13 1847

Memphis daily COMMERCIAL. d Je? 1865-66||
DLC F 2-O 26 1866
ICHi S 24,N 25 1865
MBAt N 3-4,7-8,15,19-22,25,D 5,7 1865;Ja 31, F 3,27, Je 26 1866
TM N 24 1865-Je 26 1866

Memphis daily COMMERCIAL. d 1889-94. *See* Memphis commercial appeal

Memphis COMMERCIAL APPEAL. d 1889+
1889-Je 1894 as Memphis daily commercial (title varies slightly)
pub 1889+
A My-D 1899;Ap 1906-Je 1908
DLC 1894-[1918]+
ICM My 15 1902
ICU 1935+
IU 1926[27-28]
M D 9 1926;O 13 1928;My 21 1930
MWA My 7 1925;D 9 1926;O 13 1928
MsHi My 1902-10
MsSM [O 1897-1916]+
MsU [1891-92]-[1912]-[23]-[28]+
NcD My 28-29 1901;My 19,31 1903;N 20,29 1905
T S 1893-[98]+
TKL F 14 1895
TM 1890;O 10 1892-[93]-[1910-11]+
TMP 1910+
TMS 1890+
TSS 1895-98[1900]
TU [1923]-[29]+
TxU [1931-32]
VU Jl 11,Ag 24,S 12,27-28,O 1-2,5-6 1934
WHi My 21 1930

Memphis weekly COMMERCIAL APPEAL. w 1890-1929||?
1890-Je 1894 as Memphis weekly commercial
MsHi My 1902-10
NcD D 26 1899

Memphis weekly EAGLE and enquirer. w Ja 25 1842-61||
1842-D 9 1851 as American eagle. Merged with Memphis weekly avalanche
CtY Mr 17 1843
MWA Ag 3 1843;Ja 17,31 1855;My 7,28 1856
T My 7 1856
TKL O 4 1854
TM 1842-Ja 1,My 19 1848-49;D 31 1851-Ja 7 1852
TxU F 9 1844;S 17 1851
WHi S 26 1852

Memphis daily EAGLE and enquirer. d N 9 1843-Je 30 1858||
1843-D 1851 as Memphis daily eagle. Followed by Memphis morning enquirer
DLC 1843-45;N 2 1846;Ja-D 9 1851;52-54;Ja-Je,Ag 14-D 14 1855;Jl 1856-58
MWA Je 1 1853;S 15,18,20 1857
NcD F 8 1852-53
TM 1846-50;Ja 1,13-Je 1852

Tri-weekly EAGLE and enquirer. tw N 6 1843-58||?
1843-51 as Tri-weekly eagle
DLC N 6-7,D 20-21 1843;[44-45]My 14-17,Ag 11-12 1851;D 25 1852;Jl 2,26,S 20 1853
MWA Jl 30/31,Ag 6/7 1856;Ja 14/15 1857
NcD My 12,Je 23,Ag 23,S 6,O 4 1853

Memphis ENQUIRER. w Mr 19 1836-D 9 1851||
DLC Ap 2 1841
InSHi Ap 26 1844
MWA My 12 1843
TM 1836-Je 19 1840
TxU Mr 15 1844;O 17 1845

ENQUIRER. sw O 31 1837-
DLC O 31 1837;N 27,D 4 1840

Tri-weekly Memphis ENQUIRER. tw 1842-D 9 1851||
DLC D 7 1843-D 12 1844;46;My 29-30 1847; Ja 14,S 3,D 3 1848;Jl 4,S 7,O 7 1849;S 27, N 16-24,D 18 1850;Jl 3,D 9 1851
TM Jl 15 1845;46;F 26,Ag 16 1850

Daily Memphis ENQUIRER. d 1847-D 9 1851||
United with Memphis daily eagle to form Memphis daily eagle and enquirer
DLC 1845;Jl-D 1849;Jl 1850-51
MWA Ja 19 1851
TM 1847-48;F 29-Jl,S-D 1849

Memphis morning ENQUIRER. d Jl 3 1859-Mr 8 1861||
Follows Memphis daily eagle and enquirer Merged with Memphis daily avalanche, later Memphis avalanche
DLC Complete

Daily EXPRESS. d Ap? 1851-
MWA Ja 1 1851
TM F 26 1850;My 12 1851

Memphis evening LEDGER. d
TM O 16 1857-F 18 1858

Weekly LEVEL. w Ja 4-18 1858||?
TM Ja 4-18 1858

MERCHANTS' exchange prices current. w N 30? 1866-
MWA Mr 23 1867

Memphis weekly MONITOR. w
TxU My 20 1847

Memphis morning NEWS. d My 1 1902-D 24 1904||
United with Evening scimitar to form Memphis news-scimitar, later Memphis press-scimitar
MWA 1902-Je 1903;04
MsHi 1902-Je 1903;04
T [1903-04]
TM complete

Memphis NEWS-SCIMITAR. *See* Memphis press-scimitar

Memphis weekly POST. w 1863-D 23 1869||
DLC Ap 28,My 5,Je 30,Jl 14,S 8 1866; S 16-D 23 1869
MBAt Je 11,O 8 1868;Ag 12,S 16-D 23 1869
MWA N 4 1869

Memphis evening POST. d Ja 14? 1865-S 11 1869||
Title varies: Memphis post; Memphis daily post; Memphis morning post.
DLC 1868-S 11 1869
MBAt [Ja 23 1866-S 11 1869]
MH Mr 19-Jl 1868
MWA Ja 28 1866;My 31 1869
TM F 11 1866-S 11 1869
WHi Mr 7,9,13 1867

TENNESSEE (*Continued*)

MEMPHIS—*Continued*

Memphis PRESS-SCIMITAR. d 1880+
1880-D 24 1904 as Evening scimitar; D 25 1904-N 15 1925 Memphis news-scimitar
D 1891 is Souvenir ed
pub 1893+
LNH My 27 1903
MoHi Je 8 1899
MsHi 1905-Ap 1907
NcD Je 8 1901;S 16 1906;F 17 1907
T 1905+
TKL D 1891
TM Ap 1894-Je,O 1905-O 3,N 1917+
TMS 1913-Je 1915
TU D 30 1906;O 30 1934

Memphis PRICE CURRENT and commercial letter sheet. w 1853-
MWA Ja 10,O 29,N 26,D 10 1853-Ja 14,F 11, Mr 18 1854

Memphis PRICE CURRENT and merchants' exchange reporter. w N 10 1860-
MHi O 20,N 10-17 1860;F 16,Mr 23 1861
MWA Mr 2 1861

PUBLIC ledger. d Jl 18 1865-93‖
CaOTA My 6 1868
DLC Jl 18 1871-Je 29 1872;73-D 19 1893
MBAt S 12,15,18,23,O 6 1865
TM Mr 7-S 3 1866;Mr 1867-[85]-[92-93]
TMS 1875-79;S 1889-F 1891

Weekly PUBLIC ledger. w 1870-90‖
T Jl 7 1885-[86]
TM Mr 1870-F,S 1871-F 24 1880;Mr 1882-F 21 1888;Mr 26-Ag 1889;F 11-Ag 1890

Weekly REPUBLICAN. w 1863-
DLC Mr 1,22,Ap 14,28-My 5,Je 18,S 28 1866
MBAt F 8 1866

Memphis weekly REVIEW. w My 22 1864-
DLC My 29-Je 5,Jl 2,23-Ag 6,20-S 3 1864

Memphis daily REVIEW. d S 4 1865-
DLC O 20 1865
ICHi S 5 1865

Evening SCIMITAR. *See* Memphis press-scimitar

SOUTHERN loyalist. w O 21 1865-
ICHi O 21-28 1865
MBAt O 21-28 1865;Ja 17 1866
PHi O 28 1865

Memphis daily SOUTHERNER. d
TM N 22,D 16 1850

SUN. d N 6? 1852-
MWA N 18 1852

Daily SUN. d Ja 1869-70‖?
MBAt F 5,17,Mr 10-11 1869

Memphis daily TIMES. d
TM N 5 1849

Memphis TIMES. w 1899-1910‖?
NcU Ja 24 1904

Memphis daily TRIBUNE. d Ja 5? 1866-
DLC Ja 30-31,F 3 1866
MBAt Ja 30,F 3-4 1866

Memphis UNION appeal. d
Pub by Union troops from Memphis appeal office
MWA Jl 13 1862
TM Jl 3-Ag 1862

UNION reveille.
InMovHi Ja 25 1862

WESTERN world and Memphis banner of the constitution. w Ja 8 1839-40‖?
Followed by Memphis weekly appeal, later Weekly appeal-avalanche
DLC Ja 8 1839
MWA My 8-15 1840

Memphis daily WHIG. d,tw 1852-56‖
d 1852-55
MWA Ap 18/19 1856
T D 31 1855
TM Je 17 1853
TMS Mr 11 1853-Jl 17 1856

MILAN

Milan EXCHANGE. w 1874+
pub 1874+

MORRISTOWN

Morristown GAZETTE. w 1866-1922‖?
United with Daily mail to form Daily gazette and mail
MWA N 10 1875
OClWHi Ap 27,My 10,Ag 30,S 13,O 4,18,D 28 1871;F 7,Ag 14,S 25,O 9,N 13,D 11 1872;Ja 8 1873
TKL O 8,N 12 1873;F 11,My 6,S 30,N 11,D 2-9 1874;Ja 6,20,F 10,N 3,D 22 1875;Ja 12 1876; Ap 3,Je 26,O 30,N 6 1878;Mr 5,28,Jl 16 1879;N 2 1881

Daily GAZETTE and mail. d 1916+
1916-22 as Daily mail
T Ap 19 1923

Daily MAIL. *See* Daily gazette and mail

Morristown REPUBLICAN. w 1887-1920‖?
TU N 26 1887;My 7 1915

Morristown SUN. w 1907+
TU [1909-11;14-16]29[30-32]+

Morristown TIMES. w 1877-82‖?
TKL O 29 1881

MOUNTAIN CITY

JOHNSON county news. w Ap 7 1915+
pub 1915+
TU [1931-34]+

MURFREESBORO

CENTRAL monitor. w Je? 1833-34‖?
DLC Ja 18-25,My 14,Je 28,Jl 12-19,S 6,O 11-18 1834
TU [Ag 23 1834]

*Murfreesborough COURIER. w Je 16 1814-
DLC S 27 1827
MBAt Ap 15 1824

DOLLAR weekly. w N 26 1857-
TC Mr 19 1858

FREE PRESS. w 1879-1906‖?
NcD N 19 1880;Jl 29 1881;F 3 1882
T Ap 8 1881
TXU Jl 7 1882

HOME journal. w 1886-1930‖
United with News-banner to form Daily news-journal
T My 23 1890;Jl 17 1908;Ap 27 1923

MONITOR. w Ag 12 1835-
DLC Ag 19 1835

MONITOR. w Jl 1 1865-76‖?
DLC D 11 1873
ICHi O 7,N 4-11 1865
MWA Mr 9 1867
TxU S 9 1865

NATIONAL vidette. w Ja 10 1828-
T Ja 10 1828

NEWS-BANNER. w 1866-1930‖
1866-99 as Murfreesboro news
T My 24 1876

NEWS-BANNER. d 1927-30‖
United with Home journal to form Daily news-journal
TU O 22,D 9,19 1930

Daily NEWS-JOURNAL. d 1931+
Formed by the union of News-banner and Home journal
pub 1931+
T Jl 23 1932
TMuT 1934+
TU [1932+]

Daily REBEL banner. d
T D 23 1862

RUTHERFORD courier. w 1931+
pub 1931+
TMuT current issues only

RUTHERFORD telegraph. w 1838-
1838-S 11? 1845 as Tennessee telegraph
DLC Mr 14 1838;N 21 1840
MWA O 23 1841;D 6 1856;Ja 17 1857
N N 13 1845
NcU My 2-16 1840;F 6 1841
TU N 10 1860

TENNESSEE telegraph. *See* Rutherford telegraph

Weekly TIMES. w 1837-41‖?
DLC S 19 1840;Mr 27 1841

NASHVILLE

ADVANCE guard of democracy. w Ap 23-N 25 1840‖?
DLC Ap-O 1840
T [Ap-N 1840]
TxU* Ap-O 1840
TxHuS My 7,29-Je 12,Jl 17,31,Ag 14,O 23 1840
WHi Ap-O 1840

Nashville AMERICAN. d Ap 26 1848-My 1 1853‖
1848-O 1849 as Daily centerstate American and Nashville American. United with Daily union to form Nashville union and American
ICHi Ag 2 1848
TN [1849-53]

Nashville AMERICAN. w 1848-Ag 1853‖
United with National union to form Nashville union and American
DLC N 2 1852

Nashville AMERICAN. d S 1 1875-Je 1910‖
Formed by the union of Republican banner and Nashville union and American. 1875-F 17 1876 as American; F 18 1876-S 29 1894 Daily American United with Nashville Tennessean to form Nashville Tennessean and Nashville American, later Nashville Tennessean
A Jl 1879-Ap 1883;84-Je 1887;O-D 1901;Ap-O 1902;Jl 1906;Ja 1909
DLC 1875-Ag 17 1899;My 1900-Ap 15 1901; My 1902-10
IC Ap 30-My 1 1889
ICM F 8 1881
MWA Ja 28,O 5,7 1876;Je 26 1910
MsHi F 21 1888
MsU [1887]88
N My 4 1880
NcD Jl 18,Ag 5 1880;O 14 1882;My 18 1903
T 1876-81;83-88[91-1910]
TKL My 30,Ag 30 1878;Ja 22,24 1879;O 6 1880;Ja 15,Ap 26,29 1882;Je 22,24 1884;S 1, 5-7,12,O 2,4-5,N 11,17,27-29 1887;Mr 21,Ag 21, 23 1894;Ja 8,Mr 20 1895;Ja 8,Mr 19-20,My 9 1895;My 1 1897
TN 1876-98;1903-09
TU My 2 1880;S 14,O 8 1881;Je 23 1887
TU-J Ag 15 1883;D 29 1889;O 12 1902
VU Mr 31 1903
WHi Je 26 1910

Weekly AMERICAN. w 1875-1910‖
Formed by the union of Republican farmer and Nashville union and American
MsHi 1888
TU S 13 1901
TU-J [1876;78;82-85;1902]

Nashville weekly BANNER. w 1876-1905‖?
TU My 25 1882

Nashville BANNER. d Ap 10 1876+
pub Ja-Ap 1893;94-1918;Je 1919+
DLC N 18,D 3 1878;S 23 1899-Ag,N 1918+
OClWHi Je 22 1897
T My 15 1880-Ap 1898;99+
TKL Ag 21 1878;Ja 30 1879;Ap 12 1882;F 9 1884;Ag 21-22 1894;F 16,Mr 20-21 1895
TM N 30 1899
TN [1876;81-82;85]86;1901+
TSE 1931+
TU [1910-11;25;30-33]
WaPS [1916]

Nashville BANNER and Nashville whig. w 1822-37‖
1822-My 1826 as Nashville banner. United with Nashville republican (1824-37) to form Republican-banner
NNHi N 1 1826
OClWHi Je 2 1827;Ap 8 1828
T F 14 1827
TKL My 2 1828;D 13 1830
TN [1826;31]

Nashville BULLETIN. w O 31 1870-75‖
1870-Ag 1 1872 as Tennessee tribune
T D 17 1874-75
TKL S 4-11 1872;F 6,Ag 14,N 20 1873;Ja 1, Ap 23,My 3,16,27,Jl 18,30 1874;My 6 1875
TN D 1870-D 11 1871;Ja 8-N 18,D 1872
TU Ag 14 1873

Daily CENTER-STATE American and Nashville American. *See* Nashville American

Morning CHRONICLE and Nashville commercial daily advertiser. d D 14 1835-
DLC D 14 1835

CITIZENS appeal. d 1928-My 3 1933‖
T Jl 25,30 1928[29-32]
TN [1929]-[31]-33

*Nashville CLARION and Tennessee gazette. w Ja 26 1806-24‖
1806- as Clarion; Democratic clarion and Tennessee gazette; F 9-O 21 1813,N 9 1819-F 20 1821 Clarion and Tennessee gazette; O 28 1813-N 2 1819 Clarion and Tennessee state gazette. Followed by Nashville republican (1824-37)
DLC Ja-Ag 15 1821
MWA F-Ag 1821

COLORED Tennessean. *See* Tennessean

Nashville COMMERCIAL and legal reporter. w 1869-78‖?
1869-74? as Nashville commercial reporter
THi 1873-74
TKL Ap 14 1873;My 17,Jl 26,Ag 9-16 1876; Ap 4-1877
TMS Je 23 1875-F 28 1877
TU Je 28 1876

COMMERCIAL transcript. w 1835-
TU [F 14 1835]

CONSTITUTIONAL advocate. w Jl 23 1822-24‖?
DLC Jl 30 1822-Ja 17 1824

DAVIDSON county news. w 1928-
T Jl 28 1928

Nashville daily DEMOCRAT. d 1860-61‖?
OCHi F 27-Mr 3,5-6,24,26-30 1861

Nashville DEMOCRAT. w S 20 1911-N 2 1913‖
Merged with Nashville Tennessean
MWA N 2 1913
T complete

DEMOCRATIC clarion and Tennessee gazette. *See* Nashville clarion and Tennessee gazette

DEMOCRATIC statesman. w Ap 12 1845-48‖?
Campaign paper
DLC Ap-Jl 2 1845
T Ap 12-S 6 1845
TU S 12 1848

Nashville DEMOKRAT. d S 15 1866-71‖
In German
MBAt S 15-O 4,6-11,18-21 1866

Nashville DISPATCH. d Ap 14 1862-N 23 1866‖
United with National union and American to form Nashville union and dispatch, later Nashville union and American
CtY Je 25,S 25 1865
DLC O 14 1862-S 17 1865;Ja 9,11,13-14,17,31,F 13 1866
ICHi Ag 12 1864;Jl-N 1865
MB complete
MBAt My 7-15,18,23,Je 15,Jl 8 1862;S 16-22, 24-O 3,7-23,25-N 22,25 1863-Je,D 18 1864;Ja-F 15,17-Mr 9,11-Ap 12,14-18,21-30,My 3-7,10-13,16,18-24,27-Je 1 1865
T [1862-64]F 27 1866
TN [Ap-D 1862]-S 17 1865;66
TxU Je 18,Jl 7,9,23,Ag 27,S 20 1864

*Nashville GAZETTE. sw,w My 26 1819-27‖
Merged with Nashville republican
sw My 26-D 8 1819,F-Je 1820
DLC Ja 16,F 13,My 7,Jl 16 1824;Ap 22,My 13, O 26 1825;Ap 5 1826;extra O 12 1824
MWA Ja-Je 1821;Jl 25 1823;Ag 13,S 17-24 1824;Ap 22 1825;Mr 1,O 25 1826
N Mr 21(extra)1823
NcU D 3 1824
T [1821]Jl 15 1825;F 14 1827
TKL Mr 21,Je 6 1823;F 18,My 6,S 23 1825;F 1 1826

Nashville daily GAZETTE. d 1844-68‖
Merged with Nashville union and American
Suspended 1862-65
DLC Mr 30 1844;F 1 1862;D 29 1867
ICHi Jl 13,O 21-N 28 1865
MBAt Ja 25 1862;Ap 15 1866
MWA Jl 8 1857
T N 12 1865
THi O 1857-61
TN [1848-53]-[55]-[61;65-68]
TxU F 21-22 1867
WHi Ag 13 1852

TENNESSEE (*Continued*)

NASHVILLE—*Continued*

Nashville GLOBE. w 1906+
title varies: Globe-independent
Negro
TNF 1936+

Nashville HERALD. w 1831-32||
DLC Jl 21 1831
ICHi My 30 1832
MWA Ja 5,My 16,30 1832
TKL D 8 1831
WHi F-Je 6 1832

Evening HERALD. d 1880-92||?
NcU N 14 1889
THi 1889-Je 1892
TKL Ja 24 1880

JACKSONIAN. w Ja 8-Jl 21 1932||
T complete

JEFFERSONIAN. w 1832||
T S-O,N 11 1832

JEFFERSONIAN. w 1933+
TN 1933+

LEGISLATIVE union and American. w O 12 1857-Mr 16 1858||?
MH O 12,D 14 1857;Ja 4,F 1,Mr 1-16 1858
MWA Ja 4,Mr 1 1858

NATIONAL banner and Nashville whig. d,sw,tw D 23 1825-Ag 21 1837||
Title varies: National banner, and literary, political and commercial gazette; National banner and daily advertiser. United with Nashville republican to form Republican banner
CSmH Ag 13 1830
Ct [1826-37]
DLC D 23 1825;Ja 13-20,F 10-Mr 10,24,Ap 7-14,My 3 1826-Ja 3 1831;O 30 1832;34-37
ICHi D 7 1830
MBAt S 23 1828
MWA Ja 13,F 3-10,24,Jl 26,N 11 1826;Ja 20, Ag 11-18,S 22-29,N 10,24,D 8 1827-[Ja-O]N 18 1828;F 21,Jl 18-Ag 1,22-29,S-O 17,31,N 21 1829;Mr 25,My 3 1831;Ja 10,Mr 31,Ag 18 1832;Mr 16 1837
MiU [1835]-[37]
NNHi O 31 1828;My 7 1830
NcD Je 14,Jl 5,26,Ag 2 1831
OC Jl 31,Ag 14 1833
T F 14 1827
THi complete
TN [1826]33
TxU My 13 1831

NATIONAL pathfinder. w F 3 1860-62||?
TU Jl 28 1860

NATIONAL review. w Je 14 1885-89||?
TKL S 11 1886;S 3,17-O 8,N 5,26 1887

NATIONAL union. *See* Nashville union and American

Daily evening NEWS. d 1851-Ag 1855||
WHi O 14 1853

Nashville daily NEWS. d Ag 22 1857-60||
DLC Je 2 1860
MWA Ag 22,S 16,20 1857
NjWdHi O 5 1858
T O 7 1857-60
TN Ag 15 1857-Ja 6 1860
TxU Ap 10-D 1858
WHi Ap 10 1858-Je 2 1860

Nashville daily NEWS. d 1901-05||
T 1902-04
TN [1901]-[05]

OPPOSITION. w My-Jl 1859||
T My 2,Jl 29 1859

Daily ORTHOPOLITAN. d O 1 1845-S 30 1846||
DLC O 28 1847
T [1845-46]
THi Ja-Je 1846
TKL Ag 22 1846
TN 1845
TxU My 18 1847

Nashville PATRIOT. w 1855-62||
Title varies slightly. Follows Nashville true whig
DLC Ap 17 1856;Mr 9 1859
KHi Ap,D 3 1857
MWA Ag 21 1856
NNHi F 9 1861
OClWHi Mr 28 1861
T Ap 7 1859
THi 1857-60
TN [1855-56]-[60-61]
TU Jl 18,Ag 25 1860

Daily Nashville PATRIOT. d 1856-62||?
Follows Nashville daily true whig
DLC O 15 1861
ICHi Mr 18 1862
MBAt Ap 20 1861;Ja 24 1862
MWA D 5,10,12 1856
OCHi Ja 30-31,My 7,13,Ag 13 1861
OClWHi Mr 29 1861
T [1857]-[61]
WHi My 11 1861

PLAIN DEALER. w Mr-Ag 1841||
T Mr-Jl 24 1841

POLITICIAN and weekly Nashville whig. w Ap 18 1845-52||?
1845-Ap 9 1847 as Politician
NcD 1845-Mr 1849
T 1845-Ap 10 1846
THi 1845-O 1847
TKL 1845-Mr 1849
TN 1845-[47-48]
TU Ja 26-F 2,Ap 6 1849
WHi 1845-Ap 10 1846;Ap 16 1847-Mr 1848

Nashville daily PRESS and times. d My 4 1863-O 9 1869||
1863-My 1865 as Nashville daily press
CtY Ap 9 1864[Je-D 1865]F 24,27-28,Mr 10 1866
DLC My 19-S 23 1863;My 12 1865-66;Jl 1867-69
ICHi [My-D 1865]-[Ja-Jl 1867]Ja 23,Mr 25, Ap 3 1868;Ap 10 1869
MBAt Ja 31-F 6,8-12,Ap 16 1866;Jl 12 1869
MWA [My 8-S 18 1866]
T Ja 11 1864;Ja 17 1867-N 1868
TC Ag 25 1864
TKL F 23 1864;My 12 1866;My 22,N 6 1867 [68]Ja 9,Ap 10,28,My 1,3,6,Je 12,27 1869
TN [1863]-[65-66]-[68-69]
TU S 23 1865;Ja 23,Je 11 1868
TxU D 3 1863;F 23,Ap 19,Je 27,Ag 12,S 12 1864
WHi Je 23 1864

Nashville weekly PRESS and times. w 1863-69||
DLC My 21-Je 11 1865;Ja 7-28,F 11-18,Mr 4-Ap 1,15 1866; S 24 1868
ICHi Jl 2,Ag 27,O-N 6,19 1865;66-Mr 1867

Evening REPORTER. d 1849-50||
TN [1850]

Nashville REPUBLICAN. w,sw,tw 1824-Ag 21 1837||
Follows Nashville clarion and Tennessee gazette 1824-N 12 1834 as Nashville republican and state gazette. United with National banner and Nashville whig to form Republican banner
CSmH Ag 21 1830
Ct [1828]Ja 16 1835
DLC Mr 27 1824-Ap 21,D 28 1827;Mr 11,14, 18,S 12 1828-36;Mr 16,25,30-Ag 5 1837
MWA Ag 7,O 2-9,30-N 6 1824;O 8,29 1825;O 21 1826;Ap 2,15,Jl 1,D 9 1831;Ja 27,O 11 1832
MiU 1833;35[36]1837
N O 16 1833
NNHi F 1,Mr 7,Ap 12,S 12,26,D 5,28 1828
OOxM O 3 1828
T Ap 23,S 17 1825;Ja 6 1826;F 10,Je 12,O 2 1827;Ag 15 1828;Jl 5,Ag 26 1833;Ap 27 1837
THi 1830-36
TKL Ap 16,Jl 9,O 22 1825;O 21 1826;Ap 7 1827;Ap 11,Jl 8,Ag 29 1828;F 10 1829; Jl 30 1831;Ap 26 1836
WHi Ap 16 1825;F 3-10,24,Mr 9-16,30-Ag 2 1832

Nashville REPUBLICAN. . . For the country. tw 1826?-Mr 1837||
Title varies: Nashville republican and state gazette
DLC Jl 24/27 1827;Mr 4/7 1828;Je 3 1831
MWA Mr 24 Ag 19,S 12,D 12,26 1828;Ja 13, Mr 20,Je 19-30,Jl 7,17-21,O 20,D 11-15 1829; Ja 1,15-19,O 27,N 20,D 11-25 1830;Ja 4 1831; Ag 22 1832;Jl 5,Ag 2,9,S 4,16,20,O 2 1834; F 10 1835;F 9-18 1836
TU Ap 19 1836

Nashville daily REPUBLICAN. sw,d Jl 18-D 1868||?
Title varies slightly
DLC Jl 18,S 23,O 15,24,D 4 1868
MBAt Jl 15,29,Ag 6-S 9,11-23,25-O 13,15-19, 21-23,27-31,N 4-6,9-16 1868
TKL O 7 1868
TU [1868]

Nashville REPUBLICAN. w 1893-97||?
DLC O 26 1894
TKL Ag 17 1894

REPUBLICAN banner. d,tw Ag 22 1837-Ag 31 1875||
Formed by the union of National banner and Nashville whig and Nashville republican. Title varies: Daily republican banner; Daily republican banner and Nashville whig. United with Nashville union and American to form American, later Nashville American
tw 1842-Mr 1849
CtY F 26,Mr 1 1860;Mr 2 1866
DLC 1837-61 Mr 18 1862;S 27 1865-75
ICHi S 27-N 5 1865
MBAt S 28,O 24-25 1865;Ap 18,D 5-8,11-12, 14-19,21-25,27-30 1866;Ja 1-2,4-6,9,11-20,23 1867
MWA My 17,Je 22 1838;F 8 1840[Ja-Jl 15 1841]Je 15-D 1850;O 24 1854;My 20 1855;F 12,Mr 18,Je 27 1858;My 2 1861;F 18,Ap 21, My 16[Jl-D]1866;Ap 23 1867;Mr 19,My 12,26, Je 14,D 29 1871;Je 2 1874;Mr 3 1875
NNHi Je 17 1871;My 3,10 1872;F 20,My 3,Jl 1 1873
NcD [1839;51]
OCHi [My 23 1859-Ap]-[N 1861-F 13 1862]
OClWHi O 7,N 6,12,28,D 20,24-25,28 1861;Ja 2,11,20-22,30,F 14 1862;My 15,31,Je 13,29,D 7, 12 1867;Ja 11,O 30 1868
T [1857-61;66-68;70-71]-[74-75]
THi 1837-40;53
TKL N 3 1842;Jl 24 1851;F 14 1856;F 27,O 29, D 19,22 1869[70]Ja 3,5,18,22-23,Mr 9-10 1871 [Je 1872-74]Ja 1,7,15-16,21 1875
TN [1838-39]41[45]47-[53-61]67-[70]-[75]
TU [1844;61;65-66]
WHi Ja-Je 1840;41;Ag 7 1852

REPUBLICAN banner. w Ag 22 1837-75||
Follows Nashville republican. United with Nashville union and American to form Weekly American
sw and tw during sessions of the legislature
DLC Mr 11 1839-40;My 18,Jl 23 1841;D 23 1844;N 18 1858;Ap-D 1849
MWA S 7 1838;My 1 1840;42;My 1,10,Jl 12 1843[45-60]O 30 1848;Ja 1-19,24-31,F 5-19, 23-Mr 1849;Jl 7 1850
MiU [1837-41]43-45;47-49[51;55-56]
NcD Mr 25 1837-
NcU O 26,N 30,D 14 1838-Ja 4 1839;Je 5-12 1840
WHi 1839

REPUBLICAN banner (for the country). tw
DLC Je 15/16,Jl 25/26,Ag 5 1860
MWA N 30/D 2 1856;Ja 7/8,11/13,Ag 16/18 1857

SPIRIT of '76. 1840-41;44-45||
PUn Jl 20 1844
T Ap 25 1844;Ap 5 1845
Tx My 11,Je 1,20-Ag 10,24-S 28,O 19 1844

STAR spangled banner. w My 25-O 26 1844||
Campaign paper
DLC complete
ICU [1844]
TxU [1844]

STATE sentinel and Tennessee organ. w O 14 1853-
1853 as State sentinel
MWA F 18 1854

Nashville daily SUN. d 1895-97||
T D 19,31 1895-97
TN [1895-97]

TENNESSEAN. w Je 23? 1865-
1865-66? as Colored Tennessean
Negro
MBAt Mr 24-31 1866;Jl 18 1867
NNHi O 7-14 1865

Nashville TENNESSEAN. (morning) d 1907+
Jl 1910-Jl 14 1918 as Nashville Tennessean and Nashville American
O 28 1928 is Prosperity ed
DLC Jl 1910+
IU S 16 1924-Je 17 1925
M O 28 1928
MWA Jl 15,Ag 19,S 16 1917-Ag 14 1919;O 28 1928
T 1907-Je,O 1917+
TN 1907+
TNB 1922+
TSE 1931+
TU [1911;13]31+
TxGR O 28 1928;Je 15 1930
VU D 2 1934
WHi N 9 1907;15+

Evening TENNESSEAN. d 1919+
T Ap-Je, O-D 1920;22+

TENNESSEE constitution. w My 5 1933-
TU My 5 1933

TENNESSEE organ. w 1847-54||
United with State sentinel to form State sentinel and Tennessee organ
MWA D 24 1851;Ja 28 1852
TM F 23 1853

TENNESSEE post. w 1873-76||?
In German
MWA Ag 26 1876

TENNESSEE staats zeitung. w Mr 17 1866-69||
In German
MBAt Mr 24,31-Ap 4,Ag 9-12,14-15,18,22-24,O 26,D 5-11,13-25,27-30 1866;Ja 1,3-6,9,11,13,16-19,22-26,30,S 5,10,20,23,27-28 1867
MWA Mr 17 1866
THi Mr-S 1866;O 1867-Mr 1869

TENNESSEE star. w 1886-91||?
Negro
TKL N 25 1887

Daily TENNESSEE state journal. d Je 21? 1869-
MBAt Je 24-26,30,Jl 3,6-10 1869

TENNESSEE tribune. *See* Nashville bulletin

Nashville TIMES. d F 28- N 1862||
MB F 28-Mr 16 1862
MBAt Mr 15 1862

Nashville daily TIMES and true union. d F 20 1864-My 9 1865||
United with Nashville daily press to form Nashville daily press and times
DLC complete
MBAt Mr 29,Ap 16,My 9,O 22 1864;Mr 1 1865
MWA Je 22,D 1 1864;Ap 21 1865
TKL Ap 25,N 7 1864
TN [1864-65]

Nashville weekly TIMES and true union. w F 26 1864-65||?
DLC Mr 12,Jl 2 1864
MWA N 13 1864
TxU My 21,Jl 4,Ag 4 1864

Nashville daily TRUE whig. tw,d Ja 6 1838-55||
1838-Mr 31 1849 as Nashville whig. Followed by Daily Nashville patriot
tw 1838-Ja 7 1849
CSmH Ag 26-27 1853
DLC 1838-N 3 1841;Mr 31,Ap 9 1842;Mr 9, Ap 4,My 20-25 1843;49-[51]
MWA N 26 1855
NEh Ag 23 1839
T [1839-40;43;45-47]
THi 1838-44;46
TKL Jl 23 1842;O 19 1847;Jl 24 1855
TN D 30 1845-49

Nashville TRUE whig (for the country). tw 1838-
1838-49 as Nashville whig
DLC Ja 11-Ag 14 1851
MWA Je 17,N 23 1840;Ap 23,Je 5 1841;My 20, N 14 1843;Mr 4 1851;Mr 8,Jl 11 1855
WHi O 19 1844

Nashville TRUE whig. w Ja 6 1838-55||
1838-Mr 31 1849 as Nashville whig. Followed by Nashville patriot
MWA Je 7-14 1850;Ag 14 1851;F 13 1852;Ja 12 1855
THi Ap 1850-Mr 1851
TN 1850[51]-[54-55]
TU [Ap-O 12 1849]
WHi 1839;Ap 27 1849-Mr 1852

Nashville weekly UNION. w 1885-87||
T complete
TKL Je 17 1886

TENNESSEE (*Continued*)

NASHVILLE—*Continued*

Nashville UNION and American. d 1835-Ag 31 1875||
1835-Ag? 1837 as Union; S? 1837-My 17 1853 Nashville union (title varies: Scattered numbers as National union; National union and American); N 1866-Ag 1868 Nashville union and dispatch. United with Republican banner to form Nashville American
CoHi Mr 5 1863
CtY N 24 1863-65
DLC Ap 1835-[36]F 25 1837-41;D 20 1842; Ja-D 19 1843;Ja 23 1844-48;O 19-N 1 1852; Ja 24,26,Mr 7 1853-Mr 8 1861;62-66;My 17 1867;Mr 13 1868;O 2 1869;70-F 13,18,20,My 25 1872;Jl 11 1874-75
ICHi Mr 3 1836;Jl 13,S 15,O 21,25-27,29,N 7, 25,28 1865
KHi [S 1856-My 6 1861]
MB 1858-F 16 1862;Jl-S,D 29-31 1864
MBAt Mr-Jl 18,21-Ag 6,8-O,N 3-D 2,4-19,22 1863-[64-65]-Je 17 1866;Jl 11,13-14,17,23-26,28-Ag 1,3,7-10,13-14,16,21,31,S 3-4 1867
MWA O 4,14 1844;Je 8,15 1850;Je 22,N 7 1855; Mr 16, Ap 30,D 7 1856;N 11 1859;My 27,Jl 26 1862;Mr 25,N 10 1863;Ap 8-9 1864;Je 8,22, 24,29,Ag 6,29,D 10,17 1865;N 10,17,21,23,30,D 14,21-22,29 1867
MeBa [F 25-Ap 8 1863]
MsHi Ag 5,24 1853
N Je 29 1870
NNHi Ap 25,Jl 8 1862;Ap 11,Je 14,N 22 1863
NcD [1840;45;Ja-Ap 1 1848]Je 13 1850;O 19 1853;F 23 1855[F-Ap,Je,Ag 1856;Ag,O-N 1858]F 25 1866
NcU Ag 10,14,30 1861
OCHi D 18 1860;Ja 21,28,Mr 10,24,Jl 10,27[Ag 23-D 19 1861]Ja 4-5,28-29,F 1 1862
OCl Jl 10 1864
OClWHi Ag 9,14 1845;Mr 29,D 10 1861;Ja 17, My 21,28,Je 8 1862;My 2,O 9,D 7-8 1863;Ja 12-13,15 1864;S 19 1865;Ap 30,My 4,Jl 25 1866
OHi Jl 3,7 1863
PHHi Jl 2 1865
PHi Je 17 1862
PLhT Mr 7,Ap 11,S 12,N 28 1864
T D 18 1845[53-54;57]-[62-63;65-66]70-71;73-75;extra S 19 1836;D 10 1844
THi 1835-40;55;O 1857-Mr 1858;Ja-Je 1875
TKL Je 29,Jl 15,Ag 10 1855;Je 17 1864;Ja 6 1866;S 11,17 1873;Je 25 1874;My 7 1875
TN [1835-36]37;39-42;44;48-[54-55]-[59-61;65-68]-[72]-[75]
TU N 21 1861;Ja 10,17 1862
TxU My 1 1862;Mr 30 1864
WHi F 3 1864;Ap 14 1865

Nashville UNION and American. w 1835-Ag 31 1875||
Title varies: Union; Nashville union; National union; Weekly union and American sw and tw during sessions of legislature
Ct [1835]
DLC Jl 19 1843;Ja 15 1845-46;Ap 1847-Mr 20 1848;Jl 17,O 7,D 11 1853;O 15,N 19-26 1855; Mr 4,6 1857;Jl 7,D 9 1861
GU My 19 1835-My 4 1843;Jl 15 1865
MBAt Je 23-30 1866
MH Ja 6-Ap 7 1847
MWA Jl 10,D 3 1835;Mr 5,Ag 18,S 1 1836;Mr 26 1839;O 5,N 10 1840[Ja 11-N 1 1841]S 20 1842;Ap 14,My 9-12,23,Je 2 1843;Ap 20,Ag 6 1844[46-47]F 14 1848;Je 10 1852;Ap 27 1854; Mr 12,My 21 1860;Ap 29 1861
MeBa [Mr 23 1863-Je 13 1864]
NcD O 7 1861
OClWHi Mr 23 1863;Jl-N 3 1866;N 17-24 1867
PLhT Mr 11-17,Ap 11,S 12,N 28 1864
TKL N 13,14 1867
TU Ja 31,F 23,Ap 18-19,21 1868
TxU Ap 16 1849;Ag 29 1853

***Nashville WHIG.** w Ag 26 1812-Ag 22 1826||?
Ag 25 1817-Ag 14 1819 as Nashville whig and Tennessee advertiser. United with National banner to form National banner and Nashville whig
DLC 1821-Ag 22 1826
KyLo Mr 8 1824-Jl 1826
MWA Jl 14 1823;Ag 9,O 27,D 13 1824;Ja 31 1825
N Ja 31 1825
NcD Ja 17 1821
T Jl 30 1825
THi 1823-24
TKL F 21 1825

Nashville WHIG. 1839-49 *See* Nashville true whig

WHIG banner. w 1843-
PUn Jl 20 1844
T My 13-Je 10,24-Jl 9 1843
TU 1843-44
Tx My 13,Je 10-Jl 1,15,29 1843;My 11,Jl 20-Ag 17,31-S 14,O 5-12 1844

Daily WORLD. d 1881-84||
1882 as Morning world
T My 10 1882-Je 1883;Jl-D 1884
TKL Jl 18 1883
TxU Jl 6,Ag 12 1882

WORLD. w 1881-84||
TU-J O 15 1884

NEW MARKET

EAST TENNESSEAN. *See under* Rogersville

NEW TAZEWELL

New Tazewell ENTERPRISE. w 1930+
TU [1931]+

NEWBERN

Newbern TENNESSEAN. w Mr 17 1888+
pub 1888+

NEWPORT

COCKE county tribune. w,sw 1918+
1918-F 25 1932 as Optimist
TU [1930-32]+

OPTIMIST. *See* Cocke county tribune

Newport PLAIN TALK. sw 1900+
T N 8 1922;Ja-Je,N 13 1923;Ja 8 1926
TU Ja 19-23,F 2 1934

OLIVER SPRINGS

Oliver Springs NEWS. w Je 22 1887-
TKL S 14,N 16,30 1887

ONEIDA

SCOTT County news. w 1915+
pub 1915+
T My-Je 1923;Ap 4 1924

ORLINDA

Orlinda OBSERVER. w Je 1928+
pub Jl 1928+

PARIS

GAZETTEER. w Ag 3? 1848-
MWA Jl 28 1849

Paris INTELLIGENCER. *See* Post-intelligencer

PARISIAN. w 1895+
pub 1913+
TU Je 29 1934+

Paris POST. w 1872-84||?
United with Paris intelligencer to form Paris post-intelligencer

Paris POST-INTELLIGENCER. w,d 1866+
1866-84? as Paris intelligencer
w 1866-My 1930
pub 1915+
T S 6 1929
TU Ja 2 1934

WEST-TENNESSEAN. w 1827-
DLC O 19-26 1838
T N 19 1827;Mr 10 1837;Je 29-Jl 6,20,O 26 1838;F 8-15,Mr 29,Ap 12,26,Jl 12,N 1 1839

WEST Tennessee whig. w
DLC Ag 28 1840

PARSONS

NEWS-LEADER. w 1925+
pub Mr 17 1925+
T S 10 1926

PETERSBURG

HERALD. w 1928-32||

PIKEVILLE

BLEDSONIAN. w 1891+
TSE 1932+

PITTSBURG

Pittsburg HUSTLER. w
TSE 1932+

PULASKI

Pulaski CHANTICLEER. w?
MWA Ja 7 1863

Pulaski CITIZEN. w 1854+
A 1897-98
TSE 1932+
VHi Ap 22-My,Je 10,24,S 23,N 4-11,D 16 1897; F 24,Ap 7 1898

CRANE'S Tennessee democrat. w Ap 15 1852-
DLC O 21-28 1852

GILES county record. w 1894+
pub 1894+
T Mr 26 1924
TSE 1932+

INDEPENDENT citizen. w 1854-61||?
T Mr 1 1861

Pulaski RECORD. w 1894+
TU [1931;34]+

TENNESSEE beacon and farmers' advocate. w 1831-34||?
DLC S 26,O 17 1834
MWA Je 16-23 1832

WESTERN star. w 1849-51||?
T [1849-50]51

WHIG courier. w D 15 1838-43||?
DLC D 15 1838;Ja 12,26 1839;Je 3,Jl 30,S 24 1841;Ja 27,Ap 28 1843
T S 20 1839

PURDY

WHIG banner. w
T Ag 20 1859

RANDOLPH

Randolph RECORDER. w Je 21 1834-36||?
TM 1834-Jl 10,S 25 1835-S 23 1836

Randolph WHIG. Ja 6-Ap 7 1838||?
DLC Ja 6 1838
T Ap 7 1838

RIPLEY

Ripley ENTERPRISE. *See* Lauderdale county enterprise

LAUDERDALE county enterprise. w Ag 1885+
1885-87? as Ripley enterprise
pub 1900+

ROCKWOOD

Rockwood TIMES. w 1880+
pub 1906+
T Jl 23 1921;F 2 1928
TKL D 11 1880;O 5 1883;Ag 30,S 27 1884; S 10-24,O 22,N 12-26 1887
TU O 22 1887;O 15 1908[31]

ROGERSVILLE

EAST TENNESSEAN. w 1834-40||?
1834-36? pub at New Market
DLC Ap 2 1839;Ap 25 1840
ICHi F 10 1836
MWA N 23 1839;Ap 4 1840
T Mr 7 1840

Rogersville HERALD. w 1886+
TKL O 8 1887
TU Je 22,Ag 17 1933

HOLSTON journal. w Ap 9-Je 18 1870||?
T Je 18 1870
TKL Je 18 1870

HOLSTON review. See Rogersville review

INDEPENDENT. w Ja 28 1858-
NcD Mr 11 1858

Weekly REPORTER. w 1871-72||?
NcD S 13 1872
TKL S 27 1872

Rogersville REVIEW. w 1885+
1885-87? as Holston review
NcD Ag 6 1885;Mr 31 1892
T Ag 1934
TKL D 3 1885

Rogersville SPECTATOR. w Ja 4? 1877-81||?
MWA Je 7 1877

STAR. w 1893-1918||?
TKL Ag 22 1894

Rogersville TIMES. w 1850-
MWA Jl 7 1853;S 6 1855;D 4 1856
T Ag 14 1851

ROSS' LANDING

HAMILTON gazette. w Jl 19 1838-
DLC Jl 26 1838

RUGBY

Rugby GAZETTE and East Tennessee news, m,w Ja 1881-N 15 1890||
1881-N 17 1883 as Rugbeian; N 24 1883-Ag 9 1884 Plateau gazette and East Tennessee news. Followed by Rugby news
TKL Ja,Ap 1881;Ap 1 1882
TR 1881-82
TU D 12 1885

Rugby NEWS. w N 22 1890-F 21 1891|| ?
Follows Rugby gazette and East Tennessee news

PLATEAU gazette and East Tennessee news. *See* Rugby gazette. . .

RUGBEIAN. *See* Rugby gazette. . .

RUSHVILLE

Rushville JACKSONIAN. w 1863-80||
NbHi Ap 23 1874;F 5 1880

RUTHERFORD

Rutherford REGISTER. w N 22 1889+
pub 1889+

SAVANNAH

COURIER. 1885+
pub 1885+
T S 5 1930
TU [1930+]

SEVIERVILLE

Sevierville ENTERPRISE. w Je 1 1882-83||?
TU Je 1 1882(facsimile)

MONTGOMERY'S vindicator. w 1897+
TU Mr 6 1907;D 6,20 1933

RECORD republican. w Ag 19 1914+
1914-Ag 25 1915 as Sevier county record; S 1 1915-27? Sevier county republican and the Sevier county record
pub 1914+
TU 1914-Ag 1915;Ag 12 1925;34+

REPUBLICAN. *See* Sevier county republican

SEVIER county record. *See* Record republican

SEVIER county republican. w 1883-1915||
1883-S 1887? as Republican. United with Sevier county record to form Record republican
DLC D 19 1885;Je 26 1886
TKL Ap 17,D 24 1886;S 23,O 28,N 4,18 1887

SEVIER county republican and the Sevier county record. *See* Record republican

TENNESSEE (*Continued*)

SHELBYVILLE

AMERICAN union. w Jl 29 1865-
ICHi S 16 30 1865
MWA F 24 1866
OHi Ag 5,19,27 1865

BEDFORD county times. w 1886+
pub S 20 1926+

EXPOSITOR. w 1848-
1848-51 as Shelbyville expositor
Ja 4 1852 never pub
MWA D 10 1850;S 24 1851;Ja 12 1852
OClWHi S 10 1851

Shelbyville GAZETTE. w 1873+
pub 1888+
DLC Ag 22,S 5 1879;Mr 10 1881

IMPARTIAL Compiler. w
T F 25, 1827

Shelbyville INTELLIGENCER. w 1842-
T D 20, 1842

Tri-weekly NEWS. tw My 3? 1862-
MWA Je 21 1862

Daily REBEL banner. d Ja? 1863-
OClWHi Ap 4 1863

REPUBLICAN. w Ag 17 1866-
MWA O 19 1866

WESTERN freeman. w O 30? 1831-35||?
DLC N 27-D 4,18 1832;Ja 8,Je 4 1833;Mr 27, My 29,Je 12-19,Jl 10 1835
MWA Mr 6 1832
T Ja 1833
TKL F 20 1835

WESTERN intelligencer.
DLC Ag 29,S 12 1828

SMITHVILLE

Smithville REVIEW. w 1891+
TSE 1932+

SOMERVILLE

Somerville FALCON. *See* Fayette falcon

FAYETTE falcon. w 1866+
1866-82? as Somerville falcon; 1883?-1907? Reporter and falcon
pub 1901+-
ICM My 5 1886
T Je 3 1875
TSo 1933+

Somerville REPORTER. w 1836-47||?
DLC Je 5 1847
MWA Jl 3 1852
T Ap 9 1842
TM Mr 9 1839-F 1840

Somerville REPORTER. w 1880-82||?
United with Somerville falcon to form Reporter and falcon, later Fayette falcon

REPORTER and falcon. *See* Fayette falcon

SOUTH PITTSBURG

South Pittsburg HUSTLER. w 1899+
T Jl 16 1931
TU My 19 1932;Jl 27 1933;Ja 18 1934

MARION county record. w O 19 1932-
TU O 19 1932

SPARTA

Sparta EXPOSITOR. w 1877+
pub 1877+
TU Mr 2 1934

Sparta GAZETTE. w
DLC Jl 31,Ag 14 1841

Sparta NEWS. w Ap 1 1915+
pub 1915+

Sparta RECORDER. w Je 9? 1831-
MWA Mr 24,Ag 5 1832
TKL [S 24 1831-Ag 24 1833]

Sparta REVIEW. w 1821-27||?
DLC F 11 1824-D 28 1825
MWA Jl 21 1824
T O 26,D 28 1827

SPARTONIAN and Mountain district advertiser. w Ja 3 1829-
DLC Je 20,Jl 4-18,Ag 29,S 19-26,O 17 1829; Ja 2,16 1830

Sparta TIMES. w Ag 4 1846-
OClWHi Ag 8 1846

WHITE county favorite. w 1896-1917||
Merged with Sparta expositor

SPRING CITY

Spring City SENTINEL.
T Jl 23 1925;F 2 1928

SPRINGFIELD

Springfield HERALD and Robertson county news. w 1889+
1889-Jl 17 1917 as Springfield herald
pub 1923+
TU [1932-34]

Springfield RECORD. w 1869-1919||?
T 1888-Ag 1889

ROBERTSON county times. w 1922+
TSpH 1929+
TU D 6 1934

SUNBRIGHT

Sunbright DISPATCH. w 1883-1906||?
TKL Je 12 1886;S 3-10,24,O 29,N 12-19 1887

SWEETWATER

Sweetwater DEMOCRAT-NEWS. w,sw 1876-96||
1876-90 as Monroe democrat
w 1876-94?
DLC O 9 1879
TKL S 26 1878

Sweetwater ENTERPRISE. w 1867-76||?
TKL Ag 26,D 15 1870;My 4,25,Je 29,Ag 24 1871

MONROE county times. w 1928-34||?

MONROE democrat. *See* Sweetwater democrat-news

TAZEWELL

CLAIBORNE progress. w O 5 1887+
T N 19 1930;Jl 20 1932
TU Ap 19,Je 21 1933;Ja 10-24 1934

TRACY CITY

CUMBERLAND outlook. w
TU Ja 23 1931;Je 3 1932

TRENTON

Daily BULLETIN. d Jl 1 1931+
pub 1931+
TTH 1931+

GIBSON county herald. *See* Herald-democrat

HERALD-DEMOCRAT. w F 13 1885+
1885-94 as Gibson county herald
pub 1885+
TU N 26 1931;Ag 23,D 20 1934;35+

SOUTHERN standard. w 1856?-
MBAt Ja 4 1862

STAR-SPANGLED banner. w
TM My 3 1850

WESTERN union. w
T Mr 29 1838

TULLAHOMA

Tullahoma GUARDIAN. w D 15 1880+
1880-81 as Manchester guardian (Manchester)
pub Jl 1919+
T Je 19 1931
TSE 1932+
TU F 26 1932

UNION CITY

COMMERCIAL. w 1888+
CtY Ag 15,20 1915;F 4-11 1916
TU [Ag,D 1934]+
TU-J Ag 8 1902

Union City daily MESSENGER. d S 3 1927+
TU S 1933+

OBION democrat. w 1886-1910||?
TU Jl 26 1901

WARTBURG

MORGAN county news. w 1917+
TU F 1 1934

MORGAN dispatch. w 1876-79||?
TKL Mr 23 1878

WAYNESBORO

WAYNE countian. *See* Wayne county news

WAYNE county news. w 1883+
1883-S 1933 as Wayne countian
pub 1915+
TU [1931;34]+

WHITE PINE

EASTERN progress. w 1878-84||
TKL F 7 1884

WHITESBURG

Whitesburg TIMES. w 1878-79||
TKL Je 12,Jl 3 1879

WINCHESTER

Winchester ARMY bulletin. w
DLC Jl 11,17 1863
MnHi Jl 12,Ag 8,15 1863
OClWHi Ag 16 1863

Daily BULLETIN. d N? 1862-
OClWHi Ja 17,My 7 1863

FAMILY messenger. w F 25 1843-
DLC F 25 1843

FRANKLIN county truth. *See* Truth and herald

Winchester HERALD. w 1906-12||?
United with Franklin county truth to form Truth and herald

Winchester INDEPENDENT. w Ap 5 1850-51||?
NNHi Ap 12 1850
TxU Mr 14 1851

TRUTH and herald. w 1893+
1893-1912? as Franklin county truth
TU S 13,D 20 1934;35+

WOODBURY

CANNON courier. w 1884+
pub 1930+
T Mr 23 1923;Mr 19 1927;Ag-O 1930;Mr-D 1931;32
TU Ja 20 1933

TEXAS

ABILENE

Abilene morning NEWS. d S 1 1926+
Sunday ed as Abilene reporter-news
pub 1926+
TxAM 1926+
TxAS O 1926—

Abilene semi-weekly REPORTER. w,sw 1884-1920||?
1884-Mr 3 1911 as Abilene reporter (w)
CU-B Mr 20 1885
Tx Ap 1911-15
TxU Je 24 1904-Mr 13 1908

Abilene daily REPORTER. d 1888+
Sunday ed as Abilene reporter-news My 25 1930 is West Texas Chamber of Commerce ed
pub 1888+
M My 25 1930
T My 25 1930
TxAS Jl 1921+
WHi My 25 1930

TAYLOR county news. w 1885-1908||?
CU-B O 30 1885
TxAM 1885-98
TxU S 23 1898-Mr 10 1899;Jl 8 1905-Ag 1906

Abilene TIMES. w,d 1909+
1927? as Abilene evening times; Ja 2-F 27 1928 Abilene morning times
d 1927?-F 27 1928
TxU Ap 1927-Mr 1928

ALBANY

Albany ECHO. w 1875-F 8 1884||
1875-78? as Frontier echo (Jacksboro); 1879-My? 1883 Fort Griffin echo (Fort Griffin). United with Albany star to form Albany news
TxU Je 30 1875-D 6 1878;79-Ja 21 1882;Je 1883-84

Albany NEWS. w F 1884+
Formed by the union of Albany echo and Albany star
CU-B Jl 11-25 1889
TxU O 14 1898-O 13 1899;Je 24 1904-Ag 4 1911

Albany STAR. w D 25 1882-D 21 1883||
United with Albany echo to form Albany news
TxU complete

ALEXANDER

Alexander NEWS. w S 1889-92||?
CU-B N 29,D 19 1889;Ja 2-16 1890

Alexander TRIBUNE. w 1884-86||?
Tx Ja 28 1886

ALICE

Alice ECHO. w D 5 1894+
pub [1895-1901;08-11;16+]
TxU O 20 1898-Je 1 1899;Je 30 1904-F 1 1906;My-Jl 3 1913;Ja-S 1928;Ja-Ap 1929

Alice NEWS. w Je 1913+
pub 1913+

ALLIGATOR BAYOU

MUD TURTLE.
MWA Jl 18 1864

ALPINE

Alpine REVIEW. 1889-
CU-B Ag 2 1889

TEXAS (*Continued*)

ALPINE—*Continued*

Alpine TIMES. w 1904-08||?
TxU [Je 22 1904-Mr 1907]

ALTO

Alto HERALD. w 1901+
Tx 1908-16;Je 23 1921

ALVARADO

Alvarado BULLETIN. w Ag 1880+
pub 1880+
CU-B Ag 23,N 1,D 20 1889-Ja 3 1890

ALVIN

COMMONER. w 1899-1900||?
TxU O 1899-Je 23 1900

GULF COAST review. w O 4 1929-32||?
TxGR O 18 1929;S 1931-My 13 1932

Alvin SUN. w 1890+
pub 1903+
KHi S 16-D 16 1892
TxGR S 28 1900;Ja 26,Mr 9 1917;Jl 12 1929+

ALVORD

Alvord NEWS. w 1909+
TxU Je 9 1927-F 20 1930

AMARILLO

Amarillo GLOBE. d F 1924+
pub [1924+]
KHi F 29 1924-25;Je 30 1927
TxAM 1924+
TxU [1929-Je 1935]

Amarillo daily NEWS. d N 4 1909+
pub [1909+]
KHi N 7 1920;Mr 27 1926
Tx S 27-O 1924;N 1927+
TxAM 1923+
TxAS N 1925+
TxBroH Ja 19-30 1933
TxCA 1928+
TxLT O 7 1927+
TxU Ap 28-Jl 8 1913;Jl 18-Ag 9 1918;S 1928+

Daily PANHANDLE. d 1906-20||?
TxU [O 6 1908-O 26 1914]

SOUTHWESTERN plainsman and panhandle weekly. w Ap 1915+
TxU 1918-19

ANAHUAC

Anahuac PROGRESS. w 1908+
TxU 1914-19;Ja 30 1925-28

ANDERSON

GRIMES county journal. w 1871-74||?
1871-72? as Home journal
NNHi Je 27 1872

GRIMES county record. w 1900-05||?
TxU Je 23-O 20 1904

HOME journal. *See* Grimes county journal

ANGLETON

Angleton TIMES. w 1894+
Tx S 3 1897;Mr 1908-12
TxU Je 13 1919-24

ANSON

Anson ENTERPRISE. w 1908-12||?
United with Western reporter to form Western enterprise

JONES county news. w 1897-99||?
United with Texas western to form Western news, later Western enterprise
TxU S 23-D 9 1898

Anson REPORTER. w 1903-05||?
United with Western news to form Western reporter, later Western enterprise

TEXAS western. . . *See* Western enterprise

WESTERN enterprise. w 1883+
1883-89? as Texas western and the Jones county calliope; 1890-99? Texas western; 1900-05? Western news; 1906-12? Western reporter
pub 1923+
CU-B Ag 15-22,S 5 1889
TxU Ja-F 3,S 30-D 16 1898[F 17 1899-O 1901; My 9-Ag 7 1913]

AQUILLA

Aquilla TIMES. w 1905-16||?
TxU 1908-Ap 14 1911

ARANSAS HARBOR

Aransas Harbor HERALD. *See* Aransas Pass herald (Aransas Pass)

ARANSAS PASS

Aransas Pass HERALD. w 1890-97||?
1890-92? as Aransas Harbor herald (Aransas Harbor)
Tx Mr 17 1892

Aransas Pass PROGRESS. w My 30 1910+
pub 1910+
TxGR O 21 1927
TxU My 9-Jl 1913

ARCHER CITY

ARCHER county news. w 1908+
TxU My-Je 1913

ARLINGTON

Arlington JOURNAL. w 1896+
TxU F 28 1927-29

Arlington NEWS-WORLD. w 1887-88||?
1887? as News
Tx Mr 29-Ap 19 1888

Arlington WORLD. w 1884-87||?
United with News to form Arlington news-world

ASHERTON

Asherton NEWS. w 1909-13||?
TxU Je-Ag 2 1912

ASPERMONT

Aspermont STAR. w Jl 1898+
pub F 1917+
Tx F 13 1908-13
TxU 1930-Ag 1932

ATHENS

Athens weekly REVIEW. w 1885+
pub [1885+]
TxGR Mr 29 1928
TxU 1908-Mr 4 1909

Athens daily REVIEW. d 1900+
pub [1900+]
TxU F 6 1925-S 1927;Mr 3 1928-29

ATLANTA

CITIZENS journal. w Mr 1879+
Tx D 1882
TxU Jl 21 1904-Ja 23 1908

AUBREY

Aubrey GRAPHIC. w 1904-16||?
1904-13? as Aubrey herald
TxU My-Jl 3 1913

Aubrey HERALD. *See* Aubrey graphic

AUSTIN

Sunday morning ADVERTISER. w 1903-12||?
TxU Jl 14,Ag 25 1906

Austin AMERICAN. d 1914+
Sunday ed as Sunday American-statesman
pub My 1914+
Tx 1914;Ap 1915+
TxGR N 26 1916;N 27 1922;Ag 14 1927;Je 1 1930
TxU N 8 1914+
WHi Mr 1917-19

Austin ARGUS. w 1882-83||?
Tx S 30-N 4 1882

Austin ARGUS. w Jl 10 1894-
Tx Jl-O 1894

Daily BULLETIN. d N 1841-
Tx Ja 11-15,18 1842

CAMPAIGN intelligencer. w 1859||?
TxU Je 11-18,Jl 16-23 1859
See also Southern intelligencer

Daily CAPITAL. d Mr 6-D 31 1884||?
Tx Mr-Jl 1884
TxU Ag-D 1884

Evening CAPITOL. m
TxU S 1890-Ag 1891

Evening CAPITOLIAN. d 1890-91||?
TxU S 15-N 19 1890

Weekly CAPITOLIAN. w 1890-92||?
TxU O 29,D 3 1891;Ja 28 1892

Austin CITY gazette. w O 30 1839-42||
DLC My 19-26 1841;Ja 19,Ag 17 1842
NN 1839-Mr 2 1842
PWCl My 6 1840
Tx 1839-Ap 8,N 11 1840-Mr 1842
TxWM Ag 12(extra) 1840;D 15 1841

COMMERCIAL journal. w 1877-81||?
TxU Mr 6-20 1879

DEMOCRATIC platform. ir 1859||
Tx Je 28 1859
TxU Je 2,Jl 14,26 1859

Weekly DEMOCRATIC statesman. *See* Austin semi-weekly statesman and diversified farmer

DEMOCRATIC statesman. tw 1871-72||?
TxU Jl 26 1871-72

Daily DEMOCRATIC statesman. *See* Austin statesman

Austin daily DISPATCH. d 1880-89||?
1880-86? as Dispatch; 1887 Evening dispatch
CU-B Jl 9-13,16-18 1889
TxU Je 4 1880;D 20 1881;Jl 17 1882;Ap 19,O 15,17,31 N 25 1883;Mr 12 1884;Je 1,28,O 15,17,31,N 2,15 1889

Austin daily DISPATCH. d 1931+
pub [1931]+
Tx O 23 1932

FERGUSON forum. w N 8 1917+
1917-30? pub in Temple
Tx 1917+
TxGR [O 21 1920-Je 1 1933]Mr 28,Je 4-11 1935
TxH Jl 1926+
TxHuS Ja 31 1918-Ag 1930
TxU 1917-Jl 1933
WHi Jl 11-D 12 1918

Austin FORUM-ADVOCATE. w 1901+
1901-19? as Austin forum (1909?-13? Austin forum and sifter)
Tx D 8-15 1911;Ja 5-19 1912;Ap 28 1921
TxU [Je 1901-S 1916]

FREE man's press. *See under* Galveston

FREEDMAN'S press. *See* Free man's press (Galveston)

Austin daily GLOBE. d
TxU [N-D 16 1889]

GOLD dollar. Ag 1876-
Negro
CSt Ag 1876(photostat)
DLC Ag 1876(photostat)

Sunday HERALD. w
TxU My 21 1876

HERALD. w 1890-1930||?
Negro
TxU [Mr 10 1917-Je 21 1919]

HORNET. w N 15 1918-
TxU N 22-D 21 1918

Tri-weekly INTELLIGENCER. tw N 25 1856-67||?
Tx N 25 1858;Ja 23,30,F 13,20,Mr 6-Ap 10, 17,My-Je 12,Jl 10-24 1861
—w ed *See* Southern intelligencer

INTELLIGENCER-ECHO. w O 21 1874-75||?
TxU [1874-Ag 14 1875]

LONE STAR ranger. w 1849-73||?
1849-51? as Texas ranger; 1852? Lone star and southern watch tower; 1853?-67? Texas ranger and lone star
1849-56? pub in Washington; 1857?-71? also dated in Navasota, Brenham, Chapel Hill and Washington
MWA O 16 1866
NNHi O 28 1854
Tx N 19 1850;Je 26 1852;Mr 25-Ap 1,25,My 26-Je 23,Jl 14,23,Ag 15-N,D 15 1853-N 23,D 28 1854;Ja 23-My 24,Je-O 13,N 10 1855-Mr 2,N 15 1856
TxGR O 12 1849
TxU Ap 30,My 17 1851-S 12,O 23-N 1852;F 2 1854;Ag 29 1857;F 25 1859;S 14,D 17 1860;S 9 1865;Jl 27 1867[70-F 17 1873]

LONE STAR weekly. w,sm 1893-
O 1901?-Je 1908? as Lone star (sm)
Tx O 2 1894
TxU [S 24 1898-Je 8,O 15 1901-Je 15 1908]O 15 1909-Ja 15 1910

Evening NEWS. d 1875-76||?
TxU My 2-11,Je 3-20 1875

Evening NEWS. w 1883||?
TxU Mr 14-Je 27 1883

Austin evening NEWS. d Jl 1891-1903||?
Tx Jl 1892-Jl 1893;Jl 1894-Jl 1896;Jl 1897-Jl 1898
TxU Jl 15 1891-Jl 9 1892;Jl 12 1893-Jl 10 1894;Jl 15 1895-Jl 10 1896;Jl-D 1903

PEOPLE'S advocate. w S 21 1893-95||?
Tx O 12,N 9,D 7-14 1893-[94-Ja 3 1895]

RAMBLER. w S 14? 1858-
TxU N 9 1858;Mr 8,Je 3 1859

RANGER. w 1895?-
TxU N 1897-Je 9 1900

RECORD. w Je 4 1869-
TxU 1869-Ja 21 1870

RECORD. w Mr 17 1886-87||?
CU-B Je 19 1886
TxU 1886-D 6 1887

RECORD. w F 20 1930-
Tx F-Ag 15 1930

REFORMER. w Je 17 1871-
TxU Je-O 14 1871

Daily Austin REPUBLICAN. tw,d 1867-71||?
1867-My 1868 as Tri-weekly Austin republican (tw)
DLC F 6,Mr 7-10,14-19,24,31-Ap 2,7-11,18-30,My 5-9,18-D 1868;Ja 22 1869
MWA Je 11 1870
Tx Je 11-20,23-26,29-Jl 3,6-7,16,18-Ag 1,6,8-13,15-27,29,31,S 28,O 27,N 16,18,D 4,7,17-18, 22-23,29 1868; Ja-Je,S 30,O 1 1869;Ja 7-8,Mr 29,Ap 22,My 18,Je 6 1870
TxU [N 1867-My 1868]-Ja 1871

Weekly Austin REPUBLICAN. w Je 13 1867-71||?
Tx Mr 18,Ap-Je 10,24,Jl 8,N 18 1868-Ja 11 1871
TxU 1867-S 1868

Weekly REVIEW. w 1879-80||?
TxU O-N 1879

Austin daily REVIEW. d
TxU Mr 20 1880

Austin REVIEW. w 1894||?
TxU F 10-S 1 1894

TEXAS (*Continued*)

AUSTIN—*Continued*

SOUTHERN intelligencer. w Ag 27 1856-67||
Followed by Norton's union intelligencer (Dallas)
DLC Ag-S 17,O 28 1856;Ap 8,My 20-Je 10,24, Jl 1,15,29,Ag 19-O 21,N 4-11,25 1857-F 17,Mr 3-17,31-Je 2,16-30,Jl 14-21,Ag 11,S-D 1858;Ja 12,F 9 1859-F,Mr 14 1860;extra Ap 4 1860
PHi extra Ap 4 1860
Tx N 12,26,D 10 1856-Mr 18,Ap 29-My 20,Je 10,N 7,D 9-16 1857;Ja 4(extra)20-27 1858
TxH D 12 1860
TxU N 19 1856-Ag 17 1859;Jl 21 1865-Ap 1867
WHi Mr 23,Ap 13 1859
—tw ed *See* Tri-weekly intelligencer
—campaign ed *See* Campaign intelligencer

SOUTHWESTERN American. w 1849-O? 1853||
Followed by Tri-weekly state times, later Tri-weekly times
Tx N 20 1851
TxU S 2 1850[My 1851-O 1853]
WHi Ap 13,My 11,Je 8 1853

STATE democrat. w Je 15? 1911-19||?
Tx D 21 1911;Ja 25 1912

Tri-weekly STATE gazette. tw 1849?-73||?
Title varies: Texas state gazette
MBAt Je 27,Jl 7-9,14 1863
NjP [Je 18-O 12 1863]
Tx N 19-21,D 2,8,23 1853;Ja 4,18-20,F 11-Mr 3,31,Ap 15 1854;N 9 1857-F 19 1858;S 21,O 5 1866;N 25 1867-N 26 1869;My 27 1872
TxU Jl-D 22 1855;F 8-Mr 27 1866;Ja 25 1869-Ja 10 1873
WHi N 26 1855

STATE gazette. sw Je 24 1857-
Tx Je 24,Jl 1,8-18,25-29 1857;My 27(extra) 1858

STATE gazette (for the campaign). sw Je 24-1857||?
DLC Je-Jl 1,11-15,22,29 1857

Daily STATE gazette. *See* Texas state gazette

Weekly STATE gazette. *See* Weekly Texas state gazette

Daily STATE journal. d Ja 31? 1870-74||?
DLC Ja 15 1874
NNHi Ja 27 1871
Tx [F 1870-71]-Mr 27,29 1872[Mr 1873-Ap 1874]
TxU [F 1870-72]

Weekly STATE journal. w F 3? 1870-74||?
Tx D 15 1870;F 26,Ap 9-My 23 1874

Tri-weekly STATE times. *See* Tri-weekly times

Austin STATESMAN. d Je 1871+
1871-80 as Daily democratic statesman
Sunday ed as Sunday American-statesman
pub My 1914+
CU-B O 22,30 1884;Ap 21 1885;Jl 15,D 25 1886; Ap 2,My 13 1887;D 18-30 1917
NcU Ag 24 1881
Tx Ap 21,28-29 1874;Ja 19,24,F 10,N 7 1875; Je 17 1882;83+
TxGR N 29 1905-S 6 1916;Mr 4 1923
TxH Ja 5-Je 18 1876
TxU O 5-18 1871;73+
WHi Je 8 1893
—tw ed *See* Democratic statesman

Austin semi-weekly STATESMAN and diversified farmer. w,sw 1871-1916||?
1871-83? as Weekly democratic statesman; 1884-97? Austin weekly statesman; 1898?-My 2? 1906 Austin weekly statesman and diversified farmer
w 1871-My 2? 1906
CU-B Ag 29-S 19 1889
MWA Je 25 1874;Ag 26 1875
NcU Ag 25 1881
Tx D 16 1875;76-F 15,Mr,Ap 12,My-Je 7 1877;Je 15 1882;F 21,Je 30 1884
TxGR D 13 1905-D 11 1906
TxU My 1873-O 4 1877;78-S 1883;84;86-97

Daily SUN. d Ja 1885?-
Tx F 16 1885
TxU Ja-Mr 31 1885

Austin evening TELEGRAPH. d
TxU Ag 4-5,25-26 1870

TEMPERANCE banner. S 2 1872-
TxU S 2 1872

TEXAS almanac-extra. tw O 1 1862-
MHi [1863]
NNHi Ja 24,29-31,F 5,23-24 1863
Tx D 13 1862;Ja 6,17,Mr 7,24,Ap 7-30,Mr 7 (supp)12-16,21-28,Je(supp)Jl 6 1863
TxGR O 11 1862
TxU N 1862-Je 1863

TEXAS bladet. *See under* Georgetown

TEXAS capital. w S 9 1877-81||?
Suspended Ja 4-Mr 1 1880; D 19 1880-O 31 1881
Tx 1877-N 22 1881
TxU Ja 27 1878;Ag 22 1880

TEXAS centinel. *See* Texas sentinel 1840

TEXAS democrat. w,sw Ja? 1846-63||?
w Ja?-Ap 8 1846
OClWHi F 4 1846
Tx Ja 21,F 11,Mr,Ap 8-15,My-Jl,Ag 8,19,S 9-23,O 7-D 2,16-30 1846;Ja 6-27,F 10,20-Mr 6,20,Ap 3,10,24 1847;Ja 12,Mr 18,Ag 16,30,S 13,20,O 11-D 10 1848;Ja 28-Mr 10,Ap 3-7, 21,28,My 19,Je 2,16-Jl 21,Ag 4,18 1849
TxU Ja 21-F 4,Mr 11,My 6,Je 17,Jl 29,Ag 26,S 16-23,D 16 1846;Jl 24,D 15,28 1847;F 12,Ap 22,Je 10,20,Jl 19 1848;Je 19,Ag 19,27,D 10 1862;Ja 28,Mr 4 1863

TEXAS land register. w Mr 9 1872-
TxU [Mr-O 12 1872]

TEXAS posten. w 1896+
In Swedish
IRA 1898-1922
MnHi D 26 1912+
TxU Ap 18 1896-My 12,S 29 1898-F 1909; My 19 1910-Ag 10 1911;My 16 1912-Jl 12 1913;My 30-Ag 8 1916;My 20 1926-33

TEXAS ranger. *See* Lone star ranger

TEXAS republican. w S 3 1898-
TxU S 10 1898

TEXAS sentinel. sw,w Ja 15 1840-
Early issues as Texas centinel
sw Ja-F 12 1840
DLC F 5,Ap 15 1840
ICN Ja 22,S 26 1840
NcU Ap 29 1840
Tx Ja 25,Mr 4, 1840;Ja 23-30,F 18,Ap 22-My 13,Jl 8,22-29,Ag 16,19-26 1841
TxU 1840-N 11 1841
TxWM Ja-My,Je 13,Ag 1,15-D 12,26 1840;Ja 9-Mr 11,25-S 9,23,O 7-14,28-N 11 1841(extras: Mr 23 1840;Jl 15 1841)

TEXAS sentinel. w. Je 20? 1857-
MWA O 17 1857
Tx D 19 1857;Ja 2,23,F 6 1858
TxU Jl 1857-Jl 24 1858

TEXAS siftings. w My 9 1881-95||?
CU-B Ag 25,S 22-29,O 13,N 10-17,D 15-22 1883;Ja 5 1884
KHi Jl 22 1882
NcD F 25,S 16 1882
Tx My 9,28-Je 4,18-Jl 2,16-S 3,17 1881-S 9 1882;My 12 1883-My 2 1885;My 8 1886-O 1887; My-O 1888;My-O 1889;My 1890-Ap 1891
TxGR Ag 19 1882;Ja 6,Jl 14 1883;O 3 1885
TxU 1881-Mr 10 1888;Ja 12 1889-Ja 16 1892

TEXAS state democrat. w Ja 21- 1893||?
TxU Ja 28,Mr 11 1893

TEXAS state democrat. w Mr? 1897-1902||?
TxU Ap 19 1897-[1900-Ag 1902]

Weekly TEXAS state gazette. w Ag 25 1849-79||?
Title varies: Texas state gazette; Weekly state gazette; State gazette
DLC Ag 1853-60
MWA O 27 1849;F 14 1852; N 19 1859
NN 1849-Ag 16 1851
NcD Ja 26,Ap 19 1856
NjP [Jl 20 1861-S 10 1862]
TSS Ag 10 1861-Jl 1862
Tx 1849-Mr,Ap 1852-Ag 13,S 13 1853;Ja 3-17 1854;Ja 10,Mr 17,31,Ap 28,S 16-D 6 1856[57-60]-Mr 7 1862;S 30-O 14 1863;Ag 24,O 26,N 9,23-D 21 1864[Ja-Ag 1 1865]Ja 12 1867;D 4 1869
TxGR N 17 1855
TxHuS Ag 20 1853-Ag 19 1854
TxSI Ag 30 1854-Ag 18 1855
TxU 1849-[Jl 1857-Ag 15 1868]
WHi D 8 1855
—sw ed *See* State gazette
—tw ed *See* Tri-weekly state gazette

TEXAS state gazette. d 1869?-79||?
Title varies: Daily state gazette
Tx Ap? 1874;Ja?,F 17 1875
TxH D 15 1874
TxU O 2-19 1870;S 11-30 1871;Ja-My 22 1873; Ag 22 1875-[76]
—tw ed *See* Tri-weekly state gazette
—sw ed *See* State gazette

TEXAS state times. w D 3? 1853-
Tx D 31 1853-Ja 7 1854[Mr 10-D 1855]-Mr 22,Jl 12 1856
TxU O 1854-Je 1857
WHi D 22 1855
—sw ed *See* Semi-weekly *times*
—tw ed *See* Tri-weekly *times*

TEXAS vorwärts. w O 26 1883-1914||?
In German
Tx O,N 9 1883-F,Mr 14-My 2,16-23 1884;Jl 18 1890
TxCoE Mr 1 1889
TxU 1883-O 17 1884;O 23 1885-S 4 1914

Daily TEXIAN. d N 1841-
DLC D 11 1841
Tx Ja 11,13,18,F 2 1842
TxU F 2 1842

Weekly TEXIAN. w N 25 1841-
DLC D 22 1841
TxWM N,D 15,29 1841-F 16,Mr 9 1842

Tri-weekly TIMES. tw N 1853-
Follows Southwestern American. 1853-54? as Tri-weekly state times
Tx N 16,D 1 1853;Ja 17,28,F 2,11-22,Mr 2,9,16 1854;O 2 1855
TxU Ja-Ap 13 1854
WHi D 4,11 1855
—w ed *See* Texas state times

Semi-weekly TIMES. sw
TxU Jl 21-23 1855;Ag 13,O 24 1856;Jl 14 1867
—w ed *See* Texas state times

Austin daily TRIBUNE. d 1891-1915||?
TxU Ap 4 1893-99;1901-02[Ja 19 1911-S 1913]-[14-My 1915]

VORWÄRTS. w Ja 6 1871-75||?
In German
Tx Ja-Je 16,Jl 28-Ag,S 8,22,O 1871-Ja 11,25-F 1,22-My 3,17-24,Je 7-14,Jl 12-19 1873

WESTERN advocate. w F 18 1843-
Suspended from Ap 1-15 1843
ICN Ap 1-15 1843
Tx Je 24 1843

Austin WOCHENBLATT. w 1879-86||?
In German
Tx Je 17 1882;Ap 5 1884

Das WOCHENBLATT. w 1891+
1891-Jl 29 1909 as Bellville wochenblatt (Bellville)
In German
Tx 1912-16;23-25
TxH My 18 1934+
TxU S 17 1891-Mr 1925

YEOMAN. sm Ja 15? 1916-
Tx F 3-Mr 11,Ap 23-My 6 1916

BAIRD

Baird STAR. w 1887+
CU-B Jl 11-Ag 1 1889
TxU Jl 1904

BALLINGER

BANNER. *See* Banner-leader

BANNER-LEADER. w 1890-Ja 24 1913||
Not to be confused with Banner ledger. 1890? as Banner. United with Runnels county ledger to form Banner ledger, later Ballinger ledger
Tx 1908-13
TxU Ag-O 20 1906;10-12

BANNER LEDGER. *See* Ballinger ledger

GOSSIP. *See* Ballinger weekly news

LEADER. w 1882-90||?
United with Banner to form Banner-leader

Ballinger LEDGER. w,sw,d Mr 14 1890+
1890-Ja 23 1913 as Runnels county ledger; Ja 30 1913-31? Banner ledger
sw 1931?;d 1932?;sw 1933?
pub 1900+
MWA Mr 14 1890
Tx Ja 30 1913-S 15 1916
TxU Ja 24 1908-D 17 1909;My 9-Jl 4 1913

Ballinger weekly NEWS. w F 22 1933+
F-Ap 7 1933 as Gossip; Ap 14 1933-Ja 18 1934 Weekly visitor
pub 1933+

RUNNELS county ledger. *See* Ballinger ledger

Weekly VISITOR. *See* Ballinger weekly news

BANDERA

Bandera BUGLE. w 1880-90||?
CU-B Jl 11-S 12,N 21 1889

Bandera ENTERPRISE. w 1883-1915||?
TxU Jl-S 1906

BANGS

ADVOCATE. w 1908-22||?
1908-19? as Bangs enterprise
NN O 15 1915

Bangs ENTERPRISE. *See* Advocate

BARDWELL

Bardwell HERALD. w 1900+
TxU 1928

BARSTOW

WEST Texas journal. w 1902-13||?
TxU Je 24 1904-Je 12 1908

BASTROP

Bastrop ADVERTISER. w 1853—
KHi D 7 1922
Tx My 28 1870;My 1 1871;My 8-15 1875;Ap 25 1929
TxU My 31 1873-Je 6,O 24 1874-D 18 1875; Ja 18-N 22 1878;F 23-Je 1880;Mr 1881-D 19 1885;My 29-O 1886;My 28-D 10 1887;Ap 21-Ag 22 1888;Jl 20-D 14 1889;Ag 30 1890-Ja 22 1892

COLORADO reveille.
Tx Je 24 1852

BATESVILLE

Batesville HERALD. w 1901-16||?
TxU Je 18 1904-Jl 4 1913

BAY CITY

Bay City BREEZE. w 1894-97||?
NcD My 14 1896

MATAGORDA county news. w,sw 1912-21||?
1912-14? as Matagorda county news; 1915-17? Matagorda county news and mud-coast farmer; 1918-19? Matagorda county news and new era
sw 1915-17?
TxU Ag 15 1912-Je 1917

MATAGORDA county tribune. w 1846+
pub [1904+]
—d ed *See* Daily tribune

Daily TRIBUNE. d 1903?+
pub [1904+]
TxU [Je 1903-O 19 1912]
—w ed *See* Matagorda county tribune

BAYTOWN

Daily SUN. *See under* Goose Creek

TRI-CITIES sun. *See* Daily sun (Goose Creek)

TEXAS (*Continued*)

BEAUMONT

Beaumont ENTERPRISE. w N 6 1880-1901‖?
CU-B [N 1889-N 1 1890]
MWA N 6 1880
TxU O 14-D 9 1882

Beaumont ENTERPRISE. d D 1897+
Jl 22 1930 is golden anniversary ed
pub Jl 1899+
CU-B [N 1889-N 1 1890]
MWA Jl 22 1930
Tx O 1908-Je 1918;O 1922+
TxB 1926+
TxGR [1922-32]
TxPa 1926+
TxU [S 23 1898-Jl 1901;Ag 26-O 14 1904]Ap-O 26 1906;Ag 10 1910-Ag 5 1911;Ja-N 14 1912;16-17;Jl 18-Ag 10 1918[Mr 1929+]

Beaumont daily EVENTS. d Ag 1 1900-
KHi [Ag-S 27 1900]

Beaumont JOURNAL. w,sw 1889-1903‖?
sw 1900-02?
TxU O 1898-Jl 15 1899

Beaumont JOURNAL. d S 1 1899+
pub 1899+

BEEVILLE

Beeville BEE. w 1886-My? 1928‖
United with Beeville picayune to form Bee-picayune
CU-B Ag 22 1889
TxU My 27 1886-My 22 1891;Je 1896-My 1897;Je 1898-[Jl 1908-09]Ap 21 1911-Ap 3 1919;Ap 8 1920-Mr 8 1928

BEE-PICAYUNE. w 1890+
1890-My 31 1928 as Beeville picayune
CU-B S 23-O 6,20,N 10-17,D 1,22 1893;F 16 1894
NcD O 23 1891
Tx Ja 24 1908-15
TxU Jl-D 9 1892;Ja 19 1895-1909;11-15;17-21;23;F 12-D 1925;29-33

BELDEN

Belden MONITOR. w 1883?-94‖?
CU-B Ag 6,20 1889;My 6 1890

BELLVILLE

AUSTIN county times. *See* Bellville times

Bellville COUNTRYMAN. w My 29? 1861-
MBAt Jl 19 1864
TxU Ag 21 1861-Ag 21 1865

Bellville STANDARD. w 1882-91‖?
United with Austin county times to form Times-standard, later Bellville times
Tx Jl 16-23,Ag 6,20 1886

Bellville TIMES. w 1879+
1879-91? as Austin county times; 1892?-93? Times-standard
CU-B Ja 25,F 8,22 1890
Tx Jl-Ag 7 1886;Ja 23 1908-15
TxU Ap 17,My 1,Je 3 1886;Ja 30-D 1893;F 23 1894

Bellville WOCHENBLATT. *See* Das Wochenblatt (Austin)

BELTON

BELL county democrat. w,sw 1896-1910‖?
w 1896-1908?
TxU Ja 30-D 1908

Belton COURIER. w 1878-81‖?
TxU Je 28 1881

Belton DEMOCRAT. w? 1860?-
Tx S 27 1861

Belton INDEPENDENT. w 1856?-
TxU My 1857-Ap 16 1859(photostat)

Belton JOURNAL. w 1866+
Mr 21 1898-Ap 1911? as Journal-reporter
pub 1914+
NcD My 5 1899
TxBe 1915+
TxU Ja 31 1862[Mr 19-N 20 1870;S 30 1898-1903]-Ap 7 1911
WHi N 5 1870[O 18 1877-Ap 6 1882]

Belton NEWS. d 1884-1922‖?
1898-1903? as Evening news
CU-B N 16 1889;Ja 11 1890

Belton NEWS. w 1885-95‖?
1885-89? as Progressive news
CU-B Ag 27 1889

PROGRESSIVE news. *See* Belton news

Belton REPORTER. w Ja 1881-Mr 14 1898‖
United with Belton journal to form Journal-reporter, later Belton journal

BENAVIDES

Benavides FACTS. w 1926+
TxOgO 1926+
TxSdF 1926+
TxU F 11 1931-32

BERCLAIR

Berclair HERALD. w 1892-94‖?
CU-B S 15,29-O 6,20,N 2,10-17,D 1,22 1893;F 16,Mr 2,16-23,Ap 6 1894

BERTRAM

Bertram ENTERPRISE. w 1916+
pub Je 1925+

BIG LAKE

Big Lake NEWS. w 1915-26‖?
1915-24? as Big Lake news and oil review
TxGR Ap 19 1924

BIG SPRING

Big Spring ENTERPRISE. w 1898-D 29 1911‖
Tx 1908-11

Big Spring HERALD. w 1904+
pub 1928+
TxCA 1921+

Big Spring daily HERALD. d Je 1 1928+
pub 1928+
TxU 1930+

BIRTHRIGHT

LONE STAR appeal. m 1887?-
CU-B Ag,O 1890

BLANCO

Blanco NEWS. w 1883-1909‖?
TxU Je 30 1904-S 13 1906

BLOOMING GROVE

SUN. w Mr- 1889‖?
CU-B Ag 16-23,N 22 1889

BLOSSOM

Blossom BEE. w,sw 1884-1927‖?
1925? as Blossom review
sw 1919?-23?
CU-B Ja 24-31,F 28 1890

Blossom REVIEW. *See* Blossom bee

BLUFF DALE

Bluff Dale SUN. w? 1911?-
Tx Ja 10,My 9 1913

BLUM

Blum BULLETIN. w 1909-31‖?
KHi Je 16 1927

BOERNE

Boerne POST and the San Antonio critic. w 1883-1901‖?
1883-1900? as Boerne post 1901? also dated in San Antonio
CU-B Ag 24 1893
TxU [S 22 1898-Ag 23 1900]

Boerne STAR. w 1906+
TxU Ja 24 1908-09

BONHAM

Bonham ADVERTISER. w 1850-
DLC Jl 8 1851

FANNIN county favorite. w,sw 1874-1921‖?
United with Bonham news to form Bonham news and Fannin county favorite
Tx S 29 1898-Jl 6 1899

FARMERS' review. w 1884-1901‖?
CU-B D 6 1889;Ja 10-24,F 21 1890
WHi Mr 2,My 4,O 12,N 23-20 1900;F 28 1901

Bonham daily FAVORITE. d 1892+
TxU [Ag 9 1905-Je 12 1906]F 6 1925
—w ed *See* Bonham news and Fannin county favorite

Bonham HERALD. w 1927+
TxCeC 1930-Je 1931

Bonham NEWS and Fannin county favorite. w,sw 1866+
1866-73? as Texas news; 1874?-1921? Bonham news
w 1866-1904
CU-B Jl 12-26,D 6 1889
TxU Ja 9-Jl 16 1869;Ag 5 1870[99-1903]-Mr 1914
—d ed *See* Bonham daily favorite

NORTH TEXAS enterprise. w 1870?-76‖?
TxU [D 1872-Ja 15 1875]

TEXAS news. *See* Bonham news and Fannin county favorite

BONITA

Bonita ENTERPRISE. w? 1910?-
MWA Ja 5 1912

BORGER

Borger daily HERALD. d O 15 1926+
pub 1926+

HUTCHINSON county herald. w 1926+
pub 1926+

BOWIE

Bowie BLADE. w 1891+
TxU [My 31 1901-05]

Bowie BOOSTER. w F 9 1922+
pub 1922+
TxU 1932

MONTAGUE county independent. *See* Texas independent

TEXAS independent. w 1886-91‖?
1886-90? as Montague county independent
CU-B Ja 1 1890
NbHi Ag 12 1891

BOYD

Boyd INDEX. w 1893-N 1 1907‖
United with Bridgeport index (Bridgeport) to form Wise county index, later Bridgeport index
TxU S 22 1905-07

BRACKETT. *See* BRACKETTVILLE

BRACKETTVILLE

To 1917? as Brackett

Brackettville NEWS-MAIL. w 1880+
1880? as Fort Clark news (Fort Clark); 1881?-1908? Brackett news
CU-B Jl 1889
TxU [F 25-D 23 1899]

BRADY

Brady ENTERPRISE. w 1895-My 2 1910‖
1895-1904? as McCulloch county enterprise. Merged with Brady standard
TxU 1908

McCULLOCH county enterprise. *See* Brady enterprise

Brady SENTINEL. w 1880-1927‖?
CU-B Jl 13-27,Ag 17 1889;Ja 18-25 1890

Brady STANDARD. w,sw Mr 25 1909+
w 1909-10?
pub 1909+
KHi My 2 1910
TxU Ap 29-Jl 24 1913;F 24 1925-26;30-33

BRAZORIA

ADVOCATE of the people's rights. w 1834‖?
TxU F 22 1834

BRAZOS city independent. w 1880-
1880-88? as Independent
CU-B N 9-23 1889;Ja 11 1890
TxU Ap 15,Ag 26 1881;N 24 1882

BRAZOS courier. w 1839-41‖?
TxU [D 1839-N 24 1840]

CONSTITUTIONAL advocate and Texas public advertiser. w,ir S 25 1829-Jl 1833‖?
1829-Ja? 1831 as Texas gazette; F-D 19? 1831 Mexican citizen; D 26? 1831-F 18? 1832 Texas gazette; Mr-Jl? 1832 Texas gazette and Brazoria commercial advertiser
1829-F 18? 1832 pub in San Felipe de Austin
CU-B 1829-F 13,27-Ap,My 8-29 1830(photostat)
CtY Mr 17-24,Ap 21,My 26 1831;Ja 10,F 18 1832
DLC Je 15 1833
NN S-N 7 1829;Ja 23-F 13,27-Ap,My 8-S 6,25-N 1830;Ja 15 1831(photostat)
Tx Je 12 1830(photostat)
TxGR S 5 1832
TxU 1829-F 18,Jl 23 1832

INDEPENDENT. *See* Brazos city independent

TEXAS gazette. . . *See* Constitutional advocate and Texas public advertiser

TEXAS planter. w 1852?-
TxU Jl 28 1852;N 30,D 14 1853;S 20 1854

TEXAS republican. w D 17 1834-Ag 1836‖
CtY Jl 25,Ag 22 1835
TxU Jl 5,O 25-N 8 1834[F 14-N 14 1835]

BRECKENRIDGE

Breckenridge daily AMERICAN. d 1920+
pub 1920+
—w ed *See* Breckenridge democrat

Breckenridge DEMOCRAT. w 1899-1933‖
TxU S 20 1900-F 12 1903
—d ed *See* Breckenridge daily American

BREMOND

Weekly CENTRAL Texan. w My- 1870‖?
Tx N 11 1870
TxU My 30-Je 4 1870

BRENHAM

Brenham BANNER-PRESS. w Ap 1866+
1866-70 as Southern banner; 1871-1912? Brenham banner
pub 1876+
MWA Mr 19,My 21,Je 11,Jl 16,D 24 1868
Tx N 19 1869
TxCA 1866+
TxU O 15 1868;74-F 9 1877;78-80;S 22 1881-Je 8 1882;O 1898-N 16 1899

Brenham daily BANNER-PRESS. d 1876+
1876-1912? as Brenham daily banner
pub 1876+
Tx S 18 1924;Ap 14 1925
TxCA 1924+
TxCoE F 4 1922
TxGR S 10 1925
TxU My 15 1879;My 8-Je 13 1880;81-[S 1882-My 1 1884;98-F 1900]Mr 22 1919

TEXAS (*Continued*)

BRENHAM—*Continued*

Brenham weekly INDEPENDENT. w 1878-83||?
TxU F 9,23,Ap 6,20 1882

Brenham INQUIRER. w 1853-71||?
MWA Ja 19,F 2 1867;S 5,O 31 1868
TxH Je 23 1861
TxU Ja 27-F 3 1854;D 5 1856;Jl 16 1858

Brenham daily PRESS. d 1894-D 31 1912||?
1894?-F 28 1912 as Brenham evening press
United with Brenham daily banner to form Brenham daily banner-press
Tx 1908-12
TxU My 10 1905

Weekly REPORTER. w 1879-81||?
TxU D 24 1880

Daily SENTINEL. d 1879-81||?
TxU Ap 30,My 6,31,Je 11 1879
—w ed *See* Texas sentinel

SOUTHERN banner. *See* Brenham banner-press

TEXAS ranger and lone star. *See* Lone star ranger (Austin)

TEXAS sentinel. w 1879-82||?
TxU S 28,N 23 1881;Ag 17,N 9,30 1882
—d ed *See* Daily sentinel

TEXAS volksbote. w 1873-1918||?
Title varies: Volksbote
In German
TxU S 30 1898-N 17 1911[18-Je 16 1918]

VOLKSBOTE. *See* Texas volksbote

BRIDGEPORT

Bridgeport INDEX. w 1902+
N 8 1907-12? as Wise county index; 1913?-16? Times
Tx F 14 1908-N 1 1912

TIMES. *See* Bridgeport index

WISE county index. *See* Bridgeport index

BRONTE

Bronte ENTERPRISE. w 1918+
TxU 1927-28

BROWNSVILLE

AMERICAN flag. Cameron county and Matamoras advertiser. sw,w 1844?-
Title varies: American flag
sw 1844?-N 1? 1848
1846?-47? pub in Matamoras, Mexico
CtY S 23(extra)1846;Ja 3,Mr 3,10-13,20-24 1847;N 1 1848
DLC N 22-D 6 1848
MWA N 14 1846;Ap 24 1847
TxU My 19 1855
WHi Ag 28 1847

La BANDERA. w 1848?-
In Spanish
DLC S 25 1863
ICHi S 4 1863
MBAt S 18 1863
TxU Jl 31 1862

BOLETIN estraordinario.
In Spanish
MWA N 3,5,D 7,12 1865

CORREO del Rio-Grande. d 1866?-
In Spanish
CtY Ja 8 1867

Daily COSMOPOLITAN. d 1876-93||?
TxU Ag 22 1883-Ag 18 1885;Ag 20-S 1893

El CRONISTA del valle. d,w D 1 1917-
d 1917-S 23 1927
In Spanish
TxU O 8 1924-S 23,O 2 1927-F 1930

DEMOCRAT and ranchero. sw 1875-80||?
1875-79? as Rio Grande democrat
—Spanish ed *See* El Democrata

El DEMOCRATA. sw 1875-80||?
CU-B F 28 1880
—English ed *See* Democrat and ranchero

FORT BROWN flag. w
S 4-25 1863 printed on back of La Bandera
DLC S 25 1863
MBAt S 18 1863
TxU Ap 17,My 4 1862

Brownsville HERALD. d Jl 4 1892+
pub 1892+
KHi Mr 9 1928
Tx N 12 1902
TxGR D 21 1924
TxH My 20 1930+

JOURNAL. w Ap? 1864-
MBAt Jl 13-20 1864
NNHi Jl 13 1864
PHi Jl 13 1864

Daily LOWER Rio Grande. d 1893-96||?
TxU N 17 1893-Je 1 1896

LOYAL national union journal. w Mr 5 1864-
NN Ap 2 1864
NNHi Ap 30-My 7 1864
PHi Jl 13 1864
WHi Mr-Ap 10 1864

Daily METROPOLITAN. d 1893||?
TxU Ag 20-S 1893

MODERN Americans.
Tx My 15 1852

El MUNDO. sw 1885-87||?
In Spanish
TxU D 7 1886

Weekly RANCHERO. w O? 1859-79||?
United with Rio Grande democrat to form Democrat and ranchero
1859-60? pub in Corpus Christi; 1862?-65? in Matamoras, Mexico
MBAt Je 15-29,Jl 20 1867
MWA Ag 31 1867
TxU Mr 10 1860

RANCHERO. tw,d 1866-79||?
Title varies: Daily ranchero; Daily ranchero and republican; Evening ranchero. United with Rio Grande democrat to form Democrat and ranchero
tw 1866?-68?-70?;77?-79?
LNC Mr 23 1867
MWA Ag 14-15 1872;Ap 26,29,My 1-3 1873
PPiHi O 11 1877
TxU S 18 1871;Ap 24 1872;Ja 10 1877

REPUBLICAN. El Republicana. sw 1865-
In English and Spanish
MWA My 23,30,Je 6-13,20 1867
NjWdHi S 20 1865

RIO bravo. w 1851-
In Spanish and English
DLC My 19 1852

RIO GRANDE courier. d 1866-
MBAt F 20 1867;Mr 17 1868
OCHi Ap 6 1866

RIO GRANDE democrat. *See* Democrat and ranchero

SENTINEL. w 1868-76||?
TxU Ag 8 1870

El ZARAGOZA. w D 20 1865-
In Spanish
DLC D 20 1865
MWA D 27 1865

BROWNWOOD

Brownwood BANNER. w 1876-96||?
1876-90? as Brown county banner. United with Bulletin to form Banner-bulletin
CU-B Jl 12,26 1889

BANNER-BULLETIN. w 1885+
1885-96? as Bulletin
—d ed *See* Brownwood bulletin

BROWN county banner. *See* Banner

BULLETIN. w *See* Banner-bulletin

Brownwood BULLETIN. d 1900+
TxBroH Ja 31 1931-N 1933
—w ed *See* Banner-bulletin

BRYAN

Bryan APPEAL. w 1869-77||?
Follows Weekly news-letter?
Tx N 25 1869

BRAZOS pilot. w 1876-Ja 14 1909||
Merged with Bryan weekly eagle to form Eagle and pilot, later Bryan weekly eagle
CU-B Jl 19,Ag 2-16 1889
KHi Je 27 1882
MWA Je 30 1882
TxU Ag 17 1905-Je 18 1908

Bryan weekly EAGLE. w 1889+
1889-Ja? 1909 as Bryan weekly eagle; F? 1909-Ag 1910 Eagle and pilot; S 1910-S 25 1913 Bryan eagle
pub 1889+
Tx F 20 1908-16
TxCA 1921+
TxU O 29 1891-N 17 1892;S 30 1898-Mr 4 1903;Ja 28 1904-N 1906

Bryan daily EAGLE. d 1893+
1893-Ja? 1909 as Bryan morning eagle; F? 1909-Ag 1910 as Eagle and pilot
pub 1893+
TxCA 1921+
TxGR My 6 1929
TxU [O 1898-Ja 1900]-Je 26 1901[D 19 1905-My]-[Ag-N 17 1906]Ap 10 1929+

Weekly NEWS-LETTER. w 1867-69||?
Followed by Bryan appeal?
MBAt Ag 28 1869

BURKBURNETT

Burkburnett STAR. w 1907+
pub 1920+

BURKEVILLE

NEWTON county record. w 1884-1909||?
CU-B N 7,21,D 12-19 1889;Ja 2-9,23-30,F 20 1890

BURNET

Burnet BULLETIN. w 1873+
pub 1920+
MWA Mr 14 1895
Tx N 6 1881;My 4,S 28 1882;My 17,D 3 1883;O 11 1888;Ja 3,O 24 1889;Mr 13,Ap 3,17-24,My 15,S 24,N 29 1891;Ja 20 1893;Je 17 1926;Ag 27 1931
TxU Mr-N 10 1874;Jl 8 1876-F 9 1877;Je 19 1878-Ja 10 1882;O 20-D 22 1898;F 9-Mr,O 1902-Ap 2,Jl 30 1908-Jl 3 1913;Ag 1929-32

BYERS

Byers HERALD. w 1907+
TxU 1926-27

CALDWELL

BURLESON county ledger. *See* Caldwell news. 1897+

Caldwell NEWS. 1886-96 *See* Caldwell news chronicle

Caldwell NEWS. w 1897+
1897-1927? as Burleson county ledger; 1928?-31? Caldwell news; 1932? News and Burleson county ledger

Caldwell NEWS CHRONICLE. w 1886?-1911||?
1886?-96? as Caldwell news
TxU Ja 1904; Je-Ag 24 1905;08-F 1911

Caldwell REGISTER. w My 25 1879-86||?
Tx My 25 1879

CALVERT

ALLIANCE citizen. *See* Calvert tribune 1892+

CENTRAL Texan. w 1871-78||?
CU-B O 26-N 2,30 1878
TxU D 20 1872

Calvert CHRONICLE. *See* Calvert tribune 1892—

CITIZEN-DEMOCRAT. *See* Calvert tribune 1892+

Calvert COURIER. w 1878-99||*
United with Calvert chronicle to form Courier-chronicle, later Calvert tribune

Calvert COURIER. 1917-19 *See* Calvert tribune 1892+

Calvert PICAYUNE. *See* Calvert tribune 1892+

Calvert TRIBUNE. sw,w 1870-72||?
sw 1870-71?
DLC Mr 30 1872

Calvert TRIBUNE. w 1892+
1892? as Alliance citizen; 1893?-97? Citizen-democrat; 1898?-99? Calvert chronicle; 1900?-My 19 1911 Courier-chronicle; My 26 1911-16? Calvert picayune; 1917?-19? Calvert courier
Tx F 1908-13
TxU [N 11 1898-My 1900]-My 1908;My 23 1912-Je 1913;14-Ag 1915;Ag 21 1925-26;My 16 1929-33

CAMERON

Cameron ENTERPRISE. w 1905+
1905-19? as Milam county enterprise
TxCA 1923+
TxU 1908;31-33

MILAM county enterprise. *See* Cameron enterprise

CANADIAN

Canadian CRESCENT. w 1887-90||?
KHi Ja 26 1888-Je 22 1889

Canadian ENTERPRISE. w 1890-Ja 1894||
United with Canadian free press to form Canadian record

Canadian FREE press. w Ag 22 1887-Ja 1894||
United with Canadian enterprise to form Canadian record
KHi 1887-Ja 17 1890

Canadian RECORD. w Ja 20 1894+
Formed by the union of Canadian free press and Enterprise
pub 1920+
TxCA 1894+
TxU Je 12 1919-Jl 21 1921
WyToT 1918-22

CANTON

FREE state enterprise. *See* Canton herald

Canton HERALD. w 1882+
1882-85? as Texan-telephone; 1886-95? Telephone; 1896-1904? Free state enterprise; 1905-10? Van Zandt enterprise
pub 1913+
CU-B Ag 8,N 8-15,D 6-13 1889

TEXAN-TELEPHONE. *See* Canton herald

VAN ZANDT enterprise. *See* Canton herald

CANYON

Canyon NEWS. w 1896+
1896-1925 as Randall county news
pub 1906+
KHi Ap 3 1919;Mr 19 1925

RANDALL county news. *See* Canyon news

CARBON

HERALD. *See* Carbon messenger

Carbon MESSENGER. w 1901+
1901-Ja? 1908 as Herald; F? 1908-16? Carbon news
TxU Je 24 1904-Ja 24,F 14 1908-D 16 1909

Carbon NEWS. *See* Carbon messenger

CARRIZO SPRINGS

Carrizo Springs JAVELIN. w 1884+
TxU 1932
—Spanish ed *See* La Javelina

La JAVELINA.
In Spanish
TxU [Mr 9 1895-1909]

TEXAS (*Continued*)

CARROLLTON

Carrollton CHRONICLE. w 1904+
Tx Mr 10-17 1933

CARTHAGE

Carthage BANNER. w 1887-92||?
CU-B N 15,D 6-20 1889;Ja 3-24 1890

EAST Texas register. w Ja 11 1904-24||?
Tx Ja 24 1908-15

PANOLA watchman. w Jl 2 1873+
CU-B Jl 10-31 1889
Tx 1873-S 7 1881;Ja 22 1908-D 20 1916
TxU 1926;Je 20-D 1927;29

CASTROVILLE

Castroville ANVIL. *See* Hondo anvil herald (Hondo)

Castroville ERA. w 1876-79||?
TxU Mr 30 1877

CELESTE

Celeste COURIER. w 1893+
pub 1922+
TxU Je 24 1904-08

CENTER

Center CHAMPION. w N 29? 1877+
1877-83 as Laborers champion; 1884?-95? Champion press
pub Ag 1910+
KHi D 21 1921
TxU D 6 1877;F 21-28 1878;S 22 1879

LABORERS champion. *See* Champion

SHELBY reporter. w 1925+
pub 1925+

CENTREVILLE

Centreville DEMOCRAT. w 1883-1908||?
1883-85? as Democratic farmer
CU-B D 5 1889
Tx Ap 19-26 1884

DEMOCRATIC farmer. *See* Centreville democrat

LEON pioneer. w Je? 1852-
Tx Je 9-D 15 1852;Ja-Mr,Je 15-O 19,N 1853-D 6 1854;F 27-Ap 11,My-Je 13 1855
TxU Ag 25 1852;Ag 16 1854

CHANNING

Channing COURIER. w 1898-1917||?
TxU Je 24 1904-My 5 1905;My 16 1908-Ap 13 1912

CHAPEL HILL

TEXAS ranger and lone star. *See* Lone star ranger (Austin)

CHILDRESS

CHILDRESS county news. w O 1 1929+
1929-Je 22 1933 as Childress news
pub 1929+

Childress INDEX. w,sw,tw,d Jl 28 1888+
w 1888-1917?;sw 1918-25?;tw 1926?
CU-B Ag 9 1889
KHi F 22 1924
Tx Ja 24 1908-D 20 1916
TxU Ap 30-Jl 12 1913

Childress NEWS. *See* Childress county news

CHILLICOTHE

CHILLICOTHE VALLEY news. w 1898+
pub O 1922+

CISCO

Cisco APERT. w 1892-1914||?
TxU [Je 23 1904-Ag 1913]

Cisco NEWS. w 1881-1923||?
1881-1920? as Cisco round-up
TxU S 24 1898-99;1904;Mr-Jl 5 1907;My-Jl 4 1913

Cisco ROUND-UP. *See* Cisco news

CLARENDON

BANNER-STOCKMAN. w 1891-1910||?
1891-98? as Banner
TxU Je 24 1904-S 1909

CHRONICLE. *See* Clarendon news

DONLEY county leader. w 1929+
pub Mr 12 1929+

INDUSTRIAL west. *See* Clarendon news

Clarendon NEWS. sw,w 1889+
1889-1903? as Industrial west; 1904-09? Chronicle
sw 1904?-16?
pub Jl 19 1917+

CLARKSVILLE

ALLIANCE journal. w 1888-90||?
CU-B N 13-D 11 1889

Clarksville MESSENGER. *See* McKinney messenger (McKinney)

NORTHERN standard. *See* Standard

RED RIVER county review. sw 1921-26||?
TxU F 13 1925-Jl 15 1926

STANDARD. w Ag 20 1842-88||?
1842-57? as Northern standard
DLC O 15 1842;Mr 1848-S 1849
MBAt Ag 12-26,O 21 1865
Tx Ap 28 1849;Jl 2 1853;S 4 1869;N 11-D 23 1881;82-Ap 10,Je-N 13,D 25 1885
TxCoE O 23 1847;N 17 1855
TxU 1842-46;Ap 29 1847-65[Mr 21 1868-S 11 1869;71]-S 1873;80-Ag 1888

Clarksville TIMES. w,sw 1873+
w 1873-1902?
KHi Mr 18 1921
Tx Ja 21 1908-O 25 1910
TxU Ag 1 1890

CLAUDE

Claude NEWS. w 1902+
pub 1932+
KHi Ag 19 1921;My 7 1926
Tx 1908-15

CLEBURNE

Cleburne CHRONICLE. w,sw 1868-1913||?
w 1868-93?
CU-B [1889-90]
TxCl O 21 1868-S 12 1874
TxU [F-D 1890]S 30 1898-Jl 7 1899;Mr 14-S 1902

Daily ENTERPRISE. tw,d 1888-1923||?
1888-94? as Tri-weekly enterprise
tw 1888-94?
TxCl 1890-S 24 1896;1901-Ja 1923
TxU Mr 14-My 1 1916;Jl 17-Ag 7 1918

ENTERPRISE. w,sw 1890-1923||?
1890-1914? as Weekly enterprise
w 1890-1914?
Tx 1908-10
TxCl 1890-S 24 1896
TxU Jl 14 1904-N 14 1912

JOHNSON county review. w 1891-1928||?
TxCl Ap 1891-Ap 18 1902
TxU 1899-1907
—d ed *See* Cleburne times-review

Cleburne TIMES-REVIEW. d 1904+
1904-S 1928 as Cleburne morning review; O 1928-Ja 18? 1930 Cleburne times-review; Ja 19-S 1? 1930 Cleburne morning review
pub 1928+
TxCl My 25 1905-Mr 20 1934
TxU Mr 15-Ap 26 1916;Jl 16-Ag 9 1918
—w ed *See* Johnson county review

Cleburne TRIBUNE. w 1887-94||?
CU-B Ag 24,S 14,O 5,19 1893;F 15,Mr 31-My 12 1894

WATCHMAN. w 1900-07||?
TxU Je 23 1904-Je 21 1907

CLEVELAND

Cleveland ADVOCATE. w 1917+
pub Ap 1932+
TxU F 1925-28

COLEMAN

Coleman DEMOCRAT. w 1897-Ja? 1910||
United with Coleman voice to form Democrat-voice

DEMOCRAT-VOICE. w 1881+
1881-99? as Coleman voice; 1900?-04? Voice and review; 1905?-F 4 1910 Coleman voice
pub 1916+
Tx 1908-D 2 1911

Coleman REVIEW. w 1896-99||?
United with Coleman voice to form Voice and review, later Democrat-voice

Coleman VOICE. *See* Democrat-voice

COLORADO

Colorado CLIPPER. w 1882-93||?
CU-B D 25 1884;O 31 1885

Colorado RECORD. w 1905+
pub 1905+
NN N 26 1920
Tx Ag 14 1931
TxU O 20-D 22 1905;My-Jl 4 1913;Ja 22-Ag 1926;F-O 21 1932

WEST Texas stockman. w 1897-1903||?
TxU S 27-N 1 1898

COLUMBIA

DEMOCRAT and planter. w D 21 1852-
1852-Jl? 1855 as Columbia democrat
TxGR N 20 1860
TxU O 18,N 8 1853;F 11-18,N 25 1854;Ja-F,Jl 24,O 9,23 1855;Jl 8-N 18 1856[Ja 20-N 10 1857]D 21 1858;Ag 16 1859;Jl 3,24 1860;D 3 1861

OLD capitol. w 1887-89||?
Tx Jl 20 1889
TxU D 17 1887-D 8 1888

TELEGRAPH and Texas register. *See* Weekly Houston telegraph (Houston)

COLUMBUS

COLORADO citizen. *See* Colorado county citizen

COLORADO county citizen. w 1857+
1857-1927 as Colorado citizen
pub 1909+
CU-B O 29 1885
Tx D 2 1869;F 2,O 19,N 2,23-30,D 21 1871;Ja 18,F 1,15,29-Mr 1872;My 28 1874;F 24 1876-[77]-F 5,Mr 25-N 4,18 1880-F 14 1889;Mr 13 1890-Ja 2 1894;Mr 1896-Ja 1900;Mr 2 1905
TxGR Ag 24 1923
TxU N 24 1858;D 1 1881;D 24 1904;Mr 12-D 1908;Ja 27-D 1927
WHi Ja 30 1858

Columbus weekly TIMES. w 1867-70||?
Tx Ag 21,O 30,N 27 1869

COMANCHE

Comanche CHIEF. w 1873+
S 1 1912-19? as Comanche chief and pioneer exponent
pub 1912+
Tx F 29 1908;S 17 1910;Mr 18,Ap 1,Je 10,S 23,O 28 1911[14-O 1920;O 14 1921-O 1922;Ap 11 1924-My 1929]
TxBroH D 1928-Mr 2 1934
TxU Ap 1879-N 11 1882

Comanche ENTERPRISE and weekly Wilsonian. w Ja 4 1919-25||?
Tx [1919]-Jl 3,Jl 17,Ag 21 1924;Ja 1-15,Mr 12,Ap 16,30-Je 1925

Comanche PIONEER exponent. w 1887-Ag 1912||
United with Comanche chief to form Comanche chief and pioneer exponent, later Comanche chief
Tx Ja 24 1908-10

TOWN and country. w My 13- 1886||?
Tx Je 3,17-Jl 8,22-Ag 12,S 9,23,O 7 1886

Comanche VANGUARD. w Je 28 1913-D 27 1918||
Tx 1913-D 20 1918
TxU complete

COMFORT

Comfort NEWS. w Mr 25 1904+
pub 1904+
TxU Jl 1904-Mr 3 1905

COMMERCE

Commerce weekly FARM journal. w 1889+
1889-F 1929 as Commerce journal; Mr 1929-My 1931 Commerce herald
pub 1901+
TxCoE 1901-06;08-10;13-17;19;21;23;27;32
TxGR Ag 26 1932
—d ed *See* Daily journal

Commerce HERALD. *See* Commerce weekly farm journal

Commerce weekly JOURNAL. *See* Commerce weekly farm journal

Daily JOURNAL. d O 25 1910+
1910-Ja 2 1911 as Commerce daily journal
Suspended from Ja 2 1911-Ja 1915
pub 1915+
TxCoE 1910-11;16-24;27-28;32
TxU Ap 8 1929-32
—w ed *See* Commerce weekly farm journal

CONROE

MONTGOMERY county news. w 1921+
TxU F 1925-26

COOLIDGE

Coolidge HERALD. w 1904+
TxU F 12 1925-33

COOPER

Cooper COURIER. *See* Delta courier

DELTA county banner. *See* Cooper review

DELTA courier. w 1885+
1917?-24? as Cooper courier
TxU Je 1904-Jl 13 1906

PEOPLE'S voice. *See* Cooper review

Cooper REVIEW. w 1879+
1879-91? as Delta county banner; 1892-1900? Peoples voice
CU-B F 5 1887;Ag 9,D 6-13 1889;Ja 10,Ap 4,Je 20-Jl 11,Ag 15 1890
TxU 1908-N 12 1909

CORPUS CHRISTI

Corpus Christi weekly ADVERTISER. w 1866-72||?
Tx My 20 1870

TEXAS (*Continued*)

CORPUS CHRISTI—*Continued*

Corpus Christi CALLER. d 1883+
1911?-18? as Corpus Christi caller and daily herald
Sunday ed as Corpus Christi caller-times
pub 1883+
MWA N 8 1890
TxGR S 8 1926;N 26 1933
TxU Je 4 1914-16;Je-N 13 1919;D 1929+

Corpus Christi CALLER. w 1883-1915||?
TxU Ja 21 1883-88;O 14 1898-N 6 1908
WHi D 21 1900

Corpus CRONY. w 1901-14||?
TxH S 21 1907[Ap 18 1908-Jl 3 1909]
TxU Ag 1903-Jl 1913

Corpus Christi DEMOCRAT. d 1911-15||?
TxU S-D 1915

Corpus Christi FREE press. *See* Corpus Christi press

Corpus Christi GAZETTE. w Ja 1- 1846||
DLC Ja 8,Mr 8(extra)1846
MWA Ap 2 1846
WHi F 12 1846

Corpus Christi daily HERALD. d 1908-10||?
United with Corpus Christi caller to form Corpus Christi caller and daily herald, later Corpus Christi caller
Tx S 13 1910

El HORIZONTE. *See under* San Diego

NUECES county news. w
OkScN D 14 1934+

NUECES VALLEY. w 1850-
TxU My 25,Jl 13 1850;O 1857-S 1858

NUECES VALLEY. 1870-74 *See* Corpus Christi times 1870-78

El PALADIN. w 1925+
In Spanish
CU-P N 1929-[30-31;33-35]+

Corpus Christi PRESS. w 1930+
1930-31? as Corpus Christi free press
TxU F 13-D 1931

Weekly RANCHERO. *See under* Brownsville

SOUTH Texas news. sm Jl 8 1930+
TxU 1930

Corpus Christi STAR. w S 12 1848-
TxU S 19 1848-S 8 1849

Corpus Christi STAR. w 1892-94||?
CU-B S 29-O 6,N 10-17,D 1,22 1893;F 16-23 1894

Corpus Christi TIMES. w,sw Mr? 1870-78||?
1870-74? as Nueces Valley; 1875? Valley times
w 1870-76?
Tx Ag 27 1870-72;Ja-O 1874

Corpus Christi TIMES. d 1912+
Sunday ed as Corpus Christi caller-times
pub 1912+
KHi Mr 6,Jl 30 1919;N 16 1921;My 24 1922
TxCA 1920+
TxU 1916-N 12 1917

VALLEY times. *See* Corpus Christi times 1870-78

CORSICANA

Daily COURIER-LIGHT. d 1884-1916||?
1884-90? as Daily courier; 1891?-92? Daily observer; 1893?-94? Courier-observer
TxU Jl 8 1904-F 21 1905
—w ed *See* Corsicana observer

Corsicana DEMOCRAT and truth. w N 7 1885+
1885-1904? as Corsicana democrat
CU-B N 7 1885;Ag 1 1889
Tx Ja 23 1905-13
TxU F 26 1925-27

Corsicana INDEX. w 1879||?
United with Corsicana observer to form Observer and index, later Corsicana observer

Corsicana semi-weekly LIGHT. sw 1886+
pub F 1918+
KHi Ja 23,O 26 1923
TxU [Jl 12 1904-Je 9 1908]
—d ed *See* Corsicana daily sun

NAVARRO express. w 1859?-
Tx D 3 1863
TxU Ja 7,Mr 17 1860

Corsicana OBSERVER. w 1856-1916||?
1880? as Observer and index; 1881? Observer-index
Tx O 14 1881-O 6 1882
TxGR D 15 1893

Daily OBSERVER. *See* Daily courier-light

OIL CITY Afro-American. w 1898-1901||?
Negro
DLC Ja 27 1900

Corsicana daily SUN. d 1898+
pub F 1918+
TxCor 1910+
TxU [O 24 1904-Ag 11 1906]
—sw ed *See* Corsicana semi-weekly light

COTULLA

Cotulla TIMES. w 1887-92||?
CU-B Ag 10 1889

CRAWFORD

Crawford SUN. w 1928+
TxU 1929-32

CROCKETT

Crockett COURIER. w 1890+
Tx Ja 23 1908-D 8 1910
TxU Je 23 1904-Je 18 1908;11-Ja 1915

Crockett ENTERPRISE. w 1896-1905||?
TxU S 1893-Mr 22 1899

HOUSTON county times. w 1906+
Tx N 24 1927

Crockett PRINTER. w 1860?-
MWA Mr 13 1861
TxU N 14 1860

Crockett SENTINEL. w 1866-69||?
Tx Jl 13 1869

CROSBYTON

Crosbyton REVIEW. w Ja 14 1909+
pub 1909+
TxU F 13 1927-29

CUERO

DEUTSCHE rundschau. w,sw 1891-1918||?
sw 1900-14?
In German
TxU O 1893-Jl 1901;Jl 1904-O 1907;Ag 1908-Ap 22 1911;Ap 11-N 7 1918

Daily RECORD. d Jl 30 1894+
Title varies: Cuero daily record
pub 1894+
TxGR O 24 1923;Ap 13 1927;N 20 1929
TxU Mr 21 1930+

Cuero STAR. w 1873-1918||?
Tx Ja 9 1874
TxU Ap 21 1881;Mr 10 1883

Cuero daily STAR. d 1897?-1918||?
Tx 1908-16

CUMBY

Cumby RUSTLER. w 1892+
Tx F 1908-13

DAINGERFIELD

MORRIS county news. w 1889-1929||?
TxU My 15-Jl 3 1913

DALHART

Dalhart TEXAN. w,sw,d My 1901+
w 1901-29?;sw 1930-32?
Tx F 1908-O 13 1916
TxDa Je 1923+

DALLAS

ADVANCE. w,ir Ap 9 1928-
Tx 1928-Je 15 1929

BULLETIN. 1922||?
Tx O 25,30,N 1 1922
TxGR N 1 1922

Dallas daily COMMERCIAL. d 1873-80||
Merged with Dallas daily herald
TxU F 8-Ag 1874

Daily CONSTITUTION. d
TxU Je 20,Ag 21 1890

Dallas DEMOCRAT. w 1892-1923||?
C [1913-14]Mr 18 1916-[20-21]
MWA Ja 4 1919
M 1914-19
MnHi 1920[21]
MnU Mr 18 1916-19
PP [1914]Ja 19,S 28 1918
T Ag 14-21 1920
Tx My 13-20,Je 10-17,O-N 15 1922
TxU Ag 18 1903-07
WHi N 29 1913-N 21 1914;17-N 13 1920

Dallas DISPATCH. d S 16 1906+
pub Mr 17 1918+
TxD 1906-Mr 16 1918

EVERYBODY'S business. w Ap 24? 1925-
Tx My 22-Je 5 1925

Dallas EXPRESS. w 1893+
Negro
DLC Ja 13 1900
TxU 1919-28

Semi-weekly FARM news. w,sw O 8 1885+
1885-Ja? 1894 as Dallas weekly news; Ja 16 1894-S 1908 Dallas semi-weekly news
w 1885-Ja 1894
pub 1885+
TJT F 4 1892
TxGR Je 28-Ag 9 1898
—d ed *See* Dallas morning news

Dallas HERALD. w 1848-D 31 1887||
Suspended for a time during the Civil War
TxU [D 1855-O 4 1856]Jl 1858-Je 20,O 10 1860-S 1863;Jl 1864-Je 8 1878;81-85;87

Dallas daily HERALD. d 1873-D 28 1887||
United with Times to form Daily times herald
CU-B N 8 1885
Tx N 9,13,16-17,19-20,23,27,29-D 28 1881;F 1882-N 1885
TxDT [1876-86]
TxU F 11 1873-Je 13 1878;F 1880-[83]-85;O 1886-87
WHi Je 24,26 1877

INDEPENDENT democrat. *See under* Houston

ITEM. w 1891-1900||?
Negro
DLC Ja 27 1900

Dallas JEFFERSONIAN.
TxU O 9 1909;Ap 16,My 2,S 25,O 9 1910

JEWISH examiner. w F 23 1934+
TxGR 1934+

Dallas JOURNAL. d Ap 17 1914+
1914-D 31 1919 as Evening journal
pub 1914+
Tx 1914-Je,S 1915+
TxDM Je 1924-Ja 1930

Morning MAIL. d 1876-78||?
1873? as Evening mail
Tx Mr 8 1877
TxH N 25 1876

Weekly MAIL. w 1876-78||?
TxH N 25 1876

Dallas MERCURY. w 1882-87||?
CU-B 1886-Ja 14,Mr 18 1887
Tx Ag 5/7,21 1885-Mr 5,19 Ap 2,23,My 1886
TxU Ag 27 1886

Dallas morning NEWS. d O 1 1885+
O 1 1925 is 40th anniversary ed
O 1 1935 is 50th anniversary ed
pub 1885+
ArT 1928+
CU-B N 8 1885;Mr 20,22,Ap 2,4-5 1886;Ag 5-S 23 1917
CtY [1935+]
DLC Jl 1910+
ICU 1935+
IHi F 12 1909
InRE Ag 17 1890
M Ap 30 1932
MWA O 1 1889;Ja 1 1916;My 12(extra)O 1 1925;O 1 1935
MnU Ja-Mr,Je-Jl 1920
OkDS 1933+
PP Ja 1 1929;34+
Tx D 9 1885-D 15 1886;96+
TxAM 1923+
TxAS Mr 11 1925+
TxBroH Ap 1930-Mr 9 1934
TxCA 1919+
TxD 1902+
TxDM [F 1894-1911]Je 1923+
TxDeN Ag 1919+
TxE Jl 1917+
TxF 1904+
TxGR Ag 1-4 1893;Ap 16 1895;Mr 8-10 1898; Je 21 1904+
TxGa Ja 11 1916+
TxHuS 1924+
TxLT Jl 1905+
TxNS 1926+
TxU 1885-Ag,O 1887+
TxW 1930+
TxWB 1924-Ap 1932
WHi Ap 23 1902;Ja 1 1907;F 13 1917-20
—w,sw ed *See* Semi-weekly farm news

NORD Texas presse. w 1891-1918||?
In German
Tx 1912-16
TxU Ap 25-Jl 18 1918

NORTON'S intelligencer. *See* Norton's union intelligencer (d)

NORTON'S union intelligencer. w 1867-98||?
Follows Southern intelligencer (Austin)
DLC O 12 1878-D 1880;My 28 1885-Ag 24 1895
MBAt N 22 1867
OClWHi Ja 8,22-Ap 16,30,Je 4 1887
TxU Ja-My 24 1873;Ap 24-Jl 24 1875

NORTON'S union intelligencer. d 1876-85||?
1876-Je 15 1881 as Norton's daily intelligencer; Je 16 1881-N 3 1883 Norton's daily union intelligencer
DLC O 19 1880-My 12 1885

OAK CLIFF tribune. w Ja 1902—
pub [1902+]
TxD [1902+]

Dallas SATURDAY night. w 1919-
TxGR Ja 10[Mr 13-Je 19]1920

SOUTHERN advocate. *See* Independent democrat

SUNNY clime. 1878-91||?
CLM Ag 31 1889

TEXAS advance. w 1890?-
TxU S 16 1893-Ag 1894

TEXAS citizen. ir Jl 16 1932-
Tx Jl 16 1932;Je 15 1933

Die TEXAS post. *See under* Galveston

TEXAS tribune. *See under* San Antonio

TEXAS volksblatt. w 1877-88||?
In German
KHi O 5 1888

Daily TIMES HERALD. d 1876+
1876-87 as Times; Ja 1 1888-Je? 1893 Dallas daily times-herald; Jl? 1893-F 17 1891 Times herald
pub [1876-87]+
CU-B My 25 1882
Tx Ap-S,O 20 1890;Ja-Mr 1891;92-Je,Ag 1893-Mr 1894;O 1897+
TxD 1910+
TxDM Je 1924+
TxU Ag 19 1889-91;Mr 8-Ag 22 1892

La TRIBUNA italiana. w Je 21 1913+
In Italian
pub 1913+
IU D 8 1917+

DAWSON

COTTON belt. w 1888-91||?
CU-B Ag 3,24,N 9,23,D 14 1889 Ja 4,25-F 1, 15 1890

TEXAS (*Continued*)

DECATUR

Decatur NEWS. w 1881+
TxU Ja 24 1908-16
TxU 1889-1915;F 13 1925-31

WISE county messenger. w 1880+
CU-B Ag 31 1889
TxU O 26 1906-D 9 1910;O 13 1922-33

De LEON

De Leon FREE press. w 1890+
pub Jl 1923+

DELLA PLAIN

Della Plain REVIEW. w 1888-92||?
CU-B Ag 27,S 10,D 6-13,27 1889;Ja 3 1890

DEL RIO

FARM and stock record. *See* West Texas news

NEWS. *See* West Texas news

Del Rio evening NEWS. d 1900+
pub Mr 20 1929+
TxU Jl 31,N 4,D 30 1903
—w ed *See* West Texas news; Val Verde county herald

Del Rio RECORD. *See* West Texas news

VAL VERDE county herald. w 1904+
pub 1908+
TxU 1905-S 13 1907
—d ed 1930+ *See* Del Rio daily news

WEST Texas news. w 1887-1929||?
1887-92? as Del Rio record; 1893?-1901? Farm and stock record; 1902?-04? Record-news; 1905?-06? News
pub 1907-29
CU-B Ag 10-31 1889
TxU Jl 21 1887
—d ed *See* Del Rio evening news

DENISON

GATE CITY guide. w 1887-92||?
CU-B Ag 24,N 9-30 1889;Ja 18,F 22-Mr 1,My 17,Jl 12,26-Ag 2,23,S 20,O-N 1 1890

GAZETTE. *See* Gazetteer

GAZETTEER. w,d 1882-1929||?
1882-1914? as Sunday gazetteer; 1915-19 Gazette
d 1915?-19
CU-B Ag 4,25 1889;Ja 5,19 1890
TxU S 25 1898-O 19 1902;Jl 10 1904-Jl 1913

Denison daily HERALD. d 1889+
MWA O 1889
Tx S 1908-Ag 1909;10-D 1 1911
TxCA 1921+
TxU Jl 4 1904-Mr,My 30 1905-Ja 17,Ap 1907-My 1908;O 15 1909-Ja 15 1910;My 16 1912-Jl 24 1916

Denison semi-weekly HERALD. w,sw 1889+
1889-1904? as Denison herald
w 1889-1904?
Tx Mr 27 1908-15

Denison JOURNAL. w S 1872-73||?
KHi D 21 1872

Denison daily NEWS. d 1872-80||?
Tx Ja 9 1873
TxU F 22 1873-80

Denison weekly NEWS. w 1872-80||?
TxU D 27 1872-D 18 1873

Daily NEWS and advertiser. d 1908-15||?
TxU 1911;My 15 1912-Jl 7 1913

DENTON

Denton CHRONICLE. *See* Record-chronicle

DENTON county news. w,sw 1892-1912||?
sw 1904?-11?
TxU [S 29 1898-Mr 1 1900]08-N 23 1912

DENTON county record. *See* Record-chronicle

Denton MONITOR. w My 30 1868-1906||?
TxU My-N 1868;Mr 19,My 21 1870

RECORD-CHRONICLE. w,sw 1882+
1882-97? as Denton chronicle; 1898-99? Denton county record and chronicle; 1900-01? Denton county record; 1902?-03? Denton county record and chronicle; 1904?-20? Record and chronicle
w 1882-93?;95?-99?;1904?-20?
CU-B Jl 13 1889

Denton RECORD-CHRONICLE. d Ag 15 1903+
1903-20? as Denton record and chronicle
pub 1910+
Tx Ja 23 1908-D 21 1916
TxDeN 1929+
TxGR My 1 1922
TxU [Je 27 1906-Je 16 1908]Je 9-D 1909

DEPORT

Deport TIMES. w F 10 1909+
pub 1909+
TxU N 29 1929-Jl 1930

Deport TRIUMPH. w 1902-05||?
TxU Jl 14 1904-Ja 19 1905

DEVINE

Devine NEWS. w 1897+
Tx Ja 23 1908-16

WIDE awake. w S 21 1889-92||?
CU-B S 28 1889

DICKINSON

Dickinson GAZETTE.
OkScN 1932-[34]

MAINLAND messenger. w Jl 9 1913-15||?
TxGR 1913-Jl 1915

DONNA

ADVOCATE. *See* News-advocate

NEWS. w 1918-Ja 1935||
United with Advocate to form News-advocate
TxDoN [1920-35]

NEWS-ADVOCATE. w N 6 1931+
1931-Ja 1935 as Advocate
pub 1931+

DUBLIN

Dublin PROGRESS. w 1888+
1917?-22? as Progress and telephone

Dublin TELEPHONE. w 1885-1916||?
United with Progress to form Progress and telephone, later Dublin progress
Tx N 21 1891

DUMAS

MOORE county news. w Je 17 1927+
pub 1927+
TxGR N 13 1931

EAGLE LAKE

Eagle Lake HEADLIGHT. w Mr 3 1903+
pub 1903+
TxGR Ag 25 1923

EAGLE PASS

Eagle Pass GUIDE. *See* News-guide

Eagle Pass daily GUIDE. d 1917+
In English and Spanish
TxU F 7 1925-Je 1929;30-Je 1934
—w ed *See* News-guide

NEWS-GUIDE. w Ag 25 1888-1932||?
1888-1909? as Eagle Pass guide
CtW S 1 1888
NbHi Ap 29 1893
TxU S 24 1898-F 8 1902
—d ed *See* Eagle Pass daily guide

RIO GRANDE news. w 1906-09||?
United with Eagle Pass guide to form News-guide

Eagle Pass TIMES. w 1887-90||?
CU-B Jl 20,Ag 3-17 1889;Ja 4-11,F 1-8 1890

EASTLAND

Eastland ARGUS-TRIBUNE. d 1920-28||?
1920-O 28? 1927 as Eastland daily tribune
TxU N 9 1926-My 31 1928
—w ed *See* Eastland tribune

OIL BELT news. *See* Eastland tribune

Eastland TELEGRAM. d 1923+
TxU Je 1928-Mr 1929

Eastland TRIBUNE. w O 4 1918-27||?
1918-26? as Oil belt news
Tx 1918-Ag 1 1919

Eastland daily TRIBUNE. *See* Eastland argus-tribune

EDINBURG

El DEFENSOR. w F 7 1930-D 18 1931||
In Spanish
TxU complete

EDINBURG VALLEY review. w 1914+
1914-16 as Revista del valle (In Spanish)
pub 1916+
TxU F 8 1932-33

EDINBURG VALLEY review. d F 22 1927+
pub 1927+
TxU F 8 1932-33

HIDALGO county independent. w 1927+
TxH Ag 23 1929+
TxU Ag 23 1929-33

REVISTA del valle. *See* Edinburg Valley review (w)

EL CAMPO

El Campo CITIZEN. w O 15 1901+
1901-F 4? 1905 as El Campo news
pub 1901+

El Campo NEWS. *See* El Campo citizen

EL DORADO

SUCCESS. w 1906+
TxU S 1914-18

ELECTRA

HARROLD howler. *See* Electra news

Electra NEWS. w 1906+
1906 as Harrold howler
pub 1923+
TxU Ja 15-My 1926;30-32

Electra STAR. w 1920+
pub 1925+

ELGIN

Elgin COURIER. w 1890+
pub 1909+
Tx N 3 1904;Ja 23 1908-09;F 13,Mr 10 1910;Mr 16,Je 15 1911;N 28-D 5 1912;F 13,O 9 1913;14-16;D 1 1921;Mr 2,Ap 6,My 25-Je 1 1922;My 13,Ag 26 1926;Ja 27,Je 9 1927;Mr 1,17 1928;Ja 23-30,Mr 13,Ap 10-17,My 22,Je 5-19,Jl 17,S 25 1930;F 12,Mr 5-12,Je 25 1931;Mr 17,Je 23,D 29 1932;Ja 12,F 2,16-Mr 1,23-Ap 13,27, 30,O 26-N 2,16-D 7,21 1933;Ja 25,F 8,Mr 29 1934;Je 15 1935
TxU [S 17 1898-F 10 1900]

TEXAS bladet. *See under* Georgetown

EL PASO

El Paso CITY and county advocate. w F 1909+
pub 1909+

El CONTINENTAL. w,d Ja 16 1925+
Ja-N 26 1925 as El Paso times. Edicion en español (w)
In Spanish
pub 1925+
MWA Ja 1925
—English ed Ja-N 26 1925 *See* El Paso times

EL PASO del Norte. d 1906-18||?
In Spanish
DLC Jl 28 1917

Monday GRAPHIC. w Mr 1 1897-F 28 1898||
TxE complete

El Paso HERALD. w 1881-1917||
1881-94? as Sunday herald
CU-B S 7 1881
TxET [1881]Ja-Je 1896;O-D 1898;Jl 1900-Ap 1910
TxU Jl 1906-Ap 17 1907

El Paso HERALD. d 1887-Ap 2 1931||
United with El Paso post to form El Paso herald-post.
N 9 1931 is combination ed Herald-times-post
KHi O 6-18 1920[D 1921-Jl 3 1922]F 19 1926
M Ap 30 1930
MWA Jl 6,10 1916;N 9 1931
TxE Ja-Je 1893;Jl 1895-Je 1896;1900-31
TxEH 1889-Je 1891;92-93;Jl 1894-O 22 1898;99-Jl 1930
TxU [1904-Jl 1905]F-Je 15,D 10 1913-Je 21,S 6 1914-My 1915
—evening ed. *See* El Paso news herald

El Paso HERALD-POST. d Ag 21 1922+
1922-Ap 2 1931 as El Paso post
pub 1922+
Tx O 1922+
TxE 1922+

LONE STAR. sw 1876-86||?
CSmH F 23 1884
CU-B Jl 30 1884;O 28 1885
TxE D 16 1882-Ja 6 1886

El Paso daily NEWS. d 1899-Mr 1909||?
Title varies: El Paso evening news
MWA O 30 1906
TxE 1901-09
TxU Jl 26 1904-Je 17 1908

El Paso NEWS-HERALD. d Ja 27-D 1925||
MWA Ja 27 1925
TxE Ja-N 1925
TxET complete
—morning ed *See* El Paso herald

La PATRIA. d 1919-24||?
In Spanish
CU-B N 2-22 1919

El Paso POST. *See* El Paso herald-post

La REPUBLICA. d 1917-29||?
In Spanish
CU-B [N 1919-My 22 1920]

El Paso TIMES. d Ap 2 1881+
Ag 1887 trade ed
pub My 1884-Je 1885;S 20 1887+
CSmH Ag 1887
CU-B Ap 2,Je 3,10 1881;Ja 1 1882;O 21,23 1885
KHi Ap 11-D 16 1883;Je 26-28 1922
MWA Ag 1887
Tx 1904-Je 1905
TxE [Ap 7 1884-Je 1889]90+
TxEB Ja-Je 1888;Jl 1889+
TxGR My 21 1933
TxU Je 11 1919-Ja 27 1920
WHi My 16 1923
WaPS [D 1922]
—Edicion en español. *See* El Continental

El Paso evening WORLD news. d My 9 1932+
pub 1932+
MWA My 9 1932
TxE 1932+

EMORY

Emory NEWS. w 1887-93||?
1887-90? as Rains county record
CU-B S 27,O 11,N 8,22-D 6 1889;F 1890

RAINS county leader. w 1897+
TxU F 13 1925-Ap 16 1926

RAINS county record. *See* Emory news

TEXAS (*Continued*)

ENNIS

Ennis ARGUS. w 1873-75||?
NcD N 2? 1873

Ennis weekly LOCAL. w,sw 1886+
sw during Jl-Ja,1887-91?
CU-B N 3-17,D 8 1889
TxU F 9 1901-S 5 1902;Jl 21 1904-Je 8 1905;Je 26 1919-Ja 21 1926;Ja 19-N 1928
—d ed *See* Ennis daily news

Evening METEOR. *See* Ennis daily news

Ennis daily NEWS. d 1892+
1892-96? as Evening meteor
KHi Ag 1? 1927
TxU Jl 20 1904-Je 23 1906
—w ed *See* Ennis weekly local

Saturday REVIEW. w 1875-94||?
CU-B Ja 4-11 1890

FABENS

RIO GRANDE review. w 1923+
TxU Ap 1929-32

FAIRFIELD

Fairfield RECORDER. w 1876+
TxU S 1906-Je 1907

TEXAS pioneer. w 1856?-
NNHi Ap ? 1863
Tx Je 3 1859

FALFURRIAS

BROOKS county Texan. w 1927+
TxU F 13 1931-32

Falfurrias FACTS. w 1907+
KHi Mr 14 1918

FARMERSVILLE

Farmersville TIMES. w 1884+
TxU 1908-Ag 5 1910

FARWELL

Farwell GRAPHIC. w 1888-89||?
TxU S 22 1888

STATE line tribune. w 1911+
TxU F-N ? 1932

FERRIS

SENTINEL. *See* Ferris wheel

Ferris WHEEL. w 1893+
1893-94? as Sentinel
pub 1901-[31-34]+
TxU Jl 22 1904-Mr 1906;08-Ap 1909

FLATONIA

Flatonia ARGUS. w 1877+
Tx 1879-83;Mr 6-20,Ap 24 1884
TxU Ag 1914-18

FLORESVILLE

Floresville CHRONICLE-JOURNAL. w 1877+
1877-80? as Western chronicle; 1881?-84? Western Texas chronicle; 1885?-1912? Floresville chronicle
CU-B Ag 22,S 5 1889
TxU 1908-Mr 16 1912

WESTERN chronicle. *See* Floresville chronicle-journal

WESTERN Texas chronicle. *See* Floresville chronicle-journal

WILSON county journal. w,sw 1903-12||?
United with Floresville chronicle to form Floresville chronicle-journal
sw Ag 9 1905-O 2 1907
TxU Jl 21 1904-Ap 3 1912

FLOYDADA

FLOYD county hesperian. w 1896+
1896-1903? as Hesperian gazette; 1904?-05? Hesperian
pub Mr 10 1913+
TxU Jl 27-N ? 1905

HESPERIAN. *See* Floyd county hesperian

FOLLETT

LIPSCOMB limelight and Follett times. w 1912+
1912-18? as Follett times
TxU F 1925-29

Follett TIMES. *See* Lipscomb limelight and Follett times

FORNEY

Forney MESSENGER. w 1896-1918||?
TxU Ag 12 1904-My 1906

Forney MESSENGER. w 1915+
1915-21? as Forney news

Forney NEWS. *See* Forney messenger. 1915+

FORT CLARK

Fort Clark NEWS. *See* Brackettville news-mail (Brackettville)

FORT GRIFFIN

Fort Griffin ECHO. *See* Albany echo (Albany)

FORT McKAVETT

Fort McKavett BREEZE. w 1887-91||?
CU-B Ag 3-10 1889

FORT STOCKTON

Fort Stockton PIONEER. w 1909+
pub 1910+

FORT WORTH

Fort Worth ADVANCE. d 1880-81||?
United with Fort Worth democrat to form Democrat-advance, later Fort Worth gazette

CITIZEN-STAR. w 1891-1916||?
1891-1903? as Citizen (North Fort Worth)
NN F 22 1906
TxU Jl 29 1904-Je 18 1908;My 23 1912-O 1916
—d ed *See* Fort Worth star-telegram

Fort Worth DEMOCRAT. *See* Fort Worth gazette

Fort Worth GAZETTE. w,sw 1871-98||?
1871-81? as Forth Worth democrat; 1882?-85? Democrat-advance
w 1871-82?
NcD N 3 1877
TxF 1873-Je 24 1876;83-Je 1890

Fort Worth GAZETTE. d 1876-98||?
1876-82? as Fort Worth daily democrat; 1883-85? Democrat-advance; 1886?-Mr 13 1891 Fort Worth daily gazette
CLM Ag 13 1890
CU-B N 3-4,D 31 1885;My 10 1886;Ja 4,Mr 3,Ap 24 1887;Ja 1 1889
DLC F 5-Je 1891
ICM Ap 29-30,My 3 1895
KHi My 25 1887
OkHi [1894-95]
Tx 1883-Je 21 1896
TxF Jl 4 1876-Je 29 1882;87-F,Jl-S 1889;90;Ap 1891-Mr 1892
TxU F 23 1885

JEWISH monitor. w 1914-30||?
TxU Je 20 1919-O 1929

Evening MAIL. *See* Fort Worth telegram

MEXICAN world. w O 23 1923-
TxH 1923-Ag 12 1924

Fort Worth PRESS. d O 1 1921+
pub 1921+
CU-B Ag 11 1932-[33-34]
TxF 1921+
TxGR F 22 1933
TxU F 7-Mr 1925

Fort Worth RECORD. *See* Fort Worth star-telegram [morning ed]

Fort Worth morning REGISTER. *See* Fort Worth star-telegram. [morning ed]

Fort Worth STAR-TELEGRAM. [morning ed] d 1896+
1896-1902? as Fort Worth morning register; 1903?-25? Fort Worth record; 1926?-Mr 31 1931 Fort Worth record-telegram
KHi Jl 17 1918[Mr-Ap 1921]
MWA My 12 1926
Tx Ja-Je 1898;Ap 1906-O 1925;D 1926+
TxF O 15 1903+
TxGR O 15 1932
TxU O 10 1898-O 18 1899;Ja 24-Je 22,O 4 1904-F,Ap 1912-Jl 1916

Fort Worth STAR-TELEGRAM. [afternoon ed] d 1906+
1906-D 31 1908 as Fort Worth star
Ja 31 1926 is 20th anniversary ed
pub [F 1906-08]+
MWA S 22 1915;My 29 1921;D 8 1924;Ja 31 1926
Tx S 1917+
TxAM 1923+
TxAS 1925+
TxBroH D 1913-Ja 1925
TxF 1909+
TxGR Mr 22 1924;My 21 1927
TxLT 1926+
TxU O 8 1912[Ja-S 1915]17+
—w ed *See* Citizen-star

Fort Worth TELEGRAM. d 1883-D 31 1908||
1883-90? as Evening mail; 1891-94? Mail; 1895-1901? Mail-telegram
United with Fort Worth star to form Fort Worth star-telegram. [afternoon ed]
CU-B N 4, D 29 1885;Ja 2 1886;Ja 23 1896
TxF Jl 1905-08
TxFS 1902-08
TxU Je 3-23 1908

TEXAS republican counselor. w O 7? 1918-29||?
Tx N 18 1918

TORCHLIGHT appeal. w 1886-93||?
Negro
CU-B Ja 17-F 8,22 1890

WESTERN world. w 1921+
TxH Ag 23 1924-S 19 1925
TxU S 18 1925-28

Fort Worth WHIG chief.
TxU S 12 1871

FRANKLIN

CENTRAL Texan. *See* Franklin Texan

Franklin TEXAN. w 1884+
1884-1920? as Central Texan
TxU Ja-O 1932

FRANKSTON

Frankston CITIZEN. w 1910+
TxU Ja-O 1932

FREDERICKSBURG

GILLESPIE county news. w 1888-1907||?
TxU Jl 9 1904-Jl 22 1905

LIMELIGHT. w Ja 29 1926-
Tx Ja-O 8 1926

RADIO post. w S 22 1922+
pub 1922+
Tx D 6 1929;S 1930+
TxU 1928-33

Fredericksburg STANDARD. w 1907+
TxU Je 1919-33

Fredericksburg WOCHENBLATT. w 1877+
In German
TxU Jl 24 1919-33

FREEPORT

Freeport FACTS. w 1912+
TxGR [My-Ag 1931]D 22 1932;Ja 19 1933

FRISCO

Frisco JOURNAL. w 1902+
TxU Ag 14-N 13 1912;27-28

FROST

ENTERPRISE. w Mr 1923+
pub Ag 1931+

GAIL

BORDEN citizen. w 1900-19||?
TxU Ap 28-D 1904;O 12 1905-N 1909

GAINESVILLE

COOKE county signal. *See* Gainesville signal

Daily HESPERIAN. d O 2 1879-1924||?
TxGa 1917-Je 1919
TxGaR 1888-97
TxU Ja 14-S 21 1906[D 10 1907-Mr 25 1908]

Gainesville evening MIRROR. d 1905?-08||?
TxU [F 14 1907-Je 3 1908]

Gainesville weekly REGISTER. w 1878+
pub Jl 1921+

GAINESVILLE daily REGISTER. d 1886+
pub Jl 1921+
CU-B Ja 4 1887
Tx O 11 1926
TxGa F 1917+

Gainesville SIGNAL. w 1889+
1889-92? as Cooke county signal
pub 1889+
TxGa F 28 1913+

GALVESTON

Daily ADVERTISER. d 1841-
DLC F 26 1842

ADVOCATE. w Je 10 1916-
TxGR Je 17 1916

Galveston BANNER. w 1925?+
Negro
TxGR Ja 18 1930; My 11 1935

BUSINESS budget. w 1888-
TxGR F 9 1889

Evening CALL. d 1882-
TxGR Je 3 1882

CITIZENS' bulletin. w Ap 17 1909-
TxGR My 1-2 1909

CITY times. w 1898-1930||?
Negro
TxGR [S 29 1900-Je 4 1927]
TxU Je 11 1904-O 14 1905

CIVILIAN. w S 28 1838-77||
1838-39 as Civilian and Galveston City gazette; 1840-51? Civilian and Galveston gazette; 1852?-60? Civilian and gazette
Suspended from My? 1862-65
DLC O 19 1838;Ja 11,My 17 1839
Tx F 14 1860;Jl 16 1861; My 27-O 14,28-D 16,30 1869;Ja 13-F 3,24,Mr 10-Ap 7,21-N 10,D 1,15-29 1870; Ja 12,26-Ap 1871
TxCA 1860-61
TxGR [1857-Mr 1859]
TxU Je 1,12 1844;Je 26,Jl 10,N 20 1847[Ap 15-Je 9 1848;My 27-S 2 1851]N 9-16,D 13 1861;Ja 15 1862

Semi-weekly CIVILIAN. sw 1838-My 1862||?
1838-S 1843? as Civilian and Galveston city gazette; O 1843?-52? Civilian and Galveston gazette; 1853?-56? Civilian and gazette; 1857?-F? 1862 Semi-weekly civilian and gazette
DLC N 5 1840[42-43]Ja 6,24,31 Ap 17,Jl 13 1844;Jl 19,D 10 1845
ICN Jl 2,27,Ag 10-13,O 1 1842;F 18,My 20, 27,Je 24 1843
RW Ja 1,My 28 1850
TxGR N 12 1842[43-44]S 21 1852;Mr 21,Ap 15 1856;F 14,Mr 7,17,24,31 1862
extras:Ag 5,25,31,S 4,N 12,D 7,10 1861;My 8,19 1862

TEXAS (*Continued*)

GALVESTON—*Continued*

Galveston daily CIVILIAN. d My 5 1857-85||?
Suspended from My? 1862-65
MBAt O 15,N 23-25,28,30,D 4,7-14,16-19,24-25, 28-31 1869
Tx [My 10 1869-O 1872]
TxGR N 21,D 3,8,11,13 1860;Ja 4,23,F 22,My 15,24 1861;N 12(supp)1867;O 25 1870;Ag 23,S 23,D 29 1871;F 9-Mr 28 1872;Jl 24 1873;S 15,N 23, 1877;N 7 1878;Ap 18 1879;Mr 29 1882;Jl 15 1885
TxU O 7 1872-My 21 1873

CIVILIAN and gazette. tw -1873||?
-Ag? 1861 as Tri-weekly civilian; S? 1861-62? Galveston tri-weekly civilian
Suspended from My? 1862-65
NjP Ag 6-8 1861
Tx Ag 6,N 23,D 16 1869
TxGR Jl 3,Ag 8,10,27,O 22-24,N 12,D 11,18 1861;Ja 6,10-15,31,F 3 1862

Galveston CLIPPER. w 1891-92||?
TxGR My 7 1892

COLORED American. w Jl 1920-25||?
Negro
TxGR N 20 1920

Galveston COMMERCIAL. w O 9? 1854-
TxU D 14 1854;Ja,S 6,N 22-D 19 1856

Galveston daily COMMERCIAL. d Ag 3 1873-
TxGR S 5 1873
TxH Ag-O 12 1873

COMMERCIAL bulletin. w 1865-69||?
Tx Ag 31 1867-Ag 22 1868;Ap-My 15 1869
TxGR S 1866-67
TxU F 10 1866-Ag 1869
—d ed *See* Flake's daily bulletin

Galveston COMMERCIAL gazette. w 1881-85||?
TxGR Mr 22 1884

COMMERCIAL intelligencer. w Jl 1838-40||
TxGR Jl 27 1838

COMMERCIAL weekly and prices current. w
Tx My 2 1857

COMMONER. w 1875?-
Tx My 21 1876

Weekly CONFEDERATE. w Je 26? 1855-
Tx O 2 1855
TxU Ja 5 1856

Galveston COURIER. w D 1904-06||?
TxGR [1905-Ag 11 1906]

Galveston COURIER. w My 7 1909-
TxGR My-Jl 2 1909

CRISIS. w Jl 23 1860-
ICHi S 17 1860
Tx Ag 13,S 10-17,O 8 1860
TxU Ag 27 1860

DEMOCRAT. Jl 15 1932-
TxGR Jl 15 1932

Daily DISPATCH. d 1867-69||?
MWA Ag 4 1868
TxGR Jl 21,D 24 1868

Semi-weekly FARM news. w,sw 1844-1922||?
1844-93? as Galveston weekly news; 1894?-1907? Galveston semi-weekly news
1861-My? 1866 pub in Houston
w 1844-93?
DLC Mr 3 1873
MBAt Ap 1,My 27 1863;Mr 6 1868
N Ag 31 1858
NNHi S 4 1860
NjP [1862-F 15 1865]
OClWHi F 5 1861
ODW Mr 23 1864
TJT Ja 4 1875
Tx My 30 1846;Ja 17 1854;Mr 13-S 4,18,N 13 1855-Ja 12(extra)15-Mr 11,Ap 22 1856;My 5 1857;Ap 24,N 2,D 15(extra)1858;My 24-31, Je 21,Ag 9,S 27-O 4 1859;Ja 10,Mr 6,Ag 14 1860;Ag 20,S 3 1861;Ja 14 1862;Jl 1,O 21 1863;My 23,Je 27,Ag 8 1866;Je 19-26 1876; Ap 18 1907;N 5-12,D 7,14-17 1909;F 15 1910
TxGR Je 18,Jl 23,Ag 6 1862;Mr 4,My 6 1863; S 24 1900
TxH Jl 24 1855-Ap 3 1860
TxU My 6-S 9 1851;N 18 1853-Ja 24 1854;My 1855-Mr 10 1857[Ja 16 1862-O 1865]Jl-D 1873; Je 1881-S 1 1882;87-88;90-1922
WHi Mr 5 1861
—d ed *See* Galveston daily news

FLAKE'S daily bulletin. d 1863-O 22 1872||
Title varies: Flake's daily Galveston bulletin
DLC Je 29,D 26 1865-Je 3,Jl 14 1868;Jl 23, 28 1869
LU O 1867-Mr,O-D 1868;Jl-S 1869;Ap-Je 1870
MBAt Jl 14 1865[F-D 1869]
MoSj Ap-S 1867
NbHi Je 29 1865
Tx Ja 10,F 8,Ag 10 1863[Ag 5-D 1865]-Mr,My 19 1866;Ja-S 1868;Ja-S 1869;Ja-Mr,Ap 2,Jl-S 10 1870-S 1871;Ja 3-Mr 1,3-7,9-10,12-31 1872
TxDN [D 1865-72]
TxGR Jl 4 1863;D 27 1865-S 1870[71-72]
TxHuS N 17 1865-69;Ap-Ag 1870
TxSI [Je 5-Ag 28 1868]
TxU Je 8 1865-Mr,O 1871-Mr 1872
—w financial ed *See* Commercial bulletin

FLAKE'S semi-weekly bulletin. w,sw Mr 7 1863-O 22 1872||
1863- as Flake's weekly bulletin; -My 22 1867 Flake's weekly Galveston bulletin
w 1863-My 22 1867
CtY Ja 31 1864
DLC [1866]-70;Ap 21 1871
MBAt Je 12 1864;Jl 12 1865;Je 12 1867
MWA Je 8(supp)1865
NNHi Jl 11 1863
NcD [Ap 18 1867-Mr 1868]
Tx Ap 11-Je,S 19-O 17,31-N 7,D 5 1866[67-69]-Ag 1872
TxGR Ap 19,Jl 4 1863;Mr 20-27,S 28-O 30 1864;Ap 30 1865;Mr 1867-F 1868;F 17-D 1869; D 24 1870;S 23 1871
TxH Ag 23 1872
TxU Mr 1866-67;F 29 1868-69

FLAKE'S tri-weekly bulletin. tw 1863-70||?
MWA Je 8 1865
TxGR Ja 6,Mr 22 1864

FLAKE'S evening bulletin. d 1866-71||?
Tx Ap 2-Je 23 1869;Ap-Je 29 1871
TxGR Jl-D 1867

FREE man's press. w Jl 18 1868-
Jl 1868 as Freedman's press
Jl-S 12? 1868 pub in Austin
Negro
MBAt Jl-Ag 1,15-S 12,O 24 1868
TxU Ag 1 1868

FREEMAN'S journal. w 1887-91||?
Negro
CU-B Ag 17 1889

Daily GALVESTONIAN. d Ap 1838-40||?
DLC Ap 4 1840

GALVESTONIAN. tw Ap 1839-40||?
IU My 16 1839
TxGR Mr 27 1839(photostat)

Daily GALVESTONIAN. d Mr 30 1841-
DLC Mr 31-Ap 1,D 6 1841

Weekly GALVESTONIAN. w My 8 1841-
DLC My 8 1841

GULF CITY herald. sw O 1884-
TxGR O 4,15 1884

Galveston HERALD. w My 2 1857-
TxU My 2 1857

Galveston daily HERALD. w,d Ag 3 1912-1912-F? 1913 as Galveston labor herald
w 1912-F? 1913
TxGR 1912-S 27 1913

Galveston HERALD. w Ja 18 1917-18||?
1917-Mr 7 1918 as Galveston herold
1917 in German and English
TxGR 1917-Ag 1918

Galveston HEROLD. *See* Galveston herald 1917-18

Galveston INDEPENDENT. w 1893-1901||?
ICHi Ap 1898-[Ja-Jl 9 1898]
TxGR S 1 1895;My 31 1897

Semi-weekly JOURNAL. sw 1842?-
DLC F 9,Mr 22,My 10,Je 24 1842

Weekly JOURNAL. w 1850?-
DLC [Mr 19-N 5 1852]
TxU [D 20 1850-S 9 1853;Ap 14-Jl 14 1854]
WHi Ja 28 1853

Galveston JOURNAL. w 1898-1908||?
TxGR Mr 9 1901-F 21 1908
TxU Jl 23 1904-Je 14 1907

Galveston JOURNAL. w Ag 1 1913-16||?
In English and German
TxGR 1913-D 22 1916

Galveston daily JOURNAL. *See* Daily journal of commerce

Daily JOURNAL of commerce. d 1880-82||?
1880-Ap 10 1882 as Galveston daily journal
TxGR O 4 1880-My 16 1882
—w ed *See* Texas journal of commerce

Galveston LABOR herald. *See* Galveston daily herald

Galveston daily MERCURY. d 1874-75||?
Follows Houston daily union (Houston)
Tx Ag 13-27,29,S 1-17,19-O 30,N 3-10,12-D 8,10-13,15-25,27 1874-Ja 1,5,7-16,19 1875
TxGR N 12-14,17-18,20,22 1874

Galveston Sunday MERCURY. w N 1890-92||?
1890-91? as Galveston mercury
TxGR F 14 1891

Il MESSAGGIERO italiano. *See under* San Antonio

Galveston NEW idea. w 1897-1922||?
Negro
TxGR [Jl 30 1904-F 1908]Ap 17 1920

Galveston daily NEWS. d Ap 11 1842+
Early years as Daily news
Mr? 1862-My? 1866 pub in Houston
Ap 11 1917 is 75th anniversary ed
A O-D 1882;My-D 1883;My-Je 1884;Ja-S 1885; Ap-Je 1886
CSmH Ap 19 1842(facsimile)S 13 1900
CU-B Ag 23 1883;D 1 1884;Mr 4,Ap 3 1887;S 1 1892
DLC Ap 30 1842;Ja 16,S 11 1870;Mr 5 1873; 74-Ag 18 1897;99+
KHi D 29 1879;S 12-27 1900;Ap 11 1917;Ap 7 1920;Ap 7 1921;Jl 11 1922;Je 16 1927
M O 1 1929
MBAt Je 14 1866;Je 1,D 11 1867;Ap 11 1917
MWA Je 8 1865;F 13 1866;Mr 5 1871;S 1 1880; Je 25 1882;My 1915(supp)
MiU Ap 11 1917
NNHi Ap 6 1873;O 1 1876
NbHi S 1 1877
NcD Ag 18 1867;Je 25 1882
NcU Ag 21 1881
P Jl 1890-Je 1895
TSS O-D 1884;Jl-S 1 1886
Tx Je 27,S 21 1865;Je 26 1866;69+
TxE Ag 25 1878-Je 1917
TxGR Ag 19 1842(reprint);Jl 5 1862[Mr 1865-S 1867;Ap 1868-69]Ja 7-8,19-20,Mr 1870+ suppAg 6 1861;Mr 18 1864;broadside O 18 1870
TxH O 31,N 7 1871;Ap 21,Ag 30 1872;D 18 1873;Ja 7 1874;S 5 1875;Je 29,Jl 18 1876;D 12 1880;Jl 1881+
TxSI [Ap-D 1880]
TxU Ap 19 1842;73;S-D 1874;Ap 7-Je,Ag 9 1876-Ap 18,Jl 1884+
VU S 1 1880
WHi Jl 20 1893;S 1 1899;S 1 1907
—w,sw ed *See* Semi-weekly farm news
See also Galveston news and price current; News' bulletin

Galveston tri-weekly NEWS. tw 1842-D 31 1873||
D 14? 1861-My? 1866 pub in Houston
DLC Ja 3,O 19 1863;F 3 1865;My 31 1869-73
IU N 11 1848
LNC S 12 1862
MBAt Jl 13,29,Ag 5,S 9 1863;N 22-24,29-D 8,29 1865;Ja 1,12,17,31,F 16,19,23,28,Mr 2,12-14,30,Je 15 1866
MHi [1862-63]
MWA Mr 23 1863;Mr 4,My 4,16-18, Jl 15 1864
NNHi F 9,Jl 4,S 15 1863
OClWHi [Ja-S 4 1863]
TSS Ag 15-31 1862;Ja-Ap 13 1863
Tx Ap 8,My 1,6,Je 10,O 20,D 24 1862;Ja 26,Je 17,20,24,S 18,O 5-7,21,N 6-11,18-23,27,D 23,30 1863[64-65]Ja 4,D 11 1867;D 11 1868;N 26,D 1-15 1869;N 18,25 1872
TxCA 1863
TxGR N 10,D 20 1855-O 4 1856;57;N 20-22,D 8 1860;Ja 22,Ap 6,My 7,Jl 18,Ag 27,S 24,O 17,N 19,D 4,14,19 1861[62-63]-64;Ja 27,F 10, 17-20,S 6,15-O 6,D 29 1865;F 28-Mr 2,19 1866;Jl 3 1868
TxH Je 22,D 30 1863;F 10,Mr 23-25,Ap 1,6-11,Je 6,S 7 1864;N 3 1865;O 31 1873
TxU Jl 15-17,Ag 16 1862;F 2-16 1863[64-N 6 1865]Ja 3-5 1866
WHi Mr 2-4,16-23,27,Ap 17,22-27,Ag 7,26,S 4 1863

Galveston NEWS. sw 1842-
MWA F 24-27,Mr 3 1846
TxGR Ag 17,27 1852;N 22 1853

Galveston NEWS and price current. w 1861-
Title varies: Galveston news price current and market review
TxGR Mr 12(supp)1870
TxU Je 6 1872

NEWS' bulletin. tw 1863-
pub in Houston 1863-F 1865?
MWA Ap 9 1864
Tx Ja 31-F 2 1865
TxGR [Ap 30-D 15 1864]F 16 1865

OPERA glass. w 1879-1915||?
S 12 1900 extra as Texas post-opera glass
Tx D 21 1884;Ap 14 1888
TxGR N 7(extra)1882[Ag 26 1883-Je 1905]-14;Ap 3,My 22-29 1915
TxU Ag 22 1885

Sunday morning PIONEER. w D 21 1913-
TxGR 1913-Ja 4 1914

Die Galveston POST. w 1903-09||?
In German
TxGR D 1904-O 16 1908

PRESS. w Mr 20 1920-
TxGR Mr-Je 5 1920

Daily PRINT. *See* Galveston tribune

PUBLIC opinion. w? Jl? 1874-
TxGr Ag 23 1874

PUBLIC opinion. w F 4 1883-
TxGR F 4 1883

Daily RECORD. *See* Galveston tribune

Galveston RECORD. w Ja 25 1935+
Ja-F 1 1935 as Galveston shopping news; F 8-Ap 5 1935 as Galveston record and shopping news
TxGR 1935+

Galveston REPUBLICAN. w Mr 9 1868-
MBAt Mr 16,Ap 6-20,My 4,25,Je 8-28,Jl 13,27, Ag 17 1868
TxU Mr 9-16 1868

Saturday REVIEW. w S 4 1897-1902||?
TxGR [1897-Jl 12 1902]

RIP-SAW. w My 2 1883-
TxGR My 2 1883

Daily SEA Gull. d Ap- 1891||?
TxGR Ap 4,10 1891

SEARCHLIGHT. *See* Spotlight

Galveston SENTINEL. w O 1 1932+
Negro
TxGR [1932-O 6 1934]F 22 1935+

Galveston SHOPPING news. *See* Galveston record

SPOTLIGHT. w Ap 20 1935-
Ap 20 1935 as Searchlight
TxGR Ap-My 11 1935

Galveston STANDARD. w 1871?-73||?
Tx O 14 1872
TxU Je 3 1872;Ap 14 1873

Galveston STANDARD. w My 1 1897-
TxGR My 15 1897

Galveston STAR. d Ap 12 1915-
TxGR Ap-My 10 1915;second and third extras Ag 19 1915;Ag 22(extra)1915
—w ed *See* Galveston Sunday star

Galveston Sunday STAR. w Ag 8 1915-17||?
TxGR Ag 8 1915

La STELLA del Texas. w 1912-18||?
In Italian
TxGR Mr 29 1913-Ja 26 1918

STING. w 1885||?
TxGR F 7 1885

TEXAS journal of commerce. w 1876-82||?
TxGR My 7,D 3 1881;Mr 4 1882
TxU Jl 1878-My 20 1882
—d ed *See* Daily journal of commerce

TEXAS (*Continued*)

GALVESTON—*Continued*

TEXAS portfolio. w 1856?-
TxU Ap 15 1857

Die TEXAS post. w 1869-1901||?
Follows Der Texas demokrat (Houston)
Title varies: Wöchentliche Texas post; Wochenblatt der Texas post; etc.
S 12 1900 is Texas post-opera glass
1872-73? pub in Houston; 1888?-92? in Dallas
CU-B Ag 18,S 8-15 1889
MWA Ag 24 1876
Tx O 30-D 18 1870;Ja-O 1,22 1871;O 27-D 22 1872;Ja,F 9-Ap,My 28-Jl 13,27-Ag 21,S-O 23 1873;O 28 1875-O 1876;Mr 8-O 11 1877
TxGR [My 17 1900-Jl 1901]

TEXAS times. *See* Times

THUNDERBOLT. 1876||?
TxH F 6 1876

TIMES. w,ir D? 1841-
Follows San Luis advocate (San Luis)
1841-Ap 22 1843 as Texas times
DLC N 6,D 7 1842;Ap 22 1843
ICN D 1842-Mr-My 16 1843
Tx N 30 1842
TxU N 2 1842

Galveston TIMES. w Mr 29 1873-
MB Mr 29-My 18 1873

Galveston daily TIMES. w 1874?-
Tx F 13 1875

Galveston TRIBUNE. d 1882+
1882-84? as Daily print; Ja 1?-22 1885 Daily record; Ja 23-Ap 11 1885 Evening record; Ap 13 1885-F 28? 1894 Evening tribune
MoHi My 16 1912
NN Ag 17 1915(photostat)
OClWHi My 16 1912
Tx Ap 14,21,28 1884
TxGR [Ap 17-N 8 1883;Je 6 1884-F,Jl 1894-95]-[1900]+
TxH S 12 1900;My 16 1912
TxU Je 20 1898-S 1915
WHi N 24 1904;My 16 1912

Die UNION. tw 1859?-70||?
Title varies: Dreimalwöchentliche union; Galveston union dreimalwöchentliche
In German
Tx Jl 17 1860-Jl 18 1861;D 30 1865-O 25 1866

Wochenblatt der UNION. w 1859?-71||?
In German
Tx O 25 1868-Ja 2 1870

Galveston UNION. Extra
TxGR Jl 8,16-17,Ag 6 1862
TxU Ag 13,17 1862

Galveston daily UNION. d O 1892-
TxGR N 2 1892

Galveston VOICE. w Ja 1931-
Negro
TxGR [O 1931-O 1932]

Evening WORLD. d 1891-
TxGR Ag 5 1891

GARLAND

Garland NEWS. w 1887+
CU-B Ag 22 1889
Tx S 20 1907-15;22-23

GATESVILLE

Gatesville FORUM. w 1887-99||?
United with Gatesville star to form Gatesville star-forum

Gatesville MESSENGER and star-forum. w 1892+
1892-1907? as Gatesville messenger
TxU Je 13 1906-Je 14 1907;08-Je 1910

Gatesville STAR-FORUM. w 1885-1907||?
1885-99? as Gatesville star. United with Gatesville messenger to form Gatesville messenger and star-forum
CU-B Ag 7-14 1889;Jl 21,Ag 11-18 1892

GEORGETOWN

Georgetown COMMERCIAL. w 1898-1917||?
TxU Je 1904-O 13 1911

Georgetown INDEPENDENT. w S 17 1856-
TxU 1856-F 21 1857

Georgetown RECORD. w 1872-85||?
1872-83 as Williamson county record
TxU F 15 1879;Ag 8 1885

Georgetown SENTINEL. w 1871?-
TxU O 17 1872

SUN. *See* Williamson county sun

TEXAS bladet. w 1901-Ap 28 1909||
1901-My 6 1908 pub in Elgin; My 13-N 4 1908 in Austin. Merged with Texas posten (Austin)
In Swedish
IRA 1907-09
MnHi [Mr 1908-09]

Georgetown WATCHMAN. w 1867-72||?
TxU Mr 23,Ag 24 1867;Mr 20-Je 19 1869;Ap 23-Je 1870

WILLIAMSON county record. *See* Georgetown record

WILLIAMSON county sun. w Ap 1877+
1877-80? as Sun
pub Ap 16 1877+
CU-B [1886]My 5 1887;Ag 1,15 1889;Ja 16,30-F 6 1890
Tx 1908-13
TxU Ag 1904-Je 18 1908;My 16 1912-18

GEORGE WEST

George West ENTERPRISE. w 1919-32||?
TxU N 8 1929-Je 2 1932

George West NEWS. w
TxU F 10 1928-My 3 1929

GIDDINGS

Giddings ADVOCATE. w 1885-88||?
Tx Jl 15 1886

Giddings DEUTSCHES volksblatt. w S 1899+
In German
pub 1899+
Tx 1911-16
TxU Jl 28 1904-Mr 1920

Giddings weekly TRIBUNE. w Ap? 1874-77||?
Tx S 10,24-O 1 1874

GILMER

Gilmer MIRROR. w 1877+
1877-90? as Texas mirror
pub 1920+
CU-B Ag 3 1889;Ja 9-23 1890
NcD N 15 1888;My 7 1889

TEXAS mirror. *See* Gilmer mirror

UPSHUR county echo. w 1897-1925||?
KHi S 7 1922
Tx 1908-16
TxU Je 11 1914-Jl 1925

GLADEWATER

Gladewater JOURNAL. w 1931+
Tx Jl 8,Ag 12 1932;Mr 10 1933

GLEN ROSE

Glen Rose CITIZEN. w 1885-86||?
CU-B Mr 1883

Glen Rose HERALD. w 1890-1916||?
TxU Jl 1904-Je 4 1908

GODLEY

Godley TIMES. w 1924-30||?
TxU Jl 21 1927-N 1928

GOLDTHWAITE

Goldthwaite EAGLE. w 1894+
KHi D 18 1920
Tx Ja 25 1908-D 21 1910
TxU 1911-12;F 21 1925-O 12 1928

GOLIAD

Goliad ADVANCE. w 1905-15||?
United with Goliad guard to form Advance and guard, later Goliad advance guard

Goliad ADVANCE guard. w 1855+
1855-1915? as Goliad guard; 1916- Advance and guard
CU-B S 7 1889;Ja 18-F 1, Jl 5 1890
TxU Je 8 1889;Ja 29-F 5 1920

Goliad GUARD. *See* Goliad advance guard

Goliad MESSENGER. w 1859?-
ICHi Jl 23 1863
MBAt Jl 16 1864
MWA Je 25 1863
WHi S 10 1863

GONZALES

Gonzales INQUIRER. w Je 1853+
Tx Jl 3 1883
TxGR Jl 19 1923
TxSO 1853-My 1854
TxU Ja 15 1859;Je 16 1904-S 6 1906

Daily INQUIRER. d Je 1 1897+
TxGR Jl 19 1923
TxU Ap 18 1931-33

SOUTHWESTERN index. w 1869-75||?
Tx Jl 7,D 8 1869;O 9 1874
TxU Je 3 1870

GOOSE CREEK

Daily DEMOCRAT. d 1930+
TxGR Ag 6-7 1930

Daily SUN. d 1918+
1918-31 as Tri-cities sun
also dated in Baytown and Pelly
pub 1931+

TRI-CITIES sun *See* Daily sun

GORDON

Gordon COURIER. w 1884-1914||?
CU-B Ag 9,D 6-13 1889

GORMAN

Gorman PROGRESS. w 1898+
TxGR O 11 1918
TxU F 11 1925-N 11 1926;N 14 1929-Ja 8 1931

GRAFORD

Graford MONOGRAM. w 1907-12||?
TxU 1911-N 15 1912

GRAHAM

Graham LEADER. w Ag 16 1876+
pub 1876+
CU-B Ag 8,22-29,N 7-21 1889
Tx D 12 1894
TxU S 23 1898-O 1909;My 8 1913-Ap 1914

GRANBURY

Granbury DEMOCRAT. w 1872-1906||?
United with Graphic-truth to form Graphic-democrat, later Hood county herald

Granbury GRAPHIC. *See* Hood county herald

HOOD county herald. w 1872-1921||?
1872-83? as Vidette; 1884?-97? Granbury graphic; 1898?-1906? Graphic-truth; 1907?-16? Graphic-democrat
CU-B Jl 6,20-27,Ag 10,24-31 1889

HOOD county truth. w 1894-97||?
United with Granbury graphic to form Graphic-truth, later Hood county herald

Granbury NEWS. w 1886+
pub O 1891+
Tx Je 11 1881
TxU Jl 21 1904-Ap 1907

VIDETTE. *See* Hood county herald

GRAND PRAIRIE

GRAPHIC hustler. w 1902-07||?
1902-06? as Grand Prairie hustler
TxU Ag 11 1904-Ag 3 1906

Grand Prairie HUSTLER. *See* Graphic hustler

Grand Prairie TEXAN. w 1908+
TxU 1925-28

GRAND SALINE

Grand Saline SUN. w 1894+
Tx 1908-13
TxU F 28 1929-30

GRAND VIEW

Grand View SENTINEL. w 1887-93||?
CU-B D 7-21 1889;Ja 8-15 1890

GRANGER

Granger NEWS. w 1893+
TxU F 12 1925-O 20 1927

GRAPELAND

Grapeland MESSENGER. w Mr 1898+
pub 1905+
TxU F 12 1925-29

GREENVILLE

Greenville BANNER. w 1872-1926||?
CU-B Jl 10-24 1889
Tx Ja 22 1908-16
TxCoE F 3 1909;Je 12 1913

Greenville evening BANNER. d 1894+
TxU S 22 1898-My 24 1902;My 16-Jl 4 1913

Greenville HERALD. w 1869-1925||?
CU-B O 22 1886;Ja 24,F 28 1890
TxU Jl 22 1904-Jl 7 1905;Ap 23-Jl 4 1913

Greenville INDEPENDENT. w 1867-69||?
Tx F 22,Ap 11,My 2 1868

Greenville MESSENGER. w Ag 1 1894+
pub 1894+
Tx Ja 21 1910-15
TxU My 16-Je 1913

Greenville evening NEWS. d
TxU 1900-Je 1901

GROESBECK

Groesbeck JOURNAL. w 1892+
Tx 1908-15
TxU Ap 1905-My 9 1907

LIMESTONE new era. w 1876-19__||?
CU-B N 6 1885

GROVETON

Groveton GRAPHIC. w Ja 3- 1890||?
CU-B Ja 24 1890

TRINITY county news. w 1915+
TxGR [Ja 31-O 10 1929]

TRINITY county star. w 1898-1919||?
Tx Ja 24 1908-14

TEXAS (*Continued*)

GRUVER

HANSFORD county news. w 1929+
TxU My 31 1929-My 1930

HALLETTSVILLE

Hallettsville HERALD. w,sw 1872-1929||?
1872-87? as Herald and planter. United with Semi-weekly new era to form New era-herald
w 1872-1923?
KHi D 20 1921
Tx Jl 29 1886;1908-15
TxU Ag 27 1874[My 24-D 1906]

LAVACA county nachrichten. w 1896-1926||?
In German
TxU S 16 1904-N 22 1905;Mr 29 1918-19

LAVACA county tribune. *See* Tribune

LONE STAR. w 1860?-
OClWHi N 12 1860

NAŠINEC. sw 1914-16||?
In Bohemian
TxU O 14 1914-My 1916

NEW ERA-HERALD. w,sw 1889+
1889-Mr 22 1912 as Hallettsville new era; Ap 2 1912-29? Semi-weekly new era
w 1889-Mr 22 1911
CU-B Ja 22-29 1890
Tx 1908-12
TxGR Ja 22 1929
TxU Mr 10 1899-Je 22 1900;Ag 19 1904-Je 19 1907;Ap 29-Jl 4 1913

NOVÝ domov. w,sw Mr 1895+
Follows Obzor (not in this list)
w 1895-S 1911
In Bohemian
pub Mr 1906-F 19 1914;F 22 1915-F 1930;F 25 1931+
IU [1917]-Jl 17 1922
TxGR Mr 19 1928
TxU Je 16 1919-Ja,My 1921-23;Ja 29 1925-S 1926

REBEL. w 1911-17||?
TxU 1912-Je 1914;16-Je 2 1917

TRIBUNE. sw Ja 8 1932+
1932 as Lavaca county tribune
pub 1932+

HAMILTON

Hamilton HERALD-RECORD. w Ja 1 1876+
1876-Je 20 1920 as Hamilton herald
pub [1876-1911]+

RECORD and rustler. w 1899-Je? 1920||
1899-1912? as Hamilton rustler. United with Hamilton herald to form Hamilton herald-record
TxU [F 16 1904-O 1 1905]

Hamilton RUSTLER. *See* Record and rustler

HANSFORD

HANSFORD county herald. w 1888-89||?
CU-B Jl 31,Ag 21-28 1889

HARLINGEN

Harlingen NEWS. w F 23 1929+
pub 1929+

STAR. *See* Valley morning star

VALLEY morning star. w,sw,d 1908+
1908-27? as Star
w 1908-25?;sw 1926-27?
KHi D 28 1926
TxU D 1931+
WHi F 28 1930

HARPER

Harper HERALD. w 1915+
TxU S 9 1927-32

HARRISBURG

TELEGRAPH and Texas register. *See* Weekly Houston telegraph (Houston)

HASKELL

Haskell FREE press. w Ja 1 1886+
pub 1886+
Tx Ja 25 1908-13
TxU Ag 20 1904-N 2 1907

HEARNE

Hearne ADVOCATE. *See* Hearne democrat

Hearne DEMOCRAT. w 1889+
1889-My 1911 as Hearne advocate
pub My 1911+
TxU Je 13 1919-Ap 22 1921

HEBBRONVILLE

JIM HOGG county enterprise. w My 5 1926+
pub 1926+

Hebbronville NEWS. w 1923-32||?
TxU F 11 1925-My 4 1932

HEMPSTEAD

Hempstead weekly COUNTRYMAN. w 1860-69||?
Title varies: Texas countryman
Tx N 26 1869

Hempstead COURIER. w 1854?-
TxU Je 1,Ag 6 1859;My 26 1860;Ap 6 1860

Hempstead NEWS. w 1891+
TxU O 22 1891-93;My 17-N 22 1894;Jl 15 1904-N 22 1907

TEXAS countryman. *See* Hempstead weekly countryman

HENDERSON

Henderson DEMOCRAT. w F 3? 1855-
TxU Je 2 1855;N 29 1856;Je 27 1857

EAST Texas times. *See* Henderson times

FLAG of the union. w F 2? 1854-
TxU F 2 1854

Henderson daily NEWS. d 1931+
TxGR My 25 1932
—w ed *See* Rusk county news

RUSK county news. w 1882+
TxU F 1908-N 2 1910
—d ed *See* Henderson daily news

SOUTHERN beacon. w Ja 1858-
DLC Ja 15-F 5,Ap 23-30, My 28-Jl 2 1859

Henderson TIMES. w 1853+
1853-62? as East Texas times
CU-B Ag 22,O 31-D 19 1889;Ja 9-23,F 20-27 1890
MWA F 6 1864;My 15 1868
Tx Ja 16 1864;Jl 28,Ag 25 1869;N 9 1870;Ja 30,Jl 17,Ag 14,O 30 1879;Ja 8,29,Mr 4 1880; Ap 21 1881;Ap 14,D 8 1898;Ja 2 1908
TxGR [F 17 1863-Je 4 1864]S 23 1865
TxU Mr 1,Jl 18 1862;Ag 29 1863;Ja 16,My 21, S 19 1864;F 4-11 1865;S 29 1898-N 1900;08; F 12 1925-26;Mr 1929-32

HENRIETTA

Henrietta INDEPENDENT. w 1884+
CU-B Ja 10-24,D 13-20 1890
TxU Ag 19 1904-Je 19 1908;My 17 1912-Ag 21 1914

PEOPLE'S review. w 1893-1927||?
TxU 1908-My 24 1912

HEREFORD

Hereford BRAND. w F 23 1901+
1901-F 21 1902 as Hereford reporter
pub 1901+
KHi Ja 11 1924
Tx 1908-11
TxHe N 21 1929+
TxU Ag 26 1904-Je 5 1908

Hereford REPORTER. *See* Hereford brand

HICO

Hico NEWS-REVIEW. w 1899+
1899-1906? as Hico news
pub 1929+
KHi Ap 1913-Jl 19 1918
NbHi Jl 25,Ag 8 1913
TxU Jl 30 1909-19

Hico REVIEW. w Ap 1 1885-1906||?
United with Hico news to form Hico news-review

HIGGINS

Higgins NEWS. w 1897+
Tx Ja 30 1908-16
TxU 1914-O 1919

HILLSBORO

HILL county visitor. w 1884-85||?
TxU S-N 19 1884

Hillsboro MIRROR. w 1881+
CU-B Jl 10-17,31 1889;Ja 8-29 1890
Tx Ja 22 1908-15;Je 18 1930
TxGR Je 18 1930
TxU Ag 17 1904-Jl 7 1908;Ap-D 1909;My 15 1912-Ag 1916

Hillsboro MIRROR. d 1896+
Title varies slightly
NN O 6 1915
TxU My 12-29,N 1907-Ja 20 1908;F 9 1925+

HITCHCOCK

STORM drift. N 1900-
TxGR N 1900

HOLLAND

Holland PROGRESS. w 1889+
pub Mr 1933+
Tx 1908-10

HONDO

Hondo ANVIL herald. w 1886+
1886-O 9 1903 as Castroville anvil (Castroville)
pub 1886+
Tx 1908-16;28-30
TxU Jl 22 1932-33

Hondo HERALD. w 1891-S 1903||
United with Castroville anvil (Castroville) to form Hondo anvil herald
TxHoA complete

HONEY GROVE

Honey Grove CITIZEN. w,sw 1886-Ja 1929||
1886-D 24 1915 as Texas citizen. United with Honey Grove signal to form Honey Grove signal-citizen
sw N? 1889-90?
CU-B Ag 17-28,N 22,29 1889;Ja 31,F 14,21 1890
Tx 1908-16

Honey Grove ENTERPRISE. w Je 17 1870-
TxU 1870-F 18 1871

Honey Grove SIGNAL-CITIZEN. w 1891+
1891-Ja 1929 as Honey Grove signal
pub 1895+

TEXAS citizen. *See* Honey Grove citizen

HOUSTON

ADVANCE. 1892?-
Tx Ag 10 1892

Houston AGE. d 1871-96||?
Title varies: Age; Houston daily age; Houston morning age; Houston evening age
CU-B Jl 2-3 1889
Tx Je 17 1882
TxH [F 7 1873-74]My 22,N 17,D 21 1875;Ja 11,25,31,F 9,12,16-17,21-23,Ap 18,Jl 17,S 18,O 18-19,21,30 1876;My 18,S 28,O 2,11-12,14,N 4, 14 1877;Ag 12 1878;F 13 1879;O 29,N 19 1880; F 17,Ap 18 1881;N 24,D 7 1882;My 12,O 11,N 8 1884;Ap 1,Ag 14,S 21 1885;supp My 13 1884

Weekly Houston AGE. w My 15 1871-94||?
Title varies: Age; Houston weekly age
TxH My 15 1874;My 27 1885
TxU N 24,D 27 1871

Weekly AGE of commerce. w
Tx Ap 22 1857

L'AURORA. w Je 2 1906-19||?
In Italian
IU D 8 1917-Je 1918
TxGR O 1916-D 22 1917
TxH [Je 30 1906-S 13 1919]

BEACON. w
TxU Ag 15 1851

BRYANT'S merchant's transcript. w
TxU Ap 20 1867

Houston BULLETIN. w 1911-23||?
TxH [Je 20 1912-D 8 1923]

Houston morning CHRONICLE. d O 1884-Ja? 1885||
Replaces Houston post
CLU [O 26 1884-Ja 17 1885]
TxH N 3-15 1884
TxU D 9 1884-Ja 14 1885

Houston CHRONICLE. d O 14 1901+
pub 1901+
MWA N 27 1927;D 30 1928
MnU Je 1918-Mr,Ag-D 1919
Tx Jl 1907-Je,O 1912-Je,S 1913+
TxGR O 14 1902;My 15 1906+
TxH N 28 1903+
TxU Je-Ag 1904;Je 18-Jl,S 1905-06;Mr 8 1907-Ag,O-N 1908;N 1909-Mr 1916

COLUMBIAN. w Mr 26 1925-
TxH Ap 30-My 21 1925

Houston COMMERCIAL bulletin. w 1855?-
TxU Ap 1 1855

Weekly COMMERCIAL telegraph and business register. w Ja 8 1857-
Ja-Ap 23 1857 as Houston price current and business register
Tx Mr 26,My 7 1857
TxH 1857-59
TxU F 12 1857[Mr 11-Jl 22 1858]

Houston COURIER. d Ag? 1872-
TxU O 10-N 29 1872

Houston DEFENDER. w O 11 1930+
Negro
pub 1930+
TxH 1930+

DEMOCRATIC telegraph and Texas register. *See* Weekly Houston telegraph

DEUTSCHE zeitung und anzeiger. *See* Texas deutsche zeitung

DISMUKE dug-out. w F 14 1924-
TxH F-My 1924

Houston DISPATCH. d S 4 1923-Jl 31 1924||
United with Houston post to form Houston post-dispatch, later Houston post
TxH complete

ECHO. w 1885-91||?
CU-B Ja 4-11,25 1890

FACTS. d D 26 1922-
TxH D 26-28 1922

FIFTH WARD digest. w Ja 24 1914-
TxH [Ja-Ap 4 1914]

Houston FREE telegram. *See* Houston telegram 1912-15

FREEMAN'S champion.
Tx Ap 10 1865

GALVESTON news. *See under* Galveston

Sunday GAZETTE. w
TxU My 1-8 1870

HARRIS county suburbanite. w Ja 28 1905-28||?
1905-20? as Suburbanite (Houston Heights)
TxH [1905-F 6 1920;F 10 1922-Ag 23 1923]

TEXAS (*Continued*)

HOUSTON—*Continued*

Houston daily HERALD. d 1885-O 1902||
Early issues as Evening times. Merged with Houston chronicle
TxGR Ja 21 1896;F 5,19,26 1897
TxH D 1,19,22 1885

HOOVER herald. O 18- 1928||?
Tx O 1928

HOUSTONIAN. tw 1841-
TxWM Ag 16(extra)18(extra)20 1841

Weekly HOUSTONIAN. w 1841-
DLC My 27,Jl 22 1841
Tx Ja 27 1842

INDEPENDENT. w 1898-1905||?
Negro
DLC Ja 27 1900

INDEPENDENT democrat. w Jl 19 1929-
1929-S 19 1930 as Southern advocate
Also dated in Dallas
Tx Jl-Ag 2 16,S 20,O 11 1929-S 19 1930
TxH 1929-[S 26 1930-Ja 1931]

Houston INFORMER. w My 24 1919+
Ja 10 1931-Jl 28 1934 as Houston informer and Texas freeman
Negro
TxH [1919-Je 14 1924]Ag 1930+

INVESTIGATOR. w D 15 1921-
Tx D 31 1921-Ja 20,F 3 1922
TxH 1921-Mr 10 1922

JEWISH herald. *See* Texas Jewish herald

Daily JOURNAL. d 1867||?
OClWHi Ap 13 1867

Evening JOURNAL. d F 12-D 31 1884||?
Merged with Houston morning chronicle
TxH F 13-D 1884

MERCANTILE advertiser. w D 1848-
DLC Ap 14,My 5,26,Je 9,Jl 21,Ag 11-16,S-O 8,19-D 15,29 1849

Houston daily MERCURY. d 1868?-74||?
TxH O 4 1873
TxU Jl 4 1873-F 1874

NATIONAL banner. w Ap 25 1838-
DLC Ap 25 1838
GDE O 5 1838

NATIONAL intelligencer. w 1838-
DLC Mr 1,28,Ap 18,My 2-9,Jl 4 1839
GDE Je 27,Ag 22 1839
NcD Ap 18 1839
TxU Je 20 1839

NEWS. 1861-66 *See* Galveston news (Galveston)

Houston daily NEWS. d Mr 1886-
DLC Ap 26 1886

Houston OBSERVER. w 1916-Je 18 1921||
Negro
TxH [Ja 27 1917-21]

PEOPLE'S advocate. d S 19 1878-
TxH S 19,21,26,O 3,5,17 1878

PILOT. w 1925+
TxH N 23,D 21 1928;Je 21[D 27 1929-Ag 1932]

Houston POST. d F 19 1880+
Ag 1 1924-Ja 31 1932 as Houston post-dispatch (other variations slight)
Suspended from O 14? 1884-Ja? 1885 (for this period *See* Houston morning chronicle)
pub 1900+
A My-Ag 1901;01-02
CoU 1901;05-My 1910
DLC 1898-F 1903;Jl 1930+
KHi Je 19 1882-Jl 17 1906;F 20 1922
MWA Mr 1 1882-My 15 1888;N 14 1924;Ap 26, My 14 1925;Mr 3,O 29 1926
NbHi [Ag 28-O 2 1907]
NcD 1906-My 1908
Tx F 1882-Je 1884;87-1913;Mr 1914+
TxGR F 3 1884;O 14 1886;Mr 23 1891;Ap 20-21 1895;96-F 25 1899[S 10 1900-Ap 21 1934]
TxH 1880-O 1883[Mr 26-O 14 1884]Ap 2,My 21,Jl-D 1885;90+
TxHuS O 1919-N 1923
TxU Jl-D 1895[97-98]-My 28,Jl 17 1900-Je 10 1905;Mr-D 1907;F 1908-Je 1909;Ap-Jl,O 1916-S 23,N 21 1922+
VU Ap 18 1902
WHi 1917+

Houston evening POST. d My 8 1922-24||?
TxGR N 26 1923
TxH 1922-Mr 1924

Houston PRESS. d 1911+
pub 1911+
TxGR [Ap 1919-F 1934]
TxH [D 1911-13]+
TxU Jl 1919-Jl 14 1921;Ag 5 1924+

Houston PRICE current and business register. *See* Weekly commercial telegraph and business register

PROGRESS. w F 28 1912-
TxH My 11-Jl 20 1912

Houston RECORD. d Mr 28 1910-
TxH Mr-Jl 28 1910

Houston REPUBLIC. w Jl 4 1857-
TxH 1857-Je 1858
TxU Jl 11 1857;Ap 23,N 12 1859

Houston SENTINEL. w Je 24 1927-O 31 1930||
Negro
TxH [1927-30]

SOUTHERN advocate. *See* Independent democrat

Morning STAR. d,tw Ap 8 1839-50||?
Followed by Telegraph, later Houston tri-weekly telegraph
d 1839?
DLC Ap 15,17,19,N 5 1839
MWA Mr 10-12 1846
Tx Ap 10-Ag 14 1839;43-[45]-Ja 1,6-20,27-F 3 1846;D 27(extra)1849
TxH 1839-O 26 1844
TxU Ap-O 8 1839

Daily evening STAR. d Mr 28 1866-
Title varies slightly
Tx Mr-Ap 28,My 17 1866

Houston semi-weekly STAR. sw Ap 2 1866-
Title varies slightly
Tx Ap,My 5-Jl 14 1866

STAR. w Ag 2? 1884-
Tx Ag 16,O 11,25-N 1,15 1884;Ja 17-24,My 16-30,Jl 11,Ag 1,15,S 12,26,O 17 1885

SUBURBAN record. w Ap 21 1916-
TxH [Ap-O 13 1916]

SUBURBANITE. *See* Harris county suburbanite

SÜD Texas post. w My 11 1910-11||?
In German
TxGR My 13-O 20 1910

Houston daily SUN. d N 1-D 31 1882||
Merged with Houston age
TxH complete

El TECOLOTE. w,sw,tw D 24 1924+
w 1924-2?;tw 1927?-28?;w 1928?-30?
In Spanish
pub 1925+
TxGR Mr 7 1932
TxH [F 1925]+

Houston daily TELEGRAM. d Ap 1877-N? 1880||
Follows Houston daily telegraph. Ap-My? 1877 as Daily telegram
Tx S 12 1880
TxH My 6,12,S 28-29,O 11,N 14 1877;Ap 13, 18 1878-Ap 16, S 2 1879;F 21,Mr 12,My 22, S 10,12,O 2?,N 2,7,10 1880

Houston weekly TELEGRAM. w Ap 1877-N? 1880||
Follows Weekly Houston telegraph
TxH Ap 19 1878-Ap 15,N 18 1880

Houston TELEGRAM. d D 1912-15||?
1912-Ap 30 1913 as Houston free telegram
TxH [1913-Mr 22 1915]

Weekly Houston TELEGRAPH. w,sw O 10 1835-F 11 1877||
1835-45? as Telegraph and Texas register; 1846?-51? Democratic telegraph and Texas register. Followed by Houston weekly telegram
sw during sessions of legislature
1835-Mr 24 1836 pub in San Felipe de Austin; Ap 14 1836 in Harrisburg; Ag 2 1836-Ap 11 1837 in Columbia
Suspended from Mr 24-Ap 14, from Ap 14-Ag 2 1836 from Ap 11-My 2 1837; from N 6-20 1839; from F 5-Ap 8, from Je 10-24, from Je 24-Jl 10 1840; from O? 1873-Ap? 1874
DLC F 20,S 13 1836-N 1837;My 12,30,D 19,29 1838-[Ap-N 1839]-Ja 1,Ap 8-29,N 4,18 1840; Ag 24,S 14,O 26,D 14-21 1842[43]-Ja 2,17-24, F 21,Mr 6,Je 26 1844; Ja 8,Ap 23,D 24-31 1845[Mr-D 1847]-50;Je 1858-Ag 21 1860
GDE Jl 21,Ag 25 1838
ICN D 13 1843
MBAt Ap 7 1863;Jl 19 1864
MH N 9 1836[37]-Jl 21 1838
MWA D 16 1837;D 20 1843;Mr 11 1846
MeBa F 7 1844
NN Ja 21,Mr 7,O 11,21,D 2-9 1837;Ja 6,F 24, My 12-26 1838
NNHi F 12 1862;Ap 14 1863
NcU S 29 1835
NjP [S 24 1862-Mr 4 1863]
OClWHi Ja 21,F 7,18,Mr 4-11 1863
Tx 1835-Ja 16,Ag 9 1836-Ja 6,18-27,F 10-21, Mr 7 1837-Ag 4 1838;My 29-Jl 3,17-Ag 7, 21-S 4,18,O 2-23,N 6-20,D 11-25 1839;Ap 8-S 2,O 7-14,28-N 18,D 9-16,30 1840;Ja 13-F 17,Mr 24-My 12,26-Je 2,16-Ag 11,25 S &O-D 8,22 1841-Ja,F 16 1842;43-F 11 1846; F 22,Ap 26,Ag 2 1847;Ap 6-13,Je 8,O 5 1848; Ja 25,F 22 1849;Mr 7,Ag 14 1850;Ap 25,My 31-Je 6 1851; F 13[Mr 1852-56]Ja 29,F 12,D 10,19 1862;Ja 21,Mr 11,Ap 21-My 12,Je 2,Jl 14-21,Ag,S 8,22,O 13-27,N 10 1863;Ap 19,Je 21 1864;D 2-9 1869
TxDN O 1856-60
TxGR Ag 1836-Ag 4,O 20 1838
TxH 1835-Ap 14 1836[Ag 11 1838-F 18 1854]F 1856-Mr 22 1864;S 3,N 5 1867;Je 25,S 17-O, D 3-24 1868[69-O 2 1873]Ap 25 1874-Ja,Mr, Ag 4 1876
TxU 1835-Ap 14,Ag 9 1836-[Mr 1846-48]Ja-N 1850;My 28 1858-My 1869
TxWM Ag 11 1838-Ja 20,F,Mr 10-Ag 18,S,O 12,D 22 1841-D 14 1842

Houston tri-weekly TELEGRAPH. sw,tw 1850?-77||?
Follows Morning star. 1850?-Ap 28 1855 as Telegraph(sw)Ap 30 1855-63? Tri-weekly telegraph
DLC Ag 28-S 1,6-22,O 2-18,23,27-N 13,24-D 8,21,27 1860;O 8 1862;F 2 1863;Ja-O,N 6-8,17, 22-D 1 1865
ICHi O 19 1863
MBAt Mr 23 1863
MH [1863]
MWA Ja 28,F 2,Mr 16,25-27,Ap 3,10,D 7,18 1863;N 30,D 14,21,26-30 1864;Ja 6-F 24,Mr 3-Ap 7,12-19,My 1-5,10-12,Je 9,Jl 19-21 1865
NBHi Ag 17 1863
NN Ap 3 1867
NNHi Ap 2 1861;My 23,Ja-S 3,15,26-D 8,12-15, 22 1862;Ja 5-9,14,18,F 2-4,11,16-23,Mr 23,30-Ap 8,13-29,My 6,11-13,20,25,Je 30,Ag 22-25,S 11 O 9 1863
NjP [Ap 1862-63]
OClWHi Ja 23-28,F 2-13,Mr 6-18,25-27,Ap 3, 8-10,15-17,22-27,My 1-2,9 1863;Ja 1 1864
TSS S 23,30,O 28,N 4 1861
Tx [Ja-S 1862]-[F-D 1863]Ja 11-15,22-F 5,N 2-18,21-23,28-D 19,30 1864[65]-Ja 5 1866;S 6, N 24,D 10,15,20 1869
extras:N 21,24,26,D 7,25,31 1861;Ja 2,4,7,24, 28,F 1,6,25,Mr 4,11,17,Ap 5,15,17,19,22,26,29 1862
supps:F 22,Mr 17 1862
TxCA 1864-66
TxGR N 15 1861-Mr 16,20,25,Ap 13,24-27,Jl 1,S 14,21,O 16,N 23,27,D 16-18,30 1863;Ja 6-13,18-23,27-F 1,13,N 4-11,16(supp)-D 1864; Ja 11,F 3,S 6,15-18,22-25,O 2-4,N 1 1865
extras:Mr 17,My 17,Jl 12,S 8,O 1,3,N 29 1862
TxH Ap 25-N 12 1855;F 18 1856-O 1860;N 29, D 13,18 1861;Ja 27,F 3,Mr 3,Je 11-13, 1862; F 13,Mr 16,23,Ap 13,My 8,O 2,N 18,23,27,D 7,25 1863;Ja 30,F 3 1865;S 18 1867;My 18-20,25 1870
TxU Ja 6 1864-Ap 24[My-D]1865
TxWM Mr 20 1863-F 5 1864
WHi O 22 1862-My 29,Je 15-N 23 1863

Houston daily TELEGRAPH. d F 6 1864-F 11 1877||
Title varies slightly. Followed by Daily telegram, later Houston daily telegram
Suspended from O? 1873-Ap? 1874
DLC Ap 22,My 29,Je 1,3 1864;Je 15-16,22,27 1865
KHi Ap 11 1875
MBAt Jl 22,Ag 18 1864;S 20 O 14 1865;Mr 24 1866;Je 2 1867
MWA F 10,12,19,Mr 4-5,30,Ap 1,6,My 16-17, 20,26,Jl 4,12,14-18,20 1864;Je 6-7 1865;Jl 16 1868
NNHi Mr 7-8,11,Jl 18 1864;Jl 22 1865
Tx [F-D 1864]F 21,Mr 22,Ap 7,My 22,25 1865; 67;Ap 20,31,S 9,28,N 30,D 3 1869[70]-[Ja-Je 1872;Ja-O 1873;Ap-D 1875]-77
TxGR [1864-S 4 1865]Ap 12 1866;Ag 11 1874;
extras: F 27 1863;My 16,19,25 Je 4,21,22 1864; Ap 12,24,29 1865
TxH F 12,29,Mr 18,21,23,25,Ap 13,19,28,My 13, 20,Ag 10,S 26,O 31 1864[Mr 25 1868-O 16 1873]Ap 16 1874-77
TxU My 6-Jl[D 1866-Je 14 1867]Ja 8-S 12 1870
TxWM F-Mr 23 1864
WHi My 24 1864

TEXAN. w 1908+
In Bohemian
IU D 13 1917-[30-31]+
TxH Jl 8 1915+

TEXAS anzeiger. w Je 23 1892-94||?
United with Texas deutsche zeitung to form Deutsche zeitung und anzeiger, later Texas deutsche zeitung
In German
TxH 1892-Je 15 1893

Der TEXAS demokrat. w 1861-69||
Followed by Die Texas post (Galveston)
1861-Je? 1863 pub in Victoria
In German
Tx D 9-16 1862;Ja 27,F 10-17,Mr,Ap 13,28,My 25-N,D 11-25 1863;Ja,F 10-Ap 15,Je 17-Jl 8,25-Ag 22,S-O,N 28 1864-F 9 1866
WHi Je 26 1863

TEXAS deutsche zeitung. w 1873-1917||?
1895?-1901? as Deutsche zeitung und anzeiger; 1910-15? alternate issues as Beilage der Texas deutsche zeitung
In German
Tx Ja 27 1910-15
TxU D 25 1875[S 26 1907-17]

TEXAS freeman. w 1899-D 27 1930||
United with Houston informer to form Houston informer and Texas freeman, later Houston informer
Negro
TxH Mr 1908-Ja 9 1909[17-30]

TEXAS gazette. w? D 31 1875-
TxH D 31 1875

TEXAS daily gazette. ir Ja 1 1876-
TxH Ja 2,6,20,25,F 9-11 1876

TEXAS Jewish herald. w 1907+
1907-11 as Jewish herald
pub 1907+
TxGR N 26 1908+
TxH [Je 17 1909-N 9 1911]Jl 26 1917-Ag 1 1918;Ap 10-My 1 1919;Mr 16 1922+
TxU Je 29-Ag 24 1916;Je 14 1917-Jl 1918

TEXAS plain dealer. sm 1932?-
Tx Mr 15 1933;F 11-Mr 1,Je 1 1934

Die TEXAS post. *See under* Galveston

TEXAS weekly record. w Ap 14 1865-
TxGR Ap 14 1865

TEXAS tribune. *See under* San Antonio

TEXAS world. w Mr 16 1890+
pub 1890+
TxGR Ag 19-S 9 1932
TxH Mr 12 1898;O 21,N 18 1899[1900-10]+
TxU [Ap 24 1892-Ap 2 1893]S 24 1898-Ja 1908

TEXIAN democrat. w D 1843-
DLC Ja 20,Mr 16,My 15,Je 19-23 1844

Weekly TIMES. w Ap 2 1840-
DLC Ap 30,Je 4 1840
Tx Ap 9 1840

Houston daily TIMES. d S 11 1868-72||?
1868-S 18 1869 as Houston daily times; S 19 1869-70? Times
TxGR S 16 1871
TxH 1868-Ag 2 1870;O 29,N 18 1871
TxU [S 10-O 12 1870]

TIMES. w,sw 1868-72||?
sw 1869?
Tx S 5,N 7,23 1869;N 26 1870

Evening TIMES. *See* Houston daily herald

TEXAS (*Continued*)

HOUSTON—*Continued*

Houston TRANSCRIPT. tw 1865?-
MWA Ag 24 1867

La TRIBUNA. d Je 30- 1924||?
In Spanish
TxGR Jl 4,S 24 1924
TxH [Jl 19-D 9 1924]

TRUE southron. 1860?-
Tx Je 16 1860

Tri-weekly Houston UNION. tw S 2 1868-71||?
1868-N 13 1869 as Houston union; D 5-9 1869 Tri-weekly union
Tx 1868-Jl 2,15,21-N 13,20 1869-F 26 1870
TxU [Je 1869-F 1870]

Houston UNION. w S 2 1868-73||
DLC S 23 1868-F 1870

Houston daily UNION. d Mr 10 1870-74||
Title varies: Daily union. Followed by Galveston daily mercury (Galveston)
DLC 1870-71
Tx Mr-My 1,3,24-Jl 9,12-O 7,11-28,31-N 1,3-4,7 1870-Mr 1872
TxGR F 8 1873
TxU [Mr-S 25 1870]

WASHINGTON SQUARE news. w Je 11 1926-
TxH [Jl 16 1926-Ja 23 1931]

HOUSTON HEIGHTS

Papers published in Houston Heights are listed under Houston

HUBBARD CITY

Hubbard City NEWS. w 1883+
1893-1901? as Texas pick and pan-news
CU-B My 24,Jl 12,Ag 9,30 1889;Ja 10-24 1890
Tx 1908-10
TxU Ag 26 1904-Mr 17 1905

TEXAS pick and pan. w -1893||
United with Hubbard City news to form Texas pick and pan-news, later Hubbard City news

HUMBLE

HARRIS county sun. w S 30 1909+
1909-32 as Oil city news
pub 1909+

OIL CITY news. *See* Harris county sun

HUNTSVILLE

Huntsville ITEM. w 1850+
pub 1926+
DLC Ja 5-19,F 9,Mr 1-8,22,Ap 19-My 3,17,Je 7 1856;Mr 16 1860
MWA Je 29,Jl 13 1882
Tx Ag 13 1869
TxHuS 1906[20-22]+
TxU Jl 24 1858

PATRIOT. w
TxGR Jl 14 1846

Huntsville RECORD. w 1856-
TxHuS Jl 23 1857
TxU O 15 1857

TEXAS banner. w S 1846-
DLC Mr 30, 1848;Ap 14-Je 23,Jl 14-28,Ag 25-S 1,O 5,20,N 3,17,D 1 1849
TxGR D 8 1846
TxU O 21 1847;My 26,N 24 1849

UNION republican. w 1867-73||?
TxU Je 2 1869;Ap 5 1871

IDALOU

Idalou ECHO. w 1914+
TxU F 1930-31

INDIANOLA

Indianola BULLETIN. w 1852?-
NcD My 17 1854
TxDN Mr 11 1852-My 24 1854
TxU Ap 26-Ag 1855

Indianola BULLETIN. w 1867-75||?
TxU Mr 27-D 12 1871

Indianola COURIER. w
TxU [My 21-N 22 1859]O 27-D 1 1860;Ja 5,My 25 1861

INDIANOLAN.
TxU Jl 18 1857

Indianola TIMES.
MWA D 23 1865

IOWA PARK

Iowa Park REGISTER. w 1898-1908||?
TxU Ag 12 1904-Je 19 1908

IRENE

Irene NEWS. w 1929-31||?
TxCeC 1929

IRVING

Irving INDEX. *See* Irving news

Irving NEWS. w Jl 23 1904-1916||?
1904-O 15? 1915 as Irving index
Tx 1908-O 15,D 16 1915-16

ITALY

Italy HERALD. w 1893-97||?
United with Italy news to form Italy news herald

Italy NEWS HERALD. w 1891+
1891-97? as Italy news
pub 1900-05;07-08;15;28-32;34+
TxU My 1929-32

ITASCA

Itasca ITEM. w 1887+
TxGR O 26 1923

JACKSBORO

FRONTIER echo. *See* Albany echo (Albany)

Jacksboro GAZETTE. w 1880+
pub S 1880+
Tx Ja 23 1908-15
TxU S 29 1898-O 10 1907;Ja-Ap 1913;16

Jacksboro NEWS. w 1893-1918||?
TxU Ag 25 1904-Ja 11 1918

JACKSONVILLE

Jacksonville BANNER. *See* Cherokee county banner

BOOMER. *See* Cherokee county banner

CHEROKEE county banner. w Mr 1888+
1888-Je 21 1889 as Boomer; Je 28 1889-D 20 1895 Jacksonville banner
pub Je 28 1889+
TxU Jl 15 1904-Je 18 1908;My 16-D 1912
—d ed *See* Jacksonville daily progress

Jacksonville JOURNAL. w,sw Jl 13 1934+
Follows Daily news
w 1934-Mr 5? 1935
pub 1934+
TxJ 1934+

Daily NEWS. d Ja 8-Je 30 1934||
Followed by Jacksonville journal
TxJ complete
TxJJ complete

Jacksonville daily PROGRESS. d Je 1910+
pub 1910+
TxJ 1934+
—w ed *See* Cherokee county banner

JASPER

EAST Texan clarion. w 1859-61||?
Follows Eastern Texian (San Augustine)
TxU Jl 21 1860

Jasper NEWS-BOY. w 1865+
CU-B Ag 21-28,D 4-11 1889;Ja 22 1890
MWA Ja 11 1868
NbHi Ag 12 1891
TxU Ag 17 1904-Ag 1918;32-33

JAYTON

Jayton CHRONICLE. w Ja 1 1921+
pub 1933+

JEFFERSON

COMMERCIAL bulletin. w 1864?-
MBAt My 4-18 1866

Weekly CONFEDERATE news. *See* Jefferson news

EASTERN Texas gazette. w 1857?-
TxU Mr 14,N 7 1857

Jefferson JIMPLECUTE. *See* Jefferson journal

Jefferson JOURNAL. w,sw,d 1865+
1865-F 25 1925 as Jefferson jimplecute (1868?-69? Semi-weekly jimplecute)
w 1865-67?;sw 1868?-69?;w 1870?-1925?;sw 1926?
pub Je 1925+
CU-B Jl 10-24 1889;Ja 15-22,F 5 1890
MWA My 12 1868
Tx S 4 1869;1908-16
TxU Ap 30 1867;O 30 1875;Jl 23 1904-Je 19 1908;My 16 1912-D 6 1917

Jefferson NEWS. w 1852?-
1861- 1865? as Weekly confederate news
TxU Ag 16,N 29 1861;My 16 1862;Mr 14,28,My 16 1863;Ag 11 1865

Jefferson RADICAL. w Ag 4 1869-71||?
MBAt Ag 11-18,S 18 1869
MWA O 16 1869
TxU N 13 1869-Ja 8 1870

TEXAS iron news. w 1881-91||?
CU-B D 7-21 1889

Weekly TIMES and republican. w 1867?-73||?
1867-68? as Jefferson times
MWA Jl 4 1868
Tx Jl 29-Ag 1869
TxU Ap 21 1870

JEWETT

Weekly MESSENGER. w 1885+
CU-B N 8,22,D 13 1889;Ja 3-10,24 1890
Tx My 29 1891

JOHNSON CITY

BLANCO county record. *See* Record-courier

RECORD-COURIER. w 1903+
1903-27? as Blanco county record
Tx O 9-D 13 1925

JOURDANTOWN

ATASCOSA county monitor. w 1873?+
1873-1916? as Atascosa monitor; 1917-31? Atascosa news-monitor
TxCeC 1916
TxU S 23 1909-O 12 1911

ATASCOSA monitor. *See* Atascosa county monitor

ATASCOSA news-monitor. *See* Atascosa county monitor

Jourdantown NEWS. w 1914-16||?
United with Atascosa monitor to form Atascosa news-monitor, later Atascosa county monitor

JUNCTION

CLIPPER. w 1884-92||?
CU-B Ag 29-S 12,O 3,N 7,21-D 12 1889;Ja 9, 23,F 6 1890

Junction EAGLE. w 1910+
TxBroH O 29 1931-F 18 1932

KARNES CITY

Karnes City CITATION. w 1896+
1896-1900 as Kicker; 1901-24 Karnes citation
pub 1901;05;29+
Tx Ja 23 1908-26
TxU Ja-O 9 1930

KICKER. *See* Karnes City citation

KAUFMAN

Kaufman HERALD. w 1886+
TxU F 1931-32

Kaufman daily HERALD. d 1923+
KHi O 16 1926
TxU Je 18 1929-Je 1931

Kaufman SUN. w,tw 1880-1911||?
w 1880-D 31 1909
Tx Ja 31 1908-D 15 1910
TxU S 1898-S 6 1911

KERENS

Kerens ENTERPRISE. 1888?-
CU-B Ag 29 1889

KERRVILLE

Kerrville EYE. *See* Kerrville mountain sun

Kerrville MOUNTAIN sun. w 1884+
1884-88? as Kerrville eye; 1889?-1907? Kerrville paper
pub [1884-1915]+
CU-B Mr 5 1887
Tx 1908-09
TxU Jl 17 1930-33

Kerrville PAPER. *See* Kerrville mountain sun

KILGORE

Kilgore daily NEWS. d Ja 1 1931+
pub 1931+

KILLEEN

HERALD and messenger. w,sw 1890+
1890-1908? as Killeen herald
sw 1906-08?
TxU Ag 12 1904-O 1905

KIMBALL

Kimball HERALD. w My 19 1860-
TxU My 19 1860

KINGSVILLE

Kingsville RECORD. w Ag 1906+
pub 1927+
TxGR D 20 1922
TxK 1934+
TxKC 1927+
TxKT Jl 1925+

KNOX CITY

Knox City JOURNAL. w 1909-25||?
1909-24? as Southwestern journal
TxU 1911-Ag 22 1913

KNOX county herald. w 1902+
KHi My 27 1927

KNOX county news. w 1905-13||?
TxU Ja 24 1908-Ag 1913

SOUTHWESTERN journal. *See* Knox City journal

KOSSE

Kosse CYCLONE. w 1883+
Tx S 1896-1915
TxU Ag 18 1904-08;My 16 1912-D 16 1920;Je 9 1921-O 1 1925

TEXAS (*Continued*)

LADONIA

Ladonia ENTERPRISE. w My 27? 1871-
Tx Je 17 1871-Je 15 1872

Ladonia NEWS. w 1886+
Ja 1 1909-O 28 1910 as Ladonia news and Pecan Gap tribune
pub Ja 1896;1921-Ja 1924;S 1931+
CU-B Ag 30,S 13,D 13 1889;Ja 3 1890
Tx 1908-10
TxU 1926-30

LA FERIA

La Feria NEWS. w D 23 1923+
pub [1923-24]+

LA GRANGE

La Grange DEUTSCHE zeitung. w 1890-1926||?
In German
TxU O 1924-Je 10 1926

FAR west. w F 13 1847-
Tx F-Mr 20,Ap-My 22 1847

FAYETTE county neue aera. w -1878||?
In German
Tx N 9-D 14 1876;Ja 11,25 1877
—English ed *See* Fayette county new era

FAYETTE county new era. w 1865?-78||?
1865?-O 18 1872 as La Grange new era
Tx N 20,D 4-18 1868[69-70]My 5,Jl 28,O 13 1871;72-73;Mr 26,Je 25,Jl 30-Ag 20 1875;76;Ja 11,25,F 8-My 24 1877
TxH Ja 14-28,Jl 22-29,Ag 19-26,S 9-23 1870
TxU D 1 1871
—German ed *See* Fayette county neue aera

FAYETTE county record. w 1873-79||?
1873? as Our county record
TxU Ap 15-22,D 16 1873;Ja 8 1874;My 18 1876

FAYETTE county record. tw N 1 1922+
pub [1922-25]+

La Grange INTELLIGENCER. w Ja 1844-
Tx F 15 1844-Jl 7,Ag 19-N 5,18-D 1845;Ja 10-S 19 1846

La Grange JOURNAL. w F 18 1880+
pub 1884+
CU-B Jl 11 1889
Tx Je 16 1880;86+
TxCA 1921+
TxGR Ap 2,Jl 23 1931[D 1932-33]Mr 8 1934+
TxU 1880-My 18 1882;Mr 8-D 1883

La Grange NEW era. *See* Fayette county new era

OUR county record. *See* Fayette county record

La Grange PAPER. w F 24- 1855||?
Tx F 24,Ag 4 1855

PATRIOT. w Ap 23? 1863-
Not pub O 22,29,D 31 1863;Ja 7,F 11,18,My 25 1865
Tx Je,Jl 16,30 1863-F 5,25-Mr 24,Ap 21-My 5,19,Je-S 3,24-O 15,N 19,D 10 1864-Ja 21,F-Je 3 1865
TxU [Ja-Jl 1865]

STATES rights democrat. w 1859?-70||?
Tx F 21,Mr 7,21,My 16 1861;Ag 25,S-O,N 16-D 14 1866[67]Ja-F 14,Mr 6-13,My 1-8,Je 12 1868;O 29,N 12-26,D 10 1869;Ja 21-F 4 1870

SVOBODA. w,sw D 10 1885-1930||?
w 1885-1926?
In Bohemian
Tx Mr 8 1907-16
TxU 1885-1926

TEXAS monument. w Jl 20 1850-55||
Tx Jl-S,O 9-N 6,D 1850-Ap 12,26-My 3,17-24, Je 7-14,28,Jl 14,Ag-N 7 1854
TxH N 20 1850;Jl 28 1852;Je 21,Ag 1 1854
TxU O 2 1850;Je 25-Jl 1851

TRUE issue. w 1850?-
Tx O-D 22 1855;56[57]-N 1861;Ja 1,F 5-19,Mr 12,26-Ap 2,18,My 2,16,Jl 23,Ag 1 1863;Mr 26-31,My 14,26,S 24-O 22,D 10-24 1864;Ja 7, 21-28,Mr 4,18-Je 17 1865
TxGR D 22 1860
TxH D 22 1860;F 4,14,Mr 14 1861
TxU Ja 14 1855;D 12 1857;Ag 21 1858;F 12 1859

LAMESA

Lamesa REPORTER. w 1905+
TxU S 1931-32

LAMPASAS

Lampasas BLADE. *See* Lampasas record

BRANDON'S weekly. *See* Lampasas record

Lampasas CHRONICLE. w 1859?-
TxU O 1 1859

Lampasas DISPATCH. w 1870-92||?
Tx Ap 6 1882
TxU O 31 1870;N 9,D 14 1872

Lampasas LEADER. w 1888+
pub 1888+
KHi N 30 1917
TxU My 1904-Je 23 1905;S 1932-33

Lampasas daily LEADER. d 1904+
pub 1904+
KHi F 13,S 1 1925
Tx Je 3 1919

Lampasas weekly NEWS. w 1904?-06||?
TxU Ag 12 1904-O 20 1905

OUR county record. w Ap 15 1873-
TxU Ap 15 1873

PEOPLE'S journal. w 1892-96||?
TxU Ag 1892-Ja 1893

Lampasas RECORD. w 1906+
1906-18? as Lampasas blade; 1919? Brandon's weekly
pub Ag 1920+

LANCASTER

Lancaster HERALD. w 1887+
KHi N 17 1927
Tx 1908-16

LA PORTE

La Porte CHRONICLE. w Ja 26 1893-1910||?
United with LaPorte herald to form Chronicle-herald, later La Porte chronicle and herald
KHi 1893-Jl 5 1894
TxU Ag 25 1904-Je 18 1908;09-10

La Porte CHRONICLE and herald. w,sw 1901-33||?
1901-10? as La Porte herald; 1911-21? Chronicle-herald; 1925-26? La Porte chronicle?
w 1901-25?
TxU F 1925-D 2 1926

La Porte HERALD. *See* La Porte chronicle and herald

LAREDO

El BOLETIN fronterizo comercial. d 1930-
In Spanish
LNT-M [Ag 2 1930-Ja 8 1931]

La COLONIA mexicana. sw 1886-91||?
In Spanish
CU-B Ag 24 1889

El DEMOCRATA fronterizo. w,d 1891-1920||?
w 1891-My 3 1919
In Spanish
DLC O 28-29 1919
IU D 8 1917-Je 6 1919

GATE city. d 1888-91||?
CU-B S 12-13,15,O 2,6 1889

Laredo weekly LEDGER. w 1922-23||?
Followed by Oil ledger (not in this list)
TxGR My 31-Jl 12 1923

El MUNDO. w 1888-91||?
In Spanish
IaDH F 22 1891

NEWS. d 1892-96||?
CLM Mr 22,24 1892

SOUTH Texas citizen. w D 1 1932+
pub 1932+

Laredo weekly TIMES. w 1881-1926||?
Tx Ja 28 1908-15
TxU S 11 1893-Je 14 1908;Je 13 1909-Ja 23 1910;My 19 1912-Jl 6 1913;F 8 1925-Mr 1926

Laredo TIMES. d 1883+
pub 1915+
TxU 1929-33

LAVACA

COMMERCIAL. w
TxU N 30 1850

Lavaca HERALD. w 1856?-
TxU S 13-20 1856;D 5 1867

Lavaca JOURNAL. w Jl 29 1847-
Tx Jl-S 1847;Ja 14-28 1848
TxU Ja 14 1848

LEAGUE CITY

League City LEADER. w Jl 9 1914-
TxGR [Jl 16 1914-My 13 1915]

League City NEWS. w 1911-29||?
TxGR My 25 1912[Ag 22-N 14 1914]Je 1924-Ja 4 1929

TEXAS COAST promoter. w My 1 1896-1907||?
TxGR My 1 1896;S 28 1900[Ap 15 1904-S 21 1907]

LEONARD

Leonard GRAPHIC w Ap 5 1890+
pub Ap 1924+
TxU O 1898-S 1901;Ja 24 1908-11;My 16-Jl 1915

LEWISVILLE

ENTERPRISE. w 1892+
pub 1918+
TxU 1918-Je 12 1919

LEXINGTON

Lexington ENTERPRISE. w 1899+
1899-F? 1903 as Lexington progress
Tx Ag 7 1903
TxU F 1925-Mr 1926

Lexington PROGRESS. *See* Lexington enterprise

LIBERTY

Liberty GAZETTE. w 1860-69||?
NcD F 7,Ap 10 1868 Ja 15 1869

Liberty VINDICATOR. w 1886+
CU-B Ag 23,S 6-13,O 4 1889
TxGR N 20 1931
TxU Ag 12 1910

LINDALE

Lindale NEWS. w 1922+
pub 1922+

LINDEN

ALLIANCE standard. *See* Cass county sun

CASS county sun. w 1876+
1889?-91? Standard; 1892?-97? Alliance standard
TxU Jl 31 1883;O 26 1895;Ag 23 1904-D 5 1905

STANDARD. *See* Cass county sun

LIPSCOMB

PANHANDLE interstate. w 1887-93||?
CU-B Ag 23-30 1889

LITTLEFIELD

LAMB county leader. w My 24 1923+
pub 1923+

LIVINGSTON

EAST Texas pinery. w 1882-95||?
CU-B Ja 9,23-30 1890

POLK county enterprise. w 1903+
Tx F 20 1908-16

LLANO

Llano IRON city news. *See* Llano news

Llano NEWS. w 1888+
1888-91? as Llano iron city news
CU-B Ja 16-30 1890
Tx N 6 1890

Llano TIMES. w 1892-1911||?
TxU Ja 23 1908-S 2 1909

LOCKHART

Weekly NEWS echo. w 1872-80||?
NcD Je 6 1873
TxU Ap 27 1872

Lockhart POST-REGISTER. w 1899+
1899-F 3 1916 as Lockhart post
pub 1899+
Tx 1908-16;24-25;30+
TxU [O 1906-S 23 1915]O 25 1917;Jl 17-25,Ag 8 1919

RAMBLER. w My 30? 1859-
TxU Jl 1 1859

Lockhart REGISTER. w 1879-F 4 1916||
United with Lockhart post to form Lockhart post-register
TxLoP complete
TxU Ag 12 1904-16

SOUTH and west. w D 19 1865-
TxU D 19 1865

SOUTHERN watchman. w 1856?-
TxU Je 5 1857

LOCKNEY

Lockney BEACON. w 1901+
TxU N 23 1929-30

LONE OAK

Lone Oak BANNER. *See* Lone Oak news

Lone Oak NEWS. w 1896+
1896-1902? as Lone Oak banner
CU-B Ja 1-8,24-31,F 28 1890
TxU N 1-8 1900

LONGVIEW

Longview DEMOCRAT. w 1880-85||?
TxU [Ag 26 1881-Mr 13 1885]

GREGG county clarion. *See* Times clarion

Longview morning JOURNAL. d 1931+
Sunday ed as News-journal
pub 1931+

Longview daily NEWS. d 1928+
Sunday ed as News-journal
pub 1928+
TxU Je 15 1933+

TIMES CLARION. w 1886-1921||?
1886-93? as Gregg county clarion
TxU Jl 19-O 18 1900;N 1902-Mr 12,Jl 23 1903-Je 6 1912

LORAINE

Loraine LEADER. w 1920-30||?
TxU F 13 1925-S 21 1928

TEXAS (*Continued*)

LOVELADY

Lovelady STAR. w 1927+
TxU F 17 1928-31

LUBBOCK

Lubbock morning AVALANCHE. d 1923+
Sunday ed as Avalanche-journal
pub S 1926+
TxLT S 1925+
—w ed *See* South Plains farmer

AVALANCHE-JOURNAL. w *See* South Plains farmer

AVALANCHE-JOURNAL. Sunday *See* Lubbock morning avalanche; Lubbock evening journal

Lubbock evening JOURNAL. d 1923+
Sunday ed as Avalanche-journal
KHi My 4 1927
TxLT N 1932+
—w ed *See* South Plains farmer

Lubbock NEWS. w 1931-
TxGR Ja 29 1932

PLAINS journal. w 1922-Mr 1928‖?
Merged with Lubbock avalanche to form Avalanche-journal, later South Plains farmer
TxU N 8 1923-S 16 1926

SOUTH PLAINS farmer. w 1900+
1900-25? as Lubbock avalanche; 1926-Mr 9? 1928 Avalanche-journal
TxCA 1929;32+
TxGR Je 6 1930
TxU O 1926-33
—d ed *See* Lubbock morning avalanche; Lubbock evening journal

LUFKIN

Lufkin daily NEWS. d 1916+
TxGR Ap 18 1932
TxU [Jl 16-D 1927]

LULING

Luling SIGNAL. w 1878+
Tx Jl 8-16 1886
TxGR O 24 1930

MABANK

Mabank BANNER. w Ag 14 1908+
pub 1909+

McALLEN

DELTA irrigation news. m,sm,w Jl 1921-27‖?
1921-Mr? 1922 as Lower Rio Grande Valley news; Ap? 1922-My 1926? Gravity irrigation news
m 1921-Mr? 1922;sm Ap? 1922-My 5? 1924
TxH O 1921-Mr[O 1922-N 1927]
TxU O 1921-Mr 1922;O 15 1923-25;Je 1926-F 1927

GRAVITY irrigation news. *See* Delta irrigation news

LOWER Rio Grande Valley news. *See* Delta irrigation news

McAllen MONITOR. w D 18 1909+
TxCA 1921+
TxU F 20 1925-32

McAllen daily PRESS. d N 20 1920+
pub Mr 1924+
TxU 1930-Je 1934

McKINNEY

McKinney ADVOCATE. *See* Black waxy

BLACK waxy. w Ap 3 1877-84‖?
1877-83 as McKinney advocate
Tx My 31 1884

COLLIN county citizen. w 1882-83‖?
United with McKinney advocate to form Black waxy

McKinney daily COURIER-GAZETTE. d Mr 4 1897+
1897-Jl 14? 1906 as Daily courier
pub 1897+
TxU 1930+
—w ed *See* Weekly democrat-gazette

Weekly DEMOCRAT-GAZETTE. w F 7 1884+
1884-Jl 8? 1906 as McKinney democrat
pub [1884-93]+
CU-B S 1889
TxU 1930-32
—d ed *See* McKinney daily courier-gazette

McKinney EXAMINER. w 1886+
pub 1900+

McKinney GAZETTE. w My 4 1886-Jl 1906‖
United with McKinney democrat to form Weekly democrat-gazette
Suspended from Ja 21 1887-O 1889

Daily GAZETTE. d 1899-Jl 1906‖
United with Daily courier to form Daily courier-gazette

McKinney MESSENGER. w 1855-74‖?
1855-58 as Clarksville messenger (Clarksville)
Tx O 18 1861;D 23 1864
TxGR S 11 1863
TxU F 2 1866;My 31 1867;F 28 1868;Je 19 1869;Jl 16 1870;Mr 19 1874

MADISONVILLE

Madisonville METEOR. w 1894+
pub 1894+
TxU 1928

MANGUM

Mangum STAR. 1887-90‖?
CU-B Ag 1,8,N 7,12,14,D 12 1889

MANOR

Manor COMMUNITY news. w O 1 1924-
TxU O 1924-Je 1925

MANSFIELD

Mansfield HAWKEYE. *See* Mansfield sun

Mansfield MESSENGER. w 1886-87‖?
CU-B F 26 1887

Mansfield SUN. w 1894-1912‖?
1894? as Tarrant county banner; 1895?-96? Mansfield hawkeye
Tx Ja 18-F 14 1895
TxU Ag 11 1904-Je 17 1910

TARRANT county banner. *See* Mansfield sun

MARBLE FALLS

Marble Falls MESSENGER. w 1899+
Tx Ja 23 1908-15

MARFA

BIG BEND sentinel and Marfa new era. w Mr 1926+
1926-F? 1927 as Big Bend sentinel
pub Mr 13 1927+

Marfa NEW era. w 1887-1927‖?
United with Big Bend sentinel to form Big Bend sentinel and Marfa new era
TxU Ja 25 1908-Je 8 1912;F 1925-26

MARLIN

BALL. w 1874-1905‖?
Title varies slightly
Tx O 1890
TxU N 26 1903-Ag 1905

Marlin DEMOCRAT. w,sw 1890+
w 1890-Je 27 1907;Ap 1908-24?
Tx 1908-15
TxU N 26 1903-Mr 1908

MARSHALL

Weekly HARRISON flag. w Jl? 1856-70‖?
1856-O 22 1868 as Harrison flag
Tx Jl 10 1858-Ja 12 1861;N 15 1865-O 14,N 25 1869
TxU F 21 1857

Tri-weekly HERALD. tw 1875-88‖?
TxU Jl 25 1876;Mr 29 1877

Marshall MERIDIAN. w
TxU Je 28 1854

Marshall MESSENGER. w,sw 1877-1925‖?
sw 1911?-21?
CU-B Ag 9-23,S 6-13,O 18,N 15,29-D 20 1889
KHi O 19 1920;Ag 16 1921
TxU Ap 20 1878;Ap 11 1889

Marshall MESSENGER. d 1919+
pub 1925+

Marshall NEWS. d 1919+
pub 1925+

STAR state patriot. w 1848-
DLC Mr 20-Ap 17,My 8-15,29-Je,Jl 10;24-31,Ag 14,S-O 23 1852
TxU Ag 23 1851;Ja 10-Jl 13 1852

TEXAS republican. w Mr 30 1849-69‖?
DLC D 23 1864;Ja 13 1865
Tx My 26 1849-S 10 1859;Je 2,S 22 1860-Jl 1863;S 9 1864-Je 4 1869
TxGR Ja 29 1863
TxU Je 29 1849;Ag 12 1858;Ja 22,Mr 3,My 30 1863;Je 30 1865
WHi F 11 1859

MART

Mart HERALD. w 1901+
TxU Je 13-D 1919

MASON

MASON county news. w 1877+
Tx 1908-N 10 1916;Mr 14 1935
TxU S 30 1898-S 1907;O 15 1931-32

MATADOR

Matador MAVERICK. *See* Texas maverick

TEXAS maverick. w 1892-1908‖?
1892-1905? as Matador maverick
TxU Ag 12 1904-Je 9 1905

MATAGORDA

Matagorda BULLETIN. w Ag 2 1837-
DLC Mr 14 1839
Tx S-N 22,D 6,20 1837-Ag,S 27-N 22,D 1838-Ap 4,My 1-9 1839
TxU [1837-Ap 1838]

CHRONICLE of the times. w 1855-
TxGR Ja 28 1856
TxU Mr 6 1858

COLORADO gazette and advertiser. w My 16 1839-43‖?
DLC Mr 27,Ap 17 1841
Tx Je-Ag 1,22-D 7,21 1839;Ja-F 8, Mr 14,28, Ap 11-My 8,23-Ag 8,22-S 5,19-O 24,N 7,28-D 5,19 1840;Ja 23-F,Mr 20-My 1,15-Jl 10, 24-Ag 7,21-S 11,O 2,31 1841-Ja 15,My 28,Jl 9,30 1842
TxGR S 26 1840

COLORADO herald. w Jl 1846-
TxGR Ag 26-S 2,N 14,28 1846
TxU Ap? 1847

COLORADO tribune. w 1848-
Tx Je 4,Ag,S 20,O 1-8,22-N 12,26-D 24 1849; Ja-F,Mr 11-Je 3,17,Jl 5,19-O 11,25,N 8,30,D 21 1850;Ja 4-11,Ap 19,My 10-Je 23,Jl 14-21, Ag 25-29,O 27-D 15,25 1851;Ja-F 2,Ap-My 10,27-S 6,27-28 1852;53;Ja 18-Jl 1854
TxU Ap 17,Je 1 1848[My 10-Jl 21 1861]

Weekly DESPATCH. w D 1843-
TxGR Ja 6,20-N 23,D 7 1844

Matagorda GAZETTE. w Jl 31? 1858-
TxU [O 16 1858-S 12 1860]

MAYPEARL

Maypearl HERALD. w 1903-28‖?
1903-05? as Maypearl messenger
KHi Ap 13 1925

Maypearl MESSENGER. *See* Maypearl herald

Maypearl NEWS. w 1928-30‖?
TxCeC Jl 1928-Mr 1 1930

MENARD

To 1910? as Menardville

Menard MESSENGER. w 1913+
pub 1914+

Menardville RECORD. w Ag 22? 1889-90‖?
CU-B D 5,19 1889;Ja 2,16 1890

MERCEDES

Mercedes NEWS-TRIBUNE. w,sw 1923+
1923-27? as Mercedes news item; 1928-30? Mercedes news
sw 1926-29?
Tx 1928-29
TxGR N 16 1934;current year only
TxU Ap 15 1927-Je 19 1928

MERIDIAN

BOSQUE beacon. 1866?-
MWA Ja 20 1868
N Ja 6-20 1868

BOSQUE blade. *See* Bosque citizen

BOSQUE citizen. w 1878-93‖?
1878-84? as Independent blade; 1885?-86? Bosque blade
1891-92? pub in Morgan
CU-B Jl 11,Ag 1 1889
Tx D 14 1882;D 19 1891
TxGR My 11 1882

INDEPENDENT blade. *See* Bosque citizen

PEOPLE'S tribune. *See* Tribune

TRIBUNE. w 1894+
1894-1896 as People's tribune
pub 1896+

MERKEL

Merkel MAIL. w 1890+
pub [1890-1909]+

MERTENS

Mertens NEWS.
TxCeC Jl 1928-Mr 1 1930

MESQUITE

TEXAS Mesquiter. w 1882+
CU-B Ag 23,D 20 1889;F 14 1890
Tx 1911-13
TxU Ag 26 1904-Je 9 1905

MEXIA

Mexia DEMOCRAT. w 1887-93‖?
CU-B Ag 22-29 1889

Mexia weekly HERALD. w 1890+
1890-99? as Herald-echo; 1900?-F 27 1908 State herald; Mr 5 1908-16? Weekly herald
Tx F 1908-16

Mexia LEDGER. w 1898?-1904‖?
1898? as Weekly news; 1899? News-ledger
TxU Mr 1898-Ja 5 1899
—d ed *See* Mexia daily news

Weekly NEWS. *See* Mexia ledger

Mexia daily NEWS. d Ja 4 1899+
1899-1922 as Mexia evening news
pub [1899+]
—w ed *See* Mexia ledger

STATE herald. *See* Mexia weekly herald

MIAMI

Miami CHIEF. w 1899+
KHi Je 1 1922;Ja 26 1928

TEXAS (*Continued*)

MIDLAND

Midland GAZETTE. w 1889-1905||?
CU-B N 9 1889;F 7 1890
TxU S 9 1898-Ap 11 1902

Midland LIVESTOCK reporter. *See* Midland reporter

Midland REPORTER. w,sw 1895+
1895-1905 as Midland livestock reporter
sw 1926-Mr? 1929
pub [1909-24]
TxU Ag 13 1909-O 8 1909;S 1932-33
—d ed *See* Reporter-telegram

REPORTER-TELEGRAM. d Mr 10 1929+
pub 1929+
TxM Ap 11 1929+
TxU S 1932+
—w ed *See* Midland reporter

Midland daily TELEGRAM. d Jl 1927-Mr 9 1929||?
United with Midland reporter to form Reporter-telegram
TxMR [1927-29]

MIDLOTHIAN

Midlothian ARGUS. w 1892+
1902?-13? as Midlothian argus-news
TxU Ag 19 1904-Jl 20 1913

Midlothian NEWS. w 1900-01||?
United with Midlothian argus to form Midlothian argus-news, later Midlothian argus

MILFORD

Milford COURIER. *See* Milford news

Milford NEWS. w 1890+
1890-1913? as Milford courier
TxU Ag 18 1904-10

MINEOLA

Mineola HAWKEYE. *See* Mineola monitor

Mineola MONITOR. w 1875+
1875-81? as Mineola monitor; 1882? Monitor-hawkeye; 1883? Mineola hawkeye
pub 1922+
CU-B Ja 16 1890
Tx S 23 1882

WOOD county record. w Ap 1 1928+
pub 1933+

MINERAL WELLS

HERALD. *See* Mineral Wells news

Mineral Wells INDEX. d My 5 1900+
pub 1900+
KHi O 2 1925

Weekly INDEX. w 1900-28||?
KHi My 26 1922;My 4 1923

Mineral Wells NEWS. 1886-95||?
1886-91? as Herald
CU-B Ag 16,30,S 6,N 8,13,15,22,D 20 1889;Ja 18,25,F 1,8 1890

MISSION

Mission ENTERPRISE. w 1926+
pub S 1926+
TxMi Je 1933+
TxU 1933

MISSIONITE. *See* Mission times

Mission TIMES. w 1909+
1909 as Missionite
pub 1926+
TxGR N 14 1930;Mr 18 1932;D 7 1934
TxMi Je 1933+
TxU Je-D 1931

MOBEETIE

PANHANDLE. *See* Texas panhandle

TEXAS panhandle. w 1881-93||?
1881-83? as Panhandle
MWA F 25 1882

MONTAGUE

Montague DEMOCRAT. w 1887-1910||?
IaHi Mr 26 1892-O 21 1893

MONTGOMERY

MONTGOMERY county news. w 1917?-
TxU F 1925-26

MOODY

Moody COURIER. w 1890+
TxU Jl 25 1903-Je 8 1906

MORGAN

BOSQUE citizen. *See under* Meridian

Morgan NEWS. w O 4? 1889-1909||?
CU-B N 8 1889

MOULTON

Moulton EAGLE. w 1900+
TxU Ja 10 1908-Je 7 1912;F 15 1925-N 5 1926;My-O 1932

MOUNT CALM

Mount Calm BANNER. w 1899-1915||?
TxU S 1904-F 7 1908

MOUNT ENTERPRISE

Mount Enterprise PROGRESS. w 1919+
TxU 1926-29

MOUNT PLEASANT

SOUTHERN patron. *See* Times-review

TEXAS and St. Louis news. *See* Times-review

TIMES-REVIEW. w 1873+
1873-79? as Southern patron; 1880?-85? Texas and St. Louis news; 1886? Titus times; 1887?-92? Titus county times
CU-B Jl 5-19,Ag 2-9,23,D 6 1889;Ja 31-F 7 1890

TITUS county times. *See* Times-review

MOUNT VERNON

FRANKLIN herald. *See* Mount Vernon herald

Mount Vernon HERALD. w O 1874-1905|
1874-98? as Franklin herald. United with Mount Vernon optic to form Mount Vernon optic-herald
CU-B F 20 1890

Mount Vernon OPTIC-HERALD. w 1894+
1894-1905? as Mount Vernon optic
pub 1913+

MULESHOE

Muleshoe JOURNAL. w 1924+
pub 1927+
TxU Mr-D 1925;Mr 1928-31

NACOGDOCHES

CAMPAIGN chronicle. w 1859||?
TxU Je 14-Jl 26 1859

Nacogdoches CHRONICLE. w 1852-69||?
DLC Ag 1852-O 17 1854
Tx Ap 3 1855;Mr 2 1858
TxU My 31 1853;N 10 1857
—campaign ed *See* Campaign chronicle

PHONE. *See* Sentinel

Nacogdoches PLAINDEALER. *See* Redland herald

REDLAND herald. w 1897+
1897-1907? as Nacogdoches plaindealer
TxNS 1913+
TxU Ag 18 1904-My 17,O 18 1906-F 21 1907

Daily SENTINEL. d Jl 1899+
1899-Ja? 1900 as Daily phone
Tx Ag 9,23-30,S 16,D 11-12,27 1899;Ja 1-2,5-6,F 14,19,Mr 6 1900;O 20 1902;My 17,20,27 1903;D 8 1923
TxNS N 9 1923+
TxU F-D 10 1925

Weekly SENTINEL. w 1899+
1899-Ja? 1900 as Weekly phone
Tx F 15 1900;08-16
TxU F 15 1900-Je 18 1908;My 16 1912-O 14 1913;16-F 1 1917

TEXAS chronicle. w 1836?-
TxU F 28 1838

Nacogdoches TIMES. w O? 1847-
Tx Ap 22-My 6,20-Je,Jl 8,22-Ag 5,S 2-9,23,O 12-21,N,D 9-16 1848;Ja 13-27,F 24,Mr 10-31, Ap 28-My 5,19,Je 2,16-Jl 7,Ag 4 1849

NAPLES

Naples MONITOR. w 1886+
TxU F 20 1925-29

NAVASOTA

Navasota daily EXAMINER. d 1895+
1895-1905? as Daily examiner; 1906-21? Examiner-review
TxGR Mr 25 1932
TxU S 20-D 13 1898;Ja-Jl 22,S 19 1899-F[Ap 1900-F]Jl 22 1903-04
—w ed *See* Grimes county review

EXAMINER-REVIEW. w *See* Grimes county review

GRIMES county review. w 1894+
1894-1905 as Review; 1906-21? Examiner-review
Suspended from 1921-24?
TxGR Ja 18-My 1906;F 1908-Ag 8 1912;31-32
—d ed *See* Navasota daily examiner

LONE STAR. . . *See* Lone star ranger (Austin)

REVIEW. *See* Grimes county review

Navasota weekly TABLET. w 1868-1904||?
Tx N 25 1869;O 22 1870
TxU [Je 14 1877-Ja 1879]

TEXAS ranger and lone star. *See* Lone star ranger (Austin)

NEW BRAUNFELS

COMAL current. w Jl 20 1895-
TxU 1895-N 14 1896

New Braunfels HERALD. w 1890+
pub 1905-06;Ja 10 1908-09;Ja 9 1914-18;F 1920+

Neu-Braunfelser ZEITUNG. w 1852+
In German
CU-B Ag 1 1889
Tx Ja 21 1853-S 20 1872;D 15 1932;Ap 19 1934
TxGR Jl 22 1926
TxU F 8 1917-N 1922;26-33

NOCONA

Nocona NEWS. w Je 15 1905+
pub 1905+

NORDHEIM

Nordheim VIEW. w 1902+
TxU Ag 11 1904-F 1913;Je 19 1919-N 1930

NORTH FORT WORTH

Papers published in North Fort Worth are listed under Fort Worth

ODESSA

Odessa HERALD. w 1910-21||?
TxU Je 14 1919-20

Odessa NEWS-TIMES. w 1925+
Tx D 7 1934
TxU S 16 1932-33

OLDEN

Olden ADVANCE. w Mr 6 1920-
Tx Mr-My 22,Je 5,19-Jl 17,31 1920

OMAHA

Omaha BREEZE. w 1886+
TxU 1908-Je 5 1912

ORANGE

Orange LEADER. w 1891-1918||?
1908-Je 2 1911? as Orange leader and weekly tribune
TxU S 30 1898-F 13,Jl 24 1903-S 1905;06-Je 2 1911

Orange daily LEADER. d 1902+
1902-Je 1911? as Orange daily tribune
KHi My 1 1920;Ja 6 1921;S 19 1922

Weekly Orange TRIBUNE. w 1877-96||?
TxGR S 12 1879

Orange daily TRIBUNE. *See* Orange daily leader

ORANGE GROVE

Orange Grove OBSERVER. w 1925+
pub 1927+
TxU F 13 1931-32

OVERTON

Overton RECORD. 1885?-
CU-B O 31-N 7 1889

OZONA

Ozona STOCKMAN. w 1913+
KHi Ja 14 1926

PADUCAH

Paducah POST. w My 11 1906+
pub 1906+
KHi My 26 1927

PALESTINE

Weekly ADVOCATE. w 1850+
1850-60? as Palestine advocate; 1861?-75? Trinity advocate
DLC Ap 22 1857-D 12 1860
Tx Je 19 1852;S 29 1893-Je 1 1899;Ja 24 1908-16

EAST Texas news. w 1878-98||?
1878-80? as Palestine news; 1881? Eastern Texas news; 1882-84? Texas news
TxU Mr 17,Ap 23,My 14 1881

Palestine daily HERALD. d 1901+
pub 1905+

Palestine NEWS. *See* East Texas news

Palestine PRESS. d 1898+
1898-1925? as Visitor
pub 1898+
TxGR My 13 1928
TxU S 1926-28

TEXAS news. *See* East Texas news

TRINITY advocate. *See* Weekly advocate

VISITOR. *See* Palestine press

PALMER

Palmer RUSTLER. w 1896+
TxU F 12 1925-26;28

TEXAS (*Continued*)

PALO PINTO

PALO PINTO county star. w 1876+
Title varies: Palo Pinto star
pub 1879+
TxU [1896-1907]-My 24 1912

Palo Pinto STAR. *See* Palo Pinto county star

PAMPA

Pampa daily NEWS. w,d Ap 7 1906+
1906-Mr 10 1927 as Pampas news?
w 1906-Mr 10 1927
pub 1925+
TxU Je 4 1927-Ag 1929;F 11-Ap 24,Je 5 1930-My 12,Je 23 1933+

Pampa morning POST. d 1930-31||?
TxU F 24-D 28 1931

PANHANDLE

Panhandle HERALD. w Jl 22 1887+
pub 1914+
TxPnB Jl 22 1887
TxU 1908-Ag 15 1912;29-32

PARIS

Paris daily ADVOCATE. d 1892-1918||?
TxU Ja 22-Mr 14 1907;My 13-Jl 6 1913

Paris EXAMINER. *See* Paris news

FARM labor echo. *See* Lamar county echo

LAMAR county echo. w 1922+
1922 as Farm labor echo
pub 1925+

LAMAR enquirer. w Je 29? 1856-
TxU S 14,O 16 1856

Paris weekly NEWS. w Jl 10 1869+
1869-71? as Paris examiner; 1872?-86? North Texan; 1877?-90? News and North Texan
pub 1916+
Tx Ja 30 1908-Mr 18 1909

Paris evening NEWS. d 1885+
Title varies: Paris morning news
pub 1916+
Tx Mr 24 1909-D 5 1911;Jl 1921-23
TxU Ja 6-30,Jl 2-Ag 23 1916;Jl 18-Ag 9 1918; F 7 1925+

NORTH Texan. *See* Paris weekly news

Paris PRESS. w 1864-84||?
Tx N 6 1869

Paris daily PRESS. d 1873-76||?
DLC O 8 1874

TEXAS times. w? F 1849-
IU F 20 1849

TEXAS vindicator. w F 27? 1867-71||?
MWA Ap 24,My 15,Je 26,Jl 10-17,31-O 9,29 1867;Ja 11,F 2,15,Ap 25,Ag 29 1868;Je 21 1871
MiU-C Jl 17 1867
TxU Ap 24 1869

WESTERN star. w 1848-
DLC Ja,F 16-Ap 12,My 10-24,Je,Jl 19-26,Ag 9-16,30,S 13-27,O 11-25,N 8,22,D 20 1851

PARK PLACE

Papers published in Park Place are listed under Houston

PEARSALL

Pearsall LEADER. w 1895+
Tx Ap 30 1908-16

PECAN GAP

Pecan Gap TRIBUNE. -O 1910||?
United with Ladonia news to form Ladonia news and Pecan Gap tribune (Ladonia)

PECOS

Pecos ENTERPRISE and gusher. w 1911+
1911-Mr 7 1917 as Pecos enterprise; Mr 14 1917-21? Enterprise-times; 1922?-My 9 1925 Pecos enterprise
pub 1911+
TxU S 9 1932-33

Pecos GUSHER. w 1921-My 1925||?
United with Pecos enterprise to form Pecos enterprise and gusher

NEWS. *See* Pecos Valley news

PECOS VALLEY news. w 1889-1904||?
1889-90? as News
NcD F 5 1892

Pecos TIMES. w 1898-F? 1917||
United with Pecos enterprise to form Enterprise-times, later Pecos enterprise
TxU 1908-Je 1910

PELLY

Daily SUN. *See under* Goose Creek

TRI-CITIES sun. *See* Daily sun (Goose Creek)

PERRYTON

OCHILTREE county herald. w F 1918+
pub [Ap 22 1921+]

PETROLIA

Petrolia ENTERPRISE. w,sw 1908+
1908-12? as Round-up
sw 1914?
TxU F 1925-27

ROUND-UP. *See* Petrolia enterprise

PHARR

HIDALGO county news. w Mr 22 1934+
pub 1934+

PILOT POINT

MIRROR. *See* Pilot Point post-signal

Pilot Point POST-SIGNAL. w 1886+
1886? as Mirror; 1887?-97? Post-mirror
TxU Ag 26 1904-Ag 9 1914;D 14 1926-29

Pilot Point SIGNAL. w 1897||?
United with Post-mirror to form Pilot Point post-signal

PITTSBURG

Pittsburg GAZETTE. w F 13 1884+
pub 1884+

Pittsburg TELEGRAM.
TxBroH Ag-N 5 1930

PLAINVIEW

HALE county herald. *See* Plainview evening herald

Plainview evening HERALD. w,sw,tw,d 1889+
1889-My 29 1913 as Hale county herald
w 1889-Je 3 1913;sw Je 6 1913-Je 16 1914;tw Je 23-D 29 1914;sw Ja 5 1918-28?
Tx F 14 1908-15
TxU S 15 1905-S 21 1906;N 1912-O 12 1917;Je 13-Ag 19 1919

PLANO

Plano COURIER. w 1894-1902||?
United with Plano star to form Star courier

STAR COURIER. w 1888+
1888-1902? as Plano star
TxU Ag 18 1904-F 2 1905;Ja 23 1908-10

PLEASANTON

Pleasanton MONITOR. w 1880-1914||?
CU-B Jl 12-Ag,D 13-20 1889
Tx Jl 10 1886
TxU F 1908-S 16 1909

PORT ARTHUR

Port Arthur HERALD. w 1897-1906||?
TxU S 22 1898-Mr 21,Jl 25 1903-O 14 1905

Port Arthur NEWS. w 1887-1918||?
TxGR Jl 23 1898

Port Arthur NEWS. d 1901+
pub Ap 1921+
KHi D 9 1920
Tx O 1922+
TxGR Jl 1 1923;Jl 19 1925
TxPA Ja 18 1926+

PORT ISABEL

Port Isabel PILOT. w Ap 10? 1929+
TxU O 23 1929+

PORT LAVACA

PORT LAVACAEN. w 1891-1902||?
TxU S 22 1898-Je 14 1900

PORTLAND

Portland ADVOCATE. w 1892-94||?
CU-B S 29-O 6,20-N 17,D 1,22 1893;F 16,Mr 9,Ap 20-27 1894

PYOTE

Pyote SIGNAL and Ward county news. w 1901+
TxU Mr 8-D 1929

QUANAH

Quanah CHIEF. w 1890-96||
United with Weekly tribune to form Weekly tribune chief

Quanah OBSERVER. w 1897-1921||?
Tx 1911-13
TxH Mr 13,Ap 2,S 6,20,O 4 1911

Quanah TRIBUNE CHIEF. w,sw Je 1889+
1889-96 as Weekly tribune
w 1889-1920?
pub 1889+
TxU S 29 1898-Jl 1899;1908-My 18 1911

RALLS

Ralls BANNER. w O 1911+
pub 1911+

RANGER

EASTLAND county news. w 1926+
TxBroH 1931-Mr 4 1932

Ranger RECORD. w 1910-18||?
TxGR O 11 1918

Ranger daily TIMES. d Je 1 1919+
pub 1919+
KHi Je 22 1926

Ranger weekly TIMES. w Je 1 1919+
pub 1919+

RANKIN

UPTON county journal. w O 10 1927+
pub O 24 1927+

RAYMONDVILLE

WILLACY county news. w 1917+
pub 1926+

RICE

Rice RUSTLER. w 1901+
TxU Ag 12 1904-Mr 8 1907;25-26

RICHARDSON

Richardson ECHO. w 1902+
TxU Ja 25 1908-10

RICHMOND

BRAZOS signal. w 1866-70||?
MnHi Ap 25 1868
TxU S 28 1867;Ag 1,22,O 17-24,N 7 1868;Ag 13,27 1870

Richmond DEMOCRAT. w
Tx Jl 21,O 6 1888

FORT BEND flag. w 1877-79||
TxU Ag 11 1877

FOUR counties. w 1873-78||?
TxU Ag 30 1873;Ja 8 1874;Mr 25,O 14 1875; Jl 4 1878

NATION. *See* Richmond opinion

Richmond OPINION. w 1881-88||?
1881-Ap? 1885 as Nation
NcD Ag 10 1883
TxU S 23 1883;Ag 8-22,S 19-O 3 1884;F 13, 27-Mr 6,Ap 24,Je 26,S 18 1885;Ja 28 1887

Richmond REFLECTOR.
TxU Ap 23 1879

Richmond REGISTER. w 1889-91||?
TxU Jl 12 1890

Richmond REPORTER. w 1855?-
OClWHi Ag 13,27 1859
TxU D 10 1859

SOUTH-TEXAN. w 1891-93||?
TxU Mr 11 1893

Richmond TELESCOPE. w Ap 27 1839-Ap 11 1840||
DLC Je 22 1839(photostat)
Tx Ap 27,My 25-Je 1,15-Jl 17,31-Ag 7,21,S-N 6,D 21 1839;Ja 11,25,Mr-Ap 11 1840

TEXAS coaster. w Ja 1895+
TxU 1908-Je 7 1912

TEXAS sun. w 1854?-
TxU F 17 1855-Ap 1856

RIESEL

Riesel BREEZE. *See* Riesel rustler

Riesel RUSTLER. w N 7 1895+
1895-1900? as Riesel breeze
pub 1923+
Tx 1908-O 2 1913
TxU Ag 12 1904-Je 19 1908;My 17 1912-S 1919

RISING STAR

Rising Star RECORD. w 1899+
1899-1924 as Rising Star X-ray
pub 1900+
TxBroH D 1928-S 15 1932

Rising Star X-RAY. *See* Rising Star record

ROBSTOWN

Robstown RECORD. w 1919+
pub 1926+
TxU Ag 25 1927-28

ROBY

FISHER county call. w 1888-93||?
CU-B S 19,D 12 1889

Roby STAR-RECORD. w 1912+
1912-30 as Roby star
TxU Ja 14-N 18 1926;Jl-D 1927;30-31

ROCHESTER

Rochester REPORTER. w 1921+
pub Je 20 1927+

TEXAS (*Continued*)

ROCKDALE

Rockdale MESSENGER. w 1873-1908||?
United with Rockdale reporter to form Reporter and messenger
TxU S 22 1898-Ja 1902;Ag 19 1904-Je 1 1905

REPORTER and messenger. w 1892+
1892-1908? as Rockdale reporter
pub Je 1911+
Tx Ja 23 1908-Ag 3 1916
TxU My 29 1902-N 1906

ROCKPORT

ENTERPRISE. *See* Rockport pilot

Rockport PILOT. w 1888+
1888-1915? as Enterprise; 1916-18? Pilot and enterprise; 1919-26? Pilot; 1927-30 Register-pilot
TxCeC 1911;18;20
TxU F 1917-18

REGISTER-PILOT. *See* Rockport pilot

TIMES. w 1893?-
CU-B S 29-O 6,20,N 10-17,D 1,22 1893;F 16, Ap 13 1894

Rockport TRANSCRIPT. w 1869-86||?
VU Jl 8 1876

ROCKSPRINGS

Rocksprings LEADER. w 1894-1927||?
1894-1908? as Rocksprings Rustler; 1909?-14? Rustler-standard
TxU O 1903-S 1905

Rocksprings RUSTLER. *See* Rocksprings leader

ROCKWALL

ROCKWALL county news. w 1887-92||?
CU-B O 6,N 14-D 12 1889;Ja 2-9, 23,F 6,27 1890

Rockwall SUCCESS. w Mr 1883+
pub 1883+

ROGERS

Rogers weekly NEWS. w 1893+
TxU F 1925-S 17 1926

ROSCOE

Roscoe TIMES. w 1905+
TxU Ap 8 1927-Ag 17 1928

ROSEBUD

Rosebud NEWS. w Jl 1893+
pub 1893+
TxU F 13 1925-N 5 1926

ROUND ROCK

Round Rock LEADER. w 1896+
1896-1900? as Round Rock searchlight
TxCeC 1897-Jl 1902
TxU Ag 12 1904-N 17 1905

Round Rock SEARCHLIGHT. *See* Round Rock leader

ROYSE CITY

ALTA. w 1889-91||?
CU-B F 8 1890

RULE

Rule REVIEW. w 1906+
TxU F 11 1927-28

RUNGE

KARNES county news. w 1887+
pub [1887+]
TxU O 1898-Ap 1910;F 12 1925-N 4 1926

RUNNELS

RUNNELS county record. w 1882-85||?
Tx Ag 4 1883

RUSK

CHEROKEE herald. w 1884-91||?
United with Standard enterprise to form Standard herald, later Industrial press
CU-B Jl 31 1889
TxU S 4 1889;F 27-Mr 13,27,My 1,Jl 31,S 11-18 1890

CHEROKEE sentinel. w 1850-
DLC My 17-24,Je,Jl 12,Ag 2,30-S 13,27-O 2,18-25,N 15-22 D 6-20 1856;Ja 3,17-24,Mr 28 1857

CHEROKEE standard. *See* Industrial press

Rusk CHEROKEEAN. w 1919+
TxU F 8 1929-30

INDUSTRIAL press. w 1882-1904||?
1882-Ja 7? 1888 as Cherokee standard; Ja 1888-91? Standard enterprise; 1892?-96? Standard herald. United with Weekly journal to form Press journal
TxU 1887-O 24 1888;96

IRON clad. w 1888||?
TxU O 27 1888

Weekly JOURNAL. *See* Press journal

Rusk OBSERVER. w 1865-81||?
1865-78? as Texas observer
MBAt Ap 28 1866

Rusk PIONEER. w 1848-
DLC Ap,Je 20,Jl 25-Ag 22,O 31-N 7 1849
Tx Ag 8 1849

PRESS JOURNAL. w 1896-1922||?
1896-1904? as Weekly journal
TxU D 1901-Ja 2 1903

STANDARD . . . *See* Industrial press

TEXAS observer. *See* Rusk observer

SABINAL

Sabinal SENTINEL. w 1893+
Tx 1908-16
TxCeC N 1904-N 1906

SABINE

NEWS. *See under* Sabine Pass

SABINE PASS

Sabine Pass BEACON. w 1868-72||?
NNHi Je 10 1871

Sabine Pass NEWS. w My 8 1897-1903||?
Some years pub in Sabine?
KHi Jl 3 1897
Tx [Ap 14-N 17 1898]-[1900-O 19 1901]Jl 12, N 1902

SAINT JO

Saint Jo TRIBUNE. w 1896+
TxU Je 13-D 1919

SALISBURY

HALL county record. w Je 1889-90||?
CU-B S 19,N 21-D 5 1889

SAN ANGELO

San Angelo ENTERPRISE. w 1882-98||?
CU-B Ag 1,22,N 7,28 1889;F 13 1890

San Angelo PRESS-NEWS. w 1897-1910||?
1897-1906? as San Angelo press
TxU S 27 1901-S,O 18-D 6 1906

San Angelo PRESS-NEWS. d
TxU Ja 21-My 13 1908

San Angelo STANDARD. w 1884+
pub 1914+
KHi Je 22 1923
TxSaM 1884-1913
TxU Jl 9 1904-Je 20 1908;My 16-Jl 4 1913

San Angelo daily STANDARD. d 1905+
Sunday ed as San Angelo standard-times
My 5 1935 National wool and mohair ed
pub 1914+
TxGR My 22 1923;My 3 1934;My 5 1935
TxSa 1929-N 1933
TxSaM 1905-13
TxU 1910;Mr 26 1924-Ja 12,Mr 6 1928+

San Angelo morning TIMES. d 1928+
Sunday ed as San Angelo standard-times
pub 1928+
TxSa 1929-N 1933
TxU 1930+

SAN ANTONIO

Weekly ALAMO express. w Ag 18 1860-Ag-N? 1860 as Alamo express
MH Ag-N 1860;F 16-My 4 1861
Tx S 10 1860;F 16 1861
TxCA 1860

Tri-weekly ALAMO express. tw D 1860?-
Tx My 3 1861

El BEJARENO. w F 7 1855-
In Spanish
Tx F 7,Mr-Jl 21 1855
TxU F 1855-Jl 1856

BOERNE post and the San Antonio critic. *See under* Boerne

La EPOCA. w 1916-31||
In Spanish
IU D 16 1917-Je 7 1931
NN Ja 21-28,F 11-Mr 4,My 27-Je 2,Jl 7-22,Ag 19,S 2,16-30,O 21 1917-My 4 1919

San Antonio EXPRESS. d 1865+
Title varies: Daily San Antonio express; San Antonio daily express
My 20 1915 is 50th anniversary and industrial ed; Ja 21 1927 is Southwest Texas, historical ed
pub [1865-Ap 15 1867]+
A Je 1927
CU-B D 20,23,25 1885
CoU 1902;06-My 1910
DLC 1867-74;Jl-D 1875;98+
IC My 20 1915
M Ag 21 1928
MB My 20 1915
MBAt [Mr 27-S 5 1869]
MWA Mr 14 1912;D 8 1931
MoHi N 19 1911
NcD D 21 1870;Je 24,28,Ag 1 1871
NcU Ag 23 1881
T Ja 21 1927
Tx O 11,N 21,30 1871;N 9,15-D 3,6-22,24-29 1881;82-1917;Mr 1918+
TxBroH Je 21 1927-F 9 1934
TxCA 1898;O 1904-09;My 20 1915;My 10 1918
TxGR O 30 1912-Jl 23 1918;Je 16 1919;Ja 17 1923;D 14 1924;Je 21 1927;O 29 1929;D 3 1930; D 8 1931;Ja 6 1935
TxHuS Je 21 1927
TxS [1865-Ja 1889;Ag-O 1890;O-D 1903;O-D 1911;F-My,Ag-O 1916;Mr 1917;Ap 1925]
TxSI Je 21 1927;O 29 1929
TxSO Ja 21 1927;O 29 1929;D 3 1930
TxU [Je 1898-1900]-F,Ap 22 1901+
WHi 1917-19
—w,sw ed *See* Farm express

FARM express. w,sw 1865-1923||?
1866-1920? as San Antonio express
w 1866-85?
DLC My 23,Je 20,O 24,N 21,D 5 1867
MBAt O 8,22 1868
NjR Mr 11 1875
TxSI Ap 25 1867-S 17 1874
—d ed *See* San Antonio express

FREIE presse für Texas. w,sw 1865+
w 1865-1922?
In German
pub 1865+
IU Ag 29 1917-Jl 1918
MWA Ag 18 1876
Tx Ag 17-31,S 14-O 5 1867;F 1-8,29,Ap 6,Je 15,S 26,O 17,31-N 7 1868;Ja 31 1878
TxGR My 14 1913
TxH 1929+
TxHR 1927-Ap 1931;My 1932-Ap 1933

FREIE presse für Texas. tw,d D 1866-1912||?
In German
tw 1866-75?
Tx [D 27 1866-D 24 1868]

San Antonio GAZETTE. d Ap 11 1904-Ap 28 1909||
United with San Antonio light to form San Antonio light and gazette, later San Antonio light
NcD Ag 8 1905
TxS complete
TxU [Je 22 1904-D 14 1906]09

San Antonio weekly HERALD. *See* San Antonio times

San Antonio tri-weekly HERALD. tw Ag 29 1865 -
Tx Ag-N 11 1865

San Antonio daily HERALD. *See* San Antonio daily times

Sunday HERALD. w Mr 18 1900-
TxS Mr 18-S 9 1900

El IMPARCIAL de Texas. w 1908-24||?
In Spanish
IU D 13 1917-Mr 1921

JEWISH record. w,bw Je 27 1924-32||?
w 1924-31?
TxGR [1924-Ja 15 1932]

JEWISH recorder. bw Je 10 1932-
TxGR Je 10,Ag 19,S 30 1932;Mr 17 1933

San Antonio JEWISH weekly. w 1923?-O 28 1927||
Merged with Jewish record
TxU S 1925-Ap 23 1926;27

Weekly LEDGER and Texan. w 1849-65||?
1849-59 as San Antonio ledger; Ja 7-D 1 1860 San Antonio ledger and Texan weekly. Merged with San Antonio news
DLC Ag 12 1852-S 1854;Ja 24 1857-58;Je 29-Jl 13,27-Ag 24,S 10-31,O 8,29-D 10,24 1859-60
Tx My 15 1851;O 13 1855;Ja 14 1860;F 2,Jl 27 1861
TxU My 22-O 1851;Jl 1855-Mr 8 1856
WHi Jl 28,Ag 18 1855

San Antonio LIGHT. d 1881+
1881-Ap 2 1883 as Evening light; Ap 3? 1883-Ap 28 1909 San Antonio light; Ap 29 1909-Mr 31 1911 San Antonio light and gazette
pub 1881+
IU [Ag 7 1915-D 14 1916]
Tx Ap 2 1883
TxGR O 9 1928;F 26 1931;S 29 1932
TxS 1882-[91]-[96]-[1908-11]-[18-26]+
TxSI [Ja 21 1882-Mr 1883]
TxU S-N 4 1898;Ja 11-Jl 1899;Ag 10 1904-S 2 1911;My 15 1912-Ap,Je-O 1915

Il MESSAGGIERO italiano. w 1906-14||?
In Italian
also dated in Galveston
TxGR Ja-F 21 1914
TxU S 8 1906-Ag 3 1907;Ja 25 1908-13

San Antonio NEWS. w 1861?-66||?
NNHi Mr 10 1864
NjP My 28-N 1864

Semi-weekly NEWS. sw
NNHi F 12 1863
Tx Mr 27 1862

San Antonio evening NEWS. d 1918+
pub 1918+
TxGR O 2 1918

PASSING show. w N 17 1906-09||?
Tx Je 8,29-Jl 6,Ag 6,S 7,N 9 1907[08-My 7 1909]
TxU 1906-N 9 1907

La PRENSA. d F 13 1913+
In Spanish
pub 1913+
CU-P D 1929+
IU D 20 1916-Ja 17 1928
Tx O 1916+
TxGR current year only
TxU F 7-Mr 9,Je 15-30 1915;Jl 1919-33

La PRENSA. w 1913+
pub 1913+

TEXAS (*Continued*)

SAN ANTONIO—*Continued*

El REGIDOR. bm,w 1888-1916||?
In Spanish
Tx 1907-15
TxU F 25 1904-Je 22 1905

San Antonio REGISTER. w Ap 10 1931+
Negro
pub 1931+

La ROZA. d Ja 4 1915-
In Spanish
DLC O 26,D 11 1915;Ja 12,My 7 1916

SCRIBBLER'S Saturday night. w 1923?-
Tx Ap 12-26,My 10 1924

San Antonio daily evening STAR. d 1869-
Title varies slightly
Tx O 25 1869;Ja 21 1870

San Antonio TEXAN. w 1848-59||?
1848-54? as Western Texan. United with San Antonio ledger to form San Antonio ledger and Texan weekly, later Weekly ledger and Texan?
CSmH Ja 12 1854
DLC My 29-Je 5 1851;O 14 1852
Tx Je 1 1854;F 8 1855
TxCA 1855
TxU My 15-O 1851;S 23 1852-Ja 6 1853;F 1856-F 4 1858

TEXAS courier. w
CU-B prospectus Ap 9 1823

TEXAS republic. w 1907-25||?
Tx N 4 1911

TEXAS staats zeitung. w 1856?-
In German
Tx Ap 9 1859-Ja 5 1861

TEXAS tribune. w 1887-91||?
Also dated in Dallas and Houston
CU-B Jl 27-Ag 10,D 25 1889;Ja 18-25 1890

San Antonio TIMES. w 1855-92||?
1855-80? as San Antonio weekly herald
MBAt O 19,N 2-16,30,D 21 1867
NNHi F 21 1863;Mr 5 1864;Mr 8 1873
NjP Mr 7,My 2,O 3-10 1863
Tx N 6 1869;S 30 1871
TxSE Mr 27 1857-Mr 19 1859
WHi O 10 1863

San Antonio daily TIMES. d 1857-92||?
1857-80? as San Antonio daily herald
MWA Je 17 1871
OClWHi Jl 19(extra) 1862
Tx [Ag 4 1857-59]-Ja 4,F 17,21-Mr 23 1860;N 14 1865-Je 1867[68-74]-Je 1876;Ja-Je 1878; Ja-Je 1879;Ap 8,15,17,22,24,Je 17,Ag 1-28 1884;Jl-S 1885;87-91
TxS Je 1889-Mr 1890
TxSI 1879-Je 1880

La VOCE della patria. w 1927-
In Italian and English
TxGR D 18 1930

WESTERN Texan. *See* San Antonio Texan

San Antonio ZEITUNG. w Jl 5 1853-
In German
Tx 1853-Mr 1856

SAN AUGUSTINE

San Augustine ADVERTISER. w N? 1870-71||?
Tx Ja 14,Je 10 1871

EASTERN Texian. w Ap 4? 1857-59||
Followed by East Texan clarion (Jasper)
OClWHi Jl 31 1858
Tx Ap 11-18,My,Je 20-Ag 15,29-S 19,O 3-10,24-31,N 21-D 1857;Ja 16-F 6,20,Mr-Ap, My 8-Je 5,26-Ag 21,S-D 4,25 1858;Ja 15,29-F 19,Mr 12,25-Ap 2,16-23,My 21,Je-Jl 23,Ag 20-S 10,O 1 1859

San Augustine HERALD. 1851?-
Tx Ap 1 1854

JOURNAL and advertiser. *See* Red-lander

RED-LAND beacon. 1869?-
Tx Jl 31 1869

RED LAND express. w My 5? 1860-
Tx My 19,Je 9-Jl 7,21-Ag,S 8-O 20,N 3-10, D 22 1860-F 2,23,Mr 16-Ap 6,20-My 4,18-25, Je 8,22,Jl 6-20,Ag-S 20,O 9,18-25, N 15-22 1861;Ja 3,F 8,Mr 14 1862

RED-LANDER. w,ir My 28? 1840-
1840-Ap 1841 as Journal and advertiser ir Ja-F 1847
DLC O 7 1843;F 26 1846;Ja 14-19,F-My 8,Jl 10-Ag 7 1847
Tx Je,Jl 9-16,Ag 6-13,N 5-19,D 10 1840-[41]-Ja 6,Ap 14,Ag 27-S 15,29-N 17,D 8 1842-[43]-F 8,22-Ap 12,26-My,Je 12,S 11 1845;Jl 15-29,Ag 12-19,S 9,N 11-18,D 2-9,23 1854
TxU [O 1845-Ap 9 1846]
TxWM Jl 8 1843(photostat)

SOUTH east Texan.
MWA Ag 24(extra)1867

TEXAS union. w O 9 1847-
DLC O 16-D 5 1847;Ja 8-Ap 1 1848
Tx Ag 18,S 8-O 6 1849
TxU Ap 1,29-My 6,27 1848

San Augustine TRIBUNE. w 1909+
TxGR O 29 1925

SAN DIEGO

DUVAL county facts. w 1925+
1925 as San Diego journal
pub 1926+
TxOgO 1926+

El HORIZONTE. sw N 1879-82||?
1879-Ap? 1880 pub in Corpus Christi
In Spanish
CU-B N 5 1879-Ap 24,My 8-12,19,N 13 1880

San Diego JOURNAL. *See* Duval county facts

SAN FELIPE DE AUSTIN

MEXICAN citizen. *See* Constitutional advocate and Texas public advertiser (Brazoria)

TELEGRAPH and Texas register. *See* Weekly Houston telegraph (Houston)

TEXAS gazette. *See* Constitutional advocate and Texas public advertiser (Brazoria)

SAN JUAN

San Juan SENTINEL. w 1922+
pub 1922+

SAN LUIS

San Luis ADVOCATE. w Ag 31 1840-41||?
Followed by Texas times, later Times (Galveston)
DLC S 14,D 11 1840
TxGR Je 22 1841(photostat)

SAN MARCOS

San Marcos FREE press. *See* People's era

HAYS county times. w 1886-1912||?
1886-92? as Hays county times and farmers' journal
TxU Ag 12-O 7 1904; Ja-O 20 1905

San Marcos daily HERALD. d Ap? 1905-11||?
United with San Marcos times to form San Marcos times-herald, later San Marcos times
Tx My 12-15 1905

LIGHT. *See* People's era

San Marcos daily NEWS. d My 5 1932+
pub 1932+

PEOPLE'S era. w 1871-99||?
1871-73? as San Marcos times; Ja?-F 28 1874 West Texas free press and San Marcos Valley times; Mr 1874-85? West Texas free press; 1886?-91? San Marcos free press; 1892? Light; 1893? People's era and free press
CU-B D 16 1886;F 3 1887;Jl 11,25-Ag 1 1889
N Jl 8 1876
Tx S 27 1873-Ag 7 1890;S 29 1898-O 5 1899

San Marcos RECORD. w O 12 1913+
pub 1913+
TxU Mr 13 1931-32;Je 28 1935+

San Marcos TIMES. 1871-73 *See* People's era

San Marcos TIMES. d,tw,w 1910-23||?
1912?-15? as San Marcos times-herald d 1910-19?; tw 1920-21?

WEST Texas free press. *See* People's era

SAN SABA

San Saba NEWS. w 1873+
Title varies: San Saba county news
pub Ag 12 1876;N 30 1915;Ap 1 1930
CU-B Jl 26-Ag 2,23-30 1889
KHi My 4 1922
Tx Ja 23 1905-15
TxU N 27 1880-Ja 20 1883;Jl 21 1904-Jl 1 1908

SAN SABA county news. *See* San Saba news

San Saba STAR. w Ja 1902+
pub 1902+
Tx Ja 22 1908-Je 1 1916;27-28
TxBroH Mr 1929-S 1932
TxU Ag 12 1904-O 18 1905;Je 1913-O 21 1915

SANDERSON

Sanderson TIMES. w 1907+
pub Je 1922+

TRANS-PECOS news. w 1902-08||?
TxU O 10 1903-Ja 1906

SANTA ANNA

NEWS. w Ja 1886+
pub 1920+

SAVOY

Savoy STAR. w 1902+
Tx 1908-D 8 1916

SCHULENBURG

Schulenburg STICKER. w 1894+
Early years as Schulenburg sun
pub 1916+
Tx 1908-13
TxU O 1898-Jl 4 1913

Schulenburg SUN. *See* Schulenburg sticker

SEAGRAVES

Seagraves SIGNAL. w 1923-31||?
TxU Ja-O 24 1930

SEALY

Sealy NEWS. w 1886+
Title varies slightly
Tx 1908-16
TxU F 1925-29

SEGUIN

Seguin ENTERPRISE. w 1888+
pub 1926+
Tx 1910-16
TxU S 20 1898-Ap 16 1909;My 17 1912-Je 1913;F 13 1925-33

Seguin JOURNAL. w N? 1856-
Tx Jl 11-Ag 1 1857;My 27 1858

Seguin MERCURY. w Je 17? 1857-
Follows Texas mercury?
Tx Jl 8-23 1857;Mr 3,Jl 14 1858;Ap 20-27,My 18-25,30 1859;My 30 1860

Seguin RECORD. w 1886-93||?
CU-B Ag 6-13;27-S 3 1889
Tx Jl 22-29 1886

SOUTHERN confederacy. w F 8 1861-
Tx F-Mr 22,Ap-My 17,31-Je 21,Jl,Ag 26-S 20,O 4-18 1861

TEXAS mercury. w
Followed by Seguin mercury?
Tx Je 16 1855
TxU S 24 1853-Je 1854

SEYMOUR

BAYLOR county banner. w S 1 1895+
pub 1895+
Tx Ja 24 1908-16
TxU F 1914-18;F 12-N 1931

Seymour CRESSET. w D 1879?-89||?
CU-B D 30 1886;Ja 13-Ap 14,28-My 19,Je 2-9,30,Jl 21-28,S 15-22 1887;Ja 12 1888

Seymour NEWS. w 1889-1903||?
TxU O 21 1898-Je 14 1901

SHAMROCK

Shamrock TEXAN. w 1902+
1902-27 as Wheeler county Texan
pub 1922+

WHEELER county Texan. *See* Shamrock Texan

SHERMAN

Sherman COURIER. w,d 1867-1921||?
w 1867-O 29 1916
CU-B Ja 31-F 7 1890
TxU Jl 1916-19

Sherman weekly DEMOCRAT. w 1879+
KHi S 14 1922
TxU O 1898-Jl 3 1913

Sherman daily DEMOCRAT. d Jl 26 1881+
TxGR Mr 27 1932
TxSh Jl 1914+
TxU F 17 1929+

Sherman daily REGISTER. d O 20 1885-1906||?
TxSh 1885-My 15 1906

SHINER

Shiner GAZETTE. w 1892+
TxU 1923-30;32

SINTON

SAN PATRICIO county news. w 1909+
Tx 1910-16
TxU O 1929-33

SIPE SPRINGS

CYCLONE. w 1887-92||?
CU-B Ja 2,D 6,19-26 1889;Ja 23-30 1890

SKIDMORE

Skidmore SENTINEL. w 1892-94||?
CU-B S 29-O 6,20,N 10-17,D 1,22 1893;F 16 1894

SLATON

SLATONITE. w 1911+
WyToT 1911-18

Slaton TIMES. w 1924-26||?
TxU F 12 1925-D 23 1926

SMITHVILLE

TIMES. w 1894+
pub 1894+

Smithville TRANSCRIPT. w 1895-1903||?
TxU S 9 1898-Mr 1899

SNYDER

SCURRY county citizen. w 1888-91||?
CU-B Ag 3 1889

SCURRY county times-signal. w 1923+
1923? as Scurry county times

TEXAS (*Continued*)

SNYDER—*Continued*

Snyder SIGNAL. w 1887-1923||?
United with Scurry county times to form Scurry county times-signal
KHi Ja 26 1923

WESTERN light. w 1898-1910||?
TxU Ja 31 1908-Mr 4 1910

SOMERVILLE

Somerville NEWS-TRIBUNE. *See* Somerville tribune

Somerville TRIBUNE. w 1912+
1925?-32 as Somerville news-tribune
pub Je 1928+

SONORA

Sonora SUN. w 1899-1912||?
TxU Ag 13 1904-My 1909

SOUR LAKE

OIL city visitor. sw 1908+
KHi O 12 1921

SOUTHLAND

Southland SUN. w D 17 1927+
pub 1927+

SPEARMAN

Spearman REPORTER. w 1908+
TxU 1930

SPUR

DICKENS county times. w O 1924+
pub [1924-34]+

TEXAS spur. w D 12 1909+
pub 1909+

STAMFORD

AMERICAN. w Ap 1924+
pub 1924+
TxU D 1929-O 10 1930

Stamford LEADER. w,sw 1900+
1905-10? as Stamford news; 1911?-12? News-tribune
sw 1922?-30?
TxU Ag 11 1904-Je 5 1908

Stamford NEWS. *See* Stamford leader

Stamford TRIBUNE. w 1905-10||?
United with Stamford news to form News-tribune, later Stamford leader

STEPHENVILLE

EMPIRE-TRIBUNE. w 1871+
1871-1930 as Stephenville empire
pub 1888+
CU-B Jl 13-Ag 17,S 7-14,N 2-16 1889
Tx F 17 1911;O 11 1912;N 21 1913;S 8 1914
TxStJ [1922+]
TxU Mr 17 1893

Stephenville ENTERPRISE.
TxU [Ag 26 1904-06]

ERATH appeal. w 1898-1906||?
TxU Jl 14 1898-N 7 1904

ERATH county democrat.
TxU My 16 1890

ERATH county enquirer.
TxU Ja 7 1891

TRIBUNE. w 1890-1930||
United with Stephenville empire to form Empire-tribune
Tx 1908-16
TxStE complete
TxStJ [1922-30]

STERLING CITY

Sterling City NEWS. w 1880-1901||
United with Sterling county record to form Sterling City news-record

Sterling City NEWS-RECORD. w 1899+
1899-1901 as Sterling county record
Tx Ja 31 1908-16;Ag 23 1929
TxU Ag 12 1904-Je 12 1908;My 17 1912-18;Jl 29 1919-20;Ap-S 1921;22-32

STERLING county record. *See* Sterling City news-record

SULPHUR SPRINGS

Sulphur Springs GAZETTE. w 1862-My 15 1928||
Merged with Hopkins county echo
CU-B Jl 5,S 6,O 4-11,N 8 1889
Tx Ja 24 1908-16
TxU Jl 17 1903-My 1906

HOPKINS county echo. w 1881+
pub S 1917+
—d ed *See* Daily news-telegram

INDEPENDENT monitor. 1859?-
Tx D 1 1860

Daily NEWS-TELEGRAM. d 1898+
1898-1913? as Evening news
pub Jl 28 1914+
—w ed *See* Hopkins county echo

SUTHERLAND SPRINGS

WESTERN chronicle. w 1877||?
TxU S 7 1877

SWEETWATER

Sweetwater ADVANCE. *See* Nolan county record

NOLAN county news. w F 9 1925+
pub 1925+

NOLAN county record. w Mr 1 1882-91||?
Mr-S? 1882 as Sweetwater advance
TxSwP Mr 31 1882

Sweetwater REPORTER. w 1897+
pub 1897+

Sweetwater daily REPORTER. d 1914+
Suspended from 1916-18
pub 1914+
TxAS N 1925+
TxU F 8 1925+

TAHOKA

LYNN county news. w 1904+
Tx Ap 1908-16

TAYLOR

Taylor daily DEMOCRAT. d 1903-25||?
TxU [My 3-Jl 5 1913]Jl 17-Ag 10 1918
—w ed *See* Taylor weekly Texan

Taylor JOURNAL. w 1890-1916||?
Tx F 13 1908-14
TxU S 29 1898-O 23 1908

NASINEC. w 1914+
In Bohemian
TxU O 3 1918;F 14 1919

Taylor weekly TEXAN. w 1880-1926||?
CU-B Jl 26,Ag 9 1889;Ja 24,F 21 1890
Tx 1908-13
TxU S 23-D 2 1898
—d ed *See* Taylor daily democrat

Taylor TRIBUNE. w 1897-1900||?
TxU [O 14 1898-F 2 1900]

TEAGUE

Teague CHRONICLE. w Jl 27 1906+
pub 1906+

TEMPLE

FERGUSON forum. *See under* Austin

Temple MIRROR. w 1896-1922||?
Tx 1911-15

Saturday SUN. w 1888-94||?
TxU Ag 10-24,N 9-16 1889

Temple daily TELEGRAM. d N 19 1907+
pub 1907+
TxCA 1925+
TxGR Je 29 1923
TxU 1916-D 10 1917;F 8-D 1919;Mr 1927-Je 1929;30+

Temple TIMES. w 1881-1910||?
CU-B Mr 15 1895
Tx 1908-D 18 1910

Daily TRIBUNE. d 1895-Ja 1910||
Merged with Temple daily telegram
TxGR Ap 21 1899

TERRELL

KAUFMAN star. *See* Terrell times-star

STAR *See* Terrell times-star

TEXAS star. *See* Terrell times-star

Terrell TIMES. w 1879-90||?
CU-B Mr 11 1887;Jl 12,Ag 23,D 13 1889;Ja 3 1890

Terrell TIMES-STAR. w 1866-1912||?
1866-79? as Kaufman star; 1880?-88? Star 1889?-90? Texas star
CU-B Jl 6,27,Ag 10,31,N 2 1889
TxU S 30 1898-Ap 12 1901;Ja 29-O 21 1904

Terrell TRANSCRIPT. w,sw 1897+
O 25 1901-My 26 1905? as Twice-a-week transcript(sw)
suspended 1905-08?
TxU S 20 1898-My 26 1905

Terrell daily TRANSCRIPT. d 1899-1923||?
KHi Mr 15,19,Jl 27 1921
TxU Jl 17-Ag 8 1918;Jl-D 1919

Terrell daily TRIBUNE. d 1916+
TxU F 4 1931-Je,O-D 1932

TEXARKANA *See* TEXARKANA, ARKANSAS

TEXAS CITY

GALVESTON county sun. *See* Texas City sun

GALVESTON county times. w Ja 8-Jl 22 1932||
TxGr complete

PROVOST guard. w Ja 9 1913-
1913-F 1914 as Provost guard and Texas City messenger
TxGR 1913-Jl 2 1915

Texas City STAR. . . *See* Texas City times

Texas City SUN. w 1913+
Title varies: Texas City weekly sun; Texas City-mainland sun; Galveston county sun; Texas City sun and League City gazette
pub My 1933+
TxGR D 17 1920;Jl 13 1923+
TxU Je 29 1928-29

Texas City TIMES. w,d My 1 1909-18||?
1909-Ja 1913 as Texas City times;F 1913-O 22 1914 Texas City daily times; O 23-26 1914 Texas City star and times; O 27 1914-Ap 9 1915 Texas City star
d F 1913-Ap 9 1915
TxGR 1909-[Ja-Jl 1918]

TEXLINE

Texline NEWS. w Je 14 1929-
TxGR Jl 12 1929

Texline TRIBUNE. w 1931+
TxU 1932

THROCKMORTON

Throckmorton TIMES. w 1886-1916||?
CU-B Ag 16-23 1889

TRENTON

Trenton TRIBUNE. w O 22 1909+
pub 1909+

TROUP

Troup BANNER. w 1894+
pub 1902+
TxCA [1919-23]+
TxTJ 1903+

Troup VERBENA. w
TxU Ja 25 1889

TROY

Troy ENTERPRISE. w 1888-1926||?
CU-B Jl 26,Ag 9 1889

TULIA

Tulia HERALD. w Ja 1 1909+
pub 1909+

Tulia STANDARD. w 1892-1910||?
NcD My 19 1909
TxU Ja 31 1908-10

TURKEY

Turkey ENTERPRISE. w 1926+
TxU N 1929-32

TYLER

Tyler AMERICAN. w 1922-28||?
TxGR Ap 15 1927

Tyler weekly COURIER-TIMES. w,sw 1877-1929||?
1877-1906? as Tyler weekly courier (title varies with frequency)
sw 1905?-10?
KHi D 3 1920
TxU O 6 1909-10

Tyler daily COURIER-TIMES. d 1898+
1898-1906? as Tyler courier; 1907?-08? as Courier and times
Sunday ed as Courier-times-telegraph
TxT Mr 1905-[15]-18;O-N 1919;20-[22-23]+

Tyler DEMOCRAT. *See* Smith county times

DEMOCRAT-REPORTER. d *See* Evening times

GRANGE reporter. w 1854-76||?
1854-75? as Tyler reporter. United with Tyler democrat to form Democrat and reporter, later Smith county times
OClWHi Jl 29 1871
Tx Ag 21 1869
TxGR Ap 16 1863
TxU Mr 31 1864

Tyler JOURNAL. w My 1 1925+
pub 1925+
TxCA 1925+

NATIONAL index. w 1866-76||?
Tx Ag 14 1869

OLD flag. ir F 17-Mr 13 1864||?
pub by Union prisoners at Camp Ford
CSmH F-Mr 13 1864(reprint)
DLC F-Mr 13 1864
ICHi F-Mr 13 1864
NHuHi F-Mr 13 1864
NNHi F-Mr 13 1864
OClWHi F 17,Mr 1,13 1864

Weekly RECORD. w 1887-93||?
CU-B Ja 11-18,Mr 1,Je 28-Jl 12,26,Ag 30, O 11-N 1 1890
Tx Ag 10-17 1889

Tyler REPORTER. *See* Grange reporter

SMITH county times. w,sw 1873-1906||?
1873-76? as Tyler democrat; 1877?-91? Democrat and reporter; 1892?-1905? Democrat-reporter. United with Tyler weekly courier to form Tyler weekly courier-times
sw 1905?
CU-B Jl 20-Ag 3 1889
Tx Mr 15 1884
—d ed *See* Evening times

TEXAS (*Continued*)

TYLER—*Continued*

Tyler TELEGRAPH.
Tx My 31 1851

Evening TIMES. d 1887-1906||?
1887-1905? as Democrat-reporter. United with Tyler courier to form Courier and times, later Tyler daily courier-times
—w ed *See* Smith county times

UVALDE

LEADER-NEWS. w 1898+
1898-1933? as Uvalde leader
TxU S 20 1929-S 1934

Uvalde NEWS. w My 20? 1886-1933||?
United with Uvalde leader to form Leader-news
CU-B D 16 1886;Jl 25-Ag 8 1889

VALLEY MILLS

Valley Mills NEWS. w 1888-93||?
1888-92? as Valley news
CU-B Ag 29 1889

VAN ALSTYNE

Van Alstyne LEADER. w S 3 1892+
pub 1892+
TxU O 1898-S 22 1906;My 25 1907-Je 20 1908

Van Alstyne NEWS. w 1881-1905||
Merged with Van Alstyne leader
CU-B Ag 2-9,23 1889
TxU O 1898-My 27 1900

VEGA

Vega SENTINEL. w Mr 12 1909+
pub 1909+

VELASCO

Velasco TIMES. w S 1891-1916||?
KHi N 14 1891-My 11 1893

Velasco daily TIMES. d D 1891-92||?
KHi D 24 1891-Je 11 1892

Velasco WORLD. w Ag 8 1891-1913||?
DLC My 20 1892

VERNON

Vernon CALL. w 1889-1917||?
Followed by Vernon times?

Vernon GLOBE. w 1894-99||?
Merged with Vernon call
TxVT Mr 1894-99

Vernon daily RECORD. w,sw,d 1908+
1908-24? as Vernon record
w 1908-16?;sw 1917-24?
pub 1918+
KHi F 6-Jl 6 1920
TxU F 1930+

Vernon TIMES. w 1918+
Follows Vernon call?
pub 1918+

VICTORIA

Victoria ADVOCATE. w 1846+
1846-51? as Texian advocate
S 28 1934 is 88th anniversary ed
CU-B Ja 8,Ap 2 1887
DLC Ja 20-F,Mr 9-30,Ap 13-Jl 6,20-N 16,30,D 21 1848;Ja 4-11 1849;Ja 25 1850-N 8 1851
KHi Jl 1 1928
MWA D 15 1860
OClWHi D 26 1863
PMilD Ag 13 1864
Tx F 7-14,28-Mr 7,21-Ap 4 1863;Jl 16-30 1864;Ja 3 1932;My 28 1934
TxDN N 12 1846-Ja 11 1850
TxGR S 28 1934
TxU Mr 2 1849;O 24,N 7,D 5 1850;Mr 13,15,Je 5,Jl 24,D 13 1851;Ja 3,F 14,Mr 6,Ap 3,My 22,Je 12,Jl 10,Ag 21,S 4,O 23,N 27 1852;Mr 19-26,Ap 30,Je 18,S 24,O 15 1853;Ap 8,S 23 1854;Jl 20-D 23 1876

Victoria ADVOCATE. d 1897+
pub My 15 1932-33
Tx O 18 1906

Victoria REVIEW. w 1889-96||?
CU-B Ja 22 1890

Der TEXAS demokrat. *See under* Houston

TEXIAN advocate. *See* Victoria advocate

WACO

Waco ADVANCE. w 1879-87||?
CU-B F 17 1887

Waco AMERICAN. d S 23-D 6 1928||
TxW complete

ARTESIA. w N 13 1892-O 28 1900||
TxW complete

CENTRAL Texan. w 1893?-98||?
WHi My 15 1893

Waco daily DAY-GLOBE. d S 1 1884-D 30 1893||
1884-92? as Day
TxW 1884-O 1890;Ja,Ag,N-D 1893

Waco weekly EXAMINER. w 1867-87||?
1867-74? as Waco weekly examiner; 1875-84? Waco weekly examiner and patron
Tx N 26 1869
TxW Jl 30-D 1875;78

Waco daily EXAMINER. d 1872?-88||?
Suspended Je 26-Jl 1 1884
CU-B My 21 1885-O 26 1887
Tx N 12,15-16,19-20,26-28 1881;82-S 30,D 24-26,28 1886;Ap 1887-Mr 1888
TxU S 1884-Je,O 1886-Mr 15 1887
TxW 1874-Je 1886

Waco GLOBE. d 1892||?
United with Day to form Waco daily day-globe

Waco MESSENGER. w Mr 25 1932+
Negro
pub 1932+

Waco morning NEWS. d Jl 16 1888-Je 30 1895||
1888-My 1889 as Waco evening news; Je 1889-S 1891 Waco daily news; O 1891-94? Waco evening news
Tx 1893-Mr,My 3-9 1894
TxU Ap 2-S 19 1894
TxW 1888-S 21 1894;Ap-Je 1895

Waco weekly NEWS. w,sw My 11 1889-D 29 1893||
w 1889-92?
Tx Je 6 1891
TxW complete

Waco NEWS-TRIBUNE. d O 14 1911+
1911-My 19 1918 as Waco morning news
pub 1917+
TxU O 24-D 1911;Je 8-D 1919
TxW O-N 26 1911;12+
TxWB N 1923-Je 1927;Ap 1928-Ap 1932

Waco PLAINDEALER. w 1882-91||?
CU-B Jl 27-Ag 1889

Semi-weekly REGISTER. sw 1865-72||?
Tx Ag 29 1869

Waco REGISTER. w 1865-79||?
DLC F 13 1875

SOUTHERN democrat. 1858?-
Tx Ap 22 1858

Waco morning STAR. d
TxU S 13-D 12 1907

Waco TIMES-HERALD. d 1888+
1888-97? as Waco morning times
pub 1926+
KHi S 26 1924
Tx S-O 1910;O 1923+
TxGR My 12 1928
TxU O 17 1898-1906;Ap-S 18 1907;11-27
TxW Ag 18 1895-Je 1896;98+

Waco semi-weekly TRIBUNE. w,sw 1895-Ja 19 1918||
1895-O 14 1905 as Waco weekly tribune (w) United with Waco morning news to form Waco news-tribune
Tx Ap 10 1909-16
TxW Ja 28 1905-F 3 1906;Ja 16 1907-18

Waco daily TRIBUNE. d My 21-Je 17 1907||
TxW complete

WALNUT SPRINGS

BOSQUE citizen.
TxU Je 24 1886

WASHINGTON

Washington AMERICAN. w N 1 1855-
TxH 1855-O 1856
TxU N 8 1855-Ag 18 1857

LONE star . . . *See* Lone star ranger (Austin)

NATIONAL register. w D 7 1844-46||
Tx S 18,N 15 1845-Ja 3 1846
TxU [1844-D 17 1845]

NATIONAL vindicator. w Ag 1843-
DLC Jl 6 1844
TxU D 16 1843

TEXAS emigrant. 1859?-
Tx Ag 31 1859

TEXAS ranger. *See* Lone star ranger (Austin)

TEXIAN and Brazos farmer. w Je 1842-
DLC Ap 15 1843
ICN Ap 22 1843
TxU S 10 1842

WAXAHACHIE

ELLIS county herald. w 1881-1912||?
1881-1910? as Ellis county mirror
CU-B Jl 31,Ag 21,S 4 1889;F 12 1890;Mr 1-8 1898

ELLIS county mirror. *See* Ellis county herald

Waxahachie ENTERPRISE. w 1875+
CU-B Jl 12-26 1889
Tx Ja 24 1908-11
TxU O 1898-N 17 1905;12-15
—d ed *See* Waxahachie daily light

Waxahachie daily LIGHT. d 1894+
pub 1894+
TxWx 1906+
—w ed *See* Waxahachie enterprise

WEATHERFORD

Weatherford CONSTITUTION. w 1889-90||?
CU-B Ja 1-8 1890
TxU O 16 1889

Weatherford DEMOCRAT. w 1895+
TxU S 29 1898-Je 15 1899; 1931-32

Weatherford ENQUIRER. w 1892||?
TxU F 11 1892

Weatherford NEWS.
TxBroH S 15 1932-Ja 1934

PARKER county news. w 1882-1901||?
CU-B F 21 1890

SUN. w 1883-89||?
VU My 5,Je 16 1887

WEIMAR

Weimar GIMLET. w 1885-87||?
Tx Jl 29-Ag 5,19 1886

Weimar MERCURY. w O 1888+
pub 1888+
CU-B Ja 4,D 21-28 1889

WELLINGTON

COLLINGSWORTH standard. w N 1924+
pub 1924+

WEST

West NEWS. w 1889+
1889-1909 as West times
pub 1910-12;14-15;17;19-21;26-27;30+
Tx Ja 24 1908-10
TxU S 30 1898-N 1900;Ag 12-D 23 1904;Ja 19-D 20 1912

West TIMES. *See* West news

WHARTON

INDEPENDENT. w 1880-89||?
Tx Jl 19,Ag 21 1886

Wharton SPECTATOR. w 1889+
pub 1915+
TxH [N 13 1931-Jl 1933]

WHITEWRIGHT

PLOW and hammer. w 1886-98||?
CU-B Ag 3,17,31 1889;Ja 11,25 1890

Whitewright SUN. w 1895+
pub 1912+

WHITNEY

Whitney MESSENGER. w N 2 1883+
pub 1883+
CU-B Ag 14-21,N 6-13 1889;F 26-Mr 5 1890
TxU 1931-32

WICHITA FALLS

Wichita HERALD. w 1882-1908||?
NcD N 22 1884

Wichita Falls RECORD-NEWS. d Jl 1919+
pub 1919+
ASIT N 17 1921

Wichita TIMES. w 1889-1918||?
Follows Hodgeman county scimitar (Jetmore, Kansas)

Wichita daily TIMES. d My 1907+
pub 1907+
KHi Mr 27 1921
Tx S 1927+
TxCA 1925+
TxWf 1919+

WILLIS

Willis INDEX. w 1884-1901||?
TxHuS My 27 1887

WILLS POINT

Wills Point CHRONICLE. w,sw 1876+
w 1876-S 1931
pub 1894+
CU-B S 5 1889
TxGR Ap 28 1927
TxU S 1904-Jl 6 1905;F 1929-33

WINNSBORO

Winnsboro FREE press. *See* Winnsboro weekly news

Winnsboro weekly NEWS. w 1893+
1893-1905? as Winnsboro wide-awake; 1906?-18? Winnsboro free press
TxWi 1920+

Winnsboro WIDE-AWAKE. *See* Winnsboro weekly news

WINTERS

Winters ENTERPRISE. w 1905+
TxGR S 15 1927

WOLFE CITY

Wolfe City SUN. w 1891+
pub 1891+

WOODSBORO

Woodsboro weekly TIMES. w 1925+
TxU 1930-31

TEXAS (*Continued*)

WOODVILLE

EUREKA. w 1882-96||?
CU-B Ag 3,S 7,N 2 1889

Woodville REPUBLICAN. w
TxGR N 14,28 1863

TYLER county booster. w D 11 1930+
pub 1930+

YOAKUM

Yoakum HERALD. d Ap 1 1897+
pub Ap 1920—
TxU [S 27 1898-Ag 8 1899]F 6-D 1925

Yoakum weekly HERALD. w 1897+
Tx Ja 23 1908-15
TxU [My 1904-S 9 1905]

Yoakum weekly TIMES. w 1891+
TxU Je 9-Ag 18 1906;Mr 1909-Ag 12 1911

Yoakum daily TIMES. d 1900?+
KHi N 17 1927

YORKTOWN

Yorktown NEWS. w Je 1895+
pub Je 1912+
TxGR O 4-18 1923
TxU 1908-Je 6 1917

UTAH

ALTA CITY

COTTONWOOD observer. sw Jl 13? 1873-
CU-B Jl 16-19,26-30 1873

BEAVER CITY

BEAVER county news. w Mr 1881-97||?
1881-89? as Southern Utonian; 1890?-96? Utonian
CU-B Mr 7,N 21 1889;Ja 9 1890;O 6 1893

SOUTHERN Utonian. *See* Beaver county news

UTONIAN. *See* Beaver county news

BRIGHAM

BOX elder journal. w 1905+
pub 1910+

BOX elder news. w,sw 1895+
NN S 16 1908

BRIGHTON

RECORD. w 1890-92||
CU-B Mr 19,Ap 30 1892

CAMP DOUGLAS

Daily UNION vedette. *See under* Salt Lake City

CASTLE DALE

EMERY county progress. w S 1 1900+
pub S 8 1900

CEDAR CITY

IRON county record. w 1897+
UU D 11 1908-D 2 1910;D 18 1914-D 12 1924

COALVILLE

SUMMIT county bee. w D 24 1924+
pub 1932

CORINNE

JOURNAL. d Mr ? 1871-
CU-B [My-Jl 1871]

MAIL. d S 2? 1874-75||?
CU-B [S 7-D 1874]-O 12 1875

Corinne daily REPORTER. sw,tw,d O 16 1869-73||?
sw O 1869;tw N 1869-My 1870
CU-B [1869-70]71;Jl 1872-Jl 19,O 8,15 1873
DLC F 10-D 1870;Ja 13,F 23-24,Ap 10 1871-Jl 19 1873

UTAH reporter. w 1869-71||?
CU-B My 27-Ag 1871
CtY Jl 1,4 1869
TxU D 18 1869;Ja 22 1870

DELTA

MILLARD county chronicle. w 1909+
CU-B Ja 25-F 1 1934

EPHRAIM

COUNTY register. *See* Ephraim enterprise

Ephraim ENTERPRISE. w Je 4 1890+
Je-S? 1890 as County register
pub [1890-1923]+

EUREKA

REPORTER. w 1900+
pub 1900+

TINTIC weekly miner. w 1891-1903||?

HEBER

WASATCH wave. w Mr 1889+
pub 1889+
CU-B Ja 4-12,26-F 2,23-Mr 1,15-Ap 5,19-26 1892
CoU 1899-My 1910
KHi Ap 17 1896-My 13 1910

KAYSVILLE

DAVIS county clipper. w F 1 1892-D 26 1924||
F-Ap 23 1892 as Little clipper
UO Mr 1892-My 5 1899
UU complete

LITTLE clipper. *See* Davis county clipper

Weekly REFLEX w 1905+
pub Ap 1912+

LOGAN

CACHE American. sw O 31 1931+
pub 1931+

HERALD-JOURNAL. d 1909+
1909-Ag 1928 as Logan herald
ULA S 1928—

Logan JOURNAL. w,sw,tw,d S 11? 1879-Ag 1928||
1879-Jl 1882 as Logan leader; Ag 1882-84? Utah leader; 1885-1919? Utah journal. United with Logan herald to form Herald-journal
w 1879-82; sw 1883-99?;tw 1900-16
CU-B F 13 1880;Mr 2,Je 29 1889
NN Ag 1882-Jl 1884
ULA S 1917-28

Logan LEADER. *See* Utah journal

Logan NATION. sw 1891-1904||?
KHi F-Ap 2 1895

UTAH journal. *See* Logan journal

UTAH leader. *See* Logan journal

MANTI

Manti HERALD. ir
US Ja 31-My 18 1867

HOME sentinel. *See* Sentinel

Manti MESSENGER. w 1893+
KHi Ja 25 1895

SENTINEL. w,sw 1885-91||?
1885-90 as Home sentinel
sw 1885-91
CU-B Mr 20 1889;Ag 12,N 21-D 9 1890

MOAB

GRAND Valley times. *See* Times-independent

TIMES-INDEPENDENT. w My 30 1896+
1896-S 25 1919 as Grand Valley times
pub 1896+

MORGAN

MORGAN county news. w
pub 1933+

MOUNT PLEASANT

Mt. Pleasant PYRAMID. w 1890+
M My 19 1933

NEPHI CITY

ENSIGN. w,sw 1884-92||
CU-B Ag 30,N 1 1889;Ag 30,S 3,13,O 4,18, 22,29 1890;Ag 13,27 1892

OGDEN

Ogden ADVANCE. w
UO Mr 14 1912-F 27 1913

COMMERCIAL. d 1889-90||?
CU-B O 24-25,28 1890

Ogden EXAMINER. d 1902-Mr 1920||
United with Ogden standard to form Ogden standard-examiner
UO 1912-13

Ogden FREEMAN. sw,w S 5 1876-81||?
United with other journals to form Inter-mountains freeman (Butte, Montana)
sw 1876-O? 1878
CU-B 1876[77-78]-Je 1879

Ogden FREEMAN. d D 9 1876-
CU-B D 9 1876

Ogden HERALD. *See* Ogden standard-examiner

Ogden JUNCTION. sw Ja 1 1870-79||?
CU-B [S 30 1871-O]D 25-28 1872;Ja 1-4,O 1 1873;Ag 22 1874;S 25 1875
MWA Mr 12 1870

Ogden JUNCTION. d *See* Ogden standard-examiner

ONCE a week. w
UO 1890-N 19 1892

Ogden STANDARD-EXAMINER. d Ja 1 1870+
1870-80 as Ogden junction; 1881-87 Ogden herald; 1888-Mr 1920 Ogden standard
CU-B S 21 1872-Ja 14,F 17 1873-74;Ja 24 1875;Jl 30-D 1879;Jl 7-10,12-13,15,19-20 1880
DLC Ja-Je 1898
NN Ag 30 1876
UHi 1870+
UO 1883-89;1914+
WHi My 18 1888

STATE journal. d 1896-1909||?
1896-1908? as Utah state journal
UO N 8 1904-O 1905

TELEGRAPH. *See under* Salt Lake City

UTAH state journal. *See* State journal

UTAH union. d My 1888-90||?
CU-B Je 11-20,22-23,30 1888

PARK CITY

Park MINING record. *See* Park record

Park RECORD. w F 7 1880+
1880-81? as Park mining record
pub 1880+
CoU F 1899-1903;06-Je 1910
KHi Je 24 1899

PAROWAN

Parowan TIMES. w O 27 1915+
pub 1915+

PLEASANT GROVE

Pleasant Grove weekly PYRAMID. w
CoU F 1899-F 1903

PRICE

CARBON county news. *See* News-advocate

EASTERN Utah advocate. w 1895-1914||?
United with Carbon county news to form News-advocate
CoU Ap 1899-Ja 1903

NEWS-advocate. w 1907-18||?
1907-14? as Carbon county news. United with Price sun to form Sun-advocate

SUN-advocate. w 1915+
1915-18 as Price sun

PROVO

AMERICAN. w 1888-89||
CU-B Mr 28 1889

Provo ENQUIRER. sw Jl 4 1876-1909||?
Follows Utah county times. 1876-Ag 1877 as Utah county enquirer; S 1877-87 Territorial enquirer; 1888-97? Utah enquirer
CU-B D 14 1878[Ja 28-Ag 11 1880]
UP 1877;79-89

Provo daily ENQUIRER. d N 30 1889-1908||?
UP 1889-My,D 1894-N 1897

Morning GAZETTE. *See* Utah Valley gazette

Provo HERALD. tw,d 1885+
pub Ja 6 1913+
UP 1921+
UPB 1926+

Provo POST. sw 1909-24||?
UP [1912-21]

TERRITORIAL enquirer. *See* Provo enquirer

Provo daily TIMES. *See* Utah county times

UTAH county enquirer. *See* Provo enquirer

UTAH county times. d,tw Ag 1 1873-76||
1873-S 10 1874 as Provo daily times; Provo tri-weekly times. Followed by Utah county enquirer, later Provo enquirer
CU-B D 26 1873[Ap 14-D 1874]Mr 16,18,Ap 10,27 1875
UP Ag 1 1873

UTAH enquirer. *See* Provo enquirer

UTAH daily gazette. *See* Utah Valley gazette

UTAH Valley gazette. d 1888-90||
Title varies: Utah daily gazette; Morning gazette
CU-B Je 28,Jl 5,Ag 30,S 13 1889;Ja 3,10 1890

RANDOLPH

RICH county reaper. w F 1 1928—
pub 1928+

UTAH (*Continued*)

RICHFIELD

ADVOCATE. *See* Richfield reaper

Richfield REAPER. w 1888+
1888-98 as Advocate
pub 1915+
CU-B Jl 3-17,O 30,N 20,D 4 1889;Ja 1-15,Ag 13,27 1890
CoU 1899;1904-Ja 1910
KHi F 6 1895-Ja 9 1910

ST. GEORGE

ENTERPRISE. m 1870-74||?
CU-B Ap-My,Jl,N-D 1872;My,D 1873;Ja-F, Jl 1874

OUR Dixie times. w N 12? 1867-
CU-B Ja 22-Ap 22 1868

RIO virgin times. w F? 1868-N 24 1870||?
CU-B My 13 1868-Mr 1869;My 12-N 24 1870

WASHINGTON county news. w 1908+
pub 1908+

SALT LAKE CITY

BEEHIVE. *See* Bikuben

Salt Lake BEOBACHTER. w 1891+
In German
pub 1891+
IU S 1917-O 3 1935
UHi 1905+

BIKUBEN. (Beehive). w Ag 1 1876+
In Norwegian and Danish
CU-B [Mr-D 1889]Ja 16-30,F 13,S 18,O 9,30 1890[Ja-O 6 1892]
IU D 1917-Ja 22 1925
IaDeL S 10 1896-Je 3,Jl 8-S 9 1897;D 21 1899;D 23 1925+
MnHi Ap 25 1918+
UHi 1876+

Salt Lake evening CHRONICLE. d 1881-85||?
KHi Mr 13 1885
US N 2 1882-My 16 1885

CIRCULAR. *See* Daily press

CITIZEN. w My 17 1902-My 18 1929||
1902-Je 1918 as Goodwin's weekly
US 1902-[Ap 20 1912-Ap 12 1913]-29

Salt Lake evening DEMOCRAT. d Mr 2 1885-Jl 16 1887||
KHi Mr 6 1885
US 1885-[F 28-D 1886]87

DEMOCRAT. w
US Ap 4-O 3 1914

DESERET news. w,bw,w Je 15 1850-99||?
No issues between Jl 30-O 1 1853;Jl 10-S 11 1861, and only one issue between O 23 and D 25 1861
bw O 19 1850-53
CSmH 1850-Mr 8 1855;Ap 20 1859
CU-B Ag 6 1862;O 12 1865-[69]-Ja 8 1879;F 1880-N 23 1881 [86-Mr 16 1887]
CoHi Je 15 1850
CtY F 18 1869;My 15 1872-Ja 29 1878
DLC Je 15 1850 (facsimile);N 15 1851-S 14,D 14 1859
ICN N 15 1851-53;Mr 14 1855-Jl 10,S 11-O 2, 23,D 25 1861-Je 1863;Ag 15 1870;Je 4 1873
MWA Mr 5 1853;Je 8-Jl 6,D 28 1854;Ja 18-28,F 15-22,Je 6 1855;N 11 1857;Mr 30,Jl 6 1859
NN [1851]-[57-68;77;84;86-88]-91
NNHi Je 29 1850;D 4 1855-Mr 3 1858
NjR O 5 1864
OClWHi Je 15 1850;O 14-N 4,D 9-16,29 1857-Mr 1858;Ap 20 1859
Tx Mr 12 1856-Mr 3 1858
UHi 1850-N 21 1867
UPB [1850]N 15 1851-Mr 4 1857;Mr 9 1859-F 27 1861;D 29 1888-D 10 1898
US Je-S,O 19 1850-[57-F 1858]-[N-D 1861]-[Ja-F 1866]-O 9 1867
WHi Mr 12 1856-Mr 3 1858

DESERET news. sw O 8 1865-1922||
CtY Mr 9 1894
NN Ag 31 1880;Mr 9 1888-Je 2 1891;Ja 1-5 1892;Mr 9,Jl 31-Ag 16,S 13-O 4 1900
NbHi Jl 1909-Ag 15 1918
UH complete
WHi 1899-O 1901

DESERET news. d N 22 1867+
1867-Je 12 1920 as Deseret evening news
C O 17 1868
CClP 1920-Jl 1921
CLM Jl 25,27 1907
CU-B [Ap 25-D 1868]-Ag 25,D 31 1870-Je[O 15-D 1873]1912-Jl 1921;O 7 1922-Ag 16 1925; Jl 1926-Je 1928
Ct [Ap 16-My 4 1901]
DLC Jl 1874-Ap,S 1897-1902
ICHi My 28 1870
IU S 7 1917-Jl 1921
MWA Jl 6 1868;My 9 1870;Mr 6 1872;Ja 6 1873;Ag 6 1919-Je 1921;Ap 5 1930
N D 17 1917-Jl 1921
NN D 4 1867;Ap 1-2 1870;Ag 28,O 1875;Mr 31,My 12,Je 2,Ag 4,S 3,10 1877;N 21 1878;O 16 1880;O 3 1881;My 4,6,D 2 1882;F 16 1883;O 25 1884;My 12,O 7 1885;My 18 1886;Ja 20,Mr 1,Ap 8,Jl 29,Ag 6 1887;O 1892-N 1898;1908+
NjP O-D 1913;16-18;20
OClWHi Ag 24 1881
P 1900-Je 1917
PU [1912-15]
Tx My 1919-Jl 1921
TxU Ja 30-Ag 1912[Ja 6-Jl 5 1913]
UHi 1867+
UPB [1916-21]+
US 1867+
UST N 23 1871+
UU Jl 1896+
WHi My 18 1903-Jl 29 1921

GOODWIN'S weekly. *See* Citizen

Salt Lake HERALD. d Je 5 1870-Jl 18 1920||
Ag 14 1909-Jl 7 1918 Herald-republican
CU-B [1870]-78;Mr 25 1879-80;86-Je 1887
CtY D 25 1889
KHi Mr 14 1885
MWA D 25 1887;D 25 1890;D 25 1891
NN My 18,O 5 1884;Jl 27 1887;D 25 1889
PPL D 25 1889
UHi complete
US 1870-[1904]-20
WHi Mr 21-30 1915

HERALD-REPUBLICAN. d *See* Salt Lake herald

Salt Lake HERALD-REPUBLICAN. sw S 2 1870-1916||
1870-Ag 1909 as Salt Lake semi-weekly herald (title varies slightly)
CU-B Mr 21 1874-[Je,Ag-D 1880]
NN S 5 1877;O 5 1881
UHi complete
US 1870-Je 1904
UST Ja 15 1909-16
WHi Mr 3 1896-98

HERALD-REPUBLICAN. w Mr 4 1880-1916||?
1880-1909 as Herald
CU-B [Mr 11 1880-Ja,Mr-Ag 3 1882]

Salt Lake daily INDEPENDENT. d Ja 2 1878-
CU-B Ja 9-11,F 16-17,19-22,24,26-27,Mr 1-3,5, 7 1878
US Ja-Mr 13 1878

INTER-MOUNTAIN advocate. *See* Living issues

INTER-MOUNTAIN republican. d F 12 1906-Ag 13 1909||
UHi complete
US complete

JOURNAL. d Je 1872-73||?
1872-My 21 1873 as Utah mining journal
CU-B F 20,Mr 13-Ag 14 1873
US Je 26 1872-Mr 1 1873

Salt Lake JOURNAL of commerce. sm 1881-94||?
US Jl 15 1887-Jl 1 1888

KIRK Anderson's Valley tan. *See* Valley tan

LEADER. w 1870?-73||
Merged with Salt Lake tribune
CU-B Ag-O 1873

LIVING issues. w D 14 1894-N 17 1900||?
1894-F 19 1897 as Inter-mountain advocate
ICJ 1898-N 17 1900
ICU Je 18,Jl 2-S 3,17,O 8,29-N 5 1899
KHi 1894-Ap 13 1900
US 1894-F 19,My 7 1897-F 23 1900

MORMON tribune. *See* Salt Lake tribune. w

MOUNTAINEER. w Ag 27 1859-61||?
CSmH 1859-Ag 11 1860
MWA O 29 1859
NN F 2 1861
UHi 1859-61

PONY dispatch. w
NN O 3 1861

Daily PRESS. w,d Ag 30 1873-Ag 17 1874||
Ag-N 3 1873 as Real estate circular; N 10 1873-My 11 1874 Circular
US complete

PROGRESSIVE. w,m 1912-17||?
w 1912-My? 1915
US N 30 1912-My 8,Jl 1915-Je 1916

PROGRESSIVE independent. *See* Public opinion

PUBLIC opinion. w D 2 1931+
D 2-15 1933 as Progressive independent
pub 1931+
CU-P D 2 1932;F 10 1933-[34]
CtY [1932]

PUBLIC welfare. w
US S 20 1901-Ja 10 1902

REAL estate and mining gazette. m,sm F 1875-
m F-Jl 1875
CU-B [My-D 1875]

REAL estate circular. *See* Daily press

REFUGEE. w
NN Jl 4-11 1885

Salt Lake daily REPORTER. d My 11 1868-70||?
C D 19 1868
CU-B 1868[Ja-S 1869]
UHi 1868-70

Daily REPORTER. d 1890-1907||?
US Ap 26-N 21 1901

Salt Lake daily REVIEW. d Ag 9 1871-72||
CU-B 1871-F 14 1872
N N 24,D 1,4,9 1871

SPECTATOR. w 1901-02||?
US Ag 31 1901-Je 1902

SVENSKA härolden. w Je 4 1885-92||
In Swedish
IRA [1885-90]
UHi complete

Salt Lake TELEGRAM. d Ja 28 1902+
pub 1902+
CU-B Mr 18-31,Ap 20 1915
UHi 1902+
US 1902[03-My 2 1907]-[Ja-Ag 1913]+
WHi Mr 18-30 1915

Salt Lake daily TELEGRAPH. d Jl 4 1864-My 15 1870||?
Title varies slightly
CU-B Jl 3 1867[Ap 1868]-[69]Mr 8,21-26,29-Ap 14,16-30,My 4-5,7-15 1870
KHi O 18 1867
NN Je 25 1868
UHi 1864-67
US 1864-[66]-69

Semi-weekly TELEGRAPH. sw 1864-D 30 1869||?
Jl 5-29 1869 pub at Ogden
Suspended Jl 29-Ag 23 1869
C O 26 1868
CU-B F 14 1867;Ap 16-20,27,My 4-7,18,25-Je 11,18,Jl 16 1868;Jl-S,O 28-D 13,20-30 1869
NNHi D 15 1864
UHi O 10 1864

Salt Lake TIMES. d 1886-92||?
CU-B Ap 18 1891
KHi D 29 1888;Jl 3 1889
US 1891-N 23 1892

Sunday TIMES. w
DLC O 1909-My 1910

Salt Lake TIMES. w 1921+
pub 1921+

Salt Lake TRIBUNE. d Jl 2 1870+
Title varies: Salt Lake daily tribune; Salt Lake tribune and Utah mining gazette, etc.
pub 1871+
CLM Jl 2 1870;Jl 18 1897;D 30 1898
CU-B Ap 15 1871-F,Je-S,O 26-D 1878;Mr 25 1879-Ja 1,F 17 1881;Ja 1 1882;Je 1883-[86]-[92-98]-[1900-01]Mr 18-22,24,26-28,30-Ap 2,8 1915;Jl 13 1927-O 1929;30-Mr 13,Je 19 1931-Je 21,Jl 31 1932
DLC F 8-D 1874;89-1902
ICM Mr 24,26,29-30 1878;S 4 1884
IdU [Ja 1929]
KHi [Mr 1885-Ap 1909]
MWA Ag 24 1878;Mr 28,Ap 4 1898
NN 1884-O 14 1887
NbHi Ap 23,Jl 16-17 1897[Ag-S]-D 1901;My 30-Ag 9,S 1-19,N 29 1908;F-Mr,Jl-S,D 6-17 1909;Ja,Ap 1910-Ag 21 1913
NvR [1930-31]+
OClWHi Je 29 1879;Je 17 1881
OHi F 1919-22
UHi 1870+
UPB [1919-25]+
US My 4 1872-[78-79]-[My-Ag 1895]-[Jl 1904-06]+
UST 1871+
UU 1883-87;Ap 23 1892+
WHi 1924+

Salt Lake TRIBUNE. w Ja 1 1870-1930||?
Ja-Ap 15 1870 as Mormon tribune; Ap 22 1870-Ap 13 1872 Weekly Salt Lake tribune and Utah mining gazette (other slight changes)
CLM Je 18 1870
CSmH N 6 1875
CU-B Mr 19-26 1870;Ag 5,19-S 23,O 7-14,D 2 1871;Mr 16-Jl,N 1872-[75-Jl 22 1876]F 24 1877-80
DLC 1872
MWA F 19 1870
N O 15,D 24-31 1870;O 28,N 11,D 30 1871;Ja 27,Mr 2,23 1872
NN Ja 1-8,22-F 19,Mr-Ap 1870;D 30 1871;F 17 1872;S 6,27-O 4,N 1 1873
OClWHi Ja 15 1870
PU My 21-N 11 1895
UHi Ja-Je 1870
WHi 1896-1923

TRUTH. w 1901-08||?
US S 21 1901-Mr 7 1908

Daily UNION vedette. d 1863-67||?
1863-My 1865 pub in Camp Douglas
CU-B O 17 1865-N 27 1867
DLC Ja 19,F 10,15,My 4-5,8-9,15,Je 6-D 1865
NN Ag 1 1866
NNHi O 12,N 15,22 1864
UHi 1864-71
US N 20 1863-Jl 28 1867

UNION vedette. w Mr 1 1866-67||?
CU-B [1866-N 1867]

UTAH freie presse. w N 21 1889-94||?
UHi 1889-91

UTAH independent. w 1908-11||?
US N 19 1908-Ag 10 1911

UTAH korrespondenten. w 1892-1915||
1892-F 3 1894 as Korrespondenten
In Swedish
CoU 1899-My 1910
IRA 1896-1915
MnHi [Ap 10-D 1908]-[15]

UTAH evening mail. d D 20 1875-76||
CU-B D 21 1875-Je 1876
US 1875-Je 24 1876

UTAH miner. w D 12 1875-76||?
CU-B Ja 24 1876

UTAH mining gazette. w 1873-74||
United with Salt Lake tribune to form Salt Lake tribune and Utah mining gazette, later Salt Lake tribune
US Ag 30 1873-Ag 22 1874

UTAH mining journal. *See* Journal

De UTAH Nederlander. w Ap 2 1914+
In Dutch
pub 1914+
UHi 1914+

UTAH nippo. (Japanese daily news) 1915?+
In Japanese
IU Mr 4 1918-[Ap 24 1925-Je 5 1926]

UTAH posten. w D 20 1873-S 5 1874||
In Norwegian
UHi complete

UTAH posten. w Ja 1- 1885||
In Danish
UHi [1885]

UTAH (*Continued*)

SALT LAKE CITY—*Continued*

UTAH posten. w S 20 1900+
In Swedish
IRA 1901-27;30+
IU 1918+
MnHi [Ag 12-D 1909]-11[15]17+
UHi 1900+

VALLEY tan. w N 6 1858-F 29 1860||
1858-My 17 1859 as Kirk Anderson's Valley tan
CU-B N 6,19,D 1858-Ja,F 8-Ap 1859
DLC 1858-My 17 1859;F 29 1860
IC N 12 1858-N 9 1859
ICHi Ja 18-25 My 22 1859
MWA D 3 1858 [F 15-Ag 1859] Ja 11-25 1860
UHi complete
US complete

WARREN Foster's paper. *See* Living issues

WESTERN mining gazette. w Ag 18 1880-F 19 1881||
CU-B Ag 25,S 1-15,29,O 6,20-27,N 10,20,D 25 1880
US complete

WESTERN weekly. w
US S 8 1888-Mr 2 1889

WOMAN'S exponent. sm 1872?-1916||?
CU-B D 1873[1877-78]-Jl 1 1880;S 1-15 1885

SILVER REEF

MINER. w,sw,tw 1878-83||
sw 1878-F 7 1880; tw F 18-Ap 3 1882
CU-B [Ap 12 1879-F 1883]

SPANISH FORK

Spanish Fork PRESS. w 1892-93||?
USpP My 1892-My 1893

Spanish Fork PRESS. w Ja 23 1902+
pub 1902+

TOOELE

Tooele TRANSCRIPT-BULLETIN. w 1894+
1894-1925? as Tooele transcript
KHi 1895-1924

TREMONTON

BEAR River Valley leader. w S 1925+
pub O 1927+

VERNAL

Vernal EXPRESS. w 1891+
pub 1891+
CoU 1898-Jl 1900

VERMONT

BARRE

GRANITE CITY leader. w Ja 12 1892-96||
VtBa complete

Barre morning TELEGRAM. d Ja 1 1898-1905||
1898-1902 as Barre evening telegram
VtBa Ap 1898-1902
VtU [1904]Mr 11,My 31,Je 24 1905

Barre TIMES. m F 1 1871-F 1 1872||
Not pub Mr 1871
VtBa complete

Barre daily TIMES. d Mr 16 1897+
pub 1929+
Vt 1910+
VtBa 1905+
VtMoC 1928+

BARTON

ORLEANS county monitor. w 1872+
Follows Orleans independent standard
pub 1872+
Vt S 19 1881
VtNp 1879-1929

ORLEANS independent standard. w 1856-71||?
Followed by Orleans county monitor
1856-65 pub in Irasburgh
MWA Ag 21 1857;Mr 9 1860;Je 17 1864;S 4 1870
Vt Ag 14 1857
VtBO 1856-59
VtU O 17 1856;D 11 1857;F 12 1858

BELLOWS FALLS

Bellows Falls ARGUS. w 1850-Ja? 1863||
United with Vermont patriot (Montpelier) to form Argus and patriot (Montpelier)
DLC Ag 30 1855 Jl 17 1856;Ja 13 1859-60;Ja 10,F 28-Mr,Ap 11-18,My 2-23,Je 6-20,Jl 18-25,Ag 8-15 1861
OClWHi Ag 18 1862
Vt D 1853-55;Ja 17,N 20 1856[61-62]

Bellows Falls GAZETTE. w N 24 1838-57||
DLC D 8 1838;Ja 2 1841
MWA D 8 1838-Mr 2,My 18-25,S 1839-O 1843; My 25,D 1844-Jl 5 1845;Ja 3,17,My 22-29,Je 12-19,S 11,N 20-27,D 11-25 1846[47-48]-My 1850;Ja 23-My 1851
MiU-C O 19 1839
N Ja 24 1846
NNHi Ja 20 1844;Ap 26 1845[48-49]D 7(extra) 1848
NSchU Jl 2 1842
NhD Ja 2 1841
OClWHi Mr 13,Ap 10 1841
Vt Ag 10,S 14,N 2 1839;Ja 20 1840;F 6,Mr 13,D 27 1841[42]Mr 11,Je 17,S 16,O 14,D 16 1843;Ja 27,Je 22,D 28 1844;Je 28-Jl 5,Ag 30,O 11 1845;Mr 7 1846;Ap 16 1847;O 25 1849
VtBf 1838-Ja 10,24,F 7,Mr-Ap 2,My 14-24 1850;Ja 23-My 1851
VtBr D 1838-[40-44;46]Mr 12,Ap 2,O 5 1847;F 3,Je 1,Jl 13,27-Ag 3,31,S 14 1848;Mr 29,My 17,Jl 5,N 22 1849;Je 4 1850

Bellows Falls INTELLIGENCER. *See* Vermont intelligencer

Bellows Falls JOURNAL. w Ag 8 1835-
DLC Ag 15,29,S 12 1835
MWA S 12 1835;S 30,O 28 1836;Jl 8 1837
Vt Ag 8,22-S 19 1835;Ja 15,Ag 5 1836;Ag 19 1837

Bellows Falls MONDAY nite. w
NhD 1928-29

REPUBLICAN standard. w 1850-53||
Merged with Bellows Falls argus
N Mr 31,Je 2 1853
NNHi Ag 18 1853
P-M Ja 29 1852

Bellows Falls TIMES. w Ag 6 1856+
pub 1890+
ICHi Ag 10 1877-78;80-[83]-89
MWA Ja 16 1890
NhD 1911+
Vt O 1-8,22 1856;Ap 9 1858;59-63;S 16 1864[65]-88;Mr 19 1891[1903-07]-32
VtBf 1856+
VtBr Ag 6 1856

Bellows Falls TIMES. d
OClWHi Ja 13 1865

VERMONT chronicle. *See under* St. Johnsbury

***VERMONT intelligencer.** w Ja 1 1817-35||?
1817-Ja 28? 1822 as Vermont intelligencer and Bellows Falls advertiser; F 4 1822-30? Bellows Falls intelligencer
CSmH S 6 1830
DLC Ap 7,Je 2-16,S 15,O-D 1 1823;Ja 9,F 13-27,Jl 31 1826;D 31 1827;F 25 1832-F 15 1834
MBAt S 8 1828
MH [O 20 1823-Jl 19 1824]
MWA Ja-D 17 1821;Ap 14 1823;Ap 25,Je 13 1825;O 29 1827;Mr 15,Ap 5,19-26,S 6 1830;My 31 1831;O 12 1833-O 11 1834
MSaE Ag 4 1823
MiU-C O 11 1834
N Ja-D 17 1821
NN Ag 25 1823;F 28,Mr 13-20,Ap 10-My 8,23 1826
NNHi N 3 1823;N 5-12 1831
NhD D 24 1821-D 16 1822
P-M F 22 1834
Vt Mr 26 1821;O 16,D 18 1826;Ag 31 1827[28]Ja 3-10,24-F 21 1830[31]
VtBf F-D 16 1822[23]-D 12 1825
VtBr Ap 23,Jl 9,N 19 1821-[22]
WHi Ag 31 1829

VERMONT republic. *See* Vermont republican (Brattleboro)

VERMONT republican. *See under* Brattleboro

BENNINGTON

Bennington daily BANNER. d Ag 10 1877-
MWA Ag 10-21 1877
NNHi [Ag 1877]
NcD Ag 15,17 1877

Bennington evening BANNER. d D 9 1903+
pub 1903+
VtBeM Jl 1903-22

BANNER and reformer. w,sw F 27 1841+
1841-43? as State banner; 1844?-Mr 8 1851 Bennington state banner; Mr 15 1851-F 11 1859 Vermont state banner; F 18 1859-Ap 1894 Bennington banner; My 1894-1902 Bennington semi-weekly banner
sw My 1894-1902
CtY Ja 14 1875
DLC 1841-N 1842;Ap 19 1843;S 22,O 20-D 1,29 1849
IU Je 1 1841
MWA Ag 16-23 1877;Ag 21 1891
MWo Ag 21 1891
NNHi S 24 1844
NbHi S 19 1872;F 6 1879
NhC Ja 22,F 12 Mr 26,N 10,24 1843
NhD Ja 8,22,F 12,Mr 26 1841;N 10,24 1843;D 31 1858;Jl 25 1861;O 28,D 23-30 1869;Mr 3,Ap 14,My 19,Je 19,Ag 4,18,O 13-27,D 1-8,29 1870; Mr 2,30,My 11,O 5,N 2,D 14 1871;Ja 4-11,F 1-8,22,Mr 28,My 2,16,30-Je 6,Jl 4, 18-Ag 15 1872;Ja 8,My 21 1874;Ja 21 1875;Ja 6,27-F 3 1876;Ag 21,S 6 1877;O 3,17 1878;S 18,O 2-16 1879;F 5-19,Mr 18,Ap 1-22 1880;F 17,Ap 14-21 1881;N 9 1882;Ja 4-18,F 1,15,D 13 1883;Ja 3,F 21,Ap 10,24-My 1,22,S 4-18 1884;F 18,Ap 8,29 1886;F 12 1897;Ap 14 1899
Vt [1842-86]
VtBeC 1850+
VtBeM 1841-1901
VtMoM Ap 23 1858 D 13 1866

BENNINGTON county reformer. See Reformer

BENNINGTON county whig. w?
Vt Ag 9 1837;Ja 1,Jl 15 1839

EPITOME of the world. *See* Vermont gazette. 1783-1847

Bennington FREE PRESS. d 1871-72||
NNHi Ag 26 1871
VtBeM Ja 6-O 19 1872

GREEN-MOUNTAIN farmer. *See* Vermont gazette. 1783-1847

HASWELL'S Vermont gazette. *See* Vermont gazette. 1783-1847

JOURNAL of the times. w O 3 1828-Jl? 1829||
CtY Ja 9-16 1829
DLC O 3-17,N 14,28,D 12 1828-Ap 22,My 6-13, Je 10,Jl 1 1829
MHi 1828-Mr 1829
NNH 1828-Ap 1 1829
Vt [1828-29]
VtBeM 1828-Jl 8 1829

Bennington daily NEWS. d Je 7-S 25 1875||?
Vt Je 11-S 4 1875

OUR continent. w F 15 1882-
VtBeM F-Jl 5 1882

REFORMER. w 1876-D 31 1902||
1876-Mr 7 1884 as Bennington county reformer; Mr 14 1884-Jl 29? 1892 Bennington reformer. United with Bennington semi-weekly banner to form Banner and reformer
MWA Jl 16 1886;Ag 19 1891
Vt Ap 2-16 1880
VtBeM Ag 17 1883-1901;Mr-D 1902

ROUND table. w 1862?-
VtBeM Ja-S 21 1867

STATE banner. *See* Banner and reformer

TABLET of the times. *See* Vermont gazette. 1783-1847

***VERMONT gazette.** w Je 5 1783-F 16 1847||
1783-My 31 1784 as Vermont gazette; or, freeman's depository; Ja 5-Ag 31 1797 Tablet of the times; Mr 30-S 21 1801 Haswell's Vermont gazette revived; S 28 1801-Ap 12 1802 Haswell's Vermont gazette; Ja 13 1806-F 3 1807 Vermont gazette, an epitome of the world; F 10-O 12 1807 Epitome of the world; O 19 1807-Ap 11 1809 World; Ap 17 1809-Je 10 1816 Green-Mountain farmer
Suspended from Ja 9-Mr 6 1800; from Mr 9?-30 1801; from N 8-D 8 1804; from D 1810?-Mr 20 1811
CSmH S 7 1830
Ct [1828-31]
DLC 1821-[27-29]F 9 1830-32;34-40;Ja 26,Mr 2,16,Ap-My 18,Jl 1 1841;Je 23 1846;Ja 5,19,F 9-16 1847
ICN Ag 2 1831
InI Ag 29 1837
MHi N 16 1844
WMA Jl 17 1821;S 14,O 26 1824;My 17,31,Jl 5 1825;27-28;Ap 27 1830;O 18,D 27 1836;D 26 1843
N O 15 1833
NNHi Je 4 1822;Mr 3,Ag 25,N 3 1829;Jl 6-20 1830[31]Ja 3 1832[33-35]Mr 22 1836[38-43;45]
NcD My 25,O 26 1824;F 28,Je 6 1826;N 7 1832
NhD Ap 1823-My 2 1826
PEL My 4 1830
Vt Je 24,Ag 12 1823;Je 29,N 2,23 1824;Ja 10,Ap 11,Je 20,D 12 1826;Ja 8,N 6 1827;Ja 1,Je 10,Ag 12,26 1828;Ja 27,F 10 1829;Mr 22 1831; Ap 9,My 7,Je 4 1833;Ja 14 1834;N 10 1835; My 2 1837;Jl 21 1840;N 18 1842;Mr 4 1845
VtBeM 1821-47
VtBr My 31 1836
WHi D 11 1821

VERMONT gazette. (Haswell) w Mr 17 1847-53||?
Claims to follow Vermont gazette 1783-1847
DLC [Mr 17 1847-My 3 1848]
NNHi Mr 14 1850
VtBeM 1847-O 10 1850

VERMONT gazette. (Robinson) w
Claims to follow Vermont gazette 1783-1847
DLC Je 1-8,N 16 1847
NNHi [Ja-S 19 1848]
WHi F 15 1848

VERMONT gazette. w 1872-80||
NNHi Ap 5 1873
Vt 1872-80
VtBeM 1873-My 5 1876

VERMONT state banner. *See* Banner and reformer

VERMONTER. w? Je 16 1835-
DLC Jl 28 1835

WORLD. *See* Vermont gazette. 1783-1847

BRADFORD

AMERICAN protector. *See* Vermont family gazette

AURORA of the valley. *See* Aurora and cultivator (Newbury)

Bradford JOURNAL.
VtU F 6,My 6,27,Je 1,29 1871;Mr 16,Ag 7,31-S 7 1872;F 1,N 15 1873[74-77]My 18 1878; O 15,29 1881;Je 11-18 1904;F 25,My 13 1905; Ag 11 1906;Mr 23,Jl 13,Ag 24,S 7,28 1907

VERMONT (*Continued*)

BRADFORD—*Continued*

NATIONAL opinion. *See* United opinion

NORTHERN inquirer. *See* Orange county journal

Bradford OPINION. w (Cobb) 1879-81||
Claims to follow National opinion. United with Bradford opinion (Stanton) to form United opinion

Bradford OPINION. (Stanton) *See* United opinion

ORANGE county journal. w 1851-57||
1851-54 as Northern inquirer. Merged with Aurora of the valley, later Aurora and cultivator (Newbury)
Ct D 23 1854;Ja 20 1855
NhD Ja 19 1856
Vt D 17 1853

ORANGE county telegraph. w 1857-
1857-60? as Telegraph
DLC [Mr 18 1859-N 9 1860]
NhD My 3 1861
Vt [1861-62]

TELEGRAPH. *See* Orange county telegraph

UNITED opinion. w Je 25 1866+
1866-My 30 1874 as National opinion; Je 6 1874-81 Bradford opinion (Stanton)
pub 1866+
MWA Mr 3 1871;Ag 16 1895
NhD N 22 1872[S-D 1888]-[96-98]-1904;My 12 1905-Ap 19 1907
OClWHi Mr 8 1889
Vt Je 14,Jl 12-Ag 9 1879;Ag 7 1880
VtU Ja 23-D 5 1874;Ja 2 1875;Ja 20 1877;Ag 24 1878;Mr 29,My 24 1879;F 14,28,O 23-30 1880;Mr 27 1885;Ag 12,S 2,16 1887;Mr 27,My 8 1888;S 13,O 11 1889;Mr 21,Ag 22,O 31,D 5 1890;Ag 21-28 1891;Ja 15-22,Je 17,D 9 1892;Ja 26,Ap 23 1894;Ja 4,F 1,22,Mr 29,Jl 5,26,Ag 16,30,S 13,O 25 1895;Je 5,19,Jl 10-17, Ag 14-21 1896;Ja 1-8,Mr 12-19,Ap 9,Je 25,Ag 27-S 3,17,O,N 19 1897;F 11-Mr 11,Ap 29-My 6,S 20 1898;Ag 4,S 15,O 27,D 15 1899[1900]Ag 16 1901;F 7,S 5 1902;Ap 3,S 25 1903;F 5,Mr 18,O 7 1904;Je 2,16 1905;Mr 9,Ap 6 1906

VERMONT cultivator. *See* Aurora and cultivator (Newbury)

VERMONT family gazette. w Ja 1843-52||
1843-47 as American protector
DLC Mr 19,Ap 6,20,Je 1 1844
IaDH 1843-S 1852
MWA Mr 25 1843
NNHi F 18,S 30 1843
NhD N 11 1843;My 11 1844;F 15 1845;Ja 21 1846
NjR Ap 18 1849
Vt Mr 19 1844;Ag 5,S 9 1846;N 10 1847;My 5,O 16 1850

BRANDON

Brandon GAZETTE. w My 30 1861-
Follows Northern visitor
MWA N 14 1861
Vt [1861-62]
VtBn Je 6,S 12-26,O 10,N 21,D 26 1861;F 20-27,Mr 13,Ap 10,24,My 8,29,Je 12 1862

Brandon MONITOR. w Jl 4 1862-Jl? 1863||
Followed by Vermont record, later Vermont record and farmer (Brattleboro)
MWA S 12 1862
Vt [1862]Ja 1 1863
VtBn Jl,Ag 8-N,D 12-26 1862
VtMiS 1862

NORTHERN visitor. w Ja 6 1859-Ap? 1861||
Follows Northeastern Christian advocate (not in this list)
Followed by Brandon gazette
Vt [1859-61]
VtBn Mr 22,D 27 1860;Ja 24 1861
VtMiM [Je 1859-F 1861]
VtMiS 1860

OTTER CREEK news. w O 1876-
Vt Ja 16 1880
VtBn [1876-81]

Brandon POST. w 1849-
DLC N 11 1852
DHU-M Ja 6 1853
Vt S 27,D 6 1849;My 16 1850;N 13,D 12 1851; Ag,S 9 1852;Jl 23,S 15,D 15 1853;Mr 9,Ap 20,Jl 13,27,Ag 31 1854;Ja 4,18,F 15-22,Mr 29, Ap 12-19,Je 14,Jl 5-19,Ag 16,S 6,27-O 4 1855
VtBn F 7,My 9 1850;D 2 1852;Mr 17-24 1853;Ap 20,Ag 3 1854;Mr 15 1855
VtMiS O 10 1850
VtRC 1852-53

RUTLAND and Addison county whig. w Mr 5 1840-
DLC S 10,O 1 1840
MWA Jl 9,Ag 20 1840

Brandon UNION. w N 30 1872+
N O 25 1889
Vt Jl 4 1879;F 20 1880;N 24 1882;N 28 1884; Ag 24 1894;N 1920+
VtBn 1872-[N 1893-Mr 1895]-[Mr 1897-Mr 1898]-[Mr 1903-Mr 1904]-[Ap 1911-Ja 1913] 14+
VtMiS 1873-74;76-91
VtRC 1921+

VERMONT record. *See* Vermont record and farmer (Brattleboro)

VERMONT telegraph. w S 30 1828-43||
DLC 1828-S 1830
MWA F 3,My 26 1829;F 16,S 14 1830
MdBJ Ag 24,S 14 1842
NIC O 1835-O 1843
NN Ag 30 1837
NNHi O 26 1830;Mr 10 1841
NSyU O 28 1840
NhD D 30 1840
P-M Ja 23 1834
Vt D 9-30 1828[29]S 25 1832-F 12,Mr 6 1833; Ja 2-23 1834[F-Ag 1843]
VtBn S 28 1830-S 20 1831;O 30,N 20 1832; S 10 1833;O 23,N 13 1834;Je 4-11,Ag 6, S 3, 17 1835;D 21 1836;Mr 22,Jl 12,S 12, O 25 1837;Ja 10-17,31,F 14-Mr 7,Ap 25 1838;O 4 1843
VtBr Je 18 1833;Ja 27,Mr 6 1834;Ja 18,F 8, Je 6 1837;F 21,Ap 11,Je 6,Jl 18,Ag 15-22,S 12-19 1838;F 9,N 6,D 3 1839;Jl 1,15,Ag 26 1830
VtMiM [D 15 1829-O 4 1843]
WHi Ja 20 1829;My 7,21-28,Je 25,O 1835-S 20 1837;N 18 1840

VERMONT union whig. w Je 21 1848-
Also dated in Rutland
MH Ap 18 1849
MWA My 1,Je 19 1850
Vt D 20-27 1848;Je 6-13,Jl 16-23 1849;50-Ja 1 1851
VtBn O 11 1848;Mr 28 1849
VtNp 1850-51

BRATTLEBORO

AURORA of the valley. *See* Aurora and cultivator (Newbury)

Weekly EAGLE. sw,w Ag 10 1847-54||
1847-D 9? 1852 as Semi-weekly eagle. United with Vermont phoenix to form Republican, later Vermont phoenix
sw 1847-52
CtY S 27 1852
DLC Je 10-13 1850;F 26 1852
MBAt N 27 1848-D 22 1854
MWA Ja 4 1848;Je 17 1850;F 11 1853
NNHi N 8 1852
Vt 1854
VtBeC N 1849-D 9,31 1852-54
VtBr 1847-D 9 1852;53-54

FARMERS' weekly messenger. *See* Brattleboro messenger

FLAIL. w 1840||
DLC S 8,O 6,20,N 10 1840
MWA S 1 1840
Vt S 1 1840

INDEPENDENT inquirer. w S 14 1833-S 6 1834||
United with Brattleboro messenger to form Vermont phoenix
DLC D 7,28 1833;Ja 18,F 8,Je 7,28,Jl 12-19,Ag 2-9 1834
NN Ja 18 1834
VtBr complete
VtBrR Ja 25-S 1834

Brattleboro MESSENGER. w D 10 1821-S 5 1834||
1821-D 1 1823 as Farmers' weekly messenger; My 14 1825-N 23 1827 Brattleboro messenger and farmers' and manufacturers' publick journal. United with Independent inquirer to form Vermont phoenix
Ct [1830-31]
DLC 1821-Ap 4,25,My 9,23,S 19,O 24-N 7,21-28 1828;Ja 2,Ap 3,Je 5,26-Jl 17,Ag 14-21,S 4,25-O 2,23-30,N 13-20 1829;30-Ja 22,F 12,Ap 16 1831-34
MWA O 13 1823;S 15,29 1826;Ja 18,Je 13 1828-Ja 22 1830
MiU-C Ag 18 1826
NN Je 11 1831
NNHi Ja 7,28 1832
Vt Je 7,N 29 1824;Ap 6,S 14 1827;Jl 27,Ag 10 1833;Ap 25 1834
VtBr Ap 22,Jl 15 1822;O 13,D 22 1823;Ja 22, S 4,O 1,D 10-24 1825;Ja 7,Mr 4-11,Ap 1, 26,Je 9,23,O 27,N 3-17,D 8 1826-[28-Jl 13 1834]

Evening PHOENIX. d Ap 27-S 27 1898||
NhD complete
VtBrR complete

Brattleboro PHOENIX. w See Vermont phoenix

Brattleboro daily REFORMER. w,sw,d 1876+
1876-1906? Windham county reformer (F 15 1898-F 14 1902 Semi-weekly reformer); 1907?-F 28 1913 Brattleboro reformer
w 1876-F 28 1913 (sw F 15 1898-F 14 1902)
pub Ag 15 1884+
MWA Jl 30 1886;Ag 1 1930
NcD Ag 20 1880;Ja 6 1888
NhD D 13 1878;My 30 1879
Vt D 12 1879;Je 29,Jl 13 1894;O-D 1906;O 1910+
VtBr Mr 1913+
—w ed *See* Vermont phoenix

***REPORTER.** w F 21 1803-26||
Merged with Brattleboro messenger
VtBr S 25,O 16,N 27 1821

REPUBLICAN. *See* Vermont phoenix

Daily evening TIMES. d Ap 28-Ag 4 1891||
VtBr complete
VtBrR complete

VERMONT cultivator. *See* Aurora and cultivator (Newbury)

VERMONT journal. w 1846?-82||?
VtBr O-D 1869;73

VERMONT phoenix. w S 12 1834+
Formed by the union of Brattleboro messenger and Independent inquirer. S 12 1834 as Brattleboro phoenix; Ja 1-29 1855 Republican; 1859-60? Vermont phoenix and Vermont republican; Ja 3 1861 Vermont phoenix and republican; My 1 1880-Ap 24 1891 Vermont phoenix and record farmer
Ag 20 1880 is Whittingham's centennial ed
CtY Je 23 1893
DLC 1834-Ja 15 1836;S 15 1837;Mr 1 1839;D 10 1841;Je 7,S 13 1844;Ap 15 1847;D 15 1855;Mr 29 1856;Ap 16,Jl 16 1859;Mr 10 1860;Ja 8 1864;Mr 17 1865
M Ag 20 1880
MB Jl 22,Ag 5 1847;F 1855-61;63-64;Ag 7-14 1868;My 17 1872
MWA O 10,24-N 7,21,D 12,26 1834;O 9 1835;F 12,Je 24,N 4 1836;Ap 13,D 21 1838;F 14,Jl 3 1840;F 5,Ap 9 1841;Ag 26 1842;Ja 3 1845; Ja 14 1847;O 27,N 3,17 1860;Jl 7 1865;S 13 1867;F 28-S 1868;Ap 7 1871;Ag 23 1872;Jl 10-17 1874;Mr 3,S 15 1876;Ag 20 1880;S 26 1884;Mr 20 1936
MiU-C O 9 1835
N Ja 15 1863
NN D 7 1849
NNHi O 9 1835;F 28 1873
NcD Ag 20 1880
NhD Ja 8 1841;Ja 22,F 12-Mr,N 10,24 1843; 1911;13
OClWHi S 22 1837
OHi O 8 1859;Mr 17 1865
Vt O 1 1841;43-1909;D 21 1917
VtBr O 24-N 7,D 12 1834[35]-[37]-F 2 1838 [40-41]-Ja 1842[49]Ap 26,My 24,S 20,O 11 1850;Je 5 1851+
VtBrR 1834-38;40-42;Ag 24 1849-D 6 1851;61+
VtU Je 1917+
WHi Ap 15 1842
—d ed *See* Evening phoenix; Brattleboro daily reformer

VERMONT semi-weekly record. sw Ja 1865-
MWA Ja 24,Mr 7,30,Ag 8,S 5,D 19 1865

VERMONT record and farmer. w Jl 17 1863-Ap 28 1880||
Follows Brandon monitor (Brandon) 1863-65? as Vermont record. United with Vermont phoenix to form Vermont phoenix and record farmer, later Vermont phoenix
1863-Ja 14 1865 pub in Brandon; 1867 in Springfield
ICHi Mr 18 1864
MB Ja 29 1869-73
MWA F 5,O 21-28 1864;Mr 11,Ag 19,O 14,28 1865-[66]F 9,23,Ap 6-13,My 18-Je,Jl 20-O 19, N 16-D 7,21 1867;Ja 1 1868;Je 4 1869
MiU-C [1865-67]
NNHi S 10 1869;My 16 1873
NhD F 12 1864-66;Ag 31 1867
OClWHi 1863-64;Jl 15,S 1 1865
Vt [1863]-74;Ag 17-24 1877;Ap 18,Je 5-19,Jl 10 1879
VtBn 1863-64[67]
VtBr 1863-Jl 8 1864;68-80
VtMiM [N 27 1863-Ap 13 1867]
VtMiS 1863;65-66;68
VtWoC Ap 1866-67
WHi Mr 14 1879

VERMONT republican. w 1838-
1838-51? as Vermont republic?
Also dated in Bellows Falls and Ludlow
DLC Je 15 1855
MWA Je 11 1850-Ja 14 1851
VtBr Jl 16,Ag 13,O 22 1850[F 1855-56]My 8, Je 26 1857

VERMONT statesman. w 1852-Ja 1855||
Merged with Republican, later Vermont phoenix
MWA Ag 11 1854
VtBr Ja 24 1852;S 2 1853;O 13-27,D 8,22 1854;Ja 5-19 1855

WINDHAM county democrat. w O? 1836-53||
DLC Ag 11-18,D 22-29 1837;Mr 23,D 13 1838;My 23,Ag 1,O 10 1839;Ja 28 1841;Ap 7 1842;Je 22 1853
MWA O 6,N 17,D 29 1837;My 11 1838;My 14 1851;Mr 2 1853
MnHi N 26 1840;N 3 1842
NNHi O 27 1852
Vt Ag 20 1840;Je 9 1842;Jl 16 1851;Jl 7 1852
VtBr My 19 1842;F 7,Je 20 1849

WINDHAM county reformer. *See* Brattleboro daily reformer

BRISTOL

GAZETTE. w?
VtMiS 1861

GAZETTE. w 1876-79||?
VtMiS 1876-78

Bristol HERALD. w 1879+
pub Jl 12 1891+
Vt Ap 10 1884;1921+
VtBri O 21 1909[10]13-[21-22]+
VtMiC 1908+
VtMiS [1879-96]
VtU Ap 1,My 6 1880;Jl 1 1886[87-88]Ja 24, F 14,My 9 1889[90-97]-[1914]

Bristol NEWS. w 1900-06||?
VtMiS 1901-[F-O 1906]
VtU Ap,My 23,Jl 12-19,S 27,D 27 1900;F 28, Ap 25,Ag 29-S 5,19 1901;F 20 1902;Ja 22,F 2-7,Mr 6,27,Je 19-26,S 4,O 2-8 1903;F 12,Mr 11,Ap 15,29,My 27-Je 3,S 16 1904

BURLINGTON

AMERICAN repertory. *See* Repertory(St. Albans)

CENTINEL. *See* Burlington weekly sentinel

Burlington CLIPPER. w 1875+
N My 6 1875
Vt 1920+

Burlington COURIER. w 1846-53||
1846-48? as Free soil courier
DLC Mr 14 1850
MWA 1851
Vt Ag 8 1848;Je 27 1850

VERMONT (*Continued*)

BURLINGTON—*Continued*

Burlington DEMOCRAT and weekly sentinel. w 1871-80||?
1871-74 as Burlington democrat
N My 15 1875

DEMOCRAT and sentinel. d *See* Burlington sentinel. 1874-76

Burlington FREE PRESS. w Je 15 1827-1928||
pub 1878-1928
CSmH Jl 2 1830
CU-B D 21 1849
DLC Ag 31,N 30,D 7 1827[28-29]Ja 8,22,Ag 6 1830;Ap 19 1839[51]N 5-12 1852;My 27,Jl 22 1853;N 3 1854;My 11,Jl 13,S 21,N 2 1855;O 28 1859;D 27 1860
IaDH My 18 1905-14
MBAt S 5 1828;S 27 1850-Je 1858;Ap 21 1865
MWA Je 15 1827;Ja 4 1828;Jl 31 1829;F 19,My 6,20,Ag 12,26,S 16 1831;Ja 27 1832;Je 14 1833;Ag 28-S 18 1835;Jl 3,17 1840;My 28-Je 4 1841;Je 2(extra)1843;D 12 1851;Mr 15 1861;My 11,N 2,D 28 1866;Ag 6,S 10 1869;1908;Mr 24 1910-11
NChM F 12 1830;My 30 1856
NNHi [Ag 1838-Ja 1839[Jl 17,31 1863
NhD Jl 17 1846-50
NjR Ag 27 1847
Vt Mr 2 1832;Mr 29 1833;O 8 1846;F 29 1856;N 13 1861;Jl 25,Ag 13 1862;Ap 26 1865;Ja 9 1869;Je 30 1882
VtBu complete
VtMiS 1900-05
VtU Jl 10 1846-[51-52]

Burlington FREE PRESS. d Mr 15 1848+
1848-68 as Burlington daily free press; 1869-D 12 1885 Burlington free press and times
Je 12 1927 is centennial ed
pub 1878+
Ct My 2 1903
DLC Jl 11 1874+
M F 22 1886-Ag 25 1931
MHi Je 23 1925;F 11 1927
MWA O 12 1859;O 10,N 23 1860;F 27 1872;Jl 7 1873;O 6 1880;Jl 1,Ag 10 1885;N 5-6 1886;Je 23,Jl 1-2 1887;Mr 23,N 27 1889;Mr 8 1890; 1920+
N Ap 28,My 5-12 1875
NChM Ag 25 1868;Ap 25 1870
NN Je 15 1927
NNHi S 22 1870;My 1 1873
P-M Ja 16,29 1913
Vt [Ap-O 1848]Ja 17 1852[55-92]-1910
VtBri [Ap 1931-32]33
VtBu 1848+
VtNU 1904+
VtSa Ap-N 22 1898;N 3-D 7 1927
VtU 1848+
VtV 1915+
WHi Ap-Je 1848

FREE SOIL courier. *See* Burlington courier

Burlington daily NEWS. d Je 23 1894+
Ag 22 1935 is special historical tabloid
pub 1894+
MWA Ag 22 1935
Vt F 26 1902[06-18]+

NORTHERN sentinel. *See* Burlington weekly sentinel

PATRIOTE canadien. w? Ag 7 1839-F 5 1840||
In French
CaO complete

Burlington Sunday REVIEW. *See* Rutland Sunday review (Rutland)

Saturday evening REVIEW. *See* Rutland Sunday review (Rutland)

***Burlington weekly SENTINEL.** w Mr 19 1801-69||
1801-D 6 1810 as Vermont centinel; D 13 1810-D 10 1812 Northern centinel; D 17 1812-Ja 7 1814 Centinel; Ja 14 1814-D 25 1829 Northern sentinel; Ja 1 1830-My ? 1844 Burlington sentinel; Je ? 1844-67 Sentinel and democrat
CSmH Jl 2 1830
Ct [1828]Ag 6 1830[31;34-38]
DLC Mr 19,Ap 16,N 5,26 1824;N 11 1825;Mr 31,S 8 1826;F 2,My 18,Je 1,Ag 24,S 21-28 1827 [28-29]Ja 1 1830;Ja 3 1839[Mr-O 1840;Ja-My 1841]Je 26 1846;F 22 1850[51-53]-56;D 18 1857[Ap-D 1858]-[Ja-Ag 1861]
MBAt Ap 16 1830
MHi N 23-30 1821;Ja 18 1822;F 16 1827
MWA Ap 20-27 1821;Mr 1 1822;F 6 1824;My 13 1825;Ap 28-O 27,N 10,D 14-22 1826;Ja 19 1828-Je 10 1831;Mr 20 1835;Ag 5 1842;O 11 1844[Ap 19-Je Jl 12 1855-56;Mr 23 1860
MiU-C D 28 1827;Jl 11 1828;N 12 1830
NN Mr 6 1828
NNGe 1838-39;42
NcD My 18,N 2 1821;N 1 1822;Jl 4 1823;S 3 1824;My 18,S 28 1827;My 30,Jl 4 1828;Ap 1 1836;O 23 1840;Ap 30-My 14,D 3,24 1841-Ja 7 1842;Ap 7,28 Je 23 1843;Ja 5-12,26,F 9 1844
Vt Ag 24 1827;Je 19 1835;Mr 29 1839;Ag 6-20, S 3,O 1-8,N 5,D 24-31 1841;Ja 14,F 18-24,Mr 11,Jl 8-15,D 30 1842;Ja 21,F 25 1848;F 2,16-23, Mr 16,Ap 27 1849;Mr 29,My 17-24,S 20 1850 [52-53]Ja 11,F 15-Mr 1,D 20-27 1855;Mr 12,Ap 9,N 25 1858
VtBu 1821-30;41;51-53;57-58;60

Burlington SENTINEL. sw Ja? 1838-
N 1838

Burlington daily SENTINEL. d 1848-
Vt [Ap 28-Ag 16 1848]
VtBu 1851-52;61-64
VtU Je 19 1848
WHi Je 16-Ag 16 1848;49-50

Burlington SENTINEL. d 1874-76||?
1875? as Democrat and sentinel
N My 12 1875
—w ed *See* Burlington democrat and weekly sentinel

Burlington weekly SENTINEL. w 1874||?
United with Burlington democrat to form Burlington democrat and weekly sentinel

Burlington daily TIMES. d Je 1858-D 31 1868||
United with Burlington daily free press to form Burlington free press and times, later Burlington free press
DLC N 10,15-19,28-30,D 2,6 1859;N 15 1860;67-68
MBAt Ap 17,20 1865
MWA O 12,18,21,25,29-N 1,5,7-8,12 1859;N 19 24-26 1860;S 18 1861;Jl 10,D 23 1864;Ag 27,O 25 1867
NChM Ja 6 1868
OClWHi Jl 14 1865
Vt D 1 1858[59-67]
VtBu 1858;61-62;65-68
VtBuF 1860-65
VtU N 19 1860;My 18 1861-My 20,D 30 1865;Ap 20 1867;Mr 21 1868

Burlington TIMES. w Je 1858-D 1868||
Merged with Burlington free press
DLC O 3-20,N 24,D 1,15,29 1860;F 2,Mr 30, My 11,23,Je 15-22 1861;Mr 17-N 3 1866;67
VtBu 1858;61-62;65-68
VtU N 9 1860-68

TRUE democrat. w 1843-My 1844||?
United with Burlington sentinel to form Sentinel and democrat, later Burlington weekly sentinel
Vt Ag 16 1843;F 21 1844
VtBu Je 7 1843-My 1 1844

VERMONT centennial. d Je 16-S 4 1877||
VtBeM complete

VERMONT centinel *See* Burlington weekly sentinel

VERMONT witness. w?
Vt Jl 1,Ag 5 1875;D 15 1877

CAMBRIDGE

Cambridge TRANSCRIPT. w 1887+
VtWcC 1890-[1927-30]

CASTLETON

GREEN-MOUNTAIN eagle. w 1831?-
MWA Jl 31,O 2,D 18 1832

VERMONT statesman. w 1826?-55||
CSmH S 1 1830
Ct F 21 1838
DLC Mr 28 1827;Mr 26 1828;D 5 1832
ICN Jl 28-O 20 1830;N 30-D 7 1831;Ja 4 1832
MWA N 28 1827;O 27 1830;O 3 1832;O 24 1838; Je 30,S 29,D 8-22 1841
Vt N 8 1826;My-Je,Jl 11,25-Ag 4,N 7 1827;O 1 1828;Ap,N 24-D 8 1830;Mr 23,Je 22,Ag 10-31 1831;Je 11,Jl 30,D 3-17 1833[34]35[37-38]Ja 23-30,S 11 1839;Jl 28-Ag 18 1840;Mr 10,My 5 1841;F 2-16, Je 8,29,Jl 13-27 1842;My 22,D 11 1852;D 23 1853;Mr 9,Je 1 1855

CHELSEA

FREEDOM'S banner. w My 28 1828-29||?
MH Jl 2 1828
NNHi F 11 1829
Vt D 3 1828;Ja 14,Mr 25,Ap 8,22,My 27 1829
VtBr Jl 2,16-Ag 20,S 10-O 22,N 5,19-D 24 1828;Ja 7-21,F-My 20,Je 3-10 1829
VtCh [Je 25 1828-29]

Chelsea HERALD. w 1888?+
VtCC O 1905+
VtU O 20-N 3 1892; D 5 1895;Ja 4 1900;Ag 18 1904;Je 8,Jl 25 1905

ORANGE county republican. w Jl 1840-
MWA O 8 1840

VERMONT advocate and state paper. w D 1826-
1826-F 2 1830 as Vermont advocate; Jl 20 1830-Jl 22 1831 Vermont advocate and White River advertiser
Suspended from F 2-Jl 20 1830
1825-F 2 1830 pub in South Royalton
CSmH S 6 1830
DLC O 20 1829
MWA N 24 1829-O 18 1830
NNHi S 6 1830;Ja 26 1832
NhD N 8 1832;F 7-14,28,My 27,Je 26-Jl 3,Ag 7 1833
Vt N 21 1827;Mr 11 1829[30-32]F 14,Mr 2, 14,O 16,30,D 4-18 1833[34]
VtSr N 3 1827

VERMONT Thursday news. w 1837-39||?
NhD O 4,N 8 1838
Vt S 14 1837

CHESTER

Chester ADVERTISER. w N 18 1893-Ag 22 1908||
MWA Ag 25 1894
VtCh complete

FREEDOM'S banner. w My 28 1828-
MWA My 18,O 15,N 12-26,D 10 1828-My 20 1829

CONCORD

PEOPLE'S advocate. w? Ag 5 1841-
MnHi Ag 5 1841

DANBY

OTTER CREEK VALLEY news. w 1872-80||?
Vt [1878-80]

DANVILLE

***NORTH STAR.** w Ja 8 1807-91||
Ct N 28 1836
DLC Ap 10 1832;Je 15-Jl 20,Ag 10-S 21 1835; Ap 27-My 18 1839[58]D 10 1864;Ja 1 1869
ICHi Ja 8-15 1859
MBAt 1851-58
MWA S 13,27,N 15 1821;O 3 1822;N 22 1825; D 11 1827;Ja 8,F 12,26,Ag 26 1828;F 17,Mr 10,Jl 21,Ag 18-25,S 17 1829;N 5,19-D 3,17-31 1832[36-Ap 7 1838]D 21 1839; Je 20 1840[Ap-D 1841]My 1,O 9 1843;S 23 1844;Ja 6,Ag 4 1845[Ja-Ap 20 1846]Ap 5[Je-N 15]1847;Ja 31 1848[Ja 19-O 19 1850]Ag 14,D 4 1858;Je 2 1860[61]Ja 18,F 8,Mr 22,My 17 1862;Jl 18, N 7-14,D 5,19 1863;Mr 26,My 14 1864;Ap 29,Je 24 1865;Je 30,Jl 28 1866[73-81]-[Ja-N 1883]
MnHi Je 12 1832
N S 6-13 1825;Ja 17 1826;Ag 26-D 9 1828;Je 21,O 25 1831;Ja 17,Ap 3,Jl 10,Ag 13,O 8,D 24 1832;Ja 21,My 6,S 3 1833
NNHi Ja 25 1831;My 1 1852;Mr 21 1873
NhD D 9 1828;Ja 13 1829;Ja 24,F 10,24-Mr 3,Jl 13 1830;Je 1831-32;Ja 14,Ap 1 1833;Ja 5 1839;Ja 1 1840;N 27 1843
NhM Ag 17-S 21 1835
P-M C 8 1832
Vt Ap 27-Je 8,22-Jl,S 7,O 19 1846;Ag 30 1847;Ag 24 1850;Mr 9 1867;Mr 28,Ap 11 1879; Ja 4,F 8,22,Mr 7-14,28,Ap 11,25,Ag 15,29,O 3,N 28 1884;My 12 1887
WHi Jl 22 1854

DERBY

NORTHERN oziris. w D 15 1831-45||?
NNHi Ja 26 1832
Vt [1831-32]

EAST HARDWICK

HARDWICK reporter. w 1870-73||?
MWA Jl 14 1871

EAST POULTNEY

VERMONT observer. w 1846-
VtBr Jl 29,Ag 19,S 30-O 2 1846

EAST RANDOLPH

VERMONT luminary. w Ja 7-D 30 1829||
Followed by American whig (Woodstock)
DLC F 18,S 30 1829
MWA Je 3 1829
NNHi D 23 1829
Vt My 13-O 1829
VtHi complete

ENOSBURG FALLS

Enosburg STANDARD. w Ag 2 1895+
pub 1895+

ESSEX JUNCTION

ADVANCE. w Ja 17 1914-16||?
Vt 1914-16

Essex RECORD. w,sw 1891?+
w 1891?-1903?
pub 1904+
VtMiS O 8 1903

FAIR HAVEN

Fair Haven ERA. w 1879+
MWA Mr 8 1928
Vt Jl 20-27,O 26 1881;Ap 5 1882
VtFM 1901+
VtRC 1900+

Fairhaven JOURNAL. w 1868-70||*
Vt Jl 2,S 3,14 1870

VERMONT record. w 1887-98||?
VtRC 1894-98

FAYETTEVILLE. *See* NEWFANE

GROTON

Groton TIMES. w Ja 1 1897+
NhD F 1900-04;S 27 1912
Vt N 1920+
VtU Ap 10 1897;F 11,Mr 11,Jl 1,15,29,S 9,23,D 30 1898;Je 30,Ag 18,S 15,O 27-N 3,23,D 8,15 1899;Ja-F 9,23,Mr 9-30,Ap 13,My 25,S 28,D 28 1900;Ja 18,My 10,31,Jl 12 1901;Je 27 1902; Ja 30-F 6,Jl 10 1903;F 5,Mr 4,18,O 7 1904;O-D 1930

GUILDHALL

ESSEX county herald. *See under* Island Pond

HARDWICK

Hardwick GAZETTE. w Jl 1889+
pub Jl 1897+
Vt N 1920+
VtU Jl 1917-Jl 1918

VERMONT (*Continued*)

HYDE PARK

LAMOILLE news. w N 30 1860-D 1881||
1860-Mr 21 1877 as Lamoille news dealer. United with Vermont citizen (Morrisville) to form News and citizen (Morrisville)
MWA Jl 16,Ag 20 1879
VtHpC N 23 1864-75;93
VtHpM complete
VtMor [1860-77]

LAMOILLE RIVER express. *See* Vermont state paper. . . (Johnson)

NEWS and citizen. *See under* Morrisville

IRASBURGH

ORLEANS county gazette. w My 11 1850-55||?
Merged with North union (West Charleston)
ICHi 1850-My 1 1852
MWA S 6 1851
NNHi N 6 1852
Vt [1850-52]

ORLEANS independent standard. *See under* Barton

YEOMAN'S record. w 1845-50||
Vt Mr 6 1850

ISLAND POND

ESSEX county herald. w Ja 11 1873+
Also dated in Guildhall
pub [1873+]
Vt [1873-1919]+

JOHNSON

BANNER of LaMoille. w F 29 1844-
DLC F 29 1844
NhD Mr 21 1844

FAMILY visitor. w Jl 13?- 1843||?
MWA Ag 24 1843
NhD N 23 1843

LAMOILLE RIVER express. *See* Vermont state paper and Lamoille and Orleans county democrat

LAMOILLE standard. w Jl 2 1842-43||?
Vt [1842-43]

LAMOILLE whig. w Je 6 1840-
DLC Je 19 1841
MWA Je-Ag 1,O 24 1840
NhD D 19 1840;Ja 9 1841
Vt [1840-42]

SCORPION. w Je 25-Ag 30 1839||
NhD Je 25 1839
Vt Je 25,Jl 9 1839

VERMONT state paper and Lamoille and Orleans county democrat. w Je 1 1838-My? 1840||
1838-Mr 5 1839 as LaMoille river express also dated in Hyde Park
DLC S 10 1839;My 12 1840
MWA F 4 1840
NNHi [1838-F 1 1839]
Vt [1838-40]
VtHi 1838-Je 4 1839

LUDLOW

BLACK RIVER gazette. w D 19 1866-N 2 1876||
Followed by Ludlow tribune, later Vermont tribune
Vt My 1 1867;My 16 1873;Ap 17 1874;O 13 1876
VtLu 1866-71;73-My 7,O 29 1875
VtLuT 1867-My 7 1875
VtWoC N 1867-76

BLACK RIVER transcript. w Ap 17 1866-
Vt Je 26 1866

Ludlow BLOTTER. w S 1854-
1854-O 23 1856 as Blotter
P-M N 23 1854
Vt O 4 1855;S 25 1856
VtLu S 27 1855-Mr 19 1857

GENIUS of liberty. w Ja 15? 1847-
WHi Ag 26 1847

Ludlow TRIBUNE. *See* Vermont tribune

VERMONT republican. *See under* Brattleboro

VERMONT star. *See under* Rutland

VERMONT tribune. w N 21 1876+
Follows Black River gazette
1876-D 14 1877 as Ludlow tribune
pub 1898+
NhD Je 29 1900;N 8 1901;Ap 27 1903;Ja-Je 3, Ag 5,D 9 1915-Je 1929
Vt [1879-1919]
VtLu 1876-77;79-[81]N 30 1883-N 16 1888;N 22 1889-N 8 1895;N 13 1896-Ap 16 1897[Mr 23 1923-24]27+
VtWoC S 14 1877-1923

VOICE among the mountains. w Ja 12 1860-
Vt [1860-62]
VtLu 1860-Ja 16 1862;F-O,D 1863-Ja 1864
VtWoC My 16 1861-62

LYNDONVILLE

Lyndonville JOURNAL. w 1889-O 1905||
United with Vermont union to form Vermont union-journal

VERMONT union-journal. w F 1 1865+
1865-O 1905 as Vermont union
pub 1865+
MWA [My 22 1874-75]-[Ja-Ag 10 1877]Jl 18, Ag 22 1879;Ja 16,30[Jl-O 1880;Ap 22 1881-84]-[Ja-N 20 1891]Mr 3 1893;Je 21-28,Jl 12, Ag 30,N 29 1895;Je 19-26,Jl 10-17,D 11 1896; My 28,Je 4,Ag 20 1897;N 4-11 1898[99-1900]-[03]-Mr 17 1905
MiU-C F 19 1886;Je 1 1888
Vt [1865-1905]
VtU Ap 3 1875;Ag 29,S 12 1890;Ja 2 1891;Ap 23 1897;N 18 1898;Ap 21 1905

MANCHESTER

BENNINGTON county whig. w My 31 1837-39||?
Vt Ag 16 1837

HORN of the Green Mountains. w Mr 23 1830-
CSmH S 7 1830
MWA Ap 27 1830
Vt O 5 1830;Mr 22-My 17 1831

Manchester JOURNAL. w My 28 1861+
pub 1905+
MWA Ag 31 1871
Vt O-N 4 1862;Jl 25,Ag 29 1865
VtBeC 1861+
VtM 1861-My 16 1865;Ja-My 22 1866;87;Jl 8 1897+
WHi O 7 1862

VERMONT express. w Ag 23 1836-
MWA Ag 30 1836

MIDDLEBURY

ADDISON county journal. w Ap 22 1876-83||?
United with Middlebury register to form Register and Addison county journal, later Middlebury register
Vt F 18 1881
VtMiM D 17 1880
VtMiS 1878-80

AMERICAN and gazette. w Ap 16 1828-
1828-31? as Vermont American; 1831?-34? American
DLC Ap 16 1828;Mr 18,Ap 8-22,My 6-20,Je 3,24,Jl 8-15,Ag 5,S 2,30,D 2 1829;Ja 13-20 1830
MWA Ap 30 1828;Ja 3,O 2 1832;N 18 1834;S 1 1835
NNHi D 27 1831
P-M Ap 30 1833
Vt [1828-29]Ag 4 1830;Ap 21,D 8 1835;My 25 1836
VtMiM Ag 13 1828;F 18 1829;Ag 25 1830
VtMiS 1832-36

ANTI-MASONIC republican. w O 1829-N 1830||?
Followed by Middlebury free press
CSmH Jl 1 1830
NNHi Mr 11 1830
VtMiM N 24 1830
VtMiS 1829-30

Middlebury ARGUS. *See* Green Mountain argus and Middlebury free press

BEE. m 1855?-
MWA Mr 1857

COLUMBIAN patriot. *See* National standard

DEMOCRATIC ploughman. w 1842-
VtMiM Mr 13 1843

Middlebury FREE PRESS. w D 1830?-S 26 1837||
Follows Anti-masonic republican. United with Vermont argus to form Vermont argus and free press, later Green Mountain argus and Middlebury free press
DLC O 10 1832;O 4 1836
MBAt N 24 1835
MWA O 19 1831
MnHi Ag 31 1831
Vt Ag 10 1831;Ag 13,S 11,26 1832;Je 23,O 27-N 3 1835;My 30 1837
VtMiM [Ap 25 1832-Mr 1833]
VtMiS 1830-37

Middlebury FREE PRESS. w My 5 1840-
MWA O 6 1840
Vt Ag 4,S 15 1840;F 2 1841

Middlebury GALAXY. w Ap 1836-49||?
1836-My? 1838 as People's press; Je? 1838-Jl 7 1840 People's press and Addison county democrat; Jl 14 1840-N 15 1843 Middlebury people's press; N 22 1843-Ja 31 1844 Northern galaxy and Middlebury people's press F 7? 1844-Ja 4 1848 Northern galaxy. Merged with Middlebury register?
CtY Ap 2 1839;Mr 8 1843
DLC [Jl 27 1841-42]
GAtCo Jl 7 1840
MWA S 18 1838;My 11 1841-Ap 24 1849
N Ja 6 1846
NNHi [Je 1838-F 5 1839]
NcD Jl 28 1846;F 2,Ag 3,S 21,O 5,N 3,30 1847; S 19 1848
NjR My 15 1849
Vt Jl 3 1838;Ja 3 1843;O 9 1844;Mr 9 1847
VtMiM Je 6 1836;Mr 7,O 17 1837;S 7 1841;Ja 31 1844

GREEN MOUNTAIN argus and Middlebury free press. w O 1831-
1831-Ja? 1832 as Northern argus; F 7-D 1832? Middlebury argus; 1833?-S 26 1837 Vermont argus (Je 21 1836-Mr 7 1837 Argus) O 3 1837-38? Vermont argus and free press
Ct [1831-37]Ja 16 1838
CtY S 17 1839
DLC Ja 4-11,F 28 1832;36-S 18,O 9-D 5 1838 [39]
MWA S 21-O 5 1831;My 10,Ag 2 1836
N N 4 1833
Vt Ja 1,Ap 16,Je 4,N 12 1839;Mr 10 1840
VtMiM N 24 1837
VtMiS 1830-33
WHi Mr 14-S 12,O 1837-S 18 1838

***NATIONAL standard.** w S 1 1813-
1813-Ag 23 1815 as Columbian patriot
CSmH Je 22 1830
Ct Jl 15 1828[31]
DLC 1821-30
MWA Jl 17 1821;My 13 1823;D 28 1824;Ja 11, My 17 1825;D 18 1827;S 16 1828;Mr 31 1829; Ap 27,N 16 1830
NNHi Mr 13-D 4 1821;Mr 2 1822
OClWHi Mr 22 1831
Vt Ag 27 1822;Ag 22 1826;Ja 5 1830

NORTHERN argus. *See* Green Mountain argus and Middlebury free press

NORTHERN galaxy. *See* Middlebury galaxy

PEOPLE'S press. *See* Middlebury galaxy

Middlebury RECORD. w 1901?+
VtMiS 1906-08

Middlebury REGISTER. w 1836+
1884?-85? Register and Addison county journal
pub 1871-75;83-94;97+
DLC My 28 1850;Mr 3-17 1877
MWA F 5 1850;Ja 1,F 12,Ap 2,Je 11,Ag 27,O 22,D 24 1851;Ap 21,Je 23-30,S 8,22,N 3 1852;N 1,D 27 1854;Ja 10 1855;N 5 1856;S 2 1857;Je 8 1859;O 14(supp)1898
NcD D 24 1851;Je 30 1852
NhD S 11,O 30 1885-89
Vt My 28,Jl 2,O 1 1850;Ap 1 1857;Mr 16 1869; S 12 1871;O 1 1872;Jl 22 1876;F 13 1881;Ap 13-20,Jl 27 1883[86-87]Ag 3,31 1888;Ap 5,1889; Ap 25 1890;N 27 1891;My 20-Je 10,Jl 8-15,Ag 5,26 1892
VtMiC 1850+
VtMiM Ap 1880-82
VtMiS 1839-[71]-79;81+
VtU Je 29 1859;Jl 29,S 9 1873;My 18,Jl 27,D 4 1875;F 3-10 1877;Je 27 1890;N 9 1896;N 5,D 31 1897;Ag 23 1918
WHi My 20 1863

TOPAZ. w Mr 28 1842-
CtY My 16,Je 6-20,Jl 4-18 1842
DLC Mr 28 1842
MWA Mr 28,My 16-23,Je 13,Jl 1,25,Ag 15 1842
NcD Mr 28,My 16 1842
Vt Je 6-13,Jl 18 1842
VtMiM My 23 1842

VERMONT American. *See* American and gazette

VERMONT argus. *See* Green Mountain argus and Middlebury free press

MILTON

Milton HERALD. w Ja 29 1844-
DLC Mr 5 1844

MONTPELIER

Montpelier evening ARGUS. d O 21 1897+
N 11-23 1927 are flood issues
pub 1897+
DLC D 1918+
MWA N 11,14,21-23 1927;Ja 30 1928
NhD O 4 1905
OHi O 12-13 1899
Vt O 4 1905;N 11 1918
VtMo 1928+

ARGUS and patriot. w F 1863+
Formed by the union of Bellows Falls argus (Bellows Falls) and Vermont patriot
DLC 1877-1917
MWA Mr 12 1863;S 16 1869;Jl 13 1871
NNHi Ag 10 1865;Jl 4,Ag 22 1867;O 20,D 15 1870;Mr 2-9,Je 22,D 28 1871;N 7 1872;My 8 1873
NhD Mr 5 1863;S 14 1865;Mr 1 1866
Vt Jl 9 1863;My 18 1865;N 1 1866;S 27 1867; Je 11 1868;S 8,29-O 6,N 3-17 1870;Je 8 1876; supp My 6 1875
VtMiS Ja 25 1872;Ag 7 1873;O 7 1875;Jl 2 1879;Mr 17,Jl 26 1882;Ja 20 1886;N 7 1888
VtMoC 1876-77;80-82;94-1917;28+
VtU S 13 1865;My 16 1867;O 9 1873;Je 1-8, 21,O 11,N 8 1876;Ja 17,31,F 14,Ap 18-My 2, Je 6,Jl 11,N 25 1877;N 9-D 7,21 1881;N 12, 26-D 3 1884;Mr 11,D 10 1885;S 19 1888;Ag 20-27,D 10 1890;O 5 1892;D 23 1896;O 13,27-N 3,D 1-8 1897;supp F 5 1893

Daily ARGUS and patriot. d -1879||?
pub only during session of legislature
OClWHi Je 25,Jl 2 1879
Vt O 24 1866

GREEN MOUNTAIN freeman. w Ja 6 1844-85||
Follows Vermont freeman
DHU-M Jl 15 1847
DLC 1846-48;O 4 1855;Mr 20 1856;Jl 14,Ag 4-18,S 29,D 1 1859;O 18,D 13,27 1860;Ja 10-24, Ap 4,23,Je 4,18,Jl 9,Ag 13-20 1861
MBAt 1854-D 9 1858;Ap 18 1865
MWA Jl 27 1848;Ap 12 1854;O 20,N 1859;Ag 1 1865;D 28 1870;Jl 12 1871;Je 18 1873;S 21 1881
NNHi Ja 10,Ap 25 1850;S 15,O 15,29-D 10 1857;Ag 19 1858;Jl 9 1861;Je 16,Jl 28 1863; O 15,19-26,N 9,23,D 7-21 1870;Ja 11-18,F 1-15 Ap 19,1871;F 19,O 15,N 19-26 1873;My 1-8,Jl 31 1878
NhD Mr 16 1844;Ap 4,S 18 1845;F 10,Je 15, Jl 27 1848;50;53-54[56-57]Mr 20 1866
OClWHi Ja 27 1844;Jl 5 1864
Vt F 7,Mr 21,Jl 11,O 16-23,S 18 1845;S 10,24 1846;N 25 1847[49-51]N 11 1852;Mr 10 1853;Ja 4,Mr 1,Jl 26,Ag 16,N 29 1855;N 27,D 18 1856; Ja 15,Ag 13,D 31 1857;Mr 10,D 30 1858[59] Ag 23,N 15 1860-Ap 4,D 17 1861;Mr 17,O-D 1863;N 18 1868;Ag 24 1870[72-76]
VtMoC 1878
VtU D 2 1852;Ap 23-My 21,Jl 9-23,Ag 13-20, S 3 1857;Ap 22 1858;Ap 30 1861
WHi 1848-55

VERMONT (Continued)

MONTPELIER—Continued

Daily GREEN MOUNTAIN freeman. d Ap 15 1861-65‖
Vt Jl 3,17,31,O 18 1861;Ap 12 1862;S 17,19 1863

HARRISONIAN. w Mr 10-N 1840‖
MWA [Mr-Jl 1 1840]
OClWHi [1840]
Vt Jl 8 1840

Daily JOURNAL. d 1835?-98‖?
Title varies: Walton's daily journal; Walton's legislative journal; Walton's morning journal; etc. pub only during sessions of legislature
DLC O 14,N 2 1836;N 8 1849;N 10,12-14,16-19 1859
MH [O 29-N 11 1857]N 3-9 1866
MWA F 18-28,O 9-N 11 1857;O 14,N 1,22 1859;N 21,24 1860;O 18 1861;F 21 1863;N 17 1864;N 21 1867;68;O 19 1869;S 30-N 26 1884;O 5-N 24 1886;O-N 27 1888;O 4-N 23 1892;O-N 28 1894;O 6-N 25 1896;O 5-D 1 1898
MiU-C [1868;84;86;88;92;94;98]
NNHi [O-N 1868;O-N 1872]
NcD F 21 1857
NhD O 11-N 14 1850
OClWHi Ja 5 1866
P-M N 7 1854
Vt O 17 1835[O-N 1841]O 15-N 14 1842;44-49;N 13 1856 [57-68]N 15-19,21-23 1870[74;76;78;80;82;84;86;88;90;92]-98
VtMiM O 14 1859
VtU [O 14 1841-Mr 3 1868]S 30,O 4 1888
—w ed *See* Vermont watchman

Montpelier daily JOURNAL. d N 6 1897-S 5 1914‖
1897-Ap 30 1899 as Montpelier daily record
MWA Ja 15 1899-1904;F 1909-14
MiU-C [1901-03]04
Vt [1897-99]-[1901-14]
VtU N 9,29-D 3,6-8 1904
—w ed *See* Vermont watchman

PRECURSOR. *See* Vermont watchman

Montpelier daily RECORD. *See* Montpelier daily journal

REFORMER and democrat.
Vt Ag 27 1839;Ag 20 1840

RURAL Vermonter. w 1883-88‖?
DLC Mr 16-Ap 27 1888
MWA My 21 1886-87
Vt [1886-88]

STATE journal. w O 31 1831-O? 1836‖
United with Vermont watchman and state gazette to form Vermont watchman and state journal, later Vermont watchman
DLC O 8 1832
MHi Jl 7 1835;Je 28 1836
MWA Ja 9 1832;Ja 13 1834;O 13 1835;Je 1 (extra)O 25 (extra)1836
MiU-C O 25(extra)1836
Vt O 31,N 15 1831;D 29 1834;Ag 4 1835

VERMONT chronicle. *See under* St. Johnsbury

VERMONT freeman. w N 11 1842-43‖?
Followed by Green Mountain freeman
MWA N 25 1842
NhD D 10 1842

VERMONT news. w My 28-N 1 1880‖
NhD Je 18,Jl 2-16,30-Ag 13,27,S 3 1880
Vt Jl 9 1880

VERMONT patriot. w Ja 17 1826-62‖
1825-38;46-57 as Vermont patriot and state gazette. United with Bellows Falls argus (Bellows Falls) to form Argus and patriot
CSmH S 6 1830
Ct [1827-37]
DLC My 4,Je 22-29 1829;Ag 1832-My 1841;Mr 8-Ap 12,26 1845;Jl 16 1846;Ja 14 1847-Je 1 1849;Mr 10 1853-55;Ja 25,F 8-15,Mr 28,Ap 11-18,My 16-23 Ag 22,N 7-14 1856;58-D 22 1860;Ja 12-F 16;Mr 30 1861
MBAt Mr 1 1830;D 26 1850-D 16 1852
MWA 1826-Ja 5,N 9 1829;N 22 1830;N 14 1831;O 14,D 30 1833;F 17,Ap 7,21-28,Je 30,Ag 11,25-S 15,29-N 24,D 8 1834;Ja 5,26,Mr 2,Ap 12,My 4-11,S 28,O 26-N 2 1835;Jl 10,N 13-20 1837;Ag 5 1839;N 9 1840;Jl 24 1841;D 18 1845;Ap 7 1854;F 16,Je 29 1855;O 15 1858;Mr 24,S 8 1860;Jl 20 1861
MnHi Ag 26 1833
N Ja 24 1826;O 14 1833;Ag 27 1838
NNHi Ag 29 1826;Ag 23 1830;Ap 13 1848;N 24 1860
NhD O 20 1834;Ap 18 1837;Ja 9,My 22 1838;Ja 21 1839;My 8-15 1841;F 26,My 14,N 12,D 3 24 1842;Mr 13,O 7 1843;Mr 2-9,23,Ap 13,Je 8,Jl 13,Ag 3,S 28 1844;Ag 7,28,D 25 1845;My 4 1848
NjR N 14 1826
Vt Je 2,Jl 4,18-Ag 1,O 24,N 7 1826;Mr 12,Ap 2-9, Jl 6,N 5 1827[28-29]Mr 8,Ap 19,Jl 26,Ag 9 1830;Mr 7 1831;Mr 25,S 30,O 21 1833;O 24 1836;Jl 2,D 1838-[40-50]S 18,N 27-D 4 1851;Ag 12,26-S 2 1852;D 8 1853;Ap 7,Je 16,O 20 1854;My 4,25-Je 1,Ag 17 1855;Ja 9-16 1857;Je 29 1858;O 22-N 19 1859;N 17 1860;Jl 6 1861
VtNp 1850-51
WHi 1840-45

Daily VERMONT patriot. d
OClWHi S 20 1860
Vt O 14-15,17-22,24-26,28-29,31-N 5,7-10,12,14-18 1836;O 11,13-14,16-25,27-31 1837;O 3,24-28,30-31,N 12,14,18-20,22 1838;O 10-12,14-20,22,24-N 2,4-9,11-14,16,18,20 1839

VERMONT precursor. *See* Vermont watchman

VERMONT watchman. w N 22 1806-1911‖?
1806-N 13 1807 as Vermont precursor (Ja 26-Je 25 1807 Precursor) N 20 1807-25? Watchman; 1826-O 1836 Vermont watchman and state gazette; N 1836-My 1883 Vermont watchman and state journal
DLC Ag 17 1824;O 25,N 1 1825;Ja 3,17 1826-D 15 1829;Ja 5-12,26 1830;Ap 22 1833;D 22 1834;Ja 19,F 2-9,Je 23,O 13,N 24 1835;My 2,Je 7,N 8 1836;D 10 1838;N 9 1840;Mr 22 1841-Mr 10 1843;F 25 1847;51-53;F 13 1863-N 2 1866;69-70My 20 1874;D 20 1876;O 16 1889;Ag 19-S 2 1891
ICHi Ag 8 1877-S 4 1892
InRE Mr 1 1871
MBAt Jl 24 1821;Ja 8,29 1822;N 13 1827;Ag 5,S 9 1828;D 1850-N 19 1858
MWA N 6-13 1821;S 9 1823;O 5 1824;S 6-20,O 4-18 1825;O 17-N 21 1826;Jl 3,O 16-N 1827;Ag 18 1829;Ap 27 1830;Ap 5,O 24-N 7 1831;O 22 1832;Mr 23 1835;O 18,N 8 1836;Jl 31,Ag 21 1837;N 11 1839;F 10,Ag 3,S 7-14;28-N 16 1840;O 18,N 1-15 1841;Ap 25,O 14-21 1842;46-52;54-64;N 15 1865;66;68-69;Mr 9,N 16 1870;71-1904;09-10
MiU-C [1826-27;74]76-[80-81]84-[92]-98;1901-04
N O 21 1823;Ag 11 1842
NNHi My 18,Je 1 1824;O 12 1830 D 27 1844;Ap 25 1850;F 3,24,Mr 10,Ap 7 1860;D 4 1872;Ap 30 1873;Mr 17 1875
NSchU F 7 1842
NcD D 2 1859;79-80;84;86-95
NhD My 29,Jl 31,Ag 28,O 16-23,D 4 1821;Ap 16 1822;Ja 9 1827;O 7 1828;F 23,Je 2,16,O 13 1829;Ja 12 1830;Mr 19 1832;46-54;N 28 1856-[57;Mr 1853-N 18 1859]
NjR N 21 1826;Mr 29 1849
OClWHi Jl 29 1823;O 26 1824;Jl 26 N 15 1825;Ag 4 1829;Ja 4-11 1831
P-M O 22 1832
Vt S 23,O 14-21 1823;S 24 1824[25]Mr 23,Ag 15,O 17 1826;Je 12,O 16-N 6,20-27 1827;Jl 15,Ag 26,O 14,N 4-11 1828;O 13-N 2 18 1829;Ja 3,O 18-25,N 16-30 1830[31-42]F 1843[44-59]N 4 1864;N 15 1866;F 3 1875;D 9 1885;Ag 7 1901;extra Jl 19 1861
VtBeC 1851-Je 1864
VtBr O 22 1822;N 1823-[24-O 1829 O 19 1830
VtHpC O 20 1875-94
VtMiC 1850-1906
VtMiM Ag 5 1859
VtMiS 1848-52;55-56;60-65;70-72
VtMcC 1879 84-86;89-1902
VtNp O 17,N 7 1826
VtU Ag 22 1862;My 28 1896;S 15,O 15,O 6,27-D 1897;Ja 26-Mr 23 1898;My-N 1899;D 19 1900[01-My 1902]Ja 7-14,Ag 25 1904;Ap 5 1907;Ap 29,My 7 1909
—legislative ed *See* Daily journal
—d ed *See* Montpelier daily journal

Daily VERMONTER. d O 5-N 24 1886‖?
MWA O-N 24 1886
MiU-C O-N 24 1886
NhD O 8-29,N 3,5,8,10,12-24 1886
Vt [O-N 24 1886]

WALTON'S . . . journal. *See* Daily journal

WATCHMAN. *See* Vermont watchman

MORETOWN

ENTERPRISE. O 20 1876-
Vt O 20 1876

MORRISVILLE

AMERICAN observer.
Vt N 25 1852

Morrisville MESSENGER. w Ja 1 1858+
pub [1904-22]+
Vt 1920-22
VtHpC 1901+
VtMor 1915+

NEWS and citizen. w D 1881+
Formed by the union of Vermont citizen and Lamoille news (Hyde Park)
Also dated in Hyde Park
NN Jl 4 1889
NhD My 1 1890
Vt 1920+
VtHpC 1881+
VtHpM 1881+
VtMor 1881+
VtMorM 1884+
VtU My 7 1896;F 23 1898

VERMONT citizen. w Ap 3 1873-D 1881‖
United with Lamoille news (Hyde Park) to form News and citizen
Vt [1873-81]
VtHpC complete

NEWBURY

AURORA and cultivator. w,sm Mr 4 1848-Ag 1868‖?
1848-66 as Aurora of the valley; 1867? Vermont cultivator. Merged with Vermont journal (Windsor)
Also dated in Brattleboro, Windsor and Bradford
DLC Ja 9 1864
MBAt 1856
MWA F 17,Mr 17,Ap 14,My 12 1849;Mr 5 1853
NNHi N 4 1852;D 8 1855
NhD 1848-F 17,Mr 17 1849;My 7,Je 11,N 19 1864[69]
Vt [1848-F 17 1849]My 30,Je 27 1850 Jl 24,N 1851-55;59-[68]

VERMONT cultivator. *See* Aurora and cultivator

NEWFANE

Early years as Fayetteville

GREEN MOUNTAIN democrat. w F 6 1835-
DLC Mr 20,Ap 17-My 1 1835
MWA Mr 11 1836
NNHi Mr 27-Ap 10,24-My 8 Je 5-12,Jl-O 9,23-D 11 1835
Vt Mr 27 1835
VtBr [F 13 1835-Je 17 1836]

VERMONT free press. w Je 7 1834-F 14 1835‖
ICHi complete
Vt complete
VtBr [1834]Ja 17 1835

NEWPORT

EXPRESS and standard. w Mr 1 1865+
1865-71? as Newport express
pub [1920]+
MWA S 27 1865
OClWHi S 5 1865
Vt O 4,18 1865;Mr 6-13,Ap 10,24,My 15,29-Je 5,N 27 1866;S 15 1867;Mr 17,My 12-Jl 21,N 24 1868

Newport NEWS. w 1919-21‖
United with North Troy palladium (North Troy) to form Palladium and news (Newport)

PALLADIUM and news. w 1874+
1874-1921 as North Troy palladium (North Troy)
VtNp 1922-29
VtNpE 1922+

WHIP and spur. w
DLC Mr 19 1839;S 28 1840;N 15 1856
NN Ja 22 1839
NhD Ja 1,15,29,Mr 5,26 1839
NhHi [Ja-Mr 1839;S-N 1840]Ag 28-N 13 1852[Ag 30-N 15 1856]

NORTH TROY

North Troy PALLADIUM. *See* Palladium and news (Newport)

NORTHFIELD

NEWS and advertiser. w 1878+
1878-My? 1932 as Northfield news
Vt 1932+
VtMoC 1895
VtNN 1890+
VtNU 1880+

STAR of Vermont. w O 21 1854-
Title varies: Star of Vermont and farmers' register
MBAt 1854-O 20 1855
Vt F 3 1855

NORWICH

CITIZEN soldier. *See under* Windsor

COLUMBIA enquirer, Windham, Windsor and Orange county gazette. w Mr 8 1830-
1830? as Vermont enquirer; 1831? Vermont enquirer and democratic phoenix
CSmH Ag 19 1830
DLC Ja-F 2,Mr 1 1832
MWA Ja 27 1831
MsHi Mr 10 1831
NNHi S 2 1830
NhD [Mr 8 1830-O 1831]Ja 8 1833
Vt D 30 1830

VERMONT enquirer. *See* Columbia enquirer, Windham, Windsor and Orange county gazette

VERMONT freemen. w N? 1842-
NcD Je 24,Jl 8-S, O 14,28-D 16 1843
VtBr Mr 18-Ap 15,My 8,20,Je 3-17,Jl 1-8,29-Ag 12,26-S 2,16-23 1843

POULTNEY

Poultney BULLETIN. w Mr 19 1868-D 10? 1873‖
United with Rutland county journal to form Poultney journal
MWA My 14 1868
Vt D 23 1871
VtPJ [1868-69]

Poultney GAZETTE. *See* Northern spectator

Poultney JOURNAL. w D 1873-Mr 1933‖
Formed by the union of Poultney bulletin and Rutland county journal
M Jl 7 1876
VtRC 1893-1932
VtSj [1878]80-1933

NORTHERN spectator. w O 29 1822-Jl 1830‖
1822-23 as Poultney gazette
CSmH Je 23 1830
DLC Mr 3 1824;Je 7 1826;D 25 1827;Ja 30,F 13,Mr 9-26,Ap 9-23 1828
ICN Je 20-Jl 21 1830
MBAt N 26 1822
MWA N 5,19,D 3-11,25 1822-[23]-S 8,N 24,D 29 1824;Ja 19 1825;Jl 12 1826;My 7 1828
NcD S 21 1828
Vt N 12,D 11-18 1822[23-24]Ap 6,18,My 11,D 7 1825[26]Ja 3-10 1827;Jl 15 1829

RUTLAND county journal. w 1867-D? 1873‖
United with Poultney bulletin to form Poultney journal
MWA S 23 1871

VERMONT (*Continued*)

RANDOLPH

HERALD and news. w O 1873+
1873-77? as Green Mountain herald
pub 1878+
Vt Je 20 1878;1910+

RICHFORD

Richford GAZETTE. w O 1 1878-S? 1927‖
United with Richford journal to form Journal-gazette
MWA O 3 1889
NbHi Mr 13 1884
Vt 1910-27
VtMiS S 22 1881;1901-O 1906;F 12 1909

JOURNAL-GAZETTE. w O 15 1878+
1878-O 1 1927 as Richford journal
pub [1878-1927]+

ROYALTON

VERMONT advocate and White-River advertiser. w D 5? 1826-
MBAt S 10 1828
MWA N 14 1827;Mr 26,My 7 1828;Ag 26 1829

RUTLAND

COMMERCIAL advertiser.
Vt Mr 23, Ap 6 1852

Rutland COURIER. w Ag 12 1857-Ap 14 1873‖
DLC N 16 1860;My 10 1861
Vt 1857-Jl 1864;Mr 10,Je 16,N 17 1865;Mr 16 1866;Ap 19,S 20 1867;Jl 3,D 4 1868;O 1,29,N 19,D 31 1869;F 11,Mr 11 1870;N 17 1871;My 24,Ag 9,30,S 13 1872
VtMiM Ja 9 1858
VtRC 1857-Jl 19 1872

Rutland daily GLOBE. d My 1 1873-Ag 31 1877‖
United with Rutland daily herald to form Rutland daily herald and globe, later Rutland daily herald
MWA Ja 14 1874;Ja 1 1876
Vt 1873-77
VtMiS 1873-Je 10,Jl-S 1876;Je-Jl 1877

Rutland weekly GLOBE. w My 1873-Ag 28 1877‖
United with Rutland weekly herald to form Rutland weekly herald and globe, later Rutland weekly herald
MWA Ag 8 1873;Ag 17 1877
Vt My 23,Jl 11,Ag 15,O 24,N 14 1873;F 6,Mr 13 1874;F 11,My 19,Jl 29,S 29,N 10 1876
VtRC complete

GUARD of American liberty. w? Ja 6 1855-
MWA Ja 6 1855
P-M F 24 1855

***Rutland HERALD.** w D 8 1794-Je 24 1920‖
Follows Farmers' library (not in this list) 1794-Je 22? 1795 as Rutland herald: or, Vermont mercury; Je 29 1795-Ag 1798 Rutland herald: a register of the the times; Je 18 1808-21? Rutland Vermont herald; 1822?-Ag 1877 Rutland weekly herald (N 20 1852-54? Rutland county herald) S 1877-84 Rutland weekly herald and globe
pub 1823-27;39-41;43-47;51-1920
CSmH Jl 27 1830
CtY N 30 1871
DLC [1821-27]-[30-35]Jl 19 1836;Jl 24 1838;Jl 5 1842;Jl 22 1858;O 11-N 8 1860;Ap 18 1861-65;67-68
ICN Jl 27 1830
MBAt Ag 5 1828;Ja 16 1851-Ag 1854;Ap 6,O 26,D 7 1855
MWA Mr 27 1821[22-S 16 1823;Ja-Je 15]O 12-19,N 16-D 7 1824;Ja 11-18,F 22-Mr 1,Ap 19,Jl 26,N 8-15,D 6 1825[Ja 10-My 16 1826]Mr 20,My 29,S 11 1827;Ja 8 1828;S 8 1829;Je 1,O 5 1830;Mr 13 1832;Ja 1(extra)1833;O 4 1836; Mr 7-21,My 16,Ag 15 1837;S 25,O 23 1838;Jl 21,Ag 25-S 1,O 27 1840[Je 29-D 1841]Ja 11-F 8 1842;F 14 1843[My 11-N 1855]O 28 1858;Ja 5 1860;Mr 12,S 24 1863;O 6 1864;My 25 1865;F 15,Ag 9 1866;N 25 1869;F 9 1871;F 7 1884;D 15 1904
N O 25 1825;Ag 9 1842;F 8 1844;Mr 21 1872
NCanHi N 10 1840
NN D 26 1821
NNHi Mr 20,Ag 7,O 16-N 13,D 11,25 1838-Ja 7,22-F 5 1839;D 1 1840;O 21 1852;Je 25 1863; Mr 27 1873
NhD S 15,N 24-D 1 1840
NjR D 3 1846;N 10 1847
P-M O 23 1832
Tx Ag 22 1844
Vt F 27 1822;Ap 30-My 7,27-Je 3,24 1823;N 15 1825;S 26,N 7 1829:Mr 20 1830;N 29-D 6 1831; N 13 1832;N 17 1834;Je 19,D 18 1838;39-40;O 19 1841[42]-[47]Mr 22.Jl 12,S 6,O 4 1848;Je 6 1849;Ap 26,Jl-N 21,D 5 1850[51-54]-Ja 1856; 57-S 1862[63-67]F 6,O 1,15-22,D 19 1868 [69-70]Jl 13,O 26,N 13 1871;Mr 21 1872;N 20 1873;Mr 25,Ap 15,Jl 8-15,29,D 25 1875;Ja 3 1876[78-Mr 1879]Jl 17 1884;Ag 28 1886
VtMiM [1828-F 16 1830]
VtMiS O 30 1873;S-N 1877[78-79]Ja 1880;Ja, Ap,Jl 1891;F 18 1909
VtRC 1850-54;56-1920

Rutland daily HERALD. d Ap 29 1861+
S 1 1877-85? Rutland daily herald and globe
pub 1861+
DLC Ap 22 1865;O 10-22,N 1,6,19-20 1867;My 13-14 1868;O 6 1870;86-88;98+
MWA Jl 29 1863:Ap 9 1868;O 11 1870;S 5 1871;F 27,D 27 1872:Ja 8 1873;Ja 15 1874;Ja 14,Jl 23 1875;Mr 29 1876;Ag 26 1878;Mr 5-7 1881;Ap 28 1884
N S 26 1862;Jl 7 1869;Je 25 1870;F 27,Mr 16 1872;O 6 1874;N 18 1875;N 13 1880
NhD My 4,6,9-13 1861
OClWHi F 19 1869
Vt Je 7,11,13,24,S 3 1861;Ja 1,14,F 11,My 27,S 26,O 28,N 21,D 6,9 1862;Mr 4,Ap 13,17,O 14-15,N 6,D 30 1863,Ja 9,F 5,20,22,24-25,Mr 7, 10-11,17,Je 4,Jl 6,O 24,D 30 1864;Mr 11,Ap 1,3-6,20,29,My 13,Jl 6,Ag 24,S 7,N 21 1865;F 22,27,Ap 2,4,16,18,23,My 8 1866;O 9-10,16,28,D 26 1867;My 19,Je 6,Jl 6,Ag 12,17,19,22,O 13, 19-20,22,23 1868;70-[72]My 6,24,26,Jl 24,O 8, 17 1873;F 11,Je 29,Jl 20,Ag 4,20,S 3 1874;Ja 5,Ap 15,My 17,31,Je 11,Ag 16,S 29,D 31 1875; F 1,11,Mr 2,17,30,Ap 1,Jl 19,22,S 26-27,D 28 1876;Mr 14,17,20,22,26,28-29,Je 8,Ag 14,D 6 1877;Ap 24-25 1878;Ja 14,Ap 16,S 4,8 1880; Mr 2,D 13 1882;Ap 19,My 21,Jl 20,O 11 1883;F 13,Mr 1,17,My 1,Je 2,4,7,D 17 1884;Ja 24, Ap 3,9,20,Jl 4,N 28,D 19,30-31 1885;Ja 9,18, 21,26-27,Mr 22 1886;My 9,19,21,25,Je 8,Jl 21, 23,27,Ag 14,16-17 1888[Ja-F 1889]
VtMiS Ap 4 1863[82-83]Je-Jl 1884;Ap 1885;Je, S,D 1886;F,Je-Jl 1887;My,Ag,O-D 1888[Je, Ag-O 1889]1904-05;S 1906-Ja 10 1912
VtU Ag 3 1867;Ja 21 1928+
WHi D 8 1894

Rutland INDEPENDENT. w?
Vt Ja 31,Ap 18,My 30,Jl 4,Ag 15,S 12,O 31,D 13,26 1849;D 30 1853

Rutland INDEPENDENT. w Jl 4 1866-My 1 1873‖
1866-Je 1868? as Rutland county independent. Merged with Rutland weekly globe
Suspended from Jl 4-21 1866
MWA D 1 1866;S 16 1871
Vt 1866-[68]-73
VtRC 1868-Jl 9 1870;Jl 22 1871-73

Rutland LEADER. w S 28 1877-S 1 1879‖
Followed by Rutland weekly times
MH S 28 1877
NN N 2-16,29-D 14 1877;Ja 25 1878
Vt D 7 1877

Rutland NEWS. w
Vt Mr 18 1822

Rutland evening NEWS. d F 1899-1927‖?
1899-1904? as Rutland daily news
VtMiS Ap 14 1899;Ag 30 1902;F 2 1903;Ag 15 1904
VtU [D 1924-27]

Rutland Sunday REVIEW. w Ap 21 1878-85‖?
1878 as Burlington Sunday review; 1878-79 Burlington Saturday night review; 1879-80? Saturday evening review
1878-80? pub in Burlington; 1881-85? dated in Burlington and Rutland
Vt [1878-79]F 1,22 1885

Rutland evening REVIEW. d 1878-86‖
1878-79 as Rutland evening review; 1880? Review-inquirer. Followed by Rutland evening telegram
Vt Ja 14 1880;N 24 1882;Jl 20 1883;Je 8,Ag 20,S 1,D 29 1885
VtMiS Ap 28 1882

RUTLAND county democrat.
Vt Ag 27 1851

RUTLAND county herald. *See* Rutland herald

RUTLAND county independent. *See* Rutland independent 1866-73

RUTLAND county record. w
Vt Ag 13 1887;F 4-18,Mr-Ap 14,My 26 1888

Rutland evening TELEGRAM. D 1886-91‖
Follows Rutland evening review.
Merged with Rutland daily herald
Vt Je 30 1887;D 24 1888;Jl 28 1890
VtMiS F 5 1887

Rutland weekly TIMES. w O? 1879‖?
Follows Rutland leader

Rutland VERMONT herald. *See* Rutland herald

VERMONT star. w Ag 22 1849-50‖
Ag-D 5 1849 pub in Ludlow
Vt N 14 1849
VtMiM S 26 1849

VERMONT union whig. *See under* Brandon

ST. ALBANS

St. Albans daily ADVERTISER. d 1878-80‖
United with St. Albans daily messenger to form Messenger and advertiser, later St. Albans daily messenger
MB Je 11 1878-79

AMERICAN repertory. *See* Repertory

L'AVENIR national. *See under* Troy, N.Y.

St. Albans DEMOCRAT. w
Vt N 17 1852

DEMOCRAT. w 1858-
DLC N 22 1859;Ja 31-F 7,Je 5,O 9-16,N 23, D 14 1860;Ja 18-25;F 22,Mr 1,15-Ap 5,My 10-17,Je 14-Jl 5,19,Ag 2,16 1861
Vt [1859-61]

FRANKLIN journal. w Je 13? 1833-
MWA D 19 1833
NNHi D 17 1835

FRANKLIN messenger. *See* St. Albans weekly messenger

St. Albans weekly MESSENGER. w D 14 1837+
1837-42? as Franklin messenger; 1870-73? St. Albans messenger and transcript; 1881-91? Messenger and advertiser
DLC Ap 3,My 15,N 27 1844;45-46;F 21,Mr 6, Ap 3,Jl 17 1856;Ag 3-18,N 10 1859;O 4-11, 25,D 6,27 1860;Ja 24-31,Ap 25,My 9,23-30, Jl 4,18-25 1861;N 17,D 22-29 1865;Ja 19,F 9, Mr 2,16,30,Ap 13-20,My 11,25,Je 8,22-Jl 13, Ag 10,24 1866;F 5,19 1869;Je 17 1870;85-87
ICHi Mr 7 1865
MWA D 28 1837-Ja 4,F 1,22,Mr 8-Ap 19 1838;Mr 4 1846;S 30 1870
NNHi [O 18 1838-F 7 1839]
NhD D 6 1843;O 11 1849
PPL N 28 1850
Vt F 8-15 1838;My 9,S 4,18 1839;Mr 23,Je 1 1842;49;Jl 18 1850;Ag 26,D 30 1852-D 1 1853; N 16 1854[55-92]1917;20-25

St. Albans daily MESSENGER. d 1861+
1861-63 as St. Albans daily telegraph; 1881-91? Messenger and advertiser
DLC [Ja-Je 1869;F-D 1870]
MWA F 18 1915-16;N 4 1927
NhD S 7 1878
Vt [1861-1912]-[27]+
VtMiS My 22 1888;S 15 1891;Ja 2 1901;Je 25 1903;N 14 1904;Ag-D 1906
VtSa [1862]Je 12-S 14 1863;93;N 4-D 7 1927
VtU S 11 1900;Je 1917+

Le PROTECTEUR Canadien. w 1868-71‖
Followed by L'Avenir national (Troy, N.Y.)
In French
MWA Jl 27 1871

REPERTORY. w O 2 1821-
1821-26? as American repertory
1821? pub in Burlington
CSmH S 16 1830
CtY Ap 11 1833
DLC O 9,D 4 1823;Mr 2,Jl 20,Ag 24-31,S 21,N 2 1826;Ap 26,Jl 12,Ag 23,S 13,O 4,D 6 1827; Ja 7,Mr 6,My 1,15,Ag 14,28,O 2 1828;Ja 1, F 12,Mr 26,Jl 9-30,S 3,24 1829;Ja 15 1835
ICN N 17 1831
MSaE Ag 28 1823
MWA D 4 1821;D 27 1827;F 19 1829;Je 19 (extra)1832
Vt Ja 31 1823;Ag 2 1832;Ja 1 1835
VtBr D 9 1830;Je 14 1832

St. Albans daily TELEGRAPH. *See* St. Albans daily messenger

VERMONT republican. w Jl 1839-
DLC S 10 1839
NNHi Jl 16 1847
P-M S 14 1841
Vt [1841-47]

VERMONT transcript. w Mr 18 1864-76‖
United with St. Albans weekly messenger to form St. Albans messenger and transcript, later St. Albans weekly messenger?
DLC 1864-Mr 10 1865;Ja 26 1866
OClWHi S 14 1866
Vt Mr 18 1864

ST. JOHNSBURY

St. Johnsbury CALEDONIAN. w Ag 8 1837-1920‖?
1837-66? as Caledonian
DLC N 13 1852[67-68]-70
MB Ag 14 1884-90
MBAt Jl 17 1852-Je 1858
MWA Jl 28 1840;Jl 3 1858;Mr 12,O 8 1859;Mr 20 1863;My 20,Je 17,Ag 5 1864;S 4 1874
NNHi [Je 1838-41]-N 1842;S 2 1844;Jl 11 1846; N 6 1852;D 9 1854
NhD S 3 1839;Jl 21,Ag 11,D 29 1840;Ja 12 1841;Mr 13,N 27,D 25 1847[48]D 17-24 1885; Ja 7 1886[89-93]My 17 1899;O 31 1906
NjR D 17 1891
OClWHi O 14 1864-67
OHi My 31-Jl 5 1905
Vt [1844]Ja 6,My 19,Je 2,O 25,D 27 1845; Ja 3,F 7,21,D 26 1846;Ja 2,D 25 1847-54;O 22-1859;N 18 1864;S 8 1865;Ag 31 1866;74-76; 82;86;1911;13;15[16]
VtSj complete
VtU Jl 13,N 9 1841

Tri-weekly CALEDONIAN. tw My-Je 17 1861‖
NNHi Je 10-12 1861
OClWHi Je 10-17 1861

Daily CALEDONIAN. d Je 19 1861-
MWA Jl 6 1861
OClWHi Je 19,21-22,24-26,28-29,Jl 2-5,8-12,20-21 1861
Vt Je 22,Jl 2-3,6(extra)20(extra)1861

CALEDONIAN-RECORD. d 1916+
1916-20 as Daily Caledonian
VtSj 1921+
—w ed *See* St. Johnsbury republican

FARMERS herald. w Jl 8 1828-Je 27 1832‖
Followed by Weekly messenger, and Connecticut and Passumpsic River Valley advertiser
MBAt S 9 1828
MWA Jl 15 1828;N 10 1830
Vt [1828-32]
VtSj complete

FRIEND. w Jl 22 1829-Ja 6 1830‖
Vt Ag-S 16,O 14-28,N 11,D 2,16 1829
VtSj complete

St. Johnsbury INDEX. w N 28 1879-84‖?
NhD N 28 1879;Ja 9,My 7,28 1880

Weekly MESSENGER and Connecticut and Passumpsic River Valley advertiser. w Jl 10 1832-O 1833‖
Follows Farmers herald
CSmH O 23 1832
MWA Je 18 1833
NhD O 9 1832;Jl 23,S 3 1833
OClWHi S 11 1832
Vt [1832-33]

St. Johnsbury REPUBLICAN. w Mr 26 1885+
NhD My 1 1890
Vt [1885-92]
VtLW 1885-Mr 1892
VtSj 1918;21+
VtU My 16 1889;My 22,Je 12 1890;S 18,N 6,D 1 1895;Ja 22,Mr 4 1896;Mr 2 1898;My 23, N 28 1900
—d ed *See* Caledonian-record

St. Johnsbury TIMES. w 1869-72‖?
Vt D 24 1869

VERMONT (*Continued*)

ST. JOHNSBURY—*Continued*

VERMONT chronicle. w Ap 14 1826-99||? 1826-O 3 1828 pub in Bellows Falls; O 10 1828-74 in Windsor; 1874-95? in Montpelier
CSmH Ag 13 1830
CoD N 13-D 1829
CtY Je 29,Jl 7,20 1832;My 9-Ag 22 1838;Ja 12 1842-S 18 1855
DLC Je 2 1826;27[28-29]-[39]-[47-50]-[52]F 27 1885-F 19 1886
MB S 25-O 2 1839;43[45-47;50-51]My 18 1852
MBC 1826-[73-74]-Ag 2 1895
MH [1827-88]
MWA 1825-[81-82]-Mr 9,N 23 1883;84-92;Ja 12 1894
MiU-C Je-Jl 11 1828[32-33;35-38;40-46]77-80
NN D 22 1832;D 22 1836;Mr 5 1839;My 6 1840
NNHi Mr 1827-35;Ap 30-Je,Ag 6 1850
NcD O 10 1828;Jl 8,S 2,23-30 1831[32-34]-[36-38]My 29 1839[40-41]-[45-46;48]-[50-51]-[54]-[57-60]-[62-64]Je 3,Jl 15 1865;F 10,Ap 28 1866 [67]Jl 24 Ag 14 1869;My 7,Jl 2,D 3 1870;F 11,Ap 15 1871;N 14,D 26 1874[75]-[77-78]-80; Mr 18,D 15 1882[87]Je 28 1889;O 10,D 12-19 1890
NhD 1826-63
PPL O 25 1850
Vt 1826-28;Ja 8,F 19,Mr 26,Ap 30 1830;Ja 5,9, N 16,D 23 1831[32-34]Ap 30,My 21,Jl 23 1835 [36-37]Ag 1,N 28 1838;Ag 13 1850;My 15 1869; 97
VtBr 1826-Ap 13,D 7 1827[28;42-43]
VtMiM [1826-65;75-Ap 1898]
VtWi 1845-52
VtWoC 1850-52
WHi My 14,O 22 1835;Ja 21,F 4 1836

SOMERSWORTH

GREAT FALLS transcript. w 1844-
1844-45? as Strafford transcript and Great Falls advertiser; 1846-49? Great Falls transcript and Strafford and York advertiser
DLC Mr 29 1850
NhHi D 13,27 1845[My 29 1847-48]-F 15 1851

STRAFFORD transcript and Great Falls advertiser. *See* Great Falls transcript

SOUTH LONDONDERRY

Londonderry **SIFTER.** w 1883-1923||?
VtSlM 1885-98

SOUTH ROYALTON

VERMONT advocate. *See* Vermont advocate and state paper (Chelsea)

VERMONT journal. w 1871?+
VtSr 1871-73

SPRINGFIELD

Springfield **POST.** w 1873-75||?
Vt 1874-Je 4 1875

RECORD of the times. w N 11? 1833-
DLC F 4-11 1834
MWA Ap 1 1834
Vt Mr 14 1835

Springfield **REPORTER.** w Ja 4 1878+
NN Je 28 1889
NhD Mr 8 1889
Vt Je 28 1878;1910+
VtS 1878-87;89+
VtSr 1878+

Springfield **TELEGRAPH.** w 1853-
DHU-M Ja 20 1854
Vt S 30 1853

VERMONT record and farmer. *See under* Brattleboro

SWANTON

AMERICAN journal. w Mr 10 1855-
MWA 1855-Ap 3 1857
Vt Ag 17 1855

Swanton **COURIER.** w Mr 10 1877+
pub 1887-[1921]

FRANKLIN county herald. w 1852-
1852 as Swanton herald?
Vt N 20 1852;D 31 1853;Ap 18 1862

Swanton **HERALD.** *See* Franklin county herald

NORTH AMERICAN. w Ap 11 1839-41||
DLC Ap 18 1839-My 1840
MB [1839-Ag 12 1841]

VERGENNES

CHAMPLAIN VALLEY record. w O 25 1878-79||?
Vt N 1,21 1878

Vergennes **CITIZEN.** w My 11 1855-
MBAt 1855-D 15 1856
MWA S 25 1857

Vergennes **CITY news.** *See* Enterprise and Vermonter

Vergennes **ENTERPRISE.** w 1900-Ag 1901||?
United with Vergennes Vermonter to form Enterprise and Vermonter
VtMiS [Ja 11-Mr 4 1900]

ENTERPRISE and Vermonter. w Jl 1 1824+
1824-33 as Vermont aurora; 1833-35 Vergennes gazette; 1836 Vergennes palladium and Addison county advertiser; 1837-F 1 1838 Vergennes city news; F 8 1838-S 15 1901 Vergennes Vermonter (Je 15 1854-My 11 1855 Vermont independent; My 18 1855-O 2 1860 Vermonter and citizen; O 9 1860-N 21 1862 Vermonter)
pub 1901+
CSmH Jl 1 1830
Ct [1827;36]
CtY My 19 1825;Ag 6,21 1828
DHU-M Je 24 1892
DLC Jl 1-15,29-S 2,23,N 4 1824;D 1 1825;Mr 9 1826;My 3, 24-31 1827;Ap 24,My 15,Je 19, N 6 1828;Ja 29,Ap 30, Je 18,Jl 16,Ag 13,S 3,O 1,29,N 19-26 1829;Ja 7 1830;Ap 19 1838;D 2 1840;Jl 27 1842;O 22 1845
ICU Ag 25-S 1 1825
MBAt D 4 1828
MWA Jl 15,S 9,23-O 7,28-D 1824[Ja 13-Je 23] S 22 1825;My 11 1826;Mr 8 1827;Ag 29 1838; My 15 1839-My 11 1842;Ja 12,My 17,Jl 5 1848;Ja 10,Mr 7,O 23,N 21 1849;F 6,Mr 6 1850;Ap 26,My 10 1854;Mr 6 1863
N [Ap 19-N 8 1895]
NBHi Ja 26 1826
NN F 8 1838-Ja 1839
NNHi Ja 13 1831;F 8 1838-Ag 14 1839;Ap 12 (extra)1838
NcD S 2 1824;Ja 27,Ap 7-14 1825
NhD D 2,30 1840;Jl 16 1845
Vt [1824-31] Mr 22 1838;Je 14 1843;My 10 1848;Mr 19,My 21,Je 11-18 1851;Jl 6 1855; Mr 7 1856;Ja 16 1857;Ap 8-15 1859;Ag 19 1864;Ja 23 1866;My 5,S 22 1871;F 4,My 5 1876;D 13 1878;S 8-D 1904;07-08
VtMiC Je 15 1854+
VtMiS 1842-43;65-78;My 5 1882;Ag 19 1892; 97-[1904-08]
VtU [1824]-[31-34;36-37]F 8 1838-Jl 10 1839; 1930-Ja 1 1932
VtV [1824]-[31-34;36-38]-[42-43;49-50;52-55]-[62-76]83-85;87-97;1908+

Vergennes **GAZETTE.** *See* Enterprise and Vermonter

Vergennes **INDEPENDENT.** w Je 16? 1854-Ap 19 1855||
MBAt D 8 1854-55
P-M N 17 1854

Vergennes **PALLADIUM and Addison county advertiser.** *See* Enterprise and Vermonter

VERMONT aurora. *See* Enterprise and Vermonter

VERMONT independent. *See* Enterprise and Vermonter

Vergennes **VERMONTER.** *See* Enterprise and Vermonter

WALLINGFORD

Wallingford **STANDARD.** w Mr 10 1876-78||?
1876-S 21 1877 as Wallingford standard and Rutland county advertiser
MWA 1876-Ag 30 1878
NN Ag 25 1876-N 1877;Ja 17 1878
NcD F 23,Mr 9 1877
VtMiS Je 18 1878

WATERBURY

INDUSTRIAL excelsior.
Vt Ja 11 1851

Waterbury **RECORD.** w Ap 1884+
pub 1884+
Vt S 14 1903;D 1920+
VtW 1933+

WELLS RIVER

RIVERSIDE. w 1878-80||?
NhD Ja 11,Mr 15,Je 21 1879;Ja 17-24,F 7,Je 19 1880

WEST CHARLESTON

NORTH union. w Je 10 1854-
MBAt 1854-D 5 1856
P-M My 5 1855

WEST RANDOLPH

GREEN MOUNTAIN aegis. 1851-
Vt D 31 1851;F 4,18,Jl 1,Ag 25,N 17 1852

GREEN MOUNTAIN herald. w
Vt Ja 26-F 16,Mr 16,O 12-26,D 28 1853;F 8,Ap 19,Je 7 1854

ORANGE county eagle. w 1865-73||?
Vt Mr 13 1873

VERMONT journal. w -1883||?
DLC Mr 18 1871;Ja 4 1873

WHITE RIVER JUNCTION

L'INFORMATORE del Vermont, New Hampshire, e Maine. w Ap 12 1930+
In English and Italian
NhD 1930+
Vt 1930+

LANDMARK. w Mr 18 1882+
pub 1882-1900;1923+
NhD Je 14 1884
Vt [1882-88]
VtWoC 1925+

REPUBLICAN observer. w 1878-80||?
NhD F 9 1878
Vt Mr 2 1878;Ja 31 1879;Mr 5 1880

WILMINGTON

DEERFIELD VALLEY times. w 1888+
pub [1923+]

GREEN MOUNTAIN eagle and even fellow's gazette. w F 9 1850-F 13 1851||
MWA F 9 1850
VtWil [1850-51]
WHi complete

WINDSOR

AURORA of the valley. *See* Aurora and cultivator (Newbury)

CITIZEN soldier. w Jl 22 1840-Jl 30 1841||
1840-F 3? 1841 pub in Norwich
NNH complete
NhD complete
Vt [1840-41]
VtWi 1840

DEMOCRATIC statesman. *See* Windsor statesman

SPIRIT of seventy-six. w O 22 1835-37||
Ct Jl 21 1836
MWA D 31 1835;Ap 7-14 1836;Jl 20-O 5 1837
Vt O 22 1835;D 8 1836
VtWi F-N 1836;Ag 31 1837

SPOONER'S Vermont journal. *See* Vermont journal

Windsor **STATESMAN.** w Ja 1833-40||
1833-O? 1835 as Statesman and Jackson republican; N? 1835-O? 1836 Democratic statesman
Ct [1833-38]
DLC O 1 1835;Jl 19,Ag 2-9 1838
MWA Mr 27 1834;D 3 1835;Ag 25-S 15,29,O 13-27,N 21,D 12-19 1836;Ja 25,Mr 8-Ap 5,19, My 17,31-Je 14,28,Jl 12-Ag 23,S 4,8(extra)13 1837-Ja 3,Ap 5,Je 28,Ag 2,O 12(extra)1838;Ap 18 1839
MiU-C S 29 1836
NhD O 25 1838
Vt O 10 1833;D 6 1838;Ja 17 1839

VALLEY farmer. *See* Vermont journal

VERMONT chronicle. *See under* St. Johnsbury

VERMONT cultivator. *See* Aurora and cultivator (Newbury)

***VERMONT journal.** w Ag 7 1783+
1783-Mr 13 1792 as Vermont journal and the universal advertiser; Mr 20 1792-Ag 3 1818 Spooner's Vermont journal; Ag 8 1829-D 28 1834 Vermont republican and journal, Windham, Windsor and Orange county advertiser; Ja 9 1835-Ag 18 1836? Vermont republican and courier (also dated in Woodstock) 1868?-69? Valley farmer
pub 1909+
CSmH Jl 31 1830
CtY Jl 7 1836
DLC My 5,26 1823;O 25,N 22 1824;Jl 15 1826; Ap 23,N 10,24 1827[28-29]Ja 2-9,D 25 1830;O 27 1832;Je 20 1844;O 12,D 21-28 1849;51-S 2 1853;O 29,N 19 1859;Jl 20 1861-N 3 1866;68-S 1869
ICHi 1858-60
MBAt F 13-20 1830;Je 24 1853-Je 12 1857
MSaE Je 9 1823
MWA 1821-24;Ja 27,Mr 7,Jl-S 19,O 10-N 14,28 1825-F 17,My 19,Je 9-16,S 22,N 3 1827;Ap 5, My 10,24,Ag 9 1828-32;N 1 1833;O 9 1834;35-Ag 18 1836;Je 20 1844-Ja 3 1846;Ag 6 1864;S 14,O 5,19,D 28 1867-Ja 11 1868;F 15 1873
MiU-C [1821;25;34-35]Jl 25 1844
NNHi Mr 15 1873;N 18 1876
NhD Mr 26 1821;Ja 28 1822;N 29 1843[61-63]F 13,S 17,O 15,N 12 1864;Mr 11,Ap 15-22,O 7 1865;Ag 17-31 1867;F 1 1868;Jl 17 1869;71-76; 82-96;98-1909
OClWHi Ag 14 1835
Vt Ja 16,30,Je 19,S 11,25,O 9,N 20-27 1835[36] O 29,D 19 1844;My 22,Je 1847-[51]Ag 26,D 16 1853;Ja 7,F 3,Je 9,Ag 25 1854[57-60] 61; Mr 1,Ap 19 1862;Mr 21,Jl 4,Ag 8,S 5,O 17-24,N 21,D 12-19 1863;64[65]-[67]Ja 25,D 19 1868;Ap 10-24 1869;Ap 30 1870;71-72;74;76-Ja 1878;Ja 1879[80;83-85;87-89]95-1902;Jl 18 1925
VtBr 1869-71
VtNU 1823-25
VtSj 1871-73
VtU 1830-31
VtWi Ag 9 1828-Ag 1,D 1829-Je 1 1835;49;Je 1851-Je 1854;Je 1855-[Jl-D 1861]-[Ag-D 1862]-[Ja-Je 1864]+
VtWoC Je 24 1853-54;57+
WHi 1821

***VERMONT republican and American yeoman; Windham, Windsor and Orange county advertiser.** w Ja 2 1809-Ag 1 1829||
1809-F 9 1818 as Vermont republican; F 16 1818-26? Vermont republican and American yeoman. United with Vermont journal to form Vermont republican and journal, Windham, Windsor and Orange county advertiser, later Vermont journal
Ct [1826-27]
DLC 1821-29
ICHi Ap 24 1826
MBAt Je 24,D 23 1826
MWA Ja 22,O 22,D 10,12(extra)24 1821;F 11, 25,Ap 22-D 1822;O 6 1823;Ja 19,Ap 26,Ag 16,S 20 1824;F 28 1825;Mr 27,Je 24 1826;N 24 1827
N My 26 1827
VtBr [1822-23]
VtWi 1821-D 9 1822;D 1823-29

VERMONT republican and courier. *See* Vermont journal

VERMONT republican and journal. *See* Vermont journal

VERMONT (*Continued*)

WINDSOR—*Continued*

VERMONT times. w Je 21 1839-My 1841||
DLC 1839-My 21 1841
ICHi D 18 1840
MWA 1840-My 21 1841
NhD Ja 8 1841
Vt Ap 3 1840

WOODSTOCK

Woodstock AGE. *See* Spirit of the age

AMERICAN whig. w Ja 6 1830-36||
Follows Vermont luminary (East Randolph). 1830 as American whig, Vermont luminary and equal rights
CSmH My 19 1830
DLC Mr 24,Je 16,Jl 7 1830;Je 22,O 5 1832
ICHi My 5 1830
MWA 1830;Ag 6,S 24,O 15,D 17 1831;F 18 1832;Mr 1-8,Ag 30-S 6,N 29-D 6 1833;F 21,Jl 4 1834;Je 12,Ag 7,O 8 1835
N O 25 1833
NcD Jl 14 1830
NhD O 31-N 7 1834
NhK Je 22 1832
Vt Ja 3 1831;Ja 14 1832;Je 28 1833;D 12-26 1834
VtBr [Je 1832-33]F 21,Je 27 1834

CONSTITUTION. w Jl 28 1836-
MWA Ag 18,S 1 1836
MiU-C S 1 1836

COON hunter. w Jl 6-N? 1844||
MWA O 12 1844
MoSM S 14 1844

GREEN MOUNTAIN farmer. w Ap 11? 1855?-
MBAt Mr 14 1856-F 27 1857
NhD Ap 11-18 1856

HENRY CLAY and advocate of the American system. *See* Vermont courier

Woodstock MERCURY and Windsor county advertiser. w Ap 6 1837-Mr 8 1855||
1837-Mr 1849 as Vermont mercury;Ap 1849-53 Woodstock mercury
CtY Mr 3-10,Ap 14 1843
DLC Ja 5 1838;My 21,Je 25 1841;Ap 19,Ag 2 1844;Je 13 1845
GAtCo Je 12 1840
MWA 1837-Mr 19 1847;Mr 24 1848-Mr 16 1849; Ja 6,Ap 21 1853
MiU-C [1842-43]
NNHi [My-D 1838]-F 8 1839;N 4 1852
NhD F 11 1840;F 11,Mr 11,Je 17 1842;Je 24-Jl 1,Ag 4,O 28 1843;D 6 1844;Mr 17 1853
Vt [1837-44]Ap 4,D 5 1845;Ap 3,Jl 3,24,N 20 1846[47]Mr 17,Je 16,Jl 17 1848;Ja 12,Ag 10 1849;Mr 4,18,Jl 29,N 25 1852;Mr 17,My 12,D 15 1853
VtWo complete
VtWoC Mr 20 1851-53

NORTHERN farmer. w Ap 6 1855-
MBAt 1855-Mr 7 1856
Vt O 5,N 30 1855;F 15-29 1856

*Woodstock OBSERVER and Windsor and Orange county gazette. w Ja 11 1820-33||
1820-Ja 1823 as Woodstock observer
Ct [1831]
DLC Mr 30,Ap 13-20,Je 1-8,O 26 1824;Ja 10 1826;Ap 24-My 1,D 25 1827[28-29]
ICHi D 30 1823
InI N 16 1824
MBAt Ag 5 1828
MSaE My 27 1823
MWA Ja 2,F 20-27,Ap 20-24,My 1-8,22,N 20-D 18 1821[22-23]Ja 20-27 1824;Ja 24-Ag 1 1826;F 6,S 25,N 27,D 11 1827;Ja-Ap 15,My 13,D 20 1828;29-My 10[24-N 15]1831;Mr 27-Je 5 1832
MiU-C Mr 26 1822[27;30-31]
NNHi Je 20 1826
NhD 1824-25
P-M F 22 1830
Vt F 4 1823;Ag 17 1824;O 25 1825;N 27 1827; O 21 1828;S 15 1829;Ag 31 1830;Ja 31 1832
VtWo 1821-23;27-[29-32]

OTTA-QUECHEE post. *See* Woodstock post

Woodstock POST. w S 15 1871-Je 4 1875||
1871-Ag 1872 as Otta-Quechee post
NhD 1871-S 6 1872
Vt [1871-75]

PULSE of the people. w Jl 25-O 24 1840||
MWA Jl 25,Ag 8-O 1840
Vt Ag 8 1840

SPIRIT of the age. w My 8 1840-Jl 1913||
1844? as Woodstock age. Followed by Elm tree monthly (not in this list)
DLC My 29 1840;N 30 1843;Mr 14,D 5 1844;S 25 1845;Ja 13 1848-Ja 11,My 17,Je 14-28 1849
MSaE N 4 1842
MWA My 21,O 1 1841;F 18,S 2 1842;S 26 1844;Mr 22 1860;D 19 1866
MnHi Ja 22 1841
NNHi Ja 3 1850;Ap 17 1873
NhD D 9 1842;Ag 17 1843;63-90
NhM F 1842
Vt D 25 1840;Mr 21,N 28 1844;Mr 27,Ag 28 1845;D 15 1853;D 13 1855;F 24,S 8 1859;Ap 14,S 15 1875;Ja 12 1876;Ag 6-13,S 17 1879;Je 30,S 1-8 1880;Ag 4 1884;Jl 15,D 15 1885;F 10,My 19,Ag 25 1886;Mr 2 1887;Ap 16 1895;F 19 1910
VtWo 1896-1913
VtWoC 1850-58;68-86

VERMONT courier. w S 4 1830-Ag 24 1837||
1830-Ag 26 1831 as Henry Clay and advocate of the American system; S 2 1831-N 8 1833 Vermont courier and farmers, manufacturers and merchants advocate (title varies slightly) Merged with Vermont mercury, later Woodstock mercury For 1835-Ag 18 1836 *See* Vermont journal (Windsor)
CSmH S 4 1830
DLC D 31 1830;Ja 28 1831
MWA 1830-[S 1831-Jl 6]Ag 1832-37
MiU-C D 18 1830[32-33;37]
P-M O 17 1833
Vt D 25 1830;Ja 28,My 20 1831;Jl 12 1833;My 9,Je 20-27,Ag 1,S 12,N 21 1834
VtWo S 1831-Ag 1832;Ja 25 1833-D 19 1834; Ja 9 1835-Ag 10 1837

VERMONT mercury. *See* Woodstock mercury and Windsor county advertiser

VERMONT republican and courier. *See* Vermont journal (Windsor)

VERMONT standard. w Ap 29 1853+
1853-Jl 26 1860 as Vermont temperance standard
DLC Mr 4 1846
MWA N 19 1845;N 17 1846-F 1,Mr 7 1848;Jl 8,29,S 30,N 25,D 23 1859;Ja 27,F 17,Mr 16, 30 1860;Jl 4,18,Ag 22 1862;Ap 7 1865;F 29 1866;Ja 16-23,F 6-13,27 1868;F 20 1873;O 19 1876;Je 13 1878;Ja 29 1879
NhD N 18 1853;Je 17,Jl 12-26,S-N,D 9 1860-79;Ja 9-23 1888
NjN Ag 6 1868
Vt Mr 31 1854;F 16,Jl 27,S 11,N 23,D 14 1855; My 2,Ag 22,D 26 1856;D 10 1858;S 28-O 5, D 14,28 1860;Ap 19,S 6,N 15 1861[62]-Ja 1, 22,F 5 1864;F 3 1865;Ja 25,N 11 1866;F 6,Je 16,30,D 24 1868;S 15 1870;Je 22,O 5 1871;My 30,Jl 18,Ag 29,S 12 1872;Mr 27 1873;F 19,My 28,Ag 6,S 10,24-O 1,22-29,D 10 1874[75]My 16 1878;Ap 8,S 23 1880[81-82]Jl 16 1885;Ja 21 1886;Ja 20,F 24 1887;Mr 26 1891;Jl 9 1896
VtMiM [1853-Jl 1855]
VtWo 1853+
VtWoC Ap 24 1857+

VERMONT temperance standard. *See* Vermont standard

WHIG advocate. w Je 22-S 19 1842||
MWA complete
NhD S 19 1842
Vt Jl 4 1842

WORKINGMAN'S gazette and journal of useful knowledge. w S 23 1830-Ag 1831||?
1830-Mr 29 1831 as Workingman's gazette. United with Henry Clay and advocate of the American system to form Vermont courier and farmers, manufacturers and merchants advocate, later Vermont courier
Vt [1830-31]
VtWo 1830

VIRGIN ISLANDS

To Mr 31 1917 as Danish West Indies

CHARLOTTE AMALIE. *See* SAINT THOMAS

CHRISTIANSTAED

DANSK vestindisk regierings avis. *See* St. Croix avis

HERALD. d 1915-24||?
DLC Ap 2 1917-O 3 1921;Mr 15-My 10 1922; Jl 1922-23;Mr-Je 6 1924

OFFICIEL tidende for de dansk-vestindiske besiddelser. Official gazette for the Danish West India possessions. 1852-55||?
In Danish and English
DLC 1852-55

ROYAL Danish-American gazette. sw 1770?-
In English and Danish
CU-B Ag 30,S 13,O 4 1788;Mr 10 1790;S 5 1792; O 29,N 1 1794;F 8-15,Ap 15 1797;Jl 21 1798; Ap 6-13 1799;Je 14-21,N 19 1800
MWA S 11 1776;Je 1 1796

ST. CROIX avis. sw,w 1799+
1821-44? as Dansk vestindisk regierings avis
In English and Danish
CU-B N 5 1802;Mr 23-30,Jl 5-12 1804;F 28,Jl 14-21 1806;F 2-9,23-Mr 2,My 14-21,Jl 13,27-30 1807;Ja-F 1816;F 8-22,Mr 12,26,Je 25 1822; Jl 31 1826;D 17 1827;N 12 1840
CtY Jl 17,21 1845
DLC 1821-24;My 3 1847-66;68-1904
*MWA My 29,Je 26 1823
NN F 12 1835
NNHi Ag 21,25,28 1823

SAINT CROIX gazette. sw F 1801-
In English and Danish
CU-B Ag 15-22,D 12 1801;Je 27-Jl 4,Ag 11-18 1809;Jl 24-31,D 28 1810;Ap 16 1811;F 25,28, Mr 3 1812
MWA O 26,N 2 1810

ST. CROIX tribune. d 1922+
Suspended S 12-15 1928
DLC Ap 1926+

FREDERICKSTED

WEST END news. d 1912+
DLC Jl 9,19,24-27,29,Ag 6 1926
MWA Jl 26 1926

SAINT THOMAS

To 1920 as Charlotte Amalie

St. Thomas Monday's ADVERTISER. w Ap 30 1810-
MWA O 1-22 1810

BULLETIN. d 1875+
DLC [1877-86]F 2 1900;Jl 17-22,24,27-31 1926
MWA Ap 2 1913;Jl 27 1926;Ap 3 1929
NN Ja 29 1901

EMANCIPATOR. tw 1920+
DLC Jl 3,14-24,Ag 2-23,28 1926
MWA Jl 19,Ag 11 1926

Saint Thomas GAZETTE. w 1809-
DLC Ap 21 1814
MWA Ag 23,O 25 1810

St. Thomas HERALD. sw 1882-
DLC Jl 19 1882-D 29 1884

LIGHTBOURN'S mail notes. d
MWA Mr 1,Ap 2 1913

St. Thomas MAIL notes. d,w 1919+
d 1919-28
DLC Jl 3,10,17-24,27-28 1926;Mr 16,23 1929

Saint Thomas TIDENDE. sw 1818-1918||?
Title varies: Sance Thomas tidende; St. Thomas tidende; etc.
CSmH My 28 1853
CU-B Mr 19-26,D 28 1819
CtY Ag 3 1844;Je 11 1845
DLC 1873-1904
MHi Ja 4 1826;Ap 12 1828;Je 13,23 1832;Je 11 1845;F 27 1889
MWA N 16 1825;S 13,17,24 1825;S 19-N 11 1835;Mr 19 1836;Ap 2 1913
N Mr 13,D 4,21 1833
NNHi N 20 1821;F 15 1822

VIRGINIA

ABINGDON

BANNER. *See* Jacksonian

CITIZEN. w Ag? 1886-98||?
1886-97 as Glade Spring citizen (Glade Spring)
VAbS Ap 1,O 13 1898
VHi Ja 13 1893

Abingdon DEMOCRAT. w F 24 1849-61||
Suspended from Je 7-Ag 28 1852
NcD [Mr 17 1849-D 4 1852]O-D 1855;F 23,Je 7-14,S 20,D 13 1856[Ja 10-N 1857]Jl 15 1859
NcU Ap 9 1859
VAbS F 15,Ap 19,N 29 1851[52-F 12 1853;My 12 1855-D 20 1861]
VU My 5,Je 9,23,Jl 21 1849
VWW O 4 1861
VWn Je 26 1858

JACKSONIAN. w O? 1841-47||
Follows States-rightsman. 1841-42? as Banner
MWA D 17 1842
VAbS Mr 26 1842;Jl 31 1847

JOURNAL-VIRGINIAN. w Ag 6 1897+
1897-Ag 3 1917 as Washington county journal
1897-1905 pub in Glade Spring
pub [1910-17]
NcD [F 14-Jl 10 1908]Ag 3 1917
VU N 22 1918;Mr 7-21,Je 6,Jl 25,D 12 1919;N 10-17 1922;D 25 1925;Ag 3 1928;F 20,Mr 27,My 22-29 1930;Je 20,Jl 11-Ag 8,22 1935
WaPS [1920]D 16 1921;Jl 28 1922;F 8 1924

LITTLE Tennesseean. *See* States-rightsman

PEOPLE'S friend. *See* Abingdon Virginian

VIRGINIA (*Continued*)

ABINGDON—*Continued*

Abingdon SOUTHWEST examiner. w Ap 18 1885-S? 1887||
VAbS 1885-S 2 1887

SOUTHWESTERN Virginian. *See* Abingdon Virginian

Abingdon STANDARD. w S 25? 1876-90||?
Merged with Abingdon Virginian
NcD Ja 3-11,F 8,N 1 1877;Mr 10 1881;Ja 12, Ap 20 1882
VU O 31 1878;Mr 4,D 23 1880;S 3 1884;O 4 1889

STATES-RIGHTSMAN. w N 1840-O 5 1841||?
1840-Ap 10 1841 as Little Tennesseean. Followed by Banner, later Jacksonian
NhD Ja 23 1841
VAbS Ja 2,Mr 27,Ap 3-10,Je 22,O 5 1841

TIMES. *See* Virginia statesman

VIRGINIA republican. w Mr 5 1831-Jl 28 1834||
Followed by Times, later Virginia statesman
Ct Mr 13,Ap 2 1831
DLC O 20 1832
MWA Mr 5 1831
VAbS F 2 1833

VIRGINIA republican. w Je 1906-30||
VAbS [1906-14;17-24]

VIRGINIA statesman. w Ag 2 1834-38||
Follows Virginia republican. Ag 2 1834 as Times
DLC Ag 4,S 20 1834
MWA Ag 25 1838
VAbS Ag 16 1834;Je 20 1835;O 8-22 1836;Jl 1 1837

Abingdon VIRGINIAN. w S 7 1839-Ag 1917||
S-N 2 1839 as People's friend; N 9 1839-46? Southwestern Virginian. United with Washington county journal to form Journal-Virginian
Suspended from D 15 1864-D 1865;My?-S? 1898
CSmH Ja 30 1858
DLC Ja 2 1841;Ap 18,My 16,Ag 8 1862
MWA S 14,O-N,D 14 1839-Ja 4,25-F 1,15-29 1840;O 18 1853;Ja 13 1887;F 26 1904
NNHi Mr 14 1873
NcD [My 15-Ag 1847;S 1854-Ag 1 1857]My 23,Je 27,S 12,N 21 1862;Jl 29 1864;Ap 28 1871; Ap 28 1873;My 9 1879;O 22 1880
OClWHi Ja 14 1876
TKL Mr 20,Ag 7 1863
TxU F 26 1904
VAbS [F 17 1840-D 8 1849;50-57]Ja 13 1860[D 8 1865-1900]F 14 1901-Jl 1905
VHi F 24 1893
VU Mr 25 1870;Jl 2,16,S 3 1880;My 20,Je 17,O 7 1881;F 24,S 1,15 1882;Ja 5 1888;S 29 1893
WHi [O 28 1870-O 6 1871]D 10 1880

WASHINGTON county forum. w Ap 10 1935+
VU Ap 17-Jl 10,24-31 1935

WASHINGTON county journal. *See* Journal-Virginian

ACCOMAC

PENINSULAR enterprise. w Je 30 1881+
pub 1881+
VU 1935+

ALEXANDRIA

Alexandria ADVOCATE. tw Ag 15- 1840||
DLC S 3,N 5 1840

*ALEXANDRIAN: a commercial, agricultural and literary journal. tw N 16 1820-Mr 31 1821||
Merged with Alexandria herald
DLC 1821

Daily COMMERCIAL advertiser. d Ag 2? 1868-
MBAt [Ag-S 1868]

COMMONWEALTH. tw S 30?- 1865||
MBAt O 26 1865

CRIPPLE. (U.S.General Hospital) w O 8? 1864-
CP Ap 15 1865
CtHT F 4 1865
OHi N 19 1864-Ja 14,F-Mr 4,25-Ap 1865

*Alexandria GAZETTE. tw,d Jl 11 1808+
Follows Alexandria daily advertiser (not in this list). Title varies: Alexandria daily gazette, commercial and political; Alexandria gazette and daily advertiser; Alexandria phoenix gazette
Suspended Ag 23-S 8 1814; Je? 1861-My 13 1862
tw S? 1813-Ap 1815; 1822-D 3 1825
pub 1826;Ja-Jl 1828;Ag-S 1831;32-Je 1833;Ap 1835-36;Jl 1837-49;Jl-D 1850;Jl-D 1851;60-66; 1902-04;07;11;15;Jl 1918+
CSmH Je 23 1830;O 11 1851
DLC F 7-8 1821;F 13-27,Mr 1-2,5-8,20,O 1,5, 17,22 1822[23-Ja,Je 1830-My 1861]My 13 1862-Ja 1864;65+
ICHi F 22 1832
ICU N 23 1858;My 14 1859;O 11,N 24,D 1,8, 11,18,22,25 1860;Ja 3,12,19,F 5,9,26,Mr 5,16,19, 21,26,28,Ap 5,9 11,27,My 2,4,7,11,14 1861
MBAt O 1 1828;Ag 5 1865
MHi O 17 1821;Mr 19,22,31 1825;F 25,D 5 1826;Mr 7 1833[Ja-F 1932]
MWA Ap 1831-My 25 1861;My 13 1862-Ja 24 1911;F 22 1928;F 22 1930;F 22 1932
MdHW F 4 1843
MdHi N 27 1863
MiU-C My 25,D 9,12-13 1826;D 8 1827;Jl 4 1828;Je 2,D 9 1831;D 29 1843;Mr 17 1849[Ja-My 24 1861]Ag 20 1868
N Mr 15-My 1825;F 22 1834;Ja 12,Ap 29,My 27,Je 6,Jl 13,27,29,O 7,N 16,D 9,14,18 1837;Ja 11,16,27,Jl 2-3 1838;Mr 25-26 1839;Je 12-13 1840;N 15-16 1842
NNHi Ag 6 1873;Ja-F 1932
NcD My 17-18 1821;Ap 13 1836;My 29-30 1846; Mr 5-6 1847;Mr 9-10 1853;Ja 22 1858[Jl 23-S 14 1860]Ja-Je 1863;S 17 1870;N 23,25 1871;Mr 15,18,Ag 16,S 18 1873;Mr 5,N 27 1875;O 19 1876;Ja 6 1883;F 22-23 1932
NcU My 10,Je 21,S 4,25,O 9,N 13 1845[46]Ja 16 1847
NdHi 1932-Ja 4 1933
NjE Ap 21 1826;S 16 1893;Mr 25 1840;Ja-F 1932
OCHi [Ja 30-Mr 7 1822]O 30 1826;Ag 27 1832; O 29,N 19 1840
OClWHi Ap 18 1822;Ap 22 1824;F 12 1864
PBloHi My 23 1846
PDoHi Jl 21 1826
PPot O 17 1854
TxHuS F 22 1932
V My 25 1859;My 10-11 1861;Ap 30 1867;N 30 1878;Ag 11 1879;1905+
VAA Jl 1898-1920
VAM 1821;23-Je 1824;25-S 1826;27-32;34-37;Jl 1838-Jl 1842;43-59;Je 1869-94;My 5 1862-S 4 1863[Mr-My 21 1864;Ap 21-Je 13 1865;Mr-Ap 1869]-1920
VHH Jl-D 1828
VHi Ap 14 1825;S 15 1858;D 1 1875;D 31 1892; Ja 7 1893;Jl 30 1903
VRB Ag 14 1918
VRC Ja 15,F 25 1861
VU Jl 11 1831;Jl 4 1854;Ag 26 1895;N 4 1902; N 15 1915;Mr 21 1924
WHi Ag 28 1843-49;Ja-F 27 1932
See also Local news

GEORGE WASHINGTON bi-centennial news m O 1930-D 1931||
MWA complete
NdHi complete

*Alexandria HERALD. sw,tw Je 3 1811-N 15 1826||
Merged with United States telegraph (Washington, D.C.)
sw Je-O 1811
DLC 1821-25,Jl 21,Ag 11,22,N 15 1826;Je 15 1828
MWA Jl 18 1821;Je 1822-Je 2,Ag 1,S 1,O 17,N 5 1823;My 20,Je 29 1825
N Ja 10,19,F 11,S 26,O 26,N 11 1825;O 13,31, N 7,15 1826
OCHi Mr 4 1822
OClWHi [F 1821-N 1825]
PP [1821;Ja-N 15 1826]
PPL 1821;Ja 2 1825[Ja-N 1826]
T N 7 1821;Ja 14 1822
V Jl 30 1821[F 15 1822-Ag 20 1824]My 18 1825
WHi Je 6 1821-Jl 2 1824;Je 6 1825-Je 2 1826

HERALD. w Ap 6? 1927-28||?
DLC Je 15 1928

HOME. w Ja 1888-94||
VHi Ja 7 1893

INDEX. *See under* Washington, D.C.

LEADER. *See under* Washington, D.C.

LEADER and clipper. *See* Leader (Washington, D.C.)

LIBERAL citizen. w Je 3 1871-
MH Je 17 1871

LOCAL news. d O 7 1861-F 10 1862||
Replaces Alexandria gazette for this period
DLC O 15,17,19-23,25 1861-62
MWA complete
OClWHi O 7 9-10,14 1861-62

LOTTERY register. m,sm
Title varies: Runnell's lottery register
MWA O 31 1825
MeU Ag 1 1825

NATIONAL watchman. w 1892-97||
VU Jl 27,Ag 17-23,S 28 1894;Ja 18,Je 21-28, Jl 12-Ag 9 1895
WHi Jl 27,Ag 17,S 28 1894;Ja 18 1895

Alexandria daily NEWS. d 1912-Jl 1918||
MWA Ja 10 1913

PENNSYLVANIA fifth. (Camp McDowell) ir Je 10-17 1861||?
MHi Je 10 1861
MWA Je 17 1861
OClWHi Je 10 1861
PHi Je 10 1861
PPGr Je 12 1861

Alexandria PHOENIX gazette. *See* Alexandria gazette

Daily PRESS. d Mr? 1877-
MWA S 22 1877

REPUBLICAN and Alexandria commercial and general advertiser. tw Mr 24- 1829||
DLC Mr 24 1829

RUNNELL'S lottery register. *See* Lottery register

Evening SENTINEL. *See* Evening Virginia sentinel

SIGNS of the times. w Ja? 1833-39||?
GAtCo Jl 27 1838
MWA Ja 15 1839

Daily STATE journal. d O? 1862-S? 1868||
1862-68? as Virginia state journal. Followed by Daily state journal, later Evening journal (Richmond)
CSmH [Ap 15-Jl 21 1864]Ja 24-F 21,23-Mr 1,3-4,7-14,16-Je 2 1865;My 19 1868
DLC F 24,Ap 15(extra)1865
MBAt [Ag 17-D 1865]-Ja 2,5-16 1866
MWA Jl 14,Ag 25 1864
OClWHi Ag 25 1865

Evening SUN. d 1892-93||
MWA N 8 1892;F 10,14 1893
VHi Ja 6 1893

Sunday TIMES. d,w 1894?-1916||?
1894-1903 as Alexandria times
Suspended from 1904-05?
d 1894-1903
MWA D 30 1896;Mr 18,31 1897
VU C 12-13 1899

Daily VIRGINIA chronicle. d F 26 1862-
DLC F 27 1862
OClWHi F 29 1862

VIRGINIA post and national echo. w My 21? 1880-81||
1880-82? as Virginia post
1880? pub in Harrisonburg
NcD Ag 20 1881

VIRGINIA sentinel. tw S 13 1853-61||
DLC S 17 1853;D 4 1855
ICU D 1 1859
NcU Mr 28 1861
V [S 13 1853-S 13 1856]Ja 26,N 29,D 1,13,15, 22 1860;Ja 10,15,Ap 1,16 1861
WHi Ap 18 1854;My 17-18,21-22 1861

Evening VIRGINIA sentinel. d Mr 1 1856-61||
Title varies: Evening sentinel
DLC S 23 1857[58-59]
MWA N 15 1860
V [Mr 3 1857-Mr 2 1858]
VWa Ja 13 1860
WHi Mr 28,Ap 5,Ag 11 1860;Mr 1,5,7,12,14-15, Ap 2-3,11-13,17 1861

VIRGINIA sentinel. w 1856-My 22 1861||?
DLC Ag 9,S 13-27 1860;Ja 24,F 28,Mr 7 1861
NcU Mr 28 1861

VIRGINIA sentinel. d 1871-76||
NcD Ap 17,S 1,10 1873;Ag 27 1874;Ja 16,19,F 17,Je 28 1875
VHi D 1 1874

VIRGINIA sentinel. w 1871-76||
MWA Je 16,O 17 1876
NNHi Ag 28 1873

VIRGINIA state journal. *See* Daily state journal

ALTAVISTA

Altavista JOURNAL. w 1909+
pub [1915-19]+
VLy 1935+
VU Jl 14 1916[18-19]+

TRI-COUNTY democrat. sw Je 24 1924-25||?
VU Je 24,Jl 1-Ag 5,12,19,22 1924

AMHERST

Amherst ENTERPRISE. w 1871-81||
CSmH D 14 1876
MWA Ag 10 1876
NNHi Mr 21 1873
V Jl 17,Ag 7,28,S 4-18 1879
VHi N 14 1873;Je 18 1875

Amherst NEW ERA-PROGRESS. w 1881+
1881-Je 19 1924 as Amherst new era
pub D 28 1922+
VSbC 1935+
VU O-N 14 1907

Amherst PROGRESS. w 1903-24||
United with New era to form Amherst new era-progress
VU Ja 6,F 17,Ap 13,My 11,25-Je,D 22 1904; F 2,Mr 9,23,Ap 6-20,My 4,18-Je 8,22,Jl 13,Ag 17-24 1905;Ja 4,18,F 8,Mr 1,15,Ap 19,My 3,17 1906;S 26,O 10,N 14,D 26 1907;Je 11,Jl 30-Ag 20 1908

VIRGINIA republican. w S 22- 1933||?
VU S-N 18 1933

APPALACHIA

Appalachia INDEPENDENT. w Ja 5 1920+
pub 1920+
VU Jl 12-26 1933;Jl 17-Ag 7,21 1935

APPOMATTOX

SOUTHSIDE Virginian. w 1902-09||
United with Appomattox and Buckingham times to form Times-Virginian
V My 10 1905
VRB Ag 8 1903
VU Ap 30 1908

TIMES-VIRGINIAN. w 1892+
1892-94 as Times; 1894-1909 Appomattox and Buckingham times
pub 1892+
V Ap 12,My 10 1905
VU Ap 30 1908;O 8 1919;Je 9-D 22 1920;Ja-Je 1,15-29 1921[F 15 1923-D 9 1926]S 1 1927;Jl 1935

ARVONIA

JAMES RIVER clarion. *See* Farmer-leader (Farmville)

ASHLAND

Ashland weekly ENTERPRISE. w S 1 1888-94||
VAsH Ag 28 1889
VU N 27 1890

HANOVER and Caroline news. w Ap? 1881-86||?
1881-84 as Hanover news
Suspended from Ag 25- 1882?
VU Ag 25 1882

HANOVER herald. *See* Herald-progress

VIRGINIA (*Continued*)

ASHLAND—*Continued*

HANOVER progress. w D 1913-20||
United with Hanover herald to form Herald-progress
VU Mr 6,N 20 1914;Ja 1 1915;Ag 9 1917;Ap 19 1918

HERALD-PROGRESS. w 1881+
1881-1920 as Hanover herald
pub 1924+
DLC F 1926
V 1922+
VAsR 1923+
VHi Ag 24-S 14 1923
VU Je 23 1911;Jl 12 1912;Jl 1935+

Ashland NEWS. m Ag 1- 1876||
VU Ag 1 1876(photograph)

AUGUR GENERAL HOSPITAL

SOLDIERS journal. F 17 1864-Jl 12 1865||?
MH Ap 26 1865
NNHi F 17-Je 8 1864
OClWHi F 17 1864;Je 7 1865
PSuHi Je 7 1865
VU Jl 12 1865(photograph)
WHi F 17 1864

BANISTER. *See* HALIFAX

BASIC CITY

Basic City ADVANCE. *See* Progress w (Charlottesville)

BEDFORD

To 1890 as Liberty

Bedford BULLETIN. w Ap 12 1895+
Follows Bedford index
pub 1895+
NcD My 16 1918
VRB Ag 1 1918
VU [1895]-Ap 1 1897;Ap 20-D 7,21 1899;1900-Ap 9 1903;Ap 20 1905-[11]-Mr 1916;O,N 8-D 20 1917;18-Mr 1926;Mr 31-Ag,S 8 1927+

Bedford CHRONICLE. *See* Bedford sentinel 1867-84

Bedford DEMOCRAT. w My 22? 1857-61||
VBeD 1857-60

Bedford DEMOCRAT. w Ap 1886+
pub 1886+
NcD My 16 1918
V My 7 1891;Mr 21 1895;Mr 26 1896;Ag 18 1904;My 28 1908;Ja 24 1929+
VHi Ja 12 1893
VU F 2,N 7 1890[F-S 1891]Ja 5,19-F 9,23-S,O 12,26-N 9,23-D 7 1893;94-97;99;1902[03]-Ag 18, S-D 8 1904;Ja 12-Je 1,15-Ag 17,31-S 7,21-N 2,16-D 7 1905[Ja-N 15 1906;07-N 19 1908]

Bedford INDEX. w Ap 1886-95||?
Followed by Bedford bulletin
VU Ap 12 1888;Ag 13 1891

LIBERTY news. w Je 7 1870-73||
United with Bedford sentinel to form Sentinel and news, later Bedford sentinel
NNHi Mr 21 1873

Bedford SENTINEL. w Ag? 1850-61||
CSmH S 11 1868
MWA Ja 16 1857;Ap 5 1861

Bedford SENTINEL. w Ag 9 1867-84||
1867-Ag 28 1868 as Bedford chronicle; 1873-74 Sentinel and news. United with Bedford star to form Bedford star and sentinel
CSmH S 11 1868
MWA F 18 1876
V My 2 1879
VU N 12 1869
WHi Jl 16 1880

Bedford STAR and sentinel. w My 26 1874-87||
1874-84 as Bedford weekly star
MWA Jl 21 1876
NcD O 11 1878
VBeD [1882]

BERKLEY

Berkley daily NEWS. d O? 1890-94||?
VHi F 22 1893

BERRYVILLE

CLARKE courier. w F 19 1869+
Follows Clarke journal
pub 1869-70;73-75;79-81;91-99;1902+
MWA S 14 1876;Je 9 1887
NNHi Ja 9 1873;My 31 1923
NbHi Ja 1 1880
NcD Je 30 1892;Ap 15 1920;Ag 11,S 22,O 20,D 15-22 1921;Ap 6-13,My 18-25,Ag 24,S 28,N 9 1922;F 14,Ag 7,21-28,O 9-16 1924;Je 25,Jl 9, 23-30,D 10 1925;F 18-Mr 11,25,My 6,Ag 5,N 25,D 16 1926;Ja 13-27,F 10,Mr 3,17,Ap 21,Je 23,Ag 4-11,O 6-13,N 3 1927;Mr 15 1928
VHi Ja 5 1893
VU N 15,D 13 1928;Ag 13,27,S 17-O,N 12-D 3,24 1931;D 8 1932;Jl 27,Ag 24,D 7 1933;Jl 11-18,Ag 1-8,22 1935

CLARKE journal. w S? 1856-F? 1869||
1856-58 as Clarke journal and advertiser. Followed by Clarke courier
Suspended from My? 1861-65
NcD My 13 1859
VWn [N 27 1857-My 14,S 17 1858;Mr 18-My 6 1859;Ja-Jl 20]N 23 1860;Mr 8,Ap 1 1861

Berryville CONSERVATOR. w S 13 1859-Mr 12 1862||
The last issue was never completed. The Union troops captured the town and published the First Minnesota on the incompleted issue
DLC Mr 12 1862
IHi Mr 12 1862
MWA Mr 12 1862
MnHi Mr 12 1862
OClWHi Mr 12 1862
PHi Mr 12 1862
PP Mr 12 1862

FIRST Minnesota. Mr 11 1862||
Issued by the First Minnesota regiment as a part of the incompleted issue of the Mr 12 Berryville conservator
A second ed was issued Mr 13? 1862
DLC Mr 11 1862
MSaE Mr 11 1862
MWA Mr 11 1862
MnHi Mr 11,13 1862
NcD Mr 11 1862
NdHi Mr 11 1862
OClWHi Mr 11 1862
VRC Mr 13 1862

HAVERSACK. d Mr 25?-26 1862||?
pub by the 27th regiment, Indiana volunteers on the press of the Berryville conservator
VRC Mr 26 1862

BIG LICK. *See* ROANOKE

BIG STONE GAP

POST. w 1890+
pub 1895+
V D 20 1934+

BLACKS AND WHITES. *See* BLACKSTONE

BLACKSTONE

COURIER-RECORD. w O 30 1890+
1890-Mr 1931 as Blackstone courier
pub 1924+
V N 6-13,D 11 1890;Ja 22,My 7-14,D 17 1891; Ja 21-28,F 18-25,Jl 7,O 27,D 22 1892;Mr 16-23,Ap 27 1893;Jl 5,O 18-25,N 8 1894;My 23 1895
VHi Jl 19 1901
VU O 30-N 20,D 4-11,25 1890;Ja 22,F 5,19-26, Mr 26,Ap 30-My 21,D 3,17 1891;Ja 21-Mr 10, Je 30-Jl 14,O 20-N 3,D 22 1892;Mr 2-23,Ap 27,D 7-21 1893;Mr 1,Jl,O 18-N 15 1894;Ja 3-10,My 9-23 1895;Jl-Ag 9,23 1935

NEW ERA. w 1884-91||
VHi Jl 21 1888

BLAND

To 1924 as Seddon

BLAND county gazette. w My 31? 1877-
ICM Ag 2 1877

Bland MESSENGER. w 1904+
Suspended 1919-21
pub [1928+]
VU Jl 11-Ag 1,22 1935

SOUTH-WEST. w 1877-1903||
VHi Ja 5 1893

BLUEFIELD

To Mr 14 1924 as Graham

POCOHONTAS headlight. *See under* Pocohontas

BOYDTON

EXPOSITOR and southern advocate. *See* Virginia expositor and southern advocate

MECKLENBURG democrat. w 1877-90||
Followed by Mecklenburg news
OClWHi [O 19 1881-Jl 11 1884]

MECKLENBURG news. w 1890-98||
Follows Mecklenburg democrat
VHi Ja 6 1893

MECKLENBURG sentinel. *See* Southside Virginian

MECKLENBURG times. w N 1928+
pub 1928+
VU Je 16 1933;Jl 5-12,26-Ag 2,23 1935

MESSENGER. w 1930-32||
VBoB complete

MIDLAND express. w Ap? 1891-95||?
Negro
VHi Mr 3 1893

Boydton NEWS. w F 6-Je 26 1914||
VU F 13-Mr,Ap 10-My,Je 12,26 1914

ROANOKE VALLEY. w Ag? 1869-78||?
1869-71?;73?-Ap 1874 pub at Clarksville
MWA Ag 11 1876
NNHi Mr 28 1873
OClWHi [S 16 1871-My 4 1872]Mr 18-25,Ap 8,29-My 6,Je 3 1874

SOUTHSIDE Virginian. w 1853-Ap? 1875||
1853-71 as Tobacco plant; 1871-72 Mecklenburg sentinel
1853-69 pub in Clarksville; scattered issues 1873-75 in Christiansville and Chase City
Suspended from 1861-64?
MWA Ja 4 1867
NcD [F 10 1860-O 18 1861]O 13-20,D 8 1869
VFaC N 15,D 13-27 1872[Ja 16 1873-Ap 15 1875]

TOBACCO plant. *See* Southside Virginian

VIRGINIA expositor and southern advocate. w F 23 1835-36||
F-My? 1835 as Expositor and southern advocate
DLC F 23 1835
VHi My 8,D 25 1835-Ja 13,27 1836

BOWLING GREEN

CAROLINE progress. w 1919+
pub S 5 1919+
VF 1935+

CAROLINE sentinel. w Ap? 1883-95||
VU D 24 1890

BRIDGEWATER

Bridgewater ENTERPRISE. *See* Bridgewater journal

Bridgewater JOURNAL. w Jl? 1878-N 1885||
1878-Ag 28 1879 as Bridgewater enterprise
NcD Ag 13,D 17 1880;Je 24,O 21,N 4,18 1881; N 10-17 1882;Ja 12,26,F 23 1883;O 3 1884;Je 19,Jl 10 1885
VU Jl 12 1878;Ag 4 1882
WHi My 28 1879

BRISTOL

Bristol COURIER. w S 8 1870-1907||
DLC O 2 1904
MWA Ag 3 1876
VAbS [S 15 1871-F 16 1872]S 19-26 1888;S 9 1890

Daily COURIER. d S 15 1888-F 1907||
United with Bristol herald to form Bristol herald-courier
Suspended from 1899-1900?
VAbS Je 12,18,Ag 4,9,12,18,20 1891;S 30 1892

Bristol GAZETTE. *See* State line gazette

GOODSON democrat. w My? 1885-86||
VAbS N 20 1885
VU N 20 1885

Bristol HERALD. sw *See* News and herald-courier

Bristol HERALD-COURIER. d 1903+
1903-Ja 1907 as Bristol herald
pub 1907+
TBrK Mr 1928+
TU Jl 17 1931;F 10 1935
VBrS 1934+
VU D 6 1924;Je 14-15,17-20,Jl 12 1934;Jl 10,15 1935

NEWS. w My? 1857-62||
VAbS Je 3-10 1859;Jl 13 1860

Bristol NEWS. w Ag 9 1865-1911||
ICHi S 15-22 1865
MWA Je 2 1874;Jl 11 1876
NNHi Ap 8 1873
NcD O 29 1872;Mr 4 1873;Ja 2,30,F 13 1877; Mr 8 1881
TKL Mr 7 1867
VAbS My 18,S 28 1866;Ap 25,Ag 1867-O 1875 [Ag 22 1876-S 18 1888]Je 18,Ag 1,3,4,7,S 12, 18,O 27-31 1891
VBrH D 1925-Ap 1926
VHi F 25 1893
VU Jl 1 1870;Je 19 1877;O 29 1878;S 26,N 28 1882;Ja 9,F 20,My 15,Je 26,Jl 10,S 18,O 2,N 20 1883;F 5,Ap 8,Jl 1,S 16,O 28 1884;O 27 1885;Ja 4 1887

Evening NEWS. d Mr? 1890-1910||
United with Bristol herald-courier to form News and herald-courier

NEWS and herald-courier. sw 1904-19||
1904-Ja 1907 as Bristol herald; F 1907-10 Bristol herald-courier
pub Ja-Je 1913

NEWS-BULLETIN. d My 1926+
VBrH 1926+
VU Ag 1,3 1935

SOUTHERN advocate. w Mr 27 1862-Mr? 1863||
Followed by Bristol gazette, later State line gazette
VAbS Mr-My,Je 12-S 4,25,O 9,N 6,D 25 1862; Ja 22,F 26,Mr 12 1863

STATE LINE gazette. w Mr? 1863-67||
Follows Southern advocate? 1863-64 as Bristol gazette
DLC F 18,Mr 31,My 19 1864
MWA Mr 24 1864
VAbS Mr 6,Je 22,30,Jl 21-27,Ag 10,S 21-28,N 15-D 19 1866;Ja 9,30-Mr 20 1867

BROADWAY

Broadway ENTERPRISE. *See* Valley voice

VALLEY voice. w Ja 1888-96||?
1888-F? 1895 as Broadway enterprise
NcD Ja 8 1892
VHi F 17 1893

BROOKNEAL

Brookneal SENTINEL. *See* Union star

UNION star. w D 1906+
1906-Ag 1912 as Brookneal sentinel
pub 1931+
VU My 10,Je 14 1907;16-Mr 18,Ap 1,15 1921-30;My 29-S 18,O 1931+

VIRGINIA (*Continued*)

BUCHANAN

Buchanan ADVOCATE and commercial gazette. w S? 183?-36||
VHi D 23 1835
VU F 24 1836

Buchanan BANNER. w 1893-1905||
1893-94? as Botetourt and Buchanan banner
NcU Ja 1?,Mr 30 1895

BOTETOURT and Buchanan banner. *See* Buchanan banner

Buchanan COMMERCIAL journal. w S 20 1839-40||
DLC O 11 1839;D 11 1840

Buchanan DEMOCRAT. w O 1 1880-81||
ICM Ja 21 1881

Buchanan GAZETTE. w O? 1887-89||?
NcU F 2 1888

Buchanan NEWS. w Ap? 1905+
pub [1908-?7]+
VHH 1935—
VU Je 5 1908;S 3,17 1909;F 27-Ag 7,21 1930-F 1932;Jl 11-18,Ag 1-8,22 1935

BUENA VISTA

Buena Vista ADVOCATE. w D 13 1889-1906||
Suspended 1897-99; - 1902
ICM Ja 17,My 23,O 17 1890[91-Ag 12 1892]D 18 1895;Jl 2 1897;Je 29-Ag 3 1900;Ja 25,Je 14 1901
NcD D 13 1889
NcU D 4 1895
VU D 13 1889-O 24,N 7,21 1890-D 18 1891;92-D 5 1894;D 13 1895;Jl 6,20-Ag 3 1900;Ja 25 1901

Buena Vista HERALD. w O? 1890-98||
ICM Ap 22 1898

Buena Vista HERALD. w S 10 1914-17||?
ICM S 24 1914

Buena Vista JOURNAL. w Ap- 1891||
ICM Jl 16 1891

Buena Vista NEWS. w Ap 14 1916+
pub 1921+

BURKEVILLE

SOUTHSIDE sentinel. w Mr? 1872-86||?
MWA O 20 1876
NNHi Mr ?,Je 13 1873
NcD Je 27 1873;Ap 5 1878

CAMP McDOWELL

PENNSYLVANIA fifth. *See under* Alexandria

CAMP WILKES

REGIMENTAL flag. w Ja 16?- 1862||
pub by 2nd regiment, Delaware volunteers
DLC F 6-20,Mr 6 1862
NNHi Ja 23 1862

CAPE CHARLES

EASTERN SHORE news. w 1920-24||?
V Ap 1923-D 19 1924
VOnE [Jl 1920-D 5 1924]

ECHO. w 188?-89||
Followed by Cape Charles headlight, later Cape Charles light

Cape Charles HEADLIGHT. *See* Cape Charles light

Cape Charles LIGHT. w 1889-1901||
1889-97? as Cape Charles headlight. United with Cape Charles pioneer to form Northampton times
VHi Ja 10 1893

NORTHAMPTON times. w 1902+
Formed by the union of Cape Charles pioneer and Cape Charles light
pub [1902-1?]+

Cape Charles PIONEER. w F 10 1882-1900||?
United with Cape Charles light to form Northampton times
TxU D 23 1891
VHi Ja 5 1893

CHARLOTTE COURT HOUSE

Charlotte GAZETTE. *See under* Drake's Branch

CHARLOTTESVILLE

ADVANCE. *See* Progress w

Charlottesville ADVOCATE. *See* Virginia advocate

ALBEMARLE news. w Ja 8 1931+
Ja-S 3? 1931 as Charlottesville shopping guide; S 10 1931-D 30 1932 Charlottesville guide
Suspended Ja-Je 1933
VU 1931-32;Jl 7,21-Ag 4,O 27-D 1933;Ja 12-Je 8,29-Jl 3,Ag 24,S 7 1934+

CENTRAL gazette. w Ja 29 1820-Jl? 1827||
Followed by Virginia advocate
DLC N 19,D 25 1824-Ja 8,22-F 19,Ag 20-27,S 10 1825;Ja 6-20,Mr 24 1827
MWA Ag 1 1823;Ja 13 1827
VU 1821-S 20 1822;N 19 1824;Jl 22,Ag 19 1826

Daily CHRONICLE. d D? 1863-Je? 1865||
DLC F 19,Mr 10,27,29-31,Ap 3,7,O 18,D 22,24 1864;Ja 1,F 15,22,26,Mr 1-2 1865
MB [F 17-N 16 1864]
VRC S 22 1864;Mr 3 1865
VU Je 22 1864

Charlottesville CHRONICLE. tw,sw Je 1865-73||
1865-Ja? 1866 as Tri-weekly chronicle
sw Jl-Ag 1865?
MBAt S 12,23,28,O 7,12,21-31,N 21,D 5 1865; Ja 13-16,25,Mr 13 1866
NcD Jl 26-29,Ag 23,S 2-[12 1865-Jl 6 1866]Ap 18 1867;Jl 18 1870
V Ap 18 1867
VU Jl 14 1866-[Ja-Je 1871]Ja 17 1890

Charlottesville CHRONICLE. w,sw N? 1869-1925||
sw 1904-13
DLC My 17 1878;97[99-1902]08-19;21-22
ICM Ag 23 1878
MBAt Mr 13 1866
MWA Mr 24 1876
N O 31 1883
NNHi Ap 25 1873
TxU [My 10 1878-F 4 1887]
VChP 1897[99-1902]08-19;21-22
VHi F 14 1893
VU My 13,N 18 1870;Je 2 1871;Ja-Mr 22,Ap-N 22 1872;Ja 31 1873;Ja 17 1890;S 23 1897
WHi [Ap 1878-Ap 14 1882]

Charlottesville GUIDE. *See* Albermarle news

JEFFERSONIAN republican. w,sw O 21 1835-Mr? 1862;Ap 10 1873-94||
w 1836-71
CSmH Mr 30 1847
Ct N 11 1835
DLC Ag 2 1860;Ja 10-17,D 21 1861
ICM Jl 16 1879
MB Ap 18,D 28 1861;Ja 18 1862
MWA D 5 1850;Ap 25 1860;D 1 1875;D 25 1889-My,Je 8-29 1892
NNHi Ja 17 1861;My 28 1873
NcD O 24 1850;D 23 1852;O 12 1854
PP N 28 1850
PPL N 28 1850
V N 27 1845;O 8-15 1873[Mr 10 1880-Ja 1885] N 27 1889
VHi Jl 8,O-N 1847
VRN N 2 1836
VU 1873-Mr 1888;My 25-O 5,19-D 7,21 1892-D 1,10-Jl 7,18-D 22,29 1893-Mr 2 1894
VWW Ap 11 1861
WHi D 22 1880

NELSON examiner. *See under* Lovingston

Morning NEWS. *See* Old Dominion news

OLD DOMINION news. d,w N? 1905-07||
1905-06 Title varies: Morning news; Daily news
Suspended 1906- 1907
d 1905-06
VU Ja 31 1906

PROGRESS. w My? 1890-96||?
1890-92 as Basic City advance (Basic City); 1893-95 Advance
pub [1893-95]
ICM Je 11 1891
NcD My 1,Ag 7,D 25 1890;Mr 19,My 7 1891

Daily PROGRESS. d S 14 1892+
pub 1892+
M N 19 1929
MWA Je 1 1923
NN Mr 13 1919
TxU My 2 1905
V 1905+
VHi Ja 6-7 1893
VU [Ja-Jl 1896]S 22 1897;D 3 1900;Mr 14,Je 27,Ag 26-27 1901;S 1,O 3 1904;Mr 7,D 27 1907;Ag 13,S 8 1908;Ja-Je,O 1909+

REVIEW. w Ap 13? 1860-Jl 12? 1861||
NcD My 18-25 1860;F 15,Ap 12,My 24,Jl 12 1861
V [Ap 20 1860-Jl 12 1861]

Charlottesville SHOPPING guide. *See* Albemarle news

VIRGINIA advocate. w Jl 28 1827-61||
Follows Central gazette. 1860 as Charlottesville advocate
CSmH Ag 27 1830
Ct [S 29 1827-Ap 11 1829]
DLC Ag 25-S 1,D 1,15 1827;Mr 22-29,My 10,Je 7,Je 12-Ag 9,S 6,N 15 1828;Mr 7,21,Jl 17-24, Ag 7,S 11,O 2-9,N 6,20-27,D 11 1829-30;D 12 1840
ICHi S 17 1830
MBAt Ag 16-23 1828;My 16 1829;F 19 1830
MWA My 31,N 8 1828
NcD Mr 5 1858;Mr 16 1860
OClWHi Ja 8-15,Ja 4 1830
V [O 9 1835-Ap 7 1837]O 21 1880
VHi F 12 1829[Mr 9 1832-Ap 1836]O 16 1847
VRB Ja 21 1859
VRN N 18 1836
VU Jl 26 1828-Jl,O 15 1830;F 8,Mr 1,22 1833; Ja 22 1858
WHi Ja-F,O 1828-F,D 1829-31

VIRGINIA'S advocate. w Je 10? 1880-81||
NcD Ag 12,N 11 1880

CHASE CITY

Chase City ENTERPRISE. w S? 1875-76||
MWA My 18 1876

PROGRESS. w 1888+
pub [1907-Je 1917]+
VHi Ja 6 1893
VHsC F 1935+
VU Jl 11-18,Ag 1 1935

SOUTHSIDE Virginian. *See under* Boydton

CHATHAM

To as Pittsylvania Court House

ENTERPRISE. w 1911-19||
United with Pittsylvania tribune to form Tribune-enterprise

PITTSYLVANIA courier. w Ja?-D? 1876||
United with Chatham tribune to form Pittsylvania tribune, later Tribune-enterprise
MWA S 9 1876

PITTSYLVANIA courier. w 1927-Mr 23 1933||
VAlJ complete

PITTSYLVANIA tribune. *See* Tribune-enterprise

TRIBUNE-ENTERPRISE. w D? 1869+
1869-76 as Chatham tribune; 1877-1919 Pittsylvania tribune
pub Jl 1929+
MWA Jl 27 1876
NNHi Mr 5 1873
VHi Ja 27 1876;F 24 1893
VU D 20 1878;My 7 1886;Ap 18 1924;O 1 1926
WHi My 23 1879

CHESTER

CHESTERFIELD county gazette. w F 22 1935+
pub 1935+
VU F 22,Mr 1,Je 28 1935

CHRISTIANSBURG

MONTGOMERY messenger. *See* Montgomery news-messenger

MONTGOMERY news. w 1924-Mr 1931||
United with Montgomery messenger to form Montgomery news-messenger
VSaT 1928
VU N 15 1928

MONTGOMERY news-messenger. w D 1 1869+
1869-Mr 1931 as Montgomery messenger
pub N 1929+
ICM Ja 5-12,D 2-9 1870;N 17 1871;Ja 9-16,31 1874;Je 21 1878;My 16,30-Je 6,Jl 25 1879;F 11-D 2 1887;N 11 1904;Mr 15 1907;Ja 12-D 6 1918[Je-N 1928]
MWA F 18 1876
NNHi F 21 1873
NcD [1918]
VBP Ap 1933+
VU Ja 5-12,Mr 2,16,Jl 6,O 1-,D 2-9 1870[F 24-D 15 1871]O 4-11,25-N 1 1872;73[74]Jl 2-9 1875;Je 2 1876;Ja 5,Mr 9,Jl 27,D 14 1877;Ja 25,O 4-11 1878[Ja-Ag 1 1879]F 20,Mr 12,Ap 2,Ag 13,D 24 1880;F 4,Mr 4 18,Ap 1,D 2 1881; 87;Ap 22 1892;F 8,My 31,Jl 26,Ag 23 1895;Je 12 1896;Je 4,Jl 9,Ag 6,27-S 3,O 22,N 5,26 1897[38-N 1900;Ja-O 1901]Ag 8-15,N 21 1902; Ja 9,Mr 13 1903;Mr 4,Ap 15 Jl 8-15,29,S 23,O 7,N 11 1904;F 3,D 8 1905;Ap 20,N 30-D 21 1906[Ja-N 1 1907]Ap 3 1908;Ag 27 1909;D 2 1910;Je 9,D 8 1911;Jl 26 1912;F 14,S 5 1913; Jl 24 1914;O 8 1915;Ja 7,D 21 1916;Ja 5,O 19, N 2,D 21 1917;Ja 12,D 20 1918;Ja 3,31,F 14, N 21,D 5,19 1919;Ja 2,16,30-My 21,Je 25 1920; Jl 24 1925;Je 14-21,Jl 12,Ag 2,16,30,S 13,N 22 1928;Jl 17-24 1935

NEW star. w Je? 1855-My? 1861||
Je?- 1855 as Western star; 1855-Ag 11 1860 Star and herald
V [Ag 1860-My 1861]
VU Ag 18-S 1,15-29,N 10-24 1860;F 16,Ap 13 1861

STAR and herald. *See* New star

WESTERN star. *See* New star

CHRISTIANSVILLE

SOUTHSIDE Virginian. *See under* Boydton

CLAREMONT

Claremont HERALD. *See* Surry county herald (Surry Court House)

JAMES RIVER herald. *See* Surry county herald (Surry Court House)

CLARENDON

ARLINGTON county record. w Jl 29 1932-Je 28 1933||
VFcI complete

CHRONICLE. w N 1920+
V [F 24 1928+]

CLARKSVILLE

Clarksville NEWS. w S 30 1927+
pub 1927+

Clarksville VIRGINIAN. w Ag 1882-85||?
V S 29 1883

ROANOKE VALLEY. *See under* Boydton

TOBACCO plant. See Southside Virginian (Boydton)

CLIFTON FORGE

Clifton Forge REVIEW. w,d,sw 1890+
1890-91 as Clifton Forge and Iron Gate review
pub [1902-Jl 1913]+
VHi Mr 10 1893
VU Ag 25 1905

VIRGINIA (*Continued*)

CLIFTON FORGE—*Continued*

VALLEY Virginian. w N 29 1865-95||?
1865-My? 1891 pub in Staunton
DLC My 26 1881-Mr 1884;Ap 1886-Ap 23 1891
GAA Ja 16 1873
ICM Je 25,D 10 1885;Ap 2,16 1891
MWA O 16,30 1873;Jl 20 1876
NNHi Ja 16 1873
NcD My 4 1876;S 13 1877;S 2 1880[Ag 1887-Jl 7 1892]
V [1865-81]
VHi F 16 1893
VSC [Ja 10 1866-73]-90
VU D 12-27 1865;Ja 10-Je 20,Jl 1866-Jl 10 1867;Mr 16 1868;Je 8 1876;O 3 1878;Jl 22 1880; Je 7 1883;Mr 6 1884;Jl 2 1885;My 12 1887;Je 21 1888
WHi Ap 19,D 13 1877;Ja 17 1878;Ja 9,Ap 3,S 25 1879;S 30 1880;Jl 21 1881

CLINTWOOD

DICKENSON county news. w 1929-33||?
VHi Jl 31 1930

COLONIAL BEACH

POTOMAC interest. w Jl 1928+
pub Je 1932+
VU F 22 1932;Ja 26,F 16-Je 22 1933;Jl 4-11, 25-Ag 1,22 1935

COLUMBIA

Columbia BULLETIN. w Mr? 1886-92||
Followed by Midland Virginian (Palmyra)
VWW Jl 1 1887

MIDLAND Virginian. *See under* Palmyra

CONVALESCENT CAMP. *See* AUGUR GENERAL HOSPITAL

COVINGTON

Covington DISPATCH. w 1908+
pub 1926+

Evening VIRGINIAN. d Ag 3 1914+
pub 1923+
VHi O 21 1922
VU Je 28,Jl 27 1935

CREWE

Crewe CHRONICLE. w Je 21 1935+
VU 1935+

Crewe HEADLIGHT. w Je? 1892-97||?
VU Ap 21 1894(photograph)

NOTTOWAY record, Amelia farmer and southern Virginian. w N? 1908-Ja 1931||
1908-15 as Record; 1915-22 Nottoway record; 1923-28 Nottaway record and the Amelia farmer. United with Blackstone courier to form Courier-record (Blackstone)
V 1925-27
VFaC 1928-29

RECORD. *See* Nottaway record. . .

SOUTHERN Virginian. w 1926-28||
United with Nottoway record and the Amelia farmer to form Nottoway record, Amelia farmer and southern Virginian

CULPEPER

To Je 8 1870 as Fairfax

Weekly ENTERPRISE. w 1891-1920||
NcD My 12,O 27 1892

Culpeper EXPONENT. w Ap 15 1881+
1881-1904? as Exponent and general advertiser
pub 1897+
NcD F 1 1884;O 4 1889;N 11,25 1892;Jl 21 1893;Ap 6,20 1894;Mr 23 1933
VHi F 10 1893
VU Ag 12 1905;Jl 30 1909;Mr 8-15 1912;Ja 26 1916;F 2-9,23-Ap 20,Je-Jl 5,19-O 4 1917;Ap 25,My 9,Je 6 1918[Mr-N 1919]Jl 22 1920;D 10-17,31 1925;Mr 11,My 27,Jl 15,Ag 5,26,D 2,16-23 1926;O 20 1932;N 9 1933;Ap 11,Je 27 1935+

Culpeper GAZETTE. w My 16 1827-36||?
Ct N 15 1833;My 2,Ag 1,O 3 1835;My 28 1836
DLC Mr 23 1827
N O 11 1833

Culpeper OBSERVER. w Ja 1852-77||
1858-59 as Culpeper weekly observer and general advertiser
Suspended from 1863?-65?
MWA F 21 1876;Ag 25 1882
NNHi Ja 11,Mr 8 1861
NcD My 10 1861;O 15 1869
VU S 10 1852;F 10 1854;Jl 1 1859;Ap 19 1861; S 18-25 1868;O 22 1869;Ja 23,F 6-13,25-Ap 9,24-D 1874;Ja 15,Mr 5,19-26,Ap 9,23-My 14,S 10 1875;Ja-Jl 7,21-N 3,24,D 15 1876

PIEDMONT news. w Mr? 1877-78||
VU Ja 25 1878

Culpeper TIMES. w Ap 1874-85||
MWA Mr 28 1876;Ag 25 1882
V Ap 23 1880
VU O 23 1874;D 5 1879;Ja 13 1882

VIRGINIA star. w Je 27 1919+
pub 1919+
VU Ja 27 1921[Jl 1922-32]-Ja 4,25-F 15,Mr 8-15,Ap 5,Je 28 1934;My 9,Je 6-13,Ag 22 1935

DANVILLE

Danville APPEAL. sw,w F 1 1860-S? 1865||
Formed by the union of Semi-weekly transcript and Danville republican. 1860-Ap? 1861 as Democratic appeal. Followed by Danville times
Suspended from 1861-My 1863
sw 1860-S 1864?
DLC Ap 8 1865
MH Ap 26 1861;F 11 1865
NcD Jl 7 1860;My 17 1863;S 10 1864
NcU O 7 1862
VU Jl 18 1860;Ja 14 1865

BEE. d Ja 25 1899+
Title varies: Danville daily bee; Evening bee
pub [1900-15]+
Ct S 12 1906
NcD Ap 18,22,24,My 3 1899
VD 1928+
VU F 17 1900;S 26 1907

BORDER daily express. d F? 1876-S 1877||
Followed by Spirit of the Valley (Harrisonburg)
MWA O 7 1876
NcD Jl 18,S 3 1876

Danville COMMERCIAL news. d
NN D 16-22,24,27-29 1928;Ja 1-4,6-17,F 4-28 1929

DEMOCRATIC appeal. *See* Danville appeal

FAIRBROTHER'S farrago. w 1897-1900||
Merged with Danville register
NcD My 12 1898

HERALD. w Jl 10? 1846-Ja 16? 1848||
Follows Danville reporter. Followed by Danville register
NcU N 6 1846

Danville HERALD. w Ja 24 1935+
VU F 1935+

INDEPENDENT statesman and Roanoke commercial gazette. w My 14- 1830||
DLC Jl 23 1830

Danville MONITOR. w S? 1863-64||?
NNHi O 7 1864

Daily NEWS. d N 23- 1865||
MBAt N 23 1865

Danville weekly NEWS. w 1874-80||
MWA Ag 19 1876

Daily Danville NEWS. d Ag? 1875-80||
MWA O 20 1876
NcD Ag 26,29 1876
VU D 10 1880

NEWS. d Ja 1923-O 1925||
VD Je 12 1923-25
VU S 22 1923

Danville OBSERVER. w My? 1834-35||?
VHi Mr 28 1835

Danville daily POST. d Jl 29? 1879-80||
NcD O 7,D 25 1879;S 2 1880
VU O 7,D 25 1879

Danville REGISTER. w Ja 23? 1848-1921||?
Follows Herald (1846-48)
Suspended Ap 27-My? 1865
DLC Mr 24,Ap 7 1865
MH F 3,17,Mr 31 1865
MWA Je 14 1876
NN D 5 1862
NNHi D 25 1873
NcD F 5,Jl 21 1848;N 7 1851;S 2,23 1864;Ja 27 1865;O 5 1870;S 18 1872;D 23 1874;Ag 30 1876
VRC Mr 24 1865
VU D 20 1851;Ap 10 1863;Ap 17 1867;O 19 1870;O 30 1872;My 25 1898

REGISTER. d 1864-Ap 1865||
DLC Mr 1,3,7,21,27-28 1865

Danville REGISTER. d F 1882+
Je 1885-96? as Danville daily register
pub [1900-15]+
NcD Jl 25,D 23 1882;F 5,N 10 1883;Ja 21 1884; O 3,6 1885;O 5 1886;Ap 7,My 3 1887;N 15 1888;My 14-23 1889;My 13 1890;Ag 25 1891;Ap 1,25,Jl 16,O 27 1892;Jl 23,O 6,10-11 1893[Ja 24-Mr 7 1896]F 16,Ap 10,O 6 1897;Ap 23 1898;Ap 30,O 17-18 1899;F 19 1901;Jl 23 1902; Ag 29 1907;Ag 15 1914
NcU N 8 1903
V Ap 1-2 1892;1905+
VD 1928+
VHi Ja 1 1893;Mr 11 1923
VU Ap 4 1882;Mr 31 1888;My 21 1890;S 16 1891;Ap 1-2 1892;O 17 1899;S 26 1907;My 13 1928;Jl 1-4,6,28,Ag 3 1934;Je 28 1935

Danville REPORTER. w Je? 1831-46||?
Title varies: Danville reporter and Roanoke commercial gazette; Danville reporter and internal improvement advocate. Followed by Herald
ICHi Mr 12 1836
N O 12 1833
NcD Ap 30,Ag 27 1836;Ag 21 1840;Je 24 1842
NcU My 29,Je 19-Jl 3,Ag 14 1840

Danville REPUBLICAN. w My? 1852-Ja 1860||
United with Semi-weekly transcript to form Democratic appeal, later Danville appeal
NcD My 24 1856;N 19 1857
VU Ja 27,My 12 1854;O 22 1857

RIVERSIDE headlight. w? D 1- 1894||
NcD D 22 1894

ROANOKE sentinel. *See* Telegraph

SIXTH corps. d Ap 27-My 10? 1865||
pub by the Sixth [U.S.] army corps on the press of Danville register
CSmH Ap 28 1865
DLC Ap 27,My 1-4,9-10 1865
IHi My 10 1865
MHi My 5 1865
MWA Ap 29 1865
MnHi My 2,5 1865
NN My 8 1865
NNHi Ap 28,My 2,5 1865
NcD Ap 27,My 4 1865
OClWHi My 3,10 1865
OHi My 5 1865
PWcHi My 1 1865
PYHi My 4 1865
TxU Ap 28 1865
VRC My 8 1865
VU Ap 27,My 3,10 1865(photograph)

Danville evening STAR. d Ap? 1893-96||?
NcD Jl 22 1893

TELEGRAPH. w My? 1822-30||?
1822-26? as Roanoke sentinel
DLC Mr 20,Ap 10,My 8,Ag 14 1824;D 8 1827
V Je 21 1823

Danville TIMES. w O? 1865-94||?
Follows Danville appeal
MWA F 25 1876;My 18 1877
NNHi F 1 1873
NcD F 15 1887
VHi F 9 1893
VRB My 23,Je 6 1874

Semi-weekly TRANSCRIPT. sw Ag 11? 1858-Ja 1860||
United with Danville republican to form Democratic appeal, later Danville appeal
VU F 5 1859

DAYTON

ROCKINGHAM outlook. w Mr? 1915-16||
MWA N 5 1915
VU Ap 23,Jl 9,23,Ag-S 3,24-O,N 12,26-D 10,24 1915-Mr 24,Ap 7,21-My 5,19-26,Je 9-Jl,Ag 11-S 15,29 1916

DILLWYN

BUCKINGHAM news. w Ja 5? 1929+
VAmN 1929+
VSbC 1935+

JAMES RIVER clarion. *See* Farmer-leader (Farmville)

VIRGINIA union-farmer. *See* Farmer-leader (Farmville)

DRAKE'S BRANCH

CHARLOTTE gazette. w My 8 1873+
1873-1915 pub in Charlotte Court House; 1916-19 in Phenix
pub 1920+
MWA Je 24 1876
NcD Ag 6 1874
VChC [My 8 1873-75]-[89-91]-[96-97]-My 1908;My 1910-My 1912
VHi My 1881-Ap 1883
VHsC F 1935+
VRB My 28 1874
VU D 10 1925;Jl-Ag 17,31-D 14 1933;34+

EASTVILLE

EASTERN SHORE herald. w O 1880+
pub [1918-28]+
V O 1904+
VHi O 19 1906

EDINBURGH

Edinburg SENTINEL. w 1893-Jl 22? 1920||
1893-1918? as Sentinel and Valley adviser. United with Woodstock times to form Woodstock times and Edinburg sentinel (Woodstock)
VStN [1900-19]

SHENANDOAH democrat. w Mr? 1870-72||
NcD Ag 23,S 12 1872

EMPORIA

INDEPENDENT-MESSENGER. sw,w Ap 1908+
1909-O 1919 as Independent (North Emporia)
sw 1909-13?
pub 1911+

MESSENGER. w 1896-O 1919||
United with Independent to form Independent-messenger

Emporia VIRGINIAN. w Mr? 1892-1908||
VHi F 3 1893

ESTILLVILLE

SCOTT banner. w 1875-92||
MWA Je 15 1876
TKL N 25 1885

FAIRFAX (CULPEPER COUNTY) *See* CULPEPER

FAIRFAX (FAIRFAX COUNTY)

FAIRFAX county independent. *See* Independent record

FARMER'S intelligencer. w O 14- 1843||
DLC O 21 1843

VIRGINIA (*Continued*)

FAIRFAX (FAIRFAX COUNTY)—*Cont.*

Fairfax HERALD. w Je? 1882+
pub 1914+
MWA My 5 1893
VHi My 3 1901
VU N 28,D 12 1884-Ja 9,23-My 15,29 1885; 1900;D 1 1905;Ap 5,19,My 17 1912;S 12 1913; Jl 16,Ag 20,S 24,O 8,N 26 1915[Ja-N 3 1916; 17-19]-[21 22]-[32]-Ja 1933;35+

INDEPENDENT record. w Ap 3 1929+
1929-Je 17? 1933 as Fairfax county independent
pub 1929+
VU D 22 1932;Ja-F 16,Mr-Je,Jl 12-S,O 20-27, N 10-17,D 1 1933

Fairfax NEWS. w Ag? 1849-60||?
DLC O 30 1852

Fairfax NEWS. w Mr? 1871-75||
NNHi F 28 1873

FALLS CHURCH

COMMONWEALTH. *See under* Rosslyn

Falls Church MONITOR. *See* Monitor (Rosslyn)

FARMVILLE

APPOMATTOX bulletin. w Jl 30- 1841||
DLC Ag 6 1841

Farmville CHRONICLE. w D 14 1833-48||
Followed by Farmville republican
DLC D 21 1833

Farmville COMMONWEALTH. *See* Farmville mercury

FARMER-LEADER. w 1906-Jl 1934||
1906-18 as James River clarion; 1919-30 Virginia union-farmer
1906-12 pub in Arvonia; 1913-19 in Dillwyn
V 1926-28
VFaH 1923;25;27-29;31-34

Farmville HERALD. w S 1890+
pub 1930+
V N 24 1933+
VFaC 1893-1905;08-20;23+
VHsC 1927+
VU Mr 29 1934;Jl 12-26,Ag 23 1935

Farmville JOURNAL. w S? 1848-69||
Follows Farmville republican. Followed by Farmville news
Suspended from 1861- 1865
OClWHi Mr 21 1861
TxGR My 16 1861;Mr 22 1866
VFaH S 23 1858;Mr 15-22 1866
VU S 3 1865

Farmville JOURNAL. w Ja? 1879-98||
VFaH My 2 1880[82-83]My 20,Jl 1 1886;Ja 27, Mr 31,S 22-29 1887;Ja 31,My 23,N 7 1889;S 18 1890;Ap 22 1897

Farmville LEADER. w F? 1915-30||
United with Virginia union farmer (Dillwyn) to form Farmer-leader
VFaH 1927;29-30

Farmville MERCURY. w Jl 7 1870-81||
Follows Farmville news. 1870- 1872 as New commonwealth; 1872-Jl? 1873 Farmville commonwealth
NNHi Mr 12 1873
VFaH Jl 10,S 18 1873-F 3 1876;Ja 7 1880
VU Jl 7,Ag 4 1870;O 26 1871;Ap 6 1876

NEW commonwealth. *See* Farmville mercury

Farmville NEWS. w 1869-70||
Follows Farmville journal 1848-69. Followed by New commonwealth, later Farmville mercury
MWA My 5 1870

Farmville REPUBLICAN. w 1848-49||?
Follows Farmville chronicle. Followed by Farmville journal 1848-69

FINCASTLE

Fincastle DEMOCRAT. w N 14? 1834-50||?
Follows Virginia patriot
DLC [S-D 1835]
MWA N 17 1849
NhD Ja 22 1841
VHi D 26 1835;D 25 1835;Ap 13,My 1[D 1846-My 1 1847]
VRo D 8 1845
VU N 11 1845;Ag 24,D 21 1850

Fincastle EXPRESS. sw F? 1862-65||
1862-63? as Southern express
CSmH Ag 14 1862
MH N 29 1864;Ja 31,F 3,14-17,21 1865

HERALD. w Ja? 1866+
pub 1915+
ICM Mr 25-Je 3 1880
MWA Jl 6 1876
NNHi F 13 1873
NcD Mr 19 1874[Je-Ag 19 1875]N 2 1876[Mr 27 1879-Ag 25 1921]
V Je 9 1881;S 7 1882;Ja 15,Ag 20 1885;Mr 3,S 15 1887;Ja 5 1888;D 19 1889;My 21 1891[Jl 1892-O 1895]Ja 16,Mr 12,26 1896;Ap 8,Je 17-24,O 14,D 2-9 1897;Je 22,Jl 27 1899;Mr 1,My 31 1900[F 14-Ag 8 1901]Jl 10 1902;Ap 7,My 26 1904;My 4 18-25 1905;Jl 11,Ag 6,29,S 19 1907;F 20,Ag 6 1908;O 19 1916;Mr 28,Ap 18 1918;Jl 7 1921
VU O 31 1878;Ja 2 1879;Ag 12 1880;Mr,Ap 21, My,Je 9-23 1881[82]Mr 1,Ap 26,My 24,Ag 23-30 1883;Ag 14 1884;Ja 15,Ag 20-27,S 17 1885; Ap 8,My 13,D 16 1886[Ja-S 1887]Ja 5,O 4 1888[89]Ap 30-My 7,21-28,Je 11 1891[F 1892-O 1893;94-Ap]N 5,D 3 1896[F-D 1897]Mr 3, Ap 20-27,Je 8-22,Jl 27-Ag 3 1899[1900-Ag 15 1901]F 6,Jl 10,Ag 7 1902;Je 18-25,Jl 9,O 1 1903;F 11,Mr 24-Je 16,N 17 1904[F-Je 1906] Ja 25,Ap 5,My 24,Je 7,O 4 1907;F 20,Je 1_, Ag 6,S 24 1908;D 22 1910;S 21 1911;O 19 1916; Mr 28,Ap 11-18,My 23 1918;Jl 7 1921;35+

HERALD of the Valley. w Jl? 1820-23||
Followed by Mirror
V [S 14 1822-Jl 4 1823]

MIRROR. w Jl 11 1823-29||
Follows Herald of the Valley. 1823-24 as Fincastle mirror. Followed by Virginia patriot
DLC D 5 1823;Ap 9,My 21-28 1824;Jl 25,Ag 8,S 5-19,O 3 1829
V [1823-F 18 1825]

SOUTHERN express. *See* Fincastle express

VALLEY whig. w 1845?-61||?
VU O 22 1858

VIRGINIA patriot. w D 26 1829-34||
Follows Mirror. Followed by Fincastle democrat
CSmH Ag 27 1830
DLC D 26 1829
NcD D 26 1829
VHi D 26 1834

FLOYD

To Ja 23 1896 as Jacksonville

MOUNTAIN boomer. w S? 1891-93||
VHi Mr 16 1893

PRESS. w 1891+
pub 1893+
VU S 15 1932;Mr 9 1933

Floyd REPORTER. w N? 1873-85||
MWA Je 5 1876

FRANKLIN

BLACKWATER courier. w 1891-99||
VHi F 22 1893

Franklin GAZETTE. *See* Southampton democrat

MONITOR. *See* Seaboard and Roanoke times

SEABOARD and Roanoke times. w 1873-79||
1873-28 as Monitor. Followed by Franklin gazette, later Southampton democrat

SOUTHAMPTON democrat. w 1880-1928||
Follows Seaboard and Roanoke times. 1880-86 as Franklin gazette
NcU Ag 26 1881
VHi F 23 1893

TIDEWATER news. w O 20 1905+
pub 1905+
VU Ja 4,18-Ap 5,My 17,Je 1935

FREDERICKSBURG

Weekly ADVERTISER. w Ja 8 1853-61||?
DLC O 19 1861
VF 1853-54;57-60

CHRISTIAN banner. w,sw D? 1848-62||
Suspended from My 9 1861-My 9 1862
w 1848-My 9 1861
A Je 14 1862
CSmH Je 18-24 1862
DLC My 20,31,Je 11,24,Ag 6-13 1862
ICHi Je 14,26 1862
MBAt Je 11-26,Jl 5 1862
MH Jl 2 1862
MHi Je 26-Jl 2,Ag 13 1862
MWA F 22 1850;My 20,Je 7-14,24-26,30,Ag 13 1862
MdHW Ag 13 1862
MnHi Je 11 1862
NBHi Je 26 1862
NBuG Je 26 1862
NKenHi Je 26 1862
NN Je 18 1862
NNHi My 20,Je 7-14,18 1862
NUHi My 31 1862
NcD Jl 14,26 1862
NdU My 17 1862
NjR My 17 1862
OCHi My 31 1862
OClWHi Je 18,24-26 1862
RP Je 11 1862
TxU Je 24 1862
V Je 24 1862
VHi Je 7 1862
VRC Je 7 1862
WHi My 20,Je 7-11,18,24-26 1862

DEMOCRATIC recorder. sw,tw S 9 1842-62||
Followed by Fredericksburg ledger
tw S-D 1843?
DLC Ja 1 1861;Ja 21,F 4,O 17,N 4 1862
MWA F 14 1843
NjHi F 14 1843
TxU Jl 21 1856
V Mr 8,Ap 2 1855;Mr 19 1861
VF S 9 1842;Je 23,Ag 11,15,S 6,29,D 15-22 1843;Ja 9,My 14,N 1 1844[Je 16-D 18 1846]Ja 5,Ap 2,Je 22 1847;Je 12,S 4 1848
VU Je 14 1849

DEMOCRATIC recorder. w F? 1844-
VF My 11,Je 29,Jl 27,Ag 17,D 14 1844;D 5 1845;Ja 9,30,F 20,My 29,Jl 3-10,24,Ag 14,S 4,O 23,D 11 1846;Ja 29,F 19-26,Mr 26-Ap 2,30,My 21,Je 25-Jl 2,16,Ag 6,27-S 3 1847

FREE LANCE-STAR. sw,tw,d Ja 27 1885+
1885-1902 as Free lance
sw 1885-94;tw 1895-Ag 1926
D 1907 is industrial no.
pub 1885-Ja 23 1894;Ja 28 1896-1900;02-27;Jl 1928+
DLC D 1907
M F 22 1932
MWA D 1907
NN D 1907
V D 1907;S 1926+
VFE 1899
VHi Ja 4 1902
VRB D 10 1901;Ap 29 1909
VU D 22 1891;O 21 1892;Je 16,S 5,15 1893;S 28,O 26,N 6-13 1894;N 29 1895;My 31 1900;Ja 29,F 2 1910;Je 7,28,Jl 12,15,Ag 22-23 1935

Weekly INDEPENDENT. w Mr 1875-76||
MWA Ja 14 1876

Fredericksburg evening JOURNAL. d 1904-18||?
VU O 24 1912

Fredericksburg LEDGER. sw 1865-74||
Follows Democratic recorder (1842-62)
CSmH My 19 1868
DLC Ja 16 1866
NNHi Mr 11 1873
TxU Jl 3 1866
VF My 30 1865-N 1874

NEW ERA. *See* News

NEWS. d,sw Jl 1 1847-62;65-86||
Jl 1-7 1847 as Daily whig news; Jl 8 1847-Ja 1848 Semi-weekly news; F 1848-Je 1872 Fredericksburg news (My 23 1865-Jl 1866 New era)
Suspended from O? 1862-My 23 1865
CSmH S 13 1861;O 29 1862;Je 11 1868
DLC N 11 1859
ICU 1847-Je 1848[Jl 20 1849-Je 1853]Jl 1854-Je 1860[Jl 23 1865-Jl 1 1882]
MWA S 11 1876
NNHi Mr 31 1873
TxU My 11,Jl 10 1866
V O 17 1870;S 1 1873[My 20-Jl 8 1886]
VF Jl 1853-Je 1861;S 1873-[Jl 1874-76]-Ap 1878;83-Je 1884
VFE My 23 1865-My 22 1886

PENNSYLVANIA reserve. ir Je 14 1862-
DLC Je 14 1862

POLITICAL arena. sw Jl 4 1827-45||?
1827-S 12 1828 as Political arena and literary museum
A Mr 24 1837
CSmH S 10 1830
DLC Mr 14,21-25,S 12-16 1828;Jl 14-17,30,Ag 7,D 4,22,29 1829;Ja 5-8,26-29 1830;Ja 21 1831; N 9 1832;N 20 1840;Ap 9 1841
MHi S 8 1835
MWA Jl 4 1827[Mr 10-Ap 21 1829]Je 5,Jl 28,Ag 26-28,D 4-8 1840;Ja 22,Mr 30,Ap 6 1841
VHi Jl 1830-41
VU Ja-F 16,Je 27,Jl 21-25,Ag 8,25-29,S 8,12, 26-D 1,8,12,15,22 1837;F 20-Mr 6,13-Ap 13,20, 27-S 11,18,O-D 4,11-18 1838

Weekly RECORDER. w Ja 23? 1844-
MWA Jl 27 1844;Ja 11 1845

STAR. sw w My 1869-N 1 1902||
1869-Mr 5 1884 as Virginia star. Merged with Free lance-star
DLC S 19 1894
MWA Ja 12 1876
NNHi My 14 1873
NcD N 24 1877
VFE 1877[78-80]-99
VFF 1898-1900
VHi Jl 26 1890

Daily STAR. d Je 24 1893-S 1926||
United with Free lance to form Free lance-star
DLC My 10 1894
V 1905-S 1 1926
VFE 1911-26
VFF Jl 1893-Je 1894;95-1912;14-Ag 1926
VU S 6 1923

***VIRGINIA herald.** w,sw Je 7 1787-1875||
1787- 1795 as Virginia herald and Fredericksburg advertiser; 1795-Ap 1797 Virginia herald and Fredericksburg and Falmouth advertiser
Suspended from N 29? 1862-Ja 1866?
w 1787-My 5 1795
A F 19 1842
CSmH S 11 1830
DLC [D 29 1821-36]D 16 1840;N 12 1859;O 21 1862;Ja 15-22,F 26,S 17 1866
ICU Ag-D 1826[29]
MBAt D 12 1821;Ap 6,10 1822
MWA Mr 14 1827;Ag 26 1840;O 20 1856;N 21 1862;N 16 1874
MnHi N 21 1862
N Ag 15 1827;F 17,Ag 12 1837
NN My 10 1861
NNHi Mr 11 1862;Ap 3 1873
OClWHi Mr 20,31-Ap 3,Je 16 N 27 1824
P-M O 17,D 12 1838
V 1858
VFE 1867[68]-[70-74]-76
VFF 1833
VU 1854;57;Je 25 1866

VIRGINIA star. *See* Star

Daily WHIG news. *See* News

FRONT ROYAL

Front Royal and Riverton GAZETTE. w O? 1890-94||
VHi Ja 5 1893

Front Royal RECORD. sw Ag 6 1920-S 15 1932||
Merged with Northern Virginia daily (Strasburg)
VStN complete

VIRGINIA (*Continued*)

FRONT ROYAL—*Continued*

WARREN sentinel. w Ap 9 1869+
pub Jl 1876-Je 1877;Jl 1880-Ap 1884;1914+
DLC [Ap 16-D 10 1869]O 9 1874;Ag 25 1876-Ag 22 1884
ICM Ag 10 1883
MWA Jl 7 1876
NcD Ag 8,29 1890[Mr 17-D 22 1922]Ap 20,Jl 6,S 14 1923;F 29,Mr 14,Je 13,Jl 4,Ag 8,29,O 10 1924
VHi Ja 13 1893
VLe F 28 1879
VU My 8 1885[My 25 1900-01]-[03]Ap 1,22,Je 17 1904;Mr 31 1905[06;Mr 1907-10]F 10,Mr 24,My 12-19,Je 16,S 1,D 8 1911[12;F-D 1913]-Mr 1923;35+

GALAX

CARROLL-GRAYSON gazette. w,sw Jl? 1874+
1874-85? as Grayson clipper; 1886?-1924 Grayson gazette
1874-1924 pub in Independence
w 1874-Jl 1931
pub 1925+
MWA Jl 18 1876
VU Ap 25 1884;F 26 1935

POST-HERALD. w 1908+
pub [1930+]
VRaT F 1935+
VU My 23 1935

GATE CITY

HERALD. w 1903+
pub [1906-28]+
VBrS S 1934+
VU S 27 1934;Jl 18-25 1935

GILES COURT HOUSE. *See* PEARISBURG

GLADE SPRING

Glade Spring CITIZEN. *See* Citizen (Abingdon)
JOURNAL-VIRGINIAN. *See under* Abingdon
WASHINGTON county journal. *See* Journal-Virginian (Abingdon)

GLASGOW

Glasgow HERALD. w My 20? 1890-91‖
V My 21 1891
VU My 21 1891

GLOUCESTER

CHESAPEAKE current. w O? 1870-76‖
MWA F 26 1876

GAZETTE. w Ja 9 1919+
pub [1919+]
V O 16 1924
VU [1919-22]-[25-26]+

Gloucester HERALD. w D? 1870-75‖?
NNHi F 22 1873

NEWS-REPORTER. w N? 1912-18‖?
VU S 16 1915;D 20 1917;Ja-My 1918

TIDEWATER Virginian. w D? 1886-89‖
TxU Ag 4 1887
V My 9 1889

GOOCHLAND

GOOCHLAND county times. w Ap 25 1930+
VAmN 1930+
VSbC 1935+

GOODSON-BRISTOL. *See* BRISTOL

GORDONSVILLE

Gordonsville GAZETTE. *See* Orange county news
NATIVE Virginian. *See* Piedmont Virginian (Orange)
NEWS and Virginian. *See* Orange county news

ORANGE county news. w S 4 1873+
1873-1917 as Gordonsville gazette; 1920-22 News and Virginian
1921 pub in Orange
pub [1923-27]+
MWA Je 21 1876
NcD Mr 18 1874;Ja 20 1876
VHi Ja 6 1893;Mr 4 1904
VU S 1873-F 10 1876;S 4 1919;Je 14,S 20 1934; Ja 24-31,Jl-Ag 1,22 1935

SUN-HERALD. w Ap 24? 1891
VU Jl 24 1891

GRAHAM. *See* BLUEFIELD

GREENVILLE

Greenville BANNER. w Je 9 1882-85‖
NcD Ag 18,D 15 1882
V 1882-Je 6 1883
VU 1882-F 1885

GRUNDY

VIRGINIA vidette. w N? 1879-86‖?
VU Ja 5,Mr 1,Je 14,Ag 30 1884

HAGUE

POTOMAC progress. w O 21? 1902-04‖?
VHi Je 18 1903

HALIFAX

To 1890 as Banister; 1890-1907? as Houston

Halifax ADVERTISER. w N 18? 1882-91‖?
United with Halifax record to form Halifax record-advertiser (South Boston)
NcD Ap 23 1883
VU Ja 21 1888

PEOPLE'S advocate. w Mr? 1855-60‖?
NcD Ag 15 1856

Halifax RECORD. *See* Halifax record-advertiser (South Boston)

RECORD-ADVERTISER and the Week-end. w 1927‖
An edition of Halifax record-advertiser (South Boston)
DLC My 12,Je 16 1927

VIRGINIA echo. w Jl 29 1859-61‖
NcD [1859-Ja]Mr 16,Ag 10 1860;Mr 22 1861
VU Ja 6 1860

HAMILTON

ENTERPRISE. *See* Blue Ridge herald (Purcellville)

LOUDOUN enterprise. w Ja? 1871-77‖?
MWA Ja 31 1871;Ag 3 1876
NNHi Ap 8 1873
NcD My 20 1873;Ja 27 1876

LOUDOUN telephone. w Ap? 1878-S? 1901‖
DLC 1881-Ap 1893;My 1894-Ap 24 1896
NbHi F 6 1880
NcD F 21 1879
VHi D 9 1892

HAMPTON

Hampton MONITOR. w 1876-1919‖?
1890-91 as Monitor-advance; 1892-96 Hampton news
NN Ag 1907(industrial no)
V N 18 1901[17-O 25 1918]

Hampton NEWS. *See* Hampton monitor

TRUE southerner. w N 24 1865-66‖
MBAt D 28 1865
MH N 24 1865
VWW 1865-Ap 19 1866

HARRISONBURG

AMERICAN union. w F 17 1866-F 15 1868‖?
MWA [F 24 1866-F 15 1868]

FARM and home. *See* Virginia farm and home

Harrisonburg FREE PRESS. w,d My? 1892-1906‖?
w 1892-Mr? 1904
VHi Ja 5 1893

Evening GLANCE. d Je 17? 1895-Ja 8 1896‖
VU Ag 8-10,12,S 4-5,O 5,23,29 1895

Daily INDEPENDENT. d Ap 15 1916-20‖?
VHarT [Ja-Mr 1918]F-Mr 1919
VU [1916-17]-Je 1919

Daily NEWS-RECORD. d 1898+
1898-My 1913 as Harrisonburg daily news
pub N 8 1906-10;My 1912-Ag 1913;Ja-Ag 1914; Ja-Je 23 1915;23+
NcD Ja 8,My 14 1901[N 17 1905-F 21 1906; 09-Je 1 1911]
VBrgC [S 30 1918+]
VHarT [Ja-Mr 1918]F-Mr 1919;Ja-My 1923; 35+
VU Ap 6,11,22,N 8-22,25 1907-My 7 1908;My 10-N 6 1909[Jl 1913-17]-[Ja-Je 1919]Ap 26-27 1921;Jl 23 1925;Mr 20 1928;D 2 1932;Je 27-28,Jl 12-13,Ag 28 1935
—w ed 1913-14 *See* Rockingham register

OLD commonwealth. w O 21? 1865-F 21 1884‖
MWA Mr 16 1876
NNHi Ja 30 1873
NcD [Ag 27 1867-F 21 1884]
V F 2 1870;Ja 14,My 20 1875;Ap 5,D 13,27 1877;Ja 17,31 1878[Mr-Ap 1879]Ja 22,Ag 12 1880;Ag 25,S 22 1881;82[My 31-D 1883]
VHarT O 9 1867-83
VRB Je 4 1874
VU O 1866-83
WHi My 3,Ag 30-S 13 1877[78-N 1881]Ja 12 1882

OLD Virginia. w Je 11? 1897-98‖?
VU O 15 1897

PEOPLE. *See* State republican

Harrisonburg REPUBLICAN. w Je 18 1844-54‖?
DLC Je 18 1844
NcD Ag 27-S 17,O 1-22,N 5 1844;My 31,Je 14, 28-Jl 5,Ag 30-S 6 1845
VHi S 28 1850

ROCKINGHAM daily record. d S? 1911-My 1913‖
United with Harrisonburg daily news to form Daily news-record
NcD S 16-D 1911
VHarN N 8 1912-My 1913
VU D 23 1911;Ja 15-16 1912

ROCKINGHAM register. w,sw Jl 27 1822-1914‖
Subtitle varies: Rockingham register and valley advertiser; Rockingham register and advertiser
sw My 1903-11
CSmH S 7 1829;Ag 21 1830
DLC Ap 19 1845;N 4 1848;Ag 3,O 26,D 14,28 1860;Ja 11,25,F 8,Mr 15,29,Ap 5,26,My 31,Ag 9-16,S 20,O 4,N 1 1861;F 21,Je 20,Jl 25,Ag 22-29,S 5,O 3-10,N 14 1862;F 13,Ap 24,My 15 1863;Ap 1 1864;Mr 31,Ap 21 1865[O 14 1869-O 17 1873]N 14 1878-Je 23 1881;O 23 1884-O 14 1886;O 20 1887-O 11 1889
ICHi S 1 1865
IU D 11 1863;Ja 22-F 5 1864
MH F 3,17 1865
MWA Mr 30 1860;Je 24 1864;F 24 1865;S 16 1869;Je 29 1876
NNHi Mr 7 1873
NcD Mr 10 1838;Ja 4 1840[N 1855-N 11 1886]O 27 1887;F 23 1888[Mr 1889-O 21 1892;Ap 19 1895-F 21 1896]
NjR Mr 24 1849
OHi My 26-Je 9 1865
TxU Je 13 1856
V O 18 1861[66-My 1906]
VHarN Ja-D 21 1906;Ja-N 8 1907
VHarT My 12 1825;My 12 1827;Ja 19,Ap 13,N 30-D 7 1833;Mr 23,D 21 1839;F 20 1841;My 7 1842;My 4,N 16 1844;Ja 2,D 18 1863[66-S 1870]O 24 1873-N 7 1878;O 13-D 1881[O 1883-S 1887]90-S 1897;98-Je 6 1906
VRC N 27,D 4 1863;Mr 31 1865
VU My 17 1823;My 27 1851;Je 3 1859;Je 29,O 12,D 14 1860;S 19 1862;Mr 9,Je 19 1863;Ap 8 1864;Ag 25,O 22,D 8 1865[66;F 1867-S 1868] My 13-20,Je 14,Jl 15,29 1869;F 17,Mr 3,31-Ap 7,My 19,S 8,29,O 27-N 1870;Ja 19,F 2,My 25,Je 22,Ag 2 1871;Ap 10 1874[Jl 1875-My 1878]Jl 11,25 1879;O 13 1881-S 1882;S 13 1883-O 9 1884;F-Jl 9,Ag 13-27 1885;O 21 1886-O 6 1887;Ja 19,Ap 5 1888;N 1889-My[Jl 1903-Je 1 1906]
WHi Ja 4,Mr 21,Ap 4-11,25-My 2,N 1878-Je 23 1881;O 23 1884-O 15 1885;O 18 1888-O 11 1889

SENTINEL. w S 18- 1885‖
NcD S 25-O 9,23-30 1885

SPIRIT of the Valley. w S 28? 1878-1909‖?
Follows Border daily express (Danville)
NcD [1879-Jl 13 1894;My 1896-N 22 1901]
V [1879-My 1883;Ja 16 1885-S 6 1889]O 29 1897;Mr 11 1898;O 13 1899
VU Ja 29 1881
WHi O 12-D 7,21 1878[Ja 18-Jl 1879]
—d ed *See* Harrisonburg daily times

STATE republican. w D 8 1883-1900‖?
1883-Je 1886 as People
NcD D 15 1883;Jl 26,S 6,N 16,D 27 1884;Ja 24,Ag 28 1885;Jl 29 1886;My 5,O 13-N 3 1887;Mr 15,Ap 12,S 20,N 1,29 1888;O 31 1889
VHi F 16 1893
VU [Jl 1884-85]F 26,Mr 5 1886;N 29 1888

STONEWALL. w D 1 1862-63‖?
VU Ja 15 1863

Harrisonburg daily TIMES. d 1905-12‖?
—w ed *See* Spirit of the Valley

UNION American. w N 21? 1855-56‖?
NcD Ja 16,F 13 1856
VU Ja 16 1856

VALLEY democrat. w D 8 1849-61‖?
1849-54? pub in New Market
DLC O 23 1852
ICHi N 6 1852
MWA O 8 1853
NcD F 15 1861

VIRGINIA citizen. w Je 7- 1859‖
NcD Jl 12 1859

VIRGINIA farm and home. w F? 1885-86‖
1885? as Farm and home
VU O 10 1885;Mr 13 1886

VIRGINIA post. *See* Virginia post and national echo (Alexandria)

HEATHSVILLE

ECHO. *See* Northumberland echo

NORTHUMBERLAND echo. w D 19 1902+
1902-12? as Echo
pub 1902+

HERNDON

NEWS-OBSERVER. w 1903+
1903-23? as Observer
V 1925+
VHi O 14 1916
VMJ D 1924+
VU S,O 13-20,N 10-D 8,22 1927-Ja 19 1928

OBSERVER. *See* News-observer

HILLSVILLE

CARROLL weekly news. w S? 1870-75‖
NNHi F 28 1873

CARROLL news. w 1921+
VU My 23,Jl 18 1935
VWy 1935+

Hillsville VIRGINIAN. w Ja? 1871-94‖
MWA My 11 1876
VHi Mr 2 1893

WYTHEVILLE dispatch. *See under* Wytheville

HONAKER

Honaker HERALD. w Ag 1909+
pub [1925+]
VU Jl 11-18,Ag 1,22 1935

VIRGINIA (*Continued*)

HOPEWELL

CITY and tri-county news. *See* News

NEWS. d,sw,w Je 11 1926+
1926-28? as City and tri-county news d 1928-2?,Ja-Je 1933;sw 1929-31
pub 1926+
VU S 9-16 1930;Ag 7-14,N 25 1931[My-N 1932; 33;F-D 1934]+

Hopewell NEWS-HERALD. d Ag? 1915-18||
1915-Ap 1916 as Hopewell daily news; My 1-13 1916 Hopewell news and press; My 15 1916-S 1917 Hopewell daily press
V N 1915-Je 1916;17

Hopewell daily PRESS. *See* Hopewell news-herald

HOT SPRINGS

DAY LETTER. *See* Homestead news

HOMESTEAD news. d My? 1917+
1917-23 as Day letter; 1923-24 Swallow
MWA My 11 1918

SWALLOW. *See* Homestead news

HOUSTON. *See* HALIFAX

INDEPENDENCE

GRAYSON clipper. *See* Carroll-Grayson gazette (Galax)

GRAYSON ensign. w Ja 8?- 1873||
NNHi My 22 1873

GRAYSON gazette. *See* Carroll-Grayson gazette (Galax)

MOUNTAIN news. w N? 1860-61||?
VWW N 8 1861

IRVINGTON

VIRGINIA citizen. w D? 1891-1921||
VHi D 23 1892;Ja 6 1893

JACKSONVILLE. *See* FLOYD

JEFFERSONVILLE. *See* TAZEWELL

JONESVILLE

LEE county republican. w F? 1889-99||
VHi Ja 12 1893

LEE county sentinel. w N? 1873-84||
MWA Je 23 1875

KENBRIDGE

FREE STATE news. w Ag? 1913+
pub [1913-29]+
VFaT 1935+

KEYSVILLE

Keysville PROGRESS. w Ja 5 1893-94||
VHi F 2 1893

KILMARNOCK

INDEPENDENT press. w 1930-My? 1932||
VCoP 1930-32

RAPPAHANNOCK record. w S 1917+
pub 1918+
VU Jl-Ag 1,22 1935

LAWRENCEVILLE

BRUNSWICK advocate. w My? 1874-79||?
MWA Jl 20 1876

BRUNSWICK gazette. w Ja? 1890-Ap 1915||?
United with Brunswick times to form Brunswick times-gazette
NcD S 27 1900
VU Ja 6-20,F-Jl 7,21-O 6,20-N 3,17,D 1-22 1898;D 7 1899;Ja 25,Jl 26,S 27,N 29 1900;Ja 17,My 16 1901;Ap 9 1903

BRUNSWICK times-gazette. w 1910+
1910-Ap? 1915 as Brunswick times
pub [1925-30]+
VLa D 1932+
VU Ja 13,27-F 17,Mr 17 1922-O,N 21-D 1930; N 7-14 1931

LEBANON

NEWS. w 1882+
pub [1930+]
VHi Ja 5 1893
VU Ja 3,My 30-Je 13,Jl 18,Ag 1,S 5,O 17 1902;My 12-26 1905;Ap 10 1908;Ag 11;Jl 12-Ag 2,23 1935

RUSSELL progress. w Ja? 1874-76||
MWA Ja 15 1876

LEESBURG

ADVANCE guard. w? Mr 12 1862-
Pub by officers of the 28th Pennsylvania regiment
CSmH Mr 12 1862

DEMOCRATIC mirror. *See* Loudoun times-mirror

*Leesburg GENIUS of liberty. w Ja 18 1817-41||?
DLC Ja,F 13,27-My 22,Je-Ag 7,21-O 23,N 6, 20-D 4 1821;N 14 1840;Ap 10 1841
ICHi Ja 15 1831
KHi [Ap 20-D 7 1824]
N F 6 1836
NcD O 23 1830;F 22 1840;F 13 1841
V F 17 1824;Mr 6 1827

INDEPENDENT. sm,w 1875-76||
sm. 1875
MWA Jl 21 1876

LOUDOUN chronicle. w Ja? 1846-53||?
DLC Ja 10 1851
NcD Je 7,Ag 23-30,S 27,O 25 1850;Ja 3-10, F 7-14 1851;Ap 22-29,My 20,Je 3 1853

LOUDOUN democrat. w Jl 6- 1853||
NcD Jl 20,S 7 1853

LOUDOUN mirror. *See* Loudoun times-mirror

LOUDOUN republican. w Ap 1869-72||
NcD O 7 1870;Ap 20,My 11 1872
FcU Je 23 1871

LOUDOUN times. w Jl 1916-24||
United with Loudoun mirror to form Loudoun times-mirror
pub 1920-25
NcD Mr 9,Ap 6,20,My 18-25,Je 8 1922;Je 7 1923;F 28,Jl 10,Ag 28,O 10,14 1924;Mr 2 1928
VU Jl 11-O 24,N-D 1917;F 20-27,Jl 24 S 25,N 13-27,D 11 1918;Ag 4,18,S 29-N 17,D 1921 [22-23]-O 1924

LOUDOUN times-mirror. w S 12? 1855+
1855-61? as Democratic mirror; Je 14 1865-1903 Mirror; 1904-05? Washingtonian mirror; My? 1907-24 Loudoun mirror
pub 1920+
MBAt N 2,22-30 1865;Ja 24-31,Mr 21 1866
MWA S 14 1876
NN Je 14 1865
NNHi F 5 1873
NbHi F 7 1878
NcD F 13 1856;F 27 1861;Jl 19 1865;Mr 21 1866;O 23,N 13 1867;Je 22 1870;F 7 1872;F 5,Je 11,Jl 9,S 3,O 1,29 1873;F 4,Mr 4,18,Ap 22,Ag 20 1874;F 25 1875;O 25 1877;My 9,O 3,31 1878;Ja 30 1879;Ja 27 1887;D 25 1890;My 28 1918;Je 19-26,D 24 1919;Ap 6-13,23 1920;Mr 9,N 17,D 22 1921[Mr-N 1922]F 7,Mr 20,My 22,Jl 3-10,Ag 28,O 9-16 1924[25]Mr 4,25-Ap 1,15,My 20,Je 3,Jl 29 1926;Ja 6,27,Mr 10,Je 30,Ag 11,S 22-29 1927;Ja 19 1928
VLe [S 19 1850-61]Je 21 1871-Je 7,O 4 1883; Mr 26,Je 1885-Je 6 1895;N-D 1901;S 15,29 1904;My 7 1909[F 25 1910-N 17 1911]
VU O 1 1873,Ag 20 1874;Ag 4,18,S 29-D 1,15, 29 1921-[22-23]-Ap 3,17-My 8,22-S 4,18-25,O 9-16,N 13 1924[25-29]30;S 1-13 1932;Ap 13,Jl 6,S 7 1933;Jl 11-25,Ag 22 1935

MIRROR. *See* Loudoun times-mirror

Leesburg OBSERVER. w Jl 5- 1828||
MWA O 18 1828

RECORD. w N 15 1901-07||
Merged with Loudoun mirror, later Loudoun times-mirror
VLe N 15-22,D 13-20 1901

SPIRIT of democracy. w Jl 21- 1840||
DLC Jl 21,D 15 1840
NHD O 6 1840

*WASHINGTONIAN. w D 1808-1902||
United with Loudoun mirror to form Washingtonian-mirror, later Loudoun times-mirror
DLC Jl 11 1840;D 27 1867;Ja 31,My 15-22,Je 26,Jl 17-24,Ag 7,S 18,O 23-N 6 1868;Ja 29,F 26 1869
MBAt S 8-22 O 13-27,N 17 1865;Mr 2 1866
MWA Je 24 1876
NNHi Mr 8 1873
NbHi My 16,S 12-19,N 14 1874;Ja 3 1880
NcD Ap 24 1842;N 1 1850;Ja 10,F 21,Mr 7 1851;Mr 25,Ap 29,My 20,Je 3,Jl 8,29,N 25 1853;Mr 9 1855;Jl 1 1859 S 9,23 1870;Ap 21 1871;Ag 16,30,S 13 1873;Mr 21,Je 13,S 19,N 21,D 5 1874;Je 26 1875;Mr 4,S 2 1876;F 3,Ap 7 1877;O 25-N 1 1890
VHi O 23 1857;F 18 1893
VLe Mr 28 1874;Mr 6 1875;Ja 22 1876;Ja 11 [My 10-D]1879;Mr 3 1883;Ja 16 1886;Ag 20-27 1887[Ap 27 1889-F 22 1890]N 9-D 14 1901
VU D 22 1854;Ag 30 1873;S 19 1874;F 3 1877

WASHINGTONIAN mirror. *See* Loudoun times-mirror

LEXINGTON

Lexington GAZETTE. w,sw Je 23 1832+
1832-Jl 10? 1835 as Union; Jl 17 1835- title varies: Lexington gazette; Lexington gazette and Rockbridge farmer; Gazette; Gazette and banner; Virginia gazette
Suspended Je - 1864
sw Jl-Ag 1864
CSmH Jl 31 1845;Ag 19 1868
DLC D 10 1839;D 10 1840;Ap 5 1860;My 25, Ag 2,S 16 1864
ICM O 7 1852[63]My 6,Ag 12,O 21 1870;Je 22(supp)1871[My 31 1872-O 15 1888]N 12,D 11 1891;O 27 1897;S 14-O 5 1898;Ap 5,Je 7 1899;Ja 31 1900;N 12 1902;Jl 1 1903;D 28 1904[Ja 21 1914-Mr 17 1915]Ag 6 1929;D 29 1931
MWA S 1 1876;S 10 1880
NNHi Mr 28 1873
NcD Je 24,Jl 29 1863;Ag 19,S 2 1864;D 12 1873;Ja 26 1877;Mr 29 1878
TxU Mr 6-13 1912;S 2 1930
TxGR My 18 1865;Je 7 1927
V Je 29 1843;F 6-13,S 4 1845;My 15 1850;Mr 17 1853;My 22 1856;Ap 29 1863;My 9,11 1866;Jl 22 1868;D 12 1873;N 29 1878;F 10-17,Mr 3 1881
VHi D 4 1835;Je 28 1881;Je 28 1887;My 3 1911
VLC [Jl-N 1853]54-57;59-61;Ja 30 1862-[64-65]+
VLW Je 23 1832-35[39-40]-[45]-[59-65]-71
VRC My 20,Je 24 1863;Jl 12,Ag 9,30 1864;Ja 15 1875
VU N 24 1824;S 28 1854;Jl 15 1864;O 9,N 6 1867;Ap 1 1870;My 23,D 12 1873;Je 26,S 4 1874;My 14,S 3 1875;N 24 1876;Je 29 1877;Jl 26,N 29 1878;F 21,Mr 14,My 1,Jl 24 1879;Ja 29,Mr 25-Ap 1,My 13,S 2 1880;F 10-17,Mr 3,24 1881;S 3,O 4 1883;S 14-28 1898;Ap 5 1899;Ag 5 1914;F 17 1915;Je 14 1916;S 26 1917;Mr 4,Ag 12-26 1930
WHi F 21-28,Mr 21-Ap 11,My 30 1873;Je 29 1877;Ap 1 1880

INTELLIGENCER. *See* Rockbridge intelligencer

MOUNTAIN laurel. w Mr 12- 1831||
VLW Mr 12-S 3 1831

ROCKBRIDGE citizen. w N 8 1871-74||
ICM Ja 31,Jl 10,24,Ag 7 1872;F 5,Ap 23,My 14 1873
NNHi F 10 1873
NcD D 13 1871
V S 17,O 8-15 1873
VLC N 15 1871-My 6 1874
VU F 21,Jl 10,24 1872

ROCKBRIDGE county news. w N 7 1884+
pub [1884+]
ICM N 14,D 19 1884[Ja-O 1885;86-87]Je 6-20 1889;D 25 1890;Ap 20,Ag 20,S 3-10,24,O 29,N 12-19 1891;Ap 27 1893 F 1 1894;Je 27 1895;Mr 12,Ap 30-My 7,Jl 2 1896;My 20,N 18 1897;S 15,29 1898;Je 13,Ag 8 1901;My 28 1903;O 13 1913[14]Ja 21,F 18,Mr 4-11 1915;N 4 1920
NcD [N 1884-N 5 1886]Jl 6 1888;N 14 1889;N 5 1908;N 14 1912;O 21 1915;F 10,Jl 13 1916; Ja 17,Ag 15,S 19,O 24 1918;N 18 1920;O 20 1921;Mr 16,Jl 27,N 2 1922;N 22,D 6 1923;Mr 27,Ag 21,S 25 1924;N 19 1925;F 25,My 6 1926; Ap 19-26,Jl 19 1928;Ja 24-31, Mr 14,28 1928
VHi Ja 5 1893
VLC 1884+
VLW 1927+
VU D 9,30 1887;Jl 6 1888;Mr 28,N 14,D 5-12 1889;Jl 23-30,Ag 20 1891;Ag 11-18 1892;S 10-17 1896;N 18 1897;D 24-31 1903;My 3 1906[08] Ag 5-19,S 9,23,O 7-14,28-N 18 1909[11-12]Ja 30,Jl 3,17-Ag 7,O 23 1913[14-18]Ja 16,F 6,Mr 27,My 8-15,29 1919[20;Ja-N 1922]Ag 9-O 4,18-N 22,D 6,20 1923-[24-26]-[28-Ag 4 1932]S 28 1933

ROCKBRIDGE weekly enterprise. w My? 1879-83||
ICM D 4 1879;Ja 22,Mr 18,Ap 22-29 1880;F 4-11,Mr 4,My 13 1881

ROCKBRIDGE intelligencer. w My 25? 1823-32||
1823-Ap 9? 1831 as Intelligencer. Followed by Union, later Lexington gazette
VLW Ja 10,Mr 27,Ap 24,S 11 1824;Je 3,O 7 1825;Mr 23 1826-Ap 12,S 20 1827;Ap 10,My 1,O 9 1828;Mr 26 1829;Ag 20 1831;Ja 28,Ap 2,Je 2 1832

UNION. *See* Lexington gazette

VALLEY star. w My? 1838-62||?
DLC Ap 15 1841;Ja 12,Ap 13,Ag 17 1843;My 9,30,O 24 1844;My 8 1845;Je 13,S 10 1846 Mr 4,N 4 1847;Ap 13 1848;Ja 10,Ap 25 1850;Ja 30 1851;Ja 19 1854
NcD [F 15 1844-N 11 1847]Ja 21-F 7 1850;Ap 15,Jl 1-8,S 16 1852;Ag 25 1853;Ag 14 1856;Ja 28 1858;Mr 17 1859
VHi [Ag 9 1849-My 2 1850]
VLC Jl 1853-My 2 1861
VRC Ap 3 1862
VU Ja 14 1842;Ja-Ap 20,My-Je 8,22-D 21 1843;F 13-Ap 17,My,Je 12-O 22,N-D 18 1845; Je 7,Ag 30 1849;Ja 3,17-24,F 14,28,Mr 21-Ap 4,18-My 16,Je 6-13,27-Ag 15,29,S 19-26,O 31,D 11 1850

VIRGINIA gazette. *See* Lexington gazette

LIBERTY. *See* BEDFORD

LOUISA

CENTRAL Virginian. w 1912+
pub 1928+
V Jl 19 1928+
VU N 29 1934;Ja 17-F 7,Jl 11-18,Ag 1-8 1935

Louisa ENTERPRISE. w Je? 1903-F 1913||
Follows Louisa county news. 1903-08? as Louisa-Goochland enterprise. Merged with Central Virginian
VHi Ag 17-25 1905
VLoC Ag 17-S 22 1905
VU Ag 17 1905

Louisa-Goochland ENTERPRISE. *See* Louisa enterprise

LOUISA county news. w D? 1879-1903||
1879-91 as Louisa news and farmer. Followed by Louisa enterprise
VLoC My 22 1903
VU Ag 10 1883

Louisa weekly RECORD. w Ja? 1876-77||
MWA My 27 1876

LOVINGSTON

NELSON county times. w 1896+
Follows Nelson examiner
VAmN 1926+
VSbC 1935+

NELSON enterprise. w Ap 21- 1860||
VU Ap 28 1860

NELSON enterprise. w D? 1879-97||
VU Ag 10 1883;N 28 1884;My 1,Je 5,O 23 1891;Ag 13 1896;Jl 9 1897

VIRGINIA (*Continued*)

LOVINGSTON—*Continued*

NELSON examiner. w S? 1875-96‖
1875? as Nelson county examiner. Followed by Nelson county times
1892-96 pub in Charlottesville
MWA S 15 1876

LURAY

Luray ADVANCE. *See* Page news

PAGE county news and courier. *See* Page news and courier

PAGE courier. *See* Page news and courier

PAGE news. w 1880-My 13? 1911‖
1880? as Luray advance; Ag 22? 1890-92 Luray times. United with Page courier to form Page county news and courier, later Page news and courier
pub [1898-1911]
ICM S 12,26 1890
NcD My 30 1888;Jl 19 1889
VU Jl 19 1889;S 12,26 1890;O 24,D 19 1902

PAGE news and courier. w,sw Mr 15 1867+
1867-N 12 1869 as Page Valley courier; N 17 1869-My 13? 1911 Page courier; My 20-D? 1912 Page county news and courier
w 1867-Mr 27 1923
pub [1911-24]+
MWA Je 1 1876;Ag 14 1890;Ap 24 1902
NNHi Ja 23 1873
NcD D 18 1884
VU Ag 5,S 9 1870;Jl 20 1876;Ag 21 1884;N 30 1917;Mr 7 1919;My 21 1920;My 19 1922;N 12 1929;Ap 24,Jl 28 1931;Je 28 1932;Jl 31 1934; Ja 22-Mr 15,26-Je 14,28,Jl 9 1935+

PAGE VALLEY courier. *See* Page news and courier

PAGE VALLEY record. w Ag 1912-Ap 1914‖
Suspended from Ag-D 1913
VU Ap 2 1913

Luray TIMES. *See* Page news

Weekly UNION. w Ap? 1890-98‖
VHi Ja 4 1893
VU S 13 1893

LYNCH STATION

CAMPBELL county record. *See under* Rustburg

LYNCHBURG

ADVANCE. d My 6 1880+
1880-1903 as Daily advance; 1904-07 Evening advance
NcD Jl 26 1883;F 11 1884
NcU S 10 1888;My 4,D 6-7,14 1889
VLy 1910-[18]-22;Jl 1923-30
VU Jl 26,N 9 1883;Je 8 1887;O 30 1888

Lynchburg ADVANCE. sw,tw 1880?-1902‖
sw 1880?-95

Weekly ADVANCE. w Jl? 1880-1902‖
NNHi F 25 1881;Ap 19 1882;Ag 23 1883;Ja 1, Ap 24,My 4,15-22,Je 5,26,Ag 21,S 4,18,O 9 1884;O 29 1885;F 11,25,O 21,N 25 1886
NcD Mr 15 1883
NcU S 20,N 6,D 4,25 1894-Ja 8,Ap 18,My 9,Je 20,Ag 1,S 5-12,O 3,N 21 1895

Lynchburg BOOMER. ir 1883?-90‖?
VU 1890

CAMPAIGN. w Ag 27 1883-85‖
Ag 28-N 26? 1883 as Democratic campaign
DLC Ag-N 5,19[D 1883-Je 1884]
NcD O 15,29,D 22 1883
V N 12,D 22 1883
VU O 1,29,D 22 1883;Ja 5,F 9-16 1884;S 26 1885

Lynchburg daily COURIER. d Je 3 1857-58‖?
MWA Je 3 1857

Lynchburg DEMOCRAT. sw,w D 1 1834-36‖?
1834-D 7 1835 as Virginia democrat
sw 1834-N? 1835
Ct Ag 10 1835;S 26 1836
TxU 1834-N 16,D 14 1835-[Ja-Ap 11 1836]
VRN D 8 1834

DEMOCRATIC campaign. *See* Campaign

Lynchburg daily EXPRESS. d 1853-54‖?
NN F 15,Mr 1 1853

Lynchburg HERALD. sw My?-N? 1824‖
DLC O 19,22 1824
N N 16,19 1824

Lynchburg INTELLIGENCER. w Mr? 1867-69‖
1867-F? 1869 as Piedmont intelligencer
MBAt N 29-D 20 1867;F 21,Mr 6,Je 1868;Mr 15 1869

JEFFERSONIAN. w,sw Mr 28 1828-32‖?
1828-O 22? 1830 as Jeffersonian republican. Followed by Richmond Jeffersonian (Richmond)
w 1828-Ag? 1830
Ct Ap 11-18,My 23 1828;Je 21[S 9-23]O 14-[25 1830-N 23 1831]
DLC Ja 15 1829;My 5 1831
MWA Mr 28-Ap 4 1828;Mr 11 1830
VU S 21 1831

NEWS. d Ja 15 1866+
O 11 1936 is Sesqui-centennial ed
A My 18 1886
CLM Ja 1-4,7,13-15,22 1891
DLC 1898
MWA Je 10 1870;Jl 8 1876;O 11 1936
NNHi My 1 1873;O 15 1879
NcD F 24 1872;Ap 15 1878;F 22 1911;Jl 21 1916
V S 24,29,N 3,D 8 1866[Ja-O 18 1867]1905+
VHi Ja 6 1893
VLy [Ja-Jl 1866]69-1901;S 1902-Ap,Jl-D 1903; Mr 1904-05;15-Mr,My 1913-17;Mr-Je,S 1918-22;My 1923+
VLyR Mr 30 1876
VRC F 2 1866
VSbC [1932+]
VU D 25 1868;My 11-12,16,Je 8,Ag 24 1870; My 24,26-27 1879;Ag 17 1889;Ja 27-28 1892;Ag 23 1896;Mr 16 1900;Ag 27 1901[My 1904-06;Mr-D 1907;Mr-Ag 1908]My 17 1910;Ja 27-28,Mr 12,My 30,Je 4,7,17 1916;Je 8,23-24,26,28-Jl 1, 3-5,11 1934
WHi O 4 1874;S 4 1878;O 5 1880

Tri-weekly NEWS. tw 1866-1904‖
MWA S 14 1870;S 8 1876
NNHi D 28 1866;Ag 1 1873
NcD N 25 1870;Ja 5,8,11 1872;N 7 1879
V F 21 1873
VU O 16,N 4-6,11,18 1874;D 29 1889

Lynchburg weekly NEWS. w D? 1874-1907‖?
ICM My 15 1896
MWA Ag 24 1876;S 20 1877
NNHi N 2-9 1893;Ap 17 1894
NcD F 8 1877;Ap 28 1881
VU My 29 1879

PIEDMONT intelligencer. *See* Lynchburg intelligencer

*Lynchburg PRESS. w,sw My 6 1809-Ag 2 1822‖
S 21 1818-S 21 1820 as Lynchburg press and public advertiser. United with Lynchburg gazette to form Virginian, later Lynchburg daily Virginian
w 1809-S 14 1818
DLC F 13,16 1821

*Lynchburg PRESS (for the country) w S 1818-Ag 5 1822‖
DLC [1821-22]
MHi Ja 4,D 14-28 1821
VLy Ap 20 1821-22

Lynchburg PRESS. d,tw,sw Je 1869-75‖?
d 1870?;tw 1871
DLC S 18 1869
ICM Ag 16 1871
NNHi Ap 9 1873

Lynchburg PRESS. w 1869-78‖?
Title varies: Lynchburg weekly press and Marion record; Weekly press and record
ICM Ag 16 1871
MWA Jl 8 1876
NNHi F 12 1873
PPL My 17 1870
VU S 6 1873

Lynchburg RADICAL record. w S 28- 1867‖
MBAt O 5 1867

Lynchburg RADIO news. w F 19-Je 25 1933‖?
VU F 19-Mr 12,Ap-My 21,Je 25 1933

Weekly REGISTER. w Ja 2 1864-65‖
CSmH 1864
MBAt Ap 9,D 24 1864;F 4 1865
OClWHi Ja-O 1 1864
VLy 1864
WHi Mr 19-D 1864

Lynchburg REPUBLICAN. sw,d Je 5 1840-O 31 1875‖
Title varies: Republican; Daily Lynchburg republican; Daily republican; etc. Merged with Lynchburg daily Virginian
Suspended Ap-My 12 1865
sw 1840-O 16? 1858
CSmH Ja 25 1862;D 17,30 1865;S 25 1868
DLC Jl 2 1840[45-48]O 28,N 4 1852;S 22 1857; Ag 30,S 23 1859;My 7,26,Ag 10 1860[61-65;My 6-O 1875]
MB Jl 16 1861
MBAt Mr-D 1869
MH S 27,N 26,D 17-18 1864;F 9-12,14 1865
MWA My 12 1863;S 1 1865;Je 15 1870
NN F 17,21 1853;My 31,O 15 1864;Mr 10 1867
NNHi [Mr 1848-F 1849;52;54;56]N 16 1858;Jl 6 1860[61-Mr,Ag 1863-Mr 1865]O 24,D 25 1866; D 29 1867
NcD S 12 1844;Je 19,Ag 5,O 3 1862[Ja-S 22 1863;Ja 19-Je 6 1865]O 31,N 7 1866;Ap 10 1867
NcU N 3 1842
NhD Ja 21 1841
OCHi Jl 22-[S-D]1862;Ja 12-Ag 4,25 1863
OClWHi Ja 19,Je 21,Ag 27,D 25 1860;Je 1,11 1861;O 2,7,9,21-23,25,N 20,24-25,D 13 1862;Mr 13,Je 16,Ag 20 1863
PArL [1861]Ja 15,Ap 2,Jl 10,S 25 1862;Je 9,Jl 1 1863;N 1 1864;N 20 1865
TU O 1,9,28 1862
TxGR My 9,20 1861;N 18 1864
V Ja 28 1841;S 3,N 25 1862
VHi [S-O 4 1862]
VLy My 31 1855
VLyR Je 4 1862;Ja 12 1866
VRC S 23,27 1861;S 6,O 22,D 22 1862;My 18 1863
VU Je 24,S 10,O 6 1862;Ag 15 1863;Ap 13,O 25 1864;O 29 1867;My 12,Ag 18,O 8 1870
VWW Mr 12 1846;D 22,28-31 1871;Ja 2-3 1872

Tri-weekly REPUBLICAN. tw Ja? 1850-75‖
DLC My 14-16,Jl 2-4,S 12 1875
MBAt Mr 31,Ap 30,Jl 11 1869
NNHi [1850;Ja-Je,Ag 1860-Ag 1861;Ag 1866-My,Ag 1867-Je 1868]O 8 1871;My 14 1873; Ap 12 1874
VU Ap 17 1861
VWW My 30 1866

Lynchburg REPUBLICAN. w 1873‖
NNHi My 1 1873

ROBERTSON'S real estate journal and Virginia advertiser. w,m O? 1867-71‖?
1867-70? as Virginia advertiser(w)
MWA My,Je 4 1869;Jl 1871
NcD O 30 1868
VWW My 7 1869

SOUTHERN manufacture. My 16 1883-
NNHi My 16 1883

Evening STAR. d Ap 1876-77‖
Merged with Lynchburg Virginian
MWA Je 28 1876

VIRGINIA advertiser. *See* Robertson's real estate journal and Virginia advertiser

VIRGINIA democrat. *See* Lynchburg democrat

VIRGINIA patriot. tw F 22 1848-60‖?
1848- as Virginia patriot and southwestern advocate
TxU 1848-F 21 1850
VU D 8 1848;Jl 15 1850

Lynchburg daily VIRGINIAN. w,sw,d Ag 9 1822-F 21 1893‖
Formed by the union of Lynchburg press and Lynchburg gazette. Title varies: Virginian; Lynchburg Virginian; etc. Merged with News
1862-Mr 1865 printed on half sheets (1864-65 without caption title)
w 1822-D 6 1827;sw D 10 1827-Ag 7 1852
CSmH Ag 3,7 1848-Ag 13 1849;Ap 25,My 28 1864
DLC S 6 1822-D 17 1827;Ag 18-21,S 11 1828; Mr 5,Jl 2-9,23,27,Ag 6,S 10,17,28,O 1,5,29,N 19,23,30,D 3,24,31 1829;Ja 4-14,25-28,D 20 1830;Ja 13,17,Je 9 1831;Jl 26,N 1 1832;Je 23 1834;Je 4,N 5 1840;Jl 11 1844;Ag 14(supp) 1851;Je 8,Jl 29,S 5 1863;Ja 14 Mr 26,30-Ap 2, Je 9,N 9,D 8 1864;Ja 16,23,F 28,Mr 2,5,13-21, 23-29,31,Je 9,30 1865;Ap 27 1866;My 2 1877;S 5 1879
ICHi N 25 1830
ICM Je 6 1850;F 17,O 14-15,18 1870[Je-N 13 1885]F 4 1886;S 6 1887;My 2,Ag 13 1891
InI Ag 11 1825-Ag 2 1827;Ag 7 1828-D 23 1841
LNC My 13 1863
MBAt Ja 7,21 1830;S 5 1844;My 3 1864[Jl 4 1865-Mr 12 1866]
MWA Mr 2,S 13,N 15 1827;Ag 26 1856;Je 22 1857;Ap 1 1865;Ag 5 1869;S 12 1874;Ja 10 1876
N Je 6,O 3,17 1823;N 16,26 1824;Mr 18 1825
NNHi Jl 19 1865;Ap 28 1873
NcD Ap 28 1834;D 17 1835;Je 15 1837;Mr 11 1841;Mr 21 1850;Je 26 1860;S 7 1863;Je 14 1865
NcU Je 4,25 1840;O 13,27 1842;Je 12 1887;D 11, 13 1889
OCHi Je 2[Jl 22-S 16]29-N 21,25-27,D 1,3-5,8-11 1862;Ja 17-[F 19-Ag 5]1863
OClWHi F 20 1860;Jl 3,N 6 1861;Ap 3,18,Jl 8,D 1,23 1862;F 17 1863;Mr 22-23,Ap 23,25, My 16 1864;Je 22,25 1866;N 27 1877
OHi My 7-8 1863
V F 20 1824;Jl 6 1863;Ap 22,My 2 1864
VHi D 24,31 1835;Ja 4,F 4 1836;Ag 24 1852; Ja 1 1893
VLy 1822-F 21 1893
VLyR Jl 1 1833;Ag 25 1855
VRC My 28,S 2 1862;Ja 9,13 1863;My 22 1865
VU S 20 1862;My 20,23,Je 15,S 16 1870;Ja 30,F 24 1871;O 15 1883
VWn Ag 20 1829
WHi Ag 20 1832-Ag 19 1833[73-77]

Lynchburg VIRGINIAN. tw Ag 4 1855-87‖?
CSmH F 26 1866
IU Mr 15 1858
MWA Ap 28 1856;Ja 16 1857;Ja 12 1876
NNHi Jl 14 1856;Mr 5 1858;Mr 31 1865;Ja 1,F 19 1872;My 23,D 1,31 1873[Ja 12,F-Ap 1874] Ja 23,Ap 12,30 1880;N 21 1883
NcD N 10 1862;Ap 11 1873[Ag 1876-F 1878]Ja 15 1879;Jl 15 1885
OClWHi Ja 13 1862
VU S 4 1861;Ja 19 1885

Weekly VIRGINIAN. w 1876?-93‖
ICM F 6 1884
MWA O 5 1876
NcD Mr 4 1884
VU D 28 1876;Mr 4 1884

MADISON

AMERICAN eagle. w N 5 1859-O 29 1860‖?
Followed by Southern citizen?
MHi O 29 1860
MWA N 5 1859

Madison EXPONENT. *See* Madison county eagle

MADISON county eagle. w 1910+
1910-22 as Madison exponent
pub 1923+
VU O 21 1910-[11-12]Ja 10,F 21,Mr 7-14,My 16 1913;Jl 5-12,Ag 2,23 1935

SOUTHERN citizen. w N 2? 1860-61‖?
Follows American eagle?
MHi N 23 1860

MANASSAS

Manassas GAZETTE. w Mr? 1869-Jl 10 1896‖
MWA Je 10 1876
NNHi Mr 29 1873
V Je 5 1869
VU Jl 3-10 1896
WHi Ja 6 1877

Manassas JOURNAL. w My 24 1895+
pub 1930+
CtW N 8 1895
DLC My 19 1911
P-M F 7 1913
VHi My 21 1897;My 19 1911
VMH 1895-My 24 1897
VU D 20 1907;Ap 12-19,My 3,17-Ag 9,23-D 6,20 1934+

MANCHESTER

Papers published in Manchester are listed under Richmond

VIRGINIA (*Continued*)

MARION

CONSERVATIVE democrat. *See* Marion democrat

Marion DEMOCRAT. w 1881+
1881-89? as Conservative democrat
pub 1921+
MWA Ap 28-My 19 1931
VU N 29 1933;Jl 16 1935+

HARRISONIAN. w Ja 1- 1841||
DLC Ja 1 1841

Marion HERALD. w Je 1869-72||
Merged with Southern patriot to form Patriot and herald
VU Mr 30 1871;My 30,Jl 25 1872

Marion NEWS. *See* Smyth county news

PATRIOT and herald. w Ag? 1872-90||
Formed by the union of Southern patriot and Marion herald
1889?-90? pub in Wytheville
MWA Je 15 1876
NNHi Mr 10,F 20 1873
VU Ag 22,S 26,D 5 1872;Je 12-19 1873;F 11,Mr 18,Jl 8,Ag 19,S 2-9,N 18-D 9 1875;Mr 30,My 18,Je 8,Jl 13 1876;Ap 26,Je 7,N 1,D 20 1877

Marion RECORD. w D? 1866-70||?
United with Lynchburg weekly press to form Lynchburg weekly press and Marion record, later Lynchburg press (Lynchburg)
MWA Je 13,Jl 9 1867

SMYTH county news. w 1889+
1889-My 15 1896 as Southwestern news; My 22 1896-1926? Marion news
pub 1921+
MWA 1927+
VU Jl 18,Ag 15 1935+

SOUTHERN patriot. w 1871-72||
Follows Southern star. United with Marion herald to form Patriot and herald

SOUTHERN star. w F 21? 1868-70||?
Followed by Southern patriot
VU Ag 1,28,D 30 1868

SOUTHWESTERN news. *See* Smyth county news

MARSHALL

CHIEF JUSTICE. w 1928-S 8? 1932||
United with other papers to form Northern Virginia daily (Strasburg)
VStN 1928-S 1932
VU Mr 27 1929

PIEDMONT news. w Ag? 1922-26||
VU Je 19-O 16 1923

MARTINSVILLE

HENRY bulletin. w,sw,tw,d Mr? 1889+
w 1889-F 1921;sw Mr 1921-Ag 24? 1934;tw Ag 27 1934-Ap 12 1935
pub 1915+
VHi Ja 18 1901
VU F 1 1895;1922;Ag 27 1934

HENRY news. w F 5 1885-88||?
NcD Je 18 1885

Martinsville STANDARD. w My? 1898-1904||?
VHi Mr 12 1902
VRB Ag 23 1899
VU O 24 1900

MATHEWS

Mathews JOURNAL. w Ap 1903+
pub Ap 1904
V [Jl 21 1927+]

Mathews NEWS reporter. w O 24? 1912-18||?
VU O 24,N 14-D 19 1912;Ja 2,16-F 20,Mr 6-13,27-Ag 7,21-O 9,23-N 6 1913;S 16 1915;D 20 1917;Ja-My 1918

MIDDLETOWN

VALLEY echo. w Jl 1883-85||?
NcD D 20 1884

MILNES. *See* SHENANDOAH

MONTEREY

HIGHLAND recorder. w 1878+
pub 1905+
NcD Je 23 1891
VHi Ja 6 1893
VU Jl-Ag 2,23 1935

NEW MARKET

SHENANDOAH press. w Jl 4 1883-Ap 3 1902||
VU O 20 1893

SHENANDOAH VALLEY. w Ja 17 1868+
Follows Spirit of democracy
pub 1925+
ICM Mr 21 1884
MWA Mr 13 1868;S 22 1876
NNHi D 5 1872
NcD [Je 26 1868-N 14 1873;75;77-79;81-86]-1914;O 9 1924

SPIRIT of democracy. w O 14 1854-61||?
Followed by Shenandoah Valley
NcD My 1 1857;Ap 2 1858;Ap 26 1861
VU Ap 26 1861
V Je 3 1869;D 21 1871;Mr 21 1879;N 21 1884;My 30 1889;N 19 1891[92]Jl 28 1904:D 20 1906[S 1909]
VHi Ja 5 1893
VRB Ag 28 1917
VU O 27-N 3,17-24 1870;Je 15-Jl,S 14-28,O 19-N 23,D 14 1871;Ag 13 1875;Ag 4,18,S 1 1876;O 5,N 9 1877;O 19-D 21 1883;N 7 1884[F-O 1885]86-87;Ap 19 1888;O 24-31 1889;90-1924;28;D 27 1934+

VALLEY democrat. *See under* Harrisonburg

NEWBERN

PEOPLE. *See* News-review (Pulaski)
PULASKI people. *See* News-review (Pulaski)
VIRGINIA people. *See* News-review (Pulaski)

NEWCASTLE

Newcastle RECORD. w Ap? 1885+
VHH Mr 23 1935+
VHi Ja 7 1893
VU Mr 19 1898;Ja 30,Mr 13,Je 19,S 25-O 2,16,30-N 13 1909;Ap 30,My 14,Je 4,18,Jl 2,23,Ag 20-27,S 17 O 1,15,N 5,D 3-10,24 1910;Ja 7,F 11,Je 3,Jl 15 1911;Ap 27,Je 8,Ag 31,O 12,N 2 1912;Ja 25 1913;Ap 15-29,My 20-Jl 8 1916;Mr 1 1919

NEWPORT NEWS

Newport News COMMERCIAL. w D? 1881-99||
MWA Je 8 1889
VHi Ja 7 1893

Morning HERALD. d Ap 3 1900-D 25 1901||
United with Evening times to form Times-herald
VNT complete

Daily PRESS. d Ja 1896+
pub Jl-D 1899;1905-Je 1908;Jl 1909-Je 1913;14-16;F 1917+
MWA F 24 1934
TxGR O 16-18 1931
V N 23 1919;20+
VHaH Ja-O 1916;F 3,Mr 25-Je 1917;Ja-F,My-Ag,N 1918-F 1919;30+
VN N 1929—
VU My 7 1910;My 20,22 1915;Je 28,Ag 16,18-19 1935
VWW Ag 1922+

Evening RECORDER. w,d 1893-1901||
1893-97? as Recorder (Norfolk). Followed by Newport News star
w 1893-97
Negro

Newport News STAR. w 1901+
Follows Evening recorder
Negro
pub 1915+
VHaH 1935—
VU F 24 1921;S 3 1931;Mr 17-Ap 7 1932;Mr 30,Je 15,O 26,D 7 1933;Ag 17,31 1935+

TIMES-HERALD. d Ap 1900+
1900-D 25 1901 as Evening times
pub 1900-Mr,O 1901-Je 1902;Ja-Je 1908;09-Je 1912;13-16;F 1917-Je 1918;19+
TxGR O 17,21 1931
VHi My 30 1902
VN N 1929+
VNoL Ja-Je 1903
VU Ag 25 1909;Ag 15-17 1935

NORFOLK

*AMERICAN beacon. d Ag 1815-61||?
Title varies: American beacon and commercial diary; American commercial beacon and Norfolk and Portsmouth daily advertiser; American beacon and Virginia and North Carolina gazette; etc.
CSmH Ag 28 1830
CtY Jl 11 1828;Ja 12-13 1832
DLC [F-D 1824]Ja 3 1825;Ja 16,My 10 1828;N 29,D 5-6,12 1828;Jl 29,S 26,30,O 3,N 20,D 4,25,28 1829;Ja 8,25,29,F 5 1830;Ja 21 1831;N 9 1832;Mr 18 1833;N 30 1840;Ag 1 1843;Ap 18 1844;Ag 23,27 1852
ICHi Ja 21 1831;Ja 9 1836
MBAt Ap 8 1822;F 5 1823;Ja 16 1844
MHi N 2 1821;Mr 15,Ap 2,Jl 3,5-6,23 1824;Ja 29,Mr 9,15,24,Ap 15,Ag 1 1825
MWA Ag 5,7 1822;O 17 1826;F 28 1827;My 14 1840;N 1 1845
NhD Je 5 1841
T [1821]-Ja 8,12-15 1822
V Ja 23 1823
VNo 1821-31;Jl 1832-Je 1854;Ja-Je 1855
VU Ja-F 12,14-Je 29 1850

*AMERICAN beacon and Virginia and North Carolina gazette. tw 1815?-61||?
Title varies: American beacon for the country
MHi Ag 31 1824
MWA Ap 4,Jl 28 1823;Jl 22 1829;My 4 1831;S 19 1834
NcD D 18 1827;My 8 1837;My 26 1851
NcU Je 1 1830-Ja 27 1831;N 25,D 9,12 1842;Je 23,Jl 26,S 15 1843;O 11 1844;Jl 14,Ag 31 1846;Ag 16 1847;Ja 19,F 5,Je 7,Jl 7,10,17 1848
V Jl 1833-Ap 1 1834;Mr 6 1855
VHi O 22 1834;Jl 15 1850
VNo 1821-31;Ja-Je 1833;Ja-S 1834
VWW S 12 1846

AMERICAN commercial beacon. *See* American beacon

Norfolk and Portsmouth evening BULLETIN. d O 8- 1829||
DLC O 8 1829

Daily COURIER. d Ja 1844-Je 1865||
1844-46? as Evening courier. Followed by Norfolk post
VWW Ap 2 1846

Norfolk DAY BOOK. d O 3 1857-Jl 1880||
1857-67 as Day book
Suppressed by Federal authorities several times during the Civil War
CSmH F 1 1868
DLC O 5 1857-Mr 29 1858;O 5 1859-Mr 1860;F 3,5,25,Mr 12 1862[Jl 25 1865-N 2 1866]S 3 1867[Ap 9-N 18 1869]
KHi Ap 17 1862
MBAt [Ap 26-My 1862;S 16 1865-Mr 1866]S 25,O 22 1867;Ap 10 1868
MWA S 22 1858;My 30 1862;O 14 1876
NN N 11 1861;My 10 1862
NNHi F 14,27,Ap 29,My 3 1862;F 20 1869;Mr 24 1873
NcU Ja 24,F 1,4-6,8,15,17,20,Ap 9,18 1862
OClWHi My 9 1862
P-M [1862]
V Mr 25,N 20 1861
VRC My 8 1862
VU Ja 22 1866

Weekly DAY BOOK. w
NNHi Ap 30 1862
NcD My 16 1866;S 24 1868

Norfolk DEMOCRAT. w
CtY Ja 25 1840

Norfolk DISPATCH. d N 7 1896-Ap? 1906||
United with Norfolk public ledger to form Ledger-dispatch
VNo 1896-F,Jl-N 6 1902
VNoL 1896-My 6,N 1897-N 1901;N 10 1902-N 4 1905

Daily DISTRICT whig. *See under* Portsmouth

Norfolk EXAMINER. w Ap? 1856-61||?
OClWHi Ja 26-Mr 1861

Weekly GAZETTE. w Ap? 1912-13||?
VU Mr 22-Ap 19 1913

*Norfolk and Portsmouth HERALD. tw,sw,d Ag 13 1794-Ja 25 1861||?
Title varies: Herald, and Norfolk and Portsmouth advertiser; Herald; Norfolk herald; Norfolk and Portsmouth herald and daily commercial advertiser; Norfolk, and Portsmouth herald; etc.
tw 1794-Ag 10? 1840(sw for short periods in 1824;28-29)
CSmH Ag 8 1827
CtY Ap 16 1828-Ag 6 1832
DLC [1821-26]Ja 1,3,8,24,F 5,7,Mr 28,Ap 6,9,13,18-27,My 14,D 24 1827[Ja-N 1829]Ja 18,D 8 1830;O 3 1832;Ap 9 1834;D 7 1840[44-45;49-52]-Ap 15 1853
MBAt Mr 13 1822
MHi D 5 1823;Mr 18,21 1825
MWA Jl 26,S 6,O 18 1822;Je 2,7,16,28 1824;My 11 1825;F 28 1827;Mr 10 1830;Ja 25 1861
NcD [1821-24]F 17 1834;Ap 24 1840;F 25 1858;Ja 28-29,F 1-4 1859;F 12 1861
NcU Jl 31 1857
NhD F 23 1841
V My 25 1838[47]Jl 26 1854
VHi Je 23 1834;Ag 2,4,16,D 7,21 1835-Ja 1,4,29,F 1,3,12 1836
VNo 1821-F 1823;Mr 1824-29;Ja 30 1830-31;33;35-37;39;Ja-Je 1845;Ja-Je 1852;Jl-D 1859
VRC O 29,31,D 6 1860
VRN O 7 1836;My 22 1837
VU S 10,15-22,29,O 1,8,10,15-N 7,D 10,15 1823;Ja 23-24 1824;F 21-Ap 25 1827;My 15,Ag 5,7,12-24,S 30-O 5,9,N 4 1829-Ag 2 1830;Ja 31 1831;S 10 1834-[35]Mr 2 1836;Ja-F 13,18-O 7,11-D 4,9-11,18-23 1839;Ag 14-O 16,19-D 1840;My 4-Je 2,Jl 3,6 1841[Ja-N 18 1842;43-Jl 1844]Ag 26-N 9 1846;Ja-Je 8,10-12,15-25,28,Jl 1-5,7-10,12-S 8,10 1847-48;Je 21-29,Jl 15-26,29-31,Ag 13-26,S 2 1850;51;Jl-D 1852;Ja 19-F 5,8-My 4,9-19,21-Je 1853[Ja-Jl 4 1854;Jl-D 1855]-Je 1856;Ja 22,F 24-Mr 4,D 21 1857[Ja-Je 1858]-Je 1859;Ja 9-11,F 9,11,13,22-23,25-Mr 4,9-28,30-Ap 1 1861
VWW My 24 1824

Norfolk JOURNAL. d D 4 1866-74||
Merged with Norfolk landmark
CSmH F 4 1868
MBAt [1866-68]69
NNHi My 15 1873
NcD S 1 1870;Jl 6 1871
NcU O 5 1871
V Jl 6 1871
VNo 1866-Jl 22 1871;72-Mr 1874
VNoL 1867-D 1 1868;Ja-Je 4,Jl 23 1871
VU Mr 17,Jl 22,S 15,O 26 1870;Jl 6 1871

Norfolk JOURNAL. tw 1866-74||
NNHi F 15,Je 24 1873

Norfolk JOURNAL. w 1866-74||
NcD F 17,Mr 17-24 1870
NcU O 5 1871

JOURNAL and guide. w 1901+
Negro
pub S 1916+
TNF 1923[34]+
TNY [Ap 1928-O 15 1932]
VHaH 1935+
VPC S 1931+

Norfolk JOURNAL of commerce. w,tw Jl 5- 1866||
w Jl-O 1866
MBAt Jl 5,19-26,Ag 9-30,S 13-O 25,N 5,10-17 1866

VIRGINIA (*Continued*)

NORFOLK—*Continued*

Norfolk JOURNAL of commerce. w S 1887-1902‖
United with Virginian-pilot(sw) to form Norfolk journal of commerce and Twice-a-week Virginian pilot, later Journal of commerce and Virginian-pilot
NcD Mr 24 1894;Ag 8 1902
VNo S 1900-Ag 1901
VNoL S 1888-1901

JOURNAL of commerce and Virginian-pilot. sw Ja 29 1901-D 1916‖
1901-O 17? 1902 as Twice-a-week Virginian pilot. Title varies: Norfolk journal of commerce and Twice-a-week Virginian pilot
NcD D 9 1902;Ag 7-10,S 25,O 19 1906;My 17-24,28,Jl 9 1907
VNo Jl 1903-Je 1905;Ja-Je 1906
VNoL Ja 29 1901-16

Norfolk LANDMARK. d O 3 1873-D 31 1911‖
United with Virginian-pilot to form Virginian-pilot and Norfolk landmark
DLC 1887[88-93]-[95-96]Jl-D 1897;Ap 1903-11
MWA F 21 1875;O 19 1876;S 18 1877
NN [My-S 1877]
NNHi F 19 1874
NcD N 11 1873;S 13,20 1874;Ja 3 1875;Mr 17,25,S 18,N 7 1877[78-81]Je 29 1901
NcU Ag 21 1881
TxU F 4,Mr 28 1885
V Je 29,Jl 1 1890;Ja 20 1892;D 7 1904;05-11
VHi O 9 1873;S 25 1875;Je 19 1883;S 21 1887; F 22 1888;Ja 1 1893;My 25 1895
VNo Ap-S 1874;Ap 1875-Je 1882;83-Je 1888;89-Je 1893;94-Je 1895;96-S 1898;99-1911
VNoL O 1878-Mr,S 1879-My,Jl 1880-82;84-Mr, My-Ag,O 1898-1911
VRC N 19 1875
VU D 7 1904;My 17 1910
VWW S 7,N 29 1876;Ap 19,Jl 15,S 11 1877[Ag-S 15 1878]My 1,O 30 1879
WHi [O 9 1873-F 22 1874]

Norfolk weekly LANDMARK. w 1870-97‖
DLC O 14 1891
MWA Jl 6 1876
NcD Ja 1 1880;Ja 10 1883
V O 31,N 21,D 19 1878

LEDGER-DISPATCH. d 1876+
1876-Ap 17? 1906 as Public ledger
pub Ag 3 1876-F,Ag 1879-Ag 1881;Ag 1882-Ag 1904;F 1905+
CSmH My 8 1884
CoU S 1906-Je 1910
GAtCo Je 7 1907
MWA Jl 9 1877;O 25 1879;My 25 1881;O 8 1902
NcD Mr 8 1898
VHi D 20 1892;Ap 27 1907;D 31 1924
VNo Ag 1876-F 2,Ag 2 1915-Ag 3 1916;Ap 4 1919+
VU F 9 1905;Ag 12 1930;Je 28 1935

NEW daily pilot. d My 1894-Mr 1898‖
1894-S 12 1895 as Norfolk daily pilot. United with Norfolk Virginian to form Virginian-pilot, later Virginian-pilot and Norfolk landmark
VNoL Ag 1895-F,Ap,My 3-Ag 20,N 1895

NEW regime. d F 29 1864-F 15 1865‖
DLC S 22,26,N 6,16,29,D 1,14-15,23,29 1864;Ja 8,10,12-17,19-27,29-F 1 1865
MBAt Mr 8,D 9 1864
MDeHi Mr 8 1864
MH My 28 1864
MHi Ag 23 1864
MSaE Ap 16 1864
MWA complete
MiU-C Ja 22 1865
NNHi S 17 1864
NjP complete

Daily NEWS. d Ja 1 1851-56‖?
DLC N 5,8 1852

Evening NEWS. d D? 1882-87‖
MWA N 25 1884

Evening NEWS. d,w N? 1890-96‖
1890-95? as Norfolk news and courier
MWA Ap 17 1891;O 11 1895
TxU Ja 9 1891

Norfolk NEWS. sw 1910-16‖?
VNo O 1912-Ja 1914

Norfolk NEWS and courier. *See* Evening news

Norfolk OLD DOMINION. d 1863-D 3 1866‖
Title varies: Daily Old Dominion
1863-64? pub in Portsmouth
DLC [D 25 1863-S 1864;Mr 22-Je 3]Ag 25 1865 [Ap 20-N 3 1866]
MB N 28 1863
MBAt [S 1865-66]
MWA F 16,S 15 1864;Mr 6,Jl 22 1865
NNHi Mr 25,Ap 11-12 1865
VHi My 4 1866

OUR day. w Mr 3-My 19 1866‖?
V [Mr-My 19 1866]

PEOPLE'S free press. sw O? 1829-30‖?
CSmH S 4 1830
Ct S 18,25,N 13,17 1830

Norfolk and Portsmouth PHENIX. tw Ja 8? 1841-Je 13 1844‖?
CSmH Je 26,Ag 10 1841
DLC Ja 26 1841
NN My 20 1841
NSchU Ja 29 1842

Norfolk daily PILOT. *See* New daily pilot

Norfolk POST. d,w Je 22 1865-Je 28 1866‖
Follows Daily courier
d 1865-Ap 5 1866
DLC Je 22-Ag 18,20 1865;Ap 5 1866
MBAt [Jl 25-D 1865]-66
NjP 1865-Ap 5 1866
OClWHi O 23 1865
VU Ja 22 1866

POST. d Je 13 1921-F 4? 1924‖
VNo 1921-F 1 1924

PUBLIC ledger. *See* Ledger-dispatch

RECORDER. *See* Evening recorder (Newport News)

Daily REVIEW. sw,d Mr 8? 1882-Ap 1883‖
Mr-My 1882 as Norfolk review(sw)
MWA Ap 19 1882

SHIPPING news. d Mr 1?- 1921‖
MWA Mr 3 1921

SOUTHERN argus. d Ja 8 1848-Ag? 1861‖
Ja 10-Mr 20 1848 as Southern argus and Virginia and North Carolina advertiser; Mr 21 1848-S 4 1855 Daily southern argus (Mr 1 1855 Southern argus)
Suspended from S 6-O 15 1855
DLC Ag 24,26,30 1852[55-60]
MWA N 29 1852
NcD Ag 16 1852;Jl 19 1856
NcU O 11-12,16 1860
V Ap 2 1849;My 25,Ag 1,D 10 1850;Jl 25 1854; Jl 8 1856
VNo 1848-52;Jl 1853-Je 1855;Ja-Je 1856;57-60
VU O 30 1855

SOUTHERN argus (for the country) tw
DLC My 13,22,N 4 1857;O 2 1858;D 15 1860; My 28 1861

TIDEWATER times. *See* Times-advocate

Evening TIMES. d My? 1875-76‖
MWA Ap 3 1876

TIMES-ADVOCATE. w 1912+
1912-22 as Tidewater times
pub 1930+

Norfolk UNION. d Je 2- 1862‖
Title varies slightly
MBAt Je 3-4,9 1862
MH D 19 1862
MWA Jl 15 1862
PWcHi Ag 9 1862
VU Je 3-4,9(photograph)1862

UNION republican. w Ag? 1866-67‖?
CSmH Jl 18 1867

VIRGINIA palladium. tw My 9? 1827-28‖?
My-S? 1827 as Virginia palladium and Portsmouth commercial advertiser (Portsmouth)
MWA My 15,S 29 1827;Jl 1 1828
NcD Je 2-14 1827

VIRGINIA seaport. w Mr 1 1884-85‖?
V Mr 15-Ap 19,My 3-10,Je 7 1884

Weekly Norfolk VIRGINIAN. w 1870-82‖?
1870-D 30 1871? as Weekly Virginian and Carolinian
NNHi N 9 1872
NcD Ja 27 1872;S 29 1881
V D 6 1877;Ja 3,O 24,N 28 1878;Ja 23,D 25 1879;Jl 14 1881
VNoL 1875-My 23 1876
VWW Mr 18 1880;Ag 11 1882

Norfolk VIRGINIAN. d *See* Virginian pilot and Norfolk landmark

Twice-a-week VIRGINIAN pilot. *See* Journal of commerce and Virginian-pilot

VIRGINIAN-PILOT and Norfolk landmark. d N 21 1865+
1865-Mr 30? 1898 as Norfolk Virginian; Mr 31 1898-1911 Virginian pilot
pub 1912+
DLC Mr 23 1871;Ag 1899-[1902]-[05]-[23]-[27-28]+
MBAt [N 1865-Mr 1866]O 12,N 10 1869
MWA Jl 4 1870;Ap 11 1873;O 14 1876;Ag 5 1879
NNHi N 22 1865;My 1 1873
NcD Jl 7 1871;O 8 1884;My 13 1885;D 16 1886;F 17 1887;Ja 19 1897;Je 1900;My 27 1914
NcEloC F 1924+
NcU Ap 19 1872
PPL Ja 22 1875
V Ap 15 1867;1912+
VHaH 1930+
VHi Ap 11,O 23 1873;O 23 1875;Je 18-19 1884;F 7 1892;Ja 1 1893;Ja 27 1912
VNo N 22 1867-N 20 1869;My 21 1870-My 20 1871;D 6 1872-My 10 1873;My 25-N 20 1878; Je 4-N 20 1884;N 21 1891-My 20,N 21 1895-N 21 1896;Ja-S 1899;Ap-S 1900;01-19;Ap 1920+
VNoL D 16 1865-Mr 19 1898;99-1911
VU Ja 20,F 9 1866;D 2 1869;Ja 19,Mr 24,My 12-13,Ag 18 1870;Ap 23 1872;Mr 30 1879;Jl 16, 22-26,28,30,Je 9,11-13,Jl 11,Ag 29,S 2 1934;Je 28,Ag 19 1935
VWW Mr 18 1880;Ag 11 1882;Je 1902-11
—sw ed *See* Journal of commerce and Virginian-pilot
—w ed *See* Weekly Norfolk Virginian

NORTH DANVILLE

Papers published in North Danville are listed under Danville

NORTH EMPORIA

Papers published in North Emporia are listed under Emporia

NORTON

COALFIELD progress. w Ja 1912+
pub D 1923+
VU F 9,14,Jl 18 1935

CRAWFORD'S weekly. w Jl? 1919-F 9 1935‖
Merged with Coalfield progress
V [Ap 30-D 1921]-35
VU [1921-N 17 1923;24-29]Ja 11-25,F 8-Ap 5, N 15,D 20 1930-F 8 1935

VIRGINIA digest. w Jl 24- 1926‖
VU Jl-S 18,O 2-16,30-N 13,27,D 11 1926

ONANCOCK

ACCOMACK news. *See* Eastern Shore news

EASTERN SHORE news. w Jl? 1897+
1897-1924 as Accomack news; 1925-33? News
pub 1905+
V 1925+

EASTERN VIRGINIA. w S? 1873-88‖
MWA S 15 1876

NEWS. *See* Eastern Shore news

ORANGE

Orange CHRONICLE. w 1857-61‖?
1857- as Southern chronicle
V Ja 17 1861

Orange EXPOSITOR. w My?-N 8? 1867‖
Followed by Native Virginian, later Piedmont Virginian

Orange EXPRESS. *See* Orange press. 1831-32

NATIVE Virginian. *See* Piedmont Virginian

NEWS and Virginian. *See* Orange county news (Gordonsville)

Orange OBSERVER. w 1881+
pub [1920+]
VHi Ja 6 1893;F 8 1895
VU Je 28 1929;Ja 13 1933;O 19-N,D 14-21 1934

ORANGE county news. *See under* Gordonsville

PIEDMONT Virginian. w N 15 1867-1909‖
Follows Orange expositor. 1867-Je? 1870 as Native Virginian
D 1869-Je? 1870 pub in Gordonsville
CSmH N 15,D 13 1867
MWA Je 23 1876
NNHi Ja 31 1873
V [N 15 1867-My 13 1870]
VU Ag 18 1876

Orange PRESS. w My 27? 1831-32‖?
Follows Reporter? 1831? as Orange express
DLC O 5 1832
VU Jl 1 1831

Orange PRESS. 1911-12 *See* Orange review

REPORTER. w Ap 24? 1830-31‖?
Followed by Orange express, later Orange press?
VU O 23 1830

Orange REVIEW. w Mr? 1911+
1911-12? as Orange press
Suspended from 1918-Mr 5 1931
pub Mr 3 1914-17;Mr 1931+
VU Ag 13 1933;Je 14-21,Jl 5-12,Ag 30 1934;Jl 4,25-Ag 8,22 1935

SOUTHERN chronicle. *See* Orange chronicle

PALMYRA

MIDLAND Virginian. w Ja 1895+
Follows Columbia bullet (Columbia)
1895 pub in Columbia
pub O 1930+
ICM O 26 1895
InRe Mr 23 1899
VU O 26 1895;D 22 1898;S 6 1923;Ag 22 1929;Je 6,Ag 1,S 5 1935

PEARISBURG

To 1835? as Giles Court House

Pearisburg GAZETTE. *See* Virginian

SOUTHWEST. w D? 1857-60‖
Followed by Pearisburg gazette, later Virginian

VIRGINIAN. w Jl 23 1886+
Follows Southwest. 1866-76? as Pearisburg gazette; 1885-1929 Weekly Pearisburg Virginian
pub 1866-69;1931+
ICM Ap 16,Ag 27,S 17 1886;Ap 7-14,Je 16,Ag 11,S 29,N 3,D 1 1887
MWA Je 16 1876
NNHi F 15 1873
V [Ag 21 1869-O 1874]
VU [1869-1930]Jl 23 1931;]Jl 3,Ag 22 1935+

PENNINGTON GAP

POWELL VALLEY news. w Ja? 1921+
VU N 26-D 3,17 1931+

PETERSBURG

ALLIANCE farmer. *See* Rural messenger

AMERICAN constellation. tw My 24 1834-38‖?
MWA N 25 1834;Mr 14,26 1835
NcD Ap 18 1837
VHi D 13 1834;F 17 1835
VP My 24-D 1834;My 10-D 21 1838
VWW Mr 10 1835

AMERICAN statesman. tw,sw D 3 1839-43‖
tw during sessions of the legislature;
DLC D 17 1839;Ja 3,D 4 1840
NcU My 26 1840
NhD Ja 26 1841

VIRGINIA (*Continued*)

PETERSBURG—*Continued*

Petersburg daily **APPEAL.** d N 7 1872-Jl 22 1873||
Follows Petersburg progress. United with Petersburg index to form Index and appeal, later Progress-index
NN N 7,11 1872;Mr 27,Je 20 1873
NNHi My 1 1873
OClWHi N 13,D 6,11,15-16 1872

ARMY and navy messenger. sm My 1 1863-65||
"Printed at the Enquirer job office in Richmond."
CSmH My 1 1863;Ja 1,F 1,Mr 1,Ap 1 1864
CtY F 23 1865
ICHi My 22 1863
NNHi My 1,Jl 1,Ag 1,S 1863;Mr 15-Ap 1864
NcD Mr 15 1865
PHi O 1 1863;My 26 1864(extra)
PP O 1 1863;My 26 1864(extra)
V Je 15 1863;D 16 1864;Mr 3 1865
VRC My 1,22,Je 15,Jl 1,Ag 15,S 15,D 15 1863

Petersburg daily **BULLETIN.** d Jl 30-N 1860||
Follows Press
DLC Jl 31 1860
NcU N 1 1860

Petersburg **CHRONICLE** and the Jacksonian republican. tw Ag? 1832-33||?
NcU Ja 4 1833

COMMERCIAL record. sw,w 1890?-1900||?
1890?-98 as Semi-weekly record(sw)
NcD D 22 1890;Ja 3,24,26,O 31,N 7,23,D 12-19 1891;Ja 2-4,9,N 19 1892;Mr 12,Ap 21,Je 18 1894;F 20 1897;Mr 19,My 28,N 19 1898;F 25, Mr 11,Ap 22,S 9,O 16,D 16 1899;N 24 1900
VU My 28 1898;F 25 1899

Daily **COURIER.** d O 16? 1869-Jl 25? 1871||
Follows Daily express
Jl 4 1871 never issued
MBAt [O-D 1869]
VP 1870-71

Daily **DEMOCRAT.** *See* Southside democrat

Petersburg **ENTERPRISE.** w Ag 6? 1890-95||?
NcD S 8 1894
VHi F 25 1893

Petersburg daily **EXAMINER.** d 1873||?
OClWHi [Ja 9-Jl 22 1873]

Daily **EXPRESS.** d Ap 24 1852-O 9? 1869||
Followed by Daily courier
Suspended from Ap 3-15 1865
CLM N 12 1861
CSmH [1855;D 1860-Je 11 1863]
CtHT Jl 20 1864
IC Je 14,22 1864
ICHi S 19,O 14 1865
ICN S 27-29 1864
MB N 20 1861
MBAt 1862-[65-69]
MWA Ja 25 1861;F 21 1862
MiG Mr 26 1862
N [1861]-[Ja,Mr-Ag 1864]-[Mr 1865]
NNHi [Ja-My]Jl 27,Ag 26,O 10 1861;Mr 10 1862;Je 12-13 1863;O 7 1864;Mr 28 1865
NcD [S 13 1860-N 6 1861]Ja 22,F 19,S 12 1862; My 20,Je 3,N 17 1863;F 6,16,Je 10-11,Ag 1,5 1864;Ja 18,23,F 1 1865;Ap 25 1866
NcU Ja 13,S 11,N 1,19-20,D 14 1860[Mr 1861-S 1862]
NjN My 27 1865
NjWdHi Je 13 1864
OClWHi [S 7-D 16 1861]Ja 10,14-16,Mr 20,Jl 12,23 1862;F 25 1863;Ag 16 1864;Ja 16 1865
PHi Ag 22 1863
TxGR Mr 22,Je 18 1862;Mr 22,Ag 8,24,S 20-21, 26 1864;Mr 7 1865
TxU N 13 1861
V Ap 24-O 23 1852;D 2 1858;F 22,Ap 13,Je 26 1860[Jl 22 1861-My 16 1862]Je 13 1864
VHi F 23 1858;Mr 5 1860;Je 8,10 1863[Ap 20-Ag 22]D 29 1864
VP My 13,S 23 1852;My 8 1855;56-59;Je 13 1868-Je 1869
VRC Ap 13,N 1,13,D 5 1860;My 4,Jl 24 1861; F 8 1862;N 13 1863;Mr 31,N 11 1865
VU N 9,25,D 28 1861;Ja 3,F 20,Ap 16 1862
WHi [S 17 1861-O 6 1865]

Weekly **EXPRESS.** w 1855-64||?
CSmH Ag 11-S 1,22 1855
MBAt My 13-20 1864
NcD Ja 25 1862
NcU D 8 1860
V Jl 19 1862

FARMERS' journal. w Ag 20- 1859||
MWA S 17 1859

GRANT'S Petersburg progress. tw Ap 3-10? 1865||
pub by officers of the 37th Wisconsin volunteers, and the 8th Michigan veteran volunteers on the press of Daily express
CSmH Ap 3 1865
DLC Ap 3-5 1865
MBAt Ap 7 1865
MWA Ap 5-7 1865
MnHi Ap 3 1865
NN Ap 5-10 1865
PToHi Ap 3 1865
VHi Ap 3-5(photograph)7,10 1865
VU Ap 5 1865
WHi Ap 3,7 1865

Petersburg **HERALD.** w Ap? 1888-99||
Negro
VHi D 31 1892

Petersburg **INDEX.** *See* Progress-index

Daily **INTELLIGENCER.** d Ja 2 1850-60||
NcD Mr 9,11-12,Ap 30,My 4,7,9,21,25 1850;My 1-3 1851;S 17 1859;Ag 24 1860

*INTELLIGENCER and Petersburg commercial advertiser. w,sw,tw Jl 6 1786-1860||
1786-Ap 1800 as Virginia gazette and Petersburg intelligencer; Ap 1800-17 Petersburg intelligencer (Je 7 1808-09 Petersburg Virginia intelligencer)
w 1786-Mr 1793;sw Ap 1793-1840
CSmH Je 5 1821;S 7 1830;O 6 1855
DLC N 5,13 1824[Mr 22-Jl 1825]-26;Ag 31 1827;D 5 1828;O 9,N 3,27 1829;N 9 1832;D 3 1840
ICHi N? 1835
MHi F 20 1821
MWA N 13 1830;N 3 1834
N D 3 1823;O 17 1833
NcD N 11 1825;My 11,Ag 17,27 1835;Ja 25 1836; F 25,O 10 1840;Ag 28 1841[Ap 23-Jl 16 1844]Jl 22 1845;F 7 1850
NcU My 21,28-30,Je 6-9,23-25,S 29 1840
NhD Je 5 1841
OClWHi Je 25 1822
OHi O 30 1845
V Mr 2 1827
VP [Ag 31 1824-Ag 12 1828]
VRN Je 29,Jl 3,6 1837
WHi Mr 11 1825

NATIONAL pilot. w 1886-1900||?
DLC F 1 1900

Daily **NEWS.** d My 13-Je 23 1865||
Followed by Petersburg index, later Progress-index
NN My 22-Je 1,5,8-9 1865
V Je 22 1865
WHi Je 8-9 1865

Daily **NEWS.** d N 26? 1873-76||
Followed by Daily post
NcD Mr 2 1876
V Ap 24 1874
VRB My 20-21,23,25-27,Je 3,6,8-9,11,15,17,19 1874

OLD DOMINION. sw O 27 1827-30||?
Follows Petersburg republican
CSmH S 1 1830
Ct [N 1827]F 23,Ap 2-5 1828
DLC D 6 1828;My 30,O 3,24 1829
MWA O 27 1827
VP N 20 1830

Daily **POST.** d My? 1876-Jl 1879||
Follows Daily news (1873-76)
VP 1877-Jl 9 1879

PRESS. d O 5 1858-Jl 1860||
Followed by Petersburg daily bulletin
NcD Ap 9 1859
VP 1858-Ap 4,N 21 1859-My 19 1860
VRC Ja 3 1860

Daily **PROGRESS.** d Jl 26 1871-72||?
Follows Daily courier
VP 1871

Evening **PROGRESS.** w,d Ag 6 1888-F 5 1922||
United with Index-appeal to form Petersburg progress and the index-appeal, later Progress-index
w Ag-S ? 1888
VPP 1903;Je 1904-06;08-Je 1911;12-22

PROGRESS-INDEX. d Jl 4 1865+
Follows Daily news. 1865-Jl 22? 1873 as Petersburg index; Jl 23 1873-Mr 17? 1878 Index and appeal; Mr 18 1878-F 5 1922 Progress and index-appeal
pub 1865+
A Je 20 1932
ICHi S 23,O 14 1865
MB S 5 1915
MBAt [S 8 1865-68]69
MH O 23,25,N 8-10,13,15 1865
MWA D 8 1875;O 16 1876;S 5 1915;Je 20 1932
NN S 12 1867[70-75;83]O 16 1885
NNHi Ap 24,Jl 9 1873;Ap 26 1875
NcD Ja 8 1868;S 4 1869;F 25 1870;S 11 1879; Jl 22 1881;Mr 31 1888;D 12 1896
NcU N 20,D 4 1866;F 19,22,Mr 4 1867;Ag 18 1881
OClWHi [1878-79]84-94
V [Jl 8 1865-Ja 18 1867]F 8,Mr 7,Ap 25,My 23,28,Jl 2 1870;Jl 22 1881;D 19 1884[92-1902]05+
VHi S 27 1865;O 30 1885;O 27 1892;Ja 1 1893
VP 1868-72;Jl 23 1873-Je 1911;Jl 1927+
VRB F 26 Mr 29-30,Je 7 1866
VRC Ag 12,O 21 1865
VU My 6,Jl 13,Ag 19,N 17 1870;Ja 24 1871;Jl 22 1881;D 7 1889;O 27-29 1892;Ap 12-17,19-My 28,30-Je 18 20-25,Jl 11,Ag 26,31,S 2 1934;Jl 4,20 1935+

RALEIGH register. *See under* Raleigh, N.C.

Evening **RECORD.** d N 26 1910-12||?
VPP 1910-Je 1911

Semi-weekly **RECORD.** *See* Commercial record

Daily **REGISTER.** d O 6 1863-64||
DLC O 8,19-21,24,N 6,D 4 1863;F 10-11,19,22, Mr 18,Ag 1,4,6 1864
IC Je 25 1864
MBAt Ap 11 1864
MHi Jl 11 1864
MN [Ja-Ag 1864]
NNHi Ag 25 1864
Nc N 20 1863
NcD F 19,Je 17 1864
NcU N 27 1863
NjP F 23 1864
OClWHi [Mr 23-Ag 27 1864]
VHi Mr 15,Ap 23,Je 16,18,29 1864

Weekly **REGISTER.** w
MnU N 6 1863
V F 26 1864

*Petersburg **REPUBLICAN.** sw 1799-O 16 1827||
Followed by Old Dominion
Ct Ag 11 1826
MWA [My 17-D 24 1822]
NcD F 1 1822;F 25,Jl 25 1823;O 28,N 1,15,22,D 2-9 1825
OHi N 23,D 2 1823
V Ja-S 25 1821;Mr 6 1827
VP Mr 14 1826
VU N 1 1825;Jl 7,18 1826

REPUBLICAN. d,tw F 15 1843-50||?
ICU Mr 19,S 29 1844
NcD O 7 1843;O 28 1846
VHi Ja-F 1850
VP 1843-F 10 1844;Ap 8 1846-Mr 1848
VRC Mr 2 1844[S-D 12 1845;My 15-O 26 1846]

RURAL messenger. w Ja 7 1871-92||
1887?-N? 1890 as Alliance farmer; D? 1890-91 Alliance farmer and rural messenger
MWA Ja 14 1871;S 9 1876
V S 14,O 12,D 14 1872;Ap 5,My 24,Ag 9 1873; O 10 1874
VP 1872-76;78-84
VRB Je 5 1875
VU N 22-29 1890

SOUTHERN farmer. w Ja 1854-D 18 1858||
NcD F 2-16 1856
V O 31 1857;Ja 9,30,Ap 10 My 8,29,O 16,30,N 13,27-D 4,18 1858
VWW Ag 25 1855

SOUTHSIDE democrat. d,sw,tw 1849-O 6 1858||
1855-56 as Daily democrat. Merged with Press
CtY Ag 23 1851
DLC Mr 5 1858
ICHi N 4,6 1852
NcD S 1,O 7 1853;Ja 17 1854;F 27,Je 5 1856
VHi O 1853-Mr 1854
VP C 1853-Ja 19,Jl 1857-Mr 11 1858

SOUTHSIDE news. *See* Southside Virginia news

SOUTHSIDE sentinel. w 1851?-52||?
VHi N 5 1851-N 2 1852

SOUTHSIDE Virginia news. w Jl 28 1927+
1927-Ap 1928 as Southside news
pub My 1928+
VU Jl-N 17,D 1927-Je 7,21-Jl 19,O 18-N 1,15 1928-Ja,F 14,28,Mr 14-Jl 18 1929;Jl 13 1933;Ap 26(supp)1934;Ag 8,S 1935+

STAR. 1840-45 *See under* Richmond

Evening **STAR.** d Mr 13 1875-76||?
MWA O 5 1875
OClWHi [Mr 14-O 17 1875]

SUN. d Ag 15 1877-Ja 14 1878||
VP complete

Th' **TIME** o'day! tw Ag 17-O 1 1839||
WHi complete

TIMES. w O 6 1828-31||
Merged with Intelligencer and Petersburg commercial advertiser
DLC O 6 1828
NcD Ja 3 1831

Petersburg daily **TIMES.** d N 6 1868-69||
MBAt N 7,12-17,19-23,25-26,28,D 1-2,4,7,9-21, 23,26-28,31 1868-Ja 14,18 1869
PHi 1868-Jl 10 1869

Weekly **TIMES.** w Ag 15 1868-69||
MBAt Ag 15-22,S 5 1868
PHi Ja 17 1869
V Ag 22 1868

VIRGINIA citizen. w My 1- 1876||
VWW My-O 28 1876

VIRGINIA gazette and Petersburg intelligencer. *See* Intelligencer and Petersburg commercial advertiser

VIRGINIA index. sw,w Ja 20 1859-60||
Dated also in Richmond
CSmH Mr 15,18,My 31,Je 7,24,Jl 1,8,15,22,26,Ag 19,23,S 6,16,O 4,7,N 15,29,D 20 1859;Mr 13,20, O 12,N 23 1860
DLC S 9 1859;Mr 13,27,N 6 1860
MWA Ap 10 1860
TxU [1859-Mr 13 1860]
V Ja 3,6,13,F 24,28,Mr 6,9,23,Jl 3,31,Ag 3 D 23,30 1859
VRB N 23 1860

Petersburg **VIRGINIA** intelligencer. *See* Intelligencer and Petersburg commercial advertiser

VIRGINIA star. w,sw Mr 4 1840-41||?
w 1840
DLC Mr 18 1840;Ja 9 1841

PHENIX

CHARLOTTE gazette. *See under* Drake's Branch

PITTSYLVANIA COURT HOUSE.
See CHATHAM

POCAHONTAS

Pocahontas **HEADLIGHT.** w Je? 1886-1911||
Suspended from 1897-1905
1886-95 pub in Graham (now Bluefield)
ICM F 10 1887

Pocahontas **OUTLOOK.** w Jl 20 1883-
VU O 19 1883

PORT REPUBLIC

INDEPENDENT. w Ja 2 1886-87||
NcD F 6,My 22-Jl,Ag 14-O 2,16-N 27 1886

VIRGINIA (*Continued*)

PORTSMOUTH

CHRONICLE and Old Dominion. tw,d Ap 18 1839-D 1848||
Ap 18-S 18 1839 as Commercial chronicle; S 20 1839-Ap 1840? Commercial chronicle, and the Portsmouth and Norfolk tri-weekly Old Dominion; My 1840?-Jl 2 1845 Chronicle and Old Dominion; Jl 7 1845-Mr 13 1847 New era
DLC 1839-Ap 20 1840;Ag 25 1843-[Mr 23 1847-48]
NN Ja 10 1842
NcD [Ja 22 1844-Jl 2,D 24 1845-N 1846]
V Ja 9 1847

CLAY banner, and commercial and naval intelligencer. tw Jl 22- 1842||
DLC Jl 27 1842

COMMERCIAL chronicle. *See* Chronicle and Old Dominion

Portsmouth and Norfolk COMMERCIAL gazette. tw N 28- 1833||
DLC D 14 1833

Daily DISTRICT whig. tw,d N 10 1849-60||?
1849-F 11? 1850 as District whig and commercial register for the Port of Norfolk and Portsmouth (tw)
NNHi 1849-Jl 2 1851

ENTERPRISE-TIMES. d Ap 14 1873-89||
1873-87? as Portsmouth daily enterprise
MWA O 3 1876
NcD N 1 1873;S 12 1879
VRB My 21,23-24,27,29,Je 2,4,6,9 1874

Daily GLOBE. d Jl 27 1853-60||?
DLC [Ag 15-D 30 1853]
V Je 7 1854

INDEPENDENT daily messenger. d S 29 1843-44||?
WHi 1843-Ap 27 1844

NEW ERA. *See* Chronicle and Old Dominion

OLD DOMINION. w O 20 1838-My 30? 1846||
DLC [1838-Mr 12 1842]
GAtCo My 30 1840
MWA O 27 1838
NN Je 15 1839;Ja 9,Ap 24,My 22,Ag 21 1841; Ja 15,Ap 16 1842
NcD S 7 1839;N 7 1840
NhD F 1,Ap 11,25 1840;Ap 10 1841;Je 11 1842
VWW Ap 11,25,My 30 1846
See also Chronicle and Old Dominion

Daily OLD DOMINION. 1863-64 *See* Norfolk Old Dominion (Norfolk)

Daily PILOT. d,tw O 1848-D 31 1850||?
not pub Ag 6-16,D 25-28 1850
tw My 17-Ag 5 1850
DLC D 15 1849-D 31 1850
MdHi D 30 1850
PP N 14 1850

Weekly PILOT. w
NN D 15 1849
NhD D 8 1849
PP N 16 1850

PUBLIC index. d Ap 10 1844||
DLC Ap 12 1844

REPUBLICAN and weekly times. *See* Times and republican

Portsmouth REPUBLICAN and Virginia commercial gazette. sw My- 1829||
DLC Jl 22 1829

SOUTHERN statesman. d My 4- 1857||
DLC My 21 1857

SOUTHERN whig. w Ja 11- 1843||
DLC Ja 11 1843

Portsmouth STAR. d S 3 1894+
pub 1894+
MWA D 6 1906
VU Je 27-28 1935

TIDEWATER times. w O? 1878-94||
V Ja 9 1879;Mr 29 1880

Portsmouth daily TIMES. d Ja? 1877-88||
MWA N 7 1880

TIMES and commercial advertiser. sw D? 1835-39||?
United with Republican to form Republican and weekly times, later Times and republican
VRN F 27 1836

TIMES and republican. w,sw,tw O 27 1838-40||?
1838? as Republican; 1838-39? Republican and weekly times
DLC D 22 1838;S 7 1839
NcD Jl 28 1840

Daily TRANSCRIPT. d O 1849-61||?
CSmH O 1850-Je 1860
MWA Ap 11 1856
NNHi 1859
NcD Ag 31 1853;Je 11 1860
TxU Ap 20-O 15 1852

Weekly TRANSCRIPT. w Ja 1857-
MWA Ja 21,Jl 22,S 16,D 2 1858

VIRGINIA farmer and granger. w S? 1879-93||?
1879-89? as Virginia granger
NcD Mr 24,Je 2 1881;D 14-21 1882;F 8-22,Mr 8-22,Ap-My 10,24,Je 7-14,28,Jl 19,Ag 2 1883; Ag 21 1884
VU F 22 1883

VIRGINIA granger. *See* Virginia farmer and granger

VIRGINIA palladium and Portsmouth commercial advertiser. *See* Virginia palladium (Norfolk)

PULASKI

Pulaski NEWS. *See* News-review

NEWS-REVIEW. Ag 16 1872-1909||
1872-79 as Virginia people; 1880-85 Pulaski people; 1886 People; 1886-92 Pulaski news. United with Southwest times to form Southwest times and news-review, later Southwest times
1872-86 pub in Newbern
w 1872-99
MWA S 7 1876
NNHi F 21 1873
VHi Mr 24 1893
VU S 6 1872-F 6 1874;S 15 1893

PEOPLE. *See* News-review

Pulaski REVIEW. w 1891-92||
United with Pulaski news to form News-review

SOUTHWEST times. sw,tw,d Mr 9 1906+
sw 1906-15?;tw 1916?-Je 1928
pub Mr 23 1906-07;Ap,Jl-Ag 1913;D 1916+
V [S 15 1916-34]+
VBP 1935+
VU N 4 1910;Mr 12,Je 27,Jl 28 1935

VIRGINIA people. *See* News-review

PURCELLVILLE

BLUE RIDGE herald. w Ja 1890+
1890-1920 as Enterprise (Hamilton)
NcD Ag 12 1921;D 25 1924;F 19,Mr 5-12,My 21,Je 11-25, Jl 23,D 10 1925[26-O 13 1927] Ja 19,Mr 15,Ap 19 1928
VLe Ag 30 1911
VPu Ag 1934+
VU Je 24 1904;S 4,18 1930;Je-Jl 9,23-Ag 20,S 1931-Je 2,23-Jl 7,Ag-S 15,29 1932+

QUANTICO

GAZETTE. w Jl 1933+
pub 1933+
VU Je 27,Jl 18 1935

RADFORD

Radford ADVANCE. sw,w D 1891-1912||
Followed by Record
VU Je 24 1898

Radford JOURNAL. w Ag? 1919-28||
Follows Record. United with Radford news to form Radford news-journal
VU Je 1926

Radford NEWS-JOURNAL. w,sw Ag 1912+
1912-Jl 1928 as Radford news
w 1912-22
pub 1928+
VHi [N 11 1918-Mr 16 1921]
VRaT F 1935+
VU D 8 1932;Je 29 1933;Je 20,Jl 11-18,Ag 1 1935

RECORD. w,sw 1912-19||
Follows Advance. Followed by Radford journal
w 1912-17

REMINGTON

Remington NEWS. *See* Tri-county herald

Remington PRESS. *See* Tri-county herald

TRI-COUNTY herald. w Ap 5 1923+
1923-Je 1930? as Remington press; Jl 1930?-My 1935 Remington news
pub My 1932+
VU Ja-F 9,23-O,N 9-D 21 1929;Je 27,Jl 18 1935

RENDEZVOUS OF DISTRIBUTION

SOLDIERS' Journal. *See under* Augur General Hospital

RICHMOND

ADVERTISER and register. d 1865||
CtY Ja 15 1865

Täglicher ANZEIGER. d,w Mr? 1853-My 1915||
1853- as Richmonder anzeiger (w)
In German
DLC Mr 26 1865
MWA Je 25 1876
NNHi Ja 25 1873
—**Sunday ed** *See* Die Virginische zeitung

ARMY and navy messenger. *See under* Petersburg

Richmond AURORA. d Je 9- 1842||
DLC Je 16 1842

BANNER of liberty. Je 16 1842-
"The second number will appear on July 4 1843"
DLC Je 16 1842

BANNER of temperance. *See* Southern era

Weekly BEE. (Manchester) w 1904-Ja 3 1912||
1904-10? as Bee
VU Ja 3 1912

BIOGRAPHICAL pen. w O 22 1862-
CSmH O 22 1862

Evening BULLETIN. d,sw O 1? 1853-D 1 1854||
CSmH O 15,N 11 1853;Ap 29,My 15 1854
ICM Jl 26-D 1 1854

Evening BULLETIN. d,sw N 21?- 1873||
VHi D 7 1873

Monday BULLETIN. w My 9?- 1898||
VHi Je 27,Ag 1,15 1898
VWW My 30,Jl 18 1898

BUSY DAY. sw,d Ja? 1857-59||?
CSmH Ap 2 1859

CAMPAIGN. w Ag ? 1883-O 17? 1885||
Followed by Reformer
NNHi Mr 29,S 6-20,O 11-18 1884
V Mr 8,22,My 10,Je 21,Jl 5-19,N 8 1884;S 5, 26-O 3,17 1885
VU S 26 1885

CITIZEN. d Ap 2 1866-
MWA Ap 3 1866
VHi Ap 4 1866

COMMERCIAL. *See* Monday commercial and tobacco leaf

COMMERCIAL and industrial South. w,m 1881-91||
1881-87? as Industrial South
m Ag 1886-Je? 1887
DLC [Ag 13 1881-84]86-Je 1887
ICM [My 26 1883-N 21 1885]
MB Je 9 1883-Ja 1885
NcD Ja 27 1883
NcU Jl 30 1881
V [Jl 30 1881-Jl 25 1885]
VU Ag 15,O 10,N 21 1885

Monday COMMERCIAL and tobacco leaf. w My? 1868-85||
1868-71 as Commercial; 1875-Je 1883 Commercial and tobacco leaf
Suspended 1872-74
NcD Jl 10 1875
V Ag 28 1869;Jl 2 1883;My 25,Je 8 1885

Evening COMMERCIAL bulletin. d,sw,w My 6-N 8? 1865||
CClP My 6 1865
CSmH My 9,24,Je 2 1865
CtY My 13 1865
DLC My 24 1865
MBAt [My 18-N 9 1865]
MWA My 9 1865
OHi Ag 18 1865
V [My 11-N 8 1865]
VHi My 22 1865
VRC [Je-O 21 1865]
WHi Jl 12 1865

Richmond COMMERCIAL compiler. *See* Richmond times d

COMMONWEALTH. d Ja 30-Jl 28 1880||
Merged with State
DLC complete
ICM Je 7,12-13,Jl 10,24 1880
MBAt complete
NN complete
V complete
VRB Ap 29 1880
VRC F 3 1880
V Ja 30-Mr 19,21-22,24,26-Ap 11,13-Jl 27 1880
WHi Mr 4,26 1880

COMMONWEALTH. w F 20- 1880||
NcD F 20,Ap 23,Jl 9 1880

COMMONWEALTH. sw,w 1908-28||
United with Monitor to form Commonwealth monitor (Rosslyn)
1908-12? pub in Falls Church (sw)
PSuHi Ap 22 1910
VU Je 23 1928

Richmond COMPILER. *See* Richmond times

CONSERVATIVE. w O 4-N 7 1872||
V N 7 1872

CONSERVATIVE-DEMOCRAT. sw Ag 26? 1880-O? 1881||
NcD Ag 27 1881

CONSTITUTIONAL whig. *See* Richmond whig

Evening COURIER. d N 5? 1864-Mr 31 1865||
CSmH D 31 1864[Ja-Mr 1865]
DLC F 24[Mr]1865
MH N 14,19,28 1864;Mr 2,4,9 1865
MWA Ja 11,Mr 2,22,28 1865
NN F 25 1865
V Ja 26-27,30,F 1-2,4,8-9,11,25,Mr 11 1865
VHi Ja 6 1865

Richmond COURIER and compiler. *See* Richmond times 1813-53

CRISIS. w Mr 7-O 28 1840||
DLC complete
NN complete
NcD Mr,Ap 11-O 1840
NcU Mr 7 1840
V complete

CRITIC. w S 12 1887-D 27 1890||
CtY Jl 23,Ag 13-20 1888
DLC [Mr 19 1888-D 6 1890]
MHi Jl 30,Ag 13-27[S 10 1888-D 6 1890]
MWA Jl 23-Ag 13,O 8,N 19 1888;Ja 20 1889
MdHi Je 18,Jl 30,Ag 13,O 1-8,N 5,26,D 9 1888
NNHi Jl 30,O 8,N 26 1888;F 17 1889
V [1887-90]
VHi D 19 1887[88-89]Ja 11,Mr 1 1890
VWW O 3,31[D 19 1887-Je 18,Jl 9 1888-Ja 11, F-Mr 15 1890]

DEBT payer. w Je 25-Ag 26? 1881||
ICM Jl 2-9,Ag 13 1881
VHi Ag 26 1881
WHi Jl 22 1881

DEMOCRAT. d S 25 1890-Ja 23 1891||
V [1890-91]

Richmond DISPATCH. d O 19 1850-Ja 25 1903||
1850-83 as Daily dispatch. United with Times to form Times-dispatch
Ja 2 1864-Ap 3 1865 only half sheets published (Mr 16-17 1865 never pub) Suspended from Ap 3-D 9 1865;Ap 1-9 1866
A Jl 26 1861;Mr-N 1866;Ap 9,Jl 9,N 20 1877; My 15,Jl 13,18,N 16 1878;Ja-Mr 1881
ArHi Je 19 1887;Mr 12 1898

VIRGINIA (*Continued*)

RICHMOND—*Continued*

Richmond DISPATCH. d 1850-1903||—*Continued*
CSmH [N 28 1850-Jl 9 1869]Jl 2(supp)1870;O 26 1875
Ct Ap 3 1865
CtY D 7 1861-Mr 16 1865
DLC S 3 1853;Ap 13,D 20 1859;My 18 [Ag] D 6 1860;Ja 7,Mr 14,25[Ap 8 1861-64]Ja 10-Ap 3 1865 Ap 10,Je 9,16,21,O 4 1866;My 21 1868;Ja 30 1869[Je 1870-Ag 1899] 1900-03
GU My 11 1859
IC My 7,Je 8 1864
ICHi Ap 25 1854;Ag 19 1861;Jl 3 1863
ICM Mr 9,Ag 16,N 6,21,D 21 1878;D 23 1879;Je 18,S 24,O 29 1881;Je 29,Jl 28 1883; Ja 9,27 1884[85-97;Ap-My 1900;01-02]
ICN [My 10-Ag 10 1864]
ICU N 13-15,23,29,D 7,12 1861[Ja-N 5 1862] Mr 27,Ap 2,Ag 25,D 14 1863
IU S 13,15 1858;My 20,25,27,Je 4,22,Jl 9,19, 24,27,31,Ag 9,O 14,21 1861;Ap 15 1862;Je 13 1863;Mr 23 25-Ap 4,8-12,15-19 1864;S 5 1871; Mr 6 1875;My 25 1890;My 31 1893
KHi [F 22 1861-S 9 1864]
LNC D 16,29 1862
LNM Ja 5 1865
LSfD S 21 1861
MB [Ja 8 1861-Je 1862]Ja 27 1863;F 23-Ap 22 1864
MBAt [F-D 1861]-Ap 1,D 14,23,27-28 1865 [Ja-Ag 15 1866;My 18 1867-69]
MH Ja 15,17-18,O 18 1862[Mr 17-D 1863;Mr 9 1864-65]
MHi My 15 1862;Ag 12 1863[64;76-79]Ja 1,Mr 29,Je 2 1881
MWA Ag 24 1853;N 17 1860;N 4,28,D 16 1861[F 14 1862-N 1898]O 8 1902
MdHi Jl 5 1862;Ja 1 1877;My 28-30 1890
MiU-C [1861-65]
NBHi S 16 1863;Ag 12 1864
NBuG Ja 1 1878
NN My 18-19 1859[Ap 1861-O 17 1862]Je 9, 23,Jl 9,N 9 1863[64-Ap 1 1865]F 19,Je 28, Jl 6 1867;Ap 18,20 1868;Ja 23,F 17,Mr 7,Je 15,19,21,Jl 17,24,Ag 5,S 16,N 7-9,23,25,27 1872 [F 1873-O 1874]
NNC Ap 12-15 My 4,Jl 25 1861
NNHi [Ja-F 1861;Mr 1862-F,Ap 1863-64]Mr 4,13,Ap 1 1865;Ap 28 1870;My 5 1873;Ja 1 1881
NbHi Ag 16 D 1 1862;Ja 1,Ap 13,Je 5,13,26, D 7,17 1863;Mr 30,S 12,D 1,12,21,31 1864; Mr-Ap,Ag,O 6-22,30,N 1873-Ap 1874
Nc My 16,19 23,31 1864;F 22 1884
NcD Ap 18 1855;Je 27,Jl 13,S 11 1856;Ja 31, F 14 1857;D 6 1858;D 1 1859[Ap 13 1861-F 1865]Ja 20 1866[Ap 1873-76]-[Jl 1877-78]-[Jl 1879-Je 22 1882]Ap 22,D 12 1883;O 6,8 1885; N 6 1886;Ag 2,Ag 28 1887;90;Jl 22 1891;N 9 1892;93;Ja 1 Mr 1,Jl-D 1894;Mr 15 1895[Ja]-D 1896;O 3 1897;Ja-S 1898;F 23,Jl-D 1899; Jl 1901-02
NcU O 11 1855;Mr 13,16,Je 4 1857;Je 11,S 11, D 22 1860 [Ap 26 1861-My 1863]Je 27,D 13 1864;Ag 18 1881;My 30 1890;Ap 8 1896
OCHi [My-Ag 1861]-[Mr-Ag 1862]-[F-Ap]Ag 28 1863;My 10 1877
OClWHi [1860-64]-Ap 1 1865;Ap 28,Je 1,4 1866;O 22 1870 [71-75]My 25 1876;My 7-8, Ag 15,S 13,O 3,N 22-23,D 5 1877;Ja 1 1882; Ag 10 1893[My 6 1894-O 29 1896]
ODW S 11 1861
OOxM My 12 1877
P 1890-Je 1895
PAtM Ja 22,29 1864
PHi Ag 27,S 9,14,22,O 31,D 21 1863
PP [Ag 24 1861-O 1863]
PU [1901-02]
Tx O 19 1869
TxGR My 20 Je 6,S 27 1861[Ja-O 2 1862]Mr 11,S 23 1863 F 26-Ag 9 1864]
TxU Ja 28,30 1860;Ag 10 1861;Ja 1,6,18,27, F 1,4,14,Ap 3 1862;D 12 1865:S 7 1876
V [Jl 21 1852-1903]
VHi Jl 22 1858[59-65]My 10,N 21,D 31 1866; D 3 1867;Ap 18 1868;Ap 28[My 17 1870-71]-Ja 1903
VP 1877-93;95-1902
VRB D 9 1865;Je 11 1866;My 18,24, 1869:Ap 28,My 3 1870;Ja 5 1871;My 22-28,Je 1-2,4,8-10,18,20 1874 O 26 1875;F 23,Je 27 1876;Ja 1 1878;Jl 30 1879;Ap 29 1880;Je 29 1883;Ja 1 1887;Ag 10 1893;My 20 1894;Mr 17 1895
VRC D 20 1859[My 7 1861-Ag 1 1866] D 19 1868;Ap 29 1870; Ap 18 1873;N 6 1874;F 10, 24-25,O 25-27 29 1875;Ja 26,F 4,8 1876;Ja 1 1877;Ja 1 1878;Ja 1,29 1879;Ja 1,Je 25 1880: Ja 1 1881;Ja 2 1883;Ja 1 1886
VRN D 9 1864-Ap 21 1866;Je 10 1867-Ja 1903
VU O 16 1855[Ap 13 1861-O 11 1864]Ja 17, 23,F 4,24,28,Mr 24,Ap 1 1865;Ja 17 1866;Je 10-O 1,3-8,10 1867-Je 29 1872;73-76;F 23,My 10,Jl-D 1877;Ja 30 1878-82;Jl 1883-Je,O 1898-1903
VWW Ap 15,17,D 20 1854;Ag 25 1858;Ag 16 1859;D 18,20-21 1860;S 30 1861[F 10-28]Ap 30,O 17 1862;Ja 26,F 6, Mr 19 1863;F 18 1870; F 8,O 16 1879 Ja 24-Mr 5,27 1880;Mr 15 1881; Je 29 1882;Ag 14,17,19 1883 Ja 1,F 26,Jl 16 1885;F 4-6[N 10 1886-Jl 5]S 15,O 4,14,D 25 1887;Ap 28,D 17 1889[Ja-Mr 1890]My 24-26 1891; My 8,2 23-24,Je 23,27-28,O 25 1892-1903
WHi [Ap 16 1861-Mr 20 1865]Ap 4 1868[Mr 16 1875-N 16 1880]81;F 25,Ap 12,Jl 1882-Je 29 1884;Ja-Je 28 1885;86;92-95

Weekly DISPATCH. w 1850-1903||
United with Weekly times to form Weekly times-dispatch
CSmH Ag 22,29 19 1851;F 22 S 17 1858[O 14 1859-Je 21 1861]D 29 1866;67-O 21 1870
CtY Mr 15 1861
DLC Ap 20 1860[Ja-Mr,My 17-S 20 1861;Ja-Ap 18 1862]
MHi Ja 7 1862
MWA [S 1861-F 7 1862]Jl 3 1868;N 14 1873; N 30 1877;F 1878;Ja 31,S 19 1879
NN Ap 27 1882
NNHi Jl 4 1872;Ja 31 1873;N 2 1888

NcD Ja 23,F 27 1857;Ap 6 1860[Mr 15 1861-My 2 1862]N 4 1870;S 15 1871;N 24 1876;Ag 22-S 5,26-O 17,31 1879; Ag 4,S 8,D 15 1882; N 16 1883;My 16 1884;My 22,D 18 1885;S 10,O 1-22,N 5,19-D 3,17 1886-[87]Jl 13,Ag 17,N 9 1888;My 17,Je 14 1889;O 11 1892;Ap 13-20,My 11,Je 5,15,D 18 1894;Jl 3 1896;S 17 1897;D 2 1899;S 20-24 1900;Ap 22 1901
NcU Ag 19 1881
NjHi S 6 1861
OClWHi Je 22 1860;Mr 15,My-D 1861;D 13 1857;Ap 24 1868;My 6,31,Je 17-24,Ag 12 S 25 1894;Ap 28-My 12,Ag 18-D 21 1895;Ja 26,Mr 1,Je 30-Jl 3,O 29 1896
TxU S 13 1872;S 5 1890
V Jl 12 1889
VHi F 22 1858;D 16 1859;D 2 1870;Ag 10 1897
VRB Ag 6 1852;Mr 17,Jl 7 1854;Ap 24 1868
VU S 6-13,O 4,25,N 29 1861;Ja 10,Mr 14,Ap 4-11,My 2 1862;O 29 1875;My 16 1884;My 22, Ag 14-21 1885;F 1886-D 18 1891;Ja-F 12,26 1892;Mr 25 1903
WHi Ag 1,N 14 1873;My 21,28 1875

Semi-weekly DISPATCH. sw Jl 10 1857-1903||
A Jl 23 1861-Je 13 1862
CSmH N 18 1859;Ja 13,My 11,Jl 10-13 1860; Je 25-28 1861;Ap 26 1867
DLC S 22 1863;Je 12 1866
MB S 3 1861;Ap 19,D 24 1862
MWA N 11 1870;N 3 1876;F 13 1877;My 14 1878
NN My 8 1874
NNHi My 20 1862
NcD [1862]Ja 3,Mr 14 1863;N 13 1874;Je 11, Jl 16 1875;Mr 12,22,Ap 26,S 3,O 4 1878;N 16 1880;F 4,D 2 1881;Ja 13 1882;D 9 1884;N 5 1886;Mr 15,Ap 8,Jl 1,N 29,D 9,16,30 1887;Ja 6,10,F 3,17 1888;My 17 1889;Ap 28 1891;Mr 1, Je 3,14-28,Jl 24 1892[Mr-D 1899]
NcU O 1,15,D 10 1861;Ja 14-17,Ap 4,My 2,13, Je 3,Jl 29,Ag 1,S 12,O 31 1862;Ja 20,27,F 6, 24,Ap 7 1863 Ja 13 1888
OClWHi Ap 5,19-Je 21 1861
TxU Ap 3,My 15,22-Je 2 1885
VRB Ja 1877-D 30 1881;Ja 26 1892
VRC [Ja]Ag 23,S 10 1861;My 11 1866
VU Ag 8,S 23,O 11-15,31 1862;Jl 12 1889;Jl 29-Ag,S 9 1892-Ja 17,F 14-28 1893;F 20-27 1894;My 26-Je 9,Ag 4,14-18,25-S 1,8,25,O 2,D 18 1896;F 12,22 1898;D 13 1900;O 17,N 25,D 5 1901;S 11,N 6,13,20-24 1902
WHi S 22 1874;My 14 1878

Evening DISPATCH. d S 27 1920-N 9 1923||
Follows Evening journal. S 27-O 5 1920 as Evening dispatch and journal
V complete
VRN O 1920-23
VU 1920;Ja 3-11,Ag 5,11-23,S 1-19,21-23,26-D 1921;Ja 4,6-19,Jl 16,18-22,24-26,Ag-D 23,27-30 1922;Ja 15-27,Mr 9,15-19,Ap,Ag-N 1923

Evening DISPATCH and journal. *See* Evening dispatch

***Richmond ENQUIRER.** sw,tw My 9 1804-N 28 1877||
Follows Richmond examiner (1789-1804. Not in this list). 1804-S 18? 1815 as Enquirer; Jl 16? 1867-Ja 30 1870 Enquirer and examiner
Mr 20 1862-Ap 11 1865 only half sheets published.
Suspended from Ap 1-O 30 1865; S 10-D 2 1876
tw during sessions of legislature
CSmH Ap 9 1822;Jl 29,Ag 1,12-19 1823;F 12 1824;25;Jl 27 1827;Ja 31,F 9,O 25-28,N 4-11 1828:Ap 7,D 12-15,22(extra)1829;My 7,O 15,D 9 1830;Ap 9,18 1844;F 6(extra)Ap 25 1845;My 29 1846;N 2,6,27 1860;F 5,19-28,Mr 7-23,26-30,Ap 1-9,13-15,20,My 7,14,Jl 2,O 22 1861:Ja 8 1864;Je 21 1867
CSt [1821-34]
Ct O 3 1823;Ap 27,Je 8 1827;Ja 31 1835;D 24 1836
CtHi F 16 1823-42
CtY O 19 1824;D 9 1828;Ja 3,F 5,Mr 3 1829;S 28(extra)1832
DLC [1821-F 21 1865]Ja 4,8 1867
GAtCo F 5 1839
GDE [1826]27
GU 1821[22-25]-41[63]
ICHi S 30 1830;My 17 1831[Jl 4-S 1859]Mr 30 1863;O 31 1865
ICN Mr 2,23,Ap 25,My 3,Ag 6-9,S 13,O 11-15, N 1-5,D 13 1861;My 9 1862
ICU O 19,26,N 2-23,D 4-7 1824
IU Ja 22,31,F 3,21,Mr 4,19,Ap 6,23,My 14 1824; My 17,S 27,O 18,25 1831;F 28,Ap 13,Ag 28,D 20 1832;Ag 19 26-29,S 5 1834;Je 6,N 21-24 1837;N 6 1838;My 1 1840;O 16 1868;S 10 1869
KyLo Jl 9 1824;F 25,Jl 18 1826
LSfD O 22 1861
LU Ja-Jl 23 1824;My 12,S 5[O 1823-My 8 1827;My 23-D 1828]
MB 1828-29;Je 25 1830-My 10 1831;My 15 1832-Jl 24 1846;F 8 1850[F 16 1855-D 21 1861]O 1863-Je 1864;Ja-Je 1877
MBAt [1821-76]
MH N 24 1863;S 30 1864
MHi [1821-23]Mr 25,Ap 5,N 4 1825[Ja 12-F 25]My 12,D 5 1826[Ja 30-My 1827]F 21 1865
MSaE 1837-40;S 7,28-O 1 1841
MWA 1821-[41]42;Ja 12,F 9 1843;44-[Ja-Jl 1845;Ap 10-D 1846]S 9 1853;D 5 1854;58-Ag,O 9 1860;O 3,N 4,28 1862;S 15,O 20,D 25-29 1863; Ja 5,15,My 10,Je 21,Ag 30 1864;Jl 14,21,Ag 22 1876
Md Ap 8 1823-N 12 1830
MiU Jl-D 1825;29;My 1830-My 1832;33-35
MiU-C F 6,Mr 4 1823;D 20 1825;Mr 28,My 16 1826;Jl 31,Ag 31,O 19,N 6,D 28 1827;Ja 17,My 20-23,Jl 8,Ag 26,D 23 1828;Ag 14 1829 Mr 23, D 3 1830;Ja 29,F 10,My 6,S 13,O 7,D 10 1831; Ja 17,24,F 4,24,Mr 6,13,S 4,O 19 1832;Je 21,S 27,D 7 1833;Ja 17 1835;O 19,30 1838
MnHi Ja 18 1833
MnM Ap 1825-F 1826
MsHi 1837-45
N D 8 1825;Ja 14-Ap 14,Jl 25,Ag 1826-[Ja-N 1827]Je 13 1834;Ja 19 1837

NCH 1841;Ja-Je 1843
NIC 1824-62
NN Ja 11,Mr 1-3,9,20,My 25,Jl 3,S 4 1821-Ag 1824;Ja 4,8,29,F 10,Mr 15-18,Ag 29-S,O 7-N 25,D 1825-Ag,O 26,N 20-23,D 4-6,11 1827;28-Ag 1830;S 1831-S 1832;O 1833-Ag 18,O 3 1837-F 22,Mr 8-My,Je 26-S 4,O 1838-S,O 4,18,25 1839-O 1 1844;Ap 30 1861;S 2 1862;Je 19-22 1866;Je 4 1867;Je 11 1873
extras:N 14,D 22 1829;Mr 14 1834
NNHi F 13,S 21[O 1821-Ja 2 1823]My 11 1824-My 9 1826;F 28,Mr 13-17,O 8-10,17-22,N 24 1829;My 11 1830-My 8 1840;My 10 1841-Ap 1851;Ja 8 1861;Mr 18 1862;Mr 10 1863;Ag 24 1864
extras:S 30,O 7,14,21,28,N 4,11,18,25 1825;Ag 24,S 21 1830;Jl 27 1831;Ap 13,Ag 17,28 1832; Mr 14 1834
NSchU D 19 1835
NUHi 1838-45
NcD 1821-Ag 26 1864]O 14,N 4 1870;O 25 1872;Je 2,28 1877
NcU N 1-8 1822;Mr 3,Jl 3 O 30 1827;Je 28 1836;F 14 1839;My 12,N 10,D 31 1840;N 19 1841;Ja 20 1842;F 8,Ap 20,26,My 10,Jl 30,S 13 1844;Ap 10 1846;S 3,28 1847;F 22,S 19 1848; Mr 16 1849;Ja 18,F 15,Je 11 1850;S 16 1851; Mr 16-19,S 21 1852;Ap 3,My 4,Je 5,29 1855;Ja 18 1856;N 30 1860;S 9-13;23-26,O 10-14,N 21, D 5-9,16-19 1862;Ja 9-16,F 10,17,My 15 1863
NhD 1829[Ja-Jl 9 1830]Je 1 1841
NjHi F 26 1831
NjR D 9 1826;Ap 6 1827;Jl 12 1831
OCl Mr 30 1863
OClWHi Mr 23 1844[Jl 4-N 1848]Ag 17 1852; My 30 1854[Je 10 1856-57]D 31 1858;Ap 17,S 1860-My 17,Je 13 1861-My 9,Jl 11,S 19,O 14, N 11,28 1862;Jl 3 1863;O 21 1877
OHi F 27-N 20 1821;Ja 26-O 4 1822;F 15,Je 13-17,N 18,D 20 1823;Ja 11-Ag 27 1824;N 25, D 8 1828;F-N 1829;30-My 1 1832;Ag 27,S 6, 10-13,20,O 1,8,15,25 1833;Mr 21-D 9 1834;Ja-Ap 1835;Ja 7-O 14 1836;Ja-N 21 1837;Mr-O,D 14 1838;39;F 19,My 18,Je 15 O 22 1847;Ag 15 1854;N 10 1857-Ag 1 1860;F 17 1864
OOxM F 13,22-24 1827[O 29 1829-O 1 1830]My 10-13 1877
PBL [1821]
PDoHi Ja 29,My 24 1825
PEL Ja-Je 5 1821
PHi S 22 1863
PUnR [1831]-[33]
PWaHi Ag 30,S 3 1839
T D 17 1844
TKL My 19 1862;Je 2 1863
TxGR D 9 1862
TxU 1821[F 20 1823-Mr 9]-D 1824;26-Ag 1827 [28-29]-32;O 1833-34;My 8 1835-[My 6 1836-O 20 1837]41-[Ja-Jl 22 1842]My 13 1845-Ap 2,N 1847-56;58-Jl 15 1864;Ja-Mr 2 1865
V [1821-72]
VHi [1821-76]
VHo [1858-61;63-64]
VP [Ag 31 1824-O 14 1828;Mr-D 18 1830]36-39;41
VRB D 6 1821;Jl 25 1828;Mr 14 1834;Mr 12 1850;Jl 25 1856
VRC [1861]
VRN F 24 1821;Mr 14 1834
VU [1821]-[39-N 6 1840;41-Jl 1842]Ja 19-21,F 11-14,Mr 18,25,Ap 7,Jl 11 1843;F 23-Ap 9,16-18,23-My 7,14,Ag 9,20 1844;Ja 14,F 26,Mr 4 1845;My 1846-[58]-[62-64]Ja 3,13 1865;68;71; Mr-Ap 23,30-My 21,28-S 24,O 4-D D 1872
VWW [Jl 1822-25]F 12 1831;Ap 20-23,Ag 27, N 30 1858[Ag 16-N 4 1859]Ap 24-N 20 1860;Jl 23,D 31 1861;F 25-O 14 1862;Ap-Je 19 1863 [Ja 15-Mr 1 1864]D 6 1866;My 23,Jl 18 1867; Ap 30 1873;Je 1877
WHi 1821-Je,O 6 1829-31;D 4 1832-33;D 6 1834-D 2 1836;40-42[Ag 26 1862-Mr 25 1865] Ap 23,S 17 1872

Richmond ENQUIRER. d S 18 1844-N 28 1877||
1844-Jl 15 1867 as Daily Richmond enquirer; Jl 16 1867-Ja 30 1870 Daily enquirer and examiner
A Ap 7 1863
CSmH Jl 10 1848;Ja 13,Je 5 1852;Ag 2 1853;F 24 1858;Je 10,S 19 1859;N 27 1860[F 21 1861-D 9 1863]F 15[Ap 25-D 24]1864[Ja-Mr 15 1865] Je 1,11 1866[My 14-D 1867]F 5 1868;Ja 25,30 1874;O 26 1875;My 31(supp)1876
Ct Ap 1 1865
CtHT Jl 19 1864
CtY F 12,16,28,Mr 5,Ap 22 1863;Mr 31,Ap 8, 16-My 7,23,Je 4,O 31,N 7,9-12,D 5,20 1864;Ja 5,1865;Ag 17 1867
DLC [S 28 1844-48;My 6 1853-Mr 27]N 7 1865; Mr 3,Ap 10,25 1866-Je 1869[F 27 1871-N 28 1877]
IC S 24,D 14 1864;F 8,25 1865[Ja 14-Jl 12 1873]
ICM F 24 1876;My 13 1877
ICN [Mr 27-N 26 1861]62[63-O 21 1864]
ICU O 17 1851
IHi S 10 1850;S 6 1864
IU F 17 1864
KHi S 7 1864
LNH Jl 3 1821-Je 27,Ag 29 1823-25;27-Je 4 1830;42-46
LSfD O 22 1861
MB 1850[55-61]Ja 3,Je 23,27,N 25 1862[F 18-Jl 27 1863;Ja 14-D 1864]Mr 4 1865;77
MBAt [1861-68]70-71;73-76
MDeHi Ap 1 1865
MH [1853-65]
MHi Ag 6 1864
MWA S 18 1844;N 27 1852;Ap 7 1853[My 17 1856-Ag 1 1868]D 9 1873;My 3 1874;Ap 4,14,O 7,17-19 1875
MdHi N 18 1863
MnHi Mr 3,Ap 22 1863;F 27,N 9 1864
NBHi Ap 16 1864
NN Ap 8 Ag 13,28-31,S 4-6 1861;Jl 25 1862;My 4,14 1863;Ag 9,15,17,30,S 28,O 15,26,N 25,D 3, 12,27-28 1864;F 9,15,Mr 22 1865;D 15 1866;Je 11,13-14,22,25-26,29,Jl 2,5,8-12,Ag 14,S 10,30 1867
NNHi S 25 1854-Ja 8,Mr 2,Je 7[Jl-O,D 1861-Mr,My 1863-Ja 1865]-70;Jl 1871-Jl 2,D 9 1873
NNS N 19 1839-Je 1846

VIRGINIA (*Continued*)

RICHMOND—*Continued*

Richmond ENQUIRER. d 1844-77||—*Continued*
NPrH Mr 30 1863
NSyU Ap 20 1860
NbHi [Ag-S 9 1872;Mr-Ap,O 1873]-[Ja-Ap 1874]
Nc Je 1860;Je 29,S 14,D 19-20,23-25,30 1861 [Ap 23 1862-Mr 1865]
NcD [F 17 1845-D 11 1849]Ap 11 1854;My 21, D 4 1855;Ja 2,Mr 24,Jl 9,Ag 29 1856;O 16,20, N 10 1857[59-Ja 7 1865]Mr 16,O 28 1868;F 17, Mr 9,Ap 22,Je 10 1869;Ap 27,29-30,My 2,6,O 14,N 4 1870;Mr 29,Ap 6,Jl 29 1871;Je 29,S 17 1872;Ap 29 1874;O 27 1875
NcU F 14 1855;Mr 25,Jl 4,22,S 18,O 4,14-15,D 24,30 1861[62-64]
OC Ag 14 1861-Ag 27 1863
OCHi Je 11 1822;Ag 9 1825;My 12 1835;My 17 1836;Jl 18 1861;Ap 8,My 27,Ag 5,15 1863
OClWHi O 16 1854;Ja 3 1858;Ap 30,D 2,17 1859[Ja-O 1860]Ap 2,8,Je 27,Ag 13 1861;Ja 1, 3,7,23,F 7,17,S 19,O 30 1862;Je 29,Jl 4,7,O 28 1863[64-Ap 1 1865;Je 1 1866;Je 25 1869
OHi Ag 18 1863
PHi Ag 8,20,S 19,N 14,23 1863;Ap 14 1864;Ja 23 1865
PP Ag 10 1863
PPGr Jl 12 1864
PPL Ag 10 1863
PWaHi S 19 1862
PWcHi Ag 18 1856
RP [1862]
TU N 5 1861
Tx Ap 30 1844[Mr 31-D 1864]Ja 3,5,13,16,18-19,F 25 1865
TxGR [Ap 1861-64]Ja 12-13,16,19,25 1865
TxU [My 13 1845-Mr 2 1865]
V [Mr 18 1845-N 28 1877]
VHi Ap 24 1862;S 2,Jl 6 1863;Ag 29 1868;F 15,27 1871;My 16 1873;N 18,25 1874;Je 19 1875;F 23,Mr 8 1876
VHo Ap 19,30 1859
VRB My 19-20,22,24,26-28,30-31 1874;S 17,O 10, 31 1875;Ag 18 1876
VRC [Ag 24 1860-Mr 15 1866]My 10,N 27 1867; Ap 28-29 1870;Ag 17 1873
VU [Jl 1857-S 17 1859;F 1861-S 8 1862;63-64] Ja 16-21,23,26-28,F 1,9-10,14,O 30-D 11,13,16, 21,30 1865[66]68;Je 10 1869;Je 13,Ag 13,S 6 1870[71]Ag 7,N 22-23 1872;S 4,10,15,19 1874
VWW N 5 1857;S 18,O 1,D 31 1861;D 7 1866 [Ap 4-Je 26]Ag 23,28[O 24 1867-Je 24,S 16-N 27 1869[F 1870-N 1871]Ap 20[S-D]1872;Ja 14 1873
WHi [Ag 5-D 29 1863]Mr 6 1863-Mr 21 1865; Ap 23,S 17 1872[Mr 16 1873-D 3 1875]

Weekly Richmond ENQUIRER. w Mr 7 1855-N 28 1877||
1867-70 as Enquirer and examiner
A [O 31 1829-S 11 1840]Jl 1,Ag 1-8,S 26 1851; Ja 13-20,Je 11,Ag 10,S 7,21 1852
CSmH Ja 16,My 29 1861;My 7,Ag 27 1868
CoHi O 14 1863
DLC Jl 10,31,N 27-D 4 1861;Ja 8-15,S 17 1862; D 30 1863;Ja 27,Mr 30,S 7,N 2-16,D 7-14,28 1864;Mr 25 1865;Ja 10 1867
ICN D 11 1861;N 5 1862;O 21 1863
IU My 28-Ag 20,S 10-O 8,22 1868-F 18,Mr 4-11,25-Jl 15,29-S 2,16-30 1869
IaDH [S 13 1866-68]
IaU 1829-34
MBAt Ag 19 1864;Ja 3 1867;Ja-Mr 4,18-D 23 1869
MH Ag 27 1856;Ja 11,Mr 11,25-Jl 15,Ag 5 1857
MWA Ja 21 1875
NNHi Mr 6-13,27,Ap 17-24 1861;Ag 24 1864; Ap 24 1873
Nc Jl 11 1855
NcD Jl 4-11 1855;Mr 4-N 3,D 29 1857;O 24,D 12 1860;Ag 7 1861;My 1866-N 6 1873
NcU D 26 1855;O 12 1859;Jl 10-17,Ag 14-21,S 4,30,O 12 1861;D 10 1862
OClWHi D 10 1856;D 19 1860
PBf S 23,O 22,N 11-25,D 11 1856-[Ja-S 1858] My 2-16,Je,Ag 8 1860[Ja-N 1861]
TxGR Ja 8 1862
V [Jl 18 1867-68;71-72]
VU Ag 30 1861
WHi D 10 1862

Daily Richmond ENQUIRER. d
Tx Ja-F 1886
VU D 15,18,20-21,31 1886

Saturday ENQUIRER. w F 19 1898-99||?
VWW Mr 26 1898

EVERY Saturday journal. w S? 1879-1903||
1879-81? as Every Saturday; 1882-84? Every Saturday commercial advertiser
ICM Ja 21 1882
NcD Jl 17 1880
V Je 6,Jl 4 1885;O 9 1886;S 29 1888

Richmond semi-weekly EXAMINER. sw N 4 1847-62||?
CSmH Mr 9,Je 15,N 6 1849-[50-51]-N 1 1853; F 26,Ap 16,My 13 1858
DLC O 6 1848[Ja 23-N 20 1849]F 25 1851;O 28 1853;Je 19 1853;Ag 6 1858;D 30 1859;Je 1,Ag 3,O 26,D 25 1860;Ja 1,15,F 12,Mr 15,22 1861
InNcHi Ag 14 1855
LNC Mr 12 1861
MWA Ja 4 1853;My 27 1859
NN Ap 23,Ag 13,S 3 1861
NNHi N 28,D 1 1848
NcD O 23 1849[Mr 22 1850-My 1852]Jl 15 1853; Mr 20,Je 19 1855[F 12 1856-O 1857]Mr 16,O 16 1860;Ap 5,16,23,My 17,Je 4-7,21,Ag 30 1861;Jl 11,Ag 8,S 16,30 1862
TxU Ap 20 1849-Ap 7 1861
V [Ap 10 1849-61]
VHi [1847-61]
VNo N 1854-56
VU 1850;N 21 1851;D 7,31 1858;Ja 21-25,F 1-8,15-Mr 22,29-Ap 22,29-Jl 8,15-26,Ag-N 8,15-25,D 2-13,27-30 1859
VWW Jl 6 1852;Mr 13 1855;Ja 4 1859

Richmond weekly EXAMINER. w F 3 1848-66||?
CSmH Ag 16 1850;Jl 4 1851;F 10,My 18-25,Je 8-15 1860
DLC Ag 4-18,S 15,29,O 13-27,N 10 1848;Ap 7, 27-My 4,18 1849;Ja 14,28-F 1853
MWA S 15,O 27,N 10 1848
NNHi My 17-24,Jl 12-26 1850;My 2-9 1851
NcD Mr 8 1850;My 9,Ag 1,S 12,O 3,24,N 14 1851;My 27 1853[F 10 1854-My 1857]Ag 30,D 20 1861;Ja 17,Mr 14 1862[Ja-S 1863]
TxU Ap 20 1849-My 10 1850
V S 22 1848
VWW N 16 1866

Richmond EXAMINER. d Ap 25 1859-Jl 15 1867||
1859-My 28 1864 as Daily Richmond examiner. United with Daily Richmond enquirer to form Daily enquirer and examiner, later Richmond enquirer
Suspended from Mr 31-D 9 1865
CSmH Je 3,Ag 23,S 23 1859;Je 5-6 1860[61-O 3 1866]Je 1 1867
CtHT Jl 9,13,21 1864
CtY Mr 13 1862-Mr 10 1865
DLC D 3,5 1860[Mr 12 1861-Mr]D 17 1865[My 14-N 3 1866]
GSD N 12 1861
ICHi F 15,Mr 16 1864;D 17 1865
ICN [F 28-D 6 1861]F 3,Ap 28,Je 3,9,18,Jl 8-10,19,Ag 2,30,S 2,N 10 1862;Ja 1,S 1,7-8,26, 30-O 1,10,D 10,14,22 1863[64]Ja 4,23,27-28,F 18,20-21,25,28,Mr 3,13,20,31,D 10-11 1865
ICU [My 29 1863-O 1864]Ja 16-17,Mr 20,24 1865
IU Ja 11 1864
KHi Mr 30 1863
LNC F 25 1863;F 2,My 14 1864;Mr 9 1865
MB My 12-D 1861;63-64;Ja 10-Mr 9 1865
MBAt F 28-D 24,27 1861-Mr,D 9-12,14-21 1865; Mr 28,Ap 12-13,My 16-18,Je 9,Jl 2,Ag 18 1866
MH Mr 27,D 24 1861;Mr 19 1862;Je 27,O 28-29,31,N 30,D 12-13,19,23,28 1864;Ja 5,13,30,F 20,Mr 1,6,15,21,23-25,27-30,Ap 3,D 12-17,19-20, 22-23,25,27-28 1865;Ja 3 1866
MHi [Jl 7-N 7]9-11,14-16,18-22,30 1864
MWA Ap 8,S 19-20,O 1,7 1861;Ja 10,Ap 1,20, 22,My 1,4-8,12,16,19-22[Je 15-Ag 26]O 1,5 1863;Ap 18,20,23[Je-D]1864;Ja 4,6,23-24,F 7, 20-21,23,Mr 1,7,18,24-27,Ap 3 1865
MdBP 1859-60;F 1861-Je 1863;Jl-D 1864
MiU Je 6 1864
MiU-C My 23 1861;S 25,O 19-21 1863;Mr 9-10, 14 1864;Ja 13,F 7,11,14-16,18,20,25,27-28,Mr 9, 14-15,23 1865
MnHi Je 5 1863
N Jl 1861-Ja 2 1863
NBHi Jl 13,S 16 1863
NN [Ag 9 1861-N 19 1862]-64;Ja 2-19,21,F 16, 18,28 1865;Ja 6 1866;F 15,My 20,Je 18-21,24, Jl 1,3 1867
NNHi [F 28-D 1861;F 1862-Ap 1865]My 10 (extra)1866
NbHi Ja 3,Ap 11,Ag 18,O 21,N 2,20 1863;Ja 22,Je 6,20,25,Jl 22,Ag 2,26,29-30,S 9,O 3,17, 28,D 6 1864;F 22,28,Mr 28 1865
Nc [Jl 13 1861-My 1862]My 11,13 1863;F 12, 17,My 24 1864;My 10 1866
NcD D 24,31 1859;D 29 1860[Mr 9 1861-F 1865] Ap 10,Je 1,Jl 3 1866;Mr 6,8,11-18,20-23,29-31 1867
NcU Je 3,12,15,21[Ag 1861-64]F 2,7,11,23,27 1865;My 10 1866
OCHi Jl 19[Ag-D]1861;Ja 10-[O 13-N]1862-[Ap-Ag 1863]Ja 1-2 1864
OClWHi [F 1862-Je 1863]Ja 27,F 5,8,18,26,Mr 8,14,16,19,21 1864-[Ja-Mr 1865]Ap 28,My 29 1866
OHi N 17 1863-F 23 1865
PEL My 12 1863
PHi Ag 21,N 26-27,D 17,23 1863;Ja 16,18-19, Mr 2,Ap 20 1864;My 10 1866
PPL Ja 15 1863;Mr 7 1864
TU F 18 1862
TxGR [1862-64]Ja 14,F 8,22,Mr 24 1865
TxU Mr 1861-Ja 20,Mr 6-15,20-31 1865
V Je 17 1859[F 6 1860-Ap 20 1867]
VHi [1859-Je 16 1866]
VRB Jl 18 1862;My 10-11 1866
VRC Ja 30 1857;Ja 14 1860[61-66]
VU [1861-66]Ap 2 1867
VWW O 9 1861;Mr 12,Ag 1 1862;Ja 1 1863;F 27[D 12 1865-D 6 1866]Ap 3-4,Je 20 1867
WHi [Jl 16 1861-Ag 29 1866]

EXCHANGE reporter. *See* Virginia sun

Richmond FAMILY visitor. *See* Southern religious telegraph

GUIDE and news. w,d 1867-80||
1867-70 as Merchants' and travelers' guide; 1872-F 1875 Richmond daily-weekly guide
d 1867-75
MWA Je 3 1876
NNHi Mr 3 1873
V S 18 1871;My 22-23,Je 7 1876
VHi My 5 1873
VU O 29 1875

HORNET. w N 2? 1822-Ap 11 1823||?
NN Ap 11 1823
NcD D 7 1822

INDEPENDENT republican. w Mr 20-Je 26? 1869||
Campaign paper
MWA My 1 1869
V Mr 20,Ap 10-17,My 1-8,22-Je 1869
VU My 22 1869

INDEPENDENT Virginian. d O 25-N 7? 1921||
V O 25,N 7 1921
VHi O 25 1921

Richmond INDEX. sw,w Ja 20? 1859-N 23? 1860||
Campaign paper
OClWHi [Ja 31-N 23 1860]

INDUSTRIAL South. *See* Commercial and industrial South

Richmond JEFFERSONIAN. sw,w Ag 2 1832-D 10 1833||
Follows Jeffersonian (Lynchburg) 1832-Ap? 1833 as Jeffersonian and Virginia times (sw). Merged with Richmond whig
IU Ja 17 1833
N Ag 30 1833
NcU D 17 1832
NjR My 31 1832
VHi [Ag 20-D 10 1833]
VU O 1 1832
VWW D 13,17 1832-Mr,Ap 3,10-19,26-30,Ag 20, 27-N 12,19-D 10 1833

Evening JOURNAL. d O 26 1868-F 23? 1876||
Follows Daily state journal (Alexandria). 1868-Je? 1874 as Daily state journal
CSmH F 1870
DLC Jl 8 1871;Ja 24,My 15,17,N 6,D 21 1872; D 10 1873
MBAt [1868]69
MWA Je 13 1870
NNHi Ap 2 1873
NbHi Ap 12 1871;F 5,Mr 24,Ap 27-29,My 2 1874
V D 16 1868;F 18,My 10,31,Je 15 1869[Ja-N 4 1870]Ap 6,My 26,Jl 17 1871;Ja 2,29,31 1874
VHi Ja 13,21 1870;Je 11 1873;F 23 1876
VRC Ap 25,27,30 1870
WHi [Ap-D 1871]

Richmond JOURNAL. w F? 1881-92||
V Ap 24,My 8 1886;F 12-Mr 5,26,My 14,O 1,N 19 1887

Evening JOURNAL. d Je 5 1905-S 26? 1920||
Followed by Evening dispatch and journal, later Evening dispatch
Je 15 1915 is a special ed Richmond and Virginia in 1915
IC Je 15 1915
MB Je 16 1916
MoS Je 15 1915
NN Je 15 1915
NcD Je 21 1912;Je 14 1917
NcU Je 2 1915
NjH Je 15 1915
RP Je 15 1915
TxGR Je 15 1915
V 1905-S 1920
VHi Ja 4 1906;F 15 1913;Ap 3 1915;Mr 14,17 1917
VRN O 1905-Mr,Jl 1906-Mr,Jl-D 1908;Jl 1909-Je,O 1912-Mr 1917;Ja-Je 1920
VU 1905-Mr,O 1906-Mr,Jl 1907-Je,S 21-22,30 1908-Je,O 1909-10;Mr-My,Jl 1911-[12;Ap-D 1913;F-D 1914;F-N 1915;F-D 1916;Jl 1917-18; Je 30 1919-S 5 1920]

JOURNAL of industry. w Ja 25- 1873||
VRC F 1 1873

JUSTICE. w O 8- 1898||
WHi O 8 1898

Evening LEADER. d Je 2 1888-Ja 24 1903||
1888-N 1896 as Leader (Manchester). United with Richmond news to form News-leader, later Richmond news-leader
DLC Jl-D 1898
V [N 30 1896-03]
VHi Je 12-19 1888[N-D 1897]-1900;N 26 1901
VRB N 26 1901
VRN N 1896-My,Jl 1897-98;1900-03
VU N 26 1901;02

MAGNOLIA weekly. w O 1 1862-65||
CSmH D 6 1862;Mr 7-14,My 9,23-30,Je 27,Jl 25-Ag 1,29,O 17 1863;F 20,Mr 12-19,Ag 6,S 24,D 3 1864
CtY D 12 1863-Ja 16 1864;Mr 11 1865
DLC [O 4 1862-O 1 1864]
MBAt O 4 1862-Ap 1 1865
MH F 4-18,Ap 1 1865
MWA S 10 1864
NN Ap 1 1865
NNHi O 18-N 8 1862;Ja,Mr 1863-64;F 4 1865
NcD [Je 1863-Ap]Ag 13 1864
NcU Ap 2,N 12 1864
OClWHi N 28 1863;Mr 12,Ap 9 1864
PHi O 17-24 1863;F 13 1864
TxU Jl 4-D 5 1863;S 3 1864
V [N 15 1862-Ag 1864]Ja 7 1865
VRC Je 27,S 26-O 10,N 28 1863
VU Ap 25,Je 6,27-Jl 11,25,N 7 1863;Ja-F,Mr 12 1864
WHi [Ja 24 1863-Ap 9 1864]

Morning MAIL. d Mr 30 1853-S 30? 1854||
Follows Richmond daily Republican
CSmH 1853-Je 1854
CaOTA Je 25 1853

Morning MAIL. sw Ap 1? 1853-
CSmH My 13 1853
NcD Ap 5 1853

Morning MAIL. w Ap 1? 1853-
CSmH Je 4 1853
NcD My 7 1853
VHi My 21 1853

MANCHESTER courier. *See* Virginia courier

*Richmond daily MERCANTILE advertiser. sw,d D 26 1809-D? 1822||
1809-Ag 10? 1816 as Virginia patriot; Ag 12 1816-Ap 2 1821 Virginia patriot and Richmond daily mercantile advertiser
sw 1809-Ag 10? 1816
DLC F 20-25 1822
MWA F 6,Mr 6,N 26 1821
OClWHi O 3-5 1821
V [1821-D 19 1822]
VHi Ap 19 1822

MERCHANTS' and travelers' guide. *See* Guide and news

Weekly NATIONAL American. w Ag 31 1855-
MWA Ag 31 1855

NATIONAL American. d Jl 5 1855-60||?
1855? as Daily National American
NcD N 2 1855
V S 20,22,O 15 1855;Ap 4 1856;Ja-Je 1857
VU Ag 17 1855

VIRGINIA (*Continued*)

RICHMOND—*Continued*

Semi-weekly NATIONAL American. sw S? 1855-
DLC O 17 1856
TxU S 9 1856
V Jl 4,S 19 1856

NATIONAL Virginian. sw,w D 23? 1870-72||?
sw 1870-Je? 1871
DLC F 11 1871
MWA Ja 2?,O 14 1871

Weekly NEW NATION. w O 5 1865-D 4 1868||?
1865-Mr 14 1867 as New nation
CSmH Ag 23,S 27 1866;Mr 7,Ag 15 1867
MBAt O 5 1865;Mr 29-Ap,My 10-17,Ag 16 1866;Ap 18,19(extra)Jl 18-Ag 1,29-S 5,19,O 17, 31-N 21,D 12 1867;Ja 23,Ap 16 1868
MHi Mr 22,Jl 12,Ag 9,S 1866-[Mr 21 1867-D 4 1868]
MWA O 5 1865;Ap 19,S 27,N 22 1866
V [Mr 22 1866-D 18 1867]

Daily NEW NATION. d Ap 22? 1867-N 28 1868||
CSmH Ja 7,Ag 14 1868
DLC My 9 1867
MBAt [Je 29 1867-68]
MHi N 23 1867
MWA Mr 31,Ap 11 1868
NN My 1 1868
V [Ja 4-O 28 1867;Ja 23-N 14 1868]

Morning NEWS. d Jl 2? 1859-60||
CSmH S 12 1859
MWA D 20 1859
OClWHi Ja 5 1860
TxU D 13 1859
VHi D 8 1859

Evening NEWS. d Mr 30? 1868-Jl 30? 1875||
CSmH Mr 30 1868;Ag 3,O 21,D 6 1869
MWA Mr 2? 1875
NNHi Mr 1? 1873
NcD D 9,29 1868;My 7,17,Je 1,17,21,24,D 6 1869
V Ap 4,15,17,23-24,28,Jl 8,D 9-10,29 1868[Ap 20 1869-D 5 1870]Jl 19,N 3 1871;My 4 1872;Jl 7,O 9,14,20,23,N 7 1873
VRC Ja 21 1874;Jl 31 1875
VWW D 2 1870

Richmond NEWS. d O 5 1899-1903||
United with Evening leader to form News-leader, later Richmond news-leader
NcD N 2,5 1902
V 1899-[Ja 1903]
VHi D 1899-1900;Ja 7,F 16,Je 8,S 17,N 13 1901
VRN Ap 1900-02

Daily NEWS and star. d 1846||
Follows Star (1840-45)?
CSmH Mr 3 1846

Weekly NEWS and star. w 1846||
Follows Star (1841-45)?
VU F 9 1846

Richmond NEWS-LEADER. d Ja 26 1903+
Formed by the union of Evening news and Evening leader. 1903-Ja 3 1925 as News-leader
O 16 1931 has Yorktown sesqui-centennial supp
pub [1903-O 1918;19-20]+
A Je 20-25 1932
CL O 16 1931
ICU 1930-N 1934;35+
MWA Ja 17(extra)1916;F 6(extra)1925
NcD Ag 2 1913;Je 22 1918;Ag 23 1926
NcU Mr 24,My 27,Je 2-3,Ag 4 1915;Je 7,Jl 12, 20 1916
OClWHi O 25 1906
V 1903+
VHi My 29 1905;My 2 1914;F 26,Ap 3,9,Je 1-3, O 8,D 18 1915;Mr 7,My 16,Je 19 1916;Mr 14, Ap 2[Jl 7-18 1917;N 9,11 1918[O 10 1921-N 23 1923]Mr 7,D 29 1924;D 31 1925
VRN 1903-06;Ap 1907-Ag,O 1918;Ja-Mr,My,Jl, S 1919-F,Ap,Je,S 1920+
VU Ja 26-Je,S 3 1903;04-S,N 9-11,26,D 1914-Je,S 1-10,13-N 29,D 1915-F,Ap 27-My 2,4-26 1917-[18]F 1919-Ja,Mr 1923-Mr,My-D 1925;F 1926-Ag,O 1928-N 29 1930;31-N 1932;Ag 28 1933;O 20,30-N 3,5,8,15-17,20-22 1934

OLD DOMINION. w Ap 1? 1882-84||
ICM Jl 8 1882

Richmond OMNIBUS. w Ja 10- 1846||
VWW Ja 10 1846

Richmond PATRIOT. w My 28? 1869-Jl 20 1872||?
Merged with Virginia staats-gazette
In German
V Jl 23-30,Ag 13,27,S 24-O 15,N 5-12 1869

PAUL PRY. w 1849-50||
CSmH F 23 1850

PENNY post. d,sw,w D 20? 1853-Je 30? 1855||
CSmH O 27 1854;Mr 27,My 11 1855
NcD [Je 6-23 1855]
TxU Mr 10,Ap 6 1855
V My 4 1854[F 26-Je 1855]
VU My 21-22,28-29,31-Je 1,7 1855
VWW D 19 1854

Richmond PHENIX. sw N? 1823-24||?
DLC Ap 6,23-27 1824
MWA My 7,14,22-25 1824

Richmond PHEONIX. d D 29 1823-24||?
DLC [D 19 1823-My 1824]
MWA Mr 9,24,Ap 8-9,My 14 1824

Richmond PHOENIX (for the country. w 1823?-24||?
DLC Mr 10 1824

Richmond PLANET. w D? 1883+
Negro
pub 1926;N 1931+
DLC Ja 13 1900
MH 1890-1913[25-30]
MWA Je 12 1886

V Je 8 1889[95-Je 1901]My 12[Jl-D]1917-Mr 1931;35+
VHaH 1935+
VU N 26 1932;Je 16,30-S 22,O 13-N 10,24 1934+
WHi Je 26 1919

POLITICAL expositor. tw Mr 30?- 1821||
NcD Jl 2 1821

POLITICAL reformer. w My 16?- 1840||
Campaign paper
Also dated at Portsmouth and Washington, D.C.
NcU My 5 1840
VHi My 23-[Jl-N]1840

POPULAR messenger. sm Ja- 1883||
NNHi Ap 1 1883
VU Mr 1 1883

Daily RECORD. d O 14 1878+
pub 1924+
V Ap 1916+

RECORD of news, history and literature. w Je 18-D 10 1863||
CSmH complete
DLC complete
LNH Je 18 1863
MWA complete
NN complete
NNHi complete
NcU Jl 23 1863
NjP Je-Ag 20,S-D 3 1863
OClWHi [1863]
PHi Ag 27 1863
TxU [1863]
V [1863]
VHi complete
VRC [1863]
VSbC [1863]
VU D 10 1863
WHi complete

REFORMER. w N 6? 1885-86||
Follows Campaign
V F 13 1886

REFORMER. w 1895-1931||?
DLC Ja 27 1900
TxU My 24 1913

Richmond REGISTER. d,sw,w Ja 6-F 28? 1868||
CSmH Ja 11,F 3 1868
MBAt [Ja-F 11 1868]
MWA Ja 6 1868

REPUBLIC. d My 10 1865-66||
CSmH [My-D 1865]F 28,Mr 12 1866
DLC [My 15-D 1865]Ap 10 1866
ICHi S 23 1865
MBAt 1865-My 21 1866
MH [My-D 21 1865]
MWA My 19,30 1865
MWo N 24 1865
MnHi My 30 1865
N Jl 1 1865
NBHi My 17 1865
NN [Jl 20-D 13 1865]
NcD Je 5,Jl 17-18 1865
OClWHi My 27 1865
OHi My 25,Jl 26,Ag 18 1865
TxGR Ag 30 1865
V [1865-Ap 14 1866]
VHi [1865-Mr 11 1866]
VRC [My 17-D 14 1865]Ja 2,Mr 8,11 1866
VU O 6 1865

Weekly REPUBLIC. w F 2- 1866||
MBAt F 2 1866
NcD Mr 2 1866
VHi F 23-My 11 1866
VU Mr 2 1866

Richmond daily REPUBLICAN. d Jl 1 1846-53||
Followed by Morning mail
CSmH Ag 29 1848;My 23 1849;F 25,Ag 21 1850;Je 18,Jl 1 1851;Ja-Mr 25 1853
DLC N 20 1846;F 16,S 6 1847[Mr 8 1849-50]
ICM Jl 1849-51
NcD Jl 3 1846;Je 8 1850;F 28 1851;Jl 30 1852
V Ag 23 1848;My 8,D 2 1850;F 4,S 16 1851[52-Mr 26 1853]

REPUBLICAN advocate. w Ja 6- 1851||
ICM Ja 6 1851
NN My 4 1851
NcD Mr 4 1851

Richmond REPUBLICAN and general advertiser for the country. w 1847-53||
CSmH Jl 27 1846
DLC O 16 1846;Ja 2 1847;F 14 1848;Mr 9,20, My 14 1849
ICM Ag 17 1849;S 17 1850;F 18,21,Mr 25,My 16,N 21 1851
NcD Jl 3 1852
VHi Jl 9 1850
VWW Je 1,S 14 1846

REPUBLICAN sentinel. w Mr 16-O 30 1844||
Campaign paper
DLC complete
ICU complete
NcD [1844]
V complete
VHi S 21 1844
VU Jl 6 1844

RICHMONDER. *See* Täglicher anzeiger

SENTINEL. d Mr 11 1863-Mr 2 1866||
Follows Virginia sentinel (Alexandria). Merged with Richmond enquirer
CSmH [Mr-N 1863;Mr 1864-Ap 1865]F 28 1866
DLC [1863-Mr 16]-D 1865
IC My 7 1864;F 24 1865
ICN Mr 23 1863-Ap 1 1865
ICU S 25 1863;Jl 20 1864;Mr 4 1865
LNC Je 6 1864;F 14,Ap 1 1865
MB O 25 1863-Ap 18,My 25 1864
MBAt [Mr 31 1863-F 13 1866]
MH Je 6,O 14,N 26,D 9-10 1863;Jl 26,Ag 13, 15-20,22-24 1864
MWA Je 25,D 28-29 1863[Mr 22-Je 13,S 7 1864-Ap 3 1865]
MiU-C D 31 1863
NBHi N 9-11 1864
NN [Je 20 1863-Mr 20 1865]
NNHi Je 20,22,O 6 1863;Mr 7,30,Ag 8 1864
Nc [My 11 1863-Ag 13 1864]
NcD Ap 2 1862;Ap 14,30,My 14,Je 17,Ag 27 1863;F 19,Ap 18 1864;F 14,22,Mr 2,4 1865
NcU Ap 25[Jl 16 1863-My 24]Jl 30,O 15[D 1864;F 1-14 1865]
OClWHi Mr 12 1863-Ap 1 1865
PHi My 2,Ag 26,S 24,O 1,10,N 13 1863;Ap 5 1864
PP Jl 5 1864
PPL [Jl 7 1863-Ap 1 1865]
TxGR [Ap 1863-O 17 1864]
V [1863-Mr 1865]
VHi [1863-65]
VU Ja 28,F 23,Jl 16,S 13,O 10,18,D 14 1864;F 13 1865
VWW [My 15-Jl 24]D 22 1863[Ja 8-O 15 1864]
WHi Jl 2 1863[Mr 22 1864-Mr 1865]

SENTINEL. sw Mr 17?1863-66||?
Merged with Richmond enquirer
DLC Ja-[Mr 18 1864-Mr 1865]
ICN Ag 30-S 2,23,N 11,D 6,20-30 1864;F 16, Mr 14 1865
MBAt Ap 7,Je 12,Ag 21,O 16 1863;Ja 26,My 3,31 1864
MWA Jl 21 1863;N 19 1864 Mr 17 1865
NcD F 19,Jl 22 1864;Ja 3-6,Mr 10-17 1865
VRB O 23,D 11 1863;Mr 15-18,Jl 19 1864

SENTINEL. w Ag 20 1863-66||?
ICN My 5 1864;Ja 5 1865
IU F 15 1864
MBAt O 8 1863
MWA D 10 1863
NcD Je 23,Jl 14,N 17 1864;F 9 1865
VU My 1 1863;Mr 3 1864

Daily Richmond SHIELD. d,sw N 13-20? 1841||
DLC N 13-20 1841

SOLDIERS journal. *See under* Augur General Hospital

SOLDIER'S paper. sm Ag 1 1863-Ap 1 1865||
CSmH F 15 1864
CtHT Je 1 1864
DLC Mr 1,Ap 1 1865
MWA N 1 1863;Ap 1 1865
NNHi Ag 15-S 1,N 1 1863;Ja 12,F 5-15,Mr 15 1864
NcD Mr 15 1864
OClWHi Ag 1 1863
TxGR My 1 1864
VRC Ap 1 1865

SOLDIER'S visitor. m Ag 1863-
MBAt Je 1864
MnHi Ag 1864
NNHi Ag 1863-Mr 1864;Ja-F 1865

SOUTH. d Mr 28 1857-N 19 1858||
CSmH [Ap 1857-Mr 1858]
DLC N 2 1858
ICM complete
NcD S 15 1857;Ag 26 1858
TxU D 1 1857[F 10-N 2 1858]
V [1857-58]
VHi Ag 6 1857

SOUTH. sw S 8? 1857-N 19 1858||
CSmH [S 1857-Mr 1858]
ICM Jl 14 1857
NcD S 22,D 15 1857;F 23,Jl 9,N 5 1858

SOUTHERN era. w Ja? 1846-S 1854||?
1846-Je 14? 1850 as Banner of temperance
NcD Je 14,O 25 1850
NcU Jl 6 1849

SOUTHERN illustrated news. w S 13 1862-S 3? 1865||
A Jl 4 1863;Mr 5 1864
CSmH 1862-My 14,Je 11,S 3-10 1864
CtHT Mr 5,Je 20 1864
CtY O 11,25,N 29,D 6 1862;Mr 14,Ag 1 1863
DLC 1862-My 14,Je 11,Ag 20,S 10-17,O 1,N 26 1864
GAA S 20 1862-Ap 16 1864
GU Mr 7 1863
ICHi F 27 1864
MH O 4,18 1862;F 21,Ap 11,My 2,16,30,Je 27 1863 Ja 14 1865
MWA Ap 11-N 14 1863;Ap 30-My 7 1864
MsHi [1862-63]
NN 1862-O 1864
NNHi 1862-Je 11,Jl 9,Ag 20,S 3 1865
Nc F-Mr 14,Jl 25-Ag 15,S 2,19-26 1863
NcD [S 27 1862-S 10 1864]
NcU S 6,D 1862[Ja-O 24 1863]Jl 9,O 1,N 5 1864
NjP 1862-Jl 11 1863
OClWHi [1862-O 1864]
OHi O 4 1862;Ja 31 1863;Ja-Ap 2 1864
PHi N 15 1862;Ap 25,O 24,N 21 1863
RP Ja 2 Mr 5-19 1864
TxU [O 18 1862-Je 11 1864]
V 1862-N 5 1864
VRC [1862-O 1864]
VU O 4,18-N 1,15,D 13 1862;Ja-Mr 14,28-My, Je 13-Jl 4,25-Ag 1,15,29,S 26,O 17,D 12 1863; F 13,Ap 23,Jl 30 1864
WHi O 25 1862;F 14-21,Mr 21 1863;Mr 5,26, Ap 16-30,Ag 15 1864

SOUTHERN intelligencer. w 1879-80||
ICM Je 7,D 8 1879;F 9,Mr 8,22,Je 7,S 13 1880
NcD S 13 1880
V Ja 26-O 18 1880
VU Jl 26 1879

SOUTHERN news. w Ag 20 1892-94||?
Negro
CSmH O 15 1892

SOUTHERN opinion. w Je 15 1867-My 1 1869||
CSmH 1867-N 21,D 5 1868;Ja-My 1 1869
DLC Jl 27 1867-N 21 1868
MBAt [Je 15-D 1867]
MWA Je-D 21 1867;My 16 1868
NN D 5,1868;F 6 1869
NcD S 7,12 1867;Ja 25,F 22,28,Ap 11,My 2-9 1868

VIRGINIA (*Continued*)

RICHMOND—*Continued*

SOUTHERN opinion. w 1867-69||—*Continued*
OClWHi Je 22-Jl 6,N 16,D 21 1867;F 22 1868
TxU Je 22 1867
V [1867-69]
VRC D 5 1868
VWW 1867-Ja 11,Jl 25,Ag 8 1868[F 27-Ap 10 1869]
WHi complete

SOUTHERN portfolio. w My 12-19? 1866||
V My 12-19 1866
VRC My 12-19 1866

SOUTHERN punch. w Ag 15 1863-65||?
CtHT Mr 5 1864
CtY F 13-Je 25 1864
DLC [1863-64]
ICN [1863]
MH F 13 1865
NNHi Ag 15,S 19-O 10,31,N 14-27,D 12-19 1863;Ja 2,F 18,27,Ap 9,Jl 9 1864
NcD O 10 1863
OClWHi 1863-O 2 1864
PPGr Mr 12 1864
PPL S 26-O 3,24,D 5 1863
VRC [O-N 1863;Ja-N 1864]

SOUTHERN religious telegraph. w Ap 6 1822-39||?
1822-26 as Richmond family visitor; 1827-29 Visitor and telegraph
A Ap 4 1837
CSmH Ap 13-D 21 1822;23-Ap 3 1824;Ap 16 1825;S 4,18 1830;Ap 18,N 7,28 1834;N 20 1835
CtY O 15 1825;Jl 5,Ag 9,23,S 13 1828
DLC Jl 24,Ag 14-28,S 25,O 30 1824
MDeHi O 1 1825
MWA Ap 16 1825;My 27,Jl 22,D 9 1826;Je 2,16 1827;F 23 1828;F 14,28,Mr 21 1829;Ja 25 1833-Mr 28 1839
N F 19 1825
NN Ap 10 1824-Ap 1 1826
NcD [Ap 25 1834-N 24 1837]
NhD Ja 29 1827;Jl 5,O 18,D 6 1833
V Ap 13,Ag 10-24,O 5,D 21 1822[Ja 25-Mr 15]O 11 1823;Jl 10 1824;Jl 19 1828-33[Mr 1834-35]
VHi Ap 1822-Mr 1824
VRU Ap 1822-Mr 1823;27-29
WHi [N 27 1824-Ag 6 1825]Jl 31 1835;Ja 15, Je 10 1836

SOUTHERNER. w D 4 1846-Jl 29 1848||?
CtY Mr 4,Je 10 1848
DLC S 25 1847;F 26-Jl 29 1848
ICU Ja 23-30 1848
MHi D 19 1846
MWA F 26-Jl 29 1848
Nc Ag 28 1847
NcD [1846-Ag 5 1848]
NcU Ag 7 1847

SOUTHSIDE news. w Ag 1928+
pub [1928+]
VU Je 1935

Richmond STANDARD. w S 7 1878-F 18 1882||
A S 4,O 26-D 4 1878
DLC complete
MB 1878-F 11 1882
MH [1879-81]
MHi [S 21 1878-82]
MWA complete
MdHi O 9 1880
MiU-C S 7 1878
N Ja 28-F 4 1882
NN S 1879-82
NNHi [1878-F 11 1882]
NcD [S 21 1878-N 6 1880]
P S 20 1879-82
V [1878-82]
VHi S 21 1878-Ag 1881
VWW [1879-82]
WHi [1878-82]

STAR. d Jl? 1840-45||?
Ap 1 1840-Jl 6 1841? as Daily evening star and transcript. Title varies; Star; Daily star; etc. Followed by Daily news and star?
Dated also at Petersburg
CSmH Jl 9 1842;N 16 1844
DLC My 6 1840;Ja 21-Jl 6 1841;My 21,Ag 18 1842
MWA Ag 15 1842
VU S 8 1845

Richmond weekly STAR. w Ja 4? 1841-45||?
Followed by Weekly news and star?
CSmH F 22 1841
NhD My 24 1841

Richmond STAR. d,sw Ag 31 1893-O 23 1896||
Merged with State
NNHi F 23 1894
V [1893]-96
WHi N 14 1893;Mr 10 1894-Je 1896

Daily evening STAR and transcript. *See* Star 1840-45?

STATE. d Mr 11 1876-N 20 1897||
DLC N 3,D 20 1877-97
IC Ap 30 1889
ICHi My 24 1890
ICM Ag 12 1876;My 6,Ag 13,20,S 16-17,O 6,19, N 17 1880;Ja 23,31-F 1,26[Mr 11-29]Ap 2,7-8, D 27 1881;Je 20 1882;F 3,My 5 1886;My 29 1894
KyU D 13 1879
LNC My 24 1890
MHi My 23 1881
MWA O 6,N 3 1876;Mr 24 1880;Ap 25 1881;S 22 1892
MdHi S 10 1885
Nc Mr 25-O 1 1886[87-Ja 1892]
NcD O 7 1878;D 3-4,17 1879;Ja 20,22,Mr 5 1880;Je 28 1881;S 22 1882;Ja 22-27 1894
NcU Je 23 1884;Mr 10 25,Ag 24,S 2,13,O 7, 27,D 16 1886;F 22,Mr 1,4 1887
V [Mr 20 1876-N 20 1897]
VHi Ag 22 1881;N 19 1884;My 7 1885;F 6, 16,O 26 1886;Ja 14,N 16 1892;Jl 1893-Je 1897
VRB N 26 1879;N 19 1884;S 2 1886
VRC O 14 1881
VRN Mr 19-Jl 1880
VU 1878-N 18 1880;Ag 9 1881;F 27,Mr 1-11, 16-Ap 13,15 1882-[96]-O 1897
VWW Ja 26 1880;Mr 11 1882
WHi Jl 1 1879;O 24 1896-My 24 1897

STATE. w 1876-97||
DLC N 22 1885-My 2 1886
NcD Mr 1,Je 21 1878;S 19 1879;Ag 20,O 15,N 5,D 3-10 1885;Ja 28,F 25,Mr 11-18,My 13,Je 3,24,Ag 12 1886;F 24 1887;Jl 14 1892
VU Ja-My 2 1886
WHi [Jl 26 1878-Ja 1880]

STATE. sw Ag? 1880-88||?
NcD Ap 30 1883;Ja 15,Jl 13 1885
VU My 7,O 19-D 1885

Daily STATE journal. *See* Evening journal (1868-76)

Weekly STATE journal. w 1863-74||
DLC O 8 1873;Ja 7 1874
ICM Je 25 1873
MBAT Je 4 1869
MWA Je 23[O-D]1871;Ja 31[Mr-Ap 3]O 2 1872[Ag 20 1873-Ap 22 1874]
NbHi N 15 1871;Mr 13,Ap 24 1872;F 18,Mr 11,Ap 9-15,My 13-27 1874

Semi-weekly STATE journal. sw Mr 1870-74||
DLC Jl 4 1873
MWA O 10,21,N 21,,D 16 1873
NNHi My 6 1873
NbHi N 14,Je 8 1874
VRB My 21,25,Je 1-11 1874

STATE rights republican, journal of education and Constitutional reformer. w Ja 3-29? 1842||
DLC Ja 3 1842
MDeHi F 5 1842
NcU Ja 29 1842
OClWHi Ja 8 1842

SUN. d Ag 29? 1878-79||
V N 3 1878;Ja 27 1879

Evening TELEGRAM. d Mr 14?-Ap? 1878||
V Ap 11 1878

Richmond TIMES. d My 1 1813-S 2? 1853||
1813-Ag 4? 1816 as Daily compiler and Richmond commercial register; Ag 5 1816-F 7 1835 Richmond commercial compiler; F 8?-My 4? 1835 Richmond compiler; My 5 1835-Je 1837 Richmond courier and daily compiler; F 1837-Ag 27 1844 Richmond compiler; Ag 28? 1844-Jl 1849 Times and compiler
CSmH Je 23 1821;My 1 1824;Mr 23 1826;Jl 26 1827;F 29 1844;Mr 13 1846;Je 19 1849;My 24 1850;My 26,29,Je 23 1851;Ja 13,Mr 18,O 16,22,D 29 1832;Mr 2,26,Ap 14,My 2,10,Je 18,Ag 16,S 2 1853
Ct Mr 30-31 1827
DLC N 17 1824;Mr 17,31 1825;Mr 28 1827;N 28,D 9 1828;Jl 7,11,S 15,21,O 6,N 25,27 1829; Je 25 1831;S 29,N 17 1832;D 3 1840[Je 18-O 4 1849]
ICM N 21 1831-My 19 1832;Jl 9-D 1852
ICN Jl 23,Ag 13,O 8,26,D 28 1852
MBAt Mr 30,My 13 1822;Jl 23-24 1828
MHi Ja 9 1822;D 25 1823;Ja 13,Mr 6,My 8,14 1824;Ja 12-13,15 1825;F 5,Ap 13 1826
MWA Je 26 1828;Mr 13 1832;My 20 1840;N 29 1852
MoSM 1845-Je 1846
N D 1 1824;N 1 1833;Mr 30 1834
NNHi S 18 1827
NcD N 7 1821
NhD Je 10 1841
OClWHi F 15,Je 4,15 1822;Ap 6 1841
PDoHi Jl 20-21,23,S 18-19 1826;Jl 14 1827
T [S 13 1821-Ja 17 1822]
V [1821-O 1825;My 6-Je 22 1826]Mr 2 1827 [My 21 1828-My 20 1831;F 9 1835-36;38-47; 50-Je 1852;Ja-Je 20 1853]
VHi Ag 1835-Je 1837[N 1844-Jl 1849]F 28,Ag 2 1851;Mr 3,18,D 25 1852;Mr 5 1853
VRN Mr 17 1830;O 24 1834;Ap 8,Je 26,28, 30 1837
VU Je 29 1849
VWW S 26 1834;O 28 1842;D 5-19 1843;Ja 16-19 1844

Richmond TIMES (for the country) tw,sw 1813?-40||
1813?-Je 12? 1833 as Commercial and Richmond commercial register; Jl 15 1833-My 4? 1835 Richmond compiler; My 5 1835-Ja 1837 Richmond courier and daily compiler; Ja 1837-Ag 27 1844 Richmond compiler
tw 1813-F 7 1835?
DLC N 20,D 23,28 1829;Ja 15 1841;Ag 23 1844; S 3,17 1847;Ap 6,24-27,Jl 20-24 1849
MWA Je 12-15 1821;Je 1,Ag 17 1822;Ag 26 1823;O 7,D 11 1824;Ja 15,Mr 19 1825;Jl 14 1826;N 24 1827
NN F 5,Ap 12 1836
NcD Ag 21-S 5,11-14,18-19,25-26 1833;D 11 1835;Mr 5 1841[S 15 1843-Ap 16 1844]
VHi D 1835-F 12,Mr 1-25,Ap 1-5,15,26,My 3-10 1836;Ag 13 1839;Mr 4 1841;Ap 1845-Ap 1846
VRB Ap 13 1847

Sunday morning TIMES. w Jl 12 1863-64||?
Followed by Richmond times (1865-67)
OClWHi Jl 19-26 1863

Richmond TIMES. d Ap 21 1865-Je 10 1867||
Follows Sunday morning times.
Merged with Daily dispatch
CL My 10 1865
CSmH [1865]Mr 3,Ap 27,My 11,16,24,Je 1,7, Ag 18 1866
CtY My 27,Je 21-22 1865
DLC [1865-67]
IF Ap 21-22,24 1865
MBAt [1865-66]Ja 2-7,10,12-15,17-Mr 26,28-My 13,15-18,21-Je 1867
MH 1865-Mr 6 1866;Ap 23 1867
MWA 1865-Ap 21,Ag 10 1866
MiU-C Ap 21-26,28,My 6,11 1865
MnHi My 20 1865
N My 29,31 1865
NN Jl 19,N 27-30,D 2-7,9 1865-Ja 5,8-22,24-25,F 7 1866-67
NNHi Ap 21,My 1,4-5,Je 21 1865
NcAsS Ap 28 1865
NcD Ap 22,24,O 7 1865;Ap 15 1867
NjP My 1 1865
OClWHi [1865]My 30,Je 12,15 1866
OHi Jl 26,Ag 18 1865
PAtM Ap 21-22,24-26 1865
TxGR Ag 1,S 21 1865
V [My 1865-67]
VHi Ap 21-26[Ag-D 20]1865;Je 5,9,16,O 5 1866;Ap 1 1867
VRC [1865-Ja 3 1866]
VU 1865-Mr,Ap 9-21 1866;Ap 15 1867
VWW [My 13-Jl 27 1865]
WHi Je 7,Jl 13-14,19,Ag 30,O 28 1865;Mr 21 1867

TIMES. d O 22 1886-Ja 25 1903||
1886-89 as Daily times. United with Richmond dispatch to form Richmond times-dispatch
A Jl-D 1898;Mr 1901-03
DLC D 1893-1903
ICM N 1,15,19,29 1891;My 17,Je 4,10 1892;Ja 4,Mr 26,Ap 23 1893;Je 14 1896;Ja 27,Mr 18, D 7 1900;Je 12 1901
LNC Ap 29 1890
MH [1889]-Mr 25 1891
MWA Jl 14,16-18 1901;O 7 1902
MdHi My 30 1890
NNHi My 10 1891
NcD O 31 1889;Je 20,N 6 1890;Je 16 1891;F 7 1892;Jl 23 1893;F 6,N 21 1897
NcU My 30 1890
OClWHi Ja 7,Jl 1 1894;Je 9-13,30-Jl 2 1896
V [1888-1903]
VHi Jl 24 1888;Mr 10 1889;My 25,29-30,Je 6,O 8 1890;F 22 1891;Jl 24 1892;F 5,Mr 5,Jl 1893-1902
VRN Mr-Je 1900;S 1901-03
VU F 3 1888;My 1 1889;My 29-30 1890;O 4,D 23 1891[Mr-D 1892]Jl 7,14 1893[Jl 1894-Jl 24 1895;My 30-N 1896]F 11 1898;Ap-D 1902

Weekly TIMES. w 1886-1903||
United with Weekly dispatch to form Weekly times-dispatch
NcD N 5,19,D 1-22,24 1886;Ja 14,F 4,18,Ap 8-15,Je 24-Jl 22,Ag 5,19,21,O 28,N 11-18,D 16 1887-Ja 6 1888; N 6 1890;F 20 1901
NcU My 30 1890
OClWHi Mr 1895;F 24 1896
VU F 8,Jl 16-23,Ag 13 1894
WHi Jl 1893-94;F 10 1896-Ja 8 1902

TIMES and compiler. *See* Richmond times (1813-53)

TIMES-DISPATCH. d Ja 26 1903+
Formed by the union of Richmond dispatch and Times (1886-1903)
pub 1910+
A 1905-Je 1907
DLC 1903+
ICM (Mr-S 1903]F 26,D 14 1904;O 26 1913; Ja 8,Mr 1,8,N 29,D 6 1914;Ja 3 1915;D 12 1920;Mr 22-23 1931
ICN D 9 1917-D 17 1918;Ja 28-29,F 12 1919-Ap 1920
IaDH Mr 15 1905-Ag 1907
LNH Je 4 1907
MWA Ap 22 1906
MoHi D 30 1908-Ja 1 1909
NcD [My-S 1903]Mr 1 1904;06;My 16-17,30 1907[D 8 1910-N 4 1912]Ja 30 1916;My 9 1919;F 28,Jl 27 1926;S 1930+
NcU F 7,S 13 1904;My 30 1907;Ja 16 1910[Mr-O 1915]Ap 8,19,Jl 8,10,12,17 1916
OClWHi My 31 1907;Mr 2,19 1922
PAtM Ap 21-26 1865
TxU F 23,Ap 5,Je 15 1908;Je-D 21 1913[Ja 11-Jl 1914]Ap 25 1915
V 1903+
VAsR 1901+
VHarT Mr-My 1919;Ja-Mr 1920[Ja 23 1923-My 10 1924]
VHi 1903+
VP 1903-11
VRN Ja-S 1903;04-Je,O 1906-S 1908;Ja-Je,O 1909-S 1916;17-S 1918;Ap 1919+
VRV [1930-N 1932]33+
VU My 2 1903;F 28-Mr 1,3-4,7-11,14-15,17,24-25,28,30 1905+
VWW 1903-O,D 1920-N 1921;Ja-S,N 1922+
VWn S 1913+
WHi 1915+

Weekly TIMES-DISPATCH. w 1903-12||?
Formed by the union of Weekly times and Weekly dispatch
VRN 1903-11
VU Ap 1,15,S 2,16,O 14,D 16 1903[04]F 8,S 13,N 15 1905;Ja 10,F 28,Jl 18,Ag 8,D 19 1906;Ja 9,F 13, Ag 14,D 18 1907;Ja 8 1908; Jl 14,S 1-15,O 13-20 1909;Ja 26,F 16,Mr 23, Ap 13-27,My 11 1910

Daily Richmond TRANSCRIPT. d Ag 1? 1835-Mr 1840||
United with Star to form Daily evening star and transcript, later Star
CSmH Ag 22 1835

Sunday TRANSCRIPT. w D 22? 1877-78||?
V Ja 27 1878

Evening TRUTH. d Je 1-Ag? 1887||
V Je-Ag 1887

VIRGINIA courier. (Manchester) w Jl 1874-80||?
1874-78 as Manchester courier
ICM D 9 1876
MWA Jl 15 1876;Ap 27 1878
V My 29,Je 5-12,29,Jl 3,17-24,Ag 14,28 1875; Jl 26 1879

VIRGINIA (*Continued*)

RICHMOND—*Continued*

VIRGINIA farm journal. w 1859-60‖?
MWA S 17 1859
NcD Jl 23 1859
V Ja 14 1860

VIRGINIA index. *See under* Petersburg

VIRGINIA Jackson republican and literal construction advocate. w S 18 1826-27‖?
Ct O 2 1826;Ap 30,My 14 1827
DLC O 2 1826;F 12 1827
MWA Mr 12-19 1827
N S 4 1826
VHi S 4 1826

VIRGINIA patriot. *See* Richmond daily mercantile advertiser

VIRGINIA patron. w Ap 2 1875-78‖?
MWA Jl 29 1876
NcD F 9-16,My 4,Je 1 1877
TJT D 10 1875
VU Ap 2 1875;Je 30 1876

VIRGINIA register. w Jl 7 1860-
CSmH Jl 21 1860

VIRGINIA staats-gazette. d,w Ap? 1870-1904‖
In German
MWA S 10,N 3 1876
NNHi F 13 1873

VIRGINIA star. w Ap? 1877-88‖?
Negro
CSmH S 8 1877
V My 11,D 14 1878;Mr 27 1880;Ap 30,Ag 27 1881;N 11-18,D 9-23 1882

VIRGINIA sun. sm,w Jl 11 1891-97‖
1891-Ja 1892 as Exchange reporter
sm Jl-N 28 1891
NcD O 17,N 14 1891;Ja 23,F 27,Mr 12,26,Ap 9,27,My 18,Jl 13,O 5-12,26 1892;My 17,Je 28 1893
V O 17,N 14,D 12 1891;Ja 23,Je 1,Jl 13,O 12,26 1892;My 1893
VU Jl 25 1881;Jl 11,25,O 3,17,N 14 1891;Ja 2,23,F 13-Mr 5,26,Ap 20,My-Je 1,Jl-Ag 3,S 14,O,N 16 1892;Mr 15,Ap 5,My 3,17-31,Je 14,28-Jl 5,Ag 9,23,N 2 1893;Ja 31,F 13,Mr 5,D 20 1894

Daily VIRGINIA times. sw,d F 14-Ag 25? 1823‖
sw F 14-21 1823
DLC [1823]
MHi F 28 1823
V F 14-18 1823

VIRGINIA tribune. w Jl 29? 1922-25‖?
V S 16 1922

Richmond VIRGINIAN. d Ja 28 1910-My 15 1920‖
Merged with Evening journal
NcD [1910-12]F 21,Mr 28,30[Ap 2-19 1915;Je 1916-S 1917]
NcU Je 3 1915
V complete
VHi Mr 7 1916
VRN Ap 1910-Ja,Mr-D 1911
VU [Mr 11-D 1910;Mr 1911-13]-Jl 1918
VWW D 22 1916

Die VIRGINISCHE zeitung. d,w 1859-My 22 1926‖
1861-77 merged with Richmond enquirer
d 1859-60
In German
IU Ag 26 1917-26
VU My 1 1926
—d ed *See* Täglicher anzeiger

VISITOR and telegraph. *See* Southern religious telegraph

Richmond WHIG. sw Ja 27 1824-D 27 1888‖
1824-32 as Constitutional whig; 1833-67? Richmond whig and public advertiser; 1868- Richmond whig and advertiser
Half sheets only issued 1863-64
Suspended from D 23 1885-Ja 27 1886
CSmH F-Ag 23,30-D 23,30 1825-Ja 24 1826;Ja 9 1827;Jl 2 1828;O 19 1844;49-Je 1850;Ag 20,N 15 1861;My 26 [Je 1862-N 1863]My 17,N 23,D 5-12,26 1864;Ja 28-31,F 21,Mr 2,10,22-27 1865;Je 1 1866[68]
Ct Mr 22 1831
CtW [S 1833-S 2 1834]
CtY Ja 30 1827-Ja 23 1838;F 4 1832
DLC [F 10 1824-29]Ja 1,Ag 27 1830[F 21 1831-Ag 14;O 12 1832;Jl 25 1835;Ja-[S 1840-Jl]-D 1841;O 31,N 17,D 29 1843;Ja 26 1844;Ap 22-25 1845;Je 26 1846;F 6,Jl 24 1849;Ja 5,Je 29 1855;Ap 25,Je 6 1856;Ap 14 1857;F 28,S 14 1860[61-Mr]-D 1865;N 30 1866;O 15 1869
GAtCo Mr 15 1839
ICHi N 19 1830
ICM Mr 12,26 1830;D 4-8 1874
ICU Ja 1 1830;O 29 1850
IU D 24 1830;Je 12 1832
KyLo Ag 18-22,S 1,19-29,O 17,24-27 1826
LNC [My-D 1861]-Mr 1865
MB Ja 8 1839;49-Mr 12 1852
MBAt F 25 1825;F 16 1833[61-62]-65;O 27 1868
MH Mr 2 1827;Je 21 1864
MHi F 13-17 1824;Ag 11,O 31 1831;Mr 18 1836
MSaE Ap 12 1865
MWA My 11,O 22 1824[25-Je 1826;27-29;F-S 1830]Ag 7 1832;Ap 3,Jl 10 1835;F 2,Jl 22-29,Ag 19,S 6,20 1836[Je 23-D 1 1837]Mr 29-Ap 2,O 11 1839;Ap 14-21 1840[41-Mr 8 1842]F 13 1844-Ja 14 1845;Jl 23 1852; N 24 1854[Je 18 1861-Je 9 1863]O 14,N 18,D 30 1864;F 7-10,Mr 3 1865
N N 16 1824;O 10 1826-D 8 1827
NIC O 6 1829-Ja 16 1830
NN Jl 30 1841;Ja 31,F 14,Mr 7,Ap 18,Jl 1 1862;Ja 16,F 6,Mr 13,Je 16,O 23 1863
NNHi 1824-76;Jl 1877-85
NSchU Ap 19,My 17-24 1842
NcD F 17,24-27 1824[Ap 25 1826-Ap 8 1831;32]Ap 12,N 19 1833;Je 9 1835;Ja 23,Mr 6,My 1,Je 26 1838;Ap 2 1839[Ag-S]N 24,D 15 1840;Je 4 1841;Ag 23,S 23,O 18,N 4 1842;F 17,Mr 7,14,My 26,N 24 1843;F 23,Je 4 1844[Jl-D 1848;50-55]S 19 1856;F 10,D 4,11 1857;Ja 28,Ap 5,S 23,D 23 1859;Ag 14,S 14,D 11 1860[F 26 1861-Mr 1865]Jl 3 1866;Ap 5,12,26,My 3,Je 18 1867[68-Ap 23 1875]Ag 10 1877;O 11 1878
NcU My 22,Je 5 1840;My 31 1859;N 16 1860;Ja 15,F 19,Mr 6,26,Ap 9,23,Je 7-14,25,Jl 16,O 15-18,D 7-10,27 1861[62-64]Ja 27 1865
NjR Jl 27 1824
OClWHi Ap 19,O 1 1861;Ap 11,20,28-30,My 12,Je 24,O 20 1863;Ja 8,F 26,Mr 8-15,25 1864;O 1-4 1870
OHi Ja 16 1829;Jl 1835-Je 1836;Jl 12-D 1837;Jl 1838-Ap 1842;Jl 24 1863;My 27 1864
PDoHi F 1 1825
PHi F 20 1827-My 24 1828
PP F 20 1827-My 24 1828
PU [1825-35]
TKL Jl 20 1829
Tx O 6 1829-Ja 16 1830;N 2 1860
TxU O 6 1829-30;D 1835-S 1836[Jl 1856-Je 24 1860]
VHi Je 8 1827[Mr 24-N 1829]D 20 1831[My 11-Jl 1832;33-Ap]Jl 30 1834;Ja 22,Jl 1 [S 15 1835-Ap]My 3,S 30 [O-D 1836;D 1843]Mr 1844[Jl-Ag 26 1845]D 31 1847;S 4 1855;Jl 4,Ag 6-9,O 1 1861;Ja 17 1862;My 15,S 29 1863;Ja 31,Ap 18,N 20 1865;F 21,Je 19 1866;Ja 7 1870
VLyR Ag 14 1834
VRB My 26 1843;Mr 19-22 1844[Je 15 1847-S 3 1850]Je 21,Jl 29,S 9 1853;N 21 1854;Ag 31 1855[Je 22 1858-N 22 1861]F 19,Mr 11-15,Jl 29 1864
VRN Ap 21 1834;D 16 1836;Ap 21,Je 14,Jl 7 1837
VU Jl 7-11 1826;F 13 1836;F 14,Je 2,O 20 1837[F-D 11 1838]Ja 1,Mr 1-5,Ap 2,N 8 1839 [My-D 1840]-Mr 24,My 9 1843;My 14 1844;My 20 1845;Ja 20 1846;D 31 1847[Jl-N 1852] Ag 17,S 14,N 9 1858;Ag 9 1859;Mr 2,13 1860;S 10 1861;O 20 1863;F 19,Ap 8,12,22,Jl 22,S 23,O 4,25,D 13 1864;Ja 3 1865;Ap 5 1867
VWW S 3[D 13 1833-Je 23 1837;Ag 20 1841-Je 16 1843]D 5 1854;Mr 13,20 1855[O 17 1856-Je 12 1857;58-Je 21 1861]O 14,D 25 1862 [63-Ap 15 1864]F 4 1873
Vt [1861-65]
WHi Je 22,D 21 1824;Ap 27,Je 26 1827-Jl 2 1830;S 1831-Ja,Je 26-Jl 1861]Ag 1862-Ag 1863;64-Mr 1865[Ja 26 1869-F 17 1882]

Richmond daily WHIG. d N 11? 1828-D 27 1888‖
Title varies: Daily Richmond whig; Richmond whig and commercial journal; Richmond whig and public advertiser
CSmH 1829-33;35-37;D 14,31 1850;My 27 1851;S 8 1852;F 11,Mr 28,Jl 13,S 29 1853;Ja 20,28,S 8 1857;F 25,Ap 3 1858;Ag 2-3,9,22-27,30-31 1859;F 28,My 22,Ag 22 1860;Je 8,Jl 18,Ag 8-9,12,20,30,O 11,25,29,31,D 28 1861;Ja 6,8-9,24,31,F 4-5,7,11-12,Mr 10,Ap 8,22,25,My 1-3,5,7-9,19,23 1862;Ap 20 1863;Jl 25,28,Ag 2,8,24,S 10 1864;F 7,Ap 7,10-11,13,17-19,21,26,28-29,My 10,13,Je 1,Jl 8,O 7,N 2 1865;F 3,7,S 14 1868;Jl 13 1869
CtW O 24 1833
CtY My 2 1864;Ap 15,My 13 1865;Ag 12 1868
DLC [1829-F 10]Je 11,23 1831;S 29 1832;Ap 15,N 21 1840[Jl 19 1841-Ag 10 1842]F 18,Mr 8-9,15-16,18,20,N 30,D 3 1847[Mr 10 1849-52]D 30 1858;F 6,D 12 1860 [Jl 10-O 1861]-[Ja-My]Je 4,24,O 30 1865;Ap 10 1866 [Ap 13 1867-74]D 21 1878[Mr 1879-Ja 18 1887]88
IC D 29 1864
ICHi Ja 1 1831;S 6 1848
ICM O 14 1870;Jl 10 1872;Ap 3 1874;Ja 19,Ag 10 1876;Ag 8 1877;Ag 3,19,N 4,D 24-25,28 1878;Ja 14-15,S 24 1879[80-Ag 1883]
ICN My 10-27,30-31,Je 6,8,11-16,18-25,Jl 2,5-6,9,23 1864;Ap 12 1865
ICU Je 5 1869
IU [Mr-S 1864]Ja 11,13,16,19-20,23 1865
KHi Je 4 1877
KyLo F 7 1834
LNH Ag 2 186_
MB S 9-O 11 1861;S 30 1865
MBAt [Ap 12 1865-69]
MH Ag 19 1846;N 22 1850;Mr 27 1861[Ap 15 1862-65]
MHi Jl 23 1833[Mr 1864]
MWA Mr 13[Je 29 1829-Ja 28]Ag 7,D 10 1830;Ja 5,17 1831;Ap 15 1840;Ap 15 1841;Ja 20,24,F 8 1860;D 9,20 1861[F-My,Jl-D 1862]Ja 10,Mr 4,Ap 17,Jl 25,N 2-6,18-19,30 1863[64-Je 20 1865]Ja 4,My 1869; Ap 22,S 8-9 1871;Ap 5 1872;Ap 5,S 19,N 2 1876;My 7,Je 4 1877;Ja 26 1880;N 3 1882;S 28 1885
MWo Ap 18 1861
MdHi D 28 1863-Ja 1,4,6-8,12-14 1864;Ap 22,26 1865
MnHi Ap 25-26 1864;Ap 24,My 30 1865
MsHi O 22 1861
N O 15 1833;Ap 12,17,My 29,31,Jl 1 1865
NBHi F 6 1860;N 24 1864;My 15 1865
NIC D 23 1835;Ja 9,27 1836;My 18-20,S 2 1859;D 16 1861;Mr 29,Ap 18-19,My 18,Jl 21,Ag 9,17,24,26,S 5-6,14,19,27,D 8 1864;My 11 1866;Ja 6-Je 10 1867
NNHi N 11 1828-N 6 1829;Ja-Je 1840;43-Je 1861;My 28 1862-64;Ap 6 1865-76;Jl 1877-Je 1886;Ja-Je 1887 My 9,Jl 1[N-D]1888
NtHi [F 1873-Ap 1874]
Nc D 23 1868
NcGrW S 5 1862
NcD D 18 1830;My 3 1831;S 9 1834;Jl 27 1838;Mr 20 1840;Mr 19 1844;Ja 26 1847;S 25 1856;Mr 31,D 8 1857;Ap 18-20,26,Je 26,S 5 1861;F 19[Je 30-D 1862;Mr 6 1863-Ap 22]My 2 1865;Mr 26,My 30 1866;Ag 1 1868;Mr 1,Ap 2,Jl 10,S 15 1869;Mr 1870;Ja 16,27,F 13,Ap 17,Ag 8,D 25 1871;Jl 29,Ag 8,16,S 30 1872;D 31 1873;F 12,My 7,S 1 1874[75-78]Ap 5 1879;O 24-26,28,N 2-7,24,D 9,12,16 1881;My 11 1883;My 22,Jl 25,S 18,O 9,27,N 12 1886;Je 12 1888
NcU N 21 1860[61-64]Ja 27 1865;O 15 1870
NdU Ap 22 1865
NjN Ap 18 1865
NjP D 11 1863;Ap 25 1865
OCHi Ap 25 1865;Ap 9,My 7,Je 4 1877
OClWHi Ja 5,Mr 20 1860[62-Ap 26]S 30 1865
OOxM My 12,14 1877
PAltHi Ap 10 1865
PAtM Ap 15,18-22 1865
PDoHi Ja 23 1863
PHi Ag 7,S 5,23 1863
PHoHi Ap 10 1865
PPL Ap 11,24 1865
PPGr Ja 16 1865
PUn Ap 20 1865
PWcT [1825-35]
Tx [Mr-O 1864]
TxGR Je 17,D 23 1861;Ja 27,Ap 25,Jl 9,Ag 5,7,23,S 27, O 4,6-7,10,20,28,N 5 1862;Ja 13,Je 9,23,Ag 31,S 24 1863[My 18-D 14 1864] Ja 16-19,Mr 20-21,31,Ap 1 1865
TxU [D 14 1863-Ag 11 1864]
V [1829-My 21 1831;41-43;45-Je 1847;56;S 9 1859-88]
VHi Jl 5-S 1831;Jl 2-S 8,N 1835-[Ja-F 13 1836]My 26 1841;D 5 1843 D 19 1846-51;Mr 5,Je 6 1853;Ja 16,Ag 27 1856;F 14,16,S 21 1857;Ja 12 1858;S 21 1859; Ja 19,26[F 1860;61-66]Ja 12,Ap 30 1870;S 6,9,12,O 5,12,18,21,N 1 1875;Jl 8 1886;Je 2 1891;S 28 1893
VRB Mr 1 1869;Ap 29 1870;My 20-26,28,31,Je 5,9-10,12,16 1874;S 15,20,O 4-5,12,N 1 1875
VRC Jl 2 1852;D 5 1853;Ja 19 1860-Ag 27 1866;Ja 25,Ap 28,O 14,18 1870;Mr 15,28 1871
VRN Ag 31,S 12 1830;Je 22 1832
VU My 22,O 8 1833;S 30 1856;F 1,D 3 1860;Ag 3 1863;Ap 3,My 2,Je 30,Ag 25 1864;O 21-28,31,N 10,D 6 1865; Ja 17 1866[Ja 28-S 1870;Ja-N 1871;72-77]F 12,25 1878;Ag 21 1879;D 3 1880;F 1,17 1883;My 31 1887
VWW Ag 19 1859;Je 13 1860;Mr 5 1862;Ap 10-11,13,15,17-18,O 11 1865;Mr 10,Ap 9,11,Je 1,27,S 24,N 19,D 1,10 1866;Ag 27 1867;N 26 1868;N 16 1872[Ja-Ap 1873; 78-85]
Vt [1865]
WHi [Ag 27 1862-Ag 10 1863;Mr 22 1864-Je 27 1865;Ag 4 1873-Ap 26 1881]

Weekly WHIG. w D? 1842-D 27 1888‖
Suspended from 1862-Ap 30 1867
CSmH S 9,O 14 1868
DLC Ja 25 1845[Ag 8 1846-O 23 1847]S 25,N 13 1852;Ja 22 1853;O 26,D 28 1877
ICM 1874
MB 1849-Ja 2 1852
MDeHi Ap 17-25 1865
MH Ja 6 1869
MHi Mr 3 1860
MWA F 19 1844;S 22 1876
NNHi Ap 1849-N 9 1850;My 1867-85;F 14 1886-88
NcD Mr 18,My 6,Je 24-Jl 1,15 1844;Ag 21 1858;S 8 1860;F 9-16,My 11,Ag 31-S 7,N 23-30 1861;Ap 13,S 7 1870;D 10 1873;Je 28,Jl 26,N 10,D 15 1876;N 26 1880;My 19 1882;Je 19-N 23,D 1883;Jl 25,Ag 15,O 3 1884;O 9,23 1885
OClWHi O 6-13 1860;Mr 14,Ap 11 1863
TU Ag 26 1860
Tx F 1-8,Mr 1,16,29,Ap 5-12,26,My 3-17,Je-Jl 19,Ag 2-16,30-S 6,20,O 11-25 1862;Ja 24-F 7,21,N 12 1863;O 1 1864
VHi F 4 1860[Je 1863-Je 1864]
VRB O 6 1875
VU S 16-23 1881;S 7 1883;Mr 28 1884;D 9 1887;My 4 1888
VWW D 3 1859

Evening WHIG. d O 1 1864-Ap 28 1865‖
CoHi N 29 1864
Ct Ap 4,8 1865
CtY Ap 4-28 1865
DLC O 12,15,19,22,D 8,19 1864;Ja 30,Mr 17,25,Ap 4,6-8 1865
IC D 23 1864
MBAt Ap 6,8 1865
MH D 16 1864;Ja 9,F 9,15-17,22,28,Mr 2,14,23-24,28,Ap 6-8 1865
MHi Ap 6 1865
MMarHi Ap 6 1865
MWA Ja 27,F 22,Mr 4,Ap 4-8 1865
NN O 6-7 1864;Mr 18 1865
NNHi Ap 4-7 1865
VHi O 1,N 3 1864
VWW Ap 6-8 1865

Richmond Sunday WORLD. w S 1-D? 1935‖
VU N 24 1935

YEOMAN. w Ja 29-D 25 1840‖
Campaign paper
CSmH F 26 1840
DLC 1840
ICM Ja-O,D 16-23 1840
MWA complete
NNHi complete
NcD F 5,19-O 1,27 1840
NjR [1840]
OClWHi My 18 1840
OHi My 18 1840
V [1840]
VHi complete
VU Ja-O 22,D 25 1840
WHi complete

ROANOKE

To F 3 1882 as Big Lick

BIG LICK news. *See* Roanoke Saturday review

Roanoke daily HERALD. d Ja 15 1889-93‖
ICM N 22 1891
VRo [Ap 29-N 1890;Mr 19-S 1891;Ap-Ag 1892]
VU Ap 9,23-24,My 24,28,Je 3-_,Jl 11 1890;Ja 17,Mr 14,29,Ap 14,Je 20,28,Ag 12 1891

Roanoke HERALD. w 1889-93‖
VU Jl 14,Ag 19 1891;Ag 31 1892

Roanoke LEADER. w S 7 1882-87‖
NcD D 7 1882;D 13 1884;F 20,Mr 13 1886
VRo Ag 5 1887

VIRGINIA (*Continued*)

ROANOKE—*Continued*

Roanoke NEWS. d 1901-Mr 1913‖
United with Evening world to form World-news
NcD Ap 18 1904;N 2 1909
VRoW complete

Saturday evening NEWS. *See* Roanoke Saturday review

Public journal. w 1917-24‖
1917? as Roanoke public ledger
VU Je 7 1924

Roanoke PUBLIC ledger. *See* Public journal

Roanoke daily RECORD. d Ag 2? 1892-94‖
VHi Ja 5 1893
VRo [N 26 1892-Ja 1894]
VU D 30 1893

Roanoke Saturday REVIEW. w My 12? 1877-86‖
1877-81 as Big Lick news; 1881-82 Saturday Evening news
VRo Ap 28 1883
VRoW S 22 1877
VU S 22 1877(photograph)Jl 16 1881

Roanoke weekly SUN. w Jl? 1887-89‖
VRo F 11 1888;Ja 19,F 23 1889

Roanoke TIMES. d N 30 1880+
pub [1891-92]+
DLC 1898-Je 1900
ICM My 25 1891;F 27 1892;N 9,D 3 1913;Mr 8,10-11,19,My 15 1914
MWA Ja 28 1934
N O 16 1890
NcD F 28 1918;Ja 28 1934
V 1905+
VRaT 1928[29+]
VRo Ap 4,D 7 1889;D 3 1890[Ja 24 1891-N 21 1893]Ja 24,D 5 1894;O 6,D 14 1895;My 13-14, Je 13-14,S 30,O 27,D 24 1896;F 23,25 1897;Mr 8,Je 26,S 21,O 23 1898;Mr 21,N 3,D 26,29-30 1899;Ap 21 1900;My 15,Jl 25 1901;Ap 11 1902; 23+
VU Jl 21 1889;Ap 23,My 17,31,N 2 1890;Ja 17, Je 28,Jl 3,Ag 8 1891;Ja 1 1893;Ja 24,Mr 22 1894;O 6,22 1895;My 3 1896;My 26,Je 7,19,Jl 1,D 15 1898;Mr 4 1903;N 29 1907;Ap 30 1910; Ag 29 1911;Ja 15 1922;N 30 1926;Ap 18-20 1929;Ag 14 1930[Ja-S 3 1934]Je 28,Ag 1 1935

Roanoke TRIBUNE. *See under* Salem

VIRGINIA weekly press. w 1904-05‖?
VU S 29,O 13 1904

WORLD-NEWS. d D 23 1889+
1889-Mr 1913 as Evening world
pub 1901+
VHi Ja 5 1893
VRo O 14 1892;Je 11,S 22 1898;Ap 27 1905;N 11 1918;23+
VU Je 23 1898;D 3 1907;O 8 1917;Je 8,11 1934; Je 28,Jl 31 1935

ROCKY MOUNT

COUNTY news and Franklin chronicle. w S 6 1923+
1923-29 as County news
pub 1923+
VU [1923-24]Ap 12 1934

FRANKLIN chronicle. w N 1905-29‖
VU Ja 6,Ap 21-My 5 1910;F 21,S 5,O 10 1918; Jl 24 1919;F 24,Ag 11 1921;My 18,Jl 20,O 26,D 7 1922;Ja 11,Mr 1,15 1923;Je 12 1924;Je 24 1926

FRANKLIN gazette. *See* Virginia monitor

VIRGINIA monitor. w O 1872-My 1876‖
1872-75? as Franklin gazette. United with Conservative (Salem) to form Conservative and Monitor
MWA My 26 1876

ROSSLYN

ALEXANDRIA county monitor. *See* Monitor

CHRONICLE. w S 1920+
pub 1920+
VU Ag 2 1935

COMMONWEALTH monitor. w 1928+
Formed by the union of Commonwealth (Richmond) and Monitor
pub 1928+
VU Ag 3 1935

MONITOR. w 1898-1928‖
1898-1906? as Falls Church monitor (Falls Church) 1907?-17? Alexandria county monitor. United with Commonwealth (Richmond) to form Commonwealth monitor

RURAL RETREAT

Rural Retreat TIMES. w F? 1892-1918‖
VHi F 17 1893

RUSTBURG

CAMPBELL county record. w My 25? 1883-91‖?
1883-N 1886 pub in Lynch Station
NNHi Ag 31,S 14-21,O 5,N 23 1883;Ap 11,My 9,Je 4-11,Jl 2-9,Ag 6,S 10,24-O 1,22,N 19-D 3 1884;Ja 9,Je 11,N 5,19 1884;F 11-18,N 25 1886
NcD Ag 24 1883

CAMPBELL county times. w Ag? 1929+
VAmN 1929+
VLy 1935+

SALEM

CONSERVATIVE and monitor. w Ap 13 1876-D 16? 1880‖
Ap-My 1876 as Conservative
DLC [Ap 20 1876-D 13 1877;79-D 16 1880]
ICM Je 27 1878
MWA F 25 1879
NbHi Jl 6 1876
VRo O 29 1879;F 18,S 30 1880
VU Je 15-22,Jl 13,Ag 17,S 14,O 19 1876;F 15, Mr 1,Ag 9,23,S 27,D 20 1877;Ja 3,F 28,Mr 26, My 23,Jl 18,S 5 1878;N 26,D 3 1879;Ja 14,F 25,S 16 1880

Salem LEDGER. *See* Roanoke times (1866-75)

Salem REGISTER. w Ag? 1854-Ag 30 1861‖
Follows Roanoke republican
MWA Ja 25 1861
VU Jl 20 1860

Salem weekly REGISTER. w O 4 1873-84‖
United with Roanoke times to form Salem times-register, later Times-register and sentinel
DLC [N 18 1873-76]Mr 16,Je 15,S 28,O 12,26 1877;78[80]Jl 29[S 9 1881-82]
MWA Ag 4 1876
V My 16 1876
VRo Ag 25 1876
VU O 1 1870;Jl 27-Ag 3,17,N 2,D 3-17 1875;F 25,My 5,Je 2,Ag 25,S 22 1876;Mr 2,Ap 6-13, Je 29,N 2,D 21 1877;Ja 4 1878;Ja 10,F 14,Jl 11,Ag 8,S 19 1879;Ap 2,Ag 6 1880

ROANOKE beacon. w Jl 1851-D? 1853‖
Followed by Roanoke republican
VRo Mr 18-Ap 1,29,Jl 29,D 23 1852;Ja 20-27,F 24,Ag 11-18 1853

ROANOKE republican. w Ap?-Ag? 1854‖
Follows Roanoke beacon. Followed by Salem register

ROANOKE times. w Je 8 1866-D 23 1875‖
Je 18-O 15? 1870 as Salem ledger
Suspended during Ja 1875
DLC [Je 15 1866-71]73-75
MWA Mr 18 1875
NNHi Ja 16 1873
VRo [Ag 8 1868-N 6 1869]F 1,Ap 4,O 3,31 1872;My 15,S 4 1873
VU [Je-D 11 1866]Ja 8,22,N 23 1867[Ap 1870-N 1871]Ja 18,Je 20,Jl 4,O 10,24 1872;My 1,N 20 1873;Ag 20,S 10 1874[F-D 23 1875]

ROANOKE times. w Ag 3 1881-Ag 10 1883‖
United with Salem weekly register to form Salem times-register, later Times-register and sentinel

ROANOKE tribune. w Ag 24- 1929‖
Ag 24-S 7 1929 pub in Roanoke
VU Ag 24-S 7,O 11 1929

Salem SENTINEL. w My 7 1894-N 16 1903‖
United with Times-register to form Times-register and sentinel
VRo Ag 13,D 3 1895;Ag 18,D 22 1896;My 2 1899;Ja 16,D 4 1900;D 10 1901
VU D 13 1898

Saturday SUN. w N 1891-92‖
VRo F 27,O 8 1892

TIMES-REGISTER and sentinel. w,sw Ag 15 1883+
Formed by the union of Roanoke times and Salem register. 1883-N 9 1903 as Salem times-register
w 1883-1920?
pub 1928+
NcD N 28 1890
VRo Ag 8 1884;Jl 12 1885;Mr 25,Jl 1,O 14 1887;Ja 6,S 21,O 5 1888;Ap 26,O 25 1889[90-Mr 9 1894]Je 10,23 1898;N 17 1899;F 25,Mr 17 1904
VSaR 1935+
VU Ag 31 1883;S 9 1887;N 15 1889;Ag 17 1934

SCOTTSVILLE

Scottsville COURIER. w 1859-S? 1906‖
1859-Ag? 1872 as Scottsville register; 1872-77? Weekly courier. Followed by Scottsville enterprise, later Scottsville news
MWA My 4 1876
NNHi Ap 17,N 6 1873
NcD Ap 20 1861;S 12 1872;Ja 3,S 26,O 10 1878; Je 11 1885;Ja 27 1887
VU Je 7,N 17,29 1877;F 27 1890;F 14,Ap 4,Jl 15 1895;O 3 1902;Ag 11,O 20,N 3 1905;S 7 1906
VWW D 8 1881;F 17,Mr 24-31 1887

Scottsville ENTERPRISE. *See* Scottsville news

Scottsville NEWS. w O? 1906+
Follows Scottsville courier. 1906-F? 1920 as Scottsville enterprise
pub Mr 1920+
VU Ap 23 1915;Mr 31,Jl 21 1916;F 12 1918;Ap 8 1920;Mr 17 1921;Jl 4-18,Ag 15 1935+

Scottsville REGISTER. *See* Scottsville courier

SEDDON. *See* BLAND

SHENANDOAH

To F 6 1890 as Milnes

Shenandoah ARGUS. w D 17 1892-97‖
VHi F 18 1893

MILNES weekly. w N 4 1882-
VU N 11 1882

SHENDUN

Shendun NEWS. w,sm Ja 1891-Mr 1893‖
w 1891-My 1892
VHi Ja 5 1893

SMITHFIELD

TIMES. w 1920+
pub [1930+]
VU Mr 21 1929

SOUTH BOSTON

HALIFAX gazette. w,sw S? 1903+
sw 1914-25?
pub 1904-08;19+
V 1923+
VU Ja 8 1931;Jl 11-Ag 8,22-29 1935

HALIFAX record-advertiser. w S 1 1870+
1870-91 as Halifax record
1870-79 pub in Halifax
pub 1927+
MWA Ag 16 1876
NNHi Mr 5 1873
NcD S 8 1870;O 4 1872;Jl 23 1873;Ap 18 1879; N 27 1885;Ap 2 1886;Mr 11 1891
NcU Jl 28 1875
VSo 1935+
VU S 1 1875;F 19 1886

NEWS. w S 5 1890+
pub S 5 1890(photograph)Ja 12 1899;Ja 3-17, N 14 1901;F 2 1911;27+
NcD Ja 3 1895;Ja 6 1910
VHi F 23 1893
VSo 1935+
VU S 5 1890;S-N 23,D 7-21 1899;Ja 4,18-F 22 1900;S-D 21 1905;Ja 4-18,F 8-Mr 8 1906;Ja 4-11,25-Ag,S 12-N 1907;N 3 1910;Jl 13-Ag 24 1911

RECORD-ADVERTISER and the week-end. *See under* Halifax

South Boston TIMES. w 1890-1903‖
NcD D 8,22 1899;Ja 12,26,F 9,Ap 27,Jl 16,20, O 4-18 1900;Ja 24,F 14,Mr 28,My 30,Je 13,S 26,O 3 1901

SOUTH HILL

South Hill ENTERPRISE. w 1911+
pub 1916+
V Ja 27,Jl 21,Ag 1927+
VHi Mr 2 1922
VU N 8 1934

STAFFORD COURT HOUSE

Stafford ranger. w Ag 1 1931+
VFT My 1935+
VMJ 1931+

STANARDSVILLE

GREENE county record. w Mr? 1911+
VMaM 1911+
VU Je 4,Ag 13,S 3 1931;My 5,Je 9-23,Ag 11-25,S 22,O 6 1932[Ja-O 1933;Ja-S 13 1934]+

STANLEY

Stanley HERALD. w Mr 26? 1891-99‖
VU Ap 9 1891;My 13 1897

STAUNTON

AUGUSTA county argus. w,sw D 20 1887-1915‖
w 1887-1908
NcD Jl 30 1889;My 27,Jl 22 1890;My 26 1891
VHi Ja 10 1893
VSC 1888-1907;09;12
VU 1887-1900;03-Mr 1915

AUGUSTA democrat. *See* Staunton vindicator

DISPATCH. d D 1 1903-Je 1904‖
United with Staunton news to form Dispatch and news, later News-leader

Staunton DISPATCH and news. w,sw 1891-1909‖?
1891-Mr 13 1903 as Staunton news
w 1891-95
NcD Mr 7,Ap 14-My 12,O 6 1892;F 16-Mr 2 1893;My 31 1894;Mr 21,Je 6,23[Ag]S 19,O 3, 13,D 15 1899;Mr 12 1901
VU [Ag 18 1892-93]Ja 4 1894[Mr-D 1895]Ag 11-18 1903;Ja 1 1904

Staunton DISPATCH and news. d *See* News-leader

LEADER. d (evening) D 15 1904+
Title varies: Staunton daily leader
pub 1904+
ICHi Je 13 1911
VU My 3,1905;Je 13 1912;S 12 1916;Ap 20-21, Je 6,Jl 10,D 2-3,21 1917[Ja 22-N 9 1918]O 1934+

Morning LEADER. d 1908-N 14? 1919‖
United with Daily news to form News-leader
pub 1908-19
VU Je 4-5,Jl 16,Ag 9,13,15-16,18-19,S 30,O 10, 20,23,N 14 1914;Ap 20,Ag 4,8-9,11,15,S 29,O 12,17-18,N 4,16-17,28,30 1917[Ja 22-D 1918]-Ja 2,F 15,Mr 4,8,My 2,15,Jl 27 1919

Staunton NEWS. w *See* Staunton dispatch and news

NEWS-LEADER. d Ag 3 1891+
1891-Mr 13? 1903 as Daily news; Mr 14 1903-09 Staunton dispatch and news; 1909-12 Dispatch-news; 1913-N 14? 1919 News
Ja 1 1906 is industrial number
pub [1906-12]19+
DLC Ja 1 1906
ICHi Je 24 1911
ICM S 7 1912;D 23 1913;My 28 1914;Ja 4 1917; My 2 1928
NN Ja 1 1906

VIRGINIA (*Continued*)

STAUNTON—*Continued*

NEWS-LEADER. d 1891+—*Continued*
V 1905+
VHi Ja 7 1892;Ag 11 1923
VS Ja 19 1935+
VSC Jl 1902-03;35+
VSMb 1935+
VU Ap 23,Ag 15 1895;D 28 1900;My 3-6 1905; Ja 1 1906;S 8,D 22 1907;Ap 24,Je 23-27,Ag 1, 10,O 27 1909;F 26,Mr 4,Ap 26,28,30,My 3-8,11 1910;My 9,11-12 1912;Je 25 1913[Mr-O 20 1914]My 20,23,26,Je 11 1915;My 20,26,Je 11, Jl 14,22,N 30 1916[Mr 20 1917-D 7 1918]Ja 1,23,Mr 15,My 9,16,Jl 15,Ag 26 1919;S 9,O 5, N 13 1920;My 9,16,18-27,Ag 23-24 1923;Ag 19, 22,25-30,D 29 1925;S 19 1926;S 12-16,O 7 1927; My 15,Jl 15 1928;D 15 1929[Mr-D 1932]Ja 3, 22,My 10,O 15,D 11,16 1931[Mr 1933-My]O 1934+

OLD DOMINION sun. w 1900-10||
VSN 1904-05

OLD VIRGINIA. *See under* Harrisonburg

POST. w 1882-86||
A [Ja 16-S 4 1886]

***REPUBLICAN farmer.** w 1808-23||
Followed by Staunton spectator, later Staunton spectator and vindicator

REPUBLICAN vindicator. *See* Staunton vindicator

Staunton SPECTATOR and vindicator. w D? 1823-1916||?
Follows Republican farmer. 1823-S 9 1896 title varies: Staunton spectator and republican farmer; Staunton spectator; Staunton spectator and general advertiser
Suspended from Je 7 1864-Je? 1865
CSmH Ag 3 1853;Ag 4 1863
DLC Ap 25 1828;Jl 10,24,Ag 7-14,S 4,25-O 2, 30,N 20-27,D 25 1829;Ja 15 1830;O 5 1832;Jl 23 1836;N 5 1840
ICHi My 16,Je 26,Jl 10,Ag 14,S 11 1834
ICM S 12 1865;O 3-10,N 21,D 5,26 1876-Ja 9, 30-F 6,20-Mr 13,Ap 10-17,My 22,Je 19,Jl 3 1877;Jl 15 1879;Jl 22 1884-Ap 11 1891;D 7 1892;Ja 4 1893;Ja 2,Ag 21,O 16 1895;F 5,Mr 11,S 30 1896;My 19 1898
MWA Jl 16 1835;Ja 26 1843;S 19 1876
N Ja 21 1825
NNHi D 31 1872
NcD S 5 1828;N 2 1837;Mr 11 1841;Ap 13,Je 1 1843[Ap 24 1850-O 1892]Je 7 1833;Mr 14 1894;Je 26 1895;Jl 19 1901;Mr 25 1904
NcU Ap 24 1850-51;56-59
OClWHi Ag 15 1849[Mr 12 1861-My 1864]N 21 1865;O 18 1870
V Mr 2 1827;N 26 1851;Je 1,N 16,D 28 1858 [63-81]
VLC 1888-89
VRC S 3 1861[62-63]
VSC [S 1836-53;60-My 1864;Jl 11 1865-My 1913]
VU My 16 1849;N 26 1851;My 4,D 28 1853;S 24 1856;Mr 29-Ap 1859;Ja 22,F 21,Ag 7,S 4-18,N 27 1860;F 5,Mr 1,Ap 2,My 7,28-Je 4,N 19,D 3,31 1861[Mr 1862-My 1864]Ag 15-S 5, 19-26,O 10-17 1865[Ja-N 1866;67;F-D 1868; Mr-N 3 1869]O 18,N 1870-[F 1871-S 3 1872] Ag 1873-O 17 1876[F-Je 1877]My 7,Je 25-Jl 9,30-Ag 13,D 10 1878;Ja 28,F 11 1879[Ja-N 16 1880;Ja-N 8 1881]S 12-O 3,17,31,N 21 1882-Ja 23,F 13-20 1883;Ag 5,S 30,O 29-N 5 1884; Jl 22,Ag 5-12 1885;Je 8,D 7 1887;S 5,D 12 1888;Mr 27 1889;O 17,29 1890;S 2,16 1896;My 20 1897;F 10 1898;Ap 7 1905;Ja 1 1906
WHi [My 31 1864-F 1882]

Staunton TRUE American and Virginia advertiser. w Ja 25 1855-Ap 25 1857||
Follows Virginia messenger and general advertiser. Ja-N 22 1855 as True American. Merged with Staunton spectator, later Staunton spectator and vindicator
CSmH F 21 1857
NcD N 15 1856
VSC [1855-56]
VU O 1855-Ap 18 1857

VALLEY Virginian. *See under* Clifton Forge

Staunton VINDICATOR. w Ja 1 1845-S 1896||
1845-48 as Augusta democrat; 1849-57 Republican vindicator. United with Staunton spectator to form Staunton spectator and vindicator
CSmH Ap 24 1863
DLC [Jl 13 1846-48]Ja 8 1864
ICM O 26 1883;Mr 20,F 5-12,Je 11,O 29 1886;F 11,D 30 1887;F 17,Ag 31 1888;Ap 11,Ag 1 1890;F 6,20,Ap 3-17,My 8 1891;D 9 1892;Jl 24 1896
MWA S 8 1876
MsHi 1889
NNHi F 28 1873
NcD O 30 1848;My 6,O 14 1850;F 24,O 6 1851; D 27 1852;Ap 14 1855;Mr 29,Ap 12,My 3,31 1856;Jl 10 1858;Mr 26,Ap 23 1859;Mr 23,Jl 20, S 7,21,N 16,D 7 1860;F 1-8,Mr 1-8,22 1861;My 15 1863;O 13 1865;S 21 1866;Je 14-21,S 13 1867;Ja 3 1868;O 1 1869;Ja 24 1873;Jl 10-N 13 1874;S 15 1873;O 27,D 1-14 1882;Ja 19,N 30 1883;Mr 7,My 2,O 10 1884;O 16 1885;Mr 12 1886;D 30 1887;Ja 6-20,F,N 2-9 1888;Ap 11,Jl 11,N 7 1890;F 13-20 1891
NcU Je 10 1881;D 13 1889
V [Jl 1865-81]
VHi D 23 1892
VRC F 26 1864;Mr 24-31 1865
VSC [1849]50;54-[Ja-Je 1861;F 20 1863-66]-[68-96]
VU Ja 3 1848;D 3 1849;F 29 1863;N 14 1873;Jl 24,Ag 7-O 16,N 6 1874;D 27 1878;Ap 23,My 28 1880;My 20-27,Je 17,O 21,N 25-D 9 1881 [Mr 1883-S 1885;Mr 1886-88;Mr-N 1 1889;90; Je-O 16 1891]Ag 19-26,S 9-O 21,N-D 2 1892; Ap 21,My 5,Je 9,23-30,Jl 21-28,Ag 25-S 1,D 22 1893-F 9,O 19-26,N 9 1894-F 1,22,Mr 1 1895;Ag 28 1896
WHi S 22 1865;Mr 16 1866;S 13 1867;Ja 30 1874;N 23-30 1877;Ja 18 1878;Ag 8,O 31 1879; Jl 15,D 23 1881

VIRGINIA enterprise. *See* Yost's weekly

VIRGINIA messenger and general advertiser. w N? 1849-Ja 18 1855||
Followed by True American, later Staunton true American and Virginia advertiser
OClWHi Ag 12 1851
VSC [1854-55]
VU Jl 8 1851

YOST'S weekly. w Ag 11 1892-D 24 1896||
1894-S 20 1895 as Virginia enterprise
ICM Jl 4 1895
VSC Ag 11 1892-93;95-96

STRASBURG

Strasburg weekly DOTS. w Jl 28- 1888|
V S 15 1888(photograph)

Strasburg NEWS. *See* Northern Virginia daily

NORTHERN Virginia daily. w,sw,d Je 8 1882+
1882-S 14 1932 as Strasburg news (1887-91 Virginian and news)
1887-90 pub in Woodstock
w 1882-1906?;sw 1907?-S 14 1932
pub [1893-1911]+
MWA Je 24,Ag 12,S 2,30,D 2 1882
NcD Je 8 1883;F 6,20-27,Ap 10-17,Jl 31 1885;F 12 1886;O 7 1887
V Je 27 1934+
VHi Ja 5 1893
VU Mr 18-21,Ap 3,15-17,Je 21,Ag 19,26-S 22, 27-D 6,12-23,27,29-30 1933[Ja-O 8 1934]Jl 5-6,12-15,24-25,31-Ag 3,7,22 1935

VIRGINIAN and news. *See* Northern Virginia daily

STUART

ENTERPRISE. w 1884+
1884-90 as Patrick press
pub [1884]1915+
VSaR 1935+

PATRICK press. *See* Enterprise

SUFFOLK

Suffolk HERALD. w,tw Ja 3? 1873-1927||
United with Suffolk news to form News-herald
w 1873-1916
MWA Ag 30 1876
NNHi Je 13 1873
VRC My 27-Je 3 1874
VSuN 1882-83;94-95
VU S 7 1923
VWW S 7,D 14 1923

NANSEMOND enquirer. sw Mr 23?- 1852||
DLC O 19,29 1852

NEWS-HERALD. d Ja 1923+
1923-27 as Suffolk news
pub [1929]+
NcD [Je 26 1923-Ap 17 1924]
VHi D 20,30 1924
VU Je 30 1931;Jl 20,O 15 1932

Weekly OBSERVER. w O? 1889-97||
VHi Ja 4 1893

SURRY COURT HOUSE

JAMES RIVER herald. *See* Surry county herald

SURRY county herald. w 1879+
1879-84 as James River herald; 1885-Jl 20? 1935 Claremont herald
1879-Mr 1931 pub in Claremont
VU 1905;Jl 25,Ag 8 1913-31;Ag 30 1935

Surry TIMES. w My 12 1893-97||
VU Je 2-23,Ag 25-S 15,29 1893

TAPPAHANNOCK

ESSEX gazette. *See* Tidewater index

RAPPAHANNOCK times. w S? 1896+
1896-1923 as Tidewater democrat
pub Ag 1930+
VHi Ag 27 1897
VRB Ag 20 1897;D 23 1898
VRC 1906-07
VU Jl 15-22 1898

RURAL southerner and Eastern Virginia advertiser. w S? 1848-60||?
MWA Mr 31 1860

TIDEWATER democrat. *See* Rappahannock times

TIDEWATER index. w 1869-87||
1869-71 as Essex gazette
MWA My 19 1876
NNHi F 15 1873
NcD Mr 28 1874
V My 7 1886
VRB My 31 1873

TAZEWELL

To F 29 1892 as Jeffersonville

CLINCH VALLEY news. w O? 1869+
pub My 1897+
ICM Ag 12-19 1881;Ja 13,O 6 1882;Jl 17,S 25 1885;Ap 5 1889;N 8 1901;Mr 20,S 18,N 27 1903;Mr 7 1913
NNHi Ja 16 1873
VBP 1935+
VU N 16 1906;My 17-24 1907

REPUBLICAN. w 1892-1919||?
ICM Je 4 1896

SOUTHWEST Virginia. w N? 1869-76||
MWA Mr 16 1876

SOUTHWESTERN advocate. w D? 1851-60||?
DLC O 16-23 1852

Tazewell TIMES. w Ja 18 1882-85||
ICM Ja 18 1882

VIRGINIA appeal. w F 19?- 1881||
ICM Jl 23 1881
VU Jl 23 1881

URBANNA

MATHEWS-MIDDLESEX herald. *See* Southside sentinel

SOUTHSIDE sentinel. w 1896+
1896-99 as Mathews-Middlesex herald
pub 1930+

VICTORIA

Victoria DISPATCH. w 1913+
1913-15 as Lunenburg call
pub 1917+

LUNENBURG call. *See* Victoria dispatch

VIRGINIA BEACH

Virginia Beach NEWS. w Ag? 1925+
1925-29 as Virginia Beach weekly
pub 1932+
VNo 1935+
VU N 9,23 1934-Ja 18 1935

Virginia Beach WEEKLY. *See* Virginia Beach news

WACHAPREAGUE

FARMER and fisherman. w S 19? 1891-93||
VU Ja 23 1892

WAKEFIELD

TRI-COUNTY news. w S 21 1928+
pub 1928+
VU 1928-D 19 1930;31-Ja 1933

WARM SPRINGS

BATH county enterprise. w Je 16 1897+
Title varies slightly: Bath county enterprise, news and herald
VU Ag 4,D 16 1897;My 19,Jl 21,Ag 25,S 1898; Mr 2,16,Ap 13,27,Ag 10 1899;Ja 11,Je 13-27 1900;Ja 2-9,Jl 24,S 25 1901;Ag 27-S 3 1902[03; Mr 1904-N 1905]Ja 10,24,F 14,28,Ap 11-18,My 2-16,Je 13,27 1906;Ja 30,Mr 5,N 29 1907[Ja-N 13 1908]Ap 16,Je 25,Jl 23,S 24 1909;Ja 14,S 2,N 4 1910[12-15]Mr 17,31,Ap 21-My 12 1916 [Mr-Jl 12 1917]Mr,Ap 11-18,My 23,Jl 18,Ag 8 1918;Ja 23,Ap 10 1919;N 8 1923;Ap 29 1926; My 3,Ag 30 1928;D 11-18 1930;Ap 13 1933;Jl 11-Ag 1,22 1935

BATH news. w Ag 7? 1894-97||
VU Jl 11,Ag 8,S 5-12,26-O 3,D 12 1895;My 14-21,Je 4,O 8 1896;Jl 22-Ag 5 1897

WARRENTON

BANNER. d My 25?- 1897||
VU Je 22 1897

Warrenton ENTERPRISE. w My 16 1878-S 1879||
NbHi Je 13,27 1878

FAUQUIER democrat. w,sw D 16 1905+
Follows True index
w 1905-Ap 10 1926
pub 1925+
NcD D 3 1910;D 2 1911;Jl 27 1912;Jl 24 1916; Mr 2 1918;Mr 15,Jl 12,Ag 23 1919;My 14,Je 25,N 26 1921;Ja 7,Jl 1,S 23,O 28-N 4,18,D 23 1922[23-Ja 17 1925]Jl 24 1926 S 24,D 10 1927 [Mr 21-O 10 1928;29-S 23 1933]
VU Ap 6,Je 15-22 1907;Mr 6 1909;Ja 29,D 17 1910;O 28 1911;Ja 20,Je 15,Ag 3,S 14 1912;F 15,Mr 29 1913;Ag 15 1914[Ja-N 18 1916]Ap 21,Je 13,O 13,N 3,D 8 1917[18-22]-[24-S 18 1929]F 1,Jl 19 1933+

FLAG of '98. w Je? 1842-61||?
DLC Ap 6 1844;F 20 1847
MWA Ja 24 1861
NcD Ap 2 1853
VWa Je 13 1861
WHi N 30 1844;F 6 1847;Je 17 1848;Ja 5 1850; Je 18,Ag 27-S 3 1853;Je 16 1855;Ja 22 1857; Mr 11,My 27 1858;F 16,Ap 19,My 3,17,D 6 1860;Mr 14,My 9,21,Je 6-13,27,Jl 11,Ag 1 1861

INDEPENDENT register. w Ap 12 1834-35||?
DLC My 3 1834
VHi Ja 24 1835

JEFFERSONIAN. w Jl 16 1836-41||?
Ct Jl 16 1836
DLC Ag 13 1836;Je 22 1839
V [F 15 1840-O 16 1841]
VWa F 23,Ap 27 1839

NEW YORK ninth. w Jl 31- 1862||
pub by the 9th regiment, New York state Militia on the press of the Warrenton whig
DLC Ag 7 1862
MWA Jl 31 1862
NN Ag 7 1862

***PALLADIUM of liberty.** w Mr 1817-21||?
DLC [Ja 19-S 1821]

PIEDMONT whig. *See* Warrenton weekly whig

Warrenton REPUBLICAN. w F? 1849-51||?
NcD My 3 1851

VIRGINIA (*Continued*)

WARRENTON—*Continued*

Warrenton REVIEW. w F 12-Ap 9? 1909||
VU F-Mr 26,Ap 9 1909

SOLID SOUTH. *See* Warrenton Virginian

TIMES. w O? 1844-45||?
Running title: Warrenton times and Virginia advertiser
MWA O 11 1845

Warrenton TIMES. w Je 1915-25||
Follows Warrenton Virginian. Merged with Fauquier democrat
NcD Mr 29 1917;D 30 1920;Mr 6-13,My 8 1924
VU Ja 13-Mr 16,30 1916;N 8 1917;Ja 10 1918; Jl 6 1922;Je 5 1924

TRUE index. w N 11 1865-D 9? 1905||
Followed by Fauquier democrat
DLC My 16 1868;My 29,O 30,N 20-27,D 11 1869;Ja 15-22 1870;Mr 30 1872
NNHi F 22 1873
NbHi My 5 1877;Ap 27-My 4,Jl 6 1878;F 28, Ap 10,Ag 21,O 22 1880;N 17 1883;Mr 15,Ag 30 1884;S 11,O 16,D 11 1886;Je 22-29 1889
NcD Mr 16,Ap 6 1878;Mr 7,My 19 1896;Mr 20, Je 19,D 4 1897;F 26,Mr 5-12,Ap 16,30 1898; Mr 4,My 13 1899
V F 18 1871
VLe Ap 5,Ag 23 1879
VU Ap 26-My 3 1873;Mr 23 1878;D 1 1894;Mr 9,Ap 20,My 4,N 23-D 7,21 1895[Ja-S 12 1896; 97-1900]Ag 17 1901
WHi 1865-Ag 18,S,D 8 1866;Ja-Jl 13,Ag 10-O 12 1867;Ja-Mr 21,Ap-My,S 19-O 10,24-N 14, 28-D 12 1868;Je 19 1869;Ap 19 1870

VIRGINIA gazette. w Ja 7? 1826-29||?
DLC S 1 1827;Jl 5 1828;O 24,N 21,D 5-12 1829
MWA O 11 1828
VU Ja 7 1826

VIRGINIA sentinel. w O 28 1865-71||
WHi D 23 1865;Mr 29 1866;Je 27 1867;F 20,Je 25 1860

VIRGINIA times. w Jl 8 1837-Ja 2 1841||
Suspended from D 12?-26? 1840
DLC Jl 8 1837;Je 15 1839;Ag 8 1840;Ja 2 1841
N Je 10 1837

Warrenton VIRGINIAN. w Je 1877-My 1915||
1877-82 as Solid South. Followed by Warrenton times
DLC S 11 1879
NcD Mr 10 1881
VHi Ja 5 1893
VU Jl 17 1879;S 22 1887;O 19,N 9 1893;My 9 1901;N 20 1913

Warrenton weekly WHIG. w F? 1849-60||?
1849-56? as Piedmont whig
NcD Je 8 1850;Mr 13 1852;Mr 12,Ap 16,My 14, Jl 2,23,Ag 13,S 10 1853
WHi Ap 16,Ag 20,S 3 1853;F 4 1854;Ja 20 1855;Ag 15 1857;Mr 24,My 5,19-26 1860

WARSAW

NORTHERN NECK news. w My 16 1879+
pub 1879+
MWA My 25 1928;My 31 1929
NcD My 25 1928;My 31 1929
VHi Ag 6 1899
VRB Ap 30 1909
VU 1879+

WASHINGTON

BLUE RIDGE echo. w 1878-85||?
Follows Rappahannock news. 1883? as Call

BLUE RIDGE guide. w Je 21 1888+
pub [1898+]
VU O 27 1898;Je 14,S 6 1917;N 14,D 5 1918 [19-S 13 1923;F 1924-N 10 1927;28-S 1934]Jl 12,Ag 2 1935

CALL. *See* Blue Ridge echo

RAPPAHANNOCK news. w S 21 1877-78||
Followed by Blue Ridge echo
VU S 21 1877(photograph)

WATERFORD

Waterford NEWS. w O 22?- 1864||
VU N 26 1864

WAVERLY

DISPATCH. w F 1888+
1888-97 as Sussex gazette; 1897 Sussex recorder; 1898-1913 Sussex standard; 1913 Southside Virginia dispatch
pub [1912+]
VHi F 17 1893

SOUTHSIDE Virginia dispatch. *See* Dispatch

SUSSEX gazette. *See* Dispatch

SUSSEX recorder. *See* Dispatch

SUSSEX standard. *See* Dispatch

WAYNESBORO

NEWS. sw 1928-N 18 1929||
United with Valley Virginian to form Waynesboro news-Virginian
VWbN 1929

Waynesboro NEWS-VIRGINIAN. w,d 1896+
1896-1900? as Valley herald; 1901?-N 12 1929 Valley Virginian
w 1896-1929
pub 1919-20;22-26;Ap 1929+
ICM F 14 1919;Ja 21 1927
V O 1,D 5 1932;My 2,N 1934+
VU S 18 1931+

Waynesboro SENTINEL. w F 10? 1892-99||
ICM O 27 1892

SOUTH RIVER advertiser. w S 16? 1880-82||
WHi [D 2 1880-O 20 1881]

Waynesboro TIMES. sw Ja 6 1891-92||?
ICM Ja 6,13,20,S 4 1891
VU Ja 20 1891

Weekly TRIBUNE. w N 1877-Jl 1879||
ICM Ap 17-24 1878
WHi [Mr 20 1878-Ap 25 1879]

VALLEY herald. *See* Waynesboro news-Virginian

WEST POINT

NEWS. w Ag? 1889-1928||
1889-1913 as Plain dealer (Title varies: Plain dealer and Southern immigrationist; Plain dealer and Caroline news; Weekly news). Followed by Tidewater review
VHi Ja 26 1893
VRB F 14,S 12 1919

PLAIN DEALER. *See* News

West Point STAR. w N? 1871-89||
MWA Ja 20 1876
NNHi Mr 27 1873
V Ja 17 1889
VRB Jl 10 1884

TIDEWATER review. w 1928+
Follows News
pub 1928+
V F 21 1929+
VAsR 1929+
VU My 30 1935

TIDEWATER Virginian. *See* West Point Virginian

West Point VIRGINIAN. w,d D 4 1886-99||
1886-88? as Tidewater Virginian
w 1886-94

WILLIAMSBURG

CAVALIER. *See under* Yorktown

Williamsburg weekly GAZETTE. w Ag 24 1853-61||?
1853-54? as Virginia gazette. Title varies: Williamsburg weekly gazette; Weekly Williamsburg gazette; Williamsburg weekly gazette and Richmond and Norfolk mercantile advertiser; Weekly gazette and Eastern Virginia advertiser; etc. Suspended from D 1858-F 1859
V Jl 27 1854
VWW Ag-S 15,29-N 10,D 1,15 1853;N 1854-Ag 11 1858;Mr 2-16,30 1859-O 24 1860

Williamsburg GAZETTE and James City county advertiser. w O 1 1884-89||
V [Mr 31-D 15 1886]
VHi D 24 1884

PHOENIX. *See* Phoenix gazette and Williamsburg intelligencer

PHOENIX gazette and Williamsburg intelligencer. sw 1824-Je 11? 1828||
1824-Ap 2? 1825 as Phoenix. United with Virginia plough-boy and Williamsburg weekly advocate to form Phoenix ploughboy, later Virginia phoenix
MWA Ap 13,30 1825
V [Ap 9-S 1825]
VHi Ag 13 1825
VWW Ap 15,30(photostat)1825

PHOENIX ploughboy. *See* Virginia phoenix

Weekly REVIEW. w O 4- 1865||
MWA O 4 1865
VWW O 4 1865(photostat)

SPECTATOR. w Ag 22-N 14? 1929||
VWW Ag-N 14 1929

VIRGINIA gazette. 1853-54? *See* Williamsburg weekly gazette

VIRGINIA gazette. w Ja 21? 1869-71||?
MWA F 25,Je 3,24-Jl 1 1869
VWW F 18-Jl 1 1869

VIRGINIA gazette. w My 20 1893-1922||?
VWW [1893-Jl,S-N 24 1921]

VIRGINIA gazette. w Ja 8 1926-
My 15 1926 contains a reprint of the Virginia Resolutions for independence as passed by the Virginia Convention My 15 1776
GAA My 15 1926
MBAt Ja 15 1926
VU My 15 1926
VWW Ja 22-29,F 12,Ap 9 1926

VIRGINIA gazette. w Ja 10 1930+
Ag 7 1936 is 200 anniversary ed, and contains reprint of S 10 1736 number
DLC O 19 1934
KHi Jl 3 1931
MHi F 19-26 1932
MWA Ag 7 1936
NjR Mr 17 1933;Mr 29-O 4 1935
TxGR O 16 1931
V 1930+
VHi [1930-31]
VWW [1930+]
WHi Jl 29,Ag 26 1932

VIRGINIA phoenix. w Je 16 1828-29||
Formed by the union of Phoenix gazette and Williamsburg intelligencer, and Virginia plough-boy and Williamsburg weekly advocate. 1828-Je? 1929 as Phoenix ploughboy
DLC [Jl 16-N 12 1878]Jl 8,22 1829
MWA Je 10 1829
MeU F 11 1829
NN Jl 23 1828

VIRGINIA plough-boy, and Williamsburg weekly advocate. w Ag 25 1827-Je 11? 1828||?
United with Phoenix gazette and Williamsburg intelligencer to form Phoenix plough-boy, later Virginia phoenix
MWA Ag 25 1827

WINCHESTER

CONNECTICUT fifth. Mr 18- 1862||
pub by Fifth regiment, Connecticut volunteers, on the press of the Winchester Virginian
OClWHi Mr 18 1862
V Mr 18 1862

DEMOCRATIC platform. w Jl 3?-17? 1852||
Campaign paper
NcD Jl 17 1852

*Winchester GAZETTE.** w Ap 2 1788-1825||?
1788-Je 7? 1808 as Virginia centinel; Je 14 1808-09? Centinel, and Winchester gazette. Followed by Winchester Virginian
DLC D 6 1823;N 26 1824

Daily INDEPENDENT. d Jl 23? 1923-S 9 1925||
VU Ag 16 1924
VWn Jl 23 1923-25

INDEPENDENT leader. w 1884-99||
1884-94? as Winchester leader; 1894?-95? Republican leader
NcD [Ag 12 1887-Ja 23 1891]
VWn F 5 1886

Evening ITEM. *See* Evening news-item

Winchester JOURNAL. w S 1? 1865-69||
CSmH Je 12 1868
DLC Je 11 1869
NcD Ja 29 1869
VWn [Ja 26 1866-Jl 23 1869]

Winchester LEADER. *See* Independent leader

Morning MAIL. d Jl 1?-O? 1895||
VWn Jl 27 1895

Winchester NEWS. w Jl 7 1865-1909||
CSmH S 18 1868
MWA Ja 2 1876
NNHi N 15 1872
NcD [1865-67]Ag 2 1872;Jl 28 1882
V S 1,15-22,O 13,27 1865;Ja 12,Mr 23-30 1866
VWn S 28 1866;Ja 25,My 31,N 15 1867;Je 11 1869;F 18 1870;Ag 18,S 1 1871;My 17,Jl 12 1872;Ap 11-25,Jl 18,O 24,D 5 1873;Ja 30 1874; F 26,Ap 2,D 24 1875;My 19 1876[77-79]Je 11-18,N 5 1880;81-[83]84;F 13,Je 12 1885[86]F 2 1890;F 11 1895;Ja 19 1898[1909]

Evening NEWS-ITEM. d Ja 12 1895-My 17 1907||
1895-F 15? 1897 as Evening item. Merged with Winchester evening star
MWA S 11 1905
VWn Ja 14,F 13-20,Mr 7,Ag 10 1895;F 14 1896;F 15,Ap 14 1897;F 15 1902[Ja]Mr 21 1905

*Winchester REPUBLICAN.** w Ja 1810-Mr 7? 1862||
1810-18? as Republican constellation
CSmH Jl 18 1851
DLC Ja 31,F 28,My 1,15-22,O 2-9,N 26,D 3, 24 1824;Mr 18,D 16 1825[Je 1826-27]Mr 21, Je 20,N 28 1828[Jl 1829-Ja 1830]My 10 1853
MBAt My 18 1822
MWA My 5 1821[Ap 20-D 14 1822]Ja 19,Ag 31 1827;N 6 1829;Ja 22 1830;My 10 1853;S 11 1857
MsHi Ag 30 1861
N Ag 6,N 19 1824;Ja 5 1844
NN My 12,Ag 4,S 1 1831;S 22 1848;Ja 25-F 1, 2,My 31 1850;Ja 14,Mr 14,D 12 1851
NNHi O 31 1845
NcD Ag 20 1852;S 6 1861
OClWHi Mr 7 1862
PPL N 8 1850
VU N 24 1831;Ja 26 1832;Je 6 1854
VWn N 8 1823;O 1-22 1830[31]Jl 26,Ag 16 1844;My 21,S 3 1847;Mr 3 1848;S 26 1851; Ap 29,O 21 1853;Je 22,Jl 6,S 21,D 14 1855 [56-My 10 1861]

REPUBLICAN leader. *See* Independent leader

Winchester SENTINEL. w S 17 1869-Ja 3 1871||
Merged with Winchester times
VWn S 24,N 23-30 1869;Ja 11,F 1,Mr 8,O 11,25-N 8 1870

Winchester evening STAR. d Jl 4 1896+
pub 1914+
MWA Ag 20 1904
NcD D 2 1917;Mr 5,27,Ap 18,24,My 17,,23-24,31,Je 24-25,Jl 18,Ag 8,12,16[S]1918;Mr 1, 20,22[Ap 11-My]1922
V 1905+
VHi N 7-8 1901
VU Je 28,Jl 19,Ag 22 1935
VWn Jl 6 1896+

Winchester TIMES. w S 17? 1865-Mr 29? 1905||
ICM Ja 29,F 5 1890
MWA S 13 1876
NNHi Ap 9 1873
NcD D 25 1867;My 17 1871;Ag 17 1898
OClWHi [Ag 20-D 17 1873;F 18-D 9 1874]Mr 10,Jl 28 1875;Ja 26,My 24,Je 6,Ag 2-9 1876; Ag 8,22-29,N 14 1877;Mr 20 1878;Ap 2,8,Jl 24-31 1879
V Je 13 1877
VLe F 5 1873
VWn S 26 1866;F 20,O 23 1867;Mr 4 1868[69-70]-[73-76;78-79]Ja 7 1891[1904-Mr 29 1905]

VIRGINIA centinel. *See* Winchester gazette

Winchester VIRGINIAN. w N? 1826-F 5? 1862||
Follows Winchester gazette
Ct [Ap 18 1828-Ag 1831;Mr 1833-S 6 1836]
DLC D 16 1840;Jl 2 1851
IU N 21 1861
MWA Jl 4 1828;D 1 1852
N O 9 1833
NN Ag 29 1849;Ap 16,Ag 7,O 16-23 1850;D 17 1851

VIRGINIA (*Continued*)

WINCHESTER—*Continued*

Winchester **VIRGINIAN.** w 1826-62||—*Continued*
NNHi Ja 29 1862
NcD My 23 1838;Ja 23,F 13,Mr 6-13,27-Ap 3 1839;Ap 15,Jl 29,N 4 1840;Ja 13 1841;Ap 26, O 18-D 20 1843[44-Je 17 1846]O 13 1847;Jl 5,S 13 1848;Ja 17,Je 6 1849;Mr 5,Jl 30,Ag 13,O 18,D 17-18 1851[Mr 24-S 1 1852;Ja 12-Mr]Ap 13,Ag 31 1853;Ag 15 1855;S 24 1856
OClWHi My 8 1861
V Ag 17,S 28 1859[Ja-N 1860]F 5 1862
VHi O 16 1902
VWn S 17 1830;S 10 1845;My 28 1851;Mr 31, S 21 1852;Mr 8-15,S 22,N 22 1854;Ja 24,F 21 1855[F-D 1856]N 17,21 1858;D 7 1859;Jl 18, Ag 29-S 5,26 1860;Ja 30,Mr 6 1861

WOODSTOCK

COUNTY and Valley. w 1876||
NcD Mr 9 1876

Woodstock **HERALD.** *See* Shenandoah herald

SENTINEL of the Valley. *See* Shenandoah herald

SHENANDOAH county record. w Ag? 1891-94||?
VHi Ja 6 1893

SHENANDOAH democrat. w Mr? 1870-76||
MWA Ag 10 1876
NNHi Ja 23 1873
NcD S 10 1874;Mr 16 1876

***SHENANDOAH herald.** w N 1817+
1817-21? as Woodstock herald; 1821?-My 1823 Woodstock herald and Shenandoah weekly advertiser; N 5 1825-Je 15 1848 Sentinel of the Valley; Je 22 1848-N 1868 Tenth legion
pub ir 1861-65
pub 1821-26;36-[39]-45[47-49;90-1925]+
DLC N 19 1823[N 1825-O 1826]N 3 1832
IU Ag 15-22,S 19-26,O 31 1844
MBAt D 1 1865
MWA Jl 31 1822;My 8 1829;Jl 12 1834;N 3 1865;Ja 19-26,Ap 5,26 1866;O 9 1873;Ja 27,Mr 2-9,Ap 6,Ag 17 1876;Ja 18,Ap 25,My 16 1877 [Ja 23-Jl 1878]F 26,Mr 12 1879
NNHi Ap 10 1873
NcD O 5 1838;Ja 15,Ap 30 1857;Je 30 1859;S 5,N 28 1867;Ja 23 1868;Mr 11,My 27,Jl 1,Ag 12,S 16 1869;Mr 7,Je 13,S 2,D 5 1872;O 2 1873;Mr 2-9 1876;N 14 1877;Ja 3,N 21 1883

V Mr 3 1827;Ag 20 1926
VHarT 1935+
VHi Ja 6 1893
VU Je 30 1859;Ag 20 1926;S 5-12 1930;Je 8 1931;Je 28 1935

TENTH legion. *See* Shenandoah herald

Woodstock **TIMES and Edinburg sentinel.** w Je 24 1919-S 8? 1932||
1919-Jl 29 1920 as Woodstock times. United with Strasburg news to form Northern Virginia daily (Strasburg)
VStN 1918-32

VIRGINIAN. w My 1880-85||?
United with Strasburg news to form Virginian and news later Northern Virginia daily (Strasburg)
MWA [F 3-S 22 1882]
NcD N 11,D 2 1881;O 31 1884;Ja 23,F 13,My 22 1885

VIRGINIAN and news. *See* Northern Virginia news (Strasburg)

WYTHEVILLE

Wytheville **DISPATCH.** w Ja? 1862-1909||
Suspended from Jl 25? 1863-Ag 26 1865
MH N 25-D 2 1864;Ja 20,F 10-17 1865
MWA Jl 20 1876
NNHi Ja 3 1873
NcD [Ag 26 1865-My 10 1867]N 30-O 7 1876; Ja 4,Mr 8,29 1877
TxU O 31 1878
VU Jl 25(extra)1863(photograph);S 9-16,30-N,D 9,23-30 1865;Mr 29 1867;Je 1 1876;Ag 30 1877

ENTERPRISE. *See* Southwest Virginia enterprise

Wythe **GAZETTE.** w N? 1821-27||?
DLC N 22 1823
NcD My 11 1827

INDUSTRIAL journal. *See* Wytheville journal 1890-95

Wythe **JOURNAL.** w Ja? 1840-42||?
DLC D 24 1842
NcD My 14-21,Jl 23,Ag 27,S 17-24,N 26 1842

Wytheville **JOURNAL.** w My? 1890-95||
1890-Ja? 1893 as Industrial journal
VHi F 16 1893

PATRIOT and herald. *See* under Marion

REPUBLICAN and Virginia Constitutionalist. w Ja 1 1844-55||?
DLC Mr 20-Ap 3,My 1-8,22-29,S 11 1844;Ja 1-22,F 5,15 1845;F 20 1847
NcD [Ja 15 1844-S 4 1847]
VU F 26 1844;Jl 10 1847

SOUTHERN banner. 1860?-65||?
VU Ap 10 1865(photograph)

SOUTHWEST VIRGINIA enterprise. w,sw Mr 2 1870+
1870?-72? as Enterprise
w Mr- 1870
pub 1918+
MWA Jl 13 1870;S 9 1876;O 25,N 15 1879
NNHi F 12 1873
NcD Je 15 1872;O 18-29,N 19 1873[Jl 12 1876-My 18 1878]
VU Je 8,Jl 6 1870;Mr 18 1871;Ja 17 1877;F 1 1888;D 1-5 1933;F 6,20,Mr 9,13,My 29,Je 12-19, Jl 13,24,Ag 10,S 11,21 1934;F 22,Jl 2-9,16-30 1935
VWy 1935+

Wytheville **TIMES.** w Jl? 1856-59||?
VU Ap 25 1857-58

VIRGINIA alliance news. w My? 1891-95||?
VU Ja 7 1892

WYTHE county news. sw,w O 2 1925+
pub 1925+
VU My 23,Jl 1935
VWy 1935+

YORKTOWN

CAVALIER. w Je 25 1862-Ap 11? 1864||
Je-N 1862 pub in Williamsburg
DLC Mr 17 1863
MBAt D 21 1863
MHi Jl 9 1862(photostat)
MWA Jl 9 1862;Mr 10,Ap 14 1863
NNHi Je 2 1863
PHi F-Ag 17 1863
PNoHi Je 25 1862
PPG My 6 1863
PPGr My 6 1863
PSF My 5 1863
VWW Je-Jl,Ag 20 1862;Mr 3,17,Ap 14,My 12, Je 23,Jl 14,Ag 31,S 21-28,O 12 1873;Ap 11 1864

WASHINGTON

ABERDEEN

Aberdeen weekly **BULLETIN.** w Jl 31 1889-1902||?
CU-B My 14 1890
WaAW [1901-02]

Daily **BULLETIN.** *See* Aberdeen daily world

GRAY'S HARBOR post. w Ja 1 1904+
WaA 1904+
WaPS O 21 1922-[24]-33

Aberdeen **HERALD.** w 1886-Je 29 1917||
CU-B O 2-9,23-30 1890
WaA O 16 1890-S 1916;Mr 23-Je 1917
WaPS [1915-16]17

Aberdeen **TRIBUNE daily.** d Ap 12-S 7 1910||?
WaAW [Ap 12-S 7 1910]

Aberdeen daily **WORLD.** d 1900+
1902-Je 1903 as Daily bulletin
pub 1901-06;Jl 1908+
MWA Mr 10 1926
OrU [1933]
Wa 1902-Je 1903;04-Ag,O 1914-Ag,O 1917-N 1919;20-Ap,Jl 1922-S,N 1923-S,N 1924-Ag,N 1928+
WaA D 27 1911-D 10 1916;17-S 1919;20+
WaPS [1916-18]O 1920+

ADDY

STEVENS county farm news. w 1919+
pub Ag 1919+
WaPS [1922-23;29]-33

ALBION

Albion **GRAPHIC.** *See* Albion journal

Albion **JOURNAL.** w 1915-17||?
1915? as Albion graphic
WaPS [1916]

ALMIRA

BIG BEND outlook. w 1900+
WaPS [1915-16]-[19-21]-[26]28-29

ANACORTES

Anacortes **AMERICAN.** w Ag 15 1890+
WaPS [1920]-[22-23]N 1929-33

Anacortes **CITIZEN.** *See* Anacortes daily mercury

Anacortes daily **MERCURY.** w,sw,d 1906+
1906-27? as Anacortes citizen; 1928?-31? Mercury-citizen
sw 1906-11? w 1912?-27?
WaPS F 3 1915[16]Mr 1 1917[21]-[23]-[26-27]N 12 1929-33

NORTHWEST enterprise. w Mr 25 1882-F 20 1887||
WaU [1882]-Mr 13 1886

Anacortes **PROGRESS.** w Ag 3 1889-Ja 22 1892||
WaU [1889-92]

ANATONE

Anatone **TIMES.** w?
OrWT 1903

ARLINGTON

To 1890 as Haller City

Arlington **EAGLE.** w
WaPS [1928-29;32]

STILLAGUAMISH times. *See* Arlington times

Arlington **TIMES.** w 1888+
1888-90? as Stillaguamish times; 1891?-Jl 10 1897 Haller City times
1888-89 pub in Stanwood
pub Ap 1895+
WaPS [1916-25]25[26-27]-[31]-33

ASOTIN

ASOTIN county sentinel. w 1883+
Follows Pataha city spirit (Pataha) 1883-84? as Asotin spirit
CU-B S 13 1889;Ja 10-31,O 10-31 1890
Wa Ag 1891-O 1901;02+
WaPS N 26 1915-Je 1916[17-18;22-25;27:29]-32

Asotin **SPIRIT.** *See* Asotin county sentinel

ATTALIA

NEWS-TRIBUNE. w 1909-Ag 1930||?
WaPS [1916-19]-[21-22]-[27-28]-Ag 1930

AUBURN

To 1892 as Slaughter

Auburn **ARGUS.** *See* Auburn globe-republican

Auburn **GLOBE-REPUBLICAN.** w Mr 24 1888+
1889-My 2 1893 as Slaughter sun; My 9 1893-O 11 1913 Auburn argus; O 18 1913-Ja 1916 Auburn globe
pub 1888+
CU-B S 19 1889;O 9-16 1890
WaAu S 6 1906+
WaPS [1916]S 26 1919-[23]-[26-27]+

Auburn **NEWS-SHOPPER.** w
WaPS [1933]

Auburn **REPUBLICAN.** w Ap 7 1911-Ja 1916||
United with Auburn globe to form Auburn globe-republican
WaAu complete
WaAuG complete

SENTINEL. w 1921-27||?
1921-24 as Washington co-operator
WaAu D 1922-N 1924
WaPS [1923-26]-Mr 3 1927

SLAUGHTER sun. *See* Auburn globe-republican

WASHINGTON co-operator. *See* Sentinel

BALLARD

Papers published in Ballard are listed under Seattle

BATTLEGROUND

BULLETIN. *See* Vancouver optimist (Vancouver)

BELLINGHAM

AMERICAN reveille. *See* Bellingham reveille

ARGUS. w 1912-18||?
WaPS [My 1916-My 26 1917]

BELLINGHAM BAY express. tw,d Ap 1890-94||?
tw 1890?
CU-B Ag 2,11 1892

BELLINGHAM BAY mail. *See* Puget Sound mail (La Conner)

BELLINGHAM BAY reveille. *See* Reveille

FAIRHAVEN herald. *See* Bellingham herald

FAIRHAVEN record. w
WaPS F 21 1929[30-31]

FARM bureau news (Whatcom Skagit). w 1917+
Follows Whatcom-Skagit-San Juan farm bureau news m (not in this list). 1917-Ja 15 1931 as Whatcom-Skagit-San Juan farm bureau news
WaPS [1926-28]-33

Bellingham **HERALD.** d 1890+
1890? as Fairhaven herald
Suspended 1894-Mr 13 1900
pub 1890+
MWA D 29 1890
Wa O 1903-Mr 1927
WaPS [1918-27]D 1929[30-33]+
—w ed *See* World-herald

JOURNAL progressive. w 1906-19||?
Wa Ap 1913-Je 1918
WaPS [1915]-[18]

WASHINGTON (*Continued*)

BELLINGHAM—*Continued*

NYA världen. w 1904-09||?
In Swedish
IRA 1904-09

REVEILLE. w,sw Je 15 1883-1922||?
1883-89? as Whatcom reveille; 1890?-1903? Benningham Bay reveille
sw 1903-04?
CU-B Ja 3-17 1890
KHi [Jl 27-D 1883]-Mr 12 1886
MnHi Ap 19 1889
Wa My-Ag 1914;F-Mr 1917;Ja-Mr,Jl 1918-Mr,D 1919-Mr,Jl-S,D 1920-F 1921;Jl-S,N 1922
WaPS Ja 10 1917;Ja 19,F 9,23 1919;Mr 19 1921

Bellingham REVEILLE. d 1890-Mr 13 1927||
1890-Je 1920 as American reveille. Merged with Bellingham herald
Wa Ja-O 1892;Ja-Je,S 1893-Jl 1899;F 1901-Mr 1907;F-Ap,S 1914-Mr,Jl 1915-Ja 1917;Ap-Je 1918;Ap-D 1919;Ap-Je,O 1920-Ag,N 1921-S 1922;23-27

Bellingham SENTINEL. w 1911-19||?
1911-17? as South Bellingham sentinel
NN Ap 28 1916
Wa Ag 1912-13

SOUTH BELLINGHAM sentinel. *See* Bellingham sentinel

WHATCOM reveille. *See* Reveille

WHATCOM-Skagit-San Juan farm bureau news. *See* Farm bureau news (Whatcom Skagit)

WHATCOM world. w
WaPS [1927-30]

WORLD-HERALD. w 1889-1911||?
1889-93? as Weekly world
CLM Ja 1891
—d ed *See* Bellingham herald

BINGEN

Bingen HERALD. w 1923-O 16 1925||?
WaPS Jl 1923-[25]

BLAINE

Blaine JOURNAL PRESS. w Ap 23 1885+
1885-Ja 24 1924 as Blaine journal
CU-B Mr,S 12,N 21,D 5 1889;Ja 16-30,Ag 14,O 9-30 1890
MWA S 17 1891
Wa 1910-16;D 1917-28;S 1929-Mr 1931
WaPS O 20 1922-[24]28-[31]

Blaine PRESS. w 1907-Ja 1924||?
United with Blaine journal to form Blaine journal press

BOSSBURG

Bossburg HERALD.
WaColE 1910

BREMERTON

Bremerton daily NEWS SEARCHLIGHT. w,sw,tw,d 1901+
1901-20 as Bremerton news
w 1901-14?;sw 1915?-18?;tw 1919?
pub 1901+
Wa Ap 1922+
WaB Je 1931+
WaPS D 31 1915-Je 1919[22]-32

Bremerton daily PRESS. d Ag 24 1928-O 25 1930||
WaB [1929-30]

Bremerton evening SEARCHLIGHT. w,sw 1903-20||
United with Bremerton news to form Bremerton daily news searchlight
w 1901-12?
Wa N 1903-20
WaPS [1916-20]

BREWSTER

Brewster HERALD. w 1901+
WaPS [1915-19;21-26]Mr 23 1927[29]-32

BRIDGEPORT

DOUGLAS county journal. *See under* East Wenatchee

Bridgeport REPUBLICAN. *See* Douglas county journal (East Wenatchee)

BUCKLEY

Buckley BANNER. w D 17 1889+
WaPS Mr 7 1924;Ap 9 1931[33]

BUCODA

Bucoda ENTERPRISE. w N 1 1889-94||
CU-B O 3-24 1890
Wa N 1 1889;Ag 1 1890;F 13 1891

Bucoda PRESS. w 1924-29||?
WaPS [Jl 11-D 1924]25

BURLINGTON

Burlington JOURNAL. w 1899+
1899-My 1911 as Burlington tribune
pub [1899-1906]+
Wa S 1908-Je 1918
WaBu F 1930+
WaPS [1922]-[24-26]-[31]32

Burlington TRIBUNE. *See* Burlington journal

CAMAS

Early years as La Camas

COLUMBIA pilot. w 1916-17||?
WaPS Je 8-22 1916;F 2,Mr 16 1917

Camas NEWS. w My 6 1887-Ja 22 1892||?
CU-B D 23 1887;Ja 6-13,F 17-Je,Ag 17 1888;Ja-My 10,Je 28-Jl 12,Ag 30-S 6,O 4-11,D 13-20 1889;Ja 3,17,F 7-14,Ag 15 1890;Ja 22 1892

Camas POST-Washoughal record. w 1908+
1908-Je 20 1930 as Camas post
pub 1908+
Wa Ag 1913-14
WaCa 1933+
WaPS N 26 1915-[16]-[18-21]-[23-26]-33

CAMP LEWIS. *See* FORT LEWIS

CARNATION

Carnation ENTERPRISE. w 1912-30||?
WaPS [1918-22]-[24]-[27]-Ap 1929

CASHMERE

CASHMERE VALLEY record. w 1907+
pub 1907+
WaPS [1927]N 1929-33

CASTLE ROCK

COWLITZ advocate. *See* Cowlitz county advocate

COWLITZ county advocate. w Jl 10 1886+
1886-1906? as Cowlitz advocate
pub 1912+
CU-B O 2-16 1890
MWA N 1916;Ja 18 1917
WaPS [1916-27]-33

INDEPENDENT. w 1910-20||?
WaPS D 27 1915[16-My 18 1917]O 24 1919

CATHLAMET

COLUMBIA RIVER breeze. w F 15 1889-1902||?
1889-1901? as Cathlamet gazette
CU-B Ag 15-22 1890;Ag 5,19-26,S 9-16 1892

COLUMBIA RIVER sun. w 1902+
OrHi Ag-D 1908
WaPS [1916]-[18-28]Je 25 1931

Cathlamet CRITERION. w Ap 3? 1914-15||?
MWA My 29 1914
OrHi Ag 28 1914-Ag 13 1915

Cathlamet GAZETTE. *See* Columbia River breeze

CENTRALIA

Centralia daily CHRONICLE. d Jl 1889+
1913-15? as Chronicle-examiner
pub 1923+
Wa Jl 1891-My 1892;N 1901-Ag 1918;O 1919+
WaPS Ap-D 1916;F 1917-Ap 1918[24]-[26-27]-33
—w ed 1912-17 *See* News-examiner

Centralia CHRONICLE. w Jl 4 1889-1912||?
CU-B Ag 21-S 4,18 1890;My 6 1892

Centralia daily HUB. sw,d 1913-20||?
1913-18? as Hub
sw 1913-18
WaPS O 26 1914-Ag 1918;S 12 1919-Ja 12 1920

Centralia daily NEWS. d Jl 15 1889-91||?
CU-B [S 11 1889-O 3 1890]D 17 1891
Wa Jl 29 1891

NEWS-EXAMINER. w Ap 1 1887-1917||?
1887-1900? as News. Merged with Centralia daily chronicle
CU-B Mr 29-Ap 5,Je 28-Jl 5,S 12 1889;S 4 1890;D 31 1891-Ja 7,21-28,Mr 24,Ag 19,S 2-23 1892;My 12-Je 2,16-30,Jl 14 1893
—d ed 1912-17 *See* Centralia daily chronicle

Centralia TRIBUNE. w 1922+
WaPS N 1922-[24-27]-30[32]33

CHARLESTON

AMERICAN. *See* Kitsap American

Charleston BREEZE. w 1925-29||?
WaPS [1925]

KITSAP American. w 1903-30||?
1903-16? as Navy Yard American; 1917-Ap 1917? American
Wa My 1917-Je 1923;24-F 1925
WaPS [1915-16]

NAVY YARD American. *See* Kitsap American

Charleston RECORD. w 1904-16||?
WaB S 19 1904[05-07]-D 2 1910

CHEHALIS

Chehalis BEE. sw,w Je 6 1884-N? 1898||
1884-Ap 6 1888 as Lewis county bee. United with Chehalis nugget to form Chehalis bee-nugget
sw Ag 1884
WaC 1884-Jl[S 1897-N 1898]
WaPS Ag 1891-Ap 1893;Mr 1894-S 1895
WaU [Ap-N 1886]N 25 1887-[88-89]O 10-D 5 1890[Ja-My 1891]Ap 28 1893-F 1894

Chehalis BEE-NUGGET. w Jl 14 1883+
1883-Ap 20 1888 as Nugget; Ap-Jl 1888 Lewis county nugget; Jl 1888-N? 1898 Chehalis nugget
pub 1883+
CU-B Ja 20 1888-[89]S-O 24 1890
DLC Jl 10 1885-Je 1888;F 14 1890-Je 1894
NbHi N 24 1899-Jl 13 1906;09-19
Wa Ag 1891-N 1892;94-N 1898;Ap 1901+
WaC Je 14-21,Jl 12 1884[Jl 1885-Je 1886]-Jl 1888[Jl 1889-Jl 1892]-[Jl 1893-Je 1902]+
WaPS [1914]S 24 1915-[18-19]+
WaU Mr 8 1884;Ag 1 1885[F-N 1886]F 18,Mr 4 1887;Je 5 1891;O 28 1898

LEWIS county advocate. w 1893+
pub 1895+
WaC Ag 21 1908;My 28-Je 4 1909;Mr 1911+
WaPS S 29 1922+

LEWIS county bee. *See* Chehalis bee

LEWIS county nugget. *See* Chehalis bee-nugget

Chehalis NUGGET. *See* Chehalis bee-nugget

CHELAN

CHELAN VALLEY mirror. w 1891+
WaPS S 1925-[26]Ap 5 1928[29]-33

LAKE CHELAN news. w 1911-15||?
United with Chelan leader to form Lake Chelan news leader, later Chelan leader

LAKE CHELAN news leader. *See* Chelan leader

Chelan LEADER. w 1891-1927||?
1891-92? as Chelan Falls leader; 1916? Lake Chelan news leader; 1917?-18? Chelan news-leader
1891-92? pub in Chelan Falls
InRE D 3-24 1891;Ja 7 1892
WaPS N 16 1922-[23-24]-Ag 1927

Chelan NEWS-LEADER. *See* Chelan leader

CHELAN FALLS

Chelan Falls LEADER. *See* Chelan leader (Chelan)

CHENEY

Cheney FREE press. w 1896+
1932+ part of paper called Medical Lake press
WaPS O 26 1922-[23-27]-33

NORTHWEST tribune. *See* Northwest tribune rural (Spokane)

Cheney SENTINEL. w Ap 1882-1901||?
CU-B S 6-13,27,D 6-20 1889;Ja 3-24,F 20,Je 6 1890

CHESAW

MYERS CREEK news. *See* Chesaw news

Chesaw NEWS. w 1902-19||?
1902-07? as Myers Creek news
WaPS Je 19,Jl 3 1914[16-17]

CHEWELAH

Chewelah INDEPENDENT. w 1903+
Wa D 1912-S 1924
WaColE 1907+
WaPS My 26 1916;Jl 7 1922[23;25-29]-33

Chewelah RECORDER. w 1909||?
WaColE Ap-S 1909

CHINOOK

Chinook OBSERVER. w 1900+
WaPS Ja 11 1927;N 1929-[30-31]-33

CLARKSTON

Clarkston HERALD. w 1901+
1901-06? as Clarkston republican; 1907-27? Clarkston republic
WaPS [1915-16;19;22-27;29]-33

Clarkston REPUBLIC. *See* Clarkston herald

Clarkston REPUBLICAN. *See* Clarkston herald

CLAYTON

Clayton MOOSE BULLETIN. w
WaPS [1929-30]-My 17 1932

Clayton NEWS-LETTER. w 1912-13||?
WaColE Jl 1912-Ag 1913

CLE ELUM

Cle Elum ECHO. *See* Miner-echo

MINER-ECHO. w 1901+
1901-Jl 1922 as Cle Elum echo
pub 1902+
Wa O 1905+
WaPS Ja 14 1916-[17-19]-[27-28]-33

WASHINGTON (*Continued*)

COLFAX

Colfax COMMONER. w O 2 1885-D 8 1932||
United with Colfax gazette to form Colfax gazette-commoner
CU-B N 22,D 13 1889-Ja 3,17-F 7,Je 6,Jl 11,Ag 8,22-29,S 12,26-O 10,24-31 1890
Wa Jl 1891-Je 1896;Ap 1897-F 1915;Jl 1931-32
WaCoG complete
WaPS [1891;93;1904;16]-[25]-32

Colfax GAZETTE-COMMONER. w S 29 1877+
1877-Ja 23 1893 as Palouse gazette; Ja 30 1893-D 9 1932 Colfax gazette
pub 1877+
CU-B O,N 10-24,D 15 1877;F 23 1878;Mr 8 1889;Mr 7 1890
Wa O 1907-Ja 1912;N 1913+
WaPS [1896;1914]S 24 1915-[17]-[25]-33
WaU [1877-F 1884]

NORTHWEST tribune. *See* Northwest tribune rural (Spokane)

PALOUSE gazette. *See* Colfax gazette-commoner

PALOUSER. sw 1915-S 14 1918||
WaPS S 29 1915-18

Weekly VIDETTE. w Ap 5 1883-My 1884||
Merged with Palouse gazette, later Colfax gazette-commoner
WaU [Ap-Je 1883]

WASHINGTON democrat. w Mr 23 1881-Ag 9 1882||
WaU [O 1881-82]

COLTON

Colton EAGLE. w My 1887-89||?
CU-B D 8 1887[88]-Ja 16,30,Ap 6 1889

Colton NEWS-LETTER. w 1891+
CU-B Ag 13,27 1892
WaPS [1915-16;18;21-23]-[29-30]D 31 1931-33

COLVILLE

Colville EXAMINER. w O 31 1907+
pub 1907+
WaPS [1916]-[20]-[22]-[25]-33

Colville INDEX. *See* Statesman-index

Colville PATRIOT. w,sw,tw 1914?-23||?
1914?-18? as Statesman-index (city ed)
United with Statesman-index to form Statesman-index-patriot, later Statesman-index
tw 1914?-15?;sw 1916?-18?

Colville REPUBLICAN. *See* Statesman-index

STATESMAN-INDEX. w 1889+
1889-O 1893 as Colville republican; O 1893-S 1896 Colville index; S 1896-Mr 1897 Stevens county statesman-index; Ap 1897-1923? Statesman-index; 1924-27? Statesman-index-patriot
Wa Ap 1927+
WaColE 1892-1900;07+
WaPS [1916-18;21;23;29]-33
—city ed *See* Colville patriot

STEVENS county miner. w O 5 1885-S 1893||
Merged with Colville republican to form Colville index, later Statesman-index
CU-B Ja 12-19,Mr 29-Ap 12,My 24-Je,Jl 12, 26,Ag 16-23,O 4,D 6,20 1888-F 15,Mr-Ap,My 10,31-Je 7,21 1889

STEVENS county standard. w 1892-94||?
WaColE D 31 1892

STEVENS county statesman-index. *See* Statesman-index

CONCONULLY

OKANOGAN record. w 1903-15||?
United with Tonasket times (Tonasket) to form Tonasket times and Okanogan record (Tonasket)
Wa O 1908-Ap 1915

CONCRETE

Concrete HERALD. w 1901+
KHi Je 7 1913
WaPS [1915;17-19]-[21-23]-[26]-33

CONNELL

Connell GLOBE. w 1921-31||?
WaPS [1923-24;28;30]

COULEE

Early years as Coulee City

Coulee City DISPATCH. w 1905+
WaPS [1916-18;23-25]N 15 1929-Ja 17 1930;Mr 24 1933

Coulee NEWS. w Je 20 1890-93||?
CU-B O 3,17 1890

COULEE CITY. *See* COULEE

COUPEVILLE

ISLAND county times. w 1891+
WaPS [1915-18;21-22]My 29 1925;N 12 1929-33

CRESTON

Creston NEWS. w 1901+
Suspended 1925-27?
WaPS S 24 1915-[18-20;24-25;29]

CUSICK

CALISPELL VALLEY times.
WaColE F-Mr 1907

DAVENPORT

LINCOLN county times. *See* Davenport times-tribune

Davenport TIMES-TRIBUNE. w Je 1884+
1884-86 as Harrington times (Harrington) 1886-Ag 1918 Lincoln county times
pub Je 1893+
Wa D 1909-O 1923
WaPS S 1918-[19]-[21]-[24-27]-33

Davenport TRIBUNE. w S 1889-Ag 29 1918||
United with Lincoln county times to form Davenport times-tribune
WaDT 1889-1918
WaPS [1915-17]-18

DAYTON

CHRONICLE-DISPATCH. sw,w Ap 20 1878+
1878-Ag 13 1926 as Columbia chronicle
sw 1909?-25?
CU-B Mr 2-16 1889;Ja 11,F 1-8,O 18-25 1890
WaPS D 28 1918-[19]D 21 1921;Ag 20 1926-[27]+
WaU [Ap 27 1878-F 1884]

COLUMBIA chronicle. *See* Chronicle-dispatch

COLUMBIA county dispatch. sw 1902-Ag 17 1926||
United with Columbia chronicle to form Chronicle-dispatch
WaPS Ja-Ag 20 1917;Je 18 1918;F 18 1919[20] D 13-20 1921[22-23]-26

DEMOCRATIC state journal. w Ag 4 1882-Ag 1884||
CU-B Ja 12-F 16 1883
WaS [1882-84]

INLANDER. w 1884-93||?
CU-B O 24 1885;Ja-O 15 1887;Je 29,Jl 13-27 1889

Dayton weekly NEWS. w S 1874-Ag 12 1882||
1874-Ap 12 1878 as Dayton news
CU-B D 21 1877-Ja 4,F 1,Mr 1,29,Ap 13-Ag 3,S 21 1878-Ja 10,Mr-My 22 1880
WaU [Ja 15-Ap 22,D 16 1876-Ap 1 1882]

DEEP CREEK FALLS

GATE CITY herald. w Ag 21 1890-91||?
CU-B O 23-30 1890

DEER PARK

Deer Park UNION. w 1907+
WaPS [1915-19]-Ja 22 1920;N 9 1922-[24]-[27]-33

DEMING

Deming PROSPECTOR. w 1897+
WaPS O 22 1922-[25]-[27]-33

DOUGLAS

Douglas RECORD. w 1910-13||?
WaPS F 10 1911-F 9 1912;Mr 14-Je 20 1913

DUNGENESS

Dungeness BEACON. w Je 24 1892-
KHi 1892-Je 16 1893

EAST STANWOOD

East Stanwood BULLETIN. w 1914-16||?
Wa S 1914-15

East Stanwood PRESS. w 1921-N 29 1922||
WaPS [1922]

EAST WENATCHEE

DOUGLAS county journal. w 1905+
1905-S 8 1928 as Bridgeport republican
1905-O 1934 pub in Bridgeport
pub 1928+
WaPS [1929-30]-33

EATONVILLE

Eatonville DISPATCH. w 1893+
F 26-D 1926 as Pierce county journal
WaPS [1916-18]N 17 1922-[23]-[25]-[27]-[29-31]-33

PIERCE county journal. *See* Eatonville dispatch

EDMONDS

Edmonds REVIEW. w 1904-10||?
United with Edmonds tribune to form Edmonds tribune-review
OrHi S 1908-Ag 18 1910
Wa 1905-F 1910

Edmonds TRIBUNE-REVIEW. w 1904+
1904-10? as Edmonds tribune
Wa F 1910
WaPS N 21-D 19 1924[29]-33

ELK

Elk SENTINEL. w 1926+
WaPS D 1929-33

ELLENSBURG

Ellensburg CAPITAL. w O 15 1887+
CU-B N 28-D 5 1889;Ag 14 1890
Wa Mr 1896-F 1898;1903-N 1916;17-18
WaEl 1888-O 1914;23+
WaPS D 16 1915[16-22]-[24]-[26-27]-33

Ellensburg DAWN. *See* Inter-mountain register

Ellensburg DEMOCRAT. *See* Inter-mountain register

INTER-MOUNTAIN register. w 1894-1917||?
1894-1913 as Ellensburg dawn; 1914-15 Ellensburg democrat
Wa 1902-03;Je-D 1904;Mr 1905-My 1915
WaU [Ja-Ag 1902]-13

KITTITAS standard. w Je 6 1883-85||?
WaU [Je 23 1883-F 1884]

Ellensburg LOCALIZER. w Jl 14 1884-1918||
WaElR [Jl 1909-13]-18

Ellensburg daily LOCALIZER. *See* Ellensburg evening record

Ellensburg evening RECORD. d 1905+
1905-Je 1909 as Ellensburg daily localizer
pub [1909-13]+
WaPS [1915-16]-[18-23]32-33
WaU Jl 21 1905
—w ed *See* Ellensburg localizer

Ellensburg REGISTER. d 1889-90||?
CU-B D 20 1889-Ja 2 1890

Ellensburg daily TRIBUNE. d Mr 20 1911-
WaU Mr-Ap 10 1911

ELMA

CHEHALIS county chronicle. *See* Elma chronicle

Elma CHRONICLE. w My 17 1889+
1889-91? as Chehalis county chronicle
OrHi S 1901-Mr 15 1925
Wa F 1927+
WaPS [1915-16;18;22-23]-[25-26]-[31]-33

ENDICOTT

Endicott INDEX. w 1904+
WaPS S 24-D 1915;N 10 1922-Ap 8 1927

ENTIAT

Entiat TIMES. w 1913+
WaPS N 9 1922;Mr 6 1924-S 29 1927;D 6 1928[29]N 13 1930

ENUMCLAW

Enumclaw COURIER-HERALD w 1900+
1900-33 as Enumclaw courier
pub 1900+
WaEn 1900+
WaPS [1929]+

Enumclaw HERALD. w Je 1908-33||
United with Enumclaw courier to form Enumclaw courier-herald
WaEn complete
WaEnC complete
WaPS D 1922[23-28]-33

EPHRATA

GRANT county journal. w F 1 1896+
pub 1893+
WaPS D 17 1915-[19-21]D 1922-[25;29]-33

EVERETT

To 1892 as Port Gardner

Everett HERALD. w 1890-1919||?
WaE D 10 1891-Ja 14 1897

Everett daily HERALD. d 1897+
Wa Je 1901-O 1916;Ap 1917+
WaE Jl 14 1905-[08]-[10]-[17]+
WaPS [1916-S 1924]+

LABOR journal. w 1912+
NNRa [1926]+
WaE [1920]-23;25+

Everett NEWS. w S 11 1891-Ag 29 1896||
S-N 1891 as Port Gardner news
WaE complete

Everett NEWS. d 1901+
1901-29 as Everett morning tribune
WaE Ag 1905-Jl,D 1908-[22]-[24]-[26]+
WaPS [1915-18;D 1931]Ja 2-3 S 28 1932

PORT GARDNER news. *See* Everett news

SNOHOMISH county democrat. w 1891-Ja 16 1897||
WaE O 26 1895-97

Everett TIMES. w 1891-1903||?
WaE D 17 1891-D 9 1896

Everett morning TRIBUNE. *See* Everett news

EVERSON

EVERSON VALLEY home. w 1908-Mr 13 1931||
Merged with Everson-Nooksack news
WaPS [N-D 1929]-31

EVERSON-NOOKSACK news. w 1907+
WaPS Mr 20 1931-33

FAIRFIELD

Fairfield STANDARD. w 1896+
WaPS [1915-18]-[20-21]-[25-26]N 21 1929-33

WASHINGTON (*Continued*)

FAIRHAVEN

Papers published in Fairhaven are listed under Bellingham

FALL CITY

Fall City SPIRIT. w
WaPS [1920]O 28 1921[22-23]

FARMINGTON

Farmington INDEPENDENT. *See* Farmington times

Farmington POST. w 1929+
WaPS Ja 10 1930+

Farmington TIMES. w 1908-23||?
1908-20 as Farmington independent
WaPS Jl 10 1914[15-21]F 24 1922

FERNDALE

Ferndale RECORD. w 1903+
pub 1904+
WaPS [1915]-[17;19]N 24 1922-33

FORT LEWIS

To 1926 as Camp Lewis

Bugle. w Je 7 1918-19||?
WaU [1918-Je 13 1919]

Ivy leaves. w 1921||?
WaU Jl 1 1921-Ag 26 1921

FRANKFORT

Frankfort CHRONICLE. w My 10 1892-
OrHi My-[Ag]1892

FREMONT

Papers published in Fremont are listed under Seattle

FRIDAY HARBOR

Friday Harbor JOURNAL. w 1906+
Wa S 1906-D 1926,Ag 1927+
WaPS Je 1916-[18]-[23-25]-33

GARFIELD

Garfield ENTERPRISE. w Jl 1887+
CU-B Ja 31 1890
WaPS S 24 1915-O 5,D 6 1918[24-25]-33

GEORGETOWN

Papers published in Georgetown are listed under Seattle

GIG HARBOR

BAY ISLAND news. *See* Peninsula gateway

PENINSULA gateway. w 1917+
1917-Ag 17 1923 as Bay Island news
WaPS [1918-20]-[22-33]

GOLDENDALE

Goldendale COURIER. w Mr 1 1890-93||?
CU-B Ag 15-22 1890

Goldendale GAZETTE. w 1881-My 1884||?
United with Klickitat sentinel to form Goldendale sentinel
CU-B Mr 16 1882

INDEPENDENT. w 1909-15||?
Wa My 1912-O 1914

KLICKITAT county agriculturist. w 1890+
pub 1900+
Wa D 1908-22;Je 1923+

KLICKITAT sentinel. *See* Goldendale sentinel

Goldendale SENTINEL. w 1879+
1879-My 1884? as Klickitat sentinel
pub [1879-1904]10+
CU-B Mr-Ap 21 1883;Jl 11-18 1889
Wa Je 1910-22;24+
WaPS [1916]-[18]-[20-21]-[25-26]+
WaU D 10 1881[Mr 1883-Mr 1884;N 28 1889-Jl 1 1893]

GRANDVIEW

Grandview HERALD. w 1909+
WaPS O 5 1917[21-27]-33

GRANITE FALLS

Granite Falls POST. w 1902-22||?
WaPS D 20 1918-[19]

Granite Falls RECORD. *See* Snohomish county forum

SNOHOMISH county forum. w 1922+
1922-Ja 1931? as Granite Falls record
WaPS [1922-24]-[26]-Ja 15,F 22 1931+

GREEN LAKE

Papers published in Green Lake are listed under Seattle

HALLER CITY. *See* ARLINGTON

HANFORD

Hanford COLUMBIAN. w 1908-F 11 1916||?
WaPS D 1915-16

HARRINGTON

Harrington CITIZEN. w 1898+
WaPS [1916-18]-[20]-[23]Mr 28 1924[29]+

Harrington TIMES. *See* Davenport times-tribune (Davenport)

HARTLINE

Hartline STANDARD. w 1918+
WaPS N 14 1929+

HILLYARD

Papers published in Hillyard are listed under Spokane

HOQUIAM

Hoquiam AMERICAN. w 1921-32||?
1921-N,D 21 1922 as American
WaPS S 29 1922-[23-24]-Mr 1925;Ja-My 1929

GRAYS HARBOR Washingtonian. w,d Je 5 1889+
1889-Mr 1903 as Hoquiam Washingtonian (w) Mr 1903-Ap 10 1906 Daily Washingtonian
Wa Ag 1891-Ag 1899;Ap 1901-Je,Ag 1917-Mr,Jl 1918+
WaAW S 8 1916+
WaH [1893]-[98]-[1905-07]+
WaPS [1917-18;22-23]-[26-27]+

OLYMPIC oil record. w 1902-20||?
1902-19? as Hoquiam record
WaPS [1915-17]

Hoquiam RECORD. *See* Olympic oil record

SOUTHWEST Washington labor press. w 1912-27||?
WaPS [1922]-[27]

Hoquiam WASHINGTONIAN. *See* Grays Harbor Washingtonian

HUNTERS

Hunters MESSENGER. w 1919+
WaPS N 23 1922[23-28]-33

ILWACO

NORTH Beach tribune. *See* Tribune

PACIFIC journal. w 1883-1906||?
1883-91? pub in Sealand
CU-B Ag 8-23,S 26,O 3-10,24 1890[92]Ja 6,26,F 16 1893

TRIBUNE. w 1911+
1911-Je 1932 as North Beach tribune
OrHi Je 26 1925+
WaPS Jl 3 1925-[33]

ISSAQUAH

Issaquah PRESS. w 1916+
WaPS [1922-27]

KALAMA

Kalama BEACON. w My 1870-75||?
CU-B Ap 26-My 17,31-Je 14,Jl-Ag 4,N 24 1873;Ja 20,F 10 1874
NNHi F 8 1873

Kalama BULLETIN. w Mr 15 1889+
1889-91? as Cowlitz bulletin
CU-B D 6 1889;F 28 1890
Wa D 1912-Je 1919;Ap 1925+
WaPS [1922-23]-[30-31]-N 1932

COWLITZ bulletin. *See* Kalama bulletin

COWLITZ county news. w 1906-25||?
Wa 1910-19
WaPS [1915-16]S 28 1917[22-25]

KELSO

Kelso weekly COURIER. *See* Kelso journal

COWLITZ VALLEY journal. *See* Kelso journal

Kelso JOURNAL. w.sw S 28 1888-1912||?
1888-93? as Kelso weekly courier; 1894-1906? Cowlitz Valley journal
sw 1908-09?
CU-B N 22,D 6,27 1889[90]Ja 22-F 12 1892;Mr 10 1893

KELSONIAN. *See* Daily tribune and Kelsonian

Daily TRIBUNE. d 1923-N 1924||
United with Kelsonian to form Kelsonian-tribune, later Daily tribune and Kelsonian
Wa D 1923-24

Daily TRIBUNE and Kelsonian. sw,w,d 1906+
1906-N 26 1924 as Kelsonian, N 28 1924-My 1929 Kelsonian-tribune
sw 1906-N 26 1924. w N 28 1924-1925?
OrHi F 13 1925-Ag 1926
Wa N 1924-[27]+
WaL Ap 26 1926+
WaPS D 25 1915-18[22-23]-[27]-Ap,Jl 1929+

KENNEWICK

Kennewick COURIER-REPORTER. w Mr 27 1902+
1902-14 as Kennewick courier
pub 1902+
OrHi 1902-S 1903
WaPS [1915-16]-[18-19]-[21]-[24-27]-33

Kennewick REPORTER. w 1908-14||
United with Kennewick courier to form Kennewick courier-reporter
WaKeC complete

KENT

Kent ADVERTISER JOURNAL. w Ag 14 1890+
1890-1914? as White River journal. 1915-F 14 1918 as Kent journal
WaK Ap 8 1920+
WaPS [1915-22]-[24-26]+

Kent JOURNAL. *See* Kent advertiser journal

KENT VALLEY news. w Jl 1924+
pub 1924+
WaK D 28 1928+
WaPS [1925-30]-33

WHITE RIVER journal. *See* Kent advertiser journal

KETTLE FALLS

Kettle Falls PIONEER. w 1890-95||?
CU-B S 14 1893

Kettle Falls SCIMITAR. w 1908-12||?
Merged with Colville examiner (Colville)
WaColE 1908-12

Kettle Falls VALLEY tribune. w 1905-09||?
WaColE 1907-08

KIRKLAND

EAST SIDE journal. w 1918+
WaPS [1922-25]-[27]-32;Mr 23 1933

LA CAMAS. *See* CAMAS

LaCONNER

PUGET SOUND mail. w Jl 5 1873+
1873-S 6 1879 as Bellingham Bay mail (Bellingham)
CU-B Jl 19 1873-80;Mr 14-Ap 4,Jl 4-18,O 3 N 28-D 12 1889;Ag,O 2,16 1890
Wa My 19 1877;Jl 13 1878
WaS [D 1874-F 1884]

LaCROSSE

LaCrosse CLIPPER. w 1905+
WaPS D 24 1915-Ap 28 1916;Je 3 1921;N 24 1922-Mr 9 1923[24-26]-33

Lacrosse HERALD. w
OrHi Jl 1907-My 1910

LATAH

Latah CITIZEN. w 1927+
WaPS [Ja-F 1930]

Latah TIMES. w Mr 1889-92||?
CU-B Jl 8-15,29 1892

LEAVENWORTH

Leavenworth ECHO. w 1904+
Wa 1904-D 1921;Ap 1922+
WaPS [1915-16]-[18-19]-[21-22]-[26-27]-33

LIND

Lind LEADER. w 1902+
WaPS [1916]Je 28 1919;D 14 1922-[24]-[26]-33

LITTLE FALLS

Little Falls GAZETTE. w Mr 18 1892-
CU-B Ap 1-8,My 6 1892

LONGVIEW

Longview ENTERPRISE. w Mr 7 1930+
WaL Mr 21 1930+

Longview HERALD. w D 21 1928-D 27 1929||
WaPS complete
WaU complete

Longview daily NEWS. d Ja 26 1923+
pub 1923+
OrHi O 1925+
WaL 1926+
WaLC 1925-30
WaPS [1924-29]Jl 1930+

LOON LAKE

Loon Lake TIMES. w 1910-13||?
WaColE My 1911-N 1913

WASHINGTON (*Continued*)

LYNDEN

Lynden TRIBUNE. w 1905+
Wa My 1912+
WaPS [1915-16]-[19-22]-33

MABTON

Mabton CHRONICLE. w 1904+
WaPS [1915-18]D 1922-[24-F 1929]

MALDEN

Malden REGISTER. w 1909-Je 1 1923||
WaPS N 17 1922-23

MAPLE FALLS

Maple Falls LEADER. w 1902+
Wa Jl-D 1910;Jl-D 1911;Jl 1912-N 1919;20-Ap 1921
WaPS [1915-18;20;22-23]-[25-26]-33

MAPLE VALLEY

Maple Valley MESSENGER. w 1921-25||?
WaPS [1923-24]

MARCUS

COLUMBIA courier. w 1925-28||?
WaPS Jl 2 1925[28]

Marcus MESSENGER. w 1910-20||?
WaColE Je 1910-My 1912

MARYSVILLE

Marysville GLOBE. w 1892+
Wa F-D 1907 F-O 1908
WaPS [1920-30]31

MEDICAL LAKE

Medical Lake ENTERPRISE. w 1922-Ja 8 1932||
Followed by Medical Lake press (part of Cheney free press)
WaPS N 23 1922-[24]-[26-27]-32

Medical Lake LEDGER. w Je? 1888-98||?
CU-B Ja 3,N 22 1889;Ja 10-17 1890

Medical Lake PRESS. *See* Cheney free press (Cheney)

METALINE FALLS

Metaline Falls NEWS. w 1929+
WaPS [1929-30]-33

MEYERS FALLS

COLUMBIA gateway. w 1908||?
WaColE Mr-N 1908

MILLWOOD

WEST VALLEY news. w
WaPS D 16 1927[28-29]D 12 1930

MOLSON

Molson LEADER. w 1908-24||
WaPS [1915-17]S 17 1919-Ja 2 1924

MONROE

Monroe MONITOR. w Ja 12 1899+
1910-16? as Monitor-transcript
WaM [Ja 19 1910+]
WaPS [1922-23]-[25-27]-33

Monroe TRANSCRIPT. w 1899-1909||?
1899-1907? as Washington transcript. United with Monroe monitor to form Monitor-transcript, later Monroe monitor

WASHINGTON transcript. *See* Monroe transcript

MONTESANO

CHEHALIS county vidette. *See* Montesano vidette

CHEHALIS VALLEY vidette. *See* Montesano vidette

Montesano VIDETTE. w F 1 1883+
1883-89 as Chehalis Valley vidette; 1890-Mr 1902 Weekly vidette; Ap 1902-D 24 1915 Chehalis county vidette
pub 1883+
CU-B Mr 15-29,Ap 12,Jl 5-19,Ag 9 1889;Ja-F 21,Mr 14-Ap 4 1890
OrHi 1905+
Wa Jl 1891-O 1898;99-Jl,D 1904+
WaPS [1915-16]-[18-22]-[24-27]-33
WaS 1883-F 1884

MORTON

Morton MIRROR. w 1912+
WaPS [1917-19]-My 27 1921[23-24]N 22 1929-33

MOUNT VERNON

Mount Vernon ARGUS. w 1891+
1891-97 as Mount Vernon post
pub 1903+
Wa Jl 1898-Jl 1900;Ja-Jl 1901;02+
WaPS [1916-20]-[23-26;28;32-33]

Mount Vernon HERALD. w Mr 4 1884-1922||?
1884-96? as Skagit news; 1897-1908? Skagit news-herald
CU-B Je 24 1889

Mount Vernon HERALD. d 1921+
WaPS [1922-24]-33

Mount Vernon POST. *See* Mount Vernon argus

SKAGIT news. *See* Mount Vernon herald w

NACHES

Naches REVIEW. w
WaPS [1917]

NEPPEL

Neppel RECORD. w 1912-18||?
WaPS [1914-17]

NEW WHATCOM

Papers published in New Whatcom are listed under Bellingham

NEWPORT

Newport MINER. w 1897+
WaPS N 16 1922-Mr 24 1932[33]

NOOKSACK

EVERSON-NOOKSACK news. *See under* Everson

NOOKSACK VALLEY farm review. w 1922+
1922-Ja 1931 as Nooksack sentinel
WaPS N 23 1922-[32]

Nooksack REPORTER. w 1906-20||?
WaPS [1915]

Nooksack SENTINEL. *See* Nooksack Valley farm review

NORTH BEND

North Bend ECLIPSE. w
WaPS D 6 1921[1922-24]

NORTH BONNEVILLE

BONNEVILLE index. w O 1933-Ag 1934||
OrHi complete

NORTH YAKIMA. *See* YAKIMA

NORTHPORT

Northport NEWS. w Jl 7 1892+
CU-B Ag 25,S 15-22,O 6,N 3 1892
WaColE 1907+
WaPS [1919]

Northport REPUBLICAN. w 1898-1910||?
WaColE 1907-10

OAK HARBOR

ISLAND county farm bureau news. w 1911+
1911-1916 as Island county news; 1916-Ja 16 1920 as Oak Harbor news
WaPS [1915-24]-[26-27]-33

ISLAND county news. *See* Island county farm bureau news

Oak Harbor NEWS. *See* Island county farm bureau news

OAKESDALE

Oakesdale BREEZE. *See* Oakesdale sun

Oakesdale SUN. w S 27 1888-98||?
1888-Mr 1889 as Oakesdale breeze
CU-B Ja 3,O 3 1890

Oakesdale TIDINGS. *See* Oakesdale tribune

Oakesdale TRIBUNE. w 1901+
1901-09? as Oakesdale tidings
WaPS [1915-16]-[18]-[21-23]-[33]

OAKVILLE

Oakville CRUISER. w 1900+
WaPS D 3 1915-[17-22]-33

OCOSTA

Ocosta PIONEER. w F 6 1891-95||?
MnHi F 6,Ap 3,17 1891;Ja 29 1892

ODESSA

Odessa RECORD. w 1901+
WaPS [1915-18;23-27]

OKANOGAN

Okanogan INDEPENDENT. w,sw 1905+
w 1905-15?
WaPS [1915-16]-[19-21]-[29-31]-33

OLYMPIA

ANTI-IMPERIALIST. 1900||?
Wa O-N 1900

Weekly CAPITAL. *See* Olympia state capital

Olympia CHRONICLE. w 1899-1929||?
Wa Je 1901-21;23-Mr 1927
WaPS [1915]-[18;20-23]-Mr 5 1927

COLUMBIAN. *See* Pioneer and democrat

COMMERCIAL age. w Ag 10 1868-Je 25 1870||
1868-Ag 16 1869 as Territorial republican
Suspended from Ag 16-O 2 1869
CaB complete
CU-B 1868-Mr 1,15,29,Ap 12-Je 14,Jl 12-Ag 9,O 9-N,D 11 1869-Mr,Ap 9-16,30-Je 1870
OrHi [1868]-Ag 9 1869
Wa Je 21 1869
WaU complete

Olympia daily COURIER. d Ja 1 1872-O 6 1877||
1872-74 as Puget Sound daily courier. Suspended from 1874-Mr 2 1877, and replaced by Daily Olympian
CU-B Ja 18-19,Ap 25 1872-[73]-D 13 1874[Mr-Jl 16]Ag 13 1877
DLC [1873]74-77
OrHi N 4 1872
Wa My 16,D 28 1872-[Ap 28-My 1873]
WaS 1872[73-77]
WaU 1872-[74-S 7 1877]
—w ed *See* Puget Sound weekly courier

ECHO. w S 24 1868-Mr 22 1877||
Followed by Tacoma herald 1877-80 (Tacoma). Title varies: Weekly echo; Temperance echo
CU-B O 8 1868-S,O 28 1869 Ag 18,O 13,27,N 24-D 1 1870;Ap 1871-75
OClWHi Ap 20 1871
OrHi 1868-S 22 1870
Wa 1868-N 1873
WaS [O 1868-77]
WaU O 1868-[O 1870-76]

Morning ECHO. d S 14 1875-Mr 1877||?
MWA F 6 1877
Wa Ja 25 1876
WaS [1875-Ja 19 1877]
WaU [1875-Ja 1877]

Olympia INDEPENDENT. w 1911-15||?
Wa 1911-F 1915

NEW transcript. *See* Olympia state capital

Olympia NEWS. w 1923+
pub 1926+
Wa S 1924+
WaPS Ja 4 1929;Je 26 1930[31]

Daily OLYMPIAN. d F 28 1876-F 7 1877||
Replaces Puget Sound daily courier, later Olympia daily courier
DLC [Mr-Jl]-N 24,D 5 1876
Wa [Ap-N 1876]
WaS [1876]
—w eds *See* Puget Sound weekly courier; Washington standard

Weekly OLYMPIAN. w 1890-1907||?
My 1893?-Je 1894? as Olympian tribune
Wa supp O 1890
WaPS [1894-95]

Daily OLYMPIAN. [morning ed] d 1891+
1891-Ap 1893? as Morning Olympian; My? 1893-Je 1894? Morning Olympian tribune
CU-B Jl 27 1893
Wa Ag 1891-92;F 1893-Mr,Ag 1900-S 1916;17+
WaPS Ap 20 1912-[15-23]-My,S 1927-33
WaU [Je-S 1891;Mr-O 1892;Je-Jl 1893]

Daily OLYMPIAN. [evening ed] d Ja 1 1903+
Ja 1-10 1903 as Washington recorder; Ja 11 1903-Ja 1924 Olympia recorder; F 1924-N 1927 Olympia evening recorder
Wa 1903-N 1905;06-My,S 1908+
WaPS [1918]F 4 1921[23]-My 1927

OVERLAND press. *See* Weekly Pacific tribune (Seattle)

Weekly PACIFIC tribune. *See under* Seattle

Olympia daily PACIFIC tribune. *See* Tribune (Seattle)

PARTISAN. *See* Republican partisan

PIONEER and democrat. w S 11 1852-My 31 1861||
1852-N 26 1853 as Columbian; D 1853-Ja 1854 Washington pioneer. Followed by Overland press, later Weekly Pacific tribune (Seattle)
CU-B Mr 9 1860
DLC Je 15 1855-F,Mr 8 1861
MWA F 5,My 21,D 31 1853;F 11-18,Mr 4,18,S 23 1854
NNHi D 1852-N 19 1853
OrHi 1852-[56-57]-[59-61]
P-M F 11,My 13 1854
WHi Ap 2 1854;N 27 1857-Ja 22 1858
Wa D 11 1852;Mr 26,My 7,21,Je 11,Jl,D 1853-Ja[Mr,My]Je 24,S 16,O 1854-59[Je-O 1860]Ja 4,25,Mr 22-29 1861
WaU 1852-Ja 1854

PUGET SOUND weekly courier. w Ja 6 1872-85||?
Followed by Partisan, later Republican partisan
CU-B [1872]-[75-Mr 9,My 18-D 1877]-80
CaB O 6,N 3-10,D 8-15,29 1862
CtY My 1873-Ja 1877;78-N 1880;81-82;Ja-F 1884
DLC 1872-Mr 9 1877;78-82;Ja-Je,S 9-O 22,N 4-11,25-D 16 1884;Ja 6-13 1885
MWA [1872-74]Ja 29 1876
OrHi 1872-75
Wa Je 7[Ag]D 3 1873[My-D 1874;F 27 1875-F 9 1877;Ja 11 1878-Ja 8 1884]
WaS [1872-Mr 4 1884]
WaU [Ja 13-D 14 1872]Ag 16 1873-Ap 22 1884
—d ed 1876-77 *See* Daily Olympian

PUGET SOUND daily courier. *See* Olympia daily courier

Olympia RECORDER. w 1901-Ap 6 1922||?
Mr 29 1917-Ap 7 1921 as Olympia weekly recorder
OrHi S 1913-Ap 6 1922

WASHINGTON (*Continued*)

OLYMPIA—*Continued*

Olympia daily RECORDER. *See* Daily Olympian [evening ed]

REPUBLICAN partisan. w 1885-89||?
Follows Puget Sound weekly courier. 1885-87? as Partisan. Followed by Olympia tribune

Olympia REVIEW. *See* Olympia state capital

Olympia daily STANDARD. d 1905-22||?
suspended 1907-20?
Wa 1905-N 1906;21-Mr 1922
—w ed *See* Washington standard

Olympia STATE capital. w Ag 1886-1908||?
1886-O 1888 as New transcript; N 1888-90? Olympia review; 1891-1904? Weekly capital
CU-B Mr 8,Ap 26-My 3,24-31,Jl 5-12,29 1889; Ja 17,F 14 1890[92-93]
OrHi 1907-Ap 3 1908
Wa Jl 1897-1901
WaPS [1890]
WaU [My-Ag 1891;Je-O 1892;My-Ag 1893]

STATE capital record. w 1909-18||?
Wa O 1909-F 1918

TEMPERANCE echo. *See* Echo

TERRITORIAL republican. *See* Commercial age

Olympia TRANSCRIPT. w N 30 1867-85||
C D 12 1868
CU-B Mr 7,Jl 25-Ag 1,15 1868-Mr 18,S 16,30,O 14 1871-S 21,O-N 2,D 14 1878-D 18 1880
MWA Jl 3 1875
NN D 23 1876;Je 8 1878
OClWHi D 3,17 1870;Ja 7,F 4,Ag 26 1871
OrHi 1867-82
Wa [N 21 1868-74]
WaU 1867-[D 1875-78]-[80-Ap 19 1884]

Olympia TRIBUNE. d 1890-Ap 1893||?
Follows Republican partisan. United with Morning Olympian to form Morning Olympian tribune, later Daily Olympian [morning ed]
CU-B F 29 1892
WaU [Ag 4 1890-Ja,Jl-S 1891;Mr-Jl 1892]

Olympia weekly TRIBUNE. w 1890-Ap 1893||?
Follows Republican partisan. United with Weekly Olympian to form Olympian tribune, later Weekly Olympian
CU-B F 20 1892
WaPS [1890-91]Jl 27 1892

UNION guard. tw My 21- 1866||?
Wa My 21-31 1866
WaU My 25,28 1866

WASHINGTON democrat. w O 17 1864-Jl 15 1865||
CU-B Ap 15 1865
CaB D 24 1864
NN O 24 1864
OrHi [1864-65]
WaU complete

WASHINGTON pioneer. *See* Pioneer and democrat

WASHINGTON recorder. *See* Daily Olympian [morning ed]

WASHINGTON Saturday review. w 1909-10||?
Wa Jl 1909-Je 1910

WASHINGTON standard. w,sw N 17 1860-S 23 1921||
Suspended Ja-Ap 1911
sw 1921
CU-B D 26 1863[64-79]Jl 11 1884[86-87]Ja 4 1889;D 25 1891
DLC D 7 1861;62-S 15 1866;D 14 1867-Ap 4,My 16 1868
MWA Jl 3 1875
NN Jl 3 1875;Ja 29 1876
OClWHi Ja 14,F 25,Ag 26 1871
OrHi [1861-62;67;69]Ag 21 1903-21
Wa complete
WaPS [1885;87-89]N 29 1901;My 26 1916-[18]-[20]21
WaU complete
—d ed *See* Olympia daily standard; Daily Olympian 1876-77

OMAK

Omak CHRONICLE. w,sw 1910+
w 1910-Je 1928
WaPS [1916-18]-[33]

OROVILLE

Oroville GAZETTE. w Je 1905+
pub 1905+
WaPS [1915-18]-32

ORTING

Orting ORACLE. w Ja 11 1889+
pub 1903+
CU-B O 3 1890;Ja 8-15,29,F 12,Mr 4,18,Ap-My,Ag 12,26,S 9-16,30-O,N 11-18,D 1892;Ja 13-27,F 10-Ap 7 1893
WaPS [1923-26]N 21 1929+
WaU Ja 22 1897-Ap 22 1898

OTHELLO

Othello TIMES. w 1908-18||?
WaPS [1915-18]

PALOUSE

To 1884? as Palouse City

BOOMERANG. w S 13 1882-89||
Merged with Palouse news
CU-B [Jl-D 1888]
WaS [S 30 1882-84]

Palouse NEWS. w My 1884-97||?
1884? as Palouse City news
CU-B S 20 1889[92-O 1893]F 16 1894
NcD F 1-8 1889

Palouse REPUBLIC. w 1892+
1892-97? as Palouse republican
WaPS [1915-16]-[18]-[20]-[22-23]-33

Palouse REPUBLICAN. *See* Palouse republic

PALOUSE CITY. *See* PALOUSE

PASCO

Pasco EXPRESS. *See* Pasco herald

Pasco HEADLIGHT. w F 10 1888-92||?
CU-B S 6-13 1889
OrHi F 10 1888[89]

Pasco HERALD. w 1902+
1902-My 1918 as Pasco express
pub 1905+
KHi N 1914-S 8 1916
Wa D 1908-S 1911;12+
WaPa 1925+
WaPS [D 17 1915-My 1918]+

PATAHA

Pataha CITY spirit. w Ja 25 1881-83||
Followed by Asotin spirit, later Asotin county sentinel (Asotin)
WaU [1881-S 1883]

PATEROS

Pateros REPORTER. w 1909+
WaPS Mr 2 1923-[26;29]-33

PE ELL

Pe Ell TRIBUNE. w 1913+
WaPS [1922-24]

POMEROY

EAST Washingtonian. w D 10 1881+
1881-Jl 19? 1884 as Pomeroy republican. Suspended Ja-F 1882?
WaPS [1915]-[18-21]-[23]-[25-27]-[29]+
WaU Ag 5,O 28 1882-[83]-F 23 1884

Pomeroy REPUBLICAN. *See* East Washingtonian

WASHINGTON independent. w Ag 12 1880-1904||?
Suspended from Jl 18 1900-Mr 1901
CU-B S 9 1880-O 1887;F 9,Ap 19,S 6,20,N 8 1888;F 7,Mr 14-21,Ap 4-18,My 9,Je 13-20,Jl 4,25-Ag 1,22,O 10 1889;Ja-N 20 1890;My 21 1891;Ja 21 1892;O 26 1893;Je 14 1894
WaU [1880-F 14 1884]

PORT ANGELES

DEMOCRAT-LEADER. *See* Olympic tribune

Daily HERALD. d 1915-23||?
Wa S 1920-F 1921
WaPS Jl 1 1916;N 22 1922-My 7 1923

Port Angeles evening NEWS. d Je 1916+
pub 1916+
WaPo Jl 1 1932
WaPS [1923]-Ag 1930;31-33

Port Angeles OLYMPIC leader. *See* Olympic tribune

OLYMPIC tribune. w 1891+
1891? as Port Angeles democrat; 1892?-Ap 1904 Democrat-leader; My 1904-18? as Port Angeles Olympic leader
CU-B D 3 1892
WaPS [1915-22]-33

Port Angeles TIMES. *See* Tribune-times

TRIBUNE-TIMES. w 1890-1918||?
1890-91? as Port Angeles times. United with Port Angeles Olympic leader to form Olympic tribune
WaPS [1915-16]-[18]

PORT BLAKELY

BAINBRIDGE review. w My 22 1924+
1924-32? as Bainbridge Island review also dated in Rollingbay
pub 1924+
WaPS [1928]-[33]

BAINBRIDGE ISLAND review. *See* Bainbridge review

PORT CRESCENT

LEADER. w 1890-91||?
United with Port Angeles democrat (Port Angeles) to form Democrat-leader, later Olympic tribune (Port Angeles)

PORT GARDNER. *See* EVERETT

PORT ORCHARD

Port Orchard INDEPENDENT. w Ag 1 1888+
WaPS [1922-23]-[25]26;O 13 1927

PORT TOWNSEND

CALL. w Ap 11 1885-1914||?
CU-B F 26 1890

CYCLOP. d O 11-N 3 1871||?
CU-B O 11-20,25-N 3 1871

DEMOCRATIC press. w Ag 31 1877-81||?
CU-B O 3,31,N 14 1878-F 13,27,My 1,15-Ag 14,S-O,N 13-D 18 1879;Ap 22-Jl 22,S 9,O 14-D 9 1880
WaU 1877-Ja 13 1881

Port Townsend LEADER. w,sw O 2 1889+
1889-N 1928 as Port Townsend weekly leader
sw D 1928-Jl 1 1932
pub 1889-[1903-16]+
CU-B O 8 1890;My 12 1893
Wa Ap 1903-My 1906;D 1909+
WaPS [1915-16]-[20-23]-S 1931[32]

Weekly MESSAGE. w My 6 1867-Ag 1871||
Merged with Puget Sound argus
CU-B [1867-Jl 1869]-71
OrHi [1868-70]
Wa My 27,S 26 1867;Ja 23 1868
WaU 1867-68;Ja 14,Mr 24,My 5 1869

NORTH-WEST. w Jl 5 1860-N 20 1862||
Suspended from N 30-D 28 1861
CSmH 1860-Ap,My 9-S 12,26,O 10-N 9,23,D 28 1861;Ja 11-Mr,Ap 19,My 24,Je 14,28-Jl,Ag 9,21,O 16,30,N 20 1862
CU-B N 20 1862
Wa Jl 26,N 29 1860
WaU complete

PUGET SOUND argus. w Jl 21 1870-90||
Title varies: Puget Sound weekly argus
Suspended from O 31-N 11 1872
sw F 20-Ag 29 1873
CU-B Ag 4,D 29 1870[71]F 22-29[My-O 1872;F 20 1873-F 12,S 1876-80;Ap 1882-S]N 22 1883[86-Je 1888;Ja 17-D 19 1889]
Wa Jl 31 1879
WaU O 31 1874;Ja-N 20 1875;76-[82]-Mr 20 1884;D 24-31 1885[F 1886-89]

PUGET SOUND morning argus. d Je 1882-90||?
CU-B Ja 2-31 1889

REGISTER. w D 23 1859-S 18 1861||
1869-Jl 1860 as Port Townsend register
Suspended from Jl 26-N 14 1860
DLC N 14 1860-Mr 13 1861
WaU [Ja 18-Jl]N 14 1860-61

POULSBO

KITSAP county herald. w 1900+
OrHi Mr 10 1916+
WaPS [1916-18]-[21]-[24-26]-33

Poulsbo RECORD. w 1916-27||?
WaPS [1922-23]-N 6 1925

PRESCOTT

SPECTATOR. w 1902-Ap 27 1928||
1902-22 as Walla Walla Valley spectator
WaPS [1921-22]-[24]-28

WALLA WALLA VALLEY spectator. *See* Spectator

PROSSER

BENTON county independent. w 1923+
pub 1932+

INDEPENDENT. w 1909?-Ap 1913||
United with Prosser record to form Independent-record, later Prosser record-bulletin
Wa My 1912-13

INDEPENDENT-RECORD. *See* Prosser record-bulletin

Prosser RECORD-BULLETIN. w 1892+
1892-Ap 1913 as Prosser record; My 1913-Je 1920? Independent-record
Wa O 1906-15
WaPS [1916-19;21-23]-[27-30]-33

REPUBLICAN-BULLETIN. w 1902-Je 24? 1920||
1902-08? as Prosser bulletin United with Independent-record to form Prosser record-bulletin
WaPS [1915-Je 1920]

PULLMAN

Pullman HERALD. w N 3 1888+
pub 1888+
CU-B O 11 1890
WaPS Ja 20 1893;F 29 1896;S 7 1907[09-10]-33

Pullman TRIBUNE. w 1891-1919||?
WaPS O 28 1892[95-97]O 27 1904[Ag 1907;09-15]-[17-18]

PUYALLUP

Puyallup CITIZEN. w My 10 1889-98||?
CU-B [1892-S 1894;My-Ag 1895]

COMMERCE. *See* Puyallup Valley tribune

Puyallup HERALD. *See* Puyallup press

Puyallup INDEPENDENT. *See* Puyallup Valley tribune

WASHINGTON (*Continued*)

PUYALLUP—*Continued*

Puyallup PRESS. w D 1905+
1905-13? as Puyallup republican; 1914?-S 1930 Puyallup herald
pub 1905+
WaPS [1915-23]-[27;29]Ja 3[O-D 1930]-33

PUYALLUP VALLEY tribune. w My 5 1886+
1886-98? as Commerce, 1899?-Ag 3 1903 Puyallup independent
1886-Jl 1888 pub in Tacoma
pub Ag 10 1903+
CU-B S 6,D 27 1889;O 10-17 1890;Ja 22,Mr 18 1892
Wa S 1903+
WaHi 1886-Ag 1 1888
WaPS Ja 7 1911;Je 9-Ag 11 1917[22-23]-33

Puyallup REPUBLICAN. *See* Puyallup press

QUEEN ANNE

Papers published in Queen Anne are listed under Seattle

RAYMOND

Raymond ADVERTISER. w O 6 1922+
Title varies: Advertiser
pub 1922+
WaPS [1925]-[27]-[29-33]

Raymond HERALD. w 1906+
pub 1913+
WaPS [1922-23]-33

REARDAN

Reardan GAZETTE. w 1901+
WaPS [1919;21-25;27-30]-33

RENTON

Renton BULLETIN. w 1913-Mr 30 1923||
WaPS N 17 1922-23

Renton EAGLE. *See* Renton news record

Renton weekly NEWS. w 1907-14||?
Wa Jl 1909-Jl 1911

Renton NEWS RECORD. w S 1924+
1924-25 as Renton eagle
pub S 1932+
WaPS [1929-30]-33

Renton SENTINEL. w? 1898-
CU-B Ja 13 1899

REPUBLIC

Republic NEWS-MINER. w D 14 1904+
Wa F 1914-Je 1916
WaPS [1915-16;22-23]-33

RICHLAND

Richland ADVOCATE. *See* Benton county advocate

BENTON county advocate. w 1905+
1905-F 20 1925 as Richland advocate
WaPS [1916-19]-[23]-32

RICHMOND BEACH

Richmond Beach HERALD. w 1924-My 14 1931||
Merged with Edmonds tribune-review (Edmonds)
WaPS D 19 1929-31

RIDGEFIELD

Ridgefield REFLECTOR. w 1909+
WaPS [1922-23]-S 4 1924;Ag 20 1925-[26-27]-[30]-33

RITZVILLE

ADAMS county times. *See* Times

Ritzville JOURNAL TIMES. w 1898+
1898-1911? as Washington state journal; 1912-17 Washington state journal and times; 1918-F 16 1928 Journal-times
WaPS [1915-22]-[24-27]-33

TIMES. w Jl 2 1887-1912||?
1889 as Adams county times. United with Washington state journal to form Washington state journal and times, later Ritzville journal times
CU-B S 7,D 28 1889;O 7 1893

WASHINGTON state journal. *See* Ritzville journal times

RIVERSIDE

Riverside ARGUS. *See* Riverside tribune

Riverside TRIBUNE. w 1904-22||?
1904-16? as Riverside argus
WaPS [1915-21]

ROCKFORD

Rockford ENTERPRISE. w Ag 1885-1900||?
CU-B Mr 9,30-Ap 13,Je 29,S 7,N 16 1889;Jl 26-Ag 1890

Rockford REGISTER. w 1901+
WaPS [1922-24]

ROLLINGBAY

BAINBRIDGE review. *See under* Port Blakely

BAINBRIDGE ISLAND review. *See* Bainbridge review (Port Blakely)

ROSALIA

CITIZEN-JOURNAL. w 1889+
1889-1909? as Rosalia citizen
WaPS [1914;16;18;22]-[27]-33

Rosalia RUSTLER. w Jl? 1888-94||*
CU-B S 5,13 1889;Ja 23-F 20 1890

ROY

PIERCE county recorder. w 1924+
1924-28? as Roy record
WaPS [1930]-My 19 1932

Roy RAY. w O 17 1889-90||?
CU-B O 2,30 1890

Roy RECORD. *See* Pierce county recorder

ST. JOHN

St. John JOURNAL. w 1902+
WaPS [1918;23-29]-33

ST. MARIES

St. Maries GAZETTE-RECORD. w
WaPS [1919]Jl 17 1924;My 12 1927;D 12 1929

SEALAND

PACIFIC journal. *See under* Ilwaco

SEATTLE

A. Y. P. daily news. d Je 1- 1909||?
WaU Je-Jl 2 1909

ALASKA dispatch. *See* Alaska weekly

ALASKA times. *See* Territorial dispatch and Alaska times

ALASKA weekly. w N 17 1919+
Follows Daily Alaska dispatch (Juneau, Alaska) 1919-F 1923 as Alaska dispatch
pub Mr 1923+
AkHi 1919-Je 1922
CtY [1931-33]
DLC 1919-[22-F 1923]+
WaPS O 1923-[24]-[27-30]-Mr 18 1932
WaS 1925+

Seattle AMERICAN. d My 2-28 1923||
WaS complete

AMERICAN citizen. w 1905-Mr 28 1918||?
1905-Ja 24 1918 as Washington democrat
Wa Je 1910-Ag,N 1913-O 1915
WaS [F 12 1915-Je 1917]Ja 31-Mr 1918

AMERICAN union. w O 1 1919-Ja 21 1920||?
O 1-8 1919 as Newsboy's American
WaS 1919-Ja 21 1920

ARGUS. w F 17 1894+
pub 1894+

ASAHI news. d 1905-18||?
In Japanese
IU S 11 1917-Mr 10 1918
WaPS [1917]

BALLARD news. w
WaPS [1931]
WaU Je 15 1933+

BALLARD tribune. w 1920+
WaU Je 22 1933+

Seattle BUDGET. w 1888-90||?
CU-B Ja 18-25,F 15-22 1890

Seattle daily BULLETIN. *See* Seattle daily journal of commerce and the daily bulletin

Seattle daily CALL. d My 5 1885-My 3 1886||
United with Seattle chronicle to form Seattle press
WaU [S 17 1885-Mr 12 1886]

CALL. w 1891-98||?
1891-S 5 1895? as People's call
CrHi [S 12 1895-N 3 1898]
WaU My 19,Je 2 1892;Ap 4 1896

Seattle daily CALL. d Jl 28 1917-Ap 22 1918||
WaU [1917-18]

CAPITOL HILL times. w
WaU Mr 24,N 3 1932;My 18 1933+

CAYTON'S weekly. w 1916-
Wa Jl 1917-20:F-Mr 1921

Seattle CHRONICLE. d O 10 1881-My 1 1886||
United with Seattle daily call to form Seattle press
Wa Jl 9 1883
WaU [1881-O 1882]Ap 9 1883;Mr 24,29 1884; Ap 22,My 1 1886

COMMONWEALTH. w Jl 26 1916-
WaU 1916-F 28 1917

Morning DISPATCH. d Jl 1 1871-Je 1 1877||
CU-B Jl-Ag 1 1871
WaU [My 5-Je 1877]
—w ed *See* Puget Sound dispatch

Evening DISPATCH. d S 1872-S 1878||
WaU O 7-9,D 24 1872;N 22-28 1873[74;F 1875-O 1876]Je 2,7,Jl 23 1877[Jl 31-S 9 1878]
—w ed *See* Puget Sound dispatch

DUWAMISH VALLEY news. w 1903+
1903-N 1906 as South Seattle news; D 1906-13 Georgetown gazette-news
pub 1911+
Wa Mr 1911+
WaU Je-Ag 24 1934

ENSIGN.
WaU Jl 2 1886

ENTERPRISE. *See* Northwest enterprise

Daily FIGARO. d Jl 28 1876-
WaU Ag 7 1876

Daily evening FIN-BACK. w,m,tw,d D 8 1879-O 4 1881||
1879-Je 1881 as Seattle fin-back
suspended from Je 28-Ag 31 1881
w 1879-N 1880;m D 1880-F 1 1881;tw F 5-Je 28 1881
WaU complete

FREMONT times. w
WaPS D 5 1929[30]

FULLER'S daily report. d -Mr 7 1916||
Merged with Seattle daily bulletin, later Seattle daily journal of commerce and the daily bulletin
WaPS [1916]

Seattle GAZETTE. *See* Puget Sound gazette

GAZZETTA italiana. w 1910+
In Italian
pub 1920+
WaS [N 30 1917-21]-[24]-[26-27]+

GEORGETOWN gazette-news. *See* Duwamish Valley news

Seattle GERMAN press and Pacific German press. d 1913?-Jl 20 1915||
United with Washingtoner staatszeitung (d) to form Seattle German press and Washingtoner staatszeitung
WaS [Ja-Jl 1915]

Seattle GERMAN press and Washingtoner staatszeitung. w *See* Washington staatszeitung

Seattle GERMAN press and Washingtoner staatszeitung. d 1909-Ja 15 1918||
1909-Jl 20 1915 as Washingtoner staatszeitung
IU S 1917-18
WaPS [1917-18]
WaS D 7 1914-Ap 16,Jl 21 1915-18
WaSS complete

GRAND COULEE record. w O 25-D 27 1933||?
WaU N-D 27 1933

GREAT NORTHERN daily news. d 1909+
In Japanese
IU S 1917-Je 1918
WaPS [1917;21-22]
WaU O 2 1933+

GREEN LAKE-North End reporter. w
WaU Je 9 1933+

GREENWOOD-PHINNEY herald. w
WaU Je 15,N 9 1933+

Seattle daily HERALD. d Jl 5 1882-O 8 1884||
WaU [Jl-S 1882]F 8,D 21 1883

Seattle weekly HERALD. w O 21 1882-O 8 1884||
WaU 1882-Ag 11 1883

HERALD w 1898-99||?
United with Saturday mail to form Seattle mail and herald
WHi D 16 1899

HERALD. w 1912-17||?
WaPS [1916]

Daily INDEX. w,d 1888+
1888-1904 as Seattle index (w)
WaU N 1933+

Seattle weekly INTELLIGENCER. *See* Seattle post-intelligencer

Tri-weekly INTELLIGENCER. tw Ag 9 1870-F 4 1871||
CU-B [1870-71]
OClWHi S 11,D 10-27 1870
WaU complete

Daily INTELLIGENCER. *See* Seattle post-intelligencer

JAPANESE-AMERICAN courier. w 1928+
In English
WaU Mr 10 1934+

JEWISH chronicle. w Mr-D 29 1932||?
Merged with Jewish transcript
WaSJ Mr 24-D 1932

JEWISH transcript. w Mr 6 1924+
pub 1924+
WaU Ap 1935+

Morning JOURNAL. d Ag 13 1888-90||?
1888-89 as Daily trade journal
CU-B Jl 26 1890
WaU Je 25-28 1890

Seattle daily JOURNAL of commerce and the daily bulletin. d Je 1893+
1893-Ap 1907 as Seattle daily bulletin; My 1907-08 Morning times and Seattle daily bulletin; 1909-D 23 1919 Seattle daily bulletin
pub Ag 1913+
C Mr 1916-Ja 15 1917
Wa D 1922-Je,Ag 1924-O 1927;S 1933+
WaPS [1916-17]O 5,D 5 1932;My 20,Ag 19 1930;Jl 11 1931
WaS D 24 1919+
WaU C 9 1895-[96-97]-O 24 1902;Ja 31,F 4 1907;F 1913

LEADER. w Ap 11 1889-90||?
WaU Ag 22,S 5-12,O 10,24-31 1889;Ja 23-F 6,20,Mr 13-My 8,22,Je 5-19 1890

WASHINGTON (*Continued*)

SEATTLE—*Continued*

MAGNOLIA news. w,ir 1933-Ja 31 1935||
WaU D 13 1933-35

Seattle MAIL and herald. w 1898-My 25 1907||
1898-99? as Saturday mail
OrHi Ap 14 1900-Ap 18 1903
WHi Je 23 1900
WaS 1901-07

MASONIC tribune. w D 14 1916+
Wa Jl 1917-22;Ag 1923-28;Ap 1930+
WaU 1916-O 1928;Je-Jl 6,N 23 1933+

MIRROR. w N 10 1883-S 14 1884||
WaU Ja 12,Mr 20,29 1884

Seattle weekly NEWS. w 1894-1930||?
WaPS D 20 1918[19;20-30]

Seattle NEWS. d 1904-S 28 1907||
WaS My 1905-07

NEWSBOY'S American. *See* American union

NEXT. . . *See* Workingman's paper

NORTH AMERICAN times. d 1902+
In Japanese
IU D 14 1917-Mr 1920

NORTH CENTRAL outlook. w
-F 21 1935 as Wallingford outlook
WaU Je 1933+

NORTH END herald. w 1926+
WaU Je 23 1933+

NORTH UNIVERSITY times. *See* Roosevelt way times

NORTHERN light. *See under* Tacoma

NORTHWEST enterprise. w 1920+
1920-30 as Enterprise
Negro
CU-B Ja 14-Ap 22,My 6,27-Je 3,S 23 1927
WaPS O 8 1926;27+
WaU Je 15 1933+

NOVAГA zarГa. *See under* San Francisco

Thursday noon OUTLOOK. w Mr 30-My 11 1934||
Follows Vanguard. Merged with Voice of action
WaU complete

PACIFIC tribun. *See* Svenska Pacific tribunen

Weekly PACIFIC tribune. sw,w Jl 29 1861-Mr 30 1879||
Follows Pioneer and democrat (Olympia). 1861-Ap 1864 as Overland press; My 1864-67? Pacific tribune. Merged with Seattle weekly intelligencer, later Seattle post-intelligencer
1861-Ag 9? 1873 pub in Olympia; Ag 16 1873-Je 11 1875 pub in Tacoma.
sw O 1861-F 1862
CSmH Jl 21 1862
CU-B S 8 1862;S 30 1865;Jl 1886-70;O 28 1871; My 18-25 1872;Ag 16 1873-F 2 1879
CaB S 30-N 4,21,D 2,9,19 1861;Ja-F,Mr 17-24,Ap 14,28-My 19,Je 2-23,Jl 14,S 1,29-O 6, 20,N 17,D 29 1862-Ja 12,Mr-Ap,N 16,30 1863
DLC Jl 22-29 1865;Ap 21-Jl 7,21-Ag 11,S 1,15-22 1866;My 1868-D 18 1869;Jl 17 1874-F 2 1879
NN My 14,Je 4 1864;Ag 5,S 2 1865
OrHi [1861-70]
Wa N 14 1861;F 17,29,N 10,D 15 1862[63;F-N 1864;F-O 1865;Mr 1866]O 31 1872
WaU 1861-[Ja-N 1870;Ap-D 1871]72;Ag 16 1873-Je 11 1875;Ja 25 1877-[78]79

Daily PACIFIC tribune. *See* Tribune

PEOPLE'S call. *See* Call

PHILIPPINE advocate. m D 1934+
WaU 1934+

PHILIPPINE-AMERICAN chronicle. bw
WaU F 15 1935+

Seattle daily POST. d N 15 1878-S 1881||
Follows North Pacific rural (not in this list)
United with Daily intelligencer to form Seattle post-intelligencer
CU-B N 12 1879-[80]

Seattle POST. w 1878-S 1881||
United with Seattle weekly intelligencer to form Seattle post-intelligencer
CU-B My 10,Je 14 1879-Mr 20 1880

Seattle POST-INTELLIGENCER. w,sw Ag 5 1867-1907||?
Follows Puget Sound gazette. 1867-S 1881 as Seattle weekly intelligencer; O 1881-My 10 1888 Seattle weekly post-intelligencer; My 17 1888-N 14 1889 Seattle post-intelligencer; N 21 1889-1901? Weekly post-intelligencer
w 1867-1901?
CU-B 1867-[75-76]-80;Ja 6,F 3 1882;O 22 1891
DLC Ap 12 1879-Jl 10 1890
OClWHi [1871]S 30-O 7 1872;My 3 1873
OrHi [1870]
WHi 1896
WaS 1867-[S 1869-Je 3 1876]
WaU 1867-O 1879;Mr 27 1880;D 27 1894;Je 9 1898
—tw ed *See* Tri-weekly intelligencer

Seattle POST-INTELLIGENCER. d Je 5 1876+
1876-O 2 1881 as Daily intelligencer
Suspended from Ag 13 1936-N 30 1936
O 13 1897 is special Klondike ed
pub 1876+
A Jl-O 1900;S 1901+
C Jl 1904+
CL Ja 31 1922
CLM S 16 1902
CU-B S 22 1877-78;Ap 1879-80;Ja 25,29,F 1,8, 13,16 1881;D 31 1885-91;S 22 1907-Ag 28 1911
CaB 1931+
CoU 1905-My 1910
CtY O 13 1897
DLC Jl 1890-Je 1899;1900-07
ICN Ja 15 1918-Ja 15 1919
IU N 10-D 29 1909;Ja 26-29 1910
M O 13 1897
MWA Ja 1 1889;O 13 1897
MnU [1918-21]
NcD* My 1905;06-My 1908
OHi Mr 1923-[25-26]-[29-30]
OrHi [1893-1903]
WHi Ja 2 1887;1915-O 1919;Ja 9,O 18 1920+
Wa S 8-9,11 1885;Ag 12 1888;Ag 1891-Mr,My 1892-My,Ag 1893+
WaPS [1893-99;1902;04-12]-[15]-[18]-[22-24]+
WaS 1891-93;Ap 1894+
WaU Ap 5 1878[My-Ag 1882]Ja 1,13 1883;Ja 1,20[Mr]1884;Jl 13,S 20,27-30,O 6,10,N 26,D 8,23 1885[Ja-Ag 1886;Je-O 1889]F-O 1890; Ja 25,Ap 5,Ag 23,N 29 1891;Jl 14,Ag 31 1892; F 25,My 21,Je 25,S 3,O-N 1893[F 25 1894-Ag 1895]Ja 3,27,My 16 1897;Je 21 1898;1900+
WaWW Jl 1906+
—Panama Pacific ed
NN F 19 1899;Ap 20 1913

POST of progress and western states technocrat. w F 19 1934+
1934-Je 11 1935 as Western states technocrat
WaU 1934+

Seattle PRESS. d My 5 1886-F 10 1891||
Former by the union of Seattle daily call and Seattle chronicle. United with Seattle daily times to form Seattle press-times, later Seattle daily times
CU-B My 16,Je 13 1889;My 29,Jl 11 1890
Wa Ag 18,29 1888
WaU [1886-N 1888;My-Je 1889]Jl 16 1890;Ja 7-28 1891

Seattle PRESS-TIMES. *See* Seattle daily times

PROMPTER. w Ja 10-My 18 1878||
WaU complete

PUGET SOUND daily. d Ap 23-Ag 11 1866||
WaU complete
—w ed *See* Puget Sound gazette

PUGET SOUND dispatch. w D 4 1871-80||?
Merged with Seattle weekly intelligencer, later Seattle post-intelligencer
CU-B D 18 1871[72]-O 22 1874[76-Ag 1878]
MWA Mr 24 1877
OClWHi Mr 28-Ap 4,18 1872;Ap 25 1875
WaU 1871-D 5 1872[73-Ag 1875;76]Ja 6,Mr 3,Je 23,N 10 1877-[Ja-S 1878]N 24,D 29 1879 [Ja 26-O 24 1880]
—morning ed *See* Morning dispatch
—evening ed *See* Evening dispatch

PUGET SOUND gazette. w,sw Ag 15 1863-Je 17 1867||?
Ag 15 1863 as Washington gazette (numbered prospectus) D 10 1863-Jl 1864 Seattle gazette; Ag 1864-Mr 3 1866 Seattle weekly gazette; Ap 5-19 1866 Puget Sound semi-weekly; Ap 30 1866-Mr 18 1867 Puget Sound weekly. Followed by Seattle weekly intelligencer, later Seattle post-intelligencer
Suspended from Ag 15-D 10 1863;Mr 3-Ap 5,Ap 19-30 1866
sw Ap 5-19 1866
CU-B D 10-17 1863;Ag 19,N 11-D 22 1865;Ja-F,Ap-O,D 31 1866;Ja 14-My 13,27-Je 17 1867
DLC Jl 6-13,Ag 26-S 2,16-30,O 14-21,N 4-18 1865
NN Mr 11 1867
WaS Ag 1864-Je 17 1867
WaU 1863-Je 17 1867
—d ed *See* Puget Sound daily

PUGET SOUND semi-weekly. *See* Puget Sound gazette

PUGET SOUND weekly. *See* Puget Sound gazette

QUEEN ANNE news. w
WaPS [1930-31]
WaU Je 15 1933+

RAINIER VALLEY citizen. *See* Rainier Valley times

RAINER VALLEY times. w 1908+
1908-18? as Rainier Valley citizen
WaPS [1918]S 3 1919;Jl 17-24 1920[21-30]
WaU [Ag 10 1933-Mr 17 1934]

RECORD. d S 27 1893-O 8 1895||
S-N 22 1893 as Seattle transcript. Merged with Daily bulletin, later Seattle daily journal of commerce and the daily bulletin
WaU 1893[94-95]

Seattle REPUBLICAN. w 1894-1915||?
Negro
DLC Ja 19 1900
Wa 1908-Ap 1913

ROOSEVELT district tribune. w
WaU [Mr-S 21 1933]

ROOSEVELT WAY times. w Mr 17 1932+
Title varies: University district times; North university times
WaU 1932-Ag 24[O 12 1933-34]

SEARCHLIGHT. w 1904-27||?
Also dated in Tacoma
WaS [My 1919-20]

SOCIALIST. *See* Workingman's paper

SOCIALIST world. w 1916-17||?
WaPS [Jl 21 1916-Mr 1917]

SOUTH SEATTLE news. *See* Duwamish Valley news

SPECTATOR. w 1891-95||?
WaU Jl 23 1892

Seattle Sunday STAR. w N 11 1883-90||?
WaU Mr 23 1884;O 29-N 5 1887

Seattle STAR. d 1899+
pub 1902+
OHi Ja-Mr 1919;F 1920-22
WaPS N 2 1917[18-19]O 15 1924[25]Jl 20 1926; Ag 1 1927;Ap 11 1928;O 24 1929;O 12 1932
WaS 1901+
WaU [Ap-My 1899]Ap 28,O 16 1900[My]N 19 1901;Je 1-5 1909

Seattle SUN. d F 3 1913-Ag 28 1915||
Suspended from D 30 1914-Ap 21 1915
MWA F 3 1914
Wa 1913-14
WaS complete
WaU 1913-Je 28,Jl 17-Ag 1915

SVENSKA journalen. *See* Svenska posten

SVENSKA Pacific tribunen. w Je 20 1902+
Formed by the union of Westra posten and Tacoma tribunen (Tacoma). 1902-1903 as Westerns tribun; 1903-14 Pacific tribun
In Swedish
IRA 1902-[17-18]

SVENSKA posten. w 1926+
1926-Ja 23 1936 as Svenska journalen
Ja 30 1936+ also dated in Tacoma and Portland
In Swedish
MnHi Ap 1928+
WaS S 1933+

SVENSKA pressen. *See* Swedish Pacific press

SWEDISH Pacific press. Svenska pressen. w 1902-14||?
1902-08 as Väktaren
In English and Swedish
IRA 1902-14

Seattle TELEGRAPH. d Ag 11 1890-D 8 1894||
DLC 1894
Wa My 6 1892
WaS 1890-92
WaU [My,Ag 1891-93]Mr 15,29 1894

Seattle TELEGRAPH. d F 1896-
WaU F 25 1896

TERRITORIAL dispatch and Alaska times. w O 1 1870-72||?
Follows Alaska times (Sitka) 1870-My 14 1871 as Alaska times
CU-B [1870]-Mr 19,My 14-22 1871
DLC O 23-N 6,27-D 1870;Ja 8-F 12,Mr 5-21,My 14 1871(photostat)
OClWHi Ap 16,Ag 28 1871
WaU Ap 7,My 22-Je 5,19-26,Jl 17-Ag 14,28,S 11,25,O 9 1871

Seattle daily TIMES. d My 3 1886+
1886-F 10 1891 as Seattle daily times; F 11 1891-My 10 1895 Seattle press-times; My 11-D 1895? Seattle daily times; 1896? Seattle evening times
F 25 1906 is silver jubilee ed
DLC 1898+
MWA Je 8 1913;Ja 11 1928
NN F 12 1905;Je 8 1913
OrHi O 1896-Mr 1902[05-09]
PP [1927]+
TJT N 23 1898
WHi D 21 1895;97-Ja 15 1902;F 25 1906
Wa Ag 1891-Mr,O 1892-Mr 1893;94-Ap,Jl 1898+
WaPS [1893]-[1900-08]F 1-13 1917[18-21]-[32]
WaS Jl 1891-S 1893[94-95;Je-S 1896;Ap 1897-Mr 1898]Ja-Ag 1900
WaU Mr 25,Ap 24,My 5-22,O 24 1891;My 7,Jl 14,N 5 1892;S 26 1893;Je 28,Jl 5[Ag-O 1894; 95-1911]-Mr 19 1919;Ap 1923-Ag 1931

Morning TIMES and the Seattle daily bulletin. *See* Seattle daily journal of commerce and the daily bulletin

Daily TRADE journal. *See* Morning journal

Seattle TRANSCRIPT. *See* Record

Die Seattle TRIBUNE. *See* Washington staatszeitung

TRIBUNE. d D 16 1867-Mr 15 1879||
1867-Ja 11 1868 as Olympia daily Pacific tribune; Ja 12 1868-S 14 1878 Daily Pacific tribune
1867-Jl 1873 pub in Olympia; Ag 19 1873-My 24 1874 in Tacoma
Suspended from Ja 11 1868-O 4 1869;My 24 1874-Je 15 1875
CSmH F 19 1877
CU-B N 28,D 6-7,9-10 1870;72-My 24 1874;O 1,N 22-23,D 1-2,28-30 1875[Mr 24 1876-Ja 22,Ap 5-My 21 1877;My 2-S 16 1878]-79
DLC Ap 5 1870-D 15 1871
MWA Ap 2 1872
WaU 1867-Ap 16[Ag 20 1873-My 1874]Je 15-N 24 1875;Ja 4,8,11,My 19,30 1876-S 14 1878
—w ed *See* Weekly Pacific tribune

TRUE tone. w O 17 1885-Je 12 1886||
WaU complete

UNEMPLOYED citizen. *See* Vanguard

Seattle UNION record. w 1900-23||?
IU Je 10 1916-Ja 20 1923
WHi D 19 1903;Ja 25,Je 20-N 1908;Je 12 1915;N 24 1917
WaS 1914-19

Seattle UNION record. d Ap 24 1918-F 18 1928||
CU-B [F-My 13 1919]
ICU 1921-My 1 1926
IU [1923-28]
NN [Ja 1921]
NNRa Jl-S 1926
OrU 1922[23-24]-[26]
WHi [Ja 26 1923-Ap 15]Jl 18 1924-F 17 1928
WaPS [1919-20]O 13 1921-[27-28]
WaS complete
WaU complete

UNIVERSITY district herald. sw
WaU [O-D 1928]Ja 4,Ag 20 1929+

UNIVERSITY district times. *See* Roosevelt Way times

VÄKTAREN. *See* Swedish Pacific press

WASHINGTON (*Continued*)

SEATTLE—*Continued*

VANGUARD. m,w Ja 1930-N 24 1933||
Some issues as Unemployed citizen. Followed by Thursday noon outlook
Suspended from Je-Ag 12 1932
m 1930
WaU complete

VOICE of action. w Mr 25 1933+
WaU 1933—

WACHT am sunde. *See under* Tacoma

WALLINGFORD outlook. *See* North Central outlook

WASHINGTON commonwealth builder. bw S 18 1934+
WaU 1934+

WASHINGTON democrat. *See* American citizen

WASHINGTON gazette. *See* Puget Sound gazette

WASHINGTON posten. w My 17 1889+
In Norwegian
pub 1892+
IU D 14 1917+
IaDeL Je 19 1890[S 1896-S 10 1897;D 22 1899-Ap 6 1906;Ap 20 1917-Mr 1918]D 25 1925+
MnHi Ja 8 1915
WHi My 22 1925
WaS 1922+

WASHINGTON posten (Swedish) *See* Westra posten

WASHINGTON staatszeitung. w 1878+
1878-89 as Die Seattle tribüne; 1890-1902? Washingtoner staatszeitung; 1903?-Ja 10 1918 Washingtoner staatszeitung und presse; Ja 17-My 9 1918 Seattle German press and Washingtoner staatszeitung
Suspended from My 9 1918-My 1922
In German
pub 1888+
IU Ja 17-My 9 1918
WaS [Mr 29 1917-18]-[23]-[26]-[28-29]+

WASHINGTONER staatszeitung. w *See* Washington staatszeitung

WASHINGTONER staatszeitung. d *See* Seattle German press and Washingtoner staatszeitung

WASHINGTONIAN. d F 10-S 26 1902||
WaS complete

WATERFRONT worker. w D 1 1934?+
WaU D 15 1934+

WEST COAST populist. w 1895-97||?
WHi D 10 1897

WEST SEATTLE herald. w Ja 1923+
pub 1923+
WaU Ag 11 1933+

WEST SEATTLE times. w
WaU Ja 19-Mr 9 1934

WESTERN states technocrat. *See* Post of progress and western states technocrat

WESTERNS tribun. *See* Svenska Pacific tribunen

WESTRA posten. w 1889-Je 13 1902||
1889-Jl? 1890 as Washington posten. United with Tacoma tribunen (Tacoma) to form Westerns tribun, later Svenska Pacific tribunen
also dated in Tacoma
In Swedish
CU-B Ag 29 1890
IRA 1894-1901
WaTS [1889-90]

WHITE CENTER news. w
WaU Ag 11 1933-Jl 1934

WHITE CENTER record. w
WaU [Ag-N 1933]Ja 25 1934

WORKINGMAN'S paper. w 1900-O 1 1910||
1900?-Jl 1904 as Socialist, the Workingman's paper; Ag 1904-Ja 1 1905 Next; or, the socialist; Mr 1905-Ag 13 1910 Socialist
Mr 1905-Je 2 1906 pub in Toledo, Ohio; Jl 7 1906-D 8 1906 in Caldwell, Idaho
Suspended from Ja 1-Mr 1905?;D 8 1906-Ap 7 1907
NNC [1902-10]
WHi S 2 1900;F 10,Mr 3 1901;My 4,O 12,N 23 1902;Ja 18 1903-Ag 1904;Mr 18 1905-10
WaU [Mr 24-N 1901;Ap 13 1902-My 1 1904;05-N 1906;Mr 1907-Ag 20 1910]

WORLD. w 1898-1903||?
Negro
DLC Ja 4 1899

SEDRO

Papers published in Sedro are listed under Sedro-Woolley

SEDRO-WOOLLEY

Formed by the union of Sedro and Woolley in 1898

COURIER-TIMES. w 1900+
1900-14? as Skagit county courier; 1915?-My 13 1920 Sedro-Woolley courier
WaPS [1915-22]-[24-27]-33

SKAGIT county courier. *See* Courier-times

SKAGIT county times. w 1891-My 1920||
United with Sedro-Woolley courier to form Courier-times
WaPS F 22 1917;D 19 1918;Ja 9-16 1919

SEHOME

Papers published in Sehome are listed under Bellingham

SELAH

YAKIMA VALLEY optimist. w 1911+
pub 1917+
WaPS [1923-24]-33

SEQUIM

Sequim PRESS. w Ap 8 1911+
pub 1911+
WaPS N 29 1929-My 9 1930

SHELTON

MASON county journal. *See* Shelton-Mason county journal

SHELTON-MASON county journal. w,sw D 31 1886+
1886-N 1927 as Mason county journal
w 1886-N 1927
pub 1886+
CU-B Mr 23-29,Jl 5,S 13-20,N 29,D 13 1889;Ja 3,F 7,28,Jl 25-Ag 1,15-22,O 3-24 1890;Ja 22 1892
OrHi My 20 1902-N 1909;10-25
Wa Ag 1891+
WaPS [1915-16]-[18]-[23]-[26-Mr 4 1927]+

SIDNEY

PEOPLE'S broadax. w O 27 1889-91||?
CU-B Ag 2-9 1890

SILVERDALE

KITSAP county journal. w 1929-33||?
WaPS [1929-30]-My 18 1933

SKAMOKAWA

Skamokawa EAGLE. w 1891+
MWA My 19 1892
WaPS Ja 4 1917;D 19-26 1918[22-23]+

SLAUGHTER. *See* AUBURN

SNOHOMISH

Snohomish ADVANCE. w 1913-18||?
WaPS [1916-17]

EYE. w Ja 11 1882-97||
WaU S 1882-F 1884

NORTHERN star. w Ja 15 1876-My 3 1879||
CU-B Ap 8,22,My 13,Je 24-Jl 8,S 2,O 28,D 16,30 1876;Mr 3-17,31-My 5,Je 16-23,Jl 28,S 8,29,O 6,D 1 1877;My 8-15,29-Je 12,26-Jl 13,27-Ag 10,24-S 1,O 5,N 2 1878;F 1-15,Mr 8,22,Ap 5 1879
DLC [Ja-N 1876;77]
MWA F 19 1876
Wa [Ja 22-N 18 1876;Ja 13-S 22 1877]
WaS [Ja-N 9 1878]-79
WaU 1876-Ap 14,Je 9-D 22 1877

SNOHOMISH county tribune. w 1887+
1887-Jl 1892 as Snohomish sun
pub [1889-95]+
WaPS Mr 16 1916-[18]-[20-S 16 1925]+

Snohomish SUN. *See* Snohomish county tribune

SNOQUALMIE

Snoqualmie POST. *See* Snoqualmie Valley record

SNOQUALMIE VALLEY record. w 1913+
1913-Je 1924 as Snoqualmie post
pub 1913+
WaPS Mr 2 1917;D 20-27 1918;Ap 8 1921[22-24]N 28 1929+

SOUTH BELLINGHAM

Papers published in South Bellingham are listed under Bellingham

SOUTH BEND

South Bend JOURNAL. w F 4 1890+
pub 1890+
MnU [1890-91]
Wa 1907+
WaPS D 10 1915[16-17]My 6 1921[22-23]24

WILLAPA HARBOR pilot. w Ap 16 1891+
Wa Je 1910-S 1918
WaPS [1915-16]-[18-21]-[24]+

SPANGLE

Spangle RECORD. w F 1887-95||?
CU-B Mr 7-21 1889;O 9-23 1890

Spangle SPIRIT. *See* Spokane county news (Spokane)

SPOKANE

To 1892 as Spokane Falls

CHAT. w N 14 1915-
WaSp N-D 18 1915

Spokane weekly CHRONICLE. w Je 29 1881+
1881-91? as Spokane Falls chronicle
NcU F 1 1884
TJT Ag 9 1900
WaU Je-S 14,N 15 1881;Je 20-Jl 1882;Ja 4 1883

Spokane daily CHRONICLE. d S 21 1886+
Early years as Spokane Falls evening chronicle
CU-B Jl 12 1894;Je 19, 21 1895
CoU S 1906-My 1910
DLC 1898
MWA S 21 1886(reprint)
Wa Ja-My 1898;Ap-Je 1903;Jl-Ag 1906;Ja 1912
WaPS N 12 1891[1904-10]+
WaSp F 1895-Ja 1898;99+
WaSpS 1926+

COEUR D'ALENE miner. w Ja 26 1884-
KHi Ja 26 1884

FORUM. w 1920-21||?
WaPS O 27 1920-Jl 6 1921

Spokane GLOBE. w,d 1888-91||?
1888-Ja? 1890 as Sunday globe (w)
CU-B Ja 4-11,D 8,21-28 1889;Ja 18,Jl 26,29-30 1890

Spokane HERALD. w
WaPS [1918]

HILLYARD news. *See* Inland empire news

INLAND EMPIRE news. w 1900+
1900-12 as Hillyard news
pub 1912+
WaPS Ag 29 1923;N 13 1929-Jl 1930

INLAND herald. d F 8 1910-My 6 1911||
WaSp complete

NEW state news. d,w O 11 1886-90||?
O-N 1886 as Daily evening news; N 1886-88? News-democrat; 1889? Spokane news
d O-N 1886
CU-B Je 29 1889

NEWS. *See* New state news

NORTHERN light. *See under* Tacoma

NORTHWEST tribune rural. w Je 16 1880-98||?
1880-93? as Northwest tribune
Je-O 6 1880 pub in Colfax; O 13 1880-S 1885 in Cheney
CU-B Jl 5-19 1889
WaSp Je 23 1880-Je 7 1895
WaU [1880-F 1884]

ORATOR-OUTBURST. w 1892-1910||?
1892-Je 1906 as Outburst
WaSp 1906-Je 1908

OUTBURST. *See* Orator-outburst

Spokane PRESS. d 1902+
WaPS O 17 1919[21-33]
WaSp Je 1925+

Spokane RECORD. w F 1887-
CU-B Mr 7-21 1889;O 9-23 1890

Spokane REGULATOR. w Ja 3-? 1892||
WaSp Ja 3-24 1892

REVIEW. *See* Spokesman-review

Spokane SKANDINAV. w 1906-24||?
In Norwegian and English
IU [1918-My 1919;Mr 1920-F 3 1922]
IaDeL [D 1914-Ag 1915;My 23 1917-Mr 15 1918]
MnHi [My-D 1918]-[21]

SPOKANE county news. w 1918+
1918-F 1922 as Spangle spirit (Spangle)
pub 1918+
WaPS [1919-22]-[26-29]+

SPOKANE VALLEY herald. w Mr 1920+
pub 1920+
WaPS [1920-33]+

Morning SPOKESMAN. d Mr 9 1890-F 22 1893||
United with Morning review to form Spokesman-review
Wa Ag 1891-93
WaU [1890-Jl 4 1891]

Twice-a-week SPOKESMAN-REVIEW. w,sw My 19 1883-1928||?
1883-F 1893? as Spokane Falls review (other slight title variations)
w 1883-F 1893?
CU-B O 14 1886-87;My 31,Jl-S 6,27-N 8,23-D 6,20 1889;F 1890-F 5,Mr-D 1891
NcD N 2 1903
OrHi Ja 14 1897-98
WHi S 15 1908-S 1915
WaPS [1916-25;27-28]

SPOKESMAN-REVIEW. d Je 1884+
1884?-F 22 1893 Morning review
Jl 22 1933 is golden anniversary ed
pub 1917+
CL Jl 22 1933
CU-B Ja 1,F[Jl]1890-[My 1891]My 15 1897
DLC Jl 1893+
MWA Ag 5 1890;Ja 1 1891;Jl 22 1933
NN My 14,Ag 28 1895-Je 1896
NcD D 20 1888
OrCA 1928+
TJT Je 17 1909
Wa Ag-N 1891;Ja-Mr,Jl 1892+
WaPS [1894]-[1900]-[03]-[06]-[08-09]-[11]+
WaSp S 1894+
WaSpG Mr 1914-17
WaU [My-Je,D 1886;F-Ap,N 1887-Je,N 1889-Je,N 1890;My,Jl 1891-Je]O 1894+
WaWW S 1906-Je 1930

Spokane Sunday SUN. w Ap 3 1892-96||?
WaSp 1892-S 22 1894

WASHINGTON (*Continued*)

SPOKANE—*Continued*

SVENSKA nordvästern. w 1907-22||?
Followed by Svenska pressen?
In Swedish
IRA 1910-20
IU 1917-S 23 1920
WaPS [1915-16]

SVENSKA pressen. w 1923+
Follows Svenska nordvästern?
In Swedish
MnHi 1931+
WaPS [1924]D 7 1932

Spokan TIMES. w Ap 24 1879-82||
CU-B Ap 8,Ag 7-21,S 11-O 2 1880
WaU F 5,Mr 4,Ap 1[My 15-D 1880;F 1881-Ap 1882]

WASHINGTON leader. w
WaPS [1920]

WASHINGTON post. d 1889+
1889-1900? as Washington Spokane post
In German
WaPS S 23 1915-[20]-F 19 1925

WASHINGTON Spokane post. *See* Washington post

SPOKANE FALLS. *See* SPOKANE

SPRAGUE

Sprague ADVOCATE. w Ap 19 1888+
1888-Ag 1899 as Sprague herald; S 1899-1905 Sprague times; 1906-F 1909 Independent times; Mr-Ag 13 1909 Inland advocate
pub 1888-89;91-94;99+
CU-B Ap 4,Jl 4,S,O 10-17,N 28,D 12 1889-Ja 2,23,F 27,Mr 20,Ap 17,Je 19-26,Jl 9-16,Ag 20,O 8-15,29 1890

Sprague HERALD. *See* Sprague advocate

INDEPENDENT times. *See* Sprague advocate

INLAND advocate. *See* Sprague advocate

Sprague JOURNAL. w Ja 16 1885-87||?
CU-B Mr 5,Ap 9,Jl 2-9,23,Ag 6,20,S 10,N 19 1886;Je 17-24,Jl-Ag 5 1887

Sprague daily MAIL. d 1892-94||?
WHi Mr 1 1894

Sprague TIMES. *See* Sprague advocate

SPRINGDALE

Springdale REFORMER. w 1905-23||?
WaColE 1907-11

Springdale REPORTER. w 1924+
WaPS N 28 1929+

STANWOOD

Stanwood NEWS. *See* Twin City news

STILLAGUAMISH times. *See* Arlington times (Arlington)

Stanwood TIDINGS. *See* Twin City news

TWIN CITY news. w 1905+
1905- 1920 as Stanwood tidings; 1920-Ja 23 1930 Stanwood news
pub 1912+
WaPS [1915-21]-[23-24]+

STARBUCK

Starbuck STANDARD. w 1914-19||?
WaPS [1916]

STEILACOOM

Steilacoom NEWS. w Je 6 1890-91||?
WaU [1890-O 31 1891]

PUGET SOUND courier. w My 19 1855-57||
CU-B D 14 1855
OrHi 1855-Ap 25 1856
WaU [1855-F]Ap 20 1856

PUGET SOUND express. w N 21 1872-80||?
Suspended from O 18 1877-Jl 13 1878
CU-B D 1872-Ja 2,16,30,F 21-Ap 3,My 1873-F 23,Mr 9-Ap,My 17-Ag 23,S 6,27,O 18 1876-O 18 1877;Ja-S 11 1880
NNHi Jl 17,Ag 7 1873
WaHi 1872-N 13 1873
WaU Ja 1,O 15,D 10 1874[75-Jl 1878]D 20 1879

PUGET SOUND express. d Ja 1877-
CU-B F 6-16 1877

PUGET SOUND herald. w Mr 12 1858-64||
Suspended from Mr 2-My 1860
CU-B D 12 1863
CaB 1858-My 22 1862
OrHi F 13 1864
Wa 1858-My,Je 11 1863
WaHi 1858-Mr 2 1860
WaU 1858-My 9[D 1863-N 7 1864]

TRUTH-TELLER. F 3-10 1858||?
WaU F 3 1868

WASHINGTON republican. w Ap 3-Jl 24 1857||
NNHi Je 12 1857
OrHi complete
WaU [1857]

WESTERN star. w Jl 17 1869-My 1870||?
OrHi Ag 28 1869

STEVENSON

SKAMANIA county independent. w S 1914-17||?
Wa 1914-16

SKAMANIA county pioneer. w 1886+
Wa F 1907+
WaPS [1916-24]+

SULTAN

SKYKOMISH VALLEY star. *See* Valley news

Sultan STAR. *See* Valley news

VALLEY news. w 1905+
1905-S 1921 as Skykomish valley star; O 1921-23? Sultan star
WaPS Ap 29 1921-[22-23]-[26-28;30]

SUMAS

Sumas ADVOCATE. w 1915-F 1916||?
United with Sumas news to form Advocate-news, later Sumas news

ADVOCATE-NEWS. *See* Sumas news

INTERNATIONAL vidette. w? 1891-96||?
CU-B S 29 1892

Sumas NEWS. w 1889+
Mr 1916-22? as Advocate-news
WaPS Je 12 1914[15-18;23]-33

SUMNER

AMERICAN standard. *See* Sumner standard

Sumner INDEX. *See* Sumner news index

Sumner NEWS index. w 1900+
1900-15? as Sumner index
WaPS [1916-23]+

Sumner STANDARD. w Je 1915+
1915-17 as American standard
Suspended from Mr 1917-19
pub 1915+
WaPS Ag 1916-Mr 13 1917[21]+

SUNNYSIDE

NORTHWEST forum. *See* Sunnyside observer

Sunnyside OBSERVER. w 1906-15||?
1906-11? as Northwest forum
WaPS Ag 1910-N 1913

Sunnyside SUN. w 1901+
Wa Jl 1909-S 1911
WaPS [1915-24]+

Sunnyside TIMES. w N 1 1915+
pub 1915+
WaPS [1919]-[21-23]

TACOMA

Tacoma evening CALL. d S 20 1891-92||?
WaU S 25 1891-Ja 30 1892

COMMERCE. *See* Puyallup Valley tribune (Puyallup)

EVERY Sunday. w Mr 3 1889-F 20 1892||?
Wa Mr 10 1889
WaHi 1889-F 20 1892

FORUM. w 1903-20||?
Wa Ap 1907-15

Tacoma weekly GLOBE. w Ja 18 1887-92||?
Suspended from Ja-Ag 1889?
MWA S 13 1889
WaU F 28 1890-F 19 1892

Morning GLOBE. d O 3 1888-Je 30 1895||
O 3-21 1888 as Daily world
WaHi complete
WaU O 22 1888-My,N 1889-F 23 1892

Tacoma HERALD. w Ja 6 1877-Mr 26 1880||
Follows Echo (Olympia)
CU-B Ag-D 1878
WaU Ap 1877-80

Tacoma HERALD. w 1891+
1891-1931 as Tacoma new herald
pub 1915-32
Wa My 1905-20;22-32
WaPS Ap 5 1919[29-30]
WaU 1892-Ap 23 1898
—annual numbers.
WaT 1905-06;08-09

Tacoma JOURNAL. w Ag 27 1926+
1926-F 1 1929 as Pierce county journal
pub 1926+

Tacoma weekly LEDGER. w Ap 21 1880-86||?
CU-B Ap 21-My 7,Jl 23,Ag 27,S 10,O 1-8 1880;F 25,My 20 1881;Jl-N 12 1886
MWA N 5 1886
Wa S 30 1881
WaHi 1880-Ap 1883
WaT 1880-Ap 14 1882
WaU 1880-Mr 1884

Tacoma daily LEDGER. d Ap 7 1883+
CU-B Ag 1,N 11 1886;Ja 12,Jl 31-N 20 1887;Ja 1 1889;Je 14 1890;Mr 18,S 2 1892
Ct Ja 13 1909
DLC 1893+
M S 19 1931
TJT D 25,28 1898;My 1-2 1899
TxGR Ja 13 1909
WHi Ja 13 1909
Wa Ja 16 1885;Jl 5 1887;Ag 1891-Je,S 1892-Ap,Jl 1896-Ja,Mr 1922-O,D 1924-Ap,Je 1925-Jl,S 1928+
WaHi 1883+
WaPS 1904-[16-19;22-23;25]My 3 1928;My 1 1931;Je 18,Jl 5 1932
WaT 1883-[91]-[97-98]+
WaU [1883-Mr 1884]Mr 27 1886;Ja-Je,Ag 26 1892;Ja 9,My 2,Jl-S 1893;Ja 11-Mr,Je 19,Jl 1894-Ap 1895;96;F 10 1897;O 1918-S 1920

NEW era. bw Jl 1932-Ap 1933||
Some numbers as U.C.L. chronicle
WaU Ag 1932-33

Tacoma NEW herald. *See* Tacoma herald

Tacoma NEWS. w Ag 10 1881-1909||?
1881-Ag 4 1882 as Pierce county news
CU-B Ag 18-25 1882;Mr 1 1883;Ja 20-Je 1,15-Jl 6,20-Ag,S 21-N 2,D 4 1888;89-91;F 19 1892
WaHi 1881-O 19 1882
WaU D 28 1881-S 20 1883
—d ed *See* Tacoma news-tribune

Tacoma NEWS-TRIBUNE. d S 25 1883+
1883-Je 16 1918 as Tacoma daily news
CLM S 20 1902
CU-B Ja 24 1885
DLC Ag 25 1890-98
ICHi Ja 16 1905
TJT Je 29 1905
Wa Ja-Mr 1903;Ja-Mr,Jl 1904-Ap,Jl 1909-F,My-Jl,N 1910-Ap,Jl 1911-Mr,My 1912-Mr,My 1913-F,My-Je 1918;31-S 1932;N 1933+
WaHi 1883+
WaPS [1904-11]-[16-18]-[20-23]-[25-27]-[29]+
WaT [Ap 1900-02]+
WaU Mr 21-S 24 1884;O 8 1891;Jl 4,Ap 29 1892;Ap 7 1893;94-Mr 1895;1917;Jl 1918-Mr,S 22-D 1919

NORTH END news. w Je 1922+
pub 1922+

NORTH Pacific times. w Ag 15 1878-79||?
WaU 1878-Ja 10 1879

NORTHERN light. w Jl? 1889-91||?
1889? pub in Spokane. Also dated in Seattle
CU-B O 11-N 1 1890

Weekly PACIFIC tribune. *See under* Seattle

Daily PACIFIC tribune. *See* Tribune (Seattle)

PIERCE county journal. *See* Tacoma journal

PIERCE county news. *See* Tacoma news

Tacoma POSTEN. *See* Puget Sound posten

PUGET SOUND posten. w N 10? 1905-Ja 1936||
1905-Ag 1907 as Tacoma posten. United with Svenska journalen (Seattle) to form Svenska posten
In Swedish and English
IRA 1907-18;21-36
MnHi D 31 1908-[20]Mr 2 1928
WaTS [1905-36]

RYAN'S weekly. w Ap 1920+
pub 1921+
WaPS O 23-30,N 13-27 1926

SEARCHLIGHT. *See under* Seattle

SIXTH AVENUE news. w 1922+
Title varies: Sixth Avenue news district
pub 1922+

SOUTH SIDE advertiser. *See* South Tacoma star

SOUTH TACOMA star. w O 4 1922+
1922-My 14 1926 as South Side advertiser
pub 1922+
WaPS [1929-31]+

SPIRIT of '76. w
WHi D 3,17-24 1898;F 25 1899

Tacoma SUN. w 1892-1903||?
WaT [D 1893]Ja 12 1894
WaU Ag 4-11 1893;Mr 20 1897-Ap 28 1898

SVENSKA posten. *See under* Seattle

TACOMIAN. w N 26 1892-F 25 1893||
WaHi complete

Tacoma TIDENDE. *See* Western viking

Tacoma Sunday TIMES. w Je 10 1888-90||?
CU-B N 24 1889;Ag 9-16 1890

Tacoma TIMES. d 1903+
pub 1903+
WaPS [1918-19]Ja 3 1922;N 13 1923[24] [30-33]
WaT 1909+

Tacoma TRIBUNE. d 1907-Je 16 1918||
United with Tacoma daily news to form Tacoma news-tribune
Wa Ap 1913-18
WaHi Je 12 1908-18
WaPS [1916-18]
WaT Je 1908-18
WaTW Jl 1914-18
WaU 1917

Tacoma TRIBUNEN. w Ap 17 1890-Je 13 1902||
United with Westra posten (Seattle and Tacoma) to form Westerns tribun, later Svenska Pacific tribunen (Seattle)
In Swedish
IRA 1895-1900

U.C.L. chronicle. *See* New era

Tacoma morning UNION. d N 21 1893-Jl 31 1897||
CU-B O 1 1896
WaHi 1893-Je 1895
WaT [1894-96]-Je 1897
WaU complete

VESTKYSTEN. *See* Western viking

WACHT am sunde. w F 2 1884-1929||
pub in Seattle 1884-Ag 1885
WaPS [1917-20]-29

WASHINGTON posten. *See* Westra posten (Seattle)

WASHINGTON (*Continued*)

TACOMA—*Continued*

WESTERN viking. w Jl 5 1890+
1890-1925 as Tacoma tidende (1912-16 Tacoma tidende og vestkysten) 1925-D 18 1931 Vestkysten-Tacoma tidende
In Norwegian and English
pub [1890-1931]+
IaDeL O 20 1894[Mr 14 1896-97]D 23 1899 [1900-02]My 12 1905
WHi My 17 1896;O 1898-Je 17 1899
WaPS D 1913-O 14 1932

WESTRA posten. *See under* Seattle

Daily **WORLD.** *See* Morning globe

TEKOA

Tekoa **BLADE.** w 1903+
WaPS [1915-18]-[21]-[24]-33

GLOBE. w Mr 29 1889-97||?
CU-B [1892-93]F 17,Mr 10,31-Ap 1894

TENINO

Tenino **INDEPENDENT.** *See* Thurston county independent

Tenino **NEWS.** w 1904-24||?
WaPS [1916]-[18-24]
WaTeT [1904-10]

THURSTON county independent. w Je 1922+
1921-27 as Tenino independent
pub 1922+
WaPS [N 24 1922-24]-33

TOLEDO

COWLITZ RIVER pilot. *See* Winlock news and live wire (Winlock)

Toledo **MESSENGER.** w 1910+
WaPS D 15 1915-[18]F 26-D 1926;28-33

TOLT

Tolt **ENTERPRISE.** w 1912-31||?
WaPS [1916-18]My 10 1929-Ja 23 1931

TONASKET

Tonasket **TIMES and Okanogan record.** w 1913+
1913-15? as Tonasket times
WaPS [1915-19]-[21-33]

TOPPENISH

Toppenish **REVIEW.** w 1904+
pub 1910+
Wa 1910+
WaPS [1915]-[18]-33

Toppenish **TRIBUNE.** w 1910+
pub 1917+
WaPS [1916-17;19]Ja 9 1929

TOUCHETT

WALLA WALLA county enterprise. w O 14 1927+
pub 1927+
WaPS D 21 1928-33

TWISP

METHOW VALLEY news. w 1903+
Wa Mr 1913-S 1917;Ja-S 1918

UNIONTOWN

Uniontown **JOURNAL.** w 1920+
WaPS N 25 1922-33

VALLEY

Valley **RECORD.** w 1920+
WaPS N 12-19 1925;30-33

VALLEYFORD

Valleyford **REPORTER.** w 1926+
WaPS [1931]-33

VANCOUVER

Vancouver **CHRONICLE.** 1860-61 *See* Vancouver telegraph

Vancouver **CHRONICLE.** w 1905-10||?
United with Vancouver independent to form Independent-chronicle

CLARKE county register. w N 17 1881-F 28 1884||?
Not to be confused with Vancouver register
WaS [1881-F 1884]

CLARKE county sun. w 1906+
1906-13? as Washougal sun (Washougal)
pub F 21 1913+
WaPS [1917-27]-Mr 20 1931

Vancouver **COLUMBIAN.** w S 27 1889-1926||?
pub complete
CU-B O 17 1870
Wa Jl 1901-O 1908

Vancouver evening **COLUMBIAN.** d O 21 1906+
1906-My 10 1921 as Daily Columbian
pub 1906+
OrHi My 1911-26
Wa O 1908-21
WaPS [1919-23]-N 10 1926

DOWNEY'S weekly bulletin. *See* Vancouver optimist

Vancouver **INDEPENDENT-CHRONICLE.** w S 4 1875-1913||?
1875-1910? as Vancouver independent
CU-B 1875-O 1877;Ap 25 1878-D 11 1879;Je 17 1880;Mr-Ag 3 1882;Ja-Je 1886;Ag-D 1888; F 1889-Je 1891
OrHi Jl 22 1876-Ja 10 1878
WaU [S 11 1875-F 1884]
WaVD 1875-1910

Vancouver **OPTIMIST.** w 1909-21||?
1909-Ja 1918 as Bulletin; F 1918-20? Downey's weekly bulletin
1909-Ja 1918 pub in Battleground
WaPS [1915-20]

PACIFIC weekly censor. w My 1 1881-82||?
CU-B Je 26 1881

Vancouver **REGISTER.** w S? 1865-O 10 1890||
Not to be confused with Clarke county register. 1873-74? as Register and home
C D 12 1868
CU-B S 30,N 11-25,D 9-16 1865;Ja-Mr 24,Ap-S 1,29-O,N 17,D 8-22 1866;Ja 9,F 9,Mr 9,Ap 27-My 4,18-25,Je 8-15,Jl 20-27,Ag 24 1867;Mr 21,Je-Jl 4,18-Ag 1,15 1868-Jl 10,24-S 18,O 9-23,N 20-27,D 11 1869-70;Ja 14-Jl 1,15,29-Ag 5 1871;F 10,N 23 1872;Mr 27,My 8-O 23,N 20-D 4,18 1874-Ja 15,F 12-Ap 2,16-Je,Jl 9-S 24,O 15 1875;Je 5 1889
DLC Ap 24 1869-70
OrHi [1865-70]
WaU Mr 17-24 1866;My 22,Je 19 1869;Ja 8,F 5 1870;D 25 1874;F 19-O 1875
WaVD 1865-69

Vancouver **TELEGRAPH.** w Jl 1860-
1860-N 1861 as Vancouver chronicle
DLC S-N 15,D 14-27 1861;F-Mr,Ap 11-My 2 1862

VASHON

VASHON ISLAND news-record. w 1916+
1916-20? as Vashon Island record
WaPS [1929]-33

VASHON ISLAND record. *See* Vashon Island news-record

WAITSBURG

Waitsburg **TIMES.** d,w Mr 11 1878+
d 1889?
pub Mr 11 1884+
CU-B D 13 1878-F 21,Je 20-Jl 4,18,Ag-S 12, 26 1879-Ja 23 1880;Mr 1-22,Je 28,Jl 5 1889;Ja 10,24,F 21 1890
WaPS Mr 21-28 1919;Ap 2 1920;D 5 1924;N 26 1926;Mr 20,N 29 1929-33

WALLA WALLA

Walla Walla **ARGUS.** w 1898-1908||?
OrHi [1898-1906]

Walla Walla daily **BULLETIN.** d F 12 1906+
1906-10? as Evening bulletin
pub 1906+
Wa Mr 1909-S 1911
WaPS [1916-21]Mr 3 1923;24-[32-33]
WaW 1906+
WaWW 1912+

INLAND journal. w 1916-19||?
WaW [Mr-Jl 5 1918]

Morning **JOURNAL.** d Je 2 1881-90||
United with Walla Walla daily union to form Union morning journal, later Walla Walla union
CU-B Ja 2 1889;Ja 4,6 1890
OrHi 1881-86

JOURNAL and watchman. w 1883-90||?
1883-Ap? 1885 as Walla Walla watchman. United with Walla Walla union to form Weekly union-journal, later Walla Walla union
CU-B Ap 24 1885-Ap 20,S 23-30,O 21 1887

Saturday **RECORD.** w 1894-1908||?
OrHi 1900-06

SPIRIT of the west. w,sw D 1872-Ap? 1876||
Followed by Walla Walla watchman
w 1873-N? 1875
CU-B Ap 24-My 15,Je 5 1873;74-Ap,My 14,28-Jl 1875
NNHi Jl 17 1873

Walla Walla **STATESMAN.** w N 29 1861-Ap 1910||
1861-N 9 1865 as Washington statesman
C F 19 1869
CU-B N 22,D 6-13 1862;My 9,30-S 5,19-O 17,N 14,28 1863;Ja 30-Ap 15,My-Jl 8,29-Ag 12,26 1864-Je 9,Jl 7,Ag 18,S 29,N 24 1865;Ja 19,F 9-My 11,25-Je 22,Jl 13-O 5,19,N 1866-67;70-F 17,N 3 1877;F 8 1879-D 18 1880;89
DLC D 27 1867[68]
MWA Jl 26 1862
OrHi [1861-63]-[65]-[71-73]-80;Ap 1882[84;86] Ag 15 1891-Ja 6 1900
WaU Ap 19,S 1862-[68-69;75-82]-F 1884;Ja 28,O 1904-[05]07

Evening **STATESMAN.** d F 1880-1911||?
CU-B Ag 19 1880-Ja 1 1881;86-91
OrHi Je 17 1882-N 22 1883[91-92]-99;S 8 1900-Ag 1903;04-F 1906
Wa Jl 1891-94;1903-Ap 1910;Ja-Mr 1911
WaU F 6-29 1904;F,Ap-My,Jl-S 1905;Jl,S,N 1907,S-N 1908;Je 1909
WaW [Mr 1906-Ap 16 1910]

Walla Walla **TIMES.** d 1922-25||?
WaPS [1923-24]
WaW [O 1922-N 2 1924]

Walla Walla **UNION.** w Ap 17 1869-1908||?
1890?-1903? as Weekly union-journal
CU-B 1869-[Ja-Jl 9 1870]My 27 1871;Ap 11 1874
DLC Mr 9 1872-74
OrHi [1894-1901]
WaU My 22,D 4,18 1869;Je 18 1870[N 1871-73]-77[84]-O 23 1886;Je 25 1887-89[Ap 16 1892-Ag 12 1893]

Walla Walla **UNION.** d O 10 1881+
1891?-92? as Morning union-journal (other slight variations)
pub 1881-95]+
CU-B O 1 1885;D 27 1886
OrHi [D 15 1881-99;1901-03]05-Je 14 1913
Wa Ag 1891-Ap 1894;1904-10;F 1911-Jl,O 1914+
WaPS My 1912-15;My 30 1916[18-19]S 21 1920;Ap 19 1924;Ap 24 1925[26-28]My 24 1929; Ap 12 1930;Je 10 1933
WaU [Mr 1884]My 20 1891;Ja 9 1892
WaW [D 15 1905+]

WASHINGTON democrat. d 1882-Je? 1883||
OrHi [Ja 10-Je 8 1883]

WASHINGTON statesman. *See* Walla Walla statesman

Walla Walla **WATCHMAN.** sw,w My 27 1876-Ap 17? 1885||
Follows Spirit of the west. United with Walla Walla journal to form Journal and watchman
sw 1876-Ja 6 1877
CU-B Je 22 1877;O 22 1880;Je 27,Ag 1884-Ap 10 1885
DLC Ja 6 1877
OrHi Je 24 1876-Ap 7 1882;Ja 26 1883-Ap 17 1885
WaU O 28 1876;Ag 17 1877;Mr 1[Jl-S]1878;N 7,D 19 1879[80-Ap 10 1885]

Walla Walla **WATCHMAN.** w 1894-1900||?
OrHi My 14 1897-S 4 1900

WALLULA

Wallula **GATEWAY.** w 1905+
WaPS N 24 1922-[24]-[27-28]S 1930-33

Wallula weekly **HERALD.** w N 30 1888-
CU-B S 6-13,N 15 1889;Ja 3 1890

WAPATO

Wapato **INDEPENDENT.** w Mr 1906+
pub 1906+
WaPS N 24 1922-33

WARDEN

Warden **HERALD.** w 1910-22||?
WaPS N 17 1915;Ja 21-F 1916

WASHOUGAL

Washougal **RECORD.** w 1919-Je 1930||
United with Camas post (Camas) to form Camas post-Washougal record (Camas)
WaPS [1922-23]-F 19 1930

Washougal **SUN.** *See* Clarke county sun (Vancouver)

WASHTUCNA

Washtucna **ENTERPRISE.** w 1902-25||?
WaPS F 20 1914[15-16]-[18 21-24]

Washtucna **RECORDER.** w 1927+
WaPS 1930-33

WATERVILLE

BIG BEND empire. *See* Waterville empire-press

DOUGLASS county press. w 1902-My 1921||?
United with Big Bend empire to form Waterville empire-press
WaPS O 1915-[16-20]-My 1921

Waterville **EMPIRE-PRESS.** w Ja 1888+
1888-My 1921? as Big Bend empire
CU-B N 28-D 12 1889
Wa S 1909+
WaPS [1915-18]O 26 1922;F 26 1925[27]S 25 1930

WENATCHEE

Wenatchee **FRUIT GROWER.** w 1923-D 4 1931||
Merged with Wenatchee sun
WaPS Mr 5(supp)1926[27-31]

Wenatchee **PRESS.** w 1924-25||?
WaPS D 26 1924[25]

Wenatchee **REPUBLIC.** w 1898-1914||?
Wa Ag 1901-S 1903;O 1904-10
WaWe 1903-10

Wenatchee **REPUBLIC.** d 1911-14||?
Wa 1911-Mr 1914
WaWe 1911-13

WASHINGTON (*Continued*)

WENATCHEE—*Continued*

Wenatchee SUN. w,d 1920+
w 1920-24;26-S 19 1933
pub 1920+
WaPS [1925-26]+
WaWe My 21 1921+

Wenatchee daily WORLD. d 1905+
pub 1905+
WaPS [1914+]
Wa F 1911+
WaWe 1912+

WEST SEATTLE

Papers published in West Seattle are listed under Seattle

WHATCOM

Papers published in Whatcom are listed under Bellingham

WHITE BLUFFS

White Bluffs SPOKESMAN. w 1907+
WaPS D 3 1915-[1916-19]Ja 2 1920;N 24 1922-[24]+

WHITE SALMON

White Salmon ENTERPRISE. w 1903+
WaPS [1917-31]+

WILBUR

Wilbur REGISTER. w Mr 1889+
pub 1889+
CU-B Ag 8-15 1890
Wa D 1909-13;Jl 1915-Ag 1916;17-20
WaPS [1918-24]-[27-30]+

WILSON CREEK

Wilson Creek WORLD. w 1907+
WaPS O 1915-[17-24;29-30]

WINLOCK

Winlock NEWS and live wire. w 1886+
1886?-87? as Cowlitz River pilot; 1888?-F 1908 Winlock pilot
1886-87? pub in Toledo
pub [1895-1919]+
WaPS [1921-24]26+

Winlock PILOT. *See* Winlock news and live wire

WINONA

Winona NEWS. w 1907-20‖?
WaPS [1915-16]

WINSLOW

BAINBRIDGE ISLAND beacon. w 1921-25‖?
WaPS Je 30 1922[23-24]

WINTHROP

METHOW VALLEY journal. w Ag 1 1912+
pub 1912+
WaPS [1916-17;22-27]+

WITHROW

Withrow BANNER. w 1910-24‖?
WaPS Jl 4 1913-[15]-O 12 1923

WOODLAND

LEWIS RIVER news. w 1919+
Wa Mr 1919-Ag 1929;Ap 1930+
WaL F 13 1929+
WaPS N 30 1922-[25]+

WOOLLEY

Papers published in Woolley are listed under Sedro-Woolley

YACOLT

LEWIS RIVER times. w 1923-29‖?
WaPS [1923-25]F 16 1929

YAKIMA

To D 31 1917 as North Yakima

Yakima DEMOCRAT. w 1895-1910‖?
1895-98? as Epigram
CU-B F 26 1898

EPIGRAM. *See* Yakima democrat

Yakima weekly HERALD. w F 2 1889-D 25 1912‖
pub complete

Yakima morning HERALD. d Ja 2 1906+
1906-17 as Yakima daily herald
pub 1906+
WaPS D 1915-Ag 1916;D 1918-Mr 1919;S 1921-My 1922;F 3 1923;Mr-O 1924;25;N 1926-My 1927;28-33
WaY Je 1915+

Yakima INDEPENDENT. w 1893+
WaPS D 17 1915[16;23-30;32-33]

Yakima RECORD. *See* Yakima weekly republic

Yakima weekly REPUBLIC. w S 6 1879-1919‖
1879-F 1884 as Yakima record
pub O 11 1899-S 1903
CU-B Mr 1-22,Ap-My 3,17 1889;Ja 10-24,F 7,My 16,O 3-10,24 1890
Wa N 1902-Mr 1919
WaU S 6 1879;F 1880-Ja 22,My 28,O 1[D 1881-My]N 10 1883-F 1884

Yakima daily REPUBLIC. d O 12 1903+
pub 1903+
Wa D 2 1907
WaPS S 23 1914[16;18-19;21-23]Ap 1926-S 1927;S 1928-33
WaY Ap 1 1905+

North Yakima SIGNAL. w Ja 6 1883-88‖
1883-84 as Yakima signal
WaU [1883-F 9 1884]

YAKIMA VALLEY farm news. *See* Yakima Valley farmer

YAKIMA VALLEY farmer. w 1918?+
Title varies: Yakima Valley farm news; Yakima Valley news-review and Yakima Valley farm news
WaPS [1918-19;23-25;27-28]

YAKIMA VALLEY news-review and Yakima Valley farm news. *See* Yakima Valley farmer

YELM

NISQUALLY VALLEY news. w 1922+
WaPS [1923]Mr 31 1927;Mr 6 1930+

ZILLAH

Zillah MIRROR. w 1920+
WaPS N 30 1922+

WEST VIRGINIA

ALDERSON

Alderson ADVERTISER. w 1897+
pub 1897+
Wv My 1913-F 1917

BECKLEY

MESSENGER. w 1910-17‖?
Wv Mr 1910-17

Beckley POST-HERALD. d 1924+
1924-25 as Evening post
pub Jl 1931+
WvU F 1924+

RALEIGH county index. *See* Raleigh register

RALEIGH herald. w,sw 1900-25‖
United with Evening post to form Beckley post-herald
w 1900-23?
Wv O 1907-18

RALEIGH register. w,sw,tw,d 1880+
1880-1898 as Raleigh county index
w 1880-1921?;sw 1922?;tw 1923?-27?
pub 1914+
Wv 1911-19;21-30
WvU 1907-S 1921

BELINGTON

CENTRAL republican. w 1901-10‖?
WvBelC 1901-10

CENTRAL-STATE news. w Ap 1912+
1912-27 as Belington progressive
pub 1912-27;30+

Belington OBSERVER. w 1904-09‖?
WvBelC 1903-08

Belington PROGRESSIVE. *See* Central-state news

BENWOOD

Benwood ENTERPRISE. w 1895-1920‖?
Wv My 1913-19

BERKELEY SPRINGS

MORGAN mercury. w 1869-93‖?
InRE O 19 1889
NcD S 5 1874

MORGAN messenger. w 1893+
pub 1893+
Wv N 1912-19;21+

Berkeley Springs NEWS. w 1885+
pub 1933+
NcD O 10 1924
WvBerM 1886+

POST. w 1906-16‖?
Wv 1907-16

BLUEFIELD

SUNSET news and times leader. d S 1926+
1926? as Sunset news
pub 1926+

Bluefield daily TELEGRAPH. d 1893+
pub 1893+
VHi Ag 20 1916
VU F 1 1907
Wv 1911-23;29+
WvAC 1933+
WvBl 1916-Ag 1933
WvU 1932+

TWIN CITY advance and Mercer recorder. w 1921+
1921-32 as Mercer recorder (Matoaka)
pub 1933+

BRAXTON

SUTTON mountaineer. w 1876-83‖?
1876-82? pub in Sutton
DLC Mr 18 1881

BUCKHANNON

Buckhannon BANNER. *See* Buckhannon record

DELTA. *See* Republican-delta

KNIGHT-ERRANT. w 1897-98‖?
United with Delta to form Delta and knight-errant, later Republican-delta

Buckhannon NEWS. sw 1929+
Wv 1929+

Buckhannon RECORD. w 1876+
1876-Mr 1914 as Buckhannon banner; Ap 1914-21? Upshur record
DLC My 27 1881
Wv 1907-19

REPUBLICAN-DELTA. w 1869+
1869-1928? as Delta (1899?-1917? Delta and knight-errant)
pub 1929+
DLC Jl 8 1880

UPSHUR record. *See* Buckhannon record

UPSHUR republican. w 1901-28‖?
United with Delta to form Republican-delta
Wv Je 1913-19

BUFFALO

Buffalo INDEPENDENT. w 1866?-
MWA Ja 3 1867

STAR of the Kanawha Valley. *See* Kanawha Valley star (Charleston)

BURNSVILLE

Burnsville ENTERPRISE. w 1913?-14‖?
Wv My 1913-Je 1914

CABELL COURT HOUSE

CABELL democrat. w Ja 6?- 1881‖?
DLC F 3 1881

CAIRO

Cairo ENTERPRISE. w 1904-29‖?
Wv 1911-12

RITCHIE democrat. w 1877-89‖?
DLC Ag 14 1880

CEREDO

Ceredo ADVANCE. w S 18 1885+
pub 1885+
Wv Jl 1916-19;21;36+

Ceredo CRESCENT. w O 24 1857-
MWA O 24 1857;My 15,Je 26-Jl 10,Ag 7,D 11-18 1858;Jl 9,Ag 20 1859;O 13-20 1860

CHARLES TOWN

FARMERS' advocate. w 1885+
pub 1885-1931
NcD [1908-09;18;20-27]Mr 3 1928
Wv 1913-19

FARMERS' repository. w Ap 1 1808-Mr 1 1827‖
1808-20? as Farmer's repository. United with Virginia free press to form Virginia free press and farmers' repository, later Virginia free press
DLC 1821-Mr 1827
NcD Jl 24 1822;S 14 1825

WEST VIRGINIA (*Continued*)

CHARLES TOWN—*Continued*

GUIDON. (Camp of 12th Pennsylvania Cavalry) w D 1? 1864-
WHi D 29 1864

SPIRIT of Jefferson. w Jl 17 1844+
DLC 1844-Ja 8,Ap 5 1853-Jl 17 1855;N 7 1865-1902;Ja-Je 18 1920
MWA Ag 22 1854;My 18 1869
MsHi 1844-61
NbHi S 3,N 5 1872;Ag 12 1873;Ap 7,My 26,Je 30,S 22 1874;D 28 1875;O 16 1877
NcD [1844-47;49-53;55-57;67-68;70;72-73;81;86-89;92-93;1900;07-10;17-29]
OClWHi O 7 1925
Wv Je 1906-19;21

VIRGINIA free press. w Je 23 1821-1918||?
1821-24? as Harpers-Ferry free press; Mr 7 1827-32? Virginia free press and farmers' repository
1821-27? pub in Harpers Ferry
Suspended from 1862?-Ag 24 1865?
CSmH Ja 2 1844
DLC Mr 31,D 1 1824;Mr 7,Ag 29 1827;D 3(extra)1828;Je 24,Jl 15-22,Ag 26,S 23,D 2 1829;Ja 6-13 1830;Je 23,Ag 25 1831;N 8 1832;N 12 1840;Ap 22 1841;Mr 3 1842;O 27 1847;F 21 1851;My 6 1852;Ag 10,N 23 1854;Ap 26 1855;F 19 1857;Mr 4 1858;Ap 28,S 1,O 6,27,D 1,22 1859;Ja 5,My 9 1860;Ag 24 1865-1902
IU S 28 1843;My 2 1844;N 3 1847;Ap,Je 6-14 1848;N 5 1857;Ja 28 1858;My 2,30,Je 13 1861
MBAt Ja 15 1822
MWA Je 30,Jl 17 1821;S 29,D 22 1824;O 18-25 1826;Jl 8,29 1829;F 17-24,Mr 17,Jl 7 1830;My 19,Jl 7 1831;Mr 8,Ag 9,S 20,O 11,N 15 1832;F 14-21,Ap 11,Ag 15,O 17,D 5 1833;Mr 6,Ap 17,My 1,Je 12,26,Ag 7,N 6,D 4 1834;O 15 1835;Ja 14,Ap 21,S 15,O 13 1836;Mr 2-9,S 7,N 23,D 14 1837;Ap 12,Je 14,Jl 12,S 6,O 18,N 29-D 6 1838[39-41]Mr 17-31,Ap 28,Jl 21-28,S 15,29,N 3 1842;D 5,19 1844;My 25 1848;O 6 1859;Ja 23 1862;F 10 1877
MsHi Ag 13 1857;S 16 1871
NN Ap 15 1841;F 4 1858;F 27 1862
NbHi O 19 1872;D 26 1874[75-78]Ap 19,My 31,Jl 12 1879;Jl 8 1882[83-84;86-87]Ja 5 1888;My 2 1889;Ap 2 1890;F 25,My 27 1891;Ja 25,F 8,22-Mr 1 1893;Mr 14,S 12-17 1894;Ag 3,31,S 21 1898;S 6,N 8,29,D 20 1899[1900-05]F 15,My 10 1906
NcD Ag 9 1832;Jl 17 1834;Mr 3 1836[Mr 1837-Ap 1861;Ag 1865-68;72-1910]F 9 1911;Jl 8 1915
NcU O 4 1826
OClWHi F 27 1862
OHi My 12,Je 30 1853;Ap 26,Je 28 1866
V Ja 15 1862;Jl 26 1866
VU Jl 22 1876
Wv Mr 1911-18

WEST VIRGINIA democrat. w 1855-89||?
NcD Je 25 1886;My 6 1887;Jl 19 1889

CHARLESTON

Charleston ARGUS. w Ap 24 1835-
DLC My 22 1835
NcD My 15,S 4 1835

BIMETALIST. w 1895-96||?
Wv N 22 1895-O 1896

Charleston GAZETTE. w 1877-1915||?
1877-99? as Kanawha gazette
DLC N 24 1880
NcD F 6-20 1878;F 2 1881;O 1 1884;Ja 27 1886;D 7,21 1887;Ja 11,25-F 1,Ap 25,S 26,O 31 1888

Charleston GAZETTE. d 1887+
1887-O 22 1905? as Charleston daily gazette Je 19 1932 is capitol dedication ed
pub Je-Ag,O 1920-N 1932;24-Mr,My 19 1925-O,D 1929-Ja,Mr,My 1934-Jl,O 1935+
DLC 1898+
M Je 19 1932
NNHi Je 19 1932
NcD Je 30 1899;Jl 22 1900;O 22 1905;D 19 1919
PPiHi Je 19 1932
T Je 19 1932
WHi Je 19 1932
Wv O 1891-Mr 1892;1906+
WvAC Je 1936+
WvU Mr 1934+

GREENBACK league and courier. w 1878-80||?
1878-79? as Greenback league

HERALD. *See* Charleston sun herald

INDEPENDENT democrat. w O 4 1859-
DLC 1859-Ag 21 1860
IU F 21 1860

JEFFERSONIAN. *See* Kanawha Jeffersonian

KANAWHA banner. *See* Kanawha patriot

KANAWHA chronicle. d,w 1871-77||?
1871-72? as Kanawha daily (d)
NcD Jl 2,Ag 13 1873;Ap 1 1874;Ja 17 1877
Wv Ja-Ap 1872;Mr 1873-77

KANAWHA citizen.
Wv Jl 1912-Ap 1914

KANAWHA daily. *See* Kanawha chronicle

KANAWHA gazette. *See* Charleston gazette (1877-1915)

KANAWHA Jeffersonian. w My 2? 1840-
1840-Ja? 1841 as Jeffersonian
CSmH Mr 30(extra)1847
DLC My 16,Jl 11 1840
NcD S 4 1841
NhD Ja 23 1841

KANAWHA patriot. w 1826?-
1826?-Jl 10? 1829 as Western Virginian; Jl 17? 1829-My? 1830 Western register; Je?-Ag? 1830 Kanawha register; S? 1830-Ap 1835? Kanawha banner
CSmH Je 4 1830
DLC N 1 1832;Jl 18 1833;Ap 3 1834;Jl 29 1840
MBAt O 4 1832
MWA F 18 Ag 14 1829
Wv Jl 1826-32;N 1833-Ap 1835

KANAWHA register. *See* Kanawha patriot

KANAWHA republican. w 1842-73||?
DLC Mr 14-O 24 1866
NcD S 27,D 4 1854;Je 20,Jl 10,O 16 1855;F 18,Mr 24,My 15 1860
Wv [1842-50]

KANAWHA VALLEY gazette. w Ap 25 1839-
DLC Ap 25,My 2 1839

KANAWHA VALLEY star. w Ja 3 1855-61||
1855-Ap? 1856 as Star of the Kanawha Valley
Ja-Mr? 1855 pub in Buffalo
NcD My 9,Je 13 1855;Mr 19 1856;My 4 1858;Jl 9 1860;Ap 30 1861
Wv Je 1857-Jl 1861
WvU 1855-Jl 1861

Charleston LEADER. w 1879-84||?
DLC D 23 1880

Charleston LEADER. d 1917-18||?
Wv 1917-N 1918

Charleston MAIL. w,sw 1881-1922||?
1881-91? as State tribune; 1892?-98? Star-tribune; 1899-1901? Mail-tribune
w 1881-1901?
ICM Je 2 1883
NcD D 11 1887
Wv 1881-S 1883;F 1900-22

Charleston daily MAIL. d Je 22 1893+
1898-1901? as Mail-tribune; Je 19 1932 is capitol dedication ed
pub 1921+
M Je 19 1932
NNHi Je 19 1932
NcD Je 15 1904;O 24 1926
T Je 19 1932
WHi Je 19 1932
Wv D 1893-Je 1896;1902-18;20+
WvAC Je 1935+
WvU Ag 1931+

Charleston morning NEWS. d 1905-07||?
Wv Jl 1906-Jl 1907

Charleston POST. d 1915?-17||?
Wv F 1915-Je 1917

SPIRIT of the times. w
NhD Ap 3 1841

STAR of the Kanawha Valley. *See* Kanawha Valley star

Charleston STAR-TRIBUNE. d 1881-97||?
1881-91? as Charleston star
ICM Ag 28 1885
NcD Mr 11 1887

STAR-TRIBUNE. w *See* Charleston mail

STATE tribune. *See* Charleston mail

Charleston SUN herald. w 1913-17||?
1915? as Herald
Wv Ap 1916-Ja 1917

WEST VIRGINIA courier. w 1869-79||?
United with Greenback league to form Greenback league and courier
NcD My 3 1871;D 11 1872;Ap 10 1878
Wv [1876-78]

WEST VIRGINIA journal. w 1864-78||?
NcD My 17 1871;Ja 31,F 21,D 11 1872;Ja 15-22,F 12,Mr 12-Ap 2 1873;Ja 12,Mr 8,My 10,24,Je 14 1876

WESTERN courier. w 1822?-
DLC D 2 1823;F 10,Mr 25,Je 8 1824;Ag 6 1828 Jl 15,24,Ag 7,14,28,O 30,D 4 1829
N Mr 2 1825
Wv Jl 11 1822-Jl 1 1823

WESTERN register. *See* Kanawha patriot

WESTERN Virginian. *See* Kanawha patriot

CLARKSBURG

CONSERVATIVE. w 1866-74||?
WvU F 1866-S 1868

COOPER'S Clarksburg register. w 1851-
DLC N 3 1852
WvU N 1851-N 1858

Clarksburg ENQUIRER. w 1827-
DLC Jl 4,18,S 5-19,O 31,N 21-28-D 12,26 1829;Ja 1-9,23 1830

Clarksburg EXPONENT. d My 10 1910+
Sunday issues as Exponent-telegram
pub 1910+
Wv 1911+

EXPONENT-TELEGRAM. *See* Clarksburg telegram; Clarksburg exponent

Clarksburg GAZETTE. w Je? 1822-
DLC O 19-26 1822

HARRISON republican. w 1843?-48||?
V D 29 1843[44-48]
Wv D 1843-D 1844

HARRISON whig. w Ag 20 1840-
DLC Ag 27 1840

*INDEPENDENT Virginian. w Ag 4 1819-
DLC O 14 1824

Clarksburg INTELLIGENCER. w 1823-
DLC S 20,N 1,15 1823-25
N S 10,O 1,15,29 1825
NcD My 15,29,Je 5,Jl 3 1824

NATIONAL telegraph. *See* Clarksburg telegram

Clarksburg NEWS. w
Wv [1866-67]

Clarksburg NEWS. w 1876?-1910||?
DLC Jl 10 1880
Wv 1878-79;91-92;99;1904-S 1910

Clarksburg daily POST. d 1902||?
Wv S-D 1902

SCION of democracy. w
NhD Ap 23 1841

Clarksburg TELEGRAM. w,d 1861+
1861-75? as National telegraph
w 1861-N 1902
Sunday issues as Exponent-telegram
pub Ag 9 1867+
DLC Ja-D 5 1862;My 27-Je 10,29 1864;Ja 20-27,Mr 10,My 5,Je 30 1865;68;N 27 1880
Wv Mr 1865-Ag 1906;My 1922+

Clarksburg VIRGINIAN. w
NhD Ja 16 1841

WESTERN enquirer. w My 1832-
DLC N 10 1832
MWA Ag 18 1832

CLAY

CLAY county press. w 1905+
pub O 1932+

Clay MESSENGER. w 1903+
Wv 1911-Ag 1917

DANVILLE

Danville PROGRESS. w 1910-27||?
Wv My 1913-19

DAVIS

Davis NEWS. w 1897+
Wv My 1913+

DUNBAR

Dunbar ADVANCE. *See* Kanawha Valley news

KANAWHA VALLEY news. w 1917+
1917-33? as Dunbar advance
Wv Je 1917-21
WvU 1934+

EAST RAINELLE

GREENBRIER despatch. w Ja 1930+
pub 1930+

ELIZABETH

Elizabeth GAZETTE. w
WvEK 1867-Ja 1 1868

KANAWHA news. w Ja 1 1893+
pub 1915+

Elizabeth MESSENGER. w 1886-1918||?
1886-99? as Elizabeth times; 1900?-04? Times-messenger. Merged with Kanawha news
Wv 1911-18

MOUNTAIN messenger. w 1896-99||?
United with Elizabeth times to form Times-messenger, later Elizabeth messenger

Elizabeth TIMES. *See* Elizabeth messenger

WIRT county journal. w 1908+
pub 1917+
Wv My 1913-19

ELIZABETHTOWN

MARSHALL beacon. *See under* Moundsville

WESTERN VIRGINIAN and people's press. w N 28 1833-
DLC D 19 1833;F 6,Mr 6 1834

ELK GARDEN

Elk Garden NEWS. w 1889-94||?
WvU [1889-92]

ELKINS

Elkins INTER-MOUNTAIN. w 1892-1929||?
Title varies slightly
WvU 1893-1903;09-27

Elkins INTER-MOUNTAIN. d O 1907+
Title varies slightly
pub 1924+
Wv 1911-Mr 1923;Ap 1929+

RANDOLPH enterprise. w My 1874+
pub 1874+
Wv 1911-S 1917;20+
WvU 1874+

RANDOLPH review. w My 1913+
pub 1913+

FAIRMONT

DEMOCRATIC banner. w
V My 18,Je 15 1850

FARMERS free press. w 1892-1934||?
1892-1911? as Fairmont free press
Wv My 1913-19

Fairmont FREE PRESS. *See* Farmers free press

INDEX. w 1873-1917||?
DLC Jl 2 1880

WEST VIRGINIA (*Continued*)

FAIRMONT—*Continued*

Fairmont TIMES. d 1900+
Sunday issues as Times-West Virginian
pub Jl 1902+
Wv D 11 1907-Ja 10 1908;My 10 1913-16;Ap 1929+

TIMES-WEST VIRGINIAN. *See* West Virginian; Fairmont times

Fairmont TRUE Virginian. w 1851?-
NcD F 11 1860
V S 15 1855;F 16 1856;My 15 1858;Ja 8 1859

WEST VIRGINIAN. w 1868-1906||?
DLC D 24 1880

WEST VIRGINIAN. d 1904+
Sunday issues as Times-West Virginian
Wv 1921+

FAYETTEVILLE

Fayetteville DEMOCRAT. w 1883+
pub 1884+
Wv Ap 1916+

Fayette ENTERPRISE. w 1875-86||?
DLC Je 15 1880
VU O 19 1877

FAYETTE free press. *See* Fayette tribune

FAYETTE journal. w 1890+
1890-95 as Fayette county journal
Wv Je 1906-Ag 1916

FAYETTE sun. w 1906-14||
Wv 1911-Jl 1914

FAYETTE tribune. w 1898+
1898-1908? as Fayette free press; 1909?-20? Tribune and free press
Wv 1913-19
WvAC Je 1936+
WvU Ap 1932-33

PICK and shovel. *See* State sentinel

STATE sentinel. w Ap 1920+
1920-Ja 1929 as Pick and shovel
pub 1920+
Wv current issues only

FELLOWSVILLE

BROAD-AX. w Ag 11? 1880-
DLC O 6 1880

FETTERMAN

UNION vanguard. w N 23 1866-
MWA N 23 1866

FOLLANSBEE

Follansbee REVIEW. w 1911+
1911-15 as Millstown and Follansbee review
pub Jl 1923+
Wv 1913+

FORT GAY

WAYNE advocate. w 1874?-
DLC Jl 1 1880

FRANKLIN

HERALD. w 1929+
pub 1929+

PENDLETON news. w 1875-79||?
DLC Ja 6 1876

PENDLETON times. w F 13 1913+
pub My 1924+
NcD O 10 1924
Wv My 1916-19

SOUTH BRANCH review. w 1894-1913||?
Wv 1911-O 1912

GERARDSTOWN

Gerardstown TIMES. w 1873?-1905||?
DLC Ag 28 1880

GLENVILLE

GILMER county review. w My? 1880-
DLC O 11 1880

GILMERITE. w 1879-83||?
DLC Jl 3 1880

Glenville PATHFINDER. w 1892+
pub 1926+
Wv 1911+

GRAFTON

EAGLE. w 1878-87||?
Merged with Sentinel
DLC My 20 1880

Grafton NEWS. w 1927+
1927-Ap 10? 1934 as Grafton press
pub Ap 17 1934+
Wv Ag 1934+
WvU S-O 1934

Grafton PRESS. *See* Grafton news

Grafton daily REPUBLIC. d 1907-10?
Wv Mr 4 1909-N 19 1910

SENTINEL. w 1868?+
DLC S 1 1877;My 29 1880
Wv 1868+

Grafton daily SENTINEL. d 1903+
Title varies slightly
pub 1907
Wv 1912-Mr 1921;Ap 1929+
WvU O 1907-Mr 1915;Jl 1916+

GRANTSVILLE

CALHOUN chronicle. w 1883+
pub 1900-03;06+
Wv 1911+

Grantsville NEWS. w 1898+
Wv 1911+
WvGS 1898+

GUYANDOTTE

Guyandotte HERALD and Cabell and Wayne advertiser. w 1853-
NcD Je 30 1854

INDEPENDENT. w Ap- 1871||?
NcD My 11 1871

WEST VIRGINIA chronicle. w Ag 23 1870-
MH Ag 1870

HARPERS FERRY

CONSTITUTIONALIST. w Ap 20 1839-
DLC Ap 20,My 8 1829;S 10 1840
NcD My 1,23-Je 12 1839;Ja 8-15,Jl 23,S 11,24 1840
NhD Ja 28 1841

Harpers-Ferry FREE PRESS. *See* Virginia free press (Charles Town)

Harpers Ferry SENTINEL. w 1887-97||?
1891?-94? as Saturday sentinel
MWA N 8 1890;Jl 9 1892

VIRGINIA free press. *See under* Charles Town

HARRISVILLE

Harrisville GAZETTE. w 1873+
1873-1903? as Ritchie gazette
DLC Jl 1 1880
Wv 1913-19

RITCHIE gazette. *See* Harrisville gazette

RITCHIE press. w 1859?-
DLC F 11-D 15 1864
MH S 4 1863;Ja 14 1864

HINTON

Hinton INDEPENDENT. w,sw 1884-90||?
United with Mountain herald to form Independent-herald
sw 1890?

INDEPENDENT-HERALD. w Ag 10 1872+
1872-90? as Mountain herald
pub Ag 1904+
DLC Jl 22 1880
NcD My 30 1878
Wv 1882-84;N 1891;My 1893-My 1894;My 1896; My 1913-19;21;36+

Hinton LEADER. w 1894+
Wv 1899+
WvU 1906+
—d ed *See* Hinton daily news

Hinton LEADER. d 1908-10||?
WvU 1908-10

MOUNTAIN herald. *See* Independent-herald

Hinton daily NEWS. d My 1902+
WvU 1902-Jl 1927
—w ed *See* Hinton leader

HUNTERSVILLE

POCOHONTAS times. w 1883-91||?
VU S 18-O 2,16-N,D 11-25 1884;Ja 15-22,F 12,Mr 4-12 1885

HUNTINGTON

Huntington ADVERTISER. w S 2 1869-1920||?
DLC Jl 10 1880
NNHi Ap 18 1878
Wv 1885-88

Huntington ADVERTISER. d S 2 1889+
Sunday issues as Herald-advertiser
pub 1889+
NcD Ag 7 1914
V Ap 27 1916
Wv S 1889-Ja 2 1891;Mr 1913-S 1923;Ap 1929+

Huntington ARGUS. w Ap 24 1872-1905||?
DLC Je 2 1880
OClWHi Jl 31 1872

CABELL county press. w
Wv Jl 1869-73

Huntington COMMERCIAL. w 1874-92||?
DLC Jl 9 1880

Huntington DISPATCH. d 1904-08||?
United with Huntington herald to form Huntington herald-dispatch

HERALD-ADVERTISER. *See* Huntington advertiser; Huntington herald-dispatch

Huntington HERALD-DISPATCH. d 1891+
1891-1908 as Huntington herald
Sunday issues as Herald-advertiser
pub 1909+
Wv 1911+

Huntington INDEPENDENT. w 1871-73||?
NcD Ja 23-30,Ap 3 1873

Huntington REVIEW. w 1902-09||?
WHi D 9 1903[Je 1907-Jl 3 1909]

Huntington TRIBUNE. w 1922+
pub 1927+

HURRICANE

Hurricane BREEZE. w 1900+
Wv My 1913;19+

JACKSON

Jackson HERALD. w 1876-97||?
DLC Ag 20 1880

KENOVA

Kenova REPORTER. w 1892+
Wv Jl 1916+

KEYSER

MINERAL news. d 1912+
pub 1912+
—w ed *See* Keyser tribune

MOUNTAIN echo. w 1876+
pub 1916+
DLC Ag 5 1880
KHi Mr 1889-N 7 1890
Wv My 1911-19;21

Keyser TRIBUNE. w 1869-1927||?
1869-80? as West Virginia tribune
DLC Ag 14 1880
Wv 1911-16
—d ed *See* Mineral news

WEST VIRGINIA tribune. *See* Keyser tribune

KEYSTONE

MCDOWELL times. w 1913+
Negro
Wv My 1913+

KINGWOOD

Kingwood CHRONICLE. w
Wv Ja 26-Ag 3 1861

PRESTON county journal. w 1866+
pub 1866+
DLC Ag 12 1880
Wv 1870+

PRESTON news. w 1909-16||?
Wv Je 1913-15

WEST VIRGINIA argus. w 1877+
DLC Ag 28 1880
Wv 1911-18

LEWISBURG

ALLEGHANIAN. w 1832-
DLC N 16 1832

BORDER journal. *See* Greenbrier independent

GREENBRIER independent. w 1866+
1866-71 as Border journal
pub S 1893+
DLC Jl 1 1880
ICM O 3 1878
MWA Ag 14 1879
NcD Ag 31 1893;My 7,S 20 1894;Ap 16 1896; O 20,N 24 1904-Mr 9,Ap 6-13,My 25-Je,Jl 13-27 1905;Ag 9 1906
VU S 25 1875
WHi [1880]
Wv Je 1866-89;1910-N 1918
WvU Je 1873-Je 1881;Ap 1932+

OBSERVER and western advertiser. w Mr 14 1844-
DLC Ap 11 1844
VU Mr 14 1844;Mr 6 1845

PALLADIUM of Virginia and the Pacific monitor. w N 18 1823-
CSmH S 3 1831
DLC F 11,O 18 1824;Jl 12,Ag 9,30,S 13,N 29 1828;Jl 11,25,S 12-19,O 3,N 23,D 19 1829;Ja 2-9,23 1830
N Ag 15,S 11 1825
NcD Ja 2 1830

Lewisburg TIMES. w 1865-70||?
V My 25 1867;Ap 22 1868

WESTERN enquirer and Virginia Spring gazette. w 1838?-
DLC Ap 24 1840

WESTERN whig. w Ag 14 1840-
DLC S 11,O 2 1840;Je 26 1841

LOGAN

Logan BANNER. w,sw,d 1889+
1889-1903? as Logan county banner; 1913?-15? Banner and republican
w 1889-1925?;sw 1926?-Ja 1935?
pub Ap 1921+
Wv Mr 1889-Jl 1904;Mr 24 1911-Je 11 1915
WvU F 1935+

Logan DEMOCRAT. w,sw 1906+
w 1906-22?
pub 1906+
Wv 1911-19
WvU 1934+

LOGAN county banner. *See* Logan banner

WEST VIRGINIA (*Continued*)

MADISON

BOONE democrat. w 1891-1912||?
Wv 1911-12

COAL RIVER news. w 1905-22||?
1905-21? as Coal River republican
Wv F-D 1911

COAL RIVER republican. *See* Coal River news

MANNINGTON

Mannington TIMES. w 1928+
pub 1928+

MARLINTON

Marlinton JOURNAL. w 1910+
1910-Mr 1915 as Pocohontas independent
Wv My 1913-O 1917

Marlinton MESSENGER. *See* Republican news

POCAHONTAS independent. *See* Marlinton journal

POCAHONTAS times. w 1881+
VU Mr 25,My 6-20 1898;Ja 31-F 7 1901;Je 7 1934
Wv 1911+

REPUBLICAN news. w 1900-14||?
1900-N? 1911 as Marlinton messenger
Wv 1906-07;11-Ja 1914

MARTINSBURG

AMERICAN union. Jl 4 1861-
pub by Federal troops
DLC Jl 4,6 1861
NNHi Jl 4-5,9,11 1861
PScrG Jl 4 1861
WHi Jl 9 1861

BERKELEY and Jefferson intelligencer. *See* Martinsburg gazette. 1799-

BERKELEY county news. *See* Martinsburg news

BERKELEY union. w 1865-72||?
DLC Ja 4 1867[68]

Martinsburg DEMOCRAT. w 1894-1906||
United with Martinsburg statesman to form Martinsburg Statesman-democrat

*Martinsburg GAZETTE. w Ap 3 1799-
1799-1809? as Berkeley intelligencer (title varies: Berkeley and Jefferson intelligencer; Berkeley and Jefferson intelligencer and Northern Neck advertiser) 1810?-29? Martinsburg gazette and public advertiser
CSmH Ag 26 1830
DLC D 4 1823;F 19 1824;S 8,23-N 3,17-D 1, 15-29 1825;Ag 30 1827;Jl 1,30,S 3-O 1,29-N 5,19,D 31 1829;Ja 28 1830;N 8 1832;D 3 1840
IU Ap 10,Je 5 1823
MnHi F 20 1845
NcD O 15 1829;Ja 21,F 11 1830
NhD Je 3 1841
OOxM Ap 30,Je 4,Jl 2,16 1829
PPL D 24 1850
Wv 1834-Ja 1843
WvMaC 1821-Ja 1826;27-34;F 26 1835-Mr 7 1855

Martinsburg daily GAZETTE. m,w,d 1886-Jl 30 1887||
1886-Mr 4? 1887 as Martinsburg gazette m 1886?;w Ja 7-Mr 4? 1887
WvMa O 30-D 11 1886;Ja 7-Mr 4,21-Jl 1887

Martinsburg HERALD. w 1881-1920||?
NbHi S 22 1883
NcD S 18 1886
WvMaC S 1884-1913

Martinsburg INDEPENDENT. w 1873-1900||?
WvMaC 1874-99

Martinsburg JOURNAL. d My 1 1908+
Title varies slightly
pub 1908+
NcD Ap 25,S 30 1911[18;22;25-26;28]
Wv 1914-Mr 1921
WvMa 1908+
WvMaC Jl 1927-Mr 1929
WvU 1932-34

Martinsburg NEWS. w 1931+
1931-My? 1934 as Berkeley county news
pub Je 1934—

PIONEER press. w 1882-1918||?
Negro
Wv 1911-S 1917

Martinsburg STATESMAN-DEMOCRAT. w 1869-1920||?
1869-1906 as Martinsburg statesman
DLC D 9 1880
N Je 6 1871
NcD Je 10 1880;Ja 20,F 3 1887;Ag 16 1888
WvMaC Ja 24 1907-13

VIRGINIA republican. w My 1832-
Ct My 6 1835
DLC O 11 1832
IU Ja 8 1845;Ag 9 1851
NcD [Ag 1832-37;41-Je 1846]Ag 8 1849
OHi N 8,29 1832;N 23-30,D 14 1837[N-D 1841]-N 16 1842;F 15,Ap 26-My 3,31,Ag 23,N 15 1843;Ja 10 1844
PHi Je 15 1861

Martinsburg WORLD. d Ag 31 1891-1920||?
1897-1910? as Evening world
NcD My 17 1907;D 21 1914[F-D 1915]
Wv 1912-20
WvMa 1891-S 23 1893

Martinsburg WORLD. w,sw N 13 1891-1908||?
w 1891-97?
WvMa 1891-S 1893

MATOAKA

MERCER recorder. *See* Twin City advance and Mercer recorder (Bluefield)

MIDDLEBOURNE

TYLER county journal. w 1902+
Wv 1911+

TYLER county news. w 1909-17||?
United with Tyler county star to form Tyler star-news

TYLER county star. *See* Tyler star-news

TYLER star-news. w 1877+
1877-1917? as Tyler county star
DLC Jl 9 1880
Wv My 1913-Ag 1918;19+

MILTON

CABELL record. w 1898+
pub 1898+

MONTGOMERY

Montgomery NEWS. w,sw,d 1903+
d 1903?;w 1904-31?
pub 1903+

MOOREFIELD

Moorefield EXAMINER. w 1874+
pub 1896+
DLC O 22 1880
NcD Ag 17-31 1922;O 16 1924
Wv My-D 1910;My 1916-20

HARDY county news. w 1929+
pub 1929-32
WvU Ap 1932+

HARDY whig. w? Mr 7 1851-
NN Mr 7 1851

MORGANTOWN

AMERICAN union. w 1849?-
1849?-51? as Monongalia mirror
DLC Ja 18-D 1851
PPL D 14 1850
V F 23-Mr 1 1856
WvU Je 1855-Mr 1859

Morgantown CHRONICLE. d 1904-07||?
United with Morgantown post to form Post-chronicle, later Morgantown post

DEMOCRATIC republican. w Ja 10 1835-
DLC F 21 1835;S 25 1840;O 21 1852
NcD Ag 5 1852

Morgantown DOMINION-NEWS. d 1897+
1897-1929? as New dominion
pub 1897+
Wv O 4 1913+
WvU 1897+
—w ed *See* New dominion

MONONGALIA chronicle. w
DLC Ag 11 1827
InI My 21 1825-Je 16,Ag-D 22 1827

MONONGALIA mirror. *See* American union

MONONGALIAN. w
V Ja 12-Mr 2 1833

NEW dominion. w 1876-1922||?
DLC F 5 1881
WvU 1877-1917

NEW dominion. d *See* Morgantown dominion-news

NORTH western journal. w O 15 1842-
DLC O 15 1842

Morgantown weekly POST. w Mr 12 1864-1934||?
1864-66? as Morgantown weekly post and Monongalia and Preston county gazette
pub 1879-1934
DLC Jl 10 1880
DHi My 5 1866
NNHi N 23 1872
NcD Ag 7 1875;Jl 15 1876
OCHi Jl 22-29 1876
WvU 1864-86;1905;12-32;34

Morgantown POST. d 1904+
1908-Je 29 1918 Post-chronicle
CtY Ja 16 1913
PUn [1913]
Wv 1911-Mr 1921;Ap 1929+
WvU 1904+

Morgantown TELEGRAPH. w?
V F 15,My 3 24 1855

MOUNDSVILLE

Moundsville COMMERCIAL. w 1879-80||?
DLC Jl 9 1880

CRISIS. w
CtY Ap 20 1848

Moundsville ECHO. w O 21 1891-Ag 1 1929||
pub complete

Moundsville daily ECHO. d Mr 17 1896+
pub 1896+
Wv 1911-Je 1923;Ap 1929+

Moundsville JOURNAL. d 1910+
Wv My 24 1916-23;Ap 1929+
WvMoE 1910+

MARSHALL beacon. w
-Je 26 1841 pub in Elizabethtown
DLC Je 5,19,Jl 3,17-Ag 31,O 19 1841

NATIONAL. w Ag 9? 1866-
MWA O 4 1866

NEW state gazette. w 1874-81||?
DLC Jl 8 1880

Moundsville REPORTER. w 1870-85||?
DLC Jl 2 1880

MULLENS

Mullens ADVOCATE. w 1914+
pub 1925+

NEW CUMBERLAND

HANCOCK county courier. w 1869?+
WvU F 1915-34

NEW MARTINSVILLE

MESSENGER. w 1876-85||?
DLC Jl 23 1880

WETZEL democrat. w 1877+
DLC D 17 1880
Wv 1911-18

WETZEL republican. w 1888+
pub 1898+
Wv Ja-O 1911

NORTHFORK

TRI-DISTRICT news. w 1926+
pub 1926+

PARKERSBURG

DEMOCRAT and examiner. sw 1873-74||?
1873? as Parkersburg orthopolitan; - 1874 Examiner?
WvP 1873-74

Parkersburg DISPATCH. d 1904-15||?
United with Parkersburg news to form Parkersburg dispatch news, later Parkersburg news

Parkersburg DISPATCH news. *See* Parkersburg news

EXAMINER. *See* Democrat and examiner

Parkersburg FREEMAN. w 1881-89||?
1881-84? as West Virginia freeman
Negro
NbHi My 5 1888
WvP 1883-88

Parkersburg GAZETTE. *See* Times and gazette

GREENBACK standard. *See* State standard

Parkersburg NEWS. d 1897+
1897-1915? title varies slightly; 1916?-My 9 1918 Parkersburg dispatch news
MWA O 3 1902
Wv 1906-14;16-My 9 1918;My 1923+
WvP 1898-1907
WvU Ap 1905+

Evening NORTH AMERICAN. tw
WvP Mr 10-D 1868

Parkersburg ORTHOPOLITAN. *See* Democrat and examiner

Parkersburg SENTINEL. w,sw Jl 17 1875-1923||?
w 1875-1894?
pub 1875-Jl 14 1877
DLC My 28 1881
KHi 1875-Jl 1876;Jl 1877-F 1916
WvU 1876-F 1916

Parkersburg daily SENTINEL. d O 1889+
pub 1926+
Wv 1911-N 1916
WvU 1889-1925

STATE journal. w,sw S 1869-1917||?
w 1869-1911?
DLC S 2 1880
NcD Jl 17 1890
Wv 1912-N 17 1917
WvP My 26 1870-Jl 1 1904
WvU 1869-1914

Daily STATE journal. d 1883-1918||?
DLC 1898-Je 29 1901
Wv F 13-D 1911
WvP 1895-1905
WvU 1883-Je 1918

STATE standard. w 1880-88||?
1880? as Greenback standard
DLC O 1 1880;Je 4 1881

STATE weekly and gazette. w 1911-13||?
Wv Ag 1911-Je 1913

Parkersburg daily TIMES. d 1865-74||?
MBAt Jl 20 1866
WvP Ag 12 1865-Je 8 1872
WvPS Ja 18-Jl 28 1869
—w ed *See* West Virginia weekly times; Times and gazette

TIMES and gazette. w 1833?-79||?
1833?-F 1834? as Western republican and Parkersburg gazette; Mr 1834?-73? Parkersburg gazette (1850? Parkersburg gazette and Western Virginian courier)
DLC F 14 1834;D 3 1840;Ja 7,D 17 1863;Ja 21-F 18,Mr 3 1864;68;Ap 14 1870
IU Ag 30,S 13-27,O 11 1843;Ja 11-18,F 1-15, 29,S 26 1844;Ag 5 1847
MWA D 7 1861
NcD S 22 1860;Je 1 1871
PPL D 21 1850
WvP Mr 11 1869-My 11 1871

WEST VIRGINIA freeman. *See* Parkersburg freeman

WEST VIRGINIA (*Continued*)

PARKERSBURG—*Continued*

WEST VIRGINIA weekly times. w 1865-73||?
United with Parkersburg gazette to form Times and gazette
MBAt Ag 4,S 29 1866
MWA My 12 1866
WvP S 28 1865-71
—d ed *See* Parkersburg daily times

WESTERN republican and Parkersburg gazette. *See* Times and gazette

WIRT county democrat. w
WvP 1868

PARSONS

Parsons ADVOCATE. w 1896+
Wv 1911+

MOUNTAIN state patriot. w 1902-17||?
Wv My 1913-17

TUCKER democrat. w 1901?+
Wv 1936+

PENNSBORO

Pennsboro NEWS. w 1891+
pub 1915-19;21+
Wv My 1913-Ap 1915;My 1916+

PETERSBURG

GRANT county press. w 1896+
pub 1896+
NcD S 1 1922
Wv 1911+
WvU Ap 1932+

SOUTH BRANCH gazette. w 1878-93||?
DLC Ag 20 1880

PHILIPPI

BARBOUR democrat. w 1893+
pub 1894+
Wv 1911-18

BARBOUR Jeffersonian. w 1857-84||?
United with Plain dealer to form Jeffersonian-plain dealer, later Plain dealer
DLC Ag 25 1880
NcD Ap 12 1861

PLAIN DEALER. w 1873-1905||?
1885?-99? as Jeffersonian-plain dealer
DLC Ja 22 1880

Philippi REPUBLICAN. w 1880+
Wv 1911-19;21

PIEDMONT

Piedmont HERALD. w 1881+
pub 1888+
Wv 1913-19
WvU 1906-32

PENNSYLVANIA reserve. (5th regiment)
P Jl 25 1861

PINEVILLE

INDEPENDENT herald. w 1899+
1899-1912? as Wyoming tribune
pub 1932+

WYOMING citizen. w 1905-18||
1905-15? as Wyoming mountaineer
Wv 1906-15

WYOMING mountaineer. *See* Wyoming citizen

WYOMING tribune. *See* Independent herald

POINT PLEASANT

Point Pleasant CITIZEN. w N 1931+
pub 1931+
Wv 1934+

ELEVENTH Ohio. 1862?-
Ohi Mr 14 1862

INDEPENDENT republican. w 1855-
NcD F 8,Ap 5,Jl 26,Ag 16,O 25,D 20 1855;O 30,N 6,27 1856;Mr 12,Ag 13 1857;My 2 1860

MASON county journal. w 1866-72||?
NcD Ag 19 1868

MASON republican. w 1907-24||?
Wv Ap 1908-15

Weekly REGISTER. w Mr 1862-1924||?
DLC My 4 1881
NcD F 13 1878;My 16 1883;Ja 18 1888;O 11 1893;Je 13 1894;F 3 1897
OClWHi N 13 1862;O 15-22 1874
Wv 1862-93;95-1910;My 1913-15
WvU 1862-N 1923

Point Pleasant daily REGISTER. d 1921+
pub Mr 1933+
WvU Ag 1916-Mr 1925

STATE gazette. w 1881+
pub 1925+
Wv 1888+
WvU 1888-1904;06-14

WEST VIRGINIA monitor. w 1874-80||?
OHi O 20 1876

WESTERN review. w Ag 30? 1860-
NcD O 25 1860;F 7,My 2,23 1861

WESTERN Virginia. w 1858?-
NcD O 10 1860

PRINCETON

Princeton GAZETTE. w 1912-13||?
Wv N 1912-My 1913

Princeton JOURNAL. w 1879-1902||?
DLC F 9 1881

MERCER progress. w 1911-22||?
1911-15? as Princeton progress
Wv Je 1914-15

MERCER republican. w 1899-1913||?
Wv 1911-S 1912

Princeton OBSERVER. w 1928+
Follows Evening press
pub 1928+
ICM Jl 16,Ag 6 1931;O 5-12 1933
Wv 1928+

Princeton PRESS. w 1914-15||
Wv Je 1914-O 1915

Evening PRESS. d,w 1917-28||
Followed by Princeton observer
d 1917-18?

Princeton PROGRESS. *See* Mercer progress

PRUNTYTOWN

FAMILY visitor. w 1858-
NcD Ja 20 1860

VIRGINIA patriot. w Ja 4 1861-
MWA Ja 11 1861

RALEIGH

RALEIGH county index. *See* Raleigh register

Raleigh REGISTER. w 1880-95||?
1880-92? as Raleigh county index
DLC S 14 1880

RAVENSWOOD

JACKSON bugle. w 1883-90||?
WvRC 1883-90

JACKSON county news. *See* Ravenswood news

Ravenswood NEWS. w 1868+
1868-72? as West Virginia news; 1873?-78? Jackson county news
DLC Jl 8 1880
Wv 1873-75;1911-19
WvRC 1884-1900

WEST VIRGINIA news. *See* Ravenswood news

REEDY

Reedy NEWS. w 1909+
Wv Ap 1913+

RICHWOOD

NICHOLAS republican. w 1903+
pub 1930+
Wv S 1911-19

RIPLEY

JACKSON herald. w 1876?+
Wv 1914+
WvRC 1877+

MOUNTAINEER. w 1892+
pub 1892+
Wv 1911-15
WvRC 1893-1900
WvU 1934+

ROMNEY

HAMPSHIRE and Hardy intelligencer. *See* South Branch intelligencer

HAMPSHIRE review. w 1884+
pub 1884+
Wv 1911-18
WvU Ap 1932+

SOUTH BRANCH intelligencer. w 1829-D 1896||
1829 as Hampshire and Hardy intelligencer. Merged with Hampshire review
DLC N 6 1840;F 14 1845;Jl 9 1880
NcD Jl 1 1853;O 27 1882;Ja 11 1884;Ag 24 1888;My 15 1891
WvU D 1866-Mr 1893

SOUTH BRANCH record. w 1929+
pub 1929+

VIRGINIA argus and Hampshire advertiser. w 1851?-
MWA Je 24 1852
NcD Je 13,27,Jl 11,Ag 1-8 1861

RONCEVERTE

Ronceverte TIMES. w 1911-19||?
Wv Je 18 1914-O 1919

WEST VIRGINIA news. w 1898+
pub N 1898+
Wv My 1913+

SAINT ALBANS

Saint Albans ADVERTISER. w 1925+
pub 1930+

Saint Albans EXPRESS. w 1879-81||?
DLC Jl 9 1880

St. Albans HERALD. w,sw 1910-20||
sw 1915?-19?
Wv 1911-19

St. Albans PIONEER. w 1874-78||?
NcD S 8 1877

ST. GEORGE

TUCKER county pioneer. w 1878-94||?
DLC Ag 27 1880

TUCKER democrat. w My 1880-91||?
DLC O 8 1880

SAINT MARYS

OBSERVER. w O 10 1877-81||?
DLC S 23 1880;Je 4 1881

Saint Marys ORACLE. w 1881+
pub 1881+
Wv 1911+

PLEASANTS county leader. w 1898+
pub 1898+
Wv 1911+

SALEM

Salem EXPRESS. w 1900-15||?
United with Salem herald to form Salem express and herald, later Salem herald
Wv S-D 1901;My 1913-15

Salem EXPRESS and herald. *See* Salem herald

Salem HERALD. w 1904+
1916? as Salem express and herald; 1917?-S 1918? Herald-express
pub 1904+
Wv Ja-Ag 1910;My 1913-15;17-S 1918

SHEPHERDSTOWN

EASTERN pan-handle. w S 1903-08||
Followed by Independent
NcD Ag 17 1904

INDEPENDENT. w 1908+
Follows Eastern pan-handle
NcD [1920-27]
Wv 1911-15;Je 28,N 11 1916-20
WvU 1934+

POTOMAC pioneer. w Jl 8 1829-
CSmH Ag 25 1830
DLC Jl 8 1829

Shepherdstown REGISTER. w D 4 1849+
Suspended during Civil war
pub 1882-1932
DLC D 11 1880
MWA Ja 29 1892
NbHi Ap 1 1876
NcD [1865;67;70;73;80;82;86-87;94;96;1901;19-28]
V Je 6 1857;D 24 1859;Ja 14,Ap 21 1860;Mr 31 1866;Je 12 1869;Jl 4-11 1874

SHINNSTON

Shinnston NEWS. w 1897+
pub 1897+
Wv 1916+

SIMPSON'S

NEW ERA. w My 8 1880-81||?
DLC Jl 17 1880

SISTERSVILLE

INDEPENDENT. *See* Tyler independent

Sistersville daily REVIEW. d 1895+
Wv My 14 1913-Je 1920

TYLER independent. w 1878-86||?
1882-84? as Independent
DLC Jl 9 1880

SPENCER

Weekly BULLETIN. *See* Roane county reporter

INTERIOR. *See* Roane county reporter

ROANE county record. w 1888-1912||
United with Spencer times to form Spencer times-record

ROANE county reporter. w 1879+
1879-80? as Interior; 1881-Ja 1 1915 Weekly bulletin
pub 1898+
DLC Je 24 1880
Wv My 1913-F 1917;18+

Spencer TIMES-RECORD. w 1911+
1911-12 as Spencer times
pub 1918+
Wv 1911-19;21+
WvSR 1928+

SUMMERSVILLE

NICHOLAS chronicle. w 1880+
pub [1882-My 20 1926]+
DLC Ap 8 1881
Wv 1911+

WEST VIRGINIA (*Continued*)

SUTTON

BRAXTON central. w 1883+
Wv 1911+

BRAXTON democrat. w 1883+
Wv Mr 1914+
WvU Ap 1932+

Sutton MOUNTAINEER. *See under* Braxton

TERRA ALTA

ORACLE. *See* Preston republican

PRESTON republican. w 1891+
1891-98 as Oracle
pub 1921+
Wv Mr 1909+

UNION

BORDER watchman. *See* Monroe watchman

MONROE county watchman. *See* Monroe watchman

MONROE mail. w Ag 4 1927+
pub 1927+

MONROE watchman. w 1872+
1872-84 as Border watchman; 1884-98 Monroe county watchman
pub 1872+
DLC F 4 1881
ICM N 10 1921
NcD My 24,Jl 5 1917
Wv 1911-19;21
WvU F 1872-85;87-1900;04-12

WAYNE

Wayne ADVOCATE. *See* Wayne county news

Wayne NEWS. *See* Wayne county news

WAYNE county news. w 1874+
1874-86? as Wayne advocate; 1887?-1918? Wayne news
pub 1919+
NcD S 18 1890
Wv 1911+

WEBSTER SPRINGS

WEBSTER echo. w 1879+
pub 1896+
Wv 1911+

WEBSTER republican. w 1904+
Wv 1911+

WEIRTON

Weirton daily TIMES. d Je 1928+
pub Mr 1931+
WvU Mr 1935+

WELCH

MCDOWELL recorder. w 1891+
pub [1911+]
Wv 1911-19;21+
—d ed *See* Welch daily news

Welch daily NEWS. d D 3 1923+
pub 1923+
—w ed *See* McDowell recorder

WELLSBURG

BROOKE republican. *See* Western transcript

*Wellsburg GAZETTE. w Ja 1816-
CSmH Ag 20 1830
DLC O 21 1821;Jl 20 1822
ICHi Mr 10 1836
PWCl Ag 16 1835

Wellsburg weekly HERALD. w D 1846-1928||?
Title varies slightly
DLC Jl 2 1880
NcD F 17 1849;Mr 5 1852
OClWHi Ja 12 1855;F 6 1874
PUn O 8 1897
Wv 1911
WvU F 1850-Je 1909

Wellsburg daily HERALD. d 1897+
Wv O 1899-Je 1909;Ap 1912-F 1913
WvU O 1899—

Wellsburg NEWS. w 1868-1918||?
1868-1913? as Pan-handle news
DLC Jl 23 1880
Wv 1907-11;Ag 1914-Ap 1918

PAN-HANDLE news. *See* Wellsburg news

TRUE republican and Wellsburg advertiser. w Ja 1 1835-
DLC Ja 1 1835

WESTERN transcript. w My 25? 1833-
1833-S 1835? as Brooke republican
DLC Je 13 1833;F 1,15 1834;D 22 1840
WvU 1833-Je 7 1837

WEST COLUMBIA

VIRGINIA telescope. w D? 1854-
DLC Ja 25,Mr 7,My 23 1855

WEST UNION

DODDRIDGE county republican. w 1909+
pub 1929+
Wv Je 1913+
WvU Ap 1932-33

West Union HERALD. w 1885+
pub 1921+
Wv 1911-19

West Union RECORD. w 1878+
pub 1900-[15-27]+
Wv 1911;19+

WESTON

Weston DEMOCRAT. w 1867+
pub 1881-Je 1883;87
DLC Ap 23 1881
OClWHi F 13 1871
OClWHi F 13 1871
Wv 1885-99;1911-19;21
WvU Mr 1919-20

Weston FREE PRESS. w 1915-17||?
Wv 1915-Ap 10 1917

Weston HERALD. w
P-M Ja 3 1855

Weston INDEPENDENT. w 1894+
pub 1894+
Wv 1911-O 8 1918
WvU 1916-Mr 1917;Jl 1919-23;Ja-O 1926;28-29

OHIO seventh. ir Jl 4 1861-
N Jl 4 1861
OClWHi Jl 4 1861

Weston REPUBLICAN. w 1879-1919||?
DLC Ag 21 1880
Wv 1914-15

Weston SENTINEL. w Je 19 1846-
DLC Je 26 1846

WHEELING

Wheeling ARGUS. w 1838?-
Title varies: Weekly Western Virginia argus
DLC Ja 8,F 19-Ap 2,23-Je 4,18,Jl 2-16,30-S 16,30,O 14-N 5,18-D 2,16-23 1847;O 21 1852
TKL Mr 28 1856

ARGUS. (Country ed) tw
DLC Ap 21 30,My 26,D 27 1855

Wheeling COMPILER. w Jl 1? 1829-
DLC N 18-D 2,23 1829-Ja 6,27 1830
MBAt My 26 1830

*ECLECTIC observer and working people's advocate. w Ja? 1830-
CSmH Jl 1 1830

*Wheeling GAZETTE. w Ap 23 1818-
1818-My 1 1824 as Virginia northwestern gazette
CSmH Ap 24 1830
DLC Ag 13 1821-25;O 14-21 1826;Ag 16,S 13 1828;Jl 11-18,O 24-31 1829;Ja 2 1830
IU S 28 1844
MWA Je 6 1829;Jl 9 1857
N Jl 3,N 13 1824
OCHi N 12 1825
PWaHi Ja 20 1827

Wheeling daily GAZETTE. d Ja 1 1835-
DLC Ja 1 1835

Wheeling tri-weekly GAZETTE. tw 1835?-
DLC N 4 1840
MWA Je 6 1838
WvW Ag 24 1835-Ap 1836;38;My 1839-42;49-50

Daily Wheeling GAZETTE. d 1849-
DLC Mr 7-D 1849

Wheeling INTELLIGENCER. d Ag 24 1852+
Title varies slightly
DLC N 1 1852;Ja 29 1853-Ja 25 1854;Jl 27 1861-73;Jl 9 1874-Ag 1916
ICM S 22 1890
MBAt Ap 17-19 1865[Mr 1866-68]Mr 6,Je 11,N 5,12,23,26 1869
MWA Mr 3 1888;O 13 1893
NNHi Jl 1 1863
NcD Ja 31 1833;Mr 12,S 1 1888
OClWHi Ja 22,Mr 20 1862;Ag 29 1865;N 6 1878;Ap 1,Ag 8 1885
PPM O 7 1864
PWaHi Je 16 1891
Wv 1852-1900;11-16;24+
WvU Je 1861-Ja 1884;1905-Ja 1914;15+
WvW 1852-53;60+

Weekly INTELLIGENCER. w 1852-1925||?
Title varies slightly
DLC Jl 22 1880
MWA D 2 1853
MeBa [1861-Mr 1865]
TJT Mr 23 1876
WvU 1883-Je 1886

INTELLIGENCER. tw,sw -1890||?
tw -1869?
MBAt Ja 1 1867

Sunday LEADER. w 1875-83||?
DLC Jl 4 1880

Evening LEADER. d Jl 1880-
DLC Ag 26 1880

Wheeling MAJORITY. w Mr 1907-20||?
IU Je 15 1916-Ap 1920
WHi Ja 14 1908;D 16 1909-Ag 10 1916
Wv S 1916-18

Wheeling NEWS-REGISTER. d 1890+
1890-Ag 27 1935 as Wheeling daily news
pub 1904+
OClWHi Mr 16 1907
PP 1934+
Wv 1911-Ag 1916

Daily PRESS. d 1861-
WvU Jl 1861-S 1862

QUEST. w 1890-92||?
PPCHi [1890-92]

Wheeling REGISTER. d Jl 9 1863-Ag 27 1935||
1863-N 6 1878 as Wheeling daily register
United with Wheeling news to form Wheeling news-register
CoU 1903-04;06-09
DLC Jl 1874-1935
ICHi Je 16 1864
KHi N 9 1864
MWA My 1 1896
NcD [1866;73;76;86;88;93]
Wv Ja-Je 1872;84-94;1911-S 1923;Jl-D 1928;29-35
WvW 1863-77;83-1935

Wheeling tri-weekly REGISTER. tw 1864-81?
NcD Mr 27,My 31,N 10 1866;Ja 24,F 12 1867;Ja 27 1874

Wheeling REPORTER. 1837?-
OClWHi Ja 28 1838

Wheeling evening STANDARD. d 1873-79||?
Wv O 1877-Jl 1878

Wheeling TELEGRAPH. d 1902-28||?
Wv 1911-19

Wheeling TIMES and advertiser. tw 1833?-
1833?-37? as Wheeling tri-weekly times
DLC F 1,6 1834;Jl 14,N 28 1840
WvW 1838-39;42-48

WHEELING TIMES and advertiser. d
MWA Ag 5 1843

Daily Wheeling TIMES and gazette. d
MWA O 4 1853

TIPPECANOE flag and peoples advocate. sw Ja 15- 1840||?
DLC Ja 15 1840

VIRGINIA northwestern gazette. *See* Wheeling gazette

VIRGINIA statesman. w Ja 2 1828-
MWA Ja 2 1828

Wheelinger VOLKSBLATT. sw,w 1880-87||?
sw 1880?
In German
DLC Jl 3 1881

WEST VIRGINIA state journal. w 1863?-
MWA Ap 9 1864

WESTERN transcript. w? 1842?-
OClWHi Ap 23 1843

Weekly WESTERN Virginia argus. *See* Wheeling argus

WESTERN Virginia times. w 1831?-
DLC O 31 1832
MWA D 12 1832;Mr 6 1833;Ag 6 1834;My 27 1835
NhD Je 16 1841

Daily YOUNG America. d
CtY Ja 6 1854

WILLIAMSON

MINGO republican. w 1904+
pub 1918+
ICM N 12 1914
Wv 1911-N 1917

Williamson Daily NEWS. d 1912+
pub 1927+
Wv 1912-Je 1920;29+

WILLIAMSTOWN

WOOD county news. w 1910-
Wv 1911-Mr 1912

WINFIELD

Winfield INDEPENDENT. w 1875-77||?
DLC O 14 1875;Jl 27,N 16 1876

IRREPRESSIBLE. *See* Putnam review

PUTNAM democrat. w 1876+
DLC Mr 11 1881
NcD [1878-80;82-84;86;88;91-92;94;96;98]
OClWHi Ag 29-O 1879
Wv 1911-15

PUTNAM leader. w 1882+
NcD S 8 1927
Wv O 1913-18

PUTNAM review. w 1879-1913||?
1879-Ja 1913 as Irrepressible
Wv 1911-O 1913

WIRT COURT HOUSE

WIRT county appeal. w 1875-81||?
DLC S 10 1880

WISCONSIN

ABBOTSFORD

Abbotsford **TRIBUNE.** w 1923+
pub 1923+

ADAMS

Adams **ADVERTISER.** *See* Adams county times

ADAMS county times. w 1914+
1914-23 as Adams advertiser; 1924-26 Adams times
pub 1914+
WHi F 23 1918

Adams **TIMES.** *See* Adams county times

AHNAPEE. *See* ALGOMA

ALBANY

Albany **GAZETTE.** w
WLc 1842

Albany **HERALD.** w N 1883+
1883-1924 as Albany vindicator
pub S 1933+
WHi 1885+

Albany weekly **JOURNAL.** w O 12 1865-My 3 1866||
Follows Albany times
WHi complete

Albany **JOURNAL.** w Je 1876-O 31 1891||
Suspended Jl 27? 1889-O 11? 1890
WHi F 12 1879-91

Albany **JOURNAL.** w N 7 1895-F 27 1896||
Follows Belleville news (Belleville) Followed by Waunakee news (Waunakee)
WHi complete

Albany **TIMES.** Je 1858-Ag 1862||
Follows Independent press (Monroe) Followed by Albany weekly journal

Albany **VINDICATOR.** *See* Albany herald

ALGOMA

To S 1897 as Ahnapee

AHNAPEE record. *See* Algona record-herald

Algoma **HERALD.** w 1913-F 1 1918||
United with Algoma record to form Algoma record-herald
WAlR N 1914-18

Algoma **PRESS.** w 1897-1901||?
WAlR O 1897-S 1901

Algoma **RECORD-HERALD.** w Je 12 1873+
1873-S 16 1897 as Ahnapee record; S 23 1897-F 3 1918 Algoma record
pub 1886-My 1896;Je 1898+
WHi Ja 8 1874-N 9 1876;Mr 1882+

ALMA

Alma **BLÄTTER.** w Ja 4 1889-S 22 1892; N 29 1894-Je 9 1910||
S 29 1892-N 22 1894 merged with Buffalo county republikaner (Fountain City)
In German
WHi 1889-S 22 1892;95-1910

BUFFALO county journal. w Ap 27 1861+
1861-Je 18 1863 as Buffalo county journal; Je 25 1863-68 Alma journal; 1868-Jl 22 1869 Alma journal and beef slough advocate; Jl 29 1869-My 29 1879 Alma weekly express
pub My 1868+
WHi 1861-D 1 1864;Jl 29 1869-D 15 1870;Ja 15 1874+

Alma weekly **EXPRESS.** *See* Buffalo county journal

Alma **JOURNAL.** *See* Buffalo county journal

ALMA CENTER

Alma Center **HERALD.** w F 2 1898-S 20 1899||
WHi complete

Alma Center **NEWS.** w D 7 1901-Ag 17 1933||
WHi Jl 1906-33

ALMOND

Almond **PRESS.** w N 21 1924-O 30 1931||
WHi 1924-Je 12,O 16-30 1931

AMERY

Amery **ECHO.** w Je 14 1889-Jl 30 1891||
Follows Barron county independent (Barron)
WHi complete

Amery **FREE press.** w 1891+
pub 1893+

AMHERST

Amherst **ADVOCATE.** w F 22 1893+
pub 1893+
WHi Ap 17 1919+

ANTIGO

Antigo **BANNER.** w D 5 1919+
In German
WHi 1919+

FARMERS' journal. w 1909-26||?
WHi O 1911-23

FORWARD. *See* Antigo republican

Antigo **HERALD.** w O 1888-D 28 1923||
1888-N 28 1919 as Antigo herold (in German)
WHi S 13 1901-23

Antigo **HEROLD.** *See* Antigo herald

Antigo **JOURNAL.** w S 18 1898+
pub 1898+
WHi S 29 1911-23

Antigo daily **JOURNAL.** d S 1 1904+
pub 1904+
WAn 1904-05;07+
WHi Ja 3 1924

LANGLADE county republican. *See* Antigo republican

NEW county republican. *See* Antigo republican

Antigo weekly **NEWS item.** w Ag 26 1882+
pub [1884+]
WAn 1882-Ag 7 1897;F 19-Je 25 1898;N 24 1900-01
WHi 1882+

Antigo **REPUBLICAN.** w Ja 1880-S 14 1911||
Ja-F 1880 as New county republican; Mr 1880-Ag 1884 Langlade county republican; Ag 1884-Mr 1886 Forward. Merged with Antigo journal
WAn 1902-07;09-11
WHi F 1889-1911

APOLLONIA

Weekly **BUDGET.** See Ladysmith news (Ladysmith)

APPLETON

Appleton **CRESCENT.** w F 10 1853-1919||?
DLC Ja 20,Mr 3-10,My 26 1855;Ap 25,Jl 11-25, O 10 1857;Ja 14-Mr 31,My 12,Jl 14,Ag 4,D 22 1860;F 2,23-D 28 1861
KHi [Ag 11-N 3 1888]
MWA Ap 19 1856;Je 4 1864
N Jl 2 1859
NNHi N 6-16,30-D 7 1867
WAL 1860-O 10 1869;N 16 1878-F 9,Jl 2-Ag 10 1879
WAP 1867-1917
WHi 1853-1906

Appleton **CRESCENT.** d O 1890-Ja 31 1920||
United with Appleton daily post to form Appleton post crescent
WA 1899-1918;20
WAP complete
WHi Ap 16 1897-1920

DEMOCRATIC free press. w My 15 1856-
KHi Je 26,O 2-9 1856

FOX RIVER journal. w,d 1902-17||?
1902-03 as Fox River journal and weekly advertiser
w 1902-S 7 1916
WHi F 27 1905-[16-17]

Daily **FREE PRESS.** d Jl 12? 1856-
N Jl 31 1856

GEGENWART. w,sw 1889-Je 12 1916||
w 1889-98
In German
WHi N 1898-1916

MONTAGS-BLATT. w Mr 1890-S 13 1920||
1890-O 9 1894 as Volksfreund und haus schatz
WHi D 22 1891-1920
—w ed *See* Appleton volksfreund

Appleton **MOTOR.** w Ag 18 1859-S 13 1866||
Merged with Appleton post
MWA Ja 25 1866
WHi complete

PEOPLE'S champion. w S 12 1877-Jl 24 1880||
Merged with Oshkosh standard (Oshkosh) 1877-O 1879 pub in Fond du Lac
WHi D 1877-80

Appleton **POST.** w 1858-1914||?
ICHi D 21 1882
NNHi Ap 18 1872
WAL 1866-83
WAP 1875-1912
WHi S 20 1866-1912

Appleton **POST-CRESCENT.** d My 1883+
1883-Ja 31 1920 as Appleton daily post
pub 1883+
WA F 1920-Jl,S 1922+
WAL 1900+
WHi [1913-Ag 12 1918]-20

Appleton **REVIEW.** sw Ja 16 1930-Ja 15 1932||
WA complete
—w ed *See* Week end review

Appleton **VOLKSFREUND.** w Ja 8 1870-1932||
Subtitles vary
WHi 1874-1929
WS Ag 29 1890
—**Literary and family ed.** *See* Montags-blatt

WEEK END review. w O 24 1930-My 15 1931||
Friday ed of Appleton review
WA complete

ARCADIA

ARCADIAN. w My 23 1895-Ag 9 1907||
WAr 1903-05
WHi complete

LEADER. w Jl 1 1875+
1875-N 29 1877 as Arcadia leader; D 7 1877-D 30 1880 Trempealeau county republican and Arcadia leader; Ja 6-F 10 1881 Republican-leader of Trempealeau county; F 17 1881-Ja 30 1890 Republican and leader
pub 1904+
WAr 1909-10;12;29+
WHi 1875+

Arcadia **RECORD.** w N 24 1911-My 9 1913||
WHi complete

REPUBLICAN and leader. *See* Leader

REPUBLICAN-LEADER of Trempealeau county. *See* Leader

TREMPEALEAU county republican and Arcadia leader. *See* Leader

ARENA

RURAL eye. *See* New star (Dodgeville)

Arena **STAR.** *See under* Dodgeville

ARGYLE

Argyle **ATLAS.** w D 16 1884+
pub 1884+

ASHLAND

Ashland **APPEAL.** m Ag 15-O 15 1894||
Followed by Ashland commonwealth
WHi complete

Ashland **BLADET.** w 1900-07||
1900-01 as Ashland posten. Merged with Svenska Amerikanska tribunen (Superior)
In Swedish
IRA 1902-07

Ashland **CHRONICLE.** w Ap 11 1913-S 23 1916||
Ap 11 1913-S 2 1916 as Odanah star (Odanah)
WHi complete

Ashland **COMMONWEALTH.** w N 3 1894-1895||?
Follows Ashland appeal
WHi 1894-Ja 12 1895

Weekly **LEADER.** w F 11-Jl 29 1899||
WHi complete

Ashland **NEWS.** d 1887-My 21 1915||
Merged with Ashland daily press
WHi 1896-1915

Ashland **POSTEN.** *See* Ashland bladet

Ashland weekly **PRESS.** w Je 22 1872-O 7 1916||
Continues Bayfield press (Bayfield). 1872-S 1893 as Ashland press
pub complete
MnHi 1872-73;80-[1904]
NIC Ja 19 1907-16
NNHi Ap 23 1887
WHi complete

Ashland daily **PRESS.** d 1888+
pub 1888+
WHi Ja 12 1898-Mr 22 1906;My 24 1915+

AUGUSTA

Augusta **EAGLE.** *See* Union

Augusta **EAGLE-TIMES.** *See* Union

EAU CLAIRE county union. *See* Union

Augusta **HERALD.** *See* Herald (Eau Claire)

TIMES. w Ag? 1886-N 28 1919||
United with Eau Claire county union to form Augusta eagle-times, later Union
Suspended Ag 1888-Ja 10? 1889

UNION. w Jl 11 1874+
1874-N 28 1919 as Augusta eagle; D 5 1919-Ja 23 1920 Eau Claire county union; Ja 13-Mr 10 1927 Augusta eagle-times
pub 1900+
WHi 1874+

BALDWIN

Baldwin **BULLETIN.** w N 11 1873+
N 28 1879-Ja 20 1881 as Independent
pub 1875+
WHi 1874+

INDEPENDENT. 1879-81. *See* Baldwin bulletin

Baldwin **INDEPENDENT.** 1900-01. *See* St. Croix observer (Hudson)

BALSAM LAKE

POLK county ledger. w 1897+
WHi Ag 18 1921+

BARABOO

Baraboo **BULLETIN.** w D 23 1879-Mr 24? 1883||
1879-O 5 1880 as Sauk county republican; O 15 1880-My 26 1882 Baraboo weekly bulletin; Je 2-Jl 28 1882 Wisconsin prohibitionist and Baraboo bulletin. Merged with Sauk county democrat
WHi 1880-D 22 1882

DOLLAR times. *See under* Spring Green

FORD'S Sauk county democrat. *See* Sauk county democrat

WISCONSIN (*Continued*)

BARABOO—*Continued*

INDEPENDENT. w Jl 16 1866-Je 1869||
Followed by Sauk county herald
WHi 1867-D 9 1868

Baraboo weekly **NEWS.** w My 1884+
1884-1911 as Baraboo news
pub 1884+
WHi F 1906+

Baraboo **NEWS-REPUBLIC.** d Je 4 1894+
1894-F 1929 as Baraboo daily news
pub 1894+
WHi 1894-1905

Baraboo **REPUBLIC.** w 1855-1924||?
KHi F 6 1889
MWA F 7 1866;D 4 1867

Baraboo daily **REPUBLIC.** d 1892-F 1929||
United with Baraboo daily news to form Baraboo news-republic
WBN complete

SAUK county democrat. w Je 25 1850-N 1856||
1850-Jl 30 1855 as Sauk county standard
MWA S 1[illegible] 1851
WHi Ap 17,Jl 24 1856

SAUK county democrat. w Ja 31 1880-D 30 1920||
My 19 1883-Je 26 1886 as Ford's Sauk county democrat
WB complete
WHi Mr 1880-1920

SAUK county herald. Ja 6-Jl 1870||
Follows Independent

SAUK county republican. *See* Baraboo bulletin

SAUK county standard. *See* Sauk county democrat

BARRON

BARRON county gazette. *See* Rice Lake chronotype

BARRON county independent. w Ag 1886-My 24 1889||
Followed by Amery echo (Amery) Ag-S 1886 pub at Cumberland; O 1886-F 1888 at Cameron
WHi Ap 2[illegible] 1888-89

BARRON county news. w 1900-O 24 1918||
United with Barron county shield to form Barron county news-shield

BARRON county news-shield. w N 1 1918+
Formed by the union of Barron county news and Barron county shield
WHi 1918—

BARRON county shield. w O 6 1878-O 31 1918||
United with Barron county news to form Barron county news-shield
WHi complete

BARRON county tribune. w S 15 1926-N 14 1929||
Merged with Barron county news-shield
WHi complete

BAYFIELD

BAYFIELD county press. w 1859+
1859-N 18 1882 as Bayfield press
pub 1870+
WBf 1919-21
WHi Je 20 1877-[79]Jl 1881+

Bayfield **MERCURY.** w Ap 18-O 1857||
MnHi Ap-S 5 1857
WHi Ag 22 1857

Bayfield **PRESS.** w O 13 1870-Je 15 1872||
Followed by Ashland press (Ashland)
KHi O 13 1870
MnHi complete
WHi complete

Bayfield **PROGRESS.** w Je 3 1909-Mr 30 1927||
WHi complete

BEAR CREEK

Weekly **ECHO.** w Ap 5 1917-My 9 1918||
WHi [1917-18]

BEAVER DAM

Beaver Dam **ARGUS.** w D 7 1860+
Formed by the union of Dodge county excelsior and Horicon argus (Horicon). Jl 27 1864-Mr 10 1866 as Beaver Dam argus and farm mortgage league
pub D 1863—
OClWHi Mr 31 1866
WBdA 1860-D 2 1863
WHi 1860+

Daily **CITIZEN.** d F 21 1911+
pub 1911+

Beaver Dam **DEMOCRAT.** *See* Whig of seventy-six (Juneau)

DEMOCRATIC post. Mr-My 1857||
Follows Beaver Dam republican. Merged with Dodge county citizen

DODGE county citizen. w Ap 10 1856-1929||?
Suspended Je 6 1861-O 1 1862
Issued d ed during political campaign of 1856, and again in winter of 1857-58
MWA Ap [illegible] 1861;F 8 1866
NNHi N 11-D 2 1869
WHi 1856-Ap 16 1924

DODGE county excelsior. S-D 1860||
United with Horicon argus (Horicon) to form Beaver Dam argus

Beaver Dam **REPUBLICAN and sentinel.** Mr 1853-Mr 5 1857||
1853-Ap 1855 as Beaver Dam republican. Followed by Democratic post
WHi Mr 22 1854-57

Beaver Dam **SENTINEL.** w N 1854-Ap 1855||
United with Beaver Dam republican to form Beaver Dam republican and sentinel

WHIG of seventy-six. *See under* Juneau

BELLEVILLE

Belleville **NEWS.** w Ja 24-O 18 1895||
Followed by Albany journal (Albany)
WHi complete

Belleville **RECORDER.** w Mr 1886+
1886-O 3 1902 as Sugar River recorder
Issued as supplement to New Glarus post (New Glarus) Jl 11 1924-Je 3 1926
pub Je 10 1926+
WHi D 20 1889+

SUGAR River recorder. *See* Belleville recorder

BELMONT

Belmont **BEE.** w Mr 1 1894-Ag 22 1901||
Follows Montfort monitor (Montfort)
WHi [Mr-Ag 1894]My 26 1898-1901

Belmont **GAZETTE.** w O 25 1836-Ap 12 1837||
Follows Galenian (Galena, Ill). After first session of Wisconsin territorial legislature removed to new seat of government, Burlington (now in Iowa). Continued as Wisconsin territorial gazette, later Burlington gazette (Burlington, Iowa)
DLC Ja-Ap 12 1837
MnHi Ap 12 1837
WHi complete

Belmont **SUCCESS.** w My 20 1903+
pub 1922+

BELOIT

Beloit **ARGUS.** *See* Beloit citizen

Beloit **CITIZEN.** w F 7 1880-93||?
1880-D 26 1884 as Beloit weekly outlook; Ja 2 1885-My 1888 Beloit argus
WHi 1880-S 10 1886

Morning **CITIZEN.** *See* Beloit daily news

Beloit weekly **COURIER.** w N 1856-Ap 1860||
1856-Ap 13 1859 as Beloit herald; My-D 1859 Beloit herald and times. United with Beloit journal to form Journal and courier, later Beloit free press

Beloit **FREE PRESS.** w Je 22 1848-D 25 1902||?
1848-Ap 1871 as Beloit journal (Ap 5 1860-Je 2 1864 Journal and courier; Ag 1867-Ag 1869 Beloit free press)
KHi Ja 26 1865
MWA Ja 11 1866
NNHi My 31 1863
NbHi Mr 26 1874
NjR Jl 9 1863
P-M My 10 1855
WHi Je-Jl 20 1848;56-S 21 1865;Ja 12 1871-1902

Daily **FREE PRESS.** d Ag 7 1878-Mr 15 1915||
Ag 7-Mr 1879 as Daily phonograph. Merged with Beloit daily news
WHi F 1878-1915

Beloit **GRAPHIC.** w Ja 13 1877-Jl 28 1880||
Merged with Beloit outlook
NbHi O 26 1878
WHi complete

GRIT. *See* Beloit daily news

Beloit **HERALD and times.** *See* Beloit weekly courier

Beloit **JOURNAL.** 1848-60;69-71. *See* Beloit free press

JOURNAL and courier. *See* Beloit free press

Beloit daily **NEWS.** d My 1888+
1888-91? as Morning citizen; 1892? Grit
pub 1888+
KHi S 22 1888
WBel 1888+
WHi Mr 16 1915+

Beloit **OUTLOOK.** d D 20 1881-D 1 1882||
WHi Ja 5 1882

Beloit weekly **OUTLOOK.** *See* Beloit citizen

Daily **PHONOGRAPH.** *See* Daily free press

BENTON

Benton **ADVOCATE.** w S 12 1901+
WHi 1901+

MINING times. D 6 1894-1901||?
WHi 1894-D 28 1900

BERLIN

Berlin **CITY courant.** *See* Berlin courant

Berlin **COURANT.** w Je 1854-Ja 27 1916||
Follows Marquette mercury. 1854-My 26 1864 as Berlin city courant. United with Berlin journal to form Journal-courant
MWA F 1 1866
WHi Ag 25 1859-D 13 1888;Mr 23 1911-D 23 1915

Berlin evening **JOURNAL.** d Ja 1 1881+
pub 1881+
Whi 1883-F 1899;Mr 15 1917+

JOURNAL-COURANT. w Ag 30 1870-Je 29 1922||
1870-Ja 27 1916 as Berlin journal
WHi S 20 1876-1922

MARQUETTE mercury. w N 1850-Je 1854||
Followed by Berlin courant
Suspended F-Ap 1853
WHi Je 13 1853

BIRCHWOOD

Birchwood **BULLETIN.** w 1916-19||?
WHi F 8-S 27 1918

BLACK CREEK

Black Creek **TIMES.** w Ja 1 1904-28||?
WHi 1904-Ap 12 1928

BLACK EARTH

ADVERTISER. w Mr 1 1868-S 15 1888||
1868? as Monthly budget; 1869? Monthly advertiser and produce reporter; Mr 1870-82 Black Earth advertiser. United with Saturday evening news (Madison) to form News-advertiser (Madison)
MWA My 20 1887
WHi Ag 11 1870-88

Monthly **BUDGET.** *See* Advertiser

DANE county news. w 1901+
1901-13 as Black Earth times; 1914-Ag 1915 Black Earth news
pub 1918+
WHi Je 1915+

Black Earth **NEWS.** *See* Dane County news

Black Earth **TIMES.** *See* Dane county news

BLACK RIVER FALLS

BADGER state banner. *See* Banner-journal

BANNER-journal. w Ag 14 1856+
1856-Mr 28 1868 as Jackson county banner; Ap 4 1868-Mr 4 1926 Badger state banner
pub 1856+
WHi Ja 25 1868+

JACKSON county banner. *See* Banner-journal

JACKSON county journal. w F 1886-Mr 3 1926||
United with Badger state banner to form Banner-journal
WHi Jl 27 1898-1926

NORTHWESTERN democrat. *See under* Prairie du Chien

Friday evening **POST.** *See* Fairchild graphic (Fairchild)

WISCONSIN independent. w Jl 26 1872-N 7? 1888||
Followed by Fairchild graphic (Fairchild)
Jl 26 1872-75 pub in Viroqua
DLC Mr 22,My 31 1876
WHi 1872-N 7 1888

BLAIR

Blair **PRESS.** w 1896+
pub Mr 1915+

BLOOMER

Bloomer **ADVANCE.** w Jl 27 1880+
1880-My 1886 as Bloomer workman
pub 1880+
WBl 1923-27;29;31+
WHi My 1881+

Bloomer **WORKMAN.** *See* Bloomer advance

BLOOMINGTON

Bloomington **RECORD.** w Jl 15 1880+
pub 1880+
WHi Jl 29 1880-D 14 1882;Ag 1897+

REVEALER. w Jl 31 1894-95||*
WHi Ag 28-O 1894

WEST GRANT advocate. w Je 18 1873-O 1874||
Followed by Grant county advocate (Lancaster)
WHi 1873-My 20 1874

BLUE MOUNDS

Blue Mounds weekly **NEWS.** *See* Mount Horeb weekly news (Mount Horeb)

BOSCOBEL

BOSCOBELLIAN. *See* Boscobel broad-axe

Boscobel **BROAD-AXE.** w D 18 1862-My 31 1866||
D 18 1862 as Boscobellian; D 27 1862-Je 20 1864 National broad-axe; Jl 20 1864 Boscobel hatchet
Mr-Jl 1864 pub in Prairie du Chien
MWA Ja 18 1866
WHi Je 25 1863-66

Boscobel weekly **DEMOCRAT.** D 1859-My 1860||
Followed by Boscobel express
WHi Ja 28 1860

Boscobel **DIAL.** w D 25 1872+
Ag 20 1919 as Dial enterprise
pub 1872-76;Mr 1911+
WHi 1874+

ENTERPRISE. w My 1892-O 9 1895||
1892-My 1893 as Grant county leader. United with Dial to form Dial-enterprise, later Boscobel dial
WHi F 13 1895

WISCONSIN (*Continued*)

BOSCOBEL—*Continued*

Boscobel EXPRESS. O 1860-Ja 2 1862||
Followed Boscobel weekly democrat

GRANT county leader. *See* Enterprise

Boscobel HATCHET. *See* Boscobel broad-axe

NATIONAL broad-axe. *See* Boscobel broad-axe

Boscobel SENTINEL. w D 19 1900-Ag 6 1919||
Merged with Boscobel dial
WHi Ja 30 1901-19

BRANDON

Brandon TIMES. w Jl 9 1863+
pub N 1914+
MWA Ag 31 1876
WHi Mr 9 1867+

BRILLION

Brillion NEWS. w S 4 1894+
pub 1894+
WHi Ja 31 1913+

BRODHEAD

BUSY citizen. w My 1893-99||?
WHi O 10 1893-D 23 1898

INDEPENDENT-register. w Mr 1 1860+
1860-Jl 15 1909 as Independent
MWA Ag 19-26 1881
WBr 1861-63;65-70;76+
WHi Mr 1867-68;My 15 1885+

Brodhead NEWS. w S 16 1909-N 27 1930||
Merged with Independent-register
WBr 1920-26
WHi D 9 1909-30

REGISTER. N 1 1883-Jl 14 1909||
United with Independent to form Independent-register
WBr 1907-09
WHi Ja 5 1898-1909

Brodhead weekly REPORTER. w Ap 26 1859-
Suspended N 13 1861-Mr 25 1862
WHi 1859-Ap 15 1862

BROOKLYN

Brooklyn NEWS. w 1897-1905||?
WHi O 14 1898-N 1 1905

Brooklyn TELLER. w 1908+
pub S 1918+
WHi Ja 13 1915+

BRUCE

Bruce NEWS-letter. w O 1900+
pub 1906+
WHi O 27 1905-O 1 1909;F 1920-O 20 1921

BUFFALO CITY

BUFFALO county republikaner. *See* Buffalo county republican (Fountain City)

BURLINGTON

Burlington FREE PRESS. w N 1879+
pub 1881+
WHi My 17 1881-Mr 30 1892

Burlington GAZETTE. w My 14 1859-D 11 1860||
Followed by Horicon gazette (Horicon)
WHi complete

STANDARD democrat. w O 14 1863+
1863-Ap 3 1886 as Burlington standard
pub 1863+
MWA Ap 6-13,Jl 27,Ag 31 1876
NbHi D 16 1875
WHi Je 22 1864-My 15 1886;Mr 21 1891+

STANDARD democrat. German ed. w D 12 1896-1911||?
WHi 1897-Mr 1905

BUTTERNUT

Butternut BULLETIN. w F 20 1922+
pub 1922+

CADOTT

Cadott BLADE. *See* Cadott sentinel

Cadott SENTINEL. w 1891+
1891-Ap 1914 as Cadott blade
pub Ap 1914+

CAMBRIA

Cambria NEWS. w 1883+
WHi O 4 1895-1920

CAMBRIDGE

Cambridge NEWS. w F 1 1886+
pub 1886+
KHi S 13,27 1888
WHi Jl 16 1897,D 3 1926

CAMERON

BARRON county independent. *See under* Barron

CAMPBELLSPORT

Campbellsport NEWS. w 1908+
pub 1908+
WHi Je 11 1908-S 7 1916;Ja 11 1917

CASHTON

Cashton RECORD. w 1896+
pub [1896+]
WHi 1903+

CASSVILLE

Cassville INDEX. w Mr 8 1888-Ag 9 1917||
Merged with Bloomington record (Bloomington)
WHi complete

CAZENOVIA

Cazenovia REPORTER. w O 1910+
WHi Mr 1911+

CEDARBURG

Cedarburg ENTERPRISE. *See* Ozaukee county enterprise

Cedarburg NEWS. w Ja 7 1883+
1883-1893 as Cedarburg weekly news
WHi 1883+

OZAUKEE county enterprise. w My 1879-My 31 1881||
My 1879-D 29 1880 as Cedarburg enterprise
WHi Mr 10 1880-Ap 20 1881

CENTRALIA

Papers published in Centralia are listed under Wisconsin Rapids

CENTURIA

Centuria OUTLOOK. w F 14 1902-O 8 1909||
WHi complete

CHETEK

Chetek ALERT. w S 15 1882+
pub 1882+
WHi S 29 1882+

CHILTON

INDEPENDENT journal. w 1916-F 1933||
United with Chilton times to form Chilton times-journal
WChiT complete

Chilton TIMES-JOURNAL. w S 26 1857+
1857-F 23 1933 as Chilton times
pub 1857+
CoFc O 1857-Je 18 1870
LSfD D 11 1858;N 10 1860;Je 8 1861;Ap 5-12 1862
WHi S 26,D 24 1857+

WISKONSIN demokrat. w 1873-78||?
In German
MWA Ag 26 1876

CHIPPEWA FALLS

CATHOLIC sentinel. w Ag 1889-My 25 1916||
1889 as Chippewa sentinel
WCh 1902-16
WHi Ja 21 1892-1916

CHIPPEWA county independent. w Ap 1881-D 11 1889||
Merged with Chippewa times
NNHi D 31 1885;Mr 4 1886;Mr 12 1888
WHi D 29 1881-Ap 17 1884

CHIPPEWA Valley union. *See* Chippewa union and times

Chippewa Falls DEMOCRAT. w My 6 1869-D 1872||?
WHi Je 3 1869-N 14 1872

Chippewa daily GAZETTE. *See* Chippewa telegram

Chippewa weekly HERALD. w Ja 29 1870-1918||?
Ja 29 1870-Je 22 1894 as Chippewa herald
ICM Je 2 1876
KHi Je 15,Ag 3 1888
NNHi Ag 1 1879;Jl 8 1881;Je 11 1886
WCh 1870-71;73-80;83-84;86;88-92;1900-18
WHi F 19 1870-Ag 1917

Chippewa HERALD-TELEGRAM. d Je 25 1894+
1894-D 4 1926 as Chippewa herald
pub D 1926+
WCh 1919+

Evening INDEPENDENT. *See* Chippewa telegram

Chippewa OBSERVER. w 1896-O 4 1899||
WHi 1898-99

PEOPLE'S paper. w Ag 11 1894-95||?
WHi Ag-N 17 1894

Chippewa SENTINEL. *See* Catholic sentinel

Chippewa TELEGRAM. d O 2 1887-D 4 1926||
1887-1920 as Evening independent; 1921-22 Wisconsin press; 1923-24 Chippewa daily gazette. United with Chippewa herald to form Chippewa herald-telegram
NNHi Jl 10 1901
WCh 1903-24
WChH complete
WHi Ag 16 1916-S 27 1919(Sunday ed only)

Chippewa Falls TIMES. My-Jl 1866||
United with Chippewa valley union to form Chippewa union and times

Chippewa TIMES. w O 6 1875-Ag 15 1916||
D 18 1889-Ap 5 1892 as Chippewa times and independent. Merged with Daily independent, later Chippewa telegram
NNHi Ag 19 1885
WHi D 1875-1916

Chippewa UNION and times. w S 1861-D 7 1869||
1861-Jl 1866 as Chippewa valley union. Merged with Chippewa Falls democrat
WHi Ja 12 1867-Ja 9 1869

WISCONSIN press. *See* Chippewa telegram

CLAYWOOD

MAPLE Valley educator. w Ap 8 1893-
WHi My 20,Jl 1,15 1893

CLEAR LAKE

NORTH Wisconsin news. *See under* Hayward

CLINTON

Clinton HERALD. w N 12 1874-O 1 1907||
1874-F 25 1880 as Independent; Mr 4-Ag 11 1880 Rock county republican; O 1 1880-N 23 1881 Weekly herald
WClT [1885-1907]
WHi Ja 13 1875-Ag 11,O 1880-N 23 1881;Ag 1882-1907

INDEPENDENT. *See* Clinton herald

ROCK county republican. *See* Clinton herald

Clinton TIMES-OBSERVER. w 1923+
pub Ag 1923+
WHi Ag 21 1925+

Weekly WITNESS. My 19 1893-Jl 1894||?
WHi 1893-Je 22 1894

CLINTONVILLE

DAIRYMAN-gazette. w Je 5 1919+
1919-F 22 1923 as Clintonville gazette
WHi 1919+

Clintonville GAZETTE. *See* Dairyman-gazette

Clintonville HERALD. w S 5? 1878-O 10 1879||?
WHi Mr 14-O 10 1879

Clintonville TRIBUNE. w Ag 11 1881+
pub 1881+
WHi My 17 1918+

COCHRANE

Cochrane RECORDER. w D 14 1914+
pub 1914+

COLBY

LANGLADE enterprise. *See* Enterprise (Neillsville)

Colby PHONOGRAPH. w S 11 1878+
1878-Mr 14 1918 as Phonograph
pub 1878+
WHi F 19 1879+

COLFAX

Colfax MESSENGER. w Ap 30 1897+
pub 1897+

COLUMBUS

Columbus DEMOCRAT. w S 10 1868+
Follows Transcript
pub 1868+
WHi Mr 1871-Je 13 1873;Ja 16 1874-1903

Columbus weekly JOURNAL. w F 27 1855-N 6 1864||
1855-My 30 1861 as Republican journal
WHi 1855-63

Columbus REPUBLICAN. w O 7 1868+
MWA Jl 14 1869
WHi N 18 1871-O 1872

REPUBLICAN journal. *See* Columbus weekly journal

TRANSCRIPT. w Ja 1865-Ag 1868||
Followed by Columbus democrat

Columbus UNION banner. w Je 19 1862-
WHi Je 26-Ag 7 1862

COPPER HARBOR

LAKE Superior news and miners' journal. w Jl 25 1846-
DLC Ag 22,O 10 1846

CORNELL

CHIPPEWA Valley courier. w 1912+
WCor 1922+

WISCONSIN (*Continued*)

CRANDON

FOREST echo. w Ag 1906-15||?
WHi Ag 28 1906-1914
FOREST leaves. *See under* North Crandon
FOREST republican. w O 14 1886+
pub 1925+
WHi 1886-1905

CUBA CITY

Cuba City HERALD. w 1904-06||
United with Cuba City news to form Cuba City news-herald
Cuba City NEWS-HERALD. w 1894+
1894-1906 as Cuba City news
pub [1894+]
WHi F 22 1918

CUDAHY

Cudahy ENTERPRISE. w 1908+
WHi S 6 1912-N 9 1918
Cudahy TIMES. w O 29 1893-94||?
WHi [1893-Mr 21 1894]

CUMBERLAND

Cumberland ADVOCATE. w My 22 1881+
1881-Mr 1885 as Cumberland herald
pub 1885[87]-[1910-11]+
WCu O 8 1908-My 1910;F 8 1912+
WHi Ag 14 1890+
BARRON county independent. *See under* Barron
Cumberland HERALD. *See* Cumberland advocate
Cumberland JOURNAL. My 26 1911-Ja 1 1915||
WCu complete

CURTISS

Curtiss ADVANCE. w 1923+
pub 1923
WAbT 1924-26

DALE

Dale RECORDER. w Ag 3 1899-1919||?
WHi 1899-Jl 26 1918

DALEYVILLE

Daleyville DOINGS. *See* Parish doings (Mount Horeb)

DARIEN

Darien NEWS. w Ag 1858-
WHi Ap 26 1859

DARLINGTON

Darlington DEMOCRAT. w N 1 1865+
Follows Southwestern local (Shullsburg). 1865-O 6 1882 as Lafayette county democrat; O 13 1882-My 4 1888 Democrat; My 11 1888-D 29 1893 Democrat and register
WHi N 1866+
DEMOCRAT and register. *See* Darlington democrat
DEMOCRATIC register. w N 5 1885-My 4 1888||
Merged with Darlington democrat
WHi complete
Darlington JOURNAL. w D 1885-Ja 3 1900||
United with Darlington republican to form Republican-journal
WHi S 28 1887-1900
LAFAYETTE county democrat. *See* Darlington democrat
LAFAYETTE county independent. *See* Republican-journal
LAFAYETTE county union. *See* Republican-journal
REPUBLICAN-JOURNAL. w My 11 1861+
1861-Ja 12 1865 as Lafayette county independent; Ja 19 1865-Ap 8 1869 Lafayette county union; Ap 15 1869-Jl 4 1879 Republican; Jl 11 1879-Ja 5 1900 Darlington republican
pub 1873+
MWA Ja 22 1886
WHi F 1871+

DARTFORD

GREEN Lake spectator. w O 1864-Ag 1866||
Followed by Prison City leader, later Waupun leader news (Waupun)

DEERFIELD

ENTERPRISE-leader. w Jl 1891-1905||?
1891-Ap 1892 as Deerfield tobacco journal; My 1892-D 1898 Deerfield enterprise
WHi My 21 1892-Ag 26,D 29 1898-F 23 1900
Deerfield TOBACCO herald. w S 18 1885-Ap 6 1888||
Merged with Lake Mills leader (Lake Mills)
WHi complete
Deerfield TOBACCO journal. *See* Enterprise-leader

DE FOREST

De Forest TIMES. w Ag 23 1895+
WHi 1897+

DELAVAN

Delavan ENTERPRISE. w Ag 8 1878+
Formed by the union of Sharon inquirer (Sharon) and Delavan tribune. 1878-O 19 1893 as Delavan enterprise
pub 1893+
WHi Ag 15 1878+
Delavan MESSENGER. *See* Walworth county journal
NORTHRON. *See* Walworth county journal
PATRIOT. w N 1861-D 1864||
Merged with Delavan republican
DLC Mr 6 1862
ICHi Jl 26 1862
Delavan REPUBLICAN. w O 1863+
pub 1863—
OClWHi Ja 4-25 1906
WHi Ap 23 1868+
Delavan TRIBUNE. My-Ag 1878||
United with Sharon inquirer (Sharon) to form Delavan enterprise, later Enterprise
WALWORTH county journal. w D 1855-O 1860||
1855-Jl 1856 as Family messenger (Janesville); Ag 27 1856-F 18 1857 Wisconsin messenger; F 25 1857-F 1858 Delavan messenger; Mr 1858-My 1860 Northron
WHi Ag 27 1856-Je 3 1857;Ag 31 1859
WISCONSIN messenger. *See* Walworth county journal

DE PERE

BROWN county democrat. *See* De Pere journal-democrat
BROWN county journal. *See* Brown county journal-news
BROWN county journal-news. w N 10 1916-Mr 13 1919||
1916-Ap 12 1918 as Brown county journal. United with Brown county democrat to form De Pere journal-democrat
WDp complete
WGb 1916-F 20 1919
WHi complete
De Pere FACTS. *See* Twin city index
De Pere JOURNAL-democrat. w Ja 1877+
1877-Mr 13 1919 as Brown county democrat
pub 1890+
WDp 1877+
WGb [1912-Mr 13 1919]-N 4 1920
WHi 1896+
De Pere NEWS. w Ap 8 1871-Ap 11 1918||
O 5 1878-84 as De Pere news and Brown county herald. United with Brown county journal to form Brown county journal-news
KHi Ag 11,O 13 1888;Ja 5,26 1889
WDp complete
WGb N 1899-O 1900;Ap 1902-N 1905;Ja 24 1906-D 18 1912;13;Ja 14 1914-15;Jl 1916-18
WHi 1873-N 17 1883;Ja 24 1885-1918
ONZE standaard. w 1878-1907||?
1878-1896 as De Pere Standaard
In Dutch
WHi F 23 1884
De Pere STANDAARD. *See* Onze standard
TWIN CITY index. w Ja 1877-1886||?
1877-N 1883 as De Pere facts
Suspended F?-? 1877
WHi F 1879-D 8 1881
De VOLKSSTEM. w 1890-Jl 1 1919||
Merged with Gazette van Moline (Moline, Ill.)
In Dutch
IU Ap 1918-Je 1919
WHi Ja 21 1919

DE SOTO

De Soto CHRONICLE. w Je 12 1886-Ag 16 1889||
Merged with Kickapoo transcript, later Kickapoo scout (Soldiers' Grove)
WHi complete
De Soto LEADER. *See* Vernon county leader
VERNON county leader. w Ap 1872-Ap 8? 1876||
1872-Je 26 1875 as De Soto leader
WHi F 13 1875-76

DODGE CENTER

DODGE county gazette. w My-Je 9? 1852||
Followed by Dodge county gazette (Juneau)

DODGEVILLE

Dodgeville CHRONICLE. w Ag 19 1858+
1858-S 1862 as Iowa county advocate
MWA F 21 1867
WHi S 10-24 1859;S 17 1863+
EYE and star. *See* New star
IOWA county advocate. *See* Dodgeville chronicle
IOWA county republic. *See* Weekly republic
NEW star. w D 1886-Ap 27 1900||
1886-Ag 29 1889 as Rural eye; S 5 1889-D 6 1895 Eye and star. Followed by Iowa county republic, later Weekly republic
1886-N 23 1888 pub at Arena
WHi 1887-1900
Weekly REPUBLIC. w,sw My 2 1900-F 28 1906||
Follows New Star. My 2 1900-N 17 1904 as Iowa county republic. United with Dodgeville sun to form Dodgeville sun-republic
WHi complete
RURAL eye. *See* New star
Dodgeville STAR. w Je 1874-S 1889||
1874-N 23 1883 as Arena star (Arena). United with Rural eye to form Eye and star, later New star
WHi Ja 12 1877-Mr 12 1886
Dodgeville SUN-REPUBLIC. w Jl 4 1881-My 7 1931||
1881-Mr 3 1906 as Dodgeville sun. Merged with Dodgeville chronicle
WHi F 23 1882-Jl 6 1888;N 22 1895-1931

DORCHESTER

Weekly CLARION. w Jl 16 1899+
pub My 1923+

DOUSMAN

Weekly INDEX. w Mr 22 1907+
pub 1907+

DU BUQUE. *See* DUBUQUE, IOWA

DURAND

ALEMBIC. *See* Durand weekly times
COURIER-wedge. w D 22 1877+
1877-Ap 18 1918 as Pepin county courier; D 20 1878-D 12 1879 Pepin county times and courier; My 2-Jl 4 1918 Entering wedge and Pepin county courier
pub 1918+
WDu 1878-84;86-1901;05-10;My 1918+
WHi 1877-Jl 18 1918
ENTERING wedge. w Jl 6 1893-Ap 25 1918||
United with Pepin county courier to form Courier-wedge
WDu 1904-18
WHi complete
HOME mirror. *See* Durand weekly times
LEAN wolf. *See under* Menomonie
PEPIN county courier. *See* Courier-wedge
PEPIN county news. w S 11 1884-Jl 4 1906||
1884-Mr 24 1904 as Pepin star (Pepin); Ap 1 1904-Mr 27 1906 Pepin county news and Pepin star. Merged with Pepin county courier, later Courier-wedge
WHi Ap 1895-Je 1906
PEPIN county times. *See* Courier-wedge
Durand weekly TIMES. w O 1861-D 13 1878||
1861-O 1862 as Home mirror; D 1862-63 Alembic; 1863-Ap 25 1871 Durand times. Merged with Pepin county courier, later Courier-wedge
WDu 1865-69;71-76
WHi Mr 19 1870-78

EAGLE RIVER

Eagle River DEMOCRAT. *See* Vilas County news-review
Eagle River REVIEW. w 1890-Je 23 1927||
United with Vilas county news to form Vilas county news-review
WErV complete
WHi Ja 28 1916-27
VILAS county news-review. w Ap 22 1893+
1893-Ag 3 1896 as Eagle River democrat; Ag 10 1896-Je 23 1927 Vilas county news
pub Je 30 1927+
WHi 1893-1905;Je 30 1927+
Eagle River VINDICATOR. *See* Rhinelander news (Rhinelander)

EAST TROY

East Troy GAZETTE. w Jl 9? 1879-83||
WHi Ja 21 1880-Ag 9 1882
East Troy NEWS. w F 1 1893+
pub 1893+

EAU CLAIRE

ARBEIDEREN. *See* Reform
Eau Claire ARGUS. w My 7 1879-F 23 1881||
WHi complete
Eau Claire daily ARGUS. d My 5 1880-Mr 1 1881||
WHi My 5 1880
CHIPPEWA valley news. *See* Eau Claire news
COMMERCIAL index. m D 1871-72||?
WHi O 19 1872
Sunday morning FORUM. w 1891-94||?
WE 1892-Jl 9 1893
Eau Claire FREE PRESS. w S 23 1858-D 5 1901||
Merged with Weekly telegram
Suspended Je-? 1864;Ja 18-F 1866
WE 1858-88
WHi [Ap 28 1859-Ap 6 1865]Ap 11 1867-1901
Eau Claire FREE PRESS. d Ja 1 1873-D 7 1901||
Merged with Daily telegram
WE Jl 1873-1900
WHi N 19 1883-My 5 1885

WISCONSIN (*Continued*)

EAU CLAIRE—*Continued*

GAZETTE. w F 26 1885-Jl 15 1898||?
1885-S 25 1896 as Workman's gazette
WHi [O 1896-Jl 15 1898]

Eau Claire **HERALD.** w F 25-D 1862||
WHi Mr 6,15,O 1 1862

HERALD. w Ap 3 1869-N 8 1873||
1869-Mr 1872 as Augusta herald
1869-Jl 1873 pub in Augusta
WHi S 23 1871-73

Eau Claire **LEADER.** d Ap 27 1881+
WE 1896-97;Je 1898-1900;Jl 1901-S 1905;06+
WHi Jl 24 1883-N 1885;Ja 24-Ap 1900;N 23 1905+

Eau Claire weekly **LEADER.** w Ap 27 1881-1913||?
WHi My 16 1889-Je 24 1905

Eau Claire **NEWS.** w O 23 1869-D 2 1892||?
Follows West Eau Claire argus. 1869-My 8 1875 as Chippewa valley news
WHi Jl 23 1870;F 19 1874;Ja 22 1876-Jl 6 1878;Jl 21 1883-D 2 1892

REFORM. F 9 1886+
1886-Jl 1888 as Arbeideren
In Norwegian
pub 1888+
IaDeL Jl 23 1889-[99]-[1902-16]-[31]+
MnHi 1903+
MnU Ag 1924+
WHi O 29 1895-Ag 4 1896[Je 18-S 24 1925;Ja 1-Jl 1 1926;S 12-26 1929]

Sunday **SENTINEL.** Je 27 1883-84||?
Je 27 1883-N 18 1884 as Eau Claire weekly sentinel

Daily **TELEGRAM.** d D 16 1894+
D 16 1894-Je 20 1897 as Morning telegram (F 25-Ap 6 1895 Evening telegram)
MWA O 31 1906
WE 1896-97;O 1903-Mr 17 1904;O-D 1905
WHi F 1895+

Weekly **TELEGRAM.** w D 16 1894-1906||?
WE 1897-98
WHi S 1898-1905

Eau Claire city **TELEGRAPH.** w My 25 1857-Mr 3 ? 1859||
Merged with Eau Claire free press
WHi My 25,D 28 1857;Jl 10 1858

Eau Claire **TIMES.** w My 16 1857-Ja 2 1858||?
Merged with Eau Claire city telegraph
WHi [My 23-N 28 1857]D 26 1857;Ja 2 1858

WEST Eau Claire argus. w N 9 1865-Je? 1869||
Followed by Chippewa Valley news, later Eau Claire news
WHi D 14 1865-D 23 1868

WORKMAN'S gazette. *See* Gazette

EDGERTON

Edgerton **INDEPENDENT.** *See* Wisconsin tobacco reporter

Edgerton **UNION.** w Ap 26 1866-
WHi Je 7-28;Jl 12 1866

WISCONSIN tobacco reporter. w D 4 1874+
1874-Ap 6 1877 as Edgerton independent
pub 1880+
WHi My 19 1876+

ELKHORN

BLADE. w Ap 17 1891-N 28 1905||?
WHi 1891-N 28 1905

Elkhorn **CONSERVATOR.** m S 15 1857||
Cover title incorrectly dated as O 10 1857
ICN complete
OClWHi complete
WHi complete

CONSERVATOR. w Je 28 1859-
WHi Je 28 1859

Elkhorn **INDEPENDENT.** w My 1853+
1853-55; Je 10 1868-F 4 1892 as Walworth county independent
pub 1853+
MWA Ja 18 1861
WHi Ag 26 1859-Ag 13 1874[1875]F 23 1882+
WEl N 1926+

Elkhorn **LIBERAL.** w O 25 1873-Ja 7 1876||
1873-Jl 16 1875 as Walworth county liberal
WHi D 20 1873-76

WALWORTH county democrat. w My 26 1847-49||?
WHi Ja 19,Ag 4 1848

WALWORTH county independent. *See* Elkhorn independent

WALWORTH county liberal. *See* Elkhorn liberal

WALWORTH county reporter. w Ag 8 1845-N 1856||
1845-Mr 1853 as Western star. Merged with Elkhorn independent
WHi [1849-56]

WESTERN star. *See* Walworth county reporter

ELLSWORTH

Ellsworth **GLEANER.** *See* Ellsworth record

PIERCE county herald. w Ja 16 1868+
pub 1868+
DLC S 28 1871
WHi Ag 28 1872-S 24 1884;F 13 1896+

Ellsworth **RECORD.** w 1894+
1894-1904? as Ellsworth gleaner
pub 1925+

ELMWOOD

Elmwood weekly **ARGUS.** w N 20 1920+
pub 1920+

ELROY

Elroy **CHRONICLE.** *See* Juneau county chronicle (Mauston)

Elroy **HEADLIGHT.** w Ap 30 1874-My 11 1867||
WHi S 10 1874;F 1875-76

JUNEAU county chronicle. *See under* Mauston

JUNEAU county plain-talker. *See* Plain talker

LEADER. *See* Elroy leader-tribune

Elroy **LEADER-TRIBUNE.** w 1898+
1898-My 4 1922 as Leader
WHi My 11 1922-Jl 12 1928

PLAIN talker. w O 4 1876-S 27 1883||
1876-Ja 25 1878 as Juneau county plain talker. Merged with Elroy leader-tribune
WHi 1877-83

TRIBUNE. w N 2 1881-My 4 1922||
O 5 1883-N 7 1884 as Elroy tribune and plain talker. United with Leader to form Elroy leader-tribune
WHi Ja 11 1882-1922

Elroy **UNION.** w Ja 11 1873-Ja 8 1874||
WHi complete

WISCONSIN statesman. w O-D 1875||
Campaign paper
WHi O 12-26 1875

EUREKA

Eureka **JOURNAL.** w My 10 1867-My 6 1868||
MnHi My 10,N 1 1867
WHi complete

EVANSVILLE

BADGER. w O 13 1894-Ap 7 1906||
Merged with Evansville review
WHi complete

CITIZEN. *See* Evansville review

Saturday **ENTERPRISE.** *See* Tribune

ENTERPRISE and tribune. w Je 1881-Ja 18 1911||
Je-N 1881 as Pudding-stick; D 1881-My 15 1908 Enterprise
WHi F 28 1882-1911

INDEPENDENT. *See under* Madison

PUDDING-STICK. *See* Enterprise and tribune

Evansville **REVIEW.** w Ja 3 1866+
1866-Mr 3 1870 as Citizen
pub 1927+
MWA Je 30 1883
WHi Mr 15 1870-My 17 1894;Ap 1895+

TRIBUNE. w 1882-My 12 1908||
1882-83? as Saturday enterprise. United with Enterprise to form Enterprise and tribune
WHi Ag 5 1886-1908

FAIRCHILD

Fairchild **GRAPHIC.** w Je 1890-O 21 1895||
Follows Wisconsin independent (Black River Falls). Je 1890-Ag 1895 as Friday evening post (Black River Falls)

Fairchild **OBSERVER.** w D 23 1897-O 10 1918||
WHi Ag 1905-18

FAIRWATER

Fairwater **REGISTER.** w Ap 24 1903-05||?
WHi 1903-Jl 1 1904

FALL RIVER

NEW ERA. w D 29 1905-Mr 1 1912||
Merged with Columbus republican (Columbus)
WHi 1906-12

FENNIMORE

Fennimore **TIMES.** w Ag 30 1889+
My 1893-D 5 1900 as Times-review
DLC Ag 7 1907
WHi O 1895+

TIMES-REVIEW. *See* Fennimore times

FIFIELD

Fifield **ADVOCATE.** w O 25 1883-95||?
WHi O 25 1883

FLORENCE

Florence **MINING** news. w Ja 1881+
MiHoM 1886+
WHi D 3 1881+

FOND DU LAC

COMMONWEALTH. w N 9 1852-1920||?
1852-S 2 1856 as Fountain City herald. Title varies: Fond du Lac commonwealth; Fond du Lac weekly commonwealth
DLC O 19,N 16-D 14,28 1859;Ja-O 3 1860
KHi Ag 10 1864
MB [1852-54]
MWA F 21 1866
N Ap 2 1862
WF 1852-O 1854;O 15 1856-S 23 1863;O 12 1864-67;Ap 5-Je 13 1868;Ag 29-D 14 1870;Mr 1872-F 17,Ag 28 1885-1920
WHi 1852-1906

Daily **COMMONWEALTH.** *See* Fond du Lac commonwealth-reporter

Fond du Lac **COMMONWEALTH**-reporter. d Ag 22 1870+
Follows Fountain city daily herald. 1870-S 30 1926 as Daily commonwealth
pub 1926+
WF 1870+
WHi F 27 1902+

DAHEIM. w 1884-Ag 4 1918||
Sunday ed of Nordwestliche courier
In German
WHi N 25 1917-18

DEMOCRATIC press. w My 29 1858-N 3? 1866||
Formed by the union of Fond du Lac union and Fond du Lac journal (1857-58)
WHi Je 5,Jl 9,D 15 1858
—d ed. *See* Daily Fond du Lac press

FOUNTAIN CITY. w O 2 1841-Ap 23? 1851||
1841-N 5 1844 as Green Bay republican; N 1844-Jl 1850 Wisconsin republican. Followed by Patriot, later National democrat
1841-D 1847 pub at Green Bay
DLC Ap 2,My 28,Je 21,Jl 16,30,Ag 13,27 1849
ICHi Mr 4 1845
NNHi Mr 5,My 7 1844
NcD N 20,D 11 1841
WHi D 18 1841;S 10 1842;Ja 28,Ag 26,O 17 1843-N 5 1844;Ja 21,Ap 29,S 23 1845;F 8 1847; Jl 2 1849

FOUNTAIN CITY daily herald. d Jl 25 1854-S 1856||
Followed by Daily commonwealth, later Fond du Lac commonwealth reporter
DLC Jl-N 10 1854
WHi Jl-O 20 1854;Mr-S 1856

FOUNTAIN CITY herald. w *See* Commonwealth

Fond du Lac **JOURNAL.** w O 1 1846-Je 23 1853||
United with National democrat to form Fond du Lac union
DLC Ag 19 1852;F 10,24-Mr 3,Ap 7-15,28-My 5,19-Je 2 1853
WF O 8 1846-Je 16 1853
WHi 1850-53

Fond du Lac **JOURNAL.** w F 21 1857-My 22 1858||
United with Fond du Lac union to form Democratic press
WHi [1857-58]

Fond du Lac **JOURNAL.** w My 2 1867-94||
Merged with Saturday reporter
WF 1867-92
WHi Ag 31 1874-F 3 1881;Mr 1882-N 11 1886

NATIONAL democrat. w Ap 30 1851-Je 23? 1853||
Follows Fountain city. 1851-Ja 31 1852 as Patriot. United with Fond du Lac journal (1846-53) to form Fond du Lac union
DLC O 13 1853
WHi F 9 1853

NORDWESTLICHE courier. w My 4 1871-1920||?
In German
WHi Ja 29 1874-O 14 1875;Ap 8 1896
—**Sunday ed.** *See* Daheim

PATRIOT. *See* National democrat

PEOPLE'S champion. *See under* Appleton

Daily Fond du Lac **PRESS.** d F 7 1865-N 3? 1866||
d ed of Democratic press
WHi Jl 23-25,S 25-N 3 1866

Daily **REPORTER.** d Mr 1883-S 30 1926||
1894-Mr 30 1901 as Daily reporter and Fond du Lac journal. United with Daily commonwealth to form Fond du Lac commonwealth reporter
1883-1913? as d ed of Saturday reporter
KHi N 21 1888;Jl 23 1889
WF Ap 1898-1926
WHi Je 8 1894-1926

Saturday **REPORTER.** w Ag 25 1860-1913||?
DLC Jl 1 1876
MWA D 11 1875
OClWHi Ap 4,S 26 1863;Ja 1,Mr 19,Jl 9,S 10 1864;Mr 11 1865
WF Ag 23 1862-69;F 16 1878-79
WHi Ja 26 1861-Ja 5 1889

TRIBUN. *See under* Sheboygan

Fond du Lac **UNION.** w Je 23 1853-My 20 1858||
Formed by the union of Fond du Lac journal (1846-53) and National democrat. United with Fond du Lac journal (1857-58) to form Democratic press
WF 1853-Je 14 1855
WHi complete

WESTERN freeman. w O? 1853-S 3 1856||
1853-S 28 1854 as Free press (Sheboygan Falls). United with Fountain city herald to form Commonwealth
P-M My 9 1855
WHi D 1854-56

WISCONSIN (*Continued*)

FOND DU LAC—*Continued*

Fond du Lac WHIG. w D 14 1846-D 17 1847||
WHi complete

WISCONSIN republican. *See* Fountain city

FORT ATKINSON

CAYUGA chief. *See* Wisconsin chief

Fort Atkinson CHRONICLE. w O 31 1895-D 19 1899||?
WHi 1895-D 19 1899

Fort Atkinson HERALD. w Ag 25 1866-S 4 1873||
Followed by Sharon inquirer (Sharon)
MWA S 1 1866
WHi Je 29 1872-73

JEFFERSON county union. w Mr 17 1870+
1870-My 1873 pub at Lake Mills
pub Mr 24 1871+
WHi F 1878+

Fort Atkinson STANDARD. w S 1 1859-63||?
MWA My 10 1860
WHi 1859-Ag 13 1863

WISCONSIN chief. w Ja 4 1849-
1849-56 as Cayuga chief
1849-Jl? 1856 pub in Auburn, N.Y.
DLC Ap 4 1854
MWA Jl 8 1856 O 15 1856;Jl 22 1857-My 19, Ag 11,S 15 1858;Ja-Mr,Ap 20,My 11,Je-Jl 27 1859
NAub 1849-[52]
NN O 8 1850
NcD F 20 1855
WHi My 3 1853;O 31,N 21-28,D 12-19 1854; Ja 1855

FORT HOWARD

BROWN County herald. w N 1872-S 1878||
1872-Mr 1878 as Fort Howard herald. Merged with Depere news (De Pere)
WHi Ag 13 1874-Mr 29 1877

Fort Howard HERALD. *See* Brown county herald

Fort Howard JOURNAL. w N 2 1878-O 1880||
WGb 1878-N 21 1879
WHi F 1879-Ap 24 1880

Fort Howard MONITOR. w O 10 1872-Ja 4 1877||
Merged with Fort Howard herald
WHi Ja 27 1876-77

Fort Howard REVIEW. *See* Green Bay review (Green Bay)

FORT MADISON

Fort Madison PATRIOT. w Mr 28 1838-
DLC Ap 4 1838

FORT WINNEBAGO. *See* PORTAGE

FOUNTAIN CITY

Fountain City BEACON. w Jl 18 1856-O 1858||
D 1856- ? as Fountain City beacon and Buffalo, Dunn, Chippewa, Trempealeau, and Clark counties advertiser
WHi [Ag-D 13 1856]

BUFFALO county republican. w Mr 15 1861+
1861-Ja 31 1924 as Buffalo county republikaner (S 29 1892-N 22 1894 as Buffalo county republikaner und Alma blaetter)
1861-My 1864 pub at Buffalo City
1861-192? in German
pub 1861;75+
WHi Ap 16 1870+

BUFFALO county republikaner. *See* Buffalo county republican

FOX LAKE

GAZETTE. *See* Fox Lake record

JOURNAL. *See* Fox Lake record

Fox Lake RECORD. w D 1854-Ag 1866||
1854-Jl 1856 as Times; Jl 1856-Mr 1858 Journal; Mr 1858-Mr 8 1865 Gazette. Followed by Fox Lake representative
Suspended Mr 15-My 7 1865
WHi Ap 1858-Mr 8 1865

Fox Lake REPRESENTATIVE. w O 1 1866+
Follows Fox Lake record
pub 1866+
WFo 1900—
WHi Je 16 1871-Ap 1881;D 15 1911-Ja 19 1912;Ag 7 1930+

TIMES. *See* Fox Lake record

FREDERIC

Frederic STAR. w F 26 1903+
WHi 1903+

FRIENDSHIP

ADAMS county press. w Jl 1861-F 16 1918||
MWA F 16 1866
WHi Je 30 1865-1918

GALESVILLE

Galesville INDEPENDENT. w O 1874-1908||
Merged with Galesville republican
WGR 1890-94;1905
WHi Ja 13 1876-F 10 1887

Galesville JOURNAL and record. w My 6 1870-Ag 7 1874||
1870-Ja 2? 1873 as Galesville journal. Followed by Trempealeau county messenger, later Whitehall times (Whitehall)
WHi complete

Galesville REPUBLICAN. w S 30 1897+
pub 1897+
WHi O 28 1897+

Galesville TRANSCRIPT. *See* Trempealeau county record (Trempealeau)

GENEVA

WISCONSIN standard. w
DLC Ap 21-Jl 14 1849

GENOA JUNCTION

Genoa Junction JOURNAL. w D 1890-S 4 1895||
Merged with Lake Geneva news-tribune (Lake Geneva)
WHi F 22-S 4 1875

GILLETT

Gillett TIMES. w 1900+
WHi Jl 29 1926

GLENWOOD CITY

To 1910 as Glenwood

Glenwood GLEANER. *See* Glenwood City tribune

Glenwood City TRIBUNE. w 1889+
1889-91 as Glenwood gleaner; 1891-Ja 4 1912 Glenwood tribune
pub 1889+
WHi Ag 14 1903-Jl 18 1918;Ja 20 1921+

GLIDDEN

Glidden ENTERPRISE. w Je 4 1906+
pub 1906+

Glidden PIONEER. w N 29 1884-Mr 16 1889||
WHi complete

GRAFTON

Grafton ENTERPRISE. w Jl 27 1927-Ap 13 1928||
United with Port Washington pilot, and Port Washington star to form Port Washington pilot, Port Washington star and Grafton enterprise (Port Washington)
WHi Jl 27,Ag 3 1927

GRAND RAPIDS. *See* WISCONSIN RAPIDS

GRANTON

Granton NEWS. w 1904-My 6 1921||
United with Republican and press (Neillsville) and Neillsville times to form Neillsville press (Neillsville)

GRANTSBURG

BURNETT county sentinel. w F 12 1875-Ja 27 1910||
Merged with Journal of Burnett county

JOURNAL of Burnett county. w Ag 7 1895+
F 14 1910-Mr 28 1929 as Journal of Burnett county and Burnett county sentinel
pub 1895+
WHi 1895+

GRAVESVILLE

CALUMET republican. w Ag 4 1859-D 1861||
WHi 1859-Jl 1861

GREEN BAY

Green Bay ADVANCE. *See* Sunday advance

Sunday ADVANCE. w Ja 1883-Mr 15 1885||
Follows Green Bay data. 1883? as Green Bay advance
WHi Je 15-Jl 6 1884

Green Bay ADVOCATE. w,sw,tw Ag 13 1846-D 18 1906||
Merged with Green Bay gazette
sw 1899-S 13 1901,Ja 17 1905-06;tw S 17 1901-O 1903
DLC O 21 1852;Je 1,N 30 1854;Ja 4-11,Mr 9,Jl 19,D 6 1855;D 24 1857;Ag 26 1858;Ja 13-My 5,S 15 1859
MWA Je 17 1847;N 18 1852;F 16 1854;F 22, Ap 12,My 3,24,Je 14,27,Jl 12-19 1855
OClWHi Ja 24,My 15 1856
WGb 1846-Jl 13 1848;Je 28,Ag 2 1849;Ag 29 1850-Ag 12 1852;Ap 7,D 15 1853-S 1856;Ag 4,25,S 22,O 6,N 24 1859;Ap 14,My 5-11 1865; Ap 11 1867;Je 18,N 25 1868;Ap 8 1869;Jl 7 1870-Je 1871;Ag 22 1872;Mr 25 1875;My 24 1877;Ap 1889;1902;Mr 31 1904-Je,N 14 1905-06
WHi [1846-53]Mr 30 1854-59;Ja-Je 1861;Ag 21 1862-D 23 1897;99-1906

Green Bay ADVOCATE. d C 1894-D 31 1898; 1902-D 15 1906||
1894-Ja 14 1898 as Green Bay daily advocate; Ja 15-S 27 1898 Evening advocate; S 28-D 31 1898 Advocate
WGb S 16 1896-98;O 8 1902-06
WHi 1897-98;N 19 1903-06

ADVOCATE daily bulletin. d Ap 21? 1861-Ag 1862||
WHi Je 22 1861

Green Bay BANNER. w
In German
WGb N 19-O 21 1859

Bay City PRESS. w Je 30 1860-Ap 19 1862||
WHi complete

CONCORDIA. *See* Green Bay courier

Green Bay COURIER. w O 1874-Jl 1883||
1874-D 1 1881 as Concordia. Followed by Der landsmann
1874-Jl 1875 pub at Manitowoc
In German
WHi Ag 1875-81

Green Bay DATA. d,tw D 26 1881-Ja 1883||
1881-D 9 1882 as Daily data. Followed by Green Bay advance, later Sunday advance
d 1881-D 9 1882
WHi Ja 6 1882-Ja 11 1883

FREE PRESS. d My 14 1914-Je 28 1915||
United with Green Bay gazette to form Green Bay press-gazette
WHi complete

Green Bay semi-weekly GAZETTE. w,sw Mr 3 1866-O 15 1915||
1866-Ag 6 1870 as Green Bay gazette; Ag 13 1870-Ag 1 1894 State gazette; Ag 8 1894-My 20 1899 Green Bay weekly gazette
MWA D 11 1869
WGb N 3 1866;My 11 1867;My 30 1868;Mr 5-19,Ap 16-My 7 1870;Mr 1873-F 19 1876;91-Je 1906;Ap 1908-Mr,O 1909-Je 1913;Ag 1914-Je 1915
WHi complete

Green Bay GAZETTE. d Mr 4 1871-Je 28 1915||
1871-Ag 1894 as Daily state gazette. United with Free press to form Green Bay press-gazette
WGb 1871-F 19 1876;F 12 1889-Ap 1897;98-1915
WHi N 6 1871-Mr 8,Ap 16 1872;Mr 1 1876

Green Bay GLOBE. w F 1875-Ag 22 1883||
WHi My 1 1877-83

Green Bay daily HERALD. d 1900-01||
WGb Je 12 1900-F 21 1901

Green Bay INTELLIGENCER and Wisconsin democrat. ir D 11 1833-Je 1 1836||?
1833-Je 13 1835 as Green Bay intelligencer. United with Wisconsin free press to form Wisconsin democrat
First paper in Wisconsin territory
CSmH D 11 1833
DLC D 11 1833
MWA D 11 1833(facsimile)
NN Mr 19,Ap 5,Ag 11 1834;S 5-12 1835;F 3,24 1836
WHi 1833-Mr 9,Ap 13,My 11,Je 1 1836

Der LANDSMANN. w N 1883-1923||?
Follows Green Bay courier
In German

PHOENIX. w Ag 20-D 23 1841||
WHi O 8 1841

Green Bay POST. w
In German
WGb O 20-N 10 1858

Green Bay PRESS-gazette. d Je 29 1915+
Formed by the union of Free press and Green Bay gazette
Jl 18 1934 is Tercentennial ed
IU N 1917+
MWA Ag 6 1924
MiG Jl 18 1934
WGb Jl 1915+
WHi 1915+

Green Bay REPUBLICAN. *See* Fountain City (Fond du Lac)

Green Bay REVIEW. m,w,sw S 1875-Ja 11 1919||
1875-Je 1895 as Fort Howard review (Fort Howard) m 1875-N 1876; sw Mr-Je 1895
WGb 1897-D 22 1900;Ja 19 1901-D 14 1918
WHi F 13 1877-Mr 1895;96-1919

Green Bay SPECTATOR. w Ag 2? 1852-
DLC Ja 3-F 14,28,Mr 13,27 Ap 3,Je 15,Jl 13-N 30 1853
MWA S 7 1852
WHi F 21,Ap 24 1852

Daily STATE gazette. *See* Green Bay gazette

STATE gazette. w *See* Green Bay semi-weekly gazette

Green Bay daily TIMES. d 1899-1902||
WGb N 26 1899-Je 10 1900;My 8,10-12 1902

WISCONSIN democrat. w Ag 1836-Mr 31 1840||
Formed by the union of Green Bay intelligencer and Wisconsin democrat and Wisconsin free press. Followed by Southport telegraph, later Telegraph-courier (Kenosha)
DLC O 6 1838-S 3 1839
WHi [S 1836-Mr 24 1840]

WISCONSIN free press. w Ag 1 1835-Mr 30 1836||?
United with Green Bay intelligencer and Wisconsin democrat to form Wisconsin democrat
WHi O 1835-Mr 30 1836

WISCONSIN republican. *See* Fountain City (Fond du Lac)

WISCONSIN (*Continued*)

GREEN BAY—*Continued*

WISCONSIN staats zeitung. w Jl 1868-Jl 29 1875||
Merged with Concordia, later Green Bay courier
In German
WHi Ja 15-Ap 2,Jl 16 1874-75

GREEN LAKE

GREEN LAKE county reporter. w 1894+
pub [1908-O 1934]+
WHi S 13 1928-Ap 19 1934

GREENWOOD

Greenwood GLEANER. w 1891+
pub 1933+
WGr My 21 1929+
WHi F 1900+

HALES CORNERS

TRI-COUNTY news. w My 5 1927+
pub 1927+

HAMMOND

Hammond INDEPENDENT. w Jl 23 1875-O 19 1877||
WHi complete

HANCOCK

Hancock NEWS. w D 3 1897+
pub 1897+
WHi 1897+

HARTFORD

HOME league. w Ag 11 1860-Mr 5 1864||
NNHi My 3,S 13 1862;Je 27 1863
WHi complete

Hartford PRESS. w My 30 1867-
WHi S 5 1867

Hartford PRESS. w S 13 1872-O 23 1934||
1872-Jl 14 1876 as West Bend republican (West Bend); Jl 21 1876-Ja 3 1883 Washington county republican. United with Times to form Times-press
MWA Ap 21 1876
NNHi 1872-Ja 2 1874
WHT [1874-1934]
WHi Mr 1873-Ap 1926

TIMES-PRESS. w 1894+
1894-O 23 1934 as Times
pub 1894+

WASHINGTON county republican. *See* Hartford press

HARTLAND

Hartland NEWS. w D 15 1893+
1893-97? as News and dairyman
WHi D 15 1894-S 1895;N 1910+

HAYWARD

Hayward JOURNAL. w O 1889-My 1890||
United with North Wisconsin news to form Hayward journal-news

Hayward JOURNAL-NEWS. w My 23 1890-Je 1895||
Formed by the union of Hayward journal and North Wisconsin news
WHi 1890-94

NORTH Wisconsin news. w Ja 8 1878-My 17 1890||
United with Hayward journal to form Hayward journal-news
1878-Je 29 1883 pub in Clear Lake
WHi complete

Hayward REPUBLICAN. *See* Sawyer county record and Hayward republican

SAWYER county record. w 1904-14||?
United with Hayward republican to form Sawyer county record and Hayward republican

SAWYER county record and Hayward republican. w 1893+
1893-1914? as Hayward republican
pub 1893+
WHi D 30 1915+

HIGHLAND

Highland weekly PRESS. w 1894+
WHi S 15 1899;My 2 1900

HILLSBORO

Hillsboro ENTERPRISE. w 1901-02||
United with Hillsboro sentry to form Hillsboro sentry-enterprise

Hillsboro SENTRY-enterprise. w 1885+
1885-1902 as Hillsboro sentry
pub Ap 1902+
WHi Mr 12 1895-Mr 1900;29+

HOLLAND

WARE burger. *See under* Waupun

HOLLANDALE

Weekly REVIEW. w Ja 21 1898+
pub [1898+]

HORICON

Horicon ARGUS. w S 7 1854-N 30 1860||
United with Dodge county excelsior to form Beaver Dam argus (Beaver Dam)
DLC Ap 1857-Mr 1858
WBdA complete
WHi complete

Horicon GAZETTE. w Ja 9 1861-Ja 1 1862||
Follows Burlington gazette (Burlington)
WHi complete

Horicon REPORTER. w F 1894+
pub 1900+

HORTONVILLE

Weekly REVIEW. w 1890-D 26 1935||
WHi My 6 1915-35

HUDSON

Hudson BROADCASTER. bw F 15-Mr 1 1927||?
WHi F 15,Mr 1 1927

Hudson CHRONICLE. *See* Hudson city times

Hudson DEMOCRAT. w O 1868-D 30 1874||
Merged with True republican
WHi Ja 10 1872-74

Hudson JOURNAL. *See* Hudson republican

NORTH star. *See* Hudson star-observer

PATHFINDER. *See* Hudson city times

Hudson REPUBLICAN. w Ag 4 1853-Mr 1855||
1853-Jl 20 1854 as Hudson journal; Jl 27-Ag 1854 St. Croix republican
MWA Mr 2 1854
NNHi Mr 2 1854
WHi S 8-15 1853;Je 22,Jl 6,20 1854

ST. CROIX county forum. w Mr 10 1927-Mr 29 1928||
Merged with Hudson star-observer
WHi complete

ST. CROIX inquirer. w Ag 29 1850-
MnHi Ag 29,S 19 1850

ST. CROIX observer. w Ag 1900-F 1909||
Ag 1900-Mr 1901 as Baldwin independent (Baldwin). United with Hudson star-times to form Hudson star-observer

ST. CROIX republican. 1854 *See* Hudson republican

ST. CROIX republican. Ag 1869 *See* New Richmond news (New Richmond)

SHIELD and banner. *See* Hudson city times

STAR and times. *See* Hudson star-observer

Hudson STAR-OBSERVER. w,sw N 30 1854+
1854-S 1864 as North star; S 1864-My 6 1898 Star and times; My 13 1898-F 12 1909 Hudson star-times
Suspended My-Je 1857
sw N 1903-F 17 1905
KHi Je 27-Jl 6 1888
N O 2 1861
OClWHi D 15 1869
WHi 1854-55;Ag 17 1859;My 24 1866+

STAR-TIMES. *See* Hudson star-observer

Hudson city TIMES. w Ag 1856-S 1864||
1856- as Shield and banner; - Pathfinder; D 1856-Jl 1860 Hudson chronicle. United with North star to form Hudson star and times, later Hudson star-observer
CtY D 20 1856
N O 26 1861
WHi My 7 1859

TRUE republican. w N 6 1871-1916||
WHi 1872-Jl 27 1916

HUMBIRD

Humbird ENTERPRISE. w O 4 1904+
pub S 1905+

HURLEY

GOGEBIC iron tribune. w My 8 1886-D 2 1893||
Merged with Montreal River miner
WHi complete

IRON county citizen. w Ja 7 1905-Ap 1910||
Merged with Montreal River miner
WHi Ja 14-21,F 4 1905

IRON county news. w 1903+
pub S 12 1913+

IRON county republican. w Je 8 1894-O 31 1903||
Merged with Montreal River miner
WHi complete

MONTREAL River miner. w O 5 1885+
pub 1885+
WHi 1885+

La NOSTRA terra. Ja 23 1904-14||
First Italian newspaper in Wisconsin
WHi Ja 23 1904

INDEPENDENCE

Independence NEWS-WAVE. w Mr 9 1878+
1878-Mr 1892 as Independence weekly news (Ap 26 1879-Ap 1880 Weekly news-bulletin)
pub 1920+
WHi 1878-O 1879;Ap 1892+

WAVE. w My 1888-Mr 26 1892||
United with Independence weekly news to form Independence news-wave
WHi Mr 23 1889-92

INMANSVILLE

EMIGRANTEN. *See under* Madison

IOLA

Iola HERALD. w N 1891+
WHi My 16 1918+

IRON RIVER

Iron River PIONEER. w 1894+
pub 1894+

Iron River TIMES. *See* Washburn times (Washburn)

JANESVILLE

BADGER state. w Ag 1846-D 1851||
1846-N 1848 as Rock county democrat; D 1848-F 1849 Free soil democrat; Mr 1 1849-O 20 1850 Rock county badger. Merged with Democratic standard
Suspended Ja-F 1849
MWA F 15 1851

Janesville DEMOCRAT. *See* Rock county republican

DEMOCRATEN. w Je 8 1850-O 29 1851||
Follows Nordlyset (Norway).
1850-Je 18 1851 pub at Racine
In Norwegian
IaDeL [Je 20 1850-Ap 1851]
MnSL complete

DEMOCRATIC standard. w O 11 1851-O 7 1858||
Followed by Janesville weekly times
DLC N 3 1852
MnHi Ap 22-O 20 1856
WHi complete

FAMILY messenger. *See* Walworth county journal (Delavan)

Janesville weekly FREE PRESS. w Ja 6 1853-Mr 3 1857||
1853-D 25 1855 as Janesville free press. Merged with Janesville gazette
ICHi O 16 1855
MWA F 24 1857
WHi Ja 24 1854-57

Janesville FREE PRESS. d F 1855-Mr 4 1857||
Merged with Janesville gazette
WHi Ap 10 1856-57

Janesville GAZETTE. w,sw Ag 14 1845-1916||
Mr 9? 1857-Ja 15 1864 as Weekly gazette and free press
w 1845-94
pub complete
MWA My 22 1852;Je 10 1854
WHi [Ja 24 1846-N 22]D 20 1849-Mr 14 1857; My 8 1858;Ja 22 1864-Je 1865;Jl-D 1866;69

Janesville daily GAZETTE. d Jl 11-O 7 1854; Mr 9 1857+
1857-Mr 17 1860 as Janesville morning gazette
pub 1857+
Ct Ap 30 1921
DLC N 9 1867-Je 1868
MWA S 9 1859-S 6 1862;Mr 8-S 8 1863;Jl-D 1864;Jl-D 1865;Jl-D 1866;Jl 1867-Je 1868;Ja-Je 1869
WHi 1854;57+

Janesville INDEPENDENT. w O 26 1901+
pub Mr 4 1904+

Janesville daily RECORDER. d Mr 11 1878-S 21 1913||
Merged with Janesville daily gazette
WHi Jl 21 1879-My 1 1887;Ja 1892;My 1893; Mr 27-S 21 1913

Janesville weekly RECORDER. *See* Janesville recorder and times

Janesville RECORDER and times. w S 1 1869-Mr 20 1913||
1869-O 30 1885 as Rock county recorder; N 6 1885-Ap 16 1886 Janesville recorder; Ap 23 1886-Ap 20 1893 Janesville weekly recorder and times
WHi Ja 15-Ag 1870;Ja 23 1874-1913

Evening REPUBLICAN. d 1894-1900||?
WHi Je 15 1898

ROCK county Sunday mirror. w D 16 1894-F 1895||
WHi D 16 1894

ROCK county recorder. *See* Janesville recorder and times

ROCK county republican. d,w S 7 1860-D 1861||
S-D 7 1860 as Janesville democrat
WHi 1860-S 1861

SIGNAL. w S 5 1886-O 1892||
WS Ag 9,30 1890

Saturday morning SUN. w My 1881-Je 8 1889||?
1881-D 26 1885 as Janesville weekly sun
WHi Je 17 1882-Je 8 1889

Janesville weekly SUN. *See* Saturday morning Sun

Janesville weekly TIMES. w F 8-D 22? 1859||
Follows Democratic standard
Suspended Jl 8-O 12 1859
WHi F 15-D 22 1859

WISCONSIN (*Continued*)

JANESVILLE—*Continued*

Janesville city TIMES. w Ag 1869-Ap 22 1886||
United with Janesville weekly recorder to form Janesville recorder and times
Suspended N 16 1870-Mr 1871
WHi 1873-86

JEFFERSON

Jefferson BANNER. w Jl 6 1860+
Follows Weekly Jeffersonian. 1860-S 1863 as Jefferson county republican
pub 1860+
MWA S 26 1860
WHi 1864+

Jefferson INDEPENDENT. *See* Monroe gazette (Monroe)

JEFFERSON county republican. w O 16 1855-56||?

JEFFERSON county republican. w 1860-63. *See* Jefferson banner

Weekly JEFFERSONIAN. w My 5 1853-Je 29 1860||
1853-N 16 1854 as Jeffersonian. Followed by Jefferson banner
WJeB [1853-60]

JENNY. *See* MERRILL

JUDA

Juda HOME news. w Jl 26-N 14 1907||
WHi complete

JUDEAN. *See* Latest news

LATEST news. w Jl 13 1877-S 13 1884||
1877-Mr 31 1878 as Judean
WHi F 15 1879-84

JUNEAU

BURR oak. w O 7 1853-D 29 1854||
Follows Dodge county gazette
P-M Je 30 1854
WHi complete

DODGE county democrat. w Je 1869-F 5 1879||
Merged with Juneau telephone
WHi 1876-79

DODGE county gazette. w Je 16 1852-S 23 1853||
Follows Dodge county gazette (Dodge Centre). Followed by Burr oak
MWA Jl 28 1852
WHi complete

Juneau INDEPENDENT. w D 15 1893+
WHi Je 9 1899+

Juneau TELEPHONE. w Jl 27 1877-Mr 15 1918||
1877-N 5 1880 as Telephone. Merged with Independent 1877-F 5 1879 pub at Mayville
NbHi Je 27 1879
WHi complete

WHIG of seventy-six. w N 1858-S 15 1863||
1858-D 28 1861 as Beaver Dam democrat; Ja 4-Mr 22 1862 Whig of seventy-six and Beaver Dam democrat
1858-F 12 1863 pub in Beaver Dam
WHi Ap 16 1859-63

KAUKAUNA

OUTAGAMIE county chief. w Ja 25-N 1 1894||
WHi Ja 25,N 1 1894

Kaukauna SUN. w Jl 1885-D 6 1917||
Merged with Kaukauna times
WHi D 15 1886;Je 30 1888-1917

Kaukauna TIMES. w N 1 1880+
pub 1880+
WHi N 15 1889+

Kaukauna ZEITUNG. w Mr 23 1894-S 11 1896||
Merged with Volksfreund (Appleton)
In German
WHi complete

KENDALL

KEYSTONE. w 1904+
pub 1904+

KENNAN

Kennan BANNER. m Ag 1890-Ap 1891||
WHi complete

KENOSHA

To Mr 1850 as Southport

Aigredoux and illustrated dime. ir D 18? 1857-
WHi D 25 1857

CHRONICLE. w D 16 1877-78||?
WHi D 23-30 1877;Ja 13-20,F 10 1878

Kenosha COURIER. w O 18 1879-S 27 1888||
1879-D 2 1880 as Kenosha democrat. United with Kenosha telegraph to form Kenosha telegraph-courier
WHi 1879-Ja 31 1884
WKN complete

Kenosha DEMOCRAT. sw,w Ap 23 1850-N 26 1856||
Suspended from Ja 31-Je 13 1851
sw Jl 8 1852-F 15 1853
MWA My 1 1852
WHi Je 1851-Ja,Mr 1854-56

Kenosha DEMOCRAT. w S 9 1859-Ag 30 1861||
WHi S-D 1859

Kenosha DEMOCRAT. w 1879-80. *See* Kenosha courier

Kenosha tri-weekly EXPERIMENT. tw
WHi F 26 1850

Kenosha evening HERALD. d F 22 1919-S 24 1921||
WKN complete

INDEPENDENT. w D 25(?) 1893-96||?
WHi Ja 16 1894

KENOSHA county republican. w Ja 24 1872-73||?
WHi 1872-Jl 9 1873

Daily LEDGER. d O-N 1851||?
Campaign paper
WHi O 30,31,N 1,1851

Kenosha evening NEWS. d S 22 1894+
pub 1894+
WHi Ja 11 1895+
WK S 1900+

SOUTHPORT American. w S 23 1841-O 10 1849||
DLC S 30-N 18,D 9-21,30 1841-Ja 6,Je 16,Ag 18 1842
ICHi F 10 1844
MWA N 18 1843;D 26 1846;O 10 1849
WHi Je 29 1843-49
WKN O 1845-S 1846

SOUTHPORT telegraph. *See* Telegraph-courier

Kenosha daily TELEGRAPH. d F 14-D 29 1854||
ICHi complete
WHi complete
WK complete
WKN F 17-D 28 1854

TELEGRAPH-courier. w Je 16 1840+
Follows Wisconsin democrat (Green Bay). 1840-Mr 29 1850 as Southport telegraph; Ja 4 1855-Je 9 1859 Kenosha tribune and telegraph; Je 16 1859-Je 7 1860 Kenosha telegraph and tribune; Je 14 1860-S 28 1888 Kenosha telegraph
DLC S 24 1849
ICHi S 15 1840;Ap 30 1844
MWA D 8 1840;Ag 27 1852
NSchU D 21 1841
WHi 1840-N 12 1891;95+
WK D 1848-Je 17 1853;Je-D 1871
WKN Je 1847-Je 13 1851;Je 25 1852-Je 17,D 30 1853-Ja 4 1855;Je 1858-D 7 1883;Je 1884-My 1887;Je 15 1888+

Kenosha TIMES. w Jl 2 1857-Ap 29 1859||
DLC Jl 1858-59
WHi complete
WK complete
WKN complete

Kenosha TRIBUNE. w Jl 8 1852-D 28 1854||
United with Kenosha telegraph to form Kenosha tribune and telegraph, later Telegraph-courier
Suspended S 15-O 13 1853 during which time Kenosha telegraph was sent to subscribers
WHi complete

Kenosha TRIBUNE and telegraph. *See* Telegraph-courier

Kenosha UNION. w Je 28 1866-Ap 30 1909||
WHi complete
WK 1866-Je 1 1876
WKN Mr 12 1868-Mr 11 1869;Je 1881-N 1890;Je 9 1892-Ap 23 1909

Kenosha VOLKSFREUND. w F 1892-1919||
In German
WHi Ap 1893-O 1 1896

KEWASKUM

STATESMAN. w Ja 1895+
pub 1895+

KEWAUNEE

Kewaunee ENTERPRISE. w Je 1 1859+
O 26 1859-63? as Kewaunee county enterprise
pub 1859+
WHi Je 22 1859-Ap 8 1863;Ja 26 1875+

KEWAUNEE county banner. w 1887-1926||?
In German
WHi F 1906-Ag 20 1925

KEWAUNEE county enterprise. *See* Kewaunee enterprise

KEWAUNSKÉ listy. w Ja 27 1892-1917||?
Bohemian
WHi 1892-Ap 11 1917

NEW era. w 1891-95||?
WHi Ap 4(extra)1892

KIEL

NATIONAL zeitung. *See* Tri-county record

TRI-COUNTY record. w Ja 1 1893+
1893-S 1918 as National zeitung
pub 1897+
WHi O 10 1918+
WKi Ap 30 1925+

KILBOURN. *See* WISCONSIN DELLS

KNAPP

Knapp NEWS. w O 2 1902-11||?
WHi 1902-D 6 1906

LA CROSSE

ABEND stern. d S 1892-1912||?
In German
—sw ed *See* Nordstern
—w ed *See* Volks post

AMERIKA. w Je 18 1868-D 30 1872||
In Norwegian
MnSL Ag 27 1868-72
NbHi O 15 1868

La Crosse weekly APPEAL. w Mr 13-Ap 1861||
WHi Mr 13 1861

La Crosse ARGUS. w 1897-S 26 1913||
1897-Mr 19 1904 as Weekly argus
WHi 1898-1913

La Crosse daily BADGER. D 11-31? 1895||
WHi D 11-12,19 1895

BOYCOTT'S news budget. w N 1892-1902||?
WHi My 20,1893;O 14,N 11 1899;Mr 10,31, Ap 7,Ag 4 1900

La Crosse morning CHRONICLE. d Ag 1 1878-Je 30 1912||
Follows Morning liberal democrat. Merged with La Crosse leader-press
WHi 1879-Jl 1 1880;91-S 1893;Ag 29 1894-1912
WLc complete

La Crosse Sunday CHRONICLE. w N 8 1878-Ja 14 1917||
Follows Liberal democrat. 1878-S 14 1882 as Chronicle; S 21 1882-Je 28 1906 Weekly chronicle; Jl 5 1906-12 La Crosse weekly chronicle. United with La Crosse leader-press and La Crosse tribune to form La Crosse tribune and leader-press
WHi F 14 1879-1906;Je 30 1912-17
WLc Jl-D 1912

La Crosse COURIER. w 1885-94||?
1885-Jl 1894 as La Crosse
MnHi Jl 8 1892-[94]

La Crosse DEMOCRAT. w Ap 8 1852-Jl 1872||
1852-Ap 19 1853 as Spirit of the times; Ap 26 1853-My 1 1854 La Crosse democrat; Jl 6 1854-N 22 1859 La Crosse national democrat; N 29? 1859-Mr 1861 Union and democrat; Ap 1861-My 10 1864 La Crosse weekly democrat. Followed by Liberal democrat
CtY O 8 1867;S 9 1868
DLC My 12,Je 23,O 28,D 9 1868
KHi Jl 29 1868
MWA O 27 1855;Je 11 1866;D 24 1867;Mr 24, My 5,Jl 29-S 2,16-23,O 7 21-N 25 1868
MoS O 27 1855-O 1859
MsHi O 15 1867
N Ag 20,N 26-D 3,24 1867-N 1868
NN S 30 1868
NbHi Ja 14,Ap 21,N 11,25 1868
NcD O 8 1867;Je 2,Jl 22,Ag 19-S,O 21,N 11,25 1868
PDoHi S 9 1868
PWCl F 25-Mr 3 1868
TKL F 4,18 1868
WHi 1852-My 1 1854;Mr 21 1856-O 18 1859;S 1861-Ap 10 1866
WLc 1864-Jl 11 1865;68

La Crosse DEMOCRAT. d,tw O 5 1859-Jl 1872||
O 5-N 13 1859 as La Crosse daily union; N 16 1859-My 25 1860 Daily union and democrat; Je 6 1860-My 31 1861 La Crosse tri-weekly union and democrat; Je 3 1861-Je 2 1863 La Crosse tri-weekly democrat; Je 3 1863-D 30 1868 La Crosse daily democrat; 1869 Daily democrat; 1870-71 La Crosse evening democrat. Followed by Morning liberal democrat
MnHi Ag 20 1862
MsHi O 15 1867
N O 11 1861
OClWHi Je 18 1866;Mr 24,O 21,N 25 1868
PDoHi S 9 1868
WLc 1859-N 14 1864;65;Ja-D 12 1867;68-71

La Crosse daily DEMOCRAT. Ap 1879-Ap 1880||
Followed by La Crosse daily news (1880-81)
WLc My 27-Ag 1879;Mr 2-18 1880

La Crosse DEMOCRATIC journal. w Ja 1-D 30 1863||
Merged with La Crosse democrat
WHi Je 17-D 1863

FAEDRELANDET og emigranten. *See under* Minneapolis, Minn.

FOLKEVENNEN. w 1893-95||
In Norwegian
IaDeL Ag 11 1893-F 9 1895

La Crosse FREE PRESS. w N 5 1876-S 1877||
Follows North La Crosse star. 1876-F 25 1877 as Sunday morning free press. Followed by Northwestern teetotaler
WHi F 25-Jl 21 1877

HEROLD und volksfreund. w D 22 1876-O 16 1920||?
1876-91 as Sauk county herald. Merged with Westlicher herold, Winona, Minn.
D 1876-91 pub in Reedsburg
Jl 28 1906 is jubilee ed
In German
MnHi O 26 1918-O 16 1920
NN Jl 28 1906
WHi Ja 15 1898-O 26 1918
—Wednesday ed *See* La Crosse volksfreund

La Crosse INDEPENDENT republican. *See* Republican and leader

WISCONSIN (*Continued*)

LA CROSSE—*Continued*

La Crosse evening JOURNAL. d Mr 14-Ap 16 1904||?
WHi Mr 14-Ap 16 1904

LA CROSSE. *See* La Crosse courier

La Crosse morning LEADER. d Ag 10 1869-Ag 1871||
United with La Crosse daily republican to form Daily republican and leader, later La Crosse tribune and leader-press
WHi 1869-Ap 1871

La Crosse LEADER. w Ag 14 1869-Ag 11 1871||
United with La Crosse weekly republican to form Republican and leader
WHi complete

La Crosse LEADER-PRESS. *See* La Crosse tribune and leader-press

Morning LIBERAL democrat. d Jl 11 1872-Jl 31 1878||
Follows La Crosse democrat (1859-72). 1872-Ap 15 1876 as Daily liberal democrat; Followed by La Crosse morning chronicle
WHi Ap 1875-77
WLc 1872-Ap 1874;Ap 1875-78

LIBERAL democrat. w Jl 1872-Ag 1878||
Follows La Crosse democrat. Followed by Chronicle, later La Crosse Sunday chronicle

La Crosse weekly MIRROR. w S 3 1860-Mr 4 1861||
WHi S 10,D 10 1860

MORGENSTERN. w Mr 10 1891-S 13 1921||?
1891-F 3 1914 as Nordstern blätter
In German
WHi F 10 1914-21

La Crosse NATIONAL democrat. *See* La Crosse democrat

La Crosse daily NEWS. d Jl 13 1880-D 31 1881||
Follows La Crosse daily democrat (1879-80)
WHi O 27 1880-81
WLc 1880-Je 4 1881

La Crosse NEWS. w Mr 26 1882-Ap 11 1891||
1882-83 as Sunday morning news; Ja-D 21 1884 Sunday news. Merged with Sun
WHi complete
WLc Ja-Jl 1 1883

NORDSTERN. w N 29 1856-S 23 1921||
Ap 10 1908 is jubilee number
In German
NN Ap 10 1908
WHi Ja 16 1874-1921

NORDSTERN blätter. *See* Morgenstern

NORTH La Crosse star. w O 28 1875-O 29? 1876||
Followed by Sunday morning press, later La Crosse free press
DLC D 23 1875;Ja 13 1876

NORTHWESTERN teetotaler. w S 15 1877-S 14 1878||
Follows La Crosse free press. S 15-D 1 1877 as Northwestern teetotaler and free press
WHi complete

PECK'S sun. *See under* Milwaukee

La Crosse daily PRESS. d O 24 1889-Je 13 1903||
Ja 12 1891-O 22 1893 as Daily press. United with Daily republican and leader to form La Crosse leader-press, later La Crosse tribune and leader-press
WHi 1889-My 19 1892;Ja 28 1893-1903

La Crosse daily REPUBLICAN. *See* La Crosse tribune and leader-press

La Crosse tri-weekly REPUBLICAN. Je 6 1860-Jl 1864||
N O 15 1861
WHi Mr 30 1861

REPUBLICAN and leader. w Ag 16 1854-Je 13 1903||
1854-61 as La Crosse independent republican; 1862-Ag 11? 1871 as La Crosse weekly republican
DLC My 30-Je 13,Jl 4,18-Ag 29,S 19,O 3-10, 24-31,N 14-28,D 12,26 1855;Ag 7,21,S 4,18-25 1867;Ap 13 1872
ICHi D 4 1860
MnHi N 1 1865
P-M Ag 16 1854
WHi 1854-59;Jl 15 1863-Ag 17 1864;S 18-D 25 1867;74-99

Daily REPUBLICAN and leader. *See* La Crosse tribune and leader-press

La Crosse weekly REVIEW. w My 10 1917-My 10 1923||
WLc complete

SAUK county herald. *See* Herold und volksfreund

Den SKANDINAVISKE demokrat. w Je 18 1868-
In Norwegian
MnSL Je 18-Ag 20 1868

SPIRIT of the times. *See* La Crosse democrat

Evening STAR. d 1885-86||?
WHi N 23-24,28 1885

SUN. w F 22-Jl 1891||?
WHi Ap 18-Jl 11 1891

TELESCOPE. sm F 15 1874-
MnHi F 15 1874

La Crosse TIDENDE. sw S 4 1895-O 20? 1897||
In Norwegian
IaDeL S 18 1895-S 1897
WHi O 16 1895-O 20 1897

La Crosse TRIBUNE. d My 16 1904-Ja 20 1917||
United with La Crosse leader-press and La Crosse Sunday chronicle to form La Crosse tribune and leader-press
WHi 1904-05;Jl-D 1906;Mr 25 1907-17
WLc complete

La Crosse TRIBUNE and leader-press. d 1854?+
1854?-Ag 11 1871 as La Crosse daily republican; Ag 13 1871-Je 13 1903 Daily republican and leader; Je 15 1903-Ja 20 1917 La Crosse leader-press
DLC Jl 24 1867-D 23 1870
MWA O 9 1874
WHi Je 22-Jl 1868;Ag 13 1871-Je 1872;75-77; Jl 1880-Je 1882;D 24 1894+
WLc 1891+

UNION. *See* La Crosse democrat

UNION and democrat. *See* La Crosse democrat

VARDEN. w Ag 10 1881-Ap 10 1883||
IaDeL complete

La Crosse VOLKSFREUND. w Ja 22 1891-O 23 1918||
Wednesday ed of Herold und volksfreund
In German
WHi 1898-1918

VOLKSPOST. w 1901-S 21 1921||
In German
IU Jl 4 1917-Ag 7 1918
WHi Jl 8 1903-21
—d ed *See* Abend stern

LA FARGE

La Farge ENTERPRISE. w 1898+
pub 1898+

LADYSMITH

To D 1900 as Warner

Weekly BUDGET. *See* Ladysmith news

GATES county journal. *See* Rusk county journal

Weekly JOURNAL. *See* Rusk county journal

Ladysmith NEWS. w Ap 19 1895+
1895-1907 as Weekly budget; 1907-Ap 8 1927 Ladysmith news-budget
1895-Jl 1902 pub at Apollonia
pub 1895+
WHi F 1927+

Ladysmith NEWS. w Mr 11 1905-07||
United with Weekly budget to form Ladysmith news-budget, later Ladysmith news

Ladysmith NEWS-BUDGET. *See* Ladysmith news

RUSK county journal. w,sw My 5 1900-Ja 27 1927||
1900-D 21 1901 as Weekly journal; D 28 1901-N 18 1905 Gates county journal. Merged with Ladysmith news
sw F 2-N 30 1915
WHi My-Je 1900;01-Ja 1927

LAKE GENEVA

To 1882 as Geneva Lake

Lake Geneva CISCO. w Je 1879-94||?
Summer ed of Lake Geneva herald
CoDL Je 17-S 2 1882
ICHi Jl 8 1882
ICM S 3 1881
OClWHi Ag 9 1879

Geneva weekly EXPRESS. w S 22 1855-Ap 1857||
Merged with Elkhorn independent (Elkhorn)
WHi O 20 1855-Ag 9 1856;O 25 1856

GENEVA Lake herald. *See* Lake Geneva herald

GENEVA Lake mirror. w F 1 1860-Mr 1861||
WHi Ap 26 1860

GENEVAN. w Je 3 1858-59||
WHi O 28 1858

Lake Geneva HERALD. w Ap 1872-Ap 11 1919||
1872-My 17 1879 as Geneva Lake herald. Merged with Lake Geneva news-tribune, later Regional news
CoDL F 10-Ag 11 1882
WHi Ja 10 1874-1919
—Summer ed. *See* Lake Geneva Cisco

Lake Geneva NEWS. *See* Regional news

Lake Geneva NEWS-TRIBUNE. *See* Regional news

REGIONAL news. w 1879+
1879-D 4 1924 as Lake Geneva news; D 11 1924-S 28 1933 Lake Geneva news-tribune
pub 1910+
DLC Ja 1-22 1885
MWA D 29 1882
WHi D 1891-N 11 1897;O 11 1906-33

Lake Geneva TRIBUNE. w Ap 1923-D 4 1924||
United with Lake Geneva news to form Lake Geneva news tribune, later Regional news

WISCONSIN standard. w Jl 1848-Jl 1849||
WHi Jl 7 1849

LAKE MILLS

JEFFERSON county union. *See under* Ft. Atkinson

Lake Mills LEADER. w N 12 1878+
1878-S 28 1882 as Lake Mills spike
pub 1882+
WHi F 1879+
WLa O 16 1902+

Lake Mills SPIKE. *See* Lake Mills leader

LAKE NEBAGAMON

Nebagamon ENTERPRISE. w O 15 1898-N 30 1907||
United with Solon Springs star (Solon Springs) to form Star enterprise
WHi D 1898-1907

STAR-enterprise. w D 7 1907-11||?
Formed by the union of Solon Springs star (Solon Springs) and Nebagamon enterprise
1907-S 12 1908 pub at Solon Springs
WHi 1907-O 30 1909

LANCASTER

GRANT county advocate. w O 14 1874-D 19 1877||
Follows West Grant advocate (Bloomington). Merged with Grant county argus
WHi Ja 13 1875-77

GRANT county argus. w Jl 31 1876-Je 1878||
Merged with Grant county gazette, later Inter-county gazette (Prairie du Chien)
WHi S 11 1876-Ap 8 1878

GRANT county gazette. *See* Inter-county gazette (Prairie du Chien)

GRANT county herald. w Mr 18 1843+
O 12 1844-45 as Wisconsin herald and Grant county advertiser; 1846-49 Wisconsin herald
pub 1915+
MWA My 31 1883
NbHi N 15 1852
WHi 1843-Mr 17 1849;S 26-D 5 1850;My 22 1866-80;S 1881-Jl 17 1918

GRANT county independent. w F 24 1927+
1927-O 17 1935 as Muscoda leader-press (Muscoda)
pub 1927+

GRANT county witness. *See* Platteville witness (Platteville)

Lancaster REGISTER. w O 5-D 1923||?
Follows Lancaster teller
WHi O 12-19 1923

Lancaster TELLER. w F 17 1883-S? 1923||
1883-Je 10 1915 as Weekly teller. Followed by Lancaster register
WHi 1883-My 16 1923

WISCONSIN herald. *See* Grant county herald

LAONA

FOREST county tribune. w 1919+
WLao 1919+

LINDEN

CONSERVATIVE. *See* Linden reporter

Linden REPORTER. w N 1908-12||?
1908-F 9 1911 as Conservative
WHi Ap 22 1909-11

SOUTHWEST Wisconsin. w F 21 1894-O 11 1907||
1894-N 1895 also issued at Montfort
WHi complete

LODI

Lodi ENTERPRISE. w F 16 1894+
pub 1894+
WHi S 10 1925+

Lodi weekly HERALD. w F 25 1863-N 9 1864

Lodi weekly JOURNAL. w O 20 1870-Ap 16 1873||
Merged with Jefferson county union (Ft. Atkinson)
WHi 1871-73

LODI valley news. w Ap 22 1874-Ap 7 1904||
MWA O 13 1883
WHi complete
WLoE complete

LONE ROCK

DOLLAR times. *See under* Spring Green

INTER-COUNTY times. *See* Dollar times (Spring Green)

Lone Rock JOURNAL. w O 25 1931+
pub 1931+

Lone Rock REPUBLICAN. w My 15 1886-My 28 1887||
WHi O 1886-87

LOYAL

Loyal TRIBUNE. w 1894+
pub 1929+
WHi Ja 19 1905+

LUXEMBURG

Luxemburg NEWS. w 1909+
pub 1909+
WHi D 27 1918+

WISCONSIN (*Continued*)

MADISON

AMERIKA. w 1884-Jl 28 1922||
O 20 1897-D 28 1898 as Amerika og norden
1884-96 pub in Chicago
In Norwegian
IaDeL complete
MWA 1891-93
MnHi 1885-1922
WHi 1897-1922

Daily ARGUS. *See* Wisconsin daily argus

Tri-weekly ARGUS. O 19 1847-Mr 11 1848||
tw ed of Wisconsin argus issued during last territorial legislature and second constitutional convention
DLC O 19-28,D 16 1847-Ja 20,F 8-24 1848
WHi complete

Daily ARGUS and democrat. *See* Wisconsin daily argus

Weekly ARGUS and democrat. w Je 15 1852-Je 28 1859||
Formed by the union of Weekly Wisconsin argus and Wisconsin democrat (1846-52). Merged with Wisconsin state journal
MB My 18 1858;Ja-Je 21 1859
MWA D 12 1854
MnHi 1855-[59-60]Ja 1 1861
WHi 1852-Ja 4 1853;55-59

Madison BOTSCHAFTER. *See* Wisconsin botschafter (Monroe)

CAMPAIGN express. *See* Wisconsin express

Madison CAPITAL times. d D 13 1917+
DLC 1917+
WHi 1917+
WM Jl-Ag 1923;25+
WMJ Current 10 months

CITIZEN. d Mr 31-Ap 2 1894||
campaign paper
WHi complete

Madison CITIZEN. w Mr 4 1933-Mr 31 1934||?
campaign paper
WHi Mr 4-11,Ap 1 1933;Mr 10-31 1934

Madison CITY express. *See* Wisconsin express

DANE county advocate. w O 2 1902-03||
WHi O-D 19 1902

DANE county populist. *See* Wisconsin populist

Daily DEMOCRAT. d Ja 10-Mr 17 1851;Ja 14-Je 11 1852||
United with Daily argus to form Daily argus and democrat, later Wisconsin daily argus
d ed of Wisconsin democrat (1846-52) issued during legislative sessions
WHi complete
—w ed *See* Wisconsin democrat (1846-52)

Madison DEMOCRAT. w My 21 1868-1900||?
WHi Ap 16 1874

Madison DEMOCRAT. d My 21 1868-F 27 1921||
Follows Wisconsin union. Not to be confused with other papers bearing title of Wisconsin democrat. 1868-Jl 19 1890 as Madison daily democrat. Merged with Wisconsin state journal
DLC 1871-82;84-1920
IaDeL Mr 1901-14
KHi [Ap 19 1895-Mr 1896]
WHi complete

Madison DEMOKRAT. w F 2 1858-N 2 1860||?
Merged with Wisconsin staatszeitung (1854-61)
In German
WHi 1858-N 2 1860

EAST SIDE news. w O 12- 1912||?
WHi O 12-19 1912

EAST SIDE news. w D 4 1924+
WHi Jl 15 1926+

EMIGRANTEN. w Ag 1852-S 1868||
United with Faedrelandet (La Crosse) to form Faedrelandet og emigranten (Minneapolis, Minn.)
Suspended Jl-S 1854
1852-56 pub at Inmansville; 1856-My 1857 at Janesville
In Swedish
IaDeL D 24 1852;F 4,18 1853;Ja 20 1854[56]-67[F 29-Ag 24 1868]
MWA F 26 1866
MnHi [Je-D 1857]59[61]62;64-65
MnSL 1852-[63]-68
WHi D 26 1859-61;Ag 11,S 8,N 3 1862;63-65

Madison EXPRESS. *See* Wisconsin express

Tri-weekly EXPRESS. D 16 1847-F 3 1848||
WHi complete
—w ed *See* Wisconsin express

GAUKEN. *See* Wisconsin nordmanden

INDEPENDENT. w F 29 1878-D 11 1879||
F-Je 1878 pub in Evansville
WHi My 1878-79

Weekly MADISONIAN. w Je 23 1894-N 9 1920||
WHi complete

MANDT'S weekly. *See* Scandinavian American (Stoughton)

Madison evening NEWS. d Jl 16 1887-Ag 19 1889||
1887-S 15 1888 as Evening news
WHi complete

Saturday evening NEWS. w 1887-S 16 1888||
United with Advertiser (Black Earth) to form News-advertiser

NEWS-ADVERTISER. w S 21 1888-Ag 23 1889||
Formed by the union of Advertiser (Black Earth) and Saturday evening news
WHi complete
—d ed *See* Madison evening news

NON-PARTISAN. tw Mr 27-Ap 6 1896||
campaign paper
WHi complete

NORDSTJERNEN. w Je 10 1857-O 10 1860||
Follows Den Norske Amerikaner. Merged with Emigranten
Suspended D 1857-Ag 1858
In Swedish
IaDeL 1857-My 1858
MnSL complete

NORDVESTEN. w S 17 1875-D 15 1876||
WHi complete

Der NORSKE Amerikaner. w D 1854-My 1857||
Followed by Nordstjernen
In Swedish
IaDeL [Mr 21-N 17 1855]56-57
MnSL 1855-[57]

NORSKE immigrant. w Ja 19-My 11? 1871||
In Swedish
WHi Ja 26-My 11 1871

De NORSKES ven. w Ja 1850-
In Swedish
MnSL Ja 14-28 1851

OLD Dane. *See* State

Daily Madison PATRIOT. d Ap 19 1876-Mr 8 1877||
Numbered consecutively with Wisconsin daily patriot (1854-64)
WHi complete

Weekly PATRIOT. w Ap 22 1876-Mr 10 1877||
WHi complete

PROGRESSIVE weekly. w D 7 1929+
pub 1929+
CtY 1929+
M 1929+
MnHi 1929-31
MnU D 14 1929+
NNRa 1930+
OCl 1929-31
WaU Ja 27 1934+

Madison daily RECORD. d S 19 -1871||?
WHi S 19-O 12 1871

SCANDINAVIAN American. *See under* Stoughton

Daily STAR. d Mr 19-N 17 1877||
WHi complete

Weekly STAR. w Jl 1877-Ag 3 1878||
WHi D 8 1877-78

STATE. w Ja 22 1897-1920||?
1897-Mr 4 1898 as Old Dane
WHi 1897-Ja 5 1917

Tri-weekly STATE journal. tw 1852-
MWA Ag 17 1865;F 17 1868;Ja 16 1871;Ja 15 1872
NNHi F 17 1868
NcD Jl 25 1866;F 17 1868;Ja 15,Jl 5 1872
—w ed *See* Wisconsin state journal

Daily STATESMAN. d Ja 14-Ap 16? 1852||
d ed of Wisconsin statesman (1850-52)
WHi Ja-Ap 16 1852
—w ed *See* Wisconsin statesman (1850-52)

SUBURBAN post. w N 13 1931-N 25 1932||
WHi complete

Madison TIMES. w Je 22 1892-Jl 19 1893||
Followed by Milwaukee times (Milwaukee)
WHi complete

TRUE American. w Ap 28 1855-O? 1855||
WHi Ap-My 12,Je 2,Jl 14 1855

UNCENSORED news. w F 11-N 2 1932||
WHi complete
WM complete

Madison daily UNION. *See* Wisconsin daily union

VIKINGEN. w Ag 11 1888-Je 1 1889||?
In Norwegian and English
WHi Ag 18 1888-Je 1 1889

WEST SIDE news. w F 9 1928-F 21 1929||
WHi complete

WESTERN fireside. w Jan 31 1857-Ja 8 1858||
MWA F 7,Mr 7,Jl 4 1857
WHi complete

WINGRA Park booster. ir D 18 1926-F 28 1927||?
WHi 1926-F 28 1927

Weekly WISCONSIN argus. w Ag 22 1844-Je 9 1852||
1844-S 17 1851 as Wisconsin argus. United with Wisconsin democrat (1846-52) to form Weekly argus and democrat
DLC 1844-F 9 1847
ICHi My 26 1846
MB O 3-10,N 21 1844[Ja 12-Ag 12 1845]-Ja 19 1847
MWA 1844-S 17,D 3 1851;F 11,My 12,Je 2 1852
MnHi 1844-[51]
NcD Ja-F 9 1847
PWCl F 16 1847
WHi complete

WISCONSIN daily argus. d Ja 8 1852-Ja 4 1862||
Title varies: Daily argus; Daily argus and democrat; Evening argus and democrat; etc
Suspended Jl 7 1859-Mr 26 1860
DLC Ja 17-Ap 20 1852[Mr-N 1856]Mr 5,11,15,18 1859;My 10 1861
ICHi D 6 1854;Ja 8 1855
MHi [Ja-Jl 2 1854]
MWA F 28,Mr 8,D 20 1855 Mr 25 1856;F 1,Ag 5 1858;Je 11 1859;Ag 4,N 1 1860
MnHi Ja-Ap 20 1852[Ap 30-D 1855]-[59-61]
OClWHi Mr 4,13 1861
WHi Ja-Ap 20,Je 15 1852-62

WISCONSIN weekly argus. w Ap 10 1860-Je 10 1862||
1860-O 1 1861 as Wisconsin argus and democrat
WHi 1860;Je 25 1861-62

WISCONSIN weekly blade. *See* Wisconsin enterprise-blade (Milwaukee)

WISCONSIN botschafter. *See under* Monroe

WISCONSIN daily capitol. d Ap 17 1865-Ap 5 1866||
Ap-Je 5 1865 as Daily Wisconsin capitol. United with Wisconsin democrat to form Daily Wisconsin union, later Wisconsin daily union
MB Ja 17-Ap 1866
WHi complete

Weekly WISCONSIN capitol. w Ap 28 1865-Ap 10 1866||
MB complete
WHi complete

WISCONSIN democrat. w O 18 1842-Mr 14 1844||
DLC D 13 1842;(F 1843-Mr 1844)O 3-10,31-N 14 1846(47-48)Ja 13-20,F 17,S 1,22,O 13 1849;My 15,Je 1-22,Jl 6,Ag 3 1850;Ap 10 1852
OHi Ja 11 1844
WHi complete
WM 1842-F 1843

WISCONSIN democrat. w Ja 10 1846-Je 8 1852||
Follows Mineral Point democrat (Mineral Point). United with Weekly Wisconsin argus to form Weekly argus and democrat
MnHi 1846-47
WHi 1846-Ja 11 1851
—d ed *See* Daily democrat

WISCONSIN daily democrat. d O 5 1865-Ap 5 1866||
United with Wisconsin daily capitol to form Wisconsin daily union
WHi complete

WISCONSIN weekly democrat. w O 13 1865-Ap 7 1866||
MB complete
WHi complete

WISCONSIN enquirer. *See* Wiskonsan enquirer

WISCONSIN express. w D 2 1839-Je 3 1852||
My 1842-My 23 1844 as Madison city express; My 30 1844-O 5 1848 as Madison express; O 12-N 2 1848 as Campaign express. United with Wisconsin statesman (1850-52) to form Wisconsin state palladium, later Wisconsin state palladium and statesman
Suspended My 9-O 5 1848
DLC F 1,Mr 14,Ap 4,N 28 1840;Ja 12-29,My 11 1843;Ja 15,29,F 5 1850
IU Ap 3 1849
MWA Ap 8,29 1852
NN D 12,26 1840;Mr 16-Ap 6 1843;Ap 17,O 9 1845;N 11 1846
NcD Je 9 1841
WHi complete
WM N 16 1848-N 7 1850
—tw ed *See* Tri-weekly express

WISCONSIN daily express. d Ja 12-Ap 9 1852||
MWA Mr 29 1852
WHi complete

WISCONSIN granger. *See* Wisconsin statesman (1873-76)

WISCONSIN leader. w,bw,m Ap 24 1920-26||?
w Ap 24-S 11 1920;bw S 25 1920-Mr 26 1921
Ap 1922 not pub
WHi 1920-Ag 1922

WISCONSIN nordmanden. w 1886-97||
1886-1889 as Gauken; 1890-O 1894 Normannen; O 1894-O 1895 Wisconsin normannen; O 1895-Mr 1896 Wisconsin normanden. Merged with Amerika
1886-O 25 1895 pub at Stoughton
In English and Norwegian
IaDeL Ag 29 1890-Jl 22 1891[93-Mr 13 1896]
WHi D 12 1890-Mr 6 1896

WISCONSIN daily palladium. d Je 21-Ag 16 1852||
DLC Je-Ag 11 1852
WHi complete

WISCONSIN patriot. w Je 17 1854-N 14 1864||
Title varies: Wisconsin weekly patriot; Weekly Wisconsin patriot
CtY Je 30 1860-63
DLC Mr 10 1855;Ag 1856-My 1857;Je 30 1860-Je 1861;63;Ap 22,Je 3,Jl 1,22 1876
ICHi N 11 1854;My 26 1855
MB O 1854-Je 1861;63-N 12 1864
MHi Ja-N 12 1864
MWA Ag,N 1-8,22-D 6,27 1856;Ap 18,My 1857-Ap 9 1859;Mr 3 1860;O 8 1864
NcD [My-O 1857]
PU [1858-59]
WHi Jl 8 1854-63
WM S 23 1854-Je 2,16 1855-Jl 19,Ag 1856-Je 1859;Ap-S 1860;61-62

WISCONSIN daily patriot. d N 1 1854-N 14 1864||
1854-Jl 22 1859 as Daily Wisconsin patriot
CtY Ja-O 11 1855;62
DLC Jl-N 1858
ICN Jl-D 1862
MB 1854-O 16 1855;Mr 31-D 1859;Jl-D 1861;Jl-D 1862;Jl-D 1863
MH 1863
MWA N 13 1856;Ja 16,31,F 17 1857
PU [1858]Ja-Je 1862;Ja-Je 1863
WHi complete

WISCONSIN (*Continued*)

MADISON—*Continued*

WISCONSIN populist. w S 10-N 8 1892||
S-O 25 1892 as Dane county populist
WHi complete

WISCONSIN staats-zeitung. w Ag 1854-61||
In German
CtY Ja 12(extra),F 19,Mr 5 1855

WISCONSIN staats-zeitung. w D 4 1878-Jl 23 1918||
Suspended F 7-Je 18 1912
Je 25 1912-18 issued as Friday ed of Wisconsin botschafter
In German
IU Jl 24 1917-Mr 1918
WHi D 11 1878-S 11 1889;Ap 15 1891-1918

WISCONSIN state journal. w S 1852-1909||
ICHi N 7,21 1865
MWA F 17-24 1857;F 2 1869;S 13-D 1870;Ja-Ap 2 1872
NN S 15 1868-Ag 1875
NNHi Je 4,13 1863;Ap 29 1873
NcD N 1 1864;F 2 1869;Ja 11 1870
WHi Ja 9 1855-1906
WM Mr 10 1857-S 20 1859;S 22 1863-S 10,24 1867-Ag 1875;S 1878-Ag 12 1883;Ag 22 1884-Ag 9 1889
—tw ed *See* Tri-weekly state journal

WISCONSIN state palladium and statesman. w Je 10-S 28 1852||
Formed by the union of Wisconsin express and Wisconsin statesman (1850-52). Je-Ag 1852 as Wisconsin state palladium. Followed by Wisconsin state journal
WHi complete
—d ed. *See* Wisconsin daily palladium

WISCONSIN statesman. w Ag 1 1850-Je 1 1852||
United with Wisconsin express to form Wisconsin state palladium, later Wisconsin state palladium and statesman
MB Ag 8 1850-My 11 1852
MWA Ap 20,Je 1 1852
WHi complete
—d ed. *See* Daily statesman

WISCONSIN statesman. m,w Ap 1873-O 28 1876||
Ap 1873-Je 1875 as Wisconsin granger
1873-S 1874 pub in Beaver Dam
WHi Jl 1875-76

WISCONSIN daily union. d Ap 17 1866-F 5 1868||
Formed by the union of Wisconsin daily capitol and Wisconsin daily democrat (1865-66). 1866-Mr 1867 as Daily Wisconsin union; Ap-S 30 1867 Madison daily union. Followed by Madison democrat
WHi complete

Weekly WISCONSIN union. Ap 17 1866-F 5 1868||
WHi Ag 14 1866

WISKONSAN enquirer. w N 8 1838-Je 15 1843||
1838-Je 25 1842 as Wisconsin enquirer
DLC [Ap 1839-N 1841]Jl 2,23 1842-My 11 1843
MWA 1838-[40]-Mr,Ap 17-Ag 25,S 29,N-D 4 1841
MnHi 1838-[43]
NSchU F 23 1842
WHi complete
WM 1838-Je 15 1842

MAIDEN ROCK

Weekly PRESS. w S 24 1892-S 16 1897||
Followed by Osceola sun (Osceola)
WHi complete

MANAWA

Manawa ADVOCATE. w Ap 18 1895+
pub 1895+

MANITOWOC

Manitowoc CITIZEN. w Ap 24 1879-1909||?
1879-S 22 1898 as Manitowoc tribune
WHi 1879-Jl 29 1909
WMa Mr 29 1900-Ap 1908

CONCORDIA. *See* Green Bay courier (Green Bay)

Manitowoc HERALD. w N 30 1850-Mr 26 1863||
1850-Mr 25 1854 as Manitowoc county herald. Merged with Manitowoc tribune
DLC D 22 1855
WHi complete

Manitowoc HERALD-TIMES. d O 19 1898+
1898-S 30 1918 as Manitowoc daily herald; O 1918-Ap 1932 Manitowoc herald-news
pub 1898+
WHi 1899+
WMa 1898-Mr 24,1901;O 19 1902+
WMaB O 19 1898-O 24 1899;O 13 1900-O 17 1903

JOURNAL. w O 1853-77||
1853-Ap 1854 as Wisconsin's demokrat; My 1854-Ag 1864 Union demokrat; 1866-Je 1875 Zeitung
Suspended Ag 1864-65
In German
MWA F 10 1866;Ag 24 1876
WHi Jl 1854-D 3 1855
WMa Mr 13 1862-My 12 1864

LAKE Shore times. w O 4 1881-S 24 1889||
WHi complete

MANITOWOC county herald. *See* Manitowoc herald

Manitowoc daily NEWS. d My 12 1900-S 30 1918||
United with Manitowoc daily herald to form Manitowoc herald-news, later Manitowoc herald-times
WMa complete

NORD-WESTEN. w S 8 1855-1910||
Suspended 1861-F 1865
In German
Whi Ja 15 1874-1909
WMaB 1906

Manitowoc PILOT. w Je 14 1859-Je 9 1932||
WHi 1859-75;F 1877-1932
WMa 1859-Jl 21 1865;Ag 1872-Ag 6 1874;Mr 7 1878-1932

Manitowoc POST. w,sw 1881-N 29 1924||
1923-24 pub by Westliche herold, Winona, Minn.
sw Ap 9 1910-O 19 1916
In German
IU D 1917-24
MnHi 1923-My 1924
WHi Ja 26 1899-1924
WMa Jl 1881-Je 11 1896;Jl 8 1897-Je 7 1900; Je 4 1908-Je 10 1910

Manitowoc PRESS. *See* Manitowoc times-press

Evening TIMES. d Ja 7 1920-Ap 30 1932||
1920-F 19 1931 as Manitowoc times. United with Manitowoc herald-news to form Manitowoc herald-times
WMa complete
WMaM Ap 1931-32

Manitowoc TIMES-PRESS. w 1893-1913||?
1893-99? as Manitowoc press
WMaM O 25 1899-D 7 1904;D 12 1906-D 9 1908

Manitowoc TRIBUNE. w,sw Ap 25 1854-Ap 18 1878||
Merged with Manitowoc pilot. Je 4 1858-65 as Manitowoc weekly tribune
sw Ja 2-S 1 1874
MWA Ja 17 1866
NNHi Je 3 1863
WHi 1854-Jl 12 1865;Mr 21 1867-F 20,Ag 21 1874-78
WMa 1869

Manitowoc TRIBUNE. d,tw My 31 1858-Ag 7 1863||
d 1858-N 5 1861;tw N 7 1861-S 23 1862
WHi complete

Manitowoc TRIBUNE. w 1879-98. *See* Manitowoc citizen

Daily TRIBUNE. d 1905-Ap 7 1910||
WHi [Je 26 1909-10]

UNION demokrat. *See* Journal

Die WAHRHEIT. w Je 2 1896-Jl 19 1921||
Merged with Manitowoc post
In German
WHi N 10 1896-1921
WMa Ap 27 1897-Jl 5 1921

WISCONSIN'S demokrat. *See* Journal

ZEITUNG. *See* Journal

MARATHON

Marathon TIMES. w Ja 28 1909+
pub 1909+
WHi 1909-Ag 13 1920

MARINETTE

EAGLE. *See* Weekly eagle-star

Weekly EAGLE-STAR. w,sw Je 24 1871-1909||
1871-O 9 1886 as Marinette and Peshtigo eagle; O 13 1886-Mr 9 1901 Eagle
sw O 13 1886-Ag 11 1888;Mr 15 1901-Ag 4 1903
WHi S 9 1871-Jl 2 1907
WManE 1871-Je 1879;81-1903

Marinette EAGLE-STAR. d 1892+
1892-Ag 5 1909 as Daily eagle; Ag 6 1903-Ag 26 1913 Daily eagle-star
pub 1903+
WHi D 27 1894+
WMan 1902+

FÖRPOSTEN. w 1892-Je 25 1909||
Merged with Marinette tribunen
In Swedish
IRA complete
WHi D 5 1894-1909

INDEPENDENT. w Ag 14-N 4 1886||
WHi complete

NORTH star. *See* Marinette star

Marinette STAR. w O 1880-Jl 30 1903||
1880-1901 as North star. United with Weekly eagle to form Weekly eagle-star
WHi F 24 1882-[83]-F 6 1885[Ag 29 1901-03]

Marinette daily STAR. d My 1895-Ag 5 1903||
United with Daily eagle to form Marinette eagle-star
WHi O 1901-03

Marinette TIMES. w My 27 1893-94||?
WHi Ag 12 1893;F 10 1894

Marinette TRIBUNEN. w 1894-S 28 1917||
Merged with Medborgaren (Escanaba, Mich.)
In Swedish
IRA 1896-99;1901-17
WHi Jl 2 1909-17

MARKESAN

GREEN Lake county democrat. w Jl 1876-1886||?
Jl-S 1876 as Independent (Princeton); S 1876-Je 2 1881 Green Lake county democrat (Princeton)
WHi F 13 1879-S 16 1885

Markesan JOURNAL. w N 1859-S 1862||
Suspended O 1861-F 1862
WHi F-O 1861

MARSHALL

Marshall RECORD. w S 1 1895+
pub 1886+

MARSHFIELD

DEMOKRAT. *See* Wochenblatt

Marshfield GAZETTE. w Je 17 1882-Je 1883||
Merged with Marshfield times

Marshfield HERALD. w My 6 1911-Ag 1927||
United with Marshfield daily news to form Marshfield news-herald

Marshfield NEWS and Wisconsin hub. w Ag 1889-1927||?
1889-F 24 1921 as Marshfield news
WHi Mr 10 1921-O 5 1927
WMar O 31 1901-S 28 1927

Marshfield NEWS-HERALD. d Mr 7 1921+
1921-Ag 6 1927 as Marshfield daily news
WHi Ag 1927+
WMar O 15 1927+

Marshfield TIMES. w N 1879-Mr 31 1920||
Je 1883-My 16 1885 as Times and gazette. Followed by Wisconsin hub
WHi S 15 1883-1920

WISCONSIN hub. w Ap 7 1920-F 23 1921||
Follows Marshfield times. United with Marshfield news to form Marshfield news and Wisconsin hub
WHi complete

WOCHENBLATT. w 1884- 1928||?
1884-Ja 1920 as Demokrat
In German

MATTOON

SHAWANO county press. w N 6 1919-20||?
WHi N 13 1919-Ap 1 1920

MAUSTON

JUNEAU county chronicle. w Mr 19 1890+
1890-N 30 1892 as Elroy chronicle (Elroy)
1890-D 7 1892 pub at Elroy
pub 1895+
WHi 1890+

JUNEAU county sun. w Ja 28 1885-N 19 1890||
Follows Yellow River lumberman (Necedah). Merged with Mauston star
WHi Mr 13 1885-90

Mauston STAR. w Je 10 1857+
DLC Mr 23,Jl 27 1876
MWA F 21 1867
WHi Je 17-N 20 1857;Je 22 1859+

MAYVILLE

DODGE county banner. w 1897-D 4 1919||
1897-1901? as Dodge county post
1897-Mr 28 1918 in German
WHi F 14 1918-19
WMayB 1902-[04]14-18
WMayF 1906-14

DODGE county pionier. w 1876+
In German
pub 1883+

DODGE county post. *See* Dodge county banner

Mayville NEWS. w 1892+
pub 1907+
WHi O 4 1917;Ap 18 1918

TELEPHONE. *See* Juneau telephone (Juneau)

MAZOMANIE

Mazomanie SICKLE. w Mr 21 1874+
1874-F 23 1884 as Mazomanie weekly sickle
pub [1880+]
WHi 1874-Mr 10 1888

MEDFORD

TAYLOR county leader. w D 1883-Jl 11 1929||
1883-Je 26 1919 as Waldbote. Merged with Taylor county star-news
WHi F 16 1895-1929
WMe Jl 20 1916-28

TAYLOR county news. w Mr 31 1875-D 22 1877||
United with Taylor county star to form Taylor county star-news
WHi complete

TAYLOR county news. w Ja 5 1878-Ap 27 1881||
Continues numbering of Taylor county news (1875-77)
WHi complete

TAYLOR county star-news. w 1876+
1876-77 as Taylor county star (title varies slightly)
pub 1886+

WALDBOTE. *See* Taylor county leader

WISCONSIN (*Continued*)

MELLEN

Mellen weekly RECORD. w D 27 1901+
1901-N 25 1926 as Mellen weekly
pub 1901+
WHi D 1923+

Mellen RECORD. w My 28 1925-N 25 1926||
United with Mellen weekly to form Mellen weekly record
WHi complete

Mellen WEEKLY. *See* Mellen weekly record

MELROSE

Melrose CHRONICLE. w O 1896+
pub 1896+
WHi Jl 1930+

MENASHA

Menasha ADVOCATE. w O 1853-O 1856||
WHi Je 12 1854-S 25 1856

Menasha evening BREEZE. *See* Menasha record

Menasha CONSERVATOR. w My 14 1856-Mr 17 1860||
1856-S 1859 as Conservator
pub also in Neenah
WHi complete

ISLAND city times. *See* Menasha press

Saturday evening PRESS. *See* Menasha press

Menasha PRESS. w O 22 1863-98||?
1863-Ja 15 1870 as Island city times; Ja 22 1870-D 30 1871 Winnebago county press; Ja 6 1872-D 2 1886 Menasha press; D 11 1886-Jl ? 1896 Saturday evening press
1863-S 23 1871 pub at Menasha and Neenah
CSmH O 23 1869;Ja 22 1870-O 14 1871
MWA F 18 1871;Ap 26 1883
WHi My 15-D 1866;Ja 22 1870-Jl 3,S 12-19 1896
WMe 1870-91

Menasha RECORD. d Je 20 1894+
1894-1903 as Menasha evening breeze
WHi Mr 31 1897-N 1900;Ag 18 1930+
WMe 1894-1903

TWIN CITY daily news. *See* Daily news-times (Neenah)

WINNEBAGO anzeiger. 1881-1909||
Merged with Appleton volksfreund (Appleton)
WHi D 15, 29 1883

WINNEBAGO county press. *See* Menasha press

MENOMONEE FALLS

Menomonee Falls NEWS. w 1889+
pub [1900-30]+
WHi Je 4 1915

MENOMONIE

DUNN county lumberman. *See* Dunn county news

DUNN county news. sw,w Ap 1860+
1860-Ap 1866 as Dunn county lumberman
sw S 17 1912-O 10 1913
pub 1871+
WHi My 19-D 22 1866;Ag 12 1871+
WMeno Ap 19 1862-Ap 15,N 25 1865+

LEAN wolf. w O 1869-Jl 1870||
1869-F 1870 pub in Durand

Menomonie NORDSTERN. w D 1887-F 5 1904||
In German
WHi N 1894-1904

Menomonie TIMES. w
DLC Ap 12 1867

Menomonie TIMES. w Ja 1876-Ja 1 1909||
WHi F 21 1877-Je 1891;98-1909

WISCONSIN signal. w 1891-98||?
WHi 1894-N 17 1898

MERRILL

To 1881 as Jenny

Merrill ADVOCATE. w F 6 1875-Ag 10 1909||
1875-O 10 1893 as Lincoln county advocate. United with Merrill star to form Merrill star-advocate
DLC My 6,Jl 8 1876
WHi complete

Merrill daily HERALD. d 1908+

LINCOLN county advocate. *See* Merrill advocate

LINCOLN county anzeiger. w F 4 1888-1900||?
In German
WHi 1888-N 13 1900
—Friday ed *See* Wisconsin thalbote

Merrill NEWS. w 1878-1918||
1878-1894 as Northern Wisconsin news
WHi Jl 20 1883-Ja 1890;S 18 1903-N 1904

NORTHERN Wisconsin news. *See* Merrill news

Merrill STAR-ADVOCATE. w D 31 1908-Jl 2 1935||
1898-Ag 10? 1909 as Merrill star
WHi Ag 25 1909-35

WEST MERRILL herald. *See* Rhinelander herald (Rhinelander)

WISCONSIN leader. w My 5 1877-Ag 16 1929||
Merged with Banner-journal (Black River Falls)
WHi complete

WISCONSIN thalbote. w S 21 1900-Ag 27 1920||
Friday ed of Lincoln county anzeiger
In German
WHi 1900-Jl 1918

MIDDLETON

Middleton TIMES-tribune. w 1894+
1894-Ag 18 1898 as Middleton times; Ag 26 1898-Mr 21 1930 Middleton times-herald
WHi F 1897+

VERONA herald. w O 1894-Ag 1898||
United with Middleton times to form Middleton times-herald, later Middleton times-tribune
WHi Mr 1895-98

MILAN

Milan SENTINEL. w 1923+
pub 1923+
WAbT 1924-26

MILLTOWN

Milltown HERALD. w 1910+
Ja 11 1923-Ap 29 1926 as Milltown newsman
WHi My 29 1919-Ap 13 1922;Ja 11 1923-F 14 1929

Milltown NEWSMAN. *See* Milltown herald

MILTON

Milton EXPRESS. *See* Milton Junction telephone (Milton Junction)

Milton JOURNAL. w 1894-Jl 25 1912||
Merged with Milton Junction telephone (Milton Junction)

Weekly TELEPHONE. *See* Milton Junction telephone (Milton Junction)

MILTON JUNCTION

JOURNAL-telephone. *See* Milton Junction telephone

Milton Junction TELEPHONE. w Jl 1879+
1879-Je 1882 as Milton express; Jl 1882-Jl 27 1905 Weekly telephone; Ag 3 1905-Je 25 1912 Telephone; Ag 1 1912-Ag 25 1927 Journal-telephone
1879-Ag 10 1899 pub in Milton
WHi Mr 17 1880-Je 14,Jl 20 1882+

MILWAUKEE

ABEND POST. d 1879-My 16? 1897||
Follows Vorwärts. 1879-Je 11 1890 as Milwaukee freie presse. United with Germania to form Milwaukee Germania abendpost
In German
WHi F 1 1879-Mr 1885;S 22 1892-Ap 1897
—Sunday ed *See* Sonntagsblatt der Freie presse; Nordwestliche post

Milwaukee ADVANCE. *See* National advance

Milwaukee ADVERTISER. w Jl 14 1836-Mr 20 1841||
Followed by Milwaukee courier
CSmH D 24 1836
DLC F 11,25,D 30 1837;Ja-Mr 23,Ag 10,S 14-28,N 9,23-D 7,28 1839-Ja 4,25-F 29,Ap 4,25-My 2,16-30,Je 27,Jl 18,Ag 1,22,O 24-31,N 21-28 1840
IU S 1 1838
MWA Je 3,17-Jl 8,22 1837;Mr 21 1840
WHi 1836-Jl 1[S 16 1837-40]41

Milwaukee daily ADVERTISER. d O 12 1874-Mr 18 1875||
Merged with Daily commercial times
WHi complete

Milwaukee AMERICA. w,sw Je 18 1873-N 25 1924||
1873-S 27 1918 as Germania. United with Westlicher herold (Winona, Minn) to form America-herold (Winona, Minn.)
w 1873-O 9 1889
In German
MWA Ag 26 1876
Tx Mr 14-21 1877
WHi F 5 1879-1924

Milwaukee daily AMERICAN. d Jl 1855-N 1857||
WHi S 10 1855-O 11 1856

Milwaukee AMERICAN. w Jl 1855-N 1857||
Merged with Daily Milwaukee news
WHi Ag 12-O 28 1857

AMERICAN freeman. *See* Wisconsin free democrat

AMERIKANISCHE turnzeitung. w Ja 4 1885-1917||
In German
ICN My 13 1894-S 18 1904
MB 1885-87
NN 1900-Ap 26 1908
PPG 1885-90;93-1900[02]-06
TxU 1885-86;88-Je 1891
WHi 1885-89;91-1909
WM complete

Milwaukee ARBEITER-zeitung. *See* Wisconsin vorwärts

ARMINIA. *See* Wisconsin vorwärts

ATLAS. w N 15 1856-Ap? 1861||
Followed by Milwaukee herold
WHi 1856-O 17 1857

ATLAS. d N 29 1858-Ap 1861||
Followed by Milwaukee herold
WHi 1858-N 1860

BANNER und volksfreund. d Ja 15? 1850-My 11 1880||
1850 as Wisconsin banner; 1851-Ap 9 1855 Tägliche banner. Merged with Freie presse later Abend post
MWA Ag 26 1876
WHi Mr 11-Je,Ag 1850-Je 1? 1852;Ap 10 1855-62;O 1879-My 11 1880
WM D 30 1866

BODOČNOST. *See* Jugoslovenski obzor

Evening CHRONICLE. d Jl 24 1879-N 16? 1881||
1879-My 29 1880 as Evening signal
WHi Ag 1879-N 16 1881

COLUMBIA. w Ja 1873+
In German
MnHi S 20 1922-Ja 2 1923;D 29 1926-D 19 1928
PPCHi [1894]-[97;1900]-[04;06]-[13;18-19]-[22]
WHi Ja 15-Je 1874;F 14 1875-F 26 1930

Milwaukee daily COMMERCIAL advertiser. *See* Milwaukee daily news (1848-81)

COMMERCIAL advertiser. w *See* Milwaukee weekly news

Daily COMMERCIAL and price current. *See* Daily commercial letter

Milwaukee COMMERCIAL herald. tw My 17 1843-D 27 1844||
Merged with Milwaukee sentinel
Suspended from D 1 1843-Mr 18 1844
DLC S 1 1843
IU O 23 1843
NNHi Je 3 1844
WHi Jl 1843-44
WM Ag 12-D 1844

Daily COMMERCIAL letter. d 1865?-1906||?
1865?-Mr 1880 as Daily commercial and price current
WM My 1865-95;1906

Daily COMMERCIAL times. d 1870-My 2 1878||
1870-74 as Evening times. Merged with Milwaukee daily news
DLC F 21,Mr 30-Jl 26 1873;F 23-24 1877
WHi 1875-78
WM 1875-77

Milwaukee COURIER. w Mr 27 1841-Je 2 1847||
Follows Milwaukee advertiser. Followed by Weekly Wisconsin
DLC Ag 4 1841;Ja 6,F 25,Mr 4,O 14,28 1846-My 12 1847
MWA Jl 7 1841;My 15 1844
WHi complete
WM 1841-D 13 1843;My 10 1844-Mr 4 1846

Milwaukee daily COURIER. d Mr 19-Jl 14 1846||
Followed by Evening courier
WHi Mr 19-Jl 8 1846
WM Mr-My 15 1846

Evening COURIER. d F 22-My 18 1847||
Followed by Evening Wisconsin, later Wisconsin news
WHi complete

Milwaukee COURIER. w N ? 1868-
In English and German
DLC N 7 1868

CREAM CITY courier. *See* Milwaukee gazette

CZECHOSLOVAK. w Ag 1 1918+
In Bohemian and Slovak
pub 1918+

DELAVEC. *See* Jugoslovenski obzor

DELAVSKA slovenija. *See* Jugoslovenski obzor

Milwaukee DEMOCRAT. w Ag 11 1843-F 23 1844||
Followed by American freeman, later Wisconsin free democrat
WHi complete

Milwaukee DEMOCRAT. w D 25 1897-Ap 2 1898||
WHi complete

Milwaukee DEUTSCHE zeitung. d 1933+
In German
WM Ja 24 1933+

DOMACNOST. *See under* Chicago

Milwaukee daily ENQUIRER. Jl 18 1860-
campaign paper
WHi Ag 10 1860

Milwaukee ENTERPRISE. 1872-73. *See* Milwaukee gazette

Milwaukee ENTERPRISE. w 1923?-Ja 1925||
United with Wisconsin weekly blade (Madison) to form Milwaukee enterprise-blade
Negro

Milwaukee ENTERPRISE-BLADE. w 1916+
1916-Ja 1925 as Wisconsin weekly blade (Madison)
Negro
WHi Je 8 1916-Ap 10 1920;Je 29-S 2 1922;Ja 10 1925-O 23 1926;S 1927-N 10 1928;Ja 16-N 5 1932

EVENTS. w Ap 5 1885-D 25 1897||
1885-Ja 24 1886 as Yenowine's Sunday news; Ja 31 1886-N 1895 Yenowine's news (N 30 1890-S 1894, D 7 1895-Ja 16 1897 Yenowine's illustrated news) Ja 23-O 1897 Illustrated news
CLM My 30 1886
WHi complete
WM 1885-Ja 9 1897

EXCELSIOR! für den Katholischen familien kreis. w S 8 1883+
In German
IU Mr 1918-Je 1927
WHi O 1895+

FRAM. w 1894-S 1897||
Merged with La Crosse tidende (La Crosse)
In Norwegian
IaDeL S 25,N 20 1896[Ja-Je 1897]
WHi N 1895-Jl 2 1897

WISCONSIN (*Continued*)

MILWAUKEE—*Continued*

Milwaukee daily FREE democrat. d S 16 1850-O 1861||
1850-57 as Daily free democrat. Merged with Evening Wisconsin, later Wisconsin news
MWA Je 27 1860
WHi 1850-Ap 1851;O 1854-55;S 3 1856;Mr 19,S 17 1859-F 1860
WM 1850-Mr 15 1859

Milwaukee FREE press. d Je 18 1901-D 1 1918||
Merged with Wisconsin news
ICU O 1917-N 1918
WAL 1901-17
WHi complete
WM complete

FREIDENKER. *See under* New Ulm, Minn.

Milwaukee FREIE presse. *See* Abend post

FREMAN. *See under* Chicago, Illinois

GAZETA Wisconsinska. *See* Kuryer tygodniowy i gazeta Wisconsinska

Milwaukee daily GAZETTE. d O 21 1845-F 14 1846||
Merged with Milwaukee sentinel
WHi complete

Milwaukee semi-weekly GAZETTE. sw O 22 1845-F 17 1846||
Merged with Milwaukee sentinel
WHi N 26 1845-46

Milwaukee GAZETTE. w D 1872-Jl 24 1880||
1872-Jl 1873 as Milwaukee enterprise; Ag 1873-S 20 1879 Cream City courier
WHi Ja 17 1874-Jl 22 1876;Ja-F 1877;Je 15 1878-80

GERMANIA. d *See* Milwaukee Germania abend post

GERMANIA. w *See* Milwaukee America

Milwaukee GERMANIA abend post. d 1891-D 31 1912||
1891-Ap 1897 as Germania; My 1897-N 2 1901 Germania und abend post. United with Herold to form Germania-herold, later Milwaukee herold
In German
WHi My 17 1897-1912

GERMANIA sonntagspost. *See* Milwaukee-sonntagspost

GERMANIA und abend post. *See* Milwaukee germania abend post

GERMANIA-HEROLD. *See* Milwaukee-herold

HEROLD. w,sw S 21 1861-1911||?
Follows Atlas
sw 1889-1906
WHi Ja 22 1871-F 9 1906

Milwaukee-HEROLD. d S 21 1861-O 1 1932||
Follows Atlas. 1861-Jl 1899 as Der herold: Ag 1899-D 31 1912 Herold und seebote; Ja 2 1913-My 25 1918 Germania-herold
Suspended Ag 1862-65
DLC My 13 1890-Je 19 1891;My-D 1898
IU Jl 1917-32
KHi O 25 1888
NNHi O 3 1872;My 22 1873
WHi O 12 1866-D 14 1867;86-Je 1890;94;Jl 1896-Je 1897;Ap 1899-1932
WM S 19 1863-S 1866;O 1897-1932
WaPS [1916-17]-My 11 1921

HEROLD und seebote. *See* Milwaukee-herold

INDEX. w D 22 1877-78||?
WHi 1877-F 9 1878

IRREPRESSIBLE conflict. w Ja 11 1860-
WHi Ja 11 1860

ITALIAN leader. m,sm D 1933+
m 1933-N 1934
WHi 1933+

JEWISH press. d,w 1919-31||?
1919-23? as Jewish daily press
d 1919-23
In Yiddish and English
WHi Ap 22 1919;Ap 18 1928-S 2 1931
—w ed *See* Milwauker wochenblatt

Milwaukee JOURNAL. w Ag 27 1841-F 16 1842||
Follows Tribune (Chicago). Followed by Workingman's advocate
DLC S 29,O 20-27,N 3,D 29 1841-Ja 12,F 9 1842
WHi Ja 19,F 9 1842
WM complete

Milwaukee daily JOURNAL. d 1851-
DLC D 18,20 1851;Ja 2-Mr 18 1852
WHi N 16 1850

Milwaukee JOURNAL. d N 16 1882+
1882-My 11 1883 as Daily journal; My 12 1883-Je 7 1890 Milwaukee daily journal
pub 1890-S 1892;93;Ap 1894-S 1896;97-S 1902; 03;Ap 1904-Je,O 1905-Mr,Jl 1908-Mr,Jl 1913+
DLC Jl 1891+
KHi S 5 1923
MWA N 17 1914;Je 11-16 1922
MnU 1916-[19-21]
VU N 16 1932
WAL O 1917-F 14,Ap 1920-25
WHi 1882+
WM 1882+

Milwaukee JOURNAL of commerce. w N 7 1866-80||?
Mr-D 1880 as Journal of commerce
NjR N 19 1873
OClWHi F 20 1867
WHi Jl 10 1872-Ja 1874;Ja 29 1879-D 22 1880
WM N 17 1866-73

JUGOSLOVENSKI obzor. w Mr 21 1913+
1913-O 1915 as Bodočnost; N 1915-D 2 1921 Slovenija; D 9 1921-S 2 1926 Delavaska slovenija; S 9 1926-D 12 1928 Delavec; D 19 1928-Ja 3 1929 Vestnik
In Slovenian
pub 1913+
IU D 7 1917-Je 1 1928

KRYTYKA. w N 1885-Je 1888||
Followed by Kuryer polski
In Polish

KURYER polski. d Je 23 1888+
Follows Krytyka
First Polish daily in the U.S.
In Polish
pub 1888+
IU D 5 1917-Je,N 1919-Ap 7,Jl-O 1920
WHi 1894-S 1931
—agricultural ed *See* Kuryer tygodniowy i gazeta Wisconsinska

KURYER tygodniowy i gazeta Wisconsinska. w 1892-1914||?
1892-93 as Przeglad tygodniowy; 1894-1911? Gazeta Wisconsinska
Agricultural ed of Kuryer polski
In Polish

Milwaukee LABOR review. w 1885-90||?
WHi Ag 27-S 10,O 1,N 5 1887;Je 16-23 1888
WM Ap 1886-Mr 1888
—d ed *See* Milwaukee daily news

Milwaukee LEADER. d D 7 1911+
Barred from the mails O 3-5 1917
pub 1911+
CU-B D 1927-F 17 1928
CtY S 23 1913-Ap 2 1914;N 16,24 1915
DLC Je 1928+
ICM N 7 1912
ICU D 7 1920-D 7 1924
IU Ap 25 1932+
NN Ja-N 1912;Ja-N 1913;14-N 9 1918;Ja 5-8, 10-16,18-25,27 1920;D 6-7 1921;Jl 8 1922+
NdU 1923-Jl 1932
TxU [Ja 7-S 28 1916]Ja 5-O 3 1917;Ja 5-My 10 1918;Ja 3-Ap 23 1920;Ja 5-Je 16 1921
WHi 1911+
WM 1911+
WMJ Jl-D 1914;Je-D 1915;Ap-My 1916;17;Ap 1918-28
WaU D 9 1927+
—w ed *See* Wisconsin leader

Daily LIFE. d,tw,w Ag 1861-Ap 1865||
Merged with Daily Wisconsin, later Wisconsin news
d Ag-S 1861; tw O-? 1861
DLC Mr 11 1865
WM 1864

Milwaukee MAIL. w My 26-? 1894||
WHi My-Ag 18 1894

MILWAUKEE'R socialist. d 1875-S 3 1878||
1875-76? as Der Socialist. United with Vorwärts to form Vorwärts (Milwaukee'r socialist)
In German
NN D 9-10 1875;Ag 12-16,21,24-28 1876[Je 1877-Ag 1878]

MILWAUKER wochenblat. w 1914+
w ed of Jewish press
In Yiddish and English
pub 1915+
WHi Mr 8 1917-Mr 1 1918[26-29]S 11 1931+

MILWAUKIEAN. w 1843-44||
Merged with Milwaukee commercial herald
WHi O 28-N 4 1844

Daily NATIONAL. d S 10-N 6 1859||
WHi complete

NATIONAL advance. w Ja 1890-1909||?
1890-Je 2 1894 as Milwaukee advance (scattered numbers as National advance)
WHi Ap 5 1890;Ap 1892-S 8 1900

Milwaukee daily NEWS. d 1848-Ja 1 1881||
1848-My 1852 as Milwaukee daily commercial advertiser; 1852-Je 1 1856 Milwaukee news; Je 2 1856-Je 28 1874 Daily Milwaukee news (D 1860-Jl 1861 Daily people's press and news) Followed by Daily republican and news
Suspended N 1853?-Jl 1854
DLC [Ja-Ap]D 13 1854;55-56;Mr 6 1867-70;Jl 11 1874-N 6 1877
ICHi Jl 10 1865
KHi N 3 1851
MBAt Ap 11,16 1865
MWA S 21 1859;O 18 1860;Ja 26-[Jl-D 1865]-Ag,O 1867-72;Jl-D 1873;S 8 1878
WHi [Ap 16-N 16 1850]Ap 8 1851;Ja 14-15 1852;S 23-24,O 1,5 1853;My 16 1856-Mr 5 1858;Ja 15,Mr-D 1859;S 2 1862;Ap 1864-81
WM 1855-80

Milwaukee weekly NEWS. w 1848-Ja 1 1881||
1848-My 1852 as Commercial advertiser
DLC Mr 1,D 7 1853
MiU-C Ap 15 1863
WM Jl 1861-Je 1865;66;Jl 1867-68;Ja 19 1870-O 18 1871;72-75;77-78

Semi-weekly Milwaukee NEWS. sw My 1852-Ja 1? 1881||
WHi Mr 6,8,S 4 1867

Milwaukee NEWS. Country edition. tw
DLC Ap 25-26,My 4-5,11-12,30-31 1853
N Mr 13-14 1854

Milwaukee daily NEWS. d Mr 3 1887-O 15 1918||
1887-My 26 1889 as Daily review; My 27 1889-S 16 1891 Milwaukee daily news and review. United with Evening Wisconsin to form Wisconsin-news
OClWHi O 18 1864
WHi My 30 1889-1918
WM complete
—w ed *See* Milwaukee labor review

NORDWESTLICHE post. w D 1891-My 1897||?
Follows Sonntagsblatt der Freie presse
In German
—d ed *See* Abend post

NORTH Milwaukee review. w Mr 1917-1918||?
WM 1917-F 1918

NORTH Milwaukee times. w Ag 8 1918-31||?
WM 1918-Ja 1920

NORTHWESTERN recorder. w,m,ir Ap 1892-Mr 1893||?
Ap -N 26 1892 as Wisconsin Afro-American
WHi Ag 13 1892-93

NOWINY polskie. (Polish news) d 1906+
In Polish
pub 1906+
IU D 6 1917+
PP O 1934+

PECK'S sun and Saturday star. w My 1874-1900||?
1874-D 22 1894 as Peck's sun
1874-Mr 1878 pub at La Crosse
DLC Ja-Mr 1886
KHi Jl 15 1882
MWA N 25 1882;F 2 1884
WHi D 29 1894-Mr 20 1897

Daily PEOPLE'S press. d Ag 16-D 14 1860||
United with Daily Milwaukee news to form Daily people's press and news, later Milwaukee daily news
WHi N 13 1860
WM complete

Daily PEOPLE'S press and news. *See* Milwaukee daily news (1848-81)

POLISH news. *See* Nowiny polskie

PROHIBITIONIST. *See* Northwestern mail (Madison)

PRZEGLAD tygodniowy. *See* Kuryer tygodniowy i gazeta Wisconsinska

Milwaukee RECORD. w Ap 23-My 7 1892||
WHi complete

Milwaukee daily RECORD. d O 30 1895-Mr 23 1897||
WHi N 11 1895-97

Daily REPUBLICAN and news. d Ja 3 1881-My 20 1882||
Follows Milwaukee daily news. Merged with Milwaukee sentinel
DLC 1881
ICHi Je 27 1881
WHi Mr 27 1881-82
WM complete

Daily REPUBLICAN-SENTINEL. *See* Milwaukee sentinel

Daily REVIEW. *See* Milwaukee daily news

ROVNOST. d S 7-D 21 1892||?
In Bohemian
WHi S 7-D 21 1892

Der SEEBOTE. w,sw D 1851-1925||?
1851-D 6 1875 as Der Milwaukee see-bote
sw Ap 1 1890-Mr 6 1906
S 23 1922-25 pub in Winona, Minnesota
In German
MnHi 1871-[73]-77;S 30 1922-N 1924
WHi 1865-N 1924
WM S 24 1863-66;Jl-D 1870;Jl 1890-94;96-99
—Sunday ed *See* Sonntagsbote

Milwaukee SEEBOTE. d Ja 1852-Ag 1899||
Merged with Der Herold to form Herold und seebote, later Milwaukee-herold
In German
MWA Ag 25 1876

SEMI-CENTENNIAL (1846-96) O 16 1895||
Special ed of Milwaukee dailies bound together
WHi complete

Milwaukee SENTINEL. w Je 27 1837-1903||?
Title varies slightly: Milwaukee sentinel and Wisconsin farmer; Sentinel and farmer; Weekly sentinel and Wisconsin farm journal. Mr 13 1846-O 1851 as Milwaukee sentinel and gazette
DLC Mr 12,Je 18 1839;D 29 1840[Ap 13 1841-Ag 19 1843]My 31 1865
ICN [1863]-[65]
IU Ap 12 1843;Ap 22 1873
KHi Ag 1 1861;Jl 26 1888;Ja 25 1889;S 4 1923
MWA Jl 25-Ag 1,29,N 21 1837;Mr 24 1840;N 14 1848;Ja 1,Je 25 1851
WHi Je 27 1837;Ja 23 1838-Ag 11 1847;D 17 1860;Je 3 1861;Ja 10 1871-72;80;91-94
WM 1837-Je 1841;43-Mr 1844;45-Je 1850;76-79

Milwaukee SENTINEL. d D 4 1844+
1844-F 14 1846 as Milwaukee daily sentinel; F 16 1846-O 11 1851 Daily sentinel and gazette; My-D 30 1882 Daily republican-sentinel
CoU 1901-02;05;S 1906-07
DLC Mr 11 1850-O 11 1851;Mr 16 1861-81;84-85;Ap-S 1887;O-D 1888;Ja-S 1890;98+
ICHi Ag 2 1845;Je 20 1854;Jl 4 1857;O 12 1871;Ja 25 1903
ICM F 16,My 28 1883;My 14 1884
ICN Mr 1863-65
IP O 12 1871
MNaHi Ap 9 1863
MWA Jl 30 1852;F 6,Ap 3,12-D 1854;Jl 4 1857;S 9 1860;Je 8 1861;S 12 1867;O 10-12,14, 23 1871;Mr 25,Ag 23 1876
MiU [1885]
NNHi Jl 20 1863;Ap 10,17 1873
NcD Ag 25-26 1851
OClWHi Jl 10 1846;Ap 4,O 2 1863;Ja 21,Mr 6,28 1865;Mr-D 21 1870

WISCONSIN (*Continued*)

MILWAUKEE—*Continued*

Milwaukee **SENTINEL.** d 1844+—*Continued*
OOxM N 9 1876;N 19 1880;Ja 11-17,19-20,26,F 1,6 1883
P Jl 1890-Jl 1917
WAL 1899-1901
WHi D 10 1844+
WM Je 27 1838-Je 22 1841;Ja 25 1843-My 9,Je 8 1878;79+
WMJ 1919+

Sunday SENTINEL. w Mr 30-O 5 1873; N 9 1879-S 1 1929||
S 8 1929+ the Sunday ed is included in regular issue with no change of title
MWA Ap 22 1906
WHi Ap 24 1881-1929

SHOREWOOD herald. w Je 28 1929+
1929-Je 15 1933 as Shorewood suburban herald
pub 1929+

SHOREWOOD suburban herald. *See* Shorewood herald

Evening **SIGNAL.** *See* Evening chronicle

SLOVENIJA. *See* Jugoslovenski obzor

Der **SOCIALIST.** *See* Milwaukee'r socialist

SONNTAGSBLATT der Banner und volksfreund. w
Sunday ed of Wisconsin banner und volksfreund
In German
WHi F 16 1879-My 9 1880

SONNTAGSBLATT der Freie presse. w 1880-Ja 1890||
Followed by Nordwestliche post
In German
WHi My 16 1880-Je 14 1885
—d ed *See* Abend post

SONNTAGSBOTE. w Mr 11 1906-S 3 1922||
In German
WHi complete
—Sunday ed *See* Der Seebote

Milwaukee-**SONNTAGSPOST.** w 1858+
1858?-1905 as Germania sonntagspost. 1858?-O 1932 included in numbering of daily
In German
pub 1896+
IU My 16 1897+
WaPS 1918-My 15 1921

SOUTH Milwaukee star. w N 26 1892-D 1894||
United with Peck's sun and Saturday star to form Peck's sun and Saturday star

STADT und land. w Ag 1875-D 29 1880||?
Literary supplement of Wisconsin banner und volksfreund
WHi F 12 1879-80

Saturday **STAR.** My 18 1889-D 22 1894||
United with Peck's sun, and South Milwaukee star to form Peck's sun and Saturday star
WHi complete

Milwaukee **STATE journal and South side advocate.** w F 6 1879-80||?
WHi F-D 6 1879

Milwaukee **SUN.** m,sm Ja 1924-
WHi [My 1924-Ja 1928]

TÄGLICHE banner. *See* Banner und volksfreunde

Milwaukee **TELEGRAPH.** w D 1 1878-N 25 1899||
1878-Ap 26 1891 as Milwaukee Sunday telegraph
DLC Mr 30,Je 8,Jl 6,27,Ag 15,S 7,21,N 23 1879;S 25 1880
WHi complete
WM complete

Milwaukee Sunday **TELEGRAPH.** *See* Milwaukee telegraph

Evening **TIMES.** *See* Daily commercial times

Milwaukee **TIMES.** w 1888—
pub [1888—]
WM 1917-S 11 1919

Milwaukee **TIMES.** d O 10-N 14 1893||
Follows Madison times (Madison)
WHi complete

UNION signal. w Ag 1892-1907||?
WHi Ja 6 1893;N 1894-1902

VESTNIK. 1928-29. *See* Jugoslovenski obzor

VOICE of the people.
campaign paper
WHi O-N 1910

Milwaukee **VOLKSBLATT.** w 1882-90||?
In German
WHi [1883-88]

VOLKSFREUND. w F 1847-Ap 11? 1855||
United with Wisconsin banner to form Wisconsin banner und volksfreund
In German
MWA N 24 1852
WHi Jl 15 1847-F 13 1850

Täglicher **VOLKSFREUND.** d F 11 1850-Ap 9? 1855||
United with Tägliche banner to form Banner und volksfreund
WHi 1850-52

Milwaukee **VOLKSZEITUNG.** *See* Wisconsin vorwärts

VORWÄRTS (Milwaukee'r socialist). d Ja 1878-Ja? 1879
Ja-S 3 1878 as Vorwärts. Followed by Milwaukee freie presse, later Abend post
In German
NN Ag 24,28-31,S 3-4,10-16 1878

VORWÄRTS! Unabhängige sozialistische zeitung. w 1832?-D 31 1932||
In German
MWA D 31 1932

WHITEFISH Bay herald. w Je 12 1930+
pub 1930+

Daily **WISCONSIN.** *See* Wisconsin news

Weekly **WISCONSIN.** w Je 2 1847-1904||?
Follows Milwaukee courier
DLC Je 23-D 29 1847;O 13 1852-Ag 10 1853;F 27 1867-Ag 30 1871
IU Ap 19 1854
MWA Jl 1 1857
WHi Je 9 1847-My 13 1857;D 31 1862;Jl 25 1863-Ap 1? 1886
WM 1847-Mr 1848;81-1900

Semi-weekly **WISCONSIN.** sw N 4 1862-Ag 9 1882||
WHi complete

WISCONSIN weekly advocate. w My 7 1898-1915||?
Negro
WHi 1898-S 19 1908

WISCONSIN Afro-American. *See* Northwestern recorder

WISCONSIN banner. d *See* Banner und volksfreund

WISCONSIN banner und volksfreund. w,sw S 1844-1914||?
1844-Ap 18 1845 as Wiskonsin banner; Ap 25 1845-Ap 11 1855 Wisconsin banner
In German
WHi S 14-21 1844;Mr-Ag 1845;Mr 1846-Ag 1847;S 15 1849-S 1 1858;F 13 1879-O 14 1913
WM 1895
—Sunday ed. *See* Sonntagsblatt der banner und volksfreund
—Literary supplement. *See* Stadt und land

WISCONSIN barnburner. tw Ag-S? 1848||
campaign ed of Wisconsin free democrat
WHi Ag 31,S 1 1848

WISCONSIN bulletin. m Mr 1912-D 1916||?
WHi 1912-16

WISCONSIN free democrat. w Mr 6 1844-F 1862||
Follows Milwaukee democrat. 1844-Ag 1848 as American freeman; Ag 30 1848-1849 Wisconsin freeman
1844-My 3 1848 pub in Waukesha
ICHi O 31 1855
MWA Ap 14 1846;S 1 1852
WHi S 9 1845;N 1846-S 20 1848[53-58]
—campaign ed *See* Wisconsin barnburner

WISCONSIN free democrat. tw S 1850-O 1861||
Merged with Evening Wisconsin, later Wisconsin news
DLC D 12 1855

WISCONSIN freeman. *See* Wisconsin free democrat

WISCONSIN greenback. *See under* Sparta

WISCONSIN Jewish chronicle. w D 16 1921+
pub 1921+
WHi 1921+

WISCONSIN leader. w Jl 13 1934+
WHi 1934+
—d ed *See* Milwaukee leader

WISCONSIN news. d Je 8 1847+
Follows Evening courier. 1847-68 as Daily Wisconsin; 1868-N 24 1918 Evening Wisconsin; N 25 1918-My 1924 Wisconsin news; Je-S 1924 Wisconsin news and evening sentinel
CL F 2-18,Ap 1920-21;Ja 31 1922
DLC Jl 25,27,29 1847;Ja 22-D 1848;[Ap-N 1853]Ja 18 1861-62;S 14 1865;F 21 1868;Ag 24 1869;D 1-23 1890;91-92;98
ICM My 13 1884
IU D 1916-My 26 1917
MBAt Ap 15 1865
MWA Ag 15,N 2 1859;Ja 6,S 8 1860;D 24 1879;O 27 1883
NNHi Ap 5,Ag 26 1865;Ap 25,Je 30 1873;Ag 20 1889
NcD Ja 22,Mr 24-25 1848;My 20 1853
OHi S 22 1869
WHi Ap 27 1848-Ap 1851[53-54]Ja 11-D 1855; My 15 1857-58;S 1859-S 9 1865;66-Je 1867;70; O 1881-1918
WM Ag 15 1848;Je 8 1849-Je,O 1854-68;Jl 1869-Je 1897;98+
WMJ 1919+

WISCONSIN patriot. w My 1893-Je 1898||
Merged with Altruist (not in this list)
KHi My 22 1897-Ap 16 1898
WHi Ag 11 1894-Ap 23 1898

WISCONSIN sentinel. w
NhD Ap 13 1844

WISCONSIN standard. w F 16(?) 1878-82||
F-O 11 1878 as Greenback standard; O 18 1878-Jl 29 1880 as Oshkosh standard
1878-S? 1881 pub in Oshkosh (Oshkosh)
WHi Mr 22 1878-Ag 11,O 20 1881

WISCONSIN statesman. w,m 1925+
1925-28 pub in Port Washington
WHi Ag 31,D 31 1927;O 1929;F 1933+

WISCONSIN vorwärts. m,w,tw,d Ja 1882-Ag 17 1898||
1882-My 1886 as Arminia; My 1886-D 1889 Milwaukee arbeiter-zeitung; D 1889-D 31 1892 Milwaukee volkszeitung
m 1882-85;w 1886?;tw My 1886
NN Ja 9-10 1890;F 20,24 1892
WHi My 4,29,D 28 1886;Ja 28 1887;93-98
WM 1893-98

WISCONSINI magyarsag. w Mr 21 1924+
In Hungarian
pub 1924+
WHi Ag 2 1929

WISKONSIN banner. *See* Wisconsin banner und volksfreund

WORKINGMAN'S advocate. w Ap 1842-
Follows Milwaukee journal (1841-42)

YENOWINE'S news. *See* Events

MINERAL POINT

Mineral Point **DEMOCRAT.** w Ap 11-D 10 1845||
Follows Mineral Point free press. Followed by Wisconsin democrat (Madison)
NN My 30,Jl 23,Ag 6,S 24 N 5,19 1845
WHi complete

Mineral Point **DEMOCRAT.** w Jl 27? 1852-
MnHi Mr 23 1853
WHi N 2 1853;Jl 5,Ag 16,30 1854

Mineral Point **DEMOCRAT.** w Jl 1855-
WHi O 17 1855;N 5 1856

Mineral Point **FREE PRESS.** w D 28 1841-45||?
Follows Miner's free press. Followed by Mineral Point democrat
WHi D 28 1841[42-43]

HOME intelligencer. w My 26 1859-Je 22 1865||
OClWHi My 7,21 1861;N 15 1862
WHi complete

IOWA county democrat. w S 1 1866+
1866-D 7 1877 as National democrat
WHi S-N 3 1866;Ja 11-N 18 1868;Ag 25 1869+

MINERS' free press. w Je 13 1837-Mr 1838||
Followed by Galena democrat (Galena, Ill)
DLC Je 23,Jl 14-Ag 18,S 1-8,22-O 6,20,N 3 1837
WHi [1837]

MINER'S free press. w 1838-41||?
Followed by Mineral Point free press
NN N 20,D 11 1838;Ja 22 Mr 5,12,Ap-Je 11 1839;Jl 7 1840
NcD Ja 19 1841

NATIONAL democrat. *See* Iowa county democrat

REPORTER. w,sw Ap 18 1912-13||?
w Ap 18-Jl 19 1912
WHi Ap 18-D 6 1912

Mineral Point **TRIBUNE.** w S 3 1847+
1847-51 as Wisconsin tribune
pub 1847+
NN S 17,O 1,29 1847;F 25 1848
OClWHi My 22 1860;Jl 9,O 8 1861;D 16 1863; O 19-N 9 1864
WHi 1847-S 1 1848;O 12 1849-O 23 1851;Ap 20 1854-59;61+

WISCONSIN tribune. *See* Mineral Point tribune

MINOCQUA

Minocqua **TIMES.** w Ap 1891+
WHi 1896-Jl 1911

MONDOVI

BUFFALO county herald. *See* Mondovi herald-news

BUFFALO county news. w 1898-Jl 6 1923||
United with Mondovi herald to form Mondovi herald and Buffalo county news, later Mondovi herald-news

Mondovi **HERALD and Buffalo county news.** *See* Mondovi herald-news

Mondovi **HERALD-NEWS.** w F 4 1876+
1876-Je 6 1890 as Buffalo county herald; Je 13 1890-Jl 6 1923 Mondovi herald; Jl 13 1923-Ja 1 1926 Mondovi herald and Buffalo county news
WHi O 5 1876-Ag 23 1879 Ja 13 1882+

MONROE

Monroe **GAZETTE.** w Jl 23 1879-Jl 17 1896||
1879-Jl 1881 as Jefferson independent (Jefferson); N 1881-82 Gazette. United with Monroe sun to form Monroe sun-gazette
WHi Mr-N 1882

GREEN county herold. w S 15 1877+
In German
pub 1877+
WHi Je 15 1927+

GREEN county reformer. w Ja 1870-My 6 1880||
1870-S 23 1873 as Green county republican; O 3 1873-Ja 8 1874 Green county republican and Liberal press
WHi Jl 25 1871-80

GREEN county republican. *See* Green county reformer

GREEN county union. *See* Monroe sentinel

INDEPENDENT press. O 1857-My 1858||
Follows Jeffersonian democrat. Followed by Albany times (Albany)

JEFFERSONIAN democrat. Ag 14 1856-Ap 1857||
Followed by Independent press
WHi 1856-Mr 26 1857

Monroe daily **JOURNAL.** d 1898-Je 15 1927||
Merged with Monroe evening times
WHi 1899-1927

JOURNAL-GAZETTE. w 1888-Jl 15 1927||
1888-Jl 19 1898 as Monroe county journal
WHi Jl 26 1898-1927

LIBERAL press. w 1872-S 1873||
Merged with Green county republican, later Green county reformer

MONROE county journal. *See* Journal-gazette

WISCONSIN (*Continued*)

MONROE—*Continued*

Monroe SENTINEL. w Ap 16 1850-N 2 1912||
1850-Ap 1851 as Green county union
MWA Ja 24 1866
NNHi My 8 1861-My 16 1866
WHi Ja 7,F 4 1852;My 25 1853;My 10 1854-1912
WMoT complete

Monroe SUN. *See* Monroe sun-gazette

Monroe SUN-GAZETTE. w Ja 23 1875-Jl 16 1898||
1875-Jl 18 1896 as Monroe sun. United with Monroe county journal to form Journal-gazette
Suspended from 1876?-N 1881
WHi Mr-N 18 1882;Mr 24 1883-98

Monroe evening TIMES. d O 13 1898+
pub 1898+
ICHi Jl 18 1892
WHi 1899+

WISCONSIN botschafter. w My 4 1869-Je 9 1927||
My 4-Jl 6 1869 as Madison botschafter. Merged with Green county herold
1869-O 21 1926 pub in Madison
In German
IU Ja-F 15,Jl 20-D 1917
WHi Ja 16 1874-1927

WISCONSIN state rights. *See under* Stevens Point

MONTELLO

Montello EXPRESS. w Mr 1859+
Mr-D 1859 as Oxford republican express; 1860-Mr 1 1861 Republican express; Mr 8-My 31 1861 Oxford express; Je 7 1861-72 Marquette weekly express; 1873-Ja 15 1876 as Montello weekly express
1859-Je 20 1862 pub in Oxford
WHi S 23 1859+

MARQUETTE weekly express. *See* Montello express

Montello SUN. w D 31 1881-N 2 1883||
Followed by Sun (Plainfield)
WHi complete

MONTFORT

Montfort INDEPENDENT. Mr 31 1881-Ap 1882||
Followed by Montfort monitor

Montfort MAIL. w Ja 21 1899+
pub 1899+

Montfort MONITOR. w My 17 1882-F 1894||
Follows Independent. Followed by Belmont bee (Belmont)
WHi 1882-92

SOUTHWEST Wisconsin. *See under* Linden

MONTROSE

WESTERN adventurer and herald of the upper Mississippi. w
NN S 30 1837

MORRISONVILLE

Morrisonville TRIBUNE. w D 5 1903+
pub 1903+

MOSINEE

Mosinee TIMES. w 1895+
pub 1895+
WHi Mr 13 1913-Jl 1918;Ag 1930+

MOUNT HOREB

BLUE MOUNDS weekly news. *See* Mount Horeb weekly news

DOINGS. *See* Parish doings

Mount Horeb MAIL. w N 13 1901+
pub 1901-02[20-21]24+

Mt. Horeb weekly NEWS. w My 1881-Je 8 1887||
1881-Jl 1885 as Blue Mounds weekly news (Blue Mounds) Merged with Black Earth advertiser (Black Earth)
WHi Jl 31 1883-87

PARISH doings. w
1907(?)-F 9 1921 as Daleyville doings (Daleyville) F 16 1921-Je (?) 1923 as Doings
WHi Ap 17 1912-Mr 28 1923;Jl 4 1923-Jl 29 1925

Mt. Horeb TIMES. w My 1887-Je 7 1932||
1887-N 21 1901 as Mount Horeb times. Merged with Mount Horeb mail
WHi Ag 8 1895-1932

MUKWONAGO

Mukwonago CHIEF. w Ja 1 1889+
pub [1889-1925]+

MUSCODA

GRANT county democrat. w O 1895-Ja 10 1919||
O 1895-1904? as Muscoda watchman; 1904?-Ja 1906 Valley voice. Merged with Muscoda progressive
WHi Jl 16,N 19 1896;O 18 1906-19

Muscoda LEADER-PRESS. *See* Grant county independent (Lancaster)

Muscoda NEWS. w D 4 1874-92||
Suspended My 1-S 1 1877; and for some time in 1891-92
WHi Ja 15 1876;Ja 18 1879-D 18 1880

Muscoda PROGRESSIVE. w 1913+
Ja 16-D 25 1919 as Muscoda progressive and Grant county democrat
pub 1931+
WHi Ja 16 1919+

VALLEY voice. *See* Grant county democrat

Muscoda WATCHMAN. *See* Grant county democrat

NAVARINO. *See* GREEN BAY

NEBAGAMON. *See* LAKE NEBAGAMON

NECEDAH

Necedah REPUBLICAN. w Ag 1 1884+
pub 1884+
WHi S 1884-Ap,D 11 1885+

Necedah SIGNAL. *See* Yellow River lumberman

YELLOW River lumberman. w O 13 1881-D 1884||
1881-Ja 18 1883 as Necedah signal. Followed by Juneau county sun(Mauston)
WHi O 13 1881-O 25 1883;Mr 6,13,27-Ap 10, Je 26,Jl 3 1884

NEENAH

Neenah BULLETIN. w *See* Neenah and Menasha examiner

Neenah BULLETIN. m 1875?-
KHi Je 1877

CONSERVATOR. *See* Menasha conservator (Menasha)

DANSKEREN. w Je 1892-99||?
In Danish
WHi O 11 1894-98

Neenah and Menasha EXAMINER. w My 14 1856-My 1857||
My-O 1856 as Neenah bulletin
WHi My 21-S 17 1856

Neenah GAZETTE. w 1871-98||
Merged with Neenah daily times
MWA Ja 8 1876
NNHi Ap 26 1872
WHi Ja 10 1874-S 4 1880;F 19 1881-Je 17 1882

ISLAND city times. *See* Menasha press (Menasha)

Neenah NEWS. *See* Daily news—times

Daily NEWS-TIMES. d 1880+
1880-Je 18? 1881 as Neenah news; Je 20 1881-My 17 1919 Twin City daily news
Early yours dated also at Menasha
pub 1881+
WHi F 11-My 14 1895;My 19 1919+

Neenah city TIMES. w O 15 1875-My 1919||
WHi F 4 1882

Neenah daily TIMES. d 1882-My 17 1919||
Merged with Twin City daily news to form Daily news-times
WHi Mr 25 1912-O 1913;F 21 1916-19

TWIN CITY daily news. *See* Daily news-times

WINNEBAGO county press. *See* Menasha press (Menasha)

NEILLSVILLE

CLARK county advocate. w 1862?-67||
MWA F 8 1866
WHi Ap 19 1866

CLARK county courier. w Je 1879-81||?
WHi Ja 27 1880-F 1 1881

CLARK county press. w Je 27 1873-Ap 8 1876||
United with Clark county republican to form Clark county republican and press, later Neillsville press
WHi complete

CLARK county republican and press. *See* Neillsville press

DEUTSCH-Amerikaner. w 1880-O 7 1920||?
Merged with Westlicher herold, later America-herold (Winona, Minn.)
In German
WHi F 17 1916-O 7 1920

ENTERPRISE. w F 12 1876-My 4 1878||
1876-Mr 17 1877 as Langlade enterprise. Merged with Republican and press, later Neillsville press
1876-Ja 19 1878 pub in Colby
WHi Mr 25-Je 17,D 30 1876-78

LANGLADE enterprise. *See* Enterpise

Neillsville PRESS. w O 25 1867+
1867-Ap 7 1876 as Clark county republican; Ap 15 1876-My 5 1921 Republican and press (Je 14 1876-78 as Clark county republican and press)
pub [1867-99]+
WHi S 6 1871+

REPUBLICAN and press. *See* Neillsville press

Neillsville TIMES. d D 1881-My 5 1921||
United with Republican and press and Granton news (Granton) to form Neillsville press
WHi Mr 21 1882-87;97-1921

TRUE republican. w Jl 1879-D 15 1887||
Merged with Neillsville times
WHi Mr 18 1880-87

NEKOOSA

Nekoosa TRIBUNE. w 1895-Jl 1 1922||
1895-F 27 1903 as Yellow River pilot; Mr 6 1903-F 11 1904 Pittsville Wisconsin times and the Yellow River pilot; F 18 1904-S 1 1905 Pittsville times and the Yellow River pilot; S 7 1905-D 30 1906(?) Wood county times and the Yellow River pilot
1895-S 1 1905 pub in Pittsville
WHi N 1897-Mr 16 1922

WOOD county times and the Yellow River pilot. *See* Nekoosa tribune

NEOSHO

Neosho STANDARD. w 1900-08||?
WHi My 19 1905-Je 26 1908

NEW GLARUS

DEUTSCH schweizerischer courier. w 1897-Ap 3 1917||
Merged with New Glarus post
In German
WHi 1916-17
WNgP complete

New Glarus POST. w 1912+
In English and German
Supplement 1924-26. *See* Belleville recorder (Belleville)
pub 1912+
WHi Ap 12 1917+

NEW HOLSTEIN

New Holstein REPORTER. w 1902+
pub 1902+

NEW LISBON

JUNEAU county argus. w 1856-D 16 1908||
Merged with New Lisbon times
Suspended N 1862-Mr 1863
NNHi D 25 1872
WHi N 8 1858[59]F 22-N 6 1862;S 28 1864-Ja 5 1888

New Lisbon REPUBLICAN. w Je 1855-Ja 1863||
WHi Je 20,N 7 1860

New Lisbon TIMES. w Mr 13 1895+
WHi 1895+

NEW LONDON

New London NEWS. w Jl 1874-76||
Merged with New London times
WHi Ag 11 1875-Jl 19 1876

New London NEWS. w Je 10-Ag 14 1885||?
WHi [Je-Ag 1885]

New London PRESS-republican. w,sw Jl 20 1893+
1893-S 7 1928 as New London press (title varies slightly)
sw S 13 1928-Jl 8 1929
pub 1893-1911;13-23;25-N 1926;S 20 1928+
WHi 1893+

New London REPUBLICAN. w Je 17 1897-S 7 1928||
United with New London press to form New London press-republican
WHi 1897-Ja 7 1915
WNlP Jl 19 1917-27

New London TIMES. w O 3 1856-Ap 1858||
Followed by Waupaca county register (Waupaca)
WHi 1856-O 2 1857

New London TIMES. w N 1870-S 11 1891||
Mr 26 1881-D 2 1882 as New London times and tribune
WHi 1876-91
WNlP [Jl 13 1871-N 5 1872]-My 11,N 13 1875-Jl 1877

New London TRIBUNE. w D 1880-Mr 1881||
Merged with New London times

New London TRIBUNE. w 1890-99||?
WNlP Ja 25 1895-Ja 17 1896

NEW RICHMOND

New Richmond DEMOCRAT. w Ag 1878-Ap 11 1881||
1878-S 19 1879 as New Richmond greenbacker
WHi F 1879-81

New Richmond GREENBACKER. *See* New Richmond democrat

New Richmond NEWS. w,sw Ag 14 1869+
1869-Je 29 1899 as St. Croix republican; Jl 7 1899-D 28 1907 Republican voice; 1908-My 1 1924 New Richmond news and republican voice
Ag 1869 pub in Hudson
w 1869-1907; Ja 31 1923-My 1 1924
pub Ja 20 1913+
MnHi 1869-N 1870
WHi F-Je 1870;Ja-My 1874;F 1875-S 1876;F 26 1879+

New Richmond NEWS. w 1904-07||
United with Republican voice to form New Richmond news and Republican voice, later New Richmond news

REPUBLICAN voice. *See* New Richmond news

ST CROIX republican. *See* New Richmond news

WISCONSIN (*Continued*)

NEW RICHMOND—*Continued*

New Richmond VOICE. w 1886-Je 27 1899||
United with St. Croix republican to form Republican-voice, later New Richmond news
WHi 1898-99

NEWPORT. *See* WISCONSIN DELLS

NIAGARA

Niagara JOURNAL. w D 12 1930+
pub 1930+
WHi Ap 1 1932

NORTH CRANDON

FOREST leaves. w Ap 8 1885-1912||
1885-91 pub in Crandon; 1892-97 in Three Lakes
WHi 1885-Ag 20 1891;Ja 13-Ag 25 1898

NORTHERN citizen. w 1910-18||
MWA Ja 5 1912;Mr 14 1913
WHi D 5 1911-Ap 12 1918

North Crandon REPORTER. w S 1892-Jl 1893||
WHi Ja 26-Je 29 1893

NORTH LA CROSSE

Papers published in North La Crosse are listed under La Crosse

NORTH MILWAUKEE

Papers published in North Milwaukee are listed under Milwaukee

NORWAY

NORDLYSET. w Jl 22 1847-My 18 1850||
Followed by Democraten (Racine, later Janesville)
First Norwegian newspaper in America
In Norwegian
IaDeL 1847[48]N 8 1849;F 23,My 18 1850
MnSL [1847-50]
WHi S 9 1847

OCONOMOWOC

Oconomowoc BADGER. *See* Badger state

BADGER state. w My 11 1866-1869||
1866-S 1867 as Oconomowoc badger. Followed by La Belle mirror, later Oconomowoc times
WHi [My-O 1866]

Oconomowoc CLARION. w O 1933-34||?
WHi Ja 18-S 27 1934

Oconomowoc DEMOCRAT. *See* Oconomowoc republican

Oconomowoc ENTERPRISE. w O 26 1900+
pub 1900+
WHi Mr 8 1901+

FREE PRESS. w O 14 1858-S 1862||
1858-60 as Oconomowoc free press
WHi 1858-Jl 19,O 3,25 1860;F 15 1861-Ag 16 1862

Oconomowoc FREE PRESS. sw,w My 15 1875-D 1 1910||
1875-O 8 1908 as Wisconsin free press. Merged with Oconomowoc enterprise
sw My-O 1875
WHi Je 12 1875-1910
WOcF [1875-1910]

LA BELLE mirror. *See* Oconomowoc times

Oconomowoc LOCAL. w S 4 1874-85||
WHi Mr 1875-F 6 1885

Oconomowoc REPUBLICAN. w 1888-Mr 2 1901||
1888-95 as Oconomowoc democrat. Merged with Oconomowoc enterprise
WHi Je 1896-1901

Oconomowoc TIMES. w Je 1869-1877||?
Follows Badger state. 1869-Ag 24 1870 as La Belle mirror
N F 25 1874
WHi S 6 1871-Je 4 1873

WISCONSIN free press. w 1875-1908. *See* Oconomowoc free press

OCONTO

ENQUIRER. w Jl 1881-Ag 29 1924||
Merged with Oconto county reporter
WHi F 25 1882-Ag 19 1886;Jl 21 1905-Jl 7 1911

Oconto LUMBERMAN. w Mr 1864-1920||
WHi Ag 18,S 9 1864;N 22 1873-D 19 1874

OCONTO county democrat. w Ag 1859-Ja 1860
Printed at Madison, but issued from Oconto

OCONTO county enterprise. w 1898-Ap 2 1920||
Merged with Oconto county reporter
WHi D 16 1913

OCONTO county reporter. w N 10 1871+
Ap 8 1920-Ag 28 1924 as Oconto county reporter enterprise; S 4 1924-My 28 1925 Oconto county reporter enterprise-enquirer
DLC Ap 8 1876
WHi F 7,28,Ag 22 1874+

Oconto PIONEER. w Je 25 1859-N 1875||
Merged with Oconto lumberman
WHi 1859-[63]-O 12 1865

OCONTO FALLS

FARMER-herald. *See* Oconto Falls herald

Oconto Falls HERALD. w Jl 1898+
1898-Jl 18 1902 as Herald; Mr 28 1912-Ap 28 1916 Union farmer-herald; My 5 1916-My 21 1920 Farmer-herald
pub 1922+
WHi 1899+

UNION farmer. w Je 1911-Mr 22 1912|
United with Herald to form Union farmer herald, later Oconto Falls herald
WHi Ag 19 1911-12

UNION farmer-herald. *See* Oconto Falls herald

ODANAH

Odanah STAR. *See* Ashland chronicle (Ashland)

OJIBWA

Ojibway COURIER. w 1909+
pub [1909-30]+

OMRO

Omro HERALD. w My 11 1894+
WHi 1894+

Omro JOURNAL. w O 1865-Ja 20 1916||
1865-72 as Omro union; 1872-O 31 1878 Omro weekly journal
NbHi O 19,N 2,16 1876
WHi Ag 1874-1916

Omro UNION. *See* Omro journal

ONALASKA

LA CROSSE county record. w N 6 1885+
pub 1885+

OREGON

Oregon OBSERVER. w S 22 1880+
pub 1880+
WHi Je 28 1883+

VILLAGE record. w O 29 1875-76||?
WHi 1875-My 12 1876

ORFORDVILLE

Orfordville JOURNAL. w 1908+
pub 1908+
WHi Ag 5 1925+

OSCEOLA

POLK county press. *See under* St. Croix Falls

Osceola SUN. w O 6 1897+
Follows Weekly press (Maiden Rock)
pub 1897+
WHi 1897+

OSHKOSH

AGE of labor. w F 1892-Je 3 1893||
Merged with Labor advocate
WHi Ap 1-Je 1893

Oshkosh CITY times. *See* Oshkosh weekly times

Oshkosh COURIER. w My 1852-Ag 6 1864||
1852- as Fox River courier. Merged with Weekly Northwestern
WHi Je 29,Ag 3,S 7 1853;My 1854-D 19 1863;Je 18-Ag 1864

Oshkosh daily COURIER. d F 10 1854-D 1857||
WHi My 17-N 11 1854
WO My 11-N 21 1854;S 1855-Ap,D 11 1856-Je 16 1857

Oshkosh DEMOCRAT. w F 9 1849-O 3 1860||
1849 as Oshkosh true democrat. Merged with Weekly northwestern
MWA Jl 4 1851
WHi 1849-F 25,My 20,Je 17,Ag 5,N 18 1853; Jl 21 1854

Oshkosh daily DEMOCRAT. d Je?-O 25 1865||
WHi O 4-25 1865

Oshkosh DEMOCRAT. w 1865-67 *See* Oshkosh weekly times

DEUTSCHE volksblätter. m,w F 1858-O 1866||
1858-S 1860 as Wächter am Winnebago. Followed by Wisconsin telegraph
In German

Oshkosh DEUTSCHE zeitung. w F 1857-60||
In German
WHi S 1857-59

DIENSTAGS-BLATT. w N 14 1905-N 13 1917||
Tues ed of Wisconsin telegraph
In German
WHi complete

EARLY dawn. w 1875-Ap 9 1880||
Followed by Reflector
WHi F 13 1879-80

ENTERPRISE. d 1897-99||?
WO 1898-Je 1899

FOX RIVER courier. *See* Oshkosh courier

GREENBACK standard. *See* Wisconsin standard (Milwaukee)

Oshkosh INDEPENDENT. w N? 1874-Ap 28 1875|
WHi D 26 1874-75

Oshkosh JOURNAL. w Ag 8 1868-Ap 12 1873||
Merged with Weekly northwestern
CSmH [Ag 1868-D 4 1869]
DLC 1868-Jl 30 1870
WHi complete
WO F 19-D 1870

LABOR advocate. w Ja 1893-1904||
Je 10-D 29 1893 as Labor advocate and age of labor
WHi Je 10 1893-Je 1895

Oshkosh NEWS. w Jl 11 1868-69||?
WHi Jl-O 10 1868

Weekly NORTHWESTERN. w My 18 1860-1909||?
Title varies: Northwestern; Oshkosh northwestern, etc.
WHi 1860-Je 13 1862;Ag 18 1864-D 6 1866;O 20 1870-My 23 1872;My 13 1875-94
WO 1860-S 1 1864

Daily NORTHWESTERN. d Ja 12 1861+
Title varies: Oshkosh daily northwestern; Daily northwestern, etc.
Suspended Ag 29 1861-67
DLC Jl 1 1898-Je 29 1901
WHi [1874-81]95+
WO Ja 12-Ag 1861;My 1882-91;95+

OBSERVER. w D 1929+
pub 1929+

Oshkosh RECORD. w My 1887-89||
Merged with Signal
WHi [N 19 1887-F 4 1888]

REFLECTOR. w Ap 16 1880-81||?
Follows Early dawn
WHi Ap-My 21 1880

Oshkosh REFORMER. w Ja 1898-D 28 1900||?
WHi O 28 1899-1900

SIGNAL. w 1884-97||?
1889-90 as Signal record
WHi [Mr 1886-My 19 1887]

SIGNAL-RECORD. *See* Signal

Oshkosh STANDARD. *See* Wisconsin standard (Milwaukee)

Oshkosh weekly TIMES. w O 7 1864-Ap 15 1905||
1864-Ja 27 1865 as Oshkosh union; F 1865-S 1867 Oshkosh democrat; O 1867-My 1872 Oshkosh city times; Je 1872-O 8 1904 title varies: Weekly times; Oshkosh times; etc.
MWA Ap 2 1873
WHi 1864-Ja,My-N 3 1865;Je-D 8 1866;Mr 9 1867-Ja 1883;91-1905

Oshkosh TIMES. d 1883-Ap 1905||?
MWA Ap 18 1886
WO Ja 28 1885-Mr 1901

Oshkosh TRUE democrat. *See* Oshkosh democrat

Oshkosh UNION. *See* Oshkosh weekly times

WÄCHTER am Winnebago. *See* Deutsche volksblätter

WINNEBAGO telegraph. w D 20? 1849-51||
WHi Ja 3,S 14 1850

WISCONSIN telegraph. w O 1866-1920||
Follows Deutsche volksblätter
—w ed *See* Dienstags-blatt
WHi Ja 9 1874-Ap 16 1920

OSSEO

Osseo-Eleva JOURNAL. w Je 25 1896-
WHi Je 25-S 3 1896

Osseo NEWS. w My 3 1912+

OXFORD

Oxford EXPRESS. *See* Montello express (Montello)

MARQUETTE weekly express. *See* Montello express (Montello)

REPUBLICAN express. *See* Montello express (Montello)

Oxford TIMES. w N 23? 1911-O 28 1920||
Merged with Central union (Westfield)
WHi D 7 1911-20

PALMYRA

Palmyra ENTERPRISE. w Mr 25 1874+
pub 1928+
WHi 1874+
PWa 1903-05
WS Ag 6 1890

PARDEEVILLE

CRANK. w Mr 30 1898- 1901||
WHi 1898-O 9 1901

Pardeeville TIMES. *See* Pardeeville-Wyocena times

Pardeeville-Wyocena TIMES. w D 1888+
1888-1924 as Pardeeville times
pub 1920+
WHi D 1889-Je 7 1890;N 25 1892-O 1900

WISCONSIN (*Continued*)

PARK FALLS

INDEPENDENT. *See* Park Falls leader

Park Falls **HERALD.** w S 21 1900+
pub 1900-Ja 11 1901;02+
WHi My 28 1926+

Park Falls **LEADER.** w 1915-S 20 1934||
1915-1926 as Independent
WHi Ag 28 1930-S 22 1932

PEPIN

ERA of progress. bw D 25 1861-
WHi D 25 1861

Pepin **HERALD.** w F 13 1908+
WHi My 12 1927

Pepin **INDEPENDENT.** w Ja 1857-O 25 1859||
1857-? as North Pepin independent
WHi Ap 16 1858-59

NORTH Pepin independent. *See* Pepin independent

PEPIN county press. w Je 2 1860-My 17 1862||
WHi complete

Pepin **STAR.** *See* Pepin county news (Durand)

PERRY

DALEYVILLE doings. *See* Parish doings (Mt. Horeb)

DOINGS. *See* Parish doings (Mt. Horeb)

PARISH doings. *See* Parish doings (Mt. Horeb)

PESHTIGO

Peshtigo **EAGLE.** *See* Weekly eagle-star (Marinette)

NEW Peshtigo times. w Ap 1894+
1894-Jl 25 1929 as Peshtigo times
pub 1894+
WHi N 1894-O 31 1918;F 13 1919+

Peshtigo **TIMES.** *See* New Peshtigo times

PEWAUKEE

Pewaukee **STANDARD.** w 1877-My 27 1880||
Merged with Waukesha freeman (Waukesha)
WHi F 20 1879-80

PHILLIPS

Phillips **BADGER.** w Jl 6 1881-My 21 1884||
Merged with Phillips times
WHi complete

BEE. w O 1884+
WHi 1898+

Phillips **TIMES.** w Ja 6 1877-Ap 22 1932||
Merged with Bee
WHi complete
WPh 1877-1931

PINE RIVER. *See* WAUTOMA

PITTSVILLE

Pittsville **RECORD.** w Ag 1908+
pub 1908+
WHi Jl 31 1930+

Pittsville **TIMES and the Yellow River pilot.** See Nekoosa tribune (Nekoosa)

Pittsville **WISCONSIN times and the Yellow river pilot.** *See* Nekoosa tribune (Nekoosa)

YELLOW River pilot. *See* Nekoosa tribune (Nekoosa)

PLAINFIELD

SUN. w N 23 1883+
Follows Sun (Montello)
WHi N 1883+

PLATTEVILLE

Platteville **EXAMINER.** w D 17 1857-Je 10 1858||
Follows Independent American
N My 13 1858
WHi F 11-My 1858
WPlW complete

GRANT county democrat. *See* Grant county news

GRANT county news. w S 26 1884+
1884-Ja 18 1890 as Grant county democrat
pub Je 1897+
WHi Jl 16 1885+

GRANT county witness. *See* Platteville witness

INDEPENDENT American. w Ja 11 1845-O 30 1857||
1845-Ja 6 1849 as Independent American and general advertiser. Followed by Platteville examiner
Suspended from Ja 6 1849-S 13 1851
DLC Ja 15 1847-Ja 7 1848
WHi Ja 11 1845-O 23 1857
WPlW complete

Platteville **JOURNAL.** w F 25 1899+
pub 1899+
WHi S 18 1912+

NORTHERN badger. w Jl 30 1840-S 1841||
Followed by Wisconsin whig
WHi Ja 8,29,F 19 1841

WISCONSIN whig. w S 22 1841-43||
Follows Northern badger
DLC S 22 1841
WHi Ap 27,S 14 1842

WISKONSAN standard. w Ag 4 1843-
DLC Ag 11-19 1843

Platteville **WITNESS.** w My 26 1859+
1859-F 14 1906 as Grant county witness; F 21 1906-D 3 1919 Platteville witness and mining times
Mr 26-Jl 14 1859 pub in Lancaster
pub 1859+
IaGG Ap 20 1865
NNHi Jl 23 1863;Ap 24 1873
WHi 1859-My 8 1862;Jl 1863-Je 4 1868;Mr 25 1870+

PLOVER

PORTAGE county republican. w -Ja 1861||
United with Stanton weekly times to form Stanton times and republican, later Plover times

Plover **HERALD.** *See* Plover times

Plover **TIMES.** w Ag 7 1856-81||
1856-57,? as Plover herald; 1857-60? Stanton weekly times (Stanton); 1861- Stanton times and republican; -My 9 1868 Plover times and republican
MWA Ja 6 1866
WHi Ag 7,S,O 30 1856;Ag 26,O 18-25 1859[F 10-My 1860] Jl 4 1863;Mr 1866-Ap 1881

PLUM CITY

Plum City **NEWS.** w Jl 9 1931+
pub 1931+

PLYMOUTH

Plymouth **REPORTER.** w O 8 1872-Ja 21 1927||
1872-My 14 1874 as Plymouth weekly reporter. United with Plymouth review and Sheboygan herald to form Review herald reporter, later Plymouth review
WHi complete

Plymouth **REVIEW.** w,sw N 6 1895+
Ja 13 1927-D 29 1930 as Review herald reporter
w 1895-Ja 13 1927
NdHi Je 22 1905-Mr 6 1907
WHi 1895+

REVIEW herald reporter. *See* Plymouth review

SHEBOYGAN herald. w S 1867-Ja 10 1927||
Follows Northwestern record (Sheboygan Falls). 1867-Ap 7 1871 as Sheboygan county herald; N 1882-84 Sheboygan sun and herald. United with Plymouth review to form Review herald reporter, later Plymouth review
1867-Ja 14, 1870 pub in Sheboygan Falls; Ja 21 1870-S 20 1919 in Sheboygan
WHi Jl 16 1869-N 1871;O 17 1873-O 1882;Ja 2-10 1892

PORT WASHINGTON

ADLER. w Ja 4 1860-
In German
WHi Ja 4,18 1860
—English ed *See* Ozaukee county eagle

Port Washington **HERALD.** w Ap 1895+
pub 1895+

OZAUKEE county advertiser. w My 1854-Ja 1913||
Title varies slightly: Ozaukee county advertiser and democrat. United with Port Washington star to form Port Washington star and Ozaukee county advertiser
WHi Je 13-27 1855;Mr-Ap 10,Ag 7 1856

OZAUKEE county blade. See Ozaukee county times

OZAUKEE county democrat. w Jl 25 1857-Je 1858||
Merged with Ozaukee county advertiser
WHi S 19,O 24-N 14,D 5-19 1857

OZAUKEE county eagle. w Ja 4 1860-
WHi F 23 1860
—German ed *See* Adler

OZAUKEE county times. w Ap 1849-Jl 1854||
1849-F 1853 as Washington county blade. Mr-S 1853 Ozaukee county blade
WHi F 20 1851;Ag 19 1852;Ap 20, S 29,D 8 1853-F 2,Ap 27,My 11,25,Je 8,29 1854;Ap 14-21 1859

Port Washington **PILOT, Port Washington star and Grafton enterprise.** w 1895+
1895-Ap 19 1928 as Port Washington pilot
pub 1900+
WHi Ap 26 1928+

Port Washington **STAR and Ozaukee county advertiser.** w N 1 1879-Ap 20 1928||
1879-95 title varies: Weekly star; Port Washington star; etc. United with Port Washington pilot and Grafton enterprise to form Port Washington pilot, Port Washington star, and Grafton enterprise
WHi 1879-F 16 1889;F 9 1895-1928

WASHINGTON county blade. *See* Ozaukee county times

WASHINGTON county democrat. w Ag 1847-1849||
1847-48? as Washington democrat. Merged with Washington county blade, later Ozaukee county times
WHi O 19 1848

WASHINGTON democrat. *See* Washington county democrat

WISCONSIN statesman. *See under* Milwaukee

Port Washington **ZEITUNG.** w Ja 1 1855-S 6 1928||
In German
WHi Ag 25 1859;F 14 1895-1928

PORTAGE

To 1852 as Fort Winnebago; 1852-Mr 19 1844 Portage City

Portage **ADVERTISER.** *See* Monroe county republican (Sparta)

BADGER state. w O 1 1853-D 10 1859||
Follows River times
MWA F 1 1856
WHi Mr 11 1854-Jl 2 1858
WP complete

Portage **CITY record.** w Ap 29 1857-Ap 17 1861||
Follows Independent. Merged with Wisconsin state register
N Ja 20 1858
WHi Ap 29-My 27 1857;Ag 31 1859-61
WP complete

Portage **weekly DEMOCRAT.** w Mr 23 1877-Ap 4 1919||
1877-Ja 8 1892 as Portage democrat. Merged with Wisconsin state register
NbHi N 9 1877
WHi complete
WP 1887-93;96-1918

Portage **daily DEMOCRAT.** d Mr 1 1886-Ap 4 1919||
United with Portage daily register to form Portage daily register-democrat
WP 1886-Jl 15 1892;S 12 1894-1919

Portage **HERALD.** w S 1885-S 6 1888||
United with Portage advertiser to form Herald-advertiser, later Monroe county republican (Sparta)

HERALD-ADVERTISER. *See* Monroe county republican (Sparta)

INDEPENDENT. w F 3 1855-Ap 14 1857||
Followed by Portage City record
WP complete

NORTHERN republic. *See* Republic

Portage **REGISTER-DEMOCRAT.** d Mr 1886+
1886-Ap 4 1919 as Portage daily register
d ed of Wisconsin state register
WHi My 1-2,Je 6 1891;Jl 5 1892
WP 1886+

REPUBLIC. w D 20 1851-D 1854||
1851-52? as Northern republic
WHi D 20 1851;Ag 27 1853

RIVER times. w Jl 4 1850-S 17 1853||
Followed by Badger state
WHi complete
WP complete

WESTERN advance. w 1872-Mr 26 1879||
Merged with Independent (Madison)
WHi 1874-79

WISCONSIN state register. w Mr 16 1861+
Title varies slightly: Wisconsin state register democrat, etc.
NbHi N 10 1877
WHi Ap 20-27,Je 29 1861;Jl 1863-My 16 1919; Ap 16 1920+
WP 1861+

POTOSI

Potosi **REPUBLICAN.** w My 27 1847-Ag 14 1855||
Merged with Potosi signal Ag 1852. Revived My 1853
WHi S 1847-48;Ap 29 1854-55

Potosi **SIGNAL.** w Jl 13-D 1852||
DLC O 20 1852

POYNETTE

Poynette **PRESS.** w Ap 1884+
pub 1888+
WHi N 1885+

PRAIRIE DU CHIEN

COURIER. w My 19 1852+
1852-53? as Crawford county courier. Title varies slightly: Prairie du chien weekly courier; Prairie du chien courier
pub 1856+
WHi 1852-My 24 1853;My 22 1856-D 20 1866;F 11 1873+

CRAWFORD county courier. *See* Courier

CRAWFORD county democrat. *See* Crawford county press (1870-73)

CRAWFORD county press. w Ja 1870-My 23 1873||
Follows Northwestern democrat. 1870-Ag? 1871 as Crawford county democrat. Merged with Prairie du Chien union
WHi S 8 1871-73

CRAWFORD county press. w Ja 13 1904+
pub 1904+
WHi 1904+

INTER-COUNTY gazette. w Je 5 1878-Ap 2 1880||
1878- D19 1879 as Grant county gazette (Lancaster)
Suspended F-Mr 1880
NbHi Je 19 1878
WHi complete

WISCONSIN (*Continued*)

PRAIRIE DU CHIEN—*Continued*

Prairie du Chien LEADER. w Jl 18 1857-Ap 1861||
WHi 1857-D 8 1859

NATIONAL broad-axe. *See* Boscobel broad-axe (Boscobel)

NORTHWESTERN democrat. w S 1868-D 1869||
Followed by Crawford county democrat, later Crawford county press (1870-73)
1868? pub in Black River Falls

Prairie du Chien PATRIOT. w S 15 1846-Ag 13? 1851||
First paper on the Upper Mississippi
MWA Je 23 1847
WHi complete

Prairie du Chien UNION. w Mr 18 1864-Ja 1 1914||
OClWHi Mr 11-18 1877
WHi Ap 1 1864;Ja 27 1871-1914

PRAIRIE DU SAC

SAUK county news. w O 21 1876+
pub Ag 17 1899+
WHi F 24 1877-O 1 1889;S 18 1924+

PRAIRIEVILLE. *See* WAUKESHA

PRENTICE

Prentice CALUMET. w Je 1892-S 29 1911||
United with Prentice news to form Prentice news-calumet, later Price county news
WHi Ja 25 1895-1911

Prentice NEWS. *See* Price county news

Prentice NEWS-CALUMET. *See* Price county news

PRICE county news. w 1902-29||?
1902-Jl 15 1927 as Prentice news (O 6 1911-My 1927 Prentice news-calumet)
WHi O 19 1911-Ja 11 1918;Mr 28 1919-Jl 15,O 28 1927-Mr 7 1929

PRESCOTT

Prescott weekly CLARION. *See* Prescott journal

Prescott DEMOCRAT. w O 26 1858-N 14 1860||
1858-Ap 4 1860 as North-western democrat
MnHi D 14 1858-[59]
WHi Jl 27 1859-N 7 1860

Prescott JOURNAL. w Ap 1857-Jl 12 1871||
1857-F 27 1861 as River Falls journal (River Falls)
Suspended Mr 6-My 1 1861
MWA Ja 27 1866
MnHi 1868-[71]
NBuG S 30-D 9 1857
NNHi D 23-30 1865
WHi Je 29 1859-71
WMen N 3 1868-69

Prescott JOURNAL. w Ap 4 1874+
1874-Je 19 1875 as Prescott weekly clarion; Je 29 1875-93 Pierce county plain-dealer; 1893-D 27 1923 Prescott tribune
Suspended for a time in 1924
WHi 1874-Ja 8,Ap 15 1892-Ja 6 1893;F 14 1896-Jl 14 1910;Jl 17 1919-23;Ag 14 1930+

NORTH-WESTERN democrat. *See* Prescott democrat

Prescott PARACLETE. *See* Prescott transcript

Prescott PATRIOT. w S 20 1871-
MWA S 27 1871

PIERCE county plaindealer. *See* Prescott journal

Prescott TRANSCRIPT. w F 14 1855-S 21 1861||
F 14-S 21 1855 as Prescott paraclete.
Merged with Prescott journal
ICHi Jl 27 1855
NNHi Jl 2 1859;Je 21 1861
WHi complete

Prescott TRIBUNE. *See* Prescott journal

PRINCETON

GREEN LAKE county democrat. *See under* Markesan, Wis.

INDEPENDENT. *See* Green Lake county democrat (Markesan)

Princeton REPUBLIC. w F 21 1867+
MWA F 21 1867
WHi F 13 1869-D 22 1904

Princeton STAR. w Mr 5 1902-1905||?
WHi 1902-Jl 12 1905

RACINE

Racine ADVOCATE. w N 23 1842-88||?
N 29 1853-D 26 1866 as Weekly Racine advocate
DLC D 12 1843;Ja 19 1848-Mr 14 1849;51-58;S 14,N 9,D 28 1859;Jl 25,D 19 1860;F 27,Ap 10, My 1-8,Jl 10,Ag 28,S 25,O 9-23,N 6,20 1861; F 5,19,Mr,Je 4,Ag 6 1862;Jl 19 1865
MWA Ag 9 1853
WHi 1842-Mr 24 1847;51-Ja 1 1855;Je 22 1859-F 10 1872;Je 15 1878-My 24 1888
WR 1842-Mr 10 1843;60-Ap 17 1884

Racine ADVOCATE. d
Title varies: Daily Racine advocate; Daily morning advocate
DLC D 12 1853-Mr 24 1855
WR My 9 1853-54

Racine ARGUS. w F 14-O 6 1838||
Suspended Ag 22-S 29 1838. 18 nos were pub
DLC Je 9 1838
WHi complete

Racine ARGUS. w S 1 1868-D 16 1880||
1868-D 6 1877 as Racine county argus
WHi 1874-80
WR F 25 1869-Ag 17 1876;Ap 19 1877-S 3 1880

Racine daily ARGUS. d Ag 1-D 31 1880||
Followed by Racine daily journal, later Racine journal-times
WRJ complete

Racine daily CALL. d Ag 6 1913-N 20 1915||
United with Racine daily times to form Racine times-call
WRJ complete

Racine CORRESPONDENT. w 1883-Je 29 1918||
WHi Jl 21 1900-18

Racine DAY. w D 9 1932+
1932-Ag 3 1934 as New day
pub [1932-D 22 1933]+
WHi Ag 11 1933

Racine DEMOCRAT. w Ap 1852-S 1861||
1852-? as Racine county democrat.
"Suppressed for treasonable utterances"
P-M O 3 1854
WHi Jl 16,3 17 1853;S 12,N 21 1854;D 1 1856; Ag 24 1859-Ag 21 1861
WR My 11 1857-My 17 1858;My 18 1859-My 16 1860

DEMOCRATEN. *See under* Janesville

DOLLAR weekly. w,sw Ap 24 1884-Ag 18 1911||
1884-Je 25 1901 as Utley's dollar weekly; Ag 9 1901-Ja 8 1909 Semi-weekly times
WRJ complete
—d ed *See* Racine times-call

FOLKETS avis. w, 1876- 1919||?
In Swedish
MnHi [1915]
WHi 1900-03

Racine daily HERALD. *See* Racine daily news

INDEPENDENT news. w S 2 1932-
WHi S 2-O 21 1932

Racine JOURNAL. w,bw N 1856-F 18 1913||
Title varies: Racine weekly journal
Suspended from O 1857-N 1858
w 1856-Ag 1901
WHi D 11 1856-D 2 1857[F 10-Jl 27 1864] Ja 27 1869-1913
WR S 29 1859-61;My-D 1862;Ja 25 1865-Je 5 1872;Ap 30 1873-Ap 8 1874;75-N 26 1912
WRJ Jl 12 1865-1912

Racine daily JOURNAL. *See* Racine journal-times

Racine JOURNAL-NEWS. *See* Racine journal-times

Racine JOURNAL-TIMES. d N 25 1856-64; Ja 3 1881+
1856-64 as Racine journal; 1881-Ja 6 1912 Racine daily journal; Ja 8 1912-Je 25 1932 Racine journal-news.
Suspended 1864-80
pub 1881+
MWA Mr 11 1922
OClWHi N 29 1865
WHi 1856-N 17 1857;Jl 14-O 1897;1900-04;Jl-S 1906; Mr-Ap 1921;Je 27 1932+
WR 1856-O 3 1857;My 9 1859-Ap 27 1861;81+
WRD Jl 1934+

NATIONAL demokrat. w My 1859-Je 1860||
In German
WHi S-O 1859

NEW day. *See* Racine day

Racine daily NEWS. d D 16 1878-83||?
1878-Ap 24 1879 as Racine daily herald.
Title varies: Racine evening news
WHi F 6-Mr 19 1879
WR Mr 8 1858-Ja 9 1859;Ja 4-Ap 27 1881

Racine NEWS. d 1895-Ja 6 1912||
United with Racine daily journal to form Racine journal-news
WHi Jl 1902-03
WR Jl 19 1900-Je 11 1904
WRJ 1896-1912

RACINE county argus. *See* Racine argus

RACINE county democrat. *See* Racine democrat

SLAVIE. *See under* Chicago, Ill.

SLOVAN amerikansky. w Ja 1 1860-O 30 1861||
Followed by Slavie (Chicago, Ill)

Racine daily TIMES. *See* Racine times-call

Semi-weekly TIMES. *See* Dollar weekly

Racine TIMES-CALL. d N 1883-Je 25 1932||
1884-N 20 1915 as Racine daily times (title varies slightly: Racine times; Racine evening times). United with Racine journal-news to form Racine journal-times
WHi Ap 10 1884-1932
WR 1890-My 26 1906;Mr 1923-32
WRJ Ja 1? 1884-1932
—w ed *See* Dollar weekly

UTLEY'S dollar weekly. *See* Dollar weekly

WISCONSIN aegis. w D 1843-
First anti-slavery paper in Wisconsin
WHi Mr 2 1844

RANDOLPH

Randolph ADVANCE. w N 11 1893+
pub 1893+

Randolph ENTERPRISE. *See* Lively times

LIVELY times. w Ja 3 1873-D 15 1877||
1873-76 as Randolph enterprise. Followed by Monroe county democrat (Tomah, later Sparta)
WHi complete

RANDOM LAKE

Random Lake TIMES. w My 1 1918+
pub 1918+

RED GRANITE

Red Granite TIMES. w S 15 1927+
pub 1927+

REEDSBURG

Reedsburg FREE PRESS. sw,w Je 25 1860-S 7 1861;Mr 22 1872+
sw O 30-D 20 1894
pub 1872+
WHi 1860-61;72-77;Jl 19 1883+
WReF 1860-61

Reedsburg HERALD. w O 21 1856-F 1858||
Suspended Ja 2-16 1858
WHi 1856-Ja 23 1858

SAUK county herald. *See* Herold und volksfreund (La Crosse)

Reedsburg TIMES. w 1888+
WHi O 28 1904-S 8 1916;N 9 1917+

REEDSVILLE

Reedsville REPORTER. w 1909-21||?
WHi Mr 13 1913-O 12 1916

REESEVILLE

Reeseville REVIEW. w Mr 5 1889+
Ag 13 1931 is Diamond jubilee edition
pub 1889+
WHi Ag 13 1931

RHINELANDER

Rhinelander HERALD. w Ap 1885-1912||
1885-Je 1886 as West Merrill herald (Merrill); Jl 1886-Ag 5 1893 Oneida county herald
WHi O 24 1891-O 2 1909
WRh S 1892-1906

NEW North. w D 7 1882+
WHi 1912+
WRh 1882-87;1901+

Rhinelander NEWS. w D 30 1886-1920||
1885-Jl 24 1890 as Eagle River vindicator (Eagle River) Jl 31 1890-Ag 10 1910 Vindicator
WHi Ja 20-Jl 21 1887;Jl 24 1890-Ap 1920
WRh 1905-15;17

Rhinelander daily NEWS. d Mr 1 1917+
pub F 2 1925+
WRh 1917+

ONEIDA county herald. *See* Rhinelander herald

VINDICATOR. *See* Rhinelander news

RICE LAKE

BARRON county chronotype *See* Rice Lake chronotype

Rice Lake CHRONOTYPE. w Je 1874+
Je-S 1874 as Barron county gazette (Barron) 1874-Jl 1882 as Barron county chronotype
pub Jl 1882+
DLC Ap 22,Je 10 1876
WHi Mr 1875-Jl 1882;D 18 1896+
WRi 1897+

Rice Lake INDEPENDENT. w S 17 1931-My 11 1933||
Merged with Rice Lake chronotype
WHi complete

Rice Lake LEADER. w Jl 2 1896-F 26 1909||
Merged with Rice Lake chronotype
WHi complete

RICHLAND CENTER

INDEPENDENT. w Mr -D 1872||
Follows Richland county recorder
WHi Ag 3-D 13 1872

LIVE republican. w D 13 1863-Ag 8 1867||
United with Observer to form Richland county republican, later Republican observer
WHi complete

OBSERVER. w D 21 1876-D 30 1880||
United with Richland county republican to form Richland county republican and observer, later Republican observer
WHi complete

REPUBLICAN and observer. *See* Republican observer

WISCONSIN (*Continued*)

RICHLAND CENTER—*Continued*

REPUBLICAN observer. w N 20 1855+
1855-Ag 8 1867 as Richland county observer; Ag 15 1867-D 30 1880 Richland county republican; Ja 6 1881-Ja 3 1889 Richland county republican and observer
pub 1865+
MWA Ap 22,My 13 1856;Je 2 1864
NNHi Jl 9 1863
WHi 1855-Ap 12 1859;My 1 1860;61-F 22,Ag 16,O 18 1866;Ag 15 1867+

RICHLAND county observer. *See* Republican observer

RICHLAND county recorder. w Mr 1868-1871||?
1868-Mr 1871 as Richland county sentinel. Followed by Independent
WHi F 16 1870

RICHLAND county republican. *See* Republican observer

RICHLAND county sentinel. *See* Richland county recorder

RICHLAND democrat. w 1880-81 *See* Richland rustic

RICHLAND democrat. w S 1892+
pub 1892+
WHi My 18 1904

RICHLAND democrat and farmer. *See* Richland rustic

RICHLAND farmer. *See* Richland rustic

RICHLAND rustic. w Ag 13 1880-1924||
1880-Ap 22 1881 as Richland democrat; My 6 1881 Richland farmer; My 13-Je 3 1881 Richland democrat and farmer
WHi O 15 1880-D 13 1918

RICHLAND union democrat. w Ja 3? 1884-85||?
WHi Mr 13 1884

RICHLAND zouave. w S 14 1861-Jl 17 1862||
WHi complete

RIDGEWAY

BARNEVELD banner. w 1892-O 13 1899||
Merged with Mount Horeb times (Mount Horeb)
WHi Je 25 1897-99

ENTERPRISE. w 1882-93||?
WHi Je 7-D 6 1889

RIO

BADGER blade. w Mr 13 1902-25||?
WHi 1902-O 23 1925

COLUMBIA county reporter. w S 10 1886-D 28 1906||
Merged with Badger blade
WHi complete

Rio JOURNAL. w 1925+
WHi Jl 31 1930+

RIPON

ADVANCE. w -N 18? 1896||
United with Ripon free press to form Ripon advance-press, later Ripon weekly press

ADVANCE press. *See* Ripon weekly press

Ripon COMMONWEALTH. w Ja 22 1864+
Follows Prairie city record
WHi 1864-66;Jl 29 1887+
WRip 1864-Ap 10 1874;S 1882-N 1884;D 19 1890-1903;05+

Ripon FREE PRESS. w *See* Ripon weekly press

Ripon HERALD. w D 14 1853-Jl 1855||
Followed by Ripon spur, later Ripon home
P-M S 16 1854
WHi Ag 12,26,D 2-9 1854;Ja 11,Mr 8 1855
WRip Ja-D 9 1854

Ripon HOME. w Ag 4 1855-Jl 1857||
Follows Ripon herald. Followed by Ripon weekly times. Ag 4 1855-O 1856 as Ripon spur. Title varies: Ripon weekly home; etc.
WHi 1855-S 1856;Ja 9-Je 1857
WRip 1855-Ap 4 1856

Ripon NEWS. sw D 1 1898-My 27 1899||
WRip complete

PRAIRIE city record. w My 1-D 17? 1863||
Follows Ripon weekly times. Followed by Ripon commonwealth
WHi My 14-D 17 1863
WRip My-D 2 1863

Ripon semi-weekly PRESS. sw D 4 1905-F 28 1908||
WHi complete

Ripon weekly PRESS. w Ap 1870+
1870-N 18 1896 as Ripon free press (Ja 8-Jl 25 1885 Ripon republican, pub in opposition to Stone's free press); N 25 1896-Ap 26 1900 Ripon advance-press; My 3 1900-N 30 1905 Ripon press
N Ja 29 1885
WHi Ja 7 1875+
WRip 1888;97-98;1901+

Ripon REPUBLICAN. *See* Ripon weekly press

Ripon SPUR. *See* Ripon home

Ripon STAR. w Mr 31 1857-D 1862||
Suspended My 19 1857-58;N 1861-Mr 1862
WHi Mr-My 12 1857

STONE'S free press. d My 28-Jl 29 1885||
pub in opposition to Ripon republican
WHi complete

Ripon weekly TIMES. w N 1857-Ap 17 1863||
Follows Ripon home. 1857-58 as Western times. Followed by Prairie city record
WHi Jl 23 1858;Ap 29,Ag 26 1859-63
WRip Ap 29 1859-Ap,Je 28 1861-Ag 22 1862

WESTERN times. *See* Ripon weekly times

RIVER FALLS

River Falls ADVANCE. w Jl 1 1874-Ja 31 1876||
WHi complete

CITIZEN'S reporter. w 1863-
MWA Je 27 1863

River Falls JOURNAL. 1857-61 *See* Prescott journal (Prescott)

River Falls JOURNAL. w Ag 23 1872+
WHi 1872+

River Falls PRESS. w Jl 30 1874-Je 14 1883||
DLC Ja 11 1877-D 25 1879
WHi complete

ROSENDALE

Rosendale JOURNAL. w My 15 1903-18||?
WHi 1903-Jl 1 1904

ROSHOLT

Rosholt COMMUNITY press. w N 25 1926-Ja 1 1931
WHi complete

Rosholt REVIEW. w O 22? 1920-O 31 1924||
WHi D 3 1920-24

ST. CROIX FALLS

DALLES of St. Croix. w Ja 1881-N 28 1884||
MnHi complete
WHi Ap 8 1881-84

PEOPLES advocate. w O 18 1884-
WHi O 18,25,29 1884

POLK county press. w D 1860-1908||
1860-D 1861 as St. Croixian; D 1861-Ag 12 1904 Polk county press (Osceola). United with St. Croix Valley standard to form Standard-press
MWA Mr 28 1863
MnHi [D 11 1867]-[1907]
WHi [D 1863-Je 11]D 1864-1906
WOsS complete

ST. CROIX Valley standard. *See* Standard-press

ST. CROIXIAN. *See* Polk county press

STANDARD-press. w 1885+
1885-Mr 13? 1908 as St. Croix Valley standard
WHi D 15 1887;F 1895-Mr 13 1908;Ja 13 1916+
WOsS 1908-S 15 1913

ST. NAZIANZ

St. Nazianz WEEKLY. w 1895-S 1898||
United with Manitowoc tribune (Manitowoc) to form Manitowoc citizen (Manitowoc)

SAUK CITY

PIONIER am Wisconsin. *See* Pionier press

PIONIER press. w N 23 1853+
1853-98 as Pionier am Wisconsin; 1898-S 12 1929 Sauk City pionier presse
Suspended 1854-Ap 1855
In German
WHi Ja 14 1865-Je 1897;Ap 12 1917+

Sauk City PRESSE. w 1890-98||
United with Pionier am Wisconsin to form Sauk City pionier presse, later Pionier press
In German

SEYMOUR

Seymour PRESS. w 1886+
pub [1886+]

SHARON

Sharon INQUIRER. w S 25 1873-Ag 8 1878||
Follows Ft. Atkinson herald (Ft. Atkinson). United with Delavan tribune (Delavan) to form Delavan enterprise (Delavan)
WHi O 23 1873-78

Sharon REPORTER. w 1878+
pub 1878+
WSha Ap 1930+

SHAWANO

Shawano ADVOCATE-dispatch. *See* Shawano evening leader

Shawano DISPATCH. w 1897-D 1898||
Merged with Shawano county advocate, later Shawano evening leader

Shawano evening LEADER. w,d D 8 1881+
1881-Ja 2 1929 as Shawano county advocate (D 1898-F 1903 Shawano advocate-dispatch); Ja 9 1929-Ag 16 1934 Leader-advocate
w 1881-Ag 16 1934
pub 1881+
WHi 1881-D 1 1908;D 29 1904+

LEADER-ADVOCATE. *See* Shawano evening leader

SHAWANO county advocate. *See* Shawano evening leader

SHAWANO county demokrat. *See* Shawano county wochenblatt

SHAWANO county journal. w Jl 23 1859+
Follows Shawano venture. My 30 1894-Mr 1895 as Shawano county journal and transcript
Suspended Ja-Mr 1861
DLC Jl 8 1876
WHi Jl 30-S 17 1859;Mr 9 1865-Jl 1888;S 26 1889-O 10 1894;Mr 28 1895-98;Ag 7 1930+

SHAWANO county leader. w My 6 1920-Ja 3 1929||
United with Shawano county advocate to form Leader-advocate, later Shawano evening leader
WHi 1920-D 16 1926

SHAWANO county wochenblatt. w 1884-Je 7 1901||
1884-85 as Shawano county demokrat. United with Shawano volksbote to form Volksbote-wochenblatt
In German
WHi complete

Shawano TRANSCRIPT. w My 1894||
Merged with Shawano county journal

Shawano VENTURE. w Ag 1858-Jl 1859||
Followed by Shawano county journal
WHi O 8-29,N 12-19,D 3 1858;Ja 21 1859

Shawano VOLKSBOTE. *See* Volksbote-wochenblatt

VOLKSBOTE-wochenblatt. w N 12 1897-Ja 3 1935||
1897-Je 7 1901 as Shawano volksbote
In German
pub complete
WHi complete

WISCONSIN post. w My 1872-D 30 1874||
In German
WHi F 18-D 1874

SHEBOYGAN

Sheboygan AMERIKA. d 1903+
In German
pub 1903+
IU D 1917+
WHi Jl 15 1932+

Weekly CHRONICLE. w Ja 1853-Ja 1854||
Follows Sheboygan mercury. Followed by Evergreen city times, later Shelboygan times

Sheboygan DEMOCRAT. w Jl 1849-Je 1851||
Follows Spirit of the times. United with Sheboygan lake democrat to form Sheboygan lake journal, later Sheboygan journal
WHi Je 3 1851

DEMOCRATIC secretary. w Je 1853-Je 1854||
Suspended "for lack of an editor."
WHi O 7 1853

EVERGREEN city times. *See* Sheboygan times

Sheboygan HERALD. w 1867-1909||?
DLC S 24 1875-S 14 1877;S 20 1878-S 10 1880

Sheboygan JOURNAL. w Jl 9 1851-O 1868||
Formed by the union of Sheboygan democrat and Sheboygan lake democrat. 1851-Je 10 1856 as Sheboygan Lake journal
Suspended Jl-Ag 1865
pub ir Je 17-D 18 1856
DLC [1854-55]
MWA My 1-8 1855
WHi Ja 26 1853-Jl 13 1865
WSh 1851-Ap 21, Jl 14 1852-F 16,Ap 4 1853-O 11 1854;N 16 1855-Je 10,Jl 17-31 1856;59-Ja 26 1860

LAKE shore advocate. w Mr 23 1859-F? 1860||
WHi S-O 1859
WSh Mr-O 12 1859

Sheboygan MERCURY. w F 1847-N 1852||
Followed by Weekly chronicle
WHi F 24-Ag 11 1849

NATIONAL demokrat. w,sw S 1857-Jl 14 1932||
Follows Sheboygan republicaner. Inside pages called Plymouth correspondent. Merged with Sheboygan amerika
w 1857-99
In German
WHi Ag 31 1901-32

NIEUWSBODE. w O 16 1849-My 8 1861||
First Dutch paper in the United States. 1849-54 as Sheboygan Nieumsbode. Merged with Sheboygan zeitung
MiG 1849-Ja 19 1858
WHi Mr 1854-61

PLYMOUTH correspondent. *See note under* National demokrat

Sheboygan PRESS. w D 1906+
Ag 3 1921-D 16 1924 as Sheboygan press-telegram
MWA Mr 7 1925
WHi Jl 24 1919+
WO N 1933+

Sheboygan PRESS. w D 17 1907+
pub 1907+

WISCONSIN (*Continued*)

SHEBOYGAN—*Continued*

Sheboygan REPUBLIKANER. w O 1851-57||
Followed by National demokrat

SHEBOYGAN county herald. *See* Sheboygan herald (Plymouth)

SHEBOYGAN county news. *See under* Sheboygan Falls

SHEBOYGAN Lake democrat. w -Je 1851||
United with Sheboygan democrat to form Sheboygan Lake journal, later Sheboygan journal

SHEBOYGAN Lake journal. *See* Sheboygan journal

SPIRIT of the times. w My 1848-Ap 1849||
Followed by Sheboygan democrat

Sheboygan SUN and herald. *See* Sheboygan herald (Plymouth)

Sheboygan TELEGRAM. d S 6 1887-Ag 2 1921||
Merged with Sheboygan press
WHi Ap 29 1897-1921

Sheboygan times. w F 4 1854-98||
Follows Weekly chronicle.
F 1854-Ja 1869 as Evergreen city times
MWA Ag 26 1854
WHi Mr 24 1854-O 22 1898
WSh 1854-62;Mr 8 1873-F 1875;F 21 1885-86

TRIBUN. w Ag 14 1874-D 1881||
United with Zeitung to form Zeitung und tribun, later Sheboygan zeitung
1874-Ap 1875 pub in Fond du Lac
In German

VOLKSBLATT. w 1895-1905||
In German
WHi D 24-31 1898;Ap 14 1900;Je 20 1903;Mr-My 1905

Sheboygan ZEITUNG. w Je 1860-S 1872||
In German

Sheboygan ZEITUNG. w,sw Je 1880-Je 1927||
1882-87? as Zeitung und tribun. Merged with National democrat
w 1880-98
WHi S 10 1901-Ap 1927

SHEBOYGAN FALLS

FREE PRESS. *See* Western freeman (Fond du Lac)

NORTHWESTERN record. Mr-Ag 1867||
Followed by Sheboygan county herald, later Sheboygan herald (Plymouth)

SHEBOYGAN county herald. *See* Sheboygan herald (Plymouth)

SHEBOYGAN county news. w 1876+
Title varies slightly
1876-Ap 1878 pub in Sheboygan
pub 1876+
NcD S 28-O 5,19-26,N 1921;Ja 4,Ap 19,My-S 20 1922
WHi Ja 29 1879+

SHELL LAKE

WASHBURN county register. w 1889+
pub D 1936+
WHi F 15 1896+

Shell Lake WATCHMAN. w Je 1882-Jl 21 1910||
Merged with Washburn county register
WHi Mr 1881-1910

SHIOCTON

Shiocton NEWS. w Je 11 1897-1928||?
WHi Je 11 1897-Ap 12 1928

SHOREWOOD

Papers published in Shorewood are listed under Milwaukee

SHULLSBURG

Shullsburg FREE PRESS. w Jl 1881- Ap 11 1884||
Merged with Pick and gad
WHi Mr 1882-84

LAFAYETTE county herald. w F 1 1855-Mr 19 1858||
Follows Pick and gad (1853-54). Followed by South Western local
DLC F 15-Mr 1 1855
WHi N 29 1855;Ap 10 1856-57

LAFAYETTE republican. w My-Ag 1848||
Followed by Telegraph

Shullsburg PATRIOT and flag. w Mr 27-Ag 29 1855||
WHi Ag 8 1855

PICK and gad. w Je 28 1853-D 1854||
Followed by Lafayette county herald
WHi O 4 1853

PICK and gad. w Jl 1882+
WHi Ap 17 1884+

SOUTH western local. w Mr 26 1858-Mr 17 1865||
Follows Lafayette county herald. Followed by Lafayette county democrat, later Darlington democrat (Darlington)
NNHi Ap 1860-Je 1862;Ja 9 1863
WHi Ja 21 1859-65

SOUTHWESTERN local. w F 1886-N 28 1902||
WHi Ja 15 1887-Ja 27 1889;95-1902

TELEGRAPH. w Ag 1848-
Follows Lafayette republican
WHi [Mr 13-N 17 1849]

SLADES CORNERS

MUGWUMP. w S 9 1892+
pub 1892+

SOLDIERS GROVE

ADVANCE. *See* Kickapoo scout

CRAWFORD county advance. *See* Kickapoo scout

CRAWFORD county journal. *See* Kickapoo scout

KICKAPOO scout. w Ja 1882+
1882-88 as Crawford county journal. Jl-Ag 1889;F 1890-D 1893 Kickapoo transcript. Ag 23 1889-F 1890 Kickapoo transcript and De Soto chronicle. Ja 1894-F 1898 Crawford county advance. F 1898-1902 Advance. 1902-O 1907 Kickapoo valley journal
pub O 7 1907+
WHi Ap 1883-88;Ag 23 1889-O 19 1892[Ja-S 1893]Jl 1894+

KICKAPOO transcript. *See* Kickapoo scout

KICKAPOO valley journal. *See* Kickapoo scout

SOLON SPRINGS

Solon Springs STAR. w -D 1907||
United with Lake Nebagamon enterprise (Lake Nebagamon) to form Star enterprise (Lake Nebagamon)
WHi note

STAR ENTERPRISE. *See under* Lake Nebagamon

SOUTH KAUKAUNA. *See* KAUKAUNA

SOUTH MILWAUKEE

South Milwaukee JOURNAL. w F 25 1893+
pub [1893-1904]+
WM Ap 1917-Mr 1919

SOUTH SUPERIOR

Papers published in South Superior are listed under Superior

SOUTH WAYNE

South Wayne HOMESTEAD. w F 16 1905+
Follows South Wayne news. 1905-S 8 1910 as Homestead
WHi 1905+

South Wayne NEWS. w -F 9? 1905||
Followed by South Wayne homestead

SOUTHPORT. *See* KENOSHA

SPARTA

Sparta ADVERTISER. *See* Monroe county republican 1885-1911

Sparta DEMOCRAT. w Je 29-N 9 1859||
WHi complete

Sparta DEMOCRAT. (1867-69) *See* Sparta herald

Sparta DEMOCRAT. 1885-95 *See* Monroe county democrat

DEMOCRAT enterprise. *See* Monroe county democrat

Sparta EAGLE. *See* Monroe county republican

Sparta HERALD. w Ag 1855+
1855-Je 1856 as Sparta watchman; Je 1856-58 Monroe county freeman; 1867-Ap 6 1869 Sparta democrat
WHi Jl 11 1861-D 10 1862;Ap 13 1869+
WSp 1903+

HERALD-ADVERTISER. *See* Monroe county republican

Sparta INDEPENDENT. w Jl 5 1890-Jl 1894||
Merged with Sparta herald
WHi N 1890-Je 1894

MONROE county democrat. w My 9 1863-1865||
WHi 1863-D 5 1864

MONROE county democrat. w Ja 5 1878+
Follows Lively times (Randolph). Ja 10-Ag 22 1879 as Monroe county republican; Ja 10-N 14 1885 Democrat enterprise; N 21 1885-Je 14 1895 Sparta democrat
1878-Ja 4 1879 pub in Tomah
WHi complete
WSp 1903+

MONROE county freeman. *See* Sparta herald

MONROE county republican. w Je 1861-Ja 3 1879||
1861-My 1862 as Sparta eagle. Merged with Monroe county democrat
MWA Ja 31 1866
WHi Ja 3 1862;Ag 25 1864;Jl 11 1866-S 19 1867;Ja 13-My 12 1871;76-78

MONROE county republican. w Mr 1885-O 26 1911||
1885-S 5 1888 as Portages advertiser (Portage); S 12 1888-Ja 1894 Herald-advertiser (Portage; Tomah); 1894-1901? Sparta advertiser; 1902?-09 Herald-advertiser
WHi N 10 1886-Je 12 1890 F 11 1892;Ap 26 1901
WP D 21 1887-88

Sparta WATCHMAN. *See* Sparta herald

WISCONSIN greenback. w Je 29 1876-S 18 1879||
Jl 28-N 10 1877 also dated in Milwaukee
Suspended N 17-D 13 1877;My 29-S 11 1879
DLC 1876-N 10 1877;78-My 22 1879
MnHi [Jl-D 1877]-[79]
WHi complete

SPENCER

Spencer ADVANCE. w Ja 20-Jl 14 1881||
WHi complete

Spencer TRIBUNE. w O 1881-94||?
WHi Ap 1882-Je 11 1886

SPRING GREEN

DOLLAR times. w D 1877-My 1880||
1877-S 10 1878 as Inter-county times
1877-S 10 1878 dated in Lone Rock; S 17 1878-F 18 1879 in Baraboo
WHi Mr 19 1878-My 4 1880

Weekly HOME news. w O 14 1881+
1881-82? as Times; 1883-84 Spring Green news
WHi S 26 1895+

INTER-COUNTY times. *See* Dollar times

Spring Green NEWS. *See* Weekly home news

TIMES. *See* Weekly home news

SPRING VALLEY

SUN. w D 15 1892+
1892-Je 22 1916 as Spring Valley sun; Je 29 1916-Jl 31 1919 Spring Valley sun and leader
pub 1892+
WHi 1905+

STANLEY

Stanley REPUBLICAN. w My 16 1896+
pub 1902+
WHi 1896+
WSt 1920+

STANTON

Stanton weekly TIMES. *See* Plover times (Plover)

STEVENS POINT

Stevens Point DEMOCRAT. w F 21 1880-Ag 1885|
WHi 1880-Jl 4 1885

GAZETTE and Stevens Point journal. w Jl 17 1878-Mr 21 1923||
1878-85? as Portage county gazette; 1886?-Ja 11 1921 Gazette
WHi complete
WSteJ 1882-1923

GWIAZDA polarna. w 1908-N 25 1933||
In Polish
IU D 1917-33
MnHi D 20 1924-33

Stevens Point JOURNAL. w Mr 8? 1870-Ja 14 1921||
1870-71 as Point. United with Gazette to form Gazette and Stevens Point journal
pub 1873-1919
DLC Ap 8,My 13-20,Je 3-10 1876;S 1 1877
WHi Jl 1871-1921

Stevens Point JOURNAL. d O 23 1895+
pub 1895+
WHi Mr 29 1923+

POINT. *See* Stevens Point journal

PORTAGE county gazette. *See* Gazette and Stevens Point journal

ROLNIK. w 1892+
In Polish
IU D 1917-Ja 14 1921

WISCONSIN eagle. w N 3 1884-N 2 1885||
WHi complete

WISCONSIN lumberman. w D 16 1863-68||
WHi D 23 1863-Jl 17 1868

WISCONSIN pinery. w Ja 14 1853-Jl 8 1893||?
DLC D 16 1875;F 17,Mr 16,Ap 20,My 18,Je 29,Jl 13,Ag 31 1876
WHi 1853-Ap 1 1859;Ag 23 1877;Jl 18 1884-O 1 1886

WISCONSIN state rights. w Mr 16 1859-Mr 1862||
1859-F 1861 pub in Monroe
Suspended D 1860-Ap 1861
WHi 1859-D 4 1861

STONE LAKE

Stone Lake SUN. w 1916-18||
WHi Ap 12,O 4 1917

WISCONSIN (*Continued*)

STOUGHTON

Stoughton weekly COURIER-HUB. w F 2 1876+
Follows Stoughton signal. 1876-Jl 9 1909 as Stoughton courier
pub 1885-1904
WHi D 13 1876+

Stoughton COURIER-HUB. d O 20 1906+
1906-Jl 2 1909 as Stoughton daily hub; Jl 3 1909-N 17 1925 Stoughton daily courier-hub
pub 1906+
WHi My 7 1924+

Stoughton weekly HUB. w 1880-Jl 2 1909||
1880-Mr 19 1885 as Hub; Mr 26 1885-O 19 1906 Stoughton hub. United with Stoughton courier to form Stoughton weekly courier-hub
WHi Jl 19 1883-1909

Stoughton HUB. sw S 3 1886-87||?
WHi 1886-My 5 1887

Stoughton daily HUB. *See* Stoughton courier-hub

Stoughton INDEPENDENT. w S 22-29 1857||
Followed by Wisconsin signal
WHi S-D 15 1857

NORMANNEN. *See* Wisconsin nordmanden (Madison)

Stoughton REPORTER. w F 23 1863-75||
WHi 1863-S 1869;Ja 22-Ag 20 1874

SCANDINAVIAN American. w D 10 1898-1905||?
1898-O 31 1902 as Mandt's weekly
1898-N 20 1903 pub in Madison
WHi 1898-Ag 17 1905

Stoughton SIGNAL. w 1873-Ja 1876||
Followed by Stoughton courier, later Stoughton weekly courier-hub

WISCONSIN nordmanden. *See under* Madison

WISCONSIN normannen. *See* Wisconsin nordmanden (Madison)

WISCONSIN signal. w Ja 14-Je 10 1858||
Follows Stoughton independent
WHi complete

STRATFORD

Stratford JOURNAL. w 1913+
WHi Mr 30 1917-N 1918

STURGEON BAY

Sturgeon Bay ADVOCATE. *See* Door county advocate

DEMOCRAT w O 24 1873-Mr 7 1895||
1873-Je 25 1880 as Expositor; Jl 2 1880-F 26 1886 Weekly expositor; Mr 5 1886-Je 27 1890 Independent; Jl 3 1890-D 22 1893 Republican. Merged with Door county democrat
WHi complete

DOOR county advocate. w Mr 22 1862+
F 6 1897-O 3 1912 as Advocate; O 10 1912-Jl 25 1918 Sturgeon Bay advocate
pub 1862+
WHi 1862+

DOOR county democrat. w Ja 28 1893-Jl 26 1918||
Merged with Door county advocate
WHi Mr 16 1895-1918

DOOR county news. w Jl 1 1914+
WHi D 14 1922+

EXPOSITOR. *See* Democrat

INDEPENDENT. *See* Democrat

REPUBLICAN. *See* Democrat

SUN PRAIRIE

Sun Prairie COUNTRYMAN. w D 6 1877+
1877-S 28 1882 as Countryman
pub 1877+
WHi 1877+

Sun Prairie LEDGER. w D 24? 1868-69||?
WHi Ja 14-F 25 1869

Weekly NEWS. w D 12 1903-O 29 1904||
WHi complete

SUPERIOR

Saturday evening CALL. *See* Sunday morning call

Sunday morning CALL. w Jl 31 1887-Jl 27 1890||
Title varies: Saturday evening call; Sunday evening call
WS S 22 1888-Ja,Jl 1889-Jl 13 1890

Superior daily CALL. d 1890-94||
WHi D 17 1891
WS [Mr 18 1890-F 21 1894]

Superior CHRONICLE. w Je 12 1855-Ag 29 1863||
Followed by Superior gazette
DLC Je 19,D 11 1855;Ja 20 1857;O 1,D 24 1859;Ja 7-21,F 4-11,25,Mr 17-31,Ap 28,My 5 1860
InLHi Ag 21 1855
MnHi [S 16 1856-59;61]
N My 13 1856
OClWHi Ag 7 1855;N 1856-N 3 1857
WHi 1855-[59-61]D 20 1862
WS 1860-63

Superior CITIZEN. w 1892-99||
WS [Jl 16 1892-S 2 1899]

Sunday morning FORUM. w 1892-1900||?
Title varies: French's Sunday forum; Sunday forum
WS S 16 1894-S 6 1896

Superior GAZETTE. w Ja 30 1864-F 5 1870||
Follows Superior chronicle. Merged with Superior tribune
DLC D 16 1865
MnHi [Ap 16-D 1864]N 16 1867;68[69]
NN Ap 29 1869
WHi [Ag 1864-70]
WS [1864-Ja 6 1866]

INLAND ocean. w N 8 1891-1903||
Follows Superior inter-ocean
WHi Mr 28 1896-Ag 6 1903
WS 1891-Je 7 1902

Superior INTER-OCEAN. w Mr 1882-N 1891||
Je 17 1886-88? as Wisconsin inter-ocean. Followed by Inland ocean
WHi My 3,Jl 19 1883-Ag 7 1886
WS S 10 1887-Mr 24,O 20-N 3 1888

Superior daily INTER-OCEAN. d
WS Mr 16-My 26 1885;Mr 1-S 29 1888

JOURNAL. w 1903+
1903-19 as Leader-clarion; 1919-21 Leader; 1921-31 Labor journal
WHi 1904-O 1913;F 7-14,My 2-7 1914

LABOR journal. *See* Journal

LAKE SUPERIOR miner and telegram. w 1889-F 15 1899||
WHi 1898-99

Superior LEADER. d My 1890-S 30 1903||
Title varies: Daily leader; Morning leader. United with Clarion-citizen to form Leader-clarion, later Journal
MWA Ja-Je 1898
MiU [1895]-1900
WHi F 15 1891-Mr 3 1901
WS My 1891-93;95-1903

LEADER. w *See* Journal

LEADER-clarion. d Ag 26-S 30 1903||
WS complete

LEADER-CLARION. w *See* Journal

Sunday MERCURY. w Mr 5 1892-
Mr 5-My 14 1892 as New northwest
WHi Mr-Je 26 1892

NEW northwest. *See* Sunday mercury

Daily NEWS. d Mr 15-Ag 27 1894||
Merged with Evening telegram
WS complete

POSTEN. *See* Superior tidende

Superior REPUBLICAN. w S 10 1857-
MiG O 1 1857

SCANDIA. *See under* Chicago, Ill.

Superior SENTINEL. w My 9 1888-D 11 1889||
WHi complete

Daily SHORT LINE. *See under* Duluth, Minn.

SOUTH Superior sun. *See* Superior sun

Superior STAR. w S 24-O 22 1904||
WS complete

Superior SUN. w 1891-F 22 1907||
1891-Jl 5 1902 as South Superior sun
WS Je 10 1893-1907

Superior Sunday SUN. w
WS Ag 7-O 22 1905

SVENSKA Amerikanska tribunen. *See* Svenska Amerikanska posten (Minneapolis, Minn)

Evening TELEGRAM. d Ap 21 1890+
MWA Jl 18 1891
MnHi [1890]-[1915]
WHi My 7 1890+
WS [1891-1918]+

Superior weekly TELEGRAM. w My 31 1892-93||
WHi 1892-Ap 18 1893

Superior TIDENDE. w S 1888+
1888-Jl 1893 as Posten
In Norwegian-Danish
IU D 1917+
IaDeL N 24 1892-Je 1893
MnHi Mr 12 1909+
WHi Jl 21,O 6 1892-Je 1893;N 1895-Jl 13 1934

Superior TIMES. w S 8 1870-1912||?
MnHi S 29[O-D 1870]-[1901]
WHi [N 12 1870-D 13 1873]-D 13 1879[Ap 10-S 11 1880]81-99
WS [S 15 1870-Ap 24 1909]

Superior TRIBUNE. w Jl 1869-Ap 1870||
WHi [S 4 1869-Ap 9 1870]

TYÖMIES. w,tw,d 1903+
1903-O 11 1914 pub in Hancock, Michigan
w 1903-08?; tw 1908?-Mr 4 1911
In Finnish
IU D 7 1917-Mr 22 1932
MnHi [Ap-D 1917]My 19 1921+
PP [1930]+
WHi N 23 1909+

TYÖVÄEN osuustoimintalehti. w Ja 9 1930-
In Finnish
MnHi Ja-Mr 27 1930

UNION label advertiser. *See* Vindicator

UUSI kotimaa. (New Homeland) sw 1881+
In Finnish
MnHi S 27 1928-31

VINDICATOR. w 1897-99|||
1897-Je 1898 as Union label advertiser
WHi Je 10 1898-Ja 27 1899

VOLKSFREUND. *See* Duluth-Superior volksfreund (Duluth, Minnesota)

Superior WAVE. w Je 24 1886-My 31 1902||
1886-Mr 16 1888 as West Superior wave
WHi complete
WS Ag 16,30 1889;N 28 1891-N 5 1892;Ap 8-D 23 1893

WEST Superior wave. *See* Superior wave

WISCONSIN inter-ocean. *See* Superior inter-ocean

WISCONSIN Sunday times. w Ap 1920-N 1924||
WS complete

WISCONSIN svenska tribunen. *See* Svenska Amerikanska posten (Minneapolis, Minn)

THORP

Thorp COURIER. w N 23 1883+
1883-My 23 1895 as Courier
pub 1883+
WHi Je 18 1891+

THREE LAKES

FOREST advance. w 1904-12||?
WHi My-D 1911

FOREST leaves. *See under* North Crandon

Three Lakes NEWS. w D 1931+
pub 1931+
WHi Mr 9 1933+

TIFFANY

NEWS. w Je 2 1925-27||?
WHi Je-N 5 1925

TOMAH

BADGER state monitor. *See* Monitor-herald

Tomah CHIEF. w My 28 1859-60||
WHi 1859-Ja 14 1860

HERALD. w 1884-1904||
United with Monitor to form Monitor-herald

HERALD-ADVERTISER. *See* Monroe county republican (Sparta)

Tomah JOURNAL. w Jl 24 1867+
WHi N 20 1867-Ap 27 1872[74]+

MONITOR-HERALD. w Jl 1 1880-1929||
1880-88 as Badger state monitor; 1889-1904 Monitor. Merged with Tomah journal

MONROE county democrat. *See under* Sparta

TOMAHAWK

Tomahawk LEADER. w Jl 4 1896+
pub 1896+
WHi S 26 1913-S 12 1918;S 25 1919+
WTo 1912+

TOMAHAWK. w Je 1887-S 17 1913||
Merged with Tomahawk leader
WHi F 9 1895-1913
WTo 1912-13

TREMPEALEAU

Trempealeau GAZETTE. w 1890-1910||?
WHi [Jl 17 1903-06]-Ag 20 1909

Trempealeau HERALD. w D 1885-1920||?
WHi F 8 1895-Ap 30 1920

Trempealeau REPRESENTATIVE. w Ag 5 1859-1861||
WHi Ag 12 1859-60

TREMPEALEAU county record. w Mr 16 1860-Ja 1873||
1860-N 8 1867 as Galesville transcript (Galesville). United with Galesville journal to form Journal and record (Galesville)
DLC Mr-Je 8 1860;F-Ap 8,22-D 2,16-20 1864; Ag 23 1861-62
MWA Mr 21 1862-Mr 11 1864;F 23 1866
NN 1860-Mr 11 1864
WHi 1860-Ag 1869

TREMPEALEAU county republican. w Mr 14 1873-N 30 1877||
United with Arcadia leader (Arcadia) to form Trempealeau county republican and Arcadia leader, later Leader (Arcadia)
WHi complete

TWO RIVERS

CHRONICLE. *See* Two Rivers reporter and chronicle

MANITOWOC county chronicle. *See* Two Rivers reporter and chronicle

REPORTER. w Mr 1905-Ap 15 1927||
United with Chronicle to form Two Rivers reporter and chronicle
WHi D 1906-27

Two Rivers REPORTER and chronicle. w,d Ap 1872+
1872-Je 27 1899 as Manitowoc county chronicle; Jl 4 1899-Ap 13 1927 Chronicle; Ap 22 1927-Ag 9 1928 Reporter-chronicle
w 1872-Ag 9 1928
WHi Ja 20-Ap 14,D 8 1874-Ag 9 1928;S 13 1930+

UNION GROVE

Union Grove ENTERPRISE. w O 11 1877-Mr 29 1923||
WHi F 13 1879-1923

WISCONSIN (*Continued*)

VALLEY JUNCTION

Valley ADVOCATE. w Mr 3 1898-S 13 1900||
Merged with Warrens index (Warrens)
WHi complete

WISCONSIN valley settler. w Ap 1 1905-07||?
Ap 8 1905 never pub
WHi Ap-Je 3 1905

VESPER

STATE center. w O 1 1911+
pub 1911+

VIOLA

INTELLIGENCER. w O 1890-O 25 1911||
Merged with Viola news
WHi Ap 1897-O 1911
WViN complete

Viola NEWS. w 1897?+
1897?-1908? as Wisconsin leaf tobacco news
pub N 1911+
WHi N 1911+

WISCONSIN leaf tobacco news. *See* Viola news

VIROQUA

Viroqua EXPOSITOR. w,sw Ag 28 1858-My 9 1863||
Ag 27 1859-60? as Viroqua expositor and Badax reporter. Merged with Northwestern times, later Vernon county censor
sw My 25-O 5 1861
WHi Ja 15-D 1859;61-Ja 11,Ag 30 1862-Ap 18 1863

NORTHWESTERN times. *See* Vernon county censor

Viroqua REPUBLICAN. w Ag 7 1894-Mr 2 1911||
WHi complete

VERNON county broadcaster. w 1925+
WHi Ap 13 1933+
WVV 1932+

VERNON county censor. w Je 7 1856+
Ja 7 1856-D 16 1857 as Western times; Ja 6 1858-Ag 16 1865 Northwestern times
D 23-30 1857 never pub
CSmH N 7 1860
MWA Ja 24 1866
NNHi My 20 1863
WHi 1856+
WVV 1905+

VERNON county leader. w Ag 20 1880-1923||?
WHi Ag 15 1884-Jl 19 1889;O 20-27 1882;My 11 1883;Je 20 1884;Ja 11 1918-Jl 18 1919

WESTERN times. *See* Vernon county censor

WISCONSIN independent. *See under* Black River Falls

WALWORTH

Walworth TIMES. w 1904+
WHi F 28 1918;S 20 1928+

WARNER. *See* LADYSMITH

WARRENS

Warrens INDEX. w O 2 1896-S 1910||
WHi Ja 13 1899-N 15 1901

WASHBURN

Washburn bee. w Mr 14 1885-S 10 1887||
WHi complete

Washburn TIMES. w Mr 1892+
1892-Ap 1895 as Iron River times (Iron River); Ap 10 1895-D 9 1896 Times
WHi Ap 10 1895+

WATERFORD

Waterford POST. w N 21 1877+
pub 1878+
WHi F 1879+

WATERLOO

Waterloo COURIER. w 1885+
1885-N 17 1922 as Waterloo democrat
WHi Je 9 1905+

Waterloo DEMOCRAT. *See* Waterloo courier

Waterloo ENTERPRISE. w Ja 4 1917-N 16 1922||
United with Waterloo democrat to form Waterloo courier

Waterloo JOURNAL. w D 4 1870-Ap 16 1908||
Merged with Waterloo democrat, later Waterloo courier
WHi S 1871-1908

WATERTOWN

ANZEIGER. w S 27 1853-F 1858||
United with Weltbürger to form Weltbürger und Anzeiger, later Watertown weltbürger
In German

Watertown CHRONICLE. w Je 23 1847-N 1857||
MWA Ja 10 1849;N 24 1852
WHi 1847-O 11,[N 8 1854-Mr 7 1855]

Watertown DEMOCRAT. w O 26 1854-Mr 1883||
Merged with Watertown gazette
Suspended Ag 19-O 12 1882
NNHi [N 1854;Ja-Ap 1855;Ap 1856-57;F-N 1858;59-F,Ap-Jl,S 1861]Ja 9,23 1862
OClWHi [1854-61]
WHi 1854-F 22 1883
WWa 1854-Jl 13 1876
WWaG 1855-83

DEMOCRATIC state register. *See* Watertown weekly register

Watertown GAZETTE. w Je 24 1879+
pub N 15 1880+
WHi Jl 22 1879-F 3 1880;My 1881+

Watertown weekly LEADER. *See* Watertown news

Watertown NEWS. w,tw Je 15 1860-Ja 15 1919||
1860-Ap 5 1906 as Watertown republican; Ap 13 1906-My 23 1917 Watertown weekly leader. Merged with Watertown daily times
w 1860-My 18 1917
MWA F 22 1866
WHi Ap 24 1867-1919
WWa 1860-Je 6 1862

Watertown weekly REGISTER. w Mr 5 1850-N 4 1854||
Follows Rock River Jeffersonian. 1850-S 3 1853 as Democratic state register
Not pub during O 1854
DLC O 18-25 1852
MWA D 15 1852
WHi Mr 12 1850-N 4 1854

Watertown REPUBLICAN. *See* Watertown news

ROCK RIVER Jeffersonian. w O 13 1847-F 1850||
1847-49 as Rock River pilot. Followed by Democratic state register, later Watertown weekly register
WHi 1847-O 4 1848

ROCK RIVER pilot. *See* Rock River Jeffersonian

Watertown daily TIMES. d N 23 1895+
WHi Ja 15 1919+

Watertown TRIBUNE. w O 12 1934+
WHi O 26 1934-D 20 1935

Watertown TRANSCRIPT. w Ja 15-Mr 16 1859||
Followed by Waukesha freeman (Waukesha)

Watertown WELTBÜRGER. w Ag 27 1853-D 2 1932||
1857-F 1858 as Weltbürger;F-O 1858 Weltbürger und anzeiger
Mr 7 1930-D 2 1932 pub in Winona, Minnesota, for Watertown subscribers
Suspended O-D 1858
In German
WHi Je 26 1858;S 7 1901-D 2 1932
WWa 1853-F 1855;Ag 1860-1904

WAUKESHA

To 1847 as Prairieville

AMERICAN freeman. *See* Wisconsin free democrat (Milwaukee)

Waukesha CHRONOTYPE. *See* Waukesha plain-dealer (1848-57)

Waukesha DEMOCRAT. *See* Waukesha plain-dealer

Waukesha DISPATCH. w,sw F 1891-O 30 1920||
Merged with Waukesha freeman
MWA Jl 9 1891
WHi 1894-1920
WWak 1919-20

Waukesha FREEMAN. w Mr 29 1859+
Follows Watertown transcript (Watertown)
d during summer of 1881-83; 85; 87-88
MWA Ja 23 1866
WHi Ap 19-D 13 1859[60-69]F 10 1870-Jl 4 1929

Waukesha daily FREEMAN. d 1920+
WHi Ja 23 1930+
WWak 1920+

Waukesha daily HERALD. d 1919-20||
WWak complete

INDEPENDENT press. w Jl 1853-Mr 1854||
Followed by Waukesha county democrat

Waukesha JOURNAL. w 1887-90||?
MWA Je 30 1888

Waukesha PLAIN-DEALER. w Jl 20 1848-Ja 13 1857||
1848-52 as Waukesha democrat. 1853-Jl 5 1854 Waukesha chronotype. Merged with Waukesha republican
WHi complete

Waukesha PLAIN-DEALER. w Jl 25 1865-S 19 1876||
Follows Waukesha county democrat (1854-65). Merged with Waukesha county democrat (1872-1900)
WHi complete

Waukesha PRESS. w 1898-My 30 1906||
Merged with Waukesha freeman
WHi 1903-06

Waukesha REPUBLICAN. w Ag 6 1856-Ja 4 1859||
Suspended from N 1856-Ja 20 1857
WHi Ja 20 1857-59

WAUKESHA county democrat. w Mr 1 1854-Jl 1865||
Follows Independent press. Followed by Waukesha plain-dealer
WHi 1854-Ja 3 1865

WAUKESHA county democrat. Ja 6 1872-1900||?
DLC O 18 1879;My 15,O 16 1880
NNHi D 28 1872;Mr 15 1873
WHi Ja 13 1872-Mr 1894

WAUNAKEE

Waunakee INDEX. w D 6 1907-1918||?
Suspended My 28-N 19 1914
WHi 1907-D 20 1918

Waunakee NEWS. w Mr 20 1896-1901||?
Follows Albany journal (Albany)
WHi 1896-Ag 17 1900

Waunakee TRIBUNE. w 1920-Mr 20 1930||
United with Middleton times-herald to form Middleton times-tribune

WAUPACA

EXCELSIOR. *See* Waupaca county post

Waupaca LEADER. w N 15 1911-S 18 1912||
United with Waupaca record to form Waupaca record-leader

Waupaca POST. w Ja 19 1878-D 24 1908||
United with Waupaca republican to form Waupaca republican-post, later Waupaca county post
WHi complete

Waupaca RECORD-LEADER. w 1894-My 31 1917||
1894-S 19 1912 as Waupaca record. United with Waupaca republican-post to form Waupaca county post
WHi D 1894-1917
WWap 1912-17

Waupaca REPUBLICAN. *See* Waupaca county post

Waupaca REPUBLICAN-POST. *See* Waupaca county post

Waupaca SPIRIT. *See* Waupaca county post

WAUPACA county news. w S 1 1921+
WHi S 22 1921-N 11 1926

WAUPACA county post. w N 1853+
1853-66 as Waupaca spirit (Je 1858-60 Excelsior); 1867-D 24 1908 Waupaca republican; D 31 1908-My 31 1917 Waupaca republican-post
pub 1911+
DLC Ap 6,My 18 1876
WHi O 2 1855;S 9 1857;Ap 2,Ag 27 1874+
WWap 1915+

WAUPACA county register. w My 28 1858-Jl 1860||
Follows New London times (New London) Followed by Waushara county republican (Wautoma)
WHi My-S 17 1858

WAUPACA county republican. *See* Waupaca county post

WAUPUN

Waupun DEMOCRAT. *See* Waupun news

Waupun weekly ITEM. m,w Jl 1858-S 1861||
1858-Je 8 1861 as Prison City item
m 1858-Mr 1860
WHi Ag 1860-Jl 1861

Waupun LEADER-NEWS. w,sw Ag 28 1866+
Follows Green Lake spectator (Dartford). 1866-S 22 1870 as Prison city leader; S 29 1870-Ja 1929 Waupun leader
w 1866-Je 1929
pub Jl 1924+
DLC Ja 30 1868-Jl 23 1897
WHi Jl 11 1867+
WWau 1897+

Waupun NEWS. w Mr 1900-Ja 31 1929||
1900-F 1923 as Waupun democrat. United with Waupun leader to form Waupun leader-news
WWau 1900-O 1925

PRISON City item. *See* Waupun weekly item

PRISON City leader. *See* Waupun leader

Waupun TIMES. sw,w S 17 1857-F 10 1903||
sw during summer of 1861
DLC Jl 11 1876
MWA F 1 1866
WHi My 25-Ag 24 1859;Ja 13 1874-1903
WaU [1857-1901]

WARE burger. w Ja 1859-1860||
Ja-S 1859 pub in Holland
In Dutch
WHi S 13-O 4 1859

WAUSAU

CENTRAL Wisconsin. *See* Wausau sun

DEUTSCHE pionier. w,sw Ap 1882-Ja 6 1917||
United with Wausau wochenblatt to form Wausau wochenblatt und pionier, later Wisconsin wochenblatt
w 1882-D 30 1899
In German
WHi O 18 1884-O 1 1887 Ap 13 1889-1917

Wausau HERALD. w Mr 3 1893-D 1907||
United with Wausau record to form Wausau record-herald

WISCONSIN (*Continued*)

WAUSAU—*Continued*

Wausau daily **HERALD.** 1906-D 1907||
United with Wausau daily record to form Wausau daily record-herald

MARATHON county record. w Ja 9 1862-F 1863||
WHi Ja-Mr 1862

Wausau **PILOT.** w D 1865+
1865-Ag 16 1884 as Wisconsin river pilot; Ag 19 1884-Je 22 1886 Pilot and review; Je 29 1886-Jl 21 1896 Pilot review
pub 1881+
WHi Jl 1867-My 18 1915;Ap 1917-D 3 1918;Jl 8 1919+

Wausau daily **PILOT.** d Jl 25-N 7 1896||
WHi complete

Daily **PILOT** and review. d S 1-N 8 1884||
WHi complete

Wausau **RECORD.** w Ag 1877-D 27 1907||
1877-Ap 25 1895 as Torch of liberty; May 2 1895-D 10 1896 Wausau weekly record. United with Wausau herald to form Wausau record-herald
WHi Mr 14 1878-1906

Wausau daily **RECORD.** d My 14 1895-N 30 1907||
United with Wausau daily herald to from Wausau daily record-herald
WHi complete

Wausau daily **RECORD-HERALD.** d D 2 1907+
Formed by the union of Wausau daily herald and Wausau daily record
pub 1907+
WHi 1907+

Wausau **RECORD-HERALD.** w D 1907-14||?
Formed by union of Wausau record and Wausau herald

Wausau weekly **REVIEW.** w 1882-Ag 11 1884||
Merged with Wisconsin river pilot, to form Pilot and review, later Wausau pilot
WHi Mr 26 1883-84

Wausau **SUN.** w Ap 22 1857-1917||?
1857-F 5 1910 as Central Wisconsin
Suspended ? 1867-O 1868
MWA D 17 1873
WHi Ap 22 1857-Jl 19 1862;O 21 1868;Mr 29 1870-Mr 23 1917

TORCH of liberty. *See* Wausau record

WISCONSIN River pilot. *See* Wausau pilot

WISCONSIN wochenblatt. w Ja 1871-O 3? 1924||
1871-Ja 1917 as Wausau wochenblatt; F 1917-O 15 1920 Wausau wochenblatt und pionier. Merged with Westlicher herold (Winona, Minn.)
Mr 28 1919-24 printed in Winona, Minn.
In German
MnHi O 22 1920-O 3 1924
WHi Mr 1876-D 12 1879;Ap 1917-N 28 1924

WAUSAUKEE

INDEPENDENT. w O 20 1895+
pub 1895+

WAUTOMA

Wautoma **JOURNAL.** w Ag 19 1856-My 8 1860||
Merged with Waushara county argus, later Waushara argus
KHi 1856-O 25 1859
WHi [S 1856-Mr 20]My 1 1860

PINE river argus. *See* Waushara argus

WAUSHARA argus. w Mr 10 1859+
Mr-My 1859 as Pine river argus; Je 2 1859-Mr 18 1863 Waushara county argus
pub 1931+
KHi 1859-Ag 3 1860
WHi Jl 9 1859+

WAUSHARA county argus. *See* Waushara argus

WAUSHARA county republican. w Ag 11 1860-
Follows Waupaca county register (Waupaca)

WAUWATOSA

Wauwatosa **NEWS.** w 1895+
WHi N 20 1930
WM 1916-Ap 4 1919

WAUZEKA

Wauzeka **CHIEF.** w D 1 1894+
1894-1915 as Kickapoo Chief
pub 1894+
WHi 1925+

KICKAPOO chief. *See* Wauzeka chief

WEBSTER

BURNETT county enterprise. w 1913+
WHi Je 1917-N 7 1929

WEDFORD

TAYLOR county star-news. w Mr 18 1876+
1876-Ag 10 1878 Taylor county star and Taylor county news; Ag 17 1878-Ja 3 1902 Taylor county star and news
pub [1874-88]+
WHi F 16 1878+
WMe Ag 1916-33

WELCOME

Welcome **INDEPENDENT.** w Ag 25 1905-Je 21 1912||
WHi complete

WEST ALLIS

West Allis **PRESS.** w 1912-19||
WM 1917-Jl 4 1919

West Allis **STAR.** w 1916+
WM 1917-Jl 3 1919
WWe Jl 1934+

WEST BEND

West Bend **DEMOCRAT.** *See* West Bend news

West Bend **NEWS.** w Ja 1855+
1855 as Washington county organ; 1856-60 Washington county democrat; 1861-S 1875 West Bend post; S 1875-1902 West Bend democrat
pub [1860-65;75-80;83+]
NNHi N 29 1862;N 28 1863
WHi Je 27 1859-Je 8 1867;F 21 1877+
WWb 1904+

West Bend **PILOT.** w F 24 1892+
1892-Ja 30 1907 as Washington county pilot
WHi Ap 6 1892+
WWb 1903-30

West Bend **POST.** *See* West Bend news

West Bend **REPUBLICAN.** *See* Hartford press (Hartford)

West Bend **TIMES.** w Je 3 1880-O 27 1887||
Merged with West Bend democrat, later West Bend news
WHi 1881-87

WASHINGTON county democrat. *See* West Bend news

WASHINGTON county organ. *See* West Bend news

WASHINGTON county pilot. *See* West Bend pilot

WEST EAU CLAIRE

Papers published in West Eau Claire are listed under Eau Claire

WEST SALEM

NONPAREIL-journal. w 1886+
pub Jl 1911+
WHi Ag 1913+

WEST SUPERIOR

Papers published in West Superior are listed under Superior

WESTBY

Westby **TIMES.** w 1899+
WHi Mr 8-O 11 1918

WESTFIELD

CENTRAL union. w Je 1877+
pub Jl 20 1919+
WHi F 13 1879-N 16 1882;Ja 9 1919+

MARQUETTE express. w -1858||
Followed by Oxford weekly express (Oxford) later Montello express (Montello)

MARQUETTE independent. w Ag 1871-Je 2 1874||
WHi Ja 13-Je 1874

WEYAUWEGA

Weyauwega **CHRONICLE.** w Mr 17 1877+
pub 1906+
WHi 1877-1905;Jl 30 1930+
—German ed *See* Deutsche chronik

DEUTSCHE chronik. w 1898-1910||?
WHi Ja 28 1898-1905
—English ed *See* Weyauwega chronicle

Weyauwega **HERALD.** w Jl 26 1855-59||
1855-58 as Weyauwegian; 1858-Ja 1859 Wolf River herald
Suspended Ja-Ap 1859
WHi Jl 26 1855-My 19,O 22 1858-Ja 13,My-O 5 1859

Weyauwega **TIMES.** w F 1869-D 16 1876||
Merged with Waupaca republican (Waupaca)
WHi S 1870-76

WEYAUWEGIAN. *See* Weyauwega herald

WOLF RIVER herald. *See* Weyauwega herald

WHITEFISH BAY

Papers published in Whitefish Bay are listed under Milwaukee

WHITEHALL

Whitehall **TIMES.** w Ag 1874+
Follows Galesville journal and record (Galesville). 1874-Ja 7 1880 as Trempealeau county messenger; Ja 14 1880-82 Whitehall times and Trempealeau county messenger; N 5 1891-Ja 20 1916 Whitehall times and Blair banner; Ja 27 1916-Ja 17 1924 Whitehall times-banner
pub 1880+
WHi 1876-Ag 17,D 14 1882;Jl 26 1883-S 4 1884;N 21-D 19 1889;S 22 1921+

TREMPEALEAU county messenger. *See* Whitehall times

WHITEWATER

Whitewater **GAZETTE.** w Jl 1854-Ja 1 1857||
WHi Ag 2,N 22,D 1855-57

Whitewater **GAZETTE.** d,w Mr 1889-S 26 1918||
Second paper of this name. 1889-Ja 18 1899 as Gazette (My 1891-93? Weekly gazette). Merged with Whitewater register
d 1889-My 1891
WHi [Jl 13-N 1892]Ag 1894-1918

Whitewater **PRESS.** w Ja 1 1924+
pub 1924+

Whitewater **REGISTER.** w Mr 1 1857+
pub 1857+
MWA F 23 1866;My 24,N 22,D 27 1867;Ja 10, F 14,Ap 10,My 15,Je 12,Jl 10,Ag 7,O 9,N 20, D 18 1868;Ap 2 1869
MiU-C Ag 7 1868
NNHi O 22 1869
WHi Ag 8 1857;Jl 24 1858-Je 1 1866;Ja 25 1871+

WILD ROSE

Wild Rose **TIMES.** w 1901-N 20 1919||
WHi Ap-N 1919

WILLIAMS BAY

OBSERVER. w 1896-S 23 1898||
Merged with Enterprise (Delavan)
Whi 1898

WILMOT

AGITATOR. w Ja 11 1901-F 8 1913||
OrMnH complete
WHi complete

WILSON

Wilson **PIONEER.** w Ag 1875-77||?
WHi F 7 1876;Ja 15-S 24 1877

WINDSOR

Windsor **HERALD.** w Ja 4 1899-1900||?
WHi 1899-F 9 1900

WINNEBAGO

WINNEBAGO county press. w
CSmH Jl 1 1871

WINNECONNE

Winneconne **GLOBE.** w Mr 10 1921-My 18 1922||
WHi complete

Winneconne **HERALD.** w S 26 1874-
Follows Winneconne item
WHi S 26 1874

Winneconne **ITEM.** w Ja 1871-Ag 28 1874||
Followed by Winneconne herald
WHi S 9 1871-74

Winneconne **ITEM.** w Ap 15 1876-79||?
Revival of Winneconne item (1871-74)
WHi Ap 15 1876;Ja 13 1877-Mr 29 1879

Winneconne **LOCAL.** w 1886-1928||
WHi Jl 1912-D 2 1920

WINTER

SAWYER county gazette. w Mr 8 1908+
Suspended S 12 1918-Ja 23 1919
pub 1908+
WHi F 17 1916+

WISCONSIN DELLS

To Je 10 1856 as Newport; 1856-1931? Kilbourn

Wisconsin Dells **EVENTS.** ir,w N 1903+
1903-04 as Illustrated events; Je 1905-Je 1907 Kilbourn weekly illustrated events; Jl 1907-Ap 2 1931 Kilbourn weekly events
pub 1925+
ICHi Jl 7,21 1906;F 9 1907
WHi 1903+
WWd 1903+

KILBOURN city guard. w N 15 1876-Ap 30 1879||
Follows Wisconsin mirror (1868-76)
WHi complete

KILBOURN gazette. Ja 1882-Ap 1885||
United with Wisconsin mirror to form Mirror gazette

MIRROR-GAZETTE. w O 1884-1911||
O 1884-Ap 1885 as Wisconsin mirror, a revival of Wisconsin mirror (1868-76)
WHi Ap 1887-Mr 2 1911
WWd 1895-1902;04

WISCONSIN (*Continued*)

WISCONSIN DELLS—*Continued*

WISCONSIN mirror. w Ja 1 1856-N 12 1860||
Suspended from Je 20 1859-My 14 1860
WHi 1856-F 14,Je 20 1859-60

WISCONSIN mirror. w Je 17 1868-S 29? 1876|| D 31 1870-D 1871 as Mirror. Followed by Kilbourn city guard. Revived under original name in 1884
NNHi D 14 1872
WHi complete

WISCONSIN RAPIDS
To Ag 4 1920 as Grand Rapids

CENTRALIA enterprise. w My 22 1879-My 28 1887||
United with Grand Rapids tribune to form Centralia enterprise and tribune, later Wood county tribune

CENTRALIA enterprise and tribune. *See* Wood county tribune

GRAND RAPIDS leader. *See* Wisconsin Rapids daily tribune

GRAND RAPIDS pilot. w Je 20 1863-
WHi Jl 11 1863

GRAND RAPIDS daily tribune. *See* Wisconsin Rapids daily tribune

GRAND RAPIDS tribune. w *See* Wood county tribune

Daily REPORTER. d 1906-My 31 1917||
Merged with Daily leader, later Wisconsin Rapids daily tribune
d ed of Wood county reporter
WHi Jl 1914-17

Wisconsin Rapids daily TRIBUNE. d My 25 1914+
1914-F 28 1920 as Grand Rapids leader; Mr 1-Ag 4 1920 Grand Rapids daily tribune
pub 1914+
DLC Ap 1,15,Je 3,Jl 15,29 1876
NcD S 15,17,19,22-23,25 1924
WHi complete
WWr 1922+

WISCONSIN Valley leader. w 1902-F 21 1918||
WWrT Mr 2 1911-18

WOOD county reporter. w D 9? 1857-1924||
KHi Ja 28 1860
MWA Ag 12 1858
MnHi 1879-85
WHi F 17-O 1858;Ja 8-My 7 1859;Ja 28 1860-64;Je 19 1873-N 1 1923
—d ed *See* Daily reporter

WOOD county tribune. w Ag 30 1873-D 27 1923||
1873-F 1920 as Grand Rapids tribune (Je 4 1887-Ap 14 1900 Centralia enterprise and tribune)
WHi 1873-Ja 3 1903
WWrT 1873-N 21 1874;90;1904-23

WITHEE

CLARK county journal. *See* Withee journal

Withee JOURNAL. w 1902+
1902-31? as Clark county journal
WAbT 1915-25

WITTENBERG

Wittenberg ENTERPRISE. w N 15 1893+
pub [1893-1919]+
WHi Ap 3 1919

WONEWOC

Wonewoc ENTERPRISE. w O 5 1881-O 29 1885||
Merged with Juneau county sun (Mauston)
MWA complete
WHi complete

Wonewoc GAZETTE. w O 17 1894-Ja 1901||
Mr 13 1895-O 15 1896 as Wonewoc gazette and herald statesman. Merged with Wonewoc reporter
WHi F 1895-D 13 1900

Wonewoc REPORTER. w Ap 1876+
pub [1905-12;16-17]+
WHi S 1900-My 31 1917

WOODVILLE

Woodville TIMES. w N 20 1913-N 14 1929||
WHi complete
WSvS 1913-25

WYOCENA

Wyocena ADVANCE. w Jl 1 1910-Jl 30 1920||
WHi complete

WYOMING

AFTON

STAR Valley independent. w N 3 1905+
WyHi My 5,1905-Ja 1915;Je 1926+

ALBIN

Albin JOURNAL. *See* Wyoming statesman and Albin journal

WYOMING statesman and Albin journal. w Jl 17 1931+
1931-O 11 1934 as Albin journal
pub 1931+
WyHi 1931+

BAGGS

SNAKE River sentinel. w 1906-28||?
NN N 25 1921
WyHi Jl 12-S 18 1926

BASIN

BIG HORN county rustler. *See* Basin republican-rustler

Basin REPUBLICAN. w O 1905-28||?
United with Big Horn county rustler to form Basin republican-rustler
NN F 25 1916
WyHi My 24 1905-N 1907

Basin REPUBLICAN-RUSTLER. w 1889+
1889-My 1928 as Big Horn county rustler
WyHi My-Ag 1905;Ap 1914+

BEAR RIVER CITY

FRONTIER index. *See under* Knight

BESSEMER

WYOMING Bessemer journal. w 1889-90||?
WyHi Ag 1 1889

BIG PINEY

Big Piney EXAMINER. w 1911+
pub 1918+
WyHi Je 1912-Ja 1914;F 1915+

BOTHWELL

SWEETWATER chief. *See* Rawlins republican (Rawlins)

BOYSON

COPPER mountain miner. w F 22 1907-
WyHi Mr 1907-Je 1911

BRYAN CITY

SWEETWATER mines. *See under* South Pass City

BUFFALO

Buffalo BULLETIN. w 1890+
WyHi My 18 1905+

Buffalo NEWS. w 1892-1927||?
1892-99? as People's voice; 1900?-My 1925 Buffalo voice
WyHi My 6-S 2 1905;My 1914-My,S 1925-26

PEOPLE'S voice. *See* Buffalo news

Buffalo VOICE. *See* Buffalo news

BURLINGTON

Burlington POST. w 1903-06||?
WyHi My 1905-Mr 1906

BURNS

GOLDEN Prairie herald. *See* Laramie county news

Burns HERALD. *See* Laramie county news

LARAMIE county news. w 1908+
1908-Jl 1918 as Golden Prairie herald; Ag 1918-Je 1926 Burns herald
WyHi Ag 1918-Ja 6 1927;28+

CASPER

Casper HERALD. d 1919-Ap 30 1931||
United with Casper daily tribune to form Casper tribune-herald
WyHi O 10,N 1924-31

Casper INDEPENDENT. *See* Casper times

Casper weekly MAIL. w N 22 1888-91||?
WyC Ja 25-N 8 1889

NATRONA county tribune. *See* Casper tribune-herald. w

Casper PRESS. w 1908-18||
WyC My 15 1908-My 22 1914
WyHi N 1913-16;Ag-D 1918

Casper RECORD. w S 12 1911-19||?
WyC 1911-S 2 1913
WyHi Ap 1914-18

Casper TIMES. d 1925+
1925-30? as Casper independent
pub 1931+
WyHi D 20 1929+

Casper TRIBUNE-HERALD. w Jl 15 1891+
1891-O 15 1914 as Natrona county tribune
pub 1891+
WyC 1891-O 15 1914
WyHi My 25-Ag 5 1905;My-Je 1926;29-Mr 1931

Casper TRIBUNE-HERALD. d 1916+
1916-F 27 1931 as Casper daily tribune
pub 1916+
DLC S 1921+
WyC [F-O 1917;F-Ag 1918]Ap 1919-Je 1920; Ja-Je,N 7 1921+
WyHi Jl 1918+

WYOMING democrat. w 1922-27||?
1922-25? pub in Cheyenne
WyHi Je-N 1922;O 7 1926-F 10 1927

WYOMING derrick. w Je 5 1890-1906||?
NcD Jl 3,S 18,O 2-16,N 13-20 1902
WyC 1890-My 5 1892;Je 10 1897-Mr 2 1906
WyHi My-Ag 1905

CENTENNIAL

Centennial POST. w 1902-14||?
WyHi My 6 1905-Ag 22 1914

CHEYENNE

Cheyenne daily ARGUS. d O 25 1867-69||
NcU S 8 1868
WyHi N 12 1869

BIG HORN basin savior. sw 1894-95||?
DLC N 19-22,29-D 6,27 1894-Ja 3 1895

DEMOCRATIC leader. *See* Cheyenne weekly leader

Cheyenne daily LEADER. *See* Cheyenne state leader

Cheyenne weekly LEADER. w S 19 1867-93||?
Ja 19 1884-Je 9 1887 as Democratic leader. United with Cheyenne weekly sun to form Cheyenne weekly sun-leader
CU-B N 4-6,D 4 1884
CoHi S 19 1867
DLC S 25 1875-Ja 17,31 1884-Ag 1890
NbHi Ap 13 1869
WyHi 1869:82-83

MAGIC City record. w 1890-91||?
WyHi Ja 19 1891

Cheyenne daily NEWS. d 1874-75||
Merged with Cheyenne daily sun
WyHi Ag 31, 1874;Ja 11-Jl 9 1875

Daily ROCKY Mountain star. d
DLC My 2,16,18 1869

Weekly ROCKY Mountain star. w D 8 1867-
DLC Ja 13,27,My 26-Je 9 1869

Cheyenne STATE leader. d S 19 1867-D 30 1921||
1867-Ja 18 1884 as Cheyenne daily leader. Ja 19 1884-Je 12 1887 Democratic leader; Je 13 1887-Je 23 1895 as Cheyenne daily leader. Je 24 1895-My 22 1900 as Cheyenne daily sun-leader; Je 1900-My 1909 Cheyenne daily leader. United with Wyoming state tribune to form Wyoming state tribune-Cheyenne state leader
DLC Ap 21-D 1869;Ja-Je 1871;Ag 24 1890-94; Je 24 1895-1902
MWA Ap 17 1875(extra);O 19-23 1906
WyHi 1867-94;N 14,28,D 25 1895;S 20 1897-Ag 4,N 10 1898;D 12,22 1899;D 11 1900;Ja 24 1903; My-Ag 1905;O 1906-Mr 1921
WyU N-D 1891;Jl-Ag 1894;Ja,My-D 1896;F, Jl-Ag 1897;O 1898-My 1899;My-Jl 1900;Ja-Mr,N 1901; Ja-Mr,S-O 1902; S-N 1903;F-Je, S-O 1904;Ja-Mr,My-D 1905;Mr,S 1906-Mr, Je 1908-Mr 1921

Cheyenne daily SUN. d Mr 2 1876-Je 23 1895||
Follows Laramie daily sun (Laramie)
CU-B Ja 3,N 2-3,6 1884
CtW Mr 28 1890;Ap 21 1891;My 19 1893
DLC Mr 1891-95
ICM Ja 2 1883
WyHi Mr-S 23 1876;77-Ag 21 1890
WyU Ja-Je 1894;My-Je 1895

Cheyenne weekly SUN. *See* Cheyenne weekly sun-leader

Cheyenne daily SUN-LEADER. *See* Cheyenne state leader

Cheyenne weekly SUN-LEADER. w 1877-99||?
1877-93? as Cheyenne weekly sun
WyHi Mr 20 1890;S 30 1897;N 16 1899

WYOMING (*Continued*)

CHEYENNE—*Continued*

WYOMING commonwealth. w Jl 20 1890-92||?
KHi 1890-N 14 1891
WyHi Ja 4,D 5 1891

WYOMING democrat. *See under* Casper

WYOMING eagle. w My 28 1925+
WyHi 1925+

WYOMING state tribune-Cheyenne state leader. d N 20 1869+
1869-Mr 23 1918 as Wyoming tribune
pub 1885+
DLC 1871-N 2 1872
IaDH N 1907-14
MWA Jl 20 1929
NbHi My 25 1908-F 1910
WHi 1917-21
WyHi 1869-Ap 15 1871;Ag 10 1892;S 20 1897;S 14,18,O 25 1901;04+
WyU [1895-1908]+

WYOMING tribune. *See* Wyoming state tribune-Cheyenne state leader

CHUGWATER

Chugwater NEWS. w F 3 1928+
pub 1928+

CODY

Cody ENTERPRISE. w 1899+
1899-1921 as Park county enterprise
pub 1899+
WyHi My 4-S 28 1905;F 4 1910+

NORTHERN Wyoming herald. *See* Park county herald

PARK county enterprise. *See* Cody enterprise

PARK county herald. w 1907-26||?
1907-S 20 1912 as Wyoming herald; S 27 1912-Mr 1924 Northern Wyoming herald
WyHi [F 1911-S 1912]-26

WYOMING herald. *See* Park county herald

COKEVILLE

Cokeville REGISTER. w 1911+
WyHi Mr 1914-15;17-Jl 1922;31+

COLONY

Colony COYOTE. w Jl 7 1920-My 3 1934||
1920-22 as Colony weekly news; 1923-Jl 8 1926 Colony news
WyHi complete

Colony NEWS. *See* Colony coyote

COWLEY

Cowley weekly PROGRESS. w Je 1906+
WyHi 1906-16;18-21;Jl 1922+

DEAVER

Deaver SENTINEL and Frannie independent. 1913+
WyHi Jl 18 1930+

DILLON

Dillon DOUBLEJACK. w 1902-09||?
WyHi D 27 1902;F 2 1903;F 7 1909

DOUGLAS

BILL Barlow's budget. *See* Douglas budget

Douglas BUDGET. w 1886+
1886-O 1914 as Bill Barlow's budget
Suspended Ag 1930-Ap 12 1934
pub 1886+
MWA O 17 1906
WyHi Jl 9 1890;1905-Jl 1930;Ap 19 1934+

Douglas ENTERPRISE. w My 1906+
pub 1907+
WyHi Ap 7 1914+

DUBOIS

COURIER DuBois. *See* DuBois frontier

DuBois FRONTIER. w 1919+
1919- 28 as Courier DuBois
WyHi S 17 1926;27-28;31+

DuBois GUIDE. *See* Fremont county independent (Pavillion)

EDGERTON

Edgerton INDEPENDENT. w 1925-28||?
WyHi Je 11 1926;27-S 1928

ENCAMPMENT

Encampment ECHO. w 1919+
WyHi My 21 1925;Je 9 1926+

GRAND Encampment herald. w 1898-1913||?
WyHi F 27 1903-F 1913

EVANSTON

NEWS register. w 1888-1908||?
1888-92 as Evanston news
CoU 1899-N 1907
WyHi My 8 1897

Evanston REGISTER. w 1879-92||?
United with Evanston news to form News-register

UINTA county argus. w Ap 4 1878-
CU-B My 9-S 5 1878

WYOMING press. w 1896+
WyHi My 1905-N 1913;N 1927+

WYOMING times. w 1908+
pub 1908+
WyHi Ap 1914+

FORT BRIDGER

SWEETWATER mines. *See under* South Pass City

Daily TELEGRAPH. d Je-Jl 1863||
NN Je 26 1863 (photostat)
OkTE Jl 26 1863

FORT LARAMIE

Fort Laramie SCOUT. w Mr 1920-27||
United with Goshen news to form Goshen news and Fort Laramie scout (Torrington)
WyHi O 1925-27

FORT SANDERS

FRONTIER index. *See under* Knight

GARLAND

Garland GUARD. w 1901-07||?
WyHi My 5 1905-Jl 7 1906

GILLETTE

CAMPBELL county record. w 1914-Ap 23 1925||
United with Gillette news to form Gillette news-record
WyHi Je 27 1918-25

HOMESTEADER. w
WyHi Je 1919-25

Gillette daily JOURNAL. d 1930+
pub 1930+
WyHi Ja 16-Je 1931

Gillette NEWS-RECORD. w 1906+
1906-Ap 1925 as Gillette news
pub 1913+
WyHi Ap 10 1915+

GLENDO

Glendo PIONEER. w 1919-25||?
WyHi Jl 6 1921-24

GLENROCK

Glenrock GAZETTE and Green River news. w Mr 1916-O 1925||
1916-24 as Glenrock gazette
WyHi Ap 24 1919-25

Glenrock GRAPHIC. w 1886-89||
CU-B S 13 1889

Glenrock INDEPENDENT. w Mr 30 1922+
WyHi 1922+

GREEN RIVER

FRONTIER index. *See under* Knight

WYOMING star. w 1901?+
WyHi My 5-S 1 1905

GREYBULL

Greybull STANDARD. w My 20 1920-Jl 1925||
United with Greybull tribune to form Greybull standard-tribune
WyGbS complete
WyHi D 9 1921-22

Greybull STANDARD-TRIBUNE. w Jl 3 1903+
1903-Jl 1925 as Greybull tribune
pub 1903+
WyHi 1922+

GUERNSEY

Guernsey GAZETTE. w 1899+
1899-1905? as Iron gazette
WyHi My 5 1905+
WyW 1899+

IRON gazette. *See* Guernsey gazette

HARTVILLE

Hartville UPLIFT. w 1910-18||?
WyHi F 1910-O 1913

HILLSDALE

Hillsdale REVIEW. w Mr 15 1917-27||?
WyHi Ja 4 1924;25-Je 1926;Ap 15-My 27 1927

Weekly REVIEW. w S 16 1931-Je 1933||
WyHi complete

HUDSON

MINER. w Je 12 1907-18||?
WyHi Jl 7 1911-Jl 1918

HULETT

CROOK county news. w Jl 23 1925+
WyHi Je 10-Jl 1926;Jl 10 1930+

INTERMOUNTAIN globe. w Ja 1 1906-21||?
WyHi Ap 9 1914-21

WYOMING blade. w 1911-18||?
1911-15 pub in Sundance
WyHi 1913-17

JACKSON

GRAND Teton. w D 29 1931-My 19 1934||
Merged with Jackson's Hole courier
WyHi complete

JACKSON'S Hole courier. w 1909+
WyHi Ap 2 1914+

JIREH

Jireh TRIBUNE. w 1913-15||?
WyHi Ap 4 1914-Ja 1915

KAYCEE

Kaycee HOMESTEADER. w
WyHi N 13-27 1925

Kaycee INDEPENDENT. w 1915-19||?
WyHi Ap 16 1916-My 1919

Kaycee OPTIMIST. w 1919-27||?
WyHi D 4 1925-Ja 14 1927

KEMMERER

Kemmerer CAMERA. *See* Kemmerer gazette

Kemmerer GAZETTE. w 1898+
1898-Ap 1924 as Kemmerer camera
pub 1898-1911;13+
WyHi My 6 1905-[Mr 1908-11]-[17-20]+

Kemmerer REPUBLICAN. w 1913-Ap 1924||
United with Kemmerer camera to form Kemmerer gazette
WyHi Ja 16-D 1914;Je 1918-24

KNIGHT

FRONTIER index. sw Je 4? 1867-N 17 1868||
Place of pub varies: Fort Sanders; Laramie City; Green River; Bear River City
C O 30 1868
CU-B Jl 26 1867;Mr 6,24-28,My 5,19-Jl 7,Ag 11-O 13,30-N 17 1868

LANDER

CLIPPER. w 1887-1907||?
1887-98 as Fremont clipper
WyHi D 29 1893;Ja 6 1899;My-Jl 1905

Lander EAGLE. w 1911-15||?
WyHi Ap 10 1914-Ap 1915

FREMONT clipper. *See* Clipper

Lander evening POST. d Ag 19 1918+
WyHi N 17 1921-Mr 1923

WIND River mountaineer. w 1884+
WyHi My 5 1905-18;Ag 1929+
WyL F 1898-Mr 1899[1912-24;28-35]+

WYOMING state journal. w 1884+
pub 1927+
WyHi My 1914-20;Jl 1922+
WyL [1912-16;18-24;26-35]

LARAMIE

Laramie BOOMERANG. *See* Laramie republican boomerang

FRONTIER index. *See under* Knight

Laramie daily INDEPENDENT. *See* Laramie daily sun

Laramie LEADER and Rock River review. w 1927-31||?
Follows Rock River review (Rock River)
WyHi 1928-31

Laramie REPUBLICAN. d 1890-S 29 1923||
United with Daily boomerang to form Laramie republican-boomerang
WyHi 1905-23

Laramie REPUBLICAN. w,sw Ag 11 1890-S 30 1923||
United with Semi-weekly boomerang to form Laramie republican-boomerang. w
WyHi Je 29,Jl 10,N 13 1897;O 16 1902;My-Ag,D 1905-23
WyU Ja-Ap 1894;N-D 1895;Mr-Ap,Jl 1896-Ja, Mr-Ap,S-N 1897;Jl 1898-Mr,D 1899-F,My-Jl, S 1900-Ja,Je,S-O,D 1901;F-Je,N 1902-Mr,N 1903;F-Je,D 1904-F,Ap-Je,S-D 1905;F,S,N 1906-Ja,Mr 1907-23

Laramie REPUBLICAN-BOOMERANG. d Mr 11 1881+
Title varies: 1881-S 29 1923: Daily boomerang; Laramie boomerang; Laramie daily boomerang; etc.
CU-B O 21,N 2 1885;N 12 1886
DLC [1923]+
MWA Ag 29 1883
WyHi F 20 1902;My 1905
WyU 1884-87;Jl 1888-Je 1897;98-N 1911;Ja-My 1912;13-S 1915;N 1916-Mr,Jl 1917-Je 1918; Ja-My,Jl-D 1919

WYOMING (*Continued*)

LARAMIE—*Continued*

Laramie REPUBLICAN-BOOMERANG. w,sw Mr 11 1881+
1881-Jl 30 1908 as Weekly boomerang; Ag 5 1908-S 28 1923 Semi-weekly boomerang sw Ag 5 1908-Je 3 1933
CU-B [S 24 1885-O 1887]Ja 12,F 9,S 6,N 1-8,22 1888
CoU 1899-1904;F 1906-Ag 1908
DLC 1898-O 16 1899
KHi Ag 23 1889-Je 1904
WyHi Ap 24 1884;My 1905+
WyU 1885-97;1900-04;07-10;Je 12-Jl,S 18 1913-15;17-19;O 1923+

Laramie daily SENTINEL. d My 1 1869-D 30 1878||
DLC Mr 14 1871-74
WyU My 1875-Jl 1878

Laramie weekly SENTINEL. w My 1 1869-Ap 1895||
CU-B [Jl 1885-86]Ja 1-22,F 5,19,Ap 2,30-Je 4,S 3 1887;Mr 2,S 7 1889;Ja 11 1890
WyHi Ag-O 1877;My 1885-Ap 1886;My 1890-95
WyU 1879-Ap 1889

Laramie daily SUN. d D 26 1871-Ap 1876||
1871-Mr 21 1875 as Laramie daily independent. Followed by Cheyenne daily sun (Cheyenne)
WyHi complete

Daily WYOMING state tribune. d
WyU O 1-3,5,8,1891

LIGHTNING FLAT

Lightning Flat FLASH. w Ja 6 1922-25||
Followed by Crook county flash (Sundance)
WyHi 1922-23;Ag 1924-25

LINGLE

FAMILY news-review. *See* Lingle review

Lingle REVIEW. w N 18 1917+
1919-24 as Family news-review
pub 1917+
WyHi Mr 16 1922+

LOST SPRINGS

Lost Springs TIMES. w 1914+
WyHi Je 27 1918-Je 1931

LOVELL

Lovell CHRONICLE. w My 1 1906+
pub My 8 1928+
WyHi [1917]-Ap 1920;N 23-My 1928

LUSK

CONVERSE county herald. *See* Lusk herald-standard

Lusk HERALD-STANDARD. w 1886+
1886-1922 as Lusk herald (1897?-1906 Converse county herald)
MWA O 11 1906;Ap 4 1907
WyHi Ap 30 1914;16+

Lusk STANDARD. w 1910-22||
United with Lusk herald to form Lusk herald-standard
WyHi O 17 1917-Mr 10 1922

LYMAN

BRIDGER Valley enterprise. w 1912+
WyHi Je 24-N 18 1926;Ja 27-D 8 1927;My 17 1928+

MANVILLE

Manville NEWS. w 1911-24||?
1911-Ap 1918 as Niobrara county news
WyHi Ap 1914-23

NIOBRARA county news. *See* Manville news

MEETEETSE

BIG Horn county news. *See* Meeteetse news

Meeteetse NEWS. w 1896-1932||?
1896-1912 as Big Horn county news
WyHi My-S 2 1905

WYOMING standard. w 1903-08||?
WyHi Ap 27-Ja 12 1907

MOORCROFT

Moorcroft DEMOCRAT. *See* Moorcroft leader

Moorcroft DEMOCRAT-LEADER. *See* Moorcroft leader

Moorcroft LEADER. w O 1913+
1913-21 as Moorcroft democrat; 1922 Moorcroft democrat leader
WyHi Mr 13 1914+

NEWCASTLE

Newcastle JOURNAL. w 1889-91||?
United with Newcastle news to form News-journal, later Newcastle news letter-journal

Newcastle NEWS-JOURNAL. *See* Newcastle news letter-journal

Newcastle NEWS-LETTER. w 1909-Ag 1924||
United with Newcastle news-journal to form Newcastle news letter-journal
WyHi Ag 1922-24'

Newcastle NEWS-LETTER-JOURNAL. w 1890+
1890-F 1908 as Newcastle news; Mr 1908-Ag 1924 News-journal
pub 1898+
MWA F 14-Ap 10 1896
WyHi N 6 1903;My 1905-20;Jl 1922+

Newcastle TIMES. w 1902-07||?
WyHi My-Ag 1905

WESTON county leader. w 1898-1903||?
WyHi Ag 11 1899

PAVILLION

FREMONT county independent. w 1926+
1926-27? as DuBois guide; 1927?-F 23 1928 DuBois guide and Fremont county independent (DuBois)
WyHi F 17 1927;1928-Je 1933

PINE BLUFFS

Pine Bluffs POST. w Ap 3 1908+
pub 1908+
WyHi Jl 1918+

PINEDALE

Pinedale ROUNDUP. w 1904+
WyHi My-Ag,S 13 1905-18;F-N 1920;24+

POWELL

Powell TRIBUNE. w 1909+
WyHi Ap 17 1914-S 1918;Ag 1919+

RAWLINS

CARBON county journal. w Jl 19 1879-1919||?
MWA My 11 1889
WyHi My 11 1889;My 1905-Jl 1917

CARBON county news. w
WyHi Ja 19-Ap 27 1878

Rawlins REPUBLICAN. w,sw D 20 1889+
1889 as Sweetwater chief (Bothwell)
pub 1891+
WyHi Jl 2 1897;My 3 1905+
WyR Ap 15 1926+

WYOMING reporter. w 1923-27||
WyHi Je 15 1926-Jl 19 1927
WyR My 4 1926-Ja 18 1927

RIVERTON

Riverton CHRONICLE. w 1911-29||
United with Riverton review to form Riverton review-chronicle
WyHi F 12 1926;Je 15-D 1928
WyRiR 1917-29

Riverton REVIEW-CHRONICLE. w 1907+
1907-29 as Riverton review
pub 1907—
WyHi Ja 16 1914+

ROCK RIVER

Rock River REVIEW. w Ap 11 1919-27|
Followed by Laramie leader and Rock River review (Laramie)
WyHi Ja 9 1920-21;Jl 1922-27

ROCK SPRINGS

Rock Springs INDEPENDENT. *See* Rock Springs rocket

Rock Springs MINER. w 1881+
WyHi My-S 2 1905;My 30 1914-Ag 1918;Jl-D 1921;27-32

Rock Springs ROCKET. w 1885+
1885-O? 1907 as Rock Springs independent
MWA [Ja 18-My 1929]
WyHi My 6 1905-Ap,N 28 1907+

SALT CREEK

Salt Creek GUSHER. w 1922-
WyHi 1926-Je 1930

SARATOGA

PLATTE Valley lyre. w Jl 7 1888-Je 6 1901||
WySS complete

Saratoga SUN. w Jl 14 1891+
pub 1891—
WyHi My-Ag 1905;Je 13 1918+

SHERIDAN

Sheridan ENTERPRISE. w,sw,d 1887-1924||
United with Sheridan post to form Sheridan post-enterprise
WyHi My 1905-24

Sheridan JOURNAL. w S 3 1925-30||
WyHi 1925-N 1930

Sheridan NEWS. w S 1932+
pub 1932+

Sheridan POST-ENTERPRISE. w,sw,d 1887-1930||?
1887-Je 1923? as Sheridan post
WyHi My 1905-Mr 1925;Je 1926-30

Sheridan PRESS. d 1930+
WyHi 1931+

SHOSHONI

Shoshoni ENTERPRISE. w Ap 5 1913-
WyHi S 2 1927-F 17 1928

SOUTH PASS CITY

SWEETWATER mines. sw,w,r F 14 1868-Je 19 1869||
Place of pub varies: Fort Bridger; Bryan City
CU-B Mr 21-Ap 15,My 27-Ag 8,N 25,D 2-5,23 1868-Ja 9,23,Ap 7,Je 19 1869

SUNDANCE

CROOK county flash. w
Follows Lightning Flat flash (Lightning Flat)
WyHi 1926-27

CROOK county monitor. w 1895-1924||?
WyHi My-Ag 1905;Ag 1913-Ag 1918

Sundance GAZETTE. w 1884-99||?
WyHi O 25 1884

Sundance TIMES. w 1909+
Follows Times (Welcome)
WyHi My 17 1928+

WYOMING blade. *See under* Hulett

THERMOPOLIS

BIG Horn River pilot. w 1895-1904||?
WyHi F 2-Mr 2 1898

Thermopolis INDEPENDENT-RECORD. w 1906+
1906-Ap 13 1928 as Thermopolis independent record
WyHi My 22 1914;15+

Thermopolis JOURNAL. w 1929+
WyHi S 17 1931+

Thermopolis RECORD. w 1901-Ap 1928||
United with Thermopolis independent to form Thermopolis independent-record
WyHi My 1905-19

TORRINGTON

GOSHEN county journal. w 1913-1925||
Merged with Torrington telegram
WyHi 1925
WyTcT 1917-25

GOSHEN Hole news. *See* Goshen news and Fort Laramie scout

GOSHEN news and Fort Laramie scout. w 1918+
1918-23? as Goshen Hole news; 1924?-27 Goshen news
NbHi Ag 25-S 8,29 1927-28
WyHi Jl 5 1922-23;28+

Torrington TELEGRAM. w Ag 1 1907+
pub 1918+
WyHi Mr 6 1919+

UPTON

WESTON county gazette. w 1912+
pub 1926+
WyHi Ag 13 1914+

VAN TASSELL

Van Tassell PIONEER. w 1912-18||?
WyHi Mr 28 1914-S 1917

WELCOME

PROSPECTOR. *See* Times

TIMES. w 1893-1908||
1893-94 as Prospector. Followed by Sundance times (Sundance)

WHEATLAND

LARAMIE county times. *See* Wheatland times

PLATTE county record. w 1925+
WyHi Ap 11 1929+
WyW Mr 22 1928+

Wheatland TIMES and Wheatland world. w 1902—
1902-17 as Laramie county times; 1918-21 Wheatland times
WyHi Ja 10 1913+
WyW 1918+

Wheatland WORLD. w 1894-1921||
United with Wheatland times to form Wheatland times and Wheatland world
WyHi My-Ag,N 14 1905-Ap 1920
WyW complete

WORLAND

Worland GRIT. w D 28 1905+
pub N 1906+
WyHi 1916+

WRIGHT

HOMESTEADER. w Je 6 1919-26||?
WyHi 1919-25

CANADA

ALBERTA

ACADIA

Acadia REVIEW. w
CaA Ag-D 1914

ACME

Acme NEWS w Ag 1910-F 4 1914||
CaA complete
CaAAS complete

Acme SENTINEL. w 1914+
pub 1914+
CaA Je 24 1914-17

Acme TELEGRAM-TRIBUNE. w
CaA F 11-Ap 22 1914

AIRDRIE

Airdrie NEWS. w 1908-12||?
CaA Jl 1908-09

ALDERSON

Alderson NEWS. w 1916-17||?
Follows Carlstadt news (Carlstadt)
CaA Ja-D 14 1916;Ja 11-D 1917

ALIX

Alix FREE PRESS. w Mr 11 1909+
CaA 1909-17

ALLIANCE

Alliance TIMES. w S 23 1916+
pub 1916+
CaA 1917+

ALSASK

Alsask NEWS. w
CaA My 1914-20

AMISK

Amisk ADVOCATE. w S 1921+
pub 1921+

ARROWWOOD

BOW Valley resource. w Ag 20 1931+
pub 1931+

ATHABASCA

Athabasca ECHO. w Jl 1928+
pub 1928+

Athabasca HERALD. w 1908-18||?
CaA Je-D 13 1917;18

NORTHERN news w 1908-16||?
CaA Ja 17 1909-Ja 1916

Athabasca TIMES w 1913-14||?
CaA 1913-S 1914

BANFF

CRAG and canyon. w 1898+
pub only My-Sept, 1900-20
pub Ap 1903+
CaA 1901-21

BARONS

Barons ENTERPRISE. w
Followed by Barons globe
CaA 1911-12

Barons GLOBE. w 1919-23||?
Follows Barons enterprise
CaA 1920

BARRHEAD

Barrhead LEADER. w
pub Ap 21 1932+

BASHAW

Bashaw RECORD. w 1911-17||?
CaA My 19 1911-Jl 5 1912;Ja 8-Ap 13 1915;17

BASSANO

Bassano MAIL. w Jl 23 1912+
pub 1912+
CaA F 26 1914+

Bassano NEWS. w 1910-14||?
CaA Ap 15 1910-[13-14]

BAWLF

Bawlf SUN. w 1908-30||?
CaA S 13-O 1907;Mr 1908-20

BELLEVUE

Bellevue TIMES. w 1910-18||?
CaA S 22 1910-Je 1918

BIG VALLEY

Big Valley JOURNAL. w O 15 1924+
pub 1924+
CaA 1924+

Big Valley NEWS. w 1916-24||
CaA N 9 1916-20

BLAIRMORE

Blairmore ENTERPRISE w S 1909+
pub 1909+
CaA N 25 1909+

BOW ISLAND

Bow Island REVIEW. w 1910+
CaA Je 25 1910-20

BOWDEN

Bowden NEWS w 1909-12||?
CaA Ag 13 1909-11

BROOKS

Brooks BANNER. *See* Brooks bulletin

Brooks BULLETIN. w 1910+
1910-11 as Brooks banner
pub [1912-14]+
CaA 1910+

BRUCE

Bruce NEWS. 1911-15||?
CaA Ag 10 1911-12;My 1913

CALGARY

ALBERTA tribune. *See* Albertan. w

ALBERTAN. w,sw S 16 1885-1925||?
1885-F 9 1895 as Calgary tribune; F 11 1895-D 23 1899 Alberta tribune; 1900-02 Albertan and Alberta tribune
CaM 1885-1906
CaO 1885-Ap 1 1887;95-D 16 1899
WHi N 9 1895

Calgary ALBERTAN. d 1902+
1902-07? as Morning bulletin; 1908?-10? Morning Albertan
pub [1913]20+
CaA 1906-07;Mr 1908+
CaB N 1909-Je 1910;28-Mr 1932
CaM 1900-06

Morning BULLETIN. *See* Calgary Albertan

Calgary CANADIAN. d 1907-S 1918||
1907-09 as Calgary daily news; 1910-Ap 10 1918? Calgary news-telegram
CaA Mr-O 1907[08]09;N 26 1910;11-17;Ap 17-S 1918
WaPS [1918]

Der DEUTSCH-Canadier. w 1909-14||
In German
CaA F 11 1909-Ag 15,S 5 1912-14

Calgary daily HERALD. d 1883+
pub [Ag 31 1883-1911]+
CaA 1896-98;1900-Je 1904;05-S,N 1906+
CaB N 3 1909-[S 1910-27]+
CaM 1910+
CaO D 25 1884-Je 29 1901
DLC 1931+
WHi N 30 1912-13

Calgary weekly HERALD. w 1883-1918||?
CaM 1883-1906

MARKET examiner. w 1917+
pub My 18 1918+
CaA Ag 1918+

Calgary daily NEWS. *See* Calgary Canadian

Calgary NEWS-TELEGRAM. *See* Calgary Canadian

NOR'WESTER. w Ap 22 1884-My 14 1885||
CaM complete
CaO Ap 29 1884-85

Calgary STANDARD. *See* Western standard

Calgary TRIBUNE. *See* Albertan. w

WESTERN standard. w 1911-18||
1911-F 1913 as Calgary standard
CaA Ag 1912-F 22,Mr 20 1913-N 1918

CAMROSE

Camrose CANADIAN. w D 10 1908+
pub 1908+
CaA 1908+

Camrose MAIL. w 1906-08||?
CaA My 1-O 23 1907;Mr-D 1908

CANMORE

Canmore TIMES.
pub 1932+

CARDSTON

ALBERTA star. *See* Cardston news

Cardston GLOBE. *See* Cardston news

Cardston NEWS. w 1898+
1898-1901? as Cardston record; 1902?-10? Alberta star; 1911?-21? Cardston globe 1922?-24? Cardston review
pub [1908-S 1925]+
CaA 1907-10;Jl 12 1911+

Cardston RECORD. *See* Cardston news

Cardston STAR. *See* Cardston news

CARLSTADT

Carlstadt NEWS. w 1911-15||
Followed by Alderson news (Alderson)
CaA Ag 1912-Ap 10 1913;14-15

Carlstadt PROGRESS. w
CaA 1911-Jl 25 1912

CARMANGAY

Carmangay SUN. w Mr 4 1910+
pub [1910-N 1922]My 1923+
CaA 1910-[18]O 1920+

CARSTAIRS

Carstairs JOURNAL. *See* Carstairs news

Carstairs NEWS. w 1905+
1905-Jl 1924 as Carstairs journal
pub D 1906-23;Ag 1924+
CaA My-O 1907;Mr 1908+

CASTOR

Castor ADVANCE. w N 26 1909+
pub 1909+
CaA 1909+

CAYLEY

Cayley HUSTLER. w 1910-15||?
CaA D 19 1909[10]Ja-N 1913

CEREAL

Cereal REVIEW. w 1914-18||?
CaA 1915

CHAMPION

Champion CHRONICLE. w Je 1 1919+
pub 1919+
CaA Jl 1919+

Champion SPOKESMAN. w
CaA Ap 29-S 4 1914

CHAUVIN

Chauvin ADVANCE. w 1912-13||?
CaA Mr 7-S 19 1912

Chauvin CHRONICLE. w 1914+
pub Mr 1919+
CaA Mr 26 1914+

Chauvin GAZETTE. w 1912-13||?
CaA S 13 1912-S 1913

CHINOOK

Chinook ADVANCE. w Ag 1 1914+
pub 1914-[Ap 18 1920-Jl 1920]
CaA Ag 26-D 1915

CLAIRMONT

Clairmont INDEPENDENT. w
CaA Jl 20 1916-Ap 6 1917;N-O 1918

ALBERTA (*Continued*)

CLARESHOLM

Claresholm ADVERTISER. w 1914-16||
United with Claresholm review to form Claresholm review and advertiser
CaA Ap 15-D 23 1914;15-16
CaALS [1914-16]

Claresholm LOCAL press. w O 1926+
pub 1926+
CaA 1926+
CaALS 1926+

Claresholm REVIEW-ADVERTISER. w 1904-My 1928||
1904-16 as Claresholm review
CaA My 3-O 18 1907;Mr 1908-20
CaALS [1904-18]-28

CLIVE

Clive NEWS-RECORD. w 1914-18||
CaA 1916-18

COCHRANE

Cochrane ADVOCATE. w 1909-28||?
CaA Mr 11-D 1909;Ap 1910-15

COLEMAN

Coleman BULLETIN. w 1912-18||
CaA Ja 31-O 1913;14-15;18

Coleman JOURNAL. w S 1921+
pub 1921+
CaA 1921+

Coleman MINER. w 1908-13||?
CaA 1908-11;13

CONSORT

Consort ENTERPRISE. w 1912+
pub D 1913+
CaA 1914+

CORONATION

Coronation REVIEW. w 1911+
pub [S 27 1913-20]+
CaA [1912]+

COWLEY

Cowley CHRONICLE. w
CaA D 1909-Ja 1910

CROSSFIELD

Crossfield CHRONICLE. w 1907+
CaA Mr 1908+

CZAR

Czar CLIPPER. w 1919+
pub S 1921+

DAYSLAND

Daysland PRESS. w 1907-29||?
CaA My 30-O 1907;F 1908-My 20 1909;10-17

DELBURNE

Delburne PROGRESS. w 1912-18||?
CaA My 1912-18

DELIA

Delia TIMES. w 1918+
pub [1918-26]-[32-34]+
CaA F 1919+

DIDSBURY

Didsbury PIONEER. w F 1 1903+
pub 1903+
CaA S 13-N 1 1907;F 1908+

DONALDA

FREE Lance. w 1915-16||?
CaA O-D 1916

DRUMHELLER

Drumheller MAIL. w My 2 1918+
Follows Munson mail (Munson)
pub 1918+
CaA 1918+

Drumheller REVIEW. w D 13 1913+
pub 1913+
CaA Ap 10-Je 19 1914;18+

EDMONTON

ALBERTA gazette. sm O 31 1905+
CaB Ja 15 1906+
CaOOA 1905+
CaOT Ja 15 1907+
CaQMM 1905+
DLC 1905+
NN 1905+

ALBERTA herold. w 1903-15||
In German
CaA Ap 13-Ag 1907;F-D 1908;N 5 1909-Mr 1915
NdHi S 1905-D 1910

Edmonton BULLETIN. w,sw,d 1880+
w 1880-92;sw 1892-1903
pub 1890+
CaA [1880-82]-[84-86]88[89-90]-[98-1905]+
CaAEO 1880-90
CaM 1880-1925
CaO 1888+
CaOOA N 12 1881-O 10 1885
CaOT [1884-92]

Edmonton CAPITOL. d 1909-
CaA 1910-N 1914

Le COURRIER de l'ouest. w 1905-15||?
CaA Ap 11-Ag 8 1907;08-15
CaQ O 14 1905-11

Edmonton FREE press. w 1919-20||?
CaA Ap 1919-20

GREAT West Saturday night advance. w
CaA 1913;F-Mr 1914

Edmonton JOURNAL. d 1903+
Follows Edmonton post
pub N 4 1903+
CaA 1906+
CaB N 4 1909-[S 1910-27]+
CaM 1925-32
TxU Je 11 1925-Je 1928

Edmonton NEWS. sw Ja 3-S 23 1913||?
Follows Strathcona plaindealer (Strathcona) Ja-Ag 1913 as Edmonton news-plaindealer
CaA Ja-S 23 1913

Saturday NEWS. w 1905-16||?
CaA Ap 20-Ag 1907;F 1908-Jl 1912

NOWYNY. sw,w 1912-15||
In Ukrainian
CaA N 12 Jl 15 1915

L'OUEST Canadien. w F 3 1898-1911||?
CaA 1911
CaO 1898-F 22 1900

Edmonton POST. sw 1889-1902||
Followed by Edmonton journal

PROGRES Albertain. w 1909-16||?
1909-14? as Progres
In French
CaA 1911-Ag 15 1916

RUSSIAN voice. w
CaA 1915

STATESMAN. w 1917-20||?
CaA S-N 1917;My-N 1919

La SURVIVANCE. w N 1928+
In French
CaQQL 1928+

L'UNION. w 1918-29||?
In French
CaA 1918;My 1919-20

WESTERN News. w 1927+
In Ukranian
CaA 1927+
CaAE Jl 1927+

WESTERN weekly. w
CaA Ja 22-Je 25 1915

EDSON

Edson HERALD. w 1911-17||
1911-My 1913 as Western star; Je-D? 1913 Edson critic; 1914-16 Western leader; Ja?-Je? 1917 Edson leader
CaA Mr 13-Ag 1913;Ja 22 1915-17

EMPRESS

Empress EXPRESS. w Je 6 1913+
CaA 1913+
CaAE [1913-32]+

ENTWHISTLE

Entwhistle ENTERPRISE. w 1912-13||?
CaA F 10 1912-F 8 1913

ERSKINE

Erskine REVIEW. w 1911-24||?
1911-13? as Erskine times
CaA 1918-24

Erskine TIMES. *See* Erskine review

FAIRVIEW

NORTHERN review. w
pub 1923-33

FORESTBURG

Forestburg ADVANCE. w 1916-20||
Followed by Forestburg home news
CaA Jl 28 1916-17;19-20

Forestburg HOME news. w 1921-22||?
Follows Forestburg advance

FORT SASKATCHEWAN

Fort Saskatchewan CHRONICLE. w 1910-12||?
CaA 1910-Je 1911

Fort Saskatchewan CONSERVATOR. w 1913-22||
CaA Mr 27 1913-21

Fort Saskatchewan RECORD. w Ap 1 1922+
pub 1922+
CaA 1922+

Fort Saskatchewan RECORDER. w 1912||?
CaA 1912

Fort Saskatchewan REPORTER. w 1902-09||
CaA My-O 24 1907;F 1908-09

FRANK

Frank PAPER. w 1905-09||
Followed by Frank vindicator
CaA My-O 1907;Mr 1908-N 24 1909

Frank VINDICATOR. w 1910-15||?
Follows Frank paper
CaA S 22 1910-Ag 1913

GLEICHEN

BOW Valley call. *See* Gleichen call

Gleichen CALL. w 1907+
1907 as Bow Valley call
CaA My-O 1907;F 1908+

GRANDE-PRAIRIE

FRONTIER-Signal. w
CaA S 28 1914-Ag 3 1916

Grande Prairie HERALD. w 1913+
pub 1913+
CaA Ap 8 1913-Ag 1919,20+

NORTHERN tribune. w Je 30 1932+
pub 1932+
CaB 1932+

GRANUM

Granum NEWS. w 1909-12||?
1909-10 as Granum press
CaA Jl 1909-12

Granum PRESS. *See* Granum news

GRASSEY LAKE

Grassey Lake GAZETTE. w 1911-13||?
1911-12 as Grassey Lake pilot and gazette
CaA 1911-13

Grassey Lake PILOT and gazette. *See* Grassey Lake gazette

GROUARD

Grouard NEWS. w 1912-17||?
CaA 1912-N 1915

HANNA

Hanna HERALD. w D 24 1912+
pub 1912-[31-32]+
CaA 1913+

HARDISTY

Hardisty MAIL. *See* Hardisty world

Hardisty WORLD. w 1910+
1910-21 as Hardisty mail
pub Ag 12 1910-21;S 1923+
CaA 1911+

HIGH RIVER

High River TIMES. w D 7 1905+
pub 1905+
CaA Ap 25-Ag 22 1907;F 1908+

HOLDEN

Holden HERALD. w 1910+
CaA Ap 1910-26;Ag 16 1932+

HUGHENDEN

Hughenden NEWS. *See* Hughenden record

Hughenden RECORD. w 1916+
1916-17 as Hughenden news; 1918-20 Ribstone record
pub 1916-Ag 1920;21+
CaA 1916-Jl 1919

RIBSTONE record. *See* Hughenden record

HUXLEY

Huxley NEW era. w
CaA S 25-O 9 1915

INNISFAIL

Innisfail PROVINCE. w 1905+
pub 1905+
CaA Ja 31-O 24 1907;F 1908+

IRMA

Irma TIMES. w 1916+
pub 1916+
CaA 1918+

IRVINE

Irvine INDEX. w
CaA 1912-13

ALBERTA (*Continued*)

KILLAM

Killam NEWS. w 1911-F 14 1930||
CaA [1911-12]-18;20-30

LACOMBE

Lacombe GUARDIAN. w 1913-16||?
CaA 1913-Ag 25 1916

Lacombe WESTERN globe. w 1904+
CaA Ap 20-O 1907;F 1908+

LAMONT

Lamont GAZETTE. w 1918-19||?
CaA S 1918-19

Lamont TRIBUNE. w 1914-16||?
CaA Ja 21 1915-16

LANGDON

Langdon LEADER. w 1911-12||?
CaA Mar-O 1912

LEDUC

Leduc REPRESENTATIVE. w 1906+
pub 1906+
CaA My 17-N 1 1907;F 1908+

LETHBRIDGE

Lethbridge HERALD. w N 8 1905+
pub 1905+

Lethbridge HERALD. d 1907+
pub D 11 1907+
CaA Ap 11-Jl 18 1907;F 1908+
CaAL Jl 1918+

Lethbridge NEWS. w N 1885-1913||?
CaA [1885-1910]
CaM 1885-1906
CaO Jl 1889-1900

Lethbridge morning NEWS. d 1910-13||?
CaA Jl 1-31 1913

LLOYDMINSTER

Lloydminster TIMES. w
CaA Ap 30-Jl 1907;08-20

LOMOND

Lomond PRESS. w 1916-26||?
CaA 1918-19

LOUGHEED

Lougheed EXPRESS. w 1912-22||?
CaA 1913-17;19

Lougheed JOURNAL. w 1925+
pub 1925+

MACLEOD

Macleod ADVANCE. *See* Macleod advertiser

Macleod ADVERTISER. w 1899-1913||?
1899-Ap 1909 as Macleod advance
CaA Ap 30-O 1907;F 1908-13
CaAMG 1909-12
CaM 1904-06

Macleod BUZZER. w
CaA O 22 1910-11

Macleod CHRONICLE. w Jl 1 1882-1910||?
1882-85? as Fort Macleod gazette; 1886?-1908 Macleod gazette
CaA 1882-S 1907;Ja 14-28 1909
CaAMG [1883]Jl 11 1888-Je 20 1889[93-94]
CaM 1884-1906

Macleod GAZETTE. 1882-1908. *See* Macleod chronicle

Macleod GAZETTE. w 1920+
1920-30 as Macleod times and news
pub 1920+
CaA 1920+

Macleod NEWS. w 1916-20||
Followed by Macleod times and news later Macleod gazette
CaAMG complete

Macleod SPECTATOR. w 1912-16||
CaA complete
CaAMG complete

Macleod TIMES and news. *See* Macleod gazette

MAGRATH

Magrath PIONEER. w 1906-14||?
CaA My-O 9 1907;08-O 1912;13

MANVILLE

Manville EMPIRE. w 1908-21||?
CaA D 9 1908;Ja-Ap 27 1909;O 20 1910-15,19

Manville TELEGRAM. w
CaA [1908-09]

MAYERTHORPE

Mayerthorpe TIMES. w 1931+
CaA Ja 25 1934+

MEDICINE HAT

ALBERTA farmer. w 1913-16||?
CaA O 1913-14

LABOR day bulletin.
Probably only one pub
WHi S 2 1912

Medicine Hat NEWS. w 1883+
pub 1883+
CaA Ap 19-O 4 1906;My-O 1907;F 1908-Jl 7 1910
CaO 1897-1900

Medicine Hat NEWS. d 1910+
pub 1911+
CaA 1911-17

Medicine Hat TIMES. w D 1885-95||?
CaM 1885-95
CaO Jl 1890-92

Medicine Hat TIMES. w 1903-16||?
CaA Ap 30-N 5 1907;F 1908-14;Ja-O 19 1916

MIRROR

Mirror JOURNAL. w 1911-24||
CaA [1911-12]-16;O 1919-S 1924

MONITOR

Monitor ENTERPRISE. w 1915-24||?
1915-22? as Monitor news
CaA 1916-19

Monitor NEWS. *See* Monitor enterprise

MUNDARE

POSTUP. (Progress) w 1914-17||?
In Ruthenian
CaA 1916-17

MUNSON

Munson MAIL. w Ja 4 1912-Ap 1918||
Followed by Drumheller mail (Drumheller)
CaA 1913-18
CaADM 1912-Ag 4,O 1914-18

NANTON

Nanton NEWS. w Je 25 1903+
pub 1903+
CaA My-O 1907;F 1908-N 4 1909;10-13

OKOTOKS

Okotoks ADVANCE. w 1909-14||
CaA complete

Okotoks REVIEW. w 1901+
pub 1901+
CaA 1908+

OLDS

Olds GAZETTE. w 1891+
pub 1922+
CaA My-N 1907;F 1908+

OYEN

Oyen NEWS. w 1914+
CaA Je 25 1914+

PEACE RIVER

NORTHERN gazette. w S 9 1932+
CaAPR 1932+

Peace River RECORD. w Jl 23 1914+
pub 1914+
CaA Jl 30-D 1914;16+
CaB D 27 1929-32

Peace River STANDARD. w 1917-23||?
CaA 1918-20
CaAPR [1917-23]

PINCHER CREEK

Pincher Creek ECHO. w Ag 1900+
pub 1900+
CaA My 3-N 1907;08+

PONOKA

Ponoka HERALD. w Ag 27 1900+
pub [1900-07]+
CaA My-O 1907;08+

PROVOST

Provost NEWS. w My 8 1910+
1910-16 as Provost star
pub 1910+
CaA 1911-16;18+

Provost STAR. *See* Provost news

RED DEER

Red Deer ADVOCATE. w 1901+
1901-05 as Alberta advocate
pub 1901;04-05;N 1906+
CaA Ap 11-N 1 1907;08+
WaPS Ag 1925-F 3 1927

ALBERTA advocate. *See* Red Deer advocate

Red Deer NEWS. w 1905-26||
CaA Ap 16 1907-My 1926

REDCLIFFE

Redcliffe REVIEW. w 1910+
pub 1923+
CaA [1911-12]+
WHi O 11 1912

RIMBEY

Rimbey RECORD. w Jl 1930+
pub 1930+
CaA 1934+

ROCKY MOUNTAIN HOUSE

Rocky Mountain House ECHO. w
CaA 1911-12

Rocky Mountain GUIDE. w 1909-17||?
CaA D 20 1912;13;Mr 31-S 1914;15-16;Ja 19-F 23 1917

RYLEY

Ryley TIMES. w 1909-16||
CaA [1911-12]-Mr 1916

ST. ALBERT

L'ETOILE de St. Albert. w
In French
CaA N 12-D 31 1912

St. Albert STAR. w
CaA 1913-Ap 22 1914

ST. PAUL

St. Paul CANADIAN. w 1925+
1925-33? as St. Paul journal
pub My 1934+

SEDGEWICK

COMMUNITY press. w 1908+
1908-31? as Sedgewick sentinel
CaA Jl 16 1908-20

Sedgewick SENTINEL. *See* Community press

SPIRIT RIVER

Spirit River ECHO. w 1917-20||
pub [1915-16]
CaA S 1917-18;20

STAVELEY

Staveley ADVERTISER. w Ap 9 1914+
CaA Ap-S 2 1914;Jl 28-D 1916;S 1918+

Staveley STANDARD. w 1909-17||?
CaA Ag 10 1910;14;16-17

STETTLER

Stettler INDEPENDENT. w 1906+
CaA My-O 1907;08-15;18+

STONY PLAIN

Stony Plain ADVERTISER. w 1909-13||?
CaA D 1909-Ap 26 1913

MIRROR. w 1914-17||?
CaA My-D 1915;F-My 1916

RURAL weekly news. w 1912-17||?
CaA Ja 15 1915-16

SUN. w Ag 5 1920+
pub 1920+
CaA 1920+

STRATHCONA

Strathcona evening CHRONICLE. d 1907-11||?
CaA Ap 26-O 1907;My-O 9 1908;Ja-Mr 5 1909

Strathcona PLAINDEALER. sw 1894-1912||
Followed by Edmonton news-plaindealer, later Edmonton news
CaA My 3-N 1 1907;Mr 1908-S 5 1911;12

STRATHMORE

Strathmore STANDARD. w 1909+
1909-33? as Strathmore and Bow Valley standard
pub 1909+
CaA O 9 1909;10-Mr 1918;19

STROME

Strome DISPATCH. w 1910-29||?
CaA D 1910-20

TABER

Taber FREE press. w 1907-10||?
CaA S-O 1907;F 1908-09;F-Ag 1910

Taber TIMES. w 1910+
CaA 1913+

ALBERTA (*Continued*)

THREE HILLS

Three Hills CAPITAL. w 1912+
pub 1912+
CaA 1916+

TOFIELD

Tofield MERCURY. w Ag 28 1918+
pub 1918+
CaA 1918+

Tofield STANDARD. w 1907-16||?
CaO O 1907-08;10-14;16

TROCHU

Trochu TRIBUNE. w 1911+
CaA [1911]+

VEGREVILLE

Vegreville OBSERVER. w Mr 1906+
pub 1906+
CaA My-O 1907;08+

VERMILLION

Vermillion SIGNAL. w 1906-11||?
CaA My-Jl 18 1907;08-[Ja-Ap 1910]

Vermillion STANDARD. w My 19 1909+
pub 1909+
CaA My 19 1909+

VIKING

Viking NEWS. w My 15 1913+
pub 1913+
CaA 1913+

VULCAN

Vulcan ADVOCATE. w 1913+
CaA Ag 6 1913+

Vulcan REVIEW. w 1912-14||?
CaA 1912-Ap 2 1913

WAINWRIGHT

Wainwright RECORD. w
pub Ag 1933+
CaA My 1933+

Wainwright STAR. w N 1 1908+
pub 1908+
CaA Jl 16 1919+

WARNER

Warner RECORD. w 1910-18||?
CaA Je 9-N 17 1910;Mr 1911-O 1914;15;F 11-Ag 25 1916

WESTLOCK

Westlock WITNESS. w S 1919+
pub 1919+
CaA O 1919+

WETASKIWIN

Wetaskiwin ALBERTA tribunen. w
In Swedish
CaA Mar 31-My 5 1914

Wetaskiwin CENTRAL Albertan. w 1904-11||
1904-Ag 11 1910 as Wetaskiwin post
CaA Ap 11-O 1907;F 1908-11

Wetaskiwin FREE press. w 1909+
CaA Ag 11 1912+

Wetaskiwin POST. *See* Wetaskiwin central Albertan

Wetaskiwin TIMES. w Mr 20 1901+
pub 1901+
CaA Ap 11-O 1907;08+

WHITECOURT

NEWS-RECORD. w 1914-17||?
CaA Ag 27 1914-17

YOUNGSTOWN

PLAINDEALER. w Ap 3 1913+
pub 1913+
CaA Je 25 1914+

BRITISH COLUMBIA

ABBOTSFORD

ABBOTSFORD, Sumas & Matsqui news. w 1922+
CaB N 6 1929+

Abbotsford POST. w My 6 1910-F 8 1924||
CaB complete

AGASSIZ

Agassiz RECORD. w 1923-24||?
CaB Ja 2-Ag 20 1924

ALBERNI

Alberni ADVOCATE. w Mr 6 1912-O 8 1915||
CaB Mr 22 1912-15

Alberni PIONEER news. *See* Port Alberni news (Port Alberni)

ALDERMERE

INTERIOR news. *See under* Smithers

ALICE ARM

Alice Arm and Anyox herald. w Je 4 1921+
CaB 1921+

ANACONDA

Anaconda NEWS. w D 11 1900-05||?
CaB [Jl 9 1901-Jl 19 1905]

ARMSTRONG

Armstrong ADVERTISER. w 1901+
CaB My 22 1902+

ASHCROFT

BRITISH Columbia mining journal. *See* Ashcroft journal

Ashcroft JOURNAL and Lillooet district news. w My 9 1895+
1895-Ap 29 1899 as British Columbia mining journal; My 6 1899-Jl 7 1934 Ashcroft journal
CaB 1895+
CaO 1897

ATLIN

CLAIM. w Ap 29 1899-1908||?
CaB 1899-Ap 11 1908

BARKERVILLE

CARIBOO sentinel. sw,w Je 6 1865-O 30 1875||
Suspended from O 14 1865-My 1866
CU-B Jl 4,Ag 5 1867
CaB Je 6 1865[68-My 1869]-75
CaBV [Je 17 1865-Ap 1867]-75
MWA Jl 15 1865;My 21 1866;Jl 11-18,29 1867
NN Je 6 1865(facsimile)
WaSp S 16 1865[67]Ag 5 1868

BELLA COOLA

Bella Coola COURIER. w 1912-17||?
CaB Ag 12 1916-O 6 1917

BROOKLYN

Brooklyn NEWS. w 1898||?
CaB Jl 9-N 12 1898

BURNABY

Burnaby BROADCAST. w My 27 1926+
CaB 1926+

Burnaby POST. w 1922+
CaB My 31 1934+

BURNS LAKE

INLAND independent. w 1922+
1922-O 26 1933 as Observer
CaB Ap 1927+

OBSERVER. *See* Inland independent

CAMBORNE

Camborne MINER. w 1902-06||
CaB Jl 16 1904-S 15 1906

CANTERBURY

OUTCROP. *See under* Wilmer

CASCADE

Cascade RECORD. w N 12 1898-1901||
CaB 1898-Jl 6 1901

CHILLIWACK

FRASER advance. w 1907||?
CaB F 16-Jl 27 1907

Chilliwack FREE press. w S 7 1911-O 25 1912||
CaB complete

Chilliwack PROGRESS. w 1891+
CaB 1894+

CLANWILLIAM

Clanwilliam HUSTLER.
pub "whenever trains are delayed by slides"
CaB My 26 1894

CLOVERDALE

SURREY leader. w Jl 17 1929+
CaB 1929+

SURREY times. w Ap 5-O 25 1895||
CaB complete

CODY

PAYSTREAK. *See under* Sandon

COURTENAY

COMOX argus. w My 3 1917+
CaB 1917+

COMOX district free press. w Jl 14 1927+
1927-Jl 23 1931 as Courtenay free press
CaB 1927+

Courtenay FREE press. *See* Comox district free press

Weekly NEWS. *See under* Union

PARKSVILLE-Qualicum journal. w
-Mr 14 1930 pub at Parksville
CaB F 1930-Ja 9 1931

REVIEW. w D 5 1912-Ag 29 1918||
CaB complete

CRANBROOK

Cranbrook COURIER. w N 7 1919+
CaB 1919+

Cranbrook HERALD. w Ap 5 1898-My 26 1927||
CaB complete

PROSPECTOR. w N 9 1895-D 26 1914||
1895-My 1905 pub at Fort Steele
CaB complete

Daily TRIBUNE. d N 11 1931-My 2 1933||
CaB complete

CRESTON

Creston REVIEW. w 1908+
CaB Ja 28 1909+

CROFTON

Crofton GAZETTE. w F 27-O 15 1902||
CaB complete

CUMBERLAND

ISLANDER. w Je 11 1910-Jl 21 1931||
Title varies: Cumberland Islander
CaB complete

Cumberland NEWS. w 1892-1915||
CaB Ja 24 1898-N 24 1915

DAWSON CREEK

PEACE River block news. w My 6 1930+
1930-Ap 19 1932 pub at Rolla
CaB 1930+

DONALD

TRUTH. w
CaB Jl 28,O 20 1888

DUNCAN

COWICHAN leader. w Ap 28 1905+
CaB My 1905+
WaPS [1923-24]Jl 1 1926[28-30]

SPOKESMAN. w Ja 4 1930-Ja 10 1931||
Ja-S 1930 pub in Victoria
CaB complete

EMORY

INLAND sentinel. *See* Kamloops sentinel (Kamloops)

ENDERBY

Enderby COMMONER. w Ag 27 1908+
1908-F 1909 as Walker's weekly; Mr 1909-Mr 1918 Enderby press and Walker's weekly; Ap 1918-Ap 1930 Okanagan commoner
CaB 1908+

EDENOGRAPH. *See* Enderby progress and Northern Okanagan herald

BRITISH COLUMBIA (*Continued*)

ENDERBY—*Continued*

OKANAGAN commoner. *See* Enderby commoner

Enderby PRESS and Walker's weekly. *See* Enderby commoner

Enderby PROGRESS and Northern Okanagan herald. w My 18 1904-08||?
1904-05 as Edenograph
CaB 1904-S 13 1907

WALKER'S weekly. *See* Enderby commoner

FAIRVIEW

ADVANCE. *See* Midway dispatch (Midway)

FERGUSON

EAGLE. *See* Lardeau eagle

LARDEAU eagle. w F 14 1900-O 7 1904||
F 14 1900 as Eagle; F 21-My 30 1900 Ferguson eagle
CaB complete

FERNIE

DISTRICT ledger. w 1893-Ag 1 1919||?
1893-Ag 2 1905 as Ledge; Ag 9 1905-Ja 11 1908 Fernie ledger
1893-Ag 4 1904 pub at New Denver; Ag 15-O 20 1904 at Nelson
CaB 1897-[Ag 1915-F 1917]-Ag 1 1919
CaO Ap 22 1897-1900

Fernie FREE press. w My 4 1899+
CaB 1899-[1908]+

LEDGE. *See* District ledger

Fernie LEDGER. *See* District ledger

MORRISSEY mention. w Ag 12 1916-Ja 6 1917||
Ag 12-S 21 1916 pub at Morrissey
CaB complete

FORT STEELE

PROSPECTOR. *See under* Cranbrook

GLENORA

Glenora NEWS.
CaB S 16 1898

GOLDEN

EAST KOOTENAY miner. w Ag 29 1897-D 23 1898||
CaB complete

Golden ERA. w 1891-Ap 25 1902||
CaB My 1893-1902

Golden STAR. w 1902+
CaB Ja 22 1904+

Golden TIMES. w D 28 1907-Mr 10 1909||
CaB complete

GRAHAM CENTRE

QUEEN Charlotte islander. *See under* Massett

GRAND FORKS

Grand Forks GAZETTE. d,w 1896+
1896-1900 as Grand Forks gazette; Ja-S 1901 Grand Forks gazette and weekly miner; O 1901-My 10? 1902 Miner-gazette; My 17? 1902-Ap 1 1905 News-gazette
d 1896-Je 12 1900
CaB 1900+

Grand Forks MINER. w 1896-D 24 1898||
United with Grand Forks gazette to form Grand Forks gazette and weekly miner, later Grand Forks gazette
CaB 1897-98

MINER-GAZETTE. *See* Grand Forks gazette

NEWS. w Ag 3 1901-My 17 1902||
United with Miner-gazette to form News-gazette, later Grand Forks gazette
CaB Ag 17 1901-02

NEWS-GAZETTE. *See* Grand Forks gazette

Grand Forks SUN. d,sw,w 1901+
1901-My 3? 1902 as Evening sun
d 1901-My 3? 1902; sw My 6 1902-F 1? 1907
CaB 1902+

GREENWOOD

BOUNDARY creek times. w S 12 1896-D 31 1909||
1900 as Greenwood weekly times
CaB complete

Greenwood LEDGE. w 1894-My 23 1929||
CaB My 17 1906-29

Greenwood MINER. w Ja 1899-Jl 12 1901||
CaB Jl 15 1899-1901
CaO Jl 28 1899-1900

Greenwood weekly TIMES. *See* Boundary Creek times

HAZELTON

OMINECA miner. w S 2 1911-Ag 31 1918||
CaB complete
See also New Hazelton

Hazelton QUEEK. w D 18 1880-Mr 12 1881||
CaB complete

HEDLEY

Hedley GAZETTE and Similkameen advertiser. w Ja 19 1905-Ag 16 1917||
CaB complete

HOPE

Hope NEWS. w O 18 1903-N 7 1903||
CaB complete

KAMLOOPS

INLAND sentinel. *See* Kamloops sentinel

LITTLE Joker. sw Je 22 1898-
CaB Je 22-25 1898

Kamloops SENTINEL. w,sw,tw My 28 1880+
1880-My 15? 1916 as Inland sentinel; My 22? 1916-Jl 10 1924 Kamloops standard sentinel
1880-My 1884 pub at Yale; Je 1884- at Emory
CaB 1880+
CaBV 1880-[Ag 1886-87]-1901

Kamloops STANDARD. w,sw Jl 22 1897-My 26 1916||
United with Inland sentinel to form Kamloops standard-sentinel, later Kamloops sentinel
w 1897-Mr 15 1910
CaB complete
DLC Jl 1903-Je 22 1907

Kamloops STANDARD-SENTINEL. *See* Kamloops sentinel

Kamloops TELEGRAM. w Je 16 1916-Jl 11 1924||
Merged with Kamloops standard-sentinel, later Kamloops sentinel
CaB complete

Kamloops WAWA. m,w,q My 2 1891-D 1904||
In Chinook and shorthand
m 1891-Ja 1892, 94-1900; w 1892-93
CaB 1891-S 1901
CaBV complete

KASLO

BRITISH Columbia news. w,d Jl 9 1897-O 29 1898||
My 1-Jl 10 1898 as Kaslo morning news (d)
CaB complete

Kaslo CLAIM. *See* Kootenaian

KOOTENAIAN. w My 12 1893+
1893-Ap 25 1896 as Kaslo claim
CaB 1893+
CaO My 1896-99

Kaslo morning NEWS. *See* British Columbia news

PROSPECTOR. *See* Rossland prospector (Rossland)

KELOWNA

Kelowna CLARION. . . *See* Kelowna courier . . .

Kelowna COURIER and Okanagan orchardist. w Jl 28 1904+
1904-N 1905 as Kelowna clarion and Okanagan advocate
CaB 1904+

ORCHARD City record. *See* Kelowna record

Kelowna RECORD. w D 3 1908-S 30 1920||
1908-Ja 7 1915 as Orchard City record
CaB complete

KIMBERLEY

Kimberley COURIER. w 1931+
CaB N 5 1931+

PRESS. w Ja 23 1925-My 19 1933||
CaB complete

KINCOLITH

Kincolith TIMES. ir
Typewritten
CaB N 15 1929-F 3,Jl 26-Je 1931;Jl 15 1932-Ja 6 1933

LADNER

DELTA news. *See* Delta times

DELTA times. w F 22 1902-D 25 1909||
1902-Ag 8 1903 as Delta news
CaB 1902-Ag 8,N 21 1903-09

Weekly OPTIMIST. w 1921+
CaB 1922+

SURREY gazette. *See under* White Rock

NEW MICHEL

MICHEL reporter. w 1909||?
CaB Ap 3-D 25 1909

NEW WESTMINSTER

BRITISH Columbia commonwealth. w Ap 20-D 24 1892||?
CaB Ap 27-D 24 1892

BRITISH Columbian. sw,w F 13 1861+
Mr 16-Jl 25 1869 pub at Victoria
sw 1861-Jl 1886
CU-B D 5 1863;F 18-23,28-Mr 2,Ap 27-29,My 18-23,30-Je 1865;Mr 13-16,30-Ap 3,10,17-20,27 My 1,8-15,22,29-Je 1867;Jl 1886-[87-88]89[F 26 1890-91]
CaB 1861-[62-81]+
CaBNH 1861+
CaBVi F 1864-F 1868[69-Je 1890;1900-02;04;Jl 1914-Ja 1915;Jl 1916-20;27]+
CU-B O 1,26,N 2 1886
CaO D 1897-Je 1901

BRITISH Columbian examiner. w,sw N 9 1866-D 28 1868||
My 18 1868 pub in Yale
w 1866-Jl 20 1868
CU-B [Je 29 1867-Je 1868]
CaB N-D 16 1866;Mr 11,Jl 20,D 7,28 1868

DOMINION Pacific herald. w 1870-D 24 1881||
CU-B [Ja 13 1872-N 1873;Mr 21 1874-F 3,Je 6 1877;Ja 23 1878-S 1879;Jl-D 1880]
CaB F 22 1873;Je 21 1876;79-81
CaBNH O 16 1880-81

EXPRESS. w Ag 25 1905-D 27 1910||
CaB complete

FRASER River champion. w 1895-96||?
CaB 1896-S 12 1896

GOVERNMENT gazette. *See* British Columbia gazette (Victoria)

Morning LEDGER. d S 5 1889-91||
1889-90 as Truth
CaB 1889-90;Jl 3-D 6 1891

MAINLAND guardian. sw,d 1869-89||
sw 1869-73
CU-B Ja 23 1878-S 27 1879;Jl 7 1888-Ja 2 1889
CaB Mr 30,S 30,O 4 1871[72-73]-[75-78]-Ag 21 1889
CaBNH Ag 28 1869-Ag 27 1870
CaBVR [Ap 3 1872-Ag 27 1873]-[Ap 8-O 7 1874]
CaBVi Ag 1870-85
CaO Ag 28 1869-86

Daily NEWS. d Mr 5 1906-S 4 1914||
CaB 1906-Je 1908[09]-14

NORTH Pacific times and British Columbian advertiser. sw,tw N 2 1864-
tw 1864-F 27 1865
CaB 1864-My 5 1865

PACIFIC Canadian. w S 16 1893-My 19 1894||
CaB complete

PACIFIC Canadian. w Mr 10 1916-Mr 30 1917||
CaB complete

SCORPION. sm Mr 11 1864-My 16 1864||
CaB complete
CaBNH complete

New Westminster daily SUN. d Ap 9 1898-Je 30 1898||
CaB complete

New Westminster TIMES. w S 17 1859-
O 4-D 3 1859 as New Westminster times and Vancouver Island guardian
1859-Mr 10 1860 pub in Victoria
CaB 1859-[Mr 17-Ag 8 1860]-F 1861

TRUTH. *See* Morning ledger

NICOLA

Nicola HERALD. *See* Merritt herald (Merritt)

NORTH VANCOUVER

NORTH Shore press. sw 1905+
CaB 1913+
WaPS [1925]-[27-30]-33

PARKSVILLE

Parksville-QUALICUM journal. *See under* Courtenay

PENTICTON

Penticton HERALD. w Jl 2 1910+
CaB Jl 9 1910+

Penticton PRESS. w 1905-09||?
CaB N 2 1907-D 25 1909

PHOENIX

Phoenix PIONEER. w 1899-My 27 1916||
CaB 1900-16

POPLAR

NUGGET. w D 4 1903-N 25 1904||
CaB complete

PORT ALBERNI

ALBERNI pioneer news. *See* Port Alberni news

Port Alberni NEWS. w Ag 17 1907+
1907-F 24 1913 as Alberni pioneer news
1907-N 1910 pub at Alberni
CaB 1907+

WEST Coast advocate. w 1930+
CaB 1934+

PORT COQUITLAM

COQUITLAM herald. w 1929+
CaB Je 14 1934;Ap 1935+

COQUITLAM-Moody news. *See* Coquitlam times

COQUITLAM news. *See* Coquitlam times

COQUITLAM star. w 1909-15||?
CaB S 8 1911-N 12 1915

BRITISH COLUMBIA (*Continued*)

PORT COQUITLAM—*Continued*

COQUITLAM times. w 1921-29||
1921-24 as Coquitlam news; 1925-26 Coquitlam Moody-news
CaB [1921-25]-My 1929

Port Coquitlam REVIEW. w O 16 1914-Jl 16 1915||
CaB complete

PORT ESSINGTON

Port Essington LOYALIST. w 1908-09||?
CaB Ja 30 1909-Ag 7 1909

SKEENA district news. w 1903-04||
CaB Ja 9-Ag 22 1904

SUN. w My 18 1907-Ja 25 1908||
CaB complete

PORT HAMMOND

HAMMOND, Haney and Coquitlam gazette. *See* Maple Ridge and Pitt Meadows gazette (Port Haney)

PORT HANEY

AGASSIZ advance. w
CaB Je 1930-Mr 21 1933

HAMMOND, Haney and Coquitlam gazette. *See* Maple Ridge and Pitt Meadows gazette

MAPLE Ridge and Pitt Meadows gazette. w 1918+
1918-Ap 26 1923 as Hammond, Haney and Coquitlam gazette (Port Hammond)
CaB Mr 23 1922+

LADYSMITH

Ladysmith CHRONICLE. sw,w N 21 1908+
sw 1908-N 1918
pub D 7 1918+
CaB 1908+

Ladysmith LEADER and Wellington extension news. sw
CaB 1902

Ladysmith daily LEDGER. d 1903-D 29 1906||
CaB O 1904-05

Ladysmith STANDARD. sw 1908||?
Merged with Ladysmith chronicle
CaB Ja 11-D 27 1908

LANGLEY PRAIRIE

Langley ADVANCE. w 1931+
CaB Ja 19 1933+

VALLEY sentinel. w
CaB Mr 26-My 24 1921

LARDO

Lardo REPORTER.
Printed on wall-paper
CaB Jl 24 1893

LILLOOET

Lillooet ADVANCE. w 1910-11||
CaB Ja 14-Ag 26 1911

BRIDGE River-Lillooet news. w Mr 1 1934+
CaB 1934+

Lillooet PROSPECTOR. w Je 14 1898-Ap 24 1917||
CaB 1898[Mr 12-D 1904]-[D 14 1905-N 17 1911]-17
CaO Jl 22 1898-1900

McBRIDE

JOURNAL. w 1914-D 22 1933||
CaB My 14 1914[My 1917-N 1931]-33

MASSETT

QUEEN Charlotte islander. w Ag 24 1911-O 17 1914||
1911-Mr 4 1914 pub at Queen Charlotte; Mr 11-Ap 1914 at Graham Centre
CaB complete

MERRITT

Merritt HERALD and Nicola Valley advocate. w My 18 1905+
1905-Ag 20 1909 as Nicola herald (Nicola)
CaB 1905+

NICOLA Valley news. w F 18 1910-S 29 1916||
CaB complete

MIDWAY

ADVANCE. *See* Midway dispatch

Midway DISPATCH. w Ap 26 1894-S 3 1904||
1894-Je 30 1902 as Advance
Ap-Ag 5 1894 pub at Fairview
CaB complete
CaO 1897-1903

MISSION CITY

FRASER Valley Record. w Je 18 1908+
CaB 1908+

MORRISSEY

Morrissey MENTION. *See under* Fernie

Morrissey MINER. w 1902-Ap 25 1903||
CaB Ja 31-Ap 25 1903

MOUNT PLEASANT

Mount Pleasant ADVOCATE. w 1899-1909||?
CaB 1904-D 14 1907

MOYIE

Moyie LEADER. w Ap 16 1898-Ap 28 1911||
CaB Ap 23 1898-1911

NAKUSP

ARROW Lakes news. w Je 28 1922+
CaB 1922+

Nakusp LEDGE. w O 5 1893-D 26 1895||
CaB complete

NANAIMO

Nanaimo COURIER. d D 20 1888-Jl 31 1889||
CaB complete

Nanaimo FREE press. sw,d Ap 15 1874+
sw 1874-N 1888
CU-B Ap-Ag 15 1874;S 18-D 1878;S 20-D 1879;My 12,19 1880;Jl 1887-Je 1888[F 1889-Jl 1890]
CaB 1874-[Jl-D 1878]+
OClWHi Ag 8 1888

Nanaimo GAZETTE. *See* Nanaimo tribune

Daily HERALD. sw,d Jl 22 1899+
1899-F 1901 as Nanaimo herald (sw)
CaB 1899+

Nanaimo MAIL. w,sw
w -My 16 1896
CaB F 15-D 1896

REVIEW. w,sw Ap 17 1897-D 24 1898||
w Ap-N 23 1897
CaB complete

Nanaimo TRIBUNE. w Jl 10 1865-Ag 31 1867||
1865-Jl 7 1866 as Nanaimo gazette
CU-B Ap-Je 2,Ag 25 1866-[67]
CaB 1865-[Je-Ag]-D 8 1866;Jl 20 1867

WESTWARD ho! ir
CaB Mr 4-Ag 21 1886

NELSON

Nelson CANADIAN. d Je 4 1906-My 2 1908||
CaB complete

Nelson ECONOMIST. w Jl 14 1897-D 30 1905||
CaB 1897-[1900]-[02]-05

KOOTENAY times. w
CaB My 4-N 2 1923

LEDGE. *See* District ledger (Fernie)

Nelson daily MINER. w,d Je 1890-Ap 20 1902||
1893-My 7 1898 as Miner (w)
CaB Ag 19 1893-1902
CaO 1896-Je 1901
MnHi S 18-25 1897

Daily NEWS. d Ap 22 1902+
CaB 1902+

TRIBUNE. w,d Ja 5 1892-N 11 1905||
w 1892-Ja 14? 1899
CaB 1892-[95-96]-1905

NEW DENVER

LEDGE. *See* District ledger (Fernie)

SLOCAN herald. w My 4-D 15 1933||
CaB complete

SLOCAN mining review. w Ag 31 1906-N 5 1908||
1906-O 1907 pub at Sandon
CaB S 1906-08

SLOCAN times. w
CaB Ag 25-D 27 1894

NEW HAZELTON

OMINECA herald. w 1907+
CaB 1908+

PORT MOODY

Port Moody ADVOCATE. w S 10 1925-Mr 30 1929||
CaB S 17 1925-29

Port Moody GAZETTE. w D 15 1883-My 14 1887||
CaB [1883-87]
CaBNH complete
CaBVR D 22 1883-87

PORT SIMPSON

NORTH coast. w
CaB [Ag 15 1907-Ap 18 1908]

POWELL RIVER

Powell River NEWS. w N 3 1927+
CaB 1927+

PRINCE GEORGE

Prince George CITIZEN. w My 17 1916+
CaB 1916+

Prince George HERALD. w Ag 20 1910-Ja 29 1916||
1910-My 14 1915 as Fort George herald (South Fort George)
CaB complete

LEADER. w Mr 11 1921-Mr 15 1923||
CaB Mr 18 1921-23

Prince George POST. w N 21 1914-O 9 1915||
CaB complete

Prince George STAR. w 1916-17||?
CaB O 1916-My 22 1917

PRINCE RUPERT

EMPIRE. w Jl 20 1907-Ja 30 1932||
CaB 1907-[10-17]Mr 1918-32
CaM 1909-17

Evening EMPIRE. d 1909+
CaB F 1911+

Daily NEWS. d My 2 1910+
1910-Ap 29 1911 as Prince Rupert optimist
CaB 1910+

Prince Rupert OPTIMIST. *See* Daily news

PLAIN dealer. w
CaB F-Ap 9 1921

PRINCETON

SIMILKAMEEN star. *See* Princeton star

Princeton STAR. w Mr 31 1900+
1900-My 10 1918 as Similkameen star
CaB 1900+

WRANGLER. w My 13 1933-
CaB My 13,29 1933

QUEEN CHARLOTTE

Queen Charlotte ISLANDER. *See under* Massett

Queen Charlotte NEWS. w Ap 4 1908-16||?
CaB 1908-D 20 1913

QUESNEL

CARIBOO observer. w Ag 29 1908+
CaB S 1908+

REVELSTOKE

HERALD. sw Ja 18 1897-D 28 1905||
United with Kootenay mail to form Mail herald
CaB complete

KOOTENAY mail. *See* Mail herald

KOOTENAY star. w Je 7 1890-94||
CaB 1890-Mr 31 1894

MAIL-HERALD. sw,w Ap 14 1894-D 30 1916||
1894-1905 as Kootenay herald
sw 1906-15
CaB complete

OBSERVER. w D 4 1908-Ag 20 1909||
CaB complete

Revelstoke REVIEW. w 1913+
CaB Ag 1916+

ROLLA

PEACE River block news. *See under* Dawson Creek

ROSSLAND

Rossland LEADER. d Je 21-N 1 1898||
CaB complete

Rossland MINER. w,sw,d Mr 28 1895+
d 1896-Ja 1919
CaB 1895[96]+
CaO 1896-Je 1901

MINING review. w 1896-97||?
CaB Ja-Ap 1897

Rossland PROSPECTOR. w Ja 4-D 27 1895||?
Ja-Mr 1895 as Slocan prospector (Three Forks); Ap-Ag 1 1895 Prospector (Kaslo)
CaB Ja-Mr 23,Ap 11-Ag 1,28-D 1895

Evening RECORD. d 1896-1900||?
CaB Ja 23 1897-D 7 1900

ROSSLANDER and Kootenay mining journal. w 1893-98||
1893-Jl 13 1897 as Rosslander
CaB 1897-Jl 12 1898

Rossland STAR. d 1905-06||
CaB D 1 1905-F 1 1906

TIMES. w O 30 1897-99||
CaB 1897-F 18 1899

Evening WORLD. d Ja 1901-04||?
CaB Jl 1901-Je 1904

SALMON ARM

Salmon Arm OBSERVER. w O 10 1907+
CaB 1907+

BRITISH COLUMBIA (*Continued*)

SANDON

MINING review. w Je 12 1897-1903||?
CaB 1897-Jl 18 1903
CaO 1897-1900

Sandon **MINING** standard. w Ja 2 1904-Ag 2 1906||
1904-My 6 1905 as Sandon standard
CaB complete

SLOCAN mining review. *See under* New Denver

Sandon **STANDARD.** *See* Sandon mining standard

SIDNEY

SAANICH Peninsula and Gulf Islands review. *See* Sidney and Islands review

SIDNEY and Islands review. w 1912+
Ag 19-D 12 1918 as Saanich Peninsula and Gulf Islands review
CaB 1914+

SILVERTON

Silverton **SILVERTONIAN.** w 1897-1901||
CaB 1898-S 14 1901

SLOCAN

Slocan **DRILL.** w Ap 6 1900-My 12 1905||
CaB complete

Slocan **ENTERPRISE.** w 1924+
1924-D 7 1933 as Silver standard
CaB Ap 1929+

Slocan **NEWS.** w D 1896-98||?
CaB Ja 23 1897-S 3 1898

Slocan **PIONEER.** w My 1-D 25 1897||
CaB complete

SILVER standard. *See* Slocan enterprise

SMITHERS

INTERIOR news. w 1908+
1908-Ag 12 1915 pub at Aldermere
CaB 1910+

Smithers **TRIBUNE.** w Ag 16 1913-14||?
Ag-O 18 1913 as Telkwa tribune (Telkwa)
CaB 1913-S 5 1914

SOUTH FORT GEORGE

FORT George herald. *See* Prince George herald (Prince George)

STEWART

CASSIAR news. *See* Stewart news

Stewart **NEWS.** w My 30 1919+
My 30-Ag 1 1919 as Cassiar news; Ag 8 1919-Mr 31 1928 Portland canal news
Suspended from D 2 1932-Je 22 1934
CaB 1919+

NORTHERN argonaut. w My 30 1934+
CaB 1934+

PORTLAND Canal miner. w F 5 1910-1914||?
CaB 1910-S 1911

PORTLAND canal news. *See* Stewart news

SUMMERLAND

Summerland **REVIEW.** w O 30 1908-O 1 1929||
Merged with Penticton herald (Penticton)
CaB complete

TELKWA

Telkwa **TRIBUNE.** *See* Smithers tribune (Smithers)

THREE FORKS

SLOCAN prospector. *See* Rossland prospector (Rossland)

TRAIL

Trail daily **BULLETIN** and the Trail news. *See* Trail news

Trail **CREEK** miner. w My 5 1897-N Jl 14 1897

Trail **CREEK** news. *See* Trail news

Trail **NEWS.** d 1895+
1895-N 5 1904 as Trail Creek news; N 12 1904-D 3 1925 Trail news; D 10 1925-Ap 21 1928 Trail daily bulletin and the Trail news
CaB F 1896-[1900-Ja 16 1904]+
WaPS [1924-26]

TROUT LAKE CITY

LARDEAU mining review. w O 21 1897-S 5 1907||
1897-N 4 1904 as Trout Lake topic
CaB 1897-[1902]-07

Trout Lake **TOPIC.** *See* Lardeau mining review

UNION

Weekly **NEWS.** w 1892-97||
1892-O 10 1894 pub at Courtenay
CaB 1893-N 29 1897
MWA Jl 20 1897

VANCOUVER

ADVERTISER. w 1931+
CaB Mr 22 1935+

AL. HARDY'S green sheet. w 1920-
CaB N 26 1929-Mr 23 1930

ALMADENE-DUNBAR news. w S 22 1927-29||?
S 22-O 13 1927 as Dunbar district news
CaB 1927-Ap 1929

BRITISH Columbia budget. w Mr 24 1894-Jl 13 1895||
Mr-S 15 1894 as Light; S 22 1894-Mr 16 1895 Mainlander
CaB complete

BRITISH eye-opener. w Jl 30 1932-
CaB Jl-D 10 1932

CANADA Skandinaven. w N 29 1911-28||?
Ja 31 1919-O 12 1923 as Norseman
In Swedish
CaB 1911-O 12 1923;N 20 1925-N 1928

CANADA tribunen. w 1918-19||?
In Swedish
CaB My 9-S 9 1919

Saturday **CHINOOK.** *See* Standard

CITIZEN-GAZETTE. w 1906-31||?
1906-27? as Citizen
CaB D 1907-[10-22]

COMMONWEALTH. d My 17 1933+
CaB 1933+

CRITIC. w Ag 11 1917-19||?
CaB 1917-O 1919

DUNBAR district news. *See* Almadene-Dunbar news

EXPRESS. sw Ag 25 1905-D 30 1910||
CaB complete

FINANCIAL news. w 1927+
CaB Je 1930+
CaQME Ap 1934+

Weekly **GAZETTE.** *See* Point Grey news-gazette

GREATER Vancouver chinook. *See* Standard

Daily **HERALD.** d 1887-88||
CaB Jl 22 1887-Je 30 1888

HOOK. *See* Western tribune

J.P.'s weekly. w Ja 1-O 7 1916||
CaBVR complete

JEWISH western bulletin. w 1930+
CaB Mr 28 1935+

KITSILANO times. w
CaB Mr 23 1918-[N 30 1922-S 13]-[D 20 1924-Ag 1]-[S-D 1925]-Ag 3 1929

Vancouver daily **LEDGER.** d 1901-04||?
CaB D 29 1902-Mr 1903

LIBERAL advocate. w F 12 1935+
CaB 1935+

LIGHT. *See* British Columbia budget

MAINLANDER. *See* British Columbia budget

MARPOLE-Richmond review. w 1932+
CaB Mr 28 1935+

MONITOR. w D 24 1892-93||?
CaB 1892-Ap 8 1893

MOUNT Pleasant herald. w 1926-27||?
CaB S 30 1926-D 23 1927

MOUNT Pleasant news. w 1920+
CaB Ja 26 1928-My 17 1928

Vancouver **NEWS.** d N 1 1932-Ap 8 1933||
CaB complete
CaBV complete

Daily **NEWS-ADVERTISER.** d Je 1 1886-Ag 31 1917||
1886-Mr 29 1887 as Vancouver news; Mr 31-My 12 1887 Vancouver news and daily advertiser. Merged with Vancouver daily sun, later Vancouver morning sun
CU-B D 31 1889-Ja 1,3-4 1890
CaB 1886-[Ja-Je 1888]-[89;Ap-Je 1903]-17
CaBU 1886-1915
CaBV Jl 1899-[1902]-17
CaO 1909-17
DLC D 1899-1917

Weekly **NEWS-ADVERTISER.** w S 19 1888-1913||?
CaB F 25-Je 24 1902
CaBU 1888-Ag 17 1909

NEWS-HERALD. d Ap 24 1933+
CaB 1933+
CaBV 1933+

NORSEMAN. *See* Canada Skandinaven

PEOPLE'S journal. w F 18 1893-
CaB F 18-Je 3 1893

POINT Grey gazette. *See* Point Grey news-gazette

POINT Grey news-gazette. w 1908+
1908-Je 12 1930 as Point Grey gazette (F 27 1915-Jl 30 1921 Weekly gazette)
CaB Ja 9 1909+

Vancouver **POSTEN.** w 1929+
In Swedish
CaB F 1930+

Vancouver **PROVINCE.** w Mr 3 1894+
1894-D 25 1897 as Province (Victoria)
CaB 1894-97
CaBV [1894]F 2,My 18 1895[96-Mr 1898]
CaO 1897-Je 1901

Daily **PROVINCE.** d Mr 26 1898+
Mr 26 1928 is sesqui-centennial no.
CSt Je 1933+
CU-B Je 27 1927
CaB 1898-[Ja-Je 1904]+
CaBU 1906-[16-25;29-31]+
CaBV Ap 1898;Jl-D 1899;F 1900-Ja,Mr-Ap,Je 1902-O,D 1904+
CaO Mr 1930+
CaQ 1927+
MWA Mr 26 1928

REVIEW. w 1926+
CaB S 15 1932+

Vancouver **SOUTH** echo. w 1931+
CaB [S 3 1931+]

SOUTH Vancouver leader-advocate. w 1919-23||?
CaB S 1922-[Ap-N 6 1923]

SOUTH Vancouver news. w 1927+
CaB Mr 28 1927+

STANDARD. w 1912-D 30 1916||
1912-S 11 1915 as Greater Vancouver chinook; S 18 1915-Ap 15 1916 Saturday chinook
CaB 1913-16

Vancouver morning **STAR.** d Je 2 1924-F 12 1932||
CaB complete
CaBV complete
DLC F 1926-Ag 11 1930

STATISTIC news-advertiser. sm
CaB Ja 18-D 4 1895

Vancouver **SUN.** d S 29 1888+
1888-Mr 11 1924 as Vancouver daily world
CaB 1888-[Ja-Je 1903]+
CaBU 1906-[16-30]+
CaBV [Jl 1899-1900]-My,Jl 1902-O,D 1904-Mr,My 1905+
CaO 1889-Je 1901
DLC 1930+
KHi Jl 6-N 9 1897;D 4 1898
NbHi Ja 6 1893

Vancouver morning **SUN.** d F 12 1912-Ja 31 1926||
1912-Ap 18 1920 as Vancouver daily sun; Ap 19 1920-My 15 1924 Vancouver sun
CaB complete
CaBU Ja 1913[16-26]
CaBV complete
CaO S 1917-21
DLC Jl 1918-26

SVENSKA Canada kuriren. 1914||
In Swedish
IRA complete

SVENSKA pressen. w D 24 1928+
In Swedish
CaB F 1929-[D 1933-Mr 8 1934]+

SVENSKA Vancouver posten. w 1910-14||
In Swedish
IRA [1910-14]
MnHi Mr 3 1912;F 24,Mr 17,31,Ap 14,28 1914

Daily **TELEGRAM.** d 1890-94||
CaB Jl 31 1890-My 1 1894
NbHi Ag 31 1892

Saturday **TRIBUNE.** *See* Western tribune

WEST Vancouver leader. w 1934+
CaB Ja 24 1935+

WEST Vancouver news. w 1926+
CaB Mr 20 1931+

WESTERN call. w 1909-16||
CaB Ja 7 1910-Je 30 1916

WESTERN idea. w Je 25-S 3 1920||
CaBVR complete

WESTERN tribune. w Je 22 1923+
1923-S 26 1924 as Hook; O 4 1924-D 29 1928 Saturday tribune
CaB 1923-N 2 1929

Vancouver daily **WORLD.** *See* Vancouver sun

Vancouver semi-weekly **WORLD.** sw
CaB 1902[03-05]-09
CaBV [Jl 27 1897-Mr 1900]

YALE review. w F 18-My 27 1905||
CaB complete

VANDERHOOF

Vanderhoof **HERALD.** w 1914-20||
CaB D 1917-F 21 1920

NECHAKO chronicle. w Mr 20 1920+
CaB 1920+

VERNON

Vernon **NEWS.** w My 14 1891+
CaB My 21 1891+

OKANAGAN. sw 1905-09||
CaB Mr 13 1906-D 30 1909

VICTORIA

ADVERTISER. w D 2 1874-
CaB D 2,29 1874

Daily **BRITISH** colonist. *See* Daily colonist

Weekly **BRITISH** colonist. *See* Colonist

BRITISH COLUMBIA (*Continued*)

VICTORIA—*Continued*

BRITISH Columbia gazette. w Ja 3 1863+
1863-70 as Government gazette
1863-My 23? 1868 pub at New Westminster
CU-B 1863-My 1864;O 15 1870;Ag 9 1873
CaB 1863+
CaOOA 1907+
CaOT 1919+
CaQMM 1899-1915
DLC 1866-85;90+
NN 1900+

BRITISH Columbian. *See under* New Westminster

Victoria daily CHRONICLE. d O 28 1862-Je 23 1866||
United with Daily British colonist to form Daily British colonist and Victoria chronicle, later Daily colonist
CU-B F 27 1866
CaB complete
CaBV Mr-O 27 1864

Victoria weekly CHRONICLE. w 1862-66||?
CU-B Je 22 1866
CaB My 3 1864;Jl 26-Ag 2,23-30 1864;Jl 4,Ag 22,D 19-26 1865

Daily COLONIST. tw,d D 11 1858+
1858-Jl 28 1860 as British colonist; Jl 31 1860-Je 23 1866 Daily British colonist; Je 25 1866-D 31 1886 Daily British colonist and Victoria chronicle
tw 1858-Jl 28 1860
D 10 1933 is 75th anniversary number
CL D 10 1933
CSmH D 11 1858
CSt-H [1915-16]
CU-B [D 21 1863-79]Ap 27,O 21-23 1880[86-Je 1888;89-91]
CaB D 11 1858[65;68]+
CaBU Je 13 1859-62
CaBV D 1859[60]-Je 10 1861[Je-O 1862]
CaBVi 1882-[Ja-Je 1890]+
CaM 1910-23
CaO 1863+
CaOOA 1859-62;Ag 11,18,25 1918
DLC D 8 1899+
KHi Jl 15-22 1897
OrHi Je 13 1859-Je 10 1862
WHi Ag 11,18,S 22,28,N 28 1912+
WaPS F 7-20,Mr 1913-33
WaU 1858-D 10 1862

COLONIST. w,sw D 3 1859-1917||?
1859-88 as Weekly British colonist; 1896- Semi-weekly colonist
C O 31 1868
CU-B [1864-65;Ap 1866-Ag 21]S 8-N 20,D 22 1869-Je 14,D 20 1871;Ja 17-Ap,O 23-D 18 1872;Ja-My 21,S-N 1873;Ja 14-D 9 1874;O 1875-79;Ap 23-My 19 1880;Ap 18-25,My 23,S 19 1883;My 7 1884;Ja 17,31,Je 27 1890;O 7 1892
CaB 1859-N 8 1864
CaBU D 10 1859-N 11 1862
MWA Ap 16 1859
WHi Ja 21 1896-Ag 9 1912
WaU Jl 17,31 1869[Ja 19 1870-Ag 7 1872]

Le COURIER de la Nouvelle Caledonia. ir S 11 1858-
In French
CaB S 11-O 9 1858

Daily evening EXPRESS. d Ap 27 1863-F 12 1865||
United with Vancouver times to form Vancouver times and evening express, later Vancouver daily post
CU-B Je 22 1864
CaB complete

Daily Victoria GAZETTE. tw,d Je 25 1858-N 24 1859||
Je 25-Jl 23 1858 as Victoria gazette
tw Je 25-Jl 23 1858
CU-B 1858-Je 23 1859
CaB complete
CaBNH [Jl 28-O 25]-D 1858
CaBV [Jl 1858-59]
MWA S 9 1858

Weekly Victoria GAZETTE. w Ag 13 1858-N 26 1859||
CaB Ag 14[D]1858-59
CaBV Ag 21-S 4 1858;Ja 15-22 1859
MWA S 25 1858
N Ag 14 1858
WHi Jl 21 1858
—Steamer ed. ir
CaB F 5,Ap 8,Je 9,Jl 5,Ag 20 1859

Victoria GAZETTE. tw,w D 5 1859-S 29 1860||
not to be confused with Victoria gazette 1858-59
w Ag 4-S 29 1860
CU-B N 5 1859
CaB complete

Victoria daily GLOBE. d F-S 21 1899||
CaB Mr 10-S 1899

HONEST Injun; delate wa-wa tolo. ir
CaBVR O 23,N 6 1897

ISLANDER. w Ja 13-Ap 21 1867||
CaBVR complete

LANCE. w Je 13-N 7 1925||
CaB complete

NEW Westminster times. *See under* New Westminster

Morning NEWS. d
CaB Mr 29,Je 5 1867

Daily NEWS. d F 9-S 11 1892||
CaB complete

NEWS letter for Vancouver Island and New Caledonia.
CaB S 25 1858

Daily evening POST. d My 20 1882-My 7 1887||
CaB complete
CaBVi complete

Evening POST. d Ap 1-N 29 1909||
CaB complete

Saturday POST. w F 16-N 9 1901||
Scattered numbers as Victoria post
CaB complete

PRESS. d Mr 9 1861-O 16 1862||
CU-B Jl 3 1862
CaB [1861-62]

Victoria PRICES current and shipping list.
Pub. in time for every mail steamer
CaB D 27 1865-Mr 26 1866

PROGRESS. *See* Week

PROVINCE. *See* Vancouver province (Vancouver)

SPOKESMAN. *See under* Duncan

Evening STANDARD. d Je 20 1870-Ag 31 1889||
1870-Ag 4 1888 as Victoria daily standard
CU-B Ag 23 1876-78;Ap-D 1879
CaB complete
CaBVi 1882-[Jl-D 1883]-Je 1888;Ja-Je 1889
WaU [Je 22-D 10 1870]

Victoria weekly STANDARD. w 1870-89||?
CU-B S 24 1873-My 12 1880
CaB Ja 20 1886-Ag 2 1889
CaOTA D 9 1874

SUBURB and country. w Jl 30-D 21 1904||
CaB complete

Evening TELEGRAPH. d Jl 3 1866-
CaB Jl 5-N 13 1866

Victoria daily TIMES. d Je 9 1884+
CaB 1884-[Ja-Je 1888]+
CaBU N 1927+
CaBVi 1884+
CaO D 22 1885+

Semi-weekly TRIBUNE. sw O 7 1918-N 3 1919||
CaB complete

TRUTH. w Ja 8-Ap 8 1904||
CaB F 5-Ap 8 1904

VANCOUVER Island gazette. ir Jl 28 1858-S 1859||
Merged with New Westminster times (New Westminster)
CaB Jl 28,Ag 4,9 1858

VANCOUVER daily post. d S 5 1864-Ap 29 1866||
1864-Mr 31 1865 as Vancouver times; Ap 9-Ag 10 1865 Vancouver times and evening express
CaB complete

VANCOUVER times. *See* Vancouver daily post

WEEK. w Ap 16 1904-My 8 1920||
Ap-D 17 1904 as Progress
CaB 1904-[Jl 20 1918-Ap]My 1920

WARDNER

INTERNATIONAL. w Je 17 1897-Je 23 1898||
CaB S 23 1897-98

WELLINGTON

ENTERPRISE. w 1894-D 30 1898||?
CaB 1895-98

Wellington NEWS. w Jl 20 1894-O 12 1894||
CaB complete

WHITE ROCK

SEMIAHMOO gazette. *See* Surrey gazette

SURREY gazette. m,sm,w 1912-O 17 1929||
1912-S 1915 as Semiahmoo gazette.
Merged with Surrey leader (Cloverdale)
no 1-3 pub at Ladner
CaB F 1923-29
CaBVR Mr 1913-My 2 1918

WILLIAMS LAKE

TRIBUNE. w Ap 23 1931+
CaB 1931+

WILMER

OUTCROP. w 1900-D 27 1906||?
1900-My 1902 pub at Canterbury
CaB 1901-06

YALE

BRITISH Columbia tribune. w Ap 10 1865-O 8 1866||
CaB complete

BRITISH Columbian examiner. *See under* New Westminster

INLAND sentinel. *See* Kamloops sentinel (Kamloops)

Yale REVIEW. *See under* Vancouver

YMIR

Ymir HERALD. w 1901-05||?
1901-Ap 30 1904 as Ymir mirror
CaB 1904-D 30 1905

Ymir MIRROR. *See* Ymir herald

MANITOBA

ARNAUD

Arnaud ADVANCE. w My 6 1904-06||?
In French and English
CaM 1904-Jl 27 1906

BALDUR

Baldur GAZETTE. w 1898+
pub 1898+
CaM 1898+

BEAUSEJOUR

Beausejour NEWS. w My 7 1920-My 21 1926||
CaM My 21 1920-26

Beausejour TIMES. w O 11 1909-My 13 1911||
CaM 1910-11

BELMONT

Belmont EYE. w S 5 1902-03||?
Followed by Belmont news
CaM N 22 1902-Mr 7 1903

Belmont NEWS. w My 8 1903+
Follows Belmont eye
CaM 1903-D 17 1931

Belmont STAR. w Ja 5 1899-Ap 20 1900||
CaM complete

BINSCARTH

Binscarth EXPRESS. w 1910+
CaM 1917+

BIRTLE

Birtle EYE-WITNESS. w 1891+
CaM 1891+

BOISSEVAIN

Boissevain GLOBE. w S 4 1890-D 25 1913||
Merged with Boissevain recorder
CaM complete

Boissevain RECORDER. w 1899+
CaM 1899+

BRANDON

Brandon BLADE. w O 4 1883-Mr 27 1884||
CaM N 1883-84

Brandon INDEPENDENT. w N 27 1897-Ap 23 1903||
Some numbers as Brandon independence
CaM My 5 1898-1903

Brandon daily MAIL. d D 19 1882-98||
CaM 1883-97
CaO S 28 1883-86

Brandon daily SUN. d Ja 13 1882+
pub S 1897;99;1906+
CaM 1884+
CaMB 1932+
CaO Mr 2 1882-Je 29 1901
CaOOA 1917+
WHi N 2 1912

Brandon weekly SUN. w 1882+
CaOOA [1912]+
Ct [S 1912-13]-20
DLC Je 30 1927
MnHi [My 20-D 1915]-[20]
WHi S 5 1912-N 18 1913

MANITOBA (*Continued*)

BRANDON—*Continued*

Brandon TIMES. w Je 10 1886-1913||
CaM 1886-1908
CaO Je 17 1886-1900
Ct [1912-13]

CARBERRY

Carberry EXPRESS. w 1892-1909||
United with Carberry news to form Carberry news-express
CaM complete

Carberry NEWS-EXPRESS. w 1889+
1889-1909 as Carberry news
CaM 1889+

CARMAN

DUFFERIN leader. w 1898+
CaM 1898+

Carman STANDARD. w Jl 15 1890-S 28 1916||
CaM complete

CARTWRIGHT

ROCK Lake review. *See* Southern Manitoba review

SOUTHERN Manitoba review. w 1899+
1899-1903 as Rock Lake review
CaM 1899+

CRYSTAL CITY

Crystal City COURIER. w 1897+
CaM 1898+

CYPRESS RIVER

Cypress River WESTERN prairie. w My 21 1897-N 30 1922||
CaM complete

DARLINGFORD

Darlingford COMET. w Ap 28 1910-Ap 24 1913||
CaM My 1910-13

DAUPHIN

Dauphin HERALD and press. w 1899+
1899-1917 as Dauphin herald
CaM 1899+

Dauphin weekly NEWS. w Mr 3 1899-Jl 16 1902||
CaM complete

Dauphin PRESS. w 1891-Ap 5 1917||
United with Dauphin herald to form Dauphin herald and press
CaM complete

DELORAINE

Deloraine ADVERTISER. w Ap 27 1899-Je 24 1908||
Follows Deloraine advertiser and Napinka gazette
CaM complete

Deloraine ADVERTISER and Napinka gazette. w Jl 7 1898-Mr 23 1899||
1898-Ja 12 1899 as Napinka gazette (Napinka) Followed by Deloraine advertiser
CaM complete

Deloraine TIMES and Waskada news. w N 1887+
CaM 1887+
CaO Jl 4 1889-D 28 1893

DOMINION CITY

Dominion City ECHO. w D 8 1898-D 7 1923||
Merged with Dominion City star
CaM D 22 1898-1923

Dominion City STAR. w 1904+
CaM 1926+

ELGIN

Elgin BANNER. w Mr 21 1901-D 21 1916||
CaM complete

Elgin LANCET. w 1917+
CaM Ja 14 1920-28

ELKHORN

Elkhorn ADVOCATE. w O 13 1892-D 22 1910||
CaM complete

Elkhorn MERCURY. w 1908+
CaM 1908+

ELMWOOD

Papers published in Elmwood are listed under Winnipeg

EMERSON

Emerson INTERNATIONAL. w D 26 1878-89||
CaM 1883-89
CaO D 26 1878-Ag 10 1882

Emerson JOURNAL. w 1895+
CaM 1895+

SOUTHERN Manitoba times. w 1881-Je 30 1893||
CaM Ap 22 1886-93

FLINFLON

Flinflon MINER. w 1931+
CaM 1931+

GILBERT PLAINS

MAPLE leaf. w 1901+
pub 1901+
CaM 1917+

GIMLI

GIMLUNGUR. w Mr 30 1910-
In Icelandic
CaM 1910-S 16 1911

GLADSTONE

Gladstone AGE. w My 1884+
CaM 1884+
CaO Ja 31 1885-86

GLENBORO

Glenboro GAZETTE. *See* Western prairie gazette

WESTERN prairie gazette. w Ag 25 1892+
1892- 1922 as Glenboro gazette
CaM S 1 1892+

GRANDVIEW

Grandview EXPONENT. w Mr 7 1901+
pub 1901+
CaM 1902+

GRISWOLD

Griswold LEDGER. w F 8 1899-1905||
CaM F 22 1899-O 28 1905

HAMIOTA

Hamiota ECHO. w 1893+
1893-99 as Hamiota hustler; 1900-02 Hamiota herald
CaM 1893+

Hamiota HERALD. *See* Hamiota echo

Hamiota HUSTLER. *See* Hamiota echo

HARTNEY

Hartney STAR. w 1892+
CaM 1893+

HOLLAND

Holland NEWS. w O 12 1894+
1894-N 23 1922 as Holland observer
CaM 1894-N 23 1922;F 1923-28

Holland OBSERVER. *See* Holland news

HOLMFIELD

Holmfield PRESS. w My 31 1906-D 23 1909||
CaM complete

KILLARNEY

Killarney GUIDE. w 1894+
CaM 1896+

LANGRUTH

Langruth HERALD. w Ap 18 1914-My 5 1927||
CaM Je 6 1914-27

McCREARY

McCreary TIMES. w 1924+
CaM 1925+

MacGREGOR

MacGregor HERALD. w 1897+
CaM 1897+

MANITOU

Manitou ADVANCE. m My 25 1895-D 1896||
1895 as Manitou independent
CaM My-N 1895;96

Manitou INDEPENDENT. *See* Manitou advance

Manitou MERCURY. w Ja 23 1885-Ap 27 1899||
CaM F 27 1885-99

Manitou SUN. w My 4 1899-D 27 1906||
CaM complete

Manitou WESTERN Canadian. w 1900+
CaM 1900+

MELITA

Melita ENTERPRISE. w N 12 1891-D 25 1913||
CaM complete

Melita NEW ERA. w 1915+
CaM 1915+

Melita PROGRESS-REVIEW. w Ja 11 1899-S 9 1915||
1899- 1908 as Melita western progress
CaM complete

Melita WESTERN progress. *See* Melita progress-review

MIAMI

Miami DESPATCH. w Mr 22-? 1901||
CaM [1901]

Miami HERALD. w 1903+
CaM 1903+

MINIOTA

Miniota HERALD. w 1906+
pub Jl 1913-Ag 1914;O 1919+
CaM 1906+

MINNEDOSA

MANITOBA mercury. w F 22-My 24 1894||
CaM complete

Minnedosa MERCURY. w Ag 17 1905-D 31 1908||
CaM complete
CaM 1905-08

Minnedosa TRIBUNE. w Ap 6 1883+
pub Ap 1884+
CaM 1883+
CaO Ap 6 1883-D 27 1900

MINTO

Minto PACKET. w My 2 1907+
D 20 1917-29? as Whitewater packet
CaM 1907-22

RIVERSIDE review and Dunrea advertiser. w My 2 1908-S 30 1911||
CaM My 23 1908-11

WHITEWATER packet. *See* Minto packet

MORDEN

Morden CHRONICLE. w Ja 7 1897-1911||?
CaM 1897-1909

Morden EMPIRE. w Ag 4 1898-1911||?
CaM Ag 11 1898-N 25 1909

Morden HERALD. w F 25 1892-D 25 1896||
CaM complete

MANITOBA news. w O 31 1884-87||?
CaM 1884-Mr 26 1887

Morden MONITOR. w Ap 7 1887-D 31 1896||
CaM complete

Morden TIMES. w 1910+
pub 1910+
CaM 1910+

MORRIS

Morris HERALD. w Je 1880+
CaM 1903+
CaO Mr 17 1881-S 6 1883

NAPINKA

Napinka GAZETTE. *See* Deloraine advertiser and Napinka gazette (Deloraine)

Napinka NEW CENTURY. w Ap 20 1899-1917||?
1899-1900 as Napinka standard
CaM 1899-F 9 1900;03-Je 29 1917

Napinka STANDARD. *See* Napinka new century

NEEPAWA

Neepawa CANADIAN. w Ja 24 1884-D 25 1885||
CaO complete

Neepawa HERALD and news. w My 28 1891-96||
1891-S 12 1894 as Neepawa herald
CaM complete

Neepawa NEWS. w O 13 1894-F 9 1895||
United with Neepawa herald to form Neepawa herald and news
CaM complete

Neepawa PRESS. sw 1895+
CaM 1895+

Neepawa REGISTER. w 1884-1928||?
CaM 1884-1926
CaO Ja 8 1886-D 19 1900

NELSON

MANITOBA mountaineer. w 1880-84||
CaM S 15 1883-O 11 1884

NORWOOD

Norwood PRESS. w 1905+
1905-1927? as Norwood press and St. Boniface echo
pub Ag 1927+
CaM 1932+

MANITOBA (*Continued*)

OAK LAKE

Oak Lake NEWS. w 1898+
CaM 1898+

OAK RIVER

Oak River POST. w Jl 1912+
pub 1912+
CaM 1917+

PILOT MOUND

Pilot Mound SENTINEL. w 1889+
CaM 1899+

Pilot Mound SIGNAL. w 1882-85||?
CaM 1884-Ja 10 1885

PLUMAS

Plumas STANDARD. w 1906+
CaM 1906[07-09]+

Plumas TIMES. w Ja 20-Mr 24 1905||
CaM complete

PORTAGE LA PRAIRIE

Daily GRAPHIC. d 1895+
CaM 1906;23+
CaMP 1918+
WHi O 23 1912

MANITOBA liberal. w Ap 1883+
CaM 1884+
CaO Ag 21 1885-86
WHi O 24 1912

MARQUETTE review. *See* Weekly review

NEWS. *See* Weekly review

PATRONS sentinel. w Mr 13 1896-97||?
CaM 1896-Ja 6 1897

Weekly REVIEW. w Ja 17 1879-1917||?
1879-F 8 1884 as Marquette review; F 15 1884-86 Tribune-review; 1887-99 Weekly review; 1900?-05? News
CU-B S 4 1889
CaM 1886-1913
CaO Ja 24 1879-Mr 1883;89-96

Weekly TRIBUNE. w S 9 1881-D 24 1886||
United with Weekly review to form Tribune-review, later Weekly review
CaO complete

TRIBUNE-REVIEW. *See* Weekly review

RAPID CITY

MARQUETTE reporter. *See* Rapid City reporter

NORTHWEST vindicator. w 1884-Jl 5 1890||
CaM Ag 13 1887-90

Rapid City PATRONS advocate and sentinel. w 1892-Ja 29 1896||
CaM Je 27 1894-96

Rapid City REPORTER. w 1884+
1884-1909 as Marquette reporter
pub [1891-97]+
CaM D 15 1892+

Rapid City SPECTATOR. w D 16 1886-F 13 1896||
CaM D 30 1886-96

Rapid City STANDARD and Northwest advocate. w Ap 8 1881-My 28 1886||
CaM N 1883-Mr 19 1886
CaO complete

RESTON

Reston RECORD. w 1905+
CaM 1906+

RIVERS

Rivers GAZETTE. w Jl 1908+
pub 1908+
CaM 1917+

ROBLIN

Roblin MESSENGER. w Je 7 1906-D 4 1909||
CaM complete

Roblin REVIEW. w 1912+
CaM 1917+

ROLAND

Roland NEWS. w 1895+
CaM 1899+

RUSSELL

Russell BANNER. w 1897+
CaM O 17 1899-D 25 1913

Russell CHRONICLE. w Je 15 1893-Ap 30 1898||?
CaM Je 22 1893-Ap 30 1898

ST. BONIFACE

Le MANITOBA. w Je 1 1871-1926||
1871-S 29 1881 as Metis
In French.
CaO 1871-1904
CaOTA Ag 17,S 21 1871;Ap 18 1874
CaQ 1876-80;O 13 1881-1909
CaQQL 1871-1921

METIS. *See* Le Manitoba

ST. JAMES

St. James LEADER. w Ap 10 1913+
pub 1913+
CaM Mr 12 1915+

ST. VITAL

St. Vital LANCE. w D 17 1931+
pub 1931+

SELKIRK

Selkirk EXPOSITOR. w D 7 1899-D 31 1909||
CaM 1900-09

Selkirk HERALD. w S 11 1882-86||
CaM 1884-86
CaO N 17 1882-O 3 1885

Selkirk JOURNAL. w Ap 22 1897-1902||?
CaM 1897-99

Selkirk RECORD. w N 26 1885+
pub Je 26 1896+
CaM 1885+
CaO 1885-D 21 1900

SHOAL LAKE

Shoal Lake ECHO. w Ap 30-O 22 1886||?
CaM My 14-O 22 1886

Shoal Lake STAR. w 1898+
CaM 1899+

SIDNEY

Sidney NEW ERA. w Mr 2 1900-03||?
CaM 1900-My 15 1903

SOMERSET

Somerset CENTURY. w 1901-09||?
CaM [1902-07]

Somerset NEWS and Swan Lake echo. w 1915+
In French and English
CaM 1915+

SOURIS

Souris PLAINDEALER. w 1892+
CaM 1892+

STEINBACH

Steinbach POST. w 1913+
In German
CaM 1920+

STONEWALL

Stonewall ARGUS. w 1893+
CaM 1893+

Stonewall GAZETTE. w O 3 1895-F 10 1915||
CaM O 24 1895-1915

Stonewall NEWS. w 1883-Jl 24 1891||
CaM [1884]-91

STRATHCLAIR

Straithclair PLAIN talk. w 1910+
CaM 1910+
WaPS [1923]Mr 14 1924

SWAN LAKE

Swan Lake ECHO. w 1903-14||?
United with Somerset news to form Somerset news and Swan Lake echo (Somerset)

SWAN RIVER

Swan River GIMLET. w Mr 23 1906-D 20 1907||
CaM complete

Swan River STAR and Valley times. w 1900+
1900-19 as Swan River star
pub [1900-03]+
CaM 1900+

THE PAS

The Pas HERALD. w D 7 1911-F 15 1929||
Merged with Northern mail
CaM complete

NORTHERN mail. w 1928+
CaM 1928+

TRANSCONA

Transcona and Eastern Manitoba NEWS. w Ja 23 1931+
pub 1931+
CaM 1931+

TREHERNE

Treherne TIMES. w 1899+
pub S 27 1918+
CaM 1899+

VIRDEN

Virden ADVANCE. *See* Virden empire-advance

Virden BANNER and news. w Je 27 1895-My 13 1897||
CaM complete

Virden CHRONICLE. w My 12 1892-Je 14 1894||
CaM complete

Virden EMPIRE-advance. w 1885+
1885-1907? as Virden advance
CaM 1885+
CaO 1885-D 21 1899

WAWANESA

Wawanesa ENTERPRISE. w D 16 1892-O 21 1895||
CaM complete

Wawanesa INDEPENDENT. w 1898+
CaM 1904+

Wawanesa WORLD. w S 12 1896-Mr 5 1897||
CaM complete

WEST LYNNE

SOUTHERN Manitoba times w S 18 1880-91||
CaO O 2 1880-D 25 1890

WINNIPEG

ADVANCE. w Jl 11 1908-18||?
CaM Ag 1 1908-S 4 1914

ASSINIBOIA news. w 1920-23||?
CaM Jl 21 1922-Ap 13 1923

Morning CALL. d Ap 18 1887-F 11 1889||
CaM 1887-88
CaMW complete
CaO [1887-89]
CaOOA Jl 1887-88

CANADA nyheter. w D 18 1919-20||?
In Swedish
IRA 1920
MnHi D 18 1919-[20]

CANADA posten. w 1904+
In Swedish
CaM 1907+
IRA [1905-27]
MnHi [1920]-23

CANADA tidningen. w D 1892+
1892-S 1893 as Sions väktare; S 1893-95 Väktaren; 1895-1907 Canada; 1908-31 Svenska Canada tidningen
In Swedish
pub 1892-99;1904+
CaM 1897+
IRA 1893-[1910-19;27-28]
MnHi 1918+

CANADIAN farmer. w 1900+
In Ukrainian
CaM 1923+
NdHi Jl 27 1905-Je 7 1907

CANADIAN Israelite. *See* Der Idische wort

CANADIAN ranok. w 1904+
In Ukrainian
CaM 1923+

CANADIAN Scotsman. w 1904-08||?
CaM Je 30 1906-F 8 1908

CANADIAN Ukrainian. w My 27 1911-D 31 1930||
In Ukrainian
CaM Je 3 1911-30

Le COURIER et Nord Ouest. w Mr 31-D 1888||?
In French
CaM 1888

CZAS. w 1913+
In Polish
CaM 1920+

L'ECHO de Manitoba. w Ja 27 1898-1908||?
In French
CaM 1898-1905
CaO 1898-1902

ELMWOOD advance. w 1903-14||?
CaM Jl 27 1906-S 4 1914

ELMWOOD advertiser. *See* Elmwood herald

ELMWOOD herald. w O 6 1920+
1920-28 as Elmwood advertiser
pub 1925+
CaM 1920-My 13 1921;S 5 1929+

FARMERS life. w 1925+
In Ukrainian
CaM My 22 1929-31

Winnipeg FREE press. d N 9 1872+
1872-D 1 1931 as Manitoba free press (title varies slightly)
N 9 1922 is 50th anniversary number
CSt-H [1915-17]
CaB Jl 9 1908-[S 1910-27]+
CaM 1872+
CaMP 1926+
CaMW 1875+
CaMWP 1872+
CaO Ap 12 1873+
CaOKU 1884-85;90-92[1919]-[24]-[29]-31
CaOOA 1889-1910;31+
CaOTA O 27-28 1881;Ap 13 1883
DLC D 4 1899+
InRE Ja 15,Mr 10,24,26,Ag 11,14,16 1877
MnHi Je 24 1876;Ja 10,23 Ap 3,7,30,S 9,27, D 1 1880;Mr 18,O 13 1881;Ja 30 1882;Jl 22 1890;N 21 1894+
NNC N 9 1922
NdHi Jl 15 1905-[My 1908-N 1909]-Ja 25 1911
NdU My 31 1915-Jl,O 1916-S 1917
WHi Mr 30 1901-Ja 17 1902

MANITOBA (*Continued*)

WINNIPEG—*Continued*

Weekly FREE PRESS. *See* Free press prairie farmer

FREE PRESS evening bulletin. d 1930+
Evening ed of Winnipeg free press. 1890-S 1894 as Evening free press and sun
pub 1890+
CSt-H [1916]
CaMW F-Ap 1890;1895-1926
NdHi My 1907-Ap 1908

FREE PRESS home journal. w
Thursday ed. of Free press
WHi Ap 21 1898-Mr 28 1901

FREE PRESS prairie farmer. w,sw N 1873+
1873-1917 as Weekly free press (title varies slightly)
sw 1896-1901
pub 1873+
CaOOA 1883-85
NcD Jl 17 1880
WHi F 13 1896-Mr 28 1901

GAZETA katolicka. w 1907+
In Polish
pub 1907+
CaM 1908+
IU Mr 13 1918-F 4 1925

GERMANIA. w S 22 1904-Ap 6 1911||
In German
CaM complete
NdHi 1904-[Je-Jl 1905]-F 9 1911

HEIMSKRINGLA. w S 1886+
In Icelandic. Suspended Je-O 1897
pub 1886+
CaM 1886+
DLC 1906-08;Je 29 1927
IU D 1917-O 21 1925
MH S 1931+
NdHi Mr 24 1904-S 1913;Ja 21-O 21 1925

Der IDISHE wort (Israelite press) w,d,sw 1910+
1910-S 1913 as Der Yid (Israelite); O 1913-Ag 6 1915 Der Keneder Yid (Canadian Israelite)
w 1910-S 11 1913; Ja-Ap 14 1916; d F 1914-15; 30-32
In Yiddish
pub 1911+
CaM 1928+
IU Ja 4,F 1918-S 1920
NN My 1911-[14]-16;30+

INDUSTRIAL news. w My 15 1886-S 28 1887||
CaM My 22 1886-87

ISRAELITE. *See* Der Idishe wort

ISRAELITE press. *See* Der Idishe wort

KANADAI magyar ujsag (Canadian Hungarian news). w 1924+
In Hungarian
CSt-H [1930-31]

KANADEETIS. bm Ja 30 1913-
In Lettish
WHi Ja 30-D 15 1913

KANADSKII gudok; organ russkikh rabochikh Kanady. bw Je ? 1931+
In Russian
CSt-H [1931-32]-[34]

Der KENEDER Yid. *See* Der Idishe wort

LEIFER. w Mr 5 1883-86||?
In Icelandic
CaM 1883-Je 4 1886

La LIBERTÉ. w 1913+
In French
pub 1913+
CaM 1913+
CaQQL Jl 22 1913+
IU Mr 13 1918-My 4,Jl 6,Ag 3 1920

LÖGBERG. w Ja 14 1888+
In Icelandic
pub 1888+
CaM 1888+
IU 1918-S 8 1927
NdHi Mr 24 1904-[15-24]-34
WHi Jl 12 1928; Ja 9 1930;Ja 1-8 1931

Winnipeg MAIL. w O 11 1928-D 24 1931||?
CaM 1928-31

Le MANITOBA. w 1880-Jl 29 1925||
In French
CaM O 13 1881-1925

MANITOBA free press. d *See* Winnipeg free press

MANITOBA free press. w N 1873-1910||?
Title varies slightly
CaOOA 1883-85
NcD Jl 17 1880

MANITOBA gazette. w O 22 1871+
CaB 1899+
CaM 1878-79
CaMW Mr 9-S 7 1872;Ja 14-S 9 1874
CaOOA 1883+
CaOT 1907+
CaOTU 1909-12
CaQMM 1883;88-90;1902;04-05;08+
CaQQL 1881-82;88-92
DLC 1903+
NN [1876-81]+

MANITOBA herald. d Ja 1-Jl 30 1877||?
CaM Ja 1-27;Jl 12-30 1877

MANITOBA liberal. w Jl 11 1871-72||?
Follows Manitoba news letter
CaMW Jl 11-Ag 20 1871
DLC [My-N 1872]

MANITOBA news-letter. tw S 13 1870-Jl 1 1871||
Followed by Manitoba liberal
CaMW complete
MnHi Ja 14 1871
OClWHi O 1 1870

MANITOBA Scotsman. sm Ja 13-D 30 1905||?
CaM 1905

Weekly MANITOBAN. w 1870-87||
CaM 1870-87
CaMW N 5 1870-Jl,N 30 1872-Ag 22 1874
CaMWP O 1870-O 1871;76
CaO S 30 1871-N 21 1874
CaMW N 5 1870-Jl,N 30 1872-Ag 22 1874
MnHi Je 10 1871;S 12,O 17-N 14 1874
OClWHi N 26 1870

Daily MANITOBAN. d Jl 6 1885-Ap 16 1887||
CaMW complete
CaO complete
CaOOA 1885-86

Le METIS. w My 27 1871-79||?
In French
CaMW 1871-Ap 24 1872

La MINERVE. d
In French
CaM 1885-86

MIRROR. w Mr 5 1890-1902||?
CaM 1890-95

Winnipeg MIRROR. w 1922+
CaM 1926+

NEW nation. w Ja 7-S 1870||
CaM complete
CaMW Ja 14 1870
CaQMM complete
MnHi Ja-Je 1870

Evening NEWS. d S 5 1885-Ap 20 1886||
CaM complete
CaMW S 29 1885-86

Weekly NEWS. w Mr 6 1925+
CaM 1925+

NOR' WEST advertiser. w
WHi Ag 23-O 18 1912

NOR'-WESTER. sm,w D 28 1859-N 1869||
A prospectus was issued Ag 22 1859
sm 1859-O 1864
CaB D 28 1859;Mr 14,28,My 28-Jl 1860
CaMW Mr 1864-[65;67-Jl 1868]
CaQMM [Ja 19 1868-69]
DLC D 28 1859;Ja 11-My 14,Jl 14-Ag 1860; Ap 15-My 1 1861;Jl 23 1862;My 24-Ag, S 25-O 6,N-D 15 1866;Ja 19,Mr 2,30,Jl 27-N 2 1867
MnHi Ag 22 1859;Je 14 1860;Je 11,O,N 4, D 1862;Ja 24-Ap 13,My 12-Je 11 1863
N Je 1 1861
WHi D 11 1865

NOR'WESTER. w Je 29 1874-D 20 1875||
CaM complete

Daily NOR'-WESTER. d F 23 1894-Je 9 1898||
CaM complete
CaMW complete

Der NORDWESTEN. w 1888+
In German
CaM 1897+
NdHi Jl 20 1905-Ap 16 1913

NORRONA. w 1910+
In Norwegian
pub 1910+
CaM 1915+
IaDeL 1925-[Ja-Ag 8 1929]
MnHi Ja 10 1918+

NORTH-ENDER. w 1901+
CaM 1921+
WHi F-O 17 1912

NORTHWEST banner. w Ap 23 1892-Jl 22 1896||
CaM complete

NORTHWEST review. w Ag 29 1885+
pub 1885+
CaM 1885+
CaO Ag 29 1885-Ag 4 1906
IU Mr 16 1918-My 9 1925
PPCHi [1889;92;1912]

OPINION. w Jl 1 1922-
CaM Jl-S 23 1922

La PATRIE. d 1879?-86||?
In French
CaM 1885-86

Winnipeg Saturday POST. w D 21 1907-O 13 1917||
CaM complete

QUIZ. w O 19 1878-Ja 11 1879||?
CaM 1878-Ja 11 1879

RED River pioneer. D 1 1869||
CaM complete
CaQMM complete

RUSSKII narod. (Russian people) w 1914-18||?
In Russian
DLC My 6-N 12 1915;Ja 10-O 3 1918

SAINT Peters bote. w
In German
NdHi Jl 25 1905-My 23 1907

Saturday REVIEW. w O 1933+
pub 1933+
CaM 1934+

Winnipeg SIFTINGS. w Mr 30 1883-D 27 1890||
CaM complete

SIONS väktare. *See* Canada tidningen

SKANDINAVISKE Canadienseren. m,w 1887-95||
Merged with Canada, later Canada tidningen
m 1887-S 1892
In Swedish
CaM complete
CaMWD O 1892-93
MnHi N 16 1895

SOUTHENDER. w
only 6 issues in 1930
pub [1930]+
CaM 1928+

Weekly SPECTATOR. w
CaM Ap 16-N 28 1885

SPECTATOR. w Mr 6 1925-30||?
CaM 1925-Mr 20 1926

STANDARD. w N 28 1874-Ag 30 1879||
CaM 1874-75
CaMW 1877-78
CaO complete
MnHi Mr 15,Ap 5 1879

STANDARD. w Jl 11 1924-25||?
CaM 1924-F 20 1925

STAR. w Mr 1-14 1890||?
CaM Mr 1-14 1890

STATESMAN. m Ag 28 1913-18||?
CaM 1913-16

SUN. d Ag 1881-D 1 1889||
Followed by Evening free press and sun, later Free press evening bulletin
CaM complete
CaMW O 4 1881-89
CaMWT Ja-F 1889
CaO F 20 1882-89
CaOOA Mr-D 1889
CaQMG D 1886
ICM My 15 1884

SVENSKA Canada tidningen. *See* Canada tidningen

Winnipeg TELEGRAM. (morning) d 1894-1920||
CaMW 1898-1920

Winnipeg TELEGRAM. (evening) d 1901-20||
CaMW complete

Winnipeg TELEGRAM. w F 3 1894-O 16 1920||
CaM 1898-1920
CaO 1901-20

Winnipeg daily TIMES. d Ap 12 1879-Jl 30 1885||
CaM complete
CaMW complete
CaO complete
CaOOA 1883-85
CaOTA Ja 12,17[Jl-O,D 1882;F-Mr 1883]
MnHi N 6,11,15,D 28 1880;S 22 1881

Winnipeg weekly TIMES. w 1879-85||
CaM complete
CaOTA Jl 29,O 28-N 18,D 1881-Ja 13,F, My 12-19,Je 2,Jl 21-28 1882
DLC N 5 1880
MnHi Mr 4 1881

Winnipeg evening TRIBUNE. d Ja 28 1890+
pub 1890-Je 1891;93;Jl 1895-Je 1896;Ja-Je 1897;Ap,Jl 1899-S 1913;14+
CU-B Ap 3,9 1895
CaB 1930+
CaM 1890+
CaMW 1906+
CaO 1890+

UKRANIEN voice. w 1909+
In Ukrainian
CSt-H [1933]
CaM 1920+

VÄKTAREN. *See* Canada tidningen

VOROLD. w F 5 1918-20||?
In Icelandic
CaM F 12 1918-Mr 4 1920

WAR cry. w
Printed in Toronto
CaM [1887]

WEST Canada. w 1907-18||?
In German
CaM F 3 1907-17
IU Mr 13-S 18 1918

WESTERN banner. w D 7 1905-N 15 1906||?
CaM 1905-N 15 1906

WESTERN Canadian. w Mr 25 1897-Jl 8 1899||?
CaM [1897-Jl 8 1899]

Der YID. *See* Der Idishe wort

NEW BRUNSWICK

BATHURST

COURRIER des provinces maritimes. w Ag 26 1885-1908||?
In French
CaO D 24 1885-Jl 6 1899
CaQQL 1885;88-92

BROCKVILLE

Brockville **RECORDER.** w Ja 16 1821-
NR Ja 30-Ap 1821

CAMPBELLTON

Campbellton **GRAPHIC.** w N 7 1907+
pub Jl 1910+

CHATHAM

COMMERCIAL-world. w 1898+
1898-Mr 19 1929 as Commercial
pub 1898+

GLEANER. w 1826-80||?
1826-65? pub at Miramichi
CaNS Jl 28 1829-Ag 1835;S 15 1840-S 12 1842;43-64;66;68
CaO S 30 1854-64
CaOOA 1834-60;66-67

WORLD. w 1882-Mr 26 1929||
United with Commercial to form Commercial-world

EDMUNDSON

Le **MADAWASKA.** w D 4 1913+
In French and English
pub 1913+
CaQQL Ap 25 1914-33

FREDERICTON

Fredericton evening **CAPITAL.** tw 1880-88||?
CaNU S 12 1882-My 8 1886

CAPITAL. m 1880-1909||?
CaNU D 20 1902

Daily **GLEANER.** d 1880+
pub 1915+
CaB 1928+

HEAD quarters. w 1844-76||?
CSmH F 13 1847
CaNS Ap-O 1844;46;49-50;Ap 19-26 1854;O 24 1855;56-O 1860;64-66[Ap-D 1867]-N 1868;Ag 7 1876
CaNU Jl 3,S 11,O 9,D 18 1861;S 17 1862;Jl 1 1863;Je 29 1864;S 12 1866;Jl 3,N 13 1867; Mr 11 1868 Je 30 1869
CaOOA D 1844-46
DLC O 12 1853-55;61-62

HERALD. tw My 2-Je 12 1865||
CaN complete
NN complete

LOYALIST and conservative advocate. w
CSmH Je 18 1846
CaOOA 1844-45
CaOT My 30 1844-45

NEW BRUNSWICK reporter. sw,w 1844-1904||?
CaNU My 2 1862
CaOTA N 12-26 1858

ROYAL gazette and New-Brunswick advertiser. w Ja 4 1808+
CSmH Ag 11 1830
CaB 1916+
CaNU Ja 24 1820-F 1828;30-32;34-46
CaNWC 1916+
CaOOA 1830-33
CaOT 1932+
DLC N 1826-O 1838;1903-24
ICHi D 18 8-S 1819
MWA N 5 1810
NN Ap 20 1812;1902+
NjHi [1862-13]

SENTINEL and New Brunswick general advertiser. w
DLC N 13-D 25 1841

MIRAMICHI

GLEANER. *See under* Chatham

MERCURY. w
CaNS F 1826-F 1829
CaOOA D 1826-Mr 1829

MONCTON

L'EVANGELINE. w 1887+
In French
CaNM F 1927+

Moncton **TIMES.** w 1868-1930||?
Title varies slightly
MWA D 21 1871

Moncton daily **TIMES.** d D 10 1877+
CaNM F 12 1927+
CaO Ja 5 1885-Je 29 1901

Moncton **TRANSCRIPT.** d 1882+
CaNM F 12 1927+
CaO Ja 2 1886-Je 30 1901

NEWCASTLE

NORTH Shore leader. w Je 1906+
pub 1906+

SACKVILLE

CHIGNECTO post. *See* Sackville post

Sackville **POST.** sw 1869+
1869-97? as Chignecto post
CaOOA 1872;78-86;88-91;93-95

SAINT ANDREWS

St. Andrews **BEACON.** w 1889-1919||?
MWA Je 26 1890

CHARLOTTE gazette.
CSmH Je 28 1853

Saint Andrews **HERALD.** w 1819-
Title varies
CSmH Ag 24 1830
MHi Ja 30,F 13,Mr 12,My 14 1827
MWA O 16 1821;Je 5 1826;Jl 28 1829
NjHi S 22 1829

NEW BRUNSWICK standard. w 1833-80||
CaOOA complete
MWA Ap 20 1864

ST. GEORGE

GRANITETOWN greetings. w 1906-12||?
CaNS Jl 17 1907-S 6 1912

ST. JOHN

BRITISH colonist. w 1827-34||?
CSmH Ag 27 1830
CaOOA Jl 1828-S 1834

Weekly **CHRONICLE.** w 1836-
CaNS S 1836-F,Ap 1837-[42-43]-Je 1845[46]-Je 1847[48-57]
CaOOA 1850-58
MWA Ap 30 1841
MiU-C D 27 1844

CITY gazette. w 1812-35||?
CSmH Ag 18 1830
CaNS Mr 1821-My 1824;Mr 29 1827-28[30-31]Ja 19,F 2-9 1832;Ja 16,N 27 1834
CaOOA Je 1832-Jl 1835
ICHi Mr 3 1819
MWA Mr 14-Ap 4,18-25,Je 20-Jl 4 O 17 1815;Jl 2 1821
NNHi My 21 1828
NjHi N 18 1829

COLONIAL empire. tw 1861-63||?
CaO Mr 28 1862-Ja 17 1863
CaOOA 1862
MWA S 10 1862

COMMERCIAL news and general advertiser. *See* St. John daily news

COURIER. w 1810?-65||?
1810-29? as New Brunswick courier
CaNS Je 1827-Mr 3 1832;33-Ag,O 1836-38;F-Ap 1839;40;Je-D 1843;Ja 20-D 21 1844;F 22-D 1845;Jl 1846-Jl 1851;52-Je 1854;56;Ag 21,N 6 1858;Ja-Je,Jl 16-30,S 17-24,O 22-29,N 2-9 1859;D 8 1860[Mr-S]-D 1861[Mr-S]-D 1862;Ja 6,Mr 26 1864;Ja-Je 1865
CaNU 1839-46
CaO N 24 1860-Ap 1862
CaOOA 1838-39
CaOTA F 21 1835;Mr 6 1841
CaQMG D 30 1820
DLC S 7 1816
MBAt N 10 1827;S 20 1828;S 26 1829
MHi Ap 9,S 3 1825;Ja 7 1826
MWA Mr 18,Ap 1,Je 24-Jl 8 1815;F 17,S 14 1816;Je 29-26,Jl 10-Ag 21,S-O 2 1819;Je 9 1821;S 4 1841
N Ja 17 1829

FREEMAN. w 1850-84||
CaNS 1851-64;66-84
CaO Ap 17 1862-83
CaOTA Ap 30,Ag 26 1864-Je 23 1865

Morning **FREEMAN.** tw 1851-78||?
MWA Jl 31 1852;Mr 15 1862;Mr 14 1867;Jl 30 1874

St. John **GAZETTE.** w 1786?-
-1803 as St. John gazette and general advertiser
DLC S 12-19 1788
MWA N 5-12 1803;Ja 2,F 13,27-Mr 5 1804;F 3,S 8-15,29 1806
NjHi Ap 11 1800-N 21,D 5 1802-Ja 22 1803 [04-07]

Saturday **GAZETTE.** w 1887||?
CaOOA Ap-My 1887

GAZETTE. d 1888-1904||?
CaNS 1888-S 1904

GLOBE. d 1858-Ap 1927||
United with Times-sun to form Times-globe
CaNS 1852-67;Ap 1879-83;87-Ja 1927
CaOOA 1876
MWA F 13 1867;O 20 1871

Saint John **HERALD.** tw Ag 13? 1842-
MWA S 23,28 1842

HOME journal. *See* Morning journal

Morning **JOURNAL.** tw,w 1865-68||
1865 as Home journal (inside sheets as Provincial home journal)
CaNS My 1865-Ja,Mr 23,S 10 1866;F 13,Mr 23,S 10 1867;Mr 18,Ap,D 2 1868
MWA F 9 1865;Jl 23,S 5 1866;Ap 22 1867

Daily **JOURNAL.** d 1922?-Jl 1923||
United with Telegraph and sun to form Telegraph-journal
CaNS 1922-23

St. John **LIBERATOR.** w 1844-
CSmH Ap 11 1846

LOYALIST.
CaNS O 13 1842-My 4,Je 1843-My 16 1844;Ja 1-8 1845;46[47]
CaOOA Ja-Je 1848

MARITIME broadcaster. w N 29 1930+
pub 1930+

NEW BRUNSWICK courier. *See* Courier

NEW BRUNSWICKER. tw
CaNS Ag 5,S 16,D 9,16,23,30 1841-Jl 1842;O 24,D 14 1844;Je 17,N 11 1845;My 2 1846;My 18 1847;Ap 7,Jl 5,N 3 1849;Ja 17 1850;My 15-17,24,Ag 23,O 7 1851;F 24,Ag 16,27,S 8-13,N 3-8 1853;F 23,Mr 16,25,Ap 15,Ag 5,S 23-26,O 14,31,N 23,30,D 21,30 1854[55]Ja 29,Ap 25,My 16,Jl 21,Ag 27,S 5-8,D 3,24 1857;Ap 6,My 20, Je 3,19,Jl 29 1858;Ja 22,F-Jl 1859;Jl-S 1860;F-Ag,N 26-D 1861;Ja 9-11,18,Ap 1862-F 1863
CaOOA Mr-My 1842
MWA Ag 5 1852;Ja 26 1854

St. John daily **NEWS.** d S 16 1839-Ap 8 1884||
1839-Ag 17 1840 as Commercial news and general advertiser; Ag 19 1840- Morning news
CSmH Jl 29 1846
CaN 1839-[Jl 1855-Ja 11 1856]D 31 1862
CaNS Ap 1840-41;58-83
CaO N 30 1860-84
CaOOA 1854-F 1855
MWA Mr 26,Ag 25-27 1841;Jl 16,Ag 20 1856;S 5 1866

Weekly **OBSERVER.** w My 1828-53||?
Follows Star
CSmH Ag 24 1830
CaNS My 19,N 10 1829;F 1,N 8-D 6 1831;Ja 3, F 28,D 10 1832;F 11,Jl 22,Ag 19 1834-[35-36] Ag 20-D 1839;Mr 10,O 20,D 1840[41]Ag 16 1842 Ag 20,S 3 1844;47[48-52]
CaOOA Jl 1836-Je 1837;38-39;My 12 1840-D 3 1844
CaOTA Jl 12 1853
MWA S 30,O 21-N 4 1828;Mr 17 1829

PROGRESS. w My 12 1888-1902||?
CaOOA N 16-23 1887;My 5-D 1 1888
MWA O 13 1888

PROVINCIAL home journal. *See* Morning journal

RECORD. d 1893-99||?
CaNS 1894-Ag 1899
CaOOA O-D 1896

ROYAL gazette. w 1787?-
MWA Ja 25,F 8-22,My 2,Jl 11 1804;Ja 29,S 10-17,O 1 1806

ROYAL gazette. 1808+ *See under* Fredericton

STANDARD. d 1909-Je 1922||
CaNS Mr 25-D 1909;Ap 1910-22

STAR. w My 19 1818-Ap 1828||?
Followed by Weekly observer
CaOOA 1818-My 1819;Mr-Jl 1827;Ja-Ap 1828
MWA Je 16 1818;Ja 30 1821
NjHi Jl 20 1819

STAR. d 1900-10||
United with Evening times to form Evening times and star later Times-globe
CaNS 1901-03

SUN. d 1878-Mr 12 1910||
1878-My 4 1906 as St John daily sun. United with Telegraph to form Telegraph and sun, later Telegraph-journal
CaNS O 1878-1904
CaO 1884-Mr 12 1910
CaOOA 1883-Ap 1884;98-[1904]-[08]-10
DLC N 29 1899-Je 1909
NjHi F 23,Mr 15 1884

St. John **TELEGRAPH** and news. w,sw S 27 1862-1924||?
1862- as St. John telegraph
w 1862-99?
CaNS 1862-64;Ag 1865-S 1868;Ja 21-Je 3 1869
CaO 1865-68
CaOTA Mr 29 1865
MWA Mr 13 1867;F 28 1872;My 23 1883

TELEGRAPH and sun. *See* Telegraph-journal

TELEGRAPH-JOURNAL. d 1868+
1862-1910 as Daily telegraph; 1911-Jl 1923 Telegraph and sun
CaNS Ap 1870+
CaNSa 1930+
CaNU Je 24 1876
CaO 1868+
CaOCA 1910-20
DLC N 1878-85;Ag 3 1900-01
MWA Ag 1-2 1870;Ag 26,O 20 1871

TEMPERANCE telegraph. w
CaOOA 1845-Ja 1846;55-Jl 1860

TIMES and star. *See* Times-globe

TIMES-GLOBE. d 1904+
1904-10 as Evening times; 1911 Evening times and star; 1912-Mr 1927 Times-star
CaNS Jl 1916+

Daily **TRIBUNE.** d 1872-75||
CaNS 1872-My 1875

WESTERN recorder. w
CaOOA 1859-Jl 1860

ST. STEPHEN

PROVINCIAL patriot. w
CaOOA My 1853-My 1854

ST. CROIX courier. w 1865+
CaOOA 1892-94
MWA F 10 1866

NEW BRUNSWICK (*Continued*)

SHEDIAC

Le **MONITEUR** acadien. w Jl 1 1867-O 25 1918||
In French
CaO D 13 1883-1918
CaOOA 1881-1918
CaQ Ap 26 1883-1908
CaQQL 1868-74;77-82;87-92

WOODSTOCK

CARLTON sentinel. w 1837+
1837- as Woodstock times; - Telegraph
pub 1855+
CSmH Je 25 1853
CaNS Jl 27-D 21 1839;Ja-Je 1840;F 18-O 8,N 16,D 21 1844-Ja 11,25 1845;F 12 1850-O 13 1860;F 3 1928+
IU D 19 1840
MWA F 3 1866;Mr 2 1872

DISPATCH. w 1894-1918||
CaNWA complete

Woodstock **JOURNAL.** w
CaNW Ja 6-My 19,S 29 1859-Ja 9 1862

PRESS. w 1879+
pub 1924+
CaNW S 4 1905-Ag 1906;Mr 20 1923+

TELEGRAPH. *See* Carlton sentinel

Woodstock **TIMES.** *See* Carlton sentinel

NOVA SCOTIA

AMHERST

Amherst **GAZETTE.** w,sw 1866-1907||?
w 1866-99?
NN Ag 27 1903

Amherst daily **NEWS.** d 1893+
pub 1893+

Amherst **NEWS-SENTINEL.** sw 1867+
pub 1867+

ANNAPOLIS ROYAL

SPECTATOR. w 1882+
pub [1882+]
MWA O 19,N 9 1933
NN N 23 1916

ANTIGONISH

AURORA. w D 8 1881-My 20 1885||
CaNsAS [1881-85]

CASKET. w Jl 1852+
CaNsAS [1852]+
CaQQL Je 19 1890+

BADDECK

ISLAND reporter. w 1884-87||?
NIC Ag 20 1885

BERWICK

Berwick **REGISTER.** w Je 13 1891+
pub 1896+
CaNsBrH 1891-96

STAR. w 1866-79||?
CaNs Je-D 1866
MWA Ja 16 1879

BRIDGETOWN

Weekly **MONITOR.** w Mr 22 1873+
pub [1873-1916]+

BRIDGEWATER

Bridgewater **BULLETIN.** w Je 1888+
pub [1888+]

CALEDONIA

GOLD hunter and farmers' journal. w 1888+
pub 1888+

CANSO

Canso **BREEZE** and Guysboro county advocate.
w 1920+
CaNsTN 1920+

DARTMOUTH

ATLANTIC weekly. *See* Patriot

PATRIOT. w 1893+
1893-1901? as Atlantic weekly
NN D 23 1899

DIGBY

Digby **COURIER.** w S 18 1874+
pub [1874+]

GLACE BAY

Glace Bay **GAZETTE.** w,d 1900+
w 1900-01
pub [1901+]
CaOOA 1900-Ap 1925

NOVA SCOTIA miner. w
WHi Mr 15,My 17,31,Je 7 1930

HALIFAX

ACADIAN. w
CaNS [1827-29]34
MBAt Ag 28 1829

ACADIAN recorder. d 1813-My 1930||
CaNs Ja 16 1813-Ja 15,F 5 1814-1930
CaOOA 1817-19;21-23
CaQMG Ag 12 1820;F 17 1821
MH Ja 16,Ap 5 1913;Ja 31 1914[17-20;Ja 8-Ag 27 1921]
MHi Mr 31,Je 9 1821;Ja 16 1913[17-27]
MWA D 10,12 1917;Ap 7,9 1930
NNHi F 1 1876

ACADIAN recorder. w Ja 16? 1813-My 1930||
CSmH Je 12 1830
DLC Ap 8 1815
MBAt My 23 1829
MWA D 25 1813;My 7 1814;My 20 1815;Ja 22 1825;N 8-15 1828;Mr 19 1842
NjHi S 12 1829

ACADIAN telegraph.
CaNs [1836-37]

BRITISH colonist. tw,w My 16 1848-74||
Follows Times
CaNs Ag 29 1848-74
CaO 1865-74
CaOTA Mr 5 1853;Ag 9,23,S,O 18,N 15,D 6-13 1858;Ja 3,F 14-Mr 7,Ap 25,My 16-30,Jl 11 1859
MWA Je 7 1852
MiU-C S 29 1864

Weekly **BRITISH** North American. w 1850-
CSmH Jl 14 1853

BULLFROG.
CaNs 1864-65

Weekly **CHRONICLE.** w
CaNs 1805-16;19-22
CaNsHD 1821
MHi Je 15 1821;Je 3,S 9 1825
MWA Mr 3 1804;F 24(supp)Je 15 1810;D 17-31 1813;F 4-11,25,Mr 25,Ap 29,S 30-O 7 1814

Halifax **CHRONICLE.** d Ja 24 1844+
1874-Ja 21 1927 as Morning chronicle
Ja 1 1925 is Centenary ed
CaNs 1845;51+
CaNsHD F 17 1859-[87-88]-[98-1900]-[06-07]-[11-12]-[14]-[18]+
CaNsWA 1922+
CaO D 1860+
CaOOA 1883-92
CaOTA Ap 9 1853;N 25 1862
DLC Jl 14 1874+
MH [1907-19]Ja 1 1920
MWA Ag 8 1874;D 7,9-10 1917;Mr 30 1918;Ja 1 1925
—evening ed *See* Citizen and evening chronicle

Morning **CHRONICLE.** tw Ja 24 1844-1900||?
CaNs 1862;Ja-Je 1867;68;70-74
MWA Jl 31 1852;Jl 14 1863
N F 25 1858

Halifax **CITIZEN.** tw,w 1863-77||
CaNs 1864-67;71-73
CaNsHD 1873
CaO 1868-77

CITIZEN. w 1919+
CaOOA [1926-27]

CITIZEN and evening chronicle. d 1866-88||
Followed by Daily echo
CaNs Jl 7-D 16 1870;Jl 27-S 24 1874;Ag 27 1877-Je 1882;83-Je 1888

Morning **COURIER.**
CaNs O 25-D 1847

CRITIC. w 1884-93||
CaNs complete

CROSS.
CaNs 1847

Daily **ECHO.** d F 1 1888-1926||?
Follows Citizen and evening chronicle
CaNs Jl 1888-96;Jl-D 1897;99-Je 1903;04-Je 1907;Ja-Je 1908;Ja-Je 1909;10-24
CaQMG Mr 28 1890
MWA D 7-11 1917

Evening **EXPRESS.** tw Ja 4 1858-76||?
CaNs 1858-59;62;64-[71]-74
CaO 1858-73
CaOTA Jl 6 1863
MWA Jl 6 1863

FREE press. w 1816-30||?
CSmH Jl 13 1830
CaNs 1819,21-29
CaOOA 1817-22
MHi Ap 25 1820;Ap 15 1823;F 20 1827
MWA Je 15 1819;Ag 14 1827

City **GAZETTE.**
CaNs 1814

Halifax **GAZETTE.** *See* Royal gazette

Halifax **HERALD.** d Ja 14 1875+
1875-1910 as Morning herald (title varies slightly)
CaB 1928+
CaNs Ja 22 1876-80;84-Je 1887;88-Je 1889;Jl-D 1890;Jl 1891-Je 1899;1900+
CaNsHD Jl 6 1880-1928
CaO Ja 19 1875+
CaOOA 1883+
DLC 1880-85;Je 28 1927
MWA S 18-19 1911;D 10-11 1917;N 8 1932

Morning **HERALD** and general advertiser. tw 1839-
CSmH Je 8 1846
DLC Je 24-27 1842
MWA Je 14 1841;F 23,My 16 1842

Halifax **JOURNAL.** w Ag 6 1810-
CSmH Ag 30 1830
CaNs 1810-16;19-20[23-26]31-Ag 12 1833;39
CaNsHD Ap 1811-39
MWA N 19 1810;Ja 7 1811
NN N 19 1827

Morning **JOURNAL** and commercial advertiser.
tw Ap 12 1854-
CaNs 1854-62;Ag 3 1863-D 9 1864
CaNsHD 1854

Evening **MAIL.** d 1878+
CaNs 1917-Je,O 1918-S 1921;22-24
MWA S 21 1898;S 19-20 1911;D 7-11 1917

Weekly **MIRROR.** w
CaNs 1835-36;43

Weekly **MISCELLANY.** w
CaNs Je 1863-F 1864

NEW times and reporter. w
CaNs 1879-80

NOVA Scotia citizen. w 1923-25||?
CaOOA Ap 1923-25

NOVA SCOTIA gazette and weekly chronicle.
See Royal gazette

NOVASCOTIAN. w D 29 1824-1926||?
Title varies: Novascotian or Colonial herald; Novascotian and weekly chronicle
CSmH N 2 1837;My 25 1853
CaNs 1824-60;63-68;1907-25
CaNsHD Ja 28 1829-31;39
CaNsWA [1830-68]
CaO Ja 19 1825-70
CaOOA My-Jl 1851
MBAt Ap 23 1829
MWA O 30 1828;Je 8 1842

OLIVE branch. w
CaNs 1843-45

Halifax morning **POST** and parliamentary reporter. w 1841-
CSmH S 26 1846
CaNs O 5 1841-47
MWA My 14 1842
MiU-C N 18 1843

REGISTER. w Ag 4 1841-
MWA Ag 18,S 15 1841

Halifax evening **REPORTER.** d 1860-O 11 1879||
CaNs 1860-64;67-79
CaO 1875-79
CaOTA N 13 1860;Mr 15 1862;Jl 7 1863
MWA Jl 7 1863;My 14 1872

ROYAL gazette. w Mr 27 1752+
1752-Ag 7 1766 as Halifax gazette; Ag 14 1766-Ag 1770 Nova Scotia gazette and weekly chronicle
CSmH S 3 1830
CaB Ap 19 1916+
CaNs 1800-21;23;39-41;65;89
CaNsHD 1800;08-09
CaNsWA 1813;20-23;25;27-48;50-56;58-60;62;68
CaOT 1932+
CaOTA Ag 9 1815
DLC S 25 1792;Ap 30 1793;1849-54;58-68;70;99+
MBAt O 17 1827
MWA S 24 1801;Jl 29,O 7 1802;S 29 1803;F 9,Mr 8,Ap 19-26,My 31 1804;F 7 1805;S 1 1807;N 21-28 1810;D 22-29 1813;F 9-23,Mr 30,S 28-O 5 1814;S 1 1841
NN 1873;1903+

STANDARD and conservative advocate. w
CaNs [1847-48]

Halifax daily **STAR.** d 1873+
CaNs [1873+]
CaNsHD Jl 2 1888;Ja 1 1920;Ja 22 1927-28

Halifax morning **SUN.** d 1845-S 5 1867||
Title varies
CSmH Ja 20 1847
CaNs Mr 19 1845-D 6 1848;50[55-64]
CaNsHD Ja 2 1850;52-67
CaO D 3 1860-64
MWA Ag 5 1852

TIMES. w Je 3 1834-46||?
Followed by British colonist
CSmH N 7 1837
CaNs Je 10,N 18,D 30 1834;F 10,D 1 1835;36-46
CaNsWA 1835-42;44;46
CaOT 1837
MWA Mr 1-8,Je 28 1842;Mr 14 1843

NOVA SCOTIA (*Continued*)

HALIFAX—*Continued*

Evening TRANSCRIPT. w
CaNs [185?-60]

UNIONIST and Halifax journal. w
CaNs 1865-69

KENTVILLE

Kentville ADVERTISER. w 1877+
pub 1926+

DANSKE herold. sm Mr 15 1932+
In Danish
pub 1932+

LIVERPOOL

Liverpool ADVANCE. w Mr 1878+
pub [1878-79]+
MWA Jl 13 1932

LUNENBURG

PROGRESS-enterprise. w D 10 1878+
1878-99? as Progress
pub [1878+]

MAHONE BAY

SOUTH Shore record. w D 8 1932+
pub 1932—

NEW GLASGOW

EASTERN chronicle. w,sw O 4 1843+
w 1843-1903
pub [1843+]
CaOOA [1866-67;69-70]

FREE lance. w 1894+
CaOOA 1914-17;19;21;24-25

Evening NEWS. d 1911+
CaOOA Ag 1911-Je,Ag 1913-25

NEW WATERFORD

New Waterford TIMES. w My 15 1930+
pub 1930+

NORTH SYDNEY

North Sydney HERALD. w 1872+
CaO 187?-1903

OXFORD

Oxford JOURNAL. w F 3 1897+
pub [1897+]

PICTOU

Pictou ADVOCATE. w 1893+
pub 1893+

BEE. w 1835-37||?
CSmH Je 21 1837

COLONIAL patriot. w 1828-30||?
CSmH Je 12 1830

COLONIAL standard. w
MiU-C O 4 1864

EASTERN chronicle. w 1843-
CSmH Jl 23 1846
MWA My 14 1863

Pictou OBSERVER. w
CaNs [1832]-33[38,40]

SPRINGHILL

Springhill RECORD. sw,w 1914+
sw 1914-O 1928
pub N 1928+

SYDNEY

CAPE Breton news. w 1851-
DLC Je 4 1864
MWA F 7 1857

TRURO

CITIZEN-SUN. w My 25 1871+
1871-1924? as Colchester sun
CaOOA 1871-75;80;84-86;94;Ja-My 1907

GUARDIAN. w 1879-92||?
CU-B My 21 1889

COLCHESTER sun. *See* Citizen-sun

NEWS. d O 23 1891+
CaOOA O 1892-99;Jl 1900-Je 1901;03-Je 1904;05-32

Weekly NEWS. w O 28 1892+
CaOOA 1892+

VICTORIA-INVERNESS bulletin. w Ja 26 1926+
pub 1926+

WESTVILLE

FREE lance. w 1896-1925||?
CaOOA 1908-22;24-25

WEYMOUTH

L'EVANGELINE. w N 23 1887-D 30 1909||
In French
CaO complete
CaQ N 20 1890-1909
CaQQL complete

WINDSOR

Windsor COURIER. w F 1 1865-
MHi S-N 21 1885

WOLFVILLE

Wolfville ACADIAN. sm,w Ap 1883+
sm 1883-84?
pub 1883+

YARMOUTH

ARGUS (vox populi) w Jl 27? 1867-
CaNsY Ag 31 1867

CONSERVATIVE. sw S 15 1839-Ap 10 1840||
CaNsY S 19 1839-40

Yarmouth COURIER. sw N 21 1843-Ap 6 1848||
Followed by Courier and temperance gazette, later Temperance gazette
CaNsY Je 17 1844

COURIER and temperance gazette. *See* Temperance gazette

Yarmouth HERALD. w Ag 9 1833+
pub 1833+
CaNsY 1833+
CaOOA 1834-43;45-52;67-1912
MH 1856-61
NHuHi Ap-D 1842
NN Ag 9 1833(facsimile) Jl 26 1834;D 23 1844

Yarmouth LIGHT. w 1890+
pub 1890+

Yarmouth daily NEWS. d O 24 1896-N 3 1899||
Suspended from S 23-O ? 1899
CaNsY 1899

Yarmouth TELEGRAM. w My 1 1885+
CaNsY 1885+
CaNsYH 1885+
CaOOA Mr-D 1891;96-1912
ICN 1899-1900

Yarmouth TELEGRAPH. w N 25 1831-
CaNsYH 1831-O 26 1832

TEMPERANCE gazette. w Ap 13 1848-
Follows Yarmouth courier. Ap 13- 1848 as Courier and temperance gazette
CaNs 1849-50
CaNsYH My 17 1849

Yarmouth TIMES. sw,d F 17 1883-1923||
CaNsY 1883-92;94-1901;04-15;18
CaOOA 1883-84;88

Yarmouth TRIBUNE. sw,w S 1 1855-My 15 1883||
sw 1855-58
CaOOA 1855-58;60-83
DLC Ag 30 1856-Ag 22 1857
MH 1855-My 8 1883

ONTARIO

ALEXANDRIA

GLENGARRIAN. w 1884-1909||?
1884-88 as Glengarry review
CaOOA 1889-90
CaOTA My 13 1887;F 24 1888

GLENGARRY review. *See* Glengarrian

AMHERSTBURG

Amherstburg ECHO. w 1874+
CaOWi S 25 1896-1902;04-18

ANCASTER

GORE gazette, and Ancaster, Hamilton, Dundas and Flamborough advertiser. w Mr 3 1827-Je 8 1829||
CaOHV [1827-28]29
CaOTA Mr 17 1827;My 31-Je 21,Jl 12,Ag 2,16 D 27 1828
DLC Mr 3 1827

ARTHUR

Arthur ADVOCATE, Mount Forest express Luther, and Minto journal. w 1861-
CaOTA Mr 22-29,Je 7 1862

AURORA

Aurora BANNER. w F 12 1864+
Title varies: Aurora; Aurora banner and county of York general advertiser and news-letter; etc.
CaOTA F 12-S 16,O 7,N 11 1864;Ja 20,F 10, My 10,Je 9 1865;Ja 18 1867-Ja 15,F 12,Mr 26 1869;Ja 21 1870-My 6,S 30 1870;Ja 3,Ap 4,S 19,D 5 1873;F 20,Mr 27,Jl 31,Ag 21,S 25,O 9,30,D 18 1874-Ja 1,F 5-12 1875;Mr 24-31,My 26,D 22 1876;F 23,Mr 23,Ap 8,Jl 13,N 9 1877;Je 7-21 1878;D 26 1879;Ja 23,O 8,D 24 1880;Je 29 1883;My 16 1884;Ag 7 1885;Ja 22 1886

AYLMER

OTTAWA argus. w D 5 1849-
CaOTU D 12 1849[50]

BARRIE

EXAMINER. w 1863+
pub 1900+
CaOB 1896;98-1901;05;07;09-10
CaOTA [1867]-Je 2 1870;F 15 1872

Barrie GAZETTE. w Je 19 1868-1916||?
1868-75? as Northern gazette
CaOTA Je 19-D 10 1868

Barrie HERALD. w F 3 1852-
Subtitle varies
CaOTA Ap 21,Jl 28[S 1852-F,My-Jl,S 1853-S 2 1857]

Barrie MAGNET. w Ag 13 1847-
Subtitle varies
CaOTA Ag 27[O 1847-Mr,Jl 1848-Je,Ag,N 1849-Jl,S-D 1851]

NORTHERN advance. w 1846+
pub 1846+
CaOTA Ag 16 1855;Ag 27 1857;O 20 1858;Ag 17,O 5,26,N 9,D 7 1859[Mr 1861-Ag 1864]D 6 1865[66-68]D 23 1869[Ja,Mr-Je 1870]

SPIRIT of the age, and Canadian general advertiser and intelligencer. w Mr 3 1858-
CaOTA Ap 21,N 3,D 1 1858;Ag 10-24,S 7,O 26 1859 O 10,24 1860;D 4 1861;Ja 15,F 12,Ap 2,My 14,Jl 30,O 8,N 26 1862;Mr 25 1863;Ja 20,Mr 9,My 4 1864

BELLEVILLE

ANGLO-CANADIAN. *See* Hastings times

HASTINGS times. w F 24 1831-36||?
F-Je 1831 as Anglo-Canadian; Je 1831-Jl 3 1832 Phoenix
CaOT Mr 23,O 5 1831

INTELLIGENCER. w S 13 1834-1924||?
Title varies
CaOTA S 23 1848
DLC S 13 1834

Daily INTELLIGENCER. d 1867-1929||?
United with Ontario to form Ontario-intelligencer
CaOTA F 17 1868

ONTARIO-intelligencer. d 1870+
1870-1929? as Ontario

PHOENIX. *See* Hastings times

BERLIN. *See* KITCHENER

BOWMANVILLE

CANADIAN statesman and news. w 1855+
Title varies
CaOTA Ja 22-F 12,O 30 1856;D 9,30 1858;S 8 1859;My 23 1861;Jl 24-31,Ag 14,N 13-20,D 25 1862-Ja 1,F 5,Mr 12-19,Ap 2,My 21,S 3,D 24 1863;Ag 9 1866
MWA Ja 9,F 6,Ag 28 1862;Ja 1,Mr 5 1863;O 20 1864;O 19 1865;Ja 18,Mr 8,Je 7 1866;Ap 11 1867

STAR. w 1854-
CaOTA F 9 1855

BRACEBRIDGE

NORTHERN advocate, and general advertiser for the free grant districts of Parry Sound, Muskoka and Nipissing. w S 21 1869-74||?
1869-My? 1870 pub in Parry Sound
CaOTA D 14-21 1869;Ja,Mr 15,Ap 19,My 3,O 21 1870

BRADFORD

Bradford CHRONICLE and general advertiser. w O? 1853-
CaOTA S 27 1854;Je 13 1855;N 4 1857;S 1 1858;Ap 27,O 12 1859;Je 5-12,26,Jl 3,S 4,18, O 2-16,30,N 13-D 1861;Ja 8-22 1862

SOUTH Simcoe news. *See* Bradford witness and South Simcoe news

SOUTH Simcoe times. w F 6 1862-
CaOTA F 6,27-Mr 6,Ap 10,My 8,29-Je 5,19, Jl 17,Ag 14,28-S 4,O 2-16,N 6 1862;F 26,Je 25 1863

Bradford WITNESS. A conservative journal and South Simcoe general advertiser. w 1879-92||?
United with South Simcoe news to form Bradford witness and South Simcoe news
CaOTA My 20 1880

Bradford WITNESS and South Simcoe news. w 1866+
1866-92? as South Simcoe news
CaOTA S 3 1868

ONTARIO (*Continued*)

BRAMPTON

Brampton BANNER and times. w Ja 1 1868+
1868-1902? as Peel banner; 1903?-06? Peel banner and times
CaOTA My 28-Je 4 1868

PEEL banner. *See* Brampton banner and times

PROGRESS. w O 3 1873-74||
CaOTA O 3,24-F,Mr 13-20,Ap 3,24-My,Jl 10, Ag 14,S 18 1874

Brampton STANDARD. w Mr 6 1855-
Title varies
CaOTA Mr 27,S 4 1855;Jl 23-30,S 3,O 22 1857

Brampton TIMES. w S? 1854-1902||?
Title varies slightly. United with Peel banner to form Peel banner and times, later Brampton banner and times
CaOTA O 16 1855;Jl 11-Ag 8,S 19 1856; Mr 13-Ap 10,Ag 7-14,31,S 25,D 18 1857; Ja 15,Je 11-18,Jl 30-Ag 6 1858;F 11 1859; Ja 18 1861;F 7-14,Mr 21 1862

BRANTFORD

Brantford daily COURIER. d 1861-1918||
CaOBr [1900-03]-[05]-[15]-18

Brantford EXPOSITOR. d 1850+
pub 1852+
CaOBr [1904]-[10]-[13]+
CaOOA 1892-1902

BROCKVILLE

ANTIDOTE. w 1833-37||
Follows Brockville gazette. Followed by Brockville statesman

Brockville GAZETTE. w Ag 22 1828-32||
CSmH S 4 1830
CaOBkR complete
CaOTA Ag 22 1828

Brockville RECORDER. w Ja 16 1821+
pub 1830-32;49+
CSmH Ag 31 1830
CaOOA [1830-39;43-47;1913-15]Mr 1916+
CaOTA N 18 1823(extra);Mr 12 1827

RECORDER and times. d N 1873+
1873-1918 as Evening recorder
pub 1881+

Brockville SENTINEL. w 1830-32||
Merged with Antidote

STATESMAN. w 1837-51||
Follows Antidote
CSmH Jl 21 1846
CaO O 27 1838;Jl 12,S 20 1843

Brockville TIMES. d 1882- 1918||
United with Brockville times to form Recorder and times.
CoOBleR 1897-1906;09-15

BYTOWN. *See* OTTAWA

CHATHAM

Evening BANNER *See* Chatham daily news

Chatham BANNER-NEWS. w 1865-1921||?
1865-96? as Chatham banner
CaOTA Jl 19 1866;S 17 1868

Chatham daily NEWS. d 1894+
1894-99? as Evening banner; 1900?-02? Chatham banner-news
CaOC 1897+

Chatham weekly PLANET. w 1840-1922||?
CaOTA D 24 1874

Daily PLANET. d 1851-1922||
Merged with Chatham daily news
CaOC 1897-1922
CaOCN complete
DLC Je 26 1857

CLINTON

Clinton NEW ERA. w Jl 6 1865-1924||
Title varies slightly. Merged with Clinton news record
CaOTA Jl 20 1865
MWA F 21 1867

HURON news-record. *See* Clinton news-record

Clinton NEWS-RECORD. w 1878+
1878-98? as Huron news-record

COBOURG

REFORMER. w Je 1832-37||
CaOT D 13 1832-35

Cobourg SENTINEL. w My 17 1861-78||
United with Cobourg star to form Cobourg sentinel-star
CaOTA Je 8,Ag 24 1861;F 1,Mr 8-15,My 3,17-24,Jl 19,Ag 16-23,S 6-20,O,D 6 1862;Ja 3,31-F 14,Ap 18-My 2,23,Je 27 1863;F 12,26,Ap 1 1876;S 29 1877;Ja 12 1878
MWA Je 4 1864

Cobourg SENTINEL-STAR. w Ja 11 1831+
1831-78 as Cobourg star (title varies)
CSmH Mr 11 1840
CaOCb My 18 1861+
CaOT 1831-Ap 24,My 8-S 11,O 9 1833-O,N 16 1842-S 16 1846
CaOTA Ja 18,F-S 1831;Mr 28 1838;Jl 23 1845; Ja 19-26,Mr 1, My 31-Je 7,Jl 19,Ag 9-23, S 20-27,O 18-N 8,22 1848;Ja 24,Mr 7-14,28, Jl 18,S 5,O 10-17,N 12,21-28,D 12-26 1849; Ja 9-16,F 20-27,Mr 20,Ap,My 15-22,Je 19-Jl 3 1850;My 15 1861

Cobourg STAR. *See* Cobourg sentinel-star

Cobourg WORLD. w 1864+
CaOTA N 10 1865

COLBORNE

Colborne EXPRESS. w 1866+
Title varies
N Ja 8,Jl 9,D 10 1874;N 23 1876;F 22,My 10 1877;Mr 7 1878;Ag 12 1880

NORTHUMBERLAND pilot. w 1856-
CaOTA Ap 9,Ag 30 1857

Colborne TRANSCRIPT. w Ja 25? 1856-
N Ag 23 1856

COLLINGWOOD

Collingwood BULLETIN. *See* Enterprise-bulletin

Collingwood ENTERPRISE. w 1855-1931||
Subtitle varies. United with Collingwood bulletin to form Enterprise-bulletin
Suspended from Je 11 1863-Ja 20 1864?
CaOCo 1908-31
CaOTA Jl 28 1859;Je 20 1861;Ja 23,Jl 24-31,S 11,O 23-N 13,D 4 1862;Ja 22,F 5-12,Ap 9,My 7,Je 11 1863;Ja 20 1864;N 8 1866;Jl 24 1873; Ja 22,Je 25 1874;Ja 7-14 1875;Jl 6 1876

ENTERPRISE-BULLETIN. w 1870+
1870-1931 as Collingwood bulletin
CaOCo 1899-1900;02+
DLC Je 30 1927

MESSENGER. w 1877-81||
United with Collingwood enterprise to form Collingwood enterprise-messenger, later Collingwood enterprise
CaOTA Mr 17 1881

COOKSTOWN

BRITISH standard. w O 29 1869-70||
CaOTA D 31 1869;Ja 21 1870

CORNWALL

Cornwall CHRONICLE. w F 8 1845-
CaOTA F 8 1845

Cornwall ECONOMIST. w 1860-
CaOTA Mr 14 1861

Cornwall FREEHOLDER. *See* Cornwall standard-freeholder

Cornwall OBSERVER and eastern district general advertiser. w 1832-48||?
Title varies slightly
CSmH Jl 21 1837
CaO 1833-35
CaOTA Ag 21 1835-Ja[My,Jl-S]1836-Ja 9,O 5, D 28 1837-Ja 4,18,S 27,O 11,25,D 20-28 1838[39-42]Ja 5,Mr 2,16-23,My 11-18,N 16 1843;O 2-17 1844[Ja-Ap,Jl]O 30,N 13 1845 [46]Ap 3,My 29,Je 17,Jl 22,Ag 12-19,S 23, N 27,Ja 8 1848

Cornwall REPORTER and Eastern counties gazette. w 1876-85||?
Title varies slightly
CaOOA N 1880-My 1882
CaOTA Je 21,Jl 5-12,O 11-18 1879;O 24 1885

Cornwall STANDARD. w My 13 1886-1932||?
United with Cornwall freeholder to form Cornwall standard-freeholder
N Jl 1 1886

Cornwall STANDARD-FREEHOLDER. w 1846+
1846-1932? as Cornwall freeholder

DEER PARK

RECORDER of North Toronto. *See* Recorder (Toronto)

YORK gazette. w 1895-
CaOTA Mr 12 1896

DRUMMONDVILLE

REPORTER and Welland county farmer's friend. w 1853-
CaOTA Ag 16 1855;Je 12 1856;Mr 10 1859

DUNDAS

Dundas BANNER. w F 19 1858-1914||?
1858-1908? as True banner
CaOD 1858-Je 11 1868;72-73;77-81[84]-S 14 1885

Dundas weekly POST. w Ap 1834-Jl 26 1836||
CaOT Ag 18 1835;Jl 26 1836

TRUE banner. *See* Dundas banner

UPPER CANADA phoenix. w Ag 21 1818-19||?
CaONHi Je 26 1818

Dundas WARDER and Halton county general advertiser. w Ap 24 1846-52||?
CSmH Je 26 1846
CaOT [1848-51]
CaOTU S 7,N 9 1849[50-51]My 28 1852

DUNNVILLE

Dunnville INDEPENDENT.
CaOTA My 28 1864

DURHAM

Durham STANDARD, and county of Grey advertiser. w 1859-
CaOTA Jl 26,N 22 1861;Ja 10,Ap 4,25-My 2, 16,Jl 11-25,Ag 8,S 12,O 10,N 7-14,D 12,26 1862;Ja 30,F 13,Mr 27,Je 19,S 11-25 1863

ELMIRA

Elmira SIGNET. w 1893+
CaOKi 1893;1916-19

ELORA

Elora EXPRESS. w 1852+
1852-80? as Elora lightning express
CaOTU [1869]Ja 6 1870

Elora LIGHTNING express. *See* Elora express

Elora OBSERVER. w 1860-77||?
CaOTA Jl 17 1868

EXETER

Exeter ADVOCATE. d 1887-1924||?
United with Exeter times to form Exeter times-advocate

Exeter TIMES-ADVOCATE. w 1873+
1873-1924? as Exeter times
CLM S 19-26 1889

FORT WILLIAM

Weekly HERALD. w
CaOFw Ap 15 1882-D 29 1894

Morning HERALD. d 1905-My 30 1914||
CaOFw My 1907-14

JOURNAL. *See* Daily times-journal

Daily SENTINEL. d
CaOFw Ag 11 1884-[92]Ap 5-29 1893

Weekly SENTINEL. w
CaOFw Jl 29 1875-Jl 28 1883,Ag 4 1885-D 27 1895

Daily TIMES-Journal. w,sw,d F 1887+
1887-99 as Journal
w 1887-91;sw 1892-S 1893
pub 1887-1910
CaM 1910-31
CaOFw 1892;1908+

GALT

DUMFRIES reformer. *See* Weekly reformer

Weekly REFORMER. w 1848-1911||?
1848-99 as Dumfries reformer
CaOKi 1856-62;67;69-70;72-73;75-76;78-(99)

Galt REPORTER. d 1896+
CaOKi 1912+

Galt REPORTER and Waterloo county advertiser. w 1847-1924||?
Title varies slightly
CaOTA F 5 1858;Mr 26 1869

GODERICH

HURON signal. *See* Goderich signal

Goderich SIGNAL. w 1848+
1848-90? as Huron signal
CaOOA 1861-66

GRAVENHURST

Gravenhurst BANNER. w 1878+
NN Ap 21-28 1927

GUELPH

Guelph ADVERTISER and county of Waterloo advocate. w
Merged with Guelph weekly mercury
CaOT [1848-51]

Guelph HERALD. w 1847-1923||?
CaOG Je 1850-Je 1851
OClWHi Ap 9 1850

Guelph daily HERALD. d 1871-1923||?
WaPS [1915-18]

Guelph weekly MERCURY. w 1854-1927||?
CaOTA Ag 27-S 3,O 1,15,29,D 17 1874;F 24, Mr 2 1876;F 22 1877;Ja 17,Ap 11,Jl 11,S 5, N 28,D 12-18 1878;Mr 6,27,Je 5-12,Jl 10-24, N 13 1879;Mr 31 1881;S 3 1885

Guelph evening MERCURY. d Ag? 1867+
Title varies
CaOG 1923+
CaOGA F 1933+
CaOTA O 24-25,N 19 1867;Ja 20,F 7 1868; Je 3,Jl 31,N 9,16,D 22 1869;Ja 6-7,28,F 10,23, O 19,27 1870;F 18,Mr 10[Ap-My]Je 9,27, Ag 17,N 22,D 9 1871[Ja-F]Mr 1,22 1872
WaPS [1915]Je 7 1924

HAGERSVILLE

INDIAN. w D 30 1885-D 29 1886||?
NNHi 1885-86

HALLOWELL. *See* PICTON

HAMILTON

Morning BANNER. d 1854-
CaOTA Je 12 1857

BEE. w D 24 1844-
CaOH D 24 1844;Ja 1 1845
CaOOA D 24 1844-Ap 18 1845

COMMERCIAL advertiser. w 1846-
CaOH N 27 1846

Hamilton FREE press. w Je 27 1831-37||?
CaOH Je 27-Jl 7 1831;Je 23 1836
CaONHi D 11 1833
CaOTU N 1-8 1832

ONTARIO (*Continued*)

HAMILTON—*Continued*

Hamilton GAZETTE. sw 1835-S 1 1856||
Title varies
CSmH Mr 1 1837
CaO F 6 1836-F 8 1841
CaOT [1849-50;52-55]
CaOTA My 19 1845;F 19 1846[Mr 25-D 1847] F 24,Ap 10,O 23-D 1848[N 1849-O 1850;Ag-D 1851]F 9,Jl 29,N 1,15 1852[Ja-My 1853] Mr 9,Ag 10,S 4,O 19 1854;Mr 8-19,Ap 2,Ag 23,D 13 1855;Jl 17,Ag 4-7 1856
CaOTU N 8,D 6 1841;F 2 1854
N S 8 1853;Ap 27 1854

GORE balance. *See* Western mercury

Daily HERALD. d My 1861-
NSyU Je 5 1861

Hamilton HERALD. d 1889+
pub 1925+
CaOH [1907-08]-[11-15]-[17]-[23]-[25]

JOURNAL express.
CaOTA N 2 1849

PROVINCIALIST. w 1848-
CaOH Ja 15 1849

Hamilton SPECTATOR. w,sw Jl 15 1846-1921||?
Title varies: Hamilton spectator and journal of commerce; Semi-weekly spectator and journal of commerce
w 1846-Je 1855
CSmH Je 16 1853
CaOTA Mr 16,Ag 19 1854-Ag 11 1855;D 25 1856;Ja 1-22 1857;N 6 1858;O 18 1860;Mr 13 1862;N 19 1863;F 14 1867
CaOTU Ag 11 1848;Ja 11 1849
N F 24 1855

Hamilton SPECTATOR. d 1852+
Jl 15 1926 is 80th anniversary no.; Je 29 1927 is Diamond jubilee no.
CaM 1874
CaOH [1914]+
CaOTA My 17 1854;D 21 1857;My 20 1858; Je 8,O 12,N 9 1859;Ja 4 1860;Ja 25 1862;Jl 21 1863
CaOTU Je 12-15 1883
MWA Mr 19 1857;Jl 15 1926;Je 29 1927
NBu Je 2-3,5-30 1866
TxGR Je 29 1927

Hamilton TIMES. d 1850-
1850-91? as Evening times
CaOH Ap 3 1888

Hamilton TIMES. w,sw Ja 9 1858-1919||?
CaOTA F 20 1858

WESTERN mercury. w,sw N 1829-35||?
1829-Ja 13 1834 as Gore balance
w 1829-Mr 1834
CSmH Jl 1 1830
CaOH Je 3 1830
CaOOA Mr 18 1830
CaOT [1831]-[33]-Jl 10 1834
CaOTU N 8,D 27 1832;Ja 17-31,Mr 21,My 2 1833

HESPELER

Hespeler HERALD. w 1894+
CaOKi 1919+

INGERSOLL

Ingersoll CHRONICLE and county of Oxford intelligencer. w 1853-1921||?
Title varies slightly
CaOTA F 13 1863;Jl 7,O 27 1865;Mr 2,My 11-N 2 1866;D 8 1870;My 7 1874

Ingersoll ENQUIRER. w N 6 1863-
CaOTA N 20 1863

Ingersoll NEWS. w Ap 24 1867-
CaOTA Ap 24 1867

OXFORD herald. w S 7 1859-
CaOTA Ja 12 1860;Je 13,Jl 4,Ag 22,S 5,19-25, O 17,N-D 5 1861;Ja 9,F 6,20,Mr 6,20,My 15-29 1862

KENORA

To 1905 called Rat Portage

ARGUS. w
CaOOA S 21-N 23 1883

MINER and news. sw 1894+
CaOKe 1930+

NORTH star. w O 14 1879-
CaB O 14(supp)1879

PROGRESS. w Ja 1 1881-
CaOTA F 26,Ap 16,Ag 13 1881;Mr 25,Ap 22 1882

RAT PORTAGE news. w Ja 29 1881-D 27 1895||
1881-86? as Rat Portage progress
CaM D 19 1885;F 20 1886;S 16 1887-95
CaO 1881-Je 17 1882

RAT PORTAGE record. sw Jl 18 1891-97||?
CaM 1891-D 28 1895

KINCARDINE

BRUCE reporter. *See* Kincardine reporter

BRUCE review. *See* Kincardine review-reporter

Kincardine REPORTER. w 1866-1924||?
1866-85? as Bruce reporter. United with Kincardine review to form Kincardine review-reporter
CaOTA Mr 25 1869;Ja 27 1870

Kincardine REVIEW-REPORTER. w 1863+
1863-72? as Bruce review; 1873?-1924? Kincardine review
CaOTA Mr 8 1867

WESTERN Canadian commonwealth, and Kincardine and county Bruce advertiser. w S 1857-
CaOTA S 3,14,D 30 1858;Ja 13,20,Ag 25,S 15 1859

KINGSTON

ARGUS; a commercial, agricultural, political and literary journal. w 1846-
CaOKU 1846-[51]62
CaOOA [1862]
CaOTA D 10 1852;Ja-N,D 24 1862

BRITISH whig. d See Whig-standard

BRITISH whig. sw,w Ja 1834-1926||
Title varies slightly
sw 1834-49
CaOKU 1844-[48]61;63-64;69;73;77;80;84-91;94-99;1901-08
CaOTA S 9-29,O 11-21,28,N-D 6 1842;Mr 13, Ap 10,My 11,20,Je 1-5 1846;Mr 8 1861;Ja 23 1862;O 19 1876;Ja 16,N 27 1879;Ap 1 1880
MWA Ag 1 1872
N F 20 1844

CANADA gazette. *See under* Ottawa

CANADIAN freeman and Catholic observer. w 1883+
Title varies
pub 1918+
CaOTA D 22 1886-N 1887;Ja-F 1888
IU Mr 21 1918-Je 1926
PPCHi [1885;87-89;92]

CANADIAN mirror of Parliament.
CaQMG Je 19,23,26,30 1841

CANADIAN watchman. w Ag 13 1830-32||
Followed by Kingston spectator
CaOTA Ag 13 1830-F 18 1831
N Ja 14 1831
NNHi Mr 18-Ap 15,My 13-Jl 22 1831
P-M Ag 9 1832

Kingston CHRONICLE. *See* Standard

COLONIAL standard. w
CaO 1892-Je 28 1895

Kingston GAZETTE. 1810-18. *See* Standard

Kingston GAZETTE and religious advocate. w My 15 1828-Ag 6 1830||
Merged with Kingston chronicle, later Standard
CaOTU [S 1828-N 6 1829]
NNHi Jl 3,O 3,N 7-14,D 5 1828;Ja 9-30, Mr 13,Je 12-19,Ag 7,S 4-11 1829

Kingston HERALD. w
CaOKU Ap 23 1844-45;D 15 1846;O 20 1847; Ap 26 1848
DLC My 2 1843

NEWS. sw 1841-O? 1847||
United with Chronicle and gazette to form Chronicle and news, later Standard
CaOT N 1843-O 1844
CaOTA Mr 16 1843

Daily NEWS. *See* Daily standard

PATRIOT and farmers' monitor. *See under* Toronto

Kingston SPECTATOR. w Ja 1833-36||
Follows Canadian watchman
CaOOA 1833-34

STANDARD. w,sw S 25 1810-1926||
1810-18 as Kingston gazette; 1819-Je 1835 Kingston chronicle; Jl 1835-O ? 1847 Chronicle and gazette; N? 1847-99? Chronicle and news; 1899?-1905? News; 1906-07 News and times
sw Jl 1835-O? 1847
CSmH Mr 8 1838
CaO Jl 1840-Je 1842
CaOKU [1810-12;15-18]-20;N 1824-Je 1825;Jl 1826-Je 22 1827;Jl 19 1828-[29-30]-Je 23 1832; Jl 1835-Je 1837;Jl 1838-Je 1840[41-47]-N 3 1849;54-S 2 1859
CaOOA 1818;21-23;41-42
CaOTA D 12 1812-My 1815;Ap 25,O 25 1828; Jl 9 1831
CaQMG Ja 28 1840;My 8,22 1844
MWA 1810-N 19,D 1811-Mr 24,Ap 28-Je 9,23 1812

Daily STANDARD. d 1851-D 1 1926||
1851-1905 as Daily news; 1906-07 News and times. United with British whig to form Whig-standard
CSmH My 31 1853
CaOKU 1851-[55]-[58-59]-82;84-1902[08-11]-Ap 23 1921 22-[24]-26

Kingston STATESMAN. w -1845||
CaOT My 8 1844

Evening TIMES. d 1897-1903||?
United with Daily news to form News and times, later Daily standard
CaOKU [1897-98]

UPPER Canada herald. w Mr 9 1819-51||
CSmH S 15 1830
CaOKU Mr 26 1822-F 18 1823
CaOOA 1819;21-[23-24]
CaOT D 16 1823;Ag 16 1825;Ag 27 1828;Ja 20, F 3 1830;Ap 4,Je 27,S 12 1832;Ap 3,Jl 3 1833; F 19 1834;Ag 4,18 1835;Ag 7,25 1840
CaOTA Mr-D 6 1825;N 27 1827;My 8 1833; Ja 28-Ag,S 17-O,D 1839
DLC Ag 21 1827;Ja 1,Je 3,24,Jl 8 1828;Ag 26, S 23-30,O 21 1829;Ja 5-12 1831
MWA My 7 1822
WHi Jl 2 1822

WHIG-STANDARD. d 1849+
1849-N 1926 as British whig
pub 1912+
CaOKU 1854-55;61;63-64;69;73;76-77;79-80;82; 84-86[88]96-[1908-09;14-17]18[25]D 1926+
CaOT [Ag 10 1850-F 26 1851]
CaOTA S 11 1852;F 21 1854
MH N 14 1899[1915]

KITCHENER

To 1918? as Berlin

BERLIN chronicle and Waterloo county reformers' gazette. w 1856-
CaOKi 1856;58-[60]69

BERLIN daily news. *See* Daily record

BERLIN news-record. *See* Daily record

BERLIN telegraph. w Ja 7 1853-99||?
CaOK 1853;56-64;66[69]

BERLINER journal. *See* Ontario journal

CANADA museum and Allgemeine zeitung. w Ag 27 1835-40||?
In German
CaOT Je 23 1836

Der DEUTSCHE canadier. w 1840-59||
In German
CaOKi 1844-45;48-49;50-59

DEUTSCHE zeitung. w N 3 1891-1905||?
United with Canadischer bauernfreund (Waterloo) to form Canadischer bauernfreund und Deutsche zeitung (Waterloo)
In German
CaOKi 1891-98

FREIE presse. w Ag 6 1886-87||?
In German
CaOKi 1886-Jl 1887

ONTARIO glocke. w
In German
CaOKi 1883-87,89-98,1910

ONTARIO journal. w D 29 1859-My 10 1924||
1859-1916 as Berliner journal
In German
CaOKi 1861-1909;11-18
CaOLU 1860-98

Daily RECORD. d F 9 1878+
1878-Ja 31 1897 as Berlin daily news; F 1 1897-1919? as News-record
pub 1915+
CaOKi [1878-79;93]-[1906-07]
NN F 9 1878

Daily TELEGRAPH. d My 1896-1922||
CaOKi [1898-99]-[1901]-[21]
CaOLU 1909-Jl 1922

LAKEFIELD

Lakefield CHRONICLE. *See* Lakefield news

Lakefield NEWS. w 1887+
1887-92? as Lakefield chronicle
CU-B Jl 4,O 3-10,24 1890

LANARK

Lanark OBSERVER. w
CaOOA Ag 14 1850-Ag 1853

LANCASTER

GLENGARRY times. w 1880-82||?
CaOOA 1881-82

LEWISTON

NIAGARA sentinel. w
N D 30 1825;Ja 6,20,F 17 1826

LINDSAY

Weekly CANADIAN post. w 1857?-1920||
CaOLi 1875-1920
CaOTA O 8 1880

VICTORIA warder. *See* Watchman-warder

Weekly WARDER. *See* Watchman-warder

WATCHMAN warder. w 1856+
1856- as Weekly warder; - 1899 Victoria warder
CaOLi 1879-1930

LISTOWEL

Der PERTH volksfreund. w 1878-82||?
In German
CaOS Jl 22 1881-D 22 1882

LONDON

London ADVERTISER. d O 28 1863+
O 27 1933 is 70th anniversary number
pub 1900+
CL O 27 1933
CaO 1889+
CaOL 1894+
CaOLU O 1864-[66]S 1868-[72]-[97]-[1919-20]
CaOTA Mr 13,Ag 9 1866

London ADVERTISER. w 1863+
Title varies: Liberal and western advertiser; Western advertiser and liberal; etc.
Suspended from 1915-28?
CaOLU S 1869-F 1873;75-F 1883;86-87;91-98; 1900-14
CaOOA F-Je 1875
CaOTA N 5,19,D 1875;Mr 31 1876;O 5 1877
InRE My 25 1881
TJT N 16 1883

ONTARIO (*Continued*)

LONDON—*Continued*

CANADA inquirer. w 1839-
MWA S 8-29,O 13-20 1841

CANADIAN free press. w 1849-
CaOTA Je 8,29 1854;Ag 16 1855;F 1 1861; Ja 1 1864

ECHO. w 1879+
MWA Mr 5 1886

London FREE press. d Ja 2 1849+
CaO 1889+
CaOL 1894+
CaOLU [1874]1921
CaOTA N 9 1855;My 22 1857;N 18 1859;S 28 1861;Ap 21,My 9,N 30,D 9 1863
MBAt Ap 20 1865
NbHi F 27 1877

London HERALD and London and western districts advertiser. w Ja 7 1843-
CaOLU Ja 7-Jl 12 1843

LIBERAL and western advertiser. *See* London advertiser

London NEWS and western reformer. w 1861-
CaOTA F 7 1862

London TIMES and Canada general advertiser. w Mr 1845-
Title varies
CaOLU [1846-48]
CaOT [1848-51]
CaOTA D 22 1854

WESTERN advertiser and liberal. See London advertiser

WESTERN globe, or London western and Huron districts' advertiser. w
CaOT [1846-47]

L'ORIGINAL

NEWS, Eastern Ontario and Ottawa Valley advocate. w 1876-83||?
CaOTA N 6 1877

MADOC

Madoc MERCURY. w 1864?-68||
Subtitle varies
CaOTA S 22 1866;Ja 18,F 8 1868

MARKHAM

Markham ECONOMIST and sun. w Jl 3 1856+
1856-1916? as Markham economist
Suspended from Je 30 1864-Je 14 1866(for this period *See* Rural economist)
CaOT [1856-59]
CaOTA 1856-O 15 1868;Ja 14,O 28,D 6 1869; Ja-F 3,17,Mr,My 5-12,26-Je 2,30,S 1 1870; S-D 1872;Jl 25 1878;My 1,15 1879;Je 1 1882; S 25 1884

RURAL economist. w O 25 1864-My 31 1866||?
Replaces Markham economist. O 25-D 1 1864 as Ruralist and economist
CaOTA 1864-My 1866

RURALIST and economist. *See* Rural economist

Markham SUN. w 1881-1916||?
United with Markham economist to form Markham economist and sun
CaOTA F 19-26 1885;Jl 15 1886;F 17 1887; My 21 1891

MEAFORD

Meaford MONITOR. w 1868-1919||?
Subtitle varies
CaOTA Ja 6,Mr 31-Ap 14,28-My 5 1870;S 21 1877

MERRICKVILLE

Merrickville CHRONICLE. w 1856-69||?
CaQMG My 28 1867

MILTON

CANADIAN champion and county of Halton intelligencer. w 1861-
CaOTA Mr 5,Ap 2,My 14,Je 5,18,Jl 10,Ag 13, N 5 1862

HALTON new era. w 1860-
CaOTA Ap 24 1862

MITCHELL

Mitchell ADVOCATE. w 1860+
Subtitle varies
CaOTA Ap 13,Je 15,Jl 6-13,O 26,D 14-21 1866; Mr 15,Ap 19-Ag,S 13-O 18,N-D 6 1867;Ja 21,F 25-Mr 11,Ap 1-8,29-My 6 1870;My 1,Je 5,Ag 21,O 16 1874;F 5,26 1875

MORPETH

PROGRESSIONIST. w Ja 11 1861-
CaOTA My 24 1861

MORRISBURG

Morrisburg COURIER. w 1862-1900||?
1863-Je 21 1867 as Dundas courier. Title varies
CaOTA Ag 10 1866;Ja 11,My 3-24,Je 21,Jl 5,19-26,S 13,27,N 1,29-D 13 1867;Ja 10-17,F 14,Mr 13,Jl 3,Ag 7,S 4-11,O 2 1868;Ja 28,Ag 15,29 1870

LEADER. w 1889+
CaOOA N-D 1908;F 1909-11;16+

MOUNT FOREST

CONFEDERATE. w 1867+
Title varies: Confederate and examiner; Confederate and representative; etc.

EXAMINER and general advertiser for the counties of Grey and Wellington. w Ap 17 1862-79||?
United with Confederate to form Confederate and examiner, later Confederate
CaOTA My 8-29,N 6,D 4 1862;Ja 8 1863
MWA Ag 31 1865

Mount Forest EXPRESS; Arthur, Luther, Proton, Egremont, Normanby and Minto advocate. w Jl 1860-
CaOTA Je 5-12,26,O 2-9,N 6,27-D 18 1861;Ja 8 1862

NAPANEE

Napanee BEAVER. w 1870+
1870-76? as Ontario beaver
CaOTA Jl 13 1872
MH D 29 1911;Ja 26-F 2 1912[15]-Mr 10 1916
MWA Ag 19 1898

Weekly EXPRESS. w 1864+
Title varies
CaOTA Je 28 1872

ONTARIO beaver. *See* Napanee beaver

Napanee STANDARD. w 1854-86||?
Title varies
CaOTA O 18 1866
P-M Jl 4 1854

NEW HAMBURG

CANADISCHES volksblatt. w 1854-1909||?
In German
CaOKi [1858-62;65-66;76;84]

HAMBURGER beobachter. w
In German
CaOKi [1855]

New Hamburg INDEPENDENT. w 1879+
CaOKi 1917+

NEU Hamburger neutrale. w
In German
CaOKi 1855;57

NEW TORONTO

New Toronto and Mimico ADVERTISER. w S 21 1917+
pub 1917+

NEWMARKET

Newmarket COURIER. *See* North York reformer

Newmarket ERA. w F 5 1852+
1852-Jl 12 1861 as New era
CaOTA S 3 1852;S 22 1854-Ja 1,Ap 30,S 1858-[59]Ja 6,Mr 2-16 1860[Je 21 1861-63]Jl 8,S 9,23 1864;Ja 13,31,Jl 21 1865[Ja-Jl 1866]-Ja 15,Je 11,D 31 1869-Jl 15 1870;O 20 1871;My 24 1872-Je 1876;Mr 9,Ag 3 1877;Jl 4,Ag 29-O 10, 31,N 14,28,D 12 1879;Ja 16,Jl 16,O 8 1880;Je 24,Ag 5 1881

Semi-weekly ERA. sw D 28 1874-78||?
CaOTA 1874-Ja 13 1875

NEW ERA. *See* Newmarket era

NORTH YORK reformer. w 1867-89||?
1867-74 as Newmarket courier
CaOTA O 15 1868;S 8 1876;N 19 1880

NORTH York sentinel. w D 19 1855-
CaOTA F 14-N 13 1856

NIAGARA

CANADA constellation. w Jl 19 1799-1800||?
CaOOA Ag 1799-Ja 18 1800

CANADIAN. w Ag 11 1824-1825||?
CaONHi Ag 17 1825

CANADIAN argus, and Niagara spectator. w N 18 1819-
DLC N 18,D 2-9 1819

Niagara CHRONICLE. w S 2 1837-54||
CSmH S 4 1846
CaONHi [1838-54]
CaOTA Jl 24 1851;Je 17 1853;My 19 1854
NNHi D 16 1837

GLEANER and Niagara newspaper. w D 4 1817-37||
CaOH F 3,Mr 3 1827
CaONHi Ja 6 1819;D 1831-33
CaOOA [1827-30]
CaOT F 11 1819;O 23 1824
CaOTA D 10 1818;Ag 5,O 28 1819

Niagara HERALD. w Ja 17 1801-Ag 28 1802||
CaO [1801-02]
CaOTA O 24 1801

Niagara HERALD. w Ja 1828-30||?
CSmH S 2 1830
CaONHi [1828-30]

Niagara MAIL. w 1844-70||?
CaOTA Mr 14,Je 13,O 17 1855;Ja 2,Mr 12 1856; Jl 17 1861;Ap 2 1862;F 14-21,Mr 14,Ap 11,My 9-16,Jl 4,Ag 8-15,S 12,N 7,D 5-19 1866;Ja 16,F 27 1867
MWA Mr 26 1851

Daily RECORD. d Ja 1900-D 1917||
Merged with Evening review
CaON 1915-17

Niagara REPORTER. w My 10 1833-42||?
CaONHi [1835-37;41]
CaOTA Ap 30 1841

Evening REVIEW. d O 5 1914+
pub 1914+
CaON 1915-19;23-29;Je 1931+

Niagara SPECTATOR. w Mr 1816-19||
CaONHi [1816-19]
CaOTA O 1,D 3-17 1818;Ja 28,My 27,Jl 8,29 1819
MWA Ap 30 1818

SPIRIT of the times. w Ja 1830-31||?
CaONHi Ja 24 1830

UPPER Canada gazette. *See under* Toronto

UPPER Canada guardian; or, Freeman's journal. w 1807-Je 1812||
CaOTA Ja 22 1808;Ap 14 1810
CaOTU Ag 27,N 5 1807;D 30 1809[10](photostat)
WHi N 24 1810

NORTH BAY

NUGGET. tw 1909+
CaONb 1931+

OAKVILLE

EXPRESS and county of Halton advertiser. w Ja 6 1875-82||?
CaOTA Ja 6,Ap 15,Jl 29 1875;F 24,Mr 16 1876;Je 7,Jl 26 1877

Oakville SENTINEL. sw,w 1854-
CaOTA D 14-21 1855;O 7 1856;S 11 1857

Oakville STANDARD. w 1878-82||?
CaOTA My 7 1880

OIL SPRINGS

Oil Springs CHRONICLE and petroleum advocate. w 1862-
CaOTA O 25 1866

ORANGEVILLE

SUN. w 1860+
Title varies
CaOTA Ap 24,Je 19,Jl 17,Ag 28,S 18,O 9 1862;Je 25 1863;O 5 1865;Ja 18,F 15,My 24,Ag 2,23,S 6-13,27-O 4,25,D 20 1866;Ja 10-17,F 28-Mr 7 1867[68] Ja 7 1869;F 17,Mr 10,24-Ap 7,My 5 1870;O 22,D 24 1874;Mr 4 1875

ORILLIA

Orillia EXPOSITOR. *See* Orillia packet and times

Orillia NEWS LETTER. w 1884+
CaOTA My 14,Je 11,Jl 9 1886;S 16 1887

NORTHERN light. w S 17 1869-72||?
CaOTA D 31 1869;Mr 4-18,Ap 15,29,My 20-27 1870;Mr 24 1871

Orillia PACKET and times. w 1867+
1867-77? as Orillia expositor; 1878?-87? Times and expositor; 1888?-1925? Orillia times
CaOTA D 19 1873;O 22,N 5 1874;Ja 1,F 4,25-Mr 4,O 7 1875;My 12 1876;N 14 1879;Ja 2,Ap 16,Jl 2,Ag 6,S 3-17,O 1-8,N 26-D 17 1880;Ja 7,28,F 11-25,Ap 8-Jl 8,22,Ag,S 9-23,O 14-21,N,D 16 1881-Ja 13,27,My 5,Je 9,S 8,22-O 1882;Mr 9,Ap 27-My 4,25-Je 1,Jl 6-20,Ag 31-S,N 23,D 28 1883;Ja 11,Mr 14,Ap 25,My 16,Jl 11,O 17 1884;Je 26 1885

Orillia TIMES. *See* Orillia packet and times

TIMES and expositor. *See* Orillia packet and times

OSHAWA

ONTARIO reformer. *See* Oshawa daily times

Oshawa REFORMER. *See* Oshawa daily times

Oshawa TELEGRAM. w,d,tw My 1920-O 8 1925||
Merged with Oshawa reformer, later Oshawa daily times
w 1920-O 1923; d N-Ag 22 1923
CaOOsT 1923-25

Oshawa daily TIMES. w,sw,tw,d Ap 14 1871+
1871-Je 30 1927 as Ontario reformer
w 1871-S 1919; sw O 1919-S 1920; tw O 1920-S 1925
pub 1871-83;91;93;95;1909-11;13-14;16+
CaOOs 1922;26-Je 1932

Oshawa VINDICATOR. w O 1 1855-1917||
CaOOsT 1857-71;75-1905;07-10;14-17
CaOTA [Jl 1860-Je 1864]My 9,Je 27 1866;Mr 28 1877;S 25,O 30 1878
MWA My 27 1863

OTTAWA

To 1858? as Bytown

Ottawa ADVOCATE, and Dalhousie and Sydenham advertiser. w 1842-
CSmH F 13 1844

ANGLO-SAXON. m,ir 1887-1900||?
CaOOA D 1898-Mr 1899
CaQMM 1887-[89]-92;94[95-Je 1900]

BEE. w My 19 1866-
CaOTA Je 23 1866

ONTARIO (*Continued*)

OTTAWA—*Continued*

BYTOWN gazette, and Ottawa and Rideau advertiser. w F 2 1836-
F-Ap? 1836 as Bytown independent and farmers' advocate
CaOTU [1836-37]Ja 24 1838[43-44]Mr 20 1847 [48]

BYTOWN independent. *See* Bytown gazette

BYTOWN packet. *See* Packet and weekly commercial gazette

Le CANADA. tw D 21 1865-D 21 1869||
In French
CaO Ja 13 1866-69
CaQMS [1865-69]
CaQQL complete

CANADA gazette. w O 2 1841-D 11 1869||
1841-44 pub in Kingston; 1845-51 in Montreal; 1852-55; 60-65 in Quebec; 1856-59 in Toronto
CaOKU 1857-69
CaOOA complete
CaOT 1841-O 1869
CaOTU [1842]F 18,D 16 1843;F 3,Mr 2,Je 29 1844[45]Ja-My 6 1848;Ap 27,O 19 1850;Ap 19 1851;S 30 1854;D 29 1855;Ag 15,29 1857;N 19 1859;N 3-7 1860
CaQMM complete
DLC [1841-68]
IU 1866-68

CANADA gazette. w Jl 1 1867+
CaB Jl 1 1867[73;Ja-Je 1897]+
CaOKU 1867+
CaOOA 1867+
CaOT 1867+
CaOTU 1916+
CaOTV [1879;89-1903]-[05]-[08-09]-[25]-[31]+
CaQMM 1867+
DLC Jl-D 1868;Jl 1871-Je 1873;Jl-D 1887;Jl 1892+
IEN 1928+
IU 1867-Je 1869;Jl 1878+
NN My 14 1881,[92]+
WaU O 19 1935+

CANADIAN citizen. w,sw 1844-1916||?
1844-1908 as Ottawa citizen;1909-12 Central Canada citizen
CaOO 1854[60-61]-63
CaOOA O 1859-My 1860;1909;12-Mr 1913
CaOTU [1851-54]Ja 27,F 3-10 1855
MH N 24 1914-Mr 21 1916

Le CANADIEN. N 28 1924-Ja 29 1926||
In French
CaO complete

CENTRAL Canada citizen. *See* Canadian citizen

Ottawa CITIZEN. w 1844-1908. *See* Canadian citizen

Ottawa CITIZEN. d 1864+
pub both a morning and evening ed (title varies slightly)
pub 1877;79-82;88;90-96;98-1900;02;07+
CaB D 1 1908[Mr]-My 1910
CaO Jl 1 1865+
CaOO 1865-66;69-72;74-84;87-(1908-09)-(19)-(21-22)-(28)+
CaOOA My 1871-Ap 1872;75 (80)84-85 (89;92) 1912+
CaQ 1910-Ag 1913
CaQMF 1879-81
DLC Mr 1898+

Le COURRIER d'Ottawa. w Ap 3 1861-
In French
CaO 1861-Mr 27 1862
CaQMS [1861-Mr 5 1864]

Le COURRIER federal. w My 21 1887-Jl 5 1888||
In French
CaO complete

Le COURRIER federal. w Ag 3 1917-Mr 27 1925||
In French
CaO complete

Le DROIT. d Mr 27 1913+
In French
pub 1913+
CaO Ap 1913+
CaOOU 1913+
CaQ 1925+
CaQMS [1913-32]
CaQMSm 1914+
CaQQL 1913+

Ottawa FREE press. d 1866?-1916||
United with Ottawa journal to form Ottawa journal-press
CaB Ag 10[O]1908-Ag 1910
CaO 1877-1916
CaOO 1866-67;71;73-[80]-96[98]1901;03-[07-08]-[16]
CaOOA [1875-88;90-96]D 1899[1903;12]
CaOTA Ap 6,Je 22,Jl 3,19,Ag 16,S 26,O 29 1877;F 28 1878
N Jl 9 1872
—morning ed *See* Ottawa journal

GAZETTE d'Ottawa. D 27 1878-F 28 1898||
In French
CaO complete

Ottawa JOURNAL. d D 10 1885+
pub both a morning and evening ed. 1918-19 evening ed as Ottawa journal-press
pub 1885+
CaB 1928+
CaO 1885+
CaOO 1885-1903;06[07-08]-19;22[23]-[27]-33
CaOOA 1917+
CaQ 1926+

JUSTICE. w Je 1 1912-S 25 1914||
In French
CaO complete
CaOOA complete

Weekly LETTER. w
CaB F 29 1908-F 27 1909

Evening MAIL. d Ja 1870-72||?
CaOTA Mr 30 1870

PACKET and weekly commercial gazette. w 1844-F 15 1851||
CaO [1844-51]
CaOO N 1849-51
CaOTU Ap 17,Je 19,D 4 1847[48-50]Ja 18-F 15 1851

Le PROGRES. w
CaQMS Je 3 1858-D 1 1858

Ottawa daily SUN. d 1884-85||?
CaOOA My 19-D 10 1884

Le TEMPS. d N 3 1894-Mr 4 1916||
In French
CaO 1894-1915
CaQ D 1894-N 23 1912

TIMES. w D 18 1865-Ja 9 1877||
CaO complete
CaQ 1866-67;69-70;75
N Jl 8 1872

Ottawa daily TIMES. d D 18 1865-Ja 9 1877||
CaO complete
CaOO 1866-67;71;73[76]
CaOTA D 25 1865;Mr 6-15,Je 27 1866;Ap 1 1868
CaQ 1866-67;69-70;75
N Jl 8 1872

Ottawa TRIBUNE. w Jl 23 1854-Ap 25 1862||
CaO complete
CaOTA Ja 2 1857

UNION. w Mr 1858-Ja 24 1866||
CaO Mr 30 1859-66

UNITED Canada. w 1888+
CaOTA Ag 31-S 14,28 1889;F 18 1893

La VALEE d'Ottawa. w
In French
CaQ O 20 1884-Jl 3 1888

OWEN SOUND

Owen Sound COMET. w 1853-
Title varies: Owen Sound comet and general advertiser; Owen Sound comet, Grey and Bruce chronicle; etc.
CaOTA [Je 1866-S 1867]

Weekly PROGRESS and counties of Grey and Bruce advocate and advertiser. w Ag 7 1857-
Titles varies slightly
CaOTA Ja 30-F 20 1857

Owen Sound SUN-TIMES. sw,d 1890+
1890-1919? as Owen Sound sun (sw)

Owen Sound TIMES. w,sw 1854-1919||
Title varies slightly. United with Owen Sound sun to form Owen Sound sun-times
w 1854-1916?
CaOTA O 2,23-N 3 1857;Ja 15 1858;S 30-O 21 1859;Jl 19,N 1 1861;Ja 10-17,F 14,Je 27,Ag 29,O 17,N 28 1862;Jl 13-20,Ag 10 1866;Ja 11 1867;Je 12 1868

PAISLEY

Paisley ADVOCATE. w 1863+
CaOTA S 18 1874

PALMERSTON

Palmerston PROGRESS. w O 22 1874-75||
CaOTA D 17 1874;Ja 7,F 4 1875

PARKDALE

TIMES. w 1883-92||?
CaOTA Ja 18 1889

PARRY SOUND

NORTHERN advocate. *See under* Bracebridge

PERTH

BATHURST courier and Ottawa gazette. *See* Perth courier

BATHHURST gazette. . . *See* Perth courier

Perth COURIER. w Ag 8 1834+
1834- as Bathurst courier and Ottawa gazette; - Bathurst gazette and Ottawa general advertiser
CaOOA [1835-60]-1901
CaOTA [Ag 29 1834-D 15 1837]

INDEPENDENT examiner, and Bathurst district advertiser. w 1828-
CSmH S 10 1830

PETERBOROUGH

BACKWOODSMAN and Peterboro sentinel. w 1833-
CaOTA Ap 22(extra)My 20,Je 3 1840

Peterborough EXAMINER. w 1847-1930||?
pub 1890-1930
CaOTA Ap 15,D 9 1858;Ag 2 1860

Peterborough EXAMINER. d 1835+
pub 1890+

Peterborough GAZETTE. w Ag 15 1845-
CaOOA Ag 15 1845-My 2 1846
CaOTU 1845-[46]Ja 2-9 1847

Peterborough REVIEW. w 1853-1919||?
CaOTA O 13 1876

PETROLIA

Petrolia SENTINEL. w Mr 27? 1866-
CaOTA O 9 1866

PICTON

1835?-44 as Hallowell

Picton GAZETTE. w D 13 1830+
1830-35 as Hallowell free press; Ja 29 1836-39 Prince Edward gazette; 1840-49 Traveller; or Prince Edward gazette; 1840-49 Traveller; or Prince Edward gazette
pub 1830+
CaO My 13 1836
CaOKU [1830-31]
CaOT F 1836-My 1837
CaOTA O 9,D 25 1832-D 16 1833

HALLOWELL free press. *See* Picton gazette

PRINCE Edward gazette. *See* Picton gazette

SUN. w 1844-
CaOTA My 5 1846

Picton TIMES. w 1854+
CaOTA My 1 1866

TRAVELLER. *See* Picton gazette

PORT ARTHUR

Weekly HERALD and Algoma miner. w 1882-1905||?
CaOT [1890-1901]

PORT HOPE

BRITISH Canadian. w 1862-
CaOTA My 31 1866

Port Hope TIMES. w 1862-1926||?
Title varies slightly
CaOTA N 23 1882

PORT PERRY

Port Perry STANDARD. *See* Port Perry star

Port Perry STAR. w Ag 16 1866+
1866-1907? as Port Perry standard
CaOTA Ag 16,N 29 1866-Ag 20 1868

PRESCOTT

CONSERVATIVE messenger. *See* Messenger

GRANVILLE gazette. w Ja 1832-37||
Follows Prescott telegraph
CaOTU O 1 1833(photostat)

Prescott JOURNAL. w 1847+
1847-89 as Prescott telegraph and Grenville weekly advertiser (title varies)
CaOTA Mr 19 1851;Je 1 1864;Ja 29,D 2 1868;N 3 1871
N F 2 1876

MESSENGER. w 1855-1900||?
1855-61? as Conservative messenger
CaOTA Je 21 1861

Prescott TELEGRAPH. w 1830-32||
Followed by Grenville gazette

Prescott TELEGRAPH. 1847-89 *See* Prescott journal

PRESTON

Preston PROGRESS. w 1886-1922||?
CaOKi 1916-17

PRINCE ALBERT

ONTARIO observer. w D 12 1857-
Title varies slightly
CaOTA D 12 1857-Ja 3,D 2 1858;Ja 27 1859;N 22 1860;Jl 18,Ag 22,S 5,O 17,N 14-21,D 19-26 1861;Mr 20,Ap 3,My 22,Je 12,26,Jl 31,Ag 28,S 11,O 9,N 13 1862;Ja 29-F 5,26,Ap 16,My 28 1863

QUEENSTOWN

COLONIAL advocate. *See* Advocate (Toronto)

RAT PORTAGE *See* KENORA

RICHMOND HILL

BRITISH tribune and York Ridings gazette. w Je 12 1857-
Je 12-D 4 1857 as York Ridings gazette and Richmond Hill advertiser
CaOTA 1857-D 25 1858

LIBERAL. w 1878+
CaOTA [My 27 1881-83]-D 6 1888

YORK commonwealth. *See* York herald

YORK herald. w D 3 1858-89||?
1858-Ap 1 1859 as York commonwealth (subtitle varies)
CaOTA 1858-60

YORK RIDINGS gazette and Richmond Hill advertiser. *See* British tribune and York Ridings gazette

ONTARIO (*Continued*)

ROND EAU

Rond Eau NEWS. w 1873-75||
CaOTA S 24,D 24 1875

ST. CATHARINES

BRITISH American journal. w Ag 6 1833-35||
1833-Ja 21 1834 as British colonial argus
CaOOA 1833-S 24 1835
CaOT Ja 28-O 14 1834
CaOTA Ja 11 1834

BRITISH colonial argus. *See* British American journal

St. Catharines CONSTITUTIONAL. w 1850-68||
CaOTA Ja 2 1856;Ja 14,Jl 29 1857;N 1 1860;Mr 21,Je 20,Jl 25[O 17 1861-63]S 7 1865[Ap-D 1866]F 7 1867;Jl 23 1868

FARMERS' journal and Welland Canal intelligencer. *See* St. Catharines journal

St. Catharines JOURNAL. w F 1 1826-1915||?
1826-37? as Farmers' journal and Welland Canal intelligencer; 1838?- St. Catharines journal and Welland Canal advertiser (Ja 28 1834 united with British colonial argus to form British American journal. Resumed pub 1835)
CSmH S 3 1846
CaOOA [1835-40;44-55]-[58]-[63]-My 1869
CaOTA Ap 11 1827;Mr 26 1828;D 27 1855;Jl 30 1857;D 2-9 1858;My 30,Jl 11,S 11,O 17,N 7-21, D 5-12,26 1861[62]Ja 1,F 5-12,Mr 19,Je 11,O 1-8 1863;Ja 14,F 25,Ap 7,My 12 1864;S 3-17,D 3,17,31 1874;Mr 4 1875
NNHi My 3,31,Jl 5-19,Ag 16-23,S 6 1838

St. Catharines evening JOURNAL. d 1859-1919||?
CaOTA N 23 1863;Je 23,30,Ag 11,13,O 4,D 22 1866;F 20-21,Mr 6 1867

St. Catharines NEWS. w O 17 1872-90||?
CaOOA O 1872-S 1874;75-N 1877;81-86
CaOTA D 19 1872

Semi-weekly POST. sw 1854-
CaOTA Ag 24 1858;D 13 1861

Weekly POST. w 1856-68||?
CaOTA F 20 1867

St. Catharines STANDARD. d Ap 21 1891+
pub 1892-1908;10+
CaOSc 1913+

ST. DAVIDS

SPECTATOR. w Ja 1816-17||
CaONHi Jl 19 1816
DLC Ap 5,Jl 19 1816

ST. THOMAS

Weekly DISPATCH. w 1853-76||?
CaOTA S 3,17,O 29 1857;Je 3,24 1858

St. Thomas JOURNAL. sw,d 1859-Je 29 1918||
1859?-Ap 18 1909 as Evening journal. United with St. Thomas daily times to form St. Thomas times-journal
sw 1859?-82?
CaOSt [1878-79]1906-18

LIBERAL. w S 20 1832-37||
CaONHi Ja 29,Mr 26 1835
CaOOA 1832-O 10 1833
N O 10 1833

St. Thomas TIMES-JOURNAL. d 1873+
1873-Je 29 1918 as St. Thomas daily times
CaOSt 1906+

Weekly TIMES-JOURNAL. w 1873-1924||?
1873-1918? as Weekly times
CaOTA D 4 1874;Jl 8 1875;S 30 1880

SANDWICH

CANADIAN emigrant and western district commercial and general advertiser. w Ja 6 1832-
CaOTA Ap 28,O 13 1832;S 28 1833;Je 14 1834; Ag 8,S 12 1835

VOICE of the fugitive. *See under* Windsor

WESTERN standard and Western general advertiser. w 1843-
CaOTA S 16 1848

SARNIA

CANADIAN observer. w 1854-1920||?
1854-1916? as Sarnia observer
CaOTA Ag 10-17 1866

Sarnia OBSERVER. *See* Canadian observer

SAUGEEN

BRUCE vindicator and general advertiser for the counties of Huron and Grey. w
CaOTA F 6,My 1 1862

SAULT STE. MARIE

ALGOMA pioneer, and district general advertiser. w 1875-1904||?
CaOTA Ap 24 1885

SAULT star. d S 1901+
pub 1901+
CaOSm [1924-25]+

SCHOMBERG

Schomberg STANDARD. w S 6 1867-68||?
Title varies slightly
CaOTA 1867-O 30 1868

SEAFORTH

HURON expositor. w 1867+
CaOTA Jl 22,O 14,N 11,D 30 1870-Ja 6,20 1871

HURON express, Seaforth, Harpurphay, and Egmondville advertiser. w Ja 16 1862-
CaOTA My 15 1862

SIMCOE

LONG POINT reformer. w O 3 1853-
CaOTA Ja 24 1854

NORFOLK messenger. w 1851-
CaOTA D 3 1857;N 8-15,29 1860;Je 6,20 1861

STOUFFVILLE

ALERT. w Jl 4 1877-78||
CaOTA Mr 21 1878

Stouffville TRIBUNE. w 1888+
CaOTA N 29 1894

STRATFORD

ADVERTISER. w 1880-Mr 27 1890||
CaOTA Jl 3 1884

BEACON. *See* Stratford beacon-herald

Stratford BEACON-HERALD. w Ja 5 1855-1928||?
1855-Ap 1923 as Weekly beacon
CaOS 1855-63;65-70;72-92

Stratford BEACON-HERALD. d Mr 14 1887+
1887-Ap 30 1923 as Daily beacon
Suspended Mr 1888-Ap 1891
CaOS S 1887+
CaOSB 1923+

Der CANADISCHE kolonist. w 1863-1906||
Merged with Berliner journal (Kitchener) later Ontario journal
In German

Stratford EXAMINER. w 1852-63||
CaOTA My 15,Ag 13,27,O 15,29,D 3 1862
NSyU My 23 1861

Stratford HERALD. w Jl 1 1863-1923||
United with Weekly beacon to form Stratford beacon-herald
CaOSB 1869-1923

Daily HERALD. d Mr 17 1887-Ap 30 1923||
United with Daily beacon to form Stratford beacon-herald
CaOS Jl 1890-Je 1897;98-Je 1902;03-Je 1905; [06]-Je 1914;15-21;Jl 1922-23

Stratford TIMES. w 1874-Je 1892||
Merged with Stratford herald
CaOSB 1877-89

STREETSVILLE

Weekly REVIEW. w 1846+
CSmH Je 11 1853
CaOT [1854-59]
CaOTA Ap 9,My 28 1853;Jl 8 1854;Je 2,Jl 7,Ag 18,O 6,N 17 1855;Jl 12,Ag 2-9 1856;F 8,Mr 21,Ap 4,Je 13,Ag 29,O 17 1857;Je 12,Ag 21 1858

TEESWATER

Teeswater NEWS. w 1872+
CaOTA Je 22,Jl 27,O 26 1883

TORONTO

To Mr 6 1834 as York

ADVOCATE. w My 18 1824-N 4 1834||
1824-N 1833 as Colonial advocate. United with Canadian correspondent to form Correspondent and advocate
My-O 1824 pub in Queenstown
CSmH Mr 9 1826;S 2 1830
CaOOA [1824-28;32-34]
CaOTA D 15 1825;My 18 1826;Je 12,D 25 1828 [29-30]-D 4,18 1834
CaOTU [1824-27]-[29-34]
DLC F 21 1828;S 3 1829
N Je 3-10,Jl 8-D 1824;Ja 13-Ap 7,D 8-29 1825; F 2 1826;O 17-26 1833
NNHi Ag 26,O 28 1824;Je 16 1825

ALBION of Upper Canada. w 1836-Mr 1837||
CaOTA S 17 1836

Daily ATLAS. d Jl 9- 1858||
United with Daily colonist to form Daily colonist and atlas
CaOTA Jl 9-27,Ag 13 1858

Weekly ATLAS. w Jl 16- 1858||
CaOTA Jl 16,30-Ag 20,S-O 15 1858

BANNER. w Ag 18 1843-48||?
United with Globe to form Globe and banner, later Globe and Canada farmer
CaOT 1843-Ap 12 1844
CaOTA N 24 1843;Ja 19 1844;Ap 25 1845
CaOTL D 1843-Ap 1848

BRITISH American cultivator. w
CaOOA 1843-44

BRITISH Canadian and Canada west commercial and general advertiser. w Jl 27 1844-
Title varies slightly
CaOTA [Ag 10 1844-N 11 1848]S 26 1854

BRITISH colonist. sw,w F 1 1838-Jl 5 1859||?
F 1-8 1838 as Scotsman. 1857?-Je 1859 merged with Leader
Jl 5 1859 numbered v 1 no 1
w 1840-Jl 1843
CSmH My 28 1844
CaO complete
CaOT [1842-53]
CaOTA Ja 29,Jl 1,Mr 24-D 1840;42-Mr 1844;Ja 14,Ag 12 1845;F 17,S 11 1846;Mr 19,S 24,O 8-15,N 5 1847;Mr 17[My-D 1848]F 23,Mr 6,16, Je 29,N 9,13,D 28 1849;Ja 3,Ap 11,My 27,Je 3,N 11,21,D 5,30 1851;Ja 6,My 14,Je 4,S 21,D 24 1852;S 23 1853;Ap 14,Jl 11,18,Ag 8-11 1854; Ja 12,30,Mr 20,Ap 17,S 21,O 26,N 2-13,D 20-28 1855;Ja 8,18-24,F 1,26Mr 11-Ap 18,My 5,21,Je 3-6,Ag 12-21,N 4,D 27 1856;Jl 5 1859
CaOTU 1840;S 26-30,O 3 1845;Jl 3 1846
NSchU Je 1 1842

BRITISH constitution. w D 6 1866-
CaOTA D 27 1866;Ja 3,17 1867

CANADA gazette. *See under* Ottawa

CANADIAN correspondent. *See* Correspondent and advocate

CANADIAN freeman. w Je 1825-34||
CSmH S 16 1830
CaOOA 1827-34
CaOTU Mr 1 1832[33]

CANADIAN freeman. w Ja 5 1854-72||
1854-Jl 15 1858 as Catholic citizen
CaOOA My 4 1854;F 7,Je 5,D 11-18 1856;Mr 26,Ap 9,Ag 13 1857;My 13,Jl 1,15 1858-Je 1859; Jl 1860-Je 1867;Jl 1868-Je 1869
CaOT 1859-62;64-65;68
CaOTA [Jl-D 1858]My 6,S 2,N 4-11,D 9,30 1859;60;F 14-Mr 21,Je 28,Jl 11-25,S 19-O 3 1861;Ja 23,F 20,Je 5 1862;63;Ja 5,Je 22,N 16 1865;66-67;69-Mr 7,28,Ap 18,Je 13-Ag 15,S 5,D 5 1872
NSyU Je 13 1861

CANADIAN mail. w Je 5 1857-
CaOTA Je 5 1857

CATHOLIC citizen. *See* Canadian freeman

CITIZEN and country. w 1898-1901||?
ICJ Ja-O,D 7,21 1900-Ja 4,18 1901
NN Ag 11 1898[S 1899-Mr 1900]
WHi Mr 11 1899-O 12, D 7 1900

Daily CITY press and commercial and general advertiser. d N? 1870-71||
CaOTA Mr 7 1871

COLONIAL advocate. *See* Advocate

Daily COLONIST. d N 15? 1851-S 13 1860||
N? 1858-Jl? 1860 title varies: Daily colonist and atlas; Evening colonist and atlas
CaO Je 1852-60
CaOT [1852-56]
CaOTA D 1 1851;F 7,S 22 1852[F 28 1854-Ag 1857]-[Ap-My,Jl-O 1858;Ja-Mr,Je-N 1859]Ja 6,My 5,Je 27,Ag 6,22 1860
MWA Ag 13 1859

Weekly COLONIST; or News of the week. *See* News of the week; or Weekly colonist

COMMERCIAL herald. *See* Toronto herald

COMMONWEALTH. w Jl 22 1880-
CaOTA Jl 29,Ag 5,26 1880

CONSTITUTION. w Jl 6 1836-D 6 1837||
CaOTA Mr-Ag,S 13-N 1837
CaOTU Jl 27 1836-[37]

CONSTITUTION. w Ja 14 1843-
CaOTA Ja 28,F 11 1843

CORRESPONDENT and advocate. w N 10 1832-37||
1832-N 4 1834 as Canadian correspondent
CSmH Mr 3 1836
CaOT [1834-37]
CaOTA D 8 1832[33-34]-D 7,21(supp)1836;F 22,Je 14,Ag 2,N 22 1837;extras:Ja 25-Ap 18 1836;supps:F 2 1835;Je 17 1836
CaOTU [1833;36]N 29 1837

COURIER of Upper Canada. sw,tw 1828-37||
Followed by Palladium of British America
tw N 1833-34
CSmH S 11 1830
CaOT [1835-36]
CaOTA F 18-D 1 1832;O 21 1834;Ap 11,21 1835;F 11 1837
CaOTU D 1,12,29 1832[33]Ja 14,18 1834

EMPIRE. d D 27 1887-F 6 1895||
United with Toronto daily mail to form Daily mail and empire, later Mail and empire
CaM 1888-95
CaOOA 1888-94
CaOT complete
CaOTL complete
CaOTU 1888-95
CaQ Ap 28 1888-95
CaQMF Jl 1888-Je 1894
DLC 1889-Je 1892
MnU N 20 1894-95
WHi [Ja 12-Ap]My 30 1894-95

EXAMINER. w Jl 3 1838-55||
Merged with Globe
CaO N 27 1844-Ag 22 1855
CaOT [1840-55]
CaOTA Ap 10,Jl 24,N 13-27,1839;My 20 1840-F,Jl 7,S 15-29,N 3,D 22 1841;42-F 8 1843;My 22,Je 19-26,Jl 24-31,S 4-18,O 23-30 1844;Ap 23,Je 4,O 15,D 10,24 1845[Ja-O 1846]Ja 20,Mr 17,Ag 25,O 20 1847;F 14,My 9,Ag 1,O 10[N 1849-Ag 29 1855]
CaOTU [1838-45;47-48]

EXPRESS. d Je 1871-
MWA Je 30 1871

FARMERS' sun. *See* Weekly sun

ONTARIO (*Continued*)

TORONTO—*Continued*

GLOBE and mail. tw,d Mr 5 1844+
1844-N 23 1936 as Globe
pub 1909+
CU Ja 17 1917+
CaB Ja 4 1879;D 19-30 1889;N 16-17 1896;Ja-[Ap-My,Jl 1901-02;Mr-Ap 1903;Jl 1911;Je 18-Ag 26 1920]+
CaM 1884-1931
CaNs 188--1920
CaO N 1849+
CaOCo 1908-[10]-32
CaOGA 1933+
CaOKU 1848-93[95]+
CaOL 1895+
CaOOA 1858[59]-76;78-F 1880;Jl 1883-[1909]+
CaOT [1848-55]-[66]D 1868+
CaOTL 1844+
CaOTU F 8 1867-[68]-Ja 29 1869;Mr 8 1884 [85]Ag 1891;95[1914]-18
CaOWi 1895[96]-[1909]-33
CaOWo Mr 1904-05
CaQ 1883-S 1913
CaQMF 1864-65;72-84;89-1900
CaQMS 1861
DA 1917-21
DLC O 14,21 1852;D 1874-96;Jl 1897-Jl 22,S 1899+
ICHi Ag 22 1864;Ap 17 1865
ICN 1864-65
ICU [O 27 1925-Jl 1933]35+
IU Je-Jl 4,25-29,Ag 10-S 25,29,O 3-6,16 1908; 09+
IaU F 1925-Je,Ag,O-N 1929;Ja-Ag 1930;Ap-My,Jl 1931+
InU O 1919-O 1930
MWA Jl 27 1861;O 14 1862;Mr 12,Ag 13 1863; D 16 1870
MnU 1890-91
NBu Je 2 1866-F 1867
NcD O 18 1916
OClWHi Mr-S 1870
ODW O 27 1925-Jl 26 1933
PP Ap 30 1850
WHi 1864-F 18 1896
WaPS 1913;S 1914;15[16-17]-[20]-Ja 20 1922
WvU F 1925-1936

GLOBE and Canada farmer. w 1844-1914||?
Title varies: Globe and banner; Weekly globe; etc.
CaOHU 1876-[80]
CaOOA 1876-78;1906-08
CaOS 1876-78
CaOT [1852-67]76-79
CaOTL D 1844-Je 1850;66-83
CaOTU [1869-75]-[78-79;85]
CaQQL 1884;87
ICN Mr 18 1865
MWA Je 30 1871
MiU-C Ap 3,8 1851
N Ag 29-S 5,26 1862
OCl 1877;80
WHi 1877-79

HEBREW journal. *See* Der Idisher zshurnal

Toronto HERALD. sw 1837-48||
1840-41? as Commercial herald
CSmH Ap 6 1840;Mr 23 1844
CaOTA Ja 31,Mr 17 1842;Mr 31,Ap 3 1842;My 8,18,25,Je 22 1848
MBAt Je 23 1842

HOME news. w D 7 1872-
CaOTA D 21 1872

Der IDISHER zshurnal. (Hebrew journal) d 1913+
Title varies slightly
In Yiddish
IU D 1917+
NN 1915-[25-27]+

INDEPENDENT. w O 25 1849-
CaOTA N 1 1849
CaQMS 1849-Ap 17 1850

IRISH Canadian. w Ja 7 1863-1901||?
CaO 1886-88
CaOTA S 30 1868;O 8 1873;Jl 22 1874;N 10 1875;Ja 5,26,Mr 8,22 1876;Ja 14,F 25 1880;F 17 1881;O 9 1884;Mr 12,Ap-Ag,O-N 12 1885; Ja-N 1886;Ap 18 1889;F,Ap-My,Je 19-Jl 3,S 11 1890;Jl 23 1891;Jl 14-D 1892;Jl 12 1900;Ja, Mr-Je 1901

Toronto evening JOURNAL. d 1861-
MWA Ap 19 1862

LEADER. sw Jl 1 1852-S 30 1864||
CaOOA N 1855-56;58-60;63-64
CaOT complete
CaOTA N 20 1855;Ja-Ap,My 7,Jl 8,S 3,D 12 1856 D 24 1858;Ag 1859-Ag 7,S 18 1860;Je 13-Jl 4,O 17 1862;F 13-20 1863

LEADER. w Jl 7 1852-78||?
CaOKU Jl 13 1852-Jl 7 1853
CaOOA 1852-70
CaOT 1852-67;71-73
CaOTA Mr 14,N 14,D 12 1855-Ja 2,30 1856;Mr 10,Ap 21,D 8-15,29 1858[Ja-Je,S 1859-F]Ag 1860-S 2,16-30,O 14 1864
CaOTL O 1866-67;70-72
CaQMF 1864-65
N N 3 1852;S 24 1862

LEADER. d Jl 11 1853-O 5 1878||
CaO 1856-78
CaOKU 1859-61;64;66-68;71-Jl 1875
CaOOA 1853-63;65-76
CaOT 1853-68;70-77
CaOTA N 3 1855;Ja 10,F 16,Mr 18,Ap 3,Jl 11-15 S 20[D]1856;F 17,Jl 11,D 1,10,24 1857;58-[S 1859-Je,Ag-D 1860]
CaOTL Ag 12 1853-67;Jl 1869-Je 1873
CaOTU [N 12 1867-My 1868]Ja 20,27-28,30 1869
CaQMM [1871]-Ja 17 1872
MBAt Ap 17-18,20 1865
MWA Ap 24 1857;O 23 1863
WHi My 2 1864-65

Weekly LIBERAL. w 1863-75||
United with Western advertiser to form Western advertiser and weekly liberal

LIBERAL. d Ja 27-Je 25 1875||
CaOLU complete
CaOOA F-Je 1875
CaOTA [Ja 29-F 11,Ap-Je 1875]

LOYALIST. w Je 7 1828-
CaOTA Je 7,28,Jl 26 1828;Mr 14 1829
CaOTL Je 7-S 13,27-D 27 1828

MACKENZIE'S weekly message. w Ja 27 1853-Ag 15 1856-Jl 2 1859 as Toronto weekly message
CaOT 1853-F 9 1855
CaOTA [1853-54]Ja 5-12,F 9,D 7 1855-Jl 2,16, Ag 6,27,N 26,D 24 1858;Je 10 1859-S 15 1860

MAIL and empire. d Mr 30 1872-N 23 1936||
1872-F 7 1895 as Toronto daily mail; F 8 1895-S 16 1929 Daily mail and empire
United with Globe to form Globe and mail
CSt-H [1914-17]
CaB Ja 1[D 1900;Jl-D 1901;Mr-My 1903;F 16-Mr 19 1904;15-27]-36
CaM 1884-1931
CaNs 1895-1920
CaOCo 1908-[10]-36
CaOH Ag 1914-[15]-36
CaOKU Ap 1872-Mr 1879
CaOL 1895-1936
CaOOA complete
CaOT complete
CaOTL complete
CaOTU 1872-77[95]Ag 1914-18
CaOWi 1895-[1908]-[10]-33
CaOWo 1904-05
CaQ 1880-Ag 1913;25-36
CaQMF 1874-98
CtY 1872-81
DLC 1887-1936
ICM Jl 25 1903
IU Ja 5,8-16,18-31,Mr 1-6 1883
InRE Je 5-7 1889
MH [1912-18]
MiU 1931[32]-36
MnU F 7 1895-1912
WHi F 7 1895-1936

MAIL and empire. w 1872-1917||?
1872-95 as Toronto weekly mail
CaOTU 1872-79
CaQMM Ap 21 1881
CaQQL 1884-88

Toronto weekly MESSAGE. *See* MacKenzie's weekly message

Toronto MIRROR. w Je 1837-62||
1837-41 as Mirror
CSmH O 12 1838
CaOT [1837-58]
CaOTA O 19,D 14 1838;F 1,Je 21,Ag 23,N 1,D 27 1839;Ap 3,Jl 4 1840;55-56;Mr,Jl 3,31,S 1857-N 1858;F 4,25,Mr 11-18,My-Je,S-O 7,28,N 11,D 2 1859;Jl 20,N 23 1860;S 20,O 4-18 1861
CaOTU Ap 3-10,Je 5 1846;Ap 14 1848 (49-51)
NSyU My 24,Je 14-21,Jl 19 1861

NATION. w Ap 2 1874-S 29 1876||
CaO complete
CaOOA complete

NATIONAL. w Ja 22 1874-80||
CaOTA Ja 22-29,Jl 9-16,Ag 6,27,N 19 1874;Ja 14,Ap 15-22,S 16,D 3 1875;N 28 1878;Mr 27,Je 14,O 4,D 6 1879;Ja 31,Ag-S 11,25,N 6-13,27 1880

NEWS. *See* Times

NEWS of the week; or Weekly colonist. w Ag 21 1852-
Ap 9-N 12 1858 as Weekly colonist; or News of the week
CaOTA 1852-Ja 7,Mr,Ap 22-My 20,Je 10,Jl-S 2,O 1854-O 23 1861

OBSERVER. w My 22 1820-31||
CaOOA [Jl 19 1830-Mr 14 1831]
CaOT O 23 1820;Ja 13 1823;D 19-26 1825;Ap 14,Je 16-23 1828;Mr 1 1830
CaOTA D 5 1825;Ap 20 1829
N My 29 1820;O 4 1824;N 20 1826

ONTARIO gazette. w Mr 7 1868+
Follows Upper Canada gazette
CaB S 15 1900+
CaOOA 1868-81;1921+
CaOT 1884+
DLC 1868+
MWA Je 20 1868
NN 1868[69-72]-74;Jl 1875-Jl 1880;Ja-Ag 1881; Ja,Je 1882;Ag 1883-87;89-90;93-94;Jl 1902+

ONTARIO tribune. *See* Toronto tribune

ORANGE sentinel. . . *See* Sentinel

PALLADIUM of British America. w D 20 1837-39||
Follows Courier of Upper Canada
CSmH Ag 29 1838
CaOTA 1837-Ap 11,Je 27 1838;My 17 1839

PATRIOT. d *See* Toronto daily patriot and express

PATRIOT. w *See* Patriot and farmers' monitor

Toronto daily PATRIOT and express. d Ap 1850-54||?
1850- as Patriot
CaOT [1851-55]
CaOTL Ja 14 1852-F 13 1854

PATRIOT and farmers' monitor. sw,w S 1828-64||
1828-44? as Patriot. Merged with Leader
1828-D 10 1832 pub in Kingston
sw 1828-44?
CSmH Je 29 1830
CaO Jl 28 1835-Ap 4 1848
CaOOA 1829-32[37-38;41;44-45;47]D 1854-N 1855
CaOT [1832-38;40-44]57-64
CaOTA 1838;F 15 1839;Ag 21,N 10-20 1840;F 15 1842[My 1845;Ap 1846;Je-S,N-D 1848]
CaOTU O 23 1832[33]Ja 3,17 1834
CaQMG My 7 1844
CaQQL [1829]
DLC My 2 1843
P-M O 16 1832

PROVINCIAL freeman. w Mr 25 1854-
NSyU N 18 1854
P-U [1854-55]-[57]

RECORDER. w 1889-95||?
1889-93? as Recorder of North Toronto (Deer Park)
CaOTA Jl 2-23,Ag 13 1891;Mr 24 1892;N 23 1893

Toronto RECORDER and general mercantile advertiser. sw Jl 1834-35||
CaOT Jl 30 1834

ROYAL standard. d N 9 1836-F 11 1837||
CaOT 1836-F 8 1837

SATURDAY night. w 1887+
CaB Ja 2[Ap 15-Ag 5]1932+
CaNSa Ap 10 1926+
CaOTU 1887-91;1933+
ICM Ap 30,My 14 1892
TxU Je 20-O 24 1925

SCOTSMAN. *See* British colonist

SENTINEL and Orange and protestant advocate. w 1875+
1875-78? as Orange sentinel and Protestant advocate
CaCTA N 23 1876;Ja 30 1879;My 27 1886;Ag 9 1888;O 1890-N 1892;Ja 12-19,F 23,Mr 2,30,Ap 6 1893;Jl 26,Ag 23,S 13,O 11 1894

SPIRIT of the age. w Ja 24 1868-69||
CaOTA F 21,Mr 6,20,Ap 3-17 1868;D 9 1869

Daily STANDARD. d Ja 24 1887-
CaOTA Ja 27,F 7-8 1887

Toronto STAR. sw 1839-Jl 29 1846||
CaOTA My 8 1844;Jl 26 1845-46

Toronto STAR. tw 1841-
1841-42 as Morning star
CaOT [1841-46]

Toronto daily STAR. d N 3 1892+
1892-Ja 24 1900 as Evening star
pub N 3 1892;95+
CaOT 1894-1908;10+
MH [Ag 4 1914-Ja 17 1916]
NNHi N 23 1897

Toronto STAR weekly. w Ap 9 1910+
pub 1910+
CaOT 1910+

SUN. w 1872-76||
CaOTA F 20,D 22 1873;Je 19 1874;Mr 4,Ap 2 1875;Ja 21 1876

Weekly SUN. w 1891+
1891-F 1933 as Farmers' sun
CaO Je 1894-97
CaOGA 1931+

Evening TELEGRAM. d Ap 18 1876+
Follows Daily telegraph
pub 1876+
CaOOA 1876-Mr 1883
CaOT 1876+
CaQ 1876-Je 1908
DLC Ap-Je 1896
MnU [1876-83]D 1884-85
NcD O 25 1927

Daily TELEGRAPH. (evening ed) d 1866-76||
Followed by Evening telegram
CaOT My 21-D 1866;Jl 2 1867-Je 1 1872
CaOTA [Mr,My-N 1869;Je-S 1870]Ap 11 1871

Daily TELEGRAPH. (morning ed) d Ag 31 1868-72||
CaOTA [Ap,Je-Jl,D 1869-Je,O 1870-Mr,My-Ag 1871;Ja-My 1872]

Weekly TELEGRAPH. w Ap 4 1868-72||
CaOTA Ap 4,S 25 1868;Mr 18-25,Ap 15-22 1860;My 12 1871;F 2,Mr 22,My 3,31 1872

TIMES. d My 2 1881-Je 30 1919||?
1881-Mr 26 1919 as News
CaOOA 1906-F 1912
CaOT Ap 4 1882-Je 30 1919
CaOTA My 2 1881
DLC 1881;Jl 1884-88;Jl 1889-My 1890;Ja-Je 1891;Ja-Jl 18 1892;Ja-F,Ap 1895-Je 1898;Ja-Mr,Jl 1899-Mr,O-D 1900;Ap-S 1900;Ja-Mr 1902

Toronto TRIBUNE. w Ag 27 1874-86||?
Ag 1874-Ja 14 1875 as Ontario tribune
CaOTA Ag-S 17,N 12 1874-Mr 4,Ap 29,My 6, Jl 16,Ag 5 1875;78;My 20,Je 24 1881
PPCHi [1886-87]

U.E. loyalist. w Je 3 1826-29||?
1826-My 24 1828 as a supp to Upper Canada gazette
CaOT 1826-Je 6 1829
CaOTL Jl 1827-My 24 1828
MWA S 15 1827;F 2,Mr 15 1825

UNITED empire.
CaOTA O 4 1852

UPPER Canada gazette. w Ap 18 1793-My 1 1845||
Ap 22 1807-17 as York gazette. Followed by Ontario gazette
1793-O 20 1798 pub in Newark, now Niagara
Suspended 1813-15
Issued under government auspices 1793-1840
CSmH S 2 1830;D 28(extra)1837
CaO Ja 14 1815-My 1 1845
CaOOA 1804;10-11;17-18;20-22;24-25[30]-34;36-41;43-44
CaOLU 1829-30
CaOT [1824-42]

ONTARIO (*Continued*)

TORONTO—*Continued*

CaOTA Ap 13 1811;My 29 1816
CaQMG Ap 18 1793(facsimile)
DLC S 1826-Je 1829
IU [Je 24 1826-My 17 1828]
MWA Jl 2,1803;F 11,My 5-19 1804;Mr 16,30-Ap 6 1805;S 15 1827;F 2,Mr 15 1828
NN My 18(supp)1820;S-O,D 1829-Ap 1831

VICTORY telegraph. First and last edition. N 28 1921||
Pub to promote the sale of Victory bonds
MWA complete

WAR cry. w 1885-87||?
An edition was also printed and sent to Winnipeg
CaM N 6 1886-O 29 1887

WATCHMAN. w Ja 21 1850-
CaOT 1850
CaOTA 1850-Ja 13 1851

WEEK. w D 6 1883-N 20 1896||
CSmH 1883-N 1888
CaNs complete
CaOOA 1883-87;92-94
CaOT complete
CtY 1883-93
KHi D 21 1888-Je 1889

WELLAND Canal. w D 16-30 1835||
CaOT complete

Toronto WORLD. d Ap 19 1880-Ap 11 1921||
Merged with Mail and empire
CaO 1895-Ap 10 1921
CaOH Jl 1912-[14-15]-[20]
CaOT F 1881-Ap 9 1921
CaOTL 1895-Je 1906
CaQ F 7 1896-Ap 1908
DLC 1888-90
MH [Jl 23 1914-Mr 23 1916]
MiU 1911-[15]-21

YORK gazette. *See* Upper Canada gazette

YORK weekly post. w
CaOOA [1821]

YORK tribune. (West Toronto Junction) sw Ja 1888-92||?
CaOTA D 21 1888

UNIONVILLE

PROGRESS. w Ap 12 1877-
CaOTA Ap 12-19,My-N 8,D 6-13 1877

UXBRIDGE

NORTH Ontario advocate. w N 27? 1861-
CaOTA Mr 27,Ap 10,My 8,Je 12-19,Jl 10-17,Ag 28,S 4-11,O 23 1862

Uxbridge TIMES-JOURNAL. w 1869+
1869-1929? as Uxbridge journal (title varies slightly)
CaOTA Ja 26,Mr 16-23,Ap 6,20-My 4 1870;Mr 28 1872;O 2 1873[74]Ja 14-21,F-Mr 1 1875;O 19,N 2,16 1876[77]Ja 31-F 7,Jl 11,Ag 29 1878; Jl 3-10,Ag 21-S 4,18-O 9,N 20,D 1879;Ja 1 1880

VAN KLEEK

ECONOMIST. w Ap 1 1858-
CaOTA D 9 1858

WASHAGO VILLAGE

Washago PIONEER. sw Ap 15? 1872-
CaOTA Ap 18,25 1872

WATERLOO

CANADISCHER bauernfreund und Deutsche zeitung. w 1850-1909||?
1850-1905? as Canadischer bauernfreund
In German

Waterloo CHRONICLE. w 1856+
1856-93? as Waterloo chronicle (title varies slightly); 1894?-Ap 6 1899 Waterloo county chronicle; Ap 13-Je 1 1899 Waterloo county chronicle and weekly telegraph; Je 8 1899-Jl 13 1922 Chronicle-telegraph
pub 1893+
CaOKi 1868;1917-29;32+
CaOTA Jl 13 1864;Ap 30,O 8,D 17 1874;Mr 4,S 9 1875;Mr 30 1876

CHRONICLE-telegraph. *See* Waterloo chronicle

Waterloo SENTINEL. d 1909-12||
CaOKi complete

WATERLOO county chronicle. *See* Waterloo chronicle

WEST TORONTO JUNCTION

Papers published in West Toronto Junction are listed under Toronto

WELLESLEY

Wellesley MAPLE leaf. w 1900-21||?
CaOKi 1900-04;07-08

WESTON

Weston TIMES. *See* York times and guide

YORK times and guide. w 1859+
1859-99? as Weston times; 1900?-32? Weston times and guide
CaOTA S 12 1890;Je 4,D 3,24 1891;Mr 17,31,Je 30-Jl 7,21-28,Ag 11 1892[Ap 1893-94]

WESTPORT

Westport MIRROR. w 1893+
CaOTA N 15 1894;D 5 1895

WHITBY

Whitby CHRONICLE. w Ja 22 1857-1900||?
United with Ontario county gazette to form Whitby gazette and chronicle
CaOTA Ja 18-25,Ag 20,S 17-24,D 10 1857;58-Mr,O 1-8 1859;Ja 12,Ag 11-18,S 8,22,O 11 1860-Ja 7,D 30 1869-O 6,N 3,17 1870;F 9,Mr 23 1871-Ja 11,F,Mr 14-21,Ap 11-18,My 9,S 12,O 1872-Mr,Ag 28,D 18 1873;Mr 5, Je 11-18, S 10,O 8,D 31 1874;F 4,Mr 4 1875;Je 29,S 28, O 5,N 29 1876;Ap 12 1877;Jl 17,N 20-27 1879;F 12,Ap 1,S 9 1880;F 10 1881

Semi-weekly CHRONICLE. sw Ap 2? 1859-
CaOTA My 17-14,21,Jl 8 1859;S 18 1860

COMMONWEALTH. w 1855-
CaOTA Je 18,Ag 27 1857

Whitby GAZETTE and chronicle. w O 29 1862+
1862-98? as Whitby gazette; 1899?-1904? Ontario county gazette
CaOTA N 5 1862;F 4,Ap 29,S 30 1863;Ag 16 1866

ONTARIO county gazette. *See* Whitby gazette and chronicle

ONTARIO times. w O 9 1857-
CaOTA Mr 13,27,Ap 3-17,My 1,D 25 1858;Ap 30 1859

Whitby PRESS. w F 27 1861-
CaOTA Jl 31 1861

Whitby SATURDAY night. w 1879-82||?
TJT Mr 11 1882

Whitby WATCHMAN. w Ag 25 1859-
CaOTA Ag 25,S 29,D 8,29 1859;My 17 1860;Ap 4,Je 27-Jl 4,Ag 22 1861

WINDSOR

BORDER cities star. d 1890+
1890-Ag 31 1918 as Windsor record
CaOWi Mr 28 1890-91;93+

ESSEX record. *See* Weekly record

ESSEX review. *See* Windsor review

LE PROGRÈS. w 1881-1920||?
In French
CaQQL 1888-91

Windsor RECORD. d *See* Border cities star

Weekly RECORD. w 1860-1917||?
1860-85? as Essex record
CaOWi N 16 1871-[76-77]-N 9 1882;88;90;92-1901;03-09;11-17

Windsor REVIEW. w 1876-
1876-90? as Essex review
CaOWi 1895-96

VOICE of the fugitive. sw Ja 1 1851-53||?
Title varies
Imprint reads: Sandwich and Windsor
CSmH Je 21 1853
MWA Jl 2 1851
MiD-B 1851-D 16 1852
MiU 1851-52]
OClWHi Je 7 1853

WOODBRIDGE

Woodbridge ENTERPRISE and West York general advertiser. w N 14 1873-
CaOTA D 19 1873;Ja 9 1874

WOODSTOCK

Woodstock EXPRESS. w 1898-1924||?
CaOWo My 1904-Je 1908

GOOD templar. w Ja 6 1863-
CaOTA 1863-Ag 30 1864

Woodstock HERALD and Brock district general advertiser. w Jl 1840-46||?
CSmH Ag 28 1846

OXFORD star and Woodstock advertiser. w
CaOT [F 4 1848-Ja 19 1849]

Weekly REVIEW. w 1869-78||?
United with Weekly sentinel to form Weekly sentinel-review

Weekly SENTINEL-REVIEW. w 1854+
1854-78? as Weekly sentinel
pub 1870-86

Daily SENTINEL-REVIEW. d 1886+
pub 1886+
CaOOA 1897-1901
CaOWo My 1904-Je 1908

TIMES. w 1855-1902||?
CaOTA F 13 1863

YORK. *See* TORONTO

PRINCE EDWARD ISLAND

ALBERTON

PIONEER. *See under* Summerside

CHARLOTTETOWN

Weekly ADVERTISER and colonial times. w 1847-
CaP S 18 1847-Ja 3 1849
MWA Je 5 1856

COLONIAL herald and Prince Edward Island advertiser. w
CaOT 1841-42
CaP Ag 5 1837-Jl 27 1844
N 1840

CONSTITUTIONAL. w
CaP Ap 27-O 17 1846

Charlottetown EXAMINER. d Ag 7 1847-My 22 1922||
CaO Ja 12 1850-1922
CaOOA 1847-F 1849[51]55
CaP 1847-1919
DLC Jl 11 1864
MWA Ag 29 1859

Charlottetown GUARDIAN. w 1887-1920||?
1887-1903? as Island guardian
CaP Jl 2 1887-98

Charlottetown GUARDIAN. d 1891+
CaP Jl 3 1899+

HANSARD'S gazette. Farmers' journal, and commercial advertiser. sw,w 1853-
CSmH Je 1 1853
CaOOA 1853-56
CaP Ag 26 1851-D 1 1856
MiU-C Ag 27 1853

Charlottetown HERALD. w 1862-1924||?
CaOOA O 1865-O 1866;83-88;90-93
CaP O 12 1864-94

ISLAND argus. w 1869-F 25 1881||
CaO 1879-81
CaP N 8 1870-O 31 1876
MWA Ap 15 1873

ISLAND guardian. *See* Charlottetown guardian w

ISLAND patriot. *See* Patriot d

ISLANDER. w 1842-72||?
CaO N 1860-70
CaP D 1842-71
MWA D 18 1863

MONITOR. w
CaP My 23 1857-64

NEW ERA. Ap 18 1874-83||?
MWA Ag 1 1874

Morning NEWS, and semi-weekly advertiser. sw S 5? 1843-
CaP S 9 1843-Ja 3 1849
MWA S 9 1843

PALLADIUM.
CaOOA Jl-Ag 1844

PATRIOT. w 1861-1913||
CaO 1874-1913
CaP Jl 1864-1913
MB Ag 2,N 6 1873[Ag 1874-My 1875]

PATRIOT. d 1881+
1913?-25 title varies: Island patriot; Prince Edward Island patriot
CaO 1881+
CaOOA 1883-85;89-S 12 1892
CaP 1881+

PEOPLE'S journal. w
CaP Jl 16 1866-My 24 1869

PRINCE Edward Island register. Jl 27 1823-
CSmH Ag 17 1830
CaO Ja 3 1826-Ap 7 1829
CaOOA 1823-27;29-31

Weekly RECORDER of Prince Edward Island. w S 29 1810-
MWA O 13 1810

ROSS'S weekly. w 1858-
MWA O 8 1860;Ag 18 1864

ROYAL gazette. w 1791+
CSmH Ag 24 1830
CaB 1913-[20-27]+
CaO Ag 24 1830+
CaOOA 1814-21;Je 1826-Jl 1829;32-54
CaOT Ag 24 1830-32;1932+
DLC 1903-06;10;12-19;21+
MWA Je 14,28 1842
NN D 28 1901+

VINDICATOR. w
CaQQL O 17 1862-64

WATCHMAN. w 1889-1921||?
CaP Je 12 1889-Ja 21 1921

GEORGETOWN

EASTERN advocate: or, King's County gazette. w O 5 1870-71||?
MWA D 4 1870

MONTAGUE

PIONEER. w 1879-82||?
CaP S 13 1879-My 29 1880

SUMMERSIDE

Summerside JOURNAL. w 1865+
Title varies slightly
CaP O 8 1868+
MWA Ja 4 1872;Ag 6 1874

PIONEER. w 1876+
1876-79 pub in Alberton
CaP Jl 1876-F 1879;S 15 1880+

Summerside PROGRESS. w 1866-82||?
CaP Jl 16 1866-S 1880
MWA Ja 15 1872;Je 7 1880

QUEBEC

AGNES

Le Travailleur du Lac Mégantic. w 1898-1906||?
CaQQL 1898

AMOS

L'ABITIBI. *See* La Gazette du Nord

La GAZETTE du Nord. w Ja 22 1920+
1920-Je 22 1922 as L'Abitibi
pub 1920+

ARTHABASKA

L'ECHO des bois-francs. *See under* Victoriaville

Le JOURNAL d'Arthabaskaville. w
CaQQL 1877

L'UNION des cantons de l'Est. w 1866+
CaQ D 24 1881-1906
CaQQL 1867-71;73-76;89+

La VOIX des bois-francs. *See under* Victoriaville

ATHELSTAN

Athelstan SUN. w Mr 14-My 6 1885||
Followed by Sun of Fort Covington (Fort Covington, N.Y.)
CaQHC complete

BAIE ST. PAUL

Le COURRIER de Charlevoix. w
CaQ Je 4 1896-S 3 1897
CaQQL 1895-96

L'ECHO de Charlevoix. w 1898-1907||?
CaQ Ja 5 1898-D 26 1907

BEAUCEVILLE

L'ECLAIREUR. w O 1 1908+
pub 1908+
CaOOA N 1924-Mr 1932
CaQQL 1908-O 1911;O 17 1918+

BEAUHARNOIS

Le COURRIER de Beauharnois. w 1867-71||
CaQQL complete

BERTHIER

L'ECHO des campagnes. w
CaQMS [N 21 1846-S 21 1848]Mr 22 1855-Mr 29 1856
CaQQL 1846-47

La GAZETTE de Berthier. w 1888+
1912+ printed in Sorel as an ed of Courrier de Sorel
CaQ Jl 16 1897-1906

BUCKINGHAM

Buckingham POST. w 1895+
pub [1895+]

CAUGHNAWAGA

Caughnawaga GAZETTE. sm
NN Mr 15-My 11 1905

CHICOUTIMI

La DÉFENSE. w Ja 18 1898-F 2 1905||
CaO 1898-1903
CaQMS 1898

Le JOURNAL de Chicoutimi. w
CaQ Ag 16 1899-My 29 1902

L'OISEAU mouche. w 1893-D 27 1902||
CaO complete

Le PROGRÈS du Saguenay. w,d Ag 16 1887+
d F 25 1927-My 14 1932
pub 1887+
CaQ 1887-1909
CaQQL 1887-92;1910+
WHi 1889-90;Ja 14 1892-O 1897;Je 14 1900

Le PROTECTEUR du Saguenay. w
CaQ S 17 1896-Ap 29 1899

Le REVEIL du Saguenay. w Ag 12 1886-Ag 4 1887||
CaQ complete

LE SAGUENAY. w
CaQQL [1882]

LE TRAVAILLEUR. w 1905-12||?
CaQQL 1905-10

COATICOOK

L'ETOILE de l'Est. w S 1927+
pub 1927+

Coaticook OBSERVER. w N 1869+
pub 1900-01[03-10]27+

COWANSVILLE

COTTON'S weekly. w 1870-1914||?
1870-1908? as Cowansville observer
CaOT S 17 1908-S 14 1911;N 7 1912-D 10 1914
CaQMM Jl 17 1884

Cowansville OBSERVER. *See* Cotton's weekly

DRUMMONDVILLE EAST

La PAROLE. w Mr 1926+
pub 1926+

SPOKESMAN. w 1927+
pub Je 26 1928+

FRASERVILLE

Le BULLETIN politique. w F 25 1899-1900||?
CaQQL 1899-Je 8 1900

Le COURRIER de Fraserville. w 1886-D 26 1890||
CaQ N 16 1887-90
CaQQL 1888-89

Le JOUR. *See* Le Journal de Fraserville (Rivière du Loup)

Le JOURNAL de Fraserville. *See under* Rivière du Loup

Le PROGRES. *See* Le Journal de Fraserville (Rivière du Loup)

Le SAINT-LAURENT. *See under* Rivière du Loup

FRELIGHSBURG

MISSISKOUI standard. w 1835-38||?
Printed in Montreal
CaQMM Ap 1835-Mr 1838

GRANBY

Granby GAZETTE, and Shefford county advertiser. w 1856-78||?
CaOTA Jl 27 1866-D 13 1867;Je 19,Jl 10,Ag 7, 28,S 25,O 16,30,D 18 1868;D 21-28 1870;Mr 11-18,Ap 1-8 1871;My 22,Je 12 1874

Granby LEADER-MAIL. w 1891+
1891-1903 as Granby leader
pub [1891-1910]+

Granby MAIL. sw 1895-1903||
United with Granby leader to form Granby leader-mail

Le MONITEUR. w 1865-68||
MWA [1867]68

GRAND'MERE

Le COURRIER de Grand'Mère. *See* La Semaine

La SEMAINE. w 1909-18||?
1909-14? as Le Courrier de Grand'Mère
CaQQL Je-D 1911;N 21 1912-Ag 3 1917

HULL

Le PIONNIER Canadien. w 1902-05||?
CaQ F 3 1904-Mr 2 1905

Le SPECTATEUR. w My 4 1889+
CaQ 1889-D 2 1899
CaQQL 1890-91

HUNTINGDON

Huntingdon ADVOCATE. w N 1883-D 24 1885||
1883-Je 1884 as Farmer's advocate and Beauharnois district news
CaQHC complete

CANADIAN gleaner. *See* Huntingdon gleaner

FARMER'S advocate and Beauharnois district news. *See* Huntingdon advocate

Huntingdon GLEANER. w S 18 1863+
1863-Ja 29 1912 as Canadian gleaner
pub 1863+
NNHi O 24 1872
OCl Je 18 1872;D 20 1888;N 16 1893

Huntingdon HERALD. w 1860-
CaOTA Mr 15,Ap 26,Jl 19,Ag 16,D 13 1861; Ja 3,F 28,Mr 14,28 1862

Huntingdon JOURNAL. w My 16 1862-69||?
CaOTA My 30-Je 6,Jl 18,O 31,N 14 1862;F 6, 20-27,Je 5-19,S 4,N 20,D 11 1863

SOUTH Shore gleaner. w Jl 1919-Jl 1923||
CaQBE complete

JOLIETTE

L'ACTION populaire. w S 6 1913+
pub [1913-Ag 1923]+
CaQMS [1913-Ja 1926]
CaQQL 1913+

L'ETOILE du Nord. w 1884+
CaQ D 19 1895-1909
CaQQL 1916-21

La GAZETTE de Joliette. sw,w 1866-95||?
CaQ Ja 12 1882-Jl 1895
CaQMS [1879-88]

Le MESSAGER de Joliette. sw
CaQMS [Jl 7 1863-Je 13 1864]

LAC-AU-SAUMON

L'ECHO du lac. w O 1919-26||?
CaO 1919-Ap 1926

LAC MEGANTIC

L'ECHO de Frontenac. w 1929+
pub 1929—

La PAIX. w
CaQQL Je 21-D 13 1902

LACHINE

Le MESSAGER de Lachine. w 1931+
CaQVP 1933+

LACHUTE

WATCHMAN. w 1875+
pub S 1877+

LA MALBAIE

Le COURRIER du nord. w 1928+
CaQQL D 1928+

L'ECHO des Laurentides. w 1884-87||
CaQ Ja 6-O 27 1887

LEVIS

L'ECHO de Lévis. tw Ap 15 1871-Jl 12 1876||
CaQ complete
CaQQL complete

Le MONITEUR. w
CaQ My 5 1893-Je 20 1896

Le PROGRÈS de Lévis. w
CaQ N 11 1867-Jl 23 1869

Le QUOTIDIEN. d Je 26 1879+
CaQ 1879-1912
CaQMS Jl 7 1883-Jl 5 1884
CaQQL 1879-81;88-91

Le TRAVAILLEUR de Lévis. w 1890-92||?
CaQ F 19 1890-Jl 23 1892

L'UNION canadienne. w
CaQ Jl 8-O 19 1891

LOUISEVILLE

Le COURRIER de Maskinongé. w Mr 7 1878-96||?
CaO Mr 14 1878-O 27 1881

L'ECHO de Louiseville. w Ap 27 1894-Jl 31 1897||
CaQ complete

MONT LAURIER

La VOIX du Nord. w
CaQBE 1933+

MONTMAGNY

Le COURRIER-Sentinelle. w 1891+
1891-94 as La Sentinelle; 1894-1901? L'Echo de Montmagny; 1902-26? Le Courrier de Montmagny
CaQ 1906-08
CaQQL 1891-1900;05-12

L'ECHO de Montmagny. *See* Le Courrier-sentinelle

Le PEUPLE. w 1900-27||?
CaQ Ag 25 1905;D 31 1909
CaQQL 1906-Ap 8 1910

La SENTINELLE. w 1891-94 *See* Le Courrier-sentinelle

La SENTINELLE. w 1922-26||?
United with Le Courrier de Montmagny to form Le Courrier-sentinelle

MONTREAL

L'ACTION. w Ap 15 1911-Ap 29 1916||
CaQ complete
CaQMF Ja 1904
CaQMS [1911-16]
CaQQL 1911-Je 14 1913
CaQShS 1911-Je 8 1912

Der ADLER. *See* Der Kenader adler

Daily ADVERTISER. d 1833-34||?
CSmH Je 5 1833
CaQMM [1834]
DLC My 28 1833;Mr 24 1834
N O 11 1833
NCHM N 27 1834

L'AMI du peuple. sw 1831-40||?
CaOOA 1835-40
CaQ Jl 25 1832-Jl 21 1839
CaQMS [Jl 21 1832-Jl 18 1838]
DLC O 27 1832
PHi Je 19,N 6 1833

ANTIDOTE. w Je 18 1892-Je 10 1893||
CSmH complete

L'ARALDO del Canada. w 1906+
In Italian
pub 1926+

QUEBEC (*Continued*)

MONTREAL—*Continued*

ARGUS. tw,d 1854-58||?
CaQMM 1855-N 15 1858
CaQQL [1857]
DLC Ja 16-D 8 1855;Mr 4,7,My 29,Jl 1,O 3, 28,D 3 1856;Mr 19,S 11 1857

L'AURORE des Canadas. w,sw Ja 15 1839-49||?
CaO 1839-N 25 1845
CaOLU [1843-45]
CaOOA [1840-45]
CaQMS [Je 24 1841-Ap 1843]Ag 22 1845-Ag 18 1846
CaQQL 1839-49

L'AUTORITÉ. w D 28 1913+
1913-32 as L'Autorité nouvelle
pub 1913+
CaQMF 1914-15;18
CaQMS [1913-21]

L'AVENIR. sw Jl 16 1847-57||?
CaO Ag 1847-Jl 7 1852
CaOOA Ag 1848-57
CaQ Ag 9 1848-F 16 1850
CaQMF Jl 16-O 23,N 6 1847-Ag 2 1848;O 1849-Jl 4 1851
CaQMS [N 1847-N 1852]

Le BIEN publique. w Ap 10 1874-My 20 1876||
CaO complete
CaQMF complete

Le BULLETIN. w 1902+
pub 1902+
CaQ S 1904-08

Le CANADA. d Ap 4 1903+
pub 1903+
CaO 1903+
CaQ 1903+
MWA Ja 22,24,28 1913

CANADA first. w D 17 1881-85||?
CaO 1881-O 10 1885
CaQMM [1881-83]
CaQMS 1881-N 17 1882
DLC 1881-S 16 1882
MWA Ag 26 1882(photostat)
NChM D 24 1881

CANADA gazette. *See under* Ottawa (Ontario)

CANADIAN courant and Montreal advertiser. sw My 11 1807-Mr 22 1834||
CSmH My 23 1829
CaO 1819-26
CaOOA 1807-11;F-Jl 1819;20-21;30-31
CaOT My 27 1829-34
CaQMG N 13 1809;S 9 1815;F 21 1818;D 3 1828;Ja 17 1829
CaQMM Ja 29-F 5 1825;My 1829-34
MBAt My 27-Je 3 1811;Ag 10 1812
MHi Mr 24 1821;F 11,Mr 13 1824
DLC O 16 1822
MWA Jl 27-Ag 10 1807;Mr 20-27,My 1-22, Je 19-26,Jl 17,Ag 14,O 9,N 20,D 25 1809; Ja 15-22,F 19,My 7,Jl 23,S 17,O 15,29 1810; F 25-Mr 11 1811;Ja 27 1812;N 20 1813;Ap 3 1819;Ag 3 1822;Ja 11,Ap 5,Jl 26 1823;F 19, Ap 16 1825
N Je 18 1810;N 2 1831;O 16 1833
NChM N 3 1832
NN D 4 1809;N 26 1810
NNHi My 11-Ag 10 1807;Ja 5 1828
WHi Ja 29 1810

CANADIAN mail; or, Montreal gazette for Europe. w Ja 8? 1855-
CaOTA F 26 1855

CANADIAN spectator. sw O 9 1822-29||?
CaO 1822-N 5 1828
CaQ 1822-O 8 1823
CaQMF 1822-Ja,Jl 5-D 27 1829
CaQMM Jl 19 1828
CaQMSm 1825-26
CaQQL [1822]
MWA Ap 29,Je 10 1826
N Ja 16 1828

Le CANADIEN. w D 1906-D 4 1909||
CaQQL complete

La CANADIENNE. sw 1840||?
CaQQL [1840]

Le CANARD. w O 6 1877+
CaO 1877-Jl 25 1885

La COLONISATEUR. w Ja 2 1862-Je 27 1863||
CaO complete
CaOOA complete

Le COMBAT. w O 11 1903-Ja 24 1904||
CaQMF complete
CaQMS complete

COMMERCIAL advertiser. tw,d 1835-62||
1835-O 22 1849 as Morning courier; O 26 1849-Je 7 1852 Montreal courier; Je 8-Ag 13 1852 Montreal courier and commercial advertiser
tw 1840-Ap 29 1848
CSmH Jl 14 1835
CaOTA Mr 26 1845
CaQMG My 8,25 1844
CaQMM [1836-41;45;48-50]F 5 1861;Mr 11 1862
DLC Jl 8-9 1835;40-58
MWA Jl 24 1838;F 15 1841
NCanHi O 19 1838
NChM Jl 3,O 11 1838
WHi Ja 29,F 2 1838

Le COMPOSITEUR. w F 21 1925-Je 4 1926||
CaO complete

Morning COURIER. *See* Commercial advertiser

Montreal COURIER and commercial advertiser. *See* Commercial advertiser

Le COURRIER canadien. sw
CaQMS Ja 30-Mr 6 1838
CaQQL [1838]

Le COURRIER de Montréal. w S 17 1874-O 6 1876||
CaO O 14 1874-My 17 1876
CaOOA complete
CaQ complete
CaQMS O 14 1874-D 9 1875

Le COURRIER de Montréal. d My 26 1879-Ap 12 1883||
CaO complete
CaOLU 1879-80
CaOOA 1879[80]-Mr 1883
CaQ complete
CaQMS [1879-83]
CaQMSm 1879-82
WHi Ag 7 1879

La CROIX de Montréal. *See* La Croix du Canada

La CROIX du Canada. sw,d My 30 1893-My 31 1895||
1893-Jl 27 1894 as La Croix de Montréal
CaO complete
CaQMS complete
CaQQL 1893-94
CaQShS complete

Les DÉBATS. w D 3 1899-O 4 1903||
CaQ 1899-S 1900
CaQMF complete
CaQMS [1899-1903]

Le DEVOIR. d Ja 10 1910+
pub 1910+
CStH 1910-19
CaO 1910+
CaOLU 1910-Je 1919
CaOOA 1910-F 1913
CaOOU 1910+
CaQ 1910+
CaQMS 1910+
CaQMSm 1910+
CaQQL 1910+
CaQSaC 1910+
CaQShS 1910+
WHi Ja 29-Ap 1918;Ja,F 26-27 1919

EAGLE. *See* Der Keneder adler

L'ETENDARD. d Ja 23 1883-Mr 20 1893||
CaO complete
CaQ complete
CaQMS [1883-92]
CaQMSm 1886-93
CaQQL complete

FAMILY herald and weekly star. w 1869+
1869-74? as Montreal star
pub 1869+
Ct S 9 1903
CaOTA Ap 24 1873;Je 19 1876
DLC F 6 1901
KHi N 14 1923-Mr 26 1924

FINANCIAL times. w Je 21 1912+
pub 1912+
CaB 1927+
CaQME 1922+
IEN-C Je 22 1928+

Le FRANC parleur. w Jl 28 1870-Ap 30 1878||
CaO [1870-78]
CaOOA Ag 1872-My 1875
CaQ O 31 1872-78
CaQMS [1870-O 1876]
CaQQL 1870-77

FREE lance. w
CaQMF Ag 28 1867-D 13 1873

FREE press. w
CaQQL [1822]

GAZETTE. d Je 3 1778+
1778-1866? as Montreal gazette. French title La Gazette de Montréal
pub 1816-17;26[27-32]36;39;Ja 1840;F 9 1852 [60-72]+
CSmH S 6 1830
CaB 1928+
CaM 1885+
CaO N 9 1804+
CaOKU 1924+
CaOOA [1827]-[33]-[40;64-65]-72;74-75;79-80; 83+
CaOT [1836]
CaOTL 1867[68]-[71]Jl-Ag 1882
CaOTU Ja 26,F 21,Mr 16,Je 27 1833
CaQ 1880+
CaQM Ap 1878+
CaQME 1928+
CaQMF S 14 1795-F 29 1796;1810-11;64-65;71; 74;76;88
CaQMG F 3,17 1779;N 5,9,12 1829;Ja 4 1871;Ja 18,S 4 1872
CaQMR Je 1931+
CaQMS [1837;85-Je 1888;S 1919]+
DA 1912+
DLC D 13,27 1792;Ja 3 1793;S 22 1800;S 29 1832;F 4,Mr 6-7,13,26,My 21,N 13,D 16,24 1856;Ja 20,F 5,Mr 17,19,S 11 1857;Mr 16,26 1864;Ap 4,S 5 1865;Ja 12-D 1866;Jl 11 1874-Je 1909
ICM S 3,O 29 1903
MWA Je 23 1828;F 5 1831;F 4, 7,9,11,14,16,18, 21 1837;Ag 12-18 1857;D 5 1864;O 18 1870;Ap 23 1886
MdEmJ N 11 1830
MiU 1880-97
N O 12 1833
NChM My 6 1845
NN My 4 1807;Ag 8(extra)1859;N 30 1931
NcD F 18 1861
NcU Jl 1876-[78]S 3 1879
NjR S 6 1878
OClWHi Ag 25 1800
WHi [1885;87-90;94]96+

GAZETTE. w 1778-1910||?
Title varies. Some years tw or sw during sessions of legislature
pub [1850-60;72-73]83-86;97-Je 1902
CaQMS Ag 14 1822-Jl 9 1823
MBAt Ja 7,Ag 4,S 22,O 20-27 1828;O 26,D 24 1829;F 8,11,S 16-23 1830;66-O 17 1870
MHi Jl 26 1823;Ja 10-17,31 1824;My 7,O 29 1825;Ja 7,20 1826;Ap 9 1827
MWA N 2 1801;Ag 31 1807;Ap 21,My 12-19 1808;Mr 20,N 13 1809;F 19,Mr 5-12,Jl 2,Ag 6,S 17,O 8,29 1810;Mr 11,25-Ap 1,My 13 1811;Ap 6 1812;F 24 1819;Je 23 1828;F 5 1831;F 4-21 1837[55-57]Ag 27 1860
WHi Ja 22 1810;Ja 30,F 1 1838

La GAZETTE canadienne. w
CaQMS Ag 14 1822-Jl 9 1823

La GAZETTE de Montréal. *See* Gazette

GAZETTE officielle de Quebec. 1869+
CaOT 1931+
CaQMM 1883;1915
DLC 1903+
NN 1869+

GOGLU. w Ag 8 1929+
CaO 1929+

La GUÊPE. w Ja 1858-64||?
CaO Jl 1858-61
CaQQL 1858-64

Montreal HERALD. sw,w 1808-1908||?
Title varies: Montreal herald for the country; Montreal weekly herald
CaOTA Mr 15 1845;My 16 1851;S 2,11 1854;Je 26 1857;F 24,Je 30 1860;Jl 1,S 12,13 1865;Mr 28,O 6 1868;Mr 18-25,Ap 29,N 1,19 1869;S 23,O 3 1870;My 6 1872;Ag 21,S 9,O 9,D 28 1874;My 15,16,29-30,D 11,24 1876;My 2,Je 4 1878;Ja 3,Mr 26,Ap 25,My 26,Je 28,Jl 11,25,O 2,11 1879
CaOTU D 11,29 1834[35]F 1,Mr 3,17 1836;Ap 11,15,25,29,My 6 1839[41]Ja 3,13,17,20,27,F 3 1842;Ja 17 1843;Ja 24 1844[48-51]
CaQMS [1849-60;62-63]
DLC N 19 1852
MBAt My 7 1863;Ap 21 1865
MHi Je 10 1820;My 12,26 1821;Ap 14 1824;Ag 14(extra)1861
MWA O 19,N 9-16 1811;F 29,Ap 4 1812;S 17 1814;Ap 15,My 4,13-20 1815;Mr 7(and supp) 1818;D 22 1849;Ag 18 1857;Ap 6 1861;Jl 15 1871-94
N Mr 9 1837
NChM Jl 16 1853

Montreal daily HERALD. d O 19 1811+
1811-Mr 29 1919 as Montreal herald (title varies slightly: Montreal herald and daily commercial gazette; Montreal herald and daily telegraph; etc.)
pub Ap 1912+
CSmH Ag 4 1812(extra)My 16 1829
CaO F 7 1818+
CaOOA [1811-16;18-21;24-39;75]83-F 5 1910;12-F 8 1913;Mr 1914+
CaOTL Ag 1816-O 1820
CaQ 1889+
CaQM Ap 1878-97;Ja 29-31 1914
CaQMA N 1822-O 1823
CaQMF 1861;63-65;69;71-72;79-83;93-95;97-1900
CaQMG S 19 1812;N 15,19,26 1838;D 5 1848;N 13 1856;S 15 1863;Ja 4 1873
CaQMM [1912-13;16-26;35-38;42-43;45-47;50;52-53;60-61;65;69;71-73;76;81;84-88;92;97;1901]
CaQMS [1849-69]Ja-Ap 1898
CaQMSm 1823-27
DLC Je 1 1816;Jl 9 1835;Ja 26,Mr 7,13,22,My 20,28-29,S 1,18,23,N 21,D 3,16 1856;Ja 20,Ap 25,My 1,4,8,19,Je 11 1857;O 24 1873
MWA Mr 17 1864;S 1908-Ja 26 1922
MnU O 1894-1912
NChM D 25 1855;N 26 1856;Ja 22,My 17 1859;D 9 1864
NNHi N 10 1824
OClWHi [Mr-D 1870;Ja-O 1873]
WHi D 27 1883;Je 19,Jl 6,N 13,D 30 1885;D 24 1886;Mr 11 1887

L'ILLUSTRATION. d Jl 4 1930+
pub 1930+

L'INFORMATION financiere. w N 4 1920+
pub 1920+
CaQME 1920+

IRISH vindicator. sw
CaQQL D 12 1828-D 9 1831

L'ITALIA. w 1916+
In Italian
pub 1924+

JEWISH eagle. *See* Der Keneder adler

Le JOURNAL. d D 16 1899-Mr 3 1905||
CaO complete
CaQ complete
CaQMF 1899-D 15 1900
CaQMS [1899-1905]
CaQQL complete

Der KENEDER adler. (Jewish eagle) d Ag 1907+
Title varies: Der Adler (The Eagle)
In Yiddish
pub O 1907+
IU D 12 1917-My 18,O 26 1921+
NN O 2 1908-[25]+
NNJHi [1932]+

Montreal daily MAIL. d 1913-17||?
MH Jl 22 1914-S 18 1917

La MINERVE. sw,tw,d O 4 1826-My 27 1899||
CSmH S 13 1830
CaO complete
CaOKU 1835-36;46-48[50-56]60-63;65-78;82-89; 98-99
CaOLU 1856-57
CaOOA 1827-37;43-[78]-97
CaOT [1826-35]
CaQ F 12 1827-99
CaQMF 1826-77;79-91
CaQMG F 12 1827-F 11 1828;Je 21,Ag 12,S 23,N 15,D 9 1830;O 8 1832;F 13-N 16 1837;S 9 1842-S 7 1843

QUEBEC (*Continued*)

MONTREAL—*Continued*

La MINERVE. sw,tw,d 1826-99||—*Continued*
CaQMS [F 12 1827-N 9 1837;O 13 1842-My 27 1899]
CaQMSm 1841-94
CaQQL N 9 1828-99
MB [1842-53]
MWA Jl 1,27 1841;Jl 14 1871-My 3 1872

La MINERVE. w 1918-29||?
CaQ N 1918-D 26 1925

Le MIROIR. *See* Le Patriote

MISSISKOUI standard. *See under* Frelighsburg

Le MONDE. d 1867-98||
CaQ Ja 25 1889-N 25 1897
CaQMS [1882-Ag 1 1898]
CaQQL 1881-83

Le MONDE. w *See* Le Monde Canadien

Le MONDE Canadien. w 1867-1900||
1867-97? as Le Monde
CaQ Ag 1897-Jl 5 1900
CaQMS [1882-Ag 1 1898]

Le MONITEUR Canadien. w S 1 1849-O 4 1855||
CaOOA S 1854-55
CaQ 1849-F 1851
CaQMF My 10-25 1850;53-55
CaQMS [1849-55]

MONITOR. w S 17 1925+
pub 1925+

Le NATIONAL. d Ap 24 1872-F 22 1879||
CaO [1872-79]
CaOOA My 1872-74
CaQMF 1872-76
CaQMS [1872-Mr 1875;Ap 1876-79]
MWA My 23-Ag 1 1872

Le NATIONAL. d D 14 1889-96||?
CaO 1889-D 21 1895
CaQ 1889-Mr 7 1896

Le NATIONALISTE. w Mr 6 1904-S 24 1922||
CaO complete
CaOLU [1904-06]-[14-16]-[19]
CaOOA [1906-11]
CaQ complete
CaQMS [1904-F 5 1922]
CaQMSm 1904-21
CaQShS Ag 23 1908-Mr 12 1916
DLC Mr 11 1906-Mr 1908

Le NÉGOCIANT canadien. w O 12 1871-73||
CaQQL 1871-73

NEW ERA. d My 26 1857-
CaOTA My 27,29,Je 1,15,S 17 1857;Ap 24 1858

NEW Montreal gazette. w Jl 16 1827-31||?
CaQMM 1827-[29-30]
MWA Ja 13 1831

Daily NEWS. d 1835-71||
CaOTA D 10 1869;N 21,23-24,26,D 3,5-6 1870
CaQMM [1868-71]

Evening NEWS. d 1914-18||?
CaQMM My 1914-Ap 1916

Le NOUVEAU monde. d,tw S 19 1867-Jl 5 1900||
CaO complete
CaOOA 1867-Ag 1871
CaQ 1868-88
CaQMF 1869-73;76
CaQMS [1867-Ja 3 1874]
CaQMSm 1867-78
CaQQL 1867-82

Les NOUVELLES. w S 1 1895-F 6 1898||
CaO complete

OBSERVER. w Ja 9 1845-
CSmH Ja 16 1845

L'ORDRE. tw N 23 1858-O 23 1871||
CaO complete
CaOOA complete
CaOLU 1860-69
CaQMF 1859-62
CaQMS [1858-71]
CaQMSm 1858-70
CaQQL complete

L'ORDRE. d Mr 10 1934+
CaQMF 1934+
CaQMS 1934+

La PATRIE. tw S 26 1854-Jl 17 1858||
CaO complete
CaOOA O 1854-[56]-[58]
CaOLU [1854-58]
CaOTA F 27 1855
CaQMF 1854-55;Je 12 1856-Ap 24 1857
CaQMS [1854-58]
CaQQL complete

La PATRIE. d F 24 1879+
pub 1879+
CaO 1879+
CaOOA 1883+
CaQ 1879+
CaQMF 1884-90
CaQMS 1879-F 23 1880;Jl 1888-Mr 1890[1900-31]
CaQQL 1879-1901
DLC O 9 1901-09
MWA S 11 1902
WHi 1882-85

Le PATRIOTE. w 1929—
1929-Mr 1933 as Le Miroir
pub 1929+

Le PAYS. sw Ja 15 1852-D 26 1871||
CaO complete
CaOLU [1856-57]
CaOOA 1856-[68]-71
CaQ 1852-Ja 16 1866
CaQMF 1852-55;59;61-63;65-67;70-71
CaQMS [1852-71]
CaQQL 1852-60
MWA S 13 1871

Le PAYS. w Ja 15 1910-D 3 1921||
CaO complete
CaQ complete
CaQMF 1910-16
CaQMS [1910-N 1921]

Le PETIT journal. w O 1926+
pub 1926+

PILOT. tw,w Mr 5 1844-62||?
1845-48? as Pilot and journal of commerce
CaO 1844-Mr 25 1862
CaOKU 1849-55
CaOOA 1844-47
CaOTA My 18,S 2,4-6 1844;Ja 4,Mr 6,25,Ap 5,My 10 1845;F 6[Ap-Je 11]1846;D 2 1848;Jl 31,O 15 1856
CaOTU N 3 1844[45-49]
CaQMG Jl 29 1853
CaQMM Ag 26 1845;Mr 14 1859
CaQMS [1847-Ag 1848]
MWA Jl 26-Ag 6 1857;Mr 5-N 19 1859
OClWHi Ag 17 1850
P-M Jl 8 1855
PPot Ag 15 1855

Le POPULAIRE. tw Ap 10 1837-N 3 1838||
CaQ complete
CaQMS complete
CaQQL complete

Montreal daily POST. d Je 10 1878-88||
CaOTA Je 15 1878;O 14 1879
CaQM Je 15 1878-D 17 1888
CaQMM Ap 19 1881
CaQMS Jl-D 1881;Ja-Je 1885
WHi Jl 4 1885
w ed. *See* True witness

La PRESSE. Journal français quotidien. d S 8 1863-S 1 1864||
Followed by L'Union nationale
CaQQL O 1 1863-64

La PRESSE. d O 15 1884+
pub 1884+
CSt-H [1915-16]
CaNU 1934+
CaOKU 1926+
CaO 1884+
CaQ O 20 1884+
CaQMS Ap 20-O 19 1885;N 1894-Ap 1895;D 1897-F 1898;Mr-Ag 1899[1900-30]
CaQQL O 20 1884-Je 5 1920
DLC My 2 1901+
IaHi S 29 1898-N 16 1899
MWA D 11 1931
OkU [1918-24]

QUEBEC gazette. w 1764-O 30 1874||
CaQQM [O 23 1823-24;26;49;64]
DLC [1803]
NN [1787;89-90;1809-14;25-26;42]

La QUOTIDIENNE. ir
CaQMS [1838]
CaQQL [1837]

Le RAPPEL. w
CaQQL S 14 1902-04

Le RÉVEIL. w Mr 11 1871-D 23 1876||
My 27-S 16 1876 pub in Quebec
CaQMF Mr-My 13 1871;My 27-D 1876
CaQQL My 27-D 1876

La RIPOSTE. w 1927+
CaQBE Je 1934+

Le SOIR. d
CaQQL Ap 24-Ag 31 1896

Le SPECTATEUR canadien. w 1815-43||?
CaOOA [1816-21;23-43]
CaQMF D 8 1821-F 5 1825;F 17 1827-F 1829
CaQMG S 2,16,O 14-21,N 11,25 1816;supp F 28,My 9 1815
CaQMSm 1815-27
CaQQL 1820
NN My 19 1814

SPIRIT of our times. 1861-
CaOTA My 18,Je 1 1861

Montreal STANDARD. w S 1 1905+
pub 1905+
CaOOA 1905-N 1906;07+
CaQ S 23 1905-13;17

Montreal STAR. w
CaNW Ja 21-D 16 1865

Montreal daily STAR. d Ja 16 1869+
pub 1869+
CL Je 29 1927
CSt-H [1914-17]
CaB Jl 1901[Ja-F 1909;F-Ag 1918]-Ap 19 1932
CaNSa 1930-33
CaNU 1934+
CaO Jl 1896+
CaOOA 1912-Ap 1913[15]+
CaOT S 1899[1900]-Jl 1902
CaOTA [Ja 26-Mr 16 1878]
CaQ 1881+
CaQM 1878+
CaQMF Jl 1874-Mr 1875;77;79-93;95-1900
CaQMG D 13,19,1870;Ja 25 1871;Ap 14 1877;Je 26 1886;Mr 2,6 1891
CaQMH F 1931+
CaQMM My 12 1879;Ap 19 1881;Je 25-26 1884;[Ap]My 15 1885;Ap 19-20 1888;Ja 5,Mr 18,30,N 20 1889;Jl 26,N 14 1893;Ja 22 1901;Ag 8-11 1902;Jl 23 1908;My 6-7,10-21 1910
CaQMS [1885-87;89-Mr 1890]
DLC Je 1898-N 9 1899;Mr 22 1905+
ICM F 24 1882
MWA Ja 27 1922
NNHi Ag 11,S 10 1902
WHi [1885;87-93;96]
—w ed. *See* Family herald and weekly star

Montreal STAR. w 1869-74. *See* Family herald and weekly star

SUN. w Je 1 1816-
MWA S 21 1816;Mr 8,Ag 2 1817

SUN. tw 1853-
CaOTA Ag 7 1854
MiU-C Je 2 1853

Montreal SUN. d 1875-76||
CaOTA Ja 21-26 1876

Evening TELEGRAPH. d
CaQMG Ja 12 1869

Daily TELEGRAPH. d Jl 12 1913-Ja 27 1914||
Follows Daily witness. Jl-N 28 1913 as Montreal daily telegraph and witness. Merged with Montreal daily herald
CaOOA complete
CaQ Ag 1913-14
CaQM complete

Le TEMPS. d,ir 1883||
CaQ Jl 31-O 16 1883
CaQMS Jl 28-O 15 1883
CaQQL Jl 18-O 30 1883

La TERRE de chez nous. w F 15 1929+
pub 1929+

TIMES. d S 13 1884-O 3 1885||
CaO complete
CaQMM [1885]

TIMES and commercial advertiser. tw 1841-44||?
CaQMM [1842-44]
CaQMS Mr 13 1841-F 15 1842
NChM Jl 1 1843

Montreal TRANSCRIPT. w,tw,d 1836-65||?
CaOOA 1836-37[39]41-[62]-65
CaOT [1836-41]
CaOTA Jl 28 1846
CaOTL 1842-Ap 1843
CaQMF O 20 1836-S 1837
MWA N 23 1837;S 30,O 10 1857
N O 10 1857
NN O 1837-Ap 14,21,26-My 17,24,Je 7-12,16,21-Ag 18,28-S 1838
WHi Ap 12 1838

La Tribune. w O 23 1880-My 8 1884||
CaO 1880-81
CaQMS [1880-83]
CaQQL 1880-83

TRUE witness and Catholic chronicle. w Ag 16 1850-Jl 28 1910||
CaO O 12 1892-1910
CaOT 1850-Ag 11 1876
CaQ 1850-1908
CaQMF 1851;54-57;59-70;72-73
CaQMS [1850-Ag 12 1870]
CaQMSm 1850-59
CaQQL complete
MWA O 12 1892-94
—d ed *See* Post

L'UNION nationale. w S 8 1864-67||?
Follows La presse
CaO 1864-N 7 1867

VINDICATOR and Canadian advertiser. sw D 12 1828-37||?
CSmH Ag 27 1830
CaO Ap 17 1829-O 1836
CaOOA 1833-36
CaOT N 1832-[33-34]
CaQ Ja-Jl 13 1832
CaQMF 1831-N 1837
CaQMM Jl 30 1833;O 17 1837
CaQMS Mr 28-O 13 1837
Ct [1836]
DLC N 9 1832
NChM S 2 1834

Le VIOLON. w S 25 1886-Ja 28 1888||
CaO complete
CaQ N 13 1886-88

WESTERN star. sw Mr 23 1819-
MWA Mr 30,My 28 1819

Daily WITNESS. d Ag 13 1860-Jl 11 1913||
Followed by Montreal daily telegraph and witness, later Daily telegraph
CaOOA [1875]My 1877-Je 1883;Jl 1902-[13]
CaQ 1893-1913
CaQM 1878-1913
CaQMM [1861-62;64;68-69;73;75;80-81;84-88;92-93;99;1901]08;Mr 1909-13
CaQMS [1864-65]
CaQMW complete
DLC 1898-Je 1900
ICM Je 12-14,16 1884
MWA Ap 4 1863;F 25 1864;Ja 10 1867;S 28 1870;Ap 10 1871
NChM F 14,N 8,10-11 1862;Je 30,D 9 1864
OClWHi D 3 1864
WHi D 30 1861

WITNESS and Canadian homestead. sw,tw,w 1845+
1845-Ja 31 1905 as Montreal weekly witness (title varies: Montreal witness; Montreal witness weekly review and family newspaper, etc.)
w 1845-S 1856;sw N 1856-71;tw 1872-My 1877
pub 1845+
CaOHU [1862-67]
CaOKU 1846-92
CaOOA 1846-My 1848;51-62
CaOT 1846-50;54[57]
CaOTL 1846-50;53-54;57
CaOTU 1846-[48]49
CaOWi 1846-48;50-51;55-56
CaQMG 1848;My 21 1864;O 28 1871;S 6 1872;Je 13 1873;D 12 1878
CaQMM 1846-53;55-[61-62;67-73]
CaQQF 1848;74-81;83-93;95-99
IAC O 18,N-D 20 1933;Ja 3 1934
MWA Jl 28,Ag 13 1859;S 15 1871;O 24 1873
NSyU Ag 30 1847
NcU Mr 24 1880
NjR Ag 7,O 9 1935
TxU Je 10 1925-27

QUEBEC (*Continued*)

ORMSTOWN

Ormstown COURIER. w
CaQHC D 21 1882-O 14 1886

NEW dominion of Ormstown. w
CaQHC D 17 1874-Jl 5 1882

OUTREMONT

Outremont EXAMINER-courier.
CaQMM 1930+

QUEBEC

L'ABEILLE. w Jl 27 1848-Je 23 1881||
CaO [1848-81]

L'ACTION Catholique. d D 21 1907+
1907-Je 9 1915 as L'Action sociale
pub 1907+
CaO 1907+
CaOOU 1907+
CaQ 1907+
CaQMSm 1911+
CaQSaC 1907+
CaQShS 1907+

L'ACTION sociale. *See* L'Action Catholique

Weekly ADVERTISER. w Mr 22 1861-
CaOTA Mr 17,31 1861

L'AMI de la religion et de la patrie. w D 18 1847-Mr 13 1850||
CaO complete
CaQMS 1847-N 1848

ARROW. w
CaQQL [1864]

L'ARTISAN. sw O 10 1842-
CaO 1842-Jl 13 1843
CaQQL 1842-Jl 20 1843;Ja-S 26 1844

L'AVANT-GARDE. d D 5 1896-Ap 26 1898||
CaQ D 9 1896-98
CaQMS [1896-98]
CaQQL 1896-Jl 14,N 22 1897-98

BEREAN. w
CaQ Ap 3 1845-Mr 1847

BOURRU. w F 1 1858-60||
CaO 1859-Ja 28 1860

Saturday BUDGET. w N 12 1870-1906||?
CaQ 1870-D 8 1906

CANADA gazette. *See under* Ottawa (Ontario)

Le CANADIEN. w,sw,tw,d N 22 1806-D 11 1909||
w 1806-30?;sw My 8 1831-My 2 1832;tw My 9 1832-My 6,N 9 1857-1909?;d My 8-N 6 1857
CSmH S 2 1846
CaO complete
CaOLU 1831-[46-49;58-61]
CaOOA 1832-43;83-91
CaQ 1806-Ja 16 1822;My 7 1831-F 11 1893
CaQMF D 6 1806-Mr 14 1810;34-42;51-53
CaQMG [1837-39]
CaQMS [Ja 19 1820-Ja 1824;My 7 1831-My 7 1858;My 8 1861-88]
CaQMSm 1831-46
CaQQL 1806-25;31-93
CaQShS Ja 23 1837-D 20 1839
DLC 1806-Mr 14 1810;Ja 23 1822-F 16 1825;My 7 1831-My 5 1862
—w ed *See* Le Cultivateur

Le CANADIEN indépendant. w
CaQMS [My 21 1848-O 31 1849]
CaQQL [1849]

Le CASTOR. bw N 7 1843-45||
CaO N 21 1844-Je 16 1845
CaQ N 7-14 1844
CaQQL complete

Quebec CHRONICLE. d My 18 1847-Ap 30 1924||
United with Quebec gazette to form Quebec chronicle and Quebec gazette
CaO 1861-1924
CaOOA 1883-1905
CaOTA My 28 1853
CaQ Jl 4 1860-1924
CaQMM [1864-74]Ap 21 1888
CaQQH 1847-1923
CaQQL 1850-1924
DLC D 1899-1924
MWA N 22 1851;Ap 23 1857;Ja 1 1876
NNHi Je 23 1902
NjR Ag 1 1879

Quebec CHRONICLE and Quebec gazette. d My 1 1924-Je 30 1925||
United with Quebec telegraph to form Quebec chronicle-telegraph
CaO complete
CaQ complete
CaQMM complete
CaQQL complete
DLC complete

Quebec CHRONICLE-TELEGRAPH. d Jl 2 1925+
Formed by the union of Quebec chronicle-Quebec gazette, and Quebec telegraph
pub 1925+
CaO 1925+
CaOOA 1925+
CaQ 1925+
CaQMM 1925+
CaQQL 1925+
DLC 1925+

Le CLAIRON. w
CaQ Ja 30-My 14 1897

Quebec COMMERCIAL list. w
CaQM My 15-N 13 1828
CaQQL 1815-35

COURRIER de Quebec. sw Ja 3 1807-D 31 1808||
CaO complete
CaQ complete
OClWHi Ja 28,F 11-25,Mr 14-18,Ap 4,My 2,9-27,Je 6-17 1807;Ja 20,F 3,13-27,Mr 2,26-30, Ap 2-18,Jl 2,9-20,Ag 24,S 3-7 1808

COURRIER du Canada. d F 2 1857-Ap 11 1901||
CaO complete
CaOLU 1857[77]-[79]
CaOOA 1857-[64]-66[68]-71
CaQ complete
CaQMS [1857-Ja 1859;F 1861-62;74-75;78-95]
CaQMSm 1857-1900
CaQQL 1857-1900
CaQSaC complete
CaQShS complete

Le CULTIVATEUR. w S 3 1874-90||?
CaO My 9 1885-87
CaQMF D 24 1881-82
—d ed *See* Le Canadien

L'ECHO du pays. w F 28? 1833-
PHi Jl 18,Ag 1 1833

L'ECLAIR. d
CaQ Ja 16-F 17 1906
CaQQL 1906

L'ECLAIREUR. d 1875-79||
CaQQL Ag 4 1877-F 22 1879

L'ELECTEUR. w
CaQQL Jl 16-Ag 27 1827;My 19 1866-67

L'ELECTEUR. w 1879-D 26 1896||
CLM Ag 26 1891
CaQ Je 24 1880-96

L'ELECTEUR. d Jl 15 1880-D 26 1896||
CaO O 1880-96
CaOOA 1883-96
CaQQL 1889-96
WHi 1880-82;Jl 16-S 26 1883;84;Ap 10 1885-N 27 1895

L'ETOILE et journal du commerce. *See* Star and commercial advertiser

L'EVÈNEMENT. d,tw My 13 1867+
CaO 1867+
CaQ 1867+
CaQMS [Ag 5 1871-My 1877;79;87;1901;03-08]
CaQQL 1867+
MWA Jl 5 1871-94
WHi Ap 27,29-30,O 1 1918

Le Fantasque. w,bw Ag 1 1837-58||?
CaO [1837-49]
CaQMF Ap 7-S 11 1842
CaQMS [F 1838-F 1849]
CaQQL 1837-My 24 1845;Je 10 1848-F 24 1849; N 19 1857-Je 23 1858

Le FRANC-PARLEUR. w 1914-25||?
CaQMS [S 1915-Je 13 1919]
CaQQL Jl 10 1915-Ag 5 1921

Le GASCON. w
CaQQL [1848]

Quebec GAZETTE. w,sw,tw,d,w Je 21 1764-Ap 24 1924||
Official through 1817. Bi-lingual English and French through Ap 1832. United with Quebec chronicle to form Quebec chronicle and Quebec gazette
My 1832-O 29 1842 pub Monday, Wednesday and Friday in English; Tuesday, Thursday and Saturday in French
CSmH S 2 1830;D 21 1836
CaO 1800-Je 24 1864
CaOKU [1839-41]
CaOOA 1800-50;54-55;64
CaOT [1823;32;34-35;37-40;49]
CaQ Ja 7 1796-Ja 14 1901
CaQM 1849
CaQMF 1807-09;O 30 1823-O 28 1824;Jl 7 1836-Ag 17 1837
CaQMG Je 21 1764(reprint)D 1-8 1791;My 10 1792;Ap 22,My 13 1813;Jl 14 1823;Ap 28 1825; Mr 10 1828;Mr 7 1832;Jl 29 1847
CaQMM Je 21 1764[81-82]86[90-92]1823-49;[58] Je 6 1862;83-1924
CaQMS [1820-46]
CaQMSm 1818-64
CaQQH 1764-76;79-80;84-94;97-1804;08-13;15-29;32-47;49-50;54-73
CaQQL 1820-55;1900-01
DLC Je 21 1764[facsimile]My 29 1766-67;My 1791-N 1798;Ja 3-24,Jl 11-18 1799;S 16-23 1802;Mr,S,D 1 1803;Mr 8-15,29,My 17,Ag 2,23,S 6-20,N 8,D 6-13 1804;Mr,D 19 1805;06-35;Ag 1,5,S 26,D 28 1836;Ap 26,O 11,N 15,17-24,D 15 1837;38-49;Ap 15,20,22,My 2 1854;O 21-30,N 25,D 16 1864;Je 6,10,15,Ag 19,29,31 1863[65-67]Ja 17,31,F 7,28,Mr 28,Ap 11,Jl 25, Ag 22-29,S 12-19,D 19 1894;Jl 3,17,Ag 7,S 4-18 1895;Jl 29 1896
ICH Je 21 1764
MB Je 21 1764;My 7 1767;Jl 8 1839;Je 21 1864
MBAt F 7,S 18 1828;F 4,Jl 29 1830;Je 21 1864
MH [1764-Je 24 1864]
MHi Ag 14,S 11,25-28 1820;Ap 23,D 13-20 1821;F 28 1822;Ja 22,F 9,Mr 18-22,Ap 5 1824; Mr 28,My 5,S 5 1825;Ap 6 1826;F 8,Mr 15 1827
MWA Ja 20,F 10-17,Ag 25,S 1-8,N 29 1804;Ag 15 1805;Ap 6,20-My 4,N 2 1809;Ja 11,F 15,S 13,27,O 11,25, D 13 1810;F 14-21,Ap 4,My,Je 27,Jl 18-25,Ag 8-15,S 12,26,O 17,D 5,26 1811;O 28, D 16 1813;F 3,S 15 1814;Ap 13-20,Je 29,N 16-30,D 14 1815-Ja 11,F 1,15,Mr 21,Ap 4,18-25, My 16 1816;Ap 16,Je 25,Jl 30(supp)S 7,O 1 1818;Mr 29,Ap 1 1819;N 4 1824-O 27 1825;26-27;S 18 1828[Ja-N 1838;39-40]My 1-3 1843;Ja 5,F 28,Ag 28,D 18 1844;Mr 28,Jl 30,O 29 1845; Jl 23 1847
MiD-B Ja 5 1775-Mr 21 1776
MiU-C [1766-67]
N D 27 1827;O 14 1833;S 19 1842
NN [1787;89-90;1809-11]F 27 1812;13-14;N 1825-O 1826[42]
NNHi Je 21 1864(centennary ed)
NcD S 30 1802[06-07;09;11]O 6,D 8 1814[15-16] Jl 4,O 31 1822;Ja 29,Mr 11,N 18,D 27 1824[25; 32]Mr 11 1835; Mr 28 1845
WHi Mr 31-Ap 7,Je 9-16,S 29,O 13 1808;N 4 1813
—French tw ed *See* La Gazette de Quebec

La GAZETTE de Quebec. tw My 2 1832-O 29 1842||
DLC 1834-[38]-42
MiU 1830

La GAZETTE du commerce et de l'industrie. w
CaQ My 12-Jl 20 1866

La GAZETTE officielle de Québec. *See* Quebec official gazette

GRIDIRON. w
NN Ag 20 1859

Quebec HERALD. bw
CaQM N 24 1788-N 8 1790
CaQQL O 19 1843-F 3 1844

Morning HERALD and commercial advertiser. tw 1837-
CSmH Ag 21 1837
CaQQL Ap 25-D 1837

Le JOURNAL. w D 14 1929+
CaO 1929+
CaQQL 1932+

Le JOURNAL de Quebec. w,sw,tw,d D 1 1842-O 1 1889||
CaO complete
CaOKU 1862-71;74-75
CaOT [1845]
CaQ 1842-S 1889
CaQMF 1853;61-64
CaQMS [1842-N 1850;53-54;57-60;62-73;75-77; 79;81-86]
CaQQL complete
CaQSaC 1847-64
WHi 1851-55;57 61;63-82;Je 10 1885-89

Le JOURNAL de St. Roch. w D 14 1874-F 5 1876
CaQ complete

Le JOURNAL des campagnes. w
CaQ F 9 1882-D 28 1901
CaQMS [Ja 19-N 15 1888]
CaQQL 1882-94

Le JOURNAL des etudiants. w
CaQQL D 12 1840-F 27 1841

La JUSTICE. d Ja 9 1886-Mr 24 1892||
Merged with L'Evènement
CaO 1886-91
CaQ 1890-92
CaQMS [Ap 26-Je 18 1886;Ap 30-N 23 1887]
CaQQL complete

Le LIBÉRAL. bw
CaQQL 1837

La LIBRE parole. w Je 17 1905-D 14 1912||
CaO complete
CaQQL 1905-11

LITERARY transcript and general intelligencer. ir
CaQMM [Ja 13 1838-D 28 1839]

La MASCARADE. w
CaQQL [1863]

Le MATIN. d Ja 13-S 19 1892||
CaQ complete
CaQMS [Ja-S 17 1892]

Le MENESTREL. w Je 20 1844-45||
CaO [1844-45]

Quebec MERCURY. sw,tw.d 1805-1903||?
sw 1805?-31?;tw 1832-50?
CaQ Ja 5 1805-O 17 1903
CaQM Je 23 1818;35
CaQMF 1814-20;22
CaQMG N 13 1809;Ja 6,Ap 6 1812;F 8 1814;D 21(supp)1821;S 20(supp)1822;Mr 31,Je 16 1827;Mr 7,O 3 1829;Mr 15 1831;Jl 19 1838;Je 3 1839(extra)F 26 1850
CQMM 1886
CaQMS [Jl 6 1824-25;N 24-D 15 1832;Ja-S 1833;37;Ja-Mr 26 1839]
CaQQH 1805-07;10;14;16-18;20;22-24;26;29-30; 33-36;38-51;53-63
CaQQL 1820-55;93-1902
PPAm [Ja-N 1814]

Quebec MERCURY. w Ja 5 1805-O 17 1903||
CSmH Je 1 1833
CaO complete
CaOLU N 1806-07
CaOOA 1805;09-15;31-33;Ap 18 1837
CaOT 1816
CaOTA Je 23 1829;D 15 1835;Ag 12 1837;My 3 1842;S 16-23 1852;My 12 1857
CaQMS [1821-23]
DLC 1808-09;Ja 10-D 1815
MBAt Jl 25,Ag 29 1808;Mr 20,Ap 17,My 8-15 1809;Jl 1-8,29,S 16,N 18 1811;My 4,Ag 4 1812
MWA Ja 5,19,Ag 10 1805;Ag 25 1806;Je 25-Jl 2,S 17 1810;N 25(supp)1811;D 28 1813;Ja 18, F 8 1814;Ap 9 1825
MiU-C Je 4 1853
NNHi 1811
WHi Ja 5 1807;09-10;Ja 13-Ag 18 1812;F-D 1813;Ja 25 1838

MIRROR of parliament. ir
CaQQL [1860]

Le NATIONAL. sw,tw N 20 1855-Je 10 1859||
sw in winter; tw in summer
CaO 1855-N 19 1858
CaQ complete
CaQMS [1855-59]
CaQQL complete
WHi N 23 1855-O 16 1856;O 21 1858

QUEBEC (*Continued*)

QUEBEC—*Continued*

Quebec daily NEWS. d My 1862-70||?
CaOOA 1862-Ap 18 1865
CaOTA My 14 1864
CaQ My 20 1867-F 17 1870
CaQMM My 1864-Ap 1865

Le NOUVELLISTE. d N 27 1876-O 23 1886||
CaO complete
CaQ complete
CaQMS [Jl 12 1877-O 1881;My 8-Ag 23 1883]
CaQQL complete

L'OBSERVATEUR. w
CaQMF Mr 9 1858-Ap 6,20 1859-My 17 1860
CaQQL 1858-59

Quebec OFFICIAL gazette. w 1869+
In French and English
CaB Ja 2 1897[1901;09-O 1913]+
CaOOA 1869-Je 1882
CaOT 1932+
CaQMM 1883;1915+
DLC 1903+
NN 1869+

PEOPLE'S sentinel. w Mr 26 1850-
CaQMF Mr-Je 21 1850
—French ed *See* La Sentinelle du peuple

Le QUEBEC. w
CaQ O 28-N 25 1889

La RÉFORME. bw Je 9 1860-Ag 18 1863||
CaO [1860-63]
CaQMF 1860-Jl 9 1861
CaQMS [1860-My 8 1862]

Le RÉVEIL. 1876. *See under* Montreal

Le RÉVEIL. w
CaQ D 24 1891-F 25 1892

La SCIE. w O 29 1863-Mr 12 1865||
CaO [1863-65]

La SCIE illustree. w F 11 1865-My 29 1866||
CaO [1865-66]
CaQQL complete

La SENTINELLE du peuple. w Mr 26 1850-
CaQMF Mr-Je 7 1850
CaQQL [1850]
—English ed *See* People's sentinel

Le SOLEIL. d 1882+
CaQ D 28 1896+
CaQQL 1897+
PP D 18 1928+
WHi D 28 1896-Je 1897

Le SOLEIL. w D 28 1896+
CaO 1897+
CaOOA 1897;1902-[04]-[06;10-11]-13[16;18-19]+

Quebec SPECTATOR. tw
CaQQL My 3-O 30 1848

STAR and commercial advertiser. L'Etoile et journal du commerce. w,sw D 5 1827-D 4 1830||
1827- as Quebec star
In French and English
CSmH Ag 25 1830
CaO complete
CaQM complete
CaQMS [D 1828-Je 10 1829]
DLC Ja 2 1830
MBAt O 1,N 22 1828
MWA Ap 2-9 1828
NNHi My 10 1828

Quebec TELEGRAPH. w My 11 1816-
MWA Ag 31-O 12 1816

Quebec daily TELEGRAPH. d 1872-Je 30 1925||
United with Quebec chronicle and Quebec gazette to form Quebec chronicle-telegraph
pub 1908-25
CaOOA 1914-16;18-25
CaOTA Je 3 1882
CaQ N 13 1875-Ap 1925
CaQQL 1906-25

Le TÉLÉGRAPHE. The telegraph. w Mr 22 1837-
In French and English
CaQQL [1837]

Le TRAVAILLEUR. w 1922-23||?
CaQQL 1922-Ag 30 1923

Le TRAVAILLEUR illustré.
CaQQL O 19 1878

La TRIBUNE. d,tw
CaQQL Ag 25 1863-Ag 22 1864

L'UNION liberale. w My 3 1888-N 28 1896||
CaO 1888-Mr 2 1895
CaQ complete
CaQMS [My 11 1888-Mr 13 1891]
CaQQL 1888-Mr 13 1891;D 29 1892-96

La VÉRITÉ. w Jl 14 1881+
pub My 1923+
CaO 1881-Je 16 1923
CaOLU 1881-1920
CaOOU 1881+
CaQ Jl 28 1881-1913
CaQMSm 1887-1911
CaQQL 1881-Je 16 1923
CaQSaC 1883-1906
CaQShS Jl 28 1881-Je 16 1923

La VIGIE. w,sw,d Je 30 1906-My 31 1913||
CaQ complete
CaQQL 1906-10

Quebec VINDICATOR. w 1857-
CaOTA Je 18 1859;Mr 15 1860

VRAI Canadien. Mr 10 1810-Mr 6 1811||
CaO complete

RIMOUSKI

Le COURRIER de Rimouski. sw
CaQMS [S 2 1871-N 11 1873]

L'ECHO du Golfe. w
CaQ Je 2 1885-N 18 1886

Le NOUVELLISTE de Rimouski. w 1878-
CaQQL N 28 1878-Je 16 1881

Le PROGRÈS du Golfe. w Ap 15 1904+
pub 1929+
CaQ 1904-08
CaQQL O 18 1912-N 1914;19+
CaQRS 1904+

La VOIX du golfe. w
CaQQL 1867-71

RIVIERE DU LOUP

Le JOUR. *See* Le Journal de Fraserville

Le JOURNAL de Fraserville. w Ja 2 1885-1927||?
1885-Mr 16 1888 as Le Jour; Mr 23-O 19 1888? Le Progres; O 26 1888?- as Le Journal
1885-1920 pub in Fraserville
CaQ 1885-O 19,N-D 1888

Le PROGRES. *See* Le Journal de Fraserville

Le SAINT-LAURENT. w N 19 1895+
1895-1920 pub in Fraserville
pub 1895-Mr 21 1902;Je 1927+
CaQ D 11 1896-1909
CaQQL 1895+

ROBERVAL

Le COLON. w Mr 1 1917+
pub 1917+

Le DEFRICHEUR du lac St. Jean. w
CaQ O 24 1901-Je 12 1902

Le LAC Saint-Jean. w 1902-16||?
CaQ D 11 1902-08

ROCK ISLAND

STANSTEAD journal. w 1845+
CaQRi 1907+
WHi Jl 22 1847

SAINT-CHARLES DE RICHELIEU

L'ECHO du pays. w F 28 1833-
CaO 1833-My 26 1836
CaOOA 1833-Ap 1836
CaQQL 1833-36

ST. HYACINTHE

Le CLARION. w Ja 1912+
Follows L'Union
pub 1912+

Le COURRIER de Saint-Hyacinthe. w F 24 1853+
pub [1853]-69;71+
CaO F 28 1868-F 23 1872
CaQ 1853-1911
CaQMF Mr-D 1853
CaQML 1870
CaQMS [My 1920-30]
CaQQL 1853-80;88+
MWA Je 3 1864;S 22 1871

La GAZETTE de St.-Hyacinthe. sw,tw 1868-70||?
CaQSiC Ag 13 1868-D 22 1870

Le JOURNAL de St.-Hyacinthe. w
CaQSiC My 3 1866-Ag 3 1868

La TRIBUNE. w 1888-1922||?
CaQ Mr 16 1888-1908
CaQQL Ap 27 1888-Jl 24 1891;1914-D 29 1922

La TRIBUNE. d
CaQSiC My 1 1899-Ja 31 1900

L'UNION. w O 1873-D 28 1911||
Followed by Le Clarion
CaQ Ap 21 1883-1911
CaQQL 1888-1891
CaQSiC 1909
CaQSiD complete
MWA My 1 1886

ST. JEAN

To 1913 as St. Johns

L'ALLIANCE. w Mr 30 1893-F 23 1894||
CaQ complete

Le CANADA-FRANÇAIS. w Je 1 1860+
1860-93 as Franco-Canadien
pub [1860-My 1 1920]+
CaQ 1883-1909
CaQMS [Je 1862-N 1863]
CaQQL 1862-67;88-92
MWA Jl 7 1871

Le COURRIER de St. Jean. w My 1 1896-1915||?
CaQ 1896-Mr 5 1909

FRANCO-CANADIEN. *See* Le Canada-Français

NEWS and Eastern townships advocate. w 1848+
pub 1848+

ST. JEROME

L'AVENIR du Nord. w Ja 10 1897+
pub 1897—
CaQ 1897-1909
CaQMS [Ja 28 1898-1932]
CaQQL 1897+

La CAMPAGNE. w
CaQ S 2 1886-Ap 28 1887

La NATION. w Jl 18 1901-08||?
CaQ 1901-D 26 1908
CaQQL 1901-06

Le NORD. w 1878-99||?
CaQ 1882-D 22 1899
CaQMS [Mr 23 1893-F 1895]
CaQQL 1882-93

ST. JOHNS. *See* ST. JEAN

ST. JOSEPH

La VALLÉE de la Chaudière. w Ap 1932+
pub 1932+

ST. JUSTIN

L'ECHO de Saint-Justin. m,w N 2 1921+
m 1921-N 1932
pub 1921+
CaO 1921+

STE. MARIE BEAUCE

Le GUIDE. w My 1 1930+
pub 1930+
CaQQL Ag 1931-33

SHAWENEGAN FALLS

L'INDUSTRIEL. w 1902-16||?
CaQ Ap 1906-08

SHAWVILLE

EQUITY. w Je 15 1882+
pub 1882+

SHERBROOKE

Sherbrooke EXAMINER. w,sw 1878-1907||
Merged with Sherbrooke daily record
CaQShE complete
NNHi S 8 1902

Le FORUM. *See* Sherbrooke weekly telegram

Sherbrooke GAZETTE. w 1838-1908||
Merged with Sherbrooke daily record
CaQShS complete

Le MESSAGER de Saint-Michel. w Mr 10 1917+
CaQQL 1917+
CaQShS 1917+

Le PIONNIER de Sherbrooke. w 1866-1902||
CaOOA N 1874-O 1878;79-N 1882
CaQ F 1869-My 11 1902
CaQQL 1888-90;My 12 1901-02
CaQShS O 13 1866-Mr 30 1902
MWA F 16 1872

Le PROGRÈS de l'est. sw 1883-1924||?
CaQ S 1 1883-1906
CaQQL 1888-Mr 1891;O 7 1902-23
CaQShS Ag 25 1883-1907

Sherbrooke daily RECORD. d F 9 1897+
pub 1897+
CaQShS 1897+
MWA Mr 23 1911
NNHi Ap 26 1902

ST. FRANCIS courier, and Sherbrooke gazette. w Ag 1831-
MBAt My 22,Jl 17 1832

Sherbrooke weekly TELEGRAM. w Je 1924+
1924-Ap 1925 as Le Forum; My 1925-31 Forum
pub 1924+

La TRIBUNE. d 1910+
CaQ F 21-D 1910
CaQShS F 21 1910+

SOREL

Le COURRIER de Sorel. w Ja 1900+
pub 1900+
CaQ Mr 15 1901-04
See also Gazette de Berthier (Berthier)

La GAZETTE de Sorel. w,sw,tw Ag 13 1857-82||
CaO 1874-Ag 12 1875
CaOOA Ag 1864-78
CaQ 1880-O 1881
CaQQL 1857-79

Le JOURNAL de Sorel. w
CaQMF 1867-68

Le PATRIOTE. w Jl 15 1887-D 31 1891||
CaQ complete

PILOT. w 1868-82||?
CaOOA O 1871-O 1873;76-79

Le SORELOIS. w 1879+
CaQ Ja 31 1882-1908
CaQQL 1889-91;1917-Je 1920

Le SUD. d D 1 1887-Ap 9 1892||
CaQ complete

QUEBEC (*Continued*)

STANBRIDGE

MISSISKOUI post, and Canada record. w Ja 1835-
MWA S 23 1835

STANSTEAD

BRITISH colonist and Saint Francis gazette. w My 1 1823-
CaQMM 1823-[25]-[27]
MBAt F 21-Mr 6 1828
MWA Ag 28 1823

THETFORD MINES

Le Thetford **CANADIEN.** w Je 1915+
1915-Jl 1934 as Le Canadien
pub 1915+
CaQQL S 18 1918+

Le **MÉGANTIC.** w 1925+
CaQQL S 25 1925-31

THREE RIVERS

Le **BAS-CANADA.** sw Ap 22-N 14 1856‖
CaQMS [1856]
CaQQL complete

Le **BIEN** public. sw 1909+
pub S 14 1933+
CaQQL 1911+
CaQTS 1909+

Le **CLAIRON.** d 1884‖
CaQQL complete

La **CONCORDE.** sw My 2 1879-84‖
CaO 1879-Ap 1883
CaQ 1879-My 2 1884
CaQMS [My 3 1880-Ap 24 1884]
CaQQL 1882-83

Le **CONSTITUTIONNEL.** w
CaQMF Mr 11 1823-S 21 1824
CaQQL Mr 1823-Ag 1824

Le **CONSTITUTIONNEL.** tw,d 1868-83‖?
CaQ Je 4 1868-D 31 1883
CaQQL 1872-77

L'**ECHO** du Saint-Maurice. w
CaQQL 1858

L'**ERE** nouvelle. sw Jl 13 1884-S 29 1885‖
CaO complete
CaOOA complete

L'**ERE** nouvelle, journal du district des Trois-Rivières. w,tw D 9 1852-
CSmH F 2 1853
CaQMS [Mr 16 1853-N 26 1857]
CaQQL 1852-63

INQUIRER and Three Rivers commercial advertiser. sw 1855-
CaOOA 1860-61
MWA My 31 1856

Le **JOURNAL** des Trois-Rivières. sw My 19 1865-My 19 1891‖
CaO [1865-91]
CaQ 1873-91
CaQMS [My 22 1866-My 8 1871]
CaQQL 1847-53;65-81;87-91

La **LIBERTE.** w O 1 1884-O 30 1886‖
CaO complete
CaQ complete

Le **MOUVEMENT** Catholique. w
CaQQL 1897-1901

La **PAIX.** sw N 10 1887-90‖?
CaQ 1887-89
CaQQL 1887-90

Le **TRIFLUVIEN.** sw O 31 1888-1908‖
CaO 1888-96
CaOOA Ap 1906-Je 1908
CaQ N 19 1890-1907
CaQQL 1888-91

VALLEYFIELD

Le **PROGRES** de Valleyfield. w 1878+
pub 1878+
CaQ F 1887-1909

VERDUN

CITY of Verdun messenger. *See* Messenger

Verdun **GUARDIAN.** w 1928+
CaQMM 1931+

MESSENGER. w 1912+
1912-18 as Messager de Verdun; 1918-29 City of Verdun messenger
pub 1912+

VICTORIAVILLE

L'**ECHO** des bois francs. w Je 2 1894-1917‖?
1894-1909? pub in Arthabaska
CaQ 1894-1909
CaQLL 1894-95

La **VOIX** des bois-francs. w 1928+
1928-31? pub in Arthabaska
CaQQL 1928+
CaQShS D 9 1932+

VILLAGE DEBARTZCH

L'**ECHO** du Pays. w
CaQMS [F 28 1833-F 1834;Jl 9 1835-Je 1836]

WATERLOO

Le **JOURNAL** de Waterloo. w 1882+
CaQ Mr 12 1885-1909
CaQQL 1888-91;1903-05;21-22

SASKATCHEWAN

ALAMEDA

Alameda **DISPATCH.** w Ja 1902+
pub 1902+

ARCOLA

MOOSE MOUNTAIN star-standard. w N 10 1900+
1900-Je 1922 as Moose Mountain star
pub Jl 1922+

ARRAN

Arran **ARROW.** w Je 22 1922+
pub 1922+

ASSINIBOIA

Assiniboia **TIMES.** w N 28 1912+
pub 1912+

BATTLEFORD

SASKATCHEWAN herald. sm,w Ag 25 1878+
sm 1878-84
CaM 1878-1921
CaO 1878-1900
CaOOA 1878-S 1880
MH 1878-1905

BIGGAR

Biggar **INDEPENDENT.** w Ap 1911+
pub 1911+

BLAINE LAKE

ECHO. w Je 15 1923+
1923-S 1925 pub in Leask
pub 1923+

BROADVIEW

Broadview **EXPRESS.** w Jl 6 1906+
pub 1906+

CANWOOD

Canwood **TIMES.** w Mr 29 1923+
pub 1923+

CARLYLE

Carlyle **OBSERVER.** w 1936+
pub 1936+

CLIMAX

CLIMAX. w F 23 1925+
pub 1925+

CRAIK

Craik weekly **NEWS.** w D 17 1908+
pub 1908+

CUPAR

Cupar **HERALD.** w N 30 1906+
pub 1906+

EASTEND

Eastend **ENTERPRISE.** w Je 11 1914+
pub 1914+

ELBOW

Weekly **COURIER.** *See under* Riverhurst

ESTERHAZY

Esterhazy **OBSERVER.** w 1907+
CaSE Mr 10 1907+

ESTEVAN

Estevan **MERCURY.** w Jl 1903+
pub Mr 1 1925+

GRAVELBOURG

L'**ETOILE** de Gravelbourg. *See* Gravelbourg star

Gravelbourg **STAR**; L'Etoile de Gravelbourg. w 1921+
In English and French
pub 1928+

GRENFELL

Grenfell **SUN.** w 1894+
pub 1901-12;21+
CaM 1894-99

GUERNSEY

Guernsey **STANDARD** and Lanigan ledger. w Jl 1908+
1908-14? as Guernsey standard
pub 1908+

HARRIS

GOOSE LAKE herald. w Ja 1912+
pub 1916+

HUDSON BAY JUNCTION

JUNCTION Judge. w N 30 1931+
pub 1931+

HUMBOLDT

Humboldt **JOURNAL.** w S 5 1905+
pub 1905+

INDIAN HEAD

Indian Head **VIDETTE.** w 1884-1913‖?
CaM 1905-08

KAMSACK

Kamsack **TIMES.** w Je 5 1908+
pub 1908+

KELVINGTON

Kelvington **RADIO.** w N 30 1922+
Suspended during Jl 1932
pub 1922+

KERROBERT

Kerrobert **CITIZEN.** w D 24 1910+
pub 1916+

KINDERSLEY

Kindersley **CLARION.** w Ap 22 1910+
pub 1910+

KISBEY

Kisbey **STANDARD.** w 1914-Je 1922‖
United with Moose Mountain star to form Moose Mountain star-standard (Arcola)

LASHBURN

Lashburn **COMET.** w Mr 12 1908+
pub 1908+

LEASK

ECHO. *See under* Blaine Lake

LIBERTY

Liberty **PRESS.** w Jl 1 1912+
pub 1912+

LLOYDMINSTER

Lloydminster **TIMES.** w Ap 25 1905+
pub 1905+

LOVERNA

BORDERLINE budget. w Jl 3 1914+
pub 1914+

LUCKY LAKE

Weekly **BROADCAST.** w Ap 1927+
pub 1927+

LUMSDEN

NEWS-RECORD. w Je 8 1904+
pub 1904+

MACKLIN

Macklin **TIMES.** w Mr 11 1910+
pub 1910+

SASKATCHEWAN (*Continued*)

MAPLE CREEK

Maple Creek NEWS. w 1903+
1903-Mr 1909? as Ranching news
pub Ap 1909+

RANCHING news. *See* Maple Creek news

MARYFIELD

Maryfield NEWS. w Ag 5 1909+
pub 1909+

MELFORT

CARROTT River journal. *See* Melfort journal

Melfort JOURNAL. w Ag 1908+
1908-09? as Carrott River journal

MOOSE JAW

MERCHANTS' weekly. *See* Western spotlight

Moose Jaw NEWS. My 1883-85||
CaM 1884
CaO N 1883-F 20 1885

SASKATCHEWAN liberal. w S 15 1932+
pub 1932+

Moose Jaw evening TIMES. *See* Moose Jaw times-herald

Moose Jaw TIMES-HERALD. w,sw,d Ap 1889+
1889-Je 1935 as Moose Jaw evening times
w 1889;sw 1890-F 20 1906
pub [1894-95]—
CaM 1892-1908
CaO Ja 10 1890-99

WESTERN spotlight. w D 21 1925+
1925-S 4 1931 as Merchants' weekly
pub 1925+

MOOSOMIN

Moosomin COURIER. w O 1884-D 1 1892||
Followed by Spectator
CaM complete
CaO 1889-92

SPECTATOR. w D 8 1892-1909||
Follows Moosomin courier. United with World to form World-spectator
CaM 1892-99
CaO 1892-1900
CaSMW [1904;10]

WORLD-SPECTATOR. w 1900+
1900-09 as World
pub 1904;07-09;11+

MORSE

Morse NEWS. w 1910+
pub [1911-14]+

MUENSTER

PRAIRIE messenger. w My 24 1923+
1923-Ja 18 1928 as St. Peter's messenger
pub 1923+
CaSMuS 1923+

ST. PETER'S bote. w F 11 1904+
In German
CaSMuS 1904+

ST. PETER'S messenger. *See* Prairie messenger

NAICAM

LAC VERT leader. w My 1 1934+
pub 1934+

Naicam PROGRESS. w Jl 2 1922+
pub 1922+

NOKOMIS

Nokomis TIMES and Lockwood news. w My 10 1908+
1908-26? as Nokomis times
pub [1908?-]

NORTH BATTLEFORD

North Battleford NEWS. w Jl 3 1905+
pub Ja 10 1907+

North Battleford OPTIMIST. w Ja 1 1911+
pub 1912+

OUTLOOK

NORDEN. w My 15 1918-22||?
In Norwegian
MnHi My 15 1918-Ag 2 1922

OUTLOOK. w F 9 1909+
pub 1909+

PENSE

Pense HERALD. w S 7 1912+
pub Je 31 1931+

PRINCE ALBERT

Prince Albert ADVOCATE. w 1894-1909||?
CaM O 6 1895;Ja 19 1897-1904

FARM labor news. *See* North star

NORTH STAR. w Jl 1 1933+
1933-Jl? 1934 as Farm labor news
pub 1933-Jl,S 21 1934+

Le PATRIOTE de l'ouest. w Ag 25 1910+
In French
CaO 1920+
CaQMS [1910+]
CaQQL My 25 1911+

SASKATCHEWAN. w Jl 25 1889-Je 29 1892||
CaO Ag 1889-92

Prince Albert TIMES. w O 1882-1912||
CaM 1882-95
CaO Je 6 1884-D 21 1900

PUNNICHY

TOUCHWOOD times. w Ja 8 1920+
pub 1920+

QU'APPELLE

Qu'Appelle PROGRESS. N 13 1885+
CaM 1886-99
CaO 1885-D 27 1900
CaOTA Jl 27 1887

Qu'Appelle VIDETTE. w O 9 1884-99||?
CaM 1888-99
CaO O 9 1884-97

RADVILLE

Radville NEWS. *See* South Saskatchewan star

SOUTH SASKATCHEWAN star. w Jl 10 1911+
1911-23 as Radville news
pub 1915+

REGINA

Regina JOURNAL. *See* Regina standard

LEADER. w Mr 1 1883-1915||?

Evening LEADER. d D 30 1910-Ja 12 1915||
CaSRL complete

Morning LEADER. *See* Leader-post

LEADER-POST. d N 10 1905+
1905-Ap 5 1930 as Morning leader
pub 1907+
CaB N 3 1909[10-27]+
CaSR 1909+
CaSU F 1931+
TJT N 1 1900
WHi Jl 1,S 25,O 2 1912

NORTHWEST territories gazette. sm 1883-Ag 31 1905||
Followed by Saskatchewan gazette
CaB Ja 15 1898[99]-1905
CaOOA complete
CaSRK complete
DLC 1888-92;94-1905
ICU [1888;92;1905]
NN Mr 12 1887;90-93;97-1905

Evening POST. d D 14 1910-Ap 5 1930||
1910-D 4 1913 as Daily province; D 5 1913-O 18 1913 Evening province and standard; O 19 1918-20? Regina daily post. United with Morning leader to form Leader-post
CaSR [D 17 1910-S 1913]

Daily PROVINCE. *See* Evening post

PROVINCE and standard. w Ap 27 1899-1914||?
1899-D 17? 1910 as West; D 14 1910-13? Province

Evening PROVINCE and standard. *See* Evening post

SASKATCHEWAN gazette. w S 30 1905+
Follows Northwest territories gazette
pub 1905+
CaB 1905+
CaOOA 1905+
CaOT 1905+
CaQMM 1905+
DLC 1905+
ICU [1907-09;11-18]-[20]-23
NN 1911+

SASKATCHEWAN standard. sw 1905-13||?
1905-10? as Standard. United with Province to form Province and standard
CaM 1905-08

Regina STANDARD. w 1886-1904||
CaM complete
CaO Jl 1889-90;Jl 1891-99

STANDARD. d 1904-D 4 1913||
United with Daily province to form Province and standard, later Evening post

STANDARD. sw *See* Saskatchewan standard

Regina daily STAR. d Jl 16 1928+
pub 1928+
CaSR [O-D 1930]+

WEST. *See* Province and standard

RIVERHURST

Weekly COURIER. w N 3 1914+
1914-N 4 1915 pub in Elbow
pub 1914+

ROCKGLEN

CORONACH courier. w D 22 1927+
pub 1927—

Rockglen REVIEW. w 1926+
pub 1926-Jl 1 1936

ROSETOWN

Rosetown EAGLE. w D 10 1909—
pub 1909—

ROSTHERN

Der BOTE: ein mennonitisches schrift. w Ja 14 1924+
1924 as Der Mennonitische immigrantenbote
In German
pub 1924+
CSt-H 1929-30

Der MENNONITISCHE immigrantenbote. *See* Der bote. . .

ROULEAU

Rouleau ENTERPRISE. w Mr 11 1906+
pub [1906]+

ST. WALBURG

St. Walburg ENTERPRISE. w S 7 1933+
pub 1933+

SALTCOATS

Saltcoats OBSERVER. w Je 9 1932+
pub 1932+

SASKATOON

Saskatoon CAPITAL. tw,w 1906-12||
tw 1906?
CaSU Jl-D 1909;N 1911-Ja 1912

Saskatoon evening CAPITAL. d 1908?-12||
CaSU O 1909-Je 1911

NEW PATHWAY. (Novy shlakh) w O 30 1930+
In Ukrainian
pub 1930+

NOVY shlakh. *See* New pathway

Saskatoon PHENIX. w *See* Saskatoon star-phoenix

PROGRESSIVE. *See* Western producer

Saskatoon daily STAR. d 1912-S 11 1928||
United with Saskatoon phoenix to form Saskatoon star-phoenix
CaSS [1918]20-28
CaSSS 1912-17
CaSU 1923-28
MiG Je 30 1927
WHi N 9 1912-O 21 1918

Saskatoon STAR-PHOENIX. w,d O 17 1902+
1902-06 as Saskatoon phenix(w);1907-S 11 1928 Saskatoon phoenix
Je 30 1927 is Diamond jubilee ed
CaSS 1902-17;20+
CaSSS [1911]-19
CaSU [1908-15]29+
MiG Je 30 1927
WHi N 9 1912-O 21 1918

WESTERN producer. w Ag 27 1923+
1923-S 11 1924 as Progressive
pub 1923+
CaM 1930+
CaSU 1925+

SHAUNAVON

Shaunavon STANDARD. w S 18 1913+
pub 1913+

SHELLBROOK

Shellbrook CHRONICLE. w My 11 1912+
pub 1912+

SPIRITWOOD

Spiritwood HERALD. w S 5 1933+
pub 1933+

STAR CITY

Star City ECHO. w O 4 1918+
pub Ap 1920+

STRASBOURG

Strasbourg MOUNTAINEER w My 13 1906+
pub 1906+

SWIFT CURRENT

ADVOCATE. w Ag 20 1936+
Follows Swift Current herald
pub S 17 1936+

Swift Current daily EXPRESS. d 1912||
CaSScA Ag 27-O 10 1912

Swift Current HERALD. w Ja 7 1915-S 10 1936||
Followed by Advocate
CaSScA complete

Weekly NEWS. w Je 8 1911-N 12 1914||
CaSScA Je 29 1911-14

Swift Current SUN. w Ap 1903+
pub Ja 1 1909+

SASKATCHEWAN (*Continued*)

TISDALE

Tisdale RECORDER. w D 20 1906+
pub 1914+

TURTLEFORD

Turtleford SUN. w S 11 1929+
pub 1929+

WADENA

Wadena HERALD. w 1909-28||
Followed by Wadena news

Wadena NEWS. w Je 19 1929+
Follows Wadena herald
pub 1929+

WAKAW

BROADCAST. w O 19 1936+
pub 1936+

Wakaw RECORDER. w Jl 14 1912+
pub 1912+

WATROUS

Watrous SIGNAL. w Je 21 1908+
pub Je 21 1910+

WATSON

Watson WITNESS. w S 13 1907+
pub 1907+

WAWOTA

Wawota REPORTER. w Ag 15 1934+
pub 1934+

WHITEWOOD

Whitewood HERALD. w 1892+
pub N 1900+
CaM 1893-95

WYNYARD

Wynyard ADVANCE. w Ag 1911+
pub 1911?+

YORKTON

Yorkton ENTERPRISE. w Ag 2 1896+
pub 1896+

YUKON TERRITORY

DAWSON

Sunday GLEANER and Klondike miner. w
CaB S 17-D 10 1899

KLONDIKE miner and Yukon advertiser. w
CaB Ja 27 1899

Semi-weekly KLONDIKE nugget. sw Je 16 1898-Jl 1903||?
1898-Ja 10 1900 as Klondike nugget
CaB O 1[N 1898-F,Ap-My,Jl 1899]-Ja 3 1900
CaQMM [1898-99]
IEIC Mr 29 1899
WaS Ag-D 7 1898
WaU 1898-Ja 1 1902;My 27,Je 27-Jl 1 1903

Daily KLONDIKE nugget. d Ja 8 1900-Jl 14 1903||?
CaB Ja 11-Mr 22 1900

Dawson daily NEWS. d 1899+
CaB Ag 17 1899-Mr 20 1900
WaPS [1919]

YUKON daily news. d
OrHi O 26 1901

YUKON sun. w Je 1898-1906||?
1898 as Yukon midnight sun. Subtitle varies
CaB O 22 1898;N 13 1899;Ja 17,27,Mr 20 1900
WaS Ag-N 4 1898

WHITEHORSE

Whitehorse STAR. w 1898+
pub 1925+
CaB Mr 21 1924+

NEWFOUNDLAND

HARBOR GRACE

Harbor Grace STANDARD. w 1859+
CaO Mr 14 1888-1903

ST. JOHN'S

COLONIST. d 1886-Jl 8 1892||
CaO Mr 13 1888-92

COMMERCIAL journal, prices current & shipping list. w 1856-
MWA My 12 1857

Morning COURIER and general advertiser. w 1815-16||?
CSmH Je 16 1816

Evening HERALD. d 1882-1924||?
1882-89 as Evening mercury
CaO Mr 13 1888-89;Ja 13 1890-Je 1907

Evening MERCURY. *See* Evening herald

NEWFOUNDLAND express. tw 1852-79||?
CSmH Jl 19 1853

NEWFOUNDLAND gazette. w O 7 1924+
Follows Royal gazette. . .
CaO 1924+
DLC 1924+
NN 1924+

NEWFOUNDLANDER. sw 1806-84||
CaO O 24 1861-84

Daily NEWS. d F 15 1894+
CaO 1894-Je 1907

NORTH star and St. John's Newfoundland news. w 1870-80||?
CaOT [1874-79]

Morning POST and shipping gazette. tw,sw Je? 1843-
CSmH Je 23 1846
MWA Ag 15,19 1843;My 12 1857

PUBLIC ledger, and Newfoundland general advertiser. sw,tw 1821-74||?
CSmH Je 17 1853

ROYAL gazette and Newfoundland advertiser. w 1806-O 4 1924||
Followed by Newfoundland gazette
CSmH Jl 20 1830
CaO Ja 8 1888-1924
DLC 1903-24
MWA Mr 31,Ap 21 1818
NN Je 23 1903-S 1924

STAR and Newfoundland advocate. w 1841-45||?
CSmH S 4 1845

Evening TELEGRAM. d Ap 3 1879+
CSt-H [1915-16]
CaO Mr 13 1888+
DLC D 1899+

TIMES, and general commercial gazette. w 1832-Mr 23 1895||
Title varies
CSmH Je 11 1853
CaO Mr 14 1888-95
MWA Mr 30 1836

TRADE review. w S 1892+
CaO O 3 1892-D 27 1902

Daily TRIBUNE. d N 4 1892-93||?
CaO N 4 1892-93

A Bibliography of Union Lists of Newspapers

Compiled by KARL BROWN and DANIEL C. HASKELL,
The New York Public Library

This list, like its predecessors in the "Union List of Serials," 1927, and the Supplement, 1931, has been compiled primarily to serve two interests. Academically, it brings together a record of similar, earlier lists; practically, it gathers location-lists which cover sources possibly not in the present publication—foreign, private, and smaller American collections. No attempt, however, has been made to be exhaustive.

Lists devoted to, or including newspapers, have been taken from the earlier compilations mentioned, with the addition of such lists as have appeared since the publication of the earlier bibliographies. Some lists of doubtful usefulness have been included, principally those (a) listing a relatively small number of titles, (b) giving little or no detail of holdings, or (c) having unsystematic recordings of the collections represented. In such cases, the academic interest generally justified their inclusion. The "List of Serial Publications of Foreign Governments, 1815-1931" has been included on account of the records of government newspapers and gazettes which it listed.

The arrangement of the titles is geographical, the United States first, followed by other countries in alphabetical order. Under each country the general lists come first followed by those of individual cities, states and provinces in one alphabetical arrangement. Under the specific locality the arrangement is chronological.

UNITED STATES

General

Nelson, William.
American newspapers of the eighteenth century. Chronology and history; lists of files, and libraries in which they may be found. I-III. (Documents relating to the colonial history of the state of New Jersey. Paterson, N.J., 1894-97. 8°. v. 11, p. ix-cxxvi; v. 12, p. cxxvii-cclxviii; v. 19, p. vii-lxxviii.)
Part I. Alabama-Maryland.
Part II. Massachusetts.
Part III. Michigan, New Hampshire.

James, Edmund Janes, and M. J. Loveless.
A bibliography of newspapers published in Illinois prior to 1860. Springfield, Ill.: Hillips Bros., state prtrs., 1899. 94 p. 8°.
Arranged by place of publication. Files not located in all cases.

Ayer, Mary Farwell.
Check-list of Boston newspapers, 1704-1780, by Mary Farwell Ayer, with bibliographical notes by Albert Matthews. Boston: Published for the Society, 1907. 3 p.l., (i)viii-xvii (i) p., 1 l., (1)4-527 p. 8°. (The Colonial Society of Massachusetts. Publications. v. 9.)
Gives detailed holdings of fourteen American libraries.

Thwaites, Reuben Gold.
The Ohio valley press before the War of 1812-15. Worcester, Mass.: Davis Press, 1909. 62 p., 5 facsims. 4°.
Appendix, p. 48-62.
"On the following pages [of the Appendix] are listed in detail files of the newspapers of the Ohio River valley—western Pennsylvania, Kentucky, Ohio, Indiana, and Missouri—from the beginnings of the press in each state through the year, 1812, as reported by the various libraries cited."
Gives exact statement of files.
Originally appeared in the Proceedings of the American Antiquarian Society, new series, v. 19, p. 354-368.

Cook, Elizabeth Christine.
Newspapers in the American colonies, 1704-1750. (In her: Literary influences in colonial newspapers, 1704-1750. New York, 1912. 8°. p. 268-272.)
Chronological list, with location of files. Exact holdings not given.

Brigham, Clarence Saunders.
Bibliography of American newspapers, 1690-1820. (American Antiquarian Society. Proceedings. Worcester, Mass., 1913-28. 8°. new series, v. 23-37.)
Part 1. Alabama, Arkansas, Connecticut, Delaware, District of Columbia, Florida, Georgia, Illinois, Indiana. new series, v. 23, p. 247-403.
Part 2. Kentucky, Louisiana, Maine. new series, v. 24, p. 363-449.
Part 3. Maryland, Massachusetts (Boston). new series, v. 25, p. 128 293.
Part 4. Massachusetts (except Boston). new series, v. 25, p. 396-401.
Part 5. Michigan, Mississippi, Missouri, New Hampshire. new series, v. 26, p. 80-184.
Part 6. New Jersey. new series, v. 26, p. 413-460.
Part 7. New York (A-L). new series, v. 27, p. 177-274.
Part 8. New York City. new series, v. 27, p. 375-513.
Part 9. New York (M-W) excepting New York City. new series, v. 28, p. 63-133.
Part 10. North Carolina. new series, v. 28, p. 291-322.
Part 11. Ohio. new series, v. 29, p. 129-180.
Part 12. Pennsylvania (A-N). new series, v. 30, p. 81-150.
Part 13. Pennsylvania (Philadelphia). new series, v. 32, p. 81-214
Part 14. Pennsylvania (Pittsburgh to York). new series, v. 32, p. 346-379.
Part 15. Rhode Island. new series, v. 34, p. 79-137.
Part 16. South Carolina. new series, v. 34, p 259-300.
Part 17. Tennessee and Vermont. new series, v 35, p. 79-160.
Part 18. Virginia and West Virginia. new series, v 37, p. 63-162.
To be issued later as a separate.
"Attempts, first, to present a historical sketch of every newspaper printed in the United States from 1690-1820; secondly, to locate all files found in the various libraries of the country; and, thirdly, to give a complete check list of the issues in the library of the American Antiquarian Society."

Cundall, Frank.
The press and printers of Jamaica prior to 1820. (American Antiquarian Society. Proceedings. Worcester, Mass., 1916. 8°. new series, v. 26, p. 290-412.)
Bibliography. Jamaica newspapers, 1722-1820, p. 355-373.
Locates copies in nine English libraries and eight American libraries, besides those in the Library of the Institute of Jamaica.

Princeton University.—Library.
A joint finding list of foreign newspapers. Princeton: The University Library, 1918. 2 p.l., 5-12 p. 4°.
At head of title: Uncorrected proof. Prefatory note signed: Anson Ely Morse. "A joint list of foreign newspapers currently taken, bound and kept on file in American libraries during the present war."
Indicates holdings.

Knauss, James Owen.
Table of German American newspapers of the eighteenth century. (In his: Social conditions among the Pennsylvania Germans in the eighteenth century. [Lancaster, Pa., 1922.] 8°. p. 160-202.)
Lists all copies located.
First printed in v. 29 of the Proceedings of the Pennsylvania-German Society.

Wagner, Henry Raup.
California imprints, August, 1846-June, 1851. Berkeley, Cal.: Privately printed, 1922. 4 p.l., 87 p. 8°.
Newspaper entries scattered among other imprints in chronological order; alphabetical list in classified index, p. 91-92.

Wroth, Lawrence Counselman.
A history of printing in colonial Maryland, 1686-1776. Baltimore: The Typothetae of Baltimore, 1922. 3 p.l., v-xiv p., 1 l., 275p. illus. 8°.
Includes entries for newspapers in the chronological list "Maryland imprints, an annotated bibliography of books, broadsides and newspapers printed in Maryland from 1689 to 1776," p. 155-256. Exact holdings not always given for scattered copies, but a reference to Brigham's bibliography.

Meany, Edmond Stephen.
Newspapers of Washington Territory. (Washington historical quarterly. Seattle, 1922-35. 8°. v. 13, p. 181-195, 251-268; v. 14, p. 21-29, 100-107, 186-200, 269-290; v. 26, p. 34-64, 129-143.)
Arrangement alphabetic by town. Discursive; "whenever important and interesting facts are obtained about the publications, these are set down with the bibliographic data." Not all files are located, and holdings are not exact for those libraries and collections represented.
The supplementary notes in v. 26 are by Douglas C. McMurtrie.

Brigham, Clarence Saunders.
Wall-paper newspapers of the Civil War. (In: Bibliographical essays; a tribute to Wilberforce Eames. [Cambridge, Mass.,] 1924. 8°. p. 203-209.)
Locates copies in seven American libraries.

Rusk, Ralph Leslie.
[Bibliography of] newspapers and magazines. (In his: The literature of the middle western frontier. New York, 1925. 8°. v. 2, p. 145-184.)
Locates copies in American libraries.

Knauss, James Owen.
A chronological list of Florida newspapers published before July, 1845, with a checklist of all copies located. (In his: Territorial Florida journalism. Deland, 1926. 4°. p. 86-128.)
Locates copies in the American Antiquarian Society, the Library of Congress, the New York Historical Society, and the private library of P. K. Yonge and J. C. Yonge, Pensacola, Fla.

Crane, R. S., and F. B. Kaye.
A census of British newspapers and periodicals, 1620-1800. Chapel Hill, N.C.: University of North Carolina Press, 1927. 395 p. 8°.
First published in Studies in philology, Chapel Hill, N.C., v. 24, p. 1-205.
Gives exact statement of holdings.
Sixty-two libraries represented.

Fox, Louis Hewitt.
New York City newspapers, 1820-1850. A bibliography. Chicago: University of Chicago Press, 1928. 5, 131 p. 8°. (Bibliographical Society of America. Papers. v. 21, part 1-2, 1927.)
Holdings of The New York Public Library, the New York Historical Society Library, the American Antiquarian Society Library, and the Library of Congress. If files in these libraries are very incomplete or lacking, full files elsewhere are given.

Brantley, Rabun Lee.
Georgia journalism during the Civil War period. Nashville, Tenn.: George Peabody College for Teachers, 1929. 4 p.l., xi-xvi p., 1 l., 134 p. 8°. (George Peabody College for Teachers. Contributions to education. no. 58.)
Gives exact holding in American libraries.

McMurtrie, Douglas Crawford.
Early printing in New Orleans, 1764-1810, with a bibliography of the issues of the Louisiana press. New Orleans: Searcy & Pfaff, Ltd., 1929. 4 p.l., 11-151 p. 4°.
Includes newspapers. Exact holdings not given.

Cappon, Lester Jesse.
Bibliography of Virginia history since 1865 . . . University, Va.: Institute for Research in the Social Sciences, 1930. xviii, 900 p. 8°. (University of Virginia. Institute for Research in the Social Sciences. Institute monograph no. 5.)
Newspapers, p. 805-817. Holdings of twenty-eight libraries.

Nolan, James Bennett.
The first decade of printing in Reading, Pennsylvania. Published and distributed by Reading National Bank and Trust Company. [Reading, Pa.: Reading Eagle Press,] 1930. 64 p. illus. 8°.
"Bibliography of the first decade of printing in Reading, Pennsylvania," p. 19-32.
Lists four Reading newspapers, with exact statements of holdings in public and private collections.

Brigham, Clarence Saunders.
Bibliography of Winchester newspapers printed prior to 1820. (Winchester, Virginia, Historical Society. Annual papers. Winchester, 1931. 8°. v. 1, p. 233-239.)
"All files [of nine titles] found in the various libraries of the country."

Craig, Mary Elizabeth.
The Scottish periodical press, 1750-1789. Edinburgh: Oliver and Boyd, 1931. vii, 113 (1) p. 8°.
"Bibliography: Scottish periodicals: 1750-1789," p. 95-104.
Locates files in thirty-two libraries in Great Britain and the United States. Includes newspapers.

McMurtrie, Douglas Crawford.
Newspaper record [of Michigan newspapers, 1796-1850]. (In his: Early printing in Michigan, with a bibliography of the Michigan press, 1796-1850. Chicago: John Calhoun Club, 1931. 8°. p. 227-320.)
Thirty-three public and private collections listed. Exact holdings given.

Emig, Elmer J.
A check-list of extant Florida newspapers, 1845-1876. (Florida Historical Society. Quarterly. Gainesville, Fla., 1932. 8°. v. 11, p. 77-87.)
Locates copies in American collections and the British Museum. Exact holdings given.

Fassett, Frederick Gardiner, jr.
A history of newspapers in the district of Maine, 1785-1820. Orono, Maine: University Press, 1932. 242 p. illus. 8°.
"Bibliography: newspapers", p. 225-227.
Locates files in six American libraries, but does not give statement of holdings.

List of the serial publications of foreign governments, 1815-1931, edited by Winifred Gregory. . . New York: The H. W. Wilson Company, 1932. 5 p.l., 720 p. f°.
Included for its records of government newspapers and gazettes.

Tinker, Edward Larocque.
Bibliography of the French newspapers and periodicals of Louisiana. (American Antiquarian Society. Proceedings. Worcester, Mass., 1933. 8°. new series, v. 42, p. 247-370.)
Includes a history of French journalism in Louisiana, a list of general reference books, etc., and an alphabetical list of newspapers, with historical notes and locations of copies.

McMurtrie, Douglas Crawford.
A bibliography of Nevada newspapers, 1858 to 1875 inclusive. (Gutenberg-Jahrbuch. Mainz [1935]. 4°. 1935, p. 292-312.)
Locates copies in American libraries. Exact holdings given.

The French press of Louisiana. Notes in supplement to Edward Larocque Tinker's "Bibliography of French newspapers and periodicals of Louisiana." (Louisiana historical quarterly. New Orleans, 1935. 8°. v. 18, p. 947-965.)
Locates additional copies.

McMurtrie, Douglas Crawford, and Albert H. Allen.
A record of early Colorado newspapers [through 1876]. (In their: Early printing in Colorado. Denver, Col., 1935. 8°. p. 223-286.)
Locates copies in seventeen public and two private collections. Exact holdings given.

Cappon, Lester Jesse.
Virginia newspapers, 1821-1935. A bibliography with historical introduction and notes. New York: D. Appleton-Century Company, Incorporated, for the Institute for Research in the Social Sciences, University of Virginia, 1936. xiii, 299 p. 8°. (University of Virginia. Institute for Research in the Social Sciences. Institute monograph no. 22.)
Holdings of over eighty collections listed. Arranged alphabetically by name of town.

Boston, Mass.

Boston Public Library.
A list of periodicals, newspapers, transactions, and other serial publications currently received in the principal libraries of Boston and vicinity. Boston: The Trustees of the Public Library, 1897. 3 p.l., 143 p. 4°.
Thirty-six libraries represented.

Homer, Thomas Johnston.
A guide to serial publications founded prior to 1918 and now or recently current in Boston, Cambridge, and vicinity. Compiled and edited by Thomas Johnston Homer, with the co-operation of a committee of librarians and other scholars. Part 1-5. Boston: Published by the Trustees of the Public Library, 1922-32. 4°.
Part 1-5: A-New.
Indicates approximate completeness of files. Includes newspapers.
Eighty-five libraries represented.

Buffalo, N.Y.

Severance, Frank Hayward.
The periodical press of Buffalo, 1811-1915. (Buffalo Historical Society. Publications. Buffalo, N.Y., 1915. 8°. v. 19, p. 177-280.)
Includes newspapers. Notes existence of files in the Buffalo Public Library and the Library of the Buffalo Historical Society, but does not give statement of files.

California

Chandler, Katherine.
List of California periodicals issued previously to the completion of the transcontinental telegraph (August 15, 1846-October 24, 1861.) San Francisco: [The Hicks-Judd Press,] 1905. 1 p.l., (1)4-20 p. 8°. (Library Association of California. Publications. no. 7.)
Locates copies in twenty-five public and private collections in California.

Chicago, Ill.

University of Chicago.—Library.
Newspapers in libraries of metropolitan Chicago, a union list prepared by the University of Chicago Libraries, Document Division. [Chicago,] 1931. v, 89 p. ob. 4°.
Autographic reproduction of type-written copy. "Preliminary edition."

Newspapers in libraries of Chicago, a joint check list. The University of Chicago Libraries, Document Section. Chicago, 1936. iv, 257 f. 4°.
Lists the holdings of the University of Chicago Libraries, the Newberry Library, the Chicago Public Library, the Chicago Historical Society Library, the John Crerar Library, the Northwestern University Library, Evanston, Ill., and the McCormick Historical Association Library.

Illinois

A **List** of Illinois newspapers and periodicals in Illinois libraries arranged alphabetically by towns, to which are added lists of Illinois newspapers and periodicals in the Library of Congress, the Library of the State Historical Society of Wisconsin, the Mercantile Library, St. Louis, the Library of the American Antiquarian Society, Worcester, Mass., and others. (In: F. W. Scott, Newspapers and periodicals of Illinois, 1814-1879. Springfield, 1910. 8°. p. 363-413. Illinois State Historical Library. Collections. v. 6.)
Gives statement of files.

Indiana

A **List** of Indiana newspapers available in the Indiana State Library, the Indianapolis Public Library, the Library of Indiana University, and the Library of Congress, Washington, D.C. [Indianapolis?] 1916. 1 p.l., 3-31 p. 8°. (Indiana State Library. Bulletin. v. 11, no. 4.)

Kentucky

Kinkead, Ludie, and T. D. Clark.
Check list of Kentucky newspapers contained in Kentucky libraries. . . Lexington, Ky., 1935. 4 p.l., 44 [correctly 42] f., 10 l. 4°.
Mimeographed. Holdings of twenty-two libraries.

Ohio

Ohio.—State Library.
Newspapers and periodicals in Ohio State Library, other libraries of the state, and lists of Ohio newspapers in the Library of Congress and the Library of the Historical Society of Wisconsin. Compiled by C. B. Galbreath, state librarian. Columbus, Ohio: Fred J. Heer, state printer, 1902. 2 p.l., (1)4-268 p., 1 facsim. illus. 8°.
Gives statement of holdings.
Twenty Ohio libraries represented.
Also issued, as a separately paged appendix, in Ohio.—Library Commission. Sketches of Ohio libraries. Columbus, 1902.

Pittsburgh, Pa.

Historical Society of Western Pennsylvania.
. . .Inventory of files of American newspapers in Pittsburgh and Allegheny county, Pennsylvania. Pittsburgh, Pa., 1933. vii,34p. 4°. (Western Pennsylvania historical survey. Bibliographical contributions. no. 2.)
Multigraphed.
"Based upon a careful listing of all files . . . in the possession or custody of the Historical Society of Western Pennsylvania, and upon a canvass, by letter . . . of other known or likely possessors of similar files in Pittsburgh and other parts of Allegheny county."
Lists holdings of twelve libraries and some holdings of newspaper publishers.

Richmond, Va.

Minor, Kate Pleasants, and Susie B. Harrison.
A list of newspapers in the Virginia State Library, Confederate Museum and Valentine Museum. Compiled by Mrs. Kate Pleasants Minor and Miss Susie B. Harrison under the direction of Earl G. Swem. Richmond, Va., 1912. 3 p.l., (1)285-425 p. 8°. (Virginia State Library. Bulletin. v. 5, no. 4.)
Gives statement of holdings.

Rochester, N.Y.

Rochester Public Library.
Union list of serials in the libraries of Rochester, including periodicals, newspapers, annuals, publications of societies and other books published at intervals. Rochester, N.Y.: Rochester Public Library, 1917. 2 p.l., 5-147 p. 8°.
Gives statement of holdings.
Twenty-six libraries represented.

San Francisco, Cal.

Special Libraries Association of San Francisco. Union List Committee.
Preliminary union list of periodicals in the libraries of the San Francisco Bay region. San Francisco: Special Libraries Association, 1931. 3 p.l., 103 f. 4°.
Mimeographed; printed on one side of leaf, only. Exact holdings of twenty libraries.
Includes "essential Proceedings, Transactions and Yearbooks," with separate list of newspapers.

AUSTRIA

Zenker, Ernst Victor
Geschichte der Wiener Journalistik von den Anfängen bis zum Jahre 1848. Wien und Leipzig: Wilhelm Braumüller, 1892. xi, 159(1) p. 8°.
Chronologisches Verzeichnis der bis zum Jahre 1700 in Wien gedruckten Relationen und Newen Zeitungen, p. 127-142.
Chronologisches Verzeichnis der in Wien seit dem Beginn des 17. Jahrhundertes erschienenen periodischen Zeitungen, p. 143-158.
Files located for many titles; exact holdings not given.

BRITISH GUIANA

Rodway, James.
The press in British Guiana. (American Antiquarian Society. Proceedings. Worcester, Mass., 1919. 8°. new series, v. 28, p. 274-290.)
"British Guiana newspapers before 1820," p. 288-290.
Locates files in three collections in British Guiana. Exact holdings given.

CANADA

Wallace, W. S.
A check-list of Upper Canadian periodicals, 1793-1840. (Canadian historical review. Toronto, 1931. 4°. v. 12, p. 11-22.)
Locates files in Canadian libraries; statement not always detailed.

GERMANY

Klawitter, Willy.
Die Zeitungen und Zeitschriften Schlesiens von den Anfängen bis zum Jahre 1870 bezw. bis zur Gegenwart. Breslau: Trewendt & Granier, 1930. xvi, 251 p. 8°. (Verein für Geschichte Schlesiens. Darstellungen und Quellen zur schlesischen Geschichte. Bd. 32.)
Locates files in Silesian libraries. Exact holdings given.

Deutsches Institut für Zeitungskunde, Berlin.
Standortskatalog wichtiger Zeitungsbestände in deutschen Bibliotheken, herausgegeben vom Deutschen Institut für Zeitungskunde. Leipzig: K. W. Hiersemann, 1933. xxxi, 254 p. 4°.

GREAT BRITAIN

Cundall, Frank.
The press and printers of Jamaica prior to 1820. (American Antiquarian Society. Proceedings. Worcester, Mass., 1916. 8°. new series, v. 26, p. 290-412.)
Bibliography. Jamaica newspapers, 1722-1820, p. 355-373.
Locates copies in nine English libraries and eight American libraries, besides those in the Library of the Institute of Jamaica.

Couper, William James.
The Glasgow periodical press in the eighteenth century. (Glasgow Bibliographical Society. Records. Glasgow, 1930. 8°. v. 8, p. 99-135.)
Locates files in ten Scottish and English collections, but does not give statement of holdings.

Craig, Mary Elizabeth.
The Scottish periodical press, 1750-1789. Edinburgh: Oliver and Boyd, 1931. vii, 113(1) p. 8°.
"Bibliography: Scottish periodicals: 1750-1789," p. 95-104.
Locates files in thirty-two libraries in Great Britain and the United States. Includes newspapers.

HUNGARY

Zuber, Marianne.
. . .A hazai németnyelvű folyóiratok története 1810-ig. (Irodalomtörténeti tanulmány.) . . . Budapest: Pfeifer Ferdinánd könyvkereskedése, 1915. 121 p., 2 l. 8°. (Német philologiai dolgozatok. . . [kötet] 17.)
"A hazai németnyelvü folyóiratok bibliografiája és kronologiai jegyzéke 1810-ig," p. 109-114.
Locates files in Hungarian libraries. Holdings not given.

IRELAND

Dix, Ernest Reginald McClintock.
Tables relating to some Dublin newspapers of the 18th century, shewing what volumes, &c., of each are extant and where access to them can be had in Dublin. Dublin: Hanna & Neale, 1910. 2 p.l., 3-12 p. 4°.
Seven libraries checked.
Gives statement of holdings.

Casaide, Séamus Ó.
A guide to old Waterford newspapers. Waterford, Ireland: Waterford News, 1917. 30 p., 1 l. 8°.
Appendix gives holdings of fourteen libraries and three collectors; arranged by collection.

ITALY

Manno, Antonio.
Bibliografia di Genova. Genova: Libreria R. Istituto Sordo-Muti, 1898. 539 p. 8°.
"Giornali," p. 450-480. Chronological; locates rare copies, only.

Boselli, Antonio.
La stampa periodica siciliana del Risorgimento. (Rassegna storica del Risorgimento. Roma, 1931. 8°. anno 18, fasc. 1, supplemento, p. 299-359.)
Arranged chronologically, with an alphabetical index. Includes newspapers. Lists holdings of ten Italian libraries, all but two in Sicily.

NORWAY

Oslo.—Universitet: Bibliotek.
Norske aviser, 1763-1920; fortegnelse over aviser som finnes i Universitetsbiblioteket og andre samlinger. Kristiania: Grøndahl & Søns Boktrykkeri, 1924. viii, 84 p. 8°. (Oslo.—Universitet: Bibliotek. Årbok for 1923, [del] II.)
A national as well as a union list; geographic arrangement of about nine hundred newspapers, with exact holdings of Norwegian libraries and private collections.

SCOTLAND

Aberdeen

Bulloch, John Malcolm.
Files of the local [Aberdeen] press, past and present. (Scottish notes and queries. Aberdeen, 1896. 8°. v. 9, p. 170-171.)
Seven collections listed, arranged by repository. Holdings not always exact.

SWEDEN

Sweden.—Kungliga Biblioteket.
Sveriges offentliga bibliotek. Accessionskatalog. v. 1-date. Stockholm, 1887-date. 8°.
Beginning with v. 44, 1926, a union list of newspapers currently received by Swedish libraries is included. No details given.

SWITZERLAND

Brandstetter, Joseph Leopold.
Bibliographie der Gesellschaften, Zeitungen und Kalender in der Schweiz. Bern: K. J. Wyss, 1896. 2 p.l., (i)vi-xix, 302 p. 8°. (Zentralkommission für schweizerische Landeskunde. Bibliographie der schweizerischen Landeskunde. Fascikel Ib.)
Indicates libraries in which files are located, but does not give statement of holdings.

Faessler, Oscar.
Die st. gallische Presse; Zeitungen, Zeitschriften und einige andere Periodica. . . St. Gallen: Verlag der Fehr'schen Buchhandlung, 1926-28. 2 v. illus. f°. (Historischer Verein des Kantons St. Gallen. Neujahrsblatt. [Nr.] 66, 68.)
Teil 1: Bis zur Mitte des 19. Jahrhunderts.
Teil 2: Von der Mitte des 19. Jahrhunderts bis in die achtziger Jahre.
Liste der st. gallischen Zeitungen und Zeitschriften in chronologischer Anordnung, Teil 1, p. 40-53; Teil 2, p. 44-68.
Locates copies in Swiss libraries for many titles. Exact holdings not given.

Notes on newspapers published in foreign countries found in the libraries of the United States and Canada

It is with the keenest regret that it has been found impossible to give in detail the titles and holdings of newspapers published in foreign countries that have been reported to us. As was stated in the Introduction, all reports have been filed in a special division of the Union catalogue at the Library of Congress, where they may be examined.

The following notes are made up from an examination of the records. Any omissions, or errors are the fault of the Editor alone, as with few exceptions the libraries were not asked for a statement.

In general, the collections in the Library of Congress and the New York Public Library are the largest in point of volumes owned, and in the number of titles represented. Since the Library of Congress has recently issued its list of foreign newspapers, we shall not attempt to evaluate their collection under specific headings. A note from the New York Public Library states: "We have tried for some twenty or thirty years to acquire at least one good newspaper from each of the important foreign countries and to keep it on file." In addition, this library contains an exceptionally complete file of official municipal papers from most of the larger European cities.

The Hoover War Library at Stanford University has an outstanding collection of papers from most of the countries of Europe covering the period of the World War.

Huntington is rich in specimen numbers of early papers from most of the important cities abroad.

The Historical Society of Massachusetts owns a unique collection of Prices—current for most of the countries of Europe, covering the years 1822-38.

Other special collections are listed under country:

AUSTRALIA

The Boston Athenaeum owns a collection of South Australian papers for 1912-14; Huntington has scattered files covering 1825-53; Columbia University, specimen copies of papers published O 31-N 6 1877, also for F 17 1872.

Stanford University reports practically complete files of papers published in Melbourne and Sydney for 1894-1920, with some scattered earlier issues, and a number of current files.

Columbia has specimen numbers of 88 papers published in New South Wales in 1875.

AUSTRIA

Harvard reports roughly 1865-74;81+ of the Neue freie presse; the University of Minnesota has 1873-76;88+ New York Public Library 1895+; Library of Congress 1900+.

BULGARIA

Columbia University has a collection of papers published in Sofia Je-Jl 1922.

CENTRAL AMERICA

The Bancroft Library, University of California has outstanding files. Other important collections are the Pan American Union Library in Washington, The Department of Middle American Research of Tulane University, and Yale University.

CHINA

The Hoover War Library has specimen numbers of papers published in Harbin, 1919+

CZECHOSLOVAKIA

Columbia reports a collection of scattered issues published in 1922.

DENMARK

Columbia reports issues for August 1922.

FRANCE

Harvard's collection covering the French Revolution and the subsequent period, 1789-1815 is noteworthy. Both Harvard and the New York Public Library report valuable collections covering the Revolution of 1848, and the beginning of the Second Republic. Columbia also reports a rare collection covering 1848, as well as a special collection of French trench papers.

The Boston Athenaeum, the French Institute in the United States (New York City) the Chicago Public Library, Howard University, Vassar College, Princeton University and the Universities of Chicago, Illinois, Michigan and Minnesota have extensive holdings.

The following are some of the files reported for Le Temps: Boston Athenaeum, 1890+; Boston Public Library, 1897+; University of Chicago, 1861-1934; Cleveland Public Library, 1914-19;27+; Dartmouth College, 1915-18;23+; Duke University [1902-03]14-18[29]31+; Harvard University [1865-67]1914+; University of Illinois, 1914-18;26+; Library of Congress, 1870-71;1900+; Los Angeles Public Library, 1913+; University of Michigan, 1912-18;20+; New York Public Library [1900-01;11-12]+; Newberry Library, 1918+; Rice Institute, Houston, 1913+; Smith College, 1913+; Stanford University, 1909+; University of Wisconsin, 1913+; Yale University, 1888;97-99; 1902;03;05+; University of California, Columbia University, Johns Hopkins, University of Minnesota, Princeton University and the University of Texas all have practically complete files 1914+.

GERMANY

There are several special collections of papers published in Germany during the World War, notably in the Hoover War Library and in the Universities of Illinois, Nebraska, Chicago, Michigan, Minnesota and Princeton University. Columbia has a special file of papers published Je-Ag 1922.

Files of the Allgemeine Zeitung (Munich) are reported by Library of Congress as 1798;1826-1915;17;19-1929; Harvard 1872-1929; University of Cincinnati [1820-1900]; University of Minnesota 1814-1912; Newberry Library 1888-1914; New York Public Library 1851-55;79-1929; Boston Public Library [1854-1922]; University of Chicago 1813-1929.

For the Frankfurter Zeitung, Harvard has 1859+; New York Public Library 1904-07;09+; University of Illinois and Columbia each 1914+; Library of Congress 1900+.

GREAT BRITAIN

The Clements Library, University of Michigan, and Huntington Library each have considerable collections of early and rare papers. Other outstanding collections are at Yale University, Boston Athenaeum, New York Historical Society and the Universities of Chicago and Wisconsin.

Only the longer runs of the London Times can be mentioned: McGill University, 1847-51;54+; University of Toronto, 1859-87 [1914-18]+; Legislative Library, Toronto, 1831+; Provincial Library, Victoria, 1839+; Queens University, Kingston, 1883+; Library of Parliament, Ottawa, 1848+; Boston Athenaeum [1789-99]1824;30+; Boston Public Library, 1809-23;25+; Brown University, 1838-56;1911+; California State Library, 1819+; University of California, 1811-1911;14+; Chicago Public Library [1873-74]+; University of Chicago [1794-96]1829-31;34+; University of Cincinnati, 1821+; Cleveland Public Library [1835-36]72+; Dartmouth College, 1869+; Duke University [1810-69]+; Harvard University [1789-1845]-76;80+; Huntington Library [1801-25]37-43;47-1900; University of Illinois [1817;24-25]33+; Iowa University, 1866+; Library Company of Philadelphia, 1820-25;31+; Library of Congress, [1791]96+; Maryland Historical Society [1828-57]; Mercantile Library, Philadelphia, 1861+; University of Michigan, 1817+; University of Minnesota [1803;13]28-Je 1847[51-54]+; New York Public Library, 1805+; New York State Library, 1830+; Newberry Library, Chicago, 1828-32;34+; Ohio Historical Society, Columbus, 1888-1911;14+; University of Oregon, 1871-92; 1912-18[30-32]+; Peabody Institute, Baltimore, 1821; 27-1922; University of Pennsylvania, 1877-82;90-95;99+; Peoria Public Library, 1844-70;1914-16; Princeton University, 1812+; Purdue University, 1877+; Rice Institute, Houston, Texas, 1877+; St. Louis Public Library, 1879-99;1910+; Stanford University, 1811-22;46+; Union Theological Seminary, N.Y.C., 1877+; University of Wisconsin, 1879+; Yale University, 1807-22;30;38+.

GREECE

Yale University has scattered issues covering 1839-45; Columbia specimen issues for Jl 1922; Huntington a collection for 1829-38; Wisconsin Historical Society, 1893-1900.

ICELAND

Harvard reports "Our collection of the newspapers printed in Iceland is said to be practically complete." Cornell University has a valuable collection.

ITALY

The University of Illinois, Columbia and the Boston Public Library all report important files. Harvard is particularly rich in papers of the Risorgamento period which include rare local political sheets.

The longer runs of L'Osservatore Romano are: Columbia 1861-65;1930+; Yale 1861-65; Boston Public Library 1912+; Harvard 1849-52;61-76;1929+.

MEXICO

Thousands of titles of Mexican papers were reported, the bulk of them represented by only one issue. It is evident that a number of libraries are making determined efforts to build up a working library in this field. Foremost are Bancroft Library at the University of California, Stanford University, Texas University, Department of Middle American Research, Tulane University, Yale University, Los Angeles Museum Library and the Pan American Union.

POLAND

Columbia has a collection of papers published in Warsaw and Vilna issued Je-Ag 1922.

RUSSIA

The New York Public Library, Stanford University, University of California and Columbia University all report valuable and extensive holdings.

SCANDINAVIAN COUNTRIES

The University of Minnesota has outstanding files.

SOUTH AMERICA

The largest collections are reported from Pan American Union, Huntington Library, Stanford University and Yale University.

SPAIN

The Boston Public Library and Bancroft Library, University of California have special collections

WEST INDIES

The American Antiquarian Society have added considerably to their holdings since the publication of their titles in their Proceedings, v36, p 130-65.

YUGOSLAVIA

Columbia University has specimen numbers published in Jl 1922.

Miscellaneous Collections

A number of special collections, which from their very nature it has seemed unwise to list by item are noted below:

The New York Historical Society has a collection of American newspapers published in late 1872 and early 1873. These are specimen numbers used in compiling the 1873 volume of Rowell's newspaper directory.

The Essex Institute, Salem has a collection of single issues for 1874.

The New York Public Library has a collection of scattered issues for 1876, also a volume relating to the assassination of President McKinley containing specimen numbers dated about S 14 1901, printed in the United States and abroad, also a collection relating to the obsequies of President Lincoln published in April 1865.

The State Library of Michigan has specimen numbers of 163 newspapers published in Michigan in 1876.

The Historical Society of Ohio has a large collection of Ohio papers issued in Ja 1901.

The Kansas Historical Society has a collection (usually one issue of each paper) for 1887-89.

The Nebraska Historical Society has specimen numbers for S-O 1881.

Papers collected for the Centennial Exposition by G. P. Rowell in 1876 were divided, those for the eastern United States being given to the American Antiquarian Society, for the western part to the Chicago Historical Society.

The Wisconsin Historical Society has a number of miscellaneous collections. These cover Agricultural papers, 1866-68, Insurance journals, 1871-77; Liberia colonization papers, 1830-63, Religious newspapers, 1861-69, Second Adventist papers, 1842-47, and other collections covering practically the entire country. These are not separately listed here, but may be found in their Newspaper Catalogue, issued by the Society in 1911, pp498-501.

Columbia University has 28 volumes of first issues of papers from 1827-1927, mainly American and English.

We have not attempted to list trench and camp papers of which several libraries notably Columbia University has a considerable file. Notes of these have all been kept, and anyone considering work in this field may have access to them.